Who'sWho in America®

Published by Marquis Who's Who®

Titles in Print

Who's Who in America®
Who's Who in America Junior & Senior High School Version
Who Was Who in America®
  Historical Volume (1607–1896)
  Volume I (1897–1942)
  Volume II (1943–1950)
  Volume III (1951–1960)
  Volume IV (1961–1968)
  Volume V (1969–1973)
  Volume VI (1974–1976)
  Volume VII (1977–1981)
  Volume VIII (1982–1985)
  Volume IX (1985–1989)
  Volume X (1989–1993)
  Volume XI (1993–1996)
  Index Volume (1607–1996)
Who's Who in the World®
Who's Who in the East®
Who's Who in the Midwest®
Who's Who in the South and Southwest®
Who's Who in the West®
Who's Who in American Education®
Who's Who in American Law®
Who's Who in American Nursing®
Who's Who of American Women®
Who's Who in Finance and Industry®
Who's Who in Medicine and Healthcare™
Who's Who in Science and Engineering®
Index to Marquis Who's Who® Publications
The *Official* ABMS Directory of Board Certified Medical Specialists®

Available on CD-ROM

The Complete Marquis Who's Who® on CD-ROM
ABMS Medical Specialists *PLUS*™

Who's Who in America®

1997

51st Edition

Volume 2
L–Z

MARQUIS
Who'sWho®
121 Chanlon Road
New Providence, NJ 07974 U.S.A.

Who'sWho in America®

Marquis Who's Who®

Published by Marquis Who's Who, a division of Reed Elsevier Inc.

Library of Congress Catalog Card Number 4-16934
International Standard Book Number 0-8379-0175-8 (set, Classic Edition)
0-8379-0177-4 (volume 2, Classic Edition)
0-8379-0179-0 (set, Deluxe Edition)
0-8379-0181-2 (volume 2, Deluxe Edition)
International Standard Serial Number 0083-9396

Manufactured in the United States of America

Table of Contents

Preface

"**WHO'S WHO IN AMERICA** *shall endeavor to list those individuals who are of current national reference interest and inquiry either because of meritorious achievement or because of the positions they hold."*

Albert Nelson Marquis
Founder, 1899

A Standard Reference Work

When the first edition of *Who's Who in America* appeared in 1899, it presented itself as a new and untried experiment in the field of American reference book publishing. It was the first publication ever issued which claimed to be, in any comprehensive degree, a general biographical directory of notable American contemporaries. During the generations that have passed, *Who's Who in America* has garnered a worldwide reputation for presenting the most accurate, current biographical data available. Quickly establishing itself as a standard reference work, it has grown steadily in public favor, and today is recognized globally as the premier reference pertaining to notable living Americans.

The 51st Edition continues to uphold the guiding principle set forth by A.N. Marquis in 1899: The editors of *Who's Who in America* continue to strive to identify and chronicle the achievements of men and women who have become the leaders in our society's political, cultural, and economic affairs.

One Principle Governs Selection

In 1899, Marquis Biographees numbered 8,602, or one person per 10,000 of U.S. population. In this 51st Edition, Marquis Who's Who proudly presents the biographies of over 100,000 outstanding individuals. While our Biographees have grown in number, our selection standards remain stringent. Fewer than four in 10,000 people are included in *Who's Who in America.*

Selection is based solely on reference value. Individuals become eligible for listing by virtue of their positions and/or noteworthy achievements that have proven to be of significant value to society. An individual's desire to be listed is not sufficient reason for inclusion. Similarly, wealth or social position are not criteria. Of course, Marquis Who's Who has never charged a fee for publishing a biography, nor is purchase of the book ever a factor in the selection of Biographees.

Compiling the Most Accurate Biographical Data

Through fifty-one editions, the basic *Who's Who in America* compilation process has remained unchanged. Potential Biographees are identified by Marquis researchers and editors. Candidates are sent data forms and are invited to submit complete biographical and career information. These data are reviewed to confirm that candidates meet the stringent selection criteria. Sketches are then prepared and sent to Biographees for prepublication checking.

In some cases, Marquis staff members compile and/or verify the biographical data through independent research. Sketches compiled in this manner are denoted by asterisks. For a small number of cases, where detailed information is not available at publication, the editors have written brief sketches with current career information; these are also indicated by asterisks.

To maintain its reputation for currency, and at the same time to adhere to space limitations, *Who's Who in America* undergoes meticulous review of selection criteria with each edition. Deletion of some names is inevitable; such deletion is not arbitrary. For example, if a Biographee has retired from active participation in a career or public life, the sketch may be excluded. In large part, it is career development that determines inclusion and continuation.

Annual publication enables *Who's Who in America* to bring users more new names and update more existing entries each edition. In all, over 21,500 new names appear in the 51st Edition.

Responding to Your Reference Needs

Who's Who in America provides a number of useful reference features. As a complement to the biographical profiles, the Geographic and Professional Indexes make *Who's Who in America* an even more productive research tool. Through these indexes, users can identify and locate individuals in any of thirty-eight categories, as well as by country, state, or city.

This edition also contains a cumulative Retiree Index of persons whose names were deleted from the 48th through 50th Editions because they have retired from active work. This index enables the user to locate the last published biographical sketch of each listee.

There is also a Necrology of Biographees whose sketches appeared in the 50th Edition and whose deaths were reported prior to the closing of this edition. The sketches have been removed from the book. (For those Biographees whose deaths were reported prior to July 1996, complete biographical information, including date of death and place of interment, can be found in Volume XI of *Who Was Who in America.*)

Finally, many of the women and men profiled in *Who's Who in America* have included in their biographies a listing of their avocations, thus providing additional insights into their personal lives and interests. Some of the sketches also end with an italicized feature, "Thoughts on My Life." The statement is written by the Biographees and reflects their own principles, goals, ideals, and values that have been guidelines for their success and achievement.

Our Challenge

Putting together a reference source as comprehensive as *Who's Who in America* is a monumental challenge. Over our long history, Marquis Who's Who researchers and editors have exercised diligent care in preparing each sketch for publication. Despite all precautions, however, errors do occasionally occur. Users of this directory are invited to notify the publisher of any such errors so that corrections can be made in a subsequent edition.

Standards of Admission

The foremost consideration in determining who will be admitted to the pages of *Who's Who in America* is the extent of an individual's reference interest. Reference value is based on either of two factors: 1) the position of responsibility held or 2) the level of significant achievement attained in a career of noteworthy activity. The majority of Biographees qualify for admission on the basis of the first factor, a specific position of responsibility. Incumbency in the position makes the person someone of high reference interest. The factor of position includes the following categories:

1. High-ranking members of the executive, legislative, and judicial branches of the United States government. This group includes, for example, the President of the United States, members of Congress, cabinet secretaries, chief administrators of selected federal agencies and commissions, and justices of the federal courts.

2. Military officers on active duty with the rank of Major General or higher in the Army, Air Force, and Marine Corps, and of Rear Admiral or higher in the U.S. Navy.

3. Specified state government officials. Among these are governors, lieutenant governors, secretaries of state, attorneys general, and treasurers. Also included under this standard are presidents of state senates, state university system administrators, chief state health officers, and officials of American territories.

4. Judges of state and territorial courts of the highest appellate jurisdiction.

5. High-level officials of principal cities, based on population. These officials include mayors, police chiefs, school superintendents, and other selected positions.

6. Leading government officials of Canada and Mexico. In Canada, this group includes the prime minister, premiers of the provinces, ministers of departments of the federal government, and justices of the highest courts. Examples in the Mexican government are the president of the country and cabinet secretaries of the national government.

7. Principal officers of major national and international businesses as defined by several quantitative criteria.

8. Ranking administrative officials of major universities and colleges. Some of the officers included in this category are president, provost, dean, and selected department heads.

9. Heads of leading philanthropic, cultural, educational, professional, and scientific institutions and associations. These institutions include, for example, selected foundations, museums, symphony orchestras, libraries, and research laboratories.

10. Selected members of certain honorary and professional organizations, such as the National Academy of Sciences, the National Academy of Design, the American College of Trial Lawyers, and the Royal Society of Canada.

11. Chief ecclesiastics of the principal religious denominations.

12. Recipients of major national and international awards, such as the Nobel and Pulitzer Prizes, the Academy Awards and the Antoinette Perry, or Tony Awards. Also included are winners of important professional awards, such as the American Institute of Architecture's Gold Medal for Architecture.

Admission by the second factor—significant achievement—is based on the application of objective criteria established for each field. An artist whose works are included in major museums qualifies for admission for noteworthy accomplishment. The professor who has made important research contributions in his field is of reference interest because of his outstanding achievements. Qualitative standards determine eligibility for every field.

In many instances there is considerable overlap between the two factors used for inclusion in *Who's Who in America*. For example, the head of a major library is in the book because of position, but reaching that responsibility also signifies important achievement. Similarly, a state governor not only holds a position that warrants inclusion; attaining that post also represents significant achievement in the political world. In both cases, the reference value of the biographical sketch is significant. Whether the person has been selected because of position or as a mark of achievement, the Biographee in *Who's Who in America* has noteworthy accomplishments beyond those of the vast majority of contemporaries.

Key to Information

[1] GIBSON, OSCAR JULIUS, [2] physician, medical educator; [3] b. Syracuse, N.Y., Aug. 31, 1937; [4] s. Paul Oliver and Elizabeth H. (Thrun) G.; [5] m. Judith S. Gonzalez, Apr. 28, 1968; [6] children: Richard Gary, Matthew Cary, Samuel Perry. [7] BA magna cum laude, U. Pa., 1960; MD, Harvard U., 1964. [8] Diplomate Am. Bd. Internal Medicine, Am. Bd. Preventive Medicine. [9] Intern Barnes Hosp., St. Louis, 1964-65, resident, 1965-66; clin. assoc. Nat. Heart Inst., NIH, Bethesda, Md., 1966-68; chief resident medicine U. Okla. Hosps., 1968-69; asst. prof. community health Okla. Med. Ctr., 1969-70, assoc. prof., 1970-74, prof., chmn. dept., 1974-80; dean U. Okla. Coll. Medicine, 1978-82; v.p. med. staff affairs Bapt. Med. Ctr., Oklahoma City, 1982-86, exec. v.p., 1986-88, chmn., 1988—; [10] mem. governing bd. Ambulatory Health Care Consortium, Inc., 1979-80; mem. Okla. Bd. Medicolegal Examiners, 1985—. [11] Contrb. articles to profl. jours. [12] Bd. dirs., v.p. Okla. Arthritis Found., 1982—; trustee North Central Mental Health Ctr., 1985—. [13] Served with U.S. Army, 1955-56. [14] Recipient R.T. Chadwick award NIH, 1968; Am. Heart Assn. grantee, 1985-86, 88. [15] Fellow Assn. Tchrs. Preventive Medicine; mem. Am. Fedn. Clin. Research, Assn. Med. Colls., AAAS, AMA, Masons, Shriners, Sigma Xi. [16] Republican. [17] Roman Catholic. [18] Avocations: swimming, weight lifting, travel. [19] Home: 6060 N Ridge Ave Oklahoma City OK 73126 [20] Office: Bapt Med Ctr 1986 Cuba Hwy Oklahoma City OK 73120

KEY

[1] Name
[2] Occupation
[3] Vital statistics
[4] Parents
[5] Marriage
[6] Children
[7] Education
[8] Professional certifications
[9] Career
[10] Career-related
[11] Writings and creative works
[12] Civic and political activities
[13] Military
[14] Awards and fellowships
[15] Professional and association memberships, clubs and lodges
[16] Political affiliation
[17] Religion
[18] Avocations
[19] Home address
[20] Office address

Table of Abbreviations

The following abbreviations and symbols are frequently used in this book.

*An asterisk following a sketch indicates that it was researched by the Marquis Who's Who editorial staff and has not been verified by the Biographee.
A Associate (used with academic degrees only)
AA, A.A. Associate in Arts, Associate of Arts
AAAL American Academy of Arts and Letters
AAAS American Association for the Advancement of Science
AACD American Association for Counseling and Development
AACN American Association of Critical Care Nurses
AAHA American Academy of Health Administrators
AAHP American Association of Hospital Planners
AAHPERD American Alliance for Health, Physical Education, Recreation, and Dance
AAS Associate of Applied Science
AASL American Association of School Librarians
AASPA American Association of School Personnel Administrators
AAU Amateur Athletic Union
AAUP American Association of University Professors
AAUW American Association of University Women
AB, A.B. Arts, Bachelor of
AB Alberta
ABA American Bar Association
ABC American Broadcasting Company
AC Air Corps
acad. academy, academic
acct. accountant
acctg. accounting
ACDA Arms Control and Disarmament Agency
ACHA American College of Hospital Administrators
ACLS Advanced Cardiac Life Support
ACLU American Civil Liberties Union
ACOG American College of Ob-Gyn
ACP American College of Physicians
ACS American College of Surgeons
ADA American Dental Association
a.d.c. aide-de-camp
adj. adjunct, adjutant
adj. gen. adjutant general
adm. admiral
adminstr. administrator
adminstrn. administration
adminstrv. administrative
ADN Associate's Degree in Nursing
ADP Automatic Data Processing
adv. advocate, advisory
advt. advertising
AE, A.E. Agricultural Engineer
A.E. and P. Ambassador Extraordinary and Plenipotentiary
AEC Atomic Energy Commission
aero. aeronautical, aeronautic
aerodyn. aerodynamic
AFB Air Force Base
AFL-CIO American Federation of Labor and Congress of Industrial Organizations
AFTRA American Federation of TV and Radio Artists
AFSCME American Federation of State, County and Municipal Employees
agr. agriculture
agrl. agricultural
agt. agent
AGVA American Guild of Variety Artists
agy. agency
A&I Agricultural and Industrial
AIA American Institute of Architects
AIAA American Institute of Aeronautics and Astronautics
AIChE American Institute of Chemical Engineers
AICPA American Institute of Certified Public Accountants
AID Agency for International Development
AIDS Acquired Immune Deficiency Syndrome
AIEE American Institute of Electrical Engineers
AIM American Institute of Management
AIME American Institute of Mining, Metallurgy, and Petroleum Engineers
AK Alaska
AL Alabama
ALA American Library Association
Ala. Alabama
alt. alternate
Alta. Alberta
A&M Agricultural and Mechanical
AM, A.M. Arts, Master of
Am. American, America
AMA American Medical Association
amb. ambassador
A.M.E. African Methodist Episcopal
Amtrak National Railroad Passenger Corporation
AMVETS American Veterans of World War II, Korea, Vietnam
ANA American Nurses Association
anat. anatomical
ANCC American Nurses Credentialing Center
ann. annual
ANTA American National Theatre and Academy
anthrop. anthropological
AP Associated Press
APA American Psychological Association
APGA American Personnel Guidance Association
APHA American Public Health Association
APO Army Post Office
apptd. appointed
Apr. April
apt. apartment
AR Arkansas
ARC American Red Cross
arch. architect
archeol. archeological
archtl. architectural
Ariz. Arizona
Ark. Arkansas
ArtsD, ArtsD. Arts, Doctor of
arty. artillery
AS American Samoa
AS Associate in Science
ASCAP American Society of Composers, Authors and Publishers
ASCD Association for Supervision and Curriculum Development
ASCE American Society of Civil Engineers
ASHRAE American Society of Heating, Refrigeration, and Air Conditioning Engineers
ASME American Society of Mechanical Engineers
ASNSA American Society for Nursing Service Administrators
ASPA American Society for Public Administration
ASPCA American Society for the Prevention of Cruelty to Animals
assn. association
assoc. associate
asst. assistant
ASTD American Society for Training and Development
ASTM American Society for Testing and Materials
astron. astronomical
astrophys. astrophysical
ATLA Association of Trial Lawyers of America
ATSC Air Technical Service Command
AT&T American Telephone & Telegraph Company
atty. attorney
Aug. August
AUS Army of the United States
aux. auxiliary
Ave. Avenue
AVMA American Veterinary Medical Association
AZ Arizona
AWHONN Association of Women's Health Obstetric and Neonatal Nurses

B. Bachelor
b. born
BA, B.A. Bachelor of Arts
BAgr, B.Agr. Bachelor of Agriculture
Balt. Baltimore
Bapt. Baptist
BArch, B.Arch. Bachelor of Architecture
BAS, B.A.S. Bachelor of Agricultural Science
BBA, B.B.A. Bachelor of Business Administration
BBB Better Business Bureau
BBC British Broadcasting Corporation

BC, B.C. British Columbia
BCE, B.C.E. Bachelor of Civil Engineering
BChir, B.Chir. Bachelor of Surgery
BCL, B.C.L. Bachelor of Civil Law
BCLS Basic Cardiac Life Support
BCS, B.C.S. Bachelor of Commercial Science
BD, B.D. Bachelor of Divinity
bd. board
BE, B.E. Bachelor of Education
BEE, B.E.E. Bachelor of Electrical Engineering
BFA, B.F.A. Bachelor of Fine Arts
bibl. biblical
bibliog. bibliographical
biog. biographical
biol. biological
BJ, B.J. Bachelor of Journalism
Bklyn. Brooklyn
BL, B.L. Bachelor of Letters
bldg. building
BLS, B.L.S. Bachelor of Library Science
BLS Basic Life Support
Blvd. Boulevard
BMI Broadcast Music, Inc.
BMW Bavarian Motor Works (Bayerische Motoren Werke)
bn. battalion
B.&O.R.R. Baltimore & Ohio Railroad
bot. botanical
BPE, B.P.E. Bachelor of Physical Education
BPhil, B.Phil. Bachelor of Philosophy
br. branch
BRE, B.R.E. Bachelor of Religious Education
brig. gen. brigadier general
Brit. British, Brittanica
Bros. Brothers
BS, B.S. Bachelor of Science
BSA, B.S.A. Bachelor of Agricultural Science
BSBA Bachelor of Science in Business Administration
BSChemE Bachelor of Science in Chemical Engineering
BSD, B.S.D. Bachelor of Didactic Science
BSEE Bachelor of Science in Electrical Engineering
BSN Bachelor of Science in Nursing
BST, B.S.T. Bachelor of Sacred Theology
BTh, B.Th. Bachelor of Theology
bull. bulletin
bur. bureau
bus. business
B.W.I. British West Indies

CA California
CAA Civil Aeronautics Administration
CAB Civil Aeronautics Board
CAD-CAM Computer Aided Design–Computer Aided Model
Calif. California
C.Am. Central America
Can. Canada, Canadian
CAP Civil Air Patrol
capt. captain
cardiol. cardiological
cardiovasc. cardiovascular
CARE Cooperative American Relief Everywhere
Cath. Catholic
cav. cavalry
CBC Canadian Broadcasting Company
CBI China, Burma, India Theatre of Operations
CBS Columbia Broadcasting Company
C.C. Community College
CCC Commodity Credit Corporation
CCNY City College of New York
CCRN Critical Care Registered Nurse
CCU Cardiac Care Unit
CD Civil Defense
CE, C.E. Corps of Engineers, Civil Engineer
CEN Certified Emergency Nurse
CENTO Central Treaty Organization
CEO chief executive officer
CERN European Organization of Nuclear Research
cert. certificate, certification, certified
CETA Comprehensive Employment Training Act
CFA Chartered Financial Analyst
CFL Canadian Football League
CFO chief financial officer
CFP Certified Financial Planner
ch. church
ChD, Ch.D. Doctor of Chemistry
chem. chemical
ChemE, Chem.E. Chemical Engineer
ChFC Chartered Financial Consultant
Chgo. Chicago
chirurg. chirurgical
chmn. chairman
chpt. chapter
CIA Central Intelligence Agency
Cin. Cincinnati
cir. circle, circuit
CLE Continuing Legal Education
Cleve. Cleveland
climatol. climatological
clin. clinical
clk. clerk
C.L.U. Chartered Life Underwriter
CM, C.M. Master in Surgery
CM Northern Mariana Islands
CMA Certified Medical Assistant
cmty. community
CNA Certified Nurse's Aide
CNOR Certified Nurse (Operating Room)
C.&N.W.Ry. Chicago & North Western Railway
CO Colorado
Co. Company
COF Catholic Order of Foresters
C. of C. Chamber of Commerce
col. colonel
coll. college
Colo. Colorado
com. committee
comd. commanded
comdg. commanding
comdr. commander
comdt. commandant
comm. communications
commd. commissioned
comml. commercial
commn. commission
commr. commissioner
compt. comptroller
condr. conductor
Conf. Conference
Congl. Congregational, Congressional
Conglist. Congregationalist
Conn. Connecticut
cons. consultant, consulting
consol. consolidated
constl. constitutional
constn. constitution
constrn. construction
contbd. contributed
contbg. contributing
contbn. contribution
contbr. contributor
contr. controller
Conv. Convention
COO chief operating officer
coop. cooperative
coord. coordinator
CORDS Civil Operations and Revolutionary Development Support
CORE Congress of Racial Equality
corp. corporation, corporate
corr. correspondent, corresponding, correspondence
C.&O.Ry. Chesapeake & Ohio Railway
coun. council
CPA Certified Public Accountant
CPCU Chartered Property and Casualty Underwriter
CPH, C.P.H. Certificate of Public Health
cpl. corporal
CPR Cardio-Pulmonary Resuscitation
C.P.Ry. Canadian Pacific Railway
CRT Cathode Ray Terminal
C.S. Christian Science
CSB, C.S.B. Bachelor of Christian Science
C.S.C. Civil Service Commission
CT Connecticut
ct. court
ctr. center
ctrl. central
CWS Chemical Warfare Service
C.Z. Canal Zone

D. Doctor
d. daughter
DAgr, D.Agr. Doctor of Agriculture
DAR Daughters of the American Revolution
dau. daughter
DAV Disabled American Veterans
DC, D.C. District of Columbia
DCL, D.C.L. Doctor of Civil Law
DCS, D.C.S. Doctor of Commercial Science
DD, D.D. Doctor of Divinity
DDS, D.D.S. Doctor of Dental Surgery
DE Delaware
Dec. December
dec. deceased
def. defense
Del. Delaware
del. delegate, delegation
Dem. Democrat, Democratic
DEng, D.Eng. Doctor of Engineering
denom. denomination, denominational
dep. deputy
dept. department
dermatol. dermatological
desc. descendant
devel. development, developmental
DFA, D.F.A. Doctor of Fine Arts
D.F.C. Distinguished Flying Cross
DHL, D.H.L. Doctor of Hebrew Literature
dir. director
dist. district
distbg. distributing
distbn. distribution
distbr. distributor
disting. distinguished
div. division, divinity, divorce
divsn. division
DLitt, D.Litt. Doctor of Literature
DMD, D.M.D. Doctor of Dental Medicine
DMS, D.M.S. Doctor of Medical Science
DO, D.O. Doctor of Osteopathy
docs. documents
DON Director of Nursing
DPH, D.P.H. Diploma in Public Health
DPhil, D.Phil. Doctor of Philosophy
D.R. Daughters of the Revolution
Dr. Drive, Doctor
DRE, D.R.E. Doctor of Religious Education
DrPH, Dr.P.H. Doctor of Public Health, Doctor of Public Hygiene
D.S.C. Distinguished Service Cross

DSc, D.Sc. Doctor of Science
DSChemE Doctor of Science in Chemical Engineering
D.S.M. Distinguished Service Medal
DST, D.S.T. Doctor of Sacred Theology
DTM, D.T.M. Doctor of Tropical Medicine
DVM, D.V.M. Doctor of Veterinary Medicine
DVS, D.V.S. Doctor of Veterinary Surgery

E, E. East
ea. eastern
E. and P. Extraordinary and Plenipotentiary
Eccles. Ecclesiastical
ecol. ecological
econ. economic
ECOSOC Economic and Social Council (of the UN)
ED, E.D. Doctor of Engineering
ed. educated
EdB, Ed.B. Bachelor of Education
EdD, Ed.D. Doctor of Education
edit. edition
editl. editorial
EdM, Ed.M. Master of Education
edn. education
ednl. educational
EDP Electronic Data Processing
EdS, Ed.S. Specialist in Education
EE, E.E. Electrical Engineer
E.E. and M.P. Envoy Extraordinary and Minister Plenipotentiary
EEC European Economic Community
EEG Electroencephalogram
EEO Equal Employment Opportunity
EEOC Equal Employment Opportunity Commission
E.Ger. German Democratic Republic
EKG Electrocardiogram
elec. electrical
electrochem. electrochemical
electrophys. electrophysical
elem. elementary
EM, E.M. Engineer of Mines
EMT Emergency Medical Technician
ency. encyclopedia
Eng. England
engr. engineer
engring. engineering
entomol. entomological
environ. environmental
EPA Environmental Protection Agency
epidemiol. epidemiological
Episc. Episcopalian
ERA Equal Rights Amendment
ERDA Energy Research and Development Administration
ESEA Elementary and Secondary Education Act
ESL English as Second Language
ESPN Entertainment and Sports Programming Network
ESSA Environmental Science Services Administration
ethnol. ethnological
ETO European Theatre of Operations
Evang. Evangelical
exam. examination, examining
Exch. Exchange
exec. executive
exhbn. exhibition
expdn. expedition
expn. exposition
expt. experiment
exptl. experimental
Expy. Expressway
Ext. Extension

F.A. Field Artillery
FAA Federal Aviation Administration
FAO Food and Agriculture Organization (of the UN)
FBA Federal Bar Association
FBI Federal Bureau of Investigation
FCA Farm Credit Administration
FCC Federal Communications Commission
FCDA Federal Civil Defense Administration
FDA Food and Drug Administration
FDIA Federal Deposit Insurance Administration
FDIC Federal Deposit Insurance Corporation
FE, F.E. Forest Engineer
FEA Federal Energy Administration
Feb. February
fed. federal
fedn. federation
FERC Federal Energy Regulatory Commission
fgn. foreign
FHA Federal Housing Administration
fin. financial, finance
FL Florida
Fl. Floor
Fla. Florida
FMC Federal Maritime Commission
FNP Family Nurse Practitioner
FOA Foreign Operations Administration
found. foundation
FPC Federal Power Commission
FPO Fleet Post Office
frat. fraternity
FRS Federal Reserve System
FSA Federal Security Agency
Ft. Fort
FTC Federal Trade Commission
Fwy. Freeway

G-1 (or other number) Division of General Staff
GA, Ga. Georgia
GAO General Accounting Office
gastroent. gastroenterological
GATE Gifted and Talented Educators
GATT General Agreement on Tariffs and Trade
GE General Electric Company
gen. general
geneal. genealogical
geod. geodetic
geog. geographic, geographical
geol. geological
geophys. geophysical
geriat. geriatrics
gerontol. gerontological
G.H.Q. General Headquarters
GM General Motors Corporation
GMAC General Motors Acceptance Corporation
G.N.Ry. Great Northern Railway
gov. governor
govt. government
govtl. governmental
GPO Government Printing Office
grad. graduate, graduated
GSA General Services Administration
Gt. Great
GTE General Telephone and ElectricCompany
GU Guam
gynecol. gynecological

HBO Home Box Office
hdqs. headquarters
HEW Department of Health, Education and Welfare
HHD, H.H.D. Doctor of Humanities
HHFA Housing and Home Finance Agency
HHS Department of Health and Human Services
HI Hawaii
hist. historical, historic
HM, H.M. Master of Humanities
HMO Health Maintenance Organization
homeo. homeopathic
hon. honorary, honorable
Ho. of Dels. House of Delegates
Ho. of Reps. House of Representatives
hort. horticultural
hosp. hospital
H.S. High School
HUD Department of Housing and Urban Development
Hwy. Highway
hydrog. hydrographic

IA Iowa
IAEA International Atomic Energy Agency
IATSE International Alliance of Theatrical and Stage Employees and Moving Picture Operators of the United States and Canada
IBM International Business Machines Corporation
IBRD International Bank for Reconstruction and Development
ICA International Cooperation Administration
ICC Interstate Commerce Commission
ICCE International Council for Computers in Education
ICU Intensive Care Unit
ID Idaho
IEEE Institute of Electrical and Electronics Engineers
IFC International Finance Corporation
IGY International Geophysical Year
IL Illinois
Ill. Illinois
illus. illustrated
ILO International Labor Organization
IMF International Monetary Fund
IN Indiana
Inc. Incorporated
Ind. Indiana
ind. independent
Indpls. Indianapolis
indsl. industrial
inf. infantry
info. information
ins. insurance
insp. inspector
insp. gen. inspector general
inst. institute
instl. institutional
instn. institution
instr. instructor
instrn. instruction
instrnl. instructional
internat. international
intro. introduction
IRE Institute of Radio Engineers
IRS Internal Revenue Service
ITT International Telephone & Telegraph Corporation

JAG Judge Advocate General
JAGC Judge Advocate General Corps
Jan. January
Jaycees Junior Chamber of Commerce
JB, J.B. Jurum Baccalaureus

JCB, J.C.B. Juris Canoni Baccalaureus
JCD, J.C.D. Juris Canonici Doctor, Juris Civilis Doctor
JCL, J.C.L. Juris Canonici Licentiatus
JD, J.D. Juris Doctor
jg. junior grade
jour. journal
jr. junior
JSD, J.S.D. Juris Scientiae Doctor
JUD, J.U.D. Juris Utriusque Doctor
jud. judicial

Kans. Kansas
K.C. Knights of Columbus
K.P. Knights of Pythias
KS Kansas
K.T. Knight Templar
KY, Ky. Kentucky

LA, La. Louisiana
L.A. Los Angeles
lab. laboratory
L.Am. Latin America
lang. language
laryngol. laryngological
LB Labrador
LDS Latter Day Saints
LDS Church Church of Jesus Christ of Latter Day Saints
lectr. lecturer
legis. legislation, legislative
LHD, L.H.D. Doctor of Humane Letters
L.I. Long Island
libr. librarian, library
lic. licensed, license
L.I.R.R. Long Island Railroad
lit. literature
litig. litigation
LittB, Litt.B. Bachelor of Letters
LittD, Litt.D. Doctor of Letters
LLB, LL.B. Bachelor of Laws
LLD, L.L.D. Doctor of Laws
LLM, L.L.M. Master of Laws
Ln. Lane
L.&N.R.R. Louisville & Nashville Railroad
LPGA Ladies Professional Golf Association
LPN Licensed Practical Nurse
LS, L.S. Library Science (in degree)
lt. lieutenant
Ltd. Limited
Luth. Lutheran
LWV League of Women Voters

M. Master
m. married
MA, M.A. Master of Arts
MA Massachusetts
MADD Mothers Against Drunk Driving
mag. magazine
MAgr, M.Agr. Master of Agriculture
maj. major
Man. Manitoba
Mar. March
MArch, M.Arch. Master in Architecture
Mass. Massachusetts
math. mathematics, mathematical
MATS Military Air Transport Service
MB, M.B. Bachelor of Medicine
MB Manitoba
MBA, M.B.A. Master of Business Administration
MBS Mutual Broadcasting System
M.C. Medical Corps
MCE, M.C.E. Master of Civil Engineering
mcht. merchant
mcpl. municipal
MCS, M.C.S. Master of Commercial Science
MD, M.D. Doctor of Medicine
MD, Md. Maryland
MDiv Master of Divinity
MDip, M.Dip. Master in Diplomacy
mdse. merchandise
MDV, M.D.V. Doctor of Veterinary Medicine
ME, M.E. Mechanical Engineer
ME Maine
M.E.Ch. Methodist Episcopal Church
mech. mechanical
MEd., M.Ed. Master of Education
med. medical
MEE, M.E.E. Master of Electrical Engineering
mem. member
meml. memorial
merc. mercantile
met. metropolitan
metall. metallurgical
MetE, Met.E. Metallurgical Engineer
meteorol. meteorological
Meth. Methodist
Mex. Mexico
MF, M.F. Master of Forestry
MFA, M.F.A. Master of Fine Arts
mfg. manufacturing
mfr. manufacturer
mgmt. management
mgr. manager
MHA, M.H.A. Master of Hospital Administration
M.I. Military Intelligence
MI Michigan
Mich. Michigan
micros. microscopic, microscopical
mid. middle
mil. military
Milw. Milwaukee
Min. Minister
mineral. mineralogical
Minn. Minnesota
MIS Management Information Systems
Miss. Mississippi
MIT Massachusetts Institute of Technology
mktg. marketing
ML, M.L. Master of Laws
MLA Modern Language Association
M.L.D. Magister Legnum Diplomatic
MLitt, M.Litt. Master of Literature, Master of Letters
MLS, M.L.S. Master of Library Science
MME, M.M.E. Master of Mechanical Engineering
MN Minnesota
mng. managing
MO, Mo. Missouri
moblzn. mobilization
Mont. Montana
MP Northern Mariana Islands
M.P. Member of Parliament
MPA Master of Public Administration
MPE, M.P.E. Master of Physical Education
MPH, M.P.H. Master of Public Health
MPhil, M.Phil. Master of Philosophy
MPL, M.P.L. Master of Patent Law
Mpls. Minneapolis
MRE, M.R.E. Master of Religious Education
MRI Magnetic Resonance Imaging
MS, M.S. Master of Science
MS, Ms. Mississippi
MSc, M.Sc. Master of Science
MSChemE Master of Science in Chemical Engineering
MSEE Master of Science in Electrical Engineering
MSF, M.S.F. Master of Science of Forestry
MSN Master of Science in Nursing
MST, M.S.T. Master of Sacred Theology
MSW, M.S.W. Master of Social Work
MT Montana
Mt. Mount
MTO Mediterranean Theatre of Operation
MTV Music Television
mus. museum, musical
MusB, Mus.B. Bachelor of Music
MusD, Mus.D. Doctor of Music
MusM, Mus.M. Master of Music
mut. mutual
MVP Most Valuable Player
mycol. mycological

N. North
NAACOG Nurses Association of the American College of Obstetricians and Gynecologists
NAACP National Association for the Advancement of Colored People
NACA National Advisory Committee for Aeronautics
NACDL National Association of Criminal Defense Lawyers
NACU National Association of Colleges and Universities
NAD National Academy of Design
NAE National Academy of Engineering, National Association of Educators
NAESP National Association of Elementary School Principals
NAFE National Association of Female Executives
N.Am. North America
NAM National Association of Manufacturers
NAMH National Association for Mental Health
NAPA National Association of Performing Artists
NARAS National Academy of Recording Arts and Sciences
NAREB National Association of Real Estate Boards
NARS National Archives and Record Service
NAS National Academy of Sciences
NASA National Aeronautics and Space Administration
NASP National Association of School Psychologists
NASW National Association of Social Workers
nat. national
NATAS National Academy of Television Arts and Sciences
NATO North Atlantic Treaty Organization
NATOUSA North African Theatre of Operations, United States Army
nav. navigation
NB, N.B. New Brunswick
NBA National Basketball Association
NBC National Broadcasting Company
NC, N.C. North Carolina
NCAA National College Athletic Association
NCCJ National Conference of Christians and Jews
ND, N.D. North Dakota
NDEA National Defense Education Act
NE Nebraska
NE, N.E. Northeast
NEA National Education Association
Nebr. Nebraska
NEH National Endowment for Humanities
neurol. neurological
Nev. Nevada
NF Newfoundland

NFL National Football League
Nfld. Newfoundland
NG National Guard
NH, N.H. New Hampshire
NHL National Hockey League
NIH National Institutes of Health
NIMH National Institute of Mental Health
NJ, N.J. New Jersey
NLRB National Labor Relations Board
NM New Mexico
N.Mex. New Mexico
No. Northern
NOAA National Oceanographic and Atmospheric Administration
NORAD North America Air Defense
Nov. November
NOW National Organization for Women
N.P.Ry. Northern Pacific Railway
nr. near
NRA National Rifle Association
NRC National Research Council
NS, N.S. Nova Scotia
NSC National Security Council
NSF National Science Foundation
NSTA National Science Teachers Association
NSW New South Wales
N.T. New Testament
NT Northwest Territories
nuc. nuclear
numis. numismatic
NV Nevada
NW, N.W. Northwest
N.W.T. Northwest Territories
NY, N.Y. New York
N.Y.C. New York City
NYU New York University
N.Z. New Zealand

OAS Organization of American States
ob-gyn obstetrics-gynecology
obs. observatory
obstet. obstetrical
occupl. occupational
oceanog. oceanographic
Oct. October
OD, O.D. Doctor of Optometry
OECD Organization for Economic Cooperation and Development
OEEC Organization of European Economic Cooperation
OEO Office of Economic Opportunity
ofcl. official
OH Ohio
OK Oklahoma
Okla. Oklahoma
ON Ontario
Ont. Ontario
oper. operating
ophthal. ophthalmological
ops. operations
OR Oregon
orch. orchestra
Oreg. Oregon
orgn. organization
orgnl. organizational
ornithol. ornithological
orthop. orthopedic
OSHA Occupational Safety and Health Administration
OSRD Office of Scientific Research and Development
OSS Office of Strategic Services
osteo. osteopathic
otol. otological
otolaryn. otolaryngological

PA, Pa. Pennsylvania
P.A. Professional Association
paleontol. paleontological
path. pathological
PBS Public Broadcasting System
P.C. Professional Corporation
PE Prince Edward Island
pediat. pediatrics
P.E.I. Prince Edward Island
PEN Poets, Playwrights, Editors, Essayists and Novelists (international association)
penol. penological
P.E.O. women's organization (full name not disclosed)
pers. personnel
pfc. private first class
PGA Professional Golfers' Association of America
PHA Public Housing Administration
pharm. pharmaceutical
PharmD, Pharm.D. Doctor of Pharmacy
PharmM, Pharm.M. Master of Pharmacy
PhB, Ph.B. Bachelor of Philosophy
PhD, Ph.D. Doctor of Philosophy
PhDChemE Doctor of Science in Chemical Engineering
PhM, Ph.M. Master of Philosophy
Phila. Philadelphia
philharm. philharmonic
philol. philological
philos. philosophical
photog. photographic
phys. physical
physiol. physiological
Pitts. Pittsburgh
Pk. Park
Pky. Parkway
Pl. Place
P.&L.E.R.R. Pittsburgh & Lake Erie Railroad
Plz. Plaza
PNP Pediatric Nurse Practitioner
P.O. Post Office
PO Box Post Office Box
polit. political
poly. polytechnic, polytechnical
PQ Province of Quebec
PR, P.R. Puerto Rico
prep. preparatory
pres. president
Presbyn. Presbyterian
presdl. presidential
prin. principal
procs. proceedings
prod. produced (play production)
prodn. production
prodr. producer
prof. professor
profl. professional
prog. progressive
propr. proprietor
pros. atty. prosecuting attorney
pro tem. pro tempore
PSRO Professional Services Review Organization
psychiat. psychiatric
psychol. psychological
PTA Parent-Teachers Association
ptnr. partner
PTO Pacific Theatre of Operations, Parent Teacher Organization
pub. publisher, publishing, published
pub. public
publ. publication
pvt. private

quar. quarterly
qm. quartermaster
Q.M.C. Quartermaster Corps
Que. Quebec

radiol. radiological
RAF Royal Air Force
RCA Radio Corporation of America
RCAF Royal Canadian Air Force
RD Rural Delivery
Rd. Road
R&D Research & Development
REA Rural Electrification Administration
rec. recording
ref. reformed
regt. regiment
regtl. regimental
rehab. rehabilitation
rels. relations
Rep. Republican
rep. representative
Res. Reserve
ret. retired
Rev. Reverend
rev. review, revised
RFC Reconstruction Finance Corporation
RFD Rural Free Delivery
rhinol. rhinological
RI, R.I. Rhode Island
RISD Rhode Island School of Design
Rlwy. Railway
Rm. Room
RN, R.N. Registered Nurse
roentgenol. roentgenological
ROTC Reserve Officers Training Corps
RR Rural Route
R.R. Railroad
rsch. research
rschr. researcher
Rt. Route

S. South
s. son
SAC Strategic Air Command
SAG Screen Actors Guild
SALT Strategic Arms Limitation Talks
S.Am. South America
san. sanitary
SAR Sons of the American Revolution
Sask. Saskatchewan
savs. savings
SB, S.B. Bachelor of Science
SBA Small Business Administration
SC, S.C. South Carolina
SCAP Supreme Command Allies Pacific
ScB, Sc.B. Bachelor of Science
SCD, S.C.D. Doctor of Commercial Science
ScD, Sc.D. Doctor of Science
sch. school
sci. science, scientific
SCLC Southern Christian Leadership Conference
SCV Sons of Confederate Veterans
SD, S.D. South Dakota
SE, S.E. Southeast
SEATO Southeast Asia Treaty Organization
SEC Securities and Exchange Commission
sec. secretary
sect. section
seismol. seismological
sem. seminary
Sept. September
s.g. senior grade
sgt. sergeant
SHAEF Supreme Headquarters Allied Expeditionary Forces
SHAPE Supreme Headquarters Allied Powers in Europe
S.I. Staten Island

S.J. Society of Jesus (Jesuit)
SJD Scientiae Juridicae Doctor
SK Saskatchewan
SM, S.M. Master of Science
SNP Society of Nursing Professionals
So. Southern
soc. society
sociol. sociological
S.P.Co. Southern Pacific Company
spkr. speaker
spl. special
splty. specialty
Sq. Square
S.R. Sons of the Revolution
sr. senior
SS Steamship
SSS Selective Service System
St. Saint, Street
sta. station
stats. statistics
statis. statistical
STB, S.T.B. Bachelor of Sacred Theology
stblzn. stabilization
STD, S.T.D. Doctor of Sacred Theology
std. standard
Ste. Suite
subs. subsidiary
SUNY State University of New York
supr. supervisor
supt. superintendent
surg. surgical
svc. service
SW, S.W. Southwest
sys. system

TAPPI Technical Association of the Pulp and Paper Industry
tb. tuberculosis
tchg. teaching
tchr. teacher
tech. technical, technology
technol. technological
tel. telephone
Tel. & Tel. Telephone & Telegraph
telecom. telecommunications
temp. temporary
Tenn. Tennessee
Ter. Territory
Ter. Terrace
TESOL Teachers of English to Speakers of Other Languages
Tex. Texas
ThD, Th.D. Doctor of Theology
theol. theological
ThM, Th.M. Master of Theology
TN Tennessee
tng. training
topog. topographical
trans. transaction, transferred
transl. translation, translated
transp. transportation
treas. treasurer
TT Trust Territory
TV television
TVA Tennessee Valley Authority
TWA Trans World Airlines
twp. township
TX Texas
typog. typographical

U. University
UAW United Auto Workers
UCLA University of California at Los Angeles
UDC United Daughters of the Confederacy
U.K. United Kingdom
UN United Nations
UNESCO United Nations Educational, Scientific and Cultural Organization
UNICEF United Nations International Children's Emergency Fund
univ. university
UNRRA United Nations Relief and Rehabilitation Administration
UPI United Press International
U.P.R.R. United Pacific Railroad
urol. urological
U.S. United States
U.S.A. United States of America
USAAF United States Army Air Force
USAF United States Air Force
USAFR United States Air Force Reserve
USAR United States Army Reserve
USCG United States Coast Guard
USCGR United States Coast Guard Reserve
USES United States Employment Service
USIA United States Information Agency
USMC United States Marine Corps
USMCR United States Marine Corps Reserve
USN United States Navy
USNG United States National Guard
USNR United States Naval Reserve
USO United Service Organizations
USPHS United States Public Health Service
USS United States Ship
USSR Union of the Soviet Socialist Republics
USTA United States Tennis Association
USV United States Volunteers
UT Utah

VA Veterans Administration
VA, Va. Virginia
vet. veteran, veterinary
VFW Veterans of Foreign Wars
VI, V.I. Virgin Islands
vice pres. vice president
vis. visiting
VISTA Volunteers in Service to America
VITA Volunteers in Technical Assistance
vocat. vocational
vol. volunteer, volume
v.p. vice president
vs. versus
VT, Vt. Vermont

W, W. West
WA Washington (state)
WAC Women's Army Corps
Wash. Washington (state)
WATS Wide Area Telecommunications Service
WAVES Women's Reserve, US Naval Reserve
WCTU Women's Christian Temperance Union
we. western
W. Ger. Germany, Federal Republic of
WHO World Health Organization
WI Wisconsin
W.I. West Indies
Wis. Wisconsin
WSB Wage Stabilization Board
WV West Virginia
W.Va. West Virginia
WWI World War I
WWII World War II
WY Wyoming
Wyo. Wyoming

YK Yukon Territory
YMCA Young Men's Christian Association
YMHA Young Men's Hebrew Association
YM & YWHA Young Men's and Young Women's Hebrew Association
yr. year
YT, Y.T. Yukon Territory
YWCA Young Women's Christian Association

zool. zoological

Alphabetical Practices

Names are arranged alphabetically according to the surnames, and under identical surnames according to the first given name. If both surname and first given name are identical, names are arranged alphabetically according to the second given name.

Surnames beginning with De, Des, Du, however capitalized or spaced, are recorded with the prefix preceding the surname and arranged alphabetically under the letter D.

Surnames beginning with Mac and Mc are arranged alphabetically under M.

Surnames beginning with Saint or St. appear after names that begin Sains, and are arranged according to the second part of the name, e.g. St. Clair before Saint Dennis.

Surnames beginning with Van, Von, or von are arranged alphabetically under the letter V.

Compound surnames are arranged according to the first member of the compound.

Many hyphenated Arabic names begin Al-, El-, or al-. These names are alphabetized according to each Biographee's designation of last name. Thus Al-Bahar, Neta may be listed either under Al- or under Bahar, depending on the preference of the listee.

Also, Arabic names have a variety of possible spellings when transposed to English. Spelling of these names is always based on the practice of the Biographee. Some Biographees use a Western form of word order, while others prefer the Arabic word sequence.

Similarly, Asian names may have no comma between family and given names, but some Biographees have chosen to add the comma. In each case, punctuation follows the preference of the Biographee.

Parentheses used in connection with a name indicate which part of the full name is usually deleted in common usage. Hence Chambers, E(lizabeth) Anne indicates that the usual form of the given name is E. Anne. In such a case, the parentheses are ignored in alphabetizing and the name would be arranged as Chambers, Elizabeth Anne. However, if the name is recorded Chambers, (Elizabeth) Anne, signifying that the entire name Elizabeth is not commonly used, the alphabetizing would be arranged as though the name were Chambers, Anne. If an entire middle or last name is enclosed in parentheses, that portion of the name is used in the alphabetical arrangement. Hence Chambers, Elizabeth (Anne) would be arranged as Chambers, Elizabeth Anne.

Where more than one spelling, word order, or name of an individual is frequently encountered, the sketch has been entered under the form preferred by the Biographee, with cross-references under alternate forms.

Who'sWho in America®

Biographies L–Z

LAABS, ALLISON C., hospital administrator; b. Milw., Nov. 30, 1944. BA, Catholic U. Am., 1967, MA, 1968; M Health Adminstrn., Cornell U., 1974. Various positions St. Anthony's Meml. Hosp., Effingham, Ill., 1968-71, asst. adminstr., 1974-75; exec. v.p. St. Mary's Hosp. Med. Ctr., Grenn Bay, Wis., 1975-84; assoc. adminstr. St. John's Hosp., Springfield, Ill., 1984-85, adminstr., 1985-90, adminstr., CEO, 1990—. Mem. Wis. Hosp. Assn. Home: 10 Danbury Dr Springfield IL 62704-5438 Office: St John's Hosp 800 E Carpenter St Springfield IL 62769*

LAALY, HESHMAT OLLAH, chemist, roofing materials executive, consultant; b. Kermanshah, Iran, June 23, 1927; came to Germany, 1951, Can., 1967, U.S., 1984; s. Jacob and Saltanat (Afshani) L.; m. Parvaneh Modarai, Oct. 7, 1963; (div. 1971); children: Ramesh, Edmond S.; m. Parivash M. Farahmand, Feb. 7, 1982. BS in Chemistry, U. Stuttgart, Germany, 1955; MS in Chemistry, U. Stuttgart, Republic of Germany, 1958, PhD in Chemistry, 1962. Chief chemist Kress Sohne, Krefeld, Germany, 1963-67; analytical chemist Gulf Oil Research Ctr., Montreal, Que., Can., 1967-70; material scientist Bell-Northern Research, Ottawa, Ont., Can., 1970-71; research officer NRC of Can., Ottawa, 1972-84; pres. Roofing Materials Sci. and Tech., L.A., 1984—; Patentee in field. Author: The Science and Technology of Traditional and Modern Roofing Systems, 1992 (World Lifetime Achievement award Am. Biog. Inst. 1992); patentee bi-functional photovoltaic single ply roofing membrane. Mem. AAAS (Can. chpt.), ASTM, Inst. Roofing and Waterproofing Cons., Single-Ply Roofing Inst., Assn. Profl. Engrs. Ontario, Am. Chem. Soc., Internat. Union of Testing and Rsch. Labs. for Material and Structures (tech. com. 75), Constrn. Specifications Inst., Nat. Roofing Contractors Assn., UN Indsl. Devels. Orgn., Internat. Conf. Bldg. Ofcls., Roofing Cons. Inst., Inst. for Roofing and Waterproofing Cons., Can. Standard Assn., Can. Gen. Standards Bd. Office: Roofing Materials Sci & Tech 9037 Monte Mar Dr Los Angeles CA 90035-4235

LAANANEN, DAVID HORTON, mechanical engineer, educator; b. Winchester, Mass., Nov. 11, 1942; s. Joseph and Helen Katherine (Horton) L.; m. Mary Ellen Storck, Sept. 9, 1967 (div. 1981); children: Gregg David, Robin Kaye; m. Delores Ann Talbert, May 21, 1988. BS in Mech. Engring., Worcester Poly. Inst., 1964; MS, Northeastern U., 1965, PhD, 1968. Project engr. Dynamic Sci., Phoenix, 1972-74; asst. prof. Pa. State U., State College, 1974-78; mgr. R&D Simula Inc., Phoenix, 1978-83; assoc. prof. Ariz. State U., Tempe, 1983—, dir. aerospace rsch. ctr., 1992—. Referee: Jour. Aircraft, Jour. Mech. Design; contbr. articles to Jour. Aircraft, Jour. Am. Helicopter Soc., Jour. Safety Rsch., Jour. Thermoplastic Composite Materials, Composites Sci. and Tech. Fellow AIAA (assoc.; design engring. tech. com.); mem. ASME, Am. Helicopter Soc., Sigma Xi, Sigma Gamma Tau, Pi Tau Sigma. Democrat. Achievements include research in aircraft crash survivability, composite structures. Office: Ariz State U Dept Mech Aerospace En Tempe AZ 85287

LAANE, JAAN, chemistry educator; b. Paide, Estonia, June 20, 1942; came to U.S., 1949.; s. Robert Freidrich and Linda (Treufeldt) L.; m. Tiiu Virkhaus, Sept. 3, 1966; children: Christina J., Lisa A. BS in Chemistry, U. Ill., 1964; PhD in Chemistry, MIT, 1967. Asst. prof. of chemistry Tufts U., Medford, Mass., 1967-68; asst. prof. of chemistry Tex. A&M U., College Station, 1968-72, assoc. prof. of chemistry, 1972-76, prof. of chemistry, 1976—, chmn. div. of physical and nuclear chemistry, 1977-87, 93-94, dir. inst. for Pacific Asia, 1987-90; assoc. dean sci., 1994—; dep. exec. dir., sr. policy advisor Tex. A&M U./Koriyama, College Station, 1990-94; editor Jour. Molecular Structure, 1994—; reviewer numerous profl. jours. and grant agys., 1968—; cons. indsl. and govt. orgns., 1970—; vis. prof. U. Bayreuth, Fed. Republic Germany, 1979-80; speaker Tex. A&M Faculty Senate, College Station, 1985-86; dir. NATO Advanced Rsch. Workshop, Ulm, Germany, 1992. Contbr. numerous articles to profl. jours.; lectr. numerous sci. presentations. Pres., founder College Station Assn. for Gifted and Talented, 1982-83. Recipient 9 rsch. grants Robert A. Welch Found., 1970-95, 9 rsch. grants NSF, 1976-97, U.S. Sr. Scientist award Alex Von Humboldt Found., Fed. Republic Germany, 1979, Disting. Tchg. award Tex. A&M Assn. Former Students; elected to Estonian Acad. Sci., 1995. Fellow Am. Inst. Chemists; mem. Am. Chem. Soc. (sect. pres. 1977-78), Am. Phys. Soc., Soc. for Applied Spectroscopy, Coblentz Soc. (bd. dirs., treas. 1986-89), Tex. A&M Faculty Club (pres. 1987-88), Phi Beta Delta (pres. 1990-91). Achievements include research in molecular spectroscopy and vibrational potential energy functions of molecules, laser Raman spectroscopy, laser induced fluorescence spectroscopy, ft-infrared spectroscopy. Home: 1906 Comal Cir College Station TX 77840-4818 Office: Tex A&M U Chemistry Dept College Station TX 77843

LAANO, ARCHIE BIENVENIDO MAAÑO, cardiologist; b. Tayabas, Quezon, Philippines, Aug. 10, 1939; naturalized U.S. citizen; s. Francisco M. and Iluminada (Maaño) L.; m. Maria Esmeralda Eleazar, May 2, 1964; 1 child, Sylvia Marie. A.A., U. Philippines, 1958, B.S., 1959, M.D., 1963; postgrad. Command and Gen. Staff Sch., Ft. Totten, N.Y., Ft. Leavenworth, Kans., 1978-79, Oxford (Eng.) U., 1985-86, Cambridge (Eng.) U., 1986-87. Diplomate Am. Bd. Internal Medicine. Rotating intern Hosp. St. Raphael, New Haven, 1963-64; resident internal medicine, 1964-65; rotating resident pulmonary diseases Laurel Heights Hosp., Shelton, Conn., 1965; affiliated rotating resident Yale-New Haven Med. Ctr., 1965; resident internal medicine Westchester County Med. Ctr., Valhalla, N.Y., 1965-66, resident cardiology, 1966-67; resident fellow cardiology Maimonides Med. Ctr., Bklyn., 1967-68; rotating sr. resident cardiology Coney Island Hosp., Bklyn., 1967-68; fellow internal medicine Mercy Hosp., Rockville Centre, N.Y., 1968-70; med. dir. 54 Main St. Med. Ctr., Hempstead, N.Y., 1971-76, Bloomingdale's, Garden City, N.Y., 1972—, Esselte Pendaflex Corp., Garden City, 1976—; attending staff Nassau County (N.Y.) Med. Ctr., Hempstead Gen. Hosp.; practice medicine specializing in cardiology, internal medicine, Nassau County, 1971—; chief med. svcs., chief profl. svcs. U.S. Army 808th Sta. Hosp., Hempstead, N.Y., 1979—; brig. gen. 1st U.S. Army AMEDD Augmentation Detachment, Ft. Meade, Md., 1989—, M.C., chief of staff, chief profl. svcs. U.S. Army Meddac Hosp., Ft. Dix., N.J., 1990—; med. dir. Cities Svc. Oil Co. (CITGO), L.I. div., 1972— ; mem. adv. bd. Guardian Bank, Hempstead, chmn. adv. coun., 1973-89; clin. prof. medicine SUNY at Stony Brook, 1979—; professorial lectr. medicine (cardiology) U.S. Mil. Acad.-Keller Army Med. Ctr., West Point, N.Y., 1979; affiliated teaching hosp. Harvard Med. Sch, 1979; vis. prof. Harvard U., 1979—; cons. physician ICC, Citgo, Liberty Mut. Ins. Co. Boston, 1972—, U.S. Dept. Transp.; post-doctoral in medicine-cardiovasc. diseases Brasenose Coll., Oxford U., U.K., 1985-65, post-doctoral in medicine-cardiology Corpus Christi Coll., Cambridge U., U.K., 1986-87; counsel White House Commn. on Mil. Medicine, 1988—. Perpetual benefactor endowed Dr. Archie B.M. Laano Professorial Chair in Cardiology, U.P. Coll. of Medicine, U.P.-P.G.H. Med. Ctr., Manila, 1983—, Permanent Endowment Fund, U. Philippines Coll. of Medicine, Manila, 1987—, Dr. Archie B.M. Laano Scholarship Fund, U. Philippines, Diliman, Quezon City, 1987—. Decorated Silver Star, Bronze Star, Legion of Merit, Soldiers medal, Joint Svc. Command medal, Army Meritorious Svc. medal, Dept. Def. Joint Svc. Achievement award, Southwest Asia Svc. award-Desert Storm, others. Fellow Internat. Coll. Angiology, Am. Coll. Angiology, Am. Coll. Internat. Physicians, Internat. Coll. Applied Nutrition, Am. Soc. Contemporary Medicine and Surgery, Acad. Preventive Medicine, Internat. Acad. Med. Preventives, Philippine Coll. Physicians, Am. Coll. Acupuncture, N.Y. Acad. of Sci.; mem. AMA, Am. Coll. Cardiology, N.Y. Med. Soc., Nassau County Med. Soc., Am. Heart Assn., N.Y. Cardiol. Soc., World Med. Assn., Royal Soc. Medicine (overseas, London), Nassau Acad. Medicine, Am., N.Y. State, Nassau Soc. Internal Medicine, N.Y. Soc. Acupuncture for Physicians, Am. Geriatrics Soc., Nassau Physicians Guild, Res. Officers Assn. U.S., Assn. Mil. Surgeons, Assn. Philippine Physicians Am. (bd. govs. rep. N.Y. State 1984-86, v.p. 1988-89, chmn. com. nominations and election 1987-88. spl. counsel to pres. 1986-87), Philippine Med. Assn. Am. (spl. counsel 1988-89, bd. dirs, 1989-90, spl. counsel to pres, 1986—, dir. continuing med. edn. 1990—, chmn. scholarship com. 1989—), Assn. Philippine Physicians of N.Y. (founding v.p., pres. 1985-87, pres. emeritus 1988—, chmn. com. on constitution and by-laws, nominations and election, med. coord. Internat. Games for Disabled Olympics 1984), Soc. Philippine Surgeons Am. (Medallion of.S. Knights of Rizal, U. Philippines Med. Alumni Soc. (pres. class of 1963, 1981—), U. Philippines Med. Alumni Soc. Am. (chmn. bd. 1985—), Royal Soc. Medicine Club, The Oxford Club, Rolls Royce Club L.I., N.Y. Club (chmn. 1987—), West Point Officers Club, Garden City Country Club, Phi Kappa Mu (overseas coord. U. Philippines 1985—), Beta Sigma (coun. advisers Ea. U.S. 1990—, program chmn. 1975—, chmn. bd. 1978—, pres. 1978-79), Lions (Garden City program chmn. 1975—, chmn. bd. 1978—, pres. 1978-79). Republican. Roman Catholic. Home: 80 Stratford Ave Garden City NY 11530-2531 Office: 230 Hilton Ave Ste 106 Hempstead NY 11550-8116

LABA, MARVIN, management consultant; b. Newark, Mar. 17, 1928; s. Joseph Abraham and Jean Cecil (Saunders) L.; m. Sandra Seltzer, Apr. 16, 1961 (div. May 1974); children: Stuart Michael, Jonathan Todd; m. Elizabeth Luger, June 11, 1974 (div. 1979). BBA, Ind. U., 1951. Buyer Bamberger's (Macy's N.J.), Newark, 1951-67; v.p., mdse. adminstr. Macy's N.Y., 1967-73; v.p., gen. mdse. mgr. Howland/Steinback, White Plains, N.Y., 1973-75, Pomeroy's, Levittown, Pa., 1975-76; v.p., gen. mdse. mgr., sr. v.p., exec. v.p. May Co. Calif., North Hollywood, 1976-79; pres., chief exec. officer G. Fox & Co. (div. of the May dept. stores), Hartford, Conn., 1979-82; pres. Richard Theobald & Asocs., L.A., 1983; pres., chief exec. officer Marvin Laba & Assocs., L.A., 1983—. With U.S. Army, 1946-48. Avocations: coins, tennis, theatre, travel. Office: Marvin Laba & Assoc 6255 W Sunset Blvd Ste 617 Los Angeles CA 90028-7407

LABADIE, GEORGE SHERMAN, retired art director; b. Dewey, Okla., Jan. 31, 1916; s. John and Minnie (Lunney) L.; m. Jeanne Elizabeth Woodson, June 24, 1939; children: John Woodson, Lynn Joyce Labadie Todd. Student, Sacramento Jr. Coll., 1934-37, Chouinard Art Inst., 1937-39, Art Ctr. Sch., 1938-39, UCLA, 1948. Art dir. Bishop-Conklin Co., L.A., 1940-42, 45-47, Mayers Co., L.A., 1947-49, Russel Harte & Assocs., L.A., 1949-52; sr. art dir. Erwin Wasey, Inc., L.A., 1952-58; exec. art dir. Donahue & Coe, Inc., L.A., 1958-62; advt. mgr. Equity Funding Corp. Am., Beverly Hills, Calif., 1964-65; pres., owner George S. Labadie Agy., Beverly Hills, 1966-72; exec. art dir. Mulle Breen & Rossi, Inc., Beverly Hills, 1972-90; retired, 1981; instr. Calif. Art Inst., Calabasas, 1987—; producer videos Art Video Prodns., Canoga Park, Calif., 1989-90; instr. workshops in field. Contbr. paintings to profl. mags. and contbr. paintings to authored art pubs. Recipient awards San Diego Watercolor Soc., 1982, Old Forge Arts Guild, 1982, 84, 86, Houston Watercolor Soc., 1987, 90, Allied Artists Am., 1987, La. Watercolor Soc., 1989. Mem. Allied Artists Am. (award 1987), Am. Watercolor Soc., Nat. Watercolor Soc. (bd. dirs., treas. 1987-88, nat. v.p. 1995—), Midwest Watercolor Soc. (award 1986, 88, 90), Watercolor West (award 1986, 88), West Coast Watercolor Soc. Republican. Avocations: chess, photography, mineral prospecting, American Indian culture. Home: 22940 Calabash St Woodland Hills CA 91364-2714

LABALME, PATRICIA HOCHSCHILD, educational administrator; b. N.Y.C., Feb. 26, 1927; d. Walter and Kathrin (Samstag) Hochschild; m. George Labalme, Jr., June 6, 1958; children: Jennifer R., Henry G., Lisa G., Victoria A. B.A. magna cum laude, Bryn Mawr Coll., 1948; M.A., Harvard U., 1950, Ph.D., 1958. Instr. history Wellesley Coll., Mass., 1952-57; tchr. history Brearley Sch., N.Y.C., 1957-59; lectr. Barnard Coll., N.Y.C., 1961-77; adj. assoc. prof. history Hunter Coll., N.Y.C., 1979; lectr. NYU, N.Y.C., 1980-82; adj. prof. history NYU, 1986-87; assoc. dir. Inst. for Advanced Study, Princeton, N.J., 1982-88; sec. corp. Inst. for Advanced Study, Princeton, 1982-92, asst. to dir., 1992—; mem. adv. bd. G. K. Delmas Found., N.Y.C., 1976-79, trustee, 1979; trustee Am. Acad. in Rome, N.Y.C., 1979—; exec. dir. Renaissance Soc. Am., N.Y.C., 1982-85, trustee, 1982-89; bd. dirs. Quantum Chem. Corp., 1990-93. Author: Bernardo Giustiniani: A Venetian of the Quattrocento, 1969; contbg. editor: Beyond Their Sex: Learned Women of the European Past, 1980, A Century Recalled: Essays in Honor of Bryn Mawr College, 1987; contbr. articles to profl. jours. and publs. Trustee Brearley Sch., 1975-83, pres., 1978-82, hon. trustee, 1983—; trustee Lawrenceville Sch., 1986-96. Recipient Caroline A. Wilby prize Radcliffe Coll., 1958. Mem. Am. Hist. Assn., Soc. for Renaissance Studies, Renaissance Soc. Am., Ateneo Veneto, Cosmopolitan Club, Harvard Club (N.Y.C.), Cream Hill Lake Assn. (West Cornwall, Conn.), Phi Beta Kappa. Office: Inst for Advanced Study Olden Ln Princeton NJ 08540-4920

LABAN, MYRON MILES, physician, administrator; b. Detroit, Mar. 9, 1936; s. Larry Max and Mary Marsha (Harris) LaB.; m. Rita Joyce Hochman, Aug. 17, 1958; children: Terry, Amy, Craig. B.A., U. Mich., Ann Arbor, 1957, M.D., 1967; M.Med. Sci., Ohio State U., Columbus, 1965. Diplomate Am. Bd. Phys. Medicine and Rehab. Intern Sinai Hosp., Detroit, 1961-62; resident Ohio State U. Hosp., 1962-65; assoc. dir. phys. medicine and rehab. Letterman Gen. Hosp., San Francisco, 1965-67; dir. phys. medicine and rehab. William Beaumont Hosp., Royal Oak, Mich., 1967—; Licht lecturer Ohio State U., 1986, clin. prof., 1993; clin. prof. Wayne State U., Detroit, 1990, clin. prof. Oakland U., Rochester, Mich., 1983; bd. dirs. Oakland County Med. Bd., Birmingham, Mich., 1982-87; rep. to Commn. on Phys. Medicine and Rehab., Mich. State Med. Soc. Contbr. chpts. in books, articles to profl. publs. Med. dir. Oakland County March of Dimes, Mich., 1969-83. Served to capt. U.S. Army, 1965-67. Fellow Am. Acad. Phys. Medicine and Rehab. (bd. dirs. 1980, pres. 1985-86, Bernard Baruch Rsch. award 1961, R. Rosenthal Rsch. award 1982, Zeiter lectureship, Disting. Clinician award 1991, "Top Doc" PM&R Detroit Monthly 1993, 96); mem. AMA, Am. Congress Rehab. Medicine, Am. Assn. Electromyography and Electrodiagnosis (program dir. 1972), Oakland County Med. Soc. (treas. 1983, pres.-elect 1987, pres. 1988-89), Mich. State Med. Soc., Mich. Acad. Phys. Med. and Rehab. (pres. 1982-84, jud. commr. 1991—, mem. editl. bd. Jour. Phys. Med. and Rehab.). Republican. Jewish. Avocations: gardening; ship modeling. Office: LMT Rehabilitation Assocs 3535 W 13 Mile Rd Rm 703 Royal Oak MI 48073-6706

LABAREE, BENJAMIN WOODS, history educator; b. New Haven, Conn., July 21, 1927; s. Leonard Woods and Elizabeth Mary (Calkins) L.; m. Linda Carol Prichard, June 27, 1959; children: Benjamin Woods Jr., Jonathan Martin, Sarah Calkins. BA, Yale U., 1950; AM, Harvard U., 1953, PhD, 1957. Instr. history Conn. Coll., New London, 1957-58; from instr. to asst. prof. history, Allston Burr Sr. tutor Harvard U., Cambridge, Mass., 1958-63; dean Williams Coll., Williamstown, Mass., 1963-67, assoc. to prof. history, 1963-77, Ephraim Williams Prof. Am. History, 1972-77; dir. Williams Coll.-Mystic Seaport Program/Mystic Seaport Mus., Mystic, Conn., 1977-89; dir. Ctr. for Environ. Studies Williams Coll., 1989-91; prof. history and environ. studies Williams Coll., Williamstown, 1989-92; prof. emeritus, 1992—; vis. prof. Trinity Coll., Conn., 1993, Williams Coll., 1994; dir. Munson Inst. Am. Maritime Studies, Mystic, 1974—; mng. editor Essex Inst. Hist. Collections, Salem, Mass., 1956-60. Author: Patriots and Partisans, 1962, The Boston Tea Party, 1964, America's Nation-Time, 1972, Colonial Massachusetts, 1979; co-author: New England and The Sea, 1972, Empire or Independence, 1976. Mem. Mt. Greylock Regional H.S. Com., Williamstown, 1971-74; bd. dirs. Neuburyport Maritime Soc., 1991—, Lowell's Boat Shop trust, 1992—. With USNR, 1945-46. Recipient Wilbur Cross award Conn. Humanities Coun., 1990, Samuel Eliot Morison award USS Constitution Mus., 1993. Mem. Am. Hist. Assn. (com. 1971-73), Am. Antiquarian Soc., Colonial Soc. Mass., Mass. Hist. Soc., Inst. for Early Am. History and Culture (coun. mem. 1983-86), others. Democrat. Unitarian-Universalist. Avocations: sailing, rowing, swimming. Home and Office: 2 Andrews Ln Amesbury MA 01913-4102

LABARGE, KARIN PETERSON, financial economics educator, researcher; b. Cadillac, Mich., Oct. 14, 1953; d. Carl Edwin Lindell and Frances Agda (Hodges) Peterson; m. Richard Allen LaBarge, June 28, 1980; 1 child; Robert Edwin Justin. BS in Edn. magna cum laude, Cen. Mich. U., 1975; MA, U. New Orleans, 1979; PhD in Bus. Adminstrn., U. Calif., Berkeley, 1986. Teaching asst. U. New Orleans, 1978-79; teaching asst. U. Calif., 1980-81, rsch. asst., 1981-83; rsch. assoc. Ctr. for Study of Futures Markets Columbia U., N.Y.C., 1983-84; asst. prof. fin. U. New Orleans, 1984-89, Rutgers U., Camden, N.J., 1989-96. Contbr. articles to internat. profl. jours. Chairperson fin. com. St. Andrew's Luth. Ch., New Orleans, 1985. Mem. Western Fin. Assn., Eastern Fin. Assn., So. Fin. Assn., Fin. Mgmt. Assn., Midwest Fin. Assn., Southwestern Fin. Assn., Phi Kappa Phi, Omicron Delta Epsilon. Republican. Lutheran. Avocations: piano, choral singing, reading, travel.

LABARGE, MARGARET WADE, medieval history educator; b. N.Y.C., July 18, 1916; arrived in Can., 1940; d. Alfred Byers and Helena (Mein) Wade; m. Raymond C. Labarge, June 20, 1940 (dec. May 1972); children: Claire Labarge Morris, Suzanne, Charles, Paul. BA, Radcliffe Coll., 1937; LittB, Oxford (Eng.) U., 1939; LittD (hon.), Carleton U., Ottawa, Ont., Can., 1976; LLD (hon.), U. Waterloo, Ont., Can., 1993. Lectr. history U. Ottawa, Carleton U., 1950-62; adj. prof. history Carleton U., Ottawa, 1983—. Author: Simon de Montfort, 1962, A Baronial Household, 1965, Gascony, 1980, A Small Sound of the Trumpet, 1987, others; contbr. articles to profl. jours. Bd. dirs. St. Vincent's Hosp., Ottawa, 1969-81; chmn. 1977-79; pub. rep. bd. dirs. Can. Nurses Assn., 1980-83; bd. dirs. Carleton U., 1984-93, Coun. on Aging, 1986-93 (pres., 1989-91). Recipient Alumnae Recognition award Radcliffe Coll., 1987. Fellow Royal Soc. Can.; mem. Medieval Acad., Order of Can., Phi Beta Kappa. Roman Catholic. Avocations: traveling, reading, walking. Home and Office: 402-555 Wilbrod St, Ottawa, ON Canada K1N 5R4

LA BARGE, WILLIAM JOSEPH, tutor, researcher; b. Portis, Kans., June 27, 1943; s. Louis Joseph and Mary Genevieve (Colton) La B. AB, Ft. Hays State U., Hays, Kans., 1966, postgrad., 1980; postgrad., Cloud County C.C., Concordia, Kans., 1984. Cert. tchr., Kans. Depot agt. Mo. Pacific R.R., Lenora, Kans., 1971-77; correctional officer Kans. Dept. Corrections, Hutchinson, 1977; prodn. worker Becker Mfg. Co., Downs, Kans., 1978-79; ind. study Downs, 1983-88; pvt. tutor world, Am., ancient and military history grade 6 to adult, Downs, 1988—. With USN, 1966-70. Mem. ASCD, Archaeol. Inst. Am., U.S. Naval Inst. Roman Catholic. Avocations: archaeology, history, toy soldiers, travel. Home and Office: 519 Blunt St Downs KS 67437-1713

LABARRE, CARL ANTHONY, retired government official; b. Sherwood, N.D., July 16, 1918; s. William Paul and Josephine K. LaB.; m. Persis Wester, Sept. 9, 1941; 1 son, William Paul, II. Student, U. Mont., 1936-40; postgrad., Naval Acad. Postgrad. Sch., 1945-46; grad., Naval War Coll., 1958-59, Advanced Mgmt. Program, Harvard U. Commd. ensign U.S. Navy, 1941, advanced through grades to capt., 1971; served in various fin., inventory control systems and purchasing assignments, to 1971; insp. gen. (Naval Supply Systems Command), to 1971; ret., 1971; dep. dir. materials mgmt. service GPO, Washington, 1971-75; dir. materials mgmt. service GPO, 1975, asst. public printer, supt. documents, 1975-82. Decorated Navy Commendation medal with V, Joint Service commendation medal, Legion of Merit with gold star; recipient Public Printers Disting. Service award, 1977, 81. Club: Harvard Bus. Sch. (Washington).

LABATH, OCTAVE AARON, mechanical engineer; b. Milw., Sept. 22, 1941; s. Octave Adrain and Bertha Jane (Johnson) LaB.; m. Carole Marion Clay, Jan. 23, 1965; children—Melissa, Michelle, Mark. B.S. in Mech. Engring., U. Cin., 1964, M.S., 1969. Registered profl. engr., Ohio. v.p. engring. Cin. Gear Co., 1972—. Contbr. articles to profl. jours. Mem. Am. Gear Mfg. Assn., ASME. Methodist. Men's Club. Home: 5105 Kenridge Dr Cincinnati OH 45242-4831 Office: Cin Gear 5657 Wooster Pike Cincinnati OH 45227

LABBE, ARMAND JOSEPH, museum curator, anthropologist; b. Lawrence, Mass., June 13, 1944; s. Armand Henri and Gertrude Marie (Martineau) L.; m. Denise Marie Scott, Jan. 17, 1969 (div. 1972). BA in Anthropology, Univ. Mass., 1969; MA in Anthropology, Calif. State U., 1986; lifetime instr. credential in anthropology, State Calif. Curator collections Bowers Mus., Santa Ana, Calif., 1978-79, curator anthropology, 1979-86, chief curator, 1986—, dir. rsch. and collections, 1991—; instr./prof. Santa Ana Coll., 1981-86, Calif. State U., Fullerton, 1982, 83, 88, U. Calif., Irvine, 1983, 87, 91, 93, Chapman U., 1996; trustee Balboa Arts Conservation Ctr., San Diego, 1989—, Ams. Found., Greenfield, Mass., 1985-94, Quintcentenary Festival Discovery, Orange County, Calif., 1990-91; mem. adv. bd. Elan Internat., Newport Beach, Calif., 1992—; trustee Mingei Internat. Mus., La Jolla, Calif., 1993—; inaugural guest lectr. Friends of Ethnic Art, San Francisco, 1988; hon. bd. dirs. Ethnic Arts Coun., L.A. Author: Man and Cosmos, 1982, Ban Chiang, 1985, Colombia Before Columbus, 1986 (1st prize 1987), Leigh Wiener: Portraits, 1987, Colombia Antes de Colón, 1988 (honored at Gold Mus. Bogotá, Colombia, 1988), Images of Power: Master Works of the Bowers Museum of Cultural Art, 1992; co-author Tribute to The Gods: Treasures of the Museo del Oro, Bogotá, 1992, Guardians of the Life Stream: Shamans, Art and Power In Prehispanic Central Panama, 1995. Hon. bd. dirs. Ethnic Arts Coun. L.A.; cons. Orange County Coun. on History and Art, Santa Ana, 1981-85; mem. Task Force on County Cultural Resources, Orange County, 1979; cons., interviewer TV prodn. The Human Journey, Fullerton, 1986-89. With USAF, 1963-67. Recipient cert. of Recognition Orange County Bd. Suprs., 1982, award for outstanding scholarship Colombian Community, 1987; honored for authorship Friends of Libr., 1987, 88. Fellow Am. Anthrop. Assn.; mem. AAAS, Am. Assn. Mus., N.Y. Acad. Scis., S.W. Anthrop. Assn. Avocations: photography, travel. Home: 2854 Royal Palm Dr # C Costa Mesa CA 92626-3828

L'ABBÉ, GERRIT KAREL, chemist; b. Oostende, Belgium, Dec. 13, 1940; s. Bertram L'abbé and Marie-Rose Coenegrachts; m. Christianne Platteau, Aug. 17, 1967; children: Annick, Caroline. Lic. in Chemistry with highest honors, U. Leuven, Belgium, 1963; Dr. in Sci., U. Leuven, 1966. Postdoctoral fellow Erlangen, Fed. Republic Germany, 1967-68, Boulder, Colo., 1969-70; docent U. Leuven, 1972-75, prof. chemistry, 1975-77, prof. ordinarius, 1977—; rsch. dir. U. Leuven, 1972—. Contbr. 200 articles to profl. jours. Recipient Belgian-BP prize, 1959, P. Bruylants prize Chemici Lovanienses, 1966, bieninial prize Jour. Industrie Chimique Belge, 1968, award Japan Soc. for Promotion Sci., 1979, EuChem award European

Cmtys. Chemistry Coun., 1993; Alexander von Humboldt fellow, 1967-68, Fulbright rsch. fellow, 1969-70, fellow Nat. Fund for Sci. Rsch., 1963-72. Fellow Brit. Royal Soc. Chemistry (chartered); mem. Am. Chem. Soc., Internat. Soc. Heterocyclic Chemistry, Belgian Royal Acad. Sci. (J.S. Stas medal 1966, Laureate 1972), Flemish Chem. Soc. (Breckpot prize 1983), Internat. Order of Merit. Home: Merellaan 33, 3210 Linden Belgium Office: U Leuven Dept Chemistry, Celestijnenlaan 200F, 3001 Heverlee Belgium

LABBÉ, PAUL, export corporation executive; b. Buckingham, Que., Can., Mar. 11, 1939; s. Arthur and Dorothy Frances (Gorman) L.; m. Kathryn Grace Cameron, July 10, 1965; Marie-Paule, Marc, Philippe, David, Robert. BA, U. Ottawa, 1961; BCL, McGill U., 1964; student, Ecole Nationale D'Administration, Paris, 1969, Harvard Grad. Sch. Bus., 1990. Bar: Que. 1965. Comml. sec. Can. Embassy, Paris, 1966-69; exec. asst. to minister Dept. Industry, Trade & Commerce, Ottawa, Ont., 1969-73; assoc. Interimco, Inc., 1973-75, pres., 1975-81; pres. CDN Indsl. Rev. Bd., 1981-85; commr. Fgn. Investment Rev. Agy., 1985; pres. Investment Can., Ottawa, 1985-91; pres., CEO Export Devel. Corp., Ottawa, 1991—. Gov. Can. Comprehensive Auditing Found. Mem. Rideau Club, Hunt Club. Home: 216 Clemow Ave, Ottawa, ON Canada K1S 2B6 Office: Export Development Corp, 151 O'Connor St, Ottawa, ON Canada K1A 1K3

LABBETT, JOHN EDGAR, senior financial executive; b. Chesham, Bucks, Eng., June 19, 1950; came to U.S., 1987; s. Gordon F. and Sylvia (Dalton) L.; m. Mary McGagh, Jan. 30, 1976; children: Jennifer F., Alexander T. Audit clk. White Withers and Co., Bexhill, Eng., 1966-71; auditor Peat Marwick Mitchell, London, 1971-73; chief acct. Guild S&V Ltd., London, 1973-74; from fin. analyst to contr. Roneo Vickers Ltd., London, 1974-81; fin. contr. Cambridge (Eng.) Instruments Ltd., 1981-82; fin. dir. Linfood C&C Ltd. subsid. Dee Corp., Milton Keynes, U.K., 1982-85; fin. controller Dee Corp., Milton Keines, 1985-87; exec. v.p., chief fin. officer Hermans Sporting Goods, Inc., Carteret, N.J., 1987-93; v.p., CFO The Petfood Giant, Inc., 1994-95; exec. v.p., chief fin. officer House of Fabrics, Inc., Sherman Oaks, Calif., 1995—. Fellow Inst. Chartered Accts. Eng. and Wales. Mem. Ch. Eng. Home: 597 Little Silver Point Rd Little Silver NJ 07739-1732

LABE, ROBERT BRIAN, lawyer; b. Detroit, Sept. 2, 1959; s. Benjamin Mitchell and Gloria Florence (Wright) L.; m. Mary Lou Budman, Nov. 12, 1989; 1 child, Bridget. BA with high honors, Mich. State U., 1981; JD, Wayne State U., 1984; LLM, Boston U., 1985. Bar: Mich. 1984, U.S. Dist. Ct. Mich. 1985, U.S. Tax Ct. 1985. Assoc. Weingarden & Hauer, P.C., Bingham Farms, Mich., 1988-92, shareholder, 1992-94; prin. Robert B. Labe, P.C., Southfield, Mich., 1994—; adj. prof. taxation and estate planning Walsh Coll., Troy, Mich., 1990-92; lectr. and presenter in field. Author: Research Edge-Taxation Guide, 1994; mem. publ. adv. bd. Isnt. Continuing Legal Edn. U. Mich., 1993—; contbr. articles to profl. jours. Avocations: tennis, spectator sports. Office: Robert B Labe P C 2000 Town Ctr Ste 1780 Southfield MI 48075-1150

LABELLE, EUGENE JEAN-MARC, airport director general; b. Montreal, Que., Can., Nov. 26, 1941; s. Paul Eugene and Pauline (Brissette) L.; m. Louise Gingras; 1 child, Anne Marie. BA in Sci. and Math., U. Montreal, 1962, BS in Applied Scis. (civil engring.), 1967; postgrad. in transp. mgmt., various colls., 1975-85. Registered profl. engr., Que.; cert. expert of Internat. Aviation Orgn., expert of World Bank. With Transport Canada, 1967—; field engr. constrn. br. Que. region, 1967-68, design engr. constrn. br., 1968-71; mgr. engring. and maintenance svcs. Dorval, 1971-75; regional mgr. airport ops. Que. Region, 1975-80; acting airport gen. mgr. Dorval, 1980-81; mgr. airport ops. & svcs. Mirabel, 1981-82; airport gen. mgr. Dorval, 1982-88; dir. gen. Montreal Airports, 1988-92; exec. v.p., COO Aeroports de Montreal, Canada, 1992-94, group v.p. planning and devel., 1994—; pres., gen. mgr. Aeroports de Montreal Svcs. Inc., group v.p., planning & devel.; mem. planning missions, aerodrome engr. and/or mgmt. cons. for Internat. Civil Aviation Orgn. and World Bank, Congo, 1981, Cameroun, 1983, Chad, 1983, 84, 85, Senegal, 1984, Kenya, 1984, Jordan, 1985, Hdqrs., Montreal, 1986, Madagascar, 1985, Sierra Leone, Qatar, 1986, Turks and Caicos Islands, program evaluation officer, Kigali, Rwanda, 1986; aerodrome mgmt. cons. study of civil aviation reorgn., Conakry, (Guinea), World Bank Mission, 1986; ICAO Program Evaluation Officer, UN Tchad, 1987; aerodrome mgmt. cons., Warsaw, Poland, 1987; aerodrome engring cons., Kuwait, 1988, St. Vincent and the Grenadines, 1989, Uruguay, 1989; lectr. Civil Aviation Acad., Leningrad, USSR, 1990; aerodrome mgmt. advisor Santo Domingo, 1990; aerodrome mgmt. and engring. advisor Trinidad and Tobago, 1991, 92; UN program evaluation officer, Mozambique, 1990; aerodrome planning engr., Lebanon, 1993; project mgr. Piarco Airport Trinidad and Tobago, 1993, UFA Airport, Bashkortostan, 1995, Macau Airport Certification Program, 1995; aerodrome gnr., project mgr. E.T. Joshua Airport, St. Vincent & Grenadines, 1995. Mem. ASCE, Chambre de Commerce de Montreal, Can. Inst.of Engrs., Am. Assn. Airport Execs., Airports Coun. Internat., Airports Conss. Coun., Can. Exporters Assn. Avocations: classical music, opera, reading, arts, golf. Home: 337 Perrault St, Rosemere, PQ Canada J7A 1C4 Office: Aeroports de Montreal, 1100 Rene-Levesque Blvd W 21st fl, Montreal, PQ Canada H3B 4X8

LABELLE, PATTI, singer; b. Phila., Oct. 4, 1944; d. Henry Holte; m. Armstead Edwards; children: Zuri, Stanley, Dodd. Singer Patti LaBelle and the Bluebelles, 1962-70; lead singer musical group LaBelle, 1970-76; solo performer, 1977—. Albums include Over the Rainbow, 1967, La Belle, 1971, Moon Shadows, 1972, Pressure Cookin', 1974, Chameleon, 1976, Patti LaBelle, 1977, Live at the Apollo, 1980, Gonna Take A Miracle-The Spirit's in It, 1982, I'm in Love Again, 1984, Winner in You, 1986, The Best of Patti LaBelle, Patti, Be Yourself, Burnin', 1991, Live (Apollo Theater), 1993, Gems, 1994; appeared in films A Soldier's Story, 1985, Beverly Hills Cop, 1985; appeared in TV movie Unnatural Causes, 1986, TV series A Different World, Out All Night, 1992. Recipient award of Merit, Phila. Art Alliance, 1987.Recipient Grammy award: best Rhythm & Blues vocal for "Burnin'", 1991, Grammy nomination (Best Rhythym & Blues Female Vocal, 1994) for "All Right Now". Home: 8730 W Sunset Blvd Ph W Los Angeles CA 90069-2210 Office: care MCA Records Inc 100 Universal City Plz Universal City CA 91608

LABELLE, THOMAS JEFFREY, academic administrator; b. Owen, Wis., Sept. 21, 1941; s. Wendell Allen and Katherine (Dolan) LaB.; m. Nancy Reik, June 16, 1966 (dec. 1981); children: Katherine Anne, Jeanette Marie. AA, Pierce Coll., Woodland Hills, Calif., 1962; BA, Calif. State U., Northridge, 1964; MA, U. N.Mex., Albuquerque, 1967, PhD, 1969. Prof. UCLA, 1969-86, asst. dean edn., 1971-79, assoc. dean grad. div., 1980-86; prof. comparative and internat. edn. U. Pitts., 1986-90, dean Sch. Edn., 1986-90; v.p. acad. programs, provost Ga. State U., Atlanta, 1990-93; provost, v.p. acad. affairs and rsch. W.Va. U., Morgantown, 1993-96; provost, v.p. acad. affairs San Francisco State Univ., Morgantown, 1996—; cons. InterAm. Found., U.S. AID, Ford Found., CBS, Acad. Ednl. Devel., Juarez and Assocs. Author: Education and Development in Latin America, 1972, Nonformal Education in Latin America and the Caribbean, 1986, Stability, Reform or Revolution, 1986, Education and Intergroup Relations, 1985, Multiculturalism and Education, 1994, Ethnic Studies and Multiculturalism, 1996. Vol. Peace Corps, Colombia, 1964-66. Grantee Fulbright Found., 1983, InterAm. Found., Latin America, 1984; recipient Andres Bello award 1st Class, Venezuela, 1987. Fellow Soc. Applied Anthropology; mem. Comparative and Internat. Edn. Soc. (pres. 1981), Coun. on Anthropology and Edn. (bd. dirs. 1977), Inter-Am. Found. (chmn. learning fellowship on social change), Golden Key, Omicron Delta Kappa, Phi Kappa Phi. Democrat. Office: San Francisco State Univ. Stewart Hall 1600 Holloway Ave San Francisco CA 94132

LABITZKE, DALE RUSSELL, chemical processing engineer; b. St. Louis, Mo., Dec. 3, 1945; s. Ralph Edgar and Thelma Lois Labitzke; m. Norine Bardill, July 1, 1994. BSChemE, Washington U., St. Louis, 1967. Registered profl. engr. Fla. Process engr. Olin Corp., East Alton, Ill., 1967-68; project engr. Olin Corp., St. Marks, Fla., 1969-71, sr. project engr., 1977; sr. project engr. Olin Corp., Tehran, Iran, 1978; sr. process engr. Olin Corp., St. Marks, Fla., 1979-81; assoc. project engr. Olin Corp., Jacksonville, Fla., 1982; project mgr. Olin Corp., Belgrade, Yugoslavia, 1983-85; process engring. mgr. Olin Corp., St. Marks, Fla., 1986-92, tech. mgr., 1993—; prin. Dale R. Labitzke and Assocs., Tallahassee, Fla., 1992—. Author: Ball Powder Theory and Practice, 1982. With U.S. Navy, 1971-76. Mem. Am. Def. Preparedness Assn., Fla. Engring. Soc. (bd. mem., rep.), AICE, Nat. Soc. Profl. Engrs. Avocations: traveling, gardening. Home: 1529 Chowkeebin Nene Tallahassee FL 32301-4705 Office: Olin Corp PO Box 222 Saint Marks FL 32355-0222

LA BLANC, CHARLES WESLEY, JR., financial consultant; b. Bayshore, L.I., N.Y., June 4, 1925; s. Charles Wesley and Anne (Dobson) LaB.; m. Marie Dolan, Oct. 26, 1963 (dec. Jan. 1985); children: Charles Wesley III, Gregory, Suzanne; m. Joan H. Trapp, Dec. 29, 1993. BS, Tufts Coll., 1949; MBA, NYU, 1952, PhD, 1956. Securities portfolio mgr. Manhattan Life Ins. Co., N.Y.C., 1952-57; asst. to pres. Magnavox Co., Ft. Wayne, Ind., 1957-60; security analyst C.W. LaBlanc & Assos., N.Y.C., 1960-62; treas. Macke Co., Cheverly, Md., 1962-72, dir., 1974-80; exec. v.p., sec.-treas., dir. After Six, Inc., Phila., 1972-84; pres. Bert Paley Ltd., Inc. subs., 1976-77; chmn. bd. Cymaticolor, 1983-84; chief fin. officer and dir. Standard Telecommunications Systems Inc., South Hackensack, N.J., 1983-87; pres. Standard Profit Sharing Fund, 1987—; bd. dirs. Acad. of Vacal Arts. Pres. Queens County Young Reps., 1955-57; bd. dirs. adv. council Temple U. With AC USNR, 1943-46. Fellow N.Y. Soc. Security Analysts; mem. Washington Soc. Investment Analysts, Fin. Analysts Phila., Fin. Execs. Inst., Am. Acctg. Assn., Am. Soc. Ins. Mgmt., Pub. Rels. Soc. Am., Nat. Assn. Bus. Economists, Nat. Investor Rels. Inst., Nat. Assn. Corp. Dirs., Phila. Securities Assn. (pres. 1991, bd. dirs.), Am. Stock Exch. Club, Union League, The Bond Club. Home: 370 Aubrey Rd Wynnewood PA 19096-1819 also:: Apt 1905 111 N Pompano Beach Blvd Pompano Beach FL 33062 also: 35487 Davis Wharf Rd Belle Haven VA 23306-1909

LA BLANC, ROBERT EDMUND, consulting company executive; b. N.Y.C., Mar. 21, 1934; s. Charles Wesley and Anne R. (Dobson) La B.; m. Elizabeth Lammers, 1962; children: Elizabeth, Robert, Jeanne Marie, Paul, Michelle. B.E.E., Manhattan Coll., 1956; M.B.A., NYU, 1962. With Bell System, 1956-69; mem. tech. staff Bell Telephone Labs., 1961-62; seminar leader AT&T Long Lines, Cooperstown, N.Y., 1965-67; mktg. supr. AT&T Hdqrs., N.Y.C., 1967-68; planning engr. N.Y. Telephone, 1968-69; mgr. Salomon Bros., N.Y.C., 1969-73; v.p. Salomon Bros., 1973-75, gen. partner, 1975-79; vice chmn. Continental Telephone Corp., N.Y.C., 1979-81; pres. Robert E. LaBlanc Assocs., Inc., 1981—; bd. dirs. Storage Tech. Corp., Titan Corp., Tribune Co., Prudential Global Fund Inc., Prudential Short-Term Global Income Fund, Inc., Purdential Pacific Growth Fund, Inc. Vice chmn. bd. trustees Manhattan Coll., 1987-93, trustee, 1994—. Served to 1st lt. USAF, 1956-59. Named Wall St. Leading Analyst Instl. Investor Mag., 1973-78. Fellow Fin. Analysts Fedn.; mem. N.Y. Soc. Security Analysts (sr.), Assn. for Computing Machinery, Univ. Club, Econ. Club. Republican. Roman Catholic.

LA BONTÉ, C(LARENCE) JOSEPH, weight management and lifestyle company executive; b. Salem, Mass., Sept. 23, 1939; s. Arthur and Alice Bella (Lecombe) LaB.; m. Donna Marie Chiaradonna, Aug. 2, 1959; children: Linda Jean, Joseph Michael. BS, Northeastern U., 1966, AME, 1968; MBA with distinction (Baker scholar), Harvard U., 1969. With H.P. Hood & Sons, Boston, 1958-63; project engr., mktg. coordinator Market Forge Co., Everett, Mass., 1963-67; with ARA Services, Inc., Phila., 1969-79, exec. asst. to pres., 1969-71, v.p., 1971-72, exec. v.p., 1976-79; pres. Western Co., Los Angeles, 1972-76; pres., chief operating officer, dir. Twentieth Century-Fox Film Corp., Beverly Hills, Calif., 1979-83; chmn., chief exec. officer The Vantage Group Inc., 1983-87, 90—; pres., chief operating officer Reebok Internat. Ltd., Stoughton, Mass., 1987-90; also bd. dirs. Reebok Internat., Stoughton, Mass.; chmn., CEO, Vantage Group, Inc., Palos Verdes, Calif., 1990-94; pres., CEO, Jenny Craig, Internat., Del Mar, Calif., 1994—, also bd. dirs., mem. exec. com.; bd. dirs. several cos.; founder, pres. Am. Bus. Initiative for Free South Africa, 1990-95; bd. dirs. U.S.-SALEP, Washington. Founding dir. South African Free Elections Fund, 1993-94; nat. bd. dirs. Big Bros. Am., 1970-74, pres., 1986-87; bd. dirs. L.A. Philharm. Assn., 1990-94, chmn. bd. dirs., 1994—; trustee Northea. U., 1974-95; mem. Harvard U. Bus. Sch. Fund, 1971—; trustee Orthop. Hosp., L.A., 1980-86. Mem. Harvard U. Bus. Sch. Assn., Husky Assocs. Northeastern U., Huntington Soc., Human Rights Watch (Calif. exec. com.), Phila. Country Club Down Town Club, Vesper Club, Bankers Club San Francisco, 100 of L.A. Office: Jenny Craig Internat 445 Marine View Ave Ste 300 Del Mar CA 92014-3951

LABOON, ROBERT BRUCE, lawyer; b. St. Louis, June 14, 1941; s. Joseph Warren LaBoon and Ruth (Aab) LaBoon Freling; m. Ramona Ann Hudgins, Aug. 24, 1963; children: John Andrew, Robert Steven. BSC, Tex. Christian U., 1963; LLB cum laude, So. Meth. U., 1965. Bar: Tex. 1965. Ptnr. Liddell, Sapp, Zivley, Hill & LaBoon, L.L.P., Houston, 1965-86, 88—; vice chmn. and gen. counsel Tex. Commerce Bancshares, Inc., 1986-88; dir. Tex. Commerce Bank, Gamma Biol. Inc., Tex. Med. Ctr. Bd. dirs. The Houston Interat. Festival, The Inst. Rehab. and Rsch., Internat. Ctr. Arbitration, The Greater Houston Partnership, Houston area ARC, Greater Houston Community Found., Med. Rsch. Found.; bd. dirs. Retina Rsch. Found.; trustee Tex. Christian U., The Kayser Found.; mem. Bd. of Visitors of the M.D. Anderson Cancer Ctr.-U. Cancer Found. Fellow Tex. Bar Found., Am. Coll. of Trust and Estate Counsel; mem. ABA, Am. Law Inst., Tex. Assn. of Bank Counsel, Houston Bar Assn., State Bar Tex.; mem. Houston Club, River Oaks Country Club. Office: Liddell Sapp Zivley Hill & LaBoon LLP 600 Travis Ste 3500 Houston TX 77002

LABORDE, ALDEN JAMES, oil company executive; b. Vinton, La., Dec. 18, 1915; s. Cliffe E. and Hilda (Moreau) L.; m. Margaret Bienuenu, Mar. 11, 1943; children: Susan, J. Monroe, John P., Stephanie, Jane. Student, La. State U., 1932-34; B.S., U.S. Naval Acad., 1938; DEng (hon.), Cath. U. Am., 1991; LLD (hon.), Loyola U., 1996; LHD (hon.), Xavier U., 1996. Engr., S.W. Richardson Oil Co., 1946-48; marine supt. Kerr McGee Oil Industries, 1948-52; pres. Ocean Drilling & Exploration Co., 1953-74, chmn. bd., c.e.o., 1974-77; offshore oil industry cons., 1977-85; chmn. bd., c.e.o. Gulf Island Fabrication Co., 1985—; chmn. All Aboard Devel. Corp. Trustee Catholic U. Am.; mem. bd. liquidation city debt, New Orleans; mem. New Orleans Sewage and Water Bd.; bd. adminstrs. Tulane U., 1975-85. Served from ensign to comdr. USNR, 1938-46. Decorated knight St. Gregory the Great, Vatican; recipient Order St. Louis medal, 1976; Disting. Achievement award Offshore Tech. Conf., 1977; St. Mary's Dominican Coll. medal, 1978; Loyola U. award; named to Fortune mag. Nat. Bus. Hall of Fame, 1985. Mem. Internat. Assn. Oilwell Drilling Contractors. (pres. 1973), Midcontinent Oil and Gas Assn. (pres. 1970-71), Nat. Petroleum Council, St. Vincent de Paul Soc. Home: 63 Oriole St New Orleans LA 70124-4517

LABORDE, JOHN PETER, retired international energy company executive; b. Marksville, La., Nov. 5, 1923; s. Cliffe E. and Hilda (Moreau) L.; m. Gene Zylks (div. 1974); children—John Tracy, Cliffe F., Gary L., John Peter, Mary Adrienne; m. Bethany Sanction Villere, 1983 (div. 1987); m. Sylvia R. McLellan, 1994. B.A., La. State U., 1947, J.D., 1949. Pvt. practice Marksville, La., 1949-50; div. land mgr. Richardson & Bass, New Orleans, 1950-56; pres., chief exec. officer Tidewater Inc. (formerly Tidewater Marine Service, Inc.), New Orleans, 1956-81, 87-94, chmn., chief exec. officer, 1968-94, cons., dir., 1995—; bd. dirs. United Gas Holding Corp. (dir. emeritus), Hibernia Nat. Bank New Orleans (dir. emeritus), Am. Bankers Ins. Group, Miami, Fla., Stolt Comex Seaway, S.A., Stone Energy Corp., Stewart Enterprises, Inc., Am. Bur. Shipping, N.Y.C.; mem. adv. council La. Sea Grant; mem. La. Oil and Gas Adv. Com. Past mem. editorial adv. bd. Offshore Mag.; mem. editorial adv. bd. Citybus. Mem. various coms., trustee Loyola U., New Orleans; mem. exec. com. So. Growth Policies Bd., 1976, 71; chmn. sustaining membership enrollment New Orleans Area council Boy Scouts Am., 1981; mem. U. New Orleans Met. Council for Continuing Higher Edn.; mem. Mayor New Orlean's Com. on Internat. Trade and Relations; mem. Mayor New Orleans' Bus. Devel. Council; mem. La. Gov.'s Energy Com. 100 Exec. Com.; mem. internat. policy forum, bd. govs. Council for Nat. Policy; bd. dirs., past v.p. and mem. exec com. Council for Better La.; bd. dirs., past pres. Campanile Charities, Inc.; bd. dirs. Met. Crime Commn. New Orleans, La Fete, Ochsner Found.; trustee Pub. Affairs Research Council La., Inc.; mem. adv. com. La. Council Music and Performing Arts, Inc.; mem. New Orleans Charity Hosp. Found. Served to capt. U.S. Army, 1943-46. Mem. Mil. and Hospitalier Order St. Lazarus of Jerusalem; recipient one of ten Outstanding Persons' award Inst. Human Understanding, 1974, New Orleans Salesman of Yr. award Sales Mktg. Execs.' Assn., 1980, Humantarian award Nat. Jewish Hosp.-Nat. Astham Ctr., 1983, Maritime Man of Yr. award Propeller Club, 1984, Significant Role Model award Young Leadership Coun., 1988, Disting. Citizen award Boy Scouts Am., 1995 ; named to Jr. Achievement Bus. Hall of Fame, 1985. Mem. ABA, La. Bar Assn., Chief Execs. Orgn., Nat. Ocean Industries Assn. (chmn. bd. 1980), C. of C. of New Orleans and River Region (chmn. nat. legis. com.), Bus. Coun. of New Orleans and River Region (past chmn.), Greater New Orleans Tourist and Conv. Commn., Inc., Nat. Coun. Fgn. Policy, World Bus. Coun., Bur. Govtl. Rsch., La. Region Regional Med. Program, Internat. House (pres. 1973), Petroleum Club New Orleans, Offshore Marine Svc. Assn. (past pres.), La. State U. Found., La. State U. Alumni Fedn. (pres. 1978-79, Disting. Alumnus award 1982, Outstanding Alumnus award 1983), La. State Law Ctr. Alumni Assn. (Disting. Alumnus award, 1993). Roman Catholic. Clubs: Plimsoll of New Orleans, City Energy Club. Office: Tidewater Inc 1440 Canal St New Orleans LA 70112-2715*

LABOVITZ, DEBORAH ROSE RUBIN, occupational therapist, educator; b. Phila., Oct. 13, 1942; d. Samuel Frank and Clara (Blank) Rubin; m. Judah Isaiah Labovitz, June 3, 1962; children: Gail Susan Labovitz Seligman, Bruce Joel, Daniel Mark. BS in Occupational Therapy, U. Pa., 1963, Ma in Sociology, 1974, PhD in Sociology, 1979. Lic. occupl. therapist Nat. Bd. for Cert. of Occupl. Therapy. Dir. occupational therapy Mercy Douglas Hosp., Dept Psychiatry, Univ. Pa., Phila., 1963-66; adj. lectr. Phila., 1967-69; adj. instr. U. Pa., Phila., 1971-72, instr., 1972-76, asst. prof., 1976-80; prof. and chair dept. occupational therapy NYU, N.Y.C., 1980—; cons. Ea. Pa. Psychiatric Inst., 1967-69, to pres. Beaver Coll., Phila., 1980; adj. lectr. U. Pa., 1980-81; mem. NYU Faculty Senate (acad. affairs com. 1987-88, faculty coun. exec. com. 1988-89, acad. affairs com. 1989=90, mandatory retirement subcom., 1988-92, fin. affairs com., 1988-90), Faculty Resource Network, Minority Conf. Com., 1991-92; Sch. of Edn. Budget Adv. Com., 1985—, chair 1992-93; Sch. of Edn. Instl. Planning and Devel. Com., 1986—, chair 1992-93; chair Sch. of Edn. Senate and Faculty Coun.; other coms. and offices. Contbr. articles to profl. jours.; presenter at numerous profl. confs. and ednl. meetings. Alt. del. Dem. Nat. Conv., Miami Beach, Fla., 1972. Grantee: N.Y.C. Bd. Edn., 1990-93, 93-96, MCH grant project, RSA long term tng. grant, AOA, 1988-90, NYU Challenge grant, 1990, and others. Fellow Am. Occupational Therapy Assn. (vice chair commn. on edn. steering com. 1991-93; reviewer conf. papers, rsch. grants, postdoctoral fellowships, various books and articles, many other coms. and com. offices, Svc. award 1986, 89, 93, Cert. of Appreciation 1991); mem. AAUP, Pa. Occupational Therapy Assn. Dist. V., World Fedn. of Occupational Therapists, N.Y. State Occupational Therapy Assn. (mem. chief's group met. N.Y. dist., Cert. Appreciation 1987). Office: NYU Dept Occup Therapy 35 W 4th St 11th Fl New York NY 10012

LABOVITZ, GEORGE HAROLD, business executive, educator; b. Boston, Apr. 19, 1940; s. Jacob and Janet (Bargad) L.; m. Susan Starr, Sept. 5, 1965; children: Elizabeth, Frank, Robert. BS, Boston U., 1961; MBA, Boston Coll., 1964; PhD, Ohio State U., 1968. Prof. Sch. Mgmt. Boston U., 1968—; pres. ODI, Burlington, Mass., 1977—. Contbr. articles to profl. jours. Trustee Children's Hosp. Meml. Ctr., Boston, 1985—. Capt. USAF, 1961-66. Recipient Disting. Alumni award Boston U., 198, Metcalf Cup and prize, 1979. Mem. APA, ASTD, Acad. Mgmt. Avocations: fishing, skiing, jogging, flying. Office: ODI 25 Mall Rd Burlington MA 01803-4100*

LABRECQUE, RICHARD JOSEPH, industrial executive; b. Lawrence, Mass., Dec. 19, 1938; s. Eugene N. and Ludivine M. (Roy) L.; m. Janet Marie Michaud, July 16, 1960; children: David R., Lisa M., Susan M. BSEE, Tufts U., 1962; MS in Indsl. Adminstrn., Union U., 1971. Mgr. mfg. engring. GE Aircraft Engine Group, Lynn, Mass., 1962-68; with Colt Industries, 1969-81; pres. FM Pump div., Kansas City, Kans., 1973-78, Quincy (Ill.) Compressor div., 1979-81; with ITT Corp., Skokie, Ill., 1982—, pres. fluid handling div., 1982-95; sr. v.p. ITT Industries, N.Y.C., 1996—; pres., CEO fluid transfer div. ITT Fluid Tech. Corp., Midland Pk., N.J., 1996—. Campaign chmn. United Way Wyandotte County, Kansas City, 1979. Mem. Hydraulic Inst. (bd. dirs. 1976—, pres. 1979-96).

LABRECQUE, THEODORE JOSEPH, lawyer; b. Portland, Oreg., Mar. 8, 1903; s. Herman F. and Clara (Thibault) L.; m. Marjorie Uprichard, Jan. 31, 1931; children: Theodore J., Katherine Labrecque Skiba, Thomas G., Jeanne M. Labrecque Gagliano, Robert S., David F., Susan Labrecque Woolley, Barbara Anne Labrecque Danowitz. Ed., Manhattan Coll., 1920-21; LLB, Fordham U., 1924; LLD (hon.), Georgian Ct. Coll., 1986. Bar: N.J. 1925, ICC 1936, U.S. Tax Ct. 1943, U.S. Supreme Ct. 1957. Gen. practice law Red Bank, N.J., 1925-60; mem. Quinn, Parsons & Doremus, 1929-37, Parsons, Labrecque, Canzona & Blair, and predecessor firms, 1937-60; mem. N.J. Divsn. Tax Appeals, 1946-60, pres., 1956-60; judge N.J. Superior Ct., 1960-73; judge appellate div. Superior Ct., 1964-73; presiding judge part D appellate div. Superior Ct., 1972-73; of counsel Parsons, Cappiello & Nardelli and predecessor firms, Red Bank, N.J., 1973—. Chmn., Monmouth County Transp. Coordinating Com., 1973—; chmn. North Jersey Transit Adv. Com., 1980-87; mem. Monmouth County Hist. Commn., 1988-90. Recipient Salvation Army award, 1982, Boy Scouting's Joshua Huddy Disting. Citizen award, 1988, N.J. Gov.'s Charles A. Lindbergh Transp. award, 1992. Fellow Am. Coll. Trial Lawyers, Am. Bar Found.; mem. ABA, N.J. State Bar Assn. (pres. 1960), Essex County Bar Assn., Monmouth Bar Assn., Am. Judicature Soc., Elks, Red Bank Lions Club (pres. 1939), Phi Delta Phi (hon.). Democrat. Roman Catholic. Home: 410 Rumson Rd Little Silver NJ 07739-1659 Office: 612 River Rd Fair Haven NJ 07704-3221 also: PO Box 770 Red Bank NJ 07701-0770

LABRECQUE, THOMAS G., banking executive; b. Long Branch, N.J., Sept. 17, 1938; s. Theodore Joseph and Marjorie (Uprichard) L.; m. Sheila English Cardone, June 16, 1962; children: Thomas, Douglas, Karen, Barbara. BA, Villanova U., 1960; postgrad., Am. U., 1962-64, NYU, 1965; D (hon.), Villanova U., U. Charleston, Drexel U., Marymount Coll. Mem. special devel. program The Chase Manhattan Corp., N.Y.C., 1964-65; with corp. portfolio adv. group portfolio and investment banking dept. The Chase Manhattan Corp., 1965-66, asst. treas., 1966-67, second v.p., 1967-69, 1967-69, v.p. and mgr. correspondent bank portfolio advisory, 1969-70; assoc. sec. planning to corp. exec. office The Chase Manhattan Corp., N.Y.C., 1970-71, sr. v.p. bank portfolio group, 1971-74, exec. v.p. treasury dept. and treas., 1974-76, mem. mgmt. com., 1976-80; vice chmn., CEO The Chase Manhattan Corp. and The Chase Manhattan Bank, N.A., N.Y.C., 1980-81, responsible for comml. banking, retail banking, trust and fiduciary investment, ops. dept. and corp. systems functon, 1980-81, pres., 1981-90, chmn., CEO, 1990-1996, also bd. dirs., 1990-1996; pres., COO, bd. dirs. The Chase Manhattan Corp., 1996—; bd. dirs. Pfizer, Inc., Alumax, Inc.; rep. on team that worked out the financial arrangements associated with the release of Am. hostages from Iran, Chase Manhattan Bank, 1980. Trustee Brookings Instn., Central Park Conservancy, N.Y. Pub. Libr.; bd. dirs. Fund for N.Y.C. Pub. Edn., United Way Tri-State, United Way N.Y.C.; bd. visitors Duke U. Fuqua Sch. Bus.; mem. Coun. Fgn. Rels., Trilateral Commn., Bus.-Higher Edn. Forum, Cystic Fibrosis Rsch. Devel. Coun.; mem. exec. com. Partnerships for Quality Edn. Mem. Bus. Coun., Bus. Roundtable, N.Y. Chamber of Commerce and Industry (bd. dirs.), N.Y.C. Partnership. Office: Chase Manhattan Bank NA 1 Chase Manhattan Plz New York NY 10081*

LABRIE, FERNAND, physician; b. Quebec, Que., Can., June 28, 1937; s. François-Xavier and Rose-Alma (Dubois) L.; m. Nicole Cantin; children: Claude, Pierre, Danielle, Anne, Isabelle. BA magna cum laude, Laval U., 1957, MD magna cum laude, 1962, PhD in Endocrinology summa cum laude, 1966; postgrad. of Biochemistry, Univ. Cambridge and Sussex, 1966-69. Jr. intern l'Enfant-Jesus Hosp., Quebec, Que., Can., 1961-62; resident internal medicine L'Hôtel-Dieu de Québec, 1962-63; asst. prof. dept physiology Laval U., 1966-69; tutor dept. biochemistry Cambridge (Eng.) U., 1966-67, Sussex (Eng.) U., 1967-68; assoc. prof. dept. physiology Laval U., 1969-74, dir. lab. molecular endocrinology, 1969—, prof. dept. physiology, 1974—; physician dept. medicine Le Centre Hospitalier of U. Laval, 1972—; dir. rsch. Laval U. Hosp. Rsch. Ctr., 1982—; head dept. physiology Laval U., 1990—; dir. med. rsch. group in molecular endocrinology Med. Rsch. Coun., 1973—; Keith Harrison meml. lectr. Endocrine Soc. Australia, 1984; mem. sci. com. Medicine-Scis., 1984-88; mem. med. adv. bd. Gairdner Found., Toronto, 1979-85; mem. adv. bd. Fondation de Recherche en Hormonologie, Paris, 1979-83; mem. selection panel Steacie Prize, 1982, 83; mem. mission of concertation minister for sci. and tech. Govt. Que., 1982-84; mem. steering com. Task Force on Methods for Regulation of Male Fertility,

WHO, Geneva, 1982; cons. study sect. Centre for Population Rsch., Nat. Inst. Childhood Diseases, NIH, Bethesda, Md., 1976, 77, 79, 80, 83, 84; mem. Sci. Coun. Can., 1984-87; mem. sci. com. 1st Internat. Congress on Neuroendocrinology, 1985-86; mem. Nat. Adv. Bd. Sci. and Tech., 1994—; invited spkr. more than 600 symposia, confs., workshops, cong., U.S., Can., Europe, Asia. Assoc. editor Can. Jour. Biochemistry, 1973-78, Jour. Molecular and cellular Endocrinology, 1973-81; mem. editorial bd. Jour. Cyclic Nucleotide Research, 1974-80, Advances in Sex Hormone Research, Urban and Schwarzenberg, 1975-81, Endocrinology, 1977-81, Maturitas, 1979-83, Jour. Andrology, 1979-83, Hormones, 1982—, Contraceptive Delivery Systems, MTP Press Ltd., 1983—, Clin. and Investigative Medicine, 1985—, Clin. Endocrinology Monographs, 1977—, Jour. Clin. Investigation, 1977—, Jour. Endocrinological Investigation, 1983-87; mem. editorial com. Interface, 1984-87, sci. com., 1984-88; mem. editorial com. Hormones-reproduction-metabolisme, 1984—; mem. editorial bd. Jour. Steroid Biochemistry and Molecular Biology, 1987—; editor: Hypothalamus and Endocrine Functions, 1976, Clinical Neuroendocrinology, a pathophysiological approach, 1979, Prolactin and Prolactinomas, 1983, (with P. Mauvais-Jarvis and R. Sitruk-Ware) Medecine de la Réproduction, Gynécologie Endocrinienne, 1982, (with A. Belanger and A. Dupont) LHRH and Its Analogues, Basic and Clinical Aspects, 1984, (with L. Proulx) Endocrinology, 1984, (with V. K. Wenderoth) A New Approach to the Treatment of Prostate Cancer, 1985, (with others) Early Stage Prostate Cancer: Diagnosis and Choice of Therapy, 1989, (with others) Advances in Diagnosis and Treatment of Early Prostate Cancer, 1993. Pres. Le fonds de la Recherche en Sante du que., 1992-95, mem. coun., 1981-87, Fondation du Centre Hospitalier de U. Lavel, 1981—; trustee Fondation Skibec Alpin, 1981—, founding mem.; chmn. Skibec Alpin, 1980-85; pres. Skibec, 1980-85, Que. Ski Show, 1980, 81, hon. pres., 1982, 84; coun. mem. Que. Zone Water Ski Assn., 1979-80; founding pres. Que. Water Ski Found., 1988; pres. organizing com., race chmn. Mont Ste.-Anne World Cup, 1983, 84; mem. coun. Can. Ski Assn., 1982-87; pres. Que. Water Ski Assn., 1987-89; coun. mem. Can. Water Ski Assn., 1987-89. Decorated chevalier Ordre de Malta, Order of Que., 1990, Order of Can., 1981; recipient medal city of Nice, 1977; award Fondation de Recherche en Hormolologie, 1981, award MDS Health Group, 1981, award Fideides of C. of C. of Ste.-Foy, 1984, 85, medal Coll. de France, Paris, 1984, Excel award, 1985, Gloire de l'Escole award Laval U. Alumni, 1991; Rsch. Coun. Can. fellow, 1962-68, Centennial fellow, 1968-69, scholar, 1969-73; named Grand Quebecois, Met. Que. C. of C., 1991, Most Cited Can. Sci., Inst. Sci. Info., 1973-88; numerous other awards, honors. Fellow Royal Soc. Can. (program com. 1983-84, com. for McLaughlin medal 1982-84, pres. com. for McLaughlin medal 1983-84, mem. coun. 1983-84); mem. Coll. des Médecins et Chirurgiens de la Province de Que., Royal Coll. Physicians and Surgeons Can. (assoc.), AAAS, Assn. des Médecins de Langue Française du Can. (Fondamental rsch. award 1972), Assn. Canadienne-Française pour l'Avancement des Scis. (Vincent medal 1976), Soc. Study Reproduction (rsch. award 1980), Internat. Soc. Neuroendocrinology (sec.-treas. 1984-92, v.p. 1992—), Internat. Soc. Endocrinology (exec. com. 1984-88), Biochem. Soc. (Gt. Britain), Endocrine Soc., Can. Biochem. Soc., Can. Physiol. Soc. (Michael Sarrazin prize 1990), Club de Recherches Cliniques du Quebec (Michel Sarrazin prize 1990), Am. Soc. Cell Biology, Am. Fertility Soc., Tissue Culture Assn., Can. Soc. Clin. Investigation (pres. 1981-82, pres. program com. 1982), Cans. for Health Rsch. (bd. dirs. 1983-88), Can. Soc. Endocrinology and Metabolism (chmn. liaison com. 1975-84, pres. 1978-79), Am. Soc. Andrology (coun. 1982-85), N.Y. Acad. Scis., Royal Soc. Medicine (affiliate), Soc. Argentina de Urologia (miembro correspondiente), Société Française d'Endocrinologie (hon.), Am. Soc. Biol. Chemists, Can. Fertility and Andrology Soc., Soc. Obstetricians and Gynaecologists Can. (assoc.), Can. Investigators in Reproduction, Internat. Menopause Club, Internat. Soc. Andrology, Internat. Study Group Steroid Hormones, Am. Soc. Clin. Investigation, Société d'Andrologie de Langue Française (hon.). Home: 2989 Rue de la Promenade, Ste-Foy, Ste-Foy, PQ Canada G1W 2J5 Office: Laval U Hosp, 2705 Laurier Blvd, Quebec, PQ Canada G1V 4G2

LA BUDDE, KENNETH JAMES, librarian; b. Sheboygan Falls, Wis., Jan. 20, 1920; s. Arno Peter and Claire (Devoy) LaB. A.B., U. Wis., 1941, B.L.S., 1942; student, U. Chgo., 1943-44; M.A., U. Minn., 1948; Ph.D., 1954. Student asst. U. Wis. Library, 1939-42; sr. library asst. Milw. Pub. Library, 1942; librarian Sheboygan (Wis.) Press, 1944-46; instr. English Milton (Wis.) Coll., 1946-47; dir. libraries U. Mo. at Kansas City, 1950-85, asst. prof. history, 1958-61, assoc. prof., 1961, prof., 1962-85, prof. emeritus, 1985—. Contbr. articles profl. jours. Served with AUS, 1942-44. Recipient Thomas Jefferson award U. Mo., 1988. Mem. ALA, Am. Studies Assn., Bibliog. Soc. Am., Mo. Libr. Assn. (chmn. coll. and univ. divsn. 1954-55), Kansas City Posse of Westerners, Wis. Meml. Union, Mid-Continent Am. Studies Assn. (pres. 1963-64, arts editor jour. 1959-63), Orgn. Am. Historians, Soc. Archtl. Historians, Garden History soc., Decorative Arts Soc., Rockhill Tennis Club, Beta Phi Mu, Phi Kappa Phi, Phi Alpha Theta. Home: 309 Brush Creek Blvd Kansas City MO 64112-1792

LABUDDE, ROY CHRISTIAN, lawyer; b. Milw., July 21, 1921; s. Roy Lewis and Thea (Otteson) LaB.; m. Anne P. Held, June 7, 1952; children: Jack, Peter, Michael, Susan, Sarah. AB, Carleton Coll., 1943; JD, Harvard U., 1949. Bar: Wis. 1949, U.S. Dist. Ct. (ea. and we. dists.) Wis. 1950, U.S. Ct. Appeals (7th cir.) 1950, U.S. Supreme Ct. 1957. Assoc. Michael, Best & Friedrich, Milw., 1949-57, ptnr., 1958—; dir. DEC-Inter, Inc., Milw. Western Bank, Western Bancshares, Inc., Superior Die Set Corp., Aunt Nellie's Farm Kitchens, Inc. Bd. dirs. Wis. Hist. Soc. Found.; chmn., bd. dirs. Milw. div. Am. Cancer Soc. Served to lt. j.g. USNR, 1943-46. Mem. Milw. Estate Planning Coun. (past pres.), Wis. Bar Assn., Wis. State Bar Attys. (chmn. tax sch., bd. dirs. taxation sect.), Univ. Club, Milw. Club, Milw. Country Club. Republican. Episcopalian. Home: 4201 W Stonefield Rd Mequon WI 53092-2771 Office: Michael Best & Friedrich 100 E Wisconsin Ave Ste 3300 Milwaukee WI 53202-4107

LABUDDE, SAMUEL FREEMAN, biologist, environmental activist; b. Madison, Wis., July 3, 1956; s. John Arthur and Bessie (Freeman) LaB. BA in Biology, Ind. U., 1986. Fisheries biologist Nat. Marine Fisheries Svc., Seattle, 1987; staff biologist Marine Mammal Fund, San Francisco, 1987—, Earth Island Inst., San Francisco, 1987-94; field biologist Earthtrust, Honolulu, 1989-90; field investigator Friends of Animals, Norwalk, Conn., 1990; EC marine policy cons. Humane Soc. of U.S., Washington, 1990-93. Contbg. author: (quar. jour.) Earth Island Jour., 1988-94. Coord. U.S. tuna boycott Earth Island Inst., San Francisco, 1988-90; lobbyist European comty. Humane Soc. of U.S., Brussels and Strasbourg, 1990-93; coord. U.S. Taiwan boycott Endangered Species Project, San Francisco and Washington, 1993-94. Recipient Goldman award for N.Am., Goldman Found., 1991, Founder's award for humane excellence ASPCA, 1989; named one of Am. Leaders under Age 40, Time Mag., 1994. Achievements include securing first documentary evidence of East Pacific dolphin slaughter by tuna industry in 1987, co-director U.S. campaign to end U.S. participation; organized and led high seas expedition in 1988 to obtain first documentary evidence of Asian driftnet fleets leading to 1989 UN resolution banning practice; organized and led successful U.S./internat. effort to implement U.S. trade sanctions against Taiwan for illegal trade in tigers and other endangered species. Office: Endangered Species Project E-205 Fort Mason Center San Francisco CA 94123

LABUNSKI, STEPHEN BRONISLAW, professional society administrator; b. Jordanow, Poland, Sept. 24, 1924; came to U.S., 1928, naturalized, 1943; s. Wiktor and Wanda (Mlynarski) L.; m. Betty E. Marley, Oct. 2, 1947 (div. June 1963); children: Linda, Richard, Roger; m. Jeralyn LeBrun, Aug. 28, 1967. Student, U. Kansas City, Mo., 1946-49, George Washington U., 1950. Adminstrv. asst. to U.S. Congressman Richard W. Bolling, 1949-51; with Storz Broadcasting Co., 1954-57; v.p. ABC radio network, 1957; head broadcast div. Crowell Collier Pub. Co., 1958; v.p., gen. mgr. WMCA Radio/Straus Broadcasting Group, N.Y.C., 1958-65; pres. radio div. NBC, 1965-69; mng. dir. WMCA Radio, 1969-71; v.p., partner Chuck Blore Creative Services, 1971-75; exec. v.p. Merv Griffin Group Radio, 1975-77; exec. dir. Internat. Radio and TV Soc., N.Y.C., 1978—; Bd. dirs. Radio Advt. Bur., 1965-69, Nat. Assn. Broadcasters, 1965-67. Chmn. adv. com. Voice of Am., 1987-89; Democratic candidate for Mo. Legislature, 1948. With AUS and USAAF, 1943-46. Mem. Advt. Council. Home: 30 E 37th St New York NY 10016-3019 Office: 420 Lexington Ave New York NY 10170-0002

LACAGNINA, MICHAEL ANTHONY, judge; b. Rochester, N.Y., July 6, 1932; s. Frank and Josephine (LoMaglio) L.; m. Mary Laura Mantle, June 8, 1952; children: John Michael, Gina Laura, Frank Anthony. B.S. in Bus. Adminstrn, U. Ariz., 1955, LL.B., 1957. Bar: Ariz. 1957. Asst. U.S. atty. Tucson, 1958-60; partner firm Bilby, Shoenhair, Warnock & Dolph, Tucson, 1960-83; of counsel Bilby, Shoenhair, Warnock & Dolph, 1983-84; judge divsn. II Ariz. Ct. Appeals, 1984-95; vice chief judge Div. II, Ariz. Ct. Appeals, 1985-87, chief judge, 1987-89. Served with USMCR, 1950-52. Fellow Am. Coll. Trial Attys., Ariz. Bar Found. (chmn. fellows 1986-87); mem. ABA, Ariz. Bar Assn., Pima County Bar Assn. (pres. 1981), Nat. Assn. R.R. Trial Attys., Am. Bd. Trial Advs. (nat. exec. com., nat. sec. 1981, nat. pres. 1983), Ariz. Judges Assn. (exec. com. 1985-95), Tucson Def. Attys. (pres.), Phi Delta Phi, Alpha Kappa Psi. Democrat. Episcopalian. Home: 7100 E River Canyon Rd Tucson AZ 85750-2110

LACAPRA, DOMINICK CHARLES, historian; b. N.Y.C., July 13, 1939; s. Joseph and Mildred (Sciascia) LaC.; m. Anne-Marie Hlasny, June 15, 1965 (div.); 1 dau., Veronique. B.A., Cornell U., 1961; Ph.D., Harvard U., 1970. Tutor Harvard U., Cambridge, Mass., 1967-69; asst. prof. history Cornell U., Ithaca, N.Y., 1969-74, assoc. prof., 1974-79, prof. history, 1979—; Goldwin Smith prof. European intellectual history Cornell U., Ithaca, 1985-92, Bryce and Edith M. Bowmar prof. humanistic studies, 1992—. Author: Emile Durkheim, 1972, A Preface to Sartre, 1978, "Madame Bovary" on Trial, 1982, Rethinking Intellectual History, 1983, History and Criticism, 1985, History, Politics and the Novel, 1987, Soundings in Critical Theory, 1989, Representing the Holocaust, 1994. Fulbright fellow France, 1961-62, Woodrow Wilson fellow Harvard U., 1962-63, sr. fellow NEH, 1979, Sch. Criticism and Theory; recipient Disting. Tchg. award Coll. Arts and Scis. Cornell U., 1979. Mem. MLA, Am. Hist. Assn., Internat. Assn. Philosophy and Lit., Soc. Phenomenological and Existential Philosophy, Soc. for the Humanities (dir.). Home: 119 Terrace Pl Ithaca NY 14850-4254 Office: Cornell U History Dept McGraw Hall Ithaca NY 14853

LACCI, JOHN, chemical company executive. BA, Georgetown U., 1974, JD, 1977. Sr. atty. FTC Bur. of Competition, Washington, 1977-86; v.p., gen. counsel Great Lakes Chem. Corp., West Lafayette, Ind., 1986—. Office: Gt Lakes Chem Corp One Great Lakes Blvd West Lafayette IN 47906-0200

LA CELLE, PAUL LOUIS, biophysics educator; b. Syracuse, N.Y., July 4, 1929; s. George Clarke and Marguerite Ellen (Waggoner) La C. A.B., Houghton Coll., 1951; M.D., U. Rochester, 1959. Resident U. Rochester Med. Center-Strong Meml. Hosp., 1960-62; asst. prof. medicine U. Rochester, 1967-70, asso. prof., 1970-74, prof., 1974—, chmn. dept. biophysics, 1977—; sr. assoc. dean for acad. affairs and rsch. Sch. Medicine and Dentistry, U. Rochester, 1993—; cons. to govt. Mem. Gates-Chili Sch. Bd., Rochester, 1964-72; trustee Houghton Coll., 1976-95. Served to lt. USNR, 1952-55. NIH spl. fellow, 1965-66; recipient von Humboldt Sr. Scientist award, 1982-83. Mem. Biophys. Soc., Microcirculation Soc., European Microcirculation Soc., Alpha Omega Alpha. Achievements include research in biophysics of blood cells, physiology of microcirculation. Office: U Rochester Dept Biophysics 601 Elmwood Ave Rochester NY 14642-8408

LACER, ALFRED ANTONIO, lawyer, educator; b. Hammonton, N.J., Feb. 14, 1952; s. Vincent and Carmen (Savall) L.; m. Kathleen Visser, June 15, 1974; children: Margaret, James, Matthew. BA in Polit. Sci., Gordon Coll., 1974; JD, Cath. U. Am., 1977. Bar: Md. 1977, U.S. Dist. Ct. Md. 1980, U.S. Ct. Appeals (4th cir.) 1980. Law clk. to Honorable Joseph A. Mattingly, Jr. Cir. Ct. St. Mary's County, Leonardtown, Md., 1977-78; ptnr. Kenney, Lacer & Sparling, Lexington Park, Md., 1978—; adj. prof. bus. law Fla. Inst. Tech., Patuxent, Md., 1989-92, 95—; vis. instr. St. Mary's Coll. of Md., 1988, 91; mem. bd. edn. St. Mary's County (Md.) Pub. Schs., 1989-94, pres., 1991-92; mem. inquiry panel Atty. Grievance Commn. of Md., 1984-90. Bd. dirs. St. Mary's Hosp., Leonardtown, 1982-88, v.p., 1985-88; bd. dirs. So. Md. Community Action, Inc., Hughsville, Md., 1982-84. Mem. ABA, Md. Bar Assn. (com. on jud. appointments 1982-85), St. Mary's County Bar Assn. (v.p. 1979-80, pres. 1980-81), Md. Trial Lawyers Assn., Rotary (bd. dirs. Lexington Park, 1985-86). Episcopalian. Office: Kenney Lacer & Sparling 100 Exploration Ste 2030 Lexington Park MD 20653 also: 65 Duke St Prince Frederick MD 20678

LACEY, BEATRICE CATES, psychophysiologist; b. N.Y.C., July 22, 1919; d. Louis Henry and Mollie (Libowitz) Cates; m. John I. Lacey, Apr. 16, 1938; children: Robert Arnold, Carolyn Ellen. Student, Columbia U., 1935-38; A.B. with distinction, Cornell U., 1940; M.A., Antioch Coll., 1958. Mem. staff Fels Research Inst., Yellow Springs, Ohio, 1953-82; sr. investigator Fels Research Inst., 1966-72, sr. scientist, 1972-82; instr. Antioch Coll., Yellow Springs, 1956-63, asst. prof., 1963-68, assoc. prof., 1968-73, prof., 1973-82; Fels prof. psychiatry Wright State U. Sch. Medicine, 1977-82, clin. prof. psychiatry, 1982-89, Fels prof. emeritus, 1989—; acting sci. dir. Fels Research Inst., 1979-82. Assoc. editor Psychophysiology, 1975-78; reviewer Jour. Abnormal Psychology, Psychophysiology, Biol. Psychology, Cognitive Psychology, Sci.; contbr. articles to profl. jours.; researcher, author numerous publs. in psychophysiology of the autonomic nervous system. Recipient Disting. Sci. Contbn. award, Am. Psychol. Assn., 1976, Psychol. Sci. Gold Medal award, Am. Psychol. Found., 1985. Fellow Acad. Behavioral Medicine Research, Soc. Exptl. Psychologists, Am. Psychol. Soc. (William James fellow 1989); mem. Soc. Psychophysiol. Research (dir. 1972-75, pres. 1978-79), Soc. Neurosci., Phi Kappa Phi. Achievements include rsch. and publs. in psychophysiology of the autonomic nervous system. Home: 1425 Meadow Ln Yellow Springs OH 45387-1221

LACEY, CLOYD EUGENE, retired insurance company executive; b. New Lexington, Ohio, Mar. 12, 1918; s. Russell Anderson and Freda (Bahr) L.; m. Jane Linn Williams, Sept. 12, 1941; children: Thomas, Melinda Lacey Houfek, Janene Lacey Paulus. B.S. in Bus. Adminstrn., Ohio State U., 1941. Acct., asst. treas. Pioneer Mut. Causualty Co., Columbus, Ohio, 1945-51; various corp. fin. positions Nationwide Ins. Cos., Columbus, 1951-73, v.p., asst. controller, 1973-75, v.p., corp. controller, 1975-78, v.p. Office of Treas., controller, 1978-81, sr. v.p. fin., 1981-82, ret., 1982. Served with U.S. Army, 1943-45. Republican. Methodist. *I believe in God and put my trust in him. I believe in treating other people fairly and in giving them credit for accomplishments. I believe in maintaining a high degree of integrity. I believe in diligence and determination in performing a task. I believe in striving for excellence.*

LACEY, FREDERICK BERNARD, lawyer, former federal judge; b. Newark, Sept. 9, 1920; s. Frederick Robert and Mary Agnes (Armstrong) L.; m. Mary C. Stoneham, May 20, 1944; children—Frederick Bernard, James, Virginia, Robert, Mary, Kathleen, John. A.B., Rutgers U., 1941; J.D., Cornell U., 1948; LL.D. (hon.), Montclair State Coll., 1971, Seton Hall U., 1973. Bar: N.Y. State bar 1948, N.J. bar 1952. Asso. firm Whitman & Ransom, N.Y.C., 1948-53; asst. U.S. atty. for N.J., 1953-55; U.S. atty., 1969-71; partner firm Shanley & Fisher, Newark, 1955-69; U.S. dist. judge for N.J., 1971-86; sr. litigation ptnr. LeBoeuf, Lamb, Greene & MacRae, N.Y.C. and Newark, 1986—. Served to lt. comdr. USNR, 1942-46. Mem. Order of Coif, Phi Beta Kappa. *

LACEY, HENRY BERNARD, lawyer; b. Aurora, Nov. 30, 1963; s. Leonard Joseph and Colleen Trece (DeRyan) L. BS, Ariz. State U., 1988, JD, 1991. Bar: Ariz. 1991, U.S. Dist. Ct. Ariz. 1991, U.S. Ct. Appeals (9th cir.) 1992. Jud. law clk. to Hon. Cecil F. Poole U.S. Ct. Appeals 9th Cir., San Francisco, 1991-92; assoc. Kimball & Curry, P.C., Phoenix, 1992-93; atty. Law Office of Henry B. Lacey, Scottsdale, Ariz., 1993-94; vis. fellow Natural Resources Law Inst. Northwestern Sch. Law, Lewis & Clark Coll., Portland, Oreg., 1994-95; pvt. practice Lake Oswego, Oreg., 1995—; counsel/environ. group adv. bd. dirs. Coalition to Reform the Ctrl. Ariz. Project, Phoenix, 1993; vol. lawyer/Ariz. bd. dirs. Land and Water Fund of the Rockies, Boulder, Colo., 1992—. Gen. counsel Maricopa County, Ariz. Dem. Party, 1992-94; counsel Carol Cure for Congress Campaign, Phoenix, 1994; vol. numerous polit. campaigns, Ariz., 1988-92. Mem. ABA (young lawyers divsn. 1991—, sec. on natural resources, energy and environ. law, 1991—), Ariz. State Bar (environ. and natural resources law sec., 1991—), Maricopa County Bar Assn. (environ. law com. 1993—), Environ. Law Inst., Am. Inns of Ct. (McFarland chpt. 1994—), Order of the Coif, Phi Delta Phi. Roman Catholic. Avocations: hiking, bicycling, reading, photography. Office: 440 North Shore Rd Lake Oswego OR 97034

LACEY, HUGH MATTHEW, philosophy educator; b. Sydney, Australia, Sept. 7, 1939; came to U.S., 1972; s. Owen Charles and Margaret Jane (Devine) L.; m. Maria Ines Rocha E. Silva, Aug. 14, 1966; children: Andrew David, Daniel Carlos. BA, U. Melbourne, Australia, 1962, MA, 1964; PhD, Ind. U., 1966. Tutor in math. U. Melbourne, 1961-63; lectr. history and philosophy of sci. U. Sydney, 1966-68; prof. philosophy U. São Paulo, Brazil, 1969-72; prof. philosophy Swarthmore (Pa.) Coll., 1972, chmn. dept. philosophy, 1973-83, Eugene M. Lang Rsch. Prof. of Philosophy, 1993—; vis. prof. Temple U., Phila., spring 1983, Villanova U., fall 1984, Instituto de Teologia, São Paulo, spring 1988, fall, 1992, Ctrl. Am. U., El Salvador, summer 1991, U.Pa., fall 1995. Author: A Linguagem Do Espaco E do Tempo, 1972; co-author: Behaviorism, Science and Human Nature, 1982; co-editor: Towards a Society That Serves Its People: The Thought of El Salvador's Murdered Jesuits, 1991; cons. editor: Jour. for Theory of Social Behavior, 1977—, Behavior and Philosophy, 1987—, Jour. for Peace and Justice Studies, 1987—. Bd. dirs. Chester-Swarthmore Coll. Cmty. Coalition, 1993—. NSF fellow, 1975, 79, 83; Fulbright grantee, 1963; Research Found. of State of São Paulo grantee, 1969, 73. Mem. Philosophy of Sci. Assn., Am. Philos. Assn., Am. Psychol. Assn. (commn. on behavior modification 1974-77), Brazilian Soc. for the Advancement of Sci. Roman Catholic. Home: 4 Whittier Pl Swarthmore PA 19081-1142 Office: Dept Philosophy Swarthmore College Ave Swarthmore PA 19081-1390

LACEY, JOHN IRVING, psychologist, physiologist, educator; b. Chgo., Apr. 11, 1915; s. David and Cecelia (Burnstein) L.; m. Beatrice Lucile Cates, Apr. 16, 1938; children—Robert Arnold, Carolyn Ellen. A.B., Cornell U., 1937, Ph.D., 1941. Instr. Queen's Coll., Flushing, N.Y., 1941-42; mem. faculty Antioch Coll., 1946-77, prof. psychophysiology, 1956-77; mem. staff Fels Research Inst., Yellow Springs, Ohio, 1946-82, chief sect. behavioral physiology, 1946-82; Fels prof. psychiatry Wright State U. Med. Sch., 1977-82, prof. emeritus, 1982—; cons. USPHS, 1957-82, FDA, 1977-82; mem. bd. sci. counselors Nat. Inst. Aging, NIH, 1977-80;. Cons. editor Jour. Comparative and Physiol. Psychology, 1953-69, Jour. Psychosomatic Medicine, 1962-65, Jour. Psychophysiology, 1964-69, Jour. Physiol. Psychology; contbr. articles to profl. jours. Served to capt. USAAF, 1942-46. Centennial scholar Johns Hopkins U., 1976; recipient Psychol. Sci. Gold medal Am. Psychol. Found., 1985. Fellow Am. Psychol. Soc. (William James fellow 1989); mem. Soc. Psychophysiol. Research (award for disting. contbns. 1970, pres. 1961-62, dir. 1965-68), Am. Psychosomatic Soc. (bd. dirs. 1959-62), Soc. Exptl. Psychologists, Am. Psychol. Assn. (pres. div. physiol. and comparative psychology 1969-70, mem. council 1964-68, 70-73, 78-79, bd. dirs. 1974-77, Disting. Sci. Contbn. award 1976), AAAS (chmn. sect. 1985-86), Psychonomic Soc., Soc. for Neurosci., Acad. Behavioral Medicine Rsch., Internat. Brain Rsch. Orgn., Nat. Acad. Scis. (chair com. new techs. in cognitive psychophysiology with NRC 1988), Sigma Xi, Phi Kappa Phi. Home: 1425 Meadow Ln Yellow Springs OH 45387-1221

LACEY, JOHN WILLIAM CHARLES, management consultant; b. London, May 1, 1930; came to U.S., 1956; s. William J. and Florence (Farbus) L.; m. Edna Winifred Burns, July 28, 1951; children: Jonathan Charles, Erika Jane. B.A. with honors, Oxford U., 1952, M.A. with honors, 1956. Sr. sci. officer Govt. of U.K., 1952-60; U.S. liaison officer Brit. embassy, Washington, 1956-60; mgr. research and devel., spl. systems Control Data Corp., Bloomington, Minn., 1960-63, dir. ops., 1963; pres. Control Data subs. Control Corp., Bloomington, 1964-65, gen. mgr. Devel. and Standard Systems div., 1965, v.p. computer equipment group, 1966-67, v.p. corp. devel., 1967-71, v.p., sr. staff officer corp. plans and controls, 1971-73, sr. v.p. corp. plans and controls, chmn. mgmt. com., 1973-77; pres. Control Data Edn. Co., 1977-79, Control Data Info. and Edn. Systems Co., 1979-82; exec. v.p. Control Data Corp., 1982-86; cons. in field, 1986—; chmn. bd. Control Corp., Adcomp Corp., 1963-66; bd. dirs. Graco, Inc., 1973-95, Instron Corp., LSC Inc. Bd. dirs. Jr. Achievement Greater Mpls., 1966-76, Mpls. Acquatennial, 1975-82, Guthrie Theater, 1983-88; bd. dirs. Computer Mus., 1982-86, trustee, 1986-93. With Brit. Royal Navy, 1948-49.

LACH, ALMA ELIZABETH, food and cooking writer, consultant; b. Petersburg, Ill.; d. John H. and Clara E. (Boeker) Satorius; diplome de Cordon Bleu, Paris, 1956; m. Donald F. Lach, Mar. 18, 1939; 1 dau., Sandra Judith. Feature writer Children's Activities mag., 1954-55; creator, performer TV show Let's Cook, children's cooking show, 1955; hostess weekly food program on CBS, 1962-66, performer TV show Over Easy, PBS, 1977-78; food editor Chgo. Daily Sun-Times, 1957-65; pres. Alma Lach Kitchens Inc., Chgo., 1966—; dir. Alma Lach Cooking Sch., Chgo.; lectr. U. Chgo. Downtown Coll., Gourmet Inst., U. Md., 1963, Modesto (Calif.) Coll., 1978, U. Chgo., 1981; resident master Shoreland Hall, U. Chgo., 1978-81; food cons. Food Bus. Mag., 1964-66, Chgo.'s New Pump Room, Lettuce Entertain You, Bitter End Resort, Brit. V.I., Midway Airlines, Flying Food Fare, Inc., Berghoff Restaurant, Hans' Bavarian Lodge, Unocal '76, Univ. Club Chgo.; columnist Modern Packaging, 1967-68, Travel & Camera, 1969, Venture, 1970, Chicago mag., 1978, Bon Appetit, 1980, Tribune Syndicate, 1982; inventor: Curly-Dog Cutting Bd., 1995. Recipient Pillsbury award, 1958; Grocery Mfrs. Am. Trophy award, 1959, certificate of Honor, 1961; Chevalier du Tastevin, 1962; Commanderie de l'Ordre des Anysetiers du Roy, 1963; Confrerie de la Chaine des Rotisseurs, 1964; Les Dames D'Escoffier, 1982, Culinary Historians of Chgo., 1993. Mem. Am. Assn. Food Editors (chmn. 1959). Clubs: Tavern, Quadrangle (Chgo.). Author: A Child's First Cookbook, 1950; The Campbell Kids Have a Party, 1953; The Campbell Kids at Home, 1953; Let's Cook, 1956; Candlelight Cookbook, 1959; Cooking a la Cordon Bleu, 1970; Alma's Almanac, 1972; Hows and Whys of French Cooking, 1974; contbr. to World Book Yearbook, 1961-75, Grolier Soc. Yearbook, 1962. Home and Office: 5750 S Kenwood Ave Chicago IL 60637-1744 *The art of cooking rests upon one's ability to taste, to reproduce taste, and to create taste. To achieve distinction the cook must taste everything, study cookbooks of all kinds, and experiment constantly in the kitchen. I stress in my writing and teaching the logic of food preparation, for the cook who possesses logic, knows how to create dishes rather than being content merely to duplicate the recipes of others.*

LACH, JOSEPH THEODORE, physicist; b. Chgo., May 12, 1934; s. Joseph and Kate (Ziemba) L.; m. Barbara Ryan, June 26, 1965; children—Michael, Elizabeth. A.B., U. Chgo., 1953, M.S., 1956; Ph.D., U. Calif.-Berkeley, 1963. Rsch. assoc. in physics Yale U., Hew Haven, 1963-65, asst. prof. physics, 1966-69; physicist Fermi Nat. Accelerator Lab., Batavia, Ill, 1969—, chmn. dept. physics, 1974-75; chmn. Gordon Rsch. Conf. in Elem. Particle Physics, 1975; mem. joint rsch. program with USSR and People's Republic of China. Fellow Am. Phys. Soc., Physicians for Social Responsibility, Ill. Geol. Survey (rsch. affiliate). Home: 28w364 Indian Knoll Trl West Chicago IL 60185-3013 Office: Fermilab PO Box 500 Batavia IL 60510-0500

LACHANCE, JANICE RACHEL, federal agency administrator, lawyer; b. Biddeford, Maine, June 17, 1953; d. Ralph L. and Rachel A. (Desnoyers) L. BA, Manhattanville Coll., 1974; JD, Tulane U., 1978. Bar: Maine 1978, D.C. 1982. Staff dir. subcom. on antitrust Ho. of Reps., Washington, 1982-83; adminstrv. asst. Congresswoman Katie Hall, 1983-84; asst. pres. sec. Mondale-Ferraro Campaign, Washington, 1984; press sec. Congressman Tom Daschle, 1985; ptnr. Lachance and Assocs., Washington, 1985-87; dir. communications and polit. action Am. Fedn. Govt. Employees (AFL-CIO), Washington, 1987-93; dir. policy and communications U.S. Office Pers. Mgmt., Washington, 1993-96, chief of staff, 1996—; vis. scholar Cornell U., 1972-73. Editor newsletter Govt. Standard, 1987-93. Mem. Delta Delta Delta, Phi Alpha Delta. Democrat. Roman Catholic. Office: US Office Pers Mgmt 1900 E St NW Washington DC 20415-0001

LACHANCE, PAUL ALBERT, food science educator, clergyman; b. St. Johnsbury, Vt., June 5, 1933; s. Raymond John and Lucienne (Landry) L.; m. Therese Cecile Cote; children: Michael P., Peter A., M.-Andre, Susan A. BS, St. Michael's Coll., 1955; postgrad., U. Vt., 1955-57; PhD, U. Ottawa, 1960; cert. in pastoral counseling, N.Y. Theol. Sem., 1981; DSc (hon.), St. Michael's Coll., 1982. Ordained deacon Roman Cath. Ch., 1977. Assigned to St. Paul's Ch. Princeton, N.J.; aerospace biologist Aeromed. Research Labs., Wright-Patterson AFB, Ohio, 1960-63; lectr. dept. biology U. Dayton, Ohio, 1963; flight food and nutrition coordinator NASA

Manned Spacecraft Center, Houston, 1963-67; assoc. prof. dept. food sci. Rutgers U., New Brunswick, N.J., 1967-72, dir. Sch. Feeding effectiveness research project, 1969-72, prof., 1972—, faculty rep. to bd. trustees, 1988-90, dir. grad. program food sci., 1988-91, chmn. food sci. dept., 1991—, chmn. univ. senate, 1990-93; faculty rep. to bd. govs., 1990-94; cons. Nutritional Aspects of Food Processing; mem. nutrition adv. com. Whitehall-Robins/ Lederle Consumer Divsn., 1989—; mem. sci. adv. bd. Roche chem. divsn. Hoffmann La Roche Co., 1976-88; mem. nutrition policy com. Beatrice Foods Co., 1979-86; trustee religious ministries com. Princeton Med. Ctr.; bd. dirs. J.R. Short Milling Co., 1990—. Mem. editorial adv. bd., Sch. Food Service Research Rev., 1977-82, Jour. Am. Coll. Nutrition, 1986—, Jour. Med. Consultation, 1985—, Nutrition Reports Internat., 1963-83, Profl. Nutritionist, 1977-80; contbr. articles to profl. jours. Served to capt. USAF, 1960-63. Recipient Endel Karmas award for excellence in teaching food sci., 1988, WilliamCruess award for excellence in teaching Inst. Food Technologists, 1991. Fellow Inst. Food Technologists, Am. Coll. Nutrition; mem. Am. Assn. Cereal Chemists, AAAS, Am. Inst. Nutrition, N.Y. Inst. Food Technologists (chmn. 1977-78), Am. Soc. Clin. Nutrition, N.Y. Acad. Sci., Am. Dietetic Assn., Soc. Nutrition Edn., Am. Public Health Assn., Nat. Assn. Cath. Chaplains, Sociedad Latino Americano de Nutricion, Sigma Xi, Delta Epsilon Sigma. Home: 34 Taylor Rd Princeton NJ 08540-9521 Office: Rutgers U Cook Coll Food Sci New Brunswick NJ 08903-0231

LACHEMANN, MARCEL, professional baseball manager; b. L.A., June 13, 1941. BSBA, U. So. Calif., 1962. Former player Kansas City A's (moved to Oakland); pitching coach Calif. Angels, 1983-92, mgr., head coach, 1994—; pitching coach Fla. Marlins, 1992-94. Office: California Angels 2000 E Gene Autry Way Anaheim CA 92806-6100*

LACHENAUER, ROBERT ALVIN, retired school superintendent; b. Newark, Apr. 1, 1929; s. Alvin Frederick and Helen Louise (Bowers) L.; m. Patricia McConnell, June 14, 1952; children: Jane, Nancy, Robert. AB, Montclair State U., 1951, MA, 1956; EdS, Seton Hall U., 1983. Diplomate in sch. adminstrn., 1988; cert. sch. adminstr., N.J., sch. bus. adminstr., N.J., tchr., N.J., supr., N.J., secondary sch. prin., N.J. Tchr. Bd. Edn., Union, N.J., 1951-52, 54-57, asst. bd. sec., 1957-61; dep. supt. New Providence (N.J.) Sch. Dist., 1961-76, supt., 1976-91, vice pres. Rigorous Ednl. Assistance Deserving Youth Found., 1991-93; treas. sch. monies Morris-Union Jointure Commn., 1987-93; pres. Union County Sch. Bus. Ofcls., 1967-68, Title IV State Adv. Council, Trenton, N.J., 1976-78, Morris-Union Consortium, N.J., 1981-83, Union County Supts. Roundtable, 1983-84; adv. bd. Summit Trust Co., 1971-86. Elder treas. Presbyn. Ch., New Providence, 1958-62; treas. New Providence Hist. Soc., 1966-76; pres. United Way, New Providence, 1978; property mgr. Providence Presbyn. Ch., Hilton Head Island, 1993, elder, 1995. Served as seaman USN, 1952-54. Named Disting. Scholar of the Acad. Nat. Acad. for Sch. Execs., 1990. Mem. N.J. Assn. Sch. Adminstrs. (exec. bd. 1986-91), N.J. Assn. Sch. Bus Officials (pres. 1974-75), Assn. Sch. Bus Officials U.S. (professionalization com. 1974, membership chmn. 1976), N.J. Assn. Ednl. Secs. (adv. bd. 1976—, Outstanding Adminstr. of Yr. 1987). Lodge: Rotary (pres. 1980-81). Home: Sea Pines Plantation 84 Governors Rd Hilton Head Island SC 29928-3032

LACHENBRUCH, ARTHUR HEROLD, geophysicist; b. New Rochelle, N.Y., Dec. 7, 1925; s. Milton Cleveland and Leah (Herold) L.; m. Edith Bennett, Sept. 7, 1950; children: Roger, Charles, Barbara. BA, Johns Hopkins U., 1950; MA, Harvard U., 1954, PhD, 1958. Registered geophysicist and geologist, Calif. Research geophysicist U.S. Geol. Survey, 1951—; vis. prof. Dartmouth Coll., 1963; mem. numerous adv. coms. and panels. Contbr. articles to sci. jours. Mem. Los Altos Hills (Calif.) Planning Commn., 1966-86. Served with USAAF, 1943-46. Recipient Spl. Act award U.S. Geol. Survey, 1970, Meritorious Service award, 1972, Disting. Service award U.S. Dept. Interior, 1978. Fellow AAAS, Am. Geophys. Union (Walter H. Bucher medal 1989), Royal Astron. Soc., Geol. Soc. Am. (Kirk Bryan award 1963), Arctic Inst. N.Am.; mem. Nat. Acad. Sci. Current work: solid-earth geophysics, terrestial heat flow, tectonophysics, permafrost; subspecialties: tectonics, geophysics. Office: US Geol Survey 345 Middlefield Rd Menlo Park CA 94025-3561

LACHENBRUCH, DAVID, editor, writer; b. New Rochelle, N.Y., Feb. 11, 1921; s. Milton Cleveland and Leah Judith (Herold) L.; m. Gladys Kidwell, Dec. 12, 1941; 1 child, Ann Leah Lachenbruch Zulawski. BA, U. Mich., 1942. Corr. Variety, also Detroit Times, 1940-42; reporter, asst. city editor, then wire editor Gazette & Daily, York, Pa., 1946-50; assoc. editor TV Digest with Consumer Electronics, Washington, 1950-58; mng. editor TV Digest with Consumer Electronics, 1959-68; editorial dir. TV Digest with Consumer Electronics, N.Y.C., 1968—; v.p. Warren Pub., Inc., Washington, 1962—. Adv. editor: Academic American Encyclopedia, 1989—; columnist Electronics Now mag., Video mag.; co-author: The Complete Book of Adult Toys, 1983; contbr. articles to consumer mags.; contbg. editor: N.Y. Times Ency. of TV; author: Videocassette Recorders—The Complete Home Guide, 1978, A Look Inside Television, 1985; cons. Acad. Am. Ency. Served with AUS, 1942-45. Inducted Video Hall of Fame, 1993. Mem. White House Corrs. Assn., Union Internat. de la Presse Electronique. Home: 77 7th Ave New York NY 10011-6645 also: 20 Cross Brook Rd Roxbury CT 06783-1211 Office: 276 5th Ave New York NY 10001-4509

LACHEY, JAMES MICHAEL, professional football player; b. St. Henry, Ohio, June 4, 1963. BA Mktg., Ohio State Univ., 1985. With San Diego Chargers, 1985-88, L.A. Raiders, 1988; offensive tackle Washington Redskins, 1988—. Named offensive tackle The Sporting News NFL All-Pro team, 1989-91. Played in Pro Bowl, 1987, 90-91. Office: Washington Redskins Dulles Intl Airport PO Box 17247 Washington DC 20041

LACHMAN, EDWARD, cinematographer; b. Morristown, N.J., Mar. 31, 1946; s. Edward and Rosabel Lachman. BA, Harvard U., 1965; BFA summa cum laude, Ohio U., 1969. presenter seminars Harvard U., Columbia U., NYU, Ohio U. Co-dir. photography: (feature films) Lords of Flatbush, 1973, Christo's Valley Curtain (Club Ribbon, Am. Film Festival 1974, Acad. award nomination), Lightning over Water, Wim Winders, 1976, 79 (feature film prize German Film Festival), Stroszek LaSoufriere Werner Herzog, 1976 (awards Cannes, Berlin and N.Y. Film Festivals), Little Wars, Maroon Baghdadi (feature film award Cannes Film Festival 1984), Mother Teresa (Acad. award nomination documentary 1987); dir. photography: Say Amen, Somebody, 1982 (awards Cannes and N.Y. Film Festival), Lightnong over Water, 1984 (Cannes, Berlin, N.Y. film festivals), Desperately Seeking Susan, 1985, Tokyo-Ga, 1985 (Cannes, Berlin, Venice and N.Y. Film Festivals), True Stories, 1986, Less Than Zero, 1987, Making Mr. Right, 1987, Mississippi Masala, 1991, London Kills Me, 1992, Light Sleeper, 1992 (IFP award for cinematography 1993), My New Gun, 1992, Dark Blood, 1993, Mi Familia, 1994. Recipient Best Cinematography award S.Am. Film Festival, 1988, Acad. award nomination for short subject, 1986, Silver Maile award for cinematography, 1994, Kodak award of excellence, 1995. Mem. ASC, Internat. Photographers (644, 659). Home: 43 E 19th St New York NY 10003-1304 also: Doug Apatow Agency 10559 Blythe Ave Los Angeles CA 90064-3338

LACHMAN, LAWRENCE, business consultant, former department store executive; b. N.Y.C., Jan. 9, 1916; s. Charles and Dorothy (Rubin) L.; m. Judith Lehman, Apr. 8, 1945; children: Robert Ian, Charles Scott. BS summa cum laude, NYU, 1936. Controller James McCreery & Co., N.Y.C., 1938-46; treas., dir. Citizens Utilities Co., Stamford, Conn., 1946-47; treas. Bloomingdale's, N.Y.C., 1947-53; v.p. personnel and ops. Bloomingdale's, 1953-58, exec. v.p. adminstrn. and personnel, 1958-64, pres., chief exec. officer, 1964-69, chmn. bd., chief exec. officer, 1969-78; chmn. bd., chief exec. officer Bus. Mktg. Corp., 1978-80; bd. dirs. DFS Group Ltd., ADVO, Inc. Trustee NYU, 1974-90. Served to maj. USAAF, 1942-46. Decorated Bronze Star; French Legion of Honor; recipient Madden award N.Y. U., 1969. Home: 104 E 68th St Apt 5A New York NY 10021-5905

LACHMAN, MARGUERITE LEANNE, real estate investment advisor; b. Vancouver, B.C., Can., Mar. 16, 1943; came to U.S., 1955; d. Wilfred Harry and Claire Elisha (Silverthorn) L. BA, U. So. Calif., 1964; MA, Claremont Grad. Sch., 1966. With Real Estate Rsch. Corp., 1965-87; sr. v.p. Real Estate Research Corp., 1977-79, pres., CEO, 1979-87; mng. dir. Schroder Real Estate Assocs., 1987—, Schroder Mortgage Assocs., 1992—; bd. dirs. Chgo. Title and Trust, Lincoln Nat. Corp., Liberty Property Trust; frequent lectr. seminars and profl. groups. Author: (with Al Smith and Anthony Downs) Achieving Effective Desegregation, 1973, (with Susan Olson) Tax Delinquency in the Inner City, 1976, Emerging Trends in Real Estate, 1981, 82, 83, 84, 85, 86, 87, Decade to Decade, 1988, Real Estate's Demographic Puzzle, 1995; contbr. articles to profl. jours. Trustee, v.p. Urban Land Inst., Urban Land Found. Mem. N.Y. Women's Forum, Inc., Comml. Club Chgo. Office: Schroder Real Estate Assocs 437 Madison Ave New York NY 10022-7001

LACHMAN, MORTON, writer, theatrical director and producer; b. Seattle, Mar. 20, 1918; s. Sol and Rose (Bloom) L.; m. Elaine Lachman, June 23, 1940; children: Joanne, Dianne, Robert. B.A., U. Wash., Seattle, 1939. Exec. producer TV series One Day at a Time, All in the Family, Archie Bunker's Place, Sanford, Gimme A Break, Kate & Allie; head writer, producer, dir. The Bob Hope Show; head writer Acad. Award shows; co-writer feature films Mixed Company, Yours, Mine & Ours. With AUS, 1942-45. Recipient Emmy award for directing The Girl Who Couldn't Lose, 1975. Clubs: El Caballero, Queens, Tamerisk, Rangoon Racquet. Address: 2780 Bottlebrush Dr Los Angeles CA 90077-2010

LACHS, JOHN, philosopher, educator; b. Budapest, Hungary, July 17, 1934; s. Julius and Magda (Brod) L.; m. Shirley Marie Mellow, June 3, 1967; children: Sheila Marie, James Richard. B.A., McGill U., 1956, M.A., 1957; Ph.D., Yale, 1961. From asst. prof. to prof. philosophy Coll. William and Mary, 1959-67; prof. philosophy Vanderbilt U., 1967—, Centennial Prof., 1993—; chair Vanderbilt U. Faculty Senate, 1990-91. Author: Marxist Philosophy: A Bibliographical Guide, 1967, The Ties of Time, 1970, Intermediate Man, 1981, Mind and Philosophers, 1987, George Santayana, 1988, The Relevance of Philosophy to Life, 1995; editor: Animal Faith and Spiritual Life, 1967, Physical Order and Moral Liberty, 1969; co-editor: The Human Search, 1981; co-translator: Fichte, Science of Knowledge, 1970; contbr. numerous articles to profl. jours. Past chmn. Tenn. Com. for Humanities. Recipient Award for Advancement of Scholarship Phi Beta Kappa, 1962, Harris Harbison award for distinguished teaching Danforth Found., 1967, Chancellor's cup Vanderbilt U., 1970, Madison Sarratt prize excellence undergrad. teaching, 1972, Alumni Edn. award Vanderbilt U., 1991. Mem. Internat. Neoplatonic Soc., World Sociology Assn. (alienation rsch. com.), Am. Acad. Polit. and Social Sci., Am. Philos. Assn., Metaphys. Soc. Am. (pres.), Royal Inst. Philosophy, Soc. Advancement Am. Philosophy (past pres.), Soc. Health and Human Values, C.S. Peirce Soc. (past pres.), Va. Philos. Assn., Tenn. Philos. Assn., So. Soc. Philosophy and Psychology, Hasting Ctr. Episcopalian. Home: 1968 Edenbridge Way Nashville TN 37215-5809 Office: Vanderbilt U 2305 W End Ave Nashville TN 37203-1700

LACITIS, ERIK, journalist; b. Buenos Aires, Argentina, Dec. 10, 1949; came to U.S., 1960, naturalized, 1965; s. Erik and Irene Z. L.; m. Malorie Nelson, Aug. 30, 1976. Student, Coll. Forest Resources, U. Wash., 1967-71. Editor U. Wash. Daily, 1970; pub. New Times Jour., 1970-71; reporter, pop-music cons. Seattle Post Intelligencer, 1972—; reporter, columnist Seattle Times, 1972; v.p., treas. Malorie Nelson, Inc., 1980—. Recipient numerous awards from Wash. State chpt. Sigma Delta Chi; Nat. Headliners Club award, 1978; winner gen. interest competition Nat. Soc. Newspaper Columnists, 1987. Lutheran. Office: The Seattle Times PO Box 70 Fairview Ave N & John St Seattle WA 98111-0070

LACK, ANDREW, broadcast executive. Office: NBC News 30 Rockefeller Plz New York NY 10112

LACK, JAMES J., state senator, lawyer; b. N.Y.C., Oct. 18, 1944; s. Harry A. and Eve (Kaufman) L.; m. Therese M. Gutleber, Jan. 19, 1969; children: Katherine Shana, Jeremy David. B.A., U. Pa., 1966; J.D., Fordham U., 1969. Bar: N.Y. 1970. Counsel to N.Y. State Consumer Protection Bd., 1970-72; prin. asst. frauds bur. dist. attys. office County of Suffolk, N.Y., 1972-73; commr. Suffolk County Dept. Consumer Affairs, Hauppauge, N.Y., 1974-77; pres. Better Bus. Bur. Met. N.Y., 1977-78; ptnr. Smyth & Lack, Huntington, N.Y., 1983—; mem. N.Y. Senate, 1979—; chmn. Senate Labor com., 1985-93, Majority Steering com., 1989-94, Senate com. on judiciary, 1994—, dep. majority whip, 1995—, Nat. Commn. Employment Policy; pres. Nat. Conf. State Legislatures, 1995—. Republican. Office: NY State Senate State Capitol Albany NY 12247

LACK, LARRY HENRY, small business owner; b. Richland, Wash., Aug. 27, 1952; s. Eugene Herman and Myrtle (Wellman) L.; m. Patricia Ann Henry, Aug. 19, 1978; children: Vicki Marie, Rachel Ann. Enlisted USAF, 1970, disabled vet., 1978; aircraft mechanic Ill., S.C., Okla. AFBs., 1970-78; inventor, prin. Lack Industries, Inc., Shreveport, La., 1978-85, Phoenix, 1985—; CEO Stellar Internat., Phoenix, 1991-92; cons. U.S. Air Force, Altus AFB, 1978-80, Cates & Phillips Patent Attys., Phoenix, 1985—; pres. La. Innovators Tech., Shreveport, 1981-82; lectr. Glendale Community Coll. 1987-88; guest lectr. Ariz. State U., 1989-90; authored legislation to regulate invention promotion cos. in Ariz., 1989. Patentee in field. Mem. Internat. Platform Assn. Republican. Achievements include inventor of the Sunflow Solar Pump, Pegasus Wind driven Pump, Compact Crude Oil Recovery System. Avocations: scuba diving, parachuting, hunting, rock climbing, flying. Home: 1433 W Islandia Gilbert AZ 85233 Office: Ste 25 1826 W Broadway Mesa AZ 85202

LACK, LEON, pharmacology and biochemistry educator; b. Bklyn, Jan. 7, 1922; s. Jacob and Yetta (Wolf) L.; m. Pauline Kaplan, Feb. 14, 1948; children: Elias David, Joshua Morris, Johanna Elaine, Adina Roberta, Evonne Clara. B.A., Bklyn. Coll., 1943; M.S., Mich. Stae Coll., 1948; Ph.D., Columbia U., 1953; postgrad. (Univ. postdoctoral fellow), Duke U., 1954-55. Instr. in pharmacology and exptl. therapeutics Johns Hopkins U. Sch. Medicine, 1955-59, asst. prof. pharmacology and exptl. therapeutics, 1959-63; asst. prof. physiology and pharmacology Duke U. Med. Center, 1964-66, prof. pharmacology, 1966-92, prof. emeritus pharmacology, 1992—, chief biochemist to clin. research, 1966-70; cons. E.I. DuPont de Nemours and Co., 1990-91, Monsanto, 1992-93. Contbr. numerous articles to profl. publs. Served with USAAF, 1943-46, PTO. Grantee NIH, 1960-90, OSHA, Ctr. for Disease Control, 1991-93. Mem. Am. Soc. Biol. Chemists, Am. Soc. Pharmacology and Exptl. Therapeutics. Jewish. Rsch. in pharmacology of cholesterol and lipids, pharmacology of intestinal bile salt transport, enzyme inhibitors relevant to prostatic cancer. Home: 2936 Welcome Dr Durham NC 27705-5556 Office: Duke U Med Ctr PO Box 3185 Durham NC 27715-3185

LACKENMIER, JAMES RICHARD, college president, priest; b. Lackawanna, N.Y., May 15, 1938; s. Harold and Margaret (Murphy) L. AB, Stonehill Coll., 1961; STL, Pontifical Gregorian U., Rome, 1965; AM, U.N.C., 1968; MA, U. Chgo., 1970. Ordained priest, Roman Catholic Ch. Tchr. English Notre Dame High Sch., Bridgeport, Conn., 1965-66, St. Peter's High Sch., Gloucester, Mass., 1966-68; chaplain St. Xavier Coll., Chgo., 1969-71; dir. collegiate formation Moreau Sem., Notre Dame, Ind., 1971-73; dir. campus ministry King's Coll., Wilkes-Barre, Pa., 1974-75, dir. devel., 1975-81, pres., 1981—. Bd. regents U. Portland, 1993—; bd. trustees Mercy Hosp., 1989-95, Mercy Hosp. South, 1995—; bd. dirs. Pa. Ednl. Telecom. Exch. Network, 1994—, Com. on Econ. Growth, Earth Conservancy, 1992—, Pa. Ind. Coll. and Univ. Rsch. Ctr., 1995—, Ctr. for Agile Pa. Edn., 1994—, Greater Wilkes-Barre Partnership, Inc.; mem. United Way Campaign Cabinet, 1995—; adv. bd. Pa. Mountains coun. Boy Scouts Am., North Tier Advanced Tech. Ctr. Ben Franklin Partnership Program, 1983—, Tuition Acct. Program, Office of Gov., Commonwealth Pa., 1992—; adv. group Coun. Higher Edn. Com., 1990; chmn. United Way Wyoming Valley, 1986. Mem. Wilkes-Barre C. of C., Westmoreland Club (bd. govs. local chpt. 1989-91), Mid. State Assn. Colls. and Schs. (commn. higher edn.), Pa. Assn. Colls. and Univs. (com. on acad. issues). Democrat. Lodges: Rotary Internat.; K.C. Office: King's Coll 133 N River St Wilkes Barre PA 18711-0801

LACKEY, ROBERT DEAN, oil company executive, consultant; b. Great Bend, Kans., Nov. 28, 1950; s. Jack Vernon and Doshia Maudine (Bowman) L.; m. Betty Lou Lilly, Apr. 28, 1967; children: Judy Carol Lackey Harris, Jim Dean Lackey. Grad. high sch., Yale, Okla. Stockman Brownlee Grocery, Cushing, Okla., 1968-70; agronomist Okla. State U., Stillwater, 1970-74; machinist Cesna Aircraft, Wichita, 1974-75; foreman Traco Oilfield Constrn., Cushing, Okla., 1975-79; downhole pump technician Fluor Corp., Cushing, Okla., 1979-83; store mgr. Your Oilfield Supply, Cushing, Okla., 1983-85; blast foreman Cushing Rail Car, 1985-89; br. mgr. Arrow Pump & Supply Inc., Stroud, Okla., 1989—. Democrat. Baptist. Avocations: family, fishing, hunting, reading. Home: RR 1 Box 287 Yale OK 74085-9762 Office: Arrow Pump & Supply 202 N 6th Ave Stroud OK 74079-4016

LACKEY, S. ALLEN, petroleum company executive, corporate lawyer. BBA, U. Miss., 1963, JD, 1968. Bar: Miss. 1968. Now v.p., gen. counsel Shell Oil Co., Houston. Office: Shell Oil Co 910 Louisiana St Houston TX 77002*

LACKLAND, JOHN, lawyer; b. Parma, Idaho, Aug. 29, 1939. A.B., Stanford U., 1962; J.D., U. Wash., 1964. Bar: Wash. 1965, U.S. Dist. Ct. (we. dist.) Wash. 1965, (ea. dist.) Wash. 1973, U.S. Ct. Appeals (9th cir.) 1965, Conn. 1981, U.S. Dist. Ct. Conn. 1983, U.S. Supreme Ct. 1973, U.S. Dist. Ct. (so. dist.) N.Y. 1988. Assoc. firm Lane Powell Moss & Miller, Seattle, 1965-69; asst. atty. gen. State of Wash., Seattle, 1969-72; asst. chief State of Wash. (U. Wash. div.), 1969-72; v.p., sec., gen. counsel Western Farmers Assn., Seattle, 1972-76, Fotomat Corp., Stamford, Conn., 1976-80; ptnr. Leepson & Lackland, 1981-88, Lackland and Nalewaik, 1988-92; pvt. practices Westport, Conn., 1992-94; prin. Lackland Assocs., Grand Junction, Colo., 1994—. Bd. dirs. Mercer Island (Wash.) United Ch., 1967-70, pres. bd. dirs., 1970; mem. land use plan steering com. City of Mercer Island, 1970-72; bd. dirs. Mercer Island Sch. Dist., 1970-73, v.p. bd. dirs., 1972, pres. 1973; trustee Mid-Fairfield Child Guidance Ctr., 1982-84, Norfield Congl. Ch., 1982-84; bd. dirs. Grand Junction Symphony Orch., 1995—.

LACKLAND, THEODORE HOWARD, lawyer; b. Chgo., Dec. 4, 1943; s. Richard and Cora Lee (Sanders) L.; m. Dorothy Ann Gerald, Jan. 2, 1970; 1 child, Jennifer Noel. BS, Loyola U., Chgo., 1965; MA, Howard U., 1967; JD, Columbia U., 1975; grad. U.S. Army Ranger Sch., 1968. Bar: N.J. 1975, U.S. Dist. Ct. N.J. 1975, Ga. 1982, U.S. Tax Ct. 1983, U.S. Supreme Ct. 1979, U.S. Dist. Ct. (no. dist.) Ga. 1982, U.S. Dist. Ct. (mid. dist.) Ga. 1985. Assoc. Dewey, Ballantine, Bushby, Palmer & Wood, N.Y.C., 1975-78; asst. U.S. atty. Dist. N.J., Newark, 1978-81; ptnr. Arnall Golden & Gregory, Atlanta, 1981-93, Lackland & Assocs., Atlanta, 1993-95, Lackland & McManus, 1995—; adj. prof. law Ga. State U. Law Sch., 1989—. Assoc. editor Columbia Human Rights Law Rev., 1974-75; contbr. articles to profl. jours. Adv. dir. Atlanta Bus. Devel. Ctr., Minority Bus. Devel. Council, Atlanta, 1983-91. Served with U.S. Army, 1967-71. Decorated Bronze Star with 1 oak leaf cluster, Purple Heart, Air Medal. Mem. ABA, N.J. Bar Assn., Ga. Bar Assn., Fed. Bar Assn., Gate City Bar Assn. Democrat. Roman Catholic. Home: 4400 Oak Ln Marietta GA 30062-6355 Office: Lackland & McManus 235 Peachtree St NW Ste 1700 Atlanta GA 30303-1405

LACKNER, JAMES ROBERT, aerospace medicine educator; b. Virginia, Minn., Nov. 11, 1940; s. William and Lillian Mae (Galbraith) L.; m. Ann Martin Graybiel, Aug. 26, 1970. BSc, MIT, 1966, PhD, 1970. Asst. prof. psychology Brandeis U., Waltham, Mass., 1970-74, assoc. prof. psychology, 1974-79, Riklis prof. physiology dept. psychology, 1977—, chmn. dept. psychology, 1975-83, provost, dean faculty, 1986-89, dir. Ashton Graybiel Spatial Orientation Lab., 1982—; research assoc. dept. psychology and clin. research ctr. MIT, Cambridge, 1970-80; sci. adv. bd. Space Biomed. Research Inst., Houston, 1982—, Aphasia Research Ctr. Boston U. Sch. Med., 1977-82, Eunice Kennedy Shriver Ctr. Harvard U. Med. Sch., Cambridge, 1980—; sci. adv. panel astronaut longitudinal health program Johnson Space Ctr., NASA, 1983, exec. sec. space adaptation syndrome steering com., 1982-84, pre-adaption trainer working group, 1986—, artificial gravity working group, 1987—; fabricant com. life scis. experiments for a space sta., 1982; space scis. bd. sensory motor panel NAS, 1984-86; com. on hearing, bioacoustics and biomechanics NRC, 1985-89, com. on vision, 1987-92, com. on space, biology and medicine, 1991—, mem. com. virtual reality rsch. and devel., 1992—. Mem. editorial bd. Presence, 1992—, Jour. Vestibular Rsch., Jour. Neurophysiology, 1995—; contbr. more than 200 articles to sci. jours. Mem. Am. Soc. for Gravitational and Space Biology, Aerospace Med. Assn. (Arnold B. Tuttle award), Soc. for Neurosci., Psychonomics Soc., Internat. Brain Research Orgn., Barany Soc. (hon.), Internat. Acad. Astronautics (hon.). Achievements include research in human sensory-motor coordination and spatial orientation. Home: Boyce Farm Rd Lincoln MA 01773-4813 Office: Brandeis U Ashton Graybiel Lab PO Box 9110/415 South St Waltham MA 02154-9100

LACKNER, RUDY PAUL, cardiothoracic surgeon; b. Queens, N.Y., July 25, 1958; s. Rudolph and Dorothy (Peplinski) L.; m. Carol Ann Cudone, May 15, 1990; children: Rudi, Pearl, Timothy. BS summa cum laude, Manhattan Coll., 1980; MD, N.Y. Med. Coll., 1985. Diplomate Am. Bd. Thoracic Surgery, Am. Bd. Gen. Surgery. Resident in gen. surgery L.I. Jewish Med. Ctr., New Hyde Park, N.Y., 1985-90; rsch. fellow in cardiothoracic surgery U. Chgo., 1990-91, resident in cardiothoracic surgery, 1991-93; fellow in thoracic transplant U. N.C., Chapel Hill, 1993-94; asst. prof. surgery, dir. lung transplant program U. Nebr., Omaha, 1994—. Recipient 1st prize ACS, 1989. Mem. Am. Coll. Chest Physicians, Am. Thoracic Soc., Assn. for Acad. Surgery, Internat. Soc. Heart and Lung Transplant, Epsilon Sigma Pi, Beta Beta Beta. Avocation: diving. Office: U Nebr Div Cardiothoracic Surgery 600 S 42nd St Omaha NE 68105-1002

LACKRITZ, MARC E., securities trade association executive; b. Columbus, Ohio, Sept. 29, 1946; m. Mary B. DeOreo, May 17, 1975; children: Anne, Katie, Sarah. AB in Pub. and Internat. Affairs, Princeton U., 1968; MPhil, Oxford U., 1971; JD cum laude, Harvard U., 1973. Asst. counsel U.S. Senate Watergate Com., Washington, 1973-74; dep. chief counsel U.S. Senate Budget Com., Washington, 1974-77; ptnr. Wald, Harkrader & Ross, Washington, 1977-84; staff dir., chief counsel U.S. Ho. Energy and Commerce subcom. telecommunications, consumer protection, fin., Washington, 1987-90; exec. v.p. Pub. Securities Assn., Washington, 1987-90; exec. v.p. Securities Ind. Assn., Washington, 1990-92, pres., 1992—; bd. dirs. Am. Coun. Capital Formation, Washington, Am. Univ. Adv. Bd. for MA in Fin. Econs. for Pub. Policy; bd. dirs., mem. adv. com. Fin. Acctg. Standards, Norwalk, Conn. Contbr. articles to profl. jours. Trustee Securities Industry Found. for Econ. Edn., Securities Industry Inst.; mem. fin. steering com. Clinton-for-Pres., Washington, 1991-92. Rhodes scholar 1968. Democrat. Jewish. Avocations: running, tennis, golf, writing. Office: Securities Industry Assn 1401 I St NW Ste 1000 Washington DC 20005-2225

LACOSTE, PAUL, lawyer, educator, university official; b. Montreal, Que., Can., Apr. 24, 1923; s. Emile and Juliette (Boucher) L.; m. Louise Marcil, Aug. 31, 1973 (div.); children: Helene, Paul-André, Anne-Marie. BA, U. Montreal, 1943, MA, 1944, Licenciate in Philosophy, 1946, Licenciate in Law, 1960; postgrad., U. Chgo., 1946-47; Docteur de l'Universite, U. Paris, 1948; LLD (hon.), McGill U., 1975, U. Toronto, 1978; D Univ. (hon.), Laval U., 1986. Bar: Que. 1960. Prof. philosophy U. Montreal, 1946-86, prof. law, 1960-68, 1985-87, vice rector, 1966-68, exec. vice rector, 1968-75, rector, 1975-85, prof. emeritus, 1987—; moderator, commentator CBC, 1956-63; mem. firm Lalande, Brière, Reeves, Lacoste et Paquette, Montreal, 1964-66; mem. Royal Commn. on Bilingualism and Biculturism, 1963-71, Que. Superior Coun. Edn., 1964-68, Que. Coun. Univs., 1969-77; mem. Conf. Rectors and Prins. Que. Univs., 1967-85, pres. 1977-79; chmn. Fed. Commn. and Coms. for Environ. Projects, 1991—. Author: (with others) La crise de l'enseignement au Canada Francais, 1961, Justice et Paix scolaire, 1962, A Place of Liberty, 1964, Le Canada au seuil du siecle de l'abondance, 1969, Education permanente et potentiel universitaire, 1977; contbr. articles to profl. jours. Mem. Corp. de l'Ecole des Hautes Etudes Commerciales, 1975-85, Ecole Polytechnique, 1975-85, Corp. du Coll. Marie de France; bd. dirs. Clin. Rsch. Inst. of Montreal, 1975-85; pres. Assn. des universités partiellement ou entièrement de langue française, 1978-81. Mem. Assn. Univs. and Colls. of Can. (mem. com. of pres. 1975-85, v.p. 1977, pres. 1978-79), Assn. Commonwealth Univs. (dir. 1977-80). Home: 356 Woodlea, Ville Mont Royal, PQ Canada H3P 1R5 Office: Université de Montréal, CP 6128 Pavillon 2910 bur 6, Montreal, PQ Canada H3C 3J7

LACOUTURE, FELIPE ERNESTO, museum consultant; b. Mexico City, Feb. 25, 1928; s. Juan and Guadalupe (Fornelli) L.; m. Josefina Dahl Cortés, Nov. 21, 1959; children: Yvonne Josefina, Jacqueline, Geraldine, Verónica, Juan Felipe. Architect's degree, Universidad Nacional Autónoma de México, 1952; postgrad., Ecole du Louvre, Paris, 1952-53, Inst. de Cultura

Hispánica, Universidad de Madrid, Spain, 1953-54; M in Visual Arts, U. Nacional Autonoma de Mexico, 1978; M in Museology, Inst. Nacional de Antropologia e Historia, 1981. Dir. Mus. Art and History in Ciudad Juárez, 1964-70; head dept. regional museums Nat. Inst. Anthropology and History, 1970-73; dir. San Carlos Mus., 1973-77; head dept. plastic arts Nat. Inst. Fine Arts, 1974-77; dir. Nat. Mus. History, Mexico City, 1977-82; permanent adv. museology Nat. Parks and Restoration of Monuments, 1983-85; prof. museology Churubusco Restoration Sch., 1971—; adviser in museology UNESCO, 1971-86; responsible for the program of integration new Mus. Documentation Ctr. (Coordinacion Nacional de Museos y Exposiciones) INAH-Mex.; expert appraiser Nat. Banking Commn. Mex., 1980-95. Decorated comendador Orden de Rio Branco, Brazil). Mem. Internat. Coun. Mus. (sec. Mexican nat. com.), Internat. Coun. Monuments and Sites, Colegio de Arquitectos de Mexico, Sociedad de Arquitectos Mexicanos. Home and Office: Edificio 21 Depto 203, Villa Olimpica, Mexico City 14020, Mexico

LACOVARA, PHILIP ALLEN, lawyer; b. N.Y.C., July 11, 1943; s. P. Philip and Elvira Lacovara; m. Madeline E. Papio, Oct. 14, 1961; children: Philip, Michael, Christopher, Elizabeth, Karen, Daniel, Andrew. AB magna cum laude, Georgetown U., 1963; JD summa cum laude, Columbia U., 1966. Bar: N.Y. 1967, D.C. 1974, U.S. Supreme Ct. 1970. Law clk. to presiding justice U.S. Ct. Appeals D.C. Cir., 1966-67; asst. to solicitor gen. U.S. Washington, 1967-69; assoc. Hughes Hubbard & Reed, N.Y.C., 1969-71; ptnr. Hughes Hubbard & Reed, N.Y.C. and Washington, 1974-88; v.p., sr. counsel GE, Fairfield, Conn., 1988-90; mng. dir, gen. counsel Morgen Stanley & Co., N.Y.C., 1990-93; ptnr. Mayer, Brown & Platt, N.Y.C. and Washington, 1993—; spl. counsel to N.Y.C. Police Commr., 1971-72; dep. solicitor gen. U.S. Dept. Justice, Washington, 1972-73; counsel to spl. prosecutor Watergate Spl. Prosecution Force, 1973-74; lectr. law Columbia U.; adj. prof. Georgetown U. Law Ctr.; vis. lectr. various colls., univs.; mem. Jud. Conf. D.C. Circuit, 1973—; chmn. commn. on admissions and grievances U.S. Ct. Appeals for D.C. Circuit, 1980-86; spl. counsel U.S. Ho. of Reps. Com. on Standards Ofcl. Conduct, 1976-77; chmn. bd. trustees Public Defender Service for D.C., 1976-81; sec. exec. com. bd. visitors Columbia U. Sch. Law; pres. Columbia U. Sch. Law Alumni Assn., 1986-88; bd. govs. D.C. Bar, 1981-84, gen. counsel, 1985-87, pres., 1988-89, mem. legal ethics com., 1976-81, chmn. code subcom., 1977-81. Contbr. articles to profl. jours. Co-chair, Washington Lawyers Com. for Civil Rights Under Law, 1982-84; mem. D.C. Jud. Nomination Commn., 1981-86; bd. dirs. Legal Aid Soc. of N.Y.C., 1992—. Fellow Am. Coll. Trial Lawyers; mem. ABA (ho. of dels. 1978-89, vice-chmn. sect. individual rights and responsibilities 1985-87, 89-91, chmn. 1991-92), Am. Law Inst., Practicing Law Inst. (trustee), Cath. Interracial Coun. N.Y., Lawyers Com. for Human Rights (trustee 1991—), Legal Aid Soc. N.Y.C. (bd. dirs. 1992—), 1925 F St. Club, Lotos Club, Knights of Malta. Roman Catholic. Home: 39 Mill Rd New Canaan CT 06840-4305 Office: 1675 Broadway New York NY 10019

LACROIX, CHRISTIAN MARIE MARC, fashion designer; b. Arles, Bouches du Rhône, France, May 16, 1951; s. Maxime and Jeannette (Bergier) L. Grad., U. Valery, Montpelier, France, 1973. Asst. Hermes Co., Paris, 1978-79, Guy Paulin Co., Paris, 1980-81; chief designer Jean Patou Co., Paris, 1982-87; prin. Christian Lacroix Co., Paris, 1987—. Decorated chevalier des Arts et Lettres, 1992; recipient Golden Thimble award, 1986, 88, Coun. Fashion Designer Am. award, 1987, Prix Balzac, 1989, Das Goldene Spinnrad award Kreffeld, R.F.A., 1990, MoliÈre Best Costumes award, 1996. Roman Catholic. Office: Christian Lacroix, 73 Faubourg Saint-Honoré, 75008 Paris France

LA CROSSE, JAMES, retail executive; b. 1932. Student, Wesleyan Univ., 1954; MBA, Harvard Univ., 1956. Miller Stevenson Chemical Co., 1956-59, Amerace-Ense Co., 1960-69, Bio-Dynamics Co. Inc., 1965-59; Nat. WIne & Spirits Corp., 1970—, CEO, 1991—. Office: PO Box 1602 Indianapolis IN 46206

LACY, ALAN JASPER, retail executive; b. Cleveland, Tenn., Oct. 19, 1953; s. William J. and Mary (Leigh) L.; m. Caron Ann Cap, May 16, 1981; children: Daniel Alan, Brian Matthew. BSIM, Ga. Inst. Tech., 1975; MBA, Emory U., 1977. Chartered fin. analyst., 1982; fin. analyst Holiday Inns, Inc., Memphis, 1977-79; mgr. investor relations Tiger Internat., Los Angeles, 1979-80, Dart Industries, Los Angeles, 1980-81; dir. corp. fin. Dart & Kraft, Northbrook, Ill., 1981-82, asst. treas., 1982-83, treas., v.p., 1984-86, v.p. fin. and adminstrn. internat., 1987-88; v.p., treas., chief fin. officer Minnetonka Corp., Bloomington, Minn., 1988-89; sr. v.p. strategy and devel. Kraft Gen. Foods, Glenview, Ill., 1989-90, sr. v.p. fin., 1990-92, sr. v.p. fin., strategy, systems, 1992-93; v.p. fin. svcs. and systems Philip Morris Cos., 1993-95; sr. v.p. fin. Sears, Roebuck & Co., 1995—. Mem. Fin. Analysts Fedn., Economic Club (Chgo.), The Res. Bd.

LACY, ALEXANDER SHELTON, lawyer; b. South Boston, Va., Aug. 18, 1921; s. Cecil Baker and Lura Elizabeth (Byram) L.; m. Carol Jemison, Aug. 8, 1952; children: John Blakeway, Joan Elizabeth Chancey, Alexander Shelton. B.S. in Chemistry, U. Ala., 1943; LL.B., U. Va., 1949. Bar: Ala. 1949, U.S. Ct. Appeals (5th, 11th and D.C. cirs.) 1981, U.S. Supreme Ct. 1979. Assoc. Bradley, Arant, Rose & White, Birmingham, Ala., 1949-54; with Ala. Gas Corp., Birmingham, 1954-86; v.p., asst. sec., atty. Ala. Gas Corp., 1969-86, v.p., sec., atty., 1974-86; with Patrick and Lacy, Birmingham, 1986—. Pres., chmn. bd. Birmingham Symphony Assn., 1964-67; chmn. Birmingham-Jefferson Civic Center Authority, 1965-71. Served with USN, 1943-46. Mem. ABA, Ala. Bar Assn. (chmn. energy law com. 1984-86), Birmingham Bar Assn., Am. Gas Assn. (chmn. legal sect. 1983-85), Fed. Energy Bar Assn., Fed. Bar Assn., Am. Judicature Soc., Mountain Brook Club, Summit Club, Phi Gamma Delta, Phi Delta Phi. Episcopalian. Home: 3730 Montrose Rd Birmingham AL 35213-3824 Office: Patrick and Lacy 1201 Financial Ctr Birmingham AL 35203

LACY, ANDRE BALZ, industrial executive; b. Indpls., Sept. 12, 1939; s. Howard J. II and Edna B. (Balz) L.; m. Julia Lello, Feb. 23, 1963; children: John Andre, Mark William, Peter Lello. BA Econs., Denison U.; DEng (hon.), Rose-Hulman Inst. Various mgmt. positions U.S. Corrugated, Indpls., 1961-69, exec. v.p., 1969-72; exec. v.p., chief ops. officer Lacy Diversified Industries, Indpls., 1972-78, chmn. bd. subs., 1973-78, pres., chief ops. officer, 1978-83; pres., chief exec. officer Lacy Diversified Industries, now LDI, Ltd., Indpls., 1983—, chmn., 1992; bd. dirs. Indpls. Power and Light, Indpls. IPALCO Enterprises, Inc., Indpls., Tredegar Industries, Inc., Richmond, Va., Albemarle Corp., Richmond, Herff Jones, Inc., Indpls., Patterson Dental Co., Mpls., Mid-Am. Capital Resources, Inc. Mem. bd. mgrs. Rose-Hulman Inst., Terre Haute, Ind.; pres. Indpls. Bd. Sch. Commn., Indpls., 1985-86; hon. mem. 500 Festival Assocs., Inc., Indpls.; chmn. United Way Greater Indpls., 1989-91; bd. dirs. Hudson Inst., Indpls. Conv. and Visitors Assn., 1996. Mem. Young Pres. Orgn., Ind. C. of C. (bd. dirs. 1989), Ind. Pres. Orgn., Kiwanis Club of Indpls., Skyline Club, Columbia Club, Meridian Hills Golf and Country Club (Indpls.), Lost Tree Club. Republican. Episcopalian. Avocation: sailing. Home: 5686 N Pennsylvania St Indianapolis IN 46220-3026 Office: LDI Ltd 251 N Illinois St Ste 1800 Indianapolis IN 46204-1945

LACY, BILL, academic administrator; b. Madill, Okla., Apr. 16, 1933; s. Leon and Eunice L.; m. Susan Cavert Butler, Dec. 27, 1992; children: Jan, Kate, Shawn, Ross, Jessica. B.Arch., Okla. State U., 1955, M.Arch., 1958; D.F.A. (hon.), Miami U., Oxford, Ohio, 1985. Design architect Caudill, Rowlett, Scott, Houston, 1958-61; prof., assoc. chmn. dept. architecture Rice U., Houston, 1961-65; prof., dean sch. architecture U. Tenn., Knoxville, 1965-70; v.p. Omniplan, Dallas, 1970-71; dir. architecture and environ. arts Nat. Endowment Arts, Washington, 1971-77, dir. fed. design program, 1972-77; pres. Am. Acad. in Rome, N.Y.C., 1977-80, The Cooper Union, N.Y.C., 1980-88, SUNY, Purchase Coll., 1993—; archtl. cons. Fgn. Bldgs. Ops., Dept. State. Author: 100 Contemporary Architects, 1991, Angels and Franciscans, 1992; contbr. articles, designs to profl. jours. Bd. dirs. Internat. Design Conf. Aspen, 1973-92; bd. dirs. Tiffancy Found., Am. Archtl. Found.; cons. Rothschild Found., J. Paul Getty Trust; exec. dir. Pritzker Prize Jury. With U.S. Army, 1955-57. Loeb fellow Harvard U., 1973. Fellow AIA; mem. Univ. Club. Office: 735 Anderson Hill Rd Purchase NY 10577-1445

LACY, HERMAN EDGAR, management consultant; b. Chgo., June 21, 1935; s. Herman E. and Florence L.; m. Mary C. Lacy; children: Frederick H., Carlton E., Douglas H., Jennifer S., Victoria J., Rebecca M. BS in Indsl. Engring., Bradley U., 1957; MBA, U. Chgo., 1966. Cert. mgmt. cons. Plant mgr., indsl. engring. supr. Hammond Organ Co., Chgo., 1961-66; mgr. corp. indsl. engring. Consol. Packaging Corp., Chgo., 1966-68; mgr. mgmt. cons. Peat, Marwick, Mitchell & Co., Chgo., 1968-70; dir. ops. Wilton Enterprises, Inc., Chgo., 1970-77; v.p., gen. mgr. Intercraft Industries Corp., Chgo., 1978-79; pres. Helmco Cons. Assocs., Glenview, Ill., 1979—; instr. Roosevelt U., Oakton Coll., Harper Coll. Served to capt. USAF, 1957-61. Mem. Inst. Indsl. Engrs. (past pres., founder north suburban Ill. chpt.), Am. Mgmt. Assn., Nat. Coun. Phys. Distbn. Mgmt., Soc. Mfg. Engrs., Inst. Mgmt. Cons. Office: Helmco Cons Assocs 1920 Waukegan Rd Ste 212 Glenview IL 60025-1700

LACY, JAMES VINCENT, lawyer; b. Oakland, Calif., May 29, 1952; s. James C. and Roma (Stetsky) L.; m. Janice Payt, 1987. B.A. in Internat. Relations, U. So. Calif., 1974; J.D., Pepperdine U., 1978; Cert. in Internat. Orgns., U. Geneva, 1973. Bar: Calif. 1978, D.C. 1983. Aide to Howard Jarvis, L.A., 1978-79; ptnr. Hoffenblum, Mollrich, Lacy, Inc., L.A., 1979-81; polit. cons. L.A., 1979-81; dep. dir. Office Bus. Liaison, U.S. Dept. Commerce, Washington, 1981-84, dir. Office Export Trading Co. Affairs, 1984-87, chief counsel for tech., 1989-91; pvt. practice, 1992—; gen. counsel U.S. Consumer Product Safety Commn., 1987-89. Contbr. articles to legal jours. Chmn. bd. Young Ams. for Freedom, Inc., Sterling, Va., 1978-83; bd. dirs. Am. Conservative Union, 1979—; mem. exec. com. Young Republican Nat. Fedn., 1979-81; trustee Young Ams. Found., 1979—, U.S. Justice Found., 1979—; del. Rep. Nat. Conv., 1976; aide to del. Rep. Nat. Conv., 1980. Mem. State Bar Calif. (com. fed. cts. 1995—). Roman Catholic. Home: 24921 Seagate Dr Dana Point CA 92629-1920

LACY, JOHN FORD, lawyer; b. Dallas, Sept. 11, 1944; s. John Alexander and Glenda Arcenia (Ford) L.; m. Cece Smith, Apr. 22, 1978. BA, Baylor U., 1965; JD, Harvard U., 1968. Bar: Tex. 1968. Assoc. atty. Akin, Gump, Strauss, Hauer & Feld L.L.P., Dallas, 1968-72, ptnr., 1973-82; pres. Ford Lacy PC (affiliated with Akin, Gump et al.), Dallas, 1982—; chmn. Normandy Capital Co., Dallas, 1978—. Contbr. articles to profl. jours. Co-founder, co-chmn. pres. rsch. coun. U. Tex. Southwestern Med. Ctr., Dallas, 1985-91; dir., Vis. Nurse Assn. Tex., 1994-96. With U.S. Army, 1968-74. Rsch. fellow Southwestern Legal Found., Dallas. Mem. ABA, Dallas Bar Assn., State Bar Tex. (coun. bus. law sect. 1992-95). Home: 3710 Shenandoah St Dallas TX 75205-2121 Office: Akin Gump Strauss et al Ste 4100 1700 Pacific Ave Dallas TX 75201-4618

LACY, JOSEPH NEWTON, architect; b. Kansas City, Mo., Oct. 6, 1905; s. John James and Theresa (Conboy) L.; m. Mary Duncan, Oct. 6, 1927 (dec. Aug. 1978); children: Mary-Louise, John Duncan, William Duncan; m. Martha E. Sadler, Apr. 19, 1980 (dec. Feb. 1987). B.Arch., U. Pa., 1927. Assoc. several archtl. firms in Phila., 1927-45; including Paul P. Cret, 1941-43, Louis I. Kahn, 1943-45; assoc. Eliel and Eero Saarinen, Bloomfield Hills, Mich., 1945-51; ptnr. Eero Saarinen & Assos., Bloomfield Hills, 1951-66; ret. Eero Saarinen & Assos., 1966. Mem. Coll. Fellows of AIA, Hon. Order Ky. Cols. Specialized in devel. of new bldg. materials. *Association with Eliel and Eero Saarinen, two of the great architects of modern times, gave me the opportunities to participate in the carrying out of my principles and goals of architecture. I became part of a team that designed such outstanding structures as the Jefferson Memorial Arch in St. Louis.*

LACY, LINWOOD A., JR., computer company executive; b. 1945. BS in Chem. Engring., U. Va., 1967, MBA, 1969. Sr. v.p., COO Micro D., Inc, 1982-83; sr. mgmt. position mktg. and merchandising Best Products, 1983-85; chmn., CEO Micro D., Inc., 1985-89, Imgram Micro, Inc., Santa Ana, Calif., 1989—. Office: Ingram Micro Inc 1600 E Saint Andrew Pl Santa Ana CA 92705-4931

LACY, MELVYN LEROY, plant pathology educator and reseacher; b. Henry, Nebr., Oct. 24, 1931; married, 1954; 2 children. BS, U. Wyo., 1959, MS, 1961; PhD in Plant Pathology, Oreg. State U., 1964. From asst. prof. to assoc. prof., 1965-78; prof. plant pathology Mich. State U., 1978—. Mem. Phytopath. Soc. (Disting. Svc. fellow, award). Research in soil-borne fungus diseases, epidemiology, and control; pesticides for disease control; epidemiology, disease forecasting and disease management. Office: Mich State U Botany & Plant Pathology Dept East Lansing MI 48823

LACY, NORRIS JOINER, French language and literature educator; b. Hopkinsville, Ky., Mar. 8, 1940; s. Edwin V. and Lillian Louise (Joiner) L. B.A., Murray State U., 1962; M.A., Ind. U., 1963, Ph.D., 1967. Lectr. Ind. U., 1965-66; asst. prof. to prof. U. Kans., Lawrence, 1966-88; prof. Washington U., St. Louis, 1988—; vis. assoc. prof. UCLA, 1975-76. Author: The Craft of Chretien de Troyes, 1980, The Arthurian Handbook, 1988, Reading Fabliaux, 1993; editor: Medieval French Miscellany, 1972, From Camelot to Joyous Guard, 1974, 26 Chansons d'amour de la Renaissance, 1975, The Comic Spirit in Medieval France, 1976, Essays in Early French Literature, 1982, L'Istoyre de Jehan Coquault, 1983, The Arthurian Encyclopedia, 1986, The Legacy of Chretien de Troyes, 1987, The Poetics of Love, 1989, Continuations: Essays in Honor of John L. Grigsby, 1989, The New Arthurian Encyclopedia, 1991, Conjunctures: Medieval Studies in Honor of Douglas Kelly, 1994, Medieval Arthurian Literature: A Guide to Recent Research, 1996; editor, translator: Tristan (Bèroul), 1989, The Vows of the Heron, 1991, Lancelot-Grail: The Old French Arthurian Vulgate and Post-Vulgate in Translation, 1993-96; editor in chief Summa Publs. Inc., 1981-86. Decorated knight Order of Acad. Palms (France); grantee Am. Philos. Soc., 1969, Am. Coun. Learned Socs., 1973, 85, NEH, 1975, 89-91. Mem. MLA, Medieval Acad. Am., Internat. Arthurian Soc. (hon. internat. pres.), Société Rencesvals, Am. Assn. Tchrs. French. Office: Washington U Dept Romance Lang Lit Saint Louis MO 63130

LACY, PAUL ESTON, pathologist; b. Trinway, Ohio, Feb. 7, 1924; s. Benjamin Lemmert and Amy Cass (Cox) L.; m. Emelyn Ellen Talbot, June 7, 1945; children: Paul E. Jr., Steven T. BA cum laude, Ohio State U., 1945, MD cum laude, MSc in Anatomy, 1948; PhD in Pathology, U. Minn.-Mayo Found., 1955; Doctor of Medicine (honoris causa), Uppsala (Sweden) U., 1977. Asst. instr. anatomy Ohio State U., Columbus, 1944-48; intern White Cross Hosp., Columbus, 1948-49; fellow in pathology Mayo Clinic, Rochester, Minn., 1951-55; postdoctoral fellow Washington U. Med. Sch., St. Louis, 1955-56, instr. pathology, 1956-57, asst. prof. pathology, 1957-61, asst. dean, 1959-61, assoc. prof. pathology, 1961, Mallinckrodt prof., chmn. dept. pathology, 1961-85, Robert L. Kroc prof. of pathology, 1985-95, prof. emeritus pathology, 1995—; pathologist-in-chief Barnes & Allied Hosps., St. Louis, 1985-95, pathologist, 1985-95, prof. emeritus pathology, 1995—. Served to capt. U.S. Army, 1949-51. Recipient Banting award Brit. Diabetes Assn., 1963, Am. Diabetes Assn., 1970, 3M Life Scis. award FASEB, 1981, Rous-Whipple award Am. Assn. Pathologists, 1984. Fellow AAAS, Am. Acad. Arts and Sci.; mem. NAS, Inst. Medicine. Avocations: horticulture, literature. Office: Washington Univ Med Sch Dept of Pathology 660 S Euclid Ave Saint Louis MO 63110-1010

LACY, ROBINSON BURRELL, lawyer; b. Boston, May 7, 1952; s. Benjamin Hammett and Jane (Burrell) L.; m. Elizabeth Coutrakon, Oct. 20, 1984. AB, U. Calif., Berkeley, 1974; JD, Harvard U., 1977. Bar: N.Y. 1978, U.S. Dist. Ct. (so. and ea. dists.) N.Y. 1979, U.S. Dist. Ct. (we. dist.) N.Y. 1992, U.S. Ct. Appeals (2d cir.) 1983, U.S. Ct. Appeals (10th cir.) 1990, U.S. Supreme Ct. 1986. Law clk. to judge U.S. Dist. Ct. (so. dist.) N.Y., N.Y.C., 1977-78; law clk. to chief justice Warren Burger U.S. Supreme Ct., Washington, 1978-79; assoc. Sullivan & Cromwell, N.Y.C., 1979-85, ptnr., 1985—. Mem. ABA, Assn. of Bar of City of N.Y., N.Y. State Bar Assn. Office: Sullivan & Cromwell 125 Broad St New York NY 10004-2400

LACY, STEVE, jazz musician; b. N.Y.C., 1934. Played soprano sax at Schillinger House, Boston; performed with Pee Wee Russell, Rex Stewart, Buck Clayton, Jimmy Rushing, Dicky Wells, Walter Page, N.Y.C., 1953-54; played with Cecil Taylor; then with Gil Evans' orch., 1957; formed quartet with Roswell Rudd, experimenting with chord-free improvisation and unusual song forms, early 1960s; formed sextet Paris, 1970; played regular duets with Mal Waldron, 1979—. Recordings include Soprano Sax (debut), 1957, Reflections: Steve Lacy Plays Thelonius Monk, 1958, Evidence (with Don Cherry), 1961, Paris Blues (with Gil Evans), Raps, 1977, Steve Lacy Three: New York Capers, 1979, The Way, 1979, Ballets, 1980, Herbe de L'Oubli & Snake Out (with Mal Waldron), 1981, Songs (with Brion Gysin), 1985, 86, Let's Call This (with Mal Waldron), Prospectus, 1986, Steve Lacy Two, Five & Six: Blinks, 1986, Steve Lacy Nine: Futurities, 1986, The Straight Horn of Steve Lacy, The Door (duos, trios, etc.), 1989, Anthem, 1990, Hot House (with Mal Waldron), 1991, Live at Sweet Basil, 1992, Steve Lacy Solo, 1993; composed/played musical score Landing live for D. Dunn, 1992. Frequent winner Down Beat Mag. poll, best soprano saxist, 1992. Office: care BMG 1133 Ave Of The Americas New York NY 10036-6710

LACZKO, BRIAN JOHN, theater director; b. Cleve., Aug. 7, 1952; s. Joseph John and Avonelle Dorothy (Toth) L.; m. Jill Maree Aude, Aug. 12, 1978; children: Brian John, Stefanie Dale. BA, Denison U., 1974; MA, W.Va. U., 1978. Prodn. mgr. Advent Theatre, Nashville, 1978-79; prodn. mgr. Tenn. Performing Arts Ctr., Nashville, 1980-81, dir. ops., 1981-82, asst. mng. dir., 1982-86; gen. mgr. Starwood Amphitheatre, Nashville, 1986-87; mng. dir. Tenn. Repertory Theatre, Nashville, 1987—; adjudicator Tenn. Arts Commn., Nashville, 1991—, chair adv. panel, 1992—, Met. Nashville Arts Commn., 1991—; mem. profl. cos. panel Opera-Musical Theatre Program NEA. Scenic and lighting dir. over 50 theater prodns. Mem. Am. Arts Alliance, Internat. Theatre Inst. of U.S., Theatre Communications Group, Nat. Alliance Musical Theatre Producers, Alliance Performing Arts Presenters, Tenn. Theatre Assn., Tennesseans for Arts, Nashville C. of C. Office: Tenn Repertory Theatre 427 Chestnut St Nashville TN 37203-4826

LADANYI, BRANKO, civil engineer; b. Zagreb, Croatia, Dec. 14, 1922; emigrated to Can., 1962, naturalized, 1967; s. Adalbert and Zora (Kniewald) L.; m. Nevenka Zilic, Dec. 14, 1946; children: Branka, Thomas, Marc. B.Civil Engring., U. Zagreb, 1947; Ph.D. in Soil Mechanics, U. Louvain, Belgium, 1959. Design engr. Dept. Transp., Zagreb, 1947-52; teaching asst. U. Zagreb, 1952-58; research engr. Belgian Geotech. Inst., Ghent, 1958-62; asso. prof., then prof. civil engring. Laval U., Quebec, Can., 1962-67; prof. civil engring. Ecole Poly., U. Montreal, 1967-94, prof. emeritus, 1994—, dir. North Engring. Centre, 1972—. Author papers in geotech. field, chpts. in books. Recipient Que. sci. award Que. Ministry Edn., 1974, De Beer Geotech. award Belgian Geotech. Soc., 1986, Elbert F. Rice Meml. award ASCE and U. Alaska, Fairbanks, 1991, No. Sci. award Govt. of Can., 1996. Fellow ASCE (amity award 1995), Royal Soc. Can., Can, Acad. Engring., Engring. Inst. Can., Can. Soc. Civil Engring.; mem. ASTM, Order Engrs. Que., Can. Geotech. Soc. (R.F. Legget geotech. award 1981, Robert J.E. Brown meml. award 1993), Can. Inst. Mining and Metallurgy. Office: Dept Civil Engring, Ecole Poly CP 6079 Succ Centre-Ville, Montreal, PQ Canada *There is no end to learning.*

LADAR, JERROLD MORTON, lawyer; b. San Francisco, Aug. 2, 1933. AB, U. Wash., 1956; LLB, U. Calif., Berkeley, 1960. Bar: Calif. 1961, U.S. Supreme Ct. 1967. Law clk. to judge U.S. Dist. Ct. (no. dist.) Calif., 1960-61; asst. U.S. atty. San Francisco, 1961-70; chief criminal div., 1968-70; mem. firm MacInnis & Donner, San Francisco, 1970-72; prof. criminal law and procedure U. San Francisco Law Sch., 1962-83; pvt. practice San Francisco., 1970-94; ptnr. Ladar & Knapp, San Francisco, 1994—; chair pvt. defender panel U.S. Dist. Ct. (no. dist.) Calif., 1980-90; chair stats. and tech. subcom. Fed. Civil Justice Reform Act Com. (no. dist.) Calif., 1990-95; ct. apptd. mem. Fed. Ct. Rules Revision Com. (no. dist.) Calif., 1994—; mem. continuing edn. of bar criminal law adv. com. U. Calif., Berkeley, 1978-83, 89—; panelist, mem. nat. planning com. ABA White Collar Crime Inst., 1995—. Author: (with others) Selected Trial Motions, California Criminal Law Procedure and Practice, 1986, (supplements to) California Criminal Law and Procedure, 1987-92, (chpts.) 2d edit., 1993, Direct Examination-Tips and Techniques, 1982; co-author: Criminal Trial Tactics, 1985, 3d edit., 1989; co-author chpts. Grand Jury Practice, California Asset Forfeiture in California Criminal Law and Procedure, 3d edit., 1996, U. Calif. Continuing Edn. of the Bar, 1994. Trustee Tamalpais Union High Sch. Dist., 1968-77, chmn. bd., 1973-74; mem. adv. com. Nat. PTA Assn., 1972-78; apptd. mem. criminal justice act com. U.S. Ct. Appeals (9th cir). Fellow Am. Bd. Criminal Lawyers; mem. ABA (co-author White Collar Crime Inst. 1995-96), San Francisco Bar Assn. (editor in Re 1974-76), State Bar Calif. (pro-tem disciplinary referee 1976-78, vice chmn. pub. interest and edn. com. criminal law sect., mem. exec. com. criminal law sect. 1980-87, editor Criminal Law Sect. News 1981-87, chmn. exec. com. 1983-84), Am. Inns. of Ct. (exec. com. 1994—). Office: 507 Polk St Ste 310 San Francisco CA 94102-3339

LADAU, ROBERT FRANCIS, architect, planner; b. N.Y.C., Jan. 31, 1940; s. A. Ralph and Marguerite Louise (de Valois-Vignand) L.; m. Anne Horton, May 30, 1970. A.B., Columbia U., 1961, B.Arch., M.Arch., 1965. Chmn. bd. dirs., chief exec. officer Environers Inc., N.Y.C., 1964-66, dir., 1966-73; assoc. Rogers, Butler & Burgun, Architects, N.Y.C., 1966-69; prin. Robert F. Ladau, AIA Architect/Planner, N.Y.C., 1969-70, pres., 1973—; ptnr. Metcalf & Assocs. Architects & Engrs., Washington and N.Y.C. and founder and ptnr. Sir Robert Matthew, Metcalf & Ptnrs., London and Edinburgh, 1970-73; v.p. architecture A.M. Kinney Affiliation Architects & Engrs., Cin., N.Y.C., Chgo., Denver, L.A., San Juan and Basel, Switzerland, 1975-80; sr. v.p. Welton Becket Assocs., N.Y.C., 1980-84; pres., chief exec. officer The Miller Orgn., 1984-90; pres. Emery Roth & Sons Interior Design/Facilities Mgmt., 1990—; lectr. on planning, design health facilities; mem. nat. panel Am. Arbitration Assn. Bd. fellows Frick Collection; chmn. long range planning com. bd. govs. Columbia U. Club N.Y.; mem. Bedford (N.Y.) Conservation Bd., 1975-78. Contbr. articles to profl. jours. Co-author: Color in Interior Design and Architecture, 1988; designer numerous office and comml., health, ednl., urban, recreational, residential and indsl. facilities. Recipient Group Exhibit award Rockefeller Found., 1964; design awards Rockefeller Found., 1962, N.Y. Soc. Architects, 1966, Internat. Conf. Med. Primatology, 1974, Carnegie Heroism medal, 1989; William Kinne Fellows traveling fellow, 1965; registered architect, N.Y., N.J., Del., D.C., Conn. Mem. AIA, N.Y. Soc. Architects, N.Y. State Assn. Architects, Nat. Council Archtl. Registration Bds. (certified), Humane Soc. N.Y. (bd. advisors 1992-93, trustee 1993—). Clubs: Princeton, Mashomack, Quaker Hill. Home: Mooney Hill Rd Patterson NY 12563 Office: 560 Lexington Ave New York NY 10022-6828

LADD, ALAN WALBRIDGE, JR., motion picture company executive; b. L.A., Oct. 22, 1937; s. Alan Walbridge and Marjorie Jane (Harrold) L.; m. Patricia Ann Beazley, Aug. 30, 1959 (div. 1983); children: Kelliann, Tracy Elizabeth, Amanda Sue; m. Cindra Kay, July 13, 1985. Motion picture agt. Creative Mgmt., L.A., 1963-69; v.p. prodn. 20th Century-Fox Film Corp., L.A., 1973-74; sr. v.p. 20th Century-Fox Film Corp. (Worldwide Prodns. div.), Beverly Hills, Calif., 1974-76; pres. 20th Century-Fox Pictures, 1976-79, Ladd Co., Burbank, Calif., 1979-83; pres., chief oper. officer MGM/UA Entertainment Co., 1983-86; chief exec. officer MGM/UA Entertainment Co, from 1986, also chmn. bd. dirs.; chmn., chief exec. officer Metro-Goldwyn-Mayer Pictures, Inc., Culver City, Calif., until 1988; pres., chmn. Pathe Entertainment, L.A., 1989-90; co-chmn. MGM-Pathe, L.A., 1990-93, MGM, L.A., 1990-93; chmn., CEO MGM-Pathe Communications, L.A., 1991-93; pres. The Ladd Co., L.A., 1993—. Prodr.: (films) Walking Stick, 1969, A Severed Head, 1969, TamLin, 1970, Villian Zee and Co., 1971, Fear is the Key, 1973, Braveheart, 1995 (Acad. award nominee for best picture of yr. 1996); exec. prodr.: (films) Nightcomers, 1971, Vice Versa, 1988, The Brady Bunch, 1995, Braveheart, 1995. Served with USAF, 1961-63. Office: The Ladd Co c/o Paramount 5555 Melrose Ave Los Angeles CA 90038

LADD, CHARLES CUSHING, III, civil engineering educator; b. Bklyn., Nov. 23, 1932; s. Charles Cushing and Elizabeth (Swan) L.; m. Carol Lee Ballou, June 11, 1954; children: Melissa, Charles IV, Ruth, Matthew. AB, Bowdoin Coll., 1955; SB, MIT, 1955, SM, 1957, ScD, 1961. Asst. prof. civil engring. MIT, 1961-64, assoc. prof., 1964-70, prof., 1970-94, dir. Ctr. Sci. Excellence in Offshore Engring., 1983-94, Edmund K. Turner prof., 1994—; gen. reporter 9th Internat. Conf. Soil Mechanics and Found. Engring., Tokyo, 1977; co-gen. reporter 11th Internat. Conf. Soil Mechanics and Found. Engring., San Francisco, 1985; mem. geotech. bd. NRC, 1992-94. Contbr. articles to profl. jours. Mem. Concord (Mass.) Republican Town Com., 1968-82; commr. Concord Dept. Pub. Works, 1965-78, chmn., 1972-74. Fellow ASCE (rsch. prize 1969, Croes medal 1973, Norman medal 1976, Terzaghi lectr. 1986,exec. com. geotech. engring. divsn. 1989—, chmn. 1993-94, hon. mem. 1995); mem. NAE, ASTM (Hogentogler award 1990), NSPE, Boston Soc. Civil Engrs. (bd. govs. 1972-81, pres. 1977-78), Transp. Rsch.

Bd., Internat. Soc. Soil Mechanics and Found. Engring., Am. Soc. Engring. Edn., Assn. Engring. Firms Practicing in the Geoscis., AAUW, Brit. Geotechnical Soc., Can. Geotechnical Soc. Home: 7 Thornton Ln Concord MA 01742-4107 Office: MIT Dept Civil & Environ Engrng Cambridge MA 02139

LADD, CHERYL (CHERYL STOPPLEMOOR), actress; b. Huron, S.D., July 12, 1951; d. Dolores Katz; m. David Alan Ladd (div. 1980); m. Brian Russell, Jan. 3, 1981; children: Jordan, Elizabeth, Lindsay. Studies with Milton Kateselas. Mem. Music Shop musical group, 1968-70; Goodwill amb. to Childhelp U.S.A. (Woman of the World award 1987); spokesperson Retinitis Pigmentosa International. TV shows and movies include (animated) Josie and the Pussycats, 1970-72, The Ken Berry Wow Show, 1972, Satan's School for Girls, 1973, Charlie's Angels, 1977-81, Cheryl Ladd, 1979, Cheryl Ladd-Souvenirs, 1980, Cheryl Ladd: Scenes from a Special, 1982, Roots, Police Woman, Happy Days, Switch, When She Was Bad, 1979, Grace Kelly, 1983, Kentucky Woman, 1983, Romance on the Orient Express, 1985, A Death in California, 1985, Crossings, 1986, Blue Grass, 1988, Deadly Care, 1987, The Fulfillment of Mary Gray, 1989, Jekyll and Hyde, 1990, The Girl Who Came Between Them, 1990, Crash: The Mystery of Flight 1501, 1990, Danielle Steele's Changes, 1991, Locked Up: A Mother's Rage, 1991, Dead Before Dawn, 1992, Broken Promises, 1993, Dancing With Danger, 1994, The Lady, 1995, Kiss & Tell, 1995, (syndicated series) One West Waikiki, 1995; stage appearances include Anything Goes, 1986, Hasty Heart; films include The Treasure of Jamaica Reef, 1975, Purple Hearts, 1994, Now and Forever, 1985, Millenium, 189, Lisa, 1990, Poison Ivy, 1992, One West Waikiki, 1994; numerous TV commls.; albums include Cheryl Ladd, 1978, Dance Forever, 1979. Mem. AFTRA, SAG, AGVA.

LADD, CULVER SPROGLE, secondary education educator; b. Bismarck, N.D., Nov. 15, 1929; s. Culver Sprogle and Eleanor (Pearson)L. BS, U. Md., 1953; MA, Am. U., 1963, PhD, 1984; postgrad., Oxford U. (Eng.), 1975-76; Degree by Correspondence, Indsl. Coll. of Armed Forces, Thailand, 1972. Clk.-photographer Dept. Justice, FBI, Washington, 1946-54; intercept controller Dept. of Def., USAF, 1954-56; asst. office mgr. Covington & Burling, Lawyers, Washington, 1956-62; tchr. Internat. Sch. Bangkok, Thailand, 1964-66; lectr. U. Md., Thailand, 1966-67, 71-74; project dir. Bus. Rsch. Ltd., Thailand, 1966-67, 72-74; spl. lectr. Payap U., Chiang Mai, Thailand, 1974-75; tchr. D.C. Pub. Schs., 1978—; cons. USAID, Thailand, 1973-74; vis. scientist Brookhaven Nat. Labs., L.I., 1988; master tchr. Woodrow Wilson Fellowship Found., 1989. Capt. USAFR, 1953-72; PTO. Recipient Appreciation award Payap U. 1987. Mem. Mid-Atlantic Region Assn. for Asian Studies, Am. Acad. Polit. and Social Scis., Nat. Capital Area Polit. and Social Scis., Nat. Coun. Tchrs. Math., Mid. States Coun. Social Studies, Aircraft Owners and Pilots Assn., Omicron Delta Kappa, Pi Sigma Alpha. Republican. Presbyterian. Avocations: gardening, flying. Home: PO Box 2084 Lusby MD 20657-1884 Office: POACRE Airfield PO Box 2084 845 Crystal Rock Rd Lusby MD 20657-1884

LADD, DIANE, actress; b. Meridian, Miss., Nov. 29, 1943; m. Bruce Dern (div.); 1 child, Laura; m. William Shay, Jr. (div.). Grad., St. Aloysius Acad. Appearances include (films) The Wild Angels, 1966, The Reivers, 1969, Macho Callahan, 1970, Rebel Rousers, 1970, WUSA, 1970, White Lightning, 1973, Alice Doesn't Live Here Anymore, 1974, Chinatown, 1974, Embryo, 1976, The November Plan, 1976, All Night Long, 1981, Something Wicked This Way Comes, 1983, Black Widow, 1987, Plain Clothes, 1988, National Lampoon's Christmas Vacation, 1989, Wild at Heart, 1990, A Kiss Before Dying, 1991, Rambling Rose, 1991, Cemetery Club, 1992, Hold Me, Thrill Me, Kiss Me, 1992, Code Name: Chaos, 1992, Carnosaur, 1993, Father Hood, 1993, Spirit Realm, 1993, Obsession, 1994, Mrs. Milnck (also dir.), 1994, The Haunted Heart, 1995; (TV series) Alice, 1980-81; (TV movies) The Devil's Daughter, 1973, Thaddeus Rose and Eddie, 1978, Black Beauty, 1978, Willa, 1979, Guyana Tragedy: The Story of Jim Jones, 1980, Desperate Lives, 1982, Grace Kelly, 1983, I Married a Centerfold, 1984, Crime of Innocence, 1985, Celebration Family, 1987, Bluegrass, 1988, The Lookalike, 1990, Rock Hudson, 1990, Shadow of a Doubt, 1991, Hush Little Baby, 1994. Recipient award Brit. Acad., Spirit award, Golden Globe award, 3 Acad. award nominations, 4 Golden Globe nominations, Emmy nomination for Guest Actress in a Comedy Series (Grace Under Fire), 1994. Office: Abrams Artists 9200 Sunset Blvd Ste 1130 Beverly Hills CA 90069*

LADD, JAMES ROGER, international business consultant; b. San Diego, Mar. 5, 1943; s. Robert Dwinell and Virginia Ruth (Dole) L.; m. Sharon Patricia Smith, Aug. 22, 1964; children—Brian Andrew, Jennifer Louise, Casey James. A.B., Duke U., 1964. C.P.A. With Deloitte Haskins & Sells, Seattle, 1964-79; mng. ptnr. Deloitte Haskins & Sells, Tokyo, 1979-84; nat. pers. ptnr. Deloitte Haskins & Sells, N.Y.C., 1984-86; area mng. ptnr. Deloitte Haskins & Sells, Seattle, 1986-89; mng. dir. Deloitte & Touche, Seattle, 1989-92; pres. Ladd Pacific Cons., Seattle, 1992—. Treas. United Way of King County, Seattle, 1977-79, 90-93; pres. Seattle Children's Home, 1979; bd. dirs. Corp. Coun. for Arts, 1986-92; bd. dirs., treas. Seattle Found., 1988—; bd. trustees Duke U., 1991-93; chair internat. bus. adv. coun. U. Wash., 1995—. Mem. AICPA, Japan Am. Soc. State Wash. (treas. 1994-96, pres.-elect 1996—), Wash. Soc. CPAs, Duke Alumni Assn. (nat. pres. 1991-92), Wash. Athletic Club, Rainier Club. Office: 1001 4th Ave Ste 3200 Seattle WA 98154-1101

LADD, JEFFREY RAYMOND, lawyer; b. Mpls., Apr. 10, 1941; s. Jasper Raymond and Florence Marguerite (DeMarce) L.; m. Kathleen Anne Crosby, Aug. 24, 1963; children: Jeffrey Raymond, John Henry, Mark Jasper, Matthew Crosby. Student, U. Vienna, Austria; BA, Loras Coll.; postgrad., U. Denver; JD, Ill. Inst. Tech. Bar: Ill. 1973, U.S. Dist. Ct. 1973. V.p. mktg. Ladd Enterprises, Des Plaines, Ill., 1963-66; v.p. mktg. and fin. Ladd Enterprises, Crystal Lake, Ill., 1966-70; ptnr. Ross & Hardies, Chgo., 1973-81, Boodell, Sears, et al., 1981-86, Bell, Boyd & Lloyd, Chgo., 1986—; spl. asst. atty. gen. for condemnation State of Ill., 1977-82. Named Chgo. Civic Club's 1995 Citizen of Yr. Mem. ABA, Chgo. Bar Assn., Nat. Assn. Bond Lawyers, Ill. Assn. Hosp. Attys., Am. Acad. Hosp. Attys., Crystal Lake Jaycees (Disting. Svc. award), Crystal Lake C. of C. (past pres.), Econ. Club, Legal Club, Union League Club, Bull Valley Golf Club, Woodstock Country Club, Alpha Lambda. Roman Catholic. Avocations: golf, hunting, fishing, tennis, skiing. Office: Bell Boyd & Lloyd 3 First National Pla # 3300 Chicago IL 60602

LADD, JOHN CURRAN, lawyer; b. Mpls., Nov. 24, 1945; s. John Greeley and Beatrice (Brand) L.; m. Karen Elizabeth Harnish, Oct. 13, 1984; children: Anne, Jessica. LLB, Yale U., 1970. Bar: Calif. 1970. Jud. law clk. to Stanley A. Weigel U.S. Dist. Ct. (no. dist.) Calif., 1970-71; from assoc. to ptnr. Steinhart & Falconer, San Francisco, 1971-82; ptnr. Morgenstein, Ladd & Jubelirer, San Francisco, 1982-86, Jackson & Ladd, San Francisco, 1988-89; pvt. practice law San Francisco, 1987, 89-90; ptnr. Ropers, Majeski, Kohn & Bentley, San Francisco, 1990—; co-chair San Francisco Lawyer's Com. for Urban Affairs, 1981-83; mem. Legal Svcs. Trust Fund Commn. of State Bar, 1982-86. Active in U.S. Masters Swimming. Home: 1616 Castro St San Francisco CA 94114-3707 Office: Ropers Majeski Kohn & Bentley 670 Howard St San Francisco CA 94105

LADD, JOSEPH CARROLL, retired insurance company executive; b. Chgo., Jan. 26, 1927; s. Stephen C. and Laura (McBride) L.; m. Barbara Virginia Carter, June 5, 1965; children: Carroll, Joseph Carroll, Barbara, Virginia, William. BA, Ohio Wesleyan U., 1950; CLU, Am. Coll., Bryn Mawr; D in Bus. Adminstrn. (hon.), Spring Garden Coll., 1985. Agt. Conn. Gen. Life Ins. Co., Chgo., 1950-53; staff asst. Conn. Gen. Life Ins. Co., 1953-54, mgr. Evanston (Ill.) br. office, 1954-60, dir. agys., 1960-62, mgr. Los Angeles br. office, 1963; v.p. sales Fidelity Mut. Life Ins. Co., Phila., 1964-67; sr. v.p. sales Fidelity Mut. Life Ins. Co., 1968, exec. v.p., 1969-71, pres., chief exec. officer, dir., 1971-84, chmn., chief exec. officer, dir., 1984-89, chmn., dir., 1989-91; ret.; bd. dirs. Corestates Fin., Phila. Suburban Corp., Phila. Electric Co. Trustee Bryn Mawr Hosp.; trustee United Way of S.E. Pa.; trustee Phila. United Way, also gen. chmn. 1978 campaign; bd. dirs. Phila. YMCA. Served with USNR, 1945-46. Recipient Civic Achievement award Am. Jewish Com., 1978, Achiever's award WHEELS Med. and Specialized Transp., 1978, Ohio Wesleyan U. Life Achievement award Delta Tau Delta, 1982, William Penn award, Greater Phila. C. ofC. and PENJERDEL Coun., 1988, Robert Morris Citizenship award Valley Forge Coun. Boy Scouts Am., 1988; named YMCA Man of Yr., 1979, William Penn Found. Disting. Pennsylvanian, 1980. Mem. Greater Phila. C. of C. (dir., chmn. 1979, 83-84), Phila. Country Club, Union League Club (Phila.), Summer Beach (Fla.) Country Club.

LADD, MARCIA LEE, medical equipment and supplies company executive; b. Bryn Mawr, Pa., July 22, 1950; d. Edward Wingate and Virginia Lee (McGinnes) Mullinix; children: Joshua Wingate, McGinnes Lee. BA, U. Pa., 1972; MEd, U. Va., 1973; MA, Emory U., 1979. Rsch. assoc. N.C. Tng. and Standards Coun., Raleigh, 1973-75; dir. counseling svc. N.C. State Youth Svcs. Agy., Raleigh, 1975-76; acad. dean Duke U., Durham, N.C., 1976-77; prin. Ladd & Assocs. Mgmt. Cons., Chapel Hill, N.C., 1979-88; v.p. adminstrn. CompuChem Corp., Research Triangle Park, N.C., 1988-91; v.p. mktg. Prentke Romich Co., Wooster, Ohio, 1991-94; v.p. ops. Exec. Staffing Svcs., Inc., Cary, N.C., 1994; pres., CEO, owner Triangle Aftercare, Durham, N.C., 1994—. Bd. dirs. Wayne County Arts Coun., Wooster, 1992, Stoneridge/Sedgefield Swim/Racquet Club, Chapel Hill, N.C., 1985-88, Oakwood Hist. Soc., Raleigh, 1981-84; mem. bd. visitors Carolina Friends Sch., Durham, 1986-89; Stephen min. Univ. Presbyn. Ch., Chapel Hill, 1994—, youth group leader, 1995—. Decorated Order of Long Leaf Pine Gov. of N.C., 1976. Presbyterian. Office: Triangle Aftercare 249 W Hwy 54 Durham NC 27713

LADDON, WARREN MILTON, lawyer; b. Washington, July 2, 1933; s. Misha and Hannah (Cooper) L.; m. Paula K. Cramer; children: Michael, Susan, Benjamin. BS, Wilson Tchrs. Coll., 1955; JD, U. Mich., 1962. Bar: Calif. 1963, D.C. 1966, Pa. 1967. Tchg. assoc. Boalt Hall U. Calif., Berkeley, 1962-63; trial and appellate atty. Dept. Labor, Washington, 1963-65; appellate atty. NLRB, Washington, 1965-67; assoc. Morgan Lewis & Bockius, Phila., 1967-71; ptnr. Morgan Lewis & Bockius, 1971-86; chief counsel CIGNA Corp., 1986—. Lt. (j.g.) USNR, 1956-59. Mem. ABA. Office: Cigna Corp One Liberty Pl 1650 Market St Philadelphia PA 19192-1520

LADD-POWELL, ROBERTA KAY, horsebreeder, marketing executive; b. Clearwater Beach, Fla., July 24, 1953; d. F. Robert and Marguerite Elizabeth (Ethier) Ladd; m. Michael Moore Powell, Jan. 13, 1992. BA in Indsl. Pyschology, Calif. State U., Long Beach, 1975. Lic. seminar facilitator. Sales trainer western region GTE Directories Corp., Los Alamitos, Calif., 1977-84; breeder, mktg. dir. Liberty West Arabians, Calif., 1978—; dir. mktg., tng. and promotions Guam Cable TV, Yellow Pages Ink, 1990—. Pub. Desert Horse Directory, 1984-86; editor Arabian Horse Jour., 1982-83, Animal Air Transport mag., 1988-89; contbr. articles to trade jours. and newspapers. Dir. promotions Ride Across Am. Benefit, Tucson, 1988-89; fund raiser Rainforest Action Network, San Francisco, 1988-89; supporter Orange County Riders, 1980-81, Therapeutic Riding Orgn. Tucson, 1988-89. Mem. NAFE, Internat. Arabian Horse Assn. (conf. del. 1987, 88), Am. Horse Shows Assn., Arabian Racing Assn. Calif. (Top 10 Arabian Race Mare award for LWA Khlassy Lady 1988, region 2 res. Champion Mare 1989, Can. Top 20 Mare 1989), Arabian Jockey Club (vice chmn., mem. exec. com. 1988—), So. Ariz. Arabian Horse Assn. (racing chmn. Tucson chpt. 1988-89), Sierra Pacific Arabian Racing Coun. (pres. 1987-88), Guam Equestrian Fedn. (bd. dirs. 1990-93), Hawaii Combined Tng. Assn., Arabian Horse Registry, U.S. Dressage Fedn. Methodist. Avocations: reading, tennis, horseback riding, golf. Home and Office: 970 S Marine Dr Apt 10303 Tamuning GU 96911-3403

LADEFOGED, PETER NIELSEN, phonetician; b. Sutton, Eng., Sept. 17, 1925; came to U.S., 1962; s. Niels Nielsen and Marie Frances (Foucard) L.; m. Jennifer Macdonald, Dec. 19, 1953; children: Lise, Thegn, Katie. M.A., U. Edinburgh, Scotland, 1951, Ph.D., 1959; DLitt (hon.), U. Edinburgh, 1993. Lectr. U. Edinburgh, 1953-61, U. Ibadan, Nigeria, 1959-60; rsch. fellow West African Langs. Survey, Nigeria, 1961-62; asst. prof. phonetics UCLA, 1962-63, assoc. prof., 1963-65, prof., 1965-91, prof. emeritus, 1991, rsch. linguist, 1991—; team leader East African Survey Lang. Use and Lang. Teaching, Uganda, 1968. Author: A Course in Phonetics; others. Served with Brit. Army, 1943-47. Fellow Acoustical Soc. Am. (Silver Speech Comm. medal 1994), Am. Speech and Hearing Assn., Am. Acad. Arts and Scis., Am. Speech Lang. and Hearing Assn.; mem. Linguistic Soc. Am. (pres. 1978), Internat. Phonetic Assn. (pres. 1986-91). Home: 10777 Massachusetts Ave Los Angeles CA 90024 Office: UCLA Dept Linguistics Los Angeles CA 90095-1543

LADEHOFF, LEO WILLIAM, metal products manufacturing executive; b. Gladbrook, Iowa, May 4, 1932; s. Wendell Leo and Lillian A. L.; m. Beverly Joan Dreessen, Aug. 1, 1951; children: Debra K., Lance A. B.S., U. Iowa, 1957. Supt. ops. Square D Co., 1957-61; mfg. mgr. Fed. Pacific Electric Co., 1961; v.p. ops. Avis Indsl. Corp., 1961-67; pres. energy products Group Gulf & Western Industries, Inc., 1967-78; chmn. bd., pres., chief exec. officer, dir. Amcast Indsl. Corp., Ohio, 1978-95, also chmn. bd. dirs., 1995—; bd. dirs. Key Bank. With USAF, 1951-54, Korea. Mem. Soc. Automotive Engrs., U. Iowa Alumni Assn., Moraine Country Club, Forest Highlands Country Club, Ventana Canyon Country Club, Alpha Kappa Psi. Republican. Home: 7211 E Desert Moon Loop Tucson AZ 85750-0921 Office: Amcast Indsl Corp PO Box 98 Dayton OH 45401-0098 also: Elkhart Products Corp 1255 Oak St Elkhart IN 46514-2277

LADEHOFF, ROBERT LOUIS, bishop; b. Feb. 19, 1932; m. Jean Arthur Burcham (dec. Feb. 1992); 1 child, Robert Louis Jr. Grad., Duke U., 1954, Gen. Theol. Sem., 1957, Va. Theol. Sem., 1980. Ordained deacon, priest The Episcopal Ch., 1957;. Priest in charge N.C. parishes, 1957-60; rector St. Christopher's Ch., Charlotte, N.C., 1960-74, St. John's Ch., Fayetteville, 1974-85; bishop, co-adjutor of Oreg., 1985, bishop, 1986—. Office: Diocese of Oreg PO Box 467 Lake Oswego OR 97034-0467

LADEN, BEN ELLIS, economist; b. Savannah, Ga., Mar. 4, 1942; s. Bernard and Fannie Rachel (Cooper) L.; m. Susan Sherman, Aug. 16, 1964; children: Francine, Jonathan, Paul. A.B., Princeton U., 1963; Ph.D., Johns Hopkins U., 1969. Asst. prof. econs. Ohio State U., 1967-71; economist Fed. Res. Bd., 1971-74; v.p., chief economist T. Rowe Price Assocs., Balt., 1974-87; dir. fin. instns. regulation staff HUD, Washington, 1990-94; pres. Bel Assocs., Washington, 1994—. Author: Economic Trend, 1974-87; also articles. Fellow Nat. Assn. Bus. Economists (dir. 1981-87, pres. 1984-85); mem. Am. Econs. Assn. Jewish. Home: 3111 Rittenhouse St NW Washington DC 20015-1614 *Each person has to find his own unique formula for success. My greatest achievements have come from the following elements. 1. A clear concept of priorities with persistent concentration on the highest priority. 2. Building structures which will continue to payoff in the future, rather than trying for immediate results. 3. Identifying those areas where my contribution could be the greatest and could be unique. 4. Always striving for the highest quality in my work. 5. Most important, learning from the experience of others and respecting the individual ways of other people.*

LADEN, KARL, toiletries company executive; b. Bklyn., Aug. 10, 1932; s. Judah and Anna (Bernstein) L.; m. Judy Talisman, June 24, 1956; children—Ben, Ethan, Adam, Noam, Zev. B.S., U. Akron, Ohio, 1954; Ph.D., Northwestern U., 1957. Cons. Indsl. Bio-Test Labs., Northbrook, Ill., 1955-57; research chemist William Wrigley Jr. Co., Chgo., 1957-58; research mgr. Toni Co., Chgo., 1959-64; with Gillette Research Inst., Washington, 1964-76, v.p. biomed. scis., 1968-71, pres., 1971-76; v.p. research and devel. Carter Products Co., Cranbury, N.J., 1976-86; cons. tech. transfer, new product devel., 1986—. Contbg. editor, Nat. Beauty Sch. Jour., 1970-77; Contbr. articles to profl. jours. Recipient award Internat. Flavors and Fragrances, 1963, 67. Fellow Soc. Cosmetic Chemists (pres. 1977, chmn. bd. 1978, editor jour. 1967-72, Mid-West chpt. award 1964, Lit. award 1969, Merit award 1972, Medal award 1979); mem. Am. Chem. Soc. Home: 31 Yafe Nof, Haifa Israel Office: PO Box 866 Freehold NJ 07728-0866

LADEN, SUSAN, publisher, consultant; b. Washington, Aug. 3, 1942; d. Louis and Irene (Berenter) Sherman; m. Ben E. Laden, Aug. 16, 1964; children: Francine, Jonathan, Paul. AB, Vassar Coll., 1964. Caseworker Dept. Welfare, Balt., 1964-66; publ. Biblical Archaeology rev., Washington, 1976-94, Bible rev., Washington, 1984-94, Moment mag., Washington, 1987-94; pres. Laden & Assocs., 1994, Jewish Family & Life, Washington, 1996—, Rejevenation, Inc., 1995—; bd. dirs. Portfolio Travel, Washington. Treas. Lafayette Home and Sch. Assn., Washington, 1973-75; v.p. Jewish Ednl. Ventures, Boston, 1987-94; sec. Jewish Coun. for the Aging, Rockville, Md., 1992-94, treas., 1994; sec.-treas., Bibl. Archeology Soc., 1977-94. Democrat. Home and Office: Jewish Family Life 3111 Rittenhouse St NW Washington DC 20015-1614

LADER, LAWRENCE, writer; b. N.Y.C., Aug. 6, 1919; s. Ludwig and Myrtle (Powell) L.; m. Jean MacInnis, Aug. 24, 1942 (div. Jan. 1946); m. Joan Summers, Sept. 27, 1961; 1 dau., Wendy Summers. A.B., Harvard U., 1941. With press dept. ABC, 1941-42; contbg. editor Coronet mag., 1946; feature editor Glamour mag., 1953; lectr. NYU, 1957-59, Philips Brooks Assn., Harvard, 1962—; regular contbr. Am. Heritage, Reader's Digest, N.Y. Times mags., others, 1941—; exec. dir. Hugh Moore Fund, 1966-67; fgn. corr. Arab-Israel War, 1948, other overseas assignments, 1951, 55, 57; adj. assoc. prof. journalism NYU, 1967-72. Author: Margaret Sanger, 1955, The Bold Brahmins, New England's War Against Slavery, 1961, Abortion, 1966; juvenile Margaret Sanger, 1969; Breeding Ourselves to Death, 1971, Foolproof Birth Control, 1972, Abortion II: Making the Revolution, 1973, Power on the Left: American Radical Movements since 1946, 1979, Politics, Power and the Church, 1987, Ru 486, 1991, A Private Matter, 1995. Chmn. exec. com. Nat. Abortion Rights Action League, 1969-72, chmn. bd., 1972-76; pres. Abortion Rights Mobilization, 1976—. Served to lt. AUS, 1942-46; officer-in-charge N.Y. Troop Information, Armed Forces Radio Service. Recipient Benjamin Franklin Mag. award, 1969, Cert. Distinction, NOW, 1989; named Feminist Majority Feminist of Yr., 1992. Mem. Authors Guild. Club: Harvard, Century Assn. (N.Y.C.). Home: 51 5th Ave New York NY 10003-4320

LADER, PHILIP, university president, government official,; b. Jackson Heights, N.Y., Mar. 17, 1946. BA, Duke U., 1966; MA, U. Mich., 1967, Oxford U., England, 1968; JD, Harvard U., 1972; LLD (hon.), Limestone Coll.; SJD (hon.), U. S.C.; LHD (hon.), Youngstown State U., Lander U. Bar: Fla. 1972, D.C. 1973, S.C. 1979. Assoc. Sullivan & Cromwell, N.Y.C., 1972; law clk. to U.S. cir. judge, 1973; ptnr. Hartzog, Lader & Richards, Washington and Hilton Head Island, S.C., 1974-89; pres. Sea Pines Co., Hilton Head Island, 1979-83, Winthrop U., Rock Hill, S.C., 1983-85, GOSL Land Assets Mgmt., Hilton Head Island, S.C., 1986-88, 1st Southern Corp., Hilton Head Island, 1989-91, Bus. Execs. for Nat. Security, Washington, 1991, Bond U., Gold Coast, Australia, 1991-93. Dep. dir. for mgmt. Office of Mgmt. & Budget, Exec. Office of the Pres.; chmn. Pres.'s Coun. Integrity and Efficiency, 1993, Pres.'s Mgmt. Coun., policy com. Nat. Performance Rev., 1993; dep. chief of staff White House, 1993-94; candidate for gov. of S.C., 1986. Mem. Chief Exec. Orgn., D.C. Met. Club, Phi Beta Kappa. Episcopalian. Office: 1st So Adminstrn Svcs Ste 500 2900 Chamblee Tucker Rd Atlanta GA 30341-4128

LADERMAN, EZRA, composer, educator, college dean; b. Bklyn., June 29, 1924. MA, Columbia U, 1952; studies with Otto Luening, D. Moore, P. Lang, Columbia U. Dir. music program Nat. Endowment for Arts, 1979-82; pres. Nat. Music Coun., 1985-89; dean Sch. Music Yale U., New Haven, 1989-95; chmn. Am. Composers Orch. Compositions include 8 symphonies, 9 string quartets, 7 operas, 150 compostions and 25 recordings; (dramatic operas) Jacob and the Indians, 1954, Goodbye to the Clowns, 1956, The Hunting of the Snark, 1958, Sarah, 1959, Air Raid, 1965, Shadows Among Us, 1967, Galileo Galilei, 1978; (orchestral) Piano Concerto, 1939, Leipzig Symphony, 1945, Piano Concerto, 1957, 9 Symphonies, 1964-84, Flute Concerto, 1968, Viola Concerto, 1975, Violin Concerto, 1978, Piano Concerto No. 1, 1978, Concert for String Quartet and Orchestra, 1981, Cello Concerto, 1984; (vocal) oratorio The Eagle Stirred, 1961, oratorio The Trials of Galileo, 1967, cantata Columbus, 1975, oratorio A Mass for Cain, 1983; (chamber) Wind Octet, 1957, Clarinet Sonata, 1958, 8 String Quartets, 1959-85, Double Helix for Flute, Oboe, and String Quartet, 1968, Partita for Violin, 1982, Double String Quartet, 1983; (film scores) The Charter, 1958, The Invisible Aton, 1958, The Question Tree, 1962, Odyssey, 1964, The Eleanor Roosevelt Story, 1965, The Black Fox, 1965, Magic Prison, 1966, The Meaning of Modern Art, 1967, Confrontation, 1968, Image of Love, 1968, The Bible as Literature, 1972, Burden of Mystery, 1972; (television movie scores) Herschel, 1959, Invisible City, 1961, The Voice of the Desert, 1962, Eltanin, 1962, Grand Canyon, 1964, The Forgotten Peninsula, 1967, Our Endangered Wildlife, 1967, California the Most, 1968, Before Cortez, 1970, In the Fall of 1844, 1971, Cave People of the Philippines, 1972, Lamp Unto My Feet, 1978. Guggenheim fellow 1955, 58, 64; recipient Rome proze, 1963; Kennedy Center Friedheim Award, 2nd place, 1981. mem. Am. Acad. and Inst. of Arts and Letters, 1991. Office: Yale U Sch Music Office of Dean New Haven CT 06520

LADERMAN, GABRIEL, artist; b. Bklyn., Dec. 26, 1929; s. Isidore and Leah (Stock) L.; m. Carol Ciavati, Feb. 12, 1953; children—Raphael, Michael. B.A., Bklyn. Coll., 1952; M.F.A., Cornell U., 1957. Faculty State U. N.Y., New Paltz, 1957-59, Pratt Inst., 1959-66; faculty Queens Coll., Flushing, N.Y., 1966—; chmn. Queens Coll., 1979-83; vis. prof. La. State U., Baton Rouge, 1966-67, Yale U., 1968, 81, 83, 89, 91, Viterbo Coll., 1969, 80, Art Students League, 1972-81, Boston U., 1973, N.Y. Studio Sch., Am. U., 1994—; dir. G.-T. Mus., 1980-84, Caumsett Summer Landscape Painting Program, 1980, 81; vis. critic, lectr. Yale U., Syracuse U., Bennington Coll., Vassar Coll., Rutgers U., Princeton, Cooper-Union, Phila. Coll. Art, Mus. Fine Arts, Boston, Md. Inst. Art, Swain Sch., Boston U., Boston Mus. Sch., Ind. U., Bard Coll., Kansas City Art Inst., Fla. State U., SUNY at New Paltz, Amherst Coll., Skowhegan Sch., Yale-Norfolk Sch., New York Studio Sch., Pratt Inst., N.Y. Inst. Tech., Boston Mus., Tyler Sch. of Temple U., U. R.I., U. N.H., Artists for Environment, Iowa State U., Hobart Coll., U. Wis., 1980, Md. Art Inst., 1980, Royal Sch. Art, Bangkok, Thailand, 1976, Nat. Art Sch., Jakarta, Indonesia, 1975, Art Sch., Surabaya, Indonesia, 1975, Victorian Coll. Art, Melbourne, Australia, 1975, Coll. Art, Ballarat, Australia, 1975, Prahran Coll., Melbourne, 1975, U. Minn., 1987, Yale U., 1987, State U. Calif. Arts seminars San Luis Obispo, 1986, Stanford U., 1987, 91, U. Calif., Santa Barbara, 1987, Calif. State U., Long Beach, 1987, Pa. Acad., 1988, Chautauqua Art Program, N.Y. Acad. Art, numerous others; USIS lectr., Japan, 1975; vis. lectr., critic Long Beach State Coll., 1987, Parsons Sch., 1991, Ox Bow Sch., 1991, N.Y. Acad., 1987, 91; vis. critic Chautauqua Art Sch., 1993; critic, lectr. Stanford U. Chautaugua Art Program, Bard Coll., Pa. Acad.; Disting. vis. prof. Am. Univ., Washington, 1994. Contbr. articles to profl. jours.; one man shows at Schoelkopf Gallery, 1964, 67, 70, 72, 74, 77, 86, 90, Hobart Coll., 1968, R.I. U., 1969, Temple U., 1971, La. State U., 1967, Bennington Coll., Ithaca Coll., R.I. U., So. U., Dart Gallery, Chgo., 1977, Savage Gallery, Boston, 1976, Meade Mus., Amherst Coll., 1983, Contemporary Realists Gallery, San Francisco, 1987, 90, Jessica Darraby Gallery, Los Angeles, 1987, Peter Tattistcheff Gallery, N.Y., 1994; exhibited in group shows at Whitney Mus., 1971, Mus. Modern Art, 1974, Corcoran Gallery, 1972, 76, Boston Mus., 1974, 75, Bklyn. Mus., 1952, 57, 59, 61, Library of Congress, 1957, 59, Gallery of Modern Art, 1972, N.Y. Cultural Center, 1972, Phila. Mus., 1970, Wadsworth Atheneum, 1976, Fogg Mus., 1976, Mpls. Inst. Arts, 1976, Milw. Art Center, 1977, Ft. Worth Art Mus., 1977, High Mus., 1977, San Francisco Mus. Modern Art, 1977, Pa. Acad., 1981, traveling shows sponsored by A.F.A., Smithsonian Instn., Library of Congress, Pa. Acad. Arts; represented in permanent collections Witherspoon Mus., Cleve. Mus., Mus. Fine Arts, Boston, Brandeis U. Art Mus., Chase-Manhattan Bank, A.D. White Mus. Cornell U., Nat. Gallery Art, Muzium Negara, Kuala Lumpur, Mead Mus. Amherst Coll., Glen S. Janss Collection Boise Art Mus., FMC Corp. Chgo., Archdiocese of Baton Rouge, Fidelity Bank Collection, Phila., Sierra Club. Recipient Research award CUNY, 1970-71, 75-76, 82, 86-87, 1988-89, Fed. Govt. Commn. through Interior Dept. for Bicentennial, 1974, award Rockefeller Found. at Bellagio, 1989, Altman Figure Painting prize Nat. Acad. Biennial, 1995; asst. Cornell U., 1955-57; L.C. Tiffany grantee, 1959; Fulbright fellow to Italy, 1962-63; Yaddo fellow, 1960, 62; Ingram Merrill fellow, 1975-76, 84, 90; J.S. Guggenheim fellow, 1989-90; NEA sr. grantee, 1983, 87-88; juror NEA, 1984, N.Y. State Council on Arts, 1985. Mem. Nat. Acad. (Proctor Portrait Prize Biennial Exhbn. 1993). Office: Queens Coll Flushing NY 11367

LADIGES, LORI JEAN, learning disabilities specialist; b. Sheboygan, Wis., Feb. 25, 1956; d. Donald William and Marion Margaret (Henning) L. BS in Edn., U. Wis., 1978; MA in Learning Disabilities, Cardinal Stritch Coll., 1984. Cert. tchr. elem. (grades 1-8), Cognitive disorders (K-12) and learning disabilities (K-12). Learning disabilities specialist Kohler (Wis.) Pub. Sch., 1978—; part-time instr. Silver Lake Coll., Manitowoc, Wis., 1984-92; tchr. Cardinal Stritch Coll., Milw., 1989, adj. assoc. prof., 1996—; sch. evaluation consortium chair spl. edn. Kohler Pub. Schs., 1989—, learning disabilities specialist, rep. long-range planning com., 1992—, cheerleading advisor, 1981-84, yearbook advisor, 1985-86; reviewer Sch. Evaluation Consortium, 1995.

Mem. Sch. to Work com., Alpha Sigma (Grace Alvord award 1978). Lutheran. Avocations: traveling, reading, fashion design/coordination. Home: 2236 N 23rd St Sheboygan WI 53083-4443

LADIN, EUGENE, communications company executive; b. N.Y.C., Oct. 26, 1927; s. Nat and Mae (Cohen) L.; m. Millicent Dolly Frankel, June 27, 1948; children: Leslie Hope, Stephanie Joy. B.B.A., Pace U., 1956; M.B.A., Air Force Inst. Tech., 1959; postgrad., George Washington U., 1966-69. Cost engr. Rand Corp., Santa Monica, Calif., 1960-62; mgr. cost and econ. analysis Northrop Corp., Hawthorne, Calif., 1962-66; dir. financial planning Communications Satellite Corp., Washington, 1966-70; treas., chief fin. and adminstrv. officer Landis & Gyr, Inc., Elmsford, N.Y., 1970-76; v.p., treas., comptroller P.R. Telephone Co., San Juan, 1976-77; v.p. fin. Comtech Telecommunications Corp., Smithtown, N.Y., 1977—; acting pres. Comtech Antenna Corp., St. Cloud, Fla., 1978-80; chmn., chief exec. officer Telephone Interconnect Enterprises/Sunshine Telephone Co., Balt., Md. and Orlando, Fla., 1980-82; pres. Ladin and Assocs., Cons. and Commodity Traders, Maitland, Fla., 1982-84; pres., chief fin. officer Braintech Inc., South Plainfield, N.J., 1984; sr. v.p. fin., chief fin. officer Teltec Savs. Communications Co., Miami, Fla., 1984-88; chief fin. officer Hurwitz Group Inc., North Miami Beach, Fla., 1988-91; cons. pvt. practice, 1991—; assoc. prof. acctg. So. Ill. U., East St. Louis, 1960; asso. prof. bus. U. Md., 1969-70; adj. prof. George Washington U., 1969-70; vis. prof. acctg. Pace U., 1970; cons. E. Ladin, Pembroke Pines, Fla., 1991—. Served to capt. USAF, 1951-60. Decorated Air Force Commendation medal; recipient Air Force Outstanding Unit award. Mem. Nat. Assn. Accts., Fin. Exec. Inst. Democrat. Jewish. Club: Flamingo Country Club. Avocations: golf, sailing. Home and Office: 13355 SW 16th Ct Apt 401E Hollywood FL 33027-2429 *An individual must have sufficient self esteem to sustain the courage of his convictions, a high degree of professional integrity, and his individual character. Society has adopted a philosophy of "walk the middle road".*

LADJEVARDI, HABIB, historian; b. Tehran, Iran, May 28, 1938; came to U.S., 1950; s. Seyed Mahmoud and Tahereh (Kashani) L.; m. Mina Nassirzadeh, Aug. 3, 1962 (div. June 1979); children: Mahmoud, Mariam, Leila. BS, Yale U., 1961; MBA, Harvard U., 1963; DPhil, Oxford U., 1981. Personnel dir. Behshahr Ind. Group, Tehran, 1963-65, mktg. dir., 1966-69; pres. Paxan Corp., Tehran, 1969-70; chmn. bd. dirs. Container Corp. of Iran, 1969-79; founder, v.p. Iran Ctr. Mgmt. Studies, Tehran, 1970-79; sr. rsch. assoc. Harvard U. Bus. Sch., Cambridge, Mass., 1980-81; rsch. assoc. Harvard U. Ctr. for Middle Eastern Studies, 1981—, assoc. dir., 1987-90, dir. Iranian oral history project, 1981—; mem. acceptance coms. Tehran Stock Exch., 1973-76; lectr. Iran Ctr. for Mgmt. Studies, 1975-79; vis. fellow Oxford (Eng.) Ctr. Mgmt. Studies, 1976-79; v.p. exec. coun. Harvard U. Bus. Sch., 1978-79; exec. sec. Soc. for Iranian Studies, Cambridge, 1982-87; chmn. Iranian Studies Harvard U. Ctr. for Middle Eastern Studies, 1990—, chmn. pubs. com., 1990—. Author: Labor Unions & Autocracy in Iran, 1985, Guide to the Iranian Oral History Collection, 1993, Memoirs of Ali Amini, 1995, Memoirs of Shapour Bakhtiar, 1996; contbr. articles to profl. jours., chpts. to books. Mem. coun. of state Adminstrv. and Employment Affairs of Iran, 1972-76; dir. devel. and investment Bank of Iran, 1972-79; mem. ctrl. coun. Pres. of Univs. and Colls. of Iran, 1971-78; pres. Tahereh Found., Lincoln, Mass., 1982—. NEH grantee, 1984-87. Mem. Am. Hist. Assn., Young Presidents Orgn., Acad. Polit. Sci., N.Y. Acad. Scis., Iranian Assn. of Boston (founder, pres. 1988-91), Yale U. Class Coun., Yale Club of N.Y., Harvard Club of Boston. Democrat. Avocations: squash, skiing, grandchildren. Office: Harvard U Ctr Mid Eastern Studies 1737 Cambridge St Cambridge MA 02138-3016

LADJEVARDI, HAMID, fund manager; b. Tehran, Iran, June 11, 1948; came to U.S., 1948; s. Ahmad and Banoo (Barzin) L.; m. Manijeh Mirdamad, July 19, 1978; children: Adella, Lilly. BA in Econs., BA in Polit. Sci., U. Calif., Berkeley, 1971; MBA, Harvard U., 1973. Dep. mng. dir. Behshahr Indsl. Group, Tehran, 1974-79; vice chmn., fin. dir. Akam Group of Cos., Tehran, 1975-79; investment mgr., v.p. Morgan Stanley & Co., N.Y.C., 1980-92; mgr. Baltic Fund 1 LLC, N.Y.C., 1992—; pres. Baltic Mgmt. LLC, 1995—; instr. Fairleigh Dickinson U., Rutherford, N.J., 1984; pres. Baltic Mgmt. LLC, 1995—. Mem. Coun. Internat. Bus. Risk Mgmt., Fgn. Policy Assn., Carnegie Coun. on Ethics and Internat. Affairs, U.S. Senatorial Club, Harvard Club. Home: 66 Brite Ave Scarsdale NY 10583-1637 Office: Baltic Fund 745 5th Ave New York NY 10151

LADLY, FREDERICK BERNARD, health services and financial services company executive; b. Toronto, Ont., Can., July 14, 1930; s. John Bernard and Olivia Montgomery (Fenimore) L.; m. Sharon Mary Davidson; children: Patricia, Elizabeth, Katherine, Martha, Sarah, Meghan. B.A., U. Toronto. Gen. mgr. internat. ops. Can. Packers Inc., Toronto, 1973, v.p., 1974-78, dir., 1975-84, exec. v.p., 1978-84; pres., CEO Extendicare Health Svcs. Inc., Markham, 1984-94, Extendicare Inc. (formerly Crownx Inc.), Markham, 1992-95; chmn. United Health, Inc., Milw., 1984—; vice chmn. Crown Life Ins. Co., Regina, 1994—; CEO, dep. chmn. Extendicare Inc., 1996—; chmn. Extendicare (Can.) Inc., Extendicare (U.K.) Ltd.; bd. dirs. Extendicare Inc., Crown Life Ins. Co., Cobi Foods, Inc.

LADMAN, A(ARON) J(ULIUS), anatomist, educator; b. Jamaica, N.Y., July 3, 1925; s. Thomas and Ida (Sobin) L.; m. Barbara Powers, 1948 (div. 1980); children: Susan Elizabeth, Thomas Frederick; m. Patricia A. Bergbauer, 1982; 1 child, Peter John. Student, Miami U., Oxford, Ohio, 1942-43; AB, NYU, 1947; postgrad., U. Cin., 1948-49; Ph.D., Ind. U., 1952. Teaching fellow anatomy U. Cin., 1948-49, Ind. U., 1949-52; with Harvard Med. Sch., 1952-61, assoc., 1955-61; assoc. prof. U. Tenn. Med. Units, 1961-64; vis. assoc. prof. Yale, 1964; prof., chmn. dept. anatomy U. N.Mex. Sch. Medicine, Albuquerque, 1964-81; prof. anatomy Hahnemann U., Phila., 1981-94; prof. anatomy Med. Coll. Pa. and Hahnemann U. Sch. Medicine, Phila., 1995, adj. prof. neurobiology and anatomy, 1995—; dean Sch. Allied Health Professions Hahnemann U., 1981-86. Assoc. editor Anat. Record, 1967-68, editor-in-chief, 1968—; contbr. articles to profl. jours. Recipient Rsch. Career Devel. award USPHS, 1962-64; rsch. fellow Am. Cancer Soc., 1952-55, spl. rsch. fellow USPHS, 1955-57, 71-72. Fellow AAAS; mem. Am. Assn. Anatomists (exec. com. 1972-76, 2d v.p. 1980-81, 1st v.p. 1981-82), Am. Soc. for Cell Biology, Nat. Inst. Gen. Med. Scis. (rsch. cancer awards com. 1967-71), Electron Microscope Soc. Am. (exec. coun. 1974-76), Coun. Biol. Editors (sec. 1977-82), Histochem. Soc. Home: 103 Arbor Way Lansdale PA 19446-6433 Office: Med Coll Pa & Hahnemann U # 408 Broad and Vine St Philadelphia PA 19102-1192

LADMAN, JERRY R., economist, educator; b. Sioux City, Iowa, Dec. 30, 1935; s. Harry L. and Amy I. (Swearingen) L.; m. Carmen Aida; children—Jeffrey, James, Michael, Stephanie. B.S., Iowa State U., 1958, Ph.D., 1968. Placement officer Coll. Agr., Iowa State U., Ames, 1963-65, research asst., 1965-67; asst. prof. Ariz. State U., 1967-72, assoc. prof., 1972-78, prof. econs., 1979—, dir. Ctr. for Latin Am. Studies, 1976-90; prof. agrl. econs. Ohio State U., Columbus, 1990—; asst. dir. LEAD program Ohio LEAD Program, Columbus, 1995—; chief of party Univ. Agribus. Partnership Project, Dominican Republic Ohio State U., Columbus, 1990-95; program asst. Ford Found., Mexico City, 1971-72; vis. prof. Nat. Sch. Agr., Chapingo, Mex., 1965-67, 71-72, Ohio State U., 1979; vis. scholar Stanford U., 1975; hon. prof. Cath. U. Bolivia, 1986; participant U.S.-U.S.S.R. Cultural Exchange, 1986. Author: The Development of Mexicali Regional Economy, 1975, United States-Mexican Energy Relationships: Realities and Prospects, 1981, Modern Day Bolivia: The Legacy of the Revolution and Prospects for the Future, 1982, Mexico: A Country in Crisis, 1987, Redemocratization in Bolivia: A Political Economic Analysis of the Siles Suazo Government, 1982-1985, 1990; contbr. articles to profl. jours., chpts. to books. Chmn. troop com. Boy Scouts Am., Tempe, Ariz., 1976-84; bd. dirs. Friends of Mexican Art, 1977-86. Served to capt. USAR, 1958-65. Fulbright lectr., Ecuador, 1974. Mem. Am. Econ. Assn., Am. Agrl. Econ. Assn., Latin Am. Studies Assn., Pacific Coast Council Latin Am. Studies (treas. 1977-86, v.p. 1986, pres. 1987), Rocky Mountain Council Latin Am. Studies (bd. dirs. 1976-90), Phoenix Com. Fgn. Relations, Ariz.-Mex. Commn. (bd. dirs. 1982-90), Assn. Borderlands Scholars (pres. 1983-85), PROFMEX (bd. dirs. 1983-90). Office: Ohio State U Dept Agrl Econs 2120 Fyffe Rd Columbus OH 43210-1067

LADNER, ANN-MARIE CALVO, special education educator; b. Hartford, Conn., Feb. 6, 1949; d. Vincent J. and Mary S. (Santangelo) Calvo; m. R. Martin Ladner, June 19, 1971; children: Mary-Lorraine Amy Cox, R. Vincent, Michelle A. AS, Belleville Area Coll., 1983; BS in Speech and Theater, So. Ill. U., Edwardsville, 1985, MS in Edn., 1986; EdS, Auburn U. Montgomery, 1993. Cert. specific learning disabilities, Ala., psychometrist, Ala., sch. adminstr., Ala. Tchr. merchandising Skadron Coll. Bus., San Bernardino, Calif., 1981-82; tchr. English as second lang. Turkish-Am. Assn., Ankara, Turkey, 1986; tchr. speech and computers Ozel Atilim Lisesi, Ankara, 1987-88; tchr. English and reading St. Jude H.S., Selma, Ala., 1989-90; tchr. spl. edn. Selma Sch. Dist., 1990-92, Montgomery (Ala.) County Schs., 1992-93, 95—, Dept. Youth Svcs., Jemison, Ala., 1993-95. Libr. bd. dirs. City of Millbrook, Ala., 1992-94; bd. dirs. Turkish-Am. Assn., Ankara, 1987-88, Millbrook YMCA, 1993—; judge, coach Nat. Forensics League, Belleville, Ill., 1985. Named Competent Toastmaster, Toastmasters Internat., 1985; mini-grantee Montgomery Area Comty. Found., 1992. Mem. NEA, ASCD, Coun. Exceptional Children, Nat. Coun. Tchrs. Math., Ala. Edn. Assn., Mensa, Kappa Delta Pi. Avocations: modeming, reading, collecting educational materials. Home: 394 Gardenia Rd Millbrook AL 36054-1320 Office: Project Upward Madison Park Alt Sch Montgomery AL 36110

LADNER, JOYCE A., academic administrator; b. Hattiesburg, Miss.. BA in Sociology, Tougaloo Coll.; MA, PhD in Sociology, Washington U., St. Louis. Assoc. prof. dept. sociology Howard U., Washington, 1971-73, v.p. acad. affairs, 1990—, interim pres., 1994—; prof. Hunter Coll. CUNY, 1973-81. Author: Tomorrow's Tomorrow: The Black Woman, 1971, Mixed Families: Adoption Across Racial Boundaries; editor The Death of White Sociology, 1973, Adolescence and Poverty: Challenges for the 1990s, 1991; contbr. chpts. to over 20 books and articles to Washington Post, N.Y. Times, Ebony, others. Chair Mayor's Blue Ribbon Panel on Teenage Pregnancy Prevention for D.C, 1984-85; past chair Bd. Trans Africa Forum; past sec. Twenty-First Century Found.; bd. dirs. Recording for the Blind. Recipient DuBois-Johnson-Frazier Outstanding Scholarship award Am. Sociol. Assn., Joseph S. Himes Disting. Career award Assn. Black Sociologists, Acad. Excellence award Nat. Congress Black Faculty. Mem. Coalition of 100 Black Women (bd. dirs.). Office: Howard Univ Office of Pres 2400 6th St NW Ste 402 Washington DC 20059-0001

LADNER, THOMAS E., lawyer; b. Vancouver, B.C., Can., Dec. 8, 1916. B.A., U. B.C., 1937; LLB, Osgoode Hall. Bar: B.C. bar 1940. Ret. partner firm Ladner Downs, Vancouver. Mem. Canadian, Vancouver bar assns., Law Soc. B.C. Office: PO Box 48600, 1200-200 Burrard St, Vancouver, BC Canada V7X 1T2

LADOW, C. STUART, consultant financial services; b. Warren, Pa., Apr. 21, 1925; s. Clyde and Glendine (Bentley) LaD.; m. Donna Elizabeth Miller, Aug. 21, 1993; 1 child, Paul Stuart. B.A., Cornell U., 1947. With Gen. Electric Co., 1947-50; mgr. N.Y. region Gen. Electric Credit Corp., N.Y.C., 1950-80; v.p. Gen. Electric Credit Corp., Stamford, Conn., 1971-80; pres. GECC Fin. Services, 1975-78, Color Tyme TV Rental div. Curtis Mathes Corp., Athens, Tex., 1980; sr. v.p. Yegen Assocs., Inc., Paramus, N.J., 1981-85; exec. v.p. Yegen Assocs., Inc., Paramus, 1985-87; pres. Yegen Equity Loan Corp., Paramus, N.J., 1987; fin. svcs. cons. Allison Park, Pa., 1988—; dir. Puritan Life Ins. Co., Providence, Am. Bankers Ins. Group, Miami, Fla., 1980-81. Vice pres., bd. dirs. Jr. Achievement of Stamford, Inc., 1973-80; mem. exec. budget com., chmn. budget panel United Way of Stamford, 1973-80; chmn. Stamford chpt. Am. Cancer Soc., 1977; pres. Spring Meadow Condominium Assn., Wyckoff, N.J., 1983, trustee, 1983-88; moderator Emmanuel Bapt. Ch., Ridgewood, N.J., 1985-86; trustee North Hills Community Baptist Ch., 1988-91; dir. Hampton Twsp. Mcpl. Authority, Allison Park, Pa., 1991—, dir., treas. Baptist Homes of Western Pa., 1992—, pres. Arbors Homeowners Assn., Allison Park, 1992-93; pres. Cornell U. Class of 1947, 1992—. Served with USN, 1944-46, ETO. Recipient Community Service award Gen. Electric Credit Corp., 1976. Mem. Nat. Second Mortgage Assn. (pres. 1987-88, Outstanding Service award, Meritorious Svc. award 1989), Nat. Consumer Finance Assn. (certificate of appreciation), Masons, Shriners, Cornell Club of Pitts. Republican. Baptist. Home and Office: 4211 Latour Ct Allison Park PA 15101-2968 *Ours is a great country that deserves the devotion and strong support of those who call it home. There can be few satisfactions in life greater than assisting in the moral, spiritual and career growth of those whom we have the opportunity to know and possibly influence.*

LA DU, BERT NICHOLS, JR., pharmacology educator, physician; b. Lansing, Mich., Nov. 13, 1920; s. Bert Nichols and Natalie (Kerr) La D.; m. Catherine Shilson, June 14, 1947; children: Elizabeth, Mary, Anne, Jane. B.S., Mich. State Coll., 1943; M.D., U. Mich., 1945; Ph.D. in Biochemistry, U. Calif., Berkeley, 1952. Intern Rochester (N.Y.) Gen. Hosp., 1945-46; research asso. N.Y.U. Research Service, Goldwater Meml. Hosp., N.Y.C., 1950-53; sr. asst. surgeon USPHS, Nat. Heart Inst., 1954-57; surgeon, later sr. surgeon, med. dir. Nat. Inst. Arthritis and Metabolic Disease, 1957-63; prof., chmn. dept. pharmacology N.Y.U. Med. Sch., 1963-74; prof. pharmacology U. Mich. Med. Sch., Ann Arbor, 1974-89, prof. emeritus, 1989—, chmn. dept., 1974-81. Contbr. articles to profl. jours. Served with AUS, 1943-45. Mem. AAAS, Am. Chem. Soc., N.Y. Acad. Sci. (pres.), Am. Soc. Biol. Chemistry, Am. Soc. Pharmacol. Therapeutics (pres.), Am. Soc. Human Genetics, Biochem. Soc. (Gt. Britain). Home: 817 Berkshire Rd Ann Arbor MI 48104-2630 Office: U Mich Med Sch 6322 Med Sci I Ann Arbor MI 48109-0572

LADUKE, NANCIE, lawyer, corporate executive; b. Mayfield, Ky.; m. Daniel E. LaDuke, 1978. BA, Wayne State U., 1962; JD, U. Detroit, 1976. Pvt. practice Detroit, 1976; atty. KMart, Troy, Mich., 1977-84, comml. law counsel, 1984-90, v.p., sec., 1991—. Office: KMart Corp 3100 W Big Beaver Rd Troy MI 48084-3004

LADWIG, PATTI HEIDLER, lawyer; b. Harleysville, Pa., Aug. 28, 1958; d. L. Donald and Joan E. (Wright) Heidler; m. Manfred Friedrich Ladwig, July 30, 1983; 1 child, Brittney Nichole. BA in Psychology, U. Miami, 1980, JD, 1988. Bar: Fla. 1988, U.S. Dist. Ct. (so. dist.) Fla. 1988. Assoc. atty. Taplin, Howard & Shaw, West Palm Beach, Fla., 1988-92; ptnr. Shaw, St. James, & Ladwig, West Palm Beach, Fla., 1992, St. James & Ladwig, P.A., West Palm Beach, Fla., 1992-93; pvt. practice Patti Heidler Ladwig, P.A., West Palm Beach, 1993—; bd. dirs. Cmty. Assns. Inst., West Palm Beach, First Wellington, Inc.; mem. condominium and planned devel. com., real property, probate and trust law sect. Fla. Bar. Pres., bd. dirs. Treasure Coast Communities Assn., West Palm Beach, 1990—, Pine Lake Condominium Assn. Inc., Pembroke Pines, Fla., 1986-88; mem. community appearance com. ACME Improvement Dist., Wellington, Fla., 1990—, Condominium Owners Fla., 1991—, Fedn. Mobile Home Owners Fla., 1990—; del. Fla. Legis. Action Com., 1989-91. Mem. Fla. Bar Assn. (bus. law sect., mem. condominium and planned devel. com. real property, probate and trust law sect.). Lutheran. Office: Ste 640 1645 Palm Beach Lakes Blvd West Palm Beach FL 33401-2216

LAEMMLE, CHERYL MARIE VICARIO, artist; b. Mpls., 1947. BA, Humboldt State U., Arcata, N.Y., 1974; MFA, Washington State U., 1978. One-woman shows at Tex. Gallery, Houston, 1982, Barbara Toll Fine Arts, N.Y.C., 1983, Sharpe Gallery, N.Y.C., 1984, 86, Hokin/Kaufman Gallery, Chgo., 1986, GregKucera Gallery, Seattle, 1988, 90, 92, Fay Gold Gallery, Atlanta, 1989, 92, Nat. Mus. Women in Arts, Washington, 989, Rena Bransten Gallery, San Francisco, 1989, Mus. Art, Washington State U., Pullman, 1990, Terry Dintenfass, N.Y.C., 1991, Allene LaPides Gallery, Santa Fe, N.Mex., 1992, Midtown Payson Galleries, N.Y.C., 1994; exhibited in group shows at Tweed Mus. Art, U. Minn., Duluth, 1989, Greg Kucera Gallery, Seattle, 1989, Art Mus. Fla. Internat. U., Miami, 1989, Terra Mus. Am. Art, Chgo., 1989, Laumeler Sculpture Park, St. Louis, 989, Grand Rapids (Mich.) Art Mus., 989, Arnot Art Mus., Elmira, N.Y., 1989, Hudson River Mus. Westchester, Yonkers, N.Y., 1989, Pa. Acad. Fine Arts, Phila., 1989, Denver Art Mus., 1989, New Orleans Mus. Art, 1989, Cin. Art Mus., 1989, Whitney Mus. Am. Art at Equitable Ctr., N.Y.C., 1990, U. Art Gallery, Calif. State U., Chico, 1990, Terry Dintenfass, N.Y.C., 1990, Mint Mus. Art, Charlotte, N.C., 1991, Visual Art Ctr., Calif. State U., Fullerton, 1991, Midtown Payson Galleries, N.Y.C., 1992, 94, Nancy Margolis Gallery, N.Y.C., 1995, others; represented in permanent collections at Dannheisser Found., Eli Broad Family Found., L.A., Frederick Welsman Collection, L.A., Met. Mus. Art, N.Y.C., Museo Rufino Tamayo, Mexico City, Walker Art Ctr., Mpls., Edward Downe Jr. Found., Corcoran Gallery Art, Washington, High Art Mus., Atlanta, Mint Mus. Art, Charlotte, N.C. Recipient Creative Artists Pub. Svc. Program fellowship, 980, Vera G. List award, 1984, painting fellowships Nat. Endowment for Arts, 1985-86, 86-87.

LAESSIG, RONALD HAROLD, pathology educator, state official; b. Marshfield, Wis., Apr. 4, 1940; s. Harold John and Ella Louise (Gumz) L.; m. Joan Margaret Spreda, Jan. 29, 1966; 1 child, Elizabeth Susan. B.S., U. Wis.-Stevens Point, 1962; Ph.D., U. Wis.-Madison, 1965. Jr. faculty Princeton (N.J.) U., 1966; chief clin. chemistry Wis. State Lab. Hygiene, Madison, 1966-80, dir., 1980—; asst. prof. preventive medicine U. Wis.-Madison, 1966-72, assoc. prof., 1972-76, prof., 1976—, prof. pathology, 1980—; cons. Ctr. Disease Control, Atlanta; dir. Nat. Com. for Clin. Lab. Standards, Villanova, Pa., 1977-80; chmn. invitro diagnostic products adv. com. FDA, 1974-75; mem. rev. com. Nat. Bur. Standards, 1983-86. Mem. editorial bd. Med. Electronics, 1970—, Analytical Chemistry, 1970-76, Health Lab. Sci., 1970—; contbr. articles to profl. jours. Mem. State of Wis. Tech. Com. Alcohol and Traffic Safety, 1970-88. Sloan Found. grantee, 1966; recipient numerous grants. Mem. Am. Assn. Clin. Chemistry (chmn. safety com. 1984-86, bd. dirs. 1986-89, Natelson award 1989, Contbns. Svc. to Profession award 1990), Am. Pub. Health Assn. (Difco award 1974), Am. Soc. for Med. Tech., Nat. Com. Clin. Lab. Standards (pres. 1980-82, bd. dirs. 1984-87), Sigma Xi. Avocation: Woodworking. Office: State Lab Hygiene 465 Henry Mall Madison WI 53706-1501 *If you are doing something you really enjoy and it affords you the opportunity to really help your fellow man--you're really blessed (like I am).*

LAESSIG, WALTER BRUCE, publishing executive; b. Englewood, N.J., Aug. 11, 1941; s. George Bruce Laessig and Eileen May (Codling) Roma; m. Susan Lamme, June 13, 1964; children: Katherine Anne, Sarah Eileen, Matthew Lamme. AB in History, Cornell U., 1963, MBA in Fin., 1966, LLB, 1966. Bar: N.Y. 1966, D.C. 1968. Atty. Nixon, Hargrave, Devans & Doyle, Rochester, N.Y., 1966-68, Martin, Whitfield & Thaler, Washington, 1968-70; minority economist, counsel Joint Econ. Com., U.S. Congress, Washington, 1971-75; minority tax counsel Com. on Ways and Means, U.S. Ho. Reps., Washington, 1975-77; gen. counsel Nat. Assn. REITs, Washington, 1977-79; atty. Laessig, Brown, Hearn & Clohan, Washington, 1979-84; v.p. Warren, Gorham & Lamont, N.Y.C., 1984-85, exec. v.p., 1986, pres., chief exec. officer, 1987-89; exec. v.p., chief oper. officer Thomson Profl. Pub., Stamford, Conn., 1989-90; pres., chief exec. officer The Argus Group, Washington, 1990—. Republican. Presbyterian. Office: The Argus Group 1101 Vermont Ave NW Ste 400 Washington DC 20005-3521

LAETTNER, CHRISTIAN DONALD, professional basketball player; b. Angola, N.Y., Aug. 17, 1969. Student, Duke U. Basketball player Minn. Timberwolves, 1992-1995; now with Atlanta Hawks. Named Most Outstanding Player in NCAA Divsn. 1A Tournament, 1991, Sporting News Coll. Player of Yr., 1992, Sporting News All-Am. First Team, 1992, Naismith award, 1992, Wooden award, 1992; mem. Gold medal Winning Olympic Team, Barcelona, Spain, 1992. Named to NBA All-Rookie first team, 1993; mem. NCAA Divsn. I Championship Teams, 1991-92. Office: Atlanta Hawks 1 CNN Ctr Ste 405 South Tower Atlanta GA 30303*

LA FALCE, JOHN JOSEPH, congressman, lawyer; b. Buffalo, N.Y., Oct. 6, 1939; s. Dominic E. and Catherine M. (Stasio) La F.; m. Patricia Fisher, 1979. BS, Canisius Coll., 1961; JD, Villanova U., 1964; LLD (hon.), Niagara U., 1979, St. Johns U., 1989; LHD (hon.), Canisius Coll., 1990; LLD (hon.), Villanova U., 1991. Bar: N.Y. 1964. Mem. N.Y. State Legislature, 1971-74, 94th-104th Congresses from 32nd (now 29th) N.Y. dist., Washington, D.C., 1975—. Capt. adj. gen. corps AUS. Democrat. Home: 35 Danbury Ln Buffalo NY 14217-2101 Office: US Ho of Reps Rm 2310 Rayburn House Office Bldg Washington DC 20515*

LAFARGE, CATHERINE, dean; b. Paris, May 22, 1935. BA, Mt. Holyoke Coll., 1957; PhD in French, Yale U., 1966. Acting instr. French Yale U., 1964-66, instr. to asst. prof., 1966-74, assoc. prof., 1974-80; prof. French Bryn Mawr Coll., 1980—, chmn. dept. French, 1979-84; dean Grad. Sch. Arts and Scis., Bryn Mawr Coll., 1985—. Author: The Emergence of the Bourgeoisie, 1964, Reverie et Realite dans les Nuits de Paris de Restif de la Bretonne, 1975, Paris and Myth: One Vision of Horror, In: Studies in Eighteenth Century Culture, vol. V, 1976, L'Anti-Fete dans le Nouveau Paris de L S Mercier, La Fete Revolutionnaire, 1977; author: (with J.P. Bouler) Les emprunts de mme Dupin L'Infortune litteraire des Dupin: Essai de bibliographie critique, Vol. CLXXXII, 1979, Studies on Voltaire & 18th Century: Catalogue topographique partiel des papiers Dupin-Rousseau disperse de 1951 à 58, Annales de la Societe Jean-Jacques Rousseau, Vol. XXXIX, 1980; editor: Dilemmes du Roman. Essays in Honor of Georges May, 1989. Bd. dirs. Grad. Record Examination, Test of English as a Fgn. Lang.; chmn. com. on langs. and lit. Yale U. Mem. Internat. Soc. 18th Century Studies, Am. Soc. 18th Century Studies, Soc. Francaise d'Etude 18th Siecle, Am. Assn. Tchrs. of French, Assn. Internat. Studies. Office: Bryn Mawr Coll Bryn Mawr PA 19010

LAFAVE, HUGH GORDON JOHN, medical association executive, psychiatrist, educator, consultant; b. Montmarte, Sask., Can., Apr. 28, 1929; s. Leslie Alexander and Mary (Flaman) L.; m. Joann Sanderson, June 1956; children: Bonnie Lynn, Leslie Hugh, Maria Delee. B.A. cum laude, U. Sask., 1951; MD, Chirurgiae Magistri, McGill U., 1953. Diplomate: Am. Bd. Psychiatry and Neurology. Intern Detroit Receiving Hosp., 1953-54; gen. practice medicine Rockglen, Assiniboia, Sask., Can., 1954-56; resident Medfield State Hosp., 1956-57, 58-60, Inst. Living, Hartford, Conn., 1957-58; chief rehab. Medfield State Hosp., Harding, Mass., 1960-61; clin. dir. Sask. Hosp., Weyburn, Can., 1962-64, supt., 1964-66; assoc. commr. dept. mental hygiene State of N.Y., Albany, 1966-69; dir. Eleanor Roosevelt Devel. Services, Schenectady, 1969-76; exec. dir. psychiat. services br. Dept. Health-Sask., Can., 1976-79; exec. v.p. Can. Assn. Mentally Retarded (now Can. Assn. Community Living), Downsview, Ont., 1979-84; pvt. practice specializing in psychiatry Red Deer Regional Hosp, 1984-85; dir. rehab. programs Brockville Psychiatric Hosp, 1985-94; assoc. prof. Albany Med. Coll., N.Y., 1968-76, assoc. prof. pediatrics, 1971-76, prof.; assoc. dean, prof. N.Y. Sch. Psychiatry, Poughkeepsie, 1969-76; clin. assoc. prof. psychiatry, U. Sask. Med. Coll., 1976-83, U. Ottawa, 1985-94; pres. Wellness Can., Hugh Lafave Holdings Ltd., 1981—; med. dir. Smokers Treatment Ctr., Ottawa, 1993—; mem., chmn. exptl., spl. tng. rev. com. NIMH, Chevy Chase, Md., 1970-74; mem. editl. bd. Can.'s Mental Health, 1978-80; mem. rehab.-cmty. psychiatry com. U. Ottawa, 1886-92; prin. investigator Health Innovation Grant Cmty. Rehab. Program, 1990-93; pres. Cmty. Living Cons., 1994—. Author: (with others) State Hospitals—What Happens When They Close?, 1976, Is the Community Ready?; contbr. numerous articles to profl. jours. Mem. awards com. Kennedy Found., 1977-78; bd. dirs. Byrd Hoffman Found., Inc., N.Y.C., 1974-80, Family Focus, Brockville, Can., 1986-90. Recipient Outstanding Achievement Amethyst award Province of Ont. Ministry of Citizenship, 1994; selected as Health Innovator by Ont. Premier's Health Coun., 1991-93. Mem. Can. Psychiat. Assn. (bd. dirs. 1976-79), Am. Psychiat. Assn., Can. Pub. Health Assn., Workshop, Inc. (profl. adv. com. 1970-75), Nat. Inst. Mental Retardation (assoc. 1984—), Can. Mental Health Assn. (Toronto) (consumer participation task force 1986-90), Royal Coll. Psychiatrists. Home: Box 424, Brockville, ON Canada K6V 5V6 Office: PO Box 13, Elgin, ON Canada KOG 1EO *People, all kinds of people, their rights, their health, their wellbeing, have been the focus of my career and my life, without regret.*

LAFAVE, LEANN LARSON, lawyer; b. Ramona, S.D., May 31, 1953; d. Floyd Burdette and Janice Anne (Quist) L.; m. Richard Curtis Finke, May 19, 1973 (div. Jan. 1978); 1 child, Timothy; m. Dwayne Jeffery LaFave, May 31, 1981 (div. 1992); children: Jeffrey, Allison. BS, U. S.D., 1974, JD with honors, 1977. Bar: S.D. 1977, U.S. Dist. Ct. S.D. 1977, U.S. Ct. Appeals (8th cir.) 1977, N.D. 1978, U.S. Dist. Ct. N.D. 1978. Asst. atty. gen. State of S.D., Pierre, 1977-78, 79-81; assoc. Bjella, Neff, Rathert & Wahl, Williston, N.D., 1978-79, Tobin Law Offices, P.C., Winner, S.D., 1981-83; assoc. dean, asst. prof. U. S.D. Sch. Law, Vermillion, 1983-86, dir. continuing legal edn., 1983-89, assoc. prof. law, 1986-89; ptnr. Aho & LaFave, Brookings, S.D., 1990-91; pvt. practice Brookings, 1991-92; asst. U.S. atty. U.S. Dist. S.D., 1992—; mem. S.D. Bd. Pardons and Paroles, 1987-90, chmn., 1989-90; comml. arbitrator Am. Arbitration Assn., 1985—; prof. Kilian C.C. Contbr. articles to profl. jours. Mem. planning coun. Nat. Identification Program for

Advancement Women in Higher Edn. Adminstrn., Am. Coun. on Edn., S.D., 1984-90; bd. dirs. Mo. Shores Women's Resource Ctr., Pierre, 1980, W.H. Over Mus., Vermillion, 1986-87, S.D. Vol. Lawyers for Arts, 1987—, Brookings Interagy. Coun., 1990-91, Brookings Women's Ctr., 1990-94; sec. Mediation Ctr., Inc. Named S.D. Woman Atty. of Yr. Women in Law U. S.D., 1985. Mem. S.D. Bar Assn. (bd. govs. young lawyers sect. 1983-84), S.D. Mediation Assn., Epsilon Sigma Alpha (S.D. coun. sect. 1985-86). Republican. Episcopalian. Avocation: reading. Home: 1808 S Jefferson Ave Sioux Falls SD 57105-2415 Office: PO Box 5073 Sioux Falls SD 57117-5073

LAFAVORE, MICHAEL J., magazine editor; b. Portland, Maine, Apr. 28, 1952; s. Joseph T. and Marion (Brown) L.; m. Trieste A. Kennedy; children: Nico, Alec. BA in English, U. Maine, 1975. Reporter Jour. Tribune, Biddeford, Maine, 1975-79; sr. editor Organic Gardening, Emmaus, Pa., 1979-84, Practical Homeowner, Emmaus, Pa., 1984-88; exec. editor Men's Health Homeowner, Emmaus, Pa., 1988—; screening com. mem. Nat. Mag. Awards, N.Y.C., 1994. Author: The Home Gym, 1978, Radon: The Invisible Threat, 1985; editor: Men's Health Advisor, 1992, 93. Author: The Home Gym, 1978, Radon: The Invisible Threat, 1985; editor: Men's Health Advisor, 1992, 93. Recipient Mont award Photo Design Mag., 1989, Mental Health Media award Nat. Mental Health Assn., 1991, Award for Excellence, Men's Fashion Assn., 1992, Editor of the Yr. award Advertising Age, 1995, Nat. Mag. awards nomination, 1995, 96. Office: Rodale Press 33 E Minor St Emmaus PA 18049-4113

LAFEBER, WALTER FREDERICK, history educator, author; b. Walkerton, Ind., Aug. 30, 1933; s. Ralph N. and Helen (Lidecker) LaF.; m. Sandra Gould, Sept. 11, 1955; children: Scott Nichols, Suzanne Margaret. B.A., Hanover Coll., 1955; M.A., Stanford, 1956; Ph.D., U. Wis., 1959. Asst. prof. history Cornell U., 1959-63, assoc. prof., 1963-67, prof., 1967-68, Noll prof. history, 1968—; Commonwealth lectr. U. London, Eng., 1973; Callander lectr. U. Aberdeen, 1987; Shaw lectr. Johns Hopkins U., 1989; Landmark prof. Am. U., 1992; Jefferson lectr. U. Calif., Berkeley, 1992; Mem. adv. com. hist. div. State Dept., 1971-75. Author: The New Empire...1860-1898, 1963, America, Russia and the Cold War, 8th edit., 1996, The Panama Canal, The Crisis in Historical Perspective, 1978, expanded edit., 1979, 2d edit., 1989, Inevitable Revolutions: The U.S. in Central America, 1983, 2d edit., 1992, The American Age...1750 to the Present, 1989, 2d edit. 1994, The American Search for Opportunity, 1865-1913, 1993, The Clash: U.S. Relations with Japan from the 1850's to the Present; co-author: The American Century, 4th edit, 1991; America in Vietnam, 1985; editor: John Quincy Adams and American Continental Empire, 1965, America in the Cold War, 1969, American Issues Forum, Vol. 2, 1976, also others; co-editor: Behind the Throne, Essays in Honor of Fred Harvey Harrington, 1993; mem. editorial adv. bd., Polit. Sci. Quar. Recipient Gustavus Myers prize, 1985; Guggenheim fellow, 1990. Mem. Orgn. Am. Historians, Am. Hist. Assn. (exec. coun. 1994—, Albert Beveridge prize 1962), Am. Acad. Arts and Scis. Office: Cornell U Dept History McGraw Hall Ithaca NY 14853-4601

LAFER, FRED SEYMOUR, data processing company executive; b. Passaic, N.J., Mar. 17, 1929; s. Abraham David and Pauline (Braer) L.; m. Barbara Bernstein, Apr. 4, 1954; children: Deborah, Gordon, Diana. BIE, NYU, 1950, JD, 1961; LHD (hon.), William Paterson Coll., 1987. Bar: N.J. 1961. Sec. to Justice Hayden Proector, N.J. Supreme Ct., 1961-62; partner firm Hoffman Humphreys Lafer, Wayne, N.J., 1962-67; sec., gen. counsel Automatic Data Processing, Inc., Clifton, N.J., 1967—; v.p. Automatic Data Processing, Inc., 1968-81, sr. v.p., 1981—; pres. N.J. Nets Profl. Basketball Team, 1984; pres. Taub Found. Chmn. United Jewish Appeal Fedn. North Jersey, 1973-74; pres. Jewish Fedn. North Jersey, 1976-77; v.p. N.J. Bd. Edn., 1967-68; bd. dirs. Chilton Meml. Hosp., Pompton Plains, N.J., 1970-72; trustee William Paterson Coll., 1974—, vice-chmn. bd., 1977, chmn. bd., 1978-80; pres. Am. Friends of Hebrew U., 1985-89; exec. com. Washington Inst. Near East Policy, sec.-treas., 1993—. Served to lt. USAF, 1951-52. Recipient honorary doctorate Hebrew U. of Jerusalem, 1995. Mem. Computer Law Assn. (pres. 1972-74), Assn. Data Processing Service Orgns. (chmn. 1983), ABA. Office: ADP Inc 1 A D P Blvd Roseland NJ 07068-1728

LAFEVER, HOWARD NELSON, plant breeder, geneticist, educator; b. Wayne County, Ind., May 13, 1938; s. Samuel L. and Flossie B. (Ellis) L.; m. Kay M. Schutz, Aug. 30, 1958; children: Julie, Jeff. BS, Purdue U., 1959, MS, 1961, PhD, 1963. Instr. Wis. State U., LaCrosse, 1963; assoc. prof. Purdue U., West Lafayette, Ind., 1963; research geneticist USDA-Agrl. Research Service, Starkville, Miss., 1963-65; plant breeder, prof. agronomy Ohio State U., Ohio Agr. Research and Devel. Ctr., Wooster, 1965-91; owner Sunbeam Extract Co., 1991—; cons. Ohio Found. Seeds, Croton, 1967—, Rohm & Haas Corp., Phila., 1975-78, Dow Chem. Co., 1987. Patentee Becker, Cardinal, Dynasty, Excel and Freedom wheats plus 14 other small grain varieties; contbr. numerous articles to profl. jours. Grantee John Deere, 1982-84, Eli Lilly, 1984, 85, Quaker Oats, 1984-91, Arrowhead Mills, Agrecol, 1992—. Fellow Am. Soc. Agronomy (bd. dirs. 1982-84, assoc. editor 1982-85); mem. Assn. Ofcl. Seed Certifying Agys., Ohio Seed Improvement Assn. (dir. 1968-83, grantee 1975-91). Presbyterian. Club: Gnat Boxers (Wooster) (treas. 1983-84). Avocations: woodworking; golf. Home: 500 Danberry Dr Wooster OH 44691-7401

LAFFERTY, BEVERLY LOU BROOKOVER, retired physician, consultant; b. Newark, Ohio, Aug. 15, 1938; d. Lawrence William and Rosie (Rey) Brookover; B.S., Ohio State U., 1959, M.D., 1963; diplomate Am. Bd. Family Practice; children—Marla Michele, William Brookover, Wesley Voris, Latour Rey. Intern Grant Hosp., Columbus, Ohio, 1963-64; practice medicine, West Union, Ohio, 1964-75, Sun City Center, Fla., 1975-79, Brandon, Fla., 1979-95; mem. staff Adams County Hosp., v.p., 1971-72, chief of staff, 1973-75; mem. staff Humana Hosp., Brandon, 1977-95, chmn. dept. family practice, 1984-86, hosp. trustee, 1984-92, chief of staff elect, 1986-88, chief of staff, 1988-90; physician adv. utilization mgmt. dept. South Bay Hosp., Sun City Ctr., Fla., 1995—. Mem. AMA, Fla., Hillsborough County med. assns., Am. Acad. Family Physicians, Fla. Acad. Family Physicians, Alpha Lambda Delta, Alpha Epsilon Iota, Alpha Epsilon Delta (sec. 1958-59). Home: 3913 John Moore Rd Brandon FL 33511-8020

LAFFERTY, JAMES MARTIN, physicist; b. Battle Creek, Mich., Apr. 27, 1916; s. James V. and Ida M. (Martin) L.; m. Eleanor J. Currie, June 27, 1942; children: Martin C., Ronald J., Douglas J., Lawrence E. Student, Western Mich. U., 1934-37; B.S. in Engring. Physics, U. Mich., 1939, M.S. in Physics, 1940, Ph.D. in Elec. Engring, 1946. Physicist Eastman Kodak Research Lab., Rochester, N.Y., 1939; physicist Gen. Electric Research Lab., Schenectady, 1940, 42-81; mgr. power electronics lab. Gen. Electric Research Lab., 1972-81; with Carnegie Instn., Washington, 1941-42; past pres. Internat. Union Vacuum Sci. Technique and Applications, 1980-83; People to People citizen ambassador program group leader for Vacuum Sci. and Tech. delegation to Europe, 1984, China, 1986, Australia, 1988, Soviet Union, 1990. Editor, contbg. author: Scientific Foundations of Vacuum Technique (Dushman), 1962; editor: Vacuum Arcs, Theory and Applications, 1980; asso. editor: Jour. Vacuum Sci. and Tech. 1966-69; Editorial bd.: Internat. Jour. Electronics, 1968-89; contbr. articles to profl. jours. Mem. greater consistory Ref. Ch.; trustee Schenectady Museum, 1967-73, sec., 1971-72, pres., 1972-73. Recipient Devel. award Bur. Naval Ordnance, 1946; Distinguished Alumnus citation U. Mich., 1953; IR-100 award, 1968. Fellow AAAS, IEEE (Lamme medal 1979), Am. Phys. Soc.; mem. Nat. Acad. Engring., Am. Vacuum Soc. (hon. life mem.; dir. 1962-70, sec. 1965-67, pres. 1968-69), U.S. Power Squadrons (comdr. Lake George squadron 1975-76, comdr. Dist. 2 1981-82, nat. rear comdr. 1987-91, treas. Ednl. Fund 1992—), Sigma Xi, Phi Kappa Phi, Iota Sigma, Tau Beta Pi. Patentee in field; inventor lanthanum boride cathode, 1950, hot cathode magnetron ionization gauge, 1961, triggered vacuum gap, 1966. Home: 1202 Hedgewood Ln Niskayuna NY 12309-4605

LAFFERTY, JOYCE G. ZVONAR, retired middle school educator; b. Balt., July 9, 1931; d. George S. and Carolyn M. (Bothe) Greener; children: Barbara Z. Gunter, John G. Zvonar, David A. Zvonar. BS, Towson State, 1963; M. equivalent, Md. Inst. Coll. of Art, 1978. Cert. tchr., Md. Tchr., dept. chmn. Hampstead Hill. Jr. High Annex, Balt.; tchr. Forest Park Sr. High, Balt.; tchr., dept. chmn. Roland Park Mid. Sch., Balt. Mem. Nat. Art Edn. Assn., Internat. Soc. Artists, Balt. Tchrs. Union. Home: 1101 Gilcrest Ct Baltimore MD 21234-5924

LAFFERTY, RICHARD THOMAS, architect; b. Allentown, Pa., Dec. 12, 1932; s. Arthur M. and Emily (May) L.; m. Janece Fiore, Apr. 28, 1962; children: Alicia, Hope. BArch, Syracuse U., 1956. Registered architect, N.Y. Draftsman Sweeney-Burden, Architects, Syracuse, 1954-56, Gordon P. Schopfer, AIA, Syracuse, 1959-63; job capt. Sargent, Webster, Crenshaw & Folley, Syracuse, 1963-75, assoc., chief estimator, 1975-88; project architect V.I.P. Archtl. Assocs., Syracuse, 1988-90, assoc., 1989-90, project architect Schopfer Architects, 1990-93; architect, Richard T. Lafferty, 1993-94; architect, Fuligni-Fragola Architects, 1994—; instr. drafting Onondaga Community Coll., Syracuse, 1968-70, instr. codes, 1972-76, curriculum adviser archtl. tech., 1986—; curriculum adviser archtl. tech. SUNY, Delhi, 1984—; mem. N.Y. State Bd. Architecture, 1990—, chmn., 1995-96; sec. region II NCARB, 1995—. Adv. mem. Onondaga County Plumbing Bd., Syracuse, 1978—; curriculum adviser Nat. Tech. Inst. for Deaf, Rochester, N.Y., 1984—, mem. Uniform Code Syracuse/Watertown Bd. Rev., 1984—. Served to capt. USAF, 1956-59. Recipient, Matthew W. Del Gaudio award, 1983. Mem. AIA (energy com. 1981-85, profl. devel. com. 1981-85), Central N.Y. AIA (treas. 1978-79, pres. 1981, sec. 1989-94, editor newsletter 1978—, chmn. code com. 1983-84, 1989—), N.Y. State Assn. Architects (dir. 1980-84, mem. handicap com. 1983-84, pres. 1987, past pres. 1988, Pres. Medal 1991), N.Y. State Assns. of Professions (pres. 1991). Republican. Roman Catholic. Home and Office: Limeledge and Glover Rds Marcellus NY 13108

LAFFITTE, HECTOR MANUEL, federal judge; b. Ponce, P.R., Apr. 13, 1934; s. Miguel and Gilda (Colomer) L.; m. Nydia M. Rossy, June 13, 1958; children: Yasmin, Hector W., Bernice M., Walter M., Giselle M. BA, Interamerican U., 1955; LLB, U. P.R., 1958; LLM, Georgetown U., 1960. Bar: U.S. Dist. Ct. P.R. 1959, U.S. Ct. Appeals (1st cir.) 1959, Supreme Ct. P.R. 1959, U.S. Mil. Appeals 1960, U.S. Supreme Ct. 1976. Assoc. Hartzell, Fernandez & Novas, 1959-64; pvt. practice law, 1965-66; ptnr. Nachman, Feldstein, Laffitte, & Smith, 1966-69, Laffitte & Dominguez, 1970-83; judge U.S. Dist. Ct. P.R., 1983—. Mem. ABA, Inst. Jud. Adminstrn. Office: US Dist Ct CH-142 Fed Bldg 150 Carlos Chardon Ave Hato Rey San Juan PR 00918*

LA FLARE, MARY J. DICKINSON, librarian; b. N.Y.C., Apr. 12, 1929; d. Lambert Francis and Mary Catherine (Mosher) Dickinson; m. Joseph P. La Flare, 1951 (div. 1969); children: Joseph P., Mary Ellen, Lizanne La Flare Krol, Patricia La Flare Santella. BA, Coll. Mt. St. Vincent, Riverdale, N.Y., 1950; MLS, St. John's U., Queens, N.Y., 1971. Cert. pub. libr., N.Y. Libr., rschr. Info. and Retrieval Ctr. Levittown (N.Y.) Union Free Sch. Dist., 1969-71; grad. asst. dept. L.S. St. John's U., 1969-71; mktg. rsch. libr. Sperry & Hutchinson, N.Y.C., 1971-76, project mgr. mktg. rsch., 1977-82; reference libr. Uniondale (N.Y.) Pub. Libr., 1985-86; reference libr., community libr. Farmingdale (N.Y.) Pub. Libr., 1986—; adj. prof. Nassau C.C., Garden City, N.Y., 1982-92, Hofstra U., Hempstead, N.Y., 1983-85; reading cons. Daleview Nursing Home, Farmingdale, 1993-94. St. Johns U. fellow, 1969-71. Mem. Coll. Mt. St. Vincent Alumnae (mem. capital fund com. 1985), Acad. St. Joseph Alumnae. Republican. Roman Catholic. Home: 142 Jervis Ave Farmingdale NY 11735-2426 Office: Farmingdale Pub Libr 116 Merritts Rd Farmingdale NY 11735-3216

LAFLEY, ALAN FREDERICK, retired banker; b. Stamford, Conn., Aug. 26, 1922; s. Alan George and Clara (Petersen) L.; m. Kathryn Margaret Irwin, Mar. 1, 1946; children: Alan George, Nora Kathryn, Jo Anne, Mary Patricia. B.B.A., Clarkson U., Potsdam, N.Y., 1946; M.B.A., U. Mich., 1948. Asst. prof. Sch. of Bus.; placement dir. Clarkson U., 1948-50, Sch. Bus., Ind. U., Bloomington, 1950-51; with Gen. Electric Co., 1951-73; mgr. exec. personnel and compensation Gen. Electric Co., N.Y.C., 1968-73; v.p. personnel Clark Equipment Co., Buchanan, Mich., 1973-75; exec. v.p. human resources Chase Manhattan Bank, N.Y.C., 1975-84; mng. dir. Korn Ferry Internat., 1984-86; exec. in residence, vis. prof. U. Mich. Sch. Bus., Ann Arbor, 1984-85; cons., advisor, lectr,. human resources mgr. Mem. adv. coun. Sch. Bus., Clarkson U. Served to 1st lt. U.S. Army and USAAF, 1942-46. Fellow Human Resources Policy Inst., Boston U.

LA FOLLETTE, DOUGLAS J., secretary of state; b. Des Moines, June 6, 1940; s. Joseph Henry and Frances (Van der Wilt) LaF. B.S., Marietta Coll., 1963; M.S., Stanford U., 1964; Ph.D., Columbia U., 1967. Asst. prof. chemistry and ecology U. Wis.-Parkside, 1969-72; mem. Wis. Senate, 1973-75; sec. state State of Wis., Madison, 1975-79, 83—. Author: Wisconsin's Survival Handbook, 1971, The Survival Handbook, 1991. Mem. Council Econ. Priorities; mem. Lake Michigan Fed., Wis. Environ. Decade, 1971, S.E. Wis. Coalition for Clean Air, Dem. candidate for U.S. Congress, 1970, for Wis. lt. gov., 1978, for U.S. Senate, 1988. Recipient Environ. Quality EPA, 1976. Mem. Am. Fedn. Tchrs., Fedn. Am. Scientists, Phi Beta Kappa. Office: Office Sec State of Wis PO Box 7848 Madison WI 53707-7848

LAFONT, LYDIA ANN, nurse manager; b. New Orleans, Mar. 13, 1955; d. Darwin Michael and Geraldine Marie (Terrebonne) L. Diploma, Charity Hosp. Sch. Nursing, 1977. RN, La. Staff nurse Charity Hosp., New Orleans, 1977-81, 97th Gen. Hosp., Frankfurt, Germany, 1981-85, Charity Hosp., New Orleans, 1985-87; staff nurse South La. Med. Ctr., Houma, 1987-90, RN mgr., 1990—. Sponsor Christian Children's Fund, Richmond, Va., 1990—. Mem. Charity Hosp. Sch. Nursing Alumni Assn. Republican. Roman Catholic. Avocations: traveling, reading, fishing, needle work.

LAFONTAINE, PAT, professional hockey player; b. St. Louis, Feb. 22, 1965. With U.S. Olympic Hockey Team, 1984, N.Y. Islanders, 1983-91, Buffalo Sabres, 1991—; player All-Star game, 1988-91, 93. Recipient Dodge Performer Yr. award, 1989-90, Michel Briere award, 1982-83, Jean Beliveau trophy, 1982-83, Frank J. Selke trophy, 1982-83, Des Instructeurs trophy, 1982-83, Guy LaFleur trophy, 1982-83; named to Sporting News All-Star Team, 1989-90, Player of the Year Canadian Hockey League, 1982-83. Office: Buffalo Sabres Meml Auditorium 140 Main St Buffalo NY 14202-4110*

LA FONTAINE, RAYMOND M., insurance company executive; b. 1926. Mem. Mass. Legislature, Boston, 1963-81; with Mass. Motor Vehicle Reinsurance Facility, Boston, 1974-84; pres. Commonwealth Auto Reinsurance, Boston, 1984—; chmn. house com. on ins. Mass. Legislature, Boston, 1963-81. Office: Commonwealth Auto Reinsurance 100 Summer St Boston MA 02110-2104*

LAFONTANT-MANKARIOUS, JEWEL (MRS. NAGUIB S. MANKARIOUS), diplomat, lawyer; b. Chgo., Apr. 28, 1922; d. Cornelius Francis Stradford and Aida Arabella Carter; m. John Rogers, 1946 (dissolved 1961); 1 child, John W. Rogers Jr.; m. H. Ernest Lafontant, 1961 (dec. 1976); m. Naguib Soby Mankarious, Dec. 17, 1989. AB in Polit. Sci., Oberlin Coll., 1943; JD, U. Chgo., 1946; LLD (hon.), Cedar Crest Coll., 1973; D Humanitarian Svc. (hon.), Providence Coll., 1973; LLD (hon.), Ea. Mich. U., 1973; LHD (hon.), Howard U., 1974; LLD (hon.), Heidelberg Coll., 1975, Lake Forest Coll., 1977, Marymount Manhattan Coll., 1978, Oberlin Coll., 1979; LHD (hon.), Governor's State U., 1980, LLD (hon.), 1980; citation for pub. svc., U. Chgo., 1980; LLD (hon.), Chgo. Med. Sch., 1982, Loyola U. of Chgo., 1982, Roosevelt U., 1990. Bar: Ill. 1947. Asst. U.S. atty., 1955-58; sr. ptnr. Lafontant, et al., Chgo., 1961-83, Vedder, Price, Kaufman & Kammholz, Chgo., 1983-89; dep. solicitor gen. U.S. Dept. State, Washington, 1972-75, amb.-at-large, U.S. coord. for refugee affairs, 1989-93; ptnr. Holleb & Coff, Chgo., 1993—; bd. dirs. Mobil Corp., Continental Bank, Foote, Cone & Belding, Equitable Life Assurance Soc. U.S., Trans World Corp., Revlon, Inc., Ariel-Capital Mgmt., Harte-Hanks Communications, Inc., Pantry Pride, Inc., Revlon Group, Howard U.; past dir. Jewel Cos., Inc., TWA, Hanes Corp.; past mem. U.S. Adv. Commn. Internat. Edn. and Cultural Affairs, Nat. Coun. Minority Bus. Enterprises, Nat. Coun. on Ednl. Rsch.; past chmn. adv. bd. Civil Rights Commn.; mem. Pres.'s Pvt. Sector Survey Cost Control; pres. Exec. Exchange; past U.S. rep. to UN. Bd. editors: Am. Bar Assn. Jour. Former trustee Lake Forest (Ill.) Coll., Oberlin Coll., Howard U., Tuskegee Inst.; bd. govs. Ronald Reagan Presdl. Found.; mem. Martin Luther King, Jr., Fed. Holiday Commn.; dir. Project Hope; chmn. Ill. adv. com. U.S. Civil Rights Commn.; mem. bd. overseers Hoover Instn.; mem. nat. adv. bd. Salvation Army. Recipient Howard B. Shepard award Protestant Found., Little Flowers Sem. Soc., Svc. award U.S. Dept. Justice, Humanitarian award Opportunities Industrialization Ctrs. of Am., Inc., Candace award Nat. Coalition of Black Women, Adlai A. Stevenson II award for svc. and support UN, Par Excellence Svc. award People United to Save Humanity, Disting. Svc. award Interracial Coun. for Bus. Opportunity, 1988, Woman of Distinction award Nat. Conf. for Coll. Women Student Leaders and Women of Achievement, 1988, Abraham Lincoln Marovitz award B'nai Brith, 1989, Disting. Svc. to Law and Soc. award Ill. Bar Found., 1989, cert. of recognition Vietnamese Community Leaders in U.S., 1990, Wiley A. Branton Issues Symposium award 1991, United Charities Legal Aid Soc. award, 1991, Spl. Recognition award Assyrian Am. Nat. Found., 1992, Chgo. Chpt. of Links, Inc. award, 1992, CARE Humanitarian award, 1994, Luminary award Girl Scouts U.S., 1995, Raoul Wallenberg award Am. Com. for Shaare Zedek Med. Ctr., Jerusalem, 1995, others; named Hon. Citizen of Abilene, Tex., 1991; named one of One Hundred Most Influential Black Ams., Ebony Mag., 1973-74. Fellow Internat. Acad. Trial Lawyers; mem. NAACP (sec. Chgo. br.), ACLU (bd. dirs.), Chgo. Bar Assn. (bd. govs., Earl B. Dickerson award 1995), Comml. Club, Econs. Club (past bd. dirs.), Rotary (hon.).

LA FORCE, JAMES CLAYBURN, JR., economist, educator; b. San Diego, Dec. 28, 1928; s. James Clayburn and Beatrice Maureen (Boyd) La F.; m. Barbara Lea Latham, Sept. 23, 1952; children: Jessica, Allison, Joseph. BA, San Diego State Coll., 1951; MA, UCLA, 1958, PhD, 1962. Asst. prof. econs. UCLA, 1962-66, assoc. prof., 1967-70, prof., 1971-93, prof. emeritus, 1993—, chmn. dept. econs., 1969-78, dean Anderson Sch. Mgmt., 1978-93; acting dean Hong Kong U. Sci. & Tech., 1991-93; bd. dirs. Rockwell Internat., Eli Lilly & Co., Jacobs Engring. Group Inc., The Timken Co., The Black Rock Funds, Imperial Credit Industries, Inc., Payden & Rygel Investment Trust, Providence Investment Coun. Mut. Funds; chmn. adv. com. Calif. Workmen's Compensation. Author: The Development of the Spanish Textile Industry 1750-1800, 1965, (with Warren C. Scoville) The Economic Development of Western Europe, vols. 1-5, 1969-70. Bd. dirs. Nat. Bur. Econ. Rsch., 1975-88, Found. Francisco Marroquin, Lynde and Harry Bradley Found., Pacific Legal Found., 1981-86; trustee Found. for Rsch. in Econs. and Edn., 1970—, chmn., 1977—; mem. bd. overseers Hoover Inst. on War, Revolution and Peace, 1979-85, 86-93; mem. nat. coun. on humanities NEH, 1981-88; chmn. Pres.'s Task Force on Food Assistance, 1983-84. Social Sci. Research Council research tng. fellow, 1958-60; Fulbright sr. research grantee, 1965-66; Am. Philos. Soc. grantee, 1965-66. Mem. Econ. History Assn., Mont Pelerin Soc., Phi Beta Kappa. Office: UCLA Anderson Grad Sch Mgmt 405 Hilgard Ave Los Angeles CA 90095-1481

LAFORCE, WILLIAM LEONARD, JR., photojournalist; b. Albemarle County, Va., Aug. 24, 1940; s. William Leonard and Florence Alberta (Sandridge) LaF.; m. Dorothy Lee Kesler, June 8, 1963 (div. 1987); children: William Perry, Glenn Edward. Student, U. Va., 1958-60; B.S., Johns Hopkins U., 1967, M.Liberal Arts, 1972. Dir. photography Balt. Sun papers, 1962-74; chief photographer, graphics editor and editl. page columnist N.J. edit. N.Y. Daily News, N.Y.C., 1974-79, photojournalist N.Y. staff, 1979-94; with N.Y. Times, AP; scholastic journalism faculty Columbia U., 1971-75; advisor Montclair U. Student Newspaper, 1980-84; lectr. to various news and photography orgns. Judge Miss Delmarva Pageant, 1969-74; planning com. Balt. City Fair, 1971; pres. Rumsey Island Residents Assn., Joppa, Md., 1969-72, Rumsey House Restoration Found., 1968-70, Mountain Lakes (N.J.) Fire Dept., 1977-79; Democratic committeeman, Mountain Lakes, 1976-78; chmn. Wildwood Sch. Bd., 1976-77; mgr. Mountain Lakes Little League, 1981, 85-86; bd. dirs. Joppatowne Civic Assn., 1969-71, vice chmn. citizens nominating com., 1977-81; mem. Pedestrian Safety Com., 1976-80; bd. dirs. Mountain Lakes Hist. Soc., 1987—, Am. Police Hall of Fame, 1987—; Morris County disability commn., 1995—. Recipient Best Fire Photo in U.S. award Internat. Assn. Firefighters, 1967, Disting. Community Service award Jaycees, 1971, 1st Pl. Annapolis Fine Arts Festival, 1971, award for disting. community service Rumsey Island Residents Assn., 1972; Best Photo of Preakness Race award City of Balt., 1972, Page One award for best news photo in N.Y.C. Newspaper Guild, 1983, One Man Exhibition, Overseas Press Club, 1983; Best News Photo award N.Y. Press Club, 1984; 1st place Spot News award N.J. Press Assn., 1985, 91, Best PIX Story award N.Y.C. Police, 1986, 1st place Gen. News award N.J. Press Assn., 1991, nominated for Pulitzer award, 1984, 91. Mem. Nat. Press Photographers Assn. (dir. Mid-Atlantic region 1977-81, Pres.'s citation 1980, Bootstrap Leadership award 1981), Photographic Adminstrs. N.Y. (bd. dirs. 1986—, v.p. 1988-95), N.Y. Press Photographers Club, N.J. Press Photographers, N.Y. Press Club. Home and Office: PO Box 31 Mountain Lakes NJ 07046-0031

LAFOREST, LANA JEAN, lawyer, real estate broker; b. Providence, Apr. 14, 1952; d. Harold Joseph Ecker and Nettie Jean (Starks) Page; children: Timothy Charles, Tisha DeAnne. AA in Humanities and Social Scis., Niagara County C. C., 1989; BA in English Lit. magna cum laude, Buffalo State Coll., 1990, MA in English Lit., 1992; JD, SUNY Buffalo Sch. Law, 1994; doctoral student, SUNY, Buffalo, 1994—. Lic. real estate broker. Property mgr. Personal Income Property Mgmt., Lockport, 1976—; sales assoc. John F. Collins Realty, Lockport, 1979-83, Town Crier Clark Nodine Realty, Lockport, 1983-90, McKnight, Hogan & Noonan, Lockport, 1990-91, H. Potter Realty, Lockport, 1991-93; advocate Family Court Resource Project Haven House, 1994—; advocate domestic violence clinic U. Buffalo Law Sch., 1994; pvt. practice East Amherst, N.Y., 1994—; owner, operator Custom Crafts by Lana, Lockport, 1975-79; adv. domestic violence clinic U. Buffalo Law Sch., 1994. Editor: (lit. mag.) Writer's Revue, 1989; corr. Union-Sun and Jour., summer 1989. Girl scouts coord. Niagara County Coun. Girl Scouts, Sanborn, N.Y., 1978-84; clover clan 4-H club leader Niagara County Coop. Extension, Lockport, 1984-87; with Project Dandelion, Neighborhood Legal Svcs., 1994—. Mem. ABA, MLA, N.Y. State Bar Assn., Niagara Linguistics Soc., Nat. Assn. Realtors, Univ. Buffalo Law Sch. Alumni Assn., Buffalo State Coll. Alumni Assn., Niagara County Community Coll. Alumni Assn., U. Buffalo Assn. Women Law Students, Erie County Bar Assn., Women's Bar Assn. Erie County, Phi Alpha Delt. Avocations: writing, sewing, gourmet cooking, painting. Office: PO Box 406 East Amherst NY 14051

LA FOSSE, ROBERT, ballet dancer, choreographer; b. Beaumont, Tex.. Student, Marsha Woody Acad. of Dance; Studied with David Howard, Harkness House, N.Y.C., 1977. With Am. Ballet Theatre, N.Y.C., 1977-86, mem. corps de ballet, 1977-81, soloist, 1981-83, prin., 1983-86; prin. N.Y.C. Ballet, 1986—. Created roles at Am. Ballet Theatre in Cinderella, Lynne Taylor-Corbett's Great Galloping Gottschalk, John McFall's Follow the Feet, Kenneth MacMillan's The Wild Boy and Twyla Tharp's, Bach Partita; other Am. Ballet repertoire includes: La Bayadere, Billy the Kid, Clair de Lune, Don Quixote, Fancy Free, Giselle, Jardin Aux Lilas, Swan Lake Act II, The Leaves are Fading, Prodigal Son, Les Rendezvous, Symphonie Concertante, Rodeo, Other Dances, N.Y. Export: Op. Jazz, Romeo & Juliet, Dim Luster, Nutcracker, La Sonnambula & Coppelia; created roles at N.Y. City Ballet include Quiet City, Piccalo Balleto, West Side Story Suite, A Fool for You, Tea Rose, Newcomers; repertoire at N.Y. City Ballet includes Slaughter on 10th Ave., Opus 19, The Dreamer, Raymonda Variations, Who Cares?, Davidsbundlertanze, Ballo del Regina, La Baiser de la Fee, Nutcracker, Prodigal Son, Dances at a Gathering, Scotch Symphony, Agon, Vienna Waltzes, Four Seasons, La Source, Union Jack, Dances Concertant, Coppelia, Valse Triste, Western Symphony, Goldberg Variations in G Major, Donizetti Variations, Afternoon of a Faun; dancer: (Broadway) leading roles in Dancin', 1979, Jerome Robbins, 1989; Dancing Hands, Live from Off Center, 1988; (Off Broadway) Splendora; choreographer Gretry pas de deux, Rappaccini's Daughter, 1985, (for Sch. Am. Ballet) Yesterdays, 1987, Woodland Sketches, N.Y.C. Ballet, 1988, Haydn Trumpet Concerto, 1989, Puss in Boots, 1990, Waltz Trilogy, 1991, I Have My Own Room, 1992, Four for 4, 1992, Danses de Cour, 1994; TV appearances: Ray Charles and N.Y.C. Ballet, PBS, 1989; also Am. Ballet Theatre at the Met (Triad), Am. Ballet Theatre in San Francisco (Jardin Aux Lilas, Great Galloping Gottschalk), Baryishnikov Dances Tharp (Push comes to Shore), Dance in America, Western Symphony, 1990, (movie) Nutcracker, 1993; author: Nothing to Hide: A Dancer's Life. Office: NYC Ballet NY State Theatre Lincoln Ctr Plz New York NY 10023

LAFRAMBOISE, JOAN CAROL, middle school educator; b. Bklyn., June 23, 1934; d. Anthony Peter and Nellie Eva (Zaleski) Ruggles; m. Albert George Laframboise, Aug. 5, 1961; children: Laura J., Brian A. BS in Edn., Springfield (Mass.) Coll., 1956. Cert. tchr. social sci., and mid. sch.; cert. tchr. support specialist. Tchr. Meml. Jr. H.S., Wilbraham, Mass., 1956-61,

Midland Park (N.J.) Jr./Sr. H.S., 1961-63, Luke Garrett Middle Sch., Austell, Ga., 1983-93; tchr. lang. arts Pine Mountain Middle Sch., Kennesaw, Ga., 1993—. Coun. pres. Knights of Lithuania, Westfield, Mass., 1973-75, Holyoke, Mass., 1975-76, New Eng. dist. pres., 1976-77; mem. Wistariahurst Mus. Assocs., Holyoke, 1975-77. Jr. League mini-grantee, 1991. Mem. ASCD, NEA, Ga. Assn. Educators, Cobb County Assn. Educators, Nat. Coun. Tchrs. English, Nat. Coun. Social Studies. Home: 2891 Dara Dr Marietta GA 30066-4009

LAFRAMBOISE, PATRICK J., trade association administrator; b. Yakima, Wash., June 19, 1951; s. Leon and Mary (Hardman) LaF. BA, Wash. State U., 1973. Dir. ops. Clapp & Poliak, Inc., N.Y.C., 1977-83; v.p. Graphic Arts Show Co., Reston, Va., 1983-94; pres., CEO Internat. Woodworking Fair, Norcross, Ga., 1994—. Mem. Internat. Assn. Exhbn. Mgrs., Major Am. Trade Show ORganizers (pres. 1990-91). Office: Internat Woodworking Fair 6525 Th Corners Pky Ste 115 Norcross GA 30092

LAFREDO, STEPHEN CHRISTOPHER, consultant; b. Norristown, Pa., Aug. 21, 1962; s. Frank Joseph and Yuriko (Mizuo) L. BS in Microbiology, Pa. State U., 1984; AAS magna cum laude, Montgomery County C.C., 1992, AS magna cum laude, 1992. Rsch. technician Thomas Jefferson Sch. Medicine, Phila., 1984-86; rsch. assoc. Temple Sch. Medicine, Phila., 1986-88, R.W. Johnson Pharm. Rsch. Inst., Raritan, N.J., 1988-91; clin. rsch. assoc. Rhone-Poulenc Rorer Ctrl. Rsch., Collegeville, Pa., 1991-93; advanced programmer/analyst Shared Med Systems, Malvern, Pa., 1993-95; sr. cons. KPMG Peat Marwick LLP, Radnor, Pa., 1995-96; staff cons. Computer Scis. Corp., Consulting & Syss. Integration, Berwyn, Pa., 1996—. Contbr. articles to profl. jours. Sgt. U.S. Army Nat. Guard, 1983-89. Mem. Assn. for Computing Machinery, Fraternal Order of Police (assoc.). Avocations: bicycling, reading, stunt-kite flying, English steel tip darts. Home: 9 Traverse Dr Norristown PA 19401-2533

LAFROSCIA, ERNEST JOHN, property management executive; b. Bklyn., Sept. 19, 1930; s. Peter and Anna (Ferraiuolo) LaF.; m. Josephine Curella, Aug. 13, 1955; children: Donna Marie, Diane Elizabeth. BSEE, CCNY, 1957. Group leader AIL divsn. Eaton Corp., Deer Park, N.Y., 1957-69; dir. data sys. Gen. Instruments Corp., Hicksville, N.Y., 1969-73; v.p. devel. Nationwide Devel. Inc., Virginia Beach, Va., 1973-74; founder, CEO LFC Nationwide Inc., Central Islip, N.Y., 1974—. Sgt. USAF, 1948-52. Named Entrepreneur of the Yr., Ernst and Young, 1991. Mem. Mortgage Bankers Assn. Am., Nat. Assn. Mortgage Field Svcs. Inc. (bd. govs. 1988—), Am. Alliance Loan Mgmt. (bd. dirs. 1992—, v.p. 1994, pres. 1995). Avocations: golf, gardening, reading. Office: LFC Nationwide Inc Loudoun Gateway 45240 Business Ct Sterling VA 20166-6703

LAFVING, BRIAN DOUGLAS, lawyer; b. Michigan City, Ind., Mar. 31, 1953; s. Allen Herschel and Barbara Joan (Rachow) L.; m. Diane Leigh Pierce, Aug. 16, 1975; children: Bridgette, Brandon, Brittany. BA, BFA, So. Meth. U., 1974, JD, 1977. Bar: Tex. 1977, U.S. Ct. Dist. (no. dist.) Tex., 1977. Assoc. Stalcup, Johnson, Meyers & Miller, Dallas, 1977-79, Baker, Glast, Riddle, Tuttle & Elliott, Dallas, 1979-80; ptnr. Glast & Miller, Dallas, 1980-83, Jones, Day, Reavis & Pogue, Dallas, 1983—. Mem. ABA, Tex. Bar Assn. Republican. Methodist. Office: Jones Day Reavis & Pogue 2300 Trammell Crow Ctr 2001 Ross Ave Dallas TX 75201-2911

LAGALLY, MAX GUNTER, physics educator; b. Darmstadt, Germany, May 23, 1942; came to U.S., 1953, naturalized, 1960; s. Paul and Herta (Rudow) L.; m. Shelley Meserow, Feb. 15, 1969; children—Eric, Douglas, Karsten. BS in Physics, Pa. State U., 1963; MS in Physics, U. Wis.-Madison, 1965, PhD in Physics, 1968. Registered profl. engr., Wis. Instr. physics U. Wis., Madison, 1970-71, asst. prof. materials sci., 1971-74, assoc. prof., 1974-77, prof. materials sci. and physics, 1977—, dir. thin-film deposition and applications ctr., 1982-93, John Bascom Prof. materials sci., 1986—, E.W. Mueller Prof. materials sci. and physics, 1993—; Gordon Godfrey vis. prof. physics, U. New South Wales, Sydney, Australia, 1987; cons. in thin films, 1977—; vis. scientist Sandia Nat. Lab., Albuquerque, 1975. Editor: Kinetics of Ordering and Growth at Surfaces, 1990, (with others) Methods of Experimental Physics, 1985, Evolution of Surface and Thin-Film Microstructure, 1993; mem. editorial bd., also editor spl. issue Jour. Vacuum Sci. and Tech., 1978-81; rpin. editor Jour. Materials Rsch., 1990-93; mem. editorial bd. Surface Sci., 1994—; contbr. articles to profl. jours.; patentee in field. Max Planck Gesellschaft fellow, 1968, Alfred P. Sloan Found. fellow, 1972, H.I. romnes fellow, 1976, Humboldt Sr. Rsch. fellow, 1992; grantee fed. agys. and industry. Fellow Am. Phys. Soc. (D. Adler award 1994, Davisson-Germer prize 1995), Australian Inst. Physics, Am. Vacuum Soc. (program and exec. coms. 1974-79, M.W. Welch prize 1991, trustee 1995-97); mem. AAAS, Am. Soc. Metals Internat., Am. Chem. Soc. (colloid and surface chemistry divsn.), Materials Rsch. Soc. (medal 1994). Home: 5110 Juneau Rd Madison WI 53705-4744 Office: U Wis Materials Sci & Engring 1509 University Ave Madison WI 53706-1538

LAGARDE, JACQUES YVES, metal products company executive; b. Rennes, Bretagne, France, May 2, 1938; m. Marie-Christine Cottard; children: Marion, Charlotte, Cecile, Antoine, Julie. MBA, Ecole des Hautes Etudes Commerciales, Paris, 1960; advanced mgmt. program, Harvard Bus. Sch., 1975. Advt. promotion mgr. Time Life Internat., London, N.Y.C., 1960-61; officer French Marine, Algeria, 1961-63; diverse positions Gillette France, Annecy, 1963-70; product line mgr. Braun AG, Kronberg, Germany, 1970-72; dean. Grad. Sch. Bus., Lyon, France, 1972-81; pres. Gillette France, Annecy, 1981-85, Oral-B Labs. Inc., San Francisco, 1985-89; v.p. Gillette Co., Boston, 1990-93, 1990—; chmn. bd. Mgmt. of Braun A.G., Germany; exec. v.p. Diversified Group/The Gillette Co., Boston, 1993—. Recipient Chevalier award Ordre Nat. du Merite. Office: The Gillette Co Prudential Twr Bldg Boston MA 02199

LAGARIAS, JOHN SAMUEL, engineering executive; b. Rochester, N.Y., July 4, 1921; s. Soterios Nicholas and Aspacia (Basil) L.; m. Virginia Jane Clark, June 16, 1947; children: Jeffrey, Peter, Clark. BS in Physics, Rensselaer Poly. Inst., 1948; postgrad., Oak Ridge Sch. Reactor Tech., 1955-56. Registered profl. engr., Md. Rsch. engr. Westinghouse Electric Rsch. Labs., Pitts., 1948-51; mgr. metal products rsch. Koppers Co., Inc., Pitts., 1951-63; mgr. R&D Am. Instrument Co., Silver Spring, Md., 1963-64; pres. Resources Rsch., Inc., Reston, Va., 1964-71; dir. environ. quality Kaiser Engrs., Oakland, Calif., 1971-84; pres. Lagarias Assocs., Moraga, 1984—; lectr. civil engring. dept. U. Md., 1970-71; mem. tech. adv. com. Washington Coun. Govts., 1968-70, Commonwealth of Va., 1969-71; conf. chmn. 2d Internat. Clean Air Congress, Washington, 1970; bd. mem. Calif. Air Resources Bd., 1985—. Contbr. articles to profl. jours.; patentee electrostatic precipitators, analytical instruments and indsl. gas cleaning equipment. Planning commr. City of Moraga, Calif., 1975-82; mem. Calif. Air Resources Bd., 1986—. With AUS, 1943-46. Fellow Air Pollution Control Assn. (hon., pres. 1968-69), Internat. Soc. Electrostatic Precipitation (bd. dirs. 1984, conf. chmn. 1st internatl conf.); mem. IEEE (sr., life), Am. Acad. Environ. Engrs. (diplomate). Home: 5954 Autumnwood Dr #5C Walnut Creek CA 94595 Office: 2020 L St Sacramento CA 95814-4219

LAGASSÉ, PIERRE PHILIPPE, exercise science educator; b. Dec. 15, 1944; s. Jacques Lagassé; m. Daniele Roberge, May. 27, 1967 (div. 1982); children: Jean-Francois, Genevieve; m. Lucille Lessard, Feb. 19, 1983; 1 child, Marie-Pier. BA, U. Sherbrooke, Que., Can., 1965; B Phys. Edn., U. Ottawa, Ont., Can., 1967; MA, Pa. State U., 1970; PhD, U. Mass., 1974. Asst. prof. exercise sci. U. Sherbrooke, 1973-75; assoc. prof. U. Laval, St. Foy, Que., 1975-83, prof., 1983—, dir. Labsap, 1977-81, 87-90, dir. dept. exercise sci., 1990—; cons. Thomson-Rogers, Toronto, Ont., 1979-81, Borden and Elliot, Toronto, 1983-84, Que. Police Commn., 1985—, Que. Min. Health, 1993—. Contbr. articles to sci. jours. Fellow Am. Coll. Sports Medicine; mem. Can. Soc. Biomechanics (sec./treas. 1975-77, pres. 1977-78). Office: U Laval, 2160 PEPS, Sainte Foy, PQ Canada G1K 7P4

LAGER, ROBERT JOHN, state agency administrator; b. Fairhope, Ala., Aug. 19, 1934; s. Edward Glen and Dorothy (Niemeyer) L. AB, Syracuse U., 1957; PhD, Georgetown U., 1970. Asst. prof. Russian Georgetown U., Washington, 1965-71, chmn. dept. Russian, 1971-78; exec. asst. Gov. Fob James, Montgomery, Ala., 1978-80; dir. Ctr. for Internat. Trade, Mobile, Ala., 1980—; exec. dir. Ala. Fgn. Trade Commn., Mobile, 1983—; dir. Coun. on Internat. Edn. Exchange, N.Y.C., 1969-78; Presdl. appointment to Ala. Export Coun.; cons. U.S. Dept. State, Voice of Am., Washington, 1969-78, Am. Coun. on Edn., Washington, 1975-78; adj. assoc. prof. Russian and Latin, U. South Ala., 1983—. Contbr. articles on Russian lang. and lit. to profl. jours. Trustee Ala. Inst. for Deaf and Blind, Talladega, 1979-86; mem. So. Growth Policies Bd.; bd. dirs. Mobile United. Served with USAF, 1956-60. Fellow Internat. Bus. Fellows; mem. Ala. World Trade Assn. (exec. dir. 1984-91), So. Ctr. for Internat. Studies (trustee 1986-95), Mobile Area C. of C. (cons. leadership program 1985, chmn. task force), Japan-U.S. Soc. Ala. (exec. com. 1989-93), Propeller Club, Phi Beta Kappa. Democrat. Roman Catholic. Avocations: sailing, tennis, reading, antique cars. Office: Ala Fgn Trade Commn 250 N Water St Ste 131 Mobile AL 36602-4021

LAGIN, NEIL, property management executive, landscape designer; b. Bronx, N.Y., Jan. 10, 1942; s. Barney and Helen (Goldberg) L.; m. Pamela C. Lagin; children: Laurence Connor, Jenny Janette. Buyer Alexanders, N.Y.C., 1961-69; sales mgr. Halldon, Ltd., N.Y.C., 1969-79; mgr., ptnr. in concession Michele Craig, Westbury, N.Y., 1979-85; ptnr. ALW Trading, "9", N.Y.C., 1985-87; owner, operator Accent Foliage, Delray Beach, Fla., 1987-89; pres. Neil Lagin Property Mgmt., Neil's Landscape Svc., Boca Raton, Fla., 1988—. Author poetry; exhibitor photography shows, Ward Nasse Gallery-Salon, 1975-79, Timothy Blackburn Gallery, 1978, Washington Art Show and others. Notary pub., Fla., 1990; mem. nursery adv. bd. Habilitation Ctr. for the Handicapped, Boca Raton, 1991—; mem. overall adv. com. Palm Beach County Ext., 1993—, sec., chair program rev. com.; bd. dirs. Greater Palm Beach Area Alzheimers Assn., 1993; mem. Environ. Resource Landscape Team; mem. Boca Raton Postal Customer Adv. Coun., 1994-96; memb. bd. dirs. Pheasant Walk Homeowners Assoc., 1996—. Named Fla. Master Gardener, Inst. Food and Agrl. Scis., U. Fla., 1989, Best Landscaper in Boca Raton, South Fla. Newspaper Network, 1991, Best Local Vol. in Boca Raton, 1994, Outstanding MAster Gardener, State of Fla., 1995. Mem. Internat. Palm Soc. (Palm Beach chpt.), Rare Fruit Coun. Internat. (Palm Beach chpt.), Boca Raton C. of C. (grad. leadership program 1991), Boca Raton Postal Customer Adv. Coun. Home and Office: 17730 Maplewood Dr Boca Raton FL 33487-2171

LAGNADO, LUCETTE, executive editor, journalist, author; b. Cairo, Egypt, Sept. 19, 1957; d. Leon Ezra and Edith (Matalon) L.; m. Douglas Michael Feiden, Dec. 31, 1995. BA, Vassar Coll., Poughkeepsie, N.Y., 1977. Investigative reporter Jack Anderson's Column, Washington, 1980-87, Th N.Y. Post, 1987-93, The Village Voice, N.Y.C., 1990-93; exec. editor The Forward, N.Y.C., 1993—. Office: The Forward 45 E 33d St New York NY 10016

LAGO, MARY MCCLELLAND, English language educator, author; b. Pitts., Nov. 4, 1919; d. Clark Russell and Olive Arabella (Malone) McClelland; m. Gladwyn Vaile Lago, Mar. 4, 1944; children: Jane Hazel, Donald Russell. BA, Bucknell U., 1940; MA, U. Mo., 1965, PhD, 1969; DLitt (hon.), Bucknell U., 1981. Editorial asst. Friendship Press, N.Y.C., 1941-43, Congl. Ch. Nat. Hdqrs., N.Y.C., 1944-47; teaching asst. U. Mo., Columbia, 1964-70, lectr. English, 1971-77, assoc. prof., 1977-79, prof. English, 1979-88, Catherine Paine Middlebush prof. of English, 1988-89, prof. emeritus, 1990—; mem. dean's adv. com. Bucknell U., Lewisburg, Pa., 1979-81; hon. vis. prof. U. Manchester, 1985-86; vis. fellow St. Edmund's House, Cambridge U., 1982-83, vis. Bye-Fellow Selwyn Coll., 1991-92. Editor: Imperfect Encounter, 1972, (with K. Beckson) Max and Will, 1975, Rothenstein, Men and Memories, 1978, Burne-Jones Talking, 1980, Forster Number, Twentieth Century Literature, 1985, (with P.N. Furbank) Selected Letters of E.M. Forster, 2 vols., 1984, 85, (with Ronald Warwick) Perspectives in Time, 1989; author: Rabindranath Tagore, 1976, E.M. Forster: A Literary Life, 1996, Christiana Herringham and the Edwardian Art Scene, 1996; editl. bd. Twentieth Century Lit., 1979—; translator (with Supriya Bari) The Broken Nest (Tagore), 1971; translator (with Krishna Dutta) Tagore Selected Stories, 1991; contbr. articles and revs. to mags. Convener community adv. bd. NPR/Sta. KBIA-FM, U. Mo., Columbia, 1979-88. Recipient Disting. Faculty award, Arts and Sci. Disting. Alumna award; rsch. grantee Am. Philos. Soc., 1966, 67, 72, NEH, 1980-83, Am. Coun. Learned Socs.; recipient summer rsch. stipend NEH, 1976. Mem. MLA, Soc. Authors (London), Univ. Women's Club (London), Phi Beta Kappa. Home: 13 Springer Dr Columbia MO 65201-5424 Office: U Mo Dept English 107 Tate Hall Columbia MO 65211

LAGORIA, GEORGIANNA MARIE, curator, writer, editor, visual art consultant; b. Oakland, Calif., Nov. 3, 1953; d. Charles Wilson and Margaret Claire (Vella) L.; m. David Joseph de la Torre, May 15, 1982; 1 child, Mateo Joseph. BA in Philosophy, Santa Clara U., 1975; MA in Museology, U. San Francisco, 1978. Exhbn. coordinator Allrich Gallery, San Francisco, 1977-78; asst. registrar Fine Arts Mus., San Francisco, 1978-79; gallery coordinator de Saisset Mus., Santa Clara, Calif., 1979-80, asst. dir., 1980-83, dir., 1983-86; dir. Palo Alto (Calif.) Cultural Ctr., 1986-91; ind. writer, editor and cons. mus. and visual arts orgns., Hawaii, 1991-95; dir. The Contemporary Mus., Honolulu, 1995—; V.p. Non-Profit Gallery Assn., San Francisco, 1980-82; bd. dirs. Fiberworks, Berkeley, Calif., 1981-85; field reviewer Inst. Mus. Services, Washington, 1985-87; adv. bd. Hearst Art Gallery, Moraga, Calif., 1986-89, Womens Caucus for Art, San Francisco, 1987—; mem. adv. bd. Weigand Art Gallery, Notre Dame Coll., Belmont, Calif. Curator exhbns. The Candy Store Gallery, 1980, Fiber '81, 1981; curator, author exhbn. catalogue Contemporary Hand Colored Photographs, 1981, Northern Calif. Art of the Sixties, 1982, The Artist and the Machine: 1910-1940, 1986; author catalogue, guide Persis Collection of Contemporary Art at Honolulu Advertiser, 1993; co-author: The Little Hawaiian Cookbook, 1994; coord. exhbn. selections Laila and Thurston Twigg-Smith Collection and Toshiko Takaezu ceramics for Hui No'eau Visual Arts Ctr., Maui, 1993; editor Nuhou (newsletter Hawaii State Mus. Assn.), 1991—; spl. exhbn. coord. Honolulu Acad. Arts, 1995. Mem. Arts Adv. Alliance, Santa Clara County, 1985-86; grant panelist Santa Clara County Arts Council, 1987. Exhbn. grantee Ahmanson Found., 1981, NEA, 1984, Calif. Arts Coun., 1985-89. Mem. Am. Assn. Mus., ArtTable, 1983—, Calif. Assn. Mus. (bd. dirs. 1987-89), Hawaiian Craftsmen (bd. dirs. 1994—), Honolulu Jr. League, Key Project (bd. dirs. 1993-94). Democrat. Roman Catholic. Avocations: dance, fiction writing. Home and Office: 47-665 Mapele Rd Kaneohe HI 96744-4918

LAGOS, JAMES HARRY, lawyer; b. Springfield, Ohio, Mar. 14, 1951; s. Harry Thomas and Eugenia (Papas) L.; m. Nike Daphne Pavlatos, July 3, 1976. BA cum laude, Wittenberg U., 1970; JD, Ohio State U., 1972. Bar: U.S. Supreme Ct. 1976, U.S. Ct. Appeals (6th cir.) 1979, U.S. Dist. Ct. (so. dist.) Ohio 1973, U.S. Tax Ct. 1975, Ohio Supreme Ct. 1973. Assoc. pros. atty. Clark County, Ohio, 1972-75; ptnr. Lagos & Lagos, Springfield, 1975—; mem. Springfield Small Bus. Council, past chmn., 1977—, Ohio Small Bus. Council, 1980—, past chmn., vice chmn.; past pres., v.p. Nat. Small Bus. United, 1982—; del. Small Bus. Nat. Issues Conf., 1984, Ohio Gov.'s Conf. Small Bus., 1984, resource person regulatory and licensing reform com., 1984. Bd. dirs., past pres. Greek Orthodox Ch., 1974—; mem. diocese council Greek Orthodox Diocese of Detroit, 1985-86; past chmn. Clark County Child Protection Team, 1974-82, Clark County Young Rep. Club, past pres., sec., treas., 1968-76, chmn. Ohio del. White House Conf. Small Bus., 1985-86, del. White House Conf. Small Bus., 1995, bd. dirs. Small Bus. Found. Am., 1993. Served as staff sgt. Ohio Air N.G., 1970-76. Recipient Dr. Melvin Emanuel award West Central Ohio Hearing and Speech Assn., 1983, Medal of St. Paul the Apostle Greek Orthodox Archdiocese of North and South Am., 1985; Disting. Service award Springfield-Clark County, 1977; named one of Outstanding Young Men of Am., 1978, Small Bus. Adv. Yr. U.S. Small Bus. Adminstrn., 1991. Mem. Am. Hellenic Inst. (pub. affairs com. 1979—, bd. dirs.), Am. Hellenic Ednl. Progressive Assn. (past treas), Small Bus. Found. of Am., (bd. dirs. 1993—), C. of C. (bd. dirs.), Jaycees (past chmn. several coms. 1973-89, Spoke award 1974), ABA, Ohio State Bar Assn., Springfield Bar and Law Library Assn. (past sec., exec. com. 1973—), West Cen. Ohio Hearing and Speech Assn. (bd. dirs., pres., v.p. 1973-84), Alpha Alpha Kappa, Phi Eta Sigma, Tau Pi Phi, Pi Sigma Alpha. Home: 2023 Audubon Park Dr Springfield OH 45504-1113 Office: Lagos & Lagos 1 S Limestone St Ste 1000 Springfield OH 45502-1243

LAGOWSKI, BARBARA JEAN, writer, book editor; b. Adams, Mass., Nov. 9, 1955; d. Frank Louis and Jeanette (Wanat) L.; m. Richard Dietrich Mumma III, Oct. 11, 1980; 1 child, Adam Dietrich. BA, U. South Fla., 1977; MA, Johns Hopkins U., 1978. Asst. editor Fred Jordan Books Grossett and Dunlap Pubs., N.Y.C., 1978-80; mng. editor Methuen Inc., N.Y.C., 1980-81; mng. assoc., sr. editor Bobb-Merrill Co Inc., N.Y.C., 1981-84; editor New Am. Libr., N.Y.C., 1984-85; poet-in-the-schs. Hillsborough County Arts Council, Tampa., Fla., 1976-77; poet-in-residence Cloisters Children's Mus., Balt., 1977-78. Author: Silver Skates series, 1988-89; co-author: Good Spirits, 1986, Teen Terminators, 1989, How to Get the Best Public School Education for Your Child, 1991, The Sports Curmudgeon, 1993, How to Attract Anyone, Anytime, Anyplace, 1993, Daily Negations: A Malcontent's Book of Mediations for Every Interminable Day of the Year, 1996. Mem. Authors Guild, Phi Kappa Phi. Home: 442 Dewey St Long Branch NJ 07740-5915

LAGOWSKI, J(OSEPH) J(OHN), chemist; b. Chgo., June 8, 1930; s. Joseph Thomas and Helen (Kaspryczski) L.; m. Jeanne Wecker Mund, Feb. 13, 1954. B.S., U. Ill., 1952; M.S., U. Mich., 1954; Ph.D., Mich. State U., 1957; Ph.D. (Marshall scholar), Cambridge (Eng.) U., 1959. Asst. demonstrator and supr. in inorganic chemistry Cambridge U., 1958-59; asst. prof. chemistry U. Tex., Austin, 1959-63; asso. prof. U. Tex., 1963-67, prof. chemistry and edn., 1967—, Piper prof., 1981. Author: (with G.W. Watt and L.F. Hatch) Chemistry, 1974, Chemistry in the Laboratory, 1964, The Structure of Atoms, 1964, The Chemical Bond, 1966, Modern Inorganic Chemistry, 1973; editor: Jour. Chem. Edn, 1979—. Recipient award Chem. Mfrs. Assn., 1981, Am. Chem. Soc. award in Chem. Edn., 1989. Fellow AAAS; mem. Am. Chem. Soc. (Union Carbide Corp. Chem. Edn. award 1989), Chem. Soc. (London), AAAS, Sigma Xi, Phi Lambda Upsilon. Office: U Tex Dept Chemistry Austin TX 78712

LAGRANGE, CLAIRE MAE, special education educator; b. Tarkio, Mo., Oct. 11, 1937; d. Floyd Gerald and Phyllis Geneva (Wilson) McElfish; m. Irving Joseph LaGrange, May 20, 1955; children: Raymond, Robert, Rhonda, Roger. BA, U. Southwestern La., 1983; MEd, Northwestern State U., 1990. Cert. English, spl. edn., K-12 mild and moderate, assessment tchr., libr. sci., La. Tchr.'s aide St. Martin Parish Sch. Bd., Cecilia, La., 1979-82; tchr. English Florien (La.) High Sch., 1984-86; tchr. Zwolle (La.) High Sch., 1986-90, Cecilia Jr. High Sch., 1990-92, Cecilia High Sch., 1992—. Den mother Cub Scouts-Boy Scouts Am., Spokane, Wash., 1967-69; Sunday sch. tchr. First Friends Ch., Spokane, 1968-69. Fellow U. S.W. La Alumni Assn., Northwestern State U. Alumni Assn.; mem. ASCD, Coun. Exceptional Children, Nat. Educators Am., Nat. English Honor Soc., Internat. Reading Assn., La. Assn. Educators, La. Ednl. Assessment Tchrs. Assn., La. Reading Assn., St. Martin Assn. Educators. Avocations: sketching, reading, writing, crossword puzzles, camping. Home: 1052 Charles Marks Rd Arnaudville LA 70512-3820

LAGRONE, ALFRED HALL, electrical engineering educator; b. DeBerry, Tex., Sept. 25, 1912; s. William Taylor and Lena Enola (Westmoreland) LaG.; m. Dixie Louise Ballard, Sept. 8, 1955; children: Carrie Sue, Howard, Tracy, Kimberly. B.S. in Elec. Engring, U. Tex., Austin, 1938, M.S., 1948, Ph.D., 1954. Distbn. engr. San Antonio Pub. Service Co., 1938-42; research engr. U. Tex., Austin, 1946-54; assoc. prof. U. Tex., 1954-60, prof., 1960-92, prof. emeritus, 1992—, dir. antennas and propagation lab., 1966—; Cons. ABC, Collins Radio Co., Honeywell, Inc., Tex. Nuclear Co.; chmn. U.S. Commn. F of Union Radio-Scientifique Internationale, 1975—. Served to capt. USNR, 1942-46. Recipient Scott Helt Meml. award I.R.E., 1960. Fellow I.E.E.E. (nat. chmn. fellow com.); mem. Sigma Xi, Eta Kappa Nu, Tau Beta Pi. Home: 3925 Sierra Dr Austin TX 78731-3911

LAGUEUX, RONALD RENE, federal judge; b. Lewiston, Maine, June 30, 1931; s. Arthur Charles and Laurette Irene (Turcotte) L.; m. Denise Rosemarie Boudreau, June 30, 1956; children: Michelle Simone, Gregory Charles, Barrett James. AB, Bowdoin Coll., 1953; LLB, Harvard U., 1956. Assoc. then ptnr. Edwards and Angell Law Firm, Providence, R.I., 1956-68; assoc. justice Superior Ct. State of R.I., Providence, 1968-86; judge U.S. Dist. Ct., Providence, 1986—; chief judge, 1992—; exec. counsel to Gov. Chafee, R.I., 1963-65. Rep. candidate for U.S. Senate, 1964; corporator R.I. Hosp., Providence, 1965—; solicitor Southeastern New Eng. Province United Way, 1957-68. Mem. ABA, Bowdoin Coll. Alumni Council (past v.p., pres.), Am.-French Geneal. Soc. Home: 90 Greenwood Ave Rumford RI 02916-1934 Office: US Dist Ct One Exchange Ter 214B US Courthouse Providence RI 02903

LAGUNOFF, DAVID, physician, educator; b. N.Y.C., Mar. 14, 1932; s. Robert and Cicele (Lipman) L.; m. Susan P. Powers, Mar. 8, 1958; children: Rachel, Liza, Michael. MD, U. Chgo., 1957. Rsch. asst. microbiology U. Miami, Coral Gables, Fla., 1951-53; intern U. Calif. San Francisco Hosp., 1957-58; postdoctoral fellow dept. pathology U. Wash., Seattle, 1958-59, trainee in pathology, 1959-60, instr. pathology, 1960-62, asst. prof., 1962-65, assoc. prof., 1965-69, prof., 1969-79; prof. dept. pathology St. Louis U., 1979—, chmn. dept. pathology, 1991-96, asst. v.p., 1989-93; assoc. dean rsch. St. Louis U. Sch. Medicine, 1989-96. Nat. Heart Inst. fellow Carlsberg Laboratorium, Copenhagen, 1962-64, Nat. Cancer Inst. fellow Sir William Dunn Sch. Pathology, Oxford, Eng., 1970. Mem. AAAS, AAUP, Am. Soc. Cell Biology, Am. Assn. Pathologists, Assn. Pathology Chmn., Am. Assn. Immunologists. Office: St Louis Univ Sch Medicine Dept Pathology 1402 S Grand Blvd Saint Louis MO 63104-1004

LAHAINE, GILBERT EUGENE, retail lumber company executive; b. Owosso, Mich., Jan. 30, 1926; s. Eric Eugene and Martha Dorothy (Wetzel) LaH.; m. Dorothy Jean Williams, July 1, 1945; children: Gilbert Eugene Jr., Susan, Karen, David, Barbara, Ruth, Marianne, Steven, Eric. BA, Mich. State U., 1949. Acct. Hazen Lumber Co., Lansing, Mich., 1949-56; pres., mgr. Gilbert Lumber Co., Lansing, 1956—, also bd. dirs.; sec. bd. dirs. Duane Bone Builder, Inc., East Lansing, Mich. Bd. dirs. Mo. Synod, Luth. Ch., St. Louis, 1987-95. With USN, 1944-46. Avocations: fishing, softball, reading, hunting. Home: 2401 Stirling Ave Lansing MI 48910 Office: Gilbert Lumber Co 3501 S Pennsylvania Ave Lansing MI 48910

LAHAY, DAVID GEORGE MICHAEL, ballet company director; b. Barrie, Ont., Can., July 15, 1949; s. George Anthony and Edna Alice (Silverberg) LaH. B.A., Trent U., Peterborough, Ont., 1971; B.F.A. with honors, York U., Toronto, 1973. Prin. dancer Les Grands Ballets Canadiens, Montreal, 1978-87, asst. ballet master, 1987-91; prin. dancer Atlanta Ballet, 1978; ballet master Ottawa Ballet, 1991. Choreographer Canadian Heritage Festival, 1989, 90, 91; balletmaster Alberta Ballet. Ont. scholar, 1968; Can Council grantee, 1973, 75, 78. Office: Alberta Ballet Nat Christie Ctr, 141 18th Ave, Calgary, AB Canada T2S 0B8

LAHEY, JOHN H., lawyer; b. Cleve., June 25, 1946. BS, Miami U., 1968; JD, Ohio State U., 1971. Bar: Ohio 1972. Ptnr. Jones, Day, Reavis & Pogue, Columbus, Ohio; adj. prof. law Capital Univ., 1980-83. Office: Jones Day Reavis & Pogue 1900 Huntington Ctr Columbus OH 43215*

LAHEY, RICHARD THOMAS, JR., nuclear engineer, fluid mechanics engineer; b. St. Petersburg, Fla., Feb. 20, 1939; married, 1961; 3 children. BS, U.S. Merchant Marine Acad., 1961; MS, Rensselaer Polytechnic Inst., 1964; ME, Columbia U., 1966; PhD in Mechanical Engring., Stanford U., 1971. Engr. Knolls Atomic Power Lab., 1961-64; rsch. assoc. Columbia U., 1964-66; mgr. core & safety devel. nuclear energy divsn. Gen. Electric, 1966-75; chmn. dept. nuclear engring. Rensselaer Poly. Inst., Troy, N.Y., 1975-87, prof. nuclear engring. and engring. physics, 1987-89, prof. dept. chem. engring., 1987-89, Edward E. Hood, Jr. prof. engring., 1989—, dir. ctr. multiphase rsch., 1991-94; dean engring. Rensselaer Poly. Inst., Troy, 1994—; mem. sci. adv. com. EG&G Idaho, Inc., 1976—; mem. Advanced Code Rev. Group & LOFT Rev. Group U.S. Nuclear Regulatory Commn., 1976-84; commr. Engring. Manpower Commn., 1981-84; pres. R.T. Lahey, Inc., 1981-83; adj. prof. U. Pisa, Italy and Claude Bernard U., France, 1987; Alexander von Humboldt Sr. scientist fellow, 1994-95. Editor: Jour. Nuclear Engring. & Design, 1983—. Recipient Arthur Holly Compton award, 1989, Glenn T. Seaborg medal, 1992, E. O. Lawrence Meml. award U.S. Dept. Energy, 1988; Fulbright fellow Magdalen Coll., Oxford U., 1983-84. Fellow ASME, AIChE, Am. Nuclear Soc. (Tech. Achievement award 1985), N.Y. Acad. Scis., Am. Soc. Engring. Edn. (Glen Murphy award 1985), Sigma Xi; mem. NAS, Nat. Acad. Engring., Nat. Acad. Sci. (fgn. mem. Bashkorstan, Russia). Research in two-phase flow and boiling heat transfer technology; nuclear reactor thermal-hydraulics and safety. Office: Rensselaer Poly Inst Dept Nuclear Engring & Physics 110 8th St Troy NY 12181-3522

LAHOOD, MARVIN JOHN, English educator; b. Auburn, N.Y., Mar. 21, 1933; s. Salem and Anna (Mahfoud) L.; m. Marjorie Braun, Aug. 22, 1959; children: John, Melissa, Mark. BS, Boston Coll., 1954; MA in English, U. Notre Dame, 1958, PhD in English, 1962. Instr. Niagara U., 1960-61, assoc. prof., 1962-64; assoc. prof. Buffalo (N.Y.) State Coll., 1964-67, prof., 1967-71, prof. ind. study, 1968-69, prof., assoc. for acad. devel., 1969-71, prof., 1978—, Disting. tchg. prof., 1995—; prof., acad. dean Coll. Misericordia, 1971-72, Salem State Coll., 1972-75; prof., dean faculty D'Youville Coll., 1975-78; chair Burchfield Poets and Writers Com., 1985—; manuscript reviewer Prentice Hall, 1986-88; lectr. U. Dortmund, Germany, 1986, Lille U., France, Cath. U. Lille, 1991. Author: Conrad Richter's America, 1974, State University College at Buffalo, A History: 1946-1972, 1980; editor: Lativan Literature, 1964, Tender is the Night: Essays in Criticism, 1969; contbr. articles to prof. jours. Pres. Mt. St. Mary Acad. Bd. Trustees, 1990-94. SUNY Faculty Rsch. fellow, 1967, 68, USOE fellow Inst. on Ednl. Media, 1967, SUNY fellow Inst. for Devel. Black Studies, 1969; SUNY Faculty Exch. scholar, 1969—. Office: Buffalo State College 1300 Elmwood Ave Buffalo NY 14222-1095

LAHOOD, RAY, congressman; b. Ill., Dec. 6, 1945; m. Kathleen (Kathy) Dunk LaHood; children: Darin, Amy, Sam, Sara. Student, Canton Jr. Coll., Ill.; BS in Edn. and Sociology, Bradley U., 1971. Tchr. Catholic and pub. jr. high schs., 1971-77; dist. administrv. asst. to congressman Tom Railsback, 1977; mem. Ill. Ho. of Reps., 1982; Chief of Staff Ho. of Reps.; mem. 104th Congress from 18th Ill. dist., 1995—; Mem. Agriculture Com., Transp. and Infrastructure Com. Bd. dirs. Economic Devel. Coun.; pres. sch. bd. Spalding and Notre Dame H.Schs., Bradley U. Nat. Alumni Bd.; svc. to Children's Hosp. Bd., Peoria Area Retarded Citizens Bd.; dir. Rock Island County Youth Svcs. Bur. Mem. ITOO Soc., Downtown Rotary Club, Holy Family Ch. (Peoria), Peoria Area C. of C. Roman Catholic. Office: US House Reps House Office Bldg 329 Cannon Washington DC 20515-1318 Office: US Rep Ray LaHood 100 NE Monroe Ste 100 Peoria IL 61602

LAHOURCADE, JOHN BROSIUS, retired service company executive; b. San Antonio, Tex., Nov. 18, 1924; s. Frederic Eugene and Hildagarde (Brosius) L.; m. Mary Lou Williamson, Sept. 6, 1947; children: Lynne Breuer, Lee A., Lance. BBA, U. Tex., 1948. CPA, Tex. Staff acct. Stanolind Oil & Gas Co., Brownfield, Tex., 1948-51, Carneiro Chumney CPA's, San Antonio, 1951-55; ptnr. Bielstein, Lahourcade & Lewis CPA's, San Antonio, 1955-69; v.p. Luby's Cafeterias Inc., San Antonio, 1969-74, sr. v.p. fin., 1974-79, exec. v.p., 1979-82, pres., chief exec. officer, 1982-88, chmn., CEO, 1988-90, chmn. bd. dirs., 1990-96; ret., 1996. Trustee S.W. Tex. Meth. Hosp., San Antonio, 1974-83; adv. council U. Tex. Sch. Bus. Adminstrn. Found., Austin, 1986-89; bd. dirs. San Antonio Econ. Devel. Found., 1984-95. Mem. Tex. Soc. CPA's (bd. dirs. 1965-68), San Antonio CPA's (pres. 1965).

LAHR, JACK LEROY, lawyer; b. Toledo, Aug. 5, 1934; s. Clarence L. and Josephine E. (Rosenbrook) L.; m. Greta Mars, Dec. 17, 1955 (div. 1987); children: Ellen, Julie; m. Joanna Risdon Hanes, Aug. 8, 1992. BS in Mech. Engring., U. Toledo, 1956; JD with honors, George Washington U., 1963. Bar: Va. 1963, D.C. 1963. Ptnr. Arent, Fox, Kintner, Plotkin & Kahn, 1971-80; ptnr. Foley & Lardner, Washington, 1980—; adj. prof. Georgetown U. Law Ctr., Washington, 1980-83. Author: (with E. Kintner) An Intellectual Property Law Primer, 2d edit., 1982. Served with USN, 1956-59. Mem. ABA (council adminstrv. law sect. 1971-74, chmn. administrv. law judges com. 1974-80), Order of Coif. Office: Foley & Lardner 3000 K St NW Washington DC 20007-5109

LAHR, JOHN, author; b. Los Angeles, July 12, 1941; s. Bert and Mildred (Schroeder) L.; m. Anthea Mander, Aug. 12, 1965; children: Christopher, David, James Anthony and Nicholas Dodds (twins) (dec.). B.A., Yale, 1963, Worcester Coll., Oxford, 1965; M.A., Worcester Coll., Oxford. Drama critic Manhattan East, 1966-68, New York Free Press, 1968-70, Evergreen Rev., 1968-71, Village Voice, 1969-72, The Nation, 1981-82, British Vogue, 1986-92, The New Yorker, 1992—; contbg. editor Harper's, 1979-83; lit. adviser Tyrone Guthrie Theatre, Mpls., 1968; lit. mgr. Repertory Theatre of Lincoln Center, 1969-71. Author: Notes on a Cowardly Lion: The Biography of Bert Lahr, 1969, Up Against the Fourth Wall, 1970, The Autograph Hound, 1973, Astonish Me, 1973, (with Jonathan Price) Life-Show, 1973, Hot to Trot, 1974, Prick Up Your Ears: The Biography of Joe Orton, 1978 (Gay News lit. prize 1979), Coward: the Playwright, 1983, Automatic Vaudeville, 1984, (play) Diary of a Somebody, 1989, Dame Edna Everage and the Rise of Western Civilization: Backstage with Barry Humphries, 1991 (Roger Machell prize 1992), Light Fantastic, 1996; Editor: (with Anthea Lahr) Casebook on Harold Pinter's The Homecoming, 1969, The Complete Plays of Joe Orton, 1976, The Orton Diaries, 1987; co-producer: (film) Prick Up Your Ears, 1987. Mem. Rockefeller Theatre panel, 1969-73, Nat. Endowment for the Arts, 1969-73, Theatre Devel. Fund, 1970-73; Bd. dirs. Choreoconcerts, 1966—. Recipient George Jean Nathan award for drama criticism, 1969, 95, ASCAP-Deems Taylor award 1980-81. Mem. P.E.N. (dir.). Address: 11A Chalcot Gardens, London NW3 4YB, England

LAHTI, CHRISTINE, actress; b. Detroit, Apr. 5, 1950; d. Paul Theodore and Elizabeth Margaret (Tabar) L.; m. Thomas Schlamme, Sept. 4, 1983; 1 child, Wilson Lahti. BA in Speech, U. Mich., 1972; postgrad., Fla. State U., 1972-73; studies with William Esper, Uta Hagen, Herbert Berghof Studios. Actress: (stage prodns.) The Woods, 1978 (Theatre World award 1979), Division Street, 1980, Loose Ends, 1981, Present Laughter, 1983, Landscape of the Body, 1984, The Country Girl, 1984, Cat on a Hot Tin Roof, 1985, Little Murders, 1987, The Heidi Chronicles, 1989, Three Hotels, 1993; regular mem. cast (TV series) Dr. Scorpion, 1978, The Harvey Korman Show, 1978, (TV films) The Last Tenant, 1978, The Henderson Monster, 1980, The Executioner's Song, 1982, Single Bars, Single Women, 1984, Love Lives On, 1985, Amerika, 1987, No Place Like Home, 1989, Crazy from the Heart, 1991, The Fear Inside, 1992, The Good Fight, 1985 (feature films) And Justice For All, 1979, Whose Life Is It, Anyway?, 1981, Swing Shift, 1984 (N.Y. Film Critics Circle award for best supporting actress 1985, Acad. award nominee 1985, Golden Globe award nominee 1985), Ladies and Gentlemen: The Fabulous Stains, 1985, Just Between Friends, 1986, Housekeeping, 1987, Season of Dreams, 1987, Stacking, 1988, Running on Empty, 1988, Gross Anatomy, 1989, Miss Firecracker, 1989, Funny About Love, 1990, The Doctor, 1991, Leaving Normal, 1992, Hideaway, 1995; prodr. short action film: Lieberman in Love, 1995 (Acad. award nominee for best live action short film 1996). Recipient Golden Globe award for Best Actress in a Miniseries or Motion picture Made for TV. Office: ICM 8942 Wilshire Blvd Beverly Hills CA 90211*

LAHTI, RICHARD IVAR, quality improvement administrator; b. East Chicago, Ind., May 16, 1943; s. Ivar John and Fannie (Panezich) L.; m. Margaret Alethe Dickson, Jan. 24, 1972; children: Sarah, Tom, David, Mari, Susan, John. Student, St. Joseph's Coll., 1969-70. Payroll analyst The Boeing Co., Seattle, 1964-69; mgr. Pare Inc., Madison, Wis., 1969-72; prodn. planner Revlon Co., Phoenix, 1973-78; mgr. The Boeing Co., Wichita, Kans., 1980—. With U.S. Army, 1961-64. Democrat. Congregationalist. Home: 6428 Rodeo St Wichita KS 67226-1414

LAI, HIM MARK, writer; b. San Francisco, Nov. 1, 1925; s. Mark Bing and Hing Mui (Dong) L.; m. Laura Jung, June 12, 1953. AA, San Francisco Jr. Coll., 1945; BS in Engring., U. Calif., Berkeley, 1947. Mech. engr. Utilities Engring. Bur., San Francisco, 1948-51, Bechtel Corp., San Francisco, 1953-84; lectr. Chinese Am. history San Francisco State U., 1969, 72-75, U. Calif., Berkeley, 1978-79, 84; researcher, writer on Chinese Am. history San Francisco, 1967—; dir. Chinese of Am. 1785-1980 Exhbn. Chinese Cultural Found. San Francisco, 1979-80; coord. Chinese Am. in Search of Roots Program, 1991—; cons. Asian Am. Studies Program Chinese Materials Rsch. Collection U. Calif., Berkeley, 1986-88, nat. edn. program Ams. All, 1992-96; adj. prof. Asian Am. studies dept. San Francisco State U., 1990—; coord. Chinese Cmty. Hour Cantonese radio program, 1971-84. Co-author: Chinese of America, 1785-1980: Exhibition Catalog, 1980, Island: Poetry and History of Chinese Immigrants on Angel Island, 1910-1940, 1980; author: A History Reclaimed: An Annotated Bibliography and Guide of Chinese Language Materials on the Chinese of America, 1986, From Overseas Chinese to Chinese American: History of Development of Chinese American Society During the Twentieth Century, 1992; assoc. editor: A History of the Chinese in California, A Syllabus, 1969; co-editor: Collected Works of Gilbert Woo, 1991; mem. editl. bd. Amerasia Journal, 1979—, Chinese America: History and Perspectives, 1986—; contbr. articles to profl. jours. Mem. Chinese Hist. Soc. Am. (pres. 1971, 76, 77, bd. dirs. 1972-81, 84, 85-91, 93—), Chinese Culture Found. San Francisco (bd. dirs. 1975-85, 87-94, 96—, pres. 1982, bd. chairperson 1983, 84, 85, 89). Home: 357 Union St San Francisco CA 94133-3519

LAI, JUEY HONG, chemical engineer; b. Taipei, Taiwan, Dec. 4, 1936; came to U.S., 1961, naturalized, 1976; s. Kwo-Wang and Chin-Fong L.; m. Li-Huey Chang, June 30, 1968; children: Eric Yo-Ping, Bruce Yo-Sheng. B.S. in Chem. Engring., Nat. Taiwan U., 1959; M.S. in Chem. Engring., U. Wash., 1963, Ph.D. in Phys. Chemistry, 1969. Rsch. specialist dept. chemistry U. Minn., 1969-73; prin. research scientist Honeywell Phys. Scis. Ctr., Honeywell, Inc., Bloomington, Minn., 1973-78, sr. prin. research scientist, 1978-83; staff scientist Honeywell Tech. Ctr., Honeywell, Inc., 1983-87; pres. Lai Labs., Inc., Burnsville, Minn., 1988—; lectr. SUNY, New Paltz, 1983. Author/editor: Polymers for Electronic Applications, 1989; contbr. articles on solid state chemistry, polymer chemistry and dental materials to tech. jours.; rschr. on polymer materials for electronics, gas removal tech., solid state chemistry and dental materials. Bd. dirs. Chinese Am. Assn. Minn., 1977-79, Minn. Taiwanese Assn., 1995-96. Recipient H.W. Sweatt Tech. award Honeywell, Inc., 1980, Small Bus. Innovation Rsch. award Dept. Health and Human Svcs., 1990, 93, 94. Fellow Am. Inst. Chemists; mem. Am. Assn. Dental Rsch., Am. Chem. Soc., Sigma Xi, Phi Lambda Upsilon. Office: Lai Labs Inc 12101 16th Ave S Burnsville MN 55337-2982

LAI, KHAI CHIN, medical physicist; b. Singapore, June 1, 1963; came to U.S., 1984; s. Lan-Fong and Fay-Fong (Chan) L.; m. Sara L. Hsueh, Jan. 23, 1988; 1 child, Ethan Z. BS, U. Wash., 1987, MS in Nuclear Engring., 1989. Grad. rsch. asst. U. Wash., Seattle, 1987-89; rsch. engr. U. Wash. Med. Ctr., Seattle, 1990-92, med. radiation physicist, 1992—; cons. Norland Corp., Ft. Atkinson, Wis., 1987-92, Philips Med. Systems, Shelton, Conn., 1993—. Contbr. articles to Calcified Tissue Internat. Lt. Singapore Inf., 1981-84. Mem. Am. Assn. Physicist in Medicine, Health Physics Soc. Achievements include development of high dose rate brachytherapy quality assurance management program for institution, quality assurance management program for multi-center/clinical trials. Home: 9228 Woodlawn Ave N Seattle WA 98103-3528 Office: U Wash Med Ctr 1959 NE Pacific St Seattle WA 98195-0004

LAI, WAIHANG, art educator; b. Hong Kong, Jan. 7, 1939; s. Sing and Yu-ching L.; came to U.S., 1964; BA, Chinese U. Hong Kong, 1964; MA, Claremont Grad. Sch., 1967; m. Celia Cheung, Aug. 13, 1966. Asst. prof. art Maunaolu Coll., Maui, Hawaii, 1968-70; prof. art Kauai (Hawaii) Community Coll., 1970—. Vis. prof. art Ariz. State U., Tempe, summer 1967. Recipient Excellence in Teaching award U. Hawaii, 1992, Nat. Inst. Staff and Orgnl. Devel. Excellence award U. Tex., 1993. Mem. Kauai (pres. 1974—) Watercolor Socs., Phila. Watercolor Club, Hawaii Computer Art Soc., Kauai Oriental Art Soc. (pres. 1981—), AM. Watercolor Soc. Author: The Chinese Landscape Paintings of Waihang Lai, 1966, The Watercolors of Waihang Lai, 1967; illustrator: The Tao of Practice Success, 1991, Advertisements for Acupuncturists, 1992. Home: PO Box 363 Lihue HI 96766-0363 Office: Kauai Community Coll Lihue HI 96766

LAI, W(EI) MICHAEL, mechanical engineer, educator; b. Amoy, Fukien, China, Nov. 29, 1930; naturalized U.S. citizen, 1967; s. Chia-pan and Shue-Chin (Lo) L.; m. Linda Yu-ling Chu, Dec. 21, 1963; children: David, Michelle. BSCE, Nat. Taiwan U., 1953; MS in Engring. Mech., U. Mich., 1959, PhD, 1962. Asst. prof. mechanics Renssalaer Poly. Inst., Troy, N.Y., 1961-66, assoc. prof., 1967-77, prof., 1978-87, acting dept. chmn., 1986-87; prof. mech. engring. and orthopaedic bioengring. Columbia U., N.Y.C., 1987—, acting chmn. dept. mech. engring., 1995-96, chmn. dept. mech. engring., 1996—. Author: Elements of Elasticity, 1965, Introduction to Continuum Mechanics, 1974, 3rd edit., 1993. Fellow ASME (Melville medal for Best Paper 1982, Best Paper award bioengring. divsn. 1991), Am. Inst. Med. and Biol. Engring.; mem. AAAS, Am. Soc. Biomechanics, Orthopaedic Rsch. Soc. Home: 215 W 95th St Apt 9H New York NY 10025-6355 Office: Columbia U Dept Mech Engring W 116th St New York NY 10027

LAIBINIS, PAUL EDWARD, chemical engineering educator; b. Wilkes-Barre, Pa., Dec. 8, 1963; s. Edward Bernard and Helen Jean (Draminski) L. BSChemE, BS in Chemistry, MIT, 1985; MA in Chemistry, Harvard U., 1987, PhD in Chemistry, 1991. Teaching/rsch. asst. Harvard U., Cambridge, Mass., 1985-91; postdoctoral fellow Calif. Inst. Tech., Pasadena, 1991-93; asst. prof. MIT, Cambridge, 1993-94, Texaco-Mangelsdorf asst. prof., 1994-96, Doherty asst. prof., 1996—; corr. Sci.-by-Mail, 1994-95; Beckman Fedn. young investigator, 1995—, Office of Naval Rsch. young investigator, 1996—. Mem. AAAS, AIChE, Am. Chem. Soc. (Victor K. LaMer award divsn. colloid and surface sci. 1994). Republican. Roman Catholic. Achievements include contributions to more than 30 sci. publs., 1 patent in area of thin films and nanotechnology. Avocations: hiking, swimming, racket sports, film, theater. Home: 56 Winslow Ave Apt 1 Somerville MA 02144-2501 Office: MIT Dept Chemical Engring Cambridge MA 02139

LAIBLE, JON MORSE, retired mathematics educator, dean; b. Bloomington, Ill., July 25, 1937; s. Russell James and Margaret (Herold) L.; m. Jo Ann Ivens, June 14, 1959; children: Kathy Jo, Kenneth Russell, Jackie Ann Laible Muhs, Michael Howard. Student, Carleton Coll., 1955-57; BS, U. Ill., 1959; MA, U. Minn., 1961; PhD, U. Ill., 1967. Asst. prof. Western Ill. U., Macomb, 1962-64; asst. prof., assoc. prof. then prof. math. Ea. Ill. U., Charleston, 1964-80, dean Coll. Liberal Arts and Scis., 1980-93, dean Coll. Scis., 1993-94; ret., 1994; vis. prof. math. Millikin U., Decatur, Ill., 1994—. Chmn. citizens cons. coun. Unit #1 Pub. Schs., Charleston, 1975-78; adv. com. Sarah Bush Lincoln Health Ctr., Charleston, 1986; bd. dirs. Ea. Ill. U. Found., 1995—. Recipient Outstanding Faculty Merit award Ea. Ill. Univ., 1978, Univ. Svc. award, 1991. Mem. Math. Assn. Am. (bd. govs. 1977-80, chmn. com. vis. lectrs. and cons. 1980-88, Disting. Svc. award Ill. sect. 1985), Ill. Sect. Math. Assn. Am. (chmn. 1975, 94), Ill. Coun. Tchrs. Math., Sigma Xi. Democrat. Avocation: photography.

LAIDIG, WILLIAM RUPERT, retired paper company executive; b. Sterling, Ill., Feb. 3, 1927; s. George and Margaret Anne (Gnewuch) L.; m. Lorraine Mae Grom, Jan. 2, 1952; children: Ann Marie, Mary Katherine, Margaret Anne, William Andrew. B.S.M.E., Marquette U., 1949. Registered profl. engr., Ga., Ala., Wis., Ark. Engr. Inland Steel Products, 1949-50; engr. Nekoosa Papers Inc., Port Edwards, Wis., 1950-62, mgr., 1962-66; mgr. Nekoosa Papers Inc., Ashdown, Ark., 1966-72; mill mgr. Nekoosa Papers Inc., Port Edwards, Wis., 1972-75; v.p., resident mgr. Gt. So. Paper Co., Cedar Springs., Ga., 1975-80, sr. v.p., 1979-80, pres., 1980-84; exec. v.p. Gt. No. Nekoosa Corp., Stamford, Conn., 1980-84, pres., chief exec. officer, chmn., dir., 1984-90; chmn. Jaakko Pöyry (USA), Inc., Raleigh, N.C., 1991-92; ret. Pres. Village of Port Edwards, Wis., 1966-67; trustee Marquette U., Milw.; bd. dirs. Tasman Chile Ltd., 1993. Lt. USN, 1952-53. Roman Catholic. Clubs: Eagle Creek Country (Fla.). Lodges: K.C., Elks. Home: PO Box 39 Manitowish Waters WI 54545-0039

LAIDLAW, ANDREW R., lawyer; b. Durham, N.C., Aug. 28, 1946. BA, Northwestern U., 1969; JD, U. N.C., 1972. Bar: Ill. 1972. Chair exec com., mem. Seyfarth, Shaw, Fairweather & Geraldson, Chgo.; CEO Seyfarth, Shaw, Fairweather & Geraldson, Chicago. Contbr. articles to profl. jours. Mem. ABA (antitrust and securities law coms. 1982—), Barristers. Office: Seyfarth Shaw Fairweather & Geraldson Mid Continental Plz 55 E Monroe St Chicago IL 60603-5702

LAIDLAW, HARRY HYDE, JR., entomology educator; b. Houston, Apr. 12, 1907; s. Harry Hyde and Elizabeth Louisa (Quinn) L.; BS, La. State U., 1933, MS, 1934; PhD (Univ. fellow, Genetics fellow, Wis. Dormitory fellow, Wis. Alumni Rsch. Found. fellow), U. Wis., 1939; m. Ruth Grant Collins, Oct. 26, 1946; 1 child, Barbara Scott Laidlaw Murphy. Teaching asst. La. State U., 1933-34, rsch. asst., 1934-35; prof. biol. sci. Oakland City (Ind.) Coll., 1939-41; state apiarist Ala. Dept. Agr. and Industries, Montgomery, 1941-42; entomologist First Army, N.Y.C., 1946-47; asst. prof. entomology, asst. apiculturist U. Calif.-Davis, 1947-53, assoc. prof. entomology, assoc. apiculturist, 1953-59, prof. entomology, apiculturist, 1959-74, asso. dean Coll. Agr., 1960-64, chair agr. faculty, staff, 1965-66, prof. entomology emeritus, apiculturist emeritus, 1974—; coord. U. Calif.-Egypt Agrl. Devel. Program, AID, 1979-83. Rockefeller Found. grantee, Brazil, 1954-55, Sudan, 1967; honored guest Tamagawa U., Tokyo, 1980. Trustee, Yolo County (Calif.) Med. Soc. Scholarship Com., 1965-83. Served to capt. AUS, 1942-46. Recipient Cert. of Merit Am. Bee Jour., 1957, Spl. Merit award U. Calif.-Davis, 1959, Merit award Calif. Central Valley Bee Club, 1974, Merit award Western Apicultural Soc., 1980, Gold Merit award Internat. Fedn. Beekeepers' Assns., 1986; recipient Disting. Svc. award Ariz. Beekeepers Assn., 1988. Cert. of Appreciation Calif. State Beekeepers' Assn., 1987, award Alan Clemson Meml. Found., 1989: NIH grantee, 1963-66; NSF grantee, 1966-74. Fellow AAAS, Entomol. Soc. Am. (honoree spl. symposium 1990, C.W. Woodworth award Pacific br. 1981); mem. Am. Inst. Biol. Scis., Am. Soc. Naturalists, Am. Soc. Zoologists, Nat. Assn. Uniformed Svcs., Ret. Officers Assn. (2d v.p. Sacramento chpt. 1984-86), Scabbard and Blade, Sigma Xi (treas. Davis chpt. 1959-60, v.p. chpt. 1966-67), Alpha Gamma Rho (pres. La. chpt. 1933-34, counsellor Western Province 1960-66). Democrat. Presbyterian. Author books including Instrumental Insemination of Honey Bee Queens, 1977; Contemporary Queen Rearing, 1979; author slide set: Instrumental Insemination of Queen Honey Bees, 1976. Achievements include determination of cause of failure of attempts to artificially inseminate queen honey bees; invention of instruments and procedures to consistently accomplish same; elucidation of genetic relationships of individuals of polyandrous honey bee colonies; design of genetic procedures for behavioral study and breeding of honey bees for general and specific uses. Home: 761 Sycamore Ln Davis CA 95616-3432 Office: U Calif Dept Entomology Davis CA 95616

LAIDLAW, ROBERT RICHARD, publishing company executive; b. Berwyn, Ill., Mar. 25, 1923; s. John and Mabel Josephine (Howard) L.; m. Evangeline Rene Harrelson, Aug. 12, 1944; children—Andrew Robert, Kimberly, Lisa. Student, Dartmouth Coll., 1941-42; A.B., U. N.C., 1947, J.D., 1950. Sales rep. Laidlaw Bros. (textbook pubs.), River Forest, Ill., 1950-58; sales mgr. Laidlaw Bros. (textbook pubs.), 1958-60, exec. v.p., 1960-68, pres., 1968-85. Served with USNR, 1942-45. Congregationalist.

LAIDLER, DAVID ERNEST WILLIAM, economics educator; b. Tynemouth, Northumberland, Eng., Aug. 12, 1938; s. John Alphonse and Leonora (Gosman) L.; m. Antje Charlotte Breitwisch, Jan. 29, 1965; 1 dau., Nicole Joanna; m. Frances Joan Hutner, Aug. 1960 (div. 1964). B.Sc., London Sch. Econs., 1959; M.A., U. Syracuse, 1960; Ph.D., U. Chgo., 1964; M.A., U. Manchester, Eng., 1973. Temporary asst. lectr. London Sch. Econs., 1961-62; asst. prof. U. Calif.-Berkeley, 1963-66; lectr. econs. U. Essex, Colchester, Eng., 1966-69; prof. econs. U. Manchester, 1969-75; vis. prof. econs. Brown U., Providence, 1973; prof. econs. U. Western Ont., London, Can., 1975—; mem. econ. adv. panel to Marc Lalonde, minister fin., Ottawa, Ont., 1982-84; research coord. Macdonald Royal Commn., 1984-85; scholar in residence C.D. Howe Inst., 1990-91, adj. scholar, 1991—; mem. econs. com. Social Sci. Research Council, Gt. Britain, 1972-75; mem. program adv. com. Carnegie-Rochester Pub. Policy Conf. Series, Rochester, Pitts., 1978-79; Lister lecter. Brit. Assn. Advancement Sci., 1972. Author: The Demand for Money - Theories and Evidence, 1969, Introduction to Microeconomics, 1974, Essays on Money and Inflation, 1975, Monetarist Perspectives, 1982, Taking Money Seriously, 1990, The Golden Age of the Quantity Theory, 1991, (with W. Robson) The Great Canadian Disinflation, 1993; mem. editl. bd. Rev. Econ. Studies, 1970-75, Am. Econ. Rev., 1976-78, Can. Jour. Econs., 1977-79, Jour. Econ. Lit., 1978-91; assoc. editor: Jour. Money, Credit and Banking, 1979—. Rsch. grantee NSF, 1964-66, Social Sci. Rsch. Coun., 1971-76, Social Scis. and Humanities Rsch. Coun. Can., 1977-81, 94-99, 94—, Bradley Found., 1991-96. Fellow Royal Soc. Can.; mem. Am. Econ. Assn., Can. Econ. Assn. (exec. com. 1980-83, pres. 1987-88, Douglas Purvis Meml. prize 1994). Home: 345 Grangeover Ave, London, ON Canada N69 4K8 Office: U Western Ont, Dept Econ, London, ON Canada N6A 5C2

LAINE, CLEO (CLEMENTINA DINAH DANKWORTH), singer; b. Southall, Middlesex, Eng., Oct. 28, 1927; d. Alexander and Minnie (Bullock) Campbell; m. George Langridge, 1947 (div.); m. John Philip William Dankworth, 1958; children: Stuart, Alec, Jackie. MA (hon.), Open U., 1975; MusD (hon.), Berklee Coll. Music, 1982. Vocalist Dankworth Orch., 1953-58; lead role in Seven Deadly Sins, Edinburgh, Scotland Festival and Sadlers Wells, 1961, in Showboat, 1972; acting roles Edinburgh Festival, 1966, 67, Colette, 1980; appeared in A Time to Laugh, Hedda Gabler, The Women of Troy, The Mystery of Edwin Drood, 1986 (Theatre World award, Tony award nomination, Drama Desk award nomination), Into the Woods, 1989 (L.A. Drama Critics award nomination); guest appearances symphony orchs. Eng. and abroad; numerous TV appearances and record albums; most recent albums That Old Feeling, 1985, Cleo Sings Sondheim, 1988, Woman to Woman, 1989, Jazz, 1991, Nothing Without You (with Mel Torme), 1992, Smilin' Through (with Dudley Moore), 1992, Cleo at Carnegie, 1993, Born on Friday, 1993, A Beautiful Thing, 1994, Blue and Sentimental, 1994; gold records: Feel The Warm, I'm a Song, Live at Melbourne; Platinum records: Best Friends, Sometimes When We Touch; author: Cleo, an autobiography, 1994. Decorated Order Brit. Empire, 1979; recipient Golden Feather award Los Angeles Times, 1973, Edison award, 1974, Grammy award for best female jazz vocal, 1985, Theatre World award, 1986; named Show Bus. Personality of Yr., Variety Club, 1977, Singer of Yr., TV Times, 1978; Tony nominee, 1986; recipient Theatre World award, 1986, Lifetime Achievement award N.A.R.M., 1990, Brit. Jazz award for best female vocalist, 1990. Office: care Sonoma-Hope Inc 179-9 Rte 46 W # 102 Rockaway NJ 07866

LAING, KAREL ANN, magazine publishing executive; b. Mpls., July 5, 1939; d. Edward Francis and Elizabeth Jane Karel (Templeton) Hannon; m. G. R. Cheesebrough, Dec. 19, 1959 (div. 1969); 1 child, Jennifer Read; m. Ronald Harris Laing, Jan. 6, 1973; 1 child, Christopher Harris. Grad., U. Minn., 1960. With Guthrie Symphony Opera Program, Mpls., 1969-71; account supr. Colle & McVoy Advt. Agy., Richfield, Minn., 1971-74; owner The Cottage, Edina, Minn., 1974-75; salespromotion rep. Robert Meyers & Assocs., St. Louis Park, Minn., 1975-76; cons. Webb Co., St. Paul, 1976-77, custom pub. dir., 1977-89; pres. K.L. Publs., Inc., Bloomington, Minn., 1989—. Contbr. articles to profl. jours. Community vol. Am. Heart Assn., Am. Cancer Soc., Edina PTA; charter sponsor Walk Around Am., St. Paul, 1985. Mem. Bank Mktg. Assn., Fin. Instn. Mktg. Assn., Advt. Fedn. Am., Am. Bankers Assn., Direct Mail Mktg. Assn., St. Andrews Soc. Republican. Presbyterian. Avocations: painting; gardening; reading; traveling. Office: KL Publs 2001 Killebrew Dr Minneapolis MN 55425-1865

LAING, PENELOPE GAMBLE, art educator; b. Dallas, July 24, 1944; d. William Oscar and Beth (Robertson) G.; m. Richard Harlow Laing, June 29, 1970; children: Scott Emerson, Lindsey Elizabeth. BA in Art, N. Tex. State U., 1966; MFA, Edinboro State Coll., 1979. Cert. tchr., Tex. (life), N.C. (Art all-level). Art cons. Lawrence (Kans.) Unified Sch. Dist., 1966-68; instr. art Ball State U., Muncie, Ind., 1969-71, Edinboro (Pa.) State U., 1976-77, Pitt C.C., Greenville, N.C., 1980-83; exec. dir. Pitt-Greenville Arts Coun., Greenville, 1983-84; free-lance designer, 1984-90; art tchr., head dept. art Pitt County Schs., 1990—; seminar participant N.C. Ctr. for Advancement of Teaching, 1993, tchr.-scholar, 1994, 95. Bd. dirs., v.p. Pitt-Greenville Arts Coun., 1979-82; mem. adv. bd. Pitt County Schs., Greenville, 1985-87; pres. PTA S. Greenville Sch., 1986-87. Named fellow Tchr. Exec. Inst., Pitts County Edn. Found., Greenville, 1992; grantee Pitt County Edn. Found., 1991, 92, 93. Mem. Nat. Art Edn. Assn., N.C. Art Edn. Assn. (bd. dirs., chmn. elem. divsn. 1992-94), Surface Design Assocs. (N.C. rep.), Phi Delta Kappa. Democrat. Avocations: travel, reading. Home: 204 Pineview Dr Greenville NC 27834-6434 Office: 1325 Red Banks Rd Greenville NC 27858-5315

LAING, ROBERT, production designer. Art dir.: (films) Travels with My Aunt, 1972 (Academy award nomination best art direction 1972), The Great Gatsby, 1974, True Lies, 1994; supervising art dir.: (films) Gandhi, 1982 (Academy award best art direction 1982); prodn. designer: (films) Frenzy, 1972, Night Games, 1980, High Road to China, 1983, The Doctor and the Devils, 1985, The Neverending Story II: The Next Chapter, 1990, (TV movies) Ellis Island, 1984, The Far Pavilions, 1984. Office: care Art Directors Guild 11365 Ventura Blvd Ste 315 North Hollywood CA 91604-3148

LAINGEN, LOWELL BRUCE, diplomat; b. Odin Twp., Minn., Aug. 6, 1922; s. Palmer K. and Ida Mabel (Eng) L.; m. Penelope Babcock, June 1, 1957; children: William Bruce, Charles Winslow, James Palmer. B.A. cum laude, St. Olaf Coll., 1947; M.A. in Internat. Relations, U. Minn., 1949. Internat. rels. officer State Dept., 1949-50; joined U.S. Fgn. Svc., 1950; vice consul Hamburg, Germany, 1951-53; 3d sec. embassy Teheran, Iran, 1953-54; consul Meshed, Iran, 1954-55; asst., then officer chargé Greek affairs State Dept., 1956-60; 2d sec., then 1st sec. embassy Karachi, Pakistan, 1960-64; with Pakistan/Afghanistan affairs bur. State Dept., 1964-67; assigned Nat. War Coll., 1967-68; dep. chief mission to Afghanistan Kabul, 1968-71; country dir. Pakistan, Afghanistan and Bangladesh; country dir. State Dept., 1971-73, India, Nepal, Sri Lanka and the Maldives, 1973-74; acting dep. asst. sec. state for Near Eastern and South Asian affairs State Dept., 1974-75, dep. asst. sec. state for European affairs, 1975-76; ambassador to Malta, 1977-79; chargé d'affaires Am. Embassy, Teheran, Iran, 1979; held hostage by Iranian student militants, 1979-81; v.p. Nat. Def. U., Ft. McNair, Washington, 1981-86; exec. dir. Nat. Commn. Pub. Service, Washington, 1987-90; pres. Am. Acad. Diplomacy, 1991—. Home: 5627 Old Chester Rd Bethesda MD 20814-1035

LAIOU, ANGELIKI EVANGELOS, history educator; b. Athens, Greece, Apr. 6, 1941; came to U.S., 1959; d. Evangelos K. and Virginia I. (Apostolides) Laios; m. Stavros B. Thomadakis, July 14, 1973; 1 son, Vassili N. B.A., Brandeis U., 1961; M.A., Harvard U., 1962, Ph.D., 1966. Asst. prof. history Harvard U., Cambridge, Mass., 1969-72, Dumbarton Oaks prof. Byzantine history, 1981—; assoc. prof. Brandeis U., Waltham, 1972-75; prof. Rutgers U., New Brunswick, N.J., 1975-79, disting. prof., 1979-81; chmn. Gennadeion com. (Am. Sch. Classical Studies), Athens, Greece, 1981-84; dir. Dumbarton Oaks, 1989—. Author: Constantinople and the Latins, 1972, Peasant Society in the Late Byzantine Empire, 1977, Mariage, amour et parenté à Byznace, XIe-XIIIe siècles, 1992, Gender, Society and Economic Life in Byzantium, 1992, Consent and Coercion to Sex and Marriage in Ancient and Medieval Societies, 1993. Guggenheim Found. fellow, 1971-72, 79-80, Dumbarton Oaks sr. fellow, 1983-88, Am. Coun. Learned Socs. fellow, 1988-89. Fellow Am. Acad. Arts and Scis., Medieval Acad.; mem. Am. Hist. Assn., Medieval Acad. Am., Societa Ligure di Storia Patria, Greek Com. Study of South Eastern Europe. Office: Dumbarton Oaks 1703 32nd St NW Washington DC 20007-2934

LAIR, ROBERT LOUIS, catering company executive; b. Albuquerque, Aug. 13, 1921; s. Louis E. and Inez B. (Mudd) L.; m. June Marie Moran, Aug. 9, 1941 (dec. Apr. 1983); children—Christopher Louis, Catherine Ann, Cynthia Susan; m. Therese C. Kronkowski, Sept. 15, 1984. With Boeing Airplane Co., 1940-53, dir. sub-contract adminstrn. USN, 1944-46, supr. materiel, 1947-53; with Cessna Aircraft Co., Wichita, Kans., 1953-83, sr. v.p., dir., 1969-83; chmn. bd. Precision Composites, Inc., 1984-87; co-owner Tee-C's Catering, 1987—. Bd. dirs. Jr. Achievement of Wichita, Midwest Cancer Inst. Mem. Falstaff Soc., Wichita Country Club, Rotary. Home: 105 N Woodlawn Ct Wichita KS 67218-1838

LAIRD, ALAN DOUGLAS KENNETH, mechanical engineering educator; b. Victoria, Can., Aug. 8, 1914; came to U.S., 1946, naturalized, 1955; s. George Alexander and Edna A (Foy) L.; m. Joyce Kathleen Morris, Nov. 3, 1941; children: William George, John Douglas, Linda Margaret. B.A.Sc. in Mech. Engring, U. B.C., 1940; M.S., U. Calif. at Berkeley, 1949, Ph.D., 1951. Engr. Def. Industries Ltd., Montreal, 1941-45, Leek and Co., Vancouver, Can., 1945-46; mem. faculty U. Calif. at Berkeley, 1948-80, prof. mech. engring., 1964-80, prof, emeritus, 1980-96, dir. Sea Water Conversion Lab., 1968-80, dir. emeritus Sea Water Conversion Lab., 1980-96. Mem. ASME, Pi Tau Sigma. Home: 860 Sibert Ct Lafayette CA 94549-4925

LAIRD, CHARLES DAVID, zoology and genetics educator, researcher; b. Portland, Oreg., May 12, 1939; s. Charles Bruce and Mary (Gray) L.; m. Judith Helen Shepherd; children: Michael, John, Andrew, Jennifer. BA, U. Oreg., 1961; postgrad., U. Zürich, Switzerland, 1961-62; PhD, Stanford U., 1966. Postdoctoral fellow in microbiology and genetics U. Wash., Seattle, 1966-68, assoc. prof. zoology, 1971-74, prof., 1975—, chmn. dept., 1985-89, adj. prof. genetics, 1975—, rsch. affiliate Child Devel. and Mental Retardation Ctr., 1988—; mem. Fred Hutchinson Cancer Rsch. Ctr., 1990—; asst. prof. zoology U. Tex., Austin, 1968-71. Contbr. articles to profl. jours. Recipient Career Devel. award NIH, 1969; fellow NSF, 1962, NIH, 1966. Fellow AAAS; mem. Am. Soc. Human Genetics, Genetic Soc. Am. Office: Fred Hutchinson Cancer Rsch Ctr 1124 Columbia St Seattle WA 98104-2015

LAIRD, DAVID, humanities educator emeritus; b. Marshfield, Wis., Oct. 17, 1927; s. Melvin Robert and Helen Melissa (Connor) L.; m. Helen Astrid Lauritzen, Sept. 10, 1955; 1 child, Vanessa Ann. PhB, U. Chgo., 1947; BA with highest honor, U. Wis., 1950, MA, 1951, PhD, 1955; postgrad., Courtauld Inst., 1953. Instr. to asst. prof. Oberlin Coll., 1955-58; mem. faculty Calif. State U., L.A., 1958—; chmn. dept. English Calif. State U., 1969-73, chmn. dept. Am. studies, 1977-79; Nat. Humanities Inst. fellow U. Chgo., 1978-79; sr. Fulbright lectr. U. Tunis, Tunisia, 1979-80; fellow Folger Shakespeare Libr., 1982; Fulbright lectr. Odense U. (Denmark), 1983-84; vis. prof. U. Ottawa, 1984-85; cons. to Choice. Mem. editorial bd. Jour. Forest History; contbr. articles on Shakespeare, Am. lit. and cultural history to profl. jours. Mem. Western Shakespeare Seminar, Friends of Huntington Libr. Recipient Outstanding Prof. award Calif. State U., 1987, Nat. Endowment for the Humanities Summer Seminar award Northwestern U., 1989; Uhrig Found. grantee, 1964-65; Fulbright fellow, 1953-54. Mem. MLA, Malone Soc., Am. Studies Assn., Phi Beta Kappa. Home: 565 N Milton Dr San Gabriel CA 91775-2203 Office: Humanities Dept Calif State U Los Angeles CA 90032

LAIRD, JEAN ELOUISE RYDESKI (MRS. JACK E. LAIRD), author, adult education educator; b. Wakefield, Mich., Jan. 18, 1930; d. Chester A. and Agnes A. (Petranek) Rydeski; m. Jack E. Laird, June 9, 1951; children: John E., Jayne E., Joan Ann P., Jerilyn S., Jacquelyn T. Bus. Edn. degree Duluth (Minn.) Bus. U., 1948; posgrad. U. Minn., 1949-50. Tchr. Oak Lawn (Ill.) High Sch. Adult Evening Sch., 1964-72, St. Xavier Coll., Chgo., 1974—; lectr., commencement address cir. Writer newspaper column Around The House With Jean, A Woman's Work, 1965-70, Chicagotown News column The World As I See It, 1969, hobby column Modern Maturity mag., travel column Travel/Leisure mag., beauty column Ladycom mag., Time and Money Savers column Lady's Circle mag., consumerism column Ladies' Home Jour. Mem. Canterbury Writers Club Chgo. (past. pres.), Oak Lawn Bus. and Profl. Women's Club (Woman of Yr. award 1987), St. Linus Guild, Mt. Assisi Acad., Marist, Queen of Peace parents clubs. Roman Catholic. Author: Lost in the Department Store, 1964; Around The House Like Magic, 1968; Around The Kitchen Like Magic, 1969; How To Get the Most From Your Appliances, 1967; Hundreds of Hints for Harrassed Homemakers, 1971; The Alphabet Zoo, 1972; The Plump Ballerina, 1971; The Porcupine Story Book, 1974; Fried Marbles and Other Fun Things To Do, 1975; Hundreds of Hints for Harassed Homemakers; The Homemaker's Book of Time and Money Savers, 1979; Homemaker's Book of Energy Savers, 1981; also 348 paperback booklets. Contbr. numerous articles to mags. Home: 10540 Lockwood Ave Oak Lawn IL 60453-5161 also: 1 Magnificent Mile Bldg Chicago IL 60600 also: Vista De Lago Lake Geneva WI 53147

LAIRD, JERE DON, news reporter; b. Topeka, Aug. 8, 1933; s. Gerald Howard and Vivian Gertrude (Webb) L.; m. Alexandra Berezowsky, Aug. 4, 1957; children: Lee, Jennifer, Christopher. BA in Journalism, U. Nev., 1960. Disc jockey Sta. KHBC Radio, Hilo, Hawaii, 1949-50; announcer, chief engr. Sta. KOLO Radio, Reno, Nev., 1951-58; program dir. Sta. KOLO-TV, Reno, 1958-60; news reporter Sta. KCRA Radio and TV, Sacramento, Calif., 1960-61, Sta. KRLA Radio, L.A., 1962-63; news reporter, editor Sta. KNXT-TV, L.A., 1964-68; news reporter, fin. editor Sta. KNX-CBS Radio, L.A., 1968—; fin. reporter Sta. KCBS-TV, L.A., 1990—; lectr. U. So. Calif., L.A., 1984-85; instr. Calif. State U., Northridge, 1978-79. Cpl. U.S. Army, 1953-55. Recipient Emmy award, L.A., 1964, Peabody award, U. Ga., 1984, Best Bus. News award, L.A. Press Club, 1983, 84, 86, 87, 88, 89, Martin K. Gainsburgh award, Fiscal Policy Coun., Fla., 1978. Mem. Radio TV News Assn. (bd. dirs. 1966-68, Golden Mike award 1984), Sigma Delta Chi. Avocation: sailing. Office: Sta KNX-CBS 6121 W Sunset Blvd Los Angeles CA 90028-6455

LAIRD, JOHN B., newspaper publishing executive. V.p. sales and marketing Houston Chronicle, Tex. Office: Houston Chronicle Pub Co 801 Texas St Houston TX 77002-2906

LAIRD, MARY See WOOD, LARRY

LAIRD, MELVIN ROBERT, former secretary of defense; b. Omaha, Sept. 1, 1922; s. Melvin R. and Helen (Connor) L.; m. Barbara Masters (dec. Jan. 1992); children: John, Alison, David; m. Carole Howard. B.A., Carleton Coll., 1942; LHD (hon.), Lincoln Coll., Ill., 1971; D Polit. Sci. (hon.), U. Pacific, 1968; HHD (hon.), St. Leo's Coll., 1969; LLD (hon.), U. Wis., 1982. Mem. Wis. Senate, 1946-52; chmn. Wis. Legis. Council; mem. 83d-91st Congresses; mem. Rep. Coordinating com. 83d-90th Congresses; sec. of def., 1969-73; dir., sr. counsellor nat. and internat. affairs Pres. Nixon, 1973-74; sr. counsellor nat. and internat. affairs Reader's Digest Assn., 1974—; bd. dirs. Met. Life Ins. Co., N.W. Airlines, IDS Mut. Fund Group, Sci. Applications Internat., Inc.; bd. dirs. COMSAT Corp., chmn. bd., 1991—; bd. dirs. pub. oversight bd. SEC practice sect. AICPA. Author: A House Divided: America's Strategy Gap, 1962; Editor: The Conservative Papers, 1964, Republican Papers, 1968. Bd. dirs. World Rehab. Fund, Boys Clubs Am., George Washington U., Airlie Found., Laird Youth Leadership Found., Pres.'s Reagan Moscow Assessment Rev. Panel, 1987; trustee Kennedy Center; chmn. Nat. Election Commn., 1986; co-chmn. platform com. Rep. Nat. Conv., 1960, chmn., 1964. Decorated Order of Merit 1st class Fed. Republic Germany; comdr. Nat. Order Legion of Honor, France; recipient 15th Ann. Albert Lasker med. award; Man of Year award Am. Cancer Soc.-Nat. Assn. Mental Health; Humanitarian award John E. Fogarty Found. for Mentally Retarded, 1974; Presdl. Medal of Freedom, 1974, Harry S. Truman award, 1985. Mem. Mil. Order Purple Heart, 40 and 8, Am. Legion, VFW, DAV. Presbyterian (elder). Clubs: Burning Tree, Augusta Nat. Golf. Lodge: Masons. Office: 1730 Rhode Island Ave NW 212 Washington DC 20036

LAIRD, ROBERT WINSLOW, journalist; b. Chgo., Sept. 25, 1936; s. Robert Winslow and Evelyn (Emerson) L.; m. Marsa Radbill, Dec. 1, 1962; children—Michael Winslow, Joshua Radbill. B.A., Yale U., 1959. Reporter World Telegram and Sun, N.Y.C., 1963-66; dep. press. sec. to Mayor John Lindsay N.Y.C., 1966-73; press sec. to Gov. Hugh Carey Albany, N.Y., 1974-76; opinions editor, weekly columnist Daily News, N.Y.C., 1977—. Vol. Peace Corps, Gebileh, Somalia, 1962-63; chmn. schs. com. Yale U Alumni, 1979-84. Recipient Editorial Writing award N.Y.C. Citizens Housing and Planning Coun., 1987; co-recipient Editorial Excellence award Nat. Assn. Edn. Writers, 1989. Mem. U.S. Paddle Tennis Assn. (bd. dirs. 1978-82, 87—). Avocations: tennis; paddle tennis. Home: 17 Stuyvesant Oval New York NY 10009-1920 Office: NY Daily News 220 E 42nd St Fl 817 New York NY 10017-5806

LAIRD, ROY DEAN, political science educator; b. Blue Hill, Nebr., July 15, 1925. B.A. in Biology, Hastings Coll., 1947; M.A. in Polit. Sci, U. Nebr., 1952; postgrad., U. Glasgow, Scotland, 1952-53; Ph.D., U. Wash., 1956. Research analyst CIA, Washington, 1956-57; asst. prof. polit. sci. U. Kans., Lawrence, 1957-62; asso. prof. U. Kans., 1962-66, prof. polit. sci. and Soviet and Eastern European area studies, 1966-90, prof. emeritus, 1990—; cons. Spl. Ops. Research Office, Washington, 1960; guest researcher Inst. for Study of USSR, Munich, W. Ger., 1963-64; founder Internat. Conf. on Soviet and East European Agriculture, 1962. Author: Collective Farming in Russia, 1958, (with Betty A. Laird) Soviet Communism and Agrarian Revolution, 1958, The Soviet Paradigm: An Experiment in Creating a Monohierarchial Polity, 1970, To Live Long Enough: The Memoirs of Naum Jasny, Scientific Analysis, 1976; editor: (with Betty A. Laird) Soviet Agricultural and Peasant Affairs, 1963, The Future of Agriculture in the Soviet Union and Eastern Europe, 1977, (with Ronald A. Francisco and Betty A. Laird) The Political Economy of Collectivized Agriculture, 1979; author: (with Ronald A. Francisco and Betty A. Laird) The Politburo: Demographic Trend, Gorbachev and the Future, 1986, A Soviet Lexicon: Important Terms Concepts and Phrases, 1988, The Soviet Legacy, 1993; contbr. chpts. to books, articles to profl. jours. Rockefeller Found. fellow, 1963-64; NSF grantee, 1966, 67-68; NDEA-Fulbright Hays fellow, 1967; NASA grantee, 1971-72. Mem. AAUP, Am. Assn. Advancement of Slavic Studies, Cen. Slavic Assn., Conf. Soviet Agrl. and Peasant Studies (founder), Am. Polit. Sic. Assn., Western Slavic Studies Assn., Western Slavic Conf. (v.p. 1975-76), Kans. Polit. Sci. Assn., Midwest Conf. Slavic Studies, Midwest Polit. Sci. Assn. Office: U Kans Dept Polit Sci Blake Hall Lawrence KS 66045

LAIRD, WALTER JONES, JR., investment professional; b. Phila., June 15, 1926; s. Walter Jones and Rebecca (Sedberry) L.; m. Antonia Valerie Bissell, Nov. 24, 1951; children: David E., William Ian, Philip L., Walter J. III, Emily B., Stephen P. BS, Princeton U., 1948; MSCE, M.I.T., 1950. Mgr. bldg. product sales E.I. duPont de Nemours, Wilmington, Del., 1951-68; exec. v.p. Laird, Bissell and Meeds, Wilmington, 1968-73; sr. v.p. Dean Witter Reynolds, Wilmington, 1973—; bd. dirs. Del. Trust Co., Wilmington, Meridian Asset Mgmt., Wentz Corp., Sinkler Corp. Trustee Winterthur Mus. and Gardens, 1969—, chmn., 1988-94, chmn. emeritus, 1994—; trustee St. Andrews Sch., Middletown, Del., 1967-92. Mem. Fin. Analysts Fedn., Wilmington Club (bd. govs. 1978—), Wilmington Country Club (v.p. 1995—), Ocean Forest Golf Club, Grand Senechal Chevaliers du Tastevin, Soc. Colonial Wars (gov. 1993—). Avocations: golf, skiing. Home: 1202 Stockford Rd Chadds Ford PA 19317-9349 Office: Dean Witter Reynolds Inc PO Box 749 Wilmington DE 19899-0749

LAIRD, WILBUR DAVID, JR., librarian; b. Kansas City, Mo., Mar. 15, 1937; s. Wilbur David and Alma Blanche (Turner) L.; children: Wendy, Cynthia, Brian Andrew, David Alexander; m. Helen M. Ingram, July 12, 1984. Student, U. Wichita, 1959-60; BA, UCLA, 1965, MLS, 1966. Reference libr. U. Calif., Davis, 1966-67; acquisitions libr. U. Utah, 1967-70, asst. dir. for tech. svcs., 1970-71, assoc. dir., 1971-72; univ. libr. U. Ariz., Tucson, 1972-90; pres. Books West S.W., Tucson, 1990—. Author: Hopi Bibliography, 1977; editor: Books of the Southwest, 1977—. Bd. dirs. Westerners Internat., 1974-87, Tucson Civic Ballet, 1975-76, S.W. Pks. and Mon. Assn., 1993—. With USN, 1955-59. Mem. ALA, Ariz. State Libr. Assn. (pres. 1978-79), Western History Assn., Western Lit. Assn., Guild Ariz. Antiquarian Booksellers. Office: Books West Southwest Inc 14 Whitman Ct Irvine CA 92715

LAIRD, WILLIAM EVERETTE, JR., economics educator, administrator; b. Hattiesburg, Miss., Feb. 4, 1934; s. William Everette and Mildred Alva (Howard) L.; m. Doris Anne Marley, Mar. 13, 1964; children: William Everette III, Andrew Marley, Glen Howard. B.S., Stetson U., 1956; M.A., George Washington U., 1958; Ph.D., U. Va., 1962. Asst. prof. Fla. State U., Tallahassee, 1960-66, assoc. prof., 1966-71, prof., 1971—; chmn. dept. econs. Fla State U., Tallahassee, 1974—. Contbr. articles to profl. jours. DuPont fellow, 1959-60; recipient awards Fla. State U. Grad. Research Council, 1965, 66, Faculty Devel. awards Fla. State U., 1971. Mem. Am. Econs. Assn., So. Econ. Assn. Democrat. Methodist. Clubs: Magna Charta Barons, Jamestowne Soc., St. Andrew Soc., Order of First Families of Va. Home: 1125 Mercer Dr Tallahassee FL 32312-2833 Office: Fla State U Dept Econs Tallahassee FL 32306

LAIRES, FERNANDO, concert piano educator; b. Lisbon, Portugal, Jan. 3, 1925; came to U.S., 1956; s. Joaquim Augusto and Clementina (Belfo) L.; m. Nelita True, Dec. 24, 1971. Artist diploma, Nat. Conservatory Music, Lisbon, 1945. Prof. piano Nat. Conservatory Music, Lisbon, 1949-56; asst. prof. U. Tex., Austin, 1956-61; artist-in-residence, prof. piano Okla. Coll. Liberal Arts, Chickasha, 1961-68; artist-in-residence, chmn. piano dept. Interlochen (Mich.) Arts Acad., Interlochen, 1968-72; prof. piano Peabody Conservatory, Balt., 1972-87; adj. prof. piano Cath. U. Am., Washington, 1978—; artist faculty Eastman Sch. Music, Rochester, N.Y., 1992-95; permanent guest prof. piano performance Shenyang (People's Republic of China) Conservatory of Music, 1989—; juror Tchaikowsky Internat. Piano Competition, Moscow, 1982, Van Cliburn Internat. Piano Competition, Ft. Worth, 1973, Gina Bachauer Internat. Piano Competition, Salt Lake City, 1978, 80, U. Md. Internat. Piano Competition, College Park, 1975, 77, 86, dir. U. Md. Internat. Piano Festival, 1979-81. Performed in cycle the 32 piano sonatas of Beethoven, 1944; dir.-founder 20-record Anthology Portuguese classical music, 1972-82; co-founder Pro-Arte Concert Soc., Portugal, 1949, The Am. Liszt Soc., 1964; contbr. articles to Clavier, The Piano Quar., Am. Music Tchr. Decorated comdr. Order of Price Henry the Navigator (Portugal); recipient Beethoven medal Harriet Cohen Internat. Music Awards, London, 1956, Franz Liszt medal Liszt Soc. Hungary, Budapest, 1984, Liszt medal for excellence Am. Liszt Soc., Inc., 1985, Liszt Commemorative medal Hungarian People's Republic, 1986. Mem. European Piano Tchrs. Assn., Am. Liszt Soc., Inc. (pres. 1976-85, 89—), Music Tchrs. Nat. Assn., Am. Liszt Soc. (pres.). Avocations: travel, reading, writing. Home: 210 Devonshire Dr Rochester NY 14625-1905

LAITIN, DAVID DENNIS, political science educator; b. Bklyn., June 4, 1945; s. Daniel and Frances (Blumenkranz) L.; m. Delia Fortune; children: Marc Oliver, Anna Elizabeth. BA, Swarthmore (Pa.) Coll., 1967; PhD, U. Calif., Berkeley, 1974. Instr. Nat. Tchr. Edn. Ctr., Afgoy, Somalia, 1969; master Grenada Boys' Secondary Sch., West Indies, 1970-71; asst. prof. dept. polit. sci. U. Calif.-San Diego, La Jolla, 1975-79, prof., 1984-87, chmn., 1986-87; reader dept. polit. sci. U. Ife, Nigeria, 1979-80; prof. polit. sci., dir. Wilder House Ctr. for Study Politics, History and Culture U. Chgo., 1987—, William R. Kenan, Jr. prof., 1992—; expert witness fgn. affairs subcom. U.S. Ho. Reps., 1981. Author: Politics, Language and Thought: The Somali Expeirience, 1966, Hegemony and Culture: Politics and Religious Change Among the Yoruba, 1986, Somalia: A Nation in Search of a State, 1987, Language Repertoires and State Construction in Africa, 1992. Fellow NEH, 1979-80, Howard Found., 1984-85, German Marshall Fund, 1984-85; co-prin. investigator award NSF, 1993-95. Mem. Am. Polit. Sci. Assn., Am. Acad. Arts and Scis. Office: U Chgo Dept Of Polit Sci Chicago IL 60637

LAITIN, JOSEPH, journalist, former government spokesman and public relations consultant; b. Bklyn., Oct. 2, 1914; s. Harry and Irene (Lubetkin) L.; m. Christine Henriette Houdayer (dec. Apr. 5, 1995), Apr. 26, 1961; children: Sigrid, Peter. Corr. United Press, Washington, 1941-45; fgn. corr. Reuters, Far East, Europe, Latin Am., 1945-50; chief corr. Research Inst. Am., Washington, 1950-52; freelance writer and broadcaster Hollywood, Calif., 1952-63; asst. to dir. Bur. of Budget, Washington, 1963-64; dep. press sec. to Pres. The White House, Washington, 1965-66; asst. to dir. for pub. affairs Office Mgmt. and Budget, Washington, 1966-74; asst. sec. pub. affairs Dept. Def., Washington, 1974-75; asst. adminstr. FAA, Washington, 1975-77; asst. sec. treasury U.S. Dept. Treasury, Washington, 1977-81; pvt. cons. govt. and pub. rels. Washington; advisor Hill & Knowlton, 1981-85; ombudsman Washington Post, 1986-88; sr. cons. Fleishman-Hillard, Inc., 1989-93; instr. Art Ctr. Sch. L.A., 1952-63, George Washington U., Washington, 1987; cons. Commn. on Selective Svc., 1966-67, Nat. Commn. on Causes and Prevention of Violence, 1968-70, Presdl. Commn. on Campus Unrest, 1970, Nat. Commn. on Exec., Legis. and Jud. Salaries, 1989, Paul Volcker Commn. on Pub. Svc., 1988-89; fellow media studies project Woodrow Wilson Ctr., 1990; mem. regional selection com. White House Fellows Program, 1994—. Recipient Calif. State Fair award for best radio documentary CBS The Changing Face of Hollywood, 1957; Disting. Public Service medal Dept. Def., 1975.

LAITNER, BILL, reporter. Health and fitness reporter Detroit Free Press. Office: Detroit Free Press Inc. 321 W Lafayette Blvd Detroit MI 48226-2705

LAITONE, EDMUND VICTOR, mechanical engineer; b. San Francisco, Sept. 6, 1915; s. Victor S. L.; m. Dorothy Bishop, Sept. 1, 1951; children: Victoria, Jonathan A. BSME, U. Calif., Berkeley, 1938; PhD in Applied Mechanics, Stanford U., 1960. Aero. engr. Nat. Adv. Com. for Aeros., Langley Field, Va., 1938-45; sect. head, flight engr. Cornell Aero. Lab., Buffalo, 1945-47; prof. U. Calif., Berkeley, 1947—; cons. aero. engr. Hughes Aircraft & Douglas Aircraft, 1948-78; U.S. acad. rep. to flight mechanics AGARD/NATO, 1984-88; chmn. engring. dept. U. Calif. Extension, Berkeley, 1979—. Author: Surface Waves, 1960; author, editor: Integrated Design of Advanced Fighter Aircraft, 1987; contbr. articles to Jour. Aero. Scis., Aircraft and Math. Jour. Named Miller Rsch. prof., 1960, U.S. Exch. prof., Moscow, 1964; vis. fellow Balliol Coll., 1968; vis. prof. Northwestern Poly. Inst., Xian, China, 1980. Fellow AIAA (San Francisco region chmn. 1960-61, assoc. fellow 1964-88); mem. Am. Math Soc., Am. Soc. for Engring. Edn. Achievements include discovery of effect of acceleration on longitudinal dynamic stability of a missile; nonlinear dynamic stability of space vehicles entering or leaving atmosphere; higher approximations to nonlinear water waves. Home: 6915 Wilson Way El Cerrito CA 94530-1853 Office: U of Calif Dept Mech Engring Berkeley CA 94720

LAJEUNESSE, MARCEL, university administrator, educator; b. Mont-Laurier, Que., Can., June 28, 1942; s. Achille and Gertrude (Grenier) L.; m. Louise Beauregard, Dec. 20, 1975; 1 child, Anne. BA, U. Laval, Que., Can., 1964; B. Bibliotheconomie, U. de Montreal, Que., Can., 1964, Licence ès Lettres, 1967, MA, 1968; PhD, U. Ottawa, Can., 1977. Prof. Coll. L'Outaouais, Hull, 1968-70, U. de Montreal, 1970—; prof., dir. Grad. Sch. Libr. and Info. Sci., 1987-94, assoc. dean for planning Faculty of Arts and Scis., 1994—; cons. Aupelf UREF, IDRC, Can. Internat. Devel. Agy., Agence de cooperation culturelle et technique, UNESCO. Author 9 books; contbr. numerous articles to profl. and scholarly jours. Mem. Conseil de la Langue Française, Que., 1987-91.—. Mem. Assn. Libr. and Info. Sci. Edn., Assn. Internat. des Écoles de Scis. de l'Information, Assn. pour l'Avancement des Scis. et des Techniques de la Documentation, Corp. des Bibliothécaires professionnels de Québec, Inst. French Am. History, Bibliog. Soc. Can. Home: 126 Dobie, Mont-Royal, PQ Canada H3P 1S4 Office: FAS-Direction, U de Montreal, CP 6128 Succ A, Montreal, PQ Canada H3C 3J7

LAJOIE, ROLAND, army officer; b. Nashua, N.H., Aug. 11, 1936; s. Ernest Joseph and Alice (Bechard) L.; m. Joann Theresa Sinibaldi, Feb. 11, 1961; children: Michelle, Christopher, Renee. BA in Govt., U. N.H., 1958; MA in History, U. Colo., 1971; diploma, Army Command & Staff Coll., 1973, U.S. Army War Coll., 1981. Commd. 2d lt. U.S. Army, 1958, advanced through grades to maj. gen., 1991; served as asst. army attache Am. Embassy, Moscow, 1973-76; commandant U.S. Army Russian Inst., Garmisch, Fed. Republic Germany, 1976-79; bn. comdr. 1st Psychol. Ops. Bn., Ft. Bragg, N.C., 1979-80; rsch. fellow U.S. Army War Coll., Carlisle, Pa., 1980-81, Harvard U., Cambridge, Mass., 1980-81; army attache Am. Embassy, Moscow, 1981-83; chief of mission U.S. Mil. Liaison Mission, Berlin, Potsdam, German Dem. Republic, 1983-86; def. and army attache Am. Embassy, Paris, 1986-88; dir. U.S. On-Site Inspection Agy., 1988-91; dep. dir. internat. negotiations J5 The Joint Staff, Washington, 1991-92; assoc. dep. dir. for ops./mil. affairs CIA, Washington, 1992-94, dep. asst. to sec. of def., 1994—. Decorated Nat. Intel Disting. Svc. medal, Def. Disting. Svc. medal, Bronze Star, Legion of Merit, Def. Meritorious Svc., Def. Superior Svc., Nat. Order Merit (France). Mem. VFW, Retired Officer Assn. Avocations: tennis, skiing. Home: 3727 Riverwood Rd Alexandria VA 22309-2724

LAJTHA, ABEL, biochemist; b. Budapest, Hungary, Sept. 22, 1922; naturalized; married; 2 children. PhD in Chemistry, Eotvos Lorand U., Budapest, 1945; MD (hon.), U. Padua. Asst. prof. biochemistry Eotvos Lorand U., 1945-47; asst. prof. Inst. Muscle Rsch., Mass., 1949-50; sr. rsch. scientist N.Y. State Psychiat. Inst., 1950-57, assoc. rsch. scientist, 1957-62, prin. rsch. scientist, 1962-66; dir. N.Y. State Rsch. Inst. Neurochemistry, 1966—; prof. exptl. psychiatry Sch. Medicine NYU, 1971—; asst. prof. Coll. Physicians & Surgeons, Columbia U., 1956-69. Zoology Station fellow Italy, 1947-48, Rsch. fellow Royal Inst. Great Britain, 1948-49. Mem. Armenian, Hungarian, Slovenian Acad. Sci., Internat. Brain Rsch. Orgn., Am. Soc. Biol. Chemists, Am. Acad. Neurology, Am. Coll. Neuropsychopharmacology, Internat. Soc. Neurochemistry (pres.), Am. Chem. Soc., Am. Soc. Neurochemistry (pres.). Achievements include rsch. in neurochemistry, amino acid and protein metabolism of the brain and the brain barrier system. Office: Ctr Neurochem Nathan S Kline Inst Psy Rsc Orangeburg NY 10962

LAKAH, JACQUELINE RABBAT, political scientist, educator; b. Cairo, Apr. 14, 1933; came to U.S., 1969, naturalized, 1975; d. Victor Boutros and Alice (Mounayer) Rabbat; m. Antoine K. Lakah, Apr. 8, 1951; children: Micheline, Mireille, Caroline. BA, Am. U. Beirut, 1968; MPh, Columbia U., 1974, cert. Mid. East Inst., 1975, PhD, 1978. Assoc. prof. polit. sci. and world affairs Fashion Inst. Tech., N.Y.C., 1978—, asst. chairperson social scis. dept., 1989-95, chairperson social scis. dept., 1995—; asst. prof. grad. faculty polit. sci. Columbia U., N.Y.C., summer 1979, vis. scholar, 1982-83, also mem. seminar on Mid. East; guest faculty Sarah Lawrence Coll., 1981-82; cons. on Mid. East; faculty rsch. fellow SUNY, summer 1982. Fellow Columbia Faculty, 1970-73, NDEA Title IV, 1971-72; Mid. East Inst. scholar, 1976; Rockefeller Found. scholar, 1967-69. Mem. European Cmty. Studies Assn., Am. Polit. Sci. Assn., Fgn. Policy Assn., Internat. Studies Assn., Internat. Polit. Sci. Assn. Roman Catholic. Home: 41-15 94th St Flushing NY 11373-1745 Office: 7th Ave At 27th St New York NY 10001-5992

LAKATTA, EDWARD GERARD, biomedical researcher; b. Scranton, Pa., May 10, 1944; s. Edward and Pauline Ann (Lucas) L.; m. Loretta Ellen Cantwell, July 27, 1968; children: Edward A., Christiana, Lucas A. BS in Biology, U. Scranton, 1966; MD, Georgetown U., 1970. Intern Strong Meml. Hosp., Rochester, N.Y., 1970-71, asst. resident, 1971-72; clin. assoc. Gerontology Rsch. Ctr. cardiovascular sect. NIH, Nat. Inst. Child Health & Human Devel., Clin. Physiology Br., Balt., 1972-74; asst. in medicine Johns Hopkins Sch. Medicine, Balt., 1973-74; fellow in cardiology Georgetown U. Hosp., Washington, 1974-75; fellow in med. sci. Am. Coll. Physicians for 1975 dept. physiology Univ. Coll., London, 1975-76; fellow in med. sci. dept. cardiac medicine Cardiothoracic Inst., London, 1975-76; chief cardiovascular sect. clin. physiology br. Gerontology Rsch. Ctr., Nat. Inst. Aging NIH, Balt., 1976-85, chief Lab. Cardiovascular Sci., Gerontology Rsch. Ctr., Nat. Inst. Aging, 1985—, acting sci. dir. Nat. Inst. Aging, 1994-95; prof. medicine Johns Hopkins Sch. Medicine, Balt., 1983—; prof. physiology Sch. Medicine U. Md., Balt., 1985—; vis. physician Bayview Med. Ctr., Balt., Md.; mem. ad hoc study sect. on animal model for study of pathogenesis of spl. heart muscle disease NIH, 1981; mem. ad hoc grant proposal reviews and site visit coms. VA and NSF; ad hoc reviewer Am. Jour. Physiology, Can. Jour. Physiology and Pharmacology, Circulation Rsch., Jour. Molecular and Cellular Cardiology, Sci.; mem. search com. for dir. Nat. Heart, Lung and Blood Inst., 1981, Gerontology Rsch. Ctr., 1988; chmn. intramural promotions and tenure review com. Nat. Inst. Aging, 1989-91; cons. in field. Editor for clin. scis. Exptl. Aging Rsch., 1982-89; assoc. editor Jour. Molecular and Cellular Cardiology, 1987—; mem. editorial bd. Jour. Gerontology, Jour. Molecular and Cellular Cardiology, Cardiosci., Current Problems in Geriatrics, Jour. Cardiovascular Electrophysiology; contbr. numerous articles to profl. jours., chpts. to books. Med. dir. USPHS, 1976. Recipient Paul Dudley White award Assn. Mil. Surgeons of U.S., 1992, Achievement in Aging award Allied Signal, 1993; Eli Lilly Med. Sci. fellow Am. Coll. Physicians, 1975. Fellow Am. Physiol. Soc. (cardiovascular sect.), Am. Heart Assn. (coun. basic sci., Cardiovascular B rsch. study com. 1987-89, application task force Mission to Elderly 1989-90, 90-91), Am. Soc. Clin. Investigation, Am. Assn. Physicians, Internat. Soc. for Heart Rsch. (coun.), Biophys. Soc.; mem. Physiol. Soc. (London). Avocation: fine wine and food. Home: 126 Briarcliff Ln Bel Air MD 21014-5553 Office: Nat Inst Aging Lab Cardiovascular Sci Gerontology Rsch Ctr Rm 3D09 Baltimore MD 21224-2780

LAKE, ANTHONY, federal official; married; 3 children. AB magna cum laude, Harvard U., 1961; PhD, Princeton U., 1974. Joined Fgn. Svc., Dept. State, Washington, 1962; U.S. vice consul Fgn. Svc., Dept. State, Saigon, Vietnam, 1963, Hue, Vietnam, 1964-65; spl. asst. to President U.S. for nat. security affairs Fgn. Svc., Dept. State, Washington, 1969-70; dep. policy planning for President U.S. Dept. State, Washington, 1977-81; Five Coll. Prof. Internat. Rels. Mount Holyoke Coll., 1981—; former sr. fgn. policy analyst Clinton-Gore Campaign; asst. to Pres. NSC, Washington, DC, 1993—. Author: The Tar Baby Option: America Toward Southern Rhodesia, 1976, Somoza Falling, 1989; co-author: Our Own Worst Enemy: The Unmaking of American Foreign Policy, 1984; editor: After the Wars, 1990; contbg. editor: Legacy of Vietnam: The War, American Society, and the Future of U.S. Foreign Policy, 1976. Office: Nat Security Coun 1600 Pennsylvania Ave NW Washington DC 20500*

LAKE, CARNELL AUGUSTINO, professional football player; b. Salt Lake City, July 15, 1967. Student, UCLA. Safety Pitts. Steelers, 1989—. Named to Coll. All-Am. 2d Team, Sporting News, 1987, NFL Pro Bowl Team, 1994. Office: Pitts Steelers 300 Stadium Cir Pittsburgh PA 15212

LAKE, CAROL LEE, anesthesiologist, educator; b. Altoona, Pa., July 14, 1944; d. Samuel Lindsay and Edna Winifred (McMahan) L. BS, Juniata Coll., 1966; MD, Med. Coll. Pa., 1970; postgrad., U. Calif., Irvine. Intern Mercy Hosp., Pitts., 1970-71, resident in anesthesiology, 1971-73; staff anesthesiologist Pitts. Anesthesia Assocs., 1973-75; asst. prof. anesthesiology U. Va., Charlottesville, 1975-80, assoc. prof., 1980-89, prof. anesthesiology, 1989-94; prof. anesthesiology U. Calif., Davis, 1994—, 1996—; sr. assoc. examiner Am. Bd. Anesthesiology, Hartford, Conn., 1981—. Author: Cardiovascular Anesthesia, 1985; editor: Pediatric Cardiac Anesthesia, 1988, 2d edit., 1993; Clinical Monitoring, 1990, 2d edit., 1994; co-editor: Blood: Hemostasis, Transfusion and Alternatives in the Perioperative Period, 1995; editor Advances in Anesthesia, 1993—. Fellow Am. Coll. Cardiology; mem. Assn. Cardiac Anesthesiologists (pres. 1987-88), Soc. Cardiovascular Anesthesiologists (bd. dirs. 1988-92), Assn. Univ. Anesthesiologists, Alpha Omega Alpha. Presbyterian. Avocations: music, entomology, gardening.

LAKE, DAVID S., publisher, lawyer; b. Youngstown, Ohio, July 17, 1938; s. Frank and Charlotte (Stahl) L.; m. Sandra J. Levin, Dec. 18, 1960 (div. Aug. 14, 1987); children: Joshua Seth, Jonathan Daniel. B.A. in Math, Youngstown State U., 1960; J.D. cum laude, Cleve. State U., 1965. Bar: Ohio 1965, D.C. 1970, U.S. Supreme Ct. 1969. Gen. counsel World Pub. Co., Cleve., 1965-68; dir. devel. Cath. U. Am., Washington, 1968-69; v.p., gen. counsel Microform Pub. Corp., Washington, 1969-70; dir. spl. projects Library Resources, Inc., Chgo., 1970-72; gen. mgr., partner Nat. Textbook Co., Skokie, Ill., 1972-76; pres. David S. Lake Pubs., Belmont, Calif., 1976-89, pres, owner, 1984-89; owner Lake Pub. Co., Belmont, 1989—. Contbr. to: Cleve. Marshall Law Rev, 1964. Served with USMC, 1960-62. Jewish. Office: Lake Pub Co 500 Harbor Blvd Belmont CA 94002-4021

LAKE, JOSEPH EDWARD, ambassador; b. Jacksonville, Tex., Oct. 18, 1941; s. Lloyd Euel and Marion Marie (Allen) L.; m. Sarah Ann Bryant (div.); children: Joseph Edward, Mary Elizabeth; m. Jo Ann Kessler, June 12, 1971; 1 child, Michael Allen. BA summa cum laude, Tex. Christian U., 1962, MA, 1967. Second sec. U.S. Embassy, Lagos, Nigeria, 1977-78; prin. officer and consul U.S. Consulate, Kaduna, Nigeria, 1978-81; with Fgn. Svc. Inst., Washington, 1981-82; first sec. U.S. Embassy, Sofia, Bulgaria, 1982-84, charge d'affaires, 1984, counselor, dep. chief mission, 1984-85; dep. dir. regional affairs , bur. East Asian and Pacific Affairs Dept. State, 1985-86; advisor U.S. delegation 41st UN Gen. Assembly, 1986; dir. ops. ctr. Dept. State, Washington, 1987-90; amb. to Rep. of Mongolia, Ulaanbaatar, 1990-93, Rep. of Albania, Tirana, 1994-96; dep. asst. sec. of state for info. mgmt. Dept. State, Washington, 1996—. Contbr. articles to profl. jours. Mem. Am. Fgn. Svc. Assn. Home: PO Box 2523 Merrifield VA 22116-2523 Office: Dept of State Tirana A/IM Washington DC 20520

LAKE, KATHLEEN C., lawyer; b. San Antonio, Jan. 11, 1955; d. Herschel Taliaferro and Virginia Mae (Hylton) Cooper; m. Randall Brent Lake, Apr. 9, 1977; 1 child, Ethan Taliaferro. AB magna cum laude in Polit. Sci. with high honors, Middlebury Coll., 1977; JD with high honors, U. Tex., 1980. Bar: Tex. 1980, U.S. Ct. Appeals (5th cir.) 1981, U.S. Ct. Appeals (D.C. and 3d cirs.) 1984. Assoc. atty. Vinson & Elkins, Houston, 1980-88; ptnr. Vinson & Elkins, LLP, Houston, 1989—. Mem. pack com., den leader Sam Houston Area Coun.-Golden Arrow dist. Boys Scouts Am., 1993— . Recipient Unit Svc. award Sam Houston Area Coun.-Golden Arrow dist. Boy Scouts Am. Fellow Tex. Bar Found., Houston Bar Found.; mem. ABA, Fed. Energy Bar Assn., State Bar Tex., Tex. Law Rev. Assn. (life), Houston Bar Assn., Middlebury Coll. Alumni Assn. (com. mem. 1980—), Phi Beta Kappa, Phi Kappa Phi, Order of the Coif. Office: Vinson & Elkins LLP 2300 First City Twr 1001 Fannin St Houston TX 77002-6760

LAKE, KEVIN BRUCE, medical association administrator; b. Seattle, Jan. 25, 1937; s. Winston Richard and Vera Emma (Davis) L.; m. Suzanne Roto, Oct. 25, 1986; children from previous marriage: Laura, Kendrick, Wesley. BS, Portland State U., 1960; MD, U. Oreg., 1964. Intern, Marion County Gen. Hosp. and Ind. Med. Center, Indpls., 1964-65; resident U. Oreg. Hosps. and Clinics, 1968-70; fellow in infectious and pulmonary diseases, 1970-71; fellow in pulmonary diseases U. So. Calif., 1971-72, instr. medicine, 1972-75, asst. clin. prof., 1975-79, assoc. clin. prof., 1979-84, clin. prof., 1986—; dir. med. edn. and research La Vina Hosp., 1972-75; dir. respiratory therapy Methodist Hosp., Arcadia, Calif., 1975—; mem. staff Los Angeles County/U. So. Calif. Med. Center, Santa Teresita Hosp., Duarte, Calif., Huntington Meml. Hosp., Pasadena, Calif.; attending physician, mem. med. adv. bd. Foothill Free Clinic, Pasadena. Mem. exec. com. Profl. Staff Assn. U. So. Calif. Sch. Medicine; 2d v.p. bd. mgmt. Palm St. br. YMCA, Pasadena, 1974, 1st v.p., 1975, chmn., 1976-78, met. bd. dirs., 1976-84; bd. dirs. Mendenhall Ministries, La Vie Holistic Ministries, Hospice of Pasadena, Hastings Found. co-pres. PTA, Allendale Grade Sch., Pasadena, 1975-76; deacon Pasadena Covenant Ch., 1976-79. Served to lt. U.S. Navy, 1965-68. NIH grantee, 1971-72. Fellow ACP, Am. Coll. Chest Physicians; mem. Am. Thoracic Soc., Calif. Thoracic Soc., Oreg. Thoracic Soc., Trudeau Soc., Am. Soc. Microbiology, N.Y. Acad. Scis., Calif. Med. Assn., Los Angeles County Med. Assn. Democrat. Contbr. articles to profl. jours. Home: 875 S Madison Ave Pasadena CA 91106-4404 Office: 50 Alesandro Pl Ste 330 Pasadena CA 91105-3149

LAKE, RUTH ELAINE, optics technician; b. San Jose, Calif., June 18, 1954; d. Charles Gregory and Beverly June (Beaudoin) Attarian; children: Michael, Christopehr (dec.). Student, Calif. State U., Fresno; cert. with honors, San Joaquin Valley Coll., 1988. Optical lab. technician Peggy's Optical Svc., Fresno; instr. in dispensing optics San Joaquin Valley Coll., Fresno; dispensing optician Frame-N-Lens, Clovis, Calif. Mem. CSCLA, OAA, FNAO, OAA, RSLD. Home: 568 W San Jose Ave Clovis CA 93612-2338

LAKE, SIMEON TIMOTHY, III, federal judge; b. Chgo., July 4, 1944; s. Simeon T. Jr. and Helen (Hupka) L.; m. Carol Illig, Dec. 30, 1970; children: Simeon Timothy IV, Justin Carl. BA, Tex. A&M, 1966; JD, U. Tex., 1969. Bar: Tex. 1969, U.S. Dist. Ct. (so. dist.) Tex. 1969, U.S. Ct. Appeals (5th cir.) 1969, U.S. Supreme Ct. 1976, U.S. Ct. Appeals (3d cir.) 1981, U.S. Dist. Ct. (no. dist.) Tex. 1983. From assoc. to ptnr. Fulbright & Jaworski, Houston, 1969-70, 72-88; judge U.S. Dist. Ct. (so. dist.) Tex., Houston, 1988—. Past editor Houston Lawyer. Served to capt. U.S. Army., 1970-71. Fellow Tex. Bar Assn., Houston Bar Assn., State Bar Tex., Am. Law Inst. Office: US Dist Ct 9535 US Courthouse 515 Rusk Ave Houston TX 77002

LAKE, WESLEY WAYNE, JR., internist, allergist; b. New Orleans, Oct. 11, 1937; s. Wesley Wayne and Mary McGehee (Snowden) L.; m. Abby F. Arnold, Aug. 1959 (div. 1959); children: Courtenay B., Corinne A., Jane S. AB in Chemistry, Princeton U., 1959; MD, Tulane U., 1963. Diplomate Am. Bd. Internal Medicine, Am. Bd. Allergy and Immunology. Intern Charity Hosp. of La., New Orleans, 1963-64, resident internal medicine, 1966-69; NIH fellow allergy and immunology La. State U. Med. Ctr., 1969-70; instr. dept. medicine Tulane U., New Orleans, 1967-69; fellow dept. medicine La. State U., New Orleans, 1969-70, instr. dept. medicine, 1970-73, asst. clin. prof. medicine, 1973-77; chief allergy clinic La. State U. Svc. Charity Hosp. La., New Orleans, 1970-77; assoc. clin. prof. medicine Tulane U., New Orleans, 1978—; temp. staff positions various hosps., 1963-70, including Baton Rouge Gen. Hosp., Our Lady of the Lake Hosp., Glenwood Hosp., St. Francis Hosp., Monroe, La., Lallie Kemp Charity Hosp., Independence, La., Huey P. Long Hosp., Pineville, La.; gen. med. officer outpatient clinic Hunter AFB, Savannah, Ga., 1964-65, gen. med. officer internal medicine svc., 1965-66; cons. physician Seventh Ward Gen. Hosp., Hammond, La., 1971-77, Slidell (La.) Meml. Hosp., 1971-89, St. Tammany Parish Hosp., Covington, La., 1977-85; cons. physician East Jefferson Hosp., Metairie, La., 1971-77, staff physician, 1990—; asst. vis. physician Charity Hosp. New Orleans, 1970-75, staff physician, 1975-77, vis. phys. Tulane divsn., 1979—; assoc. physician So. Bapt. Hosp., New Orleans, 1970-75, staff physician, 1975—, chmn. dept. medicine, chmn. internal medicine com., 1982-84, chmn. pharmacy and therapeutics, 1980-82, mem. investigative rev. com., 1984-85, mem. internat. medicine quality assurance com., 1989-94; staff physician Kenner (La.) Regional Med. Ctr. (formerly St. Jude Med. Ctr.), 1985—, chmn. quality assurance com., 1987-89. Author: (with others) Infiltrative Hypersensitivity Chest Diseases, 1975; contbr. articles to profl. jours. including Jour. Immunology, Internat. Archives Allergy and Applied Immunology, Jour. Allergy and Clin. Immunology; also chpts. in books concerning chest diseases. Fellow ACP, Am. Coll. Allergy, Sigma Xi; mem. New Orleans Acad. Internal Medicine, Musser-Burch Soc., S.E. Allergy Soc., La. Allergy Soc. (sec. 1975-76, v.p. 1976-77, pres. 1977-78). Republican. Episcopalian. Home: 1308 Bordeaux St New Orleans LA 70115 Office: 4224 Houma Blvd Ste 250 Metairie LA 70006

LAKE, WILLIAM THOMAS, financial consultant; b. Ocean City, N.J., June 14, 1910; s. William Carson and Marie Cecelia (Kaiser) L.; m. V. Blair Torbert, Nov. 25, 1933 (div.); children: Donna Blair Lake Wright, Deborah Caren Lake Coates, Darelle Dee Lake Riabov, Carson Thomas; m. Dorothy Howell Caddelle, Mar. 1, 1968; 1 stepdau., Lynne E. Caddelle (Mrs. W. Dean Boecher). Grad., Rider Coll., Trenton, N.J., 1930. C.P.A., N.J., Pa., Mich., Calif., Colo., N.Y. Pub. acct. Lybrand Ross Bros. and Montgomery, Phila., 1932-39; controller Keystone Portland Cement Co., Phila., 1939-42; controller, treas. narrow fabric div. Burlington Mills, Allentown, Pa., 1946-48; controller Rouge plants Ford Motor Co., 1948-53; comptroller Curtiss Wright Corp., Wood Ridge, 1953-61, Gen. Dynamics Corp., 1961-68; v.p. finance aerospace and systems group Rockwell Internat., 1968-70; fin. cons., 1970—; pres. Talmud Internat. Mgmt. Co., Peripheral Engring. Inc.; treas. Talmud Internat. Ltd. Served to comdr. USNR, World War II; supply officer 4th Naval Dist., Naval Ordnance Plant York, Pa. Mem. Am. Inst. Profl. Cons. (charter), Fin. Execs. Inst. (life), AICPA (50 year hon. mem. award), N.J., Calif., Colo., Pa., Mich., N.Y. socs. CPAs, Am. Ordnance Assn., Navy League U.S. Presbyterian. Clubs: Masons (N.Y.C.) (32 deg.); Shriners; Economic (N.Y.C.), Engineers (N.Y.C.); Pinehurst Country. Home: 9 Oakwood Dr Queensbury NY 12804-1327

LAKIER, NANCY S., health care consultant; b. Ft. Madison, Iowa, Nov. 17, 1952; d. Bernard A. and Ruth Mary (Dyer) Mehmert; m. Richard Stephen Lakier, Nov. 12, 1983; 1 child, Andrea. BSN, Creighton U., 1975; MBA, U. Nebr., 1985. Staff and mid. mgmt. positions various orgns., 1975-83; v.p. nursing Children's Hosp., Omaha, 1983-86, Ft. Hamilton (Ohio)-Hughes, 1986-88, San Bernardino (Calif.) Community Hosp., 1988-90; assoc. adminstr. Scripps Meml. Hosp., La Jolla, Calif., 1990-96; pres. InnoVia Health, La Jolla, 1996—. Case Mgmt. and Critical Path Documentation System, 1991, CareTracs, 1991. Pres. alumni adv. bd. dirs. Creighton U., Omaha, 1984-88. Recipient One-Calif. Nursing Leadership award. Mem. Am. Orgn. Nurse Execs., Calif. Nurses Assn. (chpt. pres.), VHA Nat. Nursing Adv. Bd. Avocations: walking, hiking, reading, gardening. Office: InnoVia Health Ste 320 9838 Genesee La Jolla CA 92037

LAKIN, EDWIN A., retail executive; b. 1923. BA, Bklyn. Coll., 1946; student, NYU, 1946-48. CPA. Pvt. practice, 1948-50; with Julius Lefkowitz & Co., CPAs, N.Y.C., 1950-56; with Boscov's Department Store, Reading, Pa., 1956—, now pres. Office: Boscov's Department Store 4500 Perkiomen Ave Reading PA 19606-3202*

LAKIN, JAMES DENNIS, allergist, immunologist, director; b. Harvey, Ill., Oct. 4, 1945; s. Ora Austin and Annie Pitranella (Johnson) L.; m. Sally A. Stuteville, July 22, 1972; children: Margaret K., Matthew A. PhD, Northwestern U., 1968, MD, 1969; MBA in Med. Group Mgmt., U. St. Thomas, 1996. Diplomate Am. Bd. Internal Medicine, Am. Bd. Allergy and Immunology. Dir. allergy rsch. Naval Med. Rsch. Inst., Bethesda, Md., 1974-76; clin. prof. U. Okla., Oklahoma City, 1976-89; dir. lab., chmn. allergy and immunology dept. Oxboro Clinics, Bloomington, Minn., 1989—; dir. Fairview Allergy and Asthma Svcs., Bloomington, 1995—; bd. dirs. Okla. Med. Rsch. Found., Oklahoma City, 1980-89; regional cons. Diver Alert Network, Duke U., Chapel Hill, N.C., 1987—; cert. diving med. officer NOAA, 1988. Co-author: Allergic Diseases, 1971, 3d edit., 1986; contbr. articles, revs. to profl. publs. Councilperson Our Lord's Luth. Ch., Oklahoma City, 1978-88, Faith Luth. Ch., Lakeville, Minn., 1990-91. Lt. comdr. USN, 1970-76. Fellow ACP, Am. Acad. allergy and Immunology, Am. Coll. Chest Physicians; mem. Am. Assn. Immunologists, Med. Group Mgmt. Assn., Am. Coll. Physician Execs. Achievements include research in characterization of the immunoglobulin system of the rhesus monkey, alterations in allergic reactivity during immunosuppression. Office: Oxboro Clinic 600 W 98th St Bloomington MN 55420-4773

LAKRITZ, ISAAC, management consultant; b. Milw., June 11, 1952; s. Jeffrey and Deborah (Margolis) L.; m. Lea Winninger, May 22, 1982; children: Eli, Jacob, Atara. BA, U. Wis., Milw., 1973, MA, 1974. Cert. secondary sch. tchr. Coordinator Jewish Student Services Hillel, Milw., 1972-74; analyst Israel Ministry Social Welfare, Jerusalem, 1975-76; exec. dir. Jewish Nat. Fund Wis., Milw., 1977; devel. dir. Milw. Jewish Home, 1977-78; asst. dir. N.Y. Assn. for New Americans, N.Y.C., 1978-81; nat. youth dir. Zionist Orgn. Am., N.Y.C., 1981-84; asst. dir. Jacksonville (Fla.) Jewish Fedn., 1984-87, exec. v.p., 1987-90; exec. dir. east cen. region Am. Soc. for Technion, Detroit, 1990-95; mgmt. cons., West Bloomfield, Mich., 1995—. Chmn. Israel com. Conf. Jewish Communal Svc., 1982-92. Recipient Top Pub. Rels. award in N.Am. Coun. Jewish Fedn. Mem. Assn. Jewish Community Orgn. Personnel, Phi Kappa Phi. Avocations: opera, stamps, computers. *Our task is to build a more just and compassionate world. With mankind's considerable technical expertise, we have shown that we can accomplish just about anything we really desire. Let us create an environment where that which is right and kind is desirable.*

LAKSHMANAN, T.R., federal agency administrator, geography and environmental engineering educator, writer; m. Lata Chatterjee; children: Srobona, Indira. Corp. v.p. CONSAD Rsch. Corp., Pitts.; sr. analyst, assoc. Alan M. Voorhees Assocs.; prof. geography and environ. engring. Johns Hopkins U., 1973-78; founder., exec. dir. Ctr. for Energy and Environ. Studies Boston U.; first dir. Bur. Transp. Statistics U.S. Dept. Transp., Washington; vis. scholar Netherlands Inst. for Adv. Studies in the Humanities and Social Scis., Internat. Inst. for Applied Systems Analysis, Austria, Cambridge U., U.K., MIT; cons. UN, The World Bank, Japan's EPA, many govts. in Europe and Asia. Author 10 books; contbr. over 60 articles to profl. jours. Recipient James Anderson medal Assn. Am. Geographers. Mem. Clare Hall Coll. Cambridge U. (elected life).. Office: Dept Transp Transp Statistics Bureau 400 7th St SW Washington DC 20590-0001

LAKSHMIKANTHAM, VANGIPURAM, mathematics educator; b. Hyderabad, India, Aug. 8, 1926; came to U.S., 1960, naturalized, 1966; s. Soroja Bukkapatnam, Feb. 22, 1942; children: Sreekantham, Neerada, Nirupama. MA, Osmania U., Hyderabad, 1955, PhD, 1958. Mem. faculty UCLA, 1960-61, Math. Rsch. Ctr., U. Wis., Madison, 1961-62; mem. Rsch. Inst. Advanced Studies, Balt., 1962-63; assoc. prof. U. Alta., Calgary, Can., 1963-64; prof., chmn. dept. math. Marathwada U., Aurangabad, India, 1964-66, U. R.I., Kingston, 1966-73, U. Tex., Arlington, 1973-88; prof., head dept. applied math. Fla. Inst. Tech., Melbourne, 1989—. Author 22 books; founder, editor: Jour. Nonlinear Analysis, Nonlinear World, Nonlinear Times and Digest, Stochastic Analysis and Applications, Mathematical Problems in Engineering; assoc. editor other jours.; contbr. over 250 rsch. articles to profl. publs. Mem. Am. Math. Soc., Indian Math. Soc., Soc. Indsl. and Aplied Math., Nat. Acad. Sci. India, Internat. Fedn. Nonlinear Analysts (founder). Office: Fla Inst Tech Dept Applied Math 150 W University Blvd Melbourne FL 32901-6982

LAKSHMINARAYANA, BUDUGUR, aerospace engineering educator; b. Shimoga, India, Feb. 15, 1935; came to U.S., 1963, naturalized, 1971; m. Saroja Lakshminarayana; children: Anita, Arvind. BME, Mysore U., India, 1958; PhD, U. Liverpool, Eng., 1963, DEng, 1981. Grad. trainee Steel Constrn. Co., Bangalore, India, 1957; asst. mech. engr. Kolar (India) Gold Mining Undertakings, 1958-60; rschr. in mech. engring. U. Liverpool, 1960-63, Leverhulme fellow, 1962-63; vis. asst. prof. aerospace engring. Pa. State U., University Park, 1963-65, asst. prof. aerospace engring., 1965-69, assoc. prof., 1969-74, prof., 1974-85, dir. computational fluid dynamics studies, 1980-87, disting. alumni prof., 1985-86, Evan Pugh prof., 1986—, dir. Ctr. for Gas Turbines and Power, 1994—; vis. fellow scientist Cambridge U., St. John's Coll., Eng., 1971-72; vis. assoc. prof. aeros. and astronautics MIT, 1972; vis. prof. dept. mech. engring. Indian Inst. Sci., 1979; aerospace engr. computational fluid mechanics group NASA Ames Rsch. Ctr., Moffett Field, Calif., 1979; CNRS vis. prof. Laboratoire de Mecanique des Fluides at d'Acoustique, Ecole Centrale de Lyon, France, 1987-88; vis. prof. Tech. U. of Aachen, Germany, 1988; adv. prof. Inst. Thermophysics Chinese Acad. Scis., 1993, Shanghai Jiao Tong U., China, 1993; cons. Pratt & Whitney Aircraft, GE Aircraft Engine Div., Garrett Turbines, Teledyne CAE, Inc.; UN, NATO/AGARD lectr.; Gen. Motors, Rolls Royce, European Space Agy.; mem. NASA adv. group on computational fluid dynamics, 1980; lectr. in field. Author: Fluid Dynamics and Heat Transfer of Turbomachinery, 1995; editor 2 books; contbr. numerous articles on fluid dynamics, turbomachinery, computational fluid dynamics, turbulence modelling and acoustics to profl. publs. Recipient Henry R. Worthington N.Am. tech. award, 1977, sr. prof. Fulbright award, 1988, Arch. T. Colwell merit award Soc. Automotive Engrs., 1992; merit scholar Mysore U., 1953-57; grantee NSF, numerous others. Fellow AIAA (chmn. Ctrl. Pa. chpt. 1970, Pendrey Lit. award 1989, Airbreathing Propulsion award 1994), ASME (Freeman Scholar award 1990, Fluids Engring. award 1996). Office: Pa State U Coll Engring 153 Hammond Bldg University Park PA 16802-1400

LAL, DEVENDRA, nuclear geophysics educator; b. Varanasi, India, Feb. 14, 1929; s. Radhe Krishna and Sita Devi (Gupta) L.; m. Aruna Damany, May 17, 1955 (dec. July 1993). BS, Banaras Hindu U., Varanasi, 1947, MS, 1949, DSc (hon. causa), 1984; PhD, Bombay U., 1960. Research student Tata Inst. of Fundamental Research, Bombay, 1949-60, research fellow, fellow, assoc. prof., 1960-63, prof., 1963-70, sr. prof., 1970-72; dir. Phys. Research Lab., Ahmedabad, India, 1972-83; sr. prof. Phys. Research Lab., Ahmedabad, 1983-89; vis. prof. UCLA, 1965-66, 83-84; prof. Scripps Instn. Oceanography, La Jolla, Calif., 1967—; fellow Phys. Rsch. Lab. Ahmedabad, 1989—. Editor: Early Solar System Processes and the Present Solar System, 1980, Biogeochemistry of the Arabian Sea, 1995. Recipient K.S. Krishnan Gold medal Indian Geophys. Union, 1965, S.S. Bhatnagar award for Physics, Govt. of India, 1971, award for Excellence in Sci. and Tech., Gedn. of Indian Chamber Com., 1974, Pandit Jawaharlal Nehru award for Scis., 1986, Group Achievement award NASA, 1986. Fellow Royal Soc. London, Indian Nat. Sci. Acad., Indian Acad. Scis.; mem. NAS U.S.A. (fgn. assoc.), Third World Acad. Scis. (founding mem.), Indian Geophys. Union, NAS India, Royal Astron. Soc. (assoc.), Internat. Acad. Aeronautics, Internat. Union of Geodesy and Geophysics (pres. 1984-87), Am. Acad. Arts and Scis. (fgn. hon. mem.), Internat. Assn. Phys. Sci. of Ocean (hon. mem., pres. 1979-83), Geol. Soc. India (hon. fellow 1992). Hindu. Avocations: chess, photography, painting, math. puzzles. Office: U Calif Scripps Inst Oceanography GRD-0220 La Jolla CA 92093-0220

LAL, RATTAN, soil scientist, researcher; b. Karyal, Punjab, India, Sept. 5, 1944; came to U.S., 1987; s. Jagan Nath and Krishna Nath (Lakhanpal) Bhakri; m. Sukhvarsha Sharma, Dec. 12, 1971; children: Priya, Pratibha, Abhishek, Vivek. MS in Soils, I.A.R.I., New Delhi, India, 1965; PhD in Soil Physics, Ohio State U., 1968. Rsch. asst. Rockefeller Found., New Delhi, India, 1963-65; rsch. assoc. Ohio Agrl. Rsch. and Devel. Ctr. Ohio State U., Wooster and Columbus, 1966-68; sr. rsch. fellow U. Sydney, N.S.W., Australia, 1968-69; soil physicist Internat. Inst. Tropical Agr., Ibadan, Nigeria, 1970-87, coord. UPS, 1985-87; assoc. prof. Ohio State U., Columbus, 1987-89, prof., 1989—; cons. World Bank, Washington, UN Devel. Program/ Food and Agrl. Orgn., N.Y.C., Rome, Tropical R&D, Gainesville, Fla.; bd. dirs. Orgn. Tropical Studies, Durham, N.C. Author: Tropical Ecology and Physical Edaphology, 1987, Soil Erosion in the Tropics-Principles and Management, 1990, Sustainable Management of Soil Resources in The Humid Tropics, 1995; editor: Soil Erosion Research Methods, 1988, 94; co-editor: Tropical Agricultural Hydrology, 1981, Soil Management for Sustainability, 1991, Soils and Global Change, 1995, others. Recipient Merit award Indian Soc. Soil and Water Conservation, Dehradun, India, 1990, Disting. Scientist award ASIO, 1990. Fellow AAAS, Am. Soc. Agronomy, Soil Sci. Soc. Am. (Internat. Soil Sci. award 1988, Soil Sci. Applied Rsch. award 1992, Internat. Svc. in Agronomy award 1995), Third World Acad. Scis. (Disting. Scholar award 1994); mem. Internat. Soil Tillage Rsch. Orgn. (pres. 1988-91), World Assn. Soil and Water Conservation (pres. 1988-91), Sigma Xi (Rsch. award 1995). Achievements include research on developing sustainable alternatives to shifting cultivation and bush fallow systems, soil erosion and its control, agricultural impact on soil and environmental degradation, soil process and greenhouse effect, soil compaction, anaerobiosis and other aspects of physical edaphology. Office: Ohio State U Dept Agronomy 2021 Coffey Rd Columbus OH 43210-1043

LALA, DOMINICK J., manufacturing company executive; b. N.Y.C., June 2, 1928; s. Joseph and Mary (Billera) L.; m. Nancy Bosco, Nov. 30, 1957; children: John, Steven, James, Thomas, Patrice. B.S., NYU, 1951. Mem. staff BDO/Seidman (CPAs), N.Y.C., 1951-62; v.p., contr. Universal Am. Corp., N.Y.C., 1962-68; sr. v.p. finance Paramount Pictures Corp., 1968-70; exec. v.p. Gould Paper Corp., 1970—. Served with AUS, 1946-47. Mem. AICPA, N.Y. State Soc. CPAs, Fin. Execs. Inst. Home: 10 Burnham Pl Manhasset NY 11030-2709 Office: Gould Paper Corp 315 Park Ave S New York NY 10010-3607

LALA, PEEYUSH KANTI, medical scientist, educator; b. Chittagong, Bengal, India, Nov. 1, 1934; came to U.S., 1963, to Can., 1967.; s. Sudhangshu Bimal and Nani Bala (Chaudhuri) L.; m. Arati Roy-Burman, July 7, 1962 (dec.); children: Probal, Prasun; m. Shipra Bhattacareya, Nov. 6, 1992. MBBS, Calcutta (India) U., 1957, PhD in Med. Biophysics, 1962. Demonstrator pathology Calcutta Med. Coll., 1959-60, NRS Med. Coll., Calcutta, 1961-62; resident research assoc. Biol. and Med. Research div. Argonne (Ill.) Nat. Lab., 1963-64; research scientist lab radiobiology U. Calif. Med. Ctr., San Francisco, 1964-66; research scientist Biol. and Health Physics div. Chalk River (Ont., Can.) Nuclear Lab., 1967-68; from asst. prof. to assoc. prof. dept. anatomy McGill U., Montreal, Que., Can., 1968-77, prof. dept. anatomy, 1977-83; prof. dept. anatomy U. Western Ont., London, 1983—, chmn. dept. anatomy, 1983-93, prof. dept. oncology, 1990—; mem. grants panel MRC Can., Ottawa, Ont., 1983-87, 93—, NIH U.S.A., Bethesda, Md., 1977-95, Nat. Cancer Inst. Can., Toronto, 1987-90, Cancer Rsch. Soc., Montreal, 1987-90; mem. Cannaught Com., Toronto, 1990-91; vis. prof. Walter and Eliza Hall Inst. Med. Rsch., U. Melbourne, Australia, 1977-78. Mem. editl. bd. Leukemia Rsch., 1977-86, Exptl. Hematology, 1974-77, Am. Jour. Reproductive Immunology, 1989-93, Early Pregnancy: Biology and Medicine, 1995—, Placeenta, 1996—; assoc. editor Am. Jour. Anatomy, 1987-90; contbr. articles to profl. jours. Chmn. Bengali Cultural Ctr., Montreal, 1978-83. Grantee MRC Can., 1968—, NCI Can., 1968—, NIH, 1976-79, Cancer Rsch. Soc., 1978—, USAMR, 1996—; Fulbright Found. fellow, 1962. Mem. Am. Assn. Cancer Research, Am. Assn. Anatomists, Can. Assn. Anatomists (chmn. awards com. 1987-89, v.p. and pres. elect 1989-90, pres. 1991-93, J.C.B. Grant award 1990), Internat. Soc. Exptl. Hematology, Soc. Leukocyte Biology, Am. Assn. Immunologists, Can. Soc. Immunologists, Internat. Soc. Reproductive Immunology (councillor 1986-89), Am. Soc. Reproductive Immunology (v.p. 1985-86). Achievements include discovery of new mode of cancer immunotherapy, resulting in a successful phase two human trial. Office: U Western Ont, Dept Anatomy, London, ON Canada N6A 5C1

LALAS, ALEXI, professional soccer player; b. Birmingham, Mich.; s. Demetrius and Anne Lalas. BA in English, Rutgers U., 1991. Mem. U.S. Olympic Soccer Team, 1992, World Cup U.S. Soccer Team, 1993-94, Football Club Padova, Italian League, 1994—, Major League Soccer, with New England Revolution, 1995—; mem. U.S. Olympic Festival Team, 1989, U.S. Pan-Am. Team, 1991. Mem. group Gypsies; rec. Woodland. Recipient Hermann trophy, 1991; named Coll. Soccer Player of Yr., 1991. Avocation: acoustic guitar. Office: New England Revolution Foxboro Stadium Rt 1 Foxboro MA 02035*

LALIBERTE, GARLAND EVERETT, agricultural engineering educator; b. Walkerburn, Man., Can., Dec. 28, 1936; m. Audry Whitlock; 2 children: Tracy, Marnie. BS in Agrl. Engring., U. Sask., Can., 1956, MS, 1961; PhD, Colo. State U., 1966. Prof. biosys. engring. U. Man., Winnipeg, 1967—; mem. Man. Econ. Innovation and Tech. Coun., 1992-94. Recipient Achievement in Academe award Colo. State U., 1994. Fellow Agrl. Inst. Can. (nat. coun. 1980-82), Can. Soc. Agrl. Engring. (charter, sr., v.p. tech. 1971-73, pres. 1978-79, Maple Leaf award 1981); mem. Assn. Faculties Agr. in Can. (charter, bd. dirs. 1974-78, sec.-treas. 1974-75, pres. 1976-78), Assn. Profl. Engrs. Man. (coun. 1984-90, pres. 1988-89, Outstanding Svc. award 1994), Can. Coun. Profl. Engrs. (bd. dirs. 1989-90, exec. com. 1991-96, pres. 1994-95), Am. Soc. Agrl. Engrs., Man. Inst. Agrologists, Prairie Agrl. Machinery Inst. (coun. 1983-85). Office: Univ Man, Pfo Biosys Engring, Winnipeg, MB Canada R3V 5V6

LALL, B. KENT, civil engineering educator; b. Feb. 4, 1939; m. Margaret Vivienne Boult, Nov. 30, 1970; 1 child, Niren Nicolaus. BS in Civil Engring., Panjab Engring. Coll., Chandigarh, India, 1961; ME in Hwy. Engring., U. Roorkee, India, 1964; PhD in Transp., U. Birmingham, Eng., 1969. Registered profl. engr. Commonwealth scholar U. Birmingham, 1966-69; lectr. Indian Inst. Tech., New Delhi, 1964-72, asst. prof., 1972-75; assoc. prof. U. Man., Winnipeg, Can., 1975-77; assoc. prof. civil engring. Portland (Oreg.) State U., 1977-84, prof., 1984—; vis. prof. U. Adelaide, South Australia, 1985; cons. Nat. Rds. Bd., Ministry of Works, Wellington, New Zealand, 1986. Editor procs., co-author: Transportation Engineering; contbr. articles to profl. jours. Vol. Meals on Wheels, Portland, 1991—. Fellow ASCE (chmn. transp. congress 1995, exec. com. urban transp. divsn. 1994-95, pub. transp. com. 1988-91, mem. high speed ground transport com.), Inst. Transp. Engrs., Transp. Rsch. Bd., Rotary (bd. dirs. S.W. Portland 1990-91, 95—). Office: Portland State U Dept Civil Engring PO Box 751 Portland OR 97207-0751

LALLEY, FRANK EDWARD, federal government official; b. Woonsocket, R.I., Jan. 11, 1944; s. Frank Edward III and Lois Eva (Parkin) L.; m. Joyce Lynne Rynkiewicz, June 11, 1983; children: Jonathan, Robert, Adrienne, Andrea. B in Mgmt. Engring., Rensselaer Poly. Inst., 1965; MBA, So. Ill. U., 1971; postgrad., George Washington U., 1972-75. Ops. rsch. analyst U.S. Army, 1969-74; energy analyst FEA, Washington, 1974-77; dir. petroleum supply div. U.S. Dept. Energy, Washington, 1977-87; dir. Office Info., Mgmt. and Stats. U.S. Dept. Vets. Affairs, Washington, 1987-90; assoc. dep. asst. sec. Info. Resources Policies and Oversight U.S. Dept. Vets. Affairs, 1990-94, assoc. dep. asst. sec. Telecom., 1994—; co-chmn. publ. U.S. Refining Industry, Nat. Petroleum Coun., 1986, govt. liaison publ. U.S. Oil and Gas Outlook, 1987; mem. Nat. Performance Review, 1993; chmn. Interagency Com. Info. Resources Mgmt., 1994-95; mem. Nat. Comm. Sys. Com. of Principals, 1996. Capt. USAF, 1965-69. Home: 13001 Shadwell Ct Woodbridge VA 22192-3364 Office: Dept Vets Affairs 810 Vermont Ave NW Washington DC 20420-0001

LALLEY, RICHARD A., school system administrator. Supt. Brick Sch., Amherst, N.H., 1975—. Recipient N.H. Supt. of the Yr. awd., Am. Assn. of Sch. Adminstrs., 1993. Office: SAU # 39 Brick Sch PO Box 849 Amherst NH 03031

LALLI, CELE GOLDSMITH, editor; b. Scranton, Pa., Apr. 8, 1933; d. Arthur Langfeld and Viola Catherine (Wolfort) Goldsmith; m. Michael Anthony Lalli, Apr. 4, 1964; children—Francesca Ann, Erica Catherine. BA, Vassar Coll., 1955. From asst. editor to editor Amazing Sci. Fiction Stories, N.Y.C., 1955-65; mng. editor Modern Bride's Guide to Decorating Your First Home, N.Y.C., 1965-69; exec. editor Modern Bride, N.Y.C., 1969-81, editor-in-chief, v.p., 1982—. Co-author: Modern Bride Guide to Your Wedding and Marriage, 1984, Modern Bride Wedding Celebrations, 1992; author: Modern Bride Guide to Etiquette, 1993. Bd. dirs. Conn. Assn. for Children with Learning Disabilities, 1984-93. Recipient Invisible Little Man award West Coast Sci. Fiction Orgn., 1961; named to YWCA Acad. of Women Achievers, 1986. Mem. Am. Soc. Mag. Editors, Fashion Group. Republican. Roman Catholic. Office: Modern Bride K-III Comms 249 W 17th St New York NY 10011-5300

LALLI, FRANK, magazine editor. Mng. editor Money mag., N.Y.C. Office: Money Magazine Time & Life Bldg Rockefeller Ctr 33rd fl New York NY 10020

LALLI, MARY SCHWEITZER, writer, artist; b. Newark, Ohio, June 24, 1925; d. Clemence Sylvester and Ethel Ann (Deem) Schilling; m. Francis Edward Schweitzer, Aug. 23, 1947 (div. Oct. 1974); children: Dale Francis, Darrell Charles, David Edward; m. Joseph G. Lalli, June 21, 1975. BA, Denison U., 1947. Lic. tchr. English. Tchr. English Ctrl. Jr. High, Newark, 1947-48; profl. artist Nat. Forum Profl. Artists, Phila., 1968-75; dir. art shows Phila., 1968—. Writer Doll Castle News, Doll Times, Doll Reader, Antique Doll World, Doll Collector's Price Guide, Doll World, 1983—; photojournalist Doll Times; columnist Doll Designs. Recipient 125 art awards Phila. Plastic Club, 1972, 73, 78, award of honor Inst. Pub. Edn., Drexel Hill, Pa., 1980. Mem. Nat. League Am. Pen Women (1st v.p. 1985-89), DaVinci Art Alliance (sec.), Plastic Club (pres., v.p.), Chester County Art Assn. Avocations: attending art shows, doll shows, classical music concerts, doing research.

L'ALLIER, JEAN-PAUL, mayor. BA, U. Montreal, 1959; LLM, U. Ottawa, 1962, diploma of superior studies, 1963. Mem. law firms Ville de Quebec, Ottawa and Hull, Ont., Can.; mem. law faculty U. Ottawa; rsch. officer Centre africain de formation et de recherches adminstratives pour le développment, Morocco, 1964-66; dir. coop. Ministry of Cultural Affairs Que., 1966-68; sec. gen. l'Office franco-que. pour la jeunesse, 1968, chmn. bd. dirs., 1970-76; mem. Deux-Montagnes Nat. Assembly Que., 1970-76; pres. Jean-Paul L'Allier & Assocs., 1976-89; mayor City of Que., 1989—; chmn. Quebec Urban Cmty.; ministe youth recreation and sports Nat. Assembly Que., 1970, minister pub. svc., 1970-72, minister communications, 1970-75, minister cultural affairs, 1975-76, mem. treasury bd. and legislative com., 1970-76; pres. ministerial com. Quality of Life,, 1970-76; gen. del. Que. in Belgium, 1981-84, hon. consul, 1985-88. Chmn. Orgn. World Heritage Cities, 1993. Decorated Légion d'honneur. Mem. Assn. internationale des maires francophones (v.p.). Office: Hôtel de Ville, 2 rue Desjardins CP 700, Quebec, PQ Canada G1R 4S9

LALLY, MICHAEL DAVID, writer, actor; b. Orange, N.J., May 25, 1942; s. James A. and Irene I. (Dempsey) L.; children: Caitlin Maeve, Miles Aaron. BA, U. Iowa, 1968, MFA, 1969. Instr. Trinity Coll., Washington, 1969-74; book reviewer Washington Post, 1974-77; editor Franklin Library div. Franklin Mint, 1976-79; editor, pub. various newspapers and presses including Iowa Defender, Some of Us Press, The Washington Review of the Arts, 1966-80, Venice mag., 1988-91, The Hollywood Review, 1991; bd. dirs. The Print Center, Bklyn., 1972-75, Washington Film Classroom, 1970-72. Actor: (films) Last Rites, 1980, The Nesting, 1981, White Fang, 1991, Cool World, 1992, Basic Instinct, 1992, (stage) The Heroes, 1981, Balm in Gilead, 1983, The Rhythm of Torn Stars, 1988-89, Short Eyes, 1994, (TV) Cagney and Lacey, 1984, Berrengers, 1985, Hardcastle and McCormick, 1986, L.A. Law, 1989, Father Dowling's Mysteries, 1991, Caught in the Act, 1993, Diagnosis Murder, 1994, NYPD Blue, 1995; freelance writer, reviewer, actor, N.Y.C., 1975-82; screenwriter, actor, L.A., 1982—; author 20 books including Rocky Dies Yellow, 1974, German edit., 1982, Dues, 1974, Catch My Breath, 1976, 95, Just Let Me Do It, 1978, Attitude, 1982, Hollywood Magic, 1982, Can't Be Wrong, 1996; author, dir. (one-act play) Four Grown Men, N.Y.C., 1982, Hollywood Magic, L.A., 1983; co-author (play) The Rhythm of Torn Stars, 1988-89; 3 short plays, 1995; recorded poems on CD, What You Find There, 1994; contbr. articles and poetry to profl. jours., newspapers, mags. Served with USAF, 1962-66. Nat. Endowment for Arts fellow, 1974, 81; recipient Discovery award N.Y. Poetry Ctr., 1972, award Poets Found., 1974, Lit. Prize award Pacificus Found., 1996. Mem. Screen Actors Guild, Writers Guild Am., AFTRA, P.E.N.

LALLY, NORMA ROSS, federal agency administrator, retired; b. Crawford, Nebr., Aug. 10, 1932; d. Roy Anderson and Alma Leona (Barber) Lively; m. Robert Edward Lally, Dec. 4, 1953 (div. Mar. 1986); children: Robyn Carol Murch, Jeffrey Alan, Gregory Roy. BA, Boise (Idaho) State U., 1974, MA, 1976; postgrad., Columbia Pacific U., 1988—. With grad. admissions Boise State U., 1971-74; with officer programs USN Recruiting, Boise, 1974; pub. affairs officer IRS, Boise and Las Vegas, 1975-94; ret., 1994; speaker in field, Boise and Las Vegas, 1977—. Contbr. articles to newspapers. Mem. task force Clark County Sch. Dist., Las Vegas. Staff sgt. USAF, 1950-54. Mem. NAFE, Internat. Assn. Bus. Communicators, Women in Mil. Svc. Assn., Mensa, Toastmasters (Las Vegas), Marine's Meml. Club (life), Am. Legion. Avocations: writing, dancing, music, golf, swimming. Home: 3013 Hawksdale Dr Las Vegas NV 89134-8967

LALLY, RICHARD FRANCIS, aviation security consultant, former association executive, former government official; b. Newark, Nov. 23, 1925; s. Francis J. and Helen (Fennesy) L.; m. Doris P. Yasko, Sept. 10, 1949; children: Barbara J. Lally-Dittler, Joan E. Lally Stalder. B.S., Upsala Coll., 1950. Spl. agt. FBI, Atlanta, Cin. and Washington, 1951-60; area dir., chief gen. investigations Dept. Labor, Newark and Washington, 1960-63; dep. dir. compliance and security FAA, Washington, 1963-65; dir. compliance and security FAA, 1965-67; dir. investigations and security Dept. Transp., Washington, 1967-70; dir. equal opportunity Dept. Transp., 1967-70, dir. civil rights, 1970-72, dir. transp. security, 1972-74; dir. civil aviation security FAA, 1974-82; v.p. security Air Transport Assn. Am., 1982-91; aviation security consultant, 1991—. Served with AC U.S. Army, 1944-46. Recipient Exceptional Svc. citation Dept. Trans., 1969, Meritorious Achievement award, 1970, Sec.'s award, 1973, Superior Achievement award, 1970, Sec.'s award, 1973, Superior Achievement award, 1973, 76, Superior Achievement in Equal Opportunity award, 1977, Disting. Alumnus award Upsala Coll., 1979, Presdl. Rank Sr. Exec. award, 1980, Extraordinary Svc. award FAA, 1991, Internat. Security Mgmt. Assn. J. Paul Breslin Recognition award, 1993. Home and Office: Bay Colony 25 Indian River Dr Dagsboro DE 19939

LALLY, VINCENT EDWARD, atmospheric scientist; b. Brookline, Mass., Oct. 13, 1922; s. Michael James and Ellen Teresa (Dolan) L.; m. Marguerite Mary Tibert, June 5, 1949; children: Dennis V., Marianne Baugh, Stephen J. BS in Meteorology, U. Chgo., 1944; BSEE, MIT, 1948, MS in Engring. Adminstrn., 1949. Engr. Bendix-Friez, Balt., 1949-51; chief metall. equip. devel. Air Force Cambridge Rsch. Labs., Bedford, Mass., 1951-58; rsch. dir. Teledynamics, Phila., 1958-61; dir. Nat. Sci. Balloon Facility Nat. Ctr. for Atmospheric Rsch., Boulder, Colo., 1961-66, sr. scientist, 1966-91, sr. scientist emeritus, 1991—. Contbr. articles to sci. jours., chpt. to handbook in field. 1st lt. USAAC, 1942-46. Fellow Am. Meteorol. Soc. (Cleveland Abbe award 1990); mem. Inst. Navigation, Sigma Xi. Achievements include 7 patents for space inflatables, superpressure balloons, rocket instruments, communications techniques; made first balloon flight around the world, longest balloon flight; pioneered technology in measurements from radiosondes, aircraft and rockets. Avocations: running, golf, application of Monte Carlo techniques to gaming. Home: 4475 Laguna Pl # 305 Boulder CO 80303 Office: Nat Ctr Atmospheric Rsch PO Box 3000 Boulder CO 80307

LALONDE, BERNARD JOSEPH, educator; b. Detroit, June 3, 1933; s. John Bernard and Fannie (Napier) LaL.; m. Barbara Elaine Eggenberger, Sept. 6, 1958; children—Lisa Renee, Michell Ann, Christopher John. A.B., U. Notre Dame, 1955; M.B.A., U. Detroit, 1957; Ph.D., Mich. State U., 1961. Asst. prof. mktg. U. Colo., Boulder, 1961-65; assoc. prof. Mich. State U., East Lansing, 1965-69; James R. Riley prof. mktg. and logistics Ohio State U., Columbus, 1969-85; Raymond E. Mason prof. transp. and logistics Ohio State U., 1985-95, prof. emeritus, 1995. Author: Physical Distribution Management, 2d edit, 1968, Customer Service: A Management Perspective, 1988; Editor: Jour. Bus. Logistics; Jour. book and monographs editor, Am. Mktg. Assn.; Contbr. articles to profl. jours. Pres. Transp. Research Found. Recipient John Drury Sheehan award, 1976; Formerly Ford scholar; Gen. Electric fellow. Mem. Am. Marketing Assn., Regional Sci. Assn., Council Logistic Mgmt., Soc. Logistics Engrs., Beta Gamma Sigma, Alpha Kappa Psi. Roman Catholic. Home: 8538 Pitlochry Ct Dublin OH 43017-9770 Office: Ohio State U Coll Bus Logistics Rsch Group 421 Hagerty Hall Columbus OH 43210

LALONDE, MARC, lawyer, former Canadian government official; b. Ile Perrot, Que., Can., July 26, 1929; s. J. Albert and Nora (St-Aubin) L.; m. Claire Tetreau, Sept. 8, 1955; children: Marie, Luc, Paul, Catherine. BA, Coll. St. Laurent, Montreal, 1950; LLB, U. Montreal, 1964, LLM, 1955; MA in Econs. and Polit. Sci., Oxford (Eng.) U., 1957; PhD honoris causa, Limburg U., The Netherlands, 1989. Bar: Que. 1955, Queen's Coun. 1971. Prof. bus. law and econs. U. Montreal, 1957-59; spl. asst. to Minister of Justice, Ottawa, Ont., Can., 1959-60; partner firm Gelinas, Bourque, Lalonde & Benoit, Montreal, 1960-68; policy adviser to Prime Minister Lester B. Pearson, Ottawa, 1967-68; prin. sec. to Prime Minister Pierre E. Trudeau, Ottawa, 1968-72; elected to House of Commons for Montreal-Outremont, 1972, minister of nat. health and welfare, 1972-77, minister of state for fed.-provincial relations, 1977-78, minister responsible for status of women, 1975-78, minister of justice and atty. gen. Can., 1978-79, minister of energy, mines and resources, 1980-82, minister of finance, 1982-84; ptnr. Stikeman, Elliott, Montreal; bd. dirs. Orleans Resources, Inc., Cedar Group, Inc., Citibank of Can., Camdev Corp.; chmn. bd. Hotel-Dieu de Montreal; advisor Internat. Coun. Presidium of Ukraine; ad hoc judge Internat. Ct. Justice, 1985—. Author: The Changing Role of the Prime Minister's Office, 1971. Decorated officer Order of Can.; recipient Dana award APHA, 1978. Mem. Internat. Coun. on Comml. Arbitration, Am. Arbitration Assn. (exec. bd. dirs.), Royal Coll. Physicians and Surgeons Can. Mem. Liberal Party. Home: 5440 Legare, Montreal, PQ Canada H3T 1Z4

LALONDE, ROBERT FREDERICK, state senator, retired; b. Bay City, Mich., Dec. 1, 1922; s. Joseph and Mildred Amanda (Brimmer) LaL.; m. Betty Ellen Schwartz, Aug. 2, 1941; 1 child, Rose Marie Tibbitts. BGE in Bus., U. Omaha, 1965. Airport mgr. Jackson Hole Airport, Jackson, Wyo., 1972-80; county commr. Teton County, Jackson, 1982-86, rental property owner, 1970-88; Wyo. state senator Jackson, 1989-95. Author: The Dangerous Trilogy, 1973. Chmn. Teton County Rep. Com., Jackson, 1975-77; del. Rep. Nat. Conv., Detroit, 1980; mem. Electoral Coll., Cheyenne, Wyo., 1980; sec. Wyo. Rep. party, 1980-82; chmn. Teton County Planning Commn., Jackson, 1973-78. Col. USAF, 1943-70. Mem. Am. Legion (comdr. 1989-94), Wyo. Airport Operators Assn. (founder, pres. 1973-75, Disting. Svc. award 1979), Jackson Hole C. of C. (pres. 1977-79, Citizen of Yr. 1975, Disting. Svc. award 1980), Rotary (pres. 1976-77). Christian Scientist. Avocations: hunting, fishing. Home: PO Box 1707 Jackson WY 83001-1707

LALOR, EDWARD DAVID DARRELL, labor and employment arbitrator, lawyer; b. Madison, Wis., Jan. 29, 1944; s. Edward Richard and Viola (Byrne) Lalor; adult adopted mother: Helen Rose (Litney) Pribble; m. Paula Sue Tompkins, Aug. 12, 1978; children. BBA, U. Wis., 1966, JD, 1969. Bar: Wis., 1969, Minn., 1980, U.S. Dist. Ct. (we. dist.) Wis., 1969, U.S. Supreme Ct., 1979. Gen. atty. NLRB, Kansas City, Mo., Kans., 1969-80; atty. advice divsn., advice br. NLRB, Washington, 1973-74; trial specialist NLRB, Kansas City, 1977-80; arbitrator labor and employment, pres. Pribble Arbitration and Mediation Svcs., Inc., Mpls., 1980-85; arbitrator, pres. Pribble Arbitration and Mediation Svcs., Inc., St. Cloud, Minn., 1985-95; CEO, pres., arbitrator Lalor Arbitration and Mediation, Inc., St. Cloud, Minn., 1995—; mcpl. judge City Countryside (Kans.), 1979-80; mem. arbitration panels Fed. Mediation and Conciliation Svc., 1982—, Am. Arbitration Assn., 1984—, Nat. Mediation Bd., 1991—, Minn. Bur. Mediation Svcs., 1982—, Iowa Pub. Employment Rels. Bd., 1983—; pvt. panel J.I. Case Corp. and I.A. Machinists and Aerospace Workers Local 2525, Fargo, N.D., 1985—; full-day moderator in arbitration, labor and employement law discrimination, alt. dispute resolution, evidence and family law programs Minn. Continuing Legal Edn., 1989—; labor and employment arbitrator Minn. Cts. Alt. Dispute Resolution, 1994—. Contbr. articles to profl. jours. Mem. Minn. Dem. Farm Labor State and Congl. Dist. Ctrl. Com., 1981—, Minn. State Platform Commn., Dem. Farm Labor Party, 1984-85, chmn. senate dist., 1984-85, fundraiser, initiator, co-founder Dr. Guy Stanton Ford Ednl. Found., 1964-69; co-founder Westport Free Health Clinic, Kansas City, Mo., 1970-80; active coun. Land of Lakes coun. Girl Scouts, Minn., 1985—, Leadership Coun. So. Poverty Ctr., Habitat for Humanity Internat. Ptnrs. Coun.; coach Girls Youth Basketball League, St. Cloud, 1992—; bd. dirs. St. Cloud Symphony Orch., 1992-94; chair New Voter registration Drives Senate Dist. 59, 1981-85, Stearns-Benton County Senate Dist.17, 1989-91; historian Lalor Clan for the Ams.; host family for Irish polit. prisoners children's holiday, 1996—; mem. Internat. Hearing Found. Mem. ABA (labor and employment law sects. 1978—), Fed. Bar Assn. (labor and employment law sects. 1974—), Minn. Bar Assn. (labor and employment law sects. 1980—, mock trial program judge 1989—), Nat. Youth Sports Coaches Assn. (cert.), Wis. Bar Assn. (labor and employment law sects. 1969—), Internat. Indsl. Rels. Assn., Soc. Profls. in Dispute Resolution Internat., Indsl. Rels. Rsch. Assn., Theta Delta Chi. Roman Catholic. Avocations: reading, family history, fishing, stock investing. Office: Lalor Arbitration & Mediation Inc 1220 N 13th St Saint Cloud MN 56303-2733

LAM, CHEUNG-WEI, electrical engineer; b. Hong Kong, Mar. 5, 1965; came to U.S., 1987; s. Yeung-Tak and Sau-Jin (Wong) L.; m. Hoi-Man Sarah Hui, May 29, 1993; 1 child, Isaac Samuel. BS, Chinese U. Hong Kong, 1987; MS, MIT, 1989, PhD, 1993. Rsch. asst. MIT, Cambridge, 1988-93; rschr. Schlumberger-Doll Rsch, Ridgefield, Conn., 1990; mem. tech. staff Quad Design Tech., Camarillo, Calif., 1993—; mem. com. Soc. Automotive Engrs./Electromagnetic Compatibility Modeling Task Force, 1994—. Contbr. articles to Jour. Superconductivity, IEEE, Jour. Electromagnetic Waves and Applications. Bank of Am. scholar, 1985, Du Pont scholar, 1986. Mem. IEEE (prize 1987), Sigma Xi. Achievements include design of efficient electromagnetic interference simulator, nonlinear models for superconducting transmission lines; research in high-speed electronic interconnection and packaging, acoustic logging in borehole structures. Home: 1395 La Culebra Cir Camarillo CA 93012 Office: Quad Design Tech 1385 Del Norte Rd Camarillo CA 93010

LAM, DAVID C., former lieutenant governor; b. Hong Kong; arrived in Can., 1967; Businessman, philanthropist; lt. gov. Province of B.C., 1988-95. Office: 400-576 Seymour St, Vancouver, BC Canada V6B 3K1

LAM, SHUI YAU STANNY, chemical engineer; b. Po On, China, Aug. 17, 1956; came to U.S., 1990; s. Ping Tai and Lam Fung (Man) L.; m. Yin Yuk Ng, Sept. 30, 1980; children: Hoi Yee, Cherk Yu. BSc, U. Birmingham, 1979. Profl. engr., Tex. Devel. engr. Fletcher & Stewart Ltd., Derby, England, 1980-81; process engr. Mass Transfer Internat., Kirkby Stephen, England, 1981-84; export mgr. trainee Magna Indsl. Co., Hong Kong, 1984; from chief process engr. to sr. process engr. Glitsch Cos., Parsippany, N.J., 1984—. Coach Randolph (N.J.) Cmty. Track Team, 1994, 95. Mem. Inst. Chem. Engrs. Home: 15 Shongum Rd Randolph NJ 07869 Office: Glitsch Tech Corp 1055 Parsippany Blvd Parsippany NJ 07054

LAM, SIMON SHIN-SING, computer science educator; b. Macao, July 31, 1947; came to U.S., 1966; s. Chak Han and Kit Ying (Tang) L.; m. Amy Leung, Mar. 29, 1971; 1 child, Eric. B.S.E.E. with distinction, Wash. State U., 1969; M.S. in Engring., UCLA, 1970, Ph.D., 1974. Research engr. ARPA Network Measurement Ctr., UCLA, Los Angeles, 1971-74; research staff mem. IBM Watson Research Ctr, Yorktown Heights, N.Y., 1974-77; asst. prof. U. Tex.-Austin, Austin, 1977-79, assoc. prof., 1979-83, prof. computer sci., 1983—; David S. Bruton Centennial prof. U. Tex., Austin, 1985-88, anonymous prof., 1988—; chmn. dept. computer sci. U. Tex.-Austin, Austin, 1992-94. Editor-in-chief IEEE/ACM Transactions on Networking, 1995—; editor: Principles of Communication and Networking Protocols; contbr. articles to profl. jours. NSF grantee, 1978—; Chancellor's Teaching fellow UCLA, 1969-73. Fellow IEEE (Leonard G. Abraham prize 1975); mem. Assn. for Computing Machinery (program chmn. symposium 1983). Avocations: tennis, swimming, skiing, travel. Office: Univ Tex Dept of Computer Sci Austin TX 78712

LAMAGRA, ANTHONY JAMES, concert pianist, television host, music educator; b. Jersey City, Sept. 27, 1935; s. Anthony Carl and Irma Assunta L.; m. Susan Kate Ford, Sept. 1, 1968; children: Michael Anthony, Janet Lynn. B.Mus., Yale U., 1956, M.Mus., 1957; Ed.D., Columbia U., 1966. Dir. instrumental music Lincoln High Sch., Jersey City, 1960-62; dir. Keyboard Assocs. Ltd., Chappaqua, N.Y., 1962-65; instr. music Columbia U., 1962-65; with Manhattanville Coll., Purchase, N.Y., 1965—, prof., 1967—, dir. music, 1975—, dept. music chmn., 1971—; host Westchester Performs, UA Columbia Cablevision. Author: (with Marwick and Nagy) Creative Keyboard Piano Series, 1975. Served with U.S. Army, 1958. Recipient Hudson County Mus. Art Club, 1952. Mem. AAUP, Music Tchrs. Nat. Assn., Music Educators Nat. Conf. Office: Music Dept Manhattanville Coll Purchase NY 10577

LAMALIE, ROBERT EUGENE, retired executive search company executive; b. Fremont, Ohio, June 3, 1931; s. Glennis and Mildred M. (Hetrick) L.; m. Dorothy M. Zilles, June 20, 1953; children: Deborah, Dawn, Elaine. BA, Capital U., Columbus, Ohio, 1954; postgrad., Case Western Res. U. Asst. dir. recruiting Xerox Corp., 1959-62; mgr. orgn. planning and profl. recruiting Glidden Co., 1962-65; search cons. Booz, Allen & Hamilton, Inc., Cleve., 1965-67; pres., chief exec. officer Lamalie Assocs., Inc., Tampa, Fla., 1967-84, chmn. bd. dirs., chief exec. officer, 1984-87, chmn. bd. dirs., 1987-88; pres. Robert Lamalie, Inc., Marco Island, Fla., 1988-90, ret., 1990. Served with U.S. Army, 1954-56, Korea.

LAMAN, JERRY THOMAS, mining company executive; b. Muskogee, Okla., Mar. 1, 1947; s. Thomas J. and Juanita J. (Pittman) L.; m. Lenora J. Laman, July 1, 1972; children: Troy T., Brian D. Silver Diploma, Colo. Sch. Mines, 1969. Refinery engr. ARCO, Torrance, Calif., 1969-71; chem. engr. Cleveland-Cliffs Iron Co., Mountain City, Nev., 1971-73, asst. mine supt., 1973-77; chief uranium metallurgist Cleveland-Cliffs Iron Co., Casper, Wyo., 1977-83; project mgr. In-Situ, Inc., Laramie, Wyo., 1983-85, v.p., 1985—; also bd. dirs. In-Situ, Inc.; pres. Solution Mining Corp., Laramie, Wyo., 1990—, also bd. dirs., 1990—. Mem. Soc. for Mining, Metallurgy and Exploration, Optimist (pres. Laramie club 1989). Avocations: golf, fishing. Home: 1085 Colina Dr Laramie WY 82070-5014

LAMANEC, TRACY, chemist, writer; b. Catskill, N.Y., Nov. 16, 1941; s. Julius Edward and Doris Irene (Gallon) L.; m. Eileen Mary Horan, June 22, 1963; children—Stephanie Jo., Michael Wright. A.A.S., Hudson Valley Community Coll., 1962; B.S., Union Coll., 1968. Chem. technician Gen. Electric Co., Schenectady, N.Y., 1962-68, analyst, 1968-79, sr. chemist, 1979-87; cons./microchem. materials characterization, Schenectady Materials and Processes Lab., Inc., 1987—; outdoor columnist, writer Schenectady Gazette, 1972-87. Author articles and weekly outdoor columns. Pres. Schenectady County Conservation Council, Inc., 1981, v.p., 1978-81, 82-87; sportsman's advocate, lobbyist, conservationist, environmentalist, youth instr. 4H; del. N.Y. State Conservation Council, Inc. Mem. Am. Soc. for Metals, Microbeam Analysis Soc., N.Y. State Outdoor Writers Assn. (dir., v.p. 1981-87), New Eng. Outdoor Writers Assn., Outdoor Writers Assn. Am. Clubs: Iroquois Rod and Gun (trustee 1978-87), Glenville Fish and Game (program dir.). Avocations: fishing; hunting; shooting sports; photography; flying.

LAMANTIA, CHARLES ROBERT, management consulting company executive; b. N.Y.C., June 12, 1939; s. Joseph Ferdinand and Catherine (Perniciaro) LaM.; m. Ann Christine Carmody, Sept. 16, 1961; children: Elise, Matthew. BA, Columbia U., 1960, BS, 1961, MS, 1962, ScD, 1965; grad. advanced mgmt. program, Harvard Bus. Sch., 1979. Cons. staff Arthur D. Little, Inc., Cambridge, Mass., 1967-77, v.p., 1977-81, pres., chief oper. officer, 1987-88, pres., chief exec. officer, 1988—, also bd. dirs.; pres., chief exec. officer Koch Process Systems, Westboro, Mass., 1981-86; mem. adv. coun. Sch. Engring. Columbia U., Sch. Mgmt. Boston Coll.; bd. dirs. State St. Boston Corp., 1993—; trustee Meml. Dr. Trust, 1988—. bd. dirs. Corp. Woods Hole Oceanog. Inst.; mem. bd. overseers Mus. Sci., Boston, 1988—, Sta. WGBH pub. broadcasting, 1991—, mem. Conf. Bd., 1989—; mem. Mass. Gov.'s Coun., Mass. Bus. Roundtable, 1992—. Lt. USN, 1965-67. NSF fellow, 1965; Sloan Found. fellow, 1962. Mem. Am. Inst. Chem. Engrs., Soc. Chem. Industries. Office: Arthur D Little Inc 25 Acorn Park Cambridge MA 02140-2390

LAMAR, HOWARD ROBERTS, educational administrator, historian; b. Tuskegee, Ala., Nov. 18, 1923; s. John Howard and Elma (Roberts) L.; m. Doris Shirley White, Sept. 3, 1959; children: Susan Kent, Sarah Howard. BA, Emory U., 1944; MA, Yale U., 1945, PhD, 1951; LHD (hon.), Emory U., 1975; LLD (hon.), Yale U., 1993; LittD (hon.), U. Nebr., 1994. Instr. U. Mass., 1945-46, Wesleyan U., Middletown, Conn., 1948-49; mem. faculty Yale U., 1949-94, prof. Am. History and history Am. West, 1964-94, W.R. Coe prof. Am. history, 1987-94, Sterling prof. history, 1987—, chmn. history dept., 1962-63, 67-70, dir. history grad. studies, 1964-67, fellow Ezra Stiles Coll., 1961-94, dean, 1979-85, pres., 1992-93, Sterling prof. history emeritus, 1994—. Author: Dakota Territory, 1861-1889, 1956, The Far Southwest, 1846-1912, A Territorial History, 1966; also articles, reviews.; Editor: (Joseph Downey) Cruise of the Portsmouth, 1958, Western Americana Series, 1961—, Reader's Encyclopedia of the American West, 1977, Gold Seeker: Adventures of A Belgian Argonaut in California, 1985; co-author, co-editor The Frontier in History: North America and Southern Africa Compared, 1981. Alderman, New Haven, 1951-53. Mem. Orgn. Am. Historians, Western History Assn. (pres. 1971-72), Am. Antquarian Soc., Elihu Soc., Phi Beta Kappa. Democrat. Home: 1747 Hartford Tpke North Haven CT 06473-1249 Office: Yale U Dept History New Haven CT 06520

LAMAR, MARTHA LEE, chaplain; b. Birmingham, Jan. 2, 1935; d. Alco L. and Anne Lee (Morris) Lee; m. William Fred Lamar, Jr., June 7, 1986; children: Barbara Gayle Martin, Owen Parker Jr. BS, Auburn U., 1955; MA, Christian Theol. Sem., Indpls., 1992. From adminstv. asst. to rsch. coord. Ala. Affiliate Am. Heart Assn., Birmingham, 1977-86; adminstrv. asst. alumni office De Pauw U., Greencastle, Ind., 1986-89; nursing home chaplain Heritage House Health and Rehab. Ctr., Greencastle, 1989—; nursing home chaplain Garfield Park Health Facility, Indpls., 1992-94, Heritage House Health and Rehab. Ctr., Martinsville, Ind., 1992-95; chaplain cons. Oakwood Corp., Indpls., 1991—. Vol. chaplain's office De Pauw U., 1986—, community work for homeless, Greencastle, 1986—, Fountain Sq. Devel. Corp., Indpls., 1992. Mem. ACA, Nat. Interfaith Coalition on Aging, Am. Soc. on Aging, Mental Health and Aging Network and Forum on Religion, Spirituality and Aging, Ind. Health Care Chaplains Assn. Methodist. Avocations: traveling, hiking, reading, entertaining. Office: Heritage House Health & Rehab Ctr 1601 Hosp Dr Greencastle IN 46135

LAMARRE, BERNARD, engineering, contracting and manufacturing advisor; b. Chicoutimi, Que., Can., Aug. 6, 1931; s. Emile J. and Blanche M. (Gagnon) L.; m. Louise Lalonde, Aug. 30, 1952; children: Jean, Christine, Lucie, Monique, Michèle, Philippe, Mireille. BSc, Ecole Poly., Montreal, Que., Can., 1952; MSc, Imperial Coll., U. London, 1955; LLD, St. Francis Xavier U., N.S., Can., 1980; D in Engring. (hon.), U. Waterloo, Ont., 1984; LLD (hon.), U. Concordia, Montreal, 1985; D in Engring. (hon.), U. Montreal, 1985; D in Applied Sci. (hon.), U. Sherbrooke, Que., 1986; D in Bus. Adminstrn. (hon.), U. Chicoutimi, Que., 1987; D in Sci. (hon.), Queen's U., Kingston, Ont., 1987; D in Engring. (hon.), U. Ottawa, Ont., 1988, Tech. U. N.S., 1989, Royal Mil. Coll., Kingston, 1990. Structural and founds. engr. Lalonde-Valois, Montreal, 1955-60, chief engr., 1960-62; ptnr., gen. mgr., pres. Lalonde, Valois, Lamarre, Valois, Montreal, 1962-72; chmn., chief exec. officer Lavalin Group, 1972-91; sr. advisor SNC-Lavalin Inc., 1991—; chmn. Ordre des Ingenieurs du Quebec, Montreal Design Inst., Soc. du Vieux Port de Montreal, Bellechasse Santé; bd. dirs. Videotron Inc., Capital Internat. CDDG. Active Telesystems Inc. Coll. Stanislas; hon. chmn. Montreal Mus. Fine Arts. Decorated officer Ordre nat. du Québec, Order of Can.; Athlone fellow, 1952. Fellow Engring. Inst. Can., Can. Soc. Civil Engring.; mem. ASCE, Order Engrs. Que., Mont-Royal Club, St. Denis Club, Laval-sur-le Lac Club. Roman Catholic. Home: 4850 Cedar Crescent, Montreal, PQ Canada H3W 2H9

LAMARRE, DANIEL, public relations company executive; b. Trois Rivières, Que., Can., July 7, 1953; s. Gilles and Pauline (Perreault) L.; m. Josette Ferron, Oct. 21, 1979; children: Sébastien, Josianne. BA in Comm., Ottawa (Ont., Can.) U., 1976. Accredited in pub. rels. Journalist Le Nouvelliste, Stas. CKTM-TV and CKSM, Trois Rivières, 1969-79, Radio Can., Ottawa, 1973-74; dir. comm. Fedn. Caisses Populaires, Trois Rivières, 1974-77; dir. pub. rels. COGECO, Trois Rivières, 1977-78; supr. Cockfield Brown, Montreal, Que., 1978-81; v.p., gen. mgr. Burson-Marsteller, Montreal, 1981-84; sr. ptnr., pres. Nat. Pub. Rels., Montreal, 1984—. Co-author: Les relations publiques: une nouvelle force de l'enterprise moderne, 1986. Bd. govs. Sports Que., Montreal, 1994; v.p. XII World Congress, Toronto, 1991. Recipient Can. award in pub. rels. Can. Pub. Rels. Soc., 1987. Mem. Montreal C. of C. (pres. membership com. 1990-91). Avocations: hockey, golf, skiing, reading, theatre. Home: 2031 des Saules St, Saint Bruno, PQ Canada J3V 3Z9 Office: Nat Pub Rels, Ste 1600, 770 Sherbrooke St W, Montreal, PQ Canada H3A 1G1

LAMAS, LORENZO, actor, race car driver; b. Santa Monica, Calif., Jan. 20, 1958; s. Fernando Lamas and Arlene Dahl; children: Alvaro Joshua, Shayne Dahl, Paton Lee. Grad., Farragut Acad., Pine Beach, N.J., 1975, Jim Russel Sch. Motor Racing, 1985. Ptnr. LeConte Driving Sch., Willow Springs, Calif., 1985—; driver Phil Conte Racing, Paramount, Calif., 1985—, driver competition in Internat. Motor Sports Assn. prototypes, 1988, 89. Appeared in films, Grease, 1978, Take Down, 1978, Tilt, 1979, Body Rock, 1984, Snake Eater, 1989, The Killing Streets, 1991, Night of the Warrior, 1991, also co-prodr. Snake Eater II: The Drug Buster, 1991, Final Impact, 1992, C.I.A., Code Name Alexa, 1992, Snake Eater III: His Law, 1992, Final Round, 1993, Bounty Tracker, 1993, The Swordsman, 1993, C.I.A. II: Target Alexa, 1994 (also dir.); (TV movies) Detour to Terror, 1980, Bad Blood, 1994; appeared in TV series, California Fever, 1979, Midland Heights, 1980, Falcon Crest, 1981-90, Dancin' to the Hits, 1986, Renegade Series, 1992. Winner Toyota Grand Prix of Long Beach, 1985. Avocations: surfing; skiing; golf; motorcycles; karate. Office: No Rain Prodns Inc care L & L Bus Mgmt 3727 W Magnolia # 807 Burbank CA 91505

LAMB, ANN MARIE, research scientist; b. N.Y.C., Oct. 14, 1938; d. Leonard Joseph Cammalleri and Angela Mirandi Cammalleri Stein; m. Jackson L. Lamb, 1964 (div. Sept. 1980); children: Judith Mirandi, Angela Holladay. BS, SUNY, Cortland, 1960; MS in Edn., Miss. State U., University, 1969, PhD, 1989; certificate, U. Ga. Drug and Alcohol Studies, Athens, 1977. Cert. psychometrist, tchr., counselor, Miss. Dir. special programs Noxubee County Schs., Macon, Miss., 1968-74; rep. region Div. Alcohol and Drugs Mental Health Agy. St. Miss., Jackson, 1974-76; dir. program Mental Health Services Sch. Age Children Amory (Miss.) Pub. Schs., 1976-78; exec. dir. 3 Rivers Area Health Services Inc., Amory, Miss., 1978-81; grad. asst. Rehabilitation Research and Tng. Ctr. Low Vision Blind Miss. State U., University, 1982-83; counselor student fin. aid Miss. Sate U., University, 1983-87; rsch. scientist Rehabilitation Research and Tng. Ctr. Low Vision/Blind Miss. State U., University, 1987—; test adminstr. Standardized Testing Program Miss. State U. 1985—. Contbr. articles to profl. jours. Mem. Concerned Citizens Clay County, pres., sec., 1980-84; mem., vice chmn. Clay County 3d Dist. Dem. Exec. Com., 1984—; trustee East Miss. C.C. Mem. Miss. Counselor Assn., Coun. Exceptional Children, Faculty and Profl. Women's Assn. (sec. 1985, chair scholarship com. 1994), Phi Delta Kappa. Roman Catholic. Office: Miss State U Rehab Rsch Trng Ctr Low Vision Blind 48-50 Magruder St Mississippi State MS 39762

LAMB, CHARLES F., minister; b. Maryville, Tenn., Dec. 18, 1934; s. C. Fred and Sadie Ellen (Tedder) L.; children: Elizabeth Susan, Linda Louise, Jennifer Janet; m. Betty Jane Zimmerman, Dec. 29, 1979. BA, Maryville Coll., 1956; MDiv, Grad. Sem. of Phillips U., 1961; D in Ministry, N.Y. Theol. Sem., 1990. Ordained to ministry Christian Ch., 1961. Pastor East Aurora Christian Ch., N.Y., 1961-71; assoc. regional min. Christian Ch., Disciples of Christ, Northeastern Region, Buffalo, N.Y., 1971-75; regional min. Christian Ch., Disciples of Christ, Northeastern Region, Buffalo, 1975—; mem. orgns. clergy and coun. of chs. Trustee Village of East Aurora, 1968-73; active environ. groups Conf. Mayors and Village Ofcls. N.Y., 1968-73. Mem. Conf. Regional Ministers and Moderators (pres.-elect). Democrat. Office: 1272 Delaware Ave Buffalo NY 14209-2401

LAMB, DARLIS CAROL, sculptor; b. Wausa, Nebr.; d. Lindor Soren and June Berniece (Skalberg) Nelson; m. James Robert Lamb; children: Sherry Lamb Sobh, Michael, Mitchell. BA in Fine Arts, Columbia Pacific U., San Rafael, Calif., 1988; MA in Fine Arts, Columbia Pacific U., 1989. Exhibited in group shows at Nat. Arts Club, N.Y.C., 1983, 85, 89, 91, 92, 93, 95 (Catherine Lorillard Wolfe award sculpture 1983, C.L. Wolfe Horse's Head award 1994, Anna Hyatt Huntington cash award 1995), N.Am. Sculpture Exhibit, Foothills Art Ctr., Golden, Colo., 1983-84, 86-87, 90-91 (Pub. Svc. Co. of Colo. sculpture award 1990), Nat. Sculpture Soc., 1985, 91, 95 (C. Percival Dietch Sculpture prize 1991), Loveland Mus. and Gallery, 1990-91, Audubon Artists, 1991, Allied Artists Am., 1992, 95, Pen and Brush, 1993, 95-96 (Roman Bronze award 1995), Colorado Springs Fine Arts Mus., 1996, others; represented in permanent collections in Nebr. Hist. Soc., Am. Lung Assn. of Colo., Benson Park Sculpture Garden, Loveland, others. Mem. Catherine Lorillard Wolfe Art Club, N.Am. Sculpture Soc. Office: PO Box 9043 Englewood CO 80111-0301

LAMB, FREDERIC DAVIS, lawyer; b. Oak Park, Ill., Nov. 23, 1931; s. Frederic Horace and Alice Emily (Davis) L.; m. Barbara Ann Bullard, Apr. 6, 1954; children: Deborah Ann Lamb Dunn, Jeffrey Davis. BA, Wabash Coll.; JD, U. Mich. Bar: Ohio 1957, Conn. 1989. Atty. Vick Chem. Co., N.Y.C. and Cin., 1956-63; v.p., counsel Merrell div. Richardson-Merrell Inc., Cin., 1964-80; asst. gen. counsel Richardson-Vicks Inc., Wilton, Conn., 1981-83, v.p., gen. counsel, sec., 1984-92; pvt. practice, 1993—. Mayor, councilman City of Forest Park, Ohio, 1971-75; chmn. Forest Park Charter Commn., 1969-70; trustee Food Drug Law Inst., mem. scholarship com., 1985-92. Mem. ABA, Ohio Bar Assn., Westchester-Fairfield Corp. Counsel Assn., Am. Soc. Corp. Secs., Silver Spring Country Club (pres. 1989-91). Republican. Avocations: golf; tennis; boating. Home: 30 Keelers Ridge Rd Wilton CT 06897-1607 Office: PO Box 7414 180 Old Ridgefield Rd Wilton CT 06897

LAMB, GEORGE RICHARD, foundation executive; b. Cleve., Aug. 15, 1928; s. Harold George and Mildred (Oller) L.; m. Edith Mathews Read, June 18, 1955; children: Graham Read, George Kinsey, Gwynne Lamb Grimes. B.S., Ohio State U., 1953; M.Sc., Yale U., 1955. Mgr. Tinicum Wildlife Preserve, Phila., 1957-60; exec. sec. Pres. Task Force on Natural Beauty, Washington, 1964; fed. coord. White House Conf. Natural Beauty, Washington, 1965; program and policy staff Outdoor Recreation Resources Review Commn., Washington, 1960-61; budget examiner Bur. Budget, Exec. Office Pres., Washington, 1961-65; pres. Jackson Hole Preserve, N.Y.C., trustee, 1978—; trustee, v.p. Am. Conservation Assn., N.Y.C., 1978-94; assoc. philanthropy L.S. Rockefeller, N.Y.C., 1975-96. Photographer (film) Birds of Tinicum, 1959. Mem. Palisades Interstate Park Commn., N.Y., N.J., 1973-75; pres. Rye Conservation Soc., N.Y., 1968; dir. Federated Conservationists Westchester County, 1965-82; pres. Audobon Soc. Cen. Atlantic States, Washington, 1964-65; trustee Coun. on Environment, N.Y.C., Greenacre Found., N.Y.C. With USAF, 1946-49. Fellow Internat. Council Bird Preservation, Cuba, P.R., 1956. Mem. Manursing Island Club, Campfire Club (Pleasantville, N.Y.), Tamarack Club. Office: 30 Rockefeller Plz Rm 5600 New York NY 10112-0001

LAMB, GORDON HOWARD, music educator; b. Eldora, Iowa, Nov. 6, 1934; s. Capp and Ethel (Hayden) L; m. Nancy Ann Painter; children: Kirk, Jon, Phillip. B in Music Edn., Simpson Coll., 1956; M of Music, U. Nebr., 1962; PhD, U. Iowa, 1973. Choral dir. Iowa pub. schs., Tama/Paullina, Sac City, 1957-68; asst. prof. music U. Wis., Stevens Point, 1969-70, U. Tex., Austin, 1970-74; prof., dir. divsn. music U. Tex., San Antonio, 1974-79, prof., v.p. acad. affairs, 1979-86; pres. Northeastern Ill. U., Chgo., 1986-95, pres. emeritus, 1996—; Disting. prof. music dept. Western Ill. U., 1996—. Author: Choral Techniques, 1974, 3d edit. 1988; editor: Guide for the Beginning Choral Director; contbr. articles to scholarly and profl. jours.; composer numerous pieces choral music. Served with U.S. Army, 1957-58. Recipient Most Supportive Pres. or Chancellor award Am. Assn. Colls. for Tchr. Edn., 1992. Mem. Am. Assn. Higher Edn., Am. Assn. State Colls. and Univs., Am. Choral Dirs. Assn. (life, chmn. nat. com. 1970-72).

LAMB, IRENE HENDRICKS, medical researcher; b. Ky., May 9, 1940; d. Daily P. and Bertha (Hendricks) Lamb; m. Edward B. Meadows. Diploma in nursing, Ky. Bapt. Hosp., Louisville; student, Berea (Ky.) Coll., Calif. State U., L.A. RN, Ky. Charge nurse, head nurse acute medicine, med. ICU, surgical ICU, emergency room various med. ctrs., 1963-67; staff nurse rsch. CCU, 1968; asst. nurse coord., nurse coord. clin. rsch. ctr. U. So. Calif./Los Angeles County Med. Ctr., L.A., 1969-74; sr. rsch. nurse cardiology Stanford (Calif.) U. Sch. Medicine, 1974-85, rsch. coord. pvt. clin., 1988; dir. clin. rsch. San Diego Cardiac Ctr., 1989-92, clin. rsch. cons., 1988—; sr. cmty. health nurse Madison County Health Dept., Berea, 1993—. Co-contbr. numerous articles to med. jours.; contbr. articles to nursing jours., chpts. to med. books. Mem. Am. Heart Assn. (cardiovasc. nursing sect.). Avocations: hand weaving, photography. Home: 107 Lorraine Ct Berea KY 40403-1317 *Choose work situations that stimulate your intellect and force learning...and when that situation becomes easy move forward to more difficult work. Along the way read, read, read.*

LAMB, JAMIE PARKER, JR., mechanical engineer, educator; b. Boligee, Ala., Sept. 21, 1933; s. Jamie Parker and Cletus (Hixson) L.; m. Nancy Catherine Flaherty, June 11, 1955; children: David Parker, Stephen Patrick. B.S., Auburn U., 1954; M.S., U. Ill., 1958, Ph.D., 1961. Asst. prof. engring. mechanics N.C. State U., Raleigh, 1961-63; faculty mech. engring. U. Tex., Austin, 1963—; prof. U. Tex., 1970—, chmn. dept., 1970-76, 96—, assoc. dean engring., 1970-76, 96—, prof. faculty aerospace engring., 1981-88, chmn. dept., 1981-88, Ernest Cockrell Jr. Meml. prof., 1981—; dir. engring. program U. Tex.-Pan Am., 1993-94; cons. LTV Aerospace Corp., Dallas, Marshall Space Flight Center, Huntsville, Ala., Tracor, Inc., Austin, Rocketdyne, McGregor, Tex., ARO, Inc., Tullahoma, Tenn., Tex. Gas Transport Co., Austin; spl. cons. U. São Paulo, Brazil, 1974; cons. Mobil Oil Corp., Dallas, Gilbarco, Inc., Greensboro, N.C.; mem. bd. boiler rules Tex. Dept. Labor and Standards, 1977-81; mem. rev. panel postdoctoral assoc. NRC, 1981—, mem. U.S. nat. com. on theoretical and applied mechanics, 1985-89; chmn. 10th U.S. Nat. Congress Applied Mechanics, 1986. Assoc. tech. editor: Jour. Fluids Engring., 1976-79; contbr. articles to profl. jours. Served to 1st lt. USAF, 1955-57. Recipient Joe J. King Profl. Engring. Achievement award U. Tex. at Austin, 1984, Disting. Alumnus award U. Ill. Dept. Mech. and Indsl. Engring., 1985, Centennial Alumnus award Auburn U. Dept. Mech. Engring., 1986. Fellow ASME (chmn. fluid mechanics tech. com. 1982-84, Founder's award Central Tex. sect. 1975, Leadership award 1976, 81, Centennial award 1980); assoc. fellow AIAA; mem. Am. Soc. Engring. Edn. (chmn. summer faculty programs com. 1978-80, chmn. mech. engring. div. 1979-80, bd. dirs. Profl. Interest Council I, 1981-82), Nat. Soc. Profl. Engrs., Sigma Xi, Pi Tau Sigma, Tau Beta Pi, Sigma Gamma Tau. Baptist. Home: 2605 Pinewood Ter Austin TX 78757-2136

LAMB, JERRY A., bishop; b. Denver, Sept. 4, 1940; m. Jane Onstad; 1 child, Katherine. BA in Philosophy, St. Thomas Coll.; MA in Theology, St. Thomas Sem. Ordained to Roman Catholic Archdiocese, 1965. Exec. asst. to Bishop of Oreg., elected 6th bishop of No. Calif., 1991—; rector Trinity Ch., Ashland, Oreg.; asst. to rector Emmanuel Ch., Coos Bay; coll. chaplain asst. All St.'s, Denver; dir. Camp St. Malo, Colo.; mem. standing com. Diocesan Coun., Commn. on Ministry; dep. 2 gen. convs. and provincial synods. Office: PO Box 131268 1322 27th St Sacramento CA 95816

LAMB, JOANN ISABEL, adult nurse practitioner; b. Ottawa, Ont., Can., Oct. 18, 1939; came to U.S., 1961; d. Joseph Gordon and Amelia Marguerite (Gillis) L. BSN, SUNY, Albany, 1980; MA in Nursing Edn., Columbia U., 1980, MSN, 1987. RN, N.Y. Surg. ICU head nurse Columbia-Presbyn. Med. Ctr., N.Y.C., 1973-79, procurement coord. Organ Bank, 1979-80, cardiac transplant coord., 1980-87, nurse practitioner Cardiothoracic Transplant Program, 1987-91, mgr. Cardiothoracic Transplant Program, 1991; v.p. patient svcs. The Dobelle Inst., N.Y.C., 1991—; co-owner Carlam Consultants, Inc., N.Y.C., 1979-83; mem. com. for the devel. of critical care stds. Emergency Med. Svcs. Sys., City of N.Y., 1978-79; mem. planning task force 3d Internat. Intensive Care Nursing Meeting, Montreal, 1985-88; site visitor U. Alta. Hosps., Edmonton, 1988; mem. expert panel selecting cardiac transplant ctrs. managed care program John Hancock Ins. Co., 1990, 91; participant Partnership for Organ Donation, Inc., Washington, 1990; lectr. in the field. Author: (with others) Cardiovascular Nursing, 1986, Pediatric Cardiology, 1986, Standrads for Critical Care Nursing, 3d edit., 1988, Organ & Tissue Transplantation: Nursing Care from Procurement through Rehabilitation, 1991, SCCM Textbook of Critical Care Medicine, 1995, Pocket Companion to: Textbook of Critical Care, 1996; mem. editl. bd. Heart & Lung: The Jour. of Critical Care, 1978-81, Life Support Nursing, 1981-83, Critical Care Communique, 1978-81; contbr. more than 30 articles to profl. jours. Recipient Norma J. Shoemaker award for Critical Care Nursing Excellence, Soc. of Critical Care Medicine, 1996. Fellow Am. Coll. Critical Care Medicine; mem. AACN (co-chair program com. N.Y.C. chpt. 1977-78, scholarship com. 1977-78, chair symposium com. 1979-80, bd. dirs. 1981-83, membership com. 1983-88), Soc. for Critical Care Medicine (external affairs com., 1980-81, chair nursing section, 1983, coun. mem., 1984-87, sec., 1987-89, selection panel 1988-89, co-chair mem. com., 1990-94), Columbia U. Sch. Nursing Alumni Assn., Ottawa Civic Hosp. Sch. Nursing Alumni Assn., Am. Assn. Neurosci. Nurses, Am. Assn. Physician Assts., Internat. Soc. for Heart Transplantation, RNs Assn. Ont. (Can.). Office: 3960 Broadway New York NY 10032

LAMB, PATRICK JOHN, research associate, accountant; b. Charleston, W.Va., Oct. 22, 1938; s. Charles Bernard and Grace Frances (Jackson) L.; m. Kathleen Campbell, May 5, 1962; children: Christine M., Mary K., Charles P., Michael J., Karen P. BSBA, W.Va. State Coll., 1962; MBA, W.Va. Coll. Grad. Studies, 1984. Auditor W.Va. Tax Dept., Charleston, 1961-63; acct. The Diamond, Charleston, 1963-66, W.Va. Water Co., Charleston, 1966-69; sr. rsch. assoc., acct. W.Va. Rsch. League, Charleston, 1969—. Author: The Economic Impact of the Arts in West Virginia. Mem. W.Va. Pub. Accts. Assn., KC (grand knight 1986-88, 94-96, Cath. layman 1981, dist. dep. 1988-93, state warden 1993-95, state advocate 1995-96, treas. 1996—). Republican. Roman Catholic. Home: 1403 Jackson St Charleston WV 25301-1909

LAMB, PETER JAMES, meteorology educator, researcher, consultant; b. Nelson, New Zealand, June 21, 1947; came to U.S., 1971; s. George Swan and Dorothy Elizabeth (Smith) L.; m. Barbara Helen Harrison, Aug. 29, 1970; children: Karen Deborah, Brett Timothy. BA, U. Canterbury, Christchurch, New Zealand, 1969; MA with honours, U. Canterbury, Christ Ch., New Zealand, 1971; PhD, U. Wis., 1976. Asst. lectr. U. Canterbury, 1971; rsch. asst. U. Wis., Madison, 1971-76, rsch. assoc., 1976; lectr. U. Adelaide, Australia, 1976-79; sr. sci. Ill. State Water Survey, Champaign, 1979-91, section head, 1984-90; prof. U. Okla., Norman, 1991—; vis. rsch. assoc. U. Miami, Fla., 1978-79; adj. prof. U. Ill., Urbana, 1983-94; dir. Coop. Inst. Mesoscale Meteorol. Studies, Norman, 1991—; dir. Internat. Ctr. Disaster Rsch., 1994—; assoc. dir. Weather Ctr. Programs, Norman, 1996—; cons. Dept. State, Dept. Energy, Agy. Internat. Devel., Nat. Oceanic and Atmospheric Adminstrn., NSF, World Meteorol. Orgn., Kingdom of Morocco, U. Wis., U. Adelaide, Univs. Space Rsch. Assn., EPA, 1983—; site sci. atmospheric radiation measurement program Dept. Energy, 1992—. Coauthor rsch. monographs, book chpt., numerous sci. papers. Coach Champaign Youth Soccer Orgn., 1983-91. Recipient more than 35 rsch. grants fro U.S. Fed. Agys. including NSF, EPA, Dept. Energy, Nat. Atmospheric & Oceanic Adminstrn., Agy. Internat. Devel.; grantee MacArthur Found., Ins. Inst. Property Loss Reduction, Japan Marine Sci. and Tech. Ctr. Fellow Am. Meteorol. Soc. (chief editor Jour. Climate 1989-95); mem. Royal Meteorol. Soc. (Margary lectr. 1991), Am. Assn. State Climatologists, Sigma Xi. Achievements include research on heat transport by the Atlantic Ocean; investigations into the role of the ocean in causing droughts in Sahelian Africa; study of N.Am. precipitation patterns; assessment of economic value of weather and climate information. Home: 3616 Burlington Dr Norman OK 73072-3647 Office: Univ of Oklahoma CIMMS-Sarkeys Energy Ctr 100 E Boyd St Rm 1110 Norman OK 73069-5816

LAMB, ROBERT EDWARD, diplomat; b. Atlanta, Nov. 17, 1936; s. T.E. and Lois (Harris) L.; m. Lucille Trujillo, Jan. 13, 1962; children: Robert Edward, Anne Gretchen, Michael David. BA in Internat. Rels., U. Pa., 1962. Joined Fgn. Service, Dept. State, 1963; dir. fin. services Dept. State, Washington, 1975-77, dir. passport office, 1977-79; adminstrv. counsellor U.S. Embassy, Bonn, Fed. Republic Germany, 1979-83; asst. sec. of state for adminstrn. Dept. State, Washington, 1983-85; asst. sec. of state Diplomatic Security, 1985-89; U.S. Amb. to Cyprus Cyprus, 1990-93; spl. Cyprus coord., 1993-94; exec. dir Am. Philatelic Soc., State Coll., Pa., 1994—. Served with USMC, 1958-61. Mem. Am. Philatelic Soc. Home and Office: PO Box 8000 State College PA 16803-8000

LAMB, ROBERT LEWIS, electric utility executive; b. Goodland, Kans., Mar. 29, 1932; s. Perl and Josephine (Cullins) L.; m. Patricia Jean Kanuch, Sept. 6, 1953; children: Nancy Jo, David Lewis. BSEE, U. Kans., 1955. Engr. The Empire Dist. Electric Co., Joplin, Mo., 1958-67, distbn. engr., 1967-69; supt. engring. The Empire Electric Co., Joplin, 1969-74; v.p. customer services The Empire Dist. Electric Co., Joplin, 1974-78, exec. v.p., 1978-82, pres., chief exec. officer, 1982—, dir., 1978—; bd. dirs. Edison Electric Inst.; chmn. Mokan Power Pool, 1986-87, S.W. Power Pool, 1989-91. Pres. Joplin United Way, 1981, Joplin Indsl. Devel. Authority, 1992-95; v.p., dir. Joplin So. Corp., 1974-90; bd. dirs. St. John's Regional Med. Ctr., Joplin, 1981-90, 91—, chmn., 1982-84, 92-94; trustee N.Am. Electric Reliability Coun., 1989-91; bd. dirs. Mo. So. State Coll., 1993—. Capt. USAF, 1955-58. Mem. Missouri Valley Elec. Assn. (pres. 1993-94), Joplin C. of C. (pres. 1979-80), Mo. C. of C. and Industry (bd. dirs. 1983—, treas. 1990-93, chmn. 1993-95), Twin Hills Country Club (Joplin), Kansas City (Mo.) Club. Republican. Lutheran. Office: Empire Dist Electric Co 602 Joplin St PO Box 127 Joplin MO 64801

LAMB, STACIE THOMPSON, elementary school educator; b. Abilene, Tex., Nov. 9, 1965; d. George Lyman and Shirley Elizabeth (Burton) T.; m. Dennis A. Lamb; children: Lane, Logann. BS in Edn., Lubbock Christian Coll., 1986; postgrad., Tex. Tech U. Elem. Edn. grades 1-6, Tex. 1st grade tchr. Lubbock (Tex.) I.S.D. Brown Elem., 1986-87; 3rd grade tchr., chairperson Morton (Tex.) I.S.D., 1987-89; 5th grade lang. arts tchr.

Whiteface (Tex.) C.I.S.D., 1990—. Mem. ASCD, Classroom Tchrs. Assn. (sec. 1988-89, elem. rep. 1991-92). Home: 2104 Tech Dr Levelland TX 79336-7035 Office: PO Box 117 Whiteface TX 79379-0117

LAMB, SYDNEY MACDONALD, linguistics and cognitive science educator; b. Denver, May 4, 1929; s. Sydney Bishop and Jean Louisa (MacDonald) L.; m. Sharon Reese Rowell, June 17, 1956 (div. 1971); children: Christina, Sarah, Nancy; m. Susan Ellen Jones, May 15, 1977. BA, Yale U., 1951; PhD, U. Calif., Berkeley, 1958. From asst. to assoc. prof. linguistics U. Calif., Berkeley, 1958-64; from assoc. to prof. Yale U., New Haven, 1964-77; mng. ptnr. Semionics Assocs., Houston, 1977-93; prof. Rice U., Houston, 1980—; fellow Ctr. for Advanced Study in Behavioral Scis., Stanford, Calif., 1973-74. Author: Outline of Stratificational Grammar, 1966, (with others) Sprung from Some Common Source, 1991; inventor associative computer memory, 1977, 80, 4 patents; contbr. articles to profl. jours. NSF grantee, 1959-64, 66-70; Am. Council of Learned Soc. grantee, 1973-74. Mem. Linguistic Soc. Am. (exec. com. 1966-68), Linguistics Assn. of Can. and U.S. (pres. 1983-84, chmn. bd. dirs. 1995—), Houston Philos. Soc. (treas. 1985-86, v.p. 1991-92, pres. 1992-93). Avocations: singing, songwriting. Office: Rice U Dept of Linguistics Houston TX 77251

LAMB, URSULA SCHAEFER, history educator; b. Essen, Germany, Jan. 15, 1914; came to U.S., 1935, naturalized, 1949; d. Waldemar Joachim and Maria Katharina (Hoffman von Fallersleben) Schaefer; m. Willis Eugene Lamb, Jr., June 5, 1939. Student, U. Berlin, 1933-35, Smith Coll., 1935-36; M.A., U. Calif., Berkeley, 1937, Ph.D., 1949. Instr. and asso. Barnard Coll., Columbia U., N.Y.C., 1943-51; tutor Brasenose Coll. and Univ. Lectures, Oxford, Eng., 1958-61; lectr., sr. lectr., advisor to library Yale U., New Haven, 1961-74; prof. history U. Ariz., Tucson, 1974-85, prof. emeritus, 1985—; Eva G.R. Taylor lectr. Royal Inst. Navy, London, 1981, AAAS, Chgo., 1991, Brit. Soc. for History of Sci., Imperial Coll., London, 1993; hon. mem. Mortar Bd., 1984. Assoc. editor Hispanic Am. Hist. Rev, 1975-80; mem. editorial bd. Terrae Incognitae, 1978-84, 93, 94; author: Frey Nicolás de Ovando, 1956, 2d edit., 1977; translator, author: intro. A Navigator's Universe: The Libro de Cosmographia of 1538 (Pedro de Medina), 1972; contbr. articles to profl. jours. Recipient Disting. Svc. award Conf. Latin Am. Studies, 1990; Social Sci. Rsch. Coun. grantee, 1943, Am. Coun. Learned Socs. travel grantee, 1947, Guggenheim Meml. fellow, 1968; NEH sr. scholar, 1972-73, Am. Philos. Soc. travel grantee, 1975, NSF grantee, 1978-79; Jeannette Black fellow Brown U., spring, 1985. Mem. Conf. Latin-Am. History, Am. Hist. Assn. Conn. Acad. Arts and Scis., Soc. History of Discovery (pres. 1975-77, coun. mem. 1993, 94), Internat. Soc. History of Nautical Sci. and Hydrography (U.S. rep. 1976), Internat. Commn. maritime History (U.S. rep. 1977, 80), Soc. Spanish and Portuguese Hist. Studies, Instituto de Cultura Hispanica (Caracas), Soc. Hist. Sci. (com. for the quincentennial of discovery of Am.). Home: 848 N Norris Ave Tucson AZ 85719-5130 Office: Univ Ariz Dept History 215 Social Sci Tucson AZ 85721

LAMB, VINCENT P., industrial executive; b. 1932. With Parsons De Leuw Inc., Washington, 1955—, now exec. v.p. Office: Parsons De Leuw Inc 1133 15th St NW Washington DC 20005-2701*

LAMB, WILLIS EUGENE, JR., physicist, educator; b. L.A., July 12, 1913; s. Willis Eugene and Marie Helen (Metcalf) L.; m. Ursula Schaefer, June 5, 1939. BS, U. Calif., 1934, PhD, 1938; DSc (hon.), U. Pa., 1953, Gustavus Adolphus Coll., 1975, Columbia U., 1990; MA (hon.), Oxford (Eng.) U., 1956, Yale, 1961; LHD (hon.), Yeshiva U., 1965. Mem. faculty Columbia U., 1938-52, prof. physics, 1948-52; prof. physics Stanford U., 1951-56; Wykeham prof. physics and fellow New Coll., Oxford U., 1956-62; Henry Ford 2d prof. physics Yale U., 1962-72, J. Willard Gibbs prof. physics, 1972-74; prof. physics and optical scis. U. Ariz., Tucson, 1974—, Regents prof., 1990—; Morris Loeb lectr. Harvard U., 1953-54; Gordon Shrum lectr. Simon Fraser U., 1972; cons. Philips Labs., Bell Telephone Labs., Perkin-Elmer, NASA; vis. com. Brookhaven Nat. Lab. Recipient (with P. Kusch) Nobel prize in physics, 1955, Rumford premium Am. Acad. Arts and Scis., 1953; award Rsch. Corp., 1954, Yeshiva award, 1962; Guggenheim fellow, 1960-61, sr. Alexander von Humboldt fellow, 1992-94. Fellow Am. Phys. Soc., N.Y. Acad. Scis.; hon. fellow Inst. Physics and Phys. Soc. (Guthrie lectr. 1958), Royal Soc. Edinburgh (fgn. mem.); mem. Nat. Acad. Scis., Phi Beta Kappa, Sigma Xi. Office: U Ariz Optical Scis Ctr PO Box 210094 Tucson AZ 85721-0094

LAMBERG, STANLEY LAWRENCE, medical technologist, educator; b. Bklyn., Oct. 2, 1933; s. Joseph and Ray C. (Miller) L.; m. Charlotte Frances Rothschild, June 15, 1963; children: Steven Kenneth, Eric Michael. BS, Bklyn. Coll., 1955; MA, Oberlin Coll., 1957; MS, Tufts U., 1962; PhD, NYU, 1968. Chief lab. tech. dept. biochemistry Sch. Medicine Cornell U., N.Y.C., 1957-58; Charleston rsch. and USPHS fellow dept. physiology Tufts U., Boston, 1958-61; NIDR predoctoral trainee NYU, 1961-66; lectr. dept. biology CCNY, 1966-67; instr. to asst. prof. dept. biology Bklyn. Ctr., LIU, 1967-70; part-time asst. rsch. scientist Guggenheim Inst. for Dental Rsch., NYU, 1968-69; asst. prof. dept. biology SUNY, Farmingdale, 1970-71, asst. prof., 1971-73, assoc. prof., 1973-75, prof., 1975-95, dept. med. lab. tech. Co-author various lab. manuals. Adv. chmn. Boy Scouts Am., Hauppauge, N.Y., 1982—. Recipient Chancellor's award for Excellence in Teaching SUNY, 1976; NSF fellow, 1971, others. Mem. N.Y. State Histotech. Soc., Nat. Soc. Histotech., N.Y. State Soc. Med. Tech. (treas. 1980-93, bd. dirs. 1980-93, 94—), N.Y. Acad. Scis., Sigma Xi.

LAMBERG-KARLOVSKY, CLIFFORD CHARLES, anthropologist, archaeologist; b. Prague, Czechoslovakia, Oct. 2, 1937; came to U.S., 1939; s. Carl Othmar von Lamberg and Bellina Karlovsky; m. Martha Louise Veale, Sept. 12, 1959; children: Karl Emil Othmar, Christopher William. A.B., Dartmouth Coll., 1959; M.A. (Wenner-Gren fellow), U. Pa., 1964, Ph.D., 1965; M.A. (hon.), Harvard U., 1970. Asst. prof. sociology and anthropology Franklin and Marshall Coll., 1964-65; asst. prof. anthropology Harvard U., 1965-69, prof., 1969-90, Stephen Phillips prof. archaeology, 1991—; curator Near Eastern archaeology Peabody Museum Archaeology and Ethnology, 1969—, mus. dir., 1977-90; assoc. Columbia U., 1969—; trustee Am. Inst. Iranian Studies, 1968—, Am. Inst. Yemeni Studies, 1976-77; dir. rsch. Am. Sch. Prehist. Rsch., 1974-79, 86—, Centro di Richerche Ligabue, 1984; Reckitt archaeol. surveys in Syria, 1965, excavation projects at Tepe Yahya, Iran, 1967-75, Sarazm, Tadjikistan, USSR, 1985, archaeol. surveys in Saudi Arabia, 1977-80, USSR, 1990-91; dir. survey and excavations Anau, Turkmenistan, 1992—; corr. fellow Inst. Medio and Extremo Orient, Italy; mem. UNESCO com. for sci. study of mankind, 1989—. Author: (with J. Sabloff) Ancient Civilizations: The Near East and Mesoamerica, 1979; editor: (with J. Sabloff) The Rise and Fall of Civilizations, 1973, Ancient Civilizations and Trade, 1975, Hunters, Farmers and Civilization, 1979, Archaeological Thought in America, 1988; author, gen. editor: Tepe Yahya: The Early Periods, 1986. Recipient medal Iran-Am. Soc., 1972; NSF grantee, 1966-75, 78-80, 93, Nat. Endowment for Arts grantee, 1977—, NEH grantee, 1977—. Fellow AAAS (chmn. USA/USSR archaeol. exch. program), Soc. Antiquaries Gt. Britain and Ireland (sec. N.Am. chpt. 1985-93), Am. Anthrop. Assn., N.Y. Acad. Sci., USSR Acad. Sci., Soc. Am. Archaeology, Archeol. Inst. Am., Instituto para Medio et Extrema Oriente; mem. German Archaeol. Inst., Danish Archaeol. Inst., Brit. Archaeol. Inst., Tavern Club (Boston). Office: Peabody Mus Archaeology & Ethnology 11 Divinity Ave Cambridge MA 02138-2019

LAMBERSON, JOHN ROGER, insurance company executive; b. Aurora, Mo., Aug. 16, 1933; s. John Oral Lamberson and Golda May (Caldwell) Tidwell; m. Virginia Lee, Aug. 10, 1957; 1 child, John Clinton. BA, U. Calif., Berkeley, 1954. Coach, tchr. Thousand Palms (Calif.) Sch., 1954-55; underwriter trainee Fireman's Fund Ins. Co., San Francisco, 1955; surety mgr. Safeco Ins. Co. (formerly Gen. Ins. Co.), San Francisco and Sacramento, Calif., 1957-61; pres., COO Willis Corroon Corp., N.Y.C., 1966-92, also bd. dirs., chmn. constrn. industry div., mem. exec. com., aquisition com.; pres., chmn., CEO Lamberson Koster & Co., San Francisco, 1992—; bd. dirs. Willis Cornoon Group PLC, London, Consumers Benefit Life Ins. Co., Nova Group, Inc.; chmn., CEO Lamberson Koster and Co. Mem. Nat. Assn. Heavy Engring. Constructors (bd. dirs. 1985—, Golden Beavers award for outstanding svc. to industry), Constrn. Fin. Mgmt. Assn. (bd. dirs. 1987-91, exec. com.), Assoc. Gen. Contractors Am. (membership devel. com., past chmn. bd. dirs. nat. assoc. mems. coun.), Assoc. Gen. Contractors Calif. (bd. dirs. 1976), Nat. Assn. Surety Bond Prodrs. (past nat. pres., regional v.p.), Am. Inst. Contractors, Soc. Am. Mil. Engrs., The Moles-Heavey Engring. Constrn. Soc., Young Pres. Orgn. (sem. leader), Bankers Club, Commonwealth Club, Sharon Heights Golf and Country Club, Bermuda Dunes Country Club, Rockaway Hunting Club, Villa Taverna Club. Home: 85 Greenoaks Dr Atherton CA 94027-2160 Office: Lamberson Koster & Co 580 California St San Francisco CA 94104-1000

LAMBERSON, MARY JANE, artist, educator; b. Logan, Iowa, Aug. 10, 1944; d. James Perry and Emma Jane (Skinner) Laughrey; m. Robert Ray Lamberson, Aug. 30, 1964; children: Courtney Kaye, Robert Russell. BFA, Kearney (Nebr.) State Coll., 1988; MA in Edn., U. Nebr., Kearney, 1991. Teaching asst. U. Nebr., Kearney, 1989-91, adj. art instr., 1991; com. chair Dannebrog, Nebr., 1991—; com. chair Art Exit 305, 1991—. Creator Dannebrog Outdoor Hist. Mural, 1991, Kearney's Mayor's Art Project Outdoor Mural, 1993; designer, cons. Cedar Rapids High Sch. Indoor Hist. Mural, 1992. Recipient art awards. Mem. Impact II, Women Artists of Nebr., Kansas City Artist Coalition, Kans. Sculpture Assn., Nebr. Crafts Coun. (bd. dirs. 1988—), Assn. Nebr. Art Club. Home: 688 Liberty Rd Dannebrog NE 68831-3163

LAMBERT, DANIEL MICHAEL, academic administrator; b. Kansas City, Mo., Jan. 16, 1941; s. Paul McKinley and Della Mae (Rogers) L.; m. Carolyn Faye Bright, Dec. 27, 1969; children: Kristian Paige, Dennis McKinley. AB, William Jewell Coll., 1963; MA, Northwestern U., 1965; postgrad., Harvard U., 1965-66; PhD, U. Mo., Columbia, 1977. Dean student affairs William Jewell Coll., Liberty, Mo., 1970-77, exec. asst. to pres., 1977-80, v.p., 1980-85; pres. College Hill Investments Inc., Liberty, 1985-87, Baker U., Baldwin City, Kans., 1987—; bd. dirs. Ferrell Co., Liberty; dir. Kansas City Bd. of Trade, 1988-90; hon. trustee Dohto U., Japan. Bd. dirs. The Barstow Sch., Kans. Ind. Colls. Assn.; mem. Big Bros. and Big Sisters; trustee Midwest Rsch. Inst. Capt. U.S. Army, 1966-70, Vietnam. Recipient Civic Leadership award Mo. Mcpl. League, 1986. Mem. Nat. Assn. Intercollegiate Athletics (dir.). Club: KC (Alvamar). Home: 505 E 8th St Baldwin City KS 66006 Office: Baker U Office of Pres Baldwin City KS 66006

LAMBERT, DEBORAH KETCHUM, public relations executive; b. Greenwich, Conn., Jan. 22, 1942; d. Alton Harrington and Robyna (Neilson) Ketchum; m. Harvey R. Lambert, Nov. 23, 1963 (div. 1985); children: Harvey Richard Jr., Eric Harrington. BS, Columbia U., 1965. Researcher, writer The Nowland Orgn., Greenwich, Conn., 1964-67; model Country Fashions, Greenwich, Conn., 1964-67; freelance writer to various newspapers and mags., 1977-82; press sec. Va. Del. Gwen Cody, Annandale, Va., 1981-82; assoc. editor Campus Report, Washington, 1985—; adminstrv. asst. Accuracy in Media, Inc., Washington, 1983-84, dir. pub. affairs, 1985—; TV producer weekly program The Other Side of the Story, 1994—; bd. dirs. Accuracy in Academia, Washington; film script cons. The Seductive Illusion, 1988-89. Columnist: The Eye, The Washington Inquirer, 1984—, Squeaky Chalk, Campus Report, 1985—; contbr. articles to various mags.; producer: The Other Side of the Story, 1993—. Co-founder, mem. Va. Rep. Forum, McLean, 1983—; mem. Rep. Women's Fed. Forum. Mem. Am. Bell Assn., Pub. Rels. Soc. Am., DAR., World Media Assn., Am. Platform Assn. Republican. Presbyterian. Home: 1945 Lorraine Ave Mc Lean VA 22101-5331 Office: Accuracy in Media Inc 4455 Connecticut Ave NW Washington DC 20008-2328

LAMBERT, DENNIS ALVIN, radio news director; b. Allegan, Mich., Sept. 14, 1947; s. Alvin Millard and Myrta Gertrude (Ellinger) L.; m. Pamela Sue Hoeksema, Dec. 20, 1969; children: Matthew Dennis, Nicole Leigh. BA, Mich. State U., 1971. Disc jockey Sta. WAOP, Osego, Mich., 1969; asst. news dir. Sta. WJIM, Lansing, Mich., 1969-75; news reporter Sta. WVIC, East Lansing, 1975-76; news and sports anchor Sta. WCAR, Detroit, 1976; news reporter, editor Sta. WXYZ, Detroit, 1976-84; mng. editor Sta. KTAR, Phoenix, 1984-85, news dir., 1985-89; ops. mgr. GO Media Cos., Phoenix, 1990—. Recipient various news-related awards including Peabody award, Scripps-Howard award, RTNDA Continuing Coverage award, Ariz. AP, 1984, 86, 87. Mem. Ariz. Press Club, Radio, TV and News Dirs. Assn. Avocations: golf, softball, little league. Office: GO Media Ste 216 6245 N 24th Pkwy Phoenix AZ 85016

LAMBERT, ELAINE L., surgical nurse, administrator; b. West Chester, Pa., Dec. 17, 1938; d. Lewis Robert and Grace Elma (Matlack) Beard; m. Dennis John Lambert, Jan. 2, 1989; children: Bruce Lewis, Brenda Elaine. Diploma, Presbyn. Hosp., Phila., 1959; B in Profl. Sci., U. Sys. of N.H., 1993. Cert. operating room nurse. Staff nurse operating room and emergency room Chester County Hosp., West Chester, 1959-71; night supr., charge nurse ICU Valley Regional Hosp., Pa., 1972-79; relief oper. rm. mgr. Pa. Valley Regional Hosp., 1979-81; nurse mgr. of surg. svcs. Valley Regional Hosp., Claremont, N.H., 1982-91, 1979-82; sr. nurse mgr. oper. rm./cen. supply Rutland (Vt.) Regional Med. Ctr., 1991-94; dir. Ortho. Surgery Ctr., Concord, N.H., 1994—. Mem. NAFE, N.H. Orgn. Nurse Execs., N.H.-Vt. Oper. Rm. Mgrs., Vt. Orgn. Nurse Execs., AORN, Fed. Ambulatory Surgery Assn., Nat. Assn. Orthopaedic Nurses. Home: HCR 64 Box 968 Wilmot NH 03287

LAMBERT, ELEANOR (MRS. SEYMOUR BERKSON), public relations executive, fashion authority, journalist; b. Crawfordsville, Ind.; d. Henry Clay and Helen Houghton (Craig) L.; m. Seymour Berkson, 1936 (dec.); 1 son, William Craig Berkson. Student, John Herron Art Inst., Chgo. Art Inst.; DFA (hon.), Parsons Sch. Design, 1993. Pioneer publicist for Am. art and artists and later for creative talents in Am. fashion; originator, coordinator Coty Am. Fashion Critics Award and Cotton Fashion Awards; originator, founder, coord. Nat. Fashion Press weeks and ann. Internat. Best Dressed polls, 1940—; original dir. ILGWU's consumer svc. program; prodr. large fashion shows; spl. cons. on uniforms WAC and U.S. Army Nurse Corps, 1943-45; mem. NRC adv. com. to q.m. on women's mil. clothing; mem. adv. com. Costume Inst., Met. Mus. Art; apptd. by Pres. Johnson as mem. Nat. Coun. on Arts, 1965-66; founder, charter mem. Coun. Fashion Designers of Am., 1963; mem. N.Y. Mayor's Com. World Fashion Ctr.; mem. Mayor's Hospitality Com., N.Y.; bd. dirs. N.Y. World's Fair, 1964; founder, organizer Fashion Inst. Tech. Sch. Author: World of Fashion, 1973, syndicated column on women's interests, 1965—. Recipient N.Y. Bd. of Trade gold medal award for outstanding contbns. to Am. fashion industries, 1960; Honor award Girls Clubs Am.; Matrix award in pub. rels. N.Y. Women in Communications, 1985; Lifetime Achievement awards Coun. Fashion Designers of Am., 1988, 94. Mem. N.Y. Fashion Group (v.p. 1961-63). Presbyterian. Home: 1060 5th Ave New York NY 10128-0104 Office: Eleanor Lambert Ltd 245 E 58th St New York NY 10022-1201

LAMBERT, ETHEL GIBSON CLARK, secondary school educator; b. Atlanta, Apr. 18, 1943; d. Robert Harold and Ethel (Gibson) Clark; m. Hugh Felder Lambert, June 27, 1964 (div. Nov. 3, 1988); children: Courtney Elizabeth, Hugh Lambert Jr. BA, Oglethorpe U., Atlanta, 1965; MEd, Kennesaw State Coll., Marietta, Ga., 1992; postgrad., West Ga. Coll., Carrollton, 1995—. Lic. tchr. T-5, Ga. Tchr. Clayton County Bd. Edn., Jonesboro, Ga., 1965-66, Fulton County Bd. Edn., Atlanta, 1966-67; tchr. pre-sch. weekday program First Bapt. Ch., Gainesville, Ga., 1984-88; tchr. remedial edn. program Riverdale High Sch./Clayton County Bd. Edn., 1990—. Author: The Impact of Geography on the Campaigns of the Civil War Fought in Georgia, 1993, The Utilization of Georgia Historical Sites as Teaching Methodology in MIddle Grades Education, 1993, (juvenile) Obnoxious Bill, 1993, Research on Academic Motivation of Elementary, Middle and Secondary School Students in America, 1993, Reading Strategies that Address the Reluctant Reader in America's Public Middle and High Schools, 1995. Den leader Cub Scouts Am., Gainesville, 1980-83; mem. Christian Businessmen's Prayer Breakfast, Atlanta, 1990-95, 96. Mem. Profl. Assn. Ga. Educators, Order Ea. Star. Baptist. Avocations: swimming, water skiing, reading, walking, genealogy. Home: 1881 Myrtle Dr SW Apt 711 Atlanta GA 30311-4919 Office: Riverdale High Sch 160 Roberts Dr Riverdale GA 30274

LAMBERT, EUGENE KENT, oncologist, hematologist; b. Hinsdale, Ill., Feb. 13, 1944; s. Eugene Nelson and Dorothy Louise (Diedrichson) L.; m. Maria Natalie Gonzalez,June 19, 1971; children: Carlotta Pilar, Danielle Suzanne, Jori Marie. BA, North Ctrl. Coll., Naperville, Ill., 1966; MD, U. Ill., Chgo., 1970. Diplomate Am. Bd. Internal Medicine, Am. Bd. Hematology, Am. Bd. Med. Oncology. Fellow in hematology Michael Reese Hosp., Chgo., 1976; fellow Northwestern U., Chgo., 1979; oncologist Wichita (Kans.) Clinic, 1979-81, Dreyer Med. Clinic, Aurora, Ill., 1981-86, Fond du Lac (Wis.) Clinic, 1986—; med. dir. at large Wis. divsn. Am. Cancer Soc., 1991—. Bd. dirs. Girl Scouts Am., Aurora, Ill., 1985-86, El Centro, Aurora, 1985-86, Fond du Lac Regional Clinic, 1992. Lt. USNR, 1971-73. Mem. AMA, ACP, Am. Soc. Hematology, Am. Soc. Clin. Oncologists. Avocations: music, volley ball, reading, cross country skiing. Office: Fond du Lac Clinic 80 Sheboygan St Fond Du Lac WI 54935-4333

LAMBERT, FREDERICK WILLIAM, lawyer, educator; b. Millburn, N.J., Feb. 12, 1943; m. Barbara E. Fogell, Aug. 13, 1965; children: Elisabeth, Mark. BA, U. Mich., 1965, JD, 1969. Bar: Ohio 1969, Fla. 1973, Calif. 1973, U.S. Supreme Ct. 1975. Law clk. to Stanley N. Barnes, U.S. Cir. Judge U.S. Cir. Ct., L.A., 1969-70; spl. asst. Office Legal Counsel U.S. Dept. Justice, Washington, 1970-71; law clk. to Justice William H. Rehnquist U.S. Supreme Ct., Washington, 1971-72; pvt. practice L.A., 1973-90; acting gen. counsel Itel Corp., San Francisco, 1981-82; ptnr. Adams, Duque & Hazeltine, L.A., 1985-90, chmn. bus. law dept., 1989-90; assoc. prof. Hastings Coll. Law, U. Calif., San Francisco, 1993—; vis. prof. U. Mich. Law Sch., Ann Arbor, 1990-91, Duke Law Sch., Durham, N.C., 1992-93. Mem. Calif. State Bar Assn. Home: 1531 Willard St San Francisco CA 94117-3708

LAMBERT, GARY ERVERY, lawyer; b. Providence, Oct. 27, 1959; s. Ervery Eldege and Melitta (Hirsch) L.; m. Lori Keller, Apr. 22, 1995. BS in Chemistry and Biology, Valparaiso (Ind.) U., 1981; JD with honors, Drake U., 1984. Bar: Iowa 1984, Mass. 1986, U.S. Ct. Mil. Appeals 1986, U.S. Dist. Ct. Mass. 1987, U.S. Ct. Appeals (1st cir.) 1987, U.S. Patent and Trademark Office 1993, U.S. Ct. Appeals (fed. cir.) 1996. Litigator Gallagher & Gallagher, P.C., Boston, 1987-89; owner Law Office of Gary Lambert, Boston, 1989-93; ptnr. Lambert & Ricci, P.C., Boston, 1993—; staff judge advocate 25th Marine Regt., Worcester, Mass., 1993—. Capt. USMC, 1984-87, Japan. Mem. Boston Bar Assn., Boston Patent Law Assn., Am. Intellectual Property Assn., Marine Corps Res. Officers Assn. (life), NRA (life). Republican. Lutheran. Home: 32 Columbia Ave Nashua NH 03060-1601 Office: Lambert & Ricci 92 State St Boston MA 02109-2004

LAMBERT, GEORGE ROBERT, lawyer, insurance company executive, legal consultant; b. Muncie, Ind., Feb. 21, 1933; s. George Russell and Velma Lou (Jones) L.; m. Mary Virginia Alling, June 16, 1956; children: Robert Allen, Ann Holt, James William. BS, Ind. U., Bloomington, 1955; JD, Ill. Inst. Tech. Chgo.-Kent Coll. Law, 1962. Bar: Ill. 1962, U.S. Dist. Ct. (no. dist.) Ill. 1962, Iowa 1984, Pa. 1988. V.p., gen. counsel, sec. Washington Nat. Ins. Co., Evanston, Ill., 1958-82; v.p., gen. counsel Washington Nat. Corp., Evanston, 1979-82; sr. v.p., sec., gen. counsel Life Investors Inc., Cedar Rapids, Iowa, 1982-88; v.p., gen. counsel Provident Mut. Life Ins. Co. Phila., 1988-95; atty.-at-law, 1995—; pres. Lambert Legal Consulting, Inc., Media, 1995—. Alderman, Evanston City Council, 1980-82. Served to lt. USAF, 1955-57. Mem. ABA (ho. of dels. 1987-89, chair life ins. law com. 1989-90, chair scope and correlation com. 1992-93, mem. tort and ins. practice sect.), Ill. State Bar Assn., Iowa State Bar Assn., Phila. Bar Assn., Pa. Bar Assn., Assn. of Life Ins. Counsel (past pres.), Am. Corporate Counsel Assn. (Del Valley chap., bd. dirs. 1992-95). Home and Office: 135 Emerald Key Ln Palm Beach Gardens FL 33418

LAMBERT, JEREMIAH DANIEL, lawyer; b. N.Y.C., Sept. 11, 1934; s. Noah D. and Clara (Ravage) L.; m. Vicki Anne Asher, July 25, 1959 (div.); children: Nicole Stirling, Alix Stewart, Leigh Asher; m. Sanda Kayden, Dec. 3, 1983; children: Clare Kayden, Hilary Kayden. A.B., Princeton U., 1955; LL.B., Yale U., 1959. Bar: N.Y. 1960, D.C. 1964, U.S. Ct. Appeals (5th cir.) 1964, U.S. Supreme Ct. 1964. Assoc. Cravath, Swaine & Moore, N.Y.C., 1959-63; pvt. practice law Washington, 1963-66; ptnr. Drew & Lambert, Washington, 1966-69; sr. ptnr. Peabody, Lambert & Meyers, Washington, 1969-84; ptnr. Lane & Mittendorf, Washington, 1991—; adj. prof. law Georgetown U., Washington, 1978-79; trustee Internat. Law Inst., Washington, 1983-88. Co-author: (with Lawrence White) Handbook of Modern Construction Law, 1982; author, editor: Economic and Political Incentives to Petroleum Development, 1990; contbr. articles to legal publs. 1st lt. USAR, 1963-66. Fulbright scholar U. Copenhagen, 1955-56. Mem. ABA, Am. Soc. Internat. Law, D.C Bar Assn., Bar Assn. of City of N.Y., Cosmos Club, Princeton Club, Yale Club, Chevy Chase Club. Office: Lane & Mittendorf 919 18th St NW Washington DC 20006-5503

LAMBERT, JOHN BOYD, chemical engineer, consultant; b. Billings, Mont., July 5, 1929; s. Jean Arthur and Gail (Boyd) L.; m. Jean Wilson Bullard, June 20, 1953 (dec. 1958); children: William, Thomas, Patricia, Cathy, Karen; m. Ilse Crager, Sept. 20, 1980 (dec. 1995). BS in Engring., Princeton U., 1951; PhD, U. Wis., 1956. Rsch. engr. E.I. DuPont de Nemours Co., Wilmington, Del., 1956-69; sr. rsch. engr. Fansteel, Inc., Balt., 1969, mktg. mgr./plant mgr., North Chicago, Ill., 1970-73, mgr. mfg. engring., Waukegan, Ill., 1974-80, corp. tech. dir., North Chicago, 1980-86, gen. mgr. metals, 1987-90, v.p., corp. tech. dir., 1990-91; ind. cons., Lake Forest, Ill., 1991—; bd. dirs. Lake Forest Grad. Sch. Mgmt., 1984-91, Delta Star, Inc., 1995—. Contbr. to profl. publs. Sec. Del. Jr. C. of C., Wilmington, 1972-74. Recipient Charles Hatchett medal Inst. Metals, London, 1986. Mem. AICE, Am. Chem. Soc., Am. Soc. Metals, Sigma Xi. Episcopalian. Achievements include patents in field of dispersion-strengthened metals, refractory metals, chemical vapor deposition, both products and processes. Home and Office: 617 Greenbriar Ln Lake Forest IL 60045-3214

LAMBERT, JOHN PHILLIP, financial executive, consultant; b. Davenport, Iowa, Aug. 17, 1944; s. Dale Edward Lambert and Phyllis Meeker; m. Carol Ann Moreira, Aug. 10, 1981; children: Dawn, Kimberly, Kim. BA, Augustana Coll., Rock Island, Ill., 1966. CPA, Ill. Sr. auditor Price Waterhouse, Chgo., 1966-71; sr. v.p. fin. Burger King Corp., Miami, Fla., 1971-82; exec. v.p., chief fin. officer W.R. Grace Restaurants, Irvine, Calif., 1983-84, Perkins Family Restaurants, L.P., Memphis, 1985-89; pvt. practice fin. cons. Sarasota, Fla., 1989—; fin. cons. to restaurant industry. Recipient All Am. Wrestler award NCAA, 1966; named one of Outstanding Young Men of Am., 1976. Mem. AICPA. Republican. Presbyterian. Avocations: reading, golf, boating, gardening. Home and Office: 3770 Prairie Dunes Dr Sarasota FL 34238-2853

LAMBERT, JOSEPH BUCKLEY, chemistry educator; b. Ft. Sheridan, Ill., July 4, 1940; s. Joseph Idus and Elizabeth Dorothy (Kirwan) L.; m. Mary Wakefield Pulliam, June 27, 1967; children: Laura Kirwan, Alice Pulliam, Joseph Cannon. BS, Yale U., 1962; Ph.D. (Woodrow Wilson fellow 1962-63, NSF fellow 1962-65), Calif. Inst. Tech., 1965. Asst. prof. chemistry Northwestern U., Evanston, Ill., 1965-69, assoc. prof., 1969-74, prof. chemistry, 1974-91, Clare Hamilton Hall prof. chemistry, 1991—; chmn. dept. Northwestern U., 1986-89, dir. integrated sci. program, 1982-85; vis. assoc. Brit. Mus., 1973, Polish Acad. Scis., 1981, Chinese Acad. Scis., 1988. Author: Organic Structural Analysis, 1976, Physical Organic Chemistry through Solved Problems, 1978, The Multinuclear Approach to NMR Spectroscopy, 1983, Archaeological Chemistry III, 1984, Introduction to Organic Spectroscopy, 1987, Recent Advances in Organic NMR Spectroscopy, 1987, Acyclic Organonitrogen Stereodynamics, 1992, Cyclic Organonitrogen Stereodynamics, 1992, Prehistoric Human Bone, 1993; audio course Intermediate NMR Spectroscopy, 1973; editor in chief Journal of Physical Organic Chemistry; editorial bd. Magnetic Resonance Chemistry, Archaeometry; contbr. articles to sci. jours. Recipient Nat. Fresenius award, 1976, James Flack Norris award, 1987, Fryxell award, 1989, Nat. Catalyst award, 1993; Alfred P. Sloan fellow, 1968-70, Guggenheim fellow, 1973, Interacad. exch. fellow (U.S.-Poland), 1985, Air Force Office sci. rsch. fellow, 1990. Fellow AAAS, Japan Soc. for Promotion of Sci., Brit. Interplanetary Soc., Ill. Acad. Sci. (life); mem. Am. Chem. Soc. (chmn. history of chemistry divsn., 1996), Royal Soc. Chemistry, Soc. Archaeol. Scis. (pres. 1986-87, assoc. editor Bull.), Phi Beta Kappa, Sigma Xi. Home: 1956 Linneman St Glenview IL 60025-4264 Office: Northwestern University Dept of Chemistry 2145 Sheridan Rd Evanston IL 60208-0834

LAMBERT, JUDITH A. UNGAR, lawyer; b. N.Y.C., Apr. 13, 1943; d. Alexander Lawrence and Helene (Rosenson) Ungar; m. Peter D. Leibowits, Aug. 22, 1965 (div. 1971); 1 child, David Gary. BS, U. Pa., 1964; JD magna cum laude, U. Miami, 1984. Bar: N.Y. 1985, Fla. 1990. Assoc. Proskauer Rose Goetz & Mendelsohn, N.Y.C., 1984-86, Taub & Fasciana, N.Y.C.,

1986-87, Hoffinger Friedland Dobrish Bernfeld & Hasen, N.Y.C., 1987-88; pvt. practice N.Y.C., 1988—. Mem. ABA, N.Y. State Bar Assn., Assn. Bar of City of N.Y., N.Y. Women's Bar Assn. (family law and trusts and estates com.), N.Y. County Lawyers Assn. Avocations: travel, music, theater. Office: 245 E 54th St New York NY 10022-4707

LAMBERT, LINDA MARGARET, reading specialist; b. Livingston County, Ky., Jan. 17, 1941; d. Wiley Jackson and Florence Allie (Davidson) Stallions; m. Leland Dawson Lambert; children: Sharon Kay, Sheila Lynn, Wiley Lee. AA, Yuba Coll., 1970; BLS, Mary Washington Coll., 1980; MEd, U. Va., 1986. Cert. tchr., Va. Elem. tchr. Stafford (Va.) County Schs., 1979-91, reading specialist, 1991—; mem. com. Devel. Elem. Counselors, Stafford, 1987-89, Devel. Appropriate Assessment, Stafford, 1993-94. Sponsor Ghostwriter Mystery Club, Garrisonwoods Estates, 1993—; mem. Falmouth Bapt. Ch. Mem. NEA, Va. Edn. Assn., Stafford County Edn. Assn., Internat. Reading Assn., Va. State Reading Assn., Rappahanook Reading Coun., Hist. Fredericksburg Antique Automobile Club. Democrat. Avocations: swimming, reading, antiques. Home: 203 Rumford Rd Fredericksburg VA 22405-3206 Office: Hampton Oaks Elem Sch 107 Northampton Blvd Stafford VA 22554-7660

LAMBERT, LYN DEE, law librarian, lawyer; b. Fitchburg, Mass., Jan. 5, 1954; m. Paul Frederick Lambert, Aug. 11, 1979; children: Gregory John, Emily Jayne, Nicholas James. BA in History, Fitchburg State Coll., 1976, MEd in History, 1979; JD, Franklin Pierce Law Ct., 1983; MLS, Simmons Coll., 1986. Law libr. Fitchburg Law Libr., Mass. Trial Ct., 1985—; instr. paralegal studies courses Fisher Coll., Fitchburg, 1989-94, Anna Maria Coll., Paxton, Mass., 1995—, Atlantic Union Coll., Lancaster, Mass., 1995—, pre-law coll. courses Fitchburg State Coll., 1995—. Mem. Am. Legion Band, Fitchburg, 1959—, Westminster (Mass.) Town Band, 1965—. Recipient Community Leadership award Phi Delta Kappa-Fitchburg State Coll. chpt., 1993. Mem. ALA, Am. Assn. Law Librarians (copyright com. 1987-89, publs. rev. com. 1990-92, state, ct. and county law librs. spl. interest sect. publicity com. 1993—), Law Librarians New Eng. (conf. com. 1988), Mass. Libr. Assn. (edn. chair 1991-93, freedom of info. com., legislation com.), New Eng. Libr. Assn., New Eng. Microcomputer Users Group (profl. assoc.), North Cen. Mass. Libr. Alliance (newsletter editor 1990—), Spl. Libr. Assn., Beta Phi Mu, Phi Alpha Delta, Phi Delta Kappa (Montachusett chpt.). Avocations: singing, guitar, clarinet, hiking, camping. Office: Fitchburg Law Libr Mass Trial Ct Superior Courthouse 84 Elm St Fitchburg MA 01420-3232

LAMBERT, MARJORY ANNE, nurse; b. Scotland, Dec. 31, 1937; came to U.S., 1961; d. Archibald Millar and Annie (Mellon) Walker; m. Howard P. Lambert, Aug. 30, 1963; children: Paul, Sarah. RN, Germiston Sch. of Nursing, South Africa, 1958; diploma in midwifery, Addington Sch. of Nursing, Durban, South Africa, 1959. Cert. psychiat.-mental health nurse; cert. gerontol. nurse; cert. vol. ombudsmen. Staff nurse Boulder Cmty. Hosp., 1987-92; pvt. duty staff developer HomeCare Boulder Cmty. Hosp., 1992-94; founder Hospice of Boca Raton, Fla., 1978.

LAMBERT, MICHAEL MALET, investment and hospitality consultant; b. Liverpool, Eng., Sept. 30, 1930; came to Can., 1956, naturalized, 1968; s. Arthur Reginald and Kathleen (Backhouse) L.; m. Sally Ann Day, May 15, 1957; children—Christopher Malet, Simon Day. Hotel gen. mgr. Western Internat. Hotels, Vancouver, B.C., Can., 1957-64; hotel gen. mgr. Calgary, Alta., 1964-68, Montreal, P.Q., Can., 1968-71, Washington, 1971-73; from v.p. to exec. v.p. Four Seasons Hotels Ltd., Toronto, Ont., Can., 1973-84; pres. Four Seasons Hotels Ltd., Singapore, 1984-85; regional v.p. Can. Pacific Hotels, 1985-95; gen. mgr. hotel, 1985-95, ret., 1995; pres. Michael Lambert and Assocs., Bowen Island, B.C., 1995—. Served to lt. Army of Gt. Britain, 1949-50. Avocations: history; antiques; tennis; gardening; bridge. Office: 1639 Old Eaglecliffe Rd, Bowen Island, BC Canada V0N 1G0

LAMBERT, NADINE MURPHY, psychologist, educator; b. Ephraim, Utah; m. Robert E. Lambert, 1956; children—Laura Allan, Jeffrey. Ph.D. in Psychology, U. So. Calif., 1965. Diplomate Am. Bd. Profl. Psychology, Am. Bd. Sch. Psychology. Sch. psychologist Los Nietos Sch. Dist., Whittier, Calif., 1952-53, Bellflower (Calif.) Unified Sch. Dist., 1953-58; research cons. Calif. Dept. Edn., Los Angeles, 1958-64; dir. sch. psychology tng. program U. Calif., Berkeley, 1964—; asst. prof. edn. U. Calif., 1964-70, asso. prof., 1970-76, prof., 1976—; assoc. dean for student svcs. U. Calif., Berkeley, 1988-94; mem. Joint Com. Mental Health of Children, 1967-68; cons. state depts. edn., Calif., Ga., Fla.; cons. Calif. Dept. Justice; mem. panel on testing handicapped people Nat. Acad. Scis., 1978-81. Author: School Version of the AAMD Adaptive Behavior Scale, 3d edit., 1993; co-author: (with Wilcox and Gleason) Educationally Retarded Child: Comprehensive Assessment and Planning for the EMR and Slow-Learning Child, 1974, (with Hartsough and Bower) Process for Assessment of Effective Functioning, 1981, (with Windmiller and Turiel) Moral Development and Socialization -- Three Perspectives, 1979; assoc. editor Am. Jour. Orthopsychiatry, 1975-81, Am. Jour. Mental Deficiency, 1977-80, others. With Hartsough and Sandoval Children's Attention and Adjustment Survey, 1990. Recipient Dorothy Hughes award for outstanding contbn. to ednl. and sch. psychology NYU, 1990, Tobacco Disease Related Rsch. award U. Calif., 1990-94, NIDA, 1994—, Dept. Transp., 1994-95; grantee NIMH, 1965-87, Calif. State Dept. Edn., 1971-72, 76-78. Fellow APA (coun. reps. divsn. sch. psychologists, bd. dirs. 1984-87, mem. bd. profl. affairs 1981-83, bd. ednl. affairs 1991-94, chmn. 1992-94, exec. com. divsn. sch. psychology 1995-96, mem. commn. for recognition of specialities and professions in psychology 1993—, Disting. Svc. award 1980, award for disting. profl. contbns. 1986), Am. Orthopsychiat. Assn.; mem. NEA, Calif. Assn. Sch. Psychologists and Psychometrists (pres. 1962-63, Sandra Goff award 1985), Am. Ednl. Rsch. Assn. Office: U Calif Dept Edn Berkeley CA 94720-1670

LAMBERT, OLAF CECIL, hotel executive; b. Sherfield-on-London, Hampshire, Eng.; came to U.S., 1946; naturalized, 1958; s. Stanilas and Jeanne Claire (Helsen) Lubienski; m. Trudy Guidroz, Sept. 2, 1995. Grad., Ecole Hoteliere, Nice, France, 1937. Gen. mgr. Queensbury Hotel, Glens Falls, N.Y., 1956-57; resident mgr. Istanbul (Turkey) Hilton, 1957-58; resident mgr., asst. project mgr. Berlin Hilton, 1958-59; v.p., gen. mgr. Royal Orleans, New Orleans, 1959-65, Americana of N.Y., N.Y.C., 1965-66; gen. mgr. Chateau Louisianne, New Orleans, 1966-68; treas. So. Motor Lodge, 1964—; pres. Dauphine Orleans Hotel Corp., Olaf Lambert and Assocs. Inc., New Orleans. served to flight lt. RAF, 1939-45; prisoner of war, 1942-45. Recipient Instns. Nat. Merit award Hotel Mgmt. Rev., 1958, Golden Host Merit award, 1964. Mem. Chaine des Rotisseurs, New Orleans Hotel Assn., Hotel Sales Mgmt. Assn., Global Hoteliers Club, Am. Hotel & Motel Assn., Internat. Coun. Hotel-Motel Mgmt. Cos., Masons, Shriners. Office: 412 Dauphine St New Orleans LA 70112-3147

LAMBERT, OLIVIA SUE, commercial artist, writer; b. Philippi, W.Va., July 10, 1939; d. Curtis Truman and Olive Virginia (Cox) L. BA in History, Alderson Broaddus Coll., 1961. Interim pub. rels. officer Alderson Broaddus Coll., Philippi, 1965; clk. Barbour County Ct. House, Philippi, 1966; free lance artist, writer Philippi, 1965—. Artist: (book jackets) History of Barbour County, 1965, History of Calhoun County, 1982; illustrator: (book) Wappatomaka, 1971; cartographer: Blue-Gray Reunion Map, 1993. Mem. Rep. Nat. Com., Philippi Sesquecentennial Com., Blue-Gray Reunion Com., Nature Conservancy. Mem. AAUW, Coll. Club, W.Va. Filmmakers Guild, W.Va. Writers Inc., Barbour County Writers Workshop, Order Eastern Star. Methodist. Avocation: stock market analysis. Home and Office: 4 Woodsboro Dr Rte 3 Philippi WV 26416

LAMBERT, RICHARD BOWLES, JR., national science foundation program director, oceanographer; b. Clinton, Mass., Apr. 20, 1939; s. Richard Bowles and Dorothy Elisabeth (Peck) L.; m. Sherrill Faye Smith, July 4, 1964; 1 child, Lisa Beth Lauren. AB in Physics, Lehigh U., 1961; ScM in Physics, Brown U., 1964, PhD in Physics, 1966; postgrad., Goethe Institut, Germany, 1966, NATO Internat. Sch., Germany, 1966, Max Planck Inst. for Physics & Astrophysics, Germany, 1966. Fulbright Postdoctoral fellow Institut fur Stromungsmechanik Technische Hochschule, Munich, Germany, 1966-67; asst. prof. Grad. Sch. Oceanography U. R.I., 1968-74, assoc. prof. Grad. Sch. Oceanography, 1974; program dir. physical oceanography program NSF, Washington, 1975-77; rsch. oceanographer Sci. Applications Internat. Corp., 1977-79, mgr. ocean physics divsn., 1979-83, asst. v.p., 1980-83, sr. rsch. oceanographer, 1983-84; assoc. program dir. physical oceanography program NSF, Washington, 1984-91, program dir. physical oceanography program, 1991—; adv. com. NOAA; assoc. dir. U.S. TOGA Project Office 1985-91; delegate Intergovernmental TOGA Bd.; delegation head Intergovernmental WOCE Panel; co-investigator R/V Trident Oceanographic Cruises, Feb. 1971 (21 days), Dec. 1971 (6 days), April 1974 (14 days), Nov. 1974 (19 days); chief scientist R/V Trident Oceangraphic Cruises, Oct. 1971 (17 days), Nov. 1971 (8 days), April 1973 (15 days); co-investigator R/V Atlantis II Oceanographic Cruises, July 1973 (18 days). Contbr. articles to Jour. Fluid Mech. and other profl. jours. Bd. dirs. Christian Performing Artist's Fellowship, Fairfax, Va., 1993—. Mem. Am. Geophys. Union, The Oceanography Soc. (life mem.), Phi Beta Kappa, Sigma Xi. Office: NSF Phys Oceanography Program 4201 Wilson Blvd Arlington VA 22230

LAMBERT, ROBERT FRANK, electrical engineer, consultant; b. Warroad, Minn., Mar. 14, 1924; s. Fred Joseph and Nutah (Gibson) L.; m. June Darlene Flatten, June 30, 1951; children—Cynthia Marie, Susan Ann, Katherine Cheryl. B.E.E., U. Minn., 1948, M.S. in Elec. Engring, 1949, Ph.D., 1953. Asst. prof. U. Minn. Inst. Tech., Mpls., 1953-54; assoc. prof. U. Minn. Inst. Tech., 1955-59, prof. elec. engring., 1959-94, prof. emeritus, 1994; dir. propagation research lab. U. Minn., 1968-87; assoc. dean U. Minn. (Inst. Tech.), 1967-68; asst. prof. Mass. Inst. Tech., 1954-55; cons. elec. engr., also in acoustics, 1953—; guest scientist Third Phys. Inst., Göttingen, Fed. Republic Germany, 1964; vis. scientist NASA, Hampton, Va., 1979; dir. Inst. Noise Control Engring., Washington, 1972-75. Contbr. numerous articles to tech. jours. Served with USNR, 1943-46. Fellow IEEE, Acoustical Soc. Am. (assoc. editor jour. 1985-93); mem. Am. Soc. Engring. Edn., Am. Soc. Engring. Sci., AAAS, Inst. Noise Control Engring. (dir., John C. Johnson Meml. award), Sigma Xi, Tau Beta Pi, Eta Kappa Nu, Gamma Alpha. Lutheran. Rsch. in acoustics, communication tech. random vibrations. Home: 2503 Snelling Curve Saint Paul MN 55113-3111 Office: U Minn Inst Tech Dept Elec Engring Minneapolis MN 55455

LAMBERT, ROBERT LOWELL, scientific investigator; b. Mpls., Jan. 3, 1923; s. Luell E. and Amy (Schwerin) L.; m. Jean Louise Zavodney, Mar. 19, 1949; children: Thomas R., John N. Student, U. Utah, 1941-42, Tex. A&M Coll., 1943-44, Biarritz (France) Am. U., 1945; B.S., UCLA, 1947, M.B.A., 1948; grad. student, U. Minn., 1948-50; Ph.D., U. Beverly Hills, 1982. Instr. bus. adminstrn. U. Minn., 1948-50; with Budget Pack, Inc., Los Angeles, 1950-55; v.p. Budget Pack, Inc., 1954-55; with Riverside Cement Co. div. Amcord, Inc., Los Angeles, 1955-61; treas. Riverside Cement Co. div. Amcord, Inc., 1960- 61; finance dir. Amcord, Inc., 1961-72, treas., 1965-72, 75-80, v.p., 1967-72, sec., 1972-74, sr. v.p., 1972-80; pres., dir. Inst. for Bus. Edn., Newport Beach, Calif., 1981-83; ind. investigator, author in field of chronobiological epidemiology, 1984—; former dir., officer various subsidiaries Amcord, Inc. Contbr. articles to profl. jours. Vice pres. Amcord Found., 1958-80. Served with inf. AUS, World War II, ETO. Decorated Combat Inf. badge, Bronze star with oak leaf cluster, Presdl. Unit citiation, Belgian Fourragere. Mem. Tau Kappa Epsilon, Beta Gamma Sigma, Alpha Kappa Psi. Lutheran. Clubs: Big Canyon Country (Newport Beach); Palm Desert Resort Country. Home: 13 Cool Brk Irvine CA 92612-3412

LAMBERT, SAMUEL WALDRON, III, lawyer, foundation executive; b. N.Y.C., Jan. 12, 1938; s. Samuel W. and Mary (Hamill) L.; m. Louisa Garnsey, Aug. 25, 1962; children—Louisa Kelly, Samuel William, Sarah Hamill. B.A., Yale U., 1960; LL.B., Harvard U., 1963. Bar: N.J. 1964, U.S. Tax Ct. 1975. Assoc. Albridge C. Smith III, Princeton, N.J., 1964-67; ptnr. Smith, Cook, Lambert & Miller, and predecessors, Princeton, 1967-80; officer, dir. Smith, Lambert, Hicks & Miller, P.C., Princeton, 1981-87; ptnr. in charge of office Drinker, Biddle & Reath, 1988—, mng. ptnr., 1994-96; pres. The Bunbury Co., Princeton. Bd. dirs. Winslow Found., Windham Found., Curtis W. McGraw Found.; capt. Princeton Republican County Com., 1967-69. Served with USAR, 1963-69. Mem. Princeton Bar Assn. (pres. 1976-77), N.J. Bar Assn., ABA.

LAMBERT, STEPHEN R., electrical engineer, consultant; b. Oct. 30, 1946. BSEE, U. Ill., 1969, MS, 1969. Sr. cons. Power Techs., Inc. Fellow IEEE (vice-chmn., sec., tech. coun. PES, past chmn. switchgear com., past chmn. high-voltage breaker sub-com., past chmn. TRV working group). Office: Power Tech Inc PO Box 1058 Schenectady NY 12301*

LAMBERT, STEVEN CHARLES, lawyer; b. Kingsport, Tenn., Aug. 22, 1947; s. M. Charles and Janet (Sultner) L.; children: Shelley Elizabeth, Charles Burnette. BA, Duke U., 1969; JD, Georgetown U., 1974. Bar: D.C. 1975, U.S. Ct. Fed. Claims, U.S. Ct. Appeals (fed. cir.), U.S. Tax Ct. Law clk. to Chief Judge Wilson Cowen, U.S. Ct. Claims, Washington, 1974-75; assoc. Wilkinson, Cragun & Barker, Washington, 1975-80; ptnr. Wilkinson, Cragun & Barker, 1980-82, Hamel & Park, Washington, 1982-88, Hopkins & Sutter, Washington, 1988—; mgr. litigation grp. Hopkins & Sutter, 1987-93; chmn. adv. coun. U.S. Ct. Claims, 1982-86, mem. adv. coun., 1986—, chmn. bicentennial commn., 1987-91. Co-author: Tax Ideas Desk Book, 1980; contbr. articles to profl. jours. Trustee Ferrum Coll.; mem. bd. pensions United Meth. Ch. With U.S. Army, 1970-72. Fellow Am. Bar Found.; mem. ABA (sec. litigation and natural resources), Am. Arbitration Assn., Claims Ct. Bar Assn. (pres. 1990-91), Fed. Cir. Bar Assn. (bd. dirs. 1986-88), Bar Assn. D.C. (bd. dirs. 1981-83). Methodist. Avocations: boating, fishing, tennis. Office: Hopkins & Sutter 888 16th St NW Washington DC 20006-4103

LAMBERT, WILLIAM G., journalist, consultant; b. Langford, S.D., Feb. 2, 1920; s. William G. and Blanche (Townsend) L.; m. Jean Kenway Mead, July 7, 1945; children: Kathryn, Heather Lambert Oxberry. Nieman fellow journalism, Harvard U., 1959-60. Reporter, news editor Enterprise-Courier, Oregon City, Oreg., 1945-50; reporter The Oregonian, Portland, 1950-59; anchor, news dir. KPTV, Oreg. Television, Inc., Portland, 1961-62; corr. Time mag., 1962-63; assoc. editor, staffwriter Life mag., N.Y.C., 1963-71; staff corr. Time-Life News Service, 1971-73; free-lance journalist, 1973; staff writer, cons. Phila. Inquirer, 1974-90; freelance journalist, libel litigation cons., 1990—; cons., U.S. commr. edn. Office of Edn., Washington, 1962. Served in U.S. Army, WWII, PTO, to maj. Res., ret. Decorated bronze star. Recipient Pulitzer prize for local reporting, 1957, Heywood Broun award, 1957, award for mag. reporting Sigma Delta Chi, 1967, Worth Bingham prize for distinguished reporting, 1967, Heywood Brown award, 1969, George Polk award for mag. reporting Abe Fortas articles, Sigma Delta Chi award, Nat. Headliners Club award, Page One award, 1970, Pa. Bar Assn. award, Phila. Bar Assn. award, Phila. Sigma Delta Chi award, AP Mng. Editors award (Pa.), 1981. Home: 529 Chandler Ln Villanova PA 19085-1026

LAMBERT, WILLIAM WILSON, psychology educator; b. Amherst, N.S., Can., May 10, 1919; s. Harry Brown and Alice Grace (Babcock) L.; m. Elisabeth Bird Carr, June 17, 1949; children: Hilary (Mrs. William M. Hopper), Holly Lee Alison (Mrs. Fred Nolting). A.B., Brown U., 1942; M.S., U. Nebr., 1943; Ph.D., Harvard U., 1951. Tech. aide NDRC, Washington, 1942-43; lectr. Harvard, Cambridge, Mass., 1949-50; asst. prof. Brown U., Providence, R.I., 1951-52; asst. prof. psychology, sociology and anthropology Cornell U., Ithaca, N.Y., 1952-55; asso. prof. Cornell U., 1955-60, prof., 1960—, dean Grad. Sch., 1974-81; cons. Fulbright Program, 1974-76; fellow Ctr. for Advnaced Study, Palo Alto, Calif., 1954-55; Fulbright lectr. Oslo (Norway) U., 1957-58, U. Padua, Italy, 1973; Rockefeller exch. prof. U. Philippines, Quezon City, 1968-69; part-time longitudinal rsch. prof. U. Stockholm, 1965-66. Author: (with W.E. Lambert) Social Psychology, 1964, rev. edit., 1973, (with L. Minturn) Mothers of Six Cultures, 1963, (with G. Lindsey and others) Handbook of Social Psychology, 1969, (with R. Weisbrod) Comparative Perspectives in Social Psychology, 1971; Editor: (with E. Borgatta) Handbook Personality Theory and Research, 1968, (with H. Triandis) Handbook of Cross-Cultural Psychology, Vol. I, 1979. Served with USNR, 1943-46. NIH fellow, 1966-67; Guggenheim fellow, 1973. Fellow Am. Psychol. Assn. (mem. bd. sci. affairs 1970-73), AAAS; mem. Am. Sociol. Assn., Soc. for Cross-Cultural Research (pres. 1975-76), Phi Beta Kappa, Sigma Xi. Home: 1676 Hanshaw Rd Ithaca NY 14850-9102

LAMBERT, WILLIE LEE BELL, mobile equipment company owner, educator; b. Texas City, Tex., Oct. 23, 1929; d. William Henry and Una Oda (Stafford) Bell; m. Eddie Roy Lambert, July 2, 1949; (dec. Mar. 1980); children: Sondra Kay Lambert Bradford, Eddie Lee. Degree in bus., Met. Bus. Coll., 1950; AAS, Coll. of Mainland, 1971; BS, Sam Houston U., 1976. Cert. hand and foot reflexologist, Hatha Yoga instr. Sec. Judges Reddell & Hopkins, Texas City, 1945-47, Charles Martin Petroleum, Texas City, 1948-50; acct. Goodyear Co., La Marque, Tex., 1968-70; serials libr. Coll. of the Mainland, Texas City, 1970-77, instr., 1971—; exec. dir., office mgr. Mobile Air Conditioning, La Marque, 1977-80; owner Kivert, Inc., La Marque, 1982—; ptnr., exec. dir. A/C Mobile Equipment Corp., La Marque, 1988—; owner Star Bell Ranch, 1985—. Vol. Union Carbide Chems., Texas City, 1970—, Carbide Retiree Corp., Inc., Texas City, 1980—, Hospice, Galveston, Tex., 1985—, various polit. campaigns, Texas City, 1951-62; v.p. Coalition on Aging Galveston County, Tex. City, 1990—; vol. Baylor Coll. Medicine, Houston, 1990—; mem. adv. coun. bd. Galveston County Sr. Citizens, Galveston, 1990—; mem. planning bd. Heart Fund and Cancer Fund, Texas City, 1953-62, Santa Fe (Tex.) St. Citizens, 1990—; benefactor mem. Mainland Mus., Texas City, Tex., 1994—; sec. YMCA, 1947-55; sec. Ladies VFW, 1950-59; leader Girl Scouts Am., 1958-65; v.p. PTA, 1957-60; counselor Bapt. Ch. Camp, 1960-64; v.p. Santa Fe Booster Club, 1963-67; mem. Internat. Platform Assn., 1995—. Named Mother of Yr. Texas City/ La Marque C. of C., 1990, Vol. of Yr. Heights Elem. Sch., Texas City Sch. Dist., 1959, Unsung Hero award Tex. City, 1995, 96, Most Glamorous Grandmother, 1985, Tex. Women's Hall of Fame, 1984. Mem. Internat. Platform Assn. Republican. Baptist. Avocations: making porcelain dolls and soft sculpture dolls, painting china portraits, sewing, needlework, volunteer work. Home: 3422 K1/2 PO Box 1253 Santa Fe TX 77510

LAMBERTH, ROYCE C., federal judge; b. 1943. BA, U. Tex., 1965, LLB, 1967. With civil div. U.S. Atty's. Office, Washington, 1974-77, asst. chief, 1977-78; chief U.S. Atty's. Office, 1978-87; judge U.S. Dist. Ct. (D.C. dist.), Washington, 1987—. Capt. (j.a.g.) U.S. Army, 1967-74. Mem. ABA (chmn. armed svcs. and vets. affairs com. sect. adminstrv. law 1983-83), Fed. Bar Assn. (chmn. fed. litigation sect. 1986—), Jud. Conf. D.C. Cir. (arangements com. 1985, D.C. Bar., D.C. Bar Assn. (Cert. Appreciatio 1977), State Bar Tex. Office: US Dist Ct US Courthouse 333 Constitution Ave NW Washington DC 20001*

LAMBERTI, MARJORIE, history educator; b. New Haven, Sept. 30, 1937; d. James and Anna (Vanacore) L. B.A., Smith Coll., 1959; M.A., Yale U., 1960, Ph.D., 1965. Prof. history Middlebury Coll., Vt., 1964—, Charles A. Dana prof., 1984—. Author: Jewish Activism in Imperial Germany, 1978, State, Society and the Elementary School in Imperial Germany, 1989; edtl. bd. History of Edn. Quar., 1992-94; contbr. articles to profl. jours. NEH fellow, 1968-69, 81-82; German Acad. Exch. Svc. rsch. grant, 1988. Fellow Inst. for Advanced Study (Princeton 1992-93); mem. Am. Hist. Assn., Conf. Group for Ctrl. European History, Leo Baeck Inst., Phi Beta Kappa. Home: 8 S Gorham Ln Middlebury VT 05753-1016 Office: Middlebury Coll Dept History Middlebury VT 05753

LAMBERT LINCOLN, BLANCHE M., congresswoman; b. Helena, Ark., Sept. 30, 1960. BA, Randolph-Macon Woman's Coll., 1982. Sr. assoc. The Pagonis & Donnelly Group, Inc., 1989-91; elected mem. 103rd Congress from 1st Dist., 1992. Office: U.S. House of Representatives 1204 Longworth Washington DC 20515*

LAMBERTSEN, CHRISTIAN JAMES, environmental physiologist, physician, educator; b. Westfield, N.J., May 15, 1917; s. Christian and Ellen (Stevens) L.; m. Naomi Helen Hill, Feb. 5, 1944; children—Christian James, David Lee, Richard Hill, Bradley Stevens. BS, Rutgers U., 1939; MD, U. Pa., 1943. Prof. pharmacology and exptl. therapeutics, prof. medicine U. Pa. Sch. Medicine, 1946-87; founding dir. Inst. for Environ. Medicine, U. Pa. Med. Ctr., 1968—, disting. prof. environ. medicine, 1985—; mem. adv. panel on med. scis. Office of Asst. Sec. Defense, 1954-61; sec. basic scis. Nat. Bd. Med. Examiners, 1955-71; mem. Pres.'s Space Panel, 1967-70; mem. oceanographic adv. bd. Office of Asst. Sec. of Navy for R & D, 1968-77; mem. marine bd. Nat. Acad. Engring., 1973-77; adviser Office of Marine Resources, NOAA, 1972-76; med. adviser Ocean Systems Inc., Houston, 1960-83; med. dir. SubSea Intern, 1984—; chmn. com. Man in Space; Space Sci. Bd., NAS, 1960-62; chmn. life scis. adv. bd. McDonnell-Douglas Aircraft Corp., St. Louis, 1960-67; mem. research adv. bd. Mead-Johnson Corp., Evansville, Ind., 1960-67; sr. life scis. adviser Union Carbide Corp., Buffalo, N.Y., Westinghouse Elec. Corp., Annapolis, Md., 1972-74, Air Products and Chemicals Corp., Allentown, Pa., 1983-87; pres. Ecosystems Inc., Phila., 1972—. Editor: Underwater Physiology Symposium, II, III, IV, V, 1963-76; mem. editorial bd. Marine Tech. Soc. Jour., 1977-85. Contbr. articles to med., sci. jours. Served to maj. AUS, 1944-46. Decorated Legion of Merit; recipient Lindback award for Disting. Teaching, 1967; Aerospace Med. Assn. Tuttle award, 1970; Undersea Med. Behnke award, 1970; Dept. Def. Disting. Pub. Service medal, 1972; Marine Tech. Soc. award in Ocean Sci. and Engring., 1972; Dept. Navy Commendation Adv. Service, 1972; award in environ. scis. N.Y. Acad. Scis., 1974; Disting. Pub. Service award USCG, 1976; NIH, USN, USAF, NASA, NOAA Research grantee. Fellow Aerospace Med. Assn. (v.p. 1968); mem. Am. Coll. Clin. Pharmacology and Chemotherapy, Am. Soc. Pharmacology and Exptl. Therapeutics, Am. Physiol. Soc., Am. Soc. Clin. Investigation, Assn. Am. Med. Colls., Phila. Coll. Physicians, Internat. Acad. Astronautics, Internat. Astronautic Fedn., Internat. Union Physiol. Scis., Nat. Acad. Engring., John Morgan Med. Rsch. Soc., Marine Tech. Soc., Peripatetic Med. Soc., Undersea Med. Soc. (founding pres.), Phila. County Med. Soc., Pa. Med. Soc., Phila. Maritime Mus., Phila. Physiol. Soc., Cosmos Club (Washington), Sigma Xi. Home: 3500 Westchester Pike No 33 Newtown Square PA 19073 Office: Inst Environ Medicine 1 John Morgan Bldg U Pa Med Ctr Philadelphia PA 19104-6068

LAMBERTSEN, ELEANOR C., nursing consultant. Nursing and health svc. cons. N.Y.C., 1988—. Mem. Inst. Medicine-NAS. Home: 510 E 77th St New York NY 10021*

LAMBERTSEN, MARY ANN, human resources executive; b. Kane, Pa., Dec. 23, 1939; d. Arthur Nathaniel and Anna Marie (Peterson) Turnquist; m. John Franklin Lambertsen, Aug. 30, 1972. BS, Carnegie-Mellon U., 1961; MA, Columbia U., 1963; MS, Pace U., 1977. Tchr. math. Cleve. Pub. Schs., 1963-64; mgr. traffic Ohio Bell Telephone Co., Cleve., 1964-68, systems analyst, 1968-70, personnel analyst, 1970-71; specialist bus. systems Bell Telephone Labs., Piscataway, N.J., 1971-72; dist. mgr. personnel AT&T, N.Y.C., 1972-78; v.p. human resources Fisher-Price, East Aurora, N.Y., 1978-89, v.p. human resources and information systems, 1989-91; v.p. human resources Goulds Pumps, Fairport, N.Y., 1991—; chmn. bd. N.Y. Fed. Res. Bank, Buffalo, 1986-91. Trustee Keuka Coll., 1994—. Office: Goulds Pumps 300 Willowbrook Office Pk Fairport NY 14450-4285

LAMBETH, THOMAS WILLIS, foundation executive; b. Clayton, N.C., Jan. 8, 1935; s. Mark Thomas and Ina Henrietta (Willis) L.; m. Donna Brooks Irving, July 18, 1964; children: Donna Catherine, Mark Hunter, Thomas Richard. AB in History, U. N.C., 1957; DHL (hon.), Pfeiffer Coll., Misenheimer, N.C., 1982. Reporter Winston-Salem Jour., 1959-60; adminstrv. asst. Gov. of N.C., 1961-65; staff mem. Smith Richardson Found., Greensboro, N.C., 1965-69; adminstrv. asst. Congressman Richardson Preyer, Washington, 1969-78; exec. dir. Z. Smith Reynolds Found., Winston-Salem, 1978—; acting dir. Kennedy Assasination Investigation, Washington, 1977; dir. Coun. on Founds., Washington, 1988-94, program chmn. ann. meeting, 1988-89, ch. family founds. com.; chmn. bd. Southeastern Coun. of Founds., Atlanta, 1985-87. Trustee, chmn. bd. U. N.C., Chapel Hill, 1969-83; chmn. Tchg. Fellow Commn., 1987-91, 93—. Recipient Disting. Alumnus award U. N.C., 1988. Mem. Alumni Assn. U. N.C. (pres. 1989-90). Democrat. Methodist. Home: 700 Yorkshire Rd Winston Salem NC 27106-5518 Office: Z Smith Reynolds Found 101 Reynolda Vlg Winston Salem NC 27106-5122

LAMBETH, VICTOR NEAL, horticulturist, researcher; b. Sarcoxie, Mo., July 5, 1920; s. Odus Houston and Carrie (Woods) L.; m. Sarah Katherine Smarr, May 24, 1946; children: Victoria Kay, Debra Jean. B.S., U. Mo., 1942, M.A., 1948, Ph.D., 1950. Asst. prof. U. Mo., Columbia, 1950-51, assoc. prof., 1951-59, prof. dept. horticulture, 1959-91, prof. emeritus, 1991—; cons. horticulture to Thailand, Taiwan, Liberia; judge All-Am. Vegetable Trials, 1985-92. Inventor plant growth media, 1979; plant breeder tomato lines and cultivars; contbr. articles to profl. jours. Mem. Fin. Com. City of Columbia, Mo., 1970, mem. Bd. Zoning Adjustment, 1973-76, mem.

Bd. Spl. Appeals, 1975-77. Served to lt. USN, 1943-46, PTO. Recipient Hort. award Mo. Hort. Soc., 1942; recipient Alumni Faculty award U. Mo. Alumni Assn., 1974; NSF grantee, 1982. Fellow Am. Soc. Hort. Sci. (grad. teaching award 1978); mem. Am. Soc. Plant Physiologists, Internat. Soc. Hort. Sci., Sigma Xi, Gamma Sigma Delta (pres. Mo. chpt. 1959-60). Methodist. Home: 1327 Lambeth Dr Columbia MO 65202-2466 Office: U Mo Dept Hort 1-87 Agrl Bldg Columbia MO 65211

LAMBIRD, MONA SALYER, lawyer; b. Oklahoma City, July 19, 1938; d. B.M. Jr. and Pauline A. Salyer; m. Perry A. Lambird, July 30, 1960; children: Allison Lambird Watson, Jennifer Salyer, Elizabeth Gard, Susannah Johnson. BA, Wellesley Coll., 1960; LLB, U. Md., 1963. Bar: Okla. 1968, Md. Ct. Appeals 1963, U.S. Supreme Ct. 1967. Atty. civil div. Dept. Justice, Washington, 1963-65; sole practice law Balt. and Oklahoma City, 1965-71; mem. firm Andrews Davis Legg Bixler Milsten & Price, Inc. and predecessor firm, Oklahoma City, 1971—; minority mem. Okla. Election Bd., 1984—, vice chmn., 1990-94; mem. profl. responsibility tribunal Okla. Supreme Ct., 1984-90; Master of Bench, sec.-treas. Luther Bohanan Am. Inn of Ct., Oklahoma City, 1986—, pres., 1994—. Editor: Briefcase, Oklahoma County Bar Assn., 1976. Profl. liaison com. City Oklahoma City, 1974-80; mem. Hist. Preservation of Oklahoma City, Inc., 1970—; del. Oklahoma County and Okla. State Republican Party Conv., 1971—; Okla. City Orch. League Inc., legal advisor, 1973—, bd. dirs., 1973—; incorporator, bd. dirs. R.S.V.P. of Oklahoma County, pres., 1982-83; bd. dirs. Congregate Housing for Elderly, 1978—, Vis. Nurses Assn., 1983-86, Oklahoma County Friends of Library, 1980-91, The Support Ctrs., Inc., 1989—. Mem. Okla. Women's Hall of Fame, 1995. Mem. ABA, Okla. Bar Assn. (pres. labor and employment law sect., bd. govs. 1992-94, pres. 1996), Oklahoma County Bar Assn. (bd. dirs. 1986—, pres. 1990), Oklahoma County Bar Found. (pres. 1988), Jr. League Oklahoma City (bd. dirs. 1973-76, legal advisor), Oklahoma County and State Med. Assn. Aux. (bd. dirs.), Seven Sisters Colls. Club (pres. 1972-76), Women's Econ. Club (steering com. 1981-86). Methodist. Home: 419 NW 14th St Oklahoma City OK 73103-3510 Office: 500 W Main St Oklahoma City OK 73102-2220

LAMBORN, LEROY LESLIE, legal educator; b. Marion, Ohio, May 12, 1937; s. LeRoy Leslie and Lola Fern (Grant) L. A.B., Oberlin Coll., 1959; LL.B., Western Res. U., 1962; LL.M., Yale U., 1963; J.S.D., Columbia U., 1973. Bar: N.Y. 1965, Mich. 1974. Asst. prof. law U. Fla., 1965-69; prof. Wayne State U., 1970—; vis. prof. State U., Utrecht, 1981. Author: Legal Ethics and Professional Responsibility, 1963; contbr. articles on victimology to legal jours. Mem. Am. Law Inst., Nat. Orgn. Victim Assistance (bd. dirs. 1979-88, 90-91), World Soc. Victimology (exec. com. 1982-94). Office: Wayne State U Law Sch Detroit MI 48202

LAMBREMONT, EDWARD NELSON, JR., nuclear science educator; b. New Orleans, July 29, 1928; s. Edward Nelson and Caroline Josephine (Joachim) L.; m. Janice P. Savoy, Apr. 6, 1990; m. Mary Chris Bittle, May 30, 1981 (dec. Jan. 1987); m. Carol Jane Annis, June 16, 1951; children: Carol, Suzanne, John, Barbara. B.S., Tulane U., 1949, M.S., 1951; Ph.D., Ohio State U., 1958. Research entomologist U.S. Dept. Agr., Baton Rouge, 1958-66; assoc. prof. nuclear sci. La. State U., Baton Rouge, 1966-73, prof., 1973—, dir. Nuclear Sci. Ctr., 1974—; councilor Oak Ridge Assoc. Univs., 1971-79, bd. dirs., 1979-84, vis. scientist med. div., 1967-87; vis. scientist Internat. Atomic Energy Agy. Lab., Seibersdorf, Austria, 1988-90; cons. nuclear-related corps., 1978—. Contbr. articles to sci. jours. Served with U.S. Army, 1951-54, col. Res. (ret.). Grantee NIH, 1964-71; grantee NSF, 1971-77, U.S. Dept. Agr., 1979-83. Mem. Am. Nuclear Soc., Entomol. Soc. Am. (Deep South chpt.), Health Physic. Home: 2913 Calanne Ave Baton Rouge LA 70820-5408 Office: La State U Nuclear Sci Ctr Baton Rouge LA 70803

LAMBRO, DONALD JOSEPH, columnist; b. Wellesley, Mass., July 24, 1940; s. Pascal and Mary (Lapery) L.; m. Jacquelyn Mae Killmon, Oct. 6, 1968; 1 son, Jason Phillip. B.S., Boston U., 1963. Reporter, Boston Traveler, 1963; freelance writer Washington, 1965-67; statehouse reporter UPI, Hartford, Conn., 1968-70; reporter UPI, Washington, 1970-80; columnist United Feature Syndicate, Washington, 1981—; commentator AP Radio Network, 1982-83, Nat. Pub. Radio, 1984-85; writer, hot TV documentary Star Spangled Spenders, 1982; host, co-writer PBS TV documentary Inside the Republican Revolution, 1995; nat. editor Washington Times, 1987-88; chief polit. corr. Washington Times, 1988—. Author: The Federal Rathole, 1975; The Conscience of a Young Conservative, 1976; Fat City: How Washington Wastes Your Taxes, 1980; Washington-City of Scandals, 1984; Land of Opportunity, 1986. Recipient Warren Brookes award for Excellence in Journalism, 1995. Albanian Orthodox.

LAMBRO, PHILLIP, composer, conductor, pianist; b. Wellesley, Mass., Sept. 2, 1935; s. Pascal and Mary (Lapery) L. Student, Music Acad. West, 1955. Piano debut Pianist's Fair, Symphony Hall, Boston, 1952; composer Miraflores for String Orchestra, Dance Barbaro for Percussion, Two Pictures for Solo Percussionist and Orchestra, Four Songs for Soprano and Orchestra, Toccata for Piano, Toccata for Guitar, Parallelograms for Flute Quartet and Jazz Ensemble, Music for Wind Brass and Percussion, Obelisk for Oboist and Percussionist, Structures for String Orchestra, Fanfare and Tower Music for Brass Quintet, Night Pieces for Piano, Biospheres for 6 Percussionists, Trumpet Voluntary, Eight Little Trigams for piano; composer, condr. for films including documentaries Energy on the Move, Mineral King; compositions performed by Leopold Stokowski, Philippe Entremont, Santiago Rodriguez, Phila. Orch., Rochester (N.Y.) Philharm., Balt. Symphony, Indpls. Symphony, Oklahoma Symphony, Denver Symphony, Europe, S.Am., Asia, Israel; condr. debut rec. of U.S. Internat. Orch. Active in population control, protection of animals, conservation; mem. NATO Tennis team, 1958-59. Served with inf. U.S. Army. Recipient award for best music for Mineral King, Nat. Bd. Rev., 1972. Mem. ASCAP, U.S. Tennis Assn., Raelian Movement, Tau Kappa Epsilon. Office: 1888 Century Park E Ste 1900 Los Angeles CA 90067-1723

LAMBROS, LAMBROS JOHN, lawyer, petroleum company executive; b. Sharon, Pa., 1935; s. John and Niki (George) L.; m. Cynthia Ryan, 1965; children: John F., Olivia W. A.B. magna cum laude in History and Lit, Harvard U., 1957, J.D., 1960. Bar: N.Y. 1961. Assoc. White & Case, N.Y.C., 1961-64; of counsel W.R. Grace & Co., N.Y.C., 1964-74, chief internat. counsel, 1970-74; v.p., gen. counsel Amerada Hess Corp., N.Y.C., 1974-76, sr. v.p., gen. counsel, 1976-80, sr. v.p., 1980-83, exec. v.p., dir., 1983-85; chmn., pres., chief exec. officer Norfolk Holdings Inc., Houston, 1986-93, also bd. dirs.; mng. dir. J.W. Childs Assocs., L.P., Boston, 1995—; bd. dirs. 1st Empire State Corp. Home: 131 Goshen Rd Norfolk CT 06058-1301

LAMBROS, THOMAS DEMETRIOS, federal judge; b. Ashtabula, Ohio, Feb. 4, 1930; s. Demetrios P. and Panagoula (Bellios) L.; m. Shirley R. Kresin, June 20, 1953; children: Lesley P., Todd T. Student, Fairmount (W.Va.) State Coll., 1948-49; LLB, Cleve.-Marshall Law Sch., 1952. Bar: Ohio 1952. Ptnr. firm Lambros and Lambros, Ashtabula, 1952-60; judge Ct. Common Pleas, Jefferson, Ohio, 1960-67; judge U.S. Dist. Ct. (no. dist.) Ohio, Cleve., 1967—, chief judge, 1990—; mem. faculty Fed. Jud. Ctr.; innovator of summary jury trial. Contbr. articles legal publs. Mem. exec. bd. N.E. Ohio coun. Boy Scouts Am.; pres. Ashtabula county chpt. National Found. With U.S. Army, 1954-56. Recipient Disting. Svc. award Ashtabula Jr. C. of C., 1962; Outstanding Young Man of Ohio award Ohio Jaycees, 1963; Man of Yr. award Delta Theta Phi, 1969; Outstanding Alumnus award Cleve. Marshall Coll. of Law, 1974. Fellow Internat. Acad. Law and Sci.; mem. ABA, Ohio Bar Assn., Ashtabula County Bar Assn. (past pres.), Atty. Gen. Advocacy Inst. Office: US Dist Ct 106 US Courthouse 201 Superior Ave E Cleveland OH 44114-1201*

LAMEL, LINDA HELEN, insurance company executive, former college president, lawyer; b. N.Y.C., Sept. 10, 1943; d. Maurice and Sylvia (Abrams) Treppel; 1 child, Diana Ruth Sands. BA magna cum laude, Queens Coll., 1964; MA, NYU, 1968; JD, Bklyn. Law Sch., 1976. Bar: N.Y. 1977, U.S. Dist. Ct. (3d dist.) N.Y. 1977. Mgmt. analyst U.S. Navy, Bayonne, N.J., 1964-65; secondary sch. tchr. Farmingdale Pub. Sch., N.Y., 1965-73; curriculum specialist Yonkers Bd. Edn., N.Y., 1973-75; program dir. Office of Lt. Gov., Albany, N.Y., 1975-77; dep. supt. N.Y. State Ins. Dept., N.Y.C., 1977-83; pres., chief exec. officer Coll. of Ins., N.Y.C., 1983-88; v.p. Tchr.'s Ins. and Annuity Assn., N.Y.C., 1988-96; dir. Seneca (N.Y.) Ins. Co. Contbr. articles to profl. jours. Campaign mgr. lt. gov.'s primary race, N.Y. State, 1974. Mem. ABA (tort and ins. sect. com. chmn. 1985-86), N.Y. State Bar Assn. (exec. com. ins. sect. 1984-88), Assn. of Bar of City of N.Y. (chmn. med. malpractice com. 1989-91), Am. Mgmt. Assn. (ins. and risk mgmt. council), Fin. Women's Assn., Assn. Profl. Ins. Women (Woman of Yr. award 1988), Phi Beta Kappa (v.p. Phi Beta Kappa Assoc. 1992—). *One's life develops much like a patchwork quilt: there are opportunities to add color, texture, and design; and there are missed stitches and uneven seams. Each result is unique and adds value.*

LAMENDOLA, WALTER FRANKLIN, human services, information technology consultant; b. Donora, Pa., Jan. 29, 1943. BA in English, St. Vincent Coll., 1964; MSWin Community Orgn., U. Pitts., 1966; diploma in Sociology and Social Welfare, U. Stockholm, 1970; PhD in Social Work, U. Minn., 1976. Community svcs. dir. Ariz. tng. programs State Dept. Mental Retardation, Tucson, 1970-73; assoc. prof. social welfare adminstrn. Fla. State U., 1976-77; pres., chief exec. officer Minn. Rsch. and Tech., Inc., 1977-81; assoc. prof., dir. Allied Health Computer Lab. E. Carolina U., 1981-84; prof., dir. info. tech. ctr. Grad. Sch. Social Work U. Denver, 1984-87; cons. info. tech., rsch. human svcs., 1987-90; v.p. rsch. The Colo. Trust, Denver, 1990-93, info. tech. and rsch. cons., 1993—; cons. European Network Info. Tech. & Human Svcs.; mem. adv. bd. ctr. human svcs. U. Southampton, Brit. Rsch. Coun. Univs., Human Svc. Info. Tech. Applications, CREON Found., Netherlands; lectr. conf., symposia, univs. U.S., Europe; mem. nat. adv. bd. Native Elder Health Resource Ctr., 1994-96; co-founder Denver Free Net, 1993—; info. tech. cons. Healthy Nations Program Robert Wood Johnson Found, 1993-96; evaluator Nat. Libr. Rsch. Program, Access Colo. grant, 1994, Nat. Info. Infrastructure grant Colo. State Libr.; cons. set up on the Internet for U.S. Cts.-Ct. for Mental Health Svcs., NIH, Frontier Mental Health Svcs. Network grant; collaborating investigator SBIR award Computerized Advance Directives, tech. plan San Mateo County and Seattle Dist. Cts.; keynote spkr. conf. Human Svc. Info. Tech. Applications, Finland, 1996. Co-author: Choices for Colorado's Future, 1993, The Integrity of Intelligence: A Bill of Rights for the Information Age, 1992, Choices for Colorado's Future: Executive Summary, 1991, Choices for Colorado's Future: Regional Summaries, 1991; co-editor: A Casebook of Computer Applications in Health and Social Services, 1989; contbr. numerous articles to profl. jours. Capt. U.S. Army, 1966-69. Recipient Innovative Computer Application award Internat. Fedn. Info. Processing Socs., 1979; Nat. Lib. Rsch. Evaluator grantee, Colo., 1994—, Nat. Info. Infrastructure grantee Dept. Edn., State Libr. and Adult Literacy, 1994-95; Funds & Couns. Tng. scholar United Way Am., 1964-66, Donaldson Fund scholar, 1965-66, NIMH scholar, 1964-66, 73-76, St. Vincent Coll. Benedictine Soc. scholar, 1963-64; vis. fellow U. Southampton. Office: 4098 Field Dr Wheat Ridge CO 80033-4358

LAMER, ANTONIO, Canadian supreme court chief justice; b. Montreal, Can., July 8, 1933; s. Antonio and Florence (Storey) L.; m. Danièle Tremblay; children: Stephane, Melanie, Jean-Frederic. BA, Licentiate in Laws, U. Montreal, 1956; LLD (hon.), U. Moncton, 1981, U. Montreal, 1991, U. Toronto, 1992; U. New Brunswick, 1995; D Univ. (hon.), U. Ottawa, 1987. Bar: Que. 1957. Justice Superior Ct. Que., 1969-78, Que. Ct. Appeal, 1978-80, Supreme Ct. Can., 1980—; vice chmn. Nat. Law Reform Commn., 1971-75, chmn., 1975-78; prof. agrege U. Montreal, 1967—; read law with Cutler, Lamer, Bellemare & Assocs.; lectr. U. Montreal, Can. Jud. Conf.; former sr. ptnr. Cutler, Lamer, Bellemare & Assocs.; Que. Bar rep. govt. interdisciplinary com. on structures U. Que.; chmn. Can. Law Reform Commn., 1975. Served with Can. Army Res., 1952, hon. lt.-col. Decorated Knight, Order of St. John, 1993; recipient Order of Merit, U. Montreal, 1991. Mem. Privy Coun. Can., Can. Jud. Coun. (chmn.), Nat. Jud. Inst. (chmn.). Office: Supreme Ct Can, Wellington St, Ottawa, ON Canada K1A 0J1

LAMIA, THOMAS ROGER, lawyer; b. Santa Monica, Calif., May 31, 1938; s. Vincent Robert, II, and Maureen (Green) L.; m. Susan Elena Brown, Jan. 10, 1969; children: Nicholas, Katja, Jenna, Tatiana, Carlyn, Mignon. Student U. So. Calif., 1956, BS, 1961; student U. Miss., 1957-58; JD, Harvard U., 1964. Bar: Calif. 1965, U.S. Dist. Ct. (cen. dist.) Calif. 1965, D.C. 1980, U.S. Dist. Ct. D.C. 1980, U.S. Tax Ct. 1982, N.Y. 1990. Assoc. McCutchen, Black, Verleger & Shea, Los Angeles, 1964-66; lectr. in law U. Ife, Ile-Ife, Nigeria, 1966-67, U. Zambia, Lusaka, 1967-68; assoc. Paul Hastings, Janofsky & Walker, L.A., 1968-72, ptnr., 1972-80, Washington, 1980-87, N.Y., 1987—. Mem. ABA (bus., banking, fed. regulation of securities com., SEC adminstrn., budget and legislation subcom., internat. law com.), Internat. Bar Assn. (product liability, false advt. and consumer protection com.), Harvard Law Sch. Assn., Nat. Aquarium Soc. (bd. dirs. 1982—). Office: Paul Hastings Janofsky Walker 399 Park Ave Fl 31 New York NY 10022-4614

LAMIRANDE, ARTHUR GORDON, editor, author, musician; b. Holyoke, Mass., July 19, 1936; s. Joseph Armand Arthur and Marion Gordon (Beaton) L. AA, Holyoke Community Coll., 1956; student, Peabody Conservatory Music, 1956-57; BA, Am. Internat. Coll., 1959. Editorial asst. Merriam-Webster Dictionary, Springfield, Mass., 1959-61; instr. English dept. Chicopee (Mass.) High Sch., 1961-62; asst. editor Hawthorn Books, N.Y.C., 1962-63; editl. cons., N.Y.C., 1963-66, 73-81, 95—, 95—; assoc. editor N.Y. Acad. Scis., N.Y.C., 1966-67; editorial cons. N.Y.C., 1995—; assoc. editor Grune & Stratton Pub. Co., N.Y.C., 1967-68, H.S. Stuttman Co., N.Y.C., 1968-70; mng. editor United Pub. Co., Washington, 1970-71, Sci. and Medicine Pub. Co., N.Y.C., 1971-73; dir. editorial dept. Profl. Exam. Svc., N.Y.C., 1981-92, exec. editor, 1992-94; titular organist St. Catherine of Siena Ch., N.Y.C., 1994-95. Contbr. articles to The Diapason, Lyrichord Discs, PES News; rec. artist (organ) Lyrichord Discs, N.Y.C., 1975; pianist. Pianist, asst. organist Christ Ch. Cathedral, Springfield, Mass., 1960-61; organist, mus. dir. Ch. of Immaculate Conception, Astoria, N.Y., 1963-66; titular organist Ch. of Holy Name of Jesus, N.Y.C., 1973-82, St. Catherine of Siena Ch., N.Y.C., 1994-95. Home and Office: 461 Fort Washington Ave New York NY 10033-4653

LAMIRANDE, EMILIEN, historian, educator; b. St. Georges-de-Windsor, Que., Can., May 22, 1926; s. Armand and Valentine (Boucher) L.; m. Claire Guillemette, Apr. 3, 1971. B.A., U. Ottawa, 1949, Licentiate in Philosophy, 1950, M.A., 1951, Licentiate in Theology, 1955; Th.D., Innsbruck U., 1960; S.T.M., Union Theol. Sem., 1965. Lectr. U. Ottawa, Ont., Can., 1954-60, assoc. prof., 1960-64, prof., 1964-65; prof. St. Paul U., Ottawa, 1965-70, dean theology, 1967-69; prof. dept. religion U. Ottawa, 1971-88, chmn. dept. religious studies, 1972-74, prof. emeritus, 1988—. Author: Un siècle et demi d'études sur l'ecclésiologie de saint Augustin, 1962, L'Eglise céleste selon saint Augustin, 1963, Etudes sur l'ecclésiologie de saint Augustin, 1969, La situation ecclésiologique des Donatistes d'après saint Augustin, 1972, Church, State and Toleration: An Intriguing Change of Mind in Augustine, 1975, Le Père Georges Simard, O.M.I. (1878-1956). Un disciple de saint Augustin à l'Université d'Ottawa, 1981, Paulin de Milan et la 'Vita Ambrosii', 1983, Elisabeth Bruyère, fondatrice des soeurs de la Charité d'Ottawa (1818-1876), 1993, English transl., 1995; also numerous articles. Fellow Royal Soc. Can.; mem. Société canadienne de théologie (v.p. 1967-70), Can. Soc. Patristic Studies (v.p. 1977-83, hon. pres. 1985-87). Home: 6467 Tellier, Rock Forest, PQ Canada J1N 3B1

LAMIS, LEROY, artist, retired educator; b. Eddyville, Iowa, Sept. 27, 1925; s. Leo and Blanche (Bennett) L.; m. Esther Sackler, Aug. 13, 1954; children: Alexander, Jonas. B.A., N.Mex. Highlands U., 1953; M.A., Columbia U., 1956. mem. faculty dept. art Ind. State U., 1961—, prof., 1972-89, retired 1989; artist-in-residence Dartmouth Coll., 1970; founder PC ART, 1983. One-man sculpture exhbns. include, Staempfli Gallery, N.Y.C., 1966, 69, 73, Gillman Gallery, Chgo., 1967, Tacoma Mus., 1970, Fort Wayne Art Mus., 1968, Des Moines Art Center, 1970, La Jolla Mus., 1970, Ind. State U., 1976, Sheldon Swope Gallery, Terre Haute, Ind., 1979; Kinetic computer art exhbns. at Ben Shahn Gallery, William Patterson Coll. N.J., Ind. State U., 1985, Bronx Mus. Art, 1986, 55 Mercer Gallery, 1990, Indpls. Art Mus., 1992, Evansvill Mus. Sci. and Art, 1994; represented in permanent collections, Albright-Knox Mus., Des Moines Art Center, Whitney Mus. Am. Art, Joseph H. Hirshhorn Collection, Washington, Indpls. Mus., J.B. Speed Mus., Louisville. Author: (computer program) Eighty 5, 1985; creator, producer various computer software. Served with AUS, 1943. Recipient Award Commn. N.Y. State Coun. of the Arts, 1970. Mem. Am. Abstract Artists. Address: 332 White Oak Ln Terre Haute IN 47804-1081

LAMKIN, BILL DAN, psychologist, educator, consultant; b. Cleburne, Tex., Feb. 26, 1929; s. Walter Lee and Evelyn Agnes (Watters) L.; m. Robbie Jane Stanley, Aug. 27, 1950; children: Louella Leigh, Rebecca Elizabeth, Melissa Jay. BA, Baylor U., 1950, MA, 1955; PhD, U. Tex., 1967. Tchr. English Bangs (Tex.) High Sch., 1950-53, Waco (Tex.) Schs., 1953-59; counselor Waco High Sch., 1959-60; dir. guidance Los Alamos (N.Mex.) Schs., 1960-65; research assoc. U. Tex., Austin, 1965-67; from asst. to assoc. to prof. Baylor U., Waco, 1967-81, prof. ednl. psychology, 1993—, dean Sch. Edn., 1981-93; cons. Region XII Edn. Svc. Ctr., Waco, 1967-79, New Horizons Residential Ctr., Goldthwaite, Tex., 1974—, Midway Home for Children, 1992—, Esperansa Home for Children, 1993—; teaching cons. Family Medicine Faculty Devel. Ctr., Waco, 1978-92. Contbr. articles to Jour. Med. Edn. Mem. APA, Assn. for Counseling and Devel., Am. Ednl. Rsch. Assn., Coll. of Preceptors. Democrat. Baptist. Home: 2608 Lake Oaks Rd Waco TX 76710-1616 Office: Baylor U Sch of Edn Waco TX 76798

LAMKIN, LESLIE LOWELL, public relations manager; b. Oak Park, Ill., July 3, 1940; d. Glenn Roy and Gertrude H. (Farrar) Lowell; m. Donald V. Lamkin, Mar. 29, 1975; 1 child, Kimberly Sue. BA in English, Fla. State U., 1961. Copywriter WGKA Radio, Atlanta, 1962-65, Liller Neal Advt., Atlanta, 1965-68; exec. sec. Atlanta Press Club, Atlanta, 1972-76; sr. pub. info. rep. Ga. Power Co., Atlanta, 1976-77, broadcast svcs. supr., 1977-80, news svcs. mgr., 1980-86, employee/external communications mgr., 1986—. Recipient Silver Quill award Internat. Assn. Bus. Communications, 1987, Gold Quill, 1990. Mem. Pub. Relations Soc. Am. (cert. in pub. relations, Ga. pres. 1989, bd. dirs. 1990 Phoenix award 1986 '87), Women in Communications, Inc. (Atlanta pres. 1979-80, Leadership award 1980), Nat. Mgmt. Assn., Women's Commerce Club (adv. bd. Atlanta 1988-89), Ga. Press Assn. (assoc. mem., pres. 1987-88). Office: Ga Power Co 333 Piedmont Ave NE Atlanta GA 30308-3308

LAMKIN, WILLIAM PIERCE, editor; b. Ansley, La., Oct. 17, 1919; s. John Mays and Carrie Ellen (Posey) L.; m. Irma Hazel Page, Dec. 30, 1948 (div.); children: John Page, Mary Jean, Carol Ellen; m. Jane Eagar Mills, Mar. 17, 1973. AB, U. N.C., 1948. Reporter Alexandria (La.) Daily Town Talk, 1941-43; copyreader Charlotte (N.C.) Observer, 1948-49, asst. city editor, night city editor, 1950-58, city editor, religion editor, 1958-61; news dir. Presbyn. Ch. U.S., 1961-78; editor Presbyn. Survey, Atlanta, 1978-80; editor and pub. Presbyn. Survey, 1980-83; editor Friendship mag., 1983—. With USAAF, 1943-45. Decorated D.F.C. (4), Air Medal (5). Democrat. Home: 4201 Ridgehurst Dr Smyrna GA 30080-3114 Office: 57 Forsyth St NW Ste 900 Atlanta GA 30303-2213 *The most critical issue facing humankind as we approach the 21st century is how to assure world peace. I am convinced that the best approach is through friendship and understanding. We need organized efforts to "walk in other people's shoes". It goes without saying that a world of friends is a world of peace.*

LAMM, CAROLYN BETH, lawyer; b. Buffalo, Aug. 22, 1948; d. Daniel John and Helen Barbara (Tatakis) L.; m. Peter Edward Halle, Aug. 12, 1972; children: Alexander P., Daniel E. BS, SUNY Coll. at Buffalo, 1970; JD, U. Miami (Fla.), 1973. Bar: Fla., 1973, D.C., 1976, N.Y. 1983. Trial atty. frauds sect. civil div. U.S. Dept. Justice, Washington, 1973-78, asst. chief comml. litigation sect. civil div., 1978, asst. dir., 1978-80; assoc. White & Case, Washington, 1980-84, ptnr., 1984—; mem. Sec. State's Adv. Com. Pvt. Internat. law, 1988-91; arbitrator U.S. Panel of Arbitrators, Internat. Ctr. Settlement of Investment Disputes, 1995—. Mem. bd. editors Can./U.S. Rev. Bus. Law, 1987-92; mem. editorial adv. bd. Inside Litigation; contbr. articles to legal publs. Fellow Am. Bar Found.; mem. ABA (chmn. young lawyers divsn., rules and calendar com., chmn. house membership com., chmn. assembly resolution com., sec. 1984-85, chmn. internat. litigation com. coun. 1991-94, sect. litigation, ho. dels. 1982—, nominating com. 1984-87, chair, past D.C. Cir. mem., standing com. fed. judiciary 1993—, com. scope and correlation of work), Am. Arbitration Assn. (arbitrator, com. on fed. arbitration act), Fed. Bar Assn. (chmn. sect. on antitrust and trade regulation), Bar Assn. D.C. (bd. dirs., sec.), D.C. Bar (bd. govs. 1987-93, steering com. litigation sect.), Am. Law Inst., Women's Bar Assn. D.C., Am. Soc. Internat. Law, Internat. Bar Assn. (bus. law sect., internat. litigation com.), Am. Turkish Friendship Coun. (bd. dirs., chair dirs., sec., gen. counsel), Nat. Women's Forum, Columbia Country Club. Democrat. Home: 2801 Chesterfield Pl NW Washington DC 20008-1015 Office: White and Case 601 Thirteenth St NW Washington DC 20005

LAMM, DONALD STEPHEN, publishing company executive; b. N.Y.C., May 31, 1931; s. Lawrence William and Aleen Antonia (Lassner) L.; m. Jean Stewart Nicol, Sept. 27, 1958; children: Douglas William, Robert Lawrence, Wendy Nicol. B.A. with high honors, Yale, 1953; postgrad., Oxford (Eng.) U., 1956. With W.W. Norton & Co., Inc., N.Y.C., 1956—; v.p. W.W. Norton & Co., Inc., 1968-76, pres., 1976-94, chmn., 1984—, also dir.; bd. dirs. W.W. Norton & Co., Ldt., London, Liveright Pub. Corp., Nat. Book Co., Scranton, Pa.; guest fellow Yale U., 1980, 85, Phi Beta Kappa lectr., 1994; Ida Beam disting. vis. prof. U. Iowa, 1987-88; guest fellow Woodrow Wilson Ctr., 1996. Author: (with others) The Spread of Economic Ideas, 1989, Beyond Literacy, 1990; mem. editorial bd. Logos. Mem. coun. Woodrow Wilson Ctr., Inst. Early Am. History and Culture, Williamsburg, Va.; pres. Yale U. Press; past mem. coun., bd. dirs. Roper Ctr. Pub. Opinion Rsch.; bd. advs. The Yale Rev., bd. control U. Cal. Press. With AUS, 1953-55. Fellow Branford Coll., Yale U. Mem. Manuscript Soc., Coun. Fgn. Rels., Phi Beta Kappa (senator 1990—). Home: 741 Calle Picacho Santa Fe NM 87301 Office: W W Norton & Co Inc 550 5th Ave New York NY 10036-5001

LAMM, LESTER PAUL, civil engineer; b. Cohasset, Mass., Jan. 18, 1934; s. Lester Paul and Mary E. L.; m. Mary Briden, Sept. 17, 1960; children: Diana, Deborah, Michael. B.S.C.E., Norwich U., 1955; postgrad., MIT, 1964-65, U. Md., 1966-67. With Fed. Hwy. Adminstrn., 1955-86, exec. dir., 1973-82, dep. adminstr., 1982-86; pres. Hwy. Users Fedn., Washington, 1986—. Served with U.S. Army, 1955-57. Mem. Internat. Pub. Works Fedn., Transp. Rsch. Bd. (exec. com.), Travel Industry Assn. Am. (bd. dirs. 1991—), Intelligent Vehicle-Hwy. Soc. Am. (pres. 1991—), Norwich U. Alumni Assn. (bd. dirs., pres. 1992—). Office: Hwy Users Fedn for Safety Mobility 1776 Massachusetts Ave NW Washington DC 20036-1904

LAMM, MICHAEL EMANUEL, pathologist, immunologist, educator; b. Bklyn., May 19, 1934; s. Stanley S. and Rose (Lieberman) L.; m. Ruth Audrey Kumin, Dec. 16, 1961; children—Jocelyn, Margaret. Student, Amherst Coll., 1951-54; M.D., U. Rochester, 1959; M.S. in Chemistry, Western Res. U., 1962. Diplomate Am. Bd. Pathology. Intern, asst. resident in pathology Inst. Pathology Western Res. U. and Univ. Hosps. of Cleve., 1959-62; research assoc. NIMH, Bethesda, Md., 1962-64; asst. prof. pathology NYU Sch. Medicine, N.Y.C., 1964-68, assoc. prof., 1968-73, prof., 1973-81; prof. dept. pathology Case Western Res. U. Sch. Medicine, 1981—; chmn. dept. Case Western Res. U. Sch. Medicine, 1981—; vis. sci. dept. biochemistry U. Oxford, 1968; vis. prof. dept. pathology U. Geneva, 1976-77; mem. cancer spl. program adv. com. Nat. Cancer Inst., Bethesda, 1976-79, mem. bd. sci. counselors divsn. cancer biology, diagnosis and ctrs., 1993-95; mem. sci. adv. com. Damon Runyon-Walter Winchell Cancer Fund, N.Y.C., 1978-82; mem. immunol. sci. study sect. NIH, Bethesda, 1988-92; mem. immunotoxicology subcom. NRC, 1989-90; mem. toxin peer rev. panel Am. Inst. Biol. Sci., 1990—; bd. dirs. Univ. Associated for Rsch. and Edn. Pathology. Mem. editl. bd. Procs. Soc. Exptl. Biology and Medicine, 1973-82, Molecular Immunology, 1979-83, Jour. Immunol. Methods, 1980—, Jour. Immunology, 1981-85, Am. Jour. Pathology, 1982-92, Regional Immunology, 1988-95, Modern Pathology, 1988—; contbr. articles to profl. jours. Recipient for excellence in teaching NYU Sch. Medicine, 1974; named Career Scientist Health Research Council, City of N.Y., 1966-75; NIH grantee, 1965—. Fellow N.Y. Acad. Scis.; mem. Am. Assn. Pathologists (councilor 1986-88, sec. treas. 1988-90, v.p. 1990-91, pres. 1991-92), Am. Assn. Immunologists, Am. Soc. Biochemistry and Molecular Biology, Coll. Am. Pathologists, U.S. and Can. Acad. Pathology, Soc. for Exptl. Biol. Medicine, Clin. Immunology Soc., Soc. Mucosal Immunology, Am. Soc. Clin. Pathologists, Harvey Soc., Sigma Xi, Alpha Omega Alpha. Home: 2856 Glengary Rd Cleveland OH 44120-1731

LAMMIE, JAMES L., financial planner, consultant; b. 1932. Grad., U.S. Mil. Acad., 1953. Active U.S. Corps of Engrs., 1953-75; CEO Parsons Brinckerhoff, Inc., N.Y.C., 1975—. Office: Parsons Brinckerhoff Inc 1 Penn Plz/ 2nd Fl New York NY 10119-0002 Office: One Penn Plaza 2nd Fl New York NY 10119*

LAMON, BEVERLY ANN, school system administrator; b. Howard Lake, Minn., Sept. 26, 1936; d. Erland Clifford and Vera Ella (Custer) Johnson; widowed, 1991; 1 child, Richard Lang. BS, Union Coll., 1959; MA, LaSierra U., 1993. Tchr. Firth Nebr.) Pub. Schs., 1962-64; tchr., libr. Brownton (Minn.) Pub. Schs., 1964-69, Maplewood Acad., Hutchinson, Minn., 1969-74, Ga.-Cumberland Acad., Calhoun, 1974-76; dean of women Dakota Adventist Acad., Bismark, N.D., 1977-79; assoc. supt. Minn. Adventist Schs., Maple Grove, 1980-87, supt., 1987—. Mem Assn. Supervision & Curriculum Devel., Assn. Seventh-Day Adventist Educators, Assn. Seventh-Day Adventist Sch. Adminstrs. Office: Minn Conf SDA 7384 Kirkwood Ct Maple Grove MN 55369-5270

LAMON, HARRY VINCENT, JR., lawyer; b. Macon, Ga., Sept. 29, 1932; s. Harry Vincent and Helen (Bewley) L.; m. Ada Healey Morris, June 17, 1954; children: Hollis Morris, Kathryn Gurley. BS cum laude, Davidson Coll., 1954; JD with distinction, Emory U., 1958. Bar: Ga. 1958, D.C. 1965. Ptnr. Booth, Wade & Campbell, Atlanta, 1992-95; of counsel Troutman Sanders LLP, Atlanta, 1995—; adj. prof. law Emory U., 1960-79. Contbr. articles to profl. jours. Mem. adv. bd. Salvation Army, 1963—, chmn., 1975-79, nat. adv. bd., 1976-94, chmn., 1991-92; mem. Adv. Coun. on Employee Welfare and Pension Benefit Plans, U.S. Dept. Labor, 1975-79; mem. Employee Benefits Reporter adv. bd. Bur. Nat. Affairs; bd. visitors Davidson Coll., 1979-89; trustee, pres. So. Fed. Tax Inst., Inc., 1965—; trustee Am. Tax Policy Inst., Inc., 1989-96, Embry-Riddle Aero U., 1989—, Cathedral of St. Philip, Atlanta, 1989-95. 1st lt. AUS, 1954-56. Recipient Others award Salvation Army, 1979, Centennial Honoree, 1990. Fellow Am. Bar Found., Am. Coll. Trust and Estate Counsel, Am. Coll. Tax Counsel, Internat. Acad. Estate and Trust Law, Ga. Bar Found.; mem. ABA, Fed. Bar Assn., Atlanta Bar Assn., Am. Bar Retirement Assn. (bd. dirs. 1989—, pres. 1994-95), Am. Law Inst. (life), Am. Pension Conf., So. Employee Benefits Conf. (life, pres. 1972), State Bar Ga. (chmn. sect. taxation 1969-70, vice chmn. commn. on continuing lawyer competency 1982-89), Am. Judicature Soc., Atlanta Tax Forum, Lawyers Club Atlanta, Nat. Emory U. Law Sch. Alumni Assn. (pres. 1967), Practicing Law Inst., ALI-ABA Inst., CLUs Inst., Kiwanis Club Atlanta (pres. 1973-74), Breakfast Club (pres. 1994), Peachtree Racket Club (pres. 1986-87), Atlanta Coffee House Club, Capital City Club, Commerce Club (Atlanta), Cosmos Club, Univ. Club (Washington), Phi Beta Kappa, Omicron Delta Kappa, Phi Delta Phi, Phi Delta Theta (chmn. cmty. svc. day 1969-72, legal commr. 1973-76, prov. pres. 1976-79). Episcopalian. Home: 3375 Valley Rd NW Atlanta GA 30305-1150 Office: Troutman Sanders LLP Ste 5200 600 Peachtree St NE Atlanta GA 30308-2216

LAMON, KATHY LYNN, nursing administrator; b. Moultrie, Ga., July 24, 1961; d. James Daniel and Sammie Ruth (Fletcher) Miles; m. Thomas Eldred Lamon, Aug. 23, 1980. BSN, Valdosta State U., 1983. RN, Fla. Surg. staff nurse Putnam Cmty. Hosp., Palatka, Fla., 1983-84, surg. charge nurse, 1984-86, surg. asst. nurse mgr., 1986-87, nurse mgr. progressive care unit, 1987-90; sr. cmty. health nurse Putnam County Pub. Health Dept., Palatka, 1990; DON Palatka Health Care Ctr., 1991-94; asst. regional nurse North Fla. region Nat. Healthcare, Ocala, 1994—. Author: Pockety Buddy for Nurses PCH, 1991. Youth group leader Palatka Bapt. Temple, 1992-95. Recipient Dr. Frist Humanitarian award Hosp. Corp. of Am., 1988; named Outstanding Young Med. Profl., Jaycees, 1988. Mem. Nat. Assn. DON, Intravenous Nurses Soc., N.E. Fla. DON. Republican. Office: Nat Healthcare 3400 SW 27th Ave Ocala FL 34474

LAMONE, RUDOLPH PHILIP, business educator; b. Wellsburg, W.Va., Dec. 20, 1931; s. Dominic and Maria (Branch) L.; m. Linda A. Hefler, Jan. 29, 1970. B.S., U. N.C., Chapel Hill, 1960, Ph.D., 1966. Instr. U. N.C., 1963-66; mem. faculty U. Md., College Park, 1966—, prof. mgmt. sci., 1971—, dean Coll. Bus. and Mgmt., 1973-92, prof., chair adv. bd. Michael Dingman Ctr. Entrepreneurship, 1993—; bd. dirs. Md. Ctr. Productivity and Quality of Working Life, EA Engring. Sci. and Tech. Inc.; chmn. govtl. rels. com. Am. Assembly Collegiate Schs. Bus., 1977-78; cons. Tatung Co., Taiwan; mem. adv. com. Md. Dept. Econ. and Cmty. Devel. Co-author: Linear Programming for Management Decisions, 1969, Marketing Management and the Decision Sciences, 1971, Production-Operations Management, 1972. Served with AUS, 1952-55. Mem. Acad. Mgmt., Inst. Mgmt. Scis., Am. Inst. Decision Scis., Md. C. of C. (dir.), Phi Beta Kappa, Beta Gamma Sigma. Democrat. Roman Catholic. Club: Annapolis Yacht (bd. dirs.). Office: U Md Dingman Ctr Entrepreneurship College Park MD 20742

LAMONICA, P(AUL) RAYMOND, lawyer, academic administrator, educator; b. Baton Rouge, June 10, 1944; s. Leonard and Olivia (Frank) L.; m. Dianne Davis, Aug. 23, 1971; children: Drew, Neal, Leigh. BA, La. State U., 1965, MA, 1966, JD, 1970. Bar, La. 1970. Law clk. to chief judge U.S. Dist. Ct. (we. dist.) La., 1970-71; assoc. Hebert, Moss & Graphia, Baton Rouge, 1971; judge pro tem 19th Jud. Dist. Ct., East Baton Rouge Parish, 1979; prof. La. State U. Law Sch., Baton Rouge, 1973-86; exec. counsel to La. Gov., 1983-84; U.S. atty. for mid. dist. La., 1986-94; vice chancellor, prof. law La. State U., Baton Rouge, 1994—; counsel La. Ho. of Reps., 1976-79, 80-83. Fellow Am. Bar Found.; mem. ABA, La. Bar Assn. (bd. govs. 1979). Republican. Roman Catholic. Office: La State U 210 LSU Law Ctr Baton Rouge LA 70803

LAMONSOFF, NORMAN CHARLES, psychiatrist; b. Bklyn., Sept. 16, 1936; s. Isidore and Kate (Wolfe) L.; m. Sheila R. Kaplan, Aug. 27, 1961; children: Karen M., Jacob D. BA, Cornell U., 1958; MD, SUNY, 1962. Diplomate Am. Bd. Psychiatry and Neurology. Medical internship Bklyn. Jewish Hosp., 1963; residency psychiatry Kings County Hosp., Bklyn., 1966-68; sr. supervising psychiatrist St. Vincent's Hosp. of Richmond, Staten Island, N.Y., 1968-70; cons. psychiatrist Staten Island Hosp., 1968-87; dir. psychiatry N.Y.C. Dept. Mental Health and Mental Retardation Svcs., 1970-74; attending psychiatrist Jersey City (N.J.) Medical Ctr., 1974-76; program dir. addiction svcs. unit Jersey City Medical Ctr., 1974-76; medical dir. Somerset County Com. Mental Health Ctr., Somerville, N.J., 1976-83, Helene Fuld Crisis Ctr., Trenton, N.J., 1984-87; chmn. psychiatry Helene Fuld Med. Ctr.; medical dir. Bristol-Bensalem Human Svcs. Ctr., Newportville, Pa., 1987—; clinical supr. residency training The Trenton Psychiatric Hosp., clinical asst. prof. N.J. Coll. Medicine. Contbr. articles to profl. jours. With U.S. Army, 1966-68. Decorated Army Commendation medal; recipient Exemplary Psychiatrist award Bucks County area chpt., Nat. Alliance for the Mentally Ill., 1994. Mem. N.Y. Soc. Clinical Psychiatry, Am. Psychiatry Assn., Am. Medical Assn., Mercer County Medical Soc. Home: 121 Trappe Ln Langhorne PA 19047 Office: 340 E Maple Ave Langhorne PA 19047 also: Bristol-Bensalem Human Svcs 340 E Maple Ave Ste 104 Langhorne PA 19047 Address: PO Box L-27 Langhorne PA 19047

LAMONT, LANSING, journalist, public affairs executive, author; b. N.Y.C., Mar. 13, 1930; s. Thomas Stilwell and Elinor (Miner) L.; m. Ada Jung, Sept. 18, 1954; children: Douglas Ranlet, Elisabeth Jung Lamont Wolcott, Virginia Alden Lamont Cazedessus, Thomas Stilwell II. A.B., Harvard U., 1952; M.S. in Journalism with honors, Columbia U., 1958. Reporter, Washington Star, 1958-59; Washington corr. Worcester (Mass.) Gazette, also other New Eng. papers, 1959-60; asst. reporter Washington bur. Time mag., 1961-63, polit. reporter, 1964-68, corr., dep. chief London bur., 1969-71, chief Can. corr., chief Ottawa bur., 1971-73; chief corr. UN bur. Time mag., N.Y.C., 1973-74; v.p., mng. dir. Can. Affairs The Americas Soc., 1981-91, sr. fellow, 1991-94. Author: Day of Trinity (alt. selection Lit. Guild Am.), 1965, Campus Shock, 1979; co-editor Private Letters of John Masefield, 1979, Friends So Different: Essays on Canada and U.S. in the 1980's, 1989, Journey to the Last Empire: The Soviet Union in Transition, 1991, Breakup: The Coming End of Canada and the Stakes for America, 1994 (Notable Books of Yr., N.Y. Times), Sand and Glitter: Exploring the Ancient Middle East, 1994-95. Mem. alumni bd. dirs. Harvard U., also chmn. nominating com. for overseers; trustee Milton Acad., Am. Mus. Natural History, N.Y.C., chmn. libr. com., fellow of libr. Nat. Inst. for Music Theatre; mem. Can.-Am. Com., 1984-94, Coun. Fgn. Rels. 1985—. Served to 1st lt., inf. U.S. Army, 1954-57. William Cullen Bryant fellow Met. Mus. Art, 1984—. Mem. Century Assn. (N.Y.C.), Harvard Club (N.Y.C.). Episcopalian. Office: 133 E 80th St New York NY 10021-0305

LAMONT, LEE, art management executive; b. Queens, N.Y.; m. August Tagliamonte, Apr. 30, 1951; 1 child, Leslie Lamont. With Nat. Concerts & Artists Group, N.Y.C., 1955-58; asst. Sol Hurok Concerts, N.Y.C., 1958-67; person rep. for concerts, rec. and TV Isaac Stern, N.Y.C., 1968-76; v.p. ICM Artists Ltd., N.Y.C., 1976-85; pres. ICM Artists Ltd. and ICM Artists (London) Ltd., N.Y.C., 1985-95, chmn. bd. dirs., 1995—; mem. adv. com. Hannover (Germany) Internat. Violin Competition. Mem. US/USSR Trade and Econ. Coun., Am. Coun. on the Arts, Japan Soc., Asia Soc., Am. Symphony Orch. League (bd. dirs.), Bohemian Club. Avocations: painting, sculpture. Office: ICM Artists Ltd 40 W 57th St Fl 16 New York NY 10019-4001

LAMONT, PETER, production designer, art director. Art dir.: (films) The Seven Percent Solution, 1976, The Spy Who Loved Me, 1977 (Academy award nomination best art direction 1977), The Boys from Brazil, 1978; prodn. designer: (films) For Your Eyes Only, 1981, Octopussy, 1983, Top Secret!, 1984, A View to a Kill, 1985, Aliens, 1986 (Academy award nomination best art direction 1986), The Living Daylights, 1987, Consuming Passions, 1988, License to Kill, 1989, Eve of Destruction, 1991, The Taking of Beverly Hills, 1992, True Lies, 1994. Office: The Lyons/Sheldon Agency 8344 Melrose Ave Ste 20 Los Angeles CA 90069-5496

LAMONT, ROSETTE CLEMENTINE, Romance languages educator, theatre journalist, translator; b. Paris; came to U.S., 1941, naturalized, 1946; d. Alexandre and Loudmilla (Lamont) L.; m. Frederick Hyde Farmer, Aug. 9, 1969. B.A., Hunter Coll., 1947; M.A., Yale U., 1948, Ph.D., 1954. Tutor Romance langs. Queens Coll., CUNY, 1950-54, instr., 1954-61, asst. prof., 1961-64, assoc. prof., 1965-67, prof., 1967—; mem. doctoral faculties, comparative lit., theatre, French and women's studies cert. program CUNY, 1968—; State Dept. envoy Scholar Exch. Program, USSR, 1974; rsch. fellow, 1976; lectr. Alliance Francaise, Maison Francaise of NYU; vis. prof. Sorbonne, Paris, 1985-86; vis. prof. theatre Sarah Lawrence Coll., 1994, 95. Author: The Life and Works of Boris Pasternak, 1964, De Vive Voix, 1971, Ionesco, 1973, The Two Faces of Ionesco, 1978, Ionesco's Imperatives: The Politics of Culture, 1993, Women on the Verge, 1993; translator: Days and Memory, 1990, Auschwitz and After, 1995; also contbr. to various books; mem. editl. bd. Western European Stages, also contbg. editor; European corr. Theatre Week: Columbia Dictionary of Modern European Literature; fgn. corr. Stages. Decorated chevalier, then officier des Palmes Academiques, officier des Arts et Lettres (France); named to Hunter Coll. Hall of Fame, 1991; Guggenheim fellow, 1973-74; Rockefeller Found. humanities fellow, 1983-84. Mem. PEN, MLA, Am. Soc. Theatre Research, Internat. Brecht Soc., Drama Desk (voting mem.), Internat. Assn. Theatre Critics, Phi Beta Kappa, Sigma Tau Delta, Pi Delta Phi. Club: Yale. Home: 260 W 72nd St Apt 9D New York NY 10023-2822 Office: CUNY Queens Coll Dept Romance Langs Flushing NY 11367 *An educator does not merely impart knowledge: he or she communicates an attitude, a way of looking at the world. So does the writer. Through each creative mind the world is born anew.*

LAMONT, SANDERS HICKEY, journalist; b. Atlanta, Nov. 9, 1940; s. Louis Earnest and Dorothy Rebecca (Strickland) LaM.; m. Patricia Jean Taylor, Aug. 5, 1966; children—Patricia Ruth, Zachary Taylor. A.A., Marion Mil. Inst., Ala., 1960; B.A. in Journalism, U. Ala., 1962; postgrad. U. Mich., 1977-78. Reporter, bur. chief Gannett News Service, various locations, 1961-74; mng. editor Ft. Myers News Press, Fla., 1974-77; exec. editor Marietta Times, Ohio, 1978-80, Modesto Bee, Calif., 1980—; chmn. AP News Execs. Council, Calif., 1984-85. NEH journalism fellow, U. Mich., 1977-78; Pulitzer prize juror, 1984-85. Served to 1st lt. U.S. Army, 1963-65. Mem. Am. Soc. Newspaper Editors, AP Mng. Editors, Soc. Profl. Journalists . Methodist. Office: The Modesto Bee PO Box 5256 Modesto CA 95352-5256

LAMONT-HAVERS, RONALD WILLIAM, physician, research administrator; b. Wymondham, Norfolk, Eng., Mar. 6, 1920; came to U.S., 1955, naturalized, 1964; s. William Fredrick L.-H.; m. Gabrielson, Oct. 16, 1965; children—Wendy, Melinda, Ian. B.A., U. B.C., 1942; M.D., U. Toronto, 1946; diploma in internal medicine, McGill U., 1953. Intern Vancouver (B.C., Can.) Gen. Hosp., 1946-48; resident in internal medicine Queen Mary Vets. Hosp., Montreal, Que., Can., 1949-51; Canadian Arthritis and Rheumatism Soc. fellow Columbia Presbyterian Hosp., Coll. Physicians and Surgeons, Columbia U., N.Y.C., 1951-53; med. dir. Canadian Arthritis and Rheumatism Soc., B.C. div., Vancouver, 1953-55, Arthritis and Rheumatism Found., N.Y.C., 1955-64; instr. in medicine Coll. Physicians and Surgeons, Columbia U., 1955-64; assoc. dir. extramural programs NIAMD, Bethesda, Md., 1964-68, dep. dir., 1972-74; assoc. dir. extramural programs NIH, Bethesda, 1968-72; acting dir., dep. dir. NIH, Bethesda, Md., 1974-76, acting dir., 1975, dep. dir., 1974-76; dep. to gen. dir. for rsch. policy and adminstrn. Mass. Gen. Hosp., Boston, 1976-87, v.p. rsch. and tech. affairs, 1987-90, sr. cons. for rsch., 1990—; dep. dir. Cutaneous Biology Rsch. Ctr. Mass. Gen. Hosp. and Harvard U., 1990—; del. USSR-Arthritis Exchange Program, 1964; U.S. coordinator U.S.-USSR Coop. Program in Arthritis, 1973-75. Served with M.C. Royal Canadian Army, 1944-46. Recipient Golden Pen award Jour. Am. Phys. Therapy Assn., 1965; Superior Service award HEW, 1973; Spl. citation Sec. HEW, 1975. Fellow Royal Coll. Physicians (Can.); mem. Am. Coll. Rheumatology (dir. Met. Washington sect. 1964-66), N.Y. Rheumatism Assn. (pres. 1960), Arthritis Found. (dir., governing mem. 1966-80, pres. Mass. chpt. 1987-89), Am. Acad. Orthopaedic Surgeons (hon.), Am. Gastroent. Assn. (affiliate), Alpha Omega Alpha. Office: Mass Gen Hosp 13th St Bldg 149 Charlestown MA 02129-2000

LA MONT-WELLS, TAWANA FAYE, camera operator and video director, public relations executive; b. Ft. Worth, May 12, 1948; d. Jerry James and Roberta Ann (Wilkinson) La M. AA, Antelope Coll., 1979; BA in Anthropology, UCLA, 1982. Forest technician, trail constrn. supr. Angeles Nat. Forest, Region 9 U.S. Forest Svc., Pear Blossom, Calif., 1974-79; trail constrn. supr., maintenance asst. Calif. State Parks, 1979-81; cable TV installer Sammons Comm., Glendale, Calif., 1981-83; camera operator Sammons Comm., San Fernando, Calif., 1984—; video studio and ENG remotes dir., mgr., program mgr. channels 6 and 21 Sammons Comm., Glendale, Calif., 1987—; video dir., prodr. LBW & Assocs. Internat., Ltd., 1988—; mem. ednl. access channel satellite program evaluation com., Glendale and Burbank, 1990-92; mem. Foothill Cmty. TV Network, Glendale and Burbank, 1987—; pres./CEO Chamblee Found., Ltd., 1995—. Prodr., dir. (homeless video) Bittersweet Streets, 1988; cameraperson Rockin in A Hard Place, 1988-93; dir., editor over 1000 videos. Active Glendale Hist. Soc., 1992—; bd. dirs. Am. Heart Assn., 1992—, comms. chair; bd. dirs. ARC, 1993—, mem. disaster svcs. team, cultural diversity chair, 1994—; mem. mktg. com. Burbank YMCA, 1994—; bd. dirs. Glendale Rose Float Assn., 1995—. Recipient award of appreciation LBW and Assocs. Internat., 1988, Bur. Census, 1990, USMC, 1991, Verdigo Disaster Recovery Project, 1995, ARC, 1995, ARC Spl. citation for exceptional vol. svc., 1995, award of outstanding pub. svc. Social Security Adminstrn. HHS, 1989, dedicated svc. award Am. Heart Assn., 1992, cert. of appreciation, 1994, 95. Mem. NFA, NRA, Am. Women in Radio and TV, Am. Bus. Women Assn., UCLA Alumni ASsn. (lfie), Wildlife Waystation, Alpha Gamma. Democrat. Avocations: photography, animals, flying, sailing, travel. Home: 46209 Kings Caynon Rd Lancaster CA 93536

LAMOREAUX, PHILIP ELMER, geologist, hydrogeologist, consultant; b. Chardon, Ohio, May 12, 1920; s. Elmer I. and Gladys (Rhodes) L.; m. Ura Mae Munro, Nov. 11, 1943; children: Philip E Jr., James W., Karen L. BA, Denison U., 1943, PhD (hon.), 1972; MS, U. Ala., 1949. Registered profl. geologist, Ga., N.C., S.C., Tenn., Ind., Ariz., Ark., Fla., Ky., Wyo., Pa. Geologist U.S. Geol. Survey, Tuscaloosa, Ala., 1943-45, dist. geologist Groundwater Office, 1945-57, div. hydrologist Water Resources Programs, 1957-59; chief Ground Water Br. U.S. Geol. Survey, Washington, 1959-61; state geologist, oil and gas supr. Ala. Geol. Survey, Tuscaloosa, 1961-76; pres. P.E. LaMoreaux & Assocs. Inc., Tuscaloosa, 1976-87, chmn. bd., 1987-90, sr. hydrologist, 1990—; lectr. Am. Geol. Inst. Coll. Program, 1969-71, Am. Geophys. Union Coll. Program, 1961—, NSF, Ala. Acad. Sci. H.S. Program, 1961—, No. Engring. and Testing, Salt Lake City, 1985, Ga. State U., Fla. State U., Vanderbilt U., Denison U., Auburn U., U. of Montpellier, France, U. Christ Church, New Zealand, University of Praetoria, Republic of South Africa; hydrogeology cons. to 30 fgn. countries. Editor in chief Jour. Environ. Geology, 1982—; editor in chief: Annotated Bibliography Carbonate Rocks, vols. 1-5; contbr. articles to profl. jours. Mem. Nat. Drinking Water Adv. Coun. EPA, 1984-88, mem. Tech. Rev. Group Oak Ridge Nat. Lab., 1984-88; trustee Denison U. Recipient Comdrs. medal C.E., 1990. Mem. NAE, ASTM, AIME, NAS (nat. rsch. coun. geotech. bd. 1990-92, water sci. and tech. bd. 1990—, bd. earth scis. and resources 1992—, earth resources com. 1995—), AAAS, Ala. Acad. Sci., Ala. Geol. Soc., Am. Assn. Petroleum Geologists (acad. liaison com., Ho. of Dels. 1970-72, com. preservation samples and cores, chmn. divsn. geosci. hydrogeology com.), Am. Geol. Inst. (chmn. com. on publs. 1968-70, pres. 1971-72, Ian Campbell award 1990, chmn. environ. geosci. adv. com. 1994—, William B. Heroy award 1995), Am. Geophys. Union, Am. Inst. Hydrology, Am. Inst. Profl. Geologists (chmn. com. on rels. with govtl. agencies 1967-70, bd. dirs. 1969-70), Assn. Am. State Geologists (statistician 1966-69, chmn. liaison com. fed. agencies 1968-70, pres.), Geol. Soc. Am. (1st chmn. hydrogeology group 1963, chmn. O.E. Meinzer award com. 1965, cons. membership S.E. sect. 1967-68, chmn. nominating com., bd. dirs., bd. trustees, publs. com.), Geol. Soc. London, Internat. Assn. Hydrogeologists (pres. 1977-80, v.p. 1973-77, com. on water rsch. 1978-80, Karst Commn. 1961—, chmn. hydrology hazardus waste commn. 1983-91, pres. 1994—, chmn. com. thermal and mineral waters 1994—), Internat. Water Resources Assn., Interstate Oil Compact Commn. (vice chmn. 1963, chmn. rsch. com.), Miss. Geol. Soc., Nat. Assn. Geology Tchrs., Nat. Rivers and Harbors Congress, Nat. Speleological Soc., Nat. Water Resources Assn., Nat. Water Well Assn., Soc. Econ. Geologists, Soc. Econ. Paleontologists and Mineralogists, Soil Conservation Soc. Am., Southeastern Geol. Soc., Ala. C. of C. (Pres.'s adv. com., Rep. of Energy 1980), Geol. Soc. Am. (chmn.); numerous others. Republican. Presbyterian. Avocations: golfing, photography, stamp collecting, coin collecting, gardening. Office: P E LaMoreaux & Assocs Inc 2610 University Blvd Tuscaloosa AL 35401-1508

LAMOREAUX, PHILLIP ADDISON, investment management company executive; b. Vallejo, Calif., May 8, 1941; s. Page Halleck and Marjorie Ruth (Nelson) L.; m. Sonia Ann Zeltin, Aug. 13, 1965 (div. 1988); children: Anne Elizabeth, Brian Brook. BA, Stanford U., 1963; MBA, Harvard U., 1967. Analyst Dean Witter & Co., San Francisco, 1963-65; portfolio mgr. Am. Express Investment Mgmt. Co., San Francisco, 1967-74; gen. ptnr. Lamoreaux, Glynn & Assocs., San Francisco, 1974-83, Lamoreaux Ptnrs., Sausalito, Calif., 1983—, Lamoreaux Ventures, San Francisco, 1983-90, New West Capital Ptnrs., San Francisco, 1990-93. Pres. Interfaith Housing Found., Mill Valley, Calif., 1970-76; bd. dirs. Marin Theatre Co., Mill Valley, 1985-91; bd. dirs., treas. Hospice Marin, San Rafael, Calif., 1978-84. Mem. Western Venture Capital Assn., Security Analysts San Francisco, Olympic Club, The Family (San Francisco), Mill Valley Tennis Club, Sausalito Yacht Club. Republican. Avocations: skiing, running, handball, tennis. Home: 1001 Bridgeway Ste 205 Sausalito CA 94965-2158 Office: 1505 Bridgeway Ste 125 Sausalito CA 94965-1967

LAMOREUX, FREDERICK HOLMES, financial executive; b. Montreal, Que., Can., Dec. 10, 1941; s. Frederick Silas and Marie Paule (Dubuc) L.; children: David, John, Jenny. B.C., McGill U., 1964; M.B.A., Columbia, 1966. Fin. planning mgr. Cummins Engine Co., Columbus, Ind., 1966-67; mgr. acquisition analysis Am. Standard, N.Y.C., 1967-69; asst. to exec. v.p. Am. Standard, 1970-71; asst. treas. Fairchild Industries, Germantown, Md., 1971-72; v.p. fin. and adminstrn. Fairchild Space and Electronics div. Fairchild Industries, 1972-74; v.p., treas. Arvin Industries, Inc., Columbus, 1974-76; v.p., treas., chief fin. officer Arvin Industries, Inc., 1976-81, chmn. fin. com., dir., 1977-81; gen. partner Wolsey & Co., St. Louis, 1981—; chmn. bd., chief exec. officer Sabreliner Corp., St. Louis, 1983—. Trustee The Hill Sch. 1992—. Talcott fellow, 1965. Mem. Phi Gamma Delta, Beta Gamma Sigma. Clubs: University (N.Y.C.); St. Louis. Home: 54 Westmoreland Pl Saint Louis MO 63108-1244 Office: Sabreliner Corp 7733 Forsyth Blvd Ste 1500 Saint Louis MO 63105-1817

LAMORIELLO, LOUIS ANTHONY, professional hockey team executive; b. Providence, Oct. 21, 1942; s. Nicholas Schiano and Rose (Ventura) L.; m. Patricia A. Renaldo, Aug. 9, 1970; children: Christopher, Heidi, Timothy. BA in Math. and Econs., Providence Coll., 1963. Hockey coach Providence Coll., 1968-82, athletic dir., 1982-87; pres., gen. mgr. N.J. Devils, East Rutherford, 1987—; commr. Hockey East Assn., Providence, 1984-87; mem. hockey com. U.S. Olympics 1984, 88; pres. Am. Hockey Coaches Assn., 1982-83. Named to Hall of Fame Providence Coll. Athletic Dept., 1982, I.T.L.U.-Am. Hall of Fame, 1986, R.I. Hall of Fame, 1987. Mem. Nat. Collegiate Athletic Assn. (profl. devel. com. 1984-87). Office: NJ Devils PO Box 504 East Rutherford NJ 07073-0504*

LAMOS, MARK, artistic director, administrator, actor; b. Melrose Park, Ill., Mar. 10, 1946; s. Gustav and Ruth (Oechslin) L. BS, Northwestern U., 1969; hon. doctorate, Conn. Coll., 1990, U. Hartford, 1990, Trinity Coll., 1993. Artistic dir. Ariz. Theatre Co., Tucson, 1978, Calif. Shakespearean Festival, Visalia, 1980-81, Hartford (Conn.) State Co., 1980—. Stage appearances include (stage debut) Lovers, Lake Forest, Ill., (Broadway debut) Pvt. Bowers in Love Suicide at Schofield Barracks, ANTA Theatre, 1971, Another Part of the Forest, Chgo., 1971-72, as Abel in The Creation of the World and Other Business, N.Y.C., 1972, as Christian de Neuvillette in Cyrano, N.Y.C., 1973, title role in Hamlet, San Diego, 1977, as Rex in City Sugar, N.Y.C., 1978, as Feste in Twelfth Night, Stratford, Conn., 1978, as Octavius in Man and Superman, N.Y.C., 1978, A Month in the Country, Princeton, N.J., 1978-79, title role in Anatol, Hartford, Conn., 1984, as Dr. Rank in A Doll House, Hartford Stage Co., 1986, as Jack Worthing in The Importance of Being Earnest, Hartford Stage Co., 1989, others; toured as Solomon Rothschild in The Rothschilds, 1972; theater dir. Dear Liar, Guthrie Theatre, 1976; (Ariz. Theatre Co.) The Threepenny Opera, 1978, The Seagull, 1979, Twelfth Night, 1979; (Calif. Shakespearean Festival) Romeo and Juliet, 1979, The Taming of the Shrew, 1979, Hamlet, 1980, A Midsummer Night's Dream, 1980; (Hartford Stage Co.) Mackerel, 1977, The Beaux Stratagem, 1980, Cymbeline, 1981, Undiscovered Country, 1981, Antony and Cleopatra, 1981, Kean, 1982, The Greeks, 1982, The Great Magoo, 1982, The Portage to San Cristobal of A.H., 1983, The Misanthrope, 1983, The Three Sisters, 1984, The Tempest, 1985, Twelfth Night, 1985, Distant Fires, 1986, The Gilded Age, 1986, Pericles, 1987, Morocco, 1987, Hamlet, 1987, Hedda Gabler, 1988, The School for Wives, 1988, A Midsummer Night's Dream, 1988, Peer Gynt, 1989, The Importance of Being Earnest, 1989, The Illusion, 1990, The Miser, 1990, Our Country's Good, 1990, The Master Builder, 1991, Julius Caesar, 1991, All's Well That Ends Well, 1991, Hidden Laughter, 1992, Tartuffe, 1992, Martin Guerre, 1993, Richard III, 1994, Arms and the Man, 1995 Dybbuk, 1995; opera dir. Don Giovanni, St. Louis Opera, 1983, Arabella, Santa Fe Opera, 1983, The Aspern Papers, Dallas Opera, 1988, La Boheme, Glimmerglass Opera Theater, 1990, Il Re Pastore, Glimmerglass Opera Theater, 1991, 94, The Turn of the Screw, Glimmerglass Opera Theater, 1992, Cosí fan Tutte, Portland Opera, 1993, Werther, Glimmerglass Opera Theater, 1993, Merchant of Venice, Hartford Stage, 1993, I Lombardi, Met. Opera, 1994, The Turn of The Screw, Seattle Opera, 1994, False Admissions, Hartford Stage, 1994, A Scourge of Hyacinths (world premiere), Munich Biennale, Germany, Ariadne Auf Naxos, 1994, Paul Bunyan, Glimmerglass Opera, 1995; also dir. The Merchant of Venice, Stratford Festival, 1984, The Voyage of Edgar Allan Poe, Stora Teatern, Goteborg, Sweden, 1985, The School for Wives, La Jolla (Calif.) Playhouse, 1987, Desire Under the Elms, Pushkin Drama Theatre, Moscow, 1988, Measure for Measure, Lincoln Ctr., N.Y.C., 1989, Our Country's Good, Nederlander Theater, N.Y.C., 1991 (Tony nomination), The End of the Day, Playwrights Horizons, N.Y.C., 1992; TV appearance in School for Scandal, Great Performances, PBS, 1975; film appearance in Longtime Companion, Am. Playhouse Theatrical Films, 1989; author: (play) Some Other Time, 1970. Mem. Theater Comm. Group (trustee 1991—). Office: Hartford Stage Co 50 Church St Hartford CT 06103-1201

LAMOUREUX, GLORIA KATHLEEN, nurse, air force officer; b. Billings, Mont., Nov. 2, 1947; d. Laurits Bungaard and Florence Esther (Nielsen) Nielsen; m. Kenneth Earl Lamoureux, Aug. 31, 1973 (div. Feb. 1979). BS, U. Wyo., 1970; MS, U. Md., 1984. Staff nurse, ob-gyn DePaul Hosp., Cheyenne, Wyo., 1970; enrolled USAF, 1970, advanced through grades to col.; staff nurse ob-gyn dept. 57th Tactical Hosp., Nellis AFB, Nev., 1970-71, USAF Hosp., Clark AB, Republic Philippines, 1971-73; charge nurse ob-gyn dept. USAF Regional Hosp., Sheppard AFB, Tex., 1973-75; staff nurse ob-gyn dept. USAF Regional Hosp., MacDill AFB, Fla., 1976-79; charge nurse ob-gyn dept. USAF Med. Ctr., Andrews AFB, Md., 1979-80, MCH coord., 1980-82; chief nurse USAF Clinic, Eielson AFB, Alaska, 1984-86, Air Force Systems Command Hosp., Edwards AFB, Calif., 1986-90; comdr. 7275th Air Base Group Clinic, Italy, 1990-92, 42d Med. Group, Loring AFB, Maine, 1992-94; 347th Med. Group, Moody AFB, Ga., 1994-96; chief nursing svcs. divsn. Hdqrs. Air Edn. and Tng. Command, Randolph AFB, Tex., 1996—. Mem. Assn. Women's Health, Obstetric, and Neonatal Nurses (sec.-treas. armed forces dist. 1986-88, vice-chmn. armed forces dist. 1989-91), Air Force Assn., Assn. Mil. Surgeons U.S., Bus. and Profl. Women's Assn. (pub. rels. chair Prince George's County chpt. 1981-82), Assn. Healthcare Execs., Sigma Theta Tau. Republican. Lutheran. Avocations: reading, needlework, piano, photography. Home: 3109 Robinson Rd Valdosta GA 31602-5501

LA MOY, WILLIAM THOMAS, library director, editor; b. Hartford, Conn., Jan. 27, 1953; s. Roy Henry and Margaret Mary (McKelligott) La M. BA in English Lang. and Lit. cum laude, Yale U., 1976; MS in Libr. and Info. Sci., Simmons Coll., 1988. Editor (with others) The Yale Edit. of Horace Walpole's Correspondence, New Haven, Conn., 1976-83; prodn. editor Garland Pub., Inc., Hamden, Conn., 1984-87; asst. libr. Essex Inst., Salem, Mass., 1989-90; dir. libr. Essex Inst., Salem, 1990-92; dir. James Duncan Phillips Libr. Peabody Essex Mus., Salem, 1992—. Recipient Publ. Design award Essex Inst. Hist. Collections, New Eng. Mus. Assn., 1991, Publ. Design award Peabody Essex Mus. Collections, New Eng. Mus. Assn., 1994, Publ. Design award (1st and 2d prize) Peabody Essex Mus. Collections, New Eng. Mus. Assn., 1995. Mem. ALA, Assn. Coll. and Rsch. Librs. (rare books and manuscripts sect.), Colonial Soc. Mass., Internat. Honor Soc. for Librarianship and Info. Svc. Office: James Duncan Phillips Libr Peabody Essex Mus East India Sq Salem MA 01970

LAMP, BENSON J., tractor company executive; b. Cardington, Ohio, Oct. 7, 1925; m. Martha Jane Motz, Aug. 21, 1948; children: Elaine, Marlene, Linda, David. BS in Agr. and B in Agrl. Engring., Ohio State U., 1949, MS in Agrl. Engring., 1952; PhD in Agrl. Engring., Mich. State U., 1960. Registered profl. engr., Ohio. Prof. agrl. engring. Ohio State U., Columbus, 1949-61, 87-91, prof. emeritus, 1991—; product mgr. Massey Ferguson Ltd., Toronto, Can., 1961-66; product planning mgr. Ford Tractor Ops. div. Ford Motor Co., Troy, Mich., 1966-71, mktg. mgr., 1971-76, bus. planning mgr., 1978-87; v.p. mktg. and devel. Ford Aerospace div. Ford Motor Co., Dearborn, Mich., 1976-78. Author: Corn Harvesting, 1962. Served to 2d lt. USAF, 1943-45. Fellow Am. Soc. Agrl. Engrs. (pres. 1985-86, Gold medal 1993), Country Club at Muirfield Village (Dublin, Ohio). Avocations: golf, tennis, bridge. Office: BJM Company Inc 6128 Inverurie Dr E Dublin OH 43017-9472

LAMP, FREDERICK JOHN, museum curator; b. Malvern, Pa., Nov. 20, 1944; s. Clyde Herman and Grace Ebersole (Landis) L.; m. Diane Frank, May 18, 1974 (div. 1984). BS, Kent State U., 1967; MA, Ohio U., 1971; PhD, Yale U., 1982. Adminstr., lectr. Mus. African Art, Washington, 1973-77; curator Balt. Mus. Art, 1981—. Author Art of Baga, La Guinee, African Art of W Atlantic Coast. Contbr. articles to profl. jours. Nat. Mus. Act degree fellow, 1977-79; rsch. grantee Nat. Endowment Arts, 1976, 85, Social Sci. Rsch. Coun., 1979-81, 88, Smithsonian Instn., 1985, Fulbright, 1991-92, Nat. Gallery Art, 1995-96. Mem. Coll. Art Assn., African Studies Assn. (Arts Council). Democrat. Avocation: collecting African Art. Office: Balt Mus Art Art Museum Dr Baltimore MD 21218-3898

LAMP, JOHN ERNEST, lawyer; b. Spokane, Wash., Jan. 17, 1943; s. Raymond Holmes and Marie (Cunningham) L.; m. Louise Edwards, June 26, 1976; children—Amanda Catherine Marie, Victoria Louise. B.A., Wash. State U., 1965; J.D., Willamette U., 1968. Bar: Wash. 1968. Asst. atty. gen. State of Wash., Olympia, 1968-69, 71-76; sr. asst. atty. gen. chief Spokane and Eastern Wash. br. Wash. State Atty. Gen.'s Office, 1976-81; U.S. Atty. Eastern Dist. Wash. State, 1981-91; spl. atty. to U.S. Atty. Gen., 1990-92. Mem. Atty. Gen.'s adv. com. U.S. Attys., 1983-86; apptd. to White House Conf. for Drug Free Am., 1987; apptd. to bd. dirs. Drug Watch Internat., Internat. Drug Strategy Inst., 1993. Capt. U.S. Army, 1969-71, Vietnam. Decorated Bronze Star; recipient Alumni Achievement award Wash. State U., 1986; recipient Medal Commitment Greater Spokane Substance Abuse Coun., 1989, Community Svc., Community Rels. Svc. award U.S. Dept. Justice, 1991. Mem. Wash. Bar Assn. Home: 11205 S Hatch Rd Spokane WA 99204 Office: Caine McLaughlin Wash Mut Fin Ctr W 601 Main Ste 1015 Spokane WA 99201

LAMPARTER, WILLIAM C., printing and publishing consultant, digital printing and information systems specialist; b. Bklyn., July 13, 1929; s. William C. and Nadine (Lesch) L.; m. Ann E. Martyn; children: Ellen, Susan, David. B.S., Springfield (Mass.) Coll., 1951; M.S., Boston U., 1952. V.p., gen. mgr. Mead Digital Systems, 1975-78; pres. Nat. Assn. Printers and Lithographers, Teaneck, N.J., 1978-82, PrintCom Cons. Group, 1982—; staff cons. Rochester Inst. Tech.'s Lab. for Quality and Productivity in the Graphic Arts, mem. adv. com. to Sch. of Printing Mgmt. and Scis., adv. to Graphic Arts Tech. and Edn. Ctr.; internat. lectr. in field. Author: Forecast of Long-Term Business and Technological Trends in the Graphic Arts, 1968, transl. into Polish, Russian, 1973, The Electronic Superhighway Revolution 1994-1997-2000-2010, 1994, The Impact of the Information Superhighway on Traditional Print Media, 1995, Critical Trends Update - An Overview of Printing Industry Trends in the Year of the Digital Drupa, 1996, Management Guide to Digital Printing, 1996; prin. economist, author Printing Industry Quar. Bus. Indicator Report, 1979-85, Ann. Tech. Impact Rev., 1985, Interpretative Tech. Analysis, 1986, Printing Industry Materials Mgmt. Newsletter, 1985-86; pub., prin. editor FYI/HarbingerWatch, 1995. Served with U.S. Army. Recipient Tech. Leadership award Nat. Assn. Printers and Lithographers, 1995. Mem. Printing Industries Am. Inc., Nat. Assn. Printers and Lithographers, Tech. Assn. Graphic Arts, Rsch. and Engring. Coun. of Graphic Arts Industry Inc. (mem. exec. com.), Assn. for Graphic Arts Tng., World Future Soc., Am. Soc. Quality Control, Soderstrom Soc., Inst. of Printing (London), Nat. Printing Equip. Assn. (former bd. mem.), Sigma Delta Chi. Home and Office: 1020 Farm Creek Rd Waxhaw NC 28173-7793 *Commitment, developing people and combining their skills with the advantages of automation in a bottom-line oriented but innovative entrepreneurial atmosphere are the keys to success in today's changing business environment.*

LAMPE, FREDERICK WALTER, chemistry educator, consultant; b. Chgo., Jan. 5, 1927; s. Joseph Dell and Christine Wood (Phillips) L.; m. Eleanor Frances Coffin, Mar. 26, 1949; children: Joan Dell, Kathy Lee, Erik Steven, Beth Ann, Kristina Jean. BS, Mich. State Coll., 1950; AM, Columbia U., 1951, PhD, 1953. Research chemist Humble Oil and Refining Co., Baytown, Tex., 1953-56, sr. research chemist, 1956-59, specialist research, 1959-60; assoc. prof. Pa. State U., University Park, 1960-65, prof., 1965-92; prof. emeritus, 1992—; head dept. chemistry Pa. State U., University Park, 1983-88; Robert A. Welch Found. lectr., Tex., 1982, J.L. Franklin Meml. lectr., 1990; cons. Mobil Oil Corp., Pennington, N.J., 1961-69, Sci. Rsch. Instruments Corp., Balt., 1967-77, IBM Corp., Yorktown Heights, N.Y., 1980-85, Chemetron Corp., PPG Biomed., St. Louis, 1982-90, Polaroid Corp., Waltham, Mass., 1986-88, Marquett Electronics Corp., 1993—. bd. dirs. Vestec Corp., Houston. Author: (with H.R. Allcock) Contemporary Polymer Chemistry, 1981, 2d edit. 1990; patentee in field; contbr. 160 articles to profl. jours. Served with USN, 1944-46, ATO. NSF sr. postdoctoral fellow, 1966-67; recipient Sr. U.S. Scientist award Alexander von Humboldt Found., 1973-74, 84. Fellow Am. Physical Soc.; mem. Am. Chem. Soc., Am. Soc. for Mass Spectrometry (bd. dirs. 1981-83). Republican. Methodist. Home: 542 Ridge Ave State College PA 16803-3441 Office: Pa State U Dept of Chemistry 152 Davey Lab University Park PA 16802-6300

LAMPEN, RICHARD JAY, lawyer, investment banker; b. New Brunswick, N.J., Nov. 12, 1953; s. J. Oliver and Miriam (Walsh) L.; m. Susan Matson, June 8, 1975; children: Katharine, Caroline. BA, Johns Hopkins U., 1975; JD, Columbia U., 1978. Bar: Fla. 1978, U.S. Dist. Ct. (so. dist.) Fla. 1978. From assoc. to ptnr. Steel Hector & Davis, Miami, Fla., 1978-86, co-chmn. corp. dept., 1992-95; mng. dir. Salomon Bros. Inc., N.Y.C., 1986-92; exec. v.p., gen. counsel New Valley Corp., Miami, Fla., 1995—; bd. dirs. New Valley Corp., Roland Internat. Corp., Thinking Machines Corp. Mem. Fla. Bar Assn. (chmn. securities law com. 1985-86), City Club, Exch. Club. Office: New Valley Corp 100 SE 2d St 32d Fl Miami FL 33131

LAMPERT, ELEANOR VERNA, retired human resources specialist; b. Porterville, Calif., Mar. 23; d. Ernest Samuel and Violet Edna (Watkins) Wilson; student in bus., fin. Porterville Jr. Coll., 1977-78; grad. Anthony Real Estate Sch., 1971; student Laguna Sch. of Art, 1972, U. Calif.-Santa Cruz, 1981; m. Robert Mathew Lampert, Aug. 21, 1935; children—Sally Lu Winton, Lary Lampert, Carol R. John. Bookkeeper, Porterville (Calif.) Hosp., 1956-71; real estate sales staff Ray Realty, Porterville, 1973; sec. Employment Devel. Dept., State of Calif., Porterville, 1973-83, orientation and tng. specialist CETA employees, 1976-80. Author: Black Bloomers and Han-Ga-Ber, 1986. Sec., Employer Adv. Group, 1973-80, 81—; mem. U.S. Senatorial Bus. Adv. Bd., 1981-84; charter mem. Presdl. Republican Task Force, 1981—; mem. Rep. Nat. Congl. Com., 1982-88; pres. Sierra View Hosp. Vol. League, 1988-89 ; vol. Calif. Hosp. Assn., 1983-89, Calif. Spl. Olympics Spirit Team. Recipient Merit Cert., Gov. Pat Brown, State of Calif., 1968. Mem. Lindsay Olive Growers, Sunkist Orange Growers, Am. Kennel Club, Internat. Assn. Personnel in Employment Security, Calif. State Employees Assn. (emeritus Nat. Wildlife Fedn., NRA, Friends of Porterville Library, Heritage Found., DAR (Kaweah chpt. rec. sec. 1988—), Internat. Platform Assn., Dist. Fedn. Women's Clubs (recording sec. Calif. chpt. 1988—), Ky. Hist. Soc., Women's Club of Calif. (pres. Porterville chpt. 1988-89, dist. rec. sec. 1987-89), Mo. Rep. Women of Taney County, Internat. Sporting and Leisure Club, Ladies Aux. VFW (No. 5168 Forsyth, Mo.), Ozark Walkers League.

LAMPERT, MICHAEL ALLEN, lawyer; b. Phila., May 6, 1958; s. Arnold Leonard and Marilyn (Sternberg) L.; m. Angela Gallicchio, Dec. 6, 1987; 1 child, David Max. AB in Econs. cum laude, U. Miami, Coral Gables, Fla., 1979, postgrad., 1980; JD, Duke U., 1983; LLM in Taxation, NYU, 1984. Bar: Fla. 1983, D.C. 1984, Pa. 1984, U.S. Tax Ct. 1984, U.S. Ct. Appeals for the Armed Forces, 1995. Assoc. Cohen, Scherer, Cohn & Silverman, P.A., North Palm Beach, Fla., 1984-88; instr. div. continuing edn. Fla. Atlantic U., Boca Raton, 1988—; prin. Jacobson & Lampert, P.A., Boca Raton, 1988-91; pvt. practice West Palm Beach, 1991—. Mem. editl. bd. Southeastern Tax Alert, 1993—. Instr., trainer, chpt. vice-chair, emergency svcs. chair ARC, Palm Beach County, Fla.; bd. dirs. Jewish Fedn. Palm Beach County, 1989-91; bd. dirs. Jewish Family and Children's Svc. Palm Beach County, 1988—, treas., 1991-94; mem. nat. planned giving com. Weismann Inst., Israel. Recipient Safety award ARC, 1989, Cert. of Merit, Am. Radio Relay League, West Palm Beach Club, 1988, Cert. of Appreciation for Leadership, ARC Disaster Svcs., Palm Beach County, 1989, Disaster Svc. award, 1994, Human Resources award, 1993, Tax Law award Legal Aid Soc. of Palm Beach County and Palm Beach County Bar Assn., 1993. Mem. Palm Beach Tax Inst. (pres., dir.), Fla. Bar (exec. coun., tax sect.), Palm Beach County Assn. (chair bus. and corp. continuing legal edn. com. 1989-90, chair legal asst. com. 1988-91). Avocations: aquatics, amateur radio, running. Office: Ste 900 1655 Palm Beach Lakes Blvd West Palm Beach FL 33401

LAMPERT, RICHARD HARVEY, book publishing company executive, editor; b. Phila., June 10, 1947; s. Harold J. and Selma (Heitzer) L.; m. Deborah J. Thorp, Mar. 26, 1988. BSChemE, Drexel U., 1969; MS, U. Calif., Berkeley, 1971. Asst. med. editor W.B. Saunders Co., Phila., 1971, biology editor, 1971-76; med. editor Appleton-Century-Crofts, N.Y.C., 1976-78, sr. editor, 1978-81, editor-in-chief, 1981-83; exec. editor Yr. Book Med. Pubs., Inc., Phila., 1983-85; editor-in-chief Yr. Book Med. Pubs., Inc., Chgo., 1985-87, v.p. editorial, 1987-89; v.p., pub. continuity pub. Mosby-Yr. Book Inc., Chgo., 1989—. Avocations: piano, swimming, running. Office: Mosby-Yr Book Inc 200 N La Salle St Chicago IL 60601-1014

LAMPERTI, JOHN WILLIAMS, mathematician, educator; b. Montclair, N.J., Dec. 20, 1932; s. Frank A. and Louise (Williams) L.; m. Claudia Jane McKay, Aug. 17, 1957; children—Matthew, Steven, Aaron, Noelle. B.S., Haverford Coll., 1953; Ph.D., Calif. Inst. Tech., 1957. Instr., then asst. prof. math. Stanford, 1957-62; research asso. Rockefeller Inst., 1962-63; faculty Dartmouth, 1963—, prof. math., 1968—; Sci. exch. visitor to USSR, 1970; vis. prof. U. Aarhus, Denmark, 1972-73, Nicaraguan Nat. U., 1990; cons. Am. Friends Svc. Com., 1980, 85, 91. Author: Probability: A Survey of the Mathematical Theory, 1966, 2d edit., 1996, Stochastic Processes: A survey of the Mathematical Theory, 1977, What Are We Afraid Of? An Assessment of the "Communist Threat" in Central America, 1988. Fellow Inst. Math. Stats.; mem. ACLU, War Resisters League, Peace Action, Amnesty Internat., Fedn. Am. Scientists. Home: Upper Loveland Rd Norwich VT 05055 Office: Dartmouth Coll Dept Math Hanover NH 03755

LAMPI, JUANITA, principal. Prin. Loggers' Run Community Mid. Sch., Boca Raton, Fla. Recipient Blue Ribbon Sch. award U.S. Dept. Edn., 1990-91. Office: Loggers' Run Community Mid Sch 11584 W Palmetto Park Rd Boca Raton FL 33428-2681

LAMPINEN, JOHN A., newspaper editor; b. Waukegan, Ill., Nov. 26, 1951; s. Walter Valentine and Patricia Mae Irene (Pruess) L.; m. Belinda Walter, Oct. 20, 1973; children: Amanda Michelle, Heidi Elizabeth. BS in Comm., U. Ill., 1973. Staff writer Paddock Cir. Newspapers, Libertyville, Ill., 1973-75; regional editor The Jour., New Ulm, Minn., 1975-76; various positions Daily Herald, Arlington Heights, Ill., 1976-90; asst. v.p., mng. editor Daily Herald, Arlington Heights, 1990—; adj. prof. Medill Sch. Journalism, Northwestern U., Evanston, Ill., 1995—. Mem. APME, SPJ. Avocations: baseball, long-distance running, coaching girls softball. Office: Daily Herald 217 W Campbell St Arlington Heights IL 60005-1411

LAMPL, PEGGY ANN, social services administrator; b. N.Y.C., Dec. 12, 1930; d. Joseph and Alice L. B.A., Bennington Coll., 1952. Dir. program devel. dept. mental health AMA, Chgo., 1962-66; spl. asst. NIMH, HEW, Washington, 1967-69; public relations dir. League Women Voters of U.S., Washington, 1969-73; exec. dir. League Women Voters of U.S., 1973-78; dep. asst. Sec. of State for congressional relations Dept. State, Washington, 1978-80; dep. dir. Iris Systems Devel., 1982-83; exec. dir. Children's Def. Fund, Washington, 1984-89, LWV, Washington, 1989—. Club: Federal City. Home: 2500 Q St NW Washington DC 20007-4373

LAMPORT, FELICIA (MRS. BENJAMIN KAPLAN), writer; b. N.Y.C., Jan. 4, 1916; d. Samuel C. and Miriam (Dworsky) L.; m. Benjamin Kaplan, Apr. 16, 1942; children: James, Nancy Mansbach. B.A., Vassar Coll., 1937. Reporter N.Y. Jour., N.Y.C., 1935-36; dialogue sub-title writer MGM, N.Y.C., 1937-49; instr. expository writing Harvard U., 1980-88; instr. creative writing Harvard U. Extension, 1988—. Freelance writer for various mags., newspapers including N.Y. Times, 1949—; columnist for Boston Globe, 1981—; author: Mink on Weekdays, 1950, Scrap Irony, 1961, Cultural Slag, 1966; Light Metres, 1982; Political Plumlines, 1984. Bd. dirs. MacDowell Colony, 1970-80, Am. Chess Found., 1965-80. Mem. PEN, Author's Guild, Nat. Writers Union. Home: 2 Bond St Cambridge MA 02138-2308

LAMPORT, LESLIE B., computer scientist; b. N.Y.C., Feb. 7, 1941; s. Benjamin and Hannah (Lasser) L.; m. Carol Dahl Crum, Oct. 31, 1968 (div. Feb. 1978); 1 child, Jason Christopher. BS, MIT, 1960; MA, Brandeis U., 1963, PhD, 1972. Mem. faculty Marlboro (Vt.) Coll., 1965-69; systems analyst Mass. Computer Assocs., Wakefield, 1970-77; sr. computer scientist SRI Internat., Menlo Park, Calif., 1977-85; sr. cons. engr. Digital Equipment Corp., Palo Alto, Calif., 1985—. Patentee in field. Mem. NAE. Office: Digital Equipment Corp Systems Rsch Ctr 130 Lytton Ave Palo Alto CA 94301-1044

LAMPTON, LESLIE B., SR., oil industry executive; b. 1926; married. Grad., U. Miss., 1947. With Joe T. Dehmer Distbr., Jackson, Miss., 1949-51, 53-54, Lampton Oil Co., Jackson, Miss., 1954-70; prin. Ergon Inc., Jackson, Miss., 1970—, now chmn. With U.S. Navy, 1947-79, 1951-53. Office: Ergon Inc 2829 Lakeland Dr Jackson MS 39208-9798*

LAMPTON, ROBERT DONALD, JR., chemical engineer, consultant; b. Newark, Ohio, Mar. 10, 1956; s. Robert Donald and Vera Nell (Smith) L.; m. Nancy Jane Cole, May 14, 1977; children: Robert Matthew, Amanda Kathryn, Michelle Erin. BS in Chem. Engring., Tex. A&M U., 1978; MBA in Mgmt., U. Houston, Clear Lake, Tex., 1984. Project leader Dow Chem. Co., Freeport, Tex., 1978-89; rsch. mgr. Internat. Paint Powder Coatings, Inc., Houston, 1989-93; cons. RDL Consulting, Friendswood, Tex., 1993—; cons. on epoxy coatings and coating processes USN, Port Hueneme, Calif., 1993—. Mem. ASTM (sec. com. epoxy coating task groups 1989—), Nat. Assn. Corrosion Engrs., Concrete Reinforcing Steel Inst. (sec. epoxy coating tech. com., sec. epoxy coating adv. com. 1989—), Beta Gamma Sigma (charter mem.). Achievements include patents for Dow Epoxy Resins for rebar coatings and pipe coatings, Dow Hardener for rebar coatings, others. Home and Office: 1402 Silverleaf Dr Friendswood TX 77546-4876

LAMSON, EVONNE VIOLA, therapist, computer software company executive, consultant, pastor, Christian education administrator; b. Ithaca, Mich., July 8, 1946; d. Donald and Mildred (Perdew) Guild; m. James E. Lamson, Nov. 2, 1968; 1 child, Lillie D. Assoc. in Math., Washtenaw C.C., Ypsilanti, Mich., 1977; BS, Ea. Mich. U., 1989; MA in Pastoral Counseling Ashland (Ohio) Theol. Sem., 1993. Lic. profl. counselor, Mich. Data base mgr. ERIM, Ann Arbor, Mich., 1978-81; mgr. product svcs. Comshare, Ann Arbor, 1981-90, project leader, tng. course designer info. techs., 1991-93; founder, pres. G & L Consultants, Brighton, Mich., 1982—; tng. specialist Comshare, Ann Arbor, 1990-93; Assoc. Pastor, dir. Christian edn. Keystone Cmty. Ch., Saline, Mich., 1993-95; founder Living Waters Counseling, 1993—. Study leader Brighton Wesleyan Ch., 1981-93; lic. minister Weseleyan Ch. Am., 1993—; program dir. Wesleyan Womens Assn. of Brighton, 1983-91; clin. staff counselor Women's Resource Ctr., Howell, Mich., 1991-94; clin. counselor Livingston Counseling and Assessment, 1994—, clin. team leader, 1995—. Mem. AACD, NAFE, AACC, Am. Mgmt. Assn., Fairbanks Family of Am., Internat. Platform Assn. Avocations: skiing, motivational speaking, reading. Home: 6708 Calfhill Ct Brighton MI 48116-7419

LAMSON, GEORGE HERBERT, economics educator; b. Hartford, Conn., Feb. 21, 1940; s. Arroll Liscomb and Marguerite (Brechbuhler) L.; m. Susan Kathryn Lippert, Sept. 7, 1968; children: Scott, Brandon. A.B., Princeton U., 1963; M.A., Northwestern U., 1966, Ph.D., 1971. Research asst. Northwestern U. Econ. Survery of Liberia, Monrovia, 1962-63; instr. dept. econs. Loyola U., Chgo., 1967-68, U. Conn., Storrs, 1968-69; asst. prof. then assoc. prof. dept. econs. Carleton Coll., Northfield, Minn., 1969-80, Williams prof., 1981—, chmn. dept., 1978-84; cons. Minn. Higher Edn. Coordinating Com., St. Paul, 1971-72; textbook reviewer John Wiley & Sons, N.Y.C., 1979-82; reviewer NSF grad. fellowship program, 1988-90; vis. prof. U. Internat. Bus. and Econs., Beijing, China, 1994. Intersocietal studies fellow Northwestern U., 1966-67; recipient Faculty Devel. awards 1979, 90-91. Mem. Am. Econ. Assn., Midwest Econ. Assn., Minn. Econ. Assn. (bd. dirs. 1981-83, pres. 1984). Republican. Home: 4485 Detelemark Rd Dundas MN 55019-4003 Office: Carleton Coll Dept Econs Northfield MN 55057

LAMSON, ROBERT WOODROW, retired school system administrator; b. L.A., Dec. 28, 1917; s. Ernest K. and Mabel (Mahoney) L.; m. Jeannette Juett, July 22, 1949; children: Robert Woodrow Jr., Nancy Virginia, Kathleen Patricia. BA, Occidental Coll., 1940; MA, U. So. Calif., 1955. Cert. tchr., prin., supt., Calif. Tchr. El Monte (Calif.) Sch. Dist., 1940-43; tchr. L.A. City Sch. Dist., 1945-49, prin., 1949-55, supr., 1955-57, adminstrv. asst., 1957-59, area supt., 1959-78; ret., 1978; agt. Keilholtz Realtors, La Canada, Calif.; instr. various colls. and univs. so. Calif.; a founder, v.p., bd. dirs. U.S. Acad. Decathlon, Cerritos, Calif., 1981-86. Bd. dirs. 10th Dist. PTA, L.A., 1965-78; chmn. Scout-O-Rama, Gt. Western coun. Boy Scouts Am., 1980. Lt. comdr. USNR, 1943-46, mem. Res. ret. Mem. Am. Assn. Sch. Adminstrs., Assn. Adminstrs. L.A., Alumni Occidental Coll. in Edn. (a founder, past pres., bd. dirs.), Town Hall, Nat. PTA (hon. life), Calif. PTA (hon. life, bd. dirs. 1978-80), 31st Dist. PTA (hon. life, bd. dirs. 1965-78, auditorium named in his honor 1978), Phi Beta Kappa, Alpha Tau Omega. Republican. Avocations: gardening, reading, coin and stamp collecting, investments. Home: 4911 Vineta Ave Flintridge CA 91011 Office: Richard Keilholtz Realtors 727 Foothill Blvd La Canada Flintridge CA 91011-3405

LAMY, MARTINE, dancer; b. Trois-Riviàres, Que., Can.. Attended, Nat. Ballet Sch. Dancer Nat. Ballet Co., Can., 1983-90, prin. dancer, 1990—. Dance performances include Swan Lake, Giselle, The Sleeping Beauty, Don Quixote, La Fille Mal Gardée, The Taming of the Shrew, Coppelia, others. Recipient medals Jr. Women's Divsn. Moscow Internat. Ballet Competition, 1981. Office: Nat Ballet Co Can, 157 King St East, Toronto, ON Canada M5C 1G9

LAN, DONALD PAUL, JR., lawyer; b. Orange, N.J., July 19, 1952; s. Donald Paul and Hannah Paula (Resnik) L.; m. Deborah Sue Rothenberg, Aug. 20, 1978; children: Jennifer Robyn, Adam Christopher, Eric Jacob. BS in Acctg., U. R.I., 1974; JD, Rutger U., 1977; LLM in Taxation, Georgetown U., 1982. Bar: N.J. 1977, D.C. 1978, Tex. 1983, U.S. Dist. Ct. N.J. 1977, U.S. Dist. Ct. (no. dist.) Tex. 1983, U.S. Ct. Claims 1978, U.S. Tax Ct. 1977, U.S. Ct. Appeals (fed. cir.) 1978, U.S. Ct. Appeals (5th cir.) 1984. Clk. to spl. trial judge U.S. Tax Ct., Washington, 1977-78; trial atty. tax div. U.S. Dept. Justice, Washington, 1978-82; assoc., ptnr. Shank, Irwin & Conant, Dallas, 1982-87; ptnr. Finley, Kumble Wagner et al, Dallas, 1987, Strasburger & Price, Dallas, 1988-96; shareholder Kroney Silverman, Mincey, Inc., Dallas, 1996—; adj. prof. law So. Meth. U., 1990—; lectr. on tax controversy and litigation, 1983—. Named Outstanding Atty. tax div. U.S. Dept. Justice, 1980. Mem. ABA (ct. procedures com. tax sect. 1987, stds. in tax practice com. tax sect. 1992), State Bar Tex. (chmn. ct. procedures com. tax sect.), Dallas Bar Assn., D.C. Bar Assn., Phi Kappa Phi, Beta Alpha Psi, Beta Gamma Sigma. Jewish. Avocation: all sports. Office: Strasburger & Price 901 Main St Ste 4300 Dallas TX 75202-3714

LANAHAN, JOHN STEVENSON, management consultant; b. Pitts., June 13, 1922; s. James S. and Katharine L. (Lauck) L.; m. Rosemary Lourdes Ford, Feb. 20, 1954; children—Margaret Kayne, Brian James, Ellen Ford. BA, Duke U., 1945; MBA, Harvard U., 1949. Sales mgr. Mid-Atlantic region Allen B. Dumont Labs., E. Paterson, N.J., 1950-53; sr. asso. Booz, Allen & Hamilton, Inc., N.Y.C., 1954-59; pres. Richmond Hotels, Inc., Va., 1959-69, Flagler System, Inc., Palm Beach, Fla., 1969-71, Carlton House Resort Inns, Inc., Richmond, 1971-73; exec. v.p. Braniff Internat. Hotels, Dallas, 1973-74; pres., chief exec. officer The Greenbrier, White Sulphur Springs, W.Va., 1975-80; sr. v.p.-comml. Chessie System, Inc., 1980-85; pres., mng. dir. Strategic Enterprises, Inc., 1986-89; dir. Figgie Internat. Inc., 1985—. Mem. adv. bd. W.Va. Found. for Ind. Colls.; chmn. bd. Richmond Forward, 1968; mem. bd. visitors Trinity Coll. Duke U., 1988-94. Served to lt. (j.g.) USNR, World War II. Named to Hotel Industry Hall of Fame, 1971; Hotel Mgr. of Yr. Am. Hotel and Motel Assn., 1979. Mem. Commonwealth Club of Richmond (bd. govs.), Rotary, Beta Theta Pi, Omicron Delta Kappa. Republican. Roman Catholic. Home: 36 E Lower Tuckahoe Rd Richmond VA 23233-6140

LANAM, LINDA LEE, lawyer; b. Ft. Lauderdale, Fla., Nov. 21, 1948; d. Carl Edward and Evelyn (Bolton) L. BS, Ind. U., 1970, JD, 1975. Bar: Ind. 1975, Pa. 1979, U.S. Dist. Ct. (no. and so. dists.) Ind. 1975, U.S. Supreme Ct. 1982, Va. 1990. Atty., asst. counsel Lincoln Nat. Life Ins. Co., Ft. Wayne, Ind., 1975-76, 76-78; atty., mng. atty. Ins. Co. of N.Am., Phila., 1978-79, 80-81; legis. liaison Pa. Ins. Dept., Harrisburg, 1981-82, dep. ins. commr., 1982-84; exec. dir., Washington rep. Blue Cross and Blue Shield Assn., Washington, 1984-86; v.p. and sr. counsel Union Fidelity Life Ins. Co., Am. Patriot Health Ins. Co., etc., Trevose, Pa., 1986-89; v.p., gen. counsel, corp. sec. Life Ins. Co. Va., Richmond, 1989—, also bd. dirs.; chmn. adv. com. health care legis. Nat. Assn. Ins. Commrs., 1985-87, chmn. long term care, 1986-87, mem. tech. resource com. on cost disclosure and genetic testing, 1993-95; mem. tech. adv. com. Health Ins. Assn. Am., 1986-89; mem. legis. com. Am. Coun. Life Ins., 1994—. Contbr. articles to profl. jours. Pres. Phila. Women's Network, 1980-81; chmn. city housing code bd. appeals Harrisburg, 1985-86. Mem. ABA, Richmond Bar Assn. Republican. Presbyterian. Office: Life Ins Co Va/GE Capital C 6610 W Broad St Richmond VA 23230-1702

LANCASTER, CAROLYN HOHN, secondary school educator; b. Harrison/Allegheny County, Pa., July 24, 1952; d. Carl Maurice Sr. and Doris Myrtle (Gilday) Hohn; m. Walter T. Johnson, Sept. 4, 1971 (dec. Oct. 1979); 1 child, David Alan Johnson; m. Ronald Lee Lancaster, Mar. 31, 1988. AAS, Cape Fear Tech. Inst., Wilmington, N.C., 1986; BS, U. Ctrl. Fla., Orlando, 1981; MS, N.C. A&T State U., Greensboro, 1993. Cert. technology, electronics tchr., N.C. Computer technician Nat. Data Processing GE, Wilmington, 1986-88; electronics technician Applied Tech. Assn.,

New Bern, N.C., 1988-89; computer tchr. Onslow County Schs., Jacksonville, N.C., 1989-90; indsl. arts tchr. Person County Schs., Roxboro, N.C., 1982-83; technology tchr. Alamance County Schs., Graham, N.C., 1993—; technology advisor Technology Student Assn., Graham, N.C., 1993—; vice chair Raleigh region Program Area Leadership Coun. for Tech., 1995—. Mem. Jaycees, Orlando, 1980. With USCG Res., 1985-88. Recipient Profl. Devel. scholarship N.C. Technology Educators Assn., 1993. Mem. NEA, N.C. Edn. Assn., Am. Vocat. Assn., Internat. Tech. Educators Assn., N.C. Tech. Educators Assn., Nat. Assn. Underwater Instrs. Methodist. Avocations: swimming, computers. Home: 114 Florence St Graham NC 27253-4002 Office: Graham HS 903 Trollinger Rd Graham NC 27253-1945

LANCASTER, CARROLL TOWNES, JR., business executive; b. Waco, Tex., Mar. 14, 1929; s. Carroll T. and Beatrice (Hollaman) L.; student U. Tex., 1948-51, 52-53; m. Catherine Virginia Frommel, May 29, 1954; children—Loren Thomas, Barbara, Beverly, John Tracy. Sales coordinator Union Tank div. Butler Mfg. Co., Houston, 1954-56, sales rep., New Orleans, 1956-57, br. mgr., 1957-60; asst. to exec. v.p. Maloney-Crawford Mfg. Co., Tulsa, 1960-62; mktg. cons., sr. asso. Market/Product Facts, Tulsa, 1962-63; market devel. asst. Norriseal Controls div. Dover Corp., Houston, 1963-66; area dir. Arthritis Found., Houston, 1966-69, dir. S.W. div., 1969-70; exec. dir. United Cerebral Palsy Tex. Gulf Coast, 1971-74; exec. dir. Leukemia Soc. Am., Gulf Coast, 1974-76, Lancaster & Assos., 1976—. Christian edn. tchr., 1966-70, supr., 1971, asst. youth football coach, Bellaire, 1967-68, 70-71; mem. Houston-Galveston Area Health Commn. Study Group, 1972-76, co-chmn., 1976; dir., essayist Tex. Low Vision Council, 1976-79, sec.-treas., 1978-81, pres., 1981-85; pres. Bellaire Civic Action Club, 1987-88; del. Houston Interfaith Sponsoring Com., 1979-81; bd. dirs. Council Chs. Greater Houston, 1966-68, v.p., 1968. Served with USNR, 1946-48, 51-52. Recipient award for securing free blood for indigent Harris County Hosp. Dist., 1968. Mem. Am. Mktg. Assn., Huguenot Soc., Military Order of Stars and Bars, San Marcos Acad. Ex-students Assn. (pres. 1982-84), SAR, Delta Sigma Phi. Episcopalian (vestryman 1975-78). Home: 4901 Holly St Bellaire TX 77401-5714 Office: PO Box 745 Bellaire TX 77402-0745

LANCASTER, CLAY, architecture/design educator, writer; b. Lexington, Ky., Mar. 30, 1917. Attended, Art Students League, N.Y., 1936; AB, U. Ky., 1938, MA, 1939; attended, Columbia U., 1944-50. Instr. in drawing Art Dept. U. Ky., 1938-39; staff theatre set design and constrn. Guignol Theatre, Lexington, Ky., 1939-43; asst. Avery Architecture Library Columbia U., 1944-45, ware librarian, 1946-49, lectr. dept. fine arts and archaeology, 1948-53; lectr. art dept. Vassar Coll., 1950-51; lectr. Cooper Union, 1951-53, Metropolitan Mus. Art/Columbia U., 1953; curator Prospect Park, Bklyn., 1966-67; lectr. Sch. Continuing Edn. NYU, 1968, 69; instr., lectr. Traphagen Sch., N.Y., 1956-58; adv. U.S. State Dept., 1951-53; vis. prof. Transylvania U., Lexington, 1979-81, U. Ky., 1979; Frederick Lindley Morgan prof. U. Louisville, Ky., 1983—; cons. Woodstock, Fayette COunty, Ky., Henry Clay Law Office, Sugar Hill, Woodford County, Big Spring Meeting House, Warwick, Mercer County, Liberty Hall, Franklin County, Ridgeway, Jefferson County, Peter Paul House, Fayette County, Mt. Hope, Robert Swain House, Nantucket, Mass., Eugene R. Black House, COlumbia Heights, N.Y., James W. Kennedy Residence, Mt. Eden, Cin., Ohio, Malverne, Va., Locust Grove, Stanardsville, Va. Author: (books) Back Streets and Pine Trees: The Work of John McMurtry, Nineteenth Century Architect-Builder of Kentucky, 1956, Architectural Follies in America, or Hammer Sawtooth and Nail, 1960, The Periwinkle Steamboat, 1961, Old Brooklyn Heights: New York's First Suburb, 1961, Ante Bellum Houses of the Bluegrass, 1961, The Japanese Influence in America, 1963, Nantucket in the Nineteenth Century, 1979, The American Bungalow, 1985, Antebellum Architecture of Kentucky, 1991, Holiday Island: Nantucket Hostelries and Summer Life, 1992; The Breadth and Depth of East and West: A Survey and an Assessment of Civilization Based on Universal Considerations, 1995; contbr. articles to numerous jours. Guggenheim fellow, 1953, 64; recipient Cert. of Merit Mcpl. Art Soc. N.Y., 1962, Spl. citation Pres. Borough of Bklyn. Heights, Hall of Disting Alumni award U. Ky., 1975, Merit award Ala. Hist. Commn., 1975, Preservation award Lexington-Fayette County Historic Commn., 1979, Profl. award Ky. Heritage Coun. Preservation, 1979, John Wesley Hunt award for Historic Preservation Blue Grass Trust, 1986. Home: Oregon Rd Salvisa KY 40372

LANCASTER, EDWIN BEATTIE, insurance company executive; b. LeMars, Iowa, Aug. 1, 1916; s. Middleton John and Rosabelle (Beattie) L.; m. Marjorie Forshey, Sept. 1, 1951; children: Craig, Susan. B.A., U. Iowa, 1938, postgrad., 1938-39. With Met. Life Ins. Co., N.Y.C., 1939-81; actuary Met. Life Ins. Co., 1964-65, v.p., 1965-69, sr. v.p., 1969-71, sr. v.p., chief actuary, 1971-73, exec. v.p., 1973-81; pres., chief exec. officer Life Investors, Inc., Cedar Rapids, Iowa, 1982-83, vice chmn., 1983; v.p. Tillinghast, Nelson & Warren, N.Y.C., 1983-85; chief exec. officer Accident Fund of Mich., 1985-88; bd. dirs. Cedar Income Fund, Ltd. Mem. Mount Kisco Village Bd., N.Y. 1959-61; mem. Mount Kisco Planning Bd., 1957-59, 61-69, chmn., 1962-69; bd. dirs. U. Iowa Found., 1971—; trustee No. Westchester Hosp., 1976—. Served with AUS, 1941-46; to lt. col. USAAF. Fellow Soc. Actuaries (pres. 1970-71, bd. govs. 1963-73), Phi Beta Kappa. Methodist (trustee).

LANCASTER, H(AROLD) MARTIN, former congressman, advisor to the President; b. Patetown Community, N.C., Mar. 24, 1943; s. Harold Wright and Eva (Pate) L.; m. Alice Matheny; children: Ashley Elizabeth, Mary Martin. AB, U. N.C., 1965, JD, 1967. Asst. staff judge adv. 12th Naval Dist., San Francisco, 1968; staff judge adv. USN, USS Hancock, 1968-70; ptnr. Baddour, Lancaster, Parker, Hine & Keller P.A., Goldsboro, N.C., 1970-86; rep. N.C. Gen. Assembly, Raleigh, 1978-86; mem. 100th-103rd Congresses from 3d N.C. dist., Washington, D.C., 1987-94; mem. armed svcs. com., readiness subcom., mil. pers. subcom.; chmn. morale, welfare and recreation panel; small bus. com. Mcht. Marine and Fisheries com.; chmn. judiciary com. N.C. Ho. of Reps., 1983-86; chmn. hwy. safety com., 1981-83; chmn. congrl. study group on German, 1994, North Atlantic Assembly, 1989-94; former mem. numerous other coms. Chmn. N.C. Arts Coun., 1977-81, Goldsboro Wayne Bicentennial Commn., 1975-76; pres. Community Arts Coun., 1973-74, Wayne Community Concert Assn., 1972-73; chmn. bd. trustees Wayne County Pub. Libr., 1979-80; chmn. Wayne chpt. ARC, 1978-79; mem. adv. bd. Z. Smith Reynolds Found.; deacon First Presbyn. Ch., 1972-75, elder, 1980-86. Recipient Disting. Svc. award Goldsboro Jaycees, 1977, N.C. Crime and Justice award Gov.'s Crime Commn., 1984, Spl. award Gov.'s Adv. Coun. for Persons with Disabilities, 1985, Valand award Mental Health Assn. N.C., 1985, Outstanding Legislators awards Neuse River Coun. Govts., N.C. Assn. Sch. Counselors, Nat. Security Leadership award, 1987, 89, 90, 91, 92, Sound Dollar award, 1988, 89, 90, Spirit of Enterprise award U.S. C. of C., 1989, 92, 93, Doer of Deeds award House Leadership, 1989, Pub. Health Svc. award N.C. Primary Care Assn., 1991, Charles Dick Medal of Merit, U.S. Nat. Guard Assn., 1992, Tad Davis Meml. award, U.S. Mil. Sports Assn., 1992; named N.C. and U.S. Alumnus of Yr., 4-H, 1987. Mem. ABA, Assn. Trial Lawyers Am., N.C. Bar Assn. (bd. govs.), Eighth Jud. Dist. Bar Assn., N.C. Acad. Trial Lawyers (Outstanding Legislator award), Wayne County Hist. Soc. Lodges: Masons, Shriners, Elks. Office: 4638 Main State Washington DC 20451

LANCASTER, JOHN HOWARD, civil engineer; b. Bklyn., July 3, 1917; s. George York and Alice Eliot (Littlejohn) L.; m. Phyllis Elaine Metcalf, June 1, 1938; children: Judith Ann, Barbara Jean, Marylin Sharon, Kathryn Joy, Debra Elizabeth. BS, Worcester (Mass.) Poly. Inst., 1939. Registered profl. engr., N.Y., N.Mex.; lic. master mariner USCG. Engr. Austin Co., N.Y.C., 1939-40; engr. C.E., N.Y.C., 1940-42, asst. to divsn. engr., 1942-43; chief engr. and constrn. AEC, Upton, N.Y., 1946-54; chief project engr. Brookhaven Nat. Lab., Upton, 1954-72; asst. dir. Nat. Radio Astronomy Obs. and program mgr. very large array radiotelescope program, Socorro, N.Mex., 1972-81; propr. John H. Lancaster & Assos. (cons. engrs.), 1950-72; cons. NRAO/Associated Univs. Inc., 1981—; cons. in field, 1970—; bd. dirs., sec. corp. Seven Seas Cruising Assn., 1970—; cons. NSF, 1970, Cornell U., 1971, Fermi Nat. Accelerator Lab., 1980. Bd. dirs. Good Samaritan Nursing Home; treas. Socorro Pub. Libr. With USNR, 1942-46. Recipient Meritorious Service award NSF, 1976. Mem. NSPE, N.Y. Soc. Profl. Engrs., N.Mex. Soc. Profl. Engrs., N.Mex. Tech. Club, Rotary, Masons, Ea. Star, Sigma Xi, Alpha Tau Omega.

LANCASTER, JOHN LYNCH, III, lawyer; b. Dallas, Nov. 10, 1936; s. John Lynch Jr. and Loretta Charlotte (Delaney) L.; m. Jane Frances Riddle, Sept. 5, 1959; children: Delaney, John, Jim. Student, Washington and Lee U., 1954-56; BA, U. Tex., 1958, LLB, 1960. Bar: Tex. 1960; diplomate Am. Bd. Trial Advs. Ptnr. Jackson & Walker, L.L.P., Dallas, 1962—. Mayor Town of Highland Park, Tex., 1984-86. Fellow Am. Coll. Trial Lawyers; mem. Inn of Ct. (master). Office: Jackson & Walker LLP 901 Main St Ste 6000 Dallas TX 75202-3748

LANCASTER, KELVIN JOHN, economics educator; b. Sydney, Australia, Dec. 10, 1924; s. John Kelvin and Margaret Louise (Gray) L.; m. Deborah Grunfeld, June 10, 1963; children—Clifton John, Gilead. BSc, Sydney U., 1948, BA, 1949, MA, 1953; BSc in Econs., London U., 1953, PhD, 1958. Asst. lectr., lectr. London Sch. Economics, 1954-59; reader economics U. London, 1959-62; prof. polit. economy Johns Hopkins U., 1962-66; prof. econs., 1966-78, John Bates Clark prof. econs., 1978—; John Bates Clark prof. econs. Columbia U., N.Y.C.; Ford faculty fellow, 1968-69, chmn. dept. econs., 1970-73, 89-90, Wesley Clair Mitchell research prof., 1973-74; vis. prof. U. Birmingham, Brown U., 1961-62, CUNY, 1965-66, NYU, Australian Nat. U., 1969-77, Ottawa U., 1972; fellow Inst. Advanced Studies Hebrew U., Jerusalem, 1976-77; dir. Nat. Bur. Econ. Rsch., 1971-73; trustee BT Investment Funds, 1986—. Author: Mathematical Economics, 1968, Introduction to Modern Microeconomics, 1969, Consumer Demand: A New Approach, 1971, Modern Economics: Principles and Policy, 1973, Variety, Equity and Efficiency, 1979, Modern Consumer Theory, 1991, Trade, Markets and Welfare, 1996; contbr. articles in econs. to profl. jours. Served with Royal Australian Air Force, 1943-45. Fellow Econometric Soc., Am. Acad. Arts and Scis., Am. Econ. Assn. (disting.); mem. N.Y. State Econ. Assn. (pres. 1974-75). Home: 35 Claremont Ave New York NY 10027-6823 also: 8 Island View Dr Sherman CT 06784-2035 Office: Columbia U Dept Econs New York NY 10027

LANCASTER, MARK, artist, stage designer; b. Holmfirth, Yorkshire, U.K., May 14, 1938; came to U.S., 1972; s. Charles R. and Muriel Lancaster. BA in Fine Art, U. Newcastle, Eng., 1965. Artist in residence King's Coll., Cambridge, U.K., 1968-70; designer Merce Cunningham Dance Co., N.Y.C., 1974-95. Recipient N.Y. Dance and Performance award, 1989. Mem. Mus. Modern Art, N.Y.C., Met. Mus. Art, N.Y.C., Ctr. Fine Arts, Miami, Fairchild Bot. Garden, Miami. Office: Cunningham Dance Found 55 Bethune St New York NY 10014

LANCASTER, RALPH IVAN, JR., lawyer; b. Bangor, Maine, May 9, 1930; s. Ralph I. and Mary Brigid (Kelleher) L.; m. Mary Lou Pooler, Aug. 21, 1954; children: Mary Lancaster Miller, Anne, Elizabeth, Christopher, John, Martin. A.B., Coll. Holy Cross, 1952; LL.B., Harvard U., 1955; LLD (hon.), St. Joseph's Coll., 1991. Bar: Maine 1955, Mass. 1955. Law clk. U.S. Dist. Ct. Dist. Maine, 1957-59; ptnr. firm Pierce, Atwood, Scribner, Allen, Smith & Lancaster, Portland, Maine, 1961—; mng. ptnr. Pierce, ATwood, Scribner, Allen, Smith & Lancaster, 1993—; condr. trial advocacy seminar Harvard U.; lectr. U. Maine; chmn. merit selection panel U.S. Magistrate for Dist. of Maine, 1982, '88; bd. visitors U. Maine Sch. Law, 1991—, chair 1991-93; spl. master by appointment U.S. Supreme Ct. in State of N.J. vs. State of Nev. et al, 1987-88; mem. 1st Ctr. Adv. Com. on Rules, 1991—, legal adv. bd. Martindale Hubbell, 1990—. Mem. Diocese of Portland Bur. Edn. With U.S. Army, 1955-57. Mem. Maine Jud. Coun., Am Coll. Trial Lawyers (chmn. Maine 1974-79, bd. regents 1982-87, treas. 1985-87, pres. 1989-90), Maine Bar Assn. (pres. 1982), Cumberland County Bar Assn., Canadian Bar Assn. (hon.). Republican. Roman Catholic. Home: 162 Woodville Rd Falmouth ME 04105-1120 Office: 1 Monument Sq Portland ME 04101-4033

LANCASTER, ROBERT SAMUEL, lawyer, educator; b. Floyd, Va., July 9, 1909; s. Robert Tazwell and Rachel Elma (Barnard) L.; m. Ernestine Martha DeSporte, June 21, 1931; children: Ulysse (Mrs. Wallace Matthews), Evelyn Rachel (Mrs. David Tyrrell); m. Elizabeth Craig, Jan. 4, 1980 (dec.). B.A., Hampden-Sydney Coll., 1929, D.Litt. (hon.), 1980; M.A., U. South, 1934, D.C.L., 1979; student, Andrew Jackson Law U., Nashville, 1937; Ph.D., U. Mich., 1952. Bar: Va. 1937. Instr. Gulf Coast Mil. Acad., Gulfport, Miss., 1929-31; instr. Sewanee (Tenn.) Mil. Acad., 1931-38, 46-49, comdt. cadets, 1941-43; pvt. practice Pulaski, Va., 1938-41; mem. faculty U. of South, 1949—, acting dir. devel., 1965-66, prof. polit. sci., 1953—, dean men, 1951-56; dean U. of South (Coll. Arts and Scis.), 1957-69; Fulbright lectr. Coll. Arts and Scis., Baghdad, Iraq, 1955-56, Coll. Arts and Scis. and Coll. of Law, Seoul (Korea) Nat. U., 1964-65. Author: The Better Parts of a Life: An Authobiography, 1990; co-author: An Introduction to American Government, 1954; contbr. articles to legal jours. Trustee Duck River Electric Membership Corp.; mem. acad. adv. bd. U.S. Naval Acad., 1970-75. Served to lt. (s.g.) USNR, 1943-46. Fellow Internat. Inst. Arts and Letters; mem. Va. Bar Assn., Tenn. Bar Assn., So. Polit. Sci. Assn., Phi Beta Kappa, Chi Phi, Phi Kappa Phi, Sigma Upsilon, Tau Kappa Alpha, Pi Gamma Mu, Pi Sigma Alpha, Blue Key. Republican. Episcopalian.

LANCASTER, SALLY RHODUS, philanthropy consultant; b. Gladewater, Tex., June 28, 1938; d. George Lee and Milly Maria (Meadows) Rhodus; m. Olin C. Lancaster Jr., Dec. 23, 1960; children: Olin C. III, George Charles, Julie Meadows. BA magna cum laude, So. Meth. U., 1960, MA, 1979; PhD, East Tex. State U., 1983. Tchr. English, Tex. pub. schs., 1960-61, 78-79; sr. advisor Meadows Found., Inc., Dallas, 1979-96, also trustee and dir.; cons. to philanthropy sector, 1996—. Trustee So. Meth. U., 1980-88, East Tex. State U., regent 1987-93; Tex. del. White House Conf. on Tourism, 1995; adv. dir. Los Caminos del Rio Inc.; dir. Inst. Nautical Archaeology; mem. adv. bd. Communities Found. Tex. Recipient Disting. Alumni award So. Meth. U., 1986, East Tex. State U., 1994, Citizenship Excellence award in philanthropy Dallas Hist. Soc., 1984. Mem. Am. Evaluation Assn., Conf. S.W. Founds., Council on Founds., Philos. Soc. of Tex., Phi Beta Kappa (assoc. pres. 1980-82, nat com. on assns. 1983-85), Am. Assn. Continuing Edn., World Future Soc. Presbyterian. Office: Meadows Foundation Inc Wilson Historic Block 3003 Swiss Ave Dallas TX 75204-6051

LANCE, ALAN GEORGE, lawyer, legislator, attorney general; b. McComb, Ohio, Apr. 27, 1949; s. Cloyce Lowell and Clara Rose (Wilhelm) L.; m. Sheryl C. Holden, May 31, 1969; children: Lisa, Alan Jr., Luke. BA, S.D. State U., 1971; JD, U. Toledo, 1973. Bar: Ohio 1974, U.S. Dist. Ct. (no. dist.) Ohio 1974, U.S. Ct. Mil. Appeals 1974, Idaho 1978. Asst. pros. atty. Fulton County, Wauseon, Ohio, 1973-74; ptnr. Foley and Lance, Chartered, Meridian, Idaho, 1978-90; prin. Alan G. Lance, Meridian, Idaho, 1990-94; rep. Idaho Ho. of Reps., Boise, 1990-94, majority caucus chmn., 1992-94; atty. gen. State of Idaho, 1995—. Capt. AUS, 1974-78. Mem. Ohio Bar Assn., Idaho Bar Assn., Idaho Trial Lawyers Assn., Meridian C. of C. (pres. 1983), Am. Legion (judge adv. 1981-90, state comdr. 1988-89, alt. nat. exec. com. 1992-94, nat. exec. com. 1994—), Elks. Republican. Avocations: hunting, fishing. Home: 1370 Eggers Pl Meridian ID 83642-6528 Office: PO Box 83720 Statehouse Rm 210 Boise ID 83720-0010

LANCE, GEORGE MILWARD, mechanical engineering educator; b. Youngstown, Ohio, Dec. 4, 1928; s. Ray Clifford and Louisa Brigetta (Emch) L.; m. Phyllis Joanne Sprague, Aug. 8, 1964; children: Kathryn, Deborah, John, Rebecca, George. B.S. in Mech. Engring, Case Inst. Tech., 1952, M.S. in Instrumentation Engring, 1954. Instr. Case Inst. Tech., Cleve., 1952-54; research engr. TRW Inc., Cleve., 1954-56; lectr. Washington U., St. Louis, 1956-60; sr. systems engr. Moog, Inc., 1960-61; asst. prof., then prof. mech. engring. U. Iowa, Iowa City, 1961-91; prof. emeritus U. Iowa, 1991—; acting chair mech. engring. U. Iowa, Iowa City, 1972-74; asso. dean engring. U. Iowa, 1974-79; cons. McDonnell Aircraft, Boeing Airplane Co., Collins Radio Co., U.S. Army Weapons Command, CADSI. Served with USN, 1946-48. Mem. ASME, Am. Soc. Engring. Edn., Sigma Xi, Tau Beta Pi, Pi Tau Sigma. Patentee in valves. Home: 609 S Summit St Iowa City IA 52240-5657 Office: Univ Iowa Coll Engring Iowa City IA 52242

LANCE, LEONARD, assemblyman; b. Easton, Pa., June 25, 1952; s. Wesley L. and Anne (Anderson) L. BA, Lehigh U., 1974; JD, Vanderbilt U., 1977; MPA, Princeton U., 1982. Law clk. to judges Warren County Ct., Belvidere, N.J., 1977-78; asst. counsel Office of N.J. Gov. Thomas H. Kean, Trenton, N.J., 1983-90; mem. N.J. Gen. Assembly, 1991—. Mem. Grandin Libr. Bd., Clinton, N.J., 1990—, N.J. Coun. for the Humanities, Trenton, 1994—; bd. trustees Newark Mus., 1995—. Mem. Princeton Club N.Y., Phi Beta Kappa. Republican. Home: PO Box 5240 Clinton NJ 08809-0240 Office: NJ Gen Assembly 119 Main St Flemington NJ 08822-1615

LANCHNER, BERTRAND MARTIN, lawyer, advertising executive; b. Boston, Oct. 3, 1929; s. Abraham Joseph and Mina (Grossman) L.; m. Nancy Nelson, Apr. 26, 1979; 1 son by previous marriage, David; 1 stepdau., Renate. B.A., Stanford U., 1951; postgrad., Columbia U. Grad. Sch. Bus., 1951-52, U. Vienna, Austria, summer 1955; J.D., Harvard U., 1955. Bar: N.Y. bar 1956. Asso. firm Sage, Gray, Todd & Sims, N.Y.C., 1955-57; atty. Warner Bros. Pictures, N.Y.C., 1957-59; asst. gen. counsel Dancer-Fitzgerald-Sample, N.Y.C., 1959-62; gen. counsel Lawrence C. Gumbinner Advt. Agy., N.Y.C., 1962-63; dir. bus. affairs and sports contract negotiations CBS-TV, N.Y.C., 1963-69; gen. counsel, exec. v.p. Videorecord Corp. Am., Westport, Conn., 1969-73; sr. v.p., sec., gen. counsel N.W. Ayer, Inc., N.Y.C., 1973—, also bd. dirs.; bd. dirs. 170 E. 79th St. Corp., Advt. Info. Services Inc., N.Y.C.; guest lectr. Yale U. Law Sch. Mem. adv. bd.: Communications and the Law. Mem. ABA, N.Y. State Bar Assn., Assn. of Bar of City of N.Y. (chmn. subcom. advt. agy. 1981-83), Copyright Soc. U.S., Am. Assn. Advt. Agys. (chmn. legal com. 1986-89, 95—), Am. Advt. Fedn. (mem. legal com.), Harvard Club N.Y.C., Bridgehampton Tennis and Surf Club, East Hampton Tennis Club, Tennisport Club. Office: N W Ayer Inc Worldwide Plz 825 8th Ave New York NY 10019-7416

LANCIONE, BERNARD GABE, lawyer; b. Bellaire, Ohio, Feb. 3, 1939; s. Americus Gabe and June (Morford) L.; m. Rosemary C., Nov. 27, 1976; children: Amy, Caitin, Gillian, Bernard Gabe II, Elizabetta Marie. BS, Ohio U., 1960; JD, Capitol U., 1965. Bar: Ohio 1965, U.S. Dist. Ct. (so. dist.) Ohio 1967, U.S. Supreme Ct., 1969, U.S. Ct. Appeals (4th cir.) 1982, U.S. Dist. Ct. (no. dist.) Ohio, 1989. Pres. Lancione Law Office, Co., L.P.A., Bellaire, Ohio, 1965-87, mng. atty. Cichon Lancione Co., L.P.A., St. Clairsville, Ohio, 1982-85, of counsel Ward, Kaps, Bainbridge, Maurer, Bloomfield and Melvin, Columbus, Ohio, 1987-88; Ohio Asst. Atty. Gen., Columbus, 1988-91; sole practice, 1991—; spl. counsel Ohio Atty. Gen's. Office, 1991-95; solicitor Bellaire City (Ohio), 1968-72; asst. prosecutor County of Belmont (Ohio), 1972-76; legal counsel Young Democrats Am., 1971-73; pack com. chmn. Pack 961, Westerville, Ohio Cub Scouts of Am., 1992-93. Mem. ABA, Ohio State Bar Assn., Assn. Trial Lawyers Am., Ohio Acad. Trial Lawyers (award of merit 1972). Democrat. Roman Catholic. Home: 1108 Acillom Dr Westerville OH 43081-1104 Office: 647 Park Meadow Rd # E Westerville OH 43081-2878

LANCLOS, RITCHIE PAUL, petroleum engineer; b. Opelousas, La., Sept. 20, 1964; s. Curley Joseph and Velma Marie (Folks) L.; m. Courtney Theresé Brennan, Mar. 26, 1994. BS in Petroleum Engring., U. Southwestern La., 1987; MS in Petroleum Engring. cum laude, Tex. A&M U., 1990. Registered profl. engr., La. Petroleum engr. exploration and prodn. Mobil Oil Corp., New Orleans, 1987-89, Conoco, Inc., New Orleans, 1990-93; petroleum engr. property acquisitions WRT Energy Corp., The Woodlands, Tex., 1994; petroleum engr. reservoir engring. Petrobras Am., Inc., Houston, 1995—; petroleum cons. The Scotia Group, Inc., Houston, 1994—. Bd. dirs. Big Bros./Big Sisters, New Orleans, 1991-94, Boys/Girls Club, Lafayette, La., 1992-94, Vol. Instrs. Teaching Adults (VITA), Lafayette, 1991-94; loaned exec. United Way, New Orleans, 1993-94. Scholar Am. Petroleum Inst., Lafayette, 1985-86, scholar Texaco Rsch. Ctr., Texaco Inc., College Station, Tex., 1989-90; fellow Petroleum Engring., 1989-90. Mem. Soc. Petroleum Engrs., Tex. A&M U. Petroleum Engring. Alumni (v.p. 1994-95, thesis adv. com.). Republican. Roman Catholic. Achievements include developments in the field of reservoir fluid characterization. Avocations: traveling, golfing, reading. Home: 37 Fallshire Dr The Woodlands TX 77381

LAND, CECIL E., electrical engineer; b. Lebanon, Mo., Jan. 8, 1926; married; 2 chilren. BS, Okla. State U., 1949; DSc (hon.), Okla. Christian Coll., 1978. Profl. engr., electronics divsn. Westinghouse Elec. Corp., Md., 1949-56; staff mem. Sandia Nat. Labs., Albuquerque, 1956-83, disting. mem. tech. staff, 1983—. Recipient award NSPE, 1973, Frances Rice Darne Meml. award Soc. Info. Display, 1976. Fellow IEEE (chmn. ferroelectrics com. 1978—), Am. Ceratmics Soc.; mem. Optical Soc. Am. Office: 2118 Gretta St NE Albuquerque NM 87112*

LAND, DAVID POTTS, lawyer; b. Lancaster, Pa., Mar. 29, 1944; s. William Ortlip and Jean (Potts) L.; m. Susan Delano, Aug. 20, 1966; children: Katherine, Stephen, Elizabeth. BA in Religion, Kenyon Coll., 1966; JD, Vanderbilt U., 1969. Bar: N.Y. 1970, U.S. Dist. Ct. (so. dist.) N.Y. 1972, U.S. Ct. Appeals (2d cir.) 1972. Assoc. Seward & Kissel, N.Y.C., 1969-71; asst. U.S. atty. State of N.Y., N.Y.C., 1971-75; assoc. Rosenman and Colin, N.Y.C., 1975-77; v.p., asst. gen. counsel Combustion Engring. Inc., Stamford, Conn., 1977-86; v.p., gen. counsel Brown Boveri Inc., White Plains, N.Y., 1986-87; v.p., sec., gen. counsel Asea Brown Boveri Inc., Purchase, N.Y., 1987-90; chief tax unit U.S. Attys. Office, N.Y.C., 1973-75. Pres. Saugatuck Shores Assn., Westport, Conn., 1982-85; mem. bd. deacons Saugatuck Congl. Ch., 1986—. Mem. ABA, N.Y. State Bar Assn., Bklyn. Bar Assn. Home: 21 Marine Ave Westport CT 06880-6922 Office: Nixon Hargrave et al 437 Madison Ave New York NY 10022-7001

LAND, GEOFFREY ALLISON, science administrator; b. Jeannette, Pa., July 9, 1942; s. Albert E. Jr. and Helene (Matthews) L.; m. Maxine McCluskey, Jan. 22, 1966; children: Kevin Jeffrey, Melissa Allison, Kyle Robert. MS in Biology (Biochemistry), Tex. Christian U., 1970; PhD in Microbiology/Immunology, Tulane U., 1973. Cert. clin. lab. dir. Am. Bd. Bioanalysis. Dir. mycology Wadley Institutes Molecular Medicine, Dallas, 1974-78; dir. mycology, assc. dir. microbiology U. Cin. Med. Ctr., 1978-81; dir. microbiology/immunology Meth. Med. Ctr., Dallas, 1981—, assoc. administrv. dir. pathology, 1990—; dir. histocompatibility Stewart Blood Ctr., Tyler, Tex., 1987—; sci. dir. pathology and labs. Meth. Med. Ctr., Dallas, 1993—; adj. full prof. biology Tex. Christian U., Ft. Worth, 1982—. Mem. rev. bd. Jour. Clin. Microbiology, 1980—, Am. Jour. Tropical Medicne and Hygiene, 1989—; author: Pictorial Handbook of Medically Important Fungi, 1982, (with others) The Dermatophytes, 1996, Handbook of Applied Mycoses, 1991, Manual of Clinical Microbiology, 1992, Clinical Microbiology Procedures Manual, 1994. Coach Denton (Tex.) Soccer Assn., 1981—; min. Tioga (Tex.) Ch. of Christ, 1985—; chmn.-elect Region 5 histocompatibility com. United Network for Organ Sharing, 1993. Recipient Svc. Above Self award Rotary Club. Mem. Mycol. Soc. Am. (pres. 1990-93, Billy H. Cooper-Meridian award 1992), Tex. Soc. Clin. Microbiology (pres. 1977-79, 81-83), N.Y. Acad. Sci., Am. Soc. Histocompatibility and Immunogenetics (commr. 1995, author procedure manual 1996), Am. Soc. Microbiology. Mem. Ch. of Christ. Office: Meth Med Ctr 1441 N Beckley Ave Dallas TX 75208-2308

LAND, GEORGE A., philosopher, writer, educator, consultant; b. Hot Springs, Ark., Feb. 27, 1933; s. George Thomas Lock and Mary Elizabeth Land; m. Jo A. Gunn, 1957 (dec. 1969); children—Robert E., Thomas G., Patrick A.; m. Beth Smith Jarman, 1987. Student, Millsaps Coll., 1952-54, U. Veracruz, Mexico, 1957-59; numerous hon. degrees U.S. and abroad. Program dir. Woodall TV Stas. of Ga., Columbus, 1951-52; ops. mgr. Lamar Broadcasting, Jackson, Miss., 1952-54; anthrop. research Cora, Huichole and Yaqui tribes, Latin Am. Mexico, 1955-60; dir. gen. Television del Norte (NBC), Mexico, 1960-62; v.p. Roman Corp., St. Louis, 1962-64; chmn. Transolve Inc., Cambridge, Mass., and St. Petersburg, Fla., 1964-68; chief exec., chmn. Innotek Corp., N.Y.C.; also pres. Hal Roach Studios, Los Angeles and N.Y.C., 1969-71; chmn. emeritus Turtle Bay Inst., N.Y.C., 1971-80; vice chmn. Wilson Learning Corp., Mpls., 1980-86; pres. Leadership 2000, Phoenix, 1986—, Inst. Transformational Research, Honolulu and Buffalo, 1980—; prof. Mankato State U., 1973-74; sr. fellow U. Minn., 1982—; cons.-in-residence Synplex Inc., N.Y.C., AT&T, Forest Hosp., Des Plaines, Social Systems Inc., Chapel Hill, N.C., Children's Hosp., Nat. Med. Ctr., Washington, Herman Miller, Inc., Arthur Anderson & Co., Intermedics Orthopedics; Mem. Nat. Action Com. on Drug Edn., 1974-75; co-chmn. Syncon Conf., So. Ill. U., 1972-74; keynoter Emerging Trends in Edn. Conf., Minn., 1974, 75, Bicentennial Conf. on Limits to Growth, So. Ill. U., 1976, No. States Power Conf., 1975, U.S. Office of Edn., Nat. Conf. Improvements in Edn., 1979, World Conf. on Gifted, 1977, S.W. Conf. on Arts, 1977, World Symposium on Humanity, 1979, Internat. Conf. Internal Auditors, 1977, Four Corners Conf. on Arts, 1977, Chautauqua Inst., 1977, 78, Conf. Am. Art Tchrs. Assn., 1979, Internat. Conf. on Gifted, 1982, Japan Mgmt. Assn., Nat. Conf. of Art Curators, Chgo, 1985, others; keynoter, Nat. Conf.

on Econ. Devel., Mex., 1988, Credit Union Roundtable, Tampa, Fla., 1988, Internat. Bihai Conf., Princeton, N.J., 1982, co-chmn. com. on society World Conf. Peace and Poverty, St. Joseph's U., Phila., 1968, Internat. Bahai Conf. Princeton U., 1987, Gov.'s Trade Corridor Conf., Phoenix, 1994, Cath. Hosp. Assn., Phila., 1994, Am. Assn. Adminstrs., 1994, Inst. Pub. Execs., 1994, Fed. Conf. Quality, Washington, 1994, MAC IS Nat. Conf., Ont., 1994, Innovative Thinking Conf., 1994, Ventaua Groupware Conf., 1994, Young Pres.' Orgn., Cannes, 1993, Assn. Convn. and Visitors Bureau, Phenoix, 1993, Profession Conv. Mgmt. Assn., Atlanta, Internat. Assn. Law Enforcement, 1995, Cath. Health Assn., 1995, Excellence in Govt. Fellows, 1996, and many others; mem. Nat. Security Seminar, U.S. Dept. Def., 1975; cons., keynoter corp. policy strategic seminars The Bell System, AT&T, 1978—; mem. faculty Edison Electric Grad. Mgmt. Inst., 1972-78; lectr., seminarian in transformation theory, strategic planning and interdisciplinary research Menninger Found., U. Ga., Emory U., Waterloo (Can.) U., Office of Sec. HEW, Jamestown (N.Y.) Coll., Hofstra U., U.S. Office Edn., Calif. Dept. Edn., St. Louis U., Coll. William and Mary, Webster Coll., St. Louis, Wash. State Dept. Edn., U. Ky., So. Ill. U., St. John's U., Harvard U., U. South Fla., MIT, U. Veracruz, Children's Hosp. D.C., Gov.'s Sch. N.C., Scottsdale (Ariz.) Ctr. Arts, Humbolt U., East Berlin, AAAS, others; advanced faculty Creative Problem Solving Inst., SUNY, 1965—, S. Conn. Coll.; disting. lectr. Northwestern State U., La., State U. Coll. N.Y., Coll. of the Lakes, Ill.; cons. govt., industry and instns. in U.S. and abroad, including AT&T, IBM, Dow Chem., Dow Corning, DuPont, Hughes, TRW, 3M, OAS, Fed. Quality Inst., U.S. Dept. Commerce, Office Patent & Trademarks, U.S. Gen. Svc. Adminstrn., Gen. Mills, Gen. Motors, Moore Corp., Branch Corp., Credit Union Nat. Assn., others. Author: Innovation Systems, 1967, Innovation Technology, 1968, Four Faces of Poverty, 1968, (as George T.L. Land) Grow orDie: The Unifying Principle of Transformation, 1973, Creative Alternatives and Decision Making, 1974, The Opportunity Book, 1980, (with Vaune E. Ainsworth), Breakpoint and Beyond, 1994, New Paradigm in Business, 1994, Community Building in Business, 1995, Forward to Basics; contbr. to profl. jours. and gen. mags. Fellow N.Y. Acad. Scis., World Bus. Acad.; mem. AAAS, Soc. Gen. Systems Rsch., Soc. Study Gen. Process (founding dir.), Am. Soc. Cybernetics (past v.p.), Creative Edn. Found. (trustee, Lifetime Achievement award 1993, New Paradigm in Bus. award 1994, colleague), Soc. Am. Value Engrs. (past dir.), World Future Soc., Com. for Future (colleague), Authors Guild, Authors League Am. Achievements include research on interdisciplinary unification, orginated transformation theory. Inventor computer-assisted group creative thinking processes, "The Innovator," "CoNexus," "TeamWare" and others. Home: 7119 N Red Ledge Dr Paradise Vly AZ 85253-2847 Office: Leadership 2000 3333 N 44th St Phoenix AZ 85018-6461 *I was fortunate enough in my youth to experience and learn what has been the most important idea and principle in my life, the natural law of enrichment through diversity. This concept means that change and growth come about more by combining differentnesses than by adding likenesses. As in the biological world, where such behavior produces the vitality of hybrids, and as in chemistry, where the co-valent bonds of carbon make life possible, in human life we can also benefit immeasurably from using our differences as a creative way to grow anew. Thus, we can evolve beyond polarizations such as nationalism, racism, sexism, institutionalism and other obstacles that separate us and stunt our ability to realize the full community of Man.*

LAND, KENNETH CARL, sociology educator, demographer, statistician, consultant; b. Llano, Tex., Aug. 19, 1942; s. Otto Carl and Tillie (Lindemann) L.; m. Jacqueline Yvette Apere, Mar. 22, 1969; 1 child, Kristoffer Carl. B.A., Tex. Luth. Coll., 1964; M.A., U. Tex., 1966, Ph.D., 1969. Staff assoc. Russell Sage Found., N.Y.C, 1969-73; lectr. Columbia U., N.Y.C., 1970-73; assoc. prof. U. Ill.-Urbana, 1973-76, prof., 1976-81; prof. sociology U. Tex.-Austin, 1981-86; prof., chmn. dept. sociology Duke U., Durham, N.C., 1986—, John Franklin Crowell prof. sociology, 1990—. Editor: Social Indicator Models, 1975; Social Accounting Systems, 1981; Multidimensional Mathematical Demography, 1982; Forecasting in the Social and Natural Sciences, 1987; contbr. articles to profl. jours. Fellow Am. Statis. Assn., Am. Assn. for the Advancement of Sci.; mem. Sociol. Research Assn., Am. Sociol. Assn., Population Assn. Am., Am. Soc. Criminology. Lutheran. Office: Duke U Dept Sociology Durham NC 27708-0088

LAND, REGINALD BRIAN, library administrator; b. Niagara Falls, Ont., Can., July 29, 1927; s. Allan Reginald and Beatrice Beryl (Boyle) L.; m. Edith Wyndham Eddis, Aug. 29, 1953; children—Mary Beatrice, John Robert Eddis. BA, U. Toronto, Ont., Can., 1949, BLS, 1953, MLS, 1956, MA, 1963. Catalogue copy editor T. Eaton Co. Ltd., Toronto, 1950-51; reference librarian Toronto Pub. Library, 1953-55; cataloguer U. Toronto Library, 1955-56, asst. librarian, 1959-63, assoc. librarian, 1963; head div. bus. and industry Windsor Pub. Library, Ont., Can., 1956-57; asst. editor Canadian Bus. Mag., Montreal, Que., Can., 1957-58, assoc. editor, 1958-59; exec. asst. to Minister Fin. of Can., Ottawa, Ont., 1963-64; prof. library sci. U. Toronto, 1964-78, part-time prof., 1978-93, prof. emeritus, 1993—, dean Faculty Library Sci., 1964-72; exec. dir. Ont. Legis. Library,, Toronto, 1978-93. Author: Sources of Information for Canadian Business, 1962, 4th rev. edit., 1985, Eglinton: The Election Study of a Federal Constituency, 1965; founder, gen. editor: Directory of Associations in Canada, 1974, 16th rev. edit., 1995. Mem., Canadian Radio-TV and Telecommunications Commn., 1973-78. Decorated Knight Hospitaller Order of St. John of Jerusalem; recipient Kenneth R. Wilson Meml. award Bus. Newspapers Assn. Can., 1959, Disting. Achievement award Ont. Library Trustees Assn., 1968, Queen Elizabeth IIs Silver Jubilee medal, 1977, Spl. Librarianship award Can. Assn. for Spl. Librs. and Info. Svcs., 1991, 125th Anniversary Confederation Can. medal, 1992, Alumni Jubilee award U. Toronto Libr. & Info. Sci. Alumni Assn., 1994. Mem. ALA (chmn. com. on accreditation 1973-74), Assn. Parliamentary Librs. in Can. (pres. 1982-84), Can. Libr. Assn. (pres. 1975-76), Ont. Libr. Assn. (1st v.p. 1962-63), Ont. Govt. Librs. Coun. (chmn. 1984-85), Assn. for Libr. and Info. Sci. Edn. (pres. 1973-74), Bibliog. Soc. Can., Can. Assn. for Grad. Edn. in Libr. Archival and Info. Studies (pres. 1966-67), Can. Assn. Univ. Tchrs., Can. Coun. Libr. Schs. (chmn. 1971-72), Ex Libris Assn. (bd. dirs. 1994—), Inst. Profl. Librs. Ont. (pres. 1961-62), Ont. Coun. Libr. Schs. (chmn. 1968-72), Spl. Librs. Assn. (Mem. of Yr. award Toronto chpt. 1986), Ont. Geneal. Soc., Ont. Coll. and Univ. Librs. Assn. (merit award 1962). Mem. Anglican Ch. Home: 18 Kirkton Rd, North York, ON Canada M3H 1K7

LAND, RICHARD DALE, minister, religious organization administrator; b. Houston, Nov. 6, 1946; s. Leggette Sloan and Marilee (Welch) L.; m. Rebekah Ruth Van Hooser, May 29, 1971; children: Jennifer, Richard Jr., Rachel. BA, Princeton U., 1969; ThM, New Orleans Bapt. Theol. Sem., 1972; D.Phil., U. Oxford, Eng., 1980. Ordained to ministry So. Bapt. Conv., 1969. Pastor S. Oxford Bapt. Ch., Oxford, Eng., 1972-75; prof. theology and ch. history Criswell Coll., Dallas, 1975-76, acad. dean, 1976-80, v.p. for acad. affairs, 1980-88; exec. dir. Christian Life Commn. So. Bapt. Conv., Nashville, 1988—; mem. exec. com. Nat. Coalition against Pornography, Cin., 1989—; bd. dirs. Bapt. Joint Com. Pub. Affairs, Washington, 1987-90, Nat. Pro-Life Religious Coun., Washington. Cons. editor Criswell Study Bible, 1979. Mem. Gov.'s Task Force on Welfare Reform, Austin, Tex., 1988, Pres.'s Campaign for a Drug-Free Soc., Washington, 1991—; bd. drs. Nat. Law Ctr., Arlington, Va., 1991—. Mem. Nat. Assn. Evangs. (Wheaton, Ill., bd. dirs. 1991—), Conf. on Faith and History, Evang. Theol. Soc., So. Bapt. Hist. Soc., Rotary. Office: Christian Life Commn 901 Commerce St Ste 550 Nashville TN 37203-3629

LANDA, HOWARD MARTIN, lawyer, business executive; b. Bklyn., Oct. 12, 1943; s. George and Lilli (Skolnik) L.; m. Nori Neinstein, Mar. 14, 1971; children—Alyson, David. B.A. (N.Y. State Regents scholar), Bklyn. Coll., 1964; J.D. (tuition scholar), U. Chgo., 1967. Bar: N.Y. 1968. Sole practice N.Y.C., 1968-69; assoc. Garfield, Solomon & Mainzer, N.Y.C., 1969-70, Szold, Brandwen, Meyers & Altman, N.Y.C., 1970-74; v.p., sec., gen. counsel IPCO Corp., White Plains, N.Y., 1974-90, also bd. dirs.; pres., mng. dir. Martin Hand Assocs., Inc., Greenwich, Conn., 1990-92, also bd. dirs.; owner Law Offices of Howard M. Landa, N.Y.C., 1990-94; counsel Rand Rosenzweig Smith Gordon & Burstein LLP, N.Y.C., 1994—; lectr. Dental Lab. Conf., 1977. Contrb. articles to profl. jours. Mem. Mayor N.Y.C. Panel to Study Dept. Gen. Services' Div. Mcpl. Supplies, 1978-79; vice chmn. So. N.Y. chpt. Nat. Multiple Sclerosis Soc., 1988—. Mem. ABA, N.Y. County Lawyers Assn., Corp. Bar Assn. Office: 605 3rd Ave New York NY 10158

LANDA, WILLIAM ROBERT, foundation executive; b. Jersey City, Dec. 4, 1919; s. G.B. and Henrietta (Elder) L.; m. Anne E. Longley, June 24, 1939; children: Susanne (Mrs. J.B. Moliere), Stephen R., Scott W., Richard W. Student, Ohio U., 1937-39. Salesman Sterling Drug, Inc., 1942-44; asst. export mgr. Taylor, Pinkham & Co., Inc., 1944-52; export mgr. Bates Fabrics, Inc., 1952-55; pres. Burlington Export Co., N.Y.C., 1955-62; v.p. Burlington Mills Corp., 1957-62, Burlington Industries, Inc., Greensboro, N.C., 1959-62, Warner Bros. Co., Bridgeport, Conn., 1962-66; pres. Warner Bros. Co. (Warner Bros. Internat.), 1962-66; exec. v.p. Turner Jones & Co., 1966-67, pres., 1967-68; group v.p. internat. Genesco, Inc., N.Y.C., 1968-70; v.p. Farah Mfg. Co., 1970-74; pres., dir. Holguin & Assos. Inc., El Paso, Tex., 1978-81; pres. Western Mktg. Corp., El Paso, 1981-85; spl. asst. to pres. Free/Congress Research and Edn. Found. Inc., Washington, 1986-89; dir. Affiliated Mfrs., Inc., North Branch, N.J., AMI-PRESCO; hon. consul of Belgium for West Tex. and State of N.Mex., 1981-86; Mem. Gen. Arbitration Council Textile Industry; mem. Nat. Export Council, 1965-66; cons. Internat. Mktg., 1988—. Decorated chevalier Order of Crown Belgium). Mem. Commerce and Industry Assn. N.Y., Internat. Execs. Assn., U.S. C. of C. (spl. adv. com. on internat. trade), Am. Arbitration Assn., Beta Theta Pi. Presbyterian. Home: 2032 Birch Dr Culpeper VA 22701-4063

LANDAHL, HERBERT DANIEL, biophysicist, mathematical biologist, researcher, consultant; b. Fancheng, China, Apr. 23, 1913; (parents Am. citizens); s. Carl W. and Alice (Holmberg) L.; m. Evelyn Christine Blomberg, Aug. 23, 1940; children: Carl David, Carol Ann Landahl Kubai, Linda C. Landahl Shidner. Student, U. Minn., 1931-32; AB, St. Olaf Coll., Northfield, Minn., 1934; SM, U. Chgo., 1936, PhD, 1941. Rsch. asst. psychometric lab. U. Chgo., 1937-39, rsch. asst. math. biophysics, 1938-41, instr., 1942-45, asst. prof. com. on math. biology, 1945-48, assoc. prof., 1949-56, prof., 1956-68, acting. chmn., 1965-67; prof. biophysics and math. U. Calif., San Francisco, 1968-80, prof. emeritus, 1980—; cons. Respiratory Project, U. Chgo., 1944-46, toxicity lab. U. Chgo., 1947-51, USAF radiation lab., U. Chgo., 1951-67, dept. biomath. U. Tex., Houston, 1968-89; mem. NIH com. on epidemiology and biometry, Bethesda, Md., 1960-64. Coauthor: Mathematical Biophysics of Central Nervous System, 1945; contbr. approximately 190 sci. papers to various jours.; chief editor Bull. Math. Biophysics, 1973-80; mem. editorial bd. Computers in Biology and Medicine, 1971-90. Recipient Career Devel. award NIH, 1962-67, Career Achievement award Soc. Toxicology, 1987; grantee NIH, 1963-67. Fellow AAAS; mem. Biophys. Soc., Biometric Soc. (charter), Bioengring. Soc. (charter), Latin Am. Biomath. Soc. (charter), Soc. for Math. Biology (founding, pres. 1981-83). Home: 472 Lansdale Ave San Francisco CA 94127-1617 Office: U Calif-San Francisco PO Box 970 San Francisco CA 94143-0001

LANDAN, HENRY SINCLAIR, lawyer; b. Chgo., Aug. 4, 1943. BS, DePaul U., 1965, JD, 1969; LLM in Taxation, NYU, 1970. Bar: Ill. 1969, N.Y. 1971, U.S. Supreme Ct. 1976. Assoc. Altman, Kurlander & Weiss, Chgo., 1969-70, Roberts & Holland, N.Y.C., 1970-72; sr. ptnr. Kamensky & Landan and predecessor, Chgo., 1972-84, Henry S. Landan, Chgo, 1984-88; of counsel Keck, Mahin & Cate, Chgo., 1988-90, ptnr., 1990—; counsel Caribbean Hotel Assn., Santurce, P.R., 1975-83. Contbg. author: Tax Planning for Professionals; contbr. articles to profl. jours. Mem. exec. com., bd. dirs. Jewish Coun. for Youth Svcs., 1972-77; mem. exec. com., bd. dirs. Men's Coun., Mus. Contemporary Art, Chgo., 1977-84, pres., 1980-82; bd. dirs. Little City, Chgo., 1977-82; bd. dirs., mem. exec. com. Renaissance soc. U. Chgo., 1984—, v.p., 1988-95; mem. Soc. Contemporary Art, Art Inst. Chgo., 1982-95; mem. Contemporary Arts Coun., Chgo., 1994—; mem. bd. mgrs. Henry Horner Boys and Girls Club, 1992—; bd. dirs., mem. exec. com. Randolph St. Gallery, Chgo., 1983-88, mem. adv. bd., 1988—. Named Life Dir., Young Men's Jewish Coun., 1980, Man of Yr., 1985. Mem. ABA, Ill. Bar Assn., N.Y. Bar Assn., Chgo. Bar Assn. Home: 120 W Kinzie St Chicago IL 60610-4508

LANDAU, BERNARD ROBERT, biochemistry educator, physician; b. Newark, N.J., June 24, 1926; s. Morris Harry and Estelle (Kirsch) L.; m. Lucille Slosberg, Jan. 11, 1956; children: Steven Brian, Deborah Louise (dec.), Rodger Martin. S.B., MIT, 1947; Ph.D., Harvard U., 1950, M.D., 1954; MD (hon.), Karolinska Inst., 1993. Diplomate: Am. Bd. Internal Medicine. Intern Peter Bent Brigham Hosp., Boston, 1954-55; clin. assoc. Nat. Cancer Inst., Bethesda, Md., 1955-57; fellow in biochemistry Harvard U., 1957-58; sr. resident Peter Bent Brigham Hosp., 1958-59; asst. prof. medicine Case Western Res. U., 1959-62, assoc. prof., 1962-67, prof., 1969—, prof. biochemistry, 1979—, physician Univ. Hosps., 1969—; dir. dept. biochemistry Merck and Co., Rahway, N.J., 1967-69. Contbr. articles to profl. jours. Fellow Commonwealth fund, 1965-66, Fogarty Sr. Internat. fellow 1986-87, 93-94; grantee Am. Heart Assn., 1959-64; recipient William B. Peck Postgrad. Research award, 1961. Fellow AAAS; mem. Am. Fedn. Clin. Research, Am. Soc. Clin. Investigation, Assn. Am. Physicians, Am. soc. Biol. Chemists, Am. Physiol. Soc., Endocrine Soc., Central Soc. Clin. Research, Am. Diabetes Assn., Am. Thyroid Assn., Sigma Xi, Alpha Omega Alpha. Home: 19501 S Woodland Rd Cleveland OH 44122-2834 Office: University Hosps Cleveland 11100 Euclid Ave Cleveland OH 44106-5000

LANDAU, DAVID PAUL, physics educator; b. St. Louis, June 22, 1941; s. Bernard Israel and Selma (Goldstein) L.; m. Heidi Humpert, Aug. 28, 1966; children: Ladina Aviva, Anya Karina. BA, Princeton U., 1963; MS, Yale U., 1965, PhD, 1967. Chargé de recherche CNRS, Grenoble, France, 1967-68; lectr. Yale U., New Haven, 1968-69; asst. prof. physics U. Ga., Athens, 1969-73, assoc. prof., 1973-78, prof., 1978-84, rsch. prof., 1984—, dir. Ctr. for Simulational Physics, 1986—. Editor books; author more than 200 sci. publs. Recipient Creative Rsch. medal U. Ga., 1981, sr. U.S. scientist prize Alexander von Humboldt Found., 1988. Fellow Am. Phys. Soc. (Jesse Beams award 1987). Jewish. Office: U Ga Ctr Simulational Physics Athens GA 30602

LANDAU, DOROTHY, psychotherapist, consultant; b. N.Y.C., Jan. 16, 1944; d. John Charles Sobczak and Evelyn (Schurstedt) Koritor; m. Sal Napolitano, May 4, 1963 (div. Sept. 1982); children: Debra, Drew; m. Jay Arthur Landau, Jan. 6, 1989. AAS, SUNY, Farmingdale, 1977; BSN, SUNY, Stony Brook, 1983, MS, 1992. Cert. clin. nurse specialist; cert. addictions RN; cert. nurse pratitioner in psychiatry. Staff nurse Suffolk Devel. Ctr., Melville, N.Y., 1978; head nurse/asst. supr. Brunswick House, Amityville, N.Y., 1978-80; nurse adminstr. C.K. Post Alcoholism Treatment Ctr., Brentwood, N.Y., 1981-89; asst. DON Kings Park (N.Y.) Psychiat. Ctr., 1989-93; dir. partial hospitalization program and inpatient mental health and substances abuse svcs. Mercy Med. Ctr., Rockville Centre, N.Y., 1993-94; psychotherapist Commack, N.Y., 1992—; pvt. cons. Smithtown, N.Y., 1994—; mem. adv. bd. Sch. Nursing, SUNY, Farmingdale, 1990—. Rschr. in field of substance abuse. Mem. N.Y. State Coalition of Nurse Practitioners, Soc. for Edn. and Rsch. in Psychiatric Nursing, Network of Clin. Specialists in Psychiatric Nursing, Nassau-Suffolk Coordinating Coun. (bd. dirs. 1990-93), Sigma Theta Tau. Avocation: sailing. Home: 41 Valley Ave Smithtown NY 11787-1114 Office: 283 Commack Rd Commack NY 11725-3400

LANDAU, ELLIS, gaming company executive; b. Phila., Feb. 24, 1944; s. Manfred and Ruth (Fischer) L.; m. Kathy Suzanne Thomas, May 19, 1968 (div.); children: Rachel, David; m. Yvette Ehr Cohen, Nov. 1, 1992. BA in Econs., Brandeis U., 1965; MBA, Columbia U., 1967. Fin. analyst SEC, Washington, 1968-69; asst. treas. U-Haul Internat., Phoenix, 1969-71; v.p., treas. Ramada, Inc., Phoenix, 1971-90; CFO Boyd Gaming Corp., Las Vegas, Nev., 1990—. Home: 7571 Silver Meadow Ct Las Vegas NV 89117 Office: Boyd Gaming Corp 2950 S Industrial Rd Las Vegas NV 89109-1100

LANDAU, EMANUEL, epidemiologist; b. N.Y.C., Nov. 28, 1919; s. Meyer and Annie (Heller) L.; B.A., CCNY, 1939; Ph.D., Am. U., 1966; m. Davetta Goldberg, Sept. 4, 1948; children: Melanie (dec.), Elizabeth. Supervisory analytical statistician Calif. Dept. Public Health, 1957-59, chief biometry sect., div. air pollution, 1959-62; head lab. and clin. trials sect. Nat. Cancer Inst., 1962-65; statis. adviser Nat. Air Pollution Control Adminstrn., 1965-69; epidemiologist Environ. Health Service, 1969-71, chief epidemiologic studies br. Bur. Radiol. Health, 1971-74; project dir., sci. cons. Am. Pub. Health Assn., 1975—; cons., adv. in field. Vol. White House Health Care Reform Corr. With AUS, 1942-46. Decorated Belgian Fourragere; recipient Superior Service award HEW, 1963. Fellow Am. Pub. Health Assn., Royal Soc. Health; mem. Soc. Epidemiologic Research, Am. Statis. Assn. (chmn. com. on stats. and environ.). Democrat. Jewish. Club: Cosmos (Washington). Author, editor articles, reports in field. Home: 4601 N Park Ave Apt 208 Chevy Chase MD 20815-4520 Office: Am Pub Health Assn 1015 15th St NW Washington DC 20005-2605

LANDAU, HENRY GROH, geoenvironmental consulting engineer; b. N.Y.C., Mar. 1, 1943; s. Henry G. and Ann Marie (Skvarich) L.; m. Joyce Kathryn Van de Merlen, July 27, 1965; children: Greg, Amy, Michael. BS in Civil Engring., CCNY, 1965; MS in Geotech. Engring., Purdue U., 1966, PhD in Engring., 1973. Profl. engr., Wash., N.Y., Alaska. Civil engr. Geotechnica, Sao Paulo, Brazil, 1966-67; officer U.S. Army C.E., South Vietnam, 1967-70; sr. engr. Dames & Moore, Seattle, 1973-82; sr. prin. Landau Assocs., Inc., Edmonds, Wash., 1982—; vis. prof. Fed. U., Paraiba, Brazil, 1978-79; mem. Gov.'s Sci. Adv. Bd., Olympia, Wash., 1987-90, chmn., 1990—. Contbr. articles to profl. jours. Tutor math. & sci. Edmonds Sch. Dist.; scout leader Boy Scouts Am., Edmonds, 1986-90. 1st lt. U.S. Army, 1967-70, Vietnam. Mem. ASCE, Soc. Am. Mil. Engrs., Assn. Groundwater Scientists & Engrs. Avocations: bicycling, sailing, nature study, water sports. Office: Landau Assocs Inc 23107 100th Ave W Edmonds WA 98020-5017

LANDAU, JACOB, artist; b. Phila., Dec. 17, 1917; s. Samuel and Deana (Kitaynick) L.; m. Frances Paul, May 5, 1949; children: Stephan Paul, Jonas Michael. Student, Phila. Coll. Art, 1936-39, New Sch., N.Y.C., 1948-49, 52-53, Acad. de la Grande Chaumiere, Paris, France, 1950-52. Prof. graphic art Pratt Inst., Bklyn., now prof. emeritus; founder, formerly learning coordinator integrative studies program; vis. scholar Memphis Acad. Arts, 1969, U. Notre Dame, Ind., 1969; graphic arts panelist N.J. Arts Council, 1969-73; vis. artist Skidmore Coll., Saratoga Springs, N.Y., 1971, Brookdale Coll., Lincroft, N.J., 1976, U. No. Mich., 1981, Ea. and Western Carolina Univs., Greenville and Cullowhee, N.C., 1982; panelist N.J. State Mus., Trenton, 1973, NYU, 1974, Rutgers U., New Brunswick, N.J., 1976; artist-in-residence U. No. Iowa, 1977; resident artist Pima Community Coll., Univ. Ariz., Tucson, 1984; tchr. Artist/Tchr. Inst., N.J. State Council on Arts, 1978-89; academician Nat. Acad. Design, N.Y.; cons. N.J. Dept. Higher Edn., 1974. One-man shows include Galerie LeBar, Paris, 1952, Art Alliance, Phila., 1954, 75, Art Ctr., New Brunswick, N.J., 1957, Samuel Fleisher Meml. Gallery, Phila., 1959, Assoc. Am. Artists Gallery, N.Y.C., 1960, 70, U. Maine, 1961, 71, Cober Gallery, N.Y.C., 1961, 63, Zora Gallery, L.A., 1964, Original Prints Gallery, San Francisco, 1965, Gallery 100, Princeton, N.J., 1966, Art Gallery, U. Notre Dame, 1969, A.A.A. Gallery N.Y., 1970, Print Club, Phila., 1970, Giraffe Gallery, L.A., 1970, Van Straaten Gallery, Chgo., 1970, Lunn Gallery, Washington, 1970, Jorgensen Auditorium, U. Conn. at Storrs, 1971, Bloomfield (N.J.) Coll., 1971, 72, Orpheus Ascending Gallery, Stockbridge, Mass., 1972, Galeria Pecanins, Mexico City, 1972, Imprint Gallery, San Francisco, 1973, Congregation Keneseth Israel, Elkins Park, Pa., 1974, ACA Galleries, N.Y.C., 1976, Woodbridge (N.J.) Cultural Arts Commn., Schneider-Sato Gallery, Karlsruhe, Germany, 1977, N.J. Mus., 1981, U. Ga., 1982, Phila. Mus. Judaica, 1983, Phila. Coll. Art, 1985, Galerie Neuheisel, Saarbrucken, Fed. Republic Germany, Galerie Michael Hagen, Offenburg, Fed. Republic Germany, 1985, Martin Sumers Graphics, N.Y., 1988, Rider Coll., Lawrenceville, N.J., 1988, The Mariboe Gallery, Peddie Sch., Hightstown, N.J., 1992, Judah L. Magnes Mus., 1993, N.J. State Mus., 1994, Kenneth Israel, Elkins Park, Pa., 1995, Brandywine workshop, Phila., 1996, (with Bernarda Shahn) Printmaking Coun. N.J., North Branch Stattion, N.J., 1996; numerous group shows, 1955—, latest include Four Painters, Art Alliance Phila., 1961, New Humanism, Nat. Sch. Plastics Arts, U. Mexico, 1963, regional exhbn., Pa. Acad. Fine Arts, 1964, N.J. and the Artist, N.J. State Mus., Trenton, 1965, Drawing Soc. Eastern Cen. Region, Phila. Mus. Art, 1965, N.J. Tercentenary Show, 1965, Contemporary N.J. Art, Newark Mus., 1965, Prize-Winning Am. Prints, circulating show, N.Y. State Council on Arts, 1967, Drawings U.S.A, St. Paul Art Ctr., 1968, Am. Prints Today, Mus. Art, Munson-Williams-Proctor Inst., Utica, N.Y., 1968, Selections from 50th Ann. Soc. Am. Graphic Artists, USIA Nr. East Traveling Show, 1970, Tamarind: A Renaissance of Lithography, circulating show, Internat. Exhbns. Found., 1971, SUNY Coll. at Brockport, 1972, Iowa State U., 1972, N.J. Arts Council, 1972, Art. Mus., Sao Paulo, Brazil, 1972, Am. Acad. Arts and Letters, 1973, 74, NAD, 1974, Washington Club, 1976, Soc. Am. Graphic Artists Show, 1976, 77, Am. Color Print Soc. 35th Exhbn., Phila., 1976, 1st Biennial N.J. Artists, 1977, State U., Potsdam, N.Y., 1978, Portsmouth Arts Ctr., Portsmouth, Va., 1979, Carnegie Mellon U., Pitts., 1980, Minn. Mus. Art, St. Paul, 1980, Worcester Art Mus., Worcester, Mass., 1981, Noyes Mus., Oceanville, N.J., 1983, 1991, Purdue U., W. Lafayette, Ind., 1986, Middlesex County Mus., Piscataway, N.J., 1987, FellowshipExhbn, The Monmouth Mus., 1988, Guild Hall Mus., East Hampton, N.Y., 1990, Rubelle and Norman Schafler Gallery, Pratt Int. 1990-91, Mercer County (N.J.) Communtiy Coll., 1991, Printmaking Coun., Sommerville, N.J., 1991, Ellarslie Mus., Trenton, N.J., 1992; numerous nat. and internat. shows, 1953—, latest include woodcut annuals, Print Club Phila., 1955, 59, 92d, 95th, 97th Am. Watercolor Soc. anns., NAD, 1954, 62, 64, 12th-17th print biennials, Bklyn. Mus., 1960, 62, 64, 66, 68, 70, Xylon Internats., 1962, 65, Recent Paintings, U.S.A-The Figure, Mus. Modern Art, 1962, nominee exhbn., Nat. Inst. Arts and Letters, 1962, 65, 156th, 158th, 160th, 162d anns., Pa. Acad. Fine Arts, 1961, 63, 65, 67, graphics U.S.A., USIA traveling exhbn., 1963—, 19th, 20th print exhbns., Library of Congress, 1963, 66, 30th ann., Butler Art Inst., Youngstown, Ohio, 1965, Smithsonian invitational exhbn., White House, 1966, Nat. Drawing Exhbn., Rutgers U., 1975, Hawaii Nat. Print Exhbn, Honolulu Acad. Arts, 1975, Nat. Coll. Fine Arts, Miami Graphics, Biennial Met. Mus., Coral Gables, Fla., Boston Printmakers, De Cordova Mus., Lincoln, Mass., Hunterdon (N.J.) Art Center, 1977; also exhibited at Mus. Modern Art, N.Y.C., 1969, Whitney Mus., N.Y.C., 1969, Mus. Art, Phila., 1970, NAD 157th Ann., Ohio State U., 1982, Utopian Visions in Modern Art, Hirshhorn Mus. and Sculpture Garden, Washington, 1984, Third Internat. Biennial Print Exhbn., Hangzhou, People's Republic of China, 1989; represented in permanent collections Whitney Mus. Am. Art, Mus. Modern Art, Met. Mus., Pa. Acad. Fine Arts, art museums in Balt., Atlanta, New Orleans, Phila., Bklyn., Norfolk, Va., San Antonio, Tucson, Ariz., Malmo, Sweden, Nuremberg, Fed. Republic Germany, Slater Mus., Norwich, Conn., Library of Congress, Joseph J. Hirschhorn collection, also univs. Princeton, Rutgers, Maine, Minn., Syracuse, Yale, Ky., U. Calif. at Berkeley, U. Mass., U. South Fla., Columbia, Butler Inst., Youngstown, Ohio, M.H. DeYoung Mus., San Francisco, N.J. State Mus., Trenton, Bibliotheque Nationale, Paris, Lessing Rosenwald Collection, also pvt. collections, commns. include sketches of participants at Pacem In Terris II, 1967; print of peace, Internat. Art Program, Nat. Collection Fine Arts, Smithsonian Instn., 1967; cycle of ten stained glass windows The Prophetic Quest, Keneseth Israel Congregation, Elkins Park, 1970; lithograph, Behold Jewish Ctr., Trenton, 1973, But if the Cause, Roten Galleries, Balt., 1976; etching, Einstein, Washington Print Club, 1982; lithograph, Thirty-Fourth Psalm, Jewish Family Svc. of Del. Valley, Trenton, N.J., 1988. Trustee N.J. Sch. Arts, 1981-85, Nat. Guild of Community Schs. of Arts; mem. nat. com. U. of Arts, Phila. Recipient Lessing Rosenwald Purchase award Print Club Phila., 1955, 59; recipient Woodcut prize Print Fair of Phila. Free library, 1960, Louis Comfort Tiffany award, 1962; recipinet hon. mention Am. Water Color Soc., 1962; recipient Paul F. Norton and Asso. Am. Artists awards Soc. Am. Graphic Artists, 1962, hon. mention Audubon Artists, 1965; named One of New Jersey's Five Finest Com. Curators and Critics, 1962; recipient Phila. Watercolor prize Pa. Acad. Fine Arts, 1963; First award N.J. Tercentenary Art Festival, 1963; fellow Tamarind Lithography Workshop, Los Angeles, 1965; Edna Pennypacker Stauffer prize Soc. Am. Graphic Artists, 1965; purchase awards Asso. Am. Artists, 1967; purchase award Dulin Gallery Art, Knoxville, Tenn.; purchase awards Drawing U.S.A. '68, St. Paul Art Center; purchase awards Contemporary Graphic Art on Contemporary Law and Justice, Assn. Bar City N.Y.; Vera List purchase prize Soc. Am. Graphic Artists, 1972; Childe Hassam purchase award Am. Acad. Arts and Letters, 1973-74; purchase prize Nat. Drawing Exhbn., Rutgers U., 1975; Purchase prize Nat. Print Exhbn., Hunterdon; Purchase prize AAA Gallery, N.Y.C., 1977; Ann. award YM-YWHA, Union, N.J., 1984; Alumni Silver Star award Phila. Colls. Art, 1985; Grantee Nat. Arts Council, 1966; Grantee N.J. State Arts Council, 1974; Grantee Ford Found., 1975; Guggenheim Found. fellow, 1968-69; recipient N.J. State Arts Coun. fellowship, 1988, Gov.'s award for disting. svc. in arts and edn., 1989. Mem. Soc. Am. Graphic Artists. Home & Studio: 30 Lake Dr PO Box 328 Roosevelt NJ 08555-0328 *For me, art is more than formal exploration or exploitation. Without it, we are endangered and endangering species.*

LANDAU, LAURI BETH, accountant, tax consultant; b. Bklyn., July 21, 1952; d. Jack and Audrey Carolyn (Zuckernick) L. BA, Skidmore Coll., 1973; postgrad., Pace. U., 1977-79. CPA, N.Y., Oreg. Mem. staff Audrey Z. Landau, CPA, Suffern, N.Y., 1976-78; mem. staff Ernst & Whinney, N.Y.C., 1979-80, mem. sr. staff, 1980-82, supr., 1982-84; mgr. Arthur Young & Co., N.Y.C., 1984-87, prin., 1987-89; sr. mgr. Ernst & Young, N.Y.C., 1989-92; prnt. Audrey Z. Landau & Co., Wilmington, Vt., 1992—, ptnr., 1995—; ptnr. Audrey Z. Landau & Co., Wilmington, Vt.; spkr. World Trade Inst., N.Y.C., 1987—, Nat. Fgn. Trade Coun., N.Y.C., 1989—. Composer songs. Career counselor Skidmore Coll., Saratoga Springs, N.Y., 1977—; mem. leadership com. Class of 1973, 83-85, pres., 1985-93, fund chmn., 1987-88, mem. planned gift com., 1989—. N.Y. State Regents scholar, 1970. Mem. Nat. Conf. CPA Practitioners, N.Y. State Soc. CPAs, Skidmore Coll. Alumni Assn. (mem. nominating com. 1989-92). Skidmore Alumni Club, German Shepherd Dog Am. Club. Democrat. Avocations: music, ballet, photography, sports. Office: Ste 205B 26 Firements Meml Dr Pomona NY 10970

LANDAU, MARTIN, actor; b. Bklyn., June 20, 1934; m. Barbara Bain (div.); children: Susie, Juliet. Student, Art Students League, Actors Studio. Staff artist, cartoonist N.Y. Daily News. Star TV series Mission: Impossible, 1966-69, Space 1999, 1974-77, others; TV appearances include Omnibus, Playhouse 90, G.E. Theatre, Gunsmoke, Twilight Zone; also TV movies Welcome Home, Johnny Bristol, 1972, Savage, 1973, The Death of Ocean View Park, 1979, The Harlem Globetrotters on Gilligan's Island, 1981, The Fall of the House of Usher, 1982, The Neon Empire, 1989, By Dawn's Early Light, 1990, Something to Live For: The Alison Gertz Story, 1992, Legacy of Lies, 1992 (Ace award), 12:01, 1993, miniseries Joseph, 1995; films include Pork Chop Hill, North by Northwest, 1959, Stagecoach to Dancer's Rock, 1961, Cleopatra, 1962, Hallelujah Trail, 1964, The Greatest Story Ever Told, 1965, Nevada Smith, 1966, They Call Me Mr. Tibbs, 1970, Operation SNAFU, 1970, A Town Called Hell, 1971, Johnny Bristol, 1971, Black Gunn, 1972, Strange Shadows in an Empty Room, 1977, Meteor, 1979, The Last Word, 1979, Without Warning, 1980, Operation Moonbase Alpha, 1980, Earthright, 1980, Beauty and the Beast, 1981, Alone in the Dark, 1982, Trial by Terror, 1983, Tucker: The Man and His Dreams, 1988 (Acad. Award nominee 1988), Crimes and Misdemeanors, 1989, (Golden Globe award 1989, Acad. award nominee 1989) Paint It Black, 1990, Real Bullets, 1990, Firehead, 1991, Eye of the Widow, 1991, Mistress, 1992, Sliver, 1993, Intersection, 1994, Ed Wood, 1994 (Best Supporting Actor Acad. award 1994, Golden Globe award 1994, SAG award 1994, Am. Comedy award 1994, N.Y. Film Critics award 1994, L.A. Film Critics award 1994, Chgo. Film Critics award 1994, Nat. Soc. Film Critics award 1994, Boston Film Critics award 1994, Tex. Film Critics award 1994, Lifetime Achievement award Houston Film Festival 1994, Lifetime Achievement award Charleston Film Festival 1994), City Hall, 1995, The Legend of Pinocchio, 1996; stage appearances include Middle of the Night, Uncle Vanya, Stalag 17, Wedding Breakfast, First Love, The Goat Song, Dracula. Recipient Golden Globe award, 1967; Emmy nominee. Mem. Acad. Motion Picture Arts and Scis., Actors Studio (W. Coast dir.). Office: 23717 Long Valley Rd Calabasas CA 91302

LANDAU, MARTIN, political science educator; b. N.Y.C., July 12, 1921; s. User Noah and Clara (Markowitz) L.; m. Bernice Feldman, July 11, 1943; children—Madeline, Claudia. A.B., Bklyn. Coll., 1947; M.A. in Pub. Adminstrn, N.Y. U., 1948; Ph.D., 1952; Docteur Honoris Causa, U. Paris, Dauphine, 1993. Vis. research prof. U. Calif. at Berkeley, 1969-71, prof. polit. sci., 1972—; Distinguished prof. City U. N.Y., Bklyn., 1970-72; lectr. orgn. and decision theory Fgn. Service Inst., U.S. Dept. State, Washington, 1969-72; cons. in field; chancellor Grad. Sch. Pub. Adminstrn., U. P.R., San Juan, 1970-71; Berkeley Exch. prof., Peking U., 1985; Phi Beta Kappa Nat. Lectr., 1984; dir. Berkeley-Hong Kong Project, 1984—. Author: Political Theory and Political Science; Studies in the Methodology of Political Inquiry, 1972; Chmn. editorial bd.: Polit. Sci, 1971—; mem. editorial bd.: Jour. Comparative Adminstrv. Studies, 1969—, Comparative Politics, 1970—, Jour. Theoretical Politics, 1988—, Jour. Behavioral Decision Making, 1988—. Served with Signal Corps AUS, 1941-45. Recipient Distinguished Teaching award Bklyn. Coll., 1963, E. Harris Harbison award gifted teaching Danforth Found., 1969-70, William E. Mosher award distinguished scholarship Soc. Pub. Adminstrn., 1970, 79; John Simon Guggenheim fellow, 1976-77; fellow Center Advanced Study in Behavioral Sci., 1976-77. Fellow Nat. Acad. Public Adminstrn.; mem. Am. Polit. Sci. Assn., Philosophy of Sci. Assn. Home: 1410 Summit Rd Berkeley CA 94708-2215 Office: U Calif Dept Polit Sci Berkeley CA 94720

LANDAU, PETER EDWARD, editor; b. N.Y.C., July 16, 1933; s. Edward and Charlotte (Schmidt) L. A.B., Duke, 1955; M.S. in Econs, Columbia, 1959. Editorial asst. Newsweek mag., N.Y.C., 1955-57, asst. editor, 1958-61, assoc. editor, 1962-67; v.p. Tiderock Corp., 1967; sr. editor Instl. Investor, N.Y.C., 1968, mng. editor, 1968-70, editor, 1971-91, editor-at-large, 1991—. Home: 300 E 51st St New York NY 10022-7806 Office: Instl Investor 488 Madison Ave New York NY 10022-5702

LANDAU, RICHARD L., physician, educator; b. St. Louis, Aug. 8, 1916; s. Milton S. and Amelia (Rich) L.; m. Claire Schmuckel, Dec. 4, 1943; children—James, Susan, Kay. B.S., M.D., Washington U., St. Louis, 1940. Intern U. Chgo. Clinics, 1940-41, resident, 1941-42; mem. faculty U. Chgo. Sch. Medicine, 1946—, prof. medicine, 1959-88, prof. medicine emeritus, 1988—; head sect. endocrinology, 1967-78. Editor: Perspectives in Biology and Medicine, 1973—; mem. editorial bd.: Jour. Lab. and Clin. Medicine, 1957-62, Ann. Rev. Medicine, 1959-68, Jour. AMA, 1981-89. Served to capt. M.C. AUS, 1943-46. Decorated Bronze Star. Mem. Endocrine Soc. (council 1962-65), Central Soc. Clin. Research, Am. Soc. Clin. Investigation, A.M.A., Chgo. Soc. Internal Medicine (pres. 1968). Spl. rsch. in endocrinologic aspects of reprodn., metabolic influence of progesterone. Home: 5732 S Kenwood Ave Chicago IL 60637-1719

LANDAU, SIDNEY I., publishing executive, lexicographer; b. N.Y.C., Apr. 11, 1933; s. Emanuel and Sadie Mildred (Halpern) L.; m. Sarah Gaston Bradford, June 19, 1959; children: Paul, Amy. BA in English, Queens Coll., 1954; MFA in Creative Writing, U. Iowa, 1959. Instr. English Miami U., Oxford, Ohio, 1959-61; editor, then editor in chief dictionaries Funk & Wagnalls, N.Y.C., 1961-70; editor in chief Doubleday Dictionary, Doubleday Roget's Thesaurus Doubleday & Co., N.Y.C., 1975-77; editor in chief Internat. Dictionary of Medicine and Biology, John Wiley & Sons, N.Y.C., 1977-88, mgr. med. jours., 1982-84, exec. editor medicine, 1985-87, pub. chemistry and life scis. sci.-tech. div., 1987-88; dir. reference, editor-in-chief Cambridge Dictionary of Am. English, N.Y.C., 1988—. Author: Dictionaries: The Art and Craft of Lexicography, 1984, paperback edit., 1989; contbr. numerous articles to profl. jours. With U.S. Army, 1954-56. Mem. Am. Dialect Soc., Dictionary Soc. N.Am. (pres. 1993-95), Am. Coun. Learned Socs. (del. 1994—). Home: 50 W 96th St Apt 2A New York NY 10025-6527 Office: Cambridge U Press 40 W 20th St New York NY 10011-4211

LANDAU, WALTER LOEBER, lawyer; b. New Orleans, Sept. 9, 1931; s. Walter Loeber and Mae (Wilzin) L.; m. Barbara Jane Gordon, June 23, 1954; children: Donna Hardiman, Blair Trippe, Gordon Loeber. BA, Princeton U., 1953; LLB, Harvard U., 1956. Bar: N.Y. 1956, U.S. Dist. Ct. (so. dist.) N.Y. 1962, U.S. Supreme Ct. 1971. Assoc. firm Sullivan & Cromwell, N.Y.C., 1959-65; ptnr. Sullivan & Cromwell, 1966—; bd. dirs. Alumax, Inc., U.S. Life Ins. Co., N.Y.C. Trustee Reece Sch., N.Y.C.; mem. Met. Opera Assn.; bd. dirs. Opera Orch. N.Y., N.Y.C. Opera; bd. dirs., sec. Manhattan Theater Club. Fellow Am. Bar Found.; mem. ABA, N.Y. State Bar Assn., Assn. Bar City N.Y., Am. Law Inst., N.Y. Law Inst. (pres.). Republican. Office: Sullivan & Cromwell 125 Broad St New York NY 10004-2400

LANDAUER, ROLF WILLIAM, physicist; b. Stuttgart, Germany, Feb. 4, 1927; came to U.S., 1938, naturalized, 1944; s. Karl and Anna (Dannhauser) L.; m. Muriel Jussim, Feb. 26, 1950; children—Karen, Carl, Thomas. SB, Harvard U., 1945, AM, 1947, PhD, 1950; DSc (hon.), Technion, 1991. Solid state physicist Lewis Lab., NACA (now NASA), Cleve., 1950-52; with IBM Research (and antecedent groups), 1952—; asst. dir. research IBM Research (T. J. Watson Research Center), Yorktown Heights, N.Y., 1966-69, IBM fellow, 1969—; Scott lectr. Cavendish Lab., 1991. Contbr. articles on solid state theory, computing devices, statis. mechanics of computational process to profl. jours. Served with USNR, 1945-46. Recipient Stewart Ballantine medal Franklin Inst., 1992, Centennial medal Harvard U., 1993. Fellow IEEE, AAAS, Am. Phys. Soc. (Buckley prize 1995); mem. NAE, NAS, European Acad. Scis. and Arts, Am. Acad. Arts and Scis. Achievements include initiating IBM programs leading to injection laser, large scale integration. Office: IBM Rsch Ctr PO Box 218 Yorktown Heights NY 10598-0218

LANDAW, STEPHEN ARTHUR, physician, educator; b. Paterson, N.J., June 20, 1936; s. Louis and Ida (Machowsky) L.; children: Jared Lawrence, Nicole Renee. B.S., U. Wis., 1955; M.D., George Washington U., 1959; Ph.D., U. Calif., Berkeley, 1969. Cert. rsch. adminstr. Intern Mt. Sinai Hosp., N.Y.C., 1959-60; resident in internal medicine Mt. Sinai Hosp., 1960-61; fellow in hematology Med. Coll. Va., 1962-63; fellow in nuclear medicine Donner Lab., U. Calif., 1963-69, asst. physician, 1970-73; chief isotope lab. Highland-Alameda County Hosp., Oakland, Calif., 1970-73; asso. prof. SUNY, Syracuse, 1973-78; prof. SUNY, 1978—; asso. chief staff research and devel. VA Med. Center, Syracuse, 1973-94; vis. prof. Rockefeller U., N.Y.C., 1988; vis. physician Rockefeller U. Hosp., N.Y.C., 1988; pres. Ctrl. N.Y. Rsch. Corp., 1989-94. Contbr. in field. Served with U.S. Army, 1961-62. VA grantee, 1973-93; NASA grantee, 1976-82; recipient NASA Kosmos Achievement awards, 1975, 77. Fellow ACP; mem. Am. Soc. Hematology, Am. Fedn. Clin. Rsch., Am. Coll. Physician Execs., Soc. Pediat. Rsch., Soc. Rsch. Adminstrs., Soc. Exptl. Biology and Medicine, N.Y. Acad. Sci., Sigma Xi, Alpha Omega Alpha. Jewish. Home: 3159 Burrwood Dr Baldwinsville NY 13027-1708 Office: VA Med Ctr 800 Irving Ave Syracuse NY 13210-2716

LANDBERG, GEORGE GUSTAF, mechanical engineer; b. Seneca Falls, N.Y., Sept. 25, 1939; s. Erik Gustaf and Darthea Elizabeth (Wilgus) L.; m. Melody Anne Moore, Oct. 21, 1961; children: Peter (dec.), Cynthia, Jennifer. BS in Mech. Engring., U. Rochester, 1961, MS in Aerospace Sci., 1964. Registered profl. engr., N.Y. Devel. engr. Allis Chalmers Mfg. Co., Cin., 1961-63; teaching asst. U. Rochester, N.Y., 1963-65; v.p. Lightnin A Unit Gen. Signal Corp., Rochester, 1965-82; pres. Aerocleve-Pentech Divsn. Clevepak Corp., Fall River, Mass., 1982-83; v.p., gen. mgr. process sealing divsn. EG&G Sealol, Cranston, R.I., 1983-84; pres. Warren (Mass.) Pumps Inc., 1984-90; pres., CEO, Valcor Engring. Corp., Springfield, N.J., 1990-96, cons. engring. and mgmt., 1996—. Recipient Nat. Design award James F. Lincoln Arc Welding Found., Cleve., 1963, Commendation Bd. Edn., Fall River, Mass., 1983, Disting. Alumni award U. Rochester, 1986. Mem. ASME, Rochester Engring. Soc. (pres. 1979-80). Episcopalian. Achievements include patents for fan-cooled electric motor, draft tube arrangement for starting in settled solids, impeller for mixing liquids or the like; recognized authority in design of high specific speed axial flow impellers.

LANDE, JAMES AVRA, lawyer, contracts manager; b. Chgo., Oct. 2, 1930; s. S. Theodore and Helen C. (Hamburger) L.; m. Ann Mari Gustavsson, Feb. 21, 1959; children: Rebecca Susanne, Sylvia Diane. BA, Swarthmore Coll., 1952; JD, Columbia U., 1955; Bar: N.Y. 1958, Calif. 1967. Assoc. Rein, Mound & Cotton, N.Y.C., 1957-59; atty. VA, Seattle, 1959-61, Weyerhaeuser Co., Tacoma, 1961-63, Lande Assoc., San Francisco, 1963-67; atty. NASA, Ames Research Center, Moffett Field, Calif., 1967-70; house counsel Syntex Corp., Palo Alto, Calif., 1970-73; dir. contracts dept. Electric Power Research Inst., Palo Alto, Calif., 1973-81; corp. atty., dir contracts Lurgi Corp., Belmont, Calif., 1981-82; contracts mgr. Bechtel Corp., San Francisco, 1982-92, sr. contract mgr. Bay Area Rapid Transit Dist., Oakland, Calif., 1992—; adj. prof. U. San Francisco Sch. Law, 1972-73; lectr. law U. Santa Clara Sch. Law, 1968-82. Pres. Syntex Fed. Credit Union, 1971-72. Served with U.S. Army, 1955-57. Mem. Calif. Bar Assn., Nat. Contract Mgmt. Assn. (past pres., dir. Golden Gate chpt.), Lawyers Club of San Francisco. Home: 1330 33rd Ave San Francisco CA 94122-1305 Office: Bay Area Rapid Transit Dist PO Box 12688 1000 Broadway 6th flr Oakland CA 94604-2688

LANDEGGER, CARL CLEMENT, machinery and pulp manufacturing executive; b. Vienna, Austria, Sept. 20, 1930; came to US., 1937, naturalized, 1947; s. Karl F. and Helena (Berger) L. BS in Social Sci., Georgetown U., 1951; children: Christine, Carl, Claudia, Cary, Celia, Gregory. Vice chmn., Parsons and Whittemore, Inc., N.Y.C., 1953—; with Black Clawson Co., N.Y.C., 1956—, exec. v.p., 1959-65, pres., 1965—, chmn., 1967—; chmn. St. Anne Nackawic Pulp & Paper Co.; vice chmn. Ala. River Pulp Co., Monroeville, Ala. chmn. Pencor First Fiber, Inc.; bd. dirs. Georgetown U., Gregorian U. Found. 1st lt. USAF, 1951-53. Mem. Explorers Club, Road Runners Club (bd. dirs.). Office: Black Clawson Co 405 Lexington Ave Fl 61 New York NY 10174-6199

LANDEGGER, GEORGE F., engineering executive; b. 1937. BS, Georgetown U., 1958. With Parsons & Whittemore Inc., Port Chester, N.Y., 1960—, now CEO. Office: Parsons & Whittemore 4 International Dr Rye Brook NY 10573

LANDEL, ROBERT FRANKLIN, physical chemist, rheologist; b. Pendleton, N.Y., Oct. 10, 1925; s. Carlisle Oscar and Grace Elisabeth (McEachren) L.; m. Aurora Mamauag; children: Carlisle P., Grace P., Hans F., Robert F. Jr., Kevin L., Matthew N. BA, U. Buffalo, 1949, MA, 1950; PhD, U. Wis., 1954. Rsch. assoc. U. Wis., Madison, 1954-55; sr. rsch. engr. Jet Propulsion Lab. Calif. Inst. Tech., Pasadena, 1955-59, sect. mgr., 1959-85, sr. rsch. fellow CIT, 1966-69, sr. rsch. scientist Jet Propulsion Lab., 1980-92; cons., 1992—; rsch. affiliate Rancho Los Amigos Hosp., Downey, 1976—; vis. prof. Ecole Poly Fed., Lausanne, Switzerland, 1984, U. Philippines, Manila, 1993-94; cons. Sandia Nat. Labs., Albuquerque, 1983; mem. NASA Aircraft Fire Safety Tech. Panel, 1973-80; mem. U.S.-U.K. Working Group on Antimisting Aircraft Fuels, 1978-82, Joint Dept. Def./NASA Working Group on Mech. Properties of Solid Propellants, 1957-78, 85-92; cons. in field. Mem. editorial bd. various polymers jours.; contbr. over 90 articles to profl. jours.; patentee in field. Mem., officer YMCA Indian Guides, Altadena, Calif., 1960-74. With U.S. Army combat infantry, 1943-45, ETO. French Govt. fellow Sadron Inst., Strasbourg, 1972, Sr. Fulbright fellow U. Naples, Italy, 1971-72; recipient Exceptional Sci. Achievement award, NASA, 1976, Exceptional Svc. medal, 1989, Humboldt Sr. Rsch. Scientist award, 1990. Fellow Am. Phys. Soc. (exec. com. high polymer physics div.); mem. Soc. Rheology (v.p. 1983-85, pres. 1985-87), Am. Chem. Soc., Sigma Xi (sec.-treas. Caltech chpt. 1974-75, v.p. 1975-76, pres. 1976-77). Avocations: backpacking, camping, photography, hiking.

LANDEN, ROBERT GERAN, historian, university administrator; b. Boston, July 13, 1930; s. Harry James and Evelyn Gertrude (Geran) L.; m. Patricia Kizzia, July 19, 1958; children—Michael Geran, Robert Kizzia, Jill Arnett, Amy Patricia. A.B., Coll. of William and Mary, 1952; M.A., U. Mich., 1953; A.M., Princeton U., 1958, Ph.D. (Ford Found. fellow), 1961. Asst. prof. social sci. Ball State U., Muncie, Ind., 1959-60; asst. prof. near eastern studies U. Mich., Ann Arbor, 1960-61; asst. prof. history Dartmouth, Hanover, N.H., 1961-66; asst. dean of freshmen Dartmouth, 1963-64, asso. prof. history, 1966-67; prof., head dept. history Va. Poly. Inst. and State U., Blacksburg, 1967-69; prof. history U. S.C., Columbia, 1969-75; asso. vice provost U. S.C., 1971-72, asso. provost, 1972-73; dean U. S.C. (Coll. of Social and Behavioral Scis.), 1972-75; prof. history U. Tex. at Arlington, 1975-77; dean U. Tex. at Arlington (Coll. Liberal Arts), 1975-77; prof. history U. Tenn., Knoxville, 1977-86; dean Coll. Liberal Arts, 1977-85; prof. history, v.p. acad. affairs, provost U. Montevallo, 1986-88; prof. history and humanities, dir. programs in the humanities Va Poly Inst. and State U., Blacksburg, 1988—. Author: Oman Since 1856, 1967, The Emergence of the Modern Middle East, 1970, (with Abid Al-Marayati) The Middle East, Its Governments and Politics, 1972; contbr. articles to profl. jours. and book revs. to hist. publs. Served with AUS, 1953-55. Am. Coun. Learned Socs. fellow, 1965-66, Comparative Studies Ctr. Faculty fellow, 1965-66, Malone fellow, 1988. Fellow Middle East Studies Assn. of N. Am.; mem. Am. Hist. Assn., Middle East Inst., Theta Delta Chi, Phi Kappa Phi. Roman Catholic. Office: Va Poly Inst Office of Dir Programs Humanities Lane Hall Blacksburg VA 24061

LANDER, DAVID ALLAN, lawyer; b. St. Louis, Oct. 2, 1944; s. Louis and Edna (Schramm) L.; m. Carole Weissman Aug. 12, 1965; children—Brad, Rachel. B.A. cum laude, Bowdoin Coll., 1966; J.D., U. Chgo., 1969. Bar: Mo. 1969, U.S. Dist. Ct. (ea. dist.) Mo. 1969, U.S. Ct. Appeals (8th cir.) 1970. Atty., exec. dir. Legal Aid Soc St. Louis City-County, 1975-80; asst. prof. law, St. Louis U., 1973-75, instr., 1980—; ptnr. Thompson and Mitchell, St. Louis, 1981—; lectr. numerous programs on secured lending, bus. bankruptcy and workouts. Exec. com. mem. Consumer Counseling Credit Service, St. Louis; dir. Legal Services Eastern Mo. Mem. ABA (chmn. com. on agrl. and agri-bus. fin.), Am. Coll. Bankruptcy, Am. Coll. Comml. Finance Attys., Am. Law Inst. (study com. on article 9 uniform comml. code), Mo. Bar Assn., Bar Assn. Met. St. Louis. Contbr. articles to profl. jours. Office: Thompson & Mitchell 1 Mercantile Ctr Ste 3300 Saint Louis MO 63101-1643

LANDER, HOWARD, entertainment newspaper publisher; b. N.Y.C., Oct. 25, 1950; s. Leo T. and Doris (Davis) L.; m. Gail Melanie Ravitz, Sept. 6, 1976; children: Aimee, Jared. BA, Rutgers U., Newark, 1972. Sportswriter Buffalo Courier-Express, 1973; reporter Amusement Bus., N.Y.C., 1973-76, sales rep., 1976-79; advt. mgr. Residential Interiors mag., N.Y.C., 1980; pub. Amusement Bus., Nashville, 1981-88; v.p., group pub. BPI Communications, 1988-90; pub. Billboard Mag., N.Y.C., 1990-91; sr. v.p. BPI Comms., 1991-92; exec. v.p., 1993—. Mem. Country Music Assn., Internat. Assn. Auditorium Mgrs., Internat. Assn. Amusement Parks and Attractions, Assn. Bus. Pubs. Lodge: B'nai Brith. Avocations: raquetball, tennis, music.

LANDERS, ANN (MRS. ESTHER P. LEDERER), columnist; b. Sioux City, Iowa, July 4, 1918; d. Abraham B. and Rebecca (Rushall) Friedman; m. Jules W. Lederer, July 2, 1939 (div. 1975); 1 dau., Margo Lederer Howard. Student, Morningside Coll., 1936-39, LHD (hon.), 1964; hon. degree, Wilberforce (Ohio) Coll., 1972, Am. Coll. Greece, 1979, Meharry Med. Coll., 1981, Jacksonville U., 1983, St. Leo Coll., 1984, Fla. Internat. U., 1984, Med. Coll. Pa., 1985, New Eng. Coll., 1985, U. Wis., 1985, Lincoln Coll., 1986, Nat. Coll. Edn., 1986, Southwestern Adventist Coll., 1987, Duke U., 1987, Rosary Coll., 1989, U. Hartford, 1989, L.I. U., 1989, Med. Coll. Ohio, 1989, Roosevelt U., 1991, Ind. U., 1991, Howard U., 1991, Bellevue U., 1992, DePaul U., 1992, Ursinus Coll., 1992, Hillsdale Coll., 1993, St. Xavier U., 1993, Chgo. Theol. Sem., 1993, Barry U., 1993, Northwestern U., 1994, Columbia Coll., 1995. Syndicated columnist Chgo., 1955—; pres. Eppie Co., Inc., Chgo. Author: Since You Asked Me, 1962, Ann Landers Talks to Teen-agers about Sex, 1964, Truth is Stranger, 1968, Ann Landers Speaks Out, 1975, The Ann Landers Encyclopedia, 1978; also pub. svc. booklets and numerous mag. articles; syndicated columnist Los Angeles Times-Creators Syndicates. Chmn. Eau Claire (Wis.) Gray-Lady Corps, ARC, 1947-53; chmn. Minn.-Wis. council Anti-Defamation League, 1945-49; asst. Wis. chmn. Nat. Found. Infantile Paralysis, 1951-53; hon. nat. chmn. 1963 Tb Christmas Seal Campaign; bd. sponsors Mayo Clinic, 1970; mem. sponsors com. Mayo Found.; nat. adv. bd. Dialogue for the Blind, 1972; adv. com. on better health services AMA; county chmn. Democratic Party Eau Claire; bd. dirs. Rehab. Inst. Chgo.; nat. bd. dirs. Am. Cancer Soc., Nat. Cancer Inst.; vis. com. bd. overseers Harvard Med. Sch.; mem. Pres.'s Commn. Drunk Driving; trustee Menninger Found., Nat. Dermatology Found., Am. Coll. Greece, Deree-Pierce Coll., Athens, Meharry Med. Sch., Hereditary Disease Found.; dirs. adv. bd. Yale Comprehensive Cancer Ctr. Recipient award Nat. Family Service Assn., 1965, Adolf Meyer award Assn. Mental Health N.Y., 1965, Pres.'s Citation and nat. award Nat. Council on Alcoholism, 1966, 2d nat. award, 1975, Golden Stethoscope award Ill. Med. Soc., 1967, Humanitarianism award Internat. Lions Club, 1967; plaque of honor Am. Friends of Hebrew U., 1968, Gold Plate award Acad. Achievement, 1969; Nat. Service award Am. Cancer Soc., 1971, Robert T. Morse award Am. Psychiat. Assn., 1972; plaque recognizing establishment of chair in chem. immunology Weizmann Inst., 1974, Jane Addams Public Service award Hull House, 1977, Health Achievement award Nat. Kidney Found., 1978, Nat. award Epilepsy Found. Am., 1978, James Ewing Layman's award Soc. Surg. Oncologists, 1979, citation for disting. service AMA, 1979, Thomas More medal Thomas More Assn., 1979, NEA award, 1979, Margaret Sanger award, 1979, Stanley G. Kay medal Am. Cancer Soc., 1983, 1st William C. Menninger medal for achievement in mental health, 1984, Albert Lasker pub. service award, 1985, Edwin C. Whitehead award, 1988, Community Svc. award Gateway Found.'s Citizen's Coun., 1989, Pub. Svc. award NIMH, 1989, award for outstanding pub. edn. Nat. Alliance for the Mentally Ill, 1990, Outstanding Pub. Svc. to Sci. award Nat. Assn. for Biomed. Rsch., 1990, World of Children award UNICEF, 1993, Auxiliary Pub. Spirit award Am. Legion, 1995. Fellow Chgo. Gynecol. Soc. (citizen hon.); mem. LWV (pres. 1948), Brandeis U. Women (pres. 1960), Chgo. Econs. Club (dir. 1975), Harvard Club (Award 1994), Sigma Delta Chi. Clubs: Chgo. Econs. (dir. 1975), Harvard, Sigma Delta Chi. Office: Chgo Tribune 435 N Michigan Ave Chicago IL 60611-4001 *Trouble is the great equalizer. It doesn't make any difference who you are, or what you have, when you and your neighbor share the same problem you become brothers and sisters under the skin.*

LANDERS, JAMES MICHAEL (JIM LANDERS), international editor; b. San Francisco, Calif., Feb. 11, 1951; s. William Edward and Loretta Mae (Fouts) L.; m. Susan Ann Moran, Dec. 26, 1981; children: Amy Foster, Noelle Christine, Jessica Elizabeth. BA in English with honors, Va. Poly. Inst. and State U., 1974. Staff writer The Washington Post, 1971-74; freelance journalist Belfast, Northern Ireland, 1974; staff writer The Richmond (Va.) Mercury, 1975, The Trenton (N.J.) Times, 1975-77; features editor Arab News, Jeddah, Saudi Arabia, 1978-79; sr. editor Saudi Bus. & Arab Econ. Report, Jeddah, 1979-80; Washington corr. The Dallas Morning News, Washington, 1981-88; internat. editor The Dallas Morning News, Dallas, 1988-94, internat. affairs corr. Washington bur., 1994—. U.S. del. French-Am. Found., Taormina Young Leaders Conf., 1989. Named Outstanding Washington corr. Nat. Press Club, 1985, Finalist Pulitzer prize for Explanatory Journalism, N.Y.C., 1990; recipient World Hunger Media award World Hunger Yr., N.Y.C., 1990, Pulitzer prize for Internat. Reporting, 1994. Mem. Coun. Fgn. Rels., Am. Coun. on Germany, Dallas Com. Fgn. Rels. Roman Catholic. Avocations: running, camping, home renovation, model railroading. Home: 5208 Knoughton Way Centreville VA 22020-3336 Office: The Dallas Morning News Communications Ctr PO Box 655237 Dallas TX 75265-5237

LANDERS, RENÉE MARIE, government lawyer; b. Springfield, Ill., July 25, 1955; d. Robert Edward and Marvel Margaret (Neal) L.; m. Thomas L. Barrette, Jr., Aug. 2, 1980; 1 child, Nelson Landers Barrette. AB, Harvard U.-Radcliffe Coll., 1977; JD, Boston Coll., 1985. Bar: Mass. 1985, U.S. Dist. Ct. Mass. 1986, U.S. Ct. Appeals (Ist cir.) 1986. Program devel. specialist Office Mass. Sec. State, Boston, 1978-79, chief adminstrv. asst. to sec., 1979-80, dep. sec. state for pub. records, acting supr. pub. records, 1980, dep. sec. state Comml. Bur., 1980-82; law clk. to chief justice Mass. Supreme Jud. Ct., Boston, 1985-86; assoc. Ropes & Gray, Boston, 1986-88; asst. prof. law Boston Coll. Law Sch., Newton, Mass., 1988-93; dep. asst. atty. gen. Office of Policy Devel. U.S. Dept. Justice, 1993-96; dep. gen. counsel U.S. Dept. Health and Human Svcs., Washington, 1996—; mem., subcom. co-chmn. gender bias study Mass. Supreme Jud. Ct., 1986-89, mem. racial and ethnic bias study, 1990-94. Mem. editl. bd. Mass. Law Rev., 1987-93, Am. Jour. Law and Medicine, 1989-93. Mem. bd. overseers Harvard U., 1991—; mem. Watertown (Mass.) Dem. Town Com., 1981-93, vice chmn., 1986-93; trustee Radcliffe Coll., 1987-89; bd. dirs., v.p. Hist. Mass., Inc., 1989—, Big Sister Assn. Greater Boston, 1990-93; bd. dirs. Mass. Eye and Ear Infirmary, 1993-96. Mem. Boston Bar Assn. (coun. 1988-91, chmn. com. on gender and justice 1989-93), Harvard U. Alumni Assn. (nominating com. for dirs. and overseers 1981-84, bd. dirs. 1990-92), Radcliffe Coll. Alumnae Assn. (pres. 1987-89, nominating com. 1983-84). Avocations: choral singing, jogging, tennis, reading. Office: Dept Justice Rm 4248 Main Bldg 10th St/Constitution Ave NW Washington DC 20530

LANDERS, STEVEN E., lawyer; b. N.Y.C., May 23, 1947. BA, Antioch Coll., 1969; JD, Harvard U., 1973. Gen. counsel N.Y. State Exec. adv. com. Sentencing, 1978-79; sec. N.Y. State adv. commn. Adminstrn. Justice, 1981-83; ptnr. Paul, Weiss, Rifkind, Wharton & Garrison, N.Y.C. and Paris. Mem. Internat. Bar Assn., Assn. Bar City N.Y., D.C. Bar, Am. C. of C. in France (chmn. pres.'s coun. 1995—). Office: Paul Weiss et al, 199 Boulevard Saint Germain, 75007 Paris France

LANDERS, TERESA PRICE, librarian; b. N.Y.C., Dec. 28, 1954; d. Stanley and June Ethel (Novick) Price; m. Gary David Landers, Sept. 2, 1979; children: Joshua Price, Alisha Rose. BA in History cum laude, Williams Coll., 1976; MA in LS, U. Denver, 1978; postgrad., Ctrl. Wash. U., 1980. Libr., asst. analyst Earl Combs, Inc., Mercer Island, Wash., 1979;

reference libr. Yakima (Wash.) Valley Regional Libr., 1981-83, coord. youth svcs., 1983-84; libr. Tempe (Ariz.) Pub. Libr., 1984-85; supervisory libr. Mesa (Ariz.) Pub. Libr., 1985-90; head telephone reference Phoenix Pub. Libr., 1990-91, head bus. and scis., 1991-95; info. svcs. mgr., 1995—; cons. Fed. Dept. Corrections, Phoenix, 1993. Mem. Ariz. Right To Choose, Phoenix, 1992—. Mem. ALA, Ariz. Libr. Assn., Phoenix C. of C. (libr. rep. 1993—), Nat. Wildlife Fedn. (life), Beta Phi Mu. Democrat. Unitarian. Avocations: cooking, camping. Office: Phoenix Libr Info Svcs Dept 1221 N Central Phoenix AZ 85004

LANDERS, VERNETTE TROSPER, writer, educator, association executive; b. Lawton, Okla., May 3, 1912; d. Fred Gilbert and LaVerne Hamilton (Stevens) Trosper; m. Paul Albert Lum, Aug. 29, 1952 (dec. May 1955); 1 child, William Tappan; m. 2d, Newlin Landers, May 2, 1959 (dec. Apr. 1990); children: Lawrence, Marlin. AB with honors, UCLA, 1933, MA, 1935, EdD, 1953; Cultural doctorate (hon.) Lit. World U., Tucson, 1985. Tchr. secondary schs., Montebello, Calif., 1935-45, 48-50, 51-59; prof. Long Beach City Coll., 1946-47; asst. prof. Los Angeles State Coll., 1950; dean girls Twenty Nine Palms (Calif.) High Sch., 1960-65; dist. counselor Morongo (Calif.) Unified Sch. Dist., 1965-72, coordinator adult edn., 1965-67, guidance project dir., 1967; clk.-in-charge Landers (Calif.) Post Office, 1962-82; ret., 1982. V.p., sec. Landers Assn., 1965—; sec. Landers Vol. Fire Dept., 1972—; life mem. Hi-Desert Playhouse Guild, Hi-Desert Meml. Hosp. Guild; bd. friends Copper Mountain Coll., 1990-91; bd. dirs., sec. Desert Emergency Radio Service; mem. Rep. Senatorial Inner Circle, 1990-92, Regent Nat. Fedn. Rep. Women, 1990-92, Nat. Rep. Congl. Com., 1990-91, Presdl. Task Force, 1990-92; lifetime mem. Girl Scouts U.S., 1991. Recipient internat. diploma of honor for community service, 1973; Creativity award Internat. Personnel Research Assn., 1972, award Goat Mt. Grange No. 818, 1987; cert. of merit for disting. svc. to edn., 1973; Order of Rose, 1978, Order of Pearl, 1989, Alpha Xi Delta; poet laureate Center of Internat. Studies and Exchanges, 1981; diploma of merit in letters U. Arts, Parma, Italy, 1982; Golden Yr. Bruin UCLA, 1983; World Culture prize Nat. Ctr. for Studies and Research, Italian Acad., 1984; Golden Palm Diploma of Honor in poetry Leonardo Da Vinci Acad., 1984; Diploma of Merit and titular mem. internat. com. Internat. Ctr. Studies and Exchanges, Rome, 1984; Recognition award San Gorgonio council Girl Scouts U.S., 1984—; Cert. of appreciation Morongo Unified Sch. Dist., 1984, 89; plaque for contribution to postal service and community U.S. Postal Service, 1984; Biographee of Yr. award for outstanding achievement in the field of edn. and service to community Hist. Preservations of Am.; named Princess of Poetry of Internat. Ctr. Cultural Studies and Exchange, Italy, 1985; community dinner held in her honor for achievement and service to Community, 1984; Star of Contemporary Poetry Masters of Contemporary Poetry, Internat. Ctr. Cultural Studies and Exchanges, Italy, 1984; named to honor list of leaders of contemporary art and lit. and apptd. titular mem. of Internat. High Com. for World Culture & Arts Leonardo Da Vinci Acad., 1987; named to honor list Foremost Women 20th Century for Outstanding Contbn. to Rsch., IBC, 1987; Presdl. Order of Merit Pres. George Bush-Exec. Coun. of Nat. Rep. Senatorial Com., Congl. cert. of Appreciation U.S. Ho. of Reps.; other awards and certs. Life fellow Internat. Acad. Poets, World Lit. Acad.; mem. Am. Personnel and Guidance Assn., Internat. Platform Assn., Nat. Ret. Tchrs. Assn., Calif. and Nat. Assn. for Counseling and Devel., Am. Assn. for Counseling and Devel. (25 yr. membership pin 1991), Nat. Assn. Women Deans and Adminstrs., Montebello Bus. and Profl. Women's Club (pres.), Nat. League Am. Pen Women (sec. 1985-86), Leonardo Da Vinci Acad. Internat. Winged Glory diploma of honor in letters 1982), Landers Area C. of C. (sec. 1985-86, Presdl. award for outstanding service, Internat. Honors Cup 1992-93), Desert Nature Mus., Phi Beta Kappa, Pi Lambda Theta (Mortar Bd., Prytanean UCLA, UCLA Golden Yr. Bruin 1983), Sigma Delta Pi, Pi Delta Phi. Clubs: Whittier Toastmistress (Calif.) (pres. 1957); Homestead Valley Women's (Landers). Lodge: Soroptimists (sec. 29 Palms chpt. 1962, life mem., Soroptimist of Yr. local chpt. 19, Woman of Distinction local chpt. 1987-88). Author: Impy, 1974, Talkie, 1975, Impy's Children, 1975; Nineteen O Four, 1976, Little Brown Bat, 1976; Slo-Go, 1977; Owls Who and Who Who, 1978; Sandy, The Coy, 1979; The Kit Fox and the Walking Stick, 1980; contbr. articles to profl. jours., poems to anthologies. Guest of honor ground breaking ceremony Landers Elem. Sch., 1989, dedication ceremony, 1991. Home: 632 N Landers Ln PO Box 3839 Landers CA 92285

LANDES, BARBARA L., management consultant. V.p., fin. CFO Wyatt Corp.

LANDES, GEORGE MILLER, biblical studies educator; b. Kansas City, Mo., Aug. 2, 1928; s. George Y. and Margaret B. (Fizzell) L.; m. Carol Marie Dee, Aug. 30, 1953; children: George Miller Jr., Margaret Dee, John Christopher. A.B., U. Mo., 1949; M.Div., McCormick Theol. Sem., 1952; Ph.D., Johns Hopkins U., 1956. Minister to youth Second Presbyn. Ch., Balt., 1952-53, Govans Presbyn. Ch., Balt., 1953-56; instr. Old Testament Union Theol. Sem., N.Y.C., 1956-58, asst. prof. Old Testament, 1958-62, assoc. prof., 1962-70, prof., 1970-95; prof. emeritus Union Theol. Sem, N.Y.C., 1995—; ann. prof. Am. Sch. Oriental Research, Jerussalem, Israel, 1967-68. Author: A Student's Vocabulary of Biblical Hebrew, 1961; editor, author: Report on Archaeological Work, 1975. Nettie F. McCormick fellow, 1952-54; Am. Council Learned Socs. fellow, 1967-68. Mem. Soc. Bibl. Lit., Amman Ctr. Archaeol. Rsch. (v.p. 1969-79), Am. Schs. Oriental Rsch. (sec. 1972-94), Phi Beta Kappa.

LANDES, ROBERT PAUL, architect; b. Houston, Jan. 29, 1926; s. Paul Washington and Walterene (Beasley) L.; m. Sarah Jeannine Early, May 22, 1954; children: Robert Paul Jr., Jennifer Lynn, Cindy Kay. BArch, U. Tex., 1950. Registered architect, Tex.; registered interior designer, Tex. Draftsman Ebasco Engrs., N.Y.C., 1948, Nunn & McGinty, Houston, 1949-50; designer, draftsman Bd. for Tex. State Hosps. and Spl. Schs., Austin, 1950-55; prin. Barnes, Landes, Goodman & Youngblood, Austin, 1955-88; prin., pres. BLGY, Inc., Austin, 1988—. Precinct chmn. Dem. Cen. Com., Austin, 1966-71; divsn. chmn. United Way, 1972; dir. Sunday sch. First Bapt. Ch., Austin, 1968-70, chmn. deacons, 1980. Cpl. U.S. Army, 1944-46. Mem. AIA (pres. Austin chpt. 1966-67), Austin Bass Club (Sportsmanship award 1981), Austin Woods and Waters Club (pres. 1965-66, Sportsman of Yr. 1976), N.E. Kiwanis (pres., bd. dirs. 1966-67, Top Fund Raiser award 1966-70), Delta Kappa Epsilon Alumni Club (v.p. 1957). Avocations: sports, fishing, music. Home: 7506 Greenhaven Dr Austin TX 78757-1706 Office: BLGY Inc 1600 W 38th St Ste 100 Austin TX 78731-6404

LANDES, WILLIAM M., law educator; b. 1939. AB, Columbia U., 1960, PhD in Econs., 1966. Asst. prof. econs. Stanford U., 1965-66; asst. prof. U. Chgo., 1966-69; asst. prof. Columbia U., 1969-72; assoc. prof. Grad. Ctr., CUNY, 1972-73; now prof. U. Chgo. Law Sch.; founder, chmn. Lexecon Inc.,1977—; mem. bd. examiners GRE in Econs., ETS, 1967-74. Mem. Am. Econ. Assn., Am. Law and Econ. Assn. (v.p. 1991-92, pres. 1992-93), Mont Pelerin Soc. Author: (with Richard Posner) The Economic Structure of Tort Law, 1987; editor: (with Gary Becker) Essays in the Economics of Crime and Punishment, 1974; editor Jour. Law and Econs., 1975-91, Jour. Legal Studies, 1991—. Office: U Chgo Sch Law 1111 E 60th St Chicago IL 60637-2702 also: Lexecon Inc 332 S Michigan Ave Chicago IL 60604-4301

LANDESMAN, FREDRIC ROCCO, theatre executive; b. St. Louis, July 20, 1947; s. Alfred and Paula (Berwald) L.; m. Heidi Prentice Ettinger, June 18, 1977; children: North, Nash, Dodge. BA, U. Wis., 1969; MFA, Yale U., 1972, DFA, 1976. Asst. prof. Sch. Drama, Yale U., New Haven, 1972-77; pres. Jujamcyn Theatres, N.Y.C., 1987—; bd. dirs. Municipal Arts Soc., 1989—; owner, mgr. The Cardinal Fund A Pvt. Hedge Fund, 1977-90; bd. dirs. Actor's Fund, N.Y.C., 1990—. Editor Yale/Theater mag., 1972-77; contbr. articles, revs. to profl. jours.; producer Broadway mus. Big River, Into the Woods, The Secret Garden. Bd. dirs. Ednl. Found. Am., Westport, Conn., 1980-87, Ettinger Found., N.Y.C., 1984—. Recipient Tony award Am. Theater Wing, 1985. Mem. League Am. Theaters and Producers (exec. bd. 1987—). Democrat. Jewish. Avocations: baseball, horse racing, country music, reading.

LANDESMAN, HEIDI, set designer. Set designs include Big River, 1984 (Drama Desk award, Set Design, Tony award, Musical, 1985, Tony award, Scenic Designer), Secret Garden, 1990 (Drama Desk award, Set Design, Tony award, Scenic Designer, 1991), A Midsummer Night's Dream, 1982 (Obie award, Design), Painting Churches, 1982 (Obie award, Design). Office: Second Stage Ansonia Sta PO Box 1807 New York NY 10023-9453

LANDESS, FRED S., lawyer; b. Memphis, Jan. 27, 1933; s. Sterling Stone and Beulah Elizabeth (Melton) L.; m. Catherine Sue Lee, Dec. 27, 1953; children—Susan Elinor, Charles Barton, Catherine Elizabeth. Student, Wake Forest Coll., 1951-53; A.B., George Washington U., 1955; LL.B., U. Va., 1958. Bar: Va. 1958. Enforcement atty. NLRB, Washington, 1958-60; assoc., then ptnr. McGuire, Woods, Battle & Boothe, Charlottesville, VA., 1960—. Sec. Bd. Zoning Appeals, City of Charlottesville, Va., 1967-69; bd. dirs. YMCA, Charlottesville, 1975, Westminister Child Care Ctr., Charlottesville, 1978. Fellow Am. Coll. Real Estate Lawyers; mem. Charlottesville-Albemarle Bar Assn. (pres. 1983-84), Va. Bar Assn. (real estate com.), Va. State Bar (7th dist. disciplinary com. 1986-88, sec. 1987, chmn. 1987-88), Charlottesville-Albemarle Bd. Realtors (assoc.), Blue Ridge Homebuilders Assn. (assoc.). Democrat. Presbyterian. Clubs: Boar's Head Sports (Charlottesville). Avocations: tennis, sailing, gardening. Home: 806 Gilliams Mountain Rd Charlottesville VA 22903-9756

LANDESS, MIKE (MALCOLM LEE LANDESS, III), television news anchorman; b. Houston, June 20, 1946; s. Malcolm Lee Jr. Landess and Joyce Ardis (Halley) Quitter; m. Mary Lou Porter, June 30, 1968 (div. Jan. 1972); children: Kristen and Jennifer; m. Madeleine Buchanan Buchholz, Aug. 17, 1986; children: Emily, Dana and Hayley Buchholz. Grad., Robert E. Lee H.S., Tyler, Tex. Radio reporter WFAA-AM, Dallas, 1969-70; TV reporter WFAA-TV, Dallas, 70-72, KTRK-TV, Houston, 1972-73; noon anchor, reporter KYW-TV, Phila., 1973-74; NBC news anchor WKYC-TV, Cleve., 1974-77; news anchor KUSA-TV, Denver, 1977-93; Gannett anchor WXIA-TV, Atlanta, 1993—. anchor, reporter, producer: (TV documentary) Wednesday's Child, 1978, Fight of His Life, 1982; anchor, reporter (TV spl.) Say "NO" to Strangers, 1979. Bd. dirs. Am. Cancer Soc., Denver, 1982-86, Colo. Head Injury Assn., Denver, 1990-93, Brain Injury Assn Ga., Atlanta, 1994—. Recipient numerous Emmy awards: Outstanding Achievement Anchor, 1988, 91, Outstanding Achievement Children's Programming, 1983, TV Programming Excellence, 1995, Outstanding Achievement award Luth. Social Svcs., Am. Cancer Soc. Mem. NATAS, Radio & TV News Dir. Assn., Atlanta Press Club, Sigma Delta Chi. Baptist. Avocations: vintage guitars, motorsports. Office: WXIA-TV 1611 W Peachtree St NE Atlanta GA 30309

LANDETA, SEAN, professional football player; b. Balt., Jan. 6, 1962. Student, Towson State U. With Phila. Stars, U.S. Football League, 1983-84, Balt. Stars, U.S. Football League, 1985, N.Y. Giants, NFL, 1985-93, L.A. Rams, NFL, 1993-94; punter St. Louis Rams, NFL, 1995—. Named to U.S. Football League All-Star Team, Sporting News, 1983-84, to NFL All-Pro Team, Sporting News, 1986, 89, 90, to NFL Pro Bown Team, 1986, 90; mem. N.Y. Giants Super Bowl Champion Team, 1986, 90. Office: St Louis Rams Matthews-Dickey Boys Club Saint Louis MO 63115-1276

LANDGREBE, DAVID ALLEN, electrical engineer; b. Huntingburg, Ind., Apr. 12, 1934; s. Albert E. and Sarah A. L.; m. Margaret Ann Swank, June 7, 1959; children: James David, Carole Ann, Mary Jane. BSEE, Purdue U., 1956, MSEE, 1958, PhD, 1962. Mem. tech. staff Bell Telephone Labs., Murray Hill, N.J., 1956; electronics engr. Interstate Electronics Corp., Anaheim, Calif., 1958, 59, 62; mem. faculty Purdue U., West Lafayette, Ind., 1962—; dir. lab. for applications of remote sensing Purdue U., 1969-81, prof. elec. engring., 1970—, assoc. dean engring., 1981-84; head sch. elec. and computer engring. Purdue U., West Lafayette, 1995—; rsch. scientist Douglas Aircraft Co., Newport Beach, Calif., 1964; dir. Univ. Space Rsch. Assn., 1975-78. Author: (with others) Remote Sensing: The Quantitative Approach, 1978. Recipient medal for exceptional sci. achievement NASA, 1973, William T. Pecora award NASA/U.S. Dept. Interior, 1990. Fellow IEEE (pres. Geosci. and Remote Sensing Soc. 1986-87, Sci. Achievement award 1992), Am. Soc. Photogrammetry and Remote Sensing; mem. AAAS, Am. Soc. for Engring. Edn., Sigma Xi, Tau Beta Pi, Eta Kappa Nu. Office: Purdue U Dept Elec Engring West Lafayette IN 47907-1285

LANDGREBE, JOHN ALLAN, chemistry educator; b. San Francisco, May 6, 1937; s. Herbert Frederick and Janet Miller (Allan) L.; m. Carolyn Jean Thomson, Dec. 23, 1961; children—Carolyn Janet, John Frederick. B.S., U. Calif.-Berkeley, 1959; Ph.D., U. Ill., 1962. Asst. prof. U. Kans., Lawrence, 1962-67, assoc. prof., 1967-71, prof., 1971—, dept. chmn., 1970-80; vis. prof. U. Calif.-Berkeley, 1974. Author: Theory and Practice in the Organic Laboratory, 1973, 4th edit., 1993. NSF fellow, 1960-62; E. Watkins Faculty fellow U. Kans., 1963. Mem. Am. Chem. Soc., Royal Soc. of Chemistry, Phi Lambda Upsilon. Republican. Lutheran. Avocations: metal enameling; painting; camping; hiking. Home: 1125 Highland Dr Lawrence KS 66044-4523 Office: U Kansas Dept Chemistry Lawrence KS 66045

LANDGREN, CRAIG RANDALL, biology educator; b. St. Paul, Dec. 20, 1947; s. C. Robert and Alice Elizabeth (Ryder) L.; m. Susan Carina Gatwood, July 23, 1983. BA summa cum laude, Albion Coll., 1969; MA in Biology, Harvard U., 1970, PhD, 1974. Asst. prof. George Mason U., Fairfax, Va., 1974-77; vis. asst. prof. U. Oreg., Eugene, 1976-77; asst. prof. Middlebury Coll., Vt., 1977-82, assoc. prof., 1982-89, prof., 1989—, chmn. dept. biology, 1982-88, 92, 93-96, dir. No. Studies program, 1984-87, chmn. natural scis. div., 1985-88; dir. SCIENS minority program, 1987-90, 92; dir. Reaccreditation Self-Study, 1989-90; dir. Freshman Seminar Program, 1990-91, 95-96, dir. Writing Program, 1992-93; dean instrnl. resources, 1995-96; rsch. assoc. U. Oreg., 1978, 79, 80; exch. scientist U.S. Nat. Acad. Scis. program, Moscow and Kiev, 1980. Author: The Trees of the Middlebury College Campus, 1981; contbr. articles to profl. jours. Auditor Addison N.E. Union Supervisory Dist., 1988-91, Lincoln Hist. Soc., 1989-92, Danforth Assocs. New Eng., 1989-93; devel. com., The Coll. Bd. ATP Biology Ach. Test, 1990-95, chair, 1992-95. Albion fellow, 1969. Mem. Sigma Xi, Phi Beta Kappa (pres. Beta of Vt. 1985-87), Omicron Delta Kappa, Phi Eta Sigma, Beta Beta Beta (founder George Mason U. chpt. 1976). Avocations: painting, cooking, stained glass, woodworking. Home: 16 Springside Rd Middlebury VT 05753-1229 Office: Middlebury Coll Dept Biology Middlebury VT 05753-6151

LANDGREN, GEORGE LAWRENCE, electrical engineer, consultant; b. Duluth, Minn., July 22, 1919; s. Clarence Robert and Bertha Elizabeth (Borgeson) L.; m. Anna Jean Sinamark, July 26, 1943; children: Karen J., Nancy E., Larry A., David G. B.E.E., U. Minn., 1941; M.S.E.E., Northwestern U., 1955. Registered profl. engr., Ill. Elec. engr. Commonwealth Edison Co., Chgo., 1941-85. Served to capt. U.S. Army, 1942-46, PTO. Fellow IEEE (life, Best Paper 1973). Republican. Presbyterian.

LANDI, DALE MICHAEL, industrial engineer, academic administrator; b. Cleve., July 8, 1938; s. Lawrence Roy and Lillian (Caramell) L.; m. Mary Margaret Lipke, Mar. 23, 1974; children: Michael Kenneth, Kristin Marie. BS, Northwestern U., 1960, MS, 1963, PhD, 1965. Systems analyst Gen. Electric Corp., Chgo., 1960-61; research specialist Rand Corp., Santa Monica, Calif., 1965-68, assoc. dept. head, 1968-70, program dir., 1973-78, v.p., 1978-87; asst. budget dir. N.Y.C., 1970-71; asst. police commr. N.Y.C., 1971-73; v.p. SUNY, Buffalo, 1987—. Home: 238 Brantwood Rd Buffalo NY 14226-4306 Office: SUNY at Buffalo 516 Capen Blvd Buffalo NY 14226-2822

LANDIN, DAVID CRAIG, lawyer; b. Jamestown, N.Y., Aug. 1, 1946; s. David Carl and Rita Mae (Felthaus) L.; m. Susan Ann Gregory, July 11, 1970; children: Mary Stuart, Alexander Craig, David Reed. BA, U. Va., 1968, JD, 1972. Bar: Va. 1972, Pa. 1991, Tex. 1992, U.S. Supreme Ct. 1979. Ptnr. McGuire, Woods & Battle, Richmond, Va., 1972-95, mgr. of product liability and litigation mgmt. group, 1987-95; gen. counsel Va. Assn. Ind. Schs., 1989—, Coun. for Religion in Ind. Schs., 1990—; ptnr. Hunton & Williams, Richmond, Va., 1995—; pres. The Landin Cos., 1994—. Trustee Va. Law Found., 1981—, v.p. 1986-87, pres. 1987-88; trustee St. Anne's Belfield Sch., Charlottesville, Va., 1984—, chmn. trusteeship com., 1985-87, exec. com. 1985—, sec. 1988—; mem. long-range planning com. Ch. Schs. of Episcopal Diocese Va., 1988-91; chmn. ctrl. Va. chpt. Nat. MS Soc., 1995-96. With USAR, 1968-74. Fellow Va. Law Found. (DRI Exceptional Performance award 1988); mem. ABA, Va. Bar Assn. (chmn. young lawyers sect. 1979-80, chmn. com. on Issues of State and Nat. Importance 1982-90, chmn. judiciary com. 1990-95, exec. com. 1994—), Va. Assn. Def. Attys. (regional v.p. 1982-84, pres. 1987-88, chmn. long range planning com. 1990—), Charlottesville-Albemarle Bar Assn. (sec., treas. 1975-77, chmn. young lawyers sect. 1975-78), Richmond Bar Assn., Def. Rsch. Inst., Country Club Va., Commonwealth Club. Roman Catholic. Avocations: squash, tennis. Home: 310 Oak Ln Richmond VA 23226-1639 Office: Hunton & Williams East Tower 951 E Byrd St Richmond VA 23219-4074

LANDINI, RICHARD GEORGE, university president, emeritus English educator; b. Pitts., June 4, 1929; s. George R. and Alice (Hoy) L.; m. Phyllis Lesnick, Nov. 26, 1952 (dec. Mar. 1992); children: Richard, Gregory, Matthew, Cynthia, Vincent. A.B., U. Miami, 1954, M.A., 1956; Ph.D., U. Fla., 1959; D.Civil Law, Quincy Coll., 1985; LLD, U. Miami, 1980, Baiko Jo Gakuin Coll., Japan, 1987; Ind. State U., 1996. From asst. prof. to prof. English Ariz. State U., 1959-70, dean, 1968-70; prof. English, acad. v.p. U. Mont., 1970-75; pres. Ind. State U., 1975-92, prof. English, 1975—. Contbr. articles on lit. and higher edn. to profl. jours. Served with U.S. Army, 1948-51. Decorated knight of the Holy Sepulchre Jerusalem, 1996. Mem. Phi Beta Kappa, Phi Delta Kappa, Phi Alpha Theta, Phi Kappa Phi, Sigma Tau Delta. Roman Catholic. Office: Ind State Univ Dept English Root Hall # A-288 Terre Haute IN 47809

LANDIS, DAVID MORRISON, state legislator; b. Lincoln, Nebr., June 10, 1948; m. Melodee Ann McPherson, June 6, 1969; children: Matthew, Melissa. BA U. Nebr., 1970, JD, 1971, M in Cmty. Regional Planning, 1995, MPA U. Nebr., Omaha, 1984. Bar: Nebr. 1972; practice law, Lincoln, 1972-74; mem. Nebr. Legislature, 1978—, chmn. govt. mil. and vets. affairs com., 1983-87, chmn. banking, commerce and ins., 1988—; instr. Coll. Law U. Nebr., 1990—; adj. faculty mem. dept. pub. adminstrn. U. Nebr., Omaha, 1984, adj. faculty mem. NE Wesleyan U., 1995—; adj. mem. bus. faculty Doane Coll., 1985-95. Named Doane Coll. Tchr. of Yr., 1987, 88, 92. Bd. dirs. Lower Platte S. Natural Resources Dist., 1971-78; officer PTA, 1979-80; adminstrv. law judge Dept. Labor, 1977-78; mem. Nebr. Humanities Council; mem. NE Repertory Theatre. Mem. The Innocents Soc. (hon.), Golden Key Soc. (hon., U. Nebr.). Office: State Legislature State Capitol Lincoln NE 68509

LANDIS, DONNA MARIE, nursing administrator, women's health nurse; b. Lebanon, Pa., Sept. 5, 1944; d. James O.A. and Helen Joan (Fritz) Muench; m. David J. Landis, 1967 (div. 1985); children: Danielle M. Landis Farley, David J., Derek J.; m. John C. Broderick, 1990 (div. 1995). Diploma, St. Joseph's Hosp. Sch. Nursing, Reading, Pa., 1965. RN, Md.; cert. densitometry technologist. Head nurse med.-surg. unit Hosp. of U. Pa., 1965-67; nurse various hosps. and physician's offices, Md., Pa., 1965-85; clin. dir., clin. study coord., dual energy xray absorptiometry technologist Osteoporosis Diagnostic and Monitoring Ctr., Laurel, Md., 1985-95, owner, 1995—; clin. dir., clin. study coord. Osteoporosis Assessment Ctr., Wheaton, Md., 1985-95; cons. on osteoporosis and DEXA, Merck Pharm., 1995. Mem. Balt. Bone Club, Soc. Clin. Densitometry (steering com. 1993-96, assoc. editor SCAN 1994—, sci. adv. bd. 1996, certification & credentialing com. technologists & physicians 1995-96), Nat. Osteoporosis Found., Sandoz Women's Speakers Bur., Allied Health Profls./Arthritis Found., St. Joseph's Hosp. Alumni Assn. Office: 14201 Laurel Park Dr Ste 226 Laurel MD 20707-5203

LANDIS, EDGAR DAVID, services business company executive; b. Myerstown, Pa., Jan. 7, 1932; s. Edgar Michael and Anna Irene (Dubble) L.; m. Patrecia Ann Leininger, June 13, 1953; children—Susan Pauline, Jean Ann. B.S., Lebanon Valley Coll., 1953; M.B.A., U. Pa., 1957. C.P.A. Acct., audit supr. Peat, Marwick, Mitchell & Co., Phila., 1957-64; corp. controller, div. exec. v.p. Carlisle Corp., Pa., 1964-73; v.p., sr. v.p., now exec. v.p. CDI Corp., Phila., 1973—, also dir.; dir. affiliates in U.S. and Europe. Bd. dirs. Carlisle Sch. Dist., 1967-71, Carlisle City Airport, 1968-71, YMCA, Ardmore, Pa., 1981-87, chmn., 1984-86, YMCA, Phila., 1988—, vice chmn. 1991—. With U.S. Army, 1954-56, Japan. Mem. Lebanon Valley Coll. Alumni Assocs. (regional chmn. 1977-82). Republican. Methodist. Home: 222 Church Rd Ardmore PA 19003-3302 Office: CDI Corp 1717 Arch St Philadelphia PA 19103-2713

LANDIS, ELWOOD WINTON, retired newspaper editor; b. Wichita, Kans., June 14, 1928; s. Jacob Harrison and Christina (Fry) L.; m. Nancy Gauss, Nov. 22, 1961; children: Frederic, Laura. B.A., Friends U., Wichita, 1950; M.S. in Journalism, Northwestern U., 1953. Reporter Wichita Eagle, 1953; copy editor Omaha World-Herald, 1955-57; publicity dir. Bethany (Kans.) Coll., 1957-61; publs. dir. tchr. edn. project Central Mich. U., 1961-64; mng. editor Voice Newspaper, Mich. Edn. Assn., East Lansing, Mich., 1965-93. Mem. Williamston (Mich.) City Planning Commn., 1972-75; bd. dirs. Lansing Ballet Assn., 1980-81. Served with AUS, 1953-55. Recipient awards Edn. Press Assn. Am. Mem. Sigma Delta Chi. Democrat. Home: 308 S Circle Dr Williamston MI 48895-1014

LANDIS, FRED, mechanical engineering educator; b. Munich, Mar. 21, 1923; came to U.S., 1947, naturalized, 1954; s. Julius and Elsie (Schulhoff) L.; m. Billie H. Schiff, Aug. 26, 1951 (dec. Jan. 10, 1985); children—John David, Deborah Ellen, Mark Edward. B.Eng., McGill U., 1945; S.M., MIT, 1949, Sc.D., 1950. Design engr. Canadian Vickers, Ltd., Montreal, Can., 1945-47; asst. prof. mech. engring. Stanford U., 1950-52; research engr. Northrop Aircraft, Inc., Hawthorne, Calif., 1952-53; asst. prof. NYU, 1953-56, assoc. prof., 1956-61, prof., 1961-73, chmn. dept. mech. engring., 1963-73; dean, prof. mech. engring. Poly. U., Bklyn., 1973-74; dean Coll. Engring. and Applied Sci., U. Wis., Milw., 1974-83, prof. mech. engring., 1984-94; emeritus prof. U. Wis., Milw., 1994—; staff cons. Pratt & Whitney Aircraft Co., 1957-88. Cons. editor, Macmillan Co., 1960-68; cons. editorial bd.: Funk & Wagnalls Ency., 1969—, Compton's Ency., 1984—; contbr. numerous rsch. articles to profl. jours. and encys., including Ency. Britannica. Mem. Dobbs Ferry (N.Y.) Bd. Edn., 1965-71, v.p. 1966-67, 70-71, pres., 1967-68; bd. dirs. Westchester County Sch. Bds. Assn., 1969-70, v.p., 1970, pres., 1970-71; bd. dirs. Engring. Found., 1986-94. Fellow AIAA (assoc.), ASME (hon. mem., divsn. exec. com. 1965-73, policy bd. 1973-89, v.p. 1985-89, 92-95, bd. govs. 1989-91), Am. Soc. Engring. Edn.; mem. Sigma Tau, Tau Beta Pi, Pi Tau Sigma. Home: 2420 W Acacia Rd Milwaukee WI 53209-3306

LANDIS, GEOFFREY ALAN, physicist, writer; b. Detroit, May 28, 1955; s. John Lloyd and Patricia (Sheridan) L. BS and BEE, MIT, 1980; MS, MEE, PhD, Brown U., 1988. Staff scientist Spire Corp., Bedford, Mass., 1977-82; rsch. assoc. Solar Energy Rsch. Inst., Golden, Colo., 1986-87, NASA Lewis Rsch. Ctr., Cleve., 1988-90; physicist Sverdup Tech., Brook Park, Ohio, 1994-95; sr. engr. NYMA, Inc., Brook Park, 1994—; adj. prof. Ohio Aerospace Inst., Brook Park, 1990-92; sr. rsch. assoc. Ohio Aerospace Inst., 1995—; trustee Nat. Assn. Rocketry, Pa., 1978-81; mem. U.S. team Spacemodeling World Championships, Jambol, Bulgaria, 1978; tech. chmn. Vision 21 Conf., Cleve., 1990, 93. Editor: (procs.) Vision 21: Space Travel for the Next Millenium, 1991, Vision 21: Interdisciplinary Science and Engineering, 1993; author: (short story collection) Author's Choice Monthly, 1991 (Hugo award for best sci.-fiction short story 1992); author over 40 pub. sci.-fiction short stories; contbr. over 100 articles to profl. jours. Mem. Am. Phys. Soc., Sic. Fiction Writers Am. (Nebula award 1990), Artemis Soc. Achievements include 4 patents; participation with MIT human-powered flight team for Chrysalis and Monarch aircraft; research in semiconductor physics, solar energy and astronautics. Office: NASA Lewis Rsch Ctr 302-1 21000 Brookpark Rd Cleveland OH 44135

LANDIS, GEORGE ARTHUR, retired career officer; b. Kane, Pa., Aug. 18, 1940; s. Norman Edward and Mazie Genetta (Shatto) L.; m. Sandra Kay Sanders, Dec. 28, 1963; children: Kirsten Kay Landis Lambert, Kelly Kay Landis Scott. BBA, Kent State U., 1963; MBA, Tex. Tech. U., 1970. Commd. 2d lt. U.S. Army, 1963, advanced through grades to brig. gen., 1990; student U.S. Army Transp. Sch., Ft. Eustis, Va., 1963, tng. officer, 1963-64; train comdr. transp. div. Hdqrs. Berlin Brigade, U.S. Army, Europe, 1964-66, rail transp. officer, 1966-67; comdr. 2d Transp. Co., 27th Transp. Bn., 8th Transp. Group, U.S. Army, Vietnam, 1967-68; hwy. ops. officer 8th Transp. Group, U.S. Army, Vietnam, 1968; student U.S. Army Transp. Sch., Ft. Eustis, 1968-69, Tex. Tech. U., Lubbock, 1969-70; ops. officer Hdqrs. U.S. Army terminal command Thailand, U.S. Pacific command, 1970-71; dep. comdr. U.S. Army terminal command, U.S. Pacific Command, 1971; instr. mgmt. tng. br. U.S. Army Transp. Sch., Ft. Eustis,

1971-72; student Cmmand and Gen. Staff Coll., Ft. Leavenworth, Kans., 1972-73; div. transp. officer Hdqrs. 82d Airborne div., Ft. Bragg, N.C., 1973-74, dep. G-4, 1974, chief plans and ops., 1974-75, security, plans and ops. officer div. support command, 1975-76; tng. with industry Nat. R.R. Passenger Corp., Washington, 1976-77; staff transp. officer Office of Dep. Chief of Staff for Logistics, Washington, 1977-78; comdr. 7th Transp. Bn., 1st Corps Support Command, Ft. Bragg, 1978-80; asst. chief of staff logistics 82d Airborne Div., Ft. Bragg, 1980-82; chief internat. logistics div. U.S. Pacific Command, Camp Smith, Hawaii, 1983-86; comdr. divsn. support command 25th Inf. Divsn., Schofield Barracks, Hawaii, 1986-88; asst. comdt. U.S. Army Transp. Sch., Ft. Eustis, 1988-90; commdg. gen. Mil. Traffic Mgmt. Command, Western Area, Oakland Army Base, Calif., 1990-91; dep. commdg. gen. for ops. and transp. 22d Theater Army Area Command, Dhahran, Saudi Arabia, 1991; spl. asst. Dep. Chief of Staff for Logistics, Dept. of the Army, Washington, 1992; commdg. gen. U.S. Army Pers. Info. Systems Command, Alexandria, Va., 1992—. Decorated Def. Supr. Svc. medal, Legion of Merit, Bronze Star, Def. Meritorious Svc. medal, Meritorious Svc. medal with three oak leaf clusters, Air medal, Army Commendation medal with three oak leaf clusters, Master Parachutist badge, Air Assault badge, Army Staff Indentification badge. Mem. Nat. Def. Transp. Assn., Assn. of the U.S. Army, 82d Airborne Div. Assn., Armed Forces Comm. and Elecs. Assn. Avocations: family, handball, golf, jogging, photography. Office: US Army Pers Info Systems Command 200 Stovall St Alexandria VA 22332-4000*

LANDIS, JAMES DAVID, publishing company executive, retired, author; b. Springfield, Mass., June 30, 1942; s. Edward and Eve (Saltman) L.; m. Patricia Lawrence Straus, Aug. 15, 1964 (div.); children: Sara Cass; m. Denise Evelyn Tillar, July 20, 1983; children: Jacob Dean, Benjamin Nicholas. B.A. magna cum laude, Yale Coll., 1964. Asst. editor Abelard Schuman, N.Y.C., 1966-67; editor-sr. editor William Morrow & Co., N.Y.C., 1967-80, editorial dir., sr. v.p., pub. Quill trade paperbacks, 1980-85; sr. v.p. William Morrow & Co., 1985-91, pub., editor-in-chief, 1988-91; pub., editor-in-chief Beech Tree Books, 1985-87. Author: The Sisters Impossible, 1979, Daddy's Girl, 1984, Love's Detective, 1984, Joey and the Girls, 1987, The Band Never Dances, 1989, Looks Aren't Everything, 1990, Lying in Bed, 1995. Recipient Roger Klein award for editing, 1973, Advocate Humitarian award, 1977, Morton Dauwen Zabel award for fiction Am. Acad. Arts and Letters, 1996. Mem. Phi Beta Kappa.

LANDIS, JOHN DAVID, film director, writer; b. Chgo., Aug. 3, 1950; s. Marshall David and Shirley (Magaziner) L.; m. Deborah Nadoolman, July 27, 1980; 2 children. Mem. crew MGM film Kelly's Heroes; stuntman, writer-dir. Schlock, 1971, An American Werewolf in London, 1981; dir. Kentucky Fried Movie, 1977, National Lampoon's Animal House, 1978, Trading Places, 1983, Into the Night, 1985, Spies Like Us, 1985, Three Amigos, 1986, Coming to America, 1988, Oscar, 1991, Innocent Blood, 1992, Michael Jackson's Black or White, 1992, Beverly Hills Cop III, 1994, The Stupids, 1995; co-writer, dir. The Blues Brothers, 1980, Michael Jackson's Thriller; writer, dir., producer The Twilight Zone, 1983; frequent dir., exec. prodr. TV series Dream On, 1991— (ACE awards); exec. prodr. (TV series) Weird Science, 1994—, Sliders, 1995—, Campus Cops, 1995. Decorated chevalier dans L'Ordre des Arts et des Lettres (France), 1985; recipient numerous awards including NAACP Image awards, W.C. Handy award, People's Choice awards, internat. film festival awards. Mem. Writers Guild Am., Dirs. Guild Am., Screen Actors Guild, Acad. Motion Picture Arts and Scis.

LANDIS, JOHN WILLIAM, engineering and construction executive, government advisor; b. Kutztown, Pa., Oct. 10, 1917; s. Edwin Charles and Estella Juliabelle (Barto) L.; m. Muriel Trayes Souders, July 5, 1941; children: Maureen Lucille, Marcia Millicent. BS in Engring. Physics summa cum laude, Lafayette Coll., Easton, Pa., 1939, ScD (hon.), 1960. Registered profl. engr., Calif. Research engr. Eastman Kodak Co., Rochester, N.Y., 1939-43; cons. Navy Dept., Washington, 1946-50; head sci. and engring. dept. Ednl. Testing Service, Princeton, N.J., 1948-50; reactor engr. AEC, Washington, 1950-53; dir. customer relations atomic energy div. Babcock & Wilcox Co., N.Y.C., 1953-55; asst. mgr. atomic energy div. Babcock & Wilcox Co., Lynchburg, Va., 1955-62, mgr. atomic energy div., 1962-65; gen. mgr. Washington ops. Babcock & Wilcox Co., 1965-68; regional v.p. Gulf Gen. Atomic Co., Washington, 1968-69; group v.p. Gulf Gen. Atomic Co., LaJolla, Calif., 1969-70, pres., dir. subs., 1970-74; pres. Power Systems Co., Gen. Atomic Partnership, LaJolla, Calif., 1974-75; sr. v.p., dir., pres. subs. Stone & Webster Engring. Corp., Boston, 1975-92, pvt. cons., 1992—; founding dir. Cen. Fidelity Banks, Inc., Richmond, Va.; founding gov. Nat. Materials Property Data Network, Inc., Phila.; chmn. adv. com. isotopes and radiation devel. and four other adv. coms. AEC, Washington, 1957-70; chmn. coms., co. rep. Atomic Indsl. Forum (now U.S. Nuclear Energy Inst.), Washington, 1953—; mem. N.Y. State Adv. Com. on Atomic Energy, 1956-59, Va. State Adv. Com. on Nuclear Energy, 1959-68; vice chmn. mgmt. com. Nat. Environ. Studies Project, Washington, 1974-89; dir., v.p., pres., chmn. bds. and coms., trustee Internat. Fund, Am. Nat. Standards Inst., N.Y.C., 1957—; vice chmn. ISO-9000 Registration Com.; dir., chmn. Fusion Power Assocs., Gaithersburg, Md., 1981—; chmn. U.S. Fusion Industry Coun., Internat. Thermonuclear Exptl. Reactor Industry Coun., 1994; chmn. com. on energy-related atmospheric pollution World Energy Conf., London, 1984-90, N.Am. coord. global energy study, 1989-93; dir., chmn. com. on protection of environ. U.S. Energy Assn., Washington, 1981—; mem. fusion adv. panel U.S. Ho. Reps., Washington, 1979-87; charter mem. magnetic fusion adv. com. U.S. Dept. Energy, Washington, 1982-84, chmn. internat. rsch. and devel. panel, chmn. civilian nuclear power panel, vice chmn., chmn. energy rsch. advisory bd., 1984-90; mem. adv. bd. Sec. of Energy, 1990-93, fusion energy adv. com., 1994—; advisor Carnegie-Mellon U., Pitts., 1971-73, Pa. State U., State College, 1980-83, U. Calif. San Diego, 1974-82; vis. and sustaining fellow MIT, Cambridge, 1971-90; chmn. bus. administrn. adv. bd. U. San Diego, 1972-75; chmn. engnring. adv. com. Lafayette Coll., 1988—. Co-author: six books; contbr. articles to profl. and trade jours. Trustee, chmn. Randolph-Macon Woman's Coll., Lynchburg, Va., 1963—; trustee Lafayette Coll., Easton, Pa., 1962—, Va. Poly. Inst. and State U., Blacksburg, 1966-70; bd. dirs. Va. Poly. Inst. Ednl. Found., Blacksburg, 1968—; mem. U. Calif. Pres.'s Coun. on the Nat. Labs., 1993—; chmn. MIT Reactor Com., 1995—; mem. Sr. Rev. Group, Amarillo Nat. Resource Ctr. for Plutonium, 1994—; mem. Va. Adv. Bd. on Indsl. Devel. and Planning, Richmond, 1962-72; bd. dirs. Va. Engring. Found., Charlottesville, 1962-65; trustee Seven Hills Sch., Lynchburg, Va., 1960-65; dir. Harvard U. Ctr. for Blood Rsch., 1992—; mem. Mayor's Com. on Energy, San Diego, 1973-75; chmn., mem. six coms. Nat. Rsch. Coun., 1976—. Served to lt. USN, 1943-36, ETO. Decorated Letter of Commendation, two battle stars; recipient Gen. of Industry award State of Okla., 1971, George Washington Kidd award, Joseph E. Bell award Lafayette Coll., Lehigh Valley Favorite Son award State of Pa., 1976, Dwight D. Eisenhower Award of Honor, 1990, Winston Churchill Medal of Wisdom, 1988, Disting. Career award Fusion Power Assocs., 1991, Howard Coonley medal Am. Nat. Standards Inst., 1991, Exceptional Pub. Dept. Energy, 1992; named Hon. Citizen City of Dallas, 1973, Alumni fellow Lafayette Coll., 1984; elected to Soc. d'Honneur Lafayette Coll., 1989; elected to Wisdom Hall of Fame, 1987. Fellow Am. Nuclear Soc. (pres. 1971-72, v.p. 1970-71, treas. 1964-68, chmn. coms. 1956—, bd. dirs. 1956-74), ASME; mem. NAE, Am. Soc. Macro-Engring. (pres. 1985-88, chancellor 1988—, charter bd. dirs. 1983—), Internat. Assn. Macro-Engring. Socs. (founding dir. 1987—, treas. 1989—), San Diego Hall Sci. (life), Phi Beta Kappa, Sigma Xi, Tau Beta Pi, Pi Delta Epsilon, Omicron Delta Kappa. Avocations: photography, landscaping, book-collecting, hiking. Home: 4 Whispering Ln Weston MA 02193-1157

LANDIS, MICHELE, sports program executive; b. Warren, Ohio, May 1, 1947; d. Sullivan and Elaine Christine (Cantelmo) Santucci; m. Russell M. Landis, Dec. 19, 1970 (div. 1995); 1 child, Julie Lee. Grad. high sch., Warren, Ohio. Pres., co-founder Upper St. Clair Tennis Devel. Program, Inc., Pitts., 1983—. Vol. Family House, Pitts., 1987-91, Hospice, Pitts., 1987-92, U.S. Tennis Assn., White plains, N.Y., 1993. Republican. Roman Catholic. Avocations: tennis, reading, cooking, theatre. Home: 1807 Tilton Dr Upper Saint Clair PA 15241-2636

LANDIS, WAYNE G., environmental toxicologist; b. Washington, Jan. 20, 1952; s. James G. and Harriet E. L.; m. Linda S.; children: Margaret Evelyn, Eva Armstrong. BA in Biology, Wake Forest U., 1974; MA in Biology, Ind. U., 1978, PhD in Zoology, 1979. Document mgr. Franklin Rsch. Ctr., Silver Spring, Md., 1979-81; rsch. biologist U.S. Army Chem. Rsch., Devel. & Engring. Ctr., Aberdeen Proving Ground, Md., 1982-89; dir., prof. Inst. Environ. Toxicology & Chemistry, Western Wash. U., Bellingham, 1989—. Contbr. numerous articles to profl. jours. Recipient Hankins scholarship Wake Forest U., 1972-74, U.S. Army Rsch. and Devel. Achievement award, 1984, Spl. Act award, 1985, Exceptional Performance award, 1986; named to Outstanding ILIR Rsch. Program, 1983, 84. Mem. AAAS, ASTM, Soc. Environ. Toxicology and Chemistry (Pacific NW chpt.), Genetics Soc. Am., Sigma Xi. Achievements include evaluation of aquatic toxicology of smoke, riot control materials and binary system compounds; devel. theory to predict response of biol. communities to chem. insults using resource competition models, of new methods for ecosystem anal. and applications of chaos theory to chem. impacts. Office: Western Wash U. Huxley Coll Environ Toxicology 516 High St Bellingham WA 98225-5946

LANDO, JEROME BURTON, macromolecular science educator; b. Bklyn., May 23, 1932; s. Irving and Ruth (Schwartz) L.; m. Geula Ahroni, Dec. 2, 1962; children: Jeffrey, Daniel, Avital. A.B., Cornell U., 1953; Ph.D., Poly. Inst. Bklyn., 1963. Chemist Camille Dreyfus Lab., Research Triangle Inst., Durham, N.C., 1963-65; asst. prof. macromolecular sci. Case Western U., Cleve., 1965-68, assoc. prof., 1968-74, prof., 1974—; chmn. dept. Case Western, Cleve., 1978-85; dir. Macro-Epic (acad.-indsl. research program), 1985—; Erna and Jakob Michael vis. prof. Weizmann Inst. Sci., Rehovot, Israel, 1987; Lady Davis vis. prof. Technion, Haifa, Israel, 1992-93. Author: (with S. Maron) Fundamentals of Physical Chemistry, 1974; editorial adv. bd. Jour. Molecular Electronics, Polymers for Advanced Technologies, Jour. Materials Chemistry. Served to lt. U.S. Army, 1953-55. Named Alexander Von Humboldt Sr. Am. Scientist U. Mainz (Fed. Republic Germany), 1974, disting. alumnus Poly. U., 1990; recipient rsch. award Soc. Plastics Engrs., 1994. Fellow Am. Phys. Soc.; mem. Am. Chem. Soc., Am. Crustallographic Assn., Soc. Plastics Engrs., Sigma Xi. Jewish. Home: 21925 Byron Rd Cleveland OH 44122-2942 Office: Case Western Res U Dept Macromolecular Sci Kent Hale Smith Bldg 321 Cleveland OH 44106

LANDOLT, ARLO UDELL, astronomer, educator; b. Highland, Ill., Sept. 29, 1935; s. Arlo Melvin and Vesta (Kraus) L.; m. Eunice Jean Casper, June 8, 1966; 1 child, Jennifer; stepchildren: Lynda, Barbara, Vicky, Debra. B.A., Miami U., Oxford, Ohio, 1955; M.A., Ind. U., 1960, Ph.D., 1963. Mem. 1st wintering-over party Internat. Geophys. Year, Amundson-Scott South Pole Sta., Antarctica, 1957; asst. prof. physics and astronomy La. State U., 1962-65, asso. prof., 1965-68, prof., 1968—, dir. La. State U. Obs., 1970-88, acting chmn. dept. physics and astronomy, summers 1972-73, pres. faculty senate, 1979-80; program dir. astronomy sect. NSF, 1975-76; mem. governing bd. Am. Inst. of Physics, 1985-91, 95—; guest investigator Kitt Peak Nat. Obs., Tucson, Cerro Tololo Inter-Am. Obs.,Las Campanas Observatory, La Serena, Chile, Dyer Obs., Vanderbilt U., Goethe Link Obs., Ind. U. Rsch. grantee NSF, 1964, 66, 69, 71, 73, 75, 92-96, NASA, 1965, 92, Rsch. Corp., 1964, Air Force Office Sci., 1977-87, Space Telescope Sci. Inst., 1985-90, 92. Fellow AAAS (sec. Sect. D 1970-78); mem. AAUP, Am. Astron. Soc. (sec. 1980-89, 95—), Internat. Astron. Union (sec. U.S. nat. com. 1980-89, 96—), Royal Astron. Soc. (Eng.), Astron. Soc. Pacific, Am. Polar Soc., Am. Philatelic Soc., Sigma Xi, Pi Mu Epsilon. Office: La State U Dept Physics And Astro Baton Rouge LA 70803-4001

LANDOLT, ROBERT GEORGE, chemistry educator; b. Houston, Apr. 4, 1939; s. Robert Garland and Mary Ella (Campbell) L.; m. Margaret Ann Brown, June 8, 1962; children: Laura, Lisa, Robert. BA, Austin Coll., Sherman, Tex., 1961; PhD, U. Tex., 1965. Rsch. assoc. U. Ill., Urbana, 1965-67; asst. prof., assoc. prof. Muskingum Coll., New Concord, Ohio, 1967-80; sr. scientist Radian Corp., Austin, Tex., 1980-81; assoc. prof. chemistry Tex. Weslayan U., Ft. Worth, 1981-89, prof., 1989—; resident cons. Battelle Meml. Lab., Columbus, Ohio, 1974-75; cons. Naval Rsch. Lab., Washington, 1982-83; dir. rsch. div. Tex. Higher Edn. Coord. Bd., 1991. Contbr. articles on chemical informatics and organic chemistry to profl. jours. Mem. AAAS, AAUP, Am. Chem. Soc. (Congl. fellow 1986-87), Sigma Xi. Office: Tex Weleyan U 1201 Wesleyan St Fort Worth TX 76105-1536

LANDON, FORREST M., retired newspaper executive; b. Pontiac, Mich., Sept. 24, 1933; s. DeWitt Dale Landon and Eleanor (Stevens) Landon Smith; m. Barbara Jean Patrick, Sept. 25, 1955; children—Jeffrey William, Tracy Alice. B. Journalism, U. Mo., 1955. Reporter Sta. WDBJ-AM-FM-TV, Roanoke, VA., 1955-59; news dir. Sta. WDBJ-AM-FM, Roanoke, VA., 1959-64; assoc. editorials editor Roanoke Times, VA., 1964-67, editorial page editor, 1967-71, assoc. editor, night mng. editor, mng. editor, 1971-82, exec. editor, v.p., 1982-95; acting dir. Va. Coalition for Open Govt., 1995—; host weekly program pub. TV, Roanoke, 1968-79; tchr. journalism Hollins Coll., Va., 1970-74. Pres. Roanoke Valley Council Community Services, 1973-74, Roanoke Valley Indsl. Mgmt. Council, 1961. Mem. Soc. Profl. Journalists (pres. Blue Ridge chpt. 1977-78, award 1988), Va. Press Assn. (pres. 1993-94, award 1974), Va. AP Newspapers (pres. 1989-90), Va. AP Broadcasters (award 1958, 60), Am. Soc. Newspaper Editors (FOI com. chmn. 1995-96), Torch Club (pres. Roanoke 1984-85). Unitarian. Home: 1603 Deyerle Rd SW Roanoke VA 24018-1313 Office: Roanoke Times PO Box 2491 201-209 W Campbell Ave Roanoke VA 24010-2491

LANDON, JAMES HENRY, lawyer; b. Atlanta, Ga., Oct. 24, 1945; s. Ralph Henry and Gertrude Leola (Rew) L. BA, Vanderbilt U., Nashville, Tenn., 1967; JD, Harvard U., Cambridge, Mass., 1970. Bar: Ga. 1971, U.S. Dist. Ct. (no. dist.) Ga. 1971, U.S. Ct. Claims 1972, U.S. Supreme Ct. 1976, U.S. Tax Ct. 1980. Assoc. Hansell & Post, Atlanta, Ga., 1971-76, ptnr., 1976-89; ptnr. Jones, Day, Reavis & Pogue, Atlanta, Ga., 1989—; Adj. prof. Emory Law School, Atlanta, Ga., 1983-84; dir. TRC Temporary Serv., Inc., Atlanta, Ga., 1987—; mem. steering com. So. Pension Conf., Atlanta, Ga., 1985-88. Co-author: Transportation Politics in Atlanta, 1970; contbr. article to profl. jour. Gen. counsel Woodruff Arts Ctr., Inc., 1993—; trustee Atlanta Symphony Orchestra, 1981-87, 89-92, The Hambidge Ctr., 1994—, Atlanta Med. Heritage, Inc., 1993—; trustee Atlanta Hist. Soc., 1983—, Ctr. for Puppetry Arts, Inc., 1995—; mem. cmty. adv. bd. Jr. League of Atlanta, 1987-90. Mem. ABA, Ga. Bar Assoc., Atlanta Bar Assoc., Explorers Club of N.Y.C., Phi Beta Kappa. Presbyterian. Avocations: mountain climbing, hiking. Home: 1327 Peachtree St NE Apt 503 Atlanta GA 30309-3254 Office: Jones Day Reavis & Pogue 3500 One Peachtree Ctr 303 Peachtree St NE Atlanta GA 30308-3201

LANDON, JOHN CAMPBELL, medical research company executive; b. Hornell, N.Y., Jan. 3, 1937; s. Earl Shephard and Eleanor (Crane) L.; m. Nancy Ann Bachenheimer, Aug. 24, 1958; children: David Bacheheimer, Martha Susan, Katherine Ellen, Peter Crane. BA in Biology, Alfred (N.Y.) U., 1959; MS in Biology, George Washington U., Washington, 1962, PhD in Biology, 1967. Biologist Nat. Cancer Inst., NIH, Bethesda, Md., 1960-65; virologist Litton Bionetics, Kensington, Md., 1965-68, dir., 1968-75; pres., dir. EG&G Mason Rsch. Inst., Worcester, Mass., 1975-82; pres., CEO Bioqual, Inc., Rockville, Md., 1982—; founder, v.p., co-owner Brewster (Mass.) Book Store, Inc., Brewster, Mass, 1982—; pres., CEO Sema, Inc., Rockville, 1986-91; pres., CEO Diagnon Corp., Rockville, 1986—, also chmn. bd. dirs.; founder, pres., CEO Enhanced Therapeutics, Inc., Rockville, Md., 1994—; cons. EG&G, Worcester, Mass., 1982-85; reviewer ad-hoc com. NIH, Bethesda, Md., 1981—; mem. exec. com., bd. dirs., v.p. bd. Nat. Assn. Life Sci. Industries, 1975-78, 79-81. Contbr. articles to profl. jours. Bd. dirs. Peirce Warwick Adoption Svc., Washington, 1970-79 (pres. 1972-75), Venture Expeditionary (pres. 1981-83), Washington, 1979-83; mem. credit com. Potomac Community Fed. Credit Union, 1982-85. Mem. AAAS, Am. Soc. Cell Biology, Am. Soc. Microbiology, N.Y. Acad. Scis., Sigma Xi. Office: Diagnon Corp 9600 Medical Center Dr Rockville MD 20850-3336 Office: Brewster Bookstore 2648 Main St Brewster MA 02631

LANDON, JOHN WILLIAM, minister, social worker, educator; b. Marlette, Mich., Mar. 24, 1937; s. Norman A. and Merle Irene (Lawraeon) L. BA, Taylor U., 1959; MDiv, Northwestern U., Christian Theol. Sem., 1962; MSW, Ind. U., 1966; PhD in Social Sci., Ball State U., 1972. Regional supr. Iowa Dept. Social Welfare, Des Moines, 1965-67; acting chmn. dept. sociology Marion (Ind.) Coll., 1967-69; asst. prof. sociology and social work Ball State U., Muncie, Ind., 1969-71; asst. prof. social work, coord. base courses Coll. Social Work U. Ky., Lexington, 1971-73, assoc. prof., coord. Undergrad. Program in Social Work Coll. of Social Work, 1974-85, prof., assoc. dean, 1985—; dir. social work edn. Taylor U., Upland, Ind., 1973-74. Author: From These Men, 1966; Jesse Crawford, Poet of the Organ, Wizard of the Mighty Wurlitzer, 1974; Behold the Mighty Wurlitzer, The History of the Theatre Pipe Organ, 1983; The Development of Social Welfare, 1986. Mem. AAUP, Coun. on Social Work Edn., Nat. Assn. Social Workers, Am. Guild Organists. Home: 809 Celia Ln Lexington KY 40504-2305 Office: U Ky Coll Social Work Lexington KY 40506-0027

LANDON, MICHAEL DE LAVAL, historian, educator; b. St. John, N.B., Can., Oct. 8, 1935; came to U.S., 1960; s. Arthur Henry Whittington and Elizabeth Worthington (Fair) L.; m. Doris Lee Clay, Dec. 31, 1959 (div. May 1980); children: Clay de Laval, Letitia Elizabeth; m. Carole Marie Prather, Feb. 28, 1981. BA, Oxford (Eng.) U., 1958, MA, 1961; MA, U. Wis., 1962, PhD, 1966. Asst. master Manor House Sch., Horsham, Eng., 1957, Dalhousie Sch., Ladybank, Scotland, 1958, Lakefield (Ont.) Coll. Sch., 1958-60; asst. prof. history U. Miss., Oxford, 1964-67, assoc. prof., 1967-72, prof., 1972—. Author: The Triumph of the Lawyers, 1970, The Honor and Dignity of the Profession, 1979, Erin and Britannia, 1980. Commr. City Housing Authority, Oxford, 1983—, chmn., 1993—; lay Eucharistic minister Episcopal Ch. Am. Philos. Soc. Rsch. grantee, 1967, 74. Fellow Royal Hist. Soc. (U.K.); mem. Am. Soc. for Legal History (sec.-treas. 1988—), Phi Kappa Phi, Eta Sigma Phi, Phi Alpha Theta. Episcopalian. Avocation: bird feeding. Home: 219 Bramlett Blvd Oxford MS 38655-3415 Office: Univ of Miss Dept of History University MS 38677

LANDON, ROBERT GRAY, retired manufacturing company executive; b. Portsmouth, Ohio, Dec. 22, 1928; s. Herman Robert and Hazel Ruth (Tener) L.; m. Sarah A. Newpher, July 2, 1954; children: Geoffrey, Suzanne. Student, Cornell U., 1947-49; BA in Econs., U. Pa., 1955; grad. advanced mgmt. program, Harvard Sch. Bus., 1978. Loan officer Nat. City Bank, Cleve., 1955-60; SEC adminstr. Smith Kline Corp., 1960-64; controller, treas. Grumman Allied Industries, Inc., Garden City, N.Y., 1964-76; v.p. Grumman Allied Industries, Inc., 1977-82; v.p. investment mgmt. Grumman Corp., Bethpage, N.Y., 1978-79; pres. Grumman Ohio Corp., Worthington, Ohio, 1979-88. Served with AC USN, 1949-53. Mem. The Oaks Club.

LANDON, ROBERT KIRKWOOD, insurance company executive; b. N.Y.C., Apr. 27, 1929; s. Kirk A. and Edith (Ungar) L.; m. Beulah Pair, Mar. 19, 1965; children: Chris, Kathleen Landon Staley, Kellyann Landon Spears. Student, U. Va., 1946-48; B.S., Ga. Inst. Tech., 1950. With Am. Bankers Life Assurance Co., Miami, Fla., 1952—; pres. Am. Bankers Life Assurance Co., 1960-74, chmn., chief exec. officer, 1974—; chmn. bd., CEO Am. Bankers Ins. Group Inc., Miami, 1980-95, chmn. bd., 1980—; pres. Landon Corp., Dover, Del., 1971—; charter mem. advisory bd. Fla. Internat. U., 1972-74. Trustee Kirk A. and Dorothy P. Landon Found., 1969—, Barry U. Served to lt. (j.g.) USNR, 1950-53. Mem. Coun. Internat. Visitors, World Bus. Coun., Scabbard and Blade, Grove Isle Club, Phi Gamma Delta. Republican. Congregationalist. Home: 2 Casuarina Concourse Coral Gables FL 33143-6502 Office: Am Bankers Ins Group Inc 11222 Quail Roost Dr Miami FL 33157-6543

LANDOVSKY, JOHN, artistic director; b. Riger, Latvia, Jan. 2, 1935; came to U.S., 1950; s. Jains and Olga (Kalnins) L. Dancer Weirtterberg Stadiis Opera House, Stuttgart, Fed. Republic Germany, 1965, Internat. Ballet Co., Chgo., 1960-70, Lyric Opera of Chgo., 1960-70; asst. prof. U. Ill., Urbana, 1976-80; director Duluth (Minn.) Ballet Co., 1980-82, Ballet Hawaii, Honolulu, 1982, Hawaii State Ballet, Honolulu, 1982—. Office: Hawaii State Ballet 1418 Kapiolani Blvd Honolulu HI 96814-3603

LANDOW-ESSER, JANINE MARISE, lawyer; b. Omaha, Sept. 23, 1951; d. Erwin Landow and Beatrice (Hart) Appel; m. Jeffrey L. Esser, June 2, 1974; children: Erica, Caroline. BA, U. Wis., 1973; JD with honors, George Washington U., 1976. Bar: Va. 1976, D.C. 1977, Ill. 1985. Lawyer U.S. Dept. Energy, Washington, 1976-83, Bell, Boyd & Lloyd, Chgo., 1985-86, Seyfarth, Shaw, Fairweather & Geraldson, Chgo., 1986-88, Holleb & Coff, Chgo., 1988—; chmn. Environ. Safety and Health Practice Group, 1993—, mem. exec. com., 1994—. Contbr. articles to profl. jours. Bd. dirs. Bernard Zell Anshe Emet Day Sch. Parent-Tchr. Orgn., 1991-95. Mem. ABA, Chgo. Bar Assn. (vice chmn. environ. law com. 1990-91, chmn. 1991-92), Am. Jewish Congress Commn. on Women's Equality (bd. dirs. 1995—). Office: Holleb & Coff 55 E Monroe St Ste 4100 Chicago IL 60603-5803

LANDRIAULT, JACQUES EMILE, retired bishop; b. Alfred, Ont., Can., Sept. 23, 1921; s. Amedee and Marie-Louise (Brisebois) L. BPh, U. Ottawa; Licence in Theology, St. Paul U. Sem., Ottawa. Ordained priest Roman Cath. Ch., 1947; curate in Noranda Que.; chancellor Diocese Timmins, Ont., 1953; bishop of Cadi, titular bishop of Alexandria Ont., 1962-64, bishop of Hearst, 1964-71; adminstr. bishop of Hearst, 1971-74, bishop of Timmins, 1971-90, bishop emeritus, 1990—; mem. Can. Conf. Cath. Bishops Commn.: Liturgy, Mission; mem. Ont. Episcopal Com. on Cath. Edn.; v.p. Ont. Cath. Episcopal Conf.; mem. Cath. Conf. Ont. Address: John Paul II Residence, 1243 Kilborn Pl Apt 206, Ottawa, ON Canada K1H 6K9

LANDRIGAN, PHILIP JOHN, epidemiologist; b. Boston, June 14, 1942; s. John Joseph and Frances Joan (Conlin) L.; m. Mary Florence Magee, Aug. 27, 1966; children: Mary Frances, Christopher Paul, Elizabeth Marie. A.B., Boston Coll., 1963; M.D., Harvard U., 1967; M.S., London Sch. Hygiene and Tropical Medicine, 1977, D.I.H., 1977. Diplomate Am. Bd. Pediatrics, Am. Bd. Preventive Medicine, Am. Bd. Occupational Medicine, Am. Coll. Epidemiology. Intern Cleve. Met. Gen. Hosp., 1967-68; resident in pediatrics Children's Hosp. Med. Ctr., Boston, 1968-70; fellow in pediatrics Harvard U. Med. Sch., Boston, 1969-70; clin. instr. pediatrics Emory U. Sch. Medicine, Atlanta, 1970-71; epidemic intelligence service officer Ctrs. for Disease Control, Atlanta, 1970-73, dir. research and devel. smallpox erradication program, 1973-74, chief environ. hazards activity, 1974-79; dir. div. Surveillance, Hazard Evaluations and Field Studies Nat. Inst. for Occupational Safety and Health, Cin., 1979-85; prof. community medicine and pediatrics Mt. Sinai Sch. Medicine, N.Y.C., 1985—; dir. div. environ. and occupational medicine Mt. Sinai Sch. Medicine, 1985-90; prof., chmn. dept. community medicine, 1990—; mem. bd. on toxicology and environ. health hazards Nat. Acad. Sci., Washington, vice chmn., 1981-86; clin. prof. environ. health Sch. Pub. Health U. Wash., Seattle, 1983—. Contbr. numerous articles on pediatrics, pub. health, epidemiology, occupational medicine and environ. medicine to med. jours.; cons. editor: Archives of Environ. Health, 1982—, Am. Jour. Indsl. Medicine, 1979—; editor-in-chief Environ. Research, 1987—. Recipient Vol. award Dept. HEW, 1973; recipient Pub. Health Service Career Devel. award, 1975, group citation as mem. of Ctr. for Disease Control beryllium rev. panel, 1978, Meritorious Service medal USPHS, 1985. Fellow Royal Soc. Medicine; mem. Inst. of MedicineInternat. Commn. on Occupational Health, Am. Pub. Health Assn., Am. Epidemiol. Soc., Soc. for Epidemiologic Research, AAAS. Home: 915 Stuart Ave Mamaroneck NY 10543-4124 Office: Mt Sinai Sch Medicine Dept Community Medicine 1 Gustave L Levy Pl New York NY 10029-6504

LANDRON, MICHEL JOHN, lawyer; b. Santurce, P.R., June 15, 1946; s. Francis Xavier and Francisca (Carretero) Healy; m. Carol McQuade, Apr. 22, 1989; children, Michael Francis, Ryan McQuade. BA, Lehman Coll., 1968, postgrad., 1969-73; JD, Fordham U., 1977. Bar: N.Y. 1978, U.S. Dist. Ct. (so. dist.) N.Y. 1978, U.S. Dist. Ct. (ea. dist.) N.Y. 1978. asst. atty. gen. Office of Atty. Gen., N.Y. State Dept. Law, N.Y.C., 1978-80; enforcement atty. N.Y. Stock Exch., N.Y.C., 1980-81; pvt. practice, Bklyn., 1981-82, 84—; mem. Leaf, Duell, Drogin P.C., N.Y.C., 1982-84; gen. counsel Rockcom, Inc., 1985-87, adminstr. law judge City of N.Y., 1987; of counsel Berger and Paul, N.Y.C., 1984-85; assoc. area counsel Digital Equipment Corp., 1988-89; adj. instr. N.Y. Law Sch., Ramapo Coll.; arbitrator U.S. Dist. Ct. (ea. dist.) N.Y.; guest lectr. Lehman Coll.; cons. in field; arbitrator Civil Ct. N.Y.C., No Fault Ins. Panel State of N.Y., Nat. Assn. Securities Dealers, Inc., Am. Arbitration Assn. Author: Conflicts of Law, 1992; (with others) Personal Injury: Actions, Defenses and Damages, 1992, Choice of Law; author chpts. to books; contbr. articles to profl. jours. Mem. ABA (forum com. on entertainment and sports law), Bklyn. Bar Assn. (past chmn. patents trademark and copyrights com., past chmn. arbitration com.), N.Y. State Bar Assn. (com. to cooperate with law revision commn.), Assn. Arbitrators City of N.Y., Am. Judges Assn., Phi Alpha Delta (Disting. Svc.

award 1977). Republican. Roman Catholic. Avocations: music, reading, sports. Office: 323 46th St Brooklyn NY 11220-1109

LANDRY, DEBBY ANN, computer programmer; b. Tacoma, July 27, 1963; d. Israel Joseph and Joyce Ann (Franzella) L.; 1 child, Jessica Elizabeth. BS, S.E. La. U., 1987; postgrad., U. So. Miss., 1994. Computer programmer Lockheed Engring. and Scis., Bay St. Louis, Miss., 1988-92; programmer/analyst I Sverdrup Techs., Inc., 1992-94; computer assoc. sr. Lockheed Engring. & Scis., Stennis Space Center, Miss., 1994—. Mem. Beta Sigma Phi. Democrat. Roman Catholic. Avocations: needlework, reading, CCD instructor. Home: 1107 Rose Meadow Loop Slidell LA 70460-5105 Office: Lockheed Engring & Scis Co Bldg 2105 Bay Saint Louis MS 39529

LANDRY, G. YVES, automotive company executive. Pres., CEO Chrysler Can. Ltd., Windsor, Ont., Can. Office: Chrysler Can Ltd, 2450 Chrysler Ctr PO Box 1621, Windsor, ON Canada N9A 4H6

LANDRY, JAMES EDWARD, trade association administrator; b. Saratoga Springs, N.Y., Nov. 3, 1928; s. Philip Joseph and May Regina (Gorman) L.; m. Judith Ann Stone, Dec. 19, 1981; children: James Jr., Christopher, Jeffrey, Carla, John Gorman. BS, Union Coll., 1949; LLB, George Washington U., 1956; diploma internat. air and space law, McGill U., 1957. Bar: D.C. Air transport examiner, trial atty. Civil Aeronautics Bd., U.S.G., Washington, 1957-61; sr. atty. dir. internat. programs Air Transport Assn. of Am., Washington, 1961-66, v.p. internat., 1966-70, gen. counsel, 1970-78, sr. vp., gen. counsel, 1978-92, pres., 1992-95; aviation expert, cons., 1996—; guest lectr. McGill Inst., Georgetown U. Sch. of Law; bd. advisors McGill's Inst. of Air and Space Law; adv. coun. Concordia U./IATA Internat. Aviation MGA programme; bus. adv. com. to the Transp. Ctr., Northwestern U.; bd. dirs. Air Cargo, Inc., Aeronautical Radio, Inc.; mem. industry sector adv. com. Svcs. for Trade Policy; exec. com. Travel and Tourism Govt. Affairs Coun. Contbr. numerous articles to profl. jours. With U.S. Army, 1951-54. Mem. ABA, D.C. Bar Assn. Roman Catholic. Home: 7305 Yates Ct Mc Lean VA 22101

LANDRY, JOEL DANIEL, II, lawyer; b. Washington, Oct. 18, 1963; s. Joel Daniel and Mary Ann (DiMario) L.; m. Lisa Roseann Giuliano, Oct. 24, 1993. BA, U. R.I., 1986; JD, New Eng. Sch. Law, 1989. Bar: R.I., 1989; U.S. Dist. Ct. R.I., 1990. Spl. asst. atty. gen. State of R.I., Providence, 1989-90; asst. city solicitor City of Providence, 1990-92; pvt. practice Providence, 1990—; ptnr. Voccola & Landry Law Offices; Bd. dirs. DiMario Motors, Inc., Providence. Vice chmn. Providence Water Supply Bd., 1992—. Mem. ABA, Am. Trial Lawyers Assn., Order Sons of Italy in Am., Nat. Italian Am. Bar Assn., Justinian Law Soc. (bd. dirs. 1994). Roman Catholic. Home: 627 Pleasant Valley Pky Providence RI 02908-4214 Office: Voccola & Landry Law Offices 454 Broadway Ste 201 Providence RI 02909

LANDRY, JOHN BERNARD, III, data processing executive; b. Oak Park, Ill., Nov. 13, 1947; s. John Bernard Jr. and Madeline Marie (Ries); m. Ann C. Outchcunis, Mar. 19, 1978; children: Adam John, Jillian Kate. BSBA, Babson Coll., 1969. Acct. Shawmut Nat. Corp., Boston, 1970-72; exec. v.p. rsch. and devel. McCormacy & Doge Corp., Naticu, Mass., 1972-85; chmn. Distbrn. Mgmt. Systems Inc., Lexington, Mass., 1985-87; exec. v.p. rsch. and devel. Cullinet Software Inc., Westwood, Mass., 1987—; bd. dirs. Cullinet Software Inc., Westwood, Language Technology Inc., Salem, Mass. Author: Software Development Technology, 1986. Served with U.S. Army, 1969-75. Mem. Mass. Computer Software Coun. (trustee 1987—), Assn. Data Processin Svc. Orgn. (dir. 1987—). Avocations: tennis, skiing. •

LANDRY, PAUL LEONARD, lawyer; b. Mpls., Nov. 23, 1950; s. LeRoy Robert Landry and Alice Ruth (Swain) Stephens; m. Lisa Yvonne Yeo, Dec. 13, 1984; children: Marc, Lauren, Matthew. BA, Macalester Coll., 1974; postgrad., Georgetown U., 1976-77; JD, Boston U., 1977. Bar: Va. 1977, D.C. 1978, Minn. 1984, U.S. Dist. Ct. D.C., U.S. Dsit. Ct. Va., U.S. Dist. Ct. Minn., U.S. Ct. Appeals (D.C., 2d, 4th and 8th cirs.). Dancer Dance Theater Harlem, N.Y.C., 1970-72; prin. dancer Dance Theatre Boston, 1972-75; atty. EPA, Washington, 1976-77; assoc. Reed, Smith, Shaw & McClay, Washington, 1977-83; officer, shareholder Fredrikson & Byron, P.A., Mpls., 1984—; adj. prof. law William Mitchell Coll. Law, St. Paul, 1985-89; mem. adv. bd. Minn. Music Acad., Mpls., 1989—. Bd. dirs. Ind. Sch. Dist. 284, Wayzata, Minn., 1989—, chmn., 1992-93; bd. dirs. Walker Art Ctr., Mpls., 1992—; advisor Kevin McCary Scholarship Fund, Flyte Tyme Found. Mem. ABA (conf. of minority ptnrs. adv. com., chmn. governance com.), Nat. Bar Assn., Minn. Bar Assn., D.C. Bar, Hennepin Conty Bar Assn., Corp. Coun. Assn. Minn. (bd. dirs.), Black Entertainment and Sports Lawyers Assn., Minn. Minority Lawyers Assn., Barristers. Avocations: golf, music, basketball. Office: Fredrikson & Byron PA 900 2nd Ave S Ste 1100 Minneapolis MN 55402-3328

LANDRY, ROGER D., publishing company executive; b. Montreal, Que., Jan. 26, 1934; s. Charle and Mabel (Desgroseillers) L.; m. Suzanne Shepherd; children—Johane, Charle, Genevieve. Student, Sir. George Williams U., Montreal, 1953, Institut des Sci. Politiques, Paris, 1956. Mgr. mktg. services Bell Can., Montreal, 1957-63; insp. Que. Provincial Police, Montreal, 1963-65; dep. dir. 1967 World Exhbn., Montreal, 1965-68, Air Can., 1968-70; pres. Beauregard, Landry, Nantel & Assocs., Montreal, 1970-75; sr. v.p., chief adminstrv. officer ITT Can., Port Cartier, 1975-77; v.p. mktg. and pub. affairs Montreal Baseball Club Ltd., 1977-80; pres., pub. La Presse Ltd., Montreal, 1980—; chmn. Can. Press. Chmn. Opéra de Montreal. Named Mktg. Man of Yr., Major League Baseball, 1980. Mem. Que. Dailies Inc. (bd. dirs.), Can. Daily Newspaper Assn. (bd. dirs.), Can. Pub. Relations Soc. (Médaille du President 1980, Médaille Edouard-Montpetit 1984), Order Can. (officer), Order Quebec (officer), Order Golden Lion, Sons of Italy, Grande Médaille de Vermeil de la Ville de Paris. Office: La Presse, 7 Rue St Jacques, Montreal, PQ Canada H2Y 1K9

LANDRY, THOMAS HENRY, construction executive; b. Detroit, Nov. 2, 1946; s. Ernest E. and Charman A. (Iles) L.; m. Eileen K. Iannucci, June 22, 1968; children: Paul T., Christine M. BSBA, U. Dayton, 1968; MBA, Wayne State U., 1972. Project adminstr. A.J. Etkin Constrn. Co., Farmington Hills, Mich., 1971-79, exec. v.p., 1979-85, pres., chief oper. officer, 1985—; chmn. Fin., Design & Build, Inc., Birmingham, Mich., 1986—. Bd. dirs. Metro Detroit chpt. March of Dimes, 1992—, United Cerebral Palsy; mem. Leadership Oakland, Mich., 1989—, Leadership Mich., 1995. Mem. Assoc. Gen. Contractors Am. (bd. dirs. Detroit chpt. 1987—), Engring. Soc. Detroit (vice chmn. constrn. activities com. 1987—), Mich. Constrn. Users Coun., Lakeland Country Club. Roman Catholic. Office: AJ Etkin Constrn Co 30445 Northwestern Hwy Ste 250 Farmington Hills MI 48334

LANDRY, TOM (THOMAS WADE LANDRY), former professional football coach; b. Mission, Tex., Sept. 11, 1924; s. Ray and Ruth (Coffman) L.; m. Alicia Wiggs, Jan. 28, 1949; children—Thomas, Kitty, Lisa. BBA, U. Tex., 1949; BS in Indsl. Engring., U. Houston, 1952. Player N.Y. Yankees All-Am. Football Conf., 1949; player N.Y. Giants, 1950-53, player-coach, 1954-55, defensive coach, 1956-59; head coach Dallas Cowboys, 1960-89; now chmn., CEO Landry Investment Group. Author: (with Gregg Lewis) Tom Landry: An Autobiography, 1990. Trustee Nat. Fellowship Christian Athletes, chmn. bd. Dallas chpt. Served with USAAF, World War II. Named to All-Pro team, 1954, to Pro Football Hall of Fame, 1990; coached winning Super Bowl teams, 1971, 77. Methodist (bd. govs.). Office: Landry Investment Group Inc 8411 Preston Rd Ste 720 Dallas TX 75225-5519•

LANDSBERG, JERRY, management and investment consultant, optical laboratory executive; b. Dallas, June 30, 1933; s. Max and Rose (Hechtman) L.; grad. So. Meth. U., 1954; m. Gloria Zale, Sept. 2, 1956; children: Steven Jay, Jeffrey Paul, Karen Beth, Ruth Ellen. Salesman, Remington Rand div. Sperry Rand, 1955-57; salesman Zale Corp., 1957-59, asst. mgr., 1959-60, mgr., 1960-63, merchandiser, 1963-67; registered rep., security analyst Silberberg & Co., 1967-69; owner Jerry Landsberg & Assocs., 1969-72; v.p. Ross Watch Case Corp., gen. mgr. Kenfield Jewelry div., Long Island City, N.Y., 1971-75; pres., chief operating officer King Optical Corp., Dallas, 1974-75; chmn., chief exec. officer Richland Optical Labs. Inc.; chief exec. officer The Richland Group, current; pres. Jerry Landsberg Assos., Great Neck, N.Y., 1975—; pres. N. Am. Vision Services, Inc., Freeport, N.Y., 1987—, chmn., chief exec. officer Tech-Optics Internat. Corp. Trustee, Village of Kensington, 1967-75, commr. police, 1967-69, commr. pub. works, 1969-75, dep. mayor, 1969-75, mayor, 1973; fin. v.p. Temple Emanuel, Great Neck, 1964-66, trustee, 1964-74; bd. dirs. Great Neck Symphony Soc., 1974—, pres., 1978-81, chmn. bd., 1981—; trustee North Shore Univ. Hosp., 1981—, Am. Friends of Haifa U., 1986-88; mem. adv. bd. Adelphi U. Sch. Nursing, 1981-86, chmn., 1986-93; trustee Parker Jewish Geriatric Inst., 1979—, treas., 1983-84; bd. dirs. Great Neck Community Fund, Sch. Opticianry Interboro Inst., chmn., 1990-92; v.p. Zale Found.; Great Neck chmn. Fedn. Jewish Philanthropies; active various community drives. Mem. So. Meth. U. Alumni Assn. (dir. nat. bd., pres. N.Y. club). Clubs: U.S. Power Squadron, Masons, Shriners. Office: 59 Hanse Ave Freeport NY 11520-4608

LANDSBERG, LEWIS, endocrinologist, medical researcher; b. N.Y.C., Nov. 23, 1938. AB, Williams Coll., 1960; MD, Yale U., 1964. From instr. to asst. prof. medicine Sch. Medicine Yale U., 1969-72; from asst. prof. to assoc. prof. Harvard Med. Sch., 1972-77, from assoc. prof. to prof., 1977-86; Irving S. Cutter prof., chmn. dept. medicine Med. Sch. Northwestern U. Med. Sch., 1990—; dir. Ctr. Endocrinology, Metabolism & Nutrition Northwestern U., 1990-93; assoc. physician Yale-New Haven Hosp., 1969-71, attending physician, 1971-72, Beth Israel Hosp., 1974-79, physician, 1979-88, sr. physician, 1988-90; attending physician West Haven VA Hosp., 1970-72; assisting physician Boston City Hosp., 1972-73, assoc. vis. physician, 1973-74; physician-in-chief dept. medicine Northwestern Meml. Hosp., 1990—. Fellow ACP; mem. AAAS, Am. Fedn. Clin. Rsch., Endocrine Soc., N.Y. Acad. Scis., AHA, Am. Soc. Pharmacology and Exptl. Therapeutics, Am. Physiology Soc., Am. Soc. Clin. Investigators, Am. Clin. and Climatological Assn., Assn. Am. Physicians. Achievements include rsch. in catecholamines and the sympathoadrendal system, nutrition and the sympathetic nervous system, obesity and hypertension. Office: Northwestern Univ Med Sch Wesley Pavilion 296 250 E Superior Chicago IL 60611

LANDSBERG, MICHELE, journalist; b. Toronto, July 12, 1939; d. Jack and Naomi Leah Landsberg; m. Stephen Lewis, May 30, 1963; children: Ilana Naomi, Avram David, Jenny Leah. BA, U. Toronto, 1962. Reporter Globe & Mail, Toronto, 1962-65, columnist, 1985-89; freelancer, 1965-71; editor, feature writer Chatelaine, 1971-78; columnist The Toronto Star, 1978-84, 89—, Globe and Mail, Toronto, 1985-88. Author: Women & Children First, 1982, Reading for the Love of It, 1986, This is New York, Honey! A Homage to Manhattan in Love & Rage, 1989. Recipient Nat. Newspaper award (columns), 1980, (feature writing) 81. Office: TorStar Newspapers Ltd, 1 Yonge St, Toronto, ON Canada M5E 1E6

LANDSMAN, STEPHEN A., lawyer; b. Chgo., Aug. 28, 1942; s. Sam W. and Jeanne N. (Engerman) L.; m. Beth Landsman; children: Mark, Scott, Sari. B.S. in Econs., Wharton Sch. Fin., U. Pa., 1964; J.D. summa cum laude, U. Mich., 1967. Bar: Ill. 1967, U.S. Dist. Ct. (no. dist.) Ill. 1967, U.S. Ct. Appeals (7th cir.) 1967, U.S. Tax Ct. 1970. Assoc. Mayer, Brown & Platt, Chgo., 1967-69; assoc. Rudnick & Wolfe, Chgo., 1969-70, ptnr., 1970—. Contbr. articles to legal jours. Bd. dirs., treas. St. Joseph Hosp. Assocs., Chgo., 1978-82. Mem. Chgo. Bar Assn., Ill. Bar Assn., Am. Arbitration Assn., Order of Coif. Office: Rudnick & Wolfe 203 N La Salle St Ste 1800 Chicago IL 60601-1210

LANDWEHR, ARTHUR JOHN, minister; b. Northbrook, Ill., Mar. 8, 1934; s. Arthur John Sr. and Alice Eleanor (Borchardt) L.; m. Avonna Lee, Sept. 19, 1953; children: Arthur J. III, Andrea Lea Askow. BA, Drake U., 1956; BD, Garrett-Theol. Sem., 1959; DD (hon.), North Cen. Coll., 1980. Ordained to ministry Meth. Ch., 1959. Pastor Lyndon (Ill.) United Meth. Ch., 1956-59, Marseilles (Ill.) United Meth. Ch., 1959-65, Faith United Meth. Ch., Lisle, Ill., 1965-69; sr. minister First United Meth. Ch., Elmhurst, Ill., 1969-75, Evanston, Ill., 1975-88; sr. minister Grace United Meth. Ch., Naperville, Ill., 1988—; trustee Garrett-Evang. Theol. Sem., Evanston, 1976—, 1st v.p. bd. trustees, 1977-86; del. to gen. conf. United Meth. Ch., 1976, 80, 84, 88, World Meth. Conf., Nairobi, Kenya, 1986; Wilson lectr., 1987; preacher Adams Sermon Bloomington, Ind., 1991, N.Mex. Ann. Conf., 1992, N.W. Tex. Conf., 1992. Author: In the Third Place, 1972; contbr. articles to profl. jours. Convenor Blue Ribbon Com. for Referendum on Expanded Gambling in Ill., 1994. Recipient citation for human rels. City of Lisle, 1969; study grantee World Coun. Chs., Sri Lanka, 1983, Ecumenical Inst. for Advanced Studies, Tantur, Israel, 1977. Mem. AAAS, Am. Acad. Religion, Am. Theol. Soc., Ill. Bar Assn. (interprofl. cooperation com. 1991-95), Order of St. Luke, Univ. Club (Evanston, Ill., pres. 1986-87). Home: Box 157 Chama NM 87520-0460 Office: Grace United Meth Ch 300 E Gartner Rd Naperville IL 60540-7424 *It is evident to me that life is a gift surrounded in mystery. Like most mysteries, we wait for the moment of revelation in which there is a profound understanding. I've learned that without a radical lane life has no future.*

LANDY, BURTON AARON, lawyer; b. Chgo., Aug. 16, 1929; s. Louis J. and Clara (Ernstein) L.; m. Eleanor M. Simmel, Aug. 4, 1957; children: Michael Simmel, Alisa Anne. Student, Nat. U. Mex., 1948; B.S., Northwestern U., 1950; postgrad. scholar, U. Havana, 1951; J.D., U. Miami, 1952; postgrad. fellow, Inter-Am. Acad. Comparative Law, Havana, Cuba, 1955-56. Bar: Fla. 1952. Practice law in internat. field Miami, 1955—; ptnr. firm Ammerman & Landy, 1957-63, Paul, Landy, Beiley & Harper, P.A. and predecessor firm, 1964-94, Steel Hector & Davis, 1994—; lectr. Latin Am. bus. law U. Miami Sch. Law, 1972-75; also internat. law confs. in U.S. and abroad; mem. Nat. Conf. on Fgn. Aspects of U.S. Nat. Security, Washington, 1958; mem. organizing com. Miami regional conf. Com. for Internat. Econ. Growth, 1958; mem. U.S. Dept. Commerce Regional Export Expansion Council, 1969-74, mem. Dist. Export Council, 1978—; mem. U.S. Sec. State Adv. Com. on Pvt. Internat. Law; dir. Fla. Council Internat. Devel., 1977—, chmn. 1986-87; mem. U. Miami Citizens Bd., 1977—; chmn. Fla. del. S.E. U.S.-Japan Assn., 1980-82; mem. adv. com. 1st Miami Trade Fair of Ams., 1978; dir., v.p. Greater Miami Fgn. Trade Zone, Inc., 1978—; mem. organizing com., lectr. 4 Inter-Am. Aviation Law Confs.; bd. dirs. Inter-Am. Bar Legal Found.; participant Aquaculture Symposium Sci. and Man in the Ams., Mexico City, Fla. Gov's Econ. Mission to Japan and Hong Kong, 1978; mem. bd. exec. advisors Law and Econs. Ctr.; mem. vis. com. U. Miami Sch. Bus.; mem. internat. fin. council Office Comptroller of Fla.; founding chmn. Fla.-Korea Econ. Coop. Com., 1982—, Southeast U.S.-Korea Econ. Com., 1985—; chmn. Expo 500 Fla.-Columbus Soc., 1985-87; founding co-chmn. So. Fla. Roundtable-Georgetown U. Ctr. for Strategic and Internat. Studies, 1982-85; chmn. Fla. Gov.'s Conf. on World Trade, 1984—; gen. counsel Fla. Internat. Bankers Assn.; dir., former gen. counsel Fla. Internat. Ins. and Reins. Assn., chmn. Latin Am. Carribbean Bus. Promotion Adv. Counc. to U.S. Sec. of Commerce and Aid Adminstr; appointee Fla. Internat. Trade and Investment Coun.; mem. steering com. Summit of Ams., 1994—, co-chair post summit planning com. Contbg. editor Econs. Devel. Lawyers of the Ams., 1969-74; contbr. numerous articles to legal jours. in U.S. and fgn. countries. Chmn. City of Miami Internat. Trade and Devel. Com., 1984-86; chmn. internat. task force Beacon Coun. of Dade County, Fla., 1985, dir., chmn., 1991—; bd. dirs., exec. com. Internat. Comml. Dispute Resolution Ctr., Miami Internat. Arbitration and Mediation Inst.; chmn. Comml. Dispute Resolution Ctr. for the Ams., Miami, 1995—; apptd. by Gov. of Fla. to Internat. Currency and Barter Commn., 1986; ectr. U. Miami Inter-Ban course for Latin Am. bankers; steering com. Summit of the Americas, Miami, 1994, co-chair post Summit Planning Com., 1994. With JACGC, USAF, 1952-54, Korea; to maj. Res. Named Internat. Trader of Yr., Fla. Council Internat. Devel., 1980, Bus. Person of Yr., 1986; recipient Pan Am. Informatica Comunicaciones Expo award, 1983, Lawyer of Americas award U. Miami, 1984, Richard L. McLaughlin award Fla. Econ. Devel. Coun., 1993; named hon. consul gen. Republic of Korea, Miami, 1983-88, recipient Heung-in medal (Order of Diplomatic Service), 1986, Ministerial Citation, Min. of Fgn. Affairs, 1988; apptd. Hon. consul Ft. Lauderdale, Fla., 1991—. Fellow ABA Found. (chmn. com. arrangements internat. and comparative law sect. 1964-65, com. on Inter-Am. affairs of ABA 1985-87); mem. Inter-Am. Bar Assn. (asst. sec.-gen. 1957-59, treas. 11th conf. 1959, co-chmn. jr. bar sect. 1963-65, mem council 1969—, exec. com. 1975—, pres. 1982-84, Diploma de Honor 1987, William Roy Vallance award 1989), Spanish Am. Bar Assn., Fla. Bar Assn. (vice chmn. adminstrv. law com. 1965, vice chmn. internat. and comparative law com. 1967-68, chmn. aero. law com. 1968-69), Dade County Bar Assn. (chmn. fgn. laws and langs com. 1964-65), Internat. Ctr. Fla. (pres. 1981-82), orld Peace Through Law Ctr., Miami Com. Fgn. Relations, Inst. Ibero Am. Derecho Aero., Am. Soc. Internat. Law, Council Internat. Visitors, Am. Fgn. Law Assn. (pres. Miami 1958), Bar of South Korea (hon. mem.), Greater Miami C. of C. (bd. govs. 1986—), Colombian-Am. C. of C. (bd. dirs. 1986—), Peruvian-Am. C. of C. (bd. dirs.), Phi Alpha Delta. Home: 605 Almeria Ave Coral Gables FL 33134-5602 Office: 200 S Biscayne Blvd Miami FL 33131-2310

LANDY, JOANNE VEIT, foreign policy analyst; b. Chgo., Oct. 15, 1941; d. Fritz and Lucille (Stearns) Veit; m. Seymour Landy, Mar., 1959 (div. 1962); m. Nelson Lichtenstein, Mar., 1972 (div. 1976). BA in History, U. Calif., Berkeley, 1968; MA in History, U. Calif., Berkley, 1970; MPH, Columbia U., 1982. Dir. N.Y. Met. Office, U. Chgo., N.Y.C., 1977-80; pres. Campaign for Peace and Democracy, N.Y.C., 1982—; bd. dirs. Human Rights Watch, Helsinki. Editor: Peace & Democracy, 1984—. Recipient grant for rsch. and writing John D. and Catherine T. Mac Arthur Fedn., Program on Peace and Internat. Cooperation, Chgo., 1990-91. Mem. Coun. on Fgn. Rels., Phi Beta Kappa. Home: 2785 Broadway Apt 7A New York NY 10025-2850 Office: Campaign for Peace and Democracy PO Box 1640 New York NY 10025-1560

LANDY, LISA ANNE, lawyer; b. Miami, Fla., Apr. 20, 1963; d. Burton Aaron and Eleonora Maria (Simmel) L. BA, Brown U., 1985; JD cum laude, U. Miami, 1988. Bar: Fla. 1988, U.S. Dist. Ct. (so. dist.) Fla. 1988. Atty. Paul, Landy, Beiley & Harper, P.A., Miami, Fla., 1988-94, Steel Hector & Davis, Miami, Fla., 1994—. Bd. dirs. Miami City Ballet, 1992—, pres., 1996; bd. dirs. Women in Internat. Trade, Miami, 1992—, pres., 1994. Mem. ABA, Inter-Am. Bar Assn. (sec. young lawyers divsn. 1992). Avocations: sports, arts, fluent in Spanish, French. Office: 200 S Biscayne Blvd Miami FL 33131-2310

LANDY, RICHARD ALLEN, geologist/mineralogist, consultant; b. Clearfield, Pa., Sept. 23, 1931; s. Gilbert Maxwell and Esther (Robinson) L.; m. Donna Jean Horst, Jan. 25, 1959; children: Richard A. Jr., Jennifer S. SB in Geology, MIT, 1953; MS in Mineralogy, Pa. State U., 1955, PhD in Mineralogy, 1961. Supervisory engr. Carborundum Co., Niagara Falls, N.Y., 1960-62; rsch. mineralogist Basic Inc., Bettsville, Ohio, 1962-63, mgr. quality assurance, 1963-65; cons., 1965-67; asst. prof. geology Allegheny Coll., Meadville, Pa., 1965-67; field officer Geol. Survey of Can., Ottawa, summer 1966, 67; rsch. mineralogist N.Am. Refractories Co., Curwensville, Pa., 1967-70; dir. rsch. N.Am. Refractories Co., State College, Pa., 1970-88; gen. mgr. N.Am. Refractories Co., Cleve., 1988-89, v.p. tech., 1989-91; dir. program devel. Ctr. for Advanced Materials, Pa. State U., 1992—; mem. bd. examiners Pa. Quality Leadership Awards, 1994; cons. in field. Contbr. articles to profl. jours.; patentee in field. 1st lt. U.S. Army, 1953-55. Fellow Brit. Ceramics Soc.; mem. ASTM (Merit award 1989). Home: 1751 Princeton Dr State College PA 16803-3260

LANE, ALFRED THOMAS, medical educator; b. Dayton, Ohio, July 17, 1947. BS, U. Dayton, 1969; MD, Ohio State U., 1973. Diplomate Am. Bd. Pediatrics, Am. Bd. Dermatology; lic. physician, Calif. Intern, resident pediatrics Children's Hosp. L.A., 1973-76; pvt. practice Pleasant Valley Pediatric Med. Group, Camarillo, Calif., 1976-79; resident dermatology U. Colo. Sch. Medicine, Denver, 1979-82; asst. prof. dermatology and pediatrics U. Rochester (N.Y.) Med. Ctr., 1982-88; attending physician Strong Meml. Hosp., 1982-90; staff dermatologist Rochester Gen. Hosp., 1985-90; dir. Dermatology Clinic VA, Rochester, 1985-90; assoc. prof. dermatology and pediatrics U. Rochester Med. Ctr., 1988-90; staff physician in dermatology and pediatrics Stanford (Calif.) U. Med. Ctr., Stanford Children's Hosp., 1990—, dir. pediatric dermatology, 1990—; assoc. prof. dermatology and pediatrics Stanford U. Med. Ctr., 1990—, acting chmn. dept. dermatology, 1995—; acting chief dermatology svc. Stanford U. Med. Ctr., Stanford Health Svcs., 1995—. Author: with W.L. Weston) Color Textbook of Pediatric Dermatology, 1991; (with W.L. Weston and J.G. Morelli) Color Textbook of Pediatric Dermatology, 1995; contbr. articles to profl. jours. Recipient Buswell fellowship U. Rochester, 1982-83, Clin. Investigator award NIH, 1983-88. Fellow Am. Acad. Pediatrics, Am. Acad. Dermatology (mem. task force on pediatric dermatology 1987-92, mem. adv. coun. 1988-90, mem. Presdl. Commn. on Melanoma/Skin Cancer 1988-92, mem. task force on youth edn. 1989-94); mem. Soc. Pediatric Dermatology (bd. dirs. 1986-93, pres. elect 1990-91, pres. 1991-92), Soc. Investigative Dermatology (com. on pub. rels. 1990-94, com. on govt. and pub. rels. 1992-94), Soc. Pediatric Rsch., Am. Dermatol. Assn., Am. Soc. Laser Medicine and Surgery. Office: Stanford U Med Ctr Dept Dermatology 900 Blake Wilbur #W0071 Stanford CA 94305-5334

LANE, ALVIN HUEY, JR., management consultant; b. Dallas, May 2, 1942; s. Alvin Huey and Marianne (Halsell) L.; m. Melanie Kadane, June 21, 1963; children—Alvin Huey, III, Michael, Lance, Marianne. B.A. (Western Electric scholar, J. Venn Leeds scholar), Rice U., Houston, 1964, B.S., 1965. Mgmt. positions with Procter & Gamble Mfg. Co., 1965-68; mgmt. cons. Ernst & Young, CPA's, Dallas, 1968-69; v.p. fin., sec. Balanced Investment Dynamics Co., Dallas, 1969-72, Dr Pepper Co., Dallas, 1972-80; sr. v.p. fin., sec. Dr Pepper Co., 1980-83; pres. Lane & Assocs., Dallas, 1983—; bd. dirs. Heartland Wireless Comms., Dallas, Love Bottling Co., Muskogee, Okla., Marketplace Christian Network, Dallas. Mem. Lakewood Country Club. Home: 3415 Colgate Ave Dallas TX 75225-4830 Office: Lane and Assocs 10440 N Central Expy Ste 610 Dallas TX 75231-2227

LANE, ALVIN S., lawyer; b. Englewood, N.J., June 17, 1918; s. Martin Lane and Nettie (Gans) Daniels; m. Terese P. Lyons, Apr. 24, 1949; children: Mary-Jo, Judith Lyons. Ph.B., U. Wis., 1940; LL.B., Harvard U., 1943. Bar: N.Y. 1947. Sr. ptnr. Wien, Lane & Malkin (now Wien, Malkin & Bettex), 1954-83; chmn. Rapidata, Inc., 1967-82; Mem. adv. bd. to N.Y. atty. gen. on art legis., 1966-71. Contbr. articles to art publs. and legal jours. Mem. bd. mgmt. Henry Ittleson Rsch. Ctr. Disturbed Children, Riverdale, N.Y., 1961-70; fellow Brandeis U., 1966—, nat. adv. coun. 20th Century Art Soc. High Mus. of Art, 1986—; sec., trustee Aldrich Mus. Contemporary Art, Inc., 1969-76; trustee Lexington Sch. Deaf, 1971; v.p., trustee Soho Ctr. Visual Artists, Inc., 1974-83; dir. Creative Artists Pub. Svc. Program, Inc., 1982-84; mem. drawing com. Whitney Mus. Am Art, 1991-93; mem. The Elvehjem Mus. Art Coun., 1992—. Served as lt. USNR, 1942-46. Mem. Assn. of Bar of City of N.Y. (chmn. com. art 1963-65), N.Y. Artists Equity Assn. (dir. 1982-84). Clubs: Harvard (N.Y.C.), Riverdale Yacht. Home: 5251 Independence Ave Riverdale NY 10471-2825 Office: 35 E 38th St New York NY 10016-2529

LANE, ARTHUR ALAN, lawyer; b. N.Y.C., Dec. 2, 1945; s. George and Delys L.; m. Jane Ficocella, Dec. 30, 1972; 1 child, Eva B. BA, Yale U., 1967; JD, Columbia U., 1970, MBA, 1971. Bar: N.Y. 1971. Assoc. Webster, Sheffield, Fleischmann, Hitchcock & Brookfield, N.Y.C., 1971-72; asst. to div. counsel Liggett & Myers Inc., N.Y.C., 1973; assoc. Wickes, Riddell, Bloomer, Jacobi & McGuire, N.Y.C., 1974-78, Morgan, Lewis & Bockius, N.Y.C., 1979; ptnr. Eaton & Van Winkle, N.Y.C., 1980-94, DeForest & Duer, N.Y.C., 1994—. Mem. ABA, Assn. of Bar of City of N.Y., Soc. of Colonial Wars. Avocation: gardening. Home: 103 Brooksite Dr Smithtown NY 11787-4456 Office: DeForest & Duer 90 Broad St New York NY 10004-2205

LANE, BARBARA MILLER (BARBARA MILLER-LANE), humanities educator; b. N.Y.C., Nov. 1, 1934; d. George Ross Rede and Gertrude Miller; m. Jonathan Lane, Jan. 28, 1956; children: Steven Gregory, Eleanor. B.A., U. Chgo., 1953, Barnard Coll., 1956; M.A., Radcliffe Coll., 1957; Ph.D., Harvard U., 1962. Tutor history and lit. Harvard U., Cambridge, Mass., 1960-61; lectr. to prof. history Bryn Mawr Coll., Bryn Mawr, Pa., 1962-75, dir. Growth and Structure of Cities Program, 1971-89, Andrew W. Mellon prof. humanities, 1981—; vis. prof. Architecture, Columbia U., 1989; cons. NEH sr. fellowships, Washington, 1971-73, Time-Life Books, N.Y.C., 1975, Bauhaus, Dessau, 1991; advisor Macmillan Ency. of Architects, N.Y.C., 1979-82; vis. examiner U. Helsinki, 1991; vis. lectr. Technische Universität, Berlin, 1991. Author: Architecture and Politics in Germany, 1968, 85, Italian and German edits., 1973, 86; co-author: Nazi Ideology Before 1933, 1978; contbg. author: Growth and Transformation of the Modern City, 1979, Macmillan Encyclopedia of Architects, 1982, Urbanisierung im 19, und 20, Jahrhundert, 1983, Perspectives in American History, 1984, The Evidence of Art: Images and Meaning in History, 1986, Art and History, 1988, Nationalism in the Visual Arts, 1991, Moderne Architektur in Deutschland: Expressionismus und Neue Sachlichkeit, 1994; contbr. editor: Urbanism Past and Present, 1980-85; mem. bd. editors

Archtl. History Found., 1988—, Ctrl. European History, 1992—; contbr. articles to profl. jours. Co-founder, dir., chmn. bd. dirs. New Gulph Child Care Ctr., Bryn Mawr, 1971-75; mem. Middle Atlantic Regional Com., Mellon Fellowships in the Humanities, 1985-87; mem. vis. com. Harvard U. Dept. History, 1986-92, Berlin Stadtforum (adv. coun. to Senator for Urban Devel. and Environment), 1991—. Fellow AAUW, 1959-60, Fels Found., 1961-62, Am. Council Learned Socs., 1967-68, John S. Guggenheim Found., 1977-78; sr. fellow Ctr. for Advanced Study in the Visual Arts, Nat. Gallery of Art, Washington, 1983; Am. Scandinavian Found. fellow, 1989; Wissenschaftskolleg zu Berlin fellow, 1990-91; NEH grantee, summer 1989; recipient Lindback award for excellence in tchg., 1988. Mem. Soc. Archtl. Historians (bd. dirs. 1977-80, Alice Davis Hitchcock award 1968, chmn. awards coms. 1976, 82, chmn. jour. com. 1982-83), Conf. Group on Central European History (bd. dirs. 1977-79, chmn. awards com. 1987, structure and planning adv. com. 1993—), Am. Hist. Assn. (mem. council 1979-82, chmn. com. on Popular Mag. of History 1982), Coll. Art Assn., Phi Beta Kappa. Office: Bryn Mawr Coll Bryn Mawr PA 19010

LANE, BERNARD BELL, furniture company executive; b. Lynchburg, Va., Nov. 23, 1928; s. Edward Hudson and Myrtle Clyde (Bell) L.; m. Minnie Matthews Bassett, June 7, 1950; children: William R., Lucy H., Douglas B., Bernard Bell. B.S., U.S. Naval Acad., 1950. With Lane Co., Altavista, Va., 1954-87; v.p., then exec. v.p. Lane Co., 1960-76, pres., chmn. exec. com., 1976-81, chmn. bd., 1981-87. Commr. Va. Port Authority, 1986-91; bd. dirs. Va. Poly. Inst. and State U. Ednl. Found., 1968-76, Food for the Hungry Inc., Scottsdale, Ariz., 1985-95 (chmn. bd. dirs. 1990); mem. Va. Gov.'s Adv. Bd. on Indsl. Devel., 1970-82, Va. Gov.'s Adv. Bd. on Revenue Estimates, 1977-86, Bd. of Project Concern Internat., 1995—; chmn. com. urol. rsch., endowment and devel. Duke U. Med. Ctr., 1974-82. Mem. Va. Mfrs. Assn. (bd. dirs. 1986-87). Methodist.

LANE, BRUCE STUART, lawyer; b. New London, Conn., May 15, 1932; s. Stanley S. and Frances M. (Antis) L.; m. Ann Elizabeth Steinberg, Aug. 10, 1958; children: Sue Ellen, Charles M., Richard I. Student, Boston U., 1948-49; AB magna cum laude, Harvard U., 1952, JD, 1955. Bar: Ohio 1955, D.C. 1966, U.S. Ct. Claims 1960, U.S. Tax Ct. 1961, U.S. Supreme Ct. 1961. Assoc. Squire, Sanders & Dempsey, Cleve., 1955-59; sr. trial atty. tax div. Dept. Justice, Washington, 1959-61; tax atty. Dinsmore, Shohl, Barrett, Coates & Deupree, Cin., 1961-65; sec., asst. gen. counsel corp. and tax matters Communications Satellite Corp., Washington, 1965-69; v.p., gen. counsel Nat. Corp. Housing Partnerships, Washington, 1969-70; pres. Lane and Edson P.C., Washington, 1970-89; ptnr. Kelley Drye & Warren, Washington, 1989-93; mng. ptnr. Peabody & Brown, Washington, 1993—. Co-editor-in-chief Housing and Devel. Reporter; author publs. and articles on tax, partnership and real estate. Incorporator, bd. dirs., past pres. D.C. Inst. Mental Health; past chmn. citizens Com. sect. 5 Chevy Chase, Md.; past mem. Montgomery County Hist. Preservation Commn., Md.; mem. chmn. coun. Crow Canyon Archeol. Ctr., Cortez, Colo. Maj. JAG, USAR, 1952-68. Mem. ABA, Am. Law Inst., Am. Coll. Real Estate Lawyers (pres. 1986-87), Anglo-Am. Real Property Inst., Phi Beta Kappa. Home: 3711 Thornapple St Chevy Chase MD 20815-4111 Office: Peabody & Brown 1255 23rd St NW Ste 800 Washington DC 20037-1125

LANE, BURTON (BURTON LEVY), composer; b. N.Y.C., Feb. 2, 1912; s. Lazarus and Frances Levy; m. Marion Seaman, June 28, 1935 (div. 1961); 1 dau.; m. Lynn Daroff Kaye, Mar. 5, 1961. Student, High Sch. of Commerce; studied piano with Simon Bucharoff. Former staff composer for Remick Music Pub. Wrote music for 2 songs in Three's a Crowd, 1930; 1 song in The Third Little Show, 1931; entire score for 9th edit. Earl Carroll's Vanities, 1931; 2 songs in Singin' the Blues, 1931; 1 song in Americana, 1932; composed mus. scores for Hold on to Your Hats, 1940, Laffing Room Only (also lyricist), 1944, Finian's Rainbow, 1947, On a Clear Day You Can See Forever (Tony nomination, Grammy award with Alan Jay Lerner 1965 Carmelina, 1979 (Tony nomination); songs for motion pictures including Dancing Lady, 1933, Babes on Broadway, 1941, Royal Wedding, 1951, Give a Girl a Break, 1953, On a Clear Day You Can See Forever, 1966; animated film Heidi, 1979; composer music for Junior Miss, TV, 1958; composer songs in revue Mighty Fine Music!, off-Broadway, 1983; songs include Everything I Have is Yours, Tony's Wife, Moments Like This, There's A Great Day Coming Mañana, On a Clear Day, The Lady's In Love With You, I Hear Music, Too Late Now, When I'm Not Near The Girl I Love, I Love The Girl I'm Near, Come Back To Me, How Are Things In Glocca Morra?, Look To The Rainbow, How Could You Believe Me When I Said I Love You When You Know I've Been A Liar All My Life, Says My Heart, Stop!, You're Breaking My Heart, (I Like New York In June) How About You?, It's Time For A Love Song, In Our United State, Old Devil Moon, What Did I Have That I Don't Have, One More Walk Around The Garden. Recipient 2 Acad. Award nominations, award for Finian's Rainbow, Essex Symphony Soc. 1947, Mercer Lifetime Achievement award, Richard Rodgers Lifetime Achievement award ASCAP, 1992; inducted into Theatre Hall of Fame, 1993. Mem. ASCAP (bd. dirs.), Am. Guild Authors and Composers (pres. 1957-67, Sigmund Romberg award), Songwriters Hall of Fame (dir.).

LANE, DAVID OLIVER, retired librarian; b. Flint, Mich., Oct. 17, 1931; s. Clinton Ellis and Mary Ailene (Sanders) L. B.A., U. Mich., 1958, A.M. in L.S, 1959; doctoral fellow, U. Chgo., 1968. Various library assignments, 1959-63; asst. dir. libraries Boston U., 1963-67; asst. univ. librarian U. Calif., San Diego, 1968-69; chief librarian, prof., dept. chmn. Hunter Coll., N.Y.C., 1969-90; Dir. NSF funded study of library acquisitions, 1967-68; chmn. Council Chief Librarians, City U. N.Y., 1972-75; trustee N.Y. Met. Reference Library Agy., 1978-87. Author: Study of the Decision Making Procedures for the Acquisition of Science Library Materials, 1968. Mem. A.L.A. (life), Assn. Coll. and Research Libraries, Beta Phi Mu. Home: 27D E Hill Dr Somers NY 10589

LANE, DIANE, actress; b. N.Y.C., 1963. Actress: (stage prodns.) Agamemnon, 1977, The Cherry Orchard, 1977, Runaways, 1978, Medea, Electra, The Trojan Woman, As You Like it, The Good Woman of Setzuan, (feature films) A Little Romance, 1979, Watcher in the Woods, 1980, Cattle Annie and Little Britches, 1981, National Lampoon Goes to the Movies, 1981, Six Pack, 1982, Ladies and Gentlemen, The Fabulous Stains, 1982, The Outsiders, 1983, Rumble Fish, 1983, The Cotton Club, 1984, Streets of Fire, 1984, Lady Beware, 1987, The Big Town, 1987, Vital Signs, 1990, Frankie & Johnny, 1991, Chaplin, 1992, Knight Moves, 1993, Indian Summer, 1993, Wild Bill, 1995, Judge Dredd, 1995; (TV movies) Child Bride of Short Creek, 1981, Miss All-America Beauty, 1982; appeared in TV miniseries, Lonesome Dove, 1989, The World's Oldest Living Confederate Widow Tells All, 1994. Mem. Actors' Equity Assn., AFTRA. Office: William Morris Agency 151 El Camino Beverly Hills CA 90212*

LANE, DOROTHY PERSON, nursing educator; b. Springfield, Tenn., Jan. 9, 1933; d. Robert Pearl and Sallie Mai (Griffin) Person; m. Fred. Leon Lane Jr., Aug. 29, 1958; children: Fred Leon III, Robert Person, Michael Wendell. BSN, Meharry Med. Coll., Nashville, 1955; MS in Health Adminstrn., Ctrl. Mich. U., 1988. Cert. HIV counselor. Staff nurse Hubbard Hosp., Nashville, 1955-56; staff nurse, asst. head nurse L.A. County Hosp., 1956-58; instr. Meharry Med. Coll., Nashville, 1958-61; staff nurse operating and emergency rm. St. Thomas Cath. Hosp., Nashville, 1961; staff nurse Murfresboro (Tenn.) Vets. Adminstrn. Psychiatric Hosp., 1961-62; staff nurse VA Med. Ctr. Bklyn., 1962-66, 81-89, headnurse med. unit, 1989, cmty. health nurse coord., 1989-92, instr. nursing, coord. career devel., 1992—; insvc. educator Bushwick Home and Hosp. for Aged, Bklyn., 1966; chair side asst., adminstrv. asst. Fred L. Lane Jr. D.D.S., Bklyn., 1966-79; nurse Beth Israel Hosp., N.Y.C., 1979-80; staff nurse Manhattan Kidney Ctr., N.Y.C., 1980-81; adj. prof. nursing N.Y.C. Technol. Coll., 1990-91. Asst. ch. clk. Cornerstone Bapt. Ch., 1989—, instr., tchr. tng. Sunday sch., 1985—; pres. parent assn. Elem. Sch. PS 91, Bklyn., 1976, Stuyvesant High Sch., N.Y.C., 1978-79; mem. exec. com., founder/pres. Troy Ave.- Rutland Rd. Block Assn., 1978—. Recipient Cert. of Merit Cmty. Sch. Bd. Bkyn., 1975-76, Ptnrs. in Edn. award N.Y.C. Bd. edn., 1977. Mem. Am. Nephrology Nursing Assn. (exec. bd. Big Apple chpt. 1993-95, coun. jour.), Nat. Nephrology Nursing Assn., Nurses Orgn. VA (news reporter 1993-94), Delta Sigma Theta Inc. Avocations: reading, flying, needle craft, biking, traveling. Home: 540 Troy Ave Brooklyn NY 11203 Office: VA Med Ctr Bklyn 800 Poly Pl Brooklyn NY 11209

LANE, DOROTHY SPIEGEL, physician; b. Bklyn., Feb. 17, 1940; d. Milton Barton and Rosalie (Jacobson) Spiegel; m. Bernard Paul Lane, Aug. 5, 1962; children: Erika, Andrew, Matthew. BA, Vassar Coll., 1961; MD, Columbia U., 1965, MPH, 1968. Diplomate Am. Bd. Preventive Medicine, Am. Bd. Family Practice. Resident preventive medicine N.Y.C. Dept. Health Dist., 1966-68; project dir. children and youth project Title V, HHS N.Y.C. Dept. Health Dist., Rockaway, N.Y., 1968-69; med. cons. Maternal and Child Health Svc. HHS, Rockville, Md., 1970-71; asst. prof. preventive medicine Sch. Medicine SUNY, Stony Brook, 1971-76, assoc. prof., 1976-92; prof., 1992—; assoc. dean Sch. Medicine SUNY, Stony Brook, 1986—; chair dept. community medicine, dir. med. edn. Brookhaven Meml. Hosp. Med. Ctr., Patchogue, N.Y., 1972-86. Contbr. numerous articles to profl. jours. Mem. exec. com. Am. Cancer Soc., L.I. divsn., 1975—; mem. nat. bd. dirs. Am. Cancer Soc.; corp. mem. Nassau Suffolk Health Systems Agy., L.I., 1977—; bd. dirs. Community Health Plan Suffolk, Hauppauge, 1986-91. Grantee HHS-USPHS, 1977-85, 83—, Nat. Cancer Inst., 1987—. Fellow APHA, Am. Coll. Preventive Medicine (regent 1988-96, sec.-treas. 1994-96), Am. Acad. Family Physicians, N.Y. Acad. Medicine, Am. Bd. Preventive Medicine (trustee), Assn. Tchrs. Preventive Medicine (pres. 1996—). Office: SUNY Sch Medicine Health Scis Ctr L-4 Stony Brook NY 11794-8437

LANE, EDWARD WOOD, JR., retired banker; b. Jacksonville, Fla., Apr. 4, 1911; s. Edward Wood and Anna Virginia (Taliaferro) L.; m. Helen Spratt Murchison, Oct. 16, 1948; children: Edward Wood III, Helen Palmer, Anna Taliaferro, Charles Murchison. A.B., Princeton, 1933; LL.B., Harvard U., 1936. Bar: Fla. 1936. Partner firm McCarthy, Lane & Adams (and predecessors), Jacksonville, 1941-60; pres. Atlantic Nat. Bank, Jacksonville, 1961-74, chmn., 1974-85; chmn. First Union Nat. Bank of Fla. (formerly Atlantic Nat. Bank), Jacksonville, 1985-86, ret., 1986. Served to lt. comdr. USNR, World War II. Mem. Phi Beta Kappa. Clubs: Florida Yacht (Jacksonville), Timuquana Country (Jacksonville), River (Jacksonville), Univ. (Jacksonville); Ponte Vedra, Sawgrass. Home and Office: 3790 Ortega Blvd Jacksonville FL 32210

LANE, FIELDING H., lawyer; b. Kansas City, Mo., May 6, 1926; s. Ralph Fielding and Nancy Lee (Greene) L.; m. Patricia Cecil Parkhurst, Jan. 25, 1980. B.S. in Bus. Adminstrn., U. Mo.-Columbia, 1948; LL.B. cum laude, Harvard U., 1951. Bar: Mo. 1951, Calif. 1956. Assoc. Watson Ess Marshall & Enggas, Kansas City, Mo., 1951-55; assoc. Thelen Marrin Johnson & Bridges, San Francisco, 1955-66, ptnr., 1967—. Served with USN, 1944-46; PTO; lt. comdr. Res. (ret.). Club: Olympic (San Francisco). Home: 165 Villa Ter San Francisco CA 94114-2213 Office: Thelen Marrin Johnson & Bridges 2 Embarcadero Ctr Ste 2200 San Francisco CA 94111-3995

LANE, FRANK JOSEPH, JR., lawyer; b. St. Louis, May 10, 1934; s. Frank Joseph and Virginia Laurette (Hausman) L.; m. Margaret Ann Dwyer, Mar. 2, 1957; children: Mary, Stephen, Thomas, Michael. BS in Commerce, St. Louis U., 1956, JD, 1956; LLM, Georgetown U., 1960; grad. Parker Sch. Internat. Law, Columbia U., 1970; cert., Coll. Fin. Planning, Denver, 1988. Bar: Mo. 1956, U.S. Dist. Ct. (ea. dist.) Mo. 1956, U.S. Ct. Appeals (8th cir.) 1960, U.S. Supreme Ct. 1959. Ptnr. Goldenhersh, Goldenhersh, Fredericks, Newman & Lane, St. Louis, 1960-64, Lane & Leadlove, St. Louis, 1964-66, Dill & Lane, St. Louis, 1978-79; counsel Ralston Purina Co., St. Louis, 1966-78; of counsel Petrolite Corp., St. Louis, 1979-83; v.p., trust officer Gravois Bank, St. Louis, 1983-85; regional v.p., trust officer Merc Bank N.A., St. Louis, 1985-89; of counsel Dill, Wamser & Bamvakais, St. Louis, 1989—; instr. internat. law St. Louis U., 1979. Bd. dirs. Met. St. Louis Sewer Dist., 1965-73, chmn., 1968-69; mem. planned giving com. Am. Heart Assn., St. Louis, 1986-88, St. Louis Soc. for Crippled Children, 1991; bd. dirs. Braille Vols., Inc., chmn., 1995—. Mem. Mo. Bar Assn., Met. St. Louis Bar Assn. (chmn. office practice com. 1963-64), Estate Planning Coun., Rotary (bd. dirs. Crestwood, Mo. chpt. 1988-89), KC (grand knight 1964-66, adv. West County 1983-90, Webster Groves 1991—). Republican. Roman Catholic. Avocations: oil painting, golf, travel, investment analysis. Home: 520 Lering Dr Ballwin MO 63011-1588 Office: 9939 Gravois Rd Saint Louis MO 63123-4211

LANE, FREDERICK CARPENTER, investment banker; b. Boston, Aug. 28, 1949; s. Francis Robert and Edith (Lent) L.; m. Wendy Jane Evrard, June 9, 1973; children—Jesse Evrard, Eliza Evrard. A.B. cum laude, Harvard U., 1971, M.B.A. with distinction, 1973. C.P.A., Mass. Supr. Coopers & Lybrand CPAs, Boston, 1973-76; sr. v.p., prin. Donaldson, Lufkin & Jenrette, N.Y.C. and Boston, 1976-88; exec. v.p. Bessemer Securities Corp., N.Y.C., 1988-89; mng. dir. and dir. mergers and acquistions dept. Donaldson, Lufkin & Jenrette, N.Y.C., 1989—. Dir. Process Tech. Holdings, Gastonia, N.C. Racquet and Tennis Club (N.Y.C.), Harvard Club (Boston), Maugus Club (Wellesley, Mass.), Doubles Club (N.Y.C.). Republican. Episcopalian. Office: Donaldson Lufkin & Jenrette Securities Corp 277 Park Ave New York NY 10172-9999

LANE, FREDERICK STANLEY, lawyer; b. Cumberland, Md., Jan. 16, 1915; s. Clifford Warren and Edith Persis (Mott) L.; m. Barbara Bentley, Mar. 6, 1943; children: Clifford Warren, Martha Cogswell, Susan Bonney, Jeffery Calvin. A.B. magna cum laude, Amherst Coll., 1936; LL.B., Harvard U., 1939. Bar: Mass. 1939. Assoc. Nutter, McClennen & Fish, Boston, 1939-50; ptnr. Nutter, McClennen & Fish, 1951-90; ret.; past trustee, clk. Hingham Instn. for Savs. Editor: Real Estate in Mid-Century, 1973; contbr. articles to profl. jours. Former trustee Social Law Library, Boston; former vice chmn. Council of Friends of Amherst Coll. Library. Served to lt. comdr. USNR, 1942-46. Recipient Richard B. Johnson Meml. award Mass. Conveyancers Assn., 1981. Fellow Am. Bar Found.; Mem. Boston Bar Assn., ABA (chmn. sect. real property, probate and trust law 1977-78), Anglo-Am. Real Property Inst. (chmn. 1982-83), Am. Coll. Real Estate Lawyers (pres. 1979-81), Mass. Conveyancers Assn. (pres. 1968-70), Abstract Club (pres. 1981-84), Phi Beta Kappa, Theta Delta Chi. Republican. Unitarian. Clubs: Union, Harvard, Fly Casters (pres. 1978-80). Home: 18 Ship St Hingham MA 02043-1816

LANE, GEORGE HOLMAN, JR., newspaper publisher; b. Lewisburg, Tenn., Oct. 18, 1945; s. George Holman and Martha Frances (Ross) L.; m. Sue Carol Colbert, Mar. 26, 1976; children—Lee Anna, Cynthia Lynn, Nathan George. announcer WCCF-AM, Punta Gorda, Fla., 1962-63, sports corr. Miami Herald, Ft. Myers, Fla., 1963-64; editor, pub. Northside Citizen, North Ft. Myers, 1964-65; news dir. WCAI-AM, Ft. Myers, 1965, news/photo stringer S.W. Fla., UPI, 1965-75; news reporter/editor WINK News, Ft. Myers, 1967-74; bur. chief St. Petersburg Times, Punta Gorda, Fla., 1967-74; legis. aide Fla. State Legislature, Ft. Myers and Tallahassee, 1974-75; gen. mgr., advt. dir. Sunshine Newspaper, Arcadia, Fla., 1976; gen. mgr., pub. Desoto Shopping Guide, Arcadia, 1976-83; gen. mgr.-pub., founder, Desoto County Times, 1983-86; roving editor Sun Coast Media Group (new owners Desoto County Times), 1986-89; roving feature writer Tampa Tribune, 1987-88, dir. Fal. Dept. Commerce Office of Comm., 1989—, cons., lobbyist freelance; ptnr. Big Red Q Quickprint Ctr., Arcadia, 1981-84. Author: A Pictorial History of Arcadia and Desoto County, 1984; editor hist. papers in Southwest Fla. history, 1980-83; Contbr. articles to profl. jours. Pres. Southwest Floridiana, Arcadia, 1980—; chmn. Desoto County Republican Com., 1977-84, precinct 10 committeeman, 1980-88, mem. state com., 1980— (exec. com. outstanding svc. award, 1985-87); chmn. Desoto County Hist. Commn., 1976—; mem. Desoto County Hist. Soc., 1986—; mem. DeSoto High Sch. Adv. Com., 1983—; chmn. Arcadia/DeSoto County Centennial Celebration Com., 1985-87; mem. Main Street Arcadia Com., 1984—, chmn., 1985-87; co-founder, charter v.p. Save Our School Com., 1985-87; chmn. pub. relations com. Fla. Rep. Party, 1984—; mem. citizens adv. com. Desoto Meml. Hosp., 1981-86; bd. dirs. March of Dimes, 1981-86; mem. vestry St. Edmunds Ch., 1978-80. Recipient Disting. Service award DeSoto Historic Commn., ABI Disting. Leadership award, 1987-88, Mem. Downtown Assn. Arcadia (pres. 1981-87), Desoto County C. of C. (Citizen of Yr. 1983, Minute Man award, 1982, pres. 1982-83), Fla. Advt. Pubs. Assn., Fla. Press Assn., Nat. Assn. Advt. Pubs., Charlotte Harbor Area Hist. Soc., Peace River Valley Hist. Soc., Fla. Hist. Soc., Ducks Unltd. Republican. Episcopalian. Clubs: Arcadia Country, others. Lodges: Odd Fellows, Moose, Rotary (pres. 1983-84, outstanding service award 1978-80), Elks. Home: PO Box 1776 Arcadia FL 33821 Office: George Lane, Jr, and Assocs PO Box 10433 200-C S Monroe St Tallahassee FL 32302-0433

LANE, GLORIA JULIAN, foundation administrator; b. Chgo., Oct. 6, 1932; d. Coy Berry and Katherine (McDowell) Julian; m. William Gordon Lane (div. Oct. 1958); 1 child, Julie Kay Rosewood. BS in Edn., Cen. Mo. State U., 1958; MA, Bowling Green State U., 1959; PhD, No. Ill. U., 1972. Cert. tchr. Assoc. prof. William Jewell Coll., Liberty, Mo., 1959-60; chair forensic div. Coral Gables (Fla.) High Sch., 1960-64; assoc. prof. No. Ill. U., DeKalb, 1964-70; prof. Elgin (Ill.) Community Coll., 1970-72; owner, pub. Lane and Assocs, Inc., San Diego, 1972-78; prof. Nat. U., San Diego, 1978-90; pres., chief exec. officer Women's Internat. Ctr., San Diego, 1982—; founder, dir. Living Legacy Awards, San Diego, 1984—. Author: Project Text for Effective Communications, 1972, Project Text for Executive Communication, 1980, Positive Concepts for Success, 1983; editor Who's Who Among San Diego Women, 1984, 85, 86, 90—, Systems and Structure, 1984. Named Woman of Accomplishment, Soroptimist Internat., 1985, Pres.'s Coun. San Diego, 1986, Center City Assn., 1986, Bus. and Profl. Women, San Diego, 1991, Woman of Yr., Girls' Clubs San Diego, 1986, Woman of Vision, Women's Internat. Ctr., 1990, Wonderwoman 2000 Women's Times Newspaper, 1991; recipient Independence award Ctr. for Disabled, 1986, Founder's award Children's Hosp. Internat., Washington, 1986. Avocations: computers, painting, writing. Home and Office: 6202 Friars Rd Apt 311 San Diego CA 92108-1008

LANE, HANA UMLAUF, editor; b. Stockholm, Mar. 14, 1946; came to U.S., 1951, naturalized, 1957; d. Karel Hugo Antonin and Anatolia (Spitel) Umlauf; m. John Richard Lane, Feb. 16, 1980; 1 stepchild, Matthew John. A.B. magna cum laude, Vassar Coll., 1968; A.M. in Russian and East European Studies, Yale U., 1970. Asst. to exec. editor Newspaper Enterprise Assn., N.Y.C., 1970-72, sr. asst., asst. editor World Almanac div., 1972-75, assoc. editor World Almanac, 1975-80, spl. project editor, 1977-80; editor World Almanac and World Almanac Publs., N.Y.C., 1980-85; editor in chief Pharos Books, N.Y.C., 1984-91; editor Pharos Books, 1991-93; sr. editor John Wiley & Sons, 1993—. Editor: World Almanac Book of Who, 1980, World Almanac and Book of Facts, 1981-85; (with others) The Woman's Almanac, 1977. Democrat. Home: 140 Fairview Ave Stamford CT 06902-8040

LANE, HAROLD EDWIN, retired management educator, consultant; b. Malden, Mass., Aug. 19, 1913; s. Edwin George and Annabel (Fraser) L.; m. Constance Mason, June 1, 1940; children: Stephen Winslow, Harold Edwin, Nancy (Mrs. John H. Piper). BS, Boston U., 1936, MA, 1940. Asst. sec. Greater Boston Community Fund, 1940-42; sr. economist Nat. War Labor Bd., Boston, also Portland, Oreg., 1943-46; dir. personnel Sordoni Industries, Wilkes-Barre, Pa., 1946-47; dir. personnel and labor relations Sheraton Corp. Am., Boston, 1947-54; v.p. Sheraton Corp. Am., 1954-68; mgmt. cons., 1968-69; v.p. Fred Harvey, Inc., Chgo., 1969-70; assoc. prof. Bus. Coll., Mich. State U., East Lansing, 1970-78; prof. Bus. Coll. Mich. State U., East Lansing, 1978-81, prof. emeritus, 1981—; founding dir., prof. Sch. Hospitality Adminstrn. Boston U., 1981-93, prof. emeritus, 1993—; summer sch. instr. Cornell U., 1946-67; spl. lectr. Harvard.; Mem. Pres.'s Adv. Com. on Occupational Safety; mem. Council on Pres.'s Plans for Progress; nat. adv. com. Job Corps, Office Econ. Opportunity; chmn. Wage Deviation Bd. State Mich., 1974-78; participant seminar Harvard Bus. Sch., 1963; cons. Ford Found. N.Y., 1963; seminar instr. Am. Mgmt. Assn., 1964. Author: (with Mark Van Hartesvelt) Essentials of Hospitality Management, 1983; (with Denise Dupré) Hospitality World, 1996; mem. editl. bd. Jour. Managerial Issues, Pitts. State U., Southwest Bus. Rev., Southwest Tex. State U.; contbr. articles to profl. jours. Mem. Soc. Advancement Mgmt., Am. Mgmt. Assn., Am. Hotel and Motel Assn., Council on Hotel, Restaurant and Instnl. Edn., Internat. Assn. Hotel Mgmt. Schs., Internat. Hotel Assn., Nat. Restaurant Assn., AAUP, Friends East-West Center Honolulu, The Conf. Bd. Unitarian. Home: 9 Nutmeg Cir Laconia NH 03246-5500 Office: Boston U Sch Hospitality Adminstrn 808 Commonwealth Ave Boston MA 02215-1206

LANE, HENRY WALLACE, physician, consultant; b. Chgo., Aug. 31, 1911; s. Henry Higgins and Mary June (Harper) L.; m. Mary Jane Whitaker, Aug. 26, 1938 (dec. Jan. 1984); children: Edwin Wallace, William Robert. AB, U. Kans., 1933, MA in Immunology, 1935, MD, 1939; MPH, Johns Hopkins U., 1951. Resident in pathology Kans. Med. Ctr., Kansas City, Kans., 1940-41; physician Student Health Svcs., Lawrence, Kans., 1946-48; dir. pub. health U.S. Civil Adminstrn., Naha Ryukyu Islands, 1954-55; assoc. prof. Dept. Preventive Medicine, Seattle, 1957-73; chief div. adult health State Dept. Health, Seattle, 1958-61; chief div. local health State Dept. Health, Olympia, Wash., 1961-68, dir., 1968-73; asst. sec. Dept. Social & Health Svc., Olympia, Wash., 1970-73; preventive medical cons. Olympia, Wash., 1973—. With M.C., U.S. Army, 1953-55. Recipient Oread medal U. Kans., 1929. Mem. AMA, N.Y. Acad. Sci., Phi Sigma, Phi Beta Kappa, Sigam Xi, Alpha Omega Alpha. Avocation: family history. Home and Office: 1817 Governor Stevens Ave SE Olympia WA 98501-3711

LANE, JAMES GARLAND, JR., diversified industry executive; b. Roxobel, N.C., Jan. 15, 1934; s. James Garl and Josie (Wembrow) L.; m. Janet Benthall Miller, Oct. 8, 1954; children—Bernice, Frances, Garland, Amy. B.S., U. N.C., 1959. Mem. audit staff S.D. Leidesdorf & Co., Greenville, S.C., 1959-65; v.p. finance Computer Servicenters, Inc., Greenville, 1965-68; exec. v.p., dir. Synalloy Corp., Spartanburg, S.C., 1968-73; pres. dir. Hewitt, Coleman & Assocs. subs. Continental Group, Inc., Greenville, 1973-86; chmn. bd., chief exec. officer Synalloy Corp., Spartanburg, 1986—, also dir.; bd. dirs. Sunbelt Cos., Inc. Served with USMCR, 1953-56. Home: 120 Pentland Ct Greer SC 29651-9137

LANE, JAMES MCCONKEY, investment executive; b. Pitts., July 9, 1929; s. Mortimer Bliss and Mary (Knapp) L.; m. Arlyne Ruth Nelson, Dec. 16, 1950; children: James, Theodore, Thomas, Karen, David. BA, Wheaton Coll., 1952; MBA, U. Chgo., 1953; postgrad., NYU, 1956, U. Buffalo, 1960. Credit corr. John Plain & Co., Chgo., 1951; trainee Chase Manhattan Bank, N.Y.C., 1953-55, account mgr. investment adv. divsn., 1955-59, investment officer, 1959-62, 2nd v.p., 1962-64, v.p., mgr. corp. pension trust investments, 1964-66, v.p. divsn. exec. pension trust investment divsn., 1966-68, chmn. investment policy com., 1968-78, sr. v.p., investment group exec., 1968-70, exec. v.p. fiduciary investment dept., 1970-78; pres., dir. Chase Investors Mgmt. Corp., N.Y.C., 1972-78; mng. dir. Cyrus J. Lawrence Inc., N.Y.C., 1978-82; sr. v.p., chief investment officer, head trust investment divsn. NBD Bank N.A., Detroit, 1982-94, mem. sr. mgmt., 1984-94; bd. dirs. Chateau Properties, Inc. Bd. dirs. Christian Camps Inc., 1978—, Baseball Chapel, 1994—, William Tyndale Coll., 1985—, chmn., 1995—; trustee Wheaton Coll., 1971—. Mem. N.Y. Soc. Security Analysts, Fin. Analysts Soc. Detroit (pres. bd. dirs.), Econ. Club Detroit, Detroit Club, Grosse Pointe Yacht Club. Home and Office: 24 Harbor Hill Rd Grosse Pointe MI 48236-3748

LANE, JEFFREY BRUCE, financial services company executive; b. Bklyn., June 25, 1942; s. Murray and Arlene (Avram) L.; m. Nancy Stern, June 24, 1982. BA, NYU, 1964; MBA, Columbia U., 1970. With Shearson Lehman Hutton, N.Y.C., CFO, vice chmn., 1983-84, COO, 1984-87, pres., 1987-90; pres. Primerica Holdings, N.Y., 1990-94; vice chmn. Smith Barney Harris Upham & Co. Inc., N.Y.C., 1991—; vice chmn. and dir. Smith Barney, Shearson Inc., N.Y.C.; vice chmn. Smith Barney, Shearson, Inc., N.Y.C.; vice chmn. bd. of govs. Am. Stock Exchange;. Bd. dirs. Woodmere Acad., N.Y., L.I. Jewish Hosp. Served to 1st lt. U.S. Army, 1966-68. Republican. Jewish. Office: Smith Barney Shearson Inc 388 Greenwich St New York NY 10013*

LANE, JERRY ROSS, human services manager, alcohol/drug abuse service professional; b. Pampa, Tex., June 3, 1944; s. Wilbur Howard and Christina Lavina (Hendrix) L.; m. Mary Lou Jetton, July 9, 1966; children: Jeffrey Ross, Tamara Noel. BS, McMurry U., 1968; MS in Counseling Psychology, Emmanuel Bapt. U., 1988, D in Counseling Psychology, 1991. Tchr. Fannin Elem., Abilene, Tex., 1968-70, Tierra Blanca Elem., Hereford, Tex., 1970-72; acctg. and sales staff Lane and Co., Inc., Panhandle, Tex., 1972-74; min. music and edn. Memphis (Tex.) United Meth. Ch., 1974-75, First United Meth. Ch., McAllen, Tex., 1975-79; chaplain cancer treatment ctr. McAllen (Tex.) Br. M.D. Anderson Hosp., 1977-79; owner, counselor Snelling and Snelling Employment, Pampa, 1979-83; tchr. Travis Elem., Pampa, 1983-89; student asst. program coord. Pampa (Tex.) Ind. Sch. Dist., 1989-92; counselor, dir. drug/alcohol program Clarendon Coll. Pampa (Tex.) Ctr., 1992—; trainer Developing Capable People, Provo, Utah, 1990—; trainer family cmty. leadership Tex. Extension Svc., Amarillo, Tex., 1990—; parenting cons. Region XVI Edn. Svc. Ctr., Amarillo, 1991—, adv. bd. drug/alcohol, 1992—; cons. Cal Farley's Family Living Ctr., Borger, Tex., 1992—. Bd. dirs. Pampa (Tex.) Fine Arts, 1980-83, Pampa United Way, 1996; chmn. bd. Salvation Army, Pampa, 1982; bd. pres. Civic Ballet, Pampa, 1984; choir mem., bd. dirs. First United Meth. Ch.; vol. grief counselor Hospice of Panhandle. Named Family of Yr., Mormon Ch., Pampa, 1981, Top Gun, Tex. Tech. Dads and Moms Assn., Lubbock, Tex., 1990; grantee Tex. Coun. Assn. Drug/Alcohol, Pampa (Tex.) Ind. Sch. Dist., 1989-93. Mem. Am. Assn. Christian Counselor, Nat. Christian Counselor Assn., Tex. Christian Counselors Assn., Panhandle Christian Counselors Assn., Tex. Jr. Coll. Tchrs. Assn., Pampa C. of C. Avocations: interior decorating, writing, horticulture. Home: 2007 Williston St Pampa TX 79065-3632 Office: Clarendon Coll Pampa Ctr 900 N Frost St Pampa TX 79065-5456

LANE, JOAN FLETCHER, educational administrator; b. San Francisco, May 7, 1928; d. Howard French and Kathryn Elizabeth (Kraft) Fletcher; m. Melvin Bell Lane, Feb. 15, 1953; children: Whitney Lane-Miller, Julie Lane-Gay. AB, Smith Coll., 1949. Staff World Affairs Coun. No. Calif., San Francisco, 1949-51, Inst. Internat. Edn., Stanford, Calif., 1952; spl. asst., dean Sch. H&S Stanford U., 1982-93, spl. asst. bd. trustees, 1993—; bd. dirs. The Brown Group, St. Louis, McClatchy Newspapers, Sacramento, The James Irvine Found., San Francisco. Trustee San Francisco Found., 1984-92; trustee Smith Coll., Northampton, Mass., 1978-85, chmn. bd. trustees, 1982-85, v.p. alumnae assn., 1975-78; bd. dirs. Internat. House, U. Calif., Berkeley, 1971-80; pres., assoc. coun. Mills Coll., Oakland, Calif., 1974-78. Recipient John M. Greene award Smith Coll., 1988. Avocations: hiking, gardening. Home: 99 Tallwood Ct Atherton CA 94027-6431

LANE, JOHN DENNIS, lawyer; b. Norwalk, Conn.; s. John J. and Theresa A. (Donnelly) L.; m. Elizabeth J. Galliher, Apr. 28, 1949; children: Elizabeth J., John Dennis, Margaret A., Robert E., Paul G. B.S., Georgetown U., 1943, J.D., 1948. Bar: D.C. 1948, Conn. 1950. Atty. Office Chief Counsel, Bur. Internal Revenue, Washington, 1948-49; exec. sec. to U.S. Senator Brien McMahon, 1949-50; adminstrv. asst., 1950-52; pvt. practice Washington and Norwalk, 1953—; partner firm Hedrick & Lane, 1954—82, Wilkes, Artis, Hedrick & Lane, 1982—. Mem. council Adminstrv. Conf. U.S., 1961; bd. regents Georgetown U., 1979—. Served to capt. USMCR, 1943-45. Recipient Citation of Merit. Fellow Am. Bar Found.; mem. Am. Bar Assn. (chmn. standing com. unauthorized practice of law 1971-73, chmn. standing com. nat. conf. groups 1973-75, D.C. Cir. mem standing com. on fed. judiciary 1984-86, Fed. cir. mem. 1987-90), Fed. Communications Bar Assn. (pres.-elect 1990, pres. 1991-92), Am. Law Inst. Clubs: Met. (Washington), Army and Navy (Washington); Columbia Country (Chevy Chase, Md.). Home: 5045 Van Ness St NW Washington DC 20016-1960 Office: 1666 K St NW Washington DC 20006-2803 also: 4 Berkeley St Norwalk CT 06850-3915

LANE, JOHN RODGER, art museum director; b. Evanston, Ill., Feb. 28, 1944; s. John Crandall Lane and Jeanne Marie (Rodger) L. Moritz; m. Inge-Lise Eckmann, 1992. BA, Williams Coll., 1966; MBA, U. Chgo., 1971; AM, Harvard U., 1973, PhD, 1976; DFA (hon.), San Francisco Art Inst., 1995. Asst. dir. Fogg Art Mus., Cambridge, Mass., 1974; exec. asst. to dir., adminstr. curatorial affairs, asst. dir. curatorial affairs Bklyn. Mus., N.Y.C., 1975-80; dir. Carnegie Mus. Art, Pitts., 1980-86, San Francisco Mus. Modern Art, 1987—. Author: Stuart Davis: Art and Art Theory, 1978; co-editor: Abstract Painting and Sculpture in America, 1927-1944, 1983, Carnegie International, 1985; exec. editor: The Making of a Modern Museum/SFMOMA, 1995. Served to lt. USNR, 1966-69. Nat. Endowment Arts Mus. fellow, 1974-75. Mem. Assn. Art Mus. Dirs., Am. Assn. Museums, Internat. Council Museums, Coll. Art Assn. Office: San Francisco Mus Modern Art 151 3rd St San Francisco CA 94103-3159

LANE, JOSEPH M., orthopedic surgeon, educator, oncologist; b. N.Y.C., Oct. 27, 1939; s. Frederick and Madelaine Lane; m. Barbara Greenhouse, June 23, 1963; children: Debra, Jennifer. AB in Chemistry, Columbia U., 1957; MD, Harvard U., 1965. Surg. intern Hosp. U. Pa., Phila., 1965-66, resident in gen. surgery, 1966-67, resident, 1969-72, chief resident, 1972-73, chief MBD sect., 1973-76; rsch. assoc. NIH, NIDR, Bethesda, Md., 1967-69; rsch. fellow Phila. Gen. Hosp., 1969-70; chief MBD unit Hosp. Spl. Surgery, N.Y.C., 1976-93, 96—, dir. rsch. div., 1990-93; dir. applied clin. orthopedic rsch., 1996—; dir. postgrad. edn. Hosp. Spl. Surgery, 1996—ž; chief orthopedic oncology Meml. Sloan-Kettering Cancer Ctr., N.Y.C., 1977-90; prof., chmn. orthopaedic surgery UCLA Med. Sch., L.A., 1993-96; prof. orthopedic surgery Cornell U. Med. Coll., 1980-93, 96—; assoc. dir. MultiPurpose Arthritis Ctr., N.Y.C., 1988-93; cons. Genetics Inst., Andover, Mass., Orquest, Mountain Side, Calif., Exogen, Piscataway, N.J.; mem. VA Merit Grant Bd. Recipient N.Y. Mayoral Proclamation, 1988. Fellow Am. Acad. Orthopaedic Surgeons (Kappa Delta award 1973); mem. Acad. Orthopaedic Surgeons, Am. Orthopaedic Assn., Am. Soc. Bone and Mineral Rsch., Med. Soc. State N.Y., Internat. Soc. Fracture Repair, Musculoskeletal Tumor Soc. (pres. 1982-83), Orthopaedic Rsch. Soc. (pres. 1984-85). Office: Hosp Spl Surgery 535 E 70th St New York NY 10021

LANE, KENNETH EDWIN, retired advertising agency executive; b. Orange, N.J., Sept. 30, 1928; s. Clarence Edwin and Erma Catherine (Kinser) L.; children by previous marriage—Kenneth, Laura, Linda, Katherine; m. Susan Spafford Zimmer, Sept. 13, 1980; stepchildren—Todd and Margaret Zimmer. B.A., U. Chgo., 1947, M.A., 1950. Mgr. media Toni div. Gillette Co., 1953-63; media dir. MacParland-Aveyard Co., 1963-64; asso. media dir. Leo Burnett Co., Chgo., 1964-71; mgr. media dept. Leo Burnett Co., 1971-75, sr. v.p. media services, 1975-84. Bd. dirs. Traffic Audit Bur. Maj. USAR ret. Mem. Am. Assn. Advt. Agys., Media Dirs. Council., Phi Beta Kappa. Office: Leo Burnett Agy Prudential Pla 35 W Wacker Dr Chicago IL 60601

LANE, LAURENCE WILLIAM, JR., retired U.S. ambassador, publisher; b. Des Moines, Nov. 7, 1919; s. Laurence William and Ruth (Bell) L.; m. Donna Jean Gimbel, Apr. 16, 1955; children: Sharon Louise, Robert Laurence, Brenda Ruth. Student, Pomona Coll., 1938-40, LLD (hon.), 1976; BJ, Stanford U., 1942; DHL (hon.), Hawaii Loa Coll., 1991. Chmn. bd. Lane Pub. Co.; pub. Sunset Mag., Sunset Books and Sunset Films; U.S. amb. to Australia and Nauru, 1985-89; ret., 1990; bd. dirs. Calif. Water Svc. Co., Crown Zellerbach Corp., Pacific Gas and Electric Co.; bd. dirs. Time Inc.; bd. dirs. Oreg. Coast Aquarium, Internat. Bd. Advice, ANZ Bank; U.S. amb. and commr. Gen. Worlds Fair, Japan, 1975-76; hon. fellow Coll. Notre Dame, 1974. Former mem. adv. bd. Sec. Interior's Bd. Nat. Parks; mem. adv. coun. Grad. Sch. Bus., Stanford U., SRI; mem. Pres.'s Nat. Productivity Adv. Com.; mem. Pacific Basin Econ. Coun.; former bd. dirs. Pacific Forum, CSI, Nat. Parks Found.; vol. The Nat. Ctr.; mem. bd. overseers Hoover Instn. War, Revolution and Peace; mem. exec. com. Ctr. for Australian Studies, U. Tex., Austin. Lt. USNR, World War II, PTO. Decorated officer Order of Australia; recipient Conservation Svc. award Sec. Interior; Theodore and Conrad Wirth award NPF, 1994; Wiliam Penn Mott Jr. Conservationist of Yr. award NPCA, 1995; named hon. prof. journalism Stanford U. Mem. Newcomen Soc. N.Am., Pacific Asia Travel Assn. (life mem., chmn. 1980-81), Coun. of Am. Ambs., Los Rancheros Vistadores, Advt. Club San Francisco, No. Calif. Alumni Assn., Bohemian Club, Pacific Union, Men's Garden Club L.A., Alpha Delta Sigma. Republican. Presbyterian. Office: 3000 Sandhill Rd Ste 215 Menlo Park CA 94025-7116

LANE, LAWRENCE JUBIN, retired electrical engineer, consultant; b. Morganton, N.C., Feb. 19, 1927; s. Lawrence and Sarah Virginia (Jubin) L.; m. Gladys Verna Lee Hock, Dec. 25, 1947 (dec. 1975); children: Priscilla Gayle Lane Purks, Richard Jubin; m. 2d Helen Elizabeth Sollazzo, Dec. 19, 1975. B.E.E., N.C. State Coll., 1950; M.S.E.E., U. Va., 1972. Lic. profl. engr., Va. Engr. GE, Schenectady, N.Y., 1950-54; class supr. GE, Phila., 1954-55; devel. engr. GE, Waynesboro, Va., 1955-63, sr. devel. engr., 1963-78; sr. systems design engr. GE, Roanoke, Va., 1978-83, cons. engr., 1983-95; ret., 1995. Patentee in field. Pres. Stuarts Draft PTA, Va., 1960, 61. Served as petty officer USN, 1944-46, 50-51. Recipient Managerial award Gen. Electric Co., 1965. Fellow IEEE (chpt. chmn. 1982-83); mem. Eta Kappa Nu, Tau Beta Pi, Phi Eta Sigma, Phi Kappa Phi. Methodist. Home: 4868 Warrior Dr Salem VA 24153-5816 *Since my occupational accomplishments have been judged to be noteworthy, I am indeed fortunate. I thank God and Jesus Christ for my abilities and for the opportunities for such accomplishments.*

LANE, LOUIS, musician, conductor; b. Eagle Pass, Tex., Dec. 25, 1923; s. William Bartlett and Virginia (Gardner) L. B.Mus., U. Tex., 1943; Mus.M., Eastman Sch. Music, 1947; Mus.D. (hon.), Akron U., 1973, Cleve. State U., 1974, Kent State U., 1988; Cleve. Inst. Music, 1995. adj. prof. music Akron U., 1969-82; vis. prof. music U. Cin., 1973-75, Oberlin Coll., 1995—; artistic advisor, condr. Cleve. Inst. Music, 1982—; sr. lectr. music U. Tex., 1989-91. Mem., Cleve. Orch., 1947-73, assoc. condr., 1960-70, resident condr., 1970-73, condr., Akron (Ohio) Symphony Orch., 1959-83, co-condr., Altanta Symphony Orch., 1977-83, prin. guest condr., Atlanta Symphony Orch., 1983-88, prin. condr., SABC Symphony Orch., Johannesburg South Africa, 1984-85, prin. guest condr., Dallas Symphony Orch., 1973-78, guest condr. in, Chgo., Seattle, St. Louis, Detroit, Houston, San Antonio, Vancouver, B.C., Can., Montevideo, Uruguay, Warsaw, Poland, Johannesburg, S.Africa, Helsinki, Finland, mus. dir., Lake Erie Opera Theatre, Cleve., 1964-72; co-dir., Blossom Festival Sch. of Cleve. Orch. and Kent State U., 1969-73; rec. artist for Columbia Records, Telarc Records. Served with F.A. AUS, 1943-46. Decorated chevalier l'Ordre des Arts et des Lettres de France; Recipient Mahler medal, 1971; Ditson award Columbia, 1972; Grammy award for best orch. rec., 1989. Home: 1808 Rockridge Pl NE Atlanta GA 30324-5264

LANE, MALCOLM DANIEL, biological chemistry educator; b. Chgo., Aug. 10, 1930; s. Malcolm Daniel Lane and Helga Sofia (Nielsen) Wilke; m. Patricia L. Sonquist, Mar. 17, 1951; children: Claudia J. Lane Fioranelli, M. Daniel Jr. BS, Iowa State U., 1951, MS, 1953; PhD, U. Ill., 1956. Assoc. prof. Va. Poly. Inst., Blackburg, 1956-63, prof. biochemistry, 1963-64; assoc. prof. biochemistry Sch. Medicine N.Y.U., 1964-69, prof. biochemistry Sch. Medicine, 1969-70; prof. biochemistry Sch. Medicine Johns Hopkins U., Balt., 1970-78, DeLamar prof., dir. dept. biol. chemistry, 1978—. Mem. editorial bd.: Jour. Biol. Chemistry, 1969-74, 79-84, Biochem. et Biophysica Acta, 1968-70, 75-79, Archives Biochemistry and Biophysics, 1977-80, Ann. Revs. Biochemistry, 1980-84; exec. editor: Biochem./Biophys. Research Com., 1986—; contbr. numerous articles to profl. jours. Fellow Am. Acad. Arts and Sci.; mem. NAS, Am. Soc. Biochem. Molecular Biology (sec. 1987-89, program chmn. 1990-91, pres., William C. Rose award 1981), Am. Soc. Cell Biology, Am. Inst. Nutrition (Mead-Johnson award 1966), Am. Chem. Soc. Avocations: chamber music, boating, fishing, photography. Home: 5607 Roxbury Pl Baltimore MD 21209-4501 Office: Johns Hopkins U Sch Medicine 725 N Wolfe St Baltimore MD 21205-2105

LANE, MARILYN EDITH, treasurer, corporate executive; b. Calif., June 17, 1931; d. Frederick Ernest and Grace (Davage) Mockridge; m. Jack William Lane, Feb. 2, 1948 (dec. Jan. 1989); children: Adrienne G. Murphy, Jack William II, Jon F. Gen. officer worker Talney Mfg. Co., Los Angeles, 1951-52; with govt. products div. Rheem Mfg. Co., Downey, Calif., 1953-58; acct. Reed Necker, San Diego, 1960; v.p., treas. Anthony Industries, Inc., L.A., 1960—. Office: Anthony Industries Inc PO Box 22252 Los Angeles CA 90022-0252

LANE, MARK, lawyer, educator, author; b. N.Y.C., Feb. 24, 1927; s. Harry Arnold and Elizabeth Lane; m. Patricia Ruth Erdner, 1987; children: Anne-Marie, Christina. LLB, Bklyn. Law Sch., 1951. Bar: N.Y. 1951, D.C. 1995. Pvt. practice law N.Y.C. and Washington, 1952—; founder Mid-Harlem Community Parish Narcotics Clinic, 1953, East Harlem Reform Dem. Club, 1959; prof. law Cath. U., Washington, 1975-76; sr. ptnr. Lane & Assocs., 1986—; founder and dir. Citizens Commn. Inquiry; founder Wounded Knee Legal Def.-Offense Com., 1973, The Covered Wagon, Mountain Home, Idaho, 1971. Author: (books) Rush to Judgment, 1966, A Citizen's Dissent, 1968, Chicago Eye-Witness, 1969, Arcadia, 1970, Conversations with Americans, 1970, Executive Action, 1973, (with Dick Gregory) Code Name Zorro, 1977, The Strongest Poison, 1980, Plausible Denial, 1991, Murder in Memphis, 1993; prodr. films Rush to Judgment, 1967, Two men in Dallas, 1987, 92; prodr. plays Trial of James Earl Ray, 1978, Plausible Denial, 1992, Winds of Doctrine, 1994; prodr. screenplays, Arcadia, 1992, Slay the Dreamer, 1992, Plausible Denial, 1993; founder publs. Citizens Quar., 1975, Helping Hand, 1971. Mem. N.Y. State Assembly, 1960-62. With AUS, 1945-47. Home and Office: 105 2nd St NE Washington DC 20002-7303 *I do not believe that our fate is pre-ordained. I do believe that women and men, working together, can determine their own destiny and that the people write their own history. What moves me most directly into action is the fact that I hate bullies. What concerns me the most in contemporary America is the influence of the police and spy organizations with the national news media. Together these are bullies to contemplate and oppose.*

LANE, MARK, museum director. BA in Visual Design, Auburn U., 1971, postgrad., 1980. Graphic designer, sculptor Anniston, Atlanta, Ga., 1972-75; curator exhibits Anniston Mus. Natural History, 1975-79, exec. dir., 1979-81; dir. Witte Mus., San Antonio, 1981—; presented and facilitated numerous workshops and projects. Recipient Imagineer award in Humanities, Outstanding Contbn. to South Tex., 1982, Exhibit on Animal Senses award Tex. Hist. Commn., 1983, Un-Sch. for Edn. award, 1983. Home: 219 E Rosewood San Antonio TX 78212 Office: Witte Museum 3801 Broadway San Antonio TX 78209

LANE, MARVIN MASKALL, JR., electronics company executive; b. Oak Park, Ill., Apr. 25, 1934; s. Marvin Maskall and Lucille Ernestine (Fischer) L.; m. Joan Agar Wheeler, June 28, 1958; children—Elizabeth Agar Anderson, Marlene Celia Christensen. B.S. in Elec. Engring, U. Wis., 1956, M.B.A. in Indsl. Mgmt, 1957. With Texas Instruments Inc., Dallas, 1958—; asst. v.p. Texas Instruments Inc., 1978-80, v.p., treas., 1980-82, v.p., controller, 1982—. Trustee, chmn. Tejas Girl Scouts Found., 1988-94; bd. dirs. Dallas Area Rapid Transit, 1986-93; mem. City of Dallas Jud. Nominating Commn. Mem. Fin. Execs. Inst. Presbyterian. Office: Tex Instruments Inc PO Box 655474 Dallas TX 75265-5474

LANE, MATTHEW JAY, lawyer; b. Cin., Mar. 6, 1955; s. Joseph Alan and Adele (Stacks) L. BA, Emory U., 1977; JD, Northwestern U., 1980. Bar: Ohio 1981, U.S. Dist. Ct. (so. dist.) Ohio 1981, U.S. Ct. Appeals (6th cir.) 1981, Fla. 1982, U.S. Ct. Appeals (11th cir.) 1982. Law clk. to chief judge U.S. Dist. Ct. (so. dist.) Ohio, Cin., 1980-82; ptnr. Lane & Guenthner Co., L.P.A., Cin., 1988-93; assoc. Conrad, Scherer & Jenne, Ft. Lauderdale, 1996—. Legal counsel Juvenile Diabetes Assn., Cin., 1984-92; legal counsel MADD, 1986-92, pres. S.W. Ohio chpt., 1988-91, pres. Palm Beach County chpt., 1993-95; mem. Cin. Bicentennial Commn., 1986-88; bd. trustees Isaac M. Wise Temple, Cin., 1987-89; mem. exec. com. leadership coun. Jewish Fedn. Cin., 1987-92, Big Bros./Big Sisters Devel. Com., 1985-88, Hamilton County Dem. Party, mem. exec. com., county, legis. and jud. selection coms., 1987-92; mem. Palm Beach County Democratic Exec. Com., 1993—; v.p., legal counsel Fetes de Jeunesse, 1984-90. Mem. ABA, Ohio Bar Assn., Fla. Bar Assn., Cin. Bar Assn. (chmn. svc. com.), Phi Beta Kappa. Home: 2840 Gettysburg Ln West Palm Beach FL 33409

LANE, MEREDITH ANNE, botany educator, museum curator; b. Mesa, Ariz., Aug. 4, 1951; d. Robert Ernest and Elva Jewell (Shilling) L.; m. Donald W. Longstreth, Apr. 6, 1974 (div. Feb. 1985). BS, Ariz. State U., 1974, MS, 1976; PhD, U. Tex., 1980. Asst. prof. U. Colo., Boulder, 1980-88, assoc. prof., 1988-89; assoc. prof., curator div. botany Natural History Mus., U. Kans., Lawrence, 1989—; vis. asst. prof. U. Wyo., Laramie, 1985-86; vis. scholar U. Conn., Storrs, 1989; cons. editor McGraw-Hill Ency. of Sci. and Tech., N.Y.C., 1985-92; program dir. Nat. Sci. Found., 1995-97; rsch. assoc. Smithsonian Inst., 1995—. Editor Plant Sci. Bull., 1990-94; contbr. over 25 articles to profl. jours. Mem. Am. Soc. Plant Taxonomists (sec. 1986-88, program dir. 1986-90, councillor 1993-96, Cooley award 1982), Bot. Soc. Am. (sect. chmn. 1984-86, sect. sec. 1986-90), Internat. Orgn. for Plant Biosystematics (councillor 1989-92), Internat. Assn. Plant Taxonomists, Calif. Bot. Soc. Avocations: reading, conversation, country dance, hiking, furniture refinishing. Office: R L McGregor Herbarium 2045 Constant Ave Lawrence KS 66047-3729

LANE, MONTAGUE, physician, educator; b. N.Y.C., Aug. 28, 1929; s. George and Ida (Korn) L.; m. Chrsitine Laura; children: Laura Diane, Adam Reuben. B.A., N.Y. U., 1947; M.B., Chgo. Med. Sch., 1952, M.D., 1953; M.S., Georgetown U., 1957. Diplomate: Am. Bd. Internal Medicine (mem. subcom. on med. oncology 1974-80, cons. 1981-83). Clin. assoc. Nat. Cancer Inst., NIH, 1954-56; sr. investigator Clin. Pharmacology and Exptl. Therapeutics Service; attending physician gen. med. br. Nat. Cancer Inst., 1957-60; assoc. in medicine George Washington U., Med. Sch., 1957-60; asst. prof., assoc. prof. depts. pharmacology and medicine Baylor U. Coll. Medicine, Houston, 1960-67; prof. depts. pharm. and medicine Baylor Coll. Medicine, 1967—, head div. clin. oncology dept. pharmacology, 1969-94, head sect. med. oncology dept. medicine, 1961-92; co-dir. cancer control sci. program Meth. Hosp. and Baylor Coll. Medicine, Houston, 1981-94; mem. study sect. Nat. Cancer Inst., 1966-69, mem. cancer clin. investigations rev. com., 1972-75; chmn. new agts. com. S.W. Cancer Chemotherapy study group; cons. drug evaluations AMA; cons. Merck Manual, U.S. Pharmacopeia, 1981-83; cons. interferon program Schering Corp., 1981-82; cons. com. on orphan drugs FDA, 1986—; cons. UNOMED, 1989-91; mem. adv. bd. Cancer Info. Dissemination and Analysis Ctr., Info Ventures, Inc., 1988-93; mem. sci. adv. bd. Health Infusion, Inc., 1991-94. Assoc. editor: Cancer Research, 1970-80. External adv. bd. Howard U. Cancer Center, 1977-83. Named Disting. Alumnus Chgo. Med. Sch., 1971, Disting. Faculty Mem. Baylor Med. Alumni Assn., 1990. Fellow ACP; mem. Am. Inst. Nutrition, Am. Soc. Clin. Oncology (program chmn. 1970), Am. Soc. Clin. Pharmacology and Exptl. Therapeutics (pres. 1971-72), Am. Soc. Pharmacology and Exptl. Therapeutics, Am. Soc. Hematology, Houston Soc. Internal Medicine (v.p. 1973-74, pres. 1984-85), Am. Assn. Cancer Rsch. (program com. 1990), Harris County Med. Soc. Home: 1514 Bissonnet St Houston TX 77005-1814 Office: 6560 Fannin St Ste 1510 Houston TX 77030-2707

LANE, NANCY, editor; b. N.Y.C., Dec. 20, 1938; d. Morton and Lillian (Gelb) L. A.B. in Am. Civilization, Barnard Coll., 1960. Mem. staff N.Y. Times, 1959-61; from asst. to assoc. editor Polit. Sci. Quar. and Procs. Acad. Polit. Sic., Columbia U., N.Y.C., 1962-70; from assoc. editor to mng. editor Am. Hist. Rev. Am. Hist. Assn., 1970-74; from sr. editor to exec. editor Oxford U. Press, N.Y.C., 1974—. Mem. Am. Hist. Assn., Orgn. Am. Historians. Home: 45 W 10th St New York NY 10011-8763 Office: Oxford U Press 198 Madison Ave New York NY 10016-3903

LANE, NATHAN (JOSEPH LANE), actor; b. Jersey City, N.J., Feb. 3, 1956. Appeared in plays (off-Broadway) A Midsummer Night's Dream, (Broadway) Present Laughter, 1982-83, Merlin, N.Y.C., 1983, Love, N.Y.C., 1984, Raving, N.Y.C., 1984, She Stoops to Conquer, N.Y.C., 1984, The Common Pursuit, New Haven, 1984-85, A Backer's Audition, N.Y.C., 1985, Wind in the Willows, 1985, Measure for Measure, 1985, The Common Pursuit, 1986-87, Claptrap, N.Y.C., 1987, Broadway Bound, New Haven, L.A., Uncounted Blessings, 1988, The Film Society, 1988, The Lisbon Traviata, 1989 (Drama Desk award best actor 1989), A Pig's Valise, 1989, Some Americans Abroad, 1990, Bad Habits , 1990, Lips Together, Teeth Apart, 1991, On Borrowed Time, 1991, Guys and Dolls, 1992, Laughter on the 23rd Floor, 1993-94, Love! Valor! Compassion!, 1995, A Funny Thing Happened On The Way To The Forum, 1996 (Best Actor Tony award 1996); (TV) (miniseries) Valley of the Dolls, 1981, One of the Boys, 1982, host the 50th anniversary Tony awards show, 1996; (films) Ironweed, 1987, The Lemon Sisters, 1990, Joe Versus the Volcano, 1990, He Said, She Said, 1991, Frankie and Johnny, 1991, Life With Mikey, 1993, Addams Family Values, 1993, (voice) The Lion King, 1994, The Birdcage, 1996. Office: William Morris Agy 151 El Camino Beverly Hills CA 90212*

LANE, NEAL FRANCIS, university provost, physics researcher, federal administrator; b. Oklahoma City, Aug. 22, 1938; s. Walter Patrick and Harietta (Hattie) Charlotta (Hollander) L.; m. Joni Sue Williams, June 11, 1960; children: Christy Lynn Lane Saydjari, John Patrick. BS, U. Okla., 1960, MS, 1962, PhD, 1964, DHL (hon.), 1995; DSc (hon.), U. Ala., 1994; ScD (hon.), Mich. State U., 1995; DHL (hon.), Marymount U., Arlington, Va., 1995. NSF postdoctoral fellow, 1964-65; asst. prof. physics Rice U., Houston, 1966-69, assoc. prof., 1969-72, prof. space physics and astronomy, 1972-84, chmn. dept. physics, 1977-82; dir. divsn. physics NSF, Washington, 1979-80; chancellor U. Colo., Colorado Springs, 1984-86; provost Rice U., 1986-93; dir. NSF, Washington, 1993—; non-resident fellow Joint Inst. for Lab. Astrophysics U. Colo., Boulder, 1984-93, vis. fellow, 1965-66, 75-76; mem. commn. on phys. sci., math. and applications NRC, 1989-93; bd. overseers Superconducting Super Collider (SSC) Univs. Rsch. Assn., 1985-93; disting. Karcher lectr. U. Okla., Norman, 1983; disting. vis. scientist U. Ky., Lexington, 1980; mem. adv. com. math. and phys. sci. NSF, 1992-93. Co-author: Quantum States of Atoms, Molecules and Solids, Understanding more Quantum Physics; contbr. articles to profl. jours. Active Cath. Commn. Intellectual and Cultural Affairs, 1991. Recipient George Brown prize for superior teaching Rice U., 1973-74, 76-77, Brown Coll. Teaching award Rice U., 1972-73; Alfred P. Sloan Found. fellow, 1967-71. Fellow Am. Phys. Soc. (councilor-at-large 1981-84, chmn. panel on pub. affairs 1983, exec. com. 1981-83, chmn. divsn. electron and atomic physics 1977-78), AAAS, Am. Acad. Arts and Scis.; mem. Am. Inst. Physics (gov. bd. 1984-87), Am. Assn. Physics Tchrs., Phi Beta Kappa, Sigma Xi (pres. elect 1992, pres. 1993). Roman Catholic. Avocations: tennis; squash. Office: NSF Office of Dir 4201 Wilson Blvd Arlington VA 22203-1803

LANE, NEWTON ALEXANDER, retired lawyer; b. Boston, June 16, 1915; s. Samuel B. and Eva (Robbins) L. AB, Harvard U., 1936, JD, 1939. Bar: Mass. 1939. Ptnr. emeritus Lane Altman & Owens, Boston. Served with AUS, 1942-46. Mem. Phi Beta Kappa. Home: 704 Dedham St Newton MA 02159-2937 Office: Lane Altman & Owens 101 Federal St Boston MA 02110-1842

LANE, PATRICIA PEYTON, nursing consultant; b. Danville, Ill., Oct. 5, 1929; d. Louis Weldon Sr. and Ruth Jeanette (Meyer) Peyton; m. H.J. Lane, Dec. 23, 1950 (div.); children: Jennifer Lane-Carr, Peter Lane, Amelia Ozog. Diploma, St. Elizabeth Hosp., 1950; BA in Psychology magna cum laude, Rosary Coll., 1974; postgrad., Lakeview Coll. of Nursing, Danville, Ill., 1987-88; student, Triton Jr. Coll., River Grove, Ill., 1969-72. Staff nurse St. Elizabeth Hosp., Danville, Ill., 1950; staff nurse nursery Ill. Rsch. and Ednl. Hosp., Chgo., 1951, charge nurse tumor clinic, 1951-54; res. sch. nurse elem. schs., Oak Park, Ill., 1969-78; sta. mgr. Oak Park-River Infant Welfare, Oak Park, Ill., 1972-76; vision and hearing screener suburban elem. schs., Ill., 1980-82; sch. nurse West Subrban Assn. Spl. Edn., Cicero, 1978-80; caseworker, counselor Vermilion County Mental Health and Devel. Disabilities, Inc., Danville, 1983-86; case coord., nurse cons. Crosspoint Human Svcs., Danville, 1986-88; staff nurse psychiat. acute care unit Community Hosp. of Ottawa, Ill., 1988-89; dir. social svcs. Pleasant View Luther Home, Ottawa, 1989-93; clin. case coord. Access Svcs., Inc., Mendota, Ill., 1993—; cmty. ombudsman LaSalle County Alternatives for the Older Adult, Peru, Ill., 1993—; cons. in field. Mem. ANA, Ill. State Nurses Assn. (cert. psychiat./mental nurse). Office: Alternatives for the Older Adult 2000 Luther Dr Peru IL 61354-1205

LANE, PATRICK, poet; b. Nelson, B.C., Can., Mar. 26, 1939; s. A. S. Red and E. M. (Titsworth) L.; m. Carol Beale, 1972 (div.); children: Mark Hayden, Christopher Patrick, Kathryn Mary, Michael John, Richard Patrick. Grad. high sch., Vernon, B.C. Editor Very Stone House in Transit, Vancouver, B.C., Can., 1966-80; tchr. creative writing course Notre Dame Coll., 1966; writer-in-residence U. Man., Can., 1978, U. Ottawa, Ont., Can., 1980, U. Alta., Can., 1982, Libr. of Saskatoon, 1983, Globe Theatre Co. of Regina, 1985, Concordia U., Montreal, 1987, U. Toronto, 1989; faculty U. Victoria; spl. lectr. U. Sask., 1988-89. Author: Letters From the Savage Mind, 1966, For Rita-In Asylum, 1967, Calgary City Jail, 1967, Sunflower Seeds, 1967, Separations, 1969, On The Street, 1970, Mountain Oysters, 1971, Hiway 401 Rhapsody, 1972, The Sun Has Begun to Eat The Mountain, 1972, Passing Into Storm, 1973, Beware The Months Of Fire, 1974, Certs, 1974, Unborn Things, 1975, For Riel in That Gawdam Prison, 1975, Albino Pheasants, 1977, If, 1977, Poems New and Selected, 1978 (Gov.-Gen. award for poetry 1978), (with Lorna Uher) No Longer Two People, 1979, There Are Still The Mountains, 1979, The Garden, 1980, The Measure, 1980, Old Mother, 1982, Woman in the Dust, 1983, A Linen Crow, A Caftan Magpie, 1985, Selected Poems, 1987, Winter, 1989, Milford and Me, 1989, Mortal Remains, 1991, How Do You Spell Beautiful, 1992, Too Spare, Too Fierce, 1995, (anthology with Lorna Crozier) Breathing Fire, 1995; contbr. to anthologies. Sr. Can. Coun. Arts grantee, 1973, 76, 83, Ont. Arts Coun. grantee, 1974, 75, 78, Man. Sr. Arts grantee, 1979; recipient Poetry award York U., 1971. Mem. League Can. Poets. (v.p.), Writer's Union Can. Office: Cultra Ave, Seanichton, BC Canada V8M 1L7

LANE, RAYMOND J., software systems consulting company executive; b. 1947. Various product and mktg. positions IBM, until 1977; divsn. v.p.

Electronic Data Sys. Corp., 1977-80; prin. inf. sys. practice in western U.S., Booz-Allen & Hamilton, 1980-83, mng. ptnr. S.W. region, 1983-86, sr. v.p., mng. ptnr. worldwide info. svcs. group, 1986-92, mem. exec. com., 1986-92, bd. dirs., 1985-88, 91-92; sr. v.p. Oracle Corp., Redwood City, Calif., from 1992, now exec. v.p. Office: Oracle Systems Corp 500 Oracle Pky Redwood City CA 94065-1600*

LANE, ROBERT CASEY, lawyer; b. 1932. JD, Loyola U., 1960. Bar: Ill. 1960, Wash. 1969. Atty. U.S. Dept. Justice, Washington, 1960-61; assoc. Lewis, Overbeck & Furman, 1962-69; atty. Weyerhaeuser Co., Tacoma, 1969-77, asst. gen. counsel, 1977-80, v.p., gen. counsel, 1980—. Office: Weyerhaeuser Co Law Dept CH 2J28 Tacoma WA 98477

LANE, ROBERT G., lawyer; b. Chgo., Mar. 9, 1938. AB, Duke U., 1960; JD with distinction, U. Mich., 1963. Bar: Ill. 1963. Ptnr. Winston & Strawn, Chgo. Mem. ABA, Ill. State Bar Assn. Office: Winston & Strawn 35 W Wacker Dr Chicago IL 60601-1614

LANE, ROBERT GERHART, lawyer; b. Long Beach, Calif., Sept. 24, 1931; s. Herman G. and Adele (Steg) L.; m. Mary Ellaine Griffith, Aug. 29, 1953; children: John, Scott, David, Mary Katherine. AB, U. So. Calif., 1953, MA in Polit. Sci., 1955, LLB, 1960. Bar: Calif. 1960, U.S. Dist. Ct. (cen. dist.) Calif. 1960, U.S. Ct. Appeals (9th cir.) 1964, U.S. Supreme Ct. 1971. Assoc. Paul, Hastings, Janofsky & Walker, Los Angeles, 1960-67, ptnr., 1967-93, mng. ptnr., 1986-91; gen. counsel U. So. Calif., L.A., 1993—. Mem. Town Hall, L.A.; bd. councilors U. So. Calif., L.A.; mem. bd. alliance Natural History Mus. Los Angeles County; mem. Fellows of the Huntington Libr.; mem. law and justice com. L.A. C. of C. Served to 1st lt. USAFR, 1954-57. Mem. ABA (Robinson Patman com. antitrust sect.), Calif. Bar Assn., Los Angeles County Bar Assn., Order of Coif. Clubs: Jonathan (Los Angeles); Balboa Bay (Newport Beach, Calif.); Annandale Golf (Pasadena, Calif.). Office: U So Calif Office of Gen Counsel University Park ADM 352 Los Angeles CA 90089-5013

LANE, ROBIN, lawyer; b. Kerrville, Tex., Nov. 28 1947; d. Rowland and Gloria (Benson) Richards; m. Stanley Lane, Aug. 22, 1971 (div. 1979); m. Anthony W. Cunningham, Nov. 22, 1980; children: Joshua Lane, Alexandra Cunningham. BA with honors in Econs., U. Fla., 1969; MA, George Washington U., 1971; JD, Stetson U. Coll. Law, 1978. Bar: Fla. 1979, U.S. Ct. Appeals (11th cir.) 1981, U.S. Supreme Ct. 1986, U.S. Ct. Appeals (D.C. cir.) 1992, U.S. Ct. Appeals (3rd cir.) N.Y. 1993. Mgmt. trainee internat. banking Gulf Western Industries, N.Y.C.; internat. rsch. specialist Ryder Systems, Inc., Miami, Fla., 1973, project mgr., 1974; assoc. Wagner, Cunningham, Vaughan & McLaughlin, Tampa, Fla., 1979-85; pvt. practice law, 1985—; guest lectr. med. jurisprudence Stetson U. Coll. Law, 1982-91, also mem. exec. coun. law alumni bd. Contbr. articles to various revs. Recipient Am. Jurisprudence award-torts Lawyers Co-op. Fla., 1979; Scottish Rite fellow, 1968-69. Mem. ABA, Acad. Fla. Trial Lawyers (mem. com. 1983-84), Assn. Trial Lawyers Am., Fla. Bar Assn., Fla. Women's Alliance, Omicron Delta Epsilon. Home: 4934 Saint Croix Dr Tampa FL 33629 Office: PO Box 10155 Tampa FL 33679-0155

LANE, RONALD ALAN, lawyer; b. Ames, Iowa, July 15, 1950; s. Raymond Oscar and Beverly (Burdge) L.; m. Eileen Smietana, June 17, 1972; children: Andrew, Audrey. AB, Miami U., Oxford, Ohio, 1972; JD, Northwestern U., 1975; MBA, U. Chgo., 1987. Bar: U.S. Dist. Ct. (no. dist.) Ill. 1975, U.S. Ct. Appeals (7th cir.) 1975, U.S. Supreme Ct. 1975. Atty. Atchison, Topeka & Santa Fe Ry. Co., Chgo., 1975-78; from asst. gen. atty. to gen. atty. Santa Fe So. Pacific Corp., Chgo., 1979-86, gen. corp. atty., 1986-87; asst. v.p. pers. and labor rels. Atchison, Topeka & Santa Fe Ry. Co., 1987-90; v.p., gen. counsel Ill. Cen. R.R. Co., Chgo., 1990—. Office: Ill Central RR Co 455 N Cityfront Plaza Dr Chicago IL 60611-5503

LANE, SYLVIA, economist, educator; b. N.Y.C.; m. Benjamin Lane, Sept. 2, 1939; children: Leonard, Reese, Nancy. A.B., U. Calif., Berkeley, 1934, M.A., 1936; postgrad., Columbia U., 1937; Ph.D., U. So. Calif., 1957. Lectr., asst. prof. U. So. Calif., Los Angeles, 1947-60; asso. prof. econs. San Diego State U., 1961-65; assoc. prof. finance, assoc. dir. Ctr. for Econ. Edn. Calif. State U., Fullerton, 1965-69, chmn. dept. fin., 1967-69; prof. agrl. econs. U. Calif., Davis, 1969-82, prof. emerita, 1982—; prof. emerita and economist Giannini Found., U. Calif.-Berkeley, 1982—; vis. scholar Stanford U., 1975-76; econ. cons. Pres.'s Com. Consumer Interests, 1966-72; cons. Calif. Adv. Commn. Tax Reform, 1963, Office Consumer Affairs, Exec. Office of Pres., 1972-77, FAO, UN, 1983. Author: (with E. Bryant Phillips) Personal Finance, 1963, rev. edit., 1979, The Insurance Tax, 1965, California's Income Tax Conformity and Withholding, 1968, (with Irma Adelman) The Balance Between Industry and Agriculture in Economic Development, 1989; editl. bd. Agrl. Econs., 1986-92; also articles, reports in field. Project economist Los Angeles County Welfare Planning Coun., 1956-59; del. White House Conf. on Food and Nutrition, 1969, Pres.'s Summit Con. on Inflation, 1974; mem. adv. com. Ctr. for Bldg. Tech., Nat. Bur. Stds., 1975-79; bd. dirs. Am. Coun. Consumer Interests, 1972-74; exec. bd. Am. Agr. Econ. Assn. 1976-79. Ford Found. fellow UCLA, 1963; Ford Found. fellow U. Chgo., 1965; fellow U. Chgo., 1968. Fellow Am. Agrl. Econ. Assn. (life, Sylvia Lane Fellowship Fund 1993); mem. Am. Econ. Assn., Am. Coun. Consumer Info., Omicron Delta Epsilon (pres. 1973-75, trustee 1975-83, chmn. bd. trustees 1982-84). Home: 1241 Grizzly Peak Blvd Berkeley CA 94708-2127 Office: U Calif Dept Agrl & Resource Econs Berkeley CA 94720 *Select goals carefully . . .*

LANE, TED, literacy education educator; b. Albany, N.Y., June 24, 1928. BS in Elem. Edn., U. N.Mex., 1951; MS in Sch. Adminstrs. and Supervision, N.Y. State Coll. for Tchrs., 1953; EdD in Elem. Edn., NYU, 1970. 5th grade tchr. South Colonie (N.Y.) Sch. Dist., 1954-57; 5th and 6th grade tchr. Levittown (N.Y.) Sch. Dist., 1957-58; fellow NYU, N.Y.C., 1958-59; prof. literacy edn. Jersey City (N.J.) State Coll., 1959—; cons. Title I various schs., N.J., 1964—; cons. adult edn. Jersey City State Coll. Adult Resource Cr., 1964—; cons. individualized lang. arts Weehawken (N.J.) Sch. Sys., 1965-75; cons. project read write Newark Sch. Sys., 1972-75. Mem. ASCD, Nat. Coun. Tchrs. English, Internat. Reading Assn., N.J. Reading Assn.; N.J. Edn. Assn. Office: Jersey City State Coll Dept Literacy Edn 2039 John F Kennedy Blvd Jersey City NJ 07305-1527

LANE, TOM CORNELIUS, lawyer; b. Borger, Tex., Dec. 3, 1948; s. Aubrey G. and Barbara Ellen (Cook) L.; m. Nanette Marie Betts, Jan. 25, 1969; children: Trevor C., Tom Cornelius Jr. BBA in Mktg., Tex. A&M U., 1971; JD, U. Tulsa, 1988. Bar: Okla. 1988, U.S. Dist. Ct. (no. dist.) Okla. 1988, U.S. Dist. Ct. (ea. dist.) Okla. 1995. Sales mgr. Sears, North Platte, Nebr., 1972-76, Motorola C&E, Laredo, Tex., 1976-79; gen. mgr. Autophone of Laredo, Inc., 1979-81; owner Laredo Comms., Inc., 1981-85; from clk. to atty. W.C. "Bill" Sellers, Inc., Sapulpa, Okla., 1987-95; prin. Tom C. Lane, Sr. & Assocs., Sapulpa, 1995—; atty. Ea. Okla. Legal Aid, Tulsa, 1990—. City commr. City Counsel, Sapulpa, 1992; fin. chmn. Boy Scouts Am., Sapulpa, 1993. With USN, 1985-92. Recipient Silver Key award ABA, Tulsa, 1988, Appreciation award Fraternal Order of Police, Sapulpa, 1992. Mem. Am. Trial Lawyers Assn. (membership com. 1993-94), Okla. Trial Lawyers Assn. (membership com.), Lions Club Internat., Masons. Democrat. Baptist. Avocations: working with youth groups, hunting, fishing, working with wood. Office: Tom C. Lane Sr & Assocs PO Box 384 Sapulpa OK 74067

LANE, WALTER RONALD, JR., advertising executive, educator; b. Wilmington, N.C., Sept. 2, 1940; s. Walter Ronald and Dorothy (Holmes) L.; m. Judy Carol Smith, Nov. 14, 1963 (dec. Oct. 1992); 1 child, Sheri Lynn Lane Bevil. AB, U. Ga., 1963, MA, 1964. Promotion mgr. Ln. Labs./Mentho-Mulsion Co., Wilmington, 1961-62; advt. copywriter LSP Advt., Wilmington, 1962; account exec. Am. Lithograph/Case-Hoyt, Atlanta, 1964-67; copywriter Rhodes Advt., Atlanta, 1967; creative dir. SLRS Comms., Athens, Ga., 1967-73, pres., 1973—; prof. U. Ga., Athens, 1973—; mktg. cons. Ga. Inst. Comty. and Area Devel., 1975-81; coord. Am. Assn. Advt. Agys. Inst. Advanced Advt. Studies, Atlanta, 1981-86; advt. mgr. Jour. Advt., 1987-90; mem. accrediting coun. Accrediting Bd. Journalism Colls., 1993—; judge Addy Awards, Peabody Screening Com. Co-author: Advertising Media Problem Solving, 1968, A Perspective for Advertising/Marketing in Emerging European Countries, 1990, Kleppner's Advertising Procedure, 10th edit., 1988, 11th edit., 1990, 12th edit., 1993, 13th edit., 1996; prodr. TV videos; contbr. articles to profl. jours. Grantee Newspaper Advt. Pubs. Assn., 1990, Warning Labels design grantee Am. Cancer Soc./Ga. Med. Coll., 1990. Mem. Am. Advt. Fedn. (bd. dirs., mem. coun. govs. 1992-93, chmn. acad. divsn. 1992-93, mem. acad. divsn. exec. com. 1993-96, Hileman Outstanding Educator award 1987, Outstanding Svc. award 1986), Am. Advt. Found. (bd. dirs. 1992-95), Am. Mktg. Assn., Am. Acad. Advt., Atlanta Advt. Club, Greater Augusta Advt. Club. Presbyterian. Avocations: photography, art, writing. Home: 193 Bent Tree Dr Athens GA 30606-1945 Office: SLRS Comms Inc PO Box 5488 Athens GA 30604-5488

LANE, WILLIAM C., JR., principal. Prin. Gulf Mid. Sch., Cape Coral, Fla. Recipient Blue Ribbon Sch. award U.S. Dept. Edn., 1990-91. Office: Gulf Mid Sch 1809 SW 36th Ter Cape Coral FL 33914

LANE, WILLIAM KENNETH, physician; b. Butte, Mont., Nov. 5, 1922; s. John Patrick and Elizabeth Marie (Murphy) L.; m. Gilda Antoinette Parision, Aug. 21, 1954; children: William S., Francine Deirdre. Student, U. Mont., 1940-41, Mt. St. Charles Coll., 1941-43; MD, Marquette U., 1946. Intern Queen of Angels Hosp., L.A., 1946-47, resident physician, 1954-56; pvt. practice internal medicine San Francisco, 1947-51; resident in urology VA Hosp., Long Beach, Calif., 1956-58; physician VA Hosp., Long Beach, Oakland and Palo Alto, Calif., 1958—; lectr. on psychology of the elderly Foothill Coll., Los Altos, 1972-74; rschr. in field. Bd. dirs., mem. No. Cheyenne Indian Sch.; mem. Josef Meier's Black Hills Theatrical Group, S.D., 1940. With U.S. Army, 1943-46, ETO, lt. USN, 1951-54, Korea. Mem. AMA, Am. Geriatrics Soc., Nat. Assn. VA Physicians, San Francisco County Med. Soc., Woodrow Wilson Ctr. (assoc.), St. Vincent de Paul Soc., Cupertino Landscape Artists (past pres.), Audubon Soc., Stanford Hist. Soc., San Jose Movie/Video Club, San Jose Camera Club. Roman Catholic. Avocations: oil and watercolor painting, hiking, mountain climbing, outdoor video camcorder photography. Home: 18926 Sara Park Cir Saratoga CA 95070-4164 Office: Stanford VA Med Ctr 3801 Miranda Ave # 171 Palo Alto CA 94304-1207

LANE, WILLIAM W., electronics executive; b. Roanoke, Va., Feb. 25, 1934; s. Melvin V. and Cecile (Lane); m. Ronnie G Lane, Sept. 14, 1978; children: Jonathan D., Drew H., Craig M. B.A., Bklyn. Coll., 1956; M.B.A., Cornell U., 1958. Vice pres. Major Electronics Corp., 1959-70, chmn., dir., 1970; v.p., dir. Internat. Transistor Corp., Burbank, Calif., 1971-73; vice chmn., dir. Internat. Chia Hsin, Taipai, Taiwan, 1973-76; chmn., dir. Emerson (H.K. Ltd.), Hong Kong, from 1976; chmn., CEO, dir. Emerson Radio Corp., North Bergen, N.J., 1974-91; pres. Majorette Enterprises, from 1961; chmn. MAJ EXCO Imports Inc., 1977-85, Emerson Computer Corp., 1989-91, H.H. Scott, Inc. Cardiac Resuscitator Corp., Portland, Oreg., Emerson Italy, Emerson Spain, Atlantic Shore 400 Cons. Corp., Emerson Investment Corp., Major Realty Corp., Emtek Tech. (U.K.) Ltd.; pres. W. Lane & Assocs. Inc., 1992—. Served with AUS, 1958-59. Mem. bus. adv. bd. U.S. Senate. Office: W Lane & Assocs 30 E 60th St 903 New York NY 10022-1008

LANEGRAN, DAVID ANDREW, geography educator; b. St. Paul, Nov. 27, 1941; s. Walter Bucannon and Lita Evangeline (Wilson) L.; children: Kimberley Rae, Elizabeth Ann, Erik David, Katherin Jane. BA, Macalester Coll., St. Paul, 1963; MA, U. Minn., 1966, PhD, 1970. Prof. geography Macalester Coll., 1969—; pres. Minn. Landmarks, St. Paul, 1988—, mng. dir., 1979-82; program assoc. Gen. Svc. Found., St. Paul, 1980-85; vis. prof. several univs., U.S., 1979-89; chmn. bd. dirs. Geographic Edn. Nat. Implementation Project, 1987—; coord. Minn. Alliance for Geographic Edn., St. Paul, 1987; v.p. Nat. Coun. Geographic Edn., 1995—. Author: The Saint Paul Experiment: Initiative of the Latimer Administration, 1989, St. Anthony Park: Portrait of a Community, 1987, Grand Avenue: Renaissance of an Urban Street, 1996; (with others) The Legacy of Minneapolis: Preservation Amid Change, 1983, (with Judith Martin) Where We Live: Residential Districts of the Twin Cities, 1983, (with Ernest Sandeen) The Lake District of Minneapolis: A Neighborhood History, 1979, (with P. Kane) St. Paul Omnibus, Images of the Changing City, 1979, (with Risa Palm) An Invitation to Geography, 1978, (with Patrice St. Peter) Geolinks: K-12 Geography Curriculum, 1994. Chmn. St. Paul City Planning Commn., 1982-87; dir. Northwest Area Found., 1988-90, St. Paul Progress Housing Corp., 1984-86. Named one of ten outstanding coll. or univ. tchrs. of geography Ednl. Change Mag., 1977; recipient Award for Excellence Minn. Soc. AIA, 1978, Burlington-No. award for teaching excellence Burlington No. Found., 1988, 96, Thomas Jefferson Teaching and Cmty. Svc. award Robert McConnell Found.; named to South St. Paul Hall of Excellence, 1989. Mem. Assn. Am. Geographers (treas. 1987-89, nat. councilor 1986-89), Nat. Coun. for Geographic Edn. (joint com. for geographic edn. 1983-85, exec. com., v.p. 1995—). Democrat. Presbyterian. Home: 140 Wheeler St S Saint Paul MN 55105-1925 Office: Macalester Coll 1600 Grand Ave Saint Paul MN 55105-1801

LANER, RICHARD WARREN, lawyer; b. Chgo., July 12, 1933; s. Jack E. and Esther G. (Cohon) L.; m. Barbara Lee Shless, Aug. 15, 1954; children: Lynn, Kenneth. Student, U. Ill., 1951-54; BS, Northwestern U., 1955, LLB, 1956. Bar: Ill. 1956. Assoc. Laner, Muchin, Dombrow, Becker, Levin & Tominberg, Ltd., Chgo., 1956-62, ptnr., 1962—. Editor Northwestern Law Rev., 1954-56; contbr. articles to profl. jours. Mem. Chgo. Bar Assn. (chmn. com. labor law 1972-73), Chgo. Assn. Commerce and Industry, Order of Coif. Home: 1300 Edgewood Ln Northbrook IL 60062-4716 Office: Laner Muchin Dombrow Becker Levin & Tominberg Ltd 515 N State St Fl 28 Chicago IL 60610-4320

LANESE, HERBERT J., air and aerospace transportation manufacturing executive; b. 1945. V.p. Newport News Shipbuilding & Drydock Co., 1983-86, Tenneco Inc., 1986-89; sr. v.p. McDonnell Douglas Corp., 1989-92, exec. v.p., CFO, 1992—; also chmn. bd. McDonnell Douglas Fin. Corp., Long Beach, Calif., 1993—; now pres. McDonnell Douglas Fin. Corp., Long Beach, CA. Office: McDonnell Douglas Corp Lambert St. Louis Airport Saint Louis MO 63103 also: McDonnell Douglas Corp PO Box 516 Saint Louis MO 63166-0516*

LANEY, JAMES THOMAS, ambassador, educator; b. Wilson, Ark., Dec. 24, 1927; s. Thomas Mann and Mary (Hughey) L.; m. Berta Joan Radford, Dec. 20, 1949; children: Berta Joan Vaughn, James T., Arthur Radford, Mary Ruth Laney Reilly, Susan Elizabeth Castle. BA, Yale U., 1950, BD, 1954, PhD, 1966; DD (hon.), Fla. So. Coll., 1977; LHD (hon.), Rhodes Coll., 1979; HHD (hon.), Mercer U., 1980; LLD (hon.), DePauw U., 1985; DD (hon.), Wofford Coll., 1986; LHD (hon.), Millsaps Coll., 1988, Austin Coll., 1990, W.Va. Wesleyan Coll., 1990, Yale U., 1993; DD (hon.), Emory U., 1994; LLD (hon.), U. St. Andrews, Scotland, 1994, Alaska Pacific U., 1994. Chaplain Choate Sch., Wallingford, Conn., 1953-55; ordained to ministry Meth. Ch., 1955; asst. lectr. Yale Div. Sch., 1954-55; pastor St. Paul Meth. Ch., Cin., 1955-58; sec. student Christian movement, prof. Yonsei U., Seoul, Korea, 1959-64; asst. prof. Christian ethics Vanderbilt U. Div. Sch., 1966-69; dean Candler Sch. Theology, Emory U., 1969-77, pres. univ., 1977-93; U.S. amb. to Republic of Korea, 1993—; vis. prof. Harvard Div. Sch., 1974. Author: The Education of the Heart, 1994; (with J.M. Gustafson) On Being Responsible, 1968; author essays. Pres. Nashville Community Rels. Coun., 1968-69; mem. Yale Coun. Com., 1972-77; bd. dirs. Fund Theol. Edn.; chmn. United Bd. Christian Higher Edn. in Asia, 1990-93; bd. dirs. Atlanta Symphony, 1979-91; chmn. bd. overseers com. to visit Harvard Div. Sch., 1980-85; mem. Yale U. Coun. Exec. Com., 1990-93; mem. Carnegie Endowment Nat. Commn. on Am. & the New World; mem. adv. com. Atlanta Project; chmn. so. dist. Rhodes Scholarship Com., 1980-90; bd. dirs. Atlantic Coun., 1987-93. With AUS, 1946-48. Selected for Leadership Atlanta, 1970-71; recipient Disting. Alumnus award Yale U. Div. Sch., 1979, 93, Kellogg award for leadership in higher edn., 1983, Wilbur Cross medal Yale Grad. Sch., 1996; D.C. Macintosh fellow Yale U., 1965-66. Mem. Am. Soc. Christian Ethics, Soc. for Values Higher Edn. (pres. 1987-91), Coun. on Fgn. Rels., Atlanta C. of C., Commerce Club, Phi Beta Kappa, Omicron Delta Kappa.

LANEY, JOHN THOMAS, III, federal judge; b. Columbus, Ga., Mar. 27, 1942; s. John Thomas Jr. and Leila (Davis) L.; m. Louise Pierce, Nov. 23, 1974; children: Thomas Whitfield, Elizabeth Davis. AB, Mercer U., 1964, JD magna cum laude, 1966. Bar: Ga. 1965, U.S. Dist. Ct. (mid. dist.) Ga. 1966, U.S. Ct. Appeals (5th cir.) 1966, U.S. Ct. Mil. Appeals 1967, U.S. Ct. Appeals (11th cir.) 1981. Assoc. Swift, Pease, Davidson & Chapman, Columbus, 1970-73; ptnr. Page, Scrantom, Harris & Chapman, Columbus, 1973-86; judge mid. dist. Ga. U.S. Bankruptcy Ct., Columbus, 1986—. Co-editor-in-chief Mercer Law Rev., 1965-66; contbr. articles to profl. jours. Former pres., dir. Metro. Boys Club of Columbus. Capt. U.S. Army, 1966-70. Mem. ABA (judge adminstrv. divsn. Nat. Conf. Fed. Trial Judges), State Bar Ga. (chmn. gen. practice and trial sect. 1983-84, chmn. state disciplinary bd. 1984-85), Am. Judicature Soc., Nat. Conf. Bankruptcy Judges, Columbus Bar Assn., Inc. (pres. 1985-86), Rotary. Presbyterian. Office: US Bankruptcy Ct PO Box 1540 Columbus GA 31902-1540

LANEY, MICHAEL L., manufacturing executive; b. Los Angeles, Sept. 10, 1945; s. Roy and Wanda Laney; m. Marti Miller, Dec. 31, 1964; children: Tynna, Kristen. BS with honors, Calif. State U., Northridge, 1967; MBA, UCLA, 1969. CPA, Calif. Sr. tax acct. Haskins-Sells, Los Angeles, 1967-69; asst. prof. acctg. Calif. State U., Northridge, 1969-72; tax prin. M. Klaiman Acctg. Corp., Beverly Hills, Calif., 1972-75; pvt. practice acctg. Beverly Hills, 1975-80; v.p., controller Ducommun, Inc., Los Angeles, 1980-87; sr. v.p., fin. and adminstrn. Monarch Mirror Door Co. Inc., Chatsworth, Calif., 1987-92; v.p. ops. feature animation Walt Disney Pictures and TV (part of The Walt Disney Co.), Glendale, Calif., 1992-93; sr. v.p. ops. Warner Bros., Glendale, Calif., 1994—. Mem. Fin. Execs. Inst., Tax Execs. Inst., Am. Inst. CPA's, Calif. Soc. CPA's. Office: Warner Bros Feature Animation 500 N Brand Blvd Ste 1800 Glendale CA 91203-1923

LANEY, STEPHEN FAYNE, art educator; b. Salt Lake City, Jan. 1, 1942; s. Fayne and Elzina (Maylett) L.; m. Iva Elizabeth Allen; children: Stephen Shon, Laura Kathleen, Michael Allen, David Brian, Patrick Henrie, Joseph Fayne. BA in Art, Brigham Young U., 1969; MA in Art Edn., Ariz. State U., 1972; postgrad., Brigham Young U., 1983-87. Art, photography tchr. Westwood High Sch., Mesa, Ariz., 1969-84; tchr. figure drawing, painting, basic design, illustration Mesa C.C., 1974-84; tchr. photography Rio Salado C.C., 1978-83; art tchr. Brigham Young U., 1983-84; art & photography tchr. Lakeridge Jr. High Sch., 1985-87, Mountain View High Sch., Orem, Utah, 1988—. Named Art Tchr. of Yr., 1992, Tchr. Artist of Yr., 1992. Mem. NEA, Utah Edn. Assn., Nat. Arts Edn. Assn. Home: 5256 W 10400 S Payson UT 84651-9608 Office: Alpine Sch Dist Mountain View High Sch 665 W Center St Orem UT 84057-5340

LANFORD, LUKE DEAN, electronics company executive; b. Greer, S.C., Aug. 4, 1922; s. John D. and Ethel W. (Ballenger) L.; m. Donna Marie Cellar, Dec. 20, 1945 (dec. Apr. 29, 1984); 1 dau., Cynthia Lea Lanford Brown; m. Jacquelyn Sue Carr Bussell, Feb. 14, 1986. B.S.E.E., Va. Poly. Inst., 1943. With Western Electric Co., Inc., 1946-78; asst. mgr. tng. Western Electric Co., Inc., N.Y.C., 1957-60; mgr. engring. Western Electric Co., Inc., Kansas City, 1960-63; asst. works mgr. Western Electric Co., Inc., Allentown, Pa., 1963-65; plant mgr. Reading, Pa., 1965-69; gen. mgr. Indpls., 1969-78; dir. Met. Indpls. Television Assn., Inc., Sta. WFYI-TV, 1970—, pres., 1975-79. Served with U.S. Army, 1943-46. Mem. IEEE, Telephone Pioneers Am., Eta Kappa Nu, Tau Beta Pi, Phi Kappa Phi. Republican. Presbyterian. Home: 7810 Camelback Dr Indianapolis IN 46250-1840 Office: 2525 N Shadeland Ave Indianapolis IN 46219-1768

LANFORD, OSCAR ERASMUS, JR., retired university vice chancellor; b. Louisa County, Va., Dec. 19, 1914; s. Oscar E. and Ruth (Miller) L.; m. Caroline C. Sherman, Aug. 24, 1937 (dec. Jan. 1990); children—Oscar III, Caroline Aldrich (Mrs. William Eastman), Henry C. Sherman, William Armistead, Virginia Bowen (Mrs. Sedruddin Hemani); m. Esther Lund Arroe, Feb. 23, 1991. B.S., Va. Mil. Inst., 1934; A.M., Columbia, 1937, Ph.D., 1939. Research chemist Gold Dust Corp., 1934-36; instr. chemistry Columbia, 1937-40; prof. chemistry, chmn. dept. State U. N.Y. Coll., Albany, 1940-52; dean coll. State U. N.Y. Coll., 1952-61; first dir. Atmospheric Scis. Research Center, 1961; pres. Fredonia Coll., SUNY, 1961-70; dir. panel on univ. purposes and goals, gen. mgr. constrn. fund, vice chancellor SUNY, 1970-83, cons. univ. planning and mgmt., 1983—. Author textbooks, articles in sci. jours. Mem. Sigma Xi, Phi Lambda Upsilon. Club: University (Albany, N.Y.). Home and Office: 2567 Brookview Rd Castleton On Hudson NY 12033-9713

LANFORD, OSCAR ERASMUS, III, mathematics educator; b. N.Y.C., Jan. 6, 1940; s. Oscar E. and Caroline Clapp (Sherman) L.; m. Regina Victoria Krigman, Dec. 29, 1961; 1 child, Lizabeth Miller. BA, Wesleyan U., Middletown, Conn., 1960; MA, Princeton U., 1962, PhD, 1966; ScD (hon.), Wesleyan U., 1990. Asst., assoc. to prof. math. U. Calif., Berkeley, 1966-87; prof. math. Swiss Fed. Inst. Tech., Zurich, Switzerland, 1987—; prof. physics Inst. des Hautes Etudes Scientiques, Bures-sur-Yvette, France, 1982-87. Recipient award in applied math and numerical analysis, U.S. Nat. Acad. Sci., 1986. Mem. Am. Math. Soc. Office: ETH-Zentrum, Dept Math, 8092 Zurich Switzerland

LANG, CAROL MAX, veterinarian, educator; b. Paris, Ill., Dec. 29, 1937; s. Acel G. and O. Nadine (Beaver) L.; m. Sylvia Smith, Jan. 10, 1965; children: Karen E., John A., Susan C. BS, U. Ill., 1959, DVM, 1961. Diplomate Am. Coll. Lab. Animal Medicine. Capt., vet. corp. Walter Reed Army Inst. Research, Washington, 1961-63; asst. prof. Pa. State U. Coll. Medicine, Hershey, 1966-69, assoc. prof., 1969-72, prof., 1972-84, George T. Harrell Jr. prof., 1984—, asst. dean continuing edn., 1984—. Contbr. more than 140 articles to profl. publs. Served to capt. U.S. Army, 1961-63. Recipient Research award Am. Assn. Lab. Animal Sci., 1980-81, Charles River award Am. Vet. Med. Assn., 1987; Bowman Gray Sch. Med. postdoctoral fellow, 1963-66. Mem. Am. Vet. Med. Assn., Am. Assn. Lab. Animal Sci., Am. Coll. Lab. Animal Medicine (past pres.). Home: 472 Hilltop Rd Hummelstown PA 17036-8512 Office: Pa State U Milton S Hershey Med Ctr PO Box 850 Hershey PA 17033

LANG, CATHERINE LOU, small business owner; b. Hugo, Okla., June 12, 1946; d. John Wilburn Sr. and Velma Lou (Evans) Freeman; m. Laurence Larry Lang, Nov. 20, 1974; children: Tana Louise, Henry Nathan, Gina Elise; 1 stepchild, Michael. BA in Sociology and Econs., Northeastern State U., 1970. Co-owner C&L Jewelry, Waterford, Mich., 1980—; landlord of rental home, Novi, Mich., 1977-93. Active Northwest Child Rescue Women Jr. League, 1975—, League of Women of Detroit; mem. PTA Mercy Sch. for Girls, Farmington, Mich., 1990-94, Walled Lake Mich. Schs., 1981—; mem. Great Decisions, active in leadership, 1988; team parent Team Elan Skating Team, 1991-92; mem. Lakes Assn., Novi, 1992; mem. Covenant Bapt. Ch., 1977—, Am. Bapt. Women. Recipient (with son) Arrow of Light pin Cub Scouts. Mem. AAUW (charter Novi-Northville br.), Internat. Fedn. Univ. Women, Nat. Assn. Investors Corp., Detroit Skating Club, Top Stock Stock Club. Democrat. Avocations: ceramic and porcelain dolls, ice skating team supporter, nat. vol. work. Home: 1369 E Lake Dr Novi MI 48377-1442 Office: C&L Jewelry 924 W Huron St Waterford MI 48328-3726

LANG, CECIL YELVERTON, English language educator; b. Walstonburg, N.C., Sept. 18, 1920; s. Wilton Earl and Lillie (Yelverton) L.; m. Violette Noelle Guérin-Lésé, Apr. 2, 1952; 1 child, François-Michel. AB, Duke U., 1941, AM, 1942; MA, Harvard U., 1947, PhD, 1949. Instr., then asst. prof. English Yale U., New Haven, 1949-57; assoc. prof. Claremont (Calif.) Grad. Sch., 1957-59; prof. Syracuse U., N.Y., 1959-65, U. Chgo., 1965-67; prof. Ctr. for Advanced Studies U. Va., Charlottesville, 1967-70, Commonwealth prof. English, 1970-84, John Stewart Bryan prof., 1984-91, prof. emeritus, 1991—. Editor: The Swinburne Letters, 6 vols., 1959-62, New Writings of Swinburne, 1964, The pre-Raphaelites and Their Circle, 1968; co-editor: The Tennyson Letters, 3 vols., 1982-90, The Letters of Matthew Arnold, 1996. Served to 1st lt. USAAF, 1942-46. Guggenheim fellow, 1951-52; Fulbright fellow, 1951-52, Morse fellow, 1956-57. Fellow Brit. Acad. (corr.), Royal Soc. Lit., Arts Club (London). Home: 2401 Old Ivy Rd Apt 1507 Charlottesville VA 22903-4860 Office: Univ Va Dept Of English Charlottesville VA 22903

LANG, DANIEL S., artist; b. Tulsa, Mar. 17, 1935; s. Irving and Dorothy D. (Lauterer) L. B.F.A., Tulsa U., 1953; M.F.A., Iowa U., 1959. Asst. prof. art SUNY, Fredonia, 1959-60, Art Inst. Chgo., 1962-64, Washington U., St. Louis, 1964-65; vis. artist Ohio State U., 1968-69, U. South Fla., 1971, U. Utah, spring 1984; adj. prof. U. Utah, 1984—. One-man shows include Boston Mus. Fine Arts, 1961, Arthur Tooth & Sons, London, 1970, 74, Alexandra Monett Gallery, Brussels, Belgium, 1973, 78, Fairweather

Hardin Gallery, Chgo., 1971, 77, 80, Il Gabbiano Gallery, Rome, 1975, DM Gallery, London, 1975, Gimpel & Weitzenhofer, N.Y.C., 1976, Fischbach Gallery, N.Y.C., 1977, 79, Graphik Internat. GMBH, Stuttgart, Germany, 1979, Richard Demarco Gallery, Edinburgh, Scotland, 1981, 83, Watson/Willour Gallery, Houston, 1981, David Findlay Gallery, N.Y.C., 1981, 83, Sherry French Gallery, N.Y.C., 1984, Meredith Long Gallery, Houston, 1984, Washington Gallery, Glasgow, 1986, Phillips Gallery, Salt Lake City, 1988, Gilcrease Mus., Tulsa, 1989, Am. Stock Exch., N.Y.C., 1991, Galleria Civica, Seregno, Italy, 1991, The Hokin Gallery, Palm Beach, Fla., 1991, Taylor's Contemporary Gallery, Hot Springs, Alaska, 1992, Galleria Delle Art, Cittá di Castello, Italy, 1992, William Hardie Gallery, Glasgow, Scotland, 1992, Civic Gallery, Urbino, Italy, 1992, London Art Fair, 1994, Elliot Smith Gallery, St. Louis, 1994; group shows include Am. Fedn. of Arts travelling exhbn., 1968-69, U. Pa. Inst. Contemporary Art, 1970, Moore Coll. Art, 1971, Boston U., 1972, Joslyn Art Mus., Omaha and Sheldon Meml. Art Galleries, Lincoln, Nebr., 1973-74, Sherry French Gallery, 1983, 85, 86, Ruth Siegel Gallery, N.Y.C., 1989, Antarctica 2-man show sponsored by NSF, organized by Smithsonian Instn., 1976-79, America 1976 travelling exhbn., 1976-78, including stops at Fogg Art Mus. Harvard U., Wadsworth Atheneum, Hartford, Conn. and, Corcoran Gallery Art, Washington, Watson/de Nagy Gallery of Houston travelling exhbn., 1978-79, Hirschl & Adler Gallery, N.Y.C., 1980, Gerald Peters Gallery, 1993, Landfall Press, Chgo., 1993, Cline Fine Art Gallery, Sante Fe, 1994, U. Tulsa, 1994, numerous others; represented in permanent collections including Bklyn. Mus. High Mus. Art, Atlanta, Denver Art Mus., Mus. Modern Art, N.Y.C., Art Inst. Chgo., Library of Congress, Boston Public Library, Calif. Palace Legion of Honor, Nelson Rockefeller Collection, N.Y.C., Victoria and Albert Mus., London, Hunterian Art Gallery, U. Glasgow, Elliot Smith Gallery, St. Louis, 1994, The Cline Fine Art Gallery, Santa Fe, 1994, R. Duane Reed, St. Louis, 1996, Galerie Hertz, Louisville, Ky., 1996, other pub. and pvt. collections; designer sets for Orfeo, Kent Opera Co., Eng., later filmed by BBC, 1976. Served with U.S. Army, 1954-56. Home (winter): 38 W 56th St New York NY 10019-3814 also: Montone (PG), 06014 Montone Italy

LANG, DOUGLAS STEWARD, lawyer; b. St. Louis, July 25, 1947; s. Ervin Jacob and Jacqueline Helen (Kratky) L.; m. Martha Kay Taylor, Aug. 25, 1973; children: Brian Chester and Christopher John (twins), Stewart Taylor. BS BA, Drake U., 1969; JD, U. Mo., 1972. Bar: Mo. 1972, Tex. 1973, U.S. Dist. Ct. (ea., we. and no. dists.) Tex. 1973, U.S. Ct. Appeals (5th cir.) 1977. Law clk. to Hon. Fred L. Henley Mo. Supreme Ct., St. Louis, 1972-73; assoc. Weber, Baker & Allums, Dallas, 1973-78; ptnr. Gardere, Porter & DeHay, Dallas, 1978-79, Gardere & Wynne, Dallas, 1979—; speaker continuing legal edn. seminars. Bd. dirs. Univ. Park Elem. Sch. Dads' Club, 1988-89, pres. 1990-91; chalice bearer and lay reader Ch. of Incarnation, Dallas, 1984—, mem. symposium on aging, 1990, co-chmn. annual ch. field day, 1988, 89, Sunday sch. tchr., 1982, 83, 90, vestry mem. 1990-95, Christian edn. com., 1992—, chair bldg. com., 1993—; baseball coach gradesch. teams YMCA, Dallas, 1988-89, football coach gradesch. teams, 1987-92, soccer coach gradesch. teams, 1983-86; campaign chmn., treas. Election Nathan L. Hecht, judge 95th dist. ct., Dallas, 1982; tribe chief Indian Guides, Dallas, 1985-87; mem. Dallas Mus. Art, 1986—; mem. Dallas County Rep. Men's Club, 1986—; bd. dirs. Girls' Adventure Trails, Inc., Dallas, 1986-92, chmn. facilities com., 1989-90, chmn. long-range planning com., 1987-88; mem. troops com. Boy Scout Troop 72, Dallas, 1989—, asst. scoutmaster, 1992—, order of arrow; v.p. Park Cities Ctrl. Dads' Club, Dallas, 1990-91; pres. Univ. Park Grade Sch. Dad's Club, 1990-91; bd. councillors U. Dallas, 1991-93. Recipient Outstanding Svc. awd. Legal Svcs. North Tex., Dallas, 1991, Alumni Achievement award, Drake U., Des Moines, Iowa, 1992, Double D award Drake U., 1993. Fellow Tex. Bar Found. (sustaining, life), Am. Bar Found., Dallas Bar Found (trustee 1991—, sec.-treas. 1994-96); mem. ABA (litigat. sect. 1974—, exec. com. Met. Bar Caucus 1991—, sec.-treas. 1992-93, pres.-elect 1993-94, pres. 1994-95), State Bar Tex. (coll. state bar Tex. 1992—, bd. dirs. 1992-95, exec. com. 1994-95, Outstanding Third Yr. Dir. award 1995), Dallas Bar Assn. (bd. dirs. 1976-78, 80—, pres. 1991, chmn. exec. dir. search com. 1994, v.p. adminstrv. 1979, 88, v.p. activities 1989, chmn. strategic planning com. 1982-84, mem. numerous coms.), Dallas Assn. Young Lawyers (bd. dirs. 1975, v.p. 1976, treas. 1976, pres. 1977, Outstanding Young Lawyer in Dallas 1981), Tex. Young Lawyers Assn. (bd. dirs. 1976-78), Tex. Assn. Bank Coun. (co-chmn. litigation com. 1989, bd. dirs. 1990-94, v.p. 1994-95, pres. elect 1995-96), Tex. Assn. Defense Counsel, Nat. Conf. Bar Pres. (ex officio, exec. cou. 1994-95, exec. counsel 1995-96), Am. Inn of Ct. (membership chmn. 1991-95, exec. com. 1991—, counselor 1995), North Tex. Drake Alumni Assn. (pres. 1974-75), Salesmanship Club of Dallas. Republican. Episcopalian. Avocations: golf, hiking, rafting, camping. Office: Gardere & Wynne LLP 1601 Elm St Ste 3000 Dallas TX 75201-4757

LANG, ERICH KARL, physician, radiologist; b. Vienna, Austria, Dec. 7, 1929; came to U.S., 1950, naturalized, 1960; s. Johann Hans and Caecilia C. (Felkel) L.; m. Nicoli J. Miller, Apr. 21, 1956; children: Erich Christopher, Cortney Alexander Johann. Arbitur, Realgymnasium, 1947; M.S., Columbia U., 1951; M.D., U. Vienna, 1953. Intern U. Iowa Hosps., Iowa City, 1954-55; resident in internal medicine U. Iowa Hosps., 1955-56; resident in radiology Johns Hopkins U. Hosp., Balt., 1956-59; radiologist Johns Hopkins U. Hosp., 1956-61; instr. radiology Johns Hopkins U., 1956-61; radiologist, acting dir. radiology Methodist Hosp., Indpls., 1961-67; prof., chmn. dept. radiology La. State U. Med. Center, Shreveport, 1967-76, New Orleans, 1976-92; prof., chmn. dept. radiology La. State U., Tulane U. schs. medicine, 1976—; dir. radiology Charity Hosp., New Orleans, 1976-92; prof. radiology LSU, 1992—; adj. prof. urology La. State U. Med. Ctr., 1987—; guest prof. U. Vienna, 1992-93; guest/vis. prof. U. Medicine and Dentistry N.J., 1995—. Author numerous articles in field. Served as maj. M.C., U.S. Army, 1961-65. Fellow ACP, Soc. Vascular Surgeons, Am. Coll. Radiology, Billroth Med. Soc.; mem. Radiol. Soc. N. Am., Am. Roentgen Ray Soc., Soc. Nuclear Medicine, Soc. Acad.; Chmn. Radiology, Soc. U. Radiologists, La. New Orleans med. socs., Crescent City Radiol. Soc. Office: 1542 Tulane Ave New Orleans LA 70112-2825

LANG, EUGENE M., technology development company executive; b. N.Y.C., Mar. 16, 1919; s. Daniel and Ida Lang; m. Theresa Volmar, Apr. 15, 1946; children: David A., Jane, Stephen. BA, Swarthmore Coll., 1938; MS, Columbia U., 1940; postgrad., Bklyn. Poly. Inst., 1941-42; LLD (hon.), Swarthmore Coll., 1981, St. Paul's Coll., 1987, Columbia U., 1988, SUNY, 1987, St. Michaels Coll., 1988; LHD (hon.), Coll. New Rochelle, 1986, Bank St. Coll., 1986, New Sch. Social Research, 1987, Trinity Coll., Hartford, Conn., 1988; Dr. Pub. Svc. (hon.), R.I. Coll., 1988, CUNY, 1989, Springfield Coll., Mass., 1989, Yale U., 1989, Hunter Coll., 1990, Hobart Coll., 1990, Glassboro State Coll., 1990; LHD (hon.), Bard Coll., 1991; LLD, Lawrence U., 1991, U. Mo., 1993; LHD (hon.), Whitman Coll., 1993; LHD, Goucher Coll., 1994. Works mgr. Aircraft Screw Products, Inc., N.Y.C., 1941-46; founder, pres. Clark Chem. Co., Long Island City, N.Y., 1946-48; co-founder, exec. v.p. Heli-Coil Corp. (now divsn. of Black & Decker), Danbury, Conn., 1948-52; founder, chmn. REFAC Technology Devel. Corp., N.Y.C., 1952—; chmn. Electronic Rsch. Assn., Inc., Winsted, Conn., 1978-90; bd. dirs. other U S. and fgn. cos. Patentee. Contbr. articles on internat. bus., small bus. issues, technology transfer and venture capital projects to profl. publs. Bus. chmn. Citizens for Humphrey-Muskie, N.Y., 1968; trustee, vice chmn. New Sch. Social Rsch., N.Y., 1978—; mng. dir. N.Y.C. Met. Opera Assn., 1978-93; bd. dirs. Columbia U. Grad. Sch. Bus., 1986—; adv. dir. Carnegie-Mellon Grad. Sch. Bus. Adminstrn., 1989—; dir. Mannes Coll. Music, 1989—; chmn. bd. dirs. Swarthmore Coll., Pa., 1981-88, emeritus, 1988—; chmn. Eugene M. Lang Found.; founding donor Eugene Lang Coll., New Sch. Social Rsch.; founder I Have A Dream program minority student edn. Recipient George Washington award Am.-Hungarian Fedn., 1982, Community Service award Booth Meml. Med. Ctr., N.Y., 1980, Disting. Service for Trusteeship Assn. Governing Bds., Washington, 1985, Brotherhood award NCCJ, 1985, John Jay award Conf. Ind. Colls. and Univs. of N.Y. State, 1986, Booth award Vols. of Am., 1986 presdl. citations, 1979, 85, Family of Man award nat. Council of Chs., 1986, Hubert H. Humphrey Humanitarian award Nat. Urban Coalition, 1986, Jefferson award Am. Inst. Pub. Service, 1986, Martin Luther King medal of Freedom, N.Y. State, 1987, Human Rights award N.J. Ednl. Assn., 1987, Front Page award N.Y. Daily News, 1987, Leadership award Nat. Urban League, 1987, Carter Humanitarian award NAACP, 1987, Salute award U.S. C. of C., 1987, Horatio Alger award Horatio Alger Found., 1987, Pub. Service award P.R. Family Inst., 1988, Friend of Edn. award NEA, N.Y., 1988, Fisher Disting. Service to Edn. award Council for Advancement and Support of Edn., 1988, Disting. Leadership award United Negro Coll. Fund, 1988, Val-Kill award Eleanor Roosevelt Found., 1988, Finley medal CCNY Alumni Assn., 1988, Evangeline Booth award Salvation Army, 1988, CESPA award Elem. Sch. Prins. Assn., 1989, Meridian award Children's Mus. Indpls., 1989, medal of distinction Barnard Coll., 1989, Leadership award Boston Partnership in Edn., Robie award Jackie Robinson Found., 1990, Point of Light citation President George Bush, Pub. Svc. award Boston Dept. Pub. Edn., 1991, Drum Major award So. Christian Leadership Conf., 1991, Trail Blazer award Assn. Negro Bus. Women, 1991, Community Svc. award U.S. Dept. Justice, 1991, Dodge award YMCA, 1992, S. Henry Smith Pub. Svc. award Alfred U., 1992, Fgn. Trade Leadership award Charlotte World Trade Assn., 1992, Champion of Mentoring award Children's Crusade of R.I., Trustee's award Spelman Coll., 1993, Youth Svc. award Upward, Inc., Nat. Caring award, Recog. award Martin Luther King Com., Norman Vincent Peale award Norman Vincent Peale Fedn., 1994, Goodworks award Theaterworks USA. Mem. Licensing Exec. Soc., Univ. Club, Century Club, Yale Club, Golden Key (Baruch Coll. chpt.). Home: 912 5th Ave New York NY 10021-4159 Office: REFhnology Devel Corp 122 E 42d St New York NY 10168

LANG, GEORGE, restaurateur; b. Székesfehérvár, Hungary, July 13, 1924; came to U.S., 1946, naturalized, 1950; s. Simon and Ilona (Lang) Deutsch; m. Jenifer Lang; children: Andrea, Brian, Simon John, Georgina Kathlyn. Student, U. Szeged, Hungary, 1945, Mozarteum, Salzburg, Austria, 1945-46, U. Stranieri, Perugia, Italy, 1950-51; LHD(hon.), Ind. Univ., 1994. Asst. banquet mgr. Waldorf-Astoria, 1953-58; v.p. sales and marketing Brass Rail Orgn., 1958-60; v.p. Restaurant Assos. Industries, 1960-71; pres. George Lang Corp., N.Y.C., 1971—; owner (with Ronald Lauder) Gundel's Restaurant, Budapest, Hungary, 1990—; co-owner Tokaj and Eger Vineyard. Author: The Cuisine of Hungary, 1971, Lang's Compendium of Culinary Nonsense and Trivia, 1980, The Cafe des Artistes Cookbook, 1984; co-author: Gundel Album, 1993; cons. editor Time-Life Book div.'s Foods of the World series, 1966-70; columnist, assoc. editor Travel and Leisure mag.; contbr. to Ency. Brit., 1974, also columnist mags. Pub. mem. Am. Revolution Bicentennial Commn., 1969—, mem. exec. com., chmn. Festival U.S.A. coordinating art, internat. exchange and spl. events for Bicentennial celebrations. Address: 33 W 67th St New York NY 10023-6224 *Almost anyone can be creative given enough time, budget and space, but the ones who succeed today have the common denominator of being poets of the possible.*

LANG, GEORGE EDWARD, lawyer; b. Peekskill, N.Y., Apr. 7, 1932; s. George Louis and Florence (Sheehan) L.; m. Rose Marie Corrao, June 8, 1953; children: G. Vincent Lang, Kathleen M. Lang. AB, U. Notre Dame, 1954, JD, 1955. Bar: Ky. 1955, U.S. Dist. Ct. Ky. 1956. City atty. Munfordville, Ky., 1958-85, Bonnieville, Ky., 1958-85; atty. Hart County, Munfordville, 1962-70; hearing officer Ky. Workmen's Compensation Bd., Munfordville, 1971-79; master commr. Hart Cir. Ct., Munfordville, 1984—; pres. South Ctr. Ky. Broadcasting Co., Munfordville, 1984-88; v.p. Cub Run (Ky.) Industries, 1986-90. Pres. Munfordville Indsl. Found., 1968-90; bd. dirs. Mammoth Cave (Ky.) Devel. Assn., 1972—; chmn. Hart County Dem. Party, Munfordville, 1972-78. Mem. Ctrl. Ky. Wildlife Fedn. (pres. 1962-64), Munfordville Lions Club (pres. 1966-68), Horse Cave Rotary Club (v.p. 1968-69). Roman Catholic. Home: 517 W Center St Munfordville KY 42765-0366 Office: 1 Corrao Bldg PO Box 366 Munfordville KY 42765

LANG, H. JACK, advertising executive, author; b. Cleve., June, June 24, 1904; s. Hascal Charles and Rosetta (Stettiner) L.; m. Frances Wise, Aug. 10, 1935; children: Wendy, John. BA, Antioch Coll., 1928. Founder, pres. Lang, Fisher Stashower Inc. (name changed to Liggett-Stashower Inc. 1988), Cleve. Author: The Wit and Wisdom of Abraham Lincoln, 1941, Lincoln's Fireside Reading, 1965, Two Kinds of Christmases, 1965, The Rowfant Manuscripts (named one of best books of yr. Am. Inst. Graphic Arts 1979), newspaper syndicated feature and book Letters of the Presidents (George Washington medal Freedoms Found.), 1964; Lincoln's Log Cabin Library (George Washington medal Freedoms Found.), 1965, Letters in American History, 1982, Dear Wit: Letters From the World's Wits, 1990; editor: The Wolf Mag. of Letters, 1934—; collector autograph letters. Past trustee Planned Parenthood Cleve., Antioch U., Yellow Springs, Ohio; trustee Mt. Sinai Hosp., Cleve., 1947-60, hon. trustee, 1973—; past mem. exec. com. ARC, Cleve. Lt. col. USAAF, 1942-46. Named to Hall of Fame Cleve. Advt. Club, 1977. Mem. Manuscript Soc., Western Res. Hist. Soc., Rowfant Club (fellow). Home: 1737 Andrews Rd Cleveland Heights OH 44118-1901 Office: 1228 Euclid Ave Cleveland OH 44115-1831

LANG, HANS JOACHIM, engineering company executive; b. Crailsheim, Germany, Nov. 17, 1912; came to U.S., 1920, naturalized, 1928; s. Karl Hermann and Marie (Muelberger) L.; m. Emily Ruth Crowl, Feb. 26, 1944; children—Helen Marie (Mrs. Fay Logan, Jr.), Jacqueline Ruth (Mrs. Kirk Weaver), Anne Michelle (Mrs. John Talbot), Robert Crowl. M.E., Stevens Inst. Tech., 1934; M.S., MIT, 1936. Registered profl engr., N.Y., N.J., Pa., Calif., Tex. Process engr. Standard Oil Co., N.J., 1936-41; chief process engr. Day & Zimmermann, Inc., Phila., 1942-50; project mgr. C.F. Braun & Co., Alhambra, Calif., 1950-59; mgr. European sales C.F. Braun & Co., 1959-62; v.p. N. Am. operations Lummus Co., Bloomfield, N.J., 1962-68; pres. J.F. Pritchard & Co., Kansas City, Mo., 1968-69; group pres. Internat. Systems and Controls Engring. Group of Cos., 1969-74; exec. v.p. Procon Inc., Des Plaines, Ill., 1974-75; pres. Procon Inc., 1975-77, Lang Assos. Inc., Tenafly, N.J., 1978—, The Pritchard Corp., Kansas City, Mo., 1978-84. Author books and articles in field. Mem. Am. Bar Assn., State Bar Calif., Am. Inst. Chem. Engrs., ASME, Am. Assn. Cost Engrs. (award of merit 1983). Home and Office: 136 Westervelt Ave Tenafly NJ 07670

LANG, JOHN FRANCIS, lawyer; b. Bayonne, N.J., June 8, 1915; s. Lewis F. and Pauline M. (Norwich) L.; m. Eleanor Bradford Cook, Jan. 26, 1952; children: Elaine L. Cornett, Anita L. Knowlton. BA, Georgetown U., 1937; JD, Harvard U., 1940. Bar: N.Y. 1941, U.S. Dist. Ct. (so. dist.) N.Y., U.S. Ct. Appeals (2d cir.), U.S. Supreme Ct., 1947. Assoc. Buckley & Buckley, N.Y.C., 1940-41, Law Office of D. J. Mooney, N.Y.C., 1946-51, Nash, Ten Eyck, N.Y.C., 1951-53; ptnr. McNutt & Nash, N.Y.C., 1953-56, Hill, Betts & Nash, LLP, N.Y.C., 1956-86; of counsel Hill, Betts & Nash, N.Y.C., 1986-96; bd. dirs. numerous corps.; chmn. biennial seminar in Paris on ship and aircraft fin. Co-editor: Maritime Law Handbook of the Internat. Bar Assn. Lt. comdr. USN, 1941-45. Decorated Knight Comdr. (Republic of Liberia). Mem. ABA, Internat. Bar Assn. (co-editor Maritime Law Handbook), Maritime Law Assn., Harvard Club of N.Y. Avocations: boating, skiing, travel, writing. Office: c/o Hill Betts & Nash LLP One World Trade Ctr New York NY 10048

LANG, K. D. (KATHERINE DAWN LANG), country music singer, composer; b. Consort, Alta., Can., 1961; d. Adam and Audrey L. Lang. Mem. Tex. swing fiddle band, 1982—; formed band The Reclines. Albums include A Truly Western Experience, 1984, Angel with a Lariat, 1986, Shadowland, 1988, Absolute Torch and Twang, 1990 (Can. Country Music Awards album of the yr.), Ingenue, 1992, Even Cowgirls Get the Blues (soundtrack), 1993; actress (film) Salmonberries, 1991. Recipient Can. Country Music awards, including Entertainer of Yr., 1989, Grammy award, 1990, 1993, Best Pop Female Vocal for Constant Craving, Grammy nomination Best Pop Female Vocal for Miss Chatelaine, 1994, William Harold Moon award Soc. of Composers, Authors and Music Publishers of Can., 1994. Office: Sire Records 75 Rockefeller Plz New York NY 10019-6908

LANG, KURT, sociologist, educator, writer; b. Berlin, Jan. 25, 1924; came to U.S., 1936; s. Ernst and Ilse (Kass) L; m. Gladys Engel, June 9, 1950; children: Glenna Engel, Kevin Engel. BA, U. Chgo., 1949, MA, 1852, PhD, 1953. Rsch. analyst Office of U.S. Milit. Govt., Berlin, 1945-47; asst. prof. U. Miami, Fla., 1953-54; rsch. sociologist Can. Broadcasting Corp., Ottawa, Ont., 1954-56; from asst. to assoc. prof. Queens Coll. CUNY, Flushing, N.Y., 1956-62, assoc. prof., chair, 1963-64; prof. SUNY, Stony Brook, 1964-84, chair, 1965-68; prof. U. Wash., Seattle, 1984—, dir. Sch. Comm., 1984-87; vis. assoc. prof. U. Calif., Berkeley, 1962-63; vis. prof. Free U., Berlin, 1992; cons. CBS, N.Y.C., 1964-65, Nat. Adv. Commn. Civil Disorder, Washington, 1967. Author: Collective Dynamic, 1961, Television and Politics, 1968, 84, Battle for Public Opinion, 1983, Etched in Memory, 1990. U.S. Army Rsch. Inst. grantee, 1975-78, NEH fellow, 1971, Woodrow Wilson Ctr. fellow, 1978-79, Nat. Humanities Ctr. fellow, 1983-84, Sr. Fullbright fellow, 1994. Mem. Am. Polit. Sci. Assn. (Disting. Career award in polit. comm. 1994), Am. Assn. Pub. Opinion Rsch. (coun. 1975-77, Disting. Contbn. award 1989), Am. Sociol. Assn. (Edward L. Bernays award 1952), Internat. Inst. Comm. Democrat. Avocations: art study, photography, jogging. Home: 1249 20th Ave E Seattle WA 98112-3530 Office: U Washington Dept Sociology Seattle WA 98195

LANG, MABEL LOUISE, classics educator; b. Utica, N.Y., Nov. 12, 1917; d. Louis Bernard and Katherine (Werdge) L. B.A., Cornell U., 1939; M.A., Bryn Mawr Coll., 1940, Ph.D., 1943; Litt.D., Coll. Holy Cross, 1975, Colgate U., 1978; L.H.D., Hamilton Coll. Mem. faculty Bryn Mawr Coll., 1943-91, successively instr., asst. prof., 1943-50, assoc. prof., 1950-59, prof. Greek, 1959-88, chmn. dept., 1960-88, acting dean coll. 2d semester, 1958-59, 60-61; chmn. mng. com. Am. Sch. Classical Studies, Athens, 1975-80; chmn. admissions and fellowship com. Am. Sch. Classical Studies, 1966-72; Blegen disting. rsch. prof. semester I Vassar Coll., 1976-77; Martin classical lectr. Oberlin Coll., 1982. Co-author: Athenian Agora Measures and Tokens; author: Palace of Nestor Frescoes, 1969, Athenian Agora Graffiti and Dipinti, 1976; Herodotean Narrative and Discourse, 1984, Athenian Agor Ostraka, 1990; contbr. articles profl. jours. Guggenheim fellow, 1953-54; Fulbright fellow Greece, 1959-60. Mem. Am. Philos. Soc., Am. Acad. Arts and Scis., German Archaeol. Inst., Am. Philol. Assn., Soc. Promotion Hellenic Studies (Eng.), Classical Assn. (Eng.). Home: 905 New Gulph Rd Bryn Mawr PA 19010-2941

LANG, MARGO TERZIAN, artist; b. Fresno, Calif.; d. Nishan and Araxie (Kazarosian) Terzian; m. Nov. 29, 1942; children: Sandra J. (Mrs. Ronald L. Carr), Roger Mark, Timothy Scott. Student, Fresno State U., 1939-42, Stanford U., 1948-50, Prado Mus., Madrid, 1957-59, Ariz. State U., 1960-61; workshops with, Dong Kingman, Ed Whitney, Rex Brandt, Millard Sheets, George Post. Maj. exhbns. include, Guadalajara, Mex., Brussels, N.Y.C., San Francisco, Chgo., Phoenix, Corcoran Gallery Art, Washington, internat. watercolor exhbn., Los Angeles, Bicentennial shows, Hammer Galleries, N.Y.C., spl. exhbn. aboard, S.S. France, others, over 50 paintings in various Am. embassies throughout world; represented in permanent collections, Nat. Collection Fine Arts Mus., Smithsonian Instn.; lectr., juror art shows; condr. workshops.; interviews and broadcasts on Radio Liberty, Voice of Am. Bd. dirs. Phoenix Symphony Assn., 1965-69, Phoenix Musical Theater, 1965-69. Recipient award for spl. achievements Symphony Assn., 1966, 67, 68, 72, spl. awards State of Ariz., silver medal of excellence Internat. Platform Assn., 1971; honoree U.S. Dept. State celebration of 25 yrs. of exhbn. of paintings in embassies worldwide, 1989. Mem. Internat. Platform Assn., Ariz. Watercolor Assn., Nat. Soc. Arts and Letters (nat. dir. 1971-72, nat. art chmn. 1974-76), Nat. Soc. Lit. and Arts, Phoenix Art Mus., Friends of Mexican Art, Am. Artists Profl. League, English-Speaking Union, Musical Theater Guild, Ariz. Costume Inst., Phoenix Art Mus., Scottsdale Art Ctr., Ariz. Arts Commn. (fine arts panel 1990-91). Home: 6127 E Calle Del Paisano Scottsdale AZ 85251-4212 *As a romantic impressionist I feel a tremendous exhilaration at being able to communicate my philosophy through my paintings. I look for God's beauty and mystery in all things, and as an artist, I feel very fortunate that I can eliminate the ugliness and the negatives and concentrate on the wonders of the universe around us.*

LANG, MARVEL, urban affairs educator; b. Bay Springs, Miss., Apr. 2, 1949; s. Otha and Hattie (Denham) L.; m. Mozell Pentecost, Sept. 15, 1973; children: Martin E., Maya S. BA cum laude, Jackson State U., 1970; MA, U. Pitts., 1975; PhD in Urban/Social and Econ. Geography, Rural Settlement and Quantitative Methods/Computer Applications, Mich. State U., 1979; postgrad., St. John's Coll., Santa Fe, 1973, Miss. State U., 1979, Murray State U., 1980. Grad. teaching fellow dept. geography U. Pitts., 1970-72; instr. geography Jackson (Miss.) State U., 1972-74, asst. prof. geography, 1978-82, assoc. prof. geography, 1982-83; assoc. prof., dir. geography program Jackson (Miss.) State U. Ctr. Urban Affairs, 1983-84; grad. teaching & rsch. asst. dept. geography Mich. State U. Computer Inst. Social Sci. Rsch., East Lansing, 1974-76; grad. teaching fellow dept. geography Mich. State U., East Lansing, 1976-78; grad. asst. to dir. Mich. State U. Ctr. Urban Affairs, Coll. Urban Devel., East Lansing, 1977-78; dir. Ctr. Urban Affairs, assoc. prof. urban affairs programs Mich. State U., East Lansing, 1986-91, dir. Ctr. Urban Affairs, prof. urban affairs programs, 1991-93, prof. urban affairs programs, 1993—; profl. geographer Bureau of the Census, Washington, 1984-85, rsch. geographer, 1985-86; instr. geography Lansing C.C., 1976-78, vis. prof., 1990-91; vis. prof. grad. sch. edn. & allied professions Fairfield (Conn.) U., 1990, 91, Egeler correctional facility prison edn. program Spring Arbor Coll., Jackson, 1990, McNair summer rsch. opportunity program, Mich. State U., 1989, 90, Wilberforce U., 1991, 92; rsch. cons. Mich. State U. Ctr. Urban Studies, 1978-79; prin. investigator NASA, 1979-81, Inst. Rsch., Devel. & Engring. in Nuclear Energy, 1980-81, U.S. Dept. Energy, 1980-82; co-prin. investigator & dir. U.S. Bureau of the Census, 1988—; mem. commn. geography & Afro-Am. fellowship U. Pitts, 1970-72; mem. numerous coms. Jackson State U., Mich. State U.; commentator on various radio and television programs; conductor seminars, workshops, and presentations; cons.; speaker in field. Author: (with others) The World at Your Fingertips: A Self Instructional Geography Handbook, 1991; editor: Contemporary Urban America: Problems, Issues and Alternatives, 1991, (with C. Ford) Black Student Retention in Higher Education, 1988, Strategies for Retaining Minorities in Higher Education, 1992; author (with others) Introduction to Remote Sensing of the Environment, 1982, Black Student Retention in Higher Education, 1988, Politics and Policy in the Age of Education, 1990, International Science, Technology, and Development: Philosophy, Theory and Policy, 1990, The Second Handbook of Minority Student Services, 1990, Contemporary Urban America: Problems, Issues, and Alternatives, 1991, The Guide to College Success: For Black Students Only, 1992, numerous tech. reports; mem. editorial bd. Jour. Urban Affairs, Urban Affairs Quarterly, 1992—; referee Urban Affairs Quarterly, Jour. Urban Affairs, Social Devel. Issues Jour., Econ. Devel. Quarterly, Urban Geography Jour.; contbr. articles and reviews to profl. jours. Mem. Gov.'s Coun. Selective Svc. in the State of Miss., 1969-80; bd. dirs. Boys and Girls Clubs of Lansing, 1986-89; chair bd. program com., bd. dirs. St. Vincent Children's Home/Catholic Social Svcs. of Lansing, 1986-89; mem. com. community rels. Tri-County Coun. Aging, 1987-89; mem. adv. com. Mich. Legis. Black Caucus Found., 1987—, hon. host Ann. Black History Month Celebration, 1989-91; mem. coordinating com. Friendship Baptist Ch. Acad. Enrichment Program, 1986-89; bd. dirs. Mich. Protection & Advocacy Svcs., 1991—; faculty advisor MSU Black Grad. Student's Assn., 1989-90; active CIC Acad. Leadership Devel. Program, 1989-90; co-founder, v.p. Black Men Inc. of Greater Lansing, 1992—. Acad. and Marching Band scholar Jackson State U., 1966-70; recipient Outstanding Leadership award Friendship Bapt. Ch. Laymen's League, 1988, Meritorious Svc. award Mich. Lelack Caucus Found., 1988; grantee Commn. on Geography and Afro-America and the Nat. Office of Edn., 1973, Jackson State U. Grad. Sch. Rsch. and Publ. Com., 1979, NASA, 1979-80, 80-81, U.S. Dept. Energy, 1980-81, 81-82, Inst. Rsch., Devel. & Engring. Nuclear Energy, 1980-81, NSF, 1980-82, Kellogg Found., 1981-84, Miss. Coun. Humanities, 1982-83, U.S. Bureau of the Census, 1988-90, C.S. Mott Found., 1990-93. Mem. Urban Affairs Assn. (nominating com. 1987-88, membership com. 1987—, site selection com. 1988-89, governing bd. 1989—, chair membership com. 1990-91, sec., treas. 1991-92, vice chair 1992—, chair 1993—), Assn. Am. Geographers (chair com. on the status of Afro-Am. geographers 1980-83, com. affirmative action 1983—, census adv. com. 1990—), Southeast Divsn. Assn. Am. Geographers (steering com. 1980-81, com. edn. 1981-86, program com. 1982), Nat. Coun. Geog. Edn. (remote sensing com. 1981-84), Assn. Advancement of Policy, Rsch. and Devel. in the Third World (conf. program planning com. 1988-89, chair health and population sect. 1988-89), Miss. Coun. Geog. Edn. (pres., chair program com. 1979-80), Population Assn. Am., Assn. Social and Behavioral Scientists, Mich. Acad. Scis., Sigma Rho Sigma Nat. Honor Soc., Gamma Theta Upsilon Nat. Honor Soc., Alpha Kappa Mu Nat. Honor Soc., Alpha Phi Alpha Frat., Inc. Home: 3700 Colchester Rd Lansing MI 48906-3418 Office: Mich State U Ctr Urban Affairs W-104 Owen Hall East Lansing MI 48824

LANG, NORMA M., dean, nursing educator; b. Wausau, Wis., Dec. 27, 1939. BSN, Alverno Coll., 1961; MSN, Marquette U., 1963, PhD, 1974. Staff nurse, asst. instr. St. Joseph's Hosp., 1961-62; instr., coord. med.-surg. nursing St. Mary's Sch. Nursing, 1964-65; instr., asst. prof. Sch. Nursing, U. Wis., Milw., 1965-69, from asst prof. to prof., 1968-92, dean, 1980-92; dean, prof. Sch. Nursing, U. Pa., Phila., 1992—; nursing coord. Wis. Regional Med. Program, 1968-73; rsch. assoc. U. Wis., Milw., 1977, ctr. sci. Urban Rsch. Ctr., 1977-79. Contbr. articles to profl. jours. Fellow Am. Acad.

Nursing; mem. ANA, NAS, AAUP, APHA, Am. Heart Assn. Office: U Pa Sch Nursing 420 Guardian Dr Philadelphia PA 19104-6096

LANG, NORTON DAVID, physicist; b. Chgo., July 5, 1940; s. Charles and Sadelle (Bilow) L.; m. Enid Asher, June 8, 1969; children: Eugenie, Aaron. A.B. summa cum laude, Harvard U., 1962, A.M., 1965, Ph.D., 1968; postgrad. (Knox fellow), London Sch. Economics, 1962-63. Asst. research physicist, lectr. U. Calif., San Diego, 1967-69; mem. staff IBM Research Center, Yorktown Heights, N.Y., 1969—; Erwin W. Mueller meml. lectr., Pa. State U., 1992. Contbr. articles on theoretical physics to profl. jours.; asso. editor: Phys. Rev. Letters, 1980-83. Fellow N.Y. Acad. Scis., Am. Phys. Soc. (chmn. fellowship com. divsn. condensed matter physics 1985-87, Davisson-Germer prize 1977, chmn. Davisson-Germer Prize com. 1990); mem. Phi Beta Kappa. Office: IBM Rsch Ctr Yorktown Heights NY 10598

LANG, OTTO E., industry executive, former Canadian cabinet minister; b. Handel, Sask., Can., May 14, 1932; s. Otto T. and Maria (Wurm) L.; m. Adrian Ann Merchant, 1963-88; children: Maria (dec.), Timothy, Gregory, Andrew, Elisabeth, Amanda, Adrian; m. Deborah McCawley, 1989; stepchildren: Andrew, Rebecca. BA, U. Sask., 1951, LLB, 1953; BCL (Rhodes scholar), Oxford (Eng.) U., 1955; LLD (hon.), U. Man., 1987. Bar: Sask. 1956, Ont., Yukon and N.W.T 1972, Man. 1988; created Queen's counsel 1972. Mem. faculty Law Sch., U. Sask., 1956-68, asso. prof. law, 1958-61, prof., dean law, 1961-68; M.P. for Sask.-Humboldt, 1968-79; Canadian minister without portfolio, 1968-69, minister for energy and water, 1969, minister of manpower and immigration, 1970-72, minister of justice, 1972-75, 78-79, minister transport, 1975-79; minister-in-charge Canadian Wheat Bd., 1969-79; exec. v.p. Pioneer Grain Co. Ltd., James Richardson & Sons Ltd., Winnipeg, Man., Can., 1979-88; chmn. Transp. Inst., U. Man., Winnipeg, 1983-93; mng. dir. Winnipeg Airports Authority, Inc., 1992-93, vice chmn., 1993—; pres., CEO Centra Gas Manitoba, Inc., Winnipeg, 1993—; mem. Queen's Privy Coun. for Can.; hon. consul gen. for Japan, 1993—; bd. dirs. Investors Group Trust Co., Winnipeg Commodity Exch. Editor: Contemporary Problems in Public Law, 1967. Vice pres. Sask. Liberal Assn., 1956-62, fed. campaign chmn., Sask., 1963-64; campaign chmn. Winnipeg United Way, 1983. Mem. St. Charles Golf Club. Roman Catholic. Office: Centra Gas, 444 St Mary Ave, Winnipeg, MB Canada R3C 3T7

LANG, PEARL, dancer, choreographer; b. Chgo., May 1922; d. Jacob and Frieda (Feder) Lack; m. Joseph Wiseman, Nov. 22, 1963. Student, Wright Jr. Coll., U. Chgo.; D (hon.), Juilliard Sch. Music, 1995. Formed own co., 1953; faculty Yale, 1954-68; tchr., lectr. Juilliard, 1953-69; tchr., lectr. Jacobs Pillow, Conn. Coll., Neighborhood Playhouse, 1963-68, Israel, Sweden, Netherlands. Soloist, Martha Graham Dance Co., 1944-54; featured roles on Broadway include Carousel, 1945-47, Finian's Rainbow, 1947-48, Danced Marth Graham's roles in Appalachian Spring, 1974-76, Primitive Mysteries, 1978-79, Diversion of Angels, 1948-70, Herodiade, 1977-79; role of Solvieg opposite John Garfield Broadway include, ANTA Peer Gynt; choreographer: TV shows CBC Folio; co-dir. T.S. Eliot's Murder in the Cathedral, Stratford, Conn., Direction, 1964-66, 67, Lamp Unto Your Feet, 158, Look Up and Live TV, 1957; co-dir., choreographer: full length prodn. Dybbuk for CBC; dir. numerous Israel Bond programs; assumed roles Emily Dickinson: Letter to the World, 1970; Clytemnestra, 1973; Jocasta in: Night Journey, 1974, for Martha Graham Dance Co.; choreographer: dance works Song of Deborah, 1952, Moonsung and Windsung, 1952, Legend, 1953, Rites, 1953, And Joy Is My Witness, 1954, Nightflight, 1954, Sky Chant, 1957, Persephone, 1958, Black Marigolds, 1959, Shirah, 1960, Apasionada, 1961, Broken Dialogues, 1962, Shore Bourne, 1964, Dismembered Fable, 1965, Pray for Dark Birds, 1966, Tongues of Fire, 1967, Piece for Brass, 1969, Moonways and Dark Tides, 1970, Sharjuhm, 1971, At That Point in Place and Time, 1973, The Possessed, 1974, Prairie Steps, 1975, Bach Rondelays, 1977, I Never Saw Another Butterfly, 1977, A Seder Night, 1977, Kaddish, 1977, Icarus, 1978, Cantigas Ladino, 1978, Notturno, 1980, Gypsy Ballad, 1981, Hanele The Orphan, 1981, The Tailor's Megilleh, 1981, Bridal Veil, 1982, Stravinsky's opera Oedipus Rex, 1982, Song of Songs, 1983, Shiru L'adonay, 1983, Tehillim, 1983, Sephardic Romance and Tfila, 1989, Koros, 1990, Eyn Keloheynu, 1991, Schubert Quartetsatz No. 12, 1993, Schubert Quartet 15 1st Mov., 1994. Founder Pearl Lang Dance Found.; mem. Boston Symphony, Tanglewood Fest. Recipient 2 Guggenheim fellowships; recipient Goldfadden award Congress for Jewish Culture, Achievement award Artists and Writers for Peace in the Middle East, Cultural award Workmen's Circle, Queens Coll. award, 1991, Jewish Cultural achievement award Nat. Found. for Jewish Culture, 1992. Mem. Am. Guild Mus. Artists. Home: 382 Central Park W New York NY 10025-6054

LANG, PHILIP DAVID, former state legislator, insurance company executive; b. Portland, Oreg., Dec. 16, 1929; s. Henry W. and Vera (Kern) L.; m. Marcia Jean Smith, May 29, 1952 (div. Oct. 1979); 1 son, Philip David, III; m. Virginia Ann Wolf, Feb. 16, 1980. Student, Lewis and Clark Coll., 1951-53, Northwestern Coll. Law, 1956. Police officer Oreg. Dept. State Police, Salem, 1953-55; claims adjuster Glenns Falls Ins. Co., Portland, 1955-57, Oreg. Automobile Ins. Co., Portland, 1959-61; adminstrv. asst. to mayor City of Portland, 1957-58; spl. agt., underwriter North Pacific Ins. Co., Portland, 1961-63; mgr. North Pacific Ins. Co., 1963-65, asst. v.p., 1965-80, v.p., 1980-95; ret., 1995; asst. v.p. Oreg. Automobile Ins. Co., 1965-80, v.p., 1980-95; ret., 1995. Mem. Oreg. Ho. of Reps., 1960-79, speaker, 1975-79; Div. leader Multnomah County (Oreg.) Democratic Com., 1956-60, mem. precinct com., 1956—. Served with USAF, 1947-50. Mem. Oreg. Ins. Underwriters Assn., Theta Chi. Roman Catholic. Clubs: VFW, Masons, DeMolay (Legion Honor). Home: 5769 SW Huddleson St Portland OR 97219-6645 *Success is achieved through commitment to, and perserverance in, all that is undertaken; balanced with tolerance and understanding of all persons.*

LANG, RICHARD A., lawyer; b. N.Y.C., Dec. 10, 1950. AB, Harvard U., 1972; JD, John Marshall Law Sch., 1975; LLM, Boston U., 1976. Bar: Ill. 1975, Mass. 1976. Ptnr. Kirkland & Ellis, Chgo. Mem. ABA, Ill. State Bar Assn. Office: Kirkland & Ellis 200 E Randolph St Chicago IL 60601-6436*

LANG, RICHARD WARREN, economist; b. Mpls., Oct. 23, 1949; s. Norman George and Mildred Elizabeth (Sundheim) L.; m. Carol Jean Nelson, July 31, 1971; children—Scott, Erik. B.A., St. Olaf Coll., 1971; M.A., Ohio State U., 1973, Ph.D., 1977. From economist to sr. economist Fed. Res. Bank St. Louis, 1976-80; rsch. officer, v.p. Fed. Res. Bank Phila., 1980-84, sr. v.p., dir. rsch., 1984—; mem. faculty Ill. Bankers Sch., Carbondale, 1977-80, Pa. Bankers Sch., Lewisburg, 1981—. Contbr. articles to profl. jours. Mem. Am. Econ. Assn., Am. Fin. Assn., Nat. Assn. Bus. Economists, Phi Beta Kappa. Office: Fed Res Bank Phila 10 Independence Mall Philadelphia PA 19106

LANG, ROBERT TODD, lawyer; b. N.Y.C., July 2, 1924; s. Charles and Selma L.; m. Joann Lang, Aug. 4, 1949; children: William Gerald, James David, Nancy Adler, Carolyn Kay. BA, Yale U., 1945, LLB, 1947. Bar: N.Y., U.S. Dist. Ct. (so. dist.) N.Y. Assoc. Weil, Gotshal & Manges, N.Y.C., 1948-56; ptnr. Weil, Gotshal & Manges (P.C. since 1981), N.Y.C., 1956—. Bd. dirs. Lawyers' Com. for Human Rights. Recipient Golden Torch of Hope award City of Hope, 1971, Community Svc. award Brandeis U., 1982, Learned Hand award Am. Jewish Com., 1991. Mem. ABA (chmn. subcom. proxy solicitations/tender offers 1985-93, chmn. task force listing standards self-regulatory orgn., chmn. task force on hedge funds, chmn. ad hoc com. on instnl. investors 1991-95, mem. task force on exec. compensation 1991-94, mem. task force on rev. of fed. securities laws, mem. adv. com.), NASD (legal adv. bd.), N.Y. County Lawyers Assn. (chmn. corp. law com. 1971-76, spl. com. on legal opinions 1977-81), Am. Stock Exch. (spl. com. shareholder voting rights), Yale Club of N.Y.C., Harmonie Club, Sunningdale Country Club. Office: Weil Gotshal & Manges PC 767 5th Ave New York NY 10153

LANG, THERESA, investment banker; b. Hochhausen, Germany, Aug. 25, 1952; d. John and Theresa (Wendler) L.; m. Scott David St. Marie, Nov. 12, 1977; 1 child, Hanna. BA in Econs., Fordham U., 1974; MBA in Finance, UCLA, 1982. Assoc. investment banking A.G. Becker Paribas, N.Y.C., 1982-84; assoc. investment banking Merrill Lynch Capital Markets, N.Y.C., 1984-86, v.p. investment banking, 1986-89, dir. investment banking, 1989-92; sr. v.p., treas. Merrill Lynch & Co., Inc., 1992—. Office: Merrill Lynch and Co World Financial Ctr 250 Vesey St New York NY 10281-1012

LANG, THOMPSON HUGHES, publishing company executive; b. Albuquerque, Dec. 12, 1946; s. Cornelius Thompson and Margaret Miller (Hughes) L. Student, U. N.Mex., 1965-68, U. Americas, Mexico City, 1968-69. Advt. salesman Albuquerque Pub. Co., 1969-70, pres., treas., gen. mgr., dir., 1971—; pub., pres., treas., dir. Jour. Pub. Co., 1971—; pres., dir. Masthead, Internat., 1971—; pres. Magnum Systems, Inc., 1973—; pres., treas., dir. Jour. Ctr. Corp., 1979—; chmn. bd., dir. Starline Printing, Inc., 1985—; chmn. bd. dirs. Corp. Security and Investigation, Inc., 1986—; pres., bd. dirs. Eagle Systems, Inc., 1986—. Mem. HOW Orgn., Sigma Delta Chi. Home: 8643 Rio Grande Blvd NW Albuquerque NM 87114-1301 Office: Albuquerque Pub Co PO Drawer JT(87103) 7777 Jefferson St NE Albuquerque NM 87109-4343

LANG, VERA, publishing company executive. U.S. treas. Reed Elsevier, Inc., N.Y.C. Office: Reel Elsevier Inc 200 Park Ave Fl 17 New York NY 10166*

LANG, WILLIAM CHARLES, retail executive; b. Bronx, N.Y., Jan. 29, 1944; s. Harold C. and Katherine L. (Pratt) L.; m. Marilyn Warshow, June 27, 1965 (dec.); children: Kenneth William, Pamela Sue. B.S. magna cum laude, Lehigh U., 1965. C.P.A. Accounting supr. Peat, Marwick, Mitchell & Co., 1965-69; contr. Pueblo Internat., Inc., N.Y.C., 1970-72, v.p. fin., 1972-77; exec. v.p. adminstrn. and fin. Kenyon & Eckhardt, Inc., 1977-85; exec. mng. dir. Finley, Kumble, Wagner, Heine, Underberg, Manley, Myerson & Casey, 1985-88; pres., chief fin. officer Furr's Inc., Lubbock, Tex., 1989-92; sr. v.p. fin. and adminstrn., chief fin. officer Duane Reade, N.Y.C., 1993—. Mem. Financial Execs. Inst., Am. Inst. C.P.A.'s, Nat. Accounting Soc., N.Y. State Soc. C.P.A.'s, Beta Gamma Sigma, Sigma Phi. Office: Duane Reade 49-29 30th Pl Long Island City NY 11101-3109

LANG, WILLIAM WARNER, physicist; b. Boston, Aug. 9, 1926; s. William Warner and Lilla Gertrude (Wheeler) L.; m. Asta Ingard, Aug. 31, 1954; 1 son, Robert. B.S., Iowa State U., 1946, Ph.D., 1958; M.S., M.I.T., 1949. Acoustical engr. Bolt Beranek and Newman, Inc., Cambridge, Mass., 1949-51; instr. in physics U.S. Naval Postgrad. Sch., Monterey, Calif., 1951-55; cons. engr. E.I. du Pont de Nemours & Co., Wilmington, Del., 1955-57; mem. research staff M.I.T., 1958; physicist IBM, Poughkeepsie, N.Y., 1958-92; program mgr. acoustics tech. IBM, 1976-90, mem. sr. tech. staff, 1990-92; pres. Internat. Inst. Noise Control Engring., Poughkeepsie, 1988—. Editor: Designing for Noise Control, 1978. Pres. Noise Control Found., Poughkeepsie, 1975-92; adj. prof. physics Vassar Coll., 1979—; chmn. working group Internat. Orgn. Standardization, 1969—; chmn. tech. com. 29 Internat. Electrotech. Commn., 1975-84. Served with USN, 1944-47, 52. Decorated Meritorious Service medal; recipient Pro Silentio medal Hungarian Optical, Acoustical and Film Tech. Soc., 1989. Fellow AAAS, IEEE (Audio and Electroacoustics Achievement award 1970, dir. 1970-71, Centennial medal 1984), Audio Engring. Soc., Acoustical Soc. Am. (Silver medal 1984), Inst. Acoustics (U.K.) (hon.); mem. Nat. Acad. Engring., Inst. Noise Control Engring./U.S.A. (pres. 1978), Rotary (pres. local club 1975-76). Episcopalian. Home: 29 Hornbeck Rdg Poughkeepsie NY 12603-4205 Office: Internat Inst Noise Control Engring PO Box 3067 Poughkeepsie NY 12603-3067

LANGACKER, PAUL GEORGE, physics educator; b. Evanston, Ill., July 14, 1946; s. George Rollo and Florence (Hinesley) L.; m. Irmgard Sieker, June 25, 1983. BS, MIT, 1968; PhD, U. Calif., Berkeley, 1972; MA, U. Pa., 1981. Postdoctoral assoc. Rockefeller U., N.Y.C., 1972-74; postdoctoral assoc. U. Pa., Phila., 1974-75, asst. prof. physics, 1975-81, assoc. prof. physics, 1981-85, prof. physics, 1985-93, William Smith Term prof. physics, 1993—, chair, dept. physics and astronomy, 1993-96; exec. com. Divsn. Particles & Fields of Am. Phys. Soc., Washington, 1989-91; mem. editorial bd. Phys. Rev., 1986-88, 91-93; sci. dir. Theoretical Advanced Study Inst., Boulder, Colo., 1990. Editor: Testing the Standard Model, 1991, Precision Tests of the Standard Electroweak Model, 1995. Recipient Humboldt award A.V. Humboldt Soc., 1987-88. Fellow Am. Phys. Soc., AAAS. Office: U of Pa Dept of Physics 2N10 David Rittenhouse Lab Philadelphia PA 19104

LANGACKER, RONALD WAYNE, linguistics educator; b. Fond du Lac, Wis., Dec. 27, 1942; s. George Rollo and Florence (Hinesley) L.; m. Margaret G. Fullick, June 5, 1966 (dec.). A.B. in French, U. Ill., 1963, A.M. in Linguistics, 1964, Ph.D., 1966. Asst. prof. U. Calif. at San Diego, La Jolla, 1966-70; asso. prof. U. Calif. at San Diego, 1970-75, prof. linguistics, 1975—. Author: Language and its Structure, 1968, Fundamentals of Linguistic Analysis, 1972, Non-Distinct Arguments in Uto-Aztecan, 1976, An Overview of Uto-Aztecan Grammar, 1977, Foundations of Cognitive Grammar I, 1987, Concept, Image and Symbol, 1990, Foundations of Cognitive Grammar II, 1991; assoc. editor: Lang, 1971-77, Cognitive Linguistics, 1989—; contbr. articles in field to profl. jours. Guggenheim fellow, 1978. Mem. Linguistic Soc. Am., Cognitive Sci. Soc., Soc. for Study Indigenous Langs. of Ams., Internat. Cognitive Linguistics Assn., AAUP, ACLU. Home: 7381 Rue Michael La Jolla CA 92037-3915 Office: U Calif at San Diego Dept Linguistics 0108 La Jolla CA 92093

LANGAN, JOHN PATRICK, philosophy educator; b. Hartford, Conn., Aug. 10, 1940; s. Eugene Edward and Sarah Cecilia (McCole) Langan. AB, Loyola U., Chgo., 1962; MA, Loyola U., 1966; BD, Woodstock Coll., N.Y.C., 1970; PhD, U. Mich., 1979. Ordained priest, Roman Cath. Ch., 1972. Instr. philosophy U. Mich., Ann Arbor, 1971-72; research fellow Woodstock Theol. Ctr., Washington, 1975-83; vis. asst. prof. social ethics Yale Div. Sch., New Haven, 1983; sr. fellow Woodstock Theol. Ctr., 1983—, acting dir., 1986-87; Rose F. Kennedy prof. Christian ethics Kennedy Inst. Ethics, Georgetown U., Washington, 1987—; bd. dirs. Georgetown U. Press, 1984—; vis. rsch. scholar Jesuit Inst. Boston Coll., 1993-94; mem. rsch. coun. Ctr. Strategic and Internat. Studies, 1993; vis. prof. philosophy Loyola U. Chgo., 1995—; cons. in field. Editor: The American Search for Peace, 1991, The Nuclear Dilemma and the Just War Tradition, 1986, Human Rights in the Americas: The Struggle for Consensus, 1982, Catholic Universities in Church and Society, 1993. Bd. dirs. Bon Secours Health System, 1990, Nat. Capital Presbytery, Health Care Ministries, Washington, 1989-92. Rackham Prize fellow, U. Mich., 1972-73. Mem. Am. Acad. Religion, Am. Philos. Assn., Cath. Theol. Soc. Am., Soc. Christian Ethics, Soc. Christian Philosophers, Soc. for Bus. Ethics (bd. dirs. 1996—), Internat. Studies Assn. Roman Catholic. Avocations: music, swimming. Office: Georgetown U 1437 37th St NW Washington DC 20007-2610

LANGBAUM, ROBERT WOODROW, English language educator, author; b. N.Y.C., Feb. 23, 1924; s. Murray and Nettie (Moskowitz) L.; m. Francesca Levi Vidale, Nov. 5, 1950; 1 child, Donata Emily. A.B., Cornell U., 1947; M.A., Columbia U., 1949, Ph.D., 1954. Instr. English Cornell U., 1950-55, asst. prof., 1955-60; assoc. prof. U. Va., Charlottesville, 1960-63; prof. English U. Va., 1963-67, James Branch Cabell prof. English and Am. lit., 1967—; vis. prof. Columbia U., summer 1960, 65-66, Harvard U., summer 1965; mem. supervising com. English Inst., 1970-71, chmn., 1972; mem. Christian Gauss Book Award Com., 1984-86; U.S. Info. Svc. lectr. Japan, Taiwan, Hong Kong, 1988. Author: The Poetry of Experience: The Dramatic Monologue in Modern Literary Tradition, 1957, The Gayety of Vision: A Study of Isak Dinesen's Art, 1964, The Modern Spirit: Essays on the Continuity of Nineteenth and Twentieth Century Literature, 1970, The Mysteries of Identity: A Theme in Modern Literature, 1977, The Word From Below: Essays on Modern Literature and Culture, 1987, Thomas Hardy in Our Time, 1995; editor: The Tempest (Shakespeare), 1964; anthology The Victorian Age: Essays in History and in Social and Literary Criticism, 1967; mem. editl. bd. Victorian Poetry, 1963—, New Lit. History, 1969—, Bull. Rsch. in Humanities, 1977—, Studies in English Lit., 1978—, So. Humanities Rev., 1979—, Studies in Browning and His Circle, 1987—, Victorian Lit. and Culture, 1991—, Symbiosis, 1995—. Served to 1st lt. M.I. AUS, 1942-46. Ford Found. fellow Center for Advanced Study, Stanford, Calif., 1961-62; Guggenheim fellow, 1969-70; sr. fellow Nat. Endowment for Humanities, 1972-73; Am. Council Learned Socs. grantee, 1961, 75-76; fellow Clare Hall, Cambridge U., Eng., 1978; U. Va. Ctr. Advanced Study fellow, 1982; resident scholar Bellagio Study and Conf. Ctr. Rockefeller Found., Italy, June 1987. Mem. MLA (del. assembly 1979-81), AAUP, PEN, Assn. Lit. Scholars and Critics, Phi Beta Kappa. Home: 223 Montvue Dr Charlottesville VA 22901-2022

LANGBEIN, JOHN HARRISS, lawyer, educator; b. Washington, Nov. 17, 1941; s. I. L. and M. V. (Harriss) L.; m. Kirsti M. Hiekka, June 24, 1973; children: Christopher, Julia, Anne. AB, Columbia U., 1964; LLB, Harvard U., 1968, Cambridge U., 1969; PhD, Cambridge U., 1971; MA (hon.), Yale U., 1990. Bar: D.C. 1969, Fla. 1970; barrister-at-law Inner Temple, Eng., 1970. Asst. prof. law U. Chgo., 1971-73, assoc. prof. law, 1973-74, prof. law, 1974-80, Max Pam prof. Am. and fgn. law, 1980-90; Chancellor Kent prof. law and legal history Yale U., New Haven, 1990—; commr. Nat. Conf. Commrs. on Uniform State Laws, 1984—; reporter Uniform Prudent Investor Act; assoc. reporter Restatement of Property (3d): Donative Transfers. Author: Prosecuting Crime in the Renaissance, 1974, Torture and the Law of Proof: Europe and England in the Ancient Regime, 1977, Comparative Criminal Procedure: Germany, 1977; (with L. Waggoner) Selected Statutes on Trusts and Estates, 1987, rev. edits., 1991, 92, 94, 95; (with B. WolK) Pension and Employee Benefit Law, 1990, 2d edit., 1995; contbr. numerous articles on law and legal history in profl. jours. Mem. ABA, Am. Coll. Trust and Estate Counsel, Am. Law Inst., Am. Soc. Legal History, Am. Hist. Assn., Selden Soc., Gesellschaft fuer Rechtsvergleichung, Am. Acad. of Arts and Scis., Internat. Acad. Estate and Trust Law, Internat. Acad. Comparative Law. Republican. Episcopalian. Office: Yale Univ Sch Law PO Box 208215 127 Wall St New Haven CT 06520-8215

LANGBO, ARNOLD GORDON, food company executive; b. Richmond, B.C., Can., Apr. 13, 1937; s. Osbjourn and Laura Marie (Hagen) L.; m. Martha Marie Miller, May 30, 1959; children: Sharon Anne, Maureen Bernice, Susan Colleen, Roderick Arnold, Robert Wayne, Gary Thomas, Craig Peter, Keith Edward. Student, U. B.C. Retail salesman Kellogg Co., Vancouver, 1956-57; dist. mgr. Kellogg Co., Prince George, B.C., 1957-60; supermarket salesman Kellogg Co., Vancouver, 1960; dist mgr. Kellogg Co., Winnipeg, Man., 1964-65; acct. mgr. Kellog Co. of Can., Ltd., Toronto, 1965-67; sales staff asst. Kellogg Co., Battle Creek, Mich., 1967-69, adminstrv. asst. to pres., 1969; exec. v.p. Kellogg Co. of Can. Ltd., London, Ont., 1970; v.p. sales and mktg. Kellogg Salada Can. Ltd., Toronto, 1971-74, sr. v.p. sales and mktg., 1974-76, pres., chief exec. officer, 1976-78; pres. food products div. Kellogg U.S., Battle Creek, 1978-81; past exec. v.p. Kellogg Co., Battle Creek, group exec. v.p., 1983-86, exec. v.p., 1986—; pres. Kellogg Internat., Battle Creek, 1986—; pres. Mrs. Smith's Frozen Foods Co. (subs. Kellogg Co.), Battle Creek, 1983-85, chmn., chief exec. officer, 1985—; pres. Kellogg Internat., 1986—, pres., COO, internat. bd. dirs., 1990—; chmn., CEO Kellogg Co., Battle Creek, 1992—, also dir.; bd. dirs. Johnson & Johnson, Grocery Mfg. Am., Gilmore Int. Keyboard Festival. Vice-pres. Hockey Internat., Battle Creek; trustee Albion Coll.; mem. Canadian-Am. Com., B.C. Premier's Econ. Adv. Coun.; mem. adv. bd. J. L. Kellogg Grad. Sch. Mgmt., Northwestern U.; bd. dirs. Gilmore Internat. Keyboard Festival. Mem. Am. Frozen Food Inst. (bd. dirs., vice chmn. 1985), Grocery Products Mfrs. Can. (bd. dirs.), Tea Council of Can. (bd. dirs.). Office: Kellogg Co Box 3599 1 Kellogg Sq Battle Creek MI 49017-3534*

LANGBORT, POLLY, retired advertising executive; b. N.Y.C.; d. Julius and Nettie (Berman) L. BA, Adelphi U. Sec. Young & Rubicam, Inc., N.Y.C., media buyer, media planner, 1960-65, planning supr., 1965-70, v.p. group supr., 1970-75, v.p. dir. planning devel., 1975-80, sr. v.p., dir. planning, 1980-85, sr. v.p. direct mktg. and media services Wunderman, Worldwide div., 1985-86, exec. v.p. dir. mktg. & media services Wunderman, Worldwide div., 1986-90; assoc. pub. Lear's Mag., N.Y.C., 1990-91; ret., 1991. Author: DMA Factbook, 1986; contbr. articles to profl. jours. Spl. gifts chairperson Am. Cancer Soc., N.Y.C., 1985-90. Jewish. Avocations: classical music, outdoor activities. Home: 7614 La Corniche Cir Boca Raton FL 33433

LANGDALE, GEORGE WILFRED, research soil scientist; b. Walterboro, S.C., Sept. 14, 1930; s. Benjamin Hayward and Hazel Ruth (Smith) L.; m. Eugenia Miles Boatwright, Aug. 28, 1955. B.S., Clemson Univ., 1957, MS, 1961; postgrad. N.C. State Univ., 1963-64; PhD, Univ. Ga., 1969. Rsch. soil scientist USDA, Agrl. Rsch. Svc., S.C., Ga., Tex., 1957-96, ret. 1996; conservation tillage and soil erosion. Contbr. book chpts. and articles to profl. jours. Served with 27th Inf. Wolfhounds U.S. Army, 1951-53, Korea. Kellogg fellow Agr. Policy Inst., 1963-64. Fellow Soil and Water Conservation Soc. (H.H. Bennett award 1993, chpt. pres. Tex. 1970-71, Ga. 1994-95), Am. Soc. Agronomy (pres. Ga. chpt. 1986-87), Soil Sci. Soc. Am.; mem. Soil Conservation Soc. Am., World Assn. Soil and Water Conservation, Internat. Soil Sci. Soc., Sigma Xi. Baptist. Avocations: conservation gardening, small game hunting, genealogy. Home: 125 Orchard Knob Ln Athens GA 30605-3427

LANGDALE, JOHN WESLEY, timber executive; b. Valdosta, Ga., Feb. 8, 1917; s. Harley and Thalia (Lee) L.; m. Margaret Irene Jones, Dec. 19, 1946; children: Lee Mikuta, John Widr., Margaret Perryman. AB in Econs., U. Ga., 1939, JD, 1940. Mem. Ga. Ho. of Reps., Atlanta, 1949-52, Ga. State Senate, Atlanta, 1957-58; pres. The Langdale Co., Valdosta, 1976-82, vice chmn., 1983—; vice chmn. Langdale Industries Inc., 1986—; chmn. bd. dirs. Valdosta Fed. Savs. and Loan Assn., 1957—. Chmn. U. Ga. Bd. Regents, 1967-69. Served to lt. comdr. USNR, 1941-46, PTO. Decorated Bronze Star. Mem. Ga. Bar Assn. Baptist. Lodge: Rotary (pres. local chpt. 1948-49, dist. gov. 1967-68).

LANGDALE, NOAH NOEL, JR., research educator, former university president; b. Valdosta, Ga., Mar. 29, 1920; s. Noah N. and Jessie Katharine (Catledge) L.; m. Alice Elizabeth Cabaniss, Jan. 8, 1944; 1 son, Noah Michael. AB, U. Ala., 1941; LLB, Harvard U., 1948, MBA, 1950; LLD, U. Ala., 1959. Bar: Ga. bar 1951. Asst. football coach U. Ala., 1942; practiced law Valdosta, 1951-57; instr., then asst. prof. econs. and social studies, chmn. dept. accounting, econs. secretarial sci., bus. adminstrn. Valdosta State Coll., 1954-57; pres. Ga. State U., Atlanta, 1957-88, Disting. univ. rsch. prof., 1988-89, ret., 1989, pres. emeritus, disting. rsch. prof. emeritus, 1989—; dir. Guardian Life Ins. Co. Am.; past mem. U.S. Adv. Commn. Ednl. Exchange; former mem. Pres.'s Commn. NCAA. Served to lt. (s.g.) USNR, 1942-46. Recipient 1st Georgian of Year award Ga. Assn. Broadcasters, 1962; Silver Anniversary All-Am. award Sports Illustrated, 1966; Mrytle Wreath award Hadassah, 1970; Salesman of Yr. award Sales and Mktg. Execs. of Atlanta, 1975; Silver Knight of Mgmt. award Lockheed-Ga. chpt. Nat. Mgmt. Assn., 1978; Humanitarian award Nat. Jewish Hosp. and Research Center/Nat. Asthma Center, 1980, Robert T. Jones award Boy Scouts Am. Mem. ABA, Ga. Bar Assn., Ga. Bar Found. (life), Ga. Assn. Colls. (pres. 1962-63), SAR (past v.p. Ga.), Gridiron Soc., Rotary, Phi Beta Kappa, Omicron Delta Kappa, Delta Chi, Phi Kappa Phi. Methodist. Office: Library North Ga State University Atlanta GA 30303

LANGDELL, ROBERT DANA, medical educator; b. Pomona, Cal., Mar. 14, 1924; s. Walter Irving and Florence Delsa (Reichenbach) L.; m. Alice E. Pritt, June 3, 1948; children—Robert Dana, Sara Ellen. Student, Pomona Coll., 1941-43; M.D., George Washington U., 1948. Intern Henry Ford Hosp., Detroit, 1948-49; mem. faculty Sch. Medicine, U. N.C., Chapel Hill, 1949—; assoc. prof. pathology Sch. Medicine, U. N.C., 1959-61, prof., 1961—; mem. hematology study sect. USPHS, 1968-71. Editor-in-chief Transfusion, 1972-82; assoc. editor Archives of Pathology and Laboratory Medicine, 1983—. Served to capt. M.C. AUS, 1955-56. USPHS sr. research fellow, 1957-61; Career Research fellow, 1962-66. Mem. Am. Assn. Blood Banks (pres. 1972-73), Am. Soc. Clin. Pathology, AMA, Coll. Am. Pathology (gov. 1977-83), N.C. Med. Assn. Episcopalian. Rsch. in blood coagulation and hemostasis. Home: 707 Williams Cir Chapel Hill NC 27516-1527

LANGDON, FRANK CORRISTON, political science educator, researcher; b. LaGrange, Ill., June 3, 1919; s. Ernest Warren and Julia Ida (Mondeng) L.; m. Virginia Irene Osborne, Nov. 11, 1922; children: Peter John, Marc Christopher. A.B., Harvard U., 1941, A.M., 1949; Ph.D., U. Calif.-Berkeley, 1953. Japanese Lang. Sch. intelligence officer U.S. Navy, Stillwater, Okla., 1945-46; econ. analyst Hdqrs. SCAP, Fgn. Trade div., Tokyo, 1946-47; instr. polit. sci. U. Calif. Far East Program, Korea, Japan, Guam, 1953-55; sr. lectr. Canberra U. Coll., Australia, 1955-58; prof. polit. sci. U. B.C., Vancouver, 1958-84, emeritus prof., 1984—, sr. research assoc., 1984—. Author: Politics in Japan, 1967, Japan's Foreign Policy, 1973, Politics of

Canadian-Japanese Economic Relations, 1952-83, 83; co-editor, co-author: Japan in the Post Hegomonic World, 1993; co-editor, contbr.: Superpower Maritime Strategy in the Pacific, 1990. Served to lt. comdr. USNR, 1941-45. Mem. Assn. for Asian Studies, Can. Polit. Sci. Assn., Can. Asian Studies Assn., Japan Studies Assn. of Can., Internat. House Japan, Am. Polit. Sci. Assn. Democrat. Presbyterian. Club: Mokuyokai (Vancouver). Home: 4736 W 4th Ave, Vancouver, BC Canada V6T 1C2 Office: U BC Inst Internat Rels, C456 1866 Main Mall, Vancouver, BC Canada V6T 1Z1

LANGDON, GLEN GEORGE, JR., electrical engineer; b. Morristown, N.J., June 30, 1936; s. Glen George and Mildred (Miller) L.; m. Marian Elizabeth Jacobsen, Aug. 10, 1963; 1 child, Karen Joan. BSEE, Wash. State U., 1957; MSEE, U. Pitts., 1963; PhD, Syracuse U., 1968. Elec. engr. Westinghouse Electric Co., East Pittsburgh, Pa., 1960-62, applications programmer, Churchill Boro, Pa., 1962-63; engr. IBM Corp., Endicott, N.Y., 1963-73, research staff mem., San Jose, Calif., 1974-87; prof. computer engring. U. Calif., Santa Cruz, Calif., 1987—; vis. prof. U. São Paulo, Brazil, 1971-72; lectr. U. Santa Clara, 1975-78, Stanford U., 1984. Author: Logic Design: A Review of Theory and Practice, 1974; (with Edson Fregni) Projecto de Computadores Digitals, 1974; Computer Design, 1982. Patentee in field. Lt. Signal Corps., U.S. Army, 1958-59. Recipient Armed Svcs. Communications award Wash. State U., 1957, outstanding innovation award IBM, 1980, 91. Fellow IEEE, Computer Soc. of IEEE (standards com. 1969-70, 74-81, sec. 1982, edn. bd. 1983-86, pub. bd. 1984-85, 87-90, bd. govs. 1984-87, v.p. edn. 1986, Compcon gen. chair 1986, Hot Chips IV Symposium gen. chair 1992); mem. Assn. Computing Machinery (vice chmn. So. Tier chpt. 1973), SPIE, SMPTE, Sigma Xi. Home: 220 Horizon Way Aptos CA 95003-2739 Office: U Calif-Santa Cruz Dept Computer Engring Santa Cruz CA 95064

LANGDON, HERSCHEL GARRETT, lawyer; b. Lowry City, Mo., Oct. 6, 1905; s. Isaac Garrett and Della (Park) L.; m. Ethel Virginia Waterson, May 26, 1931 (dec. Apr. 1979); children: Richard G., Ann Virginia (Mrs. Charles Eugene Willoughby Ward); m. Miriam Pickett, May 17, 1982. B.A., U. Iowa, 1930, J.D., 1931. Bar: Iowa 1931. Since practiced in Des Moines; mem. firm Herrick, Langdon & Langdon (and predecessors), 1935—. Fellow Am. Coll. Trial Lawyers, Am. Bar Found.; mem. Am., Iowa, Polk County bar assns., Phi Beta Kappa, Delta Sigma Rho, Phi Delta Pi. Conglist. Club: Mason. Home: 3524 Grand Ave Apt 603 Des Moines IA 50312-4344 Office: 1800 Financial Ctr 7th and Walnut Des Moines IA 50309

LANGE, BILLIE CAROLA, aquatic exercise video creator and specialist; b. Cullman, Ala.; d. John George and Josephine (richard) Luyben; m. Harry E. Lange (div.); children: JoAnne Lange Graham, Linda Jean Lange Reeve; m. Melvin A. Coble (div.). Grad., Long Beach City (Calif.) Coll.; BMus, U. So. Calif. Chief piano accompanist Long Beach Civic Opera Assn.; tchr./creator aquatic exercise program U. Ala., Huntsville, 1984-87; advisor Aquatic Exercise Assn., Port Washington, Wis., 1988—; creator, prodr. aquatic video exercise tapes Billie C. Lange's Aquatics, Palm Beach, Fla., 1979—. Creator: (aquatic exercise video tapes) Slim and Trim Yoga with Billie In and Out of Pool, 1979, Slim and Trim with Billie In Pool, 1994 (televised on Today Show, NBC 1995); pianist Organ-Piano Duo and various audio tapes; instrumental, audio Tranquility, 1992. Mem. Nat. Acad. Recording Arts and Scis. Avocations: classical pianist, aquatic tapes, politics. Home: PO Box 822 Umatilla FL 32784-0822 Office: PO Box 822 Umatilla FL 32784-0822

LANGE, CARL JAMES, psychology educator; b. Seneca, Pa., June 1, 1925; s. Otto Carl and Rose Marie (Jetter) L.; m. Veronica Szelypecz, Jan. 14, 1950; children: David Carl, Veronica Jean. B.S., Duke U., 1945; M.S., U. Pitts., 1948, Ph.D., 1951. Lic. psychologist, Va. Project dir. Human Resources Research Office, George Washington U., 1953-60, dir. research, planning, 1960-69; asst. v.p. research George Washington U., 1969-75, v.p. adminstrn., research, prof. psychology, 1975-88, v.p. rsch., prof. psychology, 1988-89, prof. emeritus, 1989—; cons. NSF, Ford Found.; bd. dirs. Sch. for Contemporary Edn., Nat. Lab. Higher Edn., Eric Clearinghouse for Higher Edn., Southeastern Univs. Rsch. Assn. Contbr. articles in field to profl. jours.; bd. editors: Research in Higher Education. Served with USN, 1943-45. Fellow Am. Psychol. Assn.; mem. AAAS, Sigma Xi. Home: 7 Clarendon Ct Williamsburg VA 23188-1513

LANGE, CLIFFORD E., librarian; b. Fond du Lac, Wis., Dec. 29, 1935; s. Elmer H. and Dorothy Brick (Smithers) L.; m. Janet M. LeMieux, June 6, 1959; children: Paul, Laura, Ruth. Student, St. Norbert Coll., 1954-57; B.S., Wis. State U., 1959; M.S.L.S. (Library Services Act scholar), U. Wis., 1960, Ph.D. (Higher Edn. Act fellow), 1972. Head extension dept. Oshkosh (Wis.) Public Library, 1960-62, head reference dept., 1962-63; asst. dir. Jervis Library, Rome, N.Y., 1962; dir. Eau Claire (Wis.) Public Library, 1963-66; asst. dir. Lake County Public Library, Griffith, Ind., 1966-68; asst. prof. Sch. Library Sci., U. Iowa, 1971-73; dir. Wauwatosa (Wis.) Public Library, 1973-75; asst. prof. U. So. Calif., 1975-78; state librarian N.Mex. State Library, Santa Fe, 1978-82; dir. Carlsbad City Library, Calif., 1982—. Served with U.S. Army, 1958. Mem. ALA, Calif. Libr. Assn. Home: 3575 Ridge Rd Oceanside CA 92056-4952 Office: 1250 Carlsbad Village Dr Carlsbad CA 92008-1949

LANGE, CRYSTAL MARIE, nursing educator; b. Snover, Mich., Aug. 22, 1927; d. Bazil H. and Crystal S. (Hilborn) Morse; m. Elmer William Lange, June 10, 1961; children: Gregory, Frederick, Helen, Charles, G. Benson, Robert, Larry. BSN, U.Mich., 1949; MSN, Wayne State U., 1961; PhD, Mich. State U., 1972. Pvt. duty nurse, Richmond, Ind., 1949-50; asst. dir. nursing, nursing supr., instr. St. Mary's Hosp., Tucson, Ariz., 1950-58; night supr. Pima County Hosp., Tucson, 1958-59; asst. dir. Sch. Nursing, Saginaw Gen. Hosp., Mich., 1959-60; instr. to prof., chmn. div. Delta Coll., University Ctr., Mich., 1962-76; dean Sch. Nursing and Allied Health Scis., asst. to v.p. acad. affairs Saginaw Valley State Coll., University Center, 1976—, prof., dean, 1989—; mem. vis. com. Med. Ctr., U. Mich., 1978-81. Author: Leadership for Quality, 1966; Instructor's Guide - Nursing Skills and Techniques, 1969; The Use of the Auto-tutorial Laboratory and the Mobile Tutorial Unit in Teaching, 1969; Instructor's Guide - Nursing Skills and Techniques - Films 76-126, 1972; Instructor's Guide - Nursing Skills and Techniques - Films 127-151, 1971; Auto-Tutorial Techniques in Nursing Education, 1971; Future Education: Diagnosis Prescriptions Evaluation, 1971. Contbr. articles to profl. jours. Bd. dirs. Saginaw chpt. ARC, 1982—, Saginaw Vis. Nurse Assn., 1980—. Recipient award Mich. Acad. Sci., Arts and Letters, 1970, Monsour Found. Lectureship award Health Edn. Media Assn., 1977; NEH fellow, 1983. Fellow Am. Acad. Nursing; mem. Am. Acad. Arts and Scis., Am. Acad. Nursing (governing council, sec. 1978-80), AAUP (chpt. v.p. 1976, award citation 1970), Am. Ednl. Scis., Am. Nurses Assn., Mich. Nurses Assn., Saginaw Dist. Nurses Assn. (bd. dirs. 1976—), U. Mich. Alumnae Assn., Wayne State U. Alumnae Assn., Phi Kappa Phi, Sigma Theta Tau. Home: 4135 Kochville Rd Saginaw MI 48604-9750 Office: Saginaw Valley State U University Center MI 48710

LANGE, DAVID L., law educator; b. Charleston, Ill., Dec. 7, 1938; s. Charles W.S. and Mary Helen Lange; m. Teresa Tetrick, July 30, 1972; children—David, Adam, Daniel, Jennifer, William. BS, U. Ill., Urbana, 1960, JD, 1964. Bar: Ill. 1964, N.C. 1989. Pvt. practice Chgo., 1964-71; gen. counsel media task force Nat. Commn. on Violence, Washington, 1968-69; gen. ptnr. Mediamix Prodns., 1970-71; assoc. prof. law Duke U., Durham, N.C., 1971-74; prof. law Duke U., 1974—; of counsel Parker, Poe, Adams & Bernstein, Charlotte, N.C., 1987-94; cons. in intellectual property Govt. of Vietname, 1994—. Office: Duke U Sch Law Durham NC 27708

LANGE, GEORGE WILLARD, JR., trust banker, lawyer; b. West Bend, Wis., Dec. 29, 1949; s. George W. and Ruth I. (Stobbe) L.; m. Joan Elizabeth Koeln, June 26, 1971; children: Matthew Ryan, Aaron Michael. BA, Southeast Mo. State U., 1972; JD, St. Louis U., 1977; postgrad., Southwestern Sch. Banking, 1981. Bar: Mo. 1977; cert. trust and fin. advisor; accredited estate planner. Assoc. Law Office Thomas Green, St. Louis, 1977-79; trust officer Merc. Bank, N.A., St. Louis, 1979-84; sr. v.p., trust officer Mark Twain Bank, St. Louis, 1984-87; v.p., sr. trust officer Am. Pioneer Savs. Bank, Orlando, Fla., 1987-90; sr. v.p., trust officer, mgr. Bancorp Trust Co. N.A., Naples, Fla., 1990-94; pres., COO, dir. Marshall & Ilsley Trust Co. Fla., Naples, 1994—; mem. adv. dir. S.W. Fla. Bus. Hall of Fame. Bd. dirs. Mental Health Assn. of Collier County, 1990-95, treas., 1992, v.p., 1993, prs., 1994; bd. dirs. Mental Health Assn. St. Louis, 1980-82, treas., 1981; bd. dirs. Mental Health Assn. Mo., 1981-82, United Arts Coun. Collier County, 1991—, v.p., 1991-92, pres., 1992-95; mem. Edison C.C. Collier County Devel. Bd.; trustee Bonita Springs Firefighter's Retirement Fund. Lt. col. N.G., 1971-94. Mem. ABA (com. adminstrn. and distbn. of trusts, chmn. com. fiduciary issues of holding closely held bus. in trust), Mo. Bar Assn., Soc. Am. Mil. Engrs., Res. Officers Assn., Corp. Fiduciaries Assn. S.W. Fla., Rotary (Paul Harris fellow), Estate Planning of Naples, Collier Athletic Club, Naples Area C. of C. (pres. club, chair edn. com. 1991-93), Leadership Collier, Leadership S.W. Fla., Leadership Lee County), Fla. Bankers Assn. (trust div., vice chmn. legis. com. 1994-95, chair 1995—, mem. state govtl. rels. com.), S.W. Fla. C. of C. (trustee rep. 1992—), Atty. for Closing-Held Enterprises, Res. Officer Assn., De Beough Soc. St. Louis U. (hon. v.p.), Phi Alpha Delta, Sigma Tau Gamma. Home: 3770 Catbrier Ct Bonita Springs FL 33923-7929 Office: Marshall & Isley Trust Co 800 Laurel Oak Dr Ste 101 Naples FL 33963-2713

LANGE, JAMES BRAXTON, chemical company executive; b. Amory, Miss., Feb. 17, 1937; s. Oliver John and Sarah Nell (Gravlee) L.; m. Margaret Terry Terrell, Aug. 9, 1969. B.S. in Psychology, Millsaps Coll., 1960; B.S. in Bus, Miss. Coll., 1970, M.B.A., 1973; postgrad., Harvard U., 1979. Indsl. rep. Miss. CD, 1971-73; sec., treas. 1st Miss. Corp., Jackson, 1973-88; dir. investor rels. and corp. affaris Himont, Inc., Wilmington, Del., 1988-90; pres., chief exec. officer Columbia Gas Found., Wilmington, Del., 1990-94; sec. Columbia Gas System Svc. Corp., Wilmington, 1990-94; v.p. corp. fin. svcs. PNC Bank, Wilmington, 1994—; bd. dirs. Primex, Inc. Charter mem. Community Action Coun., 1972-74; group leader United Way campaign, 1970-73; mem. exec. com. YMCA; mem. com. on free enterprise Miss. Econ. Coun.; trustee Grand Opera House, 1990-93. With USN, 1960-63. Mem. Am. Soc. Corp. Secs., Am. Soc. Corp. Treas., Nat. Investor Rels. Inst., Am. Soc. Pers. Adminstrn., Miss. Mfrs. Assn., Jackson C. of C., Nat. Assn. Corp. Dirs., Naval Res. Assn. (pres.), Res. Officers Assn. (past v.p.), Navy League Jackson, Lions. Republican. Home: 4 Normandy Dr Chadds Ford PA 19317-9274 Office: PNC Bank 222 Delaware Ave Wilmington DE 19801

LANGE, JESSICA, actress; b. Minn., Apr. 20, 1949; d. Al and Dorothy Lange; m. Paco Grande, 1970 (div. 1982); 1 child with Mikhail Baryshnikov, Alexandra; children with Sam Shepard: Hannah Jane, Samuel Walker. Student, U. Minn.; student mime, with Etienne DeCroux, Paris. Dancer Opera Comique, Paris; model Wilhelmina Agy., N.Y.C. Film appearances include King Kong, 1976, All That Jazz, 1979, How to Beat the High Cost of Living, 1980, The Postman Always Rings Twice, 1981, Frances, 1982 (Acad. award nominee 1982), Tootsie, 1982 (Acad. award 1983), Country, 1984, Sweet Dreams, 1985, Crimes of the Heart, 1986 (Acad. award nominee 1987), Everybody's All American, 1988, Far North, 1988, Music Box, 1989 (Acad. award nominee 1990), Men Don't Leave, 1990, Cape Fear, 1991, Night and the City, 1992, Blue Sky, 1994 (Golden Globe award Best Actress in a Drama 1995, Acad. award for Best Actress 1995), Losing Isaiah, 1995, Rob Roy, 1995; TV movies: Cat on a Hot Tin Roof, 1984, O' Pioneers!, 1992, A Streetcar Named Desire, 1995 (Golden Globe award 1996); in summer stock prodn. Angel on My Shoulder, N.C., 1980, A Streetcar Named Desire, 1992. Office: Creative Artists Agy care Ron Meyer 9830 Wilshire Blvd Beverly Hills CA 90212-1804*

LANGE, LESTER HENRY, mathematics educator; b. Concordia, Mo., Jan. 2, 1924; s. Harry William Christopher and Ella Martha (Alewel) L.; m. Anne Marie Pelikan, Aug. 17, 1947 (div. Oct. 1960); children: Christopher, Nicholas, Philip, Alexander; m. Beverly Jane Brown, Feb. 4, 1962; 1 son, Andrew. Student, U. Calif., Berkeley, 1943-44; B.A. in Math, Valparaiso U., 1948; M.S. in Math, Stanford, 1950; Ph.D. in Math, U. Notre Dame, 1960. Instr., then asst. prof. math. Valparaiso U., 1950-56; instr. math. U. Notre Dame, 1956-57, 59-60; mem. faculty San Jose State U., Calif., 1960—, prof. math., head dept., 1961-70, dean Sch. Natural Scis. and Math., 1970—, dean Sch. Sci., 1972-88, emeritus prof. math., emeritus dean, 1988—; founder Soc. Archimedes at San Jose State U., 1982; now spl. asst. to dir. Moss Landing (Calif.) Marine Labs. Author text on linear algebra; sr. editor Calif. Math, 1981-84; contbr. to profl. jours. Served with inf. AUS, 1943-46, ETO. Danforth fellow, 1957-58; NSF faculty fellow, 1958-59. Fellow Calif. Acad. Scis.; mem. Math. Assn. Am. (bd. govs., L.R. Ford Sr. award 1972, George Polya award 1993), Calif. Math. Coun., London Math. Soc., Fibonacci Assn. (bd. dirs. 1987—), Nat. Coun. Tchrs. Home: 308 Escalona Dr Capitola CA 95010-3419 Office: Moss Landing Marine Labs Moss Landing CA 95039

LANGE, MARILYN, social worker; b. Milw., Dec. 6, 1936; d. Edward F. and Erna E. (Karstaedt) L.; divorced; children: Lara McKelvie, Gregory Cash. B of Social Work, U. Wis., Milw., 1962, MSW, 1974. Cert. ind. clin. social worker. Recreation specialist Dept. Army, Europe, 1962-63; social worker Family Svc. Milw., 1967-75, dir. homecare divsn., 1975-85; nat. field rep. Alzheimers Assn., Chgo., 1986-90; exec. dir. Village Adult Day Ctr., Milw., 1991—. Mem. Nat. Coun. Aging, Wis. Adult Daycare Assn. (pres.), Dementia Care Network, Older Adult Svc. Providers Consortium, West Allis Bus. & Profl. Women, U. Wis.-Milw. Alumni Assn. Home: 5727 W Fillmore Dr Milwaukee WI 53219-2219 Office: Village Adult Day Ctr Inc 130 E Juneau Ave Milwaukee WI 53202-2552

LANGE, MARVIN ROBERT, lawyer; b. Bronx, Mar. 25, 1948; s. Arthur A. and Beatrice L. Lange; m. Ellen Metzger, Apr. 20, 1986; 1 child, Rebecca Hillary. BA, Queens Coll., 1968; JD, Harvard U., 1971. Bar: N.Y. 1972, U.S. Dist. Ct. (ea. and so. dists.) N.Y. 1975, U.S. Ct. Appeals (2d cir.) 1975, U.S. Supreme Ct. 1980, U.S. Ct. Appeals (6th cir.) 1986. Law clk. U.S. Dist. Ct., Phila., 1971-72; atty. FTC, Washington, 1972-75; assoc. Rosenman & Colin, N.Y.C., 1975-81, ptnr., 1981-93; pvt. practice law, 1993—. Editor Harvard Law Rev., 1969-71. Mem. ABA. Jewish. Office: 777 3rd Ave Fl 19 New York NY 10017-1302

LANGE, NIELS ERIK KREBS, biotechnology company executive; b. Soenderborg, Denmark, July 20, 1948; s. Erik Krebs and Estrid (Jensen) L. MSc in Engring., Denmarks Tech. U., Copenhagen, 1973. Cert. chem. engr. Rsch. scientist Denmarks Tech. U., 1974-75; rsch. chemist Novo Nordisk A/S, Bagsvaerd, Denmark, 1976-86, mgr. product devel. and process rsch., 1986-93, mgr. enzyme product devel., 1993-95; staff scientist Novo Nordisk Biochemicals, Inc., Franklinton, N.C., 1995—. Contbr. ar-ticples to profl. jours. Mem. AAAS, Am. Assn. Textile Chemists and Colorists (sr.), IEA Bioenergy Network. Avocations: golfing, badminton, amateur theatre. Home: 7212 Stonecliff Dr #5 Raleigh NC 27615 Office: Novo Nordisk Biochemicals Inc State Rd 1003 PO Box 576 Franklinton NC 27525

LANGE, PHIL C., retired education educator; b. North Freedom, Wis., Feb. 26, 1914; s. Richard Samuel and Martha (Grosinske) L.; m. Irene Oyen, June 8, 1940; children—Dena Rae, Richard (dec.). B.A., U. Wis., 1934, M.A., 1936, Ph.D., 1941. Tchr. Reeseville (Wis.) Pub. Sch., 1935-37; chmn. English dept. Wayland Jr. Coll. and Acad., Beaver Dam, Wis., 1937-39; instr. English, student teaching supr. Beloit (Wis.) High Sch., 1939-40; asst. instr. U. Wis., Madison, 1940-41, summers 1938, 39; chmn. psychology dept., dean men. Ariz. State Coll., Flagstaff, 1941-42; chmn. edn. dept. SUNY, Fredonia, 1942-50; prof. edn., coordinator student teaching Tchrs. Coll., Columbia U., 1950—; cons., expert for Dept. State, UNESCO, AID. Author, editor curriculum materials. Served with USNR, 1943-46. Recipient Filmstrip award Graphic Arts, 1966; Communication award Nat. Soc. Programmed Instrn., 1968; award Ednl. Press Assn. Am., 1969. Home: 727 Fox Hills Dr Sun City Center FL 33573-5127 Office: Tchrs Coll Columbia Univ New York NY 10027

LANGE, ROBERT DALE, internist, educator, medical researcher; b. Redwood Falls, Minn., Jan. 24, 1920; s. John Christian and Bertha Semelia (Eggen) L.; m. Mary Jane Adams, Sept. 16, 1944; children: Ruth Ann Lange Rehm, John Carl. B.A., Macalester Coll., 1941; M.D., Washington U., 1944. Diplomate: Am. Bd. Internal Medicine. Intern Barnes Hosp., St. Louis, 1944-45; asst. resident medicine U. Minn. Hosps., Mpls., 1945-46; fellow and instr. medicine div. hematology Washington U. Sch. Medicine, St. Louis, 1948-51; practice medicine specializing in internal medicine St. Louis, 1956-62, Knoxville, Tenn., 1964—; scientist Atomic Bomb Casualty Commn., Hiroshima and Nagasaki, Japan, 1951-53; rsch. assoc. VA Hosp., Mpls., 1953-54; mem. staff Eitel Hosp., Mpls., 1953-54; chief hematology Rsch. Lab. VA Hosp., St. Louis, 1956-62; asst. prof. medicine Washington U. Sch. Medicine, St. Louis, 1956-62; assoc. prof. medicine Med. Coll. Ga., Augusta, 1962-64; mem. staff Talmadge Hosp., Augusta, 1962-65, U. Hosp., Augusta, 1964-65, U. Tenn. Meml. Hosp., Knoxville, 1965; research prof. U. Tenn. Meml. Research Center, Knoxville, 1964-78; asst. dir. research U. Tenn. Meml. Research Center, 1966-76, dir. research, 1977-81; prof. medicine U. Tenn. Center for Health Services, Knoxville, 1970—; prof. U. Tenn. Meml. Research Ctr., 1978-85, prof. emeritus, 1985—; chmn. dept. med. biology, 1978-81; cons. to Oak Ridge Associated Univs., 1969-93, Abbott Labs Rev. Bd., 1974. Contbr. chpts. in hematology to med. books; contbr. numerous articles on research in hematology and exptl. medicine to profl. jours.; reviewer various med. jours., 1960—; editorial bd.: Exptl. Hematology, 1974-77. Served to maj., M.C. U.S. Army, 1954-56. Jackson Johnson scholar, 1941-44; recipient Cert. St. Paul Jr. Assn. of Commerce, 1941. Fellow A.C.P., Internat. Soc. Hematology; mem. Am. Soc. Hematology, Internat. Soc. Exptl. Hematology, Soc. of Research Adminstrs., Soc. Exptl. Biology and Medicine, Central Soc. Clin. Research, So. Soc. Clin. Investigation, Knoxville Soc. Internal Medicine, AMA (Cert. of Merit 1954), Tenn. Med. Assn., Knoxville Acad. Medicine, AAAS, AAUP, Sigma Xi, Alpha Omega Alpha, Pi Phi Epsilon. Methodist. Home: 8116 Bennington Dr Knoxville TN 37909-2301 Office: U Tenn Med Ctr 1924 Alcoa Hwy Knoxville TN 37920-1511

LANGE, ROBERT JOHN (MUTT LANGE), producer. Composer: (film score) Don Juan DeMarco, 1995. Recipient Best Prodr. Country Album Grammy award, 1996. Office: PO Box 269 Saint Regis Falls NY 12980*

LANGE, VICTOR, foreign language educator, author; b. Leipzig, Germany, July 13, 1908; came to U.S., 1932, naturalized, 1943; s. Walter and Theodora (Schellenberg) L.; m. Frances Mary Olrich, Feb. 23, 1945; children: Dora Elizabeth, Thomas Victor. Student, Thomasschule Leipzig, 1919-28, Oxford U., 1928, Sorbonne, 1929, U. Munich, 1929-30, U. Toronto; MA (Gertrude Davis exchange fellow 1930-31); Ph.D., U. Leipzig, 1934; H.L.D., Monterey Inst., 1978. Dir. Akademische Auslandsstelle, U. Leipzig, 1931-32; lectr. German, Univ. Coll., Toronto, 1932-38; asst. prof. German Cornell U., 1938-41, assoc. prof., 1941-45, prof., 1945-57; prof. German lit. Princeton U., 1957—, John N. Woodhull prof. modern. langs., 1968-77, emeritus, 1977—; hon. prof. Free U., Berlin, 1962—; vis. prof. U. Calif.-Davis, Smith Coll., U. Chgo., Berkeley, U. Cologne, U. Heidelberg, Munich, Columbia U., U. Mich., NYU, CUNY, Yale U., La Jolla, etc.; examiner in chief for German Coll. Entrance Exam. Bd., 1942-50; external examiner U. Hong Kong, 1979; vis. prof. U. Auckland, New Zealand, 1974; Guggenheim fellow, 1950-51, 67, McCosh fellow, 1966-67, Fulbright lectr., Australia, 1969, Phi Beta Kappa vis. scholar, 1968-69, Nat. Endowment Humanities sr. fellow, 1973-74; fellow Humanities Research Centre, Canberra, Australia, 1977. Author: Die Lyrik und ihr Publikum im England des 18. Jahrhunderts, 1936, Kulturkritik und Literaturbetrachtung in Amerika, 1938, Modern German Literature, 1945, Goethe's Craft of Fiction, 1953, Contemporary German Poetry, 1964, The Reader in the Strategy of Fiction, 1973, Mann: Tradition and Experiment, 1976, (with W.R. Amacher) New Perspectives in German Literary Criticism, 1979, The Classical Age of German Literature, 1982, Goethe's Faust II, 1980, Illyrische Betrachtungen. Essays und Aufsätze aus dreissig Jahren, 1989, Goethe-Studien, 1990, Bilder, Ideen, Begriffe, 1991; editor: Deutsche Briefe, 1940, The Sorrows of Young Werther, 1949, Goethe's Faust, 1950, Great German Short Stories, 1952, Lessings Hamburg Dramaturgy, 1962, Goethe's Wilhelm Meister, 1962, German Classical Drama, 1962, Goethe: Twentieth Century Views, 1968, Humanistic Scholarship in America, 1968, Goethes Werke, 1972; Munich edition Goethes Werke, vols. 6, 1 and 2, 1986; Goethe, 1992; trans.: Edith Wharton's Ethan Frome, 1948; editorial bd.: Rev. of Nat. Lits., Comparative Lit., 20th Century Lit.; contbr. to lit. jours. Decorated comdr.'s cross Order of Merit (German Fed. Republic); recipient Gold medal Goethe Inst., 1966, Friedrich-Gundolf prize German Acad. Lang. and Lit., 1966, Chancellor's citation U. Calif., 1985, Golden Goethe medal Weimar, 1993, Festschrift Aspekte der Goethezeit, editor T. Ziolkowski, 1977. Mem. Internat. Assn. Germanists (pres. 1965-70), Am. Soc. 18th Century Studies (pres. 1975-76), Goethe Soc. N.Am. (pres. 1980-89), Am. Assn. Tchrs. German, Modern Humanities Research Assn., German Acad. (Darmstadt), Am. Comparative Lit. Assn., Goethe Gesellschaft Weimar, Phi Beta Kappa. Home: 343 Jefferson Rd Princeton NJ 08540-3414

LANGEL, ROBERT ALLAN, III, geophysicist; b. Pitts., May 25, 1937; s. Robert Allan II and Fay Mildred (Harvey) L.; m. Carolyn May Wills, June 13, 1959; children: Kathleen Carol, Susan Lynn, Joy Christine. A.B., Wheaton Coll., 1959; M.S., U. Md., 1971, Ph.D., 1973. Physicist U.S. Naval Research Lab., 1959-62; physicist microwave antennas Goddard Space Flight Ctr., Greenbelt, Md., 1963-64, magnetospheric physicist, 1964-74, geophysicist magnetic fields satellite project, 1974—; vis. scholar Bullard Labs., Cambridge (Eng.) U., 1983-84, Purdue U., 1992-93, Copenhagen U., 1994; exec. com. Nat. Geomagnetic Workshop, 1992. Spl. editor: (issue) Physics of the Earth and Planetary Interiors, 1976, Geophys. Rsch. Letters, 1982, Jour. Geophys. Rsch., 1985, Jour. Geomagnetic Geoelectricity, 1992; assoc. editor Jour. Geophys. Rsch., 1991-95; contbr. articles to scientific publs., chpts. to books. Dir. youth Grace Brethren Ch., Temple Hills, Md., 1965-68; dir. coll.-career Berwyn Bapt. Ch., College Park, Md., 1975-89, dir. singles, 1989-91. Recipient Spl. Achievement award Goddard Space Flight Center, 1980, Group Achievement award, 1980, Exceptional Performance award, 1981, Medal for exceptional sci. achievement NASA, 1982. Fellow Am. Geophys. Union; mem. Internat. Assn. Geomagnetism and Aeronomy (vice chair Div. I 1983-87, chair working group on main field and secular variation 1987-91). Republican. Baptist. Home: 14910 Laurel Oaks Ln Laurel MD 20707-5518 Office: Goddard Space Flight Ctr Code 921 Greenbelt MD 20771 *My driving goal is to please God, which governs the things to which I commit myself and that I strive for integrity and faithfulness in what I do.*

LANGELLA, FRANK, actor; b. Bayonne, N.J., Jan. 1, 1940; m. Ruth Weil, Nov. 1977. Student, Syracuse U.; studies with Seymour Falk. Apprenticed Pocono Playhouse, Mountain Home, Pa., appeared Erie (Pa.) Playhouse, 1960, mem. original, Lincoln Center repertory tng. co., 1963; off-Broadway debut in The Immoralist, 1963; other stage appearances include: Benito Cereno, 1964, The Old Glory, 1964-65 (Obie award), Good Day, 1965-66 (Obie award), The White Devil, 1965-66 (Obie award), Long Day's Journey Into Night, The Skin of Our Teeth, The Cretan Woman, Yerma, all 1966, The Devils, Dracula, Iphigenia at Aulis, all 1967, A Cry of Players, 1968, Cyrano de Bergerac, 1971, A Midsummer Night's Dream, 1972, The Relapse, The Tooth of Crime, 1972, The Taming of the Shrew, 1973, The Seagull, 1974, Ring Round the Moon, 1975, Passion, 1983, Design for Living, 1984, After the Fall, 1984, Hurlyburly, 1985, Sherlock's Last Case, 1987, Booth, 1994, The Prince of Hamburg, Cleve. Playhouse Co., 1967-68, L.I. Festival repertory, 1968, Les Liaisons Dangereuses; Broadway debut in Seascape, 1974-75 (Drama Desk and Tony awards); stage directing debut in John and Abigail, 1969; performed in films Diary of a Mad Housewife, 1970 (Nat. Soc. Film Critics award), The Twelve Chairs, 1970, The Deadly Trap, 1972, The Wrath of God, 1972, Dracula, 1979, Those Lips Those Eyes, 1980, Sphinx, 1981, The Men's Club, 1986, Masters of the Universe, 1987, And God Created Woman, 1988, True Identity, 1991, 1492: Conquest of Paradise, 1992, Dave, 1993, Body of Evidence, 1993, Brainscan, 1994, Junior, 1994, Bad Company, 1995; TV appearances include: Benito Cereno, 1965, Good Day, 1967, The Mark of Zorro, 1974, The Ambassador, 1974, The Seagull, 1975, The American Woman: Portraits of Courage, 1976, Eccentricities of a Nightingale, 1976, Sherlock Holmes, Liberty, The Doomsday Gun, 1994. Bd. dirs. Berkshire Festival. Mem. Actors Equity, Screen Actors Guild. Office: Special Artists Agency 335 N Maple Dr Ste 360 Beverly Hills CA 90210*

LANGENBERG, DONALD NEWTON, academic administrator, physicist; b. Devils Lake, N.D., Mar. 17, 1932; s. Ernest George and Fern (Newton) L.; m. Patricia Ann Warrington, June 20, 1953; children: Karen Kaye, Julia Ann, John Newton, Amy Paris. B.S., Iowa State U., 1953; M.S., UCLA, 1955; Ph.D. (NSF fellow), U. Calif. at Berkeley, 1959; D.Sc. (hon.), U. Pa., 1985, MA (hon.), 1971. Electronics engr. Hughes Research Labs., Culver City, Calif., 1953-55; acting instr. U. Calif. at Berkeley, 1958-59; mem. faculty U. Pa., Phila., 1960-83; prof. U. Pa., 1967-83; dir. Lab. for Research on Structure of Matter, 1972-74; vice provost for grad. studies and research, 1974-79; chancellor U. Ill.-Chgo., 1983-90, U. Md. System, Adelphi, 1990—; maitre de conference associe Ecole Normale Superieure, Paris, France, 1966-67; vis. prof. Calif. Inst. Tech., Pasadena, 1971; guest researcher Zentralinstitut für Tieftemperaturforschung der Bayerische Akademie der Wissenschaften and Technische Universität München, 1974; dep. dir. Nat. Sci.

Found., 1980-82. Rschr., contbr. to publs. on solid state and low temperature physics including electronic band structure in metals and semiconductors, quantum phase coherence and nonequilibrium effects in superconductors, sci. and edn. policy and rsch. adminstrn. Recipient John Price Wetherill medal Franklin Inst., 1975, Disting. Contribution to Research Adminstrn. award Soc. Research Adminstrs., 1983, Disting. Achievement Citation, Iowa State Alumni Assn., 1984, Significant Sig award Sigma Chi, 1985; fellow NSF, 1959-60, Alfred P. Sloan Found., 1962-64; Guggenheim Found., 1966-67. Fellow AAAS (pres. 1990), Am. Phys. Soc. (pres. 1993), Sigma Xi. Office: U Md System 3300 Metzerott Rd Adelphi MD 20783-1600

LANGENBERG, FREDERICK CHARLES, business executive; b. N.Y.C., July 1, 1927; s. Frederick C. and Margaret (McLaughlin) L.; m. Jane Anderson Bartholomew, May 16, 1953; children: Frederick C., Susan Jane. BS, Lehigh U., 1950, MS, 1951; PhD, Pa. State U., 1955; postgrad. execs. program, Carnegie-Mellon U., 1962. With U.S. Steel Corp., 1951-53; vis. fellow MIT, 1955-56; with Crucible Steel Corp., Pitts., 1956-68, v.p. research and engring., 1966-68; pres. Trent Tube div. Colt Industries, Milw., 1968-70; exec. v.p. Jessop Steel Co., Washington, Pa., 1970, pres., 1970-75, also bd. dirs.; pres., bd. dirs. Am. Iron and Steel Inst., Washington, 1975-78; pres. Interlake Corp., Oak Brook, Ill., 1979-81, pres., chmn, chief exec. officer, 1981-91, also bd. dirs.; chmn. Langand Corp., Pitts., 1991—; bd. dirs. Carpenter Tech., Reading, Pa., The Interlake Corp., Chgo., Peoples Energy Corp., Chgo.. Contbr. articles to tech. jours.; patentee in field. Trustee Piedmont Coll., Demorest, Ga. Served with USNR, 1944-45. Named Oak Brook Bus. Leader of the Yr., 1986, Disting. Bus. Leader, DuPage County, 1988; Alumni fellow Pa. State U., 1977; recipient Disting. Alumni award, Pa. State U., 1989, Lehigh U., 1990. Fellow Am. Soc. Metals (disting. life mem. 1982, trustee, Pitts. Nite lectr. 1970, Andrew Carnegie lectr. 1976; David Ford McFarland award Penn State chpt. 1973); mem. AIME, Am. Soc. Metals, Metals Powder Industry Fedn., Phi Beta Kappa, Sigma Xi, Tau Beta Pi. Clubs: Duquesne, St. Clair Country (Pitts.), Congl., Burning Tree, Chgo. Golf, Chgo., Commercial (Chgo.), Laurel Valley, Rolling Rock (Ligonier, Pa.), Belleair County Club (Fla.), Carefree (Ariz.), Desert Mountain (Ariz.). Office: Langand Corp 2535 Washington Rd Ste 1131 Pittsburgh PA 15241-2592

LANGENDERFER, HAROLD QUENTIN, accountant, educator; b. Swanton, Ohio, July 21, 1925; s. Omer Quintan and Minnie (Buckenmyer) L.; m. Joan Mary Etzrodt, June 17, 1950; children: Thomas, Amy, Jeffry, Chris. B.S. in Bus, Miami U., Oxford, Ohio, 1949; M.B.A., Northwestern U., 1950; D.B.A., Ind. U., 1954. C.P.A., Ind., N.C. Prof. intermediate acctg. Ind. U., Bloomington, 1952-53; KPMG Peat, Marwick prof. profl. acctg. U. N.C., Chapel Hill, 1953-93, prof. emeritus, 1993—; cons. mgmt. devel. to Ford Found., Cairo, 1961-63; tax cons. Co-author: C.P.A. Examination - A Comprehensive Review, 3d edit., 1979, Principles of Accounting, 1981, 4th edit., 1993, Income Tax Procedure, 1994; contbr. articles to acctg. jours. Served with U.S. Army, 1943-46. Named Acctg. Educator of Yr., Beta Alpha Psi, 1980. Mem. AICPAs (Acctg. Educator of Yr. 1988), N.C. Assn. CPAs (pres. 1985-86, Acctg. Educator of Yr. 1986, Outstanding Svc. award 1989), Nat. Assn. Accts., Am. Acctg. Assn. (pres. 1983-84, chmn. com. on professionalism and ethics 1987-89, internat. lectr. 1992, Outstanding Acctg. Educator award 1995), Fin. Execs. Inst., Kiwanis (pres. Chapel Hill lodge 1966). Roman Catholic. Home: 1074 Canterbury Ln Chapel Hill NC 27514-5612 Office: UNC CB 3490 Carroll Hall Chapel Hill NC 27599

LANGENDOEN, DONALD TERENCE, linguistics educator; b. Paterson, N.J., June 7, 1939; s. Gerrit and Wilhelmina (Van Dyk) L.; m. Sally Wicklund, Aug. 16, 1964 (div. Mar. 1982); 1 child, David; m. Nancy Susan Kelly, July 28, 1984. BS, MIT, 1961, PhD, 1964. Asst. prof. Ohio State U., Columbus, 1964-68; vis. assoc. prof. Rockefeller U., N.Y.C., 1969-69; prof. Bklyn. C. and Grad. Ctr., CUNY, N.Y.C., 1969-88, U. Ariz., Tucson, 1988—; exec. officer grad. linguistics program, CUNY, N.Y.C., 1971-78; head dept. linguistics, U. Ariz., Tucson, 1988—; vis. scientist IBM T.J. Watson Research Ctr., Yorktown Heights, N.Y., 1986-87; sr. lectr. Fulbright, Utrecht, Holland, 1977. Author: The London School of Linguistics, 1968; co-author: The Vastness of Natural Languages, 1984; editor: Linguistics Abstracts, 1997—. Fellow N.Y. Acad. of Scis., N.Y.C., 1977; named Ptnr. in Edn., Bd. of Edn., N.Y.C., 1982. Mem. AAAS, Linguistic Soc. of Am. (sec., treas. 1984-88), Assn. for Computational Linguistics, Assn. for Linguistic and Literary Computing. Office: U Ariz Dept Linguistics Box 210028 Tucson AZ 85721-0028

LANGENEGGER, ARMIN, radiation physicist; b. Mainburg, Bavaria, Germany, Oct. 12, 1953; came to U.S., 1990; s. Kurt Andreas and Anne Maria (Sommerer) L.; m. Patricia Gail Cross, Feb. 28, 1982; children: Michael, Thomas, Elyse Beth; m. Lisa Marie Nelesen, Oct. 12, 1991; children: Nicholas Kurt, Matthew John. Diploma, Gordon Inst. Tech., Geelong, Victoria, Australia, 1975; BSc, Deakin U., Geelong, 1982; M Biomed. Engring., U. NSW, Sydney, Australia, 1988. Physics technologist Prince of Wales Hosp., Sydney, 1976-79, physicist, 1979-82; sr. physicist Royal Prince Alfred Hosp., Sydney, 1982-87, dep. chief physicist, 1987-88; chief physicist Royal North Shore Hosp., Sydney, 1988-90; physicist Waukesha (Wis.) Meml. Hosp., 1990-92, chief physicist, 1992-93; physicist St. Marys Med. Ctr., Racine, Wis., 1993—; dir., cons. Ralode Pty Ltd., Sydney, 1982-88; cons. Biotel Pty. Ltd., Sydney, 1990-91, Radiation Physics Svcs., Milw., 1990-94; invited participant Russian trip on radiation protection. Capt. Neighborhood Watch, Sydney, 1988-89. Mem. Am. Assn. Physicists in Medicine, Australasian Coll. Phys. Scientists and Engrs. in Medicine (sec. 1988-89). Anglican. Achievements include patent procs. couch mounted stereotactic head frame holder; creator inexpensive stereotactic radiosurgery package, dosimetry intercomparison group. Home: 3633 Canada Goose Xing Racine WI 53403-4504 Office: Southea Wis Regional Cancer Ctr 3809 Spring St Racine WI 53405-1667

LANGENFELD, MARY LUCILLE, healthcare facility administrator; b. St. Peter, Minn., Nov. 14, 1946; d. Leo John and Lucille (Meyer) Scully; m. Gerald W. Langenfeld, Apr. 19, 1969; children: Richard, David, Deborah, Amy Jo. Diploma, St. Mary Sch. Nursing, Rochester, Minn., 1967; BS, Bemidji State U., 1977; MS, U. Minn., 1980; MBA, Boise State U., 1989. RN, Minn., S.D., Idaho, Calif., Ohi, Wash. Staff nurse Northwestern Hosp., Mpls., 1967-68; charge nurse Meml. Hosp., Watertown, S.D., 1968-69, So. Hills Gen. Hosp., Hot Springs, S.D., 1969-70; supr., charge nurse Dakota Midland Hosp., Aberdeen, S.D., 1970-72; dir. nursing Community Mercy Hosp., Onamia, Minn., 1972-75, Madison (Minn.) Hosp. Assn., 1975-77; dir. patient care svcs. St. Ann's Hosp., Watertown, 1977-83; v.p. ops. Mercy Med. Ctr., Nampa, Idaho, 1983-89; v.p. St. Joseph Hosp. and Health Ctr., Lorain, Ohio, 1989-92, Olol Hosp., Pasco, Wash., 1992-93; CEO Life's Doors Hospice, Boise, 1994—; adj. prof. dept. nursing U. Akron, Ohio, 1991-92. Contbr. to profl. publs. Exec. bd. Lorainchpt. Arthritis Found., 1991-92. Fellow Am. Orgn. Nurse Execs.; mem. Am. Coll. Healthcare Execs., Ohio Orgn. Nurse Execs. (bd. dirs. 1992-94), Lorain C. of C., Sigma Theta Tau. Avocations: golf, music, tennis, running, reading. Office: Life's Doors Hospice 1111 S Orchard St Ste 209A Boise ID 83705-1922

LANGENFELD, NICHOLAS ALBERT, finance administrator; b. Lansing, Mich., Jan. 30, 1939; s. Cecil Augustus and Elizabeth Martha (Sumann) L.; m. Louise Lynn Patterson, Oct. 19, 1985; children: Karen, Alexandra. BA, Mich. State U., 1961. CPA, N.Y., Mich. Acct. Ernst & Young, Grand Rapids, Mich., 1960-64, BDO Seidman, Traverse City, Mich., 1964-65; v.p. mfg., fin. McInerney Spring & Wire, Grand Rapids, 1965-75; v.p. fin. River Shore Prodns., East Setauket, N.Y., 1975-83, Upjohn Healthcare, N.Y., Hicksville, 1983-87; ptnr. Seymour Rubenstein P.C., N.Y.C., 1987-89; dir. fin. Devel. Disabilities Inst. Inc., Smithtown, N.Y., 1989—; co-chmn. contr.'s Inter Agy. Coun., N.Y.C., 1994—; co-chmn. fiscal mgr.'s Long Island Devel. Disabilities Svc. Office/Office Mental Retardation Devel. Disabilities, Hauppauge, N.Y., 1993—. Mem. capital improvement com. Three Village Sch. Dist., East Setauket, 1994; treas. Minnesauke PTA, East Setauket, 1993—. Mem. AICPA, N.Y. State CPA (co-chmn. ann. conf. 1994—, not-for-profit com. 1992—). Republican. Roman Catholic. Avocations: golf, fishing, swimming, gardening. Home: 4 Old Coach Rd East Setauket NY 11733-3801 Office: Devel Disabilities Inst Inc 99 Hollywood Dr Smithtown NY 11787-3135

LANGENHEIM, JEAN HARMON, biology educator; b. Homer, La., Sept. 5, 1925; d. Vergil Wilson and Jeanette (Smith) H.; m. Ralph Louis Langenheim, Dec. 1946 (div. Mar. 1961). BS, U. Tulsa, 1946; MS, U. Minn., 1949, PhD, 1953. Rsch. assoc. botany U. Calif., Berkeley, 1954-59, U. Ill., Urbana, 1959-61; rsch. fellow biology Harvard U., Cambridge, Mass., 1962-66; asst. prof. biology U. Calif., Santa Cruz, 1966-68, assoc. prof. biology, 1968-73, prof. biology, 1973—; academic v.p. Orgn. Tropical Studies, San Jose, Costa Rica, 1975-78; mem. sci.adv. bd. EPA, Washington, 1977-81; chmn. com. on humid tropics U.S. Nat. Acad. Nat. Research Council, 1975-77; mem. com. floral inventory Amazon NSF, Washington, 1975-87. Author: Botany-Plant Biology in Relation to Human Affairs.; Contbr. articles to profl. jours. Grantee NSF, 1966-88; recipient Disting. Alumni award U. Tulsa, 1979. Fellow AAAS, AAUW, Calif. Acad. Scis., Bunting Inst.; mem. Bot. Soc. Am., Ecol. Soc. Am. (pres. 1986-87), Internat. Soc. Chem. Ecology (pres. 1986-87), Assn. for Tropical Biology (pres. 1985-86), Soc. for Econ. Botany (pres. 1993-94). Home: 191 Palo Verde Ter Santa Cruz CA 95060-3214 Office: U Calif Dept Biology Sinsheimer Labs Santa Cruz CA 95064

LANGENHEIM, RALPH LOUIS, JR., geology educator; b. Cin., May 26, 1922; s. Ralph Louis and Myrtle (Helmers) L.; m. Jean C. Harmon, Dec. 23, 1946; m. Virginia A.M. Knobloch, June 5, 1963; children: Victoria Elizabeth, Ralph Louis III; m. Shirley B. Ate, May 1, 1970; stepchildren: Judy Grigg, Lynn Ate, Kathleen Majack; m. Casey Diana, Mar. 6, 1993; stepchildren: Eric Steckler, Matthew Diana. B.S., U. Tulsa, 1943; M.S., U. Colo., 1947; Ph.D., U. Minn., 1951. Registered profl. geologist, Wyo. Teaching asst. U. Tulsa, 1941-43, U. Colo., 1947; fellow U. Minn., 1947-48, teaching asst., 1948-50; asst. prof. Coe Coll., 1950-52; asst. prof. paleontology U. Calif., Berkeley, 1952-59, curator Paleozoic and early Mesozoic fossil invertebrates, 1952-59; asst. prof. geology U. Ill., Urbana, 1959-62; asso. prof. U. Ill., 1962-67, prof., 1967-92, prof. emeritus, 1993—; also curator fossil invertebrates Mus. Nat. History, 1988-92, curator emeritus, 1993—; with Instituto Geologico Nacional de Colombia, summer 1953; Geol. Survey Can., summer 1958, Geol. Survey Iran, fall 1973, Geol. Survey Republic of China, fall 1981; ptnr. Lanman Assocs., Cons. Geologists, 1974—; cons., mem. faculty geology and mining depts. Poly. U., Albania, fall 1992; vis. disting. prof. U. Nev., Las Vegas, 1994; book rev. editor Jour. Geol. Edn., 1990—. Assoc. editor Jour. Paleontology, 1995—. Served with USNR, 1943-46; lt. comdr. Res., ret. Mem. AAAS, Nev. Petroleum Soc., Wyo. Geol. Assn., Paleontol. Soc. (sec. 1962-70), Geol. Soc. Am., Soc. Econ. Paleontologists and Mineralogists, Am. Assn. Petroleum Geologists, Soc. Geologique Suisse, Ill. Geol. Soc. (sec. 1978, v.p. 1979, pres. 1980), Internat. Assn. Cnidaria Specialists (treas. 1977-79), Nat. Assn. Geology Tchrs., Ill. Acad. Sci., Rocky Mountain Biol. Lab., Explorers Club, Sigma Xi. Rsch. and publs. in stratigraphy and paleontology. Home: 401 W Vermont Ave Urbana IL 61801-4928 Office: Univ Ill Dept Geology 245NHB 1301 W Green St Urbana IL 61801

LANGENKAMP, SANDRA CARROLL, retired healthcare policy executive; b. St. Joseph, Mo., Feb. 10, 1939; d. William Harry Minger and Beverly (Carroll) Lee; m. R. Hayden Downie, June 1, 1963 (div. Feb. 1979); children: Whitney, Timothy, Allyson. BS, Tex. Women's U., 1960. Adjunctive therapist Menninger Meml. Hosp., Topeka, 1960-66; asst. adminstr. Hillcrest Med. Ctr., Tulsa, 1977-82; dir. Vol. Action Agy., Tulsa, 1982-83; exec. dir. Tulsa Bus. Health Group, 1983—; v.p. Met. Tulsa C. of C., 1985—; exec. dir. Tulsa Program for Affordable Health Care, 1986-96; ret., 1996; cons. mem. Okla. Employment Security Commn., Oklahoma City, 1988—; exec. dir. Tulsa Cmty. Found. for Indigent Health Care, 1986-96; officer State of Okla. Basic Health Benefits Bd., 1985-96, chmn., 1992-93; exec. dir. Tulsa Program for Affordable Health Care, 1989—; mem. health benefit com. State of Okla. Ins. Commn., 1994—; Gov. Com. Health Care, 1993. Author: editorial column Point of View, 1985—, Tulsa mag., 1985—. Count commn. appointee Tulsa Met. Area Planning Commn., 1973-81; mayor's appointee Tulsa Housing Authority, 1985-88; pres. Tulsa Met. Ministry, 1980-83; bd. dirs. ARC, Tulsa, 1971-73, 84-85. Mem. Am. C. of C. (exec. dir. Okla. chpt.), Met. Tulsa C. of C. (v.p. 1983-95), Tulsa Tennis Club. Democrat. Roman Catholic. Avocations: reading, gardening, knitting, drawing, pottery. Office: Met Tulsa C of C 616 S Boston Ave Tulsa OK 74119

LANGER, ANDREW J., advertising agency executive. Formerly pres. The Marschalk Co. (now Lowe & Ptnrs.), N.Y.C.; pres., U.S. creative dir. Lowe Marschalk Inc., N.Y.C., creative dir., 1989—; CEO, vice chmn. Lowe & Ptnrs./SMS, N.Y.C.; bd. dirs. Am. Assn. Advt. Agys. *

LANGER, ARTHUR MARK, mineralogist; b. N.Y.C., Feb. 18, 1936; s. Morton Livingston and Ruth Regina (Lewitz) L.; m. Catherine Chilcott Josi, apr. 11, 1977; children: Erica Margaret, Andrew Michael, Elliott Mark, Christopher Morton. BA, Hunter Coll., 1956; MA, Columbia U., 1962, PhD, 1965. Exploration geologist Rosario Exploration Chibougamau Mining and Smelting, 1956; field asst. in geology Beartooth Mountains, Mont. Columbia U., N.Y.C., 1957-58, teaching asst. dept. geology, 1958-59, cons. mineralogist, 1960-65, rsch. asst. dept. geology, 1961-64; lectr. CUNY, 1964-65, mem. grad. faculty, 1982—; rsch. assoc. environ. medicine, dept. medicine Mt. Sinai Hosp., N.Y.C., 1965-67, asst. prof. dept. community medicine, 1967-68; assoc. prof. mineralogy, dept. community medicine Mt. Sinai Sch. Medicine, N.Y.C., 1968-86, 87-88, head phys. scis. sect., assoc. dir. Environ. Scis. Lab., 1969-86, sci. adminstr. Environ. Scis. Lab., 1983-84, assoc. prof. Ctr. for Polypeptide and Membrane Rsch., 1986-88; rsch. assoc. dept. mineral scis. Am. Mus. Natural History, N.Y.C., 1979—; dir. Environ. Scis. Lab. Inst. of Applied Scis. CUNY, 1988—, dep. dir. Ctr. Applied Studies of the Environment, 1992—; adj. assoc. prof. mineralogy grad. div. CUNY, 1968-69; expert cons. NIH, 1974—, WHO, 1975—, Nat. Heart, Lung and Blood Inst., 1975—, EPA, 1975—, Nat. Inst. for Environ. Health Scis., 1975—, Nat. Inst. for Occupational Safety and Health, 1975—, EPA Superfund cases, 1985—, other regional consultations; cons. Inst. Pub. Health, Norway, 1977, Ministry of Mines, South Africa, 1977, Internat. Agy. Rsch. Cancer, 1976, 86, Internat. Program Chem. Safety (WHO), 1985, Internat. Fedn. Bldg. Wood Workers, 1989; mem. internat. coms. on pollution and health. Assoc. editor Environ. Rsch., 1978-85, adv. editor, 1985-87; asst. editor Am. Jour. Indsl. Medicine, 1980-85, assoc. editor, 1985-86; mem. editorial rev. bd. Journ. Environ. Pathology and Toxicology, 1978-82, Jour. Environmental Pathology, Toxicology and Oncology, 1983—; mem. editorial adv. bd. Advances in Modern Environ. Toxicology, 1981-82; manuscript reviewer many jours.; reviewer, author fed. and industry documents, 1978—; contbr. chpts. to books, articles and abstracts to profl. jours. and symposia proc. Recipient award Dept. Geology, Hunter Coll., 1956, Dust Rsch. award Polachek Found., 1965-67, Career Scientist award Nat. Inst. Environ. Health Scis., 1969-74; named to Hall of Fame, Hunter College-CUNY, 1978; grantee Health Rsch. Coun., 1966-67, 75-77, Polacheck Found., 1966-68, NIH, 1967-78, Johns-Manville Corp., 1968-73, Am. Cancer Soc., 1971-74, 80-81, EPA, 1973, Ford Motor Co., 1973-75, Nat. Inst. Occupational Safety and Health, 1976-79, 82-84, Nat. Inst. Environ. Health Scis, 1978-86, Nat. Cancer Inst., 1979-81, Mobil Found., 1979—, Vanderbilt Talc Co., 1988, Battelle, Columbus, 1988—, Consumer Products Safety Commn., 1987-90, Ga. Pacific, 1989-91, others. Fellow Collegium Ramazzini, Geol. Soc. Am., Mineral. Soc. Am., N.Y. Acad. Scis.; mem. Phi Beta Kappa, Sigma Xi. Home: 6 Rochambeau Dr Hartsdale NY 10530-3008 Office: CUNY Brooklyn Coll Brooklyn NY 11210

LANGER, DALE ROBERT, electrical engineer; b. Kenosha, Wis., Dec. 21, 1947; s. Robert M. and Lucile A. (Brandt) L.; m. Sharon L. Bascombe, June 14, 1969; children: Michael J., Michelle M., Marissa K. BSEE, U. Wis., 1975. Electrical design engr. Tex. Instruments, Dallas, 1975-80; prin. engr. Zenith Data Systems, St. Joseph, Mich., 1980-83; mgr. comm. Exide Electronics, Raleigh, N.C., 1983—. Pres. locl br. Aid Assn. for Lutheran, Raleigh, 1995, Dallas, 1980. Mem. IEEE, Assn. for Computing Machinery. Achievements include patents in field of UPS system with improved network communications. Home: 8913 Lindenshire Rd Raleigh NC 27615 Office: Exide Electronics 3201 Spring Forest Rd Raleigh NC 27604

LANGER, EDWARD L., trade association administrator; b. Cleve., May 8, 1936; s. Edward L. and Evelyn (Palmer) L.; m. Sheila Mary Fitzpatrick, Nov. 5, 1957 (div. Sept. 1976); children—Dennis, Edward, Michael, Thomas, Michele; m. Carol E. Stower, Aug. 4, 1979; children—Tamara, Troy. B.S., John Carroll U., 1958, M.A., 1964; postgrad., Ohio U., 1962, 63, Cleve. State U., 1967-68. Asst. dean admissions and records John Carroll U., University Heights, Ohio, 1964-65; head guidance Wickliffe City Schs., Ohio, 1965-67; successively dir. mem. relations, mktg., planning, then asst. mng. dir. Am. Soc. for Metals, Materials Park, Ohio, 1967-84, mng. dir., 1984—. Author: Solid State Structures and Reactions, 1968. Bd. dirs., vice chmn. Cleve. Conv. Bur., 1984—. Mem. Am. Soc. Assn. Execs. (bd. dirs., vice chmn. 1988-92), Coun. Engring. and Sci. Soc. Execs. (bd. dirs. 1987-93, pres. 1992), numerous other engring. and sci. socs. Avocations: fishing; farming; golf; horses. Office: ASM Internat 9639 Kinsman Rd Novelty OH 44073

LANGER, ELAINE RUTH, computer programmer, consultant; b. N.Y.C.; d. Abraham and Goldie (Lusher) Goldsmith; m. Andre Langer; children: Karen G., Joseph. BA, NYU, 1948, postgrad., 1948-50. With systems svc. IBM Corp., N.Y.C., 1951-54; cons. N.Y.C., 1955-62; instr. computer programming Empire Tech. Sch., N.Y.C., 1968-81, Cope Vocat. Inst., N.Y.C., 1981-83; faculty dir. Internat. Computers and Comm. Sys., Inc., N.Y.C., 1984-87; sr. data processing cons. N.Y. Life Ins. Co., N.Y.C., 1987-88; mgr. computer programs divsn. continuing studies Baruch Coll., CUNY, N.Y.C., 1988—. Mem. ACM, Ams. for Israel and Torah Women (life). Office: Baruch Coll 48 E 26th St New York NY 10010

LANGER, ELLEN JANE, psychologist, educator, writer; b. N.Y.C., Mar. 25, 1947; d. Norman and Sylvia (Tobias) L. BA, NYU, 1970; PhD, Yale U., 1974. Cert. clin. psychologist. Asst. prof. psychology The Grad. Ctr. CUNY, 1974-77; assoc. prof. psychology Harvard U., Cambridge, Mass., 1977-81; prof. Harvard U., 1981—; cons. NAS, 1979-81, NASA; mem. div. on aging Harvard U. Med. Sch., 1979—, mem. psychiat. epidemiology steering com., 1982-90; chair social psychology program Harvard U., 1982—, chair Faculty Arts and Scis. Com. of Women, 1984-88. Author: Personal Politics, 1973, Psychology of Control, 1983, Mindfulness, 1989; editor: (with Charles Alexander) Higher Stages of Human Development, 1990, (with Roger Schank) Beliefs, Reasoning and Decision-Making, 1994); contbr. articles to profl. anc scholarly jours. Guggenheim fellow; grantee NIMH, NSF, Soc. for Psychol. Study of Social Issues, Milton Fund, Sloan Found., 1982; recipient Disting. Contbn. of Basic to Applied Psychology award APS, 1995. Fellow Computers and Soc. Inst., Am. Psychol. Assn. (Disting. Contributions to Psychology in Public Interest award 1988, Disting. Contributions of Basic Sci. to Applied Psychology 1995); mem. Soc. Exptl. Social Psychology, Phi Beta Kappa, Sigma Xi. Democrat. Jewish. Avocations: theater, horseback riding, tennis. Office: Harvard U Dept Psychology 33 Kirkland St Cambridge MA 02138-2044

LANGER, HORST, financial corporate executive. Chmn. Siemens Corp. subs. Siemens A.G., Munich, N.Y.C. Office: Siemens Corp 1301 Avenue Of The Americas New York NY 10019-6022*

LANGER, JAMES STEPHEN, physicist, educator; b. Pitts., Sept. 21, 1934; s. Bernard F. and Liviette (Roth) L.; m. Elinor Goldmark Aaron, Dec. 21, 1958; children: Ruth, Stephen, David. B.S., Carnegie Inst. Tech., 1955; Ph.D., U. Birmingham, Eng., 1958. Prof. physics Carnegie-Mellon U., Pitts., 1958-82, assoc. dean, 1971-74; prof. physics U. Calif., Santa Barbara, 1982—, dir. Inst. for Theoretical Physics, 1989-95. Contbr. articles to profl. jours. Vice pres. physics Com. Concerned Scientists, 1979—. Guggenheim fellow, 1974-75; Marshall scholar, 1955-57. Fellow AAAS, Am. Acad. Arts and Scis., Am. Phys. Soc. (chair elect divsn. condensed matter physics, chair nominating com.); mem. NAS, N.Y. Acad. Scis. Democrat. Jewish. Home: 1130 Las Canoas Ln Santa Barbara CA 93105-2331 Office: U Calif Dept Physics Santa Barbara CA 93106

LANGER, LAWRENCE LEE, English educator, writer; b. N.Y.C., June 20, 1929; s. Irving and Esther (Strauss) L.; m. Sondra Weinstein, Feb. 21, 1951; children: Andrew, Ellen. BA, CCNY, 1951; AM, Harvard U., 1952, PhD, 1961. Teaching fellow Harvard U., Cambridge, Mass., 1954-57; instr. English U. Conn., Storrs, 1957-58; instr. English Simmons Coll., Boston, 1958-61, asst. prof., 1961-66, assoc. prof., 1966-72, prof., 1972-76, Alumnae prof., 1976-92, Alumnae prof. emeritus, 1992—; Fulbright prof. Am. Lit. U. Graz, Austria, 1963-64. Author: The Holocaust and The Literary Imagination, 1975, The Age of Atrocity, 1978, Versions of Survival, 1982, Holocaust Testimonies, 1991 (Nat. Book Critics Cr. award for Criticism 1991), Art From the Ashes: A Holocaust Anthology, 1994, Admitting the Holocaust: Collected Essays, 1994. Sr. rsch. fellow NEH, 1978-79, 89-90. Mem. MLA, PEN. Office: Simmons Coll English 300 Fenway Boston MA 02115-5820 also: care Yale Univ Press Authors Mail 92A Yale Ave New Haven CT 06515-2251

LANGER, RALPH ERNEST, journalist; b. Benton Harbor, Mich., July 30, 1937; s. Ralph L. and Mary (Skuda) L.; m. Katherine B. McGuire, June 25, 1960; children: Terri B., Tammi L. Student, Central Mich. U., 1955-57; B.A. in Journalism, U. Mich., 1957-59. Telegraph editor, reporter Grand Haven (Mich.) Daily Tribune, 1959-60; mng. editor Port Angeles (Wash.) Evening News, 1962-66; copy desk Detroit Free Press, 1966-68; asst. mng. editor Dayton Jour. Herald, 1968, mng. editor, 1968-75; editor Everett (Wash.) Herald, 1975-81; mng. editor Dallas Morning News, 1981-83, exec. editor, 1983-86, v.p., 1986-91, sr. v.p., exec. editor, 1991—. Pres. Freedom of Info. Found. Tex., 1985-89, Nat. Freedom of Info. Coalition, 1992-93, Coun. of Presidents, 1991-92.. 1st lt. U.S. Army, 1960-62. Mem. Am. Soc. Newspaper Editors, Press Club Dallas (pres. 1985-86), A.P. Mng. Editors Assn. (bd. dirs 1980—, sec. 1989, v.p. 1990, pres. 1990-91), Coun. of Pres.'s (founding pres. 1992-93), AP Mng. Editors Assn. Found. (pres. 1991-92), Scabbard and Blade, Alpha Phi Gamma, Sigma Phi Epsilon. Office: Dallas Morning News Comm Ctr PO Box 655237 Dallas TX 75261

LANGER, RICHARD J., lawyer; b. Rockford, Ill., June 10, 1944; s. John W. and Dorothy E. (Brunn) Langrehr; m. Audrey A. Russo, Jan. 28, 1967; children: Kathleen M., Michael R. BS, U. Ill., 1967; JD, U. Wis., 1974. Bar: Wis. 1974, U.S. Dist. Ct. (we. dist.) Wis. 1974. Assoc. Ela, Esch, Hart & Clark, Madison, Wis., 1974-76; ptnr. Stolper, Koritzinsky, Brewster & Neider, Madison, 1976-91, Michael, Best & Friedrich, Madison, 1991—. Author: Guide to Property Classification, 1986, Workbook For Wisconsin Estate Planners, 1991, also articles. Sec. Combat Blindness Found., Madison, 1988—. Fellow Am. Coll. Trust and Estate Coun.; mem. ABA, State Bar Wis., Madison Estate Coun. Avocations: scuba diving, traveling, bicycling. Home: 1502 Windfield Way Madison WI 53562-3808 Office: Michael Best & Friedrich 1 S Pinckney St Madison WI 53703-2808

LANGER, ROBERT MARTIN, retired chemical engineering company executive, consultant; b. Boston, May 29, 1925; s. Samuel Morton and Ethel (Shlivek) L. B.Engring., Yale U., 1945, D.Engring., 1952; S.M., MIT, 1948. Sales mgr. The Badger Co., Inc., Cambridge, Mass., 1968-70; dep. mng. dir. Badger B.V., The Hague, The Netherlands, 1970-74, mng. dir., 1974-78; v.p., project adminstrn. The Badger Co., Inc., Cambridge, 1978-80; sr. v.p. Badger Am., Inc., Cambridge, 1981-83; v.p., treas. The Badger Co., Inc., Cambridge, 1983-87. Served to lt. j.g. USNR, 1945-46. Mem. AIChE. Home: 280 Commonwealth Ave Boston MA 02116-2422

LANGER, ROBERT SAMUEL, chemical, biomedical engineering educator; b. Albany, N.Y., Aug. 29, 1948; s. Robert Samuel Sr. and Mary (Swartz) L.; m. Laura Feigenbaum, July 31, 1988; children: Michael David, Susan Katherine, Samuel Alexander. BS, Cornell U., 1970; ScD, MIT, 1974. Rsch. assoc. Children's Hosp. Med. Ctr., Boston, 1974—; asst. prof. chem. and biomed. engring. MIT, Cambridge, Mass., 1978-81; assoc. prof. MIT, Cambridge, 1981-85, prof., 1985-89, Germeshausen prof., 1989—; bd. dirs. Alkermes, Cambridge, Acusphere, Cambridge, Focal, Lexington; tchr. Group Sch., Cambridge, 1971-73; endowed lectr. U. P.R., 1983, Case Western Res. U., 1986, U. Mich., 1987, U. Wash., 1988, U. Kans., 1989, U. Calif., San Francisco, 1991, U. Wis., 1991, Ga. Inst. Tech., 1991, Ohio State U., 1991, U. Pitts., 1992, Purdue U., 1992, U. Del., 1993, Pa. State U., 1993, Beth Israel Hosp., 1994, Cornell U., 1994, Calif. Inst. Tech., 1995, Ill. Inst. Tech., 1995, Ohio State Med. Sch., 1995, U. Calif., 1996, U. Tenn., 1996; cons. to numerous cos., including Genetech, San Francisco, 1981—, Merck Sharpe and Dohme, 1981-85; sci. advisor Cygnus, Redwood City, Calif., 1987—, Perspetive Biosys., Cambridge, 1991—. Author: (with D. Cincotta and K. Cole) Group School Chemistry Curriculum, 1972, (with W. Thilly) Laboratory in Applied Biology, 1978, Analaytical Practices in Biochemistry, 1979, (with W. Hrusheysky and F. Theeuwes) Temporal Control of Drug Delivery, 1991; editor: (with M. Chasin) Biodegradable Polymers in Drug Deliveyy, 1990, (with D. Wise) Medical Applications on Control Release, Vols. I and II, 1984, (with R. Steiner and P. Weisz) Angiogenesis, 1992;

contbr. over 700 articles to sci. jours.; patentee in field. Recipient John W. Hyatt Svc. to Mankind award Soc. Plastics Engrs., 1995, Internat. award, 1996, Ebert Prize, Am. Pharm. Assn., 1995; Union Oil fellow, 1970-71, Chevron fellow, 1971-72; cited for Outstanding Patent in Mass., Intellectual Property Owners Inc., 1989. Fellow Soc. Biomaterials (Clemson award 1990), Am. Assn. Pharm. Scis. (Disting. Pharm Sci. award 1993); mem. NAS, AIChE (Food, Pharm. and Bioengring. award 1986, Profl. Progress award 1990, Charles M. Stine Materials Sci. and Engring. award1991), Nat. Acad. Engring., Inst. Medicine of NAS, Am. Inst. Med. and Biol. Engrs. (founding fellow), Am. Acad. Arts and Scis., Am. Chem. Soc. (Creative Polymer award 1989, Phillips Applied Polymer Sci. award 1992, Pearlman Meml. Lectr. award 1992), Internat. Soc. Artificial Internal Organs (Organon-Teknika award 1991), Biomed. Engring. Soc. (bd. dirs. 1991-94, Whitaker lectr. 1994), Controlled Release Soc. (bd. govs. 1981-85, chmn. regulatory affairs com. 1985-89, pres. 1991-92, Founders award 1989, Outstanding Pharm. Paper award 1990, 92), Am. Soc. Artificial Internal Organs (mem. program com. 1984-87), Internat. Soc. Artificial Internal Organs. Avocations: magic, jogging. Office: MIT Dept Chem Engring 77 Massachusetts Ave Cambridge MA 02139-4301

LANGER, STEVEN, consultant human resources management and industrial psychology; b. N.Y.C., June 4, 1926; s. Israel and Anna (Glaisner) L.; BA in Psychology, Calif. State U., Sacramento, 1950; MS in Pers. Svc., U. Colo., 1958; PhD, Walden U., 1970; Lic. psychologist, Ill.; m. M. Jacquline White, Oct. 11, 1954 (dec. Dec. 1969); children: Bruce, Diana, Geoffrey; m. Elaine Catherine Brewer, Dec. 29, 1979 (dec. Feb. 1992). Asst. to pers. dir. City and County of Denver, 1956-59; pers. dir. City of Pueblo (Colo.) 1959-60; pers. cons. J.L. Jacobs & Co., Chgo., 1961-64, adminstrv. mgr., 1966-67; sales selection mgr. Reuben H. Donnelly Corp., Chgo., 1964-66; pres. Abbott, Langer & Assocs., Crete, Ill., 1967—; vis. prof. mgmt. Loyola U., Chgo., 1969-71; community prof. behavioral scis. Purdue U., Calumet campus, Hammond, Ind., 1973-75. Mem. Ill. Psychol. Assn. (chmn. sect. indsl. psychologists 1971-72), Chgo. Psychol. Assn. (pres. 1974-75, 94-95), Greater Chgo. Assn. Indsl./Orgnl. Psychology, Soc. Human Resources Mgmt. (accredited, chmn. research award com. 1966-69), Am. Compensation Assn., Chgo. Compensation Assn. (sec. 1976-77), Mensa (pres. Chgo. chpt. 1972-74). Unitarian. Contbr. numerous reports and articles on indsl. psychology and personnel mgmt. to profl. publs. Home: 309 Herndon St Park Forest IL 60466-1132 Office: Abbott Langer & Assoc 548 1st St Crete IL 60417-2142

LANGERAK, ESLEY OREN, retired research chemist; b. Pella, Iowa, Oct. 28, 1920; s. William Henry and Grace Dena (Vander Linden) L.; m. Elizabeth Jane Rhodes, Nov. 18, 1944; children—Kristin, Lisbeth, Peter. B.S. in Chemistry, Central Coll., Iowa, 1941; M.S., U. Del., 1947, Ph.D. in Organic Chemistry, 1949. High sch. tchr. Garden Grove Consol. Sch., Iowa, 1941-42; research chemist, supr., lab mgr. DuPont Co., Wilmington, Del., 1949-81; compensation mgr. chems. and pigments dept. DuPont Co., 1981-85; ret., 1985. Contbr. articles to profl. jours. Served with Ordnance, U.S. Army, 1942-46, PTO. Republican. Presbyterian. Club: DuPont Country. Patentee in field (3).

LANGERMANN, JOHN W. R., institutional equity salesperson; b. N.Y.C., Aug. 14, 1943; m. Karen Elizabeth Stives, Jan. 14, 1995. BA with highest honors, Lehigh U., 1965. Ptnr., sales mgr. L.F. Rothschild, Unterberg, Towbin, Boston, 1977-87; sr. v.p. County Nat. West Securities, Boston, 1987-90; v.p. Piper, Jaffray & Hopwood, Boston, 1990-92; sr. v.p. Needham & Co., Inc., Boston, 1993-94; mng. dir. instl. sales Ladenburg, Thalmann & Co., Inc., Boston, 1994—. Mem. Internat. Soc. Security Analysts, Kansas City Soc. Fin. Analysts. Avocations: vintage sports car racing, curling, sculling. Home: Stonehenge Farm Dover MA 02030 Office: Ladenburg Thalmann & Co Inc 10 Post Office Sq Boston MA 02109-4603

LANGEVIN, JAMES R., state official; b. Providence, Apr. 22, 1964; s. Richard Raymond and June Katherine (Barrett) L. B Arts and Scis., R.I. Coll., 1990; MPA, Harvard U., 1994. State rep. City of Warwick, R.I., 1988-94; sec. of state Office of the Sec. of State, Providence, R.I., 1995—. Bd. mem. United Cerebral Palsey, Pawtucket, R.I., 1993—, Tech Access, Providence, 1995, R.I. State House Restoration Com., 1995. Mem. Save the Bay R.I., K.C. Democrat. Roman Catholic. Avocations: reading, public speaking, community involvement. Office: Rm 218 RI State House Providence RI 02903*

LANGEVIN, LOUIS-DE-GONZAQUE, bishop; b. Oka, Can, Oct. 31, 1921. BA, Seminaire de Philosophie de Montreal, 1944; postgrad. in theology, Scolasticat des Peres Blancs, Ottawa, 1946-50; Lic. in Theology, Gregorian U., Rome, 1957; Lic. in Holy Scripture, Sainte a l'Institut Biblique, Rome, 1957. Ordained priest Roman Catholic Ch. Provincial priest Blancs d'Afrique, Montreal, Que., Can; aux. bishop Diocese de St Hyacinthe, 1974-79, titular bishop, 1979—; pres. Episcopal Commn. on Social Communications Conf. Cath. Bishops Can.; mem. Commn. for the Lay Apostate Conf. Bishops of Que. Decorated chevalier de l'Ordre du Saint-Sepulcre de Jerusalem lieutenance du Can., a Montreal, 1975, chevalier de Colomb du 4e Degre Assemblee Antoine Girouard de Saint-Hyacinthe Province de Que., Can. Home and Office: Eveche de Saint Hyacinthe, 1900 rue Girouard ouest CO 190, Saint Hyacinthe, PQ Canada J2S 7B4

LANGEVIN, THOMAS HARVEY, higher education consultant; b. St. Paul, Mar. 20, 1922; s. Thomas E. and Myrtle (Damsgard) L.; m. Pearl E. Mattfeld, Aug. 29, 1942; children: Dennis, Timothy. B.S., Concordia Tchrs. Coll., Seward, Neb., 1947; M.A., U. Neb., 1949, Ph.D., 1951. Quarantine insp. USPHS, 1943-45; grad. asst., asst. instr. U. Neb., 1947-51; prof. Concordia Tchrs. Coll., 1951-63, dean coll., 1961-63, acting pres., 1961-63; dir. long-range planning project Luth. Ch.-Mo. Synod, 1964-65; also cons. Bd. Higher Edn.; acad. v.p. Pacific Luth. U., 1965-69; pres. Capital U., Columbus, Ohio, 1969-79; pres. emeritus Capital U., 1979—; pres. Thomas H. Langevin Assoc., LadyLake, Fla., 1979—; prin. Registry for Interim Coll. and Univ. Pres., 1992—; chmn. Luth. Edn. Conf. N.Am., 1980-87; cons. Battelle Inst., 1979-87; cons., vis. fellow Battelle Seattle Rsch. Ctr., 1976. Co-chmn. Tacoma Area Urban Coalition Edn. Task Force, 1967-69; mem., past chmn. Ohio Com. Pub. Programs in Humanities; former exec. com. Fedn. Pub. Programs in Humanities; former mem. Ohio Higher Edn. Facilities Commn.; former mem. Commn. on Future Lutheran Edn., Luth Edn. Conf. N.Am., pres., 1977-78; bd. dirs. Nat. Urban League, 1979-80; Mem. Columbus Urban League; Former mem. Met. Columbus Sch. Com.; bd. dirs. Tacoma Citizens Com. Pub. TV, 1967-69, Design for Progress Tacoma, 1969, Tacoma Area Urban Coalition, 1967-69; bd. rev. Air U.; former adv. com. Center Sci. and Industry, Columbus; asso. in urban affairs Nat. Inst. Pub. Affairs; bd. control Concordia Coll., Portland, Oreg., 1965-69; bd. overseers Acad. Contemporary Problems, Columbus, 1972-75; trustee Columbus Symphony Orch., pres., 1979-81; past trustee Columbus Sch. Girls, Columbus Met. Area Community Action; hon. trustee Internat. Council of Mid-Ohio; past bd. govs. Goodwill Industries Central Ohio, Salesian Inner City Boys' Club; past bd. dirs., pres. Blue Cross Central Ohio; bd. dirs. Options, Learning Connections, Franklin County Heart Br., Columbus Area Mental Health Center; bd. dirs. Battelle Meml. Inst. Found., chmn., 1977-78; mem. bd. dirs. Nationwide Corp. Served with USCGR, 1943-45. Recipient Carnegie grant, postdoctoral fellow Center for Study Higher Edn., U. Mich., 1963-64. Mem. Assn. Ind. Colls. and Univs. Ohio (chmn. 1971-74), Orgn. Am. Historians, Nebr., Ohio hist. socs., Am. Assn. Higher Edn., Newcomen Soc. N.Am., Navy League U.S. (past dir. Columbus council), Columbus Area C. of C. (dir. 1971-74). Lutheran. Club: Columbus Rotary (dir.). Home: 441 San Pedro Dr Lady Lake FL 32159-8664

LANGFIELD, HELEN ELION, artist, radio commentator; b. New London, Conn., July 6, 1924; d. Harry Robert and Ida Fannie Elion; m. Raymond Lee Langfield, Oct. 6, 1952; 1 child, Joanna Langfield Rose. BA in English, Ohio State U., 1946; MA in Studio Art, Conn. Coll., 1972. Interviewer, commentator Sta. WNLC/WTYD, Waterford, Conn., 1971-88; instr. Lyman Allyn Mus., New London, Conn., 1984-86; chmn., art instr. Conn. Coll. Summer Program in Humanities, New London, 1968-72; TV interviewer, New London, 1970. Columnist New London Day, 1972; exhibited in one-woman and group shows at Wadsworth Atheneum, Hartford, 1974, Aldrich Mus. of Art, Ridgefield, Conn., 1976, 55 Mercer, N.Y.C., 1977, Whitney Counterweight, N.Y.C., 1981, Pastel Soc. Am., N.Y.C., 1982, Adam Gimbel Gallery, N.Y.C., 1982, 83, Cummings Art Ctr., New London, 1979, 83, 85, Brouhaha Gallery, Providence, 1986, Vangarde Gallery, New London, 1986, 87, 88, NOHO Gallery, N.Y.C., 1981, 85, 88, Conn. Commn. on Arts Showplace, Hartford, 1987, Lyman Allyn Mus., New London, Conn., 1988, 92, Conn. Coll., New London, 1988, MS Gallery, Hartford, 1988, Mark Humphrey Gallery, Southhampton, N.Y., 1991, Boca Raton (Fla.) Mus. Art, 1992, Hoxie Gallery, Westerly, R.I., 1994, Habitat Gallery, West Palm Beach, Fla., 1996; represented in permanent collections Michael DeSantis, Inc., N.Y.C., Radisson Hotel, New London, 1st Nat. Bank Danbury, Conn., Conn. Savings Bank, New Haven, Suisman, Shapiro, Wool, Brennan, Gray and Faulkner, P.C., New London, Citicorp, Boston, Otis Elevator, Hartford, State Ct. House, New London, pvt. collections. Commr. Conn. Commn. on the Arts, Hartford, 1983-85. Jewish. Avocations: tennis, bridge. Home: 23362 Torre Cir Boca Raton FL 33433-7026

LANGFITT, THOMAS WILLIAM, neurosurgeon, foundation administrator; b. Clarksburg, W.Va., Apr. 20, 1927; s. Frank Valentine and Veda (Davis) L.; m. Carolyn Louise Payne, Jan. 31, 1953; children: David Douglas, John Turner, Frank Davis. AB, Princeton U., 1949; MD, Johns Hopkins U., 1953; ScD (hon.), Salem (W.Va.) Coll., 1983, Phila. Coll. Pharmacy and Sci., 1984. Diplomate Am. Bd. Neurol. Surgery (chmn. 1985-86). Intern Johns Hopkins Hosp., Balt., 1953-54, resident, 1957-61; head neurosurgery sect. Pa. Hosp., Phila., 1961-68; asst., prof., assoc. prof. neurosurgery U. Pa., Phila., 1961-87, Charles Harrison Frazier prof. neurosurgery, chmn. dept., 1968-87; pres., chief exec. officer The Glenmede Trust Co., Phila., 1987—; pres. The Pew Charitable Trusts, Phila., 1987—; bd. dirs. The Glenmede Trust Co., Phila., SmithKline Beecham Corp., Phila., The Sun Co., Radnor, Pa., N.Y. Life Ins. Co., N.Y.C.; med. adv. com. Gen. Motors Corp., Detroit, 1985—. Co-author 200 articles, book chpts. and books. bd. trustees Princeton U.; capt. M.C., U.S. Army, 1955-57. Fellow Royal Coll. Surgeons, Edinburgh (hon.); mem. Inst. Medicine, NAS, Am. Philos. Soc., Soc. Neurol. Surgeons (pres. 1987-88, Grass medal 1984), Union League. Office: Glenmede Trust Co 229 S 18th St Philadelphia PA 19103-6144

LANGFORD, CHARLES DOUGLAS, state legislator, lawyer; b. Montgomery, Ala., Dec. 9, 1922; s. Nathan G. and Lucy B. (Brown) L. BS, Tenn. State U., Nashville, 1948; LLB, Cath. U. of Am., 1952, JD, 1967. Bar: Ala. 1953, U.S. Dist. Ct. (mid. dist.) Ala. 1954, U.S. Ct. Appeals (5th cir.) 1969, U.S. Supreme Ct. 1976, U.S. Ct. Appeals (11th cir.) 1982. Ptnr. Gray, Langford, Sapp, McGowan, Gray & Nathanson, Montgomery, Ala., 1968—; mem. Ala. State Senate, Montgomery, 1983—. Officer St. John A.M.E. Ch. With U.S. Army, 1943-46. Mem. Elks (past exalter ruler So. Pride lodge), Alpha Phi Alpha. Democrat. Home: 918 Grove St Montgomery AL 36104-4738 Office: 400 S Union St Ste 205 Montgomery AL 36104-4316

LANGFORD, DEAN TED, lighting and precision materials company executive; b. Princeton, Ill., June 19, 1939; s. Claude Robert and Dorothy Aczne (Tuckerman) L.; m. Nancy Hirsch; children: Douglas T., John P. B.S. in Math. and Aero. Engring., U. Ill., 1962, LHD, Salem State Coll., 1990. Regional sales mgr. IBM-N.E. Region, Westport, Conn., 1980-81, corp. dir. mgmt. devel., Armonk, N.Y., 1981-82, group dir., communications, Ryebrook, N.Y., 1982-83; v.p. mktg. GTE Communications Systems, Stamford, Conn., 1983-84; pres. GTE Elec. Products, Danvers, Mass., 1984-93, Osram Sylvania Inc., Danvers, Mass., 1993—. Mem. bd. advisers Sch. Engring., U. Ill.-Chgo., 1984-92; mem. adv. bd. Northeastern U., 1984; trustee Civic Edn. Found. Lincoln-Filene Ctr., Tufts U.; mem. corp. bd. Mass. Gen. Hosp. Mem. U. Ill. Alumni Assn. (bd. dirs.), Alliance to Save Energy (bd. dirs.), Nat. Assn. of Mfg. (bd. dirs.), Nat. Elec. Mfg. Assn. (bd. dirs.), Phys. Sci. Inc. (bd. dirs.), Salem Country Club. Avocations: biking, golf, skiing. Home: 345 Beacon St Boston MA 02116-1102 Office: Osram Sylvania Inc 100 Endicott St Danvers MA 01923-3623

LANGFORD, GEORGE, newspaper editor; b. Johnson City, Tenn., May 24, 1939; s. Norris McCormick and Sarah (Lacey) L.; m. Anne Roberta Mirgian, June 13, 1964; children: Jennie Anne, Julie Beth. BA, Vanderbilt U., 1961. Reporter UP, St. Louis, Chgo., N.Y.C., 1961-66; sportwriter Chgo. Tribune, 1966, asst. sports feature editor, 1974, now assoc. mng. editor photography art and graphics. Author: The Crimson Tide: Alabama Football, 1974; contbr. numerous articles to periodicals. Recipient Story of Yr. award in Ill., AP, 1970, Baseball Writer of Yr. award Horshoe Club Chgo., 1971. Roman Catholic. Home: Deerfield IL

LANGFORD, JACK DANIEL, elementary school educator; b. Cookeville, Tenn., Jan. 15, 1960; s. Sam Harley and Mary Delma (Carr) L.; m. Marilyn Ptricia Poteet. BS in Secondary Edn., Tenn. Tech. U., 1983, MA in Ednl. Adminstrn. and Supervision, 1987, MA, 1993, postgrad., 1993—. Lic. tchr., 17 tchg. endorsements. Bus. tchr. Dekalb County H.S., Smithville, Tenn., 1984; social studies tchr. White County Mid. Sch., Sparta, Tenn., 1985-92; 1st-6th grade title I tchr. Findlay Elem. Sch., Sparta, Tenn., 1992—; chmn. Findlay Improvement Team, Sparta, 1993—. Vice-pres. White County Natural Resource Conservation Svc. Recipient Career Ladder II State of Tenn., 1995. Mem. ASCD, NEA, Tenn. Edn. Assn., Internat. Reading Assn., Nat. Geog. Soc., White County Edn. Assn., Tenn. Cattlemen's Assn., White-Van Buren Cattlemen's Assn., White County Farm Bur., Phi Delta Kappa. Avocations: reading, movies, sight seeing, conversing with friends, visiting. Home: Rte 3 Box 197A Sparta TN 38583

LANGFORD, JAMES JERRY, lawyer; b. Birmingham, Ala., May 19, 1933; s. N.B. and Margaret Elizabeth (Fuller) L.; m. Mary Elizabeth Fryant, Mar. 21, 1958; children: Jan Carol Langford Hammett, Joel Fryant. BS, U. So. Miss., 1955; JD, U. Miss., 1970. Bar: Miss. 1970, U.S. Dist. Ct. (no. and so. dists.) Miss. 1970, U.S. Ct. Appeals (5th cir.) 1971, U.S. Ct. Appeals (11th cir.). Agt. Met. Life Ins. Co., Jackson, Miss., 1957-58; sales rep. Employers Mut. of Wausau, Jackson, 1958-64; v.p. Reid-McGee Ins. Co., Jackson, 1964-67; assoc. Wells Marble & Hurst, Jackson, 1970-73, ptnr., 1973-90, sr. ptnr., mng. ptnr., 1990—. Editor-in-chief Miss. Law Jour., 1969-70. Mem. U.S. Naval Inst., Annapolis, Md. 1st lt. U.S. Army, 1955-57. Mem. ABA, Fed. Bar Assn. (pres. Miss. chpt. 1981-82), Fedn. Ins. and Corp. Counsel, Nat. Assn. RR Trial Counsel, Miss. Bar Found., Miss. Bar Assn., Miss. Def. Lawyers Assn. (pres. 1992-93), Def. Rsch. Inst., Country Club Jackson, Phi Delta Phi, Omicron Delta Kappa, Pi Kappa Alpha. Presbyterian. Avocations: military history, baseball. Home: 12 Plum Tree Ln Madison MS 39110-9620 Office: Wells Marble & Hurst PO Box 131 Jackson MS 39205-0131 *People respect honesty, trustworthiness, hard work and sincerity. Do what you truly want to do for your vocation, for that is the secret of happiness in a business career.*

LANGFORD, JAMES ROULEAU, university press administrator; b. South Bend, Ind., June 12, 1937; s. Walter McCarty and Alice M. (Joubert) L.; m. Margaret Marie Hammerot, Aug. 30, 1968 (div. 1980); children: Jeremy, Joshua; m. Jill Ann Justice, July 16, 1981; children: Trevor J., Emily A. Ph.B., Aquinas Inst., 1960, M.A. in Philosophy, 1961, M.A. in Theology, 1964, S.T.L., 1965. Instr. theology St. Thomas Coll., St. Paul, 1965-67; editor Doubleday & Co., N.Y.C., 1967-69; exec. editor U. Mich. Press, Ann Arbor, 1969-74; dir. U. Notre Dame Press, Ind., 1974—; bd. dirs. Assn. Am. Univ. Presses, 1981-83. Author: Galileo, Science and the Church, 1966, rev., 1971, 3d edit., 1992, The Game Is Never Over, 1980, rev., 1982, The Cub Fan's Guide to Life, 1984, Runs, Hits and Errors, 1987, Rookie: The Story of a Season, 1990. Pres. There Are Children Here, 1994—. Democrat. Roman Catholic. Home: 21550 New Rd Lakeville IN 46536-9342 Office: U Notre Dame Press Notre Dame IN 46556 *My life as a scholar, publisher and writer has brought me into contact with many of the most intelligent, creative and important people of our time. Those I admire most are the ones of whom it can be said "They never lost their sense of humor.".*

LANGFORD, ROLAND EVERETT, military officer, environmental scientist, author; b. Owensboro, Ky., Apr. 11, 1945; s. John Roland and Mary Helen (Cockriel) L.; m. Son-Hee Shin, Dec. 18, 1971; children: John Everett, Lee Shin. AA, Armstrong State Coll., 1965; BS, Ga. So. Coll., 1967; MS, U. Ga., 1971, PhD, 1974; grad., U.S. Army Command and Gen. Staff Coll., 1985; PhD, U. N.C., 1996. Cert. indsl. hygienist; registered hazardous substances profl., sanitarian, Ariz.; diplomate Am. Acad. Sanitarians. Instr. Savannah (Ga.) Sci. Mus., 1971-72, Bainbridge (Ga.) Jr. Coll., 1973-74; asst. prof. chemistry Ga. Mil. Coll., Milledgeville, 1975-77; asst. prof. Ga. So. Coll., Statesboro, 1977-78; commd. capt. U.S. Army, 1978, advanced through grades to lt. col., 1992; chief chemistry sect. U.S. Army Acad. Health Scis., Ft. Sam Houston, Tex., 1978-79; sanitary engr. U.S. Army Environ. Hygiene Agy., Aberdeen Proving Ground, Md., 1979-81; comdr. environ. sanitation detachment Taegu, Republic of Korea, 1981-83; environ. sci. officer Ft. Huachuca, Ariz., 1984-88; chief occupational health rsch. U.S. Army Biomed. R&D Lab., Ft. Detrick, Md., 1991-92; comdr. med. rsch. detachment Walter Reed Army Inst. Rsch., Wright-Patterson AFB, Ohio, 1992—; panel mem. Comprehensive Assistance to Undergrad. Sci. Edn., NSF, 1975-77; judge Internat. Sci. Fair, San Antonio, 1979; mem. sci. rev. panel NIH, 1986—; adj. faculty St. Leo's Coll., San Antonio, 1978-79, U. Md., Taegu and Pusan, Korea, 1981-83, AFIT, 1993—, Purdue U., 1995—. Co-author: Hazardous Materials Training Program for International Union of Operating Engineers, 1988, Fundamentals of Hazardous Materials Incidents, 1990, Substance Abuse in the Workplace, 1994; contbr. articles to profl. jours. Active Boy Scouts Am., Ft. Sam Houston, 1978-79; mem. parish coun., lay minister Holy Family Parish, Ft. Huachuca, 1985-88, 95-96, lay min., lector 1992-96; advisor Med. Explorer Post, Ft. Huachuca, 1986-88; lay minister St. Thomas More Ch., 1988-91. Fellow Am. Inst. Chemists; mem. Am. Acad. Indsl. Hygiene (cert.), Am. Chem. Soc., Nat. Environ. Health Assn. (cert. hazardous materials profl.), Korean Chem. Soc., Royal Asiatic Soc. (bd. dirs. 1982-83), Assn. Mil. Surgeons U.S., Am. Acad. Sanitarians (cert.), Health Physics Soc., Am. Water Works Assn., Am. Indsl. Hygiene Assn., Am. Acad. Health Physics (assoc.). Republican. Roman Catholic. Avocations: ham radio, oriental studies, photography. Home: 509 Phelps Cir Dayton OH 45433-1324 Office: US Army Med Rsch Detachment Wright Patterson AFB Dayton OH 45433

LANGFORD, WALTER MARTIN, retired greeting card and gift wrap manufacturing executive; b. Steubenville, Ohio, Jan. 2, 1931; s. Martin and Ola Belle (Stiff) L.; m. Winifred Claire Major, Mar. 14, 1953; children: Martin B., Janet R., Steven M. BS in Acctg., U. Kans., 1952; JD, Ill. Inst. Tech., 1971. With Am. Can. Co., 1956-66; internal audit mgr. All-Steel, Inc., Aurora, Ill., 1966-68, div. controller, 1968-71, dir. corp. services, 1971-77; v.p. adminstrn. Gibson Greetings, Inc., Cin., 1977-79; sr. v.p. ops. Cleo Wrap Corp. div. Gibson Greetings, Inc., Memphis, 1979-87, exec. v.p., gen. mgr., 1987-90; bd. dirs., corp. sec. Gibson Greetings, Inc., Cin., 1978-90. Mem. adv. bd. State Tech. Inst., Memphis, 1986-91; bd. dirs. Jr. Achievement of Memphis, 1985-91, Theatre Memphis, 1994—; bd. trustees LeMoyne-Owen Coll., 1991—, chmn., 1994—. Lt. (j.g.) USNR, 1952-56, Korea. Mem. Ill. Bar Assn. Lodge: Rotary. Avocation: book collecting. Office: Gibson Greetings Inc 4025 Viscount Ave Memphis TN 38118-6106

LANGHAM, MICHAEL, theatrical director; b. Somerset, Eng., Aug. 22, 1919; s. Seymour and Muriel (Andrews Speed) L.; m. Helen Burns, July 8, 1948 (div. 1972); 1 son, Christopher; m. Ellin Gorky, 1972. Student, Radley Coll., Abingdon, Eng., 1933-37, London U., 1937-39; D.Lit. (hon.), McMaster U., 1962, St. Scholastica Coll., 1973; LL.D., U. Toronto, 1966. Engaged in theatrical profession, 1946—; dir. prodns. Arts Council Midland Theatre Co., 1946-48, Sir Barry Jackson's Birmingham Repertory Theatre, 1948-50, Glasgow Citizens' Theatre, 1953-54; artistic dir. Guthrie Theater, Mpls., 1971-79, including direction of Relapse, 1972, Oedipus the King, 1972, 73, The Government Inspector, 1973, The Merchant of Venice, 1973, King Lear, 1974, Love's Labor's Lost, 1974, The School for Scandal, 1974, Private Lives, Measure For Measure, 1975, The Matchmaker, 1976, Winter's Tale, 1977; dir. Theatre Center, The Juilliard Sch., N.Y.C., 1980—, Julius Caesar, Stratford-upon-Avon, 1950, Stratford, Ont., 1955, The Gay Invalid, London, 1950, Pygmalion, London, 1951, The Other Heart, London, 1951, Old Vic Co., prodn., Othello at Berlin Festival, also London, 1951; Brit. Council lectr., Australia, 1952; dir. Richard III, Belgian Nat. Theatre, 1952, The Merry Wives of Windsor, The Hague, 1953, artistic dir., Stratford (Ont.) Shakespearean Festival, 1955-67, including direction of Hamlet, 1957, Henry IV, Part I, 1958, Much Ado About Nothing, 1958, Romeo and Juliet, 1960, Coriolanus, 1961, Love's Labour's Lost, 1961, Taming of the Shrew, 1962, Cyrano de Bergerac, 1962, Troilus and Cressida, 1963, Timon of Athens, 1963, King Lear, 1964, The Country Wife, 1964; also prodns. Love's Labour's Lost and Timon of Athens at Festival Theatre, Chichester, Eng., 1964; dir. prodns. Hamlet, Stratford-upon-Avon, 1956, Merchant of Venice, 1960, Much Ado About Nothing, 1961, Henry V, Edinburgh Festival, 1956, Two Gentlemen of Verona, London, 1957, A Midsummer Night's Dream, London, 1960, Andorra, N.Y.C., 1963, Twelfth Night, Am. Place Theatre, 1982; compiler, dir. univ. tour prodns., Can. and U.S. on Shakespearean comedy, 1962; author, dir. prodns. The Affliction of Love for TV, 1963; Artistic cons. prodns., LaJolla (Cal.) Theater Project, 1965. Served with Brit. Army, 1939-45. Office: The Juilliard Sch Drama Div 144 W 66th St New York NY 10023-6502

LANGHAM, NORMA, playwright, educator, poet, composer, inventor; b. California, Pa.; d. Alfred Scrivener and Mary Edith (Carter) L. BS, Ohio State U., 1942; B in Theatre Arts, Pasadena Playhouse Coll. Theatre Arts, 1944; MA, Stanford U., 1956; postgrad., Summer Radio-TV Inst., 1960, Pasadena Inst. Radio, 1944-45. Tchr. sci. California High Sch., 1942-43; asst. office pub. info. Denison U., Granville, Ohio, 1955; instr. speech dept. Westminster Coll., New Wilmington, Pa., 1957-58; instr. theatre. California U., Pa., 1959, asst. prof., 1960-62, assoc. prof., 1962-79, prof. emeritus, 1979—, co-founder, sponsor, dir. Children's Theatre, 1962-79; founder, producer, dir. Food Bank Players, 1985, Patriot Players, 1986, Noel Prodns., 1993. Writer: (plays) Magic in the Sky, 1963, Founding Daughters (Pa. Nat. DAR awards 1991), Women Whisky Rebels (Pa. Nat. DAR awards 1992), John Dough (Freedoms Found. award 1968), Who Am I?, Hippocrates Oath, Gandhi, Clementine of '49, Soul Force, Dutch Painting, Purim, Music in Freedom, The Day the Moon Fell, Job Johnson; composer, lyricist (plays) Why Me, Lord?, (text) Public Speaking; co-inventor (computer game) Highway Champion. Recipient Exceptional Acad. Svc. award Pa. Dept. Edn., 1975, Appreciation award Bicentennial Commn. Pa., 1976, Gregg award Calif. U. of Pa. Alumni Assn., 1992; Henry C. Frick Ednl. Commn. grantee. Mem. AAUW (co-founder Calif. br., 1st v.p. 1971-72, pres. 1972-73, Outstanding Woman of Yr. 1986), DAR, Theatre Assn. Pa., Internat. Platform Assn. (Poetry award 1993-94, Monologue award 1995), Calif. U. Pa. Assn. Women Faculty (founder, pres. 1972-73), Calif. Cmty. Choir, Calif. Hist. Soc., Washington County Hist. Soc., Dramatists Guild, Ctr. in Woods, Mensa, Alpha Psi Omega, Omicron Nu. Presbyterian (elder). Home: PO Box 459 California PA 15419-0459

LANGHANS, EDWARD ALLEN, drama and theater educator; b. Warren, Pa., Mar. 11, 1923; s. Allen Milton and Frances Allen L. BA, U. Rochester, 1948, MA in English, 1949; M.A. in Theatre, U. Hawaii, 1951; Ph.D. in Theatre, Yale U., 1955. Asst. prof. drama U. Tex., Austin, 1955-57; asst. prof. drama and theatre U. Hawaii, Honolulu, 1957-64; assoc. U. Hawaii, 1964-71, prof., chmn. dept., 1971-85, assoc. dean arts and humanities, 1987, prof. emeritus, 1988—; vis. prof. Tufts U., 1967-68; rsch. prof. George Washington U., 1975-76. Author: (with Philip Highfill and Kalman Burnim) A Biographical Dictionary of Actors, Actresses, Musicians, Dancers, Managers and Other Stage Personnel in London 1660-1800, 16 vols., 1973-93, Five Restoration Theatrical Adaptations, 1980, Restoration Promptbooks, 1981, Eighteenth-Century British and Irish Promptbooks, 1987; co-author: An International Dictionary of Theater Language, 1985; contbr. articles to The New Grove Dictionary of Opera, 4 vols., 1992; dir., designer numerous plays. Bd. dirs. Honolulu Theatre for Youth, 1958-63, Hawaii Theatre Council, 1965-70, Hawaii Theatre Festival, 1978-82. Served with USAAF, 1942-47. Decorated Air medal, D.F.C.; Nat. Endowment for Humanities grantee, 1975-76, 85-86; Folger Shakespeare Library fellow, 1970-73. Mem. Am. Assn for Theatre in Higher Edn., Soc. Theatre Research, Am. Soc. Theatre Research. Home: 1212 Punahou St Apt 3402 Honolulu HI 96826-1026

LANGHENRY, JOHN GODFRED, JR., lawyer; b. Chgo., Feb. 10, 1933; s. John Godfred and Julia Margaret (Hoffman) L.; m. Eleanor L., Dec. 1, 1956; children: Barbara, John, Mark, Mary Patricia, Paul, Thomas, Matthew. BS, Loyola U., Chgo., 1954, JD, 1956. Bar: Ill. 1956, U.S. Dist. Ct. (no. dist.) Ill. 1959, U.S. Supreme Ct. 1971. Assoc. Hinshaw & Culbertson, Chgo., 1959-64, ptnr., 1965—; lectr. med. malpractice, hosp. law, civil practice and procedure Ill. Inst. Continuing Legal Edn.; lectr. med. loss prevention Ill. State Med. Soc.; faculty mem. trial advocacy workshop for practicing attys. Loyola U. Chgo. Sch. Law. Contbr. articles to profl. jours. Bus. chmn. Crusade of Mercy, Arlington Heights, Ill., 1966-67; chmn. safety commn. Village of Arlington Heights, 1967-69, mem. planning commn., 1969-72; trustee lay adv. bd. Sacred Heart of Mary High Sch.,

Rolling Meadows, Ill., 1972-76, 1st pres., 1972-73; mem. fin. com. Our Lady of the Wayside Ch., Arlington Heights, 1972-82, chmn., 1981-82; Loyola U. Sch. Law Alumni Assn., pres. 1973-74, Ill. Right to Life Com., chmn. 1975-76; chmn. fund raising St. Viator High Sch., Arlington Heights, mem. lay adv. bd., 1983-84, v.p. 1985-86. Served to 1st lt. USAF, 1956-59. Fellow Am. Coll. Trial Lawyers; mem. ABA, Ill. Bar Assn., Chgo. Bar Assn., Am. Soc. Hosp. Attys., Am. Bd. Trial Advs. (charter Ill. br., treas. 1988), Def. Rsch. Inst., Fedn. Ins. Counsel (chmn. med. malpractice com. 1979-80), Soc. Trial Lawyers Ill. (treas. 1986, sec. 1987, v.p. 1988, pres. 1989), Ill. Def. Counsel (pres. 1973-74), Trial Lawyers Club Chgo. (pres. 1970-71), Big Foot Country Club (Fontana, Wis.). Roman Catholic. Office: Hinshaw Culbertson 222 N La Salle St Ste 300 Chicago IL 60601-1005

LANGHOLZ, ROBERT WAYNE, lawyer, investor; b. Sioux City, Iowa, Jan. 17, 1930; s. Harry H. and Alvina (Bockhop) L.; m. Patricia Wilson Wheeler, Mar. 6, 1994; children: Robert Wayne, Laurence Henry, Kristofer Page. B.S. with distinction, U. Iowa, 1951, J.D., 1956. Bar: Iowa 1956, Okla. 1957. Research asst. to prof. Frank R. Kennedy, U. Iowa Coll. Law, 1955-56; trainee Gulf Oil Corp., 1956; mem. firm Carlson, Lupardus, Matthews, Holliman & Huffman, Tulsa, 1956-67; stockholder Holliman, Langholz, Runnels, Holden, Forsman & Sellers, Tulsa, 1967—; chmn. bd., chief exec. officer Skinner Bros. Co. Inc., Geophys. Research Corp., Indel-Davis Inc.; bd. dirs. F&M Bank & Trust Co. Trustee Herbert Hoover Presdl. Libr. Assn., West Branch, Iowa; nat. trustee Nat. Jewish Ctr. for Immunology and Respiratory Medicine, Denver. Served with USAF, 1951-53. Mem. ABA, Iowa Bar Assn., Okla. Bar Assn., Young Pres. Orgn., World Pres. Orgn., Summit Club, So. Hills Country Club (Tulsa), Eldorado Country Club (Indian Wells, Calif.). Methodist. Home: 4033 S Yorktown Pl Tulsa OK 74105-3412 Office: Holarud Bldg 10 E 3rd St Ste 400 Tulsa OK 74103-3618

LANGHORNE, LINDA KAY, health and physical education teacher; b. Lynchburg, Va., July 19; d. Theodore R. Sr. and Carolyn (Payne) L. BS, Hampton Inst. (Hampton U.), 1977, MA, 1984. Tchr. Lynchburg City Schs., Linkhorne Mid. Sch., 1978—. Mem. AAHPERD, NEA, Va. Edn. Assn., Va. Assn. for Health, Phys. Edn., Recreation and Dance, Va. Assn. Driver Edn. and Traffic Safety. Home: 1214 19th St Lynchburg VA 24504-3418 Office: Lynchburg City Schs Linkhorne Mid Sch 2525 Linkhorne Dr Lynchburg VA 24503-3315

LANGHOUT-NIX, NELLEKE, artist; b. Utrecht, The Netherlands, Mar. 27, 1939; came to U.S., 1968, naturalized, 1978; d. Louis Wilhelm Frederick and Geertruida Nix; m. Ernst Langhout, July 26, 1958; 1 child, Klaas-Jan Marnix. MFA, The Hague, 1958. Head art dept. Bush Sch., Seattle, 1969-71; dir. creative projects Project Reach, Seattle, 1971-72; artist-in-residence Fairhaven Coll., Bellingham, Wash., 1974, Jefferson Cmty. Ctr., Seattle, 1978-82, Lennox Sch., N.Y.C., 1982; dir. NN Gallery, Seattle, 1970—; guest curator Holland-U.S.A. Bicentennial show U. Wash., 1982; project dir. Women in Art Today, Wash., 1989, Wash. State Centennial Celebration; Washington to Washington traveling exhibition, 1989. Executed wall hanging for King County Courthouse, Seattle, 1974; one-woman shows include: Nat. Art Center, N.Y.C., 1980, Gail Chase Gallery, Bellevue, Wash., 1979, 80, 83, 84, Original Graphics Gallery, Seattle, 1981, Bon Nat. Gallery, Seattle, 1981, Kathleen Ewing Gallery, Washington, 1986, Ina Broerse Laren, Holland, 1992, Charlotte Daneel Gallery, Holland, 1992, Christopher Gallery, Tucson, 1992, Mercer Island Cmty. Arts Ctr., 1992, Lisa Harris Gallery, Seattle, 1994, Jacques Marchais Mus. Tibetan, S.I., N.Y., 1995, 4th World Conf. on Women, China, 1995, Global Focus, Beijing, 1995, Elite Gallery, Moscow, 1995; group shows include: Cheney Cowles Mus., Spokane, 1977, Bellevue Art Mus., 1978, 86, Renwick Gallery, Washington, 1978, Kleinert Gallery, Woodstock, N.Y., 1979, Artcore Meltdown, Sydney, Australia, 1979, Tacoma Art Mus., 1979, 83, 86, 87, Ill. State Mus., Springfield, 1979, Plener Sandomierz, Poland, 1980, Plener Kielce, Poland, 1980, Western Assn. Art Museums traveling show, 1979-80, Madison Square Garden, N.Y.C., 1981, Exhbn. Space, N.Y.C., 1982, Lisa Harris Gallery, 1985, 87, 88, Wash. State Centennial, Tacoma, 1989, Nordic Heritage Mus., Seattle, 1994; represented in permanent collections Plener Collection, Sandomierz, Poland, Bell Telephone Co. Collection, Seattle, Wash. U., Seattle, Children's Orthopedic Hosp., Seattle, Nat. Mus. Women in Arts, Washington; installations Tacoma Art Mus. Bd. dirs. Wing Luke Mus., Seattle, 1978-81, Wash. State Trust Hist. Preservation, 1990-93; v.p. Denny Regrade Cmty. Coun., 1978-79; mem. Seattle Planning Commn., 1978-84. Author (with others) Step Inside the Sacred Circle, 1989, An Artist's Book 1940-45 Remembered, 1991; designer, editor Papua New Guinea-Where She Invented Bow and Arow, 1996. Recipient Wallhanging award City of Edmonds (Wash.), 1974; Renton 83 merit award, 1984; Merit award Internat. Platform Assn. Art Exhibit, 1984, Silver medal 1st place, 1985, 87, Gold medal, Internat. Platform Assn., 1989. Mem. Denny Regrade Arts Coun. (co-founder), Internat. Platform Assn., Women in Arts N.Y.C., Nat. Mus. Women in Arts (founding mem., Libr. fellow, chairperson Wash. State com. 1988-89, mem. nat. adv. bd. 1993—), Internat. Platform Assn., Seattle-King County Cmty. Arts Network (bd. dirs. 1983-85, chmn. 1984-85), Nat. Artist Equity Assn. Address: PO Box 375 Mercer Island WA 98040-0375

LANGILL, GEORGE FRANCIS, hospital administrator, educator; b. Ottawa, Ont., Can., Dec. 31, 1946; s. Roy Joseph and Margaret (O'Hara) L.; m. Lorraine Diane Bavazeau, Aug. 10, 1947; children: Norman, Barbara Ann, Kendra. BSc with honors, Ottawa U., 1971, MHA, 1973. Adminstrv. coordinator N.S. Dept. Health, 1973-74; asst. exec. dir. Royal Ottawa Hosp., 1974-79; assoc. exec. dir. Rehab. Ctr., Ottawa, 1979-83; chief exec. officer Royal Ottawa Health Care Group, 1983—; adj. prof., part-time lectr. Faculty Adminstrn., Ottawa U., 1979—; mem. faculty health care adminstrn. WHO, Montreal, 1983—; bd. dirs., mem. exec. com. Can. council Rehab. of Disabled, Toronto, 1985—. Contbr. articles to profl. jours. Mem. Ottawa Bd. Trade, 1986. Mem. Can. Coll. Health Service Execs., Am. Coll. Health Execs., Am. Assn. Mental Health Adminstrs. Avocations: skiing, hockey, golf. Office: Royal Ottawa Health Care, Group, 1145 Carling Ave, Ottawa, ON Canada K1Z 7K4

LANGLAND, JOSEPH THOMAS, author, emeritus educator; b. Spring Grove, Minn., Feb. 16, 1917; s. Charles M. and Clara Elizabeth (Hille) L.; m. Judith Gail Wood, June 26, 1943; children—Joseph Thomas, Elizabeth Langland, Paul. BA, U. Iowa, 1940, MA, 1941; DLitt (hon.), Luther Coll., 1974. Instr. in English Dana Coll., Blair, Nebr., 1941-42; part-time instr. U. Iowa, 1946-48; asst. prof., then asso. prof. U. Wyo., 1948-59; mem. faculty U. Mass., Amherst, 1959-79; prof. English U. Mass., 1964-79, prof. emeritus, 1979—; dir. program for MFA in writing, 1964-70, 78-79; vis. lectr. U. B.C., U. Wash., Seattle, San Francisco State U.; guest reader, Republic of Madeconia, 1995. Author: poems For Harold, 1945, The Green Town, 1956, The Wheel of Summer, 1963, 2d edit., 1966, An Interview and Fourteen Poems, 1973, The Sacrifice Poems, 1975, Any Body's Song (Nat. Poetry Series), 1980, (poem with etchings) A Dream of Love, 1986, Twelve: Preludes & Postludes, 1988, Selected Poems, 1991, 2d edit., 1992; co-editor: poems Poet's Choice, 1962, 83, The Short Story, 1956; co-translator: poems Poetry From the Russian Underground, 1973. Served to capt., inf. AUS, 1942-46, ETO. Ford fellow in humanities Harvard-Columbia U. 1953-54; Amy Lowell Poetry fellow, 1955-56; Arts and Humanities fellow in poetry, 1966-67; recipient Melville Cane prize poetry Poetry Soc. Am., 1964; named Living Art Treasure in Lit., New Eng. Arts Biennial, 1985. Democrat. Home: 16 Morgan Cir Amherst MA 01002-1131

LANGLANDS, ROBERT PHELAN, mathematician; b. New Westminster, Can., Oct. 6, 1936; came to U.S., 1960; s. Robert and Kathleen (Phelan) L.; m. Charlotte Lorraine Cheverie, Aug. 13, 1956; children: William, Sarah, Robert, Thomasin. BA, U. B.C., 1957, MA, 1958, DS honoris causa, 1985; PhD, Yale U., 1960; DSc (hon.), McMaster U., 1985, CUNY, 1985; D in Math. (hon.), U. Waterloo, 1988; DSc (hon.), U. Paris, 1989, McGill U., 1991, Toronto U., 1993. From instr. to asso. prof. Princeton (N.J.) U., 1960-67; prof. math. Yale U., New Haven, 1968-72, Inst. Advanced Study, Princeton, 1972—. Author: Euler Products, 1971, (with H. Jacquet) Automorphic Forms on GL (2), 1970, On the Functional Equations Satisfied by Eisenstein Series, 1976, Base Change for GL (2), 1980, Les Débuts d'une Formule des Traces Stable, 1983. Recipient Wilbur Lucius Cross medal Yale U., 1975, Common Wealth award Sigma Xi, 1984, Mathematics award Nat. Acad. Sci., 1988, Wolf prize in math., 1995-96. Fellow Royal Soc. London, Royal Soc. Can.; mem. NAS, Am. Math Soc. (Cole prize 1982), Can. Math. Soc. Office: Inst Advanced Study Sch Math Olden Ln Princeton NJ 08540

LANGLEBEN, MANUEL PHILLIP, physics educator; b. Poland, Apr. 9, 1924; emigrated to Can., 1929, naturalized, 1935; s. David and Charna Molly (Shabason) L.; m. Rose Cohen, May 25, 1948; children—Adrian, David, Louise. B.Sc., McGill U., Can., 1949, M.Sc., 1950, Ph.D., 1953. Postdoctoral fellow Meterol. Office, Dunstable, Eng., 1953-54; research asso. McGill U., Montreal, Que., 1954—; asst. prof. physics McGill U., 1960-62, assoc. prof., 1962-68, prof., 1968-90, prof. emeritus, 1990—, dir. Centre for No. Studies and Rsch., 1977-80; mem. sub-com. snow and ice, asso. com. geotech. research Nat. Research Council Can., 1968-74; mem. working group on ice reconnaissance and glaciology Canadian Adv. Com. on Remote Sensing, 1971-75; mem. panel on ice, subcom. Arctic oceanography Canadian Com. on Oceanography, 1973-84; mem. adv. bd. Ea. Arctic Marine Environ. Studies, 1977-83; mem. Working Group on Arctic Regions and Atmospheric Interactions, Can. Global Change Program, Internat. Geosphere-Biosphere Programme, 1988—. Contbr. articles sci. jours. Served with Royal Can. Navy, 1941-45. Fellow Royal Soc. Can.; mem. Canadian Assn. Physicists, Royal Meteorol. Soc., Internat. Glaciological Soc., Am. Geophys. Union, Sigma Xi. Home: 4753 Grosvenor, Montreal, PQ Canada H3W 2L9

LANGLEY, GEORGE ROSS, medical educator; b. Sydney, N.S., Can., Oct. 6, 1931; s. John Goerge Elmer and Freda Catherine (Ross) L.; m. Jean Marie Ballantyne, June 22, 1957; children: Joanne Marie, Mark Ross, Richard Graham. B.A., Mt. Allison U., 1952; M.D., Dalhousie U., 1957. Intern Victoria Gen. Hosp., Halifax, N.S., 71957; resident Victoria Gen. Hosp., 1958, Toronto (Ont.) Gen. Hosp., 1960, U. Melbourne, Australia, 1961, U. Rochester, N.Y., 1962; John and Mary Markle scholar in acad. medicine Dalhousie U., Halifax, 1963-68; from lectr. to prof. medicine Dalhousie U., 1963-69, prof., chmn. dept. medicine, 1974-82; chief of service medicine Camp Hill Hosp., Halifax, 1969-74; head dept. medicine Victoria Gen. Hosp., 1974-82; chmn. clin. investigation grants com. Med. Research Council, 1976-78; chmn. clin. and epidemiol. research adv. com., bd. dirs. Nat. Cancer Inst. Can., 1978-86. Contbr. articles to sci. jours. Decorated Queen's Jubilee medal, 1977. Fellow Internat. Soc. Hematology, Royal Coll. Physicians and Surgeons (v.p., coun., Wightman vis. prof. 1990), ACP (bd. govs. 1973-78), Royal Coll. Physicians (Edinburgh); mem. Can. Hematology Soc. (pres. 1976-78), Can. Soc. Clin. Investigation, Am. Soc. Hematology, Can. Soc. Oncology, Alpha Omega Alpha. Mem. United Ch. Can. Home: 6025 Oakland Rd, Halifax, NS Canada B3H 1N9 Office: Victoria Gen Hosp, Ste 8-024, Halifax, NS Canada B3H 2Y9

LANGLEY, LYNNE SPENCER, newspaper editor, columnist; b. West Palm Beach, Fla., June 4, 1947; d. George Hosmer and Elwa June (Harries) Spencer; m. William A. Langley, Oct. 10, 1970. student, Glasgow U., Scotland, 1967-68; BA with honors, Coll. of Wooster, 1969. Feature writer, asst. women's editor Palm Beach Times, West Palm Beach, 1969-70; asst. editor Brunswick (Maine) Times Record, 1971; investigative reporter Maine Times, Topsham, 1971-75; asst. mng. editor York County Coast Star, Kennebunk, Maine, 1976-78; environ. and med. editor, nature columnist Charleston (S.C.) Post and Courier Newspapers, 1979—; editor Maine Audubon Soc. News, 1975-76; stringer Newsweek mag., 1971-75; speaker in field; freelance writer. Author: Nature Watch, 1987. Recipient Media award S.C. Assn. Mentally Retarded, 1985. Mem. Charleston Mus., S.C. chpt. Nature Conservancy. Recipient Media awards Charleston County Parks and Recreation Commn., 1985, Am. Diabetes Assn. S.C. chpt., 1989, Communicator of Yr. award S.C. Wildlife Fedn., 1983, Writing awards S.C. Press Assn., 1987. Mem. Am. Hort. Soc., Nat. Audubon Soc., Charleston Natural History Soc. (Media award 1985), Garden Writers Assn. Am., PEO (sec. chpt. D Maine 1975-76, corr. sec. chpt. J S.C. 1986-88), Sigma Delta Chi. Home: PO Box 97 Adams Run SC 29426-0097 Office: 134 Columbus St Charleston SC 29403-4800

LANGLEY, RICKY LEE, occupational medicine physician; b. Fountain, N.C., Aug. 31, 1957; s. Ernest Lee and Janie Ruth (Fulford) L.; m. Sandra Jane Ward, June 7, 1980; children: Patrick, Nicholas, Megan. BS magna cum laude, N.C. State U., 1979; MD, Bowman Grey Sch. Medicine, 1983; MPH, U. N.C., 1988. Diplomate Am. Bd. Internal Medicine, Am. Bd. Preventive Medicine. Intern East Carolina Sch. Medicine, Greenville, N.C., 1983-84, resident, 1984-86; asst. prof. dept. preventive medicine and health policy East Carolina U., Greenville, N.C., 1989-91, adj. asst. prof. dept. family medicine, 1989-91, adj. asst. prof. dept. environ. health, 1989—, asst. prof. dept. internal medicine, 1991; fellow Sch. Medicine Duke U., Durham, N.C., 1986-88, asst. cons. prof. in occupational medicine, 1989-90, asst. clin. prof. dept. community and family medicine, 1991—; pvt. practice occupational medicine Health and Hygiene, Inc., Greensboro, N.C., 1988-89; adj. asst. prof. Dept. of Biol. and Agrl. Engring. N.C. State U., 1995—; cons. in field; mem. planning com. on agrl. safety N.C. State Fair, 1991; mem. Task Force on Agri-Bus. for Gov.'s Commn. on Reduction of infant Mortality, 1992; mem. N.C. State Task Force on Blood-Borne Pathogens, N.C. Occupl. Health and Safety Adminstrn. 1991-92; presenter in field; mem. Nat. Park Producers Coun. Task Force on Worker Health and Safety, 1995; occupl. medicine residency program evaluator for NIOSH, 1992—. Guest editor N.C. Med. Jour., 1992, 93, 95; contbr. articles to profl. jours. Vol. Greenville Cmty. Shelter, 1990, Health Hotline, WITN, 1990, 91, State Employee Wellness Day 1989, Adopt-A-Hwy. Project, 1989; Doctor of the Day, N.C. State Legislature, 1991; doctor on call blood dr. ARC, Greensboro, 1989; vol. Freemont Peoples Clinic, 1993; pub. affairs officer Coast Guard Aux., 1996—, flotilla 18-11, 1995—; hunting safety educator, N.C., 1996—. Lloyd T. Weeks scholar, 1978, Benjamin Elloit Ibie and Benjamin Elliot Ibie Jr. Meml. scholar, 1976. Fellow ACP, Am. Coll. Occupl. and Environ. Medicine, Am. Coll. Preventive Medicine; mem. AMA, N.C. Med. Soc. (environ. health subcom. 1991—), Am. Occupl. Med. Assn. (mem. med. ctr. occupl. health com. 1990—), Carolinas Occupl. Med. Assn. (sec.-treas. 1991-92, pres-elect 1992-93, pres. 1993-94, del. 1995—), Am. Coll. Occupation and Environ. Medicine (del. 1995-96), Am. Biol., Safety Assn., Am. Conf. Govt. Indsl. Hygienists, Am. Indsl. Hygiene Assn., Tarheel Archaeology Soc. (program chair 1996), Sigma Xi, Phi Kappa Phi, Phi Eta Sigma, Gamma Sigma Delta, Alpha Epsilon Delta. Avocations: astronomy, archeology. Home: 1506 Miles Chapel Rd Mebane NC 27302-9008 Office: Duke U PO Box 2914 Durham NC 27715-2914

LANGLINAIS, JOSEPH WILLIS, educator, chaplain; b. San Antonio, Aug. 12, 1922; s. Joseph Willis and Marie Nellie (St. Julien) L. B.S. in Edn, U. Dayton, 1943; S.T.D., U. Fribourg, Switzerland, 1954. Joined Soc. Mary, 1940; ordained priest Roman Cath. Ch., 1952; tchr. high schs. in Mo., Ill. and Man., Can., 1943-48; dir. admissions Chaminade Coll. Prep. Sch., St. Louis, 1957-59; dir. Archdiocesan High Sch. Sodality Union St. Louis, 1958-59, Marianist Novitiate, Galesville, Wis., 1959-63; mem. faculty St. Mary's U., San Antonio, 1963—, dean Sch. Arts and Scis., 1964-75, acad. v.p., 1975-81, dir. instnl. self-study, 1970-72, 82-84, chmn. theology dept., 1981-83, dean Sch. Humanities and Social Scis., 1986, chaplain Sch. of Bus., 1988—, Univ. Prof., 1993—; pres. Cen. Cath. Marianist High Sch., San Antonio, 1987-91; dir. semester in Puebla, Mex. St. Mary's U., 1994; pres. Holy Rosary Sch. Bd., 1995—. Contbr.: Cath. Ency. Am., Encyclopedic Dictionary of Religion. Mem. AAUP, Cath. Theol. Soc. Am., Mariological Soc. Am., Archaeol. Soc. Am., Torch Internat., Rotary. Home: 1 Camino Santa Maria St San Antonio TX 78228-8518

LANG-MIERS, ELIZABETH ANN, lawyer; b. Mpls., Nov. 26, 1950. BA, U. Mo., 1972, JD, 1975. Bar: Mo. 1975, Tex. 1977, U.S. Ct. Appeals (5th cir.), U.S. Supreme Ct. Law clk. to presiding justice Mo. Supreme Ct., Jefferson City, 1975-76; ptnr. Locke, Purnell, Rain, Harrell, Dallas, 1976—. Mem. editorial bd. Mo. Law Review. Mem. Dallas County Med. Soc. Aux., bd. dirs. Met. YWCA; bd. dors., chairperson adv. bd. Women's Resource Ctr. Leadership Dallas, Leadership Tex., Leadership Am. Recipient Am. Jurisprudence awards 1973, 74. Mem. ABA, Tex. Bar Assn., Dallas Bar Assn. (chmn. media rels com. 1985, chair lawyer referral svc., v.p., sec.-treas., bd. dirs., exec. com 1987—, chmn. bd. dirs., vice-chair), Tex. Young lawyers Assn. (com. chair), Dallas Assn. Young Lawyers (com. chair), State Bar (com. chair). Office: Locke Purnell Rain Harrell 2200 Ross Ave Ste 2200 Dallas TX 75201-6766

LANGMUIR, CHARLES HERBERT, geology educator; b. Chalk River, Ont., Can., Nov. 24, 1950; came to U.S., 1954; s. David Bulkeley and Marianna (Lawrence) L.; m. Diane Marie Langmuir, Sept. 22, 1973; 1 child, Molly Kathryn. BA, Harvard U., 1973; MS, SUNY, Stony Brook, 1978, PhD, 1980. From asst. to assoc. prof. Lamont-Doherty Geol. Observatory Columbia U., Palisades, N.Y., 1981-88, prof., 1988—, Arthur D. Storke Meml. prof., 1989—; vis. scientist Inst. de Physique du Globe, Paris, 1989-90; mem. adv. com. on ocean scis. NSF, 1990-93; mem. lithosphere panel Joint Oceanographic Instns. for Deep Earth Sampling, 1984-87; chmn. Conf. on Sci. Ocean Drilling II, Work Group on Mantle-Crust Interactions, 1986-87; mem. steering com. Ridge Interdisciplinary Global Experiments, 1990-93; chmn. coord. com. Project French-Am.-Ridge Atlantic, 1989—; mem. steering com. Inter Ridge, 1992—. Editor: Earth and Planetary Sci. Letters, 1989—; mem. editorial bd. Chem. Geology, 1985—; contbr. over 40 articles to profl. jours. Alfred Sloan Rsch. fellow, 1983-85, Henry Shaw fellow Harvard U., 1974. Fellow Am. Geophys. Union (fellows com. 1995—); mem. Geol. Soc. Am. Office: 37 Iroquois Ave RFD 1 Box 86 Palisades NY 10964

LANGRAN, ROBERT WILLIAMS, political science educator; b. N.Y.C., Feb. 15, 1935; s. Robert Joseph and Leona Gertrude (Williams) L.; m. Eleanor Victoria Groh, Dec. 26, 1959; children—Irene, Elizabeth, Thomas. B.S. with honors, Loyola U., Chgo., 1956; M.A., Fordham U., 1959; Ph.D., Bryn Mawr Coll., 1965. Prof. polit. sci. Villanova U., Pa., 1959—. Author: (book) The United States Supreme Court: An Historical and Political Analysis, 1989, 2d edit. 1992, 3d edit. 1995; contbr. articles to profl. publs. Served to 1st lt. U.S. Army, 1956-58. Mem. Am. Polit. Sci. Assn., Supreme Ct. Hist. Soc. Office: Villanova Univ Political Sci Dept Villanova PA 19085

LANGRIDGE, ROBERT, scientist, educator; b. Essex, Eng., Oct. 26, 1933; came to U.S., 1957; naturalized, 1987; s. Charles and Winifred (Lister) L.; m. Ruth Gottlieb, June 26, 1960; children: Elizabeth, Catherine, Suzanne. B.Sc. in Physics (1st class honours), U. London, Eng., 1954, Ph.D. in Crystallography, 1957. Vis. research fellow biophysics Yale, 1957-59; research assoc. biophysics M.I.T., 1959-61; research assoc. pathology Children's Cancer Research Found., Boston; research assoc. biophysics, lectr. biophysics, also tutor biochem. scis. Harvard, 1961-66; research assoc. Project MAC, Lab. for Computer Sci., M.I.T., 1964-66; prof. biophysics and info. scis. U. Chgo., 1966-68; prof. chemistry and biochem. scis. Princeton, 1968-76; prof. pharm. chemistry, biochemistry and biophysics, dir. Computer Graphics Lab. U. Calif., San Francisco, 1976—; vis. prof. computer sci. Stanford U., 1983-84; mem. computer and biomath. rsch. study sect. NIH, USPHS, 1968-72, chmn., 1975-77, mem. nat. adv. rsch. resources coun., 1992—; mem. vis. com. biology dept. Brookhaven Nat. Lab., 1977-80, mem. adv. com. neutron diffraction, biology dept., 1980-83; mem. sci. and ednl. adv. com. Lawrence Berkeley Labs., 1988-92; chair U. Calif. Berkeley/U. Calif. San Francisco Grad. Group in Bioengring., 1991—; mem. computer sci. and tech. bd. NRC, NAS, 1988-91. Guggenheim fellow, 1983-84. Fellow AAAS; mem. Inst. Medicine of NAS, Am. Soc. Biol. Chemists, Am. Chem. Soc., Am. Cryst. Assn., Biophys. Soc. (editorial bd. 1970-73, council 1971-74), Assn. Computing Machinery. Office: U Calif 926 Med Sci San Francisco CA 94143-0446

LANGROCK, KARL FREDERICK, former academic administrator; b. Toeterville, Iowa, Jan. 26, 1927; s. Lee Henry and Alice Dora (Grube) L.; m. Rose Marie Meyer, June 4, 1950; children: Laura Sue, Charles Alan. BA, U. No. Iowa, 1949; MA, U. Iowa, 1951; MDiv, Luth. Sch. Theology, Chgo., 1955; LittD (hon.), Grand View Coll., 1989. Pastor Lake Park Luth. Ch., Milw., 1955-57, Resurrection Luth. Ch., Franklin Park, Ill., 1957-62, Luth. Ch. of the Holy Spirit, Deerfield, Ill., 1962-69; asst. to pres. Berea (Ky.) Coll., 1969-72; pres. Grand View Coll., Des Moines, 1972-88; free-lance writer, 1988—. Mem. Iowa Coll. Aid Commn., Des Moines, 1980-84, Luth. Social Services of Ill., Chgo., 1962-70, pres., 1968-70. Served in USN, 1945-46. Mem. Iowa Assn. Independent Colls. and Univs. (bd. dirs. 1972-87, chmn. 1986-87), Council of Luth. Ch. in Am. Colls. (pres. 1978), Phi Eta Sigma. Address: 2234 NE Douglas St Newport OR 97365-1837

LANGROCK, PETER FORBES, lawyer; b. N.Y.C., Feb. 2, 1938; s. Frank Langrock; m. Joann Murphy, July 4, 1960; children: Frank, Catherine, Eric. BA, U. Chgo., 1958, JD, 1960. Bar: Vt. 1964, U.S. Supreme Ct. 1966. State's atty. Addison County, Vt., 1960-65; sr. ptnr. Landrock Sperry Life & Wool, Middlebury, Vt., 1965—; commr. Nat. Conf. Commrs. on Uniform State Laws. Chmn. Vt. Breeders Stake Bd., 1984-90. Mem. ABA (chmn. individual rights and responsibilities sect. 1980-81, del. 1982-83, ho. of dels. 1984-96, bd. govs. 1993-96), Am. Law Inst. Avocations: horse breeding and raising, fishing, hunting. Home: Rd Lower Plains Rd Salisbury VT 05769 Office: 15 S Pleasant St PO Box 351 Middlebury VT 05753-0351

LANGSLEY, DONALD GENE, psychiatrist, medical board executive; b. Topeka, Oct. 5, 1925; s. Morris J. and Ruth (Pressman) L.; m. Pauline R. Langsley, Sept. 9, 1955; children: Karen Jean, Dorothy Ruth, Susan Louise. B.A., SUNY, Albany, 1949; M.D., U. Rochester, 1953. Diplomate: Am. Bd. Psychiatry and Neurology (dir. 1976-80), Nat. Bd. Med. Examiners. Intern USPHS Hosp., San Francisco, 1953-54; resident psychiatry U. Calif., San Francisco, 1954-59; NIMH career tchr. in psychiatry U. Calif., 1959-61; candidate San Francisco and Chgo. insts. for psychoanalysis, 1958-67; asst. prof., assoc. prof. psychiatry U. Colo. Sch. Medicine, 1961-68; prof., chmn. dept. psychiatry U. Calif., Davis, 1968-77, U. Cin., 1977-81; prof. dept. psychiatry Northwestern U. Sch. Medicine, Chgo., 1981—; mem. psychiatry edn. com. NIMH, 1969-75; exec. v.p. Am. Bd. Med. Spltys., 1981-91; trustee Ednl. Commn. for Fgn. Med. Graduates, 1983-91; mem. adv. com. on Grad. Med. Edn. Dept. Def., 1986-87; bd. govs. EcuMed, 1983-85; bd. dirs. Nat. Resident Matching Program, 1982, sec. 1984-87, 89-91, pres. 1987-89. Author: The Treatment of Families in Crisis, 1968, Mental Health Education in the New Medical Schools, 1973, Peer Review Manual for Psychiatry, 1976, Handbook of Community Mental Health, 1981, Evaluating the Skills of Medical Specialists, 1983, Legal Aspects of Certification & Accreditation, 1983, Trends in Specialization, 1985, Hospital Privileges & Specialty Medicine, 1986, 2d edit., 1991, How To Evaluate Residents, 1986, How to Select Residents, 1988, Health Policy Issues in Graduate Medicine Education, 1992; contbr. articles to med. jours. Served with AUS, 1943-46; med. officer USPHS, 1953-54. Recipient Spl. awards Colo. Assn. for Mental Health, 1968, Spl. awards Sacramento Area Mental Health Assn., 1973. Fellow Am. Psychiat. Assn. (Hofheimer award 1971, pres. 1980-81, chmn. peer rev. com. 1975-77, Kiewit lectr. 1990, Adminstrv. Psychiatry award 1993), Am. Coll. Psychiatrists; mem. Ctrl. Calif. Psychiat. Soc. (pres. 1973-74), Colo. Psychiat. Soc. (pres.-elect 1967-68), Soc. Med. Adminstrs. Home and Office: 9445 Monticello Ave Evanston IL 60203-1117

LANGSTAFF, DAVID HAMILTON, commercial industry executive; b. Paris, June 12, 1954; s. E. Kennedy and Percy (Lee) L.; m. Cynthia Shauer, Aug. 26, 1978; children: Meredith Avery, Christopher Maxim. BA cum laude, Harvard U., 1977, MBA, 1981. Assoc. First Boston Internat., Athens, Greece, 1977-78, Blyth Eastman Dillon & Co., Athens, 1978-79; prin. Langstaff Design & Mgmt., Cambridge, Mass., 1980-81; assoc. Inverness Group, Houston, 1981-82, v.p. corp. fin., 1982-83, v.p. corp. fin., mgr. mergers and acquisitions, 1983-84; sr. v.p., chief exec. officer, sec., treas. Space Industries Inc., Houston, 1984—; now pres. Space Industries, Houston. Founder, mem. bd. advisors Harvard U. Ensemble, Boston; bd. dirs. Boston Premiere Ensemble, 1981—, Houston Symphony Orch., 1987—; mem. exec. com. Houston Grand Opera, 1986-87. Democrat. Avocations: music, athletics, squash, skiing, counseling. Office: Space Industries Inc 800 Connecticut NW Ste 1111 Washington DC 20006*

LANGSTAFF, GARY LEE, food service marketing executive; b. Cherry Point, N.C., Aug. 21, 1948; s. Harold A. and Ruth (Means) L.; m. Claudia Gramps, Jan. 8, 1977; children: Danielle, Brett Allyn. BA in History, Polit. Sci., U. Calif., Santa Barbara, 1970; BS in Internat. mgmt., Thunderbird Grad. Sch. Bus., 1971, M in Internat. Mgmt., 1972. Account exec. Benton & Bowles, N.Y.C., 1972-77, v.p. account supr., 1977-79; sr. v.p., mgmt. supr. Benton & Bowles, N.Y.C. and Chgo., 1979-81; pres. Envision Systems, Inc., Westport, Conn., 1981-85; exec. v.p. Triparte Corp., Fresno, Calif., 1983-85; also bd. dirs. Triparte Corp., Fresno; gen. mgr. Wieden & Kennedy, Inc., Los Angeles, 1985; sr. v.p. mktg. Hardee's Food Systems, Rocky Mount, N.C., 1985-86, exec. v.p. mktg., 1986-89; exec. v.p. mktg. Burger King Corp., Miami, Fla., 1989-91; prin. Retail Resolve, Inc., Steamboat Springs, Colo., 1991—. Bd. Dirs. Rocky Mount Acad., 1987-88. Republican. Office:

Retail Resolve Inc 29950 Emerald Meadows Ln Steamboat Springs CO 80487

LANGSTAFF, GEORGE QUIGLEY, JR., retired footwear company executive; b. Paducah, Ky., July 28, 1925; s. George Quigley and Katherine Elizabeth (Irion) L.; m. Maureen Black, Dec. 27, 1946; children: Patricia (Mrs. Charles Poole), Lynne (Mrs. Steve Frederick), Katherine (Mrs. George Stockman). B.A., U. of South, 1948; grad., Advanced Mgmt. Program, Harvard U., 1978. Mfg. mgr. Genesco, Inc., Nashville, 1948-59; mktg. mgr. Genesco, Inc., 1959-70, group pres., 1970-73, v.p., chief operating officer, 1974-78, exec. v.p., 1978-80; pres., chief exec. officer Footwear Industries Am., Inc., Phila., 1981-85. Pres. Nashville Mental Health Assn., 1970, Episcopal Churchmen of Tenn., 1966; trustee, alumni v.p. U. of the South; mem. Rep. State Exec. Com., 1952-53; bd. dirs. United Fund, Jr. Achievement; vestry St. George's Episcopal Ch., sr. warden, 1966, 89, 90. With USNR, 1943-46. Home: 6001 Andover Dr Nashville TN 37215-5731

LANGSTAFF, JOHN MEREDITH, musician; b. Bklyn., Dec. 24, 1920; s. Bridgewater Meredith and Esther Knox (Boardman) L.; m. Diane Guggenheim; 1 child, Carol; m. Nancy Graydon Woodbridge, Apr. 3, 1948; children—John Elliot, Peter Gerry, Deborah Graydon. Student, Curtis Inst. Music, Juilliard Sch. Music, Columbia U. Author (books) Frog Went a-Courtin', 1955 (Caldecott prize 1955), Over in the Meadow, 1957, On Christmas Day in the Morning, 1959, The Swapping Boy, 1960, Ol' Dan Tucker, 1963, Hi! Ho! The Rattlin' Bog, 1969, Jim Along, Josie, 1970, Gather My Gold Together, 1971, The Golden Vanity, 1971, Soldier, Soldier, Won't You Marry Me?, 1972, The Two Magicians, 1973, Shimmy, Shimmy Coke-a-pop!, 1973, St. George and the Dragon, 1973, A-Hunting We will Go, 1974, A Season for Singing, 1974, Sweetly Sings the Donkey, 1976, Hot Cross Buns, 1978, The Christmas Revels Songbook, 1985, Sally Go Round The Moon, 1986, What A Morning!, 1987, Climbing Jacob's Ladder, 1991, I Have A Song To Sing-O, 1994, A Revels Garland of Song, 1996; recitals, U.S., Can., Eng., Iceland, Europe, rec. for, Odeon-Capital, Jupiter, RCA-Victor, Nixa, Renaissance, Tradition, HMV, Desto, Weston Woods, Revels Records, Minstrel Records; soloist with, Cantata Singers, N.Y. Philharmonic, Nat. Symphony, Montreal Symphony Orch., Little Orch. Soc., N.Y. Oratorio Soc., Collegium Musicum, Stratford Shakespeare Festival, Eng., Mpls. Symphony Orch., radio, TV in U.S., Europe, Can., BBC, Eng.; dir. music dept., Potomac Sch., Washington, 1953-68, Shady Hill Sch., Cambridge, Mass., 1969-72, faculty, Simmons Coll., Boston, 1970-86 , Wheelock Coll., Boston, 1974-79, Mass. Coll. Art, 1977, Boston Coll., 1979, U. Conn., 1977-79, Lesley Coll., 1978—, artistic dir., Young Audiences Mass., 1972-81, adv. bd., 1981—, artist-lectr., Assn. Am. Colls. Served as 1st lt., inf. AUS, World War II. Recipient Hope S. Dean Meml. award Found. for Children's Books, 1991. Mem. Actors Equity, Country Dance and Song Soc. Am., Internat. Folk Music Council, English Folk Song Soc. (founder and dir. Christmas Revels 1956, 57, 66, 70—, Spring Revels 1972—, Sea Revels 1983—). Office: Revels Inc One Kendall Sq Bldg 600 Cambridge MA 02139

LANGSTON, MARK EDWARD, professional baseball player; b. San Diego, Aug. 20, 1960; m. Michelle Langston; 1 child, Katie. Student, San Jose State U. Baseball player Seattle Mariners, 1981-89, Montreal Expos, 1989—, California Angels, 1989—. Named AL Rookie Pitcher of Yr. 1984 by the Sporting News, Am. League All-Star Team, 1987, 91-93; recipient AL Gold Glove, 1987-88, 1991-94. Office: care Calif Angels Anaheim Stadium 200 State College Blvd Anaheim CA 92806

LANGSTON, NANCY SUE FRIEDRICH, nursing educator, college dean; b. Little Rock, Dec. 14, 1944. BSN cum laude, U. Ark., 1966; M in Surg. Nursing, Emory U., 1972; PhD in Edn., Ga. State U., 1977. RN, Va. Staff RN U. Ark. Med. Ctr., Little Rock, 1966-67, Doctor's Hosp., Shreveport, La., 1967; instr. Confederate Meml. Med. Ctr. Sch. Nursing, Shreveport, La., 1967-70, Northwestern State U. Sch. Nursing, Shreveport, La., 1970-71, Emory U. Sch. Nursing, Atlanta, 1972-73; adminstrv. intern U. Tex. Sys. Sch. Nursing, Austin, 1974-75, rsch. assoc., 1975-76; assoc. prof., assoc. dean undergrad. programs U. Nebr. Med. Coll. Nursing, Lincoln, 1976-85; prof., dean U. N.C. at Charlotte Coll. Nursing, 1985-91, Med. Coll. of Va. of Va. Commonwealth U. Sch. Nursing, Richmond, 1991—; nurse-cons. Goodwill Industries of Atlanta, Inc., 1973-74; adj. assoc. prof. U. Nebr. at Lincoln Tchrs. Coll., 1983-85. Contbr. articles to profl. jours., chpts. to books; presenter in field. Mem. bd. Fan Free Clinic, strategic planning com., 1994, med. svcs. com, 1994—, chmn. 1995; mem. Richmond Rotary, med. svcs. com. 1993—, chmn. 1994; mem. adv. bd. Here's To Your Health; bd. dirs. Hospice of Charlotte, 1988-91, chair profl. adv. com., 1989-91; mem. Civitan Charlotte, 1989-91, at-large 1991—; bd. dirs. Lincoln Lancaster Commn. on Status of Women, 1983-85, edn. com. 1981-85; bd. dirs. Southeast Nebr. Health Systems Agy., 1981-82; pub. issues com. Nebr. Cancer Soc., 1978-80; adv. bd. geriat. Atlanta Regional Commn., 1973; chair nursing sect., Shreveport chpt. ARC, 1969-71. Recipient award of honor Alumni Assn. Nell Hodgson Woodruff Sch. Nursing, Emory U., 1989; Am. Nurses' Found. scholar 1972, Rockefeller scholar 1962-64. Mem. ANA, Nat. League for Nursing, So. Nursing Rsch. Coun., Phi Kappa Phi, Phi Theta Kappa, Sigma Theta Tau.

LANGSTON, PAUL T., music educator, university dean, composer; b. Marianna, Fla., Sept. 15, 1928; s. Howard McGhee and Rosa (Jeffries) L.; m. Esther Howard, Aug. 12, 1950; children: Claire Beth, Erin, Howard. Pvt. study with, Nadia Boulanger, 1962, 63; diploma, Conservatoire Americaine, France; BA, U. Fla., 1950; MS in Music, So. Bapt. Theol. Sem., 1953; SMD, Union Theol. Sem., 1963; DMus (hon.), Stetson U., 1985. Organist-choirmaster St. John's Bapt. Ch., Charlotte, N.C., 1953-60; instr. music theory Davidson Coll., 1959-60; mem. faculty Stetson U., De Land, Fla., 1960-93; dean Sch. Music, Stetson U., 1985-93, William Kenan Jr. prof. music, 1986-93, prof. and dean music emeritus, 1993—; asso. condr. Charlotte Oratorio Singers, 1954-60; dir. Fla. Internat. Music Festival, Fla. Internat. Music Festival Inst.; research fellow Inst. Sacred Music, Yale U., 1985. Composer organ, choral works.; oratorio Petros (premier Nov. 1983). Recipient Hand award for outstanding rsch., 1993. Mem. Am. Guild Organists, Hymn Soc., Coll. Music Soc., Music Tchrs. Nat. Assn., Nat. Assn. Schs. of Music (undergrad. commn., McEniry award teaching excellence), Assn. Anglican Musicians, Soc. Composers, Omicron Delta Kappa, Pi Kappa Lambda, Delta Tau Delta. Home: 313 N Salisbury Ave Deland FL 32720-4054

LANGSTON, ROY A., insurance company consultant; b. Dallas, Feb. 13, 1912; s. Lamar Q. and Gertrude (McDaniel) L.; m. Edna Earle Scott, 1936; 1 dau., Peggy Langston Schieffer. With Trinity Universal Ins. Co., 1929-33; with Traders & Gen. Ins. Co., 1933-73, dir., 1949-73, exec. v.p., 1953-56, pres., chief exec. officer, 1956-73; founder Traders Indemnity Co., 1962; past pres. Tex. Assn. Fire & Casualty Cos. Mem. Mason (32 degree, Shriner), Oak Cliff Shrine Club (pres.). Methodist. Home: 2032 W Five Mile Pky Dallas TX 75224-3608

LANGTON, BRYAN D., hotel executive. Chmn. Holiday Inns, Inc. Office: Holiday Inn Worldwide 3 Ravinia Dr Ste 2000 Atlanta GA 30346-2118

LANGTON, CLEVE SWANSON, advertising executive; b. N.Y.C., Sept. 1, 1950; s. Raymond Benedict and Viola (Swanson) L.; m. Patricia Scott, July 16, 1976; children: Elizabeth Renwick, Cleve, Jr. B.A., NYU, 1972; M.B.A., Columbia U., 1974. Product mgr. Gen. Foods Corp., White Plains, N.Y., 1974-76; sr. account exec. Dancer Fitzgerald Sample, N.Y.C., 1976-79; v.p., account supr. D'Arcy MacManus Masius, N.Y.C., 1979-83, corp. v.p. bus. devel. worldwide, DMB&B, N.Y.C., 1983-89; corp. sr. v.p. DDB Needham Worldwide, 1990-92; corp. exec. v.p. multinat. nat. client devel., 1993—. Bd. dirs. Columbia U. Grad. Sch. Bus., St. Bartholomew Sch. Club: Metropolitan (N.Y.C.). Office: DDB Needham Worldwide Inc 437 Madison Ave New York NY 10022-7001

LANGTON, RAYMOND BENEDICT, III, manufacturing company executive; b. N.Y.C., Oct. 26, 1944; s. Raymond B. II and Viola M. (Swanson) L.; m. Regina M. Rose, July 20, 1968; children: Raymond B. IV, Tyler J. BA in History, U. Va., 1966; MBA, U. Pa., 1971. Dir. sales and mktg. Continental Forest Industries (Continental Group), Greenwich, Conn., 1974-78, dir. planning and devel., 1978-79; v.p. mktg. bus. devel. Fram (Allied Signal), Providence, 1979-81, v.p., gen. mgr. div. indsl. filtration, 1981-83, v.p. ops., 1983-86; pres. SKF Automotive Products, King of Prussia, Pa., 1986-87, SKF Bearing Industries Co., King of Prussia, 1987-91; pres., chief exec. officer SKF USA Inc., King of Prussia, 1991—, also bd. dirs.; mem. regional adv. bd. First Fidelity Bank; bd. dirs. Right Mgmt. Cons., Inc. Mem. Antifriction Bearing Mfrs. Assn. (treas. 1990, vice chmn., chmn. 1993). Office: SKF USA Inc 1100 1st Ave King Of Prussia PA 19406

LANGWIG, JOHN EDWARD, retired wood science educator; b. Albany, N.Y., Mar. 5, 1924; s. Frank Irving and Arlene Stone (Dugan) L.; m. Margaret Jacquelyn Kirk, Aug. 31, 1946; 1 dau., Nancy Ann Langwig Davis. B.S., U. Mich., 1948; M.S., Coll. of Forestry, SUNY, Syracuse, 1968, Ph.D., 1971. Asst. to supt. Widdicomb Furniture Co., Grand Rapids, Mich., 1948-50; salesman John B. Hauf Furniture, Inc., Albany, N.Y., 1950-51; asst. mgr. furniture dept. Montgomery Ward Co., Menands, N.Y., 1951-52; office mgr. U.S. Plywood Corp., Syracuse, 1952-65; instr. wood products engring. SUNY Coll. Forestry, Syracuse, 1969-70; asst. prof. wood sci. Okla. State U., Stillwater, 1971-74; prof., head dept. forestry Okla. State U., 1974-81, prof. wood sci., wood products extension specialist, 1982-86, mem. faculty council, 1983-86; mem. Gov.'s Com. on Forest Practices, 1975-77. Contbr. articles to profl. jours. Served with AUS, 1943-45. NSF fellow, 1966-68. Mem. Soc. Am. Foresters, TAPPI, Forest Products Research Soc. (regional bd. dirs. 1983-89, regional rep. to nat. exec. bd. 1983-86), Soc. Wood Sci. and Tech., Okla. Acad. Sci., Okla. Forestry Assn. (bd. dirs. 1982-83), Council Forestry Sch. Execs., Sigma Xi, Xi Sigma Pi., Gamma Sigma Delta, Alpha Zeta, Phi Kappa Phi. Episcopalian. Home: 33 Liberty Cir Stillwater OK 74075-2015 Office: Okla State U Dept Forestry Stillwater OK 74078 *My graduate education began after a seventeen year career in the forest products industry. This additional education broadened my life, and opened up a rich new world of experience beyond my greatest expectations. I commend to all young people the pursuit of a maximum education, as one of life's most worthy efforts.*

LANGWORTHY, AUDREY HANSEN, state legislator; b. Grand Forks, N.D., Apr. 1, 1938; d. Edward H. and Arla (Kuhlman) Hansen; m. Asher C. Langworthy Jr., Sept. 8, 1962; children: Kristin H., Julia H. BS, U. Kans., 1960, MS, 1962; postgrad., Harvard U., 1989. Tchr. jr. high sch. Shawnee Mission Sch. Dist., Johnson County, Kans., 1963-65; councilperson City of Prairie Village, Kans., 1981-85; mem. Kans. State Senate, 1985—; alt. del. Nat. Conf. State Legislatures, 1985-87, del., 1987—, nominating com., 1990-92, vice chair fed. budget and taxation com., 1994, chair fed. budget and taxation com., 1995-96; del. Midwestern Conf. State Legislatures, 1989. City co-chmn. Kassebaum for U.S. Senate, Prairie Village, 1978; pres. Jr. League Kansas City, Mo., 1977, Kansas City Eye Bank, 1980-82, chmn., 1983-85, bd. mem., 1977—; mem. bd. Greater Kansas City ARC, 1975—, pres., 1984, chmn. midwestern adv. coun., 1985-86, nat. bd. govs., 1987-93; mem. Johnson County C.C. Found., 1989—; mem. Leadership Kans., Germany Today Program, 1991; bd. dirs. Kans. Wildlife & Parks Fund; trustee Found. on Aging, 1992—; mem. nat. adv. panel Child Care Action Campaign, 1988—; mem. adv. com. Coro Found., 1989—; mem. adv. bd. Kans. Alliance for Mentally Ill., 1994—; hon. chair Fund Raiser for Health Partnership of Johnson County, 1995. Recipient Outstanding Vol. award Cmty. Svcs. Award Found., 1983, Confidence in Edn. award Friends of Edn., 1984, Pub. Svc. award as Kans. Legislator of Yr., Hallmark Polit. Action Com., 1991, Clara Barton Honor award Greater Kans. City ARC, Intergovtl. Leadership award League Kans. Mcpls., 1994, Disting. Pub. Svc. award United Cmty. Svcs. of Johnson County, 1995, Outstanding Achievement in Hist. Preservation award Alexander Majors Hist. House, 1995, Kansas City Spirit award, 1996. Mem. LWV, Women's Pub. Svc. Network, U. Kans. Alumni Assn. Episcopalian. Avocations: hunting, running, family. Home: 6324 Ash St Prairie Village KS 66208-1369

LANGWORTHY, EVERETT WALTER, association executive, natural gas exploration company executive; b. West Springfield, Mass., Aug. 17, 1918; s. Walter Carr and Lucy Anne (Laurent) L.; m. Mary Jane Mateer, Nov. 30, 1946 (dec. Oct. 1966); children: John Alan, Jo Ann Langworthy Sears, Robert Carr; m. Joan E. Scott, Feb. 27, 1982; stepchildren: Russell, Michael, Gregory. B.A., U. Mass., 1940; M.A., George Washington U., 1964; grad., Nat. War Coll., 1964. Commd. 2d lt. U.S. Army, 1943; commd. capt. U.S. Air Force, 1947; advanced through grades to col., 1963, ret., 1972; v.p. ops. Meteor Aero Inc., Gaithersburg, Md., 1972-76; sec. contest and record bd. Nat. Aero. Assn., Washington, 1976-80; exec. v.p. Nat. Aero. Assn., 1980—; v.p. LABCO Inc., Martinsburg, W.Va., 1974—; gen. ptnr. M&E Assocs., Gaithersburg, 1976—; dir. Acad. Model Aeronautics, Reston, Va.; cons. FBI, 1992—; cons. FBI. Contbr. articles and columns on aerospace activities to profl. publs. U.S. rep. Fedn. Aeronautique Internat., Paris, 1980—. Decorated DFC, Air medal African Campaign award, Berlin Air Life medal; recipient Paul Tissandier diploma Fedn. Aeronautique Internationale, 1987. Mem. Nat. Aviation Club (elder statesman aviation 1990), Aero Club Washington, Air Force Assn., Ret. Officers Assn., Soaring Soc. Am. (bd. dirs. 1980—), U.S. Hang Gliding Assn. (bd. dirs. 1980—), VFW. Republican. Club: Lakewood Country (Rockville, Md.). Avocations: golf; writing. Home: 13701 Charity Ct Germantown MD 20874-2965 Office: Nat Aeronautic Assn 1815 Ft Myer Dr Arlington VA 22209-1805

LANGWORTHY, ROBERT BURTON, lawyer; b. Kansas City, Mo., Dec. 24, 1918; s. Herman Moore and Minnie (Leach) L.; m. Elizabeth Ann Miles, Jan. 2, 1942; children: David Robert, Joan Elizabeth Langworthy Tomek, Mark Burton. AB, Princeton U., 1940; JD, Harvard U., 1943. Bar: Mo. 1943, U.S. Supreme Ct 1960. Practiced in Kansas City, 1943—; assoc., then mem. and v.p. Linde, Thomson, Langworthy, Kohn & Van Dyke, P.C., 1943-91; pres., mng. shareholder Blackwood & Langworthy, P.C., Kansas City, Mo., 1991—; mng. mem. Blackwood & Langworthy, LC, Kansas City, Mo., 1996—; lectr. on probate, law sch. CLE courses U. Mo., Kansas City. Mem. bd. editors Harvard Law Rev., 1941-43; contbr. chpts. to Guardian Desk Book of Mo. Bar. Mem. edn. appeal bd. U.S. Dept. Edn., 1982-86; chmn. Housing Authority Kansas City, 1963-71, chmn., 1969-71; chmn. commr. Housing Authority Kansas City, 1963-71, ... Bd. Election Commrs. Kansas City, 1973-77; chmn. bd. West Ctrl. area YMCA, 1969—; mem. bd. Mid-Am. region YMCA, 1970-83, vice chmn., 1970-73, chmn., 1973-78; pres. Met. Bd. Kansas City (Mo.) YMCA (now YMCA of Greater Kansas City), 1965, bd. dirs., 1965—, mem. nat. bd. 1971-78, 79-83; bd. dirs. YMCA of the Rockies, 1974—, bd. sec., 1994—; chmn. bd. trustees Sioux Indian YMCAs, 1983—; bd. dirs. Armed Svcs. YMCA, 1984-85; pres. Met. Area Citizens Edn., 1969-72; chmn. Citizens Assn. Kansas City (Mo.), 1967, bd. dirs., 1959—; bd. dirs. Project Equality Kans.-Mo., 1967-80, pres., 1970-72, treas., 1972-73, sec., 1973-76; 1st v.p. Human Resources Corp. Kansas City, 1969-71, 72-73, bd. dirs., 1965-73; hon. v.p. Am. Sunday Sch. Union (now Am. Missionary Fellowship), 1965—; vice chmn. bd. trustees Kemper Mil. Sch., 1966-73; U.S. del. YMCA World Coun., Buenos Aires, 1977, Estes Park, Colo., 1981, Nyborg, Denmark, 1985; bd. dirs. Mo. Rep. Club, 1960—; del., mem. platform com. Rep. Nat. Conv., 1960; Rep. nominee for U.S. Congress, 1964; mem. gen. assembly Com. on Representation Presbyn., 1991—, moderator, 1993-94; commr. to gen. assembly Presbyn. Ch., 1984; moderator Heartland Presbyn., 1984. Lt. (j.g.) USNR, 1943-46; now capt. Res. ret. Mem. ABA, Kansas City Bar Assn. (chmn. probate law com. 1988-90, living will com. 1989-91), Mo. State Bar (chmn. probate and trust com. 1983-85, chmn. sr. lawyers com. 1991-93), Lawyers Assn. Kansas City, Harvard Law Sch. Assn. Mo. (v.p. 1973-74, pres. 1974-75, 85-87), Univ. Club (Kansas City), Leawood (Kans.) Country Club. Presbyterian (elder). Home: 616 W 69th St Kansas City MO 64113-1937 Office: 1220 Washington St Ste 300 Kansas City MO 64105-2245

LANGWORTHY, WILLIAM CLAYTON, college official; b. Watertown, N.Y., Sept. 3, 1936; s. Harold Greene and Carolyn (Peach) L.; m. Margaret Joan Amos, Sept. 6, 1958; children: Kenneth, Geneva. B.S. magna cum laude, Tufts U., 1958; Ph.D., U. Calif.-Berkeley, 1962. Asst. prof. Alaska Meth. U., Anchorage, 1962-65; asst. prof. chemistry Calif. State U.-Fullerton, 1965-67, assoc. prof., 1967-72, prof., 1972-73, assoc. dean Sch. Letters Arts and Scis., 1970-73; prof. chemistry Calif. Poly. State U., San Luis Obispo, 1973-76, head dept. chemistry, 1973-76; dean Sch. Sci. and Math Calif. Poly State U., San Luis Obispo, 1976-83; v.p. acad. affairs Ft. Lewis Coll., Durango, Colo., 1983-95, prof., 1995—. Author: monograph Environmental Education, 1971; contbr. articles to profl. jours. Treas. Coun. Concerned Citizens, Inc., Arroyo Grande, Calif., 1976-83; mem. Clean Air Coalition, San Luis Obispo, 1978-83; active Mozart Festival, 1981-82; b. dirs. Durango Choral Soc., 1984-93, Durango Stage Co., 1990-96, San Juan Symphony, 1995—, also pres., 1992-94. Mem. AAAS, AAHE, Am. Chem. Soc., Coun. Colls. Arts and Scis. (bd. dirs. 1982), Sierra Club, Phi Beta Kappa, Sigma Xi, Kappa Mu Epsilon, Phi Kappa Phi.

LANHAM, BETTY BAILEY, anthropologist, educator; b. Statesville, N.C., Aug. 12, 1922; d. Clyde B. and Naomi (Bailey) L. B.S., U. Va., 1944, M.A., 1947; Ph.D., Syracuse U., 1962. Mem. faculty River Falls State Tchrs. Coll., 1948-49, U. Md., 1949-50, Wakayama U., Japan, 1951-52, Randolph Macon Women's Coll., 1954-55, Oswego State Tchrs. Coll., 1956-58, Hamilton Coll., 1961-62, Ind. U., 1962-65, Western Mich. U., 1965-67, Albany Med. Coll., 1967-70, U.Guyana, 1969-70; prof. anthropology Indiana U. of Pa., 1970-88, prof. emeritus, 1988—. Contbr. articles to jours. Wenner-Gren Found. for Anthrop. Rsch. predoctoral fellow, 1951-52, AAUW predoctoral rsch. fellow, 1959-60. Mem. Am. Anthrop. Assn., Assn. Asian Studies, Soc. for Psychol. Anthropology, Caribbean Studies Assn. Democrat. Home: 2529 Willard Dr Charlottesville VA 22903-4225

LANHAM, URLESS NORTON, curator; b. Grainfield, Kans., Oct. 17, 1918; s. Urless R. and Frankie V. (Norton) L.; m. Caroline Jane Combs, Sept. 1, 1945; children: Robert, Margaret, Carl. B.A. cum laude, U. Colo., 1940; Ph.D., U. Calif., Berkeley, 1948; postgrad., UCLA, La Jolla, 1942-44, U. Chgo., 1945-46. Asst. prof., research asso. U. Mich., Ann Arbor, 1948-62; asso. prof. Monteith Coll., Wayne State U., 1959-62; vis. curator, asso. curator entomology U. Colo. Mus., Boulder, 1962-73, curator, 1973-89, prof. natural history, 1973-89, prof. emeritus, 89—, mem. Tunisian expdn., 1976; asst. prof. biophysics U. Colo. Med. Center, Denver, 1968-71; vis. lectr. Arctic-Alpine Inst., Dept. Devel. Biology, 1966-67; vis. investigator Carnegie Mus. Pitts., 1982; editor biol. sci. curriculum studies Am. Inst. Biol. Scis., 1963-66; cons. Smithsonian Instn., Washington, 1967. Author: The Fishes, 1962, The Insects, 1964, Origins of Modern Biology, 1968, German transl., 1972; The Bone Hunters, 1973, 91, The Enchanted Mesa, 1974, The Sapphire Planet, 1978, transl. into Arabic and Spanish; also tech. papers; adv. editor, Columbia U. Press, 1964-72. Served to capt. USAAF, 1942-46, PTO. Mem. Phi Beta Kappa, Sigma Xi. Home: 2670 Stephens Rd Boulder CO 80303-5762 Office: U Colo Museum Campus Box 218 Boulder CO 80309

LANIAK, DAVID KONSTANTYN, telecommunications company executive; b. Rochester, N.Y., Sept. 10, 1935; s. Konstantyn and Anastasia (Andrieve) L.; m. Carol Hammond, Sept. 19, 1959; children: Mark, Todd. BEE, Rochester Inst. Tech., 1958; MBA, U. Rochester, 1985. Elec. engr. Rochester Gas and Electric Corp., 1959-75, supt. meter dept., 1975-78, div. supt., 1978-80, v.p. electric system planning, operation, 1980-82, v.p. corp. planning, 1982-87, sr. v.p. gas, electric distbn., corp. planning, 1988-90, sr. v.p. gas, electric distbn., customer svcs., 1990-94; exec. v.p., COO, 1994-95; CEO ACC Corp., Rochester, 1995—, also bd. dirs.; bd. dirs. Telog Instruments, Inc. Mem. IEEE, Rochester Engring. Soc. Republican. Avocations: tennis, golf, fishing. Home: 10 Harvest Ln Rush NY 14543-9764 Office: ACC Corp 400 West Ave Rochester NY 14611

LANIER, ANITA SUZANNE, musician, piano educator; b. Talladega, Ala., May 21, 1946; d. Luther Dwight and Elva (Hornsby) L. BS in Music Edn., Jacksonville (Ala.) State U., 1969. Elem. music tchr. Talladega City Schs., 1969-81; librarian, elem. music tchr. Talladega Acad., 1981-84; tchr. piano and organ Talladega, 1981—. Organist Trinity United Meth. Ch., Talladega, 1981—. Recipient Commemorative Honor medallion, 1990, World Decoration of Excellence medallion, 1990; named Woman of the Yr., 1990, Rsch. Adv. of Yr., 1990, ABI, 1990. Mem. NAFE, AAUW, Am. Pianists Assn., Pilot Club (sec. 1977-78), World Inst. Achievement, Women's Inner Circle Achievement, Internat. Platform Assn., Delta Omicron. Home: 601 North St E Talladega AL 35160-2525

LANIER, BOB, former professional sports team executive, former basketball player; b. Buffalo, Sept. 10, 1948. Student, St. Bonaventure U., 1966-70. Basketball player Detroit Pistons, 1970-79, Milw. Bucks, 1980-84; actor various commls., 1984—; asst. basketball coach Golden State Warriors, 1994—; now owner Bob Lanier Enterprises, Milw. Mem. NBA All-Star Team, 1972-79, 82; named Most Valuable Player NBA All-Star Team, 1974. Office: Bob Lanier Enterprises 8316 North Steven Rd Milwaukee WI 53223*

LANIER, JAMES ALFRED, III, aquarium administrator; b. Norfolk, Va., Sept. 28, 1941; s. James Alfred and Mary Elizabeth (Baughan) L.; m. Hope Baldwin, Aug. 1, 1964; children: Hope Baldwin (Holly), David Ludwell, Andrew Lee. BA, U. Va., 1963; MA, William and Mary Coll., 1972, PhD, 1981. Commd. lt. USNR, 1963, advanced through grades to comdr. and served, to 1983; edn. program dir. Va. Inst. Marine Sci., Gloucester Pt., Va., 1971-80; dir. ednl. programs N.J. Marine Sci. Consortium, Princeton, N.J., 1980-82; dir. N.C. Aquarium Ft. Fisher, Kure Beach, N.C., 1982—; pres. Friends Pub. Radio, Wilmington, N.C., 1990-91, Greater Wilmington C. of C. Contbr. articles to profl. jours. Recipient Gov's. award, Governor N.C., Raleigh, 1990, Pres. award Nat. Marine Educators Assn., 1989. Mem. Wilmington Rotary Club. Democrat. Episcopalian. Avocations: aquariums, bonsai, gardening. Home: 140 Edgewater Ln Wilmington NC 28403-3748 Office: North Carolina Aquarium Box 1 2201 Ft Fisher Blvd S Kure Beach NC 28449-0130

LANIER, JOHN HICKS, apparel company executive; b. Nashville, Apr. 12, 1940; s. Sartain and Claudia Gwynn (Whitson) L.; m. Jane M. Darden, Oct. 15, 1966; children: Jay, Liza, Stephen. B.A., Vanderbilt U., 1962; M.B.A., Harvard U., 1964. Pres., chmn., chief exec. officer Oxford Industries, Inc., Atlanta, 1981—; bd. dirs. Shaw Industries, Inc., Dalton, Ga., Crawford & Co., Trust Co. of Ga. Assocs. Trustee, Henrietta Egleston Hosp. for Children, The Westminster Schs., Atlanta; bd. dirs. Piedmont Hosp., Atlanta. Served with USAFR, 1964-65. Mem. Am. Apparel Mfrs. Assn. (past bd. dirs.). Republican. Office: Oxford Industries Inc 222 Piedmont Ave NE Atlanta GA 30308-3306*

LANIER, ROBERT C. (BOB LANIER), mayor; b. Baytown, Tex., 1931. Student, Lee Coll., Univ. N.Mex.; grad. in law with hons., U. Tex. Former reporter The Baytown Sun and The Austin Am.-Statesman.; law assoc. Baker & Botts; then pvt. practice; mayor Houston, 1992—. Chmn. Tex. Highway and Pub. Transp. Commn., Houston Met. Transit Authority; founder Houston Community Coll.; founder, chmn. Bd. Hope Ctr. Wilderness Camp. Office: Office of the Mayor PO Box 1562 Houston TX 77251-1562*

LANIER, THOMAS, chemical and export company executive; b. Cienfuegos, Cuba, Sept. 18, 1923; came to U.S., 1938; s. Joseph and Irene (Medina) L.; divorced; children: Margie, Robert, George, Thomas Emil; m. Julie Gonzalez, May 1, 1980. Student, Bowens Bus. Coll., 1939-40, Latin Am. Inst., 1940-41; BBA, Havana U., 1948; postgrad., St. Mary's U., San Antonio, 1955. Mgr. sales Joskes of Tex., San Antonio, 1949-51; mgr. office investment corp. San Antonio, 1951-55; v.p. internat. sales Sun-X Internat. Export Corp., San Antonio, 1955-59; pres. Sun-X Internat. Ltd., Houston, 1963-66; pres., mgr. Tri-X Internat. Co., North Bergen, 1963—; pres., chief exec. officer Lanier Shipping Co., Inc., North Bergen, N.J., 1966-87; internat. trade cons. Falor Assocs. Inc., North Bergen, 1987—, Factory Assocs. & Exporters, East Hanover, N.J., 1987—. Served with USAF, 1943-45. Recipient E award U.S. Govt., 1963. Mem. Am. Soc. Internat. Execs., C. of C. of Shipping (pres. North Bergen 1982-88), Bogota (N.J.) Tenants Assn., Am. Radio Relay League. Democrat. Roman Catholic. Avocations: amateur radion, stamp collecting, lecturing. Office: Tri-X Internat Co 7500 Bergenline Ave North Bergen NJ 07047-5401

LANIER, WILLIAM JOSEPH, college program director; b. Great Falls, Mont., Dec. 20, 1963; s. Bolder Lanue and Nancy Jo (Kiszczak) L. AS, No. Mont. Coll., 1985, B Tech., 1987, MEd, 1989. Drafting intern Columbus Hosp., Great Falls, 1985-87; grad. asst. No. Mont. Coll., Havre, 1987-89; dir. student life Mont. State U. -No. (formerly No. Mont. Coll.), Havre, 1989-95, 1995—. Bd. dirs. Havre Encourages Long Range Prevention, 1992—, Hill County Crimestoppers, 1991-93; adv. bd. No. Ctrl. Mont. Upward Bound, Harlem, 1992—; mem. Nat. Eagle Scout Assn., Irving, Tex., 1991—. Recipient Golden N award student senate No. Mont. Coll., 1992. Mem. Am. Counseling Assn., Am. Coll. Pers. Assn., Nat. Assn. Student Pers. Adminstrs., No. Mont. Coll. Alumni Assn. (bd. dirs 1990—). Avocations: reading, collecting baseball cards. Home: MacKenzie Hall Havre MT 59501 Office: Mont State U - No Box 7751 Havre MT 59501

LANIGAN, DENIS GEORGE, retired advertising agency executive; b. Eng., Jan. 25, 1926; widowed; 2 children. Ed., Cambridge (Eng.) U. With J. Walter Thompson Co., 1952-87; mgr. J. Walter Thompson Co., Frankfurt, Germany, 1959-64; mng. dir. J. Walter Thompson Co., London, 1966-74; pres. European div. J. Walter Thompson Co., 1974-80; vice chmn. adminstrn. J. Walter Thompson Co., N.Y.C., 1980-82; dir., chief operating officer J. Walter Thompson Co. and JWT Group, N.Y.C., 1982-86; bd. dirs. Marks & Spencer, U.K., 1987—, TSB Bank plc, 1987-90; chmn. MM&K Ltd., U.K., 1988-91; chmn. N.Am. Adv. Group, mem. Brit. Overseas Trade Bd. Office: Michael House, 47 Baker St, London W1A 1DN, England

LANIGAN, ROBERT J., packaging company executive; b. Bklyn., Apr. 26, 1928; s. John F. and Katherine (Sheehy) L.; m. Mary Elizabeth McCormick, Dec. 30, 1950; children: Kenneth J., Betty Jane Lanigan Snavely, Kathryn Ann Lanigan Pilewskie, Jeanne Marie Lanigan Schafer, Suzanne Marie Lanigan Georgetti. A.B. in Econs., St. Francis Coll., N.Y.C., 1950; B.A. (hon.), Nathaniel Hawthorne Coll., Antrim, N.H., 1979. Pres. domestic ops. Owens-Ill., Inc., Toledo, 1976-79, pres. internat. ops., 1979-82, pres., 1982-86, chief oper. officer, 1982-84, chief exec. officer, 1984-90, chmn. bd., 1984-91, chmn. emeritus, 1991—; bd. dirs. Chrysler Corp., Detroit, The Coleman Co., Denver, Sonat, Inc., Birmingham, Ala., Dun & Bradstreet Corp., N.Y.C., Sonat Offshore Drilling, Inc., Houston. Pres. Toledo Symphony Orch.; hon. trustee Toledo Mus. Art. Recipient achievement award St. Francis Coll. Alumni Assn., 1980. Mem. Burning Tree (Bethesda, Md.) Club, Quail Creek Country Club (Naples, Fla.), Belmont Country Club (Perrysburg, Ohio). Roman Catholic. Avocations: fishing; hunting; golf; tennis. Home: 13145 Valewood Dr Naples FL 33999-8506 Office: Owens-Ill Inc 1 Seagate Toledo OH 43666-1000

LANING, J. HALCOMBE, retired computer scientist; b. Kansas City, Mo., Feb. 14, 1920; s. J. Halcombe and Mary Alice (Knox) L.; m. Betty Arleen Kolb, June 27, 1943; children: Christine, James, Susan, Linda. Student, Kansas City Jr. Coll., 1936-38; SBChemE, MIT, 1940, postgrad., 1941, PhD in Applied Math., 1947; postgrad., Brown U., 1941-42. Engr. Watertown (Mass.) Arsenal Govt. U.S., 1942-45; group leader instrumentation lab. MIT, Cambridge, 1945-73; head dept. C.S. Draper Lab., Cambridge, 1973-88, sr. tech. advisor, 1988-89. Author: Random Processes in Automatic Control, 1956; creator computer programs; patentee in field. C.S. Draper fellow, 1982-85. Mem. NAE, Assn. Computing Machinery, Am. Math. Soc., Soc. for Indsl. and Applied Math., AIAA, IEEE, Inst. Mgmt. Scis.

LANING, RICHARD BOYER, naval officer, writer, retired; b. Washington, Jan. 1, 1918; s. Richard Henry and Marguerite (Boyer) L., m. Ruth Richmond, Sept. 5, 1942; children: Christine, Lucille. BSEE, U.S. Naval Acad., 1940; MS in Biophysics & Nuclear Physics, U. Calif., Berkeley, 1950; postgrad., U.S. Nat. War Coll., 1960. Officer USS Yorktown, 1940-41, USS Hornet Doolittle Raid, Tokyo, Battle of Midway, 1941-42; exec. officer USS Salmon Pacific Fleet, 1942-44; nuclear weapons planner OPNAV, Washington, 1953-54; commdg. officer 5 subs. including commng. 2d nuclear sub. USS Seawolf, 1956; first Polaris tender USS Proteus USN, Scotland, 1960-62; asst. chief of staff Submarines Pacific USN, Pearl Harbor, Hawaii, 1962-63; ret. USN, 1963; corp. planner, mgr. biotech. programs United Aircraft Corp., Hartford, Conn., 1963-73; life ins. underwriter Equitable of Iowa, Orlando, Fla., 1973-77; writer Orlando, Fla., 1977—; cons. in field. Contbr. articles to profl. jours. Mem. U.S. Naval Inst., Naval Acad. Alumni, Fleet Res. Assn., Navy League, Adm. Nimitz Fedn., U. Calif. Alumni, Futurist Soc., Greater Orlando C. of C., Nat. Space Soc., Navy Submarine League, Univ. Club Winter Park, Mil. Order of World Wars, Retired Officers Assn. Avocations: swimming, racquetball, computer art. Home and Office: 5955 Turnbull Dr Orlando FL 32822-1740

LANING, ROBERT COMEGYS, retired physician, former naval officer; b. Haiti, Sept. 20, 1922; s. Richard Henry and Marguerite C. (Boyer) L.; m. Alice Teresa Lech, Sept. 9, 1961; 1 dau., Maria Laning LeBerre. BA, U. Va.; MA, Ohio State U.; MD, Jefferson Med. Coll., 1948. Diplomate: Nat. Bd. Med. Examiners, Am. Bd. Surgery. Intern Jefferson Hosp., Phila., 1948-50; enlisted USN, 1950, advanced through grades to rear adm., 1973, mem. astronaut recovery teams, 1960-66; chief of surgery Naval Hosp., San Diego, 1967-71; med. dir. Naval Hosp., Yokosuka, Japan, 1972-73; med. officer Pacific Fleet, 1973-75; asst. chief Bur. Medicine and Surgery for Operational Med. Support, Washington, 1975-77; dep. dir. surg. service Cen. Office, VA, Washington, 1977-79, dir. surg. service, 1979-87. Fellow ACS (gov. 1984-87); mem. AMA, Am. Assn. Mil. Surgeons, Soc. Med. Cons. to ArmedForces (pres. 1988-89, bd. dirs.), Ret. Officers Assn. Roman Catholic. Home: 6532 Sunny Hill Ct Mc Lean VA 22101-1639

LANITIS, TONY ANDREW, market researcher; b. Port Said, Egypt, May 29, 1926; came to U.S., 1929; s. Christopher and Helen (Joanides) L.; m. Anne Mortimer, Feb. 4, 1947 (div. 1951); 1 son, Philip; m. Gertrude Lettese, June 14, 1959; 1 dau., Melissa. BS in Econs., NYU, 1950, MA, 1951. Assoc. research dir. Morey, Humm & Warwick, N.Y.C., 1954-55; sr. group supr. Colgate-Palmolive Co., N.Y.C., 1955-60; sr. v.p. SSC & B: Lintas Worldwide, Inc., N.Y.C., 1960-89, dir. rsch., 1960-87, dir. market planning and rsch., 1987-89; market planning and rsch. cons. N.Y.C., 1989—; instr. Ulster County C.C., 1993—; guest lectr. NYU, 1970-72, Pace Coll., 1970-73, L.I. U., 1968-70; lectr. in field. Cons. editor Psychology and Mktg. Jour., 1983—; contbr. articles to profl. jours. Bd. dirs. Port Chester (N.Y.) Coun. Arts, 1981-89, Unison Art and Learning Ctr., New Paltz, N.Y., 1990-92. Served with U.S. Army, 1944-46. Named Marketer of Month Kansas City, Am. Mktg. Assn, 1972. Mem. Am. Mktg. Assn., Advt. Research Found., Advt. Agy. Research Dirs. Council, Am. Psychol. Assn., Inst. Mgmt. Sci., Market Research Council, Communications Research Council. Club: Commerce. Home: 59 Lake Hill Rd Kingston NY 12401-8440

LANKFORD, FRANCIS GREENFIELD, JR., education educator emeritus; b. Morattico, Va., Feb. 14, 1906; s. Francis Greenfield and Alma (Coulbourne) L.; m. Florence Fleet, June 4, 1935; children: William Fleet, Francis Greenfield III. B.S., Randolph-Macon Coll., 1928, LL.D., 1959; M.A., U. Va., 1932, Ph.D., 1938. High sch. prin., 1928-31; from instr. to prof. edn. U. Va., Charlottesville, 1932-55; dir. research Richmond Pub. Schs., 1943-44; pres. Longwood Coll., Farmville, Va., 1955-65; prof. edn., dir. office instl. analysis U. Va., 1965-72, sesquicentennial scholar, 1971-72, Commonwealth prof., 1972, prof. edn. emeritus, 1972—; ednl. adviser Ford Found.-U. Chgo. Pakistan Edn. Project, 1962-63; Dir. study high sch. edn. Va. C. of C., 1942-43; dir. div. ednl. research U. Va., 1951-55; mem. Charlottesville (Va.) Sch. Bd., 1952-55. Co-author: Mathematics for the Consumer, 1947, 2d edit., 1953, Basic Ideas of Mathematics, 1953, Algebra One and Algebra Two, 1955, Essential Mathematics, 1961, 2d edit., 1967, 3d edit., 1975, Contemporary Algebra I, 1962, Contemporary Algebra II, 1963, Algebra One, 1969, 72, Algebra Two, 1969, 72, 77, Numbers and Operations, 1970, Consumer Mathematics, 1971, 2d edit., 1974, author, 1981, also articles.; Departmental editor: Math. Tchr, 1953-57. Campaign chmn. Prince Edward Community Chest, 1958. Recipient Disting. Alumnus award U. Va. Sch. Edn., 1977; Gen. Edn. Bd. fellow U. Mich., 1939-40. Mem. Nat. Council Tchrs. Math. (v.p. 1955-57), Raven Soc., Phi Beta Kappa, Omicron Delta Kappa, Phi Delta Kappa (distinguished service award U. Va. chpt. 1944). Democrat. Home: 2600 Barracks Rd Apt 396 Charlottesville VA 22901-2196

LANKHOF, FREDERIK JAN, publishing executive; b. Mar. 4, 1949; came to U.S., 1983; s. Adriaan Pieter and Janny (Baas) L.; m. Joyce Ganimian, May 31, 1983; children: Lauren, Nora. Attended, U. Amsterdam. Editorial asst. Meulenhoff Pub. Co., Amsterdam, The Netherlands, 1968-72; free-lance copy editor, proofreader, translator The Netherlands, 1972-83; bookseller, libr. asst. N.Y.C., 1983-86; pres., owner i.b.d., Ltd., Kinderhook, N.Y., 1989—; pres. E.J. Brill (USA), Inc., Kinderhook, 1986—, Nedbook New York, Inc., Kinderhook, 1990—, Internat. Bur. Fiscal Documentation, Kinderhook, 1993—. Trustee Kinderhook Meml. Libr., 1994—. Avocations: reading, writing, translations, publishing. Home: 24 Hudson St Kinderhook NY 12106-2004 Office: E J Brill USA Inc 24 Hudson St Box 467 Kinderhook NY 12106

LANKTON, STEPHEN RYAN, family therapist, management consultant; b. Lansing, Mich., May 29, 1947; s. Stanley R. and Mary Lou (Cook) L.; children: Stephen, Shawn Michael, Alicia Michelle. Student, Lansing Community Coll., 1966-68; BA, Mich. State U., 1972; MSW (scholar), U. Mich., 1974. Diplomate Am. Bd. Examiners in Clin. Social Work, NASW, Am. Hypnosis Bd. for Clin. Social Work; lic. marriage and family therapist, Fla. Youth outreach YMCA, Lansing, 1969-70; residential youth treatment Camp Highfields, Inc., Onondaga, Mich., 1970-73; instr. psychology Jackson (Mich.) Community Coll., 1974-78; clin. social worker Family Services of Jackson, 1974-78; mem. tng. staff. Huron Valley Inst., Dexter, Mich., 1978-79; pvt. practice psychology Gulf Breeze, Fla., 1980—; adj. instr. psychology U. West Fla., 1980—. Author: Practical Magic: The Clinical Application of Neuro Linguistic Programming, 1980; editor Ericksonian Mongraphs, 1984—; author: The Answer Within: A Clinical Framework of Ericksonian Hypnotherapy, 1983, Enchantment and Intervention in Family Therapy: Training in Ericksonian Approaches, 1986, Tales of Enchantment: A Collection of Goal Directed Metaphors for Adults and Children in Therapy, 1989, The Blammo-Surprise!: A Story to Help Children Overcome Fear, 1988. Recipient Lifetime Achievement award for outstanding contbns. to the field of psychotherapy, 1994. Fellow Am. Acad. Pain Mgmt., Am. Assn. Marriage and Family Therapy (approved supr., clin. mem.); mem. Internat. Transactional Analysis Assn., Acad. Cert. Social Workers, Soc. Clin. and Exptl. Hypnosis, Am. Acad. Phychotherapists, Internat. Soc. Hypnosis, Fla. Soc. Clin. Hypnosis, Am. Soc. Clin. Hypnosis (approved cons.), Am. Family Therapy Assn. (clin. tchg. mem.). Avocation: scuba diving. Office: PO Box 958 Gulf Breeze FL 32562-0958

LANMON, DWIGHT PIERSON, museum director; b. Pueblo, Colo., July 28, 1938; s. Ira Dwight and Elaine Glea Pierson (Curtis) L.; m. Ann Lorraine Welling, Jan. 10, 1970. Student, Knox Coll., 1956-58; B.A., U. Colo., 1960; postgrad., UCLA, 1961-66; M.A., U. Del., 1968. Asst. curator, assoc. curator, and in charge of conservation Winterthur Mus., Del., 1968-73; dep. dir. Corning Mus. Glass, N.Y., 1973-81, dir., 1981-92; CEO, dir., trustee Winterthur (Del.) Mus., 1992—; trustee Rockwell Mus., Corning, 1983-92, pres., 1988-92, chmn. exec. com., 1988-92, acting dir., 1986-88; trustee Corning Mus. Glass, 1981-95. Author: (with Arlene Palmer) John Frederick Amelung, 1976, 2d edit., 1981, (with Paul Hollister) Paperweights, 1978, (with David B. Whitehouse) Glass in the Robert Lehman Collection, 1993 (Urban Glass award for best. hist./acad. publ. 1995). Winterthur fellow, 1966-68. Fellow Soc. Antiquaries of London; mem. Internat. Assn. History of Glass (sec.-gen. 1981-85), Internat. Coun. Mus., Assn. Art Mus. Dirs., Am. Assn. Mus., Census of Stained Glass (dir. 1980-92), Paperweight Collectors Assn. (bd. dirs. 1991-92), Walpole Soc., Blair House Fine Arts Com., Chevaliers de Tastevin. Office: Henry Francis Du Pont Winterthur Mus RR 52 Winterthur DE 19735

LANNAMANN, RICHARD STUART, executive recruiting consultant; b. Cin., Sept. 4, 1947; s. Frank E. and Grace I. (Tomlinson) L. AB in Econs., Yale U., 1969; MBA, Harvard U., 1973; divorced; children: Thomas Cleveland, Edward Payne, John Stewart. Investment analyst U.S. Trust Co. N.Y., N.Y.C., 1969-71; rsch. analyst Smith, Barney & Co., N.Y.C., 1973-75, 2d v.p., 1975-77, v.p. successor firm rsch. div. Smith Barney Harris Upham & Co., 1977-78; v.p. Russell Reynolds Assocs., Inc., N.Y.C., 1978-83, mng. dir. 1983-86, 87—; sr. v.p. Mgmt. Asset Corp., Westport, Conn., 1986-87. Dir. Boy's Choir Harlem. Mem. N.Y. Soc. Security Analysts, Internat. Soc. of Fin. Analysts, Assn. for Investment Mgmt. and Rsch., Inst. Chartered Fin. Analysts, Riverside Yacht Club, Yale Club of N.Y., Links Club. Home: 21 Willowmere Cir Riverside CT 06878 Office: 200 Park Ave New York NY 10166-0005

LANNERT, ROBERT CORNELIUS, manufacturing company executive; b. Chgo., Mar. 14, 1940; s. Robert Carl and Anna Martha (Cornelius) L.; m. Kathleen A. O'Toole, July 10, 1965; children: Jacqueline, Krista, Kevin, Meredith. B.S. in Indsl. Mgmt., Purdue U., 1963; M.B.A., Northwestern U., 1967; grad. Advanced Mgmt. Program, Harvard U., 1978. With Navistar Internat. Transp. Corp. (formerly Internat. Harvester), Chgo., 1963—, staff asst. overseas fin., 1967-70; asst. mgr., treas. and contr. IH Finanz AG, Zurich, Switzerland, 1970-72; mgr. overseas fin. corp. hdqrs. Navistar Internat. Transp. Corp., Chgo., 1972-76, asst. treas., 1976-79; v.p., treas. Navistar Internat. Corp., Chgo., 1979-90, exec. v.p., chief fin. officer, 1990—, also bd. dirs.; bd. dirs. NITC, Harbour Assurance Co., Bermuda, Navistar Fin. Corp., Chgo. Mem. adv. bd. to dean Krannert Sch. Purdue U. Mem. Fin. Execs. Inst. Home: 130 N Grant St Hinsdale IL 60521-3334 Office: Navistar Internat Corp 455 N Cityfront Plaza Dr Chicago IL 60611-5503*

LANNES, WILLIAM JOSEPH, III, electrical engineer; b. New Orleans, Oct. 12, 1937; s. William Joseph Jr., and Rhea Helen (Simon) L.; m. Patricia Anne Didier, Jan. 17, 1961: children: David Mark, Kenneth John, Jennifer Anne. BEE, Tulane U., 1959; MEE, U.S. Naval Postgrad. Sch., 1966; registered profl. engr. Commd. 2d lt. U.S. Marine Corps, 1959, advanced through grades to maj., 1967, served as electronics officer, ops. officer, until 1970; substation engr. La. Power & Light, New Orleans, 1970-71, utility engr., 1971-76, system relay engr., 1976-77, system substation engr., 1977-79, engring. supr. for substations, 1979-83, substation engring. mgr., 1983-86, dir. systems engring., 1986—, v.p. systems engring., 1986-88, with cen. engring., 1988-89; sr. v.p. Energy Supply Fossil, 1989-91; v.p. svc. and support Entergy Corp., 1991-92; assoc. dean rsch. & grad. studies Coll. Engring., U. New Orleans, 1992—; dir. U. New Orleans EPRI Community Initiative Ctr., 1993-95; assoc. dir. Ctr. Energy Resources Mgmt., 1993—; dir. Engring. Mgmt. Program, 1995—; instr. Delgado Jr. Coll., 1973-74; instr. elec. engring. U. New Orleans, 1979-80; dir. 5th Dist. Savs. and Loan, 1982—; speaker profl. confs. Contbr. articles to profl. jours. Committeeman New Orleans Area Coun., Boy Scouts Am., 1972-76; vol., United Way 1975, 76, 81; treas., PTA 1971; vol. tchr. Confraternity of Christian Doctrine, 1972; mem. bus. adv. coun. Our Lady of Holy Cross Coll., 1981-86; chmn. engring. adv. coun. U. New Orleans; bd. dirs. New Life in La.; vol. coach New Orleans Recreation Dept., 1973; mem. La. Employees Com. on Polit. Action, Tulane Univ. Engring. Coun., New Orleans Archiocesan Pastoral Coun., 1988-91; mem. adv. bd. Bridge House, 1992-95. Decorated Bronze Star; Cross of Gallantry Republic S. Vietnam; recipient cert. of merit, Mayor New Orleans, 1964; registered profl. engr., La. Fellow IEEE (profl. mem., Outstanding Svc. award 1976, chmn. New Orleans sect. 1981-82, Edward Freitag award 1988, Region 3 Outstanding Engr. award 1991); mem. Electric Power Rsch. Inst. (industry advisor), Edison Electric Inst. (systems and equipment com.), Soc. Power Rsch. and Implementation (chmn. 1987—), Southeastern Electric Exchange (substation com. 1977-85), Power Engring. Soc. (Prize Paper award 1988), Sigma Xi, Eta Kappa Nu. Republican. Roman Catholic. Office: Coll Engring U New Orleans New Orleans LA 70148

LANNIE, PAUL ANTHONY, lawyer; b. Hayti, Mo., Feb. 21, 1954; m. Donna Dean; children: Heather, Anthony. BA magna cum laude, Vanderbilt U., 1974, JD, 1978. Bar: Tex. Assoc. Johnson & Swanson, Dallas, 1978-83; exec. v.p. BusLease, Inc., Dallas, 1983-87, Greyhound Lines, Inc., Dallas, 1987-91; v.p. and gen. counsel Baroid Corp., Houston, 1991-94; sr. v.p., gen. counsel Tejas Gas Corp., 1994—. Bd. dirs. Dallas Indstrl. Devel. Corp., 1985-87; exec. mem. Ctrl. Dallas Assn., 1990. Mem. Order Coif, Phi Beta Kappa. Office: Baroid Corp 3000 N Sam Houston Pky E Houston TX 77032-3219

LANNON, LINNEA, newspaper editor. Book review editor Detroit Free Press. Office: Detroit Free Press 321 W Lafayette Blvd Detroit MI 48226-2705

LANO, CHARLES JACK, retired financial executive; b. Port Clinton, Ohio, Apr. 17, 1922; s. Charles Herbin and Antoinette (Schmitt) L.; m. Beatrice Irene Spees, June 16, 1946 (dec. 1995); children: Douglas Cloyd, Charles Lewis. B.S. in Bus. Adminstrn. summa cum laude, Ohio State U., 1949. C.P.A., Okla. With U.S. Gypsum Co., 1941-46, Ottawa Paper Stock Co., 1946-47; accountant Arthur Young & Co. (C.P.A.'s), Tulsa, 1949-51; controller Lima div. Ex-Cell-O Corp., 1951-59, electronics div. AVCO Corp., 1959-61, Servomation Corp., 1961; asst. comptroller Scovill Mfg. Co., Waterbury, Conn., 1961-62, comptroller, 1962-67; controller CF&I Steel Corp., Denver, 1967-69; v.p., controller CF&I Steel Corp., 1969-70; controller Pacific Lighting Corp., 1970-76; exec. v.p. Arts-Way Mfg. Co., Armstrong, Iowa, 1976-85; mgmt. auditor City of Anaheim, Calif., 1985-96; ret., 1996. Served with USMCR, 1942-45. Mem. Am. Inst. C.P.A.'s, Calif. Soc. C.P.A.'s, Inst. Internal Auditors. Home: 6274 E Calle Jaime Anaheim CA 92807-4005 Office: Civic Ctr 200 S Anaheim Blvd Anaheim CA 92805-3820

LANOIS, DANIEL, record producer, musician, popular; b. Hull, Que., Can., 1951; s. Guy and Jill Lanois. Founder, prodr. Grant Ave. Studio, Ont., Can., 1980-85; indep. prodr., 1981—. Solo albums include Arcadie, 1989, For the Beauty of Wynona, 1993; prodr. albums by Martha and the Muffins, Brian Eno, U2 (Grammy award The Joshua Tree 1987), Peter Gabriel, Robbie Robertson, Bob Dylan, The Neville Brothers. Grammy award, Best Producer (with Brian Eno for U2's Achtung Baby),1993. Office: Opal/ Warner Bros 3300 Warner Blvd Burbank CA 91505-4632

LANOU, ROBERT EUGENE, JR., physicist, educator; b. Colchester, Vt., Feb. 13, 1928; s. Robert E. and Flora G. (Goyette) L.; m. Cornelia Rockwell Wheeler, May 14, 1960; children: Katharine, Gregory, Elizabeth, Steven. BS, Worcester Poly. Inst., 1952; PhD, Yale U., 1957. Physicist Lawrence Berkeley (Calif.) Lab., 1956-59; asst. prof. physicist Brown U., Providence, 1960-63, assoc. prof., 1963-67, prof., 1967—, chair dept. physics, 1986-92; cons. Brookhaven Nat. Lab., Upton, N.Y., Los Alamos (N.Mex.) Nat. Lab.; sci. advisor Gov. State of R.I., Providence, 1986-88. Contbr. articles to profl. jours. With USN, 1946-48, ETO. Grantee Dept. Energy, 1960—, NSF, 1995—. Fellow AAAS, Am. Phys. Soc.; mem. Sigma Xi, Tau Beta Pi. Achievements include research in experimental particle physics and astrophysics. Home: 90 Keene St Providence RI 02906-1508 Office: Brown U Dept Physics Providence RI 02906

LA NOUE, TERENCE DAVID, artist, educator; b. Hammond, Ind., Dec. 4, 1941; s. George David and Lois (Lish) L.; m. Ann Marcus, Oct. 15, 1977; children: Daniel, Alexandra. BFA, Ohio Wesleyan U., 1964; Fulbright meister student, Hochschule fur Bildenden Kunste, West Berlin, 1964-65; MFA, Cornell U., 1967; DFA, Ohio Wesleyan U., 1994. Prof. Trinity Coll., Hartford, Conn., 1967-72, CUNY, N.Y.C., 1972-85, NYU, 1987. Works represented in various museums, including Whitney Mus., Guggenheim Mus., Bklyn. Mus., Albright-Knox Mus., Corcoran Gallery Art, Carnegie Inst., Power Inst. Fine Arts, Sydney, Australia, Musé d'Art et Archeologie, Toulon, France, Musée de Strasbourg, France, Mus. Contemporary Art, Teheran, Iran, Mus. Modern Art, N.Y.C.; monograph, Terence La Noue, Ashton Dore, 1992. Grantee Fulbright Found., Berlin, 1964-65, NEA, 1972-73, 83-84, Guggenheim Found., 1982-83. Office: 714 Broadway New York NY 10003-9506

LANOUETTE, WILLIAM JOHN, writer, public policy analyst; b. New Haven, Sept. 14, 1940; s. Joseph Francis and Gertrude Veronica (Thiede) L.; m. JoAnne Marie Sheldon, Apr. 12, 1969; children: Nicole Marie, Kathryn Ann. Student, USCG Acad., 1958-59; A.B., Fordham Coll., 1963; M.Sc., London Sch. Econs. and Polit. Sci., U. London, 1966, Ph.D., 1973. Researcher, reporter Newsweek, N.Y.C., 1961-64; news editor Radio Sta. WVOX AM-FM, New Rochelle, N.Y., 1964; Am. lectr. Hansard Soc. for Parliamentary Govt., London, 1965-67, 70-71; profl. staff mem., tech. programs subcom. Govt. Ops. Com. Ho. of Reps., Washington, 1967; legis. asst. to U.S. Rep. John S. Monagan, Washington, 1967-68; staff writer Nat. Observer, Washington, 1969-70, 72-77; staff corr. Nat. Jour., Washington, 1977-82, contbg. editor, 1982-83; communications dir. World Resources Inst., Washington, 1983-85, sr. assoc., 1985; Washington corr. Bull. Atomic Scientists, 1989-90; sr. evaluator energy and science issues U.S. Gen. Acctg. Office, Washington, 1991—; pres. Internat. Soc. Panetics. Author: Genius in the Shadows, a Biography of Leo Szilard, 1993. Recipient Forum award, 1974; fellow John F. Kennedy Sch. Govt., Harvard U., 1988-89; guest scholar Wilson Ctr., Smithsonian Instn., 1989. Democrat. Club: Potomac Boat (Washington). Home: 326 5th St SE Washington DC 20003-2048

LANPHER, BILL WESTON, college president, minister; b. Bernie, Mo., June 29, 1933; s. Weston and Norma Pearl (Bishop) L.; m. Janice Mae Thornhill, Aug. 28, 1954; children: David Geoffrey, James Eric. BS, Nyack Coll., 1955; BA, Wayne State U., 1956; MA, Mich. State U., 1958; D of Ministry, Drew U., 1984. Ordained to ministry Christian and Missionary Alliance, 1958. Min. various chs. Christian and Missionary Alliance, 1955-69; asst. v.p. Christian and Missionary Alliance, N.Y.C. and Nyack, N.Y., 1969-85; dean of students St. Paul Bible Coll., St. Bonifacius, Minn., 1985-87, pres., 1987—; trustee Beulah Beach Corp., 1966-68; treas. west cen. dist. Christian and Missionary Alliance, 1966-68, bd. mgrs., 1988—; mem. exec. com. Eccles. Endorsing Agts., 1978-79. Mem. Adminstrs. Higher Edn., Assn. Pres. Ind. Colls. and Univs., Nat. Assn. Evangs. (chmn. commn. on chaplains, bd. adminstrn. 1974-78, sec. commn. on chaplains 1978-80), Assn. Statisticians Am. Religious Bodies (pres. 1978-80), Nat. Conf. on Ministry to Armed Forces (chmn. com. on concerns 1983-85). Republican. Office: St Paul Bible Coll Saint Bonifacius MN 55375

LANPHIER, DAVID J., judge; b. Omaha, Feb. 7, 1945; s. Lawrence Anthony and virginia (Kelly) L.; m. Patricia Quinn, Oct. 16, 1963; children: David Lanphier, Jr., Dominic, Krista, Elizabeth. AB, Creighton U., Omaha, 1967; JD, Fordham Law Sch., N.Y.C., 1971. Law clk. to hon. John W. Delehant Omaha, 1971-72; assoc. atty. Morsman, Fike, Sawtell & Davis, Omaha, 1972-75; dir. McGill, Koley, Parsonage & Lanphier, Omaha, 1975-90, Croker, Huck, Kasher, Lanphier, DeWitt & Anderson, Omaha, 1990-92; supreme ct. judge Nebr. Supreme Ct., Lincoln, 1993—. Mem. City Omaha Pers. Bd., 1984-89, Charter Rev. Conv., Omaha, 1983, State Crime Commn., Lincoln, Nebr., 1992. Mem. Nebr. Bar Assn., Omaha Bar Assn. Office: Nebr Supreme Ct 2413 State Capitol Lincoln NE 68509

LANSAW, CHARLES RAY, sales industry executive; b. Middletown, Ohio, Mar. 5, 1927; s. Edward Curtis and Lura (Tyra) L.; m. Joan Betty Kalbaugh, July 4, 1949; children: Charles E., Gail D., Leslie J., Kristi L. Student, Miami U., Oxford, Ohio, 1947-48; student engring., U. Cin., 1949-51. Chief engr., sales mgr. Dupps Co., Germantown, Ohio, 1950-85; pres. C.R. Lansaw, Inc., Germantown, 1985—. Mem. Germantown Planing Commn.; bd. dirs. Germantown Pub. libr., 1991—; served with VOCA at Saratov and Volgograd, Russia, 1996, Internat. Exec. Svc. Corps, Alexandria, Egypt, 1993. With USNR, 1944-46; with Internat. Exec. Svc. Corp, Alexandria, Egypt, 1993. Mem. U.S. Power Squadron (past officer Dayton), Rotary (pres. Germantown 1987-88). Avocations: sailing, woodworking, tennis. Home: 73 Sue Dr Germantown OH 45327-1628 Office: 45 N Main St Germantown OH 45327-1349

LANSBURY, ANGELA BRIGID, actress; b. London, Oct. 16, 1925; came to U.S., 1940; d. Edgar and Moyna (Macgill) L.; m. Peter Shaw, Aug. 12, 1949; children: Anthony, Deirdre. Student, Webber-Douglas Sch. Drama, London, 1939-40, Feagin Sch. Drama, N.Y.C., 1940-42; LHD (hon.), Boston U., 1990. Host 41st, 42d and 43d Ann. Tony Awards, 45th Ann. Emmy Awards. Actress with Metro-Goldwyn-Mayer, 1943-50; films include: Gaslight, 1944 (Acad. award nomination), National Velvet, 1944, The Picture of Dorian Gray, 1944 (Golden Globe award, Acad. award nomination), The Harvey Girls, 1946, The Hoodlum Saint, 1946, Till the Clouds Roll By, 1946, The Private Affairs of Bel Ami, 1947, If Winter Comes, 1948, Tenth Avenue Angel, 1948, State of the Union, 1948, The Three Musketeers, 1948, The Red Danube, 1949, Samson and Delilah, 1949, Kind Lady, 1951, Mutiny, 1952, Remains to be Seen, 1953, A Life at Stake, 1955, The Purple Mask, 1956, A Lawless Street, 1956, Please Murder Me, 1956, The Court Jester, 1956, The Long Hot Summer, 1958, Reluctant Debutante, 1958, A Breath of Scandal, 1960, Dark at the Top of the Stairs, 1960, Season of Passion, 1961, Blue Hawaii, 1961, All Fall Down, 1962, Manchurian Candidate, 1962 (Golden Globe award, Acad. award nomination), In the Cool of the Day, 1963, Dear Heart, 1964, The World of Henry Orient, 1964, The Greatest Story Ever Told, 1965, Harlow, 1965, The Amorous Adventures of Moll Flanders, 1965, Mister Buddwing, 1966, Something for Everyone, 1970, Bedknobs and Broomsticks, 1971, Death on the Nile, 1978, The Lady Vanishes, 1980, The Mirror Crack'd, 1980, The Pirates of Penzance, 1982, The Company of Wolves, 1983, Beauty and the Beast, 1991; star TV series Murder She Wrote, 1984— (Golden Globe awards 1984, 86, 91, 92, 11 Emmy nominations, Lead Actress - Drama); appeared in TV mini-series Little Gloria, Happy at Last, 1982, Lace, 1984, Rage of Angels, part II, 1986; other TV movies include: The First Olympics-Athens 1896, A Talent for Murder, Gift of Love, 1982, Shootdown, 1988, The Shell Seekers, 1989, The Love She Sought, 1990, Mrs. 'Arris Goes to Paris, 1992; appeared in plays Hotel Paradiso, 1957, A Taste of Honey, 1960, Anyone Can Whistle, 1964, Mame (on Broadway), 1966, 83 (Tony award for Best Mus. Actress 1966), Dear World, 1968 (Tony award for Best Mus. Actress 1969), All Over (London Royal Shakespeare Co.), 1971, Prettybelle, 1971, Gypsy, 1974

(Tony award for Best Mus. Actress 1975, Sarah Siddons award), The King and I, 1978, Sweeney Todd, 1979 (Tony award for Best Mus. Actress 1979, Sarah Siddons award), Hamlet, Nat. Theatre, London, 1976, A Little Family Business, 1983. Named Woman of Yr., Harvard Hasty Pudding Theatricals, 1968, Comdr. of British Empire by Queen Elizabeth II, 1994; inducted Theatre Hall of Fame, 1982; recipient British Acad. award, 1991. Office: Bldg 426 100 Universal City Plz Universal City CA 91608

LANSBURY, EDGAR GEORGE, theatrical producer; b. London, Jan. 12, 1930; came to U.S., 1941, naturalized, 1953; s. Edgar Isaac and Charlotte Lillian (McIldowie) L.; m. Rose Anthony Kean, Aug. 12, 1955; children: James, Michael, David, George, Brian, Kate. Ed., UCLA. Designer stock and off-Broadway prodns., 1953-55; art dir. ABC-TV, 1955, CBS-TV, 1955-62, Channel 13, N.Y.C., 1962-63; motion picture art dir., 1963-64; formed Edgar Lansbury Prodns. Inc., for ind. prodn. in theatre and films, 1964—; chmn. The Acting Co.; bd. dirs. drama dept. Story Line Press. Producer Broadway plays: First One Asleep Whistle, 1966, The Subject Was Roses, 1964, That Summer-That Fall, 1967, The Only Game in Town, 1968, Promenade, 1970, Look to the Lilies, 1970, Engagement Baby, 1971, Godspell, 1971, Elizabeth I, 1972, The Night That Made America Famous, 1974, The Magic Show, 1974, Gypsy, 1975, American Buffalo, 1977, Broadway Follies, 1981, O, Pioneer!, 1989, Club XII, 1990, Amphigorey, 1992, Any Given Day, 1993; films The Subject was Roses, 1968, Godspell, 1973, The Wild Party, 1974, Squirm, 1976, Blue Sunshine, 1978, He Knows You're Alone, 1980, The Clairvoyant, 1982, Summer Girl, 1983, A Stranger Waits, 1986; dir. Without Apologies, 1989, All the Queen's Men, 1989, Advice from a Caterpillar, 1990, The Country Club, 1992. Pres. Agni Yoga Soc.; pres. Nicholas Roerich Museum, N.Y.C.; bd. govs. League N.Y. Theatres and Producers. Served with U.S. Army, 1951-53. Recipient N.Y. Art Dirs. award for best comml. film, 1963; N.Y. Outer Critics Circle award, 1965; N.Y. Critics Circle award, 1965; Antoinette Perry award for best produced play, 1965; nomination for Antoinette Perry award for best mus. play, 1977; N.Y. Critics Circle award for best drama, 1977. Mem. Russian Mus. Arts Soc. Am. (bd. dirs.). Office: Edgar Lansbury Prodns 450 W 42nd St Ste 2C New York NY 10036-6805

LANSDALE, DARYL L., retail executive; b. 1940. Student, Okla. State U. Pres., CEO Handy Dan, Handy City & Houseworks, San Antonio, 1976-87, Lone Star Hardware, Inc., 1987-88; chmn., CEO Scotty's Inc., Winter Haven, Fla., 1988—. Office: Scotty's Inc 5300 Recker Hwy Winter Haven FL 33880-1256

LANSDOWNE, KAREN MYRTLE, retired English language and literature educator; b. Twin Falls, Idaho, Aug. 11, 1926; d. George and Effie Myrtle (Ayotte) Martin; BA in English with honors, U. Oreg., 1948, MEd, 1958, MA with honors, 1960; m. Paul L. Lansdowne, Sept. 12, 1948; children: Michele Lynn, Larry Alan. Tchr., Newfield (N.Y.) H.S., 1948-50, S. Eugene (Oreg.) H.S., 1952; mem. faculty U. Oreg., Eugene, 1958-65; asst. prof. English, Lane C.C., Eugene, 1965-82, ret., 1982; cons. Oreg. Curriculum Study Center. Rep., Cal Young Neighborhood Assn., 1978—; mem. scholarship com. First Congl. Ch., 1950-70. Mem. MLA, Pacific N.W. Regional Conf. C.C.s, Nat. Council Tchrs. English, U. Oreg. Women, AAUW (sec.), Jaycettes, Pi Lambda Theta (pres.), Phi Beta Patronesses (pres.), Delta Kappa Gamma. Co-author: The Oregon Curriculum: Language/Rhetoric, I, II, III and IV, 1970. Home: 15757 Rim Dr La Pine OR 97739-9412

LANSER, HERBERT RAYMOND, retired financial planner; b. Hollywood, Calif., Dec. 10, 1932; s. Hugo and Anna (Strandlund) L.; divorced; children: Lynn (dec.), Deborah, Cynthia, Karen, Rick; m. Judy Kay Skousen; children: Zachary, Joshua, Ezekiel. Cert. fin. planner. With Herb Lanser Fin. Svc's., San Mateo, Calif., 1956-62, financial planner, 1962-83, cons., 1971-83; fin. planner Herb Lanser Fin. Svc's., Morro Bay, Calif., 1986-92; cons., fin. planner Lanser Vermiculture Svc's., Herb Lanser Fin. Svc's., Nurnberg, Fed. Republic Germany, 1983-85; cons. various orgns., 1975-92. Author: Profit From Earthworms, 1976; contbr. articles to profl. jours. Sgt. U.S. Army, 1953-55. Named Nat. Sales Leader Prudential Ins. Co., Europe, 1985, 1987. Mem. Assn. Life Underwriters (v.p. San Luis Obispo, Calif. chpt.), Morro Bay C. of C. (chmn. econ. devel. com., v.p. 1991, pres. 1992). Republican. Avocation: photography. Studio: PO Box 834 Morro Bay CA 93443-0834

LANSING, SHERRY LEE, motion picture production executive; b. Chgo., July 31, 1944; d. Norton and Margo L.; m. William Friedkin. BS summa cum laude in Theatre, Northwestern U., 1966. Tchr. math. public high schs. Los Angeles, 1966-69; model TV comml s. Max Factor Co., 1969-70, Alberto-Culver Co., 1969-70; story editor Wagner Internat. Prodn. Co., 1972-74, dir. west coast devel., 1974-75; story editor MGM, 1975-77, v.p. creative affairs, 1977; v.p. prodn. Columbia Pictures, 1977-80; pres. 20th Century Fox Prodns., 1980-82; founder Jaffee-Lansing Prodns., 1982—; chmn. Paramount Pictures' Motion Picture Group, 1992—. Appeared in movies Loving, 1970, Rio Lobo, 1970; exec. story editor movies, Wagner Internat., 1970-73; v.p. prodn., Heyday Prodns., Universal City, Calif., 1973-75; exec. story editor, then v.p. creative affairs, MGM Studios, Culver City, Calif., 1975-77; sr. v.p. prodn., Columbia Pictures, Burbank, Calif., 1977-80, pres., 20th Century-Fox Prodns., Beverly Hills, Calif., 1980-83; ind. producer., Jaffe-Lansing Prodns., Los Angeles, 1983-91; producer Racing With the Moon, 1984,Firstborn, 1984, Fatal Attraction, 1987, The Accused, 1988, Black Rain, 1989, School Ties, 1992, Indecent Proposal, 1993; TV exec. producer When the Time Comes,1987, Mistress, 1992. Office: Paramount Pictures Corp 5555 Melrose Ave Los Angeles CA 90038-3197*

LANSKY, ZENA, surgeon; b. Phila., Apr. 18, 1942; d. Jacob and Thelma Lansky. BA summa cum laude, U. Pa., 1963; MD, Med. Coll. Pa., 1967. Diplomate Am. Bd. Surgery, 1975. Intern Montefiore Hosp., 1968-69; resident in surgery Bellevue Hosp., 1968-72, chief resident in surgery, 1971-72, instr. surgery, 1971-72; teaching asst. NIH, 1970, 71; mem. med. staff Morton F. Plant Hosp., Largo Med. Ctr., Clearwater Community Hosp.; staff mem. Morton Plant Hosp., Largo Med. Ctr., Clearwater Cmty. Hosp., Mease Hosp., Northside Hosp., Bayonet Point Hosp., Health South Rehab. Ctr., New Port Richey Cmty. Hosp., Riverside Hosp., HCA Oak Hill Hosp., Univ. Cmty. Hosp., Dade City Hosp., Helen Ellis Meml. Hosp., St. Anthony's Hosp., St. Joseph Hosp., North Bay Hosp., Brooksville Regional Hosp., Bartow Meml. Hosp.; pres. Metabolic Cons. Inc. Infusion Co., pharmacy; mem. nat. med. adv. bd. New Eng. Critical Care, 1985. Mem. editorial bd. Nutritional Support mag., 1987; contbr. articles to profl. jours.; inventor gastrostomy tube, long term venous catheter repair kit, gastrostomy tube and percutaneous endoscopic kit. Fellow ACS, Southeastern Surg. Congress; mem. Am. Soc. Parenteral and Enteral Nutrition (bd. dirs. 1989), Fla. Med. Assn., Fla. Assn. Nutritional Support (pres. 1986-87), Pinellas County Med. Soc. Office: Metabolic Cons Inc 412 S Missouri Ave Clearwater FL 34616-5336

LANSNER, KERMIT IRVIN, editor, consultant; b. N.Y.C., May 9, 1922; s. David and Anna (Gordon) L.; m. Fay Gross, Sept. 10, 1948; children: Gabrielle, Erica. B.A., Columbia U., 1942; postgrad., Harvard U., 1947, Columbia U., 1948; Fulbright scholar, Sorbonne, Paris, 1950. Asst. prof. philosophy Kenyon Coll., 1948-50; asso. editor Art News mag., 1953-54; mem. staff Newsweek mag., 1954-73, sr. editor, 1959-61, exec. editor, 1961-65, mng. editor, 1965-69, editor, 1969-72, contbg. editor, columnist, 1972-77; editor-in-chief Newsweek Books, 1972-73; cons. Louis Harris & Assocs., 1973-76, sr. v.p., 1976-82; editor-in-chief Fin. World mag., 1983-89, editl. dir., columnist, 1989-96. Columnist; contbr. New Republic, Kenyon Rev., Art News. Served to lt. USNR, 1942-46. Mem. Council Fgn. Relations, Century Assn., Phi Beta Kappa. Home and Office: 317 W 80th St New York NY 10024-5701

LANTAY, GEORGE CHARLES (WAGNER), school psychologist, psychotherapist, environmental consultant; b. N.Y.C., Aug. 1, 1942; s. George Sylvester and Geraldine LeMae (Ogline) L.; children by previous marriage: Scott Christopher, Christina, Susan Kimberly, Erica; m. Susannah Hewson, Dec. 31, 1992; 1 child, George Mason; BA, Hope (Mich.) Coll., 1965; MA, U. Ill., 1968; postgrad. in phys. therapy NYU, 1971-72; postgrad. in phys. and recreation therapy L.I. U., 1978-79; student physician asst. program Touro Coll., 1982-83; postgrad. in U.S. customs and law World Trade Inst., 1989—; postgrad. in E. Asian and African Studies St. John's U., 1993—; postgrad in electronics engring. tech. Tech. Career Inst., N.Y.C., 1993; universal HVAC cert. Mainstream Engring. Corp., 1994; postgrad. residential and comml. air conditioning Bergen County Tech. Schs., 1994-96; cert. programs air conditioning and refrigeration York Internat. Corp., 1996. Asst. prof. psychology Westminster Coll., Princeton, N.J., 1969-70; behavioral scientist, dir. Wagner Assocs., Princeton, 1969—; mgmt. tng. assoc. Western Elec. Co., N.Y.C., 1970; phys. therapist asst. Jewish Meml. Hosp., N.Y.C., 1970-72; sch. psychologist St. Agnes Cathedral High Sch., Rockville Centre, 1976—; ednl. cons. Test Preparation Centers, Riverdale, N.Y., 1975-79; intern psychologist N.Y. State Dept. Mental Hygiene, 1973-75; psychologist Odyssey House Parents Program, Wards Island, N.Y., 1973; adj. prof. behavioral scis. N.Y. Inst. Tech., Old Westbury, L.I., 1974-75; bd. dirs. div. field services N.Y. Testing and Guidance Center, Flushing, 1976—; with Adult Edn. Program Bergen County Tech. Schs., 1994-95. bd. dir. Shangri-La Day Camps, N.Y.C., 1976—; seminar instr. Nat. Traffic Safety Inst., N.Y.C., 1988—; asst. dir. aftersch. program Pub. Sch. 234, N.Y.C., 1988; founder Separation Encounter; contbr. U.S. Postal Svc., Cit. Stamp Adv. Coun., 1975-80, Pres.'s Commn. Mental Health, 1977-78; cons. Eastern Regional Inst. Edn., N.Y.U. Med. Sch. Dept. Psychiatry, Newark Council Social Agys., N.Y.C. Bd. Edn., Astor Program Intellectually Gifted Children, N.Y.C. Bd. Edn., Evaluation and Placement Unit, 1977-78, N.Y.C. Bd. Edn. Spl. Edn. Div., Queens Region, 1983, Office Contracted Services, 1983-86, Camp Northwood for Learning Disabilities, summer 1977, Esperanza Day Treatment Center, N.Y.C., 1981-82; psychologist United Cerebral Palsy of N.Y. State, 1986; field ops. supr. N.Y. regional office U.S. Census Bur., 1990; presch. sch. psychologist and outreach coord. St. Mark's Inst. for Community Mental Health, N.Y.C., 1990—; preschool psychologist Karen Horney Clinic Therapeutic Nursery Program, N.Y.C., 1992—; contbr. Commrs. Adv. Council on Vocat. Rehab., N.Y. State Edn. Dept., 1978-79; asst. dir. after school program P.S. 234, N.Y.C., 1988; registrar Ind. Order of Forresters USA, 1991; sales coord. NSA wings program, Northeast Region, USA. Named an Outstanding Young Man of Am., 1975; cert. sch. psychologist, cert. emergency med. technician, N.Y. State; qualified mental retardation profl., N.Y. State. Mem. APA (life), AAUP, Am. Ednl. Research Assn., Am. Assn. Sex Educators, Counselors and Therapists, Am. Phys. Therapy Assn. Am. Acad. Physicians Assts., Air Pollution Control Assn, Am. Soc. Heating, Refrigerating and Air Conditioning Engrs. Clubs: St. Bartholomew's Community, Downtown Glee (N.Y.C.). Author: Activities for Learning Disabled Children, 1980, Radon in Homes & What You Can Do to Protect Your Family's Health, 1987, A Nation Bored of Education, 1996; contbr. articles to Ch. Herald mag.; research on underachievement and masculine identification. Home and Office: 28 Greenwich Ave New York NY 10011-8359

LANTHIER, JOHN SPENCER, accounting company executive; b. Montreal, Can., 1940; m. Diane Safford, Sept. 16, 1961; children: Sherrill, Suzanne, John, Sara. Student, McGill U., Montreal. Fin. chartered acct. Ontario Inst., 1982. With Peat, Marwick Mitchell & Co., Montreal, 1960-72, ptnr., 1972-77; mng. ptnr. Peat Marwick's London (merger Thorne Ernst & Whinney 1989), Ontario, Can., 1977-82; mng. ptnr. Peat Marwick's London, Can., 1982-84, Toronto, Can., 1984-89; vice-chmn. KPMG Peat Marwick Thorne, Toronto, Can., 1989-93; chmn., chief exec. KPMG Can., Toronto, Can., 1993—; past chmn. bd. Goodwill Industries Toronto. Trustee United Way Greater Toronto, 1985-90, vice chmn., treas., mem. exec. com., 1986-89; mem. exec. com., gov. coun. U. Toronto, 1989—; dir. United Way Centraide Can., 1990-92; chair area wide United Way, Toronto, 1994—. Office: KPMG Canada, 40 King St W Scotia Pla Box 122, Toronto, ON Canada M5H 3Z2

LANTHIER, RONALD ROSS, retired manufacturing company executive; b. Montreal, Que., Can., May 2, 1926; s. Emile Edgar and Edith (Martin) L.; m. Jacqueline Barbara Dyment; children: April Carolyn, Bonnie Alice, Ronald Dyment, Andrea Elizabeth, John Elliott. Chartered Accountant, McGill U., 1952. Pub. accountant, 1944-51; chief accountant St. Lawrence Flour Co., 1951-52; controller Canadian Underwriters Assn., 1952-54; div. controller Canadian Aviation Electronics Co., 1954-56; treas. Webb & Knapp, Can., 1956-62; dir. adminstrn., mem. exec. com. Greenshields, Inc. (investment dealers), 1962-67; v.p. finance, treas., mem. exec. com. Canadian Marconi Co., 1967-72; v.p. finance, dir., mem. exec. com. Macdonald Tobacco, Inc., 1972-75; pres. Lanco Mgmt. Ltd., 1975—; v.p. finance MacDonald Stewart Textiles, 1976-77; v.p. fin., mem. exec. com. Electrolux Can., 1978-79; pres. Robert R. Bramhall & Assos. (Can.) Ltd., 1980-81; sr. v.p. Camflo Mines Ltd., 1981-84; v.p. fin. Starnav Corp., 1984-86; v.p. VR Fin. Svcs., 1987—. Mem. Inst. Chartered Accts. Que. and Ont., Phi Kappa Pi. Anglican. Home: 100 Westview Dr, Aurora, ON Canada L4G 7C9

LANTIERI, MICHAEL, special effects expert. Films include Heartbeeps, 1981, The Last Starfighter, 1984, Fright Night, 1985, My Science Project, 1985, Back to School, 1986, Poltergeist, 1986, Star Trek IV: The Voyage Home, 1986, The Witches of Eastwick, 1987, Moving, 1988, Who Framed Roger Rabbit?, 1988, Twins, 1988, Back to the Future II, 1989 (Acad. award nominee for best visual effects 1989), Caddyshack II, 1989, Indiana Jones and the Last Crusade, 1989, Nothing But Trouble, 1991, Hook, 1991 (Acad. award nominee 1991), Death Becomes Her, 1992, Jurassic Park, 1993 (Acad. award 1993). Office: IATSE Local 44 11500 Burbank Blvd North Hollywood CA 91601-2308

LANTIGUA, JOSE SALVADOR, computer engineer, consultant; b. Havana, Cuba, Mar. 18, 1953; came to U.S., 1960; s. Jose Gregorio and Hilda Simona (Barrial) L.; m. Pansy Reen Fuller, Mar. 5, 1977; children: Joseph Gabriel, Christina Simone. AA, Miami-Dade C.C., 1973; BA, Northwestern State U. La., 1978, BS, 1979; MA, Pepperdine U., 1980; M Computer Engring., Fla. Atlantic U., 1989. Engr. NASA, Houston, 1973-75; mgr. automation Blue Cross-Blue Shield, Jacksonville, Fla., 1981-83; regional engring. mgr. Victor Techs., Jacksonville, 1983-84; dir. sys. integration Abacus Data, Inc., Jacksonville, 1984-85; cons. engr. IBM, Jacksonville, 1985-93; mng. dir. Furash & Co., Washington, 1993-94; pres. Epi-Tech Corp., Alexandria, Va., 1994—. Author: Knowledge Rules from Dircted Graphs, 1989; contbr. articles to various publs. Advisor Jr. Achievement, Jacksonville, 1987. Maj. U.S. Army, 1975-80, mem. USAR, 1980—. Mem. IEEE, Am. Assn. for Artificial Intelligence, Assn. for Computing Machinery, Mensa, Phi Theta Gamma. Republican. Roman Catholic. Achievements include development of knowledge acquisition software, business process reengineering methodology, financial application business system architecture. Office: Epi-Tech Corp 8305 Rampart Ct Alexandria VA 22308

LANTOS, PETER R(ICHARD), industrial consultant, chemical engineer; b. Budapest, Hungary, July 18, 1924; came to U.S. 1939; naturalized citizen; s. Ernest and Bertha (Wigner) L.; m. Janice Kirchner, Dec. 20, 1947 (div. 1982); children: Geoffrey P., Gregory P., Gabrielle, Giselle. BChemE, Cornell U., 1945, PhD in Chem. Engring., 1950. Devel. chemist GE, Pittsfield, Mass., 1946-47; rsch. engr. E. I. Du Pont Nemours & Co., Wilmington, Del., 1950-55, supr. rsch., 1955-60; mgr. application and product devel. Celanese Plastics Co., Clark, N.J., 1961-63, mgr. R & D, 1964-69; dir. devel. Sun Chem. Corp., Carlstadt, N.J., 1969-70, v.p. R & D, 1970-75; gen. mgr. div. plastics Rhodia Inc., N.Y.C., 1975-76; dir. R & D Arco Polymers, Inc., Phila., 1976-77, v.p. R & D, 1978-79; pres. Target Group, Inc., Phila., 1980—. Contbr. over 30 articles to profl. jours. Pres. Bd. Health, Kennett Square, Pa., 1955-59. Mem. Am. Chem. Soc. (chmn. div. chem. mktg. and econs. 1988-89), Am. Inst. Chem. Engrs., Assn. Cons. Chemists and Chem. Engrs., Soc. Plastics Engrs., Soc. Plastics Industry. Home: PO Box 27247 Philadelphia PA 19118-0247 Office: Target Group Inc 1000 Harston Ln Erdenheim PA 19038

LANTOS, THOMAS PETER, congressman; b. Budapest, Hungary, Feb. 1, 1928; m. Annette Tillemann; children: Annette, Katrina. B.A., U. Washington, 1949, M.A., 1950; Ph.D., U. Calif.-Berkeley, 1953. Mem. faculty U. Wash., San Francisco State U., 1950-83; TV news analyst, commentator, sr. econ. and fgn. policy adviser to several U.S. senators; mem. Presdl. Task Force on Def. and Fgn. Policy, 97th-104th Congresses from 11th (now 12th) Calif dist., 1981—; ranking minority mem., internat. rels. subcom. on internat. ops. and human rels., internat. rels. subcom. on western hemisphere, mem. gov. reform and oversight com.; founder study abroad program Calif. State U. and Coll. System. Mem. Millbrae Bd. Edn., 1950-66. Democrat. Office: US Ho of Reps 2217 Rayburn HOB Washington DC 20515-0512*

LANTRIP, SANDRA TYNES-LEBLANC, realtor; b. Baton Rouge, Dec. 9, 1948; d. Otis Calvin Tynes and Mable (Brown) Hudgins; m. Terry L. Lantrip; children: Stacey Ann, William Heath, Lawrence Lloyd LeBlanc. Student, La. State U., 1966-67, SE La. U., 1967-68. Lic. real estate agent, La.; cert. mineral lease and royalty broker. Co-owner, v.p. Unltd. Properties Inc., Ethel, La., 1978-82; co-owner Unltd. Mgmt. Inc., Zachary, La., 1979-82, Sandia Properties, Ethel, 1982-86; corp. recruiter, acct. exec. Sales Cons., Baton Rouge, 1986-87; corp. recruiter, acct. exec. mgr. Armon's Career Ctr., Baton Rouge, 1987-88; pvt. practice cons., 1988-89; agt. Farms and Acreage Real Estate, 1986-89, Town & Country Properties, 1990—; owner The Real McCoy, 1988—. Bd. dirs. Battered Womens' League. Mem. NAFE, Baton Rouge Bd. Realtors, Realtors Land Inst. (state treas. ALC designation 1994), C. of C. of Baton Rouge. Democrat. Roman Catholic. Home: 8618 Highway 955 E Ethel LA 70730-4201 Office: PO Box 135 Ethel LA 70730-0135

LANTZ, GEORGE BENJAMIN, JR., business executive, college executive, consultant; b. Buckhannon, W.Va., Feb. 6, 1936; s. George Benjamin and Georgia Myrtle (Bodkin) L.; m. Mary Sue Powell, Feb. 25, 1957; children—Mary Lynne, Marsha, Kimberly, Rebecca, Todd. AB with honors, W.Va. Wesleyan Coll., 1960; LLD, W.Va. Wesleyan Coll., 1993; STB with honors, Boston U., 1964, PhD, 1971. Minister United Meth. Pastorates, W.Va. and Mass., 1956-75; mem. faculty W.Va. Wesleyan Coll., Buckhannon, 1967-73, chmn. div. humanities, prof. humanities and religion, 1974-75; asst. to pres., ACE fellow Ohio Wesleyan U., Delaware, 1973-74; dean coll. Mount Union Coll., Alliance, Ohio, 1975-80, pres., 1980-85; v.p. adminstrn. and devel. Nesco, Inc., Hudson, Ohio, 1985-88; pres. U. Indpls., 1988—; cons. Coun. Ind. Colls., Washington, 1982—; bd. dirs. The Nat. Bank Indpls. Trustee W.Va. Wesleyan Coll., 1986-88; bd. dirs. Dollars for Scholars Program, Ind., bd. dirs. Ind. Coll. of Ind., Salvation Army Adv. Bd. Mem., Ind. Law Enforcement Tng. Bd., Ind. State chpt. Nat. Multiple Sclerosis Soc., Ind. Higher Edn. Telecomm. Sys., Bus. Encouraging Success for Tomorrow, Meridian Mut. Inst.; bd. dirs. Greater Indpls. Progress Com.; bd. dirs. Internat. Fedn. for Bus. Edn.; mem. United Way Ctrl. Ind., Indpls. Downtown Inc., Japan-Am. Soc. of Ind., Inc., Benjamin Harrison Meml. Comm., English Speaking Union, Ind. Soc. of Chgo.; bd. adv. Greater Johnson County Cmty. Found.; mem. Ind. Colls. Blue Ribbon panel Indpls. Bus. Jour., Mayor's Global Initiative Task Force, Mayor's Operation Respect Network Com., Ind., Ind. Bus./Higher Edn. Forum; bd. dirs. Indpls. Conv. and Visitors Assn.; trustee Cypress Am. Archeol. Rsch. Inst.; elder South Ind. Conf. United Meth. Ch. With U.S. Army, 1954-56. Recipient Cokesbury Grad. award Meth. Bd. Higher Edn. Fellow Am. Coun. Edn.; mem. AAUP, Nat. Assn. Ind. Colls. and Univs. (commn. on financing higher edn.), Am. Assn. Higher Edn. (bd. dirs.), Nat. Assn. Schs. and Colls. of United Meth. Ch. (pres. 1993, mem. com. on internat. edn.), Internat. Assn. Univ. Pres., Soc. Bibl. Lit., North Ctrl. Assn. Colls. and Schs. (commr. 1978-85, cons., evaluator), Indpls. C. of C., Economic Club, Columbia Club, Skyline Club, Kiwanis. Home: 4051 Otterbein Ave Indianapolis IN 46227-3618 Office: U Indpls Office Pres 1400 E Hanna Ave Indianapolis IN 46227-3697

LANTZ, JOANNE BALDWIN, academic administrator emeritus; b. Defiance, Ohio, Jan. 26, 1932; d. Hiram J. and Ethel A. (Smith) Baldwin; m. Wayne E. Lantz. BS in Physics and Math., U. Indpls., 1953; MS in Counseling and Guidance, Ind. U., 1957; PhD in Counseling and Psychology, Mich. State U., 1969; LittD (hon.), U. Indpls., 1985; LHD (hon.), Purdue U., 1994; LLD (hon.), Manchester Coll., 1994. Tchr. physics and math. Arcola (Ind.) High Sch., 1953-57; guidance dir. New Haven (Ind.) Sr. High Sch., 1957-65; with Ind. U.-Purdue U., Fort Wayne, 1965—, interim chancellor, 1988-89, chancellor, 1989-94, chancellor emeritus, 1994—; bd. dirs. Ft. Wayne Nat. Corp., Foellinger Found. Contbr. articles to profl. jours. Mem. Ft. Wayne Econ. Devel. Adv. Bd. and Task Force, 1988-91, Corp. Coun., 1988-94; bd. advisors Leadership Ft. Wayne, 1988-94; mem. adv. bd. Ind. Sml. Bus. Devel. Ctr., 1988-90; trustee Ancilla System, Inc., 1984-89, chmn. human resources com., 1985-89, exec. com., 1985-89; trustee St. Joseph's Med. Ctr., 1983-84, pers. adv. com. to bd. dirs., 1978-84, chmn., 1980-84; bd. dirs. United Way Allen County, sec., 1979-80; bd. dirs. Anthony Wayne Vocat. Rehab. Ctr., 1969-75. Mem. Fort Wayne Ind.-Purdue Alumni Soc. (hon. mem. 1987), Am. Psychol. Assn., AAUW (internat. fellowship com. 1986-88, prog. com. 1981-83, Am. women fellowship com. 1978-83, chmn. 1981-83, trust rsch. grantee 1980), Southeastern Psychol. Assn. (referee conv. papers 1987, 88), Ind. Sch. Women's Club (v.p. prog. chair 1979-81), Pi Lambda Theta, Sigma Xi, Delta Kappa Gamma (editorial bd. 1986-88, gen. chair conv. 1985-86, dir. N.E. region 1982-84, adminstrv. bd., exec. bd. 1982-84, leadership devel. com.). Avocations: swimming, reading, knitting, boating.

LANTZ, KENNETH EUGENE, consulting firm executive; b. Altoona, Pa., Mar. 9, 1934; s. William Martin and Alice Lucretia (Glass) L.; m. D. Arlene Yocum, Nov. 28, 1959; children—Antonia Marie, Theresa Antoinette. B.S. cum laude, Fordham U., 1956. Cons. Sutherland Co., 1960-62; spl. rep. IBM, Los Angeles, 1962-67; dir. info. services Loyola-Marymount U., Los Angeles, 1967-70; pres. CBIS, Los Angeles, 1970-72, Kenneth Lantz Assocs., Los Angeles, 1977-82; mgr. fin. systems Occidental Life Ins. Los Angeles, 1973-77; dir. systems Sayre & Toso, Los Angeles, 1982-83; prin. Atwater, Lantz, Hunter & Co., Los Angeles, 1983—; lectr. computing topics Technology Transfer Inst., 1987-88. Author: The Prototyping Methodology, 1984. Contbr. articles to profl. jours. Served to 1st lt. USAF, 1957-60. Mem. Future of Automation Roundtable (dir. 1983—), Ins. Acctg. and Systems Assn. (Nat. Merit award 1984). Republican. Roman Catholic.

LANTZ, PHILLIP EDWARD, corporate executive, consultant; b. Laramie, Wyo., Sept. 21, 1938; s. Everett Delmer and Elizabeth Mary (Stratton) L.; m. Paula Bogel, June 16, 1962; children: Kirk Edward, Eric William. BA in Math., U. Colo., 1960; MA in Math., U. Wyo., 1966; MS in Ops. Rsch., Johns Hopkins U., 1972. Grad. teaching asst. U. Wyo., Laramie, 1964-65; sr. engr. Applied Physics Lab. Johns Hopkins U., Silver Spring, Md., 1965-70; v.p. Ops. Rsch. Inc., Silver Spring, Md., 1970-72; dir. Tetra Tech. Inc., Arlington, Va., 1972-74; pres., chief exec. officer Systems Planning and Analysis, Inc., Alexandria, Va., 1974—, also bd. dirs.; bd. dirs. Bryce Resort, Basye, Va. Lt. USN, 1960-64. Home: 2911 Eddington Ter Alexandria VA 22302-3503 Office: Systems Planning and Analysis Inc Ste 400 2000 N Beauregard St Alexandria VA 22311-1712

LANTZ, WILLIAM CHARLES, lawyer; b. Rochester, Minn., July 3, 1946; s. Charles E. and Doris (Greenwood) L.; m. Vickie L. Erickson, May 17, 1972; children: Charles Eric, Andrew William. BA, Hamline U., 1968; JD, U. Minn., 1971. Bar: Minn. 1971. From assoc. to ptnr. Dorsey & Whitney, Rochester, 1975—. Served to lt. JAGC, USNR, 1971-75. Mem. Minn. Bar Assn., Olmsted Bar Assn. Methodist. Lodge: Kiwanis. Home: 807 Sierra Ln NE Rochester MN 55906-4230 Office: Dorsey & Whitney 201 1st Ave SW Ste 340 Rochester MN 55902-3155

LANYI, JANOS KAROLY, biochemist, educator; b. Budapest, Hungary, June 5, 1937; came to U.S., 1957, naturalized, 1962; s. Istvan and Klara (Rosthy) L.; m. Carol Ann Giblin, Sept. 15, 1962 (div. Dec. , 1984); children: Clara Aileen, Sean Renton, Gabriella; m. Brigitte Schobert, Mar. 27, 1988. Student, Eotvos Lorand U. Scis., Budapest, 1955-56; B.S., Stanford U., 1959; M.A., Harvard U., 1961, Ph.D., 1963. Postdoctoral fellow Stanford U. Sch. Medicine, 1963-65; Nat. Acad. Scis. resident assoc. NASA-Ames Research Ctr., 1965-66; sr. scientist NASA-Ames Research Ctr., Moffett Field, Calif., 1966-80; prof. physiology and biophysics U. Calif.-Irvine, 1980—, chair dept. physiology and biophysics, 1995—; vis. fellow Cornell U., 1976. Recipient NASA medal for exceptional sci. achievement, 1977; recipient H. Julian Allen award for best sci. paper Ames Research Ctr., 1978, Alexander von Humboldt award for Sr. U.S. Scientists W.Ger., 1979-80. Mem. Am. Soc. Biol. Chemists, Biophys. Soc., Am. Soc. Microbiology, Hungarian Acad. Scis. (fgn.), Phi Beta Kappa, Sigma Xi. Office: U Calif Dept Physiology Biophy Irvine CA 92717

LANYON, ELLEN (MRS. ROLAND GINZEL), artist, educator; b. Chgo., Dec. 21, 1926; d. Howard Wesley and Ellen (Aspinwall) L.; m. Roland Ginzel, Sept. 4, 1948; children: Andrew, Lisa. BFA, Art Inst. Chgo., 1948; MFA, U. Iowa, 1950; Fulbright fellow, Courtauld Inst., U. London, 1950-51. Tchr. jr. sch. Art Inst. Chgo., 1952-54; past tchr. day sch., tchr. Rockford Coll., summer 1953, Oxbow Summer Sch. Painting, Saugatuck,

Mich., 1961-62, 67-70, 71-72, 78, 88, 94, U. Ill., Chgo., 1970, U. Wis. Extension, 1971-72, Pa. State U., 1974, U. Calif., 1974, Sacramento State U., 1974, Stanford U., 1974, Boston U., 1975, Kans. State U., 1976, U. Mo., 1976, U. Houston, 1977; assoc. prof. Cooper Union, N.Y.C., 1980-93; ret., 1993; founder, sec.-treas. Chgo. Graphic Workshop, 1952-55; participant Yaddo, 1973, 75, 76, Ossobow Island Project, 1976; adj. vis. prof. So. Ill. U., 1978, No. Ill. U., 1978, SUNY, Purchase, 1978, Cooper Union, N.Y.C., 1978-79, Parsons Sch. Design, N.Y.C., 1979; disting. vis. prof. U. S.D., 1980, U. Calif. Davis, 1980, Sch. Visual Arts, N.Y.C., 1980-83; vis. artist U. N.Mex., 1981, So. Ill. U., 1984, Sch. Art Inst., Chgo., 1985, U. Tenn., Md. Inst., Northwestern Grad. Sch., 1988, U. Pa., U. Iowa, 1991, 92; instr. workshops Anderson Ranch Workshop, Snow Mass, Colo., 1994, 96, Aspen Design Conf., 1994; vis. prof. U. Iowa, 1991-92; bd. dirs. Oxbow Summer Sch. Painting, 1972-82, emeritus, 1982—, instr., 1960, 72-82, 88, 94; vis. artist, instr. workshops Vt. Studio Sch., 1995, U. Costa Rica, San Pedro and San Ramon, 1995; instr. Interlaken Sch. of Art, 1996. One woman shows, Superior St. Gallery, Chgo., 1960, Stewart Richart Gallery, San Antonio, 1962, 65, Fairweather Hardin Gallery, Chgo., 1962, Zabriskie Gallery, N.Y.C., 1962, 64, 69, 72, B.C. Holland Gallery, Chgo., 1965, 68, Ft. Wayne Art Mus., 1967, Richard Gray Gallery, Chgo., 1970, 73, 76, 79, 82, 85, Madison Art Center, 1972, Nat. Collection at Smithsonian Instn., 1972, Odyssia Gallery, Rome, 1975, Krannert Performing Arts Center, 1976, Oshkosh Pub. Mus., 1976, U. Mo., 1976, Harcus Krakow, Boston, 1977—, Fendrick Gallery, Washington, 1978, Ky. State U., 1979, Ill. Wesleyan U., 1979, U. Calif., Davis, 1980, Odyssia Gallery, N.Y., 1980, Landfall Press, 1980, Alverno Coll., Milw., 1981, Susan Caldwell, Inc., N.Y.C., 1983, N.A.M.E. Gallery, Chgo., 1983, Printworks, Ltd., Chgo., 1989, 93 Pretto Berland Hall, N.Y.C., 1989, Struve Gallery, Chgo., 1990, 93, Berland Hall Gallery, N.Y.C., 1992, Sioux City Art Mus., Iowa, 1992, U. Iowa Mus. Art, 1994, Andre Zarre Gallery, N.Y.C., 1994, TBA, Chgo., 1996; retrospective exhibitions, Krannert Art Mus., McNay Art Mus., Chgo. Cultural Ctr., Stamford Mus., U. Tenn.; exhibited group shows, 1946—, including traveling exhbns., Am. Fedn. Arts, 1946-48, 50, 53, 57, 65, 66, 69; Art Inst. Chgo., 1946-47, 51-53, 55, 57-58, 60-62, 64, 66, 67, 68, 69, 71, 73, Corcoran Gallery Art, 1961, 76, Denver Art Mus., 1950, 52, Exhbn. Momentum, Chgo., 1948, 50, 52, 54, 56, Library of Congress, 1950, 52, Met. Mus. Art, 1952, Mus. Modern Art, 1953, 62, Phila. Mus. Art, 1946, 47, 50, 54, San Francisco Mus. Art, 1946, 50, U. Ill., 1953, 54, 57, Drawing Soc., Nat. Traveling Exhbn., 1965-66, The Painter and The Photograph traveling exhbn., 1964-65; Nostalgia traveling show, 1968-69, Violence,, Mus. Contemporary Art, Chgo., 1969, Birds and Beasts,, Graham Gallery, N.Y.C., 1969-71; Ill. Painters, Ill. Arts Council, 1968-71; Ill. painters: Beyond Illustration, HMH Publs. Europe, 1971, Chgo. Imagists, 1972, Chgo. Sch, 1972, Am. Women, 1972, Artists Books, 1973; Bicentennial America 76 traveling exhibit, 1976; Chgo. Connection, 1976-77, Downtown Whitney, N.Y.C., 1978—, Queens Mus., 1978, Dayton Art Inst., 1978, Odyssia Gallery, N.Y.C., 1979, Chgo. Cultural Center, 1979, Aldrich Mus. Contemporary Art, 1980, Bklyn. Mus., 1980, Walker Art Center, 1981, also Lisbon, Venice biennales, Voorhees Mus. Rutgers U., Mus. Contemporary Art, Chgo., Milw. Art. Mus., Art of the Quilt traveling exhibition, 1985—, Made In America Berkeley Art Mus., 1987, Art of the Screen traveling exhibition, 1986—, Lines of Vision: Drawings by Contemporary Women, 1989, Symbolism: Cooper Union, 1989, Randall Gallery, St. Louis, 1991, Printworks Ltd., Chgo., 1989-96, Berland/Hall, N.Y.C., 1991, The Cultural Ctr., Chgo., 1992, Matnan Locks Gallery, Phila., 1992, Art Inst. Chgo., 1992, Andre Zarre Gallery, N.Y.C., 1993-96, Nat. Mus. Women in Arts, Washington, 1994-95, Wadsworth Atheneum, Hartford, Conn., 1996, Mus. Contemporary Art, 1996, represented in permanent collections Art Inst. Chgo., Denver Art Mus., Library of Congress, Inst. Internat. Edn., London, Finch Coll., N.Y., Krannert Mus., U. Ill., U. Mass., N.J. State Mus., Ill. State Mus., Bklyn. Mus., Mus. Contemporary Art, Chgo., Nat. Coll. Fine Arts, Walker Art Ctr., Mpls., Boston Pub. Library, Des Moines Art Center, Albion Coll., Met. Mus., McNay Art Inst., Albion Coll., Kans. State U., U. Dallas, U. Houston, Cornell U., CUNY, Nat. Mus. Women in Arts, also numerous pvt. collections.; mural paintings: Working Men's Coop. Bank Boston, 1979, State of Ill. Bldg., Chgo., 1985, State Capitol, Springfield, Ill., 1989, City of Miami Beach, Art in Public Places project, Police and Court Facility, 1993; published: Wonder Production Vol. I, 1971, Jataka Tales, 1975, Transformations, 1976, Transformations II (Endangered), 1983 ; editorial bd.: Coll. Art Jour., 1982-92; illustrator: The Wandering Tattler, 1975, Perishible Press, 1976—, Red Ozier Press, 1980—. Recipient Armstrong prize Art Inst. Chgo., 1946, 55, 77, Town and Country purchase prize, 1947, Blair prize, 1958, Palmer prize, 1962, 64, Chan prize, 1961, Vielehr prize, 1967, Logan prize, 1981; purchase prize Denver Art Mus., 1950; purchase prize Library of Congress, 1950; Cassandra Found. award, 1970; Nat. Endowment for Arts grantee, 1974, 87; Herewood Lester Cook Found. grantee, 1981. Mem. Coll. Art Assn. (dir., exec. com. 1977-80), Delta Phi Delta. Address: 138 Prince St New York NY 10012-3135 also: PO Box 1045 Stockbridge MA 01262

LANYON, WESLEY EDWIN, retired museum curator, ornithologist; b. Norwalk, Conn., June 10, 1926; s. William J. and Frances A. (Merrill) L.; m. Vernia E. Hall, Jan. 29, 1951; children: Cynthia Hall, Scott Merrill. A.B. in Zoology, Cornell U., 1950; Ph.D., U. Wis., 1955. Interpretive specialist Nat. Park Service, summers 1947-51; instr. zoology U. Ariz., 1955-56; asst. prof. Miami U., Oxford, Ohio, 1956-57; asst. curator birds Am. Mus. Natural History, N.Y.C., 1957-63, asso. curator, 1963-67, curator, 1967-88; resident dir. Kalbfleisch Field Research Sta., 1958-74; adj. prof. biology City U. N.Y., 1968-87; expdns. for mus. to, C.Am. and Mexico, 1959, 60, 63, West Indies, 1960, 65, 66, S. Am., 1967-80. Contbr. articles to profl. jours. Fellow Am. Ornithologists Union (Brewster award 1968, pres. 1976-78); mem. Cooper, Wilson ornithol. socs., Eastern Bird Banding Assn., Ecol. Soc. Am., Soc. Study Evolution, Soc. Systematic Zoology, Linnaean Soc. N.Y., Sigma Xi. Home: RR 2 Box 219 Louisa VA 23093-9405

LANZ, ROBERT FRANCIS, corporate investment and financial officer; b. Greenwich, Conn., Oct. 30, 1942; s. John Edwin and Katheryn Loretto (Jerman) L.; m. Elizabeth Kienlen, Nov. 11, 1967; children—Christopher, Jennifer. B.A., LaSalle Coll., Phila., 1964; postgrad., Law Sch., Fordham U., 1966-67; M.B.A., U. Conn., 1975. Corp. trust officer Chase Manhattan Bank, N.Y.C., 1966-71; cons. Stone & Webster, N.Y.C., 1971; sr. cons. EBASCO Services, N.Y.C., 1971-73; v.p., treas. Pacific/Corp., Inc., Portland, Oreg., 1973-93; chief investment officer Pacific/Corp., Inc., 1993—; chmn. investment com., 1993—; sr. v.p. Pacific/Corp. Credit, Inc., Portland, Oreg., 1986—; pres. Willamette Devel. Corp. Mem. legal budget com. City of Lake Oswego, Oreg., 1975-80. Served with U.S. Army, 1964-66. Mem. Edison electric Inst. (fin. com. 1980-85), Northwest Electric Light and Power Assn. Democrat. Roman Catholic. Avocations: travel; languages; golf. Home: 17351 Canyon Dr Lake Oswego OR 97034-6711 Office: PacifiCorp 700 NE Multnomah St Portland OR 97213*

LANZA, DONALD CHARLES, otolaryngologist, rhinologist; b. Yonkers, N.Y., Jan. 16, 1959; s. Donald Charles and Lenore Angela (Boccia) L.; m. Suzanne Terse Moons, Jan. 7, 1989; children: Douglas Reid, Andrew Joseph. BS in Biology, Fordham U., 1975-79; MS in Physiology, Georgetown U., 1979-80, student, 1980-81; MD, SUNY, Bklyn., 1981-85. Diplomate Am. Bds. Otolaryngology, Med. Examiners; lic. Pa., Md., N.Y. General surgery intern Albany (N.Y.) Med. Ctr. Hosp., 1987-90, gen. surgery resident, 1986-87, otolaryngology resident, 1987-90; fellow rhinology and endoscopic sinus surgery U. Pa., Phila., 1991, Johns Hopkins Med. Instns., Balt., 1990-91; instr. surgery Albany Med. Coll., 1989-90; instr. otolaryngology Johns Hopkins Med. Instns., Balt., 1990-91; lectr. U. Pa., Phila., 1991, asst. prof., 1991—; mem. numerous coms. U. Pa., 1992—, dept. otorhinolaryngology Hops. U. Pa., 1991—; guest faculty Shadyside Hosp., Pitts., 1993, Health Comms., Inc., Princeton, N.J., 1993, Albany Med. Ctr., 1990-91; course dir. U. Pa., 1991-92; instr. Med. Coll. Ga., Boca Raton, Fla., 1991, Lahey Clinic, Boston, 1990, Tulane U., New Orleans, 1990, U. Mich., Ann Arbor, 1990; advanced pediatric life support Children's Hops. Albany Med. Ctr., 1990; lectr. in field 1989—. Peer reviewer: Jour. Allergy and Clin. Immunology, 1992—, Am. Jour. Rhinology, 1991—; contbr. articles to profl. jours., chpts. to books. Recipient Otolaryngology Resident Rsch. award Albany Med. Ctr., 1988, 89. Mem. AMA, Am. Acad. Otolaryngology, Am. Acad. Otolaryngic Allergy (assoc.), Am. Rhinology Soc. (cons. to bd. dirs. 1993—), Am. Sleep Disorders Assn., Assn. Chemoreception Scis., Pa. Med. Soc., Pa. Acad. Otolaryngology, Phila. County Med. Soc., Soc. Univ. Otolaryngologists. Office: Hosp U Pa Head & Neck Surg Silverstein 5 3400 Spruce St Philadelphia PA 19104

LANZA, FRANK C., electronics executive; b. 1931. BS, Heralds Engring. Coll., 1956. Project engr. Philco Western Devel. Labs., 1957-59; v.p. Textron Corp., Providence, 1960-72; with Loral Corp., N.Y.C., 1972—, v.p., 1973-79, exec. v.p., 1979-81, corp. pres., chief operating officer, 1981—, also bd. dirs., CEO, bd. of dirs. Served with USCG, 1953-55. Office: Loral Corp 600 3rd Ave Fl 36 New York NY 10016-2001*

LANZA, ROBERT JOHN, lawyer; b. N.Y.C., June 10, 1957; s. Joseph John and Rose (LaGatta) L.; m. Ana Fatima Abraido; 1 child, Anthony Joseph. BA, Baruch Coll., 1982; JD, Yeshiva U., 1985; LLM, NYU, 1986. Bar: N.Y. 1986, Calif. 1986, U.S. Dist. Ct. (all dists.) Calif. 1986, U.S. Ct. Appeals (9th cir.) 1987. Assoc. Morgan Lewis & Bockius, Calif., 1986-89, N.Y., 1986-89; from assoc. to ptnr. Marcus Montgomery Wolfson PC, N.Y.C., 1989—; sec. com. on mcpl. affairs N.Y. City Bar Assn., N.Y.C., 1992. Contbg. author: California Labor Law, 1989. Cpl. USMC, 1974-79. Avocations: boxing, hiking. Office: Marcus Montgomery Wolfson 53 Wall St New York NY 10005

LANZA, ROBERT PAUL, medical scientist; b. Boston, Feb. 11, 1956; s. Samuel and Barbara (Corbett) L. BA, U. Pa., 1978, MD, 1983. Sr. scientist Biohybrid Techs., Shrewsbury, Mass., 1990-93, dir. transplantation biology, 1993—; clin. assoc. prof. surgery Tufts U., 1994-95; assoc. surgery Harvard Med. Sch., 1991-93. Editor: Heart Transplantation, 1984, Medical Science and the Advancement of World Health, 1985, Procurement of Pancreatic Islets I, 1994, Immunomodulation of Pancreatic Islets II, 1994, Immunoisolation of Pancreatic Islets III, 1994, One World, 1996, Tissue Engineering/Cellular Medicine Series, 1995—, Yearbook of Cell and Tissue Transplantation, 1996—, Principles of Tissue Engineering, 1996; contbr. articles to profl. jours. Prof. Howe Buck scholar, 1974-75, Benjamin Franklin scholar, 1975-78, Univ. scholar, 1976-83, Fulbright scholar, 1978-79; Hon. Christiaan Barnard fellow, 1982-84, Mry K. Iacocca Transplantion fellow, 1988-90. Home: South Meadow Pond Island 15-35 S Meadow Rd Clinton MA 01510 Office: BioHybrid Techs 910 Boston Turnpike Shrewsbury MA 01545-3303

LANZAFAME, SAMUEL JAMES, manufacturing company executive; b. Canastota, N.Y., Oct. 9, 1950; s. James Charles and Sarah Ann (Aiello) L.; m. Janet Mangan, Nov. 23, 1974; children: Bethany, Erin, John. BA, Holy Cross U., 1972; MBA magna cum laude, Notre Dame U., 1974. Project coordinator Oneida (N.Y.) Ltd., 1975-76, mgr. mktg. research and bus. devel., 1977-78, corp. mgr. spl. projects, 1979-80, br. mgr. No. Ireland subsidiary, 1980-82, sr. v.p. Camden Wire subsidiary, 1983-84, pres. Camden Wire subsidiary, 1985-86, pres. corp., 1986—. Avocations: running, gardening. Office: Ctrl Locating Svc Ltd 6489 Ridings Rd Syracuse NY 13206-1112*

LANZANO, RALPH EUGENE, civil engineer; b. N.Y.C., Dec. 26, 1926; s. Ralph and Frances (Giuliano) L. BCE, NYU, 1959. Registered profl. engr., N.Y. Engring. aide Seelye, Stevenson, Value & Knecht, N.Y.C., 1957-58; jr. civil engr. N.Y.C. Dept. Pub. Works (now N.Y.C. Dept. Water Resources), 1960-63; asst. civil engr. N.Y.C. Dept. Water Resources, 1963-68, civil engr., 1968-71, 72-77; sr. san. engr. Parsons, Brinckerhoff, Quade & Douglas, N.Y.C., 1971-72; civil engr. N.Y.C. Dept. Water Resources, N.Y. Dept. Environ. Protection, 1978-90; pvt. practice profl. engr. Huntington Station, N.Y., 1990—. Mem. NRA (life), ASCE (life), ASTM, NSPE, APHA, N.Y. Soc. Profl. Engrs., Water Environ. Fedn., Am. Water Works Fedn., Am. Fedn. Arts, U.S. Inst. Theatre Tech., Met. Mus. Art, NYU Alumni Assn., Lincoln Ctr. for Performing Arts, Film Soc. Lincoln Ctr., N.Y.C. Ballet Guild, Asia Soc., Nat. Fire Protection Assn., N.Y. Pub. Libr., Sta. WNET-TV, U.S. Lawn Tennis Assn. (life), Nat. Wildlife Fedn., Internat. Wildlife Fedn., Bible-a-Month Club, Nat. Pks. and Conservation Assn., Nat. Geog. Soc., Nat. Audubon Soc., Am. Automobile Assn., Bklyn. Bot. Garden, Am. Mus. Natural History, Paralyzed Vets. Am., Am. Soc. Prevention Cruelty to Animals, Chi Epsilon. Avocations: books, art, music, dance, theatre. Home and Office: 17 Cottage Ct Huntington Station NY 11746 .

LANZEROTTI, LOUIS JOHN, physicist; b. Carlinville, Ill., Apr. 16, 1938; s. Emanuel Louis and Mary Pauline (Orienti) L.; m. Mary Yvonne DeWolf, June 19, 1965; children: Mary Yvonne, Louis DeWolf. BS, U. Ill., 1960; MA, Harvard U., 1963, PhD, 1965. Postdoctoral fellow Lucent Technologies Bell Labs., Murray Hill, N.J., 1965-67; mem. tech. staff AT&T Bell Labs., Murray Hill, N.J., 1967-82, Disting. mem. tech. staff, 1982—; adj. prof. U. Fla., Gainesville, 1978—; mem. polar rsch. bd. NRC, Washington, 1982-91, mem. space sci. bd., 1980-84, chmn. space studies bd., 1988-94, mem. ocean studies bd., 1995—, chmn. bd. rev. Army Rsch. Lab., 1996—; mem. phys. sci. com. NASA, Washington, 1975-79, chmn. space and earth adv. commn., 1984-88, mem. adv. coun., 1984-94; mem. adv. com. on future U.S. space program, 1990, mem. v.p.'s space policy adv. bd., 1992-93, v.p. blue ribbon adv. com. on redesign of space sta., 1993-94; mem. corp. Woods Hole Oceanographic Instn., 1993—. Co-author: Particle Diffusion in Rad. Belts, 1974; co-editor 2 books related to space physics, 1977, 79; contbr. over 400 tech. papers to profl. jours. V.p. Harding Twp. (N.J.) Sch. Bd., 1982-90, com., 1993—. Recipient Antarctic Svc. medal U.S., 1979, Disting. Pub. Svc. award NASA, 1988, 94, Achievement award Blackburn Coll. Alumni Assn., 1993; mountain named in his honor in Antarctica; minor planet 5504 named in his honor. Fellow Am. Phys. Soc., Am. Geophys. Union, AAAS; mem. NAE, Internat. Acad. Astronautics, Woods Hole Oceanographic Instn. Office: Bell Labs Lucent Technologies 700 Mountain Ave New Providence NJ 07974-2008

LANZILLOTTI, ROBERT FRANKLIN, economist, educator; b. Washington, June 19, 1921; s. Vincent and Gilda S. (Incutti) L.; m. Patricia Joy Jackson, Oct. 27, 1945; children—Robert J. (dec.), Donna J. Student, Dartmouth Coll., 1943; B.A., Am. U., 1946, M.A., 1947; Ph.D., U. Calif., Berkeley, 1953; D.D.L. (hon.), Tampa U., 1979; D.D.S. (hon.), Fla. Inst. Tech., 1979. Teaching fellow U. Calif. at Berkeley, 1947-49; mem. faculty Wash. State U., 1949-61, prof. econs., 1959-61; research assoc. Brookings Instn., 1956-57, 1974-75; prof. econs., chmn. dept. Mich. State U., 1961-69; prof. econs., dean Coll. Bus. Adminstrn., U. Fla., Gainesville, 1969-86, Eminent Scholar chair in Am. econ. instns., 1986; mem. U.S. Price Commn., 1971-72; bd. dirs. Jim Walter Corp., Citizens and So. Bank Corp., Am. Birthright Corp., Fla. Power Corp., Bank of Ormond Beach, Fla., Talquin Corp., Bottom-Line Assoc., Fla. Progress Corp.; chmn. Econ. Adv. Bd. to Gov. Fla., 1973—; cons. Mich. Bankers Assn., attys. gen. Calif., Wis., Minn., Ill., Fla., Mich., Oreg., Washington; attys. gen. also Fed. Trade Commn., U.S. Dept. Justice, U.S. Govt. Acctg. Office, U.S. Comptroller of the Currency, U.S. Census Bur. Author: Hard-Surface Floor Covering Industry, 1955, Pricing, Production & Marketing Policies of Small Manufacturers, 1964, Banking Structure in Michigan, 1945-63, 1966; co-author: Pricing in Big Business, 1959, Phase II in Review: The Price Commission Experience, 1975, Economic Effects of Government Mandated Costs, 1979; editor: The Conglomerate Corporation, 1981; co-editor: Management Under Government Intervention: The View from Mt. Scopus; contbr. articles to profl. jours. Served to lt. (j.g.) USNR, 1943-45; lt. comdr. Res. Decorated Bronze Star (2); NATO fellow, 1964. Mem. Am. Econ. Assn., So. Econ. Assn. (1st v.p. 1972-73), Fla. Coun. of 100, Phi Beta Kappa (hon.), Beta Gamma Sigma, Omicron Delta Kappa.

LANZINGER, KLAUS, language educator; b. Woergl, Tyrol, Austria, Feb. 16, 1928; came to U.S., 1971, naturalized, 1979; m. Aida Schuessl, June, 1954; children—Franz, Christine. B.A., Bowdoin Coll., 1951; Ph.D., U. Innsbruck (Austria), 1952. Research asst. U. Innsbruck, 1957-67; assoc. prof. modern langs. U. Notre Dame (Ind.), 1967-77, prof., 1977—, resident dir. fgn. study program, Innsbruck, 1969-71, 76-78, 82-85; acting chmn. dept. Modern and Classical Languages, U. Notre Dame, fall 1987, chmn. dept. German and Russian, 1989-96. Author: Epik im amerikanischen Roman, 1965, Jason's Voyage: The Search for the Old World in American Literature, 1989. Editor: Americana-Austriaca, 5 vols., 1966-83. Contbr. numerous articles to profl. jours. Bowdoin Coll. fgn. student scholar, 1950-51; Fulbright research grantee U. Pa., 1961; U. Notre Dame summer research grantee Houghton Library, Harvard U., 1975, 81. Mem. MLA, Deutsche Gesellschaft für Amerikastudien, Thomas Wolfe Soc. Home: 52703 Helvie Dr South Bend IN 46635-1215 Office: Dept German Russian Langs & Lits U Notre Dame Notre Dame IN 46556

LANZL, LAWRENCE HERMAN, medical physicist; b. Chgo., Apr. 8, 1921; s. Hans and Elsa (Seitz) L.; m. Elisabeth Farber, Sept. 18, 1947; children: Eric Lawrence, Barbara Jane. B.S., Northwestern U., 1943; M.S., U. Ill., 1947, Ph.D., 1951. Diplomate: Am. Bd. Health Physics (dir. 1969-73), Am. Bd. Radiology (mem. physics exam. com. 1977-83). Asst. dept. astronomy Dearborn Obs.; interim instr. dept. physics Northwestern U., Evanston, Ill., 1941-43; jr. physicist Metall. Lab., Manhattan Project, U. Chgo., 1944, Los Alamos (N.Mex.) Sci. Lab., Manhattan Project, U. Calif., 1944-45; research asst. dept. physics U. Ill., Urbana, 1946-50; asso. physicist naval reactor div. Argonne (Ill.) Nat. Lab., 1951; sr. physicist U. Chgo., Argonne Cancer Research Hosp., 1951-55, research asso., 1955-56; asst. prof. U. Chgo., 1956-59, asso. prof., 1959-68, prof. dept. radiology and Franklin McLean Meml. Research Inst.,, 1968-80, prof. emeritus, 1980—; prof. Rush Med. Coll., Chgo., 1980—; prof., chmn. dept. med. physics Coll. Health Scis. and Grad. Coll., Rush U., Chgo., 1982—; 1st officer divsn. life scis. IAEA, Vienna, Austria, 1967-68; cons. Pan Am. Health Orgn., 1993, Internat. Atomic Energy Agy., 1994; radiation hazard control expert Ill. Bd. Radiation Physics, 1960; mem. Radiation Protection Adv. Coun. State Ill., 1966—, chmn., 1971—; mem. Med. Use Adv. Bd. State Ill., 1974—. Author: (with others) Moving Field Radiation Therapy, 1962, Radiation Accidents and Emergencies in Medicine, Research and Industry, 1965, Atlas of Radiation Dose Distributions, 1972; editor: Recent Developments in Digital Imaging, 1985; contbr. (with others) articles to profl. jours. Mem. DBM Adv. Panel for Californium Program AEC, 1969-73; cons. Nat. Cancer Inst., 1968-88; cons. therapeutic radiology service, sect. radiation physics Hines (Ill.) VA Hosp., 1969-87, chmn. adv. panel on radiation safety and protection, 1973-80; mem. coun. Marie Sklodowska-Curie Meml. Found., Warsaw, Poland, 1989—. Recipient Commendation VA, Washington, 1975, Alumni Honor award for disting. svc. U. Ill., 1984, Landauer award Midwest chpt. Am. Assn. Physicists in Medicine/Health Physics Soc., 1989; Evans scholar Northwestern U., 1940-43; Lawrence H. Lanzl Inst. of Med. Physics named in his honor. Fellow Am. Coll. Radiology (mem. commn. human resources 1976-88), Health Physics Soc. (editor assn. jour. 1979-83), Am. Assn. Physicists in Medicine (pres. 1966-67, chmn. Commn. on Accreditation 1981-89, Spl. Recognition award Midwest chpt. 1977, chmn. local arrangements 1969-86, mem. com. on tng. med. physicists 1976-90, William D. Coolidge award 1978, Farrington Daniels award 1984, Landauer Meml. award 1989, establisher Laurence H. Lanzl lecture); mem. AAAS, Am. Phys. Soc., Am. Assn. Physicists in Medicine (pres. 1990), Internat. Orgn. Med. Physics (U.S. del. 1973-85, v.p. 1982-85, pres. 1985-89, editor Med. Physics World 1982-85), Radiol. Soc. N.Am. (mem. assoc. sci. com. 1972-82), Nat. Coun. Radiation Protection and Measurements (mem. sci. coms. 1967-92), Radiation Rsch. Soc., Am. Nuclear Soc. (Midwest), Hosp. Physicists' Assn. (U.K.), Internat. Radiation Protection Assn., Assn. Med. Physicists India, Chinese Soc. Med. Physics (hon.), Internat. Union Phys. and Engring. Scis. in Medicine (coun. 1985-94, pres. 1988-91, past pres. 1991-94), Sigma Xi (Dsiting. Scientist Mem. award 1989, J.M. Paul Meml. award 1992). Unitarian. Club: Quadrangle. Office: Rush-Presbyn-St Luke's Med Ctr Dept Med Physics 1653 W Chicago IL 60612

LANZONI, VINCENT, medical school dean; b. Kingston, Mass., Feb. 23, 1928; s. Vincent and Caroline (Melloni) L.; m. Phoebe Krey, June 12, 1960; children: Karen, Susan, Margaret. BS, Tufts U., 1949, PhD, 1953; MD, Boston U., 1960. USPHS fellow Tufts U., 1953-54; intern in medicine Boston City Hosp., 1960-61, resident and fellow in medicine, 1961-65; asst. prof. pharmacology Boston U., 1964-67, assoc. prof. medicine and pharmacology, 1967-73, prof., 1973-75; assoc. dean Sch. Medicine, 1969-75; prof. U. Medicine and Dentistry N.J., Newark, 1975—, dean N.J. Med. Sch., 1975-87, interim dean Grad. Sch. Biomed. Scis., 1987—; bd. dirs., sec.-treas. Postgrad. Med. Inst., 1972-75; bd. dirs. Mass. Health Research Inst., Mass. Registration in Nursing, Roxbury Neighborhood Clinic. Served to 1st lt. USAF, 1954-56. Researcher cardiovascular pharmacology, hypertension. Office: NJ Med Sch 100 Bergen St Newark NJ 07103-2407

LAO, LANG LI, nuclear fusion research physicist; b. Hai Duong, Vietnam, Jan. 28, 1954; came to U.S., 1972; s. Thich Cuong and Boi Phan (Loi) L.; m. Ngan Hua, Dec. 22, 1979; children: Bert J., Brian J. BS, MS, Calif. Inst. Tech., 1976; MS, U. Wis., 1977, PhD, 1979. Staff scientist Oak Ridge (Tenn.) Nat. Lab., 1979-81, TRW, Redondo Beach, Calif., 1981-82; prin. scientist Gen. Atomics, San Diego, 1982—. Contbr. articles to sci. jours. Recipient award for Excellence in Plasma Physics Research Am. Physical Society, 1994. Fellow Am. Phys. Soc. (co-recipient excellence in plasma physics rsch. award 1994). Achievements include being world leader in equilibrium analysis of magnetic fusion plasma physics experiments; developed a widely used computer code essential for successful operation and interpretation of tokamak fusion experiments. Office: General Atomics 3550 General Atomics Ct San Diego CA 92121-1122

LAPALOMBARA, JOSEPH, political science educator; b. Chgo., May 18, 1925; s. Louis and Helen (Teutonico) LaP.; m. Lyda Mae Ecke, June 22, 1947 (div.); children—Richard, David, Susan; m. Constance Ada Bezer, June, 1971. A.B., U. Ill., 1947, A.M., 1950; A.M. (Charlotte Elizabeth Proctor fellow, Class of 1883 fellow), Princeton U., 1952, Ph.D., 1954; student, U. Rome (Italy), 1952-53; M.A. (hon.), Yale U., 1964. Instr., then asst. prof. polit. sci. Oreg. State Coll., 1947-50; instr. politics Princeton U., 1952; mem. faculty Mich. State U., 1953-64, prof. polit. sci., 1958-64, head dept., 1958-63; prof. polit. sci. Yale U., 1964—; Arnold Wolfers prof., 1969—, chmn. dept. polit. sci., 1974-78, 82-85; prof. Sch. of Orgn. and Mgmt., 1979-84; dir. Instn. for Social and Policy Studies, 1987-92; chmn. Council Comparative and European Studies, 1966-71; cultural attache, first sec. U.S. embassy, Rome, 1980-81; vis. prof. U. Florence, Italy, 1957-58, U. Calif.-Berkeley, 1962, Columbia U., 1966-67, U. Turin, 1974, U. Catania, 1974; cons. FCDA, 1956, Carnegie Corp., 1959, Brookings Instn., 1962, Ford Found., 1965-76, Twentieth Century Fund, 1965-69, AID, 1967-68, Fgn. Svc. Inst., 1968-72, 74-76, Ednl. Testing Svc., 1970-75, Alcoa, 1978-80, Rohm & Haas, 1975-76, GE, 1978-80, Union Carbide, 1981-82, Montedison, 1984-85, Ente Nazionale Idrocarburi, 1983-93, Guardian Industries, 1990-93, Praxair, 1992—, Swiss Bank Corp., 1994—, Athena, 1994-95, Richard Medley Assocs., 1995—; sr. rsch. assoc. Conf. Bd. N.Y., 1976-81; pres. Italian-Am. Multimedia Corp. N.Y., 1988—. Author: The Initiative and Referendum in Oregon, 1950, The Italian Labor Movement: Problems and Prospects, 1957, Guide to Michigan Politics, rev. edit, 1960, (with Alberto Spreafico) Elezioni e Comportamento Politico in Italia, 1963, Bureaucracy and Political Development, 1963, Interest Groups in Italian Politics, 1964, Italy: The Politics of Planning, 1966, (with Myron Weiner) Political Parties and Political Development, 1966, Clientela e Parentela, 1967, Burocracia y desarrolo politico, 1970, Crises and Sequences of Political Development, (with others), 1972, Politics Within Nations, 1974, (with Stephen Blank) Multinational Corporations and National Elites: A Study in Tensions, 1975, Multinational Corporations in Comparative Perspective, 1976, Multinational Corporations and Developing Countries, 1979, A Politica nos Interior das Nações, 1982, Democracy, Italian Style, 1987, Democrazia all'italiana, 1988, Die Italiener: oder Demokratie als Lebenskunst, 1988, Democratie à l'italienne, 1990; bd. editors Midwest Jour. Polit. Sci, 1956-57, Yale U. Press, 1965-72, 73-76, ABC-CL10, 1976—, Global Perspectives, 1983—; mem. editorial bd. Comparative Politics, 1968—, Jour. Comparative and European Studies, 1969—, Am. Jour. Polit. Sci, 1976-80, Italian Jour., 1988, Yale Rev., 1993—; editor series comparative politics Prentice-Hall Co., 1971-85; mem. editorial adv. bd. Jour. Comparative Adminstrn, 1970-74, Adminstrn. and Soc, 1974—; adv. bd. ABC Polit. Sci; N.Am. editor: Mediterranean Observer, 1981-86; editor in chief Italy, Italy, 1988—; contbr. articles to profl. jours. Mem. exec. com. Inter Univ. Consortium Polit. Rsch., 196-70; mem. staff Social Sci. Rsch. Coun., 1966-73; chmn. West European fgn. area fellowship program Social Sci. Rsch. Coun.-Am. Coun. Learned Socs., 1972-74; bd. dirs. Mich. Citizenship Clearing House, 1955; trustee Transparency Internat.-USA, 1994—; mem. internat. coun. Ctr. for Strategic and Internat. Studies, 1990—. Decorated knight comdr. Order of Merit, Republic of Italy, Fulbright scholar, 1952-53, 57-58, Penfield scholar U. Pa., 1953; fellow Social Sci. Rsch. Coun., 1952-53, Ctr. Advanced Study Behavioral Scis., 1961-62, Rockefeller Found., 1963-64, Ford Found., 1969, Guggenheim Found., 1971-72; recipient Guido Dorso prize, Italy, 1984, Medal of Honor, Italian Constitutional Ct., 1993, Presidency of Italian Republic, 1993. Mem. Am. Acad. Arts and Scis., Conn. Acad. Arts and Scis., Am. Acad. in Rome (trustee 1984-90), Social Sci. Research Council (com. comparative politics 1958-72), Am. Polit. Sci. Assn. (exec. coun. 1963-65, exec. com. 1967-68, v.p. 1979-80, mem. conf. group on Italian politics and soc. 1978, conf. pres. 1984-85), So. Polit. Sci. Assn., Midwest Polit. Sci. Assn., Am. Soc. Pub. Adminstrn., Am. Acad. Polit. and Social Sci., Soc. for Italian Hist. Studies, Societá Italiana di Studi Elettorali, Consiglio Italiano di Scienze Sociali, Phi

Beta Kappa, Phi Kappa Phi, Phi Eta Sigma. Clubs: Yale of N.Y., Elizabethan, Morys Assn., East India. Home: 50 Huntington St New Haven CT 06511-1333

LAPE, ROBERT CABLE, broadcast journalist; b. Akron, Ohio; s. C. Robert and Mary Elizabeth (Cable) L.; m. Marcia Lou Giesy, June 22, 1955 (div. Dec. 1969); children: Debra, Robert S., Alida, Douglas; m. Eve Bergman, Feb. 14, 1982. BS in Journalism and Radio Speech, Kent State U., 1955. Reporter, asst. news dir. WCUE Radio, Akron, 1954-56; news dir. WICE Radio, Providence, 1956-61; corr., news dir. WBZ Radio, Boston, 1961-68, WABC-TV, N.Y.C., 1968-82; critic, writer on food and travel, lectr. WABC, WCBS, Crain's N.Y. Bus., N.Y. Law Jour., N.Y. Post, N.Y.C., 1983—; bd. dirs. Internat. Food Media Conf., N.Am., 1986—. Author: Epicurean Rendezvous, 1990, (periodical) Bob Lape's Restaurant Index, 1987-91. Nat. judge food March of Dimes, 1991—; spkr., M.C. Crohn's & Colitis Found., N.Y., Nat. Cancer Soc.; judge James Beard Found. Awards. Recipient Emmy award for TV News Coverage, 1980. Mem. SAG, AFTRA, Assn. Italian Sommeliers, Wine Media Guild, Commanderie de Cordon Bleu de France, Compagnons de Beaujolais, Friars Club. Avocations: travel, reading. Office: Bob Lape Prodns 1055 River Rd Edgewater NJ 07020

LAPHAM, LEWIS HENRY, editor, author, television host; b. San Francisco, Jan. 8, 1935; s. Lewis Abbot and Jane (Foster) L.; m. Joan Brooke Reeves, Aug. 10, 1972; children: Lewis Andrew, Elizabeth Delphina, Winston Peale. Grad., Hotchkiss Sch., 1952; BA, Yale U., 1956; postgrad., Cambridge U., 1956-57; LLD, Hampden-Sydney Coll., Va. Reporter San Francisco Examiner, 1957-60, N.Y. Herald Tribune, 1960-62; author, editor USA-1, N.Y.C., 1962, Saturday Evening Post, N.Y.C., 1963-67; writer Life mag., Harper's, N.Y.C., 1968-70; mng. editor Harper's, N.Y.C., 1971-75; editor Harper's, 1975-81, 83—; TV host weekly series Bookmark, PBS, also host, author documentary series America's Century. Author: (essays) Fortune's Child, 1980, Money and Class in America, 1988, Imperial Masquerade, 1989, The WIsh for Kings, 1993, Hotel America, 1995. Mem. Coun. on Fgn. Rels., Century Assn. Office: Harper's Mag 666 Broadway New York NY 10012-2317

LAPIDES, JEFFREY ROLF, corporate executive; b. Balt., June 16, 1954; s. Morton M. and Joan Elisabeth (Sherbow) Winston; m. Kathy Lee Bortner, June 19, 1977; children: Jessica, David, Benjamin. BA, Clark U., Mass., 1976; MS in Physics, U. Md., 1979; Ph.D., U. Md., College Park, 1981. Research asst. NASA-Goddard, Greenbelt, Md., 1976-81; staff fellow NIH, Bethesda, Md., 1981-82; dir. intra-corp. devel. Allegheny Beverage Corp., Cheverly, Md., 1982-83, v.p. info. systems, 1983-85, sr. v.p. strategic planning, 1985-86; exec. v.p. Alleco, Cheverly, Md., 1986-88, pres., 1988; pres. Service Am. subs. Alleco, 1986-87, Jeffrey R. Lapides and Assocs., Inc., Columbia, Md., 1989-90; v.p. comml. products Essex Corp., Columbia, 1990—. Mem. Am. Phys. Soc., Phi Beta Kappa. Office: Essex Corp 9150 Guilford Rd Columbia MD 21046-1891*

LAPIDUS, ARNOLD, mathematician; b. Bklyn., Nov. 6, 1933; s. Morris and Mollie L. m. Nancy Beatrice Latner, Aug. 9, 1952. BS, Bklyn. Coll., 1956; MS, PhD, N.Y. U., 1967. Research scientist Courant Inst., N.Y.C., 1956-68; computer application math. analyst Goddard Inst. for Space Studies, N.Y.C., 1968-70, math. analyst programming methods, 1970-71, sr. mem. tech. staff computer scis., 1971-73; assoc. prof. quantitative analysis Fairleigh Dickinson U., Teaneck, N.J., 1973-83, prof., chair dept. computer and decision systems, 1983-85; sr. engr. Singer Electronic Systems Corp., Little Falls, N.J., 1986-87; owner Advanced Math. Co., Englewood, N.J., 1987—; pvt. practice Englewood, 1987—. Contbr. articles to profl. publs. Mem. AAAS, AAUP, Math. Assn. Am., Am. Math. Soc., Soc. Indsl. and Applied Math. Home and Office: 160 Rockwood Pl Englewood NJ 07631-5028

LAPIDUS, JULES BENJAMIN, educational association administrator; b. Chgo., May 1, 1931; s. Leo R. and Lillian D. (Davidson) LaP.; m. Anne Marie Liebman, June 8, 1970; children: Steven, Amy, Mark, Marilyn. B.S., U. Ill., 1954; M.S., U. Wis., 1957, Ph.D., 1958. Prof. medicinal and pharm. chemistry Ohio State U., 1958-84; assoc. dean Grad. Sch., 1972-74, dean Grad. Sch., 1974-84, vice provost for research, 1974-82; pres. Council Grad. Schs., 1984—; Mem. pharmacology and toxicology tng. com. NIH, 1965-67, pharmacology program com., 1971-74; mem. Grad. Record Examination Bd., 1982—. Mem. AAAS, Am. Chem. Soc. Office: Coun Grad Schs 1 Dupont Cir NW Ste 430 Washington DC 20036-1110

LAPIDUS, MORRIS, retired architect, interior designer; b. Odessa, Russia, Nov. 25, 1902; came to U.S., 1903, naturalized, 1914; s. Leon and Eva (Sherman) L.; m. Beatrice Perlman, Feb. 22, 1929 (dec. 1992); children: Richard L., Alan H. Student, NYU, 1921-23; B. Arch., Columbia, 1927. With Warren & Wetmore, N.Y.C., 1926-28, Arthur Weisner, N.Y.C., 1928-30; asso. architect Ross-Frankel, Inc., N.Y.C., 1930-42; prin. Morris Lapidus Assos., 1942-86; keynote speaker Conv. Preserving the Recent Past, U.S. Dept. Interiors, 1995. Author: Architecture-A Profession and a Business, 1967, Architecture of Joy, 1979, Man's Three Million Odyssey, 1988, A Pyramid in Brooklyn, 1989, Morris Lapidus: The Architect of the American Dream, 1992 (English and German edits. by Martina Duttmann); architect-designer: Fontainebleau Hotel, Miami Beach, Fla., 1954, Eden Roc Hotel, 1955, Lincoln Rd. Mall, Americana Hotel, Bal Harbor, Fla., 1956, Sheraton Motor Inn, N.Y.C., 1962, Internat. Inn, Washington, 1964, Fairfield Towers, Bklyn., 1966, Summit Hotel, N.Y.C., 1966, Paradise Island Hotel, Nassau, 1967, Paradise Island Casino, Nassau, 1968, Out-Patient and Rehab. Center, continuing care wing Mt. Sinai Hosp, Miami Beach, Fla., 1967, Research Bldg, 1981, congregation Beth Tfiloh, Pikesville, Md., 1967, Internat. Hdqrs. of Jr. Chamber Internat., Coral Gables, Fla., 1968, Americana Hotel, N.Y.C., 1968, Cadman Plaza Urban Redevel., Bklyn., 1969, Miami Internat. Airport, 1969-74, Penn-Wortman Housing Project, Bklyn., 1971, Bedford-Stuyvesant Swimming Pool and Park, Bklyn., 1970, El Conquistador Hotel, P.R., 1969, Trelawney Beach Hotel, Jamaica, W.I., 1973, Greater Miami Jewish Fedn. Hdgrs, 1970, Hertz Skycenter Hotel, Jacksonville, Fla., 1971, Aventura, Miami, 1971, U. Miami (Fla.) Concert Hall, 1972, Griffin Sq. Office Bldg, Dallas, 1972, U. Miami Law Library, 1975, Citizens Fed. Bank Bldg, Miami, 1975, Miami Beach Theater of Performing Arts, 1976, Ogun State Hotel, Nigeria, 1977, Exhbn. Designers, Forum Design, Linz, Austria, 1980; others; assoc. architect: Keys Community Coll, Key West, Fla., 1977, Churchill Hotel London, Grandview Apt. Complex, 1980, La Union Ins. Bldg., Guayaquil, Ecuador, 1983, Daniel Tower Hotel, Herzlea, Israel, 1983, Colony Performing Arts Ctr., 1983, Jabita Hotel, Nigeria, 1984; lectr. store, hotel design; one-man exhibit 40 Yrs. Art and Architecture, Lowe Gallery, Miami U., 1967, Fedn. Arts and Archtl. League N.Y., 1970, Weiner Galleries, 1972, Exhibit 55 Yrs. Architecture, Rotterdam, The Netherlands, 1992; exhibited at Bass Mus. of Art, 1994, Columbia U., 1995; monograph pub. in Basil's Switzerland, 1992. Mem. Miami Beach Devel. Commn., 1966-67. Winner nat. competition S.W. Urban Renewal Program in Wash.; internat. competition for trade ctr. on The Portal Site in Washington; recipinet Justin P. Allman award Wallcovering Wholesaler's Assn., 1963; Outstanding Specifications award Gypsum Drywall Contractors Internat., 1968; cert. merit N.Y. Soc. Architects, 1971;, NYU Alumni Achievement award, 1955. Mem. Miami Beach C. of C. (gov.), Kiwanis. Achievements include initial use of modern in merchandising field; areas of work include housing, hosps., hotels, shopping ctrs., office bldgs., religious instns. Home: 3 Island Ave Miami FL 33139-1363

LAPIDUS, NORMAN ISRAEL, food broker; b. N.Y.C., July 20, 1930; s. Rueben and Laurette (Goldsmith) L.;m. Myrna Sue Cohen, Nov. 20, 1960; children: Robin Anne, Jody Beth. BBA, CCNY, 1952; postgrad. internat. Relations, CCNY, NYU, 1957-60. Salesman Rueben Lapidus Co., N.Y.C., 1954-56, pres., 1960—; sales trainee Cohn-Hall-Marx, N.Y.C., 1955; salesman to v.p. Julius Levy Co., Millburn, N.J., 1964-66, pres., 1966—; salesman Harry W. Freedman Co., Millburn, N.J., 1975-76, v.p., treas., 1976-84, pres., 1984—; pres. Julius Levy/Rueben Lapidus and Harry W. Freedman Cos. div. Pezrow Corp., Millburn, N.J., 1985-86, L&H Food Brokers, Millburn, N.J., 1986-87. Mem. Maplewood (N.J.) Bd. Adjustment, 1975-82, Bedminster (N.J.) Bd. Adjustment, 1996—; gen. chmn. Maplewood Citizens Budget Adv. Com., 1977-79; chmn. Maplewood United Jewish Appeal Drive, 1975-76, 83-84; vice-chmn. Maplewood 1st Aid Squad Bldg. Fund Dr., 1978-79; co-founder Citizens for Charter Change in Essex County, N.J., 1974, mem. exec. bd., 1974—, treas., 1983-84; founder, chmn. Music Theatre of Maplewood; pres. Maplewood Civic Assn., 1983-85; mem. bd. mgrs. Essex County unit Am. Cancer Soc., v.p., 1984-87, chmn. 1991—; mem. adv. bd. Essex County Coll., West Essex, N.J., chairperson bd., 1991—; mem., sec., bd. dirs. Knollcrest Neighborhood Assn., 1994—, pres., 1991-96; active local theatricals. Recipient Leadership Medallion United Jewish Appeal, 1970, 84. Mem. Nat. Food Brokers Assn. (regional dir., Cert. Exceptionally Meritorious Svc.), Nat. Food Svc. Sales Com., Met. Food Brokers Assn. (chmn. 1982-90), Assn. Food Industries (bd. dirs.), Nat. Food Processors Assn., Young Guard Soc., Old Guard Soc., CCNY Alumni Assn., U.S. Navy Inst., Acad. Polit. Sci., Archaeol. Inst. Am., Nat. Trust for Historic Preservation, Assn. Food Distbrs., Knollcrest Homeowners Assn. (bd. trustees), LWV, Am. Legion, Lions (bd. dirs.), B'nai Brith. Republican. Jewish. Club: Maplewood Glee. Home: 9 Lockhaven Ct Bedminster NJ 07921-1728 Office: 2204 Morris Ave Ste 310 Union NJ 07083-5914

LAPIERRE, DOMINIQUE, writer, historian, philanthropist; b. Chatelaillon, France, July 30, 1931; s. Jean and Luce (Andreota) L.; m. Dominique Conchon, Apr. 5, 1980. Student (Fulbright Exchange scholar), U. Polit. Sci., Paris, 1950-51; B.A., Lafayette Coll., Easton, Pa., 1952, LittD (hon.), 1982. Editor Paris Match News mag., 1955-67. Author: The City of Joy, 1985 (Christopher award 1986), Beyond Love, 1991; co-author: Is Paris Burning?, 1964, ...Or I'll Dress You in Mourning, 1967, O Jerusalem, 1971, Freedom at Midnight, 1975, The Fifth Horseman, 1980. Founder, pres. Action Aid for Lepers' Children of Calcutta. Decorated comdr. Order of Tastevin; recipient Gold medal of the City of Calcutta for humanitarian action, 1987. Home: 26 Ave Kleber, 75116 Paris France Office: care Morton Janklow Lit Agy 598 Madison Ave New York NY 10022-1614

LAPIN, HARVEY I., lawyer; b. St. Louis, Nov. 23, 1937; s. Lazarus L. and Lillie L.; m. Cheryl A. Lapin; children: Jeffrey, Gregg. BS, Northwestern U., 1960, JD, 1963; LLB in Taxation, Georgetown U., 1967. Bar: Ill. 1963, Fla. 1980, Wis. 1985. Cert. tax lawyer, Fla. Bar. Atty., Office Chief Counsel, IRS, Washington, 1963-65; trial atty. Office Regional Csl., IRS, Washington, 1965-68; assoc., then ptnr. Fiffer & D'Angelo, Chgo., 1968-75; pres. Harvey I. Lapin, P.C., Chgo., 1975-83; mng. ptnr. Lapin, Hoff, Spangler & Greenberg, 1983-88, Lapin, Hoff, Slaw & Laffey, 1989-91, ptnr. Gottlieb and Schwartz, Chgo., 1992-93; prin. Harvey I. Lapin & Assocs., P.C., Northbrook, Ill., 1993—; instr. John Marshall Law Sch., 1969—; facility adv. lawyers asst. program Roosevelt U., Chgo.; mem. cemetery adv. bd. Ill. Comptroller, 1974-96. C.P.A., Ill. Mem. Chgo. Bar Assn. (chmn. tax exempt orgns. subcom., sect. taxation, 1988-90), Ill. Bar Assn., ABA, Fla. Bar Assn. (Fla. cert. tax specialist), Wis. Bar Assn. Jewish. Asst. editor Fed. Bar Jour., 1965-67; contbg. editor Cemetery Business and Legal Guide and Funeral Service Business and Legal Guide; contbr. articles to trade assn. jours. Office: Harvey I Lapin & Assocs PC PO Box 1327 Northbrook IL 60065

LAPINE, JAMES ELLIOT, playwright, director; b. Mansfield, Ohio, Jan. 10, 1949; s. David Sanford and Lillian (Feld) L.; m. Sarah Marshall Kernochan, Feb. 24, 1985; 1 child, Phoebe. BA, Franklin and Marshall Coll., Lancaster, Pa.; hon. degree, Franklin and Marshall Coll., 1994; MFA, Calif. Inst. of Arts, Valencia. Author, dir.: (plays) Photograph, 1977 (Obie award 1977), Table Settings, 1980 (George Oppenheimer/Newsday award), Twelve Dreams, 1983, Sunday in the Park with George, 1984 (N.Y. Drama Critics' Circle award 1984, Pulitzer prize for drama 1984), Into the Woods, 1987 (Tony award 1988, N.Y. Drama Critics' Circle award 1988, Drama Desk award 1988), Falsettoland, 1990 (2 Tony awards 1992), Luck, Pluck and Virtue (La Jolla Playhouse), 1993, Passion, 1994 (Tony award 1994); dir.: March of the Falsettos, 1982, Merrily We Roll Along (La Jolla Playhouse), A Midsummer Night's Dream, A Winter's Tale, 1988, (films) Impromptu Passion, 1990, Life with Mikey, 1993. Recipient 4 Drama Desk awards, Outer Critics Circle award, Evening Standard award, Olivier award; Guggenheim fellow. Mem. Dramatists Guild. Office: care Sam Cohn Internat Creative Mgmt 40 W 57th St New York NY 10019-4001

LAPINSKI, DONALD, elementary school principal. Prin. Dick Scobee Elem. Sch., Auburn, Wash. Recipient Elem. Sch. Recognition award U.S. Dept. Edn., 1989-90. Office: Dick Scobee Elem Sch 1031 14th St NE Auburn WA 98002-3314

LAPINSKI, TADEUSZ ANDREW, artist, educator; b. Rawamazowiecka, Poland, June 20, 1928; s. Tadeusz Alexander and Valentina (Kwiatkowska) L. MFA, Acad. Fine Arts, Warsaw, Poland, 1945. Prof. U. Md., College Park, 1973—. One-man shows include Mus. Modern Art, N.Y.C., also mus. in Washington, São Paulo and Rio de Janeiro, Brazil, Turin, Italy, Belgrade, Yugoslavia and Vienna, Austria, Regional Mus. of Torun, Poland, 1992, Plock Mus. and Libr., Poland, 1993, Regional Mus. of Zyrardow, Poland, 1994, Sci. Soc. Plock, 1993, Dist. Mus. City of Zyrardow, Poland, 1994, Zyrardow Mus. of Art, Poland, 1994; group shows include Nat. Royal Acad., London, biennial exhbns. in Venice, Italy, Paris, Buenos Aires, Argentina, John Guggenheim Gallery Exhibition, Coral Gables, Fla., 1988, Argentina, John Guggenheim Gallery Exhibition, Coral Gables, Fla., 1988, numerous others; retrospective exhibition Nat. Mus. Torun, Poland, 1956-92; represented in permanent collections Mus. Modern Art, N.Y.C., Libr. of Congress, Washington, Nat. Mus. Am. Art, Washington, mus. in São Paulo, Warsaw and Cracow, Poland, others. Recipient Gold medal Print Festival, Vienna, 1979, Silver medal World Print '80, Paris, medal City of Zamosc, Poland, 1980, UNESCO prize Paris, Statue of Victory 85 World prize, Italy, Achievement award Prince George's County, 1989, Cultural Achievement award Am. Polish Art award U. Md., 1991, Am. Polish Arts Assn. award, 1991; T. Lapinski day proclaimed by mayor of Washington, 1981; named Man of Yr. Md. Perspectives Mag., 1984, Internat. Man of Yr. Intern., Art award City Plock, Poland, 1994. Mem. Soc. Graphic Art, Painters and Sculptors Soc. N.J. Office: U Md Dept Art College Park MD 20742

LA PLATA, GEORGE, federal judge; b. 1924; m. Frances Hoyt; children: Anita J. La Plata Rard, Marshall. AB, Wayne State U., 1951; LLB, Detroit Coll. Law, 1956. Pvt. practice law, 1956-79; judge Oakland County (Mich.) Cir. Ct., Pontiac, 1979-85, U.S. Dist. Ct. (ea. dist.) Mich., Ann Arbor, 1985—; prof. Detroit Coll. Law, 1985-86. Trustee William Beaumont Hosp., 1979—, United Found., 1983—. Served to col. USMC, 1943-46, 52-54. Mem. ABA, Oakland County Bar Assn., Hispanic Bar Assn. Lodge: Optimists. Office: US Dist Ct 200 E Liberty St Ste 400 Ann Arbor MI 48104-2121 Office: US District Court US Courthouse PO Box 7760 Ann Arbor MI 48107-7760*

LAPOE, WAYNE GILPIN, retired business executive; b. Waynesburg, Pa., July 13, 1924; s. James Lindsay and Mary (Gilpin) LaP.; m. Margaret Louise Clark, Feb. 21, 1953; children: Deborah Jean, Marqui Lynne. B.A., Pa. State U., 1947. With personnel and sales depts. Armstrong Cork Co., Lancaster, Pa., 1947-53, Chgo., 1947-53, San Francisco, 1947-53; personnel dir. Safeco Ins. Group., 1953-63, v.p., 1963-86; v.p. Safeco Corp., Seattle, 1976-80, sr. v.p., 1980-86; v.p. Gen. Ins. Co. Am., 1963-86, Safeco Ins. Co. Am., 1963-86, Safeco Life Ins. Co., 1963-86, First Nat. Ins. Co. Am., Seattle, 1963-86, Safeco Nat. Ins. Co., St. Louis, 1972-86. Mem. White House Conf. Children and Youth, 1960; bd. dirs. Ind. Colls. Washington. Capt. USAAF, 1943-46, USAF, 1951-52. Decorated D.F.C.; decorated Air medal with three oak leaf clusters. Mem. Mus. Flight, Ocean Liner Mus., Am. Polit. Items Collectors (past pres.), Am. Aviation Hist. Soc., SS Hist. Soc. Am., Assn. Des Amis Des Paquebots, Nat. Trust Hist. Preservation, Phi Kappa Tau. Republican. Home: 11986 Lakeside Pl NE Seattle WA 98125-5955

LAPOINTE-PETERSON, KITTIE VADIS, choreographer, ballet school director, educator; b. Chgo., June 4, 1915; d. Samuel Joseph and Katie (Parbst) Andrew; m. Arthur Joseph LaPointe, Dec. 17, 1938 (dec. Apr. 1985); children: Janice Deane, Suzanne Meta; m. Ray Burt Peterson, Feb. 2, 1992 (dec. Nov. 1995). Studies with, Marie Zvolanek, Chgo., 1921-28, Laurent Novikoff, Chgo., 1928-35, Edward Caton, Chgo., 1928-35; student Royal Danish Ballet, Copenhagen, 1926. Dancer Chgo. Civic Opera, 1929-32, Century of Progress, Chgo., 1933-34, Stone-Camryn Ballet, Chgo., 1934-35, Mary Vandas Dancers, Chgo., 1935-38, Balaban-Katz Theaters, Chgo., 1935-36; tchr., choreographer Studio of Dance Arts, Chgo., 1952-68, Herrstrom Sch., Chgo., 1968-72; dir. Le Ballet Petit Sch., Chgo., 1972-92. Soloist in Michael Fokine's Co., 1935. Mem. Danish Brotherhood and Sisterhood (pres. 1962-65, 72-75, Midwest dist. pres. 1972-74), Chgo. Outdoor Art League (sec. 1975-79, Manor Garden Club. Avocations: cooking, writing, gardening. Home: 5843 W Peterson Ave Chicago IL 60646-3907

LAPONCE, JEAN ANTOINE, political scientist; b. Decize, France, Nov. 1925; s. Fernand and Fernande (Ramond) L.; m. Joyce Price, July, 1950; children: Jean-Antoine, Marc, Patrice; m. Iza Fiszhaut, Apr. 10, 1972; 1 child, Danielle. Diploma, Institut d'études politiques, Paris, 1947; Ph.D., UCLA, 1955. Instr. U. Santa Clara, 1956; asst. prof. polit. sci. U. B.C., Can., Vancouver, 1956-61; assoc. prof. U. B.C., 1961-66, prof., 1966—; dir. Inst. Interethnic Rels. U. Ottawa, 1993—; mem. grad. faculty Aichi Shukutoku U., 1994—. Author: The Protection of Minorities, 1961, The government of France under the Fifth Republic, 1962, People vs Politics, 1970, Left and Right, 1981, Langue et territoire, 1984, Languages and Their Territories, 1987. Fellow Royal Soc. Can. (pres. Acad. Humanities and Social Scis. 1988-91); mem. Can. Polit. Sci. Assn. (pres. 1972-73), Am. Polit. Sci. Assn., French Polit. Sci. Assn., Internat. Polit. Sci. Assn. (pres. 1973-76). Office: U BC Dept Polit Sci, Vancouver, BC Canada V6T 1Z1

LAPORTE, CLOYD, JR., retired manufacturing executive, lawyer; b. N.Y.C., June 8, 1925; s. Cloyd and Marguerite (Raeder) L.; m. Caroline E. Berry, Jan. 22, 1949; children—Elizabeth, Marguerite, Cloyd III. AB, Harvard U., 1946, JD, 1949. Bar: N.Y. 1949. Assoc. mem. firm Cravath, Swaine & Moore, N.Y.C., 1949-56; dir. adminstrn. Metals div. Olin Corp., N.Y.C., 1957-66; legal counsel Dover Corp., N.Y.C., 1966-93, sec., 1971-93. 2d lt. A.C. AUS, WWII. Mem. Harvard Club (N.Y.C.). Home: Gipsy Trail Club Carmel NY 10512

LAPORTE, GERALD JOSEPH SYLVESTRE, lawyer; b. Windsor, Ont., Can., Oct. 16, 1946; came to U.S., 1948, naturalized, 1954; s. Rosaire Joseph and Catherine Rose (Sylvestre) L. BA, Sacred Heart Sem. Coll., 1968; STB, St. Paul U., Ottawa, Ont., 1971; BTh, U. Ottawa, 1971; MA, Georgetown U., 1974; JD, George Washington U., 1976. Bar: Mich. 1976, D.C. 1977. Legis. asst. to U.S. Congressman William J. Randall, Washington, 1971-75; law clk. to U.S. Dist. Judge, Washington, 1976-77; assoc. Wilmer, Cutler & Pickering, Washington, 1977-82, Nutter, McClennen & Fish, Washington, 1987; sr. spl. counsel, Office Gen. Counsel, SEC, Washington, 1982-85; counsel to SEC Commr., 1985-87; ptnr. Patton Boggs, L.L.P., Washington, 1988—; mem. steering com. sect. corp., fin. and securities law D.C. Bar. Mng. editor George Washington Law Rev., 1975-76. Mem. ABA (sect. on bus. law, fed. regulation of securities com., subcom. SEC adminstrn., budget and legis.), Nat. Assn. Bond Lawyers (vice chmn. securities law and disclosure com.), Nat. Assn. Stock Plan Profls.. Democrat. Roman Catholic. Home: 3154 Key Blvd Arlington VA 22201-5037 Office: Patton Boggs LLP 2550 M St NW Washington DC 20037

LAPORTE, LEO FREDERIC, earth sciences educator; b. Englewood, N.J., July 30, 1933; s. Leo Frederic and Edea (Giacobbe) L.; m. Mary G. Dunlap, 1956 (div. 1983); children: Leo G., Eva R.; m. Margaret Liniecki, 1985; 1 child, Noel A. Student, Fordham Coll., 1951-53; A.B., Columbia U., 1956, Ph.D., 1960. From instr. to prof. dept. geol. scis. Brown U., Providence, 1959-71; prof. bd. earth scis. U. Calif.-Santa Cruz, 1971-94, prof. emeritus, 1994, chmn., 1972-75, dean div. natural scis., 1975-76, provost Crown Coll., 1993—, assoc. vice chancellor for undergrad. edn., 1994—; vis. prof., Yale U., 1964; geologist N.Y. State Geol. Survey, 1962-64; petroleum research cons.; mem. com. geol. scis. Nat. Acad. Sci.-NRC, 1970-72; sec. U.S. Nat. Com. Hist. Geology, 1991-93, chair, 1994—. Author: Ancient Environments, 1968, 79, 89, Encounter with the Earth, 1975; prin. author: The Earth and Human Affairs, 1972; editor: Reefs in Time and Space, 1974, Evolution and the Fossil Record, 1978, Simple Curiosity: Family Letters of George G. Simpson, 1987, Establishment of a Geologic Framework for Paleoanthropology, 1990; contbr. articles to profl. jours. Recipient President's award Am. Assn. Petroleum Geologists, 1969; U. Calif. Santa Cruz Alumni Disting. Teaching award, 1980. Fellow AAAS, Geol. Soc. Am., Calif. Acad. Sci.; mem. History of Earth Scis. Soc. (pres. 1994), Soc. Econ. Mineralogists and Paleontologists (chmn. rsch. com., paleontology councilor, editor PALAIOS 1984-89, pres. 1995—). Office: U Calif Crown Coll Santa Cruz CA 95064-1017

LAPOSATA, JOSEPH SAMUEL, army officer; b. Johnstown, Pa., Oct. 3, 1938; s. Joseph Thomas and Mary Marie (Coco) L.; m. Anita Louise Sabo, Aug. 12, 1961; children: Joseph S. Jr., David G., Matthew M. BS, Indiana U. Pa., 1960; MS, Cornell U., 1968; grad., Command and Gen. Staff Coll., Leavenworth, Kans., 1971, Indsl. Coll. Armed Forces, Washington, 1980. Commd. 2d lt. U.S. Army, 1960, advanced through grades to lt. gen., 1991; asst. chief of staff for logistics 5th Inf. Div., Ft. Polk, La., 1978-79; chief war res. div. Office Dep. Chief of Staff for Logistics, Hdqrs. Dept. Army, Washington, 1980-81; comdr. 8th Support Group, U.S. Army So. European Task Force, Livorno, Italy, 1981-84; dep. comdr., chief of staff U.S. Army So. European Task Force, Vicenza, Italy, 1984; exec. to dep. chief of staff for logistics Hdqrs. Dept. Army, Washington, 1984-86, dir. plans and ops., dep. chief of staff for logistics, 1986-88; comdg. gen. U.S. Army Material Command-Europe, Heidelberg, Fed. Republic Germany, 1988-89; dep. chief of staff for logistics U.S. Army Europe and 7th Army, Heidelberg, 1989-91; chief of staff Allied Forces So. Europe, Naples, Italy, 1991-93; Presdl. appointee as sec. Am. Battle Monuments Commn., Washington, 1994-95; ret.; mem. accrediting commn. Distance Edn. Tng. Coun.; hon. col. Quartermaster Regiment. Decorated Def. DSM, DSM (1), Legion of Merit (3), Bronze Star (2); knight comdr. Republic of Italy; recipient Man of Yr. award Interclub Coun., Johnstown, Pa., 1990, Disting. Alumnus award Ind. U. of Pa., 1992; inducted into Quartermaster Hall of Fame, 1994. Mem. Assn. U.S. Army (pres. European dept. 1989-91), Quartermaster Found. (bd. dirs.), Rotary, Phi Kappa Phi. Roman Catholic. Avocation: golf. Home: 2420 Stirrup Ln Alexandria VA 22308-2148

LAPP, JAMES MERRILL, clergyman, marriage and family therapist; b. Lansdale, Pa., July 20, 1937; s. John E. and Edith (Nice) L.; m. Nancy Swartzentruber, Mar. 1, 1936; children: Cynthia Ann, J. Michael. B.A., Eastern Mennonite Coll., 1960; B.D., Goshen Bibl. Sem., 1963; D.Min., Drew U., 1981. Ordained to ministry Mennonite Ch., 1963. Pastor Belmont Mennonite Ch., Elkhart, Ind., 1961-63; tchr. Christopher Dock Mennonite High Sch., Lansdale, Pa., 1963-70; pastor Perkasie Mennonite Ch., Pa., 1963-72, Albany Mennonite Ch., Oreg., 1972-81; dir. campus ministries Goshen Coll., Ind., 1981-87; gen. sec., gen. bd. Mennonite Ch., Elkhart, 1987-95; conf. pastor Franconia Mennonite Conf., Souderton, Pa., 1996—; moderator Pacific Coast Conf. on Mennonite Ch., Oreg., 1977-79, Mennonite Gen. Assembly, Lombard, Ill., 1985-87. Contbr. articles to Mennonite Ch. publs. Democrat. Avocations: gardening, baking, walking. Home: 61 W Park Ave Sellersville PA 18960 Office: Franconia Mennonite Conf PO Box 116 Souderton PA 18964

LAPP, JOHN ALLEN, religious organization administrator; b. Lansdale, Pa., Mar. 15, 1933; s. John E. and Edith Ruth (Nyce) L.; m. Alice Weber, Aug. 20, 1955; children: John Franklin, Jennifer Lapp Lerch, Jessica. BA, Ea. Mennonite Coll., 1954; MA, Case Western Res. U., 1958; PhD, U. Pa., 1968. From instr. to prof. history Ea. Mennonite Coll., Harrisonburg, Va., 1958-69; exec. sec. peace sect. Mennonite Cen. Com., Akron, Pa., 1969-72, exec. sec., 1985—; prof. history, dean Goshen (Ind.) Coll., 1972-79, prof. history, provost, 1979-84; rep. Ch. World Svc. and Witness, N.Y.C., 1985—; observer World Coun. Chs., Canberra, Australia, 1991. Author: Mennonite Church in India 1897-1962, 1972, The View from East Jerusalem, 1980; editor: Peacemaking in a Broken World, 1970; columnist Christian Living mag., 1963-80; mem. editorial bd. Mennonite Quar. Rev., 1972—; contbr. articles to profl. jours. Visitor N. Cen. Assn. Schs. and Colls., Chgo., 1976-84; pres. Rockingham Coun. on Human Rels, Harrisonburg, 1962-65; v.p. Va. Coun. on Human Rights, Richmond, 1965-69. Mem. Conf. on Faith and History, Mennonite Hist. Soc. (pres. 1972-84). Home: 13 Knollwood Dr Akron PA 17501-1113 Office: Mennonite Cen Com PO Box 500 21 S 12th St Akron PA 17501-0500

LAPPEN, CHESTER I., lawyer; b. Des Moines, May 4, 1919; s. Robert C. and Anna (Sideman) L.; m. Jon Tyroler Irmas, June 29, 1941; children—Jonathan Bailey, Timothy, Andrea L., Sally Morris. A.B. with highest honors in Econs, U. Calif., 1940; LL.B. magna cum laude (Faye diploma), Harvard, 1943. Bar: Calif. bar 1943. Practice in Los Angeles, 1946—; sr. partner firm Mitchell, Silberberg & Knupp, 1949—; advisory bd. Bank Am., 1962-65; chmn. bd., dir. Zenith Nat. Ins. Corp., 1975-77; bd. dirs. Arden Group, Inc. (chmn. exec. com. 1978), 1963-91, Data Products Corp. (chmn. fin. com.), 1965-93, City Nat. Bank Corp., 1967-92; trustee, pres. Citinat, Devel. Trust; bd. dirs., chmn. bd. Pacific Rim Holding Corp.

Editor-in-chief: Harvard Law Rev, 1942-43. Chmn. bd. trustees Immaculate Heart Coll., 1981-88; trustee UCLA Found.; v.p., dir. Ctr. for Childhood. Served as spl. agt. CIA AUS, 1943-46. Mem. ABA, Los Angeles Bar Assn. (dir. 1953), Los Angeles Jr. Bar Assn. (pres. 1953), Beverly Hills (Calif.) Bar Assn., Harvard Law Sch. Alumni Assn. So. Calif. (pres. 1973-82), Artus (hon.). Republican. Office: Mitchell Silberberg & Knupp 11377 W Olympic Blvd Los Angeles CA 90064-1625

LAPPIN, RICHARD C., corporate executive; b. Detroit, Dec. 16, 1944; s. Thomas Gerald and Helen Marie (Manor) L.; m. Mary Ann Hopkinson; children: Sean, Reid; children from previous marriage: Jill, Richard, Nicole. BA in Mgmt., Econs. and Psychology, U. Detroit, 1968. Corp. mgr. indsl. engring. AMC Corp., Southfield, Mich., 1972-75, corp. mgr. fin., 1975-77; internat. ops. exec. Chrysler Corp., Highland Park, Mich., 1977-79; v.p. ops. Distbn. and Controls divsn. Gould Inc., Rolling Meadows, Ill., 1979-80; gen. mgr. ball and roller divsn. Hoover Uniroyal, Ann Arbor, Mich., 1980-82; asst. to pres. Northop Def. Systems, Rolling Meadows, 1982-86; group v.p. electronics, corp. v.p. bus. devel. RTE Corp., Brookfield, Wis., 1986-88; pres. N.Am. Automotive Products Champion Spark Plug, Toledo, Ohio, 1988—; pres., chief exec. officer Doehler-Jarvis/Farley Inc., Toledo, 1989—; chief exec. officer So. Fastner/Farley Inc., Statesville, N.C., 1989—; pres., chief oper. officer Farley Industries, Chgo., 1991—; vice-chmn. Fruit of the Loom, Inc., Chgo. Office: Fruit of the Loom Inc 233 S Wacker Dr Chicago IL 60606-6306*

LAPSLEY, JAMES NORVELL, JR., minister, pastoral theology educator; b. Clarksville, Tenn., Mar. 16, 1930; s. James Norvell and Evangeline (Winn) L.; m. Brenda Ann Weakley, June 4, 1953 (dec. May 1989); children: Joseph William, Jacqueline Evangeline; m. Helen Joan Winter, Feb. 24, 1990. BA, Rhodes Coll., 1952; BD, Union Theol. Sem., 1955; PhD (Div. Sch. fellow, Rockefeller fellow), U. Chgo., 1961. Ordained to ministry Presbyn. Ch., 1955; asst. min. Gentilly Presbyn. Ch., New Orleans, 1955-57; instr. Princeton (N.J.) Theol. Sem., 1961-63, asst. prof., 1963-67, assoc. prof., 1967-76, prof. pastoral theology, 1976-80, Carl and Helen Egner prof. pastoral theology, 1980-92, acad. dean, 1984-89, prof. emeritus, 1992—; mem. editl. bd. Jour. Pastoral Care, 1966-69, 91—; bd. dirs. N.W. Maricopa UN Assn., 1994—, v.p., 1995-96. Editor: The Concept of Willing, 1967, Salvation and Health, 1972, Renewal in Late Life Through Pastoral Counseling, 1992; editor: (with B.H. Childs, D.W. Waanders), Festschrift: The Treasure of Earthen Vessels, 1994; chmn. editl. bd. Pastoral Psychology Jour., 1975-84. Bd. dirs. Westminster Found., Princeton U., 1970-76. Danforth fellow Menninger Found., 1960-61. Mem. Am. Acad. Religion, Phi Beta Kappa. Presbyterian. Home: 16610 N Meadow Park Dr Sun City AZ 85351-1758

LAQUEUR, MARIA, educational association administrator; b. San Francisco, Sept. 25, 1942; d. Gert Ludwig and Mary Alice (Murphy) L.; m. William Gerald Hamm, Feb. 12, 1983. BA German, Am. Univ., 1965, MA German/Linguistics, 1968; MPA, U. of No. Colo., 1978. German lang. cataloger Libr. of Congress, Washington, 1965-70, assoc. catalog editor, 1970-76, asst. dir. NUC proj., 1976-81; assoc. pub. Bemrose UK, Ltd., London, 1981-85; exec. dir. Assoc. of Part-time Profls., Falls Church, Va., 1988—. Author: Flexible Work Options: A Selected Bibliography, 1990; co-author: Breaking Out of 9 to 5, 1994.. Fellow U.S. Office Edn., 1967. Home: 508 Council Ct NE Vienna VA 22180 Office: Assn of Part Time Profls Crescent Plaza 7700 Leesburg Pike Ste 216 Falls Church VA 22043-2615

LAQUEUR, WALTER, history educator; b. Breslau, Germany, May 26, 1921; s. Fritz and Else (Berliner) L.; m. Barbara Koch, May 29, 1941; children: Sylvia, Shlomit. Grad., Johannesgymnasium, Breslau, 1938; student, Hebrew (Jerusalem) U., 1938-39; HHD (hon.), Hebrew Union Coll., 1988, Adelphi U., 1993, Brandeis U., 1994. Agrl. worker Palestine, 1940-44; newspaper corr., free-lance author, 1944-55; founder, editor Survey, London, Eng., 1955-67; vis. prof. Johns Hopkins, 1957, U. Chgo., 1958, Harvard, 1977; dir. Inst. Contemporary History, Wiener Library, London, 1964-92; prof. history ideas and politics Brandeis U., Waltham, Mass., 1967-72; prof. history U. Tel Aviv, 1970-80; chmn. internat. research council Ctr. Strategic and Internat. Studies, Washington, 1973—; univ. prof. govt. Ctr. Strategic and Internat. Studies Georgetown U., Washington, 1977-91. Author: Communism and Nationalism in the Middle East, 1956, The Soviet Union and the Middle East, 1959, Young Germany, 1962, Russia and Germany, 1966, The Fate of the Revolution, 1967, The Road to War, 1967, The Struggle for the Middle East, 1969, Europe Since Hitler, 1970, Out of the Ruins of Europe, 1971, Confrontation: The Middle East and World Politics, 1974, A History of Zionism, 1972, Weimar, 1975, Guerrilla, 1976, Terrorism, 1977, Guerrilla Reader, 1977, Terrorism Reader, 1978, A Continent Astray, 1979, The Missing Years, 1980, Political Psychology of Appeasement, 1980, Farewell to Europe, 1981, The Terrible Secret, 1981, America, Europe, and the Soviet Union, 1983, Germany Today, 1985, A World of Secrets, 1985, The Age of Terrorism, 1987, The Long Road to Freedom: Russia and Glasnost, 1989, Stalin, 1991, Thursday's Child Has Far to Go, 1992, Black Hundred, 1993, The Dream That Failed, 1994; co-editor, founder: Jour. Contemporary History, 1966—; founder Washington Papers, 1972—. Recipient 1st Distinguished Writer's award Center Strategic and Internat. Studies, 1969, Inter Nationes award, 1985, Grand Cross of Merit German Fed. Republic, 1987. Office: Ctr Strategic and Internat Studies 1800 K St NW Washington DC 20006-2202

LARA, ADAIR, columnist, writer; b. San Francisco, Jan. 3, 1952; d. Eugene Thomas and Lee Louise (Hanley) Daly; m. James Lee Heig, June 18, 1976 (div. 1989); children: Morgan, Patrick; m. William Murdock LeBlond, Nov. 2, 1991. BA in English, San Francisco State U., 1976. Reader Coll. of Marin, Kentfield, Calif., 1976-83; freelance editor, 1983-86; mng. editor San Francisco Focus mag., 1986-89; exec. editor San Francisco mag., 1988-89; columnist San Francisco Chronicle, 1989—. Author: History of Petaluma: A California River Town, 1982, Welcome to Earth, Mom, 1992, Slowing Down in a Speeded-up World, 1994, At Adair's House, More Columns by America's Funniest Formerly Single Man, 1995; contbr. articles to profl. publs. Recipient Best Calif. Columnist award AP, 1990. Democrat. Avocations: reading, photography, travel, softball, biking. Office: San Francisco Chronicle 901 Mission St San Francisco CA 94103-2905

LARABEE, MARCIA RAND, counselor, writer; b. Melrose, Mass., Mar. 21, 1939; d. Roger Glade and Muriel Henley (Foster) Rand; m. John Edgar Larabee, June 14, 1959 (div. June 1981); children: Jacqueline Chenot, John Robert (dec.), Michael Rand, Kyle Foster, David James. BA in English, Ohio Wesleyan U., 1960; MA in Human Devel., Fairleigh Dickinson U., 1978. Lic. clin. profl. counselor; cert. tchr., N.Y. Tchr. Cleve. Pub. Schs., 1960-61, Montessori Sch., Chatham Twp., N.J., 1976-78; tchr. Voorheesville (N.Y.) Cen. Schs., 1978-81, 82-85, sch. treas., 1981-82; counselor Al-Care, Albany, N.Y., 1985-89, pvt. practice, Schenectady, N.Y., 1989-90, Safe Harbor Miles Hosp., Newcastle, Maine, 1990-91, pvt. practice, Damariscotta, Maine, 1991-94; pvt. practice Schenectady & Saratoga Springs, N.Y., 1994—; mem. focus com., women's events com. Women's Ctr., Miles Hosp., Damariscotta, 1993-94. Researcher and writer in field; contbr. articles to profl. jours. Mem. Am. Assn. Grief Counselors, Inc., Assn. for Humanistic Psychology, Internat. Women's Writing Guild, Maine Hist. Soc., C.G. Jung Ctr. Studies in Analytical Psychology. Avocations: women's history, photography, astrology. Home: 3 Rip Van Ln Ballston Spa NY 12020-3005 Office: Tuttle Assocs 1375 Union St Schenectady NY 12308-3019

LARAGH, JOHN HENRY, physician, scientist, educator; b. Yonkers, N.Y., Nov. 18, 1924; s. Harry Joseph and Grace Catherine (Coyne) L.; m. Adonia Kennedy, Apr. 28, 1949; children: John Henry, Peter Christian, Robert Sealey; m. Jean E. Sealey, Sept. 22, 1974. MD, Cornell U., 1948. Diplomate Am. Bd. Internal Medicine. Intern medicine Presbyn. Hosp., N.Y.C., 1948-49; asst. resident Presbyn. Hosp., 1949-50; cardiology trainee Nat. Heart Inst., 1950-51; rsch. fellow N.Y. Heart Assn., 1951-52; asst. physician Presbyn. Hosp., 1950-55, asst. attending, 1954-61, assoc. attending, 1961-69, attending physician, 1969-75, pres. elect med. bd., 1972-74; mem. faculty Coll. Physicians and Surgeons Columbia U., 1950-75, prof. clin. medicine, 1967-75, spokesman exec. com. faculty coun., 1971-73; vice chmn. bd. trustees for profl. and sci. affairs Presbyn. Hosp., 1974-75; dir. Hypertension Ctr., chief nephrology div. Columbia-Presbyn. Med. Ctr., 1971-75; Hilda Altschul Master prof. medicine, dir. Hypertension and Cardiovascular Ctr., N.Y. Hosp.-Cornell Med. Ctr., 1975—, chief cardiology div., 1975-95; cons. USPHS, 1964—. Editor-in-chief Am. Jour. Hypertension, Cardiovascular Reviews and Reports; Editor: Hypertension Manual, 1974, Topics in Hypertension, 1980, Frontiers in Hypertension Rsch., 1981; editor Hypertension: Pathophysiology, Diagnosis, and Management, 1990, 1995; editorial bd.: Am. Jour. Medicine, Am. Jour. Cardiology, Kidney Internat., Jour. Clin. Endocrinology and Metabolism, Hypertension, Jour. Hypertension, Circulation, Am. Heart Jour., Procs. of Soc. Exptl. Biology and Medicine, Heart and Vessels. Mem. policy adv. bd. hypertension detection and follow-up program Nat. Heart and Lung Inst., 1971, bd. sci. counselor, 1974-79; chmn. U.S.A.-USSR Joint Program in Hypertension, 1977-93. With U.S. Army, 1943-46. Recipient Stouffer prize Med. Rsch., 1969, J.K. Lattimer award Am. Urol. Assn., 1989, Robert Tigerstedt award Am. Soc. Hypertension, 1990, John P. Peters award Am. Soc. Nephrology, 1990. Lifetime Achievement in Medicine award N.Y. Acad. Medicine, 1993, Disting. Alumnus award Cornell U. Med. Coll., 1993; subject of Time Mag. cover story, 1975; Most Frequently Cited Scientist: Top Ten Advances in Cardiopulmonary Medicine, 1946-75. Fellow Am. Coll. Cardiology; mem. ACP (Master), Am. Heart Assn. (chmn. med. adv. bd. coun. high blood pressure rsch. 1968-72), Am. Soc. Clin. Investigation, Assn. Am. Physicians, Assn. Univ. Cardiologists, Endocrine Soc., Am. Soc. Nephrology, Am. Soc. Hypertension (founder, 1st pres. 1986-88), Internat. Soc. Hypertension (pres. 1986-88), Harvey Soc., Kappa Sigma, Nu Sigma Nu, Alpha Omega Alpha, Winged Foot Golf Club (Mamaroneck, N.Y.), Shinnecock Hills Golf Club (Southampton, N.Y.). Achievements include research on hormones and electrolyte metabolism and renal physiology, mechanisms of edema formation and on causes and treatments of high blood pressure. Home: 27 Overlook Dr Southampton NY 11968-3206 Office: NY Hosp-Cornell Med Ctr 525 E 68th St (Starr 4) New York NY 10021 *In my research, a key resource has been the ability to look at everyday clinical phenomena differently, to recognize and develop new ideas and principles about human physiology. These perceptions enable hypotheses and experiments for creation and synthesis of new knowledge that redirects medical thinking.*

LARBERG, JOHN FREDERICK, wine consultant, educator; b. Kansas City, Mo., Jan. 21, 1930; s. Herman Alvin and Ann (Sabrowsky) L. AA, Kansas City Jr. Coll., 1948; AB cum laude, U. Mo., 1950, postgrad., 1955-56; MSW, Bryn Mawr Coll., 1961. Cert. social worker. With Westinghouse Electric Corp., 1953-56; dir. House of Industry Settlement House, Phila., 1957-61; asst. to exec. dir. Health and Welfare Coun., Inc., Phila., 1961-66; sr. staff cons., 1966-73, dir. Washington office, 1971-72, Nat. Assembly for Social Policy and Devel., Inc., N.Y.C.; nat. dir. community and patient services Nat. Multiple Sclerosis Soc., N.Y.C., 1974-81, nat. dir. spl. projects, 1981-82; adminstrv. v.p. Fedn. Protestant Welfare Agys. N.Y., 1982-86; sr. advisor, 1986-87; exec. dir. Am. Assn. State Social Work Bds., 1987-89; cons. The Wine Aficionado, N.Y., 1990—. Cons. exec. com. Commn. on Vol. Svc. and Action, 1967-76, cons. Met. N.Y. Project Equality, 1968-73, Encampment for Citizenship, 1973-74, Symphony for UN, 1974-77, Lower Eastside Fam. Union, 1984—, Wielenga Psych. Svc., 1993—, Malignant Hyperthermia Assn. U.S., 1994—, Internat. Fedn. Multiple Sclerosis Socs., 1995—; bd. dirs. Health Systems Agy. of N.Y., 1984-86; trustee The Riverside Ch., N.Y.C., 1985-89, worship commn., 1992-94, ordination com., 1993—, chmn., 1996—; bd. dirs., mem. exec. com. Metro Assn. United Ch. of Christ, N.Y., 1993—, dir. N.Y. state coun., 1995—; nat. dir. Coun. Social Work Edn., 1985-86. Served with AUS, 1951-53. Mem. Acad. Cert. Social Workers (charter), Nat. Assn. Social Workers (chpt. legis. com. 1968-70, nat. publs. com. 1968-71, nat. legal regulation com. 1987-89), Internat. Coun. Social Welfare (internat. com. of reps. 1980-84, U.S. com. for Internat. Coun. Social Welfare, bd. dirs. 1983-90, exec. com. 1983-90), Internat. Fedn. Multiple Sclerosis Socs. (vice chmn. patient services com. 1976-81, chmn. 1981-84, mem. individual and family services com. 1984—, non-govtl. rep. to UN, 1990—, rep. to Rehab. Internat. Med. Commn. 1976-81), Nat. Conf. Social Welfare (program com. 1966-73, chmn. combined assoc. groups 1969-70, nat. dir. 1971-73, 83-87), Fedn. of Assns. Regulatory Bds. (nat. dir. 1988-89), Malignant Hyperthermia Assn. U.S. (nat. dir. 1984-93, nat. pres. 1985-89, rep. 10th Quad. World Congr. Anesth. Hague 1992), Am. Acad. Polit. and Social Sci., Nat. Urban League (nat. trustee-at-large 1968), Hawk Mountain Sanctuary Assn., Bryn Mawr Social Work Alumni Assn. (pres. 1963-65), Mo. Soc. N.Y., Am. Mus. Natural History, Phi Beta Kappa Assn. N.Y. (pres. 1980-82), Omicron Delta Kappa, QEBH, Alpha Phi Omega, Alpha Pi Zeta, Pi Sigma Alpha, Alpha Kappa Psi. Home and Office: 400 E 58th St 2F New York NY 10022

LARCHE, JAMES CLIFFORD, II, state agency administrator; b. Mobile, Ala., Nov. 27, 1946; s. James Clifford and Alma (Dunn) L.; m. Mary Cecilia Whelchel, June 6, 1969 (div. 1972); m. Jan Pirkle, May 7, 1994. A.B., Ga. State U., 1974. Claims examiner Employees' Retirement System, Atlanta, 1969-73, div. dir., 1973-84, dep. dir., 1985—; with Nat. Conf. State Social Security Adminstrs., Atlanta, 1973—, regional v.p., 1978-80, sec., 1980-82, first v.p., 1982-83, pres., 1983-84, chmn. fed.-state procedures com., 1984-85. Served with N.G., 1968-74. Roman Catholic. Home: PO Box 38056 Atlanta GA 30334-0056 Office: State Social Security Adminstrs 2 Northside Ste 300 Atlanta GA 30318-7778

LARDIERI, ANTHONY J., school system administrator. Supt. Fontana (Calif.) Unified Sch. Dist. State finalist Nat. Supt. Yr., 1993. Office: Fontana Unified Sch Dist 9680 Citrus Ave Fontana CA 92335-5571

LARDNER, GEORGE, JR., journalist, author; b. N.Y.C., Aug. 10, 1934; s. George Edmund and Rosetta (Russo) L.; m. Rosemary Schalk, July 6, 1957; children: Helen, Edmund, Richard, Charles, Kristin (dec.). AB summa cum laude in Journalism, Marquette U., 1956, MA, 1962. Reporter The Worcester (Mass.) Telegram, 1957-59, The Miami (Fla.) Herald, 1959-63; reporter The Washington Post, 1963-64, 66—, columnist, 1964-66; bd. dirs. Fund for Investigative Journalism, Washington. Author: The Stalking of Kristin, 1995. Recipient Byline award Marquette U., 1967, Front-page Nat. News award Washington-Balt. Newspaper Guild, 1984, 86, Pulitzer Prize for feature writing, 1993. Mem. Congl. Press Gallery. Roman Catholic. Home: 5604 32nd St NW Washington DC 20015-1623 Office: Washington Post 1150 15th St NW Washington DC 20071-0001

LARDNER, HENRY PETERSEN (PETER LARDNER), insurance company executive; b. Davenport, Iowa, Apr. 5, 1932; s. James Francis and Mary Catharine (Decker) L.; m. Marion Cleaveland White, Dec. 28, 1954; children: Elisabeth, Emily Decker, David, Peter, Sarah (dec.). B.S.E. (Indsl. Engring.), U. Mich., 1954; M.A., Augustana Coll., 1982. C.P.C.U. Indsl. engr. Cutler-Hammer, Milw., 1954; Agt. H.H. Cleaveland Agy., Rock Island, Ill., 1956-60; with Bituminous Ins. Cos., Rock Island, 1960—; exec. v.p. Bituminous Ins. Cos., 1968-72, pres., 1972-95, chmn. and CEO, 1984—; pres. Bitco Corp., 1973-95, chmn., bd. dirs., 1973—; bd. dirs. Old Republic Internat., 1985—. Bd. govs. State Colls. and Univs., 1971-80; trustee Black Hawk Coll., 1964-72; mem. Ill. Bd. Higher Edn., 1976-77; chmn. Ill. State Scholarship, 1982-85. Served with AUS, 1954-56. Home: 3227 29th Ave Rock Island IL 61201-5568 Office: Bitco Corp 320 18th St Rock Island IL 61201-8716

LARDNER, RING WILMER, JR., author; b. Chgo., Aug. 19, 1915; s. Ring Wilmer and Ellis (Abbott) L.; m. Silvia Schulman, Feb. 19, 1937 (div. 1945); children: Peter, Ann; m. Frances Chaney, Sept. 28, 1946; 1 child, James; stepchildren: Katharine, Joseph. Student, Princeton, 1932-34. Reporter N.Y. Daily Mirror, 1935; press agt. Selznick Internat. Pictures, Culver City, Calif., 1935-37; screenwriter various cos., 1937-82; freelance writer, 1982—. Screenwriter: (with Michael Kanin) Woman of the Year, 1942 (Acad. award 1942), (with Leopold Atlas) Tomorrow the World, 1944, (with Albert Maltz) Cloak and Dagger, 1946, (with Philip Dunne) Forever Amber, 1947, (with Terry Southern) The Cincinnati Kid, 1965, M*A*S*H, 1970 (Acad. award 1970), The Greatest, 1977; author: (novels) The Ecstasy of Owen Muir, 1955, All for Love, 1985, The Lardners: My Family Remembered, 1976; also TV and movie pieces; collaborator Broadway mus. Foxy, 1964. Mem. Writers Guild Am. (Screen Laurel award 1989, Ian McLellan Hunter Meml. award for lifetime achievement 1992).

LARDY, HENRY A(RNOLD), biochemistry educator; b. Roslyn, S.D., Aug. 19, 1917; s. Nicholas and Elizabeth (Gebetsreiter) L.; m. Annrita Dresselhuys, Jan. 21, 1943; children; Nicholas, Diana, Jeffrey, Michael. BS, S.D. State U., 1939, DSc (hon.), 1979; MS, U. Wis., 1941, PhD, 1943. Asst. prof. U. Wis., Madison, 1945-47, assoc. prof., 1947-50, prof., 1950-88, Vilas prof. biol. sci., 1966-88, prof. emeritus, 1988—; Henry Lardy annual lectr. S.D. State U., Brookings, 1985. Edtl. bd. Archives Biochemistry and Biophysics, 1957-60, Jour. Biol. Chemistry, 1958-64, 80-85, Biochem. Preparations, Methods of Biochem. Analysis, Biochemistry; contbr. over 430 articles to profl. jours. Pres. Citizens vs McCarthy, Wis., 1950. Recipient Wolf Found. award in Agr., 1981, Nat. award Agrl. Excellence, 1982. Fellow Wis. Acad. Arts and Scis.; mem. Am. Chem. Soc. (chmn. biol. divsn. 1958, Paul-Lewis Labs. award 1949), Am. Soc. Biol. Chemists (pres. 1964, William Rose award 1988), Am. Acad. Arts and Scis. (Amory prize 1984), Am. Philos. Soc., Am. Diabetes Assn., Biochem. Soc. Great Britain, Harvey Soc., Soc. for Study of Reprodn. (Carl Hartman award 1984), Golden Retriever Club Am. (pres. 1964). Democrat. Achievements include patents for steroid compounds and lab. apparatus. Home: 1829 Thorstrand Rd Madison WI 53705-1052 Office: U Wis 1710 University Ave Madison WI 53705-4087

LARDY, NICHOLAS RICHARD, economics educator; b. Madison, Wis., Apr. 8, 1946; s. Henry Arnold and Annrita (Dresselhuys) L.; m. Barbara Jean Dawe, Aug. 29, 1970; children: Elizabeth Brooke, Lillian Henry. BA, U. Wis., 1968; MA, U. Mich., 1972, PhD, 1975. Asst. prof. Yale U., New Haven, 1975-79, assoc. prof., 1979-83, asst. dir. econ. growth ctr., 1979-82; assoc. prof. U. Wash., Seattle, 1983-85, chair China program, 1984-89, prof., 1985—, dir. The Henry M. Jackson Sch. Internat. Studies, 1991-95; sr. fellow The Brookings Instn., Washington, 1995—; bd. dirs. Nat. Com. on U.S.-China Rels., N.Y.C., Comm. in Internat. Rels. Studies with China, 1989-92, Program for Internat. Studies in Asia, 1993-95; chmn. Com. on Advanced Study in China; vice chmn. com. on scholarly comm. with China NAS, Washington, 1991-95; mem. bd. mgrs. The Blakemore Found., 1993—; founding mem. Pacific Coun. on Internat. Policy, 1995—. Author: Economic Growth and Distibution in China, 1978, Agriculture in China's Modern Economic Development, 1983, Foreign Trade and Economic Reform in China, 1978-90, 1992, China in the World Economy, 1994, (policy study) Economic Policy Toward China in the Post-Reagan Era, 1989; mem. editl. bd. The China Quar. (London), China Econ. Rev., Jour. Asian Bus. Rsch. fellow Am. Coun. Learned Socs., 1976, 78-79, 89-90, Henry Luce Found., Inc., 1980-82; faculty rsch. grantee Yale U., 1976, 78. Mem. Am. Econ. Assn., Assn. for Asian Studies (nominating com. 1986-87), Assn. for Comparative Econ. Studies (exec. com. 1986-88). Avocations: skiing, squash, tennis, sailing. Home: 2811 Albemarle St NW Washington DC 20008 Office: The Brookings Instn 1775 Massachusetts Ave NW Washington DC 20036

LARDY, SISTER SUSAN MARIE, prioress; b. Sentinel Butte, N.D., Nov. 9, 1937; d. Peter Aloysius and Elizabeth Julia (Dietz) L. BS in Edn., U. Mary, Bismarck, N.D., 1965; MEd, U. N.D., 1972. Entered Order of St. Benedict, Bismarck, 1957. Elem. tchr. Cathedral Grade Sch., Bismarck, 1958-67, Christ the King Sch., Mandan, N.D., 1967-68, 70-72, St. Joseph's Sch., Mandan, 1968-70; asst. prof. edn. U. Mary, Bismarck, 1972-80; adminstr., asst. prioress Annunciation Priory, Bismarck, 1980-84, prioress, major superior, 1984—; pres., bd. dirs. St. Alexius Med. Ctr., Bismarck, 1984—, Garrison (N.D.) Meml. Hosp., 1984—, U. Mary, Bismarck, 1984—. Chair Health Commn. of Diocese of Bismarck, 1991. Mem. Delta Kappa Gamma. Home: 7520 University Dr Bismarck ND 58504-9681

LAREAU, RICHARD GEORGE, lawyer; b. Woonsocket, R.I., June 11, 1928; s. Hector R. and Agnes P. (Valley) L.; m. Thelma Johnson, Aug. 11, 1970; 1 son, Alan Hartland; 1 son by previous marriage, William Wheeler Mohn. BA, St. Michael's Coll., Winooski Park, Vt., 1949; JD, U. Minn., 1952. Bar: Minn. 1952. Ptnr. Oppenheimer, Wolff & Donnelly, St. Paul, Mpls., 1956—; bd. dirs. Ceridan, Bloomington, Minn., Nash Finch Co., Mpls., Merrill Corp., St.Paul, No. Techs. Internat. Corp., Lino Lakes; trustee Mesabi Trust, N.Y.C.; sec. AVECOR Cardiovascular Inc., Plymouth, Minn. Sec., bd. dir. Minn. Cooperation Office for Small Bus. and Job Creation, Mpls.; bd. dirs. Minn. Project on Corp. Responsibility, Mpls. 1st lt. USAF, 1952-56. Mem. ABA, Minn. Bar Assn., Hennepin County Bar Assn., Mpls. Club. Avocation: fishing. Home: 20750 Linwood Rd Excelsior MN 55331-9386 Office: Oppenheimer Wolff & Donnelly 3400 Plz VII 45 S 7th St Minneapolis MN 55402-1614

LAREN, KUNO, investment banker; b. Tallinn, Estonia, Sept. 29, 1924; came to U.S., 1946, naturalized, 1953; s. Alexander and Jenny (Ozolit) L.; m. Mary Boondas, Nov. 18, 1950; children: Inga, Guy, Philip, Anders. Student, U. Stockholm, 1944-46; B.A., Park Coll., 1948; M.A., NYU, 1950. Securities analyst Shearson, Hammill & Co., N.Y.C., 1953-59; mgr. investment research Jesup & Lamont, N.Y.C., 1959-62; v.p. investment banking and research McDonnell & Co., N.Y.C., 1962-70; treas. Kumala Inc., N.Y.C., 1970—; pres. U.S. Securities Corp., N.Y.C., 1971—; bd. dirs., mem. exec. com. Servicemaster Industries, Inc., Downers Grove, 1962-83; pres. Pennate Corp., N.Y.C., 1983—; chmn. Quality Industries, Inc., Thibodaux, La., 1989—, Grand Enterprise Ltd., N.Y.C., 1986—; bd. dirs. Ages Health Svcs. Inc., Rockland, Mass.. Mem. Princeton Club of N.Y. State. Office: 320 Lexington Ave New York NY 10016-2645

LARESE, EDWARD JOHN, company executive; b. Kimball, W.Va., Mar. 7, 1935; s. Innocente and Velia (Pais) L.; m. Julianne Falotico, Aug. 15, 1964. Student, U. Ky., 1953-54; AB in Acctg., Duke, 1957. CPA, N.C., N.Y. Acct. Price Waterhouse & Co., N.Y.C., 1957-65; mgr.-fin. acctg. Ea. Air Lines, Inc., N.Y.C., 1965-67, asst. to sr. v.p. fin. and adminstrn., 1968-70, asst. contr. fin. planning and analysis, 1970-72; v.p., contr. Eastern Air Lines, Inc., 1972-76; v.p. planning and control IU Internat., Inc., Phila., 1976-79; CEO, pres. Altair Airlines, Inc., 1979-81; mgmt. cons. Berwyn, Pa., 1981-84; exec. v.p., CFO Finalco Group, Inc., McLean, Va., 1984-89; mgmt. cons. Warrenton, Va., 1989-91; v.p. fin. and adminstrn., CFO Star Techs., Inc., Sterling, Va., 1992-94; pres., CEO Scala, Inc., Herndon, Va., 1994—. Loaned exec. Dade County (Fla.) United Fund, 1965, corp. chmn., 1975-76. With USAFR, 1958-64. Mem. AICPA, Air Transp. Assn. (vice chmn. corp. acctg. com.), N.Y. Soc. CPAs, N.C. Assn. CPAs, Fin. Execs. Inst., Duke U. Alumni Assn., Bath Club (Miami Beach, Fla.), Radnor Hunt Club (Berwyn, Pa.), Warrenton Hunt Club, Ashland Bassetts Club, Springs Club, Fauquier Club, Sigma Nu. Republican. Episcopalian. Home: 8372 Elway Ln Warrenton VA 22186-9730 Office: Scala Inc 2323 Horse Pen Rd Ste 300 Herndon VA 22071-3405

LARGE, CORA MAYE D. RUSSELL, geriatrics nurse; b. St. Augustine, Fla., Dec. 24, 1914; d. Andrew S. and Alda Earle (Morris) Russell; m. Fred D. Large, Sept. 10, 1938. Diploma, Temple U., 1937. RN. Gen. duty nurse Flagler Hosp., St. Augustine; gen. duty nurse in obstetrics Shadyside Hosp., Pitts., Temple U. Hosp., Phila.; night supr. St. Johns County Welfare Fedn., St. Augustine. Elder, deacon United Presbyn. Ch.; former mem. Claysville (Pa.) Borough Coun.; active Am. Cancer Soc.; bd. dirs. Cross and Sword, Fla. State Play, 1995-96. Home: 36 Comares Ave Saint Augustine FL 32084-3788

LARGE, G. GORDON M., computer software company executive; b. Phila., Apr. 4, 1940; s. James M. and Sarah Morris (Ellison) L.; m. Janet G. Leith, 1964 (div. 1978); children: Christopher M., Allison G.; m. Theresa A. M. Misiorek, Nov. 30, 1978. BA, Princeton U., 1962; MBA, U. Pa., 1963. V.p. Smith, Barney & Co., Inc., N.Y.C., 1964-73; adminstr. N.J. State Energy Office, Trenton, 1974-75; exec. dir. N.J. Cabinet Energy Com., Trenton, 1974-75; v.p. Mathematica, Inc., Princeton, N.J., 1975-81, Mathematica Products Group, Inc., Princeton, 1981-84, Martin Marietta Data Systems, Greenbelt, Md., 1984-86; sr. v.p., chief fin. officer Palladian Software, Inc., Cambridge, Mass., 1986-88, Pansophic Systems, Inc., Lisle, Ill., 1988-91; sr. v.p., fin. and adminstrn. CFO Systems Ctr. Inc., Reston, Va., 1992-93; exec. v.p., CFO Card Establishment Svcs., Inc., Melville, N.Y., 1993-95; exec. v.p., CFO Interleaf Inc., Waltham, Mass., 1995—, also dir. Mem. Fin. Execs. Inst. Avocations: running, tennis, photography, music. Office: Interleaf Inc Prospect Plz 62 4th Ave Waltham MA 02154

LARGE, JAMES MIFFLIN, JR., banker; b. Phila., Mar. 15, 1932; s. James Mifflin and Sarah Morris (Ellison) L.; m. Carol E. Large, Sept. 30, 1978; children: James Mifflin III, Richard C., Ginny, Dudly, Jon. Postgrad., Stonier Grad. Sch. Banking; BSE, Princeton U. Exec. v.p., chmn. credit policy Centran Corp., Pa., 1975-82; chmn. bd., pres. First Nat. Bank, Allentown, Pa., 1982-85; vice chmn. Meridian Bancorp, Reading, Pa., 1984-85; exec. v.p., asst. to pres. 1st Interstate Bancorp, L.A., 1986, 89; chmn. chief exec. officer Anchor Savs. Bank FSB, Hewlett, N.Y., 1989—; also chmn., CEO Anchor Bancorp, Inc., Hewlett, N.Y., also bd. dirs.; CEO Dime Savings Bank (formerly Anchor Bancorp Inc.), N.Y.C. Author: Planning Secondary Defenses Against Loan Losses; contbr. articles to trade jours. Served with USN, 1955-59. Mem. Corinthian Yacht Club (Phila.), Piping Rock Club (N.Y.). Episcopalian. Home: 14 Underhill Rd Locust Valley NY 11560-2216 Office: Dime Savings Bank 589 5th Avenue New York NY 10017*

LARGE, JOHN ANDREW, library and information service educator; b. Mexborough, Yorkshire, Eng., Mar. 27, 1947; arrived in Can., 1989; s. Gordon and Winifred Mary (Tompkins) L.; m. Valerie Merle Wilson, Aug. 30, 1972; children: Amanda Fiona, Kirsty Jane. BSc in Econs., London U., 1968, diploma in libr., 1973; PhD, Glasgow U., Scotland, 1973. Asst. libr. Glasgow U. Libr., 1973-74; libr. Inst. Soviet and East European Studies, Glasgow U., 1974-78; prin. lectr. Coll. Librarianship Wales, Aberystwyth, 1978-89; prof., dir. Grad. Sch. Libr. and Info. Studies McGill U., Montreal, Que., Can., 1989—; vice chmn. U.K. Online User Group, London, 1987-89; chmn. Can. Coun. Libr. Schs., 1991-93; external examiner U. W.I., 1991—, U. Ibadan, Nigeria, 1992-95. Author: The Foreign-Language Barrier, 1983, The Artificial Language Movement, 1985, Japanese edit., 1995, A Modular Curriculum for Information Studies, 1987; co-author: Online Searching: Principles and Practice, 1990; editor: Manual of Online Search Strategies, 1988, 2d edit., 1992, CD-ROM Information Products: An Evaluative Guide vol. 1, 1990, vol. 2, 1991, vol. 3, 1992; mem. editl. adv. bd. Jour. Librarianship and Info. Sci., 1992—; editor jour. Edn. for Info., 1983—, CD-ROM Info. Products, 1993. Rsch. grantee Brit. Libr. R&D Dept., 1981-82, 85-86, European Space Agy., 1983-85; IBM Acad. Info. Exch. fellow, 1991-92, Social Sci. and Humanities Rsch. Coun. fellow, 1991-94, 96—; recipient Commemorative medal for 125th Anniversary of the Confedn. of Can., 1992. Mem. ALA, Am. Soc. for Info. Sci., Can. Libr. Assn., Assn. Libr. and Info. Sci. Edn., Que. Libr. Assn. Avocation: music listening and playing. Office: McGill U Grad Sch Libr and Info, Studies 3459 McTavish, Montreal, PQ Canada H3A 1Y1

LARGEN, JOSEPH, retailer, furniture manufacturer, book wholesaler; b. Union, N.J., June 13, 1940; s. Fred and Wilma Largen; children: Lori, Lisa. B.S. in Econs, U. Mo., 1963. Mgmt. trainee R.R. Donnelly Corp., Chgo., 1964-67; distbn. mgr., material control and distbn. Warwick Electronic Co., Niles, Ill., 1967-69; with Brodart, Inc., 1969—; v.p. prodn. Brodart, Inc., Williamsport, Pa., 1973-75; exec. v.p. Brodart, Inc., 1975-78, pres., 1978—. Served with USCG, 1963-64. Home: 2000 First Ave #2602 Seattle WA 98121 Office: Brodart Co 500 Arch St Williamsport PA 17701-7809

LARGENT, STEVE, congressman, former professional football player; b. Tulsa, Sept. 28, 1954; m. Terry Largent; children: Kyle, Kelly, Kramer, Casie. BS in biology, U. Tulsa, 1976. Wide receiver Seattle Seahawks, NFL, Kirkland, Wash., 1976-89; player Pro Bowl, 1979, 80, 82, 85-88; mktg. cons. Sara Lee Corp., 1991-94; mem. 103d-104th Congresses from 1st Okla. dist., Washington, DC, 1995—; mem. budget com., mem. health care task force, mem. sci. com., mem. energy & environ. and space & aeronautics subcoms., mem. commerce com. Holder NFL record for passes caught in consecutive games, also for career receiving yardage, receptions; named to NFL Hall of Fame, 1995. Office: US House Reps 410 Cannon House Office Bldg Washington DC 20515-3601*

LARGMAN, KENNETH, strategic analyst, strategic defense analysis company executive; b. Phila., Apr. 7, 1949; s. Franklin Spencer and Roselynd Marjorie (Golden) L.; m. Suzanna Forest, Nov. 7, 1970 (div. Nov. 1978); 1 child, Jezra. Student, SUNY-Old Westbury, 1969-70. Ind. strategic analyst, 1970-80; chmn., chief exec. officer World Security Council, San Francisco, 1980—, dir. joint project with Apple Computer to develop improved techniques for decision analysis; dir. US/Soviet Nuclear Weapons and Strategic Def. Experiment: Discovery of Unanticipated Dangers and Possible Solutions. Author: (research documents) Space Peacekeeping, 1978, Preventing Nuclear Conflict: An International Beam Weaponry Agreement, 1979, Space Weaponry: Effects on the International Balance of Power and the Prevention of Nuclear War, 1981, Defense Against Nuclear Attack: U.S./Soviet Interactions, Moves, and Countermoves, 1985, 2 vols. on U.S./Soviet options in strategic def. race, 1986, Telecomplanning: A New Field of Science: The Identification and Study of New Methods of Planning Using Interactive Collaborative Telecomputing to Detect Unanticipated Flaws, Options, Solutions, 1994. Mem. World Affairs Council. Achievements include research in experimental decision analysis, in development of new methodologies of policy analysis and decision making for use in summit negotiations, in exposure of decision making to extremely rigorous and methodical scientific examination.

LARIC, MICHAEL VICTOR, academic administrator; b. Split, Yugoslavia, Feb. 8, 1945; came to U.S., 1971; s. Joseph and Ljubica (Abraham) L.; m. Roberta Kine; children: Shai Samuel, Pnina Leora, Ari Nathaniel. BA in Econs. and Polit. Sci., Hebrew U. of Jerusalem, 1968, MA in Bus., 1971; PhD, CUNY, 1976. Economist Israel Hotel & Motel Owners, Tel Aviv, 1968-69; gen. mgr. Galia Laundries, Jerusalem, 1969-71; economist Risk Analysis Corp., Alpine, N.J., 1971-72; lectr. CUNY, N.Y.C., 1972-73; asst. prof. Rutgers U., State U. N.J., Newark, 1974-75, U. Conn., Storrs, 1975-81; prof. mktg. U. Balt., 1981—, acad. assoc. dean, 1992-95; course dir. Data Tech. Inst., Clifton, N.Y., 1986-92, Frost & Sullivan, N.Y.C. and Eng., 1990—; cons. Ecomares Internat., Ellicott City, Md., 1981—. Author: Marketing Management: Analysis Using Speedsheets, 1988, Lotus Exercises for Principles of Marketing, 1986, 14 other books; contbr. numerous articles, monographs and cases to profl. jours. Named Outstanding Young Man of The Yr. Jaycees, 1979, 80. Mem. Am. Mktg. Assn. (bd. mem. Balt. chpt. 1976-82, Outstanding Contbr. of Conn. 1978), Product Devel. and Mgmt. (bd. mem. 1981, 82), Am. Econs. Assn., Beta Gamma Sigma. Home: 4609 Morning Ride Ct Ellicott City MD 21042-5927 Office: U Balt 1420 N Charles St Baltimore MD 21201-5720

LARISON, BRENDA IRENE, law librarian; b. Springfield, Ill., Apr. 3, 1949; d. Richard Wayne and Corabell Marie (Bea) L.; 1 child, Alyce Sherbenou. BA, U. Ill., 1971; MA, Sangamon State U., Springfield, 1977; MLS, U. Mich., 1980. Corp. libr. ADP Network Svcs., Ann Arbor, Mich., 1978-86; legis. rsch. law libr. State of Ill., Springfield, 1986-91; libr. Supreme Ct. Ill., Springfield, 1992—; del. White House Conf. on Librs., 1990; midwest coord. Nat. Conf. State Legislatures, Denver, 1987-91; mem. state agy. libr. bd. State of Ill. Libr., Springfield, 1988-90. Literacy vol. Lincoln Land C.C., Springfield, 1992-95; vol. coord. Lincoln Meml. Gardens, Springfield, 1993-94. Mem. Am. Assn. Law Librs., Chgo. Assn. Law Librs., Spl. Librs. Assn. (bd. dirs. Ill. chpt. 1989-90). Avocations: gardening, birding, cycling. Office: Supreme Ct Ill Supreme Ct Bldg Springfield IL 62701

LARIVÉE, JACQUES, conservationist. Co-author: (with A. Cyr) Atlas saisonnier des oiseaux du Québec, 1995. Recipient Snowy Owl Conservation award Québec Zoological Gardens, 1993. Home: 194 Ouellet, Rimouski, PQ Canada G5L 4R5

LARIVIERE, RICHARD WILFRED, Asian studies educator, consultant; b. Chgo., Jan. 27, 1950; s. Wilfred Francis and Esther Irene (Kallestad) L.; m. Janis Anne Worcester, June 5, 1971; 1 child, Anne Elizabeth. BA, U. Iowa, 1972; PhD, U. Pa., 1978. Lectr. U. Pa., Phila., 1978-79; asst. prof. U. Iowa, Iowa City, 1980-82; prof. U. Tex., Austin, 1982—, Ralph B. Thomas Regents prof. Asian studies, 1993—; assoc. v.p. U. Tex., 1995—; ptnr. Sinha & Lariviere Internat. Comms. Cons., Austin, 1994—; dir. Ctr. for Asian Studies, Nat. Resource Ctr. for South Asia; founder Doing Bus. in India seminar; cons. Perot Sys. Corp., Dallas, 1993—. Author: Ordeals in Hindu Law, 1981, Narada Smrti, 1989; gen. editor Studies in South Asia. Fellow NEH, 1979-83. Fellow Royal Asiatic Soc.; mem. Am. Oriental Soc., Am. Inst. Indian Studies (sr.fellow 1989, 95, v.p. 1990), Assn. Asian Studies. Lutheran. Office: U Tex Asian Studies Mail Code G9300 Austin TX 78727

LARK, M. ANN, management consultant, strategic planner, naturalist; b. Denver, Feb. 28, 1952; d. Carl Eugene and Arlena Elizabeth (Bashor) Epperson; m. Larry S. Lark, Apr. 1, 1972 (div. 1979). Asst. corp. sec., savs. dir. Imperial Corp. dba Silver State Savs. & Loan, Denver, 1972-75; client svcs. mgr. 1st Fin. Mgmt. Corp., Englewood, Colo., 1977-81; regional account mgr. Ericsson Info. Systems, Chatsworth, Calif., 1981-82; ind. cons. Denver, 1982-84; regional account mgr. InnerLine/Am. Banker, Chgo., 1984-85; chief info. officer Security Pacific Credit Corp., San Diego, 1985-88; prin. The Genessee Group, Thousand Oaks, Calif., 1988—. Avocations: tennis, gardening, hiking, bicycling, writing, sketching. Home and Office: 1144 El Monte Dr Thousand Oaks CA 91362-2117

LARK, RAYMOND, artist, art scholar; b. Phila., June 16, 1939; s. Thomas and Bertha (Lark) Crawford. Student, Phila. Mus. Sch. Art, 1948-51, Los Angeles Trade Tech. Coll., 1961-62; B.S., Temple U., 1961; L.H.D., U. Colo., 1985. Ednl. dir. Victor Bus. Sch., Los Angeles, 1969-71; public relations exec. Western States Service Co., Los Angeles, 1968-70; owner, mgr. Raymond Lark's House of Fine Foods, Los Angeles, 1962-67; exec. sec. to v.p. Physicians Drug and Supply Co., Phila., 1957-61; lectr. L.A. Trade Tech. Coll., 1973, Compton (Calif.) Coll., 1972, Nat. Secs. Assn., Hollywood, Calif., UCLA, U. Utah, Salt Lake City, 1993, numerous others. One-man shows include, Dalzell Hatfield Galleries, Los Angeles, 1970-80, Arthur's Gallery Masterpieces and Jewels, Beverly Hills, Calif., 1971, Dorothy Chandler Pavillion Music Center, L.A., 1974, Honolulu Acad. Arts, 1975, UCLA, 1983, U. Colo. Mus., 1984, Albany State Coll. Art Gallery, Albany, Ga., 1988, Utah Mus. Fine Arts, Salt Lake City, 1989, Mind's Art Gallery, Dickinson U., Dickinson, N.D., 1989, Trinton Mus. Art, Santa Clara, Calif., Greenville (N.C.) Mus. of Art, 1993, Springfield (Mo.) Art Mus., 1995, Washington County Museum of Fine Arts, Hagerstown, Md., 1996; The Peninisula Fine Arts Center, Newport News, Va. others; group exhbns. include, Smithsonian Instn., 1971, N.J. State Mus., Trenton, 1971, Guggenheim Mus., N.Y.C., 1975, Met. Mus. Art, 1976, La Galerie Mauffe, Paris, 1977, Portsmouth (Va.) Mus., 1979, Ava Dorog Galleries, Munich, W. Ger., 1979, Accademia Italia, Parma, 1980, Ames Art Galleries and Auctioneers, Beverly Hills, 1980, Le Salon des Nations at Centre International d'Art Contemporain, Paris, 1983; represented in permanent collections, Library of Congress, Ont. Coll. Art, Toronto, Mus. African and African Am. Art and Antiquities, Buffalo, Carnegie Inst., numerous others; art commrs. for TV and film studios include, All in the Family, Carol Burnett Show, Maude, The Young and the Restless, Universal City Studios, Palace of the Living Arts, Movie Land Wax Mus.; author works in field; author and contbr. more than 50 scholarly treatises on art, edn. and the hist. devel. of Black Ams., chpts. to encyclopedias and textbooks, articles to jours., introductions to mus. exhbn. catalogues. Recipient gold medal Acad. Italia, 1980, also numerous gold medals and best of show awards, 3 presdl. proclamations; award Internat. Platform Assn.; Dr. Raymond Lark Day proclaimed by State of Md., 1994; grantee Nat. Endowment Arts, ARCO Found., Colo. Humanities Program, Adolph Coors Beer Found. Mem. Art West Assn. (pres. 1968-70). Address: PO Box 76169 Los Angeles CA 90076-0169 *I was telling people that I was Black, proud, and beautiful long before it became fashionable to be very dark. I never felt, "I am the greatest." However, I never had an inferiority complex. I always knew that I had God-given talent, character, and good common sense. In addition, I have always had great confidence in God and in myself. While I am not a soothsayer and never will be a braggart, I knew my art would be recognized. For whatever recognition I have received, I have worked extremely hard and have paid my dues.*

LARKIN, ALFRED SINNOTT, JR., newspaper editor; b. Boston, May 13, 1947; s. Alfred Sinnott and Lillian Louise (Brunswick) L.; children: Kristin, Jessica, Hannah, Matthew. Reporter Boston Herald, 1968-72; reporter Boston Globe, 1972-74, asst. met. editor, 1974-76, reporter, 1977-81, Sunday mag. editor, 1981-82, asst. mng. editor local news, 1982-86, dep. mng. editor, 1986-88, mng. editor Sunday edition, 1988-90, mng. editor adminstrn., 1990—. Nieman fellow Harvard U., 1977. Office: Boston Globe 135 Morrissey Blvd Dorchester MA 02125-3310

LARKIN, BARRY LOUIS, professional baseball player; b. Cin., Apr. 28, 1964; m. Lisa Davis. Student, U. Mich., 1982-85. Baseball player Cincinnati Reds, 1985—. First baseball player twice named MVP of Big Ten Athletic Conf.; two-time All-Am. honors; named MVP, Rookie of Yr. and to All-Star team, 1988-95, to Topps' Triple-A All-Star team, 1986, All-Star teams by Sporting News, 1988-92, 94-95, AP, 1990, UPI, 1990, Maj. League Baseball, 1988-91, 93, to N.L. Silver Slugger team Sporting News, 1988-92, 95; recipient Gold Glove award, 1994. Achievements include mem. U.S. Olympic Baseball Team, 1984, World Series Team, 1990. Office: Cin Reds 100 Riverfront Stadium Cincinnati OH 45202-3590*

LARKIN, EDWARD COLBY, securities analyst, financial services company executive; b. Evanston, Ill., Jan. 6, 1951; s. Edward Tyrus and Ethel (Colby) L.; m. Teresa Mary Berger, Apr. 21, 1978; children: Sean, Brian, Trent. BS, U. Colo., 1973; MBA, U. Denver, 1974. Fin. analyst, supr. Nat. Assn. Securities Dealers, Denver, 1975-80; v.p. corp. fin. Wall Street West, Englewood, Colo., 1980-86, Richard Christman Lavigne, Inc., Seattle, 1986-87; exec. v.p., dir. rsch., chief fin. officer Cohig & Assocs., Denver, 1987—, pres., 1995—. Office: Cohig & Assocs 6300 S Syracuse Way Ste 430 Englewood CO 80111-6724

LARKIN, EUGENE DAVID, artist, educator; b. Mpls., June 27, 1921; s. John Peter and Martha Lavinia (Vandevere) L.; m. Audrey Jean Krueger, Jan. 29, 1947; children: Andrew, Alan. BA, U. Minn., 1946, MA, 1949. Mem. faculty dept. art Kans. State Coll., Pittsburg, 1949-54; head printmaking dept., chmn. divsn. fine arts Mpls. Sch. Art, 1954-69; prof. design dept. U. Minn., St. Paul, 1969—, prof. emeritus design, housing and apparel, 1991—. One man exhbns. include, Mpls. Inst. Arts, 1957, 60, 68, Syracuse U., 1962, Walker Art Center, Mpls., 1967, New Forms Gallery, Athens, Greece, 1967, U. Kans., 1972, Macalester Coll., 1974, U. Minn., St. Paul, 1973, 78, 87, 91; group exhbns. include, Phila. Printmakers Club, 1966, 20 American Artists, Geneva, Switzerland, 1964, Big Prints, N.Y. U., 1968, Midwestern Printmakers, Walker Art Center, 1973, Cabo Frio Internat. Print Biennial, Brazil, 1983, Nat. Works on Paper, Minot State Coll., 1986, 17th Annual Works on Paper SW State U., San Marcos, Tex., 4th Annual North Coast Coll. Soc. Exhbn., Hiram Coll., Hudson, Ohio, 1988, 20th Annual Works on Paper Dulin Nat. Knoxville, Knoxville Mus. Art, 1988, Paepcke Meml. Bldg. Gallery, 1993, Aspen Inst. and Music Assoc. of Aspen, 1993; represented in permanent collections, Mus. Modern Art, N.Y.C., Nat. Mus. S.Africa, Capetown, Library Congress, Chgo. Art Inst., Mpls. Inst. Arts, U. Minn. Gallery, Des Moines Art Center, U. Tenn., Kans. State Tchrs. Coll., Minn. Mus. Art, Nat. Collection Fine Arts, Smithsonian Instn; author: Design: The Search for Unity, 1988. Recipient juror's award Rockford Internat. Print and Drawing Biennale, 1983. Mem. Coll. Art Assn. Am. Home: 64 Groveland Ter Minneapolis MN 55403-1103

LARKIN, JOAN, poet, English educator; b. Boston, Apr. 16, 1939; d. George Joseph and Celia Gertrude (Rosenberg) Moffitt; m. James A. Larkin, Dec. 23, 1966 (div. 1969); 1 child, Kate. BA, Swarthmore Coll., 1960; MA, U. Ariz., 1969. Asst. prof. English CUNY-Bklyn. Coll., 1969-94, ret., 1994; assoc. faculty MFA program Goddard Coll.; mem. guest faculty poetry writing Sarah Lawrence Coll., Bronxville, N.Y., 1984-86, fall 1988; vis. instr. Hartwick Coll., Manhattan Theatre Club, Gainesville, Tenants Harbor and Cummington workshops; poet-in-residence Writers Community, Manhattan, West Side YMCA. Author: (poems) Housework, 1975, A Long Sound, 1986, Cold River, 1996, (rec. poetry reading) A Sign I Was Not Alone, 1980; co-editor: Gay and Lesbian Poetry in Our Time: An Anthology, 1988 (Lambda Lit. award 1988), Amazon Poetry, 1975, Lesbian Poetry, 1981; editor: The Women Writers Calendar, 1982, 83, 84; contbr. poems to periodicals including Am. Poetry Rev., Conditions, Ms., Paris Rev., Sinister Wisdom, The Village Voice, Aphra, Endymion, The Lamp in the Spine, Global City Rev., Am. Rev., Genesis West, Sojourner. Nat. Endowment for Arts fellow in poetry, 1987-88, 96-97, N.Y. Found. for Arts fellow in poetry, 1987-88; Creative Artists Pub. Svc. Program grantee N.Y. State Coun. Arts, 1976, 80; Mass. Cultural Coun. grantee in playwriting, 1995.

LARKIN, JOHN PAUL, II, state legislator; b. Rutland, Vt., Dec. 2, 1969; s. John Paul and Ann Marie (Canfield) L. BA, U. Vt., 1992. Lic. securities broker, life and health ins. agt., Vt. Mem. Vt. Ho. of Reps., Montpelier, 1992—; state vice-chmn. Am. Legis. Exch. Coun., Washington, 1993—; chair Fair Haven Green-Up Day. Vice-chmn. Fair Haven Rep. Com., Freshman GOP, 1992-94; co-chair Vt. Rep. Youth Outreach com., 1993—; trustee pub. funds Town of Fair Haven, 1994—. Mem. Nat. Rep. Legislator's Assn., Vt. Vets. Action Group, Alzheimer's Assn. (Green Mountain chpt. 1994—), Sons of the Am. Legion. Roman Catholic. Avocations: basketball, snowboarding, golf. Home: PO Box 92 Fair Haven VT 05743-0092

LARKIN, LEE ROY, lawyer; b. Oklahoma City, Aug. 11, 1928; s. William Patrick and Agnes (Matthis) L.; m. Mary Jane Langston, Apr. 17, 1965; children—James William, John Patrick (dec.). BS, Oklahoma A&M U., Stillwater, 1950; MA, Vanderbilt U., 1952; LLB, William Mitchell U., St. Paul, 1959. Bar: Minn. 1959, Tex. 1963, D.C. 1963. Economist U.S. Dept. Agr., Washington, 1953; economist, lawyer Pillsbury, Mpls., 1953-62; ptnr. Harris & Larkin, Houston, 1963-65; sr. ptnr. Andrews & Kurth, Houston, 1966—; speaker Continuing Legal Edn. Officer Sharpstown Civic Assn., Houston, 1966-95; elder St. Philip Presbyn. Ch., Houston; moderator Presbytery of New Covenant, Houston, 1980. Served to capt. USAR, 1951-58. Fellow Tex. Bar Found., Houston Bar Found.; mem. ABA, State Bar Tex., Houston Bar Assn., Am. Intellectual Property Assn., Houston Intellectual Property Assn., Riverbend Country Club, Houston Club, Rotary (pres. 1978-79), Delta Theta Phi. Avocations: golf; tennis; ranching. Home: 3725 Wickersham Ln Houston TX 77027-4013 Office: Andrews & Kurth 4200 Tex Commerce Towers Houston TX 77002

LARKIN, LEO PAUL, JR., lawyer; b. Ithaca, N.Y., June 19, 1925; s. Leo Paul and Juanita (Wade) L. AB, Cornell U., 1948, LLB, 1950. Bar: N.Y. 1950, U.S. Dist. Ct. (so. dist.) N.Y. 1951, U.S. Supreme Ct. 1967. Assoc., ptnr., sr. counsel Rogers & Wells and predecessor firms, N.Y.C., 1950—. Served with U.S. Army, 1943-45. Mem. ABA, Fed. Bar Coun., Univ. Club, Sky Club, Delta Phi, Phi Beta Kappa, Phi Kappa Phi, Theta Delta Phi. Home: 200 E 66th St Apt 1804B New York NY 10021-6728 Office: Rogers & Wells 200 Park Ave Ste 5200 New York NY 10166-0005

LARKIN, MARY, chemist, consultant; b. Mt. Vernon, N.Y., Oct. 8, 1950; d. Frederick Joseph and Dorothy Patricia (Sillery) Larkin; m. Alfred Karl Jung, June 11, 1983 (div. Jan. 1994). BA in Chemistry, Coll. of New Rochelle, 1976. Cert. color and image cons. From technician to assoc. rsch. chemist Stauffer Chem. Co., Dobbs Ferry, N.Y., 1971-86; rsch. chemist Chesebrough-Ponds Inc., Shelton, Conn., 1986-87; tech. mktg. asst. Ganes Chems. Inc., N.Y.C., 1988; rsch. chemist Rhone-Poulenc, Cranbury, N.Y., 1989-91; devel. specialist UOP, Tarrytown, N.Y., 1991-95; sr. rsch. scientist Clairol, Inc., Stamford, Conn., 1995—. Patentee in field (2); contbr. articles to profl. jours. Mentor Pace U. Rsch. Project, Tarrytown, 1993. Mem. ASTM, Soc. Cosmetic Chemists. Roman Catholic. Avocations: cycling, sewing, reading, color analysis, computers. Office: Clairol Inc 2 Blachley Rd Stamford CT 06922

LARKIN, MICHAEL JOHN, newspaper editor, journalist; b. Boston, Sept. 27, 1950; s. Alfred Sinnott and Lillian Louise (Brunswick) L.; m. Sarah Jane Wood, July 6, 1970 (div. 1985); children—Jonathan Michael, Joshua Stuart; m. Alison Rose Biggs, June 1, 1986. B.A. in English, U. Mass., 1973. News copy editor Boston Globe, 1974-76, sports copy editor, 1976-80, asst. bus. editor, 1980-82, Sunday editor, 1982, mag. editor, 1982-85, living/arts editor, 1985-89, sr. asst. met. editor zoned editions, 1989-92, Sunday editor, 1992-95; asst. mng. editor, 1995—. Office: Boston Globe PO Box 2378 Boston MA 02107-2378

LARKIN, MICHAEL JOSEPH, retail food executive; b. N.Y.C., June 6, 1941; s. John Thomas and Mary (Finnerty) L.; m. Sandra L. Pagano, July 15, 1978; 1 child, Lisa. BBA, Iona Coll., 1963; postgrad., Cornell U., 1970. Supermarket mgr. Grand Union Co., N.Y.C., 1963-69; dist. mgr. Grand Union Co., Syracuse, N.Y., 1969-71, dir. ops., 1971-75; div. v.p. Grand Union Co., Mt. Kisco, N.Y., 1975-78; regional v.p. Grand Union Co., Elmwood Park, N.J., 1978-84; ops. v.p. Gt. Atlantic and Pacific Tea Co., Montvale, N.J., 1984-85, group v.p., 1985-87, sr. v.p. ops., 1987-89, exec. v.p. ops., 1989-95, COO, 1991-95; owner, pres. Gemini Food Mkts., L.P., Morristown, N.J., 1995—; pres. Daitch Shopwell Co., N.Y.C., 1986-95. With USMC, 1960-65. Named Man of Yr. Cath. Inst. of Food Industry, N.Y.C., 1986, Boys Town of Italy, 1993; recipient award of merit Deborah Hosp., Browns Mill, N.J., 1988. Republican. Roman Catholic. Home: 15 Windmill Dr Morristown NJ 07960-5971 Office: Gemini Food Markets LP 10 Wilmot St Morristown NJ 07960 also: Shoprite of Whitehall 2641 MacArthur Rd Whitehall PA 18052

LARKIN, MOSCELYNE, retired artistic director, dancer; b. Miami, Okla., Jan. 14, 1925; d. Reuben Frances and Eva (Matlogova) L.; m. Roman Jasinski, Dec. 24, 1943 (dec. 1991); 1 child, Roman. Studied with Serge Grigorieff, Lubov Tchernicheva, Mikhail Mordkin, Anatole Vilzak, Vincenzo Celli; hon. doctorate of Fine Arts, U. of Tulsa, 1991. With Ballet Russe, 1941-47, Ballet Russe de Monte Carlo, 1948-52; prima ballerina Radio City Music Hall, N.Y.C., 1951-52; with Alexandra's Danilova's Great Moments of Ballet touring co., 1952-54; established Tulsa Sch. Ballet, from 1956; artistic dir. Tulsa Civic Ballet, 1956-76, Tulsa Ballet Theater, 1976-91; artistic dir. emerita Tulsa Civic Ballet, 1991—. Dance performances include Mikhail Forkine's Paganini and Les Sylphides; Leonid Massine's Le Beau Danube, Symphonie Fantastique, Les Presages; George Balanchine's Concerto Barocco, Night Shadow, Cotillion; Agnes De Mille's Rodeo; David Lichine's Graduation Ball; Michael Maule's The Carib Peddler. Recipient Dance Mag. award, 1988, Gov. Arts award, 1988, Rogers State Coll. Lynn Riggs award, 1989, award of Am.,1992; named to Tulsa Press Clubb Headliner award, Okla. Hall of Fame, 1979, Tulsa Hall of Fame, 1988, Okla. Womens Hall of Fame, 1993, and numerous others. Mem. Southwestern Regional Ballet Assn. (exec. v.p. 1963-76), Nat. Assn. Regional Ballet. Home: 5414 S Gillette Ave Tulsa OK 74105-6434 Office: Tulsa Ballet Theatre 4512 S Peoria Ave Tulsa OK 74105-4563

LARKIN, PETER ANTHONY, zoology educator, university dean and official; b. Auckland, New Zealand, Dec. 11, 1924; arrived in Can., 1929; s. Frank Wilfrid and Caroline Jane (Knapp) L.; m. Lois Boughton Rayner, Aug. 21, 1948; children: Barbara, Kathleen, Patricia, Margaret, Gillian. BA, MA, U. Sask., Can., 1946, LLD (hon.), 1989; DPhil (Rhodes scholar), Oxford U., 1948; DSc (hon.), U. B.C., 1992. Bubonic plague survey Govt. of Sask., 1942-43; fisheries investigator Fisheries Rsch. Bd. Can., 1944-46; chief fisheries biologist B.C. Game Commn., 1948-55; asst. prof. U. B.C., 1948-55, prof. dept. zoology, 1959-63, 66-69; prof. Inst. Animal Resource Ecology, 1969—, also dir. fisheries, 1955-63, 66-69, head dept. zoology, 1972-75, dean grad. studies, 1975-84, assoc. v.p. rsch., 1980-86, v.p. rsch., 1986-88, univ. prof., 1988—; hon. life gov. Vancouver Pub. Aquarium; mem. Can. nat. com. Sci. Com. on Problems of Environment, WHO, 1971-72; mem Killam selection com. Can. Can., 1974-77; mem. Sci. Coun. Can., 1971-76, Nat. Rsch. Coun. Can., 1981-84, Can. Com. on Seals and Sealing, 1981-86, Can. Inst. Advanced Rsch., 1982-85, Nat. Scis. and Engring. Rsch. Coun. Can., various govtl. rsch. coms.; mem. Internat. Ctr. for Living Aquatic Resources Mgmt., 1977, chmn. bd. dirs., 1991-93; bd. dirs. B.C. Packers, 1980—; mem. bd. govs. Internat. Devel. Rsch. Coun., Can., 1987-93; mem. Nat. Sci. Eng. Rsch. Coun. Can., 1987-93; pres. Rawson Acad., 1988-91; commr. B.C.Utilities Commn., 1993—; mem. interim gov. coun. U. No. B.C., 1991-93. Contbr. articles to profl. jours. Pres. B.C. Conservation Found., 1987-90; temporary commr. B.C. Utilities Commn., 1993—; trustee Vancouver Hosp., 1994-95. Recipient centennial medal Govt. Can., 1967, silver jubilee medal, 1977, Can. Sport Fishing Inst. award, 1979, Murray A. Newman conservation award Vancouver Aquarium, 1996; Nuffield Found. fellow, 1961-62. Fellow Royal Soc. Can.; mem. Internat. Limnol. Assn., Am. Fisheries Soc. (award of excellence 1983, Carl R. Sullivan conservation award 1993), B.C. Natural Resources Conf. (pres. 1954), B.C. Wildlife Fedn., Can. Soc. Zoologists (pres. 1972, Fry medal 1978), Can. Assn. Univ. Rsch. Adminstrn. (pres. 1979), Am. Inst. Fisheries Biologists (outstanding achievement award 1986), Sci. Coun. B.C. (career achievement award 1995), Order of Can. Home: 4166 Crown Crescent, Vancouver, BC Canada V6R 2A9 Office: U BC Fisheries Ctr, 2204 Main Mall, Vancouver, BC Canada V6T 1Z4

LARKIN, SARA ANN, artist; b. Quincy, Mass., Dec. 28, 1946; d. Sydney S. and Myrtle (Harriman) Larkin; m. Richard Preston Lacey, Dec. 29, 1972 (dec. 1974). BFA, U. Pa., 1969; Cert. of Completion, Pa. Acad. Fine Arts, 1969; student, Cornell U., Syracuse U., 1964-65. Women's style editor Bangkok World Newspaper, 1970-71; owner, cons. artist Sara Larkin Gallery, Hong Kong, 1972-76; artist, art investor, cons. Sara Larkin Fine Art, Washington, 1978—; vis. artist St. John's Coll., Annapoli, Md., summer 1992; artist/pvt. tutor Sara Larkin Studio, Annapolis, 1992—. One woman shows include NASA Hdqrs., Washington, 1982, Fashion Moda, N.Y.C.,

1982, Langley Rsch. Ctr., Hampton, Va., 1983, Alpha Gallery, Rockville, Md., 1980-90, Covington-Burling, Washington, 1993; group exhibits include Danforth Mus., Framingham, Mass., 1984, El Paso Mus. Art, 1986, Expo '86, Tokyo, 1986, Mitsukoshi Gallery, Tokyo, 1986, Govinda Gallery, Washington, 1986, John F. Kennedy Space Ctr., Spaceport USA, 1987, Mass. Bay C.C., 1989; included in permanent collections at John F. Kennedy Ctr., Okla. Air and Space Mus., Fed. Res.; works include painting series Spacesacpes--An Am. Landscape, 1980s, series Baseball, 1990s. Vol. C.R.A.B. Sailing for Disabled Charity, Annapolis, 1993. Ford Found. scholar, 1968, 69; Nat. Endowment Arts grantee, 1982; recipient N.Y. State Initiative award, 1969, Commendation, Gov. Hong Kong and U.S. Consul Hong Kong, 1974, Popular prize Arts Club of Washington, 1992. Mem. Nat. Arts Club. Avocations: squash, tennis, weight lifting, flower arranging. Home: 239 Prince George St Apt 3R Annapolis MD 21401-1633 Office: Sara Larkin Fine Art 2301 E St NW Washington DC 20037-2829

LARKIN, WILLIAM VINCENT, JR., oil field service company executive; b. N.Y.C., July 19, 1953; s. William Vincent and Gloria Ann (Stone) L.; m. Margaret Catherine Gunn, Nov. 12, 1988; children: William Vincent III, Jeremy Stone. AB cum laude, Harvard U., 1976; M Pub. and Pvt. Mgmt., Yale U., 1980. Intern White House, 1975; staff acct. Price Waterhouse & Co., N.Y.C., 1976-78; mktg. asst. AMF Ben Hogan Co., Ft. Worth, 1980-81; asst. to pres. AMF Biol. & Diagnostic Co., Seguin, Tex., 1981-82; mktg. mgr. AMF Tuboscope, Houston, 1982-83, mgr. mill div., 1983-84; v.p. Tuboscope Inc., Houston, 1984-91; pres., COO Tuboscope Vetco Internat., Houston, 1991-93, pres., CEO, 1993—. Bd. dirs. Family Svc. Ctr. Mem. Young Pres.'s Orgn., Petroleum Equipment Suppliers Assn., Nomads, Yale Sch. Mgmt. Alumni Assn. (chmn. nominating com. 1980-82), A.D. Club (Cambridge, Mass.), Harvard Club (N.Y.C.), Yale Club (Houston). Republican. Episcopalian. Avocations: woodworking, golf, tennis. Home: 360 Westminster Dr Houston TX 77024-5608 Office: Tuboscope Inc 2919 Holmes Rd Houston TX 77051-1025

LARMORE, JENNIFER, mezzo-soprano; b. Atlanta, 1960. Debuted in La Clemenza di Tito, France; repertoire includes Rossini's Rosina, L'Enfant et les Sortileges, Giulio Cesare, Donna Elvira, Rossini's Isabella and Adele, Monteverdi's Ottavia, Bellini's Romeo, Cenerentola, Dorabella. Office: Columbia Artists Mgt Inc Foster Div 165 W 57th St New York NY 10019-2201

LARNER, JOSEPH, pharmacology educator; b. Brest-Litovsk, Poland, Jan. 9, 1921; came to U.S., 1921; s. George and Ida (Sobel) Likovsky; m. Frances Wolpert, Sept.7, 1947; children: Andrew Charles, James Mitchell, Paul Frederick. BS, U. Mich., 1942; MD, Columbia U., 1945; MS in Chemistry, U. Ill., 1949; PhD in Biochemistry, Washington U., St. Louis, 1951; D honoris causa, U. Barcelona, Spain, 1983. Instr. biochemistry dept. Washington U., St. Louis, 1951-53; asst. prof. chemistry dept. U. Ill., Urbana, 1953-57; assoc. prof. Pharmacology Western Res. U., Cleve., 1957-63, prof., 1963-64; Hill prof. metabolic enzymology U. Minn. Med. Sch., Mpls., 1964-69; prof., chmn. pharmacology dept. U. Va. Med. Sch., Charlottesville, 1969-90; Alumni prof. U. Va. Med. Sch., Charlotte, 1974—; dir. neurosci. program U. Va. Med. Sch., 1972-75, diabetes confs., 1974-91; prin. scientist Insmed Co., Charlottesville, 1989-91. Author: Intermediary Metabolism and Its Regulation, 1971; editor: Methods in Diabetes Research, 1985, Human Pharmacology, 1991. Capt. U.S. Army, 1946-48. Recipient Sesquicentennial Disting. Alumnus award U. Mich., 1967, Established Investigator award Am. Diabetes Assn., 1978-83, David Rumbaugh Sci. award Juvenile Diabetes Found., 1980, Banting medal and lecture Am. Diabetes Assn., 1987, Disting. Rsch. award Am. Assn. Med. Colls., 1987, Rsch. award Japan Soc. for Starch Rsch., 1985, Va. Lifetime Achievement award in Sci., 1992, U. Va. President's Report, 1992, Va. Inventor of Yr. award and Prize, 1993. Mem. Am. Soc. Pharmacology and Exptl. Therapeutics, Am. Soc. Biochemistry, Am. Soc. Chmn. Pharmacology Depts., Am. Inst. Chemists. Jewish. Office: U Va Diabetes Rsch Ctr Jefferson Park Ave Charlottesville VA 22901-9133

LARO, DAVID, judge; b. Flint, Mich., Mar. 3, 1942; s. Samuel and Florence (Chereton) L.; m. Nancy Lynn Wolf, June 18, 1967; children: Rachel Lynn, Marlene Ellen. BA, U. Mich., 1964; JD, U. Ill., 1967; LLM, NYU, 1970. Bar: Mich. 1968, U.S. Dist. Ct. (ea. dist.) Mich. 1968, U.S. Tax Ct. 1971. Ptnr., Winegarden Booth Shedd and Laro, Flint, Mich., 1970-75; sr. ptnr. Laro and Borgerson, Flint, Mich., 1975-86; prin. David Laro, P.C., Flint, 1986-92; apptd. judge U.S. Tax Ct., Washington, 1992—; of counsel Dykema Gossett, Ann Arbor, Mich., 1989-90; pres., chief exec. officer Durakon Industries, Inc., Ann Arbor, 1989-91, chmn., Lapeer, Mich., 1991—; chmn. Republic Bank, 1986—, vice chmn. Republic Bancorp, Inc., Flint, 1986—. Regent U. Mich., Ann Arbor, 1975-81; mem. Mich. State Bd. Edn., 1982-83; chmn. Mich. State Tenure Commn., 1972-75; commr. Civil Svc. Commn., Flint, Mich., 1984—. Mem. State Bar Mich., Phi Delta Phi. Republican. Office: U.S. Tax Ct 400 2nd St NW Rm 217 Washington DC 20217-0001

LA ROCCA, ISABELLA, artist, educator; b. El Paso, Apr. 14, 1960; d. Remo and Alicia Estela (Gonzalez) La R. BA, U. Pa., 1984; MFA, Ind. U., 1993. Freelance photographer N.Y.C., 1986-90; assoc. instr. Ind. U., Bloomington, 1991-93; instr. Herron Sch. Art, Indpls., 1992; vis. asst. prof. Ind. U., 1994—; asst. prof. DePauw U., Greencastle, Omd/, 1994-95; vis. asst. prof. Bloomsburg (Pa.) U., 1995—. One-woman shows include Haas Gallery, Bloomsburg, Pa., Ctr. Photography Woodstock, N.Y., Moore Coll., Pa., 1994; exhibited in group shows at Bellevue Gallery, 1992, 494 Gallery, N.Y.C., 1993. Ind. U. CIC Minority fellow, 1990-91; Jewish Found. Edn. Women scholar, 1990; recipient Friends Photography Ferguson award, 1993.

LAROCCA, JAMES LAWRENCE, lawyer; b. N.Y.C., Aug. 29, 1943; s. Elias D. and Claire (Walsh) L.; m. Dale Maizels, May 9, 1971; children: Joshua, Amy, Michael. BA, Hofstra U., 1964; JD, Cath. U. Am., 1974; LHD (hon.) Hofstra U., 1993. Bar: D.C. 1974, Fla. 1974. Mem. staff U.S. Ho. of Reps., 1969-73; counsel to vice-chmn. Nat. Commn. Water Quality, Washington, 1974-75; dep. sec. to gov., dir. N.Y. State Office Fed. Affairs, Washington, 1975-77; commr. energy N.Y. State and chmn. N.Y. State Energy R & DAuthority, 1977-83; trustee Power Authority State of N.Y., Albany, 1982-89; commr. transp. N.Y. State, 1983-85; pres., CEO L.I. Assn., Inc., 1985-93; sr. ptnr. Cullen and Dykman, Garden City, 1993—; bd. dirs. European Am. Bank. Host: (TV program) Long Island Talks Business, 1986-93. Mem. adv. council Sch. Bus. Hofstra U., 1984—; chair Touro Coll. Law Ctr., Suffolk County Comml. and Indsl. Incentive Bd.; bd. visitors Marine Scis. Rsch. Ctr., SUNY-Stony Brook; bd. dirs. Nature Conservancy Long Island; mem. Gov.'s Task Force on Coastal Resources, 1990-92; co-chmn. Suffolk Vietnam Vets. Meml. Commn.; mem. State Commn. on Constl. Revision, 1993—, Gov. Coun. Fiscal and Econ. Priorities. Mem. Temp. State Commn. on Constitutional Revision; vice chmn. L.I. Housing Ptnrship; mem. coun. of SUNY at Stony Brook, Gov.'s Sch.-Bus. Alliance Task Force . Lt. USN, 1965-68, Vietnam. Recipient George M. Estabrook award Hofstra U., 1988, Charles Evans Hughes award Am. Soc. for Pub. Adminstrn., 1985. Mem. ABA, Fed. Bar Assn., D.C. Bar, State Bar Fla. Democrat. Home: 8 Beardsley Ln Lloyd Harbor Long Island NY 11743 Office: Cullen & Dykman 100 Quentin Roosevelt Blvd Garden City NY 11530-4843

LAROCHE, ROGER RENAN, psychiatrist; b. St. Paul, July 12, 1960; s. Gerard Auguste and Carolyn Mae (Seese) L.; m. Elizabeth Ann Tollerud, June 25, 1988; children: Austin, Hope. BA, Bethel Coll., St. Paul, 1982; MD, U. Minn., 1987. Diplomate Nat. Bd. Med. Examiners, Am. Bd. Psychiatry and Neurology, Am. Soc. Addiction Medicine, Geriatric Psychiatry, Addiction Psychiatry. Med. intern Hennepin County Med. Ctr., Mpls., 1987-88; resident dept. psychiatry Mayo Clinic Grad. Sch. Medicine, Rochester, Minn., 1988-91; fellowship addiction medicine dept. psychiatry Mayo Clinic Grad. Sch. Medicine, Rochester, 1991-92; med. dir. dept. psychiatry Bradford (Pa.) Regional Med. Ctr., 1992—; rotating med. student educator Mayo Med. Sch., 1987-92; contract forensic psychiatrist U.S. Bur. Prisons, Fed. Med. Ctr., Rochester, 19890-91; prin. investigator for carbamazepine in smoking cessation Mayo Clinic, Rochester, 1991-92, psychiatric rsch. com. cons., 1991-92; pvt. and consulting psychiatrist, Bradford, Pa., 1992—; staff sec.-treas. Bradford Regional Med. Ctr., 1995—, med. staff v.p., 1996. Contbr. articles to profl. jours. County del. Rep. Party Conv., Rochester, 1990. Recipient Medtronic Corp.'s Med. Fellow scholarship of excellence in leadership and acads., 1983, Acad. Writing Excellence award Mayo Clinic, 1991; Mayo Clinic Grad. Sch. Medicine grantee, 1991-92. Mem. AMA (resident physician sect. nat. del. 1990, 91), Am. Psychiat. Assn., Am. Soc. Addiction Medicine, Minn. Med. Assn. (del. ho. of dels. 1990, 91, resident physician sect. state governing officer 1990, 91), Pa. Med. Assn., Pa. Psychiat. Soc., Pa. Soc. Addiction Medicine, McKean County Med. Soc. Avocations: violist, vocal soloist, oil painting, weight training, distance biking. Home: 46 Stone Ave Bradford PA 16701-1050 Office: Med Arts Bldg 199 Pleasant St Bradford PA 16701-1098

LA ROCHELLE, PIERRE-LOUIS, civil engineering educator; b. Quebec, Que., Can., Aug. 20, 1928; s. Emile Joseph and Juliette Marie (Coulombe) LaR.; m. Rachel Gratia Bedard, July 11, 1958 (dec. Aug. 1991); children—Judith, Sophie, Anne. B.A., Seminaire De Quebec, Can., 1950; B.Sc. in Civil Engring., U. Laval, Quebec, 1954, M.Sc., 1956; Ph.D., U. London, 1960. Registered profl. engineer, Que. Asst. prof. engring. U. Laval, Quebec, 1960-63, head dept. civil engring., 1963-67, prof. engring., 1968-96; adj. prof., 1996—; dir. grad. studies civil engring. U. Laval, Quebec, 1992-94; pres. Les Cons. PLR Inc.; cons. in geotech. engring., dam design and construction. Hydro-Quebec, SNC, Golder, others, Can. Contbr. articles to profl. jours. Recipient Can. Geotech. Soc. Prize, 1975, R.F. Leggett award, 1977, Queen Elizabeth Jubilee's medal Can. Govt., 1978. Fellow Engring. Inst. Can.; mem. ASCE, ASTM (Hogentogler award 1985), Royal Soc. Can., Can. Acad. Engring., Internat. Com. on Landslides (pres. 1981-89), Yacht Club (Sillery, Que.; commdr. 1982). Avocations: sailing, skiing, golfing, music. Home: 2528 Des Hospitalieres, Sillery, PQ Canada G1T 1V7 Office: U Laval Dept Civil Engring, Cite Universitaire, Quebec, PQ Canada G1K 7P4

LAROCHELLE, RICHARD CLEMENT, tanning company executive; b. Lewiston, Maine, July 21, 1945; s. Paul H. and Jeannette D. (Jean) L.; children—Anne Marie, Paul, Christie, Marc, Peter. B.A., U. Maine, 1971; M.B.A., Northeastern U., 1976. Cert. mgmt. acct. Prodn. scheduling mgr. A.C. Lawrence Co., South Paris, Maine, 1971-73; adminstrv. supt. A.C. Lawrence Leather Co., Peabody, Mass., 1973-76; v.p., treas. Nat. Tanning and Trading Corp., Peabody, 1976-79; exec. v.p. Hermann Loewenstein Inc., Johnstown, N.Y., 1980-82; pres. Irving Tanning Co., Hartland, Maine, 1982—, CEO, 1992—; bd. dirs. Fugua Enterprises, Inc. Com. chmn. Boy Scouts Am., Johnstown, N.Y., 1981-82; trustee YMCA, Johnstown, 1982; treas. Boys/Girls Club, Waterville, Maine, 1985; co-chmn. Maine Govs. Internat. Adv. Bd., 1995—; bd. dirs. Mid-State Econ. Devel. Corp., 1995—; bd. advisors U. Maine Sch. Bus., 1995—. Served with USN, 1965-69. Mem. Assn. Leather Industries Am. (treas. 1982-84, 92—, chmn. 1984-86, chmn. targeted export assistance com. 1986-90, exec. com. 1982—). Avocations: personal investing, personal computing. Home: PO Box 369 Hartland ME 04943 Office: Irving Tanning Co Main St Hartland ME 04943

LAROCK, BRUCE EDWARD, civil engineering educator; b. Berkeley, Calif., Dec. 24, 1940; s. Ralph W. and Hazel M. (Lambert) L.; m. Susan E. Gardner, June 17, 1968; children: Lynne M., Jean E. BS in Civil Engring., Stanford U., 1962, MS in Civil Engring., 1963, PhD, 1966. Registered profl. engr., Calif. Asst. prof. U. Calif., Davis, 1966-72, assoc. prof., 1972-79, prof., 1979—; sr. vis. fellow U. Wales, Swansea, 1972-73; U.S. sr. scientist Tech. U., Aachen, Germany, 1986-87. Author: (with D. Newnan) Engineer-in-Training Examination Review, 3d edit., 1991; contbr. over 70 tech. articles to profl. jours. Mem. ASCE, Sigma Xi, Tau Beta Pi. Lutheran. Avocation: duplicate bridge. Office: U Calif Davis Dept Civil & Eviron Engring Davis CA 95616-5294

LA ROCQUE, EUGENE PHILIPPE, bishop; b. Windsor, Ont., Can., Mar. 27, 1927; s. Eugene Joseph and Angeline Marie (Monforton) LaR. BA, U. Western Ont., 1948; MA, Laval U., 1956. Ordained priest Roman Catholic Ch., 1952, consecrated bishop, 1974; asst. parish priest Ste. Therese Ch., Windsor, 1952-54; registrar, then dean men, lectr. Christ The King Coll., U. Western Ont., 1956-64; asst. spiritual dir. St. Peter's Sem., 1964-65; prin., dean King's Coll., 1965-68; pastor St. Joseph's Ch., Rivière-aux-Canards, Ont., 1968-70, Ste. Anne's Ch., Tecumseh, 1970-74; bishop of Alexandria-Cornwall, Ont., 1974—; dean Essex County, 1970-73; trustee Essex County Roman Cath. Separate Sch. Bd., 1972-74; 1st chmn. liaison com. Can. Jewish Congress Can. Coun. Chs. and Can. Cath. Conf. Bishops, 1977-84, mem. pro-life com., 1992-94; pres. Ont. Conf. Cath. Bishops, 1992-96; pres. Fedn. Couns. Priests of Can., 1973-74. Mem. KC (3d degree, chaplain Ont. 1977-87). Address: 200 Montreal Rd, Box 1388, Cornwall, ON Canada K6H 5V4 *Belief in God, who creates my unique human life and has a loving plan and concern for each of his children, sustains me amidst the strains, challenges and turmoils of life.*

LA ROCQUE, GENE ROBERT, retired naval officer, government official, author; b. Kankakee, Ill., June 29, 1918; s. Edward and Lucile (Eddy) La R.; m. Sarah Madeline Fox, Apr. 17, 1945 (dec. Apr. 1978); children: John C., James C., Annette D.; m. Lillian Anna Kerekes Danchik, Nov. 16, 1979 (dec. Apr. 1994); stepchildren: Howard Alan Danchik, Roger Lewis Danchik. Student, U. Ill., 1936-40; B.A., George Washington U., 1958; hon. doctorate, Hanyang U., Seoul, Korea, 1975, Haverford Coll., 1987. Commd. ensign U.S. Navy, 1941, advanced through grades to rear adm., 1965, comdr. Task Group in 6th Fleet Mediterranean Sea, 1965-66, mem. faculty Naval War Coll., 1951-53; dir. Inter-Am. Def. Coll. U.S. Navy, Washington, 1969-72; ret. U.S. Navy, 1972; pres. Ctr. Def. Info., Washington, 1972—. Decorated Bronze Star with combat V, Legion of Merit; Abdon Calderon 1st Class (Ecuador); Order Naval Merit (Brazil); Mil. Order Gt. Star (Chile). Mem. Naval Inst. Clubs: New York Yacht, Cosmos (Washington). Home: 3140 Davenport St NW Washington DC 20008-2244 Office: Center For Defense Information 1500 Massachusetts Ave NW Washington DC 20005-1821

LAROCQUE, JUDITH ANNE, federal official; b. Hawkesbury, Ont., Can., Sept. 27, 1956; d. Jean Olier Edouard and Elizabeth Robina (Murray) LaR.; m. Andre Roland Lavoie, Mar. 15, 1991. BA with honours, Carleton U., Ottawa, Ont., 1979, MA, 1992. Notary Pub., Ont. Adminstrv. asst. Internal Audit Directorate, Pub. Svc. Commn., Ottawa, 1979; writer, researcher Prime Min.'s Office, Ottawa, 1979; spl. asst. Office Leader of Opposition, Ottawa, 1980-82; com. clk. coms. and pvt. legis. br. Can. Ho. of Commons, Ottawa, 1982-84, legis. asst. to Govt. House leader, 1984-85, head of House Bus. Office of Govt. House Leader, 1985-86; pres. Queen's Privy Coun. for Can. and min. responsible for regulatory affairs, Ottawa, 1985-86; exec. asst. to min. justice and atty. gen. Can., Ottawa, 1986-89; chief staff Office Leader Govt. in Senate and min. responsible for fed.-provincial rels., Ottawa, 1989-90; sec. to gov. gen. and herald chancellor Govt. House, Ottawa, 1990—; sec. Gen. Order Can., Order Mil. Merit. Fellow Heraldry Soc. Can. (hon.). Office: Govt House, 1 Sussex Dr, Ottawa, ON Canada K1A 0A1

LAROSA, GIANNI, aerospace industry administrator; b. S. Biagio Platani, Italy, Jan. 22, 1937; came to U.S., 1954; s. Alfonso and Santa (Marino) LaR.; m. Maria Cappello, Jan. 6, 1958; children: Alfonso, Sandra, Claudio, Julio. Student, Cass Tech., 1962; diploma in art, Musée de Art Modern, Tonneins, France, 1993. Owner indsl./comml. food svc. equipment mfg. business Detroit, 1970-74; supr. aerospace industry, 1985—. Exhbns. include San Bernardino County (Calif.) Mus., 1992, San Clemente (Calif.) Art Fest, 1992, Paris City Hall, 1993, Modern Art Mus., Bordeaux, France, 1993, Modern Art Mus. Unet, Tonneins, France, 1993, Soho Internat. Art Competition, N.Y.C., 1993, Wirtz Gallery, Miami, 1993, Bower Mus., Orange County, Calif., 1995. Recipient award Fine Arts Inst., 1992, award Soho Internat. Competition, 1993, award Mayor of Paris, Internat. Art Competition, 1993; named Disting. Vis., Mayor of Miami, Fla., 1994. Home: 26641 Domingo Dr Mission Viejo CA 92692-4114

LA ROSA, RICHARD, acoustical engineer, consultant; b. Oct. 4, 1925. BEE, Poly. Inst. Bklyn., 1947, MEE, 1949, DEE, 1953. Sr. cons. engr. Hazeltine Corp. Fellow IEEE (Charles J. Hirsch award 1978, Region 1 award 1977, chmn. L.I. SU group 1983-85, chmn. L.I. sect. awards nomination com. 1983-85, chmn. L.I. sect. 1985-86). Office: care Hazeltine Corp Rsch MS 1-4 Cuba Hill Rd Greenlawn NY 11740-1605*

LAROSE, NANCY JEAN, fiberglass manufacturer; b. Lowell, Mass., Nov. 9, 1949; d. George Michael and Jean E. (Coffin) LaR.; m. Michael W. Marks, Jan. 5, 1970 (div. Feb. 1972). Grad., high sch., 1967. Night supr. Swim Industries, Largo, Fla., 1980-86; asst. plant mgr. Blue Dolphin Pools, Largo, 1986-92; field cons. Fibretech, Largo, 1992-94; owner LaRose Fiberglass, St. Petersburg, Fla., 1994—. Mem. NAFE, AARP, Nat. Parks and Conservation, Smithsonian Instn., Police Benevolence Assn. Christian. Avocations: camping, fishing, boating, reading, collecting old movies. Home and Office: 3237 Prescott St N Saint Petersburg FL 33713-3044

LAROSE, ROGER, former pharmaceutical company executive, former university administrator; b. Montreal, Que., Can., July 28, 1910; s. Alfred and Anna (Contant) L.; m. Rita Dagenais, Aug. 10, 1936 (dec. Oct. 1960); 1 child, Louise Larose Cuddihy; m. Julienne Begin, Aug. 4, 1961. B.A., U. Montreal, 1929, B.Sc. in Pharmacy, 1932; Licentiate in Social, Polit., and Econ. Scis, 1934. Asst. prof. pharmacy U. Montreal, 1934; dean Faculty Pharmacy, 1960-65, vice rector, 1969-79; with Ciba Co. Ltd., Montreal, 1936-71; v.p. Ciba Co. Ltd., 1958-68, pres., 1968-71, dir., 1958-71; pres. Ciba-Geigy Can. Ltd., 1971-73, dep. chmn. bd., 1973-78, chmn. bd., 1978-82; vice chmn. bd., mem. exec. com. Bank Canadian Nat., 1969-80; mem. Sci. Council Can., 1966-71; pres. com. Sci. Council on Health Scis., 1969-73. Bd. dirs. Institute recherches cliniques de Montreal, 1968-95, pres. of found. 1995-96; bd. dirs. Hotel-Dieu de Montreal, 1969-79; pres. Hopital St. -Luc de Montreal, 1978-88; bd. govs. Can. Bankers Inst., 1973-80; pres. Montreal Symphony Orch., 1978-79, pres. and mng. dir., 1979-81; pres. Chamber Orch. I Musici de Montreal, 1984-88; bd. dirs. Que. Hosp. Assn. Decorated officer Order Can. Mem. Acad. Pharmacy (France) (hon.), Pharm. Soc. Gt. Britain (hon.), Can. Hosp. Assn. (bd. dirs. 1985-89, George Findlay Stephen award 1990), St.-Denis Club (Montreal). Home: 404-205 Côte Ste, Catherine Rd, Outremont, PQ Canada H2V 2A9

LA ROSSA, JAMES M(ICHAEL), lawyer; b. Bklyn., Dec. 4, 1931; s. James Vincent and Marie Antoinette (Tronolone) La R.; m. Gayle Marino, Sept. 20, 1958; children—James M., Thomas, Nancy, Susan. B.S., Fordham U., 1953, J.D., 1958. Bar: N.Y. 1958, U.S. Dist. Ct. N.Y. 1961, U.S. Supreme Ct. 1969. Pvt. practice law N.Y.C., 1958-62, 67-74, 76—; asst. U.S. atty. Eastern Dist. N.Y., Bklyn., 1962-65; ptnr. firm Lefkowitz & Brownstien, N.Y.C., 1965-67, La Rossa, Shargel & Fishetti, N.Y.C., 1974-76, La Rossa, Brownstein & Mitchell, N.Y.C., 1980-82, La Rossa, Axenfeld & Mitchell, N.Y.C., 1982-84, La Rossa, Cooper, Axenfeld, Mitchell & Bergman, N.Y.C., 1984-85; now ptnr. La Rossa, Mitchell & Ross, N.Y.C.; participant Debate on Legal Ethics Criminal Cts. Bar Assn. Queens County, N.Y., 1978, Criminal Trial Advocacy Workshop, Harvard U. Law Sch., 1978. Author: White Collar Crimes: Defense Strategies, 1977, Federal Rules of Evidence in Criminal Matters, 1977, White Collar Crimes, 1978. Served to 1st lt. USMC, 1953-55. Recipient Guardian of Freedom award B'nai B'rith, 1978. Mem. ABA, N.Y. State Bar Assn. (Criminal Law Practitioner of Yr. 1990), Fed. Bar Counsel, Assn. Bar City N.Y. Office: LaRossa Mitchell & Ross 41 Madison Ave New York NY 10010-2202

LAROUNIS, GEORGE PHILIP, manufacturing company executive; b. Bklyn., Mar. 19, 1928; s. Philip John and Helen (Cormentelou) L.; m. Mary G. Efthymiatou, Jan. 13, 1958; 1 child, Daphne H. B.E.E., U. Mich., 1950, postgrad. in Law; J.D., N.Y. U., 1954. Electronics engr. in research and devel. Columbia U. Electronics Research Lab., 1952-54; assoc. firm Pennie, Edmonds, Morton, Barrows & Taylor, N.Y.C., 1954-58; fgn. patent atty. Western Electric Co., N.Y.C., 1958-60; asst. dir. Bendix Internat., Paris, 1960; dir. licensing and indsl. property rights Bendix Internat., to 1974; v.p. staff ops. Bendix Europe, 1974-77; v.p. Bendix Internat. Fin. Corp.; v.p. Europe, Middle East and Africa Bendix Corp., Paris, 1977-82; pres. Bendix Internat. Cons. Corp., 1974-86; v.p., group exec. Allied Automotive, 1982-85; pres. Allied-Signal Fibers Europe S.A.; v.p. Allied-Signal Internat., 1985-93; dir. CopyTele, Inc., Delphi Soc., Greece. Served with U.S. Army, 1946-47. Chevalier French Legion of Honor. Mem. N.Y. Patent Bar Assn., Fed. Patent Bar Assn., Licensing Execs. Soc., Am. C. of C. in France and Greece (dir., pres., exec. com. European Coun.), Polo Club de Paris, Papagou Tennis Club (Athens), Tau Beta Pi, Eta Kappa Nu. Home: 15-17 A Tsoha St, Athens 11521, Greece

LARPENTEUR, JAMES ALBERT, JR., lawyer; b. Seattle, Aug. 6, 1935; s. James Albert and Mary Louise (Coffey) L.; m. Hazel Marie Arnton, Apr. 23, 1965 (div. 1983); children: Eric James, Jason Clifford; 1 adopted child, Brenda Mon Fong; m. Katherine Annette Bingham, Nov. 8, 1986. BS in Bus., U. Oreg., 1957, LLB, 1961. Bar: Oreg. 1961, U.S. Dist. Ct. Oreg. 1961, U.S. Tax Ct. 1962, U.S. Ct. Appeals (9th cir.) 1962, U.S. Supreme Ct. 1965. Assoc. Schwabe Williamson & Wyatt, Portland, Oreg., 1961-69, ptnr., 1969-82, sr. ptnr., 1982—, mem. exec. com., 1989-92. Dir. exec. com. Portland Rose Festival Assn., 1975—, pres., 1987; ex-officio dir. Portland Visitors Assn., 1981—; bd. dirs., mem. exec. com. Providence Child Ctr. Found., 1983-94, chmn. exec. com., 1986-87; bd. dirs. Willamette Light Brigade, 1987—, Cath. Charities Portland, 1989-92; bd. dirs. Albertina Kerr Ctrs., 1996—. Mem. Oreg. Bar Assn. (editor, writer, speaker numerous continuing legal edn. programs, chmn. bus. law sect. 1986-87, real estate, estate planning, securities regulation sects.), Multnomah Athletic Club (pres. 1984), Univ. Club Portland, Waverley Country Club, Arlington Club, City Club of Portland. Avocation: golf. Home: 324 NW Lomita Ter Portland OR 97210-3321 Office: Schwabe Williamson & Wyatt 1211 SW 5th Ave Portland OR 97204-3713

LARR, PETER, banker; b. Indpls., Jan. 17, 1939; s. David and Marjorie Kathleen (Hearne) L.; m. Rosamond Holmes Woodfield, July 7, 1962; children—Alexia Aisha, Diana Kirsten, David Hearne. B.A., Princeton U., 1960. Asst. mgr. London and Beirut brs. Chase Manhattan Bank, 1961-67, v.p., div. exec. land transp., 1976-78, v.p., group exec. credit tng. and devel., 1978-80, v.p., div. exec. commodity fin., 1980-83; sr. v.p., bus. exec. nat. corr. banking Chase Manhattan Bank, N.Y.C., 1983-85; sr. v.p., exec. domestic instl. banking Chase Manhattan Bank, 1985-90, sr. v.p., risk asset rev. exec., 1990-95; sr. v.p. sr. credit and porfolio mgmt. exec. Asia Chase Manhattan Bank, Hong Kong, 1995—. Assoc. vestry Christ Ch., Rye, N.Y., 1983-85; planning commr., City of Rye, 1992-95. Mem. Assn. Res. City Bankers (assoc., bank pay sys. com. 1984-90), Am. Bankers Assn. (chmn. corp. banking divsn. 1988-94), Robert Morris Assn. N.Y. (pres. 1994), Am. Yacht Club, Apawamis Club. Avocations: tennis, golf, genealogical rsch. Office: Chase Manhattan Bank, Chase Manhattan Tower, Sha Tin Hong Kong

LARRABEE, DONALD RICHARD, publishing company executive; b. Portland, Maine, Aug. 8, 1923; s. Henry Carpenter and Marion (Clapp) L.; m. Mary Elizabeth Rolfs, Oct. 9, 1948; children—Donna Louise, Robert Rolfs. Student, Syracuse U., 1941-43. Reporter Portland Press Herald, 1941-43, Syracuse Post Standard, 1943; reporter Griffin-Larrabee News Bur., Washington, 1946-54; mng. editor Griffin-Larrabee News Bur., 1954-67, bur. chief, 1967-69, owner, 1969-78; dir. Washington office, State of Maine, 1978-89; dir. Nat. Press Bldg. Corp., 1973-85. Bd. dirs. Nat. Press Found., 1978—. Served with USAAF, 1943-45. Mem. Me. Soc. Washington (pres. 1950-53), Corrs. for Congl. Press Galleries (standing com. 1959-60), White House Corrs. Assn. Conglist. (moderator 1962). Clubs: Gridiron (Washington), National Press (Washington) (sec. 1953-54, treas. 1966-67, chmn. bd. 1969, pres. 1973). Home and Office: 4704 Jamestown Rd Bethesda MD 20816-2923

LARRABEE, MARTIN GLOVER, biophysics educator; b. Boston, Jan. 25, 1910; s. Ralph Clinton and Ada Perkins Miller L.; m. Sylvia Kimball, Sept. 10, 1932 (div. 1944); 1 son, Benjamin Larrabee Scherer; m. Barbara Belcher, Mar. 25, 1944; 1 son, David Belcher Larrabee. B.A., Harvard, 1932; Ph.D., U. Pa., 1937; M.D. (hon.), U. Lausanne, Switzerland, 1974. Research asst., fellow U. Pa., Phila., 1934-40; assoc. to assoc. prof. U. Pa., 1941-49; asst. prof. physiology Cornell U. Med. Coll., N.Y.C., 1940-41; assoc. prof. Johns Hopkins U., Balt., 1949-63, prof. biophysics, 1963—. Contbr. articles to scientific jours. Mem. Am. Physiol. Soc., Biophys. Soc., Am. Soc. Neurochemistry, Internat. Neurochem. Soc., Nat. Acad. Scis., Soc. for Neurosci. (treas. 1970-75), Physiol. Soc. (asso., Eng.), Phi Beta Kappa. Clubs: Appalachian Mountain, Sierra, Mountain of Md. Rsch. on circulatory, respiratory and nervous systems of animals, especially on synaptic and metabolic mechanisms in sympathetic ganglia, 1934—; wartime research on oxygen lack, decompression sickness, nerve injury, infrared viewing devices, 1941-45. Home: Glen Meadows 11630 Glen Arm Rd Glen Arm MD 21057-9403 Office: Johns Hopkins U Biophysics Dept Baltimore MD 21218

LARREY, INGE HARRIETTE, jazz and blues freelance photographer; b. Freiburg, Germany, Jan. 21, 1934; came to U.S., 1983; d. Friedrich W. and Claerle I. (Mueller) Luger; m. Toni Halter, Aug. 5, 1967 (div. 1977); m. Louis A. Larrey, June 13, 1981. Student, N.Y. Inst. Photography, Saudi Arabia, 1983. Au Pair, Finland, 1952; Various assignments Federal Republic of Germany in Turkey, Spain, Belgium, England, 1956-82; audit student in journalism, photography U. Houston, 1984; substitute employee with consulate gen. Federal Republic of Germany, Houston, 1985; visitors' Relations German real estate company, Houston, 1985—; internat. network mktg. Interior Design Nutritionals, 1995—. Works shown in more than a dozen exhbns., 1986-91; photographs in pvt. collections, in various publs., on cassette, record covers. Vol. Houston FotoFest, Women's Caucus for Art. Mem. Nat. Mus. of Women in the Arts (charter), Am. Image News Svc., Cultural Arts Coun. of Houston, Friends of Photography, Houston Ctr. for Photography, Jazz Heritage Soc. Tex., Milt Larkin Jazz Soc. (founding). Office: Sueba USA Corp 1800 West Loop S Ste 1323 Houston TX 77027-3211

LARRIMORE, RANDALL WALTER, manufacturing company executive; b. Lewes, Del., Apr. 27, 1947; s. Randall A. and Irene (Faucett) L.; m. Judith Cutright, Aug. 29, 1970; children: Jacob, Alex. BS, Swarthmore (Pa.) Coll., 1969; MBA, Harvard U., 1971. Product mgr. Richardson-Vick, Wilton, Conn., 1971-75; sr. engagement mgr. McKinsey & Co., N.Y.C., 1975-80; pres. Pepsi-Cola Italia, Rome, 1980-83, Beatrice Home Specialties, Inc. (name changed to Twentieth Century Cos., Inc.), Skokie, Ill., 1983-87; pres., chief exec. officer MasterBrand Industries, Inc., 1988—; v.p. Am. Brands, Inc., 1988-95; chmn. Moen Inc., 1990—, chief exec. officer, 1990-94; adv. bd. Nat. Home Ctr. Show, 1990-93. Bd. dirs. Winnetka Congl. Ch., 1989-90; mem. hardware/home improvement coun. City of Hope, 1991—, pres. 1991-93; mem. adv. bd. Nat. Home Ctr. Show, 1990-93; commr. Landmark Preservation Coun., Winnetka, 1992—. Mem. Plumbing Mfg. Inst. (bd. dirs. 1991-93). Home: 830 Sheridan Rd Winnetka IL 60093-1929 Office: MasterBrand Industries Inc 510 Lake Cook Rd Deerfield IL 60015-5610 also: Am Brands Inc 1700 E Putnam Ave Box 819 Old Greenwich CT 06870

LARROCA, RAYMOND G., lawyer; b. San Juan, P.R., Jan. 5, 1930; s. Raymond Gil and Elsa Maria (Morales) L.; m. Barbara Jean Strand, June 21, 1952 (div. 1974); children—Denise Anne Sheehan, Gail Ellen, Raymond Gil, Mark Talbot, Jeffrey William. B.S.S., Georgetown U., 1952, J.D., 1957. Bar: D.C. 1957, U.S. Supreme Ct. 1960. Assoc., Kirkland, Fleming, Green, Martin & Ellis, Washington, 1957-64; ptnr. Kirkland, Ellis, Hodson, Chaffetz & Masters, Washington, 1964-67, Miller, Cassidy, Larroca & Lewin, Washington, 1967—. Served with arty. U.S. Army, 1948-49, to 1st lt., inf., 1952-54. Mem. ABA, D.C. Bar, Bar Assn. D.C., The Barristers. Republican. Roman Catholic. Clubs: Congl. Country (Potomac, Md.); University (Washington). Office: 2555 M St NW Ste 500 Washington DC 20037-1302

LARROQUETTE, JOHN BERNARD, actor; b. New Orleans, Nov. 25, 1947; s. John Edgar Larroquette and Berthalla (Oramous) Helmstetter; m. Elizabeth Ann Cookson, July 4, 1975; children: Lisa Katherina, Jonathan Preston, Benjamin Lawrence. Grad. high sch., New Orleans. Plays include: The Crucible, Enter Laughing, Endgame; numerous appearances in TV shows including Baa Baa Black Sheep; Dan Fielding in Night Court, NBC, 1983-92 (Best Actor Emmy award, 1985, 86, 87, 88), The John Larroquette Show, 1993— (Best Actor Emmy award nominee 1994); feature films include: Altered States, 1980, Stripes, 1981, Cat People, 1982, Twilight Zone: The Movie, 1983, Choose Me, 1983, Star Trek III: The Search for Spock, 1984, Hysterical, 1984, Meatballs, Part II, 1984, Summer Rentals, 1985, Blind Date, 1987, Second Sight, 1989, Madhouse, 1990, Tune in Tomorrow, 1990, Richie Rich, 1994; TV film appearance Hot Paint, 1988; narrator Texas Chainsaw Massacre, 1974, One Special Victory, NBC, 1991. Avocation: collecting first edition books. Office: care Adam Venit/CAA 9830 Wilshire Blvd Beverly Hills CA 90212

LARROWE, CHARLES PATRICK, economist, educator; b. Portland, Oreg., May 1, 1916; s. Albertus and Helen (Maginnis) L.; 1 child, Peter (dec.). B.A., U. Wash., Seattle, 1946, M.A., 1948; Ph.D., Yale U., 1952. Asst. instr. econs. U. Wash., 1946-49, Yale U., 1949-52; assoc. prof. U. Utah, 1952-56; mem. faculty Mich. State U., East Lansing, 1956-89; prof. econs. Mich. State U., 1961-89, faculty grievance ofcl., 1976-80, 88-89; cons. to govt. Author: Shape-Up and Hiring Hall, 1955, Harry Bridges, 2d edit., 1977, Lashing Out, 1982. Served with Am. Field Service, 1942-43; Served with AUS, 1943-45. Decorated Silver Star, Purple Heart with oak leaf cluster, Combat Infantryman's badge; grantee Rabinowitz Found., 1962. Mem. ACLU, NAACP, Amnesty Internat., Rolls-Royce Owners' Club. Democrat. Home: 537 Gunson St East Lansing MI 48823-3525 Office: Mich State Univ Dept Econs East Lansing MI 48824

LARRY, R. HEATH, lawyer; b. Huntingdon, Pa., Feb. 24, 1914; s. Ralph E. and Mabel (Heath) L.; m. Eleanor Ketler, Sept. 10, 1938; children: David Heath, Dennis Ketler, Thomas Richard. A.B., Grove City Coll., 1934, LL.D., 1964; J.D., U. Pitts., 1937. Bar: Pa. 1937, D.C. 1937. Pvt. practice, 1937-38; atty. Nat. Tube Co., 1938-44, sec., dir., 1944-48; gen. atty. U.S. Steel Corp., Pitts., 1948-52; asst. gen. solicitor U.S. Steel Corp., 1952-58, adminstrv. v.p. labor relations, 1958-66, exec. v.p., asst. to chmn., 1966-69, vice chmn. bd., 1969-77; pres. N.A.M., 1977-80, of counsel Reed Smith Shaw & McClay, Washington, 1980—; dir. emeritus Textron, Inc. Bd. visitors U. Pitts. Sch. Law; trustee Grove City Coll.; former trustee Conf. Bd. Mem. Am. Iron and Steel Inst. Presbyn. Clubs: Met. (Washington); Economic (N.Y.C.); Gulf Stream Golf, Delray Beach Yacht, Gulf Stream Bath and Tennis, Little; Bermuda Run Country Club. Home: 4333 N Ocean Blvd Apt A53 Delray Beach FL 33483 also (summer): Bermuda Vlg # 3107 Advance NC 27006-9477

LARSEN, ANNA KARUS, medical practice administrator; b. Howell, Mich., June 6, 1932; d. Arthur Emil Karus and Alida Lucile (Schoenhals) Loring; m. James Patrick Larsen, Apr. 22, 1955 (div. Oct. 1973); children: K. Stephan, Kirsten Larsen Babcock. Diploma, Mercy Sch. Nursing, Ann Arbor, Mich., 1953; BA, Stephens Coll., Columbia, Mo., 1979; MBA, Ariz. State U., Tempe, 1980. Nurse Houston, 1956-58, Coromoto Hosp., Maracaibo, Venezuela, 1960-62; program coord. St. Joseph's Hosp., Phoenix, 1973-79; owner Larsen & Assocs., Phoenix, 1982-89; project mgr. Harris Labs., Lincoln, Nebr., 1989-90; adminstr. Hope Eye Ctr., Phoenix, 1990—; owner, shareholder Pearlsen, Inc., Phoenix, 1994—; owner, developer Corhealth, Phoenix, 1986-88; editor, pub. Ariz. Mgmt. Newsletter, Phoenix, 1983-86; med. practice mgmt. cons., Phoenix, 1980—. Mem. Med. Group Mgmt. Assn., Am. Assn. Ophthalmic Adminstrs., Ariz. Treasury Mgmt. Assn. Avocations: watercolors, snow skiing, granddaughters. Office: Hope Eye Ctr 1530 W Glendale Ave Ste 103 Phoenix AZ 85021-8578

LARSEN, ANNE, editor; b. Blue Island, Ill., Apr. 13, 1941; d. Robert Edward and Ruth Elizabeth (Hunke) Schnare; m. Eric Everett Larsen, June 5, 1965; children: Flynn, Gavin. BA, Carleton Coll., 1963; MA, U. Wis., 1965. Support svcs., researcher Sta. WNET-TV, N.Y.C., 1972-74; freelance book reviewer, writer Village Voice, Chgo. Tribune, Parents mag., N.Y.C., 1974-76; assoc. editor fiction Redbook mag., N.Y.C., 1976-83; free-lance editor and cons. Redbook, Mademoiselle, Seventeen, Cosmopolitan, Esquire, N.Y.C., 1983-85; editor, fiction Kirkus Rev., N.Y.C., 1985-87, fiction editor, 1987-94, editl. dir., 1995—. Mem. Nat. Book Critics Circle, Am. Soc. Mag. Editors, Women's Media Group, Friends of Poets and Writers, Friends of PEN. Office: Kirkus Svc Inc Kirkus Reviews 200 Park Ave S New York NY 10003-1503

LARSEN, EDWIN MERRITT, retired chemist, educator; b. Milw., July 12, 1915; s. Howard Reynolds and Ella (Tees) L.; m. Kathryn Marie Behm, Aug. 17, 1946; children—Robert, Lynn, Richard. B.S., U. Wis., 1937; Ph.D., Ohio State U., 1942. Chemist Rohm & Haas, Phila., 1937-38; teaching asst. Ohio State U., 1938-42; group leader Manhattan Dist. polonium project Monsanto Chem. Co., 1943-46; mem. faculty dept. chemistry U. Wis.-Madison, 1942-43, 46-86, prof., 1958-86, assoc. chmn. dept., 1977-86; mem. Wis. Fusion Tech. Inst.; vis. prof. U. Fla., 1958; Fulbright lectr. Technische Hochschule, Vienna, Anorganische Institut, 1966-67. Author: Transitional Elements, 1965; contbr. articles to profl. jours. on synthesis in liquid aluminum trihalides and on role of chemistry in development of fusion energy. Fellow AAAS; mem. Am. Chem. Soc. (chmn. Wis. sect.), Am. Nuclear Soc., Wis. Acad. Scis., Arts and Letters, Sigma Xi (chmn. Wis. chpt.), Phi Lambda Upsilon. Home: 109 Standish Ct Madison WI 53705-5131

LARSEN, EINAR V., electrical and systems engineer, consultant; b. Feb. 14, 1951. BSEE, Calif. Poly. Inst., 1973; MS in Elec. Power Engring., Rensselaer Poly. Inst., 1974. Sr. cons. engr. GE. Fellow IEEE (region 1 awad 1980, chmn. Schenectady sect. Power Engring. soc. 1977, mem. edn. sys. working group, HVDC harmonics working group, HVDC control working group, chmn. FACTS working group). Office: General Electric Co. 1 River Rd #2-605 Schenectady NY 12345*

LARSEN, ERIK, art history educator; b. Vienna, Austria, Oct. 10, 1911; came to U.S., 1947, naturalized, 1953; s. Richard and Adrienne (Schapringer de Csepreg) L.; m. Lucy Roman, Oct. 4, 1932 (dec. 1981); children: Sigurd-Yves, Annik-Eve., Erik-Claude (dec.); m. Anna Gallup Moses, May 8, 1982 (div. Sept. 1986); m. Katharina Ehling, Oct. 21, 1989. Candidate, Institut Superieur d'Histoire de l'Art et d'Archéologie, Brussels, 1931; Licentiate, Louvain (Belgium) U., 1941; Docteur en Archéologie et Histoire de l'Art, 1959; D. honoris causa, Janus Pannonius U., Pécs, Hungary, 1992. Dir., editor-in-chief on semi-ofcl. cultural mission for Belgian Govt. Pictura, art. mag., Brussels, Rio de Janeiro, Brazil, 1946-47; research prof. art Manhattanville Coll. of Sacred Heart, 1947-55; instr. CCNY, 1948-55; lectr, then vis. prof. Georgetown U., 1955-58, assoc. prof. fine arts, 1958-63, prof., 1963-67, head dept. fine arts, 1960-67; prof. history of art U. Kans., 1967-80, prof. emeritus, 1980—; dir. Center for Flemish Art and Culture, 1970-80; cons. old masters' paintings, guest-prof. U. Salzburg, Austria, 1988. Author: books, the most recent being La Vie, Les Ouvrages et Les Eleves de Van Dyck, 1975, Calvinistic Economy and 17th Century Dutch Art, 1979, Anton van Dyck, 1980, Rembrandt, Peintre de Paysages: Une Vision Nouvelle, 1983, Japanese edit., 1992; Seventeenth Century Flemish Painting, 1985, The Paintings of Anthony van Dyck, 2 vols., 1988; contbr. numerous articles, revs. to profl. publs., newspapers. Mem. Kans. Cultural Arts Commn., 1971-73; mem. Kans. Cultural Arts Adv. Council, 1973-79. Served with Belgian Underground, 1942-45. Decorated knight's cross Order Leopold, knight's cross Order of Crown, officer Order Leopold (Belgium); officer Order of Rio Branco (Brazil); recipient prix Thorlet, laureate Inst. France, Académie des sciences morales et politiques, 1962; Internat. Hon. Citizen, New Orleans, 1989; named hon. Ky. col., 1977. Fellow Soc. Antiquaries of Scotland; mem. Appraisers Assn. Am., Association des Diplomés en Histoire de l'Art et Archéologie de L'Université Catholique de Louvain, Académie d'Aix-en Provence (France) (corr.), Académie de Mâcon (France) (asso.), Académie d'Alsace (France) (titular), Comité Cultural Argentino (hon.), Schweizerisches Institut fuer Kunstwissenschaft (Zurich, Switzerland), Academia di Belle Arti Pietro Vanucci (Perugia, Italy) (hon.), Royal Soc. Arts (London) (Benjamin Franklin fellow); correspondent-academician Real Academia de Bellas Artes de San Telmo (Malága, Spain), Real Academia de Bellas Artes de San Jorge (Barcelona, Spain), Accademia Tiberina (Rome), Académie Royale D'Archéologie de Belgique (fgn. assoc.). Home: 511 S Washington St Beverly Hills FL 34465-4312

LARSEN, GARY LOY, physician, researcher; b. Wahoo, Nebr., Jan. 10, 1945; s. Allan Edward and Dorothy Mae (Hengen) L.; m. Letitia Leah Hoyt, Dec. 22, 1967; children: Kari Lyn, Amy Marie. BS, U. Nebr., 1967; MD, Columbia U., 1971. Diplomate Am. Bd. Pediatrics, Am. Bd. Pediatric Pulmonology (chmn. 1990-92)/. Pediatric pulmonologist Nat. Jewish Ctr. for Immunology & Respiratory Medicine, Denver, 1978—; mem. faculty U. Colo. Sch. Medicine, Denver, 1978—, dir. sect. of pediatric pulmonary medicine, 1987—, prof. pediatrics, 1990—. Contbr. articles to prof. jours. Major M.C., U.S. Army, 1974-76. NIH med. rsch. grantee NIH, 1981—. Mem. AM. Thoracic Soc. (chmn. pediatric assembly 1987-88), Soc. Pediatric Rsch., Phi Beta Kappa, Alpha Omega Alpha, N.Y. Acad. Scis. Lutheran. Office: Nat Jewish Ctr Immunology & Respiratory Medicine 1400 Jackson St Denver CO 80206-2761

LARSEN, GLEN L., school system administrator; b. Ainsworth, Nebr., Dec. 19, 1937. BEd, Chadron State Tchrs. Coll., 1962; MEd, U. Nebr., Lincoln, 1968, EdS, 1975. Tchr. elem. sch. Brocksburg, Nebr., 1955-56; tchr. jr. h.s. Long Pine, Nebr., 1959-60; tchr., coach Ashland, Nebr., 1962-67; secondary prin. Deshler (Nebr.) Schs., 1967-68, supt., 1968-71; supt. Fullerton (Nebr.) Pub. Schs., 1971-81, Adams Ctrl. Jr./Sr. High Sch., Hastings, Nebr., 1981—. Recipient Nebr. Superintendent of the Yr. award Am. Assn. of Sch. Adminstrs., 1991. Mem. Nat. Rural Edn. Assn., Nebr. Coun. Sch. Adminstrs., Am. Assn. Sch. Adminstrs., Nebr. Assn. County Supts., Nebr. Rural Cmty. Schs. Assn. (past pres.), Nebr. Class VI Schs. Assn., Nebr. Sch. Activity Assn. (chmn. Region IV). Office: Adams Ctrl Jr Sr High Sch PO Box 1088 Hastings NE 68902-1088

LARSEN, GWYNNE E., computer information systems educator; b. Omaha, Sept. 10, 1934; d. Melvin and Vernetta (Allen) Bannister; m. John M. Larsen, June 8, 1958; children: Bradley Allen, Blair Kevin, Randall Lawrence. A in Bus. Adminstrn., Denver U., 1956, MBA, 1975, PhD, 1979; BS, Met. State Coll., 1971. Instr. Met. State Coll. Denver, 1979-81, asst. prof., 1981-85, assoc. prof., 1985-88, prof., 1989—, acting chair computer dept., 1991-92; book reviewer McGraw Hill, 1991, Harcourt Brace Jovanovich, 1991, Macmillan Pub. Co., 1993, Southwestern Pub. Co., 1993; presenter Mountain Plains Mgmt. conf., Denver, 1982, Rocky Mountain Bus. Expo, Denver, 1982, Red Rocks C.C., 1984, Colo.-Wyo. Acad. Sci. conf., 1985, Boulder, 1986, Colorado Springs, 1987; local coord. John Wiley & Sons, Denver, 1982, 83; panel chmn. on office automation Assn. for Computing Machinery, Denver, 1985; spkr. ASTD, 1986, Am. Pub. Works Assn., 1986; participant numerous presentations and confs. Author: (with others) Computerized Business Information Systems Workbook, 1983, Collegiate Microcomputer, 1992, (with Verlene Leeberg) Word Processing: Using WordPerfect 5.0, 1989, Word Processing: Using WordPerfect 5.1, 1991, First Look at WordPerfect 5.1, 1991, First Look at DOS, 1991, First Look at NetWare, 1992, Using WordPerfect for Windows, 1993, (with Marold and Shaw) Using Microsoft Works: An Introduction to Computing, 1993, Using Microsoft Works, An Introduction to Computing, 1993, First Look at WordPerfect 6.0 for Windows, 1994, Using WordPerfect 6.0 for Windows, 1994, Using Microsoft Works for Windows, An Introduction to Computing, 1996; apptd. editl. bd. Jour. Mgmt. Systems, 1988, Jour. Microcomputer Systems Mgmt., 1989, Info. Resources Mgmt. Jour., 1991; mem. editl. review bd. Jour. Info. Resources Mgmt. Systems, 1985—, Jour. Mgmt. Info. Systems, 1986—, Jour. Database Mgmt. Systems, Jour. Database Mgmt. Systems, 1987—, Jour. End User Computing, 1990—; contbr. articles to profl. jours. Mem. Info. Resources Mgmt. Assn., Colo.-Wyo. Acad. Scis., Office Automation Soc. Internat., Internat. Acad. for Info. Mgmt., panel part., 1995. Avocations: walking, aerobics, reading detective stories. Home: 8083 S Adams Way Littleton CO 80122 Office: Met State Coll Denver Campus Box 45 PO Box 173362 Denver CO 80217-3362

LARSEN, JONATHAN ZERBE, journalist; b. N.Y.C., Jan. 6, 1940; s. Roy Edward and Margaret (Zerbe) L.; m. Katharine Wilder, May 28, 1966; m. Jane Amsterdam, Aug. 31, 1985; 1 child, Edward Roy. B.A., Harvard U., 1961, M.A.T., 1963. Contbg. editor Time mag., N.Y.C., 1965-66; corr. Time mag., Chgo., 1966-68, Los Angeles, 1968-70; bur. chief Time mag., Saigon, Vietnam, 1970-71; assoc. editor Time mag., 1972-73; editor New Times mag., N.Y.C., 1974-79; Nieman fellow Harvard U., 1979-80; news editor Life mag., 1980-81, sr. editor, 1981-82; free-lance writer, 1982-88; editor-in-chief The Village Voice, N.Y.C., 1989-94. Trustee Natural Resources Def. Council., Cambridge Coll.; bd. dirs. Larsen Fund. Recipient Clarion award, 1986. Home: Finch Farm Vail Ln North Salem NY 10560

LARSEN, PAUL EDWARD, lawyer; b. Rock Springs, Wyo., Jan. 5, 1964; s. Otto E. and Linda K. (Wright) L.; m. Dawn Jannette Griffin, June 25, 1986; 1 child, Quinne Caitlin. BA, U. Oreg., 1986, JD, 1989. Bar: Nev. 1989, U.S. Dist. Ct. Nev. 1989, U.S. Ct. Appeals (9th cir.) 1994. Atty. Lionel, Sawyer & Collins, Las Vegas, Nev., 1989—, chmn. land use and planning divsn., 1995—; gen. counsel Nev. State Democrats, 1996, corp. for solar tech. and renewable resources, 1995-96. Author, editor: Nevada Environmental Law Handbook, 1991, 1st edit., 2d edit., 3rd edit.; contbg. author: Nevada Gaming Law, 2d edit., 1995; contbr. articles to profl. jours. Pres., dir. Desert Creek Homeowners Assn., Las Vegas, 1994-95; atty. Clark County Pro-Bono Project, Las Vegas, 1989-95, Nev. Dem. Party, Las Vegas, 1994. Mem. ABA (vice chair com. natural resources pub. lands sect. 1993-95, bd. dirs. young lawyers divsn. natural resources com. 1992-95, atty. young lawyers divsn. program 1989-90), Nev.-Am. Inns of Ct., Nev. Assn. Gaming Attys., Internat. Assn. Gaming Attys. Avocations: scuba diving, golf, fishing. Office: Lionel Sawyer and Collins 300 S 4th St Ste 1700 Las Vegas NV 89101

LARSEN, PAUL EMANUEL, religious organization administrator; b. Mpls., Oct. 5, 1933; s. David Paul and Myrtle (Grunnet) L.; m. Elizabeth Helen Taylor, Mar. 19, 1966; children: Kristin, Kathleen. BA, Stanford U., 1955; MDiv, Fuller Theol. Sem., 1958; STD, San Francisco Theol. Sem., 1978. Ordained to ministry Evang. Ch., 1963. Asst. pastor Evang. Ch., Eagle Rock, Calif., 1958-59; pastor Pasadena, Calif., 1963-70, Peninsula Covenant Ch., Redwood City, Calif., 1971-86; pres. Evang. Covenant Chs., Chgo., 1986—; chmn. meeting U.S. ch. leaders, 1992—. Author: Wise Up and Live, Mission of a Covenant. Home: 24 Landmark Northfield IL 60093-3452 Office: Evang Covenant Ch 5101 N Francisco Ave Chicago IL 60625-3611

LARSEN, PETER N., leisure products manufacturing executive. Chmn., CEO Brunswick Corp., Lake Forest, Ill. Office: Brunswick Corp 1 North Field Corp Lake Forest IL 60045*

LARSEN, RALPH IRVING, environmental research engineer; b. Corvallis, Oreg., Nov. 26, 1928; s. Walter Winfred and Nellie Lyle (Gellatly) L.; BS in Civil Engring., Oreg. State U., 1950; MS, Harvard U., 1955, PhD in Air Pollution and Indsl. Hygiene, 1957; m. Betty Lois Garner, Oct. 14, 1950 (dec. Feb. 1989); children: Karen Larsen Cleeton, Eric, Kristine Larsen Burns, Jan Alan; m. Anne Harmon King, Aug. 3, 1991; children: Vikki King Ball, Terri King Readling, Cindi King King. San. engr. div. water pollution control USPHS, Washington, 1950-54; chief tech. service state and cmty. svc. sect. Nat. Air Pollution Control Adminstrn., Cin., 1957-61; with EPA and Nat. Air Pollution Control Adminstrn., 1961—, environ. rsch. engr. Nat. Exposure Rsch. Lab., Rsch. Triangle Park, N.C., 1971—; air pollution cons. to Poland, 1973, 75, Brazil, 1978; condr. seminars for air pollution researchers, Paris, Vienna and Milan, 1975; adj. lectr. Inst. Air Pollution Tng., 1969—; Falls of Neuse cmty. rep. City of Raleigh (N.C.), 1974—. Recipient Commendation medal USPHS, 1979. Mem. Air and Waste Mgmt. Assn. (mem. editorial bd. jour. 1971-88), Conf. Fed. Environ. Engrs., USPHS Commd. Officers Assn. (past br. pres.), Sigma Xi. Republican. Mem. Christian and Missionary Alliance Ch. (elder). Contbr. over 55 articles to profl. jours. Home: 4012 Colby Dr Raleigh NC 27609-6045 Office: Md # 56 Epa Research Triangle Park NC 27711 *God issued me a 1928-model body. It works best, for others and me, as I read a chapter of the Owner's Manual (The Holy Bible) first thing each morning.*

LARSEN, RALPH S(TANLEY), health care company executive; b. Bklyn., Nov. 19, 1938; s. Andrew and Gurine (Henningsen) L.; m. Dorothy M. Zeitfuss, Aug. 19, 1961; children: Karen, Kristen, Garret. BBA, Hofstra U., 1962. Mfg. trainee, then supt. prodn. and dir. mfg. Johnson & Johnson, New Brunswick, N.J., 1962-77; v.p. ops., v.p. mktg. McNeil Consumer Products Co. div. Johnson & Johnson, Ft. Washington, Pa., 1977-81; pres. Becton Dickenson Consumer Products, Paramus, N.J., 1981-83; pres. Chicopee div. Johnson & Johnson, New Brunswick, 1983-85; co. group chmn. Johnson & Johnson, New Brunswick, N.J., 1985-86, vice chmn., exec. com., bd. dirs., 1986-89, chmn. bd., pres., CEO, 1989—, also bd. dirs., mem. exec. com.; bd. dirs. N.Y. Stock Exch., Xerox Corp., AT&T Corp. Bd. dirs. UNICEF. Mem. Bus. Coun. (vice chmn.), Bus. Roundtable (co-chmn. policy com.). Republican. Avocations: skiing, boating, art. Office: Johnson & Johnson 1 Johnson Johnson Plz New Brunswick NJ 08933

LARSEN, RAYMOND S., engineering executive; b. 1934. BA in Sci., U. B.C., 1956, MA in Sci., 1958; Engring. Degree, Stanford U., 1966. Pres. Analytek Ltd. Fellow IEEE. Office: Analytek Ltd 365 San Aleso Ave Sunnyvale CA 94086*

LARSEN, RICHARD GARY, accounting firm executive; b. Tampa, Fla., Nov. 28, 1948; s. Dagfinn T. Larsen and Elizabeth M. (Koch) Thompson; m. Harriet Taylor Jones, Dec. 19, 1970; children—Jonathan Daniel, Alice Taylor. BBA in Acctg., George Washington U., 1971, JD, 1974; postgrad., Columbia U., 1985. Bar: Va. 1974; CPA, D.C., Va. Mem. staff U.S. Senate, Washington, 1967-73; ptnr. Ernst & Young, Washington, 1973—; adj. prof. U. Md., College Park, 1976-78, Am. U., Washington, 1977-78. Mem. ABA, Va. Bar Assn., AICPAs, Md. Soc. CPAs, Univ. Club (Washington), Coral Beach and Tennis Club (Bermuda), Chatham Beach and Tennis Club, Eastward Ho Country Club (Chatham), Columbia Country Club (Chevy Chase), Belle Haven Country Club, Capitol Hill Club. Home: 319 S St Asaph St Alexandria VA 22314 Office: Ernst & Young 1225 Connecticut Ave NW Washington DC 20036-2604

LARSEN, RICHARD LEE, former mayor and city manager, business, municipal and labor relations consultant, arbitrator; b. Jackson, Miss., Apr. 16, 1934; s. Homer Thorsten and Mae Cordelia (Amidon) L.; m. Virginia Fay Alley, June 25, 1955; children: Karla, Daniel, Thomas (dec.), Krista, Lisa. B.S. in Econs. and Bus. Adminstrn, Westminster Coll., Fulton, Mo., 1959; postgrad., U. Kans., 1959-61. Fin. dir. Village of Northbrook, Ill., 1961-63; city mgr. Munising, Mich., 1963-66, Sault Ste. Marie, Mich., 1966-72, Ogden, Utah, 1972-77, Billings, Mont., 1977-79; mcpl. cons., 1979—, pub./pvt. sector labor relations cons., arbitrator, 1979—; mayor City of Billings, Mont., 1990-95; dep. gen. chmn. Greater Mich. Found., 1968. Bd. dirs. Central Weber Sewer Dist., 1972-77; chmn. labor com. Utah League Cities and Towns, 1973-77, Mont. League Cities and Towns, 1977-79; bd. dirs., coach Ogden Hockey Assn., 1972-77, Weber Sheltered Workshop, 1974-77, Billings YMCA, 1980-86, Rimrock Found., 1980-86; chmn. community relations council Weber Basin Job Corps Center, 1973-77. Served with USCG, 1953-57. Recipient Cmty. Devel. Disting. Achievement awards Munising, 1964, Cmty. Devel. Disting. Achievement awards Sault Ste. Marie, 1966-70, Citizen award Dept. of Interior, 1977, Alumni Achievement award Westminster Coll., 1990, Dist. award of merit Boy Scouts Am., 1993, Silver Beaver award Boy Scouts Am., 1994; named Utah Adminstr. of Yr., 1976. Mem. Internat. City Mgmt. ASsn. (L.P. Cookingham career devel. award 1974, Clarence Ridley in-service tng. award 1979), Utah City Mgrs. Assn. (pres. 1972-74), Greater Ogden C. of C. (dir.), Phi Gamma Delta. Mem. LDS Ch. Club: Rotary. Home and Office: 1733 Parkhill Dr Billings MT 59102-2358

LARSEN, ROBERT DHU, lawyer; b. Stoughton, Wis., Oct. 20, 1922; s. Hans Christian and Helen Charlotte (Sobye) L.; m. Mary Lee Matheson, May 5, 1959 (div. 1973); children: Brooke, Christopher Dhu. AB, U. Wis., 1947; JD with honors, U. N.C., 1950. Bar: N.C. 1950, D.C. 1952, U.S. Supreme Ct. 1957, N.Y. 1959. Law clk. to presiding judge U.S. Ct. Appeals (4th cir.), Charlotte, N.C., 1950-51; from assoc. to ptnr. Rogers & Wells (and predecessors), N.Y.C., 1951-90; retired, 1990. Editor-in-chief U. N.C. Law Rev., 1950. Chmn. bd. trustees Pine Manor Coll., Chestnut Hill, Mass., 1981-84. Served to capt. inf. U.S. Army, 1943-46. Mem. Order of Coif. Democrat. Episcopalian. Home: 40 E 88th St New York NY 10128-1176

LARSEN, ROBERT LEROY, artistic director; b. Walnut, Iowa, Nov. 28, 1934; s. George Dewey and Maine M. (Mickel) L. MusB, Simpson Coll., Indianola, Iowa, 1956; MusM, U. Mich., 1958; MusD, Ind. U., 1972. Music prof. Simpson Coll., 1957—, chmn. music dept., 1965—; founder, artistic dir. Des Moines Met. Opera, 1973—. Mus. coach Tanglewood, Lenox, Mass., 1963, Oglebay Pk. (W.Va.) Opera, 1965, Chgo., N.Y. studios; condr., stage dir. Simpson Coll., Des Moines Met. Opera, Miss. Opera, U. Ariz.; solo pianist, accompanism numerous recitals; adjudicator Met. auditions and competitions, Mpls., Chgo., Kansas City, Mo., Tulsa, San Antonio; stage dir., condr. operas, Simpson Coll., Des Moines Met. Opera, 1973—; editor Opera Anthologies by G. Schirmer; piano rec. artist for G. Schirner Libr. Recipient Gov's. award State of Iowa, 1974. Mem. Am. Choral Dir. Assn., Nat. Opera Assn., Music Tchrs. Nat. Assn., Pi Kappa Lambda, Phi Kappa Phi, Phi Mu Alpha Sinfonia (faculty advisor). Presbyterian. Avocations: reading, theatre, coaching students. Office: Des Moines Metro Opera 106 W Boston Ave Indianola IA 50125-1836

LARSEN, STEVEN, orchestra conductor; b. Oak Park, Ill., Feb. 10, 1951; s. Edwin Earnest and Sylvia Nila Larsen; divorced; children: Vanessa,

Krista; m. Martha Jane Bein, Mar. 21, 1993. MusB, Am. Conservatory Music, Chgo., 1975; MusM, Northwestern U., 1976. Cert. Nederlandse Dirigenten Kursus. Instr. music theory, chair instrumental dept Am. Conservatory Music, Chgo., 1976-82, orch. dir., 1978; music dir. Opera Theatre of San Antonio, 1987-90; orch. dir. Rockford (Ill.) Symphony Orch., 1991—; music dir., acting artistic dir. Chgo. Opera Theater, 1981-92; interim artistic dir. Dayton (Ohio) Opera, 1996; music dir. Champaign-Urbana (Ill.) Symphony, 1996—; lectr. opera performance Chgo. Mus. Coll., 1989—. Mem. Rockford Downtown Rotary. Office: Rockford Symphony Orch 711 N Main St Rockford IL 61103-6999

LARSEN, TERRANCE A., bank holding company executive. BA, U. Dallas, 1968; PhD, Tex. A&M U., 1971. With Phila. Nat. Bank, from 1977, sr. v.p., 1980-83, exec. v.p., from 1983; exec. v.p. Corestates Fin. Corp. (parent), Phila., 1983-86, pres., 1986—, COO, 1986-87, chmn., CEO, 1988—, also bd. dirs. Office: Core States Fin Corp NE Corner Broad & Chestnut Sts PO Box 7618 Philadelphia PA 19101-7618*

LARSEN, WILLIAM LAWRENCE, materials science and engineering educator; b. Crookston, Minn., July 16, 1926; s. Clarence M. and Luverne (Carlisle) L.; m. Gracie Lee Richey, June 19, 1954; children—Eric W., Thomas R. B.M.E., Marquette U., 1948; M.S., Ohio State U., 1950, Ph.D., 1956; postgrad., U. Chgo., 1950-51. Registered profl. engr., Iowa. Research assoc. Ohio State U., Columbus, 1951-56; research metallurgist E. I. duPont de Nemours & Co., Wilmington, Del., 1956-58; metallurgist Ames Lab., AEC, Iowa, 1958-73; assoc. prof. Iowa State U., Ames, 1958-73, prof. materials sci. and engring., 1973-93; prof. emeritus, 1993—; cons. metallurgical engring., 1960—. Contbr. articles to profl. jours. Served with USN, 1944-46. Mem. ASM Internat., ASTM, Am. Soc. Engring. Edn., NACE Internat. (cert.), The Minerals, Metals and Materials Soc., Nat. Collegiate Honors Coun. Home: 335 N Franklin Ave Ames IA 50014-3424 Office: Iowa State U Engring Dept Ames IA 50011

LARSON, ALLAN LOUIS, political scientist, educator, lay church worker; b. Chetek, Wis., Mar. 31, 1932; s. Leonard Andrew and Mabel (Marek) L. BA magna cum laude, U. Wis., Eau Claire, 1954; PhD, Northwestern U., 1964. Instr. Evanston Twp. (Ill.) High Sch., 1958-61; asst. prof. polit. sci. U. Wis., 1963-64; asst. prof. Loyola U., Chgo., 1964-68, assoc. prof., 1968-74, prof., 1974—. Author: Comparative Political Analysis, 1980, (essay) The Human Triad: An Introductory Essay on Politics, Society, and Culture, 1988; (with others) Progress and the Crisis of Man, 1976; contbr. articles to profl. jours. Assoc. mem. Paul Galvin Chapel, Evanston, Ill. Norman Wait Harris fellow in polit. sci. Northwestern U., 1954-56. Mem. AAAS, ASPCA, AAUP, Humane Soc. U.S., Northwestern U. Alumni Assn., Am. Polit. Sci. Assn., Am. Acad. Polit. and Social Sci., Acad. Polit. Sci., Midwest Polit. Sci. Assn., Spiritual Life Inst., Anti-Cruelty Soc., Nat. Wildlife Fedn., Noetic Scis. Inst., Humane Soc. U.S., Kappa Delta Pi, Pi Sigma Epsilon. Roman Catholic. Home: 2015 Orrington Ave Evanston IL 60201-2911 Office: Loyola U 6525 N Sheridan Rd Damen Hall Rm 915 Chicago IL 60626 *We are each of us mysteries to ourselves. We are on a life-long search for meaning: questions about where we have come from, what we are doing and where we are going. The deepest desires of a person embody the spiritual quest. The Kingdom of God tells us where to place our priorities. Life is short. No one is untouched by tragedy. We are reminded every day of our finiteness. We care because it is our nature to care. Christianity teaches a reverence for life that urges us to transcend narcissism and selfishness.*

LARSON, APRIL U., bishop. Pastor; bishop Southeastern Minn. Synod, Evang. Luth. Ch. in Am., 1992—. Office: Evang Luth Ch in Am SE Minn Synod Assissi Heights, Box 4900 Rochester MN 55903

LARSON, BENNETT CHARLES, solid state physicist, researcher; b. Buffalo, N.D., Oct. 9, 1941; s. Floyd Everet and Gladys May (Hogen) L.; m. Piola Anne Taliaferro, June 6, 1969; children—Christopher Charles, Andrea Kay. B.A. in Physics, Concordia Coll., Moorhead, Minn., 1963; M.S. in Physics, U. N.D., 1965; Ph.D. in Physics, U. Mo., 1970. Rsch. physicist, group leader x-ray diffraction, sect. head thin films and microstructures solid state div. Oak Ridge Nat. Lab., Tenn., 1969—. Contbr. numerous articles to profl. jours. Recipient Sidhu award Pitts. Diffraction Soc., 1974. Fellow Am. Phys. Soc.; mem. Am. Crystallographic Assn. (Bertram E. Warren Diffraction Physics award 1985), Materials Research Soc. Office: Oak Ridge Nat Lab Solid State Dv Oak Ridge TN 37831

LARSON, BEVERLY ROLANDSON, elementary education educator; b. Oklee, Minn., May 30, 1938; d. Orville K. and Belle A. (Anderson) Rolandson; m. Roland K. Larson, June 29, 1962; children: Amy Jo, Ann Marie, Carl Lee. BS, Concordia Coll., 1962; MA, Mankato State U., 1984. Cert. elem., spl. edn. tchr., Minn. Tchr. Hudson Sch. Dist., LaPuente, Calif., 1961-62, Thief River Falls (Minn.) Sch. Dist., 1962-63, Sch. Dist. 271, Bloomington, Minn., 1964-69, 71-72, Valley View Sch., Bloomington, Minn., 1989—; spl. edn. tchr. Sch. Dist. 271, Bloomington, Minn., 1975-79, 86-89. Youth leader, Sunday sch. tchr. Christ the King Luth. Ch., Bloomington, 1969-82; precinct co-chair Rep. Party, Bloomington, alt., del. Recipient Svc. award Walk for Mankind, 1976, Golden Apple Achiever award Ashland Oil, 1994. Mem. NEA, Assn. Childhood Edn. (pres. Bloomington br. 1992-94), Minn. Edn. Assn., Nat. Learning Disabilities Assn., Minn. Learning Disabilities Assn., Bloomington Edn. Assn. Republican. Lutheran. Avocations: crafts, reading, plays and musicals, golf. Home: 7800 Pickfair Dr Bloomington MN 55438-1380 Office: Valley View Sch 351 E 88th St Bloomington MN 55420-2909

LARSON, BRENT T., broadcasting executive; b. Ogden, Utah, Sept. 23, 1942; s. George Theodore and Doris (Peterson) L.; m. Tracy Ann Taylor; children: Michelle, Brent Todd, Lindsey. Student, pub. schs., Los Angeles; diploma in radio operational engring., Burbank, Calif., 1962. Owner, mgr. Sta. KAIN, Boise, Idaho, 1969-77; owner, operator Sta. KXA Radio, Seattle, 1975-83, Sta. KYYX Radio, Seattle, 1980-83, Sta. KGA Radio, Spokane, Wash., 1978-84, Sta. KUUZ Radio, Boise, 1976-82, Sta. KOOS Radio, North Bend, Oreg., 1980-81, Sta. KODL Radio, The Dalles, Oreg., 1974-80, Sta. KKWZ Radio, Richfield, Utah, 1980-94, Sta. KSVC Radio, Richfield, 1980-94; v.p. Casey Larson Fast Food Co., Oreg. and Idaho, 1976-94, Imperial Broadcasting Corp., Idaho, 1970—, KSOS Am & KLZX FM, 1983—; pres. First Nat. Broadcasting Corp., 1970—; v.p. Larson-Wynn Corp., 1974—, Brentwood Properties, Ogden, 1977—; pres. Sta. KSIT Broadcasting, Rock Springs, Wyo., 1980-90, Gold Coast Communications Corp., Oreg., 1980-81, Sevier Valley Broadcasting Co., Inc., Utah, 1980-94, Brent Larson Group Stas., Western U.S., 1969—; v.p. mktg. Internat. Foods Corp., Boise, 1969-81; ptnr. Larson Tours and Travel, Burley, Idaho, 1977-87; v.p. Harrison Square Inc., 1995—; founder 1st Nat. TV Div., 1990; bd. dirs. Casey-Larson Foods Co., La Grande, Oreg. Bd. dirs. Met. Sch., 1981-93, Children's Aid Soc., 1991-94; chmn. bd. ZLX Limited Libility Co., 1995—. Mem. Am. Advt. Fedn., Nat. Assn. Broadcasters, Nat. Radio Broadcasters Assn., Wash. Broadcasters Assn., Oreg. Broadcasters Assn., Idaho Broadcasters Assn., Utah Broadcasters Assn., Citizens for Responsible Broadcasting (bd. dirs.). Republican. Mem. LDS Ch. Home: 2613 Seashore Dr Las Vegas NV 89128 Office: First Nat Broadcasting Corp 4455 S 5500 W Ogden UT 84315-9650

LARSON, BRIAN FOIX, architect; b. Eau Claire, Wis., July 6, 1935; s. Albert Foix and Dorothy Jean (Thompson) L.; m. Mildred Anne Nightswander, Feb. 13, 1961; children: Urban Alexander, Soren Federick. BArch, U. Ill., 1959. Registered architect, Wis., Minn., Colo., Mass., N.H. Architect-in-tng. Geometrics, Inc., Cambridge, Mass., 1959-60, Bastille Halsey Assoc., Boston, 1960-62; ptnr. Larson, Playter, Smith, Eau Claire, 1962-72; v.p. Larson, Hestekins, Smith, Ltd., Eau Claire, 1962-80, Ayres Assocs., Eau Claire, 1980—; sec. Wis. Bd. Archtl. Examiners, 1985-88, chmn., 1988-89; master juror Nat. Coun. Archtl. Rev. Bd. Bldg. Design Exam, 1987—. Prin. works include One Mill Plaza, Laconia, N.H. (Honor award New Eng. Regional Council AIA 1974), Eau Claire County Courthouse, Wis., (Honor award Wis. Soc. Architects 1978), St. Croix County Courthouse, Wis. Mem. Hist. Bldg. Code Adv. Com., Wis., 1985. Mem. AIA (bd. dirs. 1996—), Wis. Soc. Architects (pres. 1983), Wis. Architects Found. (bd. dirs.), Soc. Archtl. Historians. Home: 215 Roosevelt Ave Eau Claire WI 54701-4065 Office: Ayres Assocs PO Box 1590 Eau Claire WI 54702-1590

LARSON, CHARLES FRED, trade association administrator; b. Gary, Ind., Nov. 27, 1936; s. Charles F. and Margaret J. (Taylor) L.; m. Joan Ruth Grupe, Aug. 22, 1959; children: Gregory Paul, Laura Ann. BSME, Purdue U., 1958; MBA summa cum laude, Fairleigh Dickinson U., 1973. Registered profl. engr., N.J. Project engr. Combustion Engring., Inc., East Chicago, Ind., 1958-60; sec. Welding Rsch. Council, N.Y.C., 1960-70, asst. dir., 1970-75; exec. dir. Indsl. Rsch. Inst., Inc., N.Y.C., 1975—. Assoc. editor Jour. Pressure Vessel Tech., 1973-75; mem. bd. advisors Who's Who in Am. Mem. Wyckoff (N.J.) Bd. Edn., 1973-78, pres., 1976-77; reader In Touch Networks, Inc., N.Y.C., 1979-89; chmn. 43d Nat. Conf. on Advancement Rsch. Fellow AAAS; mem. ASME, NSPE, Am. Soc. Assn. Execs., Coun. Engring. and Sci. Soc. Execs., Univ. Club, Kenwood Club. Republican. Methodist. Office: Indsl Rsch Inst Inc 1550 M St NW Washington DC 20005-1708

LARSON, CHARLES ROBERT, naval officer; b. Sioux Falls, S.D., Nov. 20, 1936; s. Eldred Charles and Gertrude Edythe (Jensen) L.; m. Sarah Elizabeth Craig, Aug. 19, 1961; children: Sigrid Anne, Erica Lynn, Kirsten Elizabeth. B.S. in Marine Engring, U.S. Naval Acad., 1958. Commd. ensign USN, 1958, advanced through grades to adm., 1990; naval aviator, attack pilot, 1958-63, nuclear power, submarine tng., 1963-64, assigned nuclear subs., 1964-76, naval aide to the Pres., 1969-71, comdg. officer USS Halibut, 1973-76, comdr. submarine devel. group one, head operational deep submergence program, 1976-78, chief naval ops. staff Strategic Submarine Programs, 1978-79; dir. long range planning group Washington, 1978-82; comdr. submarines Mediterranean, 1982-83; supt. U.S. Naval Acad. Annapolis, Md., 1983-86; comdr. 2d Fleet, 1986-88; dir. plans, policies and ops. DCNO, 1988-90; comdr. U.S. Pacific Fleet, 1990-91, U.S. Pacific Command, Hawaii, 1991-94; supt. U.S. Naval Acad., 1994—; v.p. U.S. Naval Inst., 1994—. Mem. USO Coun., Honolulu, 1990-92; mem. Honolulu area coun. Boy Scouts Am., 1990-94. Decorated Def. D.S.M. (6), Legion of Merit (3), Bronze Star, others; named Disting. Eagle Scout Balt. area coun. Boy Scouts Am., 1985; White House fellow, 1968-69. Mem. Coun. on Fgn. Rels. Home: 1 Buchanan Rd Annapolis MD 21402 Office: 121 Blake Rd Annapolis MD 21402-5000

LARSON, CLARENCE EDWARD, foundation administrator; b. Cloquet, Minn., Sept. 20, 1909; s. Louis Ludwig and Caroline Hilda (Ullman) L.; m. Gertrude Ellen Ruben, May 17, 1934 (dec. June 1952); 1 child, Robert Edward; m. Jane Ritchie Warren, Apr. 20, 1957; children—Lawrence Ernest, Lance Stafford (dec.). B.S., U. Minn., 1932; Ph.D., U. Calif.-Berkeley, 1937. Chmn. chemistry dept. Coll. of Pacific, Stockton, Calif., 1937-42; project dir., mgr. Union Carbide Corp., Oak Ridge, 1942-50; mgr. corp. research Union Carbide Corp., N.Y.C., 1955-61; pres. nuclear div. Union Carbide Corp., Oak Ridge, 1961-69; dir. Oak Ridge Nat. Lab., 1950-55; commr. AEC, Washington, 1969-74; pres. Pioneers Sci. and Tech. Hist. Assn., Washington, 1982—; chmn. Nat. Battery Adv. Commn., Washington, 1975-81. Patentee separation process for uranium. Recipient Disting. Achievement award Am. Soc. for Advancement Mgmt., 1963. Fellow Am. Nuclear Soc., Am. Inst. Chemists; mem. NAE, Am. Chem. Soc., Cosmos Club (Disting. Svc. award 1991), Knights of Malta, Rotary, Sigma Xi, Tau Beta Pi. Republican. Avocations: amateur radio; computers; scuba diving; photography; golf. Home: 6514 Bradley Blvd Bethesda MD 20817-3248

LARSON, DANIEL JOHN, physics educator; b. Mpls., Nov. 8, 1944; s. Edwin Wildridge and Verva May (Johnson) L.; m. Tanya Helen Furman, June 5, 1994. BA in Physics and Math. summa cum laude, St. Olaf Coll., 1966; MA in Phyics, Harvard U., 1967, PhD in Physics, 1971. Asst. prof. physics Harvard U., Cambridge, Mass., 1970-75; assoc. prof. physics Harvard U., Cambridge, 1975-78; assoc. prof. physics U. Va., Charlottesville, 1978-87, prof. of physics, 1987—, assoc. dean, 1989-91, chmn. dept. physics, 1991—; mem. panel on current trends in atomic spectroscopy NRC, 1982, mem. com. of atomic, molecular and optical scis., 1987-95, vice-chmn., 1991-92, chmn., 1992-94, past chmn., 1994-95, mem. panel on future opportunities in atomic, molecular and optical scis., 1991-93, mem. AMO Sics. Assessment Panel, Commn. on Phys. Scis., Math. & Applications, 1993, Workshop on Quantitative Assessment of Health of Phys. and Math. Scis., 1993; mem. program com. Gordon Conf. on Atomic Physics, 1983, 89, 91; mem. precision measurements grants outside adv. com. Nat. Bur. Standards, 1986-90; vis. scientist Nat. Bur. Standards, Boulder, Colo., 1985-86, Lab. Aimé Cotton, Orsay, France, 1991; vis. prof. Chalmers U., Gothenburg, Sweden, 1986; chmn. Com. on Atomic, Molecular and Optical Scis, NRC, Washington, 1992-94; mem. Dept. Energy rev. com. for atomic physics program Argonne Nat. Lab., 1988, Kans. State U., 1989, Oak Ridge Nat. Lab., 1990; external reviewer dept. physics Washington and Lee U., 1988; mem. acad. program rev. dept. physics and astronomy U. Nebr., 1994; mem. rev. com. dept. physics and astronomy U. Ky., 1995; mem. ad hom com. for rsch. univs. Rsch. Corp., 1993, mem. AMO faculty early career devel. program panel NSF, 1995. Contbr. articles to profl. jours.; cons. editor Am. Inst. Physics Press, 1993—. Rsch. grantee Office of Naval Rsch. NSF, 1978-95; Woodrow Wilson fellow, 1966, NSF grad. fellow, 1966-70. Fellow Am. Phys. Soc. (nominating com. divsn. atomic, molecular and optical physics 1986-87, 91-94, divsn. councillor 1991-94, exec. com. divsn. atomic, molecular and optical physics 1991-95, audit com. 1992, nominating com. laser sci. topical group 1991-92, chmn. 1992, com. on minorities 1992-94, com. on coms. 1993-94, chmn. 1994, nominating com. topical group on precision measurement and fundamental constants 1993-94, chmn. task force on forums 1995, Davisson-Germer prize com. 1995-96, exec. bd. 1993-94); mem. Optical Soc. Am., Phi Beta Kappa, Sigma Xi, Sigma Pi Sigma. Achievements include extensive contributions to the understanding of the interaction of light with atomic systems, especially negative ions. Home: 3265 Waverly Dr Charlottesville VA 22901 Office: U Va Dept Physics McCormick Rd Charlottesville VA 22901

LARSON, DAVID BRUCE, research epidemiologist; b. Glen Ridge, N.J., Mar. 13, 1947; s. John Owen and Peggy June (Asbury) L.; m. Susan Joan Slingerland, Dec. 20, 1975; children: David Chad, Kristen Joan. BS, Drexel U., 1969; MD, Temple U., 1973; MS in Pub. Health, U. N.C., 1982. Diplomate Nat. Bd. Med. Examiners, Am. Bd. Psychiatry. Intern MacNeal Meml. Hosp., Berwyn, Ill., 1973-74; resident in psychiatry Duke U. Med. Ctr., Durham, N.C., 1974-77, psychosomatics teaching fellow, 1975-77, fellow in behavioral scis., 1976-78; chief resident psychiatry Duke U. Med. Ctr. and Durham County Gen. Hosp., 1977-79; fellow in geropsychiatry Duke U. Med. Ctr., Durham, N.C., 1979-81; epidemiology fellow U. N.C., Chapel Hill, 1982-83; epidemiology fellow NIMH, Rockville, Md., 1983-85, rsch. psychiatrist, 1985-91; sr. policy researcher Office of the Sec., HHS, Washington, 1991-93; sr. analyst office of dir. NIH, 1993-94; pres. Nat. Inst. Healthcare Rsch., 1994—. Contbr. chpts. to books, articles to profl. jours. Mem. AAAS, AMA, So. Med. Assn., Christian Med. Soc., Am. Psychiat. Assn., So. Psychiat. Assn., Christian Assn. Psychol. Studies, Am. Assn. Marital and Family Therapy, Soc. for Sci. Study of Religion, Sigma Xi. Episcopalian. Avocations: reading, running, exercising.

LARSON, DAYL ANDREW, architect; b. Denver, Aug. 13, 1930; s. Andrew and Esther (Freiberg) L.; m. Kay W. Larson; children: Linda, Lesli, Lucy. BS in Architecture, BSBA, U. Colo., 1953. Pres. Haller & Larson Architects, Denver, 1962-92. Served to capt. C.E., U.S. Army, 1953-55. Fellow AIA (pres. Denver chpt. 1978, pres-elect 1986-87); mem. Colo. AIA (pres.). Home: 2153 S Beeler Way Denver CO 80231-3409 Office: Haller & Larson 1621 18th St Denver CO 80202-1266

LARSON, DONALD CLAYTON, physics educator, consultant; b. Wadena, Minn., Jan. 29, 1934; s. Clyde Melvin and Selma (Wilson) L.; m. Susan Dunnet, July 17, 1960; children: Tor Frederick, Jun Dunnet (dec.), Erika Rose. BS, U. Wash., 1956; SM, Harvard U., 1957, PhD, 1962. Asst. prof. U. Va., Charlottesville, 1962-67; assoc. prof. Drexel U., Phila., 1967-83, full prof., 1983—; vis. prof. Univ. Chile, Santiago, 1969, 73, Tel-Aviv (Israel) U., 1984, 92; vis. scientist Naval Air Devel., Warminster, Pa., summers 1981-91; cons. NIST, Gaithersburg, Md., 1984-95. Author: Physics of Thin Films, vol. VI, 1971, Experimental Methods in Preparation and Measurement of Thin Films, vol. II, 1974. Mem. Optical Soc. Am., Phi Beta Kappa, Tau Beta Pi, Sigma Xi. Home: 409 Drew Ave Swarthmore PA 19081-2407 Office: Drexel U Physics Atmospheric Sci Dept Philadelphia PA 19104

LARSON, EARL RICHARD, federal judge; b. Mpls., Dec. 18, 1911; s. Axel R. and Hannah (Johnson) L.; m. Cecill Frances Carlgren, Dec. 30, 1939; children: Jane, Earl R. BA, U. Minn., 1933, LLB, 1935. Bar: Minn. 1935. Judge U.S. Dist. Ct. Minn., Mpls., 1961-77, sr. judge, 1977—. Lt. USNR, 1943-46. Recipient Outstanding Achievement award U. Minn., 1978. Office: US Dist Ct 661 US Courthouse 110 S 4th St Minneapolis MN 55401-2221*

LARSON, ELAINE LUCILLE, nurse researcher, epidemiologist, educator; b. Douglas, Ariz., Apr. 27, 1943; d. John Earl and Jerry Lucille (Hunter) Williamson; m. Steven Mark Larson, June 14, 1965; children: Nathan, Justine. BS, U. Wash., 1965, MA, 1969, PhD, 1981. Registered nurse. Nurse specialist, instr. U. Wash. Hosp., Seattle, 1965-69, hosp. epidemiologist, 1967-70, assoc. dir. nursing., asst. prof., 1976-83; postodoctoral fellow U. Pa., Phila., 1983-85; Nutting chmn. in Clin. Nursing Johns Hopkins U. Sch. Nursing, Balt., Md., 1985—; pres. Cert. Bd. for Infection Control. Contbr. numerous articles to profl. jours. Testified in House and Senate for nursing edn. and research, 1984-85; testified in Joint Econ. Com. for testing of disinfectants. Grantee Johnson & Johnson, 1985. Fellow Am. Acad. Nursing, NSF (inst. of medicine 1986). Presbyterian.

LARSON, G. STEVEN, coach, athletic director; b. Washington, Mar. 11, 1951; s. J. Stanford and Dorothy Madeline (Schwaller) L.; m. Debra Ann Roemer Larson, Mar. 11, 1972; children: Jennifer, Joshua, Jacqueline, Ryan. BS in English, U. Wis., Oshkosh, 1974, MS in Edn. Administrn., 1980; postgrad. Sports Mgmt., U.S. Sports Acad., 1993—. Cert. Edn. Administrn. Basketball coach, athletic dir., math tchr. St. Patrick Sch., Menasha, Wis., 1967-70, 73-76; j.v. basketball coach, tchr. English St. Mary's Ctrl. H.S., Menasha, Wis., 1970-71, head varsity basketball coach, athletic dir., devel. dir., 1982-86; head varsity basketball coach Riverside Milit. Acad., Gainesville, Ga. and Hollywood, Fla., 1976-78; grad. asst. basketball coach, grad. asst. to dean of students U. Wis., Oshkosh, Wis., 1978-79; head varsity basketball coach, dean of students St. Mary's Springs H.S., Fond Du Lac, Wis., 1979-82; head men's basketball, athletic dir. Edgewood Coll., Madison, Wis., 1986—; dir. Steve Larson Basketball Sch., Madison, 1979—; dir., cons. Winning Images Network, Madison, 1988—; commr., pres. Lake Mich. Conf., Madison, 1992—, Midwest Classic Conf., 1987-89;. Author: (booklet) The Motion Offense, 1993, Basketball Drills: Fundamentals, 1994, Individual Basketball Instruction, 1979-95; contbr. articles to profl. jours. Basketball com. NAIA, Dist. 14, 1991-95; pres. Queen of Peace Sch. Bd., Madison, 1995; fund raising chair Cystic Fibrosis Found., Neenah, Wis., 1982-86; commr. Badger State Games-Basketball, Madison, 1987-88; v.p. Catholic Boys League, 1974-76. Capt. faculty ROTC, 1976-78. Recipient Award of Merit NAIA, 1993, State of Wis. Gov.'s award for athletic leadership, 1988, Gold Medal Wis.-USA Friendship Games, 1986, City of Menasha Mayor & Common Coun. Resolution of Commendation, 1986, Fond du Lac City Coun. Resolution award, 1982, State of Wis. Assembly Citation, 1982; named Coach of the Year NAIA dist. 14/Affiliatied Conf. Men's Basketball, 1991-92, 92-93, .93-94, 94-95, Lake Mich. Conf. Men's Basketball, 1991-92, 92-93, 93-94, 94-95, North Ctrl. Dist. Men's Basketball, 1987-88, 88-89, 89-90, 89-91, Dist. Basketball, 1977-78. Mem. Nat. Assn. Basketball Coaches, Nat. Assn. Dirs. Athletics, Madison Pen & Mike Club (Sportsman of the Month 1992, Hall of Fame Spl. Achievement award 1994), Red Smith (Outstanding Coaching award 1992), Fox Valley Christian Conf. (All Star Coach 1981, 82, 86, Coach of the Year 1981-82, 85-86), Wis. Basketball Coaches Assn. (Fall clinic demonstration chair, 1986-94, Appreciation award 1990, Outstanding achievement award 1986, 89, 90, 95, Recognition award 1988, 89), Fellowship Christian Athletes, Kappa Delta Pi (pres. 1978-79). Roman Catholic. Avocation: reading, movies, chess, biking, collecting pins, video movies, caps and glasses. Office: Edgewood Coll 855 Woodrow St Madison WI 53711

LARSON, GARY, cartoonist; b. Tacoma, Wash., Aug. 14, 1950; s. Vern and Doris Larson; married. BA in Communications, Wash. State U., 1972. Jazz musician, 1973-76; with music store, Seattle, 1976-77, Humane Soc., Seattle, 1978-80; cartoonist Seattle Times, 1978-79; syndicated cartoonist The Far Side Chronicle Features Syndicate, San Francisco, 1979-84, Universal Press Syndicate, Kansas City, Mo., 1984-94; prodr. books and calendars. Exhbns. include The Far Side of Sci. (exhibited at Calif. Acad. Scis., 1987, Smithsonian Instn., 1987, Denver Mus. Natural History, L.A. County Mus., Shedd Aquarium, Chgo., other mus.), The Far Side of the Zoo, Wash. Pk. Zoo, Portland, Oreg., 1987; author: (cartoon collections) The Far Side, 1982, Beyond the Far side, 1983, In Search of the Far Side, 1984, Bride of the Far Side, 1985, Valley of the Far Side, 1985, It Came from the Far Side, 1986, The Far Side Observer, 1987, Hound of the Far Side, 1987, Night of the Crash-Test Dummies, 1988, Wildlife Preserves, 1989, The Prehistory of the Far Side: A 10th Anniversary Exhibit, 1989, Weiner Dog Art, 1990, Unnatural Selections, 1991, Cows of Our Planet, 1992, The Chickens are Restless, 1993, The Curse of Madame "C", 1994, (cartoon anthologies) The Far Side Gallery, 1984, The Far Side Gallery II, 1986, The Far Side Gallery III, 1988, The Far Side Gallery IV, 1993, The Far Side Gallery V, 1995; television animation Gary Larson's Tales from the Far Side, 1994 (Grand prix Annecy Film Festival, 1995). Recipient award for Best Humor Panel, Nat. Cartoonists Soc., 1986, Reuben award for Outstanding Cartoonist of Yr. Nat. Cartoonists Soc., 1991, 94, Max and Moritz prize for best internat. comic strip panel Internat. Comics Salon, 1993, other awards. Avocation: jazz music. Office: Universal Press Syndicate 4900 Main St Fl 9 Kansas City MO 64112-2630

LARSON, GEORGE CHARLES, magazine editor, writer; b. Mar. 31, 1942; s. George Lester and Mildred Caroline (Frehner) L.; m. Valarie Ann Thompson, Aug. 20, 1946; children: Evan Richard; Alice Lynn and Keely Mae (twins). BA, Harvard U., 1964. Staff writer Scholastic Mag., N.Y.C., 1971; regional editor, mng. editor Flying Mag., N.Y.C., 1972-78; tech. editor Bus. & Comml. Aviation Mag., White Plains, N.Y., 1980-85; editor Air & Space/Smithsonian Mag., Washington, 1985—. Author: Fly on Instruments, The Blimp Book. Served with U.S. Army, 1966-70, Vietnam.

LARSON, HARRY ROBERT, investment banking executive; b. Chgo., Oct. 13, 1945; s. Harry John and Alice Marie Larson; m. Charlene Marie Grenier; children: Christopher, Elizabeth, Erik, Brandon. BSBA, Roosevelt U., 1968. Contr. Halsey Stuart & Co. Inc., Chgo., 1967-73; with dept. sales Bache Halsey Stuart Inc., N.Y.C., 1973-79; sr. v.p. 1st Interstate Bank Calif., N.Y.C., 1979-85; pres. Chem. Securities Inc., N.Y.C., 1985-89, 1st Chgo. Capital Markets, Inc., 1989—; vice chmn. Mcpl. Securities Rulemaking Bd., Washington, 1989. Mem. Pub. Securities Assn. Home: 180A Old Sutton Rd Barrington Hi IL 60010-9383 Office: First Chicago Capital Markets Inc 1 First National Plz Chicago IL 60670*

LARSON, HARRY THOMAS, electronics engineer, executive, consultant; b. Berkeley, Calif., Oct. 16, 1921; s. Harry Homer and Edna Clara (Petersen) L.; m. Merry Evelyn Otteson, Dec. 26, 1956 (div. Dec. 1975); children: Kristin Evelyn Beltz, Margit Merry Mills, Megan Marie Hoyt. BSEE summa cum laude, U. Calif., Berkeley, 1947; MSEE, UCLA, 1954. Computer engr. Inst. for Numerical Analysis Nat. Bur. Standards, L.A., 1949-51; mem. tech. staff Advanced Electronics Lab. Hughes Aircraft Co., Culver City, Calif., 1951-54; dept. mgr. bus. applications of computers Ramo-Wooldridge Co., Inglewood, Calif., 1954-56; asst. divsn. dir. command and control systems Aero. divsn. Philco-Ford Co., Newport Beach, Calif., 1956-68; asst. div. dir. software and computing ctr. TRW Systems, Redondo Beach, Calif., 1968-69; dir. planning Calif. Computer Products, Anaheim, 1969-74; sr. scientist Hughes Aircraft, Fullerton, Calif., 1978-87; pres. Larbridge Enterprises Cons., Laguna Hills, Calif., 1970—; mem. Army Sci. Bd., Washington, 1988-92; contbd. to NASA's Mission Control Ctr. in Houston for Gemini, Apollo, Skylab and shuttle missions, Field Army tactical command and control system, first random access computer memory, early airborne digital computer, first keyboard and cathode ray tube data entry device (terminal), first-of-a-kind applications of computers in banks, factories, pension trust funds, payroll, acctg., truck scheduling, R.R. car routing, car body design and manufacture, automobile assembly plant inventory control, electrical power distbn. network, steel hot roll mill, computer programming methodologies (modularization, report generator, table-driven software), founds. for display tech. and large screen displays; lectr. workshops, conf. sessions, 1954-74. Editor Proc. Inst. Radio Engrs., 1961; editor, pub. The Labridge Letter, 1973-76; co-editor Handbook of Automation, Computation and Control, 1959; contbr. articles to profl. jours., computer publs.; patentee in field. 1st lt. USAF, 1942-45. Fellow IEEE (life; Centennial medal); mem. IEEE Computer Soc. (co-founder, nat. chmn. 1954-55),

Soc. for Info. Display, Am. Fedn. Info. Processing Socs. (bd. govs. 1956-60), Los Escribientes (San Clemente, Calif.), Sigma Xi, Tau Beta Pi, Eta Kappa Nu. Avocations: writing, photography. Home and Office: Larbridge Enterprises 236 Calle Aragon Unit A Laguna Hills CA 92653-3492

LARSON, JANICE TALLEY, computer science educator; b. Houston, Sept. 29, 1948; d. Hiram Peak Talley and Jennie Edna (Forbes) Donahoo; m. Harold Vernon Larson, Apr. 8, 1977; children: Randall Neil, Christopher Lee. AA in Computer Sci., San Jacinto Coll., 1981; BA in Computer Info. Systems, U. Houston, Clear Lake, 1984, MA in Computer Info. Systems, 1988; postgrad. in instructional tech., U. Houston, 1994—. Programmer Control Applications, Houston, 1985-86, Tex. Eastern Pipeline, Houston, 1988-90; instr. computer sci. San Jacinto Coll., Houston, 1990-94; sponsor Computer Sci. Club, Houston, 1992-94. Mem. IEEE, U. Houston Alumni Assn., Phi Delta Kappa, Kappa Delta Pi.

LARSON, JERRY L., state supreme court justice; b. Harlan, Iowa, May 17, 1936; s. Gerald L. and Mary Eleanor (Patterson) L.; m. Debra L. Christensen, July 17, 1993; children: Rebecca, Jeffrey, Susan, David. BA, State U. Iowa, 1958, JD, 1960. Bar: Iowa. Partner firm Larson & Larson, 1961-75; dist. judge 4th Jud. Dist. Ct. of Iowa, 1975-78; justice Iowa Supreme Ct., 1978—. Office: Supreme Ct Iowa State Capital Bldg Des Moines IA 50319

LARSON, JOHN DAVID, life insurance company executive, lawyer; b. Madison, Wis., July 6, 1941; s. Lawrence John and Anna Mathilda (Furseth) L.; m. Evelyn Vie Smith, Jan. 22, 1966 (div. Apr. 1980); children: Eric John, Karen Annette; m. Nancy Jay With, Nov. 29, 1980; stepchildren: Andrew Zachary, Anne Elizabeth, Christopher Allen. BBA, U. Wis., 1964, JD, 1965, MBA, 1966. Bar: Wis. 1965, U.S. Ct. Mil. Appeals 1966; CPA, Wis.; CLU, chartered fin. cons. With Nat. Guardian Life Ins. Co., Madison, 1969—; exec. v.p., treas. Nat. Guardian Life Ins. Co., 1973, pres., dir., 1974—, pres., chief exec. officer, 1989—; dir. Firstar Bank Wis., TV Wis., Inc., Madison, KELAB, Inc., Madison. Chmn. Madison chpt. ARC, 1974-75; pres. United Way Dane County, 1975; pres. Wis. Nat. Guard Assn., 1992—. With U.S. Army, 1966-69, brig. gen. Wis. Army N.G. Recipient Know Your Madisonian award Wis. State Jour., 1973. Mem. ABA, State Bar Wis., Am. Soc. CLUs, Am. Soc. Chartered Fin. Cons., Madison C. of C. (dir. 1976-80), U. Wis. Bus. Alumni (bd. dirs. 1986-90). Lutheran. Clubs: Maple Bluff (dir. 1974-80), Rotary. Home: 401 New Castle Way Madison WI 53704-6070 Office: PO Box 1191 Madison WI 53701-1191

LARSON, JOHN HYDE, retired utilities executive; b. Phila., Sept. 15, 1930; s. Roy Frank and Olive (Alden) L.; m. Priscilla Hibbs Beane; children: Michael Alden, Christopher Hibbs, Cynthia Ann. BA, Trinity Coll., 1953; M City Planning, MIT, 1955. Vice-pres. The Potomac Edison Co., Hagerstown, Md., 1969-72; treas. Allegheny Power System, Inc., N.Y.C., 1973-79; v.p. fin. Conn. Energy Corp., Bridgeport, Conn., 1980-85, pres., chief exec. officer, 1985-89; exec. v.p., chief operating officer So. Conn. Gas. Co., Bridgeport, Conn., 1981-85; pres., chief exec. officer So. Conn. Gas. Co., Bridgeport, 1985-89; acting dir. fin. City of Bridgeport, 1989-90; chmn. mgmt. adv. com. City of Bridgeport, Conn., 1990-93; chmn. selectman's com. on ops. improvement Westport, Conn., 1991; bd. dirs. Bay State Gas Co., Westborough, Mass., Bolt Tech., Inc., Norwalk Conn. Vice chmn. Bridgeport Hosp., 1991-93; chmn. Nova Med. Corp., 1991-95; hon. chmn. capital funds drive Family Svcs. Woodfield, 1988. Lt. (SC) USNR. Recipient Corp. Leadership award MIT, 1987, Century Svc. award Bridgeport Boys and Girls Club, 1991, Richard P. Bodine Community Leadership award, 1993. Mem. New Eng. Gas Assn. (chmn. 1988-89). Home: Mount Hunger Rd Barnard VT 05031

LARSON, JOHN WILLIAM, lawyer; b. Detroit, June 24, 1935; s. William and Sara Eleanor (Yeatman) L.; m. Pamela Jane Wren, Sept. 16, 1959; 1 dau., Jennifer Wren. BA with distinction, honors in Economics, Stanford, 1957; LLB, Stanford U., 1962. Bar: Calif. 1962. Assoc. Brobeck, Phleger & Harrison, San Francisco, 1962-68, ptnr., 1968-71, 73—, CEO, mng. ptnr., 1988-90, chmn. of firm, CEO, 1993-96; asst. sec. Dept. Interior, Washington, 1971-73; exec. dir. Natural Resources Com., Washington, 1973; counsellor to chmn. Cost of Living Coun., Washington, 1973; faculty Practising Law Inst.; bd. dirs. Measurex Corp. Mem. 1st U.S.-USSR Joint Com. on Environment; mem. bd. visitors Stanford U. Law Sch., 1974-77, 85-87, 95—; pres. bd. trustees The Katherine Branson Sch., 1980-83. With AUS, 1957-59. Mem. ABA, Calif. Bar Assn., San Francisco C. of C. (Bay Area coun. chmn. bd. dirs.), Order of Coif, Pacific Union Club, Burlingame Country Club, Bohemian Club. Home: PO Box 349 Ross CA 94957-0349 Office: Brobeck Phleger & Harrison Spear St Tower 1 Market Plz San Francisco CA 94105

LARSON, JOSEPH STANLEY, environmentalist, educator, researcher; b. Stoneham, Mass., June 23, 1933; s. Gustave Adolph and Marian (Kelly) L.; m. Wendy Nichols, Nov. 23, 1958; children: Marion Elizabeth, Sandra Frances. BS, U. Mass., 1956, MS, 1958; PhD, Va. Poly. Inst., 1966. Registered profl. forester, Maine. Exec. sec. Wildlife Conservation, Inc., Boston, 1958-59; state ornithologist Mass. Div. Fisheries and Wildlife, Boston, 1959-60; head conservation edn. div. Natural Resources Inst., U. Md., Annapolis, 1960-62, rsch. asst. prof., LaVale, 1965-67; wildlife rsch. biologist U.S. Fish and Wildlife Svc., Amherst, Mass., 1967-69; prof., dir. The Environ. Inst., U. Mass., Amherst, 1969—; cons. in field. Contbr. articles to profl. jours. Recipient Chevron Conservation award, 1990; grantee in field. Mem. AAUP (pres. Mass. chpt. 1976-77), AAAS, Wildlife Soc. (cert. wildlife biologist), Ecol. Soc. Am. (cert. sr. ecologist), Am. Assn. Mammalogists, Nat. Wetlands Tech. Coun. (exec. chmn.), Soc. Wetland Scientists (profl. wetland scientist), Mass. Audubon Soc. (bd. dirs.), U.S. Nat. Ramsar Com. (chmn.), Internat. Union for Conservation of Nature and Natural Resources (wetland com.) (Switzerland), Faculty Univ. Club, Cosmos Club, Sigma Xi, Xi Sigma Pi, Phi Sigma. Congregationalist. Home: 27 Arnold Rd Pelham MA 01002-9757 Office: U Mass Environ Inst Blaisdell House Box 30820 Amherst MA 01003-0820

LARSON, KERMIT DEAN, accounting educator; b. Algona, Iowa, Apr. 7, 1939; s. Loren L. and Hansena Laurena (Andersen) L.; m. Nancy Lynne Weber, June 17, 1961; children: Julie Renee, Timothy Dean, Cynthia Lynne. A.A., Ft. Dodge Jr. Coll., 1960; B.B.A., U. Iowa, 1962, M.B.A., 1963; D.B.A., U. Colo., 1966. C.P.A., Tex. Mem. faculty U. Tex., Austin, 1966—; Arthur Andersen & Co. Alumni prof. emeritus U. Tex., 1975—, chmn. dept. accounting, 1971-75; vis. asso. prof. Tulane U., New Orleans, 1970-71; cons. sales tax audit litigation, pvt. anti-trust litigation, expropriation ins. arbitration. Author: Fundamental Accounting Principles, 1978, 14th edit., 1996, (with Paul Miller) Financial Accounting, 6th edit., 1995, (with Charlene Spoede and Miller) Fundamentals of Financial and Managerial Accounting, 1994; contbr. articles to profl. jours. Mem. AICPA, Am. Acctg. Assn. (v.p. 1978-79), Tex. Soc. CPAs, Beta Gamma Sigma, Beta Alpha Psi. Baptist. Home: 1310 Falcon Ledge Dr Austin TX 78746-5120 Office: 823 Congress Ave Ste 1500 Austin TX 78701-2429

LARSON, LARRY, librarian; b. El Dorado, Ark., July 18, 1940; s. Willie Lee and Myrtle Elizabeth (McMaster) L.; m. Dorothy Ann Bing, Apr 23, 1966; 1 child, Larisa Ann. BS, Ouachita Baptist U., 1962; MLS, George Peabody Coll., 1967. Asst. librarian, media specialist Hall High Sch., Little Rock, 1962-65; asst. librarian, circulation Ark. Tech. U., Russellville, 1965-67; asst librarian reference Hendrix Coll., Conway, Ark., 1967-73; head librarian U. Ark., Monticello, 1973-75; librarian, dir. N. Ark. Regional Library, Harrison, 1975-85, Ft. Smith (Ark.) Pub. Library, 1985—. Bd. dirs. Ft. Smith Hist. Soc., 1986-90; treas. bd. dirs. Pub. Awareness Com., Ft. Smith, Ark., 1986—. Mem. ALA (chair pub. libr. div. 1980), Ark. Libr. Assn. (vice chair membership com. 1968, Disting. Svc. award 1985, chair pub. libr. divsn., 1993), Ark. Libr. Devel. Dist. (chair 1985-87), Ark. Adminstrs. Pub. Librs. (chair 1988-89, del. Ark. govs.' conf. on librs. 1990), Noon Exchange Club. Democrat. Baptist. Avocations: gardening, woodworking. Home: 3114 S Enid St Fort Smith AR 72903-4445 Office: Ft Smith Pub Libr 61 S 8th St Fort Smith AR 72901-2415

LARSON, MARK ADAM, lawyer; b. Steubenville, Jan. 14, 1964. BA, U. Pitts., 1986; JD, U. Akron, 1994. Bar: Pa. 1994, U.S. Dist. Ct. (we. dist.) Pa. 1994. Surety underwriter Chubb Ins., Pitts. and Washington, 1986-89; paralegal Burns, White & Hickton, Pitts., 1989-92; law clk. Magistrate judge C. Laurie U.S. Dist. Ct. No. Dist. Ohio, Cleve., 1993; law clk. Burns, White & Hickton, Pitts., 1993-94, Bowes & Grefenstette, P.C., Pitts., 1994-95; pvt. practice law McKeesport, Pa., 1994-95; of counsel Adams, Myers & Baczkwsoki, McKeesport, 1995; asst. dist. atty. Allegheny County, Pa., 1995—. Recipient Clark Boardman Callaghan Book award Clark Boardman Callaghan Pub. Co., Deerfield, Ill., 1994. Mem. Pa. Bar Assn., Pa. Dist. Atty's. Assn., Allegheny County Bar Assn. Office: 401 Courthouse Pittsburgh PA 15219

LARSON, MARK ALLAN, financial executive; b. Milw., June 24, 1948; s. Owen Earl and Alice May (Ulmen) L.; m. Linda Rosalie Wohlschlaeger, Jan. 3, 1970; children: Craig Allan, Emily Lin. BA, Ripon Coll., 1970; postgrad., Washington U., St. Louis, 1971-74; postgrad. in bus., St. Louis U., 1974-76. Personnel supr. Barnes Hosp., St. Louis, 1970-71; various fin. and mgmt. positions Bank Bldg. Corp., St. Louis, 1971-76, G.D. Searle & Co., Skokie, Ill., Geneva, Switzerland, 1976-85; sr. v.p., chief fin. and admistrv. officer Leaf Inc., Bannockburn, Ill., 1985-89; v.p. internat. devel. and adminstrn. Carlson Cos., Inc., Mpls., 1990-91; exec. v.p. fin. and adminstrn., travel and mktg. groups, 1992-93, exec. v.p. ops. and internat., mktg. groups, 1993-95; sr. v.p. fin. Internat. Distillers & Vintners N.Am., Hartford, Conn., 1995—. Home: 40 Northgate Avon CT 06001

LARSON, MAURICE ALLEN, chemical engineer, educator; b. Missouri Valley, Iowa, July 19, 1927; s. Albert Juluis and Grace Elizabeth (Chambers) L.; m. Ruth Elizabeth Gugeler, Dec. 5, 1953; children: Richard Alan (dec.), Janet Ann, John Albert. BS, Iowa State U., 1951, PhD, 1958. Chem. engr. Dow Corning Corp., Midland, Mich., 1951-54; teaching asst. Iowa State U., 1954-55, instr. dept. chem. engring., 1955-58, asst. prof., 1958-61, assoc. prof., 1961-64, prof., 1964—, Anson Marston Disting. prof., 1977—, chmn. dept. chem. engring., 1978-83; cons. AID, Kharagpur, India, 1968, USIA, Amman, Jordan, 1983, 84, 85; Shell vis. prof. Univ. Coll., London, 1971-72; sci. exchange visitor, Czechoslovakia and Poland, 1974; vis. prof. U. Queensland, Australia, summer 1981, U. Manchester Inst. Sci. and Tech., Eng., 1984-85; guest prof. Tianjin U., Peoples Republic of China, 1982; hon. lectr. Mid. Am. State U. Assn., 1986-87; Dow Corning Australia Bicentennial lectr., Sydney, 1988. Author: (with A.D. Randolph) Theory of Particulate Processes, 1971, 2d edit., 1988; contbr. (with others) articles to profl. jours. With U.S. Army, 1946-47. Recipient H.A. Webber Teaching award Iowa State U., 1967, Western Electric Fund award Am. Soc. Engring. Edn., 1970, Faculty citation Iowa State U. Alumni, 1972, Gov.'s Sci. medal State of Iowa, 1990, D.R. Boylan Eminent Faculty award Iowa State U., 1990; NSF fellow, 1965-66. Fellow Am. Inst. Chem. Engrs. (pres. Iowa 1970-71); Mem. Am. Chem. Soc. (chmn. div. fertilizer and soil chemistry 1975), Am. Soc. Engring. Edn., Lions (pres. Ames club 1979-80), Sigma Xi, Tau Beta Pi, Phi Lambda Upsilon, Phi Kappa Phi. Democrat. Methodist. Home: 2710 Thompson Dr Ames IA 50010-4759

LARSON, MICHAEL LEN, newspaper editor; b. St. James, Minn., Feb. 3, 1944; s. Leonard O. and Lois O. (Holte) L.; m. Kay M. Monahan, June 18, 1966; children: Christopher, David, Molly. BA, U. Minn., 1966; MBA, Mankato State U., 1986. Mng. editor Paddock Circle Inc., Libertyville, Ill., 1972-74, New Ulm (Minn.) Journal, 1974-76, Republican-Eagle, Red Wing, Minn., 1976-79, Mankato (Minn.) Free Press, 1979-84, 1979-84, editor, 1984-95, editor of editl. page, 1995—. Bd. dirs. Valley Indsl. Devel. Corp., Mankato, 1985-95, also treas.; mem. adv. bd. minn. State U. Bus. Sch. Served with U.S. Army, 1966-68, Vietnam. Recipient five First Place awards for investigative reporting Minn. Newspaper Assn., 1969, 71, 72, 76, 78, First Place award for feature writing, Suburban Newspapers Am., 1974. Mem. Minn. AP (pres. 1988—), Kiwanis. Roman Catholic. Avocation: bicycling. Home: 35 University Ct Mankato MN 56001-4182 Office: Mankato Free Press 418 S 2nd St Mankato MN 56001-3727

LARSON, NANCY CELESTE, computer systems manager; b. Chgo., July 17, 1951; d. Melvin Ellsworth and Ruth Margaret (Carlson) L. BS in Music Ed., U. Ill., 1973, MS in Music Edn., 1976; postgrad., Purdue Univ., 1982-86. Vocal music educator Consol. Sch. Dist., Gilman, Ill., 1975-77; elem. vocal music tchr. Sch. Dist. 161, Flossmoor, Ill., 1977-87; instr. Vander Cook Coll., Chgo., 1980-88; systems programmer analyst Sears, Roebuck & Co., Chgo., 1987-92, tech. instr., 1989-90, project leader, 1990-91, sr. systems analyst, 1991-92; sr. systems analyst Trans Union Corp., Chgo., 1992—, project mgr., 1994, mgr., 1994—; tchr. adult computer edn. Homewood-Flossmoor High Sch., 1986-90. Chmn. Faith Luth. Ch., 1982-87, pres. bd., 1988-91, vocal soloist and voice-over performer. Mem. Ill. Music Educators Assn., Music Educators Nat. Conf., Ill. Educators Assn., Nat. Educators Assn., Am. ORFF Schulwerk Assn., Flossmoor Edn. Assn. (negotiator 1983-86). Republican. Lutheran. Avocations: swimming, skiing, reading, antique hunting. Office: Trans Union Corp 555 W Adams St Chicago IL 60661-3601

LARSON, PETER L., legal assistant, investigator; b. Chgo., June 24, 1941; s. Allan M. and Harriet G. (Lans) L.; m. Carole J. Dierking, Feb. 4, 1961; children: Lori, Lance, Lynn, Lee. Assoc. Bus. Adminstrn., Muskegon Bus. U., 1961. Bar: Tex. (legal assts. divsn.) 1992; cert. in civil trial law, personal injury trial law Tex. Bd. Legal Specialization (L.A. divsn. stds.). South Tex. area mgr. So. Detectives, Inc., Houston, 1976-78; pres. Confidential Investigation Agy., Houston, 1978-85; sr. legal asst. Leger, Coplen & Jefferson, PC, Houston, 1985—; exec. dir. Tex. Citizens' Property Rights Orgn., Houston. Chmn. Tri-County Foster Parents, Muskegon, 1974; committeeman Boy Scouts Am., Ravenna, Mich., 1972. Staff sgt. USAF, 1961-64. Mem. ATLA (paralegal affiliate), Nat. Assn. Legal Assts. (cert.), Nat. Assn. Legal Investigators (cert., Editor/Pubs. award 1994). Avocations: photography/videography, stamps, antique woodworking tools, target pistols, art. Home: 10135 Prospect Hill Dr Houston TX 77064-5439 Office: Tex Citizen Property Rights Ste 2440 5847 San Felipe Houston TX 77057 Office: Tex Citizens Property Rights Orgn 5847 San Felipe Ste 2440 Houston TX 77057

LARSON, REED EUGENE, foundation administrator; b. Smith County, Kans., Sept. 27, 1922; s. George Christian and Edith Hazel (Whitney) L.; m. Marjorie Jeanne Hess, Aug. 31, 1947; children: Patricia Kay Larson Sween, Barbara Ann Larson Finnegan, Marcia Lynn Larson Craig. Student, Kans. Wesleyan U., 1940-41, Ohio State U., 1943-44; B.S. in E.E, Kans. State U., 1947. Design engr. Stein Labs., Atchison, Kans., 1947-48; processing engr. Coleman Co., Wichita, Kans., 1948-54; exec. v.p. Kansans for the Right to Work, Wichita, 1954-58; exec. v.p. Nat. Right-to-Work Com., Washington, 1959-76, pres., 1976—; exec. v.p. Nat. Right-to-Work Legal Def. Found., Washington, 1968-73, pres., 1973—; chmn. Hallmark Bank & Trust, 1984-94, F&M Bank-Hallmark, 1994—. Served with AUS, 1943-46. Recipient Seldon Waldo award U.S. Jaycees, 1956; Silver Anvil award Public Relations Soc. Am., 1966; James J. Kilpatrick award Internat. Platform Assn., 1980; Awarded Doctor of Laws Campbell U., 1988. Mem. Mont Pelerin Soc., Phila. Soc., Eta Kappa Nu, Tau Beta Pi. Baptist. Clubs: Kansas Jaycees (pres. 1953-54), Rotary, Am. Legion. Home: 7803 Antiopi St Annandale VA 22003-1405 Office: 8001 Braddock Rd Springfield VA 22151-2110

LARSON, ROBERT FREDERICK, public broadcasting company executive; b. Detroit, Mar. 24, 1930; s. Trygve and Solveig Johanna (Larsen) L.; m. Shirley Ann Burch, Aug. 20, 1955; children: Robb Jonathan, Peer Christopher. B.A., Muskingum Coll., 1953; M.Div., Pitts. Theol. Sem., 1956, Th.M, 1960; M.A. in Communications, U. Mich, 1964, Ph.D., 1969. Ordained to ministry Presbyterian Ch. Producer, dir. WITF-TV, Harrisburg, Pa., 1964-68, asst. mgr. program devel., 1968-70, pres., gen. mgr., 1970-83; exec. sec. radio/TV Pa. Council Chs., Harrisburg, 1967-70; pres., gen. mgr. WTVS-TV, Detroit, 1983-95, pres. emeritus for humanities and cmty. devel., 1995—; pres. The Larson Comms. Group, Inc., 1996—; bd. dirs. Am's. Pub. TV Stas., Mich. Pub. Broadcasting, Interlochen Ctr. Arts, Mich's Children, New Detroit Inc., Community Telecom. Network, Neighborhood Renaissance, Inc., Ctrl. Bus. Dist. Assn., New Ctr. Area Coun., William Tynedale Coll.; former vice chmn. bd. dirs. PBS. Producer, dir. (TV program) Sons and Daughters, 1967, A Time to Act, 1968, Is Religion Obsolete?, 1969; exec. producer: All About Welfare, No Time To Be A Child, Act Against Violence: Help Wanted; producer: So Where Are You, God?. Mem. Detroit Coun. of Chs., Detroit Presbytery. Mem. Detroit Athletic Club.

LARSON, ROLAND ELMER, health care executive; b. Chgo., Jan. 21, 1939; s. Elmer Gustav and Anna (Alphida) L.; m. Noel Kathleen Brennan, June 28, 1969; children: Eric R., Jennifer L., Melissa K. BA, Augustana Coll., 1961; MHA, U. Iowa, 1963; postgrad., Harvard U., 1978. Adminstrv. asst. U. Vt. Med. Ctr., Burlington, 1962-64; assoc. adminstr. Roger Williams Hosp., Providence, 1964-73; v.p. adminstrn. Norwalk (Conn.) Hosp., 1973-81; pres., chief exec. officer Nashoba Community Hosp., Ayer, Mass., 1981-88; v.p. Charles River Assn., Boston, 1988-90; cons. Charles River Assocs., Boston, 1990-93; ind. healthcare cons. Harvard, Mass., 1990—. Chmn. Harvard (Mass.) Coalition Against Drugs and Alcohol, Opportunities, Inc., Providence, 1966-68, Greater Norwalk Community Coun., 1980; bd. dirs. Nat. Arthritis Found., N.Y.C., 1967-71, Am. Cancer Soc., Stamford, Conn., 1978-81. Fellow Am. Coll. Healthcare Execs.; mem. Cen. Mass. Hosp. Coun. (chmn. 1987-88), Rotary. Avocations: sailing, bicycling, golf, squash, woodworking. Home: 28 Candleberry Ln Harvard MA 01451-1641 Office: Larson & Assocs 28 Candleberry Ln Harvard MA 01451-1641

LARSON, ROY, journalist, publisher; b. Moline, Ill., July 27, 1929; s. Roy W. and Jane (Beall) L.; m. Dorothy Jennisch, June 7, 1950; children: Mark, Bruce, Jodie, Bradley. A.B., Augustana Coll., Rock Island, Ill., 1951; M.Div., Garrett Theol. Sem., 1955. Ordained to ministry Methodist Ch., 1956; min. Covenant United Meth. Ch., Evanston, Ill., 1963-68, First United Meth. Ch., Elmhurst, Ill., 1968-69; religion editor Chgo. Sun-Times, 1969-85; pub. The Chgo. Reporter, 1985-94; exec. dir. Garrett-Medill Ctr. for Religion and News Media, Evanston, Ill., 1995—. Home: 1508 Hinman Ave Evanston IL 60201-4664 Office: Garrett-Medill Ctr 2121 Sheridan Rd Evanston IL 60201-2926

LARSON, RUSSELL EDWARD, university provost emeritus, consultant agriculture research and development; b. Mpls., Jan. 2, 1917; s. Karl Sam and Belle (Wing) L.; m. Margaret Agnes Johnson, Aug. 19, 1939; children: Gayle Margaret, Beverly Jean, Russell Troy. BS, U. Minn., 1939, MS, 1940, PhD, 1942; DSc (hon.), Delaware Valley Coll. Sci. and Agr., 1966. Asst. prof. U. R.I., Kingston, 1941-44; asst. prof. Pa. State U., University Park, 1944-45, assoc. prof., 1945-47, prof., 1947—, head dept. horticulture, 1952-62, dean Coll. Agriculture, 1963-72, provost, 1972-77; sci. advisor Am. Cocoa Rsch. Inst., McLean, Va., 1975-87; cons. Agriculture R & D, State Coll. Pa., 1977—. Contbr. 46 tech. articles on plant sci. to profl. jours. Recipient Outstanding Alumnus award U. Minn., 1961. Fellow AAAS, Am. Soc. Hort. Sci. (pres. 1963-64, L.H. Vaughan award 1948); mem. Am. Genetic Assn., Am. Inst. Biol. Sci., Sigma Xi. Republican. Lutheran. Avocations: gardening, golf, fishing. Home: 608 Elmwood St State College PA 16801-7053 Office: Pa State U 6 Tyson Bldg University Park PA 16802-4202

LARSON, RUSSELL GEORGE, magazine and book publisher; b. Waukesha, Wis., May 4, 1942; s. George Arthur and Dorothy Edna (Hanneman) L.; m. Barbara Kay Krsek, Aug. 1, 1964; children—Eric, Craig, Denise. A.A.S., Milw. Sch. Engring., 1962. Tech. writer various publs., 1962-69; assoc. editor Model Railroader Mag., Milw., 1969-75, mng. editor, 1975-77, editor, 1977-93, v.p. editorial, 1989-93, sr. v.p. editorial, 1993—; pub. Model Railroader Mag., Trains Mag., Classic Toy Trains Mag., Collecting Toys Mag., Astronomy Mag., Earth Mag., Birder's World Mag., Kalmbach Books, Greenberg Books, Milw. Author: N Scale Primer, 1973, Beginner's Guide to N Scale Model Railroading, 1990, Beginner's Guide to Large Scale Model Railroading, 1994. Mem. Soc. Tech. Communication. Lutheran. Avocations: golf, model railroading, reading, travel. Office: Kalmbach Pub Co PO box 1612 21027 Crossroads Cir Waukesha WI 53186-4055

LARSON, SANDRA MAE, nursing educator; b. Chgo., Apr. 21, 1944; d. Richard Milward and Eldred Gertrude (Piehl) Blackburn; m. Eric Richard Larson, Nov. 25, 1967; children—Sarah, Keith. B.S., No. Ill. U., 1966, M.S., 1978. R.N., Ill. Nursing educator Lutheran Hosp., Moline, Ill., 1968-70; charge nurse ICU, Peninsula Hosp., Burlingame, Calif., 1970-72; staff nurse Illini Hosp., Silvis, Ill., 1972-76; nursing educator Black Hawk Coll., Moline, 1976—; mem. audit com. Rock Island County Health Dept., Ill., 1983—; presenter radio program on stress Sta. KIIK, Moline, 1980; interviewer Am. Cancer Soc., Moline, 1982, 84, 86. Co-author Anatomy and Physiology Testbank, 1994. Mem. Am. Nurses Assn., Ill. Nurses Assn. (bd. dirs. 5th dist. 1979-82, treas., 1982-84, pres. 1984-86, 1st v.p. 1986-87, pres. 1988-92, 2nd v.p., 1993-95), Sigma Theta Tau. Democrat. Roman Catholic. Avocations: camping; reading. Home: 3009 29th St Moline IL 61265-6950 Office: Black Hawk Coll 6600 34th Ave Moline IL 61265-5870

LARSON, SIDNEY, art educator, artist, writer, painting conservator; b. Sterling, Colo., June 16, 1923; s. Harry and Ann Levin; m. George Ann Madden, Aug. 30, 1947; children: Sara Catherine, Nancy Louise. BA, U. Mo., 1949, MA in Art, 1950. Prof. art Columbia Coll., Mo., 1951—; art curator State Hist. Soc. Mo., 1962—; painting conservator, Columbia, 1960—. Exhibited paintings and drawings in group shows in Midwest, Washington, N.Y. and Japan; executed murals Daily News, Rolla, Mo., Shelter Ins., Columbia, Mo., Guitar Bldg., Columbia, Mcpl. Bldg., Jefferson City, Mo., Centerre Bank, Columbia, chs. in Okla. and Ark. Adv. Mo. State Council on Arts, 1960, Boone County Courthouse, Columbia. Served with USN, 1943-46, PTO. Fellow Huntington Hartford Found., 1962; rRecipient Commendation award Senate of State of Mo., 1977, 87, Nat. Prof. of Yr. award, Bronze medalist, Mo. State Prof. of Yr. award Coun. for Advancement and Support Edn., 1987, Disting. Svc. award State Hist. Soc. Mo., Mo. State Arts Coun. award, 1991. Mem. Am. Inst. Conservation of Hist. and Artistic Works (assoc. mem.), Nat. Assn. Mural Painters. Avocations: world travel, reading. Home: 1408 Whitburn Dr Columbia MO 65203-5172 Office: Columbia Coll Dept Art Columbia MO 65216

LARSON, WARD JEROME, lawyer, retired banker; b. Mpls., Mar. 3, 1924; s. Philip Jerome and Inez (Sandstrom) L.; m. Phyllis Jean Lindahl, June 18, 1949; children—Eric, Peter, David, Barbara. BA, North Central Coll., Naperville, Ill., 1948; LLB, Harvard U., 1951. Bar: Ill. 1951. Atty. First Nat. Bank Chgo., 1951-56; asst. trust officer, v.p. DuPage Trust Co., Glen Ellyn, Ill., 1956-62; with Fed. Res. Bank Chgo., 1962-80, v.p., gen. counsel, sec., 1968, sr. v.p., gen. counsel, sec., 1970-80; sole practice law Glen Ellyn, 1980—; Chmn. ins. com. Fed. Res. Banks, 1968-80; mem. adminstrv. bd. Fed. Res. Employee Benefits System, 1970-74, vice chmn., 1973-74. Mem. bd. edn. Sch. Dist. 41, Glen Ellyn, Ill., 1961-67, pres., 1964-67; chmn. estate planning com. North Ctrl. Coll., 1962-68, trustee, 1980-81, planned giving officer, 1987-90; chmn. trustees 1st United Meth. Ch., Glen Ellyn, 1968-69, chmn. coun. ministries, 1969-71, chmn. membership commn., 1973-75, chmn. social concerns com., 1977, membership sec., 1985-90, lay leader, 1979, 90-93; lay mem. ann. conf. United Meth. Ch. No. Ill., 1992—, mem. conf. coun. fin. and adminstrn.; bd. dirs., v.p. B.R. Ryall YMCA, Glen Ellyn, 1968-70; bd. dirs. United Meth. Found.-North Ill. Conf., 1973-76; mem. exec. com. Chgo. chpt. March of Dimes, 1978-80; mem. Coun. Laity Garrett-Evang. Theol. Sem., 1984-90; planned giving cons. Ctrl. DuPage Hosp., 1992—. 1st lt., infantry, AUS, 1943-46. Mem. ABA, Alumni Assn. North Central Coll. (dir. 1976—, sec. 1977-78, pres. 1980-81, nat. chmn. ann. fund 1983-92, Outstanding Alumnus award 1986). Home and Office: 822 Saddlewood Dr Glen Ellyn IL 60137-3202

LARSON, WILFRED JOSEPH, chemical company executive; b. N.Y.C., July 12, 1927; s. Fred Wilfred and Mabel Louise (Messier) L.; m. Joan Jesslyn Tilford, Sept. 4, 1949; children: Linda Sue, Robert Wilfred. B.S. in Econs., U. Pa., 1951; postgrad., U. Chgo., 1958-59, Seton Hall U., 1960-61, U. Cin., 1964-65. With Ward Foods, N.Y.C., 1953-63; contr., chief fin. officer Ward Foods, 1961-63; with Drackett Co., Cin., 1963-79; fin. v.p. Drackett Co., 1966-67, adminstrv. v.p., 1967-68, exec. v.p., 1969-79; pres. Bristol-Myers Products Can., 1977-79; v.p. Bristol-Myers Squibb Co., 1981-92; pres. Westwood Squibb Pharms., Inc., 1979-92; past chmn. Western N.Y. Tech. Devel. Ctr.; bd. dirs. First Empire State Corp., MT&T Bank, Bryant & Stratton, Horus Therapeutics Inc.;. Pres., trustee Cin. Adolescent Clinic, Inc., 1968-80; trustee, past chmn. Women's & Children's Rsch. Found., Children's Hosp.; past chmn., bd. dirs. Greater Buffalo YMCA; trustee, past treas. Studio Arena Theatre; chmn. SUNY-Buffalo Sch. Pharmacy Centennial, 1986; past trustee Calspan/UB Rsch. Ctr.; past vice chmn., bd. dirs. Buffalo Children's Hosp.; chmn. bd. dirs. Buffalo Philharm. Orch. Soc., Inc., 1986-91; vice chmn. bd. dirs. Greater Buffalo Devel. Found., 1987-92; bd. dirs. Buffalo Fine Arts Acad., 1988-91, Am. Symphony Orch. League, 1989-91, U. at Buffalo Found., 1990-94; mem. cmty. coun. Roswell Park Meml. Inst., 1988-94. With USNR, 1945-47, AUS, 1951-53. Named Buffalo/Niagara Sales and Mktg. Exec. of Yr., 1985, Disting. Citizen of Yr. Boy Scouts Am., 1987, Ann. Alumni award Niagara Frontier Exec. of Yr., U. Buffalo Sch. Mgmt., 1987; recipient Disting. Pub. Svc. award SUNY Buffalo Alumni Assn., 1986, Outstanding Citizens award Buffalo News, 1987, Man of Yr. award West Side Bus. and Taxpayers Assn., 1989, Bus. Exec. of Yr. award Nat. Assn. Accts. Buffalo chpt., 1989. Mem. Fin. Execs. Inst. (treas., sec. 1965-68), Greater Buffalo C. of C. (bd. dirs. 1989-92, We. New Yorker of Yr. award 1992, Patron of Arts award 1993), Leland (Mich.) Country Club, Moorings Country Club (Naples, Fla.), Commonwealth Club Cin., Buffalo Club, Royal Poinciana Golf Club (Naples). Republican. Episcopalian (vestryman, treas. 1966-69). Home: 88 Oakland Pl Buffalo NY 14222-2030 Office: 100 Forest Ave Buffalo NY 14213-1032

LA RUE, CARL FORMAN, lawyer; b. Ann Arbor, Mich., Aug. 4, 1929; s. Carl D. and Evelina F. La R.; children: Steven, Edward; m. Ann Williams Lindbloom, June 28, 1971; stepchildren: Eric, Sarah Relyea. A.B., Harvard U., 1952; LL.B., U. Mich., 1957. Bar: Ohio 1957, Ill. 1964, Calif. 1969. Assoc. firm Fuller & Henry, Toledo, 1957-59; asst. U.S. atty. for Northwestern Ohio, Dept. Justice, 1959-61; staff atty. Trinova Corp. (then Libbey-Owens-Ford Co.), Toledo, 1961-64; v.p., gen. counsel, sec. Trinova Corp., Toledo, 1978-87; ptnr. Marshall & Melhorn, Toledo, 1988-89, counsel, 1989—; sr. atty. Armour and Co., Chgo., 1964-68; asst. gen. counsel Rockwell Internat., Los Angeles, 1968-78. With U.S. Army, 1952-54. Mem. ABA, Ohio Bar Assn., Toledo Bar Assn., Toledo Club, Toledo Tennis Club, Westowne Tennis Club. Home: 3553 Brookside Rd Toledo OH 43606-2610 Office: Marshall & Melhorn 4 Seagate Toledo OH 43604-1588

LA RUE, HENRY ALDRED, consultant, former oil company executive; b. Denver, Aug. 13, 1927; s. Robert Hughes and Leona Spencer (Wood) La R.; m. Marion Hardin Klein, Aug. 22, 1954. B.S. in Bus. Adminstrn., U. Kans., 1951. Pres. Pacific Gulf Oil Co., Tokyo, 1973-74; exec. v.p. Gulf Oil Middle East Co., Pitts., 1974-75, Gulf Sci. and Tech. Co., Pitts., 1975-82; pres. Gulf Research and Devel. Co., Pitts., 1975-82, Pitts. Applied Rsch. Corp., U. Pitts. Applied Rsch. Ctr., 1986-88; vice chmn. Pitts. Applied Rsch. Ctr., 1988-92; chief exec. officer Alle-Kiski Revitalization Corp., 1989-90; cons. in field. Bd. dirs. Gulf Oil Corp. Found., Pitts., 1976-82, Franklin Rsch. Ctr., Phila., 1981-86, Colo. Sch. Mines Rsch. Inst., Golden, 1981-87; v.p., dir. Bio Rsch. Ctr. Co., Tokyo, 1973-84; mem. adv. bd. Mellon Inst., Pitts., 1977-83;; sec. Salvation Army Greater Pitts., 1980—; mem. Bell Acres Borough Coun., 1992, vice chmn., 1994. Recipient achievement award indsl. research Slippery Rock U. Mem. Am. Petroleum Inst., Am. C. of C. (pres. Seoul, Korea 1970-71, 1st v.p. Taipei, Taiwan 1972-73), Duquesne Club, Edgeworth Club, Sewickley Heights Golf Club, Beta Theta Pi, Delta Sigma Pi. Republican. Episcopalian. Home: 129 Woodcock Drive Rd Sewickley PA 15143-8356 Office: Pitts Applied Research Corp 100 William Pitt Way Pittsburgh PA 15238-1327

LA RUE, (ADRIAN) JAN (PIETERS), musicologist, educator, author; b. Kisaran, Sumatra, Indonesia, July 31, 1918; s. Carl Downey and Evelina Brown (Forman) LaR.; m. Helen Claire Robison, Aug. 21, 1940; children: Charlotte (Mrs. Jonathan L. Isaacs), Christine (Mrs. Dan Honig). SB, Harvard, 1940, PhD, 1952; M.F.A., Princeton, 1942. Instr. music Wellesley Coll., 1942-43, 46-48, asst. prof., 1948-50, asso. prof., 1950-57, chmn. dept. music, 1950-57; prof. NYU, 1957-88; prof. emeritus N.Y. U., 1988—, exec. dean arts and sci., 1962-63, chmn. dept. music, 1970-73, dir. grad. studies in music, 1973-80; vis. prof. UCLA, 1947, U. Mich., 1962, Bar Ilan U., Israel, 1980, Queens U., Ont., 1996; first musicologist-in-residence Mozart Festival, The Kennedy Ctr., Washington, 1975. Author: Guidelines for Style Analysis, 1970, 2d edit., 1992, A Catalogue of 18-th Century Symphonies, 1988, Vol. 1, Thematic Identifier; co-author: (with M. Ohmiya) Methods and Models for Comprehensive Style Analysis, 1988; contbg. author: Die Musik in Geschichte und Gegenwart, 1968, Grove's Dictionary of Music and Musicians, 1980, Essays in Honour of Alan Tyson; editor: Congress Report of the Internat. Musicol. Soc., 2 vols., 1961, Festschrift Otto Erich Deutsch, 1963, Festschrift Gustave Reese: Aspects of Medieval and Renaissance Music, 1966; contbr. numerous articles on 18th century symphony and concerto, mus. analysis, watermarks, music manuscripts and computer applications to profl. jours. Mem. coun. Smithsonian Instn., 1967-73; mem. Zentralinstitut für Mozartforschung, Salzburg (Austria) Mozarteum, 1969—. 1st lt. Transp. Corps, AUS, 1943-46. Fellow Ford Found., 1954, Fulbright Found., 1954-56, Am. Coun. Learned Socs., 1964, Guggenheim Found., 1965; grantee NEH, 1978, 80-84; honored with publ. of Studies in Musical Sources and Style: Essays in Honor of Jan LaRue, 1990. Mem. Music Library Assn., Soc. Ethnomusicology, Am. Musicological Soc. (pres. 1966-68), Am. Soc. Eighteenth-Century Studies (exec. bd. 1978-80), Phi Beta Kappa. Home: 103 Woods End Rd New Canaan CT 06840 Office: NYU Dept Music Dept Music New York NY 10003-6757

LARUE, PAUL HUBERT, lawyer; b. Somerville, Mass., Nov. 16, 1922; s. Lucien H. and Germaine (Choquet) LaR.; m. Helen Finnegan, July 20, 1946; children: Paul Hubert, Patricia Seward,, Mary Hogan. PhB, U. Wis., 1947, JD, 1949. Bar: Ill. 1955, Wis. 1949, U.S. Supreme Ct. 1972. Instr. polit. sci. dept. U. Wis., 1947-48; mem. staff Wis. Atty. Gen., 1949-50; trial atty., legal adviser to commr. FTC, 1950-55; pvt. practice, Chgo.; mem. Chadwell & Kayser, Ltd., 1955-90; ptnr. Vedder, Price, Kaufman & Kammholz, 1990-93, of counsel, 1993—; speaker profl. meetings. Mem. Com. Modern Cts. in Ill., 1964; mem. Ill. Com. Constl. Conv., 1968, Better Govt. Assn., 1966-70, Lawyers com. Met. Crusade of Mercy, 1967-68, lawyers' com. United Settlement Appeal, 1966-68; apptd. pub. mem. Ill. Conflict of Interest Laws Commn., 1965-67. Served with AUS, 1943-45, ETO; as capt JAGC, USAFR, 1950-55. Fellow Ill. Bar Found. (life); mem. ABA (mem. council sect. antitrust law 1980-83, chmn. Robinson-Patman Act com. 1975-78), Ill. State Bar Assn., Chgo. Bar Assn. (chmn. antitrust com. 1970-71), Wis. State Bar, Met. Club. Roman Catholic. Contbr. articles to profl. jours. Home: 250 Cuttriss Pl Park Ridge IL 60068 Office: Vedder Price Kaufman & Kammholz 222 N La Salle St Chicago IL 60601-1003

LARUE, PAUL HUBERT, JR., lawyer; b. Madison, Wis., July 17, 1950; s. Paul Hubert and Helen (Finnegan) L.; m. Nancy Karen Whiting, Dec. 17, 1983; children: Madeleine, Michelle, Michael. BA cum laude, Yale U., 1972; JD, Cornell U., 1975. Bar: Ill. 1975, U.S. Dist. Ct. (no. dist.) Ill. 1975; U.S. Tax Ct. 1993. Assoc. Lord, Bissell & Brook, Chgo., 1975-83, ptnr., 1984—. Mem. Chgo. Coun. on Foreign Rels., 1993. Mem. ABA, Chgo. Bar Assn., Yale Club of Chgo., Rotary (Chgo. chpt.). Home: 124 Robsart Rd Kenilworth IL 60043-1213 Office: Lord Bissell & Brook 115 S La Salle St Chicago IL 60603-3801*

LARUSSA, JOSEPH ANTHONY, optical company executive; b. N.Y.C., May 10, 1925; s. Ignacio and Jennie (Bellone) LaR.; m. Stella M.A. Braconnier, July 2, 1946; children—Joseph, Raymond Paul, Debra Marie. BME, CCNY, 1949; M.S., Columbia U., 1955, postgrad. math., mechanics, 1955-59; postgrad. math., physics, NYU, 1959-62; diploma in Infrared Tech., U. Mich. Registered profl. engr., N.Y. V.p.- charge advanced engring. Farrand Optical Co., Inc., Valhalla, N.Y., 1952, sr. v.p., tech. dir., 1952-88; pres., chief oper. officer Tech. Innovation Group Inc, Pleasantville, N.Y., 1988-90, Electro Visual Engring. Inc., Yorktown Heights, N.Y., 1991—. Designed Mercury, Gemini, Apollo LM visual spaceflight simulators for NASA; designed space shuttle Aft and Ohd visual simulators for NASA, others for USAF. Patentee in field; contbr. articles profl. publs. Served with inf. AUS, World War II, ETO. Mem. AIAA (DeFlorez award 1968), Tau Beta Pi, Pi Tau Sigma. Home: 451 Rutledge Dr Yorktown Heights NY 10598-5011

LA RUSSA, TONY, JR. (ANTHONY LA RUSSA, JR.), professional baseball manager; b. Tampa, Fla., Oct. 4, 1944; m. Elaine Coker, Dec. 31, 1973; 2 daus.: Bianca, Devon. Student, U. Tampa; BA, U. So. Fla., 1969; LLB, Fla. State U., 1978. Bar: Fla., 1979. Player numerous major league and minor league baseball teams, 1962-77; coach St. Louis Cardinals orgn., 1977; mgr. minor league team Knoxville, 1978, Iowa, 1979; coach Chgo. White Sox, 1978, mgr., 1979-86; mgr. Oakland A's, 1986-95, St. Louis Cardinals, 1996—; mgr. A.L. champion Oakland A's, 1988, 89, 90, World champions, 1989; mgr. All-Star team, 1988, coach, 1984, 87. Named Am. League Mgr. of Yr. Baseball Writers' Assn. Am., 1983, 88, 92, AP, 1983, Sporting News, 1983, Am. League Mgr. of Yr., 1988, 92. Office: St Louis Cardinals Busch Stadium 250 Stadium Plz Saint Louis MO 63102*

LARWOOD, LAURIE, psychologist; b. N.Y., 1941; PhD, Tulane U., 1974. Pres., Davis Instruments Corp., San Leandro, Calif., 1966-71, cons., 1969—; asst. prof. orgnl. behavior SUNY, Binghamton, 1974-76; assoc. prof. psychology, chairperson dept., assoc. prof. bus. adminstrn. Claremont (Calif.) McKenna Coll., 1976-83, Claremont Grad. Sch., 1976-85; prof., head dept. mgmt. U. Ill.-Chgo., 1983-87; dean sch. bus. SUNY, Albany, 1987-90; dean Coll. Bus. Adminstrn., U. Nev., Reno, 1990-92; dir. Inst. Strategic Bus. Issues, 1992—; mem. western regional advisory coun. SBA, 1976-81; dir. The Mgmt. Team; pres. Mystic Games, Inc. Mem. Acad. Mgmt. (editl. rev. bd. Rev. 1977-82, past chmn. women in mgmt. div., managerial consultation divsn., tech. and innovation mgmt. divsn.), Am. Psychol. Assn., Assn. Women in Psychology. Author: (with M.M. Wood) Women in Management, 1977; Organizational Behavior and Management, 1984, Women's Career Development, 1987, Strategies-Successes-Senior Executives Speak Out, 1988, Women's Careers, 1988, Managing Technological Development, 1988; mem. editl. bd. Sex Roles, 1979—, Consultation, 1986-91, Jour. Orgnl. Behavior, 1987—, Group and Orgn. Mgmt., 1982-84, editor, 1986—; founding editor Women and Work, 1983, Jour. Mgmt. Case Studies, 1983-87; contbr. numerous articles, papers to profl. jours. Home: 2855 Sagittarius Dr Reno NV 89509-3885 Office: U Nev Coll Bus Adminstrn Reno NV 89557

LASAGE, JOHN DAVID, public relations firm executive; b. Gary, Ind., May 6, 1937; s. Harold and Natalie (Marich) LaS.; m. Carol Lee Monson, June 17, 1962; children: Laura, Catherine. B.A. in Journalism, U. Mich., 1959. Publicity writer U.S. Gypsum Co., Chgo., 1960-64; account exec. Burson-Marsteller, Chgo., 1964-70; supr. Burson-Marsteller, 1970-78, gen. mgr. Chgo., 1978-83, exec. v.p. central region, 1980-91, pres., CEO Chgo., 1992—. Bd. dirs. Urban Gateways, Chgo., 1978-80; bd. dirs. Community Renewal Soc., 1975-78, Eastern Seal Soc., 1980—, Boy Scouts Am., 1982—. Recipient Golden Trumpet Publicity Club Chgo., 1968. Mem. Pub. Relations Soc. Am. (accredited Silver Anvil 1972, accredited Silver Anvil 1980). Congregationalist. Clubs: Publicity (Chgo.); Chicago. Office: Burson-Marsteller 1 E Wacker Dr Chicago IL 60601*

LASAGNA, LOUIS CESARE, medical educator; b. N.Y.C., Feb. 22, 1923; s. Joseph and Carmen (Boccignone) L.; m. Helen Chester Gersten; children: Nina, David, Maria, Kristin, Lisa, Peter, Christopher. BS, Rutgers U., 1943; MD, Columbia U., 1947; DSc (hon.), Hahnemann U., 1980, Rutgers U., 1983. Asst. prof. medicine Johns Hopkins U., Balt., 1954-57, asst. prof. pharmacology, 1954-59, assoc. prof. medicine, 1957-70, assoc. prof. pharmacology, 1959-70; prof. pharmacology and toxicology U. Rochester, 1970-86, prof. medicine, 1970-86; dean Sackler Sch. Tufts U., 1984—, prof. pharmacology and psychiatry, 1984—. Author: The Doctors' Dilemmas, 1962, Life, Death and the Doctor, 1968, Phenylpropanolamine, A Review, 1988; editor: Controversies in Therapeutics, 1980,. Sr. asst. surgeon USPHS, 1952-54. Recipient Oscar B. Hunter award Am. Soc. Clin. Pharmacology, 1975, ASPET award Am. Soc. Pharmacology and Exptl. Therapeutics, 1976, Lilly prize Brit. Pharmacological Soc., 1985, Rutgers U. award, 1993, J. Allyn Taylor Internat. prize in Medicine, 1993; named Disting. prof. Tufts U., 1994. Mem. Inst. Medicine of NAS, Am. Coll. Neuropsychopharmacology (pres. 1979-80). Republican. Roman Catholic. Home: 256 Woodland Rd Auburndale MA 02166-2707 Office: Tufts U Sackler Sch Grad Biomed Sci 136 Harrison Ave Boston MA 02111-1800

LA SALLE, ARTHUR EDWARD, historic foundation executive; b. New Orleans, Aug. 9, 1930; s. Rene Charles and Jeanne Matilda (Senac) La S.; divorced; children—Carl Alan, Adam David, Jeanne Ambre Victoria. Student Holy Name of Jesus Coll. Founder, pres. Am. R.R. Equipment Assn., Asheville, N.C., 1960—; founder Trains of Yesterday Mus., Hilliard, Fla., 1964-73; owner, restorer Brush Hill mansion, Irwin, Pa., 1973-77; lessee, restorer Springfield mansion, Fayette, Miss., 1977—; founder, pres. Hist. Springfield Found., Fayette, 1977—; cons. Smithsonian Instn., 1959, 75, Japanese Nat. Rys., Tokyo, 1968, Henry Ford Mus., 1975 City of Natchez, Miss., 1985, Old South Soc., Church Hill, Miss., 1985—; cons. in field; lectr. in field. Author: The Marriage of Andrew Jackson at Springfield Plantation; contbr. articles to profl. jours. Mem. Ry. and Locomotive Hist. Soc., Nat. Trust for Historic Preservation, Natchez Hist. Soc., U.S. Naval Inst. Avocations: historical preservation and study; writing; painting. Home and Office: Springfield Plantation RR 1 Box 201 Fayette MS 39069-9527

LASAROW, WILLIAM JULIUS, retired federal judge; b. Jacksonville, Fla., June 30, 1922; s. David Herman and Mary (Hollins) L.; m. Marilyn Doris Powell, Feb. 4, 1951; children: Richard M., Elisabeth H. BA, U. Fla., 1943; JD, Stanford U., 1950. Bar: Calif. 1951. Counsel judiciary com. Calif. Assembly, Sacramento, 1951-52; dep. dist. atty. Stanislaus County, Modesto, Calif., 1952-53; pvt. practice law L.A., 1953-73; bankruptcy judge U.S. Cts., L.A., 1973-94; chief judge U.S. Bankruptcy Ct., Central dist., Calif., 1978-90; judge Bankruptcy Appellate Panel 9th Fed. Cir., 1980-82; fed. judge U.S. Bankruptcy Ct., L.A., 1973; faculty Fed. Jud. Ctr. Bankruptcy Seminars, Washington, 1977-82. Contbg. author, editor legal publs.; staff: Stanford U. Law Review, 1949. Mem. ABA, Am. Coll. Bankruptcy, Am. Bankruptcy Inst., L.A. County Bar Assn., Wilshire Bar Assn., Blue Key, Phi Beta Kappa, Phi Kappa Phi. Home: 11623 Canton Pl Studio City CA 91604-4164

LASCH, PAT, artist, educator; b. N.Y.C., Nov. 20, 1944; d. Fred and Helen Veronica L.; 1 child, Melinda. BA, Queens Coll., 1970; FAAR, Am. Acad. in Rome, 1983; MFA, Ga. State U., Atlanta, 1990. Mem. found. faculty Parsons Sch. of Design, N.Y.C., 1979-88; asst. prof. R.I. Sch. of Design, Providence, 1988-89; assoc. prof. U. Mass., Amherst, 1990—. Artist: solo exhibits include A.I.R. Gallery, N.Y.C., 1973, 77, 79, 80, 94, Zabrskie Gallery, N.Y.C., 1975, Galleriet, Lund, Sweden, 1980, Galerie Ahlner, Stockholm, 1980, Kathryn Markel Gallery, N.Y.C., 1981, 84, 85, Albright Knox Gallery, Members' Gallery, Buffalo, 1977-84, Thomas Segal Gallery, Boston, 1988, Sculpture Ctr., N.Y.C., 1993, Herter Gallery, U. Mass., Amherst, 1993; group shows inclde Inst. Contemporary Art, Phila., Street Scenes, 1981, Malmo (Sweden) Konsthall, Food, 1984, San Francisco Internat. Airport, The Right Foot Show, 1987, Thomas Segal Gallery, The Raw and the Cooked, Boston, The New Mus., N.Y.C., Bad Girls, 1994; spl. exhibition The Mus. of Modern Art (50th Anniversary), Homage 1929-79. Recipient Yaddo, 1978, 80, 94, Rome prize, 1982-83, Lilly fellowship, 1993-94, NEA-MCC fellowship, 1995-96; grantee: C.A.P.S., 1980, NEA, 1980-81, N.Y. State Coun. for the Arts, 1984-85, Ariana Found., 1987-88, Pollock-Krasner, 1987-88. Fellow Soc. of Fellows Am. Acad. in Rome; mem. Nat. Acad. Design (life). Democrat. Roman Catholic. Home: 463 West St Apt 228 G New York NY 10014 Office: Univ Mass Fine Arts Ctr Amherst MA 01002

LASCH, ROBERT, former journalist; b. Lincoln, Neb., Mar. 26, 1907; s. Theodore Walter and Myrtle (Nelson) L.; m. Zora Schaupp, Aug. 22, 1931 (dec. 1982); children: Christopher (dec. 1994), Catherine; m. Iris C. Anderson, Sept. 14, 1986. A.B., U. Nebr., 1928; postgrad. (Rhodes scholar), Oxford, 1928-31; Nieman fellow, Harvard, 1941-42. Reporter, state editor, editorial writer Omaha World-Herald, 1931-41; editorial writer, then chief editorial writer Chgo. Sun and Sun-Times, 1942-50; editorial writer St. Louis Post-Dispatch, 1950-57, editor editorial page, 1957-71, ret. Contbr. to: Newsmen's Holiday, 1942; Author: For a Free Press, 1944 (Atlantic Monthly prize), Breaking The Building Blockade, 1946. Recipient; St. Louis Civil Liberties award, 1966; Pulitzer prize for distinguished editorial writing, 1966. Home: 685 S La Posada Cir # 703 Green Valley AZ 85614-5118

LASCHER, ALAN ALFRED, lawyer; b. N.Y.C., Dec. 8, 1941; s. Morris Julius and Sadie Lillian (Chassen) L.; m. C. Amy Weingarten, July 12, 1969; children: David, Lauren, Alexandra, Carlyn. BS, Union Coll., 1963; LLB, Bklyn. Law Sch., 1967. Bar: N.Y. 1967. Assoc. Kramer, Leven et al, N.Y.C., 1969-75; ptnr. real estate dept. Weil, Gotshal & Manges, N.Y.C., 1975—; mem. law com. N.Y. Real Estate Bd., N.Y.C., 1981—. Served to sgt. USAF, 1968-69. Named Real Estate Lawyer of Yr. Am. Lawyer, 1982. Mem. Am. Coll. Real Estate Lawyers (mem. Resolution Trust Corp. and Bankruptcy coms.). Office: Weil Gotshal & Manges 767 5th Ave New York NY 10153

LASCHUK, ROY BOGDAN, lawyer; b. Saskatoon, Sask., Can., Aug. 13, 1932; s. Nicholas and Agatha (Schyhol) L.; m. Tairroyn Riley, Aug. 21, 1964; children: Tonia Jane, Stephen Clare, Graham Christopher. BA, U. Sask., 1953, LLB, 1955. Bar: Sask.; created Queen's counsel 1978. Assoc. firm Balfour, Moss, Milliken, Laschuk & Kyle (and predecessors), Regina, Sask., 1956-61; ptnr. Balfour Moss and predecessor firms, Regina, Sask., 1961-94, of counsel, 1994—; mem. Crown Investment Rev. Commn., vice chmn. 1983-84. Bd. dirs. Regina Housing Authority, 1973—; chmn. 1987-94. Mem. Law Soc. Sask., Can. Bar Assn. (council), Regina Bar Assn. (life, dir. 1975—, v.p. 1977-78, pres. 1978, chmn. health law sect. 1990-93), Canadian Petroleum Assn. (chmn. legal com. Sask. 1972-78), Can. Assn. Occupational Therapists (hon. exec. mem. 1970-75), Royal United Svcs. Inst., Sask. Track and Field Assn. (dir. 1983-85), Assiniboia Club, Rotary (pres. 1967-68). Baptist. Home: 9443 Wascana Mews, Regina, SK Canada S4V 2V6 Office: 700-2103 11th Ave, Regina, SK Canada S4P 4G1

LASH, JAMES WILLIAM (JAY LASH), embryology educator; b. Chgo., Oct. 24, 1929; s. Joseph and Alice (Smith) L.; m. Natalie Novak, Sept. 10, 1954; 1 child, Rebecca. Phd, U. Chgo., 1954; MS (hon.), U. Pa., 1981. Postdoctoral fellow NIH, Phila., 1955-57; sr. rsch. fellow NIH, London, 1986; from asst. prof. to prof. U. Pa., Phila., 1957-95, prof. emeritus, 1995—; Helen Hay Whitney fellow Helen Hay Whitney Found., Phila., 1958-61, Helen Hay Whitney Established Investigator, 1961-66; cons. NSF, Washington, 1967-70; mem. adv. bd., cons. NIH, 1970-83. Co-editor 6 books in field. Fellow Lalor Found., 1957, Paulo Found., 1969, NIH, 1986; recipient rsch. award Wellcome Found., 1960, Lindback award for disting. tchg. Avocations: watercolors, nature, reading, music, birding. Office: RR 2 Box 716 Woodstock VT 05091-9401

LASH, JONATHAN, non-profit environment/development executive; b. N.Y.C., Aug. 12, 1945; s. Joseph P. and Trude W. (Wenzel) L.; m. Eleanor Scattergood, Apr. 27, 1968; children: Elissa, Matthew, Emily. BA, Harvard Coll., 1967; MA in Edn., Cath. U., 1971, JD, 1974. Atty. Natural Resources Def. Coun., Washington, 1978-85; commr. Vt. Dept. Environ. Conservation, Waterbury, 1985-87; sec. Vt. Agy. Natural Resources, Waterbury, 1987-90; dir. Environ. Law Ctr. Vt. Law Sch., South Royalton, 1990-93; pres. World Resources Inst., Washington, 1993—; cons. sci. adv. bd. EPA, Washington, 1989-90, Inst. for Sustainable Cmts., South Royalton, 1991-92; co-chmn. President's Coun. on Sustainable Devel., Washington, 1993—; chmn. Nat. Commn. Superfund; mem. adv. bd. Tata Energy Rsch. Inst.; mem. internat. adv. bd. Keidanren Com. on Nature Conservation; bd. dirs. Keystone Ctr. Co-author: The Synfuels Manual, 1980, A Season of Spoils, 1984. Vol. Peace Corps, Dominican Republic, 1967-70; bd. dirs. Vt. Law Sch., The Putney Sch., Alliance to Save Energy; mem. Earth Coun. Democrat. Mem. Soc. of Friends. Office: World Resources Inst 1709 New York Ave NW Washington DC 20006-5206

LASH, MYLES PERRY, hospital administrator, consultant; b. Detroit, May 31, 1946; s. Irving and Rose (Simkovitz) L.; m. Linda Pauline Borger, June 19, 1968; children: Alissa Beth, David Howard. B.S., Wayne State U., 1968; M.Hosp. Adminstrn., U. Mich., 1970. Asst. to exec. dir. Peoples Community Hosp. Authority, Wayne, Mich., 1970-72; asst. prof. Grad. Program Hosp. Adminstrn., Ohio State U., Columbus, 1970-72; adminstr. Ohio State U. Hosps., Columbus, 1973-79; exec. dir. Med. Coll. Va., Richmond, 1979-85; nat. dir. health care Arthur Young Co., Washington, 1985-86; pres. Lash Group-Health Care Cons., Washington, 1986—. Contbr. articles to profl. jours. Bd. dirs. Univ. Hosp. Consortium, 1980-85, pres., 1985. Mem. U. Mich. Hosp. Adminstrn. Alumni Assn. (pres.), Am. Hosp. Assn., Am. Coll. Hosp. Adminstrs. (Robert S. Hudgens Meml. award 1982). Home: 6708 Bonaventure Ct Bethesda MD 20817-4026 Office: 555 13th St NW Washington DC 20004-1109

LASH, STEPHEN SYCLE, auction company executive; b. Boston, Feb. 10, 1940; s. Samuel George and Carolyn Virginia (Sycle) L.; m. Wendy Lehman, Oct. 29, 1967; children: Abigail Sycle, William Lehman. BA, Yale U., 1962; MBA, Columbia U., 1966. V.p. Bali Footwear, Inc., Marlborough, Mass., 1962-64, 66-68, S.G. Warburg and Co., London, N.Y.C., 1968-76; v.p. Christies, N.Y.C., 1976-80, sr. v.p., 1980-84, exec. v.p., 1984-93, vice chmn., 1993—; also bd. dirs. Christies Internat. PLC. Founder, pres. Ocean Liner Mus., N.Y.C., 1983-88, co-chmn., 1988—; commr. N.Y.C. Landmarks Preservation Commn., 1973-76; bd. dirs. N.Y. Landmarks Conservancy, N.Y.C., 1975—, chmn., 1992-95; bd. dirs. Preservation League N.Y., Albany, 1986—. With USCGR, 1962-67. Pan Am. Union fellow, 1965. Mem. Yale U. Alumni Assn. Metro N.Y. (pres. 1987-90), River Club, Mill Reef Club, Century Assn., Wadawanuck Club (Stonington, Conn.). Home: 151 E 79th St New York NY 10021-0421 Office: Christie Manson & Woods Internat Inc 502 Park Ave New York NY 10022-1108

LASH, TERRY R., federal agency administrator; m. Elizabeth M. Vogt; children: Benjamin, Lara. BA in Physics, Reed Coll., Portland, Oreg.; MPh in Molecular Biophysics, Yale U., PhD. With numerous pub. interest orgns., 1972-84; dir. Ill. Dept. Nuclear Safety, 1984-90; spl. asst. to sec. of energy U.S. Dept. Energy; dir. office nuclear energy, sci. and tech. U.S. Dept. Energy, Washington, 1994—; cons. in field. Office: US Dept Energy Office Pub Affairs Washington DC 20585

LASHBROOKE, ELVIN CARROLL, JR., law educator, consultant; b. Dec. 14, 1939; s. Elvin Carroll Sr. and Lois Lenora (Weger) L.; m. Margaret Ann Jones, Dec. 19, 1964; children: Michelle Ann, David C. BA, U. Tex., 1967, MA, 1968, JD, 1972, LLM, 1977; PhD, Mich. State U., 1993. Bar: Tex. 1972, Fla. 1973. Legis. counsel Tex. Legis. Coun., Austin, 1972-75; pvt. practice law Austin, 1975-77; asst. prof. coll. of law DePaul U., Chgo., 1977-79, Stetson U., St. Petersburg, Fla., 1979-80; assoc. prof. sch. law Notre Dame, Ind., 1981-85; prof., chmn. bus. law dept. Mich. State U., East Lansing, 1985-95, assoc. dean adminstrn. Eli Broad Coll. Bus., 1993—; pvt. practice cons. East Lansing, 1986—; instr. St. Edward's U., Austin, 1975-76. Author: Tax Exempt Organizations, 1985, The Legal Handbook of Business Transactions, 1987; contbr. articles to profl. jours. Mem. ABA, Tex. Bar Assn., Fla. Bar Assn. Avocation: computers. Home: 6435 Island Lake Dr East Lansing MI 48823-9735 Office: Mich State U Office of Dean Eli Broad Coll Bus East Lansing MI 48824-1122

LASHELLE, CHARLES STANTON, lawyer, insurance company executive; b. Colorado Springs, Colo., June 25, 1947; s. Stanton Duane and Glenna (Bloom) LaS.; m. Pamela Montross, Aug. 24, 1968; children: Rebecca, Karen. BA, U. No. Colo., 1969; JD, Creighton U., 1972. Bar: Nebr. 1972, U.S. Dist. Ct. Nebr. 1972, U.S. Tax Ct. 1980, U.S Ct. Appeals (8th cir.) 1980, U.S. Supreme Ct. 1980; CLU. Mktg. rep. Teton Nat. Life Ins. Co., Greeley, Colo., 1968-69; v.p., asst. gen. counsel Mut. Protective & Medico Life, Omaha, 1973-83; sr. v.p. adminstrn. Am. Founders Life Ins. Co., Austin, Tex., 1983-87; exec. v.p. adminstrn. Nat. Western Life Ins. Co., Austin, 1987-92; pres., CEO Tex. Life and Health Ins. Guaranty Assn., Austin, 1992—; pres. Comml. Adjusters Inc., Austin, 1988-92. Bd. dirs. Variety Club, Omaha, 1983, Nat. Orgn. Life & Health Guaranty Assns., 1993—, chair confederation life task force, 1994—; vice chmn. Mayor's Task Force on Drugs and Drug Abuse, 1990-91. Capt. USAR, 1972-76. Mem. ABA, Nebr. Bar Assn., Am. Soc. CLUs, Am. Coun. Life Ins., Greater Austin C. of C. (legis. com.), Sertoma Club (Round Rock, Tex.). Republican. Methodist. Avocations: golf, reading. Home: 1821 Possum Trot St Round Rock TX 78681-1710

LASHER, ESTHER LU, minister; b. Denver, June 1, 1923; d. Lindley Aubrey and Irma Jane (Rust) Pim; m. Donald T. Lasher, Apr. 9, 1950 (dec. Mar. 1982); children: Patricia Sue Becker, Donald T., Keith Alan, Jennifer Luanne Oliver. Assoc. Fine Arts, Colo. Women's Coll., 1943; BA, Denver U., 1945; MA Religious Edn., Ea. Bapt. Sem., 1948; MA, Denver U., 1967. Ordained to ministry Bapt. Ch., 1988. Christian edn. dir. 1st Bapt., Evansville, Ind., 1948-52; min. Perrysburg Bapt. Ch., Macy, Ind., 1988-95; min.-at-large Am. Baptist Conv./USA, 1996—; libr. Peru (Ind.) Pub. Schs., 1990-91; sec. Ind. Ministerial Coun., Indpls., 1990-92; chairperson Women in Ministry, Indpls., 1988-93; chmn. Fellowship Mission Circle, Rochester, Ind., 1988-93; mem. Partnership in Ministry, Indpls., 1990-94; bd. mrs. Am. Bapts./Ind., 1991-93; asst. dir. Greenwood Pub. Library, 1978-84; dir. Fulton County Pub. Library, 1984-90. Pres. Toastmasters, Rochester, 1984-90, 95, edn. v.p., 1992-93; asst. dir. Greenwood Pub. Libr., 1977-85; dir. Fulton County Pub. Libr., 1985-90; bd. dirs. Manitau Tng. Ctr., Rochester, 1988-90; v.p. Mental Health Ctr., Rochester, 1987-90; founder Fulton County Literacy Coalition, Rochester, 1989-90; tutor/trainer Peru Literacy Coalition of Peru Pub. Libr., 1994-95; sec. Northwest Area ABC/IN, 1994-95; sec.-treas. North Miami County Mins. Fellowship, 1993-95; bd. dirs. Peru Civic Ctr., 1995; active CASA Lincoln County, 1995—; chair Christian Edn. Bd., 1995—. Named Outstanding Libr., Biog. Inst., 1989. Mem. Leadership Acad. (bd. dir., sec.), Bus. and Profl. Women (pres. Greenwood, Ind. chpt. 1984-86), Rochester Women's Club (pres. 1989-92), Fulton County Mins. Assn. (treas. 1993-95), Logansport Assn. Bapt. Women, Peru

Lit. Club (v.p.-elect 1995), Christian Women's Club (hostess chair 1995—), CASA Miami County, Rotary, Sigma Alpha Iota (adv.), Christian Edn. (chmn. 1996—). Republican. Home and Office: HC 64 Box 768 South Bristol ME 04568 *Wisdom is a powerful tool, without knowledge, it can entice or terrify an individual, all depending on how it is used with much forethought.*

LASHLEY, CURTIS DALE, lawyer; b. Urbana, Ill., Nov. 3, 1956; s. Jack Dale and Janice Elaine (Holman) L.; m. Tamara Dawn Yahnig, June 14, 1986. BA, U. Mo., Kansas City, 1978, JD, 1981. Bar: Mo. 1981, U.S. Dist. Ct. (we. dist.) Mo. 1981, U.S. Tax Ct. 1982, U.S. Ct. Appeals (8th cir.) 1992. Assoc. Melvin Heller, Inc., Creve Coeur, Mo., 1982; ptnr. Domjan & Lashley, Harrisonville, Mo., 1983-86; asst. gen. counsel Mo. Dept. Revenue, Independence, 1986-89, assoc. gen. counsel, 1989-92, sr. counsel, 1992—, adminstrv. hearing officer, 1995—; spl asst. atty. gen., 1986—; spl. asst. prosecutor Jackson County, Mo., 1990—; city atty., Adrian and Strasburg, Mo., 1985-86. V.p. Cass County Young Reps., Harrisonville, 1985. Mem. ABA, Kiwanis (treas. Harrisonville chpt. 1985-86, Harrisonville Disting. Svc. award 1985), NRA, Phi Alpha Delta. Republican. Presbyterian. Office: Mo Dept Revenue 16647 E 23rd St S Independence MO 64055-1922

LASHLEY, LENORE CLARISSE, lawyer; b. N.Y.C., June 3, 1934; d. Leonard Livingston and Una Ophelia (Laurie) L.; children: Donna Bee-Gates, Michele Bee, Maria Bee. BA, CUNY, 1956; MSW, U. Calif., Berkeley, 1970, MPH, 1975; JD, U. Calif., San Francisco, 1981. Bar: Calif. 1981. Atty. W.O.M.A.N., Inc., San Francisco, 1982-84; pvt. practice San Francisco Law Office, 1984-87; dep. dist. atty. Monterey Dist. Atty., Salinas, Calif., 1987-89; trial atty. State Bar of Calif., L.A., 1989; dep. dist. atty. L.A. Dist. Atty., 1989; city atty., dep. City Atty. L.A., 1989—; chair, bd. dirs. St. Anthony's Dining Room, San Francisco, 1986-87; sec., bd. dirs. NAAC, Monterey, 1987-88; bd. dirs. Childrens Home Soc., Oakland, Calif., 1966-68. Recipient Cert. of Merit, Nat. Assn. Naval Officers, 1987. Mem. NAACP, L.A. County Bar Assn. (del. to state bar 1992, 93). Roman Catholic. Avocations: running, reading, animal welfare. Office: City Atty LA 200 N Main St 1700 CHE Los Angeles CA 90065

LASHLEY, VIRGINIA STEPHENSON HUGHES, retired computer science educator; b. Wichita, Kans., Nov. 12, 1924; d. Herman H. and Edith M. (Wayland) Stephenson; m. Kenneth W. Hughes, June 4, 1946 (dec.); children: Kenneth W. Jr., Linda Hughes Tindall; m. Richard H. Lashley, Aug. 19, 1954; children: Robert H., Lisa Lashley Van Amberg, Diane Lashley Tan. BA, U. Kans., 1945; MA, Occidental Coll., 1966; PhD, U. So. Calif., 1983. Cert. info. processor, tchr. secondary and community coll., Calif. Tchr. math. La Canada (Calif.) High Sch., 1966-69; from instr. to prof. Glendale (Calif.) Coll., 1970—, chmn. bus. div., 1977-81, coord. instructional computing, 1974-92, prof. emeritus, 1992—; sec., treas., dir. Victory Montessori Schs., Inc., Pasadena, Calif., 1980—; pres. The Computer Sch., Pasadena, 1983-92; pres. San Gabriel Valley Data Processing Mgmt. Assn., 1977-79, San Gabriel Valley Assn. for Systems Mgmt., 1979-80; chmn. Western Ednl. Computing Conf., 1980, 84. Editor Jour. Calif. Ednl. Computing, 1980. Mem. DAR. NSF grantee, 1967-69, EDUCARE scholar U. So. Calif., 1980-82; John Randolph and Dora Haynes fellow, Occidental Coll., 1964-66; student computer ctr. renamed Dr. Virginia S. Lashley Ctr., 1992. Mem. AAUP, AAUW, DAR, Calif. Edn. Computing Consortium (bd. dirs. 1979—, v.p. 1983-84, pres. 1985-87), Orgn. Am. Historians, San Marino Women's Club, Colonial Dames, XVII Century, Phi Beta Kappa, Pi Mu Epsilon, Phi Alpha Theta, Phi Delta Kappa, Delta Phi Upsilon, Gamma Phi Beta. Republican. Congregationalist. Home: 1240 S San Marino Ave San Marino CA 91108-1227

LASHMAN, SHELLEY BORTIN, judge; b. Camden, N.J., Aug. 18, 1917; s. William Mitchell and Anna (Bortin) L.; m. Ruth Horn, Jan. 3, 1959; children—Karen E. Lashman Hall, Gail A. McBride; children: Mitchell A., Christopher R. B.S., William and Mary Coll., 1938; postgrad. Columbia U., 1938, 39; J.D., U. Mich., 1946. Bar: N.Y. 1947, N.J. 1968. Judge N.J. Workers Compensation, 1981—. With USNR, 1940-70. Mem. Atlantic County Bar Assn., Am. Judges Assn., Atlantic County Hist. Soc., Am. Judicature Soc., Ret. Officers Assn., U.S. Navy League, Fleet Res. Assn., USS Yorktown Club, Mil. Order World Wars, Atlantic City Country Club, Greater Atlantic City Yacht Club. Republican. Home: 1209 Old Zion Rd Egg Harbor Township NJ 08234-7667 Office: Workers Compensation Ct 518 Market St Camden NJ 08102

LASHOF, JOYCE C., public health educator; b. Phila.; d. Harry and Rose (Brodsky) Cohen; m. Richard K. Lashof, June 11, 1950; children: Judith, Carol, Dan. AB, Duke U., 1946; MD, Women's Med. Coll., 1950; DSc (hon.), Med. Coll. Pa., 1983. Dir. Ill. State Dept. Pub. Health, 1973-77; dep. asst. sec. for health programs and population affairs Dept. Health, Edn., and Welfare, Washington, 1977-78; sr. scholar in residence IOM, Washington, 1978; asst. dir. office of tech. assessment U.S. Congress, Washington, 1978-81; dean sch. pub. health U. Calif., Berkeley, 1981-91, prof. pub. health Sch. Pub. Health, 1981-94, prof. emerita, 1994—; co-chair Commn. on Am. after Roe vs. Wade, 1991-92; mem. Sec.'s Coun. Health Promotion and Disease Prevention, 1988-91; pres. APHA, 1992; chair Pres.'s Adv. Com. on Gulf War Vets. Illnesses, 1995-96. Mem. editorial bd. Wellness Letter, 1983—; mem. editorial com. Ann. Rev. of Pub. Health, 1987-90. Recipient Alumni Achievement award Med. Coll. Pa., 1975, Sedgewick Meml. medal APHA, 1995. Mem. editl. bd. Wellness Letter, 1983—, editl. com. Ann. Rev. of Pub. Health, 1987-90. Avocation: hiking. Home: 601 Euclid Ave Berkeley CA 94708-1331 Office: U Calif-Berkeley Sch Pub Health 19 Earl Warren Hall Berkeley CA 94720

LASHUTKA, GREGORY S., mayor, lawyer; b. N.Y.C., 1944; m. Catherine Adams; children: Stephanie, Michael, Nicholas, Lara. BS, Ohio State U., 1967; JD, Capitol U., 1974. Bar: Ohio, 1974, Fla., D.C., 1975. Former ptnr. Squire, Sanders & Dempsey, Columbus, Ohio; elected mayor City of Columbus, 1991—; former Columbus City Atty. Past chmn. Columbus-Area Sports Devel. Corp.; 1st v.p. Nat. League of Cities; comentator of the Ohio State U. Football Color, 1983-90; active civic and charitable orgns. including Charity Newsies Assocs., Nat. Football Found., Ohio State U. Varsity "O". Served to lt., USN. Named Mcpl. Leader of the Yr., Am. City and County mag., 1993. Office: Office of the Mayor City Hall Room 247 90 W Broad St Columbus OH 43215-9000*

LASICH, VIVIAN ESTHER LAYNE, secondary education educator; b. Hopewell Twp., Pa., Dec. 17, 1935; d. Charles McClung and Harriette Law (George) Layne; m. William G. Lasich, Apr. 10, 1958; children: C. Laurence, Celeste M., Michelle R. AB, Geneva Coll., 1956; MA in Edn., No. Mich. U., 1970, postgrad. Secondary tchr. Freedom (Pa.) High Sch., 1956-57; elem. educator Gilbert Elem. Sch., Gwinn, Mich., 1967-69; lang. arts educator Gwinn Mid. Sch., 1970—; adv. bd. comty. arts panel Coun. for Arts, Mich., 1979-81; at-large rep. U. Peninsula adv. panel Mich. Dept. Edn./Arts, 1976-79; mem. sch. improvement team, 1988-91, 93-94, mid. sch. concept team, 1992—, co-chair, 1995—, mid. sch. at-risk coord. dist. curriculum coordinating coun., 1995-96; dist. curriculum strategy action team, 1993-94; dist. profl. devel. strategy action team, 1993-94; mem. sounding bd. Mid. Sch., 1994—, dist. sch. improvement team, 1994—; rep. Gwinn Edn. Assn. Mid. Sch., 1995—. Author: Prophets Without Honor: Teachers, Students, & Trust, 1991. V.p. Marquette (Mich.) Community Theatre, 1962-63 bd. dirs. 1963-74, mem. 1961-92; pres. Marquette Arts Coun. 1973-74, v.p. 1972-73, bd. dirs. 1970-78, mem. 1970-84; pres. Upper Peninsula Arts Coordinating Bd. 1976-78, v.p. 1974-76, bd. dirs. 1978-84; bd. dirs. Mich. Community Theatre Assn. 1972-73; bd. dirs. Mich Community Arts Agys., 1976-79. Recipient Committment to Excellence award Marquette Community Theatre, 1965. Devotion to Arts Development award Upper Peninsula (Mich.) Arts Coord. Bd. 1979. Mem. ASCD, NEA, AAUW, Mich. Edn. Assn., Phi Delta Kappa. Presbyterian. Avocations: rsch., writing, theatrical direction and performance, vocal music. Home: 508 Pine St Marquette MI 49855-3838 Office: Gwinn Area Community Schs Gwinn MI 49841

LASKAWY, PHILIP A., accounting and management consulting firm executive; b. 1941. With S. D. Leidesdorf & Co., 1961-78, ptnr., 1971-78; ptnr. Ernst & Whinney (acquired S. D. Leidesdorf 1978), 1978-85, vice chmn., mng. ptnr. N.Y. region, 1983-93; chmn., CEO Ernst & Young (merger of Ernst & Whinney and Arthur Young 1993), 1993—, also bd. dirs. Office: Ernst & Young 277 Park Ave New York NY 10172-0099*

LASKER, DAVID RAYMOND, newspaper editor, musician; b. N.Y.C., Apr. 21, 1950; arrived in Can., 1974; s. Joseph Leon and Mildred (Jaspen) L. BA in History of Art cum laude, Yale U., 1972, MMus, 1974. Double-bassist Winnipeg (Man., Can.) Symphony Orch., 1974-84; freelance archtl. journalist, Toronto, Ont., Can., 1984-89; editor Contract mag., Toronto, 1989-91; editor fashion and design The Globe and Mail, Toronto, 1991—; prin. double-bassist North York Symphony Orch. Author: (children's book) The Boy Who Loved Music, 1979 (ALA Notable Book award). Avocations: collecting classical vinyl records, high-end audio, bodybuilding. Home: 533 Logan Ave, Toronto, ON Canada M4K 3B3 Office: The Globe and Mail, 444 Front St W, Toronto, ON Canada M5V 2S9

LASKER, GABRIEL WARD, anthropologist, educator; b. York, Eng., Apr. 29, 1912; s. Bruno and Margaret Naomi (Ward) L.; m. Bernice Kaplan, July 31, 1949; children: Robert Alexander, Edward Meyer, Ann Titania. Student, U. Wis., 1928-30; A.B., U. Mich., 1934; A.M., Harvard U., 1940, Ph.D., 1945. Instr. English Chiao T'ung U., Peking, China, 1936-37; teaching fellow in anatomy Harvard Med. Sch., 1941-42; mem. faculty dept. anatomy Wayne State U. Sch. Medicine, Detroit, 1946—, asst. prof., 1947-55; assoc. prof., 1955-64; prof. Wayne U. Sch. Medicine, 1964-82, prof. emeritus, 1982—; fellow commoner Churchill Coll. Cambridge U., 1983-84; conducted Wayne U.-Viking Fund field trip to Mexico to study effects of migration on phys. characteristics of Mexicans, 1948. Author: Physical Anthropology, The Evolution of Man, Surnames and Genetic Structure; editor: Yearbook of Phys. Anthropology, 1945-51, Human Biology, 1953-87, Research Strategies in Human Biology: Field and Survey Studies, 1993; contbr. articles to profl. jours. Fellow Am. Anthrop. Assn., AAAS (v.p. 1968); mem. Am. Assn. Phys. Anthropologists (sec.-treas. 1947-51, v.p. 1960-62, pres. 1963-65, Charles Darwin award 1993), Am. Assn. Anatomists, Human Biology Council (pres. 1982-84), Soc. Study Human Biology (U.K.), Asociación Mexicana de Antropología Biológica, Sigma Xi. Office: 540 E Canfield St Detroit MI 48201-1998

LASKER, JONATHAN LEWIS, artist; b. Jersey City, July 30, 1948; s. Lester and Henrietta Selma (Gross) L. Student, Sch. Visual Arts, N.Y.C., 1975-77, Calif. Inst. Arts, 1977. One-man exhbns. include Landmark Gallery, N.Y., Gunnar Kaldewey, Dusseldorf, Fed. Republic Germany, 1981, Annette Gmeiner, Kirchzarten, Fed. Republic Germany, 1984, Tibor de Nagy, N.Y.C., 1984, 86, Michael Werner, Cologne, Fed. Republic Germany, 1986, 87, 90, Massimo Audiello, N.Y.C., 1986, 88, 89, Anders Tornberg, Lund, Sweden, 1987, 90, Gian Enzo Sperone, Rome, 1988, 91, Sperone Westwater Gallery, N.Y.C., 1991, 93, 95, Lars Bohman, Stockholm, 1991, 94, Inst. Contemporary ArtU. Pa., Phila., 1992, Thaddaeus Ropac Gallery, Paris, 1992, Witte de With Ctr. Contemporary Art, Rotterdam, 1993, Rhona Hoffman Gallery, Chgo., 1993, Soledad Lorenzo, Madrid, 1995, L.A. Louver Gallery, 1995, numerous others; selected group exhbns. include Mus. Ludwig, Cologne, Wacoal Art Ctr., Tokyo, 1985, Rose Art Mus. Brandeis U., Waltham, Mass., 1986, Corcoran Gallery Art, Washington, 1987, Aldrich Mus. Contemporary Art, Ridgefield, Conn., 1987, Roos Mus., Malmo, Sweden, U. N. Tex., Denton, J.B. Speed Mus., Louisville, Alta. Coll. Art., Edmonton, Can., Contemporary Arts Ctr., Cin., Santa Fe Community Coll., Gainesville, Fla., Met. Mus. Art, N.Y.C., 1988, Stedelijk Mus., Amsterdam, The Netherlands, 1989, Marc Richards Gallery, L.A., Scott Hansen Gallery, N.Y.C., 1990, Pace Gallery, N.Y.C., 1990, Sperone Westwater Gallery, N.Y.C., 1991, 94, Gallery Modern Art, Bologna, Italy, 1991, Hirshhorn Mus. and Sculpture Garden, Washington, 1991, Mus. Contemporary Art of Dayton Art Inst., 1992, Documenta IX, Kassell, Germany, Gallerie Nächst Sankt Stefan, Vienna, 1992, Thaddaeus Ropac, Paris, 1992, Ruth Bloom Gallery, L.A., 1993, Hayward Gallery, London, 1994, Ctr. for the Fine Arts, Miami, 1994, Va. Mus. Fine Arts, Richmond, 1995, Mus. Contemporary Art, Helsinki, Folkwang Mus., Essen, Germany, 1995, numerous others; in pub. collections Corcoran Gallery, Hirshhorn Mus. and Sculpture Garden, Washington, Mus. Ludwig, Cologne, Wacoal Art Ctr., Tokyo, Whitney Mus. Am. Art, N.Y.C., Moderna Museet, Stockholm, Fond Nat. d'Art Contempor Ain, Paris, High Mus., Atlanta, Museo De Arte Contemporaneo, Seville, Spain, La Fundacion Caja De Pensiones, Madrid; critiqued numerous art books, catalogs, mags. including Beyond Boundaries: New York's New Art (Jerry Saltz), N.Y. Art Now, The Saatchi Collection (Dan Cameron), The Silent Baroque (Christian Leigh editor), Interpreting Contemporary Art (Rainer Crone and David Moos), Art at the End of the Social (Collins and Milazzo), Art Since Mid-Century: 1945 to the Present (Daniel Wheeler), Art News (Feb. 1990, Apr. 1992), Le Monde (June 1992). NEA fellow, 1987, 89. Office: care Sperone Westwater Gallery 142 Greene St New York NY 10012-3236

LASKER, MORRIS E., judge; Fed. judge, U.S. Dist. Ct. (so. dist.) N.Y.; fed. judge, U.S. Dist. Ct., Boston, Mass., 1994—. Office: US Dist Ct 90 Devonshire St Boston MA 02109

LASKEY, RICHARD ANTHONY, biomedical device executive; b. N.Y.C., Oct. 24, 1936; s. Charles Lewis and Gertrude Ann (Stolzenthaler) L.; m. Frances M. Pollack, June 29, 1975; children: Victoria Ann, Deborah Lea. Student CCNY; BS in Chemistry, Ohio, MS in Organic Chemistry; PhD in Organic Chemistry, Sussex (Eng.) U., 1970; LLB, U. Chgo., 1972; MD (hon.), Med. Coll. S.A., 1975, fellow, Psychiatry 1976; postgrad. in ob-gyn, U. Pa., 1989-94. Diplomate Am. Bd. Examiners in Psychotherapy. Head sec. med. products, lab. mgr. Hydron Labs., North Brunswick, N.J., 1967-73; v.p. biomed. rsch. Datascope Corp., Paramus, N.J., 1973-82; pres. rsch. Millbrook Labs., Inc., Rochelle Park, N.J., 1982—; cons. in field. Recipient Doctor's award Chgo. Med. Coll., 1975; fellow Am. Acad. Behavioral Sci., 1976. Fellow Am. Inst. Chemist; mem. NRA, AAAS, Md. Med. Soc., Idaho Med. Soc., Nat. Med. Soc., Internat. Coll. Physicians and Surgeons, Am. Inst. Chemist, Am. Psychotherapy Assn., Nat. Psychol. Assn., Assn. Advancement Med. Instrumentation, Soc. Rsch. Adminstrs. Biomed. inventor, patentee. Home: PO Box 133 Washington NJ 07882-0133 Office: PO Box 125 Rochelle Park NJ 07662-0125

LASKIN, BARBARA VIRGINIA, legal association administrator; b. Chgo., July 2, 1939; d. Cyril Krieps and Gertrude Katherine (Kujawa) Szymanski; children: Dawn Katherine Doherty, Amy Lynn Anderson. BA, U. Ill., Chgo., 1967; MA, Am. U. Beirut, 1978, Georgetown U., 1985. Asst. buyer Carson, Pirie, Scott & Co., Chgo., 1967-69; fgn. svc. officer Dept. State, Washington, 1969-79; mgr. gift shops Marriott Hotels, Washington, 1979-81; office mgr. Robt Schwinn & Assoc., Bethesda, Md., 1983-85; exec. dir. Internat. Acad. Trial Lawyers, San Jose, Calif., 1985—. Fellow Rotary Club San Jose; mem. AAUW (v.p. 1987), Am. Soc. Assn. Execs., Meeting Planners Internat., Internat. Spl. Events Soc. (v.p. edn. 1995), Internat. Spl. Events Found. (dir.), Profl. Conservation Mgrs. Assn. Roman Catholic. Office: Internat Acad Trial Lawyers 4 N 2nd St Ste 175 San Jose CA 95113-1306

LASKIN, DANIEL M., oral and maxillofacial surgeon, educator; b. Ellenville, N.Y., Sept. 3, 1924; s. Nathan and Flora (Kaplan) L.; m. Eve Pauline Mohel, Aug. 25, 1945; children: Jeffrey, Gary, Marla. Student, NYU, 1941-42; BS, Ind. U., 1947; MS, U. Ill., 1951. Diplomate Am. Bd. Oral and Maxillofacial Surgery. Mem. faculty U. Ill., Chgo., 1949-84; prof. dept. oral and maxillofacial surgery U. Ill., 1960-84, head dept., 1973-84, clin. prof. surgery, 1961-84, dir. temporomandibular joint and facial pain research center, 1963-84; prof., chmn. dept. oral and maxillofacial surgery Med. Coll. Va., 1984—; dir. temporomandibular joint and facial pain rsch. ctr. MCV, 1984—; head dept. dentistry MCV Hosp., Richmond, 1986—; former attending oral surgeon Edgewater, Swedish Covenant, Ill. Masonic, Skokie Valley Community hosps., all Chgo.; former chmn. dept. oral surgery Cook County Hosp., Chgo.; cons. oral surgery to Surgeon Gen. Navy, 1977—; dental products panel FDA, 1988-92, cons., 1993—; Francis J. Reichmann Lectr., 1971, Cordwainer lectr., London, 1980. Author: Oral and Maxillofacial Surgery, Vol. I, 1980, Vol. II, 1985; contbr. articles to profl. jours.; editor-in-chief: Jour. Oral and Maxillofacial Surgery, 1972—; mem. editorial bd. Internat. Jour. Oral and Maxillofacial Surgery, 1978-88, Topics in Pain Mgmt., Densat, Internat. Jour. Oral and Maxillofacial Implants, Quintessence Internat., Revista Latino America Cirugia Traumatologia Maxilofacial, Virginia Dental Jour., Jour. Dental Rsch.; mem. internat. editorial bd. Headache Quar. Nat. hon. chmn. peer campaign A.A.O.M.S. Edn. and Rsch. Found., 1990. Recipient Disting. Alumni Svc. award Ind. U., 1975, William J. Gies editl. award hon. mention, 1975-77, 80, 88, 90, 91, 93, 95, 1st prize, 1978-79, 84, 87, 89, 92, Simon P. Hullihen Meml. award, 1976, Arnold K. Maislen Meml. award, 1977, Thomas P. Hinman medallion, 1980, W. Harry Archer Achievement award for rsch., 1981, Heidbrink award, 1983, Disting. Alumnus award Ind. U. Sch. Dentistry, 1984, Rene Lefort medal, 1985, Semmelweis medallion Semmelweis Med. U., 1985, Golden Scroll award Internat. Coll. Dentists, 1986, Internat. award Friends Sch. Dental Medicine, U. Conn. Health Ctr., Donald B. Osborn award, 1991, Achievement medal Alpha Omega, 1992, Norton M. Ross Excellence in Clin. Rsch. award, 1993, Va. Commonwealth U. Faculty award of Excellence, 1994; named Zendium Lectr., 1989, Edward C. Hinds Lectr., 1990, Disting. Practitioner Nat. Acads. Practice, 1992, Hon. Diplomate, Am. Soc. Osseointegration (hon.), 1992; fellow in gen. anesthesia Am. Dental Soc. Anesthesiology, fellow in dental surgery Royal Coll. Surgeons Eng. Fellow AAAS, Am. Coll. Dentists, Internat. Coll. Dentists, Am. Acad. Implant Prosthodontists (academia), Acad. Internat. Dental Studies (hon.), Glasgow Royal Coll. of Physicians (hon.), Internat. Assn. Oral and Maxillofacial Surgeons (hon., exec. com. 1980—, pres. 1983-86, sec. gen. 1989-95, exec. dir. 1995—); mem. Ill. Splty. Bd. Oral Surgery, ADA (adv. com. advanced edn. in oral surgery 1968-75, cons. Council on Dental Edn. 1968-82, mem. Commn. on Accreditation 1975-76), Am. Assn. Oral and Maxillofacial Surgeons (editor Forum 1965-95—, disting. service award 1972, pres. 1976-77, research recognition award 1978, William J. Gies award 1979, dedication 73d ann. meeting and sci. sessions 1991; editor AAOMS, 1996—), Internat. Assn. Dental Research, , Am. Dental Soc. Anesthesiology (pres. 1976-78), Am. Soc. Exptl. Pathology, Am. Assn. Dental Editors, Royal Soc. Medicine, Brazilian Coll. Oral and Maxillofacial Surgery and Traumatology (hon.), Chilean Soc. Oral and Maxillofacial Surgery (hon.), Hellenic Assn. Oral Surgery (hon.), Sadi Fontaine Acad. (hon.), Internat. Congress Oral Implantologists (hon.), Soc. Maxillofacial and Oral Surgeons South Africa (hon., assoc. life), Am. Dental Bd. Anesthesiology (pres. 1983-92), Nat. Chronic Pain Outreach Assn. (adv. bd.), Japanese Soc. for Temporomandibular Joint (hon.), Am. Soc. Laentistry (hon. life), Internat. Study Group for the Advancement of TMJ Arthroscopy (hon.), William F. Harrigan Soc., Odontographic Soc., Can. Assn. Oral and Maxillofacial Surgeons (hon.), Hungarian Dental Assn. (hon.), Sigma Xi, Omicron Kappa Upsilon. Rsch. and publs. on connective tissue physiology and pathology, particularly cartilage and bone metabolism, craniofacial growth, oral maxillofacial surgery, and pathology of temporomandibular joint. Office: Med Coll Va Dept Oral/Maxillofac Surg PO Box 980566 Richmond VA 23298-0566

LASKIN, LEE B., lawyer, state senator; b. Atlantic City, June 30, 1936; student Am. U., Temple U.; Rutgers U., 1960; m. Andrea Solomon; 1 dau., Shari. Bar: N.J.; asst. atty. City of Camden (N.J.), from 1962; asst. U.S. atty. N.J., 1964-68; mem. N.J. Gen. Assembly, 1968-70; mem. Camden County Bd. Chosen Freeholders, 1970-73; mem. N.J. Senate, 1977-92; judge N.J. Superior Ct., 1994—; mcpl. atty. Audubon, Berlin Borough, Berlin Twp., Clementon, Laurel Springs, Mt. Ephraim and Waterford, N.J., and Winslow Twp.; counsel Bellmawr Bd. Edn., Berlin Zoning Bd., Camden County Welfare Bd., Non-Resident Taxpayers Assn., Animal Welfare Assn., Brith Sholom Fed. Credit Union, Camden Hebrew Fed. Credit Union, Union Fed. Savs. and Loan Assn., Div. 880 Amalgamated Transit Union, Local 18 of Am. Fed. Tech. Engrs., Camden Fire Officers Assn., Am. Postal Workers Union, Fuel Mchts. Assn., Glendale Nat. Bank; field counsel Fed. Nat. Mortgage Assn.; founder, 1st chmn. Glendale Nat. Bank; del. Rep. Nat. Conv., 1984. Served with USMCR. Office: NJ State Senate 1878 Route 70 E Cherry Hill NJ 08003-2090

LASKO, WARREN ANTHONY, mortgage banker, economist; b. Bklyn., June 29, 1940; s. Albert Anthony and Mildred (Hoyer) L.; m. Lorraine Gevertz; children: Karen, Erika. AB in Econs., Columbia U., 1962, MA in Econs., 1969. V.p. mortgage backed securities Govt. Nat. Mortgage Assn., Washington, 1977-81, 81-82, exec. v.p., 1982-85; v.p. strategic planning Fed. Nat. Mortgage Assn., Washington, 1981; exec. v.p. Mortgage Bankers Assn. Am., Washington, 1985—. Bd. dirs. Boys & Girls Homes Montgomery County, Chevy Chase, Md.; mem. Greater Washington Research Ctr., Washington, Chesapeake Bay Found., The Nature Conservancy, Chevy Chase. Recipient Cert. of Merit, U.S. Dept. Housing and Urban Devel., 1979, Disting. Svc. award U.S. Govt., 1982. Mem. Columbia Club. Home: 3211 Leland St Bethesda MD 20815-4009 Office: Mortgage Bankers Assn of Am 1125 15th St NW Washington DC 20005-2707

LASKOWSKI, EDWARD JOHN, chemist; b. Milw., Dec. 24, 1950; s. Ervin Joseph and Florence Margaret Laskowski; m. Mary Ann Rizzo, July 16, 1988. BS with honors in Chemistry, U. Wis., 1972; PhD in Inorganic Chemistry, U. Ill., 1976. Postdoctoral rsch. asst. Stanford U., Palo Alto, Calif., 1976-78; mem. tech. staff AT&T Bell Labs., Murray Hill, N.J., 1978—. Contbr. articles to profl. jours. Mem. Environ. Def. Fund, 1990-95, Humane Soc. U.S., 1990-95; leader Boy Scouts Am., 1981-88. Mem. Am. Chem. Soc., Alpha Chi Sigma. Roman Catholic. Achievements include patents relating to etching of compound semiconductors, patent for fabrication of an electro-optic sampling probe. Avocations: golf, nature study, minerology, gardening, wildlife protection. Office: AT&T Bell Labs 600 Mountain Ave New Providence NJ 07974-2008

LASKOWSKI, LEONARD FRANCIS, JR., microbiologist; b. Milw., Nov. 16, 1919; s. Leonard Francis and Frances (Cyborowski) L.; m. Frances Bielinski, June 1, 1946; children—Leonard Francis III, James, Thomas. B.S., Marquette U., 1941, M.S., 1948; Ph.D., St. Louis U., 1951. Diplomate: Am. Bd. Microbiology. Instr. bacteriology Marquette U., 1946-48; mem. faculty St. Louis U., 1951—, prof. pathology and internal medicine, Div. Infectious Diseases, 1969-90, prof. emeritus, 1990—, assoc. prof. internal medicine, 1977-90—; dir. clin. microbiology sect. St. Louis U. Hosps. Labs., 1965—; cons. clin microbiology Firmin Desloge Hosp., St. Louis U. Group Hosps., St. Marys Group Hosps.; cons. bacteriology VA Hosp.; asst. dept. chief Pub. Health Lab., St. Louis Civil Def., 1958—; cons. St. Elizabeths Hosp., St. Louis County Hosp., St. Francis Hosp. Contbr. articles to profl. jours. Health and tech. tng. coordinator for Latin Am. projects Peace Corps, 1962-66. Served with M.C. AUS, 1942-46. Fellow Am. Acad. Microbiology; mem. Soc. Am. Bacteriologists, N.Y. Acad. Scis., Am., Mo. pub. health assns., AAUP, Med. Mycol. Soc. Am., Alpha Omega Alpha. Home: 6229 Robertsville Rd Villa Ridge MO 63089-2617 Office: 1402 S Grand Blvd Saint Louis MO 63104-1004

LASKOWSKI, MICHAEL, JR., chemist, educator; b. Warsaw, Poland, Mar. 13, 1930; came to U.S., 1947, naturalized, 1955; s. Michael and Maria (Dabrowska) L.; m. Joan Claire Heyer, Nov. 29, 1957; children: Michael Christopher, Marta Joan. B.S. magna cum laude, Lawrence Coll., 1950; Ph.D. (NIH fellow), Cornell U., 1954, postgrad., 1954-55; postgrad., Yale U., 1955-56. Research asst. Marquette U., 1949-50; instr. Cornell U., 1956-57; asst. prof. chemistry Purdue U., 1957-61, asso. prof., 1961-65, prof., 1965—; chmn. Gordon Rsch. Conf. Physics and Phys. Chemistry Biopolymers, 1966, Proteolytic Enzymes and Their Inhibitors, 1982; mem. study sect. NIH, 1967-71, NSF, 1989, sci. adv. bd. Receptor, Inc., 1993-94, Khepri Pharms., Inc., 1993-95. Mem. editorial bd. Archives Biochemistry and Biophysics, 1972-90, Biochemistry, 1973-78, Jour. Protein Chemistry, 1981—, Jour. Biol. Chemistry, 1983-88; contbr. articles to profl. jours. Recipient McCoy award Purdue U., 1975; co-recipient award in biol. scis. Alfred Jurzykowski Found., 1977. Mem. Am. Chem. Soc. (chmn. sect. 1968-69, treas. div. biol. chemistry 1981-84, councillor 1985-88), Am. Soc. Biol. Chemists, Biophys. Soc., Protein Soc., AAAS, AAUP, Polish Acad. Arts, Sci. Am., ACLU, Sigma Xi. Home: 222 E Navajo St West Lafayette IN 47906-2155 Office: Purdue U Dept Chemistry West Lafayette IN 47907 *A scientist who claims a small subfield of science as his personal fief should strive to leave it simpler and more coherent than he originally found it.*

LASKOWSKI, RICHARD E., retail hardware company executive; b. 1941. With Ace Hardware Corp., Oak Brook, Ill., 1962—, now chmn. bd. dirs., also pres. subs. Office: Ace Hardware Corp 2200 Kensington Ct Oak Brook Mall IL 60521*

LASKY, DAVID, lawyer, corporate executive; b. N.Y.C., Nov. 12, 1932; s. Benjamin and Rebecca (Malumed) L.; m. Phyllis Beryl Sumper, Apr. 14, 1957; children—Jennifer Lee, Robert Barry. BA, Bklyn. Coll., 1954; LLB, Columbia U., 1957. Bar: N.Y. 1957. Atty. N.Y.C. R.R. Co., 1957-62; with Curtiss-Wright Corp., N.Y.C., 1962—, corp. counsel, 1966-67, gen. counsel, 1967-93, v.p., 1972-80, sr. v.p., 1980-93, sec., 1989-93, pres., 1993—, chmn., 1995—. Chmn. zoning bd. appeals, Ramapo, N.Y., 1968-72; dir., v.p. Oak

Trail Homeowners Assn., 1987-90. Mem. ABA (chmn. com. corp. gen. counsel 1992-93), N.Y. Bar Assn., Phi Beta Kappa. Office: 1200 Wall St W Ste 501 Lyndhurst NJ 07071-3616

LASKY, LAURENCE D., lawyer; b. Chgo., June 26, 1940. BA, DePaul U., 1962; JD magna cum laude, Northwestern U., 1965. Bar: Ill. 1965. Ptnr. Sidley & Austin, Chgo. Office: Sidley & Austin 1 First Nat Plz Chicago IL 60603*

LASKY, MOSES, lawyer; b. Denver, Nov. 2, 1907; s. Juda Eisen and Ida (Grossman) L.; m. Ruth Helen Abraham, July 6, 1933; children: Morelle, Marshall. A.B. magna cum laude, U. Colo., 1926, J.D., 1928; LL.M., Harvard U., 1929. Bar: Calif. 1930, U.S. Supreme Ct 1947. Asst. dept. econs. U. Colo., 1925-26; salesman, local sales mgr. R.C. Barnum Co., Cleve., 1927-28; asso. Brobeck, Phleger & Harrison, San Francisco, 1929-41; partner Brobeck, Phleger & Harrison, 1941-79, Lasky, Haas, Cohler & Munter, San Francisco, 1979-94; Lasky, Haas & Cohler, San Francisco, 1994—; instr. Golden Gate Law Sch., 1934-35; sr. adv. bd. U.S. Ct. Appeals (9th cir.), 1984-90, chmn., 1989-90; vis. prof. law as disting. practitioner in residence Sch. Law, U. Colo., 1995. Contbr. articles in legal field and on Jewish life to jours. and mags. Pres. bd. dirs. San Francisco Mus. Modern Art, 1963, 64, now life trustee; pres. Regional Arts Coun. San Francisco, 1963-64; v.p. bd. dirs. San Francisco Art Inst., 1964; trustee War Meml. San Francisco, 1969-75; co-chmn. San Francisco Crime Com., 1968-71; bd. dirs. The Exploratorium, San Francisco, 1979—; bd. overseers L.A. br. Hebrew Union Coll.; nat. exec. com. Am. Jewish Com., 1947-55. Recipient Disting. Alumnus award U. Colo. Law Sch., 1977, U. Colo. medal, 1983, 50 Yr. award Am. Bar Found., 1989. Fellow Am. Coll. Trial Lawyers; mem. ABA, Phi Beta Kappa, Delta Sigma Rho. Home: 10 Mountain Spring Ave San Francisco CA 94114-2118 Office: 505 Sansome St Fl 12 San Francisco CA 94111-3106

LASLO, LAURA ELIZABETH, technical librarian, security manager, artist; b. Cleve., June 27, 1953; d. George Edward and Elizabeth Ann Laslo. AA, Grossmont Jr. Coll., El Cajon, Calif., 1974; BA, San Diego State U., 1976, cert. in tchg. Art tchr. Cajon Valley Sch. Dist., El Cajon, 1978-79; San Diego County sr. clk. Registrar of Voters, 1979-82; security mgr. Nat. Advanced Sys., San Diego, 1982-83; tech. libr. IVAC Corp., San Diego, 1983-86; tech. libr., security mgr. Logicon, Inc., San Diego, 1987—. One-women shows include All Media Student Art Exhibit, 1976, Bastille Gallery, 1977, Extra Ordinaire Gallery, 1981, San Diego and Mex. Art Exchange, 1982, The Right Bank Art Gallery, 1983, 1620 Lewis St. Gallery, 1986. Hist. commr. La Mesa (Calif.) City, 1990—; mem. San Diego Mus. of Art. Recipient commendation City of La Mesa, 1991. Mem. San Diego Artist Guild. Avocations: tennis, music, historical preservation.

LASORDA, THOMAS CHARLES (TOMMY LASORDA), professional baseball team manager; b. Norristown, Pa., Sept. 22, 1927; s. Sam and Carmella (Covatto) L.; m. Joan Miller, Apr. 14, 1950; children: Laura, Tom Charles. Student pub. schs., Norristown. Pitcher Bklyn. Dodgers, 1954-55, Kansas City A's, 1956; with L.A. Dodgers, 1956—; mgr. minor league clubs L.A. Dodgers, Pocatello, Idaho, Ogden, Utah, Spokane, Albuquerque, 1965-73; coach L.A. Dodgers, 1973-76, mgr., 1976—. Author: (with David Fisher) autobiography The Artful Dodger, 1985. Served with U.S. Army, 1945-47. Named Pitcher of Yr. Internat. League, 1958; L.A. Dodgers winner Nat. League pennant, 1977, 78, 81, 88, winner World Championship, 1981, 88; 2d Nat. League mgr. to win pennant first two yrs. as mgr.; named Nat. League Mgr. Yr. UPI, 1977, AP, 1977, 81, Baseball Writers' Assn. Am., 1988, Sporting News, 1988, Baseball Writers Assn. Am., 1983, 88; recipient Milton Richman Meml. award Assn. Profl. Baseball Players Am.; coach Nat. League All-Star team, 1977, 83-84, 86, 93. Mem. Profl. Baseball Players Am. Roman Catholic. Club: Variety of Calif. (v.p.). Office: care Los Angeles Dodgers 1000 Elysian Park Ave Los Angeles CA 90012-1112*

LASPINA, PETER JOSEPH, computer resource educator; b. Bay Shore, N.Y., June 28, 1951; s. Peter Celestine and Barbara Elizabeth (Rodee) L.; m. Julia Mary Gunther, July 10, 1982; 1 child; Joseph Peter. BMus with high honors, N.Y. State Coll., Potsdam, 1973, Performer's Cert. on Piano, 1973; MS in Music Edn., L.I. U., 1978; MS in Tech. Sys. Mgmt., SUNY, Stony Brook, 1987; postgrad., Nova Southeastern U., 1995—. Tchr. music E. Meadow (N.Y.) pub. schs., 1974-75, Northport-East Northport pub. schs., 1975-86; computer resource tchr. Northport-East Northport Pub. Schs., 1986—; adj. faculty SUNY, Stony Brook, 1991—; writer master trainer N.Y. State Edn. Dept., Albany, 1987—; cons. ednl. tech., Smithtown, N.Y., 1987—; invited del. U.S./China Joint Conf. on Edn., Beijing, 1992, 95-96, and conf. presenter. Contbr. articles to profl. jours. Mem. Am. Fedn. Tchrs., N.Y. State United Tchrs., Suffolk County Music Educators Assn., Nat. Assn. Sci., Tech. and Soc., N.Y. State Assn. Computers and Techs. (mem. conf. com. 1994), Internat. Soc. for Tech. in Edn., Computer Profls. for Social Responsibility. Presbyterian. Avocations: reading, oenology, home repair, travel. Home: 749 Meadow Rd Smithtown NY 11787-1621 Office: SUNY Dept Tech and Soc Stony Brook NY 11794

LASRY, JEAN-MICHEL, mathematics educator; b. Paris, Oct. 29, 1947; m. Elisabeth du Boucher; children: Laura, Romain, Julien. M in Econs., U. Paris-Assas, 1970; these d'etat in math., U. Paris IX, 1975. Rsch. fellow Ctr. Nat. Recherche Scientifique, Paris, 1971-78; prof. Paris-Dauphine U., 1978—, chmn. math. dept., 1980-83; cons. Compagnie Bancaire, Paris, 1988-91; mem. exec. bd. Caisse des Depots, 1991-94; CEO Caisse Autonome de Refinancement. Contbr. articles to profl. jours. Mem. Am. Math. Soc., Soc. Mathematique apliquies et industrielles (bd. dirs.), Soc. Mathematique de France, Assn. Francaise de Finance, Ecole de la Cause Freudienne.

LASS, E(RNEST) DONALD, communications company executive; b. Neptune N.J., Jan. 15, 1938; s. Ernest W. and Frances F. (Felger) L.; m. Elsa Green, Aug. 6, 1960 (div. 1968); children: Deborah, Mark Donald; m. 2d Jean L. Taylor, Dec. 17, 1978. B.A., Lafayette Coll., 1960; M.S. in journalism, Columbia U., 1961. Asst. mng. editor Asbury Park Press, N.J., 1968-74, exec. editor, 1974-80, editor, 1980—, pub., 1990—; pres. Asbury Park Press Inc., 1980—, Press Broadcasting Co., Asbury Park, 1980—. Bd. dirs. Shore Area YMCA, Asbury Park, 1978—, pres., 1981-83; bd. dirs. Monmouth Boys Club, 1977—, Monmouth coun. Boy Scouts Am., 1985-89, Journalism Resource Inst., Rutgers U., 1983—, Am. Cancer Soc., Monmouth, 1985—; chmn. Monmouth Coll. Assocs., 1985-86; bd. visitors Columbia U. Grad. Sch. Journalism; bd. overseers Rutgers U.; mem. Monmouth Coll. Coun. Pub. Affairs. Recipient Editorial Comment award N.J. Press Assn., 1980, Disting. Service award Greater Asbury Park Jaycees, 1968, Meritorious Service award Monmouth-Ocean Chiropractic Soc., 1976; Disting. Pub. Service award Monmouth council Boy Scouts Am., 1985. Mem. Am. Soc. Newspaper Editors, Newspaper Assn. Am., Nat. Conf. Editorial Writers (pres. 1987, chmn. 1988), N.J. Press Assn., Nat. Assn. Broadcasters, Nat. Assn. TV Programming Dirs., Greater Asbury Park C. of C. (pres. 1972-74), Sigma Delta Chi, Delta Upsilon. Presbyterian. Office: Asbury Pk Press Inc PO Box 1550 3601 Hwy 66 Neptune NJ 07754-1550 also: Sta WTKS-FM 600 Courtland St Ste 100 Orlando FL 32804-1313

LASSAR, SCOTT R., lawyer; b. Evanston, Ill., Apr. 5, 1950; s. Richard Ernest and Jo (Ladenson) L.; m. Elizabeth Levine, May 22, 1977; children: Margaret, Kate. B.A., Oberlin Coll., 1972; J.D., Northwestern U., 1975. Bar: Ill. 1975. Former dep. chief spl. prosecutions divsn. no. dist. Office U.S. Atty., Chgo.; former ptnr. Keck, Mahin & Cate, Chgo.; now 1st asst. U.S. atty. no. dist. Office U.S. Atty., Chgo. Office: US Attys Office 219 S Dearborn St Chicago IL 60604-1702

LASSER, HOWARD GILBERT, chemical engineer, consultant; b. N.Y.C., Nov. 24, 1926; s. Milton and Tessie (Rosenthal) L.; m. Barbara Ann Katz, Aug. 24, 1950; children: Cathy, Ellen Lasser-LeVee, Alan. BSChemE, Lehigh U., 1950; postgrad., Columbia U., 1951; Dr.Ing., Darmstadt Tech. Inst., Germany, 1956. Registered profl. engr., D.C., Va., Calif. Chem. engr. Belvoir Rsch. Engring. & Devel. Ctr., Ft. Belvoir, Va., 1951-55, 58-72; materials engr. Naval Sea Systems Command, Washington, 1956-57, chem. engr., 1955-56; materials engr. Naval Facilities Engring. Command, Alexandria, Va., 1972-82; chem. engr. Materials Rsch. Cons., Alexandria & Springfield, Va., 1982—. Author: Design of Electroplating Facilities, 1990; contbr. articles to profl. jours. Fellow AAAS, Oil and Colour and Surface Finishers Chemists Assn., Am. Inst. Chemists; mem. Am. Electroplaters Soc., AIChE, NACE Internat. (cert.), ASM INternat., Steel Structures Painting Coun., Tau Beta Pi, Sigma Xi, Alpha Chi Sigma, Pi Delta Epsilon. Achievements include 6 patents in electroplating and metal finishing; description of thermodynamic properties of carbon dioxide; development of thermotropic dyes for aluminum oxides; development of dyes to match laser wavelengths to enhance etching of substrates used in the electronics industry and medicine; over 500 publs. in materials and chemical engineering. Home: 5912 Camberly Ave Springfield VA 22150-2438 Office: Materials Rsch Cons 1121 King St Alexandria VA 22314-2924

LASSER, JOSEPH ROBERT, investment company executive; b. N.Y.C., Sept. 25, 1923; s. Milton and Tessie (Rosenthal) L.; m. Ruth Jean Pollak, May 4, 1925; children: James, Carol Lasser Kornblith, Jean. BS, Lehigh U., 1946; MBA, NYU, 1951. Sr. analyst Lewisohn and Co., N.Y.C., 1946-51; dir. research Walston and Co., N.Y.C., 1951-55, Wertheim and Co., N.Y.C., 1956-67; ptnr. Shufro, Rose, Ehrman and Stanley Marks, Lasser & Co., N.Y.C., 1967-75; sr. portfolio mgr. C.J. Lawrence, N.Y.C., 1975-76; ptnr., sr. portfolio mgr. Neuberger & Berman, N.Y.C., 1977—. Treas. Bronx House, N.Y., 1978-95; past trustee United Jewish Appeal/Fedn. Jewish Philanthropies, mem. bd. overseers. 1st lt. USAF, 1943-45. Decorated Air medal with three bronze oak leaf clusters, one silver oak leaf cluster; recipient 1st Lit. award Soc. Paper Money, 1976. Mem. Am. Numismatic Soc. (councillor 1990-93), N.Y. Soc. Security Analysts, Chartered Fin. Analysts Assn., N.Y. Stock Exchange (allied), Phi Beta Kappa, Princeton Club (N.Y.C.), Quaker Ridge (Scarsdale N.Y.). Home: 119 Cushman Rd Scarsdale NY 10583-3405 Office: Neuberger & Berman 605 3rd Ave New York NY 10158

LASSERS, WILLARD J., judge; b. Kankakee, Ill., Aug. 24, 1919; s. Henry and Sylvia (Oppenheim) L.; m. Elisabeth Stern, June 30, 1946; 1 dau., Deborah. A.B., U. Chgo., 1940, J.D., 1942. Bar: D.C. 1941, Ill. 1942, U.S. Supreme Ct. 1965. Practiced in Chgo., 1946-78; practice with Alex Elson, Chgo., 1946-48, Elson and Cotton, 1948-49; atty. RFC, Chgo., 1950-51, Office Price Stablzn., Chgo., 1951-53; individual practice law Chgo., 1953-60; partner Elson, Lassers and Wolff, Chgo., 1960-78; judge Circuit Ct. Cook County, Chgo., 1978—; lectr. taxation U. Chgo., 1954-55. Author: (with Alex Elson and Aaron S. Wolff) Civil Practice Forms Annotated, Illinois and Federal, 1952, 65, Scapegoat Justice: Lloyd Miller and the Failure of the Legal System, 1973; reviser: Fletcher Corporation Forms, 5 vols, 1957-60. Mem. Gov.'s Com. to Study Consumer Credit Laws, 1962-63; chmn. Com. Ill. Govt., 1962-63; Bd. dirs. Ill. div. ACLU, to 1978. Served with AUS, 1943-46. Mem. Ill., Chgo. bar assns., Am. Arbitration Assn. (mem. panel labor arbitrators 1965-78). Home: 1509 E 56th St Chicago IL 60637-1910 Office: Richard J Daley Center Chicago IL 60602

LASSETER, KENNETH CARLYLE, pharmacologist; b. Jacksonville Fla., Aug. 12, 1942; s. James and Retta (Shad) L.; BS, Stetson U., 1963; MD, U. Fla., 1967; m. Kathy G. Marks, Aug. 6, 1977; children: Kenneth C. III, Susan, Frank L. Diplomate Am. Bd. Clin. Pharmacology. Intern, resident in medicine U. Ky. Med. Ctr., 1967-71; asst. prof., assoc. prof. pharmacology and medicine U. Miami Med. Sch., 1971-81, clin. assoc. prof., 1981—; adj. assoc. prof. pharmacology, Barry U., 1986—; v.p., dir. Clin. Pharmacology Assos., Inc., Miami, 1981—. Served with USAR, 1971-76. Recipient William B. Peck Sci. Rsch. award Interstate Postgrad. Med. Assn., 1976, rsch. award Alpha Omega Alpha, 1967. Fellow Am. Coll. Clin. Pharmacology; mem. ACP, Am. Soc. Pharmacology and Exptl. Therapeutics, Am. Soc. Clin. Pharmacology and Therapeutics, Sigma Xi. Republican. Contbr. articles to profl. jours. Home: 552 Ocean Dr Key Largo FL 33037-4345 Office: Clin Pharmacol Assocs 2060 NW 22nd Ave Miami FL 33142-7338

LASSITER, CHARLES WHITFIELD, construction executive; b. Unice, N.Mex., Aug. 16, 1952; s. James Edward and Lollie (Barber) L.; m. Donna Jean Young, Mar. 1, 1979; children: Belinda Dawn Watts, Kimberly Renee Watts, Charlene Michelle. BS in Mech. Engring., Kensington U., 1982; postgrad., U. Tex., 1982, Pa. State U., 1990. Welder, pipefitter, supt. Modern Welding, Plano, Tex., 1970-73; welder, pipefitter, owner C&J Svcs., Garland, Tex., 1973-75, C.W. Lassiter Constrn. Svcs., Garland, 1975-81; supt., estimator, engr. F.P. Ross Inc., Houston, 1981-82; owner, welder, pipefitter C.W. Lassiter Svcs., Arlington, Tex., 1982-83; v.p., project mgr., estimator RECC, Crowley, Tex., 1984-85; project mgr., engr. Gallagher Engring., Houston, 1985-88; project mgr., v.p. fabrication and constrn. Petrofac Inc., Tyler, Tex., 1989-92; project mgr., v.p., owner Engring. Procurement and Constrn., Inc., Tyler, 1992—; mem. adv. bd. ASHRAE, N.Y.C., 1991-92. Mem. adv. bd. Indsl. Coop. Tng. program Plano H.S., 1972-73. Mem. ASME, Am. Welding Soc. Avocations: snow skiing, motorcycling, sailing, family activities. Office: EPC Inc 11182 Us Highway 69 N Tyler TX 75706-8743

LASSITER, KENNETH T., photography educator, consultant; b. Richmond, Va., Jan. 2, 1935; s. B. Taylor and Euzelia (Duke) L.; m. Carol Lester, Apr. 9, 1960; children: Karen, Keith. BS, Va. Poly. Inst. and State U., 1957; MS (hon.), Brooks Inst. Photography, 1992. Engr. Eastman Kodak Co., Rochester, N.Y., 1957-60, tech. editor, 1960-69, dir. publs., 1970-84, dir. photo trade rels., 1984-93, mgr. photo edn., 1986-93; retired, 1993; mng. dir. Palm Beach (Fla.) Photo Workshops, 1993-94; mem. pres.'s coun. Internat. Ctr. Photography, N.Y.C., 1985-93; dir. Photographic Art & Sci. Found., Oklahoma City, 1984-95. Author: Executive Producer: Techniques of the Masters Videoconference Series; author or editor numerous Kodak publs. Mem. Soc. for Imaging Sci. and Tech. (sr., bd. dirs. 1965—), Friends of Photography, Nat. Press Photographers Assn., Soc. for Photographic Edn. Republican. Presbyterian. Avocations: boating, photography, music, computers.

LASSITER, PHILLIP B., insurance company executive. Chmn., CEO, pres. Ambac Inc., N.Y.C.; bd. dirs. HCIA, Inc., Diebold, Inc. Office: Ambac Inc One State Street Plaza New York NY 10004

LASSITER, RONALD CORBETT, oil company executive; b. Houston, Aug. 2, 1932; s. Mance and Pauline Marie (Lloyd) L.; m. Ella Lee Moechel, Dec. 26, 1951; children: Rona Lee, James Mance, Jennifer Lynn, Lynda Fay. B.A., Rice U., 1955; M.B.A., Harvard U., 1964. Sr. v.p. corp. devel. Zapata Corp., Houston, 1970-71, exec. v.p. natural resources, 1971-74, chief oper. officer natural resources products, 1974-77, dir., sr. exec. v.p. natural resource products, 1977-78, pres., chief operating officer, 1978-83, chief exec. officer, 1983, chief exec. officer, chmn. bd., 1986—, also dir.; bd. dirs. Zapata Off-Shore Co., Zapata Haynie Corp., Pesquera Zapata, Tidewater, Inc., Zapata Exploration Co., Daniel Industries, Inc. Mem. editorial bd. Offshore mag. Mem. dean's adv. bd. Coll. Bus. Adminstrn., U. Houston. Mem. AIME, Soc. Mining Engrs., Petroleum Club, Forum Club. Office: Zapata Corp Zapata Tower PO Box 4240 Houston TX 77210-4240*

LASSLO, ANDREW, medicinal chemist, educator; b. Mukacevo, Czechoslovakia, Aug. 24, 1922; came to U.S., 1946, naturalized, 1951; s. Vojtech Laszlo and Terezie (Herskovicova) L.; m. Wilma Ellen Reynolds, July 9, 1955; 1 child, Millicent Andrea. MS, U. Ill., 1948, PhD, 1952, MLS, 1961. Rsch. chemist organic chems. div. Monsanto Chem. Co., St. Louis, 1952-54; asst. prof. pharmacology, divsn. basic health scis. Emory U., 1954-60; prof. and chmn. dept. med. chemistry Coll. Pharmacy, U. Tenn. Health Sci. Ctr., 1960-90, Alumni Disting. Svc. prof. and chmn., dept. medicinal chemistry, 1989-90, professor emeritus, 1990—; cons. Geschickter Fund for Med. Research Inc., 1961-62; rsch. contractor U.S. Army Med. R & D Command, 1964-67; dir. postgrad. tng. program sci. librarians USPHS, 1966-72; chmn. edn. com. Drug Info. Assn., 1966-68, bd. dirs., 1968-69; dir. postgrad. tng. program organic medicinal chemistry for chemists FDA, 1971; exec. com. adv. council S.E. Regional Med. Library Program, Nat. Library of Medicine, 1969-71; chmn. regional med. library programs com. Med. Library Assn., 1971-72; mem. pres.'s faculty adv. council U. Tenn. System, 1970-72; chmn. energy authority U. Tenn. Center for Health Scis., 1975-77, chmn. council departmental chmn., 1977, 81; chmn. Internat. Symposium on Contemporary Trends in Tng. Pharmacologists, Helsinki, 1975. Producer, moderator (TV and radio series) Health Care Perspective, 1976-78; editor: Surface Chemistry and Dental Intequments, 1973, Blood Platelet Function and Medicinal Chemistry, 1984; contbr. numerous articles in sci. and profl. jours.; mem. editorial bd. Jour. Medicinal and Pharm. Chemistry, 1961, U. Tenn. Press, 1974-77; composer (work for piano) Synthesis in C Minor, 1968; patentee in field. Trustee 1st Bohemian Meth. Ch., Chgo., 1951-52, mem. bd. stewards, 1950-52; mem. ofcl. bd. Grace Meth. Ch., Atlanta, 1955-60; mem. adminstrv. bd. Christ United Meth. Ch., Memphis, 1964-72, 73-75, 77-79, 81-83, 88-90, chmn. commn. on edn., 1965-67, chmn. bd. Day Sch., 1967-68. 1st lt. USAR, 1953-57, capt., 1957-62. Recipient Research prize U. Ill. Med. Ctr. chpt. Sigma Xi, 1949, Honor Scroll Tenn. Inst. Chemists, 1976, Americanism medal DAR, 1976; U. Ill. fellow, 1950-51; Geschickter Fund Med. Research grantee, 1959-65, USPHS Research and Tng. grantee, 1958-64, 66-72, 82-89, NSF research grantee, 1964-66, Pfeiffer Research Found. grantee, 1981-87. Fellow AAAS, Am. Assn. Pharm. Scientists, Am. Inst. Chemists (nat. councilor for Tenn. 1969-70), Acad. Pharm. Rsch. and Sci.; mem. ALA (life), Am. Chem. Soc. (sr.), Am. Pharm. Assn., Am. Soc. Pharmacology and Exptl. Therapeutics (chmn. subcom. pre and postdoctoral tng. 1974-78, exec. com. ednl. and profl. affairs 1974-78), Sigma Xi (pres. elect U. Tenn. Ctr. for Health Sci. chpt. 1975-76, pres. 1976-77, Excellence in Rsch. award 1989), Beta Phi Mu, Phi Lambda Sigma, Rho Chi. Methodist. Achievements include 7 U.S. and 11 foreign patents in field; identification of platelet aggregation-inhibitory specific functions in synthetic organic molecules; design and synthesis of novel human blood platelet aggregation inhibitors, novel compound for mild stimulation of central nervous system activity; research on relationships between structural features of synthetic organic entities, their physicochemical properties and their effects on biologic activity. Home and Office: 5479 Timmons Ave Memphis TN 38119-6932 *Of all the pleasures a human being can savor, none exceeds the satisfaction of a genuine sense of accomplishment. It undergirds all elements of creative living and surmounts vicissitudes exceeding conventional human endurance.*

LASSMAN, MALCOLM, lawyer; b. Bklyn., June 9, 1938; M. Barbara Turley (div.); children: Scott, Robin, Amy; m. Vivienne McIntosh; 1 child, Justine. BA, Washington & Lee U., 1960, LLB cum laude, 1963. Bar: Va. 1963, D.C. 1965. Ptnr. Akin, Gump, Strauss, Hauer & Feld, Washington. Jewish. Lodge: Masons. Home: 2883 Audubon Ter NW Washington DC 20008-2309 Office: Akin Gump Strauss Hauer & Feld Ste 400 1333 New Hampshire Ave NW Washington DC 20036-1564*

LASSNER, FRANZ GEORGE, educator; b. Leipzig, Germany, May 6, 1926; s. Oscar and Marga (Treskow) L.; m. Marguerite Sansone, Aug. 18, 1961; children: Alexander Nicholas, John Paul. A.B. in History, Rutgers U., 1947; M.A. in History, Georgetown U., 1951, Ph.D. in Govt., 1960. With various research projects Georgetown U., Washington, 1951-62; research supt. Russian Studies Project, Washington, 1956-57; research assoc., curator spl. collections Hoover Inst., Stanford, Calif., 1962-63; dir. Herbert Hoover Presdl. Libr., West Branch, Iowa, 1963-67; dir. archives Hoover Inst., Stanford, 1969-74, spl. rep., 1974—; dir. devel. Phila. Coll. Textiles and Sci., 1974-76; sr. v.p. programs Freedoms Found., Valley Forge, 1977-91; adj. prof. history Temple U., Phila., 1992-93, Atlantic C.C., N.J., 1992-95. Mem. adv. bd. Internat. Telecommunications Inst., Houston, 1984-89; bd. dirs. St. Lawrence Inst., Montreal, 1985-89. Mem. World Affairs Coun. Greater Valley Forge (bd. dirs. 1991-93), Lambda Chi Alpha, Delta Phi Alpha. Roman Catholic. Home: 1069 Michigan Ave Cape May NJ 08204-2541

LASSNER, KEITH MICHAEL, publishing executive; b. Santa Monica, Calif., Apr. 21, 1949; s. Nathan and Mildred (Feldstein) L.; m. Jane Robin Wagner, June 1, 1969; children: Bryan, Craig. BS in History, Calif. State U., Northridge, 1971; MS in Info. Sci., U. So. Calif., 1973. Acquisitions chief Calif. Inst. Tech., Pasadena, 1973-76; mktg. mgr., nat. libr. dir. Prentice-Hall, Inc., Englewood Cliffs, N.J., 1976-81; v.p. mktg. Birkhauser Boston, Inc., Cambridge, Mass., 1981-82; exec. dir. Springhouse (Pa.) Pub. Co., 1982-87; pres., chmn. Rsch. Publs. Inc., Woodbridge, Conn., 1991—; exec. v.p. mktg. Gale Rsch. Inc., Detroit, 1987-91, pres., CEO, 1992-95; group CEO Thomson Corp. Pub. Internat. Ref./Libr. Group, Detroit, 1995—.

LASSWELL, MARCIA LEE, psychologist, educator; b. Oklahoma City, July 13, 1927; d. Lee and Stella (Blackard) Eck; m. Thomas Lasswell, May 29, 1950; children: Marcia Jane, Thomas Ely, Julia Lee. B.A., U. Calif., Berkeley, 1949; M.A., U. So. Calif., 1952; postgrad., U. Calif., Riverside, U. So. Calif., U. N.C. Individual practice psychotherapy, marriage/family therapy Claremont, Calif.; asst. prof. Pepperdine Coll., Los Angeles, 1959-60; asst. prof. psychology behavioral sci. dept. Calif. State U., Pomona, 1960-64; asso. prof. Calif. State U., 1965-69, prof., 1970—, chmn. dept., 1964-69; asso. clin. dir. Human Relations Center, U. So. Calif., 1975—; vis. assoc. prof. Scripps Coll., 1968-69, U. So. Calif., 1969-70, Occidental Coll., 1971-72; lectr. various Calif. univs.; mem. staff spl. project alcoholics and narcotics offenders Calif. Prison System, 1970-73; mem. Calif. Accreditation Com. Secondary Schs. and Colls., 1965—; mem. commn. accreditation for marriage and family tng. U.S. Dept. Edn., 1981-87. Author: College Teaching of General Psychology, 1967, Love, Marriage and Family, 1973, No-Fault Marriage, 1976, Styles of Loving, 1980, Marriage and Family, 1982, rev. edit., 1987, 91, Equal Time, 1983. Recipient Outstanding Tchrs. award Calif. State U., 1971, Outstanding Contbn. to Marriage and Family Therapy, 1991, Disting. Clin. Mem. award Calif. Assn. Marriage and Family Therapists, 1995. Fellow Am. Assn. Marital and Family Therapy (bd. dirs. 1970-72, 87-91, pres. elect 1993-95, pres. 1995-97); mem. AAAS, Nat. Coun. Family Rels. (exec. com. 1978-80), Am. Acad. Family Therapy, So. Calif. Assn. Marital and Family Therapy (pres. 1972-73), Alpha Kappa Delta, Phi Delta Gamma, Pi Gamma Mu. Home: 800 W 1st St #2908 Los Angeles CA 90012

LAST, MICHAEL P., lawyer; b. Chgo., July 31, 1946; s. Jules Hilbert and Muriel Esther (Ruekberg) L.; m. Yong-Hee Chyun, Dec. 1970 (div.); m. Jane Antoinette Nooy Bunnell, May 29, 1983. BA magna cum laude, Lawrence U., 1968; JD cum laude, Harvard U., 1971. Bar: Mass. 1971. Ptnr., head Real Estate, Environ. Law Dept. Warner & Stackpole, Boston, 1972-84; ptnr., head Environ. Law Dept. Gaston & Snow, Boston, 1984-91; ptnr., co-chair Environ. Law sect. Mintz, Levin, Cohn, Ferris, Glovsky and Popeo P.C., Boston, 1991—; mng. dir. ML Strategies, Inc., Boston, 1991—; bd. dirs. Newell Enterprises Inc., 1983-87; co-chair Am. Law Inst./ABA Ann. Course Study Minimizing Liability for Hazardous Waste Mgmt.; lectr. in field. Contbr. articles to profl. jours. Chair wetlands regulation rev. bd. Mass. Dept. Environ. Quality Engring., 1983-85, Town Wellesley Wetlands Protection Com., 1980-82; mem. Town Wellesley Planning Bd., 1983-88; rep. Town Meeting, Wellesley; mem. rev. bd. Mass. Dept. Environ. Protection, 1991-92; mem. bd. environ. mgmt. Mass. Dept. Environ. Mgmt., 1991—, chmn., 1994—; founder, pres. Santa Fe Coun. Environ. Excellence, 1991—; mem. corp. gifts com. Boston Mus. Fine Arts Capital Fund Dr., 1979; vice chair open space plan implementation com. Town Wellesley, 1978-79; trustee, bd. govs. New Eng. Aquarium, 1995—, Mass. Eye and Ear Infirmary, 1990—; trustee, bd. govs., exec. com. Newton-Wellesley Hosp., 1987-94, chmn. joint trustee staff com., 1992-93. 1st lt. USAF, 1971-72. Warren Hurst Stevens scholar Lawrence U., 1964. Mem. ABA (standing com. environ. law 1989-91, natural resources sect., corp., banking, bus. law sect., real property, probate, trust law sect.), Boston Bar Assn. (bd. dirs. 1984-87, chair environment com. 1979-81, chair urban affairs sect. 1983-87, co-chair mcpl. planning process com. 1983-87), Greater Boston C. of C. (real estate devel. com. 1979-80, co-chair Boston 2000 project review com. 1982-90, Boston 2000 steering com. 1983-90, co-chair adv. com. Devel. Design Guideline Study Downtown Boston 1983-92), Phi Beta Kappa. Avocations: canoeing, cross country skiing, camping. Office: Mintz Levin Cohn Ferris Glovsky & Popeo PC One Financial Center Boston MA 02111

LASTER, DANNY BRUCE, animal scientist; b. Scotts Hill, Tenn., Nov. 29, 1942; married 1960; 2 children. BS, U. Tenn., 1963; MS, U. Ky., 1964; PhD in Animal Breeding, Okla. State U., 1970. Rsch. specialist U. Ky., Lexington, 1965-68; asst. prof. endocrinology Iowa State U., 1970-71; rsch. leader reproduction rsch. unit, Clay ctr., agr. rsch. svc. USDA, Nebr., 1971-78; nat. program leader, assoc. dep. adminstr. beef and sheep USDA, 1981-88; dir. Roman L. Hruska U.S. Meat Animal Rsch. Ctr. Clay Ctr., Nebr., 1988—. Mem. Am. Soc. Animal Sci. Office: USDA Roman L Hruska US Meat Animal Rsch Ctr (MARC) PO Box 166 Clay Center NE 68933-0166

LASTER, LEONARD, physician, consultant, author; b. N.Y.C., Aug. 24, 1928; s. Isaac and Mary (Ehrenreich) L.; m. Ruth Ann Leventhal, Dec. 16, 1956; children: Judith Eve, Susan Beth, Stephen Jay. AB, Harvard U., 1949, MD, 1950. Diplomate Nat. Bd. Med. Examiners, Am. Bd. Internal Medicine (gastroenterology). From intern to resident in medicine Mass. Gen. Hosp., Boston, 1950-53; fellow gastroenterology Mass. Meml. Hosp., 1958-59; vis. investigator Pub. Health Rsch. Inst., N.Y.C., 1953-54; lt. commd. USPHS, 1954, advanced through grades to asst. surgeon gen. (rear adm.), 1971; mem. staff Nat. Inst. Arthritis, Metabolic and Digestive Diseases, NIH, Bethesda, Md., 1954-73, chief digestive and hereditary diseases br., 1969-73; spl. asst., then asst. dir. human resources President's Office Sci. and Tech., 1969-73; exec. dir. Assembly Life Scis., also div. med. scis. NAS-NRC, 1973-74; ret. USPHS, 1973; v.p. acad. affairs and clin. affairs Med. Ctr., also dean Coll. Medicine, prof. medicine Downstate Med. Ctr., SUNY, Bklyn., 1974-78; pres. Oreg. Health Scis. U., Portland, 1978-87, prof. medicine, 1978-87; chancellor U. Mass. Med. Ctr., Worcester, 1987-90, disting. univ. prof. medicine and health policy, 1990—, chancellor emeritus, 1990—; bd. dirs. Thermo Cardiosystems, Inc., Woburn, Mass.; cons. mgmt. and productivity of R & D programs for numerous pharm. corps., R & D strategic planning, orgn. corp. health care programs for multinat. paper corp. and pvt. rsch. found.; lab. investigator Marine Biol. Lab., Woods Hole, Mass., summers, 1962-69, chmn. organizer symposia on nat. policy and biomed. scis., summers, 1971-72, libr. reader, summers, 1973-76, chmn. steering com. Falmouth Forum, 1994—. Author: Life After Medical School, 32 Doctors Describe How They Shaped Their Medical Careers, 1996; contbr. articles on gastrointestinal disease, inborn errors of metabolism, devel. biology to profl. jours.; contbr. op-ed column and other pieces to Washington Post, essays to Hosp. Practice and MD Mag. Active Found. Advanced Edn. Scis., Bethesda, 1965-69, Bedford Stuyvesant Family Health Ctr., Bklyn., 1975-78, Med. Rsch. Found., Oreg., 1979-87, Oreg. Symphony, 1979-85, Oreg. Contemporary Theatre, 1981-83; pres. Burning Tree Elem. Sch. PTA, Bethesda, 1972-73; bd. dirs. Internat. Artists Series, Worcester, 1988-91, Mass. Biotech. Ctrs. for Excellence, Boston, 1988—, Mass. Biotech. Rsch. Inst., Worcester, 1988-90, Worcester Bus. Devel. Corp., 1988-91; co-chmn. United Way Ctrl. Mass., COMEC Campaign, 1989; mem. exec. com. Worcester Econ. Club, 1988-91; mem. citizen gov. bd. Worcester Fights Back, 1990-95; chmn. corp. liaison com. Marine Biol. Lab., 1991—; mem. Worcester Com. Fgn. Rels. (affiliated with Coun. Fgn. Rels.), 1992—. Fellow ACP; mem. Am. Fedn. Clin. Rsch., Am. Gastroenterol. Assn., Am. Soc. Biol. Chemists, Am. Soc. Clin. Investigation (emeritus), Marine Biol. Lab. Corp., Harvey Soc. N.Y., Portland C. of C. (dir. 1980-84), Mass. Med. Soc. (pub. rels. com.), Worcester Dist. Med. Soc., Worcester Club, Cosmos Club (Washington), Harvard Club (N.Y.C.), Univ. Club (Portland, Oreg.), Phi Beta Kappa, Sigma Xi. Home: 47 Pine Arden Dr West Boylston MA 01583-1024 Office: U Mass Med Ctr 120 Front St Ste 800 Worcester MA 01608-1404 *Education is nurturing excellence in others and facilitating its spread as an infectious disease.*

LASTER, RALPH WILLIAM, JR., insurance company executive, accountant; b. Hutchinson, Kans., Oct. 4, 1951; s. Ralph William Sr. and Peggy Edith (O'Connell) L.; m. Jerri Laster, May 26, 1971; children: Tarissa Marie, Damian Michael. BSBA, Emporia (Kans.) State U., 1974. Staff acct. Deloitte, Haskin & Sells, Kansas City, Mo., 1974-76, Mize, Houser, Mehlinger & Kimes, Topeka, 1976-78; ptnr. Gregg, Prichard & Laster CPA's, Winfield, Kans., 1978-81; v.p., chief fin. officer, sec. Am. Investors Life Ins. Co., Inc., Topeka, 1981-84, exec. v.p., chief fin. officer, sec., 1985-88, also bd. dirs.; exec. v.p. chief fin. officer, sec., treas. AmVestors Fin. Corp., Topeka, 1986-88, vice-chmn., chief exec. officer, 1988, chmn., chief exec. officer, 1988—; bd. dirs. AmVestors Fin. Corp., Topeka, AmVestors Investment Group, Topeka, Am. Investors Sales Group, Topeka. Methodist. Home: 5646 SW 33rd St Topeka KS 66614-4517 Office: Am Investors Life Ins Co Inc 415 SW 8th Ave Topeka KS 66603-3913*

LASTER, RICHARD, biotechnology executive, consultant; b. Vienna, Austria, Nov. 10, 1923; came to U.S., 1940; naturalized, 1944; s. Alan and Caroline (Harband) L.; m. Liselotte Schneider, Oct. 17, 1948; children: Susan Laster Rubenstein, Thomas. Student U. Wash., 1941-42; BChE cum laude, Poly. Inst. Bklyn., 1943; postgrad. Stevens Inst. Tech., 1945-47. With Gen. Foods Corp., 1944-82, corp. rsch. and devel., Hoboken, N.J., 1944-58, ops. mgr. Franklin Baker divsn., Hoboken, N.J., Atlantic Gelatin divsn., Woburn, Mass., 1958-64, mgr. rsch. devel. Jell-O divsn., White Plains, N.Y., 1958-64, corp. mgr. quality assurance, White Plains, 1964-67, ops. mgr. Maxwell House divsn., White Plains, 1967-68, exec. v.p. Maxwell House divsn., 1968-69, pres. Maxwell House divsn., 1969-71, corp. group v.p., White Plains, 1971-73, exec. v.p. Gen. Foods Corp., 1974-82, also dir., rsch., devel. and food-away-from-home, 1975-82; bd. dirs. DNA Plant Tech. Corp., 1982-94, chmn., 1988-94, CEO, 1982-92, pres. 1982-91; mgmt. cons., 1994—; bd. dirs. RiceTec, Peptor Ltd.; mem. sch. bd. Chappaqua, N.Y., 1971-74, pres., 1973-74; chmn., mem. bd., 1st v.p. United Way of Westchester, 1978; chmn. adv. com. Poly. Inst. Westchester, 1977; trustee Poly. Inst. N.Y.,1978—; mem. coll. coun. SUNY, Purchase, Purchase Coll. Found, 1986—; mem. corp. N.Y. Botanical Garden; mem. subcom. Export Adminstrn. Pres.'s Export Coun., 1995; chmn. Westchester Edn. Coalition, 1992—; dir. Westchester Holocaust Commn., 1994; chmn. Am. Soc. of Plant Physiologists Edn. Found., 1995; mem. New Castle Town Bd. Recipient Disting. Alumnus award. Fellow Poly. Inst. N.Y. Mem. AAAS, N.Y. Acad. Scis., AIChE (Food and Bioengring. award 1972), Am. Chem. Soc., Am. Inst. Chemists, Tau Beta Pi, Phi Lambda Upsilon. Contbr. articles on food sci. to profl. publs. Patentee in field. Home: 23 Round Hill Rd Chappaqua NY 10514-1622 Office: Richard Laster 103 S Bedford Rd Mount Kisco NY 10549-3440

LASTINGER, ALLEN LANE, JR., banker; b. Atmore, Ala., Aug. 16, 1942; s. Allen Lane and Sue Belle (Bevis) L.; m. Shirley Delores Taylor, May 1, 1965; children—Randall Lane, Lindsey Kathleen, Amy Delores. B.B.A., U. Fla., 1965, 1971; postgrad. Stonier Grad. Sch. Banking, Rutgers U., 1979-81; A.M.P., Harvard U., 1982. Fin. analyst Barnett Banks Fla., Inc., Jacksonville, 1971-75, asst. v.p., 1975; pres., chief exec. officer Barnett Bank, Gainesville, Fla., 1976-80; exec. v.p. community banking Barnett Banks Fla., 1980-82, sr. exec. v.p. community banking, 1982-84, vice-chmn., 1984-88, vice chmn., chief banking officer, 1988-91, pres., chief oper. officer, 1991—; dir. Barnett Banks, Inc.; vice-chmn. Enterprise Florida, Inc. Served with USN, 1966-70. Mem. Bankers Roundtable. Republican. Episcopalian. Office: Barnett Banks Inc PO Box 40789 Jacksonville FL 32203-0789*

LASTMAN, MELVIN D., mayor; b. Toronto, Ont., Can., Mar. 9, 1933; s. Louis and Rose L.; m. Marilyn Lastman, Nov. 15, 1953; children—Dale, Blayne. Pres. Bad Boy Furniture & Appliances, Toronto, 1955-76; mayor North York, Ont., 1972—; bd. govs. North York Gen. Hosp.; commr. York-Finch Gen. Hosp. Found. Active Pride of Israel Synagogue, North York br. Can. Red Cross, Sunnybrook Med. Ctr., Ont. Men's ORT, Can. ORT Orgn., Parents Against Drugs, North York YMCA, Vol. Ctr. Met. Toronto, North York Mental Health Coun., North York Srs. Ctr., North York Hydro Commn., North York chpt. Heart and Stroke Found. Ont., Can. Found. for Ileitis and Colitis, Ont., March of Dimes, Shalom Food Project, Good Cheer Russian Lang. Radio Program, Can. Assn. for Riding for the Disabled, St. John Ambulance Canine Therapy Program, Metro Toronto; patron Kidney Found. Can.; hon. chmn. Children's Wish Found. Ont., Drug and Alcohol Network North York, Bloorview MacMillan Ctr., Leukemia Rsch. Fund, St. John's Rehab. Hosp.; active Chi-Ping Dance Group, North York Singers. Recipient Ursaki award Can. Sales and Mktg. Execs., C. of C. Lifetime Achievement award, 1995; named Temple Sinai Brotherhood Humanitarian of Yr., 1995. Mem. North York C. of C., Older Adult Ctrs. Assn., B'nai Brith Can., Juvenile Diabetes Found. Can., Can. Cancer Soc. (Willowdale Unit), Caritas Project, Can. Soc. Yad Vashem (bd. dirs.), Assn. Children with Learning Disabilities, North York Symphony, Kiwanis Club of North York, Kinsmen Club, North York Civitan Club, Rotary. Home: 19 Widefird Pl, North York, ON Canada M2M 4H3 Office: City of North York, 5100 Yonge St, North York, ON Canada M2N 5V7

LASTOWKA, JAMES ANTHONY, former federal agency executive, lawyer; b. Chester, Pa., Oct. 1, 1951; s. Joseph Edward and Mary A. (O'Malley) L.; m. Sandra L. Pugh, Apr. 28, 1979; children: Conor David, Carey Anna, Austin Tucker. BA in Econs. cum laude, Syracuse U., 1973; JD, Georgetown U., 1976. Bar: Pa. 1976, D.C. 1990, U.S. Ct. Appeals (a4th, 5th, 9th, 10th, 11th, D.C. cirs.) 1981. Staff atty. U.S. Occupational Safety and Health Rev. Commn., Washington, 1976-78, asst. gen. counsel, 1979-80; supervisory atty. Fed. Mine Safety and Health Rev. Commn., Washington, 1978-79, dep. gen. counsel, 1980-81, gen. counsel, 1981-84, commr., 1984-90; with Jones, Day, Reavis & Pogue, Washington, 1990-92, McDermott, Will & Emery, Washington, 1992—. Contbr. editor Occupational Hazards Mag. Mem. ABA (mem. labor law sect., com. occupational safety and health law, com. natural resources, energy and environ. law). Office: McDermott Will & Emery 1850 K St NW Washington DC 20006-2213

LATAIF, LAWRENCE P., lawyer; b. Fall River, Mass., Nov. 1, 1943; s. Louis and Linda Adele (Salwan) L.; m. Noha Nader, Dec. 29, 1979; children: Nicole, Lawrence Jr., Diana. BA, Brown U., 1965; JD, Georgetown U., 1968, LLM, 1970. Bar: D.C. 1969, U.S. Ct. Appeals (D.C. cir.) 1969, U.S. Ct. Mil. Appeals 1969, U.S. Supreme Ct. 1973, Va. 1974, U.S. Tax Ct. 1979. Asst. U.S. atty. U.S. Dept. Justice, Washington, 1970-73; pvt. practice Arlington, Va., 1974-75; ptnr. Lataif & Bernsen, Arlington, 1976-77; pvt. practice Fairfax, Va., 1978-85; of counsel Jones, Day, Reavis & Pogue, Washington, 1986-88, ptnr., 1989-91; ptnr. McDermott, Will & Emery, Miami, Fla., 1991-95; prin. Lawrence P. Lataif, P.A., Ft. Lauderdale, Fla., 1995—. Bd. advisors: Corp. Counsel's Guide to Business-Related Immigration, 1989—; contbr. articles to Wall St. Jour. and profl. jours. Mem. bd. overseers Children's Hosp., Boston, 1993—; mem. bd. Symphony of Americas, 1995—. Prettyman fellow Georgetown U. Law Sch., 1968. Mem. Am. Immigration Lawyers Assn. Office: Ste 202 5100 N Federal Hwy Fort Lauderdale FL 33308

LATANÉ, BIBB, social psychologist; b. N.Y.C., July 19, 1937; s. Henry Allen and Felicite Gillman (Bibb) L.; m. Deborah Ruth Richardson; children by previous marriage: Julia Gillman, Claire Augusta, Henry Arbiter. B.A., Yale U., 1958; Ph.D., U. Minn., 1963. Mem. faculty dept. social psychology Columbia U., N.Y.C., 1962-68; prof. psychology, dir. behavioral scis. lab. Ohio State U., Columbus, 1968-82; prof. psychology, dir. Inst. Research Social Sci. U.N.C.-Chapel Hill, 1982-90; prof. psychology Fla. Atlantic U., Boca Raton, 1990—. Contbr. articles to profl. jours. Guggenheim fellow, 1974-75; James McKeen Cattell fellow, 1981-82; NSF, Office of Naval Research grantee. Mem. Am. Psychol. Assn. (council rep. 1971-75), Soc. Personality and Social Psychology (pres. 1976-79, Campbell award 1986), Midwestern Psychol. Assn. (pres. 1981-84), Acad. Mgmt., AAAS (Socio-Psychol. prize 1968, 80), Am. Sociol. Assn., Animal Behavior Soc., Internat. Assn. Applied Psychology. Home: 4521 S Ocean Blvd Boca Raton FL 33487-4235 *We know so much, yet have so much to learn about each other that the science of behavior will continue to vitalize and be vital.*

LATANISION, RONALD MICHAEL, materials science and engineering educator, consultant; b. Richmondale, Pa., July 2, 1942; s. Stephen and Mary (Kopach) L.; m. Carolyn Marie Domenig, June 27, 1964; children: Ivan, Sara. BS, Pa. State U., 1964; PhD in Metall. Engring., Ohio State U., 1968. Postdoctoral fellow Nat. Bur. Standards, Washington, 1968-69; research scientist Martin Marietta, Balt., 1969-73, acting head materials sci., 1973-74; dir. H.H. Uhlig Corrosion Lab. MIT, Cambridge, 1975—, Shell Disting. prof. materials sci. and engring., 1983-88, dir. Materials Processing Ctr., 1984-91; co-founder ALTRAN Materials Engring. Corp., Boston, 1992—; mem. tech. adv. bd. Modell Devel. Corp., Framingham, Mass., 1987—; sci. advisor com. on sci. and tech. U.S. Ho. of Reps., 1982-83; chmn. ad hoc com. Mass. Advanced Materials Ctr., Boston, 1985—; mem. adv. bd. Mass. Office Sci. and Tech.; co-PI, NSF/SSI project PALMS; chmn. MIT Coun. on Primary and Secondary Edn. Editor: Surface Effects in Crystal Plasticity, 1977, Atomistics of Fracture, 1983, Chemistry and Physics of Fracture, 1987, Advances in Mechanics and Physics of Fracture, 1981, 83, 86; contbr. articles to profl. jours. Recipient sr. scientist award Humboldt Found., 1974-75, David Ford McFarland award Pa. State U., 1986; named Henry Krumb lectr. AIME, 1984, Disting. Alumnus, Ohio State U. Coll. Engring., 1991; hon. alumnus MIT, 1992. Fellow Am. Soc. Metals Internat. (govt. and pub. affairs com. 1984), Nat. Assn. Corrosion Engrs. (A.B. Campbell award 1971, Willis R. Whitney award 1984); mem. New Eng. Sci. Tchrs. (founder, co-chmn.), Nat. Acad. Engring., Nat. Materials Adv. Bd. Roman Catholic. Office: MIT Materials Sci & Engring 77 Massachusetts Ave Rm 8202 Cambridge MA 02139-4301

LATCHUM, JAMES LEVIN, federal judge; b. Milford, Del., Dec. 23, 1918; s. James H. and Ida Mae (Robbins) L.; m. Elizabeth Murray McArthur, June 16, 1943; children: Su-Allan, Elizabeth M. A.B. cum laude, Princeton U., 1940; J.D., U. Va., 1946. Bar: Va. 1942, Del. 1947. Assoc. Berl, Potter & Anderson, Wilmington, 1946-53; partner Berl, Potter & Anderson, 1953-68; judge U.S. Dist. Ct. Del., Wilmington, 1968-73; chief judge U.S. Dist. Ct. Del., 1973-83, sr. judge, 1983—; New Castle County atty. Del. Hwy. Dept., 1948-50; asst. U.S. atty., 1950-53; atty. Del. Interstate Hwy. Div., 1955-62, Delaware River and Bay Authority, 1962-68. Chmn. New Castle County Democratic Com., 1953-56, Wilmington City Com., 1959-63. Served to maj. Insp. Gen. Corps AUS, 1942-46, PTO. Mem. ABA, Del. Bar Assn., Va. Bar Assn., Order of Coif, Sigma Nu Phi. Presbyn. Clubs: Wilmington, Univ. Office: US Dist Ct 844 N King St # 34 Wilmington DE 19801-3519

LATHAM, ALLEN, JR., manufacturing company consultant; b. Norwich, Conn., May 23, 1908; s. Allen and Caroline (Walker) L.; m. Ruth Nichols, Nov. 11, 1933 (dec. 1992); children: W. Nichols, Harriet Latham Robinson, David W., Thomas W.; m. Charlotte T. Goldsmith, July 4, 1992. B.S. in Mech. Engring, MIT, 1930, Sloan fellow, 1936. Devel. engr. E.I. duPont, Belle, W.Va., 1930-35; engr., treas. Polaroid Corp., Cambridge, Mass., 1936-41; engr., v.p. Arthur D. Little, Cambridge, 1941-66; pres. Cryogenic Tech., Waltham, Mass., 1966-71; founder Haemonetics, Braintree, Mass., 1971—. Recipient New Eng. Inventor award, 1987, Morton Grove-Rasmussen award Am. Assn. Blood Banks, 1989; named Engr. of Yr. Socs. New Eng. Engring., 1970. Mem. AAAS, ASME (hon.), AIChE, Instrument Soc. Am., Nat. Acad. Engring. Club: Country (Brookline, Mass.). Patentee in blood processing equipment and processes. Home: 143 Whitcomb Ave Jamaica Plain MA 02130-3436 Office: Haemonetics 400 Wood Rd Braintree MA 02184-2486

LATHAM, ELEANOR RUTH EARTHROWL, neuropsychology therapist; b. Enfield, Conn., Jan. 12, 1924; d. Francis Henry and Ruth Mary (Harris) Earthrowl; m.Vaughan Milton Latham, July 20, 1946; children: Rebecca Ann, Carol Joan, Jennifer Howe, Vaughan Milton Jr. BA, Vassar Coll., 1945; MA, Smith Coll., 1947, Clark U., Worcester, Mass., 1974; EdD, Clark U., Worcester, Mass., 1979. Lic. psychologist, Mass. Guidance counselor Worcester Pub. Schs., 1967-74, sch. psychologist, 1975-80; pvt. practice neuropsychology Worcester, 1981—; postdoctoral trainee Children's Hosp.-Harvard Med. Sch., Boston, 1980-81; mem. staff The Med. Ctr. of Ctrl. Mass. Meml.-Hahnemann, Worcester, St. Vincent Hosp., Worcester; assoc. in pediats. U. Mass. Med. Ctr. and Med. Sch., Worcester, 1982—. Author: Neuropsychological Impairment in Duchene Muscular Dystrophy, 1985, Motor Coordination and Visual-Motor Development in Duchenne Muscular Dystrophy, 1991, Developmental Considerations in Educational Planning for Boys with Duchenne Muscular Dystrophy; contbr. chpt.: Children and Death, 1987. Mem. Internat. Neuropsychology Soc., Am. Psychol. Assn. Republican. Unitarian. Avocations: chamber music, piano, travel, swimming, gardening. Home: 59 Berwick St Worcester MA 01602-1442 Office: Vernon Med Ctr 10 Winthrop St Worcester MA 01604-4435

LATHAM, JAMES DAVID, lawyer; b. Lowell, Mass., Apr. 18, 1942; s. Ernest Hargreaves and Anne Crowdis (MacIvor) L.; m. Pauline Page, Apr. 14, 1972; children: James Benjamin, Timothy David. AB, Dartmouth Coll., 1964; LLB, Boston U., 1967. Bar: Mass. 1967, U.S. Dist. Ct. Mass. 1968. Assoc. Goldman & Curtis, Lowell, 1967-72; ptnr. Goldman, Curtis, Leahey & Latham, Lowell and Boston, 1972-74; assoc. counsel ITT Sheraton Corp., Boston, 1974-78, sr. counsel, 1978-80, asst. gen. counsel, 1982-84, v.p., 1984-92, sr. v.p., sec., gen. counsel, 1992—; gen. counsel Sheraton Mgmt. Corp., London, 1980-84. Chmn. Lowell Rep. City Com., 1972. Mem. Vesper Country Club, The Internat. Club. Episcopalian. Office: ITT Sheraton Corp 60 State St Boston MA 02109-1803

LATHAM, JAMES RICHARD, research scientist; b. Pomona, Calif., July 1, 1946; s. James Richard and Norma Elizabeth (Mills) L.; m. Pamela June Staley Latham, Aug. 31, 1968, 1 child, Joan Elizabeth Latham. Student, U. Calif., Berkeley, 1964-65, Chabot Coll., Hayward, Calif., 1965-72. Technician Coast Mfg./Hexel Co., Livermore, Calif., 1966-69, Crown Zellerbach Co., San Leandro, Calif., 1969-70; sr. rsch. technician Kaiser Aluminum & Chem. Corp., Pleasanton, Calif., 1970-82; sr. technician Clorox Tech. Ctr., Pleasanton, Calif., 1982—. Patentee in field. Named Merit Scholarship Finalist; recipient NROTC scholarship. Mem. AAAS, Am. Chemical Soc., Div. Chemical Technicians (treas.), N.Y. Acad. Sci. Mem. LDS Ch. Avocations: sailing, amateur radio (KE6QJV). Office: Clorox Technical Ctr 7200 Johnson Dr Pleasanton CA 94588-8004

LATHAM, JOSEPH AL, JR., lawyer; b. Kinston, N.C., Sept. 16, 1951; s. Joseph Al and Margaret Lee (Tyson) L.; m. Elaine Frances Kramer, Dec. 19, 1981; 1 child, Aaron Joshua. BA, Yale U., 1973; JD, Vanderbilt U., 1976. Bar: Calif. 1976, U.S. Dist. Ct. (cen. dist.) Calif. 1977, U.S. Ct. Appeals (9th cir.) 1977, U.S. Dist. Ct. (no. and so. dists.) Calif. 1978, Ga. 1980, U.S. Dist. Ct. (no. dist.) Ga. 1981, U.S. Ct. Appeals (5th and 11th cirs.) 1981, U.S. Dist. Ct. (mid. dist.) Ga. 1982, D.C. 1984. Assoc. Paul, Hastings, Janofsky & Walker, Orange County and L.A., 1976-80, Atlanta, 1980-83; ptnr. Paul, Hastings, Janofsky & Walker, Orange County and L.A., 1987—; chief counsel to bd. mem. NLRB, Washington, 1983-85; staff dir. U.S. Commn. on Civil Rights, Washington, 1985-86; instr. advanced profl. program U. So. Calif. Law Ctr., 1988, lectr. law, 1989—. Articles editor Vanderbilt Law Rev., 1975-76; editorial asst. Employment Discrimination Law, 2d edit., 1983; contbr. articles to Barron's, ABA Jour., Litigation, Employee Rels. Law Jour. Mem. ABA (labor and employment law sect.), Calif. Bar Assn., Ga. Bar Assn., D.C. Bar Assn., Order of Coif. Republican. Episcopalian. Office: Paul Hastings Janofsky & Walker 555 S Flower St Fl 23 Los Angeles CA 90071-2300

LATHAM, LARRY LEE, state administrator, psychologist; b. Dallas, June 27, 1945; s. James L. Latham and Sara B. (MacClaine) Dulaney; m. Helen Marie Bumpass, Dec. 19, 1966; children: Wade Lee, Ryan Justin. BS in Psychology, U. North Tex., 1966, MS in Psychology, 1967; PhD in Psychology, U. Ala., 1977. Lic. psychologist, Ala. Psychologist Outwood State Sch., Dawson Springs, Ky., 1967-69; psychologist, unit coord. Denton (Tex.) State Sch., 1969-72; dir. habilitation W.D. Partlow Devel. Ctr., Tuscaloosa, Ala., 1972-77; dir. applied rsch. Ala. Dept. Mental Health and Mental Retardation, Tuscaloosa, 1977-81; dir. L.B. Wallace Devel. Ctr. Ala. Dept. Mental Health and Mental Retardation, Decatur, 1981-84; assoc. commr. for mental retardation Ala. Dept. Mental Health and Mental Retardation, Montgomery, 1984-91; dir. Bur. Orgnl. Devel., Montgomery, 1991—; dir. Greil Psychiat. Hosp./ Ala. Dept. Mental Health and Mental Retardation, 1993—; cons. Latham & Assocs., 1969-72, Tex. Dept. Mental Health and Mental Retardation, 1987; pres. Human Svcs. Pers. Specialist, Inc. Bd. dirs. Foster Grandparents Ky., 1967-69, Ala. Spl. Olympics, 1984-91, Ala. Devel. Disabilities Coun., 1984-91. Fellow Am. Assn. Mental Retardation (pres. Ala. chpt. 1988-89). Avocations: woodworking, golf. Office: Greil Meml. Psychiat Hosp 2140 Upper Wetumpka Rd Montgomery AL 36107-1342 *In this age it is best to remember that just because your values are not valued does not mean that you are wrong.*

LATHAM, LAVONNE MARLYS, physical education educator; b. Garrison, Iowa, Mar. 17, 1942; d. Harry August and Vona Irene (Loveless) Hilmer; m. Robert Allen Latham Jr., July 21, 1979. BA, U. Iowa, 1964; postgrad., No. Ill. U., 1985, Western Ill. U., 1970-88, Bemidji State U., 1979. Cert. tchr., Ill. Tchr. phys. edn., elem. computer coord. Erie (Ill.) Community Unit 1, 1964—; head counselor Camp Lenore Owaissa, Hinsdale, Mass., 1964-78. Mem. NEA, AAHPER, Ill. Assn. Health, Phys. Edn. and Recreation, U. Iowa Alumni Assn., Ill. Edn. Assn., Erie Tchrs. Assn. (pres. 1982-83), Nat. Audubon Soc., Nature Conservancy, Delta Kappa Gamma. Baptist. Avocations: violin, computers, photography, travel, outdoor activities. Home: 1002 6th St Erie IL 61250 Office: Erie Community Unit 1 605 6th Ave Erie IL 61250-9452

LATHAM, PATRICIA HORAN, lawyer; b. Hoboken, N.J., Sept. 5, 1941; d. Patrick John and Rosemary (Moller) Horan; m. Peter Samuel Latham, June 12, 1965; children: John Horan, Kerry Patricia. BA, Swarthmore Coll., 1963; JD, U. Chgo., 1966. Bar: D.C. 1967, U.S. Dist. Ct. D.C. 1967, U.S. Ct. Appeals 1967, U.S. Supreme Ct. 1970, Va. 1989, U.S. Dist. Ct. (ea. dist.) Va. 1989, U.S. Dist. Ct. Md. 1991. Assoc. Fried Frank Harris Shriver & Kampelman, Washington, 1966-69; atty. Office of Gen. Counsel, SEC, Washington, 1969-71; assoc. Martin & Smith, Washington, 1971—, ptnr., 1974-85; ptnr. Latham & Latham, Washington, 1986—; lectr. Columbus Sch. Law, Cath. U. Am., Washington, 1978-92; mem. panel of arbitrators N.Y. Stock Exch., 1985—; co-founder, co-dir. Nat. Ctr. Law and Learning Disabilities, 1992—. Co-author: Attention Deficit Disorder and the Law, 1992, Learning Disabilities and the Law, 1993, ADD and the College Student, 1993, Succeeding in the Workplace, 1994, Higher Education Services for Students with Learning Disabilities and Attention Deficit Disorder: A Legal Guide, 1994, A Comprehensive Guide to Attention Deficit Disorder in Adults, 1995. Legal advisor League of Rep. Women of D.C., 1988-90; co-founder, trustee Beacon Coll., 1989-93, chmn. bd. trustees, 1990-92; mem. nat. adult issues com. Children and Adults with Attention Deficit Disorders. Mem. ABA, D.C. Bar, Am. Arbitration Assn. (panel arbitrators and mediators 1982—), Nat. Attention Deficit Disorders Assn. (bd. dirs.), City Tavern Club. Roman Catholic. Home: 7000 Loch Edin Ct Potomac MD 20854-4844

LATHAM, PETER SAMUEL, lawyer; b. Boston, July 23, 1940; s. Earl Gansen and Margaret (Perrier) L.; m. Patricia Ann Horan, Sept. 5, 1941; children: John Horan, Kerry Patricia. BA with honors, Swarthmore Coll., 1962; LLB, U. Pa., 1965. Bar: D.C. 1966, U.S. Ct. Appeals (D.C. cir.) 1982, U.S. Dist. Ct. Md. 1991. Atty. SEC, Washington, 1965-66; assoc. firm Vom Baur, Coburn, Simmons & Turtle, Washington, 1969-71; mem. firm Wachtel, Ross and Matzkin, Washington, 1971-80; ptnr. Latham & Latham and predecessor firms, Washington, 1980—; arbitrator Am. Arbitration Assn., 1978—. Author: Government Contract Disputes, 1981, 86; co-author: Attention Deficit Disorder and the Law: A Guide for Advocates, 1992, Learning Disabilities and the Law, 1993, Succeeding in the Workplace, 1994, Higher Education Services for Students with Learning Disabilities and Attention Deficit Disorder: A Legal Guide, 1994; producer, dir. The ABC's of ADD, other videos on legal topics. Co-founder, trustee Beacon Coll., 1989-93; co-founder, co-dir. Nat. Ctr. for Law and Learning Disabilities. Lt. USN, 1966-69. Decorated Navy Achievement medal with combat V. Mem. ABA, City Tavern Club. Republican. Roman Catholic. Avocations: tennis, swimming. Home: 7000 Loch Edin Ct Potomac MD 20854-4844 Office: Latham and Latham 1016 16th St NW Fl 7 Washington DC 20036-5703

LATHAM, TOM, congressman; b. Hampton, Iowa, July 14, 1948; s. Willard and Evelyn L.; m. Kathy Swinson, 1975; children: Justin, Jennifer, Jill. Student, Watrburg Coll., Iowa State U. Bank teller, bookkeeper Brush, Colo., 1970-72; ind. ins. agent Fort Lupton, Colo., 1972-74; mktg. rep. Hartford Ins. Co., Des Moines, 1974-76; with Latham Seed Co., Alexander, Iowa, 1976—; now v.p., co-owner Latham Seed Co.; mem. 104th Congress from 6th Iowa dist., 1995—; Mem. congressman Fred Grandy's agriculture com.; sec. Republican Party of Iowa; rep. 5th dist. Republican State Ctrl. com.; co-chair Francklin County Republican Ctrl. com.; whip Iowa del. Republican Nat. Conv., 1992. Past chair Franklin County Extension Coun.; mem. Nazareth Lutheran Ch., past pres.; citizens adv. coun. Iowa State U. Mem. Am. Soybean Assn., Am. Seed Trade Assn., Iowa Farm Bur. Fedn., Iowa Soybean Assn., Iowa Corn Growers Assn., Iowa Seed Assn., Agribusiness Assn. of Iowa. Lutheran. Office: US House Reps 516 Cannon House Office Bldg Washington DC 20515-1505

LATHAM, WELDON HURD, lawyer; b. Bklyn., Jan. 2, 1947; s. Aubrey Geddes and Avril (Hurd) L.; m. Constantia Beecher, Aug. 8, 1948; children—Nicole Marie, Brett Weldon. BA, Howard U., 1968; JD, Georgetown U., 1971; postgrad. George Washington U., 1975-76. Bar: D.C. 1972, U.S. Ct. Appeals (D.C. cir.) 1972, U.S. Ct. Mil. Appeals 1974, U.S. Ct. Claims 1975, U.S. Supreme Ct. 1975, Va. 1981, U.S. Ct. Appeals (fed. cir.) 1988. Mgmt. cons. Checchi & Co., Washington, 1968-71; atty. Covington & Burling, Washington, 1971-73; sr. atty. Fed. Energy Adminstrn., Washington, 1974; asst. gen. counsel Exec. Office Pres., Office Mgmt. and Budget The White House, 1974-76; atty. Hogan & Hartson, Washington, 1976-79; gen. dep. asst. sec. HUD, 1979-81; v.p., gen. counsel Sterling Systems, Inc. (subs. PRC), exec. asst., counsel to chmn., CEO, and assoc. gen. counsel Planning Rsch. Corp., McLean, Va., 1981-86; mng. ptnr. Reed Smith Shaw & McClay, McLean, Va., 1986-91; sr. ptnr. Shaw, Pittman, Potts & Trowbridge, Washington, 1992—; adj. prof. Howard U. Law Sch., Washington, 1972-82; guest prof. U. Va., Charlottesville, 1976-90; mem. Va. Gov.'s Bus. and Industry Adv. Com. on Crime Prevention, 1983-85, Va. Gov.'s Regulatory Reform Adv. Bd., 1982-84; chmn. task force SBA, 1982; legal counsel Md. Mondale for Pres. Campaign, 1984. Columnist Minority Bus. Entrepreneur (MBE) Mag., 1991—. Mem. Washington steering com. NAACP Legal Def. Fund, 1975-95, Fairfax County Airports Adv. com., 1987-88; bd. dirs., gen. counsel Northern Va. Minority Bus. and Profl. Assn., 1985-92;

trustee Va. Commonwealth U., Richmond, 1986-90; bd. dirs. Washington Urban League, 1986-90, U. D.C. Found., 1982-87, Washington Coun. Lawyers, 1973, bd. dirs. Profl. Svcs. Coun., 1983-88; bd. dirs. Minority Bus. Legal Def. and Edn. Fund, 1989-91; appointee Greater Washington Bd. Trade, Blue Ribbon Task Force on Home Rule, 1985-86, bd. dirs., exec. com., chmn. regional affairs com., corp. sec. Greater Wash. Bd. Trade, 1990-95; trustee George Mason U., Fairfax, Va., 1990-94; mem. adv. bd. First Union Nat. Bank, 1995—; civilian aide Sec. of Dept. of Army, 1995—; mem. Clinton Small Bus. Adminstrn. Nat. Adv. Coun., 1993—; prin. coun. for Excellence in Govt., 1989—; mayor D.C. Internat. Ins. Adv. Commn., 1994-95; chair D.C. Mayor's bus. adv. coun., 1994—; mem. nat. adv. coun. Clinton Adminstrn., 1993—; co-chair UNCF Sportsfest Fundraiser, 1994; gen. counsel's Honors Program Office of Sec. Capt. USAF, 1973-74. Recipient SES Effective Mgr. award HUD, 1980, Nat. Assn. for Equal Achievement Opportunity in Higher Edn. award, 1987. Mem. ABA (vice-chmn. subcom. pub. contract law sect. 1988-93), Fed. Bar Assn., Nat. Bar Assn., D.C. C. of C. (gen. counsel 1979), State Va. Bar Assn., Washington Bar Assn., Bar Assn. D.C., Nat. Contract Mgmt. Assn. Mem. editorial adv. bd. Washington Bus. Jour., 1985-87. Home: 7004 Natelli Woods Ln Bethesda MD 20817-3924 Office: Shaw Pittman Potts & Trowbridge 2300 N St NW Washington DC 20037-1122

LATHAM, WILLIAM PETERS, composer, former educator; b. Shreveport, La., Jan. 4, 1917; s. Lawrence L. and Eugenia (Peters) L.; m. Joan Seyler, Apr. 18, 1946; children: Leslie Virginia, William Peters, Carol Jean. Student, Asbury Coll., Wilmore, Ky., 1933-35, Cin. Conservatory Music, 1936-38; B.Sc. in Music Edn, U. Cin., 1938; B.Mus., Coll. Music Cin., 1940, M.Mus., 1941; Ph.D., Eastman Sch. Music, 1951; pupil composition with, Eugene Goossens, Howard Hanson, Herbert Elwell. Mem. faculty N. Tex. State Tchrs. Coll., 1938-39, Eastern Ill. State Tchrs. Coll., 1946; mem. faculty State Coll. Iowa, 1946-65, prof. music, 1959-65; prof. composition Sch. Music, U. N. Tex., Denton, 1965-84; dir. grad. studies Sch. Music, U. N. Tex., 1969-84, disting. prof., 1978-84, prof. emeritus, 1984—. Composer numerous works, 1938—, including works for orch., band, chorus, chamber groups, soloists, one opera and one ballet; compositions since 1980 include (chorus) Gaudeamus Academe, 1981, Bitter Land, 1985, My Heart Sings, 1988, Missa Novella, 1989, Only in Texas!, 1994; (chamber music) Ion, The Rhapsode for clarinet and piano, 1985, Metaphors, three songs for soprano, 1988, A Green Voice, cantata for soprano and tenor, 1989, The Sacred Flame, cantata for baritone and orch., 1990, Vital Signs for chorus of unchanged voices, Tex., 1991, Excelsior K-2 for orch., 1994, Requiem for My Love, three songs for high voice, 1994, Suite Summertime, three movements for band, 1995. Served to 2d lt. AUS, 1942-46. Scholar in composition Cin. Coll. Music, 1939-41; recipient numerous awards and commns. Mem. ASCAP (ann. awards 1962—), Coll. Mus. Soc., Phi Mu Alpha, Pi Kappa Lambda. Home: PO Box 50373 Denton TX 76206-0373

LATHE, ROBERT EDWARD, management and financial consultant; b. Balt., Apr. 8, 1945; s. Warren Calvin Sr. and Margaret Mary (Cavey) L.; m. Hermina Yeghnazarian, Apr. 13, 1967; children: Michelle Gayaneh, Mellina Margaret. MSc in Mgmt., U. Dublin, 1985. Metrology/field engr. Bendix Field Engring. Corp., Balt., 1967-68; quality assurance supr. space seismology lab. Bendix Aerospace Systems Divsn., Ann Arbor, Mich., 1968-72; programs mgr. Iran Aircraft Industries, Tehran, 1972-76; mgmt. cons. Alexander Proudfoot Co., Chgo., 1977-78; program mgr., field engr. Harris-PRD Electronics Divsn., Syosset, N.Y. & Isfahan, Iran, 1978-80; ops. dir. Airmotive Ireland Ltd., Dublin, 1980-84; project mgr. Handley-Walker Co., Inc., Valencia, Calif., 1986-87; owner, pres. Hyrel Bus. Svcs., Glendale, Calif., 1987-90; fin. planner, investment advisor IDS Fin. Svcs. Inc., Glendale, 1990-94; co-founder, sr. ptnr. Calif. Connection, Glendale, 1994—. Sgt. USAF, 1963-67, Vietnam. Mem. Am. Legion, La Crescenta C. of C. Avocations: microcomputers, golf, swimming, ten-pin bowling. Home: 543 Milford St # 4 Glendale CA 91203-1697

LATHI, BHAGAWANDAS PANNALAL, electrical engineering educator; b. Bhokar, Maharashtr, India, Dec. 3, 1933; came to U.S., 1956; s. Pannalal Rupchand and Tapi Pannalal (Indani) L.; m. Rajani Damodardas Mundada, July 27, 1962; children: Anjali, Shishir. BEEE, Poona U., 1955; MSEE, U. Ill., 1957; PhD in Elec. Engring., Stanford U., 1961. Research asst. U. Ill., Urbana, 1956-57, Stanford (Calif.) U., 1957-60; research engr. Gen. Electric Co., Syracuse, N.Y., 1960-61; cons. to semicondr. industry India, 1961-62; assoc. prof. elec. engring. Bradley U., Peoria, Ill., 1962-69, U.S. Naval Acad., Annapolis, Md., 1969-72; prof. elec. engring. Campinas (Brazil) State U., 1972-78, Calif. State U., Sacramento, 1979—; vis. prof. U. Iowa, Owa City, 1979; founder, sole proprieter Berkeley-Cambridge Press. Author: Signals, Systems and Communication, 1965, Communication Systems, 1968 (transl. into Japanese 1977), Random Signals and Communication Theory, 1968, Teoria Signalow I Ukladow Telekomunikacyjnych, 1970, Sistemy Telekomunikacyjne, 1972, Signals, Systems and Controls, 1974, Sistemas de Comunicacion, 1974, 86, Sistemas de Comunicacao, 1978, Modern Digital and Analog Communication Systems, 1983, 89 (transl. into Japanese 1986, 90), Signals and Systems, 1987, Linear Systems and Signals, 1992; contbr. articles to profl. jours. Fellow IEEE. Avocations: swimming, poetry. Office: Calif State U 6000 J St Sacramento CA 95819-2605

LATHLAEN, ROBERT FRANK, retired construction company executive; b. Phila., May 25, 1925; s. Clarence Delcamp and Anna Marie (Schwab) L.; m. Nancy Nichols, May 1948 (div. July 1983); children: Margaret, Gail, Carol Sue; m. Margot von Harten, May 4, 1985. BSCE, Drexel U., 1945; SMCE, MIT, 1946. Registered profl. engr., N.Y. With W.J. Barney Corp., N.Y.C., 1946-94, pres., 1972-91, chmn. bd., 1991-94; vis. prof. Ea. Carolina U., 1993; adj. assoc. prof. NYU, 1984-91. Trustee St. Vincent's Hosp. and Med. Ctr., N.Y.C., 1986-90. Mem. ASCE (life), Assoc. Gen. Contractors (bd. dirs., chmn. various coms. 1976—, chmn. bldg. divsn. 1991), Gen. Bldg. Contractors N.Y. State (pres. 1975-76), N.Y. Bldg. Congress (bd. dirs. 1975-80), Am. Arbitration Asssn. (dir. 1986-94, exec. com. 1987-93, chmn. nat. constrn. industry arbitration com. 1989-90). Mem. Ch. of Christ. Avocations: writing fiction; bicycle riding; swimming; bird watching.

LATHROP, ANN, librarian, educator; b. L.A., Nov. 30, 1935; d. Paul Ray and Margaret (Redfield) W.; divorced; children: Richard Harold, John Randolph, Rodney Grant. BA in History summa cum laude, Ea. N.Mex. U., 1957; MLS, Rutgers U., 1964; PhD, U. Oreg., 1988. Cert. elem. tchr., Calif.; cert. libr., Calif; adminstrv. credential, Calif. Elem. sch. tchr. Chalfont (Pa.) Boro Sch., 1960-61, Livingston Elem. Sch., New Brunswick, N.J., 1961-63, Rosedale Elem. Sch., Chico, Calif., 1964-65; libr. Chico (Calif.) H.S., 1965-72, Princeton (Calif.) H.S., 1972-73, Santa Maria (Calif.) H.S., 1973-77; libr. coord. San Mateo County Office Edn., Redwood City, Calif., 1977-89; assoc. prof. Calif. State U., Long Beach, 1989-92, prof., 1993—; dir. Calif. Software Clearinghouse, Calif. State U. Long Beach. Author: Online Information Retrieval as a Research Tool in Secondary School Libraries, 1988; co-author: Courseware in the Classroom, 1983; editor: Online and CD-ROM Databases in School Libraries, 1989, The 1988-89 Educational Software Preview Guide, 1988, Technology in the Curriculum Resource Guides, 1988; editor, founder: (jours.) The Digest of Software Reviews: Education, 1983-86, Software Reviews on File, 1985-86; editor: (database) California Online Resources in Education, 1989-94, Technology in the Curriculum Online, 1995—; contbr. chpts. to books, articles to profl. jours. Mem. ALA, NEA, Am. Assn. Sch. Librs., Assn. State Tech. Using Tchr. Educators, Calif. Faculty Assn., Calif. Sch. Libr. Assn., Computer Using Educators, Internat. Soc. for Tech. in Edn. Avocations: traveling, camping. Office: Calif State U 1250 N Bellflower Blvd Long Beach CA 90840-0006

LATHROP, GERTRUDE ADAMS, chemist, consultant; b. Norwich, Conn., Apr. 28, 1921; d. Williams Barrows and Lena (Adams) L. B.S., U. Conn., 1944; M.A., Tex. Woman's U., 1953, Ph.D., 1955. Devel. chemist on textiles/Alexander Smith & Sons Carpet Co. Yonkers, N.Y., 1944-52; research assoc. textiles Tex. Woman's U., 1952-56; chief chemist Glasgo Finishing Plant div. United Mchts. & Mfrs., Inc., Conn., 1956-57; chief chemist Old Fort Finishing Plant div. United Mchts. & Mfrs., Inc., N.C., 1957-63; research chemist United Mchts. Research Ctr., Langley, S.C., 1963-64; lab. mgr. automotive div. Collins & Aikman Corp., Albemarle, N.C., 1964-78; chief chemist, lab. mgr. Old Fort Finishing Plant div. United Mchts., 1979-82. Treas. 1st Congl. Ch., Asheville, N.C., 1985-87, bd. deacons, 1990-93; tax-aide counselor to elderly IRS, 1984—, Am. Assn. Ret. Person, Widowed Person Svcs., Asheville-Buncombe County, Inc., 1990-91, pres. Widowed Persons Svcs., 1992—; active RSVP Land of Sky, 1989-92; pub. Rels. com. Swannanoa Valley, N.C., Am. Assn. Ret. Persons, 1984-92, v.p., 1992, treas., 1993-94. Recipient Nat. Cmty. Svc. award Am. Assn. Ret. Persons, 1989, 96, Widowed Person's Outstanding Individual Achievement award, 1994, Disting. Alumni award U. Conn. Sch. Family Studies, 1980-81, Woman of Yr. award, 1979, Bus. and Profl. Women's Club, Albemarle, Woman of Yr. award Bus. and Profl. Women's Club Asheville, 1980. Mem. ASTM (chmn. transp. fabrics on flammability com. 1973-75), Am. Chem. Soc. (emeritus), Am. Assn. Textile Chemists and Colorists (emeritus, sec., rsch. chmn., treas., vice chmn. 1962-64, chmn. edn. com. Piedmont sect. 1977-78), Bus. and Profl. Women's Club (chpt. pres. 1974-76), Iota Sigma Pi (emeritus mem.-at-large). Home and Office: PO Box 1166 Black Mountain NC 28711-1166

LATHROP, IRVIN TUNIS, retired academic dean, educator; b. Platteville, Wis., Sept. 23, 1927; s. Irvin J. and Marian (Johnson) L.; m. Eleanor M. Kolar, Aug. 18, 1951; 1 son, James I. B.S., Stout State Coll., 1950; M.S., Iowa State U., 1954, Ph.D., 1958. Tchr. Ottumwa (Iowa) High Sch., 1950-55; mem. faculty Iowa State U., 1957-58, Western Mich. U., 1958-59; mem. faculty Calif. State Coll., 1959-88, prof. indsl. arts, 1966-88, chmn. dept. indsl. edn., 1969-88, assoc. dean extended edn., 1978-88, prof. emeritus, 1988—; cons. Naval Ordnance Lab., Corona, Calif., 1961-63. Author: (with Marshall La Cour) Photo Technology, 1966, rev. edit., 1977, Photography, 1979, rev. edit., 1992, The Basic Book of Photography, 1979, Laboratory Manual for Photo Technology, 1973, (with John Lindbeck) General Industry, 1969, rev. edit., 1977, 86, (with Robert Kunst) Photo-Offset, 1979; Editorial cons.: (with Robert Kunst) Am. Tech. Soc; Contbr. (with Robert Kunst) articles to profl. jours. Mem. adv. com. El Camino and Orange Coast Coll.; mem. Orange County Grand Jury, 1989-90, Orange County Juvenile Justice Commn., 1991—. Mem. Nat. Soc. for Study Edn., Am. Council Indsl. Arts Tchr. Edn., Am. Vocat. Assn., Nat. Assn. Indsl. and Tech. Tchrs., Internat. Tech. Assn., Am. Ednl. Research Assn., Epsilon Pi Tau, Psi Chi, Phi Delta Kappa, Phi Kappa Phi. Home: PO Box 3430 Laguna Hills CA 92654-3430 Office: 1250 N Bellflower Blvd Long Beach CA 90840-0006

LATHROP, MITCHELL LEE, lawyer; b. L.A., Dec. 15, 1937; s. Alfred Lee and Barbara (Mitchell) L.; m. Denice Annette Davis; children: Christin Lorraine Newlon, Alexander Mitchell, Timothy Trewin Mitchell. B.Sc., U.S. Naval Acad., 1959; J.D., U. So. Calif., 1966. Bar: D.C. 1966, Calif. 1966, U.S. Supreme Ct. 1969, N.Y. 1981; registered environ. assessor, Calif. Dep. counsel Los Angeles County, Calif., 1966-68; with firm Brill, Hunt, DeBuys and Burby, L.A., 1968-71; ptnr. Macdonald, Halsted & Laybourne, L.A. and San Diego, 1971-80; sr. ptnr. Rogers & Wells, N.Y.C., San Diego, 1980-86; sr. ptnr. Adams, Duque & Hazeltine, L.A., San Francisco, N.Y.C., San Diego, 1986-94, exec. com., 1986-94, firm chmn., 1992-94; sr. ptnr. Luce, Forward, Hamilton & Scripps, San Diego, N.Y.C., San Francisco, L.A., 1994—; presiding referee Calif. Bar Ct., 1984-86, mem. exec. com., 1981-88; lectr. law Calif. Judges Assn., Practicing Law Inst. N.Y., Continuing Edn. of Bar, State Bar Calif., ABA. Author: State Hazardous Waste Regulation, 1991, Environmental Insurance Coverage, 1991, Insurance Coverage for Environmental Claims, 1992. Western Regional chmn. Met. Opera Nat. Coun., 1971-81, v.p., mem. exec. com., 1971—, now chmn.; trustee Honnold Libr. at Claremont Colls., 1972-80; bd. dirs. Music Ctr. Opera Assn., L.A., sec., 1974-80; bd. dirs. San Diego Opera Assn., 1980—, v.p., 1985-89, pres.-elect, 1993, pres., 1994—; bd. dirs. Met. Opera Assn., N.Y.C.; mem. nat. steering coun. Nat. Actors Theatre, N.Y. Capt. JAGC, USNR, ret. Mem. ABA, N.Y. Bar Assn., Fed. Bar Assn., Fed. Bar Council, Calif. Bar Assn., D.C. Bar Assn., San Diego County Bar Assn. (chmn. ethics com. 1980-82, bd. dirs. 1982-85, v.p. 1985), Assn. Bus. Trial Lawyers, Assn. So. Calif. Def. Counsel, Los Angeles Opera Assos. (pres. 1970-72), Soc. Colonial Wars in Calif. (gov. 1970-72), Order St. Lazarus of Jerusalem, Friends of Claremont Coll. (dir. 1975-81, pres. 1978-79), Am. Bd. Trial Advocates, Judge Advocates Assn. (dir. Los Angeles chpt. 1974-80, pres. So. Calif. chpt. 1977-78), Internat. Assn. Def. Counsel, Brit. United Services Club (dir. Los Angeles 1973-75), Mensa Internat., Calif. Soc., S.R. (pres. 1977-79), Calif. Club (Los Angeles), Valley Hunt Club (Pasadena, Calif.), Met. Club (N.Y.C.), The Naval Club (London), Phi Delta Phi. Republican. Home: 455 Silvergate Ave San Diego CA 92106-3327 Office: Luce Forward Hamilton and Scripps 600 W Broadway Fl 26 San Diego CA 92101-3311 also: Citicorp Ctr 153 E 53rd St Frnt 26 New York NY 10022-4611

LATHROPE, DANIEL JOHN, law educator. BSBA, U. Denver, 1973; JD, Northwestern U., 1977; LLM, NYU, 1979. Bar: Ariz. 1977, Calif. 1978. Assoc. Evans, Kitchel & Jenckes, Phoenix, 1977-78; instr. law NYU, 1979-80; assoc. prof. U. Calif. Hastings Coll. Law, San Francisco, 1980-86, prof., 1986-95, assoc. acad. dean, 1986-87, acting dean, 1987-88, acad. dean, 1988-90; prof., assoc. dean, dir. grad. tax program U. Fla. Coll. Law, Gainesville, 1995—. Co-author: (with Lind, Schwarz and Rosenberg) Fundamentals of Corporate Taxation, 3d edit., 1991, (with Lind, Schwarz and Rosenberg) Fundamentals of Partnership Taxation, 4th edit., 1994, (with Schwarz) Black Letter on Federal Taxation of Corporations and Partnerships, 1991, 2d edit., 1994; author: The Alternative Minimum Tax-Compliance and Planning with Analysis, 1994. Mem. Order of Coif, Beta Gamma Sigma. Office: U Fla Coll Law Holland Hall Gainesville FL 32611

LATIES, VICTOR GREGORY, psychology educator; b. Racine, Wis., Feb. 2, 1926; s. Simon Gregory and Rima (Kapnik) L.; m. Martha Ann Fisher, July 29, 1956; children: Nancy, Andrew, Claire. A.B., Tufts U., 1949; Ph.D., U. Rochester, N.Y., 1954. Ford Found. teaching intern Brown U., 1954-55; instr., asst. prof. dept. pharmacology Johns Hopkins U. Sch. Medicine, 1955-65; asso. prof. U. Rochester Sch. Medicine and Dentistry, 1965-71, prof. dept. biophysics, psychology, pharmacology, 1971-93, dir. toxicology tng. program, 1978-91, 95-96, dir. environ. studies program, prof. dept. environ. medicine, 1992—; mem. preclinical psychopharmacology research rev. com. NIMH, 1967-71; mem. bd. on toxicology and environ. health hazards Nat. Acad. Sci.-NRC, 1977-80, mem. toxicology info. program com., 1981-85; mem. sci. rev. com. for health research EPA, 1981-89. Editor: Jour. Exptl. Analysis of Behavior, 1972-76, exec. editor, 1966-72, 76—; editor: (with B. Weiss) Behavioral Toxicology, 1975, Behavioral Pharmacology, 1976; mem. editorial bd.: Jour. Pharmacology and Exptl. Therapeutics, 1965-71, Psychopharmacology, 1968-78, 81-89, The Behavior Analyst, 1980-82, Experimental and Clinical Psychopharmacology, 1993—; contbr. articles to profl. jours. Served with USN, 1944-46. Fellow Am. Psychol. Assn. (pres. div. psychopharmacology 1968-69, div. exptl. analysis of behavior 1979-82, bd. sci. affairs 1983-85), Behavioral Pharmacology Soc. (pres. 1966-68), Am. Soc. Pharmacology and Exptl. Therapeutics, Assn. for Behavior Analysis, Soc. Toxicology, Am. Psychol. Soc., Soc. for Exptl. Analysis of Behavior (sec.-treas. 1966—). Home: 55 Dale Rd E Rochester NY 14625-2137 Office: U Rochester Medical Ctr Dept Environ Medicine Box EHSC Rochester NY 14642

LATIMER, ALLIE B., lawyer, government official; b. Coraopolis, Pa.; d. Lawnye S. and Bennie Latimer. BS, Hampton Inst., 1947; JD, Howard U., 1953, MDiv, 1986, DMin, 1988; LLM, Cath. U., 1958; postgrad., Am. U., 1960-61. Bar: N.C. bar 1955, D.C. bar 1960. Vol. in projects Am. Friends Service Com., N.J. and, Europe, 1948-49; correctional officer Fed. Reformatory for Women, Alderson, W.Va., 1949-51; personnel clk. NIH, Bethesda, 1953-55; realty officer Mitchell AFB, N.Y., 1955-56; with Office Gen. Counsel, GSA, Washington, 1957-76; chief counsel Office Gen. Counsel, GSA, after 1966, asst. gen. counsel, 1971-76, gen. counsel, 1977-87; asst. gen. counsel NASA, 1976-77; spl. counsel Gen. Svcs. Adminstrn., Washington, 1987—; past chmn. central office com. Fed. Women's Program, GSA; mem. membership and budget com. Health and Welfare Council, 1967-72. Bd. dirs. D.C. Mental Health Assn., pres., 1977-79; bd. dirs. Friendship House, Washington; elder Presbyn. Ch.; pres. Interacial Council, 1964-75; chmn. Presbyn. Econ. Devel. Corp., 1975-81; mem. governing bd. Nat. Council Chs. of Christ in U.S.A. Recipient GSA Sustained Superior Service award, 1959, Meritorious Service award, 1964, Commendable Service award, 1964, Pub. Service award, 1971, Outstanding Performance award, 1971, Presdl. Rank award, 1983, Disting. Service award, 1984. Mem. ABA, Nat. Bar Assn. (sec. 1966-74), Fed. Bar Assn., Washington Bar Assn., N.C. Bar Assn., Nat. Bar Found. (dir. 1970-71, pres. 1974-75), Hampton Alumni Assn. (pres. Washington chpt. 1970-71), Howard Law Alumni Assn. (v.p. 1962-63) alumni assns), Links (pres. Washington chpt. 1971-74, nat. v.p. 1976-80), Federally Employed Women (founder, 1st pres.). Home: 1721 S St NW Washington DC 20009-6117

LATIMER, BEN WILLIAM, healthcare executive; b. Lawrenceville, Ga., Aug. 3, 1940; married. BA, Ga. Tech, 1962, MA, 1965. Dir. mgmt. sys. Meth. Hosp., Memphis, 1965-69; various positions to CEO Carolinas Hosp., Charlotte, N.C., 1969-81; pres., CEO SunHealth Corp., Charlotte, 1982—. Contbr. articles to profl. jours. Mem. AHA (del. 1980-87), HIMSS (pres. 1973—). Office: SunHealth Corp Box 668800 Charlotte NC 28266-8800*

LATIMER, HELEN, information resource manager, writer, researcher; b. Elizabeth, N.J.; d. Raymond O. and Minna A. Mercner; divorced; children: Alexander, Victoria. AB, Duke U.; MS in Journalism, Columbia U.; cert. in bus. adminstrn., Harvard-Radcliffe; MBA in Mktg., Am. U.; postgrad., U. Calif., Berkeley, Rutgers U.; MBA, Syracuse U., 1995. Instr. mktg. Am. U., Washington; mgr. info. resources Burdeshaw Assocs., Ltd., Bethesda, Md., 1985-94, assoc., 1994—; acting commr. Commn. for Women, Washington, 1996—; initiated publ. specialists program George Washington U., Washington; officer alumni bds. Harvard-Radcliffe Program in Adminstrn., Am. U.; comm., info. resource mgmt. cons., tech. editor MIT Servomechanisms Lab.; AA to editor Reinhold Pub. (former subs. McGraw-Hill); facilitator, subgroup on mktg. The White House Conf. on Libr. and Info. Svcs., 1991. Contbr. articles to newspapers and mags. Past leader Troop 1907, Girl Scouts Am.; mem. Troop 100 com. Boy Scouts Am. Named to D.C. Commn. for Women, 1996. Mem. Spl. Librs. Assn., Harvard Bus. Sch. Club D.C. (initiated admission of women, v.p., bd. dirs.).

LATIMER, KENNETH ALAN, lawyer; b. Chgo., Oct. 26, 1943; s. Edward and Mary (Schiller) L.; m. Carole Ross, June 23, 1968; children: Cary, Darren, Wendy. BS, U. Wis., 1966; JD with honors, George Washington U., 1969. Bar: D.C. 1969, Ill. 1970. Atty. U.S. Office of Comptroller, Washington, 1969-70; assoc. Berger, Newmark & Fenchel, Chgo., 1970-74, ptnr., 1975-86; ptnr. Holleb & Coff, Chgo., 1986—; guest speaker Ill. Inst. for Continuing Legal Edn., Chgo., 1975-87. Pres. North Suburban Jewish Cmty. Ctr., Highland Park, Ill., 1985; bd. dirs. Jewish Cmty. Ctrs. Chgo., 1985-95. Mem. Ill. Bar Assn. (chmn. sect. coun. on comml. banking and bankruptcy 1990-91), ABA (com. on banking and comml. finance), Chgo. Bar Assn. (com. on fin. instns.), Comml. Fin. Assn. Ednl. Found. (governing bd.), Assn. Comml. Fin. Attys., Am Coll. Comml. Fin Attys., Standard Club. Avocations: jogging, travel, tennis. Office: Holleb & Coff 55 E Monroe St Ste 4100 Chicago IL 60603-5803

LATIMER, PAUL JERRY, non-destructive testing engineer; b. Springfield, Tenn., July 21, 1943; s. Paul Daniel and Juanita Inez (Richey) L.; m. Sylvia Susan Cole, June 6, 1966; children: Zachary Nathaniel, Matthew Jason. BS in Physics with honors, U. Tenn., 1966, MS in Physics, 1979, PhD in Physics, 1983. Cert. level III ultrasonic testing methods. Devel. engr. Oak Ridge (Tenn.) Nat. Lab., 1980-81; faculty rsch. assoc. Ohio State U., Columbus, 1981; rsch. asst. U. Tenn., Knoxville, 1981-83; sr. rsch. engr. Babcock and Wilcox, Lynchburg, Va., 1983—. Contbr. articles to profl. jours.; patentee in field. Co-leader cub pack Lynchburg Area coun. Boy Scouts Am., 1983-84; vol. United Way, 1994; mem. Pacer Club for United Way Support, 1993-96. Mem. Am. Soc. Non-destructive Testing (cert. Level III untrasonic methods), Sigma Pi Sigma. Avocations: martial arts, hiking, lapidary, mineral collecting. Home: 303 Juniper Dr Lynchburg VA 24502-5661 Office: Babcock and Wilcox Lynchburg Rsch Ctr Lynchburg VA 24506

LATIMER, ROY TRUETT, museum executive; b. Albany, Tex., Aug. 23, 1928; s. Charles Lee and Zora Neil (Brock) L.; m. Judith Gail Johnson, Nov. 26, 1955 (div. 1975); children: Jeff, Laura, Tiffany; m. Harriet Calvin, Nov. 20, 1976. BA, Hardin-Simmons U., 1951, LLD, 1996. Owner Gen. Ins. Agy., Abilene, Tex., 1951-55; alumni dir. Hardin-Simmons U., Abilene, 1955-62; dir. pub. relations Tex. Assn. of Realtors, Austin, 1962-65; exec. dir. Tex. Hist. Commn., Austin, 1965-81, Tex. Hist. Found., Austin, 1972-81; v.p. pub. relations and mktg. Spaw Glass, Inc., Houston, 1981-85; pres. Houston Mus. Natural Sci., Houston, 1986—; pres. Nat. Conf. State Hist. Preservation Officers, 1974-75; bd. advisors Nat. Trust for Hist. Preservation, Washington, 1981-88. Mem. Tex. Ho. Reps., Austin, 1952-62; bd. devel. Hardin-Simmons U., 1974—; bd. dirs. Downtown Houston Assn., 1983—, past pres.; bd. dirs. Rice Design Alliance, Houston, 1983-87; chmn. S. Main Ctr. Assn., 1991-93. Mem. Houston C. of C., South Main Ctr. Assn. (bd. dirs. 1988—), Internat. Space Theatre Consortium (treas. 1995-96). Presbyterian. Avocations: running, canoeing, backpacking, travel. Home: 2807A Midlane St Houston TX 77027-4909 Office: Houston Mus Natural Sci 1 Hermann Circle Dr Houston TX 77030-1749

LATINI, ANTHONY A., financial services company executive; b. Chester, Pa., June 8, 1942; s. Angelo and Mildred (Gardner) L.; m. M. Katherine Kraft; children: Anthony A., Diane Marie. B.S., St. Joseph U., 1964. Tax mgr. Price Waterhouse & Co., Phila., 1971; dir. taxes Colonial Penn Group, Phila., 1971-76, treas., 1976-79, sr. v.p., treas., 1979-86, exec. v.p. fin. ops., 1987; chief fin. officer Pa. Conv. Authority, 1988; v.p., asst. comptr. Prudential Ins. Co. Am., South Plainfield, N.J., 1988-91, v.p. investment ops., systems and reporting, 1991—. Bd. mgrs. Children's Hosp. of Phila., 1985—, mem., chmn. long range planning com. Mem. Fin. Execs. Inst., Tax Execs. Inst., Soc. Ins. Accts., Nat. Assn. Corp. Treas., Internat. Assn. Fin. Planners, Am. Inst. C.P.A.s, Pa. Inst. C.P.A.s. Avocations: skiing; boating; tennis. Office: Three Gateway Ctr 12th Fl Prudential Ins Co Am 100 Mulberry St Newark NJ 07102-4004

LATIOLAIS, RENÉ LOUIS, natural resources company executive, chemical engineer; b. New Orleans, July 21, 1942; s. Lewis W. and Elise (Kernion) L.; m. Joan Filizola, Mar. 31, 1962; children: Renelle Latiolais Brame, Craig A., Christopher A. BChemE, La. State U., 1965; grad. mgmt. devel. program, Harvard U., 1978. Registered profl. engr. Chem. and prodn. engr. Freeport Sulphur Co., Port Sulphur, La., 1965-68, prodn. supt., 1968-74, ops. mgr., 1974-78; asst. to pres. Freeport Sulphur Co., New Orleans, 1978-79; asst. mgr. corp. devel. Freeport Minerals Co., N.Y.C., 1979, exec. v.p., 1984; pres. Nat. Potash Co. (sub. Freeport Minerals Co.), N.Y.C., 1979-84; v.p., dir. ops. rev. and investor relations Freeport Minerals Internat., N.Y.C., 1982; sr. v.p. Freeport-McMoRan Inc., New Orleans, 1986-92; exec. v.p. and COO Freeport McMoRan, Inc., New Orleans, 1992-93, pres. and COO, 1993-95, pres. and CEO, 1995—. Patentee sulphur well sealing method, apparatus and method mining of subterranian sulphur. Mem. Am. Soc. Petroleum Engrs. Republican. Roman Catholic. Avocations: golf, tennis, sailing, skeet shooting. Office: Freeport-McMoRan Inc 1615 Poydras St New Orleans LA 70112-1254

LATNO, ARTHUR CLEMENT, JR., telephone company executive; b. Ross, Calif., May 14, 1929; s. Arthur Clement and Marie (Carlin) L.; m. Dorothy Sheldon Guess, June 27, 1953; children—Jeannine Marie, Michele Claire, Arthur Clement III, Mary Suzanne, Patrice Anne. B.S., Santa Clara U., 1951. With Pacific Tel. & Tel. Co., San Francisco, 1952-92; v.p. Pacific Tel. & Tel. Co., 1972-78, exec. v.p., 1978-92; former amb. accorded by Ronald Reagan, 1988; chmn. U.S. Delegation to World Telecom. Conf., Australia; bd. dirs. WestAm. Bank, WestAm. Bancorp. Bd. dirs. Marin Gen. Hosp.; bd. dirs., former chmn. Calif. Inst. Fed. Policy Rsch.; chmn. adv. bd. Berkeley program in bus. and social policy U. Calif.; trustee St. Mary's Coll. Calif. Mem. Meadow Club, Knights of Malta, Alpha Sigma Nu. Home: 67 Convent Ct San Rafael CA 94901-1333

LATORRE, L. DONALD, chemical company executive; b. Amsterdam, N.Y., Sept. 19, 1937; s. Matthew Albert and Nancy (Donato) LaT.; m. Gloria Jean Lojpersberger, Nov. 5, 1940; children: L. Donald Jr., David S., Craig M., Amy E. BS, Lowell Tech. Inst., 1960; MS, Union Coll., 1967. Tech. sales rep. Ritter Chem. Corp., Amsterdam, 1960-66; market research, planning mgr. Diamond Shamrock, Cleve., 1967-69; market mgr. Diamond Shamrock Splty. Chems. Div., Cleve., 1969-73; comml. devel. mgr. BASF Wyandotte (Mich.) Corp., 1973-74; mktg. mgr. BASF Wyandotte Corp. Urethanes Div., 1974-79; div. mgr. BASF Wyandotte Corp. Styropor Div., Parsippany, N.J., 1980-82; exec. v.p., bd. dirs. Velcro, U.S.A., Manchester, N.H., 1982-84; sr. v.p. gen. mgr. splty. chems. div. Engelhard Corp., Menlo Park, N.J., 1984-88, v.p., pres. pigments and additives div., 1988-90, sr. v.p., COO, 1990-95, pres., COO, 1995—, also bd. dirs.; bd. dirs. N.E. Chemcat Corp.; bd. dirs. engring. adv. bd. Mercer U., Macon, Ga., 1987—, chmn., 1995—. Officer Jr. C. of C., Amsterdam, 1962; bd. dirs. Manchester C. of

C., 1982-84; sd. dirs. engring. adv. bd. Mercer U., Macon, Ga., 1987—, chmn., 1995—;strustee Ind. Coll. Fund N.J., 1991—, Bloomfield Coll., 1996—. Mem. Nat. Assn. Corp. Dirs., Mfrs.' Alliance for Productivity and Innovation. Office: Engelhard Corp 101 Wood Ave S Iselin NJ 08830-2703

LATORRE, ROBERT GEORGE, naval architecture and engineering educator; b. Toledo, Jan. 9, 1949; s. Robert James and Madge Violette (Roy) L. BS in Naval Architecture and Marine Engring. with honors, U. Mich., 1971, MS in Engring., 1972; MSE in Naval Architecture, U. Tokyo, 1975, PhD. in Naval Architecture, 1978. Asst. prof. U. Mich., Ann Arbor, 1979-83; assoc. prof. U. New Orleans, 1984-87, prof. naval architecture and marine engring., 1987, prof., 1989—, chmn. dept., 1989-95; assoc. prof. mech. engring., U. Tokyo, 1986-87; rsch. scientist. David Taylor Naval R & D Lab., Bethesda, Md., 1980, 81, Bassin d'Essais des Carenes, Paris, 1983; cons. in field. Contbr. to profl. publs. Mem. Soc. Naval Architects, Royal Inst. Naval Archtects Gt. Britain, ASME, Soc. NAval Architects Japan, Am. Soc. engring. Edn. (program chmn. ocean engring. divsn. 1989-93O, Japan Club New Orleans. Roman Catholic. Home: 300 Lake Marina Dr New Orleans LA 70124-1676 Office: U New Orleans 911 Engring Bldg New Orleans LA 70148

LA TOURETTE, JOHN ERNEST, academic administrator; b. Perth Amboy, N.J., Nov. 5, 1932; s. John Crater and Charlotte Ruth (Jones) LaT.; m. Lillie M. Drum, Aug. 10, 1957; children—Marc Andrew, Yanique Renee. B.A., Rutgers U., 1954, M.A., 1955, Ph.D., 1962. From asst. prof. to prof. Rutgers U., New Brunswick, N.J., 1960-61, SUNY, Binghamton, 1961-76; chair dept. econs. SUNY, 1967-75, provost grad. studies, 1975-76; dean grad. sch., vice provost grad. studies Bowling Green (Ohio) State U., 1976-79; v.p., provost No. Ill. U., DeKalb, 1979-86; acting pres. No. Ill. U., 1984-85, pres., 1986—; vis. prof. Karlsruhe (W. Ger.) U., 1974; research prof. Brookings Inst., 1966-67; vis. scholar Ariz. State U., 1969, 70; lectr. Econs. Inst., U. Colo., 1966; dir. NSF Departmental Sci. Devel. Grant, 1970-75, First Am. Bank, DeKalb, 1985—, Higher Edn. Stategic Planning Inst., Washington, 1984-88; cons. North Cen. Assn., 1983—. Contbr. articles to profl. jours. Served to capt. USAF, 1955-58. Ford Found. grantee, 1963; SUNY Found. grantee, 1963, 65, 70. Mem. Am. Econ. Assn., Can. Econ. Assn. (fin. acctg. adv. standards coun. 1991-94). Office: No Ill U Office of Pres De Kalb IL 60115

LATOURETTE, STEVEN C., congressman; b. Cleve., July 22, 1954; m. Susan LaTourette; 4 children. BA in Hist., U. Mich., 1976; JD, Cleve. State U., 1979. Asst. pub. defender Lake County Pub. Defender's Office, 1980-83; assoc. Cannon, Stern, Aveni & Krivok, Painesville, 1983-86; with Baker, Hackenberg & Collins, Painesville, 1986-88; prosecuting atty. Lake County Prosecutor Office, 1988-93; mem. U.S. Ho. of Reps., Washington, 1994—; mem. com. on Transp. & Infrastructure, subcom. pub. bldgs. & econ. devel., surface transp., & water resources and environ. U.S. Ho. of Reps., also vice-chmn. investigations and oversight subcom., mem. com. Reform and Oversight, D.C. subcom., mem. com. Small Bus., subcoms. Tax & Fin. and Govt. Programs, mem. U.S. Holocaust Meml. Coun., 1995—. Office: US House Reps 1508 Longworth House Office Bldg Washington DC 20515-3519

LATOURRETTE, JAMES THOMAS, retired electrical engineering and computer science educator; b. Miami, Ariz., Dec. 26, 1931; s. Emery Everest and Carrie D. (Hoffman) LaT.; m. Muriel Ashe, Aug. 28, 1955; children: Mary Beth, John Emery, James Thomas, Joanne. B.S., Calif. Inst. Tech., 1953; M.A. (Gen. Communication Co. fellow), Harvard U., 1954, Ph.D. (NSF fellow), 1958. Research assoc., lectr. physics Harvard U., 1957-59; physicist Gen. Electric Research Lab., Schenectady, 1960-62; sr. supervisory scientist TRG, Inc., Melville, N.Y., 1962-66; sect. head TRG div. Control Data Corp., Melville, 1966-67; prof. elec. engring. and computer sci. Poly. U. (formerly Poly. Inst. Bklyn. and Poly. Inst. N.Y.), Farmingdale, N.Y., 1967-93, prof. emeritus, 1993; assoc. dir. Weber Rsch. Inst., Poly. U., 1987-90. Contbr. articles to profl. jours. NSF postdoctoral fellow Physikalisches Institut der U. Bonn, Germany, 1959-60. Mem. AAAS, IEEE, IEEE Computer Soc., N.Y. Acad. Sci., Assn. for Computer Machinery, Sigma Xi, Tau Beta Pi. Home: 2 Candlewood Ct Huntington NY 11743-1827 Office: Poly Univ Rt 110 Farmingdale NY 11735

LATSCHAR, JOHN A., historic site administrator. Supt. Gettysburg (Pa.) Nat. Mil. Park. Office: Gettysburg Nat Mil Park 97 Tareytown Rd Gettysburg PA 17325

LATSHAW, JOHN, entrepreneur; b. Kansas City, Dec. 10, 1921; s. Ross W. and Edna (Parker) L.; m. Barbara Haynes, Nov. 13, 1954 (div. Dec. 1975); children: Constance Haynes, Elizabeth Albright Latshaw Reid-Scott. Student, Kansas City Jr. Coll., 1938-40; BS, Mo. U., 1942. Mgr. trading dept. Harris, Upham & Co., 1943-49; ptnr. Uhlmann & Latshaw, 1949-53; ptnr. E.F. Hutton & Co. (merger with Uhlmann & Latshaw), 1954-87, exec. v.p., mgn. dir., 1987—; chmn. bd. dirs., chief exec. officer B.C. Christopher & Co., 1987-89, chmn. emeritus, 1989-90; chmn., chief exec. officer Conchemco Inc.; chmn., chief exec. officer, mng. dir. Latshaw Enterprises, 1990—; chmn. bd. dirs. Bus. Communications, Inc., Install, Maintain and Repair, Inc., Interior Designs, Inc.; mem. Kansas City Bd. Trade; gov. Midwest Stock Exchange, 1966-68; moderator, opening speaker Plenary Panel on Needs and Opportunities in Key Bus. Sectors, Miami Conf. on the Caribbean, 1980; pres. World Cable Ltd. Past Chmn. Key Men's Council; past pres. Friends of Zoo, 1970; mem. exec. com. Religious Heritage Am., Starlight Theatre, Performing Arts Kansas City; v.p., mem. exec. bd. Am. Cancer Soc., 1970, 71; mem. Jackson County and Crusade Adv. Com., Gov.'s Com. on Higher Edn.; bd. dirs. Kansas City Theatre Guild Council, The Curry Found., Am. Urban Devel. Found., Kansas City Crime Commn.; trustee City Employees Pension Plan, St. Andrew's Episcopal Ch. Meml. and Res. Trust Fund, U. Mo., Kansas City; bd. govs. Am. Royal, Agrl. Hall of Fame, 1976-77; exec. bd. Kansas City Area council Boy Scouts Am., 1970-72, adv. bd., 1973, chmn. patriotism program, 1970; hon. bd. dirs. Rockhurst Coll.; past pres. Kansas City Soccer Club, Inc.; mem. exec. com. N.Am. Soccer League, 1968, 69; bd. govs. Invest-In-Am. Nat. Council; mem. Central Region exec. com.; regional chmn. Invest-in-Am. Week Liaison, 1958—; mem. fin. com. Mayor's Profl. Theater; mem. Univ. Assos. of U. Mo. of Kansas City; chmn. hon. trustees YWCA, 1968-69; trustee Midwest Research Inst.; mem. chancellor's adv. council Met. Community Colls., 1976-77; mem. pres.'s council bd. hon. trustees Kansas City Art Inst.; mem. Pres.' Scholarship Club Avila Coll.; bd. dirs., mem. fin. com. Mayor's Christmas Tree Assn.; chmn. bd. trustee Conservatory of Music; community adv. com. U. Mo. Kansas City Sch. Nursing; mem. Civic Council Greater Kansas City; chmn. Brotherhood Citation Dinner for NCCJ, 1980; trustee Westminster Coll., 1981; hon. bd. govs. Hyman Brand Hebrew Acad.; adv. com. Metro Energy Ctr., 1982; mem. NASA adv. bd. to Pres. U.S., 1983-86. Recipient citation of merit U. Mo., 1957, Golden Eagle award Nat. Invest in Am. Coun., 1970, Chaturathabhorn of Most Exalted Order of White Elephant award, Thailand, 1983; named hon. consul Thailand, Royal Consulate Gen., 1986, The Knight Comdr. of the Most Noble Order of the Crown of Thailand, 1993; decorated Knight Hospitaller of Malta Sovereign Order St. John Jerusalem. Mem. Internat. Trade Assn. (chmn. bd.), Kansas City C. of C. (dir., past pres.), Bus. and Profl. Assn. Western Mo. (mem. adv. bd.), Kansas City Security Traders Assn. (past pres.), Nat. Security Traders Assn. (past exec. v.p.), Wine Soc. of World, Order Jim Daisy, Sigma Nu. Episcopalian (trustee). Clubs: Carriage, Mission Hills Country. Home and Office: 5049 Wornall Kansas City MO 64112

LATT, PAMELA YVONNE, school system administrator; b. Mineola, N.Y., Mar. 24, 1952; d. Michael and Irene (Pearlman) Vuicich; m. James Michael Latt, Aug. 31, 1974; 1 child, Jeremy Jacob. BA in Secondary Edn./English, SUNY, Fredonia, 1973, MA in English, 1974. Lectr. Adam Mickiewicz U., Poznan, Poland, 1972-74; English/reading specialist Halifax County (Va.) Pub. Schs., 1974-76; ESL tchr., grades K-6 Fairfax County (Va.) Pub. Schs., Baileys X-Roads, Va., 1976-79; ESL tchr., grades 7-8 Fairfax County (Va.) Pub. Schs., Vienna, Va., 1979-80; coord. of cen. registration Fairfax County (Va.) Pub. Schs., Falls Church, 1980-89, dir. of ... 1989-92; subsch. prin./Lake Braddock Secondary Fairfax ...ub. Schs., Burke, Va., 1992-93; prin. Centreville High Sch. ..., Clifton, Va., 1993—; spl. adjunct to U. Va., Falls Church, ... State Dept., Arlington, Va., 1990—; adv. bd. Am. Overseas ...l. Bd., Washington and N.Y., 1989—. Author/editor: School ...Emergencies, 1990, Handbook for School Health Risks, 1990; contbg. author/cons. Cross-Cultural Learning in K-12 Schools: Foreign Students as Resources, 1982. Cons., focus group Human Svcs./Fairfax County, 1988—. Adam Mickiewicz U. scholar, Poznan, 1970-72; named one of Outstanding Young Women of Am., 1979, Super Boss of Yr., Fairfax Assn. Ednl. Office Pers., 1989. Mem. ASCD, Nat. Assn. Sch. Prins. Secondary Schs., Nat. Assn. Fgn. Student Affairs (region 8 rep. 1987-89). Democrat. Roman Catholic. Avocations: sculpting, golf, reading and writing poetry. Office: Centreville High Sch 6001 Union Mill Rd Clifton VA 22024-1128

LATTANZIO, STEPHEN PAUL, astronomy educator; b. Yonkers, N.Y., June 29, 1949; s. Anthony Raymond and Anella Lattanzio; m. Barbara Regina Knisely, Aug. 14, 1976; children: Gregory Paul, Timothy Paul. BA in Astronomy, U. Calif., Berkeley, 1971; MA in Astronomy, UCLA, 1973, postgrad., 1973-75. Planetarium lectr. Griffith Obs., Los Angeles, 1973-75; instr. astronomy El Camino Coll., Torrance, Calif., 1974-75; planetarium lectr. Valley Coll., Los Angeles, 1975; prof. astronomy Orange Coast Coll., Costa Mesa, Calif., 1975—, planetarium dir., 1975—; mem. adv. commn. Natural History Found. Orange County, Calif., 1988-91; scientific advisor instructional TV series Universe: The Infinite Frontier, 1992—. Co-author: Study Guide for Project: Universe, 1978, 2d rev. edition 1981; textbook reviewer, 1978—; co-screenwriter Project: Universe instructional TV series episode, 1979; contbr. articles to profl. jours. Mem. Astron. Soc. Pacific, The Planetary Soc., Sigma Xi (assoc.), Phi Beta Kappa. Avocation: astronautics. Office: Orange Coast Coll 2701 Fairview Rd Costa Mesa CA 92626-5563

LATTES, RAFFAELE, physician, educator; b. Torino, Italy, May 22, 1910; came to U.S., 1940, naturalized, 1947; s. Attilio Marco and Dolce (Noemi) L.; m. Eva H. Hahn, 1936; children—Conrad George (dec.), Robert George. M.D., U. Torino, 1933; D.M.S., Columbia, 1946. Diplomate: Am. Bd. Pathology. Tng. surgery, surg. pathology U. Torino Med. Sch., 1934-38; instr. pathology Woman's Med. Coll. Pa., Phila., 1941-43; asst. prof. pathology N.Y. Postgrad. Hosp. and Med. Sch., 1946-48; instr. surg. pathology Coll. Phys. and Surg., Columbia, 1943-46, asst. prof., 1948-49, asso. prof. surgery, surg. pathology, 1949-51, prof. surgery, surg. pathology, 1950-78, prof. emeritus, 1978—, spl. lectr. in surgery, 1978, dir. lab. surg. pathology, 1951-78. Fellow AMA, Coll. Am. Pathologists, N.Y. Acad. Medicine, Internat. Acad. Pathology; mem. AAAS, N.Y. Path. Soc., Am. Assn. Pathologists and Bacteriologists, Am. Assn. Cancer Rsch., Am. Soc. Clin. Pathologists, Arthur Purdy Stout Soc. Surg. Pathologists. Home: 597 Rutland Ave Teaneck NJ 07666-2947 Office: Coll Physicians and Surgeons 630 W 168th St New York NY 10032-3702

LATTIMER, GARY LEE, physician; b. Nanticoke, Pa., Dec. 4, 1939; s. Paul Floyd and Gene Elizabeth L.; m. Patricia Sara Weise, June 14, 1958; children: Toni Jo, Gregory Weise. M.D., Temple U., 1966; postgrad., Jefferson Med. Coll., 1970-72. Intern Allentown (Pa.) Hosp.; resident Presbyn.-Univ. Hosp., Phila., 1969-70; resident Jefferson Med. Coll. Hosp., Phila., 1970-71, chief med. resident, 1971-72; chief infectious diseases Allentown-Sacred Heart Hosp. Center, 1972-80; assoc. prof. medicine U. N.D., 1980-81, chief infectious diseases, 1980-81; chief infectious diseases New Britain (Conn.) Gen. Hosp., 1981—; assoc. prof. medicine U. Conn., 1981-83; dir. infectious diseases Williamsport Hosp., Divine Providence Hosp., 1983—. Author: Legionnaires' Disease, 1981; contbr. articles to profl. jours. Served with M.C. U.S. Army, 1967-69. Decorated Bronze Star; recipient Disting. Service award Pa. chpt. Am. Legion. Fellow ACP; mem. Am. Soc. Microbiology, AAAS, Nat. Found. Infectious Diseases, Am. Legion. Office: 904 Campbell St Williamsport PA 17701

LATTIMER, JOHN KINGSLEY, physician, educator; b. Mt. Clemens, Mich., Oct. 14, 1914; s. Eugene and Gladys Soulier (Lenfestey) L.; m. Jamie Elizabeth Hill, Jan. 1948; children: Evan, Jon, Gary. AB, Columbia U., 1935, MD, 1938, ScD, 1943; student, Balliol Coll., Oxford (Eng.) U., 1944, Med. Field Svc. Sch., Paris, 1945. Diplomate Am. Bd. Urology. Surg. intern Meth.-Episcopal Hosp., N.Y.C., 1938-40; urol. resident Squier Urol. Clinic Presbyn. Hosp., N.Y.C., 1940-43, dir. Squier Urol. Clinic, 1955-80, dir. urol. svc., 1955-80, also dir. urology Sch. Nursing; staff asst., instr. urology Columbia Coll. Physicians and Surgeons, 1940-53, asst. prof. clin. urology, 1953-55, prof. urology, chmn. dept. urology, 1955-80; vis. prof. Med. Coll. S.C., Med. Coll. Va., Mayo Clinic Med. Sch., Rochester, Minn., 1977, Boston U., Tufts U., U. Oreg., Ind. U., UCLA, Leeds Med. Sch. U. Witwatersrand, South Africa; guest lectr. Akron City Hosp., 1977, Reno Surg. Soc., 1977; chief urology Babies Hosp., Vanderbilt Clinic, Frances Delafield Hosp., N.Y.C., 1955; cons. urology VA, N.Y.C., 1947-80, USPHS Hosp., S.I., N.Y.C., Meth. Hosp., Bklyn., Englewood (N.J.), Yonkers (N.Y.) gen. hosps., Harlem, Roosevelt, St. Lukes hosps. (all N.Y.C.); mem. com. surgery in Tb, genito-urinary Tb, VA; med. cons. Time mag.; cons. to com. on therapy Nat. Tb Assn.; mem. expert adv. panel biology human reprodn. WHO; mem. N.Y. Supreme Ct. Med. Arbitration Panel, 1975; Am. Urol. Assn. rep. to NRC-Nat. Acad. Scis.; mem. tng. grants com. NIH, 1968-72. Contbr. over 350 articles on urology and history to various publs., also chpts. in books; guest author New Eng. Jour. Medicine; rschr., writer, speaker on assassinations of Pres. Lincoln and Kennedy, and Nuremberg Trials. Trustee Presbyn. Hosp., 1974-78; mem. vis. com. Ft. Ticonderoga Mus.; mem. vis. com. sect. arms and armour Met. Mus. Art, 1978, Abraham Lincoln U., Harrogate, Tenn.; chmn. book com. Englewood Hist. Soc., 1984—; mem. Dallas Coun. World Affairs, Phila. Coun. World Affairs; ofcl. historian City of Englewood, N.J. Maj. M.C., AUS, 1943-46; med. officer at Nuremberg Trials, 1945-46. Decorated Croix de Guerre (France and Belgium); recipient Joseph Mather Smith prize for kidney disease rsch. Columbia U., 1943, honor award for meritorious work in field Tb, Am. Acad. Tb Physicians, also prizes for sci. exhibits, gold medal Coll. Physicians and Surgeons Alumni Assn., 1971, Disting. Svc. award, 1993, Hugh Young medal for outstanding work in infectious diseases, 1973, Belfield medal Chgo. Urol. Soc., Bureau medal N.J. Acad. Medicine, Edward Henderson gold medal Am. Geriat. Soc., 1978, Gt. medal City of Paris, 1979, Normandy Liberation medal Soc. French War Vets., Paris Liberation medal French Govt., medal Nat. Kidney Fedn., 1987, Am. Acad. Pediatric Urology, 1987; Richard Chute lectr., 1973, Stoneburner lectr. Med. Coll. Va., 1973. Fellow ACS (chmn. adv. com. urology 1962-64, gov. 1966-79, com. on undergrad. tng. 1967-80, chmn. nominating com. 1976-77, com. to study size and composition of bd. govs.), AMA (prize rsch. kidney Tb 1953), Am. Acad. Pediatrics (chmn. com. on pediatric urology, pres. sect. urology 1973-79); mem. AAAS, Am. Assn. Clin. Urologists, Assn. Am. Med. Colls., Clin. Soc. Genito-Urinary Surgeons (pres. 1984), N.Y. Acad. Sci. (trustee), N.Y. Acad. Medicine (chmn. genito-urinary surg. sect. 1956-57, trustee 1978-84, v.p. 1986-87, chmn. bldg. com. 1982-87), Am. Assn. Genito-Urinary Surgeons (pres. 1982), Am. Urol. Assn. (pres. 1975-76, chmn. com. on pediatric urology, pres. N.Y. sect. 1966, exec. com. 1967-80, com. on surgery, rev. and long range planning com., editorial bd. Jour. Urology 1965-68, chmn. com. to gather info. about urology, chmn. coordinating coun. for urology, chmn. nominating com. 1976-77, 1st prize for clin. rsch. 1950, 60, Ramon Guiterez medal 1980, Keyes medal 1996), Am. Thoracic Soc., AAUP, Soc. U. Urologists (pres. 1969), Nat. Inst. Social Scis., St. Nicholas Soc., Assn. Mil. Surgeons Harvey Soc., Nat. Tb ssn., N.Y. State Pediatrics Soc., N.Y. Med. Socs., New York County Med. Soc., Soc. Pediatric Urology (pres. 1961-62), Brit. Assn. Urol. Surgeons (corr.), N.Y. Soc. Surgeons, N.Y. Soc. Professions, Internationale Société d'Urology (v.p. 1967-73, pres.1973-79), Assn. Pediatric Urology (pres. 1961), Spanish Urol. Assn. (hon.), Paleopathology Assn., Charles A. Lindbergh Soc. (ofcl. historian City of Englewood 1990), Dallas Surgical Soc., Japanese Urol. Assn. (hon.), Italian Urol. Assn. (hon.), SAR, Assn. Mil. Historians, Soc. War 1812, Mil. Order Fgn. Wars U.S., Order of Founders and Patriots, Arms and Armour Soc. N.Y., Arms and Armour Soc. Eng., Arms and Armour Soc. Gueurnsey, Soc. Colonial Wars, Englewood Hist. Soc., Manuscript Soc., Revolutionary War Round Table of N.Y., Abraham Lincoln Soc., Lincoln Soc. N.Y., Wis., Ill., Fla., Washington, Civil War Surgeons (hon.), Am. Legion, 82d Airborne Div. Assn., 101st Airborne Div. Assn., Res. Officers Assn., Metropolitan Club, Sigma Xi. Office: Columbia U Med Sch New York NY 10032

LATTIMORE, JOY POWELL, preschool administrator; b. Goldsboro, N.C., Jan. 18, 1954; d. Albert and Zudora (Baldwin) P.; m. Vergel L. Lattimore, Dec. 16, 1978; children: V. Alston, Adam V., Alia Joy. BS in Early Child Edn., Barber-Scotia Coll., 1976; MEd in Early and Mid. Child Edn., The Ohio State U., 1977. Dir. alumni affairs Barber-Scotia Coll., Concord, N.C., 1977-79; tchra. Concord Mid. Sch., 1979-80; asst. dir. admissions Kendall Coll., Evanston, Ill., 1980-83; dir. pre-K program Dunbar Ctr. United Way Agy., Syracuse, N.Y., 1987-89; tchr. Hughes Magnet Sch., Syracuse, 1989-90; dir. Busy Bee Day Care, Westerville, Ohio, 1991—. Mem. race adv. com. United Way, 1995-96; vol. benefit com. Columbus Works. Mem. Nat. Assn. Edn. of Young Children, AAUW, NAFE, Internat. Reading Assn., Phi Delta Kappa. Methodist. Avocations: reading, volleyball, tennis, science fiction, coin collecting. Home: 610 Olde N Church Dr Westerville OH 43081 Office: Busy Bee Day Care Busy Bee Day Care 610 Olde N Church Dr Westerville OH 43081

LATTIN, ALBERT FLOYD, banker; b. Everett, Wash., May 23, 1950; s. Albert S. and Erma Victoria (Hunt) L. Student, U. Nairobi, Kenya, 1970-71, Am. U. Cairo, Egypt, 1972; BA, Antioch U., 1973; MA, NYU, 1979; MBA, Columbia U., 1984. Asst. curator The Bklyn. Mus., 1973-76, assoc., 1976-79; sec. of the mus. Solomon R. Guggenheim Mus., N.Y.C., 1979-80, cons. in arts, 1980-83; banker Bankers Trust Co., N.Y.C., 1984-93; v.p. CS 1st Boston, N.Y.C., 1993-95, CS First Boston Corp., N.Y.C., 1995—; Chief investment officer Praedrem Recovery Fund, N.Y.C., 1994—. Editor, researcher book and catalogue Africa in Antiquity: The Arts of Ancient Nubia and the Sudan, 1978; organizer exhibition/movie The Heritage of Islam, 1982. Dir., trustee Mus. Holography, N.Y.C., 1980-87; mem. bd. advisors Gallery Assn. N.Y. Stte, 1988—; treas. Theban Found., 1991—; mem. Bklyn. Hist. Soc., Brooklyn Heights Assn., 1986—. Mem. Am. Banking Assn., Urban Land Inst., Internat. Council of Mus., Am. Assn. Mus., Internat. Assn. Egyptologists, Roundout Valley Country Club, Columbia Club. Home: 242 Henry St Brooklyn NY 11201-4662 Office: CS First Boston Corp 55 E 52nd St New York NY 10055-0002

LATTIS, RICHARD LYNN, zoo director; b. Louisville, May 31, 1945; s. Albert Francis and Jean Elizabeth (Baker) L.; m. Sharon Louise Elkins, June 22, 1968; children Michael David, Robert Brian, Theodore James. BS in Biol., U. Louisville, 1967, MS in Ecol., 1970. Asst. curator edn. Bronx (N.Y.) Zoo, 1974-75, curator edn., 1975-78; chmn. edn. The Wildlife Conservation Soc., 1978-80; dir. city zoos N.Y. Zoological Soc., 1980-93, v.p. conservation parks and aquariums, 1993—; lectr., cons. zoos, aquariums, nature ctrs.; past cons. Time-Life Wild Wild World Animals film series; appeared Who's Who in the Zoo WNBC-TV, N.Y.C. Sgt. USAR, 1970-76. Mem. AAAS, Am. Assn. Zool. Parks and Aquariums (bd. dirs., bd. regents, govt. affairs. com.), Nat. Hist. Soc., Soc. Conservation Biol., Zoo Biol., Sigma Xi. Avocations: fishing, photography, golf, gardening, bird watching. Home: 1650 Maxwell Dr Yorktown Heights NY 10598-4802 Office: Wildlife Conservation Soc The Bronx Zoo Bronx NY 10460

LATTMAN, LAURENCE HAROLD, retired academic administrator; b. N.Y.C., Nov. 30, 1923; s. Jacob and Yetta (Schwartz) L.; m. Hanna Renate Cohn, Apr. 12, 1946; children—Martin Jacob, Barbara Diane. BSChemE, Coll. City N.Y., 1948; MS in Geology, U. Cin., 1951, PhD, 1953. Instr. U. Mich., 1952-53; asst. head photogeology sect. Gulf Oil Corp., Pitts., 1953-57; asst. prof. to prof. geomorphology Pa. State U., 1957-70; prof., head dept. geology U. Cin., 1970-75; dean Coll. of Mines U. Utah, 1975-83, dean Coll. Engring., 1978-83; pres. N.Mex. Tech., Socorro, 1983-93, pres. emeritus, 1993—; bd. dirs. Pub. Svc. Co. of N.Mex.; cons. U.S. Army Engrs., Vicksburg, Miss., 1965-69, also major oil cos. Author: (with R.G. Ray) Aerial Photographs in Field Geology, 1965, (with D. Zillman) Energy Law; Contbr. articles to profl. jours. Served with AUS, 1943-46. Fenneman fellow U. Cin., 1953. Fellow Geol. Soc. Am.; mem. Am. Assn. Petroleum Geologists, Am. Soc. Photogrammetry (Ford Bartlett award 1968), Soc. Econ. Paleontologists and Mineralogists, AIME (Disting. mem. 1981, Mineral Industries Edn., award 1986—), Assn. Western Univs. (chmn. bd. dirs. 1986-87), Sigma Xi. Home: 11509 Penfield Ln NE Albuquerque NM 87111-6506

LATTO, LEWIS M., JR., broadcasting company executive; b. Duluth, Minn., Jan. 21, 1940; s. Lewis M. and Ethel S. L.; divorced; children: Aaron, Caroline. B.A., U. Minn., 1963. Owner, mgr. Sta. KXTP, Duluth, 1965-94, Sta. WAKX-FM, 1974-94; owner Sta. WEVE AM-FM, Eveleth, Minn., 1978—, Sta. KGPZ-FM, Grand Rapids, Minn., 1995—. Mem. Duluth City Council, 1969-75, pres., 1974. Mem. Nat. Radio Broadcasters Assn. (dir.), Minn. Broadcasters Assn. (pres. 1992-93). Republican. Methodist. Office: Northland Radio Stas 5732 Eagle View Dr Duluth MN 55803-9498

LATZ, G. IRVING, II, manufacturing company executive; b. Ft. Wayne, Ind., Feb. 12, 1920; s. G. Irving and Carrie (Stiefel) L.; m. Janet Horwitz Simon, Oct. 16, 1949; children: Sara Rose, G. Irving III. BS in Econs., U. Pa., 1941; MBA, U. Chgo., 1971. Trainee F.R. Lazarus Co., Columbus, Ohio, 1941; with Wolf & Dessauer Co., Ft. Wayne, 1946-66, treas., 1947-66, pres., 1957-66; dir. Model Cities, Columbus, 1967-68; cons. urban affairs Michael Reese Hosp. and Med. Ctr., Chgo., 1973-74; cons. econ. urban affairs, 1974-80; prin. Latz Assocs., Ft. Wayne, 1974-80; pres. Sci-Agra, Inc., Ft. Wayne, 1980—; exec. dir. Ft. Wayne Future, Inc., 1980-84; hon. bd. dirs. Ft. Wayne Nat. Bank. Gen. chmn. Ft. Wayne Fine Arts Found., 1958-67, pres., 1967-69; gen. chmn. Ft. Wayne United Fund; pres. Ind. Retail Coun., 1965-66; bd. dirs. Ft. Wayne Jewish Fedn., United Community Svcs. With AUS, 1941-46. Mem. Ft. Wayne C. of C., Ft. Wayne Country Club. Home: 6801 Covington Creek Trail Fort Wayne IN 46804

LATZA, BEVERLY ANN, accountant; b. Pompton Plains, N.J., June 10, 1960; d. George and Helen Mae (Ryan) L. BA in Acctg., Bus. Administrn., Thiel Coll., 1982. Internal auditor Monroe Systems for Bus., Morris Plains, N.J., 1983-85; acct. Am. Airlines, Tulsa, 1985-86, Accountemps, Tulsa, 1986-87; credit investigator Denrich Leasing, Inc., Kansas City, Mo., 1987-89; tax examining asst. IRS, Kansas City, Mo., 1989—. Lutheran. Avocations: singing, counted cross-stitch. Home: 13148 W 88th Ct Apt 141 Lenexa KS 66215-4923 Office: IRS 2306 E Bannister Rd Kansas City MO 64131-3011

LATZER, RICHARD NEAL, investment company executive; b. N.Y.C., Jan. 6, 1937; s. Paul John and Alyce A. Latzer; B.A., U. Pa., 1959, M.A., 1961; m. Ellen Weston, Sept. 5, 1965; children—Steven, David. Security analyst Mut. Benefit Life Ins. Co., Newark, 1963-66; portfolio mgr. Equitable Life Ins., Washington, 1966-68; securities analyst Investors Diversified Services, Mpls., 1968-69, dir. cert. and ins. investments, 1969-77, v.p. cert. and ins. investments, 1977-84; v.p. cert. and ins. investments IDS Fin. Services, Inc., 1984-86, IDS Fin. Corp., 1987-88; v.p. investments, IDS Reins. Co., 1986-88; asst. treas. Investors Syndicate Life Ins. & Annuity Co., Mpls., 1969-72; v.p. IDS Life Ins. Co., Mpls., 1973-80, v.p. investments, 1980-88; v.p. Investors Syndicate of Am., 1973-77, v.p. investments, 1977-84; v.p. Investors Syndicate Title & Guaranty Co., 1977-83, investment officer IDS Life Ins. Co. of N.Y., 1977-88; v.p. investments IDS Life Capital Resource Fund I, Inc., 1981-88 , IDS Spl. Income Fund, Inc., 1981-88, Am Enterprise Life Ins. Co., 1986-88, Reinsurance Co. 1986-88; IDS Life Series Fund, 1986-88; IDS Life Managed Fund, Inc., 1986-88, IDS Property Casualty, 1987-88; v.p. IDS Realty Corp., 1987-88; pres., chmn. bd., bd. dirs. Real Estate Svcs. Co., 1986-88; IDS Life Moneyshare Fund, Inc., 1981-88 ; IDS Cert. Co., 1984-88 ; chmn. bd., dir. IDS Real Estate Services Co., 1983-86; v.p. Fireman's Fund Am. Life Ins. Co., 1985-86; dir. Investors Syndicate Devel. Corp., Mpls., 1970-88 , Nuveen Realty Corp., Mpls., 1976-80; sr. v.p., chief investment officer Transamerica Corp., San Francisco, 1988—, pres., CEO Transamerica Investment Svcs., Inc., San Francisco, 1988—; dir., chief investment officer, chmn. investment com. Transamerica Occidental Life Ins. Co., L.A., 1989—, Transamerica Life Ins. and Annuity Co., L.A., 1989—; dir., chief investment officer, mem. investment com. Transamerica Ins. Group, Woodland Hills, 1988-93; bd. dirs., mem. exec. com. Transamerica Realty Svcs., Inc., San Francisco, 1988—, pres., CEO, 1996—; dir. Transamerica Realty Investment Corp., San Francisco, 1988—; chmn. pension investment com. Transamerica Corp., San Francisco, 1988—, dir. Transamerica Cash Res. Inc., L.A., 1989-90, Transamerica Income Shares, 1989—; dir., mem. investment com. Transamerica Life Ins. Co. Can., Toronto, 1991—; chief investment officer, mem. operating com. ARC Reinsurance Corp., Honolulu, 1993—. Served to lt., USN, 1960-63. Chartered fin. analyst. Mem. Security Analysts San Francisco, Chartered Fin. Analysts. Office: 600 Montgomery St San Francisco CA 94111-2702

LAU, CHARLES KWOK-CHIU, architect, architectural firm executive; b. Hong Kong, Oct. 19, 1954; came to U.S., 1973; s. Oi-Ting and Wai-Han L. BFA in Environ. Design, U. Hawaii Manoa, Honolulu, 1977. Registered architect, Hawaii. Designer CJS Group Architects, Honolulu, 1977-78, Fox

Hawaii, Honolulu, 1978-80, Wimberly Allison Tong & Goo, Honolulu, 1980-82, Architects Hawaii, Honolulu, 1982-84; assoc., designer Stringer & Assocs., Honolulu, 1984-85; pres. AM Ptrns., Inc., Honolulu, 1985—; instr. U. Hawaii, Honolulu, 1987. Principal works include Crystal Fantasy, Hyatt Regency Hotel, Honolulu, 1988 (Merit award Hawaii chpt. AIA 1988), Dole Cannery Sq., Honolulu, 1989 (Merit award Hawaii Renaissance 1989), Danelle Christie's, Ala Moana Hotel, Honolulu, 1989 (Hawaii Region award Illuminating Engring. Soc. N.Am. 1989, Grand and Nat. Grand awards Hawaii Renaissance 1989, Tiger Restaurant, Lahaina, Hawaii, 1990 (Gold Key Excellence in Interior Design award Am. Hotel and Motel Assn. 1990, Nat. and Merit awards Hawaii Renaissance 1990), La Pierre du Roi, ANA Kalakaua Ctr., Honolulu, 1990 (Grand and Nat. Grand awards 1990), Crazy Shirts, Honolulu, 1991 (Grand and Overall awards Hawaii Renaissance 1991), Grand Hyatt Wailea, Maui, Hawaii, 1992 (Merit award Hawaii chpt. AIA 1992), Carrera y Carrera, Ala Moana Ctr., Honolulu, 1992 (Merit award Hawaii chpt. AIA 1992), Danelle Christie's, Outrigger Waikiki Hotel, Honolulu, 1992 (Merit award Hawaii Renaissance 1992), Exec. Ctr. Hotel, Honolulu, 1992 (Merit award Hawaii Renaissance 1992), Centre Ct. Restaurant, Honolulu, 1993 (Merit award Hawaii Renaissance 1993), Lani Huli, Kailua, 1993 (Spl. Recognition award Parade of Homes 1993), 218 Plantation Club Dr., Kapalua, Maui, 1993 (Interior Design award Am. Soc. Interior Design 1993), Royal Garden Restaurant, Alamoana Hotel, Honolulu, 1994 (Brand and Overall award Hawaii Renaissance, 1994, Lani Huli, Kailua, Hawaii (Project of Yr., City and County of Honolulu 1994). Recipient 1994 Best in Am. Living award Profl. Builders, Kapalua Residence in Maui. Mem. AIA (mem. design award jury selection com. Honolulu chpt. 1990), C. of C. Hawaii, Chinese C. of C. Hawaii, Pacific Club. Office: AM Partners Inc 1164 Bishop St Ste 1000 Honolulu HI 96813-2824

LAU, CLIFFORD, electrical engineer, researcher; b. Nov. 6, 1942. BS, U. Calif., Berkeley, 1966; MS, U. Calif., 1967; PhD, U. Calif., Santa Barbara, 1978. Electronic engr. Office of Naval Rsch. Fellow IEEE (assoc. editor IEEE Control Sys. Mag. 1985-88, publicity chmn. NIPS conf. 1988, treas. NIPS conf. 1989, tech. assoc. editor IEEE Transactions on Cirs. and Sys. 1989-90, tech. assoc. editor IEEE Transactions on Neural Networks 1991-92, editl. bd. mem. Procs. of the IEEE 1991—, mem. bd. govs. Cirs. and Sys. Soc. 1991—, gen. chmn. IJCNN 1992). Office: Office of Naval Rsch Code 1114se/800 N Quincy St Arlington VA 22217*

LAU, ELIZABETH KWOK-WAH, clinical social worker; b. Hong Kong, Jan. 7, 1940; m. Edmond Y. Lau, June 5, 1965; children: Melissa, Ernest. BA, Brigham Young U., 1963; MSW, U. Kans., 1965. Supr. N.E. Community Mental Health Ctr., San Francisco, 1968-73; clin. dir. Chinatown Child Devel. Ctr., San Francisco, 1973-75; program specialist Kai Ming Head Start Program, San Francisco, 1975-77; clin. social worker VA Hosp., Palo Alto, Calif., 1977-86; social work coord. VA Hosp., San Francisco, 1986-95, managed care coord., 1995—; tour dir. Pacific Delight Co., N.Y., 1984—; host, interviewer Sta. KTSF-TV, San Francisco, 1982-94, Jade Channel, San Francisco, 1994—; bd. dirs. Kai Ming Head Start Program. Author: Innovative Parenting, 1980, How to Love Your Children, 1983, How to Raise a Successfull Child, 1984, How to Train a Bright Child, 1985, Understanding Your Children, 1987, The Art of Child Rearing, 1989, Getting to Know Americans, 1990, Providing Guidance to Teenagers, 1991, The Art of Parenting I & II, 1994, The American Welfare System, 1996, The Social Service for Chinese Americans, 1996. V.p. Parents-Tchrs. League Zion Luth. Sch., San Francisco, 1981-83; bd. dirs. Christ Found., 1990—, Kai Ming Head Start Program, 1985—; chairperson bd. deacons Zion Luth. Ch., 1990-91. Recipient Performance award VA Med. Ctr., Palo Alto, 1979, 83, Social Wokr Research award VA Med. Ctr., Palo Alto, 1985, named Fed. Employee of Yr., 1990. Mem. Nat. Assn. Social Workers (cert.). Home: 470 Ortega St San Francisco CA 94122-4622 Office: VA Med Ctr 4150 Clement St San Francisco CA 94121-1545

LAU, H. LORRIN, physician, inventor; b. Honolulu, Hawaii, Apr. 21, 1932; s. Henry S. and Helen (Lee) L.; m. Maureen Lau; children: David, Marianne, Mike, Mark, Linda. AB cum laude, Harvard U., 1950-54; MD, Johns Hopkins U., 1954-58, MPH, 1970-71. Asst. prof. Sch. Med. Johns Hopkins U. (Balt.), 1964-82; assoc. prof. U. Hawaii, 1982-84; chief ob-gyn. St. Francis West Hosp., Honolulu, 1980-92, Kuakini Hosp., Honolulu, 1994-95. Fellow AMA; mem. ACOG, Internat. Soc. Biology and Medicine. Inventor pregnancy tests, introduced alpha-fetoprotein tests into obstetrics in USA, 1971. Home: 925 14th Ave Honolulu HI 96816-3627 Office: 1010 S King St Honolulu HI 96814-1701

LAU, HENRY, mechanical engineer, consultant; b. Hong Kong, Feb. 4, 1941; s. Mo Ngok and Julia (Seto) L.; m. Bing Sin, June 6, 1970; 1 child, Ryan. BS, U. Tenn., 1966; MS, Duke U., Durham, N.C., 1969, PhD, 1973. Rsch. assoc. Duke U., Durham, 1973-74; mech. engr. Ayres & Hayakawa Energy Mgrs., L.A., 1974-77; tech. dir. Ayres Assocs., L.A., 1977-85; prin. and tech. dir. Ayres, Ezer, Lau Inc., L.A., 1985-92; sr. engr. So. Calif. Edison, San Dimas, 1992—; cons. Lawrence Berkeley (Calif.) Lab., 1978-84, Calif. Energy Commn., Sacramento, 1978-82, Martin Marietta, L.A., 1981. Contbr. articles to profl. jours. Grantee Dow Chem., 1965, ASHRAE, 1974, U.S. Army Rsch., 1969. Mem. ASHRAE, ASME, Sigma Xi. Roman Catholic. Achievements include research in building energy systems, computer energy simulations, energy efficiency standards, indoor air quality, energy conservation, solar energy, thermal storage systems, load management. Home: 1948 Crest Dr Los Angeles CA 90034 Office: Southern Calif Edison Co 300 N Lone Hill Ave San Dimas CA 91773

LAU, IAN VAN, safety research engineer, biomechanics expert; b. Macao, Apr. 4, 1950; came to U.S., 1969; s. Wai-Hung L.; m. Helen Ting, Jan. 5, 1973; 1 child, Lisa Alison. BS, U. Mass. at Lowell, 1973; PhD, Johns Hopkins U., 1977. Rsch. engr. GM Rsch. Labs., Warren, Mich., 1978-86, sr. staff engr., 1986—; head dept. automotive safety and health GM, 1993—; mgr. USCAR safety consortium for Gen. Motors, Ford and Chrysler. Contbr. articles on injury prevention in car crashes (Caldwell award 1988, 89, 91); discoverer viscous injury index (Hwy. Safety award 1988); inventor safety steering wheel (McCuen award 1989), side impact dummy. Mem. Soc. Automotive Engrs. (Isbrandt Safety Engring. award 1986, 87, 91), Biomed. Engring. Soc. Republican. Roman Catholic. Avocation: racquetball. Office: GM Rsch Labs Automotive Safety & Health Warren MI 48090

LAU, LAWRENCE JUEN-YEE, economics educator, consultant; b. Guizhou, China, Dec. 12, 1944; came to U.S., 1961, naturalized, 1974; s. Shai-Tat and Chi-Hing (Yu) Liu; m. Tamara K. Jablonski, June 23, 1984. BA with great distinction, Stanford U., 1964; MA, U. Calif.-Berkeley, 1966, PhD, 1969. Acting asst. prof. econs. Stanford U., Palo Alto, Calif., 1966-67, asst. prof., 1967-73, assoc. prof., 1973-76, prof., 1976—, Kwoh-Ting Li prof. econ. devel., 1992—; co-dir. Asia/Pacific Rsch. Ctr., 1992—; cons. The World Bank, Washington, 1976—; vice chmn. Bank of Canton of Calif. Bldg. Corp., San Francisco, 1981-85; dir. Bank of Canton of Calif., San Francisco, 1979-85; dir. Property Resources Equity Trust, Los Gatos, 1987-88; vice-chmn. Complete Computer Co. Far Eat Ltd., Hong Kong, 1981-89. Co-author: (with D.T. Jamison) Farmer Education and Farm Efficiency, 1982, Models of Devlopment: A Comparative Study of Economic Growth in South Korea and Taiwan, 1986, rev. edit., 1990; contbr. articles to profl. jours. Adv. bd. Self-Help for Elderly, San Francisco, 1982—; bd. dirs. Chiang Chiang-Kuo Found. for Internat. Scholarly Exch., 1989—; govs. coun. econ. policy advisors State of Calif., 1993—. John Simon Guggenheim Meml. fellow, 1973; fellow Ctr. for Advanced Study in Behavioral Scis., 1982; Overseas fellow Churchill Coll., Cambridge U., Eng., 1984. Fellow Econometric Soc.; mem. Academia Sinica, Conf. Research in Income and Wealth. Republican. Episcopalian. Office: Stanford U Dept Econs Stanford CA 94305

LAU, MARY APPLEGATE, lawyer; b. Washington, Dec. 17, 1952; d. Robert Lee and Barbara Edith (Pressler) Applegate; m. James Victor Lau, Apr. 1, 1982; 1 child, Chelsea Nicole. BA magna cum laude, Mich. State U., 1974; JD with honors, Fla. State U., 1976. Bar: Fla. 1977, U.S. Dist. Ct. (mid. dist.) Fla. 1977, U.S. Ct. Appeals (11th cir.) 1977. Assoc. atty. Holland and Knight, Tampa, Fla., 1977-82, ptnr., 1982-86; shareholder Lau, Lane, Pieper, Conley & McCreadie, P.A., Tampa, 1986—. Mem. Fed. Bar Assn., (treas. Tampa Bay chpt. 1993), Hillsborough County Bar Assn. Republican. Roman Catholic. Office: Lau Lane Pieper Conley & McCreadie PA 100 S Ashley Dr Tampa FL 33602-5360

LAU, MICHELE DENISE, advertising consultant, sales trainer, television personality; b. St. Paul, Dec. 6, 1960; d. Dwyane Udell and Patricia Ann (Yri) L. Student, U. Minn., 1979-82. Pub. rels. coord. Stillwater (Minn.) C. of C., 1977-79; asst. mgr. Salkin & Linoff, Mpls., 1982, store merchandiser, sales trainer, 1982-83; rental agt. Sentinel Mgmt. Co., St. Paul, 1983-84; account exec. Community Svc. Publs., Mpls., 1984-85, frwy. news supr., 1985, asst. sales mgr., 1985-86; asst. sales mgr. St. Paul Pioneer Press Dispatch, 1986-91; pres. Promotional Ptnrs., Eden Prairie, Minn., 1991-96; on-air show host Home Shopping Network, Eden Prairie, 1996—; on-air personality Sta. WCCO II Cable TV Mpls., 1988-89, co-host Afternoon Midwest, 1989-93; co-host Home Shopping Show, host Minn. Voices, Fox 29, 1995; cons. U. Minn. Alumni mag., 1986-89. Author mechandising and sales tng. manuals. Fund-raiser sustaining program YMCA, Mpls., 1986, Jr. Achievement, St. Paul, 1988; cons. Muscular Dystrophy Assn., St. Paul, 1988-89; bd. dirs. St. Paul Jaycees. Mem. NAFE, Nat. Assn. Home Builders, Mpls. Builder Assn. (amb.), Metro-East Profl. Builders Assn. (spl. events com.), Advt. Fedn., The Newspaper Guild, Internat. Platform Assn., Speakeasy Club. Lutheran. Avocations: tennis, golf, aerobics. Home: Bldg D # 101 4750 Dolphin Cay Ln S Saint Petersburg FL 33711

LAU, ROBERT KEITH, production manager, musician, actor; b. Hackensack, N.J., Oct. 20, 1958; s. Grant Franklin and Mary Teresa (Lee) L. BA, U. Md., 1981; profl. cert., Convergence Corp., N.Y.C., 1984; quality improvement cert., Phil Crosby and Assocs., 1986; MGA, U. Md., 1995. Intern, prodn. asst. PM Mag., camera operator asst. Eyewitness News Sta. WDVM-TV (now WUSA), Washington, 1981; sr. engr., staff announcer The Washington Ear, Inc.-Radio Reading Service for Blind & Handicapped, Silver Spring, Md., 1981-84; tech. dir. NUS Tng. Corp., Gaithersburg, Md., 1984-86, assoc. dir., sr. video editor, 1986-90, dir., editor, 1990-94; sys. operator IICS-DC BBS, 1991—; prodn. mgr. Thunderwave, Inc., Rockville, Md., 1994-95; distance edn. telecom. planning coord. U. Md., 1995—; audio cons. Fine Arts div. U. Md., College Pk., 1981, communications dept. Montgomery Coll., Rockville, Md., 1983, Arena Stage Theater, Washington, 1984, U.S. Holocaust Meml. Mus., Washington, 1994-95; video editor pub. service announcement Am. Lung Assn., 1985, tng. video Digital Circuits 5, 1985 (Merit award), sales video NUS Tng. Corp., 1986 (Merit award), computer graphics animation Sta. WETA, 1987 (Merit award), Atlas Video, Inc., Hyattsville, Md., 1986, Hyattstown Vol. Fire Dept., Germantown, Md., 1987, Montgomery County Police Dept., 1987; video tech. PM/Evening Mag., San Francisco, 1987; music cons. The Source Theater, Washington, 1986. Keyboardist, vocalist, Rockville, Md., 1973-85; extra actor feature films, 1986—; actor The Wash, Studio Theatre, 1994; composer music Chlorep Theme, 1987 (Merit award); composer music series opening Microprocessor Series, 1985, photographer textbook and catalog, 1987 (Merit award), video photographer Washington Grove Heritage com., Gaithersburg, 1987. Elections judge Montgomery County, Rockville, 1977-79; mem. Nat. Rep. Congl. Com., Washington, 1979-85. Dist. winner nat. auditions Nat. Guild Piano Tchrs., 1970-76, state winner 1977-79; recipient Nebr. Interactive Videodisc award, 1987. Mem. AFTRA, SAG, Internat. TV Assn. (award of Excellence 1986), 2 Merit awards 1986, Golden Reel of Excellence award 1987), Hawaii State Soc. Washington, Am. Film Inst., Friends of Kennedy Ctr., Interactive Multimedia Assn., Internat. Interactive Comm. Soc. (bd. dirs. Washington chpt. 1991—, Internat. 1992-95), U. Md. Alumni Assn. (life), Internat. Platform Assn., Alpha Epsilon Rho. Lutheran. Avocations: music, photography, travel, electronics. Home: 12034 Winding Creek Way Germantown MD 20874-1954

LAUB, ALAN JOHN, engineering educator; b. Edmonton, Alta., Can., Aug. 6, 1948; came to U.S., 1970; naturalized, 1984; BSc with honors, U. B.C., 1969; MS, U. Minn., 1972, PhD, 1974. Asst. prof. Case Western Res. U., Cleve., 1974-75; vis. asst. prof. U. Toronto, Can., 1975-77; rsch. scientist MIT, Cambridge, Mass., 1977-79; assoc. prof. U. So. Calif., L.A., 1979-83; prof. U. Calif., Santa Barbara, 1983—, chmn. dept. elec. and computer engring., 1989-92. Contbr. articles to profl. jours. Fellow IEEE; mem. IEEE Control Systems Soc. (pres. 1991, Disting. Mem. award 1991, Control Systems Tech. award 1993), Soc. Indsl. Applied Math., Assn. Computing Machinery. Avocations: bridge, tennis. Office: U Calif Dept Elec & Computer Engring Santa Barbara CA 93106-9560

LAUB, WILLIAM MURRAY, retired utility executive; b. Ft. Mills, Corregidor, Philippines, July 20, 1924; s. Harold Goodspeed and Marjorie M. (Murray) L.; m. Mary McDonald, July 26, 1947; children: William, Andrew, Mary, David, John. BSBA, U. Calif., Berkeley, 1947, LLB, 1950. Bar: Calif. 1951. Practice law Los Angeles, 1951-55; with Southwest Gas Corp., Las Vegas, Nev., 1948-88; v.p., gen. counsel Southwest Gas Corp., 1958-60, exec. v.p., 1960-64, pres., chief exec. officer, 1964-82, chmn., chief exec. officer, 1982-88. Pres. Boulder Dam Area council Boy Scouts Am., 1967-69, So. Nev. Indsl. Found., 1967-68, So. Nev. Meth. Found., 1967-74; chmn. Nev. Equal Rights Commn., 1966-68; Chmn. Clark County Republican Central Com., 1964-66; nat. committeeman Nev. Rep. Com., 1968-80; trustee Sch. Theology at Claremont, Calif., 1977—; trustee Inst. Gas Tech., 1983-89; nat. bd. advisors, coll. bus. and pub. adminstrn. The U. Ariz., 1985-89; bd. dirs. Alliance for Acid Rain Control, 1985-89. Served to lt. (j.g.) USNR, 1941-45. Mem. ABA, Am. Gas Assn. (bd. dirs., chmn. 1986-87), Pacific Coast Gas Assn. (chmn. 1983), Calif. Bar Assn., Nat. Coal Coun., Jonathan Club, Pauma Valley Country Club, Spanish Trail Golf and Country Club, Las Vegas Country Club. Office: 2810 W Charleston Blvd Ste 53 Las Vegas NV 89102-1906

LAUBACH, ROGER ALVIN, accountant; b. Riegelsville, N.J., July 3, 1922; s. Harry and Daisy (Cyphers) L.; diploma in bus. adminstrn. Churchman Bus. Coll., Easton, Pa., 1941; B.S. cum laude in Acctg., Rider U., 1949. CPA, N.Y., N.J. Acct., Coopers & Lybrand, C.P.A.s, N.Y.C., 1949-60; asst. to treas. Coca-Cola Bottling Co. N.Y., N.Y.C., 1960-63; mgr. audits and systems Atlantic Research Corp., Alexandria, Va., 1964-65; controller Ely-Cruikshank Co., Inc., realtors, N.Y.C., 1965-71, asst. treas., 1966-67, treas., dir., 1967-71; dir. N.Y. Federal Savings & Loan Assn., 1970-71; dir. Phila. Acctg. Center, Ogden Food Service Corp., 1971-72, treas., 1972-77; dir. corp. auditing Ogden Corp., N.Y.C., 1977-79; contr. Burlington County Community Action Program, Burlington, N.J., 1981-84. Served with U.S. Army, 1942-46; ETO. Decorated Bronze Star. Mem. AICPA, Am. Red Cross (vol. bloodmobile 1986-96), Inst. Internal Auditors, N.Y. State, N.J. socs. CPAs, Real Estate Bd. N.Y., SAR (registrar, geneal., 1995-96), VFW, Am. Legion, 100th Inf. Div. Assn., Soc. Colonial Wars, Delta Sigma Pi (pres. 1948). Lutheran (treas., council). Home: 39 Southgate Rd Mount Laurel NJ 08054-2932

LAUBACHER, STEVE, professional society administrator; b. Canton, Ohio, May 11, 1947. BA in Psychology, U. Dayton, 1969; MA in Sociology and Psychology, Duquesne U., 1972; PhD in Pub. Policy and Orgnl. Behavior, U. Houston, 1990; MPA, Harvard U., 1994. Instr. U. Dayton, Ohio, 1973-75; dir. outpatient svcs. Bur. Alcoholism and Drug Abuse, Dayton, 1975-77; exec. dir. ARC of Montgomery County, Dayton, 1977-82; dep. exec. dir. Mental Health and Mental Retardation Authority, Houston, 1983-89; exec. dir. ARC of Ill., Chgo., 1989-91, Spina Bifida Assn. Am., Washington, 1992-93, Orton Dyslexia Soc., Balt., 1994-96, Seneca Mental Health/Mental Retardation Coun., Summersville, W.Va., 1996—. Mem. Am. Soc. of Pub. Adminstrn., Washington Soc. of Assn. Execs. Home and Office: 302 E Joppa Rd #1908 Baltimore MD 21286-3131

LAUBE, ROGER GUSTAV, retired trust officer, financial consultant; b. Chgo., Aug. 11, 1921; s. William C. and Elsie (Drews) L.; m. Irene Mary Chadbourne, Mar. 30, 1946; children: David Roger, Philip Russell, Steven Richard. BA, Roosevelt U., 1942; postgrad., John Marshall Law Sch., 1942, 48-50; LLB, Northwestern U., 1960; postgrad., U. Wash., 1962-64. Cert. fin. cons. With Chgo. Title & Trust Co., Chgo., 1938-42, 48-50, Nat. Bank Alaska, Anchorage, 1950-72; mgr. mortgage dept. Nat. Bank Alaska, 1950-56, v.p., trust officer, mgr. trust dept., 1956-72; v.p., trust officer, mktg. dir., mgr. estate and fin. planning div, Bishop Trust Co., Ltd., Honolulu, 1972-82; instr. estate planning U. Hawaii, Honolulu, 1978-82; exec. v.p. Design Capital Planning Group, Inc., Tucson, 1982-83; pres., sr. trust officer, registered investment adviser Advanced Capital Advisory, Inc. of Ariz., Tucson, 1983-89; registered rep., pres. Advanced Capital Investments, Inc. of Ariz., Prescott, 1983-89; pres., chief exec. officer Advanced Capital Devel., Inc. of Ariz., Prescott, 1983-89; mng. exec. Integrated Resources Equity Corp., Prescott, 1983-89; pres. Anchorage Estate Planning Coun., 1960-62, Charter mem., 1960-72, Hawaii Estate Planning Coun., 1972-82, v.p., 1979, pres., 1980, bd. dirs., 1981-82; charter mem. Prescott Estate Planning Coun., 1986-90, pres. 1988. Charter mem. Anchorage Community Chorus, 1946, pres., 1950-53, bd. dirs., 1953-72, Alaska Festival of Music, 1960-72; mem. Anchorage camp Gideons Internat., 1946-72, Honolulu camp, 1972-82, mem. Cen. camp, Tucson, 1982-85, Prescott, 1985-90, Port Angeles-Sequim Camp, 1990—; mem. adv. bd. Faith Hosp., Glenallen, Alaska, 1960—, Cen. Alaska Mission of Far Ea. Gospel Crusade, 1960—; sec., treas. Alaska Bapt. Found., 1955-72; bd. dirs. Anchorage Symphony, 1965-72; bd. dirs. Bapt. Found. of Ariz., 1985-90; bd. dirs., mem. investment com. N.W. Bapt. Found., 1991—; mem. mainland adv. coun. Hawaii Bapt. Acad., Honolulu, 1982—; pres. Sabinovista Townhouse Assn., 1983-85; bd. advisers Salvation Army, Alaska , 1961-72, chmn., Anchorage, 1969-72, bd. advisers, Honolulu, 1972-82, chmn. bd. advisers, 1976-78; asst. staff judge adv. Alaskan Command, 1946-48; exec. com. Alaska Conv., 1959-61, dir. music Chgo., 1938-42, 48-50, Alaska, 1950-72, Hawaii, 1972-82, Tucson, 1982-85, 1st So. Bapt. Ch., Prescott Valley, Ariz., 1985-90; 1st Bapt. of Sequim, Wash., 1990—; chmn. bd. trustees Hawaii, 1972-81, Prescott Valley, 1986-89, Sequim, Wash., 1991—; worship leader Waikiki Ch., 1979-82. 1st lt., JAGD, U.S. Army, 1942-48. Recipient Others award Salvation Army, 1972. Mem. Am. Inst. Banking (instr. trust div. 1961-72), Am. Bankers Assn. (legis. com., trust div. 1960-72), Nat. Assn. Life Underwriters (nat. com. for Ariz.), Yavapai County-Prescott Life Underwriters Assn. (charter), Anchorage C. of C. (awards com. 1969-71), Internat. Assn. Fin. Planners (treas. Anchorage chpt. 1969-72, exec. com. Honolulu chpt. 1972-82, Ariz. chpt. 1982-90, del. to World Congress Australia and New Zealand 1987), Am. Assn. Handbell Ringers. Baptist. Home: Sunland Country Club 212 Sunset Pl Sequim WA 98382-8515

LAUBER, JOHN K., research psychologist; b. Archbold, Ohio, Dec. 13, 1942; s. Kenneth Floyd and Fern Elizabeth (Rupp) L.; m. Susan Elizabeth Myers, Sept. 16, 1967; 1 stepchild, Sarah H. BS, Ohio State U., 1965, MS, 1967, PhD, 1969. Rsch. psychologist U.S. Naval Tng. Equipment Ctr., Orlando, Fla., 1969-73; chief aero. human factors office NASA Ames Rsch. Ctr., Moffett Field, Calif., 1973-85; mem. Nat. Transp. Safety Bd., Washington, 1985-95; v.p. corporate safety and compliance Delta Air Lines, Atlanta, 1995—; mem. Rsch., Engring. and Devel. adv. com. FAA, 1995—; mem. aero. adv. com. NASA, 1987—, USAF Studies Bd., NAS, Washington, 1987-89; bd. govs. Flight Safety found., 1995—. Contbr. articles to profl. jours. Recipient Industry Svc. award Air Transport World, N.Y.C., Disting. Svc. award Flight Safety Found., Tokyo, 1987, Joseph T. Nall Meml. award Nat. Air Traffic Contrs. Assn., 1992, Paul T. Hansen Lectureship award, 1993, Forrest & Dominique Bird award Civil Aviation Med. Assn., 1994. Fellow Aerospace Med. Assn. (chmn. aviation safety com. 1978-82, R. F. Longacre award 1990),; mem. Human Factors Soc. Democrat. Avocations: sailing, flying, amateur radio, cooking.

LAUCHENGCO, JOSE YUJUICO, JR., lawyer; b. Manila, Philippines, Dec. 6, 1936; came to U.S., 1962; s. José Celis Sr. Lauchengco and Angeles (Yujuico) Sapota; m. Elisabeth Schindler, Feb. 22, 1968; children: Birthe, Martina, Duane, Lance. AB, U. Philippines, Quezon City, 1959; MBA, U. So. Calif., 1964; JD, Loyola U., L.A., 1971. Bar: Calif. 1972, U.S. Dist. Ct. (cen. dist.) Calif. 1972, U.S. Ct. Appeals (9th cir.) 1972, U.S. Supreme Ct. 1975. Banker First Western Bank/United Calif. Bank, L.A., 1964-71; assoc. Demler, Perona, Langer & Bergkvist, Long Beach, Calif., 1972-73; ptnr. Demler, Perona, Langer, Bergkvist, Lauchengco & Manzella, Long Beach, 1973-77; sole practice Long Beach and L.A., 1977-83; ptnr. Lauchengco & Mendoza, L.A., 1983-92; pvt. practice L.A., 1993—; mem. commn. on jud. procedures County of L.A., 1979; tchr. Confraternity of Christian Doctrine, 1972-79; counsel Philippine Presdl. Commn. on Good Govt., L.A., 1986. Chmn. Filipino-Am. Bi-Partisan Polit. Action Group, L.A., 1978. Recipient Degree of Distinction, Nat. Forensic League, 1955. Mem. Criminal Cts. Bar Assn., Calif. Attys. Criminal Justice, Calif. Pub. Defenders Assn., L.A. County Bar Assn., Assn. Trial Lawyers Am., Calif. Trial Lawyers Assn., L.A. Trial Lawyers Assn., Philippine-Am. Bar Assn. (bd. dirs.), U. Philippines Vanguard Assn. (life), Beta Sigma. Roman Catholic. Lodge: K.C. Avocations: classical music, opera, romantic paintings and sculpture, camping, shooting. Office: 3545 Wilshire Blvd Ste 247 Los Angeles CA 90010-2305

LAUCK, ANTHONY JOSEPH, artist, retired art educator, priest; b. Indpls., Dec. 30, 1908; s. Anthony Peter and Marie Elizabeth (Habig) L. Diploma in fine arts, John Herron Art Sch., 1936; AB, U. Notre Dame, 1942, DFA (hon.), 1980; cert. in carving, painting, Corcoran Sch. Art, 1948. Entered Congregation of Holy Cross, 1937; ordained priest Roman Catholic Ch., 1946; priest aux. St. Martin's Ch., Washington, 1946-48, Holy Cross Ch., N.Y.C., 1948-49; priest aux. univ. ch. U. Notre Dame, Ind., 1950, mem. faculty dept. art univ. ch., 1950-82, assoc. prof. sculpture univ. ch., 1958-70, prof. sculpture, 1970-72, emeritus prof., 1973—, head dept. art, 1960-67, dir. Univ. Art Gallery, 1962-74, dir. emeritus, 1974—; Chmn. art jury Nat. Sacred Heart Drawing Competition, Xavier U., 1956. Exhibited, John Herron Art Inst., Ind. State Fair, Indpls., Corcoran Gallery Art, Nat. Mus. Art, Washington, N.A.D., Audubon Artists, N.Y.C., Pa. Acad. Fine Arts, Phila., Conn. Acad. Fine Art, Hartford, Provincetown (Mass.) Art Assn., Newport (R.I.) Art Assn., sculpture retrospective, U. Notre Dame, 1980-81, Snite Mus.Art, 1993; represented permanent collections, Phila. Mus. Art, Corcoran Gallery Art, Pa. Acad. Fine Arts, Norfolk Mus. Art, South Bend Art Ctr., Indpls. Mus. Art, Snite Mus. Art, Notre Dame U., Ind. State Museum, Indpls., Grand Rapids Art Mus., Evansville Mus. Arts and Sci., Ball State U. Art Mus., Gary Art Center, Hartwick Coll., Krasl Art Ctr., Midwest Mus. of Am. Art, Ind., St. Joseph, Mich., Midwest Mus. of American Art, Elkhart, Ind. ,also pvt. collections.; contbr. articles on sacred art to jours. and mags. Recipient Fairmount Park purchase prize Third Sculpture Internat., 1949, George D. Widener Gold medal for sculpture Am. art exhbn. Pa. Acad. Art, 1953, John Herron Art Inst. citation, 1957, 1st prize for sculpture Newport Art Assn., Peterson Sculpture Purchase award, 1991, Sculpture Purchase prize Midwest Mus. Am. Art, 1992; inducted medalist Ind. Acad., 1973. Mem. Audubon Artists, St. Joseph Valley Watercolor Soc., No. Ind. Artist, Ind. Artists Club, Nat. Sculpture Soc. N.Y. Home: Moreau Seminary Notre Dame IN 46556 Office: U Notre Dame Snite Mus Art Notre Dame IN 46556 *My work does not enter vitally into the main currents of American life, this busy, mechanized, space-oriented, scientific world of the late 20th century. What interest can such a world have in these silent little sacred images? It's up to them, nevertheless, to exercise some aesthetic attraction upon those who can see what I've tried to reveal. I do hope, of course, that these images may implant a warm, deep reminder into a few hearts and minds.*

LAUDA, DONALD PAUL, university dean; b. Leigh, Nebr., Aug. 7, 1937; s. Joe and Libbie L.; m. Sheila H. Henderson, Dec. 28, 1966; children: Daren M., Tanya R. B.S., Wayne State Coll., 1963, M.S., 1964; Ph.D., Iowa State U., 1966. Assoc. dir. Communications Center U. Hawaii, 1966-67; assoc. prof. indsl. arts St. Cloud (Minn.) State Coll., 1967-69; asst. dean Ind. State U., 1970-73; chmn. tech. edn. W.Va. U., 1973-75; dean Sch. Tech., Eastern Ill. U., Charleston, 1975-83, Calif. State U., Long Beach, 1983—; cons. in field. Author: Advancing Technology: Its Impact on Society, 1971, Technology, Change and Society, 1978, 2d edit., 1985; contbr. articles to profl. jours. Pres. Council on Tech. Tchr. Edn.; dir. Charleston 2000 Futures Project, 1978-81. Served with USAR, 1957-59. EPDA research fellow, 1969-70; Eastern Ill. U. faculty research grantee, 1971. Mem. Future Soc. Internat. Tech. Edn. Assn., Coun. Tech. Tchr. Educators (pres., Tchr. of Yr. award 1978), World Future Soc., Internat. Tech. Edn. Assn. (pres. 1990), World Coun. Assn. Tech. Edn., Am. Vocat. Assn., Phi Kappa Phi (pres. 1993), Epsilon Pi Tau (Laureate citation 1982), Long Beach C. of C. (bd. dirs. 1995—), Japan Am. Soc. (adv. bd.). Office: Calif State U Coll Health & Human Svcs Long Beach CA 90840 *Jobs and careers come through a great deal of effort, education, but, most importantly, through the help of others. It is this input that helps one clarify goals, gain new insights, and synthesize information. The process is reciprocal in that one helps others grow. Reflecting on the past always brings to mind people rather than degrees, positions, salaries, etc. When one loses sight of this, he/she is missing the greatest achievement of life.*

LAUDEMAN, LESLIE, nursing administrator, oncological nurse; b. Santa Monica, Calif., Nov. 6, 1960; d. Hal Cella and Janet (Graham) L. BSN, U. Ariz., 1982; MSN, UCLA, 1988. RN, Calif.; ANA advanced adminstr. cert. Staff nurse St. Joseph Med. Ctr., Burbank, Calif., Kenneth Norris

So. Calif. Cancer Ctr., L.A.; nurse mgr. bone marrow transplant, oncology unit UCLA Med. Ctr.; nurse adminstr. Revlon/UCLA Breast Ctr. Mem. Am. Orgn. Nurse Execs. (coun. nurse mgr. affiliates), Oncology Nurses Soc. (cert.).

LAUDER, ESTÉE, cosmetics company executive; b. N.Y.C.; m. Joseph Lauder (dec.); children: Leonard, Ronald. LLD (hon.), U. Pa., 1986. Chmn. bd. Estée Lauder Inc., 1946—. Author: Estée: A Success Story, 1985. Named One of 100 Women of Achievement Harpers Bazaar, 1967, Top Ten Outstanding Women in Business, 1970; recipient Neiman-Marcus Fashion award, 1962; Spirit of Achievement award Albert Einstein Coll. Medicine, 1968; Kaufmann's Fashion Fortnight award, 1969; Bamberger's Designer's award, 1969; Gimbel's Fashion Forum award, 1969; Internat. Achievement award Frost Bros., 1971; Pogue's Ann. Fashion award, 1975, Golda Meir 90th Anniversary Tribute award, 1988; decorated chevalier Legion of Honor France, 1978; medaille de Vermeil de la Ville de Paris, 9, 1979; 4th Ann. award for Humanitarian Service Girls' Club N.Y., 1979; 25th Anniversary award Greater N.Y. council Boy Scouts Am., 1979; L.S. Ayres award, 1981; Achievement award Girl Scouts U.S.A., 1983; Outstanding Mother award, 1984; Athena award, 1985; Pres. award Cosmetic Exec. Women, 1989, Neiman-Marcus Fashion award, 1992; honored Lincoln Ctr., World of Style, 1986; 1988 Laureate Nat. Bus. Hall of Fame. Office: Estée Lauder Cos 767 Fifth Ave New York NY 10153-0002*

LAUDER, EVELYN, cosmetics executive; b. Vienna; m. Leonard Lauder, 1959; children: William, Gary. Attended, Hunter Coll.; hon. degree, Muhlenberg Coll., 1996. Sr. corp. v.p. Estée Lauder Cos., N.Y.C. Photographer: (book) The Seasons Observed, 1994. Founder Breast Cancer Rsch. Found., 1993. Named one of 75 most influential bus. women Crain's Newspaper, 1996. Office: Estée Lauder Cos 767 Fifth Ave New York NY 10153

LAUDER, LEONARD ALAN, cosmetic and fragrance company executive; b. N.Y.C., Mar. 19, 1933; s. Joseph H. and Estée (Mentzer) L.; m. Evelyn Hausner, July 5, 1959; children: William Phillip, Gary Mark. BS, Wharton Sch., U. Pa., 1954. With Estée Lauder, Inc., N.Y.C., 1958—, exec. v.p., 1962-72, pres., 1972-82, pres., chief exec. officer, 1982—; vice chmn. bd. CFTA, N.Y.C., 1976-79. Trustee Aspen Inst. for Humanistic Studies, 1978—, U. Pa., Phila., 1977—; pres. Whitney Mus. Am. Art, 1977—; bd. dirs. Adv. Commn. on Trade Negotiations, Washington, 1983-87; bd. govs. Joseph H. Lauder Inst. Mgmt. and Internat. Studies, 1983—. Lt. USNR, 1955-58. Mem. Chief Execs. Orgn., French-Am. C. of C. in U.S. (coun. frn. relations). Office: Estée Lauder Cos 767 5th Ave New York NY 10153-0001*

LAUDER, RONALD STEPHEN, investor; b. N.Y.C., Feb. 26, 1944; s. Joseph H. and Estee (Josephine) (Mentzer) L.; m. Jo Carole Knopf, July 8, 1967; children: Aerin Rebecca, Jane Alexandra. Degree in French lit., U. Paris, 1964; B.S. in Internat. Bus., U. Pa., 1965. With Estee Lauder, Inc., Brussels, Paris, N.Y.C., 1965-83, also bd. dirs.; chmn. Estee Lauder Internat., Inc., 1980-83; dep. asst. Sec. of Def., Washington, 1983-85; ambassador to Austria Vienna, 1986-87; chmn., pres. Lauder Investments, Inc.; pvt. investor Ea. and Cen. Europe; founder, chmn. Cen. European Devel. Corp. Author: Fighting Violent Crime in America, 1985. Mem. N.Y. State Econ. Devel. Bd., 1972-78; fin. chmn. N.Y. State Republican Com., 1979-82; chmn. 500 Club of N.Y. Rep. Com., 1979-83; trustee Mus. Modern Art, 1975—, Mt. Sinai Med. Ctr., 1981—; Rep. candidate, Conservative nominee for Mayor of N.Y.C., 1989. Recipient Ordre De Merit, France, 1985, Disting. Pub. Svc. medal award Dept. Def., 1986; decorated Great Cross of the Order of Aeronautical Merit with White Ribbon, Spain, 1985; Ronald S. Lauder Drawing Gallery at Mus. Modern Art named in his honor, 1984. Office: Lauder Investments Inc 767 5th Ave Ste 4200 New York NY 10153

LAUDER, VALARIE ANNE, editor, educator; b. Detroit, Mar. 1; d. William J. and Murza Valerie (Mann) L. AA, Stephens Coll., Columbia, Mo., 1944; postgrad. Northwestern U. With Chgo. Daily News, 1944-52, columnist, 1946-52; lectr. Sch. Assembly Svc., also Redpath lectr., 1952-55; freelance writer for mags. and newspapers including N.Y. Times, Yankee, Ford Times, Travel & Leisure, Am. Heritage, 1955—; editor-in-chief Scholastic Roto, 1962; editor U. N.C., 1975-80, lectr. Sch. Journalism, 1980—; gen. sec. World Assn. for Pub. Opinion Rsch., 1988-95; nat. chmn. student writing project Ford Times, 1981-86; pub. rels. dir. Am. Dance Festival, Duke U., 1982-83, lectr., instr. continuing edn. program, 1984; contbg. editor So. Accents mag., 1982-86. Mem. nat. fund raising bd. Kennedy Ctr., 1962-63. Recipient 1st place award Nat. Fedn. Press Women, 1981; 1st place awards Ill. Women's Press Assn., 1950, 1951. Mem. Pub. Rels. Soc. Am. (treas. N.C. chpt. 1982, sec. 1983, v.p. 1984, pres.-elect 1985, pres. 1986, chmn. council of past pres., chmn. 25th Ann. event 1987, del. Nat. Assembly 1988-94, S.E. dist. officer, nat. nominating com. 1991, 1st Pres.'s award 1993), Women in Communications (v.p. matrix N.C. Triangle chpt. 1984-85), N.C. Pub. Rels. Hall of Fame Com., DAR, Soc. Mayflower Desc. (bd. dir. Ill. Soc. 1946-52), Chapel Hill Hist. Soc. (bd. dir. 1981-85, 94—, chmn. publs. com. 1980-85), Chapel Hill Preservation Soc. (bd. trustees 1993-96, nominating com. 1994), N.C. Press Club (3d v.p. 1981-83, 2d v.p. 1983-85, pres. 1985, 1st pl. awards 1981, 82, 83, 84), Univ. Woman's Club (2d v.p. 1988), The Carolina Club, The Nat. Press Club. Office: U NC Sch Journalism and Mass Comm CB 3365 Chapel Hill NC 27599-3365

LAUDISE, ROBERT ALFRED, research chemist; b. Amsterdam, N.Y., Sept. 2, 1930; s. Anthony Thomas and Harriette Elizabeth (O'Neil) L.; m. Joyce Elizabeth DeSilvia, Aug. 24, 1957; children: Thomas Michael, Margaret Joyce, John David, Mary Elizabeth, Edward Robert. B.S. in Chemistry, Union Coll., Schenectady, N.Y., 1952; Ph.D. in Chemistry (A.D. Little fellow), M.I.T., 1956. Mem. Tech. staff Bell Telephone Labs., Murray Hill, N.J., 1956-60; head crystal chemistry rsch. dept. Bell Telephone Labs., 1960-72, asst. dir. materials research lab., 1972-74, dir. materials research lab., 1974-77, dir. phys. and inorganic chemistry research lab., 1977-87, dir. materials chemistry rsch. lab., 1988-90, dir. materials and processing rsch. lab., 1990-92, adj. dir. chem. rsch., 1994—; vis. prof. U. Aix, Marseilles, France, 1971, Hebrew U., Jerusalem, 1972, Shandong U., China, 1980; cons. Pres.'s Sci. com., 1960-64; adv. com. Nat. Bur. Standards, 1970-78; solid state scis. com. NRC, 1977-81; adv. com. NASA, 1977-82; chair Nat. Math. Adv. Bd., 1996—; adj. prof. MIT, 1988—, Rutgers U., 1991—. Author: The Growth of Single Crystals, 1970; editor: Jour. Crystal Growth, 1978-94, Jour. Materials Rsch., 1994—; contbr. articles to sci. jours. Recipient Sawyer award, 1974, Eiler award U. Toledo, 1996. Fellow AAAS, Am. Mineral Soc., Am. Ceramic Soc. (Orton award lectr. 1994); mem. NAS, NAE, Internat. Orgn. Crystal Growth (pres. award 1981), Am. Assn. Crystal Growth (pres. 1971-77), Am. Chem. soc. (Materials Chemistry prize 1990), electrochem. Soc., Am. Crystal Soc., Fedn. Math. Soc. (pres. 1995—), The Mariner's Soc. Roman Catholic. Patentee in field. Home: 65 Lenape Ln Berkeley Heights NJ 07922-2333 Office: Bell Telephone Labs 600 Mountain Ave New Providence NJ 07974-2008

LAUDONE, ANITA HELENE, lawyer; b. Boston, Sept. 14, 1948; d. Vincent A. and Wanda L.; m. Colin E. Harley, May 20, 1978; children: Clayton Thomas, Victoria Spencer. A.B., Conn. Coll., 1970; J.D., Columbia U., 1973. Bar: N.Y. 1974. Law clk. to judge Fed. Dist. Ct., N.Y.C., 1973-74; asso. Davis Polk & Wardwell, N.Y.C., 1974-78; assoc. Shearman & Sterling, N.Y.C., 1978-79; with Phelps Dodge Corp., N.Y.C., 1979-85; corp. sec. Phelps Dodge Corp., 1980-85, v.p., corp. sec., 1984-85. Editor: Columbia Law Rev., 1973. Home: 510 North St Greenwich CT 06830-3439

LAUENSTEIN, MILTON CHARLES, management consultant; b. Webster Groves, Mo., Feb. 16, 1926; s. Milton Charles and Helen (Scholz) L.; m. Helen Smith, Feb. 5, 1949; children: Paul C., Kurt, Maria, Fritz. BS, Purdue U., 1945; MBA, U. Chgo., 1960. Tech. svc. engr. Norton Co., Worcester, Mass., 1948-51; with silicone products dept. GE Co., Waterford, [illegible] Cleve. and Chgo., 1951-57; cons. mktg. and corp. planning A.T. [illegible] Chgo., 1957-60; dir. long range planning Bell & Howell Co., [illegible] res. Ventron Corp., Beverly, Mass., 1962-76, Lauenstein & [illegible] nt. cons.), Wenham, Mass., 1977-91, Telequip Corp., Lit- [illegible] 79-80; chmn. Telequip Corp., Nashua, N.H., 1989—; bd. [illegible] Corp., Waltham, Mass., Tech/Ops. Sevcon Corp., Boston; [illegible] Chgo., 1961-62, 79-80; adj. prof. mgmt., 1983-85; exec.-in- [illegible] Bus. Adminstrn., Northeastern U., Boston, 1980-83. Author: What's Your Game Plan?, 1986; contbns. editor Jour. Bus. Strategy. Trustee, treas. Vt. Studio Ctr., Johnson; chm., Wenham Dem. Town Com., 1967-72. With USNR, 1943-46. Fellow emeritus Am. Inst. Chemists. Avocations: painting, sailing. Home and Office: 90 Hesperus Ave Gloucester MA 01930-5273

LAUER, CLINTON DILLMAN, automotive executive; b. Joliet, Ill., Dec. 8, 1926; s. Thomas Ayscough and Francis (Dillman) L.; m. Lea Merrill, Dec. 9, 1950; children: Joanne L. Gunderson, John C. BS, U. Ill., 1948; MBA, U. Pa., 1950. Supply mgr. automotive assembly div. Ford Motor Co., Dearborn, Mich., 1971-76, dir. body and assembly purchasing N.Am. automotive ops., 1976-83, exec. dir. N.Am. Automotive Ops. prodn. purchasing, 1983-87, v.p. purchasing and supply, 1987-92; pres. Lauer and Assocs., Inc., Bloomfield Hills, Mich., 1992—; bd. dirs. Masland Corp., Top Source Techs., Inc., Mexican Industries. Mem. exec. bd. Detroit Area coun. Boy Scouts Am., pres., 1990-92; mem. fin. com. Meadowbrook-Oakland U., Rochester, Mich.; bd. dirs. nat. and S.E. Mich. Jr. Achievement, Boys and Girls Club of S.E. Mich. With U.S. Army, 1944-46, 50-52. Mem. Soc. Automotive Engrs., Oakland Hills Country Club, Bear Creek Golf Club, Sea Pines Country Club. Republican. Episcopalian. Avocation: golf. Home: 4053 Hidden Woods Dr Bloomfield Hills MI 48301 also: 4053 Hidden Woods Dr Bloomfield Hills MI 48301 also: 26 Marsh View Rd Hilton Head SC 29926

LAUER, ELIOT, lawyer; b. N.Y.C., Aug. 17, 1949; s. George and Doris (Trenk) L.; m. Marilyn Steinberg, June 5, 1977; children: Tamar Rachel, Ilana Jennifer, Michael Jonathan, Samuel Geoffrey. BA, Yeshiva U., 1971; JD cum laude, Fordham U., 1974. Bar: D.C. 1975, N.Y. 1975, U.S. Dist. Ct. (so. and ea. dists.) N.Y. 1975, U.S. Ct. Appeals (2d cir.) 1975, U.S. Supreme Ct. 1984. Assoc. Curtis, Mallet-Prevost, Colt & Mosle, N.Y.C., 1974-82, ptnr., 1982—. Counsel Keren-Or Inc., N.Y.C., 1985—; bd. dirs. Hebrew Acad. Long Beach, N.Y., 1985—, Young Israel Lawrence, Cedarhurst, N.Y., 1984—. Mem. ABA, N.Y. State Bar Assn., Assn. of Bar of City of N.Y., Fed. Bar Council, Am. Arbitration Assn. (arbitrator 1979—), Nat. Futures Assn. (arbitrator 1983—). Republican. Office: Curtis Mallet-Prevost Colt & Mosle 101 Park Ave New York NY 10178

LAUER, JAMES LOTHAR, physicist, educator; b. Vienna, Austria, Aug. 2, 1920; came to U.S., 1938, naturalized, 1943; s. Max and Friederike (Rappaport) L.; m. Stefanie Dorothea Blank, Sept. 5, 1955; children: Michael, Ruth. A.B., Temple U., 1942, M.A., 1944; Ph.D., U. Pa., 1948; postgrad., U. Calif., San Diego, 1964-65. Scientist Sun Oil Co., Marcus Hook, Pa., 1944-52; spectroscopist Sun Oil Co., 1952-64, sr. scientist, 1965-77; asst. prof. U. Pa., 1952-55; lectr. U. Del., 1952-58; research fellow mech. engring. U. Calif., San Diego, 1964-65; research prof. mech. engring. Rensselaer Poly. Inst., Troy, N.Y., 1978-85; prof. mech. engring. Rensselaer Poly. Inst., 1985-93, prof. mech. engring. emeritus, 1993—; rsch. sci. Ctr. Magnetic Recording Rsch. U. Calif., San Diego, 1993-95, vis. scholar, 1995—; sr. faculty summer rsch. fellow NASA-Lewis Rsch. Ctr., 1986, 87; vis. prof. Ctr. for Magnetic Rec. Rsch., U. Calif., San Diego, 1991; cons. Digital Equipment Corp., 1992—, NASA-Lewis Rsch. Ctr., 1993—. Author: Infrared Fourier Spectroscopy—Chemical Applications, 1978; author numerous tech. papers. Active Penn Wynne Civic Assn., 1959-77, Country Knolls Civic Assn., 1978-93. Sun Oil Co. fellow, 1964-65, Air Force Office Sci. Rsch. grantee, 1974-86, NASA Lewis Rsch. Ctr. grantee, 1974-86, Office Naval Rsch. grantee, 1979-82, Army Rsch. Office grantee, 1985-89, NSF grantee, 1987—. Mem. Am. Chem. Soc. (emeritus), Am. Phys. Soc., Soc. Applied Spectroscopy, Materials Rsch. Soc., Optical Soc. Am. (emeritus), Sigma Xi. Jewish. Patentee in field. Home: 7622 Palmilla Dr Apt 78 San Diego CA 92122-5049 Office: U Calif San Diego La Jolla CA 92093 *My advice to those contemplating a career in experimental research is to give much thought to these points: (1) interest, enthusiasm, willingness to work are only basics, (2) a loving and understanding wife is essential, and (3) the knowledge that one can create one's own success at any time is the driving force.*

LAUER, JEANETTE CAROL, college dean, history educator, author; b. St. Louis, July 14, 1935; d. Clinton Jones and Blanche Aldine (Gideon) Pentecost; m. Robert Harold Lauer, July 2, 1954; children: Jon, Julie, Jeffrey. BS, U. Mo., St. Louis, 1970; MA, Washington U., St. Louis, 1973, PhD, 1975. Assoc. prof. history St. Louis Community Coll., 1974-82; assoc. prof. history U.S. Internat. U., San Diego, 1982-90, prof., 1990-94; dean Coll. of Arts and Scis., San Diego. Author: Fashion Power, 1981, The Spirit and the Flesh, 1983, Til Death Do Us Part, 1986, Watersheds, 1988, The Quest for Intimacy, 1991, 2d edit., 1993, No Secrets, 1993, The Joy Ride, 1993, For Better of Better, 1995, True Intimacy, 1996, Intimacy on the Run, 1996. Woodrow Wilson fellow, 1970, Washington U. fellow, 1971-75. Mem. Am. Hist. Assn., Orgn. Am. Historians. Democrat. Presbyterian. Home: 18147 Sun Maiden Ct San Diego CA 92127-3102

LAUER, MATT, broadcast journalist; b. Dec. 30, 1958. University of Ohio. Producer WOWK-TV, Huntington, W.Va., 1979-80; program host various locations, 1980-88; host Day's End, ABC-TV, 1989, Esquire Show, King Prodns./Lifetime, 1988-89, 9 Broadcast Plaza, WWOR-TV, N.Y.C., 1989-91; with WNBC, N.Y.C., 1991—; news anchor NBC News' Today Show, N.Y.C., 1994—; co-anchor News 4/Live at Five, N.Y.C., 1994—. Office: NBC News 30 Rockefeller Plz Rm 1420 New York NY 10112

LAUER, MICHAEL THOMAS, software company executive; b. Lehighton, Pa., Feb. 13, 1955; s. Thomas Lee and Dorothy Ruth (Rehrig) L.; children from previous marriage: Michael T. Jr., Matthew T.; m. Donna Marie Baker, May 19, 1990; 1 stepchild, J. David Beales. Cert. computer analyst. Programmer/analyst Informatics, Linthicum, Md., 1977-78; systems analyst Nat. Security Agy., Annapolis Junction, Md., 1978-79; mgr. Compuware Corp., Landover, Md., 1979-82; exec. v.p., owner Lamarian Systems, Inc., Greenbelt, Md., 1982-90; exec. v.p. Nynex World Trade, Landover, Md., 1990-92; cons. The Harmic Group, Budapest, Hungary, 1993-94; div. mgr. global platform support AT&T, Silver Spring, Md., 1995—; cons. MCI Telecomm., Arlington, Va., 1982-85, U.S. Dept. Transp. Maritime Adminstrn., Washington, 1986-91, Jacksonville (Fla.) Port Authority, 1987-88, Hungarian Customs & Fin. Guard, Budapest, 1992-94. Author rsch. reports in field. Sgt. USAF, 1973-77. Republican. Home: 2503 Prospect Grn Mitchellville MD 20721-2527

LAUER, RONALD MARTIN, pediatric cardiologist, researcher; b. Winnipeg, Man., Can., Feb. 18, 1930; m. Eileen Pearson, Jan. 12, 1959; children: Geoffrey, Judith Lauer. BS, U. Man., 1953, MD, 1954. Diplomate Am. Bd. Pediatrics. Asst. prof. pediatrics U. Pitts., 1960-61; asst. prof. pediatrics U. Kans., 1961-67, assoc. prof. pediatrics, 1967-68; prof. pediatrics, dir. pediatrics cardiology U. Iowa, 1968—, vice chmn. pediatrics, 1974-82, prof. pediatrics and preventive medicine 1980—. Home: RR 6 Iowa City IA 52240-9806 Office: U Iowa Coll Medicine Div Pediatric Cardiology Iowa City IA 52242

LAUERSEN, NIELS HELTH, physician, educator; b. Denmark, Sept. 10, 1939; came to U.S., 1967, naturalized, 1977; s. Bernhard and Maria L. M.D. cum laude, U. Copenhagen, 1967, Cornell U., 1968. Diplomate: Am. Bd. Ob-Gyn. Intern, then resident in ob-gyn N.Y. Hosp.-Cornell U. Med. Center, 1968-72, assoc. prof., 1972-79; assoc. prof. ob-gyn Mt. Sinai Sch. Medicine, N.Y.C., 1979-83; prof. ob-gyn N.Y. Med. Coll., 1983—. Author: It's Your Body, A Woman's Guide to Gynecology, 1978, new version, 1993, Clinical Perinatal Biochemical Monitoring, 1981, Principles of Microsurgical Techniques in Infertility, 1982, Listen to your Body, 1982, Childbirth With Love, 1983, Modern Management of High-Risk Pregnancy, 1983, PMS: Premenstrual Syndrome and You, 1984, It's Your Pregnancy, 1987, The Endometriosis Answer Book, 1988, A Woman's Body, 1989, Getting Pregnant, 1990, You're in Charge, 1993; also numerous articles. Served with Danish Air Force, 1958-60. Recipient Profl. Service award AMA, 1979, 80, 82, 84, 86, 88, 92. Fellow Am. Coll. Obstetricians and Gynecologists (award 1977), Soc. Gynecol. Investigation, Am. Fertility Soc., N.Y. Obstet. Soc., N.Y. Gynecol. Soc., Soc. of Perinatal Medicine; mem. AFTRA, N.Y. Gynecol. Soc., N.Y. Soc. Reproductive Medicine, Author's Guild Am. Home: 750 Park Ave New York NY 10021-4252 Office: 784 Park Ave New York NY 10021-3553 *Through helping others, you will help yourself.*

LAUFER, BEATRICE, composer; b. N.Y.C.; d. Samuel and Fanny (Silverman) L.; m. Theodore Lassoff, Oct. 2, 1940 (dec. 1955); 1 child, Samuel; m. Seymour H. Rinzler, Oct. 19, 1969 (dec. 1970). Student Julliard Sch. Music, 1944. Composer: Symphony No. 1 (performed by Eastman-Rochester Symphony Orch., 1945-46, performance Germany and Japan under auspices of State Dept., 1948, performed by Nat. Gallery Orch., Washington, 1982), Dance Festival (performed by Eastman-Rochester Symphony, 1946-47); choral compositions include: Under the Pines, Spring Thunder performed Tanglewood, 1949, Song of the Fountain, inter-racial chorus, UN Freedom celebration, 1952; Small Concerto for Chamber Orch. performed McMillan Theatre, Columbia, 1949-50; Ile, opera, world premiere Royal Opera Co., Stockholm, Sweden, 1958, recorded by Yale U. Orch. 1978, Broadcast Nat. Pub. Radio, 1980, 87, performed in Chinese at Nanjing U. World Conf. on O'Neill, Shanghai Opera House, June 1988; Second Symphony performed by Oklahoma City Orch., 1961; premiere concerto at Donnell Library Ctr., 1962; premiere performance Prelude and Fugue for Orch., Brevard Music Ctr., N.C., 1964, Cry! orchestral prelude, Orch. of Am., Town Hall, 1966, Lyric string trio, 1991, Bowdoin Coll. Contemporary Music Festival, 1966, performed with Eastman-Rochester Symphony, 1968, Shreveport Symphony Orch., 1978, Berkshire Symphony Orch., 1981; In the Throes performed Shreveport Symphony, 1980, New Orleans Symphony Orch., 1982, Berkshire Symphony Orch., 1985; Conn. Found. of Arts grantee for performance And Thomas Jefferson Said (symphonic version performed by S.W. Floridan Symphony Orch., 1987), Norwalk Symphony Orch., 1976, 3 excerpts performed by USAF Chamber Players, Washington, 1985, premiere version for concert band baritone solo performed by The Goldman Meml. Band, 1986, also at the Aspen (Colo.) Music Festival, 1987, orchestral performance We Hold These Truths, S.W. Fla. Symphony, Nov. 1987; master ceremonies Young Am. Artists, radio sta. WNYC; hostess The Conductor Speaks series sta. WNYC. Mem. ASCAP, Am. Symphony Orch. League, Am. Music Ctr. Address: PO Box 3 Lenox Hill Sta New York NY 10021

LAUFER, DONALD L., lawyer; b. Neptune, N.J., May 31, 1933. AB, Columbia U., 1955, LLB, 1957. Bar: N.Y. 1958, U.S. Dist. Ct. (so. dist.) N.Y. 1961. Law clk. to Hon. Harold R. Medina U.S. Ct. Appeals (2nd cir.), 1957-58; counsel Faust, Rabbach, Stanger & Oppenheim, N.Y.C., 1995—. Mem. ABA, N.Y. County Lawyers Assn., Assn. Bar City N.Y. Home: 345 E 80th St Apt 29B New York NY 10021 Office: Faust Rabbach Stanger & Oppenheim 488 Madison Ave New York NY 10022

LAUFER, HANS, developmental biologist, educator; b. Germany, Oct. 18, 1929; s. Sol and Margarete (Freundlich) L.; m. Evelyn Green, Oct. 31, 1953; children: Jessica, Marc, Leonard. B.S., CCNY, 1952; M.A., Bklyn. Coll., 1953; Ph.D. (James fellow), Cornell U., Ithaca, N.Y., 1957. Research and teaching asst. Cornell U., 1953-57; NRC fellow Carnegie Instn. of Washington, 1957-59; asst. prof. biology Johns Hopkins U., 1959-65; assoc. prof. U. Conn., Storrs, 1965-72; prof. U. Conn., 1972—; vis. prof. Karolinska Inst., Stockholm, 1972, Charles U., Prague, 1974, Yale U., 1980, Harvard U., 1987-89; participant Nat. Acad. Scis.-Czechoslovak Acad. exchange program, 1974, 77; ad hoc mem. study sect. tropical medicine NIH, 1981, mem., 1982-85; Conklin Meml. fellow Marine Biology Lab., Woods Hole, Mass., 1956, Lalor fellow, 1962, 63, mem. staff, embryology course, 1968-72, mem. corp., 1962—, corp. trustee, 1978-82, mem. exec. com., 1979-80; vis. scholar Case Western Res. U., 1962; mem. NSF-NATO Fellowship Rev. Panel, 1974, 76. Contbg. author numerous books; assoc. editor Jour. Exptl. Zoology, 1969-73, 90-93, archives Insect Physiology and Biochemistry, 1983-95, Invertebrate Reprodn. and Devel., 1984-86, mng. editor, 1991—; contbr. numerous articles to profl. jours. Recipient Rsch. Svc. award NIH, 1989, Marcus Singer medal for rsch., 1986, 95; NATO sr. fellow Lady David Trust, Hebrew U., 1988; Japan Soc. Promotion of Sci. fellow, 1980; Rosenstiel scholar Brandeis U., 1973. Fellow AAAS (chmn. sect. biology 1975), Royal Entomology Soc. London (fgn. fellow, elected); mem. Internat. Soc. Devel. Biology, Assn. Rsch. Couns. (nat. bd. on grad. edn. of conf. bd. 1971-75), Am. Soc. Zoology (chmn. divsn. developmental biology 1981-82), Soc. Devel. Biology, Am. Soc. Cell Biology, European Soc. Comparative Endocrinology, Am. Assn. Advancement Aging Rsch., Internat. Soc. Differentiation, Tissue Culture Assn. (coun. 1979-82), World Agrl. Soc. Home: Aquaculture 57 Davis Rd Storrs CT 06268 Office: U Conn Dept Molecular & Cell Biology U-125 Storrs Mansfield CT 06268

LAUFF, GEORGE HOWARD, biologist; b. Milan, Mich., Mar. 23, 1927; s. George John and Mary Anna (Klein) L. B.S., Mich. State U., 1949, M.S., 1951; postgrad., U. Mont., 1951, U. Wash., 1952; Ph.D., Cornell U., 1953. Fisheries research technician Mich. Dept. Conservation, 1950; teaching asst. Cornell U., 1952-53; instr. U. Mich., 1953-57, asst. prof., 1957-61, asso. prof., 1961-62; research asso. Gt. Lakes Research Inst., U. Mich., 1954-59; dir. U. Ga. Marine Inst., 1960-62; asso. prof. U. Ga., 1960-62; research coord. Sapelo Island Research Found., 1962-64; dir. Kellogg Biol. Sta., 1964-90; prof. dept. fisheries and wildlife and zoology Mich. State U., East Lansing, 1964-91, prof. emeritus, 1991—; mem. cons. and rev. panels for Smithsonian Inst., Nat. Water Commn., NSF, Nat. Acad. Sci., Am. Inst. Biol. Sci., U.S. AEC, Inst. Ecology, others. Editor: Estuaries, 1967, Experimental Ecological Reserves, 1977. Served with inf. U.S. Army, 1944-46. Office of Naval Research grantee; U.S. Dept. Interior grantee; NSF grantee; others. Fellow AAAS; mem. Am. Inst. Biol. Sci., Am. Soc. Limnology and Oceanography (pres. 1972-73), Ecol. Soc. Am., Freshwater Biology Assn., INTECOL, Societas Internationalis Limnologiae, Orgn. Biol. Field Stas., Sigma Xi, Phi Kappa Phi. Home: 3818 Heights Dr Hickory Corners MI 49060-9504 Office: 3700 E Gull Lake Dr Hickory Corners MI 49060-9505

LAUFMAN, HAROLD, surgeon; b. Milw., Jan. 6, 1912; s. Jacob and Sophia (Peters) L.; m. Marilyn Joselit, 1940 (dec. 1963); children: Dionne Joselit Weigert, Laurien Laufman Kogut; m. June Friend Moses, 1980. BS, U. Chgo., 1932; MD, Rush Med. Coll., 1937; MS in Surgery, Northwestern U., Chgo., 1946, PhD, 1948. Diplomate: Am. Bd. Surgery. Intern Michael Reese Hosp., Chgo., 1936-39; resident in gen. surgery St. Marks Hosp., London, Northwestern U. Med. Sch., Cook County Hosp., Hines VA Hosp., 1939-46; mem. faculty Northwestern U., 1941-65; from clin. asst. to prof., attending surgeon Passavant Meml. Hosp., Chgo., 1953-65; prof. surgery, history of medicine Albert Einstein Coll. Medicine, N.Y.C., 1965-82, prof. emeritus, 1982—; dir. Inst. Surg. Studies, Montefiore Hosp. and Med. Center, Bronx, N.Y., 1965-81; pvt. practice gen. and vascular surgery Chgo., 1941-65, N.Y.C., 1965-81; ret. professorial lectr. surgery Mt. Sinai Sch. Medicine, N.Y.C., 1979-83, emeritus, 1983—; attending surgeon Mt. Sinai Hosp., N.Y.C., 1979-83; cons., lectr. in field; chmn. FDA Classification Panel Gen. and Plastic Surgery Devices, 1975-78; pres. Harold Laufman Assocs., Inc., 1977—, sr. ptnr., 1988—; pres. HLA Systems. Author: (with S.W. Banks) Surgical Exposures of the Extremities, 1953, 2d edit., 1986, (with R.B. Erichson) Hematologic Problems in Surgery, 1970, Hospital Special Care Facilities, 1981, The Veins, 1986; chmn. editorial bd.: Diagnostica, 1974-79; mem. editorial bd.: Surgery, Gynecology and Obstetrics, 1974-92, Infection Control, 1980-88, Med. Instrumentation, 1972-83, Med. Rsch. Engring., 1972-79; contbr. articles to sci. publs. Chmn. bd. dirs. N.Y. Chamber Soloists, 1974-80, Chamber Music Conf. and Composers Forum of the East, 1975-91. Maj. AUS, 1942-46. Named Disting. Alumnus Rush Med. Coll., 1993. Fellow ACS; mem. Assn. Advancement Med. Instrumentation (pres. 1974-75, chmn. bd. 1976-77), Am. Assn. Hosp. Cons., Am. Med. Writers Assn. (pres. 1968-69), Am. Surg. Assn., Société Internationale de Chirurgie, Western Surg. Assn., Cen. Surg. Assn., N.Y. Surg. Soc., Soc. Vascular Surgery, Internat. Cardiovascular Soc., Soc. Surgery Alimentary Tract, Surg. Infection Soc. (councillor 1980-84), Sigma Xi, Alpha Omega Alpha, Phi Sigma Delta, Zeta Beta Tau. Jewish. Clubs: Standard (Chgo.); Harmonie (N.Y.C.); Willow Ridge Country (Harrison, N.Y.). Home and Office: 31 E 72nd St New York NY 10021-4146

LAUFMAN, LESLIE RODGERS, hematologist, oncologist; b. Pitts., Dec. 13, 1946; d. Marshall Charles and Ruth Rodgers; m. Harry B. Laufman, Apr. 25, 1970 (div. Apr. 1984); children: Hal, Holly; m. Rodger Mitchell, Oct. 9, 1987. BA in Chemistry, Ohio Wesleyan U., 1968; MD, U. Pitts., 1972. Diplomate Am. Bd. Internal Medicine and Hematology. Intern Montefiore Hosp., Pitts., 1972-73, resident in internal medicine, 1973-74; fellow in hematology and oncology Ohio State Hosp., Columbus, 1974-76; dir. med. oncology Grant Med. Ctr., Columbus, 1977-92; practice medicine specializing in hematology and oncology Columbus, 1977—; bd. dirs. Columbus Cancer Clinic; prin. investigator Columbus Cmty. Clin. Oncology Program, 1989—. Contbr. articles to profl. jours. Mem. AMA, Am.

Women Med. Assn. (sec./treas. 1985-86, pres. 1986-87), Am. Soc. Clin. Oncology, Southwest Oncology Group, Nat. Surg. Adjuvant Project for Breast and Bowel Cancers. Avocations: tennis, piano, sailing, hiking, travel. Office: 393 E Town St # 109 Columbus OH 43215-4741 also: 8100 Ravine'S Edge Ct Worthington OH 43235

LAUGHLIN, CHARLES WILLIAM, agriculture educator, research administrator; b. Iowa City, Iowa, Dec. 9, 1939; s. Ralph Minard and Geraldine (O'Neill) L.; m. Barbara Waln, Dec. 17, 1966; children: Shannon Morris, Charles Tudor. BS, Iowa State U., 1963; MS, U. Md., 1966; PhD, Va. Tech., 1969. Asst. extension nematologist U. Fla., Gainesville, 1968-69; asst. prof., extension nematologist Mich. State U., East Lansing, 1969-73, assoc. prof., asst. dir. acad. and student affairs, 1973-78, prof., asst. dean, dir. acad. and student affairs, 1978-80; prof., dept. head plant pathology and weed sci. Miss. State U., Starkville, 1980-83; prof., assoc. dir. Ga. Agrl. Expt. Sta. U. Ga., Athens, 1983-92; dir. co., Agrl. Expt. Sta. Colo. State U., Ft. Collins, 1992-96; dean coll. tropical agriculture and human resources U. Hawaii, Honolulu, 1996—; cons. Brazilian Ministry of Edn. and Culture, Brasilin, Brazil, 1975-77, Brazilian Nat. Agrl. Rsch. Agy., 1978, W.K. Kellogg Found., Battle Creek, Mich., 1983—, Latin Am. Inst. of Creativity, São Paulo, Brazil, 1991. Recipient Colleague award Creative Edn. Found., 1988. Mem. Soc. Nematologists, Am. Phytopathological Soc., Brazilian Soc. Nematologists. Avocations: creative problem solving, outdoors recreation. Address: 16 Administration CSU Fort Collins CO 80523-0001

LAUGHLIN, DAVID EUGENE, materials science educator, metallurgical consultant; b. Phila., July 15, 1947; s. Eugene L. and Myrtle M. (Kramer) L.; m. Diane Rae Seamans, June 13, 1970; children—Jonathan, Elizabeth, Andrew, Daniel. B.Sc., Drexel U., 1969; Ph.D., MIT, 1973. Asst. prof. materials sci. Carnegie-Mellon U., Pitts., 1974-78, assoc. prof., 1978-82, prof., 1982—; rsch. scientist Oxford (Eng.) U., 1985. Editor: Solid-Solid Phase Transformations, 1982; category editor of copper: Am. Soc. Metals-Nat. Bur. Stds. Phase Diagram Program, 1981-94; assoc. editor: Metall. Trans., 1982-87, editor, 1987—; contbr. numerous articles to profl. jours. Mem. sch. bd. Trinity Christian Sch., Pitts., 1976-85, 87-95, pres., 1978-83, sec., 1988-91, pres., 1991-94; ruling elder Covenant Presbyn. Ch., Pitts., 1982—; foster parent Children's Home of Pitts., 1984-90; bd. dirs. Christian Schs. Internat., 1991—. Recipient Ladd Teaching award Carnegie-Mellon U., 1975; postdoctoral fellow Nat. Acad. Scis., 1974. Fellow Am. Soc. Metals; mem. Metallurgical Soc. of AIME, Am. Sci. Affiliation, Materials Rsch. Soc. Orthodox Presbyterian. Avocations: sports; books. Home: 2357 Mcnary Blvd Pittsburgh PA 15235-2779 Office: Carnegie-Mellon U Dept Materials Sci Eng Pittsburgh PA 15213

LAUGHLIN, FELIX B., lawyer; b. New Orleans, Dec. 4, 1942; m. Betty Gayle Laughlin. BS with honors, U. Tenn., 1967, JD with honors, 1967; LLM, Georgetown U., 1971. Bar: Tenn. 1967, D.C. 1972, U.S. Ct. Claims 1969, U.S. Tax Ct. 1968, U.S. Dist. Ct. D.C. 1972, U.S. Ct. Appeals (D.C. cir.) 1988, U.S. Ct. Appeals (fed. cir.) 1992, U.S. Supreme Ct. 1970. With interpretation divsn. Office Chief Counsel IRS, 1967-71; assoc. Dewey Ballantine, Washington, 1972—, mem., 1975—. Dir. Friends of U.S. Nat. Arboretum, Nat. Bonsai Found. Mem. ABA (tax sect.), Fed. Bar Assn. (chmn. tax sect. 1989), Met. Club (Washington), George Town Club (Washington), Order of Coif, Sigma Alpha Epsilon, Phi Eta Sigma, Phi Kappa Phi, Phi Delta Phi. Office: Dewey Ballantine 1775 Pennsylvania Ave NW Washington DC 20006-4605

LAUGHLIN, GREGORY H. (GREG LAUGHLIN), congressman; b. Bay City, Tex., Jan. 21, 1942. BA, Tex. A&M U.; LLB, U. Tex. Asst. dist. atty. Harris County, Tex., 1970-74; pvt. practice Tex.; mem. 101st-103rd Congresses from 14th Tex. dist., Washington, D.C., 1989—. With AUS; col. USAR. Office: US Ho of Reps 442 Cannon Bldg Washington DC 20515-0003*

LAUGHLIN, HENRY PRATHER, physician, psychiatrist, educator, author, editor; b. Hagerstown, Md., June 25, 1916; s. John Royer and Myrtle Frances (Binkley) L.; m. Marion Page Durkee, June 2, 1941; children: Constance Ann Kuhn, John Royer II, Robert Scott, Barbara Hilton Galant, Deborah Page Mayer. Student, Johns Hopkins U, 1936,1938; BS, Ursinus Coll., 1937, ScD, 1976; MD, Temple U., 1941; D Social Sci., U. Louisville, 1978; LittD, Albright Coll., 1994; PSD, Washington Coll., 1995. Diplomate Am. Bd. Psychiatry and Neurology, Nat. Bd. Med. Examiners. Pvt. practice Md., 1947-92; faculty psychiatry George Washington U, 1947-83; clin. prof. psychiatry George Washington U., 1948-83; disting. vis. prof. U. Louisville, 1974-89, adj. prof. emeritus, 1989; vis. prof. 60 med. ctrs. around the world, 1950-93; pres. Nat. Psychiat. Endowment Fund, Washington, Frederick, Md.,1957-91; pres. Med. Coun. of the Washington Met. area, 1959-1961; exec. dir. Nat. Inst. of Emerging Tech., Frederick, 1989-92, mem.; bd. dirs. Ursinus Coll., Collegeville, Pa., 1967-77, life mem. 1985; cons. 14 U.S. agys., Washington, 1974-79; asst. or assoc. examiner Am. Bd. Psychiatry and Neurology, 1948-82; cons. editor in psychoanalysis Psychosomatics, N.Y., 1977-87; cons. Walter Reed Army Med. Ctr., 1949-57, Nat. Naval Med. Ctr., 1972-79; co-founder, bd. dirs. Robert R. Luce Inc. Pubs., Washington, 1957-62; owner Montgomery House, Bethesda, Md. 1959-84, owner Kings Park Plz., Hyattsville, Md., 1965—; co-developer So. Manor Country Club, Boca Raton, Fla., 1970-73; dir., sec., 1982-84, dir., 1987-94, Galaxy Cos., Frederick, Md.; bd. dirs. Frederick Trading Co., 1991—, Capital Investment Co., Washington, 1959-62; co-founder, v.p., treas. Alaska-N.Am. Investment Co., Washington, 1958-62; chief psychiatry and neurology, 1954-64, attending staff, cons. to 1977, emeritus med. staff 1977—, Suburban Hosp., Bethesda, Md.; cons., emeritus staff Frederick Meml. Hosp., 1976-94, mem. hon. staff, 1994—. Author: The Neuroses in Clinical Practice, 1956, Mental Mechanisms, 1963, The Neuroses, 1967, 70, The Ego and Its Defenses, 1970, 79, 17 other books; assoc. editor Md. Med. Jour., 1988—; assoc. editor Physician's Practice Digest, 1989-92, editor, 1992-94, editor emeritus, 1994—; contbr. more than 148 articles and revs. to profl. jours., reports, chpts. to books. Pres. CAMPER, U.S. Park Svc., Catoctin Mountain Park, 1987-90, bd. dirs., 1980-94, Md. Sheriffs Youth Ranch, Frederick County, 1989-90, bd. dirs., 1989-96; grand marshal Nat. Independence Day parade, Washington, 1988, 89, Grand Marshal emeritus, 1989—; capt. USN Admiral's Team, Lander, Wyo., One Shot Unit, 1991; bd. assocs. Hood Coll., 1988—; trustee, Francis Scott Key Meml. Found., 1988—; pres. Dr. Henry P. and M. Page Durkee Laughlin Found., 1991—. With M.C., USN, 1941-47. Decorated six medals with four battle stars; recipient Disting. Alumni award Ursinus Coll., 1966, the Laughlin prize established in his hon., Royal Coll. Physiciatrists of Great Britain, 1979—, Laughlin Profl./Ursinus Coll. faculty achievement award established in his honor, 1988, three Salute to Excellence awards, 1990-92, 6 gov.'s citations State of Md., from 1969, hon. citizenship/comms. various states, 1st Internat. Patriot's award OAS, 1993, Pres. Spl. Achievement award Md. Sheriffs Youth Ranch, 1993, others. Fellow Am. Psychiat. Assn. (life), Am. Soc. of Physician Analysts (founder, hon. lifetime pres. 1982), Royal Coll. Psychiatrists (hon.), Am. Coll. of Psychiatrists (founder, pres. 1963-65), hon. mem. National Accreditation Assn. in psychoanalysis, 1978—, Am. Coll. of Psychoanalysts (founder, 1st and 8th pres., hon. life pres. 1979, established Laughlin Fellowship program, 1994—, Laughlin fellow, 1977, Gold medals 1965, 76, plaque for significant contbns. as hon. life pres. 1994), USN Psychiatrists (commodore 1978-80, hon. life commodore 1980), USN Admirals Team (capt. 1991), Med. and Chirurg. Faculty of Medicine Md. (mem. coun. 1962-73, 88-92), emeAm. Soc. Psychoanalytic pysicians, 1987—, Montgomery County Med. Soc. (pres. 1959-60, emeritus mem. 1985), hon. mem Titus Harris Psychiatric Soc. of Tex., Frederick County Med. Soc. emeritus (pres. 1991, 92, 93), SAR (MD soc. pres. 1987-88, Md. surgeon 1994-95, v.p. gen. nat. soc. 1988, surgeon gen. 1990-91, various nat. coms. 1986—, numerous awards), Nat. Congress of Patriotic Orgns. (inaugural pres. emeritus 1991), Am. Legion, U.K. Soc. SAR (trustee 1989-91, inaugural pres. coun. of pres. Md. Soc. 1992-94, inaugural pres. emeritus, 1994—), Gov. Md. Sons and Dau. of the Pilgrims (hon. gov. 1995), Gen. Soc. War of 1812, Pan Am. Bldg. Orgn. Am. States (1st Internat. Patriots award 1993), Rotary. Avocations: philately, genealogy, philanthropy, big game hunting, marksmanship. Home: Freehold Park 7977 Timmons Rd Union Bridge MD 21791-7699

LAUGHLIN, JAMES, publishing company executive, writer, lecturer; b. Pitts., Oct. 30, 1914; s. Henry Hughart and Marjory (Rea) L.; m. Margaret Keyser, Mar. 13, 1942 (div. 1952); children: Paul, Leila; m. Ann Clark Resor, May 19, 1956 (dec. Nov. 1987); children; Robert (dec.), Henry; m. Gertrude Huston, Dec. 5, 1991. A.B., Harvard U., 1939; Litt.D. (hon.), Hamilton Coll., 1969, Colgate U., 1978; H.H.D. (hon.), Duquesne U., 1980; L.H.D., Yale U., 1982, Brown U., 1984, Bellarmine Coll., 1987, St. Joseph's Coll., Hartford, 1993. Founder New Directions (now New Directions Pub. Corp.), N.Y.C., 1936; pres. New Directions (now New Directions Pub. Corp.), 1964—, Intercultural Publs., Inc; pub. Perspectives, USA and Perspectives supplements The Atlantic Monthly Jour.; cons. Indian So. Langs. Book Trust, Madras, 1955; vis. Regents prof. U. Calif., San Diego, 1974; Ida Bean vis. prof. U. Iowa, 1981; chmn. creative writing panel Inst. Internat. Edn. Conf. on Arts Exchange, 1956—; adj. prof. English, Brown U., 1983, 85. Author: Some Natural Things, 1945, A Small Book of Poems, 1948, The Wild Anemone and Other Poems, 1957, Selected Poems, 1960, The Pig, 1970, In Another Country, 1978, Stolen and Contaminated Poems, 1984, The House of Light, 1986, Selected Poems, 1986, The Owl of Minerva, 1987, Pound as Wuz, 1987, William Carlos Williams and James Laughlin: Selected Letters, 1989, The Bird of Endless Time, 1990, Kenneth Rexnoth and James Laughlin: Selected Letters, 1991, Random Essays, Random Stories, 1991, The Man in the Wall, 1993, Delmore Schwartz and James Laughlin: Selected Letters, 1993, Collected Poems, 1994, Ezra Pound and James Laughlin: Selected Letters, 1994, (novella) Angelica, 1993, Collected Poems, 1994, Phantoms, 1995, The Country Road, 1995; profiled in New Yorker; contbr. mags. and books; collector lit. mags. (little mag. type); active prodn. documentary films on modern poets, 1983—. Bd. dirs. Goethe Bi-Centennial Found., 1949, Aspen (Colo.) Inst. Humanities, 1950; mem. Nat. Citizens Commn. for Internat. Cooperation, U.S. Nat. Commn. for UNESCO, 1960-63, Nat. Commn. for Internat. Coop. year, 1966; past trustee Allen-Chase Found.; mem. vis. com. German Princeton U; mem. vis. com. dept. Romance langs. Harvard U; co-trustee Merton Legacy Trust, 1969—; trustee Rosenbach Found., Phila., to 1981. Decorated chevalier Legion of Honor; hon. fellow Coll. Five, U. Calif., Santa Cruz, 1972—; recipient Disting. Svc. award Am. Acad. Arts and Letters, 1977, award for pub. PEN, 1979, Carey-Thomas citation Pubs. Weekly, 1978, Conn. Arts Comn. award, 1986, Nat. Book Found. medal for Disting. Contbn. to Am. Letters, 1992. Mem. Am. Acad. Arts and Scis., Am. Acad. Arts and Letters, Alta Ski Lifts Co. (formerly Salt Lake City Winter Sports Assn.; dir. 1939—, v.p. 1958), Alta Lodge Co. (v.p. 1948-58, pres. 1958-59), PEN, Asia Soc. (chmn. publs. com. 1959-67), Century Assn. (N.Y.C.), Harvard Club of N.Y.C. Office: New Directions Pub Corp 80 8th Ave New York NY 10011-5126

LAUGHLIN, JAMES HAROLD, JR., lawyer; b. Charleston, W.Va., July 18, 1941; s. James Harold and Pearl Ruby L.; m. Eleanor Blackford Watson, II Aug. 3, 1968; children: C. Michelle, Jeanette C., Cheryl Adele. B.S. in Chem. Engring., W.Va. U., 1964; J.D., Am. U., 1968. Bar: D.C. 1968, Va. 1969. Atty., Am. Cyanamid Co., Wayne, N.J., 1968-70, Xerox Corp., Rochester, N.Y., 1971-76; ptnr. Benoit, Smith & Laughlin, Arlington, Va., 1977-92, Lane & Mittendorf, Washington, 1993—. Mem. ABA, Am. Intellectual Property Law Assn. (bd. dirs. 1976-79, treas. 1982-85, councilman 1993-94), Va. State Bar, (chmn. PTC sect. 1982-83), Nat. Council Patent Law Assns. (Va. del. 1983—), Nat. Inventors Hall of Fame Found. (bd. dirs. 1988-93, pres. 1991-92). Office: 919 18th St NW Washington DC 20006-5503

LAUGHLIN, JOHN SETH, physicist, educator; b. Canton, Mo., Jan. 26, 1918; s. Sceva Bright and Catherine (Goodall) L.; m. Barbara Kester, June 14, 1943; children—Catherine Ann, Frances Elizabeth, Janet Judd; m. Eunice Chapin Beyersdorf, June 23, 1979. A.B., Willamette U., 1940, D.Sc., 1968; M.S., Haverford Coll., 1942; Ph.D., U. Ill., 1947. Diplomate: Am. Bd. Radiology. Research physicist OSRD, 1944-45; asst. prof. dept. physics U. Ill., 1946-48, assoc. prof. radiology, 1951-52; attending physicist Meml. Hosp., chmn. dept. med. physics, 1952-89; chief div. biophysics Sloan-Kettering Inst., N.Y.C., 1952-89; v.p. Sloan-Kettering Inst., 1966-72; prof. biophysics Sloan Kettering div. Cornell U. Grad. Sch., 1955—; prof. radiology Cornell U. Med. Coll., 1970—; dir. N.E. Center for Radiol. Physics, 1974-85; chmn. med. radiation adv. com. Bur. Radiol. Health, 1976-79; John Wiley Jones lectr. Rochester Inst. Tech., 1977. Author: Physical Aspects of Betatron Therapy, 1954; editor: Medical Physics, 1988—. Recipient Distinguished Service Alumni award U. Ill. Coll. Engring., 1972; Alumni citation Willamette U., 1964; Disting. Service award Health Physics Soc., 1982. Fellow Am. Phys. Soc., Am. Coll. Radiology (Gold medalist), N.Y. Acad. Scis., Am. Inst. Med. and Biol. Engring, Sigma Xi; mem. AAAS, Am. Soc. Therapeutic Radiology and Oncology (Gold medal 1993), Health Physics Soc. (pres. 1960-61), Assn. Tchrs. Physics, Radiol. Soc. N.Am., Soc. Nuclear Medicine (dir., Aebersold award 1984), Am. Radium Soc. (Gold medal 1986), Internat. Orgn. Med. Physics (v.p. 1965-69, pres. 1969-72), Radiation Research Soc. (pres. 1970-71), Am. Assn. Physicists in Medicine (pres. 1964-65, chmn. sci. com. 1968-75, Coolidge award 1974), Am. Coll. Med. Physicists (Williams award 1992). Mem. Soc. of Friends. Home: 48 Graham Rd Scarsdale NY 10583-7256 Office: 1275 York Ave New York NY 10021-6007

LAUGHLIN, LOUIS GENE, economic analyst, consultant; b. Santa Barbara, Calif., Sept. 20, 1937; s. Eston A. and Cornelia Helen (Snively) L.; student Pomona Coll., 1955-58; BA, U. Calif., Santa Barbara, 1960; postgrad. Claremont Grad. Sch., 1966-70, 85-86, Sch. Bank Mktg., U. Colo., 1974-75, Grad. Sch. Mgmt., U. Calif.-Irvine, 1983. Mgr., Wheeldex-L.A. Co., 1961-62; v.p. Warner/Walker Assocs., Inc., L.A., 1962; cons. Spectra-Sound Corp., L.A., 1964-65; rep. A.C. Nielsen Co., Chgo., 1962-64; rsch. analyst Security Pacific Nat. Bank, L.A., 1964-67, asst. rsch. mgr., 1967-68, asst. v.p., 1968-72, v.p., mgr. market info. and rsch. div., 1972-76, v.p. rsch. adminstrn., pub. affairs/rsch. dept., 1976-82, v.p. govt. rels. dept., 1982-85; dir. R & D Applied Mgmt. Systems, South Pasadena, Calif., 1986; pres. L.G. Laughlin & Assoc., Houston, 1987—; prin. Courtyard Holdings, Houston, 1988—; pres. CEO, Mastodon Capital Corp., Houston, 1988-89, 94—; mem. Nat. Conf. on Fin. Svcs., 1982-84, mem. policy coun., 1983-84; mem. policy coun. Nat. Conf. on Competition in Banking, 1978-79, 81. Sec. econs. Town Hall of Calif., 1966. Mem. Am. Econs. Assn., Western Econ. Assn., Nat. Assn. Bus. Economists, L.A. C. of C. (food and agr. adv. com. 1981).

LAUGHLIN, NANCY, newspaper editor. Nation/world editor Detroit Free Press. Office: Detroit Free Press Inc 321 W Lafayette Blvd Detroit MI 48226-2705

LAUGHREN, TERRY, marketing executive; b. Trenton, N.J., July 6, 1940; s. Donald Dunn and Hazel Melinda (Rogers) L.; children: Laurie Margot, B. Kenneth, Brandon Keith. BSBA with honors, Boston U., 1961. Brand mgr. Procter & Gamble Co., Cin., 1963-70; dir. mktg. Internat. Playtex Corp., N.Y.C., 1970-71; dir. corp. mktg. Mattel Inc., Hawthorne, Calif., 1971-72; pres., CEO Metaframe Corp. (subs. of Mattel), Elmwood Park, N.J., 1972-75; exec. v.p. J. Walter Thompson, Detroit and N.Y.C., 1976-80; pres. FTTL Media Co., 1981—; pres., mng. ptnr. Screenvision Cinema Network, N.Y.C., 1981-89, chmn., 1990. 1st lt. U.S. Army, 1961-63. Mem. Young Pres.'s Orgn., Nat. Alumni Coun. Boston U. (chmn.), Econ. Club Detroit, Adcraft Club, Friar's Club, Beta Gamma Sigma. Republican. Office: FTTL Media Co Inc Ste 302 311 W 43d St New York NY 10036-6413

LAUGHTER, BENNIE M., corporate lawyer. V.p., gen. counsel Shaw Industries, Dalton, Ga., 1990—. Office: Shaw Industries Inc 616 E Walnut Ave PO Drawer 2128 Dalton GA 30722-2128

LAUGHTON, KATHARINE L., career officer; b. L.A., Dec. 9, 1942; d. Herman and Mary-Alice (McCunniff) H.; m. Robert James Laughton, Oct. 16, 1972. Attended, Vassar Coll., 1960-61; BA, U. Calif., Riverside, 1964; dist. grad., Navy War Coll., 1986. Dep. dir. mgmt. info. svcs. Military Sealift Command, 1977-79; commdg. officer Military Sealift Command, Pt. Canaveral, 1979-82; program mgr. Naval Data Automation Command, 1982-84; spl. asst. inspector gen. U.S. Navy, 1984-86; head ADP svcs. commdr. n chief U.S. Atlantic, Norfolk, Va., 1986-87; commander Navy Space Command, Dahlgren, Va., 1995—. Recipient medal of merit for excellence in tech. Armed Forces Communications & Elecs. Assn., 1991, Parsons award for scientific and Tech. progress Navy League, 1990. Mem. AFCEA (internat. v.p.), Vassar Club. Episcopalian. Avocation, crafts. Office: Navy Dept. 5820 14 St Dahlgren VA 22448-5300*

LAUKENMANN, CHRISTOPHER BERND, lawyer; b. Aug. 15, 1962. BA, Duke U., 1984, JD, 1988, LLM, 1988. Bar: Ga. 1989, Calif. 1990, D.C. 1990, U.S. Dist. Ct. (ctrl. dist.) Calif. 1990, U.S. Ct. Appeals (9th cir.) 1990. Assoc. Kilpatrick & Cody, Atlanta, Washington, 1988-89; assoc. Loeb & Loeb, L.A., 1989-91, Hancock, Rothert & Bunshoft, L.A., San Francisco, 1991—. Asst. editor: (book) Doing Business in Japan, 1995; contbr. articles to profl. jours. Mem. ABA, Internat. Bar Assn., German-Am. C. of C., Directory of Japanese Speaking Attys. in the U.S. Avocations: languages (German, French, Japanese). Office: Hancock Rothert & Bunshoft Ste 1700 515 S Figueroa St Los Angeles CA 90071-3301

LAULICHT, MURRAY JACK, lawyer; b. Bklyn., May 12, 1940; s. Philip and Ernestine (Greenfield) L.; m. Linda Kushner, Apr. 4, 1965; children: Laurie Hasten, Pamela Hirt, Shellie Davis, Abigail Herschmann. BA, Yeshiva U., 1961; LLB summa cum laude, Columbia U., 1964. Bar: N.Y. 1965, N.J. 1968, U.S. Supreme Ct. 1976. Mem. legal staff Warren Commn., Washington, 1964; assoc. Kaye, Scholer, Fierman, Hays & Handler, N.Y.C., 1965-68; ptnr. Lowenstein, Sandler, Brochin, Kohl & Fisher, Newark, N.J., 1968-79, Pitney, Hardin, Kipp & Szuch, Florham Park, N.J., 1979—. Mem. N.J. Consumer Affairs Adv. Com., 1991-93; chmn. N.J. Commn. on Holocaust Edn., 1992-95; pres. Jewish Edn. Assn., 1981-84, Jewish Fedn. Metro West, 1996—; chmn. Cmty. Rels. Com., 1988-91. Recipient Julius Cohn Young Leadership award Jewish Fedn. Metrowest, 1976. Mem. ABA, N.J. State Bar Assn. (dist. X ethics com. 1986-89, bd. editors N.J. Law Jour. 1986-93), N.J. Lawyer Mag. (chmn. 1993-95). Democrat. Avocations: computers, communal activities. Home: 18 Crestwood Dr West Orange NJ 07052-2004 Office: Pitney Hardin Kipp & Szuch PO Box 1945 200 Campus Dr Florham Park NJ 07932-1012

LAUMAN, RICHARD H., JR., nuclear energy executive; b. Rockville Center, N.Y., Aug. 12, 1956; s. Richard H. and Joane M. (Albright) L.; m. Laura H. Cady, Aug. 28, 1982; 1 child, Richard H., III. B in Mech. Engring., Villanova U., 1978; MBA, Pace U., 1994. Field engr. Gen. Electric Co., Phila., 1979-81; mech. engr. Ebasco Svcs., Inc., N.Y.C., 1981-82; engr. nuc. ops. and maintenance N.Y. Power Authority, White Plains, 1982-86, sr. engr., 1986-88, dir. nuc. ops. and maintenance, 1988-92, dir. nuc. bus. ops., 1992—. Mem. ASME, Am. Mgmt. Assn., Planning Forum. Avocations: skiing, windsurfing, sailing. Home: 9 Serendipity Ln Wilton CT 06897-1314 Office: NY Power Authority 123 Main St White Plains NY 10601-3104

LAUMANN, EDWARD OTTO, sociology educator; b. Youngstown, Ohio, Aug. 31, 1938; m. Anne Elizabeth Solomon, June 21, 1980; children: Christopher, Timothy; children by previous marriage: Eric, Lisa. AB summa cum laude, Oberlin Coll., 1960; MA, Harvard U., 1962, PhD, 1964. Asst. prof. sociology U. Mich., Ann Arbor, 1964-69, assoc. prof., 1969-72; prof. sociology U. Chgo., 1973—, George Herbert Mead Disting. Service prof., 1985—, chmn. dept., 1981-84, dean div. of social scis., 1984-92, provost, 1992-93; bd. govs. Argonne Nat. Lab., 1992-93. Author: Prestige and Associations in an Urban Community, 1966, Bonds of Pluralism, 1973, (with Franz U. Pappi) Networks of Collective Action, 1976, (with John P. Heinz) Chicago Lawyers, 1982, (with David Knoke) The Organizational State, 1987, (with John P. Heinz, Robert Nelson and Robert Salisbury) The Hollow Core, 1993, (with John Gagnon, Robert Michael, Stuart Michaels) The Social Organization of Sexuality, 1994, (with Robert Michael, John Gagnon, Gina Kolata) Sex in America, 1994; editor Am. Jour. Sociology, 1978-84, 95—. Mem. sociology panel NSF, Washington, 1972-74; commr. CBASSE, NRC, 1986-91; v.p., trustee NORC; trustee U. Chgo. Hosps., 1992-93. Fellow AAAS; mem. Sociol. Rsch. Assn., Am. Sociol. Assn., Population Assn. Am. Office: U Chgo 5848 S University Ave Chicago IL 60637-1515

LAUN, LOUIS FREDERICK, government official; b. Battle Creek, Mich., May 19, 1920; s. Louis Frederick and Roena (Graves) L.; m. Margaret West, Jan. 25, 1947; children: Nancy, Kathryn Webb, Margaret. B.A., Yale U., 1942. Asst. advt. mgr. Bates Fabrics, Inc., N.Y.C., 1946-48; asst. to pres., indsl. and public relations Bates Mfg. Co., Lewiston, Maine, 1948-55; advt. dir., out-of-town sales mgr. Burlington Industries, N.Y.C., 1955-57; gen. merchandising mgr. Celanese Fibers Co., N.Y.C., 1957-60; v.p., dir. mktg. Celanese Fibers Co., 1960-63, exec. v.p. mktg., 1963-64; pres. Celanese Fibers Mktg. Co. div. Celanese Corp., 1964-71, also v.p. corp., 1964-71; asso. adminstr. ops. SBA, Washington, 1973; dep. adminstr. SBA, 1973-77; pres. Am. Paper Inst., N.Y.C., 1977-86; asst. Sec. Commerce for Internat. Econ. Policy Dept. of Commerce, Washington, 1986-89, exec. br. commr., Commn. on Security and Cooperation in Europe, 1988-89; cons. Nat. Exec Svc. Corp, 1989—; U.S. pulp and paper rep. food and agrl. orgns. UN; bd. dirs. Overseas Pvt. Investment Corp., Noranda Aluminum, Inc.; exec. br. mem. Commn. on Security and Cooperation in Europe (Helsinki Commn.). Bd. dirs. N.Y. Bd. Trade, Better Bus. Bur. N.Y., Alliance to Save Energy, Bus. Adv. Com. on Fed. Reports, Citizens Against Govt. Waste; indsl. asst. to chmn. Opportunities Industrialization Centers Am.; nat. adv. council SBA; chmn. Republican Industry Workshop program; field dir. Com. for Reelection of Pres., 1972; trustee Taft Sch.; mem. exec. com. President's Pvt. Sector Survey on Cost Control. Served with USMCR, 1942-46. Decorated Bronze Star; recipient Human Rights award Anti-Defamation League, 1968; Achievement award Textile Vets. Assn., 1970; named Young Man of Yr. Lewiston-Auburn C. of C., 1953, Man of Yr. Textile Salesman Assn., 1970, Man of Yr. Fabric Salesmen's Guild, 1971; Gold medal for disting. service SBA, Citation Merit Taft Sch., 1988. Mem. Color Assn. U.S. (sec.), Man-Made Fiber Producers Assn. (chmn. 1967-69), Yale Club (N.Y.C.), Sleepy Hollow Country Club (Scarborough, N.Y.), Met. Club (Washington), Mid-Ocean Club (Bermuda). Home: 25 Spring Ln Chappaqua NY 10514-2607

LAUNDER, YOLANDA MARIE, graphic design director; b. Columbus, Ohio, Mar. 21, 1957; d. Wilbur Winfield and Julia Mary (Moretti) Reifein; m. David Paul Launder, Oct. 14, 1989; 1 child, Jonathan David. BFA in Design Comm., Tex. Tech. U., 1979. Graphic designer Perception, Inc., Chgo., 1980-81; graphic designer Source, Inc., Chgo., 1982-83, assoc. design mgr., 1983-84; sr. graphic designer Oscar Mayer Foods Corp., Madison, Wis., 1984-85, design mgr., 1986-88, group design mgr., 1989-95; assoc. dir., 1995—; lectr. Wis. Dept. Agr., Madison, 1988, Design Mgmt. Inst., Martha's Vineyard, Mass., 1991, Oscar Mayer Foods Corp., Women Career Devel., Madison, 1993-94, Philip Morris Packaging Roundtable, 1995. Co-inventor in field of Oscar Mayer Lunchables Packaging, 1989—. Sunday sch. tchr. St. Bernard's Ch., Dallas, 1973-75; evaluated high sch. portfolios Tex. Tech. U., Chgo., 1982-83; poll watcher David Patt Alderman campaign, Chgo., 1982; graphic design vol. Mental Health Assn. Dane County, 1986, United Way of Wis., Madison, 1992. Recipient Snack Food Package of the Yr. award Food & Drug Packaging Mag., 1989, Sial D'or award Salon International de L'alimentation, Paris, 1990, Bronze award for Excellence in Packaging for Oscar Mayer Lunchables, The Nat. Paperboard Packaging Coun., 1990, Mktg. Creativity award Kraft U.S.A., 1992, 93. Mem. Women in Design/Chgo. (program dir. 1982-83, membership dir. 1983-84, pres. 1984-85), Madison Advt. Fedn. (Addy awards com. 1985, voluntary action com. 1986), Design Madison (programs com. 1989-92), Package Designers Coun. Internat., Design Mgmt. Inst. Avocations: travel, theater, reading, art galleries, exercising. Office: Oscar Mayer Foods Corp 910 Mayer Ave Madison WI 53704-4256

LAUNER, DALE MARK, screenwriter; b. Cleve., May 19, 1952; s. Sol John and Estelle Launer. Student, Calif. State U., Northridge. Ind. screenwriter Calif., 1986—. Screenwriter: (films) Ruthless People, 1986, Blind Date, 1987; screenwriter, exec. prodr.: (films) Dirty Rotten Scoundrels, 1988; screenwriter, dir., prodr.: (films) Love Potion #9, 1991; screenwriter, prodr.: (films) My Cousin Vinny, 1992. Democrat. Jewish. Home: 118 1/2 Pacific St Santa Monica CA 90405-2212

LAUNEY, GEORGE VOLNEY, III, economics educator; b. Ft. Worth, Feb. 8, 1942; s. George Volney and Harriet Louise (Pitts) L.; m. Sondra Ann Schwarz, May 29, 1965; children: George Volney IV, David Vincent. BBA, U. N. Tex., Denton, 1965, MBA, 1966; PhD, U. Ark., 1970. Asst. prof. econs. N.E. La. U., Monroe, 1968-70; asst. prof., assoc. prof. econs. Franklin (Ind.) Coll., 1970-83, chmn. econs. and bus. dept., 1971-81, prof. econs., Joyce and E. Don Tull prof. bus. and econs., 1983—, chmn. social sci. div., 1983—; pres. Econ. Evaluation, Inc., Franklin, 1985—; cons. Von Durpin, Div. Ingersol Rand, Bargersville (Ind.) State Bank, Ind. Dept. Ins., Med. Malpractice Bd., Indpls. Contbr. articles to profl. jours. Recipient Branigin award for teaching excellence Franklin Coll. Bd. Trustees, 1979. Mem. Am. Econ. Assn., Am. Assn. Forensic Economists, Am. Acad. Fin. and Econ. Experts (bd. editors 1988—). Avocation: coin collecting. Home: 1875 Hillside Dr Franklin IN 46131-8542 Office: Franklin Coll Dept Econs Franklin IN 46131

LAU-PATTERSON, MAYIN, psychotherapist; b. N.Y.C., May 13, 1940; d. Justin S. and Susan (Lee) Lau; m. Oscar H. L. Bing, Dec. 26, 1962 (div. Dec. 1974); children: David C., Michael H.; m. Michael Morrow Patterson, Nov. 8, 1989. BA, Goucher Coll., 1962; MA, George Washington U., 1966; postgrad., Boston Coll., 1977. Lic. psychologist, Mass.; lic. profl. counselor, Tex.; diplomate in managed mental health care; chem. dependency specialist, marriage and family therapist, criminal justice specialist; compulsive gambling counselor, hypnotherapist, Tex.; cert. criminal justice specialist. Psychologist children's unit Met. State Hosp., Waltham, Mass., 1966-67, clin. psychologist, 1967-68, prin. psychologist, 1968-70, chief psychologist, 1970-76; chief psychologist South Cove Community Health Ctr., Boston, 1976-78; pvt. practice Newton, Mass., 1974-78, Gateway Counseling, Framington, Mass., 1975-78, Alamo Mental Health, San Antonio, 1978-92, The Patterson Relationship and Counseling Ctr., San Antonio, 1992—; clin. instr. psychology Dept. Psychiatry Harvard U. Med. Sch., Cambridge, MAss., 1974-76; instr. Tufts New Eng. Med. Ctr. Hosp., Boston, 1975-78; presenter Am. Acad. Child Psychiatry, 1973, 74. Contbr. articles to profl. jours. Office: Ste 200 3510 N St Marys St Ste 200 San Antonio TX 78212-3164

LAUPER, CYNDI, musician; b. Queens, N.Y., June 20, 1953. Studied with Katie Agresta, N.Y., 1974. Toured with Doc West's Disco Band Flyer; mem. musical group Blue Angel, N.Y.C., 1980. Featured in German TV music program; rec. artist: (album) She's So Unusual, 1983, A Night To Remember, 1989, Hat Full of Stars, 1993; co-writer: (songs) Girls Just Want to Have Fun, She Bop, Money Changes Everything, Time After Time, Goonies R Good Enough, 1985, True Colors, 1986, A Night to Remember, 1989; contbr. A Very Special Christmas, 1992, vol. 2, 1993; star: (videos) Girls Just Want to Have Fun, Time After Time, others; film debut: Vibes, 1988, (other films) Life with Mikey, 1993; TV appearances include The Tonight Show, The David Letterman Show, Mad About You (Emmy award, Guest Actress - Comedy Series, 1995); concert tours in Japan, Australia, Hawaii and Eng. Named one of Women of Yr., 1984, Best Female Video Performer, MTV Video Music Awards, 1984, Best Female Performer, Am. Video Awards, 1985; recipient 6 Grammy awards, 1985, 2 Am. Video awards, 1985. Office: Epic Records care Sony Music Entertainment 550 Madison Ave New York NY 10022-3211*

LAUPUS, WILLIAM EDWARD, physician, educator; b. Seymour, Ind., May 25, 1921; s. John George and Laura Kathryne (Hancock) L.; m. Evelyn Estelle Fike, Mar. 6, 1948; children: Patricia, John Richard, Laura (dec.), William Edward. B.S., Yale, 1943, M.D., 1945. Diplomate Am. Bd. Pediatrics (ofcl. examiner 1966-90, mem. exec. bd. 1972-77, pres. 1976-77). Intern N.Y. Hosp.-Cornell Med. Center, 1945-46; resident, 1948-51; instr. pediatrics Cornell U. Sch. Medicine, 1950-52; asst. prof., then asso. prof., prof. pediatrics Med. Coll. Ga., 1959-63; prof. pediatrics, chmn. dept. Med. Coll. Va., Va. Commonwealth U., Richmond, 1963-75; pediatrician-in-chief Med. Coll. Va. Hosps.; prof. pediatrics Sch. of Medicine East Carolina U., 1975-89, dean Sch. Medicine, 1975-82, dean Sch. Medicine, vice chancellor divsn. Health Scis., 1982-89, dean emeritus, 1989—; prof. preventive medicine and pediatrics East Carolina U. Sch. Medicine, 1989-91; pres. Am. Bd. Med. Specialists, 1984-86. Contbr. to: Nelson's Textbook of Pediatrics, 1964, 69, 75, Kendig's Respiratory Diseases in Children, 1969, 72, 77, Gellis and Kagen's Current Therapy, 1969-77. Pres. Richmond Area Community Council, 1973-75. Served with AUS, 1946-48. Mem. Am. Acad. Pediatrics (past pres. Va. chpt.), Am. Pediatric Soc., AMA, N.C. Med. Soc., Pitt County Med. Soc., Alpha Omega Alpha, Phi Kappa Phi. Office: Welco Consulting PO Box 20007 Greenville NC 27858-0007

LAUR, BERNARD PAUL, radio executive; b. Milw., Feb. 5, 1964; s. Joseph Edwin and Ruth Bernadine (Beiswenger) L.; m. Kathy Ann Kossard; 1 child, Lindsay Nicole. BA, U. Minn., 1987. Program asst. WLOL Radio, Mpls., 1984-87; program producer WISN WLTQ Radio, Milw., 1987; promotion dir. WMIL WOKY Radio, Milw., 1988-89, WMYX WEMP Radio, Milw., 1989-94; account exec. WMYX/WEZW/WEMP, 1994-95, KSTP-FM, Mpls./St. Paul, 1995—; gen. ptnr. L.T. Entertainment, Milw., 1991—. Bd. dirs. Great Lakes Hemophilia Found., Milw. Roman Catholic. Avocations: football, softball, golf, hunting. Office: KSTP-FM 3415 University Ave Minneapolis MN 55414

LAUR, WILLIAM EDWARD, retired dermatologist; b. Saginaw, Mich., Nov. 17, 1919; s. Vertner Linton and Ruth Gae (Eyre) L.; m. Mary Elizabeth Kirby, Dec. 31, 1943; children: Eric, Edward, John, J. Michael. BS, Mercer U., Macon, Ga., 1941; MD, U. Mich., 1943; MS in Medicine, Wayne State U., Detroit, 1949. Diplomate Am. Bd. Dermatology. Intern John Sealy Hosp., Galveston, Tex., 1943; resident Wayne State U., Detroit, 1946-49; pvt. practice Amarillo, Tex., 1949-70; pres. High Plains Dermatology Ctr., P.A., Amarillo, 1975-90; ret.; cons. VA, USAF, 1952-90; assoc. prof. Tex. Tech. Health Sci. Ctr., Amarillo, 1965-90. Contbr. articles to profl. jours. including Archives of Dermatology, Internat. Jour. Dermatology, Cutis, So. Med. Jour., Jour. Am. Acad. Dermatology, Panhandle Med. Soc. Bull., Urologic and Cutaneous Rev. Dir. Moon Watch, NASA, Amarillo, 1956. Capt. U.S. Army, 1944-46, ETO. Fellow Am. Acad. Dermatology; mem. AMA, Tex. Med. Assn., Noah Worcester Dermatol. Soc., Potter Randall County Med. Soc. (pres. 1964). Avocations: cooking, duplicate bridge, computer activities. Home: 1607 S Fannin St Amarillo TX 79102-2412

LAURA, ANTHONY JOSEPH, lawyer; b. Bklyn., July 15, 1961; s. Andrew J. and Edda V. (DePaola) L.; m. Rosemary B. Marino, Sept. 21, 1986; children: Diana Marie, Amanda Rose. BA, Yale U., 1983; JD, Fordham U., 1986. Bar: N.J. 1986, U.S. Dist. Ct. N.J. 1986, N.Y. 1987, U.S. Dist. Ct. (so. dist.) N.Y. 1987, U.S. Ct. Appeals (3rd cir.) 1993. Assoc. atty. Kelley Drye and Warren, N.Y.C., 1986-87, Morristown, N.J., 1987-89, Parsippany, N.J., 1989—; bd. trustee Cmtys. on Cable, Summit, N.J., 1994—, United Way Summit, New Providence, N.J., 1995—. Township committeeman Rep. Com. Union County, Berkeley Hts., N.J., 1994—; trustee Runnells Specialized Hosp. Found., 1996—. Mem. The Mory's Assn., Park Ave Club (membership com. 1994—), Yale Club Ctrl. N.J. Avocation: golf. Office: Kelley Drye and Warren 5 Sylvan Way Parsippany NJ 07054

LAURANCE, DALE R., oil company executive; b. Ontario, Oreg., July 6, 1945; s. Rolland D. and Frances S. (Hopkins) L.; m. Lynda E. Dolmyer, Sept. 11, 1966; children—Catherine Megan, Brandy Nichole, Holly Elizabeth. B.S. in Chem. Engring., Oreg. State U., 1967; M.S. in Chem. Engring., U. Kans., 1971, Ph.D. in Chem. Engring., 1973. Mem. mgmt., research staff E.I. DuPont de NeMours, Lawrence, Kans., 1967-77; mgr. process technology Olin Corp., Lake Charles, La., 1977-80; bus. mgr. urethanes Olin Corp., Stamford, Conn., 1980-82, gen. mgr. urethane and organics, 1982-83; sr. v.p. Occidental Chem. Corp., Darien, Conn., 1983-84; exec. v.p. Occidental Petroleum Corp., Los Angeles, 1984-91, exec. v.p., sr. oper. officer, 1991, also bd. dirs.; chmn. adv. bd., mem. dept. chem. and petroleum engring., U. Kans., Lawrence, 1985—. Contbr. articles to profl. jours. Patentee in field. Recipient Disting. Engring. Svc. award Sch. Engring., U. Kans., 1991. Mem. Am. Petroleum Inst., Chem. Mfrs. Assn., Soc. Chem. Industry, L.A. Area C. of C. (bd. dirs.). Republican. Club: Riveria Country (Los Angeles). Office: Occidental Petroleum Corp 10889 Wilshire Blvd Los Angeles CA 90024-4201*

LAURANCE, LEONARD CLARK, marketing researcher, educator and consultant; b. Perth, Australia, Aug. 20, 1932; came to U.S., 1963; s. Thomas Clark and Lorna Ruby (Spencer) L.; m. Lorraine Joan Harwood, June 10, 1954 (div. 1960); 1 child, Beverley Lorraine; m. Judith Ellen Krickan, Sept. 8, 1962; children: Cynthia Ellen, Amanda Lee. Gen. mgr. Ketchikan & No. Terminal Co. Inc., Ketchikan, Alaska, 1963-65; regional mgr. Alaska Steamship Co., Ketchikan, 1965-68; pres. Alaska World Travel Inc., Ketchikan, 1968-72, Leisure Corp., Ketchikan, 1972-85, AlaskaBound, Inc., Ketchikan, 1985-88, Mariner Inc., Ketchikan, 1988—; faculty mem. U. Alaska SE, Ketchikan, 1987—, Juneau, 1995; dir. mktg. Taquan Air, Ketchikan, 1991—; bd. dirs. Hist. Ketchikan, Inc.; mem. Alaska Tourism mktg. commn., 1995—. Mem. Alaska Mktg. Coun., Juneau, 1979-84, chair, 1982-84; mem. SE Alaska Tourism Coun., Juneau, 1982-86, chair, 1982-83; mem. mgmt. com. Sheffield Hotels, Anchorage, 1980-85; chair Alaska Marine Hwy. Task Force, Juneau, 1983-84, UAS Coll. Coun., 1982-83; mem. Ketchikan Gen. Hosp. Adv. Bd., 1973-84, chair, 1979; assemblyperson Ketchikan Gateway Borough, 1976-82. Recipient North Star award Alaska Visitors Assn., 1977, Gov.'s award State of Alaska, 1984, Presdl. award Ketchikan C. of C., 1970. Mem. Alaska Visitors Assn. (bd. dirs. 1969-93, advisor to bd. 1994—, pres. 1972-73, hon. life 1994), Ketchikan Visitors Bur. (bd. dirs. 1980—, chair 1983-84), UAS Visitor Ind. Program (adv. bd. 1986—). Republican. Episcopalian. Avocations: sportfishing, swimming, community service, tourism research. Office: Mariner Inc 5716 S Tongass PO Box 8800 Ketchikan AK 99901-3800

LAURANCE, MARK RODNEY, optics instrumentationist; b. Seattle, Nov. 27, 1959; s. Sidney Laurance and Patricia Louise Sadlier. BS in Astronomy, U. Wash., 1984, BS in Physics, 1984, MS in Astronomy, 1992. Computer ops. programmer Seattle Police Dept., Seattle, 1980-85; researcher U. Wash., Seattle, 1984-90; lighting engr. Korry Electronics Co., Seattle, 1990-92; optics instrumentationist Can.-France-Hawaii Telescope Corp., Kamuela, Hawaii, 1992—; pres. Digitek Hawai'i, Inc., 1995—. Contbr. articles to profl. jours. Mem. chpt. mgmt. program mgr., exec. bd. dirs. Hawaii State Jaycees, 1995; exec. v.p. Kona Jaycees, 1994, cmty. fundraising dir., 1993; cert. prime trainer Jr. Chamber Internat., 1994. Recipient C. William Brownfield Meml. award for outstanding first yr. jaycee Kona Jaycees, 1994, Presdl. Excellence award Hawaii State Jaycees, 1995, First Place Speak-Up Competition award Hawaii State Jaycees, 1995; named Outstanding Young Men of Am. award Jaycees, 1989, Outstanding Exec. V.P. of Quar., Hawaii Jaycees, 1995, Ten Outstanding Young Persons of Hawaii Jaycees, 1995. Mem. S.P.I.E. Internat. Soc. Optical Engring. Avocations: bicycling, photography, guitar playing, dance choreography, hiking.

LAUREN, RALPH, fashion designer; b. Bronx, N.Y., Oct. 14, 1939; s. Frank and Frieda Lifshitz; m. Ricky Low Beer, Dec. 30, 1964; children: Andrew, David, Dylan. Student, CCNY; DFA (hon.), Pratt U., 1988. Salesperson Brooks Bros., N.Y.C.; asst. buyer Allied Stores, N.Y.C.; rep. Rivetz Necktie Mfrs., N.Y.C.; neckwear designer Polo divsn. Beau Brummel, N.Y.C., 1967-69; founder Polo Fashions, Inc., N.Y.C., 1968—; established Polo Men's Wear Co., N.Y.C., 1968—, Ralph Lauren Womenswear, N.Y.C., 1971—, Polo Leathergoods, 1978—, Polo/Ralph Lauren for Boys, 1978—, Polo/Ralph Lauren Luggage, 1982—, Ralph Lauren Home Collection, 1983—; launched fragrances Polo for Men, Lauren for Women, 1979—; chmn. Polo Ralph Lauren Corp. (flagship store N.Y.C., 65 other stores in U.S. and 140 stores worldwide); launched Safari fragrance for women, 1990, Safari for men, 1992, Polo Sport, 1994. Served in U.S. Army. Recipient Coty Am. Fashion awards, 1970, 73, 74, 76, 77, 81, 84, also Coty Hall of Fame award for Menswear and Womenswear, Tommy award Am. Printed Fabrics Coun., 1971, Neiman Marcus Disting. Svc. award, 1973, Am. Fashion award, 1975, award Coun. Fashion Designers Am., 1981, CFDA Lifetime Achievement award, 1992. Office: Polo Ralph Lauren Corp 650 Madison Ave New York NY 10022-1029

LAURENCE, DAN H., author, literary and dramatic specialist; b. N.Y.C., Mar. 28, 1920. B.A., Hofstra U., 1946; M.A., N.Y. U., 1950. Performed in profl. theatre, 1932-41; writer, performer Armed Forces Radio, 1942-45; writer for radio, TV U.S. and Australia, 1946-48; grad. asst. NYU, 1950-52, assoc. prof. English, 1962-67, prof., 1967-70; instr. Hofstra U., 1953-58; editor Readex Microprint Corp., 1959-60; lit. and dramatic adv. Estate of George Bernard Shaw, London, 1973-90; vis. prof. Ind. U., 1969, U. Tex., 1974-75; vis. fellow Inst. Arts and Humanistic Studies, Pa. State U., 1976; spl. cons. Humanities Research Center, U. Tex., Austin, 1975-77; Andrew W. Mellon prof. humanities Tulane U., New Orleans, 1981; Montgomery fellow Dartmouth Coll., 1982; disting. vis. prof. humanities Guelph U. (Ont., Can.), 1983, U. B.C. (Can.), 1984; adj. prof. drama Guelph U., 1986-91; literary advisor, mem. acting ensemble of Shaw Festival, Ont., 1982-90, assoc. dir., 1987—. Author: (with Leon Edel) Henry James: A Bibliography, 3d edit., 1981, Robert Nathan: A Bibliography, 1960, Bernard Shaw: A Bibliography, 1983; playwright: The Black Girl in Search of God, 1977; editor: Uncollected Writing of Bernard Shaw: How to Become a Musical Critic, 1961, Platform and Pulpit, 1961, (with David H. Greene) The Matter with Ireland, 1962, Selected Non-Dramatic Writings of Shw, 1965, Collected Letters of Bernard Shaw, 4 vols., 1965-88, Bernard Shaw's Collected Plays with Their Prefaces, 7 vols., 1970-74, (with Daniel J. Leary) Flyleaves, 1977, Shaw's Music, 1981, (with James Rambeau) Agitations, 1985, (with Martin Quinn) Shaw on Dickens, 1985, (with Nicholas Grene) Bernard Shaw, Lady Gregory, and the Abbey, 1993, (with Daniel J. Leary) Shaw: Complete Prefaces, vol. 1, 1993, vol. 2, 1995, Theatrics, 1995, (with Margot Peters) Unpublished Shaw, 1996. Served with USAAF, 1942-45, PTO. John Simon Guggenheim Meml. fellow, 1960, 61, 72, Pres.'s medal Hofstra U., 1990. Mem. Royal Acad. Dramatic Art (assoc.), Phi Beta Kappa, Phi Alpha Theta, Alpha Psi Omega, Phi Gamma Delta. Home: 9001 Wurzbach Rd San Antonio TX 78240-1057

LAURENCE, JEFFREY CONRAD, immunologist; b. N.Y.C., Oct. 21, 1952; s. Harry and Stephanie (Maderic) L.; m. Linda Dusenbury, July 4, 1987; children: Auden, Galen. BA summa cum laude, Columbia U., 1972; MD, U. Chgo., 1976. Diplomate Am. Bd. Internal Medicine. Rsch. assoc. Inst. for Cancer Rsch., Osaka, Japan, 1974-75; intern, resident, then hematology fellow N.Y.C. Hosp.-Cornell, 1976-79; assoc. physician The Rockefeller U., N.Y.C., 1980-84; asst. prof. Cornell U. Med. Coll., N.Y.C., 1982-87, assoc. prof., 1988-91, assoc. prof. with tenure, 1991—; dir. Lab. AIDS Rsch. Cornell Med. Coll., N.Y.C., 1986—; sr. dir. Immune Tech., Inc., N.Y.C., 1986—; sr. scientist Am. Found. AIDS Rsch., N.Y.C. and Beverly Hills, Calif., 1986—. Author: (play) Many Happy Returns, 1982; editor-in-chief The AIDS Reader, 1991—; editor AIDS Targeted Info. Newsletter, 1987-92; assoc. editor AIDS Rsch. and Human Retroviruses, AIDS, 1987-95; editor-in-chief AIDS Patient Care and STDs, 1996—; cons. editor Infections in Medicine, 1987—; patentee in field. Recipient Clinician-Scientist award Am. Heart Assn., 1980-85; William S. Paley Found. fellow, 1982-84; Henry Luce Found. scholar, 1974, Rhodes scholar-elect, 1973. Mem. NIH (mem. study sect.), AMA, Am. Fedn. Clin. Rsch., Am. Soc. Microbiology, Phi Beta Kappa. Episcopalian. Avocations: collecting ancient med. books and sci. instruments, contemporary art. Home: 86 Brookside Dr Greenwich CT 06831-5345 Office: The NY Hosp-Cornell Med Ctr Dept Medicine Lab AIDS Rsch 411 E 69th St New York NY 10021-5603

LAURENCE, MICHAEL MARSHALL, magazine publisher, writer; b. N.Y.C., May 22, 1940; s. Frank Marshall and Edna Ann (Roeder) L.; m. Patricia Ann McDonald, Mar. 1, 1969; children—Elizabeth Sarah, John Marshall. A.B. cum laude, Harvard U., 1963. Sr. editor Playboy mag., Chgo., 1967-69, contbg. editor, 1969-72, asst. pub., 1977-82; mng. editor Oui mag., Chgo., 1973-77; editor/pub. Linn's Stamp News, Sidney, Ohio, 1982—, also columnist Editor's Choice; co-founder, dir. U.S. 1869 Pictorial Research Assocs., 1975-82. Author: Playboy's Investment Guide, 1971; also articles. Editor: U.S. Mail and Post Office Assistant, 1975. Recipient G.M. Loeb award for disting. mag. writing U. Conn., 1968. Mem. Internat. Soc. Philatelic Journalists, U.S. Philatelic Classics Soc. (Elliott Perry award 1975; bd. dirs. 1975-81), Harvard Club (N.Y.C.), Collectors Club Chgo. (bd. dirs. 1978-82), Collectors Club N.Y.C. Avocations: stamp collecting; gardening. Office: Linn's Stamp News 911 S Vandemark Rd Sidney OH 45365-8974

LAURENCE, ROBERT LIONEL, chemical engineering educator; b. West Warwick, R.I., July 13, 1936; s. Lionel Gerard and Gertrude Sara (Lefebvre) L.; m. Carol Leah Jolicoeur, Sept. 7, 1959; children: Jonathan, Lisa, Andrew. BSChemE, MIT, 1957; MSChemE, U. R.I., 1960; PhDChemE, Northwestern U., 1966; DSc (honoris causa), Inst. Nat. Poly., 1989. Rsch. engr. Gen. Dynamics, Groton, Conn., 1957-59, E. I. du Pont de Nemours, Wilmington, Del., 1960-61; field svc. engr. E. I. du Pont de Nemours, Beaumont, Tex., 1961-63; asst. prof. chem. engring. Johns Hopkins U., Balt., 1965-68; rsch. engr. Monsanto Co., Springfield, Mass., 1968; assoc. prof. U. Mass., Amherst, 1968-73, head dept. chem. engring., 1982-89, prof., 1973—; vis. prof. Imperial Coll., London, 1974-75, Coll. de France, Paris, 1982-83, Ryks U., Gent; invited prof. ENSIGC, Toulouse, France, 1990; vis. rsch. fellow GE, Schenectady, 1989; cons. UN Devel. Program, Argentina, 1978, 80, Beijing, 1982; mem. Conseil Technologique Groupe Rhone-Poulenc, Paris, 1988—. Fellow Am. Inst. Chem. Engrs., Am. Inst. Chemists; mem. Am. Chem. Soc., Soc. Plastics Engrs., Am. Soc. Engring. Edn., Sigma Xi, Tau Beta Pi. Roman Catholic. Avocation: rugby. Office: U Mass Dept Chem Engring Amherst MA 01003

LAURENDI, NAT, criminal investigator; b. Sant'Eufemia d'Aspromonte, Reggio Calabria, Italy, Aug. 7, 1923; s. Domenick and Grace (Crea) L.; grad. RCA Insts., 1951; A.A.S., Coll. City N.Y., 1969; m. Laura Autelitano, Mar. 28, 1946; children: Domenick, Susan (dec.), Adrienne, Loretta, Diana, Robert. With N.Y. Police Dept., 1951-75, N.Y. Dist. Atty's Office, 1952-75, criminal investigator, 1951-75, polygraph expert, 1962-75; pres. Certified Lie Detection, N.Y.C., 1975—, Nat. Laurendi, 1975—; mem. Frank S. Hogan Assocs., Hogan-Morgenthat Assocs.; author, lectr. on polygraph. Served with CIC, AUS, 1943-46. Decorated Bronze Star medal; recipient Excellent Police Duty award N.Y. Police Dept., 1954, 62, also Meritorious Police Duty awards. Fellow Acad. Certified Polygraphists; mem. ABA (criminal justice assoc.), AAAS, Am. Bd. Forensic Examiners, Am. Soc. Criminology, Internat. Narcotic Officers Assn., Internat. Police Assn., N.Y.C. CIC Assn. (pres. 1956), N.Y. State Polygraphists (chmn. membership com., 1964—), Am. Polygraph Assn., N.Y. State Assn. Criminal Def. Lawyers, N.Y. Acad. Scis., N.Y. State Defenders Assn., Am. Assn. Police Polygraphists, Detectives Endowment Assn., N.Y. Police Dept. Patrolmens Benevolent Assn., N.Y. Police Dept. Ret. Detectives, Ret. Patrolmen N.Y. Police Dept., Am. Soc. for Indsl. Security, Nat. Law Enforcement Assos., N.Y. Vet. Police Assn., N.Y.C. Ret. Employees Assn., Soc. Profl. Investigators, Fraternal Order Police, Superior Officers Assn. Retired N.Y.C. Police Dept., Assn. Legal, Med. and Investigative Experts. Roman Catholic. Home: 108 Village Rd S Brooklyn NY 11223-5237 Office: Certified Lie Detection 299 Broadway New York NY 10007-1901

LAURENSON, ROBERT MARK, mechanical engineer; b. Pitts., Oct. 25, 1938; s. Robert Mark and Mildred Othelia (Frandsen) L.; m. Alice Ann Scroggins, Aug. 26, 1961; children: Susan Elizabeth Laurenson Matchael, Shari Lynn, Laurenson Lawson. Student, Drury Coll., 1956-58; BS in Mech. Engring., Mo. Sch. Mines, 1961; MS in Mech. Engring., U. Mich., 1962; PhD in Mech. Engring. (NASA tng. grantee), Ga. Inst. Tech., 1968. Registered profl. engr., Mo. Dynamics engr. McDonnell Douglas Corp., St. Louis, 1962-64, sr. dynamics engr., 1968-71, group engr., 1971-74, staff engr., 1974-75, tech. specialist, 1975-78, sr. tech. specialist, 1978-81, sect. chief, 1981-85, prin. tech. specialist, 1985-87, br. chief, 1987-89, prin. mgr. engring., 1989-92; prin. tech. specialist, systems engring. mgr. McDonnell Douglas Aerospace, Seabrook, Md., 1992-93, sr. mgr., 1993-95; asst. dir. engring., 1995—; participant 14th Midwestern Mechanics Conf., 1975; lectr. engring. mechanics St. Louis U., part-time 1969-71; adj. assoc. prof. U. Mo.-Rolla Grad. Engring. Ctr., St. Louis, 1980-88; lectr. mech. engring. Johns Hopkins U., 1996—; participant Symposium on Dynamics and Control of Large Flexible Spacecraft, Blackburg, Va., 1977, In-Space Tech. Experiments Workshop NASA, 1988, Damping, '89 Conf., 1989; mem. panel Am. Astronauticla Soc. Symposium on Dynamics and Control of Nonridig Spacecraft, UCLA, 1974. Contbr. articles to profl. jours.; reviewer profl. jours.; author tech. papers Jour. Engring. for Industry, 1972, Jour. Spacecraft and Rockets, 1973, AIAA Jour., 1976, 78, 80, 85; numerous papers presented at tech. confs. Vestryman Episcopal Ch., 1972-76, sr. warden, 1976, uscher chmn., 1978-80, Dunday sch. tchr., 1980-84, chmn. every mem. canvas, 1983, mem. steering com., 1983-88, chmn. steering com., 1987-88, mem. search com., 1984-85, mem. exec. com., 1991-92, warden, 1991-92; mem. Commn. on Ministry, Diocese of Mo., 1985-91, chmn., 1989-91; mem. standing com. Diocese of Mo., 1990-92; trustee Corp. of Episcopal Diocese of Mo., 1990-92; mem. seminarian com., 1993-96, chair, 1994—, engring. mentor Holy Trinity Episcopal Day Sch. Fellow ASME (structures materials com. aerospace divsn. 1975-84, com. chmn. 1979-81, session organizer, chmn. ann. meeting 1975, participant ann. meeting 1986, 89, mem. exec. com. aerospace divsn. 1980-85, sec.-treas. 1981-82, vice-chmn. 1982-83, chmn. 1983-84, Flag award aerospace divsn. 1990, mem. Guggenheim medal bd. 1989-92, mem. conf. organizing com., session chmn. Structures, Structural Dynamics and Materials Conf., 1977, chmn. tech. program 1978, gen. co-chmn. 1979, gen. chmn. 1981, mem. SDM planning com. 1978-82, chmn. 1981-82, session chmn. 1985, 88, adv. com. 1978-82, participant 1979, 83, 86, 90, mech. engring. evaluator Accreditation Bd. Engring. and Tech. 1985-91, organizer symposium on microgravity fluid mechanics 1986, mem. planning com. edn. conf. 1986, editor Advances in Aerospace Structures 1982, Procs. of 1986 Edn. Conf. The Decade Ahead, bd. engring. edn. K thru 12 task force 1992-93, bd. pre-coll. edn. 1992—, 1st alt. nat. nominating com. 1993-94, engring. accreditation com. 1993—, exec. com. 1993-96, rep. on Am. Assn. Engring. Soc.'s Precoll. Edn. Coun. 1993—, exec. com. 1993—. Dedocated Svc. award 1995); mem. AIAA (sr., gen. chmn. dynamics specialist conf. 1981, session chmn. 1987), Edison Electric Inst. (adv. com. power engring. edn. forgivable loan program 1993-94), Sigma Xi, Pi Tau Sigma, Tau Beta Pi, Phi Kappa Phi, Sigma Phi Epsilon. Home: 1104 Jasper Ct Crofton MD 21114-1658 Office: McDonnell Douglas Aerospace 7404 Executive Pl Lanham Seabrook MD 20706

LAURENT, J(ERRY) SUZANNA, technical communications specialist; b. Oklahoma City, Okla., Dec. 28, 1942; d. Harry Austin and M. LaVerne (Barker) Minick; m. Leroy E. Laurent, July 2, 1960; children: Steven, Sandra, David, Debra. AS in Tech. Writing, Okla. State U., 1986. With Technically Write, Mustang, Okla., 1960-75, acctg. adminstr., 1976-80, retail bus. mgr., 1981-87, owner, CEO, 1989-95; sr. tech. comms. specialist Applied Intelligence Group, Edmond, Okla., 1995—. Mem. Soc. Tech. Comm. (Superscript editor 1985, feature editor 1986, v.p., 1985, student chpt. pres. 1986, program coord. Okla. chpt. 1992-93, sec. 1993-94, v.p. 1994-95, state pres. 1995-96, other honors), Am. Bus. Women's Assn. (Dist. III v.p. 1988-89, conf. gen. chair 1992, editor Smoke Signals 1993-95, chmn. bd. dirs. Help Us Grow Spiritually 1993-95, Bull. award 1977, 81, 83, 84, 93, 95, Woman of Yr. 1977, 96, Bus. Assoc. of Yr. 1983-84). Democrat. Baptist. Avocations: reading, public speaking, motivating people, volunteer activities. Home: 347 W Forest Dr Mustang OK 73064-3430

LAURENT, LAWRENCE BELL, communications executive, former journalist; b. Monroe, La., Mar. 9, 1925; s. Lewis Emeal and John Ethel (Dawkins) L.; m. Margaret F. Goodwillie, Nov. 1, 1949; children—Richard Sandford, Arthur Halliday, Margaret Funsten, Elizabeth MacLean. Student, U. Va., 1946-49; pvt. study with, Dr. W.Y. Elliott, 1954-56, Dr. Franklin Dunham, 1957-58. With Bluefield (W.Va.) Daily Telegraph, 1949-50, Charlottesville (Va.) Daily Progress, 1950-51; with Washington Post, 1951-82, radio-TV editor, 1953-82, radio-TV editor emeritus, 1982—; cons. Assn. Ind. TV Stas., 1982-85, dir. communication, 1985-86, v.p. communication, 1986-91; congl. cons., 1991—; editor-in-residence Broadcast Pioneers Library, 1985-96; adj. prof. communications Am. U., Washington, 1963-85; chmn. editorial bd. TV Quar., 1963-74, bd. dirs., 1974—; guest prof. Syracuse U., 1965; vis. prof. U. Detroit, 1967, George Washington U., 1982—; formerly judge Alfred I. duPont awards, Saturday Rev. Lit. TV awards, Sigma Delta Chi pub. service TV awards, Humanitas awards. Editor, author: (with Newton N. Minow) Equal Time, 1964; Contbr. to books, mags. Trustee Human Family Edn. and Cultural Inst.; bd. dirs. Pioneers Edn. Fund, Inc., 1984-94, trustee, 1995—. With USNR, 1943-46. Recipient Front Page award Am. Newspaper Guild, 1964, Disting. Tchr. award Am. U., 1978, TV Acad.'s Silver Circle award, 1988; named to Broadcast Pioneers' Hall of Fame, 1984; du Pont Journalism scholar U. Va. Mem. AAUP, NATAS (life), VFW (life), DAV (life), Nat. Press Club, White House Corrs. Assn., Washington Post E-Streeters, Am. Legion (life), Sigma Delta Chi, Pi Delta Epsilon, Theta Chi. Episcopalian. Home: 215 Jefferson St Alexandria VA 22314-4323

LAURENT, PIERRE-HENRI, history educator; b. Fall River, Mass., May 15, 1933; s. Henri and Harriet (Moriarty) L.; m. Virginia Brayton, 1958; children: Paul-Henri, Bradford Webb, Nicole, Alexa. A.B., Colgate U., 1956; A.M., Boston U., 1960, Ph.D., 1964. Instr. polit. economy Boston U., 1961-64; asst. prof. history Sweet Briar Coll., 1964-66; vis. asst. prof. history U. Wis., Madison, 1966-67; asst. prof. history Tulane U., New Orleans, 1967-68, assoc. prof., 1968-70; assoc. prof. history Tufts U., Medford, Mass., 1970-75, prof., 1975—, chmn. dept., 1987-89, adj. prof. diplomatic history/Fletcher Sch. Law and Diplomacy, 1977, 84, chmn. Exptl. Coll., 1973-75, acting dir. internat. relations program, 1979, dir. internat. relations program, 1984-88; co-dir. Internat. Relations Inst. Tufts U., France, 1979-80; acad. dir. Tufts European Ctr., France, 1994—; mem. history devel. bd. Ednl. Testing Svc. of Princeton, 1979-82; instr. JFK Inst. Polit., Harvard U., Cambridge, 1989; mem. nat. screening com. Fulbright-Hays program Inst. Internat. Edn., 1988-91; rsch. assoc. Ctr. for Internat. Affairs, Harvard U. Mem. editorial bd. Jour. Social History, 1966-74; sect. editor Am. Hist. Rev., 1967-77; contbr. chpts. to books, articles to profl. jours., mags., encys. Served with USAF, 1956-58. NATO fellow, 1967, NEH fellow, 1969, Paul-Henri Spaak Found. fellow, 1976-77; Sweet Briar Faculty rsch. grantee, 1965, Tufts Faculty rsch. grantee, 1972, Inst. European Studies-Exxon Ednl. Fund grantee, 1983; Fulbright Rsch. scholar, 1992-93. Fellow Inst. des Rels.

Internationales, Acad. Assoc. Atlantic Coun.; mem. AAUP (exec. com. Mass. State Conf. 1974-76, pres. Tufts U. chpt. 1982-84), European Cmty. Studies Assn. (exec. com. 1988-92, 95—, chmn. 1991-92), Belgian-Am. Edn. Found. (bd. govs. 1986-90). Office: Tufts Univ Dept Of History Medford MA 02155

LAURENTS, ARTHUR, playwright; b. N.Y.C., July 14, 1917; s. Irving and Ada (Robbins) L. BA, Cornell U., Ithaca, N.Y., 1937. Radio script writer, 1939-40. Author: (novels) The Way We Were, 1972, The Turning Point, 1977 (screen plays) The Snake Pit, 1948, Rope, 1948, Caught, 1948, Anna Lucasta, 1949, Anastasia, 1956, Bonjour Tristesse, 1958, The Way We Were, 1973, The Turning Point, 1977 (Writer Guild Am. award), (plays) Home of the Brave, 1946, The Bird Cage, 1950, The Time of the Cuckoo, 1952, A Clearing in the Woods, 1956, Invitation to a March, 1960, The Enclave, 1973, Scream, Houston, 1978, The Hunting Seaston (Jolson Sings Again), 1995, The Radical Mystique, 1995, (mus. plays) West Side Story, 1957, Gypsy, 1959, Do I Hear A Waltz?, 1964, Hallelujah, Baby, 1967 (Tony award), Nick and Nora, 1991; screenwriter, co-producer (film) The Turning Point, 1977 (Golden Glove award, Nat. Bd. Rev. award); co-author, dir.: (dramatic prodns.) My Mother was a Fortune Teller, 1978 (Drama Desk award), The Madwoman of Central Park West, (radio plays in anthologies) Radio Drama in Action, 1945, Best One Act Plays of 1944-45, 1945-46, dir.: (Broadway prodns.) Invitation to a March, 1960, I Can Get It For You Wholesale, 1962, La Cage aux Folles (Tony award for Best Dir. 1984); writer, dir.: (Broadway prodns.) Invitation to the March, 1960, Anyone Can Whistle, 1964, The Enclave, 1973, (one-act play) A Loss of Memory (Best Short Plays of 1983); dir. (London prodn.) Gypsy, 1973, N.Y. revival, 1974 (Drama Desk award), La Cage aux Folles, 1983, Australian prodn. (Best Dir's. award 1985, London prodn. 1986), Birds of Paradise, 1987, Gypsy, revival, 1989, Nick and Nora, 1991. Served with AUS, 1941-45. Recipient Variety Radio award, 1945, Am. Acad. Arts and Letters award; co-recipient Sidney Howard award, 1946. Mem. Dramatists Guild Council, P.E.N., Authors League, Screenwriters Guild, Acad. Motion Picture Arts and Scis., Theatre Hall of Fame. Address: Peter Franklin care William Morris Agency 1325 Ave of the Americas New York NY 10019

LAURENZO, VINCENT DENNIS, industrial management company executive; b. Des Moines, May 31, 1939; s. Vincent C. and B.J. (Garver) L.; m. Sherrill S. Mullen, Sept. 10, 1960; children: Lisa, David, Susan, Nancy, James. B.B.A., U. Notre Dame, 1961; M.B.A., U. Mich., 1964. With Ford Motor Co., Dearborn, Mich., 1961-66; plant controller Massey Ferguson Inc., 1967-70; with parent co. Massey Ferguson Ltd., Toronto, Ont., Can., 1971—, dir. fin. Am. div., 1977-78, v.p., comptr. Massey Ferguson Ltd., 1978-80, sr. v.p. planning and adminstrn., 1980—; pres. Varity Corp. (formerly Massey Ferguson Ltd.), Toronto, 1981-88; vice chmn. bd. Varity Corp. (formerly Massey Ferguson Ltd.), Buffalo, 1988—, vice chmn., pres., 1988-94; ret., 1994, vice chair bd. dirs. Roman Catholic. Office: Varity Corp 672 Delaware Ave Buffalo NY 14209-2202

LAURET, CURTIS BERNARD, JR., international marketing professional; b. Vicksburg, Miss., Mar. 17, 1945; s. Curtis Bernard and Ora Belle (Scott) L.; m. Mary Lorraine Fontenot, Sept. 12, 1964; children: Curtis B. III, Charles E., Christopher S., Craig T. Student, La. State U., 1963—. CLU. Dist. mgr. Nat. Life & Accident Co., Baton Rouge, 1967-74; cons. Life Ins. Mktg. Rsch. Assn., Hartford, Conn., 1974-77; asst. dir., then dir. ednl. svcs. Life Ins. Mktg. Rsch. Assn., 1977-81, dir. co. rels., 1981-83; v.p. co. rels. Life Underwriter Tng. Coun., Washington, 1983-85, v.p. mktg., 1985-87, sr. v.p. mktg., 1987-94, sr. v.p. internat., 1994—; mem. faculty Life Underwriter Tng. Coun., Washington, 1970-74. Contbr. articles to profl. publs. Mem. parish coun. St. Catherine Ch., Simsbury, Conn., 1975-81; counselor Boy Scouts Am., Conn. and Md., 1975-86; mem. Intercounty Connector Task Force, Rockville, Md., 1985-87. Fellow Life Underwriter Tng. Coun., Limra Leadership Inst.; mem. Nat. Assn. Life Underwriters, Gen. Agts. and Mgrs. Assn., Internat. Ins. Soc., K.C., La. Soc. Washington, Choral Ministry of St. Patrick's, Worldwide Marriage Encounter. Democrat. Avocations: reading, computers, tennis, bicycling. Office: Life Underwriter Tng Coun 7625 Wisconsin Ave Bethesda MD 20814-3560

LAURIE, JAMES ANDREW, journalist, broadcaster; b. Eustis, Fla., June 16, 1947; s. Andrew Louis and Geneva Lavina (Pryor) L. B.A. in History, Am. U., Washington, 1970; postgrad., George Washington U. Free-lance writer Washington, 1969, 73-74, Phnom Penh, Cambodia and Saigon, Vietnam, 1970-71; reporter NBC News, Saigon, 1971-73, 75, Tokyo, 1976-78; with ABC News, 1978—, corr., bur. chief, Hong Kong, 1978-81, opened 1st Am. radio-TV bur. in Peking, 1981, bur. chief, Peking, 1981-82, chief Asia corr., Tokyo, 1983-88, corr., bur. chief Moscow, 1989-91; sr. corr. ABC News, London, 1991-96, China, 1996—; bur. chief ABC News, Hong Kong, 1996—. Writer, narrator: (ABC Closeup documentaries) Japan: Myths behind the Miracle, 1981, The Unruly Dragon: China's Yellow River, 1988, Soviet segment ABC Spl. "Beyond the Cold War", 1989; covered Mikhail Gorbachev in Cuba, East Germany, Rome, Malta, 1989, Tien An Men Crushing of Democrats Movement, 1989, Gorbachev summit in U.S., 1990, Bush-Gorbachev summit, Moscow, 1991, coup d'etat Moscow, 1991, Somalia Famine, 1992, Iraq Crisis, 1993, Bosnia Crises, 1993, Israeli-Palestinian Negotiations, 1993, Russian Crisis October, 1993, South African elections, 1994, U.S. operation in Haiti, 1994. Recipient George Foster Peabody Broadcasting award for reporting fall of Saigon, 1976; Columbia-Dupont award for ABC Closeup documentary Cambodia: This Shattered Land, 1981; award for radio news coverage of assassination of Philippine leader Benigno Aquino, Overseas Press Club, 1983; Emmy award, 1987. Office: ABC News Citibank Plz, 2307 Asia Pacific Fin Tower, Hong Kong Hong Kong

LAURIE, JOHN VELDON, business financial executive, accountant; b. Granby, Que., Can., July 2, 1952; s. Veldon Earl and Lillian Ruby (Wickens) L.; m. Linda Enrica Dominick, Dec. 6, 1952; children: Krista, Courtney. BS, Bishop's U., Lennoxville, Que., 1974; degree in acctg., McGill U., 1977. Chartered acct. Acct. Peat, Marwick Mitchell & Co., Montreal, Que., 1974-78; tax specialist Peat, Marwick Mitchell & Co., Toronto, 1978-82; tax mgr. George Weston Ltd., Toronto, 1982-84, asst. treas., 1984-86, treas., 1986-93, v.p., treas., 1993—. Mem. Inst. Chartered Accts. Avocations: golf, skiing, running, hockey. Home: 14 Squirewood Rd, Willowdale, ON Canada M2J 4T3 Office: George Weston Ltd, 22 St Clair Ave E, Toronto, ON Canada M4T 2S7

LAURIE, PIPER (ROSETTA JACOBS), actress; b. Detroit, Jan. 22, 1932; 1 child. Motion picture debut in Louisa; other motion pictures include The Prince Who Was A Thief, Until They Sail, The Hustler (Acad. award nominee 1962), Carrie, 1976 (Acad. award nominee 1976), Tim, 1978, Return to Oz, 1985, Children of a Lesser God, 1986 (Acad. award nominee 1986), Appointment with Death, 1988, Other People's Money, 1990, Rich in Love, 1992, Trauma, 1993, Wrestling Ernest Hemingway, 1993, The Grass Harp, 1995; TV appearances include Days of Wine and Roses, Playhouse 90, The Deaf Heart, The Ninth Day, G.E. Theatre, Play of the Week, Hallmark Hall of Fame, Nova: Margaret Sanger, The Woman Rebel, In the Matter of Karen Ann Quinlan, Rainbow, Skag, The Thorn Birds, 1983; TV films include The Bunker, 1981, Love, Mary, 1985, Mae West, 1985, Promise, 1986, Toughlove, 1985, Lies and Lullabies, 1993, Shadows of Desire, 1994, Fighting for My Daughter, 1995; TV series: Twin Peaks, 1990-91 (Golden Globe award 1990), Traps, 1994; appeared Broadway play Glass Menagerie, 1965, off-Broadway plays Rosemary and the Alligators, 1961, The Innocents, 1971, Biography, 1980, Zelda, 1986, The Destiny of Me, 1992, The Cherry Orchard, 1993. Recipient Emmy award Acad. TV Arts and Scis., 1987; named Woman of Yr., Harvard U. Hasty Pudding, 1962. Mem. Acad. Motion Picture Arts and Scis. Address: William Morris Agy care Jonathan Howard 151 S El Camino Dr Beverly Hills CA 90212-2704*

LAURIE, ROBIN GARRETT, lawyer; b. Mobile, Ala., June 10, 1956; s. George and Margaret Eloise (Garrett) L.; m. Deborah Dockery; children: Elizabeth Anne, Robin Garrett. AA, Marion (Ala.) Mil. Inst., 1976; BS in Bus., U. Ala., Tuscaloosa, 1978; JD, U.Ala., Tuscaloosa, 1988. Bar: Ala. 1988, U.S. Dist. Ct. (no., mid. and so. dists.) Ala. 1988, U.S. Ct. Appeals (11th cir.) 1988. Lawyer, ptnr. Balch & Bingham, Montgomery, Ala., 1988—. Lead articles editor Ala. Law Rev., 1986-88. Recipient Outstanding Svc. award Ala. Law Rev., 1988. Mem. ABA, Ala. State Bar, Montgomery County Bar Assn., Montgomery Rotary Club, Order of the Coif. Methodist. Avocations: flying small airplanes, fishing, hunting. Office: Balch & Bingham 2 Dexter Ave PO Box 78 Montgomery AL 36101

LAURIE, RONALD SHELDON, lawyer; b. San Francisco, June 30, 1942; s. Charles M. and Mimosa (Ezaoui) L.; m. Mina Heshmati, June 1, 1986. BS in Indsl. Engring., U. Calif., 1964; JD, U. San Francisco, 1968. Bar: Calif. 1969, U.S. Ct. Appeals (9th cir.) 1969, U.S. Patent Office 1969, U.S. Supreme Ct. 1971, U.S. Ct. Appeals (fed. cir.) 1972. Programmer, sys. engr. Lockheed Missiles & Space Co., Sunnyvale, Calif., 1960-64; patent atty. Kaiser Aluminum & Chem. Co., Oakland, Calif., 1968-70; ptnr. Townsend and Townsend, San Francisco, 1970-88, Irell & Manella, Menlo Park, Calif., 1988-91, Weil, Gotshal & Manges, Menlo Park, 1991-94, McCutchen, Doyle, Brown & Emersen, San Francisco, 1994—; chmn. McCutchen Computers and Software Industry Group, 1995—; lectr. computer law Stanford U. Law Sch., 1993—; advisor NAS, U.S. Copyright Office and U.S. Patent and Trademark Office, Washington, Office Tech. Assessment, U.S. Congress, World Intellectual Property Orgn., Geneva. Co-editor: International Intellectual Property, 1992; contbr. articles to profl. jours. Mem. Internat. Intellectual Property Assn. (exec. com.), State Bar Calif. (past mem. exec. com. intellectual property sect.), Computer Law Assn. (bd. dirs.). Avocation: vintage auto racing. Home: 107 Acacia Ave Belvedere CA 94920-2309 Office: McCutchen Doyle et al Three Embarcadero Ctr San Francisco CA 94111

LAURIN, CHANTELLE, airport executive. Gen. mgr. Montreal (Can.) Internat. Airport, Dorval. Office: Montreal Internat Airport, N Ste, 387 975 Romeo Vachon Blvd, Dorval, PQ Canada H4Y 1H1*

LAURIN, PIERRE, finance company executive; b. Charlemagne, Que., Can., Aug. 11, 1939. MBA, U. Montreal, 1963; D in Bus. Adminstrn., Harvard U., 1969; PhD (hon.), Concordia U., Montreal, 1983. Dean bus. sch. U. Montreal, 1975-82; v.p. planning and adminstrn. Alcan Co. of Can., 1982-87; vice chmn., dir. gen. Merrill Lynch Can. Inc., Montreal, 1987—. Author mgmt. textbook. Named officer Order Can. Office: Merrill Lynch Can Inc, 1800 McGill College Ave Ste 2500, Montreal, PQ Canada H3A 3J6

LAURITZEN, PETER OWEN, electrical engineering educator; b. Valparaiso, Ind., Feb. 14, 1935; s. Carl W. and Edna B. (Seebach) L.; m. Helen M. Janzen, Apr. 6, 1963; children: Beth K., Margo S. B.S., Calif. Inst. Tech., 1956; M.S., Stanford U., 1958, Ph.D., 1961. Asso. evaluation engr. Honeywell Aero. Div., Mpls., 1956-57; mem. tech. staff Fairchild Semiconductor Div., Palo Alto, Calif., 1961-65; asst. prof. elec. engring. U. Wash., Seattle, 1965-68; asso. prof. U. Wash., 1968-73, prof., 1973—, adj. prof. social mgmt. of tech., 1977-83; engring. mgr. Avtech Corp., Seattle, 1979-80; cons. x-ray div. Chgo. Bridge & Iron Works, 1967-71, 78, Eldec Corp., 1982-91, Energy Internat., 1986-88; conf. chair IEEE Power Electronics Specialist Conf., 1993. Pres. Coalition for Safe Energy, Wash. Citizens Group, 1975-76. Danforth asso., 1966-78; NASA-Am. Soc. Engring. Edn. summer faculty fellow, 1974. Mem. IEEE, Am. Soc. Engring. Edn., AAAS. Home: 7328 58th Ave NE Seattle WA 98115-6257 Office: U Wash Elec Engring Dept PO Box 352500 Seattle WA 98195-2500

LAURSEN, PAUL HERBERT, retired university educator; b. Ord, Nebr., Mar. 28, 1929; s. Ejvind L. and Jacobine E. (Jorgensen) L.; m. Marcia Gail Thompson, Aug. 23, 1959; children: Brett Paul, Scott Warren. B.A. cum laude, Dana Coll., Blair, Nebr., 1954; Ph.D. (duPont teaching fellow 1958-59), Oreg. State U., 1961; NSF vis. fellow, UCLA, 1967-68. Mem. faculty Nebr. Wesleyan U., Lincoln, 1959-93; prof. chemistry Nebr. Wesleyan U., 1964-93, head dept., 1961-76, chmn. div. natural scis. and math., 1966-67, 68-71, chmn. faculty, 1973-76, acad. dean, 1976-78, provost, 1978-87, trustee, bd. govs., 1973-76; dir. student sci. tng. projects NSF, 1971-75; dir. Nebr. State Sci. Talent Search, 1974-80; lectr. U. Md. Munich campus, 1987-88. Active local Boy Scouts Am., 1970-75, Habitat for Humanity, 1993—; treas. Citizens Environ. Improvement, 1971-73; co-chair Trnsition Team, Nebr. Synod of the New Luth. Ch., 1986-87; mem. com. appeals Evang. Luth. Ch. Am., 1987-93, mem. discipline com., 1993—; mem. Bd. Regents Dana Coll., 1990—, sec. 1995—. With AUS, 1951-53. Recipient Honor Faculty award Nebr. Wesleyan U. Trustees, 1969, Disting. Alumnus award Dana Coll., 1975. Mem. Am. Chem. Soc. (sec. Nebr. sect. 1989), AAAS, Nebr. Acad. Scis. (pres. 1970-71), Sigma Xi, Phi Lambda Upsilon, Sigma Pi Sigma, Phi Kappa Phi. Club: Polemic. Address: 3148 N 75th Street Ct Lincoln NE 68507-2139

LAURUS (LAURUS SKURLA), archbishop; b. Ladomirova, Czechoslovakia, Jan. 1, 1928; s. Michael Ivan and Helen Michael (Martinik) Skurla. BTh, Holy Trinity Sem., 1954. joined Holy Trinity Monastery, 1946; ordained deacon Russian Orthodox Ch. Abroad, 1950, ordained priest, 1957, consecrated bishop, 1967, elevated to archbishop, 1981. Instr. Old Testament Holy Trinity Sem., Jordanville, N.Y., 1960-65, instr. patristics, 1959-93, instr. moral theology, 1973-76, insp., 1958-67, dean, 1973-76, abbot, 1976—, rector, chmn. bd., 1976—; bishop Diocese of Manhattan, 1967-76; bishop, then archbishop Diocese of Syracuse, 1976—; sec. Synod of Bishops, 1967-77, 1986—; pres. St. John of Kronstadt Meml. Fund, 1976—. Editor Calendar, 1976—, Orthodox Life, 1991—, Orthodox Russia, 1991—; contbr. articles to ch. publs. and periodicals. Mem. Orthodox Palestine Soc., 1986—. Home: Holy Trinity Monastery Jordanville NY 13361 Office: Synod of Bishops 75 E 93rd St New York NY 10128-1331

LAUSE, MICHAEL FRANCIS, lawyer; b. Washington, Mo., Aug. 3, 1948; s. Walter Francis and Junilla Rose (Marquart) L.; m. Ann G. Hellman, Aug. 29, 1981; children: Andrew Edward, Scott Michael. BA, St. Benedict's Coll., 1970; JD, U. Ill., 1973. Bar: Mo. 1973. Ptnr. Thompson & Mitchell, St. Louis, 1973—; mem. mgmt. com. Thompson & Mitchell, St. Louis, 1988-90, co-chmn. corp. dept., 1990—. Gen. counsel Mo. Health and Ednl. Facilities Authority, 1986—. Mem. ABA, Mo. Bar Assn., St. Louis Bar Assn., Nat. Assn. Bond Lawyers, Bellerive Country Club. Roman Catholic. Home: 9822 Old Warson Rd Saint Louis MO 63124 Office: Thompson Coburn One Mercantile Ctr Ste 3400 Saint Louis MO 63101

LAUTENBACH, TERRY ROBERT, information systems and communications executive; b. Cin., Aug. 10, 1938; s. Robert C. and Frances M. (Herbert) L.; m. Carole Wuest; children: Jennifer, Susan, Julie, Martha, Mary, Anne. B in Physics, Xavier U., 1959, LLD (hon.), 1977. Pres. data processing div. IBM Corp., White Plains, N.Y., 1976-78; pres. World Trade Ams., Far East Corp. Mt. Pleasant, N.Y., 1978-83; v.p. mktg. Purchase, N.Y., 1984-85; pres. communication products div. White Plains, 1985-86, group exec., info. systems and communications group, 1986-88; sr. v.p. worldwide mfg. and devel., N.Am. mktg. and svc. IBM, 1988-92, mem. mgmt. com., 1988-92; bd. dirs. Air Products and Chem., Inc., Melville Corp., Varian Assocs., Inc.; trustee Loomis Sayles Mutual Funds. V.p. Darien Library, Conn., 1988. Mem. Sanctuary Golf Club, Wee Burn Country Club. Home: 1312 Sea Spray Ln Sanibel FL 33957

LAUTENBACHER, CONRAD CHARLES, JR., naval officer; b. Phila., June 26, 1942; s. Conrad Charles and Dorthea Henrietta (Jensen) L.; m. Susan Elizabeth Scheihing, June 20, 1964; children: Elizabeth Lautenbacher Katz, Conrad John. BS, U.S. Naval Acad., 1964; MS, Harvard U., 1965, PhD, 1968. Commd. ensign USN, 1964, advanced through grades to vice adm., 1994; aide to Vice Chief Naval Ops., Chief Naval Ops. USN, Washington, 1974-75; exec. officer USS Benjamin Stoddert USN, Pearl Harbor, Hawaii, 1975-77; program analyst Chief Naval Ops. USN, Washington, 1977-80; comdg. officer USS Hewitt USN, San Diego, 1980-82; dir. program planning Chief Naval Ops. USN, Washington, 1982-86; comdg. officer Naval Sta., Norfolk USN, Va., 1986-88; insp. gen. U.S. Pacific Fleet Hdqrs. USN, Pearl Harbor, 1988-90; comdr. Cruiser-Destroyer Group 5 San Diego, 1990-91; dir. force structure, resources and assessment J-8, Joint Staff, Washington, 1991-94; spl. asst. to asst. sec. navy USN, 1994; commdr. U.S. Third Fleet, 1994—. Decorated D.S.M., Legion of Merit with 3 gold stars, Meritorious Svc. medal with 2 gold stars, Navy Commendation medal, Navy Achievement medal. Mem. U.S. Naval Inst.. Lutheran. *Life is about people and relationships. True happiness begins with sensitivity and responsiveness to the needs of others.*

LAUTENBERG, FRANK R., senator; b. Paterson, N.J., Jan. 23, 1924; s. Samuel and Mollie L.; children: Ellen, Nan, Lisa, Joshua. BS, Columbia U., 1949; DHL, Hebrew Union Coll., Cin. and N.Y.C., 1977; PhD (hon.), Hebrew U., Jerusalem, 1978. Founder Automatic Data Processing, Inc., Clifton, N.J., 1952-55; exec. v.p. adminstrn. Automatic Data Processing, Inc., 1955-69, pres., 1969-75, chief exec. officer, 1975-82, chmn. bd.; mem. U.S. Senate from N.J., 1982—. Commr. Port Authority N.Y. and N.J., 1978-82, N.J. econ. devel. coun.; trustee Sch. Bus., Columbia U.; nat. pres. Am. Friends Hebrew U., 1973-74; former gen. chmn., pres. Nat. United Jewish Appeal, 1975-77; mem. bd. overseers N.J. Symphony Orch.; mem. Pres.'s Coun. on the Holocaust; founder Lautenberg Center for Gen. and Tumor Immunology, Med. Sch., Hebrew U., Jerusalem, 1971; mem. fin. council Nat. Democratic Com. Served with Armed Forces, 1943-46, ETO; bd. mem. Montclair Art Mus., mem. adv. bd. Interfaith Hunger Appeal; trustees Tri-County Scholarship fund. Recipient Torch of Learning award Am. Friends Hebrew U., 1971, Scopus award, 1975. Mem. Nat. Assn. Data Processing Service Orgns. (pres. 1968-69, dir. from 1974), Patrons Soc. Met. Opera. Office: US Senate 506 Hart Senate Ofc Bldg Washington DC 20510-0004*

LAUTENSCHLAGER, PEGGY ANN, prosecutor; b. Fond du Lac, Wis., Nov. 22, 1955; d. Milton A. and Patsy R. (Oleson) L.; m. Rajiv M. Kaul, Dec. 29, 1979 (div. Dec. 1986); children: Joshua Lautenschlager Kaul, Ryan Lautenschlager Kaul; m. William P. Rippl, May 26, 1989; 1 child, Rebecca Lautenschlager Rippl. BA, Lake Forest Coll., 1977; JD, U. Wis., 1980. Bar: Wis., U.S. Dist. Ct. (we. dist.). Pvt. practice atty. Oshkosh, Wis., 1981-85; dist. atty. Winnebago County Wis., Oshkosh, 1985-88; rep. Wis. Assembly, Fond du Lac, 1988-92; U.S. atty. U.S. Dept. of Justice, Madison, Wis., 1992—; apptd. mem. Govs. Coun. on Domestic Violence, Madison, State Elections Bd., Madison; bd. dirs. Blandine House, Inc. Active Dem. Nat. Com., Washington, 1992-93; com. Wis., 1989-92. Named Legislator of Yr., Wis. Sch. Counselors, 1992, Legislator of Yr., Wis. Corrections Coalition, 1992. Mem. Wis. Bar Assn., Dane County Bar Assn., Western Dist. Bar Assn., Fond du lac County Bar Assn., Phi Beta Kappa. Avocations: gardening, house renovation, sports, cooking, needlecrafts. Home: 1 Langdon St Apt 211 Madison WI 53703-1314

LAUTER, JAMES DONALD, stockbroker; b. L.A., Sept. 3, 1931; s. Richard Leo and Helen M. (Stern) L.; BS, UCLA, 1956; m. Neima Zwieli, Feb. 24, 1973; children: Walter James (dec.), Gary. Market rsch. mgr. Germain's Inc., L.A., 61; sr. v.p. investments, former branch mgr. Dean Witter Reynolds, Inc., Pasadena, Calif., 1961—. With Armed Forces, 1954-56. Recipient Sammy award L.A. Sales Execs. Club, 1961. Mem. AARP, UCLA Alumni Assn.), Pasadena Bond Club (pres. 1995—), Bruin Athletic Club. Home: 17237 Sunburst St Northridge CA 91325-2922 Office: Dean Witter Reynolds Inc 55 S Lake Ave Ste 800 Pasadena CA 91101-2626

LAUTERBACH, CHRISTINE, radio producer; b. Chgo., July 8, 1951; d. William Edward and Alberta Gertrude (Johnson) L.; m. Matthew Forest Simon, July 6, 1995. BA, Pomona Coll., 1974. Pub. affairs prodr. KSPC, Claremont, Calif., 1975-76; intern KPFK, L.A., 1976-78, news and pub. affairs prodr., 1978-79; news and pub. affairs dir. KNTF, Ontario, Calif., 1979-82; freelance news and feature reporter Calif. Pub. Radio/Nat. Pub. Radio, 1978-82; exec. producer The Broadcast Group, Washington, 1982—. Exec. prodr. In Depth Mag., 1982-84, Face-Off, 1984—, A Day's Work, Hosted by Studs Terkel, 1986, Worldtalk, 1988, Leonard Maltin on Video, 1989—, Secrets of Great Sex: The Guide to Transforming Your Intimate Relationship, 1993-94. Vol. CASA de Md., Takoma Park, 1990—. Mem. Soc. of Friends.

LAUTERBACH, ROBERT EMIL, steel company executive; b. Erie, Pa., May 31, 1918; s. Emil and Inez (Ricci) L.; m. Jane Stonerod; children: Jeffrey R., Marsha J., Mark S. BBA, Westminster Coll., 1939; postgrad., U. Pitts., 1939-41; LLD (hon.), Wheeling Coll., 1975. With Wheeling-Pitts. Steel Corp. and subs., 1939-78; treas. Johnson Steel & Wire Co., 1947-50, asst. sec. parent firm, 1950-52, sec., 1952-58, v.p., 1958-68; exec. v.p. Wheeling Pitts. Steel Corp., 1968-70, pres., 1970—, chmn., 1973-78, also bd. dirs.; bd. dirs. H.H. Robertson Co., Covenant Life Ins. Co. Bd. dirs. United Way of All County, Boy Scouts Am.; treas. local br. Am. Cancer Soc., 1953-62; pres. Mt. Lebanon Libr. Bd., 1962-73; pres. bd. trustees Westminster Coll., 1970-85. With AUS, 1943-46. Recipient George Washington Honor medal Freedoms Found. at Valley Forge. Mem. Am. Petroleum Inst., Am. Iron and Steel Inst., Duquesne Club, Laurel Valley Golf Club, Rolling Rock Club, Fox Chapel Golf Club. Home: 115 Forest Dr Pittsburgh PA 15238-2103

LAUTERBORN, ROBERT F., advertising educator; b. Albany, N.Y., Apr. 3, 1936; s. Ferdinand Raymond and Julia Marie (O'Brien) L.; m. Sylvia Ann Stebbings, Sept. 28, 1963; children: Michael Alan, David Ian. BA in English, Columbia U., 1956; postgrad., Syracuse U., 1957. Advt. sales rep. Syracuse (N.Y.) Herald Jour., 1957-60; mgr. creative programs Gen. Electric, Schenectady, N.Y., 1960-76; dir. mktg. communications, corp. advt. Internat. Paper, N.Y.C., 1976-86; James L. Knight prof. advertising U. N.C., Chapel Hill, 1986—; bd. dirs. Sawyer Riley Compton, Atlanta; prin. Morgan, Anderson & Co., N.Y.C., 1990—. Co-author: Integrated Marketing Communications, 1992; columnist (mag.) Advt. Age; radio commentator Sta. WUNC; contbr. articles to profl. jours. Mem. Bus. Mktg. Assn. (chmn. 1994-95), Advt. Rsch. Found., Am. Advt. Fedn., Assn. Nat. Advertisers (vice-chmn. 1985-86), Am. Acad. Advt., Mktg. Sci. Inst., Nat. Advt. Rev. Bd., Sigma Alpha Epsilon. Republican. Roman Catholic. Home: 1403 Graybluff Trl Chapel Hill NC 27514-9126

LAUTERBUR, PAUL C(HRISTIAN), chemistry educator; b. Sidney, Ohio, May 6, 1929. BS, Case Inst. Tech., 1951; PhD, U. Pitts., 1962; PhD (hon.), U. Liege, Belgium, 1984; DSc (hon.), Carnegie Mellon U., 1987; DEng (hon.), Corpernicus Med. Acad., Cracow, Poland, 1988; DSc (hon.), Wesleyan U., 1989, SUNY, Stony Brook, 1990; DEng (hon.), Rensselaer Poly. Inst., 1991, U. Mons., Hainaut, Belgium, 1996. Rsch. asst. and assoc. Mellon Inst., Pitts., 1951-53, fellow, 1955-63; assoc. prof. chemistry SUNY, Stony Brook, 1963-69, prof. chemistry, 1969-84, with, 1963-85, rsch. prof. radiology, 1978-85, univ. prof., 1984-85; prof. (4) depts. U. Ill., Urbana, 1985—; Disting. Univ. prof. Coll. Medicine U. Ill., Chgo., 1990—. Contbr. articles to profl. jours.; mem. editorial bds.; mem. sci. couns. Cpl. U.S. Army, 1953-55. Recipient Clin. Rsch. award Lasker Found., 1984, Nat. Medal of Sci., U.S.A., 1987, Fiuggi Internat. prize Fondazione Fiuggi, 1987, Roentgen medal, 1987, Gold medal Radiol. Soc. N.Am., 1987, Nat. Medal of Tech., 1988, Gold medal Soc. Computed Body Tomography, 1989, The Amsterdam (Alfred Heineken) prize in medicine, 1989, Laufman-Greatbatch award Assn. for Advancement Med. Intrumentation, 1989, Leadership Tech. award Nat. Elec. Mfr. Assn., 1990, Bower award and prize for achievement in sci. Benjamin Franklin Nat. Meml. Commn. of the Franklin Inst., 1990, Internat. Soc. Magnetic Resonance award, 1992, Kyoto prize, Inamori Foundation, 1994. Fellow AAAS, Am. Phys. Soc. (Biol. Physics prize 1983), Am. Inst. Med. and Biol. Engring.; mem. IEEE (sr.), NAS, Am. Chem. Soc., Internat. Soc. Magnetic Resonance in Medicine (Gold medal 1982). Office: U Ill-Urbana-Champaign 1307 W Park St Urbana IL 61801-2332

LAUTZ, LINDSAY ALLAN, retained executive search consultant; b. San Bernardino, Calif., Dec. 24, 1947; s. Carl Ernest and Carole Mae (Lindsay) L.; m. Laurie Ann Morgan, June 20, 1970; children—Christopher, Kathryn, Amy. BS, U. So. Calif., 1971, postgrad., 1971. Adminstrv. mgr. Associated Freight Lines, Los Angeles, 1969-73; with Fromm & Sichel, Inc., San Francisco, 1973-81; treas. and fin. officer Fromm & Sichel, Inc., 1977-81; co-founder, pres., CEO Positive Video, Ltd., Montreal, Que., Can., 1981-88; founder, chmn. Morgan Board Works, Inc., San Francisco, 1989-90; prin. Korn/Ferry Internat., San Francisco, 1990-92; ptnr. Wilkinson and Ives, San Francisco, 1992—. Exec. producer Makaha Skate Classic, spl. interest home video; inventor skate bd. product Instant Ollie. Founder Havens Dads Club, Piedmont, Calif. With USAR, 1971-77. Mem. Commerce Assocs. (pres.), U. So. Calif. Bay Area Alumni Assn., Pi Kappa, Alpha. Republican. Home: 321 Bedford Pl Moraga CA 94556-2106 Office: Wilkinson and Ives Ste 550 One Bush St San Francisco CA 94104

LAUTZENHEISER, BARBARA JEAN, insurance executive; b. LaFeria, Tex., Nov. 15, 1938; d. Fred E. and Verna V. L. B.A. with high distinction, Nebr. Wesleyan U., 1960. Actuarial trainee Bankers Life Ins. Co. Nebr., Lincoln, 1960-64, programmer and systems analyst, 1964-65, asst. actuary, 1965-69, assoc. actuary, 1969-70, 2d v.p., actuary, 1970-72, v.p., actuary,

1972-80; sr. v.p. Phoenix Mut. Life Ins. Co., Hartford, Conn., 1980-84; pres. Montgomery Ward Life Ins. Co., Montgomery Ward Ins. Co., Forum Ins. Co., Schaumberg, Ill., 1984-85; prin. Lautzenheiser & Assocs., Hartford, 1986—; spokesperson for ins. industry, witness U.S. Senate and Ho. of Reps. coms., commns. and state legislatures; featured on TV, nat. mags. and newspaper articles; mem. Interim Actuarial Std. Bd., 1985-88, Actuarial Std. Bd., 1988-89; chmn. Com. for Fair Ins. Rates, 1983-86; mem. adv. com. NAIC Life Disclosure (A) Com. working group; bd. dirs. LifeUSA Holding Co. Contbr. articles to profl. jours. Mem. Lincoln Electric Sys. Adminstrv. Bd., 1977-79; bd. dirs. Nebr. Wesleyan U., 1977-82, 89-93, Am. Coll., 1987—. Recipient Corp. Woman award Women Bus. Owners of N.Y., 1983, C.H. Poindexter award for disting. achievement and exceptional svc. to the assn. and ins. industry Nat. Assn. Life Cos., 1989. Fellow Soc. Actuaries (pres. 1982-83, dir. 1975-80, 81-85, exec. com. 1981-84, chmn. adminstrn. and fin. com. 1981-82, assoc. editor The Actuary 1992-93, life nonforfeiture task force 1995—), Conf. Cons. Actuaries; mem. Am. Acad. Actuaries (dir. 1974-77, chmn. com. on publs. 1980-81, com. on life ins. 1995—), Soc. of Actuaries Found. (charter trustee 1994—), Nat. Alliance Life Companies (bd. dirs. 1992—), Nebr. Actuaries Club (dir. 1969-70, 71-74, chmn. 1973-74, pres. 1972-73, sec., treas. 1971-72), Life Office Mgmt. Assn. (corp. fin. planning com. 1974-81, chmn. 1976-78), Am. Coun. Life Ins. (risk classification com. 1973-81), Greater Hartford C. of C. (nat. policies panel 1980-84). Home: 17 Huntingridge Dr South Glastonbury CT 06073-3614 Office: City Place II Fl 11 Hartford CT 06103

LAUVEN, PETER MICHAEL, anesthesiologist; b. Leverkusen, Fed. Republic Germany, May 13, 1948; s. Peter Aloysius and Katharina (Oedekoven) L.; m. Anne-Kareen Wetje, Nov. 7, 1970; children: Anne-Laureen, Lars-Peter. Diploma in Chem., U. Bonn, Fed. Republic of Germany, 1970, Dr. rer. nat., 1974, Dr. med., 1979, priv.-dozent, 1985. Teaching asst. Inst. Organic Chem. U. Bonn, Fed. Republic of Germany, 1970-76, scientist Inst. Anaesthesiology, 1976-79, physician, 1979—, anaesthesiologist, 1983—, asst. dir., 1983-85, vice-chmn., 1985-92, prof. of anaesthesia, 1986—, chmn. dept. Anaesthesiology & Surg. ICU, 1993—; mem. German Fed. Drug Admission Com., 1987—. Author, co-editor: Das Zentralanticholinergische Syndrom, 1985, Klinische Pharmakologie und rationale Arzneimitteltherapie, 1992; author, editor: Anasthesie und der Geriatrische Patient, 1989, Postoperative Schmerztherapie, 1991. Recipient scholarship Stipendien Fonds der Chemischen Inst., Frankfurt, 1970, Paul Martini award, Paul Martini Found., Bonn, 1988. Mem. Gesellschaft Deutscher Chemiker, Deutsche Gesellschaft für Anaesthesiologie und Intensiv Medizin, Am. Soc. Anaesthesiology (affiliate), Am. Soc. Regional Anaesthesia, European Acad. Anaesthesiology, European Soc. Regional Anaesthesia, European Soc. Intensive Care Medicine, European Soc. Anaesthesiology, N.Y. Acad. of Scis. Home: Haendelstr 22, D-33604 Bielefeld Germany Office: Clinic Anaesthesiology and Intensive Care, Teutoburger Str 50, D-33604 Bielefeld Germany

LAUVER, EDITH BARBOUR, health facility administrator; b. Tarrytown, N.Y., Mar. 2, 1933; d. John Alan and Adelaide Cora (Marden) Barbour; m. Robert Mitchell Lauver, Dec. 16, 1961; children: Alan Jackson, Donald Marden, Robert Barbour. BSN, Skidmore Coll., 1954; MA, Columbia U., 1957; postgrad., U. Ariz., 1980—. Sch. nurse, tchr. Pub. Schs. of Tarrytowns, North Tarrytown, N.Y., 1956-60; instr. St. Mary's Hosp. Sch. Nursing, Tucson, 1960-62; asst. prof. Coll. Nursing U. Ariz., Tucson, 1969-73, grad. teaching, rsch. assoc., 1980-85; asst. dir. nursing for pediatrics U. Ariz. Med. Ctr., Tucson, 1973-74; asst. adminstr. patient care Pima County/Kino Community Hosp., Tucson, 1974-77; asst. dir. nursing for staff devel. U. Ariz. Health Scis. Ctr., Tucson, 1978-80; dir. Interfaith Coalition for Homeless, Tucson, 1987—; mem. staff Thomas-Davis Clinic, Tucson, 1963-64; staff nurse surg. unit St. Joseph's Hosp., Tucson, 1964-65; adminstrv. asst. Tucson Ecumenical Coun., 1987; weekend relief staff nurse Handmaker Jewish Geriatric Ctr., Tucson, 1988-89. Active Accord Interfaith Soc. Action Group, 1983-94, St. Mark's Prebyn. Presch. and Kindergarten, 1965-87, St. Mark's Presbyn. Ch., 1986—, elder, 1986-92; bd. dirs. Ariz. Coalition for Human Svcs., 1987—; Mobile Meals Tucson, Inc., 1976-87, sec. 1981-83; bd. dirs. Interfaith Coalition for Homeless 1987—; participant Ariz. Women's Town Hall, 1986, 87; mem. adv. bd. Tucson Met. Ministry's Cmty. Closet, 1988-92; bd. dirs. Tucson Met. Ministry, 1989-92; active various other civic activities. Mem. ANA, Ariz. League Nursing (bd. dirs. 1982-84, legis. liaison 1984-85, long-term care task force 1986), Ariz. Nurses' Assn. (fin. com. 1985-87, ANA del. 1986-87, dist. bd. dirs. 1982-84, pres.-elect, pres. dist. 1985-87, various coms.), Skidmore Coll. Alumni Assn., Sigma Theta Tau (mem. nat. fin. com. 1981-83, treas. local chpt. 1978-81, fin. com. 1974-88, pres.-elect 1990—, pres. 1988-92), Pi Lambda Theta, Phi Delta Kappa. Home and Office: 445 S Craycroft Rd Tucson AZ 85711-4549

LAUX, JAMES MICHAEL, historian, educator; b. La Crosse, Wis., Nov. 4, 1927; s. William M. and Clara (Smelser) L.; m. Barbara I. Robertson, 1952; children: Robert James, Stephen Andrew, Frederick Lawrence. Student, Wis. State U., 1946-48; BS, U. Wis., 1950; MA, U. Conn., 1952; PhD, Northwestern U., 1957. Instr. history Wis. State U., La Crosse, 1955-57; asst. prof. U. Cin., 1957-65, assoc. prof., 1965-69, prof., 1969-89, prof. emeritus, 1989—; vis. prof. Northwestern U., Evanston, Ill. 1966-67. Author: In First Gear, 1976, The European Automobile Industry, 1992; co-author: Revolution Automobile, 1977; co-editor: French Revolution, 1968; translator Right Wing in France, 1966; co-editor French Hist. Studies, 1985-92, Napoleon, 1989. With USN, 1945-46. Fulbright scholar, France, 1954-55; recipient Rieveschl award, U. Cin., 1981. Mem. Soc. French Hist. Studies, Soc. Automotive Historians, Amis Fondation Automobile Marius Berliet. Home: 100 S Tremain Apt G-4 Mount Dora FL 32757

LAVALLE, IRVING HOWARD, decision analysis educator; b. Hancock, N.Y., Apr. 24, 1939; s. Irving Howard and Louise Hartshorne (Wood) LaV. A.B., Trinity Coll., Conn., 1960; M.B.A., Harvard U., 1963, D.B.A., 1966. Asst. prof. A.B. Freeman Sch. Bus., Tulane U., New Orleans, 1965-68; assoc. prof. A.B. Freeman Sch. Bus., Tulane U., 1968-71; prof. A.B. Freeman Sch. Bus., Tulane U., New Orleans, 1971-93; Francis Martin prof., 1993—; chmn. Decision Analysis SIG, Balt., 1980-82, So. Cons. Group, Inc., New Orleans, 1981—. Author: Introduction to Probability, Decision and Inference, 1970; Fundamentals of Decision Analysis, 1978; also articles; editor various profl. jours. Ford Found. fellow, 1964. Mem. Royal Statis. Soc., Inst. Mgmt. Scis., Ops. Research Soc. Am., Inst. Math. Stats., Econometric Soc. Episcopalian. Avocations: music; photography; woodworking. Home: 726 Foucher St New Orleans LA 70115-1311 Office: Tulane U Freeman Sch Bus St Charles Ave New Orleans LA 70118-5669

LAVALLEE, H.-CLAUDE, chemical engineer, researcher; b. Cap-Santé, Que., Can., July 28, 1938; s. Henri Lavallée and Yvonne Lavallée-Légaré; m. Ginette Morissette, June 25, 1966. BScA, Univ. Laval, Que., 1964, MScA, 1965, DSc, 1970. Rschr. Def. Rsch. Establishment of Valcartier Govt. of Can., Que., 1965-67; prof. chem. engring. U. Que. at Trois-Rivières, 1970-74; sr. engr. pulp & paper industry Ministry of Environment-Govt. of Que., Quebec City, 1974-87, head pulp & paper industry, 1980-87; dir. Pulp & Paper Rsch. Ctr. U. Que. at Trois-Rivières, 1987—; pres. H.C. Lavallée Inc., Donnacona, Que., 1989—; cons. Roche Ltée, Québec City, 1988—; adminstr. John Meunier Inc., Montréal, 1991—, Centre des technologies du gaz naturel, Montréal, 1992—. Contbr. articles to profl. jours., chpts. to books. Recipient prize Raimbeault de Montigny Conf. Technologique, Point-au-Pic, 1990, 95, prize of excellence SNC-Lavalin Assn. Que. Technique de l'eau, 1993. Mem. TAPPI, Can. Pulp and Paper Assn. (John S. Bates award 1995), Ordre des Ingènieurs du Que. Roman Catholic. Office: Ctr Rsch Pulp & Paper, 3351 Blvd des Forges, Trois Rivieres, PQ Canada G9A 5H7

LAVALLEY, FREDERICK J. M., lawyer; b. May 23, 1947; m. Christine Dengler. AB, Stanford U., 1969; JD, U. Pa., 1972. Bar: Pa. 1972. Ptnr. Morgan, Lewis & Bockius, Phila. Chmn. Francis W. Sullivan Found. Mem. Phila. Club. Office: Morgan Lewis & Bockius 2000 One Logan Sq Philadelphia PA 19103*

LAVANE, LOUISE M., medical, surgical nurse; b. Lufkin, Tex.; d. Lewis J. and Mae L. (Perry) Menefee; m. Eldridge LaVane Jr., May 4, 1983; children: Katrinka M. Jenkins, Lintonette L. Acliese. Grad., Meml. Hosp. Vocat. Nursing, Lufkin, 1971; ADN, Angelina Coll., Lufkin, 1976; BSN, Stephen F. Austin State U., 1994; postgrad., U. Tex., Tyler. LVN, RN, Tex.; cert. emergency nurse, med.-surg. nurse, ACLS, CPR instr. Dir. emergency svcs. Meml. Med. Ctr. East Tex., Lufkin, 1981-85; asst. nurse mgr. Woodland Hts. Med. Ctr., Lufkin, 1985—. Mem. ANA (med. surg. coun.), Tex. Nurses Assn., Nat. Black Nurses Assn., Emergency Nurses Assn., Stephen F. Austin State Univ. Nursing Honor Soc.

LAVATELLI, LEO SILVIO, retired physicist, educator; b. Mackinac Island, Mich., Aug. 15, 1917; s. Silvio E. and Zella (Cunningham) L.; m. Anna Craig Henderson, June 14, 1941 (dec. Sept. 1966); children: Nancy Jack, Mark Leo; m. Celia Burns, Jan. 23, 1967 (dec. May 1976); 1 stepchild, Faith Stendler (dec.); m. Barbara Gow, Nov. 22, 1976 (div. Jan. 1979); stepchildren: Ann Deemer, Lindsay Deemer; m. Olwen Thomas, Mar. 4, 1982; stepchildren: Alice Ann Williamson (Mrs. Michael W. Cone), Caroline Hill Williamson, Thomas Holman Williamson, Hugh Stuart Williamson. BS, Calif. Inst. Tech., 1939; MA, Princeton U., 1943, Harvard U., 1949; PhD, Harvard U., 1951. Instr. physics, chemistry, algebra, calculus, symbolic logic Deep Springs (Calif.) Jr. Coll., 1939-41; instr. Princeton (N.J.) U., 1941; rsch. asst. Manhattan Dist. Office Sci. R&D, Nat. Def. Rsch. Coun., Princeton, 1942-43; jr. staff mem. Los Alamos (N.Mex.) Nat. Lab. (formerly Manhattan Dist. Site Y), 1943-46; rsch. asst. Harvard U., Cambridge, Mass., 1946-50; asst. prof. physics, staff mem. Control Systems Lab. U. Ill., Urbana, 1950-55, assoc. prof., 1955-58, prof., 1958-79, prof. emeritus, 1979—; mem. measuring groups and witness for Trinity, the Alamogordo Atomic Bomb Test, 1945; mem. design team orbit plotting/control circuit logic FM new cyclotron project Harvard U., 1946; observer air/ground exercises U.S. Dept. Def., Waco, Tex., 1952; observer joint air exercises NATO, Fed. Republic Germany, 1955; mem. project quick-fix Control Sys. Lab., 1953; cons. Ill. group Phys. Sci. Study Com., 1956-57, Sci. Teaching Ctr., MIT, 1966, Teheran Rsch. unit U. Ill., 1970; participant info. theory in biology conf. U. Ill., 1952. Producer silent film cassettes on orbit graphing U. Ill., 1964; co-interviewee video tape Logical Thinking in Children and Science Education, Nat. Japanese TV, Tokyo, 1970; phys. sci. cons. The Macmillan Science Series, 1970 edit., The Macmillan Co., N.Y.C., 1967-70; contbr. articles and revs. to profl. publs. Co-moderator discussion Fedn. Atomic Scientists, 1945, 1947. Recipient U. Ill. Undergrad Teaching award U. St. Andrews, Scotland, summer 1965; John Simon Guggenheim Meml. fellow U. Bologna, Italy, 1957. Fellow Am. Phys. Soc.; mem. Harvard Faculty Club (non-resident). Avocations: music, painting, art history, books, movies. Home: 10181 Seven Paths Rd Spring Hope NC 27882-9543

LAVE, CHARLES ARTHUR, economics educator; b. Phila., May 18, 1938; s. Israel and Esther (Axlerod) L.; 1 child, Rebecca. BA, Reed Coll., 1960; PhD, Stanford U., 1968. Mem. faculty U. Calif., Irvine, 1966—, prof. econs., chmn. dept. econs., 1978-85, 89-92; vis. prof., vis. scholar Hampshire Coll., 1972, Stanford U., 1974, MIT, 1982, Harvard U., 1982, U. Calif., Berkeley, 1988, 94. Author: (with James March) An Introduction to Models in the Social Sciences, 1975, Energy and Auto Type Choice, 1981, Urban Transit, 1985, others. Trustee Reed Coll., Portland, Oreg., 1978-82; bd. dirs. Nat. Bur. Econ. Rsch., Cambrdige, 1991—; chmn. bd. Irvine Campus Housing Authority, Inc., 1982—, asst. to chancellor, 1996—. With USAF, 1957. Recipient Pyke Johnson award Transp. Rsch. Bd., 1987, Extraordinarius award U. Calif., 1993. Fellow Soc. Applied Anthropology; mem. Am. Econ. Assn., AAAS, Transp. Research Bd. Office: U Calif Dept Econs Irvine CA 92717

LAVE, JUDITH RICE, economics educator; came to U.S., 1961; d. J.H. Melville and G.A. Pauline (Lister) Rice; m. Lester Bernard Lave, June 21, 1965; children: Tamara Rice, Jonathan Melville. BA in Econs., Queen's U., Kingston, Ont., Can., 1957-61; MA in Econs., Harvard U., 1964, PhD, 1967; LLD, Queen's U., 1994. Lectr., asst. prof. econs. Carnegie Mellon U., Pitts., 1966-73, assoc. prof., 1973-78; dir. econ. analysis Office of Sec., Dep. of Asst. Sec. Planning and Evaluation, Washington, 1978-79; dir. office of rsch. Health Care Fin. Adminstrn., Washington, 1980-82; prof. health econs. U. Pitts., 1982—, co-dir. Ctr. for Rsch. on Health Care, 1996—; cons. Nat. Study Internal Medicine Manpower, Chgo., 1976, Wash. State Hosp. Assn., 1984, Horty, Springer & Mattern, Pitts., 1984, Hogan and Hartson, Washington, 1989, Ont. Hosp. Assn., Conn. Hosp. Assn., 1991; cons. various agys. U.S. HHS (formerly U.S. HEW), 1971-89; mem. adv. panel Robert Wood Johnson Found., Princeton, N.J., 1983-84, 96—, Leonard Davis Inst., Phila., 1984, U.S. Congress, 1977, 82, 83—; com. mem. Inst. Medicine Coms., Washington, 1975-91, Project 2000 Commn. on Future of Podiatry, Washington, 1985-86. Editl. bd. Wiley Series in Health Svcs., 1989-90, Health Svcs. Rsch., 1970-74, Inquiry, 1979-82, AUPHA Press, 1986, Jour. of Health Policy Politics and Law; co-author: Hospital Construction Act - An Evaluation of the Hill Burton Program, 1948-73, 74, Health Status, Medical Care Utilization and Outcome: A Bibliography of Empirical Studies (4 vols.) 1989, Providing Hospital Services, 1989; contbr. numerous articles to profl. jours. Mem. Prospective Payment Assessment Commn., 1993—, planning com. ARC, Pitts., 1986—; mem. rev. com. United Way, Pitts., 1988-90; bd. dirs. Craig Ho., Pitts., 1976-77. Woodrow Wilson fellow, 1961-62. Fellow Assn. Health Svcs. Rsch. (pres. 1977-88, bd. dirs. 1983-93); mem. Found. for Health Svcs. Rsch. (pres. 1988-89, bd. dirs. 1983—), Am. Pub. Health Soc., Am. Econ. Soc. (com. mem.), Inst. Medicine, Nat. Acad. Social Ins. Democrat. Home: 1008 Devonshire Rd Pittsburgh PA 15213-2914 Office: U Pitts A649 Pub Health Pittsburgh PA 15213

LAVECK, GERALD DELOSS, physician, educator; b. Seattle, Apr. 19, 1927; s. DeLoss Francis and Helen Marie (Keller) LaV.; m. Beverly Beers Vander Veer, July 22, 1976; children: Gerald DeLoss, Roxanne M., Julie B., Amy B., Jill M. B.S., U. Wash., 1948, M.D., 1951. Clin. dir. Rainier Sch., Buckley, Wash., 1958-62; head crippled children's service Wash. Health Dept., 1962-63; dir. Nat. Inst. Child Health and Human Devel., Bethesda, 1966-73; clin. prof. pediatrics Georgetown U., Washington, 1966-73; clin. prof. U. Wash., Seattle, 1973—; dir. research Bur. Community Health Services, USPHS, Rockville, Md., 1976-77; med. cons. Region X, USPHS, Seattle, 1977-85. With USPHS, 1953-55, 72-85, ret., 1985. Recipient Superior Service award HEW, 1966. Fellow Am. Acad. Pediatrics, Am. Pub. Health Assn., Assn. Mental Deficiency. Home: 6633 NE Windermere Rd Seattle WA 98115-7942

LAVELLE, ARTHUR, anatomy educator; b. Fargo, N.D., Nov. 29, 1921; s. Frank and Lillie (Hanson) LaV.; m. Faith Evelyn Wilson, 1947; 1 dau., Audrey Anne. B.S., U. Wash., 1946; M.A., Johns Hopkins, 1948; Ph.D., U. Pa., 1951. USPHS postdoctoral fellow U. Pa., Phila., 1951-52; mem. faculty dept. anatomy U. Ill. Coll. Medicine, Chgo., 1952—; assoc. prof. U. Ill. Coll. Medicine, 1958-65, prof., 1965-87, prof. emeritus, 1987—; vis. prof. UCLA, 1968-69; cons. Galesburg (Ill.) State Rsch. Hosp., 1965-68; mem. Biol. Stain Commn., 1953-93, trustee, 1978-93, pres., 1981-86, v.p., 1991-92. Mem. editorial bd. Biotechnic and Histochemistry, 1989-93; contbr. articles to profl. jours. USPHS research grantee, 1953-70; Cerebral Palsy Found. grantee, 1964-68; Guggenheim fellow, 1968-69. Mem. Am. Assn. Anatomists, Am. Soc. Cell Biology, Soc. Developmental Biology, AAAS, Soc. Neurosci., Sigma Xi. Office: 1853 W Polk St Chicago IL 60612-4316

LAVELLE, BRIAN FRANCIS DAVID, lawyer; b. Cleve., Aug. 16, 1941; s. Gerald John and Mary Josephine (O'Callagahan) L.; m. Sara Hill, Sept. 10, 1966; children: S. Elizabeth, B. Francis D., Catherine H. BA, U. Va., 1963; JD, Vanderbilt U., 1966; LLM in Taxation, N.Y.U., 1969. Bar: N.C. 1966, Ohio 1968. Assoc. VanWinkle Buck, Wall, Starnes & Davis, Asheville, N.C., 1968-74, ptnr., 1974—; lectr. continuing edn. N.C. Bar Found., Wake Forest U. Estate Planning Inst., Hartford Tax Inst., Duke U. Estate Planning Inst. Contbr. articles on law to profl. jours. Trustee Carolina Day Sch., 1981-92, sec., 1982-85; vice-chmn. Buncombe County Indsl. Facilities and Pollution Control Authority, 1976-82; bd. dirs. Geodetic Internat., Inc. U.S. div., Western N.C. Community Found., 1986— (sec. 1987-90); mem. Asheville Tax Study Group, 1981—, chmn., 1984; bd. advs. U.N.C. Annual Tax Inst., 1981—. Capt. JAG USAF, 1966-67. Mem. ABA, N.C. Bar Assn. (bd. govs. 1979-82, councillor tax sect. 1979-83, councillor estate planning law sect. 1982-85), Am. Coll. Trust and Estate Counsel (state chmn. 1982-85, regent 1984-90, lectr. continuing edn.), N.C. State Bar (splty. exam. com. on estate planning and probate law 1984-90, chmn. 1990-91, cert. 1987). Episcopalian (clk. vestry All Souls Ch.). Clubs: Biltmore Forest Country. Lodge: Rotary (Asheville). Home: 45 Brookside Rd Asheville NC 28803-3015 Office: 11 N Market St PO Box 7376 Asheville NC 28802

LAVELLE, PAUL MICHAEL, lawyer; b. Scranton, Pa., July 19, 1956; s. James Gregory and Helen Delores (Borys) L.; m. Sue Swan, May 24, 1980. BS, U. Scranton, 1978; JD, Loyola U., New Orleans, 1981. Bar: La. 1981, U.S. Dist. Ct. (ea., mid. dists.) La., U.S. Dist. Ct. (we. dist.) La. 1985, U.S. Ct. Appeals (5th cir.) 1981. Assoc. Montgomery, Barnett, Brown & Read, New Orleans, 1981-86, ptnr., 1986-90; ptnr. Guste, Barnett & Shushan, New Orleans, 1991—; chair Nat. H.S. Mock Trial Championship, Inc., 1991-92; mem. adv. bd. La. Ctr. for Law and Civic Edn. Mem. ABA (assembly del. young lawyers divsn. 1987-88), La. Bar Assn. (chmn. h.s. mock trial 1988, rep. exec. coun. young lawyers sect. 1988), Def. Rsch. Inst., Internat. Assn. Def. Counsel, Assn. Transp. Practitioners, Order Ky. Cols. (hon.), La. Assn. Def. Counsel. Democrat. Roman Catholic. Avocations: camping, hiking, coach LaFreniere Soccer Assn. Office: Guste Barnett & Shushan 639 Loyola Ave Ste 2500 New Orleans LA 70113-7103

LAVEN, DAVID LAWRENCE, nuclear and radiologic pharmacist, consultant; b. Detroit, Jan. 31, 1953; s. Harold Sanford and Ada Rae (Blumenthal) L.; m. Maxine Frances Miller, May 14, 1977; children: Ryan Stuart, Cameron Alexander. BA in History, Biology, Albion Coll., 1975; BS in Pharmacy, U. N.Mex., 1981. Rsch. technologist, biodistbn. specialist U. N.Mex. Coll. Pharmacy, Albuquerque, 1978-81; asst. mgr. Syncor, Inc. (formerly Pharmatopes), Miami, Fla., 1981-84; instr. nuclear pharmacy U. Miami, 1982-85; pres., owner Gammascan Cons., Bay Pines, Fla., 1982—; staff pharmacist Hollywood (Fla.) Med. Ctr., 1983-84; asst. mgr. Nuclear Pharmacy, Inc., Sunrise, Fla., 1984-85; dir. nuc. pharmacy program VA Med. Ctr., Bay Pines, 1985-96; exec. dir. Ala. Pharmacy Assn., 1996—; mem. adv. panel on radiopharms. U.S. Pharmacopeial Conv. Inc., Rockville, Md., 1985—; dir. nuclear pharmacy program VA Med. Ctr., Bay Pines, 1985-96; cons. nuclear pharmacy Nat. Assn. Bds. Pharmacy, Chgo., 1987—; adj. asst. clin. prof. U. Fla. Coll. Pharmacy, Gainesville, 1986—, Nova-Southeastern U. Coll. Pharmacy, North Miami Beach, Fla., 1990—; edn. cons. Nuclear Tech. Rev. Series Rev., Inc., 1988—; mem. splty. coun. on nuclear pharmacy Bd. Pharm. Specialties, 1988-91. Co-author: Pharmacologic Alterations in the Biorouting/Performance of Select Radiopharmaceuticals Used in Cardiac Imaging, 1990, Pharmacologic Alterations with Biorouting/Performance of Radiopharmaceuticals Used in Nuclear Medicine Abscess, Liver/Spleen, and Tumor/Inflammation Imaging Procedures, 1992, Pharmacologic Alterations in the Biorouting of Radiopharmaceuticals Used in Nuclear Medicine Adrenal, Cerebral, Hepatobiliary, Pulmonary, and Renal Scintigraphic Studies, 1993, International Handbook of Drug-Radiopharmaceutical Interactions and Incompatibilities, 1994; Pharmacologic Alterations in the Biorouting/Performance of Radiopharmaceuticals Used in Cistrnography, Ferrokinetic Studies, Gastrointestinal Imaging, Schillings Testing, Thrombus Localization, Thyroid Uptake/Imaging, and Other Nuclear Medicine Procedures, 1994; editor, co-pub. Clini-Scan Monthly, 1982-84; co-guest editor Jour. Pharmacy Practice, Radiologic Pharmacy I, 1989, II, 1989, III, 1994, mem. editorial bd., 1991—; guest editor Fla. Jour. Hosp. Pharmacy, 1990, cons. editor, 1986—; guest author In-Svc. Rev. in Nuclear Medicine, 1990—; mem. editorial bd. New Perspectives in Cancer Diagnosis and Management, 1992—; nat. field editor ASHP Signal Newsletter, 1985-87; contbr. chpt. to book. Mem. Henry Morgan chpt. B'nai B'rith, Southfield, Mich., 1975-77. Fellow Am. Soc. Hosp. Pharmacists (chmn. specialized practice group on radiologic pharmacy 1993-95, edn. program assoc. 1988-95, practice adv. panel 1992-93, mem. continuing edn. 1995—), Acad. Pharmacy Practice and Mgmt. (del. 1986—, edn. cons. 1987—, nuclear pharmacy sec. ednl. affairs com. 1983—, profl. and scientific affairs com. 1988—, regulatory affairs com. 1984—, Practitioner Merit award 1990, Presentation award 1990, 91, 94, Poster award 1990, 91, 94); mem. Am. Pharm. Assn. (chmn.-elect 1988-89, chmn. sect. on specialized pharm. svcs. 1989-90, chmn.-elect 1992-93, chmn. section on nuclear pharmacy 1993-94, edn. adv. com. 1988-89, 92-94, mem. nuc. pharmacy sect., mem. ednl. affairs com. 1983—, mem. profl. and sci. affairs com. 1988—, mem. regulatory affairs com. 1984—), Am. Assn. Colls. Pharmacy (mem. task force on residency programs and support 1990-91, mem. task force on assessment of experimental function 1994-95), Am. Soc. Pharmacy Law, Fla. Pharmacy Assn. (chmn. ednl. affairs coun. 1989-90, chmn. nuclear pharmacy section 1987-89, 91-93, chmn. acad. pharmacy practice 1988-90, 93-95, chmn. orgnl. affairs coun. 1992-93, del. 1988—, edn. cons. 1987—, exec. com. 1989—, pres. com. 1989-90, 94-95, budget and fin. com. 1989-90, 94-95, mem. conv. planning com. 1989-93, 95, mem. exec. com. 1989—, region XII rep. 1989—, mem. task force on mission of pharmacy in Fla. 1989-92, 95, gs for nuclear pharmacy lecture series 1993-96, Number 1 Club 1990, Disting. Young Pharmacist award 1990, Acad. Pharmacy Practice Practitioner Merit award 1992, Sidney Simkowitz Pharmacy Involvement award 1992, Disting. Svc. award 1993), Acad. Pharmacy Practice (chmn. 1988-90, 93-95, chmn. nuclear pharmacy sect. 1987-89, 91-93, Poster Presentation 1st Pl. award 1995), Fla. Soc. Hosp. Pharmacists, Fla. Nuclear Medicine Technologists (mem. exec. coun. 1992—, editor Proceedings 22nd ann. meeting 1993, 24th ann. meeting 1995, 25th ann. meeting 1996), Internat. Pharm. Fedn. (scientific poster award 1992, vice chmn. nuclear pharmacy subsection, 1994-95, edn. con. Pharmacy World Congress 1992, 93, 95, editor Radioimmunopharm.: Current and Future Considerations), Soc. Nuclear Medicine (mem. S.E. chpt., mem. govt. affairs com. 1985-86, program com. 1988-89, edn. cons. 1989—, chair pharmacy liaison com. 1995—, mem. Brewster Bill task force 1995, mem. NRC com. 1995—), Pinellas Pharmacist Soc. (mem. exec. com. 1989—, pres.-elect 1991-92, pres. 1992-93, newsletter editor, 1992—, Pharmacist of Yr. award 1992, Pres' award 1993, FPA Unit Assn. Recognition award 1993, 95, PPS Merit award 1994, Practice Merit award 1994, life), Pasco-Hernando Pharmacy Assn. (treas. 1990-93, mem. exec. com. 1990-94, Pharmacist of Yr. 1995), Hillsborough County Pharmacy Assn. (mem. exec. com. 1991—, sec. 1991-92, pres.-elect 1993-94, pres. 1994-95, newsletter editor, 1994—, Pres. award 1994-95, Pharmacist of Yr. 1994), Polk County Pharmacy Assn., Internat. Pharmacy Fedn. (Sci. Poster award Sect. Hosp. Pharmacists 1992, editor proceedings spl. session Pharmacy World Congress 1993, vice chmn. nuclear pharmacy group 1994—), Kappa Psi, Psi Chi, Phi Alpha Theta, Beta Beta Beta. Avocations: art collecting, intramural sports, camping, traveling, writing. Home: 5600 Carmichael Rd # 2327 Montgomery AL 36117 Office: Ala Pharmacy Assn 1211 Carmichael Way Montgomery AL 36106-3672

LAVENANT, RENE PAUL, JR., lawyer; b. Highland Park, Ill., Feb. 6, 1925; s. Rene Paul and Marie C. (Nack) L.; m. Marjorie Ann Witter; children: Hilary, Mark, Amelie. B.S., Northwestern U., 1945; LL.B., Stanford U., 1949. Bar: Calif. 1949, N.Y. 1962, Tex. 1978. Successively atty., sr. atty., regional gen. counsel Mobil Oil Corp. and affiliates, Los Angeles, 1949-73, Casper, Wyo., 1949-73, Billings, Mont., 1949-73, N.Y.C., 1949-73, Paris and London, 1949-73; ptnr. in charge London office Fulbright & Jaworski LLP, Houston, 1973-78; sr. ptnr. Fulbright & Jaworski, Houston, 1978—. Mem. ABA, Houston Bar Assn. Home: Lafayette Pl Houston TX 77036 Office: Fulbright & Jaworski 1301 Mckinney St Houston TX 77010

LAVENAS, SUZANNE, writer, editor, consultant; b. Buenos Aires, Dec. 17, 1942; came to U.S., 1955; d. Carlos Fernando and Mary (Sharp) Lavenas; m. Wesley First, Jan. 9, 1982. Student, Antioch Coll., 1960-64, 65-66. Computer programmer N.Y. Telephone, N.Y.C., 1966-68; prodn. editor, then copy editor Travel Weekly, N.Y.C., 1968-76, chief copy editor, 1976-79; mng. editor Indsl. Chem. News, N.Y.C., 1981-82; editor, writer, cons. N.Y.C., 1986—. Author numerous articles. Mem. Overseas Press Club, Soc. Silurians. Republican. Episcopalian. Avocations: reading, cooking, computer hacking, walking, cinema. Home: 236 Edgemere St Montauk NY 11954-5249

LAVENBERG, STEPHEN S., electrical engineer, researcher; b. Mar. 22, 1943. BS in Elec. Engring., Rensselaer Poly. Inst., 1963; MS in Elec. Engring., Calif. Inst. Tech., 1964, PhD in Elec. Engring., 1968. Rsch. staff mem., sr. mgr. IBM Corp. Rsch., Thomas J. Watson Rsch. Ctr. Fellow IEEE (Meritorious Svc. award 1984, Koji Kobayashi Computers and Comm. award 1991). Office: IBM Corp Rsch Thomas J Watson Rsch Ctr Yorktown Heights NY 10598*

LAVENDER, ROBERT EUGENE, state supreme court justice; b. Muskogee, Okla., July 19, 1926; s. Harold James and Vergene Irene (Martin) L.; m. Maxine Knight, Dec. 22, 1945; children—Linda (Mrs. Dean Courter), Robert K., Debra (Mrs. Thomas Merrill), William J. LL.B., U. Tulsa, 1953; grad., Appellate Judges Seminar, 1967, Nat. Coll. State Trial Judges, 1970. Bar: Okla. bar 1953. With Mass. Bonding & Ins. Co., Tulsa, 1951-53, U.S.

Fidelity & Guaranty Co., Tulsa, 1953-54; asst. city atty. Tulsa, 1954-55, practice, 1955-60; practice Claremore, Okla., 1960-65; justice Okla. Supreme Ct., 1965—, chief justice, 1979-80; guest lectr. Okla. U., Oklahoma City U., Tulsa U. law schs. Republican committeeman, Rogers County, 1961-62. Served with USNR, 1944-46. Recipient Disting. Alumnus award U. Tulsa, 1993. Mem. ABA, Okla. Bar Assn., Rogers County Bar Assn., Am. Judicature Soc., Okla. Jud. Conf., Phi Alpha Delta (hon.). Methodist (adminstrv. bd.). Club: Mason (32 deg.). Home: 2910 Kerry Ln Oklahoma City OK 73120-2507 Office: US Supreme Ct Okla Rm 1 State Capitol Oklahoma City OK 73105

LAVENGOOD, LAWRENCE GENE, management educator, historian; b. Tulsa, June 30, 1924; s. Lawrence Wilbur and Elizabeth (Gardner) L.; m. Gloria M. deLeon, Aug. 27, 1947; children: Jessica, Abigail, Timothy, Rachel. M.A., U. Chgo., 1947, Ph.D., 1953. Asst. prof. bus. history Northwestern U., Evanston, Ill., 1953-59, assoc. prof., 1959-69, chmn. dept. policy and environ., 1980-82, prof. bus. history and policy and environ., 1970-94, prof. emeritus, 1994—; mem. Com. on Ethics in Bus. Edn., 1977-79; cons. on mgmt. devel. edn. U.S. and European corps.; U.S. faculty coord. Sasin Grad. Inst. Bus. Arminstrn., Chulalongkorn U., Bangkok, 1983-95; chmn. bd. dirs. ctr. for ethics Garrett-Evang. Theol. Sem., Evanston, 1995—. Editor, contbr.: Moral Man and Economic Enterprise, 1967. Mem. Bd. Edn. Ill. elem. dist. 65, Evanston, 1967-72, 75-78; bd. dirs. Evanston Comm. Found., 1996—. Recipient Ann. Kellogg Alumni Choice award, 1992. Mem. Bus. History Conf. Democrat. Presbyterian. Office: Kellog Grad Sch Mgmt Northwestern U Evanston IL 60201

LAVENSON, JAMES H., hotel industry executive; b. Phila., 1919. Grad., Williams Coll., 1941. Chmn. CEO SYR Corp., 1976-88; pres. Lavenson Mgmt. Enterprises, Inc., N.Y.C., 1976—, Plaza Hotel, N.Y.C., 1972-75, Sunwear, Inc.; chmn. Doxsee Food Co.; pres. Lavenson Bur. Advt., Inc., 1950-64; dir. Sonesta Hotels, TLC Corp.; chmn. Pine Tree Computers, Camden, Maine; bd. dirs. Am. Field Svc., Chief Exec. Forum. Author: Selling Made Simple, Sensuous Animal, Think Strawberries, How to Earn a MBWA Degree. Trustee Thomas Coll. Office: 12 Norumbega Dr Camden ME 04843-1746

LAVENSON, SUSAN BARKER, hotel corporate executive, consultant; b. L.A., July 26, 1936; d. Percy Morton and Rosalie Laura (Donner) Barker; m. James H. Lavenson, Apr. 22, 1973; 1 child, Ellen Ruth Stanclift. BA, Stanford U., 1958, MA, 1959; PhD (hon.), Thomas Coll., 1994. Cert. gen. secondary credential tchr., Calif. Tchr. Benjamin Franklin Jr. High Sch., San Francisco, 1960; tchr. French dept. Lowell High Sch., San Francisco, 1960-61; v.p. Monogram Co., San Francisco, 1961-62; creative dir. Monogram Co., N.Y.C., 1973-86; pres. SYR Corp., Santa Barbara, Calif., 1976-89; ptnr. Lavenson Ptnrs., Camden, Maine, 1989—; mem. commn. on co-edn. Wheaton Coll., Norton, Mass., 1985-87; mem. Relais et Chateaux, Paris, 1978-89; cons. World Bank Recruit Divsn., 1993. Author: Greening of San Ysidro, 1977 (Conf. award 1977). Trustee Camden Pub. Libr., 1989-95, v.p. 1991-93; vice chair bd. trustees Thomas Coll., Waterville, Maine; trustee Atlantic Ave. Trust; founding pres. Maine chpt. Internat. Women's Forum, 1991—. Mem. Advice Inc., Camden Yacht Club, Stanford Alumni Assn., Com. of 200 (treas. 1985-86), Phi Delta Kappa. Home and Office: 12 Norumbega Dr Camden ME 04843-1746 *Three rules to remember: 1) Never take anything personally. 2) Never lose your sense of humor. 3) Keep your eye on the objective - I also like the Apocryphal writers' words: "I am not made or unmade by things that happen to me, but by my reactions to them."*

LAVENTHOL, DAVID ABRAM, newspaper editor; b. Phila., July 15, 1933; s. Jesse and Clare (Horwald) L.; m. Esther Coons, Mar. 8, 1958; children: Peter, Sarah. BA, Yale U., 1957; MA, U. Minn., 1960; LittD (hon.), Dowling Coll., 1979; LLD (hon.), Hofstra U., 1986. Reporter, news editor St. Petersburg (Fla.) Times, 1957-62; asst. editor, city editor N.Y. Herald-Tribune, 1963-66; asst. mng. editor Washington Post, 1966-69; assoc. editor Newsday, L.I., N.Y., 1969, exec. editor, 1969, editor, 1970-78, pub., chief exec. officer, 1978-86; group v.p. newspapers Times Mirror Co., 1981-86, sr. v.p., 1987-93, pres., 1987-93; pub., chief exec. officer L.A. Times, 1989-93; editor-at-large Times Mirror Co., L.A., 1994—; mem. Pulitzer Prize Bd., 1982-91, chmn., 1988-89; vice chmn. Internat. Press Inst., 1985-93, chmn., 1993-95; dir. Am. Press Inst., 1988—. Bd. dirs. United Negro Coll. Fund, 1988, Mus. Contemporary Art, L.A., 1989—, chmn., 1993—; bd. dirs. Associated Press, 1993-96, Columbia Journalism Sch., 1993—, Nat. Parkinson Found., 1993—, Saratoga Performing Arts Ctr., 1993—. With Signal Corps AUS, 1953-55. Recipient Columbia Journalism award for Disting. Svc., 1994. Mem. Am. Soc. Newspaper Editors (chmn. writing awards bd. 1980-83), Council Fgn. Relations. Clubs: Century (N.Y.C.), Regency (L.A.). Office: LA Times Times Mirror Sq Los Angeles CA 90053-3816

LAVENTHOL, HENRY L(EE) (HANK LAVENTHOL), artist, etcher; b. Phila., Dec. 22, 1927; s. Lewis Jacob and Sadye Aileen (Horwitz) L.; m. Josephine P. Weitjens, Mar. 26, 1965. B.A., Yale U., 1947; postgrad., Columbia U., 1948-51, New Sch. Social Research, 1952-53, Academia di Bell Arte, Florence, Italy, 1961-62. Sr. acct. Laventhol Horwath & Co., N.Y.C., 1948-51; v.p. Wings Shirt Co., Inc., N.Y.C., 1951-61; guest lectr. N.Y. U., 1955, Pratt Graphic Center, N.Y.C., 1974. One-man shows include John Whibley Gallery, London, 1963-69, Galerie Goldoni, Florence, 1962, Galerie de la Madeleine, Brussels, 1962, Die Brucke, Dusseldorf, Fed. Republic Germany, 1964, Galerie Ganzoni, Geneva, 1964, Galerie de Sfinx, Amsterdam, The Netherlands, 1967, Bodley Gallery, N.Y.C., 1968-71, Mickelson Gallery, Washington, 1973, Frank Fedele Fine Arts, N.Y.C., 1980, 81, 82, Werner Gallery, N.Y.C., 1989; exhibited in group shows at Phila. Mus. Art, 1969, Print Club Phila, 1969-86, Bibliotheque Nationale Paris, 1979, Associated Am. Artists, 1968-86, Shippee Gallery, N.Y.C, 1987; represented in permanent collections, Nat. Gallery Art, Washington, IBM Corp., Armonk, N.Y., N.Y. Public Library, N.Y.C., Yale U. Art Gallery, Cigna Corp., Hartford, Conn., Forbes Coll., Pepsico, Purchase, N.Y., Lowe Mus. Art, Miami, Fla., Duke U. Mus. Art, Reuben A. Donnelley, White Plains, N.Y., Free Library Phila., Citicorp Collection, N.Y.C., Erbamont N.A., White Plains, Bibliotheque Nationale, Paris, Evansville Mus., Ind., Warnaco, Bridgeport, Conn., E.M. Warburg Pincus & Co., N.Y.C., NYNEX Corp., White Plains, N.Y.; contbr. etchings to books Le Miroir Aux Alouettes, 1973, Eyedeas, 1980, Crises, 1980. Mem. Artists Equity Assn. Home: 805 Hanover St Yorktown Heights NY 10598-5904

LAVERGE, JAN, tobacco company executive; b. Amsterdam, Netherlands, Nov. 17, 1909; came to U.S., 1934, naturalized, 1942; s. Hendrik Johannes and Margaretha (Van Gelder) L.; m. Henriette Amelia Boelen, May 21, 1935; children—Bart Jan, Eva S., Charlotte M. M.E., Higher Tech. Sch., Amsterdam, 1930. With Am. Tobacco Co., Amsterdam, 1930-34; with Universal Leaf Tobacco Co., Inc., Richmond, Va., 1934—; asst. v.p. Universal Leaf Tobacco Co., Inc., 1946-51, v.p., 1951-66, sr. v.p., 1966-78, dir., 1953—, chmn. exec. com., 1974-78, cons., 1978-81, dir. emeritus, 1981—. Served to maj. AUS, 1943-46. Decorated U.S. Legion of Merit, Croix de Guerre France; Netherlands Order Orange Nassau. Home: 6120 St Andrews Ln Richmond VA 23226-3213 Office: Universal Bldg Broad and Hamilton Richmond VA 23230

LAVERNE, MICHEL MARIE-JACQUES, international relations consultant; b. Paris, June 1, 1928; s. Charles Henri Andre and Anne Marie Henriette (Bour) L.; m. Genevieve Laverne Pierès, June 29, 1963; children: Beatrice, Thierry, Loic Heaulme, Christophe, Matthieu. MBA, Ecole des Hautes Etudes Commerciales, 1953; postgrad., Centre de Perfectionnement dans l'Adminstrn. des Affaires, 1960. Various mktg., adminstrn. and fin. positions Shell Group Cos., internat. locations, 1954-73; account exec. Union d'Etudes et Investissements (subs. Credit Agricole), Paris, 1973-76; v.p. fin. Salmon et Cie, Paris, 1976-81; chief exec. officer Cartonneries de St. Germain, 1977-79, Papeteries Maunoury, 1979-80; exec. Generale Biscuit, Athis-Mons, France, 1981-83; former chmn. bd. Generale Biscuit, Italy; pres., CEO Mother's Cookies, Oakland, Calif., 1983-91, Mother's Cookies/Gen. Biscuit Am., 1990-91; assoc. MLG Plus Cons., Oakland, 1991—, Eurosite, Oakland, 1992—. Commr. Internat. Trade and Fgn. Investment Commn., City of Oakland. Mem. Conseiller du Commerce Exterieur de la France (pres. U.S.A. N.W. sect.). Roman Catholic. Avocations: sailing, skiing, photography, hunting. Home and Office: MLG Plus Cons 8 Marr Ave Oakland CA 94611-3131 Address: Grand Pas, 41230 Vernou-en-Sologne France

LAVERS, J. DOUGLAS, electrical engineer, educator. Prof. dept. elec. engrng. U. Toronto. Fellow IEEE. Office: Univ Toronto, Dept Electrical Engineering, Toronto, ON Canada M5S 1A4*

LAVERTY, BRUCE, curator; b. Phila., Nov. 20, 1958; s. John Patterson and Barbara Shirley (McKee) L.; m. Wendy S. Emrich, Sept. 14, 1985; children: Allison B., Susan L. BA, La Salle Coll., 1979. Asst. dir. N.W. Phila. Hist. Site Survey, 1979-80; manuscripts libr. Hist. Soc. Pa., Phila., 1980-83; archivist Athenaeum of Phila., 1983-88, curator of architecture, 1988—; juror Charles E. Peterson Prize Hist. Am. Bldgs. Survey, Washington, 1984—; cons. Phila. Archdiocese Hist. Resource Ctr., Phila., 1994—. Bd. dirs. Old York Rd. Christian Endeavor, Phila., 1975-93, Whosoever Gospel Mission & Rescue Home, Phila., 1992—. Grantee NEA, 1993. Mem. Soc. Am. Archivists, Mid-Atlantic Regional Archivists Conf. Democrat. Avocations: reading, travel, racquetball. Office: Athenaeum Phila 219 S 6th St Philadelphia PA 19106-3719

LAVERTY, ROGER MONTGOMERY, III, food products executive, lawyer; b. Los Angeles, June 12, 1947; s. Roger M. and Joan Ruth (Wright) L.; m. Melinda Hodell, July 10, 1970 (div. July, 1980); m. Jill B. Rosenbaum, Oct. 12, 1982; children: Rory, Geoffrey, Molly. BA, Stanford U., 1969, JD, 1972. Bar: Calif. 1972. Atty. Bodkin, McCarthy & Sargent, Los Angeles, 1975-79; gen. counsel Thriftimart, Inc., Los Angeles, 1979-82, v.p., 1982-84; sr. v.p. Smart & Final Iris Corp., Los Angeles, 1984-87, pres., 1988—. Served to lt. USN, 1972-75. Mem. Calif. Bar Assn. Republican. Clubs: Los Angeles Country, Los Angeles Athletic. Avocations: tennis, cycling, golf, fishing. Home: 320 16th St Manhattan Beach CA 90266-4621 Office: Smart & Final Stores 524 Chapala St Santa Barbara CA 93101-3412*

LAVERY, DANIEL P., management consultant; b. N.Y.C., June 28, 1932; B.S. with honors, Manhattan Coll., 1954; M.B.A., Rutgers U., 1963; m. Doris E. Guenther, Oct. 23, 1954; children—Daniel, Brian, Kevin, Michael. Mem. prodn. mgmt. staff, photo products dept. E.I. DuPont de Nemours & Co., Inc., 1954-65; div. mgr. Anken Industries, Williamstown, Mass., 1965-71; gen. mgr. Dymo Industries, N.Y.C., 1971-73; dir. cons. studies Quantum Sci. Corp., N.Y.C., 1973-79; mgr. strategic mktg. ITT, N.Y.C., 1979-80; sr. dir. market research Western Union, 1980-82; v.p. Pactel, Inc., mgmt. cons., N.Y.C., 1982-83; ptnr. Palo Alto Mgmt. Group, Wyckoff, N.J., 1983—. Served as capt. USAF, 1955-57. Mem. Inst. Mgmt. Cons. (cert. mgmt. cons.), Am. Arbitration Assn. (panel mem. 1985—). Office: Palo Alto Management Group Inc 458 Sicomac Ave Wyckoff NJ 07481-1120

LAVEY, STEWART EVAN, lawyer; b. Newark, July 24, 1945; m. Suzanne Laurence, July 9, 1972. AB, Syracuse U., 1967; JD, Fordham U., 1970. Bar: N.Y. 1971, N.J. 1987, Pa. 1988, D.C. 1988. Assoc. Kelley Drye & Warren, N.Y.C., 1970-71, Emil, Kobrin, Klein & Garbus, N.Y.C., 1971-72, Zimet Haines Moss & Goodkind, N.Y.C., 1972-75; asst. sec., asst. gen. counsel Norlin Corp., N.Y.C., 1975-78; sec., asst. gen. counsel Norlin Corp., 1978-85; of counsel Shanley & Fisher, P.C., Morristown, N.J., 1985-87, ptnr., 1987—; adj. assoc. prof. law Fordham U., N.Y.C., 1976-79, adj. prof., 1980—, lectr. Fordham U. Continuing Legal Edn., 1991-93. Mem.: Fordham Law Rev, 1968-70. Mem. Am. Bar Assn., N.Y. State Bar Assn., Assn. of Bar of City of N.Y., N.J. Bar Assn. (securities law com.), Pa. Bar Assn., D.C. Bar Assn. Office: Shanley & Fisher PC 131 Madison Ave Morristown NJ 07960-6086

LAVEZZI, JOHN CHARLES, art history educator, archaeologist; b. Chgo., July 7, 1940; s. Francis M. and Dorothy M. (Kopal) L. AB magna cum laude, Cath. U. Am., 1962; MA, U. Cin., 1965; postgrad., Am. Sch. Classical Studies, Athens, Greece, 1967-70; PhD, U. Chgo., 1973. Sec. Am. Sch. Classical Studies at Athens, 1968-70; asst. prof. Sch. Art Bowling Green (Ohio) State U., 1973-80, assoc. prof., 1980—; sr. assoc. mem. Am. Sch. Classical Studies at Athens, 1972—, rsch. assoc. Corinth Excavations, 1972—. Contbr. articles to profl. jours. Mem. Toledo Mus. Art. Recipient CUA Stratemeier award, 1962, Medici Circle teaching awards, 1986, 94; grantee Am. Philos. Soc., 1973. Mem. Archeol. Inst. Am., Midwest Art History Soc., Soc. for Preservation of Greek Heritage, Nat. Geog. Soc., Smithsonian Instn. Friends, Cyprus Am. Archeol. Rsch. Inst., Phi Beta Kappa (pres. chpt. 1992), Phi Alpha Theta, Blue Key, Delta Epsilon Sigma, Phi Eta Sigma. Roman Catholic. Office: Bowling Green State U Sch Art Bowling Green OH 43403

LA VIA, MARIANO FRANCIS, physician, pathology and laboratory medicine educator; b. Rome, Jan. 29, 1926; came to U.S., 1952; s. Vincenzo and Carmela (Carbone) La V.; m. Martha Ann Tillson, Dec. 26, 1959 (div. 1972); children: William, Maria, Charles, Jacqueline, Susan, Christopher, Thomas; m. June F.S. Bailey, Oct. 19, 1991. MD, U. Messina, Italy, 1949. Internship, residency A.M. Billings Meml. Hosp., U. Chgo., 1952-57; pathology fellow U. Rome, Italy, 1949-52; rsch. asst. pathology U. Chgo., 1952-57; resident in pathology A.M. Billings Hosp., U. Chgo., 1952-57; instr. anatomy U. Chgo., 1957-60; asst. prof. pathology U. Colo. Med. Ctr., Denver, 1960-67, assoc. prof. pathology, 1967-68; prof. pathology and lab. medicine Bowman Gray Sch. Medicine, Wake Forest U., Winston-Salem, N.C., 1968-71, Sch. Medicine, Emory U., Atlanta, 1971-79, Med. U. S.C., Charleston, 1979-95; prof. emritus U. S.C., Charleston, 1996—. Contbr. numerous articles to profl. jours. Pres. Advocacy Coun. for Persons with Disabilities, 1994. Recipient NIH Rsch. Career Devel. award, 1962-68. Fellow AAAS; mem. Am. Soc. Investigative Pathology, Clin. Cytometry Soc. (past pres.), Am. Assn. Immunologists, Clin. Immunology Soc., others. Avocations: photography, pipe collecting. Office: Med U SC 171 Ashley Ave Charleston SC 29425-0001

LA VICTORIA, ELDA G., elementary education educator. Sci. tchr. Garapan Elem. Sch., Saipan Island, Northern Mariana Islands. Named State Tchr. Yr. Mariana Islands, 1993. Office: Garapan Elem Sch CNMI Pub Sch Sys Saipan MP 96950

LAVIDGE, ROBERT JAMES, marketing research executive; b. Chgo., Dec. 27, 1921; s. Arthur Wills and Mary Beatrice (James) L.; m. Margaret Mary Zwigard, June 8, 1946; children: Margaret, Kathleen, William, Lynn Elizabeth. AB, DePauw U., 1943; MBA, U. Chgo., 1947. Analyst Pepsodent div. Lever Bros., Chgo., 1947-48, new products mktg. rsch. mgr. Pepsodent div., 1948-49; asst. dir. mktg. Am. Meat Inst., Chgo., 1950-51; ptnr. Elrick, Lavidge and Co., Chgo., 1951-56; pres. Elrick and Lavidge, Inc., Chgo., 1956-86; pres. emeritus Elrick and Lavidge, Scottsdale, Ariz., 1987—; lectr. mktg. research, sales adminstrn. Northwestern U., 1950-80; mem. Nat. Mktg. Adv. Com., 1967-71, also exec. com. Trustee Village Western Springs, Ill., 1957-61, pres., 1973-77; trustee McCormick Theol. Sem., 1981-90, 92—; mem. adv. council U. Chgo. Grad. Sch. Bus. With USNR, 1943-46. Mem. Am. Mktg. Assn. (v.p. 1963-64, pres. 1966-67, trustee found. 1992—, chmn.), Internat. Rels. Soc. (chmn. 1961-65), Internat. Trademark Assn., Econ. Club Phoenix, De Pauw U. Alumni Assn. (pres. 1967-68), Klinger Lake Club (Mich.), paradise Valley Country Club, Phi Beta Kappa, Beta Gamma Sigma, Sigma Delta Chi, Pi. Presbyterian.

LAVIGNE, LAWRENCE NEIL, lawyer; b. Newark, June 30, 1957; s. Daniel S. and Alice M. (Melon) L.; m. Benjie Panesh, Oct. 12, 1980; children: Gabriel A., Derek N. BA, Franklin & Marshall Coll., 1979; JD, Seton Hall U., 1982. Bar: N.J. 1982, U.S. Dist. Ct. N.J. 1982, U.S. Ct. Appeals (3d cir.) 1986, U.S. Supreme Ct. 1986, N.Y. 1989. Assoc. Shanley & Fisher, P.C., Newark, 1982-83; ptnr. Hanlon, Lavigne, Topchik, Herzfeld & Rubin, Edison, N.J., 1983—; instr. Am. Inst. Paralegal Studies, Mahwah, N.J., 1985-88. Mem. ABA (litigation sect.), N.J. Bar Assn. (product liability com.), Middlesex County Bar Assn., Trial Attys. N.J., N.J. Def. Assn., Assn. Trial Lawyers Am., Worrall F. Mountain Inn of Court (barrister 1991-93). Republican. Jewish. Avocations: tennis, music, computers. Office: Hanlon Lavigne Et Al 10 Parsonage Rd Ste 200 Edison NJ 08837-2429

LAVIGNE, PETER MARSHALL, environmentalist, lawyer, consultant; b. Laconia, N.H., Mar. 25, 1957; s. Richard Byrd and D. Jacquiline (Cobleigh) L.; m. Nancy Gaile Parent, Sept. 20, 1979. BA, Oberlin Coll., 1980; MSL cum laude, Vt. Law Sch., 1983, JD, 1985. Bar: Mass. 1987. History tchr. Cushing Acad., Ashburnham, Mass., 1983-84; rsch. writer Environ. Law Ctr., Vt., 1985; lobbyist Vt. Natural Resources Coun., Montpelier, 1985; exec. dir. Westport (Mass.) River Watershed Alliance, 1986-88, Merrimack River Watershed Coun., West Newbury, 1988-89; environ. cons. Mass., N.H., Vt., and Oreg., 1990—; N.E. coord. Am. Rivers, Washington, 1990-92; dir. river leadership program River Network, Portland, Oreg., 1992-95; dir. spl. programs River Network, Portland, 1995-96; dep. dir. For the Sake of the Salmon, Portland, 1996—; adj. prof. Antioch New Eng. Grad. Sch., Keene, N.H., 1991-92; mem. adv. bd. Cascadia Times, Portland, 1995—, Amigos Bravos, Taos, N.Mex., 1993—; trustee Rivers Coun. Washington, Seattle, 1993—; bd. mem. Alaska Clean Water Alliance, 1995—, Watershed adv. group Natural Resources Law Ctr. U. Colo., 1995—; coastal resources adv. bd. Commonwealth of Mass., Boston, 1987-91. Co-author: Vermont Townscape, 1987; contbr. articles to profl. jours. Dir. Mass. League of Environ. Voters, Boston, 1988-92; mem. steering com. N.H. Rivers Campaign, 1988-92; co-founder, co-chair New England Coastal Campaign, 1988-92; EMT South Royalton (Vt.) Vol. Rescue Squad, 1982-86; dir., chairperson Vt. Emergency Med. Svcs. Dist. 8, Randolph, 1984-86; co-founder, v.p. Coalition for Buzzards Bay, Bourne, Mass., 1987; housing renewal commn. City of Oberlin, Ohio, 1980-81; mem. properties com. First Unitarian Ch., 1995—. Recipient Environ. Achievement award Coalition for Buzzards Bay, 1988; land use rsch. fellow Environ. Law Ctr., Vt. Law Sch., 1984-85; Mellon found. rsch. grantee Oberlin Coll., 1980. Mem. Natural Resources Def. Coun., Conservation Law Found., League of Conservation Voters. Democrat. Unitarian-Universalist. Avocations: sea kayaking, mountaineering, woodwork, reading, photography. Home: 3714 SE 11th Ave Portland OR 97202 Office: For the Sake of the Salmon 45 SE 82nd Dr Ste 100 Gladstone OR 97027-2522

LAVIN, BERNICE E., cosmetics executive; b. 1925; m. Leonard H. Lavin, Oct. 30, 1947; children: Scott Jay, Carol Marie, Karen Sue. Student, Northwestern U. Vice chairperson of bd., sec.- treas. Alberto-Culver Co.; dir., v.p., sec.- treas. Alberto-Culver U.S.A., Inc.; sec.- treas., dir. Alberto-Culver Internat., Inc.; v.p., sec.-treas. Sally Beauty Co., Inc. Office: Alberto-Culver Co 2525 Armitage Ave Melrose Park IL 60160-1125

LAVIN, CHARLES BLAISE, JR., realtor, association executive; b. Balt., Aug. 13, 1940; s. Charles Blaise and Dorothy (Sturla) L.; m. Eileen Donohue, Sept. 3, 1966; children—Charles, Michael, Kristine, Philip. Student, U. Balt., 1958-62, U.S. Army Sch. Mil. Intelligence, 1962. Exec. dir. New Eng. chpt. Associated Builders and Contractors, Waltham, Mass., 1966-78; exec. v.p. Am. Subcontractors Assn., Washington, 1978-81; exec. asst. to dep. sec. for housing HUD, Washington, 1981-82; exec. v.p. Nat. Assn. Plumbing, Heating and Cooling Contractors, Washington, 1982-87; exec. dir. and lobbyist Nat. Burglar and Fire Alarm Assn., Washington, and Cen. Sta. Alarm Assn., Bethesda, Md., 1987-90; realtor Prudential Preferred Properties, Laurel, Md., 1990-95; exec. dir. Nat. Duckpin Bowling Congress, Balt., 1995—; trustee Assoc. Splty. Contractors, Constrn. Jurisdictional Dispute Bd., 1983-85; chmn. County Real Estate Bd., 1993-95. Vice chmn. bd. dirs., chmn. fin. com. Laurel-Beltsville Gen. Hosp. (Md.), 1982-84; mem. Budget Com. Hopkinton, Mass., 1975-77, Planning Commn., 1977-78; bd. dirs. Young Republicans Balt., 1966. Served with CIC U.S. Army, 1962-65. Mem. New Eng. Soc. Assn. Execs. (pres.), Greater Washington Soc. Assn. Execs. (dir.), Am. Soc. Assn. Execs., Am. Legion (Post 60 comdr. 1994-95), U.S. C. of C., D.C. Basketball Ofcls. Assn., Internat. Assn. Basketball Ofcls., Washington Dist. Football Ofcls. Assn., Nat. Duckpin Bowling Congress (nat. dir.), Sons of Italy, KC, Loyal Order of Moose, West Laurel Recreational Coun. (chmn. 1994—). Republican. Roman Catholic. Home: 7006 Redmiles Rd Laurel MD 20707-3244 Office: Nat Duckpin Bowling Cong 4991 Fairview Ave Baltimore MD 21090

LAVIN, FRANKLIN L., think tank executive; b. Canton, Ohio, 1957; married; 3 children. BSc in Fgn. Svc., Georgetown U., 1980, MSc in Chinese Lang. and History, 1985; MA in Internat. Econs./Internat. Rels., Johns Hopkins U., 1990; MBA, U. Pa., 1996. Mem. staff White House, Dept. State; dep. exec. sec. Nat. Security Coun.; assoc. dir. White House, Washington; dep. asst. sec. for East Asia and Pacific Dept. Commerce, Washington, 1991-93; trade economist, exed. dir. Asia Pacific Policy Ctr., Washington, 1994—; adj. fellow Ctr. Strategic and Internat. Studies; mem. U.S. Com. on Security and Cooperation in the Asia Pacific; mem. Nat. Policy Forum; mem. steering com. Am. Coun. on Germany's Young Leaders' Program. Contbr. chpts. to book, articles to N.Y. Times, Wall St. Jour., Fgn. Affairs, others. Officer USNR. Office: Asia Pacific Policy Ctr Ste 1011 1730 Rhode Island Ave NW Washington DC 20036

LAVIN, JOHN HALLEY, editor, author; b. Queens County, N.Y., Oct. 27, 1932; s. John Joseph and Dorothy Monica (Halley) L.; m. Bernadette Manning, Mar. 2, 1957; children—John Stephen, Michael James, Eileen Mary, Monica Anne. B.A., Queens Coll., 1958; health adminstrv. devel. program, Cornell U., 1969. Editor L.I. Graphic (weekly), 1958; copy editor New Haven Register, 1958-59; newsman, state news editor A.P., Newark, 1959-65; gen. news supr. A.P., N.Y.C., 1965-66; editor-writer Med. Econs. Co., mag. pubs., Oradell, N.J., 1966-82; Atlantic bur. chief Soccer Am. Mag., 1977-78; sr. editor, news div. chief. mem. editorial bd. Med. Econs., 1968-73; editor RN, 1973-75, Nursing Opportunities, 1973-75, RN Recruiter, 1974-75, Geriatric Cons., 1982-94, Pharmacy World News, 1985-86, Contemporary Sr. Health, 1989-93; with Cardiology World News, 1982—. Author: Stroke: From Crisis to Victory, 1985; contbr. articles to profl. and gen. interest publs. Publicity chmn. Glen Rock (N.J.) Cub Scouts and Boy Scouts Am., 1968-73; founder, mem., trustee Glen Rock Jr. Soccer Club, 1970-74. Served with USN, 1951-55, Korea. Recipient Jesse H. Neal award Am. Bus. Press, 1976, cert., 1976; Journalism award Am. Acad. Family Physicians, 1981. Mem. Soc. Prfol. Journalists. Roman Catholic. Home: 106 Delbrook Way Marco Island FL 33937-4605 *An editor's primary responsibility is to his reader. If he has performed his corporate duties well, endeared himself to his publisher, pleased his writers and advertisers, fed his ego among his fellow editors, but has allowed the editorial excellence of his publication to be compromised, he has not met his primary responsibility. If he loses touch with the copy or the reader, he is no longer an editor; he is a manager. And he might as well be in some other business.*

LAVIN, LEONARD H., personal care products company executive; b. Chgo., 1919; married. BA, U. Wash., 1940. With Lucien Lelong, 1940-46; with Leonard H. Lavin Co., 1951-55, Alberto-Culver Co., Melrose Park, Ill., 1955—, chmn., pres., CEO, now chmn., bd. dirs. Served to lt. commdr. USNR, 1941-45. Office: Alberto-Culver Co 2525 Armitage Ave Melrose Park IL 60160-1163

LAVIN, LINDA, actress; b. Portland, Maine, Oct. 15, 1937; d. David J. and Lucille (Potter) L. BA, Coll. William and Mary, Williamsburg, Va., 1959. Debut: (Off-Broadway) Oh, Kay!, 1960, (Broadway) A Family Affairs, 1962; appearances in revues Wet Paint, 1965, The Game Is Up, 1965, The Mad Show, 1966; with nat. touring company On a Clear Day You Can See Forever, 1966-67; mem. acting company Eugene O'Neil Playwrights' Unit, 1968; other stage appearances include It's a Bird... It's a Plane... It's Superman, 1966, Something Different, 1967, Little Murders, 1969, Cop-Out, 1969, The Last of the Red Hot Lovers, 1969 (Tony nominee), Story Theatre, 1970, The Enemy is Dead, 1973, Love Two, 1974, The Comedy of Errors, 1975, Dynamite Tonite!, 1975, Six Characters in Search of an Author, Am. Repertory Theatre, Cambridge, Mass., 1983-84 season, Broadway Bound, 1986 (Tony award 1987), Gypsy, 1990, The Sisters Rosensweig, 1993, Death Defying Acts, 1995; film appearances: See You In The Morning, 1989, I Want to Go Back Home, 1989; star: (TV series) Alice, 1976-85 (Golden Globe award 1979); star and prodr.: (TV series) Room for Two, 1992—; prodr.: (PBS TV miniseries) The Sunset Gang, 1991; other TV appearances on Phyllis, Family, Rhoda, Harry O; TV movies include: The Morning After, 1974, Like Mom, Like Me, 1978, A Matter of Life and Death, 1981, Another Woman's Child, 1983, A Place To Call Home, Lena: My One Hundred Children. Recipient Sat. Rev., Outer Critics Circle awards for Little Murders, Theater World award for Wet Paint. Office: Metropolitan Talent Agy 4526 Wilshire Blvd Los Angeles CA 90010-3801*

LAVIN, MATTHEW T., horticultural educator. Assoc. prof. biology dept. Mont. State U., Bozeman. Recipient N.Y. Botanical Garden award Botanical Soc. Am., 1993. Office: care Dept Biology 310 Lewis Hall Montana State U Bozeman MT 59717-0002*

LAVIN, ROXANNA MARIE, finance executive; b. San Antonio, Sept. 8, 1952; d. Teddy Harold and Cora Ann (Ames) Maddox; m. Michael Paul Lavin, July 11, 1971; children: Sharon Renai, Christopher Michael, Katherine Marie. Student, Ea. Mich. U., 1985, 86, 70; BBA magna cum laude, Cleary Coll., 1992; postgrad, Ctr. Mich. U., 1993, Madonna Univ., 1994; postgrad., U. Mich., 1996. Sales clk. Children's Fashion Shop, Livonia, Mich., 1970; bookkeeping clk. Ypsilanti (Mich.) Savs. Bank, 1970-73; receptionist, acctg. clk. Maize & Blue Properties, Ann Arbor, Mich., 1986-87; acctg. clk. Sensors, Saline, Mich., 1987; office supr., fin. mgr. Great Lakes Coll. Assn., Ann Arbor, 1988-94; fin., pers. mgr. Jackson (Mich.) Libr., 1994—, interim co-dir., 1995. Sec., treas. Old Mill Hills Assn., Pinckney, Mich., 1990-93; mem. Pinckney High and Mid. Sch. Parents, 1990-92; parent vol. Lincoln Cons. Schs., Ypsilanti, 1985-86; mem. Jackson County Literacy Coun. Recipient scholarship Ea. Mich. U., 1970. Mem. AAUW, Mich. Libr. Assn. Avocations: painting, sketching, gardening, reading. Office: Jackson Dist Libr 244 W Michigan Ave Jackson MI 49201-2230

LAVIN-CORTI, ROSE MAUREEN, artist; b. Perth Amboy, N.J., Oct. 16, 1952; d. James V.P. and Emma (Kiblosh) Lavin; m. Franco Casentini, Feb. 14, 1974 (div. 1984); 1 child, Franco K. Casentini; m. Stefano Corti, Oct. 24, 1984; 1 child, Sandro J. Corti. Student, Georgian Ct., 1970-72, U. Florence (Italy), 1972-73. Saleswoman Correges, Rome, 1977-78; sec. McDonnell-Douglas, Rome, 1978-80, McCann-Erickson, Rome, 1980-82, RAI TV and Radio Corp., N.Y.C., 1983-84; mgr. Benetton, Woodbridge, N.J., 1984-85; sole proprietor Art Studio LC, Woodbridge, 1990—. Artist drawing logo contest, Tarquinia, Italy (Silver medal 1978). Directress St. Peter's Altar Guild, Perth Amboy, 1991-94; mem. NOW, 1991—. Mem. Nat. Mus. of Women in the Arts, Nat. Assn. Women Bus. Owners. Democrat. Episcopalian. Avocations: karate (brown belt), swimming, cooking. Home: 677 Parker St Perth Amboy NJ 08861-2913 Office: Art Studio LC 76 Main St Woodbridge NJ 07095-2816

LAVINE, ALAN, columnist, writer; b. Sharon, Pa., Feb. 17, 1948; s. Milton and Doris (Helfman) L.; m. Gail Jeanne Liberman, Dec. 20, 1991. BA, Kent State U., 1970; MA, U. Akron, 1973; MBA, Clark U., 1981. Dir. of rsch. Donoghue Orgn., Holliston, Mass., 1981-83; nat. syndicated fin. columnist, 1983—; syndicated radio commentator Bus. News Network, 1994—; columnist Am. Online, 1995; presenter papers in field ann. meeting AAAS, 1972, ann. meeting Mass. Psychol. Assn., Wellesley, 1978, ann. meeting APA, 1979, Nat. Symposium on Rsch. in Art, U. Ill., 1980; guest lectr. Cornell U., 1990, 91, 92, 93. Author: Diversify: Investor's Guide to Asset Allocation Strategies, 1990 (alt. selection Fortune Book Club), Your Life Insurance Options, 1993 (endorsed Inst. CFPs), Improving Your Credit and Reducing Your Debt, 1994 (endorsed Inst. CFPs), Getting Started in Mutual Funds, 1994, Diversify Your Way to Wealth, 1994 (alt. selection Fortune Book Club), 50 Ways to Mutual Fund Profits, 1995, The Complete Idiot's Guide to Making Money with Mutual Funds, 1996; contbr. articles to profl. jours. Mem. Nat. Writers Union. Home: H2 3606 Alder Dr Apt H2 West Palm Beach FL 33417-1182 Office: Alan Lavine Inc 3951 Haverhill Rd N Ste 210 West Palm Beach FL 33417-8145

LAVINE, HENRY WOLFE, lawyer; b. Phila., Apr. 21, 1936; s. Samuel Phillips and Sarah Pamela (Leese) L.; m. Meta Landreth Doak, Feb. 20, 1960 (div. Feb. 1980); children: Lisa, Lindsay; m. Martha Putnam Cathcart; children: Samuel Putnam, Gwenn Cathcart. BA, U. Pa., 1957, JD, 1961. Assoc. Squire, Sanders & Dempsey, Cleve., 1961-70; ptnr. Squire, Sanders & Dempsey, Washington, 1970-85, mng. ptnr. Washington office, 1985-91; sr. mng. ptnr., 1991--; dir. Greater Washington Bd. of Trade. Trustee Fed. City Coun., Washington; bd. assocs. Gallaudet U.; mem. The Bretton Woods Com. Mem. Siasconset Casino Club, Met. Club. Office: Squire Sanders & Dempsey 1201 Pennsylvania Ave NW PO Box 407 Washington DC 20044

LAVINE, JOHN M., journalism educator, management educator; b. Duluth, Minn., Mar. 20, 1941; s. Max H. and Frances (Hoffman) L.; m. Meryl Esta Lipton, June 1, 1980; children: Miriam, Marc, Max. B.A., Carleton Coll., Minn., 1963; postgrad., U. Minn., 1963; LL.D. (hon.), Emerson Coll., Boston, 1975. Pub., editor Lavine Newspaper Group, Chippewa Falls, Wis., 1964-89; pub. Ind. Media Group, Profl. Publs., Inc., 1984-94; Cowles prof. media mgmt. and econs. U. Minn., Mpls., 1984-89; prof., dir. Newspaper Mgmt. Ctr. a joint program Northwestern U. Kellogg Grad. Sch. Mgmt./Medill Sch. Journalism, Evanston, Ill., 1989—; pres. Newspaper Cons. Inc. (NCI), Evanston, 1993—; cons., lectr. in field, vis. prof. numerous profl. and ednl. instns.; participant numerous profl. confs. Author: China, 1980; The Constant Dollar Newspaper, 1980; Managing Media Organizations, 1988; contbr. chpts. to books, articles to profl. jours. Recipient numerous awards for excellence in mgmt. and journalism. Mem. Newspaper Assn. Am., Am. Soc. Newspapers Editors, Inter Am. Press Assn., Inland Daily Press Assn. (chmn., pres. 1984-85), Wis. Newspaper Assn. (life). Home: 335 Greenleaf Evanston IL 60202-2501 Office: Newspaper Mgmt Ctr 1845 Sheridan Rd Evanston IL 60208-0815

LAVINE, LAWRENCE NEAL, investment banker; b. Providence, Sept. 20, 1951; s. Avery B. and Pearl (Burbil) L.; m. Pamela Ferne Selby, Jan. 3, 1981; 1 child, Jason. BS summa cum laude, Northeastern U., 1974; MBA with highest distinction, Harvard U., 1976. V.p. Kidder, Peabody & Co. Inc., N.Y.C., 1976-87; mng. dir. Donaldson, Lufkin & Jenrette, N.Y.C., 1987—. Dir. Nat. Downe Syndrome, N.Y.C. Mem. Harvard Club of N.Y., Harvard Bus. Sch. Club of N.Y., Sunningdale Country Club. Avocations: running, tennis, golf. Office: Donaldson Lufkin & Jenrette Securities Corp 277 Park Ave New York NY 10172

LAVINE, STEVEN DAVID, academic administrator; b. Sparta, Wis., June 7, 1947; s. Israel Harry and Harriet Hauda (Rosen) L.; m. Janet M. Sternburg, May 29, 1988. BA, Stanford U., 1969; MA, Harvard U., 1970, PhD, 1976. Asst. prof. U. Mich., Ann Arbor, 1974-81; asst. dir. arts and humanities Rockefeller Found., N.Y.C., 1983-86, assoc. dir. arts and humanities, 1986-88; pres. Calif. Inst. Arts, Valencia, 1988—; adj. assoc. prof. NYU Grad. Sch. Bus., 1984-85; cons. Wexner Found., Columbus, Ohio, 1986-87; selection panelist Input TV Screening Conf., Montreal, Can., and Granda, Spain, 1985-86; cons., panelist Nat. Endowment for Humanities, Washington, 1981-85; faculty chair Salzburg Seminar on Mus., 1989; co-dir. Arts and Govt. Program, The Am. Assembly, 1991; mem. arch. selection jury L.A. Cathedral. Editor: The Hopwood Anthology, 1981, Exhibiting Cultures, 1991, Museums and Communities, 1992; editor spl. issue Prooftexts jour., 1984. Bd. dirs. Sta. KCRW-FM (NPR), 1989—, J. Paul Getty Mus., 1990—, Am. Coun. on the Arts, 1991—, L.A. Philharm. Assn., 1994—, Endowments, Inc., Bond Portfolio for Endowments, Inc., 1994—. Recipient Class of 1923 award, 1979, Faculty Recognition award, 1980 U. Mich.; Charles Dexter traveling fellow Harvard U., 1972, Ford fellow, 1969-74, vis. rsch. fellow Rockefeller Found., N.Y.C., 1981-83. Jewish. Office: Calif Inst Arts Office Pres 24700 Mcbean Pky Santa Clarita CA 91355-2340

LAVINGTON, MICHAEL RICHARD, venture capital company executive; b. Purley, Surrey, Eng., Feb. 21, 1943; came to U.S., 1972; s. Richard H. and Patricia (Young) L.; m. June Watford, Aug. 13, 1966; children: Susan, Victoria. B.A., Cambridge U., 1964; M.A., Columbia U., 1965; Ph.D., Lancaster U., (Eng.), 1968. Dir. Ralli Australia, 1969-71, Bowater America, N.Y.C., 1971-74; pres. Kay Jewelers Inc., Alexandria, Va., 1974-90, Watford Investment Corp., Fredericksburg, Va., 1990—, Hi-Gear Auto, Capitol Heights, Md., 1996—. Chmn. St. Stephen's and St. Agnes Sch., Alexandria, 1981—; trustee Ch. Schs. in Diocese of Va., 1989—.

LAVINSKY, LARRY MONROE, lawyer, consultant; b. N.Y.C., Oct. 23, 1929; s. Isaac A. and Rose (Zuroff) L.; m. Dena Mazell, Mar. 20, 1960; children: Joshua, Avram, Ezra. Bar: N.Y. 1953, U.S. Ct. Appeals 2d cir. 1958, U.S. Ct. Appeals 3d cir. 1978, U.S. Supreme Ct. 1961. Assoc. Baer, Marks, Frieman, Berliner & Klein, N.Y.C., 1953-57; law clk. U.S. Dist. Ct. (so. dist.) N.Y., 1957-59; assoc. Proskauer, Rose, Goetz & Mendelsohn, N.Y.C., 1959-67, ptnr., 1967—; spl. cons. on desegregation N.Y.C. Bd. Edn., 1973-74. Contbr. articles to profl. jours.; pub. TV appearances, 1978, 79. Chmn. nat. law com. Anti-Defamation League, B'nai B'rith, 1972-76, chmn. nat. civil rights com., 1976-80, vice chmn. nat. com., 1980-86, sec. nat. com., 1986-88; founding mem. Com. on Equal Edn. Opportunity, 1978. Mem. ABA (Post-Bakke task force 1978-80, affirmative action com. 1981-86), New York County Lawyers Assn. (chmn. civil rights com. 1988-90), Assn. Bar City N.Y. Office: Proskauer Rose et al 1585 Broadway New York NY 10036-8200*

LAVITT, MEL S., investment banking professional; b. Denver, Sept. 9, 1937; s. Al R. and Ruth Lucille (Friedman) L.; m. Wendy Susan Adler, Sept. 10, 1959; children—Kathy, John, Meredith. A.B. in Am. Civilization, Brown U., Providence, 1959. Assoc. Bear Sterns & Co., N.Y.C., 1959-62; ptnr. C.E. Unterberg Towbin, N.Y.C., 1962-77; adminstrv. mng. dir. L.F. Rothschild, Unterberg, Towbin, N.Y.C., 1977-87; pres. Lavitt Mgmt., Park City, Utah, 1987-92; mng. dir. Unterberg Harris, 1992—; bd. dirs. St. Bernard Software, Inc., Jabil Circuit Co. Mem. Harmonie Club, N.Y. Road Runners Club. Avocations: running, skiing, biking, collecting American Indian art. Home: 15 E 91st St New York NY 10128-0648 also: 439 Woodside PO Box 74 Park City UT 84060-0074

LAVOIE, LIONEL A., physician, medical executive; b. St. Brieux, Sask., Can., Aug. 24, 1937; s. Athanase T. and Ella Marie (Mevel) L.; m. Mary Tina Luchewski, Oct. 12, 1964; children: Robert, Michelle, Nicole, Andrea. BA, Ottawa U., Ont., Can., 1958, MD, 1964. Intern, then resident Univ. Hosp., Sask.; assoc. clin. prof. family medicine U. Sask., 1978—; chief of staff Melfort (Sask.) Union Hosp., 1985-90; commr. Med. Care Ins. Commn., 1984-88. Chmn. Melfort Dist. Minor Sports, 1978-80, Melfort Pks. and Recreation, 1983-86, Sask. Summer Games 1988, 1986-88. Recipient Ramstead award Jaycees of Province Sask., 1975, Dedication award Sask. Parks, Recreation and Culture, 1988, Community Recreation award Melford C. of C., 1989, Commemorative medal 125th Anniversary Can. Confed., 1993. Mem. Can. Med. Assn. (bd. dirs. 1978-83, pres. elect 1989-90, pres. 1990-91), Sask. Med. Assn. (bd. dirs. 1971-76, v.p. 1974, pres. 1975), Can. Acad. Sports Medicine, Am. Geriatric Soc., Coll. Family Physicians Can. (sec. Sask. province 1967-70), Sask. Acad. Sports Medicine (pres. 1986-88), Coun. Med. Assn. (chmn. 1985-89), Sask. Paraplegic Assn. (bd. dirs. 1978—), Can. Cancer Soc. (adv. com. Sask. div. 1986—), Nat. Aerospace Med. Assn., KC (grand knight 1980-81), Rotary (pres. Melfort club 1987-88). Avocations: golf, curling, horticulture. Home: 402 Stovel E, Melfort, SK Canada S0E 1A0 Office: Can Med Assn, 1867 Alta Vista Dr, Ottawa, ON Canada K1G 0G8

LAVOIE, SERGE, principal dancer; b. Lachine, Que., Can., Jan. 30, 1963; s. Jean Claude and Therese (Larr) L. Student, Nat. Ballet Sch., Toronto, 1979-82. Prin. dancer Northern Ballet Theatre, Manchester, Eng., 1981, 82; dancer Nat. Ballet Can., Toronto, Ont., 1982-86, 2d soloist, 1986-87, 1st soloist, 1987-88, prin. dancer, 1988—. Appeared in Raymonda Act III, Don Quixote, La Sylphide, Onegin, Napoli, The Nutcracker, Symphony in C, Romeo and Juliet, Elite Syncopations; featured in Here We Come, Endangered Species, Reminiscence, Components; created roles in L'Ile Inconnue, Blue Snake, Pastorale, The Miraculous Mandarin, The Actress; appeared in Quartet, Khachaturian Pas de Deux, 1983; appeared with stars and soloists of Can. Ballet in Etc!, On Occasion, Pastel, Swan Lake,(Italy, 1985); debuted as Prince in Swan Lake, 1985-86; danced lead in Transfigured Night and Elite Syncopations; debuted as Solor in La Bayadere Act III, as James in La Sylphide, as guest artist with London Festival Ballet; appeared with Basel Ballet in Switzerland, 1986-87 in Coppelia and The Sleeping Beauty; performed with Berlin Opera Ballel in Theme and Variations, 1987, at La Scala in Milan in The Nutcracker, in France, Italy and the U.S. with Nureyev, at Spoleta Festival in Australia; appeared with Can. Ballet Company in Concerto Barocco, Second Movement of Barocco, Forgotten Land, Death of a Lady's Man, Song of the Earth, Symphony in C, Alice, Steptext, Diana and Acteon Pas de Deux, 1987; appeared with Boston Ballet in La Sylphide, The Nutcracker, Monotones I, Sacre du Printemps, Don Quixote, Esmeralda Pas De Deux, Coppelia, Swan Lake, 1988, 89. Recipient 1st prize Internat. Ballet Competition, Moscow, 1980, Silver medal 1st N.Y.C. Internat. Ballet, 1984. Office: National Ballet of Canada, 157 King St East, Toronto, ON Canada M5C 1G9

LAW, BERNARD FRANCIS CARDINAL, archbishop; b. Torreon, Mex., Nov. 4, 1931; s. Bernard A. and Helen A. (Stubblefield) L. B.A., Harvard U., 1953; postgrad., St. Joseph Sem., St. Benedict, La., 1953, Pontifical Coll. Josephinum, Worthington, Ohio, 1955. Ordained priest Roman Catholic Ch., 1961, consecrated bishop, 1973; editor Natchez-Jackson diocesan paper, Jackson, 1963-68; exec. dir. U.S. Bishops Com. for Ecumenical and Interreligious Affairs, 1968-71, chmn., from 1975; vicar gen. Diocese of Natchez-Jackson, 1971-73; bishop Diocese of Springfield-Cape Girardeau, Mo., 1973-84; archbishop Archdiocese of Boston Brighton, Mass., 1984—; created cardinal, 1985; mem. adminstrv. com. Nat. Conf. Cath. Bishops, from 1975; mem. communication com. U.S. Cath. Conf., 1974, mem. adminstrv. bd., from 1975; mem. Vatican Secretariat for Promoting Christian Unity, from 1976; consultor Vatican Commn. Religious Relations with the Jews, from 1976; chmn. bd. Pope John XXIII Med.-Moral Research and Edn. Ctr., St. Louis, 1980-82; ecclesiastical del. of Pope John Paul II for matters pertaining to former Episcopal priests, 1981. Trustee Pontifical Coll. Josephinum, 1974-85, Nat. Shrine of Immaculate Conception, from 1975; bd. regents Conception (Mo.) Sem. Coll., from 1975. Office: Cardinal's Residence 2101 Commonwealth Ave Brighton MA 02135-3193

LAW, CAROL JUDITH, medical psychotherapist; b. N.Y.C., May 1, 1940; d. Aldo and Jennie (Feldman) Settimo; m. Perry J. Koll, Dec. 26, 1967 (div. Nov. 1974); 1 son, Perry J.; m. Edwin B. Law, June 1, 1979. BA, Upsala Coll., 1962; postgrad., Rutgers U., 1964-66; MA, Columbia Pacific U., 1982, PhD, 1984. Diplomate Am. Bd. Med. Psychotherapy. Pers. dir. Hotel Manhattan, N.Y.C., 1961; supr. social work Essex County, Newark, 1962-67; exec. dir. USO, Vung Tau, South Vietnam, 1967-68; dir. Dept. Health and Rehab. Svcs., Pensacola, Fla., 1968-79; therapist, tchr. Franciscan Renewal Ctr., Scottsdale, Ariz., 1982-92; pvt. practice Scottsdale, 1982-92; drug free workforce cons. Pensacola C. of C., Fla., 1992—; pres. Drug Free Workplaces, Inc., 1993—; mem. Healthy Start of N.W. Fla.; dist 1 chmn. Alcohol, Drug Abuse and Mental Health Planning Coun. Mem. state adv. bd. Parents Anonymous, Phoenix, 1982; chmn. Gov.'s Adv. Commn. Drugs and the Elderly, Tallahassee, 1978; pres. Jaycettes, Pensacola, 1969; chmn. social com. United Way Fund, Pensacola, 1977; mem. adv. bd. USO, Pensacola, 1973, H.R.S. Dist. 1 Community Collaboration Project; trustee ORME Sch. Fellow Am. Acad. Polit. and Social Sci.; mem. Am. Assn. Pub. Adminstrs., Pensacola Country Club, Escambia County Drug Court Coalition, Fla. State C. of C. (drug issues com.), Nat. Drugs Don't Work (Fla. rep.), Partnership for a Drug Free Fla. (bd. dirs.), Pensacola Downtown Rotary. Roman Catholic. Home: 3386 Chantarene Dr Pensacola FL 32507-3586

LAW, CLARENE ALTA, innkeeper, state legislator; b. Thornton, Idaho, July 22, 1933; d. Clarence Riley and Alta (Simmons) Webb; m. Franklin Kelso Meadows, Dec. 2, 1953 (div. July 1973); children: Teresa Meadows Jillson, Charisse Meadows Haws, Steven Riley; m. Creed Law, Aug. 18, 1973. Student, Idaho State Coll., 1953. Sec., sub. tchr. Grand County Schs., Cedar City, Utah, 1954-57; UPI rep. newspaper agy. Moab, Utah Regional Papers, Salt Lake City and Denver; auditor Wort Hotel, Jackson, Wyo., 1960-62; innkeeper, CEO Elk Country Motels, Inc., Jackson, Wyo., 1962—; rep. Wyo. Ho. of Reps., Cheyenne, 1991—, chmn. house travel com., 1993—, mem. bank bd. State of Wyo., 1991—; bd. dirs. Jackson State Bank, Snow King Resort. Chmn. sch. bd. dirs. Teton County Schs., Jackson, 1983-86. Named Citizen of Yr. Jackson C. of C., 1976, Bus. Person of Yr. Jackson Hole Realtors, 1987, Wyo. Small Bus. Person SBA, 1977. Mem. Wyo. Lodging and Restaurant Assn. (pres., chmn. bd. dirs. 1988-89, Big Wyo. award 1987), Internat. Leisure Hosts (bd. dirs. Phoenix chpt. 1991-94), Soroptimists (charter), BPW (Woman of Yr. 1975). Republican. Mem. LDS Ch. Avocations: travel, study. Home: Box 575 43 W Pearl Jackson WY 83001 Office: Elk Country Motels Inc 43 W Pearl Jackson WY 83001

LAW, DAVID HILLIS, physician; b. Milw., July 24, 1927; s. David Hillis Law III and Hazel Janice (May) Young; m. Patricia Bicking Thornton, Sept. 14, 1949; children: Linda Clark, Wendy, David, Kimberly Rankin, Cassandra. BS, Cornell U., 1950, MD, 1954. Resident in internal medicine Cornell U. Med. Coll., N.Y.C., 1954-57, fellow in gastroenterology, 1957-59; dir. personnel health services N.Y. Hosp., Cornell Med. Ctr., N.Y.C., 1959-60; asst. adminstrn. assoc., prof. medicine, chief gastroenterology Vanderbilt U. Med. Coll., Nashville, 1960-69; prof., vice chmn. dept. medicine U. New Mex. Sch. Med., Albuquerque, 1969-85; chief med. services Vets. Adminstrn. Med. Ctr., Albuquerque, 1969-85; dir. med. services Vets. Adminstrn. Cen. Office, Washington, 1985-86, dep. asst. chief med. dir. for clin. services, 1986-89, asst. chief med. dir. clin. affairs, 1989-91, acting dep. assoc. chief med. dir. for hosp.-based svcs., 1991—, assoc. dep. chief med. dir. for clin. program, 1993—; mem. human rsch. com. Los Alamos (N.Mex.) Sci. Lab., 1972-80; sabbatical dept. clin. physiology Karolinska Inst., Stockholm, 1980; bd. dirs., officer N.Mex. Nutrition Improvement Program, 1970-75; sub-com. chmn. U.S. Pharmacopeia Commn. on Revision, 1975-80; lectr. in field. Editor, Parenteral Nutrition; mem. editorial bd., Am. Jour. Digestive Diseases, 1968-74; rev. numerous med. jours.; contbr. articles to numeous profl. jours. Bd. dirs., officer Albuquerque Friends of Music, 1975-85; mem. Nat. Digestive Disease Adv. Bd., 1989—; mem. Interdepartmental Digestive Disease Coordinating Com. Cpl. U.S. Army, 1945-46. Named Tchr. and Attending Physician of Yr. Dept. Medicine House Staff, 1985. Fellow ACP (gov. 1989—); mem. AMA (lectr.), Western Assn. Physicians, Western Soc. Clin. Rsch., Am. Gastroenterol. Assn., Am. Inst. Nutrition, Alpha Omega Alpha. Republican.. Presbyterian. Avocation: hot air ballooning. Office: Vets Adminstrn Cen Office 810 Vermont Ave NW Washington DC 20420-0001

LAW, FREDERICK MASOM, engineering educator, structural engineering firm executive; b. Newark, Mar. 8, 1933; s. Frederick T. and Evelyn (Masom) L.; m. Margaret Mary Maus, Oct. 27, 1956; children: Carolyn Jean, Frederick Masom. B.S. Engring., Princeton U., 1956; M.S., N.J. Inst. Tech., 1962; Ph.D., Rutgers U., 1965. Registered profl. engr., Mass., R.I., N.Y., N.J., Pa., Fla., S.C. Structural engr. H.N.T.& B. Engrs., N.Y.C., 1956-57, 60-61, Austin Co., Roselle, N.J., 1961-63; asst. prof. engring. Newark Coll. Engring., 1963-68; assoc. prof. Pa. State U., Middletown, 1968-70; prof., chmn. dept. civil engring. U. Mass., North Dartmouth, 1970—; prin. Frederick M. Law, P.E., South Dartmouth, 1970—; pres. Timberspan Bridges Inc., South Dartmouth, 1983—; vice chmn. Mass. Bd. Registration Profl. Engrs. and Land Surveyors, 1977-82; mem. jury Am. Inst. Steel Constrn. Prize Bridge Competition, 1982. Served to 1st lt. AUS, 1957-60, ETO. Recipient Grand Conceptor Cons. Engrs. Council Am., 1978. Fellow ASCE; mem. Nat. Soc. Profl. Engrs., Mass. Soc. Profl. Engrs. (Outstanding Engring. Achievement 1978), Am. Soc. Engring. Edn., Soaring Soc. Am. Home: 10 Swift Rd South Dartmouth MA 02748-3717 Office: U Mass Dept Civil Engring Old Westport Rd North Dartmouth MA 02747

LAW, GORDON THEODORE, JR., library director; b. Norwood, Mass., Oct. 27, 1945; s. Gordon Theodore and Laura (Andersen) L.; m. Pam Marilyn Baxter, Sept. 29, 1990;. BA in History, SUNY, Albany, 1967, MA in Social Scis., 1968, MLS, 1972. Tchr. Mynderse Acad., Seneca Falls, N.Y., 1968-71; dir. Krannert Libr., Purdue U., West Lafayette, Ind., 1983-93; head reference and info. svcs. Catherwood Libr., Cornell U., Ithaca, N.Y., 1972-83, dir. Catherwood Libr., 1993—. Author: A Guide to Information on Closely Held Corporations, 1986; editor recent publ. feature Indsl. and Labor Rels. Rev., 1974-83. Mem. ALA, Com. Indsl. Rels. Librs., Spl. Librs. Assn., Indsl. Rels. Rsch. Assn. Office: Cornell U Martin P Catherwood Libr 237 Ives Hall Ithaca NY 14853-3901

LAW, JANET MARY, music educator; b. East Orange, N.J., Mar. 8, 1931; d. Charles and Mary Ellen (Keavy) Maitland; m. William Howard Law, Dec. 13, 1952; children: Robert Alan, Gail Ellen. Lic. Practical Nurse, St. Barnabas Sch., 1971; BA magna cum laude, Fairleigh Dickinson U., Rutherford, N.J., 1981; tchr. tng. course, Westminster Choir Coll., 1990—, Queens U., Canada, 1993. Registered Suzuki tchr., Suzuki piano tchr., traditional piano tchr. Staff nurse psychiat. unit St. Barnabas Med. Ctr., Livingston, N.J., 1972-78; office nurse, asst. to pvt. physician North Arlington, N.J., 1978-79; dir., owner B Sharp Acad., Rutherford, N.J., 1979-83; founder, tchr. piano music preparatory div. Fairleigh Dickinson U., Rutherford, 1983-89; founder, coord. piano divsn. Garden State Acad. Music, Rutherford, N.J., 1989-94; tchr. piano divsn. Garden State Acad. Music, Rutherford, 1989-95; Suzuki piano coord., tchr. Suzuki piano program, coord. Suzuki piano divsn. Montclair (N.J.) State U., 1994—. Author: Keyboard Kapers, 1983; inventor music games, 1983. Mem. Music and Performing Arts Club, Profl. Music Tchrs. Guild N.J. Inc., Suzuki Assn. of the Ams. Avocation: concerts. Home: 169 Hillcrest Dr Wayne NJ 07470-5629 also: Montclair State U Valley Rd and Normal Ave Upper Montclair NJ 07043

LAW, JOHN HAROLD, biochemistry educator; b. Cleve., Feb. 27, 1931; s. John and Katherine (Frampton) L.; m. Nancy Jean Floyd, June 8, 1956. BS, Case Inst. Tech., Cleve., 1953; PhD, U. Ill., 1957; D hon. causa, U. Sofia, 1995. Postdoctoral fellow Harvard U., Cambridge, Mass., 1958-59, from instr. to asst. prof. biochemistry, 1960-65; instr. Northwestern U., Evanston, Ill., 1959-60; prof. U. Chgo., 1965-81; prof. U. Ariz., Tucson, 1981-91, Regents prof., 1991—, chmn. dept. biochemistry, 1981-86, dir. biotech. program, 1986-92; dir. Ctr. Insect Sci., 1993; assoc. dean coll. agr. U. Ariz., Tucson, 1988-90; mem. gov. bd. Internat. Ctr. Insects, Nairobi, Kenya, 1980-87; mem. bd. trust Gordon Rsch. Conf., 1992—, chmn., 1996; mem. coun. Am. Soc. Biochem. Molecular Biology, 1993-96. Recipient Gregor Mendel medal Czech Acad. Sci., 1992, J.E. Purkinje medal Czech Acad. Sci., 1994. Fellow AAAS, ESA; mem. NAS, Am. Soc. Biochem. Molecular Biology, Am. Chem. Soc., Entomol. Soc. Am. Home: 2540 E 7th St Tucson AZ 85716-4702 Office: U Ariz Dept Biochemistry Bioscis W 345 Tucson AZ 85721

LAW, JOHN MANNING, retired lawyer; b. Chgo., Dec. 5, 1927; s. Fred Edward and Elisabeth (Emmons) L.; m. Carol Lufkin Ritter, May 14, 1955; children: John E., Lucy L., Frederick R., Beth K. Student, U. Chgo., 1944-45, St. Ambrose Coll., 1945; BA, Colo. Coll., 1948; JD, U. Colo., 1951. Bar: Colo. 1951, Ill. 1952, U.S. Ct. Appeals (10th cir.) 1954, U.S. Supreme Ct. 1989. Atty. trust dept. Harris Bank, Chgo., 1951-52; assoc. Dickerson, Morrissey, Zarlengo & Dwyer, Denver, 1952-57; ptnr. Law, Nagel & Clark, Denver, 1958-84, Law & Knous, Denver, 1984-93; ret.; mem. law com. Colo. Bd. Law Examiners, 1971-81, Colo. Ofcls. Compensation Commn., 1985-89. Mem. Moffatt Tunnel Commn., Denver, 1966-90. Capt. USNR, 1945-77, ret. Fellow Colo. Bar Found. (charter); mem. ABA (chmn. com. legal assistance to mil. pers. 1973-77), Colo. Bar Assn. (bd. govs. 1968-71), Denver Bar Assn. (trustee 1971-74), Internat. Soc. Barristers, Law Club, Denver Country Club. Republican. Presbyterian. Home: 3333 E Florida Ave Apt 35 Denver CO 80210-2541

LAW, LLOYD WILLIAM, geneticist; b. Ford City, Pa., Oct. 28, 1910; s. Craig Smith and Cora Jane (Whiteley) L.; m. Bernette Bohen, May 4, 1942; children: Lloyd William, David Bradford. B.S., U. Ill., 1931; A.M., Harvard U., 1935, Ph.D. (Austin fellow), 1937; Harvard Sheldon fellow, Stanford U., 1937-38. Tchr. high sch. Charleston, Ill., 1931-34; Finney-Howell Med. research fellow Jackson Meml. Lab., Bar Harbor, Maine, 1938-41; Commonwealth Fund fellow Jackson Meml. Lab., 1941-42, research asso., 1946, sci. dir., 1947; now trustee; geneticist Nat. Cancer Inst., Bethesda, Md., 1947-52; head leukemia studies sect. Nat. Cancer Inst., 1952—, chief lab. cell biology, 1970—, mem. sci. directorate, 1970-90; Panel mem. com. on growth NRC, 1952-56; mem. pharmacology and exptl. therapeutics study sect. NIH, 1955—; mem. screening panel cancer chemotherapy Nat. Service Center, 1955—; mem. adv. bd. Nat. Blood Research Found., 1954—; adv. bd. cancer research Am. Cancer Soc., 1965—, mem. panel on etiology of cancer, 1960—; sci. bd. Children's Cancer Fund Am., 1956—; bd. sci. advisers Roswell Park (N.Y.) Cancer Inst., 1957—; expert adv. com. cancer WHO, 1960-80; mem. U.S.A. nat. com. Internat. Union Against Cancer, 1969-78; mem. bd. sci. advs. Chemotherapy Found. N.Y., 1974—; mem. bd. sci. advisers Ludwik Cancer Found., 1980—, chmn., 1985. Author: Advances in Cancer Research Vol. II, 1954, Vol. XXXII, 1980, Leukemia Research, 1955, Origins of Resistance to Toxic Agents, 1955; other books in field; editor: Tumour Antigens; contbr. articles to profl. jours., books and pamphlets. Served as capt. 2d Air Force USAAF, 1942-46. Recipient Anne Frankel Rosenthal award AAAS, 1955; USPHS Meritorious Service award, 1965; G.H.A. Clowes Meml. award in cancer research, 1965; Allesandro Pascoli prize, 1969; Disting. Service medal USPHS, 1969; G.B. Mider lecture award NIH, 1970. Mem. Soc. Exptl. Biology and Medicine, N.Y. Acad. Sci., Am. Soc. Exptl. Pathology, Am. Assn. Cancer Rsch. (dir. 1956-59, 65—, pres. 1967-68), Italian Cancer Soc., Royal Soc. Medicine, Am. Immunology Assn., Am. Assn. Cancer Rsch. (hon. 1987), Europe Assn. Cancer Rsch. (hon. 1987). Home: 9810 Fernwood Rd Bethesda MD 20817-1512 Office: Nat Cancer Inst Pub Health Service Rockville Pike Bethesda MD 20892

LAW, MARK EDWARD, electrical engineer, educator; b. St. Paul, July 19, 1959; s. Paul Rock and Bernice Edna (Brookshaw) L.; m. Alison Leigh Retz, May 30, 1981; children: Christopher, Heather. BS CprE, Iowa State U., 1981; MSEE, Stanford U., 1982, PhD in Elec. Engring., 1988. Engr. Hewlett Packard, 1982-84; rsch. asst. Stanford (Calif.) U., 1984-87, rsch. assoc., 1988; asst. prof. elec. engring. U. Fla., Gainesville, 1988-93, assoc. prof. elec. engring., 1993—; presenter, spkr. in field; vice chmn. tech. adv. bd. tech. computer aided design program Los Alamos (N.Mex.) Nat. Lab.; session chmn. various tech. meetings in field. Author: Floods/Floops User's Manual, 1993; contbr. articles to profl. jours., chpts. to books. Recipient Young Faculty Devel. award IBM, 1988, Tech. Excellence award Semicondr. Rsch. Corp., 1993, Outstanding Young Alumnus award Iowa State U., 1994, Profl. Progress award Iowa State U., 1994; Nat. Merit scholar, 1977-81; grantee NSF, 1992—, SRC, 1989—, 93—, IBM, 1991-93; NSF Presdl. fellow, 1992. Mem. IEEE (sr., guest editor publ. 1991, assoc. editor IEEE Transactions on Semicondr. Mfg.), Am. Soc. Engring. Edn., Am. Phys. Soc., Electrochem. Soc., Sigma Xi, Phi Beta Pi, Phi Kappa Phi. Avocations: soccer, beer brewing. Office: U Fla 339 Larsen Hall Gainesville FL 32611-2044

LAW, MICHAEL R., lawyer; b. Rochester, N.Y., Nov. 30, 1947; s. George Robert and Elizabeth (Stoddart) L.; m. Cheryl Heller. BS, St. John Fisher Coll., 1969; JD, U. Louisville, 1975. Bar: N.Y. 1976, U.S. Dist. Ct. (we. dist.) N.Y. 1976, U.S. Supreme Ct. 1982. Assoc., Wood, P.C., Rochester, 1976-77; pvt. practice, Rochester, 1977-78; assoc. Sullivan, Peters, et al, Rochester, 1978-80, ptnr., 1980-81; ptnr. Phillips, Lytle, Hitchcock, Blaine & Huber, Rochester, 1982—. Exec. com. Camp Good Days and Spl. Times, Rochester, 1984—. Served with USAR, 1968-74. Mem. Monroe County Bar Assn. (judiciary com. 1981-88, ethics and personal injury com. 1988—), N.Y. State Bar Assn. (trial sect., ins. negligence com.), ABA (trial law sect., trial techniques com., editor 1986 Trial Techniques), N.Y. State Trial Lawyers (bd. dirs.), Genesee Valley Trial Lawyers Assn. (treas., 1992-93, pres.-elect 1993-95, pres. 1995—), Nat. Spinal Cord Injury Assn. (bd. dirs. Rochester chpt. 1990-92). Republican. Roman Catholic. Home: 3373 Elmwood Ave Rochester NY 14610-3425 Office: Phillips Lytle Hitchcock Blaine & Huber 1400 First Federal Plz Rochester NY 14614-1909

LAW, NANCY ENELL, school system administrator; b. South Gate, Calif., Jan. 12, 1935; d. Frank Ronald Cruickshank and Grace Margaret (Wright) Brotherton; m. George Otto Enell, Aug. 26, 1955; children: George, Grace; m. Alexander Inglis Law, Feb. 1, 1987. BS, U. So. Calif., 1956, MEd, 1961, PhD, 1977. Tchr. El Monte (Calif.) City Schs., 1956-58, Pasadena (Calif.) City Schs., 1958-62; from tchr. to project cons. Fullerton (Calif.) Elem. Sch. Dist., 1966-76; evaluation specialist San Juan Unified Sch. Dist., Carmichael, Calif., 1976-84; from dir. evaluation svcs. to adminstr. accountability Sacramento (Calif.) City Schs., 1984—; officer divsn. H Am. Ednl. Rsch. Assn., 1995—. Mem. Phi Delta Kappa. Avocations: creative handiwork, piano. Home: 9045 Laguna Lake Way Elk Grove CA 95758-4219 Office: Sacramento City Schs 520 Capitol Mall Sacramento CA 95814-4704

LAW, THOMAS HART, lawyer; b. Austin, Tex., July 6, 1918; s. Robert Adger and Elizabeth (Manigault) L.; m. Terese Tarlton, June 11, 1943 (div. Apr. 1956); m. Jo Ann Nelson, Dec. 17, 1960; children: Thomas Hart Jr., Debra Ann. AB, U. Tex., 1939, JD, 1942. Bar: Tex. 1942, U.S. Supreme Ct. 1950. Assoc. White, Taylor & Chandler, Austin, 1942; assoc. Thompson, Walker, Smith & Shannon, Ft. Worth, 1946-50; ptnr. Tilley, Hyder & Law, Ft. Worth, 1950-67, Stone, Tilley, Parker, Snakard, Law & Brown, Ft. Worth, 1967-71; pres. Law, Snakard, Brown & Gambill, P.C., Ft. Worth, 1971-84, Law, Snakard & Gambill, P.C., Ft. Worth, 1984—; bd. dirs., gen. counsel Gearhart Industries, Inc., Ft. Worth, 1960-88; gen. counsel Tarrant County Jr. Coll. Dist. Chmn. Leadership Ft. Worth, 1974-90; bd. regents U. Tex. System, 1975-81, vice chmn., 1979-81. Served to lt. USNR, 1942-46. Recipient Nat. Humanitarian award Nat. Jewish Hosp./Nat. Asthma Ctr., 1983; named Outstanding Young Man, City of Ft. Worth, 1950, Outstanding Alumnus, Coll. of Humanities, U. Tex., 1977, Outstanding Citizen, City of Ft. Worth, 1984, Bus. Exec. of Yr., City of Ft. Worth, 1987, Blackstone award for contbns. field of law Ft. Worth Bar Assn., 1990. Fellow Am. Bar Found., Tex. Bar Found., Am. Coll. Probate Counsel; mem. Ft. Worth C. of C. (pres. 1972), Mortar Bd., Phi Beta Kappa, Omicron Delta Kappa, Pi Sigma Alpha, Delta Sigma Rho, Phi Eta Sigma, Delta Tau Delta. Democrat. Presbyterian. Clubs: Ft. Worth (bd. govs. 1984-90), Century II (bd. govs. to 1985), River Crest Country, Exchange (pres. 1972), Steeplechase. Lodge: Rotary (local club pres. 1960). Avocation: numismatics. Home: 6741 Brants Ln Fort Worth TX 76116-7201 Office: Law Snakard & Gambill 3200 Bank One Tower 500 Throckmorton St Fort Worth TX 76102-3708

LAWARE, JOHN PATRICK, retired banker, federal official; b. Columbus, Wis., Feb. 20, 1928; s. John Henry and Ruth (Powles) L.; m. Margery Ann Ninabuck, Dec. 22, 1952; children: John Kevin, Margaret Ann. BA in Biology, Harvard, 1950; grad., Advanced Mgmt. Program, 1975; MA in Polit. Sci., U. Pa., 1951; LHD (hon.), Suffolk U., D in Polit. Sci. (hon), Northeastern U. Trainee Chem. Bank & Trust Co., N.Y.C., 1953-54, with credit dept., 1954-56, asst. sec., 1957-60, asst. v.p., 1960-62, v.p., 1962-65, v.p. in charge mktg. div., 1965-68, sr. v.p., 1968-72; sr. v.p. in charge holding co. ops. Chem. N.Y. Corp., from 1972; pres., dir. Shawmut Corp., 1978-80, Shawmut Bank of Boston N.A., 1978-80, chmn., dir., 1980-88; pres., dir. Shawmut Assn., Inc., 1978-80; chmn., CEO Shawmut Bank Boston, 1980-88; mem. bd. govs. FRS, Washington, 1988-95, ret., 1995; pres., dir. Devonshire Fin. Svc. Corp., 1978-88; chmn., treas. Boston Clearing House Assn., Inc.; Shawmut Corp. subs.; mem. Internat. Fin. Conf.; chmn. Mass. Bankers Assn., 1982-83, Assn. Bank Holding Cos., 1986-87; dir. Liberty Mutual Ins. Co., 1981, 88, mem. compensation com. Trustee, vice chmn., chmn. fin. com. Northeastern U., 1981-88; trustee, mem. fin. com. Mt. Holyoke Coll., 1984-88; chmn. Children's Hosp. Med. Ctr., 1989-91; past chmn., bd. dirs. Mass. Bus. Roundtable; chmn. coordinating com. Boston Bus. Leaders Orgn. 2d lt. USAF, 1951-53. Recipient Disting. Citizen award Minuteman Coun. Boy Scouts Am., Chief Exec. Officer of Yr. award Northeastern U. Coll. Bus., Outstanding Citizen award B'nai B'rith-Antidefamation League. Mem. Assn. Bank Holding Cos. (past chmn. and dir.). Office: PO Box 30083 Sea Island GA 31561

LAWATSCH, FRANK EMIL, JR., lawyer; b. Avenel, N.J., May 11, 1944; s. Frank Emil and Jessie Margaret L.; m. Deanna Conover, May 25, 1969; children: Amanda, Abigail, Frank. BA, Colgate U., 1966; JD, Cornell U., 1969. Bar: N.Y. 1969, Pa. 1992, N.J. 1993. Assoc. Shearman & Sterling, N.Y.C., 1969-78; sr. v.p., gen. counsel, sec. Midlantic Corp., Edison, N.J., 1978-91; sr. v.p., gen. counsel PNC Bank Corp., Pitts., 1991-92; ptnr. Crummy, Del Deo, Dolan, Griffinger & Vecchione, Newark, 1993—. Mem. ABA, N.J. Bar Assn., Pa. Bar Assn., Assn. of Bar of City of N.Y., Am. Soc. Corp. Secs. Episcopalian. Home: 11 The Fairway Montclair NJ 07043-2533 Office: Crummy Del Deo Dolan Griffinger & Vecchione One Riverfront Plz Newark NJ 07102

LAWES, PATRICIA JEAN, art educator; b. Mathis, Tex., June 28, 1940; d. Thomas Ethan and Alma Dena (Pape) Allen; m. Elmer Thomas Lawes, Apr. 9, 1960; children: Linda Lee, Tracy Dena. BA in Art Edn., U. Wyo., 1976; MA in Curriculum and Instruction, Leslie Coll., 1988. Cert. tchr., Wyo. Elem. art tchr. Laramie County Sch. Dist. # 1, Cheyenne, Wyo., 1977—, facilitator elem. art. and gifted edn., 1979-87; ret. Laramie County Sch. Dist. #1, 1994, storyteller, 1995; owner, sec. Dundele Ltd. Liability Co., Mesa, Ariz., 1994-95; artist in the sch. Mesa, Ariz., 1994-95; judge F.W. Warren AFB Artist Craftsman Show, Cheyenne, 1988-92; adjudicator for music festival for Assn. Christian Schs. Internat., Tempe, Ariz.; storyteller Laramie County Sch. Dist. 1, 1995-96; presenter in field; artist in the sch., Tempe; instr. Smith Driving Sys. Salt River Project, Phoenix, 1996—. Author, mem. visual arts task force various curricula; Author, dir: The Apron Caper, 1989 (recognition 1990), Oh Where Oh Where Have Those Little Dawgs Gone, 1989 (recognition 1990); exhibitions include Wyoming Artists Assn., Wyo., 1977, Washington Congressional Exhibit, 1977-78. Mem. state bd. dirs. Very Spl. Arts Wyo., 1995—. Recipient Cert. of Appreciation Mayor Erickson, Cheyenne, 1986, MWR Vol. Recognition F.E. Warren Moral, Welfare, Recreation Dept., Cheyenne, 1988-93; grantee Coun. on Arts, Cheyenne, 1987-91. Mem. NEA, Am. Fedn. Tchrs., Nat. art Edn. Assn., Wyo. Assn. Gifted Edn. (bd. dirs., W.E. rep. 1986—, presenter, chmn. state ass. award 1992—), Wyo. Arts Alliance for Edn. (presenter, bd. dirs. 1987—, sec. 1988-91, visual arts task force, chmn. state arts award 1990-92), Wyo. Coun. Arts (slide bank 1986—), Wyo. Odessey of Mind (bd. dirs. 1991-92), Wyo. Women's Fedn. Club (chmn. state safety 1972-75), Order of Eastern Star (presiding officer, worthy matron 1984-85, grand officer 1990-91), Daughters of Nile, Assn. of Christian Schs. Internat. Music Festival (adjudicator 1995). Avocation: art, hiking, traveling, photography, storytelling. Address: 12231 S 44th St Phoenix AZ 85044-2403

LAWHON, JOHN E., III, lawyer, former county official; b. Denton, Tex., Dec. 14, 1934; s. John E. and Gladys (Barns) L.; m. Tommie Collins, Aug. 27, 1967; 1 son, David Collins. Student, U. N.Tex., 1951-53; BBA, U. Houston, 1958, JD, 1958. Bar: Tex. 1958; cert. specialist in estate and probate law, criminal law, family law. Asst. dist. and county atty. Denton County, Tex., 1958-61; dist. and county atty., 1961-77; dir. Southridge, Inc., Denton, 1962-72, Lawyers Title Agy. Denton, 1965-74; Legal adviser Denton City-County Day Nursery, 1972-80; tchr. bus. law U. North Tex. (formerly North Tex. State U.), Denton, 1969-71; mem. adv. bd. Tex. Criminal Justice Council, 1973-79; univ. atty. Tex. Woman's U., 1977-83, gen. counsel, 1983—, sec. bd. regents, 1987—. Bd. dirs. Denton County Welfare Coun., 1970-78, Denton Community Coun., 1978-79, 80-82; mem. Denton Forum; chmn. Denton County ARC, 1985-87, Denton County Probation Adv. Bd., 1985-92; mem. City of Denton Land Use Com., 1986-88. Mem. Tex. Bar Assn., Denton Bar Assn. (pres. 1968-69, bd. dirs. 1978-81), Tex. Dist. and County Attys. Assn. (bd. dirs. 1964-66), Denton Jaycees (sec. 1961), Denton C. of C., Tex. Assn. State Univ. Attys. (pres. 1983-84, Denton County crim. justice task force 1992-93, state bar coll. fellow 1995—). Baptist (deacon 1968—). Lodges: KP, Kiwanis (bd. dirs. 1981-86, pres. 1984-85). Home: 2810 Carmel St Denton TX 76205-8310 Office: Tex Woman's U Adminstrn Tower Bldg PO Box 23025 Denton TX 76204-1025

LAWHON, SUSAN HARVIN, lawyer; b. Houston, Oct. 10, 1947; d. William Charles and Ruth Helen (Beck) Harvin; m. Robert Ashton, July 25, 1970 (dec. Dec. 1992); children: Bryan Ashton, Harvin Griffith. AB, Smith Coll., Northampton, Mass., 1970; MEd, U. Tex., 1973; JD, U. Houston, 1990. Bar: Tex. 1990, U.S. Dist. Ct. (so. dist.) Tex. 1991, U.S. Ct. Appeals (5th cir.) 1993. Tchr. Nat. Cathedral Sch., Washington, 1970-71, Austin (Tex.) Ind. Sch. Dist., 1973-74, Spring Branch Ind. Sch. Dist., Houston, 1974-76; assoc. Fulbright & Jaworski, LLP, Houston, 1990—. Editor-in-chief: Houston Jour. Internat. Law, 1989-90. Mem. devel. coun. Tex. Children's Hosp., Houston, 1986—; mem. devel. bd. U. Tex. Health Sci. Ctr., Houston, 1984-87; sponsor Children's Fund, Inc., Houston, 1979-87; bd. dirs. Houston Child Guidance Ctr., 1977-80; bd. dirs., treas., fin. v.p. Jr. League Houston, 1984-86; docent Bayou Bend, 1977-84. Mem. ABA, State Bar Tex., Houston Bar Assn., Houston Country Club, Smith Coll. Club (Houston) (Seven Coll fund rep. 1982-87). Episcopalian. Home: 6222 Holly Springs Dr Houston TX 77057-1137 Office: Fulbright & Jaworski LLP 1301 McKinney St Ste 5100 Houston TX 77010-3095

LAWHON, TOMMIE COLLINS MONTGOMERY, child development/family living educator; b. Shelby County, Tex., Mar. 15; d. Marland Walker and Lillian (Tinsley) Collins; m. David Baldwin Montgomery, Mar. 31, 1962 (dec. Aug. 1964); m. John Lawhon, Aug. 27, 1967; 1 child, David Collins. B.S., Baylor U., 1954; M in Home Econs. Edn. in Home Econs., Tex. Woman's U., 1964, Ph.D., 1966. Cert. tchr., Tex., home economist, family life educator. Tchr., Victoria Pub. Schs. (Tex.), 1954-55; stewardess, supr. Am. Airlines, Dallas/Fort Worth, 1955-62; prof. home econs. Ea. Ky. U., Richmond, 1966-67, U. North Tex., Denton, 1968—; profl. presenter Profl. Devel. Inst., U. North Tex., 1981-84, mem. faculty senate 1984-90, chmn. com. on coms., 1987-88, com. status of women, 1984-87, mem. faculty salary study com., 1989-95, chmn., 1989-91, mem. tradition com., 1989-95, recorder, 1989-91; bd. dirs. Univ. union, 1985-88, mem. Status of Women Com., 1984-87, mem. Com. on Coms., 1986-89, chmn. 1987-88, vice chmn., 1988-89, mem. student mentor com., 1990-96, mem. benefits com., 1994—, vice chair, 1994-95, mem. faculty senate, 1996—. Co-author: Children are Artists, 1971; Hidden Hazards for Children and Families, 1982; editor: What to do with Children, 1974; Field Trips for Children, 1984; contbr. articles to profl. jours. Chmn., United Way North Tex. State U., 1980-81; chmn. crusade Am. Cancer Soc., Denton County, 1982-83; chmn. nominating com. First Bapt. Ch., Denton, 1983-84, 84-85; advisor North Tex. Student Coun. on Family Rels., 1994—. Recipient Presdl. award Tex. Council on Family Rels., 1979, Fessor Graham award North Tex. State U., 1980, Svc. award Am. Cancer Soc., 1983, Outstanding Home Economists Alumni award Baylor U., 1985, Moore-Bowman award, 1994; named Honor Prof. North Tex. State U., 1975. Mem. Tex. Council on Family Rels. (pres. 1977-79, chmn. policy advisor com. 1986-88, nominating com. 1986-88, 94-96, chair 1994-96, mem. family life edn. com. 1994—), Denton Assn. for Edn. of Young Children (pres. 1970-72, 84-85, 85-86, v.p. 1986-87), Tex. Assn. Coll. Tchrs. (nominating com. 1988-89, 89-90, v.p. 1990-92, v.p. U. North Tex. chpt. 1987-88, pres. 1988-89, 89-90), Tex. Home Econs. Assn. (chmn. FLCD nominating com. 1983-84, chmn. child devel. and family rels. sect. 1988-90, sect. rep. THEA bd. 1989-90), Nat. Council on Family Rels. (com. 1982-83, cert. family life edn. com. 1996—), Nat. Assn. Early Childhood Tchr. Educators (mem. membership com. 1995—), North Tex. Home Econs. Interorgnl. Council (adviser 1983-85), Phi Delta Kappa (pres. local chpt. 1991-92), Alpha Iota/Phi Upsilon Omicron (advisor 1970-82, chmn. nat. com. 1984-87, nat. bd. dirs. edn. found. 1990-94, com. pubs. 1991-92, vice chair edn. found. 1992-94). Democrat. Clubs: Tri D (v.p. Baylor U. 1953-54); Univ. Grad. (pres. Tex. Woman's U. 1965-66). Office: U North Tex Coll Edn Denton TX 76203

LAWHON, WILLIAM M., accounting firm executive; b. 1947. Grad., So. Meth. U., 1969. Mng. ptnr. Weaver & Tidwell Accts., Ft. Worth, 1979—. Office: Weaver & Tidwell Accts 307 W 7th St Fort Worth TX 76102

LAWI, DAVID STEVEN, energy, agriservice and thermoplastic resins industries executive; b. Baghdad, Iraq, Aug. 3, 1935; came to U.S., 1946, naturalized, 1952; s. Steven David and Marcelle (Masry) L.; m. Anne Shamash, June 9, 1968; children—Nicole, Neil. A.A. in Sci, N.Y. State Coll., 1955. Registered rep. Bear, Stearns & Co., N.Y.C., 1956-62; dir. Adobe Brick & Supply, West Palm Beach, Fla., 1962-64; v.p. Molly Corp., Reading, Pa., 1962-64; gen. mgr. United Shoe Machinery Corp., Reading, 1964-65; a founder, sec., treas., mem. exec. com., dir. Unimax Group Inc. (formerly Riker-Maxson Corp), N.Y.C., 1966-80; also dir. all subs., v.p., treas. Telepictures Corp., N.Y.C., 1980-81, chmn. fin. com., sec., 1980-86; exec. v.p., sec. Helm Resources, Inc., Greenwich, Conn., 1980—, also bd. dirs.; bd. dirs., sec. Teletrak Advanced Tech. Sys., Inc., 1983—, Continuing Care Assocs., 1982—; sec. bd. dirs., chmn. exec. com. Seitel Inc. (formerly Seismic Enterprises, Inc.), 1982-84, now bd. dirs.; advisor Lorimar-Telepictures (acquired by Warner Comm., Inc. 1989), 1986, now Time-Warner, 1990—; bd. dirs., chmn. exec. com. Intersys., Inc. (formerly Bamberger Polymers, Inc.), Unipix Entertainment, Inc. (formerly Majestic Entertainment, Inc.); chmn. exec. com., bd. dirs. Cliff Engle Ltd. Served with AUS, 1968. Home: Ramapo Trail Harrison NY 10528 Office: Helm Resources Inc 537 Steamboat Rd Greenwich CT 06830-5502

LAWING, JACK L., lawyer, corporate executive; b. 1938. A.B., U. N.C., 1960; J.D., Harvard U., 1964. Assoc., Berry & Blesoe, 1964-67; atty. Reynolds Metal Co., 1967-69; div. counsel Litton Industries, Inc., 1969-71; atty. Tenn. Eastman Co. div. Eastman Kodak Co., 1971-76; gen counsel, v.p., sec. Gold Kist Inc., Atlanta, 1976—. Office: Gold Kist Inc 244 Perimeter Center Pky NE Atlanta GA 30346-2302

LAWIT, JOHN WALTER, lawyer; b. Phila., Aug. 13, 1950; s. Alfred and Marilyn Jane (Balis) L.; m. Susan Stein, July 15, 1984; children: Andrew Alejandro, Samuel Martin, Ivan Luis (twins). Student, U. Bridgeport, 1968-70; B of Univ. Studies, U. N.Mex., 1972; JD, Franklin Pierce Law Ctr., Concord, N.H., 1977. Bar: Pa. 1978, N.Mex. 1980, Tex. 1992, U.S. Dist. Ct. (ea. dist.) Pa. 1978, U.S. Dist. Ct. N.Mex. 1980. Investigator Franklin Pierce Law Ctr., 1976-77; social researcher Commun. Svc. Coun., Concord, 1977-78; sole practitioner N.Y.C., 1978-79; atty., assoc. McCallister, Fairfield, Query, Strotz & Stribling, Albuquerque, 1979-80; sole practitioner Albuquerque, 1980—; adj. prof. immigration law U. N.Mex. Sch. Law, 1983, 84, 88; spl. immigration counsel U. N.Mex., Albuquerque, 1987—; U.S. immigration judge US. Dept. Justice, 1985; apptd. mem. N.Mex. Internat. Trade/Investment Coun., 1984-87, N.Mex. Border Commn., 1982-86; hon. cons. atty. Ministry Fgn. Affairs Republic of Mex., 1983; lobbyist, author, drafter N.Mex. Immigration & Nationality Law Practice Act. Presenter in field. Founder, profl. cons. Jewish Family Svcs. of Albuquerque, 1988—; bd. dirs., pres. Rainbow House Internat. Adoption, Belen, N.Mex., 1987—; v.p. N.Mex. Refugee Assn., Albuquerque, 1979-84; bd. dirs. N.Mex. Civil Liberties Union, 1988-90; mem. adv. bd. Healing the Children, Albuquerque, 1989—; bd. dirs. Inst. for Spanish Arts, 1994—. Recipient Disting. Svcs. award Cath. Social Svcs., 1988. Mem. N.Mex. State Bar (chair internat. and immigration lawyers sect. 1990-91, bd. dirs. 1988-90), Albuquerque Bar Assn., Am. Immigration Lawyers Assn. (nat. chair 1988-89), El Paso Assn. Immigration and Nationality Lawyers. Avocations: family activities, whitewater rafting, hiking, cross-country skiing. Office: 900 Gold Ave SW Albuquerque NM 87102-3043 also: 869 Agua Fria Santa Fe NM 87501-2010

LAWLER, JAMES EDWARD, physics educator; b. St. Louis, June 29, 1951; s. James Austin and Dolores Catherine Lawler; m. Katherine Ann Moffatt, July 21, 1973; children: Emily Christine, Katie Marie. BS in Physics summa cum laude, U. Mo., Rolla, 1973; MS in Physics, U. Wis., 1974, PhD in Physics, 1978. Rsch. assoc. Stanford (Calif.) U., 1978-80; asst. prof. U. Wis., Madison, 1980-85, assoc. prof., 1985-89, prof., 1989—; product devel. cons. Nat. Rsch. Group, Inc., Madison, 1977-78; cons. GE, Schenectady, N.Y., 1985—, Teltech, Inc., 1990—; exec. com. Gaseous Electronics Conf., 1987-89, treas., 1992-94, DAMOP program com., 1993-95. Editor: (with R.S. Stewart) Optogalvanic Spectroscopy, 1991; contbr. articles to profl. jours. Recipient Penning award Internat. Conf. on Phenomena in Ionized Gases, 1995; Schumberger scholar U. Mo., 1971-72; grad. fellow U. Wis. Alumni Rsch. Found., 1973-74, NSF, 1974-76, H.I. Romnes faculty fellow U. Wis., 1987. Fellow Am. Phys. Soc. (Will Allis prize 1992), Optical Soc. Am.; mem. Sigma Xi. Achievements include patent for Echelle Sine Bar for dye laser cavity; development of laser diagnostics for glow discharge plasmas, of methods for measuring accurate atomic transition probabilities and radiative lifetimes. Office: U Wis Dept Physics 1150 University Ave Madison WI 53706-1302

LAWLER, JAMES RONALD, French language educator; b. Melbourne, Australia, Aug. 15, 1929; married, 1954; 2 children. BA, U. Melbourne, 1950, MA, 1952; DUniv., U. Paris, 1954. Lectr. French U. Queensland, Australia, 1955-56; sr. lectr. U. Melbourne, 1957-62; prof., head dept. U. Western Australia, 1963-71; prof., chmn. dept. UCLA, 1971-74; McCulloch prof. Dalhousie U., Halifax, N.S., Can., 1974-79; prof. French U. Chgo., 1979—, Edward Carson Waller Disting. Svc. prof., 1983—; vis. prof. Coll. de France, 1985; chmn. vis. com. Romance Langs. and Lits. Harvard U., 1991-94. Author: Form and Meaning in Valery's Le Cimetiere Marin, 1959, Lecture de Valery: Une Etude de Charmes, 1963, The Language of French Symbolism, 1969, The Poet as Analyst, 1974, Rene Char: The Myth and the Poem, 1978, Edgar Poe et les Poetes Francais, 1989, Rimbaud's Theatre of the Self, 1992, Baudelaire's Moral Dialectic, 1996; co-author: Paul Valery; Poems, 1971, Paul Valery: Leonardo, Poe, Mallarme, 1972; editor: An Anthology of French Poetry, 1960, Paul Valery: An Anthology, 1977, Paul Valery, 1991; founding editor Essays in French Literature, 1966, Dalhousie French Studies. Decorated officier Palmes Academiques; Brit. Coun. interchange scholar, 1967; Australian Acad. Humanities fellow, 1970, Guggenheim Found. fellow, 1974, NEH fellow, 1985. Mem. MLA, Am. Assn. Tchrs. French, Internat. Assn. French Studies (v.p. 1974—). Rsch. in modern French poetry, poetics, 20th century novel. Office: U Chgo Dept Romance Langs & Lit 1050 E 59th St Chicago IL 60637-1512

LAWLER, RICHARD FRANCIS, lawyer; b. Providence, Mar. 24, 1945; s. Richard F. and Priscilla (Lenihan) L.; m. Jacqueline Marie Depuy, Oct. 2, 1976; children: James, Christopher. BA, Yale U., 1967; JD, Columbia U., 1973. Bar: Conn. 1974, N.Y. 1980. Assoc. atty. Wiggin & Dana, New Haven, 1973-76; asst. U.S. atty. U.S. Atty's. Office So. Dist. N.Y., N.Y.C., 1976-80; ptnr. Whitman Breed Abbott & Morgan, N.Y.C., Greenwich, Conn., 1980—. Lt. (j.g.) USN, 1969-70. Fulbright scholar Colombia, S.Am., 1967-68. Mem. Field Club Greenwich (bd. govs. 1993—). Office: Whitman Breed Abbott Morgan 100 Field Point Rd Greenwich CT 06830-6353 Also: 200 Park Ave New York NY 10166

LAWLER, RONALD DAVID, academic administrator; b. Cumberland, Md., July 29, 1926; s. Leo Thomas and Lillian Marie (Laing) Lawler. BA, St. Fidelis Coll.; MA in Philosophy, St. Louis U., 1957, PhD, 1959; postgrad., Oxford U., 1969-70. Instr. St. Fidelis Coll., Herman, Pa., 1958-59, 60-69, Capuchin Coll., Washington, 1959-60, Cath. U. Am., Washington, 1960-64, Oxford U., 1972-73, Pontifical Coll., 1975-77, U. St. Thomas, Houston, 1980-82, St. John's U., N.Y.C., 1982-88; instr. Holy Apostles Coll. and Sem., Cromwell, Conn., 1988-90, 93-95, pres., rector, 1993—; dean studies St. Fidelis Coll. and Sem., 1961-64, pres., 1964-69; dean. sch. theology Pintifical Coll. Josephinum, 1975-77; dir. ctr. Thomistic studies U. St. Thomas, 1980-82, Inst. Advanced Studies Cath. Doctrine, St. John's U., 1982-88; dir. edn. Pope John Ctr. Biol. Rsch., Braintree, Mass., 1991-93; lectr. in field. Author: Philosophical Analysis and Ethics, 1968, The Christian Personalism of John Paul II, 1981; co-author: Catholic Sexual Ethics, 1985, The Catholic Catechism, 1986; co-author and editor: Philosophy in Priestly Formation, 1978; co-author and co-editor: The Teaching of Christ, 1976, 2d edit., 1983; co-editor: Excellence in Seminary Education, 1988; contbr. articles to profl. publs. Office: Holy Apostles Coll and Sem Cromwell CT 06416

LAWLER, SUSAN GEORGE, elementary education educator; b. Evergreen Park, Ill., Jan. 20, 1940; d. Louis Lawrence and Elsie Marie (Velk) George; m. Jerome Charles Lawler, Feb. 23, 1963; children: Susan Elizabeth, Kathleen Marie. BS in Edn., Mt. Mary Coll., 1961; MEd, Nat. Louis U., Evanston, Ill., 1991. Tchr. Oak Lawn (Ill.) Sch. Dist. 123, 1961-65, Palos Community Sch. Dist. 118, Palos Park, Ill., 1975—; pres. Parent-Faculty Orgn. Sch. Dist. 230, Orland Park, Ill., 1982-85. Sec. Ishnala Homeowners Assn., Palos Heights, Ill., 1972-75; active Neighborhood Watch, City of Palos Heights, 1988—. Mem. AAUW (chair hist. 1975-77), Internat. Reading Assn., Nat. Coun. Tchrs. English, Ill. Reading Assn., Palas Edn. Assn. (pres. 1992—), Mt. Mary Coll. Alumni Assn. (co-chair Chgo. chpt. 1992—), Phi Delta Kappa. Avocations: reading, bridge, taking classes, golf, walking. Home: 12932 S Comanche Dr Palos Heights IL 60463-2618 Office: Palos Community Sch Dist 118 8800 W 119th St Palos Park IL 60464-1004

LAWLESS, JAMES L., editor, columnist; b. Des Moines, Mar. 26, 1932; s. James L. and Mary O. (Gray) L.; m. Mary Belle McPherson; children: Kathleen, Maureen, Michael, Martha, Kerry, Dan. BA, Drake U., 1954. Editor, columist Des Moines Register, Des Moines, 1956—; columnist Gannett News Svc. Alexandria, Va., 1986—. Chmn. Clive (Iowa) Planning & Zoning, 1970-80; mem. bd. adjustment, Clive, 1980-90. Lt. (j.g.) USNR, 1954-56. Nat. Press Found. fellow, 1986. Republican. Roman Catholic. Avocations: tennis, travel, swimming. Home: 6137 Pleasant Dr Des Moines IA 50312-1217 Office: The Des Moines Register 715 Locust St Des Moines IA 50309-3724

LAWLESS, ROBERT WILLIAM, academic administrator; b. Baytown, Tex., Feb. 13, 1937; s. James Milton and Belva Ambaline (Mode) L.; m. Marcella Jane Emmert; children: Christopher, Cheryl, Diana. B.S., U. Houston, 1964; Ph.D., Tex. A&M U., 1968. Instr., asst. prof. Tex. A&M U., College Station, 1967-69; prof., sr. vice chancellor U. Houston, 1969-82; v.p., chief fin. officer S.W. Airlines, Dallas, 1982-85, exec. v.p., chief oper. officer, 1985-89; cons. Tex. Hosp. Assn., Austin, 1966-82, banks, savs. and loans, 1970-72, NASA, 1970; pres. Tex. Tech U. and Tex. Tech U. Health Scis. Ctr., Lubbock, 1989—; ind. dir. Salomon Bros. Asset Mgmt. Co., 1991—, Cen. and S.W. Corp., 1991—; chmn. Coun. of Pub. Univ. Pres. and Chancellors, Tex. higher edn. sys., 1993-95, mem. NCAA Pres.'s Commn., 1994—. Contbr. articles to profl. jours. Mem. formula adv. com. Tex. State Coordinating Bd., Austin, 1977-89; chmn. bd. dirs. Coll. Football Assn., 1990-92; mem. Citizens Commn. on the Tex. Jud. System, 1991-93. Recipient Teaching Excellence award U. Houston, 1972, Disting. Faculty award Coll. Bus. Alumni, 1971, Disting. Alumni award Lee Coll., 1984, U. Houston, 1990. Office: Tex Tech U Office of President Lubbock TX 79409-2013

LAWLESS, RONALD EDWARD, retired transportation executive; b. Toronto, Apr. 28, 1924. Student, McGill U., Montreal, U. Toronto, Concordia U. Mem. express dept. CN Rail, Toronto, 1941-43, numerous positions, 1946-61, officer employee relations, 1961-62, gen. supt.-express Great Lakes region, 1962-69; system mgr. container devel. CN Rail, Montreal, Que., 1969-70; gen. mgr. express and intermodal systems CN Rail, Montreal,

Que., 1970-72, v.p. freight sales, 1972-74, v.p. mktg., 1974-79, pres., 1979-85, pres., chief operating officer, 1987; pres., chief oper. officer Can. Nat. Railways, Montreal, Que., 1985-87, pres., chief exec. officer, 1987—, also bd. dirs.; pres., chief exec. officer VIA Rail Can. Inc., Montreal, Que., 1989—, also bd. dirs.;, 1987-93; chmn., pres., chief exec. officer Grand Trunk Corp., Grand Trunk Western R.R. Co., Cen. Vt. Ry. Inc., Duluth, Winnipeg & Pacific R.R. Co.; Concordia Bd. Govs. (1987-90), Dome Consortium Investments Inc., Ry. Assn. of Can. (chmn.), Can. Transp. Edn. Found. Bursary Bd., U. Manitoba Adv. Com., Old Brewery Mission, Montreal Bd. Trade Heritage Found., Bishop's U.; bd. dirs. Assn. Am. Rys. Campaign chmn. Lakeshore Gen. Hosp. Bldg. Fund., Centraide, 1992—; co-chmn., hon. v.p. Scouts Can. With RCAF, 1943-46. Decorated Knight Order of St. John; named Can.'s Transp. Man of Yr., 1986; recipient Achievement award Nat. Transp. Week Can. (Quebec chapt.), 1990. Fellow Chartered Inst. Transport; mem. Can. Inst. Traffic and Transp. (hon.), Nat. Freight Transp. Assn., N.Y. Traffic Club, Toronto Ry. Club, Transp. Club Toronto, Montreal Bd. Trade, Can. Ry. Club, Traffic Club Montreal, Can. Club N.Y., Can. Club of Montreal, McGill Assocs., Beaconsfield Golf Club, Mount Royal Club, St. James Club, The Vancouver Club, Corp. Adv. Com. Wanuskewin Heritage Pk. Avocations: golf, reading. Home: 935 Lagauchetiere St W, Montreal, PQ Canada H3B 2M9

LAWLEY, ALAN, materials engineering educator; b. Birmingham, Eng., Aug. 29, 1933; s. Archibald and Millicent A. (Olorenshaw) L.; m. Nancy A. Kressler, Mar. 26, 1960; children—Carolyn Ann, Elizabeth Ann, Jennifer Ann. B.Sc., U. Birmingham, 1955, Ph.D., 1958. Research asso. U. Pa., 1958-61; mgr. research labs. Franklin Inst. Labs., 1961-66; A.W. Grosvenor prof. materials engring. Drexel U., Phila., 1969—; head dept. Drexel U., 1969-79, 94—; cons. to govt., industry. Editor in chief Internat. Jour. Powder Metallurgy; contbr. chpts. to books, articles to profl. jours. Recipient Disting. Svc. award Metal Powder Industries Fedn., 1991. Fellow Am. Soc. Metals; mem. AIME (pres. 1987), Minerals, Metals and Materials Soc. (pres. 1982), Am. Soc. Engring. Edn., Inst. Materials, Microscopy Soc. Am., APMI Internat., Sigma Xi, Phi Kappa Phi, Tau Beta Pi, Alpha Sigma Mu. Home: 336 Hathaway Ln Wynnewood PA 19096-1925 Office: Drexel Univ Dept Materials Engring Philadelphia PA 19104

LAWNICZAK, JAMES MICHAEL, lawyer; b. Toledo, Sept. 11, 1951; m. Christine Nielsen, Dec. 31, 1979; children: Mara Katharine, Rachel Anne, Amy Elizabeth. BA, U. Mich., 1974, JD, 1977. Bar: Mich. 1977, Ill. 1979, Ohio 1989. Law clk. to the Honorable Robert E. DeMascio U.S. Dist. Ct. (ea. dist.) Mich., Detroit, 1977-79; assoc. Levy and Erens, Chgo., 1979-83; assoc. then ptnr. Mayer, Brown & Platt, Chgo., 1983-88; ptnr. Calfee, Halter & Griswold, Cleve., 1988—. Mem. Chgo. Bar Assn. (subcom. on bankruptcy 1983-88), Cleve. Bar Assn. (bankruptcy com.). Home: 14039 Fox Hollow Dr Novelty OH 44072-9773 Office: Calfee Halter & Griswold 800 Superior Ave E Ste 1400 Cleveland OH 44114-2601

LAWRANCE, CHARLES HOLWAY, civil and sanitary engineer; b. Augusta, Maine, Dec. 25, 1920; s. Charles William and Lois Lyford (Holway) L.; m. Mary Jane Hungerford, Nov. 22, 1947; children: Kenneth A., Lois R., Robert J. BS in Pub. Health Engring., MIT, 1942; MPH, Yale U., 1952. Registered profl. engr., Calif. Sr. san. engr. Conn. State Dept. Health, Hartford, 1946-53; assoc. san. engr. Calif. Dept. Pub. Health, L.A., 1953-55; chief san. engr. Koebig & Koebig, Inc., Cons. Engrs., L.A., 1955-75; engr., mgr. Santa Barbara County Water Agy., Santa Barbara, Calif., 1975-79; prin. engr. James M. Montgomery Cons. Engrs., Pasadena, Calif., 1979-83; v.p. Lawrance, Fisk & McFarland, Inc., Santa Barbara, 1983-96; cons. engr., Santa Barbara, 1996—. Author: The Death of the Dam, 1972; co-author: Ocean Outfall Design, 1958; contbr. articles to profl. jours. Bd. dirs. Pacific Unitarian Ch., Palos Verdes Peninsula, Calif., 1956-60, chmn. bd. 1st lt. USMCR, 1942-46, PTO. Fellow ASCE (life, Norman medal 1966); mem. Am. Water Works Assn. (life), Am. Acad. Environ. Engrs. (life diplomate), Water Environment Fedn. (life). Republican. Unitarian. Home and Office: 1340 Kenwood Rd Santa Barbara CA 93109

LAWRENCE, ALBERT WEAVER, insurance company executive; b. Newburgh, N.Y., Aug. 4, 1928; s. Claude D. and Janet (Weaver) L.; m. Barbara Corell, June 28, 1950; children: David, Janet, Elizabeth. BSAE in Engring., Cornell U., 1950; grad. advanced mgmt. program, Rensselaer Poly. Inst., 1975. Ins. agt., exec., 1953—; founder, chmn. A.W. Lawrence and Co. Inc., Schenectady and Albany, N.Y., 1954-82; chmn. bd. dirs. Lawrence Agy. Corp., Albany, 1982—, Lawrence Ins. Group Inc., Albany, 1986—, Lawrence Group Inc., Schenectady, 1986—; mem. Cornell Engring. Adv. Coun.; bd. dirs. Capital Dist. Ctr. for Econ. Devel., Schenectady Indsl. Devel. Corp., Mech. Tech., Inc., Latham, N.Y. Trustee Russell Sage Coll., Troy, N.Y., Rensselaer Poly. Inst., Sunnyview Hosp. and Rehab. Ctr.; past pres. Schenectady Girls Club, Family and Child Svc. Schenectady; bd. dirs. Ind. Living for Physically Disabled, St. Clare's Hosp., Proctor's Theatre, N.Y. State Olympic Regional Devel. Authority, 1989; co-founder Lawrence Inst. for Physically Disabled Rsch.; past chmn. Schenectady United Fund Drive, Jr. Achievement Capital Dist. With U.S. Army, 1946-47. Recipient Sca-Nec-Ta-De Civic award, 1967. Mem. Schenectady C. of C. (past pres.), Schenectady Hist. Soc. (past bd. dirs.), Mohawk Golf Club, Cornell Club (N.Y.C.), N.Y. Athletic Club, N.Y. Yacht Club, No. Lake George Yacht Club (past commodore), U. Club Albany, Ft. Orange Club Albany, Rotary Club (past pres.). Republican. Mem. First Dutch Reformed Ch. Home: 708 Riverview Rd Rexford NY 12148-1433 Office: Lawrence Group Inc 430 State St Schenectady NY 12305

LAWRENCE, ALICE LAUFFER, artist, educator; b. Cleve., Mar. 2, 1916; d. Erwin Otis and Florence Mary (Menough) Lauffer; m. Walter Ernest Lawrence, Sept. 27, 1941; 1 child, Phillip Lauffer. Diploma in art, Cleve. Inst. Art, 1938; BS in Art Edn., Case Western Res. U., 1938. Grad. asst. in art edn. Kent (Ohio) State U., 1939-40; art tchr. Akron (Ohio) and Cleve. Pub. Schs.; comml. artist B.F. Goodrich Co., Akron, 1942-44; sub. art tchr. Akron Pub. Schs.; sketch artist numerous events Akron, 1945-91. Author numerous poems. Mem. Cuyahoga Valley Art Ctr., Women's Art Mus., Akron Art Mus., 1963-94. Recipient 1st pl., 2d pl. in drawing, Butler Mus. Am. Arts, 1940-41, Cleve. Mus. Art, 1944. Mem. Woman's Art League Akron (sec. 1962), Ohio Watercolor Soc., Internat. Soc. Poets (life). Republican. Avocation: writing poetry. Home: 861 Clearview Ave Akron OH 44314-2969

LAWRENCE, BRYAN HUNT, investment banking executive; b. N.Y.C., July 26, 1942; s. Bryan and Suzanne (Walbridge) L.; m. Elizabeth D. Lawrence, Sept. 25, 1965; children: Bryan R., E. Corey. BA, Hamilton Coll., 1964; MBA, Columbia U., 1966. Assoc. Dillon, Read & Co. Inc., N.Y.C., 1966-70, v.p., 1971-74, sr. v.p., 1975-81, mng. dir., 1982—; bd. dirs. Vintage Petroleum, Tulsa, Meenan Oil, Inc., Syosset, N.Y., D & K Wholesale Drug, St. Louis, Transmontaigne Oil Co., Denver, Fintube, L.P., Tulsa, Willbros Group Inc., Panama, Interenergy Corp., Denver, Benson Petroleum, Calgary, Alta. Cavell Energy, Calgary, PetroSantander Inc., Houston, Hallador Petroleum, Denver, Strega Energy, Calgary. Trustee Hamilton Coll., Clinton, N.Y., 1991-94. Republican. Home: 116 E 63rd St New York NY 10021-7343 Office: Dillon Read & Co Inc 535 Madison Ave New York NY 10022-4212

LAWRENCE, CALEB JAMES, bishop; b. Lattie's Brook, N.S., Can., May 26, 1941; s. James Otis and Mildred Viola (Burton) L.; m. Maureen Patricia Cuddy, July 18, 1966; children: Fiona, Karen, Sean. B.A., Dalhousie U., Halifax, N.S., 1962; B.S.T., U. of King's Coll., Halifax, 1964, D.Div. (hon.), 1980. Ordained priest Anglican Ch. of Canada, 1965. Missionary priest St. Edmund's Anglican Parish, Gt. Whale River, Que., Can., 1965-74, rector, 1974-79; canon St. Jude's Cathedral, Frobisher Bay, N.W.T., Can., 1974-75; archdeacon of Arctic Que. Diocese of the Arctic, Toronto, Ont., Can., 1975-79; bishop Diocese of Moosonee, Schumacher, Ont., 1980—; mem. coun. of north Anglican Ch. Can., 1979—, mem. gen. synod, 1980—; mem. Anglican Coun. N.Am. and Caribbean, 1983-86. Translator liturgical services, hymns into Cree, 1970-80. Canon W.H. Morris travelling scholar U. of King's Coll., 1964. Home: PO Box 830, Schumacher, ON Canada P0N 1G0 Office: Anglican Ch of Can, Diocese of Moosonee, PO Box 841, Schumacher, ON Canada P0N 1GO

LAWRENCE, DAVID, JR., newspaper editor, publisher; b. N.Y.C., Mar. 5, 1942; s. David Sr. and Nancy Wemple (Bissell) L.; m. Roberta Phyllis Fleischman, Dec. 21, 1963; children: David III, Jennifer Beth, Amanda Katherine, John Benjamin, Dana Victoria. BS, U. Fla., 1963; postgrad. advanced mgmt. program, Harvard U., 1983; LHD (hon.), Siena Heights Coll., Adrian, Mich., 1985; HHD (hon.), Lawrence Inst. Tech., Detroit, 1986; LHD (hon.), No. Mich. U., 1987; LD (hon.), Barry U., 1991, Fla. Meml. U., 1992, Northwood U., 1993; U. Fla., 1993. Reporter, news editor St. Petersburg (Fla.) Times, 1963-67; news editor Style/Washington Post, 1967-69; mng. editor Palm Beach (Fla.) Post, 1969-71, Phila. Daily News, 1971-75; exec. editor Charlotte (N.C.) Observer, 1975-76, editor, 1976-78; exec. editor Detroit Free Press, 1978-85, pub., chmn., 1985-89; pub., chmn. The Miami Herald, 1989—. Bd. dirs. U. Fla. Found., PBS, Fla. Coun. of 100; chmn. United Way of Dade County; chmn. Ctr. for Fine Arts. Named Disting. Alumnus, U. Fla., 1982; recipient Nat. Human Rights award Am. Jewish Com., 1986, First Amendment Freedoms award Anti-Defamation League, 1988, Ida Wells Nat. award for advancement of minorities Nat. Assn. Black Journalists and Nat. Conf. of Edit. Writers, 1988, John S. Knight Gold medal Knight-Ridder, 1988, Silver Medallion award NCCJ, 1992, Disting. Svc. award Nat. Assn. Schs. Journalism and Mass Comm., 1992, Scripps Howard First Amendment award, 1993, Nat. Assn. of Minority Media Execs. lifetime achievement award. Mem. Am. Soc. Newspaper Editors (pres. 1991-92), Inter Am. Press Assn. (pres.). Office: The Miami Herald 1 Herald Plz Miami FL 33132-1609

LAWRENCE, DAVID M., health facility administrator; b. 1940. MD, U. Ky., 1966; MPH, U. Wash., 1973. Intern in internal medicine, pediat.; with Kaiser Found. Health Plan and Hosps., Oakland, Calif., 1981—, now chmn., CEO; various professorships, directorships and fellowships with U. Wash., Johns Hopkins U., U. Ky.; dir. Pacific Gas and Electric Co., Hewlett Packard, Healthcare Forum, Bay Area Coun., Calif. Coll. Arts and Crafts, Colby Coll. Mem. APHA, Am. Hosp. Assn., Am. Coll. Preventive Medicine, Calif. Assn. Hosps. and Healty Sys., Group Health Assn. Am., Western Consortium for Pub. Health, Calif. Bus. Roundtable, The Conf. Bd. (bd. dirs.), Inst. Medicine/NAS (bd. dirs.). Office: Kaiser Found Health Plan & Hosp 1 Kaiser Plz Oakland CA 94612-3610

LAWRENCE, DAVID MICHAEL, lawyer, educator; b. Portland, Oreg., Dec. 26, 1943; s. Robert A. and Maude (Davis) L.; m. Alice Oviatt, June 18, 1966. A.B., Princeton U., 1965; J.D., Harvard U., 1968. Asst. prof. Inst. Govt., U. N.C., Chapel Hill, 1968-71, assoc. prof., 1971-76, prof. pub. law and govt., 1976-94; Kenan prof. pub. law and govt. U. N.C., Chapel Hill, 1994—; counsel N.C. Local Govt. Study Commn., 1972-73, N.C. Open Meetings Study Commn., 1978-79. Author: Local Government Finance in North Carolina, 2d edit., 1991 (award for excellence Rsch. and Publs. Govt. Fin. Officers Assn. U.S. and Can. 1991); contbr. law articles to profl. jours. Chmn. Durham (N.C.) Hist. Dist. Commn., 1985-89. Recipient Herald prize Princeton U., 1965. Mem. N.C. State Bar, Campus Princeton U. Club. Democrat. Office: University of NC Knapp Bldg Clb # 3330 Chapel Hill NC 27599

LAWRENCE, DOUGLASS RAY, radio station executive, state legislator; b. Gardner, Kans., Nov. 23, 1957; s. William R. and Phyllis A. (Douglass) L.; m. Marla A. Riebel, June 10, 1982; children: Will, Lacy, Andrew. Student, Kans. State U., 1975-79. Program dir. Stas. KIKS and KIOL, Iola, Kans., 1980-81; news dir. Sta. KMAN, Manhattan, Kans., 1981-86; ins. agt. Kans. Farm Bur., Burlington, 1986-88; owner, mgr. Computer Ctr., Burlington, 1988-90; gen. mgr. Sta. KSNP-FM, Burlington, 1990—; mem. Kans. Ho. of Reps., Topeka, 1992—; owner Creative Computer Solutions, Burlington, 1993—; Pres. Coffey County Broadcasting, Burlington, 1988—. Mem. Coffey County Coun. for Arts, 1992. Mem. Nat. Assn. Broadcasters, Kans. Assn. Broadcasters, Coffey County C. of C. (bd. dirs. 1991), Optimists (v.p. Burlington 1991). Republican. Baptist. Home: 902 Miami St Burlington KS 66839-1526 Office: Sta KSNP-FM 210 Osage New Strawn St Strawn KS 66839-9114

LAWRENCE, EVELYN THOMPSON, retired music educator, researcher; b. Marion, Va., Nov. 13, 1919; d. John Emmett and Susie Barnett (Madison) Thompson; m. Joseph John Lawrence, Oct. 5, 1946; 1 child, Sheila Ann (dec.). BS in Edn., W. Va. State Coll., 1941; student, Va. State U., 1946, Hampton U., 1948; M of Music, U. Mich., 1952. Elem. sch. tchr., music tchr. Carnegie High Sch., Marion, Va., 1941-65; tchr. Marion Primary Sch., 1965-84; judge art, storytelling, and creative writing Smyth County Schs., Marion, Chilhowie, Va., 1984-96; rocking reader Smyth County Schs., Marion, 1994—; producer, dir. plays Supporters Enriched Edn. and Knowledge, Marion, 1983-92; music and recreation dir. Douglass Ctr., Toledo, Ohio, summer, 1953; instr. ch. music Va. Union U., Richmond, summer 1960, 61; judge Sherwood Anderson Lit. Contest, 1989-91. Author: Directoty of African-American Students and Teachers in all Smyth County Schools, 1906-1965. Organist and choir dir. Mt. Pleasant Meth. Ch., Marion, 1994—; bd. dirs. Blue Ridge Job Corps., Marion, 1994—; v.p., past pres. Church Women United, Marion, 1985-86. Recipient 2 nominations Tchr. of Yr. award, S.W. Va. Coun. of Internat. Reading Assn., Abingdon, Va., 1981, 82, Svc. to Youth aard Carnegie Sch. Alumni, Marion, 1983, Citizen of Yr. award Marion Rotary Club, 1985. Mem. AAUW (chmn. cultural rels. com. 1966-96), Alpha Kappa Alpha (1940—), Alpha Delta Kappa (tchrs. sor. 1987—). Avocations: travel, children's activities, flower gardening, crossword puzzles. Home: 312 Broad St Marion VA 24354-2804

LAWRENCE, FRANCIS LEO, language educator, educational administrator; b. Woonsocket, R.I., Aug. 25, 1937. B.S., St. Louis U., 1959; Ph.D. in French and Italian, Tulane U., 1962. Mem. faculty Tulane U., New Orleans, 1962-90, chmn. dept. French and Italian, 1969-76, acting dean Newcomb Coll., 1976-78, dep. provost, 1978-81, acting provost, grad. dean, 1981-82, prof. French, from 1971, acad. v.p., provost, 1982-90; pres. Rutgers, New Brunswick, N.J., 1990—. Author numerous publs. on French 17th century lit. Contbr. articles, revs. and essays to profl. publs. Decorated chevalier, Palmes Academiques, 1977. Mem. Am. Assn. Tchrs. French, N.Am. Soc. 17th Century French Lit., MLA. Office: Rutgers U Office of Pres New Brunswick NJ 08903

LAWRENCE, GERALD, JR., lawyer; b. Phila., Jan. 10, 1968; s. Gerald and Rita Katherine (Duffy) L.; m. Andrea Stewart, Jan. 8, 1994. BSBA, Georgetown U., 1990; JD, Villanova U., 1993. Bar: Pa. 1993, U.S. Dist. Ct. Pa. 1994, U.S. Ct. Appeals (3d cir.) 1994. Clk. Commonwealth Ct. of Pa., Phila., 1992; assoc. Elliott Reihner Siedzikowski & Egan, Blue Bell, Harrisburg, Scranton, Pa. and Woodbury, N.J., 1992—; assoc. Elliott Reihner Siedzikowski North & Egan, Scranton, Pa., 1992—, Harrisburg, Pa., 1992—, Cherry Hill, N.J., 1992—; solicitor Del. County Dem. Party, 1996—. Interviewer Georgetown Alumni Admission Program, 1992—. Mem. ABA, ATLA, Pa. Bar Assn. (mem. judicial selection and adminstrn. com.), Phila. Bar Assn. Home: 349 Oak Terr Wayne PA 19087 Office: Elliot Reihner Siedzikowski North & Egan Union Meeting Corp Ctr IV 925 Harvest Dr Blue Bell PA 19422

LAWRENCE, GERALD GRAHAM, management consultant; b. U.K., June 21, 1947; came to U.S., 1962, naturalized, 1967; s. Raymond Joseph and Barbara Virginia Lawrence; 1 child, Ian Andrew; m. Julie Ann Quiram. BA in Math., Northeastern U., 1970, MA in Econs., 1973; MBA, U. Pa., 1975. Optics rsch. technologist Polaroid Corp., Cambridge, Mass., 1968-70; intern Corning Glass Works, Inc., N.Y.C., 1974; asst. brand mgr. Procter and Gamble, Cin., 1975-76; assoc. Theodore Barry & Assocs., N.Y.C., 1976-79; dir. performance improvement systems Stone & Webster Mgmt. Cons., N.Y.C., 1979-84; mgr. utility MAS Deloitte Haskins & Sells, N.Y.C., 1984-86; pres. PMC Mgmt. Cons., Inc., Three Bridges, N.J., 1986—; advisor Commerce & Econ. Devel. Dept. State of N.J.; speaker in field. Designer: auditor system nuclear power plant constrn; innovator; quality assurance for profl. cons. svcs; contbr. articles to profl. jours. Econs. fellow Northeastern U., 1973, adminstrv. fellow Wharton Sch. U. Pa., 1975. Home: 11 Thistle Ln Flemington NJ 08822-7067 Office: PMC Mgmt Cons PO Box 332 Three Bridges NJ 08887-0332

LAWRENCE, GLENN ROBERT, arbitrator; b. N.Y.C., Nov. 8, 1930; m. Nina M. Scaturro; children: David P., Eric A. JD, Bklyn. Law Sch., 1954; BA, U. Louisville, 1968; MD, Cath. U., 1977; PhD, Am. U., 1980, MA in Psychology, 1977. Bar: N.Y. 1955, D.C. 1973, U.S. Supreme Ct. 1976. Atty. N.Y.C. Legal Aid, 1955-57; ptnr. Lawrence & Lawrence, N.Y.C., 1957-64; agt. N.Y. State, Babylon, N.Y., 1964-66; atty. U.S. Army Engrs., Washington, 1966-69; assoc. chief trial atty. U.S. Dept. Navy, Washington, 1969-78; judge adminstrv. law HEW, Camden, N.J., 1978-79, U.S. Dept. Labor, Washington, 1979-93, SEC, Washington, 1993-96; mem. bd. contract appeals U.S. Dept. Labor, Washington, 1981-93; nat. arbitrator Nat. Assn. Securities Dealers, Inc., Supreme Ct., Washington, 1996—; arbitrator Superior Ct., Washington, 1996—; adj. prof. law George Mason U., Fairfax, Va., 1980-83, Ctrl. Mich. U., Washington, 1981—, Nat. Jud. Coll. U. Nev., Reno, 1984-88; lectr. Banares Hindu U., Varanasi, India, 1988, Law Coll., Ernakulum, Cohin, India, 1989, Wahsignton Lee U., Lexington, Va., 1990; mem. adv. com. Georgetown U. State Cts. and Toxic Torts, 1991; advisor judiciary Leadership Devel. Coun. Inc., 1990—; bd. dirs. Fed. Bar Found., 1994—, chmn. rsch. divsn., 1993—. Author: Condemnation Law, 1969. Bd. dirs. Democracy Devel. Initiative. Mem. ABA (chmn. nat. conf. adminstrv. law judges edn. com. 1985-90, chmn. internat. conf. jud. edn. London 1985, pres. fed. adminstrv. law judge conf. 1984-85, chmn. edn. jud. adminstrn. divsn. 1987-91, chmn. confs., chmn. jud. edn. standards program 1991-95, vice chmn. govt. lawyers com. sr. lawyers divsn. 1991-95), Fed. Bar Assn. (chmn. adminstrv. judiciary com. 1984-88, continuing edn. bd. 1988-91, chmn. judiciary sect. 1989-91, sect. coord. exec. com. 1992-94, editor Fed. Jurist 1991—, chair pub. rels. com. 1993—), Trial Lawyers Assn. (pres. adminstrv. 1970-79). Office: SEC 450 5th St NW Washington DC 20549-0002

LAWRENCE, HENRY SHERWOOD, physician, educator; b. N.Y.C., Sept. 22, 1916; s. Victor John and Agnes (Whalen) L.; m. Dorothea Wetherbee, Nov. 13, 1943; children: Dorothea, Victor, Geoffrey. AB, NYU, 1938, MD, 1943. Diplomate Am. Bd. Internal Medicine. Mem. faculty NYU, N.Y.C., 1947—; John Wyckoff fellow in medicine NYU, 1948-49, dir. student health, 1950-57, head infectious disease and immunology div., 1959—, prof. medicine, 1961-79, Jeffrey Bergstein prof. medicine, 1979—, co-dir. med. svcs., 1964—, dir. Cancer Ctr., 1974-79; dir. Ctr. for AIDS Rsch., 1989-94; vis. physician Tisch Hosp., Bellevue Hosp., 1964—; cons. medicine Manhattan VA Hosp., 1964—; infectious disease program com. VA Rsch. Svc., 1960-63; cons. allergy and immunology study sect. USPHS, 1960-63, chmn., 1963-65; assoc. mem. commn. on streptococcal and staphylococcal diseases Armed Forces Epidemiol. Bd., Dept. Def., 1956-74; mem. coms. Nat. Acad. Scis.-NRC, 1957-65, chmn. com. transplantation, 1963-65; mem. NRC, 1970-72; mem. allergy and infectious disease panel Health Rsch. Coun., N.Y.C., 1962-75, co-chmn., 1968-75; mem. sci. adv. council Am. Cancer Soc., 1973-75. Editor: Medical Clinics of North America, 1957, Cellular and Humoral Aspects of Hypersensitive States, 1959, (with M. Landy) Mediators of Cellular Immunity, 1969, (with Kirkpatrick and Burger) Immunobiology of Transfer Factor, 1983; mem. editorial bd. Transplantation, Ann. of Internal Medicine; founder, editor in chief: Cellular Immunology. Served to lt. M.C. USNR, World War II. Commonwealth Fund fellow Univ. Coll., London, 1959; recipient Research Career Devel. award USPHS, 1960-65, prize Alpha Omega Alpha, 1943; Meritorious Sci. Achievement award NYU Alumni Assn., 1970, von Pirquet Gold medal Ann. Forum on Allergy, 1972, Award for Disting. Achievement in Sci. of Medicine ACP, 1973, Sci. Achievement award Am. Coll. Allergists, 1974, Sci. medal N.Y. Acad. Medicine, 1974, Bristol Sci. award Infectious Diseases Soc. Am., 1974, Charles V. Chapin medal, 1975, Lila Gruber honor award Am. Acad. Dermatology, 1975, Alumni Achievement award NYU Washington Sq. Coll., 1979. Fellow ACP (Bronze medal 1973), Am. Acad. Allergy (hon.), Royal Coll. Physicians and Surgeons Glasgow (hon.); mem. Nat. Acad. Scis., Assn. Am. Physicians, Am. Soc. for Clin. Investigation, Am. Assn. Immunologists, Soc. for Exptl. Biology and Medicine (editorial bd. procs.), Interurban Clin. Club, Harvey Soc. (sec. 1957-60, lectr. 1973—, councillor 1974-77), Peripatetic Clin. Soc., Infectious Diseases Soc. (charter, councillor 1970-72, Bristol Sci. award 1974), Royal Soc. Medicine (affiliate) (Eng.), Internat. Transplantation Soc. (chmn. constn. com., councillor), Société Française d'Allergie (corr.), Alpha Omega Alpha. Achievements include discovery of Transfer Factor - a product of lymphocytes (T-cells) which confers and/or augments immunity to mycobacterial, viral and fungal infections when administered to non-immune individuals; research on mechanisms tissue damage and homograft rejection in man. Home: 343 E 30th St New York NY 10016-6417

LAWRENCE, JACOB, artist, educator; b. Atlantic City, Sept. 7, 1917; s. Jacob and Rose Lee (Armstead) L.; m. Gwendolyn Knight, July 24, 1941. Student, Harlem Art Workshop, N.Y.C., 1932-39; scholar, Am. Artists Sch., N.Y.C., 1938-39; DFA (hon.), Denison U., 1970, Pratt Inst., 1972, Colby Coll., 1976, Md. Inst. Coll. Art, 1979, Carnegie-Mellon U., 1981, Yale U., 1986, Spelman Coll., 1987, Rutgers U., 1988, Parsons Sch. Design, N.Y.C., 1988; LHD (hon.), Howard U., 1985, Tulane U., 1989. Artist Yaddo Found., Saratoga, 1955-56; instr. Pratt Inst. Art Sch., N.Y.C., 1955-70, Art Students League, N.Y.C., 1967-69, New Sch. Social Rsch., N.Y.C., 1966-69; artist in residence Brandeis U., 1965; coord. of the arts Pratt Inst., 1970—, prof. art, 1970; prof. art U. Wash., Seattle, 1971-83, prof. emeritus, 1983—; Disting. Faculty lectr. U. Wash., 1978. Exhibits include John Brown Series, under auspices Am. Fedn. Art, 1945, 30 paintings on history U.S., Alan Gallery, 1957; one-man shows include Migration Series, Mus. Modern Art, 1944, Downtown Gallery, N.Y.C., 1941, 43, 45, 47, 50, 53, M'Bari Artists and Writers Club, Nigeria, 1962, Terry Dintenfass Gallery, N.Y.C., 1963, Francine Seders Gallery, Seattle, 1985; works included Johnson Wax Co. World tour group exhbn., 1963, U.S. State Dept. group exhbn. in, Pakistan, 1963, retrospective exhbn., Whitney Mus. Am. Art, 1974, traveling retrospective Exhbn., Seattle Art Mus., 1986-87; commd. for graphic impressions 1977 Inauguration, Washington, mural commd., Kingdome Stadium, Seattle, 1979, Mural Howard U., 1980, 85, U. Wash., 1985, others; represented in, Met. Mus. Art, Mus. Modern Art, Whitney Mus., Phillips Meml. Collection, Washington, Portland (Oreg.) Mus., Worcester (Mass.) Mus., Balt. Mus. Art, Wichita Art Mus., Albright-Knox Art Gallery, Buffalo, AAAL, N.Y.C., Mus. Modern Art, Sao Paulo, Brazil, R.I. Sch. Design, Va. Mus. Fine Arts, Bklyn. Mus., IBM Corp., Container Corp. Am., various univs.; Author: Harriet and the Promised Land, 1968; illustrator: Aesop's Fables, 1970; (book catalogue for retrospective exhbn.: Jacob Lawrence-American Painter, 1986; executed mural Theatre, 1985; executed, instated mural Orlando Fla. Internat. Airport, 1988, GSA, Jamaica, N.Y. Mem. bd. govs. Skowhegan Sch. Painting and Sculpture; mem. Fulbright Art Com., 1966-67, Wash. State Arts Commn., 1976—; elector Hall of Fame for Gt. Americans, 1976—. Rosenwald fellow, 1940-42, Guggenheim fellow, 1946; recipient purchase prize Artists for Victory, 1942, purchase prize Atlanta U., 1948, Opportunity mag. award, 1948; Norman Wait Harris medal Art Inst. Chgo., 1948; Acad. Arts and Letters grantee, 1953; Chapelbrook Found. grantee, 1955; recipient 1st prize in mural competition for UN Bldg. Nat. Council U.S. Art, Inc., 1955, Retrospective Exhbn. with Definitive Catalogue Ford Found., 1960, Retrospective Exhbn. with Definitive Catalogue Whitney Mus. Modern Art, 1974; works selected as part of exchange exhibit with Soviet Union, 1959; Spingarn medal NAACP, 1970; ann. citation Nat. Assn. Schs. Art, 1973; recipient U.S. Gen. Svcs. Adminstrn. Design award, 1990, Nat. Medal of Arts award Pres. of U.S., 1990, Gold medal Nat. Arts Club N.Y., 1993. Mem. Artist Equity Assn. (past sec., pres. N.Y. chpt. 1957), Nat. Endowment for Arts, Nat. Inst. Arts and Letters, Nat. Coun. Arts. Address: Horizon House 900 University 16 ABC Seattle WA 98101 *As an artist, I hope to contribute something of value to life in general and to my fellowman in particular. I hope that when my life ends... I would have added a little beauty, perception and quality for those who follow. During my lifetime also...I hope to learn and add further motivation, insight and dimension as to my own thinking.*

LAWRENCE, JAMES BLAND, marketing executive; b. Houston, July 22, 1947; s. Harding Luther and Jimmie Georgia (Bland) L.; m. Marie Therese Heckethorn, Feb. 7, 1976 (div. 1981); m. Pamela Douglas Moffat, Sept. 7, 1985. BA in Psychology, U. So. Calif., 1970, MA in Comm./Cinema, 1975. Account exec. KTVV TV, Austin, Tex., 1974, KXAS TV, Dallas, 1975-77; v.p. pub. affairs Braniff Internat., Dallas, 1977-78; v.p. Pacific & Asia Braniff Internat., Hong Kong, 1978-80; v.p. govt. and internat. affairs Braniff Internat., Dallas, 1980-81; v.p. Wells, Rich, Greene, Inc., N.Y.C., 1981-82; sr. v.p., mng. dir. Wells, Rich, Greene, Inc., Detroit, 1983-88, exec. v.p., mng. dir., 1988-90; exec. v.p. Wells, Rich, Greene, Inc., N.Y.C., 1990—. Dir., producer documentary film: Honky Tonk Heros, 1975. Active Foster Parents Plan, Warwick, R.I., 1988—; mem. Met. Affairs Corp., Detroit, 1989. Mem. Detroit Inst. Arts, Am. Assn. Advt. Agencies, Wilderness Soc., Nat. Wildlife Fedn., Greenfield Village/Henry Ford Mus., Adcraft Club, Fairlane Country Club, Waccabuc Country Club (N.Y.). Avocations: tennis, sailing. Office: Wells Rich Greene Inc 9 W 57th St New York NY 10019

LAWRENCE, JAMES HUCKABEE, commercial realtor; b. Durham, N.C., Feb. 3, 1953; s. Henry Newman and Margaret (Huckabee) L.; m. Beth Hutt, June 28, 1975; children: Elizabeth, James, John. Student, Gulf Coast Community Coll., Panama City, Fla., 1971-72, Harvard Bus. Sch., 1980, Am. Mgmt. Assn., Washington, 1982. Pub. rels. profl. and sales rep. Sinclair Distbr., Panama City, 1965-69; v.p. new accounts and loans Lawrence Oil Co., Fina, Panama City, 1970-75; pres., credit factor Sports Emporium, Panama City, 1976-79; pres., gen. mgr. Lawrence & Sons Oil Co. Inc., Panama City, 1981-83; adminstr. Sun South Sch. Real Estate, Panama City, 1984-85; comml. realtor John Davidson Realty/REM Inc., Panama City, 1985—; exec. v.p., sec. Diamondhead Towers, Inc., Panama City Beach, Fla., 1990—; owner Realty Svcs. Inc. of the South, Panama City, Fla., 1993—; ptnr. Assoc. Mortgage Ventures aka AMV Inc., 1994—; bd. dirs. DHT Inc., DHT Condo Assn., Panama City Beach. State lobbyist Nat. Gasohol Commn., Tallahassee, 1977-81; mem. nat. adv. bd. Am. Security Coun., Washington, 1981-82; charter mem. Franklin Mint Assn., 1968—; asst. scoutmaster Boy Scouts Am., 1994—. With U.S. Army, 1972-78, Panama Canal. Named Aide de Camp, Ala. Gov., 1989, Ky. Col., 1989, Col. Govs.'s Staff, Tenn., 1990. Mem. Nat. Assn. Realtors, Fla. C. of C., U.S. C. of C. (state dir. 1980), Fla. Jaycees (bd. dirs. 1980-81), U.S. Jaycees (Goodwill Amb. 1974—), Am. Entrepreneurs Assn. Democrat. Episcopalian. Avocations: boating, coin collecting, antique vases, painting, tennis. Office: Realty Svcs of South Suite D 801 Jenks Ave Ste D Panama City FL 32401-2569

LAWRENCE, JAMES KAUFMAN LEBENSBURGER, lawyer; b. New Rochelle, N.Y., Oct. 8, 1940; s. Michael Monet and Edna (Billings) L.; m. George-Ann Adams, Apr. 5, 1969; children: David Michael, Catherine Robin. AB, Ohio State U., 1962, JD, 1965. Bar: Ohio. 1965, U.S. Dist. Ct. (so. dist.) Ohio 1971, U.S. Ct. Appeals (6th cir.) 1971, U.S. Ct. Appeals (4th cir.) 1978. Field atty. NLRB, Cin., 1965-70; ptnr. Frost & Jacobs, Cin., 1970—; adj. prof. econs. dept. and Coll. Law, U. Cin., 1975—, Ohio State U. Coll. Law, 1995—, Xavier U., 1995—, McGregor Sch., Antioch U., 1993—; master Potter Sewart Inn of Ct., Cin., 1987—, treas., 1988-90; tchg. fellow Harvard Negotiation Project, 1991; chmn. adv. panel on appointment of magistrate judges U.S. Dist. Ct. for So. Dist. Ohio, 1993—. Contbr. articles to profl. jours. Mem. nat. coun. Ohio State U. Coll. Law, 1974—; mem. steering com. Leadership Cin., 1985-89; mem. Seven Hills Neighborhood Houses, Cin., 1973-95, pres., 1992-94; bd. dirs. Beechwood Home, Cin., 1983-86; mem. adv. bd. Emerson Behavioral Health Svcs., 1990-95, chmn., 1995; chmn. Labor Dept., 1978-89, Providence Hosp. Devel. Coun., 1995—, chmn., 1996—; trustee Ctr. for Resolution of Disputes, Inc., 1988-91, treas., 1990-91; mem. Ohio Gov.'s Ops. Improvement Task Force, 1991. Mem. ABA, Cin. Bar Assn. (chmn. labor law com. 1979-82, comm. adv. com. 1994—), Ohio Bar Assn. (vice chmn. labor and employment law sect. 1987-90, chmn. 1990-92), Indsl. Rels. Rsch. Assn. (bd. govs. 1977-80), Alumni Assn. Coll. Law Ohio State U. (pres. 1984-85), Cincinnatus Assn. (pres. 1985-86), Univ. Club. Avocations: collecting movie posters, biking. Home: 3592 Raymar Dr Cincinnati OH 45208-1560 Office: Frost & Jacobs 2500 PNC Ctr 201 E 5th St Cincinnati OH 45202-4117

LAWRENCE, JEROME, playwright, director, educator; b. Cleve., July 14, 1915; s. Samuel and Sarah (Rogen) L. BA, Ohio State U., 1937, LHD (hon.), 1963; DLitt, Fairleigh Dickinson U., 1968; DFA (hon.), Villanova U., 1969; LittD, Coll. Wooster, 1983. Dir. various summer theaters Pa. and Mass., 1934-37; reporter, telegraph editor Wilmington (Ohio) News Jour., 1937; editor Lexington Daily News, Ohio, 1937; continuity editor radio Sta. KMPC, Beverly Hills, Calif., 1938-39; sr. staff writer CBS, Hollywood, Calif. and N.Y.C., 1939-42; pres., writer, dir. Lawrence & Lee, Hollywood, N.Y.C. and London, 1945—; vis. prof. Ohio State Univ., 1969, Salzburg Seminar in Am. Studies, 1972, Baylor Univ., 1978; prof. playwriting Univ. So. Calif. Grad. Sch., 1984—; co-founder, judge Margo Jones award, N.Y.C., 1958—; co-founder, pres. Am. Playwrights Theatre, Columbus, Ohio, 1970-85; bd. dirs. Am. Conservatory Theatre, San Francisco, 1970-80, Stella Adler Theatre, L.A., 1987—, Plumstead Playhouse, 1986—; keynote speaker Bicentennial of Bill of Rights, Congress Hall, Phila., 1991; hon. mem. Nat. Theatre Conf., 1993; adv. bd. Am. Theatre in Lit. Contemporary Arts Ednl. Project, 1993—. Scenario writer Paramount Studios, 1941; master playwright NYU Inst. Performing Arts, 1967-69; author-dir. for: radio and television UN Broadcasts; Army-Navy programs D-Day, VE-Day, VJ-Day; author: Railroad Hour, Hallmark Playhouse, Columbia Workshop; author: Off Mike, 1944, (biography, later made into PBS-TV spl.) Actor: Life and Times of Paul Muni, 1978 (libretto and lyrics by Lawrence and Lee, music by Billy Goldenberg); co-author, dir.: (album) One God; playwright: Live Spelled Backwards, 1969, Off Mike, (mus. with Robert E. Lee) Look, Ma, I'm Dancin', 1948 (music by Hugh Martin), Shangri-La, 1956 (music by Harry Warren, lyrics by James Hilton, Lawrence and Lee), Mame, 1966 (score by Jerry Herman), Dear World, 1969 (score by Jerry Herman), (non-mus.) Inherit the Wind (translated and performed in 34 langs., named best fgn. play of year London Critics Poll 1960), Auntie Mame, 1956, The Gang's All Here, 1959, Only in America, 1959, A Call on Kuprin, 1961, Diamond Orchid (revised as Sparks Fly Upward, 1966), 1965, The Incomparable Max, 1969, The Crocodile Smile, 1970, The Night Thoreau Spent in Jail, 1970, (play and screenplay) First Monday in October, 1978, (written for opening of Thurber Theatre, Columbus) Jabberwock: Improbabilities Lived and Imagined by James Thurber in the Fictional City of Columbus, Ohio, 1974, (with Robert E. Lee) Whisper in the Mind, 1994, The Angels Weep, 1992, (novel) A Golden Circle: A Tale of the Stage and the Screen and Music of Yesterday and Now and Tomorrow and Maybe the Day After Tomorrow, 1993; Decca Dramatic Albums, Musi-Plays.; contbg. editor Dramatics mag., mem. adv. bd., contbr. Writer's Digest; Lawrence and Lee collections at Libr. and Mus. of the Performing Arts, Lincoln Ctr., N.Y., Harvard's Widener Libr., Cambridge, Mass., Jerome Lawrence & Robert E. Lee Theatre Rsch. Inst. at Ohio State U., Columbus, est. 1986. A founder, overseas corr. Armed Forces Radio Service; mem. Am. Theatre Planning Bd.; bd. dirs. Nat. Repertory Theatre, Plumstead Playhouse; mem. adv. bd. USDAN Center for Creative and Performing Arts, East-West Players, Performing Arts Theatre of Handicapped., Inst. Outdoor Drama; mem. State Dept. Cultural Exchange Drama Panel, 1961-69; del. Chinese-Am. Writers Conf., 1982, 86, Soviet-Am. Writers Conf., 1984, 85; Am. Writers rep. to Hiroshima 40th Anniversary Commemorative, Japan, 1985; mem. U.S. Cultural Exchange visit to theatre communities of Beijing and Shanghai, 1985; adv. coun. Calif. Ednl. Theatre Assn., Calif. State U., Calif. Repertory Co., Long Beach, 1984—. Recipient N.Y. Press Club award, 1942, CCNY award, 1948, Radio-TV Life award, 1948, Mirror awards, 1952, 53, Peabody award, 1949, 52, Variety Showmanship award 1954, Variety Critics poll 1955, Outer-Circle Critics award 1955, Donaldson award, 1955, Ohioana award,Ohio Press Club award, 1959, Brit. Drama Critics award, 1960, Moss Hart Meml. award, 1967, State Dept. medal, 1968, Pegasus award, 1970, Lifetime Achievement award Am. Theatre Assn., 1979, Nat. Thespian Soc. award, 1980, Pioneer Broadcasters award, 1981, 95, Diamond Circle award, 1995, Ohioana Library career medal, Master of Arts award Rocky Mountain Writers Guild, 1982, Centennial Award medal Ohio State U., 1970, William Inge award and lectureship Independence Community Coll., 1983, 86—, Disting. Contbr. award Psychologists for Social Responsibility, 1985, ann. awards San Francisco State U., Pepperdine U., Career award Southeastern Theatre Conf., 1990; named Playwright of Yr. Baldwin-Wallace Coll., 1960; named to Honorable Order of Ky. Colonels, 1965, Tenn. Colonels, 1988; named to Theater Hall of Fame, 1990. Fellow Coll. Am. Theatre, Kennedy Ctr.; mem. Nat. Theatre Conf. (hon.), Acad. Motion Picture Arts and Scis., Acad. TV Arts and Scis. (2 Emmy award 1988), Authors League (coun.), ANTA (dir., v.p.), Ohio State U. Assn. (dir.), Radio Writers' Guild (founder, pres.), Writers Guild Am. (dir., founding mem. Valentine Davies award), Dramatists Guild (coun.), ASCAP, Calif. Ednl. Theatre Assn. (Profl. Artist award 1992), Century Club N.Y., Phi Beta Kappa, Sigma Delta Chi. Avocations: traveling, photography, swimming. *I want people to leave the theatre after seeing a play I have written feeling as if they were taller human beings, as if their souls had been sandpapered. A work must have meanings many layers deep so that it illumines our lives and our times.*

LAWRENCE, JOHN KIDDER, lawyer; b. Detroit, Nov. 18, 1949; s. Luther Ernest and Mary Anna (Kidder) L.; m. Jeanine Ann DeLay, June 20, 1981. AB, U. Mich., 1971; JD, Harvard U., 1974. Bar: Mich. 1974, U.S. Supreme, 1977, D.C. 1978. Assoc. Dickinson, Wright, McKean & Cudlip, Detroit, 1973-74; staff atty. Office of Judge Adv. Gen., Washington, 1975-78; assoc. Dickinson, Wright, McKean, Cudlip & Moon, Detroit, 1978-81; ptnr. Dickinson, Wright, Moon, VanDusen & Freeman, Detroit, 1981—. Exec. sec. Detroit Com. on Fgn. Rels., 1988—; trustee Ann Arbor (Mich.) Summer Festival, Inc., 1990—; patron Founders Soc. Detroit Inst. Arts, 1979—. With USN, 1975-78. Mem. AAAS, ABA, Am. Law Inst., Fed. Bar Assn., State Bar Mich., D.C. Bar Assn., Am. Judicature Soc., Internat. Bar Assn., Am. Hist. Assn., Detroit Club, Detroit Athletic Club, Econ. Club Detroit, Phi Eta Sigma, Phi Beta Kappa. Democrat. Episcopalian. Office: Dickinson Wright Moon VanDusen & Freeman 500 Woodward Ave Ste 4000 Detroit MI 48226-3423

LAWRENCE, KEN, columnist; b. Chgo., Nov. 11, 1942; s. Lawrence Edward and Mary Ewing (Glickauf) Burg; m. Patricia Rose Bridges, Feb. 6, 1964 (div. Sept. 1980); children: Vernon H. Davis, Max E.; m. Elizabeth Ann Sharpe, 1984 (div. Feb. 1993); m. Kathleen Wunderly, Feb. 24, 1995. Student, Shimer Coll., 1959-61, Roosevelt U., 1962-63, 68. Freelance film technician Chgo. and Gary, Ind., 1959-71; corr. Southern Conf. Ednl. Fund, Jackson, Miss., 1971-75; editor Greenwood Press & Univ. Press of Miss., Jackson, 1976; columnist Covert Action Info. Bull., Washington, 1979—, Stamp Collector, Albany, Oreg., 1982-86, Linn's Stamp News, Sidney, Ohio, 1987—, Am. Philatelist, State College, Pa., 1991—; dir. Am. Friends Svc. Com., Jackson, 1977-79, Anti-Repression Resource Team, Jackson, 1979-93. Author: Linn's Plate Number Coil Handbook, 1990, (booklet) The New State Repression, 1980; editor: Mississippi Slave Narratives, 5 vols., 1976, The Philatelic Communicator, 1989-94; contbr. (book) Dirty Work 2-The CIA in Africa, 1979. Trainer United Meth. Voluntary Svc., N.Y.C., 1980-83; organizer Nat. Anti-Klan Network, Atlanta, 1980-85; bd. dirs. South African Mil. Refugee Aid Fund, N.Y.C., 1977-85. Recipient Rosebud, MORE Journalism Rev., 1975, Cert. of Merit, Miss. Hist. Soc., 1976. Mem. Am. Philatelic Soc. (dir.-at-large 1991-93, sec. 1993-95, v.p. 1995—, Rsch. medal 1988), Am. Philatelic Congress, Jackson Philatelic Soc. (v.p. 1990-91, pres. 1992-93), Bur. Issues Assn. (gov. 1989—), The Manuscript Soc. Avocations: stamp collector, traveling. Office: PO Box 8040 State College PA 16803-8040

LAWRENCE, LAUREN, psychoanalytical theorist, psychoanalyst; b. N.Y.C., June 26, 1950; d. Jack and Elaine (Gaumont) Soever; m. D. Henry Lawrence, June 24, 1972; 1 child, Graham. MA in Psychology, New Sch. for Social Rsch., 1993. Psychoanalyst N.Y.C., 1992—. Contbr. articles to profl. jours. Mem. N.Y. Psychoanalytic Soc. Achievements include founding of a third person analysis, a new method of analysis in clinical practice, which provides the analysand a narrational objectivity; and the covert seduction theory, which expounds the dangers of a non-physical parental seduction. Avocations: tennis, musical composition, writing poetry, reading, studying Greek. Home: 31 E 72d St New York NY 10021

LAWRENCE, LINDA HIETT, retired school system administrator, writer; b. Phoenix, July 26, 1939; d. Lydle and Hazeldell (Sutton) Hiett; children: Pamela Lee Reardon, Annabel Virginia Urrea. BA, U. Ariz., 1961; MA, Ariz. State U., 1985, EdD, 1986. Cert. sch. supt., prin., tchr., Ariz. Prin. Washington Elem. Sch. Dist. 6, Phoenix, 1980-83; prin. Dysart Unified Sch. Dist. 89, Peoria, Ariz., 1985-87, asst. supt., 1987-88; supt. Cottonwood Ariz. Oak Creek Sch. Dist. 6, 1988-91; cons., writer, 1991—; owner Lawrence Properties and Enterprises; adj. prof. No. Ariz. U., 1990-91. Author: Adventures in Arizona, 1991; co-author: History of Jerome and Verde Valley, 1991. Trustee Marcus J. Lawrence Hosp.; pres. bd. dirs. Children's Advocacy Ctr. NSF grantee for Math; recipient USC's 100 Outstanding Supts. award. Mem. AAUW, Ariz. Hist. Soc., Ariz. Ctr. for the Book, Sacred Heart Alumni Assn., Ariz. State U. Alumni Assn. Ariz. Humanities Coun., Phoenix Zoo, Friends of Our Bros. and Sisters, Phi Delta Kappa.

LAWRENCE, MARGERY H(ULINGS), utilities executive; b. Harmarville, Pa., June 17, 1934; d. Richard Nuttall and Alva (Burns) Hulings; student Bethany Coll., 1951-52; B.S. in Mktg., Carnegie-Mellon U., 1955. Asst. mdse. buyer Joseph Horne Co., Pitts., 1955-57; home econs. editor Pitts. Group Cos. Columbia Gas System, Pitts., 1957-64, dir. home econs., 1968-72; home economist Columbia Gas Pa., Jeannette, 1964-68, dist. marketing mgr., 1972-87, div. mgr., 1987-94; dir. mktg. Columbia Gas Pa. & Columbia Gas Md., 1991—. Bd. dirs., vice chmn. Ohio Valley Gen. Hosp. Mem. DAR, NAFE, AmGas Assn. (Home Svc. Achievement award 1964), Pa. Economy League (bd. dirs. Beaver County chpt.). Office: Columbia Gas Pa Inc 650 Washington Rd Pittsburgh PA 15228-2702

LAWRENCE, MARTIN, actor, comedian; b. Frankfurt, Germany, 1966; s. John and Chlora L.; m. Patricia Southall, 1995. TV series include: What's Happening Now, 1985, HBO One Night Stand, 1989, Kid 'N' Play, 1990 (voice only), Russell Simmons' Def Comedy Jam, 1991-93 (host), Martin, 1992— (also creator and exec. prodr.); films include: Do the Right Thing, 1989, House Party, 1990, House Party 2, 1991, Talkin' Dirty after Dark, 1991, Boomerang, 1992, You So Crazy, 1994 (concert film, also exec. prodr.), Bad Boys, 1995. Office: c/o Fox Broadcasting Co 10201 W Pico Blvd Los Angeles CA 90035*

LAWRENCE, MARY JOSEPHINE (JOSIE LAWRENCE), library official, artist; b. Carbondale, Pa., Mar. 9, 1932; d. Domenick Anthony and Teresa Rose (Zaccone) Gentile; m. John Paul Lawrence, Apr. 25, 1953 (dec. June 1977); children: Mary Josephine, Jane Therese, Susan Michele. BFA, Mass. Coll. Art, 1989; postgrad, Chelsea (Eng.) Sch. Art, 1989, San Pancrazio Art Sch., Tuscany, Italy, 1990, 91, 92; cert. in grad. studies, Guangzhou Acad. Fine Arts, China, 1993; postgrad., Md. Inst. Fine Art, Sorrento, Italy, 1994. Sales clk. Gorins, 5&10, Jordan Marsh, Boston, 1946-49; clk.-typist, sec. John Hancock Ins. Co., Boston, 1950-53; machine operator, quality control supr. Rust Craft Greeting Cards, Dedham, Mass., 1961-69; restaurant hostess Tony's Villa, Waltham, Mass., 1972-73; mus. sales clk., artist John F. Kennedy Libr., Boston, 1979-87, mgr. mus. store, supr., 1988—; tchr.'s asst. San Pancrazio Art Sch., 1992. One woman shows include de Havilland Fine Art Gallery, Boston, 1993; exhibited in group shows including South Shore Arts Ctr., Cohasset, Mass., 1991, North River Arts Soc., Marshfield Hills, Mass. Recipient Outstanding Achievement awards Nat. Archives and Rsch. Adminstrn., 1989, 94, Svc. award, 1990, Hon. Mention award South Shore Arts Ctr., 1991, Best of Show award de Havilland Fine Art Gallery, 1992, Best of Show North River Arts Soc., 1994, Honorium Weymouth Art Assn., 1995. Mem. Boston Visual Artist Union, de Havilland Fine Art Gallery, South Shore Art Ctr., North River Arts Soc., Nat. Mus. Women in Arts (charter), Weymouth Art Assn. (honorium). Democrat. Roman Catholic. Office: John F Kennedy Libr and Mus Columbia Pt Boston MA 02125

LAWRENCE, MERLE, medical educator; b. Remsen, N.Y., Dec. 26, 1915; s. George William and Alice Rutherford (Bowne) L.; m. Roberta Ashby Taylor Harper, Aug. 8, 1942; children—Linda Alice, Roberta Harper Lawrence Henderson, James Bowne. A.B., Princeton, 1938, M.A., 1940, Ph.D., 1941. NRC fellow Johns Hopkins Hosp., 1941; asst. prof. psychology Princeton, 1946-50; assoc. prof., 1950-52; assoc. research Lempert Inst. Otology, N.Y.C., 1946-52; assoc. prof. dept. otolaryngology U. Mich. Med. Sch., 1952-57, prof. otolaryngology, 1957-85, prof. emeritus, 1985—; research assoc. Inst. Indsl. Health, 1952—; prof. psychology U. Mich. Coll. Lit. Sci. and Arts, 1957—; dir. Kresge Hearing Research Inst., 1961-83; mem. sci. rev. bd. Deafness Research Found., 1960-66, 82-84; Nat. Adv. Neurol. and Communicative Disorders and Stroke Council, 1976-79; mem. communicative disorders research tng. com. Nat. Inst. Neurol. Diseases and Blindness, 1961-65; mem. communicative scis. study sect. div. research grants NIH, 1965-69, chmn., 1967-69, mem. communicative disorders rev. com., 1972-76; cons. Surgeon Gen. U.S. Army office Aviation Medicine, 1963-70. Served as naval aviator USNR, 1941-46, 50-51, PTO; Served as naval aviator USNR, Korean conflict, PTO. Decorated Purple Heart, Silver Star, Disting. Flying Cross (2), Air medal with nine gold stars; recipient Sec. Navy Commendation, Disting. Svc. award Princeton Class of 1938, Achievement award Am. Acad. Audiology, 1992. Fellow AAAS, Am. Acad. Otolaryngology-Head and Neck Surgery, Otosclerosis Study Group, Am. Laryngol., Rhinolog. and Otolaryngol. Soc.; mem. Acoustical Soc. Am., Mich. Acoustical Soc. (pres. 1956), Am. Acad. Ophthalmology and Otolaryngology (Merit award 1965), Am. Otol. Soc. (Merit award 1967, cons. bd. trustees rsch. fund, guest of honor 1986), Collegium Oto-Rhino-Laryngologicum Amicitiae Sacrum, Soc. U. Otolaryngologists, Assn. Rsch. Otolaryngology (Merit award 1979), Am. Auditory Soc. (coun. 1978-82), Walter P. Work Soc., Am. Tinnitus Assn., Quarter Century Wireless Assn. Clubs: Rotary (pres. 1978-79), Centurion, Mich. Masters Swim. Home (winter): 1535 Shorelands Dr E Vero Beach FL 32963-2648 Home (summer): 2029 Vinewood Blvd Ann Arbor MI 48104-3613

LAWRENCE, MERLOYD LUDINGTON, editor; b. Pasadena, Calif., Aug. 1, 1932; d. Nicholas Saltus and Mary Lloyd (Macy) Ludington; m. Seymour Lawrence, June 21, 1952 (div. 1984); children: Macy, Nicholas; m. John M. Myers, 1985. A.B., Radcliffe Coll., 1954, M.A., 1957. With Houghton Mifflin Co., 1955-57; free lance translator, 1957-65; editor, treas., v.p. Seymour Lawrence Inc., Boston, 1965-83; pres. Merloyd Lawrence, Inc., Boston, 1983—. Translator works of Flaubert and Balzac, modern French fiction, German and Swedish children's books.; contbr. articles to nat. mags. Treas., v.p. Milford House Properties, Ltd., N.S., Can., 1975-80; trustee Milton (Mass.) Acad., 1974-82; mem. com. clin. investigations Beth Israel Hosp. Mem. Am. Translators Assn., New Eng. Forestry Found. (exec. bd. officer 1989—), Mass. Audubon Soc. (dir. 1974—, exec. com. 1992—), Phi Beta Kappa. Home: 102 Chestnut St Boston MA 02108-1120 Office: 102A Chestnut St Boston MA 02108-1120

LAWRENCE, PAUL ROGER, retired organizational behavior educator; b. Rochelle, Ill., Apr. 26, 1922; s. Howard Cyrus and Clara (Luther) L.; m. Martha G. Stiles, Dec. 14, 1948; children: Anne Talcott, William Stiles. Student, Grand Rapids Jr. Coll., 1939-41; AB, Albion Coll., 1943; MBA, Harvard U., 1947, DCS, 1950. Mem. faculty Harvard U. Bus. Sch., Boston, 1947-91, asst. prof., 1951-56, assoc. prof., 1956-61, prof. organizational behavior, 1961-68, Donham prof. organizational behavior, 1968; retired, 1991. Author: (with others) Renewing American Industry, 1983, HRM, Trends and Challenges, 1985, Behind the Factory Walls, 1990. Served to lt. USNR, 1943-46. Fellow Acad. Mgmt.; mem. Am. Sociol. Assn. Home: 17 Willard St Cambridge MA 02138-4836 Office: Cumnock Hall Soldiers Fld Boston MA 02163

LAWRENCE, RAY VANCE, chemist; b. Vance, Ala., July 6, 1910; s. William Monroe and Frances (Ray) L.; m. Barbara New, June 22, 1935; children: Robert Craig, Richard Vance. BS, U. Ala., Tuscaloosa, 1931; MS, U. Tenn., Knoxville, 1933. Instr. chemistry Marion (Ala.) Mil. Inst., 1932-33; chemist TVA, Muscle Shoals, Ala., 1933-38, Naval Stores Sta., Olustee, Fla., 1938-41, Naval Stores Rsch. Div., Washington, 1941-43; head rosin rsch. So. Regional Rsch. Lab., New Orleans, 1943-50; head rosin rsch. Naval Stores Rsch. Lab., Olustee, 1950-58, dir., 1958-73; cons. Naval Stores, Lake City, Fla., 1973—; lectr. terpene chemistry U. Fla., Gainesville, 1953-57; lectr. Nanjing (China) Forestry U., 1979. Columnist, assoc. editor Naval Stores Rev., 1977-90; contbr. articles to profl. jours.; patentee in field. Mem Am. Chem. Soc. (chmn. Fla. sect. 1965, Fla. award 1971), Am. Oil Chemists Soc. Presbyterian. Home and Office: 5900 Wilson Blvd Apt 453 Arlington VA 22205-1550

LAWRENCE, RICHARD WESLEY, JR., foundation executive; b. N.Y.C., Jan. 16, 1909; s. Richard Wesley and Ruth (Earle) L.; m. Marjorie Fitch, June 23, 1933 (dec. Feb. 1945); children: Ruth Earle Lawrence Wilson (dec.), Alida L. Currey; m. Elizabeth Hand Wadhams, Apr. 13, 1946 (dec. Nov. 1987); 1 child, Elizabeth Lawrence. B.S., Princeton U., 1931; LL.B., Columbia U., 1934. Bar: N.Y. 1935. Former chmn. bd. Printers Ink Pub. Co., Bankers Comml. Corp.; v.p., dir. Umont Mining, Inc. Chmn. Adirondack Park Agy., 1971-75; chmn. Commr. Edn.'s com. on Reference and Rsch. Libr. Resources; mem. Gov.'s Commn. on Future of Adirondacks, Gov.'s Commn. on Adirondacks in the 21st Century; past chmn. coun. State U. Coll., Plattsburgh; past chmn. bd. trustees North Country C.C.; pres. Crary Edn. Found. Capt. USAAF, 1942-44; lt. col. ret. Recipient North Country citation St. Lawrence U., 1969, Conservation award Garden Club Am., 1982, Disting. Svc. award Potsdam Coll., 1987, Founders award Adirondack Hist. Assn., 1991, Assn. for Protection of Adirondacks award, 1994. Hon. mem. N.Y. Library Assn. (Velma Moore award), N.Y. State Hist. Assn. (trustee), Essex County Hist. Soc.; mem. Explorers Club, Union League, Princeton Club (N.Y.C.), Ausable Club. Home: Elizabethtown NY 12932 Office: PO Box 427 Elizabethtown NY 12932-0427

LAWRENCE, ROBERT ALLEN, lawyer; b. Scranton, Pa., Dec. 25, 1935; s. Karl Manning and Edith Mary (Richards) L.; div.; children: Allan, Richard, Brian, Robert. BS, Columbia U., 1962; JD, George Washington U., 1966. Bar: Va. 1966. Asst. commonwealth atty. Commonwealth of Va., Fairfax, 1967-68; asst. county atty. County of Fairfax, Fairfax, 1969; ptnr. Fried, Fried, Klewans and Lawrence, Fairfax, 1970-73, Hazel and Thomas, P.C., Falls Church, Va., 1974—; counsel No. Va. Bldg. Assn., Fairfax, 1976-79; lectr. on zoning law. Chmn. planning and land use com. Fairfax County C. of C., 1985-86; bd. dirs. Southeast Fairfax Devel. Corp., 1987-88. With USAF, 1954-58. Mem. ABA (com.), Va. State Bar, Fairfax Bar Assn., Homeowners Warranty Corp. (life dir.). Avocations: music, golf. Office: Hazel and Thomas PO Box 12001 3110 Fairview Pk Dr Ste 1400 Falls Church VA 22042*

LAWRENCE, ROBERT G., insurance company executive; b. Sheboygan, Wis., Sept. 30, 1932; s. Raymond O. and Mildred (Kahr) L.; m. Phyllis A. Moos, Apr. 15, 1956; children: Cheryll, Daniel, David, Janice, Laura Beth. Grad., Purdue Profl. Mgmt. Inst., Agy. Mgrs. Tng. Coun. CLU, ChFC, fraternal ins. counsellor. Agy. mgr. Modern Woodmen of Am., Brookfield, Wis., 1956—, also bd. dirs.; instr. in field. Contbr. articles to Salesman Mag. Cub scout leader Boy Scouts Am., 1949-50, boy scout leader, 1949-50; chmn. Silver Lake Assn., 1979-84, mem., 1979—; recruiter Jesuit Retreat House, 1979—. Fellow Life Underwriters Tng. Coun. (chmn. 1984); mem. NALU (pres. Ozaukee-Washington chpt. 1968-69, pres. 1979-80, bd. dirs. Milw. chpt.), GAMA (pres. 1989-90, Hall of Fame 1994, 7 Builder of Yr. awards, 8 Nat. Mgmt. awards), Nat. Assn. Fraternal Ins. Counselors (past pres.), Wis. Gen. Agts. and Mgrs. Assn. (past sec.-treas., former bd. dirs., v.p. 1988, pres. 1989), Milw. Fraternal Underwriters Assn. (former pres., past bd. dirs.), Agy. Mgrs. Tng. Coun. (moderator 1986-87, 87-88, 94-95, chmn. 1987-88, mem. coun. Limra chpt. 1993—, chmn. region 6 1994), Pres.'s Club. Avocations: golf, fishing, boating.

LAWRENCE, ROBERT SWAN, physician, educator, academic administrator; b. Phila., Feb. 6, 1938; s. Thomas George and Catherine (Swan) L.; m. Cynthia Starr Cole, July 1, 1960; children: Job Scott, Matthew Swan, Hannah Starr, Jin Sook, Sang Bo. AB magna cum laude, Harvard U., 1960, MD, 1964. Intern, then resident in internal medicine Mass. Gen. Hosp., 1964-66, 69-70; surgeon USPHS, 1966-69; asst. prof., then assoc. prof. medicine, chief div. community medicine Med. Sch. U. N.C., 1970-74; dir. div. primary care Med. Sch. Harvard U., 1974-91, assoc. prof. medicine Med. Sch., 1980-81, Charles S. Davidson assoc. prof. medicine Med. Sch., 1981-91; chmn. dept. medicine Cambridge (Mass.) Hosp., 1980-91; adj. prof. NYU Sch. of MEdicine, 1992-95; prof. health policy & mgmt. Johns Hopkins Sch. Hygiene & Pub. Health, 1995, prof. medicine, Johns Hopkin's Sch. Medicine, 1995—; mem. com. human rights NAS; chmn. bd. health promotion and disease prevention IOM, 1981-86, chmn. com. health and human rights, 1990—; chmn. U.S. Preventive Svc. Task Force, HHS, 1984-89, active mem., 1990—; fellow Ctr. for Advanced Study in Behavioral Scis., 1988-89; dir. health scis. Rockefeller Found., 1991-95; assoc. dean for profl. edn. Johns Hopkins Sch. Hygiene & Pub. Health, 1995—. Editor Am. Jour. Preventive Medicine, 1990-92; contbr. articles and chpts. in books. Bd. dirs. Physicians for Human Rights, 1986-91, Tchrs. Coll., Columbia U., Am.'s Watch. Recipient Maimonides prize, 1964. Fellow ACP, Am. Coll. Preventive Medicine (Spl. Recognition award 1988); mem. Inst. Medicine, Am. Pub. Health Assn., Soc. Gen. Internal Medicine (pres. 1978-79), Soc. Tchrs. Preventive Medicine (Spl. Recognition award 1993), Phi Beta Kappa. Home: Highfield House 1112 4000 N Charles St Baltimore MD 21218-1737 Office: Johns Hopkins Sch Hygiene & Pub Health 615 N Wolfe St Baltimore MD 21205-2179

LAWRENCE, RUDDICK CARPENTER, public relations executive; b. Marquette, Mich., Jan. 5, 1912; s. Willard Carpenter and Verna (Ruddick) L.; m. Barbara Dole, June 5, 1937 (div. 1971); children: Dana Ann Lawrence Wetstone, Sara Hilary Lawrence Engelhardt, Megan Elizabeth Lawrence Cumming, Jean Hathaway Lawrence Petri, Ruddick C., Daniel Dole; m. Cherry McDonnell Swasey, Oct. 27, 1973; stepchildren: Leslie Denison Black, Caroline McDonnell Black Blydenburgh. B.A. in Journalism cum laude, U. Wash., 1934. Dir. publicity Detroit Inst. Arts, 1934-36; assoc. dir. World Adventure Series, Detroit, 1934-36; mgr. Western div. Am. Boy mag., Chgo., 1936-39; Phila. and So. mgr. Fortune mag., Time, Inc., 1939-44, N.Y.

mgr., assoc. advt. mgr., 1946-50; dir. sales devel. TV network, dir. promotion, planning, devel. radio and TV networks NBC, N.Y.C., 1950-53; v.p. N.Y. Stock Exchange, 1953-68, Conoco Inc. (now DuPont Co.), 1968-77; pres. Lawrence Assocs., 1977—. Trustee Sarah Lawrence Coll., 1954-69, chmn. bd. trustees, 1964-69; bd. mgrs. N.Y. Bot. Garden, 1968-92; hon. chmn., bd. dirs. N.Y. Bd. Trade, 1968-92, pres., chmn., 1978-80; bd. dirs. Internat. Film Found., 1956—, World Adventure Series, 1952-80, N.Y. State Festival, 1981-93; gov. Invest-in-Am. Nat. Coun. Inc., 1954-91; hon. pres. U.S.-Arab C. of C., pres., 1976-79, 82-83. Served from lt. (j.g.) to lt. USNR, 1944-46; staff requirements rev. bd. Office Sec. Navy, Chief Naval Ops. Decorated Star of Jordan, Cedars of Lebanon. Mem. Pub. Rels. Soc. N.Y., Pilgrims Soc., Explorers Club, Circumnavigators Club, Bronxville Field Club, Rockefeller Luncheon Club, Univ. Club, Econ. Club, Shelter Island Yacht Club, Phi Kappa Psi (chmn., trustee Endowment Fund Corp. 1960-88, Disting. Alumnus award 1988), Sigma Delta Chi. Episcopalian. Home: 3 Wellington Cir Bronxville NY 10708-3011 also: Menantic Rd PO Box 1052 Shelter Island NY 11964-1052 Office: 122 E 42nd St Rm 1700 New York NY 10168-1799

LAWRENCE, SALLY CLARK, academic administrator; b. San Francisco, Dec. 29, 1930; d. George Dickson and Martha Marie Alice (Smith) Clark; m. Henry Clay Judd, July 1, 1950 (div. Dec. 1972); children: Rebecca, David, Nancy; m. John I. Lawrence, Aug. 12, 1976; stepchildren: Maia, Dylan. Docent Portland Art Mus., Oreg., 1958-68; gallery owner, dir., Sally Judd Gallery, Portland, 1968-75; art ins. appraiser, cons. Portland, 1975-81; interim dir. Mus. Art. Sch., Pacific Northwest Coll. Art, Portland, 1981, asst. dir., 1981-82, acting dir., 1982-84, dir., 1984-94, pres., 1994—; bd. dirs. Art Coll. Exch. Nat. Consortium, 1982-91, pres., 1983-84. Bd. dirs. Portland Arts Alliance, 1987—, Assn. Ind. Colls. of Art and Design, 1991—, pres., 1995—. Mem. Nat. Assn. Schs. Art and Design (bd. dirs. 1984-91, treas. bd. dirs. 1994—), Oreg. Ind. Coll. Assn. (bd. dirs. 1981—, exec. com. 1989-94, pres. 1992-93). Office: Pacific NW Coll of Art 1219 SW Park Ave Portland OR 97205-2430

LAWRENCE, SANFORD HULL, physician, immunochemist; b. Kokomo, Ind., July 10, 1919; s. Walter Scott and Florence Elizabeth (Hull) L. AB, Ind. U., 1941, MD, 1944. Fellow in biochemistry George Washington U., 1941; intern Rochester (N.Y.) Gen. Hosp., 1944-45; resident Halloran Hosp., Staten Island, N.Y., 1946-49; chief med. svce. Ft. Ord Regl. Hosp., 1945-46; dir. biochemistry rsch. lab. San Fernando (Calif.) VA Hosp.; asst. prof. UCLA, 1950—; cons. internal medicine and cardiology U.S. Govt., Los Angeles County; lectr. Faculte de Medicine, Paris, various colls. Eng., France, Belgium, Sweden, USSR, India, Japan; chief med. svc. Ft. Ord Regional Hosp.; chmn. Titus, Inc., 1982—. Author: Zymogram in Clinical Medicine, 1965; contbr. articles to sci. jours.; author: Threshold of Valhalla, Another Way to Fly, My Last Satyr, and other short stories; traveling editor: Relax Mag. Mem. Whitley Heights Civic Assn., 1952—; pres. Halloran Hosp. Employees Assn., 1947-48. Served to maj. U.S. Army, 1945-46. Recipient Rsch. award TB and Health Assn., 1955-58, Los Angeles County Heart Assn., 1957-59, Pres. award, Queen's Blue Book award, Am. Men of Sci. award; named one of 2000 Men of Achievement, Leaders of Am. Sci., Ky. Col., named Hon. Mayor of West Point, Ky. Mem. AAAS, AMA, N.Y. Acad. Scis., Am. Fedn. Clin. Research, Am. Assn. Clin. Investigation, Am. Assn. Clin. Pathology, Am. Assn. Clin. Chemistry, Los Angeles County Med. Assn. Republican. Methodist. Avocations: bridge, comml. pilot, pianist, organist. Home: 2014 Whitley Ave Los Angeles CA 90068-3235 also: 160 rue St Martin, 75003 Paris France

LAWRENCE, STEVE, entertainer; b. Bklyn., July 8, 1935; s. Max Leibowitz; m. Eydie Gorme, Dec. 29, 1957; children: David, Michael. Former mem. cast The Tonight Show; host Steve Lawrence Show, CBS-TV, 1965; has starred (with Eydie Gorme) in TV spls. honoring Gershwin, Porter and Berlin (7 Emmy awards); TV appearances include: Police Story, Murder She Wrote; also numerous TV guest appearances; performer night clubs; made stage debut in What Makes Sammy Run, 1964; co-starred: (with Eydie Gorme) in Golden Rainbow, N.Y.C., 1967; co-host: (TV series) Foul-Ups, Bleeps and Blunders, 1984; TV miniseries: Alice in Wonderland, 1985; albums include Through the Years, At the Movies, Together Forever, The Best of Steve and Eydie, 1990. Hon. chmn. entertainment com. Cerebral Palsy; bd. govs. Brookdale Hosp., N.Y.C. Served with AUS, 1958-60. Recipient N.Y. Drama Critics award for best male performance in mus. comedy, 1964, TV Critics Circle award for achievement in music 1976-77, Grammy for album We've Got Us (with Eydie Gorme). Club: Friars (N.Y.C.) (gov.). Office: care William Morris Agy Inc 151 S El Camino Dr Beverly Hills CA 90212-2704

LAWRENCE, TELETÉ ZORAYDA, speech and voice pathologist, educator; b. Worcester, Mass., Aug. 5, 1910; d. James Newton and Cora Valeria (Hester) Lester; A.B. cum laude, U. Calif., Berkeley, 1932; M.A., Tex. Christian U., 1963; pvt. study voice with Edgar Schofield, N.Y.C., 1936-41, drama with Enrica Clay Dillon, N.Y.C., 1937-40; m. Ernest Lawrence, Oct. 9, 1939; children—James Lester, Valerie Alma. Lic. speech-lang. pathologist. Mem. Am. Lyric Opera Co., 1939—; instr. speech Sch. Fine Arts, Tex. Christian U., Fort Worth, 1959-66, asst. prof., 1966-71, assoc. prof., 1971-75, prof., 1975-76, emeritus, 1976—, speech pathologist specializing voice disorders Speech and Hearing Clinic, 1959—, faculty research leave, Gt. Britain, Western Europe, Hungary, 1968; pvt. practice speech and voice pathology, 1960—. Mem. bd. Sunshine Haven, home for retarded children, 1957-59; gen. chmn. Ft. Worth and Tarrant County, Nat. Retarded Children's Week, 1954; mem. family and child welfare div. Community Council Ft. Worth and Tarrant County, 1955-57, mem. health and hosp. div., 1959-60; mem. women's com. Ft. Worth chpt. NCCJ, 1956-59; exec. v.p. Fine Arts Found. Guild of Tex. Christian U., 1955-56, past exec. sec., past fin. sec. Recipient Faculty Research grant Tex. Christian U., 1961. Fellow Internat. Soc. Phonetic Scis.; mem. Nat. Council Chs. (bd. joint com. missionary edn. Pacific Coast area, 1952-55), United Ch. Women of Ft. Worth (chmn. Christian world missions dept. 1955-57, pres. 1957-59). Ft. Worth Area Council Chs. (v.p. 1955-57, exec. com. 1957-59, bd. dirs. 1959-60), U. Calif. Alumni Assn. (life), Am. Speech-Lang.-Hearing Assn. (life; cert. clin. competence in speech pathology), Tex. Speech-Lang.-Hearing Assn. (cert.), Ft. Worth Council for Retarded Children, Speech Communication Assn. (sec. speech and hearing disorders interest group 1962-63, mem. com. 1961-64), Am. Dialect Soc., Internat. Assn. Logopodics and Phoniatrics, Phonetic Soc. Japan (hon.), AAUP (emeritus), Lambda Ma'ams of Lambda Chi Alpha (pres. Ft. Worth 1962-63), Phi Beta Kappa Assn. (Ft. Worth chpt.), Phi Beta Kappa (Alpha of Calif. chpt.; charter mem., v.p. Delta of Tex. chpt. 1971-73, pres. 1973-74), Delta Zeta, Psi Chi, Sigma Alpha Eta. Republican. Mem. Christian Ch. Clubs: Woman's of Fort Worth, Women of Rotary. Participant, 13th Congress of Internat. Assn. Logopedics and Phoniatrics, Vienna, 1965, 14th Congress, Paris, 1968, 15th Congress, Buenos Aires, 1971, 16th Congress, Interlaken, Switzerland, 1974, 17th Congress, Copenhagen, 1977, 18th Congress, Washington, 1980, 19th Congress, Edinburgh, Scotland, 1983; participant 10th Internat. Congress of Linguists, Bucharest, 1967; participant 6th Internat. Congress of The Internat. Soc. Phonetic Scis., Prague, 1967, 7th Internat. Congress, Montreal, 1971, 8th Internat. Congress, Leeds, Eng., 1975; participant 1st Congress Internat. Assn. Sci. Study Mental Deficiency, Montpellier, France, 1967, Semmelweis Ann. Week, Budapest Acad. Scis., 1968, 3d World Congress Phoneticians, Tokyo, 1976. Author: Handbook for Instructors of Voice and Diction, 1968; contbr. articles to profl. jours. Home: 3860 S Hills Cir Fort Worth TX 76109-2757

LAWRENCE, THOMAS PATTERSON, public relations executive; b. Phila., Nov. 20, 1946; s. Granville Allen and Rebecca (Patterson) L.; m. Peggy Wilson, Nov. 1, 1986. BA in Journalism, Fla. So. Coll., 1968. Reporter Nashville Banner, 1968-70; account exec. Holder, Kennedy & Co., Nashville, 1971-78, exec. v.p., 1978-79; ptnr. Dye, Van Mol & Lawrence, Nashville, 1980—. Mem. Nat. Investor Rels. Inst., Nashville Soc. Fin. Analysts Inc., Nashville City Club, Hillwood Country Club. Republican. Presbyterian. Office: Dye Van Mol Lawrence 209 7th Ave N Nashville TN 37219-1802

LAWRENCE, VICKI SCHULTZ, singer, dancer, comedienne; b. Los Angeles, Mar. 26, 1949; d. Howard Axelrad and Ann Alene (Loyd) L.; m. Alvin Adolph Schultz, Jr., Nov. 16, 1974; children: Courtney Allison, Garrett Lawrence. Student, UCLA, 1967-70. Toured as entertainer with Johnny Grant, Vietnam, 1968. Appearances include (TV series) The Carol Burnett Show, CBS, 1967-78, Mama's Family, 1983-90, 87; hostess: (game shows) Win, Lose or Draw, 1987-89; recs. include The Night the Lights Went Out in Georgia (Gold record 1973); host Group W syndicated daytime talk show Vicki, 1992—. Recipient Emmy award for Burnett show, 1976. Republican. Lutheran. Avocations: needlepoint, sailing. Office: VICKI! Group W Productions 3000 W Alameda Ave Burbank CA 91523-0001

LAWRENCE, VICTOR B., computer engineer, systems engineer; b. Accra, Ghana, May 10, 1945. BSc, U. London, 1968, PhD, 1972. Tech. staff mem. AT&T Bell Labs. Fellow IEEE (assoc. editor IEEE Comm. Mag. 1978-81, assoc. editor IEEE Transactions on Cirs. and Sys. 1981-83, tech. program chmn. first internat. workshop on VLSI in comms. 1981, gen. chmn. fourth internat. workshop on VLSI in comm. 1986, tyech. program chmn. first internat. workshop on met. area networks 1986, chmn. tech. com. on signal processing and comm. electronics, mem. AdCom., Cirs. and Sys. Soc. 1986-89, mem. awards policy planning com. 1989-91, mem. bd. govs. Comm. Soc. 1990-92, vice-chmn. 1992-93, chmn. 1994—, Guillemin Cauer prize paper award 1981). Office: AT&T Bell Labs 200 Laurel Ave S Rm 1p-246 Middletown NJ 07748*

LAWRENCE, WALTER, JR., surgeon; b. Chgo., May 31, 1925; s. Walter and Violette May (Matthews) L.; m. Susan Grayson Shryock, June 20, 1947; children: Walter Thomas, Elizabeth, William Amos, Edward Gene. Student, Dartmouth Coll., 1943-44; PhB, U. Chgo., 1944, SB, 1945, MD with honors, 1948. Diplomate Am. Bd. Surgery (examiner 1974-78, sr. mem. 1978—). Intern Johns Hopkins, 1948-49, asst. resident, 1949-51; fellow Meml. Sloan-Kettering Cancer Center, 1951-52, 54-56, research fellow, 1956, asst. mem., asst. attending surgeon, 1957-60, asso. mem., asso. attending surgeon, 1960-66; practice medicine specializing in surgery N.Y.C., 1956-66, Richmond, Va., 1966—; instr. surgery Cornell U., 1957-58, asst. profl. clin. surgery, 1958-63, clin. assoc. prof., 1963-66; vis. investigator Queen Victoria Hosp., East Grinstead, Eng., 1964-65; prof. surgery Med. Coll. Va., Richmond, 1966—, chmn. divsn. surg. oncology, 1966-90, exec. vice chmn. dept. surgery, 1966-73, acting chmn., 1973-74, Am. Cancer Soc. profl. clin. oncology, 1972-77; dir. Cancer Ctr., 1974-88, dir. emeritus, 1988—; chmn. surgery test com. Nat. Bd. Med. Examiners, 1973-77; med. dir.-at-large Va. divsn. Am. Cancer Soc., 1967—, med. v.p. Am. Cancer Soc., 1975-77, pres., 1977-79, nat. del., 1982-85, bd. dirs., 1985—, nat. pres., 1991-92, mem. nat. coun. for rsch. and clin. investigation, 1974-78, nat. del., mem. profl. edn. com., 1982—, bd. dirs., 1985—, vice chmn., chmn. M&S com., 1986-88, chmn. M&S exec. com., 1989-90, pres. elect, 1990-91, pres., 1991-92; bd. sci. counsellors Nat. Cancer Inst., 1978-82, chmn. surg. oncology rsch. devel. com.; mem. N.c.a.b., 1988-94; governing coun. U.I.C.C., 1994—. Author: (with J.J. Terz) Cancer Management, 1977, (with J.J. Terz, J.P. Neifeld) Manual of Soft Tissue Surgery, 1983; mem. editl. bd. Va. Med., 1977-93, Jour. Surg. Oncology, 1978—, assoc. editor, 1991—; editl. bd. Jour. Cancer Edn., 1986; asst. editor Cancer, 1962-65, assoc. editor, 1991—; contbr. articles to med. jours. Served with USNR, 1942-46; Served with U.S. Army, 1952-54. Recipient Cancer Rsch. award Alfred P. Sloan Found., 1964; J. Shelton Horsley award Am. Cancer Soc., 1973; Disting. Svc. award U. Chgo., 1976; Va. Commonwealth U. Univ. Award for Excellence, 1988, Disting. Faculty award Med. Coll. Va. Alumni Assn., 1988, Va. Cultural Laureate award, 1992, OBICI award, 1992, Dean's award for Disting. Svc., 1992; named to Humera Soc. (hon.), 1992. Fellow ACS (commn. on cancer 1973-85, chmn. 1979-81), N.Y. Acad. Scis., Royal Soc. Medicine; mem. AAAS, AMA, Am. Assn. Cancer Edn., Am. Assn. Cancer Rsch., Am. Gastroenterol. Assn. (coun. on cancer 1972-76), Am. Surg. Assn., Halsted Soc. (pres. 1975), James Ewing Soc., Soc. Head and Neck Surgeons, Am. Soc. Clin. Oncology, Am. Radium Soc. (exec. coun. 1985-87), Soc. Surgery Alimentary Tract (founder), Soc. Surg. Oncology (exec. com. 1976-77, v.p. 1977-78, pres. 1979-80, chmn. exec. coun. 1980-81), Soc. Univ. Surgeons, Surg. Biol. Club III (founding mem.), Transplantation Soc., Collegium Internat. Chirurgiae Digestive, Southeastern Surg. Congress, Pan Am. Med. Assn., Sociètè Internationale de Chirurgie, Va. Surg. Soc. (v.p. 1973-74), Richmond Surg. Soc. (pres. 1986-87), Richmond Acad. Medicine (trustee 1986-87, 1st v.p. 1988), So. Surg. Assn., Argentine Surg. Assn. (hon.), Sigma Xi, Alpha Omega Alpha. Home: 6501 Three Chopt Rd Richmond VA 23226-3118 Office: Med Coll Va Hosps 1200 E Broad St PO Box 980011 Richmond VA 23298

LAWRENCE, WALTER THOMAS, plastic surgeon; b. Balt., Sept. 5, 1950; s. Walter Jr. and Susan (Shryock) L.; m. Marsha Blake, May 30, 1987. BS, Yale U., 1972; MPH, Harvard U., 1976; MD, U. Va., 1976. Diplomate Am. Bd. Surgery. Diplomate Am. Bd. Plastic Surgery. Intern and resident in gen. surgery U. N.C., Chapel Hill, 1976-78; resident gen. surgery Med. Coll. Va., Richmond, 1978-81; resident plastic surgery U. Chgo., 1981-83; expert NIH, Bethesda, Md., 1983-85; asst. prof. U. N.C., Chapel Hill, 1985-92, assoc. prof., div. chmn., 1992-95; prof., divsn. chmn. U. Mass. Med. Ctr., 1995—. Fellow Am. Coll. Surgeons; mem. Am. Assn. Plastic Surgeons, Am. Soc. Plastic and Reconstructive Surgeons, Plastic Surgery Rsch. Coun., Humera Soc., Womack Soc. Avocations: skiing, sailing, tennis. Office: U Mass Med Ctr Divsn Plastic Surgery Divsn Plastic Surgery 55 Lake Ave N Worcester MA 01655

LAWRENCE, WAYNE ALLEN, publisher; b. Cin., Dec. 11, 1938; s. Clarence E. and Edna M. (Newman) L.; m. Carol SueAnn Wisecup, July 28, 1959; children: Jeffrey Thomas, Jon Christopher, Jeremy Wayne. Student public schs., Seaman, Ohio. Advt. salesman Amos Press, Inc., Sidney, Ohio, 1957-61; v.p. Amos Press, Inc., 1973-83, sr. v.p., 1983-92, ret., 1992, also bd. dirs.; pub. Stamp World, Linns Stamp News, 1977-82; v.p. advt. Coin World, Sidney, 1973-78; advt. mgr. World Coins, Sidney, 1964-68, advt. dir., 1968-73, v.p., 1973-77; adv. mgr. Numis. Scrapbook, Sidney, 1967-68, advt. dir., 1968-73, v.p. advt., 1973-78; pub. Cars & Parts, Sidney, 1978-85; propr., dir. Sidney Camera, 1981-87; pres. Scott Pub. Co., 1984-92. Contbr. articles and editorials on coins, stamps and cars to Amos publs. Bd. dirs. Shelby County (Ohio) United Way, 1970-76, 1st United Meth. Ch., Sidney, 1982—; bd. dirs. Sidney-Shelby County United Way, 1982-85, sec., 1985; mem. U.S. Assay Commn., 1975. Mem. Am. Mgmt. Assn., Am. Numis. Assn., Am. Philatelic Assn., Numis. Lit. Guild, Am. Stamp Dealers Assn., Mag. Pubs. Assn., Am. Motorcycle Assn., Soc. Automotive Historians. Lodge: Moose. Home: PO Box 242 Anna OH 45302-2042 Office: 911 S Vandemark Rd Sidney OH 45365-8974

LAWRENCE, WILLARD EARL, mathematics, statistics and computer science educator emeritus; b. Chassell, Mich., Apr. 8, 1917; s. William and Ruth Marie (Messner) L.; m. Lorayne Adalayde Williams, June 12, 1943; children—Victoria (Mrs. Joseph C. Barton), Barbara (Mrs. Timothy F. Columbia), Joan (Mrs. James A. Wilger), Willard, Mark. Student, Ripon Coll., 1947-49; B.S., Marquette U., 1951, M.S., 1953; postgrad., U. Wyo., summer 1959, Iowa State U., summer 1961; M.S., U. Wis., 1962, Ph.D., 1964. Prof. math. and statistics Marquette U., Milw., 1953-87; prof. emeritus math., statistics and computer sci. Marquette U., 1987—, chmn. dept., 1973-79; statis. cons. Author: Introduction to the Theory of Probability, 1967, Probability: An Introductory Course, 1970. Served with USAAF, 1941-45. Decorated Bronze Star medal.; NSF faculty fellow, 1961-62. Mem. Math. Assn. Am., Wis. Geol. Soc. Roman Catholic. Home: 13865 Adelaide Ln Brookfield WI 53005-4967 Office: Marquette U Katharine Reed Cudahy Hall Milwaukee WI 53233

LAWRENCE, WILLIAM, JR., elementary education educator; b. L.A., Mar. 2, 1930; s. Willie and Nellie (January) L.; m. Elizabeth Johnson, Jan. 13, 1951; children: William III, Timothy Dwight, Walter Fitzgerald. BA in Psychology, Columbia Coll., Mo., 1981; LLB, LaSalle U., 1982; MA in Edn., Claremont Coll., 1992; postgrad., Calif. Coast U., 1992—. Enlisted U.S. Army, 1947, advanced through grades to lt., 1957, commd. sgt. maj., 1965; served U.S. Army, Vietnam, 1965-70; instr. U.S. Military Acad., West Point, N.Y., 1970-73; with Berlin Brigade, U.S. Army, Berlin, Germany, 1973-76; dep. sheriff L.A., 1958-65; probation officer San Bernardino County, Calif., 1985-89; tchr. Pomona Unified Sch. Dist., Pomona, Calif., 1989—. Decorated U.S. Army Dist. Svc. Cross for Extraordinary Heroism in Combat, Silver Star, 7 Purple Hearts. Mem. Legion of Valor, 555Th Parachute Battalion (pres.). Democrat. Roman Catholic. Avocations: photography, free fall parachuting. Home: 1456 S Lilac Ave Bloomington CA 92316-2130 Office: Pomona Unified Sch Dist 800 N Garey Ave Pomona CA 91767-4616

LAWRENCE, WILLIAM DORAN, physician; b. Tampa, Fla., Sept. 3, 1926; s. Joseph Daniel and Gladys Irene (Lamb) Lawrence; m. Mardelle Laura Wright, June 18, 1950; children: Jodi Werhanowicz, Patricia Lawrence, Susan Hunter. BA, State U. Iowa, 1948, MD, 1951. Diplomate Am. Bd. Ob-Gyn. Intern Parkland Hosp., Dallas, 1951-52; family doctor Hereford, Tex., 1952, 53, 56; resident, preceptorship Northwestern Hosp., Mpls., 1954-55, 57-61; pvt. practice Phoenix, 1957—. Contbr. articles to profl. jours. Physician World Brotherhood Exch. and So. Bapt. Mission, India, Africa, 1963-93. With USNR, 1944-46. Recipient Dr. Thomas Dooley medal Maricopa County Med. Soc., 1979. Mem. Ariz. Med. Assn. Republican. Avocations: flying, fishing, hunting. Home: 32 E Marshall Ave Phoenix AZ 85012-1318

LAWRENCE, WILLIAM JOSEPH, JR., retired corporate executive; b. Kalamazoo, Feb. 1, 1918; s. William J. and Borgia M. (Wheeler) L.; m. Doris Luella Fitzgerald, Aug. 19, 1955; children: Aaron Frances, Cleve Moren, Julie Anne, William III. A.B., Kalamazoo Coll., 1941. Engaged in personal investments; dir. emeritus, treas. Superior Pine Products Co.; chmn. bd. dir. Channel 41, Inc.; dir. LPI. Trustee emeritus, mem. fin. and adminstrn. com. Kalamazoo Found., Borgess Hosp.; trustee emeritus Kalamazoo Coll. With AUS, 1942-46. Mem. Kalamazoo C. of C., Kiwanis, Com. of Twenty-Five (Palm Springs, Calif.), Gull Lake Country Club, Park Club. Roman Catholic. Home: PO Box 37 Richland MI 49083-0037 Office: 1000 Old Kent Bank Bldg Kalamazoo MI 49007

LAWRENCE-FORREST, LORI LOUISE, restaurateur; b. Brockton, Mass., Oct. 12, 1950; d. Hallett Thompson and Dorothy Mae (McElroy) L.; m. David John Forrest, 1994; 1 child, Cameron Stuart Forrest. AA, Canada Coll., Redwood City, Calif., 1970; postgrad., Chapman Coll., 1971-72, Foothill Coll., 1973-74. Owner, operator The Natural Gourmet, Palo Alto, Calif., 1974-76, Quiche Lori, Palo Alto, 1976-81; sales assoc Williams-Sonoma, Palo Alto, 1981-86; owner, operator Lori's Kitchens, Palo Alto, 1982-91; sales assoc. Neiman-Marcus Epicure, Palo Alto, 1986-91; owner, operator The Rose & Crown, Palo Alto, 1991—; Contbr. articles to publs. Recipient award dessert category Cook Your Way to France Profl. Chef's Contest, 1990. Mem. San Francisco Profl. Food Soc. Avocations: oenology, foreign travel, sailplaning, skiing, hiking. Office: The Rose & Crown 547 Emerson St Palo Alto CA 94301-1608

LAWRIE, DUNCAN H., computer science educator, consultant; b. Chgo., Apr. 26, 1943; s. John Lawrie and Annabel (Harwood) McKenna; m. Linda K. Zapf, June 1, 1974. BA, De Pauw U., 1966; BSEE, Purdue U., 1966; MS, U. Ill., 1969, PhD, 1973. Asst. prof. U. Ill., Urbana, 1973-79, assoc. prof., 1979-84, prof., 1984—, head dept. computer sci., 1990—. Contbr. numerous articles to profl. jours.; patentee computer memory. Fellow IEEE (editor-in-chief transp. parallel and distributed systems); mem. IEEE Computer Soc. (pres. 1991), Assn. Computing Machinery. Office: U Ill Dept Computer Sci 1304 W Springfield Ave Urbana IL 61801-2910

LAWROSKI, HARRY, nuclear engineer; b. Dalton, Pa., Oct. 10, 1928; s. Alexander and Nancy (Lutchka) L.; m. Mary Ann DeWoody, Oct. 6, 1962. B.S. in Chem. Engring, Pa. State U., 1950, M.S., 1956, Ph.D., 1959. Research and devel. work in petroleum refining Pa. State U., 1950-58; instr., thesis advisor Argonne (Ill.) Nat. Lab., 1958-63; supt., asso. project dir. exptl. breeder reactor II power plant Idaho Nat. Engring. Lab., 1968-73; gen. mgr. quality assurance and environmental services Nuclear Services Corp., Campbell, Calif., 1973-76; asst. gen. mgr. nuclear fuel processing and waste mgmt. tech. Idaho chem. programs Allied Chem. Corp., Idaho Falls, 1976-79; cons., 1979—; lectr. Idaho Acad. Scis.; cons. in field; chmn. sci. and tech. project 1990 Idaho Centennial Celebration. Author. Named Outstanding Engring. Alumnus Pa. State U., 1981. Fellow Am. Nuclear Soc. (treas. 1973-77, dir. 1969-77, pres.-elect 1979-80, pres. 1980-81), Am. Inst. Chem. Engrs. (chmn. nuclear engring. div. 1974), Skull and Bones, Sigma Xi, Tau Beta Pi, Sigma Tau, Phi Lambda Upsilon. Clubs: Rotary, Elks. Patentee in field. Home: PO Box 717 Wilson WY 83014-0717

LAWRY, SYLVIA (MRS. STANLEY ENGLANDER), association executive; b. N.Y.C.; d. Jack and Sonia (Tager) Friedman; m. Michael Lawry, Mar. 1944 (div. 1946); m. Stanley Englander, Apr. 1957 (dec. 1968); children: Franklin Miles, Steven Jon. A.B., Hunter Coll., 1936. Law practice and hearing reporter for State Arbitrator, 1937-40; sponsored by N.Y.C., 1942-43; Law practice and hearing reporter for U.S. Atty.'s office, N.Y., 1943-44; asst. dir. radio prodn. Civilian Def. Reporting; founded Nat. Multiple Sclerosis Soc., N.Y.C., 1946; exec. dir. Nat. Multiple Sclerosis Soc., until 1982, now founder-dir., 1982—; sec. Internat. Fedn. Multiple Sclerosis Soc., 1967—. Mem. President's Com. on Employment of Handicapped. Recipient Disting. Svc. award Nat. Health Coun., Pres. Reagan's Volunteer Action award, 1987. Mem. APHA, Acad. Polit. Sci., Am. Judicature Soc., Rehab. Internat. Office: Nat Multiple Sclerosis Soc 733 3rd Ave New York NY 10017-3288

LAWS, ELLIOTT PEARSON, federal agency administrator; b. N.Y.C., May 4, 1956; s. James Garfield and Elvira Johanna (Freeman) L.;m. Karen Marie Jackson, June 22, 1991. BA, St. John's U., Jamaica, N.Y., 1977; JD, Georgetown U., 1980. Bar: N.Y., D.C. Law clk. Office of Chief Counsel, Army C.E., Washington, 1978-80; asst. dist. atty. N.Y. County Water Enforcement Divsn. Office Enforcement & Compliance Monitoring, U.S. EPA, Washington, 1980-84, atty., 1984-85; trial atty. environ. def. sect. Dept. of Justice, Washington, 1985-87; assoc. Patton, Boggs & Blow, Washington, 1987-91, ptnr., 1991-93; asst. adminstr. Office Solid Waste & Emergency Response, U.S. EPA, Washington, 1993—. Co-author: Clean Water Handbook, Govt. Inst., 1990, Environ. Law Handbook, 1991, Clean Air Law and Regulation, 1992; Contributing author in field. Office: EPA 401 M St SW Washington DC 20460 Office: US EPA 5101 401 M St NW Washington DC 22046*

LAWS, GORDON DERBY, lawyer; b. Dallas, Feb. 1, 1949; s. Wilford Derby and Ruby (Whiteleather) L.; m. Barbara Ruth Hill, May 9, 1974; children: Gordon Derby Jr., Stephen Richard, Ruthanne. BA in Econs., Brigham Young U., 1973, JD, 1976. Bar: Utah 1976, Tex. 1986, U.S. Supreme Ct. 1981, U.S. Ct. Appeals (5th cir.) 1982, U.S. Dist. Ct. (we. dist.) Tex. 1987, U.S. Dist. Ct. (so. dist.) Tex. 1991. Trial atty. U.S. Justice Dept., Washington, 1976-81; asst. U.S. atty. Western Dist. Tex., San Antonio, 1981-87, asst. chief, civil divsn., U.S. atty., 1985-87; assoc. Gary, Thomasson, Hall & Marks, Corpus Christi, Tex., 1987-89; ptnr./mem. Gary, Thomasson, Hall & Marks, 1989—; mem. exec. com. Gary, Thomasson, Hall & Marks,1994—. Bishop Ch. of Jesus Christ of Latter Day Saints, Corpus Christi, 1990-95. Avocations: reading, camping. Home: 4158 Eagle Dr Corpus Christi TX 78413 Office: Gary Thomasson Hall & Marks 210 Carancahua Ste 500 PO Box 2888 Corpus Christi TX 78403-2888

LAWS, PRISCILLA WATSON, physics educator; b. N.Y.C., Jan. 18, 1940; d. Morris Clemens and Frances (Fetterinan) Watson; m. Kenneth Lee Laws, June 3, 1965; children: Kevin Allen, Virginia. BA, Reed Coll., 1961; MA, Bryn Mawr Coll., 1963, PhD, 1966. Asst. prof. physics Dickinson Coll., Carlisle, Pa., 1965-70; assoc. prof. Dickinson Coll., Carlisle, 1970-79, prof. physics, 1979—, chmn. dept. physics and astronomy, 1982-83; cons. in field. Author: X Rays: More Harm than Good?, 1977, The X-Ray Information Book, 1983; contbr. numerous articles to profl. jours.; assoc. editor Am. Jour. Physics, 1989—. Vice-pres. Cumberland Conservancy, 1972-73, pres. 1973; bd. dirs. Pa. Alliance for Returnables, 1974-77; asst. sec., treas. Carlisle Hosp. Authority, 1973-76; pres. bd. Carlisle Day Care Ctr., 1973-74. Fellow NSF, 1963-64, grantee, 1989-95, Commonwealth of Pa., 1985-86, U.S. Dept. Edn. Fund for Improvement of Post-Secondary Edn., 1986-89, 89-93, AEC; recipient Innovation award Merck Found., 1989, Educom Incriptal award for curriculum innovation in sci. labs., 1989, award Sears Roebuck and Co., 1990, award Outstanding Software Devel. Computers in Physics Jour., 1991, Pioneering Achievement in Edn. award Dana Found., 1993. Mem. Am. Assn. Physics Tchrs. (Disting Svc. citation 1992, Robert A. Milliken award for Outstanding Contbns. to Physics Tchg., 1996), Fedn. Am. Scientist, Sigma Xi, Sigma Pi Sigma, Omicron Delta Kappa. Democrat. Home: 10 Douglas Ct Carlisle PA 17013-1714 Office: Dickinson Coll PO Box 1773 Carlisle PA 17013

LAWSON, A(BRAM) VENABLE, retired librarian; b. South Boston, Va., Jan. 9, 1922; s. Abram Venable and Vivien Strudwick (Moseley) L.; children—Janet Lee, Abram Venable, Mary Vivian. B.A., U. Ala., 1946; M.Ln., Emory U., 1950; D.L.S., Columbia U., 1969. Auditor Socony Mobil Oil Co., 1947-48; teller 1st Nat. Bank, Altavista, Va., 1948-49; library asst. Harvard Coll. Library, 1951-54; head reference dept. Atlanta Pub. Libr., 1954-56, coord. pub. svcs., 1956-60; asst. prof. Fla. State U., 1960-65; dir. div. librarianship Emory U., Atlanta, 1965-89; vis. prof. Clark Atlanta U., 1989-90. Active Friends of Atlanta Fulton Pub. Libr., 1987—; advisor Friends of Librs. USA, 1990-93; bd. dirs. Episcopal Chartities Found., Absalom Jones Student U., 1995—. With USAF, 1942-46. Recipient George Virgil Fuller award Columbia U., 1964, Nick Davies award Friends of Atlanta Fulton Pub. Libr., 1993. Mem. ALA, AAUP, Assn. Libr. and Info. Sci. Edn., Southeastern Libr. Assn., Ga. Libr. Assn. (Nix-Jones award for disting. svc. to Ga. librarianship 1989). Home: 1065 Briarcliff Rd NE Atlanta GA 30306-2619

LAWSON, ANDREW LOWELL, JR., defense industry company executive; b. Macon, Ga., Jan. 16, 1938; s. Andrew Lowell and Valerie Ula (Brazzeal) L.; m. Carol Belle Few, Dec. 31, 1961; children: Andrew L. III, Steven Brian. Student, Mercer U., 1955; cert., Middle Ga. Coll., 1956-58; BS in Math, U. Ga., 1960. Contract price analyst WRAMA, Robins AFB, Ga., 1960-64; with E-Systems, Inc., Greenville, Tex., various fin. positions, 1964-70; v.p. fin., div. controller Huntington, Ind., 1970-73; corp. v.p., controller Dallas, 1973; corp. v.p., div. v.p. fin. & adminstrn. Greenville, 1973-78, corp. v.p., gen. mgr. Greenville div., 1978-83; sr. v.p., group exec. aircraft systems group Dallas, 1983-87, exec. v.p., 1987—, also bd. dirs. Deacon Ridgecrest Bapt. Ch., Greenville. Served with USNR, 1955-63. Mem. Aerospace Industries Assn., Am. Def. Preparedness Assn., Armed Force Communnications and Electronic Assn., Assn. U.S. Army, Air Force Assn., Navy League, Old Crows. Office: E-Systems Inc PO Box 660248 Dallas TX 75266-0248*

LAWSON, BEN F., lawyer, international legal consultant; b. Marietta, Okla., Feb. 7, 1939; s. Woodrow W. and Lennie L. (McKay) l.; children: Nicole, Benjamin C. BBA, U. Houston, 1965, JD, 1967. Bar: Tex. 1967. Atty. Monsanto/Burmah Oil, Houston, 1967-72; mgr. internat. acquisitions Oxy (formerly Cities Svc. Co.), Houston, 1972-78; gen. atty. Damson Oil Corp., Houston, 1978-81; gen. counsel, v.p. Newmont Oil Co., Houston, 1981-86; pvt. practice internat. law Houston, 1986—; cons. internat., 1987—. Contbr. numerous articles to profl. jours. Staff sgt. USAF, 1959-65. Fellow Houston Bar Found.; mem. ABA, Am. Corp. Counsel Assn. (chmn. oil and gas com. 1986-87). Republican. Avocations: fishing, antiques. Address: 3027 Bernadette Ln Houston TX 77043-1302

LAWSON, BETH ANN REID, strategic planner; b. N.Y.C., Jan. 9, 1954; d. Raymond Theodore and Jean Elizabeth (Frinks) Reid; m. Michael Berry Lawson, Jan. 29, 1983; children: Rayna, Sydney. BA, Va. Tech., 1976; MPA, Golden Gate U., 1983. From systems analyst I to support ops. asst. City of Virginia Beach, Va., 1977-93; water conservation coord. City of Virginia Beach, 1993-94; owner Strategic Planning and Teamwork, Virginia Beach, 1993—; U.S. Army Corps. Engring. Va. Beach Cmty. Devel. Corp.; cons. Va. Beach Cmty. Devel. Corp., 1996, Lifesaving Mus. Va., 1994, Virginia Beach C.A.R.E. Com., 1995, Virginia Beach Rescue Squad, 1992—, Virginia Beach Mcpl. Employees Fed. Credit Union, 1992—, Virginia Beach Resort Area Adv. Commn., 1993, Virginia Beach Conv. and Visitors Devel. Bur., 1991-93. Sunday sch. tchr. Wycliffe Presbyn. Ch., Virginia Beach. Mem. Virginia Beach Rotary Club (Outstanding Employee 1993), Va. Tech. Alumni Assn. (pres. 1982-83). Avocations: tennis, movies, planning, writing. Home: 701 Earl Of Warwick Ct Virginia Beach VA 23454-2910 Office: Strategic Planning and Teamwork 701 Earl Of Warwick Ct Virginia Beach VA 23454-2910

LAWSON, BILLIE KATHERINE, elementary school educator; b. Cleveland, Tenn., Jan. 15, 1943; d. William Taylor and Katherine Beatrice (Kelley) L. BS in Elem. Edn., Lee Coll., 1970; postgrad., Exeter (Eng.) U., 1975; MEd, U. Tenn., 1975; postgrad., Trevecca Nazarene Coll., Nashville, 1989. Cert. elem. tchr., Tenn. Tchr. Prospect Sch., Cleveland, 1970-76, Trewhitt Elem. Sch., Cleveland, 1976—; mem. Gov.'s Coun. Gore del. 3rd Congl. Dist. Conv., Tenn., 1988. Recipient 4-H Leader award, 1985. Mem. NEA (local rep. to nat. conv.), Nat. Coun. Tchrs. of Math., Tenn. Edn. Assn. (local rep. to state conv.), Bradley County Edn. Assn. (treas., sch. rep., mem. coms.), U. Tenn. Alumni Assn., Lee Coll. Alumni Assn. Democrat. Baptist. Avocations: reading, travel. Home: 198 Charles Cir SE Cleveland TN 37323-8814 Office: Trewhitt Elem Sch 610 Kile Lake Rd SE Cleveland TN 37323-8446

LAWSON, D. DALE, public relations executive. Sr. labor policy analyst Govt. Rsch. Corp; v.p. Hill and Knowlton Pub. Affairs Worldwide; sr. prin./dir. labor policy Capitoline Internat. Group Ltd., 1991—. Office: Capitoline Internat Group Ltd 1615 L St NW # 1150 Washington DC 20036-5610*

LAWSON, DAVID E., architect; b. Eau Claire, Wis., Apr. 12, 1937; s. Ralph E. and Guida (Mahon) L.; m. Mary A. Gease, Dec. 29, 1984; children from previous marriage: Eric, Kent, Keith. BArch, U. Ill., 1960. Lic. architect Wis., Va., Iowa, Mich. Pa. Archtl. intern Tannenbaum & Koehnen, Milw., 1961-63; project mgr. Cashin & Goodwin, Madison, Wis., 1963-64; project architect Law Law Potter & Nystrom, Madison, 1964-66; exec. v.p. Potter Lawson Architects, Madison, 1966—; bd. dirs. Associated Randall Bank, Madison, Downtown Madison Ptnrs. Inc. Architect: McPhee Physical Edn. Bldg., Eau Claire, Wis., 1970 (Honor award Wis. Soc. Arch.), Wis. Power and Light Control Ctr., 1977 (Honor award Wis. Soc. Arch.). Mem. City of Madison Urban Design Task Force, 1973; chmn. Archtl. Engring. Div. Dame County (Wis.) United Way, 1981; bd. dirs. Friends U. Wis. Arboretum, Madison, 1977-80. Named Dane County's Top Architectural Exec., Madison Mags. Survey of 1000 Bus. Leaders, 1994. Fellow AIA (bd. dirs. 1983-85, v.p. 1986, chmn. govt. affairs adv. bd., nat. registration law adv. task force, 1979-88, chmn. AIA design build task force 1989-91); mem. Wis. Soc. Archs. (chmn. legis. com 1974-81, v.p., pres. elect 1977, pres. 1978, recipient first Golden award for disting. svc. to profession 1985), Nat. Archtl. Accrediting Bd. (exec. com. 1987-88), Madison Club (bd. dirs. 1988-92, v.p. 1989-90, pres. 1990-91), Nakoma Country Club. Lutheran. Home: 2145 Middleton Beach Rd Middleton WI 53562-2904 Office: Potter Lawson Inc PO Box 44964 Madison WI 53744-4964

LAWSON, DAVID JERALD, bishop; b. Princeton, Ind., Mar. 26, 1930; s. David Jonathon and Bonnetta A. (White) L.; m. Martha Ellen Pegram, July 16, 1950; children: John Mark, Karen Sue Lawson Eynon. A.B., U. Evansville, 1955; M.Div., Garrett Theol. Sem., 1959; D.D., U. Evansville, 1977. Ordained to ministry United Methodist Ch. Bishop United Meth. Ch., Wis., 1984-92, Ill., 1992—; trustee Ill. Wesleyan Coll., McKendree Coll., MacMurray Coll., Meth. Health Svcs., Peoria, No. Ctrl. Coll., Naperville, Ill., 1984-92; pres. United Meth. Bd. Discipleship, also chairperson; mem. com. theol. edn. World Meth. Coun., also mem. exec. com.; mem. originating steering com. New Africa U.; mem. Ill. Conf. of Churches, Coun. of Bishop's to Study the Ministry. Author monograph: Administrative Spirituality; contbr. articles to profl. jours.

LAWSON, DAVID LEWIS, religious organization administrator, minister; b. Hoopeston, Ill., Feb. 9, 1932; s. Moses and Mildred Grace (Hofer) L.; m. Paula Jean Laird, June 4, 1954; children: Dayla Jean, Pamali Jill. BS, Anderson U., 1959; MA, Ball State U., 1963; DD, Mid-Am. Bible Coll., 1986. Ordained to ministry Ch. of God, 1960. Interim pastor Ch. of God, Watseka, Ill., 1958-59; assoc. pastor Ch. of God, New Albany, Ind., 1959-60; from promotional sec. to exec. dir. World Svc., Anderson, Ind., 1960-88; assoc. gen. sec. Leadership Coun., Anderson, 1980—. With U.S. Army, 1951-54, Korea. Mem. Kiwanis. Home: 1303 Frances Ln Anderson IN 46012 Office: Leadership Coun Ch of God 1303 E 5th St Anderson IN 46012

LAWSON, EDWARD EARLE, neonatologist; b. Winston-Salem, N.C., Aug. 6, 1946; s. Robert Barrett and Elsie Chatterton (Earle) L.; m. Rebecca Newhall Fitts, June 21, 1969; children: Katherine Tabor, Robert Barrett II. BA magna cum laude, Harvard U., 1968; MD, Northwestern U., 1972. Diplomate Am. Bd. Pediatrics and Neonatal/Perinatal Medicine. Intern then resident pediatrics Children's Hosp., Boston, 1972-75, fellow neonatology, 1975-78; from asst. prof. pediatrics to prof. pediatrics U. N.C., Chapel Hill, 1978—, chief div. neonatal medicine, 1987-95, interim chmn. dept. pediatrics, 1993-95; v. chmn., Dept. Pediatrics, 1995—. Assoc. editor Jour. of Pediatrics, 1985-95; contbr. numerous articles to profl. jours. Recipient Sidney Farber Meml. Rsch. award United Cerbral Palsy, 1982, Rsch. Career Devel. award NIH, 1982-87; fellow E. L. Trudeau, 1978-81, Alexander Von Humboldt, 1985-86; NIH grantee, 1979—. Fellow Am. Acad. Pediatrics; mem. Am. Lung Assn. (sci. adv. com. 1989-91), Am. Thoracic Soc. (bd. dirs. 1988-90), Am. Bd. Pediatric Soc., Perinatal Rsch. Soc. Achievements include research on developmental aspects of respiratory control, particularly physiology and neurobiology. Office: U NC Dept Pediatrics CB 7220 Chapel Hill NC 27599-7220

LAWSON, ELIZABETH LOUISE, special education educator; b. New London, Conn., May 2, 1945; d. V. Francis and Susan Louise (Spilman) Reynolds; m. Vernon Grady Lawson, Aug. 24, 1968; children: Mary Elizabeth Lawson Omar, Steven Raymond. BS in Home Econs., U. Ariz., 1967; MEd summa cum laude, N.C. Ctrl. U., 1993. Clerical and ad layout technician Impressive Advt., Waynesboro, Va., 1959-67; tchr. Augusta County (Va.) Schs., 1967, Waynesboro (Va.) City Schs., 1967-68; skin care cons. Luzier Cosmetics, Titusville, Fla., 1970-72; kindergarten aide Wake County Schs., Raleigh, N.C., 1979-81; spl. edn. tchr. Spring Hill Sch., Raleigh, 1984—, mentor tchr., 1994—; tchr. of deaf adults Raleigh 1st United Pentecostal Ch., 1993—, interpreter for deaf, 1981—. Author model for interpretive dance for U. Meth. Ch. Leadership Mag., 1969. Recipient Appreciation award Brevard County coun. Girl Scouts U.S.A., 1971. Mem. Coun. for Exceptional Children (sec. N.C. fedn. of mental retardation/developmentally disabled divsn. 1995—), N.C. Registry of Interpreters for the Deaf. Republican. Avocations: knitting, crochetting, singing, musical instruments, tatting. Office: Spring Hill Sch/Dorothea Dix Hosp 820 S Boylan Ave Raleigh NC 27603-2176

LAWSON, EVE KENNEDY, ballet mistress; b. Washington, Mar. 28, 1964; d. John and Elizabeth Lawson. Student, Sch. Am. Ballet, N.Y.C., 1972-83. Prin. dancer State Ballet Mo., Kansas City, 1983-87; dancer Miami City Ballet, Miami Beach, Fla., 1988-94, coord. edn., 1993-94, ballet mistress, 1994—. Created prin. roles in ballet Voyager (Bolender), 1984, Miniatures (Gamonet), 1990, Tango Tonto (Gamonet), 1991. Office: Miami City Ballet 905 Lincoln Rd Miami FL 33139

LAWSON, F. D., bishop. Bishop Ch. of God in Christ, Stillwater, Okla. Office: Ch of God in Christ PO Box 581 Stillwater OK 74076-0581

LAWSON, FRANCIS COLIN, chemical company executive; b. Apr. 7, 1917; s. James and Alice (Gamble) L.; m. Mary Aileen Behan, Oct. 21, 1942; children: Paul, Judy, Tony, Moya, Clare, Margaret, James. From various clerical positions to asst. sales mgr. of subs. Australian Consol. Industries Ltd., Melbourne, 1932-50; sec. Gibson Chem. Industries Ltd., Melbourne, 1950-62, dep. mng. dir., 1970-75, mng. dir., 1975-83, chmn. bd., 1983—. Fellow Cert. Practising Accts., Australian Inst. Mgmt. Roman Catholic. Avocations: golf, public speaking. Home: 7 Limeburners Way, Portsea Victoria 3944, Australia Office: Gibson Chem Industries Ltd, 350 Reserve Rd/Cheltenham, Melbourne Victoria, Australia

LAWSON, FRED RAULSTON, banker; b. Sevierville, Tenn., Mar. 26, 1936; s. Arville Raulston and Ila Mary (Lowe) L.; m. Sharon Sheets, Jan. 1, 1982; children: Terry Lee Lawson Akins, Laura Ann Lawson Rathbone, Kristi Yvette. Student, U. Tenn., 1953-59, La. State U. Sch. Banking of South, 1965-68, Harvard Inst. Fin. Mgmt., 1968. From br. mgr. to exec. v.p. Blount Nat. Bank, Maryville, Tenn., 1958-68, pres., 1968-86, also bd. dirs.; pres. Tenn. Nat. Bancshares, Inc., Maryville, 1971-86, Bank of East Tenn., Knoxville, 1986-92; pres., CEO BankFirst, Knoxville, 1993—; mem. Ft. Sanders Alliance Investment Mgrs. Rev. Subcom.; bd. dirs. Areawide Devel. Corp., Fortress Corp. Mem. Blount County Indsl. Devel. bd., 1969—; chancellors assoc. U. Tenn., Knoxville, 1971-78; trustee Carson-Newman Coll., Jefferson City, 1984-94, Harrison-Chilhowee Bapt. Acad., Seymour, Tenn., 1972-85, Pellissippi State Found.; adv. bd. U. Tenn. Med. Rsch. Ctr. and Hosp.; bd. regents Mid-South Sch. banking, Memphis, 1982-90; bd. dirs. Thompson Cancer Survival Ctr., Knoxville, 1987-94, The Downtown Orgn., Tenn. Resource Valley, East Tenn. Hist. Soc., Maryville Coll., 1995—. Recipient Tenn. Indsl. Devel. Vol. award, 1977. Mem. Assn. Bank Holding Cos. (bd. dirs. 1978-82), Tenn. Bankers Assn. (chmn. state legis. com. 1980, banking practice com. 1983, bd. dirs. 1990—, pres. 1994-95). Republican. Baptist. Home: 2101 Cochran Rd Maryville TN 37803-2812

LAWSON, H(ERBERT) BLAINE, JR., mathematician, educator; b. Norristown, Pa., Jan. 4, 1942; s. Herbert Blaine and Mary Louise (Corson) L.; m. Carolyn Elaine Pieroni, June 6, 1964 (div. Sept. 1977); children: Christina Corson, Heather Brooke. AB, ScB in Applied Mat. and Russian Lit., Brown U., 1964; MS in Math., Stanford U., 1966, PhD in Math., 1968. Lectr. math. U. Calif., Berkeley, 1968-70, assoc. prof., 1971-74, prof., 1974-80, asst. dean, 1975-77; Disting. prof., chmn. SUNY, Stony Brook, 1978—; vis. asst. prof. IMPA, Rio de Janeiro, 1970-71; vis. prof. Inst. des Hautes Etudes Scientifiques, Bures-sur-Yvette, France, 1977-78, Ecole Poly., Palaiseau, France, 1983-84; bd. dirs. U.S.-Brazilian Math. Exch., Stony Brook and Rio de Janeiro; trustee Math. Scis. Rsch. Inst., Berkeley; chmn. Nat. Com. Math. NAS, Washington, 1989-91; mem. Inst. Advanced Study, Princeton U., 1973-74; lectr. in minimal submanifolds, 1971. Author: The Theory of Gauge Fields in 4 Dimensions, 1985, Spin Geometry, 1989; editor Jour. Differential Geometry, Topology, The Princeton Mat. Series; contbr. articles to profl. jours. Sloan Found. fellow, 1971, Guggenheim Found. fellow, 1983, Japan Soc. Promotion Sci. fellow, 1985. Mem. Nat. Acad. of Sci., Am. Math. Soc. (coun. 1988—, editor jour., Steele prize 1975), Math. Assn. Am. Achievements include construction of minimal surfaces in the 3-dimensional sphere, construction of foliations on higher dimensional spheres; characterization of boundaries of analytic varieties; co-creation of Calibrated Geometries; research on basic results on manifolds on non-positive curvature, on spaces of positive scalar curvature, on stability results for Yang-Mills fields, on relations between algebraic cycles and topology, and on structure of Chow Varieties. Home: 29 North Rd Stony Brook NY 11790-1009

LAWSON, JACK WAYNE, lawyer; b. Decatur, Ind., Sept. 23, 1935; s. Alva W. and Florence C. (Smitley) L.; m. Sarah J. Hibbard, Dec. 28, 1961; children: Mark, Jeff. BA in Polit. Sci., Valparaiso U., 1958, JD, 1961. Bar: Ind. 1961, U.S. Supreme Ct. 1970, U.S. Dist. Ct. (no., so. dists.) Ind. 1991, Ind. Supreme Ct., Appellate Cts. 1991. Ptnr. Dunten, Beckman & Lawson, Ft. Wayne, Ind., 1961-84; sr. ptnr. Beckman, Lawson, Sandler, Snyder & Federoff, Ft. Wayne, 1984—; seminar presenter and writer Ind. CLE Forum, Indpls., 1970—, Nat. Health Lawyers Assn., Washington, 1986. Editor-in-chief Indiana Real Estate Transactions; contbr. articles to profl. jours. Mem. Ft. Wayne C. of C., 1975—; small claims ct. judge, Allen County, Ind., 1963-67. Mem. Am. Coll. Real Estate Lawyers. Republican. Lutheran. Avocations: sailing, teaching religious seminars. Office: Beckman Lawson Sandler Snyder & Federoff 200 E Main St PO Box 800 Fort Wayne IN 40801-0800

LAWSON, JANE ELIZABETH, bank executive; b. Cornwall, Ont., Can.; d. Leonard J. and Margaret L. BA, LLB, U. N.B., Can., 1971. With law dept. Royal Bank Can., Montreal, Que., Can., 1974-78, sr. counsel, 1978-84; v.p., corp. sec. Royal Bank Can., Montreal, Que., 1988-92, sr. v.p., sec., 1992—. Mem. Can. Bar Assn., N.B. Bar Assn., Que. Bar Assn., Inst. Chartered Secs. and Adminstrs., Inst. Corp. Dirs., Inst. Donations and Pub. Affairs Rsch. (fin. com.), Am. Soc. Corp. Secs., Mt. Royal Tennis Club. Office: Royal Bank Can PO Box 6001, 1 Place Ville Marie, Montreal, PQ Canada H3C 3A9

LAWSON, JENNIFER, broadcast executive; b. Birmingham, Ala., June 8, 1946; d. Willie DeLeon and Velma Theresa (Foster) L.; m. Elbert Sampson, June 1, 1979 (div. Sept. 1980); m. Anthony Gittens, May 29, 1982: children: Kai, Zachary. Student, Tuskegee U., 1963-65; MFA, Columbia U., 1974; LHD (hon.), Teikyo Post U., Hartford, Conn., 1991. Assoc. producer William Greaves Prodns., N.Y.C., 1974-75; asst. prof. film studies Bklyn. Coll., 1975-77; exec. dir. The Film Fund, N.Y.C., 1977-80; TV coord. Program Fund Corp. for Pub. Broadcasting, Washington, 1980-83, assoc. dir. TV Program Fund, 1983-89, dir. TV Program Fund, 1989; exec. v.p. programming PBS, Alexandria, Va., 1989-95; v.p. Internat. Pub. TV, Washington, 1984-88; panelist Fulbright Fellowships, Washington, 1988-90. Author, illustrator: Children of Africa, 1970; illustrator: Our Folktales, 1968, African Folktales: A Calabash of Wisdom, 1973. Coord. Nat. Coun. Negro Women, Washington, 1969. Avocations: painting, reading. Office: 1838 Ontario Pl Washington DC 20009

LAWSON, JOHN H., university official; b. Gloucester, Mass; s. Howard Vincent and Alice Louise (Carpenter) L.; m. Helen Louise De Lotto, July 3, 1948 (dec. 1981); children—John, Paula, Jay; m. Sally W. Ward, Mar. 7, 1983. B.S., U. N.H., 1949, Ed.M., 1952; Ed.D., Boston U., 1958; postgrad., Guilford Coll., 1970; Aspen Humanities Inst., 1968, Columbia U. Supt.'s Workshop, 1963, Harvard Advanced Adminstrv. Inst., 1962-72, Northeastern U. (hon.), 1982. Tchr. sch. sci. and social studies, coach Antrim, N.H., 1949-51; supervising prin. Salisbury (Mass.) Meml. Sch., 1951-55; supt. schs. Salisbury and Newbury, Mass., 1955-57, Hamilton-Wenham, Mass., 1957-61, Hingham, Mass., 1961-65, Shaker Heights, Ohio, 1965-76, Lexington, Mass, 1976-81; commr. edn. Commonwealth Mass., Quincy, 1982-86; prof. ednl. adminstrn. U. N.H., Durham, 1986-91, officer dept. labor rels., 1991-93, assoc. v.p. for alumni affairs, 1993—; vis. lectr., adj. prof. Boston U., Northeastern U., Case Western Reserve U., Harvard U., Ind., U., Cleve. State U., U. Akron, U. Tex., U. Nebr., John Carroll U. Contbr. articles to profl. jours. Bd. dirs. Sci. Mus., Mus. Fine Arts, Bay State Skills Corp; trustee Econ. Edn. Council; mem. Boston U. Nat. Alumni Council, Cleve. Commn. on Higher Edn., N.C.A.T.E. Accreditation Com. on Sch. Adminstrn., M.I.T. Bd. Overseers, Mass. Telecommunications Commn., Bd. Library Commrs., Mass. State Consortium Com. for Gifted/Talented, Gov.'s Task Force on Edn. Job-Training Partnership Act; pres. U. N.H. Alumni Assn.; mem. state adv. com. Globe Scholastic Art Awards; founding dir. Teacher and Learning Ctr. Bd. Mem. Nat. Suburban Sch. Supts. (pres.), AASA (higher edn. com.), ASCD, Edn. Commn. of the States, Council of Chief State Sch. Officers (vice chmn. policies and priorities com.), Phi Delta Kappa. Home: 7 Bucks Hill Rd Durham NH 03824-3202 Office: U NH Elliott Alumni Ctr Durham NH 03824

LAWSON, JOHN QUINN, architect; b. Tucumcari, N.Mex., Apr. 11, 1940; s. Tom L. and Mable Marie (Hagglund) L.; m. Elizabeth Jo Waddel, June 4, 1961 (div. 1980); children: Bevan Eugene, Cary Augusta; m. Lorna Miriam Katz, Feb. 20, 1981. BA, Rice U., 1961, BSArch, 1962; MFA in Architecture, Princeton U., 1964. Registered architect, Pa., N.J. Staff architect Doxiadis Assocs., Phila., 1961, Collins, Uhl, Hoisington, Princeton, N.J., 1963, Frank Schlesinger, Doylestown, Pa., 1964, Kneedler Mirick & Zantzinger, Phila., 1964; staff architect Mitchell/Giurgola Architects, Phila., 1965-71, assoc., 1972-73, ptnr., 1974-85; ptnr. John Lawson Architects, Phila., 1986—; mem. adj. faculty Grad. Sch. Fine Arts U. Pa., 1972-87; chmn. archtl. adv. bd. Spring Garden Coll., Phila., 1986-92. Prin. works include United Way hdqrs. bldg., Phila., 1971, Lang Music Bldg. Swarthmore (Pa.) Coll., 1973, Ind. Nat. Hist. Park maintenance bldg., Phila., 1981, Columbia Ave. Sta. improvements, Phila., 1983, all recipients Pa. Soc. Architects awards. V.p. Logan Sq. Neighborhood Assn., Phila., 1971-72; mem. Community Leadership Seminar Alumni, Phila., 1982-85; cons. Friends of Starr Garden, Inc., Phila., 1989. Lowell M. Palmer fellow Princeton U., 1964, NEA Mid-Career fellow Am. Acad. in Rome, 1980. Fellow AIA (mem. architecture for edn. com. 1976-85, chmn. urban design com. Phila. chpt. 1986—); mem. Pa. Soc. Architects, Soc. Hill Civic Assn., City Pks. Assn. (bd. dirs. 1988—), Awbury Arboretum Assn. (bd. dirs. 1989—), Soc. Hill Towers (coun. 1994—). Democrat. Office: John Lawson Architects 812 Chestnut St Fl 2 Philadelphia PA 19107-5104

LAWSON, JONATHAN NEVIN, academic administrator; b. Latrobe, Pa., Mar. 27, 1941; s. Lawrence Winters and Mary Eleanor (Rhea) L.; m. Leigh Farley (div.); children: Paul, Joshua, Jacob; m. Pamela Cross. AA, York Coll. Pa., 1962; BFA, Tex. Christian U., 1964, MA, 1966, PhD, 1970. Dir. composition St. Cloud (Minn.) State U., 1971-77, assoc. dean, 1977-81; asst. vice chancellor Minn. State U. System, St. Paul, 1980-81; dean liberal arts Winona (Minn.) State U., 1981-84; dean arts and scis. U. Hartford, West Hartford, Conn., 1984-86; sr. v.p., dean of faculty U. Hartford, 1986-95; v.p. acad. affairs Idaho State U., Pocatello, 1995—. Author: Robert Bloomfield, 1980; editor: Collected Works: Robert Bloomfield, 1971; contbr. articles and papers to scholarly publs; assoc. editor Rhetoric Soc. Quar., St. Cloud, 1974-79. Mem. regional adv. bd. Greater Hartford C.C., 1992-94; mem. bd. trustees Hartford Coll. for Women, 1992-94. Mem. Am. Coun. Edn., Coun. Fellows Alumni, Coun. Liberal Learning, Assn. Gen. and Liberal Studies, Assn. Am. Colls., N.E. Assn. Schs. and Colls. (chmn. commn. on instns. higher edn. 1992—), Asian Studies Consortium (chmn. bd.), Lambda Iota Tau (hon.), Alpha Chi (hon.). Episcopalian. Avocations: fishing, camping, writing. Home: 1401 Juniper Hill Dr Pocatello ID 83204 Office: Idaho State U Campus Box 8063 Pocatello ID 83209

LAWSON, MARGUERITE PAYNE, small business owner; b. Detroit, Apr. 30, 1935; d. LeRoy and Marguerite Lenore (Archambeau) Payne; m. William Allen Stanke, Sept. 4, 1954 (div. Sept. 1962); children: Elizabeth Susan Hankey, Elaine Kathryn Dinwiddie; m. Vernon Arthur Lawson, Aug. 15, 1975. BA in Social Sci., Mich. State U., E. Lansing, 1957. Lic. real estate assoc.; cert. tax preparer. Tchr. El Segundo Unified Sch. Dist., Calif., 1957-58, Las Virgenes Unified Sch. Dist., Calif., 1962-66, Timber Unified Sch. Dist., Thousand Oaks, Calif., 1966-72, Muroc Unified Sch. dist., Edwards, Calif., 1972-78; store owner Margie Lawson's Gourmet Ctr., Lancaster, Calif., 1978—; tour leader Royal Cruise Line voyages, 1987-92; speaker various local clubs, TV sta., Lancaster and Palmdale, Calif., 1977—. Contbr. newspaper articles to Antelope Valley Press, 1975—, also photojournalist; pub. travel writer. Candidate Lancaster (Calif.) City Coun., 1977, Antelope Valley Hosp. Bd., 1982; pres. College Terrace Park Condo Assn., 1987-92; founder, chmn., judge Curtain Call, 1989—; judge Gourmet Products Show, 1992—; patron to 4 local theatrical groups, 1986—. Mem. AAUW, Mensa, Intertel, Am. Booksellers Assn., Asst. League Antelope Valley, Desert Amigas-Domestic Violence (affiliate), Alpha Charter Guild. Republican. Avocations: cruising, world travel, photography, theater, tournament poker. Home: 2849 W Avenue J4 Lancaster CA 93536-6016 Office: Margie Lawson's Gourmet Ctr 906 W Lancaster Blvd Lancaster CA 93534-2306

LAWSON, MELANIE KAY, management administrator, early childhood consultant; b. Fort Valley, Ga., Feb. 8, 1955; d. William C. and Mamie Nell (Brown) Chapman; m. Robert Scott Lawson, Dec. 18, 1975; children: Robert Scott Jr., Joshua Cody, Ashley Jeanell. AA, Cisco Jr. Coll., 1984; BE in Elem./Spl. Edn., Hardin-Simmons U., 1988, MEd in Reading, 1990; MEd in Sch. Adminstrn., Abilene Christian U., 1992; postgrad., Tex. Tech. U., 1995—. Cert. reading specialist, supr., mid-mgmt. tchr. Speech pathology asst. Head Start/Abilene Ind. Sch. Dist., Abilene, Tex., 1983-84; assoc. tchr. Head Start/AISD, Abilene, Tex., 1984-88, cert. tchr., 1988-90; English as second lang. tchr. AISD-Curriculum div., Abilene, Tex., 1990-92; kindergarten tchr. AISD-Long Elem. Sch., Abilene, Tex., 1992-93; asst. dir. Child Devel. Ctr., Dyess AFB, Tex., 1993-94; tng. mgr. 7 SVS Squadron, Dyess AFB, Tex., 1994—. Mem. Youth Task Force, Abilene City Govt., 1994-95, Higher Edn. Working Group, Tex. Head Start Collaboration Project. Recipient Key City Reading award Reading Coun., 1988. Mem. AAUW, Internat. Reading Assn., Nat. Assn. Edn. of Young Children (Membership Affiliate grant 1994), Tex. Assn. Edn. of Young Children (at-large, Tex. Affiliate grant, 1993, 94, exec. bd., chair accreditation), Big Country Assn. for Edn. of Young children (membership chair 1988-90, pres. 1992-94, state repl 1992-94), Tex. Assn. for Gifted/Talented (grant 1991), Coun. Early Childhood Profl. Recognition (rep. 1993—), Golden Key Honor Soc., Kappa Delta Phi. Baptist. Avocations: reading, sewing, walking, ceramics, wood crafts. Home: 1702 Yorktown Dr Abilene TX 79603-4216 Office: 7 SVS Squadron 309 Fifth St Dyess AFB TX 79607

LAWSON, PATRICIA GILLY, secondary education English educator; b. Texarkana, Ark., Aug. 13, 1950; d. Norbert Sidney Jr. and Ora Marie (Chiasson) Gilly; m. James Patrick Lawson Jr., May 4, 1973; children: Ryan Patrick, Christopher Michael, Colin Timothy. BA in English Edn., U. New Orleans, 1972, MEd, 1979, cert. reading cons., 1984; cert. in supervision and adminstrn., Ctrl. Conn. State U., 1993. Cert. 7-12 English tchr., K-12 reading cons., adminstr. and supr., Conn. English tchr. Cohen Sr. H.S., Orleans Parish Sch., New Orleans, 1973; chpt. 1 reading tchr. Toulminville H.S., Mobile County Sch., Mobile, Ala., 1973-74; English and reading tchr. Orleans Parish Sch., 1974-76; 5th-8th grade English and reading tchr. St. Pius X Sch., New Orleans, 1976-77; 7th-8th grade English and reading tchr. St. Rita Sch., Harahan, La., 1978-79; 6th grade reading tchr. Ellender Mid. Sch., Jefferson Parish Schs., Marrero, La., 1983-84; 9th-12th grade English tchr. RHAM H.S., Region # 8 Schs., Hebron, Conn., 1985—, 7th-12th grade coord reading, English, language arts, 1993—; state assessor State of Conn. Best Program, Hartford, 1993—; mem. com. RHAM Profl. Devel. Com., Hebron, 1991—. Publicity/sports writer Glastonbury (Conn.) H.S., 1992—, Ctrl. Conn. Youth Hockey Assn., Glastonbury, 1986-92. Mem. ASCD, Conn. ASCD, RHAM Edn. Assn. (rep. coun. mem. 1992—), Nat. Coun. Tchrs. English (mem. conf. on edn1. leadership 1993—), Conn. Coun. Tchrs. English, Conn. Reading Assn., Conn. Heads of English Depts. Roman Catholic. Avocations: reading, landscaping, interior decorating, needlecrafts. Office: RHAM HS 67 Rham Rd Hebron CT 06248-1527

LAWSON, RANDALL CLAYTON, II, financial executive; b. Wabash, Ind., June 20, 1948; s. Randall Clayton and Evelyn Beatrice (Wright) L.; m. Julie Ann Severin, June 30, 1973; children: Randall Clayton III, Erin Elizabeth. BS, Butler U., 1970. CPA, Ind., Ohio. Jr. acct. Price Waterhouse, Indpls., 1970-73; sr. acct. Price Waterhouse, Indpls. and Cin., 1973-76; audit mgr. Price Waterhouse, Cin., 1976-79; unit devel. contr. Ponderosa, Inc., Dayton, Ohio, 1979-81, asst. corp. contr., 1981-82, corp. contr., 1982-84, v.p., corp. contr., 1984-85, sr. v.p., chief acctg. officer, 1985-87, sr. v.p., CFO, 1987; v.p., CFO Tad Tech. Services Corp., Cambridge, Mass., 1988-89; v.p. fin. HydroLogic, Inc., Asheville, N.C., 1993; dir. mgmt. acctg. Rust Indsl. Cleaning Inc., Ashland, Ky., 1994-95, divsn. v.p., contr., 1996—; adj. prof. Wilmington Coll., 1991; bus. cons., 1987—. Mem. agy. audit com. United Way Greater Cin., 1975; mem. fin. and resource allocation com. United Way Greater Dayton, 1985, mem. com. on agy. fins., 1986-87. Mem. AICPA, Ohio Soc. CPAs, Fin. Execs. Inst., Phi Kappa Psi. Republican. Presbyterian. Clubs: Queen City Assn. (bd. dirs. 1978) (Cin.), Dayton Racquet. Lodge: Elks. Avocations: golf; tennis; reading; antiques; crafts. Home: 3229 Hanna Ave Cincinnati OH 45211-6848

LAWSON, RICHARD LAVERNE, trade association executive, retired military officer; b. Fairfield, Iowa, Dec. 19, 1929; s. Vernon C. and Wilma Aletha (Rabel) L.; m. Joan Lee Graber, Aug. 28, 1949; children: Leslie D., Wendy L., Richard H., Randolph S. BSChemE, Parsons Coll., 1951, MSChemE, 1951; grad., Nat. War Coll.; MPA, George Washington U., 1964; PhD (hon.), Centenary Coll., 1980; PhD in Polit. Sci. (hon.), Boston U., 1985. Enlisted U.S. Army USA, 1946, advanced through grades to sgt. maj.; transferred to USAF and advanced through grades to gen., 1951; mil. asst. to Pres. The White House, Washington, 1973-75; dir. plans HQ USAF, Washington, 1975-77; comdr. 8th Air Force, Barksdale AFB, La., 1977-78; dir. Joint Chiefs of Staff, Washington, 1978-80; U.S. rep. to milit. com. NATA, Brussels, Belgium, 1980-81; chief of staff Supreme HQ Allied Powers Europe, Mons, Belgium, 1981-83; deputy comdr. in chief HQ U.S. European Command, Stuttgart, Germany, 1983-86; retired USAF, 1986; pres. Nat. Coal Assn., Washington, 1987-95, also bd. dirs.; pres., CEO Nat. Mining Assn., 1995—; Chmn. Internat. Com. Coal Rsch., Washington, 1987—, Trade Assn. Liaison Coun., Washington, 1992-93, Bus. Com. Atlantic Coun., Washington, 1987—; chmn. global climate com. U.S. Energy Assn., 1994—. Decorated Def. DSM with 1 oak leaf cluster, DSM with 1 oak leaf cluster, Legion of Merit with 1 oak leaf cluster, Soldiers medal, Bronze Star, Air medal with 1 oak leaf cluster, USAF Commendation medal with 3 oak leaf clusters, Republic of Vietnam Gallantry Cross with Palm, Joint Chiefs of Staff Identification Badge, Presdl. Svc. Badge, Armed Forces Expeditionary medal, Vietnam Svc. medal with 4 oak leaf clusters, USAF Overseas Long Tour ribbon with 1 oak leaf cluster, USAF Longevity Svc. award ribbon with 7 oak leaf clusters. Mem. U.S. Energy Assn. (bd. dirs.), Washington Inst. Fgn. Affairs, World Energy Coun., Nat. Energy Found., World Energy Congress. Home: 6910 Clifton Rd Clifton VA 22024-1524 Office: Nat Mining Assn 1130 17th St NW Washington DC 20036-4604

LAWSON, ROBERT BERNARD, psychology educator; b. N.Y.C., June 20, 1940; s. Robert Bernard Sr. and Isabella Theresa (McPeake) L.; children: Christina Megan, Steven Robert, Jennifer Erin. B.A. in Psychology, Monmouth Coll., 1961; M.A. in Psychology, U. Del., 1963, Ph.D. in Psychology, 1965. Mem. faculty U. Vt., Burlington, 1966—; asst. prof. psychology U. Vt., 1966-69, assoc. prof., 1969-74, prof., 1974—, assoc. v.p. acad. affairs, 1978, assoc. v.p. research, dean Grad. Coll., 1978-86, dir. gen. exptl. psychology, 1988-90; chair dept. pub. adminstrn., 1990-95; cons. Mgmt. Systems, 1986—; vis. scholar Stanford U., 1986-87; pres. Alliance Mgmt. Cons. Group, Burlington, 1987—, N.E. Assn. Grad. Schs., Princeton, N.J., 1983-86; bd. dirs. Grad. Record Exams-ETS, Princeton, 1984-88. Author: (with S.G. Goldstein and R.E. Musty) Principles and Methods of Psychology, 1975, (with W.L. Gulick) Human Stereopsis: A Psychophysical Approach, 1976. Bd. govs. Univ. Press New Eng., 1978-86, dir., 1979-80. Recipient numerous grants NIH, NSF, USDA; numerous awards from Nat. Eye Inst. Mem. AAAS, Psychonomic Soc., Council Grad. Schs., N.Y. Acad. Scis., Am. Psychol. Assn., Am. Eastern psychol. assns. Avocations: running, reading, playing tennis. Office: U Vt Dept Psychology John Dewey Hall Burlington VT 05405-0134

LAWSON, ROBERT WILLIAM, JR., retired lawyer; b. South Boston, Va., Sept. 20, 1908; s. Robert William and Mary Easley (Craddock) L.; m. Virginia Peyton Broun, Nov. 19, 1938; children: Robert William III, Fontaine Broun, Lewis Peyton. BA, Hampden-Sydney Coll., 1930, LLD, 1992; LLB, U. Va., 1935. Bar: Va. 1934, W.Va. 1935, U.S. Ct. Appeals (4th cir.) 1950. Assoc. Steptoe & Johnson, Charleston, W.Va., 1935-41; ptnr. Steptoe & Johnson, Charleston, 1941-62, sr. ptnr., 1962-84, of counsel, 1984-89; dir. Fed. Res. Bank Richmond, 1967-75, dep. chmn., 1968-71, chmn., 1972-75. Trustee Episcopal H.S., 1961-67, Hampden-Sydney Coll., 1951-77; chancellor Protestant Episcopal Diocese W.Va., 1956-77. Lt. comdr. USNR, 1944-46. Fellow Am. Bar Found.; mem. ABA (state del. 1975-84, bd. govs. 1984-86), Am. Law Inst., Am. Judicature Soc. (bd. dirs. 1985-89), Rotary. Democrat. Avocations: golf; reading. Home: 10 Grosscup Rd Charleston WV 25314-1210

LAWSON, SHIRLEY ANN, food service executive; b. Gardena, Calif., Oct. 11, 1940; d. Andrew Jason and May Louise (Hudson) Rutherford; m. Gilbert Lee Anderson, May 5, 1961 (div. Aug. 10, 1986); children: Johnny Gilbert, Bret Michael, Bruce David, Richard Glen; m. Ted E. Lawson, Mar. 19, 1990. Student in history, U. Md., Spain, 1964; student in sociology, U. Alaska, 1974. Prin. sec. Pennell Elem. Sch., Fairbanks, Alaska, 1972-79; student office mgr. Shadle Park High Sch., Spokane, Wash., 1981-89; office mgr. St. Mary's Sch., Medford, Oreg., 1991-92; food svc. dir. Camp Colman, Lakebay, Wash., 1993—. Home and Office: 127 S Keeneway Dr Medford OR 97504-7509

LAWSON, SUSAN COLEMAN, lawyer; b. Covington, Ky., Dec. 4, 1949; d. John Clifford and Louise Carter Coleman; m. William Henry Lawson, June 6, 1980; 1 child, Philip. BA, U. Ky., 1971, JD, 1979. Bar: Ky. 1979. Ptnr. Lawson & Lawson, P.S.C., Harlan, 1995—; atty. Stoll, Keenon & Park, Lexington, Ky., 1979-80; atty., Harbert Constrn. Co., Middlesboro, Ky., 1980-81; ptnr. Buttermore, Turner, Lawson & Boggs, P.S.C., Harlan, Ky., 1981-94. Elder 1st Presbyn. Ch., Pineville, Ky., 1986—. Mem. ABA, Ky. Bar Assn., Harlan County Bar Assn. (pres. 1983), Order of Coif. Democrat. Avocations: tennis, golf. Home: 511 W Kentucky Ave Pineville KY 40977-1307 Office: PO Box 837 103 N 1st St Harlan KY 40831

LAWSON, WILLIAM DAVID, III, retired cotton company executive; b. Jackson, Miss., Oct. 30, 1924; s. William David Jr. and Elizabeth Vaiden (Barksdale) L.; m. Elizabeth Coppridge Smith, June 9, 1948; children: Margaret, William David IV, Susan Barksdale, Thomas Nelson. BS, Davidson Coll., 1948; MBA, U. Pa., 1949. Trainee T.J. White and Co., Memphis, 1949-52; v.p. W.D. Lawson and Co., Gastonia, N.C., 1952-70, pres., 1971-81; pres. Lawson, Lewis & Peat, Gastonia, 1981-85, Lawson Cotton Co., Gastonia, 1985-95; v.p. Hohenberg Bros. Co. div. Cargill Inc., Memphis, 1988-95; ret., 1995; hon. dir. 1st Union Nat. Bank, Gastonia. Bd. dirs. Sister Cities Com., Gastonia; elder Presbyn. Ch. 1st lt. infantry, U.S. Army, WWII. Named Cotton Man of Year Cotton Digest, 1969, 76. Mem. Nat. Cotton Coun. (pres. 1975-76), Am. Cotton Shippers Assn. (pres. 1968-69), Atlantic Cotton Assn. (pres. 1957-58), Cotton Coun. Internat. (pres. 1972-73), Am. Cotton Exporters Assn. (pres. 1979-80), Newcomen Soc., Gaston County C. of C. (pres. 1972-73), Am. Legion, Gaston Country Club, Gastonia City Club, Rotary (pres. 1964-65, dist. gov. 1995-96), Kappa Sigma. Clubs: Gaston Country, Gastonia City. Avocations: scuba diving, tennis, jogging. Home: 1341 Covenant Dr Gastonia NC 28054-3816

LAWSON, WILLIAM HOGAN, III, electrical motor manufacturing executive; b. Lexington, Ky., Feb. 3, 1937; s. Otto Kirsky and Gladys (McWhorter) L.; div.; children: Elizabeth, Cynthia; m. Ruth Stanat, 1995. B.S. in Mech. Engring, Purdue U., 1959; M.B.A., Harvard U., 1961. Gen. mgr. service div. Toledo Scale Corp., 1964-68; exec. v.p., chief ops. officer Skyline Corp., Elkhart, Ind., 1968-85; chmn. bd. dirs., chief exec. officer Franklin Elec. Co., Inc., Bluffton, Ind., 1985—, also bd. dirs.; bd. dirs. JSJ Corp., Skyline Corp., Am. Electronics Co., Plc., Sentry Ins. (a Mut. Ins. Co.); chmn. bd. Oil Dynamics, Inc.; instr. U. Toledo, 1966-67. Trustee Ind. Inst. Tech., Am. Ground Water Trust. With U.S. Army, 1961-63. Mem. Harvard U. Bus. Sch. Assn., Ft. Wayne Country Club, Summit Club Ft. Wayne, Harvard Club N.Y.C. Republican. Presbyterian. Home: 7118 Blue Creek Dr Fort Wayne IN 46804-1483 Office: Franklin Electric Co Inc 400 E Spring St Bluffton IN 46714-3737

LAWSON-JOHNSTON, PETER ORMAN, foundation executive; b. N.Y.C., Feb. 8, 1927; s. John R. and Barbara (Guggenheim) L.; m. Dorothy Stevenson Hammond, Sept. 30, 1950; children: Wendy, Tania, Peter, Mary. Reporter, yachting editor Balt. Sun Papers, 1951-53; exec. dir. Md. Classified Employees Assn., Balt., 1953-54; pub. info. dir. Md. Civil Def. Agy., Pikesville, 1954-56; sales mgr. Feldspar Corp. subs. Zemex Corp. (formerly Pacific Tin Consol.), N.Y.C., 1956-60, v.p. sales, 1961-66, v.p., 1966-72, chmn., 1972-81, bd. dirs., 1959—; v.p. Zemex Corp., 1966-72, vice chmn. 1972-75, pres., 1975-76, chmn., 1975—, also bd. dirs.; chmn. Anglo Energy, Inc., 1973-86; trustee Solomon R. Guggenheim Found. (operating Guggenheim Mus., N.Y.C. and Peggy Guggenheim Collection, Venice, Italy), 1964—, v.p. bus. adminstrn., 1965-69, pres., 1969-95, chmn., 1995—; dir. Harry Frank Guggenheim Found., 1968—, chmn., 1971—; ptnr. Guggenheim Bros., 1962-70, sr. ptnr., 1971—; ltd. ptnr. emeritus Alex. Brown & Sons, Inc.; pres., bd. dirs. Elgerbar Corp.; bd. dirs. McGraw Hill Inc., Nat. Rev. Inc. Trustee The Lawrenceville Sch., pres. 1990—; bd. dirs. Coun. for U.S. and Italy. Served with AUS, 1945-47. Recipient Gertrude Vanderbilt Whitney award Skowhegan Sch. Painting and Sculpture, 1986, Ellis Island Medal of Honor, Nat. Ethnic Coalition Orgns., 1993. Mem. Pilgrims of U.S., Carolina Plantation Soc., U.S. Srs. Golf Assn., Edgartown Yacht Club, Edgartown Reading Room Club, Green Spring Valley Hunt Club, River Club, Century Assn., Links, Nassau Gun Club, Bedens Brook Club, Pretty Brook Tennis Club, Md. Club, Seminole Golf Club, Island Club, Brook Club (N.Y.C.), Yeamans Hall Club. Republican. Episcopalian. Home: 215 Carter Rd Princeton NJ 08540-2104 Office: Solomon R Guggenheim Found 527 Madison Ave New York NY 10022-4304

LAWSON-JOWETT, M. JULIET, lawyer; b. Mobile, Ala., May 26, 1959; d. William Max Lawson and Perina Juliet (Barich) Franc. BA, U. Miss., 1981, JD, 1987. Bar: Miss. 1988, U.S. Dist. Ct. (no. and so. dists.) Miss. 1988. Tchr. Ocean Springs (Miss.) Sch. System, 1981-85; atty. Ronald W. Lewis & Assocs., Oxford, Miss., 1988-89; atty. occupl. hearing loss and hand-arm vibration syndrome Scruggs, Millette, Lawson & Dent, P.A., Pascagoula, Miss., 1989—; cons. Occupational Hearing Loss, P.A., 1989—. Contbr. articles to profl. jours. Mem. Walter Anderson Players, Ocean Springs, 1973-96. Mem. ABA, ATLA (chmn. occupational hearing loss litigation group 1990-94), Miss. Trial Lawyers Assn. (editor 1990-92), Magnolia Bar Assn. Democrat. Roman Catholic. Avocations: reading, golf, horseback riding, gardening, acting. Office: Scruggs Millette Lawson Bozeman & Dent PA 610 Delmas St Pascagoula MS 39567-4345 Office: Scruggs Millette Lawson Bozeman & Dent PA 934 Jackson Ave Pascagoula MS 39567-4345

LAWTON, ALEXANDER ROBERT, III, immunologist, educator; b. Savannah, Ga., Nov. 8, 1938; s. Alexander Robert and Elizabeth (Holdrege) L.; m. Frances Ritchie Crockett, Nov. 25, 1960; children: Julia Beckwith, Alexander Robert IV. BA, Yale U., 1960; MD, Vanderbilt U., 1964. Diplomate Am. Bd. Pediatrics. Resident in pediatrics Vanderbilt U., Nashville, 1964-66; fellow dept. pediatrics U. Ala., Birmingham, 1969-71, from asst. prof. to prof. pediatrics and microbiology, 1971-80; prof. microbiology, Edward C. Stahlman prof. pediatric physiology and cell metabolism Vanderbilt U. Sch. Medicine, Nashville, 1980—; mem. cancer spl. programs rev. com. Nat. Cancer Inst., 1981-84; mem. allergy, immunology and transplantation rev. com. Nat. Inst. Allergy and Infectious Diseases, 1985-88. Contbr. over 150 articles, book chpts. to profl. publs. Surgeon USPHS, 1966-69. Grantee NIH, March of Dimes Birth Defects Found. Mem. Soc. Pediatric Rsch., Am. Pediatric Soc., Am. Soc. Clin. Investigation, Am. Assn. Immunologists, Am. Assn. Pathologists. Episcopalian. Office: Vanderbilt U Sch Medicine D3237 Med Ctr N Nashville TN 37232

LAWTON, CHARLES See HECKELMANN, CHARLES NEWMAN

LAWTON, FLORIAN KENNETH, artist, educator; b. Cleve., June 20, 1921; s. Maximillian and Mary L.; m. Lois Mari Ondrey, June 19, 1948; children: Kenneth R., David F., Dawn M., Patricia A. Student, Cleve. Sch. Art, 1941-43, Cleve. Inst. Art, 1948-51, John Huntington Polytech. Inst., 1946-50. Instr. Cooper Sch. Art, Cleve., 1976-80, Cleve. Sch. Art, 1980-82; cons., instr. Orange Art Ctr., Pepper Pike, Ohio, 1978—; cons. in field, juror, 1968—. Exhbns. include Am. Watercolor Soc., N.Y., Cleve. Mus. Art, Butler Mus., Youngstown, Ohio, Canton (Ohio) Mus., Massillon (Ohio) Mus., Nat. Arts Club, N.Y.C., Pitts. Watercolor Soc., Audubon Artists, N.Y.C., Salmagundi Club, N.Y.C., Parkersburg (W.Va.) Art Ctr., Boston Mills Arts Festival, Peninsula, Ohio, Marietta (Ohio) Coll., many others; 25 yrs. retrospective exhbn. Amish paintings, Butler Inst. Am. Art, 1989; represented in collections including Am. Soc. Metals, Ctrl. Nat. Bank, Diamond-Shamrock, Diocese Cleve., Kaiser Found., Ohio Conservation Found., Nat. City Bank Ohio, TRW, Standard Oil Co., Huntington Bank, Nat. Mennonite Mus., Lancaster, Pa., Ohio Bell Telephone Co., Day-Glo Corp., Soc. Bank Corp., numerous others U.S. and internat., also pvt. collections; featured mags., calendars; Mill Pond Press; cons., artist (documentary) Amish Romance, 1979; official Coast Guard artist. Cons. Aurora (Ohio) Community Libr., 1990—. Cpl. USAF, 1943-46, PTO. Recipient Disting. Alumni award Garfield Hgts. (Ohio) High Sch., 1990. Mem. Ohio Watercolor Soc. (signature, charter, Grand Buckeye award 1983), Am. Watercolor Soc. (signature, Strathmore award 1977), Nat. Watercolor Soc. (signature), Akron Soc. Artists, Assoc. Audubon Artists, Artists Fellowships Inc. (N.Y.), Ky. Watercolor Soc., Midwest Watercolor Soc., Pa. Watercolor Soc., Ga. Watercolor Soc., NOVA, Whiskey Painters Am., Rotary Club Chagrin Valley (Paul Harris fellow 1989). Office: 410-29 Willow Cirle Aurora OH 44202

LAWTON, JONATHAN FREDERICK, screenwriter; b. Riverside, Calif., Aug. 11, 1960; s. Harry Wilson and Georgeann Leona (Honegger) L.; m. Teresa Ann Neely, Mar. 17, 1988. Student, Calif. State U., Long Beach, 1978-83. Freelance editor L.A., 1983-88, freelance screenwriter, 1988—. Screenwriter: (short films) The Artist, Renesance; (feature films) Pretty Woman, 1989 (Writers' Guild award nomination 1990, British Academy award nomination 1990), (with Barry Primus) Mistress, 1992, Under Siege, 1992, (with Damon Wayans) Blankman, 1994; screenwriter, dir.: (as J.D. Athens) Cannibal Women in the Advocado Jungle of Death, 1989, (as J.D. Athens) Pizza Man, 1991, The Hunted, 1995; editor: (films) Talking Walls, 1986. Mem. Writers' Guild Am., Acad. Motion Picture Arts & Scis., British Acad. Film & Television.

LAWTON, JOSEPH J., JR., lawyer; b. Syracuse, N.Y., Aug. 8, 1926; m. Mary Clarke; children: Joe, Jeff, Eileen, Dan, Sara. BS, Niagara U., 1950; JD, St. John's U., 1953. Bar: N.Y. 1953, U.S. Dist. Ct (no. dist.) N.Y. 1954, U.S. Ct. Appeals (2d cir.) 1966, U.S. Supreme Ct. 1970. Atty. Schoeneck & King, Syracuse, N.Y., 1953; Arbitrator Am. Coll. Construction Arbitrators, 1982-90; adv. com. Legal Adv. Counsel Am. Subcontractors Assn., Washington, 1974-90, chmn. 1983-85; lectr. in field. Mem. ABA (forum Constrn. Industry), Am. Arbitration Assn. (constrn. adv. counsel 1983-90, panel arbitrators), Am. Subcontractors Assn. (chpt. atty. ctrl. N.Y. chpt. 1971-93), N.Y. State Bar Assn. (ins. sect. constrn. and surety com. 1961-90, chmn. 1967-71, continuing legal edn. com. 1973-74, chmn. 1975-77, legal edn. and admission to Bar 1980-81, chmn. 1982-84), Constrn. Specification Inst. (ctrl. N.Y. chpt.). Avocations: education, golf, travel, archtl. design, photography. Home: 3371 E Lake Rd Skaneateles NY 13152-9001 Office: Bond Schoeneck & King 1 Lincoln Ctr Fl 18 Syracuse NY 13202-1324

LAWTON, KIM AUDREY, religious journalist; b. Springville, N.Y., July 21, 1963; d. David Edwin and Judith Anne (Churchill) L. BA in Communication, Messiah Coll., Grantham, Pa., 1985. Washington editor Christianity Today Mag., 1987—. Writer book chpt., Elizabeth Dole, 1991; interviewer Pres. George Bush on religion, 1991. Mem. House and Senate Periodical Press Gallery, Nat. Press Club.

LAWTON, LOIS, health facility administrator; b. Lucedale, Miss., Sept. 2, 1934; d. Floyd Jefferson and Ernestine (Cooley) Eubanks; m. Frank Willingham Lawton, Aug. 17, 1952; children: Deaver Lamar, Wesley Maxwell, Alice Sandra Lawton Hogue, Sarah Diane. Student, Clark Coll., 1952-53, Miss. Coll., 1953-54, Desoto C.C., 1969. Cert. health unit coord. Nat. Assn. Health Unit Coords. Kindergarden supr., tchr. Union Ave. Bapt. Ch., Memphis, 1967-73; health unit coord. Meth. South Hosp., Memphis, 1973-76, Richmond (Va.) Meml. Hosp., 1976-77; coord., trainer health unit coords. Henrico Drs. Hosp., Richmond, 1978-88, health unit coord., 1990—; presenter, coord. seminars in field. Editor newsletter Regional 8 Communicates, 1985-90, Chapter Chatter, 1990-93; author: The History of NAHUC, 1988. Mem. Nat. Assn. Health Unit Coords., Inc. (lead regional rep. 1985-90, regional rep. 1985-90, bd. dirs. 1985-95, treas. capital area chpt. 1989-95, chair various coms. 1990-93, mem. ad hoc task force 1990-93, mem. fiscal affairs com. 1990-95, pres.-elect 1990-93, pres., CEO 1993-95, Disting. Svc. award 1990). Baptist. Avocations: flower and vegetable gardening. Home: 11602 Lothbury Ln Richmond VA 23233-4025 Office: NAHUC Ste S-104 1821 University Ave Saint Paul MN 55104-2869

LAWTON, NANCY, artist; b. Gilroy, Calif., Feb. 28, 1950; d. Edward Henry and Marilyn Kelly (Boyd) L.; m. Richard Enemark, Aug. 4, 1984; children: Faith Lawton, Forrest Lawton. BA in Fine Art, Calif. State U., San Jose, 1971; MFA, Mass. Coll. Art, 1980. artist-in-residence Villa Montalvo Ctr. Arts, Los Gatos, Calif., 1971, Noble & Greenough Sch., Dedham, Mass., 1990. One-woman shows include The Bklyn. Mus., 1983, Victoria Munroe Gallery, N.Y.C., 1993; group shows include San Francisco Mus. Modern Art, 1973, The Bklyn. Mus., 1980, 83, Staempfli Gallery, N.Y.C., 1984, The Ark. Art Ctr. Mus., Little Rock, 1984, 88, 92, 93, Victoria Munroe Gallery, 1985, 87, 88, 92, Butler Inst. Am. Art, Ohio, 1988, Smith Coll. Mus. Art, Mass., 1988, NAD, N.Y.C., 1988, Reynolds Gallery, Richmond, 1994, Nancy Solomon Gallery, Atlanta, 1995; public collections include The Ark. Art Ctr. Mus., Art Inst. Chgo., Bklyn. Mus., Nat. Mus. Am. Art, Smithsonian Inst., Washington. Scholar Mellon Found., 1982; N.Y. State Creative Artists grantee, 1983, N.Y. State Arts Devel. Fund grantee, 1989. Home and Office: 49 Monument Rd Orleans MA 02653-3511

LAWTON, THOMAS, art gallery director; b. Somerset, Mass., Feb. 5, 1931; s. John Henry and Beatrice Alice (Miller) L. B.S., Durfee Tech. Inst., 1953; M.F.A., U. Iowa, 1959; Ph.D., Harvard U., 1970. Asst. curator Freer Gallery Art, Washington, 1967-70, curator Chinese Art, 1970-71, asst. dir., 1971-77, dir., 1977-87; concomitant dir. Arthur M. Sackler Gallery, Washington, 1982-87, sr. rsch. scholar, 1987—. Author: Chinese Figure Painting, 1973, Chinese Art of the Warring States Period, 1983, New Perspectives on Chu Culture During the Eastern Zhou Period, 1991; co-author: Freer: A Legacy of Art, 1993. Grantee Ford Found., 1959-61; grantee JDR 3d Fund (China), 1966-67; Fulbright fellow, 1963-66; scholar Harvard U., 1961-63. Club: Cosmos (Washington). Home: 420 4th St SE Washington DC 20003-2005 Office: Arthur M Sackler Gallery 1050 Independence Ave SE Washington DC 20003-3912

LAX, MELVIN, theoretical physicist; b. Bklyn., Mar. 8, 1922; s. Morris and Rose H. L.; m. Judith Heckelman, June 26, 1949; children: R. Laurie, David A., Jonathan R., Naomi A. B.A. in Physics (Charles Hayden scholar 1938-42), NYU, 1942; M.S. in Physics; M.S. (fellow in applied math. 1942-43), MIT, 1943, Ph.D. (fellow in physics 1943-46, research asso. 1946-47), 1947. Mem. faculty Syracuse (N.Y.) U., 1947-55, Princeton U., 1961, Oxford (Eng.) U., 1961-62; mem. tech. staff AT&T Bell Labs., Murray Hill, N.J., 1955-72; head theoretical physics research dept. Bell Labs., 1962-64, cons., 1972—; Disting. prof. physics CCNY, 1971—; cons. to govt. and industry. Author books and numerous papers in field; bd. editors Phys. Rev., 1958-60, 84-86; editor: Advanced Series in Applied Physics, 1988—; mem. adv. bd. Modern Physics Letters, Internat. Jour. Modern Physics; editorial bd. Quantum Optics, 1992-94. Fellow AAAS, Am. Phys. Soc. (publs. com. 1980-83); mem. NAS (sec. applied scis., math. and engring. class 1989-92, 95—), Am. Phys. Soc.-Chinese Phys. Soc. (telecom. com. 1995—), Optical Soc. Am. (publs. tech. com. 1991-94, optics letters rev. com. 1995—). Jewish. Home: 12 High St Summit NJ 07901-2413 Office: CCNY 138th St and Convent Ave New York NY 10031

LAX, PHILIP, land developer, space planner; b. Newark, Apr. 22, 1920; s. Nathan and Beckie (Hirschhorn) L.; m. Mildred Baras, Feb. 15, 1948; children: Corinne, Barbara. BS, NYU, 1940, postgrad., 1941-42. With Lax & Co., Newark, 1942-77; v.p. Lax & Co., 1950-77; pres. Chathill Mgmt., Inc., 1977—; cons. World Book of Am. Heritage, 1992; active The Albert Gallatin Assocs., N.Y.C. Pres. B'nai Brith Ctr., Rochester, Minn., 1965-70, now hon. pres.; trustee Rutgers U. Hillel; pres. B'nai Brith Rutgers U. Hillel Found. Bldg. Corp., 1969—; chmn. United Jewish Appeal, Maplewood, N.J., 1966, 76; mem. N.J. region exec. bd. Anti-Defamation League, mem. nat. community rels. bd.; mem. Gov.'s Conf. on Edn., N.J., 1966, Mayor's Budget Com., Maplewood, 1958-59; co-chmn. N.J. Opera Ball, 1977; trustee B'nai Brith Found., Washington, 1967— (Philip Lax Gallery of B'nai Brith History and Archives named for him in Philip Klutznick Mus., Room named in his honor Stern Sch. Econs.); co-chmn. B'nai Brith Internat. Coun., 1979, chmn., 1980-85, hon. chmn., apptd. chmn. internat. coun., 1990; voting del. to Jewish Agy., Jerusalem; ECOSOC mem. UN, representing coordinated Bd. Jewish Orgns.; attended UNESCO Conf. in Mex., 1982, with Internat. Coun. B'nai Brith and U.S.; trustee, mem. exec. com. N.J. sect. NCCJ, 1981; trustee Henry Monsky Found., Washington, 1968—; trustee Leo N. Levi Hosp., Hot Springs, Ark., 1968-71, B'nai Brith World Jewish Ctr., Jerusalem, 1982, Nat. Arthrities Hosp., 1976—, N.Y. Statue of Liberty Centennial Found.; hon. trustee Arts Coun. of Suburban Essex, N.J., 1980; mem. Econ. Devel. Commn., Twp. of Maplewood, 1979—; mem. steering com. to Restore Ellis Island, 1977—; nat. pres. Ellis Island Restoration Commn., 1978—, responsible for planning, funding and operating Family History Ctr. on Ellis Island; appointed to planning team of Statue of Liberty and Ellis Island by Nat. Park Service, Dept. of Interior ; mem. Statue of Liberty/Ellis Island Centennial Commn., Statue of Liberty-Ellis Island Centennial Commn., Com. of Architecture and Restoration of Statue of Liberty-Ellis Island, past chmn.. Decorated cavaliere ufficiale Order of Merit of the Republic of Italy; recipient Found. award B'nai Brith, 1968, Humanitarian award, 1969, Pres.'s Gold medal, 1975; Pro Mundi Beneficio medal Brazilian Acad. Humanities, 1976; Philip Lax chapel at Rutgers U. Hillel named in his honor; honored by N.J. State Senate; room named in his honor Stern Sch. Econs. Mem. Am. Soc. Interior Designers, Nat. Soc. Interior Designers (trustee 1970-73), Am. Arbitration Assn., Am. Jewish Hist. Com. (v.p.), Am. Jewish Hist. Soc. (trustee 1984), Am. Soc. Israel Philatelists, Albert Gallatin Assocs.-NYU, Masons (32 deg.), Shriners, B'nai Brith (v.p. Supreme Lodge 1968-71, internat. bd. govs. 1971—, mem. exec. com. of internat. coun.), NYU Club (founder 1956), Nat. Press Club). Clubs: Masons (32 deg.), Shriners, B'nai Brith (v.p. Supreme Lodge 1968-71, internat. bd. govs. 1971—, mem. exec. com. of internat. council); NYU (N.Y.C.) (founder 1956); Nat. Press Club (Washington). Room named in honor Stern Sch. Econs. Home: 35 Claremont Dr Maplewood NJ 07040-2119 Office: Chathill Mgmt 26 Main St Chatham NJ 07928-2402

LAY, DONALD POMEROY, federal judge; b. Princeton, Ill., Aug. 24, 1926; s. Hardy W. and Ruth (Cushing) L.; m. Miriam Elaine Gustafson, Aug. 6, 1949; children: Stephen Pomeroy (dec.), Catherine Sue, Cynthia Lynn, Elizabeth Ann, Deborah Jean, Susan Elaine. Student, U.S. Naval Acad., 1945-46; BA, U. Iowa, 1948, JD, 1951; LLD (hon.), Mitchell Coll. Law, 1985. Bar: Nebr. 1951, Iowa 1951, Wis. 1953. Assoc. Kennedy, Holland, DeLacy & Svoboda, Omaha, 1951-53, Quarles, Spence & Quarles, Milw., 1953-54, Eisenstatt, Lay, Higgins & Miller, 1954-66; judge U.S. Ct. Appeals (8th cir.), 1966—, chief judge, 1980-92, senior judge, 1992—; faculty mem. on evidence Nat. Coll. Trial Judges, 1964-65, U. Minn. Law Sch., William Mitchell Law Sch.; mem. U.S. Jud. Conf., 1980-92. Mem. editorial bd.: Iowa Law Rev., 1950-51; contbr. articles to legal jours. With USNR, 1944-46. Recipient Hancher-Finkbine medal U. Iowa, 1980. Fellow Internat. Acad. Trial Lawyers; mem. ABA, Nebr. Bar Assn., Iowa Bar Assn.,

Wis. Bar Assn., Am. Judicature Soc., Assn. Trial Lawyers Am. (bd. govs. 1963-65, Jud. Achievement award), Order of Coif, Delta Sigma Rho (Significant Sig award 1986, Herbert Harley award 1988), Phi Delta Phi, Sigma Chi. Presbyterian. Office: US Ct Appeals 8th Cir Rm 560 316 N Robert St Saint Paul NM 55101

LAY, ELIZABETH MARIAN, financial systems development administrator; b. Reading, Eng., Oct. 11, 1949; d. John Hunter and Brigid Mary (Maas) L. BS in Biology, SUNY, Albany, 1976; Cert. in Exec. Devel., George Washington U., 1989. mem. adv. coun. No. Va. Mental Health Inst.; puppeteer Smithsonian Instn., 1970-71. Sec. Touche Ross & Co., Washington, 1971-73, para-cons., 1974-75, assoc. cons., 1975-82; fin. systems liason Student Loan Mktg. Assn., Washington, 1982-84, mgr. fin. systems, 1985-87, dir. fin. systems, 1988-95. Mem. Am. Assn. Suicidology, Nat. Mental Health Assn. (life, pres. 1994-95), Alexandria Mental Health Assn. (pres. 1984-86, 95-96, treas. 1993-94, Disting. Svc. award 1994), Am. Mensa. Democrat. Avocations: antique Worcester collecting, pen collecting, music composition, suicide intervention training.

LAY, KENNETH LEE, diversified energy company executive; b. Tyrone, Mo., Apr. 15, 1942; s. Omer and Ruth E. (Reese) L.; m. Linda Ann Phillips, July 10, 1982; children: Robyn Anne, Mark Kenneth, Todd David, Elizabeth Ayers, Robert Ray. BA, U. Mo., 1964, MA, 1965; PhD, U. Houston, 1970. Corp. economist Exxon Corp., Houston, 1965-68; asst. prof. and lectr. in econs. George Washington U., 1969-73; tech. asst. to commr. FERC, 1971-72; dep. undersec. for energy Dept. Interior, 1972-74; v.p. Fla. Gas Co. (now Continental Resources Co.), Winter Park, Fla., 1974-76, pres., 1976-79; exec. v.p. The Continental Group, 1979-81; pres., chief operating officer, dir. Transco Energy Co., Houston, 1981-84; chmn., chief exec officer Houston Natural Gas Corp., 1984-85; pres., chief exec. officer, chief operating officer, dir. HNG/InterNorth (now Enron Corp.), Omaha, 1985—, also chmn. bd. dirs., Houston; asst. prof. George Washington U.; bd. dirs. Eli Lilly & Co., Trust Co. West, Compaq Computer Corp.; past chmn. Greater Houston Partnership; mem. President's Coun. on Sustainable Devel. Sec. Energy Adv. Bd.; former chmn. bd. regents U. Houston, Bus. Coun. for Sustainable Energy Future; Houston Host Com. for 1992 Rep. Nat. Conv.; co-chmn. 1990 Houston Econ. Summit Host Com. Decorated Navy Commendation award; N.A.M. fellow; State Farm fellow; Guggenheim fellow. Mem. Nat. Petroleum Coun. (bd. dirs.), River Oaks Country Club, Phi Beta Kappa. Republican. Methodist. Office: Enron Corp PO Box 1188 Houston TX 77251-1188

LAY, NORVIE LEE, legal educator; b. Cardwell, Ky., Apr. 17, 1940; s. Arlie H. and Opha (Burns) L.; 1 dau., Lea Anne. B.S., U. Ky., 1960; J.D., U. Louisville, 1963; LL.M. (Cook fellow), U. Mich., 1964, S.J.D., 1967. Bar: Ky. 1963. Asst. prof. law U. Louisville, 1964-67, assoc. prof., 1967-70, prof., 1970—; asst. dean U. Louisville (Sch. Law), 1971-73, assoc. dean, 1973-84, acting dean, 1981-82; vis. prof. Southwestern U. Sch. Law, summer 1983, N.Y. Law Sch., 1983-84, Coll. of Law U. Iowa, summer 1989. Author: Tax and Estate Planning for Community Property and the Migrant Client, 1970; contbr. articles to profl. jours. Trustee St. Joseph's Infirmary, 1974-78, S.W. Jefferson Community Hosp., 1979-80, Suburban Hosp., 1981-84, Humana-Audubon Hosp., 1985-88, U. Louisville Law Sch. Alumni Found., from 1982-85; bd. dirs. Louisville Ballet, from 1982-88, Louisville Theatrical Assn., 1985-88, Louisville Art Gallery, 1984-87, Watertower Art Assn., 1986-89, Chamber Mus. Soc. of Louisville, 1985-88, Louisville Chorus, 1985-88, Ky. Contemporary Theatre, 1984, Ky. Country Day Sch., 1985-88, Ky. Arts Coun., 1991—; mem. Nat. Conf. Commrs. Uniform State Laws. Recipient Scholarship Key Delta Theta Phi, 1963, Outstanding Graduating Sr. award Omicron Delta Kappa, 1963. Fellow Am. Coll. of Trust and Estate Counsel (acad.), Am. Coll. Tax Counsel; mem. ABA, Ky. Bar Assn., Louiville Bar Assn., Am. Judicature Soc. Republican. Baptist. Office: U Louisville Sch Law Belknap Campus Louisville KY 40292

LAY, THORNE, geosciences educator; b. Casper, Wyo., Apr. 20, 1956; s. Johnny Gordon and Virginia Florence (Lee) L. BS, U. Rochester, 1978; MS, Calif. Inst. Tech., 1980, PhD, 1983. Rsch. assoc. Calif. Inst. Tech., Pasadena, 1983; asst. prof. geosciences U. Mich., Ann Arbor, 1984-88, assoc. prof., 1988-89; prof. U. Calif., Santa Cruz, 1989—; cons. Woodward Clyde cons., Pasadena, 1982-84; dir. Inst. Tectonics, 1990-94, chmn. earth sci. dept., 1994—. Contbr. more than 120 peer-reviewed articles to sci. jours. NSF fellow, 1978-81, Guttenberg fellow Calif. Inst. Tech., 1978, Lilly fellow Eli Lilly Found., 1984, Sloan fellow, 1985-87, Presidential Young Investigator, 1985-90. Fellow Royal Astron. Soc., Am. Geophys. Union (Macelwane medal 1991), Soc. Exploration Geophysicist, Seismol. Soc. Am., AAAS. Home: 32 Eastridge Dr Santa Cruz CA 95060-1803 Office: U Calif Santa Cruz Earth Sci Bd Santa Cruz CA 95064

LAYBOURNE, EVERETT BROADSTONE, lawyer; b. Springfield, Ohio, Oct. 26, 1911; s. Lawrence Everett and Jean (Broadstone) L.; m. Dorrise Barclay, Sept. 19, 1936 (dec. Nov. 1973); m. Ottilie Kruger, July 31, 1974. B.A., Ohio State U., 1932; J.D., Harvard, 1935. Bar: Calif. bar 1936. Mem. firms Macdonald, Schultheis & Pettit, 1936-40; mem. firms Schultheis & Laybourne, 1940-54, Schultheis, Laybourne & Dowds, 1954-68, Laybourne, Keeley & MacMahon, 1968-69; sr. partner Macdonald, Halsted & Laybourne, Los Angeles, 1969-88; of counsel Baker & McKenzie, Los Angeles, 1988-93; dir. Viking Industries, Pacific Energy Corp., McBain Instruments, Coldwater Investment Co., Brouse-Whited Packaging Co., Calif. Energy Co. Trustee Brite-Lite Corp. Calif.; Calif. chmn. UN Day, 1960; regional vice chmn. U.S. Com. for UN, 1961-64; mem. adv. council Stamp Out Smog, 1963-75; mem. spl. rev. com. Los Angeles Air Pollution Control Dist., 1964-65. Bd. dirs. Fedn. Hillside, Canyon Assos., Los Angeles, 1952-59, chmn. bd., 1957-59; bd. dirs. WAIF, Inc., 1977—, chmn. bd., 1978—; bd. dirs. UN Assn. U.S.A., 1964-65; bd. dirs. Ralph M. Parsons Found., 1977—, v.p., 1978—; trustee, sec. Beta Theta Pi Scholastic Found. So. Calif., 1947-58. Served as lt. USNR, 1944-46. Recipient Commendation Los Angeles City Council, 1957, Ohio State U. Alumni Centennial award, 1970, Alumni Citizenship award, 1988. Mem. Big Ten Univs. Club So. Calif. (pres. 1941-42), L.A. Bar Assn. (exec. com. internat. law sect. 1968-74), World Affairs Coun., Selden Soc., Roscomare Valley Assn. (pres. 1952-54), Calif. Club, Bel-Air Country Club, Phi Beta Kappa. Republican. Episcopalian (sr. warden 1966-67). Office: 555 W 5th St Fl 35 Los Angeles CA 90013-1010

LAYBOURNE, GERALDINE, broadcasting executive; b. Plainfield, N.J., 1947; married; 2 children. BA, Vassar Coll., 1969; MS, U. Pa., 1971. Former high sch. tchr.; with Nickelodeon, 1980—, creator Nick at Nite, 1985—, pres.; also vice chmn. MTV Networks. Office: MTV Networks 1515 Broadway 38th fl New York NY 10036

LAYCOCK, HAROLD DOUGLAS, law educator, writer; b. Alton, Ill., Apr. 15, 1948; s. Harold Francis and Claudia Anita (Garrette) L.; m. Teresa A. Sullivan, June 14, 1971; children: Joseph Peter, John Patrick. BA, Mich. State U., 1970; JD, U. Chgo., 1973. Bar: Ill. 1973, U.S. Dist. Ct. (no. dist.) Ill. 1973, Tex. 1974, U.S. Dist. Ct. (we. dist.) Tex. 1975, U.S. Ct. Appeals (5th and 11th cirs.) 1975, U.S. Supreme Ct. 1976, U.S. Ct. Appeals (6th cir.) 1987, U.S. Ct. Appeals (8th cir.) 1994. Law clk. to judge U.S. Ct. Appeals (7th cir.), Chgo., 1973-74; pvt. practice Austin, Tex., 1974-76; asst. prof. U. Chgo., 1976-80, prof., 1980-81; prof. U. Tex., Austin, 1980—, endowed professorships, 1983-88, assoc. dean for acad. affairs, 1985-86, endowed chair, 1988—, assoc. dean for rsch., 1991—; vis. prof. U. Mich., 1990; reporter com. on motion practice Ill. Jud. Conf., 1977-78. Author: Modern American Remedies, 1985, 2d edit., 1994, The Death of the Irreparable Injury Rule, 1991; mem. bd. advisors Religious Freedom Reporter, 1990—; contbr. articles to law revs. Mem. adv. bd. Consumer Svcs. Orgn., Chgo., 1979-80; mem. exec. bd. Ctr. for Ch./State Studies, DePaul U., Chgo., 1982-87; mem. adv. com. on religious liberty Presbyn. Ch. U.S.A., 1983-88, advisor restatement of restitution, 1984-85; v.p. St. Francis Sch., 1990-92, pres. 1992—; mem. bd. advisors J.M. Dawson Inst. Ch./State Studies, Baylor U., 1990—. Fellow Internat. Acad. for Freedom of Religion and Belief; mem. AAUP (mem. com. on status of women in acad. profession 1982-85), Am. Law Inst., Chgo. Coun. Lawyers (v.p. 1977-78), Assn. Am. Law Schs. (chmn., sec. on remedies 1983, 94). Home: 4203 Woodway Dr Austin TX 78731-2034 Office: U Tex Law Sch 727 E 26th St Austin TX 78705-3224

LAYCRAFT, JAMES HERBERT, judge; b. Veteran, Alta., Can., Jan. 5, 1924; s. George Edward and Hattie (Cogswell) L.; m. Helen Elizabeth Bradley, May 1, 1948; children: James B., Anne L. BA, U. Alta., Edmonton, 1950; LLB, U. Alta., 1951; LLD (hon.), U. Calgary, Alta., 1986. Bar: Alta. Barrister Nolan Chambers & Co., Calgary, 1952-75; justice trial div. Supreme Ct. of Alta., Calgary, 1975-79; justice Ct. of Appeal of Alta., Calgary, 1979-85, chief justice of Alta., 1985-91, ret., 1991. Contbr. articles to law jours. Served to lt. Royal Can. Arty., 1941-46, PTO. Mem. United Ch. of Can. Avocations: amateur radio, fishing.

LAYDEN, FRANCIS PATRICK (FRANK LAYDEN), professional basketball team executive, former coach; b. Bklyn., Jan. 5, 1932; m. Barbara Layden; children: Scott, Michael, Katie. Student, Niagara U. High sch. basketball coach L.I., N.Y.; head coach, athletic dir. Adelphi-Suffolk Coll. (now Dowling Coll.); head basketball coach, athletic dir. Niagara U., Niagara Falls, N.Y., 1968-76; asst. coach Atlanta Hawks, 1976-79; gen. mgr. Utah Jazz, Salt Lake City, 1979-88, head coach, 1981-88, v.p. basketball ops., until 1988, pres., 1989—. Bd. dirs. Utah Soc. Prevention Blindness; bd. dirs. Utah chpt. Multiple Sclerosis Soc., Utah Spl. Olympics. Served to 1st lt. Signal Corps, AUS. Office: Utah Jazz Delta Ctr 301 W South Temple Salt Lake City UT 84101-1216*

LAYDEN, LYNN MCVEY, lawyer; b. Mpls., June 15, 1941; d. David Hugh and Adelyn Martha (Dvorak) McVey; m. Charles Max Layden, Jand 28, 1967; children: David Charles, Kathleen Ann, John Michael, Daniel Joseph. LBA, Carleton Coll., Northfield, Minn., 1963; JD, Ind. u., 1967. Bar: Ind. 1967, U.S. Dist. Ct. (so. and no. dists.) 1967. Assoc. Vaughan, Vaughan & Layden, Lafayette, Ind., 1967-86; ptnr. Layden & Layden, Lafayette, Ind., 1986—; guardian at litem Superior Ct. III-Juvenile Ct., Lafayette, 1986—. Pres. devel. coun. Ivy Tech. State Coll., 1993—; pres. bd. trustees West Lafayette Sch. Corp., 1988-95. Mem. ABA, Ind. Bar Assn., Tippecanoe County Bar Assn., Order of Coif, Phi Beta Kappa. Home: 2826 Ashland St West Lafayette IN 47906-1510 Office: Layden & Layden Bank 1 Bldg Ste 710 Lafayette IN 47901

LAYISH, DANIEL T., internist. BA magna cum laude, Boston U., 1986, MD magna cum laude, 1990. Diplomate Am. Bd. Internal Medicine, Nat. Bd. Med. Examiners; ACLS, Advanced Trauma Life Support. Intern/resident, dept. internal medicine Barnes Hosp., St. Louis, 1990-93; pulmonary/critical care/sleep medicine fellow Duke U. Med. Ctr., Durham, N.C., 1994—; critical care staff, assoc. med. staff Christian Hosp. Northeast, St. Louis, 1993-94; staff, Urgent Care Clinic Carolina Permanente, Raleigh, N.C., 1994—. Contbr. articles to profl. jours. Recipient Med. Grad. award, Hewlett-Packard Co., 1990, Young Investigator and Alfred Soffer Rsch. awards, Am. Coll. Chest Physicians, 1995. Mem. AMA, ACP, Am. Thoracic Soc. (assoc.), Am. Coll. Chest Physicians (affiliate), Alpha Omega Alpha. Home: 5202-B Penrith Dr Durham NC 27713-1724 Office: Duke Univ Med Ctr Divsn Pulmonary/Crit Care Durham NC 27710

LAYMAN, EMMA MCCLOY (MRS. JAMES W. LAYMAN), psychologist, educator; b. Danville, Va., Feb. 25, 1910; d. Charles Harold and Anna (Fisher) McCloy; m. James Walter Layman, Dec. 12, 1936 (dec. May 5, 1978). A.B., Oberlin Coll., 1930; M.A., NYU, 1931; Ph.D., U. Iowa, 1937; L.H.D. (hon.), Iowa Wesleyan Coll., 1981. Diplomate: Am. Bd. Examiners Profl. Psychology. Psychol. examiner Iowa Psychopathic Hosp., Iowa City, 1934-35, 37; clin. psychologist Mich. Children's Inst., Ann Arbor, 1935-36; supr. psychol. services Iowa Bd. Social Welfare, Des Moines, 1937-41; assoc. prof. psychology Woman's Coll., U. N.C., 1947-52; supervisory clin. psychologist Brooke Army Hosp., Ft. Sam Houston, 1952-54; chief psychologist Children's Hosp., Washington, 1954-60; head dept. psychology Iowa Wesleyan Coll., Mt. Pleasant, 1960-75, assoc. prof., 1960-61, prof., 1961-75, emeritus, 1975—, asst. acad. dean, 1964-65, chmn. social sci. div., 1969-75, dir. East Asian Inst., 1963-75, dir. internat. studies, 1970-75; pvt. practice clin. psychology, 1941—; lectr. U. Chattanooga, 1946-47; vis. prof. edn. Duke, summers 1948-50; adj. prof. Am. U., 1954-60; lectr. Howard U., 1956-60; cons. Walter Reed Army Hosp., 1956-60. Author: Mental Health Through Physical Education and Recreation, 1955, Airesboro Castle, 1974, Buddhism in America, 1976, also articles. Pres. Oberlin-Wellington bd. Ch. Women United; bd. dirs. Intergenerational House; pres. class of 1930 Oberlin Coll., also mem. alumni coun.; mem. Spectrum Community Club. Lt. USNR, 1943-46. Fellow APA, Acad. Clin. Psychology, Sigma Xi; mem. AAUW, Am. Assn. Chinese Studies, Phi Beta Kappa. Episcopalian. Home: 154 Kendal Dr Oberlin OH 44074-1907

LAYMAN, LAWRENCE, naval officer; b. Laclede County, Mo., Oct. 28, 1930; s. Archibald A. and Zoe Ellen (Hoke) L.; m. Carmen Elizabeth Meyer, Oct. 5, 1953; children: Linda Carmen, Lawrence, Harry Arthur, John Robert. B.S., U.S. Naval Acad., 1952; M.S. in Internat. Affairs, George Washington U., 1972. Commd. ensign U.S. Navy, 1952, advanced through grades to rear adm., 1979; service to Korea and Vietnam; dep. comdr. Naval Telecommunications Command, 1978-79; dir. command, control and communications systems U.S. European Command, 1979-81; vice dir. Def. Communications Agy., Washington, 1981-83; dir. Naval Communications, Washington, 1983-86; dir. space command and control Office Chief Naval Ops., Washington, 1986-89, ret., 1989. Decorated D.S.M., Def. Superior Svc. medal with oak leaf cluster, Legion of Merit with Gold Star, Bronze Star with combat V, Meritorious Svc. medal. Home: 3429 Silver Maple Pl Falls Church VA 22042-3545

LAYMAN, WILLIAM ARTHUR, psychiatrist, educator; b. West New York, N.J., Feb. 8, 1929; s. Frank Kyle and Lucy Geraldine (Rooney) L.; 1 child, William Kraft. Student, NYU, 1946, 48; B.S. cum laude, St. Peter's Coll., 1951; M.D., Georgetown U., 1955. Diplomate: Am. Bd. Psychiatry and Neurology. Intern Hackensack (N.J.) Hosp., 1955-56; resident in psychiatry Lyons (N.J.) VA Hosp., 1956-57, Fairfield Hills Hosp., Newtown, Conn., 1957-58; fellow in psychiatry Yale U., 1958-59; instr. psychiatry Seton Hall Coll. Medicine, 1959-61, asst. prof., 1961-65; assoc. prof. psychiatry N.J. Med. Sch., Newark, 1965-74; clin. prof. N.J. Med. Sch., 1974-77, prof., 1977—; practice medicine specializing in psychiatry Hackensack, NJ, 1959—; dep. chmn. ednl. services, dept. psychiatry and mental health sci. N.J. Med. Sch., 1976-83, acting chmn. dept. psychiatry and mental health sci., 1983-86; cons. Hackensack Hosp.; mem. staff Coll. Hosp. Contbr. articles to profl. jours. Served with U.S. Army, 1946-48. Fellow Am. Psychiat. Assn. (life); mem. AAUP, N.J. Med. Soc., Bergen County Med. Soc. Office: UMDNJ Univ Hosp G-Yellow #G/300 150 Bergen St Newark NJ 07103-2406

LAYNE, JAMES NATHANIEL, vertebrate biologist; b. Chgo., May 16, 1926; s. Leslie Joy and Harriet (Hausmann) L.; m. Louise Virginia Linderoth, Aug. 26, 1950; children: Linda Carrie, Kimberly, Jamie Linderoth, Susan Nell, Rachel Pratt. BA, Cornell U., 1950, PhD, 1954. Grad. teaching asst. Cornell U., Ithaca, N.Y., 1950-54; asso. prof. zoology Cornell U., 1963-67; asst. prof. zoology So. Ill. U., Carbondale, 1954-55; asst. prof., then asso. prof. biology U. Fla., 1955-63; asst. curator, then asso. curator mammals Fla. State Mus., Gainesville, 1955-63; research asso. Fla. State Mus., 1963-65; dir. research, then exec. dir. Archbold Biol. Sta.; Archbold curator mammals Am. Mus. Natural History, 1967-85; sr. rsch. biologist Archbold Biol. Sta., 1985-94, sr. rsch. biologist emeritus, 1994—; rsch. assoc. Fla. State Collection of Arthropods, Am. Mus. Natural History; vis. scientist primate ecology sect. Nat. Inst. Neurol. Diseases and Blindness, summers 1961-62. Contbr. articles and chpt. to profl. jours. and books. Hon. trustee Fla. Defenders of Environment; bd. dirs. Fla. Audubon Soc.; mem. Fla. Nongame Wildlife Adv. Council, Peace River Basin Bd., Fla. Panther Tech. Adv. Council. Served with USAAF, 1944-46. Fellow AAAS; mem. Am. Soc. Zoologists, Am. Soc. Mammalogists (pres. 1970-72, hon. mem. 1993, C. Hart Merriam award 1976), Ecol. Soc. Am., Soc. for Study of Evolution, Am. Soc. Naturalists, Wildlife Soc., Wildlife Disease Assn., Nature Conservancy (trustee Fla. chpt.), Fla. Acad. Scis. (pres. 1984-85, medalist 1995), Orgn. Biol. Field Stas. (pres. 1986-87), Phi Beta Kappa, Sigma Xi, Phi Kappa Phi, Phi Sigma. Office: Archbold Biol Sta PO Box 2057 Lake Placid FL 33852-2057

LAYSON, WILLIAM MCINTYRE, research consulting company executive; b. Lexington, Ky., Sept. 24, 1934; s. Zed Clark and Louise (McIntyre) L.; m. Robin Dale Fort, July 28, 1982. B.S., MIT, 1956, Ph.D., 1961; postgrad., U. Sydney, Australia, 1957-58. Research scientist European Ctr. Nuclear Research, Geneva, 1960-62; research scientist U. Calif.-Berkeley, 1962-64; mem. tech. staff Pan Am World Airways, Patrick AFB, Fla., 1964-67; research scientist Gen. Research Corp., Rosslyn, Va., 1967-70; dir. Sci. Applications Internat. Corp., McLean, Va., 1970—, sr. v.p., chmn. incentives com., 1975-93; coord. def. nuclear programs, 1975—, chmn. ethics com., 1994—; pres. Langley Sch., 1995—; dir. Langley Sch., 1992—; pres. Layson's Buffalo Trace Farms, 1976—. Fulbright scholar U. Sydney, Australia, 1957-58. Mem. Am. Def. Preparedness Assn. Democrat. Presbyterian (elder). Avocations: church activities, jogging, swimming, skiing. Home: 8301 Summerwood Dr Mc Lean VA 22102-2213 Office: Sci Applications Internat Corp 1710 Goodridge Dr Mc Lean VA 22102-3701

LAYTON, BILLY JIM, composer; b. Corsicana, Tex., Nov. 14, 1924; s. Roy William and Jimmie Vera (Franks) L.; m. Evro Zeniou, Feb. 2, 1949; children: Alexis Roy, Daphne Niobe. Mus.B., New Eng. Conservatory Music, 1948; Mus.M., Yale U., 1950; postgrad. (Alfred M. Hertz Travelling fellow), U. Calif. at Berkeley, 1954; Ph.D., Harvard U., 1960. Faculty New Eng. Conservatory Music, 1959-60, Harvard U., 1960-66; prof. State U. N.Y. at Stony Brook, 1966-92, chmn. dept. music, 1966-72, 82-85. Composer: Five Studies for Violin and Piano, 1952, An American Portrait; symphonic overture, 1953, Three Dylan Thomas Poems; mixed chorus, brass sextet, 1954-56, String Quartet in Two Movements, 1956, Three Studies for Piano, 1957, Divertmento, 1958-60, Dance Fantasy for Orchestra, 1964. Rome Prize fellow, 1954-57; grantee Nat. Inst. Arts and Letters, 1958; Guggenheim fellow, 1963; grantee Thorne Music Fund, 1968-70; Recipient Creative Arts award Brandeis U., 1961. Mem. Am. Music Center (dir. 1972-74), Am. Soc. Univ. Composers (founding), A.S.C.A.P., Am. Musicological Soc., Coll. Music Soc. (mem. council 1970-72), Internat. Soc. Contemporary Music (dir. U.S.A. sect. 1968-70), Soc. for Music Theory (founding). Home: 1105 Massachusetts Ave Apt 10A Cambridge MA 02138

LAYTON, EDWIN THOMAS, JR., science and technology history educator, writer; b. Los Angeles, Sept. 13, 1928; s. Edwin Thomas Layton and Virginia Louise (Yarnell) Meyer; m. Barbara Jean Wyman, May 2, 1952 (dec. Apr. 1978); 1 child, George Mowry; m. Margaret Ruth Brubacher Kirby, Nov. 24, 1982; 1 step-son, David Kirby. BA in History, UCLA, 1950, MA in History, 1953, PhD in History, 1956. Instr. U. Wis., Madison, 1955-56, Ohio State U., Columbus, 1956-60; asst. prof. Purdue U., Lafayette, Ind., 1960-65; assoc. prof. Case Western Res. U., Cleve., 1965-75; prof. history of sci. and tech. dept. mech. engring. U. Minn., Mpls., 1975-94, Inst. Tech. prof., 1994—; cons. Iron Bridge Trust, U.K., summer 1986. Author: The Revolt of the Engineers, Social Repsonsibility and the American Engineering Profession, 1971, rev. edit. 1985, Dexter prize 1971, A Regional Union Ctalog of Manuscripts Relating to the History of Science and Technology, 1971; author, co-editor: The Dynamics of Science and Technology, 1978, History of Heat Transfer, 1988; editor: Technology and Social Change in America, 1973; adv. editor Technology and Culture, Bus. and Profl. Ethics Jour., 1981—; contbr. chpts. to books, articles to profl. jours. Mem. nuclear manpower studies commn. NRC, Washington, 1981. AEC fellow Summer Inst. Oak Ridge, Tenn., 1963, NSF grantee 1965-70, 67-69, 71, 74-75, 77-78, 79-80, 81, 85. Fellow AAAS (chmn. sect. L 1989-90); mem. ASME (affiliate, history and heritage com. 1981), Soc. for History Tech. (numerous coms. 1971-78, 94—, pres. 1985-86, adv. editor Tech. and Culture jour. 1987-95, Leonardo da Vinci medal 1990), History of Sci. Soc. (adv. editor ISIS 1979-81), Midwest Junto for History Sci. (pres. 1985-86, pres.-elect 1995-96), Soc. for Social Studies Sci. (exec. bd. 1978-79), Faculty Club (U. Minn.). Democrat. Episcopalian. Home: 2816 Webster Ave S Minneapolis MN 55416-1846 Office: Univ of Minn Dept of Mech Engring 111 Church St SE Minneapolis MN 55455-0150

LAYTON, HARRY CHRISTOPHER, artist, lecturer; b. Safford, Ariz., Nov. 17, 1938; s. Christopher E. and Eurilda (Welker) L.; LHD, Sussex Coll., Eng., 1969; DFA (hon.), London Inst. Applied Research, 1972, DSc (hon), 1972; DD (hon.), St. Matthew U., Ohio, 1970, PhD (hon.), 1970; m. Karol Barbara Kendall, July 11, 1964 (div. Jan. 1989); children: Deborah, Christopher, Joseph, Elisabeth, Faith, Aaron, Gretchen, Benjamin, Justin, Matthew, Peter. Cert. clin. hypnotherapist. Pres. Poems, Art & Myths; pres., CEO Layton Studio Graphic Design; lectr. ancient art Serra Cath. High Sch., 1963-64, L.A. Dept. Parks and Recreation, summer 1962, 63, 64; interior decorator Cities of Hawthorne, Lawndale, Compton, Gardena and Torrance (Calif.), 1960-68; one-man shows paintings; Nahas Dept. Stores, 1962, 64; group shows include: Gt. Western Savs. & Loan, Lawndale, Calif., 1962, Gardena (Calif.) Adult Sch., 1965, Serra Cath. High Sch., Gardena, 1963, Salon de Nations Paris, 1983; represented in permanent collections: Sussex Coll., Eng., Gardena Masonic Lodge, Culver City-Foshey Masonic Lodge, Gt. Western Savs. & Loan; paintings include: The Fairy Princess, 1975, Nocturnal Covenant, 1963, Blindas Name, 1962, Creation, 1962. Elder Ch. of Jesus Christ of Latter-day Saints, Santa Monica, Calif., 1963—; works pub. in Our World's Favorite Gold and Silver Poems, 1991, Our World's Favorite Poems, 1993, World's Best Poems, 1993, Outstanding Poets of 1994, Best Poems of 1995, others; appt. dep. dir. gen. IBC for the Ams., Cambridge, Eng., 1990. Editor's Choice award Nat. Libr. of Poetry, 1994, 95. Mem. Am. Hypnotherapy Assn., Internat. Soc. Artists, Internat. Platform Assn., Am. Security Council, Soc. for Early Historic Archaeology, Am. Councilor's Soc. of Psychol. Counselors, Le Salon Des Nation Paris Geneva, Ctr. Internat. d'Art Contemporain, Internat. Soc. Poets (disting.), Internat. Masonic Poetry Soc., Am. Legion, Masons (32 deg.), Shriners, K.T., Alpha Psi Omega. Republican. Home: Layton Studio Graphic Design Inc 3654 S Centinela Ave # 10 Los Angeles CA 90066-3147 Office: Layton Studios Graphic Design 3654 S Centinela Ave # 10 Los Angeles CA 90066-3147

LAYTON, JOHN C., federal agency administrator; b. East Stroudsburg, Pa., Oct. 9, 1944; s. Charles O. and Jeanne (Carlton) L.; m. Laura Bick, June 8, 1991; children: Gwen Ann, Susan Carlton. BS in Commerce, Rider Coll., 1966. Auditor Litton Industries, East Orange, N.J., 1969-72; spl. agt. FBI, Washington, 1972-80; dep. inspector gen. NASA, Washington, 1983-84; inspector gen. U.S. Dept. Treasury, Washington, 1984-86, U.S. Dept. Energy, Washington, 1986—. Served to 1st lt. U.S. Army, 1966-69. Mem. Assn. Govt. Accts. (chmn. ethics bd. 1985), Fed. Investigators Assn. (treas. 1982, bd. dirs. 1983-85), Soc. of Former Agts. of the FBI. Methodist. Office: Dept of Energy Inspector Gen 1000 Independence Ave SW Washington DC 20585-0001

LAYTON, ROBERT, lawyer; b. N.Y.C., Feb. 19, 1931; s. Benjamin and Ruth (Beck) L.; m. Joan Levy, May 17, 1967 (div. Jan. 1876); children: Elisabeth, Julie; m. Christine Lambert, Dec. 31, 1988. BA, U. Mich., 1951; LLB, Yale U., 1954. Teaching fellow Stanford Law Sch., Palo Alto, Calif., 1957-58; atty. U.S. Dept. Justice, Washington, 1958-62; assoc., ptnr. Gilbert, Segall & Young, N.Y.C., 1962-73; ptnr. Layton and Sherman, N.Y.C., 1973-84, Surrey & Morse, N.Y.C., 1984-85, Jones, Day, Reavis & Pogue, N.Y.C., 1986-93. Mem. exec. com. Yale Law Sch. Assn., 1992-95. Served to sgt. U.S. Army, 1954-56. Club: Yale (N.Y.C.).

LAYTON, RODNEY EUGENE, controller, newspaper executive; b. Lusk, Wyo., Feb. 27, 1954; s. Raymond Dwight Layton and Mary Elizabeth (Miller) Spencer; m. Susan Carol Johnson, Jan. 8, 1977; children: Joshua, Elise, Caleb. Ba in Polit. Sci./Econs., Kearney State, 1977; student, U. Nebr., 1978-80. CPA, Nebr. Auditor State of Nebr., Lincoln, 1979-80; staff auditor Arthur Andersen, Houston, 1980-81; audit sr. McDermott & Miller, Grand Island, Nebr., 1981-82; internal audit sr. Norwest Bank Corp., Omaha, 1982-86; internal audit mgr. Berkshire Hathaway, Inc., Omaha, 1986-89; treas., controller Buffalo News, 1989—. Treas. Citizens Advocacy, Grand Island, 1981; treas., pres. Crippled Children's Camps, Inc., Buffalo, 1989-93; treas., bd. dirs. Cradle Beach Camp, Buffalo, 1989-94. Mem. AICPAs, Nebr. Soc. CPAs, Internat. Newspaper Fin. Execs. Avocations: tennis, golf, piano. Home: 3796 Teachers Ln #10 Orchard Park NY 14127 Office: Buffalo News 1 News Plz Buffalo NY 14203-2930

LAYTON, WILLIAM GEORGE, computer company executive, management consultant, human resources executive; b. Missouri Valley, Iowa, Sept. 11, 1931; s. George Holbert and Margaret (Wilson) L.; m. Caroline R. Tiffany, June 27, 1953; children: Kathleen Layton Medl, Sara Layton Howe, Thomas William. B.A., Coe Coll., 1953; M.A., U. Ill., 1955. Indsl. rels. trainee Procter & Gamble Co., Cin., 1955-57, pers. specialist, 1957-62; indsl. rels. mgr. Procter & Gamble Co., France, 1962-66; pers. mgr. European Tech. Ctr. Procter & Gamble Co., 1966-69, pers. mgr. internat., 1969-72; v.p. human resources Food Svc. div. Heublein, Inc., Louisville, 1972-77; sr. v.p.

human resources Holiday Inns, Inc., Memphis, 1977-83; pres. The Layton Group, St. Petersburg, Fla., 1983—; sr. ptnr. Johnson-Layton Co. Mgmt. Cons., L.A. and St. Petersburg, 1985-95; pres. CompCom, Inc., 1994—. Bd. dirs., pres. Jr. Achievement of Memphis, 1981-83; mem. Tenn. Jobs Tng. Coordinating Coun., 1982-88; mem. Pvt. Industry Coun. of Memphis and Shelby County, 1982-88; mem. Pres.'s Coun., Rhodes Coll., Memphis, 1983-90; mem. Tenn. Coun. Vocat. and Tech. Edn., 1984-88. Served with USAF, 1953-55. Mem. Soc. for Human Resources Mgmt., Am. Mgmt. Assn. (human resources coun. 1981-83), Inst. Mgmt. Cons. (cert. mgmt. cons.), Coun. Mgmt. Cons. (1987—, Sr. Examiner Sterling Quality award Fla. 1994), Phi Beta Kappa. Republican. Presbyterian. Lodge: Rotary. Office: 1135 Pasadena Ave S #307 Saint Petersburg FL 33707

LAYTON, WILLIAM ISAAC, mathematics educator; b. Cameron, Mo., Sept. 26, 1913; s. Joseph Evening and Mary Rebecca (Leighton) L.; m. Eva James Wade Layton, Mar. 28, 1941; children: Mary Layton Wells, Gay Layton Aycock. BS, U. S.C., 1934, MS, 1935; PhD, Vanderbilt U., 1948. Cert. tchr., S.C., Fla. Math. tchr. Greer High Sch., Greer, S.C., 1935-36, Rome High Sch., Rome, Ga., 1937-39; math. dept. head Albany Sr. High Sch., Albany, Ga., 1939-40; math. tchr. Peabody Demonstration, Nashville, Tenn., 1940-41; math. and engring. drawing tchr. Amarillo Coll., Amarillo, Tex., 1941-46; math. dept. head Austin Peay State Univ., Clarksville, Tenn., 1946-48; assoc. prof. math. Auburn Univ., Auburn, Ala., 1948-49; dean of instrn. Frostburg State Coll., Frostburg, Md., 1949-50; chmn. math. and statistics Stephen F. Austin State Univ., Nacogdoches, Tex., 1950-79; math prof. Newberry (S.C.) Coll., Newberry, S.C., 1979-92; prof. emeritus Newberry (S.C.) Coll., 1992—, chmn. math., computer sci. and physics, 1982-92, acting chair dept. maths., computer sci. and physics, 1992-93. Author: An Analysis of Certification Requirements for Teachers of Mathematics, 1949, (with others) College Algebra, 1956, Mathematics of Finance, 1958, College Arithmetic, 1959, 2d edit., 1971, Essential Business Mathematics, 1977; contbg. author to The Mathematics Teacher. Pres., founder East Tex. Council of Tchrs. of Math. Recipient Alumni Disting. Prof. award Stephen F. Austin State Univ., 1976, Meritorious Svc. award Nat. Coun. Tchrs. Math., 1984, Fifty Yrs. Teaching award, 1987; named Prof. of Yr., Newberry Coll., 1988, 92. Mem. Am. Math. Soc. (pres. Tex. sect.), Math. Assn. Am., S.C. Coun. Tchrs. Math., S.C. Acad. Sci., Rotary (pres. S.C. 1987), Phi Beta Kappa, Sigma Xi, Phi Delta Kappa, Pi Mu Epsilon. Presbyterian. Home: 2421 Fulmer Ave Newberry SC 29108-2009 Office: Newberry Coll Math Dept Newberry SC 29108 *died April 19, 1996.*

LAYZELL, THOMAS D., academic administrator. Chancellor Bd. Govs. U., Springfield, Ill.

LAZAR, AUREL A., electrical engineer, educator; b. Jan. 30, 1950. Dipl.-ing., Technische Hochschule, Darmstadt, Germany, 1976; MS, Princeton U., 1977, MA, 1978, PhD, 1980. Prof. dept. elec. engring. Columbia U. Fellow IEEE (vice-chmn. computer comm. tech. com. Comm. Soc. 1987-88, chmn. 1989-91, editor IEEE Transactions on Comm. 1989-91, area editor 1991—). Office: Columbia U Dept Electrical Engineering 1318 SW Mudd Bldg New York NY 10027*

LAZAR, LUDMILA, concert pianist, educator; b. Celje, Slovenia; married; two children. MusB, Roosevelt U., 1963, MusM, 1964; D of Musical Arts, Northwestern U., 1987. Faculty Roosevelt U., Chgo., 1967—; prof. piano Chgo. Musical Coll. Roosevelt U., 1988—; chmn. keyboard dept. Roosevelt U., Chgo., 1983—. Roosevelt U. rsch. grantee, 1988; recipient Goethe Inst. award, 1987; named to All Star Profs. Team Chgo. Tribune, 1993. Mem. AAUP, Music Tchrs. Nat. Assn. (master tchr. cert. 1991), European Piano Tchrs. Assn., Ill. State Music Tchrs. Assn., Soc. Am. Musicians (pres., v.p.), Coll. Music Soc., Mu Phi Epsilon (pres., v.p.). Office: Roosevelt U 430 S Michigan Ave Chicago IL 60605-1301

LAZAR, RANDE HARRIS, otolaryngologist; b. N.Y.C., Feb. 27, 1951; s. Irving and Dorothy (Tartasky) L.; m. Linda Zishuk, Aug. 11, 1974; 1 child, Lauren K. BA, Bklyn. Coll., 1973; MD, U. Autonoma de Guadalajara, Mexico, 1978; postgrad., N.Y. Med. Coll., 1978-79. Diplomate Am. Bd. Otolaryngology-Head and Neck Surgery; lic. physician, N.Y., Ohio, Tenn. Gen. surgery resident Cornell-North Shore Community Hosp., Manhasset, N.Y., 1979-80; gen. surgery resident Cleve. Clinic Found., 1980-81, otolaryngology-head and neck surgery resident, 1980-84, chief resident dept. otolaryngology & communicative disorder, 1983-84; physician Otolaryngology Cons. Memphis, 1984—; fellow pathology head and neck dept. otolaryngologic pathology Armed Forces Inst. Pathology, Washington, 1983; pediatric otolaryngology fellow Le Bonheur Children's Med. Ctr., Memphis, 1984-85, dir. pediatric otolaryngology fellowship tng., 1989—, chief surgery, 1989, chief staff East Surgery Ctr.; chmn. dept. otolaryngology head and neck surgery Meth. Health Systems, 1990-91; courtesy staff Bapt. Meml. Hosp., Bapt. Meml. Hosp.-East, Eastwood Med. Ctr., Meth. Hosp., Germantown, Tenn.; chief dept. otolaryngology Les Passees Rehab. Ctr., 1988—. Contbr. articles to profl. jours. Bd. dirs. Bklyn. Tech. Found. Recipient award of honor Am. Acad. Otolaryngology-Head and Neck Surgery, 1991. Fellow Internat. Coll. Surgeons; mem. AMA, Am. Acad. Otolaryngology-Head and Neck Surgery, Am. Acad. Facial Plastic and Reconstructive Surgery, Am. Acad. Otolaryngic Allergy, Centurions Deafness Rsch. Found., Am. Auditory Soc., Nat. Hearing Assn., Soc. Ear, Nose Throat Advances in Children, Am. Soc. Laser Medicine and Surgery, So. Med. Assn., N.Y. Acad. Scis., Tenn. Med. Soc., Tenn. Acad. Otolaryngology-Head and Neck Surgery, Memphis and Shelby County Med. Soc., Memphis/Mid South Soc. Pediatrics. Office: Otolaryngology Cons Memphis 777 Washington Ave Ste 240P Memphis TN 38105-4566

LAZAR, RAYMOND MICHAEL, lawyer, educator; b. Mpls., July 16, 1939; s. Simon and Hessie (Teplin) L; m. Susan Leah Krantz, Dec. 27, 1966; children: Mark, Deborah. BBA, U. Minn., 1961, JD, 1964. Bar: Minn. 1964, U.S. Dist. Ct. Minn. 1964. Spl. asst. atty. gen. State of Minn., St. Paul, 1964-66; sole practice Mpls., 1966-72; ptnr. Lapp, Lazar, Laurie & Smith, Mpls., 1972-86; ptnr., officer Fredrikson & Byron P.A., Mpls., 1986—; lectr. various continuing edn. programs, 1972—; adj. prof. law U. Minn., Mpls., 1983—. Fellow Am. Acad. Matrimonial Lawyers; mem. ABA (chair divorce laws and procedures com. family law sect. 1993-94), Minn. Bar Assn., Hennepin County Bar Assn. (chair family law sect. 1978-79). Home: 1611 W 22nd St Minneapolis MN 55405-2402 Office: Fredrikson & Byron PA 1100 Internat Centre 900 2nd Ave S Minneapolis MN 55402-3314

LAZAR, THEODORE AARON, retired manufacturing company executive, lawyer; b. Chgo., July 16, 1920; s. Philip and Rena (Goodman) L.; m. Betty Jean Papermaster, July 6, 1952; children: Mark D., Paul A., Nancy Paula. JD, John Marshall Law Sch., Chgo., 1951. Bar: Ill. 1951, Wis. 1962, Ohio 1966. Sole practice, Chgo., 1951-62; asst. corp. counsel City of Chgo., 1956-59; atty. NLRB, Chgo. and Los Angeles, 1962-65; corp. counsel Lancaster Colony Corp., Columbus, Ohio, 1965-83, v.p. law, 1983-88, ret., 1988. Served as sgt. U.S. Army, 1942-46. Mem. Columbus Bar Assn. Home: 270 Bryant Ave Columbus OH 43085-3009

LAZAROVIC, KAREN, money manager, investment consultant; b. Bklyn., June 30, 1947; d. Alex and Lillian (Kurlanchik) Schwartzberg; children: Laura, Michael. BA cum laude, Bklyn. Coll., 1968. Proofreader Consumers Handbook, Great Neck, N.Y., 1975-77; sports dept. asst. N.Y. Post, N.Y.C., 1977-78, fin. dept. asst., 1978-79, reporter fin., 1979-84, columnist and editor fin., 1984-89; editor, pub. Wall St. Monitor newsletter, 1983-88; pres., stock portfolio mgr. KLP Capital Mgmt. Inc., 1989—; adv. to various companies on corp. fin. issues. Poetry pub. various jours. Avocations: tennis, photography.

LAZARUS, ALLAN MATTHEW, retired newspaper editor; b. New Orleans, Nov. 21, 1927; s. Harry Adolph and Edna Mary (Wodiker) L.; m. Martha Elizabeth Ellis, July 26, 1946; children—Kenneth Wayne, Virginia Lynn. B.A. in History, Centenary Coll., 1951. Copy boy The Times, Shreveport, La., 1944-45, reporter, 1945-46, telegraph editor, 1947-58, news editor, 1958-69, mng. editor, 1969-90; Pulitzer Prize Juror, 1978. Served as cpl. USAF, 1946-47. Mem. AP Mng. Editors Assn. (bd. dirs. 1975-80), La-Miss. AP Assn. (pres. 1977-78), Soc. Profl. Journalists (pres. local chpt. 1971-72). Roman Catholic. Home: 7713 Tampa Way Shreveport LA 71105-5701

LAZARUS, ARNOLD ALLAN, psychologist, educator; b. Johannesburg, Republic of South Africa, Jan. 27, 1932; came to U.S., 1963; s. Benjamin and Rachel Leah (Mosselson) L.; m. Daphne Ann Kessel, June 10, 1956; children: Linda Sue, Clifford Neil. BA with honors, U. Witwatersrand, 1956; MA, U. Witwatersrand, Johannesburg, 1957, PhD, 1960. Diplomate: Am. Bd. Profl. Psychology, Am. Bd. Med. Psychotherapists (fellow), Internat. Acad. Behavioral Medicine, Counseling and Psychotherapy. Pvt. practice clin. psychology Johannesburg, 1959-63, 64-66; vis. asst. prof. dept. psychology Stanford (Calif.) U., 1963-64; prof. psychology Temple U. Med. Sch., Phila., 1967-70; dir. clin. tng. Yale U., New Haven, 1970-72; disting. prof. Rutgers U., New Brunswick, N.J., 1972—; mem. adv. bd. Psychologists for Social Responsibility, 1984—; cons. in field. Author: 15 books including Behavior Therapy and Beyond, 1971, Multimodal Behavior Therapy, 1976, The Practice of Multimodal Therapy, 1981, rev. edit., 1989, In the Mind's Eye, 1984, Martial Myths, 1985, Mind Power: Getting What You Want Through Mental Training, 1987, The Essential Arnold Lazarus, 1991, A Dialogue with Arnold Lazarus, 1991, Don't Believe It For A Minute!, 1993, Abnormal Psychology, 1995; editl. bd. sci. jours.; contbr. articles to profl. jours. Recipient Disting. Svc. award Am. Bd. Profl. Psychology, Disting. Career Achievement award Am. Bd. Med. Psychotherapists, Outstanding Contbns. to Mental Health award Psychiat. Outpatient Ctrs. of the Americas, 1991. Fellow APA (Disting. Psychologist award divsn. of psychotherapy 1992), Am. Bd. Profl. Psychology (diplomate), Internat. Acad. Eclectic Psychotherapists, Acad. Clin. Psychology; mem. Am. Acad. Psychotherapy, Assn. for Advancement Psychotherapy, Nat. Acads. Practice in Psychology (disting.), Soc. for Exploration of Psychotherapy Integration. Home: 56 Herrontown Cir Princeton NJ 08540-2924 Office: Rutgers U PO Box 819 Piscataway NJ 08855-0819 *Whatever modicum of success I may have achieved is probably due, in large part, to my view of parity as a way of life. I am committed to the notion that there are no superior human beings—we are all different, indeed unique, but equal. While some people possess superior skills and abilities, this does not make them superior human beings. To respect others for their exceptional capacities, but never to deify them, enables one to learn from others instead of envying them and denigrating oneself. This egalitarian view transforms acquisitiveness, power, and aggression into love, intimacy, and productive activity.*

LAZARUS, ARTHUR, JR., lawyer; b. Bklyn., Aug. 30, 1926; s. Arthur and Frieda (Langer) L.; m. Gertrude Chiger, Jan. 8, 1956; children: Andrew Joseph, Edward Peter, Diana Ruth. BA with honors, Columbia U., 1946; JD, Yale U., 1949. Bar: N.Y. 1951, D.C. 1952, U.S. Supreme Ct. 1954. Assoc. Fried, Frank, Harris, Shriver & Jacobson, Washington, 1950-57, ptnr., 1957-91, mng. ptnr. Washington office, 1974-86; of counsel Sonosky, Chambers, Sachse & Endreson, Washington, 1994—. Trustee Arena Stage, 1987—. Home: 3201 Fessenden St NW Washington DC 20008-2032

LAZARUS, CHARLES, retail toy company executive; b. 1923; married. With Lash Distributors Inc., 1958-67; with Interstate Stores Inc. (acquired by Toys "R" Us Inc., 1978), from 1967, sr. v.p., 1971-76, pres., chief exec. officer, from 1976; with Toys "R" Us Inc., Rochelle Park, N.J., 1970—; now chmn. Toys "R" Us Inc., Paramus, N.J.; also bd. dirs. Toys "R" Us Inc., Rochelle Park, N.J. Office: Toys R Us Inc 461 From Rd Paramus NJ 07652-3526*

LAZARUS, DAVID, physicist, educator; b. Buffalo, Sept. 8, 1921; s. Barney B. and Lillian (Markel) L.; m. Betty Jane Ross, Aug. 15, 1943; children: Barbara, William, Mary Ann, Richard. B.S., U. Chgo., 1942, M.S., 1947, Ph.D., 1949. Instr. electronics U. Chgo., 1942-43, electronics engr., 1946-49, instr. physics, 1949; research assoc. radio research lab. Harvard, 1943-45; mem. physics faculty U. Ill., Urbana, 1949—, prof., 1959—; vis. prof. U. Paris, 1968-69, M.I.T., 1978-79, Harvard U., 1978-79; vis. scientist Am. Inst. Physics, N.Y.C., 1962-69; cons. Phys. Sci. Study Com., 1957-59, Hallicrafters Co., Chgo., 1957-69, Gen. Electric Co., Cin., 1960-68, Gen. Atomic, La Jolla, Calif., 1962-63, Lawrence Radiation Lab., 1967-68, Sandia Lab., 1970-72, Addison-Wesley Pub. Co., Reading, Mass., 1964-80; dir. Council on Materials Sci., U.S. Dept. Energy, 1981-85. Author: (with H. de Waard) Modern Electronics, 1966, (with R.I. Hulsizer) The World of Physics, 1972, (with M. Raether) Practical Physics: How Things Work, 1979; also articles. Guggenheim fellow, 1968-69. Fellow AAAS, Am. Phys. Soc. (coun. 1974-78, 80-91, exec. com. 1980-91, editor-in-chief 1980-91, publs. com. 1980-91, exec. com. div. contensed matter physics 1968-70, 74-78, chmn. New Materials prize com. 1976, chmn. Buckley prize com. 1979); mem. Am. Inst. Physics (governing bd. 1981-92, exec. com. 1981-89, publs. policy com. 1981-92). Home: 502 W Vermont Ave Urbana IL 61801-4931

LAZARUS, FRED, IV, college president; b. N.Y.C., Jan. 1, 1942; s. Fred and Irma (Mendelson) L.; m. Jonna Gane, Nov. 27, 1970; children: Anna Mendelson, Fred Lazarus V. B.A., Claremont McKenna Coll., 1964; M.B.A., Harvard U., 1966. Staff assoc. Nat. Council for Equal Bus. Opportunity, Washington, 1969-71; pres. Washington Council for Equal Bus. Opportunity, 1971-74; exec. asst. to chmn. Nat. Endowment for Arts, Washington, 1975-78; pres. Md. Inst. Coll. Art, Balt., 1978—; vice chmn. 1992-95, Md. Ind. Colls. and Univs. Assn.; vice chmn. Assn. Ind. Colls. Art and Design, 1992-95; trustee Alliance for Ind. Colls. Art, 1978-91, chmn., 1984-86, 89-91; founding chmn. Nat. Coalition for Edn. in Arts, 1988-90. Trustee St. Paul's Sch.; trustee, chmn. Am. Coun. for Arts, sec., 1991-94, Md. Art Place; trustee emeritus Ptnrs. for Livable Places; bd. dirs. Afro-Am. Newspapers, Balt. Artists Housing Corp.; chmn. Balt. Coun. for Equal Bus. Opportunity Md. Art Place; mem. Thurgood Marshall Meml. Statue Commn. Recipient mayor's art award, City of Balt., 1988. Mem. Harvard Club (N.Y.C.). Office: Md Inst Coll Art 1300 W Mount Royal Ave Baltimore MD 21217-4134

LAZARUS, GEORGE MILTON, newspaper columnist; b. Worcester, Mass., June 16, 1932; s. Milton George and Urania (Costa) L.; m. Karen Jayne Sippel, Mar. 1, 1969; children: Lana Elizabeth, Tara Lisanne. BBA, Clark U., 1954; MS in Journalism, Northwestern U., 1957. Staff writer AP, Chgo., 1957-59; asst. editor Printers' Ink mag., Chgo., 1959-61; fin. news reporter Chgo. Daily News, 1961-69, mktg. news columnist, 1961-69; mktg. columnist Chgo. Today, 1969-72, Chgo. Tribune, 1972—, Adweek's Mktg. Week, 1982-90, N.Y. Daily News, 1984-90; spkr. and cons. in field; former commentator stas. WFLD-TV, WGN, WMAQ, WLAK, Chgo.; instr. advt. North Park Coll., 1957-58. Author: Marketing Immunity, 1988; contbr. articles to mags. Recipient Marshall Field award for editorial contbns., 1966-67, Nat. Headliners award, 1971, Compton Advt. award for best newspaper article on advt., 1983. Mem. Merchandising Execs. Club Chgo. (pres. 1979-80, dir.), Lambda Chi Alpha, Alpha Delta Sigma, Sigma Delta Chi. Club: Flossmoor Country. Home: 1214 Western Ave Flossmoor IL 60422-1636 Office: The Chicago Tribune 435 N Michigan Ave Chicago IL 60611-4001

LAZARUS, GERALD SYLVAN, physician; b. N.Y.C., Feb. 16, 1939; s. Joseph W. and Marion (Goldstein) L.; m. Sandra Jacob, Sept. 3, 1961 (dec. 1985); children: Mark, Elyse, Lynne, Laura; m. Audrey Fedyszyn Jakubowski, Apr. 7, 1990. B.A., Colby Coll., 1959; M.D., George Washington U., 1963. Intern, then resident U. Mich., Ann Arbor, 1963-64; resident in medicine U. Mich., 1964-65; NIH research asso. NIH, Bethesda, Md., 1965-68; resident in dermatology Harvard U., Cambridge, Mass., 1968-70; research fellow Strangeways Labs., Cambridge, Eng., 1970-72; assoc. prof. medicine, co-dir. dermatology tng. program Albert Einstein Med. Coll., N.Y.C., 1972-75; J. Lamar Callaway prof. Duke U., Durham, N.C., 1977-82; chief dermatology Duke U., 1975-82; Milton B. Hartzell prof. U. Pa. Sch. Medicine, Phila., 1982—, chmn. dept. dermatology, 1982-93; dean Sch. Medicine U. Calif., Davis, 1993—; mem. study sect. NIH, 1976-80. Author: (with L. Goldsmith) Diagnosis of Skin Disease, 1980, (with Herman Beerman) Tradition of Excellance: History of Dermatology at Univ. Pa. Sch. of Medicine; asso. editor: Jour. Investigative Dermatology, 1977-82; contbr. numerous articles to profl. jours. Served with USPHS, 1965-68. Carl Herzog fellow Am. Dermatology Assn., 1970-72; John Simon Guggenheim fellow U. Geneva, 1986; sr. investigator Arthritis Found., 1972-77; grantee NIH. Fellow ACP, Assn. Am. Physicians, Am. Soc. Clin. Investigation; mem. Am. Dermatol. Assn., Soc. Investigative Dermatology (dir., pres. 1996-97, Disting. alumnus award George Washington U. 1996), Biochem. Soc., Am. Acad. Dermatology (Sultzberger award 1986). Republican. Jewish. Office: U Calif Sch Medicine Office Of The Dean Davis CA 95616

LAZARUS, KENNETH ANTHONY, lawyer; b. Passaic, N.J., Mar. 10, 1942; s. John Joseph and Margaret (Di Cenzo) L.; m. Marylyn Jane Flemming, Aug. 13, 1966; children: Maggi Ann, John, Joseph. BA, U. Dayton, 1964; JD, U. Notre Dame, 1967; LLM in Taxation, George Washington U., 1971. Bar: N.J. 1967, U.S. Tax Ct. 1970, U.S. Ct. Claims 1970, U.S. Supreme Ct. 1971, D.C. 1976. Trial atty. U.S. Dept. Justice, 1967-71; assoc. counsel and chief counsel to Minority Com. on Judiciary, U.S. Senate, 1971-74; assoc. counsel to Pres. U.S., 1974-77; ptnr. Ward, Lazarus & Grow, Washington, 1977-91; of counsel Dixon & Dixon, Washington, 1991—; mem. adv. bd. Sch. Law Dayton U., 1975-85; adj. prof. Sch. Law Georgetown U., 1979—; mem. U.S. Adv. Com. on Trade Negotiations, 1983-87; chmn. Sailors and Mchts. Bank and Trust Co., Vienna, Va., 1987-89. Mem. adv. bd. Houston Jour. Internat. Law, 1983-90; contbr. numerous articles to profl. publs. U.S. reporter to UN, 1975-77; mem. adv. coun. Rep. Nat. Com., 1977-80; mem. Presdl. transition team Office of Pres.-Elect, 1980-81; caucus mgr. George Bush Rep. Conv., 1988; bd. trustees Internat. Law Inst., pres., 1990—. Mem. ABA, D.C. Bar Assn., Bar Assn. D.C., Fed. Bar Assn., N.J. Bar Assn., Am. Judicature Soc., Am. Law Inst. Home: Apt 716 4501 Connecticut Ave NW Washington DC 20008-3712 Office: 1850 M St NW Ste 450 Washington DC 20036-5803

LAZARUS, MARGARET LOUISE, film producer and director; b. N.Y.C., Jan. 22, 1949; d. Leon A. and Paula (Plesser) L.; children: Michael Lazarus Renner, Matthew Lazarus Renner. BA cum laude, Vassar Coll., 1969; MS in Broadcast, Film, Boston U., 1972. Researcher Westinghouse Broadcasting/Parallel Prodns., Boston, 1970-71; producer, writer Sta. WNAC-TV, Boston, 1971-72; producer, dir. Cambridge (Mass.) Documentary, 1973—, also pres., 1980-90; cons., bd. dirs. Cambridge Community TV, 1987-94. Producer, dir. (films) Taking Our Bodies Back, 1974, Rape Culture, 1976, 83, Eugene Debs and the American Movement, 1977, Killing Us Softly, 1979, Calling the Shots, 1982, Pink Triangles, 1984, The Last Empire, 1986, Still Killing Us Softly, 1987, Hazardous Inheritance, 1989, Not Just a Job, 1990, Advertising Alcohol, 1991, Life's Work, 1993, Defending Our Lives, 1993 (Academy Award, Best Documentary Short Subject); co-author: The New Our Bodies, Ourselves, 1984. Counselor, mem. Alliance Against Sexual Coercion, Cambridge, 1977-81; peace commr. City of Cambridge, 1988-91. Recipient London Film Festival award, 1982, Mannheim (Fed. Republic Germany) Film Festival award, 1982, Berlin Film Festival award, 1982, Red Ribbon Am. Film Festival award, 1983, Melbourne (Australia) Film Festival award, 1983, 1st place Am. Jour. Nursing, 1984, 1st place Nat. Council on Family Relations, 1984, 93, Blue Ribbon award Am. Film Festival, 1987, 91, U.S.A. Film Festival award 1987, World Peace Film Festival award, 1987, Global Village Film Festival award, 1985, Filmosav award India, 1988, Golden Babe award Chicago Ednl. Film Festival, 1988, Silver Apple award Nat. Ednl. Film Festival, 1991, 94, Seattle Film Festival Silver Placque award, 1993, Chgo. Internat. Film Festival award, 1993, Exceptional Merit in Media award, 1993, PASS award Nat. Coun. on Crime and Delinquency, Chris award Columbus Internat. Film Festival, 1993, Outstanding Film of the Year award New England Film and Video Festival, 1994. Mem. Acad. Motion Picture Arts and Scis.

LAZARUS, MAURICE, retired retail executive; b. Columbus, Ohio, June 27, 1915; s. Fred, Jr. and Meta (Marx) L.; m. Nancy Stix, June 7, 1942 (dec. 1985); children: Carol, Jill; m. Nell P. Eurich, Nov. 25, 1988. Student, Ohio State U.; B.A., Harvard, 1937; LL.D., Am. Internat. Coll., 1969. Div. mdse. mgr. John Shillito Co., Columbus, 1937-41; head service and control Foley's, Houston, 1945-48; exec. v.p. Foley's, 1948-58; pres., treas. Filene's, Boston, 1958-64; chmn. bd. Filene's, 1964-65; vice chmn. Federated Dept. Stores, Inc., Boston, 1965-70; chmn. finance com. Federated Dept. Stores, Inc., 1971-82, also dir. Mem. adv. com. on nat. health ins. issues HEW, 1977-78; bd. dirs. Cambridge Ctr. Adult Edn., 1974-75; mem. adv. Council Pres.'s Commn. on Status of Women, 1963-68; chmn. exec. com. Public Agenda Found., 1987—; mem. div. health scis. and tech. Harvard U.-M.I.T., 1978-87, Harvard Cmty. Health Plan Found. Bd., 1984—, chmn., 1996—; mem. adv. bd. Schlesinger Library Women's Archives, Radcliffe Coll., 1972-76; mem. bd. overseers Harvard Coll., 1977-83; mem. ethics adv. bd. HEW, 1978-80; vis. com., chmn. central services, Med. Sch. and Dental Medicine, Sch. Public Health Harvard U., 1978-85, mem. governance com., 1968-71, mem. working group div. health policy research and edn.; chmn. adv. com. Joint Center Urban Studies., 1977-82; trustee Mass. Gen. Hosp., Old Sturbridge Village, 1965-78, Marine Biol. Lab., 1977-84, McLean Hosp., 1980—, Tufts U. Civic Edn. Found. of Lincoln Filene Center for Citizenship and Public Affairs, 1972-80, New Eng. Med. Center Hosp., 1960-78, Beth Israel Hosp., 1958-65, Bennington Coll., 1965-72, Combined Jewish Philanthropy Greater Boston, 1962-65; chmn. exec. com. Pub. Agenda Found., 1977—; bd. dirs. Boston chpt. ARC, 1962-64; dir. Med. Found., 1987—; chmn. Harvard Cmty. Health Plan, 1984-93; bd. overseers Boston Symphony Orch., 1971-74; bd. dirs. Salzburg Seminars in Am. Studies, Assoc. Harvard Alumni, 1966-73; pres. Assoc. Harvard Alumni, 1972-73; mem. Mass. Higher Edn. Facilities Commn., 1970-74; mem. corp. Northeastern U., Peter Bent Brigham Hosp.; bd. overseers Boston Symphony Orch., 1971-74; mem. M.I.T. Council Arts, 1972-77, Harvard Med. Center, 1977-79; mem. adv. com. hosp. initiatives in long-term care Am. Hosp. Assn.; chmn. bd. dirs. Harvard Cmty. Health Plan, dir. emeritus, 1994—; mem. adv. bd. Brandeis U. Ctr. Social Policy in Middle East, 1978-88. Fellow Am. Acad. Arts and Scis. Clubs: Bay (Boston), Harvard (Boston, N.Y.C.); Univ. (N.Y.C.); St. Botolph (Boston), Comml.-Mchts. (Boston). Home and Office: 144 Brattle St 3d Fl Cambridge MA 02138-2202

LAZARUS, MELL, cartoonist; b. N.Y.C, May 3, 1927; s. Sidney and Frances (Mushkin) L.; m. Eileen Hortense Israel, June 19, 1949; children: Marjorie, Suesan, Catherine. Cartoonist-writer Miss Peach, 1957—, Momma, 1970—; author anthologies Miss Peach, Miss Peach, Are These Your Children?, Momma, We're Grownups Now!; novels The Boss is Crazy, Too, 1964, The Neighborhood Watch, 1986; plays Everybody into the Lake, Elliman's Fly, Lifetime Eggcreams, 1969-70; juvenile Francine, Your Face Would Stop a Clock, 1975; co-author Miss Peach TV spl. programs Turkey Day Pageant and Annual Heart Throb Ball. Trustee Internat. Mus. Cartoon Art. With USNR, 1945, USAFR, 1951-54. Mem. Nat. Cartoonists Soc. (pres. 1989-93, chmn. membership com. 1965, nat. rep., Humor Strip Cartoonist of Yr. 1973, 79, Reuben award 1981), Writers Guild Am. West, Nat. Press Club, The Century Assn., Newspaper Features Coun. (bd. dirs.), Sigma Delta Chi. Office: Creators Syndicate Inc 5777 W Century Blvd Los Angeles CA 90045-5600

LAZARUS, RICHARD STANLEY, psychology educator; b. N.Y.C., Mar. 3, 1922; s. Abe and Matilda (Marks) L.; m. Bernice H. Newman, Sept. 2, 1945; children—David Alan, Nancy Eve. A.B., City Coll. N.Y., 1942; M.S., U. Pitts., 1947, Ph.D., 1948; Dr. honoris causa, Johannes Gutenberg U., Mainz, Fed. Republic Germany, 1988, U. Haifa, Israel, 1995. Diplomate in clin. psychology Am. Bd. Examiners in Profl. Psychology. Asst. prof. Johns Hopkins, 1948-53; psychol. cons. VA, 1952—; assoc. prof. psychology, dir. clin. tng. program Clark U., Worcester, Mass., 1953-57; assoc. prof. psychology U. Calif. at Berkeley, 1957-59, prof. psychology, 1959-91, prof. emeritus, 1991—; prin. investigator Air Force contracts dealing with psychol. stress, 1951-53, USPHS grant on personality psychol. stress, 1953-70; NIA, NIDA, and NCI grantee on stress, coping and health, 1977-81, MacArthur Found. research grantee, 1981-84; USPHS spl. fellow Waseda U., Japan, 1963-64. Author 18 books, numerous publs. in profl. jours. Served to 1st lt. AUS, 1943-46. Recipient Disting. Sci. Achievement award Calif. State Psychol. Assn., 1984, Div. 38 Health Psychology, 1989; Guggenheim fellow, 1969-70; Army Rsch. Inst. rsch. grantee, 1973-75. Fellow AAAS, APA (Disting. Sci. Contbn. award 1989); mem. Western Psychol. Assn., Argentina Med. Assn. (hon.). Home: 1824 Stanley Dollar Dr Apt 3B Walnut Creek CA 94595-2833 Office: Univ Calif Dept Psychology Berkeley CA 94720

LAZARUS, ROCHELLE BRAFF, advertising executive; b. N.Y.C., Sept. 1, 1947; d. Lewis L. and Sylvia Ruth (Eisenberg) Braff; m. George M. Lazarus, Mar. 22, 1970; children: Theodore, Samantha, Benjamin. AB, Smith Coll., 1968; MBA, Columbia U., 1970. Product mgr. Clairol, N.Y.C., 1970-71; account exec. Ogilvy & Mather, N.Y.C., 1971-73, account supr., 1973-77, mgmt. supr., 1977-84, sr. v.p., 1981—, account group dir., 1984-87; gen. mgr. Ogilvy & Mather Direct, N.Y.C., 1987-88, mng. dir., 1988-89, pres., 1989-91; pres. Ogilvy & Mather, N.Y.C., 1991-94, pres. N. Am., 1991-94; pres., COO Ogilvy & Mather Worldwide, N.Y.C., 1995—. Bd. dirs. Ann Taylor, Advt. Edn. Found., YMCA, Nat. Women's Law Ctr.; mem. Com. of 200; mem. bus. com. Solomon R. Guggenheim Mus.; mem. bd. overseers

Columbus Bus. Sch.; trustee Smith Coll., Columbia Presbyn. Hosp. Recipient YWCA Women Achievers award, 1985, Matrix award, 1995. Mem. Am. Assn. Advt. Agys. (bd. dirs.), Advt. Women N.Y. (Woman of Yr. 1994), Nat. Coun. World Wildlife Fund. Home: 106 E 78th St New York NY 10021-0302 Office: Ogilvy & Mather Worldwide 309 W 49th St New York NY 10019-7316

LAZARUS, STEVEN S., management consultant, marketing consultant; b. Rochester, N.Y., June 16, 1943; s. Alfred and Ceal H. Lazarus; m. Elissa C. Lazarus, June 19, 1966; children: Michael, Stuart, Jean. BS, Cornell U., 1966; MS, Poly. U. N.Y., 1967; PhD, U. Rochester, 1974. Pres. Mgmt. Systems Analysis Corp., Denver, 1977—; dir. Sci. Application Intern Corp., Englewood, Colo., 1979-84; assoc. prof. Metro State Coll., Denver, 1983-84; sr. v.p. Pal Assocs. Inc., Denver, 1984-85; with strategic planning and mktg. McDonnell Douglas, Denver, 1985-86; mktg. cons. Clin. Reference Systems, Denver, 1986; pres. Mgmt. Sys. Analysis Corp., 1986-89, 95—; assoc. exec. dir. Ctr. Rsch. Ambulatory Health Care Adminstrn., Englewood, 1990-94; spl. cons. State of Colo., Denver, 1976-81; mktg. cons. IMX, Louisville, 1986-87; speaker Am. Hosp. Assn., Chgo., 1983—, Med. Group Mgmt. Assn., 1975—; asst. sec. Work Group for Elec. Data Interchange, 1995—. Contbr. chpts. to books; patentee med. quality assurance. NDEA fellow U. Rochester, 1968-71. Fellow Healthcare Info. and Mgmt. Systems Soc.; mem. Inst. Indsl. Engring. (sr.), Med. GroupMgmt. Assn., Optimists (program chmn. Denver club 1976-78). Home: 7023 E Eastman Ave Denver CO 80224-2845 Office: MSA Corp Ste 300 4949 S Syracuse St Denver CO 80237

LAZAY, PAUL DUANE, telecommunications manufacturing company executive; b. Phila., June 2, 1939; s. Louis and Thea (Lindberg) L.; m. Joan Elizabeth Robinson, Sept. 2, 1961; 1 child, Thomas. BS, Trinity Coll., 1961; PhD, MIT, 1968. Supr. optic measurement Bell Labs., Murray Hill, N.J., 1969-83; v.p. engring. ITT-EOPD, Roanoke, Va., 1983-86; v.p. engring. Telco Systems Fiber Optics Div., Norwood, Mass., 1986-87, v.p. mktg., 1987-88, pres., gen. mgr., 1987-88; pres., chief exec. officer Telco System, Inc., Norwood, 1988-94; v.p., gen. mgr. ATM divsn. Cisco Systems, Inc., Chelmsford, Mass., 1995—; bd. dirs. SpecTran Corp., Sturbridge, Mass. Contbr. articles on fiber optics to profl. jours.; patentee in field. Mem. IEEE, Am. Physics Soc., Optical Soc. Am., Sigma Xi.

LAZCANO, MARCO ANTONIO, orthopedic surgeon, educator, researcher; b. Mexico City, Oct. 5, 1930; s. Antonio and Carmen (Marroquin) L.; m. Susana Barrero, Dec. 19, 1937; children: Marco Antonio, Manuel, Herman. MD, U. Mexico City, 1954; MS, U. Minn., 1960. Assoc. prof. Nat. Inst. Nutricion, 1968-85; prof. Nat. Inst. Orthopedics, 1977-79; prof. orthopedics, chmn. Am. British Cowdray Hosp., 1980—; pres. Am. British Cowdray Hosp., 1967-68, Am. Coll. Surgeons, Mexico City, 1974-75, Latin Am. Orthopedic Soc., 1983-86; founder Ibero Latino Am. Orthopedic Soc., 1986; vis. prof. Mayo Clinic, 1990. Author: Low Friction Arthroplasty, 1984, Hemiarthroplasty of the Hip, 1994; contbr. 45 articles to profl. jours.; patentee new model of hemiartroplasty of the hip. Recipient award Mexican Orthopedic Soc., 1973; named hon. mem. Med. Coll., Costa Rica, 1975, Orthopedic Soc., Peru, 1985, Med. Assn., Argentina and Venezuela, 1985, Orthopedic Soc., Panama, 1986; fellow Royal Soc. Arts, England, 1972. Fellow Internat. Soc. Orthopedics Trauma, Am. Coll. Surgeons, Am. Acad. Orthopedic Surgeons, Latin Am. Orthopedic Soc. Avocations: golf, Mexican history, music. Home: Fuente Mercurio # 30, 16 Mexico City Mexico Office: Ortopedia Tecamachalco SC, Sur 136 # 116, 01120 Mexico City Mexico

LAZEAR, EDWARD PAUL, economics and industrial relations educator, researcher; b. N.Y.C., Aug. 17, 1948; s. Abe and Rose (Karp) L.; m. Victoria Ann Allen, July 2, 1977; 1 child, Julia Ann. A.B., UCLA, 1971, A.M., 1971; Ph.D., Harvard U., 1974. Asst. prof. econs. U. Chgo., 1974-78, assoc. prof. indsl. relations, 1978-81, prof. indsl. relations, 1981-85, Isidore and Gladys Brown prof. urban and labor econs., 1985-92; sr. fellow Hoover Instn. Stanford (Calif.) U., 1985—, coord. domestic studies Hoover Instn., 1987-90, prof. econs. and human resource mgmt. Grad. Sch. Bus., 1992-95; Jack Steele Parker prof. econs. and human resource mgmt. Stanford U., 1995—; econ. advisor to Romania, Czechoslovakia, Russia, Ukraine, Georgia; rsch. assoc. Nat. Bur. Econ. Rsch., Econs. Rsch. Ctr. of Nat. Opinion Rsch. Ctr.; fellow Inst. Advanced Study, Hebrew U., Jerusalem, 1977-8; lectr. Inst. Advanced Study, Vienna, 1983-84, Nat. Productivity Bd., Singapore, 1982, 85; vis. prof. Inst. des Etudes Politiques, Paris, 1987; Wicksell lectr., Stockholm, 1993. Author: (with R. Michael) Allocation of Income Within the Household, 1988; (with J.P. Gould) Microeconomic Theory, 1989, Personnel Economics, 1995; editor: Economic Transition in Eastern Europe and Russia, 1995; founding editor Jour. Labor Econs., 1982—; assoc. eidtor Jour. Econ. Perspectives, 1986-89; co-editor: Jour. Labor Abstracts, 1996—; contbr. numerous articles to scholarly jours. NSF grad. fellow, 1971-74. Fellow Econometric Soc., Soc. Labor Economists (1st v.p. 1995-96); mem. Am. Econs. Assn. Home: 277 Old Spanish Trl Portola Valley CA 94028-8129 Office: Stanford U Grad Sch Bus Stanford CA 94305-5015 Also: Stanford Univ Hoover Inst Stanford CA 94305-6010

LAZECHKO, D. M. (MOLLY LAZECHKO), former state legislator; b. Innisfail, Alta., June 3, 1926; came to U.S., 1960; d. Archibald Donald and Violet Georgina (Adams) Manuel; m. Walter Vladimir Lazechko, Apr. 16, 1960; children: William Donald, Robert James. BA, Boise State U., 1976. Cert. elem. tchr. Tchr. Olds Sch. Dist., Stewart Sch., Alta., 1945-46, Innisfail (Alta.) Sch. Dist., 1946-50; tchr., vice prin. Calgary (Alta.) Sch. Dist., 1950-59; exchange tchr. Edinburgh, Scotland, 1954-55; math tutor mgr. Title I, Boise, Idaho, 1974-76; elem. tchr. Boise (Idaho) Sch. Dist., 1976-87; jr. high tchr. Chpt. I, Boise, 1987-88; ret., 1988-90; mem. Idaho Ho. of Reps., Boise, 1991, 92; pres. div. I Alta. Tchrs. Assn., Calgary, 1958-59, Whittier PTA, Boise, 1969-70, 73-74; pres., 3d v.p. Dist. 8 Idaho State PTA, 1973-75; sec., elem. dir. Boise (Idaho) Edn. Assn., 1978-81. Treas. LWV, Boise, 1988-90, Ho. Dems. Campaign Com., Boise, 1991-92; precinct capt. Ada County Dems. Dist. 16, Boise, 1988-90; sec. Boise Ret. Tchrs., 1989-90, pres., 1993-94; bd. dirs. Boise Neighborhood Housing Svcs., 1990-92, Cmty. Contbn. Ctr., 1991-94, Idaho Housing Coalition, 1991-94, Epilepsy League Idaho, 1993-95; gubernatorial appointee to bd. dirs. Idaho Coun. on Domestic Violence, 1994—; candidate Idaho Legis. Ho. Reps., 1994. Mem. NEA, Idaho Edn. Assn., Idaho Conservation League, Idaho Women's Network, Grassroots Women's Lobby, Idaho Citzen's Network. Episcopalian. Avocations: politics, reading, swimming.

LAZENBY, FRED WIEHL, insurance company executive; b. Chattanooga, Jan. 13, 1932; s. John Wesley and Adela (Valenzuela) L.; m. Virginia Banks; children: Kathryn Wesley, Grace Woodard. BA cum laude, Vanderbilt U., 1954. CLU. With Nat. Life & Accident Ins. Co., Nashville, 1956—, from agt. to pres., 1956-83; chmn. bd., chief exec. officer Southlife Holding Co., Nashville, 1983-94; chmn., CEO SouthCap Corp., 1994—, Premier Life Ins. Co., 1995—; past chmn. Life Insurers Conf.; bd. dirs. Nashville Bank of Commerce. Trustee Life Underwriting Tng. Coun., 1978-82; mem. bd. advisors Massey Sch.; chmn. Nashville Community Found. 1st lt. U.S. Army, 1954-56. Mem. Life Ins. Mgmt. Rsch. Assn. (bd. dirs. 1985-88, past chmn. combination cos. exec. com.), Belle Meade Country Club, Cumberland Club, Carolina Yatch Club, Rotary. Republican. Methodist. Avocations: tennis, golf, skiing. Office: SouthCap Corp 211 7th Ave N Nashville TN 37219-1823

LAZENBY, GAIL R., library director; b. Charlotte, N.C., May 6, 1947; d. James Yates and Marian Elizabeth (Church) Rogers. BA, Salem Coll., 1969; MLS, U. N.C., 1971. Cert. libr., Ga. Br. libr. Atlanta Pub. Libr., 1970-77; br. coord. Dekalb Libr. System, Decatur, Ga., 1977-82; asst. dir. West Ga. Regional Libr., Carrollton, 1982-83; asst. dir. Cobb County Pub. Libr., Marietta, Ga., 1983-90, dir., 1991—. Mem. Leadership Cobb, Cobb County, 1985-86. Mem. ALA, Ga. Libr. Assn. (2d v.p. 1987-89), Southeastern Libr. Assn. (v.p.-pres. elect. 1990-92, pres. 1992-94), Urban Librs. Coun., Kiwanis Club Marietta (bd. dirs. 1991-92, sec. 1992-93, sec.-treas. 1993-94, pres. 1995-96). Office: Cobb County Public Lib 266 Roswell St SE Marietta GA 30060-2005

LAZERSON, EARL EDWIN, academic administrator emeritus; b. Detroit, Dec. 10, 1930; s. Nathan and Ceil (Stashefsky) L.; m. Ann May Harper, June 11, 1966; children from previous marriage: Joshua, Paul. BS, Wayne State U., Detroit, 1953; postgrad., U. Leiden, Netherlands, 1957-58; MA, U. Mich., 1954, PhD, 1982. Mathematician Inst. Def. Analyses, Princeton, N.J., 1960-62; asst. prof. math. Washington U., St. Louis, 1962-65, 66-69; vis. asso. prof. Brandeis U., 1965-66; mem. faculty So. Ill. U., Edwardsville, 1969—, prof. math., 1973—, chmn. dept. math. studies, 1972-73, dean Sch. Sci. and Tech., 1973-76, univ. v.p., provost, 1977-79, pres., 1980-93; pres. emeritus, 1994—. Chmn. Southwestern Ill. Devel. Authority, City of East St. Louis Fin. Adv. Authority; active Leadership Coun. Southwestern Ill., Gateway Ctr. Met. St. Louis, Inc., St. Louis Symphony Soc.; trustee Jefferson Nat. Expansion Meml. Assn., Ill. Econ. Devel. Bd. Recipient Sr. Teaching Excellence award Standard Oil Found., 1970-71. Mem. Am. Math. Soc., Math. Assn. Am., European Math. Soc., London Math. Soc., Soc. Mathematique France, Fulbright Alumni Assn., Sigma Xi. Home: 5 Hidden Valley Ln Edwardsville IL 62025-3706

LAZERSON, ELEANOR MARIE, psychiatric, mental health nurse, administrator; b. Chgo.; d. Ettore A. and Lena A. (Plastine) Ianniccari; m. Jack Lazerson, Mar. 24, 1962 (div.); children: David, Deborah, Darlene, Donna. Diploma, Presbyn. Hosp. Sch. Nursing, Chgo., 1954; BA, Northeastern U., Chgo., 1976; MS, No. Ill. U., 1978. Cert. psychiat./mental health nurse, clin. nursing supr.-adminstr. Clin. nursing supr./adminstr. Dept. Mental Health and Developmental Disabilities, Chgo.; staff nurse, patient educator VA Hosp., Chgo.; lectr. in field. Author script for audiovisual presentation on manic-depressive illness. Fellow Am. Orthopsychiat. Assn.; mem. ANA, Ill. Nurses Assn., Chgo. Nurses Assn., Am. Psychiat. Nurses Assn., Am. Nurses Found.

LAZERSON, JACK, pediatrician, educator; b. Bronx, Jan. 9, 1936; s. Mayer and Jennie (Gerson) L.; (div.); children: David, Deborah, Darlene, Donna; (div.); 1 child, Samuel. AB, NYU, 1957; MD, U. Chgo., 1961. Diplomate Am. Bd. Pediatrics. Rotating internship L.A. County Gen. Hosp., 1961-62; resident in pediatrics Stanford-Palo Alto (Calif.) Hosp., 1962-64; chief resident in pediatrics, instr. U. Wash. Hosp., Seattle, 1966-67; asst. prof. dept. pediatrics Sch. of Medicine Stanford U., 1969-72; from asst. to assoc. prof. dept. pediatrics U. So. Calif., L.A., 1972-76; assoc. prof. dept. pediatrics U. Wis., Milw., 1976-79; prof. dept. pediatrics Sch. of Medicine U. Calif., Davis, 1979-86, prof. dept. pathology, 1980-86; prof., chmn. dept. pediatrics Sch. of Medicine U. Nev., 1986-94, prof. dept. pediatrics Sch. Medicine, 1986—; chief hemophilia svc. Children's Hosp. Stanford U. Sch. of Medicine, 1969-72; assoc. hematologist div. hematology and oncology Children's Hosp. L.A., 1972-76. Contbr. numerous articles to profl. jours. Bd. dirs. hemostasis program Milw. Children's Hosp., 1976-79; med. dir. Great Lakes Hemophilia Found., 1976-79. Armour and Hyland Labs. grantee, 1969-72, 72-76, Med. Coll. of Wis. grantee, 1976-79, HEW grantee, 1976-79, Cutter Labs. grantee, 1981-82, 82-83; recipient Rsch. Funds award U. Calif.-Davis, 1981-82, Outstanding Alumnus award U. Chgo., 1981. Fellow Am. Acad. Pediatrics; mem. Am. Fedn. for Clin. Rsch., N.Y. Acad. Scis., Nat. Hemophilia Found., Am. Chem. Soc. (biochemistry sect., med. chemistry sect.), Hemostasis Assn. of Calif., Internat. Soc. Thrombosis and Hemostasis, Am. Heart Assn. Coun. on Thrombosis Basic Sci. Coun., Am. Soc. Hematology, Am. Soc. for Exptl. Pathology, World Fedn. Hemophilia, Am. Assn. Blood Banks, Am. Soc. Pediatric (hematology and oncology credentials and by-laws com., membership com.), Alpha Omega Alpha. Office: U Nev Sch Medicine 2040 W Charleston Blvd Ste 200 Las Vegas NV 89102-2206

LAZIO, RICK A., congressman, lawyer; b. Amityville, N.Y., Mar. 13, 1958; s. Anthony and Olive E. (Christensen) L. AB in Polit. Sci., Vassar Coll., 1980; JD, Am. U., 1983. Bar: N.Y. 1984, U.S. Dist. Ct. (ea. and so. dists.) N.Y., 1985. Asst. dist. atty. Suffolk County Rackets Bureau, Hauppauge, N.Y., 1983-88; exec. asst. dist. atty. Suffolk County, N.Y., 1987-88; village atty. Village of Lindenhurst, N.Y., 1988-93; mng. ptnr. Glass, Lazio and Glass, Esqs., Babylon, N.Y., 1988-93; mem. Suffolk County Legislature from 11th Dist., N.Y., 1989-93; mem. 103d-104th Congresses from 2nd N.Y. dist., Washington, 1993—, dep. majority whip; budget com. banking subcom.; chmn. subcom. on housing and cmty. opportunity; mem. capital markets, securities and govt. sponsored enterprises. Mem. admissions com. Vassar Coll., N.Y.; past pres. West Islip Rep. Club. Mem. Suffolk County Bar Assn. Roman Catholic. Avocations: numismatics, guitar. Office: US Ho of Reps 314 CHOB Washington DC 20515

LAZOR, PATRICIA ANN, interior designer; d. Charles A. and Grace E. (Siegrist) LaGattuta; m. E. Alexander Lazor, Aug. 22, 1959; children: Pamela A., Carolyn L., Charles L., Peter A. BA, Chestnut Hill Coll., 1957; MEd, Rutgers Coll., 1962; cert., N.Y. Sch. Interior Design, 1972. Tchr. Bridgewater (N.J.) Raritan Schs., 1958-69; designer Patricia A. Lazor Interior Design, Bernardsville, N.J., 1975-85; pres. Alexander Abry, Inc., Washington, 1985-87; owner, designer Patricia A. Lazor Interior Design Antiques, Inc., Bernardsville, 1985—. Rep. com. woman, Somerset County, N.J., 1978; chmn. Family Counseling Svc. Somerset County, 1972-78. Mem. Essex Hunt Club (Peapack, N.J.), Somerset Hills Country Club (Bernardsville), Garden Club Morristown, Morristown Club, Kappa Delta Phi. Republican. Avocations: horseback riding, paddle tennis, oil painting, photography, golf. Home and Office: Interior Design/Antiques Inc Roebling Rd Bernardsville NJ 07924

LAZOR, THEODOSIUS (HIS BEATITUDE METROPOLITAN THEODOSIUS), archbishop; b. Canonsburg, Pa., Oct. 27, 1933; s. John and Mary (Kirr) L. AB, Washington and Jefferson Coll., 1957, DD (hon.), 1973; BD, St. Vladimir's Orthodox Theol. Sem., 1960; postgrad., Ecumenical Inst., Bossey, Switzerland, 1961; DD (hon.), St. Vladimir's Orthodox Theol. Sem., 1986; DHL (hon.), Georgetown U., 1988. Tonsured monk Orthodox Ch. in Am., 1961, ordained priest, 1961; priest Nativity of Holy Virgin Mary Ch., Madison, Ill., 1961-66; elected bishop of Washington, 1967, Sitka and Alaska, 1967, Pitts. and, W.Va., 1972; elected primate of Orthodox Ch. in Am., Met. All Am. and Can.; archbishop of N.Y., 1977, archbishop of Washington and Met. of All Am. and Can., 1981—. Address: Orthodox Ch Am PO Box 675 Syosset NY 11791-0675

LAZORKO, ANTHONY, JR., art director; b. Phila., June 5, 1935; s. Anthony and Rose (Rudnick) L.; m. Marguerite Francis Biddle, Aug. 1, 1959; children: Jonathan, Paul, Catherine. Student, Pa. Acad. Fine Arts, U. Pa. Staff artist Phila. Bull., 1950-60, asst. art dir., 1960-74, art dir., 1974-80, asst. news art dir., 1980-82; staff artst St. Louis Post-Dispatch, 1982, asst. news art dir., 1982-85, news art dir., 1985—; art dir. Blavat Advt., Erdenheim, Pa., 1968-82. Treas. Powelton Civic Club, Phila., 1966; pres. Powelton '76, Phila., 1971. Mem. Soc. Newspaper Design, Hist. Soc. Pa. Avocations: travel, music, history. Home: 816 Ann Ave Saint Louis MO 63104-4135*

LAZZARA, BERNADETTE See PETERS, BERNADETTE

LAZZARO, ANTHONY DEREK, university administrator; b. Utica, N.Y., Jan. 31, 1921; s. Angelo Michael and Philomena (Vanilla) L.; m. Shirley Margaret Jones, Dec. 20, 1941; 1 child, Nancy. BS in Indsl. and Sys. Engring., U. So. Calif., 1948; LL.D. with honors, Pepperdine U., 1974. Registered profl. engr., Calif. Asst. bus. mgr. U. So. Calif., L.A., 1948-60, asst. bus. mgr., dir. campus devel., 1960-65, asso. bus. mgr., dir. campus devel., 1965-71, asso. v.p. bus. affairs, 1971-72, v.p. bus. affairs, 1972-86, sr. v.p. bus. affairs, 1986-88, univ. v.p., 1988-91, v.p. emeritus, 1991—; cons. HEW. Editorial cons. College and University Business, 1955-58. Mem. nat. adv. coun. United Student Aid Funds, N.Y.C., 1974-77, chmn., 1976-77; dir. Rep. Fed. Savs. & Loan Assn. and subs. corps., L.A., 1961-88; spl. studies cons. div. higher edn. Office Edn. HEW, 1956-59; mem. citizens com. Palos Verdes Bd. Edn., 1955-57; mem. Hoover urban renewal adv. com. Community Redevel. Agy. City of L.A., 1960-88. Lt. USNR, 1941-46. Mem. Nat. Assn. Coll. and Univ. Bus. Officers (pres. 1978-79, dir. 1972-80, chmn. goals and programs com. 1978, chmn. large inst. com. 1986-87, Disting. Bus. Officer award 1986), Western Assn. Coll. and Univ. Bus. Officers (pres. 1971-72), Soc. Coll. and Univ. Planning, Blue Key, Golden Key, Phi Kappa Phi, Tau Beta Pi. Club: Jonathan (Los Angeles). Home: 4012 Via Larga Vis Pls Vrds Est CA 90274-1122 Office: Los Angeles CA 90089-1454

LE, CAN, mechanical engineer, inventor, author; b. Tam Quan, Vietnam, Dec. 14, 1949; arrived in Guam, 1975; s. Trac and Phung Thi (Nguyen) L. AD, Eastfield Coll., Mesquite, Tex., 1988. Helper dept. mech. engring. U. Tex., Arlington, 1978; ind. designer and programmer Dallas, 1980—. Holder copyrights for multiplication and divsn. integrations, The Accurate PI, program P.V.T. Process, Labor Expansion; program inventor Condodrafters, others. 1st lt. Vietnamese Army, 1969-75. Roman Catholic. Avocations: guitar, keyboard, magazines, jogging. Home: 2824 San Diego Dr Dallas TX 75228-1646

LE, KHANH TUONG, utility executive; b. Saigon, Vietnam, Feb. 25, 1936; parents Huy Bich and Thi Hop; m. Thi Thi Nguyen, Apr. 22, 1961; children: Tuong-Khanh, Tuong-Vi, Khang, Tuong-Van. BS in Mech. Engring., U. Montreal, 1960, MS in Mech. Engring., 1961. Cert. profl. engr. Project mgr. Saigon Met. Water Project Ministry Pub. Works, Saigon, 1961-66; dep. dir. gen. Cen. Logistics Agy. Prime Min. Office, Saigon, 1966-70; asst. dir., chief auditor Nat. Water Supply Agy. Min. Pub. Works, Saigon, 1970-75; mgr. Willows Water Dist., Englewood, Colo., 1975—; dean sch. mgmt. scis., asst. chancellor acad. afairs Hoa-Hao U., Long-Xuyen, Vietnam, 1973-75; chmn. bd. dirs. Asian Pacific Devel. Ctr.,; adv. bd. Araphoe County Utility Douglas County Water Authority. Treas. Met. Denver Water Authority, 1989-92; mem. Araphoe County Adv. Bd., Doughas County Water Authority, 1993—; mem. Front Range Water Forum presided by Gov. Roy Romer, Colo., 1993—; vol. Water for People, 1994-95. Recipient Merit medal Pres. Republic Vietnam, 1966, Pub. Health Svc. medal, 1970, Edn. Svc. 1st class medal, 1971, Pub. Works 1st class medal, 1972, Rural Reconstrn. 1st class medal, 1972, Svc. award Asian Edn. Adv. Coun., 1989; co-recipient Engring. Excellence award Am. Cons. Engrs Coun., 1994; named to Top Ten Pub. Works Leaders in Colo., Am. Pub. Works Assn., 1990. Mem. Am. Water Works Assn., Water Environ. Fedn., Colo. Water Congress, Asian C. of C. (bd. dirs. 1993), Vietnamese Profl. Engrs. Soc. (founder), Amnesty Internat., Friendship Bridge. Buddhist. Avocations: reading, swimming, tennis, hiking. Office: Willows Water Dist 6970 S Holly Cir Ste 200 Englewood CO 80112-1066

LE, THUY TRONG, research and development engineer, educator; b. Vietnam, Jan. 20, 1958; came to US, 1980; s. Thich Trong and Le-Phi Thi (Vuong) V.; m. Nhan Thi Le, Aug. 20, 1985; 1 child, Thuy-Nhu Thi. BS in Nuclear Engring., U. Calif., 1985, MS in Nuclear Engring., 1987, PhD in Engring., 1990. Electronic technician Aertech Industry, Sunnyvale, Calif., 1982; nuclear reactor operator, health physicist assistant Nuclear Engring. Dept. U. Calif., Berkeley, 1985-88, graduate student instr.Nuclear Engring. and Physics Dept., 1987-90; rsch. asst. physics divsn. Lawrence Berkeley Nat. Lab., 1988-89; instr. physics, calculus I, II, III Dept. Applied Art and Sci. Calif. Coll. of Alameda, 1989-90; rsch. engr. scientific computation divsn.applied physics group Westinghouse Savannah River Lab., 1990-93; sr. R & D engr. SuperComputer Group Fujitsu Am. Incorporation, Calif., 1993—; cons. engr. Sierra nuclear Corp., Scotts Valley, Calif., 1989; lectr. U. S.C., Aiken, 1991-93. Contbr. numerous articles to profl. jours. Mem. Am. Nuclear Soc. (math. and computation divsn.), The Engring Soc. Advancing Mobility Land Sea Air and Space, Assn. Computing Machinery. Achievements include authoring GRIMH3 computer code: multi dimensional reactor analysis code, WINDEX System: detailed energy residence treatment code, research in parallel algorithms and mathematical schemes for the development of scientific and engineering application software. Address: 43146 Mayfair Park Ave Fremont CA 94538

LE, YVONNE DIEMVAN, chemist; b. Vietnam, Nov. 21, 1961; d. Hien Trung and Thanh-Hoa Thi (Luu) L. BA in Chemistry, Math., San Jose State U., 1984. Chem. technician Hewlett Packard Co., Palo Alto, Calif., 1983; assoc. chemist Ampex Corp., Sunnyvale, Calif., 1984-86; chemist II Info. Memory Corp., Santa Clara, Calif., 1986-88; R&D project engr. Komag, Inc., Milpitas, Calif., 1988—. Mem. Am. Chem. Soc. Roman Catholic. Avocations: skiing, tennis, piano. Office: Komag Inc 275 S Hillview Dr Milpitas CA 95035

LEA, GEORGE A., JR., retail food executive; b. Pine Bluff, Ark., Apr. 8, 1950; s. George A. and Lois (Hogg) L.; m. Martha Elizabeth Quinn Stuckey, Sept. 16, 1972 (div. 1987); children: George A. III, Robert Quinn, Lois Anne Elizabeth. BA in Econs. and Bus., Hendrix Coll., 1972. CPA, Ark. Acct. Glenn Railsback & Co., Pine Bluff, Ark., 1972-77; pres., CEO The Mad Butcher, Inc., Pine Bluff, 1977—. Elder Presbyn. Ch. Mem. AICPA, Ark. Soc. CPA, Ark. Grocers and Retail Mchts. (vice chmn. 1994). Home: 501 Carter Dr Pine Bluff AR 71602-3004 Office: The Mad Butcher Inc PO Box 1020 Pine Bluff AR 71613-1020

LEA, LORENZO BATES, lawyer; b. St. Louis, Apr. 12, 1925; s. Lorenzo Bates and Ursula Agnes (Gibson) L.; m. Marcia Gwendolyn Wood, Mar. 21, 1953; children—Victoria, Jennifer, Christopher. BS, MIT, 1946; JD, U. Mich., 1949; grad. Advanced Mgmt. Program, Harvard U., 1964. Bar: Ill. 1950. With Amoco Corp. (formerly Standard Oil Co. Ind.), Chgo., 1949—, asst. gen. counsel, 1963-71, assoc. gen. counsel, 1971-72, gen. counsel, 1972-78, v.p., gen. counsel, 1978-89. Trustee Village of Glenview (Ill.) Zoning Bd., 1961-63; bd. dirs. Chgo. Crime Commn., 1978—, Midwest Council for Internat. Econ. Policy, 1973—, Chgo. Bar Found., 1981—, Chgo. Area Found. for Legal Services, 1981—; bd. dirs. United Charities of Chgo., 1973—, chmn., 1985—. Served with USNR, 1943-46. Mem. ABA, Am. Petroleum Inst., Am. Arbitration Assn. (dir. 1980—), Ill. Bar Assn., Chgo. Bar Assn., Assn. Gen. Counsel, Order of Coif, Law Club, Econs. Club, Legal, Mid-Am. (Chgo.), Glen View, Wyndemere, Hole-In-The-Wall, Sigma Xi. Republican. Mem. United Ch. of Christ.

LEA, SCOTT CARTER, retired packaging company executive; b. New Orleans, Nov. 14, 1931; s. Leonard G. and Helen (Stoughton) L.; m. Marilyn Ruth Blair, Oct. 25, 1957; children: Scott, Nancy B., Mark S. BA, Amherst Coll., 1954; MBA, U. Pa., 1959. Sales and mktg. positions Riegel Paper, 1959-66, sales mgr. folding carton dept. southeastern div., 1966-67, gen. sales mgr., 1967-69, v.p. folding carton dept., 1969-71; v.p. bd. conversion div. Rexham Corp., Charlotte, N.C., 1971-73; v.p. packaging group Rexham Corp., 1973-74, pres., 1974-90; chmn. bd. Rexham Industries, Inc., 1990-92; bd. dirs. Lance, Inc., Speizman Industries, Inc. Trustee Johnson C. Smith U., Charlotte, N.C. With U.S. Army, 1954-57. Mem. Charlotte C. of C. (bd. dirs. 1977-78), Carmel Country Club, Quail Hollow Country Club, Wild Dunes Club (Isle of Palms, S.C.). Home: 3704 Stone Ct Charlotte NC 28226-7343 Office: 5821 Fairview Rd Ste 200 Charlotte NC 28209-3649

LEA, STANLEY E., artist, educator; b. Joplin, Mo., Apr. 5, 1930; s. Everett G. and Edna F. L.; m. Ruth Lowe, Aug. 19, 1951; children: Kristy Ruth, Kraig, Kelly B. B.F.A., Pitts. State U., 1953; M.F.A., U. Ark., 1961. Prof. art Sam Houston State U., Huntsville, 1961—, Mexican Field Sch., Puebla, Mexico, 1963-65; vis. artist prof. Mus. Fine Arts, Houston, 1968, 69, 70; prof. art study abroad program London, 1977-78. Juror various art exhibits, 1970-81; workshop demonstrator, E. Tex. State U., Commerce, 1977, 10th ann. color print symposium, Tex. Tech. U., Lubbock, 1983; one-man shows paintings and/or prints, Valley House Gallery, Dallas, 1963, Moody Gallery, Houston, 1976, Sol Del Rio, San Antonio, 1978, 89, Adelle M. Fine Arts, Dallas, 1978, Dubose Gallery, Houston, 1980, Cultural Activities Ctr., Temple, Tex., 1982, Tex. A&M U., College Station, 1986, Mus. at E. Tex., Lufkin, 1989; numerous group shows, latest being Moody Gallery, Houston, 1975, 77, Pecan Square Gallery, Austin, Tex., 1977, Waco Art Center, Waco, Tex., 1977, East Tex. State U., Commerce, 1977, Galveston (Tex.) Art Center, 1978, Twenty Five Nat. Printmaker, Lubbock, Tex., 1978, Beaumont (Tex.) Art Mus., 1978, Art League of Houston, 1978, Gates Gallery, Port Arthur, Tex., 1979, Ars Longa, Houston, 1974, Laguna Gloria Mus., Austin, 1979; represented in permanent collections, Library of Congress, Washington, Brit. Mus., London, Mus. Fine Arts, Houston, USIA, N.Y.C., N.Y. Public Library, N.Y.C., Mpls. Inst. Art, Kalamazoo Inst. Art, Boise (Idaho) Gallery of Art, Madison (Wis.) Art Center, Spiva Art Center, Joplin, Mo., Ft. Worth Art Mus., Cleve. Mus., Inst. Mexicano Norteamericana de Relationes, Mexico City, Smithsonian Inst., Washington, also corp. and pvt. collections. (Recipient numerous awards, latest being, Southwest Graphics Invitational award 1971, Dimensions IX Exhbn. award 1974, 68th Nat. Tex. Fine Arts Exhbn. 1979). Sam Houston State U. grantee, 1970, 74. Mem. Coll. Art Assn., So. Graphics Council. Home: 3324 Winter Way Huntsville TX 77340-8919 Office: Sam Houston State Univ Art Dept Huntsville TX 77341

LEAB, DANIEL JOSEPH, history educator; b. Berlin, Aug. 29, 1936; s. Leo and Herta (Marcus) L.; BA, Columbia U., 1957, MA, 1961, PhD, 1969; m. Katharine Kyes, Aug. 16, 1964; children: Abigail Elizabeth, Constance

Martha, Marcus Rogers. With Columbia U., 1966-73, Seton Hall, 1974—; pub., co-editor Am. Book Prices Current; mng. editor Labor History; dir. Bancroft-Parkman. Fellow Met. Mus. Art.; mem. Historians of Am. Communism (gen. sec.). Clubs: Century, Grolier. Home: PO Box 1216 Washington Depot CT 06793

LEACH, CHRISTINE ELAINE, technical support executive; b. Riverside, Calif., Aug. 25, 1957; d. Kenneth Orvis and Gwendolyn Eloise (Belew) T.; m. Robert Gary Leach, June 11, 1983; children: Robert Arlan, Jonathan Abraham. Enlisted USAF, 1977, advanced through grades to tech. sgt., 1980, asst. mgr., 1983, adminstrv. supr. battle staff sect., 1984, mgr. force applications adminstrn., 1984-90, resigned, 1988; facility security officer Logicon, Inc., 1990—, assoc. program asst., 1990—; instr. for software Logicon, Inc., Bellevue, Nebr., 1988—. Mem. Air Force Assn. (life). Republican. Baptist. Avocations: needlecraft, reading, gardening, animals, archeology/paleontology. Office: 1408 Fort Crook Rd S Bellevue NE 68005-2969

LEACH, FRANKLIN ROLLIN, biochemistry educator; b. Gorman, Tex., Apr. 2, 1933; s. Frank Rollin and Jewel Laurie (Casey) L.; m. Mary Kathleen Kincaid, Jan. 26, 1956 (dec. Feb. 1969); children: Carolyn Ann, Janet Lynne, Barbara Naomi; m. Anna Belle Coke, Feb. 27, 1970; stepchildren: Alan Charles Coke, Barry Neil Coke, Carol Ann Coke. BA, Hardin-Simmons U., 1953; PhD, U. Tex., Austin, 1957. Rsch. asst. U. Tex., Austin, 1953-56, Hite rsch. fellow, 1956-57; Nat. Rsch. Coun. fellow med. sci. U. Calif., Berkeley, 1957-59; then asst. prof. to assoc. prof. Okla. State U., Stillwater, 1959-65, prof. biochemistry and molecular biology, 1966—, assoc. dept. head, 1990—; rsch. fellow Calif. Inst. Tech., Pasadena, 1965-66; cons. Kerr-McGee Co., Edmond, Okla., 1970-72, 3M Co., St. Paul, 1981-85, 95—, Idexx, 1994—, Teltech, 1994—; interim dept. head biochemistry Okla. State U., 1990. Author: Biochemical Indicators of Subsurface Pollution, 1980; editor Okla. Acad. Sci., 1990—; contbr. over 90 articles to sci. jours. Pres.'s fellow, Soc. Am. Bacteriologists, 1960; recipient rsch. career devel. award, Nat. Cancer Inst., 1962-72. Mem. AAAS, Am. Soc. Biochemistry and Molecular Biology, Am. Soc. Microbiology, Am. Soc. Photobiology, Am. Chem. Soc., Coun. Biology Editors, Protein Soc., Int. Soc. Bioluminescence Chemilumin., Stillwater Flying Club (pres. 1968-86). Avocations: hunting, reading, photography. Home: 1101 N Lincoln St Stillwater OK 74075-4033 Office: Okla State U Dept Biochem/Molecular Biol 246 NRC Stillwater OK 74078-3035

LEACH, JAMES ALBERT SMITH, congressman; b. Davenport, Iowa, Oct. 15, 1942; s. James Albert and Lois (Hill) L.; m. Elisabeth Foxley, Dec. 6, 1975; 1 child, Gallagher. BA, Princeton U., 1964; MA, Johns Hopkins U., 1966; postgrad., London Sch. Econs., 1966-68. Mem. staff Congressman Donald Rumsfeld, 1965-66; U.S. Fgn. Service officer, 1968-69, 70-73; spl. asst. to dir. OEO, 1969-70; mem. U.S. del. Geneva Disarmament Conf., 1971-72, UN Gen. Assembly, 1972, UN Natural Resources Conf., 1975; pres. Flamegas Companies Inc., Bettendorf, Iowa, 1973-76; chmn. bd. Adel Wholesalers, Inc., Bettendorf, 1973-76; mem. 95th-104th Congresses from 1st Iowa dist., 1977—; chmn. banking and fin. svcs. com., mem. internat. rels. com.; mem. U.S. Adv. Commn. Internat. Ednl. and Cultural Affairs, 1975-76. Chmn. Iowa Rep. Directions '76 Com. Episcopalian. Office: 2186 Rayburn Bldg Washington DC 20515-0005*

LEACH, JAMES GLOVER, lawyer; b. Panama City, Fla., Jan. 26, 1948; s. Milledge Glover and Thelma Louise (Hamilton) L.; m. Judith A. Leach, Feb. 26, 1972 (div. 1987); children: Allison, Arica. AS, Gulf Coast Coll., 1968; BA, Duke U., 1970; MBA, Ga. State U., 1974, MI, 1976; JD, Drake U., 1989. Bar: Iowa 1990; CPCU 1977, CLU 1978. Bank officer Bank South, Atlanta, 1972-75; asst. v.p. Johnson & Higgins, Atlanta, 1975-78; pres. Nat. Gen. Ins. Co., St. Louis, 1978-85, AOPA Svc. Corp., St. Louis, 1985-87, Kirke-Van Orsdel Specialty, Des Moines, 1987-89, Gallagher Specialty, St. Louis, 1990-92; prin., dir., counsel Pauli & Co. Inc., St. Louis, 1992-93; gen. counsel Am. Safety Ins., Atlanta, 1993—; cons. McDonnell Douglas, St. Louis, 1987; dir. Gateway Ins. Co., St. Louis, 1992; corp. assembly Blue Cross/Blue Shield, St. Louis, 1991-92. Contbr. articles to profl. jours. 1st lt. USAF, 1970-72, Korea. Avocations: pilot, golf. Home: 2931 Torreya Way Marietta GA 30067 Office: Am Safety Ins Group Ste 200 1845 The Exchange NW Atlanta GA 30339-2022

LEACH, JOHN F., newspaper editor, journalism educator; b. Montrose, Colo., Aug. 6, 1952; s. Darrell Willis and Marian Ruth (Hester) L.; m. Deborah C. Ross, Jan. 2, 1982; children: Allison, Jason. BS in Journalism, U. Colo., 1974, MA in Journalism, 1979; MA in Am. Studies, U. Sussex, Falmer, Brighton, Eng., 1983. News reporter Boulder (Colo.) Daily Camera, 1974-79; news reporter Ariz. Republic, Phoenix, 1979-85, asst. city editor, 1985-93; news editor The Phoenix Gazette, 1993-94; asst. mng. editor Phoenix Gazette, 1994-95; asst. mng. editor, news ops. The Ariz. Republic and The Phoenix Gazette, 1995—; faculty assoc. Ariz. State U., Tempe, 1990—; pres., dir. First Amendment Funding Inc., Phoenix. Bd. Regents scholar U. Colo., 1970, Rotary Found. scholar, 1982. Mem. Ariz. Press Club (treas. 1984-86, pres. 1986-87), Soc. Profl. Journalists, Reporter's Com. for Freedom of Press. Home: 4313 E Calle Redonda Phoenix AZ 85018-3733 Office: Ariz Republic/Phoenix Gazette 200 E Van Buren St Phoenix AZ 85004-2227

LEACH, JOHN FRANK, transportation executive; b. New Ross, Ireland, Mar. 11, 1921; came to U.S., 1921; s. John Reginald and Evelyn Muriel (Ard) L.; m. Lee Marie Serre, Dec. 1, 1945; children: John Michael, Suzanne Lee Leach, Earnest. B.A. in Indsl. Mgmt., Wayne State U. Tool and diemaker apprentice Ford Motor Co., Dearborn, Mich., 1934-38; various mfg. positions to mgr. Ford Engine Plant, Cleve., 1938-54; dir. mfg. Studebaker-Packard Corp., Detroit, 1954-56; various positions from v.p. mfg. and pres. Amphenol Electronics Corp.; exec. v.p., chief oper. officer Bunker Ramo Corp., Chgo., 1956-72; pres., chief exec. officer Arcata Corp., Menlo Park, Calif., 1972-82, chmn. bd., 1982-85; pres., chief oper. officer Consol. Freightways Inc., Menlo Park, 1990-91; ptnr. Sequoia Assocs., Menlo Park, 1982—; chmn. bd. Acme Fixture Co., Oakland, Calif.; bd. dirs. Material Sci. Corp., Chgo., Basic Am. Foods Ind., San Francisco, Newell Industries, Lowell, Mich., Champion Rd. Machinery Co., Ltd., Goderich, Ont., Can., Snow Mountain Pine Lumber Co., Hines, Oreg. Chmn. steering com. Friends of Radiology, Stanford U. Med. Ctr.; pres. gov. bd. Filoli (Nat. Hist. Trust Property). 2d lt. USAAF. Recipient Medal of Honor Electronic Industries Assn., 1972. Mem. Elec. Industries Assn. (chmn., chief exec. officer Washington chpt. 1971-72, EIA medal of honor 1973), Desert Horizons Country Club, Menlo Country Club, Palo Alto Club, Lincoln Club of No. Calif. (past chmn.). Office: Sequoia Assocs Bldg 2 Ste 140 3000 Sand Hill Rd Menlo Park CA 94025-7116

LEACH, JUDITH I., nursing educator; b. Meadville, Pa., June 15, 1941; d. James Huth and Lois Hope (Martin) Lynn; m. Burr Lewis Leach, Aug. 27, 1965; children: Tanya, Todd, Tiffany, Troy. Diploma, Orange Meml. Sch. Nursing, Orlando, Fla., 1962; BS in Nursing, Marion (Ind.) Coll., 1980; MSN, Ind. U., 1988. Cert. nursing adminstr. Sch. nurse Marion (Ind.) Coll., 1967-70, 78-79; staff nurse Kamakwie Wesleyan Hosp. Sierra Leone, West Africa, 1970-73, 75-78; instr. traditional program Ind. Wesleyan U., Marion, Ind., 1989-90; staff nurse Veterans Affairs, Marion, Ind., 1980-81, head nurse, 1981-85, clin. coord., 1985-87, nursing QA coord., 1987-91, assoc. chief nursing svc. edn., 1991—; instr. IWU RNBS program Ind. Wesleyan U., Marion, Ind., 1993—. Mem. Ind. State Nurses Assn., Sigma Theta Tau. Republican. Home: 1707 W Lakeview Dr Marion IN 46953-5769

LEACH, MAURICE DERBY, JR., librarian; b. Lexington, Ky., June 23, 1923; s. Maurice Derby and Sallie Eleanor (Woods) L.; m. Virginia Stuart Baskett, Mar. 16, 1953; 1 dau., Sarah Stuart. A.B., U. Ky., 1945; B.L.S., U. Chgo., 1946. Bibliographer Dept. State, 1947-50; fgn. service officer Dept. State (USIS); vice consul, attache Dept. State (USIS), Cairo and Alexandria, U.A.R., Beirut, 1950-59; chmn. dept. library sci. U. Ky., 1959-66; regional program officer Ford Found., Beirut, 1967-68; univ. librarian, prof. Washington and Lee U., Lexington, Va., 1968-85, prof., asst. to pres., 1985-88; library adviser Nat. Library, Egypt, Lebanon and acad. libraries in Middle East. Contbr. articles to profl. jours. Served with AUS, 1948-49. Mem. English Speaking Union (pres. Lexington br. 1970-75), Va. Libr. Assn. (pres. 1976), Assn. Preservation of Va. Activities (dir. Lexington br. 1989-91), Rockbridge Hist. Soc., SAR (v.p. 1990-93). Episcopalian. Home: 1 Courtland Ctr Lexington VA 24450-1813

LEACH, MICHAEL GLEN, publisher; b. Chgo., Aug. 19, 1940; s. Glen E. and Sara Faith (Giarrizzo) L.; M.A., St. Mary of the Lake Coll., 1966; m. Vickie Louise Jacobi, Oct. 3, 1969; children—Christopher, Jeffrey. Adminstr., Cath. Charities of Chgo., Maryville Acad., 1966-68; v.p., sr. editor Seabury Press, N.Y.C., 1969-80; sr. v.p., asso. pub. The Crossroad Pub. Co., N.Y.C., 1981-83; pres. The Continuum Pub. Corp., N.Y.C., 1980-83; exec. v.p., assoc. pub. The Crossroad/Continuum Pub. Cos., N.Y.C., 1983-90; pres., pub. The Crossroad/Continuum Pub. Group, 1990-92; COO and pub. The Crossroad Pub. Co., N.Y.C., 1993—. Mem. Assn. Am. Pubs., Protestant Ch.-Owned Pubs. Assn., Religious Pubs. Group (pres. 1991-92), Nat. Book Critics Circle, Cath. Book Pubs. Assn. (pres. 1989-90), Riverside Acres Community Assn. (pres. 1988). Roman Catholic. Author: I Know It When I See It: Pornography, Violence and Public Sensitivity, 1975; The Boy Who Had Everything, 1977; Don't Call Me Orphan, 1979; contbr. articles to profl. jours. Home: 49 Long Meadow Rd Riverside CT 06878-1125 Office: 370 Lexington Ave New York NY 10017-6503

LEACH, NORMAN STEWART, chamber of commerce executive, management and marketing consultant; b. Canora, Sask., Can., Feb. 21, 1963; s. Clarence Milburn Leach and Olga Prokopishin. BA with honours, U. Man., Winnipeg, Can., 1987. Exec. asst. to min. Ministry of Agr., Regina, Sask., 1984; translator Govt. of Can., Tsukuba, Japan, 1985; pres. Norman Leach & Assocs., Winnipeg, 1987—; exec. v.p. Man. C. of C., Winnipeg, 1991—; lectr. U. Man., 1990—; bd. dirs. Chamber Ins. Corp. Can., Winnipeg. Bd. dirs. Man. Opera Soc., Winnipeg, 1992—, Children's Hosp. Rsch. Found., Winnipeg, 1992—; advisor to bd. Red River C.C., Winnipeg, 1992; advisor Man. Human Rights Commn., Winnipeg, 1992—. Decorated Can. 125 medal. Mem. Can. Assn. Soc. Execs., Rotary. Home: Box 171 Sta L, Winnipeg, MB Canada R3H 0Z5 Office: Manitoba C of C, 167-167 Lombard Ave, Winnipeg, MB Canada R3H 0V6

LEACH, RALPH F., banker; b. Elgin, Ill., June 24, 1917; s. Harry A. and Edith (Sanders) L.; m. Harriet C. Scheuerman, Nov. 18, 1944; children: C. David, H. Randall, Barbara E. A.B., U. Chgo., 1938. Investment analyst Harris Trust & Savs. Bank, Chgo., 1940-48, Valley Nat. Bank, Phoenix, 1948-50; chief govt. finance sect. Fed. Res. Bd., Washington, 1950-53; treas. Guaranty Trust Co., N.Y.C., 1953-59; v.p. Guaranty Trust Co., 1958-59; v.p., treas. Morgan Guaranty Trust Co., N.Y.C., 1959-62; sr. v.p., treas. Morgan Guaranty Trust Co., 1962-64, exec. v.p., treas., 1964-68, vice chmn. bd. dirs., 1968-71, chmn. exec. com., 1971-77; chmn. emeritus Energy Conversion Devices Inc. Served to capt. USMCR, 1940-45. Mem. Coral Ridge Country Club, Phi Kappa Psi. Home: 4211 NE 25th Ave Fort Lauderdale FL 33308-5706 Office: Energy Conversion Devices Inc 1675 W Maple Rd Troy MI 48084-7118

LEACH, RICHARD HEALD, political scientist, educator; b. Denver, May 30, 1922; s. Richard Edwards and Helen Caroline (Heald) L.; m. Betty Carroll, Sept. 5, 1947; 1 son, Christopher Alan. A.B., Colo. Coll., 1944; M.A., Princeton U., 1949, Ph.D, 1951. Asst. prof. Ga. Inst. Tech., Atlanta, 1949-53; staff assoc. So. Regional Edn. Bd., Atlanta, 1953-55; asst. prof to prof. emeritus Duke U., Durham, N.C., 1955—; vis. disting. prof. Citadel, Charleston, S.C., 1976; vis. scholar Australian Nat. U., 1975,83; cons. U.S. Adv. Commn. on Intergovtl. Relations, Am. Coll. Testing Program. Coauthor: In Quest of Freedom, 1959, reissued, 1981, State and Local Government: The Third Century of Federalism, 1988; author: Governing the American Nation, 1967, American Federalism, 1970, Intergovernmental Relations in the 1980's, 1983. Mem. Durham City County Merger Study Commn., 1971-73; mem. Ill. Commn. of Scholars, 1973-77. Fulbright scholar U. Amsterdam, 1967-68. Mem. Am. Soc. Pub. Adminstrn. Clubs: Cosmos (Washington); Princeton (N.Y.C.). Lodge: Rotary. Home: 1313 Woodburn Rd Durham NC 27705-5740

LEACH, ROBERT ELLIS, physician, educator; b. Sanford, Maine, Nov. 25, 1931; s. Ellis and Estella (Tucker) L.; m. Laurine Seber, Aug. 20, 1955; children: Cathy, Brian, Michael, Craig, Karen, Diane. AB, Princeton U., 1953; MD, Columbia U., 1957. Diplomate Am. Bd. Orthopedic Surgery (treas. 1986-93). Resident orthopedic surgery U. Minn., 1957-62; orthopedic surgeon Lahey Clinic, Boston, 1964-68; chmn. dept. Lahey Clinic, 1968-70; prof., chmn. dept. Boston U. Med. Sch., 1970—; head physician U.S. Olympic Team, 1984; chmn. sports medicine coun. U.S. Olympic Com., 1984-93; vice chmn. sports medicine coun. U.S. Tennis Assn., 1988—. Editor-in-chief Am. J. Sports Med.; contbr. articles to profl. jours. Served to lt. comdr. USNR, 1962-64. Am., Brit., Canadian Orthopedic Travelling fellow, 1971; Sports Medicine Man of the Yr., 1988. Mem. Am. Acad. Orthopedic Surgeons, Continental Orthopedic Soc. (sec. 1966), Am. Orthopedic Assn. (pres. 1994), Am. Orthopedic Soc. Sports Medicine (pres. 1983), Longwood Cricket Club. Home: 40 Rockport Rd Weston MA 02193-1428 Office: 230 Calvary St Waltham MA 02154-8366

LEACH, ROBIN, producer, writer, television host; b. London, Aug. 29, 1941; came to U.S., 1963; s. Douglas Thomas and Violet (Phillips) L. Diploma, Nat. Union Journalists, 1961. Reporter Harrow (Eng.) Observer, 1958-61, Daily Mail, London, 1961-63; mag. pub. GO mag., N.Y.C., 1964-67; show bus. editor The Star, N.Y.C., 1964-79; reporter Cable News Network, N.Y.C., 1979-80; entertainment reporter Entertainment Tonight, N.Y.C., 1980-83; exec. producer Leach Entertainment Enterprises, N.Y.C., 1983—. Author: The Go Rock & Roll Manual, 1966, 2d rev. edit., 1967, Lifestyles of the Rich and Famous, 1986; producer: (TV shows) Lifestyles of the Rich and Famous, 1984 (Emmy nomination), Runaway with the Rich and Famous, The Rich and Famous Worlds Best, 1985, 86, 87, 88, 89, 90, 91, Fame, Fortune & Romance; host: KNBC-TV Year in Review, 1986, (Emmy award), Supermodel of the World, 1986, Home Videos of the Stars, 1991. Mem. AFTRA, Screen Actors Guild. Avocations: tennis, gourmet cooking. Office: Leach Entertainment Features 885 2nd Ave New York NY 10017-2201

LEACH, RONALD GEORGE, university dean, librarian; b. Monroe, Mich., Feb. 22, 1938; s. Garnet William and Erma (Erbadine) L.; m. Joy Adeline Moore, Dec. 21, 1956; children—Ronald George, Debra Mabel, Catherine Louise, Shane John. B.S. in Secondary Edn, Central Mich. U., 1966; M.A. in L.S. (U.S. Office Edn. fellow 1968-69), U. Mich., 1969; Ph.D. in Higher Edn. Adminstrn, Mich. State U., 1980. Head libr. Ohio State U., Mansfield, 1969-70; asst. dir., then acting dir. libr. Lake Superior State Coll., Sault Ste. Marie, Mich., 1970-76; assoc. dir. librs. Central Mich. U., 1976-80; dean libr. svcs. Ind. State U., Terre Haute, 1980-93, assoc. v.p. info. svcs., dean of librs., 1994—; tchr. libr. sci. and edn., mem. accreditation teams N. Central Assn. Author articles in field. Served with N.G., 1955-61. Mem. ALA, INFORMA (steering com. 1990—), Assn. Coll. and Rsch. Librs., Libr. Info. and Tech. Assn., Ind. Libr. Assn., Am. Soc. Info. Sci., Libr. Adminstrn. and Mgmt. Assn. (pres. 1985-86), Online Computer Libr. Ctr. User Council (exec. com. 1986, 88). Home: 4815 E Wolf Tree Ave Terre Haute IN 47805-9414 Office: Ind State U Office Dean of Library Terre Haute IN 47809

LEACH, RUSSELL, judge; b. Columbus, Ohio, Aug. 1, 1922; s. Charles Albert and Hazel Kirk (Thatcher) L.; m. Helen M. Sharpe, Feb. 17, 1945; children: Susan Sharpe Snyder, Terry Donnell, Ann Dunham Samuelson. B.A., Ohio State U., 1946, J.D., 1949. Bar: Ohio 1949. Clk. U.S. Geol. Survey, Columbus, 1948-49; reference and teaching asst. Coll. Law, Ohio State U., 1949-51; asst. city atty. City of Columbus, 1951, 53-57, city atty., 1957-63, presiding judge mcpl. ct., 1964-66; ptnr. Bricker & Eckler, 1966-88, chmn. exec. com., 1982-87; judge Ohio Ct. Claims, 1988—. Commr., Columbus Met. Housing Authority, 1968-74; chmn. Franklin County Republican Com., 1974-78. Served with AUS, 1942-46, 51-53. Named One of 10 Outstanding Young Men of Columbus, Columbus Jaycees, 1956, 57. Mem. ABA, FBA, Ohio Bar Assn. (coun. of dels. 1970-75), Columbus Bar Assn. (pres. 1973-74, Svc. medal 1993), Am. Judicature Soc., Pres.' Club Ohio State U., Am. Legion, Delta Theta Phi, Chi Phi. Presbyterian. Home: 1232 Kenbrook Hills Dr Columbus OH 43220-4968 Office: Ohio Ct Claims 65 E State St Ste 1100 Columbus OH 43215

LEACH, SHAWNA, food service director; b. Lehi, Utah, July 9, 1949; d. Lloyd D. and Dawna Mae (Marrott) Boren; m. Micheal Merrell Wiley, Feb. 11, 1967 (div.); children: Shannon Wiley Espinoza, Cyndie Wiley Anderson, Michael Shane, Stacie Lee; m. Calvin Donald Leach, Feb. 18, 1983. Cert. in dietary managing, Ctrl. Ariz. Coll., 1993. Mgr. cafeteria Provo (Utah) Sch. Dist., 1976-86; supply clk. Bur. of Reclamation, Page, Ariz., 1987-88; dir. food svc. Page Unified Sch. Dist., 1988—. Mem. Am. Sch. Food Svc. Assn. (dir., adminstr. I 1992—, instr. 1993—), Am. Sch. Bus. Officials, Ariz. Sch. Bus. Officials, Ariz. Sch. Food Svc. Assn. (chair certification 1992, state v.p. 1995-96, state pres. elect 1996-97, state officer), Dietary Mgrs. Assn., Page Recycles. Democrat. LDS. Avocations: gardening, crocheting, pottery making, crewel embroidering. Home: PO Box 3618 Page AZ 86040-3618 Office: Page Unified Sch Dist PO Box 1927 Page AZ 86040-1927

LEACH, SHERYL, television show character creator; b. Athens, Tex.; d. B.J. Stamps; m. Jim Leach; 1 child. Sch. tchr. Tex.; writer DLM Inc., Allen, Tex.; devel. Barney & the Backyard Gang video series (now Barney & Friends) PBS-TV, 1987. Creator of Barney the Dinosaur TM, 1987; devel. Barney and the Backyard Gang video series and numerous others. Office: Lyons Group 2435 N Central Expy Ste 1600 Richardson TX 75080-2753

LEACHMAN, CLORIS, actress; b. Des Moines, June 30, 1930; m. George England, 1953 (div. 1979); 5 children. Ed., Northwestern U. Actress: (films) including Kiss Me Deadly, 1955, Butch Cassidy and the Sundance Kid, 1969, W.U.S.A., 1970, The People Next Door, 1970, Lovers and Other Strangers, 1970, The Steagle, 1971, The Last Picture Show, 1971 (Acad. award for best supporting actress 1971), Charles and the Angel, 1972, Happy Mother's Day...Love, George, 1973, Dillinger, 1973, Daisy Miller, 1974, Young Frankenstein, 1974, Crazy Mama, 1975, High Anxiety, 1977, The Mouse and His Child, 1977 (voice), Foolin' Around, 1979, The North Avenue Irregulars, 1979, The Muppet Movie, 1979, Scavenger Hunt, 1979, Yesterday, 1979, Herbie Goes Bananas, 1980, History of the World, Part 1, 1982, Shadow Play, 1986, My Little Pony, 1986 (voice), Walk Like a Man, 1987, Hansel and Gretel, 1987, Prancer, 1989, Love Hurts, 1990, Texasville, 1990, Walter and Emily, 1991, My Boyfriend's Back, 1993, The Beverly Hillbillies, 1993, A Troll in Central Park, 1994 (voice), Storytime, 1994, Nobody's Girls, 1994; TV series including Lassie, 1957, Route 66, Laramie, Trials of O'Brien, Mary Tyler Moore Show, Phyllis, 1975-77, Facts of Life, The Nutt House, 1989; (TV movies) including Silent Night, Lonely Night, 1969, Suddenly Single, 1971, Haunts of the Very Rich, 1972, Brand New Life, 1973, Dying Room Only, 1973, Crime Club, 1973, Death Sentence, 1974, Thursday's Game, 1974, Hitchhike!, 1974, The Migrants, 1974, A Girl Named Sooner, 1975, Ladies of the Corridor, The New Original Wonder Woman, 1975, Death Scream, 1975, Someone I Touched, 1975, It Happened One Christmas, 1977, Long Journey Back, 1978, Mrs. R.'s Daughter, 1979, Willa, 1979, S.O.S. Titanic, 1979, The Acorn People, 1981, Advice to the Lovelorn, 1981, Miss All-American Beauty, 1982, Dixie: Changing Habits, 1983, The Demon Murder Case, 1983, Ernie Kovacs, Between the Laughter, 1984, Deadly Intentions, 1985, Love is Never Silent, Danielle Steele's Fine Things, 1990, In Broad Daylight, 1991, A Little Piece of Heaven, 1991, Fade to Black, 1993, Without a Kiss Goodbye, 1993, Spies, 1993, Miracle Child, 1993, Double, Double, Toil and Trouble, 1993, Between Love and Honor, 1995; (TV miniseries) Backstairs at the White House, 1979; theater appearance in Grandma Moses: An American Primitive, Washington, 1990; guest appearance: The Love Boat, 1976. Recipient 6 Emmy awards.

LEACHMAN, ROGER MACK, librarian; b. Stillwater, Okla., June 3, 1942; s. Oakley Thaddeus and Mildred Violet (McNeff) L.; m. Nancy Jo Lordeman, Aug. 25, 1973; children—Emily Anne, James Oakley. A.B., U. Pa., 1967; M.S., U. N.C., 1973. Planner Pa. State Planning Bd., Harrisburg, 1967-68; rsch. libr. U. Va., Charlottesville, 1973-74, info. svcs. libr., 1974-76, dir. reference svcs., 1976-84, rare book bibliographer, 1984-88; coord. Southeast Libr. System, Rochester, Minn., 1988—. Contbr. articles to profl. jours. Served with U.S. Army, 1965-67. Gov's. fellow U. Va., Charlottesville, 1968-69. Mem. ALA, MEMO, MLA. Episcopalian. Avocations: bibliography; backpacking. Home: 822 4th St SW Rochester MN 55902-2914 Office: Southeast Libr System 107 W Frontage Rd N # 52 Rochester MN 55901-0343

LEA-COX, JOHN DEREK, plant physiologist; b. Bulawayo, Zimbabwe, Aug. 31, 1960; came to U.S., 1989; s. Nigel and Joyce (Adnams) Lea-C. BSc, U. Natal, South Africa, 1984; MSc, U. Natal, 1989; PhD, U. Fla., 1993. Mgr. nursery Amanzi Citrus Estate, Uitenhage, South Africa, 1984-86; rsch. assoc., lectr. U. Natal, 1987-89; grad. rsch. asst. U. Fla., Lake Alfred, 1989-93; assoc. nat. rsch. coun. NASA-Life Scis., Kennedy Space Center, Fla., 1993-95; rsch. scientist Dynamac Corp., Kennedy Space Center, 1996—. Contbr. articles to Jour. Am. Soc. Horticulture Sci., Fla. Horticulture Soc., Annals of Botany. With Rhodesian African Rifles, 1979. A.S. Herlong scholar, 1989-93; Nat. Rsch. Coun. fellow, 1993-95; South Africa Citrus Nursery Men's Assn. grantee, 1987. Mem. Am. Soc. Plant Physiology, Am. Soc. Hort. Sci., Fla. Hort. Soc., Crop Sci. Soc. Am. Achievements include research in nutrient movement to groundwater, nutrient uptake by plants, adaptive control systems for nutrient delivery and pH control in plant growth modules for space research, advanced life support and controlled environment agriculture. Office: NASA-Life Scis Mail Code MD-RES Kennedy Space Center FL 32899

LEADBETTER, MARK RENTON, JR., orthopedic surgeon; b. Phila., Nov. 7, 1944; s. Mark Renton and Ruth (Protzeller) L.; m. Letitia Ashby, July 28, 1973 (div. June 1990); m. Jan Saker, 1991. BA, Gettysburg Coll., 1967; MSc in Hygiene, U. Pitts., 1970; MD, Temple U., 1974. Surg. intern Univ. Hosps., Boston, 1974-75, resident in surgery, 1975-76; emergency room physician Sturdy Meml. Hosp., Attleboro, Mass., 1976-78; resident in orthopaedics U. Pitts., 1978-81; orthopaedic physician Rockingham Meml. Hosp., Harrisonburg, Va., 1981-82, courtesy staff, 1982—; pvt. practice, Staunton, Va., 1982—; mem. active staff King's Daus. Hosp., Staunton, 1982—; active staff Samaritan Hosp., Moses Lake, Wash.; courtesy staff Columbia Basin Hosp., Ephrata, Wash. Contbr. articles to med. jours.; patentee safety syringes, safety cannulas, designer of medecal equipment. Mem. Am. Coll. Sports Medicine, So. Med. Assn., So. Orthopaedic Assn., County Med. Soc., Nat. Futures Assn. (assoc.). Republican. Avocations: flying, skiing, raising bird dogs. Home: 660 Coolidge St Moses Lake WA 98837-1877

LEAF, ALEXANDER, physician, educator; b. Yokohama, Japan, Apr. 10, 1920; came to U.S., 1922, naturalized, 1936; s. Aaron L. and Dora (Hural) L.; m. Barbara Louise Kincaid, Oct. 1943; children—Caroline Joan, Rebecca Louise, Tamara Jean. B.S., U. Wash., 1940; M.D., U. Mich., 1943; M.A., Harvard, 1961. Intern Mass. Gen. Hosp., Boston, 1943-44; mem. staff Mass. Gen. Hosp., 1949—, physician-in-chief, 1966-81; resident Mayo Found., Rochester, Minn., 1944-45; research fellow U. Mich., 1947-49; practice internal medicine Boston, 1949-90; faculty Med. Sch., Harvard, 1949—, Jackson prof. clin. medicine, 1966-81, Ridley Watts prof. preventive medicine, 1980-90, chmn. dept. preventive medicine and clin. epidemiology, 1980-90, Jackson prof. clin. medicine emeritus, 1990—; Disting. physician VA Medical Ctr. Brockton/W. Roxbury Hosps., Boston, 1992—. Served to capt. M.C. AUS, 1945-46. Recipient Outstanding Achievement award U. Minn., 1964; vis. fellow Balliol Coll., Oxford, 1971-72; Guggenheim fellow, 1971-72; named Disting. Physician, VA, 1991—. Fellow Am. Acad. Arts and Scis.; mem. NAS, ACP (master), Inst. Medicine, Am. Soc. Clin. Investigation (past pres.), Am. Physiol. Soc., Biophys. Soc., Assn. Am. Physicians (Kober medal 1995). Home: 1 Curtis Cir Winchester MA 01890-1703 Office: Mass Gen Hosp Boston MA 02114

LEAF, HOWARD WESTLEY, retired air force officer, military official; b. Menominee, Mich., Sept. 22, 1923; s. Joseph Conrad and Hilda Eugene (Lavoy) L.; m. Madonna Anne Ronan, May 21, 1955; children: Mary Beth, Barbara Anne, Timothy, Anne Marie, Thomas, James. B.S., Colo. Sch. Mines, 1950; M.S., St. Louis U., 1955; grad., Command and Staff Coll., 1961, Indsl. Coll. Armed Forces, 1969. Commd. 2d lt. U.S. Air Force, 1951, advanced through grades to lt. gen., 1980, ret., 1985; aviation cadet, 1950-51; jet pilot Korea, 1952-53; test pilot, 1955-60, geophysicist, 1961-64; ops. officer (49th Tactical Fighter Wing), Europe, 1965; squadron comdr. S.E. Asia, 1966; staff officer (Hdqrs. USAF), 1966-68, 69-71; wing comdr. 1st and 366th Tactical Fighter Wings, 1971-74; dep. chief staff for requirements Tactical Air Command, 1974-76; comdr. Air Force Test and Evaluation Ctr., Kirtland AFB, N.Mex., 1976-80; insp. gen. U.S. Air Force, Washington, 1980-83, asst. vice chief of staff, 1983-85; sr. v.p. BDM Internat. Corp., McLean, Va., 1984-91; dir. test and evaluation Hdqrs. USAF The Pentagon,

Washington, 1992—; mem. Air Force Sci. Adv. Bd. Decorated D.S.M., Silver Star, Legion of Merit, D.F.C.; recipient Eugene M. Zuckert Mgmt. Award, 1978, Disting. Achievement award Colo. Sch. Mines, 1982. Mem. Internat. Test and Evaluation Assn. (sr. adv. bd., Allen R. Mattews Award, 1994). Presbyterian. Home: 8504 Brook Rd Mc Lean VA 22102-1505 Office: Hdqs USAF TE 4E-995 The Pentagon Washington DC 20330

LEAF, PAUL, producer, director, writer; b. N.Y.C., May 2, 1929; s. Manuel and Anna (Dardick) L.; m. Nydia Ellis, Oct. 22, 1955 (div. 1990); children: Jonathan, Alexandra, Ellen. BA in Drama with honors, CCNY, 1952. pres. Sea Gate Co. Dir., prodr.: 17 Broadway prodns., including The Subject Was Roses, 1964, films include: Judge Horton and the Scottsboro Boys, 1976 (Peabody award), Desperate Characters, 1972, Hail to the Chief, 1973, Sister Aimee, 1977, Every Man a King, 1977, Top Secret, 1979, God, Sex and Apple Pie, 1995, TV prodns. include Sgt. Matlovich vs. the U.S. Air Force, 1978; author: Comrades, 1985, Red, Right, Returning, 1987. Founder, chmn. Santa Monica Arts Commn., Santa Monica Arts Found.; founder, cons., bd. dirs. Santa Monica Coll. Art, Design and Architecture, 1990—; mem. grants panel Nat. Endowment for the Arts, 1993, Nat. Endowment for the Humanities, 1994. With U.S. Army, 1952-54. Decorated Meritorious Service medal; recipient 20 internat. festival and profl. awards, including Venice, 1967, London, 1967, 68, 69, N.Y., 1967, 68, 69, Berlin, 1972. Mem. Dirs. Guild Am., Writers Guild Am. Home: 2800 Neilson Way Santa Monica CA 90405-4025

LEAF, ROBERT STEPHEN, public relations executive; b. N.Y.C., Aug. 9, 1931; s. Nathan and Anne (Feinman) L.; m. Adele Ornstein, June 8, 1958; 1 child, Stuart Nathan. B.J., U. Mo-Columbia, 1952, M.A., 1954. Account exec. Herbert Kaufman, N.Y.C., 1956-57; various positions Marsteller Orgn., N.Y.C., 1957-65; v.p., gen. mgr. Marsteller Internat., Brussels, 1965-68; v.p. Marsteller Internat., Europe, 1968-70; pres. Burson-Marsteller Internat. and Marsteller Internat., London, 1970-81; chmn. Burson-Marsteller Internat., London, 1985—; dir. Burson-Marsteller Ltd., (Eng.), Burson-Marsteller Inc. (U.S.), Burson-Marsteller, (Japan), Burson-Marsteller Intermarkets, Bahrain, Burson-Marsteller S.E.A., (Singapore), Burson-Marsteller Ltd., (Hong Kong), Burson-Marsteller Gmbh, Germany; dir. Burson-Marsteller S.A., (Belgium), (France); dir. Burson-Marsteller S.P.A., (Italy), Burson-Marsteller S.A., (Switzerland), Burson-Marsteller Pty., (Australia), Burson-Marsteller, China. Contbr. articles to profl. pubs. Mem. Public Relations Soc. Am., Inst. Pub. Relations Eng., Pub. Relations Consultancy Assn. (London), Fgn. Press Assn., Pub. Relations Soc. Am., Alpha Pi Zeta, Kappa Tau Alpha. Club: Hurlingham (London). Home: 3 Fursecroft George St, London W1, England Office: Burson Marsteller Internat, 24-28 Bloomsbury Way, London WC1A 2PX, England

LEAF, ROGER WARREN, business consultant; b. New Rochelle, N.Y., Aug. 3, 1946; s. Harold Edwin and Mabel (Erickson) L.; m. Judith Blaine Edds, Sept. 23, 1978; children: Spencer W., Andrew B. BA in Econs., Heidelberg Coll., 1968; MBA, NYU, 1978. V.p. pub. fin. Dean Witter Reynolds Inc., N.Y.C., 1974-81; prin. corp. fin. Morgan Stanley & Co., Inc., N.Y.C., 1981-84; v.p. pub. fin., The First Boston Corp, N.Y.C., 1984-87, dir. mcpl. securities, 1988-91, chief oper. officer fixed income divsn., 1991-93; pres. R.W. Leaf & Co., 1993—, CFO Beverage Mktg. Techs., Inc., 1995—. Trustee All Souls Sch., N.Y.C., 1984-90, treas. 1984-88. 1st lt. USAR, 1969-72. Mem. Waccabuc Country Club (N.Y.). Office: RW Leaf & Co 100 Park Ave New York NY 10017

LEAHEY, LYNN, editor-in-chief. Editor-in-chief Soap Opera Digest, N.Y.C. Office: Soap Opera Digest 45 West 25th St 8th Fl New York NY 10010*

LEAHIGH, ALAN KENT, association executive; b. Chgo., Dec. 25, 1944; s. Leland Jean and Rena Matilda (Rodda) L.; m. Lorrie Lynn Johnson, Aug. 19, 1967; children: Matthew Alan, Nathan Andrew. BA, Ill. Wesleyan U., 1967; MA, U. Mo., 1971. Reporter, editor Daily Pantagraph, Bloomington, Ill., 1965-71; tchr. Joliet (Ill.) Pub. Sch. Dist., 1969-71; assoc. dir. pub. info. Am. Dental Assn., Chgo., 1971-75, dir. pub. edn., 1976-77, editor ADA News, 1978-80; v.p. Pub. Communications Inc., Chgo., 1981-83, sr. v.p., ptnr., 1983-90, exec. v.p., 1990-95; exec. v.p. Exec. Adminstrn., Inc., Arlington Heights, Ill., 1995—; v.p. Living Learning Devel. Corp., Wheaton, Ill., 1980-89, Marian Park Inc., Wheaton, 1980-89; lectr. workshops in field. Contbr. articles to profl. jours. Mem. Wheaton Hist. Preservation Soc., 1978—; chmn. Wheaton Community TV Cmmn., 1986—. Mem. Pub. Rels. Soc. Am. (Silver anvil award 1982, 85, 86, 93), Soc. Profl. Journalists, Am. Hosp. Assn., Am. Soc. Assn. Execs., Chgo. Publicity Club, Chgo. Headline Club, Masons. Presbyterian. Office: Exec Adminstrn Inc 85 W Algonquin Rd Arlington Heights IL 60005

LEAHY, GERALD PHILIP, hospital administrator; b. Vancouver, B.C., Canada, Feb. 16, 1936; married. B, U. Portland, 1959; MHA, St. Louis U., 1961. Adminstrv. asst. Sacred Heart Med. Ctr., Spokane, Wash., 1961-63, asst. adminstr., 1963-68, assoc. adminstr., 1968-81, exec. v.p., 1981-88, pres., chief exec. officer, 1988—. Mem. Am. Coll. Healthcare Execs., Am. Hosp. Assn. (del. 1979-81, reg. adv. bd. 1977-83) Wash. Hosp. Assn. (chmn. 1977-78, bd. dirs. 1970-82). Home: 4925 S Perry St Spokane WA 99223-6337 Office: Sacred Heart Med Ctr PO Box 2555 Spokane WA 99220-2555*

LEAHY, MICHAEL JOSEPH, newspaper editor; b. Chgo., Feb. 24, 1939; s. Joseph Michael and Elizabeth Catherine (Keefe) L.; m. Harriet Smith Friday, Sept. 18, 1971; children—Christine Elizabeth, Thomas Joseph, Christopher Michael. A.B., Georgetown U., 1961; M.S. in Journalism, Columbia U., 1966. Copy boy, news clk., copy editor N.Y. Times, N.Y.C., 1961-71, asst. to mt. editor, 1971-73, editor L.I. Weekly, 1973-77, editor Conn. Weekly, 1977-81, travel editor, 1982-86, editor arts & leisure sect., 1986-90, dep. editor The Week in Review, 1990-92, real estate editor, 1992—. Editor: (with A.M. Rosenthal, A. Gelb and N. Kerr) The Sophisticated Traveler series. Bd. advisors Georgetown Coll., 1990-96; mem. edn. com. St. David's Sch., 1991-93. 1st lt. U.S. Army, 1961-64. Pulitzer Traveling fellow Columbia U., 1967. Mem. Georgetown Libr. Assocs. (trustee 1981-94), Columbia Journalism Alumni (pres. 1981-83), Century Assn. Roman Catholic. Office: NY Times Co 229 W 43rd St New York NY 10036-3913

LEAHY, PATRICK JOSEPH, senator; b. Montpelier, Vt., Mar. 31, 1940; s. Howard and Alba (Zambon) L.; m. Marcelle Pomerleau, Aug. 25, 1962; children: Kevin, Alicia, Mark. B.A., St. Michael's Coll., Vt., 1961; J.D., Georgetown U., 1964. Bar: Vt. 1964, D.C. 1979, U.S. Ct. Appeals (2d cir.) 1966, Vt. Fed. Dist. Ct. 1965, U.S. Supreme Ct. 1968. State's atty. Chittenden County, Vt., 1966-75; U.S. senator from Vt., 1975—, ranking minority mem. com. on agrl., nutrition and forestry, subcom. on fgn. ops., jud. subcom. antitrust, bus. routes & competition, mem. judiciary com., mem. appropriations com., mem. appropriations com., vice chmn. senate intelligence com., 1985-86; mem. World Hunger bd.; bd. visitors U.S. Mil. Acad. West Point, Gallaudet Coll., Nat. Coll. Deaf, Washington; mem. Senate Dem. Steering & Coordination Com. Recipient 1st Amendment award Soc. Profl. Journalists. Mem. Nat. Dist. Attys. Assn. (v.p. 1971-74). Office: US Senate 433 Russell Senate Office Washington DC 20510*

LEAHY, T. LIAM, investments and management consultant; b. Camp Legeunne, N.C., Apr. 15, 1952; s. Thomas James and Margaret May (Munnelly) L.; m. Shannon Kelly Brooks, Apr. 21, 1990. BS, St. Louis U., 1974, MA, 1975; postgrad., Hubbard Coll. of Adminstrn., L.A., 1989. V.p. sales Cablecom Inc., Chgo., 1978-81, Kaye Advt., N.Y.C., 1981-83; group pubr. Jour. Graphics Pub., N.Y.C., 1983-85; gen. mgr. Generation Dynamics, N.Y.C., 1985-86; pres. Leahy & Assocs., N.Y.C., 1982-86, Tarzana, Calif., 1982—; assoc. Am Coun. of Execs. Assoc., Glendale, 1991—; bd. dirs. Cons. Assn. Contbr. articles to profl. jours. Fellow Success Mgmt. Ctrs. (sr.); mem. Am. Coun. Execs. (bd. dirs. 1993-95), Turnaround Mgmt. Assn., L.A. C. of C. Avocations: music, computer systems design. Office: Leahy & Assocs 19131 Enadia Way Reseda CA 91335-3827

LEAHY, WILLIAM F., insurance company executive, lawyer; b. N.Y.C., July 28, 1913; s. William F. and Anna (Murphy) L.; m. Catherine Patricia Carlin, Oct. 19, 1940; children: William C., Michael J. Pre-law certificate, Coll. City N.Y., 1936; LL.B. cum laude, Bklyn. Law Sch., 1939, LL.M., 1940. Bar: N.Y. 1940. With Met. Life Ins. Co., N.Y.C., 1932-78; assoc. gen. counsel Met. Life Ins. Co., 1962-65, v.p. real estate financing, 1965 and after, sr. v.p., 1976-78; sr. real estate cons. Goldman Sachs Realty Co., 1979-85; adv. bd. N.Y. State Tchrs. Retirement Sys. Served to lt. col. USAAF, 1941-46. Mem. ABA. Home: 6152 N Verde Trl Apt D122 Boca Raton FL 33433-2419 also: 24 Cliff Dr Sag Harbor NY 11963-1805

LEAK, MARGARET ELIZABETH, insurance company executive; b. Atlanta, Sept. 9, 1946; d. William Whitehurst and Margaret Elizabeth (Whitsitt) L. BS in Psychology, Okla. State U., 1968; postgrad., U. Okla., 1968-69, Cornell U., 1976-78; grad. advanced mgmt. program, Harvard U., 1983-84. Editor communications Eastern State Bankcard Assn., N.Y.C., 1969-71; sr. edn. specialist Citibank, N.Y.C., 1971-73; adminstr. orgn. devel. NBC, N.Y.C., 1973-74; mgr. tng. and devel. Atlantic Mut. Cos., Property/Casualty Ins., N.Y.C., 1974-76, sec. human resources, 1976-78, v.p. human resources, 1978-84, v.p. human resources and corp. communications, 1984-86, sr. v.p. adminstrv. services, 1987—. Office: Atlantic Mut Cos 3 Giralda Farms Madison NJ 07940-1027

LEAK, ROBERT E., management consultant; b. Charlotte, N.C., Sept. 15, 1934; s. James Pickett and Cornelia (Edwards) L.; m. Martha Councill, Aug. 25, 1956; children: Robert E., James Councill. B.S., Duke U., 1956; M.S., U. Tenn., 1957. With Pan Am. Petroleum Co., Lafayette, La., 1957-59, Allied Securities Corp., Raleigh, N.C., 1961-62, Cameron Brown Mortgage Co., Raleigh and Charlotte, 1962-64; with N.C. Dept. Natural and Econ. Resources, Raleigh, 1959-61, 64-76; dir. div. econ. devel. N.C. Dept. Natural and Econ. Resources, until 1976; dir. S.C. State Devel. Bd., Columbia, 1976-84; pres. Research Triangle Park Found., N.C., 1984-88; prin. Leak-Goforth Co., LLC, Raleigh, N.C., 1988—; mem. U.S. Dept. Commerce Small Bus. Adv. Council; also vice-chmn. Dist. Export Council; leader industry organized govt. approved trade and indsl. devel. missions to, Can., Europe, S.Am., Australia, Far East. Bd. dirs. Raleigh YMCA, S.C. Tech. and Comprehensive Edn., N.C. Symphony Fedn.; bd. dirs., mem. adv. bd. Duke Hosp.; bd. Duke Alumni Assn. Mem. Am. Indsl. Devel. Council (past pres.), Nat. Assn. State Devel. Agys. (past pres.). Episcopalian. Home: 3301 Landor Rd Raleigh NC 27609-7012 Office: Ste 2700 150 Fayetteville Street Mall Raleigh NC 27601-2919

LEAKE, DONALD LEWIS, oral and maxillofacial surgeon, oboist; b. Cleveland, Okla., Nov. 6, 1931; s. Walter Wilson and Martha Lee (Crowe) L.; m. Rosemary Dobson, Aug. 20, 1964; children: John Andrew Dobson, Elizabeth, Catherine. AB, U. So. Calif., 1953, MA, 1957; DMD, Harvard U., 1962; MD, Stanford U., 1969. Diplomate Am. Bd. Oral and Maxillofacial Surgery. Intern Mass. Gen. Hosp., Boston, 1962-63; resident Mass. Gen. Hosp., 1963-64; postdoctoral fellow Harvard U., 1964-66; practice medicine specializing in oral and maxillofacial surgery; asso. prof. oral and maxillofacial surgery Harbor-UCLA Med. Ctr., Torrance, 1970-74, dental dir., chief oral and maxillofacial surgery, 1970—, prof., 1974—; assoc. dir. UCLA Dental Rsch. Inst., 1979-82, dir., 1982-86; prof. extranjero Escuela de Graduados, Asociacion Medica Argentina, 1990—; cons. to hosps.; dental dir. coastal health services region, Los Angeles County, 1974-81; oboist Robert Shaw Chorale, 1954-55; solo oboist San Diego Symphony, 1954-59. Contbr. articles to med. jours.; rec. artist: (albums on Columbia label) The Music of Heinrich Schütz, Stockhausen, Zeitmasse for 5 Winds, Schönberg, Orchestra Variations-Opus 31; freelance musician various film studio orchs., Carmel Bach Festival, 1949, 52-53, 67-81, numerous concerts with Coleman Chamber Music, The Cantata Singers, Boston, Garden St. Chamber Players, Cambridge, Baroque Consortium, L.A., Corona Del Mar Baroque Festival, others; world premieres (oboe works) by Darius Milhaud, William Kraft, Alice Parker, Mark Volkert, Eugene Zádor, Robert Linn. Mem. Commn. on the Future of Rose-Hulman Inst. Tech., Terre Haute, Ind., 1992-93. Recipient 1st prize with greatest distinction for oboe and chamber music Brussels Royal Conservatory Music Belgium, 1956. Fellow ACS; mem. AAAS, Internat. Assn. Dental Rsch., Internat. Assn. Oral Surgeons, Soc. Biomaterials, Biomed. Engring. Soc. (sr. mem.), L.A. County Med. Assn., European Assn. Maxillofacial Surgeons, Brit. Assn. Oral and Maxillofacial Surgeons, Internat. Gesellschaft fur Kiefer-Gesichts-Chirurgie, Internat. Soc. Plastic, Aesthetic and Reconstructive Surgery, Phi Beta Kappa, Phi Kappa Phi. Clubs: Harvard (Boston and N.Y.C.). Achievements include patents for work related to bone reconstruction, 1974, 82, 90. Home: 2 Crest Rd W Rolling Hills CA 90274-5003 Office: Harbor-UCLA Med Ctr 1000 W Carson St Torrance CA 90502-2004 also: Harbor UCLA Profl Bldg 21840 Normandie Ave Ste 700 Torrance CA 90502-2047

LEAKE, PRESTON HILDEBRAND, tobacco research executive; b. Proffit, Va., Aug. 8, 1929; s. Perry Hansford and Lydia Viola (Cox) L.; m. Elizabeth Ann Kelly, Dec. 5, 1954; children: Luther Hildebrand, Lawrence Albert. BS, U. Va., 1950; MA, Duke U., 1953, PhD, 1954. Rsch. supr. Allied Chem. Corp., Hopewell, Va., 1954-60; asst. rsch. dir. Albemarle Paper Mfg. Co., Richmond, Va., 1960-65; asst. to mng. dir. The Am. Tobacco Co., Hopewell, 1965-68, asst. mng. dir., 1968-70, asst. R & D dir., 1970-87, dir. R & D, 1987-88, v.p. rsch., 1988-91, ret., 1991; adj. prof. organic chemistry Va. Commonwealth U., 1963-64; tobacco industry rep. to Coun. for Tobacco Rsch., 1977-88; chmn. bd. dirs. Tobacco Inst. Testing Lab., 1977-88; adv. bd. chem. abstracts Va. Jr. Acad. Sci., 1986-88, mem. planning com., 1991-95; mem. Congl. Study Com., 1984-88; expert witness patent suit Toronto, 1993-95. Patentee amino acid synthesis and tobacco cigarette filter; contbr. articles to profl. jours. Chmn. Providence Jr. High Sch. PTA, Midlothian, Va., 1968-70, Clover Hill High Sch. PTA, 1971-72; chmn. bd. trustees Chesterfield County (Va.) Pub. Librs., 1974-77; mem. County Sch. Adv. Com., Chesterfield, 1969-70; judge chemistry sect. Jr. Acad. Sci., 1991-92; mem. Hopewell Community and Indsl. Panel for Environ. Improvement, 1992—. Recipient Army Chem. Corp fellowship, 1950-52, Allied Chem. fellowship, 1952-54. Mem. Am. Chem. Soc. (treas. 1966, sec. 1967, vice chmn. 1968, chmn. 1970, mem. People to People Goodwill Tour to England, Norway, USSR, Czechoslovakia, East and West Germany 1971, Disting. Svc. award 1976), Am. Inst. Chemists (chmn. 1962), Va. Acad. Sci., Computer Users Group (pres. Richmond chpt. 1984-86), James River Catfish Club (keeper of keys 1978-80), Rotary (sec. Hopewell 1992), Sigma Xi, Phi Lambda Upsilon. Home: 401 Delton Ave Hopewell VA 23860-1815

LEAKE, ROSEMARY DOBSON, physician; b. Columbus, Ohio, July 14, 1937; d. Joseph Lawrence and Rosemary Elizabeth (Brockmeyer) Dobson; m. Donald Leake, Aug. 20, 1964; children: John, Elizabeth, Catherine. BA, Ohio State U., 1959, MD, 1962. Diplomate Am. Bd. Neonatal-Perinatal Medicine. Intern, pediatrics Mass. Gen. Hosp., Boston, 1962-63, resident, pediatrics, 1963-64; rsch. fellow Maternal Infant Health Collaborative Study The Boston Lying-In Hosp., Boston, 1965-67; neonatal fellow Stanford U. Hosp., Palo Alto, Calif., 1968-69; co-dir. NIH sponsored perinatal tng. program Harbor-UCLA Med. Ctr., Torrance, 1979, program dir. NIH sponsored perinatal rsch. ctr., 1980—; prof. pediatrics UCLA Sch. of Medicine, L.A., 1982—; dir. regionalized fellowship Harbor-UCLA/King-Drew Med. Ctr., Torrance, 1986-92; chair pediatrics Harbor-UCLA Med. Ctr., Torrance, 1992—; dir. perinatal crisis care program Harbor-UCLA Med. Ctr., Torrance, 1972-76, dir. neonatal ICU, 1974-81, assoc. prof. pediatrics, 1976-82, assoc. chief div. neonatology, 1976-77. Named UCLA Woman of Sci., 1985, Outstanding Woman Acadmician of Yr. Nat. Bd. Award of the Med. Coll. of Pa., 1989; recipient Alumni Achievement award Ohio State U. Sch. Medicine, 1987. Mem. Am. Pediatric Soc., Soc. for Pediatric Rsch. Home: 2 Crest Rd W Rolling Hills CA 90274-5003 Office: Harbor-UCLA Med Ctr 1000 W Carson St Torrance CA 90502-2004

LEAL, BARBARA JEAN PETERS, fundraising executive; b. Hartford, Ala., Oct. 24, 1948; d. Clarence Lee and Syble (Simmons) Peters; m. Michael Wayne Foster, 1966 (div.); children: Michaelle, Jonathan; m. Ramon Leal, 1991. AA, Enterprise State Jr. Coll., 1970; BA, U. South Fla., 1974; MA, Trinity U., San Antonio, 1975; postgrad. Universidad Nacional Autonoma de Mexico, 1982. Cert. fund raising exec. Instr., San Antonio Coll., 1975; planner Econ. Opportunities Devel. Corp., San Antonio, 1976, Alamo Area Council Govts., San Antonio, 1977-82; dir. planned giving Oblate Missions, San Antonio, 1982—; spkr. in field. Author: Paratransit Provider Handbook, 1978; contbg. author: Human Responses to Aging, 1976; Transportation for Elderly Handicapped Programs and Problems, 1978; contbr. articles to profl. publs. Named one of Outstanding Young Women of Am., 1985. Founding mem. Nat. Soc. Fund Raising Execs. (past pres. San Antonio chpt.), Am. Coun. on Gift Annuities, Coun. Advancement and Support Edn., San Antonio Planned Giving Coun. Democrat. Roman Catholic. Office: Oblate Missions PO Box 96 San Antonio TX 78291-0096

LEAL, HERBERT ALLAN BORDEN, former university chancellor, former government official; b. Beloeil, Que., Can., June 15, 1917; s. Frederick William and Marie Ange (Ranger) L.; m. Muriel Isobel, Mar. 21, 1942; children: Kathleen Mary Leal Clark, Allan Ross, James Frederick. B.A. with honors in History, McMaster U., 1940; LL.M., Harvard U., 1957. Bar: Called to Ont. bar 1948. Read law with Frank Erichsen-Brown, Toronto, 1945-48; mem. firm Erichsen-Brown & Leal, Toronto, 1948-50; lectr. Osgoode Hall Law Sch., 1950-56, vice dean, prof., 1956-58, dean, prof., 1958-66; dep. atty. gen. Ont., 1977-81; chancellor McMaster U., Hamilton, Ont., 1977-86; chmn. Ont. Law Reform Commn., 1966-77, vice chmn., 1981-89; spl. lectr. Law Soc. Upper Can., 1951, 57, 60, 66, 77, Faculty of Law, U. Toronto, 1972-77; mem. council Medico-Legal Soc. Toronto, 1960, 1st v.p., 1968, pres., 1969. Contbr. articles to legal and profl. jours. Mem. exec. com. Toronto br. Can. Red Cross Soc., 1959-64; co-chmn. spl. com. Assn. Am. Law Schs., Assn. Can. Law Tchrs. Can.-Am. Coop., 1962-66; commr. Ont. Uniform Law Conf. Can., 1963-86, pres., 1977-78; mem. adv. com. Can. Civil Liberties Assn. Ont., 1965-66; mem. faculty Can. Jud. Conf., 1969-73, dir., 1969-70; mem. Can. del. Hague Conf. on Pvt. Internat. Law, 1968, 72, 76, chief of del., 1980; chief Can. del. Internat. Diplomatic Conf. on Wills, Washington, 1973; chmn. spl. com. uniform law Conf. Internat. Conventions Pvt. Internat. Law, 1971-81. With Royan Can. Arty., 1943-45; reeve Village of Tweed, 1991-94. Decorated officer Order of Can.; recipient Gov. Gen. medal McMaster U., 1939; A. G. Alexander scholar, 1939; Rhodes scholar, 1940. Mem. Law Soc. Upper Can. (medal 1987), Toronto Arty. Officers Assn., Assn. Can. Law Tchrs. (pres. 1959-60), African Students Found. (bd. dirs.). Club: Masons.

LEAL, LESLIE GARY, chemical engineering educator; b. Bellingham, Wash., Mar. 18, 1943; s. Leslie Arthur and Esther Vivian (Jones) L.; m. Mary Ann Seelye, June 11, 1965; children: Heather Noel, Kameron Brie, Farrah Aimee. BS, U. Wash., 1965; MS, Stanford U., 1967, PhD, 1969. Asst. prof. chem. engring. Calif. Inst. Tech., Pasadena, 1970-75, assoc. prof., 1975-78, prof., 1978-89, Chevron Disting. prof., 1986-89; prof., chmn. dept. chem. and nuclear engring. U. Calif., Santa Barbara, 1989—; cons. Firestone Rsch., Akron, Ohio, 1981-88, Dynamics Tech., Torrance, Calif., 1982-90, Richards of Rockford, Ill., 1975-79, Dowell-Schlumbargar, Tulsa, Okla., 1985-88, U. Okla. Fracturing Fluid Characterization Facility Project, 1991—; active U.S. Nat. Com. on Theoretical and Applied Mechanics, 1991—, chmn. 1994—; lectr. in field. Assoc. editor Internat. Jour. Multiphase Flow, 1985—; mem. editl. bd. Experiments in Fluids, 1994—, Ann. Revs. Fluid Mechanics, 1985-90, Jour. Colloid and Interface Sci., AIChE Jour. Tchr.-scholar grantee Camille and Henry Dreyfus Found., 1975; fellow John Simon Guggenheim Found., 1976. Fellow Am. Phys. Soc.; mem. NAE (mem. membership policy com. 1994—), AIChE (William H. Walker award 1993, Allan P. Colburn award 1978, tech. achievement award So. Calif. sect. 1978, chmn. nat. program com. in fluid mechanics 1984-89), Nat. Rsch. Coun. (mem. space studies bd. com. on microgravity rsch. 1993—), Soc. Rheology, Am. Soc. for Engring. Edn., Phi Beta Kappa, Tau Beta Pi, Phi Sigma Upsilon. Methodist. Home: 1560 Hillcrest Rd Santa Barbara CA 93103-1841 Office: U Calif Dept Chem and Nuclear Engring Santa Barbara CA 93106

LEALE, OLIVIA MASON, import marketing company executive; b. Boston, May 5, 1944; d. William Mason and Jane Chapin (Prouty) Smith; m. Euan Harvie-Watt, Mar. ll, 1967 (div. Aug. 1979); children: Katrina, Jennifer; m. Douglas Marshall Leale, Aug. 29, 1980. BA, Vassar Coll., 1966. Cert. paralegal. Sec. to dir. Met. Opera Guild, N.Y.C., 1966; sec. to pres. Friesons Printers, London, 1974-75; guide, trainer Autoguide, London, 1977-79; ptnr. Inmark Internat. Mktg. Inc., Seattle, 1980—. Social case worker Inner London Ednl. Authority, 1975-76. Democrat. Presbyterian. Avocations: reading, making doll house furniture, painting, knitting. Home and Office: 5427 NE Penrith Rd Seattle WA 98105-2842

LEAL-QUIROS, EDBERTHO, nuclear engineer, physicist; b. Macaravita, Colombia, Apr. 7, 1952; came to U.S., 1984; s. Hector and Nohemi Leal; m. Isabel C. Escalante, Jan. 3, 1975; children: Paola X., David Alberto. BS in Physics, Nat. U. Colombia, 1973, MS in Physics, 1976; MS in Physics, UCLA, 1986; PhD in Nuclear Engring., U. Mo., Columbia, 1989. Prof. U. de Los Andes Santa Fe de Bogota, Colombia, 1974-75, U. Nacional Colombia-Santa Fe de Bogota, 1971-76, U. Simon Bolivar, Caracas, 1977-81, U. Ctrl. Venezuela, 1976-84, U. Met. Caracas, Venezuela, 1981-84, Los Alamos (N.Mex.) Nat. Lab., 1986, U. Mo., Columbia, 1987-90, Am. Tech. Inst., 1989-90; nuclear physicist North Anna Nuclear Power Sta., Mineral, Va., 1990—; presenter in nat. and internat. confs.; mem. Nuclear Quality Analysis, North Anna Nuclear Power Sta./Surry Nuclear Power Sta./Corp. Office Va. Power, Innsbrook; presenter in field. Contbr. more than 25 articles to profl. publs., including Jour. Applied Physics, Fusion Tech., Rev. Sci. Instruments, Plasma Sci., others; presenter in field. Mem. IEEE, Am. Phys. Soc., Fusion Power Assocs., Soc. Hispanics Profl. Engrs., Am. Nuclear Soc. (chmn. NAPS br. 1991-92, chmn. Va. sect. 1994-95), Sigma Xi. Achievements include research in measurements of nuclear reactor parameters and coefficients, nuclear activation analysis, several nuclear systems plant tests, in fusion and plasma physics, ECR and ICH heating, plasma diagnostics, energy analyzers, on sources and detectory; design of Cusps, Mirrors, Double Plasma Machine, CCT Tokamak Experience; 7 patents in field. Home: 10212 Spinning Wheel Way Richmond VA 23233-2750

LEAMAN, DAVID MARTIN, cardiologist; b. Lancaster, Pa., Apr. 24, 1935; s. Benjamin Denlinger and Elise Mae (Martin) L.; m. Doris Jean Heisey; children: Gretchen Jane, Heidi Jean, Erika Ingrid. Student, Franklin & Marshall Coll., 1956-58; BA, Eastern Mennonite Coll., 1960; MD, Temple U., 1964. Intern Mary Hitchcock Hosp., Hanover, N.H., 1964-66; resident U. Vt., Burlington, 1968-71; asst. prof. medicine Pa. State U., Hershey, 1971-77, assoc. prof., 1977-84, prof., 1984—, chief div. of cardiology, 1984-95, asst. dean for student affairs, 1987-91, asst. dean for admissions, 1991-94. Contbr. articles to med. jours. Sch. dir. Lower Dauphin Sch. Dist., Hummelstown, Pa., 1977-83. Served with USPHS, 1966-68. Named Alumnus of Yr. Eastern Mennonite Coll., 1985. Fellow Am. Coll. Cardiology, Am. Coll. Chest Physicians, ACP, Soc. Cardiac Angiology, Am. Heart Assn. (mem. council on clin. cardiology, Service Recognition award 1981, Disting. Service award 1985, bd. dirs. Pa. affiliate 1975—), Alpha Omega Alpha. Republican. Mennonite. Avocations: reading, photography. Office: Pa State Univ Hershey Med Ctr PO Box 850 Hershey PA 17033-0850

LEAMAN, J. RICHARD, JR., paper company executive; b. Lancaster, Pa., Sept. 22, 1934; s. J. Richard and Margaret B. (Leaman); m. Helen Brown, June 15, 1957; children: Lynda B., J. Richard, III. BA, Dartmouth Coll., 1956, MBA, 1957; PhD (hon.), Widener U., 1988. With Scott Paper Co., Phila., 1960-95, v.p. comml. products, 1975-78, exec. v.p. mktg. and sales, 1978—, pres. Packaged Products div., 1983—, vice chmn., 1991-94, dir., 1986; pres. Scott Worldwide, 1986; pres., CEO, S.D. Warren Co., 1991-95; bd. dirs. Church & Dwight Co., Inc., Pep Boys, S.D. Warren Holdings. Vice-chmn. exec. com., trustee Widener U., 1987; mem. conf. bd.'s coun. Global Bus. Mgmt., Dartmouth Alumni Coun., 1993-96. Capt. USAF, 1957-61. Recipient Disting. Performance in Mgmt. award Widener U. Mem. Conf. Bd.'s Coun. on Global Bus. Mgmt. Republican. Episcopalian. Clubs: Dartmouth (Phila.). Home: 317 Boot Rd Malvern PA 19355-3317 Office: 225 Franklin St Boston MA 02110

LEAMAN, JACK ERVIN, landscape architect, community/regional planner; b. Mason City, Iowa, Jan. 24, 1932; s. Theodore R. and Dorothy M. (Schrum) L.; m. Darlene A. McNary, June 15, 1952; children: Jeffrey A., Danna J., Jay M., Duree K. B.S. in Landscape Architecture and Urban Planning, Iowa State U., 1954, M. Community and Regional Planning, 1982. Registered landscape architect, Calif., Iowa, Minn., N.Mex. Landscape architect Sam L. Huddleston Office, Denver, 1954-55, Phillips Petroleum Co., Bartlesville, Okla., 1955-58; landscape architect for Price Tower and residence with architect Frank Lloyd Wright Bartlesville, Okla., 1957-58; planning technician Santa Barbara County, Calif., 1958-60; planning cons. Engring. Planners, Santa Barbara, 1960-63; planning dir. City of Santa Barbara, 1963-66, City of Mason City, 1966-72; landscape architect, planning cons. Midwest Research Inst., Kansas City, Mo., 1972-74, Hansen, Lind, Meyer, Iowa City, Iowa, 1974-76, Sheffler, Leaman, Rova, Mason City,

1976-78, RCM Assocs., Inc., Hopkins, Minn. and Ames, Iowa, 1978-82; planning dir. City-County Planning, Albuquerque, 1982-86, City of Colorado Springs, Colo., 1986-90; adj. prof. dept. cmty. and regional planning Coll. of Design, Iowa State U., Ames, 1990—; landscape architect, pvt. practice planning cons. Mason City, Iowa, 1990-92; assoc. ptnr., landscape architect, community/regional planner Yaggy Colby Assocs., Mason City, Iowa, 1992-95; pvt. cons. cmty. and regional planning, landscape architect Mason City, Iowa, 1995—. Recipient Residential Landscape Design award Calif. Landscape Contractors Assn., 1962, Design Achievement award Coll. of Design Iowa State U., 1988. Fellow Am. Soc. Landscape Architects (chpt. pres. 1967-68, 90-91, trustee Iowa 1980-82, N.Mex. 1982-86, Award of Excellence 1954); mem. Am. Inst. Cert. Planners, Am. Planning Assn. (chpt. pres. Iowa 1969-70), Urban Land Inst., Tau Sigma Delta.

LEAMON, TOM B., industrial engineer, educator; b. Ossett, Yorkshire, U.K., Apr. 16, 1940; came to U.S., 1980; s. Harold and Dorothy (Wilde) L.; m. Geraldine Bland, July 1, 1967; children: Amanda Charlotte, Jonathan Barton, Genevieve Emma. BS in Chemistry, U. Manchester, U.K., 1961; MS in Indsl. Engring., Inst. Tech., Cranfield, U.K., 1964; MS in Applied Psychology, U. Aston, Birmingham, U.K., 1970; PhD in Indsl. Engring. Production Mgmt., Inst. Tech., Cranfield, 1982. Chartered engr.; chartered profl. ergonomist. Indsl. engr. Ilford (Eng.) Ltd., 1961-62; mgr. ergonomics Pilkington Ltd., St. Helens, Eng., 1964-71; dir. masters course Inst. Tech., Cranfield, 1970-75; head ergonomics br. Nat. Coal Bd., Burton-upon-Trent, U.K., 1975-80; dir. grad. program in occupational safety U. Ill., Chgo., 1981-82; prof., chmn. No. Ill. U., DeKalb, 1982-87, acting dean, 1985-86; prof., chmn. Tex. Tech. U., Lubbock, 1987-91; v.p., dir. rsch. ctr. Liberty Mut. Ins. Group, Hopkinton, Mass., 1991—. Trustee Am. Soc. Safety Engrs. Found. Named 1985 Disting. Lectr., Coll. Lake County. Fellow Inst. Prodn. Engrs. (Sir Ben Williams Silver medal 1969), Human Factors Soc. (chmn. indsl. ergonomics 1983-85), Ergonomics Soc.; mem. Inst. Indsl. Engrs. (chmn. ergonomics div. 1990-91, Spl. citation for outstanding contbns. to the enhancement of ergonomics), Am. Soc. Safety Engrs., Sigma Xi. Office: Liberty Mutual Rsch Ctr 71 Frankland Rd Hopkinton MA 01748-1231

LEAPHART, W. WILLIAM, judge; b. Butte, Mont., Dec. 3, 1946; s. Charles William and Cornelia (Murphy) L.; m. Barbara Berg, Dec. 30, 1977; children: Rebecca, Retta, Ada. Student, Whitman Coll., 1965-66; BA, U. Mont., 1969, JD, 1972. Bar: Mont. 1972, U.S. Dist. Ct., U.S. Ct. Appeals (9th cir.) 1975, U.S. Supreme Ct. Law clk. to Hon. W.D. Murray U.S. Dist. Ct., Butte, 1972-74; ptnr. Leaphart Law Firm, Helena, Mont., 1974-94; justice Mont. Supreme Ct., Helena, 1995—. Home: 510 Dearborn Helena MT 59601 Office: Mont Supreme Ct Justice Bldg 215 N Sanders Helena MT 59620

LEAR, ERWIN, anesthesiologist, educator; b. Bridgeport, Conn., Jan. 1, 1924; s. Samuel Joseph and Ida (Ruth) L.; m. Arlene Joyce Alexander, Feb. 15, 1953; children—Stephanie, Samuel. MD, SUNY, 1952. Diplomate Am. Bd. Anesthesiology, Nat. Bd. Med. Examiners. Intern L.I. Coll. Hosp., Bklyn., 1952-53; asst. resident anesthesiology Jewish Hosp., Bklyn., 1953-54; sr. resident Jewish Hosp., 1955, asst., 1955-56, adj., 1956-58, assoc. anesthesiologist, 1958-64; attending anesthesiologist Bklyn. VA Hosp., 1958-64, cons., 1977—; assoc. vis. anesthesiologist Kings County Hosp. Ctr., Bklyn., 1957-80; staff anesthesiologist Kings County Hosp. Ctr., 1980-81; vis. anesthesiologist Queens Gen. Hosp. Ctr., 1955-67; dir. anesthesiology Queens Hosp. Ctr. Jamaica, 1964-67, cons., 1968—; chmn. dept. anesthesiology Catholic Med. Ctr., Queens and Bklyn., 1968-80; dir. anesthesiology Beth Israel Med. Ctr., N.Y.C., 1981—; clin. instr. SUNY Coll. Medicine, Bklyn., 1955-58; clin. asst. prof. SUNY Coll. Medicine, 1958-64, clin. assoc. prof., 1964-71, clin. prof., 1971-80, prof., vice-chmn. clin. anesthesiology, 1980-81; prof. anesthesiology Mt. Sinai Sch. Medicine, 1981-94, Albert Einstein Coll. of Medicine, 1994—. Author: Chemistry Applied Pharmacology of Tranquilizers; contbr. articles to profl. jours. Served with USNR, 1942-45. Fellow Am. Coll. Anesthesiologists, N.Y. Acad. Medicine (sec. sect. anesthesiology 1985-86, chmn. sect. anesthesiology 1986-87); mem. AMA, Am. Soc. Anesthesiologists (chmn. com. on by-laws 1982-83, dir. 1981—, ho. of dels. 1973—, editor newsletter 1984—, chmn. adminstrv. affairs com., 1987—), N.Y. State Bd. Profl. Med. Conduct, N.Y. State Soc. Anesthesiologists (chmn. pub. relations 1963-73, chmn. com. local arrangements 1968-73, dist. dir. 1972-73, v.p. 1974-75, pres. 1976, bd. dirs. 1972—, chmn. jud. com. 1977-81, assoc. editor Bulletin 1963-77, editor Sphere 1978-84), N.Y. State Med. Soc. (chmn. sect. anesthesiology 1966-67, sec. sect. 1977-81), N.Y. County Med. Soc., SUNY Coll. Medicine Alumni Assn. (pres. 1983, trustee alumni fund 1980), Alpha Omega Alpha. Address: Harriman Dr Sands Point NY 11050

LEAR, EVELYN, soprano; b. Bklyn., Jan. 8, 1930; m. Thomas Stewart; children: Jan, Bonni. Vocal student in, N.Y.C.; student, N.Y. U., Hunter Coll. Song recitals, Phillips Gallery, Washington; mem. Juilliard Sch. Music Workshop; recital, Town Hall, N.Y.C., 1955; lead in Marc Blitzstein's Reuben, Reuben; performed Strauss's Four Last Songs with London Symphony Orch., 1959; mem. Deutsche Opera, 1959, appeared in Lulu at Vienna Festival, 1962, The Marriage of Figaro at Salzburg Festival, 1962, debut, Vienna State Opera, 1964, Frankfurt Opera, 1965, Covent Garden, 1965, Kansas City (Mo.) Performing Arts Found., 1965, Chgo. Lyric Opera, 1966, La Scala Opera, 1971, also in Brussels, San Francisco, Los Angeles, Buenos Aires, debut at Met. Opera as Lavinia in Mourning Becomes Electra, 1967, mem. co., 1967—; roles include Tosca, Manon, Marshallin, Desdemona, Mimi, Dido, Donna Elvira, Marina, Tatiana: TV appearance in La Boheme, 1965; numerous solo appearances, 1960—; appeared in film Buffalo Bill, 1976; rec. artist Angel Records, Deutsche Grammophon. Recipient Concert Artists Guild award 1955, Liederabend, Salzburg Festival 1964, Grammy award for best operatic recording (Marie in Wozzeck) 1965; Fulbright scholar, 1957.

LEAR, JOHN, writer, editor; b. nr. Allen, Pa., Aug. 10, 1909; s. Charles D. and Esther M. (Sourbeer) L.; m. Dorothy Leeds, Sept. 26, 1931 (dec. May 1965); m. Marie Nesta, Aug. 28, 1966. D.Sc. (hon.), Dickinson Coll., 1968. Editor Daily Local News, Mechanicsburg, Pa., 1927-28; reporter Patriot, Harrisburg, 1928-34; editor West Shore Call, New Cumberland, Pa., 1930-33; writer-editor A.P., Phila., Chgo., N.Y.C., Washington, Buenos Aires; roving assignments A.P., Eastern U.S., Can., S.Am., 1934-42; coordinator info. staff gov. P.R., 1942-43; radio news writer Press Assn., N.Y.C., 1943; free lance mag. corr., 1944-48; mng. editor Steelways mag., 1948-49; chief articles editor Collier's mag., 1949-50, assoc. editor, 1950-53; cons. publs. IBM Corp., 1953-54; dir. spl. atomics and automation studies Research Inst. Am., 1954-55; sci. editor Sat. Rev., 1956-71, sr. editor, 1971-72; v.p. Bauer Engring., Inc., 1972; v.p., chief editor Bauer, Sheaffer & Lear, Inc., Chgo., 1972-75; chief editor Keifer & Assos., Inc., 1975-76; Am. corr. New Scientist, London, 1956-62; editorial cons. Russell Sage Found., 1967-68, Inst. for Social Research, U. Mich., 1972-73; columnist King Features Syndicate, 1973; editorial cons. Rockefeller Found., 1978-82; cons. Office of Tech. Assessment, U.S. Congress, 1975; publs. cons. Acad. Forum, Nat. Acad. Scis., 1976. Author: Forgotten Front, 1942, Kepler's Dream, 1965, Recombinant DNA—The Untold Story, 1978; contbg. editor: World Press Rev, 1976-84; sci. editor Pa. mag., 1982-83; editor Pa. Press Bur., Pa. Newspaper Pubs. Assn., 1986; columnist The Gettysburg Times, 1986-87. Recipient Disting. Svc. to Journalism medal Sigma Delta Chi, 1950, 60, Westinghouse prize AAAS, 1951, Albert Lasker Med. Journalism award, 1952. Home: 4570 Larch Dr Apt 181 Harrisburg PA 17109-5105

LEAR, NORMAN MILTON, producer, writer, director; b. New Haven, July 27, 1922; s. Herman and Jeanette (Seicol) L.; children: Ellen, Kate B. Lear LaPook, Maggie B.; m. Lyn Davis; children: Benjamin Davis, Brianna, Madeline. Student, Emerson Coll., 1940-42, HHD, 1968. Engaged in pub. relations, 1945-49; founder Act III Comms., 1987—. Comedy writer for TV, 1950-54; writer, dir. for TV and films, 1954-59; producer: films Come Blow Your Horn, 1963, Never Too Late, 1965; prodr., screenwriter: Divorce American Style, 1967, The Night They Raided Minsky's, 1968; writer, producer, dir.: film Cold Turkey, 1971; exec. prodr. film Start the Revolution Without Me, The Princess Bride, Breaking In, Fried Green Tomatoes; creator, dir.: TV shows TV Guide Awards Show, 1962, Henry Fonda and the Family, 1963, Andy Williams Spl., also Andy Williams Series, 1965, Robert Young and the Family, 1970; exec. prodr., creator-developer: TV shows All in the Family, 1971 (4 Emmy awards 1970-73, Peabody award 1977), Maude, 1972; Sanford and Son, 1972, Good Times, 1974, The Jeffersons, 1975, Hot L Baltimore, 1975, Mary Hartman, Mary Hartman, 1976, One Day At a Time, 1975, All's Fair, 1976, A Year at the Top, 1977, All That Glitters, 1977, Fernwood 2 Night, 1977, The Baxters, 1979, Palmerstown, 1980, I Love Liberty, 1982, Sunday Dinner, 1991, The Powers That Be, 1992, 704 Hauser, 1994; creator a.k.a. Pablo, 1984; exec. producer Heartsounds, 1984. Pres. Am. Civil Liberties Found. So. Calif., 1973—; trustee Mus. Broadcasting; bd. dirs. People for the American Way; founder Bus. Enterprise Trust. Served with USAAF, 1942-45. Decorated Air medal with 4 oak leaf clusters; named One of Top Ten Motion Picture Producers, Motion Picture Exhibitors, 1963, 67, 68, Showman of Yr., Publicists Guild, 1971-77, Assn. Bus. Mgrs., 1972, Broadcaster of Yr., Internat. Radio and TV Soc., 1973; Man of Yr. Hollywood chpt. Nat. Acad. Television Arts and Scis., 1973; recipient Humanitarian award NCCJ, 1976, Mark Twain award Internat. Platform Assn., 1977, William O. Douglas award Pub. Counsel, 1981, 1st Amendment Lectr. Ford Hall Forum, 1981, Gold medal Internat. Radio and TV Soc., 1981. Disting. Am. award, 1984, Mass Media award Am. Jewish Com. Inst. of Human Relations, 1986, Internat. award of Yr., Nat. Assn. TV Program Execs., 1987; inducted into TV Acad. Hall of Fame, 1984. Mem. Writers Guild Am. (Valentine Davies award 1977), Dirs. Guild Am., AFTRA, Caucus Producers, Writers, and Dirs. Office: Act III Communications 1999 Avenue Of The Stars Los Angeles CA 90067-6028

LEAR, ROBERT WILLIAM, holding company executive; b. Canon City, Colo., May 10, 1917; s. Louis and Bertha (May) L.; m. Dorothy Schureman, Sept. 16, 1941; children—William S., Andrew R. B.A., U. Colo., 1938; M.B.A. with distinction, Harvard, 1940. Market research analyst U.S. Steel Corp., 1940-43; sales promotion mgr. Duff-Norton Co., 1946-47; corp. dir. marketing services Am. Standard Co., 1947-61; v.p. marketing Carborundum Co., 1961-64, group v.p., 1964-67; pres., dir. Indian Head Inc., 1967-72; pres., chief exec. officer, chmn., dir. F. & M. Schaefer Corp., N.Y.C., 1972-77; exec.-in-residence Columbia Grad. Bus. Sch., 1977—; prin. Lear, Yavitz & Assocs., LLP, 1996—; bd. dirs. Welsh, Carson, Anderson Assocs. Venture Funds, Korea Fund, Scudder, Stevens & Clark Instnl. Funds, others; ind. gen. ptnr. Equitable Capital Ptnrs. Author: How to Turn Your MBA into a CEO, 1987, Pressure Points, 1992; chmn. adv. bd. Chief Exec. Mag., 1994—. Bd. dirs. Waveny Care Center. Served as lt. USNR, 1943-46. Clubs: Harvard (N.Y.C.); New Canaan Country, Blind Brook, Mill Reef. Home: 429 Silvermine Rd New Canaan CT 06840-4320 Office: Columbia U 206 Uris Hall # F New York NY 10027

LEARMANN, JUDITH MARILYN, secondary education educator; b. Charleston, Ill., Feb. 1, 1938; d. Charles P. and Estelle M. (DeWitt) Swan; m. Paul C. Learmann, Aug. 29, 1958 (dec.); children: Kevin L., Michael P. (dec.). BS, Wis. State Coll., Oshkosh, 1960; MA, Pacific Western U., 1994. Tchr. Monona (Wis.) Grove H.S., 1960-62, U.S. Army Coll. Program, Denver, 1967, Wood Mid. Sch., Ft. Leonard Wood, Mo., 1983-85; tchr., chmn. dept. lang. arts Waynesville (Mo.) H.S., 1985—; presenter in field; chmn. North Ctrl. Philosophy Com., Waynesville, 1987-88; reviewer textbook Adventures in English Literature, 1994; reviewer sci. curriculum, 1994-95, math. curriculum, 1995, social studies curriculum, 1996. Named Most Influential Tchr. award U. Mo., 1991; recipient influential tchr. recognition letter Westminster Coll., 1992, 95. Mem. Nat. Coun. Tchrs. English, Mo. Tchrs. Assn., Mo. Tchrs. English (meeting chmn. dist. conv. 1989, 90), Cmty. Tchrs. Assn. (chmn. legal svcs. 1991-95), Phi Delta Kappa (tchr. awards, officer nomination, constn. revision coms.). Avocation: reading. Home: 1737 J C St Waynesville MO 65583-2450 Office: Waynesville HS Historic Rt 66 West Waynesville MO 65583

LEARN, ELMER WARNER, agricultural economics educator, retired; b. Sayre, Pa., Jan. 19, 1929; s. John Walter and Naomi Ruth (Warner) L.; m. Theresa Arlene Green, Sept. 22, 1956; children—Diane Marie, Linda Jean. B.S., Pa. State U., 1950, M.S., 1951, Ph.D., 1957; student, U. Minn., 1954-55. Grad. research asst., instr. Pa. State U., 1950-51, 53-54, 55-56; successively asst. prof., assoc. prof., prof. U. Minn., 1956-69, head dept. agrl. econs., 1963-64, asst. to pres. then exec. asst. to pres., also dir. planning, 1964-69; prof., exec. vice chancellor U. Calif.-Davis, 1969-84, prof., 1984-92; cons. 9th Dist. Fed. Res. Bank, 1962, Dept. Agr., 1962-65. Contbr. articles on agrl. policy, prices, fgn. trade policy to profl. jours. Served with AUS, 1951-53. Recipient Grad. Student award Am. Farm Econs. Assn., 1956. Mem. AAUP, Am. Agrl. Econs. Assn., Phi Kappa Phi, Gamma Sigma Delta. Home: 1702 Sycamore Ln Davis CA 95616-0809

LEARNARD, WILLIAM EWING, marketing executive; b. Joliet, Ill., July 21, 1935; s. Roy Stevens and Clara (Ewing) L.; m. Susan Douglas-Willan, Oct. 1, 1960; children: Matthew, Roger, Vanessa. BA, Trinity Coll., 1957. With Smith, Kline & French, Phila., 1957-78, v.p. customer affairs, 1976-78; v.p. corp. affairs Smithkline Beckman, Phila., 1978-85; pres. Smithkline Consumer Products, Phila., 1985-89; vice chmn. Smithkline Beecham Consumer Brands, Phila., 1989-91; chmn. Coun. on Family Health, N.Y.C., 1989-91; bd. dirs. Nelson Comms., DiMark, Inc. Bd. dirs. Chestnut Hill Hosp., Phila., 1982-88, Morris Arboretum, U. Pa., Phila., 1982-92; chmn. Sta. WHYY TV & Radio, Phila., 1990-94. Capt. USAF, 1958-61. Mem. Nonprescription Drug Mfrs. Assn. (chmn. 1989-91), Phila. Cricket Club, George Town Club. Republican. Home: 48 Hillcrest Ave Philadelphia PA 19118-2620 Office: Trident Group Ste 230 Spring House Corp Ctr Ambler PA 19002

LEARNED, VINCENT R., electrical engineer , educator; b. San Jose, Calif., Jan. 21, 1917. BSEE, U. Calif., 1938; PhD, Stanford U., 1943. Prof. elec. and computer engr. emeritus San Diego State U. Fellow IRE. Office: San Diego State University 3842 Silvera Ct Paradise CA 95969*

LEARY, CAROL ANN, academic administrator; b. Niagara Falls, N.Y., Mar. 29, 1947; d. Angelo Andrew and Mary Josephine (Pullano) Gigliotti; m. Noel Robert Leary, Dec. 30, 1972. BA, Boston U., 1969; MS, SUNY, Albany, 1970; PhD, Am. Univ., 1988. Asst. to v.p. for student affairs, dir. women's programs Siena Coll., Loudonville, N.Y., 1970-72; asst. dir. housing Boston U., 1972-78; dir. residence Simmons Coll., Boston, 1978-84, assoc. dean, 1984-85; assoc. dir. The Washington Campus, Washington, 1985-86; adminstrv. v.p., asst. to pres. Simmons Coll., Boston, 1988-94; pres. Bay Path Coll., Longmeadow, Mass., 1995—. Bd. dirs. Bay State Med. Ctr., Careen Hill Girls Club, Colony Club, STCC Assistance Corp., 1996—. Fellow Ednl. Policy Fellowship Program, 1990-91. Mem. Am. Coun. Edn. (rep. Mass. divsn. 1991—), Phi Beta Kappa. Avocations: classic movies, traveling overseas, hiking. Office: Bay Path Coll Office of the President 588 Longmeadow St Longmeadow MA 01106-2212

LEARY, DANIEL, artist; b. Glens Falls, N.Y., July 20, 1955; s. John Andrew and Maud Houston (Parkhurst) L. BFA, Antioch Coll., 1979; MFA, Syracuse U., 1987. One person exhbns. include Breedlove Gallery, Westark Cmty. Coll., Fort Smith, Ark., 1984, 85, Comart Gallery, Syracuse U., 1985, 87, The Printspace, U. Ark., Fayetteville, 1985, The Fort Smith Art Ctr., 1986, Printworks, Ltd., Chgo., 1988, 95, The Hyde Collection, Glens Falls, N.Y., 1990, The Blanden Meml. Art Mus., Fort Dodge, Iowa, 1992, The Bobbit Visual Art Ctr., Albion Coll., Mich., 1993, Sharon Campbell Gallery, Greenville, S.C., 1994, We. Mich. State U., Kalamazoo, 1994; group exhbns. include East Tenn. State U., Johnson City, 1985, Gallery Sixty-Eight, Belfast, Maine, 1985, The Fort Smith Arts Ctr., 1985, Syracuse U., 1985, The Ark. Arts Ctr. and the Decorative Arts Mus., Little Rock, 1985, The Soc. Am. Graphic Artists, 1986, Westminster Coll., New Wilmington, Pa., 1986, Joe Fawbush Editions, N.Y., 1986, Cazenovia (N.Y.) Coll., 1987, Jan Turner Gallery, L.A., 1987, The Greenville County Mus. Art, 1988, The Mpls. Inst. Arts., 1988, The Munson-Williams-Proctor Inst. Mus. Art, Utica, N.Y., 1989, The Statesville Arts and Scis. Mus., 1989, The Nat. Exhbn. Ctr. Can., Alma, Quebec, 1989, The Pyramid Arts Ctr., Rochester, N.Y., 1989, The Vero Beach Ctr. For the Arts, Fla., 1989, The Jane Voorhees Zimmerli Art Mus., Rutgers U., New Brunswick, N.J., 1990, Bradford Art Galleries and Mus., England, 1990, The Contemporary Arts Ctr., Cin., 1991, Northwest Art Gallery, Ind. U. Northwest, Gary, 1993; public collections include Albion (Mich.) Coll., The Ark. Arts Ctr., The Arts Ctr., Greenville, The Boston Pub. Library, The Blanden Meml. Art Mus., The Carnegie Mus. Art, Pitts., East Tenn. State U., The Hyde Collection, Glens Falls, The Library of Congress, Washington, D.C., The Metropolitan Mus. Art., N.Y., The Milw. Art Mus., The Mpls. Inst. Arts, The Munson-Williams-Proctor Inst. Mus. Art, The N.Y. Pub. Library, The Spencer Mus. Art, U. Kans., Syracuse U., The Toledo Mus. Art, U. Ariz. Mus. Art, The Walker Art Ctr., Mpls., We. Mich. U., The Williams Coll. Mus. Art, Williamstown, Mass., Wright State U., Dayton, Ohio, The Jane Voorhees Zimmerli Art Mus., Rutgers U., New Brunswick, N.J.; gallery reps. include Sharon Campbell Gallery, Greenville, Printworks Gallery, Chgo. Recipient Visual Artists Fellowship grantee NEA, 1989; fellow N.Y. Found. for the Arts, 1988. Home: PO Box 136 Hudson Falls NY 12839

LEARY, DAVID EDWARD, university dean; b. L.A., May 5, 1945; married; 3 children. BA in Philosophy, San Luis Rey Coll., 1968; MA in Psychology, San Jose State Coll., 1971; PhD in History of Sci., U. Chgo., 1977. Instr. psychology Holy Names Coll., Oakland, Calif., 1972-74, U. Calif. Extension Svcs., Berkeley, 1972-74; counseling psychologist Howard Inst., Oakland, 1972-74; instr. psychology San Jose (Calif.) State U. Extension Svcs., 1973-74, San Francisco State U. Extension Svcs., 1973-74, U. Calif. at Santa Cruz Extension Svcs., Monterey, 1973-74, U. Chgo., 1975; asst. prof. history and philosophy of psychology U. N.H., Durham, 1977-81, co-dir. grad. program in history and theory psychology, 1977-89, assoc. prof. psychology and humanities, 1981-87, chmn. dept. psychology, 1986-89, prof. psychology, history and humanities, 1987-89; prof. psychology, dean arts and scis. U. Richmond, Va., 1989—; vis. asst. prof. psychology Grad. Theol. Union, Berkeley, 1971-72; fellow Ctr. Advanced Study in Behavioral Scis., Stanford, Calif., 1982-83, co-dir. summer inst. on history of social sci. inquiry, 1986; assoc. prof. humanities Summer Program Cambridge U., Eng., 1984; presenter in field. Author: A Century of Psychology as Science, 2d rev. edit., 1992 (Assn. Am. Pub. award 1986), An Introduction to the Psychology of Guilt, 1975; editor: Metaphors in the History of Psychology, 1990; author: (with others) The Encyclopedia of Higher Education, 1992, Writing the Social Text: Poetics and Politics in Social Science Discourses, 1992, Annual Review of Psychology, 1991, Metaphors in the History of Psychology, 1990, Reflections on The Principles of Psychology: William James After a Century, 1990, Psychology in Twentieth-Century Thought and Society, 1987, Psychology in its Historical Context, 1985, Thinkers of the 20th Century, 1984, Studies in Eighteenth-Century Culture, 1984, The Problematic Science: Psychology in Nineteenth Century Thought, 1982; contbr. articles to profl. jours. Grantee NEH, 1982-83, 91-94, Social Sci. Rsch. Ctr. Faculty Support, U. N.H., 1988, Coll. Liberal Arts Faculty Rsch. Support, U. N.H., 1987-88, Ctrl. U. Rsch. Fund, U. N.H., 1979, 87, Mellon Found., 1986, NSF, 1980-82, 82-83; rsch. fellow History Psychology Found., 1980, summer fellow NEH, 1979, U. N.H., 1978, grad. fellow U. Chgo., 1975-77. Fellow Am. Psychol. Soc.; mem. AAAS, APA (centennial lectr. on history of psychology 1979-80, 91-92, fellow divsn. 24 1988—, fellow divsn. 1 1983—, pres. divsn. 26 1983-84, fellow divsn. 26 1982—, pres.-elect divsn. 24 1993-94, pres. 1994-95), Am. Assn. Higher Edn., Am. Conf. Acad. Deans (bd. dirs. 1994—), Am. Hist. Assn., Assn. Am. Colls. (grantee 1990-91), Soc. History of Sci. in Am., Cheiron: Internat. Soc. History of Behavioral and Social Scis., Forum History of Human Sci., History of Sci. Soc., Phi Beta Kappa (hon.). Office: Univ Richmond Office Dean Arts & Scis Richmond VA 23173

LEARY, DENIS, comedian; b. 1958; m. Ann Lembeck; children: Jack, Devin. BA in English, Emerson Coll., 1979. Films: National Lampoon's Loaded Weapon I, 1993, The Sandlot, 1993, Who's the Man?, 1993, Judgment Night, 1993, Demolition Man, 1993, Gunmen, 1994, The Ref, 1994, Operation Dumbo Drop, 1995; off Broadway appearances No Cure for Cancer, 1991-92, Birth, School, Work, Death, 1993; TV spls. No Cure for Cancer, 1993, MTV Unplugged, 1993, A-hole, 1993; alkbum No Cure for Cancer, 1993. Office: c/o William Morris Agency 151 S El Camino Dr Beverly Hills CA 90212-2704

LEARY, MICHAEL WARREN, journalist; b. Rice Lake, Wis., Apr. 15, 1949; s. Warren Denis and Patricia (Berigan) L.; m. Janice Marie Kalmar, Sept. 5, 1970; children: Meghan, Evan, Kieran. Student, U. Innsbruck, Austria, 1968-69; AB cum laude, U. Notre Dame, 1971; MS, Columbia U., 1972. Reporter Phila. Inquirer, 1972—, nat. corr. Houston Bur., 1983-86, asst. city editor, Phila., 1986-87, European corr., London, 1987-90, editor Book Rev. sect., 1990-93, assoc. editor, mem. editorial bd., 1993—. Dir. Chestnut Hill Fathers Club. Recipient Silver Gavel award ABA, 1981, Gold award Best Op-Ed Page Am. Soc. Opinion Page Editors, 1995. Home: 7153 Crittenden St Philadelphia PA 19119-1217 Office: Philadelphia Inquirer PO Box 8263 400 N Broad St Philadelphia PA 19101

LEARY, THOMAS BARRETT, lawyer; b. Orange, N.J., July 15, 1931; s. Daniel and Margaret (Barrett) L.; m. Stephanie Lynn Abbott, Dec. 18, 1954, June 3, 1991; children: Thomas A., David A., Alison Leary Estep. AB, Princeton U., 1952; JD magna cum laude, Harvard U., 1958. Bar: N.Y. 1959, Mich. 1972, D.C. 1983. Assoc. White & Case, N.Y.C., 1958-68, ptnr., 1968-71; atty.-in-charge antitrust Gen. Motors Corp., Detroit, 1971-77, asst. gen. counsel, 1977-82; ptnr. Hogan & Hartson, Washington, 1983—. Served to lt. USNR, 1952-55. Mem. ABA. Office: Hogan & Hartson Columbia Sq 555 13th St NW Washington DC 20004-1109

LEARY, TIMOTHY, psychologist, author; b. Springfield, Mass., Oct. 22, 1920; s. Timothy and Abigal (Ferris) L.; m. Rosemary Woodruff, Dec. 12, 1967; m. Barbara Chase, Dec. 18, 1978; children: Susan, John Busch, Zachary; remarried Rosemary Woodruff, Mar. 21, 1995. Student, Holy Cross Coll., 1938-39, U.S. Mil. Acad., 1940-41; AB, U. Ala., 1943; MS, Wash. State U., 1946; PhD in Psychology, U. Calif. at Berkeley, 1950. Asst. prof. U. Calif. at Berkeley, 1950-55; dir. psychol. research Kaiser Found., Oakland, Calif., 1955-58; lectr. Harvard, 1959-63; first guide League Spiritual Discovery, 1964—; pres., producer Futique Inc. (electronic books), 1985—; psychol. cons. to mgmt., 1953-63; cons. Mass. Dept. Corrections, 1961-63, Afghanistan Export Assn., 1966-69; Interactive Software Cons., Xor, 1981, Electronic Arts, 1981, Activision, 1986, Epyx, 1988, Autodesk, 1989; keynote speaker Ars Futura, Barcelona, Spain, 1989, Siggraph, Dallas, 1990, Ars Electronica, Linz, Austria, 1990, Cyberthon, San Francisco, 1990, Cyberarts, Pasadena, Libertarian Party Nat. Conv., Chgo., Design Forum Symposium, Matsue, Japan, 1991, Am. Humanist Psychology Conv., 1993, Lalapaloosa Festival, 1993; founder Conscious-Net Electron Bulletin Bd., 1994. Producer: Psychedelic Celebrations, 1965-66; writer, actor: (film) Turn On, Tune In, Drop Out, 1967, Volcano of Love, 1991; author: Social Dimensions of Personality, 1950, Interpersonal Diagnosis of Personality, 1950, Multi-level Assessment of Personality, 1951, Psychedelic Experience, 1964, Psychedelic Reader, 1965, Psychedelic Prayers, 1964, High Priest, 1968, Politics of Ecstasy, 1968, The Psychology of Pleasure, 1969, Jail Notes, 1970, Confessions of a Hope Fiend, 1973, Neurologic, 1973, Terra II, 1973, The Intelligence Agents, 1978, Exo-Psychology, 1979, What Does Women Want?, 1979, Changing My Mind, 1982, Flashbacks: An Autobiography, 1983, 1983, Infopsychology, 1987, The Cybernetic Societies of the 21st Century, 1987, Greatest Hits, 1990, Virtual Reality and Telepresence, 1991, Chaos & Cyber Culture, 1994, The Adventures of Huck Getty, 1994, High Priest, 1995, Design for Dying, 1995, Quality of Life Manual, 1995; actor: (film) Cheech & Chong's Nice Dreams, 1981, Return Engagement with G. Gordon Liddy, 1984, Hard Knocks, Showscan, 1987, Moonlighting, 1988, Medium Rare, 1988, Imagine with John Lennon, 1989, Fatal Skies, 1989, Shocker, 1989, Chamelion Blue, 1990, Chill Me, 1991, Roadside Prophets, 1991, Super Force, 1991, Ted and Venus, 1991, Banana Chip Love, 1991, Volcano of Love, 1992, Roadside Prophet, 1992, Ted and Venus, 1992, Sex Police, 1993, Cyberpunk with Billy Idol, 1993, Brisco County Jr., 1994, (with Retinalogic) Chaos Engineering, 1994; (recordings) Give Peace a Chance, 1969, (with J. Lennon) Seven Up, 1973, (with Jimi Hendrix) You Can Be Anything This Time Around, 1970, TranceFormation (with Psychic TV), 1992, Brain Exchange (with Hyperdelic Video), 1992, How to Operate Your Brain, 1993, With Retinalogic, 1993, (with Richard Chase) Five Generations that Changed American Culture in the 20th Century, 1994, Gilocopter (with Ministry), 1994, (with Aileen Getty) Dying is a Team Sport, 1994; designer interactive computer programs Mind Mirror, Life Adventure, 1985, Head Coach Master Mind; designer reactive videoware program for Mental Fitness, software program Neuromancer, 1986, Intercom EDL Software, 1989; designer CD Rom program Wonderland Park, World Wide Web Site. Candidate for gov., Calif., 1969-70; mem. Alcor Cryonics Life Extension Found., 1991; sponsor Cyberspace Room, Digital Hollywood Conv., 1996. Recipient Lifetime Achievement award Acad. Interactive Arts & Scis., 1995. Mem. AFTRA, Screen Actors Guild, Am. Courseware Assn. (pres. 1989), Hemlock Soc. Address: PO Box 69886 Los Angeles CA 90069-0886 *Died May 31, 1996.*

LEARY, WILLIAM JAMES, educational administrator; b. Boston, Oct. 1, 1931; s. John Gilbert and Josephine Marie (Kelley) L.; m. Joann Linda Parodi, June 25, 1960; children: Lorraine, Lisa, Linda. S.B., Boston Coll., 1953; M.Ed., Boston State Coll., 1954; postgrad. (Fulbright fellow), Sophia U., Tokyo, 1967; cert. advanced study, Harvard U., 1972, Ed.D., 1973; Ed.D., Boston U., 1971. Tchr. pub. schs. Boston, 1957-67; chmn. dept. social studies Dorchester High Sch., Boston, 1967-68; dir. curriculum Boston Dist. Pub. Schs., 1969-72, supt. schs., 1972-75; exec. dir. Met. Planning Project, Newton, Mass., 1975-77; supt. schs. Rockville Centre, N.Y., 1977-82, North Babylon, N.Y., 1982-84, Broward County, Ft. Lauderdale, Fla., 1984-88; supt. Gloucester (Mass.) Pub. Schs., 1989-93; assoc. prof. dept. ednl. leadership U. Miss., University, 1993—; assoc. prof. dept. continuing studies Boston State Coll., 1970-72; assoc. in edn. Harvard U. Grad. Sch. Edn., 1972-75; adj. prof. edn. Boston U., 1973-75, C.W. Post Ctr., L.I. U., 1979-84, Fla. Internat. U., 1984-88, Salem (Mass.) State Coll., 1990-93; prof. Suffolk U., 1975-77; mem. meml. scholarship fund com. Harvard U., 1977-82; TV commentator Channel 5, Boston, 1975-76; prodr. edn. programs New Eng. Cablevision, 1989-93; keynote spkr. Harvard U. Grad. Sch. Edn., 1976, NYU, 1980; mem. faculty senate U. Miss., 1994—, chair subcom. on athletics, 1994-95. Edn. columnist Boston Herald, 1975-78, L.I. News, 1982-84, Gloucester Times; edn. commentator New Eng. Cablevision, 1989-93; contbr. articles to profl. jours. Edn. coord. Boston chpt. United Way, 1974, Rockville Centre United Fund, 1979-80, Broward County chpt., 1985-87; trustee Mus. Fin. Arts, Boston, 1972-77; bd. dirs. Boston Youth Symphony, 1972-77, Edn. Devel. Ctr., 1972-77, Broward Com. of 100, Boys Club Broward County, 1985-88; mem. nat. alumni bd. Boston U., 1975—; mem. vis. com. Suffolk U., 1978-80; adv. bd. Harvard N.Y. Alumni Forums, 1980-84; mem. L.I. Regional Planning Bd., 1983-84, Gov.'s Task Force on Alt. Edn., Fla., 1986-88; mem. Atty. Gen.'s edn. adv. com., Mass., 1991-93. Recipient Friend of Youth award Hayden Goodwill Boys' Home, 1973, Ida M. Johnston Outstanding Alumni award Boston U. Sch. Edn., 1976, Man of Yr. award Pope's Hill Assn., 1976, Jenkins Meml. award for ednl. leadership N.Y. State Coun., PTA, 1980, Ednl. Leadership award L.I. chpt. NCCJ, 1980, Broward County Med. Aux., 1984, Lifetime Achievement award Matignon H.S. Alumni, 1995; selected as mem. Exec. Educator 100, Nat. Sch. Bd. Assn., 1987; named to Matignon H.S. Hall of Fame, 1995. Mem. ASCD (nat. commn. on supervision 1984-85), Am. Assn. Sch. Adminstrs. (del. assembly 1991, 92, 93, resolutions com. 1988-89, 93-94, 94-95, 95—), Am. Hist. Assn., Horace Mann League, Assn. for Asian Studies, Nat. Coun. Social Studies (nat. urban affairs com. 1977-80), Miss. Assn. Sch. Supts., Mass. Atty. Gen.'s Adv. Group, Harvard Club N.Y.C., Boston Coll., Varsity Club, KC, Rotary, Am. Legion, Phi Delta Kappa. Roman Catholic. Office: Grad Sch of Edn Univ of Mississippi PO Box 563 University MS 38677-0563 *A person's ability for creative and imaginative thinking is limited only by his/her fear to dream.*

LEASE, JANE ETTA, environmental science consultant, retired librarian; b. Kansas City, Kans., Apr. 10, 1924; d. Joy Alva and Emma (Jaggard) Omer; B.S. in Home Econs., U. Ariz., 1957; M.S. in Edn., Ind. U., 1962; M.S. in L.S., U. Denver, 1967; m. Richard J. Lease, Jan. 16, 1960; children—Janet (Mrs. Jacky B. Radifera), Joyce (Mrs. Robert J. Carson), Julia (Mrs. Earle D. Marvin), Cathy (Mrs. Edward F. Warren); stepchildren—Richard Jay II, William Harley. Newspaper reporter Ariz. Daily Star, Tucson, 1937-39; asst. home agt. Dept. Agr., 1957; homemaking tchr., Ft. Huachuca, Ariz., 1957-60; head tchr. Stonebelt Council Retarded Children, Bloomington, Ind., 1960-61; reference clk. Ariz. State U. Library, 1964-66; edn. and psychology librarian N.Mex. State U., 1967-71; Amway distbr., 1973—; cons. solid wastes, distressed land problems reference remedies, 1967; ecology lit. research and cons., 1966—. Ind. observer 1st World Conf. Human Environment, 1972; mem. Las Cruces Community Devel. Priorities Adv. Bd. Mem. ALA, Regional Environ. Edn. Research Info. Orgn., NAFE, P.E.O., D.A.R., Internat. Platform Assn., Las Cruces Antique Car Club, Las Cruces Story League, N.Mex. Library Assn. Methodist (lay leader). Address: 2145 Boise Dr Las Cruces NM 88001-5149

LEASE, MARTIN HARRY, JR., retired political science educator; b. Plainfield, Ind., Aug. 15, 1927; s. Martin Harry and Beatrice Irene (Krebs) L.; m. Jeanne Marie Lachance, Sept. 6, 1969; children—Deborah Eileen, Joshua Martin. B.A., Ind. U., 1953, M.A., 1955, Ph.D., 1961. Instr. polit. sci. U. Miami, Coral Gables, Fla., 1955-56; instr. U. Minn., Duluth, 1957-61, asst. prof., 1961-65, assoc. prof., 1965-70, prof., 1970-94, asst. dean grad. sch., 1968-77, acting acad. vice-provost, 1977-79, polit. sci. dept. head, 1979-83, dir. overseas program, Eng., 1983-84; ret.; vis. lectr. Lakehead U., Thunder Bay, Ont., Can., 1975. Del. Democratic Nat. Conv., 1968; active local party offices including head of Duluth orgn.; election cons. local radio and TV, Duluth; mem. fed. dist. ct. com. on Celebration Bicentennial U.S. Constn. Nat. Ctr. for edn. in Politics fellow, 1962-63. Mem. Western Polit. Sci. Assn. (research group), Minn. Polit. Sci. Assn. (bd. dirs. 1966-68), Ctr. for Study of Presidency. Mem. Democratic Farm Labor Party. Avocations: fishing; gardening. Office: U Minn-Duluth Polit Sci Dept 302 B Cina Hall Duluth MN 55812

LEASE, RICHARD JAY, police science educator, former police officer; b. Cherokee, Ohio, Dec. 10, 1914; s. Harold and Mabelle (Fullerton) L.; m. Marjorie Faye Stoughton, Sept. 2, 1939 (div. Apr. 1957); children: Richard Jay II, William Harley; m. Jane Etta Omer, Jan. 16, 1960; stepchildren: Janet Radifera, Joyce Carson, Julia Marvin, Catherine Warren; adopted children: Alan Fudge, Stephen V. Graham. Student, Wittenberg U., 1932-33; BA, U. Ariz., 1937, MA, 1961; postgrad., Ind. U., 1950, 60, Ariz. State U., 1956, 63-65, 67—; grad., U. Louisville So. Police Inst., 1955. Grad. asst . U. Ariz., Tucson, 1937-38; with Tucson Police Dept., from 1938; advanced from patrolman to sgt., also served as safety officer Pima County Sheriff's Dept., Tucson, 1953, patrol supr., 1953-55, investigator, 1955-56; tchr. sci. pub. schs. Tucson, 1957-59; lectr. dept. police adminstrn. Ind. U., Bloomington, 1960-65; asst. prof. dept. police sci. N.Mex. State U., Las Cruces, 1965—; cons. law enforcement problems HEW, 1960, Indpls. Police Dept., 1962, Harrisburg Community Coll. Police Sci. Dept., 1967, Phoenix Police Dept., 1968—; advisor police tng. programs several small city police depts., Ind., 1960-63, Indpls., 1962; mem. oral bd. for selection chief in Bateville, Ind., 1962, oral bd. for selection sgts. and lts., Las Cruces Police Dept., 1966—. Author: (with Robert F. Borkenstein) Alcohol and Road Traffic: Problems of Enforcement and Prosecution, 1963, The Dreams, Hopes, Recollections and Thoughts of a Professional Good Samaritan; cons. editor Police, various rsch. publs. on chem. intoxification tests, psychol. errors of witnesses, reading disabilities, delinquency. Participant numerous FBI seminars; active youth work, philanthropy, among Am. Indians in Southwest; founder awards outstanding ROTC cadets N.Mex. State U., 1967—; founder Wiltberger ann. awards Nat. Police Combat Pistol Matches; scoutmaster Yucca council Boy Scouts Am., 1966—. Served to 1st lt. USMCR, 1942-45, PTO. Fellow Am. Acad. Forensic Scis. (sec. gen. sect.); mem. Internat. Assn. Chiefs of Police, Internat. Assn. Police Profs., Brit. Acad. Forensic Scis., Can. Soc. Forensic Sci., Am. Soc. Criminology, Ret. Officers Assn., Assn. U.S. Army (2d v.p. 1969—), NEA, N.Mex. Edn. Assn., N.Mex. Police and Sheriffs Assn., Internat. Crossroads, NRA (benefactor mem.), Marine Corps League (life), Sigma Chi. Lodges: Masons, Elks. Home and Office: 2145 Boise Dr Las Cruces NM 88001-5149

LEASE, ROBERT K., lawyer; b. Cleve., 1948. AB magna cum laude, Dartmouth Coll., 1970; JD cum laude, U. Conn., 1976. Bar: Ohio. Ptnr. Baker & Hostetler, Cleve. Mem. Phi Beta Kappa. Office: Baker & Hostetler 3200 Nat City Ctr 1900 E 9th St Cleveland OH 44114-3401

LEASE, RONALD CHARLES, financial economics educator; b. Davenport, Iowa, Feb. 3, 1940; s. Mace Duane and Mary Virginia (Marsh) L.; m. Judy Ellen Gifford, Aug. 24, 1962; 1 child, Tracy Rene. BS in Engring., Colo. Sch. Mines, 1963; MS, Purdue U., 1966, PhD, 1973. Metall. engr. Aluminum Co. Am., 1963-69; prof. U. Utah, Salt Lake City, 1973-86; prof., chmn. Tulane U., New Orleans, 1986-90, endowed prof., assoc. dean, 1988-90; endowed prof. U. Utah, Salt Lake City, 1990—; vis. assoc. prof. U. Chgo., 1978-79; vis. prof. U. Mich., Ann Arbor, 1985-86. Mem. editorial bd. Jour. Fin. Rsch., Phoenix, 1987-93, Fin. Mgmt., Tampa, 1986—, Jour. Corp. Fin., Pitts., 1993—; contbr. articles to profl. jours. Mem. Am. Fin. Assn., Western Fin. Assn., Fin. Mgmt. Assn. (editor Survey and Synthesis in Fin. 1984-90, pres. 1992-93), Phi Kappa Phi, Beta Gamma Sigma. Home: 1409 Spring Ln Salt Lake City UT 84117-6710 Office: U Utah Eccles Sch Bus Salt Lake City UT 84112

LEASK, JOHN MCPHEARSON, II, accountant, author, speaker; b. Bridgeport, Conn., Oct. 21, 1942; s. Haldane Burgess and Laura (Manchester) L.; m. Phoebe Kamelakis, Aug. 19, 1979; 1 child, John McPhearson III; stepchildren: Peter Rizos, Andy Rizos, Joanna Rizos Bogardus. Student U. Mich., 1961-68; AS in Acctg., Bryant Coll., 1973, BS in Acctg., 1974. CPA, Conn. Salesman for Conn. and R.I., Winthrop Lab., NYC, 1969-73; staff acct. Leask & Leask, P.C., Fairfield, Conn., 1973-75, v.p., 1976-80, audit prin., chmn. bd., mng. prin., 1980—, also dir.; adj. prof. Fairfield U., 1976—. Contbg. editor CPA Client Svc. Mem. Libr. Bldg. Com., Fairfield, 1981-83, allocations council United Way, Bridgeport, Conn., 1982-91; co-pres. Am. Field Service Parents Group, 1988-89; chmn. Fairfield Festival of Arts, 1983, 86-91; vice chmn. East Providence Town Com., 1971-73; chmn. audit com. Congregationalist Ch., 1986—. Recipient Vol. award United Way, 1983, Score Citation, SBA Citation. Fellow Conn. Soc. CPAs (mgmt. acctg. practice com. 1985-88, 90-94, mem. state taxation com. 1987-88, CPE com. 1985-86, 93-94); mem. Am. Inst. CPAs, Fairfield C. of C. (pres. 1983-84, Harold Harris Cmty. Svc. award 1991). Republican. Congregationalist. Club: Rotary (Citation Meritorious Svc. Found. Rotary Internat. 1993, Paul Harris Cmty. Svc. award 1988, Paul Harris fellow 1988, 95, Disting. Svc. award, Fairfield treas. 1983-87, v.p. programs 1987-88, chpt. 1st v.p., 1988-89, pres. 1989—, treas. dist. 798 1988-90, various dist. offices 1990-94, gov. R.I. dist. #7980 1995—). Office: Leask & Leask PC CPAs PO Box 159 Fairfield CT 06430-0159

LEASON, JODY JACOBS, newspaper columnist; b. Margarita, Venezuela, June 8, 1926; came to U.S., 1928; d. Jose Cruz Caceres and Graciela Rodriguez; m. Russell L. Jacobs (div.); 1 child, Jessica Jacobs Vitti; m. Barney Leason, Dec. 29, 1976. BA, Hunter Coll., 1940's. Assoc. fashion editor Women's Wear Daily, N.Y.C., 1969-70; West Coast fashion editor Women's Wear Daily, Los Angeles, 1957-69; London fashion editor Women's Wear Daily, N.Y.C., 1970-72; soc. editor L.A. Times, 1972-86. Author: (novel) The Right Circles, 1988. Avocations: needlework, gardening.

LEATH, KENNETH THOMAS, research plant pathologist, educator, agricultural consultant; b. Providence, Apr. 29, 1931; s. Thomas and Elizabeth (Wootten) L.; m. Marie Andreozzi, Aug. 1955; children: Kenneth, Steven, Kevin, Maria Beth. BS, U. R.I., 1959; MS, PhD, U. Minn., 1966. Rsch. plant pathologist U.S. Regional Pasture Rsch. Lab. USDA-ARS, 1966-94; prof. Pa. State U., 1966-94; pvt. agrl. cons. Boalsburg, Pa., 1994—; advisor numerous state and nat. orgns. Contbr. numerous articles to profl. jours. and chpts. to books. With USN, 1951-55. Mem. Elks. Achievements include research on root diseases and systemic wilts of forage species.

LEATHAM, JOHN TONKIN, business executive; b. Chgo., July 4, 1936; s. Chester and Betty (Collins) L.; m. Sheila K. Andersen, Sept. 13, 1958; children: Lisa M., John A., Bronwen Gay, Douglas Q. B.A., Lawrence U., Appleton, Wis., 1958. Asst. cashier, lending officer Continental Ill. Nat. Bank & Trust Co., Chgo., 1962-68; with Reliance Group, Inc., N.Y.C., 1968-79; sr. v.p., chief financial officer Reliance Group, Inc., 1971-72, exec. v.p., chief operating and chief financial officer, 1972-79, dir., mem. exec. com., 1974-79; investment and merchant banker, 1979—; chmn., dir. Security Health Managed Care, Inc., 1994—; vice chmn., dir. CliniCorp, Inc., West Palm Beach, Fla., 1992-94; pres., CEO Clinicorp Midwest, Inc., 1992-93; bd. dirs., mng. dir. Scuul Ltd.; trustee Endowment Realty Investors Inc., 1987—; nat. dir. Reading is FUN-damental, Inc., 1975-91. Trustee Lawrence U., 1981—, chmn., 1990-92; trustee The Common Fund, 1987—, Endowment Advisers, Inc., Fairfield Ptnrs., Inc., 1990—, chmn., 1992—. 1st lt. USAF, 1958-62. Decorated Air Force Commendation medal. Mem. Lawrence U. Alumni Assn. (v.p. 1963-70, dir. 1963-71). Home: 1925 Calvin Ct Deerfield IL 60015-1636

LEATHER, VICTORIA POTTS, college librarian; b. Chattanooga, June 12, 1947; d. James Elmer Potts and Ruby Lea (Bettis) Potts Wilmoth; m. Jack Edward Leather; children: Stephen, Sean. BA cum laude, U. Chattanooga, 1968; MSLS, U. Tenn., 1978. Libr. asst. East New Orleans Regional Libr., 1969-71; libr. Erlanger Nursing Sch., Chattanooga, 1971-75; chief libr. Erlanger Hosp., Chattanooga, 1975-77; dir. Eastgate Br. Libr., Chattanooga, 1977-81; dir. libr. svcs. Chattanooga State Tech. Community Coll., 1981—. Mem. Allied Arts, Hunter Mus., High Mus. Art. Mem. ALA, Southeastern Libr. Assn., Tenn. Libr. Assn. (chair legislation com.), Chattanooga Area Libr. Assn. (pres. 1978-79), Tenn. Bd. Regents Media Consortium (chair 1994-95), Phi Delta Kappa. Episcopalian. Avocations: reading, needlework, traveling.

LEATHERBARROW, DAVID, architecture department chair. Chair architecture dept. U. Pa., Phila. Office: U Pa 34th & Spruce St Philadelphia PA 19104*

LEATHERBEE, WILLIAM BELL, architect; b. Hanover, N.H., Apr. 13, 1938; s. John Howland and Helen Luscombe (Ullmann) L.; m. Tabitha Susan Allen, July 2, 1960 (div. 1987); children: Lydia Leah, Rachel Lyn. BA, Harvard Coll., 1959; MArch, U. Pa., 1963. Registered architect, Pa., N.J., Md.; lic. planner, N.J. Designer H2L2 Architects/Planners, Phila., 1963-64, Vincent G. Kling Assocs., Phila., 1964-65; architect Bower & Fradley Architects, Phila., 1965-68; project mgr. Richard Martin & Assocs., Phila., 1968-69; pvt. practice Phila., 1969—; pres. Benezet Ct., Inc., Phila., 1973-80; archtl. critic, instr. Drexel U., Phila., 1972-83. Prin. works include rehabilitation of low income single family houses Allegheny West Found., 1993, Group Home for Boys, Phila., 1991, S.W. Sr. Ctr. for Phila. Corp. for Aging, 1989; cons. architect for shopping ctrs., N.C., S.C., Kans. Dir., chmn. properties and bldgs. coms. Boys and Girls Clubs Phila., 1984—. Lt. comdr. USCGR Reserve, 1959-70. Recipient award for excellence in masonry design Delaware Valley Masonry Inst., 1978, Legion of Honor award Chapel of the Four Chaplains, 1985. Mem. AIA (dir. Phila. chpt. 1983-84, Am. Arbitration Assn., Nat. Trust for Historic Preservation, Nat. Assn. Housing and Redevel. Ofcls. (dir., treas. 1974-90), Pa. Soc. Architects AIA (Dist. Bldg. award 1972). Avocations: sailing, skiing, gardening. Office: Leatherbee & Assocs Architects & Planners 1504 South St Philadelphia PA 19146-1636

LEATHERDALE, DOUGLAS WEST, insurance company executive; b. Morden, Man., Can., Dec. 6, 1936; came to U.S., 1968; s. Walter West and Lena Elizabeth (Gilligan) L.; children—Mary Jo, Christopher. B.A., United Coll., Winnipeg, Man., 1957. Investment analyst, officer Gt. West Life Assurance Co., Winnipeg, 1957-68; assoc. exec. sec. Bd. Pensions, Luth. Ch., Mpls., 1968-72; exec. v.p., then v.p. St. Paul Investment Mgmt. Co., subs. St. Paul Cos., Inc., 1972-77; v.p.-fin. St. Paul Cos., Inc., 1974-81, sr. v.p.-fin., 1981-82, exec. v.p., 1982-89, also dir., pres., chief oper. officer, 1989-90, chmn., pres., chief exec. officer, 1990—; bd. dirs. St. Paul Fire and Marine Ins. Co., St. Paul Land Resources, Inc., St. Paul Real Estate of Ill., Inc., John Nuveen & Co. Inc., St. Paul Properties, Inc., St. Paul Oil and Gas Corp., St. Paul Fire & Marine Ins. Co. (U.K.) Ltd., St. Paul Mercury Ins. Co., St. Paul Guardian Ins. Co., St. Paul Surplus Lines Ins. Co., Nat. Ins. Wholesalers, Atwater McMillian, 77 Water St., Inc., Ramsey Ins. Co., St. Paul Risk Services, Inc., St. Paul Plymouth Ctr., Inc. Athena Assurance Co., St. Paul Fin. Group, Inc., Graham Resources, Inc., Carlyle Capital, L.P., United HealthCare Corp. Mem. Twin Cities Soc. Security Analysts, Fin. Execs. Inst. Club: Minnesota (St. Paul). Avocation: horses. Office: St Paul Cos Inc 385 Washington St Saint Paul MN 55102-1309*

LEATHERMAN, HUGH KENNETH, SR., state senator, business executive; b. Lincoln County, N.C., Apr. 14, 1931; s. John Bingham and Ada Annis (Gantt) L.; m. Jean Helms, Nov. 11, 1978; children: Sheila Dianne, Hugh Kenneth, Karen Ann, Joyce Lynn, Amy Jean, Sarah Ada. BS in Civil Engring., N.C. State U., 1953; HHD (hon.), Francis Marion Coll., 1987. Engr., then sec. Florence (S.C.) Concrete Products Inc., 1955-72, pres., 1972-93; sec. Hugh-Stan Inc., Myrtle Beach, 1974—; mem. S.C. Senate, 1980—; commr. S.C. Dept. Consumer Affairs. Deacon 1st Bapt. Ch. Named Legislator of Yr., 1982. Home: 1817 Pineland Ave Florence SC 29501-5419 Office: 205 Gressette Bldg Columbia SC 29202

LEAVENGOOD, VICTOR PRICE, telephone company executive; b. Ocala, Fla., June 2, 1924; s. Hansel Devane and Mildred (Price) L.; m. Elizabeth Lee Bird, Sept. 12, 1950; children: Sally (dec.), Ann, Hansel. BSBA, U. Fla., 1947; MBA, Harvard U., 1949. Bus. mgr. Ocala (Fla.) Star Banner (daily newspaper), 1952-59; circulation dir. Tampa (Fla.) Tribune, 1959-60, dir. community affairs, 1960-64; asst. v.p. Gen. Telephone Co. Fla., Tampa, 1964-70; sec., treas. Gen. Telephone Co. Fla., 1970-87; bd. dirs. Blue Cross Blue Shield Fla. Pres. Hills County Cmty. Coordination Coun., 1964-65, Tampa Econ. Opportunity Coun., 1965-66, Fla. Clergy Econ. Edn. Found., 1964-68, Fla. chpt. United Way, 1969-70; bd. dirs., treas. Fla. Aquarium, Hospice of Hillsborough, Fla.; bd. dirs. West Ctrl. Fla. Area Agy. on Aging, Japan-Am. Soc. Ctrl. Fla., Suncoast coun. Girl Scouts U.S.A.; bd. advisors U. South Fla. Contemporary Art Mus.; trustee Fla. Mental Health Inst.; chmn. Tampa Bay Internat. Super Task Force, Fla. Mcht. Assn., Tampa Commn. on Pub. Art; pres. United Fund Greater Tampa Inc., 1964-68, treas., 1970-75; mem. Fla. Coun. Mental Health Tng. and Rsch., 1967-74, President's Round Table, Eckerd Coll., St. Petersburg, Fla., 1969—; mem. president's coun. U. South Fla., 1974—, Hillsborough County Hosp. Authority; treas. U. South Fla. Found., 1957-80, pres., 1982-83. Comdr. USNR, 1942-47. Mem. Greater Tampa C. of C. (bd. dirs.), Fla. C. of C., edn. com. 1968-71), U.S. C. of C. (edn. com.), Phi Eta Sigma, Phi Delta Theta.; mem. Ye Mystic Krewe of Gasparilla. Democrat. Methodist (ofcl. bd.). Clubs: University (Tampa), Tampa, Tampa Yacht and Country (Tampa). Home: 4516 W Sylvan Ramble St Tampa FL 33609-4214

LEAVITT, AUDREY FAYE COX, television programming executive; b. Old Hickory, Tenn., June 1, 1932; d. James Aubrey and Bernice (Hudnall) Cox; student David Lipscomb Secondary Sch. and Coll., 1947, Tenn. Sch. Broadcasting, 1949-50, Vanderbilt U., 1948-50; children: Jack, Teresa. Woman commentator, continuity chief radio sta. WGNS, Murfreesboro, Tenn., 1949-50; announcer, continuity chief, traffic dir. Sta. KDWT, Stamford, Tex., 1950-51; sales account exec. Sta. KMAC, San Antonio, 1952; continuity chief, announcer Sta. KEYL-TV, San Antonio, 1952-54, also firm dir.; film buyer, mgr. Sta. WOAI-TV, San Antonio, 1954-68, ops. mgr. film, video-tape traffic, continuity, 1968-71; film and videotape operations mgr., film buyer Sta. KENS-TV, San Antonio, 1972-79; exec. v.p. Jim Thomas & Assocs., San Antonio, 1979-80; owner Communique Internationalé, TV programming syndication, 1981—, Faye Leavitt Advt., 1990—, Strategic Planning Services; exec. producer TV series The Lone Star Sportsman Show; writer, exec. producer and dir. TV series Weather or Not; writer, producer gourmet cooking show For Men Only, The Great Age, 1988; hostess radio series Our Turn, 1994—. Pub. rels dir., advt. dir. The Madison Retirement Community, San Antonio, 1991—. Mem. NAFE, Nat. Pub. Rels. Soc., Internat. Platform Assn., Alamo Heights C. of C. (bd. dirs.), San Antonio Conservation Soc., San Antonio Livestock and Rodeo Exposition, San Antonio Apt. Assn. (publicity chmn.), Yellow Rose Tex., World Affairs Council. Office: PO Box 6493 San Antonio TX 78209-0493

LEAVITT, CHARLES LOYAL, English language educator, administrator; b. Randolph, Maine, Apr. 30, 1921; s. Charles Warren Franklin and Alice Mabel (Sparrow) L.; m. Emily Raymond Stewart, June 12, 1951 (dec. 1966); m. Virginia Louise Kracke, Sept. 6, 1969. Diploma in Edn., U. Maine, Farmington, 1941; BS in Edn., U. So. Maine, 1946; MA in English, Boston U., 1947; PhD in English, U. Wis., 1961; MLS, Columbia U., 1969. Cert. tchr. English and history, elem., secondary, coll. Tchr. pub. schs., Vanceboro, Maine, 1941-42; tchr., prin. pub. schs., York Village, Maine, 1945-47; Instr. English and history Endicott Jr. Coll., Beverly, Mass., 1947-48; assoc. prof. English Lyndon State Coll., Lyndon Center, Vt., 1948-53, 54-55; teaching asst. in English U. Wis., Madison, 1953-54, 55-59; instr. Wayne State U., Detroit, 1959-61; assoc. prof. Montclair (N.J.) State Coll, 1961-68; v.p., sec., dir. edn. Universal Learning Corp., N.Y.C., 1968-69; assoc. dir. admissions Sarah Lawrence Coll., Bronxville, N.Y., 1970-71; dir. continuing edn., asst. dean, prof. Bloomfield (N.J.) Coll., 1971-74; chmn. liberal arts, prof. Coll. of Ins., N.Y.C., 1975-86, prof. emeritus, 1987—; adj. prof. English Fairleigh Dickinson U., Teaneck, N.J., 1988-92. Author: Ten Lit. Study Guides, 1964-66; cons. editor Monarch Lit. Guides, N.Y.C., 1963-68; author chpt. in book. Treas. Youth Community Funds, York Village, Maine, 1946-47; asst. scoutmaster Boy Scouts Am., York Village, 1946-47; v.p. Overseas Neighbors, Montclair, 1974-75; tchr. Adult Sch. of Montclair, 1963-68. With USAAF, 1942-45. Named Most Popular Prof., Montclair State Coll., 1967, Prof. of Yr., Coll. of Ins., 1978; yearbook dedications Lyndon State Coll., 1950, Bloomfield Coll., 1974, Coll. of Ins., 1987; Nat. Audubon scholar, Garden Clubs York Village, 1947. Mem. AAUP, MLA, Coll. English Assn., Internat. Platform Assn., Princeton Club (N.Y.C.), Faculty Columbia U. Club, New Eng. Soc. N.Y.C. Club, Kiwanis (trustee Manhattan found. 1989—). Republican. Baptist. Home: 93 Stonebridge Rd Montclair NJ 07042-1632 Office: One Insurance Pla 101 Murray St New York NY 10007-2132

LEAVITT, DANA GIBSON, management consultant; b. Framingham, Mass., Dec. 4, 1925; s. Luther C. and Margaret (Gibson) L.; m. Frances Smith, Apr. 12, 1952; children: Margaret Gibson, Jonathan. BA, Brown U., 1948; postgrad., Harvard U. Bus. Sch., 1954-55. Home office rep. Aetna Life Ins. Co., Boston, also Long Beach, Calif., 1949-54; v.p., sec.-treas., exec. v.p. N. Am. Title Ins. Co., Oakland, Calif., 1955-64; pres. Transam. Title Ins. Co., Oakland, 1964-72; v.p. Transam. Corp., 1969-71, group v.p., 1971-77, exec. v.p., 1977-81; bd. dirs. Chgo. Title and Trust Co., Chgo. Title Ins. Co., World Minerals, Inc., Am. Ctr. for Wine, Food and the Arts, Napa Valley, Calif., pres., 1994-66. Bd. dirs. Children's Hosp. Med. Ctr. and Found., 1969-72; trustee Lewis and Clark Coll., Portland, Oreg., 1972-75, Queen of Valley Hosp., Napa, Calif., 1988-90, Nat. Wildflower Rsch. Ctr., Austin, Tex., 1988—, pres., 1990-94, Brown U., Providence, 1973-78, trustee emeritus, 1978—. With USMCR, WWII. Mem. World Presidents Orgn. (bd. dirs. 1986), Delta Kappa Epsilon. Republican. Clubs: Brown U. of No. Calif, Harvard Bus. Sch. of No. Calif, Napa Valley Country; Bohemian (San Francisco). Office: 2201 3rd Ave N Napa CA 94558-3836

LEAVITT, DAVID ADAM, writer; b. Pitts., June 23, 1961; s. Harold Jack and Gloria (Rosenthal) L. BA, Yale U., 1983. Reader, editorial asst. Viking-Penguin Inc., N.Y.C., 1983-84. Author: Family Dancing, 1984 (Nat. Book Critics Cir. award nomination 1984, PEN-Faulkner award nomination 1985), The Lost Language of Cranes, 1986, Equal Affections, 1988, A Place I've Never Been, 1990, While England Sleeps, 1993; co-editor: The Penguin Book of Gay Short Fiction, 1994; contbr. to periodicals including Esquire, Harper's, New Yorker, N.Y. Times Book Rev., Village Voice, others. Recipient Willets prize for fiction Yale U., 1982, O. Henry Award, 1984; Nat. Endowment for Arts grantee, 1985; vis. fgn. writer Inst. Catalan Letters, Barcelona Spain, 1989; Guggenheim fellow, 1990. Mem. PEN.

LEAVITT, HAROLD JACK, management educator; b. Lynn, Mass., Jan. 14, 1922; s. Joseph and May (Lopata) L.; m. Gloria Rosenthal, Jan. 31, 1943 (dec.); children—John, Emily, David; m. Jean Lipman-Blumen. B.A., Harvard Coll., 1943; M.S., Brown U., 1944; Ph.D., Mass. Inst. Tech., 1949. Asst. prof. psychology Rensselaer Poly. Inst., 1949-50; assoc. prof. Sch. Bus., U. Chgo., 1954-58; prof. indsl. adminstrn. and psychology GSIA, Carnegie Inst. Tech., 1958-66; Walter Kenneth Kilpatrick prof. orgn. behavior and psychology Grad. Sch. Bus., Stanford U., 1966-90, prof. emeritus, 1990; vis. prof. London Grad. Sch. Bus. Studies, 1972; v.p. Nejelski & Co., 1951-53; cons. European Prod. Agy., Paris, 1956; faculty prin. Mgmt. Analysis Ctr., Inc., 1971—. Author: (with H. Bahrami) Managerial Psychology, 5th edit., 1988, (with W. Dill and H. Eyring) The Organizational World, 1973, Corporate Pathfinders, 1986; co-editor: Organizations of the Future, 1974. Served to lt. (j.g.) USNR, 1944-46. Fellow Am. Psychol. Assn. Home: 1520 E California Blvd Pasadena CA 91106-4104 Office: Stanford U Grad Sch Bus Stanford CA 94305

LEAVITT, JEFFREY STUART, lawyer; b. Cleve., July 13, 1946; s. Sol and Esther (Dolinsky) L.; m. Ellen Fern Sugerman, Dec. 21, 1968; children: Matthew Adam, Joshua Aaron. AB, Cornell U., 1968; JD, Case Western Res. U., 1973. Bar: Ohio 1973. Assoc. Jones, Day, Reavis & Pogue, Cleve., 1973-80, ptnr., 1981—. Contbr. articles to profl. jours. Trustee Bur. Jewish Edn., Cleve., 1981-93, v.p. 1985-87; trustee Fairmount Temple, Cleve., 1982—, v.p. 1985-90, pres., 1990-93; trustee Citizens League Greater Cleve., 1982-89, 92-94, pres., 1987-89; trustee Citizens League Rsch. Inst., Cleve., 1989—, Great Lakes Region of Union Am. Hebrew Congregations, 1990-93; mem. bd. gov. Case Western Res. Law Sch. Alumni Assn., 1989-92; sec. Kulas Found., 1986-88, 93—, asst. treas., 1989-92. Mem. ABA (employee benefits coms. 1976—), Midwest Pension Conf. Jewish. Home: 25961 Annesley Rd Cleveland OH 44122-2437 Office: Jones Day Reavis & Pogue N Point 901 Lakeside Ave E Cleveland OH 44114-1116

LEAVITT, JEROME EDWARD, childhood educator; b. Verona, N.J., Aug. 1, 1916; s. Thomas Edward and Clara Marie (Sonn) L.; m. Florence Elizabeth Wilkins, Aug. 23, 1963. B.S., Newark State Coll., 1938; M.A., N.Y. U., 1942; Ed.D., Northwestern U., 1952. Tchr. pub. schs. Roslyn Heights, N.Y., 1938-42; instr. Sperry Gyroscope, Bklyn., 1942-45; prin., supr. pub. schs. Los Alamos, N.Mex., 1945-49; prof. edn., exec. asst. to dean Portland (Oreg.) State U., 1952-66; prof. edn. U. Ariz., Tucson, 1966-69; prof. elem. edn., coordinator Child Abuse Project, Calif. State U., Fresno, 1969-81; pres. Jerome Leavitt, Inc., 1981—. Author: Nursery-Kindergarten Edn., 1958, Carpentry for Children, 1959, By Land, By Sea, By Air, 1969, The Beginning Kindergarten Teacher, 1971, America and Its Indians, 1971, The Battered Child, 1974, Herbert Sonn: Yosemite's Birdman, 1975, Child Abuse and Neglect: Research and Innovation, 1983, others; contbr. articles to profl. jours. Mem. ASCD (life), NEA (life), Assn. Childhood Edn. Internat. (life), Soc.Profs. Edn., Calif. Tchrs. Assn., Profs. Curriculum, Phi Delta Kappa, Kappa Delta Pi, Epsilon Pi Tau. Home and Office: Villa Campana 6653 E Carondelet Dr Apt 124 Tucson AZ 85710-2138

LEAVITT, MARTIN JACK, lawyer; b. Detroit, Mar. 30, 1940; s. Benjamin and Annette (Cohen) L.; m. Janice C. (McCreary) Leavitt; children: Michael J., Paul J., David A., Dean N., Keleigh R. LLB, Wayne State U., 1964. Bar: Mich. 1965, Fla. 1967. Assoc. Robert A. Sullivan, Detroit, 1968-70; officer, bd. dirs. Law Offices Sullivan & Leavitt, Northville, Mich., 1970—, pres., 1979—; bd. dirs. Tyrone Hills of Mich., Premiere Video, Inc., The Keim Group, Ltd., Guardian Home Warranty Corp., others. Lt. comdr., USNR, 1959-64. Detroit Edison Upper Class scholar, 1958-64. Mem. ABA, Mich. Bar Assn., Fla. Bar Assn., Transp. Lawyers Assn., ICC Practitioners, Meadowbrook Country Club, Huron River Hunting & Fishing Club (past pres.), Rolls Royce Owners Club (bd. dirs.). Jewish. Office: Sullivan and Leavitt PC PO Box 400 Northville MI 48167-0997

LEAVITT, MARY JANICE DEIMEL, special education educator, civic worker; b. Washington, Aug. 21, 1924; d. Henry L. and Ruth (Grady) Deimel; BA, Am. U., Washington, 1946; postgrad. U. Md., 1963-65, U. Va., 1965-67, 72-73, 78-79, George Washington U., 1966-67; tchr.'s cert. spl. edn., 1968; m. Robert Walker Leavitt, Mar. 30, 1945; children: Michael Deimel, Robert Walker, Caroline Ann Leavitt Snyder. Tchr., Rothery Sch., Arlington, Va., 1947; dir. Sunnyside, Children's House, Washington, 1949; asst. dir. Coop. Sch. for Handicapped Children, Arlington, 1962, dir., Arlington, Springfield, Va., 1963-66; tchr. mentally retarded children Fairfax (Va.) County Pub. Schs., 1966-68; asst. dir. Burgundy Farm Country Day Sch., Alexandria, Va., 1968-69; tchr., substitute tchr. specific learning problem children Accotink Acad., Springfield, Va., 1970-80; substitute tchr. learning disabilities Children's Achievement Center, McLean, Va., 1973-82, Psychiat. Inst., Washington and Rockville, Md., 1976-82, Home-Bound and Substitute Program, Fairfax, Va., 1978-84; asst. info. specialist Ednl. Research Service, Inc., Rosslyn, Va., 1974-76; docent Sully Plantation, Fairfax County (Va.) Park Authority, 1981-87, 88-94, Childrens Learning Ctrs., vol. Honor Roll, 1987, Walney-Collections Fairfax County (Va.) Park Authority, 1989—; sec. Widowed Persons Service, 1983-85, mem., 1985—. Mem. edn. subcom. Va. Commn. Children and Youth, 1973-74; Den mother Nat. Capital Area Cub Scouts, Boy Scouts Am., 1962; troop fund raising chmn. Nat. Capitol coun. Girl Scouts U.S.A., 1968-69; capt. amblyopia team No. Va. chpt. Delta Gamma Alumnae, 1969; vol. Prevention of Blindness, 1980—; fund raiser Martha Movement, 1977-78; mem. St. John's Mus. Art, Wilmington, N.C., 1989—, Corcoran Gallery Art, Washington, 1989-90, 94—, Brunswick County Literacy Coun., N.C., 1989—; mem. search com. St. Andrews Episc. Ch., Burke, Va., 1996. Recipient award Nat. Assn. for Retarded Citizens, 1975, Sully Recognition gift, 1989, Ten Yr. recognition pin Honor Roll, 1990. Mem. AAUW (co-chmn. met. area mass media com. D.C. chpt. 1973-75, v.p. Alexandria br. 1974-76, fellowship co-chmn., historian Springfield-Annandale br. 1979-80, 89-94, 94-95, name grantee ednl. found. 1980, cultural co-chmn. 1983-84), Assn. Part-Time Profls. (co-chmn. Va. local groups, job devel. and membership asst. 1981), Older Women's League, Nat. Mus. of Women in the Arts (charter mem.), Delta Gamma (treas. No. Va. alumnae chpt. 1973-75, pres. 1977-79, found. chmn. 1979-81, Katie Hale award 1989, treas. House Corp. Am. U. Beta Epsilon chpt. 1994—). Club: Mil. Dist. of Washington Officer's Clubs (Ft. McNair, Ft. Myer). Episcopalian. Home: 7129 Rolling Forest Ave Springfield VA 22152-3622

LEAVITT, MICHAEL OKERLUND, governor, insurance executive; b. Cedar City, Utah, Feb. 11, 1951; s. Dixie and Anne (Okerlund) L.; m. Jacalyn Smith; children: Michael Smith, Taylor Smith, Anne Marie Smith, Chase Smith, Weston Smith. BA, So. Utah U., 1978. CPCU. Sales rep. Leavitt Group, Cedar City, 1972-74, account exec., 1974-76; mgr. underwriting Salt Lake City, 1976-82; chief operating officer, 1982-84, pres., chief exec. officer, 1984—, gov., state of Utah, 1993—; bd. dirs. Pacificorp, Portland, Oreg., Utah Power and Light Co., Salt Lake City, Great Western Thrift and Loan, Salt Lake City. Utah Bd. Regents, chmn. instl. coun. So. Utah State U., Cedar City, 1985-89; campaign chmn. U.S. Sen. Orrin Hatch, 1982, 88, U.S. Sen. Jake Garn, 1980, 86; cons. campaign Gov. Norman Angerter, 1984; mem. staff Reagan-Bush '84. 2d lt. USNG, 1969-77. Named Disting. Alumni So. Utah State Coll. Sch. Bus., 1986. Mem. Chartered Property Casualty Underwriters. Republican. Mormon. Avocation: golf. Office: Office of the Governor 210 State Capitol Building Salt Lake City UT 84114-1202*

LEAVITT, MICHAEL P(AUL), performing arts manager and concert producer; b. N.Y.C., Dec. 9, 1944; s. Harry and Bertha (Mandell) L.; m. Nancy J. Redden, April 2, 1964; children: Amy, Sarah. BA, Kans. Wesleyan U., 1965; MA, Queens Coll., 1967; M in Philosophy, CUNY, 1975. Adminstrv. dir. Gregg Smith Singers, N.Y.C., 1978-79; exec. dir. Horizon Concerts, N.Y.C., 1978-79; mng. dir. Allied Artists Bur., N.Y.C., 1979—, Beethoven Soc., 1979-85, Empire Music Group, Inc., N.Y.C., 1990—; mng. dir. MPL Advt. for Arts, N.Y.C., 1981—; pres. MPL Prodns. Mem. Music Library Assn., Nat. Assn. Performing Arts Mgrs. and Agts. Home: 195 Steamboat Rd Great Neck NY 11024-1739 Office: Empire Music Group Inc 170 W 74th St New York NY 10023-2350

LEAVITT, THOMAS WHITTLESEY, museum director, educator; b. Boston, Jan. 8, 1930; s. Richard C. and Helen M. (Pratt) L.; m. Jane O. Ayer, June 23, 1951 (div. 1969); children: Katherine, Nancy, Hugh; m. Lloyd B. Carter, Sept. 14, 1978 (div. 1985); mem. Michele C. McDonald, Apr. 20, 1991; children: Zachary Leavitt, Collin McDonald. A.B., Middlebury (Vt.) Coll., 1951; M.A., Boston U., 1952; Ph.D., Harvard, 1958. Asst. to dir. Fogg Mus., Harvard, 1954-56; exec. dir. fine arts com. People to People Program, 1957; dir. Pasadena (Calif.) Art Mus., 1957-63, dir. Santa Barbara (Calif.) Mus. Art, 1963-68; dir. Andrew Dickson White Mus. Art, Cornell U., Ithaca, N.Y., 1968-73, Herbert F. Johnson Mus. Art, 1973-91; univ. prof. history art Cornell U., 1968-91, prof. emeritus, 1991—; interim dir. R.I. Sch. Design Mus. of Art, 1993-94, Newport Art Mus., 1994-95; Dir. mus. program Nat. Endowment for Arts, 1971-72, mem. museum panel, 1972-75; vice chmn. Council on Museums and Edn. in Visual Arts, 1972-76; trustee Gallery Assn. N.Y. State, 1972-78; mem. mus. panel N.Y. State Council Arts, 1975-78, 1980-82; chmn. art adv. com. Nat. Air and Space Mus., 1988—. Author exhbn. catalogs, articles. Trustee Am. Fedn. Arts, 1972-91, Newport Art Mus., 1995—; bd. dirs. Am. Arts Alliance, 1976-82, Ind. Sector, 1980-84; bd. govs. N.E. Mus. Conf., 1973-76; trustee Williamstown Regional Art Conservation Lab., 1979-91, pres., 1984-87. Mem. Assn. Art Mus. Dirs. (pres. 1977-78, trustee 1978-80), Am. Assn. Museums (council 1976-79, v.p. 1980-82, pres. 1982-85). Home: 25 Waterway Rd Saunderstown RI 02874-3906

LEAVY, EDWARD, judge; m. Eileen Leavy; children: Thomas, Patrick, Mary Kay, Paul. AB, U. Portland, 1950, LLB, U. Notre Dame, 1953. Dist. judge Lane County, Eugene, Oreg., 1957-61, cir. judge, 1961-76; magistrate U.S. Dist. Ct. Oreg., Portland, 1976-84, judge, 1984-87, cir. judge U.S. Ct. Appeals (9th cir.), 1987—. Office: US Ct Appeals Pioneer Courthouse 555 SW Yamhill St Ste 216 Portland OR 97204-1323

LEAVY, HERBERT THEODORE, publisher; b. Detroit, July 10, 1927; s. Morris and Thelma (Davidson) L.; m. Patricia J. Moran, June 20, 1953; children: Karen, Kathryn, Jill, Jacqueline. B.S. in Journalism, Ohio U., 1951. Supervisory editor Fawcett Books, N.Y.C., 1951-60; v.p., editorial dir. Davis Publs., N.Y.C., 1960-69; founder, pres. Internat. Evaluations, Haup-page, N.Y., 1969-70; pub. dir. Countrywide Publs. Inc., N.Y.C., 1970-75; pres. Communications Devel. Co., N.Y.C., 1975-79; editorial dir. Watson-Guptil Publs., N.Y.C., 1979-80; pres. Books from Mags., Inc., Smithtown, N.Y., 1980—, Resumes Unltd., Smithtown, 1984—. Author: 101 Fast Track Resumes, The Pleasure, Executive Handbook, Vegetarian Times Cookbook, McCall's Houseplant and Indoor Landscaping Guide, Working Mother Cookbook, Carpentry, Shoe and Leather Repair at Home, The Complete Book of Beards and Moustaches, Air Conditioning-Repair and Maintenance, Designing and Building Beds, Lofts and Sleeping Areas, Wallcovering, Floor Stripping and Refinishing, Packing and Moving, Recreational Vehicles, Appliance Repair, Plumbing Handbook, Successful Small Farms; numerous others. 1st sgt. USAF, 1945-47. Mem. Sales Exec. Club, Am. Soc. Mag. Editors, Nat. Sporting Goods Assn., Am. Mgmt. Assn., Mag. Advts. Sales Club, Electronics Press Club, U.S. Tennis Ct. and Track Builders Assn., Am. Motorcycle Assn., Am. Horse Council, Authors Guild, Motorcycle Industry Council, Nat. Indoor Tennis Assn., Bus./Profl. Advt. Assn., Sigma Delta Chi. Office: Resumes Unlimited 222 E Main St Ste 107A Smithtown NY 11787

LEB, ARTHUR STERN, lawyer; b. Cleve., June 26, 1930; s. Ernest A. and Bertha (Stern) L.; m. Lois Shafron, Oct. 21, 1932; children: Gerald P., Judith A., Robert B. AB, Columbia Coll., 1952; JD, Case Western Res. U., 1955. Bar: Ohio 1955, U.S. Supreme Ct., 1965. Ptnr. Leb & Halm, Canton, Ohio, 1961-84, Amerman, Burt & Jones, L.P.A., Canton, 1985-90, Buckingham, Doolittle & Burroughs, 1991—; founding mem., exec. com. Ohio Coun. Sch. Bd. Attys., 1976-84, pres. 1983. Served to 1st lt. JAGC, USAF, 1955-57. Recipient Merit award Ohio Legal Ctr. Inst., 1964. Fellow Ohio Bar Found.; mem. ABA, Stark County Bar Assn. (pres. 1985-86), Ohio Bar Assn.

LEBADANG, artist; b. Vietnam, 1922. Student, Sch. Fine Arts, Toulouse, France. Exhibited in group shows Cin. Art Mus., Newman Contemporary Art Gallery, Phila., Galerie Fontaine, Paris, Frost and Reed Gallery, London, Wonderbank Gallery, Frankfurt, Germany; represented in permanent collections Univ. Art Gallery, Lund, Sweden, Phoenix Art Mus., also pvt. and corp. collections. Address: care Circle Gallery 2501 San Diego Ave San Diego CA 92110

LEBANO, EDOARDO ANTONIO, foreign language educator; b. Palmanova, Italy, Jan. 17, 1934; s. Nicola and Flora (Puccioni) L.; came to U.S., 1957, naturalized, 1961; m. Mary Vangeli, 1957; children: Tito Nicola, Mario Antonio. Student Biennio, U. Florence, 1955; M.A., Catholic U. Am., 1961, Ph.D., 1966. Tchr. high sch., Florence, Italy, 1955-57; Italian lang. specialist Bur. Programs and Standards, CSC, Washington, 1958; lang. instr. Sch. Langs., Fgn. Services Inst., Dept. State, Washington, 1959-61; lectr. Italian, U. Va., Charlottesville, 1961-66; asst. prof. Italian, U. Wis.-Milw., 1966-69; assoc. prof., assoc. chmn. dept. French and Italian, 1969-71; assoc. prof. dept. French and Italian, Ind. U., Bloomington, 1971-83, prof., 1983—, dir. Scuola Italiana, Middlebury Coll., Vt., 1987-95. Author: A Look at Italy, 1976; Buon giorno a tutti, 1983; L'Insegnamento dell'italiano nei colleges e nelle universita del nordamerica, 1983. Contbr. articles to profl. jours. Recipient Uhrig award Faculty U. Wis., 1968. Decorated Cavaliere nell'ordine al Merito della Repubblica Italiana. Mem. MLA, AAUP, Am. Assn. Tchrs. Italian (sec. treas. 1980-84, pres. 1984-87, Disting. Svc. award 1994), Dante Soc. Am., Renaissance Soc. Am., Boccaccio Soc. Am., Nat. Italian Am. Found., Am. Italian Hist. Assn., Am. Assn. Italian Studies, Midwest MLA. Home: 715 N Plymouth Rd Bloomington IN 47408-3066 Office: Ind U Ctr for Italian Studies Bloomington IN 47405

LEBARON, EDWARD WAYNE, JR., lawyer; b. San Rafael, Calif., Jan. 7, 1930; s. Edward Wayne and Mabel Butler (Sims) LeB.; m. Doralee M. LeBaron, June 4, 1954; children: Edward Wayne, William Bruce, Richard Wilson. BA, Coll. Pacific, 1950; LLB, George Washington U., 1959. Bar: Calif. bar 1960, Tex. bar 1960, Nev. bar 1967. Football quarterback Washington Redskins, 1952-59; with Dallas Cowboys, 1960-63; exec. v.p. Nevada Cement Co., 1964-65; mem. firm Wynne & Wynne, Dallas, 1960-63, Bible, McDonald & Carano, Reno, 1966-68, Laxalt & Berry, Carson City, Nev., 1969-70; partner firm Jones, Jones, Bell, LeBaron and Brown, Las Vegas, Nev., 1970-76; gen. mgr. Atlanta Falcons Football team, 1977-85; ptnr. Powell, Goldstein, Murphy & Frazer, 1986-89, Pillsbury, Madison & Sutro, 1989-94; ret., 1994; bd. dirs. Tom Brown, Inc.; ptnr LeBaron Ranches. Served with USMC, 1950-52. Decorated Purple Heart, Bronze Star.; named Sportsman of Year in Ga., 1978-79; named to Coll. Football Hall of Fame, 1980. Mem. ABA, Sutter Club, Northridge Country Club. Republican.

LE BARON, JOSEPH EVAN, diplomat; b. Nampa, Idaho, Sept. 3, 1947; s. Carlos Stannard and Truellen Ruth (Davis) McCracken; m. Elinor Rae Drake, Mar. 3, 1973; 1 child, Petra Drake. BS, Portland State U., Oreg., 1969; MA, Princeton U., 1978, PhD, 1980. Consular officer U.S. Embassy, Doha, Qatar, 1980-82; polit. officer U.S. Embassy, Amman, Jordan, 1982-83, econ./commercial officer, 1983-84; staff aide to amb. U.S. Embassy, Ankara, Turkey, 1984-85; polit. officer U.S. Consulate Gen., Istanbul, Turkey, 1985-87; desk officer for Lebanon U.S. State Dept., Washington, 1987-89; fgn. affairs advisor to majority leader U.S. Senate, Washington, 1989-90; consul gen. U.S. Consulate Gen., Dubai, United Arab Emirates, 1991-94; dep. amb. U.S. Embassy, Manama, Bahrain, 1994-96; dep. dir. officer Iran and Iraq State Dept., Washington, 1996—. With USAF, 1970-74. Recipient Sinclaire award Disting. Lang. Study Am. Fgn. Svc. Assn., Washington, 1992; rsch. fellow for Sudan Social Sci. Rsch. Coun., N.Y.C., 1978-79; Nat. Defense Fgn. Lang. fellow Princeton U., 1976-78; Princeton U. fellow, 1976. Office: US Embassy Bahrain Dept Of State Washington DC 20520

LEBEAU, CHARLES PAUL, lawyer; b. Detroit, Dec. 11, 1944; s. Charles Henry Jr. and Mary Barbara (Moran) L.; m. Victoria Joy (Huchin), May 15, 1970; children: Jeffrey Kevin, Timothy Paul. AA, Macomb County Community Coll., Warren, Mich., 1967; BA, Wayne State U., 1969; JD, U. Detroit, 1972; grad. tax program, NYU Sch. Law, 1972-73. Bar: Mich. 1973, U.S. Tax Ct. 1973, Calif. 1987, U.S. Ct. Internat. Trade. 1988, U.S. Supreme Ct. 1988, U.S. Dist. Ct. (so. dist.) Calif. 1988. Tax atty. Ford Motor Co., Dearborn, Mich., 1973-75; assoc. Hoops & Huff, Detroit, 1975-76, Miller, Canfield, Paddock & Stone, Detroit, 1976-78; tax mgr. Oceaneering Internat., Santa Barbara, Calif., 1978-79; tax counsel Signal Cos. Inc., Beverly Hills and La Jolla, Calif., 1979-83; assoc. Gray, Cary, Ames & Frye, San Diego, 1983-84; of counsel James Watts Esq., La Jolla, 1985, Murfey, Griggs & Frederick, La Jolla, 1986; pvt. practice La Jolla and San Diego, 1987—; lectr. grad. tax program Golden Gate U., San Diego, 1979-87; adj. prof. law U. San Diego, 1982-85, 88-89; mem. Law Rev., U. Detroit, 1971-72; lectr. in taxation. Contbr. articles on internat. tax to profl. jours.; monthly tax case commentator Taxes Internat., London, 1981-85. Campaign coord. United Way, Santa Barbara, 1979. Mem. ABA, Mich. Bar Assn., Calif. Bar Assn., San Diego County Bar Assn., Pi Sigma Alpha. Republican. Roman Catholic. Avocations: sailing, tennis, walking. Home: 1999 Via Segovia La Jolla CA 92037-6441 Office: Law Offices Charles LeBeau Ste 1070 4660 La Jolla Village Dr San Diego CA 92122-4606

LEBEAU, HECTOR ALTON, JR., management consultant, former confectionary company executive; b. Hartford, Conn., July 2, 1931; s. Hector Alton and Gladys (Chester) LeB.; m. Joan Michaelson, May 31, 1955; children: Linda, Jane, Michael, Leslie. B.S., U. Tex., 1960; Program for Mgmt. Devel., Harvard U., 1965. With mktg. dept. Gen. Foods, White Plains, N.Y., 1960-73; v.p., gen. mgr. Consol. Brands div. Gulf & Western, N.Y.C., 1973-78; with sales and mktg. dept. Timex, Middlebury, Conn., 1978-80; v.p. fields ops. Schweppes U.S.A., Stamford, Conn., 1980-82, pres., 1982-84; pres. Rose Holland House, 1984-85, Cadbury U.S.A., 1985-88; sr. v.p. Cadbury Schweppes Inc., Stamford, Conn., 1985-88; pres. The Marcon Group, 1988—; pres., CEO Am. Candy Co., Selma, Ala., 1995—. Mem. Stanford Bd. Reps., 1966-69; mem. nat. com. Explorers, Boy Scouts Am., 1970-71; trustee St. Augustine Arts Assn., 1994—; pres. Marsh Creek Homeowners Assn., 1994—. Capt. USAF, 1954-58. Elected dean Nat. Candy Wholesalers Assn., 1988. Mem. Beta Gamma Sigma. Republican. Clubs: Union League (N.Y.C.); Cedar Point Yacht (Westport, Conn.); Marsh Creek Country Club (St. Augustine, Fla.). Office: PO Box 879 Selma AL 36702-0879

LEBEC, ALAIN, investment banker; b. Dunkerque, Nord, France, Apr. 25, 1950; came to U.S., 1971; m. Leah M. Koncelik, June 27, 1981; children: Gabriel, Christina, Xavier. Diplome d'Ingenieur, Ecole Poly., Paris, 1971; MBA, Northwestern U., 1973. Mng. dir. A.G. Becker & Co., N.Y.C., 1973-84; mng. dir. investment banking group Merrill Lynch & Co., N.Y.C., 1984—. 2d lt. French Army, 1971. Office: Merrill Lynch & Co World Fin Ctr North Tower New York NY 10281-1330

LEBECK, WARREN WELLS, commodities consultant; b. Chgo., Mar. 13, 1921; s. Emil and Hazel (Wells) L.; m. Dorothy Lester, Feb. 1, 1943; children: Sara Beth, Kenneth, Clayton A., Frederick E. BA, North Central Coll., Naperville, Ill., 1942. With Montgomery Ward & Co., Chgo., 1941-42, 46-54; with Chgo. Bd. Trade, 1954-79, sec., then exec. v.p., 1957-73, pres., 1973-77, sr. exec. v.p., 1977-79; pvt. practice cons. Chgo., 1979—; past dir. Bank of Hinsdale, Ill.; past chmn. bd., pres. South Loop Improvement Project; mem. U.S. Agrl. Policy Adv. Com., 1976-87; trustee Nat. Agrl. Forum, 1983-86; bd. dirs., exec. com. U.S. Feed Grains Coun., 1978-90, Agrl. Coun. Am., 1980-90; bd. dirs., exec. com. Nat. Grain Trade Coun., 1968-90, chmn., 1988-89; mem. founding com., bd. dirs., exec. com. Nat. Futures Assn., 1982—. Former mem. bd. edn. Downers Grove (Ill.) Twp. High Sch. Served with USNR, 1942-45. Home and Office: 1060 Burning Tree Rd Pinehurst NC 28374-9271

LEBEDOFF, DAVID M., lawyer, author, investment advisor; b. Mpls., Apr. 29, 1938; s. Martin David and Mary Louise (Galanter) L.; m. Randy Louise Miller, Feb. 7, 1981; children: Caroline, Jonathan, Nicholas. BA magna cum laude, U. Minn., 1960; JD, Harvard U., 1963. Bar: Minn. 1963. Spl. asst. atty. gen. Atty. Gen. of Minn., St. Paul, 1963-65; spl. counsel U.S. Senator Walter F. Mondale, Washington, 1966; pvt. practice law Mpls., 1967-81; ptnr. Lindquist & Vennum, Mpls., 1981-91, Briggs & Morgan, Mpls., 1991-95; sr. v.p. Voyageur Asset Mgmt., Mpls., 1995—; of counsel Gray, Plant, Mooty, Mooty & Bennett, Mpls., 1995—; spl. master U.S. Dist. Ct., Mpls., 1974-75. Author: The 21st Ballot, 1969, Ward Number Six, 1972, The New Elite, 1981; contbr. articles to profl. jours. Bd. regents U. Minn. , Mpls and St. Paul, 1977-89, chmn. bd. 1987-89; chmn. Mpls. Inst. Arts, 1989-91 bd. dirs. 1991—; bd. dirs. Blake Sch., U. Minn. Found. Recipient Outstanding Achievement award U. Minn., 1991. Mem. Mpls. Club (bd. dirs.), Minikahda Club, Phi Beta Kappa. Home: 1738 Oliver Ave S Minneapolis MN 55405-2222

LEBEDOFF, JONATHAN GALANTER, federal judge; b. Mpls., Apr. 29, 1938; s. Martin David and Mary (Galanter) L.; m. Sarah Sargent Mitchell, June 10, 1979; children: David Shevlin, Ann McNair. BA, U. Minn., 1960, LLB, 1963. Bar: Minn. 1963, U.S. Dist. Ct. Minn. 1964, U.S. Ct. Appeals (8th cir.) 1968. Pvt. practice Mpls., 1963-71; judge Hennepin County Mcpl. Ct., State Minn., Mpls., 1971-74; dist. ct. judge State of Minn., Mpls., 1974-91; U.S. magistrate judge U.S. Dist. Ct., St. Paul, 1991—; mem. Gov.'s Commn. on Crime Prevention, 1971-75; mem. State Bd. Continuing Legal Edn.; mem. Minn. Supreme Ct. Task Force for Gender Fairness in Cts., mem. implementation com. of gender fairness in cts.. Jewish. Avocations: reading (biographies, history), family, bridge. Office: 570 US Courthouse 110 S 4th St Minneapolis MN 55401-2221

LEBEDOFF, RANDY MILLER, lawyer; b. Washington, Oct. 16, 1949; m. David Lebedoff; children: Caroline, Jonathan, Nicholas. BA, Smith Coll., 1971; JD magna cum laude, Ind. U., 1975. Assoc. Faegre & Benson, Mpls., 1975-82, ptnr., 1983-86; v.p., gen. counsel Star Tribune, Mpls., 1989—; asst. sec. Star Tribune Cowles Media Co., Mpls., 1990—; Bd. dirs. Milkweed Editions. Bd. dirs. Minn. Opera, 1986-90, YWCA, 1984-90, Planned Parenthood Minn., 1985-90, Fund for Legal Aid Soc., 1988—, Abbott-Northwestern Hosp., 1990-94. Mem. Newspaper Assn. Am. (legal affairs com. 1991—), Minn. Newspapers Assn. (bd. dirs. 1995—). Home: 1738 Oliver Ave S Minneapolis MN 55405-2222 Office: Star Tribune 425 Portland Ave Minneapolis MN 55488-0001

LEBEL, ANDRÉ, communications executive; m. Maryse Lachance; 1 child, Jordan. Pres. Telebec Ltd.; sr. exec. Bell Can., BCE; sr. v.p. internat. diversified fin. svcs. orgn.; pres., CEO Teleglobe Can. Inc., Montreal, Que.; CEO, chmn. Teleglobe Internat. Inc., Montreal; chmn. World Telecom. Adv. Coun., UN Internat. Telecom. Union; mem. Conf. Bd. Can.; co-chairperson internat. symposium in innovative mgmt., 1994. Mem. adv. bd. Norman Paterson Sch. Internat. Affairs, Carleton U.; mem. Bus. Coun. on Nat. Issues, Ctr. Patronal de l'Environ.; chmn. bd. dirs. I Musici Montreal, 1987-89, now chmn. internat. devel. Office: Teleglobe Canada Inc, 1000 de la Gauchetiere St West, Montreal, PQ Canada H3B 4X5*

LEBEL, ROBERT, bishop; b. Trois Pistoles, Que., Can., Aug. 11, 1924; s. Wilfrid and Alexina (Belanger) L. L.Theol., St. Paul U., Ottawa, 1950; D.Theol., Athenee Angelicum, Rome, 1951. Ordained priest Roman Cath. Ch., 1950, consecrated bishop, 1974; tchr. theology Major Sem., Rimouski, Que., 1951-65; rector Major Sem., 1963-65, Minor Sem., 1965-68; tchr. domatic theology U. Rimouski, 1970-74; aux. bishop St. Jean, Que., 1974-76; bishop Valleyfield, Que., 1976—. Contbr. ch. publs. Mem. Roman Synod on the Christian Family, 1980. Mem. Assemblee de Eveques Que., Conf. Can. Cath. Bishops, Soc. Canadienne de Theologie, KC. Address: 11 de l'Eglise, Valleyfield, PQ Canada J6T1J5

LEBENZON, CHRIS, film editor. Editor: (documentary) (with Robert K. Lambert and Ian Masters) The Secret Life of Plants, 1978, (films) Demon, 1977, The Private Files of J. Edgar Hoover, 1978, (with Marshall M. Borden, Martin Bram, and Dennis Dolan) Wolfen, 1981, A Breed Apart, 1984, (with Scott Wallace and Mark Warner) Weird Science, 1985, Death of an Angel, 1985, (with Billy Weber) Top Gun, 1986 (Academy award nomination best film editing 1986), (with David Handman and Jon Poll) Weeds, 1987, (with Michael Tronick and Weber) Beverly Hills Cop II, 1987, (with Tronick and Weber) Midnight Run, 1988, Revenge, 1990, (with Weber) Days of Thunder, 1990, Batman Returns, 1992, Josh and S.A.M., 1993, Ed Wood, 1994. Office: care Lawrence Mirisch The Mirisch Agency 10100 Santa Monica Blvd Ste 700 Los Angeles CA 90067-4011

LEBER, LESTER, advertising agency executive; b. Newark, June 11, 1913; s. David and Hattie Leber; m. Ruth Schwarz, Mar. 29, 1940 (div. 1968); m. Magdalena Maurer, July 15, 1968; children: Frederick, Laura Wood, Daniel. BA, Columbia U., 1934. Various positions Grey Advt., N.Y.C., 1935-52; founder, hon. chmn. Leber Katz Ptnrs., N.Y.C., 1952-72. Columnist: Saturday Evening Post, 1950, Tide, 1952, Advertising Age, 1960. Served with USN, 1943-45; Pearl Harbor. Home: 95706 Overseas Hwy Key Largo FL 33037-2046 Office: FCB/Leber Katz Ptnrs 150 E 42d St New York NY 10017

LEBER, STEVEN EDWARD, film producer, corporate executive; b. Bklyn., Dec. 12, 1941; s. David and Selma (Teitelbaum) L.; m. Marion Susan Greiffenhagen, Feb. 6, 1966; children: Michelle, Jill, Jordan. BA in Mgmt. and Acctg., Northeastern U., 1964. Agt. William Morris Agy., N.Y.C., 1964-72; pres. Contemporary Communications Corp., N.Y.C., 1972—; producer Leber and Krebs, Inc., N.Y.C., 1972—; pres. Global Sports & Arts, Ltd., N.Y.C., 1989—; pres. Tyumen Cons. Group, Inc., cons. Tyumen region, Russia; founder Hollywood Stores; voting mem. Tony Selection Com., N.Y.C., 1977—. Producer: Jesus Christ Superstar-Touring Co., N.Y.C., 1972-78, Beatlemania-Broadway, 1977-84, 1st Pro-Skating Championships-ABC Wide World of Sports, 1981-83, Tennis Championships, 1981-83, Moscow Circus-Circus Prodn., Inc., N.Y.C., 1988— (Family Show of Yr. award Performance mag. 1989), Moscow Circus (Family Show of Yr. award Performance mag. 1990), Teenage Mutant Ninja Turtles' "Coming Out of Their Shells", 1990; producer Animated Films, Russia. Mem. H.E.L.P. (found. to aid homeless), N.Y.C., 1988—; bd. dirs. Children's Med. Ctr., Great Neck, N.Y., 1985—, Five Towns United Way; fund raiser Armenian Earthquake Fund, Washington/N.Y.C., 1988; exec. producer Concert for Bangledesh, 1971. Mem. NARAS (voting), N.Y. League Theatrical Producers, N.Y. Internat. Festival arts (bd. mem. 1989), Friars Club, Innercircle Club (Washington). Office: Circus Prodns Inc 155 E 55th St Apt 6H New York NY 10022-4040

LEBLANC, HUGH LINUS, political science educator, consultant; b. Alexandria, La., Oct. 30, 1927; s. Moreland Paul and Carmen Marie (Haydel) LeB.; m. Shirley Jean Smith, Feb. 28, 1953; children: Leslie Ann, Alexander Hugh. BA, La. State U., 1948; MA, U. Tenn., 1950; PhD, U. Chgo., 1958. Asst. prof. George Washington U., Washington, 1955-58, assoc. prof., 1959-

63, prof., 1964-90, prof. emeritus dept. polit. sci., 1991—, chmn. dept., 1963-65, 70-76, 82-88; v.p. Area Inc., Arlington, VA, 1961-63. Author: American Political Parties, 1982, (with D. Trudeau Allensworth) The Politics of States and Urban Communities, 1971; contbr. articles to polit. sci. jours. Served to lt. (j.g.) USNR, 1944-45, 52-55. Named Outstanding Prof. Interfraternity Council, George Washington U., 1963. Mem. Country Club of Fairfax (Va.). Home: 3403 Barger Dr Falls Church VA 22044-1202

LEBLANC, HUGUES, philosophy educator; b. Ste-Marie de Beauce, Que., Can., Mar. 19, 1924; came to U.S., 1946, naturalized, 1952; s. Edmond and Alice (Caron) L.; m. Virginia Southall Graham, June 10, 1950 (div. Apr. 1983); children—Gabrielle, Suzanne, Stephen. MA, U. Montreal, Que., 1946, hon. doctorate, 1980; PhD, Harvard U., 1948; hon. doctorate, Dalhousie U., 1982, U. Que., Montreal, 1985. Prof. philosophy Bryn Mawr (Pa.) Coll., 1948-67, Temple U., Phila., 1967-92, U. Que., Montréal, 1992—. Author: An Introduction to Deductive Logic, 1955, Statistical and Inductive Probabilities, 1962, Techniques of Deductive Inference, 1966, Deductive Logic, 1972, Truth, Syntax and Modality, 1973, Truth-Value Semantics, 1976, Existence, Truth and Probability, 1982, Essays on Epistemology and Semantics, 1983; also numerous papers on logic, philosophy of logic and probability theory. Fulbright fellow, 1953-54; Guggenheim fellow, 1965-66. Fellow Royal Soc. Can., Assn. for Symbolic Logic (exec. com. 1958-61, treas. 1979-91, 82-85), Soc. for Exact Philosophy (v.p. 1978-80, pres. 1980-82). Home: 460 Champ de Mars Apt 502, Montreal, PQ Canada H2Y 1B4 Office: U Que at Montreal, Dept Philosophy, Case Postale 8888, Montreal, PQ Canada H3C 3P8

LEBLANC, JEANETTE AMY, psychotherapist, educator, writer, consultant; b. Blytheville, Ark., Mar. 31, 1968; d. Bob Gene and Joan Ann (Hall) Ash; m. Robert Louis LeBlanc, May 27, 1987. BS in Liberal Arts and Psychology, SUNY, Albany, 1989; MS in Cmty. Counseling, Ga. State U., 1991; PhD in Adminstrn. and Mgmt., Walden U., 1994. Libr. technician Civil Svc., Munich, 1988-89; crisis counselor U.S. Army Community Svc., Munich, 1988-89; adolescent counselor Bradley Ctr. Hosp., Inc., Columbus, Ga., 1990-91; group therapist children of alcoholics, 1991-92; social svcs. coord., therapist Anne Elizabeth Shepherd Home, Inc., Columbus, 1991-93; instr. Upper Iowa U., Ft. Polk, La., 1993—; cons., trainer, speaker, 1995—; group therapist for womens group Vernon Cmty. Action Coun., Leesville, La., 1994-96. With U.S. Army, 1986-88. Mem. ACA, NAFE, Assn. for Counselor Edn. and Supr., Internat. Assn. Marriage and Family Counselors, Sierra Club, Toastmasters. Avocations: writing, travel, reading.

LEBLANC, LAUREEN ALISON, service company administrator; b. Santa Ana, Calif., Feb. 25, 1964; d. Thomas Albert and Kathleen Mary (Thompson) Cox; m. Mark J. LeBlanc, July 17, 1992; children: Katherine Morgan, (from a previous marriage) Robert Daniel, Alicia Michelle. Grad. high sch., Oakland Park, Fla., 1982. Horse trainer, mgr. various show horse stables, U.S. and Europe, 1975-84; office mgr. Land Title Ins. Co., Ft. Lauderdale, Fla., 1979-82; gen. mgr. Boca Travel Trailer Resort, Boca Raton, Fla., 1982-85; asst. mgr. credit Boca Raton Hotel and Country Club, 1985-90; credit and accounts receivable mgr. Callaway Gardens Resort, Pine Mountain, Ga., 1990-94; contr. Holiday Inn Denver Internat. Airport Hotel Trade & Conv. Ctr., 1994—. Mem. NAFE, Internat. Assn. Hospitality Accts., U.S. Dressage Assn., Nat. Assn. Credit Mgrs. Avocations: sailing, fishing, diving, racquetball, tennis.

LEBLANC, L(OUIS) CHRISTIAN, architect; b. Heidelberg, Bavaria, Fed. Republic Germany, July 5, 1957; s. Louis Carroll LeBlanc and Gladys Jane Everett; m. Janet Beverly Frances Mulholland; children: Jacob Bodalski (stepchild), L. Christian Jr., Francesca Helen. BS in Design, Clemson U., 1980, MArch, 1982. Architect FJ Clark Inc., Anderson, S.C., 1982-86, Freeman & Major Architects Inc., Greenville, S.C., 1987-88, Narramore & Assocs., Inc., Greenville, 1988-89, Greene & Assocs., Inc., Greenville, 1989—. Mem. AIA. Republican. Roman Catholic. Avocations: languages, sailing. Home: 213 Oregon St Greenville SC 29605-1050 Office: Greene & Assocs Architects Inc 704 E Washington St Greenville SC 29601-3035

LEBLANC, MATT, actor. TV appearances include (movies) Anything to Survive, (series) Top of the Heap, TV 101, Vinnie and Bobby, Friends. Office: care UTA 9560 Wilshire Blvd 5th Fl Hollywood CA 90212

LEBLANC, ROGER MAURICE, chemistry educator; b. Trois Rivières, Que., Can., Jan. 5, 1942; s. Henri and Rita (Moreau) L.; m. Micheline D. Veillette, June 26, 1965; children: Daniel, Hughes, Marie-Jose, Nancy. BSc, U. Laval, 1964, PhD, 1968. NRC postdoctoral fellow Davy Faraday Rsch. Lab. Royal Inst. Great Britain, London, 1968-70; prof. phys. chemistry U. Que., Trois-Rivières, 1970-93, chmn. dept., 1971-75, dir. Biophysics Rsch. Group, 1978-81, chmn. Photobiophysics Rsch. Ctr., 1981-91; prof., chmn. dept. chemistry U. Miami, Coral Gables, Fla., 1994—; hon. prof. Jilin U., Changchun, Cina, 1992. Recipient Barringer award Spectroscopy Soc. Can., 1983, Medaille du Merite Universitaire du Que. a Trois-Rivieres, 1987, Commemorative medal for 125th Anniversary of Confedn. Can., 1993. Fellow Chem. Inst. Can. (Noranda award 1982, John Labatt Ltd. award 1992); mem. Am. Chem. Soc., Assn. Canadienne Francaise pour l'Avancement des Sciences (Prix Vincent 1978), Am. Soc. Photobiology, Biophys. Soc., European Photochem. Assn. Roman Catholic. Home: 9335 SW 77th Ave Apt 251 Miami FL 33156-7925 Office: Univ Miami Dept Chemistry Cox Sci Bldg Rm 315 1301 Memorial Dr Coral Gables FL 33124-0431

LEBLANC, ROMÉO, Canadian government official; b. Memramcook, N.B., Can., Dec. 18, 1927; s. Philias and Lucie LeB.; m. Diana Fowler; 4 children. BA, St. Joseph U., 1948, BEd, 1951; postgrad., Paris U., 1953-55; DCL (hon.), Mount Allison U., New Brunswick, 1977; D Pub. Adminstrn. (hon.), U. de Moncton, New Brunswick, 1979; JD (hon.), U. Sainte-Anne, Nova Scotia, 1995. Tchr. Drummond High Sch., New Brunswick, Can., 1951-53; Prof., New Brunswick Tchrs. Coll., Fredericton, Can., 1955-59; journalist, correspondent Radio Can., Ottawa, 1960-62, United Kingdom, 1962-65, U.S.A., 1965-67; founding pres. CBC/Radio-Can. Correspondent's Assn., 1965; press sec. to Right Hon. Lester B. Pearson, 1967-68, Right Hon. Pierre Elliott Trudeau, 1968-71; asst. to pres. and dir. pub. rels. l'Universite de Moncton, Can., 1971-72; M.P. from Westmorland-Kent, New Brunswick dist. Ho. of Commons, Can., 1972-84; min. Ministry of Fisheries, 1974-76, Ministry of Fisheries and the Environ., 1976-79, Ministry of Fisheries and Oceans, 1980-82, Ministry of Pub. Works, 1982-84, Canada Mortgage and Housing Corp., 1982-84, Nat. Capital Commn., 1982-84; mem. Can. Senate, 1984-94, speaker, 1993-94; governor general Govt. Can., 1995—; ofcl. rep. Govt. Can. USSR, Poland, Cuba, The EEC, U.K., France, 1974-84; mem. del. UN Law of the Sea Conf., 1974-79; cabinet com. mem. External Affairs and Econ. Affairs, 1974-82, Comms. Com., 1974-84, chmn. Comms. Com., 1976-81, Priorities and Planning Com., 1975-84; Social Affairs, 1982-84; mem. senate com. Internal Econ., Budgets and Adminstrn., 1984-93, chmn., 1989-93, Fgn. Affairs, 1986-94, Sub. Com. on Security and Nat. Def., 1992-94; vis. scholar Inst. Can. Studies, Carleton U.; part-time faculty mem. Can. studies Concordia U., Montreal. Mem. Canada France Parliamentary Assn., Internat. Assn. French Speaking Parliamentarians. Office: Office of the Governor General, Rideau Hall 1 Sussex Dr, Ottawa, ON Canada K1A 0A1

LEBLANC, TINA, dancer; b. Erie, Pa.; m. Marco Jerkunica, May 1988. Trained, Carlisle, Pa. Dancer Joffrey II Dancers, N.Y.C., 1982-83, The Joffrey Ballet, N.Y.C., 1984-92; prin. dancer San Francisco Ballet, 1992—; guest tchr. Ctrl. Pa. Youth Ballet, 1992, 94—. Work includes roles in (with San Francisco Ballet) Con Brio, Bizet Pas de Deux, Swan Lake, Nanna's Lied, Handel -- A Celebration, La fille mal gardée, Rubies, Tchaikovsky Pas de Deux, Seeing Stars, The Nutcracker, La Pavane Rouge, Company B, Romeo and Juliet, Sleeping Beauty, The Dance House, Terra Firma, Lambarena, Fly by Night, In the Night, Ballo della Regina, The Lesson, The Tuning Game, Quartette; (with other companies) The Green Table, Les Presages, Le sacre du printemps, Les Noces, Light Rain, Romeo and Juliet, Runaway Train, Empyrean Dances, La Vivandière, L'air D'esprit, Corsaire Pas de deux, Don Quixote pas de deux. Recipient Princess Grace Found. award, 1988, Princess Grace Statuette award, 1995. Office: San Francisco Ballet 455 Franklin St San Francisco CA 94102-4438

LEBLOIS, AXEL, computer company executive; b. 1949. Student in Econs., Ecole Nationale des Sciences Politiques; student in Philosophy, U. Paris; MBA, INSEAD. With Compagnie Europeenne de Publication; pres. French ops. Internat. Data Corp., France, 1983-86; pres., CEO IDG Comm., 1986-91; vice chmn. Internat. Data Group, 1986-91; chmn., CEO Internat. Data Corp, 1986-91; pres., CEO H N Bull Info. Systems, Billerica, Mass., 1991—. Office: H N Bull Information Systems Technology Park Billerica MA 01821*

LEBLOND, CHARLES PHILIPPE, anatomy educator, researcher; b. Lille, France, Feb. 5, 1910; s. Oscar and Jeanne (Desmarchelier) L.; m. Gertrude Sternschuss, Oct. 22, 1936; children—Philippe L., Paul N., Pierre F., Marie Pascale. L.Sc., U. Lille, 1932; M.D., U. Paris, France, 1934, D. Sc., 1945; Ph.D., U. Montreal, 1942; DSc Acadia (hon.), McGill U., 1982, York U., 1985. Asst. histology U. Lille and U. Paris, France, 1934-35; Rockefeller fellow anatomy Yale, 1935-37; charge biology div. Lab. Synthese Atom, Paris, 1937-40; research fellow U. Rochester, N.Y., 1940-41; mem. faculty McGill U., Montreal, Que., Can., 1941—; prof. anatomy McGill U., 1948—, chmn. dept., 1957-75. Author: L'Acide Ascorbique dans les Tissues et sa Detection, 1936, Radioautography as a Tool in the Study of Protein Synthesis, 1965, also over 300 articles mainly on cell and tissue dynamics. Fogarty scholar NIH, 1975. Fellow Royal Soc. London, Royal Soc. Can., Am. Assn. Anatomy, Can. Assn. Anatomists, Prix. Scientifique du Que. Home: 68 Chesterfield St, Montreal, PQ Canada H3Y 2M5

LEBLOND, PAUL HENRI, oceanographer, educator; b. Que., Can., Dec. 30, 1938; s. Sylvio and Jeanne (Lacerte) LeB.; m. Josee Michaud (div. 1985); children: Michel, Philippe, Anne. BA, Laval U., Quebec, 1957; BS, McGill U., Montreal, Que., 1961; PhD, U. B.C., Vancouver, Can., 1964; DSc (hon.), Meml. U., Newfoundland, 1992. Prof. depts. oceanography and physics U. B.C., Vancouver, 1965, assoc. dean faculty of sci., 1982-85, head dept. oceanography, 1987-92, dir. program earth and ocean scis., 1992-96; chmn. Can. nat. com. World Ocean Circulation Expt., 1987-92; program leader Ocean Prodn. Enhancement Network, Can., 1991-93. Co-author: Waves in the Oceans, 1978, Cadborosaurus, 1995; contbr. articles to profl. jours. Bd. dirs. Can. Ocean Frontiers Rsch. Initiative Found., Can. Ctr. for Fisheries Innovations, 1993-96; mem. Fisheries Resource Conservation Coun., 1993—. Fellow Royal Soc. Can.; mem. Can. Meteorol. and Oceanographic Soc. (Pres.'s prize 1981, Tully medal 1991), Am. Geophys. Union. Avocations: hiking, history. Office: U BC Dept Earth & Ocean Sci, Vancouver, BC Canada V6T 1Z4

LEBLOND, RICHARD FOARD, internist, educator; b. Seattle, July 17, 1947; s. Donald E. and Ruth Elizabeth (Foard) LeB.; m. Anita Caraig Carcia, Dec. 28, 1994; children: Sueno Emmeline, Edgardo Alan. AB, Princeton U., 1969; MD, U. Wash., 1972. Diplomate Am. Bd. Internal Medicine (bd. dirs. 1993—). Intern Harlem Hosp., N.Y.C., 1972-73; resident in medicine, clin. fellow in oncology U. Wash., Seattle, 1975-78; pvt. practice, Livingston, Mont., 1978-96; dir. Livingston Meml. Hosp., 1979-91, 94-96, chmn. bd. dirs., 1984-91; clin. asst. prof. medicine Mont. State U., Bozeman, 1979-96, U. Wash., 1991-96, U. Claif., San Francisco, 1991-92; acting instr. Makerere U., Kampala, 1991-92; clin. prof. medicine U. Iowa, Iowa City, 1996—; bd. dirs. Deaconess Rsch. Found., Billings, Mont., 1993. Dir. Park County Friends of the Arts, Livingston, 1981-87, Livingston Cmty. Trust, 1986-91. Named Regional Trustee of Yr., Am. Heart Assn., 1989; recipient med. achievement award Deaconess Rsch. Found., 1995. Fellow ACP; mem. AMA, Mont. Med. Assn., Am. Soc. for Internal Medicine, Nat. Rural Health Assn. Avocations: fishing, hunting, hiking, reading, gardening. Home: Rt 62 Box 3196 Livingston MT 59047 Office: Park Clinic PC 1001 River Dr Livingston MT 59047-3716

LEBLOND, RICHARD KNIGHT, II, banker; b. Cin., Nov. 16, 1920; s. Harold R. and Elizabeth (Conroy) LeB.; m. Sara Cordial Chapman, Dec. 11, 1948; children—Mary, Richard, E. Chapman, Elizabeth, David, Virginia, William, Thomas, Sara, Joseph. B.A., Princeton U.; D.C.S. (hon.), St. John's U., Jamaica, N.Y., 1978. Exec. v.p. Chem. Bank, N.Y.C., 1968-73; vice-chmn. bd. Chem. Bank, 1973-85, sr. advisor, 1985—; chmn. bd. Chem. Bank & Trust of Fla., 1988—; bd. dirs. Ingersoll Internat., Inc., Rockford, Ill., Bedford Stuyvesant D&S Corp., Bklyn. Trustee St. Patrick's Cath., N.Y.C. 1st lt. U.S. Army, 1943-46, PTO. Mem. N.Y. State Bankers Assn. (pres. 1979-80), Harvard Bus. Sch. Assn. (pres. 1975-76). Republican. Roman Catholic. Office: Chem Bank 11 W 51st St Fl 2 New York NY 10019-6901

LEBOEUF, RAYMOND WALTER, manufacturing company executive; b. Chgo., Dec. 30, 1946; s. Raymond O'Dillon and Opal Rosalind (Powell) LeB.; m. Loralee Ann Sawyer, Jan. 24, 1968; children—Mandy, Whitney. BA, Northwestern U., 1967; MBA, U. Ill., 1970. Analyst Ford Motor Co., Detroit, 1970-73; asst. comptroller Union Bank, Los Angeles, 1973-74; mgr. banking Ford Motor Co., Detroit, 1974-80; treas. PPG Industries, Inc., Pitts., 1980-84, controller, 1984-86, v.p. purchasing, 1986-88, v.p. finance, 1988-94, exec. v.p., 1994—. Mem. Fin. Execs. Inst. (dir. 1983-84). Office: PPG Industries Inc 1 Ppg Pl Pittsburgh PA 15272-0001

LEBOR, JOHN F(RANCIS), retired department store executive; b. Portland, Oreg., Mar. 22, 1906; s. John G. and Jettie P. (Cook) L.; m. Violette Steinmetz, Oct. 7, 1931 (dec. Feb. 11, 1983); children: Andrew Scott, John Cook (dec. Jan. 1990); m. Dorothy Patrick Burns, Sept. 22, 1984. B.B.A., U. Oreg., 1928; M.B.A., Harvard U., 1930. Investment analyst Scudder, Stevens & Clark, N.Y.C., 1930-33; financial staff Radio-Keith-Orpheum Corp., 1933-40; sec.-treas. York (Pa.) Corp., 1940-46; treas. Federated Dept. Stores, Inc., Cin., 1946-51; v.p., treas., dir. Federated Dept. Stores, Inc., 1951-57, v.p., dir., 1958-60, exec. v.p., dir., 1960-65; trustee The Gateway Trust, Cin. Mem. Phi Beta Kappa, Beta Gamma Sigma, Beta Alpha Psi, Alpha Kappa Psi. Episcopalian. Clubs: Queen City (Cin.), The Beach; Old Guard Soc. Palm Beach Golfers (Palm Beach, Fla.); Turtle Creek (Tequestra, Fla.), Westchester Country (Rye, N.Y.). *An important guiding principle for evaluating myself and others has been dependability and a record of "mission accomplished," as opposed to offering alibis.*

LEBOUITZ, MARTIN FREDERICK, financial services industry executive, consultant; b. Phila., May 16, 1946; s. William and Sylvia (Magen) L.; m. Helene A. Pepe, Oct. 15, 1977; 1 child, Clarke S. BS, U.S. Air Force Acad., Colorado Springs, Colo., 1971; MA, The Fletcher Sch. of Law and Diplomacy, 1972. Asst. v.p. Bankers Trust Co., N.Y.C., 1976-82; v.p. mgr. of planning Barclays Bank of N. Am., N.Y.C., 1982-85; v.p. corp. devel. Chase Manhattan Bank, N.Y.C., 1985-88; v.p. planning and devel. Paine Webber Group Inc., N.Y.C., 1988-90; prin. DRI/McGraw-Hill, N.Y.C., 1990-91; mng. dir. Fin. Svcs. Cons., N.Y.C., 1991-95; v.p., dir. strategy wholesale oper. products The Chase Manhattan Bank, N.A., Bklyn., 1995—. Bd. dirs., chmn. sch. rels. com. N.Y. chpt. Fletcher Sch. Capt. USAF, 1971-76. Mem. Planning Forum (dir., chmn. program com. N.Y. chpt.), Assn. for Corp. Growth, Am. Mgmt. Assn., USAF Acad. Alumnae (treas. N.Y. metro area chpt.), Harvard Club, Fletcher Sch. Club N.Y. (chmn. sch. rels. com.). Office: The Chase Manhattan Bank NA 4 Chase Metrotech Ctr Fl 21 Brooklyn NY 11245

LEBOUTILLIER, JANET ELA, real estate investment asset manager, writer; b. Marshfield, Mass., May 10, 1936; d. Preston Carleton and Barbara (Higgins) Ela; m. John Walter McNeill, Oct. 10, 1959 (div. 1970); children: Duncan Davis McNeill, Sarah McNeill Treffry; m. Martin LeBoutillier, May 10, 1986. AA, Briarcliff Jr. Coll., 1956; BA in English Lit., U. Colo., 1958; postgrad. Real Estate/Mortgage Banking, NYU, 1973-78. Lic. N.Y. and Conn. real estate broker; cert. property mgr. Sales, leasing agt. L.B. Kaye Assocs., Ltd., N.Y.C., 1969-74; comml. leasing agt. Kenneth D. Laub & Co., N.Y.C., 1975; dir. leasing, asst. bldg. mgr. Douglas Elliman Gibbons & Ives Co., N.Y.C., 1975-76; adminstr. REIT adv. unit Chase Manhattan Bank, N.A., N.Y.C., 1976-78; asst. dir. real estate investments Mass. Mut. Life Ins. Co., Springfield, Mass., 1978-80; dir. real estate investments Yale U., New Haven, Conn., 1980-81; ind. cons. N.Y.C., 1981-83; sr. analyst, equity mgmt., sales and devel. Aetna Realty Investors, Inc., Hartford, Conn., 1983-84; dir. pub. involvement unit Aetna Realty Investors, Inc., 1984-86; sr. asset mgr. Cigna Investments, Inc., Hartford, 1986-87; v.p. Wm. M. Hotchkiss Co., New Haven, Conn., 1987-88; pres., prin. LeBoutillier & LeBoutillier, Inc., Lyme, Conn., 1989-93. Author: Mediations on Joy, 1995. Mem. Grace Episcopal Ch., mem. pastoral care and healing commn., coord. prayer team ministry. Mem. Internat. Coun. Shopping Ctrs., Nat. Coun. for Urban Econs. Devel., Inst. Real Estate Mgmt. (chpt. 51 pres., sec., treas., nat. asset mgmt. com.), Fin. Women's Assn., The Real Estate Exch., Urban Land Inst., Internat. Order of St. Luke the Physician (co-founder, convener Old Saybrook, Conn. area chpt. 1993). Democrat. Episcopalian. Avocations: prayer ministry, skiing, fishing, sailing, tennis. Home and Office: 8 Laurel Dr Old Lyme CT 06371-1462

LEBOVITZ, HAROLD PAUL (HAL LEBOVITZ), journalist; b. Cleve., Sept. 11, 1916; s. Isaiah and Celia (Levy) L.; m. Margie Glassman, Feb. 20, 1938; children: Neil Ross, Lynn Gail. BA, Case Western Res. U., 1938; MA, Western Res. U., 1942. Sci. tchr., coach Euclid (Ohio) High Sch., 1938-46; reporter, baseball writer, columnist Cleve. News, 1946-60; columnist Cleve. Plain Dealer, 1960-84, sports editor, 1964-84; columnist The Sporting News, 1970-92, Gannett Syndicate, 1979-82; dir. Cleve. Jewish News, 1971-89; baseball umpire, 1937-50, football ofcl., 1940-71, basketball ofcl., 1940-60; Cleve. corr. Sporting News, 1950-64. Author: Pitchin' Man, 1948; (with Phil R. Gilman) Springboards to Science, 1967; contbg. editor: Webster's New World Dictionary, 1983—; syndicated columnist several Ohio newspapers, 1984—; contbr. articles to various periodicals; inventor outdoor playground game Four Sq. Tennis. Mem. recreation com. University Heights, Ohio, 1965-75; bd. dirs. Jewish Community Ctr., Cleve., 1962-63, Alumni Assn. Adelbert Coll. Case-Western Res. U., 1969-83. Named Citizen of Yr. City of University Heights, 1964, Sportsman of Yr. B'rith Emeth Men's Club, 1964, Top Sportswriter Cotron Twelve of Atlantic Fleet, 1961, Sporting News Top Feature Writer, 1963-64; recipient ten best writing awards Cleve. Newspaper Guild, 1948-60, Greater Cleve. Football Coaches Golden Deeds award, 1987; inducted into Glenville High Sch. Hall of Fame, 1980, Ohio Baseball Hall of Fame, 1984, Greater Cleve. Softball Hall of Fame, 1989, Sport Media Assn. of Cleve. Hall of Fame, 1990, Cleve. Journalism Hall of Fame, 1991. Mem. Baseball Writers Assn. (pres. 1965-66, bd. dirs. 1966-67), Ohio Sports Editors Assn. (pres. 1965-66), Cleve. Football Ofcls. Assn., Ohio Football Ofcls. Assn., Cleve. Umpires Assn., Sigma Delta Chi (Disting. Svc. award 1981, Mel Harder Disting. Svc. award 1992). Home: 2380 Edgerton Rd Cleveland OH 44118-3726

LEBOW, BENNETT S., communications executive; b. Phila., 1938; 1 child, Geri. BEE, Drexel U.; postgrad., Princeton U. Prin. DSI Systems Inc., Rockville, Md., from 1961, B.S. LeBow Inc.; chmn. Western Union Corp., Upper Saddle River, N.J., New Valley Corp. (formerly Western Union Corp.), Upper Saddle River, 1993—, New Valley Corp., Miami, FL, 1995—. also: New Valley Corp 1 Mack Centre Dr Paramus NJ 07452*

LEBOW, IRWIN LEON, electronics engineering consultant; b. Boston, Apr. 27, 1926; s. Samuel and Ruth (Tobey) L.; m. Grace H. Hackel, July 8, 1951; children: Judith, William, David. S.B., MIT, 1948, Ph.D., 1951. Staff mem. MIT Lincoln Lab., 1951-60, assoc. leader satellite communications surface techniques group, 1960-65, leader, 1965-70, assoc. head communications div., 1970-72, assoc. head data systems div., 1972-75, mem. steering com., 1970-75; chief scientist, assoc. dir. tech. Def. Communications Agy., Washington, Dept. Def., Washington, 1975-81; v.p. engring. Am. Satellite Co., Rockville, Md., 1981-84; v.p. Systems Research and Applications Corp., Arlington, Va., 1984-87; ind. cons. Washington, 1987—. Author: (with others) Theory and Design of Digital Machines, 1962, The Digital Connection, 1990, Information Highways and Byways, 1995. Served with USNR, 1944-46. Awarded rank of Meritorious Sr. Exec., 1980; recipient Meritorious Civilian Service medal Dept. Def., 1981. Fellow Am. Phys. Soc., IEEE; mem. AAAS, Armed Forces Communications and Electronics Assn., Sigma Xi. Home and Office: 2800 Bellevue Ter NW Washington DC 20007-1366

LEBOW, MARK DENIS, lawyer; b. Harrisburg, Pa., Apr. 2, 1940; s. Sylvan and Ruth M. (Lebowitz) L.; m. Catherine Maugee, Nov. 22, 1972 (div. 1982); m. Patricia Edith Harris, Jan. 30, 1988; children: Michael, Jeffrey, Alexandra. AB, Yale U., 1961; JD, Harvard U., 1964. Bar: N.Y. 1965, U.S. Ct. Appeals (2d cir.) 1965, U.S. Dist. Ct. (so. and ea. dists.) N.Y. 1966. Assoc. Coudert Bros., N.Y.C., 1965-71, ptnr., 1972—; chmn. N.Y.C. CSC, 1979-92. Chmn. St. Francis Friends of the Poor, Inc., 1991—. Lt. USNR, 1964-71. Home: 1067 Fifth Ave New York NY 10128-0101 Office: Coudert Bros 1114 Avenue Of The Americas New York NY 10036-7703

LEBOWITZ, ALBERT, lawyer, author; b. St. Louis, June 18, 1922; s. Jacob and Lena (Zemmel) L.; m. Naomi Gordon, Nov. 26, 1953; children—Joel Aaron, Judith Leah. A.B., Washington U., St. Louis, 1945; LL.B., Harvard U., 1948. Bar: Mo. bar 1948. Assoc. Frank E. Morris, St. Louis, 1948-55; partner firm Morris, Schneider & Lebowitz, St. Louis, 1955-58, Crowe, Schneider, Shanahan & Lebowitz, St. Louis, 1958-66; counsel firm Murphy & Roche, St. Louis, 1966-67, Murphy & Schlapprizzi, St. Louis, 1967-81; partner firm Murphy, Schlapprizzi & Lebowitz, 1981-86; editor lit. quar. Perspective, 1961-80; of counsel Donald L. Schlapprizzi, P.C., 1986—, John T. Murphy, Jr., 1986-88. Author: novel Laban's Will, 1966, The Man Who Wouldn't Say No, 1969, A Matter of Days, 1989; also short stories. Served as combat navigator USAAF, 1943-45, ETO. Decorated Air medal with 3 oak leaf clusters. Mem. ABA, Mo., St. Louis bar assns., Phi Beta Kappa. Home: 743 Yale Ave Saint Louis MO 63130-3120 Office: Gateway One On The Mall 701 Market St Ste 1550 Saint Louis MO 63101-1861

LEBOWITZ, CATHARINE KOCH, state legislator; b. Winchester, Mass., June 30, 1915; d. William John and Carolyn Sophia (Kistinger) Koch; m. Murray Lebowitz, Sept. 21, 1971 (dec. Oct. 1978). Student Northeastern U., 1948-49, Boston Coll., 1949-52. Sec. ERA, Bangor, Augusta, Maine, 1935-38, WPA, Portland, Maine, 1938-42; personnel officer, exec. sec. USN, Portland, 1942-47; exec. sec. Clark Babbitt, Boston, 1947-48; adminstrv. asst. Moore Bus. Forms, Boston, 1948-52; apt. mgr., wholesale appliance div. Coffin-Wimple Inc., 1952-62, clerk U.S. Dist. Ct. Bangor (No. dist), 1962-79; sec. Portland Credit Bur., 1980-86; mem. Bangor City Council, 1985-87; mem. Maine State Legislature, 1982-92; bd. dirs. Eastern Transportation, 1989-94; mem. Bus. Adv. Coun., 1991—; active Program Rev. Subcom., 1991—; mem. adv. com. RSVP, 1987—, bd. dir., bus. adv. coun., and chmn. sub com. project with industry RSVP, 1992—; mem. adv. coun. Eastern Maine Tech. Coll., 1992—; bd. dirs. Rural Health Ctrs. Maine, Inc., 1992—; adv. bd. Maine Ctr. for the Arts, U. Maine, 1992—. Sec. Symphony Women, Bangor, 1964-84; bd. dirs. Opera House Com., Bangor, 1978-94; del. Rep. Nat. Conv., 1984, 88; mem. Spl. Task Force to Study Child Abuse, 1985-92; legis. com. United Way of Penobscot Valley, 1988-93, bd. mem., 1993—; adv. com. Maine Devel. Found., 1984-92; adv. bd. Aftercare, 1990, planning bd. St. Joseph Hosp., 1987-92, dir., v.p. St. Joseph Hosp. Aux., 1994—, Maine Ctr. Arts adv. bd., 1994; Bangor City Hosp. Aux., 1988—; bd. dirs. Penobscot Theater, 1990; accredited Beauty Pageant judge, 1986—. Recipient Civilian Meritorious Service award USN, Portland Maine, 1946; named Hon. Alumnus Secretarial Sci., Husson Coll., 1980. Mem. Credit Women Internat. (treas. 1975-77, Credit Woman of Yr. 1969), Credit Profls., 1988-92, Bangor Community Theater (treas. 1973—, award 1973), U. Maine Maine Masque Theater (judge 1983-90), Maine N.G. Assn. (hon.), Maine Air N.G. (hon.), Nat. Assn. Retired Fed. Employers (v.p. bd. dirs. 1993—, sec. 1994), Credit Women Bangor (sec. 1965-67), Bangor Dist. Nursing Assn. (corp. mem. at large), Bangor C. of C. (mem. consumer rels. coun. 1981-90, coord. 150th anniversary prodn. Music Man 1984), Bangor Hist. Soc. (bd. dirs. 1993—, exec. bd. sec. 1994—), Penobscot County Extension Svc. (bd. dir. 1995), Penobscot County Republicans, Penobscot County Rep. Women's Club (sec. 1979), Bangor City Rep. Club (bd. dirs., treas. 1993—), Newcomb Soc., Ret. Fed. Employees (v.p. 1994), Zonta Club (pres. Bangor 1962-64, 80-82, v.p. 1994, Outstanding Leader 1991), Mgmt. Club, Easdtern Maine Med. Ctr. Aux.

LEBOWITZ, JOEL LOUIS, mathematical physicist, educator; b. May 10, 1930; came to U.S., 1946, naturalized, 1951; m. Estelle Mandelbaum, June 21, 1953. BS, Bklyn. Coll., 1952; MS, Syracuse U., 1955, PhD, 1956; hon. doctorate, Ecole Poly. Federale, Lausanne, Switzerland, 1977. NSF postdoctoral fellow Yale U., New Haven, 1956-57; mem. faculty Stevens Inst. Tech., Hoboken, N.J., 1957-59; mem. faculty Yeshiva U., N.Y.C., 1959-77, prof. physics, 1965-77, acting chmn. Belfer Grad. Sch. Sci., 1964-67, chmn. dept., 1967-76; George William Hill prof math. and physics, dir. Ctr. for Math. Scis., Rutgers U., New Brunswick, N.J., 1977—. Co-editor: Phase Transitions and Critical Phenomena, 1980, editor Jour. Statis. Physics, 1975—, Studies in Statis. Mechanics, 1973—, Com. Math. Physics, 1973—; contbr. articles to profl. jours. Recipient Boltzmann medal Internat. Union Pure and Applied Physics, 1992, Max Planck Rsch. award, 1993, Delmar S. Fahrney medal Franklin Inst., 1994; Guggenheim fellow, 1976-77. Fellow

AAAS, Am. Phys. Soc., N.Y. Acad. Scis. (pres. 1979, A. Cressy Morrison award in natural scis. 1986); mem. NAS, AAUP, Am. Math. Soc., Phi Beta Kappa, Sigma Xi. Office: Rutgers U Ctr Math Sci Rsch Busch Campus-Hill Ctr New Brunswick NJ 08903

LEBOWITZ, MARSHALL, publishing company executive; b. Boston, Mar. 4, 1923; s. Max Nathan and Rissah (Zangwill) L.; m. Charlotte Lily Meyersohn, Aug. 7, 1949; children: Wendy Ann, Marian Kay, Mark Louis. AB, Harvard U., 1942. Statis. analyst U.S. WPB, Washington, 1942-43; periodicals mgr. J.S. Canner & Co. Inc., Needham Heights, Mass., 1946-68, gen. mgr., 1968-86, v.p., 1987—; v.p. Plenum Pub. Corp., 1977—. Mem. Natick (Mass.) Planning Bd., 1964-69, chmn., 1968-69; mem. Natick Town Meeting, 1954—, chmn. town by-laws revision com., 1965-67; pres. Greater Framingham Mental Health Assn., 1963-64, dir. 1954-63; mem. Greater Framingham Mental Health Area Bd., 1972-78, v.p., 1974-75, pres., 1975-77; mem. Regional Drug Rev. Bd., 1973; chmn. Natick Regional Vocat. Sch. Planning Com., 1974-77; mem. Natick Sch. Com., 1978-81, clk., 1979-81; chmn. legis. impact study commn. Town of Natick, 1980; chmn. town commn. to rev. by-laws and mcpl. charter, 1980-90; mem. trustees adv. coun. Leonard Morse Hosp., 1973-91, vice chmn., 1974-77, mem. mental health adv. com., 1972-91; chmn. Natick Land-Use Com., 1983—; mem. Mcpl. Charter Rev. Com., 1985-88, Framingham-Natick Golden Triangle Planning Com., 1988-93; trustee Morse Inst. Libr., 1989—; bd. dir. Framington-Natick Cemetery Assn., 1991—; mem. Mcpl. Facilities Planning Com., 1994—. With AUS, 1943-46. Jewish (fin. sec. temple 1954-56, treas. 1952-54, vice-chmn. bd. 1958-59). Home: 2 Abbott Rd Natick MA 01760-1913 Office: 10 Charles St Needham MA 02194-2906

LEBOWITZ, MICHAEL DAVID, epidemiologist; b. Bklyn., Dec. 21, 1939; s. Harry and Rachel (Dick) L.; m. Joyce Marian Schmidt, Sept. 9, 1960; children: Jon A., Kira L., Debra M. AB, U. Calif., 1961, MA, 1965; PhC, U. Wash., 1969, PhD, 1971. Resch. assoc. preventive medicine U. Wash., Seattle, 1967-70, rsch. assoc. environ. health, 1970-71; asst. prof. internal medicine U. Ariz., Tucson, 1971-75, assoc. prof. internal medicine, 1975-80, prof. medicine, 1980—, prof. preventive cmty. medicine, 1996—, asst. dir. div. respiratory sci., 1974-84, assoc. dir. Respiratory Sci. Ctr., 1985-96; dir., prof. epidemiol. unit Ariz. Prevention Ctr., Tucson, 1996—; dir. epidemiol. unit Ariz. Prevention Ctr. U. Ariz., Tucson, 1996—; vis. fellow Postgrad. Cardiothoracic Inst., U. London, 1978-79; vis. prof. Groningen U., The Netherlands, 1993, U. Pisa, Italy, 1993; cons. NIH, Bethesda, Md., 1985—, EPA, Washington, 1969—, WHO, 1979—, Italian Nat. Rsch. Coun., 1979—, Polish Nat. Inst. Hygiene and Acad. Scis., 1981—, Hungarian Nat. Inst. Hygiene, 1989—, Pan Am. Health Orgn., 1985—, also numerous others; co-chmn. Indoor Air Pollutants Commn., NAS-NRC, Washington, 1979-81, WHO Guidelines for Studies in Environ. Epidemiology, 1983, WHO-EURO Monographs on Air Quality, 1982-94. Mem. editl. bd.: Jour. Behavioral Medicine, 1977-93, Jour. Air Pollution Control Assn., 1984-88, Pediat. Pulmonology, 1990-95, Archives Environ. Health, 1990—, Am. Rev. Respiratory Diseases, 1993—; co-editor: WHO/Euro Biol. Contaminants, 1990, WHO Europ Priorities in Environ. Epidemiology, 1996; assoc. editor: Jour. Toxicology Indsl. Health, 1984—, Jour. Exposure Analysis Environ. Epidemiology, 1992—; contbr. numerous articles to profl. jours., chpts. to books and monographs. Chmn. Pima County Air Quality Adv. Coun., Tucson, 1975-78; cons. Ariz. State Dept. Health Svcs., 1972—, Ariz. Lung Assn., 1971—, State Dept. Environ. Quality, 1987—, Gov. of Ariz., 1987-93; senator U. Ariz. Faculty Senate, Tucson, 1976-78. Recipient Ariz. Clean Air award Ariz. Lung Assn., 1987; numerous epidemiology/disease grants and contracts, NIH, EPA, FDA, EPRI and others, 1964—. Fellow Am. Coll. Epidemiology, Am. Coll. Chest Physicians, Collegium Ramazzini, Internat. Acad. Indoor Air Sci.; mem. Am. Epidemiol. Soc., Am. Thoracic Soc., Internat. Epidemiol. Assn., European Respiratory Soc., Soc. Epidemiol. Rsch., Internat. Soc. Environ. Epidemiology, Internat. Soc. Exposure Assessment, Hungar Soc. Health (hon.). Office: U Ariz Coll Medicine Prevention Ctr 1501 N Campbell Ave Tucson AZ 85724-0001

LEBRECHT, THELMA JANE MOSSMAN, reporter; b. Indpls., Feb. 21, 1946; d. Elmore Somerville and Lois Thelma (Johnson) Mossman; m. Roger Dublon LeBrecht, May 4, 1968. BS in Journalism, U. Fla., 1968. Pub. affairs reporter WBT and WBTV, Charlotte, N.C., 1967-72; freelance reporter Toronto and N.Y.C., 1972-76; reporter KYW Newsradio, Phila., 1976-80; editor ABC Radio Network, N.Y.C., 1980-81; reporter AP Broadcast, Washington, 1981—. Bd. dirs. Washington Press Club Found., 1995—. Mem. Radio and TV Corrs. Assn. in U.S. Capitol (chmn. 1991). Office: AP Broadcast 1825 K St NW Washington DC 20006-1202

LEBRO, THEODORE PETER, property tax service executive; b. Fulton, N.Y., Feb. 12, 1910; s. Peter and Mary (Karpala) L.; BS, Syracuse U., 1954; m. Wanda Safranski, Oct. 16, 1932. Farmer nr. Fulton, 1935-76; various positions, Fulton, 1929-54; owner, operator Lebro Real Estate and Ins. Agy., Fulton, 1951—; dir., sec. Hosp. Home Health Care, 1991—. Past bd. dirs. Lee Meml. Hosp.; life mem. Polish Home; pres. Cath. Youth Orgn. Fulton, 1976—; dir. Cath. Charities. Served with 35th inf. U.S. Army, 1942-46, PTO. Certified property mgr. Recipient Bronze Star, Philippine Liberation medal, Combat Infantry Badge, Cmty. Svc. award Fulton Rotary, Outstanding Citizen award Fulton Republican City Cmty, 1995. Mem. VFW, Soc. Real Estate Appraisers, Oswego County Bd. Realtors, N.Y. State Soc. Appraisers (gov.), Assn. County Dirs., Am. Legion, St. Michael's Soc. (pres. 1960—), Beaver Meadow, Pathfinders Game and Fish (life), KC (life knight-4th degree), Elks. Republican. Roman Catholic. Home: RFD 1 Box 111 Rte 48S Phoenix NY 13135 Office: 316 W 1st St Fulton NY 13069

LE BUHN, ROBERT, investment executive; b. Davenport, Iowa, May 2, 1932; s. Dick and Mable (Blom) LeB.; m. Jo-Ann Fitzsimmons, June 19, 1954 (dec. Aug. 1991); children: Anne, Ellen, Robert, Richard; m. Elaine L. Woody, Nov. 25, 1995. B.S., Northwestern U., 1954; M.B.A., U. Pa., 1957. Security analyst Cyrus J. Lawrence & Sons, N.Y.C., 1957-62; v.p. Eppler & Co., Inc., Morristown, N.J., 1962-72; independent fin. cons., 1972-80; mng. dir. Rothschild, N.Y.C., 1980-84; chmn. Investor Internat. (U.S.), Inc., N.Y.C., 1984-94; bd. dirs. Cambrex, Inc., USAIR Group, Inc., Acceptance Ins. Cos., Inc., N.J. Steel, Enzon Corp.; pres. Geraldine R. Dodge Found. Served to lt. (j.g.) USNR, 1954-56. Home: PO Box 6287 86 St Andrews Ct Unit 72 Snowmass Village CO 81615

LE CAM, LUCIEN MARIE, mathematics educator; b. Croze Creuse, France, Nov. 18, 1924; came to U.S., 1950; s. François Marie and Marie Renée (Joanno) Le C.; m. Louise E. Romig, Aug. 19, 1952; children: Denis A., Steven D., Linda M. Licence es Scis., U. Paris, 1947; grad. student, Sorbonne, Paris, 1947-48; Ph.D., U. Calif. at Berkeley, 1952. Mem. faculty U. Calif. at Berkeley, 1952—, from asst. to assoc. prof. stats., 1953-57, prof. stats., 1961-91, Miller prof., 1971-72, prof. math., 1973-91, chmn. dept., 1961-65, prof. emeritus, 1991—. Author: Asymptotic Methods in Statistical Decision Theory, 1986, (with Grace Lo Yang) Asymptotics in Statistics, 1990. Dir. Centre de Recherches Mathématiques, U. Montreal, 1972-73. Home: 101 Kensington Rd Kensington CA 94707-1011 Office: Univ Calif Math Dept Berkeley CA 94720-3860

LECAPITAINE, JOHN EDWARD, counseling psychology educator, researcher; b. Nov. 21, 1950; s. Vincent Bernard and Evelyn Lucille LeCapitaine; m. Jessica Dale; 1 child, Katherine Briee. BS, U. Wis., 1973, MS, 1975; D, Boston U., 1980. Rsch. assoc. Dupont Psychol. Edn. Inst., Eau Claire, Wis., 1975-76; counseling and sch. psychologist Martin Luther King. Jr. Ctr., Boston, 1976-78; rsch. cons. Dept. Mental Health, 1985-90; prof. counseling psychology U. Wis., River Falls, 1990—; adj. prof. Boston U., 1981-89. Contbr. poetry, fiction, and acad. articles to profl. jours. Mem. Am. Counseling Assn., Nat. Assn. Sch. Psychologists, Internat. Coun. Psychologists, Assn. Play Therapy, Assn. Multicultural Counseling and Devel., Assn. Humanistic Devel. and Edn., Assn. Counselor Edn. and Supervision, Internat. Soc. Poets, Phi Delta Kappa. Avocation: fiction writing, poetry. Home: 731 Lumphrey Ct River Falls WI 54022-3426 Office: U Wis Ames Bldg River Falls WI 54022

LE CARRÉ, JOHN (DAVID JOHN MOORE CORNWELL), author; b. Poole, Dorset, Eng., Oct. 19, 1931; s. Ronald Thomas Archibald and Olive (Glassy) Cornwell; m. Alison Ann Sharp, Nov. 27, 1954 (div. dissolved 1972); children: Simon, Stephen, Timothy; m. Valerie Jane Eustace, 1972; 1 son, Nicholas. Student, Bern (Switzerland) U., 1948-49; B.A. in Modern Langs., Lincoln Coll., Oxford (Eng.) U., 1956; hon. doctorate, U. Exeter, 1990. Tutor Eton Coll., Berkshire, Eng., 1956-58; mem. Brit. Fgn. Service, 1959-64; 2d sec. embassy Brit. Fgn. Service, Bonn, Germany, 1961-63; consul Brit. Fgn. Service, Hamburg, Germany, 1963-64. Author: Call for the Dead, 1960, A Murder of Quality, 1962, The Spy Who Came in From the Cold, 1963 (Mystery Writers of Am. Novel of Yr., 1963, Brit. Crime Novel of Yr. award 1963), The Looking-Glass War, 1965, A Small Town in Germany, 1968, The Naive and Sentimental Lover, 1971, Tinker Tailor Soldier Spy, 1973, The Honourable Schoolboy, 1977 (James Tait Black Meml. prize, Crime Writers Assn. gold dagger), Smiley's People, 1980 (televised 1982), The Little Drummer Girl, 1983, A Perfect Spy, 1986, The Russia House, 1989 (Nikos Kasanzakis prize 1991), The Secret Pilgrim, 1991, The Night Manager, 1993, Our Game, 1995. Recipient Somerset Maugham award 1964, Edgar Allen Poe award Mystery Writers Am., 1965, Gold dagger Crime Writers Assn., 1978, Black Meml. award, 1978, Grand Master award Mystery Writers Am., 1986, Malaparte prize, 1987, Diamond Dagger award Crime Writers Assn., 1988; Lincoln Coll., Oxford hon. fellow, 1984. Office: David Higham Assocs Ltd, 5-8 Lower John St Golden Sq, London W1R 4HA, England

LECERF, OLIVIER MAURICE MARIE, construction company executive; b. Merville-Franceville, France, Aug. 2, 1929; s. Maurice and Colette (Lainé) L.; m. Annie Bazin de Jessey, Jan. 11, 1958; children: Christophe, Véronique, Nicolas, Patricia. Baccalauréat A in Philosophy, 1946; diploma Inst. Polit. Studies Paris, 1950; M. Law, U. Paris, 1950; diploma Indsl. Studies Ctr., U. Geneva, 1960. Asst. mgr. Omnium pour l'importation et l'exportation, Paris, 1951-56; asst. mgr. Ciments Lafarge, Can., 1956-57, and Brazil, 1958-59, asst. mgr. fgn. dept., 1961, adj. comml. dir., Paris, 1962-64, pres., CEO Lafarge Cement N.Am., Vancouver, B.C., Can., 1965, pres. Lafarge Can. Que., Montreal, 1968, pres. Lafarge Can. Ltd., 1969, gen. mgr. Can. Cement Lafarge, Montreal, 1970, exec. gen. mgr., Paris, 1971-73, chmn., CEO (now Lafarge), 1974—, hon. chmn., 1989—, also dir.; dir. Compagnie de St Gobain, L'Oréal, others; mem. adv. com. Morgan Stanley, dir., chmn. financière Lafarge; pres. Sicav, Saint Honoré, Marchés Emergents. With inf. French Army, 1950-51; lt. Res. Decorated officer de la Legion d'Honneur, commandeur Ordre National du Merite. Contbr. articles to profl. jours. Home: 8 rue Guy de Maupassant, 75116 Paris France Office: Lafarge, 61 rue des Belles Feuilles, 75116 Paris France

LECHAY, JAMES, artist, emeritus art educator; b. N.Y.C., July 5, 1907; s. Charles and Augusta (Wolfson) L.; m. Rose David, Mar. 26, 1934; children: Jo, Daniel. A.B., U. Ill., 1928; D.F.A. (hon.), Coe Coll., 1961. Asst. prof. art U. Iowa, 1945-49; assoc. prof. 1949-56, prof., 1956-75, prof. emeritus, 1975—; tchr. Stanford U., 1949, N.Y. U., 1953, Skowhegan (Maine) Sch. Painting and Sculpture, 1961; artist in residence Tamarind Inst., 1973; vis. artist New Asia Coll., Chinese U. of Hong Kong, 1976, Parsons Sch. Design, Provincetown, Mass., 1981—, Studio Art Sch. of Aegean, Samos, Greece, 1986, 87, 88. Exhibited in numerous one-man shows including N.Y.C., others in, Trieste, Italy, Chgo., Cedar Rapids, Iowa City, Des Moines Art Center, Louisville, Springfield, Ill., Ft. Dodge, Cedar Falls and Davenport, Iowa Wesleyan U., Sioux City, Iowa, Wellfleet, Mass., Palardy Gallery, Montreal, Que., Can., Dartmouth Coll., Hanover, N.H., SUNY, Binghamton; exhibited group shows Met. Mus. Art, N.Y.C., Pa. Acad. Fine Arts, Provincetown Art Assn., Mass., Va. Mus. Fine Arts, Bklyn. Mus., Chgo. Art Inst., Phillips Meml. Gallery, Whitney Mus. Am. Art, Corcoran Gallery Art, Carnegie Instn., Copenhagen City Gallery, Denmark, others; represented permanent collections, Nat. Collection Fine Arts Smithsonian Instn., Pa. Acad. Fine Arts, U. Ariz., U. Iowa, Bklyn. Mus., New Britain Inst., U. Nebr., Memphis Mus., Ill. Wesleyan U., Chgo Art Inst., Wichita Art Center, Philbrook Mus., Tulsa, Des Moines Art Center, Coe Coll., Joslyn Art Mus., U. No. Iowa, Springfield (Mo.) Art Mus., Rochester Meml. Gallery, others, also pvt. collections. Recipient Norman Wait Harris bronze medal, 52 ann. exhbn. Am. Painting, Art Inst. Chgo., 1941, Lambert purchase prize Pa. Acad., 1942; represented hon. mention for water color Art Inst. Chgo., 1943, prize for oil 2d Ann. Portrait of Am. Exbhn., 1945, hon. mention Denver Mus., 1946, 1st prize for oil Iowa State Fair Exhbn., 1946, 51, 53, 55, 1st prize First Biennial Walker Art Ctr., Mpls., 1947, Minn. Centennial award, 1949, Edmundson trustee prize Des Moines Art Ctr., 1950, 1st prize, 1952, 53, 1st prize Davenport Mcpl. Art Gallery, 1950, Rosenfield Collection purchase prize Des Moines Art Ctr., 1959, Childe Hassam purchase prize, 1974, Benjamin Altman prize NAD, 1977, 91, Henry Ward Ranger Fund purchase prize, 1979, 86, Edwin Palmer Meml. award, 1981, Adolph and Clara Obrig prize NAD, 1993, 95. Mem. NAD. Office: Kraushaar Galleries 724 5th Ave New York NY 10019-4106

LECHELT, EUGENE CARL, psychology educator; b. Edmonton, Alta., Can., Dec. 26, 1942; s. Adolph Carl and Natalie (Klapstein) L.; m. Sandra Dona Morris, Dec. 18, 1965; 1 child, David Patrick. B.Sc., U. Alta., 1964, M.Sc., 1966, Ph.D., 1969. Research assoc., lectr. Princeton U., N.J., 1969-72; asst. prof. dept. psychology U. Alta., Edmonton, 1972-76, assoc. prof., 1976-82, prof., 1982—, chmn., 1986—. Recipient Rutherford Teaching award, 1985, Vol. award Fed. Govt. of Can., 1994; U. Alta. dissertation fellow, 1968-69; Social Scis. Research Council Can. fellow, 1978-79. Mem. Psychonomic Soc., Can. Psychol. Assn., AAAS, N.Y. Acad. Scis., Sigma Xi. Home: 11723-91 Ave, Edmonton, AB Canada T6G 1B1 Office: U Alta, Dept Psychology, Edmonton, AB Canada T6G 2E9

LECHEVALIER, HUBERT ARTHUR, microbiology educator; b. Tours, Indre et Loire, France, May 12, 1926; came to U.S., 1948; s. Jean Gaston and Marie (Delorme) L.; m. Mary Pfeil, Apr. 10, 1950; children: Marc, Paul. L és Sci., Laval U., 1947, MS, 1948, DSc (hon.), 1983; PhD, Rutgers U., 1951. Asst. prof. Rutgers U., New Brunswick, N.J., 1951-56, assoc. prof., 1956-66, prof. microbiology, 1966-91, assoc. dir. Waksman Inst., 1980-88; prof. emeritus, 1991—; vis. scientist Acad. of Scis. USSR, Moscow, 1958-59, Pasteur Inst., Paris, 1961-62;. Author: (with others) A Guide to the Actinomycetes and Their Antibiotics, 1953, Neomycin--Its Nature and Practical Application, 1958, Antibiotics of Actinomycetes, 1962, Three Centuries of Microbiology, 1965, Hungarian transl., 1971, The Microbes, 1971, Macrophages and Cellular Immunity, 1972, Microbial Ecology, 1974, The Development of Applied Microbiology at Rutgers, 1982; contbr. numerous articles to profl. jours.; 4 patents. Trustee Am. Type Culture Collection, Rockville, Md., 1973-79. Recipient Lindback award 1976, Bergey award 1989; inducted into N.J. Inventors Hall of Fame, 1990. Mem. Soc. Française de Microbiology (hon.), Soc. for Indsl. Microbiology (Charles Thom award 1982). Home: RR 2 Box 2235 Morrisville VT 05661-9429

LECHLEIDER, JOSEPH W., computer engineer; b. Bklyn., Feb. 22, 1933; married; 2 children. BME, Cooper Union, 1954; MEE, Poly. Inst. Bklyn., 1957, PhD in Elec. Engring., 1965. Engr. Gen. Electric Co., 1954-55; mem. tech. staff Bell Telephone Labs., 1955-65, supr. transmission studies, outside plant/underwater sys., 1965-67, head loop transmission maintenance engring. dept., 1970-76, head software design dept., 1976—; bd. dirs. Bellcore. Mem. IEEE (sr.); mem. Am. Math. Soc., Sigma Xi. Office: Bellcore/445 South St Rm 21261/PO Box 1910 Morristown NJ 07960*

LECHNER, ALFRED JAMES, JR., judge; b. Elizabeth, N.J., Jan. 7, 1948; s. Alfred J. and Marie G. (McCormack) L.; m. Gayle K. Peterson, Apr. 3, 1976; children—Brendan Patrick, Coleman Thomas, Mary Kathleen. B.S., Xavier U., Cin., 1969; J.D., U. Notre Dame, 1972. Bar: N.J. 1972, N.Y. 1973; U.S. Dist. Ct. N.J. 1972, U.S. Dist. Ct. (so. and ea. dists.) N.Y. 1974, U.S. Ct. Appeals (2d cir.) 1974, U.S. Ct. Appeals (3d cir.) 1980, U.S. Supreme Ct. 1975. Assoc. Cadwalader, Wickersham & Taft, N.Y.C., 1972-75, MacKenzie, Welt & Duane, Elizabeth, N.J., 1975-76; ptnr. MacKenzie, Welt, Duane & Lechner, Elizabeth, 1976-84; judge Superior Ct. State N.J., 1984-86; judge U.S. Dist. Ct. N.J., 1986—. Mem. Union County (N.J.) adv. bd. Catholic Community Services, 1981-83, chmn., 1982. Maj. USMCR. Fellow Am. Bar Found.; mem. Assn. Fed. Bar of State N.J. Roman Catholic. Clubs: Friendly Sons of St. Patrick (pres. 1982), Union County. Note and comment editor Notre Dame Law Rev., 1972; contbr. articles to legal jours. Office: US Dist Ct Martin Luther King Jr Fed Bldg US Ct House Box 999 Newark NJ 07102

LECHNER, BERNARD JOSEPH, consulting electrical engineer; b. N.Y.C., Jan. 25, 1932; s. Barnard Joseph and Lillian Veronica (Stevens) L.; m. Joan Camp Mathewson, Nov. 21, 1953. BSEE, Columbia U., 1957; postgrad., Princeton U., 1957-60. Mem. tech. staff RCA Labs., Princeton, N.J., 1957-62, project leader, 1962-67, group head, 1967-77, lab. dir., 1977-83, staff v.p., 1983-87; cons., Princeton, 1987—; cons. expert on TV matters including high definition TV and flat-panel displays; bd. dirs. Palisades Inst., N.Y.C.; chmn. adv. commn. Mercer County Coll., Trenton, N.J., 1968-85. Contbr. articles to profl. jours.; holder 10 patents. Reader Recording for the Blind, Princeton, 1967-72. Served to cpl. U.S. Army, 1953-55. Recipient David Sarnoff Gold medal RCA Corp., 1962. Fellow Soc. for Info. Display (pres. 1978-80, other offices, Frances Rice Darne award 1971, Beatrice Winner award 1983), IEEE (chpt. chmn. 1964-66, Best Paper award Solid State Cirs. Conf. 1966); mem. Soc. Motion Picture & TV Engrs., Am. Relay Radio League, Sigma Xi, Tau Beta Pi, Eta Kappa Nu. Episcopalian. Club: Princeton Sqs. (pres. 1981-87). Avocations: amateur radio, sq. dancing, philately, sailing, swimming. Address: 98 Carson Rd Princeton NJ 08540-2207

LECHNER, JON ROBERT, nursing administrator, educator; b. Detroit, Nov. 5, 1957; s. Monroe Stanley and Helen Cecelia (Schneider) L. Cert. in practical nursing, Oakland C.C., Southfield, Mich., 1983; ADN, Mercy Coll. Detroit, 1991, BSN, 1992. Cert. EMT; RN, ANCC, Mich. Coord. emergency med. svcs., paramedic William Beaumont Hosp., Royal Oak, Mich., 1979-84, lic. practical nurse, 1986-91, RN, 1991—, asst. nursing mgr., 1992—; pastoral assoc. St. Mary's Parish & Sch., Toledo, 1984-86; adj. clin. instr. Oakland C.C., Waterford, Mich., 1993—; cert. BLS instr. Am. Heart Assn., Southfield, 1986—. Vol. Project Health-O-Rama, 1992—, Wellness Networks, Inc., 1992—; voting mem. region I State of Mich. HIV Planning & Prevention Commn., Detroit, 1994—. Mem. Am. Assembly Men Nursing, Am. Assn. Neurosci. Nurses, Acad. Med. Surg. Nurses (charter), Assn. Nurses AIDS Care, Sigma Theta Tau. Democrat. Roman Catholic. Avocations: reading, hiking, walking, cycling, theatre. Home: 28450 Universal Dr Warren MI 48092-2441 Office: William Beaumont Hosp 3601 W 13 Mile Rd Royal Oak MI 48073-6769

LECHOLOP, STEPHEN KINON, medical center administrator; b. Dillon, S.C., Sept. 11, 1953; s. Michael Stephen Lecholop and Miriam Edna Kinon Sanders; m. Carol Roberts, Nov. 26, 1976; children: Stephen K. II, Timothy R. BSBA, The Citadel, Charleston, S.C., 1975; MBA, Golden Gate U., San Francisco, 1977; MS in Health Svcs. Adminstrn., Ctrl. Mich. U., 1987. Dir. patient adminstrn. Hill Hosp., Ogden, Utah, 1978-79, dir. med. resource mgmt., 1979-80; dir. patient affairs Eglin Regional Hosp., Ft. Walton Beach, Fla., 1980-82; adminstr. Fairford (U.K.) Clinic, 1982-84; assoc. to chief Med. Svc. Corps Surgeon Gens. Office, Washington, 1984-87; chief human resources Regional Office S.W., San Antonio, 1987-91; adminstr. Bergstrom Hosp., Austin, Tex., 1991-93; regional dir. managed care Wilford Hall Med. Ctr., San Antonio, 1993-94; exec. dir. TriCare S.W., San Antonio, 1994—. Bd. dirs. McAllister Park, San Antonio, 1994—, Blue Gray Ednl. Soc., Washington, 1994—, Donald Wagner Scholarship, San Antonio, 1994—; preceptor Baylor U. Grad. Program. Col. USAF, 1975—. Named Fed. Young Healthcare Adminstr., Assn. Mil. Surgeons U.S., 1987. Fellow Am. Coll. Healthcare Execs. (regent 1993—); mem. Am. Coll. Managed care Adminstrs. (coun. regents 1993—), Helthcare Execs. Group of Wilford Hall, Gateway Hills Gold Club (chair person adv. coun.), Rotary. Avocations: golf, music. Home: 17206 Fawn Cloud Ln San Antonio TX 78248 Office: TriCare S W 7800 IH 10W Ste 400 San Antonio TX 78230-4750

LECHTENBERG, VICTOR L., agricultural studies educator; b. Butte, Nebr., Apr. 14, 1945; m. Grayce Lechtenberg; 4 children. BS, U. Nebr., 1967; PhD in Agronomy, Purdue U., 1971. Prof. agronomy Purdue U., West Lafayette, Ind., 1971—, assoc. dir. Agrl. Experiment Sta., 1982-89, exec. assoc. dean agr., 1989-93, dean agr., 1994—, exec. assoc. dean of agr., 1989-94; dean agr. Purdue U., West Lafayette, 1994—, pres., 1996; mem. land grant univ. coms. advising USDA, U.S. Congress on funding for agrl. rsch., extension, teaching. Contbr. articles to profl. jours., chpts. to books. Scoutmaster Boy Scouts Am., 1983-85. Recipient Nebr. 4-H Dist. Alumni award, 1981. Fellow Am. Soc. Agronomy (Ciba-Geigy award), Crop Sci. Soc. Am. (past pres.); mem. Crop Sci. Soc. Agrnomy, Coun. Agrl. Sci. and Tech. (pres.-elect, bd. dirs.), Am. Registry of Cert. Profls. in Agronomy, Crops and Soils, Sigma Xi, Alpha Zeta, Gamma Sigma Delta. Roman Catholic. Avocation: woodworking. Office: Purdue Univ 1140 Ag Adminstrn West Lafayette IN 47907

LECKER, ABRAHAM, former banker; b. Rumania, Mar. 29, 1916; came to U.S., 1957; s. Schaje and Lisa (Schimmel) L.; m. Minnie Kamenetzky, Aug. 29, 1954; 1 dau., Lisa Joy. MBA, Cert. Assn. Brit. Inst. Bankers, London, 1947; LLB, Sch. Law, Tel Aviv, 1957; postgrad., Harvard Bus. Sch. With banks in Palestine, 1934-36, Barclays Bank DCO, Palestine, 1936-49; dep. treas., comptroller City of Haifa, Israel, 1949-57; with Exchange Nat. Bank, Chgo., 1957-81; sr. v.p., cashier Exchange Nat. Bank, 1966-73, exec. v.p., 1973-81, dir., 1971-75. Served with Brit. Army, World War II; Served with Israeli Army, 1948-49. Former mem. Am. Jewish Com., Brit. Inst. Bankers, Am. Inst. Bankers, Ill. Mfrs. Assn., Bankers Assn. Fgn. Trade, Internat. Bus. Coun. Chgo., Ill. C. of C., Svc. Corps Ret. Execs. (vol.), Exec. Svc. Corps., Internat. Exec. Svc. Corps., B'nai B'rith. Home: 3750 N Lake Shore Dr Chicago IL 60613-4238

LECKEY, ANDREW A., financial columnist; b. Chgo., Sept. 22, 1949; s. Alexander and Ellen (Martin) L. B.A., Trinity Coll., Deerfield, Ill., 1971; M.A. in Journalism, U. Mo., 1975; postgrad., Columbia U., 1978-79, Rutgers U., 1981. Fin. editor Oreg. Statesman, Salem, 1975-76; statehouse reporter Phoenix Gazette, 1976-78; fin. columnist Chgo. Sun-Times, 1979-85, Chgo. Tribune and N.Y. Daily News, 1985—; fin. commentator Sta. WBEZ, Chgo., 1981-83, Sta. WLS-TV, Chgo., 1983—; syndicated fin. columnist Los Angeles Times Syndicate, 1983-85, Tribune Media Services, 1985—; fin. commentator WLS-TV. Author: Make Money with the New Tax Laws, 1987. Office: WLS-TV 190 N State St Chicago IL 60601 also: Chgo Tribune Co 435 N Michigan Ave Chicago IL 60611-4001

LE CLAIR, CHARLES GEORGE, artist, retired dean; b. Columbia, Mo., May 23, 1914; s. Carl Amie and Marie (Fess) LeC.; m. Margaret Foster, May 30, 1945 (dec. Nov. 1992). BS, MS, U. Wis., 1935; posgrad., Academie Ranson, Paris, 1937; grad. study, Columbia U., 1940-41. Instr. art U. Ala., 1935-36, asst. prof., head dept., 1937-42; asst. prof. art, head dept. Albion Coll., 1942-43; tchr. painting and design Albright Art Sch., Buffalo, 1943-46; assoc. prof., head dept. Chatham Coll., 1946-52, prof., 1952-60; dean Tyler Sch. Art, Temple U., Phila., 1960-74; dean emeritus Tyler Sch. Art, Temple U., 1981—, prof. painting, 1974-81, chmn. painting and sculpture dept., 1979-81; established Tyler Sch. Art, Rome, Italy, 1966. Author: The Art of Watercolor, 1985, rev. edit. full color, 1994, Color in Contemporary Painting, 1991; contbg. author: Everything You Ever Wanted to Know About Oil Painting, 1994; works exhibited Pa. Acad. Met. Mus. Art, Carnegie Inst., Whitney Mus., Corcoran Mus., Chgo. Art Inst., Richmond Mus., Butler Mus. Art, Am. Watercolor Soc., Bklyn. Mus.; one-man shows include Carnegie Inst., 1954, Salpeter Gallery, N.Y.C., 1956, 59, 65, Rochester Inst. Tech., 1958, Phila. Art Alliance, 1962, 73, Franklin and Marshall Coll., 1969, Galleria 89, Rome, 1970, Left Bank Gallery, Wellfleet, 1983, 87, 96, 40-yr. Retrospective, Temple U., 1978, Visual Images, Wellfleet, 1978, 79, 80, Am. Acad. and Inst. Arts and Letters, 1978, Gross-McCleaf Gallery, Phila., 1979, 81, 96, More Gallery Phila., 1983, 87, 89. Fellow Fund for Advancement Edn. Ford Found., 1952-53; named Pitts. Artist of Year, 1957. Subject of Elizabeth Leonard's book Painting Flowers, 1986. Home: 1810 Rittenhouse Sq Philadelphia PA 19103-5837

LECLAIR, SUSAN JEAN, hematologist, clinical laboratory scientist, educator; b. New Bedford, Mass., Feb. 17, 1947; d. Joseph A. and Beatrice (Perry) L.; m. James T. Griffith; 1 child, Kimberly A. BS in med. tech., Stonehill Coll., 1968; postgrad., Northeastern U., Boston, 1972-74; MS in Med. Lab. Sci., U. Mass., Dartmouth, 1977. Cert. clin. lab. scientist; cert. med. technologist. Med. technologist Union Hosp., New Bedford, Mass., 1968-70; supr. hematology Morton Hosp., Taunton, Mass., 1970-72; edn. coord., program dir. Sch. Med. Tech. Miriam Hosp., Providence, 1972-79; hematology technologist R.I. Hosp., Providence, 1979-80; asst. prof. med. lab. sci. U. Mass., Dartmouth, 1980-84, assoc. prof. med. lab. sci., 1984-92, prof. med. lab. sci., 1992—; instr. hematology courses Brown U., Providence, 1978-80; cons. Bd. R.I. Schs. Med. Tech., R.I. Hosp. Div. Clin. Hematology, Cardinal Cushing Gen. Hosp., Charlton Meml. Hosp., St. Luke's Hosp., VA Med. Ctr., Providence, 1984—, Nemasket Group, Inc., 1984-87, Gateway Health Alliance, 1985-87; chair hematology/hemostasis com. Nat. Cert. Agy.

for Med. Lab. Pers. Exam. Coun., 1994—. Contbr. articles to profl. jours.; contbr. articles to jours and chpts. to books; author computer software in hematology. Reviewer Nat. Commn. Clin. Lab. Scis., 1986-89; chairperson Mass. Assn. Health Planning Agys., 1986-87; bd. dirs. Southeastern Mass. Health Planning Devel. Inc., (1975-88, numerous other offices and coms.); planning subcom. AIDS Edn. (presentor Info Series). Mem. Am. Soc. Clin. Lab. Sci., Nat. Cert. Agy. for Med. Lab. Pers. (chair Hematology Com. of Exam Coun. 1994—), Am. Soc. Med. Tech. Edn. and Rsch. Fund, Inc. (chairperson 1983-85), Mass. Assn. for Med. Tech. (pres. 1977-78), Southeastern Mass. Soc. Med. Tech. (pres. 1975-76), Alpha Mu Tau (pres. 1993-94). Avocations: choral singing, cooking, reading. Office: U Mass Dept Med Lab Sci Dartmouth MA 02747

LECLERC, PAUL, library director; b. Lebanon, N.H., May 28, 1941; s. Louis and M. Juliette (Trottier) LeC; m. Judith Ginsberg, Oct. 26, 1980; 1 child, Adam Louis. BS, Coll. Holy Cross, 1963; student, U. Paris, 1963-64; MA, Columbia U., 1966, PhD with distinction, 1969; LHD (hon.), L.I. U., 1994, Coll. of the Holy Cross, 1994, Hamilton Coll., 1995. Assoc. prof. French Union Coll., Schenectady, 1969-79, chmn. dept. modern langs. and lit., 1972-77, chmn. humanities div., 1975-77; univ. dean for acad. affairs CUNY, 1979-84; provost and acad. v.p. Baruch Coll., CUNY, 1984-88; pres. Hunter Coll., CUNY, 1988-93; pres., CEO New York Public Library, 1994—; bd. dirs. N.Y. Alliance for Pub. Schs., N.Y.C., 1981-84, El Museo del Barrio, The Feminist Press; pres. N.Y. Tchr. Edn. Conf. Bd., Albany, N.Y., 1983-84. Author: Voltaire and Crebillon Pere, 1972, Voltaire's Rome Sauvée, 1992; co-editor: Lettres d'André Moreliet, vol. I, 1991, vol. II, 1994; contbr. articles to profl. jours. Decorated officier Palmes Académiques (France); grantee NEH, 1971, 79, Am. Coun. Learned Socs., 1973, Ford Found., 1979. Mem. MLA, Am. Soc. for 18th Century Studies. Office: NY Pub Libr Fifth Ave & 42nd St New York NY 10018

LECOCQ, KAREN ELIZABETH, artist; b. Santa Rosa, Calif., Nov. 4, 1949; d. Maynard Rodney and Lois May (Lessard) LeC.; m. David Lawrence Medley, Sept. 7, 1995. BA, Calif. State U., Fresno, 1971, MA, 1975; postgrad., Calif. Inst. of the Arts, L.A., 1971-72. Founding mem. Feminist Art Program, Fresno, Calif., 1971, Calif. Inst. of the Arts, L.A., 1972; One woman shows include Calif. State U. Art Gallery, Fresno, 1970, 76, Merced (Calif.) Coll., 1969, 77, 91, Calif. Inst. of the Arts, L.A., 1972, Recent Sculptures, Fresno, 1977, 78, Womanart Gallery, N.Y.C., 1980, Merced, 1987, Arts Coun. Gallery, Merced, 1989, Amos Eno Gallery, N.Y.C., 1994, 750 Gallery, Sacramento, 1995, Meridian Gallery, San Francisco, 1996, others; commissions include Absolut Vodka, 1993; vis. artist Merced County Schs., 1977-78, 79-82, 88-91; grad. instr. Calif. State U., Fresno, 1976-78, Merced Coll., 1973-76. Group shows include Womanhouse, L.A., 1972, Off Centre Centre, Calgary, Alta., Can., 1985, 86, Ryosuke Gallery, Osaka, Japan, 1986, Gallery Six Oh One, San Francisco, 1989, Fresno Art Mus., 1989, Ann Saunders Gallery, Jamestown, Calif., 1991, Pro arts Gallery, Oakland, Calif., 1991, Calif. Mus. Art, Santa Rosa, 1991, Harbs Gallery, Lexington, Va., 1992, Russell Sage Gallery, Troy, N.Y., 1992, Amos Eno Gallery, 1992-96, ARC Gallery, Chgo., 1993, 96, Lengyel Gallery, San Francisco, 1995, 750 Gallery, Sacramento, 1994-96, L.A. Mus. Contemporary Art, 1995, Armand Hammer Mus., L.A., 1996, many others. Docent Gallery Guide Art Train, Merced, 1983; artistic dir. Black and White Ball, Merced Regional Arts Coun., 1989-96. Cora T. McCord scholar; CETA grantee, Merced, 1978, Fresno, 1977; Calif. Inst. Arts scholar, 1972. Mem. Internat. Sculpture Source, No. Calif. Women's Caucus for Art, Pro Arts of Oakland, San Francisco Mus. Art. Democrat. Home and Office: PO Box 2204 Merced CA 95344

LECOMPTE, ELIZABETH, theater director; b. Summit, N.J., Apr. 28, 1944. BS, Skidmore COll., 1967. Founder, dir. Wooster Group, N.Y.C., 1980—. Director: Frank Dell's The Temptation of Saint Antony, 1987, Brace Up!, 1991, Fish Story, 1993, The Emperor Jones, 1994, The Hairy Ape, 1995. Recipient Obie award for Point Judith; MacArthur fellow, 1995, NEA Disting. Artists fellow for lifetime achievement in Am. theater. Office: The Wooster Group PO Box 654 Canal St New York NY 10013

LECOMPTE, ROGER BURTON, management consultant; b. Cin., May 22, 1942; s. Joseph Edward and Lefa May (Ayars) LeC.; m. Margaret Morgan, 1969 (div. 1971); m. Helen Lida Smits, Aug. 28, 1976; 1 child, Theodore Edward. BA, U. Cin., 1965; MBA, U. Pa., 1975. Cons. alt. delivery systems Blue Cross Assn., Chgo., 1971-73; asst. to pres. Albert Einstein Med. Ctr., Phila., 1975-77; cons. Lewin & Assocs., Washington, 1977-81; v.p. planning Middlesex Hosp., Middletown, Conn., 1981-93; prin. The Futures Group, Glastonbury, Conn., 1993-94; pres. LeCompte & Co. Healthcare Planning, 1993—; dir. network devel. Health Right, Inc., Meriden, Conn., 1995—; bd. dirs. Aetna Health Plan of So. New Eng.; vol. US Peace Corps, Kumba, Cameroon, 1965-67; vice-chmn. Vis. Nurses of Lower Valley, Essex, Conn., 1983-86. Author/editor: Prepaid Group Practice Manual, 1973. Mem. bd. edn. Essex Elem. Sch., 1985-91, chmn. sch. bldg. com., 1987-93; vestryman St. John's Episcopal Ch., Essex, 1988-92, chmn. capital fund drive, 1996. Democrat. Home: 81 Main St Ivoryton CT 06442-1032

LE COMTE, EDWARD SEMPLE, author, educator; b. N.Y.C., May 28, 1916; s. John Radway and Mary (Semple) Le C.; m. Marie Munzer, Jan. 19, 1945; 1 son, Douglas Munzer. A.B., Columbia, 1939, A.M., 1940, Ph.D., 1943. Instr. English Columbia, 1943-45; asst. prof. English U. Calif.-Berkeley, 1945-48; asst. prof. English Columbia U., 1948-56, assoc. prof., 1956-64; prof. English SUNY-Albany, 1964-81, prof. emeritus, 1981—. Author: Endymion in England: The Literary History of a Greek Myth, 1944, Yet Once More: Verbal and Psychological Pattern in Milton, 1953, A Dictionary of Last Words, 1955, The Long Road Back, 1957, He and She, 1960, A Milton Dictionary, 1961, Grace to a Witty Sinner: A Life of Donne, 1965, The Notorious Lady Essex, 1969, The Man Who Was Afraid, 1969, Milton's Unchanging Mind, 1973, Poets' Riddles: Essays in Seventeenth-Century Explication, 1975, Sly Milton: The Meaning Lurking in the Contexts of His Quotations, 1976, Milton and Sex, 1978, The Professor and the Coed, 1979, A Dictionary of Puns in Milton's English Poetry, 1981, I, Eve, 1988, Milton Re-viewed: Ten Essays, 1991, Carnal Sin, 1994; also various articles in scholarly jours. on 17th Century lit.; editor: Paradise Lost and Other Poems, 1961, Justa Edovardo King, 1978. Mem. Milton Soc. (hon. scholar), P.E.N., MLA, Phi Beta Kappa. Home: PO Box 143 North Egremont MA 01252-0143

LE COUNT, VIRGINIA G., communications company executive; b. Long Island City, N.Y., Nov. 22, 1917; d. Clifford R. and Luella (Meier) LeCount. BA, Barnard Coll., 1937; MA, Columbia U., 1940. Tchr. pub. schs. P.R., 1937-38; supr. HOLC, N.Y.C., 1938-40; translator Guildhall Publs., N.Y.C., 1940-41; office mgr. Sperry Gyroscope Co., Garden City, Lake Success, Bklyn. (all N.Y.), 1941-45; billing mgr. McCann Erickson, Inc., N.Y.C., 1945-56; v.p., bus. mgr., bd. dirs. Infoplan Internat, Inc., N.Y.C., 1956-69; v.p., bus. mgr. Communications Affiliates Ltd., Communications Affiliates (Bahamas) Ltd., N.Y.C., 1964-69; mgr. office services Interpublic Group of Cos., Inc., N.Y.C., 1971-72; bus. mgr. Jack Tinker & Ptnrs., Inc., N.Y.C., 1969-70; corp. records mgr. Interpublic Group of Cos., Inc., N.Y.C., 1972-83, mktg. intelligence data mgr., 1975-83. Mem. Alumnae Bernard Coll. Mem. Marble Collegiate Ch. Home: 136 E 55th St Apt 10Q New York NY 10022-4534

LECOURS, MICHEL, electrical engineering educator; b. Montreal, Que., Can., Aug. 1, 1940; s. Henri and Germaine (L'Archeveque) L.; m. Almut Lange, July 14, 1966; children: Christiane, Mireille, Jean-Yves. BScA, Ecole Poly., Montreal, 1963; PhD, Imperial Coll., London, 1966. Registered profl. engr., Que. Mem. sci. staff Bell-No. Rsch., Ottawa, Ont., Can., 1971-72; prof. elec. engring. U. Laval, Quebec City, Que., 1967—, head dept., 1975-77, vice dean, 1977-85; cons. Lab-Volt (Que.) Ltd., Quebec City, 1981—; vis. researcher Nippon Tel. & Tel., Yokosuka, Japan, 1986. Contbr. numerous articles on electronics and communications to sci. jours.; patentee for short range high resolution radar. Recipient ann. merit award Ecole Poly., 1986. Fellow Can. Soc. for Elec. and Computer Engring., Engring. Inst. Can.; mem. IEEE (sr.), Order Engrs. Que. (sr.). Office: Laval Univ, Dept Elec Engring, Quebec, PQ Canada G1K 7 P4

LE DAIN, GERALD ERIC, retired Canadian Supreme Court justice; b. Montreal, Que., Can., Nov. 27, 1924; s. Eric George and Antoinette Louise (Whithard) Le D.; m. Cynthia Roy, Sept. 13, 1947; children—Jacqueline, Catherine, Barbara, Caroline, Eric, Jennifer. B.C.L., McGill U., Montreal, 1949; LLD (hon.), McGill U., 1985; Docteur del'Universite, U. Lyon, France, 1950; LL.D. (hon.), York U., Toronto, 1976, Concordia U., Montreal, 1976; D.C.L. (hon.), Acadia U., N.S., 1978. Bar: Que. 1949, Ont. 1968; created Queen's counsel 1961. Asso. prof. law McGill U., 1953-59, prof., 1966-67; dean, prof. Osgoode Hall Law Sch., York U., 1967-72, prof., 1972-75; practiced law with Walker, Martineau & Co., Montreal, 1950-53; with legal dept. CDN Internet Pap Co., Montreal, 1959-61; ptnr. Riel, LeDain & Co., Montreal, 1961-66; judge Fed. Ct. of Appeal of Can., Ottawa, Ont., 1975-84; judge Supreme Ct. Can., Ottawa, 1984-88, ret., 1988. Contbr. articles to legal jours. Chmn. Commn. of Inquiry Into Non-Med. Use of Drugs (Le Dain Commn.), 1969-73. Served with arty. Can. Army, 1943-46, France, Germany. Recipient Elizabeth Torrance Gold medal McGill U., 1949, Companion of the Order of Can., 1989, Justice Gerald LeDain award, Drug Policy Found., ,1990; MacDonald Travelling scholar, 1949-50. Club: Rideau (Ottawa).

LEDBETTER, CALVIN REVILLE, JR. (CAL LEDBETTER), political science educator, university dean, former legislator; b. Little Rock; s. Calvin Reville Sr. and Virginia Mae (Campbell) L.; m. Mary Brown Williams, July 26, 1953; children: Grainger, Jeffrey (dec.), Snow. BA, Princeton U., 1951; LLB, U. Ark., 1954; PhD, Northwestern U., 1960. Bar: Ark., 1954. Pvt. practice Little Rock, 1954; mem. faculty dept. polit. sci. U. Ark., Little Rock, 1960—, now prof., head dept., 1968-78, dean, 1978-88; cons. law enforcement program, advisor pre-law program; mem. Ark. Ho. of Reps., 1967-76; chmn. spl. legis. com., com. on legis. orgn.; vice chmn. legis. com. state agys. and govt. affairs; cons. pub. schs.; mem. Nat. Adv. Com. on Criminal Justice Goals and Standards; mem. adv. com. Nat. Inst. Law Enforcement and Criminal Justice.; election night analyst for Ark. congl. and Presdl. elections ABC, 1964-84. Co-author: Politics in Arkansas: The Constitutional Experience, 1972, The Arkansas Plan: A Case Study in Public Policy, 1979, Arkansas Becomes a State, 1985, Carpenter from Conway: George W. Donaghey as Governor of Arkansas 1909-1913, 1993; contbr. articles, book reviews to profl. jours. Mem. Ark. Adv. Coun. on Pub., Elem. and Secondary Edn.; Gov.'s rep. So. Regional Growth Policies Bd.; mem. Ark. Legis. Coun.; del. Ark. Constl. Conv., 1979, v.p., 1979-80; chmn. law enforcement and criminal justice task force Nat. Legis. Conf. Former chmn. coll. and univ. sect. United Fund; del. Dem. Nat. Conv., 1968, 84; mem. exec. com. Ark. Young Dems.; bd. dirs. Health and Welfare Coun. Pulaski County; trustee Philander Smith Coll., chmn. council community advisers; sec. bd. dirs. St. Vincent's Infirmary; bd. dirs. Ark. Humanities Coun., 1989-93, v.p., 1991-93, pres. 1993-94; bd. trustees Ark. Mus. Sci. and History. Served with JAGC AUS, 1955-57. Recipient award for outstanding contbn. to humanities Little Rock Arts and Humanities Commn., 1993; named Educator of Yr., Greater Little Rock Fedn. Women's Clubs, 1968. Mem. ABA, Ark. Bar Assn. (Writing Excellence award 1985-86), Pulaski County Bar Assn., Nat. Conf. State Legislators (exec. com.), Nat. Conf. Acad. Deans (pres. 1987-88), Am. Polit. Sci. Assn., So. Polit. Sci. Assn., Ark. Polit. Sci. Assn. (pres. 1980-81), Ark. Acad. Sci., Am. Acad. Polit. and Social Sci., Ark. Hist. Assn., Ark. Edn. Assn., Pulaski County Hist. Soc. (bd. dirs. 1988-90), Ark. Hist. Commn. (v.p. 1989—, pres. 1990—), Rotary (pres. West Little Rock chpt. 1987-88). Presbyterian. Home: 4322 I St Little Rock AR 72205-2054 Office: Univ Ark Little Rock Polit Sci Dept Little Rock AR 72204

LEDBETTER, DAVID OSCAR, lawyer; b. Santa Rosa, Calif., Mar. 16, 1950; s. Oscar Smith Ledbetter and Nova Nell (Huckaby) Kramer; m. Judith Louise Fischer, Dec. 14, 1976; children: Hannah J., Jordan B. BA, U. Redlands, 1972; JD, Hastings Coll. Law, 1977. Bar: Calif. 1977, D.C. 1986, Va. 1987. Assoc. Moran, Urich & Evans, San Francisco, 1977-79; trial atty. land and natural resource divsn. U.S. Dept. Justice, Washington, 1979-85; assoc., counsel, ptnr. Hunton & Williams, Richmond, Va., 1985—; bd. adv. Chem. Waste Litigation Reporter, Washington, 1983—. Co-author: Environmental Law Practice Guide, 1996; co-author, editor: Outline RCRA, Cercla Enforcement Issues and Holdings, 1996; contbr. articles to profl. jours. Bd. dirs. John Tyler C.C. Found., Chester, Va., 1992—; ednl. adv. coun. Charles City (Va.) County Vocat., 1990—. Mem. ABA (vice chair spl. com. toxic and environ. torts), Va. State Bar Assn., Calif. Bar Assn., Bar Assn. D.C., Environ. Law Inst., Charles City Ruritan Club. Democrat. Methodist. Avocations: gardening, fishing. Home: 16530 The Glebe Ln Charles City VA 23030-3837 Office: Hunton & Williams 951 E Byrd St Richmond VA 23219-4040

LEDBETTER, DEIDRE LEDAY, special education educator; b. New Orleans, Oct. 16, 1959; d. Felton Clark Augusta and Frances Ada (Norman) Provost; m. Robert Leday, June 8, 1975 (dec. Aug. 1976); 1 child, Demetria Marie; m. George Dallas Ledbetter, Jr., Feb. 7, 1981. B Gen. Studies in Behavioral Scis., U. Southwestern La., 1982, BA in Spl. Edn., 1993, MEd in Guidance and Counseling, 1996. Resource tchr. Iberia Parish Sch. Bd., New Iberia, La., 1982-94, link cons., 1994—; mem. core com. Very Spl. Arts Festival, New Iberia, 1990-94. Active Coun. for Exceptional Children. Named Tchr. of Yr., Lee Street Elem. Sch., 1994. Mem. NEA, La. Assn. Educators, Iberia Assn. Educators (sec. 1989-90), Order Ea. Star, Order of Cyrene (royal Magdalene 1991—), Heroines of Jericho (vice ancient matron 1990—). Democrat. Methodist. Avocations: travel, sewing, cooking, photography. Home: 1007 Bank Ave New Iberia LA 70560 Office: Iberia Parish Spl Edn Dept PO Box 200 New Iberia LA 70560

LEDBETTER, RANDI RAE, obstetrician/gynecologist; b. Portland, Oreg., June 24, 1952; d. James Edward Wagenblast and Shiela Faye (Mathis) Rhyne; m. Gordon Kirk Ledbetter, Feb. 14, 1971. BA in Biology, Linfield Coll., 1974; MD, Oreg. Health Scis. U., 1978. Diplomate Am. Bd. Ob-Gyn., Am. Bd. Family Practice. Intern, resident Family Practice Residency of Idaho, Boise, 1978-81; pvt. practice Boise Family Practice, 1981-88; resident in ob-gyn. Kaiser Found. Hosp., San Francisco, 1988-91; pvt. practice Women's Healthcare Assocs., Portland, Oreg., 1991—; chmn. laparoscopy com. ob-gyn. dept. St. Vincent's Hosp., Portland, 1993—. Mem. women's task force Women's Life, Boise, 1985-88. Fellow Am. Coll. Ob-Gyn.; mem. Oreg. Med. Assn., Washington County Med. Soc. (bd. dirs.), Porsche Club Am., Sports Car Club Am., Team Continental (dir. med.). Republican. Avocations: autoracing, gardening, computers. Home: 12929 NW Laidlaw Rd Portland OR 97229-2413 Office: Women's Healthcare Assocs 9155 SW Barnes Rd Ste 340 Portland OR 97225-6630

LEDDICOTTE, GEORGE COMER, business executive, consultant; b. Oak Ridge, Tenn., May 28, 1947; s. George W. Leddicotte and Virginia (Comer) Leddicotte Stratton; m. Connie Laverne Sterrett, Jan. 25, 1969; 1 child, Matthew Sterrett. BA in Polit. Sci., U. Mo., 1970. Cert. relocation profl. Customer service supr. Crown Zellerbach, San Francisco, 1973-74; exec. recruiter Christopher & Long, St. Louis, 1974; regional ops. mgr. Curtin Matheson Scientific, Inc., Houston, 1974-80; regional mgr., mng. cons. Merrill Lynch Relocation Mgmt., White Plains, N.Y., 1980-82, regional v.p., nat. accounts, 1982-83, regional v.p. govt. svcs., 1983-84; dir. govt. svcs. Coldwell Banker Relocation Mgmt., Washington, 1984-85; dir. sales., account mgmt. Homequity, Wilton, Conn., 1985-87; v.p. nat. sales Premier Relocation Svcs., Inc., Irvine, Calif., 1987-88; v.p., sr. mng. cons. Premier Decision Mgmt., Irvine, 1988—; pres., CEO Feasiblility Relocation Mgmt. Svcs., Inc., Raleigh, N.C., 1988—; pres., COO Carolina Relocation Group, Hendersonville, N.C., 1994. Pub. Relocation Update, 1993-95. First lt. U.S. Army, 1970-72, Korea. Mem. Am. Mktg. Assn., Am. Mgmt. Assn., Soc. for Human Resource Mgmt., Employee Relocation Coun. Avocations: sailing, golf, skiing. Home and Office: Feasibility Relocation Mgmt Svcs Inc 8000 Glenbrittle Way Raleigh NC 27615-4737

LEDDY, SUSAN, nursing educator; b. N.J., Feb. 23, 1939; d. Bert B. and Helen (Neumann) Kun; children: Deborah, Erin. BS, Skidmore Coll., 1960; MS, Boston U., 1965; PhD, NYU, 1973; cert., Harvard U., 1985. Chair dept. nursing Mercy Coll., Debbs Ferry, N.Y.; dean sch. nursing U. Wyo., Laramie, dean coll. health scis.; prof. Widener U. Sch. Nursing, Chester, Pa., 1988—, dean, 1988-93. Author: (with M. Pepper) Conceptual Bases of Professional Nursing, 1985, 3d edit., 1993. Bd. dirs. Springfield Hosp., 1992-94. Postdoctoral fellow U. Pa., 1994-96. Mem. NLN (bd. dirs. and 1st v.p. 1985-87).

LEDEBUR, LINAS VOCKROTH, JR., retired lawyer; b. New Brighton, Pa., June 18, 1925; s. Linas Vockroth and Mae (McCabe) L.; m. Conne Ryan, July 3, 1969; children: Gary W., Sally, Nancy, Sandra. Student, Geneva Coll., Beaver Falls, Pa., 1943, 45-46, Muhlenberg Coll., Allentown, Pa., 1943-44; J.D., U. Pitts., 1949. Bar: Pa. 1950. Assoc., then ptnr. Ledebur, McClain & Ledebur, New Brighton, 1950-63; trust mktg. mgr. Valley Nat. Bank Ariz., Phoenix, 1963-72; ptnr. Ledebur & Ledebur, New Brighton, 1972-76; sr. v.p., mgr. state trust div. Fla. Nat. Banks Fla., Inc., Jacksonville, 1976-81; sr. v.p. Fla. Nat. Bank, Jacksonville, 1977-81; pres. Northeastern Trust Co. Fla., N.A., Vero Beach, 1982-86; exec. v.p. PNC Trust Co. Fla., N.A., 1986-87; sole practice Beaver, Pa., 1987-96; master in divorce Beaver County, Pa., 1990-96; instr. bus. law Geneva Coll., 1951-52, 88-96; past pres. Ctrl. Ariz. Estate Planning Coun. Chmn. Beaver County chpt. Nat. Found.-March of Dimes, Pa., 1950-63; chmn. com. corrections Pa. Citizens Assn., 1958-63; bd. dirs., counsel Beaver County Mental Health Assn., 1962-63; bd. dirs. Maricopa County chpt. ARC, Ariz. 1968-72. Served with USMC, 1943-45, 51-53. Mem. ABA, Pa. Bar Assn. Home: 652 Bank St Beaver PA 15009-2728

LEDEEN, ROBERT WAGNER, neurochemist, educator; b. Denver, Aug. 19, 1928; s. Hyman and Olga (Wagner) L.; m. Lydia Rosen Hailparn, July 2, 1982. B.S., U. Calif., Berkeley, 1949; Ph.D., Oreg. State U., 1953. Postdoctoral fellow in chemistry U. Chgo., 1953-54; rsch. assoc. in chemistry Mt. Sinai Hosp., N.Y.C., 1956-59; rsch. fellow Albert Einstein Coll. Medicine, Bronx, N.Y., 1959; asst. prof. Albert Einstein Coll. Medicine, 1963-69, assoc. prof., 1969-75, prof., 1975-91; prof., dir. div. neurochemistry U. Medicine and Dentistry N.J., Newark, 1991—. Contbr. articles to profl. jours.; dep. chief editor Jour. Neurochemistry. Mem. neurol. scis. study sect. NIH; mem. study sect. Nat. Multiple Sclerosis Soc. NIH grantee, 1963—; Nat. Multiple Sclerosis Soc. grantee, 1967-74; recipient Humboldt prize, Javits Neurosci. Investigator award. Mem. Internat. Soc. Neurochemistry, Am. Soc. Neurochemistry, Am. Chem. Soc., Am. Soc. Biol. Chemists, N.Y. Acad. Sci. Jewish. Achievements include discoveries in the biochemistry of brain glycolipids and myelin. Home: 8 Donald Ct Wayne NJ 07470-4608 Office: U Medicine and Dentistry NJ Dept Neurosci 185 S Orange Ave Newark NJ 07103-2714

LEDER, MIMI, television director; b. N.Y.C., Jan. 26, 1952; d. Paul and Etyl Leder; m. Gary Werntz, Feb. 6, 1986; 1 child, Hannah. Student, Am. Film Inst. Dir. TV movies A Little Piece of Heaven (also known as Honor Bright), 1991, Woman with a Past, 1992, Rio Shannon, 1992, Marked for Murder, 1992, There Was a Little Boy, 1993, House of Secrets, 1993, The Sandman, 1993; dir. TV series L.A. Law, 1986, Midnight Caller, 1988, A Year in the Life, 1988, Buck James, 1988, Just in Time, 1988, Crime Story, 1988; supervising prodr. China Beach, 1988-91 (Emmy nominations for outstanding drama series 1989, 90, and outstanding directing in drama series 1990, 91), Nightingales, 1989, ER, 1994— (Emmy award 1995). Mem. Dirs. Guild Am.

LEDER, PHILIP, geneticist, educator; b. Washington, Nov. 19, 1934; married; 3 children. A.B., Harvard U., 1956, M.D., 1960. Research assoc. Nat. Heart Inst., Nat. Cancer Inst.; lab chief molecular genetics Nat. Inst. Child Health and Human Devel., NIH, 1972-80; prof. genetics Harvard U. Med. Sch., Boston, Mass., 1980—, now John Emory Andrus prof. genetics; sr. investigator Howard Hughes Med. Inst. Co-author: Molecular Basis of Blood Diseases, 1987; co-editor: Molecular Medicine, 1994. Recipient Albert Lasker Med. Rsch. award, 1987, Nat. Medal of Sci., 1989. Mem. NAS, Inst. Medicine. *

LEDERBERG, JOSHUA, geneticist, educator; b. Montclair, N.J., May 23, 1925; s. Zwi Hirsch and Esther (Goldenbaum) L.; m. Marguerite S. Kirsch, Apr. 5, 1968; children: David Kirsch, Anne. BA, Columbia U., 1944; PhD, Yale U., 1947. With U. Wis., 1947-58; prof. genetics Sch. Medicine, Stanford (Calif.) U., 1959-78; pres. Rockefeller U., N.Y.C., 1978-90, univ. prof. Sackler Found. scholar, 1990—; adj. prof. Columbia U., 1990—; mem. adv. com. med. rsch. WHO, 1971; mem. bd. sci. advisors Affymax N.V., Palo Alto, Hewlett Packard Inc., Palo Alto, Aviron, Belmont, Calif.; cons. U.S. Def. Sci. Bd., NSF, NIH, NASA, ACDA. Trustee Camille and Henry Dreyfus Found.; bd. dirs. Chem. Industry Inst. Toxicology, N.C. With USN, 1943-45. Recipient Nobel prize in physiology and medicine for rsch. in genetics of bacteria, 1958, U.S. Nat. Medal of Sci., 1989, Alan Newell award ACM, 1996; Sackler Found. scholar, 1995—. Fellow AAAS, Am. Philos. Soc., Am. Acad. Arts and Scis., N.Y. Acad. Medicine (hon.), Acad. Universelle Cultures (Paris); mem. Inst. Medicine NAS, Coun. Fgn. Rels., Royal Soc. London (fgn.), N.Y. Acad. Scis. (chmn.), Ordre des Lettres et des Arts (comdr.). Office: Rockefeller U 1230 York Ave Ste 400 New York NY 10021-6307

LEDERER, EDITH MADELON, journalist; b. N.Y.C., Mar. 27, 1943; d. Samuel B. Weiner and Frieda (Rich) Weiner Lederer; adopted d. Irving A. Lederer. B.S. with distinction, Cornell U., 1963; M.A., Stanford, 1964. With Sci. Service, Washington, 1964-65; free-lance writer, 1965-66; mem. staff AP, 1966—, South Vietnam, 1972-73; chief bur. AP, Lima, Peru, 1975; chief Caribbean services, San Juan, P.R., 1975-78; corr. Hong Kong, 1978-81, London, 1982-90, 91—; corr. Gulf War, Saudi Arabia, 1990-91. Recipient resolution Calif. Assembly, 1974, Nat. Press Club award, 1993, Nat. Headliner award, 1994. Mem. Mortar Bd., Internat. Women's Media Found., Phi Kappa Phi, Omicron Nu, Sigma Delta Chi. Address: care Asso Press 50 Rockefeller Plz New York NY 10020-1605 *Women should take more risks to live their dreams, which otherwise turn to nightmares of frustration as empty years pass. It is better to fail and touch the essence of life than to stand forever on the threshold as a gutless spectator.*

LEDERER, MRS. ESTHER P. See **LANDERS, ANN**

LEDERER, JACK LAWRENCE, personnel director, human resources specialist; b. Oak Park, Ill., July 19, 1940; s. Ludwig George and Netta O. (Olsen) L.; m. Diane D. Lederer, Sept. 1, 1962; children: Chris, Kevin, Kathy. BA in Psychology, Ohio Wesleyan U.; MBA, George Washington U. Career devel. specialist, pers. rsch. specialist, mgmt. intern Nat. Security Agy., 1962-65; regional pers. mgr., corp. mgr. equal employment opportunity, corp. mgr., mgmt. devel. Eastern Airlines Inc., 1965-69; mgr. corp. pers. Celanese Corp., 1969-72; dir. employee rels. multigraphics div. Addressograph-Multigraph Corp., d1972-73; dir. corp. pers. Allis Chalmers Corp., 1974; corp. dir. compensation and manpower resources Fiat-Allis Inc., 1974-75; ptnr., exec. v.p. Meredith Assocs. Inc., 1975-79; pres. Meredith Assocs. Inc. (merged with Alexander & Alexander), 1979-83, Meredith, Lederer & Assocs. Inc., 1983-86; co-founder, pres. Pers. Corp. Am., Norwalk, Conn., 1986-93; pres. Compo Consulting Group, Westport, Conn., 1994—. Founder Conn. POP Warner Football, Weston; chmn. Weston Pks. and Recreation Commn. Def. Dep. fellow National Security Agency. Mem. Nat. Urban League (trustee 1979—). Republican. Office: Compo Consulting Group 495 Post Rd E Westport CT 06880-4435*

LEDERER, JEROME, aerospace safety consultant, engineer; b. N.Y.C., Sept. 26, 1902; m. Sarah Bojarsky, Nov. 1, 1935; children: Nancy, Susan. BSc in Mech. Engring., NYU, 1924, M.Engring., 1925. Registered profl. engr., N.Y. Aero engr. USAir mail svc., 1926-27; chief engr. Aero Ins. Underwriters, N.Y.C., 1929-40; dir. safety bur. CAB, Washington, 1940-42; mgr. Airlines War Tng. Inst., 1942-44, U.S. Strategic Bombing Survey, 1945; pres., Flight Safety found., 1947-67, pres. emeritus, 1967—; dir. Cornell-Guggenheim Aviation Safety Rsch. Ctr., N.Y.C., 1950-67; dir. Office Manned Space Flight Safety, NASA, Washington, 1967-70, dir. safety, 1970-72; ret., 1972; adj. prof. Inst. Safety and System Mgmt., U. So. Calif., ret.; past mem. adv. council Inst. Nuclear Power Ops., Atlanta, 1980-85; cons., Laguna Hills, Calif., 1974—. Author books and articles on aviation and space safety. Recipient NASA Exceptional Service medal, Daniel Guggenheim medal, Wright Bros. trophy, Amelia Earhart medal, Ziolkowski and Yuri Gagarin medals, Soviet Fedn. Cosmonauts, Von Baumhaüer medal Royal Dutch Aero. Soc., Laura Taber Barbour award, many others; named to Safety and Health Hall of Fame Internat., OX5 Club Hall of Fame, Internat. Space Hall of Fame. Fellow AIAA (hon.), Am. Astronautics Assn., Soc. Automotive Engrs., Royal Aero. Soc., Human Factors Soc.; mem. NAE, Airline Pilots Assn. (hon.), Mil. Order Daedalions (hon.), Wings Club (N.Y.). Home: 468 Calle Cadiz-D Laguna Hills CA 92653

LEDERER, MARION IRVINE, cultural administrator; b. Brampton, Ont., Can., Feb. 10, 1920; d. Oliver Bateman and Eva Jane (MacMurdo) L.; m. Francis Lederer, July 10, 1941. Student, U. Toronto, 1938, UCLA, 1942-45. Owner Canoga Mission Gallery, Canoga Park, Calif., 1967—; cultural heritage monument Canoga Mission Gallery, 1974—; Vice pres. Screen Smart Set women's aux. Motion Picture and TV Fund, 1973—; founder sister city program Canoga Park-Taxco, Mexico, 1963; Mem. mayor's cultural task force San Fernando Valley, 1973—; mem. Los Angeles Cultural Affairs Commn., 1980-85. Mem. Los Angeles Cultural Affairs Commn., 1980-85. Recipient numerous pub. service awards from mayor, city council, C. of C. Mem. Canoga Park C. of C. (cultural chmn. 1973-75, dir. 1973-75). Presbyn. Home: PO Box 32 Canoga Park CA 91305-0032 Office: Canoga Mission Gallery 23130 Sherman Way Canoga Park CA 91307-1402

LEDERER, PETER DAVID, lawyer; b. Frankfurt, Fed. Republic Germany, May 2, 1930; came to U.S., 1938; s. Leo and Alice (Freistadt) L.; m. Norma Jean Taylor, June, 1955 (div. 1966); 1 child, Patricia Ann; m. Midori Shimanouchi, Dec. 16, 1966. BA, U. Chgo., 1949, JD, 1957, M Comparative Law, 1958. Bar: Ill. 1959, U.S. Supreme Ct. 1966, N.Y. 1967. Law and behavioral sci. research fellow U. Chgo. Law Sch., 1958-59; ptnr. Baker & McKenzie, Zurich, Switzerland, 1960-66; ptnr. Baker & McKenzie, N.Y.C., 1966-94, of counsel, 1994—; dir. Nuc. Electric Ins. Ltd., Nuc. Mutual Ltd. Mem. vis. com. U. Miami Law Sch., Coral Gables, Fla., 1974—, U. Chgo. Law Sch., 1988-91; adv. bd. Wildlife Preservation Trust Internat., Phila.; dir. Asian-Am. Legal Def. & Edn. Fund, N.Y.C., The Midori Found.; pres. bd. trustees The Calhoun Sch., N.Y.C., 1980-83. With AUS, 1951-53. Mem. ABA, Assn. Bar City of N.Y. (chmn. com. on nuclear law 1978-81, del. to the Union Internat. des Avocats 1989—), Internat. Nuclear Law Assn. Office: Baker & McKenzie 805 Third Ave 29th fl New York NY 10022-7513

LEDERER, RICHARD HENRY, writer, educator, columnist; b. Phila., May 26, 1938; s. Howard Jules and Leah (Perry) L.; m. Rhoda Anne Spangenberg, Aug. 25, 1962 (div. 1986); m. Simone Johanna van Egeren, Nov. 29, 1991; children: Howard Henry, Anne Labarr, Katherine Lee. BA, Haverford Coll., 1959; student, Harvard U., 1959-60, M of Arts and Teaching, 1962; PhD, U. N.H., 1980. Tchr., coach St. Paul's Sch., Concord, N.H., 1962-89; lectr. in field. Author: Anguished English, 1987, Get Thee to a Punnery, 1988, Crazy English, 1989, The Play of Words, 1990, The Miracle of Language, 1991, More Anguished English, 1993, Building Bridge, 1994, Adventures of a Verbivore, 1994, Literary Trivia, 1994, Nothing Risqué, Nothing Gained, 1995, The Write Way, 1995, Pun and Games, 1996, Fractured English, 1996; weekly columnist Looking at Lang.; contbr. more than 2000 articles to mags. and jours.; broadcaster various radio stas.; numerous TV appearances. Recipient Lifetime Achievement award Columbia Scholastic Press Assn., N.Y.C., 1989; named Internat. Punster of Yr. Internat. Save the Pun Found., Toronto, Can., 1990. Mem. Am. Mensa, Phi Beta Kappa, Phi Delta Kappa. Avocations: tennis, cards, film. Home: 5 Merrimack St Concord NH 03301-3845 *Whatever you hear about the closing of the American mind and cultural illiteracy, there has never been a more passionate moment in the history of the American love affair with language than right now. I'm exceedingly fortunate to have written books that embrace that passion.*

LEDERER, WILLIAM JULIUS, author; b. N.Y.C., Mar. 31, 1912; s. William J. and Paula (Franken) L.; m. Ethel Hackett, Apr. 21, 1940 (div. Jan. 1965); children: Brian, Jonathan, Bruce; m. Corinne Edwards Lewis, July 1965 (div. May 1976). B.S., U.S. Naval Acad., 1936; assoc. Nieman fellow, Harvard U., 1950-51. Enlisted USN, 1930, commd. ensign, 1936, advanced through grades to capt., 1952, ret., 1958; Far East corr. Reader's Digest, 1958-63; lectr. colls. and univs., 1949—. Author in residence, Harvard U., 1966-67; Author: All the Ship's at Sea, 1950, The Last Cruise, 1950, Spare Time Article Writing for Money, 1953, Ensign O'Toole and Me, 1957, A Nation of Sheep, 1961, Timothy's Song, 1965, Pink Jade, 1966, (with Eugene Burdick) The Ugly American, 1958, Sarkhan, 1965, Our Own Worst Enemy, 1967, (with Don D. Jackson) The Mirages of Marriage, 1968, (with Joe Pete Wilson) Complete Cross-Country Skiing and Ski Touring, 1970, (with others) Marriage for and Against, Marital Choices, A Happy Book of Happy Stories, I, Giorghos, 1984, Creating a Good Relationship, 1984. Mem. Signet Soc., Authors Guild, Acad. Orthomolecular Psychiatry, European Acad. Preventive Medicine, Internat. Acad. Preventive Medicine, Internat. Coll. Applied Nutrition, Sigma Delta Chi. Clubs: Lotos, Trap Door Spiders, National Press, Harvard Faculty. Address: PO Box 248 Peacham VT 05862-0248 *If one works at being joyful and physically functional, almost everything else seems to come along on its own. Put energy into the "here and now" and do not distract from it by worrying about either the past or the future.*

LEDERIS, KAROLIS PAUL (KARL LEDERIS), pharmacologist, educator, researcher; b. Noreikoniai, Lithuania, Aug. 1, 1920; arrived in Can., 1969; s. Paul Augustus and Franciska (Danisevicius) L.; m. Hildegard Gallistl, Feb. 28, 1952; children: Aldona Franciska, Edmund Paul. Diploma, Tchrs. Coll., Siauliai, Lithuania, 1939; BSc, U. Bristol, U.K., 1958, PhD, 1961, DSc, 1968. Jr. lectr., then lectr. and reader U. Bristol, 1961-69; prof. pharmacology and therapeutics U. Calgary, Alta., Can., 1969-89, prof. emeritus, 1989—; vis. prof. univs. in Fed. Republic Germany, Austria, Chile, Argentina, Sri Lanka, Switzerland, Lithuania, France, , USA, USSR, 1963-79, U. Bristol, 1979, U. Kyoto, Japan, 1980; career investigator, mem., chair grants com. Med. Rsch. Coun., Ottawa, Ont., Can., 1970-89, coun. mem., exec., 1983-90; mem. internat. com. Centres Excellence Networks, Ottawa, 1988-89. Author, editor: 5 books on hypothalamic hormones; editor in chief Jour. Exptl. and Clin. Pharmacology, 1977-89; contbr. approximately 350 book chpts. and articles to profl. jours.; patentee hormonal peptides. Recipient Upjohn award in pharmacology, 1990, various fellowships and scholarships in U.K., Fed. Republic of Germany, U.S. Fellow NAS, Royal Soc. Can.; mem. Western Pharmacological Soc. (pres. 1982-83), pharm., physiol., endocrinological, biochem. socs. U.K., Can., U.S., Lithuanian Club (London), Men's Can. Club, Cabot Yacht and Cruise Club (Bristol). Avocations: music, sailing, fishing, hunting, golf. Home: 147 Carthew St, Comox, BC Canada V9M 1T4 Office: U Calgary, Health Scis Centre, Calgary, AB Canada T2N 4N1

LEDERMAN, BRUCE RANDOLPH, lawyer; b. N.Y.C., Oct. 12, 1942; s. Morris David and Frances Lederman; m. Ellen Kline, Aug. 4, 1979; children: Eric, Jeffrey, Joshua. Cert., U. London, 1963; BS Econs. cum laude, U. Pa., 1964; LLB cum laude, Harvard U., 1967. Bar: U.S. Dist. Ct. (cen. dist.) Calif. 1967. Law clk. to Hon. Irving Hill U.S. Dist. Ct. Cen. Dist., L.A., 1967-68; sr. ptnr. Latham & Watkins, L.A., 1968—. Avocations: bicycle riding, real estate investments. Office: Latham & Watkins 633 W 5th St Los Angeles CA 90071-2005*

LEDERMAN, FRANK L., scientist, research center administrator; b. Buffalo, Aug. 19, 1949; s. Sol J. and Carol S. (Dankman) L.; m. Daphna Kaplansky, Aug. 8, 1993. BS in Math., Carnegie-Mellon U., 1971, MS in Physics, 1971; MS in Physics, U. Ill., 1972, PhD, 1975. Fellow U. Pa., Phila., 1975; physicist R & D ctr. GE Corp., Schenectady, N.Y., 1976-78, mgr. ultrasound program, 1978-80, mgr. energy systems mgmt. br., 1981-82, acting mgr. liaison ops., 1983-84, mgr. power electronics systems br., 1984-87, mgr. programs and resources, 1988; v.p., dir. rsch. Noranda Inc., Pointe Claire, Que., Can., 1988-91, sr. v.p. tech., 1992-95; v.p., chief tech. officer Aluminum Co. Am., Alcoa Center, Pa., 1995—. Contbr. articles to profl. jours.; patentee in field. Mem. IEEE, Indsl. Rsch. Inst., Am. Phys. Soc. Home: 4011 Pin Oak Ln Murrysville PA 15668 Office: Alcoa Tech Ctr 100 Technical Dr Alcoa Center PA 15069

LEDERMAN, LAWRENCE, lawyer, writer, educator; b. N.Y.C., Sept. 8, 1935; s. Herman Jack and Lillian (Rosenfeld) L.; children: Leandra, Evin. B.A., Bklyn. Coll., 1957; LL.B., N.Y.U., 1966. Bar: N.Y. 1968; Law clk. chief justice Calif. Sup. Ct., 1966-67; assoc. Cravath, Swaine & Moore, N.Y.C., 1968-74; ptnr. Wachtell, Lipton, Rosen & Katz, N.Y.C., 1975-91; ptnr., chmn. corp. practice Milbank, Tweed, Hadley & McCloy, 1991—; adj. prof. law N.Y.U. Sch. Law, 1974—; Chmn. bd. Phoenix House Devel. Corp., mem. Phoenix House Found. Author: Tombstones: A Lawyer's Tales from the Takeover Decades, 1992. Bd. dirs. One to One Partnership Inc. Served with U.S. Army, 1957-59. Mem. ABA, N.Y. State Bar Assn., Order of the Coif . Contbr. articles to profl. jours. Office: Milbank Tweed Hadley & McCloy 1 Chase Manhattan Plz New York NY 10005-1401

LEDERMAN, LEON MAX, physicist, educator; b. N.Y.C., July 15, 1922; s. Morris and Minna (Rosenberg) L.; m. Florence Gordon, Sept. 19, 1945; children: Rena S., Jesse A., Heidi R.; m. Ellen Carr, Sept. 17, 1981. BS, CCNY, 1943, DSc (hon.), 1980; AM, Columbia U., 1948, PhD, 1951; DSc (hon.), No. Ill. U., 1984, U. Chgo., 1985, Ill. Inst. Tech., 1987. Assoc. in physics Columbia U., N.Y.C., 1951, asst. prof., 1952-54, assoc. prof., 1954-58, prof., 1958-89, Eugene Higgins prof. physics, 1972-79; Frank L. Sulzberger prof. physics U. Chgo., 1989-92; dir. Fermi Nat. Accelerator Lab., Batavia, Ill., 1979-89, dir. emeritus, 1989—; Pritzker prof. sci. Ill. Inst. Tech., Chgo., 1992—; dir. Nevis Labs., Irvington, N.Y., 1962-79; guest scientist Brookhaven Nat. Labs., 1955; cons. Nat. Accelerator Lab., European Orgn. for Nuclear Rsch. (CERN), 1970—; mem. high energy physics adv. panel AEC, 1966-70; mem. adv. com. to div. math. and phys. scis. NSF, 1970-72; sci. advisor to gov. State of Ill., 1989-93. Author: Quarks to the Cosmos, 1989, The God Particle, 1993; also over 200 articles. 1st lt. Signal Corps, AUS, 1943-46. Recipient Nat. Medal of Sci., 1965, Townsend Harris medal CUNY, 1973, Elliot Cresson medal Franklin Inst., 1976, Wolf prize, 1982, Nobel prize in physics, 1988, Enrico Fermi prize, 1992, Rosenblith Lectures in Science and Technology Nat. Acad. of Sciences, 1995; Guggenheim fellow, 1958-59, Ford Found. fellow European Ctr. for Nuclear Rsch., Geneva, 1958-59, fellow NSF, 1967. Fellow AAAS (pres. 1990-91, chmn. 1992-93), Am. Phys. Soc.; mem. NAS, Italian Phys. Soc., Aspen Inst. Physics (pres. 1990-92), Ill. Math. Sci. Acad. (vice chmn. 1985—), Tchrs. Acad. for Math. and Sci. in Chgo. (co-chmn. 1990—). Office: Ill Inst Tech Dept Physics 3300 S Federal St Chicago IL 60616-3732

LEDERMAN, MARIE JEAN, English language educator; b. Bklyn., Dec. 28, 1935; d. Samuel and Gladys (Leeshutz) Candel; m. Theodore Lederman, June 28, 1957 (div. 1963); 1 child, Mark; m. Martin Benis, 1977. B.S. magna cum laude, NYU, 1957, Ph.D., 1966; M.A., Bklyn. Coll., 1963. Tchr. English, N.Y.C. Bd. Edn., 1957-59, cons., 1975-76, 78-79; instr. NYU, 1965-66; asst. prof. N.Y.C. Community Coll., 1966-68; asst. prof. SEEK program CUNY, 1968-69, successively asst. prof., assoc. prof., prof. Baruch Coll., 1969-79, 88-91, prof. emerita, 1991—, cons. chancellor's SEEK task force, 1975, univ. dean acad. affairs, 1979-85; dean for freshman skills La Guardia Community Coll., Long Island City, 1985-87; cons. Mohawk Valley Community Coll., Utica, N.Y., 1980, Tex. A&I U., 1984, U. Toronto, 1984, Framingham State Coll., 1987, Woodrow Wilson Fellowship Found., 1985, Dept. Higher Edn. State of N.J., 1989-91; cons. U. Minn., 1989-90. Chgo. State U., 1991-92. Exhibited works at Cork Gallery/Lincoln Ctr., Lever House, Pen and Brush Club, Salamagundi Club; mem. editl. bd. Jour. Basic Writing, 1987-94; contbr. articles to profl. jours. Bd. dirs. Jean Cocteau Repertory Theatre, v.p., 1988—. Recipient CUNY faculty research award, 1976-78; Fund for Improvement of Postsecondary Edn. grantee, 1981-87. Mem. Internat. Sculpture Ctr., Nat. Sculpture Soc., Art Students League, Burr Artists (bd. dris.), Visual Individualists United. Democrat. Jewish.

LEDERMAN, MICHAEL WAINWRIGHT, small business owner; b. N.Y.C., Jan. 9, 1948; s. Rocky H. and Jeanette (Wainwright) L.; BS, Cornell U., 1969, MS, 1970; PhD, U. Bologna, Italy 1976; DVM, U. Parma, Italy, 1985. Founding partner Lederman Service, restoration and racing preparation of Porsche automobiles, Bologna and Parma (Italy), 1976—, sr. operating officer, 1978—; racer of Porsche in Europe, 1976—. Mem. Emergency Rescue Service, Parma. With U.S. Army, 1970-71. Registered engr., Parma. Mem. Porsche Club Am., Porsche Club Gt. Britain, Porsch Club Italia (hon. pres.), U.S. Polo Assn., Mille Miglia Racing Assn. (Italy), Clubs: Punta Ala Polo, Cornell (N.Y.C.), Gli Elefanti (Parma), Ferrari Club Am. Home: Murmuring Hollow Farm Accord NY 12404

LEDERMAN, PETER (BERND), environmental services executive, consultant; b. Weimar, Germany, Nov. 16, 1931; came to U.S., 1939, naturalized, 1945; s. Ernst M. and Irmgard R. (Heilbrunn) L.; m. Susan Sturc, Aug. 25, 1957; children: Stuart M., Ellen L. BSE, U. Mich., 1953, MSE, 1957, PhD, 1961. Instr., U. Mich., 1959-61; research engr. Esso Research Labs., Baton Rouge, La., 1961-63; sr. engr. Esso Research & Engring. Co., Florham Park, N.J., 1963-66; asso. prof. chem. engring. Poly. Inst. Bklyn., 1966-72, adj. prof., 1972-75; dir. Ind. Waste Treatment Research Lab., EPA, Edison, N.J., 1972-75, dir. indsl. and extractive processes research, Washington, 1975-76; v.p. Cotrell Environ. Scis. Div., Research Cottrell, Bound Brook, N.J., 1976-80; v.p. hazard/toxic materials mgmt. Roy F. Weston, Inc., Edison, N.J., 1980-92; dir. Ctr. for Environ. Engring. and Sci. NJIT, Newark, 1993—, rsch. prof. chem. engring., 1993—; mem. NRC-Nat. Acad. Sci. Rev. Panel, Office Recycled Tech., U.S. Bur. Standards, 1980-83; mem. com. decontamination and decomissioning nuclear gaseous diffusion plants; mem. expert panel PCBs Agy. for Toxic Substances and Disease Registry. Mem. editorial bd. Environ. Progress, Chem. Engring. Progress, Hazardous Waste Mgmt. Jour. Mem. exec. bd. Watchung Area council Boy Scouts Am., 1970-86; assoc. editor AWMA Jour., mem. affirmative action adv. com. New Providence (N.J.) Bd. Edn., 1979-83. Served with AUS, 1953-55. Recipient Silver medal EPA, 1976. Fellow Am. Inst. Chem. Engrs. (chmn. profl. devel. com., chmn. N.J. sect., chair environ. div., Larry K. Cecil award 1987, dir. AICHE Found., Gary Leach award 1995, Environ. Divsn. Svc. award 1995); mem. ASME, AAAS, Am. Chem. Soc., Am. Soc. Engring. Edn., Nat. Soc. Profl. Engrs., Am. Acad. Environ. Engrs. (diplomate, trustee, Stanley Kappe award 1993), Am. Arbitration Assn., Am. Assn. of Eng. Soc. (chair environ. comm.), U. Mich. Engring. Alumni Soc. (chair, bd. dirs.), Sigma Xi, Phi Kappa Phi, Phi Lambda Upsilon. Contbr. numerous articles on environ. regulations, solid waste mgmt., hazardous waste mgmt., computer tech. to profl. jours. Home: 17 Pittsford Way New Providence NJ 07974-2428 Office: NJIT Dept Chem Engring Newark NJ 07102

LEDERMAN, STEPHANIE BRODY, artist; b. N.Y.C.; d. Maxwell and Ann (Rockett) Brody. Student, U. Mich.; BS in Design, Finch Coll.; MA in Painting, L.I. U., 1975. One-person exhbns. Franklin Furnace, N.Y.C., 1979, Kathryn Markel Fine Arts, N.Y.C., 1979, 81, 83, Katzen/Brown Gallery, N.Y.C., 1988, 89, Real Artways, Hartford, Conn., 1984, Alfred U., 1990, Hal Katzen Gallery, N.Y.C., 1992, Hillwood Art Mus., Brookville, N.Y., 1992, Casements Mus., Ormond Beach, Fla., 1994, Broward Cmty. Coll., Ft. Lauderdale, Fla., 1994, Hebrew Home for the Aged, N.Y.C., 1994-95, Galerie Caroline Corre, Paris, 1995, La. State U., Shreveport, 1995; exhibited in numerous group shows including Newark Mus., 1983, Met. Mus. Art, N.Y.C., 1986, Queens Mus., 1989, Basel Art Fair, 1989, Caroline Corre, Paris, 1991, R.I. Mus. Art, 1991, Am. Acad. Arts & Letters, N.Y.C., 1992, Guild Hall Mus., East Hampton, N.Y., 1993, Ind. U, Terre Haute, 1993, Jewish Mus., N.Y.C., 1993, Nat. Mus. Women in Arts, Washington, 1994, Ronald Feldman Gallery, N.Y.C., 1995, Alternative Mus., N.Y.C., 1995, Eugenia Cucalon, Gallery, N.Y.C., 1995; represented in permanent collections Newark Mus., Mus. Modern Art, Prudential Ins., Bertelsmann Music Group, Guild Hall Mus., East Hampton, L.I., Chase Manhattan Bank, N.Y. Health and Hosp. Corp., Victoria & Albert Mus., London, Doubleday Books. Recipient Hassam and Speicher purchase award Am. Acad. and Inst. Arts and Letters, 1988, purchase award Arts in Hosps., Richmond, Va.; grantee Creative Artists Pub. Svc., 1977, Ariana Found. for Arts, 1985, Artists Space, 1987, E.D. Found., 1991, Lancaster Group., U.S.A. Comm. award, 1991, spl. opportunity stipend N.Y. State Coun. Arts, 1992, 94, Heuss House project Lower Manhattan Cultural Coun., 1992. Studio: 85 N 3rd St Fl 5 Brooklyn NY 11211-3923

LEDFORD, FRANK FINLEY, JR., surgeon, army officer; b. Jacksonville, Fla., Apr. 22, 1934; s. Frank F. and Hazel H. (Barrette) L.; m. Marilyn Sue Kain, Aug. 23, 1957; 1 child, Cheryl Lynn. B.S., U. Dayton, 1955; M.D., U. Cin., 1959; postgrad., Indsl. Coll. Armed Forces, 1976—. Diplomate: Am. Bd. Orthopedic Surgery. Commd. 2d lt. U.S. Army, 1958, advanced through grades to lt. gen., 1988; surgeon, 1958-69; intern Brooke Army Hosp., San Antonio, 1959-60; resident in surgery Womack Army Hosp., 1960-61; resident in orthop. surgery Letterman Gen. Hosp., San Francisco, 1961-64; resident in pediat. orthop. surgery Phoenix Crippled Childrens Hosp., 1964-65; chief orthopedic surgery (Army Hosp.), Landstuhl, W.Ger., 1969-71; dep. commr. (Army Hosp.), Heidelberg, W.Ger., 1971-72; chief surg. cons. Office of Surgeon Gen., Washington, 1972-73; chief grad. med. edn. Office of Surgeon Gen., 1973-76; comdr. U.S. Army Hosp., Fort Riley, Kans., 1977-80, Ft. Benning, Ga., 1980; dir. profl. services Office of Surgeon Gen., U.S. Army, Washington, 1980-82; comdr. Letterman Army Med. Ctr. San Francisco, 1982-85; chief surgeon U.S. Army Europe, 1985-88; The Surgeon Gen. Dept. of the Army, Heidelberg, Germany, 1988-92; pres. S.W. Found. for Biomedical Rsch., San Antonio, 1992—; clin. prof. Health Sci. Ctr. U. Tex., San Antonio, 1993—; clin prof. surgery Uniformed Services U. Health Scis. Contbr. articles to med. jours. Fellow ACS, Am. Acad. Orthopedic Surgeons, Am. Coll. Physician Execs.; mem. AMA, Assn. Mil. Surgeons, Soc. Mil. Orthopedic Surgeons. Methodist. Clubs: Bohemian. Address: SW Found For Biomedical Research PO Box 28147 San Antonio TX 78228-0146*

LEDFORD, GARY ALAN, real estate developer; b. San Diego, Dec. 30, 1946; s. Loren Oscar and Madge Francis (Condon) L.; m. Winifred Jess Ledford; children: Kelly, Jeanne, Robert. BSCE, U.S. Army Engrng. Coll., 1967. Pres. Mastercraft Contractors/Mastercraft Diversified Svcs., Inc./ Masterplan, Inc., Colo. Springs, 1969-73; v.p. K.L. Redfern, Inc., Orange, Calif., 1973-75; pres. Ledford Industries, Inc./G.A. Ledford & Assocs., 1975-82, Watt Jess Ranch, Inc., Apple Valley, Calif., 1985-94; chmn. Jess Ranch, Apple Valley, 1994—, Jess Ranch Water Co., Apple Valley, 1986—; gen. ptnr. GLBT Assocs., 1978-79; chmn. Watt-Jess/Ledford, Apple Valley, 1992-94; pres. LJ&J Investments, Inc., Apple Valley, Ledford-Schaffer/ Rogers, Apple Valley. Designer computer software, 1979. Past pres. Cultural Arts Found., 1991-92, Victorville, Calif; bd. trustees Apple Valley Christian Care Ctr., High Desert Questors, Victorville; past pres. Victor Valley Mus. Assn., Baldy View B.I.A. Capt. C.E., U.S. Army, 1967-69, Vietnam. Mem. Internat. Coun. Shopping Ctrs., Nat. Assn. Home Builders', Nat. Planning Assn., NRA (life), High Desert Constrn. Indsutry Assn. (past v.p.), Bldg. Industry Assn., VFW, Sr. Housing Coun. Republican. Avocations: hunting, chess, equestrian. Home: 11401 Apple Valley Rd Apple Valley CA 92308-7503 Office: Jess Ranch 11401 Apple Valley Rd Apple Valley CA 92308-7503

LEDFORD, JACK CLARENCE, retired aircraft company executive, former air force officer; b. Blairsville, Ga., Sept. 1, 1920; s. Jack Raymond and Clara Mae (Duckworth) L.; m. Pauline F. Knight, Dec. 9, 1973; children: Barbara Jan (Mrs. Russell J. Thomas), Jack Michael, Joseph Dan. B.S., Ohio State U.; M.B.A., George Washington U. Commd. 2d lt. Air Corps U.S. Army, 1941; advanced through grades to brig. gen. USAF, 1965; dep. chief staff Def. Atomic Support Agy., Washington, 1958-61; dir. spl. projects USAF, 1961-63; asst. dir. CIA, 1963-66; dir. inspection USAF, 1966-68; comdr. 12th Strategic Air Div., Tucson, 1968-70; ret., 1970; v.p. area devel. So. Ariz. Bank & Trust Co., Tucson., 1970-71; v.p. Hughes Aircraft Internat. Service Corp., 1971-85. Pres. Old Pueblo Boys Club.; bd. dirs. Tucson United Community Campaign, Catalina council Boy Scouts Am., Pima County Air Mus. Decorated D.S.C., D.S.M. (2), Legion of Merit, Air Medal, Purple Heart; Order of Flying Cloud and Banner China). Mem. Air Force Assn., Skyline Country Club (Tucson), Calif. Yacht Club (L.A.), Delta Upsilon.

LEDFORD, RICHARD ALLISON, food science educator, food microbiologist; b. Charlotte, N.C., June 30, 1931; s. Travis Allison and Sarah (Moon) L.; m. Martha Ann Worley, Jan. 26, 1957; children: Richard Jr. (dec.), Roeby, Ann, Jeanne, Robert. BS, N.C. State U., 1954, MS, 1958; PhD, Cornell U., 1961. Dir. food lab. N.Y. State Agr. & Markets, Albany, 1961-64; asst. prof. food sci. Cornell U., Ithaca, N.Y., 1964-70, assoc. prof., 1970-80, prof., 1980—, chmn. dept., 1972-77, 85—; dir. Inst. Food Sci., 1988—. Served to 1st lt. U.S. Army, 1954-56. Mem. Am. Soc. Microbiology, Inst. Food Technologists, Am. Dairy Sci. Assn. Lodge: Rotary. Office: Cornell U Dept Food Sci 114 Stocking Hall Ithaca NY 14853-7201

LEDFORD, RODNEY JAMES, engineering executive; b. Palmer, Mass., Nov. 29, 1946; s. Talmadge O. Ledford and Julie M. (Gralinski) Dynak; m. Martha Delano Emery, Mar. 28, 1968; children: Amy Elizabeth, Adam Michael. BS, Kennedy Western U., 1994. Elec. engr., Conn., Alaska, Mass., Iowa, Ga. Elec. engr. IBEW, Mass., 1965-90, Aramco Saudi Arabia, 1978-85, Nutrasweet, Augusta, Ga., 1985-94; pres. RJL Holdings, Inc., Martinez, Ga., 1994-95; engring. project mgr. Vector Corp., Marion, Iowa, project mgr., West Coast dist. mgr., 1994—. Sgt.-at-arms Am. Legion, Monson, Mass., 1973-74. With USN, 1965-68, Viet Nam. Mem. IEEE, Instrument Soc. Am., Internat. Soc. for Pharm. Engrs. Mem. IEEE, Instrument Soc. Am. Republican. Roman Catholic. Avocation: outdoor activities. Home: 4119 Lark Ct NE Cedar Rapids IA 52402

LEDFORD, SANDRA, principal. Prin. Harding Mid. Sch., Cedar Rapids, Iowa. Recipient Blue Ribbon Sch. award, 1990-91.

LEDGER, WILLIAM JOE, physician, educator; b. Turtle Creek, Pa., 1932. B.A., Princeton U., 1954; M.D., U. Pa., 1958; M.S., Temple U., 1964. Diplomate Am. Bd. Ob-Gyn. Intern Hamot Hosp. Assn., Erie, N.Y., 1958-59; resident Temple U. Hosp., Phila., 1961-64; attending physician Women's Hosp.-Mich. Med. Ctr., 1964-72; assoc. prof. U. Mich., Ann Arbor; prof. U. So. Calif., L.A., 1972-79; Given Found. prof., chmn. ob-gyn. Cornell U. Med. Coll., N.Y.C., 1979—. Served to capt. USMC, 1959-61. Fellow ACS, Am. Coll. Ob-Gyn. Office: NY Hosp-Cornell Med Sch 525 E 68th St New York NY 10021

LEDLEY, ROBERT STEVEN, biophysicist; b. N.Y.C., June 28, 1928. DDS, NYU, 1948; MA, Columbia U., 1949. Rsch. physicist Columbia U. Radiation Labs., Columbia, 1948-50; instr. physics Columbia U., 1949-50; vis. scientist Nat. Bur. Standards, 1951-52; physicist, 1953-54; ops. rsch. analyst Johns Hopkins U., 1954-56; assoc. prof. elec. engring George Washington U., 1957-60; instr. pediatric. Johns Hopkins U., Sch. Medicine, 1960-63; prof. elec. engring. George Washington U., 1968-70; prof. physiology, biophysics & radiology Georgetown U., from 1970; pres., rsch. dir. Nat. Biomed. Rsch. Found., from 1960; pres. Digital Info. Sci. Corp., 1970-75. named to Nat. Inventor Hall of Fame, 1990. Mem. Soc. Math Biophys., Inst. Elec. & Electronics Engrs., Biphys. Soc., N.Y. Acad. Sci., Pattern Recognition Soc. Office: Georgetown U Nat Biomed Rsch Found 3900 Reservoir Rd NW Washington DC 20007-2187

LEDNUM, FLORENCE NASH, biological sciences educator; b. Abington, Pa., May 11, 1941; d. Charles Edgar and Jane (Gessner) N.; m. Allan Alfred Rieken, June 17, 1966 (div. Dec. 1976); children: Dawn Elizabeth, Holly Raina; m. Charles Wendell Lednum, Aug. 17, 1993. BS, Wash. Coll., 1962; MS, U. Del., 1964; EdD, U. Md., 1993. Biol. oceanographer U.S. Naval Oceanographic Office, Washington, 1964-69; anatomy, physiology and microbiology instr., recruiter Macqueen Gibbs Willis Sch. Nursing, Easton, Md., 1969-82; assoc. prof. biol. scis. WOR-WIC C.C., Salisbury, Md., 1982-92; prof. biol. scis., dept. chair Chesapeake Coll., Wye Mills, Md., 1992—, coord. sci. adv. com., 1994—. Coord., editor (cookbook) Trinity's Table, 1992-93. Recipient Excellence in Tchg. award Md. State Bd. for C.C.'s, 1990. Mem. AAAS, Assn. for Advancement of County Coll. Tchg. Episcopalian. Avocations: quilting, gardening, sewing. Home: 31751 Tappers Corner Rd Cordova MD 21625-2133 Office: Chesapeake Coll PO Box 8 Wye Mills MD 21679-0008

LEDOGAR, STEPHEN J., diplomat; b. N.Y.C., Sept. 14, 1929; m. Marcia Hubert, Sept. 16, 1967; children: Lucy, Charles. BS, Fordham U., 1954, LLB, 1958. Bar: N.Y. 1959. Surety claims atty. Chubb & Son, N.Y.C., 1954-59; with Fgn. Svc., 1959—; press spokesman, U.S. del. Vietnam Peace Talks, Paris, 1967-72; with U.S. Mission to NATO, 1973-76; spl. asst. to undersec. of state, 1976-77; dir. Office of NATO Affairs, 1977-80; mem. State Dept. Senior Seminar, 1980-81; dep. chief of mission U.S. Mission to NATO, Brussels, 1981-87; amb., U.S. rep. European Conventional Stability Negotiations and Mutual and Balanced Force Reductions Talks, 1987-89, amb. and head U.S. Del. to Negotiations on Conventional Armed Forces in Europe, 1989, amb. and U.S. rep. Conference on Disarmament, 1989—. Lt. USN, 1949-52, USNR, 1954-60 (Naval Aviator). Office: US Del to Conf Disarmament, 11 Rte de Pregny, 1292 Geneva Switzerland

LEDOUX, CHRIS LEE, country musician; b. Biloxi, Miss., Oct. 2, 1948; s. Alfred Hector and Bonnie Jeanette (Gingrich) LeDoux; m. Peggy Jo Rhoades, Jan. 4, 1972; children: Clayton, Ned, Will, Cindi, Beau. AA, Sheridan (Wyo.) Coll., 1969. With rodeo, 1971-81, musician, 1972—; rancher Wyo., 1976—. Songwriter, singer 22 albums of songs with Western themes, 1972—, recent recordings include Western Underground, 1991, (with Garth Brooks) Watcha Gonna Do With a Cowboy, 1992, Under This Old Hat, 1993, (with Garth Brooks) Best of Chris LeDoux, 1994. Sculptor (Best Bronze of Show, State of Wyo. 1985, Best Art of Show, State of Nev., 1986). State spokesman, Wyo. State Centennial, 1990. Mem. Profl. Rodeo Cowboy Assn. (World Champion Bareback Broncs, 1976). Avocations: Wyo.

rancher, give music concerts with Western Underground. Office: ACS Inc 3015 Leeville Rd Mount Juliet TN 37122-3911

LEDOUX, HAROLD ANTHONY, cartoonist, painter; b. Port Arthur, Tex., Nov. 7, 1926; s. Antoine Ovide and Pauline Zulma (Bernard) LeD.; m. Jeanne Labbe, 1964 (div. 1979); children: Lorraine Marthe, Noelle Pauline. Grad., Thomas Jefferson High Sch., Port Arthur, Tex., 1944; student, Chgo. Acad. Fine Arts, 1948-49. Cartoonist, illustrator N.Am. Syndicate, 1965—. Cartoonist, Famous Funnies, N.Y.C., 1950-53; asst. cartoonist: syndicated comic strip Judge Parker, 1953-65; represented in permanent collection Mus. of Gulf Coast, Port Arthur, Tex., Internat. Mus. Cartoon Art, Boca Raton, Fla. Advisor Council for Devel. of French in La. Served with U.S. Mcht. Marine, 1944-47. Recipient Atlantic War Zone Bar War Shipping Adminstrn. Mem. Nat. Cartoonists Soc., Comics Council, Southwestern Watercolor Soc. Club: Alliance Française. Address: N Am Syndicate 235 E 45th St New York NY 10017-3305

LEDOUX, WILLIAM JOHN, lawyer; b. Bklyn., June 30, 1931; s. William Desau and Elizabeth Ann (Horton) LeD.; m. Elma Lucia Giancaterino, Feb. 27, 1954; children: John F., William M., Michael J., Susan E. AB, Boston U., 1960, JD, 1963. Bar: Mass. 1963, U.S. Supreme Ct. 1969, U.S. Ct. Appeals (1st cir.) 1982, U.S. Dist. Ct. Mass. 1964. Ptnr. Christopher & LeDoux, Worcester, Mass., 1963-67, Bowditch & Dewey, Worcester, Mass., 1967-89, Christopher & LeDoux, Worcester, Mass., 1989-95; pvt. practice William J. LeDoux, Worcester, Mass., 1996—; dir. Providence & Worcester Rail-Road, Worcester, 1990—; chmn. Clients' Security Bd. of Supreme Judicial Ct., Boston, 1988—. 1st lt. U.S. Army, 1948-54. 1st lt. U.S. Army, 1950-52, Korea. Fellow Mass. Bar Found. (life), Worcester County Bar Found. (life); mem. Worcester County Bar Assn. (fee arbitration bd. 1990—). Avocations: swimming, reading. Home: 7 Brandon Rd Worcester MA 01606-1609 Office: William J LeDoux 446 Main St Worcester MA 01608-2302

LEDSINGER, CHARLES ALBERT, JR., hotel, gaming executive; b. Memphis, Jan. 1, 1950; s. Charles Albert Ledsinger Sr. and Betty L. (Clark) Heller; m. Anita Clarendon, May 11, 1974; children: Leila Grace, Katherine Elise. BA in English, U. Va., 1972; MBA in Fin., Memphis State U., 1977. Restaurant mgr. Boudreaux and Shoup Enterprises, Atlanta, 1972-74; comml. property mgr. Hoover Morris, Enterprises, Atlanta, 1974-75; fin. analyst Holiday Inns, Inc., Memphis, 1978-79, mgr. investor rels., 1980, exec. asst. to pres., 1980-83; v.p. fin. and adminstrn. Embassy Stes., Irving, Tex., 1983-87; v.p. project fin. Holiday Corp., Memphis, 1987-90; v.p., treas. The Promus Cos., Memphis, 1990; sr. v.p., CFO The Promus Cos., Memphis, 1990-95, Harrah's Entertainment, Memphis, 1995—; bd. dirs. The Restaurant Co., Perkins Mgmt. Co., Inc., Friendly Ice Cream Corp. Mem. exec. bd. Chickasaw coun. Boy Scouts Am., 1993—; trustee St. Mary's Episcopal Sch., 1994—; bd. dirs. Memphis Devel. Found., 1992—, TBC Corp., 1996—, Sky City Ltd., Auckland, New Zealand, 1995—. Office: Harrah's Entertainment Inc 1023 Cherry Rd Memphis TN 38117-5423

LE DUC, ALBERT LOUIS, JR., computer services director; b. Montgomery, Ala., Feb. 1, 1937; s. Albert Louis and Rachel Nancy (Wineinger) LeD. Student Duke U., 1954-55; B.A., Fla. State U., 1958, M.S., 1960; m. Ellen Heath, June 18, 1960; children: Albert Louis III, Charles Andrew. Civilian mathematician Army Rocket Guided Missile Agy., Huntsville, Ala., 1958-59; mathematician analyst RCA Svc. Co., Patrick AFB, Fla., 1960-63, programming leader, 1963-67, project mgr., Eglin AFB, Fla., 1967-69, mktg. adminstr., Cherry Hill, N.J., 1969-71; tech. dir. Ind. U., Bloomington, 1971-77; dir. analysis programming Miami-Dade Community Coll., Miami, Fla., 1977-89, dir. computer svcs., 1989—; part-time instr. Fla. State U., 1958-60, Brevard Engring. Coll., 1961-62, Ind. U., 1972-77. Bd. dirs. Coll. and Univ. Machine Records Conf., 1979-87. Recipient Frank Martin award Coll. and Univ. Machine Records Conf., 1985. Mem. Assn. Computing Machinery (Best Paper award 1973), Profl. Assn. for Computing and Info. Tech. in Higher Edn. (best paper award 1986), CAUSE (bd. dirs. 1993—, Elite award 1993). Author: The Computer for Managers, 1972. Home: 10321 SW 107th St Miami FL 33176-3473 Office: 11011 SW 104th St Miami FL 33176-3330

LE DUC, DON RAYMOND, lawyer, educator; b. South Milwaukee, Wis., Apr. 7, 1933; s. Raymond Joseph and Roberta (Jones) Le D.; m. Alice Marie Pranica, Oct. 24, 1959; children—Paul, Marie. B.A., U. Wis., 1959, Ph.D., 1970; J.D., Marquette U., 1962. Bar: Wis. 1962. Assoc. firm Arnold, Murray & O'Neill, Milw., 1962-63; Ford fellow in comparative law U. Wis.-Madison, 1963-64; pvt. practice Green Bay, Wis., 1964-67; assoc. prof. U. Wis.-Madison, 1973-76, prof., 1976-84; chmn. Western European studies program U. Wis., 1979-80; Reagan prof. telecommunications U. Ala., University, 1984-86, chmn. doctoral program, 1984-86; chief counsel Wis. Dept. Ins., Madison, 1967-69; asst. prof. communications law U. Md., 1970-71; assoc. prof. Ohio State U., 1971-73; prof. U. Wis., Milw., 1986—, chmn. dept. mass comm., 1991—; dir. Comparative Telecommunications Research Center, Madison, 1974-84. Author: Cable Television and the FCC, 1973, Issues in Broadcast Regulation, 1974, Beyond Broadcasting: Patterns in Policy and Law, 1986, (with Dwight Teeter) Law of Mass Communications, 1995; editor Client mag., 1973-77; assoc. editor Jour. Broadcasting, 1974—, Jour. Comm., 1978—; contbr. articles to profl. publs. Chief counsel Wis. Gov.'s Task Force on Telecommunications, 1971-72; cable TV advisory com. mem. FCC, 1972-76. Served as spl. agt. CIC U.S. Army, 1954-57. Recipient award Ohio State U., 1971, Wis. Alumni Research Found., 1974, 75, 77; grantee Am. Philos. Soc., 1975, 77; research fellow NATO, 1979; research fellow Council European Studies, 1979. Mem. FCC, Wis. bar assns., Broadcast Edn. Assn., Internat. Inst. Communication. Republican. Roman Catholic. Home: 1800 Fairhaven Dr Cedarburg WI 53012-9100 Office: U Wis-Milw Dept Mass Communicatio Milwaukee WI 53201

LEDUC, JOHN ANDRE, lawyer; b. Oberlin, Ohio, Apr. 13, 1954. AB summa cum laude, Princeton U., 1975; JD cum laude, Harvard U., 1978. Bar: Ohio 1978, Ill. 1984. Ptnr. Winston & Strawn, Chgo., Skadden Arps & Slate, Chicago, IL, 1992—; adj. prof. law U. Chgo., 1985-91; active Fed. Income Tax Project Tax Adv. Group. Contbr. articles to profl. jours. Mem. ABA (mem. corp. tax com. tax sect. 1985—), Ill. Bar Assn., Chgo. Bar Assn., Am. Law Inst. Office: Skadden Arps & Slate 333 W Wacker Dr Ste 2100 Chicago IL 60606*

LEDWIDGE, PATRICK JOSEPH, lawyer; b. Detroit, Mar. 17, 1928; s. Patrick Liam and Mary Josephine (Hooley) L.; m. Rosemary Lahey Mervenne, Aug. 3, 1974; stepchildren—Anne Marie, Mary Clare, John, David, Sara Mervenne. A.B., Coll. Holy Cross, 1949; J.D., U. Mich., 1952. Bar: Mich. 1952. Assoc. firm Dickinson, Wright, Moon, Van Dusen & Freeman, Detroit, 1956-63; ptnr. Dickinson, Wright, Moon, Van Dusen & Freeman, 1964—. Served to lt. j.g. U.S. Navy, 1952-55. Mem. Mich. Bar Assn., Detroit Bar Assn., Am. Law Inst. Roman Catholic. Clubs: Detroit, Detroit Athletic, Detroit Golf. Home: 777 N Williamsburg Rd Bloomfield Village MI 48301-2521 Office: Dickinson Wright et al 1 Detroit Ctr 500 Woodward Ave Ste 4000 Detroit MI 48226-3423

LEDWIG, DONALD EUGENE, association executive, former public broadcasting executive, former naval officer; b. Lubbock, Tex., Mar. 2, 1937; s. Paul Lawrence and Rose L.; m. Gail Wilcox, Jan. 30, 1965; children: Donald Eugene Jr., David W. BS, Tex. Tech. U., 1959; MBA, George Washington U., 1973; Disting. Grad. Naval War Coll., 1977. Commd. ensign, U.S. Navy, 1959, advanced through grades to capt., 1980, ship's officer U.S. Pacific Fleet, 1959-65, 77-79, staff Adm. H.G. Rickover, Nuclear Propulsion Program, 1966-72, dir. contract policy Naval Material Command, Washington, 1979-81, dep. comdr. Naval Electronic Systems Command, Washington, 1981-84, ret. 1984; v.p., treas. Corp. for Pub. Broadcasting, Washington, 1984-86, pres., chief exec. officer, 1987-92; exec. dir. Am. Prodn. and Inventory Control Soc., Falls Church, Va., 1992-95; pres. Am. Logistics Assn., Washington, 1995—. Decorated Legion of Merit; recipient Barrow Meml. award Hastings Coll. Law, 1989, Nat. Captioning Inst. Award, 1990, Disting. Alumnus award Tex. Tech U., 1992. Mem. Am. Soc. Assn. Execs., Nat. Press. Club, Army and Navy Club, Army/Navy Country Club. Office: Am Logistics Assn 1133 15th St NW Ste 640 Washington DC 20005

LEDWITH, JAMES ROBB, lawyer; b. Bryn Mawr, Pa., Feb. 14, 1936; s. Richard W. (dec.) and Elizabeth T. Ledwith; children: Cheryl D., James Robb Jr., Scott W.; m. Katherine Hoffman, Dec. 2, 1978. AB, Princeton U., 1958; LLB, U. Pa., 1963. Bar: Pa. 1964. Assoc. Pepper, Hamilton & Scheetz, Phila., 1963-71, ptnr., 1971—. Bd. dirs., trustee Coll. Settlement Phila.; bd. dirs., trustee, asst. sec., treas., past pres. bd. trustees Kuhn Day Camp; sec., trustee Curtis Inst. Music, Mary Louise Curtis Bok Found. Lt. USNR, 1958-60. Fellow Am. Coll. Trust and Estate Counsel (past bd. regents, past Pa. chmn.); mem. ABA (past chmn. com. on adminstrn. estates sect. real property, probate and trust law sect.), Pa. Bar Assn. (past chmn. sect. real property, probate and trust law), Pa. Bar Inst. (bd. dirs., past pres.), Phila. Bar Assn. (past chmn., exec. com. probate and trust law com.), Nat. Assn. Estate Planning Couns. (past bd. dirs., past pres.). Republican. Presbyterian. Avocations: tennis, squash, music (piano). Office: Pepper Hamilton & Scheetz 3000 Two Logan Sq 18th Arch St Philadelphia PA 19103

LEDWITH, JOHN FRANCIS, lawyer; b. Phila., Oct. 3, 1938; s. Francis Joseph and Jane Agnes (White) L.; m. Mary Evans, Aug. 28, 1965; children—Deirdre A., John E. A.B., U. Pa., 1960, J.D., 1963. Bar: Pa. 1965, U.S. Dist. Ct. (ea. dist.) Pa. 1965, U.S. Ct. Appeals (3rd cir.) 1965, U.S. Supreme Ct. 1970, N.Y. State, 1984. Assoc. Joseph R. Thompson, Phila., 1965-71; mem. Schubert, Mallon, Wallheim & deCindis, Phila., 1971-81, LaBrum & Doak, Phila., 1981—. Author: (with others) Philadelphia CP Trial Manual, 1982. Bd. dirs. Chestnut Hill Community Assn., Pa., 1975, 76. Served to E-6 USCG, 1963-71. Mem. ABA, Phila. Bar Assn., Pa. Bar Assn., Def. Research Inst., Fedn. of Ins. Corp. Coun. Republican. Roman Catholic. Clubs: Racquet (Phila.), Phila. Cricket; Avalon Yacht (N.J.) (commodore 1982). Office: Marshall Dennehey Warner Coleman & Goggins 1845 Walnut St Philadelphia PA 19103-4797

LEDWITH, SISTER MARGARET CHRISTINE, nun, counselor; b. Longford, Ireland, Dec. 19, 1935; came to U.S., 1990; SRN, Whipps Cross Hosp., London, 1963; SCM, Dublin Nat. Maternity Hosp., Dublin, 1964; postgrad., London Hosp. and Royal Coll., 1967-69; M in Pastoral Counseling, Loyola Coll., Balt., 1991; postgrad. in urban ministry and CPE, Emmanuel Coll., 1991-92; postgrad. in Spanish, Maryknoll Inst., Bolivia, 1992—; clin. pastoral edn., Shannon Hosp., San Angelo, Tex., 1993, Meth. Hosp., Lubbock, Tex., 1994-95. Joined Missionary Sisters of the Holy Rosary, Roman Cath. Ch., 1955; cert. Coll. of Chaplains; cert. Nat. Assn. Cath. Chaplains.qq. Tutor midwifery Missionary Sisters of Holy Rosary, Nigeria, 1964, sr. ward sister, 1964-67; adminstr. pers. Missionary Sisters of Holy Rosary, Ireland, 1972-78, superior gen., 1978-89; chaplain Med. Ctr. Hosp., Odessa, Tex., 1993—; adminstr. nursing Tembisa Hosp., Johannesburg, South Africa, 1969-72; clin. pastoral edn. Shannon Hosp., San Angelo, Tex., 1993, Meth. Hosp., Lubbock, Tex., 1994-95. Fellow Coll. of Chaplains; mem. Am. Assn. Pastoral Counselors. Home: Missionary Sisters of Holy Rosary 14 Marquee West 1111 West 13th St Odessa TX 79763 Office: Missionary Sisters of Holy Rosary 741 Polo Rd Bryn Mawr PA 19010

LEDYARD, JOHN ODELL, economics educator, consultant; b. Detroit, Apr. 4, 1940; s. William Hendrie and Florence (Odell) L.; m. Bonnie Higginbottom, May 23, 1970; children: Stephen, J. Henry, Meg. BA, Wabash Coll., 1963; PhD, Purdue U., 1967; PhD (hon.), Purdue U./Ind. U., 1993. Asst. prof. Carnegie-Mellon U., Pitts., 1967-70; prof. Northwestern U., Evanston, Ill., 1970-85; prof. Calif. Inst. Tech., Pasadena, 1985—, exec. officer for social sci., 1989-92, chmn. div. humanities and social scis., 1992—. Contbr. articles to profl. jours. Fellow Econometric Soc.; mem. Pub. Choice Soc. (pres. 1980-82), Econ. Sci. Assn. (exec. com. 1986—). Office: Calif Inst of Tech Dept Econs Pasadena CA 91125

LEDYARD, ROBINS HEARD, lawyer; b. Nashville, Oct. 14, 1939; s. Quitman Robins and Alma Elizabeth (Stevenson) L.; m. Julia Bordeaux Gambill, Dec. 19, 1962; children: Stevenson Gambill, Quitman Robins II, Margaret Dabney. BA, Vanderbilt U., 1965, JD, 1966. Bar: Tenn. 1966, U.S. Supreme Ct. 1975. Atty. Nat. Life & Accident Ins. Co., Nashville, 1966-68; asst. counsel Nat. Life & Accident Ins. Co., 1968-69, asso. counsel, 1969-70, counsel, 1970-72, asso. gen. counsel, 1972-75, gen. counsel, 1975-80; partner Bass, Berry & Sims, 1980—; tchr. C.L.U.s, 1967-75. Asst. editor: Vanderbilt Law Rev., 1965-66; contbr. articles to profl. jours. Active United Way, Nashville, 1967—, Heart Fund, 1970-73; vice chmn. United Diocesan Givers, 1975; bd. dirs. St. Thomas Hosp., 1990—. With USMC, 1958-61. Recipient Bennett Douglas Bell Meml. prize, 1966; Marr scholar, 1965-66. Mem. ABA, Am. Coun. Life Ins. (chmn. tax com. 1978-80), Assn. Life Ins. Counsel (chmn. tax com. 1979-80), Tenn. Bar Assn., Nashville Bar Assn., Internat. Assn. Ins. Counsel, Global Leaders for the South, Order of Coif, Phi Delta Phi, Alpha Tau Omega. Democrat. Roman Catholic. Clubs: Belle Meade Country, Capitol of Nashville, KC. Home: 1215 Chickering Rd Nashville TN 37215-4519 Office: 2700 First American Ctr Nashville TN 37238

LEE, ADRIAN ISELIN, JR., journalist; b. Miami, Fla., Nov. 6, 1920; s. Adrian Iselin and Adriana Lanier (Owen) L.; m. Marie Lainé Santa Maria, Oct. 14, 1950; children: Adrian Iselin III, Catherine Taney, Thomas Sim, William Owen, Anne Marie, Louisa Carrell. BA, Spring Hill Coll., Mobile, Ala., 1943. With The Bulletin, Phila., 1948—; gen. assignment reporter The Bulletin, 1960—, editorial writer, 1967-72, columnist op-ed page, 1972-82; with Phila. Daily News, 1982-88; speech and op-ed writer U.S. Atty. Gen. Edwin Meese III, 1988-89; writer CBS Radio News, 1989—; tchr. editorial writing, dept. journalism Temple U. Active Chestnut Hill Community Assn. Lt. (j.g.) USNR, 1943-46, PTO. Decorated Navy Unit Commendation medal. Mem. Nat. Press Club, Pen and Pencil Club, Phila. Press Assn. (prize for coverage John F. Kennedy assassination 1963), Sigma Delta Chi (prize for column writing 1978). Republican. Roman Catholic. Home and Office: Penns Wood Apt F-20 20 E Haws Ln Flourtown PA 19031-2048

LEE, ALLAN WREN, clergyman; b. Yakima, Wash., June 3, 1924; s. Percy Anson and Agnes May (Wren) L.; m. Mildred Elaine Ferguson, June 16, 1946; 1 dau., Cynthia Ann. B.A., Phillips U., Enid, Okla., 1949; M.A., Peabody Coll. Tchrs., 1953; B.D., Tex. Christian U., 1955, D.D. (hon.), 1968. Ordained minister Christian Ch. (Disciples of Christ), 1949; pastor chs. in Tex. and Wash., 1955-60, 90—; gen. sec. World Conv. Chs. of Christ, Dallas, 1971-92; mem. gen. bd. Christian Ch., 1971-73; pres. Seattle Christian Ch. Missionary Union, 1964-66, Wash.-No. Idaho Conv. Christian Chs., 1966; TV panel mem. Am. Religious Town Hall, 1988—. Author: Bridges of Benevolence, 1962, Wit and Wisdom, 1963, The Burro and the Bibles, 1968, Under the Shadow of the Nine Dragons, 1969, Reflections Along the Reef, 1970, Disciple Down Under, 1971, Meet My Mexican Amigos, 1972, One Great Fellowship, 1974, Fifty Years of Faith and Fellowship, 1980, Recollections of a Dandy Little Up-to-Date Town, 1985, also articles. Bd. trustees N.W. Christian Coll., Eugene, Oreg., 1985-93; bd. dirs. Melissa Pub. Libr., 1992-94. With USNR, 1943-46. Recipient Disting. Service citation Children's Home Soc. Wash., 1967, Disting. Service award Bremerton Jaycees, 1959; Jamaica Tourist Bd. citation, 1984. Mem. Disciples of Christ Hist. Soc. (founder, life mem.), Religious Conv. Mgrs. Assn. (v.p. 1972-92), Am. Bible Soc. (nat. adv. coun. 1985-94), Seattle Civitan (pres. 1962-64, lt. gov. Orewa dist. 1965). Club: Seattle Civitan (pres. 1962-64, lt. gov. Orewa dist. 1965). Home and Office: 2112 Stone Creek Dr Plano TX 75075-2936 *I make every effort to live a life patterned after the life and teachings of the Man of Nazareth, Jesus Christ—that is, to be compassionate, understanding, peaceful and loving.*

LEE, ALVIN A., literary educator, scholar, author; b. Woodville, Ont., Can., Sept. 30, 1930; s. Norman Osborne and Susanna Elizabeth (Found) L.; m. Hope Arnott, Dec. 21, 1957; children: Joanna, Monika, Fiona, Alison, Margaret. B.A., U. Toronto, Ont., Can., 1953, M.A. in English, 1958, Ph.D., 1961; M.Div., Victoria U., Toronto, 1957. Teaching fellow in English U. Toronto, 1957-59; asst. prof. English McMaster U., Hamilton, Ont., 1960-65; assoc. prof. McMaster U., 1966-70, prof., 1970-92, prof. emeritus, 1990—, asst. dean Sch. Grad. Studies, 1968-71, dean Sch. Grad. Studies, 1971-73, acad. v.p., 1974-79, pres., vice-chancellor, 1980-90, pres. emeritus, 1994—; Northrop Frye prof. literary theory U. Toronto, 1992; mem. Western Ont. coun. Conf. Bd. Can., 1983-90; mem. adv. bd. Medieval and Renaissance History, 1991—. Author: James Reaney, Twayne's World Authors Series, 49, 1968, The Guest-Hall of Eden: Four Essays on the Design of Old English Poetry, 1972; editor: (with Hope Arnott Lee) Wish and Nightmare, 1972, Circle of Stories: One, 1972, Two, 1972, The Garden and the Wilderness, 1973, The Temple and the Ruin, 1973, The Peaceable Kingdom, 1974; (with Robert D. Denham) The Legacy of Northrop Frye, 1994; gen. editor: McMaster Old English Studies and Texts, Collected Works of Northrop Frye, 1995—; editl. bd. English Studies in Canada, 1982-88; contbr. articles to profl. jours. Trustee, mem. exec. com. Chedoke-McMaster Hosps., 1980-90; mem. Community Edn. Coordinating Com., 1981-90; mem. Council Ont. Univs., 1980-90, vice chmn., 1981-83, chmn., 1983-85, mem. exec. com., 1981-87; mem. Health Scis. Liaison Com., 1980-90; dir. Council Ont. Univ. Holdings Ltd., 1981-90; mem. chancellors coun. Victoria U., U. Toronto, 1983—; hon. bd. dirs. Operation Lifeline, Hamilton, 1980-90; hon. Patron Opera Hamilton, 1982-90; vice chmn. bd., mem. exec. com. Royal Bot. Gardens, Hamilton, 1980-90, chmn. provincial and fed. relations com., 1981-90, vice chmn. sci. and ednl. com., 1981-90, mem. nominating com., 1981-90; vice chmn. bus. adv. conf. Regional Municipality of Hamilton-Wentworth, 1983-90; chmn. fund-raising liaison com. McMaster Hosps. Found./McMaster U., 1983-90; hon. patron Edn. Found. of Fedn. Chinese Can. Profls., Ont., 1984-90; mem., vice chair Can. Merit Scholarship Found., 1990-93; bd. dirs. Art Gallery Hamilton, 1991-94; mem. adminstrn. bd. McMaster Mus. Art; active Hamilton Region Conservation Authority Found., 1992-94. Mem. MLA, Mediaeval Acad. Am., Assn. Univs. and Colls. Can. (coun. univ. pres. 1980—), Hamilton Assn. Advancement Lit., Sci. and Art (hon. pres. 1980-88), Can. Inst. Advanced Rsch., Internat. Assn. Anglo-Saxonists, Corporate-Higher Edn. Forum, McMaster U. Alumni Coun. (hon. pres. 1980-90), McMaster U. Letterman's Assn. (hon.), Hamilton and Dist. C. of C. (dir., mem. program com. 1982-87). Office: McMaster U, 1280 Main St W, Hamilton, ON Canada L8S 4L9

LEE, ANDRÉ LAFAYETTE, hospital administrator; b. Detroit, Aug. 14, 1943; s. Clyde and Laura D. (Davis) L.; m. Katrina (div.); children—Andre, Bryan, Tracey, Robyn. B.S., Mich. State U., 1966; M.P.A., Cornell U., 1972; D.P.A., Nova U., Fort Lauderdale, 1978. Cert. med. technologist Am. Soc. Clin. Pathologists. Adminstr., Highland Park Hosp., Mich., 1972-76; adminstr. Sumby Hosp., River Rouge, Mich., 1976-78; asst. adminstr. St. Joseph Hosp., Fort Wayne, Ind., 1978-81; adminstr. Hubbard Hosp., Nashville, 1981-87; pres. Urban Health Assocs., Nashville, 1987—; asst. prof. Shaw Coll., Detroit, 1976-77; assoc. prof. Ind. U. Grad. Sch., Fort Wayne, 1978-80; adj. prof. Eastern U., Ann Arbor, Mich., 1976-78; asst. prof. Meharry Med. Coll., Nashville, 1981—; asst. prof. Tenn. State U., 1994—. CEO United Cmty. Hosp., Detroit; owner, Friendship Hospice, Nashville, New Orleans, Natchez, Detroit. Author: Teach Your Child Healthy Habits, 1978; newspaper/cartoonist: Frost Illustrated, 1978-79. Contr. articles to profl. jours. Served to capt. U.S. Army, 1968-70. Fellow Am. Coll. Hosp. Adminstrn. (numerous coms.), Am. Acad. Med. Adminstrn. (state bd. dirs. 1981—); mem. Nat. Assn. Health Sci. Execs. (pres. 1985), NAACP. Methodist. Club: Optimist (River Rouge). Avocation: cartooning. Home: 100 Riverfront Apts #606 Detroit MI 48216 Office: United Cmty Hosp 2401 20th St Detroit MI 48216

LEE, ARTHUR VIRGIL, III, biotechnology company executive; b. Detroit, Nov. 24, 1920; s. Arthur Virgil and Emily S. (Burry) L.; m. Elizabeth Hoppin Chafee, Dec. 8, 1945 (div.); children: Arthur C., Sherrill Ann Rosoff, William J., Henry C.; m. Jean Austin LaMothe, Dec. 30, 1967. BA, Williams Coll., 1942; Indsl. Adminstr. (World War II MBA), Harvard Bus. Sch., 1943. With McKesson & Robbins, Inc., Memphis, 1946-47; ops. mgr. Providence div. McKesson & Robbins, Inc., 1947-63, v.p., mgr. Providence div., 1954-59, with Boston div., 1959-63, with Pitts. div., 1963; asst. dean Harvard U. Bus. Sch., Cambridge, Mass., 1964-65, dir. corp. rels., 1965-72, dir. resources, 1972-73; v.p. Lesley Coll., Cambridge, 1973-77; dir. corp. rels. Tufts U., Medford, Mass., 1977-79; pres. Biotec Internat., Ltd., Williamstown, Mass., 1979-95. Bd. dirs. New Eng. Drug Exchange, 1956-63; trustee Am. Coll. Switzerland, 1978-82, Williamstown Theatre Festival, 1984-94, trustee emeritus, 1994—; mem. Weston Town Fin. Com., 1961-66; mem. adv. bd. Coll. Pharmacy, U. R.I., 1957-58. Lt. USNR, 1942-46. Mem. Taconic Golf Club, Alpha Delta Phi. Congregationalist. Home and Office: 1549 Green River Rd Williamstown MA 01267-3128

LEE, BARBARA A., retired federal magistrate judge. AB, Boston U., 1959; LLB, Harvard Law Sch., 1962. Bar: Conn. 1962, N.Y. 1966. Atty. Poletti Freidin Prashker Feldman & Gartner, 1968-74, ptnr., 1974-82; pvt. practice N.Y.C., 1983-87; U.S. magistrate judge U.S. Dist. Ct. (so. dist.), N.Y., 1988-96; ret., 1996; adj. prof. law Seton Hall U., So. Orange, N.J., 1984-87. Mem. com. on ecumenical and inter-religious affairs of Roman Cath. Archdiocese of N.Y., 1983—. Mem. Fed. Magistrate Judges Assn., Assn. of Bar of City of N.Y. (mem. adminstrv. law com. 1973-74, mem. fed. cts. com. 1981-84, mem. com. on state cts. of superior jurisdiction 1984-87, mem. libr. com. 1989-92).

LEE, BARBARA ANNE, academic administrator, lawyer; b. Newton, N.J., Apr. 9, 1949; d. Robert Hanna and Keren (Dalrymple) L.; m. James Paul Begin, Aug. 14, 1982; 1 child, Robert James. BA , U. Vt., 1971; MA, Ohio State U., 1972; JD, Georgetown U., 1982; Ph.D., Ohio State U., 1977. Bar: N.J. 1983, U.S. Dist. Ct. N. J. 1983. Instr., Franklin U., Columbus, Ohio, 1974-75; rsch. asst. Ohio State U., Columbus, 1975-77; policy analyst Dept. Edn., Washington, 1978-80; dir. data trends Carnegie Found., Princeton, N.J., 1980-82; asst. prof. Grad. Sch. Edn., Rutgers U., 1982-84; asst. prof. Inst. Mgmt. and Labor Rels., Rutgers U., New Brunswick, N.J., 1984-88, assoc. prof. 1988-94, prof. 1994—, assoc. provost 1995—; mem. Study Group on Excellence in Higher Edn., Nat. Inst. Edn., 1983-84; project dir. Carnegie Corp., N.Y.C., 1982-84. Corse fellow U. Vt., 1971; recipient John F. Kennedy Labor Law award Georgetown U., 1982; grantee Bur. Labor-Mgmt. Rels. and Coop. Programs, 1985-86. Mem. ABA, N.J. Bar Assn. (exec. com. labor and employment law sect. 1987—, women's rights sect.), Am. Ednl. Rsch. Assn., Indsl. Rels. Rsch. Assn., Acad. Mgmt., Assn. Study Higher Edn. (legal counsel 1982-88), Nat. Assn. Coll. and Univ. Attys. (vice chair editl. bd. 1986-89, chair 1995—, chair publs. com. 1988-91, bd. dirs. 1990-93) Author: Academics in Court, 1987; co-author: The Law of Higher Education, 3d edit., 1995; contbr. numerous articles to profl. jours. Office: Rutgers U Provost's Office 18 Bishop Pl New Brunswick NJ 08903

LEE, BENNY Y. C., import and export company executive; b. Taipei, Taiwan, Feb. 23, 1947; s. Ko Kwan and Hsiu Yen (Huang) L.; m. Edith Y.C. Lee, June 25, 1989; children: Jenny I.S., Elizabeth Jordan, Katherine Belinda. Student, Tatung Instn. Tech., Taipei. Staff engr. Bendix Corp., Taipei, 1969-70, Philco Ford Corp., Taipei, 1970; supr. quality control Arvin Corp., Taipei, 1970-72; staff engr. Midland Corp., Taipei, 1972-74, mgr., 1974-77; mgr. elec. dept. Amerex Corp., Taipei, 1977-79; pres., owner Mitco, Taipei, 1979—, Kansas City, Mo. Mem. World Trade Ctr., Kansas City Internat. Trade Club.

LEE, BERNARD SHING-SHU, research company executive; b. Nanking, People's Republic of China, Dec. 14, 1934; came to U.S., 1949; s. Wei-Kuo and Pei-fen (Tang) L.; m. Pauline Pan; children: Karen, Lesley, Tania. BSc, Poly. Inst. Bklyn., 1956, DSc in Chem. Engring., 1960. Registered profl. engr., N.Y., Ill. With Arthur D. Little, Inc., Cambridge, Mass., 1960-65; with Inst. Gas Tech., Chgo., 1965-78, pres., 1978—; chmn. M-C Power Corp., Burr Ridge, Ill.; bd. dirs. NUI corp., Bedminster, N.J., Nat. Fuel Gas Co., Buffalo, Peerless Mfg. Co., Dallas, Energy BioSystems Corp., The Woodlands, Tex., New Eng. Gas Assn.; chmn. SGT, Shanghai, People's Republic of China. Contbr. more than 60 articles to profl. jours. Recipient Outstanding Personal Achievement in Chem. Engring. award Chem. Engring. mag., 1978. Fellow AAAS, Am. Inst. Chem. Engrs. (33d inst. lectr. 1981); mem. AIME, Am. Chem. Soc., Am. Gas Assn. (Gas Industry Rsch. award 1984), Econ. Club Chgo. Office: Inst Gas Tech 1700 S Mount Prospect Rd Des Plaines IL 60018-1804

LEE, BETTY REDDING, architect; b. Shreveport, La., Dec. 6, 1919; d. Joseph Alsop and Mary (Byrd) Redding; m. Frank Cayce Lee, Nov. 22, 1940 (dec. Aug. 1978); children: Cayce Redding, Clifton Monroe, Mary Byrd (Mrs. Kent Ray). Student La. State U., 1936-37, 37-38, U. Calif. War Extension Coll., San Diego, 1942-43; student Centenary Coll., 1937; attended Roofing Industry Ednl. Inst., 1980-82, 84, 86-88, 89-90, 93, Better Understanding Roofing Systems Inst., 1989. Sheetmetal worker Consol.-Vultee, San Diego, 1942; engring. draftsman, 1943-45; jr. to sr. archtl. draftsman Bodman & Murrell, Baton Rouge, 1945-55; sr. archtl. draftsman to architect Post & Harelson, Baton Rouge, 1955-58; assoc. arch. G. Ross Murrell, Jr., Baton Rouge, 1960-66; staff arch. Charles E. Schwing & Assos., Baton

Rouge, 1966-71, Kenneth C. Landry, Baton Rouge, 1971, 73-74; design draftsman Rayner & McKenzie, Baton Rouge, 1972-73; cons. arch. and planner Office Engring. and Cons. Svcs., La. Dept. Health and Human Resources, Baton Rouge, 1974-82; arch. roofing and waterproofing sect. La. Dept. Facility Planning and Control, 1982—. Author Instructions to Designers for Roofing Systems for Louisiana Public Buildings; co-author: Building Owners Guide for Protecting and Maintaining Built-Up Roofing Systems, 1981; designed typical La. country store for La. Arts and Sci. Ctr. Mus. Recipient Honor award Schuller BURSI Group, 1989, 90, 91, 92, 93. Mem. La. Assn. Children with Learning Disabilities, 1967-69, Multiple Sclerosis Soc., 1963—, CPA Aux., 1960-69, PTA, 1953-66; troop leader Brownies and Girl Scouts U.S.A., 1959-60; asst. den mother Cub Scouts, 1955-57. Licensed architect. Mem. ASTM, Nat. AIA, AIA La., AIA Baton Rouge (first woman mem.), DAR, Constrn. Specifications Inst. (charter mem. Baton Rouge chpt.) So. Bldg. Code Congress Internat., Miss. Roofing Contractors Assn. (first woman hon.), Nat. Roofing Contractors Assn., La. Inst. Bldg. Scis. (founding mem. 1980), Roof Cons. Inst. (govt. liaison mem.), Inst. Roofing and Waterproofing Consultants, Jr. League Baton Rouge., Le Salon du Livre Club, Kappa Delta. Republican. Episcopalian. Home: 1994 Longwood Dr Baton Rouge LA 70808-1247 Office: Capitol Sta PO Box 94095 Baton Rouge LA 70804-9095

LEE, BLAINE NELSON, educational executive, consultant, educator; b. Olympia, Wash., Apr. 3, 1946; s. Elwyn Earl and Thelma Marie (Woods) Reeder; m. Shawny Christian Lee; children: Blaine, Benjamin, Adam, Michal, Joseph, Joshua, Casey, Abraham, Eliza, Gabriel, Celeste. BS in Psychology, Brigham Young U., 1969, MS in Ednl. Psychology, 1972; PhD in Ednl. Psychology, U. Tex., 1982. Cert. ednl. specialist, secondary edn., ednl. adminstrn. Dir. instrnl. sys. USAF, San Antonio, 1972-75; assoc. prof. USAF Acad., Colorado Springs, Colo., 1975-78; edn. dir. Heritage Sch., Provo, Utah, 1978-81; asst. prof. Utah Valley State Coll., Orem, 1981-84; pres. Skills for Living, Salem, Utah, 1984-86; v.p. Covey Leadership Ctr., Provo, Utah, 1986—; ednl. cons. in field. Author: Affective Objectives, 1972, Personal Change, 1982, Stress Strategist, 1986, Principle Centered Leadership, 1990, Power Principle, 1996; contbr. articles to profl. jours. High councilman LDS Ch., mem. gen. bd., 1970-72; pres. Provo PTO. Named Outstanding Young Man in Am., U.S. C. of C., 1976, 84. Mem. APA, ASTD, Am. Mgmt. Assn., Nat. Spkrs. Assn., Phi Delta Kappa. Avocations: cmty. theatre, choir dir., camping, poetry, soccer coach. Home: 10435 S 600 E Salem UT 84653-9389 Office: Covey Leadership Ctr 3507 N University Ave Provo UT 84604-4478

LEE, BRADFORD H., physician, consultant; b. San Francisco, Sept. 4, 1952; s. William M. and Jane (Fong) L. BS, USAF Acad., 1974; MD, Howard U., 1978; JD, U. Pacific, 1991; MBA, Golden Gate U., 1994. Bar: Calif. 1991, U.S. Dist. Ct. (ea. and no. dists.) Calif. 1991. Commd. USAF, 1970, advanced through grades to col.; emergency physician USAF Hosp., Mostler AFB, Calif., 1981-83; chmn. dept. emergency medicine David Grant Med. Ctr., Travis AFB, Calif., 1983-85; dir. base med. svcs. OLAA, Osan, Republic of Korea, 1985-86; chief med. staff 652nd Med. Group, Matler AFBB, 1986-92, 9th Med. Group, Beale AFB, Calif., 1992-94; chief clin. medicine Air Combat Command Surgeon, Langley AFB, Va., 1994-95; cons. to surgeon ACC, Langley AFB, 1993—; cons. PACAF, 1985-86, Calif. Med. Bd., 1991. Fellow Am. Coll. Legal Medicine, Am. Coll. Emergency Medicine; mem. Am. Coll. Healthcare Execs., Calif. Bar Assn. Office: Hdqs ACC/SGSTZ 162 Dodd Bldg Ste 100 Langley AFB VA 23665

LEE, BRANT THOMAS, lawyer, federal official; b. San Francisco, Feb. 17, 1962; s. Ford and Patricia (Leong) L.; m. Marie Bernadette Curry, Sept. 20, 1991. BA in Philosophy, U. Calif., Berkeley, 1985; JD, Harvard U., 1990, M in Pub. Policy, 1994. Bar: Calif. 1992. Counsel subcom. on Constitution, U.S. Senate Judiciary Com., Washington, 1990-92; assoc. Breon, O'Donnell, Miller, Brown & Dannis, San Francisco, 1992—; dep. staff sec., spl. asst. to Pres. (acting) Washington, 1993; commr. San Francisco Ethics Commn., 1995—. Trustee Chinese for Affirmative Action, San Francisco, 1992—; bd. dirs. Conf. Asian Pacific Am. Leadership, Washington, 1990-92; staff mem. Dukakis for Pres., Boston, 1988. Mem. Bar Assn. San Francisco, Nat. Asian Pacfic Am. Bar Assn., Asian Am. Bar Assn. Greater Bay Area. Office: Breon O'Donnell Miller et al 71 Stevenson St San Francisco CA 94105-2934

LEE, BRENDA (BRENDA MAE TARPLEY), singer, entertainer; b. Lithonia, Ga., Dec. 11, 1944; m. Ronnie Shacklett; children: Julie, Jolie. First appeared on Red Foley Ozark Jubilee Show, 1956; appeared in Opryland USA Show, Nashville, Music! Music! Music! Starring Brenda Lee, 1988; appeared in film Smokey and the Bandit II, 1980, in cable TV spl. Legendary Ladies, 1986, in PBS spl. Shake Rattle and Roll, 1988; recs. include Brenda Lee, 1960, Sincerely, 1961, All Alone Am I, 1962, By Request, 1964, Bye Bye Blues, 1966, 10 Golden Years, 1966, Memphis Portrait, 1970, Now, 1975, and many others; recent albums include Brenda Lee, 1991, Anthology Vols. 1 & 2, 1991, Greatest Hits Live, 1992. Recipient Gov.'s award Nat. Acad. Rec. Arts and Scis., 1984. Address: Brenda Lee Entertainments care Ronnie Shacklett PO Box 101188 Nashville TN 37210-1188

LEE, BRIAN EDWARD, lawyer; b. Oceanside, N.Y., Feb. 29, 1952; s. Lewis H. Jr. and Jean Elinor (Andrews) L.; m. Eleanor L. Barker, June 5, 1982; children: Christopher Martin, Alison Ruth, Danielle Andrea. AB, Colgate U., 1974; JD, Valparaiso U., 1976. Bar: N.Y. 1977, U.S. Dist. Ct. (so. and ea. dists.) N.Y. 1978, U.S. Ct. Appeals (2nd cir. 1992). Assoc. Marshall, Bellofatto & Callahan, Lynbrook, N.Y., 1977-80, Morris, Duffy, Ivone & Jensen, N.Y.C., 1980-84; sr. assoc. Ivone, Devine & Jensen, Lake Success, N.Y., 1984-85, ptnr., 1985—. Pres., trustee Trinity Christian Sch. of Montville Inc., N.J., 1985—. Mem. ABA, N.Y. State Bar Assn., N.Y. County Lawyers Assn., Christian Legal Soc. Republican. Baptist. Home: 292 Jacksonville Rd Pompton Plains NJ 07444-1511 Office: Ivone Devine & Jensen 2001 Marcus Ave New Hyde Park NY 11042-1011

LEE, BURNS WELLS, public relations executive; b. St. Louis, July 21, 1913; s. Channing B. and Rae (Wells) L.; m. Pauline Slocum, Apr. 10, 1939 (div.); m. Kathleen Booth Strutt, July 1, 1960. A.B., Occidental Coll., 1935. Publicity dir. Benton & Bowles, Inc., N.Y.C., Hollywood, 1939-42; sr. specialist war savs. staff Treasury Dept., Washington, 1942-43; pub. relations mgr. Rexall Drug Co., Los Angeles, 1946-49; pres. Bergen & Lee, Inc., Los Angeles, 1949—. Served as pub. relations officer USMCR, 1943-46. Mem. Pub. Rels. Soc. Am. (chmn. com. standards of profl. practice 1951, regional v.p. 1952-53, chmn. pub. rels. reference round table 1954-55, chmn. eligibility com. 1962, chmn. grievance bd. 1965-66, chmn. spl. task force on pub. rels. 1975-77, 1st ann. professionalism award L.A. chpt. 1964), Regional Plan Assn. So. Calif. (dir., chmn. pub. rels. com. 1967-70), Central City Assn. (dir. 1971-84), L.A. C. of C. (chmn. pub. rels., bus. outlook conf. 1974, mem. exec. com., internat. commerce coun. 1979-83, 85-89), GrandPeople (L.A., mem. bd. dirs. 1988-92),Exec. Svc. Corps. (cons. L.A. chpt. 1991—), Publicity Club L.A., Rotary L.A. (editor weekly publ. 1993—). Home: 870 Rome Dr Los Angeles CA 90065-3215 Office: 123 S Figueroa St Ste 200B Los Angeles CA 90012-5517

LEE, CARLA ANN BOUSKA, nursing educator; b. Ellsworth, Kans., Nov. 26, 1943; d. Frank J. and Christine Rose (Vopat) Bouska; m. Gordon Larry Lee, July 8, 1967. RN, Marymount Coll., Salina, Kans., 1964; BSN, U. Kans., 1967; MA, Wichita State U., 1972, EdS, 1975, M in Nursing, 1984; PhD, Kans. State U., 1988. RN; cert. family and adult nurse practitioner, advanced nurse adminstr., health edn. specialist. Staff, charge nurse Ellsworth (Kans.) County Vet. Meml. Hosp., 1964-65; critical, coronary, and surg. nurse Med. Ctr. U. Kans., Kansas City, 1966-67; Watkins Meml. Hosp. and Student Health Ctr., 1965-55; asst. dir., chief instr. sch. nursing Wesley Sch. Nursing, Wichita, Kans., 1967-74; asst prof., chairperson Nurse Clinician/Practitioner Dept. Wichita State U., 1974-84; assoc. prof., dir. nurse practitioner program Ft. Hays State U., Hays, Kans., 1992-95; assoc. prof., coord. postgrad. nursing studies Clark Coll., Omaha, 1995—; cons. GRCI's CE Providership, 1994-96; lectr. Wichita State U., 1972-74, mem. grad. faculty, 1993-95; cons. Hays Med. Ctr.-Family Healthcare Ctr., 1993-96, Baker U., Northeastern U., Boston; mem. adv. coun. Kans. Newman Coll.; mem. adv. bd. Kans. Originals, Kans. Dept. Econ. Devel. Project, Wilson; mem. grad. faculty U. Kans. 1993-95; rschr. in field. Author: (with Stroot & Barrett) Fluids and Electrolytes: A Basic Approach, 3d edit., 1984, 4th ed., 1996 (poetry) Seasons: Marks of Life, 1991 (Golden Poet award 1991), Winter Tree, 1995 (Internat. Poet of Merit award 1995), (booklet) Czechoslovakian History, 1988 (honor room Czech Mus. and Opera House, Wilson); author, editor: History of Kansas Nursing, 1987; contbr. articles to profl. jours. Co-founder Kans. Nurses Found., pres., trustee, 1978-93, vol. ARC, 1967-92, bd. dirs., 1977-90; mem. rschr. Gov.'s Commn. Health Care, Topeka, 1990; mem. State of Kans. health care agenda Kans. Pub. Health Assn., 1995; city coord. campaign Sec. State, 1986; vol., lectr. Am. Heart Assn., Am. Cancer Soc., 1967—; election judge Sedgwick County, Kans., 1989-94; chair Nat. Task Force on Care Competence of Nurse Practitioners, 1995; mem. Nat. Task Force on Feasibility of Care Exam. for Nurse Practitioners, 1995. Nurse Practitioner Tng. grantee U.S. Health and Human Svcs.; named Outstanding Cmty. Leader, jaycees, Alumnus of Yr., Kansas U, 1979, marymount Coll., 1987, Poet of Yr., 1995; recipient Tchr. award Mortar Bd. Fellow Am. Acad. Nursing, Am. Acad. Nursing; mem. ANA (nat. and site visitor ANCC), Kans. Nurses Assn. (bd. dirs., treas.), Kans. Alliance Advanced Nurse Practitioners (founder, pres., 1986), Gt. Plains Nurse Practitioners Soc., (founder, pres. 1993), Internat. Soc. Poets (disting.), Alpha Eta (pres. Wichita State U. chpt.), Sigma Theta Tau Internat., Internat. Woman of Yr. Republican. Roman Catholic. Avocations: poetry, music, landscaping, writing, sewing. Home: 1367 N Westlink St Wichita KS 67212-4238 Office: Clarkson Coll Dept Nursing 101 S 42nd St Omaha NE 68131

LEE, CATHERINE, sculptor, painter; b. Pampa, Tex., Apr. 11, 1950; d. Paul Albert and Alice (Fleming) Porter; m. B. R. Mangham, 1967 (div. 1976); 1 child, Parker Valentine; m. Sean Scully, 1977. BA, San Jose State U., 1975. artist-in-residence Mpls. Coll. Art & Design, Minn. Inst. Art, 1982; vis. asst. prof. painting U. Tex., San Antonio, 1983; adj. asst. prof. Columbia U., N.Y.C., 1986-87. Group exhbns. include Albright-Knox Mus., Buffalo, 1987, Biennale de Sculpture, Monte Carlo, Monaco, 1991, Mus. Folkwang, Essen, Germany, 1992, Stadtische Galerie im Lenbachhaus, Munich, 1992, Neue Galerie Der Stadt Linz, Austria, 1992, Cleve. Mus. of Art, 1993, The Tate Gallery, 1994, many others. Creative Artists Pub. Svc. fellow, 1978; NEA grantee, 1989. Office: 106 Spring St New York NY 10012-3814 also: Galerie Karsten Greve, Wallrafplatz 3, 5000 Koln Germany also: Galerie Lelong 20 W 57th St New York NY 10019-3917

LEE, CHARLES, retired English language and literature educator, arts critic; b. Phila., Jan. 2, 1913; s. Benjamin and Lillian (Potash) Levy; divorced; children: Myles E., Gail M. A.B., U. Pa., 1933, M.A., 1936, Ph.D., 1955. Lit. editor Boston Herald-Traveler, 1936-40; contbg. reviewer N.Y. Times Book Review, 1942-58; Lit. editor Phila. Record, 1940-47; contbg. reviewer Phila. Evening Bulletin, 1947-49; faculty U. Pa., 1949-65, prof. communications, 1959-65, prof. English, 1959-83, emeritus prof. English, 1983—; vice dean Annenberg Sch. Communications, 1959-65; roving critic WCAU radio, 1960-65, WCAU-TV, 1965-73; entertainments editor WCAU radio, 1974-79; roving critic WFLN-AM & FM, 1979—; creative cons. Four-Star Internat., Hollywood. Exhibited: one-man art show Janet Fleisher Gallery, Phila., 1972, Faculty Club, U. Pa., 1985, 89, Designer's Corner Gallery, 1990, Burrison Gallery, U. Pa., 1991, 93; author Exile: A Book of Verse, 1936, How to Enjoy Reading, 1939, An Almanac of Reading, 1940, Weekend at the Waldorf, 1945, North East, South, West, 1945, The Twin Bedside Anthology, 1946, Snow, Ice and Penguins, 1950, I'll Be Waiting, 1958, The Hidden Public, 1958; Editor (author preface): The State of the Nation, 1963, Sevens Come Eleven, 1972, Ten Sevens, 1982, Love, Life and Laughter, 1990. Recipient 1st award for meritorious achievement in journalism U. Pa., 1944, achievement award Logan Square East, 1991, citation City of Phila., 1993. Mem. Soc. Am. Historians, A.A.U.P., Phi Beta Kappa. Office: Univ Penn English Dept Philadelphia PA 19131 *Savor the sun. Study the dust. Enjoy what you can. Endure what you must.*

LEE, CHARLES ROBERT, telecommunications company executive; b. 1940; married; 5 children. BS in Metall. Engring., Cornell U., 1962; MBA, Harvard U., 1964. Mgr. bus. research U.S. Steel Co., 1964-71; sr. v.p. fin. Penn Ctrl. Corp., 1971-80, Columbia Pictures Industries, 1980-83, GTE Corp., Stamford, CT, 1983-86; sr. v.p. fin. & planning GTE Corp., 1986-89; pres., chief oper. officer GTE Corp., Stamford, CT, 1988-92, chmn., chief exec. officer, 1992—, also bd. dirs.; bd. dirs. United Techs. Corp., Proctor & Gamble Co., USX Corp.; mem. Pres.'s Nat. Security Telecoms. Adv. Com. Trustee Cornell U.; bd. dirs. Stamford Hosp. Found., New Am. Schs. Devel. Corp.; bd. dirs. of the assocs. Harvard Bus. Sch. Mem. Fin. Execs. Inst., Nat. Planning Assn. (com. on new Am. realities, trustee), Bus. Roundtable, Stanwich Club, Blind Brook Club, Thunderbird Country Club, Laurel Valley Golf Club. Office: GTE Corp 1 Stamford Forum Stamford CT 06901-3302

LEE, CHARLES TOMERLIN, lawyer; b. N.Y.C., Feb. 20, 1950; s. Thomas Bailey and Sarah (Tomerlin) L.; m. Leslie Simmons, May 19, 1979; children: Thomas, Leslie. BA, Harvard U., 1972; JD, Columbia U., 1976. Assoc. Webster & Sheffield, N.Y.C., 1976-84; assoc., now ptnr. Paul, Hastings, Janofsky & Walker, Stamford, Conn., 1984—. Founder, pub. Noonmark mag., 1967; founder Harvard Ind., 1969. Chmn. Urban Redevel. Commn., Stamford, 1984-91; dir. Hartman Found., 1984—. Mem. Harvard Club N.Y.C. (sec. 1990—). Avocations: history, hiking, skiing. Office: Paul Hastings Janofsky & Walker 1055 Washington Blvd Fl 9 Stamford CT 06901-2218*

LEE, CHARLYN YVONNE, chemical engineer; b. Washington, May 1, 1960; d. James Charles and Beverly Mae (Williams) L. BSChemE, MIT, 1982; MSChemE, Ga. Inst. Tech., 1984. Cert. environ. mgr. Engring. intern Naval Surface Weapons Ctr., Silver Spring, Md., 1977-78; engring. aid VA, Washington, 1978-81; engr. Dupont Savannah River Lab, Aiken, S.C., 1982-83, Dupont Exptl. Sta., Wilmington, Del., 1984-86; mfg. engr. Dupont Spruance Plant, Richmond, Va., 1986-89; rsch. engr. Dupont Jackson Lab., Deepwater, N.J., 1989-91; process engr. Dupont Pontchartrain Works, LaPlace, La., 1991-93; environ. protection specialist NIH, Bethesda, Md., 1993—. Bd. mem. Richmond Area Program for Minorities in Engring., 1987-89; corp. advisor Nat. Action Coun. for Minorities in Engring., Wilmington, 1991; mem. D.C. Youth Adv. Bd. for Mental Health, Washington. Recipient Merit award VA, 1981; Proctor and Gamble grantee, 1981; Gem fellow Nat. Consortium for Grad. Degrees for Minorities in Engring., Inc., 1982, Fed. Jr. fellow, 1978. Mem. AIChE, NAFE. Home: 4812 Illinois Ave NW Washington DC 20011-4578

LEE, CHESTER MAURICE, government official; b. New Derry, Pa., Apr. 6, 1919; s. Joseph and Mary L.; m. Rose McGinnis, Apr. 18, 1942; children: Suzanne D., David J., Virginia A., Nancy M. B.S., U.S. Naval Acad., 1941; postgrad., George Washington U., 1962-63, Nat. War Coll., 1962-63. Commd. ensign U.S. Navy, 1941, advanced through grades to capt., 1961; comdg. officer U.S.S. Rodman, Charleston, S.C., 1952-53; instr. Gen. Line Sch., Monterey, Calif., 1953-56; with Spl. Projects Office, Bur. Naval Weapons, Washington, 1956-58, 60-62; comdg. officer U.S.S. Gyatt, Norfolk, 1958-60; comdr. Destroyer Div. 132, Long Beach, 1963-64; with Office Sec. Def., Washington, 1964-65; ret., 1965; with NASA, Washington, 1965-87; dir. Apollo Mission NASA, 1969-72, program dir. Apollo/Soyuz Test Project, 1973-75, dir. space transp. systems utilization, 1975-81, dir. customer services, 1981-87, asst. assoc. adminstr. Office of Space Flight, from 1987; now v.p. Spacehab Inc., Washington, president. Decorated Navy Commendation medal; recipient 2 Exceptional Service medals, 1969, 3 Distinguished Service medals, 1973, 75, 87, Distinguished Service medals NASA., Outstanding Leadership medal; Pres.' Rank of Meritorious Exec. with Sr. Exec. Service.. Fellow AIAA (assoc.), Am. Astronautic Soc. *

LEE, CHI HSIANG, electrical engineer, educator; b. Mar. 27, 1936. BS, Nat. Taiwan U., 1959; PhD, Harvard U., 1968. Prof. elec. engring. dept. elec. engring. U. Md. Fellow IEEE (chmn. 1986-89, lightwave tech. com., MTT-S, vice-chmn. LEOS Washington-No. Va. chpt. 1988-89). Office: Univ Maryland Dept of Electrical Engineering College Park MD 20742*

LEE, CHIN-TIAN, academic administrator, agricultural studies educator; b. Chiayi, Taiwan, June 22, 1940; came to U.S., 1967; s. Pau-Tong and Wu-May (Yang) L.; m. Shu-Teh Kuo, June 22, 1969; Corinna T., Frances T. BS, Nat. Taiwan U., Taipei, 1964, MS, 1967; MS, U. Wis., 1969, PhD, 1971. Rsch. asst. Nat. Taiwan U., Taipei, 1965-67; rsch. asst. U. Wis., Madison, 1967-71, biologist, 1971-74; asst. prof. U. Guam, Mangilao, 1974-80; assoc. prof. U. Guam, Manigilao, 1980-87, prof., 1987—, dean coll. agriculture, 1989—; dir. Guam Coop. Extension Svc., Mangilao, 1989—, Guam Agrl. Expt. Sta., Mangilao, 1989—; cons. South Pacific Commn., Suva, Fiji, 1978. Contbr. articles to profl. jours. Vice-chmn. bd. dirs. Chinese Sch. Guam, Harmon, 1984-88, advisor, 1989-91, chmn., 1992—. 2d lt. Taiwanese Air Force, 1965. Recipient Outstanding Prof. award 19th Guam Legislature, Faculty award for excellence in rsch. U. Guam, 1988; USDA grantee, 1974-89. Mem. Chinese Assn. Agrl. Sci., Asian Assn. Colls. and Univs. (bd. dirs. 1989—), We. Assn. Agrl. Exptl. Sta. Dirs. (exec. com. 1993), Am. Soc. Agronomy, Am. Soc. Horticultural Sci., Epsilon Sigma Phi. Avocations: reading, gardening, traveling, swimming, fishing. Home: Y-Papao Estates 156 Bengbing St Dededo GU 96912-2421 Office: U Guam Coll Agriculture Coll Agriculture UDG Sta Mangilao GU 96923

LEE, CHONG-SIK, political scientist, educator; b. Anju, Korea, July 30, 1931; came to U.S., 1954, naturalized, 1969; s. Bong-Joo and Bong-kye (Moon) L.; m. Myung-Sook Woo, Mar. 19, 1962; children—Sharon, Gina, Roger. B.A., UCLA, 1956, M.A., 1957; Ph.D., U. Calif., Berkeley, 1961. Instr. polit. sci. U. Colo., Boulder, 1960-61, Dartmouth Coll., Hanover, N.H., 1961-63; asst. prof. U. Pa., Phila., 1963-65; assoc. prof. U. Pa., 1965-73, prof., 1973—; dir. Anspach Inst. Diplomacy and Fgn. Affairs, 1980-85, chmn. grad. program internat. relations, 1980-85; chmn. joint com. on Korean Studies Social Sci. Research Council and Am. Council Learned Socs., 1970-77. Author: The Politics of Korean Nationalism, 1963, Counter-insurgency in Manchuria: The Japanese Experience, 1931-40, 1967, (with Robert A. Scalapino) Communism in Korea, 1973, The Life of Kim Kyu-sik, 1974, Materials on Korean Communism, 1945-47, 1977, The Korean Workers' Party: A Short History, 1978, Revolutionary Struggle in Manchuria: Chinese Communism and Soviet Interest, 1922-1945, 1983, Japan and Korea: The Political Dimension, 1985; (with Mike Langford) Korea: Land of Morning Calm, 1988, Recollections of Anti-Japanese Revolutionaries, 1988, Korea Briefing, 1990, 91, North Korea in Transition, 1991, In Search of a New Order in East Asia, 1991; mem. editorial bd.: Asian Survey, 1973—, Jour. N.E. Asian Studies, 1982—, Orbis, 1980-86. Mem. Task Force on Equal Ednl. Opportunity and Quality Edn., Pa. Higher Edn. Planning Commn., 1977. Social Sci. Rsch. Coun. grantee, 1963, 66-67, 72, 73-74, Rockefeller Found. grantee, 1965-66, Hoover Inst. grantee, 1980, Yonkang Found. grantee, 1990-93; Ford Found. faculty fellow, 1969-70. Mem. Am. Polit. Sci. Assn. (Woodrow Wilson Found. award for best book in polit. sci. 1974), Assn. Asian Studies. Home: 8 Cypress Ln Berwyn PA 19312-1005 Office: Univ Pa Dept Polit Sci Philadelphia PA 19104-6215

LEE, CHOOCHON, physics educator, researcher; b. Seoul, Korea, June 8, 1930; came to U.S., 1962.; s. Yoon Young and Soon Ye (Rhee) L.; m. Chung Sun Yun, Apr. 9, 1960; children: John Taihee, Jane Eun Kyoung, Carol Eunmee. BS in Physics, Seoul Nat. U., 1953, MS in Physics, 1957; PhD in Physics, U. Ill., 1968. From instr. to asst. prof. Seoul Nat. U., 1957-62; rsch. asoc. U. Ill., Urbana, 1968; rsch. physicist U. Montreal, Que., Can., 1968-75; assoc. prof. Korea Advanced Inst. Sci. and Tech., Seoul, Taejon, 1975-78, prof., 1978-92, Korea Telecom. Found. prof. physics, 1992—; pres. Korea Advanced Inst. Sci. and Tech., Seoul, 1980-92; vis. scholar Harvard U., Cambridge, Mass., 1982-83, 87-88. Author: Physics of Semiconductor Materials and Applications, 1986; contbr. over 170 articles to profl. jours. and internat. conf. procs. Decorated Order of Rose of Sharon Republic of Korea, 1995; recipient Presdl. Sci. prize Govt. of Republic of Korea, 1985, Incheon prize in acad. achievement, 1993. Mem. IEEE, Am. Phys. Soc., Korean Phys. Soc. (pres. 1991-93), Soc. Info. Display (bd. dirs. 1991—). Methodist. Achievements include discovery of negative staerble-wronski experiment; first to confirm mechanism of Controversial State III annealing in gold, to explain persistent photocontercivity in a-Si:H and a-Si:H/a-SiN multilayers; 1st observation of persistent photo conductivity in porous silicon. Home: 237 Kajong-dong KIT Apt 15-201, Yusongku Taejon 305-350, Republic of Korea Office: Korea Advanced Inst Sci and Tech, 373-1 Kusong-dong Yusong-ku, Taejon 305-701, Republic of Korea

LEE, CHRISTOPHER FRANK CARANDINI, actor, author; b. London, May 27, 1922; s. Geoffrey Trollope and Estelle Marie (Carandini) L.; m. Birgit Kroencke, Mar. 17, 1961; 1 child, Christina Erika. Student Brit. schs. With theatrical and film industry, 1947—; films include Corridor of Mirrors, 1947, The Curse of Frankenstein, 1956, Dracula, 1958, The Three Musketeers, 1974, The Four Musketeers, 1975, The Man with the Golden Gun, 1974, Airport 77, 1977, Caravans, 1978, Return from Witch Mountain, 1978, Circle of Iron, 1979, The Passage, 1979, The Wicker Man, 1979, Jaguar Lives, 1979, 1941, 1980, Bear Island, 1980, The Salamander, 1981, An Eye for an Eye, 1981, Safari 3000, 1982, The Last Unicorn, 1982, The Return of Captain Invincible, 1983, House of the Long Shadows, 1984, Murder Story, 1989, The Return of the Musketeers, 1989, Gremlins 2, 1990, Honeymoon Academy, 1990, Gremlins II: The New Batch, 1990, Police Academy: Mission to Moscow, 1994, Death Train, The Stupids, Moses, Ivanhoe, Feast at Midnight; appeared in TV miniseries: The Pirate, 1978, Captain America II, 1979, Goliath Awaits, 1981, The Far Pavilions, 1984, Roadtrip, Mio My Mio, The Girl, The Funny Man, 1993, A Feast at Midnight, 1994, The Stupids, 1995; TV movies include: Poor Devil, 1973, Once Upon a Spy, 1980, Charles and Diana: A Royal Love Story, 1982, The Disputation, Metier du Seigneur, Shaka Zulu, Around the World in Eighty Days, Treasure Island, Young Indy, 1992, Death Train, 1992, Moses, 1995; author: autobiography Tall Dark and Fearsome, 1977, The Great Villains, 1979, Archives of Evil. Served with RAF, 1941-46. Decorated Polonia Restituta, Czechoslovak Medal for Valor, officer Arts, Lettres et Scis., France. Mem. Screen Actors Guild, Brit. Actors Equity, Variety, Clubs Internat. Conservative. Mem. Ch. of Eng. Clubs: Hon. Company Edinburgh Golfers; Bucks's (London); Travellers (Paris). Office: DSA Inc Garden Office Bldg # 345 15301 Ventura Blvd Sherman Oaks CA 91403

LEE, CLEMENT WILLIAM KHAN, trade association administrator; b. N.Y.C., Feb. 7, 1938; s. William P. and Helen M. BTh, Concordia Coll., 1958; MDiv, Concordia Theol. Sem., 1962; MA, New Sch. for Social Research, 1976. Asst. exec. dir. Greater Detroit Luth. Ctr., 1962; editor Detroit and Suburban Luth. Newspaper, 1963; assoc. communications dir. Met. Detroit Council of Chs., 1964; dir. media ops. Am. Bible Soc., N.Y.C., 1967; dir. media relations Luth. Council U.S.A., N.Y.C., 1971-82, asst. exec. dir. communications and interpretation, 1977-82; dir. dept. telecommunications Luth. Ch. in Am., N.Y.C., 1983-87; dir. electronic media Episcopal Ch., N.Y.C., 1987-93, program dep. for communication, 1989-93, Episcopal telecomm. dir., 1993—; media cons. Luth. Ch.-Mo. Synod, Spaulding for Children, Metro News of Metro N.Y., Synod of Luth. Ch. Am., archtl. newsletter Window, Luth. Deaconess Assn., Concordia Coll., Bronxville, Physicians for Social Responsibility, Wheatridge Found., Luth. Sch. Theology, Chgo.; chmn. broadcast ops. com. Nat. Council Chs. of Christ U.S.A., 1976-80; vice chmn. bd. mgrs. Communications Commn., 1977-80; chmn. inter-faith Media Data System, 1981; mem. TV awards com. N.Y. Council Chs.; mgr. Lutherans-in-Media Conf. I and II, 1980, Luth. Audio-Visual Conf., 1981; project dir. Lambeth Conf. Inter-Anglican Telecommunication Network, 1988; internat. computer network resource leader Religious Communications Congress 90, 1990; bd. dirs. FACTA TV News, Inc.; pres. N.Y. chpt. Religious Pub. Rels. Coun.; telecommunication cons. World Coun. of Chs., Canberra Assembly, 1990-91, Episc. Bd. Theol. Edn., 1993—. Editor: Media Alert newsletter, 1980-86, Luth. Communication newsletter, 1983-87, Episcopal Media Adv. newsletter, 1989—; creator children's TV series Storyline; producer multi-image sequences, Augustana Jubilee, 1980, multi-image program Proclaim, 1984, multi-image effects, Milw. Conv., 1986, (films) Mission on Six Continents, 1975, Room for a Stranger, 1978, Winter Wheat, 1982; exec. producer, One in Mission, 1985, Gathering of the Family, 1988, Doers of the Word, 1988, The Tully-Freeman Report, 1988, Outpourings of Love, 1989, Faith on a Tightrope, 1989, Fresh Winds Blowing, 1989, Prophecy Fulfilled in Me, 1990, President Carter Center Health Video, 1990, To Walk in Beauty, 1990, Pathways for Peace, 1990, Word in the World, 1991, Executive Council Presents, 1991, Cantenbury in North Carolina, 1992. Mem. Metro N.Y. Synod Evangelical Luth. Ch. in Am. Communication Commn., Religious Pub. Rels. Coun.; mem. communication dept. nat. adv. com. Evang. Luth. Ch. in Am.; chair Telecomm. Task Force Lambeth Anglican Bishops Confs., 1988, Bldg. Restoration com. St. John's Episc. Ch., N.Y.C., 1993-95; gov. Inter-Anglican Info. Network Quest Internat. Mgmt. team, 1992—. Recipient award Detroit Press Club Found., 1963, silver medal Internat. Film and TV Festival, 1975, 79, Creative Excellence award U.S. Indsl. Film Festival, 1986, Brit. Telecommunications award, 1988, Polly Bond award, 1989, 90, 91, 92, N.Y. TV Festival finalist, 1990. Mem. Assn. Edn. Communication Tech., Internat. Assn. Bus. Communicators, Internat. TV Assn., World Assn. Christian Communication (chmn. N.Am. broadcast sect. 1975), Nat. Interfaith Cable Coalition VISN (members' com.), Satellite TV Network (bd. dirs.), Episcopal Cathedral Teleconferencing Network (steering com.). Office: Episcopal Ch Nat Office 815 2nd Ave New York NY 10017-4503*

LEE, DAI-KEONG, composer; b. Honolulu, Sept. 2, 1915; s. Lin Fong and Young Kun (Chang) L.; m. Dorothy Isabelle Moncur, May 16, 1974. Student in pre-medicine, U. Hawaii, 1933-36; scholarship student with Roger Sessions, N.Y.C., 1937-38; fellowship student under Frederick Jacobi, Juilliard Grad. Sch., 1938-41; fellowship student under Aaron Copland, Berkshire Music Ctr., summer 1941; M.A. under Otto Luening, Columbia U., 1951. bd. dirs. Am. Music Ctr., N.Y.C., 1960-69. Recorded Prelude, Hula, Symphony No. 1, Polynesian Suite; wrote mus. score for motion picture Letter from Australia, 1945; guest condr., ABC Symphony, Sydney, Australia, 1944-45; composer: orchestral works including Prelude and Hula, 1939, Hawaiian Festival Overture, 1940, Introduction and Allegro for Strings, 1941, Golden Gate Overture for Chamber Orch., 1941, Polynesian Suite, Symphony No. 1, 1941, revised 1947, Symphony No. 2, 1952; chamber works including String Quartet No. 1, 1947, Sonatina for Piano, 1947, Incantation and Dance for Piano and Violin, 1948, Introduction and Allegro for Cello and Piano, 1947; opera Open the Gates, produced by Blackfriars, N.Y.C., 1951; ballet Waltzing Matilda, 1951; mus. score Teahouse of the August Moon, produced by Maurice Evans-George Shaeffer, 1953; Polynesian Suite for Orch., 1958, Violin Concerto, 1947, revised 1955, Mele Olili for Chorus, Solo and Orch., 1960, Canticle of the Pacific, 1968; mus. play Noa-Noa, 1972; Mortal Thoughts of a Buddhist Monk for baritone, chorus and orch., 1976; one-act opera Ballad of Kitty the Barkeep, 1979; mus. plays Jenny Lind, 1981, Gauguin, Maker of Sea and Sky, 1994; Concerto Grosso for string orch., 1952, rev., 1985; contbr. articles to music mags., newspapers. Served with AUS, 1942-45, PTO. Received Albert Metz commn. for violin concerto, 1946; received CBS commn. for Introduction and Allegro for Strings, 1941, Inst. Mus. Art commn. for one-act opera, Poet's Dilemma, 1940; recipient hon. mention Prix de Rome competition Am. Acad. in Rome, 1942; Guggenheim fellow, 1945, 51. Mem. ASCAP, League Composers, Allied MacDowell Club, Dramatists Guild. Composer orchestral, symphonic, chamber music; 1st orchestral work Valse Pensieroso, performed Honolulu Symphony Orch., 1936; works performed by N.Y. Philharm., Eastman Rochester Philharm., Mpls., San Francisco, Cin., CBS, Nat., Montreal, Manila, N.Y.C. Phila., symphony orchs.; under direction of Kurtz, Monteux, Mitropoulos, Goosens, Barlow, Caston, Dixon, Stokowski, Stoessel, Pelletier, Wallenstein, others. Home: 245 W 104th St New York NY 10025-4249

LEE, DAN M., state supreme court justice; b. Petal, Miss., Apr. 19, 1926; s. Buford Aaron and Pherbia Ann (Camp) L.; m. Peggy Jo Daniel, Nov. 27, 1947 (dec. 1952); 1 child, Sheron Dianne, Lee Anderson; m. Mary Alice Gray, Sept. 30, 1956; 1 child, Dan Jr. Attended, U. So. Miss., 1946; LLB, Jackson Sch. Law, 1949; JD, Miss. Coll., 1970. Bar: Miss. 1948. Ptnr. Franklin & Lee, Jackson, Miss., 1948-54, Lee, Moore and Countiss, Jackson, Miss., 1954-71; county judge Hinds County, Hinds County, 1971-77; cir. judge Hinds-Yazoo Counties, Hinds-Yazoo Counties, 1977-82; assoc. justice Miss. Supreme Ct., Jackson, 1982-87, presiding justice, 1987-95, chief justice, 1995—. With U.S. Naval Air Corps, 1944-46. Mem. ABA, Hinds County Bar Assn., Miss. State Bar Assn., Aircraft Owners and Pilots Assn., Am. Legion, VFW. Democrat. Baptist. Lodges: Masons, Odd Fellows.

LEE, DANIEL, physician, public health service officer; b. Pinehurst, Ga., Apr. 28, 1918; s. Amos and Leila (Fowlkes) L.; m. Thelma Modestine, Dec. 26, 1944 (dec. Jan. 1986); children: Daniel Jr., Kenneth Amos, Sharon Diane. BA, Lincoln U., 1940; MD, Howard U., 1945. Diplomate Nat. Bd. Med. Examiners. Intern Harlem (N.Y.) Hosp., 1946; asst. prof. Coll. Hygiene Lincoln (Pa.) U., 1946-48; mem. med. staff Pottstown (Pa.) Meml. Hosp., 1948-55; mem. staff Coatesville (Pa.) and Brandywine Hosps., 1955—; sch. physician Pine Forge Acad. Seventh Day Adventists; past mem. staff Atkinson Meml. Hosp.; sch. physician Coatesville Area Schs., 1965—; hon. mem. med. staff Brandywine Hosp., Caotesville, 1992—. Bd. dirs. Western Chester Coun., Ctr. and Western Chester County Indsl. Devel. Authority and Corp., United Cerebral Palsy Assn. Chester County; mem. Pa. State bd. dirs. United Cerebral Palsy Assn.; mem. adv. bd. Sr. Citizens Coatesville, Southeastern Pa. High Blood Pressure; trustee Second Bapt. Ch., Pottstown; mem. health and safety com. 15th Continental Dist. Boy Scouts Am.; past pres., founder Pottstown Civic League; past pres. Pottstown Com. on Human Rels.; former mem. aloocations com. United Way, Pottstown; past mem. Chester County Health Dept.; adv. bd. Chester County Boy Scouts Am., Senoir Citizens, Coatesville, Pa.; sustaining mem. Coatesville YMCA; corp. bd. dirs. Coatesville and So. Chester County YMCA, 1995—; past trustee Embreeville State Hosp.; past mem. Coatesville Day Care Com.; past bd. dirs. Brandywine Red Cross, Chester County Hosp. Authority; adv. bd. Vis. Nurses of Coatesville. Maj. U.S. Army, 1955-57. Recipient Man of Yr. award So. Chester County Bus. and profl. Women, Scott Jr. High Sch. award for Community Svc., 1992, Cert. of Appreciation Coatesville Jaycees for Concern of Mankind and the Nation, 1973, Cert. of Appreciation for Vol. Svcs. Pub. Welfare Com. Southeastern Region, 1973; named to Coatesville Hall of Fame, 1977, Legion of Honor, Chapel of Four Chaplains, 1968, Laura S. Greenwood scholarship fund, 1970, 73, Black Heritage award for Bricklayers Mt. Tabor AME Ch., Avondale Pa., 1992, Be A Hero award YMCA, 1992; Gundaker Fellow Rotary Club of Coatesville, 1992; honoree Zeta Phi Beta. Fellow Am. Acad. Family Physicians, Am. Geriatrics Soc.; mem. AMA, NAACP (life, past trustee), Pa. Med. Soc., Nat. Med. Assn., Chester County Med. Soc., Howard U. Med. Alumni Assn., Rotary (pres. Coatesville chpt. 1976-77, Paul Harris fellow 1978, Gundake fellow 1992), Western Chester County C. of C. (pres. 1978-79, Joe Filoromo Cmty. Svcs. award 1983, awards com. 1992), Pottstown C. of C., Elks (health dir., Mount Vernon lodge, supr. high blood pressure clinic and annual bloodmobile), Men of Malvern (St. Joseph;s retreat), Chester County Pan Hellenic Assembly (past pres.), Club XV (chaplain), Elks (Man of Yr. 1991, Diamond Ebony award 1991), Kappa Alpha Psi (Outstanding Alumni Brother award Epsilon chpt., honoree 75th yr. celebration). Republican. Avocations: fishing, hunting, writing. Home: 1289 Lone Eagle Rd Coatesville PA 19320-4766 Office: 723 Merchant St Coatesville PA 19320-3339

LEE, DANIEL ANDREW, osteopathic physician, ophthalmologist; b. Bklyn., Aug. 20, 1951; s. Jack W. and Lily (Ho) L.; m. Janet Lynne Eng, June 14, 1975 (div. Sept. 1985); children: Jason Matthew, Brian Christopher, Joshua Daniel; m. Kelly Lynne Crego, Sept. 5, 1987; children: Joshua David, Alexandra Nicole Avetkova, Brandon Scott. BS in Psychobiology, SUNY, Stony Brook, 1973; BS in Biology, Westminster Coll., 1973; OD, Pa. Coll. Optometry, 1977; DO, Ohio U., 1984. Cert. in low vision proficiency, ophthalmology; cert. Osteopathic Academy of Opthalmology and Otolaryngology. Instr. Mohawk Valley C.C., Rome, N.Y., 1978-80; pvt. practice optometry, Utica, N.Y., 1978-80, Chauncey, Ohio, 1981-84, Dayton, Ohio, 1984—; intern Grandview Hosp., Dayton, 1984, mem. staff, 1984-85, ophthalmology resident, 1985—; ophthalmolgy chief resident, 1987-88; pvt. practice ophthalmology Corneal Cons. of Ind., Indpls.; chmn. dept. ophthalmology USNH, Okinawa; assoc. prof. Ophthalmology Ohio U. Coll. Osteopathic Medicine; cons. Rome Sch. Dist., Cen. Assn. for Blind, Utica, Kernan Sch. for Multiple Handicapped, Utica, Dept. of Defense Schs.; credentials chmn. Dayton br. Laser Ctrs. Am.; Amelia Earhart student adv. coun., Vestry-All Soul's Episcopal Ch.; speaker various profl. orgns. and confs.; mem. curriculum adv. com. Deer Creek Curriculum Rev. Conf., 1982. Contbr. articles to profl. jours. Mem. adv. bd. ARC, Rome, 1977-80; mem. Mohawk Valley Chinese Cultural Assn., Rome, 1977-80, Dayton Area Chinese Assn., 1985—; nominated People to People Optometry Delegation to People's Republic of China, 1985, India, 1986; co-chmn. Ohio Eye Injury Registry; chmn. pub. health & welfare com. Dayton dist. Acad. Osteo. Medicine. Served with USAF, 1977-80, to lt. comdr. USNR, 1988-91. Fellow Am. Acad. Optometry, Osteopathic Coll. Ophthalmology, Otolaryngology, and Head and Neck Surgery; mem. AMA, Am. Cancer Soc. (mem. bd. dirs. Miami County, Troy chpt.), Am. Osteo. Assn. (student rep. nat. com. on colls. 1984), Ohio Osteo. Assn., Am. Acad. Ophthalmology, Pediatric Keratoplasty Soc., Dayton Area Chinese Assn., Gold Key, Montgomery County Med. Soc., Ohio State Med. Assn., Am. Soc. Cataract and Refractive Surgery, Ohio Opthalmological Soc., Miami County Medical Soc., Internat. Soc. Refractive Keratoplasty, Assn. Contemporary Optholmology, Ohio Eye Injury Registry (co-chmn.), Internat. Soc. Refractive Surgery, C. of C. Huber Heights and Troy, Order of the Eastern Star, Harmony Lodge, Teikoku Lodge, Aloha and Antioch Shriner's Temples, Scottish Rite, Troy Lions Club, Beta Beta Beta. Episcopalian. Avocations: hunting, fishing, martial arts, photography, playing mandolin. Home: 1495 Fox Run Troy OH 45373-9594 Office: 7371 Brandt Pike Ste B Huber Heights OH 45424-3200

LEE, DAVID C., screenwriter. Screenwriter TV series, including The Jeffersons, 1979-85, Cheers, 1984-88, Wings, 1991; exec. prodr. Frasier, 1992— (Emmy award for outstanding comedy series 1995). Office: Broder Kurland Webb Offner Agy 9242 Beverly Blvd Beverly Hills CA 90210

LEE, DAVID DEWITT, industrial hygienist; b. Detroit, Feb. 16, 1948; s. Floyd Herbert and Anne Theresa (Damask) L.; m. Lorraine Angeline Wozniak, Sept. 6, 1969; children: Jennifer, Mary, Brian, Jonathan, Sarah. BS Psychology, No. Mich. U., 1975; M Indsl Safety, U. Minn., 1988. Cert. indsl. hygienist, safety profl. Ops. foreman Nat. Steel Pellet Co., Keewatin, Minn., 1976-78, 84-86; safety engr. Hanna Mining Co. Agts., Hibbing, Minn., 1978-81, Butler Tacconite, Nashwauk, Minn., 1981-84; indsl. hygienist Sonora (Calif.) Mining Co., 1988-89, State Indsl. Ins. System, Reno, Nev., 1990-92; indsl. hygienist, safety specialist Univ./C.C. System Nev., Reno, 1992—. Accredited vis., vis. chmn. Mended Hearts, Inc., Reno, 1993-95. With USN, 1967-70, Vietnam. Recipient scholarship Semi-Conductor Safety Assn. Mem. Am. Indsl. Hygiene Assn., Am. Conf. of Govt. Indsl. Hygienist, Am. Acad. Indsl. Hygiene, Am. Bd. Indsl. Hygiene, Am. Soc. Safety Engrs. (chpt. sec. 1994—, chpt. pres.-elect 1995, pres. 1996), Bd. Cert. Safety Profls. Republican. Roman Catholic. Avocations: weight-lifting, running, bicycling. Office: U Nev Environ Health & Safety MS 181 Reno NV 89557

LEE, DAVID MORRIS, physics educator; b. Rye, N.Y., Jan. 20, 1931; s. Marvin and Annette (Franks) L.; m. Dana Thorangkul, Sept. 7, 1960; children: Eric Bertel, James Marvin. AB, Harvard U., 1952; MS, U. Conn., 1955; PhD, Yale U., 1959. Instr. of physics Cornell U., Ithaca, N.Y., 1959-60, asst. prof. physics, 1960-63, assoc. prof. physics, 1963-68, prof. physics, 1968—; vis. scientist Brookhaven Nat. Lab., Upton, N.Y., 1966-67; vis. prof. U. Fla., Gainesville, 1974-75, 94, U. Calif., San Diego, La Jolla, 1988; vis. lectr. Peking U., Beijing, China, 1981; chair municipal Joseph Fourier U., Grenoble, France, 1994. Contbr. articles to Phys. Rev. Letters, Phys. Rev., Physica and Nature. With U.S. Army, 1952-54. John Simon Guggenheim fellow Guggenheim Found., 1966-67, 74-75, Japan Soc. Promotion of Scis. fellow, 1977; recipient Sir Francis Simon Meml. prize British Inst. of Physics, 1976. Fellow AAAS, Am. Phys. Soc. (Oliver Buckley prize 1981); mem. Am. Acad. Arts and Scis., Nat. Acad. Scis. Achievements include co-discovery of superfluid 3He, of the tricritical point of 3He-4He mixtures; co-observation of spin waves in spin polarized hydrogen gas. Office: Cornell U Physics Dept Clark Hall Ithaca NY 14853

LEE, DAVID STODDART, investment counselor; b. Boston, Jan. 12, 1934; s. George Cabot and Kathleen Bowring (Stoddart) L.; m. Lucinda Hopkins, Apr. 29, 1972; children: Alexander Putnam, Madeline Jackson, Alice Ingalls. A.B., Harvard U., 1956, M.B.A., 1960. V.p., dir. Lee Higginson Corp., N.Y.C., 1960-65; mng. dir., Scudder, Stevens and Clark, Boston, 1965—; dir., pres., asst. treas. Scudder Investor Svcs., Inc. (formerly Scudder Fund Distbrs.); prse., trustee Scudder Calif. Tax Free Trust, Scudder Cash Investment Trust, Scudder U.S. Treas. Money Fund, Scudder Mcpl. Trust, Scudder State Tax Free Trust, Scudder Tax Free Money Fund, Scudder Tax Free Trust; v.p., trustee Scudder Equity Trust, Scudder GNMA Fund, Scudder Portfolio Trust; v.p. Scudder Securities Trust, Scudder Funds Trust, Scudder Mut. Funds, Inc., Scudder Investment Trust, Scudder Variable Life Investment Fund, The Argentina Fund, Inc., The Brazil Fund, Inc., The Korea Fund, Inc., The L.Am. Dollar Income Fund, Inc., Scudder New Asia Fund, Inc., Scudder New Europe Fund, Inc., Scudder World Income Opportunities Fund, Inc.; v.p., asst. treas. Scudder Global Fund, Inc., Scudder Internat. Fund, Inc.; chmn. dir. Scudder Instnl. Fund, Inc., Scudder Fund, Inc., AARP Cash Investment Funds, AARP Growth Trust, AARP Income Trust, AARP Tax Free Income Trust; v.p., dir. Scudder Svc. Corp. Trustee Cotting Sch. for Handicapped Children, Boston, 1974—, New Eng. Med. Ctr., 1974—, The Winsor Sch., 1991—; bd. dirs. Rogerson House, 1978—; corporator Mass. Gen. Hosp., 1975—. Lt. (j.g.) USN, 1956-58. Mem. Soc. Chartered Fin. Analysts (chartered investment counsellor). Republican. Episcopalian. Clubs: Country, Somerset (Boston).

LEE, DEBORA ANN, elementary school educator, reading specialist; b. Beckley, W. Va., May 2, 1958; d. David Lavon and Edith (Graham) L. AB in Bus. Adminstrn., Beckley Coll., 1978; AB in Arts, Beckley Coll. (Coll. W. Va.), 1982; BS, Concord Coll., 1984; MA, U. W. VA., 1990. Cert. tchr. elem. edn. 1-8, reading specialist k-12, adult. Sec. United Mine Workers Assn., Mullens, W. Va., 1978; receptionist, sec. Ashland Fin., Mullens, 1978-79; tchr. Wyoming County Bd. Edn., Pineville, W. Va., 1984—. Mem. NEA, W. Va. Edn. Assn., Internat. Reading Assn., W. Va. State Reading Coun., Wyoming County Reading Coun. (charter, pres. 1990), Kappa Delta Pi. Democrat. Baptist. Avocations: reading, cooking, needlepoint, music, travel. Office: Mullens Elem Sch 300 Front St Mullens WV 25882-1304

LEE, DEBORAH ROCHE, federal agency administrator. BA, Duke U., 1979; M in Internat. Affairs, Columbia U., 1981. Intern Presdl. Mgmt. Program, Washington, 1981; profl. staff mem. House Armed Svcs. Com., Washington; asst. sec. def. for res. affairs Dept. Def., Washington, 1993—. Office: Reserve Affairs The Pentagon Washington DC 20301

LEE, DON YOON, publisher, academic researcher and writer; b. Seoul, Korea, Apr. 7, 1936; came to U.S., 1957; s. Yoo-ehn and Ch'i-ho (Kim) L. BA, U. Wash., 1963; MA, St. John's U., Jamaica, N.Y., 1967; MS, Georgetown U., 1971; MA, Ind. U., 1975, 90. Founder, pub. Eastern Press, Inc., Bloomington, Ind., 1981—. Author: History of Early Relation Between China and Tibet, 1981, An Introduction to East Asian and Tibetan Linguistics and Culture, 1981, Learning Standard Arabic, 1988, An Annotated Bibliography of Selected Works on China, 1981, Light Literature and Philosophy of East Asia, 1982, An Annotated Bibliography on Inner Asia, 1983, An Annotated Archaeological Bibliography of Selected Works on Northern and Central Asia, 1983, Traditional Chinese Thoughts: The Four Schools, 1990, others. Office: Eastern Press Inc PO Box 881 Bloomington IN 47402-0881

LEE, DONALD JOHN, federal judge; b. 1927. AB, U. Pitts., 1950; LLB, Duquesne U., 1954. Bar: Pa. Supreme Ct. 1955; U.S. Supreme Ct. 1984. Assoc. George Y. Meyer and Assocs., 1954-57; law clk. to Hon. Rabe F. Marsh Jr. U.S. Dist. Ct., Pa., 1957-58; assoc. Wilner, Wilner and Kuhn, 1958-61; ptnr. Dougherty, Larrimer & Lee, Pitts., 1961-84, 86-88; judge Ct. Commnon Pleas of Allegheny County, Pa., 1984-86, 88-90, U.S. Dist. Ct. (we. dist.) Pa., Pitts., 1990—; councilman Borough of Green Tree, 1961-63, solicitor, 1963-84, 86-88; spl. asst. atty. gen. Office of Atty. Gen. Commonwealth of Pa., 1963-74; spl. legal counsel Home Rule Study Commn., Municipality of Bethel Park and Borough of Green Tree, 1973-74, City of Pitts., 1978-80, various municipalities, 1970-86; chmn. Home Rule Charter Transition Com. Bethel Park, 1978. Mem. ad hoc com. Salvation Army. With USN, 1945-47. Mem. ABA, Allegheny County Bar Assn., St. Thomas More Legal Soc., Western Pa. Conservancy, Am. Youth Hostel, Ancient Order of Hibernians, Knights of Equity, Woodland Hills Swim Club, Gaelic Arts Soc., Tin Can Sailors. Office: US Dist Ct 7th Grant St Rm 916 Pittsburgh PA 15219

LEE, DONALD YOUNG (DON LEE), publishing executive, editor, writer; b. Tokyo, Dec. 11, 1959; s. Victor Young and Jean Ann (Kim) L. BA in English, UCLA, 1982; MFA in Creative Writing, Emerson Coll., 1986. Writing instr. Emerson Coll., Boston, 1985-89; mng. editor Ploughshares, Boston, 1988-92, dir., 1992—; panelist NEA Lit. Program, Washington, 1991-92; cons. AGNI, Boston, 1993, Asian Pacific Am. Jour., 1994. Contbr. short stories, articles to jours. St. Botolph Club Found. fellow, 1990, 91. Mem. PEN Am. New Eng. (bd. dirs.). Democrat. Office: Ploughshares Emerson Coll 100 Beacon St Boston MA 02116-1501

LEE, DONNA JEAN, retired hospice and respite nurse; b. Huntington Park, Nov. 12, 1931; d. Louis Frederick and Lena Adelaide (Hinson) Munyon; m. Frank Bernard Lee, July 16, 1949; children: Frank, Robert, John. AA in Nursing, Fullerton (Calif.) Jr. Coll., 1966; extension student, U. Calif., Irvine, 1966-74; student, U. N.Mex., 1982. RN, Calif.; cert. Intraventous Therapy Assn. U.S.A. Staff nurse Orange (Calif.) County Med. Ctr., 1966-71, staff and charge nurse relief ICU, CCU, Burn Unit, ER, Communicable Disease, Neo-Natal Care Unit, 1969-71, charge nurse communicable disease unit, 1969-70; staff and charge nurse ICU, emergency rm., CCU, med./surg. units Anaheim (Calif.) Meml. Hosp., 1971-74; charge and staff nurse, relief Staff Builders, Orange, 1974-82; agy. nurse Nursing Svcs. Internat., 1978-89; asst. DON Chapman Convalescent SNF, Orange, 1982; geriatric and pedicatrics nurse VNASS, 1985-93; hospice/respite nurse VIA Upjohn Home Healthcare Svcs and VNA Support Svcs. of Orange, 1985-93; ret.; staff relief nurse ICU/CCU various hosps. and labs, including plasmapheresis nurse Med. Lab. of Orange, 1978. Life mem. Republican, pres. task force, 1982—; past mem. Republican adv. com., Rep. Presdl. Trust; mem. Rep. Presdl. Legion of Merit. Mem. AACN, RNCC, RNSC, ADA, ASA, Inst. Noetic Scis., The Heritage Found., Aria, Am. Cancer Soc., Am. Lung Assn., Am. Heart Assn., Nat. Multiple Sclerosis Soc., Easter Seal Soc. Baptist. Home: 924 S Hampstead St Anaheim CA 92802-1740

LEE, DOUGLAS A., music educator; b. Carmel, Ind., Nov. 3, 1932; s. Ralph Henley and Flossie Ellen (Chandler) Lee; m. Beverly Ruth Haskell, Sept. 2, 1961. MusB with High Distinction, DePauw U., 1954; MusM, U. Mich., 1958, PhD, 1968; postgrad., U. Md., 1985. Instr. Nat. Mus. Camp, Interlochen, Mich., 1959-62; instr. Mt. Union Coll., Alliance, Ohio, 1959-61, chmn. keyboard instrn., 1959-61; asst. prof. Music Wichita (Kans.) State U., 1964-68, assoc. prof., 1968-74, coord. Music History and Lit., 1968-71, coord. grad. studies in Music, 1969-70, chmn. dept. Musicology, 1971-74, prof. Music, 1974-86, administrv. intern, v.p. bus. affairs, 1983; pvt. practice event coord., 1974-85; prof. Musicology Vanderbilt U., Nashville, 1986—, coord. Music History and Lit., advisor, 1987—; radio commentator Sta. KMUW-FM, 1969-76; judge various competitions, Mu Phi Epsilon, 1980, Kans. Music Tchrs. Assn., 1975-83, Baldwin Found. awards, 1979, 80; program annotator Nashville Symphony Orch., 1988—; cons. U.S. Dept. Edn. Jacob Javits fellowship program, 1988, 89, United Meth. Publishing Ho., 1988, Mayfield Pub. Co., 1990. Author: The Instrumental Works of Christoph Nichelmann: The Thematic Index, 1971, Franz Benda: A Thematic Catalogue of His Works, 1984: editor: Christoph Nichelmann: Clavier Concertos in E Major and A Minor, 1977, Six Sonatas for Violin and Bass by Franz Benda, with Embellishments, 1981; contbr. articles to The New Grove Dictionary of Music and Musicians, 1980, The New Grove Dictionary of Music in the United States, 1986; contbr. articles to profl. jours., chpts. to books. With U.S. Army, 1955-57, Japan. Rector Scholar Found., 1950-54; Rackham fellow U. Mich., 1961-65, fellow NEH, 1980, 85, Am. Philos. Soc., 1980, Kans. Arts Coun., 1985, Tenn. Arts Coun., 1988, 89. Mem. Am. Musicological Soc. (program chmn. Midwest chpt. 1984, South-Ctrl. chpt. 1989, nat. coun. 1986, pres. South-Ctrl. chpt. 1990-91), Music Tchrs. Nat. Assn. (editor 1971-90), Am. Soc. Eighteenth Century Studies, Coll. Music Soc., Sonneck Soc. Am. Music (program coord. 1987-88, editor The Sonneck Soc. Bull. 1988-1900. Episcopalian. Avocation: photography. Office: Vanderbilt U 2400 Blakemore Ave Nashville TN 37212-3406

LEE, E. BRUCE, electrical engineering educator; b. Brainerd, Minn., Feb. 1, 1932; s. Ernest R. and Hazel B. Lee; m. Judith P. Paine, Apr., 1954; children: Brian, Kevin, Timothy, Joel, Cara, Elizabeth. AA, Brainerd State Coll., 1952; BSME, U. N.D., 1955, MSME, 1956; PhD, U. Minn., 1960. Rsch. engr. Honeywell, Inc., Mpls., 1955-63; assoc. prof. U. Minn., Mpls., 1963-65, prof., 1966—, head dept. elec. engring., 1976-82, acting head elec. engring. dept., 1983-84, assoc. dir. Ctr. for Control Sci., 1984—; cons. Nat. Sci. Found., Washington, 1978-80, Fulbright (CIES), Washington, 1980-82. Author: Foundations of the Optimal Control Theory, 1986. Fellow: IEEE. Home: 1705 Innsbruck Pky Minneapolis MN 55421-2003 Office: U Minn Elec Engring Dept 200 Union St SE Minneapolis MN 55455-0154

LEE, EDNA PRITCHARD, education educator; b. Windsor, N.C., Oct. 6, 1923; d. Peter Bernard and Edna (Smith) Pritchard; m. Mack Lloyd Lee Sr., May 17, 1945 (dec. Nov. 1970); 1 child, Mack Lloyd Jr.; m. Lee Cross, June 1, 1991. BS, State U. N.C., Elizabeth City; MA, NYU, N.Y.C. Cert. N.Y. Adminstr.-Supr. Tchr. elem. schs. Windsor, N.C., 1944-61; tchr. elem. schs. Mohegan Lake, N.Y., 1961-68, asst. prin. elem. sch., 1968-82; dir. basic edn. Peekskill (N.Y.) High Sch., 1969-80; adj. prof. Mercy Coll., Peekskill, 1985—; vice chmn. bd. dirs. Peekskill Area Health Ctr.; bd. dirs. Family Resource Ctr., Montrose Child Care Ctr. Co-author: Syllabus for 4th Grade Social Studies, 1972. Named Woman of Yr., NAACP, Peekskill, 1976, Woman Engr. of Yr., Bus. and Profl. Women, Peekskill, 1980; recipient Louis Gregory award Bahai Religion, Peekskill, 1988. Mem. AAUW (v.p. 1970-72), Blacks in Govt., Delta Kappa Gamma, Alpha Kappa Alpha, Tee-Ettes (sec. 1982-88). Avocations: golf, gardening. Home: 101 Dutch St Montrose NY 10548-1517

LEE, EDWARD A., electrical engineer, educator; b. Oct. 3, 1957. BS, Yale U.; SM, MIT; PhD, U. Calif., Berkeley. Fellow IEEE (past chair VLSI tech. com., Paper award), Signal Processing Soc. Office: U Calif Electronics Dept Cory Hall Berkeley CA

LEE, EDWARD L., bishop; b. Fort Washington, Pa., 1934; m. Kathryn Fligg, 1961; 1 child, Kathryn E. Grad. cum laude, Brown U., 1956; MDiv, Gen. Theol. Seminary, 1959. Ordained diaconate, priesthood Episc. Ch., 1959. Curate Ch. Holy Trinity, Phila., 1959-64; Episc. advisor Univ. Christian Movement Temple Univ., Phila., 1964-73; rector St. James Ch., Florence, Italy, 1973-82, St. John's Ch., Washington, 1982-89; bishop Diocese We. Mich., Kalamazoo, 1989—; Sunday, pastoral asst. Ch. Annunciation, Phila.; parish cons. St. Peters Ch., Germantown; lectr. homiletics Phila. Divinity Sch.; nat. chair Episc. Peace Fellowship, 1970-73; with Convocation of Am. Chs. Europe, pres. coun. advice; dep. Gen. Conv., 1976, 79; chair Coun. Coll. Preachers; active Washington Diocesan Coun., chmn. exec. com.; com. inquiry on the nuclear issues Diocesan Peace Commn. former chair bd. advisors Am. Internat. Sch. Florence. Office: Episcopal Church Ctn 2600 Vincent Ave Kalamazoo MI 49008-3438

LEE, ELIZABETH BOBBITT, architect; b. Lumberton, N.C., July 9, 1928; d. William Osborne and Catharine Wilder (Bobbitt) Lee. Student Salem Coll., 1945-47; B.Arch. with honors, N.C. State Coll., 1952. Registered architect, N.C., 1955, S.C., 1964. Assoc. William Coleman, Architect, Kinston, N.C., 1952-55; Skidmore, Owens & Merrill, N.Y.C., 1955-56; prin. Elizabeth B. Lee, FAIA, Architect, Lumberton, N.C., 1956-73, 82—; sr. ptnr. Lee & Thompson, Architects, Lumberton, 1973-82. Bd. dirs. Robeson Little Theatre, Lumberton, 1977-80, N.C. Dance Theatre, Winston-Salem, N.C., 1980-85, Robeson County Community Concerts, Lumberton, 1980-87; trustee N.C. State U., Raleigh, 1983-92; mem. bd. endowment N.C. State U., 1993—. Recipient cert. recognition Randolph E. Dumont Design Program, 1970, Disting. Alumna award, Salem Coll., 1989. Fellow AIA (nat. dir. 1983-85; officeholder N.C. chpt., 1959, v.p., 1978, pres. 1979, bd. dirs. 1980, pres. eastern sect. N.C. chpt., 1975, bd. dirs. S. Atlantic Regional Council, 1977-79); mem. Jr. League (pres. Lumberton chpt., 1968), Robeson County Heart Assn. (pres. 1970), N.C. Design Found., N.C. Archtl. Found. (pres. 1982-83), Lumberton Jr. Service League (pres. 1968), N.C. State Alumni Assn. (bd. dirs. 1982-85, chmn. Robeson county chpt.), Phi Kappa Phi. Democrat. Presbyterian. Home: 906 N Chestnut St Lumberton NC 28358-4801 Office: 407 Elm St PO Box 1067 Lumberton NC 28359

LEE, E(UGENE) STANLEY, industrial engineer, mathematician, educator; b. Hopeh, China, Sept. 7, 1930; came to U.S., 1955, naturalized, 1961; s. Ing Yah and Lindy (Hsieng) L.; m. Mayanne Lee, Dec. 21, 1957 (dec. June 1980); children: Linda J., Margaret H.; m. Yuan Lee, Mar. 8, 1983; children—Lynn Hua Lee, Jin Hua Lee, Ming Hua Lee. BS, Chung Cheng Inst. Tech., Republic of China, 1953; MS, N.C. State U., 1957; PhD, Princeton U., 1962. Research engr. Phillips Petroleum Co., Bartlesville, Okla., 1960-66; asst. prof. Kans. State U., Manhattan, 1966-67; asso. prof. Kans. State U., 1967-69, prof. indsl. engring., 1969—; prof. U. So. Calif., 1972-76; hon. prof. Chinese Acad. Sci., 1987—; chaired prof. Yuan-ze Inst. Tech., 1993—; cons. govt. and industry. Author: Quasilinearization and Invariant Imbedding, 1968, Coal Conversion Technology, 1979, Operations Research, 1981, Fuzzy and Evidence Reasoning, 1996; editor: Energy Sci. and Tech., 1975—; assoc. editor Jour. Math. Analysis and Applications, 1974—, Computers and Mathematics with Applications, 1974—; editorial bd. Jour. Engring. Chemistry and Metallurgy, 1989—, Jour. of Nonlinear Differential Equations, 1992—, Jour. Chinese Fuzzy Systems Assn., 1995—. Grantee Dept.

Def., 1967-72, Office Water Resources, 1968-75, EPA, 1969-71, NSF, 1971—, USDA, 1978-90, Dept. Energy, 1979-84, USAF, 1984-88. Mem. Soc. Indsl. and Applied Math., Ops. Rsch. Soc. Am., N. Am. Fuzzy Info. Processing Soc., Internat. Neural Network Soc., Sigma Xi, Tau Beta Pi, Phi Kappa Phi. Office: Kans State U Dept Indsl Engring Manhattan KS 66506 *Nothing can replace hard work and persistence.*

LEE, EUN KYUNG, telecommunications professional; b. Seoul, Nov. 1, 1959; came to the U.S., 1992; d. Chan-Bok and Jin Sil (Park) L. B in Info. Sci., Yonsei U., Seoul, 1982. Dir. Dacom Corp., Seoul, 1982-91; exec. dir. Dacom Am., Fort Lee, N.J., 1992—. Recipient award Ministry of Comm., Seoul, 1986. Avocations: cooking, traveling, driving. Office: Dacom America Inc 1 Executive Dr Fort Lee NJ 07024-3309

LEE, FRED C., electrical engineering educator; b. China, 1946; naturalized; BS, Nat. Cheng Kung U., Taiwan, 1968; MSA, Duke U., 1972, PhD, 1974. Tchg. asst. Duke U., Durham, N.C., 1970-72; rsch. asst. Spacecraft Sys. Rsch. Lab., 1972-77; from asst. prof. to prof. Va. Poly. Inst. and State U., Blacksburg, 1977-86, James S. Tucker prof., 1986—, dir. Engring. Ctr., 1985—; bd. dirs. Zyetc Corp.; mem. adv. bd. Power Integrations Inc., 1988—. Fellow IEEE (William E. Newell Power Electronics award 1989, past assoc. editor Trans. on Power Electronics, mem. advt. com.), IEEE Power Electronics Soc. (chmn. meeting com., mem. advt. com., mem. fellow evaluation com., chmn. power electronics specialists conf. 1987, v.p. 1988, pres. 1993-94), IEEE Engrs. Indsl. Applications Soc., Brit. Inst. Engrs. Office: 2909 Stradford ln Blacksburg VA 24060

LEE, FRED STEVEN, telecommunications engineer; b. Wahiawa Oahu, Hawaii, June 7, 1954; s. Michael T. H. and Annette Kimiko (Ozawa) L.; m. Lynn Marie Gray, Aug. 16, 1985; children: Jennifer L. Pearce, Sandra M. Pearce, Christopher M., Nicole M. BSEE, Cornell U., 1975, MSEE, 1976. Head digital task group Watkins-Johnson, Gaithersburg, Md., 1976-78; prin. engr. Fairchild Space and Electronics, Germantown, Md., 1978-82; dir. engring. DAMA Telecom., Rockville, Md., 1982-86, Data Gen. Telecom., Rockville, 1986-87; pres., owner TransDigital Sys., Inc., Rockville, 1987—; cons. COMSAT Labs., Germantown, 1987—. Tiger Cub leader Cub Scouts Pack 178, Rockville, 1992-93. Achievements include patents for distributed switching architecture and high speed communication processing system. Avocations: scuba, backpacking, spelunking. Office: TransDigital Sys Inc 7753 Barnstable Pl Rockville MD 20855

LEE, GEORGE C., civil engineer, university administrator; b. Peking, China, July 17, 1933; s. Shun C. and J. T. (Chang) L.; m. Grace S. Su, July 29, 1961; children—David S., Kelvin H. B.S., Taiwan U., 1955; M.S. in Civil Engring., Lehigh U., 1958, Ph.D., 1960. Research assoc. Lehigh U., 1960-61; mem. faculty dept. civil engring. SUNY, Buffalo, 1961—; prof. SUNY, 1967—, chmn. dept., 1974-77, dean sch. of engring. and applied scis., 1978-95; sr. univ. advisor for technology SUNY, Buffalo, 1995—; head engring. mechanics sect. NSF, Washington, 1977-78; assoc. dir. Calspan-U. Buffalo Rsch. Ctr., 1985-89; acting dir. Nat. Ctr. for Earthquake Engring. Rsch., 1989-90, dir., 1992—; sci. cons. Nat. Heart Lung and Blood Inst., NSF. Author: Structural Analysis and Design, 1979, Design of Single Story Rigid Frames, 1981, Cold Region Structural Engineering, 1986, Stability and Ductility of Steel Structures Under Cyclic Loading, 1991; contbr. articles to profl. jours. in areas of structural design, nonlinear structural mechanics, biomed. engring. and cold region structural engring. Recipient Adams Meml. award Am. Welding Soc., 1974; Superior Accomplishment award NSF, 1977. Mem. ASCE, Am. Welding Soc., Welding Research Council, Structural Stability Research, Council, Am. Soc. Engring. Edn., AAAS, Sigma Xi, Chi Epsilon, Tau Beta Pi. Office: SUNY Buffalo 429 Bell Hall Buffalo NY 14260-0001

LEE, GEORGE TERRY, JR., lawyer; b. Dallas, Oct. 28, 1935; s. George Terry and Isabel (Breckenridge) T.; m. Natalie Blythe Henderson, Aug. 17, 1957; children: George Terry III, Blythe, Rebecca, Hamilton. BA, Yale U., 1957; LLB, Stanford U., 1960. Assoc. Goldberg, Fonville, et al, Dallas, 1960-65; gen. counsel George A. Fuller Co. and OKC Corp., Dallas, 1965-73; ptnr. Akin, Gump, Strauss, Hauer & Feld, L.L.P., Dallas, 1973—. Trustee Found. for Arts, Dallas, 1963—, St. Mark's Sch. of Tex., Dallas, 1966-72; bd. dirs. Dallas Mus. Fine Arts; pres. Brit.-Am. Commerce Assn., Dallas, 1986. Fellow (life) Tex. Bar Found.; mem. ABA, University Club (N.Y.C.), Brook Hollow Golf Club (Dallas), Koon Kreek Klub (Athens, Tex.), Crescent Club (Dallas). Home: 3101 Greenbrier Dr Dallas TX 75225-4603 Office: Akin Gump Strauss Hauer & Feld LLP 1700 Pacific Ave Ste 4100 Dallas TX 75201-4624*

LEE, GILBERT BROOKS, retired ophthalmology engineer; b. Cohasset, Mass., Sept. 10, 1913; s. John Alden and Charlotte Louise (Brooks) L.; m. Marion Corinne Rapp, Mar. 7, 1943 (div. Jan. 1969); children: Thomas Stearns, Jane Stanton, Frederick Cabot, Gilbert Eliot Frazar. BA, Reed Coll., 1937; MA, New Sch. for Social Rsch., 1949. Asst. psychologist U.S. Naval Submarine Base Civil Svc., Psychophysics of Vision, New London, Conn., 1950-53; rsch. assoc. Project Mich., Vision Rsch. Labs., Willow Run, 1954-57; rsch. assoc. dept. ophthalmology U. Mich., Ann Arbor, 1958-72, sr. rsch. assoc., 1972-75, sr. engring. rsch. assoc. ophthalmology, 1975-82, part-time sr. engr. ophthalmology, 1982—; sec. internat. dept., 23d St. YMCA, N.Y.C.; cons. W.K. Kellogg Eye Ctr., Ann Arbor, 1968—. Local organizer, moderator (TV program) Union of Concerned Scientists' Internat. Satellite Symposium on Nuclear Arms Issues, 1986; producer (TV show) Steps for Peace, 1987; designer, builder portable tristimulus Colorimeter; (videotape) Pomerance Awards, UN.; broken lake ice rescue procedure rsch., by one person in a dry suit, all weather conditions, 1966, 89-93 (videotape). Precinct del. Dem. County Conv., Washtenaw County, 1970, 74; treas. Dem. Club, Ann Arbor, Mich., 1971-72, 74-79; vice chmn. nuclear arms control com., 1979; chmn. Precinct Election Inspectors, 1968-75; scoutmaster Portland (Oreg.) area coun. Boy Scouts Am., 1932-39. Capt. AUS, 1942-46, 61-62. Mem. AAAS, Nat. Resources Def. Coun., Fedn. Am. Scientists, N.Y. Acad. Sci., Nation Assocs., ACLU, Sierra Club, Amnesty Internat. Home: 4131 E Pinchot Ave Phoenix AZ 85018-7115

LEE, GLENN RICHARD, medical administrator, educator; b. Ogden, Utah, May 18, 1932; s. Glenn Edwin and Thelma (Jensen) L.; m. Pamela Marjorie Ridd, July 18, 1969; children—Jennifer, Cynthia. B.S., U. Utah, 1953, M.D., 1956. Intern Boston City Hosp.-Harvard U., 1956-57, resident, 1957-58; clin. asso. Nat. Cancer Inst., NIH, 1958-60; postdoctoral fellow U. Utah, 1960-63; instr. U. Utah Coll. Medicine, 1963-64, asst. prof. internal medicine, 1964-68, assoc. prof., 1968-73, prof., 1973—, assoc. dean for acad. affairs, 1973-76, dean, 1978-83; chief of staff Salt Lake VA Med. Ctr., 1985-95. Author: (with others) Clinical Hematology, 9th edit, 1993; Contbr. (with others) numerous articles to profl. jours.; editorial bd.: (with others) Am. Jour. Hematology, 1976-79. Served with USPHS, 1958-60. Markle Found. scholar, 1965-70; Nat. Inst. Arthritis, Metabolic and Digestive Disease grantee, 1977-82. Mem. A.C.P., Am. Soc. Hematology, Am. Soc. Clin. Investigation, Western Assn. Physicians, Am. Inst. Nutrition. Mem. LDS Ch. Home and Office: 3781 Ruth Dr Salt Lake City UT 84124-2331

LEE, GRIFF CALICUTT, civil engineer; b. Jackson, Miss., Aug. 17, 1926; s. Griff and Lida (Higgs) L.; m. Eugenia Humphreys, July 29, 1950; children: Griff Calicutt III, Robert H., Carol E. B.E., Tulane U., 1948; M.S., Rice U., 1951. Civil engr. Humble Oil & Refining Co., New Orleans, Houston, 1948-54; design engr. J. Ray McDermott & Co., Inc., New Orleans, 1954-66; chief engr. J. Ray McDermott & Co., Inc., 1966-75, group v.p., 1975-80, v.p., group exec., 1980-83; cons. engr. Griff C. Lee Inc., 1983—; mem. vis. com. dept. civil engring. U. Tex.; mem. adv. bd. Tulane U., Rice U., MIT; mem. marine bd. NRC. Contbr. articles to profl. jours. Served with USN, 1944-46. Named Outstanding Engring. Alumnus Rice U., 1991. Mem. NAE, ASCE (hon.), Am. Bur. Shipping, Am. Concrete Inst., Am. Welding Soc., Soc. Petroleum Engrs., Am. Petroleum Inst., Internat. House Club, City Club, Bienville Club, New Orleans Country Club, Rotary. Presbyterian. Home: 6353 Carlson Dr New Orleans LA 70122-2803 Office: 1010 Common St New Orleans LA 70112-2401

LEE, HON CHEUNG, physiology educator; b. Hong Kong, May 7, 1950; came to the U.S., 1967; s. Chai Chong and Yee Chin (Ng) L.; m. Miranda Wong, Aug. 1981; 1 child, Cyrus W. BA, U. Calif., Berkeley, 1971, MA, 1973, PhD, 1978. Postdoctoral rschr. U. Calif., Berkeley, 1978-79, Stanford U., Pacific Grove, Calif., 1979-81; asst. prof. U. Minn., Mpls., 1981-86, assoc. prof., 1986-90, full prof., 1990—; mem. Reproductive Biology Study Sect., NIH, Bethesda, Md., 1993—; chmn. Reproductive Biology Spl. Emphasis Panel, NIH, Bethesda, 1994. Contbr. articles to profl. jours. Rsch. grantee NIH, Bethesda, 1983—, 94—, NSF, Washington, 1986-89. Mem. AAAS, Am. Soc. for Cell Biology. Achievements include discovery of Cyclic ADP-ribose, a messenger molecule for regulating cellular calcium; patent for Cyclic ADP-ribose antagonists. Office: Univ Minn Dept Physiology 6-255 Millard Hall Minneapolis MN 55455

LEE, HOWARD DOUGLAS, academic administrator; b. Louisville, Ky., Mar. 15, 1943; s. Howard W. and Margaret (Davidson) L.; m. Margaret Easley, Nov. 20, 1965; children: Gregory Davidson, Elizabeth Anna. BA in English, U. Richmond, 1964; ThM, Southeastern Seminary, Wake Forest, N.C., 1968; PhD in Religion, U. Iowa, Iowa City, 1971. Prof. religion, devel. dir. Va. Intermont Coll., Bristol, 1971-73; dir. univ. relations Wake Forest (N.C.) U., 1973-78; v.p. devel. Stetson U., DeLand, Fla., 1978-80, v.p. planning and devel., 1980-83, exec. v.p., 1984-86, pres.-elect, 1986-87, pres., 1987—. Contbr. articles to profl. jours. Founding dir. Atlantic Ctr. for Arts, New Smyrna Beach, Fla., 1978—; chmn. DeLand C. of C., 1994; chair Volusia Vision Com., 1994-96. Named Cen. Fla. Fundraiser of Yr. Nat. Assn. Fundraising Execs. 1985. Mem. So. Assn. Colls. and Schs. (exec. coun. 1993-94), Rotary, Deland Country Club, Omicron Delta Kappa. Avocations: running, golf, wood carving, woodworking/antiques, reading. Office: Stetson U Campus Box 8258 421 N Boulevard Deland FL 32720

LEE, HWA-WEI, librarian, educator; b. Canton, China, Dec. 7, 1933; came to U.S., 1957, naturalized, 1962; s. Luther Kan-Chun and Mary Hsiao-Wei (Wang) L.; m. Mary F. Kratochvil, Mar. 14, 1959; children: Shirley, James, Pamela, Edward, Charles, Robert. BEd, Nat. Taiwan Normal U., 1954; MEd, U. Pitts., 1959, PhD, 1964; MLS, Carnegie Mellon U., 1961. Asst. libr. U. Pitts. Librs., 1959-62; head tech. svcs. Duquesne U. Libr., Pitts., 1962-65; head libr. U. Pa., Edinboro, 1965-68; dir. libr. and info. ctr. Asian Inst. Tech., Bangkok, Thailand, 1968-75; assoc. dir. librs., prof. libr. adminstrn. Colo. State U., Fort Collins, 1975-78; dean librs., prof. Ohio U., Athens, 1978—; cons. FAO, UNESCO, U.S. AID, World Bank, Internat. Devel. Rsch. Ctr., Asia Found., OCLC; del.-at-large White House Conf. Libr. and Info. Svcs., 1991. Author: Librarianship in World Perspectives, 1991, Fundraising for the 1990s: The Challenge Ahead, 1992, Modern Library Management, 1996; exec. editor Jour. Ednl. Media and Libr. Sci., 1982—; mem. editl. bd. Internat. Comm. in Libr. Automation, 1975-76, Jour. Libr. and Info. Sci., 1975-78, Libr. Acquisition: Practice and Theory, 1976-83; adv. bd. Jour. Info., Comm. and Libr. Sci.; contbr. articles to profl. jours. Recipient Disting. Svc. award Libr. Assn. of China (Taiwan), 1989. Mem. ALA (councilor 1988-92, 93—, John Ames Humphry/Forest Press award 1991), Acad. Libr. Assn. Ohio, Am. Soc. Info. Sci., Asian-Pacific Am. Librs. Assn. (Disting. Svc. award 1991), Internat. Fedn. Libr. Assns. and Instns. (standing com. univ. librs. and other gen. rsch. librs. 1989-93), Assn. Coll. and Rsch. Librs. Chinese-Am. Librs. Assn. (Disting. Svc. award 1983), Internat. Assn. Orientalist Librs., Ohio Libr. Assn. (bd. dirs. 1991-92, Libr. of the Yr. 1987), Online Computer Libr. Ctr. (users coun. 1987-91), Ohio Chinese Acad. and Profl. Assn. (founding pres. 1988-90). Home: 19 Mulligan Rd Athens OH 45701-3734 Office: Ohio U Alden Libr Athens OH 45701

LEE, ISAIAH CHONG-PIE, social worker, educator; b. Ma-kung, Taiwan, Jan. 31, 1934; s. Ju-Nie Chen and Chioh L.; m. Ho-Mei Chen, Feb. 8, 1960; children—Jense, Jenfei. Dr.P.H., UCLA, 1972. Lic. clin. social worker, family, marriage and child counselor. Dist. dir. public health social work Los Angeles County Health Dept., 1970-72; assoc. prof. social work Calif. State U., Long Beach, 1972-78, prof. social work, 1978—, chmn. dept., 1980-86, dir. Internat. Inst. Social Work, 1982—; vis. prof. social work Tunghai U., Tai Chung, 1986-87; vis. prof. family medicine Kaoshiung Med. Coll., 1989, med. sociology, 1993-94. Author: Medical Care in a Mexican American Community, 1972, Health Care Need of the Elderly Chinese in Los Angeles, 1979, Youth Leadership in Immigrant Communities, 1986, Yin-Yang Theory in Chinese Medicine, 1987, Selective Readings in Social Work, 1988, Community Organizing--Chinese-American Perspectives, 1992, The Proceedings of the Conference on Health and Social Policy Research at Kaohsiung Medical College, 1993, The Proceedings of the Conference on Medical Care and Welfare Policy for the Elderly at Kaohsiung Medical College, 1994. Sec. bd. dirs. Oriental Healing Arts Inst., Calif.; founder Formosan Presbyterian Ch. of Orange County, 1978; pres. bd. dirs. Formosan Presbyn. Ch. Orange County, 1978-79; chmn. Asian Presbyn. Council So. Calif., 1980-81; chmn. Internat. Task Force Nat. Comm. on Self-Devel. of People United Presbyn. Ch., 1980-84; advisor social econ. group World Coun. on Chs., Geneva, 1980-84; adv. bd. Asian Am. Community Mental Health Tng. Center, Los Angeles, 1972-77; v.p. Pacific Asian-Am. Center, Santa Ana, Calif., 1981-82, pres., 1982-84; founder Calif. Inst. of Human Care, 1988. 2d lt. Chinese Army, 1954-55. Fellow Soc. Clin. Social Work; mem. Oriental Social Health Soc. (founder, pres. 1970-72), AAUP, Council Social Work Edn., Chinese-Am. Social Workers Assn. USA, (founder, pres. 1985-88), Nat. Assn. Social Workers, Acad. Cert. Social Workers, Taiwanese-Am. Profl. Assn. USA (pres. 1993—). Democrat. Office: Calif State U Dept Social Work Long Beach CA 90840

LEE, IVY, JR., public relations consultant; b. N.Y.C., July 31, 1909; s. Ivy and Cornelia (Bigelow) L.; m. Marie F. Devin, Oct. 14, 1988; children: Peter Ivy III (dec.), Jean Downey. BA, Princeton U., 1931; MBA, Harvard U., 1933. Ptnr. Ivy Lee & T.J. Ross, N.Y.C., 1933-45; with Pan Am. World Airways, Miami, Fla. and San Francisco, 1942-45; adminstrv. asst. S.D. Bechtel, Bechtel Cos., San Francisco, 1950-54; pres. Ivy Lee Jr. & Assocs., San Francisco, 1945-85; pres., cons. Ivy Lee Jr. & Assocs., Inc., San Francisco, 1985—. Trustee Princeton (N.J.) U., 1965-69; bd. dirs. San Francisco TB Assn., Bay Area Red Cross, San Francisco, Edgewood Childrens Ctr. Mem. Pub. Relations Soc. Am., Internat. Pub. Relations Assn. (pres. 1976-77). Republican. Presbyterian. Clubs: Bohemian, Pacific Union. Home: 1940 Broadway San Francisco CA 94109-2216 Office: 210 Post St Ste 609 San Francisco CA 94108-5108

LEE, J. DANIEL, JR., retired insurance company executive; b. Pitts., Mar. 11, 1938; s. John Daniel and Frances Emma (Schimid) L.; m. Betty Williams, Oct. 22, 1961; children—John, Michael, Julie. A.B., Duke U., 1960; M.B.A., U. N.C., 1963; postgrad., Dartmouth Coll., 1984. Investment analyst, gen. investment mgr. Prudential Ins. Co Am., Jacksonville, Fla., 1963-70; gen. investment mgr. Prudential Ins. Co Am., Newark, 1974-77; asst. v.p. Tchrs. Ins. and Annuity Assn. of Am., N.Y.C., 1978, 2d v.p., 1978-80, v.p., 1980-83, mgr. securities div., 1983, sr. v.p., 1983, investment area mgr., 1984, exec. v.p., chief investment officer, 1984-96; ret. Avocations: golf; salt-water fishing.

LEE, J. E., bishop. Bishop Ch. of God in Christ, Dallas. Office: Ch of God in Christ 1701 Turtle Point Dr De Soto TX 75115-2747

LEE, J. PATRICK, academic administrator; b. Leitchfield, Ky., Nov. 30, 1942; s. Herman G. and Josephine (Pearl) L.; m. Louise Sipple, June 8, 1972. BA, Brescia Coll., 1963; postgrad., U. Paris, 1966-67; PhD, Fordham U., 1971. Asst. prof. French Brescia Coll., Owensboro, Ky., Univ. of Ga., Athens, Ga.; v. p. acad. affairs Belmont N.C. Abbey Coll., Barry Univ., Miami, Fla.; researcher 18th Century French lit., Voltaire works. Woodrow Wilson fellow, 1963, Danforth fellow, 1963-67, Fulbright fellow, 1966-67. Mem. AAUA (exec. bd.), SEASECS (exec. bd., past pres.), Delta Epsilon Sigma (nat. sec./treas.), Phi Beta Kappa. Home: 1341 NE 103rd St Miami FL 33138

LEE, JACK (JIM SANDERS BEASLEY), broadcast executive; b. Buffalo Valley, Tenn., Apr. 14, 1936; s. Jesse McDonald and Nelle Viola (Sanders) Beasley; m. Barbara Sue Looper, Sept. 1, 1961; children: Laura Ann, Elizabeth Jane, Sarah Kathleen. Student, Wayne State U., 1955-57; BA, Albion Coll., 1959. Cert. radio mktg. cons. Announcer Sta. WHUB-AM, Cookeville, Tenn., 1956; news dir., program dir. Sta. WALM-AM, Albion, Mich., 1957-59; radio-TV personality WKZO-Radio-TV, Kalamazoo, 1960-62; prodn. dir. Stas. WKMH-WKNR, Detroit, 1962-63; gen. mgr. Sta. WAUK-AM-FM, Waukesha, Wis., 1963-65; asst. program mgr. Sta. WOKY, Milw., 1965-70; program mgr. Sta. WTMJ-WKTI, Milw., 1970-76; gen. mgr. Sta. WEMP-WMYX, Milw., 1976-88; pres. Jack Lee Enterprises Ltd., Milw., 1977—; pres., CEO, Milw. Area Radio Stas., 1989—; instr. dept. mass communication U. Wis.-Milw., 1972-81; adviser Nat. Baha'i Info. Office. With U.S. Army, 1959, 61-62; maj. CAP, 1964—. Decorated Army Commendation medal. Mem. AFTRA, Milw. Advt. Club, Omicron Delta Kappa, Alpha Epsilon Rho. Home and Office: 277 W N Chicory Ln # 2793 Pewaukee WI 53072 *It is a constant struggle to balance my greatest gift—the ability to express myself—with my biggest failing—the inability to keep my mouth shut.*

LEE, JAMES A., health facility finance executive; b. Red Level, Ala., Dec. 19, 1939; s. H. Alton Lee; m. Charlotte Phillips, Dec. 19, 1963 (div. July 1971); children: Phillip, Michele, Jenifer; m. Melanie Cooper, Dec. 14, 1973; children: Christopher, Amanda. BBA in Acctg., Jacksonville State U., 1964; MS in Hosp. and Health Adminstrn., U. Ala., 1980. CPA, Ala. Sr. acct. Macke, Eldredge, McIntosh, Birmingham, Ala., 1964-67, Touche, Ross, Bailey & Smart, Birmingham, 1967-68; bus. functions mgr. Druid City Hosp., Tuscaloosa, Ala., 1968-71; sr. assoc. adminstr., fin. Univ. Ala. Hosp., Birmingham, 1971-94; CFO Montgomery Cardiovasc. Assocs., PC, 1994—; asst. prof. health services adminstrn. Univ. Ala. Birmingham, 1980—; asst. prof. Dept. Pub. Health, Univ. Ala. Birmingham, 1984—. Mem. Health Care Fin. Mgmt. Assn., Ala. Soc. CPA's, Am. Inst. CPA's, Am. Hosp. Assn. Republican. Baptist. Home: 109 Pemberton Pl Pelham AL 35124-2817

LEE, JAMES EDWARD, JR., educational administrator; b. Pitts., Mar. 9, 1939; s. Willard and Gladys Hilda (Jenkins) L.; m. Daisy Mae Tibbs, June 29, 1977; children: Stephen Michael, Monica Michelle, Brian Patrick, Priscilla Demone. BS, Wayne State U., 1962, EdS, 1969; MA, U. Mich., 1964; postgrad., Mich. State U., Wayne State U., U. Minn., U. Colo., 1964-95, Ctrl. Mich. U. Cert. tchr., adminstr., Mich. Tchr. Miller, Durfee and Michael Jr. High Schs., Detroit, 1962-67; team leader Nat. Tchr. Corps, Detroit, 1967-69; dept. head Noble Jr. High Sch., Detroit, 1969-74; asst. prin. MacKenzie High Sch., Detroit, 1974-80; asst. prin. Drew Mid. Sch., Detroit, 1980, prin., 1980—; instr. Wayne State U., Detroit, 1967-69, edn. cons., 1970-71; instr. Wayne C.C., 1967-81; prin. adult evening sch., 1974-80, summer gifted program, Detroit, 1986-92; mem. profl. stds. commn. for sch. adminstrs. Mich. Dept. Edn., 1992—, mem. adminstrv. waiver com., 1992-94. Contbg. author: The Development of Micro Teaching as an Evaluative Instrument in Teacher Training, 1969, (manual) The Principalship, 1990. Co-chair ednl. audit com. Oak Park (Mich.) Sch., 1988-90; bd. dirs. Scott Community Ctr., Detroit, 1988—; adv. bd. Adrian/Scott program to inspire readiness for ednl. success, Detroit, 1990—; adv. coun. Christ Child House, Detroit, 1990-92. With USMC, 1956-58. Recipient Prins. and Educators award Booker T. Washington Bus. Assn., Detroit, 1986, 90, Citation for Outstanding Leadership Detroit Bd. Edn., 1986; named finalist Boss of Yr., Detroit chpt. Am. Bus. Women's Assn., 1987. Mem. Nat. Assn. Secondary Sch. Prins., Nat. Mid. Sch. Assn., Mich. Assn. Supervision and Curriculum Devel., Mich. Assn. Secondary Sch. Prins. (exec. bd. 1986-88, Outstanding Mid. Level Prin. of Yr. 1991), Mich. Assn. Mid. Sch. Educators (bd. dirs. 1988-91). Avocation: tennis. Home: 22580 Saratoga St Apt 2102M Southfield MI 48075-5947 Office: Charles R Drew Mid Sch 9600 Wyoming St Detroit MI 48204-4669

LEE, JAMES JIEH, environmental educator, computer specialist; b. I-Lan, Taiwan, Aug. 27, 1939; came to U.S.A. 1968; s. Yun Ping and Lien Hwa (Kuo) L.; m. Margie J. Feng, March 31, 1965; 1 child: Jean H. BA, Taiwan Normal U., Taipei, 1962; MA, U. Minn., 1970; PhD in Environ. Scis., Greenwich U., 1971. Cert. high sch., univ. tchr., Taiwan. Tchr. I-Lan High Sch., 1962-64; instr. Ta-Tung & Taiwan Normal U., 1964-68; rsch. asst. U. Minn., Mlps., 1968-71, rsch. assoc., 1971-77; computer specialist U.S. Dept. Commerce, Silver Spring, Md., 1977-83; sr. computer system analyst U.S. Pub. Health Svc., Rockville, Md., 1983-92; planning dir. Ctr. for Taiwan Internat. Rels., Washington, 1990—; pres. World Fedn. Taiwanese Assns., 1995—; with Internat. Environ. Protection Assn., Washington, 1988-90, also bd. dirs. 1986—; bd. dirs. Asia Resource Ctr., Washington, 1993—; exec. dir. Constitution Movement for Taiwan, Washington, 1993—; chmn. Formosan Human Rights Assn. Washington chpt., 1976—. Co-author: (with others) Introduction to Human Geography, 1966, Yun-Wu Social Sci., 1971; author: Minnesota Taxing Jurisdictions, 1976, Return to Nature, 1991, Taiwan's Ecological Series, Vols. 1-4, 1955. Bd. dirs. Formosan Assn. Pub. Affairs, Washington, 1982-92. Recipient automation data processing/extramural rsch. USPHS, 1991. Mem. World Watch, Nat. Resource Def. Coun., Am. Solar Energy Soc., Union of Concerned Scientists, World Fedn. Taiwanese Assns. (pres. 1995—), Sierra Club. Avocations: traveling, hiking. Home: 14306 Parkvale Rd Rockville MD 20853-2530

LEE, JAMES KING, technology corporation executive; b. Nashville, July 31, 1940; s. James Fitzhugh Lee and Lucille (Charlton) McGivney; m. Victoria Marie Marani, Sept. 4, 1971; children: Gina Victoria, Patrick Fitzhugh. BS, Calif. State U., Pomona, 1964; MBA, U. So. Calif., 1966. Prodn. and methods engring. foreman GM Corp., 1963-65; engring. adminstr. Douglas MSSD, Santa Monica, Calif., 1965-67; mgr. mgmt. systems, computer tech. TRW Systems, Redondo Beach, Calif., 1967-68; v.p. corp. devel. DataStation Corp., L.A., 1968-69; v.p., gen. mgr. Aved Systems Group, L.A., 1969-70; mng. ptnr. Corp. Growth Cons., L.A., 1970-81; chmn., pres., CEO Fail-Safe Tech. Corp., L.A., 1981-93; pres., COO The Flood Group Inc., Torrance, Calif., 1994-96, CyberSense Syss. Corp., 1996—. Author industry studies, 1973-79. Mem. L.A. Mayor's Cmty. Adv. Com., 1962-72, aerospace conversion task force L.A. County Econ. Devel. Commn., 1990-92; bd. dirs. USO Greater L.A., 1990—, v.p. personnel 1990-92, exec. v.p., 1992-93, pres. 1993-96; asst. adminstr. SBA, Washington, 1974; vice chmn. Traffic Commn., Rancho Palos Verdes, Calif., 1975-78; chmn. Citizens for Property Tax Relief, Palos Verdes, 1976-80; mem. Town Hall Calif. Recipient Golden Scissors award Calif. Taxpayers' Congress, 1978. Mem. So. Calif. Tech. Execs. Network, Am. Electronics Assn. (chmn. L.A. coun. 1987-88, vice chmn. 1986-87, nat. bd. dirs. 1986-89), Nat. Security Industries Assn. Republican. Baptist. Home: 28874 Crestridge Rd Palos Verdes CA 90275-5063 Office: CyberSense Syss Corp 3521 Lomita Blvd Ste 201 Torrance CA 90505-5016

LEE, JAMES MATTHEW, Canadian politician; b. Charlottetown, PEI, Can., Mar. 26, 1937; s. James Matthew and Catherine (Blanchard) L.; m. Patricia Laurie, July 2, 1960; children: Jason, Laurie Ann, Patti Sue. P.C., St. Dustans U., 1956. Mem. provincial parliament from, 5th Queens Riding, 1975-82; minister Health and Social Service-Province of P.E.I., Charlottetown, from 1979, Tourism, Parks and Conservation, 1980; premier, pres. Exec. Council-Province P.E.I., Charlottetown, 1981-86. Mem. Can. Pension Commn., 1986—, Privy Council Can., 1982. Mem. Can. Jaycees (internat. senate 1983), United Comml. Travellers Am. (past sr. councilor), Coun. for Can. Unity (nat. v.p. 1993). Roman Catholic.

LEE, JAMES MICHAEL, religious education educator, publisher; b. Bklyn., Sept. 29, 1931; s. James and Emma (Brenner) L.; m. Marlene Mayr, Oct. 16, 1976; children: James V, Michael F.X., Patrick John. A.B., St. John's U., 1955; A.M., Columbia U., 1956, Ed.D., 1958. Tchr. gen. sci. N.Y.C. secondary sch., 1955-56, chmn. sci. dept. and coordinator audio-visual aids, 1956-59, substitute tchr. adult edn., 1955-60; lectr. Hunter Coll. Grad. Sch., N.Y.C., 1959-60, Sch. Edn. Seton Hall U., South Orange, N.J., 1959; asst. prof. grad. dept. edn. St. Joseph Coll., West Hartford, Conn., 1959-62, U. Notre Dame, South Bend, Ind., 1962-65; assoc. prof. U. Notre Dame, 1965-68, prof., 1968-77, chmn. dept. grad. studies in edn., 1966-71, dir. religious edn. program, 1967-77; prof. U. Ala. at Birmingham, 1977—, chmn. dept. secondary instrn. and ednl. founds., 1977-79; lectr. Chaplain's Sch., Air U., 1985-88; subject matter expert, lectr. GS-16 Chaplain Corps, USN, 1990-91, hon. chaplain, 1991; mem. Birmingham Diocesan Bd. Edn., 1981-89; founder, pub. Religious Edn. Press; cons. in field. Author: Principles and Methods of Secondary Education, 1963, Guidance and Counseling in Schools, Foundations and Processes, 1966, Purpose of Catholic Schooling, 1968, Shape of Religious Instruction, 1971, The Flow of Religious Instruction, 1973, Forward Together, 1973, The Content of Religious Instruction, 1985; sr. author: The Delivery of Religious Education in the Sea Services, 1991; editor, contbr.: Seminary Education in a Time of Change, 1965, Readings in Guidance and Counseling, 1966, Catholic Education in the Western World, 1967, Toward a Future for Religious Education, 1970, The Religious Education We Need, 1977, The Spirituality of the Religious Educator, 1985, Handbook of Faith, 1990; corr. editor Panorama: An Internat.

Jour. Religious Edn. and Values. Fulbright sr. research scholar U. Munich, 1974-75; Religious Edn. Assn. Lilly research tng. fellow, 1974-75, 85. Fellow Soc. for Sci. Study Religion; mem. NEA, N.Am. Profs. of Christian Edn., Assn. Profs. and Rschrs. in Religious Edn. (exec. com. 1972-73, 78-80), Am. Ednl. Rsch. Assn., Nat. Soc. Study Edn., Religious Edn. Assn. (rsch. com. 1970-76, bd. dirs. 1979-89); Religious Rsch. Assn., Fulbright Alumni Assn. Home: 5316 Meadow Brook Rd Birmingham AL 35242-3315

LEE, JANIE C., art gallery owner; b. Shreveport, La., Apr. 22, 1937; d. Birch Lee and Joanna (Glassell) Wood; m. David B. Warren, Jan. 2, 1980. Student, Nat. Cathedral Sch., 1951-55; BA, Sarah Lawrence Coll., 1959. Asst. to Cheryl Crawford, Actors Studi o, N.Y.C., 1962-63; co-prodr. Off Broadway Theatre Co., N.Y.C., 1963-65; owner, pres. Janie C. Lee Gallery, Dallas, 1967-74, Houston, 1973—; owner, pres. Janie C. Lee Master Drawings, N.Y.C., 1983—; mem. art appraisal panel IRS, Washington, 1987-94. Prodr. ann. catalogue on 20th Century drawings, 1979-93; prodr., editor: Mark di Suvero Catalogue, Houston Graphic Soc. Mem. Alumnae Bd. Sarah Lawrence Coll. (1972-74). Mem. Art Dealers Assn. Am. (bd. dirs. 1980-88, 1992—, v.p. 1984-88). Avocation: study of Italian life and culture. Office: Janie C Lee Gallery 1209 Berthea St Houston TX 77006-6411

LEE, JEN-SHIH, biomedical engineering educator; b. Kwangtong, China, Aug. 22, 1940; parents Y. and Yao-Ze (Lai) L.; m. Lian-Pin Ma Lee, June 11, 1966; children: Lionel, Grace, Albert. BS, Nat. Taiwan U., 1961; MS, Calif. Inst. Tech., 1963, PhD, 1966. Advance rsch. fellow San Diego Heart Assn., U. Calif., San Diego, 1966-69; asst. prof. dept. Biomedical Engring. U. Va., Charlottesville, 1969-74, assoc. prof., 1974-83, prof., 1983—, chmn. dept. Biomedical Engring., 1988—. Editor: Microvascular Mechanics, 1988; assoc. editor Jour. Biomech. Engring., 1987-93; contbr. articles to Jour. Applied Physiology, Jour. Biomech. Engring., others. Recipient Rsch. Career Devel. award NIH, 1974-80. Fellow ASME, Am. Inst. Med. and Biol. Engring.; mem. IEEE, Am. Physiol. Soc., Microcirculatory Soc., Biomed. Engring. Soc. (bd. dirs. 1991-93, pres. 1994-95), Coun. of Socs. Am. Inst. Med. and Biol. Engring. (bd. dirs. 1995-97, chair 1995-97). Office: U Va Health Sci Ctr Dept Biomed Engring Box 337 Charlottesville VA 22908

LEE, JEROME G., lawyer; b. Chgo., Feb. 23, 1924; m. Margo B. Lee, Dec. 23, 1947; children—James A., Kenneth M. BSChE, U. Wis., 1947; JD, NYU, 1950. Bar: N.Y. 1950, U.S. Supreme Ct. 1964. Assoc. firm Jeffery, Kimball, Eggleston, N.Y.C., 1950-52; assoc. firm Morgan, Finnegan, Durham & Pine, N.Y.C., 1952-59; ptnr. Morgan, Finnegan, Pine, Foley & Lee, N.Y.C., 1959-86; sr. ptnr. Morgan & Finnegan, N.Y.C., 1986—; lectr. in field. Author: (with J. Gould) Intellectual Property Counseling and Litigation, 1988, USPTO Proposals to Change Rule 56 and the Related Rules Regarding a Patent Applicant's Duty of Candour, Patent World, 1992; contbr. articles to legal jours. in patent and trademark litigation splty. Served to sgt. U.S. Army, 1944-46. Fellow Am. Bar Found.; mem. ATLA, ABA (mem. coun. Intellectual Property Law sect., chmn. com. fed. practice and procedure, chmn. com. Ct. of Appeals Fed. Cir., chmn. com. on ethics and profl. responsibility, stds. com., mem. fed. cir. adv. com. 1992—), Am. Intellectual Property Law Assn. (bd. dirs. 1984-90, pres. 1991), Am. Judicature Soc., Internat. Fedn. Indsl. Property Attys., Found. for Creative Am. (bd. dirs.), N.Y. Bar Assn., Assn. of Bar of City of N.Y., N.Y. County Bar Assn., N.Y. Patent, Trademark and Copyright Law Assn. (bd. dirs. 1975-80, pres. 1981), others. Home: PO Box 8176 Longboat Key FL 34228-4259 Office: Morgan & Finnegan 345 Park Ave New York NY 10154-0004

LEE, JERRY CARLTON, university administrator; b. Roanoke, Va., Nov. 21, 1941; m. Joan Marie Leo; 1 child, Zan. BA, W.Va. Wesleyan Coll., 1963; postgrad., W.Va. U. Grad. Sch. Indsl. Relations, 1963-64, U. Balt. Sch. Law, 1967-69; MA, Va. Poly. Inst., 1975, EdD, 1977; LLD (hon.), Gallaudet U., 1986. Mgmt. trainee Gen. Motors Corp., 1964-65; v.p. adminstrn. Comml. Credit Indsl. Corp., Washington, 1965-71; dir. gen. services Gallaudet Coll., Washington, 1971-77, asst. v.p. bus. affairs, 1978-82, v.p. adminstrn. and bus., 1982-84; pres. Gallaudet U. (formerly Gallaudet Coll.), Washington, 1984-88, Nat. U., San Diego, 1989—. Hon. bd. dirs. D.C. Spl. Olympics; commn. in adminstrn. org. Rehab. Internat.; bd. dirs. People to People, Deafness Research Found.; hon. advocacy bd. Nat. Capital Assn. Coop. Edn.; mem. Personnel Policies Forum Bur. Nat. Affairs. Served with USAR, 1966-72. Recipient Nat. Service award, Hon. Pres. award Council for Better Hearing and Speech, 1986, One-of-a-Kind award People-to-People, 1987, Advancement Human Rights & Fundamental Freedoms award UN, U.S.A., Disting. Alumni award Va. Poly. Inst., 1985, Pres.' award Gallaudet Coll. Alumni Assn., Gallaudet Community Relations award, U.S. Steel Found. Cost Reduction Incentive award Nat. Assn. Coll. and Univ. Bus. Officers, award Am. Athletic Assn. Deaf, 1987. Mem. Am. Assn. Univ. Adminstrs. (Eileen Tosney award 1987), Consortium of Univs. Washington Met. Area (exec. com.), Nat. Collegiate Athletic Assn. (pres.' commn.), Nat. Assn. Coll. Aux. Services (jour. adv. bd., journalism award), Alpha Sigma Pi (Man of Yr. award 1983-84). Lodge: Sertoma (life, found. nat. adv. com.). Avocations: tennis, long distance running, weightlifting. Office: Nat Univ 4025 Camino Del Rio S San Diego CA 92108-4107

LEE, JHONG SAM, electronics company executive; b. Kiljoo, Korea, Dec. 20, 1935; came to U.S., 1955; s. Dong Kyu and Boon Don (Chung) L.;m. helen H. Chang; children: Mary, Grace, David. BSEE, U. Okla., 1959; MSEE, George Washington U., 1961, DSc, 1967. Sr. engr. FXR, Inc., Woodside, N.Y., 1960-64; asst. prof. elec. engring. George Washington U., Washington, 1965-68; expert cons. U.S. Naval Rsch. Lab., Washington, 1965-73; adv. engr. IBM Corp., Gaithersburg, Md., 1968-69; assoc. prof. elec. engring. Cath. U. Am., Washington, 1969-73; assoc. dir. Magnavox Advanced Sys. Office, Silver Spring, Md., 1973-76; pres., CEO J.S. Lee Assocs., Inc., Rockville, Md., 1976—, Dae Young Elec. Co. Ltd., Seoul, Korea, 1985-86; cons. Radiation Sys., Inc., McLean, Va., 1968-72, Comsat Labs., Washington, 1965, 71, Dae Young Electronics Co. Ltd., Seoul, 1977-84. Contbr. articles to profl. jours. NASA doctoral fellow, 1964. Fellow IEEE; mem. Am. Def. Preparedness Assn. (life), Armed Forces Comm. and Electronics Assn. Home: 11111 S Glen Rd Potomac MD 20854 Office: JS Lee Assocs Inc 451 Hungerford Dr Rockville MD 20850*

LEE, JINHO, research engineer, consultant; b. Seoul, Korea, Sept. 11, 1963; came to U.S., 1976; s. Sangawan and Junghee (Han) L.; m. Joan E. Carletta, Oct. 3, 1994. BS in Engring., SUNY, Buffalo, 1985, PhD in Engring., 1991. Asst. engr. Calspan Co., Buffalo, 1985-91; rsch. engr. Sverdrup Tech. Inc., Brook Park, Ohio, 1991-94; sr. rsch. engr. NYMA, Inc., Brook Park, Ohio, 1994—; cons. engr. Waste Minimization Co., Cleveland, 1991—. Contbr. articles to profl. jours. Mem. AIAA (sr.), ASME. Republican. Methodist. Achievements include co-development of pollution free cleaning system, co-development of NASA combustor analysis tools. Home: 4091 River Ln Rocky River OH 44116 Office: NYMA Inc at Lerc Brookpark OH 44142

LEE, JOE, federal judge. BJ, U. Ky., 1952, JD, 1955. Bar: Ky., U.S. Dist. Ct. (ea. dist.) Ky., U.S. Ct. Mil. Appeals, U.S. Supreme Ct. Law clk. to chief justice Ky. Supreme Ct.; law clk. to dist. judge U.S. Dist. Ct. (ea. dist.) Ky.; counsel to congl. subcom. U.S. Ho. of Reps.; bankruptcy judge U.S. Bankruptcy Ct., Lexington, Ky., 1961—; adj. prof. U. Ky. Coll. Law, 1972-92. Editor-in-chief Am. Bankruptcy Law Jour., 1982-90; author: Bankruptcy Practice Manual, 1981, 84-87; contbr. of more than 40 articles to profl. jours. Treas., bd. dirs. Emerson Ctr., Inc. With USAF, 1943-49. Recipient Henry T. Duncan Meml. award for disting. jud. svc. Fayette County Bar Assn., 1986. Fellow Am. Bar Found.; mem. ABA (chmn. com. on consumer bankruptcy 1977-82), Ky. Bar Assn. (Outstanding Judge award 1991), Fed. Bar Assn. Nat. Bankruptcy Conf. (chmn. com. on individual debtor 1982—), Nat. Conf. Bankruptcy Judges (pres. 1973-74, sec. 1979-90, com. on legis. 1973-77, Herbert M. Bierce Disting. Jud. Svc. award 1983). Office: US Bankruptcy Ct PO Box 1111 Lexington KY 40589-1111

LEE, JOE R., food service executive; b. 1940; married. Store mgr. Red Lobster Inns, Lakeland, Fla., 1967-69, supr., dir. ops., 1969-72, v.p. ops., 1972-75, pres., CEO, 1976-79; pres. Gen. Mills Restaurant, Inc., 1979-91; with Gen. Mills, Inc., Mpls., 1970-95, v.p., 1976-80, exec. v.p., 1980-91, exec. v.p. fin., 1991-92, CFO, 1992, vice-chmn., 1992-95; chmn. CEO Durden Restaurants, Inc., Orlando, Fla., 1995—. Office: Darden Restaurants Inc 5900 Lake Ellenor Dr Orlando FL 32859-3330

LEE, JOHN CHONGHOON, SR., financial executive, international laywer; b. Seoul, Korea, July 4, 1928; came to U.S., 1948; s. Sung Han and Song Soh (Chae) L.; m. Mary Aniela Cyrulik, May 6, 1967; children: Suzanne, Daniel, Judy, Jeannette, John Jr. BSFS, Georgetown U., 1954; univ. doctorate in laws, faculty of laws, U. Paris, 1957. Spl. asst. to Korean ambassador UN, Geneva, Switzerland, 1955; v.p. Stanford Corp., Washington, 1958-60; chmn., pres. Overseas Investment Corp., Berkeley Springs, W.Va., 1961-70, 76—; chmn. Amfico Corp./Allnations Devel. Bank, 1971-76; co-chmn. Brit. Indsl. Bank, London, 1965-68; spkr. internat. law soc. Am. U., 1987-88; founder Global Econ. Action Inst., N.Y.C., Washington; participant World Conf. Econ. and Social Order, Geneva, 1983; bd. dirs. Fulbright Assn. Fulbright scholar, 1950-54. Office: Overseas Investment Corp PO Box 691 Berkeley Springs WV 25411

LEE, JOHN EDWARD, JR., agricultural studies educator; b. Pickens County, Ala., May 29, 1933; s. John Edward and Lois Juanita (Stallings) L.; BS, Auburn U., 1957, MS, 1958; PhD, Harvard U., 1969; m. Mary Alice Herren, Feb. 8, 1958 (div. 1987); children: Mary Elizabeth, John Edward III, James Whitfield; m. Marie Elizabeth Dougan, May 28, 1988; 1 child, Anne M. Dougan Clark. Instr., rsch. asst. Auburn U., 1958-59; teaching fellow Harvard U., 1961-62; agrl. economist Econ. Rsch. Svc., U.S. Dept. Agr., Washington, 1962-67, chief agrl. fin. br., 1967-71, dir. farm prodn. econs. div., 1971-73, commodity econs. div., 1973-76, nat. econs. div., 1976-81, adminstr., 1981-93; head dept. agrl. econs. Miss. State U., 1993—; mem. Pres.'s Commn. Productivity in the Food Industry, 1971-72; mem. Joint Coun. on Food and Agrl. Scis., 1981-93; mem. exec. com. Gt. Plains Agrl. Council, 1984-89; bd. dirs. Grad. Sch. USDA, 1985-89; pres. Am. Agrl. Econs. Assn. Found., 1991-93. Served with Signal Corps, U.S. Army, 1953-55. Fellow Am. Agrl. Econs. Assn. (gov. bd. found.); mem. Agrl. History Soc., Internat. Assn. of Agrl. Economists, Internat. Agribusiness Mgmt. Assn. (bd. dirs.), Methodist. Contbr. articles to profl. jours. Home: 4 Lakes Blvd Starkville MS 39759-3157 Office: Miss State Univ Dept Agrl Econs Mississippi State MS 39762-9755

LEE, JOHN FRANCIS, international management consulting company executive, author; b. Boston, Sept. 19, 1918; s. Michael Francis and Catherine Mary (Arrigal) L.; m. Helene Zinka Comes, May 13, 1946 (div.); children: Anne-Marie Lee Buckband, Robert Paul, Virginia Louise Lee Linden, Jacqueline, Lee Arthur. S.B., The Citadel, 1947; S.M., Harvard U., 1948; Sc.D., U. London, 1968; Litt.D. (hon.), U. Malaga, 1972. Registered profl. engr., Maine, D.C. Asst. prof. to assoc. prof., U. Maine, Orono, 1948-52; Broughton disting. prof. engring. N.C. State U., Raleigh, 1952-61; pres. SUNY-Stony Brook, 1961-62; special advisor, cons. NSF, 1962; pres., chief exec. officer Internat. Devel. Services, Inc., Washington, 1962-71; pres., chief exec. officer Promotorco, S.A. (Europe), Luxembourg, 1971-79; pres., chief exec. officer, Intercontinental Mgmt. Cons., Inc., Torrance, Calif., 1979-84; pres., chief exec. officer Calif. Tech. Cons., 1984-89, ret., 1989; dir. internat. firms; vis. prof. Calif. State Univ. system. Participant White House Conf. Internat. Cooperation, 1965; ambassador ICEM-Argentina Negotiations; participant State Dept. Foreign Policy Conf., 1970-71. Served to maj. U.S. Army, 1941-45. Decorated Bronze Star, Purple Heart; order Southern Cross (Brazil), Order Bernardo O'Higgins (Chile) chevalier Legion D'Honeur (France); named Ambassador of Good Will, State of N.C., 1961. Mem. Am. Foreign Service Assn., IEEE, AIAA, Optical Soc. Am., Soc. Photo-optical Instrumentation and Engring., Internat. Soc. Hybrid Microelectronics, Sigma Xi, Tau Beta Pi, Pi Tau Sigma. Unitarian. Clubs: Cosmos, International (Washington); Jockey (Paris). Author: Theory and Design of Steam and Gas Turbines, 1954, 2nd edit., 1961; co-author: Thermodynamics, 1955, 2nd edit., 1962; Statistical Thermodynamics, 1963, 2nd edit., 1973; others; contbr. articles to profl. jours. Home: 480 N El Camino Real-213 Encinitas CA 92024

LEE, JOHN FRANKLIN, retired lawyer, retired association executive; b. Idaho Falls, Idaho, Dec. 7, 1927; s. Wilford D. and Lorine (Hutchinson) L.; m. Patricia Anne Mason, Sept. 15, 1950; children: Randall Mason, Laurelei, John F. B.A., Brigham Young U., 1950; J.D., George Washington U., 1956; diploma, Stonier Grad. Sch. Banking, Rutgers U., 1966. Bar: Utah, D.C. 1956. Atty. SEC, 1956-59; practice in Salt Lake City, 1959-64; asst. to chmn. Fed. Deposit Ins. Corp., Washington, 1964-66; gen. counsel Fed. Deposit Ins. Corp., 1966-68; pres. N.Y. Clearing House Assn., N.Y.C., 1968-93; retired, 1993. Served to lt. comdr. USNR, 1945-46, 51-54. Mem. Order of Coif.

LEE, JOHN J., petroleum, fertilizer company executive; b. 1933. With Barber Oil Co., N.Y.C., 1970-80, Fibre Sullivan Resources Co., 1980-83; pres. Lee Devel. Corp., 1983—; chmn. d., CEO Seminole Fertilizer Corp., 1989—; pres. Tosco Corp. Office: Lee Development 281 Tresser Blvd 2 Stamford Plaza Stamford CT 06901*

LEE, JOHN JIN, lawyer; b. Chgo., Oct. 20, 1948; s. Jim Soon and Fay Yown (Young) L.; m. Jamie Pearl Eng, Apr. 30, 1983. BA magna cum laude, Rice U., 1971; JD, Stanford U., 1975; MBA, 1975. Bar: Calif. 1976. Assoc. atty. Manatt Phelps & Rothenberg, L.A., 1976-77; asst. counsel Wells Fargo Bank N.A., San Francisco, 1977-79, counsel, 1979-80, v.p., sr. counsel, 1980, v.p., mng. sr. counsel, 1981—; mem. governing com. Conf. on Consumer Fin. Law, 1989-93. Bd. dirs. Asian Bus. League of San Francisco, 1981—, gen. counsel, 1981. Fellow Am. Coll. Consumer Fin. Svcs. Attys., Inc., (bd. regents 1995—), mem. ABA (chmn. subcom. on housing fin., com. on consumer fin. svcs., bus. law sect. 1983-90, vice chmn. subcom. securities products, com. consumer fin. svcs. bus. law sect. 1993-95, chmn. subcom. securities products com. consumer fin. svcs. bus. law sect. 1995—), Consumer Bankers Assn. (lawyers com.), Soc. Physics Students, Stanford Asian-Pacific Am. Alumni/ae Club (bd. dirs. 1989-93, v.p. 1989-91). Democrat. Baptist. Office: Wells Fargo Bank NA Legal Dept 111 Sutter St San Francisco CA 94104-4504

LEE, JOHN MARSHALL, mathematics educator; b. Phila., Sept. 2, 1950; s. Warren W. and Virginia (Hull) L.; m. Pm Weizenbaum, May 26, 1984; children: Nathan Lee Weizenbaum, Jeremy Lee Weizenbaum. AB, Princeton U., 1972; student, Tufts U., 1977-78; PhD, MIT, 1982. Systems programmer Tex. Instruments, Princeton, N.J., 1972-74; Geophys. Fluid Dynamics Lab., NOAA GFDL/NOAA, Princeton, 1974-75; tchr. math. and physics Wooster Sch., Danbury, Conn., 1975-77; programmer and cons. info. processing svcs. MIT, Cambridge, Mass., 1978-82; asst. prof. math. Harvard U., Cambridge, 1982-87; asst. prof. math. U. Wash., Seattle, 1987-89, assoc. prof. math., 1989—; sr. tutor Harvard U., Cambridge, 1984-87. Contbr. articles to profl. jours. Rsch. fellow NSF, 1982. Mem. Am. Math. Soc. (Centennial fellow 1989). Avocations: hiking, wine tasting. Home: 5637 12th Ave NE Seattle WA 98105-2603 Office: Univ Wash Math Dept Box 354350 Seattle WA 98195-4350

LEE, JOHN THOMAS, finance educator, financial planner; b. Cleve., May 31, 1942; s. Harry C. and Lucille B. (Varnell) L.; children: Andrea, Joanne. BS in Econs., Tenn. Tech U., 1964; MS in Fin., U. Tenn., 1966; PhD in Fin., U. Ga., 1977. CFP. Instr. fin. Tenn. Tech U., Cookeville, 1966-71, asst. prof., 1973-78, assoc. prof., 1978-84; teaching asst. U. Ga., Athens, 1971-73; prof. fin. Mid. Tenn. State U., Murfreesboro, 1984—, Weatherford prof. fin., 1984-91, chmn. dept. econs. and fin., 1991—; mem. faculty 5th Ann. Cash Mgmt. Inst. Nat. Forum, 1984, Grad. Sch. Banking of South, La. State U., 1986, 88, 89, Tenn. Bankers Sch., Vanderbilt U., 1985; spkr., discussant, moderator, presenter numerous profl. orgns. Contbr. numerous articles to profl. jours. Recipient Outstanding Faculty award Tenn. Tech. U. Coll. Bus. Found.; named Prof. of Yr. Coll. of Bus. Mid. Tenn. State U., 1988, 91; Ayers fellow ABA Stonier Grad. Sch. Banking, summer 1987. Mem. Inst. CFP's, Internat. Assn. for Fin. Planning (pres. greater Tenn. chpt. 1995-96), Fin. Mgmt. Assn., So. Fin. Assn., Ea. Fin. Assn., Midwest Fin. Assn., Southwestern Fin. Assn., Mid-South Acad. Econs. and Fin. (2d v.p. 1990-91, 1st v.p. 1991-92, pres. 1993-94), Mid. Tenn. Soc. CFP's (charter), Civitan (pres. Cookeville 1983-84, Stones River 1990-91, lt. gov. Valley dist.), Beta Gamma Sigma (pres. Mid. Tenn. State U. chpt. 1986-87, 92-94), Omicron Delta Epsilon, Sigma Iota Epsilon, Alpha Kappa Psi, Phi Delta Theta. Baptist. Home: 2522 Tomahawk Trce Murfreesboro TN 37129-6502 Office: Mid Tenn State U E Main St Murfreesboro TN 37132

LEE, JONATHAN OWEN, financial services company executive, lawyer; b. Boston, Mar. 12, 1951; s. Herbert C. and Mildred (Schiff) L.; m. Barbara Ruth Cole, Mar. 24, 1984; children: Suzanna Cole, Alexander Philip. AB in Architecture, U. Calif., Berkeley, 1973; JD, Boston Coll., 1976. Bar: Mass. 1976. Staff atty. SEC, N.Y.C., 1976-79; gen. ptnr. Lee Capital Holdings, Boston, 1979—; chmn. bd. dirs. Globe Metall., Inc., Cleve., 1986—, HSC Hospitality, Inc., Dallas, 1995—, So. Energy Homes, Inc., Adison, Ala., 1989—; bd. dirs. 1st Security Svcs., Inc., Boston, Hyde Athletic Industries, Inc., Peabody, Mass., P.A.R. Assocs., Inc., Boston. Bd. dirs. Combined Jewish Philanthropies, Boston, 1987—; mem. bd. overseers Mus. Fine Arts, Boston. Mem. Young Presidents Orgn., Explorers Club. Office: Lee Capital Holdings 1 International Pl Boston MA 02110-2600

LEE, JONG HYUK, accountant; b. Seoul, Korea, May 6, 1941; came to U.S., 1969, naturalized, 1975; s. Jung Bo and Wol Sun L. BS Han Yang U., Seoul, Korea, 1964, BA, Sonoma State U., Rohnert Park, Calif., 1971; MBA in Taxation, Golden Gate U., San Francisco, 1976. CPA, Calif.; m. Esther Kim, Jan. 24, 1970. Cost acct., internal auditor Foremost-McKesson Co., San Francisco, 1971-74; sr. acct. Clark, Wong, Foulkes & Barbieri, CPAs, Oakland, Calif., 1974-77; pres. J.H. Lee Accountancy Corp., Oakland, 1977-89, 95—, Bay Cities Restaurants, Inc. Wendy's Franchise, 1989-94; instr. Armstrong Coll., Berkeley, Calif., 1977-78; lectr. acctg., dir. sch. of bus. The U.S.-Korea Bus. Inst., San Francisco State U.; adv. bd. mem. Ctr. for Korean Studies, Inst. of East Asian Studies U. Calif, Berkeley. Bd. dirs. Korean Residents Assn., 1974, Multi-svc. Ctr. for Koreans, 1979, Better Bus. Bur., 1984-87; chmn. caucus Calif.-Nev. ann. conf. United Meth. Ch., 1977; commr. Calif. State Office Econ. Opportunity, 1982-86; pres. Korean-Am. Dem. Network; mem. Dem. Nat. Fin. Coun.; regional chmn. Adv. Coun. on Peaceful Unification Policy, Republic of Korea; commr. Asian Art Mus. San Francisco, 1988-91; bd. dirs. East Bay Asian Local Devel. Corp. With Korean Marine Corps, 1961-64; 1st lt. Calif. State Mil. Res. Mem. Am. Inst. CPAs, Nat. Assn. Asian Am. CPAs (bd. dir.), Am. Acctg. Assn., Nat. Assn. Accts., Internat. Found. Employee Benefit Plans, Calif. Soc. CPAs, Oakland C. of C., Korean Am. C. of C. (pres. Pacific North Coast, Rotary. Democrat. Author tax and bus. column Korea Times, 1980. Home: 180 Firestone Dr Walnut Creek CA 94598-3645 Office: 369 13th St Oakland CA 94612-2636

LEE, JOSEPH WILLIAM, sales executive; b. Florence, S.C., Sept. 19, 1943; s. Warner Lou and Rosalee (Hyman) L.; m. Rita Martin, Sept. 8, 1962; children: Mark Stephen, Allison Lynette. Grad. high sch., Florence. Clk. Atlantic Coast Line R.R., Florence, 1962-69; sales rep. Durham (N.C.) & So. Rwy., 1969-74; dist. sales mgr. Westmoreland Coal Sales Co., Charlotte, N.C., 1974-82; v.p. purchasing Westmoreland Coal Sales Co., Phila., 1982-85, v.p. purchasing distbn., 1985-88, v.p. purchasing and northern sales, 1988-91; sr. v.p. Westmoreland Coal Sales Co., Phila., Pa., 1991, pres., 1991-95; v.p. sales TECO Coal Corp., 1995. Mem. N.C. Coal Inst., So. Coals Conf., Inc. (trustee 1989-92), Norfolk So. Corp. Adv. Bd. Republican.

LEE, JOYCE ANN, administrative assistant; b. Safford, Ariz., Sept. 18, 1942; d. Roy and Minnie R. (Mobley) Brewer; m. Eugene W. Gaddy Jr., Mar. 16, 1970 (div. 1985); children: Carol, Kevin, Aaron; m. Glenn A. Lee, Oct. 16, 1992. AA, Ea. Ariz. Coll., 1980, AAS, 1993; BA, U. Phoenix, 1993—. Dispatcher Mohave County Sheriff's Office, Kingman, Ariz., 1969-74; sec. Globe (Ariz.) Mobile Home Sales, 1975-83; data entry supr. SMC & Assocs., Globe, 1985-88; tax preparer H&R Block Co., Globe, 1992; adminstrv. asst. Am. Pub. Co., Globe, 1994—; instr. computer, bus. classes Ea. Ariz. Coll. Gila Pueblo campus, Globe, 1996—. Girls camp dir. LDS Ch., Globe, 1985-90; mem. com. Boy Scouts Am., Globe. Mem. NAFE, Phi Theta Kappa. Democrat. Avocations: hunting, fishing, hiking, archery, camping. Home: Rte 1 CC # 179 Globe AZ 85501 Office: Am Pub Co Omni Care Ctr 1100 Monroe St Globe AZ 85501-1416

LEE, KANG-WON WAYNE, engineering educator; b. Seoul, Korea, Nov. 15, 1947; came to U.S., 1976; s. Chong-Keuk and Jung-Ki (Baik) L.; m. Jee-Bock Hong, Aug. 11, 1979; children: J. Stephen, J. Harold, Grace E. BS, Seoul Nat. U., 1974; MS, Rutgers U., 1978; PhD, U. Tex., 1982. Civil engr. Lyon Assocs., Inc., Seoul, Seoul, 1974-76; structural engr. TAMS-Engrs. and Architects, Seoul, 1976; hwy. constrn. inspector N.J. Dept. Transp., East Brunswick, N.J., 1978; rsch. engring. asst. U. Tex., Austin, 1978-82; asst. prof. Kind Saud U., Riyadh, Saudi Arabia, 1982-85; from asst. prof. to prof. dept. civil engring. U. R.I., Kingston, 1985—; vis. rsch. assoc. U. Calif., Berkeley, 1991; vis. prof. Seoul Nat. U., 1991, Korean Inst. of Sci. and Tech., Daejon, 1992; engring. cons. Lee Engring., Kingston, 1987—. Author: ASTM Special Technical Publication, 1989, 2d edit., 1991, Transportation Research Record, 1988-94, ASCE Jour. Transp. Engring., 1985-96; contbr. articles to profl. jours. Adv. com. mem. New Eng. Transp. Consortium, Rocky Hill, Conn., 1986—; policy com. mem. Region I Univ. Transp. Ctr., Cambridge, Mass., 1988—; mem. R.I. Transp. Joint Rsch. Coun., Providence, 1994—. Recipient Program Devel. award U. R.I., 1987, Murphy Award for faculty excellence, 1990. Mem. ASCE (sec. BMC), ASTM, Transp. Rsch. Bd. (chair A2D04 (3)), Chi Epsilon. United Ch. Christ. Achievements include research in areas of pavement and transportation engineering. Avocations: gardening, hiking, sports. Office: Univ of Rhode Island Dept Civil Engring Kingston RI 02881

LEE, KENNETH, physicist; b. San Francisco, July 3, 1937; s. Kai Ming and Ah See Lee; A.B. with honors in Physics, U. Calif., Berkeley, 1959. Ph.D., 1963; m. Cynthia Ann Chu, June 28, 1959; children—Marcus Scott, Stephanie Denise. Research physicist Varian Assocs., Palo Alto, Calif., 1963-68; mem. research staff, mgr. IBM, San Jose, Calif., 1968-83; dir. memory techs. Southwall Techs., Palo Alto, Calif., 1983-84; sr. v.p. product devel. Domain Tech., Milpitas, Calif., 1984-89; chief tech. officer, exec. v.p. engring. Quantum Corp., Milpitas, Calif., 1989—; chief tech. officer, pres. HCSG Bus. Group. Fellow Am. Phys. Soc.; sr. mem. IEEE; mem. Phi Beta Kappa, Sigma Xi. Contbr. articles to profl. jours.; patentee in field. Home: 20587 Debbie Ln Saratoga CA 95070-4827 Office: Quantum Corp 500 Mccarthy Blvd Milpitas CA 95035-7908

LEE, KENNETH STUART, neurosurgeon; b. Raleigh, N.C., July 23, 1955; s. Kenneth Lloyd and Myrtie Lee (Turner) L.; m. Cynthia Jane Anderson, May 23, 1981; children: Robert Alexander, Evan Anderson. BA, Wake Forest U., 1977; MD, East Carolina U., 1981. Diplomate Nat. Bd. Med. Examiners, Am. Bd. Neurol. Surgeons; med. lic. N.C., Ariz. Intern then resident in neurosurgery Wake Forest U. Med. Ctr., Winston-Salem, N.C., 1981-88; fellow Barrow Neurol. Inst., Phoenix, 1988-89; clin. asst. prof. neurosurgery East Carolina U., Greenville, N.C., 1989-93; clin. assoc. prof. neurosurgery, 1994—. Assoc. editor Current Surgery, 1990—; contbr. 30 articles to profl. jours. and 5 chpts. to books. Mem. Ethicon Neurosurgical Adv. Panel, 1989—. Bucy fellow, 1988. Fellow Am. Heart Assn. (stroke coun.); mem. AMA, N.C. Med. Soc., Am. Assn. Neurol. Surgeons, Am. Soc. Stereotactic and Functional Neurosurgery, So. Med. Assn., Congress Neurol Surgeons, N.C. Neurosurg. Soc. (sec.-treas. 1991-93, pres. 1994-95), Alpha Omega Alpha. Democrat. Baptist. Achievements include research on the efficacy of certain surgical procedures, particularly carotid endarterectomy, in the prevention of strokes. Home: 3600 Baywood Ln Greenville NC 27834-7630 Office: Ea Carolina Neurosurg 2325 Stantonsburg Rd Greenville NC 27834-7534

LEE, KEUN SOK, business educator, consultant; b. Pusan, Korea, May 12, 1954; came to the U.S., 1981; s. Namho and Okki (Ryo) L.; m. Youn Bin Lee, Apr. 15, 1980; children: Grace, Danny. BA, Hankuk U. of Fgn. Studies, Seoul, 1979; MBA, U. No. Iowa, 1983; DBA, U. Ky., 1987; postgrad., Columbia U. Rsch. cons. U. No. Iowa, Cedar Falls, 1982-83; rsch. asst. U. Ky., Lexington, 1983-84, teaching asst., 1984-85; instr. Hofstra U., Hempstead, N.Y., 1986-87; asst. prof. Hofstra U., 1987-93, tenured prof., 1993—. Author numerous publs. in mktg. jours. and confs. Recipient best article award Mu Kappa Tau, 1989, Acad. Mktg. Sci., 1991, best paper award AMS, 1991. Mem. Acad. Mktg. Svc., Am. Mktg. Assn. (assoc.). Avocation: Tae Kwon Do (2d degree Black Belt). Home: 555 North Ave Apt 2E Fort Lee NJ 07024-2406 Office: Hofstra U 141 Weller Hall Hempstead NY 11550

LEE, KUO-HSIUNG, medicinal chemistry educator; b. Kaohsiung, Taiwan, Jan. 4, 1940; came to U.S., 1965; s. Ching-Tsung Lee and Chin-Yeh Yang; m. Lan-Huei Chen; children: Thomas Tung-Ying, Catherine Tung-Ling. BS, Kaohsiung Med. Coll., Taiwan, 1961; MS, Kyoto U., Japan, 1965; PhD, U. Minn., 1968. Postdoctoral scholar dept. chemistry UCLA, 1968-70; asst. prof. Sch. Pharmacy, U. N.C., Chapel Hill, 1970-74, assoc. prof., 1974-77, prof. medicinal chemistry, 1977-91, dir. natural products lab., 1983—, Kenan prof. medicinal chemistry, 1992—; adj. prof. Koahsiung Med. Coll., 1977—; mem. devel. therapeutics contract rev. com. Nat. Cancer Inst., NIH, 1984-88, Bio-organic and natural products chemistry study sect., 1990-94, mem. reviewers res., 1994-98; cons. natural products program divsn. life scis. NSC, Taiwan, 1986-87, Food and Drug Bur., Dept. Health, Exec. Yuan of Republic of China, Taiwan, 1986-92, Genelabs, Inc., Redwood City, Calif., 1988—, Nat. Rsch. Inst., Chinese Medicine, Taiwan, 1989—, Sphinx Pharms. Corp., Durham, N.C., 1990-94; sci. advisor Nat. Lab. Foods and Drugs, Dept. Health, Exec. Yuan of Republic of China, Taiwan, 1990—; mem. sci. adv. bd. Pharmagenesis, 1992—; mem. acad. adv. com. planning sect. Nat. Health Rsch. Inst., Dept. Health, 1992—. Mem. editl. adv. bd. Abstracts of Chinese Medicines, 1986—, Oriental Healing Arts Internat. Bull., 1987—, Bot. Bull. Academia Sinica, 1988—, The Chinese Pharm. Jour., 1988—, Jour. Pharm. Scis., 1990-92, Jour. Chinese Medicine, 1990—, Internat. Jour. Oriental Medicine, 1989—, Kaohsiung Jour. Med. Sci., 1992—, Internat. Jour. Pharmacognosy, 1991—, Jour. Nat. Prod., 1994—; contbr. numerous articles to profl. jours. Grantee NIH, Am. Cancer Soc., U.S. Army, 1971—; recipient Soine Meml. award U. Minn., 1990, Achievement award Genelabs, 1993, Lifu Acad. award Chinese Medicine, 1994, T.M. Tu Sci. award, 1995. Fellow AAAS, Chem. Soc., Am. Assn. Pharm. Scientists, Acad. Pharm. Sci.; mem. Am. Chem. Soc., Am. Soc. Pharmacognosy, Am. Assn. Pharm. Sci., Am. Assn. Coll. Pharm., Phytochemistry Soc. N.Am., Soc. Syn. Organic Chemistry. Achievements include patents on synthesis of anti-cancer drugs, anti-fungal agts., anti-AIDS compounds, discovery of more than 1,000 novel plant anti-tumor agts. and synthetic analogs; elucidation of structure-activity relationships, mechanisms of action of bioactive products. Office: U NC Sch Pharmacy Chapel Hill NC 27599-7360

LEE, KYO RAK, radiology educator; b. Seoul, Korea, Aug. 3, 1933; s. Ke Chang and Ok Hi (Um) L.; came to U.S., 1964, naturalized, 1976; M.D., Seoul Nat. U., 1959; m. Ke Sook Oh, July 22, 1964; children: Andrew, John. Intern, Franklin Sq. Hosp., Balt., 1964-65; resident U. Mo. Med. Center, Columbia, Mo., 1965-68; instr. dept. radiology U. Mo., Columbia, 1968-69, asst. prof., 1969-71; asst. prof. dept. radiology U. Kans., Kansas City, 1971-76, assoc. prof., 1976-81, prof., 1981—. Served with Republic of Korea Army, 1950-52. Diplomate Am. Bd. Radiology (CAQ in pediat. radiology). Recipient Richard H. Marshak award Am. Coll. Gastroenterology, 1975. Fellow Am. Coll. Radiology; mem. Radiol. Soc. N.Am., Am. Roentgen Ray Soc., Assn. Univ. Radiologists, Kans. Radiol. Soc., Greater Kansas City Radiol. Soc., Wyandotte County Med. Soc., Korean Radiol. Soc. N.Am., Soc., Soc. Pediat. Radiology. Contbr. articles to med. jours. Home: 9800 Glenwood St Shawnee Mission KS 66212-1536 Office: U Kans 39th St and Rainbow Blvd Kansas City KS 66103

LEE, LANSING BURROWS, JR., lawyer, corporate executive; b. Augusta, Ga., Dec. 27, 1919; s. Lansing Burrows and Bertha (Barrett) L.; m. Natalie Krug, July 4, 1943; children: Melinda Lee Clark, Lansing Burrows III, Bothwell Graves, Richard Hancock. BS, U. Va., 1939; postgrad U. Ga. Sch. Law, 1939-40; JD, Harvard U., 1947. Bar: Ga. 1947. Former corp. officer Ga.-Carolina Warehouse & Compress Co., Augusta, 1957-89, pres., chief exec. officer, 1989—, co-owner Ga.-Carolina Warehouse Co. Chmn. bd. trustees James Brice White Found., 1962—; sr. warden Episc. Ch., also chancellor, lay min. Sr. councillor The Altantic Coun. of the U.S.; bd. dirs. Med. Coll. Ga. Found., Kanuga Endowment, Inc. Capt. USAAF, 1942-46. Fellow Am. Coll. Trust & Estate Counsel, Ga. Bar Found.; mem. Harvard U. Law Sch. Assn. Ga. (pres. 1966-67), Augusta Bar Assn. (pres. 1966-67), Soc. Colonial Wars Ga., Ga. Bar Assn. (former chmn. fiduciary law sect.), U.S. Supreme Ct. Hist. Soc., U. Va. Thomas Jefferson Soc. of Alumni, Internat. Order St. Luke, Augusta Country Club, Harvard Club of Atlanta, The Pres.'s Club of Med. Coll. Ga. Home: 2918 Bransford Rd Augusta GA 30909-3004 Office: Law Offices Lansing B Lee Jr First Union Bank Bldg 699 Broad St Ste 904 Augusta GA 30901-1448

LEE, LESLIE WARREN, marketing executive; b. Mpls., Nov. 21, 1949; s. Adolph Orlando and Eunice Celia (Akerson) L.; m. Kathleen Karen Frie, June 2, 1973; children: Megan Christine, Maren Elisabeth, Matthew Warren. BA in History magna cum laude, Augsburg Coll., Mpls., 1971. CLU, ChFC. Dir. YMCA, Mpls., 1971-73; dist. sales mgr. Chrysler Mtr. Corp., Marshfield, Wis., 1973-75; agt. Northwestern Mut. Life, Marshfield, 1975-81; mgr. advanced underwriting The Rural Cos., Madison, Wis., 1981-83; advanced life mktg. specialist Am. Family Ins., Madison, 1983—; instr. Dept. Bus., U. Wis., Madison, 1981-82, Dept. Econs., U. Wis., Stevens Point, 1978-91; lectr. in field; cons. in litigation involving life ins. Mem. Nat. Assn. Life Underwriters, Madison Assn. Life Underwriters, Am. Soc. CLU and ChFC. Republican. Lutheran. Avocation: philately. Office: Flexsystem TASC 2302 International Ln Madison WI 53704-3134

LEE, LILLIAN VANESSA, microbiologist; b. N.Y.C., June 1, 1951; d. Wenceslao and Ada (Otero) Cancel; B.S. in Biology, St. Johns U., 1972; M.S. in Microbiology, Wagner Coll., 1974; m. Thomas Christopher Lee, June 11, 1972; children—Tovan, John-Peter, Phillip-Michael. Grad. lab. asst. in microbiology Wagner Coll., S.I., N.Y., 1972-74; clin. microbiology technologist Queens Hosp. Center, Jamaica, N.Y., 1974-81, clin. microbiology supr., 1981-84; sect. head microbiology Nyack (N.Y.) Hosp., 1984-93, acting lab. mgr., 1992-93; microbiology mgr. Beth Israel Med. Ctr., N.Y., 1994—. Cert. registered microbiologist and specialist in microbiology, clin. lab. specialist. Mem. Am. Soc. Clin. Pathologists, Am. Soc. Microbiology (N.Y.C. br. coun. mem. 1992—, program com. chair 1993—, N.Y.C. br. nat. coun. 1996), Am. Acad. Microbiology, Med. Mycology Soc., N.Y., N.Y. Acad. Scis., N.Y.C. Soc. Infectious Diseases, Clin. Lab. Mgmt. Assn. Home: 14 Continental Dr West Nyack NY 10994-2803 Office: Beth Israel Med Ctr 1st Ave at 16th St New York NY 10003

LEE, LIN-NAN, communications engineer, engineering executive; b. Kaohsiung, Taiwan, Feb. 24, 1949. PhD in Elec. Engring., U. Notre Dame, 1976. Asst. v.p., engr. Hughes Network Sys. Fellow IEEE (past chmn. Washington/No. Va. sect. info. theory group). Office: Hughes Network Systems B 212/11717 Exploration Ln Germantown MD 20876*

LEE, LOW KEE, electronics engineer, consultant; b. Oakland, Calif., Feb. 12, 1916; s. Hing Wing and Yan Hai (Louie) L.; m. Alice Jing, Nov. 29, 1953; children: Elliott James, Elizabeth Joanne. BS, U. Calif., Berkeley, 1937, MS, 1939; PhD, Calif. Western U., 1977. Group leader Aerophysics Lab., Los Angeles, 1946-50; lab. mgr. Stanford Research Inst., Menlo Park, Calif., 1950-55; asst. to dir. Gen. Mills, Mpls., 1955-57; dept. mgr. product engring. TRW, Redondo Beach, Calif., 1957-62, asst. dir. product assurance, 1962-78, ret., 1978; cons. Omni Corp., Rancho Santa Fe, Calif., 1983—, Control Data Inc., City of Industry, Calif. Co-author: Design and Construction of Electronic Equipment, 1961; contbr. to books, encys. Fellow IEEE, Chinese Am. Inst. Engrs. and Scientists (pres. San Francisco 1945-46, trustee 1979-81, 89-91, Meritorious award 1985), Masons. Home: 4479 Deerberry Ct Concord CA 94521-4513

LEE, MARGARET BURKE, college administrator; b. San Diego, Dec. 28, 1943; d. Peter John and Margaret Mary (Brown) Burke; m. Donald Harry Lee, June 30, 1973; children: Katherine Louise, Kristopher Donald. BA summa cum laude, Regis Coll., 1966; MA with honors, U. Chgo., 1970, PhD, 1978; IEM Cert. Harvard U., 1992, Seminar for New Pres., 1996. Asst. to humanities MIT, Cambridge, 1969; instr. Dover-Sherborn High Sch., Dover, 1973-75; instr. Alpena Community Coll., Mich., 1975-80, dean liberal arts, 1980-82; dean instrn. Kalamazoo Valley Community Coll., 1982-85; v.p. Oakton Community Coll., Des Plaines, Ill., 1985—, pres. 1995—; cons. evaluator North Cen. Assn., Chgo., 1982—, commr.-at-large, 1988—, commn. on inst. of higher edn. bd. dirs., 1992—, vice chair, 1996—; cons., field faculty Vt. Coll., Montpelier, 1982—; mem. admissions com. Ill. Math and Sci. Acad., 1988—; bd. gov.'s North Cook Ednl. Svc. Ctr., 1988—; bd. dirs. North Cook Ednl. Svc. Ctr., 1989—, vice-chair, 1990-91, chair 1992-94; mem. Bd. Edn. Dist. 39, Wilmette, Ill., 1990-92, chair, 1992—; Des Plaines Sister Cities, 1995—; mem. bd. dirs. Ill. Cmty. Coll. Atty's. Assn., 1994—. Mem. Career Edn. Planning Dist., Kalamazoo, 1982, Kalamazoo Forum/Kalamazoo Network, 1982, Needs Assessment Task Force, 1984. Ford Found. fellow, 1969-73; Woodrow Wilson Found. fellow, 1975; fed. grantee, 1978-84. Mem. Am. Assn. Community and Jr. Colls., Mich. Assn. Community Coll. Instrnl. Adminstrs. (pres. 1983-85), Mich. Occupational Deans Adminstrs. Coun. (exec. bd. 1983-85), Mich. Women's Studies Assn. (honors selection com. 1984), North Cen. Assn. Acad. Deans (pres. 1988—), Kalamazoo Consortium Higher Edn. (pres.'s coun. coordinating com. 1982-85), Kalamazoo C. of C. (vocat. edn. subcom. indsl. coun. 1982), North Cen. Assn. Acad. Deans (v.p., pres. 1985-87), Des Plaines C. of C. (mem. bd. dirs. 1995—). Democrat. Lutheran. Avocations: quilt collecting, reading, listening to classical music, sports spectating, theatre-going. Home: 2247 Lake Ave Wilmette IL 60091-1410 Office: Oakton CC 1600 E Golf Rd Des Plaines IL 60016-1234

LEE, MARIANNA, editor; b. N.Y.C., Aug. 23, 1930; d. Isaac and Charlotte (Steiner) Lubow; m. Edward Lee, June 17, 1968 (div. 1978); 1 child, Susanna. BA, Smith Coll., 1952; postgrad, Columbia U., 1952-53; postgrad., Oxford (Eng.) U., 1957-58. Asst. editor Watson-Guptill Publs., N.Y.C., 1958-59; chief copy editor Grolier, Inc., N.Y.C., 1960-61; mng. editor Portfolio & Art News Ann., N.Y.C., 1961-62; assoc. editor Parade Publs., N.Y.C., 1962-66; mng. editor The Johns Hopkins Press, Balt., 1966-68, U. Tex. Press, Austin, 1968-69; sr. publs. mgr. Scripps Inst. of Oceanography, La Jolla, Calif., 1979-82; mng. editor Harcourt Brace and Co., San Diego, 1982—. Contbr. articles to profl. jours. Democrat. Jewish. Avocations: piano, painting, fell walking, speaking. Office: Harcourt Brace and Co 525 B St San Diego CA 92101-4403

LEE, MATHEW HUNG MUN, physiatrist; b. Hawaii, July 28, 1931; married; 3 children. AB, Johns Hopkins U, 1953; MD, U. Md., 1956; MPH, U. Calif., 1962. Diplomate Am. Bd. Physical Medicine & Rehab. Resident Inst. Physical Medicine & Rehab., NYU, 1962-64, assignee rehab. svc.N.Y. State Health Dept., 1964-65, from asst. prof. to assoc. prof. rehab. medicine, 1965-73, dir. edn. & training dept. rehab. medicine, 1966-68, assoc. dir., 1968, prof. rehab medicine, 1973—; dir. dept. rehab. medicine Goldwater Meml. Hosp., 1968—; assoc. vis. physician Goldwater Meml. Hosp., 1965-68, vis. physician, 1968—, chief electrodiagnosis unit, 1966—, v.p. med. bd., 1969-70, pres., 1971' asst. clin. prof. Coll. Dentistry NYU, 1966-69, clin. asst. prof., 1969-70, clin. assoc. prof., 1970—; cons. Daughters of Israel Hosp., N.Y., 1965-72, Bur. Adult Hygiene, 1965—, Human Resources Ctr., 1966—; asst. attending physician Hosp. NYU, 1968—; med. dir. dept. rehab. medicine N.Y.U., 1989; attending physician Bellevue Hosp. Ctr., 1971—; cons. World Rehab. Fund, Gordon Seagrave & Maryknoll Hosps., Korea, 1969, U.S. Dept. Interior. Fellow Am. Acad. Physical Medicine & Rehab., Am. Coll. Physicians, Am. Pub. Health Assn.; mem. AAAS, Pan-Am. Med. Assn. Office: Jerry Lewis Neuromuscular Dis Ctr Dept Rehab Medicine 400 E 34th St New York NY 10016-4901

LEE, MEREDITH, German literature and language educator; b. St. Louis, July 11, 1945; m. Anthony Battaglia, Nov. 18, 1977. BA summa cum laude, St. Olaf Coll., Northfield, Minn., 1968; MPhil with distinction, Yale U., 1971, PhD, 1976. Asst. prof. U. Calif., Irvine, 1974-81; assoc. prof. U. Calif., 1981-93; prof. U. Calif., Irvine, 1993—, dean undergrad. studies, 1984-88, assoc. dean humanities, 1982-84, chair dept. German, 1991—; sec., treas., dir. Goethe Soc. N.Am., 1979-94, exec. sec., 1994—; chair area adv. com. Coun. for Internat. Exch. Scholars, Washington, 1986-88. Author: Studies in Goethe's Lyric Cycles, 1978; co-editor: Interpreting Goethe's Faust Today, 1994; contbr. articles to profl. jours. Danforth fellow, 1968-74; Fulbright scholar, Göttingen, Fed. Republic Germany, 1972-73. Mem. Am. Assn. Tchrs. German, Am. Soc. for 18th Century Studies, Soc. For Values in High Edn., Modern Lang. Assn., German Studies Assn. (exec. com. 1983-86), Phi Beta Kappa. Lutheran. Office: U Calif Dept German Irvine CA 92717

LEE, MICHAEL HAL, lawyer; b. L.A., Oct. 12, 1955; s. Martin M. and Rose M. Lee. BA, UCLA, 1977; JD cum laude, Suffolk U., 1980; LLM, London Sch. Econs., 1984; grad. barrister program with honors, Inns of Ct. Sch. Law, London, 1987. Bar: Calif. 1980, Mass. 1982, Eng. and Wales 1987. Dep. pub. defender City of L.A., 1981; assoc. Garber & Garber, L.A., 1984-86; barrister at law Chambers of R. Thwaites, Queen's Counsel, London, 1990—; pvt. practice Inglewood, Calif., 1993—. Author: Bermuda I's Borodino, 1983. Mem. ACLU, NAACP, Amnesty Internat., B'nai Brith Youth Orgn. (internat. pres. 1973-74). Office: Atty at Law 467 S Market St Inglewood CA 90301-2309

LEE, MICHELE, actress; b. L.A., June 24, 1942; d. Jack and Sylvia Helen (Silverstein) Dusick; m. James Farentino, Feb. 20, 1966 (div. 1983); 1 son, David Michael; m. Fred Rappoport, Sept. 27, 1987. Actress roles include (Broadway play) How to Succeed in Business Without Trying, 1962-64, Seesaw, 1973, (movies) How to Succeed in Business With Really Trying, 1967, The Love Bug, 1969, Dark Victory, 1975, Bud and Low, 1976, A Letter to Three Wives, 1985, Single Women, Married Men, 1989, The Fatal Image, 1990, My Son Johnny, 1991, (TV movie) Broadway Bound, 1992, When No One Would Listen, 1993, Big Dreams Broken Hearts: The Dottie West Story, 1995, (TV series) Knots Landing, 1979-93 (Outstanding Lead Actress award Soap Opera awards 1992). Recipient Top Star of Tomorrow award Motion Picture Exhibitors of U.S. and Can., 1967, Drama Desk award Broadway Critics, 1973, Outer Critics Circle award, 1973; nominated for Antoinette Perry award, 1973-74, Emmy for Knots Landing, 1981-82.

LEE, MING CHO, set designer; b. Shanghai, China, Oct. 3, 1930; came to U.S., 1949, naturalized, 1961; s. Tsufa F. and Ing (Tang) L.; m. Elizabeth Rapport; 3 children. B.A., Occidental Coll., 1953, LHD (hon.), 1975; postgrad. in theatre arts, UCLA; student art, Chang Kuo-Nyen, Shanghai; DFA (hon.), Parsons Sch. Design, 1986. Apprentice, asst. designer Jo Mielzinger, 5 yrs.; art dir., designer in residence San Francisco Opera, fall 1961; prin. designer Juilliard Opera Theatre and Am. Opera Ctr. of Juilliard Sch. Music, from 1964; tchr. set design Yale U. Drama Sch., 1968—, co-chair, 1979—; tchr. theatre program NYU, 1967-69; set designer Yale Repertory Theatre, 1981-82; adj. prof., scene design adviser Yale U., New Haven; cons. in field; former mem. theatre projects com. N.Y.C. Planning Bd.; mem. adv. council U.S.-China Arts Exchange; trustee Nat. Design Archive. First sets designed for theatre, The Internal Machine, Phoenix, N.Y.C., 1958; designer sets: off-Broadway prodns. The Crucible, 1958, Triad, 1958, Walk in Darkness, 1963, Othello, 1964, Gandhi, 1970, Manhattan Project Seagull, 1974, Cuban Swimmer/Dog Lady, 1984; Broadway prodns. The Moon Besieged, 1962, Mother Courage, 1963, 78, Conversation in the Dark, 1963, Slapstick Tragedy, 1966, A Time for Singing, 1966, Little Murders, 1967, Here's Where I Belong, 1968, King Lear, 1968, Billy, 1969, La Strada, 1969, Lolita, 1971, Two Gentlemen of Verona, 1971, Much Ado About Nothing, 1972, All God's Children Got Wings, 1975, The Glass Menagerie, 1975, 83, For Colored Girls, 1976, Romeo and Juliet, 1977, Caeser and Cleopatra, 1977, The Shadow Box, 1977, Angel, 1979, The Grand Tour, 1978, K2, 1983, most recent work Execution of Justice, 1986; prin. designer, N.Y. Shakespeare Festival, 1962-73, designer N.Y. Shakespeare Festival various theatres and touring group shows, including The Merchant of Venice, 1962, The Tempest, 1962, King Lear, 1962, Macbeth, 1962, Anthony and Cleopatra, 1963, As You Like It, 1963, A Winter's Tale, 1963, Twelfth Night, 1963, Hamlet, 1964, 72, Othello, 1964, Electra, 1964, A Midsummer Night's Dream, 1964, Love's Labour's Lost, 1965, Coriolanus, 1965, Troilus and Cressida, 1965, The Taming of the Shrew, 1965, Henry V, 1965, All's Well That Ends Well, 1966, Measure for Measure, 1966, Richard III, 1966, The Comedy of Errors, 1967, Titus Andronics, 1967, Hair, 1967, Henry IV, Parts I and II, 1968, Romeo and Juliet, 1968, Ergo, 1968, Peer Gynt, 1969, Electra, 1969, Cities in Bezique, 1969, Invitation to a Beheading, 1969, The Wars of the Roses (Henry VI, Parts I, II, and III, and Richard III), 1970, Sambo, 1969, 70, Jack MacGowran in the Works of Samuel Beckett, 1970, Timon of Athens, 1971, Two Gentleman of Verona, 1971, The Tale of Cymbeline, 1971, Older People, 1972, Much Ado About Nothing, 1972, Wedding Band, 1972; designer sets: plays King Lear, N.Y.C., 1968, Lolita, 1971, My Love in Philadelphia, 1971, Remote Asylum, Los Angeles, 1971, Henry IV, Part I, Los Angeles, 1972, Volpone, Los Angeles, 1972, Two Gentlemen of Verona, London, 1973, Lear, New Haven, 1973, The Crucible, Arena Stage, Washington, 1967, The Tenth Man, 1968, Room Service, 1968, The Iceman Cometh, 1968, The Night Thoreau Spent in Jail, 1970, Our Town, 1972, Inherit the Wind, 1973, Julius Caeser, 1975, The Ascent of Mount Fuji, 1975, Waiting for Godot, 1976, For Colored Girls, Los Angeles, 1977, Shadow Box, New Haven, 1977, Twelfth Night, Stratford, Conn., 1978, Hamlet, Washington, 1978, Don Juan, Washington, 1978, The Glass Menagerie, Mpls., 1979, Plenty, Washington, 1980, K2, Washington, 1982, Execution of Justice, Washington, 1985, numerous others; ballets for troupes of Jose Limon, Martha Graham, Gerald Arpino, Alvin Ailey including Missa Brevis, 1958, Three Short Dances, 1959, A Look at Lightning, 1962, Sea Shadow, 1963, Adriadne, 1965, The Witch of Endor, 1965, Olympics, 1966, Night Wings, 1966, Elegy, 1967, The Lady of the House of Sleep, 1968, Secret Places, 1968, A Light Fantastic, 1968, Anim, 1969, The Poppet, 1969, Myth of a Voyage, 1973, Don Juan, 1973, Whisper of Darkness, 1974, In-Quest of the Sun, 1975, The Leaves Are Fading, 1975, The Tiller in the Fields, 1978, The Owl and the Pussycat, 1978, Dream of the Red Chamber, 1983, Les Noces, 1985, Tangled Night, 1986, Sephardic Songs, Intermezzo; set designer: opera cos., including Peabody Arts Theatre of Peabody Inst., Balt., 1959-63; designer: Peabody Arts Theatre prodns. The Turk in Italy, The Old Maid and the Thief, The Fall of the City, La Boheme, Amahl and the Night Visitors, The Pearl Fishers, Werther, Hamlet; Empire State Music Festival prodns. Katya Kabanova, 1960, Peter Ibbetson, 1960, The Pearl Fishers, 1961; Balt. Civic Opera prodns. Tristan and Isolde, 1962; Opera Co. of Boston prodn. Madama Butterfly, 1961, Turandot, 1983; Met. Opera Nat. Co. prodns. Madama Buttefly, 1965, Marriage of Figaro, 1966; Opera Soc. Washington prodn. Bombarzo, 1967; N.Y.C. Opera prodns. Don Rodrigo, 1966, Julius Caeser, 1966, Le Coq d'Or, 1967, Bombarzo, 1968, Faust, 1968, Roberto Devereaux, 1970, Susannah, 1971, Maria Stuarda, 1972, Contes D'Hoffman, 1972, Anna Bolena, 1973, Idomeneo, 1975, Attila, 1981, Alceste, 1982; Hamburgische Staatsoper prodns. Julius Caeser, Hamburg, Fed. Republic Germany, 1969, Lucia di Lammermoor, Hamburg, 1971; Juilliard Opera Theatre and Am. Opera Ctr. of Juilliard Sch. Music prodns. Katya Kabanova, 1964, Il Tabarro, 1964, Gianni Schicchi, 1964, Fidelio, 1965, The Magic Flute, 1965, The Trial of Lucullus, 1965, The Rape of Lucrezia, 1967, L'Ormindo, 1968, The Rake's Progress, 1970, Il Giuramento, 1970, also prodns. at Lyric Opera Chgo., Covent Garden, London, Houston Grand Opera, Teatro Colon, Buenos Aires, San Francisco Opera, Dallas Civic Opera, Kennedy Ctr., Washington, Chilean Opera Soc., Santiago, Associated Opera Co. Am.; one-man shows of water colors and design, Los Angeles, N.Y.C., Calif. Water Color Soc., Los Angeles County Art Show, Ohio U., Athens, Capricorn Gallery, N.Y.C., Compass Gallery, N.Y.C., Library and Mus. Performing Arts, N.Y.C., Mus. City of N.Y., Design '70; designer: Mobile Unit, N.Y. Shakespeare Festival, Florence Sutro Anspacher Theatre, N.Y. Shakespeare Festival, Estelle R. Newman Theatre, N.Y. Shakespeare Festival, Garage Theatre, Harlem Sch. Arts. Bd. dirs. Pan Asian Repertory Theatre, Chen and Dancers; mem. citizens cultural adv. com.; mem. nat. adv. bd. Drama League N.Y.; mem. adv. bd. Theatre at Storm King. Recipient 1st Joseph Maharam award for Electra, 1965, Maharam award for Ergo, 1968, Off-Broadway award Show Bus., 1969, Tony award nomination, 1970, Spl. award Nat. Opera Inst., 1980, Tony award for set design for Broadway play K-2, 1983, Outer Critics Circle award, 1983, Drama Desk award, 1983, Maharam award, 1983, Mayor's award of Honor for Arts and Culture, 1984, 1st Qinyun award for Art and Culture China Inst., 1984, Los Angeles Drama Critics Circle award for Traveller in the Dark, 1985, Hollywood Drama-Logue Critics award for Traveller in the Dark, 1985; named Man of Yr., Chinatown Planning Commn., 1986; Guggenheim fellow, 1988—. Mem. United Scenic Artists Local Union 829 (v.p. 1969-71), Mcpl. Arts Soc. (bd. dirs.). Office: care Drama Sch Yale U 205 Park St West Haven CT 06516-6044 also: 12 E 87th St New York NY 10128*

LEE, MORDECAI, religious agency administrator, political scientist; b. Milw., Aug. 27, 1948; s. Jack Harold and Bernice (Kamesar) L.; 1 child, Ethan. BA, U. Wis., 1970, MPA, Syracuse U., 1972, PhD, 1975. Guest scholar Brookings Instn., Washington, 1972-74; legis. asst. to Congressman Henry Reuss, Washington, 1975; asst. prof. polit. sci. U. Wis.-Whitewater and Parkside, 1976; mem. Wis. Ho. Reps., 1977-82; mem. Wis. Senate, 1982-89; exec. dir. Milw. Jewish Coun. Cmty. Rels., 1990—; adj. prof. govt. U. Wis.-Milw. Jewish.

LEE, NELDA S., art appraiser and dealer, film producer; b. Gorman, Tex., July 3, 1941; d. Olan C. and Onis L.; A.S. (Franklin Lindsay Found. grantee), Tarleton State U., Tex., 1961; B.A. in Fine Arts, N. Tex. State U., 1963; postgrad. Tex. Tech. U., 1964, San Miguel de Allende Art Inst., Mexico, 1965; 1 dau., Jeanna Lea Pool. Head dept. art Ector High Sch., Odessa, Tex., 1963-68. Bd. dirs. Odessa YMCA, 1970, bd. dirs. Am. Heart Assn., Odessa, 1975; fund raiser Easter Seal Telethon, Odessa, 1978-79; bd. dirs. Ector County (Tex.) Cultural Center, 1979—, Tex. Bus. Hall of Fame, 1980-85; bd. dirs., mem. acquisition com. Permian Basin Presdl. Mus., Odessa, 1978; bd. dirs., chairperson acquisition com. Odessa Art Mus., 1979—; pres. Mega-Tex. Prodns., TV and movie producers; pres. Ector County Democratic Women's Club, 1975, Nelda Lee, Inc., Odessa; appointee Tex. Commn. Arts, 1993—. Group exhbns. include El Paso, Tex., New Orleans. Recipient Designer-Craftsman award El Paso Mus. Fine Arts, 1964. Mem. Am. Soc. Appraisers (sr.), Nat. Tex. Assn. Art Dealers (pres. 1978—), Odessa C. of C. Contbr. articles to profl. jours. Office: Nelda Lee Inc PO Box 4268 Odessa TX 79760-4268

LEE, PAUL CHING-LAI, banker, real estate developer; b. Tainan, Taiwan, Republic of China, Dec. 10, 1943; came to the U.S., 1978; s. Lau Teh and Koy (Lin) L.; m. Mary S. Lin, June 8, 1966; children: Patty S., Kathy S. B in Commerce, Nat. Cheng-Kung U., Tainan, 1966. Pres. Oriental Spring Internat. Corp., N.Y.C., 1978-81, Taiwan Christian Svcs., Inc., N.Y.C., 1982—, Teco Industry (USA) Corp., N.Y.C., 1978—; vice chmn. Great Ea. Bank, N.Y.C., 1990—; bd. dirs. Five Giants, Inc., San Francisco, Seven Giants, Inc., N.Y.C., 1984—, 136-09 Realty, Inc., N.Y.C. Lt. U.S. Army, 1966-67, Taiwan. Mem. Am. Reformed Ch. Avocations: golf, travel, tai-chi, swimming, ping-pong. Home: 106 Jarvis Ave Staten Island NY 10312-5772 Office: Great Ea Bank 41-48 Main St Flushing NY 11355-3134

LEE, PAUL KING-LUNG, electronics engineer, researcher; b. Taipei, Republic of China, Aug. 7, 1942; came to U.S., 1966; s. Ching-Yuan and Chong (Chang) L.; m. Ying-Ming Yang, Aug. 8, 1970; children: Karen, Sharon. BSEE, Nat. Taiwan U., 1965; MSEE, Ill. Inst. Tech., 1968, PhD in Elec. Engring., 1972. Elec. engr. Magnavox Co., Ft. Wayne, Ind., 1968-69; instr. Ill. Inst. Tech., Chgo., 1971; mem. tech. staff MITRE Corp., Bedford, Mass., 1972-80, lead engr., 1980-86, group leader, 1986-94; chmn. internat. conf. sessions, sr. prin. systems engr. Sanders A Lockheed Martin Co., Nashua, N.H., 1995—; sys. engring, mgr. Sanders, A Lockheed Martin Co., Nashua, N.H.; mem. EIA/ NAB broadcast stds. com. Contbr. articles to profl. jours. and conf. proc. EIA/Nab broadcast standards committee member. Charter mem. Rep. Presdl. Task Force, 1990—. Inland Steel Co. fellow, 1969-70, N.Y. Acad. Scis. fellow, 1984. Mem. IEEE (sr.), AIAA (sr.), Pioneer Investment Club (pres. 1977-80). Republican. Avocations: music, photography, hiking. Home: 257 E Emerson Rd Lexington MA 02173-2110 Office: Lockheed Sanders Nashua NH 03061

LEE, PAUL LAWRENCE, lawyer; b. N.Y.C., 1946. AB, Georgetown U., 1969; JD, U. Mich., 1972. Bar: N.Y. 1974. Law clk. to Hon. Walter R. Mansfield U.S. Ct. Appeals (2d cir.), 1973-74; spl. asst. to gen. counsel U.S. Treasury Dept., 1977-78, exec. asst. to dep. sec., 1978-79; dep. supt. and counsel N.Y. State Banking Dept., 1980-81; ptnr. Shearman & Sterling, N.Y.C., 1982-94; exec. v.p., gen. counsel Republic N.Y. Corp., N.Y.C., 1994—. Editor-in-chief Mich. Law Rev., 1971-72. Office: Republic NY Corp 452 5th Ave New York NY 10018-2706

LEE, PEGGY (NORMA DELORES EGSTROM), singer, actress; b. Jamestown, N.D., May 26, 1920; d. Marvin Engstrom; m. Dave Barbour, 1943 (div. 1951); 1 dau., Nicki; m. Brad Dexter, Jan. 4, 1955 (div. 1955); m. Dewey Martin, Apr. 25, 1956; Jack del Rio, Mar., 1964 (div. 1964). Grad., high sch. Singer Sta. WDAY, Fargo, N.D.; various singing engagements Mpls.; vocalist Will Osborne's band, Doll House, Palm Springs, Ambassador Hotel West, Chgo., Americana Hotel, Basin St. East, Benny Goodman's Band, 1941-43; singer concerts with Benny Goodman at Melodyland Theatre, Anaheim, Calif., Circle-Star Theatre, San Carlos, Calif. Author: (verse) Softly, With Feeling, 1953; screen appearances include Mr. Music, 1950, The Jazz Singer, 1953, Pete Kelly's Blues, 1955; performer Revlon Revues CBS-TV, 1960; actor Gen. Electric Theater, 1960; composer for films including Johnny Guitar, About Mrs. Leslie; composer musical score (cartoon) Tom Thumb; lyricist, voice talent Lady and the Tramp; rschr., program writer, performer The Jazz Tree Philharm. Ctr. for Performing Arts, N.Y.C., 1963; recordings include Golden Earrings, You Was Right Baby, It's A Good Day, Manana, and I Don't Know Enough About You, Is That All There Is (Grammy award 1969), I'm A Woman, Mirrors, There'll Be Another Spring, 1948, 1985, You Can Depend On Me, Seductive, Peggy Lee Sings With Benny Goodman, 1988, Peggy Lee Sings the Blues, 1988, Vol. 1-The Early Years, 1990, Classics, 1993, Love Held Lightly, 1993, Moments

Like This, 1993. Named Best Female Vocalist by Metronome, Downbeat mags., 1946; recipient Most Popular Vocalist citation Billboard, 1950; Nat. Acad. of Recording Arts & Sciences Lifetime Achievement Award, 1994. Office: care Irvin Arthur & Assoc 9363 Wilshire Blvd Ste 212 Beverly Hills CA 90210-5418

LEE, PETER JAMES, bishop; b. Greenville, Miss., May 11, 1938; s. Erling Norman and Marion (O'Brien) L.; m. Kristina Knapp, Aug. 28, 1965; children: Stewart, Peter James Jr. AB, Washington and Lee U., 1960; MDiv, Va. Theol. Sem., 1967; postgrad, Duke U. Law Sch., 1963-64; DD (hon.), Va. Theol. Sem., 1984, St. Paul's Coll., Lawrenceville, Va., 1985, U. of the South, 1993. Ordained priest Episc. Ch., 1968, bishop, 1984. Newspaper reporter, editor Pensacola, Fla., Richmond, Memphis, 1960-63; deacon St. John's Cathedral, Jacksonville, Fla., 1967-68; asst. min. St. John's Ch. LaFayette Sq., Washington, 1968-71; rector Chapel of the Cross, Chapel Hill, N.C., 1971-84; bishop coadjutor Episcopal Diocese of Va., Richmond, 1984-85, bishop, 1985—; pres. trustees of the funds Diocese of Va., 1985—; dir. Presiding Bishop's Fund for World Relief, 1986-93. Rector bd. trustees Episcopal H.S., Alexandria, Va., 1985—; chmn. Meml. Trustees, Richmond, Am. Friends the Episcopal Diocese Jerusalem; bd. advisors Christian Children's Fund, Wash. Nat. Cathedral. Mem. Phi Beta Kappa, Omicron Delta Kappa. Office: Diocese Va 110 W Franklin St Richmond VA 23220-5010

LEE, PHILIP RANDOLPH, medical educator; b. San Francisco, Apr. 17, 1924; married, 1953; 4 children. AB, Stanford U., 1945, MD, 1948; MS, U. Minn., 1956; DSc (hon.), MacMurray Coll., 1967. Diplomate Am. Bd. Internal Medicine. Asst. prof. clin. phys. medicine & rehab. NYU, 1955-56; clin. instr. medicine Stanford (Calif.) U., 1956-59, asst. clin. prof., 1959-67; asst. sec. health & sci. affairs U. Calif., San Francisco, 1967-69, chancellor, 1969-72, prof. social medicine, 1969—, dir. inst. health policy studies, 1972-93; asst. sec. U.S. Dept. of Health & Human Services, Washington, D.C., 1993—; mem. dept. internal medicine Palo Alto Med. Clinic, Calif., 1956-65; cons. bur. pub. health svc. USPHS, 1958-63, adv. com., 1978, nat. commn. smoking & pub. policy, 1977-78; dir. health svc. office tech. cooperation & rsch. AID, 1963-65; dep. asst. sec. health & sci. affairs HEW, 1965, asst. sec., 65-69, mem. nat. coun. health planning & devel., 1978-80; co-dir. inst. health & aging, sch. nursing U. Calif., San Francisco, 1980—; pres. bd. dirs. World Inst. Disability, 1984—; mem. population com. Nat. Rsch. Coun.- Nat. Acad. Sci., 1983-86; mem. adv. bd. Scripps Clinic & Rsch. Found., 1980—. Author over 10 books; contbr. articles to profl. jours. Recipient Hugo Schaefer medal Am. Pharm. Assn., 1976. Mem. AAAS, AMA, ACP, Am. Pub. Health Assn., Am. Fedn. Clin. Rsch., Am. Geriatric Soc., Assn. Am. Med. Colls., Inst. Medicine-Nat. Acad. Sci. Achievements include research in arthritis and rheumatism, especially Rubella arthritis, cardiovascular rehabilitation, academic medical administration, health policy. Office: Dept of Health & Human Servs Public Health Service 200 Independence Ave SW Washington DC 20201-0004*

LEE, QWIHEE PARK, plant physiologist; b. Republic of Korea, Mar. 1, 1941; came to U.S., 1965; d. Yong-sik and Soon-duk (Paik) Park; m. Ickwhan Lee, May 20, 1965; children: Tina, Amy, Benjamin. MS, Seoul Nat. U., Republic of Korea, 1965; PhD, U. Minn., 1973. Head dept. plant physiology Korea Ginseng and Tobacco Inst., Seoul, 1980-82; instr. Sogang U., Seoul, 1981, Seoul Women's U., 1981; research assoc. U. Wash., Seattle, 1975-79. Exec. dir. Korean Community Counseling Ctr., Seattle, 1983-86. Named one of 20 Prominent Asian Women in Wash. State, Chinese Post Seattle, 1986. Mem. AAAS. Buddhist. Home: 13025 42nd Ave NE Seattle WA 98125-4624 Office: U Wash Dept Pharm SJ-30 1959 NE Pacific St Seattle WA 98195-0004

LEE, R. MARILYN, employee relations executive. BA in Polit. Sci., U. Calif., Santa Barbara, 1969; JD, U. Pacific, 1977. Dep. city atty. City of L.A., 1977-82; corp. dir. human resources The Times Mirror Co., L.A., 1982-90; v.p. employee rels. L.A. Times, 1990—; regent U. Calif. Bd. Regents, 1986-88; bd. dirs. L.A. Times Fund, L.A. Times Credit Union; mem. adv. bd. Women in Bus. Legis. aide congl. offices, Washington, 1970-74; bd. trustees U. Calif. Santa Barbara Found., Calif. Summer Sch. of Arts. Mem. Newspaper Pers. Rels. Assn., Calif. State Bar Assn., L.A. County Bar Assn. (labor and employment law com.), Soc. Human Resource Planning, McGeorge Sch. Law (alumni rep.), Alumni Assn. U. Calif. (pres. 1987-88, bd. dirs. 1983-89). Office: LA Times Times Mirror Sq Los Angeles CA 90012*

LEE, RICHARD, martial arts educational executive; b. Hartford, Conn., Feb. 5, 1942; children: Christopher Lee Cuvelier, Stacy Ann Cuvelier. Attended, Foothill Coll. Exec. v.p. U.S. Chinese Kuoshu Fedn.; founder, pres. East West Martial Arts Schs., Alamo, Calif., 1967—; pres., head instr., sys. master Internat. Chinese Bok Fu Kenpo Assn.; coach U.S. Team at 1st World Kung Fu Championships, Taiwan, 1975, U.S. Kung Fu Kuoshu Team 7th World Championships, Republic of China, 1992; founder, grand master Bok-Fu Chinese Kenpo. Achieved 10th degree Black Belt in Chinese Kenpo. Shotokan, Tai kwon do; avocations: travel, spl. interest cars, antiques. Office: East-West Karate Sch 140 Alamo Plz # C Alamo CA 94507-1550

LEE, RICHARD DIEBOLD, law educator, legal publisher; b. Fargo, N.D., July 31, 1935; s. Sidney Jay and Charlotte Hannah (Thompson) L.; m. Patricia Ann Taylor, June 17, 1957; children—Elizabeth Carol, Deborah Susan, David Stuart. B.A. with distinction, Stanford U., 1957; J.D., Yale U., 1960. Bar: Calif. 1961. U.S. Dist. Ct. (no. dist.) Calif. 1961, U.S. Ct. Appeals (9th cir.) 1961. Dep. atty. gen. Office of Atty. Gen., Sacramento, 1960-62; assoc. McDonough, Holland, Schwartz, Allen & Wahrhaftig, Sacramento, 1962-66, ptnr., 1966-69; asst. dean U. Calif. Sch. Law, Davis, 1969-73, assoc. dean, 1973-76; assoc. prof. law Temple U. Sch. Law, Phila., 1976-77, vis. prof., 1975-76, prof., 1977-89; dir. profl. devel. Baker & McKenzie, Chgo., N.Y.C., 1981-83; dir. Am. Inst. for Law Tng., Phila., 1985-89; dir. profl. devel. Morrison & Foerster, San Francisco, 1989-93; dir. Continuing Edn. of the Bar, Berkeley, 1993—; mem. Grad. and Profl. Fin. Aid Coun., Princeton, N.J., 1974-80; trustee Law Sch. Admission Council, Washington, 1976-78; mem. internat. adv. com. Internat. Juridical Org., Rome, 1977-88; mem. bd. advisors Lawyer Hiring and Tng. Report, Chgo., 1983-95; vis. prof. law sch. law Golden Gate U., San Francisco, 1988-89. Author: (coursebook) Materials on Internat. Efforts to Control the Environment, 1977, 78, 79, 80, 84, 85, 87. Co-editor: Orientation in the U.S. Legal System annual coursebook, 1982-92. Contbr. articles to profl. jours. Bd. dirs. Lung Assn. of Sacramento-Emigrant Trails, 1962-69, pres., 1966-68; bd. dirs. Sacramento County Legal Aid Soc., 1968-74, pres., 1971-72; chmn. bd. overseers Phila. Theol. Inst., 1984-88, bd. overseers, 1979-80, 84-88; mem. bd. of council Episcopal Community Services, Phila., 1984-88; trustee Grace Cathedral, San Francisco, 1989—, chair bd. trustees, 1992-95; mem. bd. visitors John Marshall Law Sch., Chgo., 1989-93; trustee Grad. Theol. Union, Berkeley, 1991—, vice-chair, 1994—. Mem. ABA (chmn. various coms., spl. cons. on continuing legal edn. MacCrate Task Force on Law Schs. and the Profession: Narrowing the Gap 1991-93), State Bar Calif. (chair standing com. on minimum continuing legal edn. 1990-92, com. mem. 1990-93), Profl. Devel. Consortium (chair 1991-93), Am. Law Inst. Democrat. Episcopalian. Club: Yale (N.Y.C.). Home: 2001 Sacramento St # 4 San Francisco CA 94109-3342 Office: Continuing Edn of the Bar 2300 Shattuck Ave Berkeley CA 94704-1576

LEE, RICHARD KENNETH, building products company executive; b. Birmingham, Eng., Dec. 10, 1942; came to U.S., 1964; s. Kenneth Jesse Lee and Eleanor Margaret (Bellsham) Dean; m. Melinda Elena Noback, Aug. 20, 1966; children: Sonja Eleanor, Alyssa Claire. BSc with upper 2d class honours, No. Poly. U. London, 1964; MS in Inorganic Chemistry, Northwestern U., 1965; PhD in Inorganic Chemistry, U. London, 1968. Various corp. rsch. positions UOP Inc., Des Plaines, Ill., 1965-74, mgr. catalyst R & D automotive products divsn., 1974-77; v.p., gen. mgr. portable battery div. Gould Inc., St. Paul, 1977-82; v.p., gen. mgr. Elgar Corp., an Onan/McGraw Edison Co., San Diego, 1982-85; v.p. R & D, Pharmaseal div. Baxter Healthcare Corp., Valencia, Calif., 1985-88; v.p. strategic bus. ops. Manville Sales Corp., Denver, 1988-92; pres., chief exec. officer Rocklite Inc., Denver, 1992—; adj. prof. masters tech. program U. Coll., U. Denver, 1993-95. Author: (videotape) U.S. Competitiveness—A Crisis?, 1992; patentee for vehicle emission control system. Chmn. Summit 91, Denver, 1991, mem. organizing com. Summit 92, Pacoima, Calif., 1992; bd. dirs. Indsl. Rsch. Inst., Inc., Washington, 1991-92. Recipient IR-100 award Indsl. R & D, 1978; Fulbright travel scholar, 1964-65. Mem. Rocky Mountain World Trade Ctr. (vice chmn. 1992-94, exec. com. 1992-94, bd. dirs. 1990-95), Denver C. of C. Office: Rocklite Inc PO Box 44423 Denver CO 80201-4423 *The quality of life for U.S. citizens in the early 21st Century will be primarily determined by the results of U.S. industry and government efforts to improve our ability to commercialize technology successfully.*

LEE, RICHARD VAILLE, physician, educator; b. Islip, N.Y., May 26, 1937; s. Louis Emerson and Erma Natalie (Little) L.; m. Susan Bradley, June 25, 1961; children: Matthew, Benjamin. BS, Yale U., 1960, MD cum laude, 1964. Diplomate Am. Bd. Internal Medicine, Am. Bd. Family Practice. Intern Grace-New Haven Hosp., 1964-65, asst. resident in internal medicine, 1965-66, 69-70; fellow in inflammatory disease Yale U., New Haven, 1970-71; practice medicine specializing in internal medicine New Haven, 1969-76, Buffalo, 1976—; family practice Poplar, Mont., 1966-68, Chester, Mont., 1968-69; asst. prof. medicine Yale U., 1971-74, assoc. prof. clin. medicine, 1974-76; prof. medicine SUNY, Buffalo, 1976—, prof. pediatrics, 1985—, adj. prof. anthropology, 1989—, prof. obstetrics, 1992—, chief div. gen. internal medicine, 1979-82, chief div. maternal and adolescent medicine, 1982—, chief div. geog. medicine, 1991—; dir. primary care ctr. Yale-New Haven Hosp., 1975-76, dir. med. clinics, 1971-75; chief med. svc. Buffalo VA Hosp., 1976-79; head dept. medicine Children's Hosp. Buffalo, 1979—; chief med. officer WHO Collaborating Ctr. for Health in Housing, 1995—; fellow WHO Collaborating Ctr. for Health and Housing, 1985—; cons. internal medicine N.Y. Zool. Soc., 1973—; cons. physician Buffalo Zool. Soc., 1980—; aviation med. examiner, 1980—; med. dir. Ecology and Environment, Inc., Lancaster, N.Y. Sr. editor Current Obstetric Medicine, 1989—; corr. editor Jour. Obstetrics and Gynecology, London, 1989—; mem. editl. bd. Internat. Jour. Environ. Health, 1994—; cons. editor Am. Jour. Medicine, 1976-86; contbr. articles on gen. medicine, infectious diseases, and med. anthropology to med. jours., also articles on med. problems during pregnancy; contbr. chpts. to books on obstetrics. Trustee Yale-China Assn., 1992—. Served with USPHS, 1966-68. Fellow ACP, Am. Acad. Family Practice, Explorers Club N.Y.C., Royal Geog. Soc., Royal Soc. Medicine; mem. AMA Am. Soc. History of Medicine, Yale China Assn. (trustee 1992—, sec. 1995—), N.Y. Acad. Sci., Am. Fedn. Clin. Rsch. Soc., Gen. Internal Medicine, Am. Soc. Tropical Medicine and Hygiene, Infectious Diseases Soc. Am., Soc. Obstetric Medicine (pres. 1991-93), Am. Coll. Occupl. and Environ. Medicine, Great Lakes Interurban Clin. Club, Alpha Omega Alpa. Home: 7664 E Quaker St Orchard Park NY 14127-2015 Office: 219 Bryant St Buffalo NY 14222-2006

LEE, ROBERT DORWIN, public affairs educator; b. Detroit, Jan. 14, 1939; s. Robert Dorwin Sr. and Virginia (Stanow) L.; m. Barbara Marvin, June 4, 1966; children: Robert, Craig, Cameron. BA, Wayne State U., 1960; MA, Syracuse (N.Y.) U., 1963, PhD, 1967. From asst. to prof. Pa. State U., University Park, 1966—, head pub. adminstrn. dept., 1988-94; prof. hotel, restaurant, and recreation mgmt., 1994—. Author: Public Personnel Systems, 3d edit., 1993; lead author: Public Budgeting Systems, 5th edit., 1994. Avocations: backpacking, swimming, bicycling. Home: 672 Devonshire Dr State College PA 16803-3231 Office: Pa State U Sch Hotel Restaurant & Rec 201 Mateer Bldg University Park PA 16802-1307

LEE, ROBERT EARL, retired physician; b. North Sydney, N.S., Can., Sept. 26, 1928; came to U.S. 1928, naturalized, 1942; s. Matthew and Amy Roberts (Moulton) L.; m. Sally Gosling, June 23, 1953 (annulled 1967); children: Diane, Cynthia, Susan, Robert; m. Elaine Katherine Chapleau, Dec. 15, 1967. AB, Colgate U., 1948; MD, Cornell U., 1952. Diplomate Am. Bd. Internal Medicine. Intern N.Y. Hosp., Cornell Med. Ctr., N.Y.C., 1952-53, resident, 1955-56, asst. clin. prof. internal medicine Med. Coll.; fellow Manhattan VA Hosp., N.Y.C., 1956-57; cons. internal medicine N.Y. Hosp., Cornell Westchester Div., 1958, dir. med. services, 1967-80, attending physician Burke Rehab., White Plains, 1957-71, cons., 1971-93; attending physician White Plains Hosp., N.Y., 1957-93, St. Agnes Hosp., White Plains, 1971-93; ret., 1993; cons. in medicine Dobbs Ferry Hosp., N.Y., 1968-90; pres. White Plains Hosp. Med. Staff, 1975-76; mem. Westchester County Bd. Mgrs., Div. Lab. and Research, 1970, chmn. 1984—. Bd. dirs. Westchester Council Social Agencies, 1972-77; sr. warden Ch. of St. James the Less, Scarsdale, N.Y., 1988; vol. vol. advisor Scarsdale Ambulance Corps., 1977—; v.p. Greenburgh Nature Ctr., Scarsdale, 1982-84. Served to 1st lt. U.S. Army, 1953-55. Named to Am. Soc. Most Venerable Order of St. John of Jerusalem, 1984 (comdr.). Mem. Westchester County Med. Soc., N.Y. State Med. Soc., ACP, Westchester County Med. Soc. (bd. dirs. 1970-72). Republican. Episcopalian. Clubs: Fox Meadow Tennis (Scarsdale) (pres. 1980-81); Union League. Home: 9 Old Windy Bush Rd New Hope PA 18938-1133

LEE, ROBERT LLOYD, pastor, religious association executive; b. Escanaba, Mich., Jan. 3, 1943; s. Lloyd Benjamin and Eleanor Mae (Leece) L.; m. Gloria Jeanne James, June 3, 1967; children: Adam Robert, Amy Vicary Lee Skogerboe. BA, Augsburg Coll., 1965; MDiv, Free Luth. Sem., 1968; ThM, Bethel Theol. Sem., 1988. Ordained min. Luth. Ch., 1968. Pastor Tioga (N.D.) Luth. Parish, 1966-72, Grace & Zion Luth. Chs., Valley City, N.D., 1972-79, Helmar Luth. Ch., Newark, Ill., 1990-92; prof. hist. theology Free Luth. Schs., Mpls., 1979-89; pres. Assn. Free Luth. Congregations, Mpls., 1992—. Author: Fever Saga, 1987, Do the Work of An Evangelist, 1990; editor The Luth. Ambassador, 1990-93. Co-chmn. Luth. Estonian Am. Friends, 1992—. Mem. Valdres Samband, Norwegian-Am. Hist. Assn., N.Am. Manx Assn. Office: Assn Free Luth Congregations 3110 E Medicine Lake Blvd Minneapolis MN 55441-3008

LEE, ROBERT SANFORD, psychologist; b. Bklyn., Nov. 16, 1924; s. Mark and Celia (Edelstein) L.; m. Barbara Kaplan, June 9, 1963 (div. 1980); children: David, Daniel. Student, U. Chgo., 1943-46; B.A., NYU, 1947, Ph.D., 1956. Psychologist, N.Y. Program dir. U.S. Bur. Census, N.Y.C., 1947-50; research assoc. NYU, 1952-58; asst. dir. The Psychol. Corp., N.Y.C., 1959-61; researh advisor for communications IBM, Armonk, N.Y., 1961-81; sr. v.p. McCann-Erickson, Inc., N.Y.C., 1981-84; assoc. prof. mktg. Lubin Grad. Sch. Bus. Pace U., N.Y.C., 1984—. Author: (with Chein, Gerard and Rosenfeld) The Road to H, 1964. Served with U.S. Army, 1943-45. Recipient Kurt Lewing award N.Y. State Psychol. Assn., 1994. Mem. AAAS, APA, Am. Assn. for Pub. Opinion Rsch. (exec. coun. 1967-68, 71-72), N.Y. Assn. for Pub. Opinion Rsch. (pres.), Am. Mktg. Assn. Home: 277 W 10th St Ph B New York NY 10014-2583 Office: Pace Univ Lubin Sch Bus 1 Pace Plz New York NY 10038-1502

LEE, RONALD BARRY, marketing company executive, former army officer; b. N.Y.C., May 26, 1932; s. Kermit James and Lillian Bryant (Jackson) L.; m. Nancy Jean Kowalk, Oct. 10, 1985; children: Brett Michael, Brooke Alexandra; 1 child by previous marriage, Dean Eric. B.S. in Engring, U.S. Mil. Acad., 1954; M.B.A., Syracuse U., 1964; PhD (ABD), Am. Univ., 1975; LL.D., Western New Eng. Coll., 1969; M.A., Am. U., 1977, postgrad., 1977-79. Commd. 2d lt. U.S. Army, 1954, advanced through grades to maj., 1965; communications officer 3d Armored Corps, 1954-56; radio and wire communications constrn. engring. Okinawa, 1956-59; part-time radio announcer Sta. KSBK, Okinawa, 1957-59; instr. orgn. and staff procedures U.S. Army Signal Sch., 1960-61, instr. plans and operations, 1961, chief operations, officer dept., 1961-62; asst. G-3 (operations) adviser Vietnamese 9th Div., 1962-63; chief electronic system sect., evaluation br. systems analysis Army Material Command, 1964-65; White House fellow, 1965-66, resigned commn., 1966; mem. staff Lawrence F. O'Brien, The White House, 1965; asst. to postmaster gen., 1965-66, dir. office planning and systems analysis, 1966-68; asst. provost, dir. Center for Urban Affairs; prof. Mich. State U., 1968-69; asst. postmaster gen. for planning and marketing, 1969-72; with Xerox Corp., Stamford, Conn., 1972-73, White Plains, N.Y., 1973-75; regional mgr. Xerox Corp., Des Plaines, Ill., 1975-78; mgr. govt., edn. and med. mktg. Xerox Corp., Rochester, N.Y., 1978-79; mgr. bus. and community affairs Xerox Corp., Washington, 1979-82; pres. Phoenix Group Internat. Ltd., Washington, 1982-89; exec. v.p. Devl. Mgmt. Group, Inc., Chgo., 1989-90; pres. Vantage Mktg. Internat. Inc., 1991—, Phoenix Group Internat., Ltd., 1991—; exec. v.p. G/DEC Internat., Ltd., 1992—; lectr. in field. Contbr. articles to profl. jours., chpts. to books; poet. Mem. Weston (Conn.) Police Commn., 1973-75; trustee Western New Eng. Coll., 1969-75; bd. advisers, trustee Woodrow Wilson Sch. (Princeton), 1969-75; bd. dirs. Zion Investment Assn., 1970-76, Jr. Achievement Greater Washington, 1979-89, NCCJ, 1980-89, Comty. Found. Greater Washington, 1980-89, Duke Ellington Sch. Arts, 1980-89, Workshops for Careers in the Arts, 1980-89; adv. bd. Nat. Assn. Sickle Cell Diseases, 1972—; chmn. bd. trustees Capital Children's Mus., 1979-89; mem. D.C. Mayor's Pvt. Industry Coun., 1979-89. Decorated Army Commendation medal with oak leaf cluster; named Neighbor of Month Springfield, Mass., June 1950; jr. singles champion New Eng. Tennis Assn., 1950; recipient Arthur S. Flemming award, 1968. Mem. NAACP, Nat. Urban League, Assn. West Point Grads., Assn. Syracuse Army Comptrs., Am. Soc. Pub. Adminstrn., White House Fellows Assn. (1st pres. 1966), Am. Acad. Polit. and Social Sci., Beta Gamma Sigma, Alpha Phi Alpha. Office: Vantage Marketing Internat Inc 4200 Wisconsin Ave NW Washington DC 20016-2143

LEE, RONALD DEMOS, demographer, economist, educator; b. Poughkeepsie N.Y., Sept. 5, 1941; s. Otis Hamilton and Dorothy (Demetracopoulou) L.; m. Melissa Lee Nelken, July 6, 1968; children: Sophia, Isabel, Rebecca. BA, Reed Coll., 1963; MA, U. Calif.-Berkeley, 1967; PhD, Harvard U., 1971. Postdoctoral fellow Nat. Demographic Inst., Paris, 1970-71; asst. prof. to prof. U. Mich., Ann Arbor, 1971-79; prof. demography and econs. U. Calif., Berkeley, 1979—, chair dept. demography, dir. Berkeley Ctr. on Econs. and Demography of Aging; cons. in field. Peace Corps. vol., Ethiopia, 1963-65. NIH fellow, 1965-67; NSF fellow, 1968-69; Social Sci. Research Council fellow, 1970-71; NIH grantee, 1973—; Guggenheim fellow, 1984-85. Mem. NAS (chair com. on population), Population Assn. Am. (pres. 1987), Am. Econ. Assn., Internat. Union Sci. Study of Population. Democrat. Author: Econometric Studies of Topics in Demographic History, 1978; Population Patterns in the Past, 1977, Population, Food, and Rural Development, 1988, Economics of Changing Age Distributions in Developed Countries, 1988, others; contbr. articles to profl. jours. Home: 2933 Russell St Berkeley CA 94705-2333 Office: U Calif Dept Demography 2232 Piedmont Ave Berkeley CA 94720

LEE, SALLY A., editor-in-chief; m. Rob Niosi. Grad., Durham U., Eng., Clark U., Mass. Reporter Worcester (Mass.) Telegram; mng. editor Worcester (Mass.) Monthly; spl. features editor Woman's World mag., N.Y.C.; articles editor Woman's Day mag., N.Y.C.; sr. editor Redbook mag., N.Y.C.; editor-in-chief YM/Young & Modern mag., N.Y.C., 1994-96, Fitness Mag., N.Y.C., 1996—; corr. E! Entertainment Network. Office: Fitness Mag 110 Fifth Ave New York NY 10011

LEE, SARAH TOMERLIN, design executive; b. Union City, Tenn.; d. Charles Granville and Dorothy (Robinson) Tomerlin. B.A., Randolph Macon Women's Coll., 1932. Copyeditor Vogue mag. JBK, N.Y.C., 1939-45; v.p. Lord and Taylor, N.Y.C., 1959-65; pres. Fashion Group, N.Y.C., 1960-63; editor-in-chief House Beautiful mag., N.Y.C., 1965-71; pres. Tom Lee Ltd., N.Y.C., 1971-93, Beyer Blinder, Belle/Tom Lee Interiors, N.Y.C., 1993—; cons. to pres. Fashion Inst. Tech., 1971-74. Editor: American Fashion. Vice pres. N.Y. Landmarks Conservancy. Recipient Penny-Mo. Magazine award, 1967, Fashion Inst. award, 1981, Women Bus. Owners N.Y. Entrepreneurial award, 1981, Am. Inst. Interior Decorators Project award, 1982, Decorators Club medal of honor, 1982, Interior Design Project award Am. Soc. Interior Designers, 1987, award of Spl. Distinction, Restaurant & Instns., 1987, 1st Pl. Resort Splty. award Restaurant Hospitality, 1988, Platinum Circle award, 1988, Interior Design award Restaurant Hospitality, 1989, Interior Design Project award Am. Soc. Interior Designers, 1990; named to Interior Design Mag. Hall of Fame, 1986; named Woman of Yr. by Exec. Women in Hospitality, 1988, Designer of Distinction, Am. Soc. Interior Designers, 1990. Mem. Decorators Club (pres. 1995-96), Craft Coun. N.Y. (bd. dirs. 1965-75, emeritus 1983), Cosmopolitan Club, Nat. Arts Club. Office: Beyer Blinder Belle Tom Lee Interiors 41 E 11th St New York NY 10003-4602

LEE, SERI, mechanical engineer, researcher; b. Seoul, Nov. 5, 1957; arrived in Can., 1974; s. Han Dong and Hwa Yon (Kim) L.; m. Nabee Han, July 28, 1979; children: Jonah Dan, Yunah Jean. BASc, U. Waterloo, Ont., Can., 1984, PhD, 1988. Design engr. Joy Mfg. Co., Kitchener, Ont., Can., 1980-82; rsch. asst. prof. U. Waterloo, 1988-93; dir. advanced thermal engring. Aavid Thermal Techs., Inc., Laconia, N.H., 1993—; cons. Thermowatt, Inc., Waterloo, 1992-93, Aavid Engring., Inc., 1992-93. Editor: (procs.) Heat Transfer in Electronic Systems, 1994; contbr. articles to profl. jours. Mem. ASME, AIAA, IEEE, Internat. Electronics Packaging Soc. Avocations: model airplanes, swimming, Tae Kwon Do. Office: AAvid Thermal Techs Inc One Kool Path Laconia NH 03247

LEE, SHERMAN EMERY, art historian, curator; b. Seattle, Apr. 19, 1918; s. Emery H. and Adelia (Baker) L.; m. Ruth A. Ward, Sept. 3, 1938; children: Katharine C. (Mrs. Bryan Reid), Margaret A. (Mrs. Stephen Bachenheimer), Elizabeth K. (Mrs. William Chiego), Thomas W. B.A., M.A., Am. U.; Ph.D., Western Res. U. Curator, Far Eastern art Detroit Inst. Art, 1941-46; with dept. arts and monuments, div. civil info. and edn. sect. Gen. Hdqrs. SCAP, Tokyo, 1946-48; asst. dir., then asso. dir. Seattle Mus. Art, 1948-52; curator Oriental art Cleve. Mus. Art, 1952-57, dir., 1958-83; prof. art Western Res. U., 1962-83; adj. prof. U. N.C., Chapel Hill,. Author: Chinese Landscape Painting, rev. edit., 1962, (with Wen Fong) Streams and Mountains Without End, 1955, Japanese Decorative Style, 1961, History of Far Eastern Art, 5th edit., 1994, (with W.K. Ho) Chinese Art under the Mongols, 1968, Reflections of Reality in Japanese Art, 1983, Past, Present, East and West, 1983; editor: On Understanding Art Museums, 1977. Trustee Amon Carter Mus. Western Art, Isamu Noguchi Found. Served from ensign to lt. (j.g.) USNR, 1944-46. Decorated Legion of Honor; Order North Star; Order of Sacred Treasure 3d class. Mem. Am. Acad. Arts and Scis., Asia Soc. (hon. trustee), Japan Soc., Century Assn. (N.Y.C.). Home: 102 Dixie Dr Chapel Hill NC 27514-6615 Office: Univ NC Dept Art Chapel Hill NC 27514

LEE, SHEW KUHN, retired optometrist; b. Balt., Apr. 24, 1923; s. Mong Har and Gum Tuey (Wong) L. OD, Ill. Coll. Optometry, 1949; postgrad. Cath. U. Am., 1957, Md. U., 1959; m. Florence Gin Toy, Oct. 29, 1949; children: Wayson Perry, Davin Jeffrey. Pvt. practice optometry, Washington, 1949-88; ret., 1988. Lectr. D.C. Traffic Safety Sch.; v.p. D.C. Bd. Optometry, 1959-65; mem. D.C. Bd. Examiners in Optometry, 1973-84, sec., 1974; mem. Eye Bank Council; vision rsch. cons. HEW, 1973. Bd. dirs. Eye Bank and Rsch. Found., Washington Hosp. Center. With U.S. Army, 1942-45. Decorated Purple Heart, Bronze Star medal with oak leaf cluster; recipient Meritorious Pub. Svc. award Govt. of D.C., 1965. Mem. Am. Optometric Assn. (life, pres. joggers 1968—, Disting. Svc. award 1974), Am. Legion (life, citation of merit 1954, post comdr. D.C. 1960), D.C. Optometric Soc. (sec. 1956-57), Lees Assn. (trustee), Chinese Consol. Benevolent Assn. (founder), Flying Optometrist Assn. Am. (bd. dir. 1974—), Beta Sigma Kappa. Lion (charter pres. Chi-Am. 1960, zone chmn. 1961, dep. dist. gov. 1963, hon. mem. Capitol Hill, Washington Host, Extension award 1960, 75, Presdl. Banner award 1975). Rsch. publs. in field. Home: 2939 McKinley St NW Washington DC 20015-1217

LEE, SHIH-YING, mechanical engineering educator; b. Peking, China, Apr. 30, 1918; came to U.S., 1942, naturalized, 1952; s. Tse-Kung and Pei-Jour (Tao) L.; m. Lena Yin, Aug. 18, 1973; children: Carol Sana, David, Linda Grace, Eileen M. Sc.D., MIT, 1945. Bridge design engr. Chinese Govt., 1940-41, hydraulic power research engr., 1941-42; design engr. Cram & Ferguson Co., Boston, 1945-47; research engr. MIT, Cambridge, 1947-52, mem. faculty, 1952-74, prof. mech. engring., 1966—; chmn., chief exec. officer Setra Systems Inc., Acton, Mass.; Mem. Nat. Acad. Engrs. Inventor field instrumentation, fluid power control. Home: Huckleberry Hl Lincoln MA 01773 Office: Setra Systems 45 Nagog Park Acton MA 01720-3413

LEE, SHUISHIH SAGE, pathologist; b. Soo-chow, Kiang Su, China, Jan. 5, 1948; came to U.S., 1972, naturalized, 1979; d. Wei-ping Wilson and Min-chen (Sun) Chang; m. Chung Seng Lee; children: Yvonne Claire, Michael Chung. MD Nat. Taiwan U., 1972; PhD, U. Rochester, 1976. Resident in pathology Strong Meml. Hosp., Rochester, N.Y., 1976-78, Northwestern Meml. Hosp., Chgo., 1978-79; dir. cytology and electron microscopy Parkview Meml. Hosp., Ft. Wayne, Ind., 1979—; clin. assoc. prof. Ind. U. Med. Sch. Contbr. articles to profl. jours. Fellow Coll. Am. Pathologists, Am. Soc. Clin. Pathologists; mem. AMA, Ind. Med. Assn., N.E. Ind. Pathologists Assn. (sec. 1984), Ind. Assn. Pathologists, N.Y. Acad. Scis., Am. Assn. Pathologists, Am. Soc. Cytology, Internat. Acad. Pathology, Internat. Acad. Cytology, Buckeye Soc. Cytology, Electron Microscopy

Soc. Am. Home: 5728 The Prophets Pass Fort Wayne IN 46845-9659 Office: Parkview Meml Hosp 2200 Randallia Dr Fort Wayne IN 46805-4638

LEE, SHUNG-MAN, nephrologist; b. Canton, Peoples Republic of China, Feb. 22, 1949; came to the U.S., 1968; s. Ning-Woo and Shui-Fong Lee; m. Ellen Poon, Aug., 1976; 1 child, Andrew. BS, U. Toronto, 1972, MD, 1976. Diplomate Am. Bd. Nephrology, Am. Bd. Internal Medicine, Nat. Bd. Med. Examiners. Intern Sunnybrook Med. Ctr. U. Toronto, 1976-77, resident, 1977-78; resident Jewish Gen. Hosp. McGill U., Montreal, 1978-79; clin. fellow in nephrology Billings Hosp. U. Chgo., 1979-81, rsch. fellow, 1981-82; pres., med. dir. Biotronics Kidney Ctr., Beaumont, Tex., 1990—; cons. nephrologist, mem. med. staff St. Elizabeth Hosp., Beaumont, Bapt. Hosp. S.E. Tex., Beaumont, Beaumont Med. Surg. Hosp., 1982-90; med. dir. Cmty. Dialysis Svcs., Beaumont, 1986-90; cons. nephrologist, mem. courtesy staff Dr.'s Hosp., Groves, Tex., Bapt. Hosp., Orange, Tex., Park Place Hosp., Port Arthur, Tex.; clin. asst. prof. U. Tex. Med. Br. at Galveston, 1991—; founder, owner Biotronics Kidney Ctr. Beaumont, Inc.; founder, Lake Charles (La.) Dialysis Ctr. Contbr. articles to profl. jours. Organizer, founding mem. Adult Indigent Clinic for S.E. Tex., Beaumont, 1992—. Rsch. fellow Chgo. Heart Assn., 1981; rsch. scholar Ontario Cancer Soc., 1974, Ann Shepard Meml. scholar in biology, 1970. Fellow ACP; mem. AMA, Internat. Soc. Nephrology, Internat. Soc. Peritoneal Dialysis, Am. Soc. Nephrology, Jefferson County Med. Soc., So. Med. Assn., Am. Soc. Internal Medicine, Tex. Med. Assn., Chinese-Am. Soc. Nephrology (pres.), New Century Health Care Internat. (pres.). Office: Biotronics Kidney Ctr 2688 Calder St Beaumont TX 77702-1917

LEE, SIDNEY PHILLIP, chemical engineer, state senator; b. Pa., Apr. 20, 1926; s. Samuel L. and Mollie (Heller) L. B.Sc., U. Pa., 1939; McMullin fellow, Cornell U., 1939-40, then M.Ch.E. Chem. engr. Atlantic Richfield Co., 1938-42; sr. chem. engr., 1942-45; pres. Dallas Labs., 1945—, Asso. Labs., Dallas, 1945—, West Indies Investment Co., 1957—; chmn. exec. com. West Indies Bank & Trust Co.; dir., mem. exec. com. Am. Ship Bldg. Co.; prin. West Indies Investment Co., St. Croix, 1956—. writer of Lee Lets Loose column for local Carribean newspapers. Mem. V.I. Senate, 1976—, now v.p.; chmn. com. govt., chmn. com. on fin. ops. V.I. Govt. Dem. nat. committeeman for V.I., 1969—; mem. V.I. Bd. Edn., 1969-76; mem. Gov.'s Blue Ribbon Commn. for Econ. Devel., 1995—. Fellow Am. Inst. Chemists; mem. AIChE (sr.), AIME (sr.), AARP (chmn. legis. com. 1984—), St. Croix C. of C. (v.p. 1995), Rotary (pres. 1971-73), Lions (pres. 1960), Tau Beta Pi, Sigma Tau. Home and Office: 135 E 54th St Apt 11C New York NY 10022-4511 Office: PO Box 15705 Dallas TX 75215 *In retrospect, elation from supposed triumphs or defeats is blurred in memory; and of greater importance is the quality of one's life or how one played the game.*

LEE, SPIKE (SHELTON JACKSON LEE), filmmaker; b. Atlanta, Mar. 20, 1957; s. William and Jacqueline (Shelton) L.; m. Tonya Lewis; 1 child: Satchel Lewis Lee. BA, Morehouse Coll., 1979; MA in filmmaking, NYU, 1983. Dir., writer films Joe's Bed-Stuy Barber Shop: We Cut Heads, 1982 (student dir. award Acad. Motion Pictures Arts and Scis.), She's Gotta Have It, 1986 (New Generation award L.A. Film Critics, Prix de Jeunesse, Cannes Film Festival 1986), School Daze, 1988, Do the Right Thing, 1989, Mo' Better Blues, 1990, Jungle Fever,1991, Malcolm X, 1992, Crooklyn, 1994; other film appearances include: Drop Squad, 1994; author: Spike Lee's Gotta Have It: Inside Guerilla Filmmaking, 1987, Uplift the Race: The Construction of School Daze,1988, Do the Right Thing: A Spike Lee Joint, 1989, Mo' Better Blues, 1990, By Any Means Necessary: The Trials and Tribulations of the Making of "Malcolm X", 1992. Trustee Morehouse Coll., 1992—. Office: 40 Acres & a Mule 124 Dekalb Ave Ste 2 Brooklyn NY 11217-1201

LEE, STAN (STANLEY MARTIN LIEBER), cartoon publisher, writer; b. N.Y.C., Dec. 28, 1922; s. Jack and Celia (Solomon) Lieber; m. Joan Clayton Boocock, Dec. 5, 1947; 2 dau., Joan C., Jan (dec.). Student pub. schs., N.Y.C.; hon. degree, Bowling Green State U. Copy writer, then asst. editor, editor Timely Comics (became Atlas Comics), N.Y.C., 1939-42; editor, creative dir. Atlas (became Marvel Comics) Comics, until 1961; creative dir., editor-in-chief Marvel Comics, 1961-70, pub., 1970—; creative dir. Marvel Prodns., 1980-89, chmn. Marvel comics, 1989—; adj. prof. popular culture Bowling Green (Ky.) State U.; coll. lectr., TV script editor. Creator, former writer and editor Fantastic Four, Incredible Hulk, Amazing Spiderman, numerous others; author: Origins of Marvel Comics, 1974, Son of Origins, 1975, Bring On The Bad Guys, 1976, Mighty Marvel Strength & Fitness Book, 1976, Mighty Marvel Superheroes Fun Book, 1976, The Marvel Comics Illustrated Version of Star Wars, 1977, The Amazing Spiderman Vol. No. 3, 1977, The Superhero Women, 1977, The Mighty World of Marvel Pin-up Book, 1978, The Mighty Marvel Superhero Fun Book Vol. No. 3, 1978, The Silver Surfer, How to Draw Comics the Marvel Way, 1978, Marvel's Greatest Superhero Battles, 1978, Incredible Hulk, 1978, Marvelous Mazes to Drive You Mad, 1978, Fantastic Four, 1979, Doctor Strange, 1979, Complete Adventures of Spider-Man, 1979, Captain America, 1979, The Best of the Worst, 1979, Marvel Word Games, 1979, Omnibus Fun Book, 1979, Dunn's Conundrum, 1985, The Best of Spider-Man, 1986, Marvel Team-Up Thrillers, 1987, The Amazing Spiderman, No. 2, 1980, Hulk Cartoons, 1980, Marvel Masterworks Vol. 2: Fantastics Four, 1987, X-Men, 1987, Marvel Masterworks, Vol. 1: Amazing Spider-Man, 1987, Masterworks, Vol. 6: Fantastic Four, 1988, Silver Surfer: Judgement Day, 1988, Silver Surfer: Parable, 1988, Spider-Man, 1988, Avengers, 1988, The God Project, 1990, Silver Surfer: The Enslavers, 1990, Marvel Masterworks, Vol. 13: Fantastic Four, 1990, Best of Marvel Comics, 1991, Night Cat, 1991, Marvel Masterworks, Vol. 17: Daredevil, 1991, Marvel Masterworks, Vol. 18: Thor, 1991, Spider-Man Wedding, 1991, Spider-Man Masterworks, 1992, Uncanny X-Men Masterworks, 1993, Marvels Greatest Super Battles, 1994, The Ultimate Spiderman, 1994, The Very Best of Spiderman, 1994, The Incredible Hulk: A Man-Brute Berserk, 1995, others. Served with AUS, 1942-45. Recipient Alley Award, 1963-68; Comic Art Award, Soc. for Comic Art Rsch. & Preservation, 1968; Eureka Award, Il Targa 1970; Publisher of the Year, Periodical & Book Assn. of America, 1978; ann. award Popular Culture Assn., 1974. Mem. (founder), Acad. Comic Book Arts (award 1973), Nat. Acad. TV Arts and Scis., Nat. Cartoonists Soc., AFTRA. Club: Friars (N.Y.C.). Office: Marvel Comics Group 387 Park Ave S New York NY 10016-8810 also: Cowles Syndicate Inc 235 E 45th St New York NY 10017-3305

LEE, STANLEY, physician, educator; b. Newburgh, N.Y., Aug. 27, 1919; s. Philip H. and Bessie (Stember) L.; m. Ann Rosenthal, Dec. 23, 1947; children: Nancy E., Edward J., Kenneth R. B.A., Columbia U., 1939; M.D., Harvard U., 1943. Diplomate: Am. Bd. Internal Medicine. Intern, resident, fellow in medicine and pathology Mt. Sinai Hosp., N.Y.C., 1943-44, 46-49; research asst., asst. attending physician Mt. Sinai Hosp., 1949-59; practice medicine, specializing in internal medicine N.Y.C.; dir. hematology Maimonides Med. Center, Bklyn., 1959-71; dir. medicine Jewish Hosp. and Med. Center, 1971-77; asso. prof. SUNY Downstate, Bklyn., 1959-69; prof. SUNY Downstate, 1969-91; Dean faculty, 1978-81, acting pres., 1979-81; dean Coll. Medicine; v.p. for acad. affairs Coll. Medicine, 1981-82, prof. emeritus, 1991—. Served with AUS, 1944-46. Decorated Combat Med. badge. Fellow A.C.P.; mem. Am. Soc. Hematology, Am. Soc. Human Genetics, Am. Soc. Clin. Oncology, Am. Rheumatism Assn., Soc. Exptl. Biology and Medicine, Harvey Soc., N.Y. Acad. Medicine, AAAS, Am. Fedn. Clin. Research. Jewish. Club: Harvard (N.Y.C.). Office: Brookdale Hosp Med Ctr Brooklyn NY 11212

LEE, STEPHEN W., lawyer; b. New Castle, Ind., Oct. 25, 1949; s. Delmer W. Lee and Loma F. (Thurston) McCall; m. Pamela A. Summers, Aug. 2, 1969; children: Erin E., Stephanie M. BS, Ball State U., 1971; JD summa cum laude, Ind. U., 1977. Bar: Ind. 1977, U.S. Dist. Ct. (so. dist.) Ind. 1977, U.S. Ct. Appeals (7th cir.) 1977, U.S. Supreme Ct. 1982. Officer, lt.(j.g.) USNR, Phila., 1971-74; law clk. U.S. Dist. Ct. (no. dist.) Ind., Ft. Wayne, 1977-78; assoc. Barnes, Hickam, Pantzer & Boyd, Indpls., 1978-82; assoc. Barnes & Thornburg, Indpls., 1982-83, ptnr., 1984—. Editor-in-chief: Indiana Law Jour., 1976-77. Dir. Ind. Repertory Theatre, Indpls., 1986-91; exec. coun. Ind. U. Alumni Assn., Bloomington, 1989; dir. Ind. U. Sch. of Law Alumni Assn., Bloomington, 1984-90, pres., 1991-92; mem. Ball State U. Coll. Bus. Alumni Bd., 1991—, Ball State U. Entrepreneurship Adv. Bd., 1994—. Mem. Ind. State Bar Assn., Indpls. Bar Assn. (chmn. bus. sect. 1985), Highland Golf & Country Club. Republican. Avocations: golf. Office: Barnes & Thornburg 11 S Meridian St Indianapolis IN 46204-3506

LEE, SUL HI, library administrator; b. Taegu, Korea, July 13, 1936; s. Sang Moo and Won Nim L.; m. Seol Bong Ryu, Sept. 6, 1962; 1 child, Melissa Jemee. B.A., Bowling Green State U., 1961; M.A., U. Toledo, 1964, U. Mich., 1966. Reference libr. Toledo Pub. Libr., 1961-67; supr. info. analysts Owens-Ill., Inc., 1967-68; dir. Ctr. for Libr. and Info. Sys., U. Toledo, 1968-70; assoc. dir. libr. Eastern Mich. U., Ypsilanti, 1970-73; assoc. dir. librs. U. Rochester, N.Y., 1973-75; dean libr. svcs. Ind. State U., Terre Haute, 1975-78; dean univ. librs. U. Okla., Norman, 1978—, prof. Sch. Libr. and Info. Studies, 1988—. Author: Library Orientation, 1972, A Challenge for Academic Libraries, 1973, Planning-Programing-Budgeting System, 1973, Library Budgeting, 1977, Emerging Trends in Library Organization, 1978, Serials Collection Development: Choices and Strategies, 1981, Reference Service: a Perspective, 1983, Library Fundraising, 1984, Issues in Acquisitions, 1984, Access to Scholarly Information, 1985, Pricing and Cost of Monographs and Serials, 1987, Acquisitions, Budgets and Materials Costs, 1988, The Impact of Rising Costs of Serials and Monographs on Library Services and Programs, 1989, Library Material Costs and Access to Information, 1990, Budgets for Acquisitions, 1991, Vendor Evaluation and Acquisitions Budgets, 1992, Collection Assessment and Acquisitions Budgets, 1993, The Role and Future of Special Collections in Research Libraries, 1993, Declining Acquisitions Budgets, 1994, Access, Ownership and Resource Sharing, 1995; editor: Collection Management, 1996—, Jour. Libr. Adminstrn., 1987—. Mem. ALA (com. on accreditation 1981-83, mem. coun. 1986-90, coun. com. on coms. 1988-89), Assn. Rsch. Librs. (chair com. mgmt. rsch. librs. 1987-89, bd. dirs. 1991-94), Greater Midwestern Rsch. Librs. Consortium (chair 1994-95), U. Mich. Sch. Libr. Sci. Alumni Soc. (pres. 1983-84, mem. edtl. com. CAUSE 1995-98). Office: U Okla 401 W Brooks St Norman OK 73069-8824

LEE, SUNG W., electronics executive. Pres., cfo Samsung Semiconductor Inc., San Jose, Calif., 1991—; with Samsung Group, Korea, 1970-91. Office: Samsung Semiconductor Inc 3655 N 1st St San Jose CA 95134-1707*

LEE, T. GIRARD, architect; b. Washington, Nov. 3, 1938; m. T. Girard and Dorothy (Thomas) L.; m. Paula Stephan, June 17, 1961; children: Kenneth Robert, Jennifer Margaret Dowd, Rebecca Susan Clark, Nancy Elizabeth. BArch, Miami U., 1961. Registered architect M.D., D.C., Va., W.Va. Architect intern various architects offices, Silver Spring, Md., 1965-68; assoc., architect Bagley & Soule Architects, Chevy Chase, Md., 1968-69; sole propriator Lee & Assoc., Bethesda, Md., 1969-71; ptnr. Bagley, Soule, Lee Architects, Chevy Chase, 1971-84, Lee Warner & Assocs., Annapolis, Md., 1984-90; v.p., treas., prin. Lee-Warner Architects, Inc., Annapolis, Md., 1990-96. Chmn. bd. mgmt. Bethesda Chevy Chase YMCA, 1976-77; bd. trustees United Way and Nat. Capitol Area, Washington, 1977-80; bd. dirs. Anne Arundel County YMCA, Annapolis, Md., 1986-91. Mem. AIA (pres. Potomac Valley chpt. 1974-75, treas. Chesapeake Bay chpt. 1985-91), Md. Soc. Architects (pres. 1978-79), Rotary (pres. club 1982-83). Republican. United Methodist. Avocations: golf, tennis, sailing, jogging. Office: 754 Robin Hood Hill Annapolis MD 21405

LEE, THOMAS ALEXANDER, accountant, educator; b. Edinburgh, Scotland, May 18, 1941; s. Thomas Henderson and Dorothy Jane (Norman) L.; m. Ann Margaret Brown, Sept. 14, 1963; children: Sarah Ann, Richard Thomas. Chartered acct., Inst. Chartered Accts.Scotland, Edinburgh, 1964; tax acct., Inst. Tax, Glasgow, Scotland, 1965; MS, U. Strathclyde, Glasgow, Scotland, 1969, DLitt, 1984. Audit asst. Edinburgh, 1959-64, Glasgow, 1964-66; lectr. U. Strathclyde, 1966-69, U. Edinburgh, 1969-73; prof. U. Liverpool, Eng., 1973-76, U. Edinburgh, 1976-90; dir. rsch. Inst. Chartered Accts. Scotland, 1983-84; prof. U. Ala., 1990—, dir. PhD program, 1991—; vis. prof. U. Md., 1986, U. Utah, 1987-88, U. Edinburg, Scotland, 1991-94, Deakin U., 1994—; hon. prof. U. Dundee, Scotland, 1995—. Editor: Internat. Jour. Auditing; assoc. editor Brit. Acctg. Rev.; mem. editl. bd. various jours., 1971—. Trustee Acad. Acctg. Historians, v.p., 1996—. Mem. Fellow Royal Soc. Arts; mem. Inst. Chartered Accts. Scotland (coun. 1989-90), Inst. Taxation. Presbyterian. Avocations: church, road running, cricket history. Office: U Ala PO Box 870220 Tuscaloosa AL 35487-0220

LEE, THOMAS HENRY, electrical engineer, educator; b. Shanghai, China, May 11, 1923; came to U.S., 1948, naturalized, 1953; s. Y. C. and Nan Tien (Ho) L.; m. Kin Ping, June 12, 1948; children—William F., Thomas H. Jr., Richard T. B.S.M.E., Nat. Chiao Tung U., Shanghai, 1946; M.S.E.E., Union Coll., Schenectady, 1950; Ph.D., Rensselaer Poly. Inst., 1954. Registered profl. engr., Pa. Mgr. research and devel. Gen. Electric Co., Phila., 1959-74; mgr. strategic planning Fairfield, Conn., 1974-78, staff exec., 1978-80; prof. elec. engring. MIT, Cambridge, 1980-84, 87—; dir. Internat. Inst. for Applied Systems Analysis, Laxenburg, Austria, 1984-87; pres. Tech. Assessment Group, Schenectady, 1980-84, Ctr. for Quality Mgmt., Cambridge, Mass., 1990—. Author: Physics and Engineering of High Power Switching Devices, 1973, Energy Aftermath, 1989; patentee in field. Recipient Davis medal for outstanding engring. accomplishment Rensselaer Poly. Inst., 1987. Fellow IEEE (Power Life award 1980, Haraden Pratt award 1983), AAAS; mem. NAE, Swiss Acad. Engring. Sci., Power Engring. Soc. (pres. 1974-76).

LEE, TOM STEWART, judge; b. 1941; m. Norma Ruth Robbins; children: Elizabeth Robbins, Tom Stewart Jr. BA, Miss. Coll., 1963, JD cum laude, U. Miss., 1965. Ptnr. Lee & Lee, Forest, Miss., 1965-84; pros. atty. Scott County, Miss., 1968-71; judge Scott County Youth Ct., Forest, 1979-82; mcpl. judge City of Forest, 1982; judge U.S. Dist. Ct. (so. dist.) Miss., Jackson, 1984—. Asst. editor: Miss. Law Jour. Deacon, Sunday sch. tchr. Forest Bapt. ch.; pres. Forest Pub. Sch. Bd., Scott County Heart Assn.; bd. visitors Miss. Coll. Law Sch.; lectr. Miss. Coll., 1993. Served to capt. USAR. Named one of Outstanding Young Men Am. Mem. Miss. Bar Assn., Scott County Bar Assn., Hinds County Bar Assn., Fed. Bar Assn., Fed. Judges' Assn., Forest C. of C. (bd. dirs.), Forest Jaycees (past pres., Disting. Service award), Ole Miss. Alumni Assn. (pres.), Miss. Coll. Alumni Assn. (bd. dirs.), Am. Legion. Office: US Dist Ct 245 E Capitol St Ste 110 Jackson MS 39201-2409

LEE, TONG HUN, economics educator; b. Seoul, Korea, Nov. 20, 1931; came to U.S., 1955, naturalized, 1968; s. Chong Su and Yun (Lee) L.; m. Yul Jah Ahn, June 11, 1960; children: Bruce Keebeck, James Keewon. B.S., Yon-Sei U., 1955; Ph.D., U. Wis., 1961. Asst. prof. econs. U. Tenn., Knoxville, 1962-64; assoc. prof. U. Tenn., 1964-67; prof. econs. U. Wis., Milw., 1967—, chmn. dept. econs., 1978-82. Author: Interregional Intersectoral Flow Analysis, 1973; Contbr. articles to profl. jours. NSF grantee, 1965-67, 73-75. Mem. Am. Econ. Assn., Am. Fin. Assn., Am. Statis. Assn., Econometric Soc. Home: 559 W Surf St # 500 Chicago IL 60657 *Success comes from determination, persistence and hard work, but the ultimate measure of success is derived from the inner life of a person.*

LEE, TUNG-KWANG, pathologist, cancer researcher; b. Wuchang, China, Oct. 6, 1934; came to U.S., 1980; s. Jie-Tsai Lee and Chong-Wen Ding; m. You-An Sun, Jan. 30, 1974; 1 child, Hao. MD, Shanghai First Med. Coll., 1955. Resident in surgery and pathology Yubei Med. Sch., Henan, China, 1957-60, tchr. pathology, 1960-78, assoc. prof., 1979-80; Bradshaw fellow Bowman Gray Sch. of Medicine, Winston-Salem, N.C., 1980-81, rsch. assoc., 1981-85; rsch. instr. East Carolina U. Sch. Medicine, Greenville, N.C., 1985-87, rsch. asst. prof., 1988-95, rsch. assoc. prof., 1996—; researcher and speaker in field. Author: (with others) Rheumatology, 1985, Ovarian Tumors, 1984, Clinical Cytology, 1981; contbr. over 60 articles to profl. jours. Bd. dirs., chmn. membership com. Eastern Carolina Multicultural Ctr., Greenville, 1992—. Brown F. Finch Found. grantee 1993. Mem. Am. Assn. Cancer Rsch., Radiation Rsch. Soc., Internat. Acad. Cytology, Internat. Soc. Comparative Oncology, Sigma Xi. Avocation: classical music. Home: 1403 Evergreen Dr Greenville NC 27858-4612 Office: Dept Radiation Oncology Sch of Medicine Leo W. Jenkins Cancer Ctr Greenville NC 27834

LEE, TUNNEY FEE, urban planning educator; b. Taishan, Guangdong, China, Oct. 22, 1931; came to U.S., 1938; s. Kwang Lien and Kam Kwai (Chan) L.; m. Irene Friedman, Apr. 18, 1957; children: Thea, Kaela, Dara. BArch, U. Mich., 1954. Registered architect, Mass. Designer Geodesics, Inc, Raleigh, N.C., 1954-55, Marcel Breuer, Architect, N.Y.C., 1955, Ulrich Franzen, Architect, N.Y.C., 1956, I.M. Pei Assocs., Architects, N.Y.C., 1958-59; chief of planning design Boston Redevel. Authority, 1960-66; chief designer Marcou O'Leary, Planners, Washington, 1966-68; prin. Tunney Lee, Architect, Washington, 1968-70; prof. dept. urban studies and planning MIT, Cambridge, Mass., 1970-93, head dept., 1986-90; prof. dept. architecture, head dept. Chinese U., Hong Kong, 1990—; coord. Citizens Adv. Com. Copley Pl., Boston, 1977-80; city rep. for Cambridge, Boston Transp. Planning Rev., 1970-72. Co-author: Development Politics, 1980; contbr. articles to profl. jours. Bd. dirs. Asian Community Devel. Corp., Boston, 1988-90, South Cove Community Health Ctr., Boston, 1981-87, Oxfam Am., Boston, 1986-88; chmn. Decennial Census Commn., Boston, 1987; dep. commr. Mass. Div. Capital Planning and Ops., Boston, 1983-86. Fulbright fellow U. Rome, 1956-57. Democrat. Office: Chinese Univ of Hong Kong, Dept of Architecture, Sha Tin Hong Kong

LEE, VERNON ROY, minister; b. Jackson, Miss., Feb. 1, 1952; s. Samuel Rayford and Evie Mae (Abel) L.; m. Rhonda Sue Parker, Nov. 6, 1970; 1 child, Shannon Grant. Pastor Mt. Moriah Bapt. Ch., Junction City, Ark., 1971-72, Pleasant Grove Bapt. Ch., El Dorado, Ark., 1972-74, Pilgrims Rest Bapt. Ch., Spearsville, La., 1974-76, Bethany Bapt. Ch., Bastrop, La., 1976-78, 1st Bapt. Ch., Taylor, Ark., 1978-83, Farmington Bapt. Ch., Corinth, Miss., 1983-86, Wyatt Bapt. Ch., El Dorado, 1986—. Trustee Southeastern Bapt. Coll., Laurel, Miass., 1983-86, Ctrl. Bapt. Coll., Conway, Ark., 1992—, asst. chmn. bd. trustees, 1993-95, chmn., 1995—; vol. Boy's Clubs, El Dorado, 1986-91, YMCA, Corinth, 1983-86. Mem. Bapt. Missionary Assn. Am. (v.p. 1986-88, pres. 1990-92, clk. missionary com. 1989-91, asst. ch. adv. com. 1992-95), Miss. Bapt. Assn. (pres. 1984-86). Avocations: golf, fishing, basketball, softball. Home: 137 S Wyatt Dr El Dorado AR 71730-6768 Office: Wyatt Bapt Ch 4621 W Hillsboro El Dorado AR 71730-6768

LEE, VIRGINIA JOHNSON, nursing administrator; b. McComb, Miss., Dec. 25, 1930; d. John Robert and Katherine A. (Hayes) Johnson; m. Edward Arlis Middleton, July 15, 1951 (dec. Feb. 1952); 1 child, Arlene MIddleton James; m. Henry Allen Lee, Nov. 3, 1956; children: David J., Mark A., Joel R., Andrew R. Diploma, McComb Infirmary Sch. Nursing, 1951; BS in Social Scis. for Nurses, Tift Coll., 1972; MEd, U. So. Miss., 1983. RN, Miss., Ga., La.; cert. nursing adminstrn. ANC. Dir. continuing edn. Med. Ctr. Ctrl. Ga., Macon, 1971-75; instr. ADN program Macon C.C., 1975-76; dir. nursing, asst. adminstr. S.W. Miss. Regional Med. Ctr., McComb, 1976-80, head dept. edn., 1980-82, clin. nurse coronary care, 1983-86, supr. relief, 1986-90, nurse mgr. med/cardiac/telemetry, 1990-93, relief supr., 1993—; staff nurse coronary care Our Lady of Lake Regional Med. Ctr., Baton Rouge, 1982-83. Chmn. bd. dirs. ARC, McComb, 1982-88, treas., 1988-91; mem. chancel choir, 2d v.p. just older youth group, mem. women's group, moderator-elect J.J. White Presbyn. Ch., McComb; past pres. Gideon's Aux. Mem. Miss. Nurses' Assn. (pres. dist. 2 1990-94, acting sec. 1994-95, Adminstrv. Nurse of Yr. 1992, Nurse of Yr. 1986, 93). Avocations: cross-stitch, home crafts, singing, sewing, fund raising. Home: 6027 Highway 48 W Summit MS 39666-9242

LEE, WALLACE WILLIAMS, JR., retired hotel executive; b. Nacogdoches, Tex., June 28, 1915; s. Wallace Williams and Caryl (Ames) L.; m. Doris Card, Sept. 19, 1942; children: Doris Lee Bessette, Frederic Williams. B.S. in Hotel Adminstrn, Cornell U., 1936; postgrad. in Advanced Bus. Mgmt, Columbia, 1954. Cert. hotel adminstr. Asst. mgr. Broadmoor Hotel, Colorado Springs, Colo., 1938-42; resident mgr. Hotel Thayer, West Point, N.Y., 1945-47; mgr. Hotel Anderson (Ind.), 1947-48; resident mgr. Hotel Roosevelt, N.Y.C., 1951-53; v.p., gen. mgr. Hotel Roosevelt, 1954; asst. mgr. Waldorf-Astoria, N.Y.C., 1948-51; mgr. Waldorf-Astoria, 1954-59, v.p., resident mgr., 1959-61; v.p., gen. mgr. The Barclay and Park Lane Hotels, N.Y.C., 1961-63; group v.p. accommodations Howard Johnson Co., 1963-80; dir. Smiley Bros., Inc., 1981-96, mem. exec. com., 1982-87. Vice chmn. AH/MA adv. com. to Statler Found., 1966-72; mem. exec. bd. Greater N.Y. coun. Boy Scouts Am., 1960-71, mem. exec. bd. Boston Coun., 1971-79, chmn. camping Northeast region, 1972-73; bd. dirs., 1960-71, v.p. bd. dirs. YMCA of Greater N.Y., 1965-71; bd. dirs. Travelers Aid Soc., N.Y.C., 1959-66; trustee Am. Hotel Found., 1973-78; pres. Hospitality, Lodging and Travel Rsch. Found., 1975-80; trustee Christ Ch. Meth. N.Y.C., 1959-64, chmn. ocfl. bd., 1963-64; trustee Congl. Ch., Sherman, Conn., 1965-68, deacon, 1981-83; assoc. 1st Presbyn. Ch., Orlando, Fla., 1990—. Served to capt. AUS, 1942-45. Recipient Silver Beaver award Boy Scouts Am., 1964, Disting. Achievement in Edn. and Advancing Profession of Innkeeping award Hotel and Restaurant Mgmt. Soc. NYU, 1964, award of merit Am. Hotel and Motel Assn., Hosp. Travel Rsch. Found., 1980; named Man of Yr. YMCA Neighbor Youth Br. Greater N.Y., 1961; named to Hall of Fame Hospitality Mag., 1965. Mem. Cornell Soc. Hotelmen (pres. 1953-54, trustee Found. 1991—), Am. Security Coun., Conn. Soc. Mayflower Desc., Ednl. Inst., Timber Trails Club (pres. 1966-67). Congregationalist. Home (summer): 172 Route 37 S Sherman CT 06784-2401 Home (winter): 1055 Kensington Park Dr Altamonte Springs FL 32714-1911

LEE, WALTER WILLIAM, JR., film writer, consultant, publishing executive; b. Eugene, Oreg., Aug. 16, 1931; s. Walter William and Okria LaVelle (Mooney) L.; m. Frances Eve Olveda, May 9, 1959; children: Cindy Lee Kimmick, Steven Marco. BS with honors, Calif. Inst. Tech., 1954; postgrad., U. Calif., Berkeley, 1954-55. Cert. Motion Picture Assn. Am. Film writer Howard Hughes, Culver City, Calif., 1955-59; v.p., dir. Tech. Communications, Inc., L.A., 1959-62; sr. project engr., film writer, coord. Hughes Aircraft Co., El Segundo, Calif., 1962-89; pres. Chelsea-Lee Books, L.A., 1972—; v.p., dir. Sci. Fiction Cons. of Hollywood, Inc., L.A., 1980-94; cons. L.A. Film Expn., 1975, Lucasfilm/20th Century Fox, L.A., 1979, 86, CBS spl. E.T. & Friends/Warner Bros., L.A. and Burbank, Calif., 1982. Editor: Pendulum mag., 1952-54, It mag., 1955-58; editor, compiler Reference Guide to Fantastic Films, 1972, vol. 2, 1973, vol. 3, 1974 (Spl. award World Sci. Fiction Conv. 1975); author: (with Richard Delap) Shapes, 1987; mem. bd. advisors Who's Who in Entertainment, 1991-93; contbr. articles to profl. jours., The New Ency. of Sci. Fiction, 1988. Mem. Community Adv. Coun., L.A., 1975-79. Recipient Film award Internat. Film Producers Assn., 1967. Mem. Am. Film Inst. Democrat. Avocation: collecting sci. fiction, fantasy and horror film reference material. Office: PO Box 66273 Los Angeles CA 90066-0273

LEE, WEN-HWA, medical educator; b. Taiwan, June 1, 1950; came to U.S., 1978; s. Suen-Yi and Chen-Jen (Shu) L.; m. Eva Y.H. Pan, Sept. 12, 1975; children: Sou-Ying, Allen. BS, Nat. Taiwan Normal U., 1972; MS, Nat. Taiwan U., 1977; PhD, U. Calif., Berkeley, 1981. Tchr. Nankung Mid. Sch., Taipei, Taiwan, 1972-73; teaching asst. Inst. Biochemistry, Nat. Taiwan U., Taipei, 1977-78; rsch. scientist Cetus Corp., Berkeley, Calif., 1982-83; asst. prof. U. Calif., San Diego, 1984-87, assoc. prof., 1987-90, prof., 1990-91; prof. pathology U. Tex. Health Sci. Ctr., San Antonio, 1991—, prof. cellular and structural biology, 1991—, chair grad. program molecular medicine, 1993—, Alice P. McDermott Disting. U. chair, prof. and dir. Ctr. Molecular Medicine/Inst. Biotech., 1991—; vis. scientist Lawrence Berkeley Lab., 1983-84; vis. prof. Inst. Molecular Biology, Sinica Academia, Taipei, 1987-88; adj. prof. Chinese U. Sci. and Tech., Hefei, China, 1991-94; chmn. sci. adv. bd. Canji, Inc., San Diego, 1990-95; dir., lectr. NIH, 1991; mem. bd. sci. advisors Hong Kong Cancer Inst., 1994—; sci. advisor for search com. Arthur G. James Cancer Hosp., Columbus, Ohio, 1994—; advisor on life scis. World Sci. Pub. Co., Singapore, 1995—. Jr. lt. Taiwan Army, 1973-75. Postdoctoral fellow U. Calif., 1981-82; Outstanding Sci. Achievement in Bioscis. award Cheng-Hsing Med. Found. and Soc. Chinese Bioscientists in Am., 1992, Rsch. award Alcon, 1994. Mem. AAAS, Am. Soc. Microbiology, Am. Soc. Human Genetics, Am. Assn. Cancer Rsch., Internat. Assn. Comparative Rsch. on Leukemia and Related Diseases, Assn. Rsch. in Vision and Ophthalmology, Soc. Chinese Bioscientists in Am., N.Y. Acad. Sci., Academia Sinica (elected). Achievements include patents in Human Esterase D, Its Uses and a Process of Purification, Phosphoprotein-The Retinoblastoma Susceptibility Gene Product. Avocations: swimming, ping-pong, movies, opera. Office: Ctr for Molecular Medicine/Inst Biotech 15355 Lambda Dr San Antonio TX 78245

LEE, WILLIAM CHARLES, judge; b. Fort Wayne, Ind., Feb. 2, 1938; s. Russell and Catherine (Zwick) L.; m. Judith Anne Bash, Sept. 19, 1959; children—Catherine L., Mark R., Richard R. A.B., Yale U., 1959; J.D., U. Chgo., 1962. Bar: Ind. 1962. Ptnr., Parry, Krueckeberg & Lee, Fort Wayne, 1964-70; dep. pros. atty. Allen County, Fort Wayne, 1963-69, chief dep., 1966-69; U.S. atty. No. Dist. Ind., Fort Wayne, 1970-73; ptnr. Hunt, Suedhoff, Borror, Eilbacher & Lee, Fort Wayne, 1973-81; U.S. Dist. judge No. Dist. Ind., Fort Wayne, 1981—; instr. Nat. Inst. Trial Advocacy. Contbd. numerous publications and lectrs. in the field. Co-chmn. Fort

Wayne Fine Arts Operating Fund Drive, 1978; past bd. dirs., v.p., pres. Fort Wayne Philharm. Orch.; past bd. dirs., v.p. Hospice of Fort Wayne, Inc.; past bd. dirs. Fort Wayne Fine Arts Found., Fort Wayne Civic Theatre, Neighbors, Inc., Embassy Theatre Found.; past bd. dirs., pres. Legal Aid of Fort Wayne, Inc.; past mem. ch. coun., v.p. Trinity English Lutheran Ch. Council; past trustee, pres. Fort Wayne Community Schs., 1978-81, pres., 1980-81; trustee Fort Wayne Mus. Art, 1984-90; past bd. dirs., pres. Fort Wayne-Allen County Hist. Soc. Griffin scholar, 1955-59; chmn. Fort Wayne Cmty. Schs Scholarship Com.; bd. dirs. Arts United of Greater Fort Wayne, Fort Wayne Ballet. Weymouth Kirkland scholar, 1959-62; named Ind. Trial Judge of the Yr, 1988. Fellow Am. Coll. Trial Lawyers, Ind. Bar Found.; mem. ABA, Allen County Bar Assn., Ind. State Bar Assn., Fed. Bar Assn., Seventh Cir. Bar Assn., Phi Delta Phi (past bd. dirs., 1st pres.), Benjamin Harrison Am. Inn of Ct., North Side High Alumni Assn. (bd. dirs. pres.), Fort Wayne Rotary Club (bd. dir.). Republican. Lutheran. Office: US Dist Ct 2145 Fed Bldg 1300 S Harrison St Fort Wayne IN 46802-3435

LEE, WILLIAM CHIEN-YEH, electrical engineer; b. London, July 20, 1932; married; 2 children. BSc, Chinese Naval Acad., Taiwan, 1954; MS, Ohio State U., 1960, PhD, 1963. Mem. tech. staff comms. Bell Labs., 1964-79; sr. scientist, mgr. def. comm. divsn. ITT, 1979-84; v.p. Pactel Cellular, Walnut Creek, Calif., 1985—, Airtouch, Walnut Creek, 1985—; affil. mem. U. Calif., Irvine, 1985—, U. Calif., Davis, 1985—; mem. Nat. Comms. Forum Overseas Coun., 1985—; state apptd. bd. mem. Calif. Sci. and Tech. Coun., 1996-99. Author 3 books on mobile comms.; contbr. over 100 articles to profl. publs. Recipient Disting. Alumni award Ohio State U., 1990. Fellow IEEE (Avante Garde award Vehicluar Tech. Soc. 1990, Contbn. award San Francisco sect. 1990); mem. Brit. Inst. Elec. Engrs., Sigma Xi. Office: Airtouch 2999 Oak Rd Rm 614 Walnut Creek CA 94596 *Use mathematics to solve problems; use physics to interpret results; use counter examples to check outcomes; use pictures to memorize the importance.*

LEE, WILLIAM FRANKLIN, III, association administrator; b. Galveston, Tex., Feb. 20, 1929; s. William Franklin Jr. and Anna Lena (Keis) L.; m. Jacqueline Tyler; children: William Franklin IV, Robert Terry, Patricia Lynn, Peggy Ann. MusB, N. Tex. State U., 1949, MS, 1950; MusM, U. Tex., 1956, PhD, 1956. Prof. music St. Mary's U., San Antonio, 1952-55; asst. to dean fine arts U. Tex., 1955-56; chmn. dept. music Sam Houston State Coll., 1956-64; dean Sch. Music U. Miami (Fla.), 1964-82, provost, exec. v.p., 1982-86, disting. prof., composer in residence, 1986-88; dir. arts Fla. Internat. U., Miami, 1988-90; dean coll. fine arts and humanities U. Tex., San Antonio, 1990-95; exec. dir. Internat. Assn. Jazz Educators, 1995—. Performances with Houston, Dallas symphony orchs., performances with Gene Krupa and Artie Shaw, guest clinician, condr., composer, 1952—; composer, author, arranger more than 100 published works.; author: Music Theory Dictionary, 1962; also articles, music publs.; biographer, discographer of Stan Kenton, 1981; editor, co-founder: Southwestern Brass Jour., 1958, Belwin New Dictionary of Music and Musicians, 1988. Mem. AAUP, ASCAP (recipient 26 awards 1968— including Deems Taylor awards 1981, 85), Nat. Assn. Am. Composers and Condrs., Music Educators Nat. Conf., Am. Fedn. Musicians, Music Tchrs. Nat. Assn., Pi Kappa Lambda, Kappa Kappa Psi, Phi Mu Alpha. Office: Internat Assn Jazz Educator PO Box 724 Manhattan KS 66502-0006

LEE, WILLIAM JOHN, petroleum engineering educator, consultant; b. Lubbock, Tex., Jan. 16, 1936; s. William Preston and Bonnie Lee (Cook) L.; m. Phyllis Ann Bass, June 10, 1961; children: Anne Preston, Mary Denise. B in Chem. Engring., Ga. Inst. Tech., 1959, MSChemE, 1961, PhD in Chem. Engring., 1963, NAE, 1993, Ga. Tech. Acad. Disting. Engring. Alumni, 1994. Registered profl. engr., Tex., Miss. Sr. rsch. specialist Exxon Prodn. Rsch. Co., Houston, 1962-68; assoc. prof. petroleum engring. Miss. State U., Starkville, 1968-71; tech. advisor Exxon Co., Houston, 1971-77; prof. petroleum engring. Tex. A&M U., College Station, 1977—, holder Noble chair in petroleum engring., 1985-93, Peterson chair in petroleum engring., 1993—; dir. Crisman Inst. for Petroleum Reservoir Mgmt. at Tex. A&M U., 1987-93; exec. v.p. S.A. Holditch & Assocs., Inc., College Station, 1979—. Author: Well Testing, 1982. Recipient award of excellence Halliburton Edn. Found., 1982, Meritorious Engring. Teaching award Tenneco, Inc., 1982, Disting. Teaching award Assn. Former Students, Tex. A&M U., College Station, 1983; Tex. Engring. Experiment Sta. fellow, 1987-88, sr. fellow 1990. Mem. Soc. Petroleum Engrs. (disting., chmn. edn. and accreditation com. 1985-86, disting. lectr. 1980, disting. faculty achievement award 1982, Reservoir Engring. award 1986, Regional service award 1987, disting. svc. award 1992, Carll award 1995, dir. 1996—). Presbyterian. Avocation: travel. Home: 3100 Rolling Gln Bryan TX 77807-3209 Office: Tex A&M U Petroleum Engring Dept College Station TX 77843

LEE, WILLIAM JOHNSON, lawyer; b. Oneida, Tenn., Jan. 13, 1924; s. William J. and Ara (Anderson) L.; student Akron U., 1941-43, Denison U., 1943-44, Harvard U., 1944-45; J.D., Ohio State U., 1948. Bar: Ohio 1948, Fla. 1962. Research asst. Ohio State U. Law Sch., 1948-49; asst. dir. Ohio Dept. Liquor Control, chief purchases, 1956-57, atty. examiner, 1951-53, asst. state permit chief, 1953-55, state permit chief, 1955-56; asst. counsel, staff Hupp Corp., 1957-58; spl. counsel City Attys. Office Ft. Lauderdale (Fla.), 1963-65; asst. atty. gen. Office Atty. Gen., State of Ohio, 1966-70; adminstr. State Med. Bd. Ohio, Columbus, 1970-85, also mem. Federated State Bd.'s Nat. Commn. for Evaluation of Fgn. Med. Schs., 1981-83; Mem. Flex 1/Flex 2 Transitional Task Force, 1983-84; pvt. practice law, Ft. Lauderdale, 1965-66; acting municipal judge, Ravenna, Ohio, 1960; instr. Coll. Bus. Adminstrn., Kent State U., 1961-62. Mem. pastoral relations com. Epworth United Meth. Ch., 1976; chmn. legal aid com. Portage County, Ohio, 1960; troop awards chmn. Boy Scouts Am., 1965; mem. ch. bd. Melrose Park (Fla.) Meth. Ch., 1966. Mem. Exptl. Aviation Assn. S.W. Fla., Franklin County Trial Lawyers Assn., Am. Legion, Fla., Columbus, Akron, Broward County (Fla.) bar assns., Delta Theta Phi, Phi Kappa Tau, Pi Kappa Delta. Served with USAAF, 1943-46. Editorial bd. Ohio State Law Jour., 1947-48; also articles. Home: Apple Valley 704 Country Club Dr Howard OH 43028-9530

LEE, WILLIAM MARSHALL, lawyer; b. N.Y.C., Feb. 23, 1922; s. Marshall McLean and Marguerite (Letts) L.; m. Lois Kathryn Plain, Oct. 10, 1942; children: Marsha (Mrs. Stephen Derynck), William Marshall Jr., Victoria C. (Mrs. Larry Nelson). Student, U. Wis., 1939-40; BS, Aero. U., Chgo., 1942; postgrad., UCLA, 1946-48, Loyola U. Law Sch., L.A., 1948-49; JD, Loyola U., Chgo., 1952. Bar: Ill. 1952. Thermodynamicist Northrop Aircraft Co., Hawthorne, Calif., 1947-49; patent agt. Hill, Sherman, Meroni, Gross & Simpson, Chgo., 1949-51, Borg-Warner Corp., Chgo., 1951-53; ptnr. Hume, Clement, Hume & Lee, Chgo., 1953-72; pvt. practice Chgo., 1973-74; ptnr. Lee and Smith (and predecessors), Chgo., 1974-89, Lee, Mann, Smith, McWilliams, Sweeney & Ohlson, Chgo., 1989—; cons. Power Packaging, Inc. Speaker and contbr. articles on legal topics. Pres. Glenview (Ill.) Citizens Sch. Com., 1953-57; v.p. Glenbrook High Sch. Bd., 1957-63. Lt. USNR, 1942-46, CBI. Recipient Pub. Svc. award Glenbrook High Sch. Bd., 1963. Mem. ABA (chmn. sect. intellectual property law 1986-87, sect. fin. officer 1976-77, sect. sec. 1977-80, sect. governing coun. 1980-84, 87-88), Ill. Bar Assn., Chgo. Bar Assn., 7th Fed. Cir. Bar Assn., Am. Intellectual Property Law Assn., Intellectual Law Assn. Chgo., Licensing Execs. Soc. (pres. 1981-82, treas. 1977-80, trustee 1974-77, 80-81, 82-83, internat. del. 1980—), Phi Delta Theta, Phi Alpha Delta. Republican. Home: 84 Otis Rd Barrington IL 60010 Office: 209 S La Salle St Chicago IL 60604-1202

LEE, WILLIAM SAUL (BILL LEE), artist, writer; b. Bklyn., Nov. 15, 1938; s. Arthur Martin and Clara (Levine) Levy; m. Dona Ruth Johnson-Lee; 1 child, Jennifer Catherine. Grad. high sch., N.Y.C. Humor editor Penthouse Publs., N.Y.C., 1976—; tchr. satiric art Sch. Visual Art; lectr. slide shows of satiric art. Author: 7 books including Insecurity is Better Than No Security at All, (comic strip and lit. format) Investigative Cartooning; featured cartoonist San Francisco Chronicle, Leescapes, The New Yorker, Playboy, Penthouse, Omni, Esquire, Cosmopolitan, Nat. Lampoon, and others; nationally syndicated cartoonist: Lee Scapes, Tribune Media Svcs.; one-man art show at Visual Arts Ctr., N.Y.C., 1974; works exhibited in group shows at Castelli Gallery, N.Y.C., 1972, Motreal Fair, 1974, Hansen Galleries, N.Y.C., 1975, Van Gogh Mus., Holland, 1975, Kew Gardens, London, 1975, Greene St. Gallery, N.Y.C., 1986, Broome St. Gallery, 1987, Atrium Gallery, 1989. Recipient Internat. Humor award Montreal Expo, 1971, 72, Metro Arts Festival, 1986, 87. Mem. Nat. TV Acad., Writers Guild, Motion Picture Acad., Mus. of Broadcasting, Nat. Cartoonist Soc., Soc. Illustrators, Am. Inst. Graphic Arts, Soc. Publ. Designers, Tareytown Group. Avocations: drawing, writing, painting, sculpting.

LEE, WILLIAM STATES, retired utility executive; b. Charlotte, N.C., June 23, 1929; s. William States and Sarah (Everett) L.; m. Janet Fleming Rumberger, Nov. 24, 1951; children—Lisa, States, Helen. BS in Engring. magna cum laude, Princeton U., 1951. Registered profl. engr., N.C., S.C. With Duke Power Co., Charlotte, 1955-94, engring. mgr., 1962-65; v.p. engring. Duke Power Co., 1965-71, sr. v.p., 1971-75, exec. v.p., 1976-77, pres., chief operating officer, 1978-82, chmn., CEO, 1982-94, also dir., mem. mgmt. and fin. coms.; retired, 1994; bd. dirs. Liberty Corp., J.P. Morgan Co., Morgan Guaranty Trust Co., Knight-Ridder, Tex. Instruments. Bd. dirs. United Cmty. Svcs., Found. of the Carolinas; trustee Queen's Coll., U. N.C., Charlotte Found., Presbyn. Hosp. Found. With C.E. USNR, 1951-54. Named Outstanding Engr. N.C. Soc. Engrs., 1969. Fellow ASME (George Westinghouse gold medal 1972, James N. Landis medal 1991), ASCE; mem. Nat. Acad. Engring., Nat. Soc. Profl. Engrs. (Outstanding Engr. award 1980), Edison Electric Inst. (dir. econs. and fin. policy com., dir.), Charlotte C. of C. (chmn. 1979), Am. Nuclear Soc., Phi Beta Kappa, Tau Beta Pi. Presbyn. (ruling elder). Office: Duke Power Co 526 S Church St EC12P Charlotte NC 28202-1802

LEE, YOUNG BIN, psychiatrist, neurologist; b. Seoul, Korea, Mar. 21, 1937; came to U.S., 1964; s. Suksin and Insik (Kim) L.; m. Moon Chin Cho, Apr. 24, 1965; children: Edward S., Susan E., Ellen M. Pre-med. study coll. sci. and engring., Yonsei U., Seoul, 1955-57, MD, 1961. Diplomate Am. Bd. Neurology and Psychiatry. Rotating intern Sibley Meml. Hosp., Washington, 1964-65; neurology resident Pa. Hosp., Phila., 1965-68; psychiatry resident Ancora Psychiat. Hosp., Hammonton, N.J., 1968-70, neurologist in charge, 1970—, asst. med. dir., 1972-88; clin. asst. prof. Robert Wood Johnson Med. Sch., Camden, N.J.; cons. in neurology West Jersey Hosp., Berlin, 1971, Vineland (N.J.) Devel. Ctr., 1971-87; cons. in neuropsychiatry Cumberland County Guidance Ctr., Millvile, N.J., 1971-86. With Korean Army, 1962-63. Named Outstanding Asian Am. N.J. Asian Am. Heritage Counsel, Hackestown, N.J., 1994. Mem. Am. Acad. Neurology, Am. Psychiat. Assn., Am. Electroencephalography Assn., The Capitol Hist. Soc., Korean Am. Assn. So. N.J. (pres. 1988-91), The Fedn. of Korean Am. Assn. N.J. (pres. 1991-93). Achievements include establishment of Korean Language Course at Rutgers U. Avocations: gardening, classical music apreciation, fishing, car repair. Home: 7 Pine Acres Dr Medford NJ 08055-9578 Office: 228 Kings Hwy E Haddonfield NJ 08033-1913

LEE, YOUNG JACK, federal agency administrator; b. Seoul, Republic of Korea, Feb. 25, 1942; came to U.S., 1969; s. Kyung Ho and Taekyo (Chung) L.; m. Kiran Jung, Mar. 31, 1967; children: Hyung Joo, Taejoo J., Minjoo L. BEE, Seoul Nat. U., 1964; MS in Stats., Ohio State U., 1972, PhD in Stats., 1974. Asst. prof. U. Md., College Park, 1974-79; math. statistician NIH, Bethesda, Md., 1979-89, br. chief, 1989—. Mem. Am. Statis. Soc., Clin. Trial Soc., Biometrics Soc. Office: NIH Bldg 6100 Rm 7B13 Bethesda MD 20892

LEE, YUNG-KEUN, physicist, educator; b. Seoul, Korea, Sept. 26, 1929; came to U.S., 1953, naturalized, 1968; s. Kwang-Soo and Young-Sook (Hur) L.; m. Ock-Kyung Pai, Oct. 25, 1958; children—Ann, Arnold, Sara, Sylvia, Clara. B.A., Johns Hopkins, 1956; M.S., U. Chgo., 1957; Ph.D., Columbia, 1961. Research scientist Columbia U., N.Y.C., 1961-64; prof. physics Johns Hopkins U., Balt., 1964—; vis. mem. staff Los Alamos Sci. Lab., 1971; vis. researcher Institut Scis. Nucléaires, Grenoble, France, 1975; cons. Idaho Nat. Engring. Lab., 1988—. Contbr. articles to profl. jours. Mem. Am. Phys. Soc. Democrat. Methodist. Club: Johns Hopkins. Home: 1318 Denby Rd Baltimore MD 21286-1627 Office: Johns Hopkins U 34th and Charles Sts Baltimore MD 21218

LEEB, CHARLES SAMUEL, clinical psychologist; b. San Francisco, July 18, 1945; s. Sidney Herbert and Dorothy Barbara (Fishstrom) L.; m. Storme Lynn Gilkey, Apr. 28, 1984; children: Morgan Evan, Spencer Douglas. BA in Psychology, U. Calif.-Davis, 1967; MS in Counseling and Guidance, San Diego State U., 1970; PhD in Edn. and Psychology, Claremont Grad. Sch., 1973. Assoc. So. Regional Dir. Mental Retardation Ctr., Las Vegas, Nev., 1976-79; pvt. practice, Las Vegas, 1978-79; dir. biofeedback and athletics Menninger Found., Topeka, 1979-82, dir. children's div. biofeedback and psychophysiology ctr. The Menninger Found., 1979-82; pvt. practice, Claremont, Calif., 1982—; dir. of psychol. svcs. Horizon Hosp., 1986-88; dir. adolescent chem. dependency and children's program Charter Oak Hosp., Covina, Calif., 1989-91; founder, chief exec. officer Rsch. and Treatment Inst., Claremont, 1991—; lectr. in field. Contbr. articles to profl. jours. Mem. Am. Psychol. Assn., Calif. State Psychol. Assn. Office: 937 W Foothill Blvd Ste D Claremont CA 91711-3358

LEEBERN, DONALD M., distilled beverage executive; b. 1938. Pres. Georgia Crown Distributing, Columbus, Ga., 1960—. Office: Georgia Crown Distributing PO Box 7908 Columbus GA 31908-7908*

LEECH, CHARLES RUSSELL, JR., lawyer; b. Coshocton, Ohio, July 29, 1930; s. Charles Russell and Edna (Henry) L.; m. Patricia Ann Tubaugh, June 20, 1953; children—Charles Russell III, Timothy David (dec.), Wendy Ann. A.B. cum laude, Kenyon Coll., 1952; J.D., Ohio State U., 1955; M.A., U. Toledo, 1969. Bar: Ohio 1955. Assoc. Fuller & Henry P.L.L. and predecessor firms, Toledo, 1957-64; ptnr. Fuller & Henry and predecessor firms, Toledo, 1964—. Mng. editor: Ohio State Law Jour., 1955. Mem. exec. com. alumni council Kenyon Coll., 1967-72, trustee coll., 1974-80. Served with USNR, 1955-57. Fellow Ohio State Bar Found.; mem. Am., Ohio, Toledo bar assns., Kenyon Coll. Alumni Assn. Maumee Valley (past pres.), Beta Theta Pi, Phi Delta Phi. Republican. Home: 10953 Springbrook Ct Whitehouse OH 43571-9674 Office: 1 SeaGate 17th Fl Toledo OH 43603-2088

LEECH, JAMES WILLIAM, technology company executive; b. St. Boniface, Man., Can., June 12, 1947; s. George Clarence and Mary Elizabeth (Gibson) L.; m. Jacqueline Roberts Hilton; children: Jennifer Hilton, Joanna Marjorie, James Andrew Douglas. BS in Math. and Physics with hons., Royal Mil. Coll. Can., 1964; MBA, Queen's U., Can., 1973. Exec. asst. to pres. Commerce Capital Corp., Ltd., Montreal, Que., Can., 1973-74, v.p., 1974-75; exec. v.p. Commerce Capital Trust Co., Calgary, Alta., Can., 1976-78; sr. v.p. Eaton/Bay Fin. Services Ltd., Toronto, Ont., Can., 1979; pres., bd. dirs. Unicorp Canada Corp., Toronto, 1979-88; pres., CEO, bd. dirs. Union Energy, Inc., Toronto, 1985-93, Disys Corp., Toronto, 1993—; bd. dirs. Harris Steel Group, Inc., 20/20 Fin. Corp., Winpak Ltd. Vice chmn. adv. coun. sch. bus. Queens U., 1979-83, mem. gen. coun., 1978—, mem. investment com. bd. trustees, 1980—, trustee, 1984—, mem. fund coun., 1988—; bd. dirs., chmn., pres., mem. exec. com. Can. Stage Co., 1989-94; bd. dirs. Toronto Arts Coun., 1994—. D.I. McLeod scholar, 1971-73; Seagram rsch. fellow, 1983, Samuel Bronfman Found. fellow, 1973, Transp. Devel. Agy. fellow, 1972. Mem. Young Pres. Orgn. (Upper Can. chpt.), The Nat. Club, Ranchmen's Club, Granite Club, Glencoe Club. United Ch. Can. Home: 70 Garfield Ave, Toronto, ON Canada M4T 1E9 Office: Disys Corp, No 10 Airport Sq, 2600 Skymark Ave, Mississauga, ON Canada L4W 5B2

LEECH, JOHN DALE, lawyer, health care/corporate consultant; b. Cleve., Apr. 3, 1939; s. George Alfred and Mary Virginia (Merrell) L.; m. Patricia Jeanne Higgins, July 15, 1961; children: Kathryn, Carolyn, Krista, Karlyn. BA with honors, Williams Coll., 1961; LLB, Duke U., 1964. Bar: Ohio 1964, U.S. Dist. Ct. (no. and ea. dists.) Ohio 1965, U.S. Ct. Appeals (6th cir.) 1968, U.S. Ct. Appeals (4th cir.) 1974, U.S. Supreme Ct. 1988. Assoc. Arter & Hadden, Cleve., 1964-72; ptnr. Calfee, Halter & Griswold, Cleve., 1972-95, mem. exec. com., 1989-92, of counsel, 1996—; chmn. health care law sect., antitrust. Councilman, pres. coun. Mayfield Village, Ohio, 1970-74, mayor, 1974-75; trustee Regional Income Tax Agy., Cuyahoga County, Ohio, 1974-75; pres. Hillcrest Hosp., Cleve., 1980-84, chmn. bd., 1986-88; bd. dirs. Cleve. Dialysis Ctr., 1984-89; del. Congress Hosp. Trustees, Chgo., 1986-94; chmn., trustee Am. Hosp. Assn., 1993-95, mem. exec. com., trustee various coms., Chgo., 1987-95, bd. mentor, 1984—; testimony House Ways and Means Subcom., 1987, 93; trustee sec. Health Hill Hosp., 1988—. Mem. ABA (various coms., antitrust and healthcare sects.), Soc. Ohio Hosp. Attys., Ohio Bar Assn., Greater Cleve. Bar Assn., Cleve. Country Club, Union Club. Republican. Avocations: golf, tennis, photography, reading, hiking. Home: 10149 Cedar Rd Chesterland OH 44026-3301 Office: Calfee Halter & Griswold 800 Superior Ave E Ste 1800 Cleveland OH 44114-2601

LEECH, NOYES ELWOOD, lawyer, educator; b. Ambler, Pa., Aug. 1, 1921; s. Charles S. and Margaret Owens (Reid) L.; m. Louise Ann Gallagher, Apr. 19, 1954; children: Katharine, Gwyneth. AB, U. Pa., 1943, JD, 1948. Bar: Pa. 1949. Assoc. Dechert, Price & Rhoads (and predecessors), Phila., 1948-49, 51-53; mem. faculty dept. law U. Pa., Phila., 1949-57; prof. U. Pa., 1957-78, Ferdinand Wakeman Hubbell prof. law, 1978-85, William A. Schnader prof. law, 1985-86, prof. emeritus, 1986—. Co-author: The International Legal System, 3d edit., 1988; gen. editor: Jour. Comparative Bus. and Capital Market Law, 1978-86. Mem. Order of Coif, Phi Beta Kappa. Office: U Pa Law Sch 3400 Chestnut St Philadelphia PA 19104-6204

LEE-DAVIS, LAURA MAE, mental health nurse; b. Miami, July 3, 1943; d. Ellison Lee and Willie Bell (Boyd) Fears; m. Isaac Davis; 1 child, Tracy Lee. Diploma, Dayton Sch. Practical Nursing, 1962; ADN, Cen. Tex. Coll., Killeen, 1972; student, U. Mary Hardin Baylor. Cert. psychiat. and mental health nurse ANCC; cert. alcohol and drug abuse counselor, social worker. Nurse VA Ctr., Dayton, Ohio, 1968; nurse, gynecol. and med.-surg. Scott and White Hosp., Temple, Tex., 1972-73; psychiat. nurse Olin E. Teague VA Ctr., Temple, 1983; nurse, substance abuse therapist Ctrl. Counties Ctr. for Mental Health and Retardation Svcs., Killeen and Temple, 1973-91; program adminstr. I, Ctrl. Counties Ctr. for Mental Health and Retardation Svcs., Killeen, 1991—. Mem. ANA, Order Eastern Star.

LEEDER, ELLEN LISMORE, language and literature educator, literary critic; b. Vedado, Havana, Cuba, July 8, 1931; came to U.S., 1959; d. Thomas and Josefina (Jorge) Lismore; m. Robert Henry Leeder, Dec. 20, 1957 (dec.); 1 child, Thomas Henry. D of Pedagogy, U. Havana, Cuba, 1955; MA, U. Miami, 1966, PhD, 1973. Lang. tchr. St. George's Sch., Havana, 1952-59; from part-time instr. to full prof. Spanish Barry U., Miami Shores, Fla., 1960-75, prof. Spanish, 1975—, chmn. dept. for lang., 1975-76, coord. of Fgn. Lang., 1976-89; dir. Spanish immersion program, 1986-88; part-time prof. Miami-Dade C.C., 1974-75; vis. prof. U. Madrid, 1982; prof. Forspro Program Studies Abroad, 1989, 90; cons. HEH, 1981-83; judge Asiación Criticos y Comentaristas del Arte, Miami, 1985—; judge Silver Knight Awards, 1979-83; oral examiner juror Dade County Pub. Schs., Miami, 1986-87. Author: El Desarraigo en Las Novelas de Angel María de Lera, 1978, Justo Sierra y el Mar, 1979, Dimensión Existencial en la Narrativa de Lera, 1992. Bd. dirs. Vis. Nurse Assn., 1978-80. Mem. MLA, South Atlantic MLA, Am. Coun. Tchg. Fgn. Langs., Am. Assn. Tchrs. Spanish and Portuguese (pres. 1978-84, v.p. 1984-87, pres. Southeastern Fla. chpt.), Fla. Fgn. Assn., Círculo de Cultura Panamericano, Assn. Internat. Hispanistas, Assn. Cubana de Mujeres Universitarias (pres.), Cuban Women Assn., Phi Alpha Theta, Kappa Delta Pi, Sigma Delta Xi, Alpha Mu Gamma, Coral Gables Country Club. Avocations: tennis, piano, singing, numismatics. Home: 830 SW 101st Ave Miami FL 33174-2836 Office: Barry Univ 11300 NE 2d Ave Miami FL 33161-6628

LEEDOM, ERIN, dancer. Attended, Am. Ballet Sch., Joffrey Ballet Sch. Dancer Oakland (Calif.) Ballet, until 1988; dancer Ballet West, Salt Lake City, 1988-90, prin. artist, 1990—. Dance performances include Giselle, Coppelia, Death and the Maiden, Green Table Cake Walk, Daphnis and Cloe, Romeo & Juliet, Anna Karenina, The Dream, The Nutcracker, The Gilded Bat, Sleeping Beauty, Rosalinda, Cinderella. Office: Ballet West 50 W 200 S Salt Lake City UT 84101-1642

LEEDOM, JOHN NESBETT, distribution company executive, state senator; b. Dallas, July 27, 1921; s. Floyd H. and Gladys Lorraine (Nesbett) L.; m. Betty Lee Harvey, Mar. 17, 1956; children: Joann, Judy, Eddie Kennedy, Danny Kennedy, Linda, John Nesbett. B.S.E.E., Rice U., 1943. Engr., Naval Research Lab., Washington, 1943-45; asst. sales mgr. Sprague Products Co., North Adams, Mass., 1945-50; founder, chief exec. officer Wholesale Electronic Supply, Inc., Dallas, 1950—; pres. Levco, Inc., 1973—; mem. Tex. Senate, 1980—. Chmn. Dallas County Republican Com., 1962-66, mem. state exec. com., 1966-68; mem. Dallas City Council, 1975-80. Author The Group and You. Served to lt. (j.g.), USNR, 1943-45. Mem. Nat. Electronic Distbrs. Assn. (pres. 1971-72), Nat. Assn. Wholesale Distbrs. (pres. 1972-73), IEEE, Mil. Order World Wars, Navy League, Tau Beta Pi. Office: 2809 Ross Ave Dallas TX 75201-2524

LEEDS, CHARLES ALAN, publishing executive; b. Mpls., Aug. 20, 1951; s. Charles Phillips and Irene (Pollard) L.; m. Karen Sue Biggs-Leeds, Aug. 2, 1986; children: Charles Austin, Tyler Dixon. BA, Drake U., 1973, MPA, 1978. Mktg. coord. Register and Tribune Syndicate Inc., Des Moines, Iowa, 1973-79; sales mgr. Washington Post Writers Group, Washington, 1979-89; pres. and editorial dir. L.A. Times Washington Post News Svc., Washington, 1989—; asst. professorial lectr. George Washington U., Washington, 1986, 88. Mem. nat. adv. bd. Sch. Journalism and Mass Comm. Drake U., 1996—. Recipient Best in Bus. award Am. Journalism Rev., 1995. Mem. Internat. Press Inst. (assoc.), Soc. Profl. Journalists, Sigma Delta Chi, Kappa Tau Alpha. Presbyterian. Avocations: jogging, tennis. Home: 4714 17th St N Arlington VA 22207-2031 Office: LA Times-WA Post News Svc 1150 15th St NW Washington DC 20071-0001

LEEDS, DOUGLAS BRECKER, advertising agency executive, theatre producer; b. N.Y.C., Mar. 15, 1947; s. Richard Henry and Nancy Ann (Brecker) L.; m. Christine Castler, Jan. 14, 1980; 1 child, Victoria Brecker. BS, Babson Coll., 1970. V.p., dir. Auto Data Systems, Inc., Natick, Mass., 1970-72; dir. leasing Beacon Cos., Inc., Boston, 1972-77; account exec. Thomson-Leeds Co., Inc. div. The WPP Group, N.Y.C., 1977-84, exec. v.p., 1985-88, pres., 1988—, chief exec. officer, 1989—; chmn. ednl. rels. com. Point of Purchase Advt. Inst., 1986—, elected bd. dirs., 1989, vice chmn., 1994—; bd. dirs. Checker Board Found. Co-producer: (Broadway musical) Streetheat, 1985; assoc. producer: (Broadway play) Sleight of Hand, 1986; patentee in field. Chmn., founder Lobby Gallery Assocs. Whitney Mus. Am. Art, N.Y.C., 1983-90; trustee Guild Hall of East Hampton (Mus. and Theatre), 1990-92, John Drew Theatre; chmn. men's com. Boys Club N.Y., 1989; bd. dirs. chmn. Friends Henry Street Settlement House, N.Y.C., 1977-80; trustee Whitney Mus. Am. Art, 1992—, co-chmn. membership com., 1993—, Worcester Acad., 1982-85, Babson Coll., 1979-86, also co-chmn. devel. and pub. affairs com.; spl. projects com., The Soc. of Meml. Sloan-Kettering Cancer Ctr.; bd. dirs. Am. Theatre Wing, 1991—, mem. adminstrn. com. Tony Awards. Mem. Babson Coll. Alumni Assn. (bd. dirs., v.p. 1975-79), Union Club, Doubles Club, Royal Tennis Court Club (Middlesex, Eng.). Office: Thomson-Leeds Co Inc 450 Park Ave S New York NY 10016-7320

LEEDS, LILO J., publishing executive; b. Frankfurt, Germany, Feb. 8, 1928; came to U.S., 1939; d. Sigmund and Caroline (Hirsch) Schott; m. Gerard G. Leeds, Apr. 1, 1951; children: Michael, Richard, Daniel, Gregory, Jennifer. BS, Queens Coll., 1948; MA, Stonybrook U., 1979. Mathematician Bell Telephone Labs., N.Y.C.; co-owner Leeds Co., Great Neck, N.Y., Data Device Co., Long Island, N.Y.; co-chair CMP Publs., Inc., Manhasset, N.Y., 1971—. Pres. Great Neck North Sr. High PTA, 1971-72; sec. United Parent Tchr. coun., Great Neck, 1973-74; trustee North Shore Hosp., Manhasset, 1987-92; bd. dirs. SUNY-Old Westbury, 1988—, Manhasset Great Neck Community Child Care Partnership, North Shore Child and Family Guidance Ctr.; mem. Nassau County Day Care Task Force, 1987—; co-chair Corp. Initiative for Child Care/Elder Care, bd. dirs. Day Care Coun.; day care advocate Helping Youth at Risk; co-chair Inst. for Cmty. Devel. Democrat. Avocation: skiing. Office: CMP Publs Inc 600 Community Dr Manhasset NY 11030-3847

LEEDS, MARGARET ANN, assistant principal; b. Memphis, Tex., Sept. 14, 1934; d. Roy Alvin and Abbie Cordelia (O'Neal) Massey; m. Charles Stanton Leeds, Nov. 3, 1959 (div. 1965). BA, Baylor U., 1956; MLA, U. So. Calif., 1976. Cert. tchr. secondary theatre arts, French, phys. edn., English. Tchr. Rexford Jr. and Sr. H.S., Beverly Hills, Calif., 1958-60; substitute tchr. Beverly Hills Unified Sch. Dist., 1960-66; tchr. phys. edn. Beverly Hills H.S., 1966-89, chair dept. phys. edn., 1981-89, asst. prin., 1989—, coach various sports incl. volleyball, gymnastics, fencing, 1966-89; cons. Calif. Dept. Edn., 1986—; ofcl. volleyball ofcl. Nat. Assn. Girls and Women's Sports, 1975-80;

presenter sessions to various confs., 1985—; conductor insvc. tng. workshops. Author: Beverly Hills Unified School District Physical Education Scope and Sequence, 1988, Beverly Hills High School Health Fitness Manual, 1987, Fight Back: A Woman's Guide to Self Defense, 1978; contbr. articles to profl. jours.; prodr. video tapes: Implementing Health Fitness in Schools, 1987, Physical Education is Alive and Well in Beverly Hills, California, 1986. Cons. Calif. Gov.'s Coun. on Phys. Fitness and Sports, 1993—; adv. bd. L.A. UNICEF, 1993—; ham radio operator Beverly Hills Disaster Comm. Sys. Vol., 1994—, L.A. County Disaster Comm. Sys. Vol., 1994—. Recipient Calif. Educator award Calif. Dept. Edn., 1987. Mem. NEA, AAHPERD (reviewer Jour. Health, Phys. Edn., Recreation and Dance 1989—, Calif. phys. best coord. 1988—, pub. rels. coord. 1987-91), Calif. Tchrs. Assn., Beverly Hills Edn. Assn. (pres. 1969-70), Calif. Assn. Health, Phys. Edn., Recreation and Dance (pres. unit 401 1986-88, dir. CORE Project 1987-91, pub. rels. chair 1987—, adminstrn. and supervision chair phys. edn. adv. com. 1994—, Honor award 1993, Outstanding Secondary Phys. Educator 1987, Calif. Phys. Educator of Yr. 1985). Baha'i Faith. Avocations: travel, folk art collecting, marathon running/jogging, backpacking, reading. Home: 1557 S Beverly Glen Blvd Los Angeles CA 90024-6141 Office: Beverly Hills High Sch 241 S Moreno Dr Beverly Hills CA 90212-3639

LEEDS, ROBERT, dentist; b. Newark, Sept. 8, 1930; s. William David and Gertrude (Greene) L.; m. Joyce Sumner, Nov. 28, 1960; children: Deborah Joyce, Robin Elizabeth. AA, U. Fla., 1950; DDS, Emory U., 1954. Gen. practice dentistry, Miami, Fla. Patentee herpes simplex method of therapy. Served to maj. USAF, 1954-56. Mem. ADA, East Coast Dental Assn., Miami Dental Soc., South Dade Dental Soc. Club: Coral Gables Country (Fla.). Lodges: Shriners, Masons. Avocations: sailing; water skiing; snow skiing. Office: 6437 Bird Rd Miami FL 33155-4827

LEEDS, ROBERT LEWIS, JR., marketing and management educator; b. N.Y.C., Feb. 9, 1930; s. Robert Lewis and Elisabeth (Bandler) L.; m. Irene Osterweil, July 9, 1958 (div.); children: Leslie Anne, Robert Lewis III; m. Joan Wrigley, Sept. 27, 1984. B.A., Amherst Coll., 1951; M.B.A., U. Pa., 1953. With Manhattan Industries, Inc. (formerly Manhattan Shirt Co.), N.Y.C., 1955-76; v.p. marketing Manhattan Industries, Inc., 1958-65, exec. v.p., 1965-66, chmn. bd., chief exec. officer, 1966-74; also dir.; v.p. corporate devel. Benrus Corp., 1976-78; adv. bd. Mfrs. Hanover Trust Co., 1973-74; part-time faculty Bklyn. Coll., 1979, Pace U., 1979-81, Marymount Manhattan Coll., 1982—; Disting. lectr. mktg. and mgmt., dir. Exec. MBA Program, U. South Fla., 1982—. Bd. dirs. Hillside Hosp., Glen Oaks, N.Y.; mem. mktg. com. Morton Plant Hosp., 1984—Served with USAF, 1953-55. Recipient award for Civic Endeavour Textile Vets. Assn., 1968; award Young Men's Assn., 1971. Mem. Men's Fashion Assn. (chmn. bd. 1972-74, dir.). Home: 215 Midway Is Clearwater FL 34630-2316

LEEDY, DANIEL LONEY, ecologist; b. Butler, Ohio, Feb. 17, 1912; s. Charles Monroe and Bernice Camilla (Loney) L.; m. Barbara E. Sturges, Nov. 25, 1945 (dec. Mar. 12, 1988); children: Robert Raymond, Kathleen Eleanor; m. Virginia Lee Bittenbender, Sept. 22, 1989. A.B. with honors, Miami U., Oxford, Ohio, 1934, B.Sc., 1935; M.Sc., Ohio State U., 1938, Ph.D., 1940. Asst. geology and zoology depts. Miami U., 1933-35; instr. wildlife mgmt. Ohio State U., 1940-42; leader Ohio Coop. Wildlife Research Unit, 1945-48; biologist charge coop. wildlife research units U.S. Fish and Wildlife Service, Washington, 1949-57; mem. biol. sci. com. Dept. Agr. Grad. Sch., 1950-75; pres. Wildlife Soc., 1952, exec. sec., 1953-57; chief br. wildlife research U.S. Fish and Wildlife Service, 1957-63; chief div. research Bur. Outdoor Recreation, Dept. Interior, 1963-65; water resources research scientist Office Water Resources Research, 1965-74; ret., 1974; sr. scientist Nat. Inst. Urban Wildlife, Columbia, Md., 1975-95. Contbr. over 100 articles to profl. publs. Served to capt. USAAF, 1942-45. Decorated Bronze medal.; Recipient cert. of merit Nash Conservation Awards program, 1953; Am. Motors Conservation award, 1958; U.S. Dept. Interior Disting. Service award, 1972; Disting. Alumni award Ohio State U., 1975; Daniel L. Leedy Urban Wildlife Conservation award established in his honor Nat. Inst. Urban Wildlife, 1985. Fellow AAAS; mem. Wildlife Soc. (hon., Aldo Leopold award for disting. service to wildlife conservation 1983), Am. Ornithologists Union (elective mem.), Wilson Ornithol. Soc., Am. Fisheries Soc., Sigma Xi. Clubs: Field Biologists, Cosmos (Washington). Home: 12401 Ellen Ct Silver Spring MD 20904-2905

LEEDY, ROBERT ALLAN, SR., retired lawyer; b. Portland, Oreg., Aug. 5, 1909; s. Harry E. and Loretta (Viles) L.; m. Annapauline Rea, Sept. 14, 1935; children: Douglas Harry, Robert Allan, Jr. J.D., U. Oreg., 1933. Bar: Oreg. 1933. Practiced in Portland, 1934-86; former mem. firm Bullivant, Houser, Bailey, Pendergrass, and Hoffman, ret.; U.S. commr., 1943-56; Mem. Oreg. Bar Examiners, 1947-48, chmn., 1949. Chancellor Episcopal Diocese Oreg., 1970-83. Mem. ABA, Oreg. Bar Assn. (pres. 1953), Multnomah County Bar Assn., Western Bar Conf. (pres. 1952), Alpha Tau Omega, Phi Delta Phi. Home: 2839 NW Fairfax Ter Portland OR 97210-2805 Office: Pioneer Towers Portland OR 97204

LEEF, JAMES LEWIS, biology educator, immunology research executive; b. San Francisco, Mar. 6, 1937; married, 1964; 4 children. BA, U. Calif., San Francisco, 1967; PhD in Biology, U. Tenn., 1974. Sr. investigator cryobiology, head Malaria Rsch. dept. Biomed. Rsch. Inst., Rockville, Md., 1976-82, exec. dir., 1982—; cons. Sci. and Indsl. Rsch. and Devel. Co., 1967-69; guest scientist Navy Med. Rsch. Inst., 1976—. U. Ill. fellow, 1973-76. Mem. AAAS, Soc. Cryobiology, Tissue Culture Assn., Am. Assn. Tissue Banks, N.Y. Acad. Sci. Achievements include research in malariology; mechanisms of freezing injury; study of various developmental stages of malaria and schistosomiasis parasites as antigens in developing a malaria and schistosomiasis vaccine and preservation of these forms at low temperatures. Office: Biomed Rsch Inst 12111 Parklawn Dr Rockville MD 20852*

LEEFE, JAMES MORRISON, architect; b. N.Y.C., Aug. 28, 1921; s. Charles Clement and Suzanne (Bernhardt) L.; m. Miriam Danziger, Oct. 31, 1949; 1 dau., Molly Elizabeth. Cert., U.S. Mcht. Marine Acad., 1943; B.Arch., Columbia U., 1950. Practice architecture San Francisco, 1955-60; chief architect power and indsl. div. Bechtel Inc., San Francisco, 1960-64; prin. urban designer Bechtel Inc., 1974-80; chief architect San Francisco Power div. Bechtel Power Corp., 1980-89; v.p., asst. sec. Bechtel Assos. (P.C.), N.Y., 1978-89; v.p. Bechtel Assos. (P.C.), D.C. and Va., 1978-89; pvt. cons. architect Sausalito, Calif., 1989—; ptnr. Leefe & Ehrankrantz Architects, San Francisco, 1964-68; v.p. Bldg. Systems Devel. Inc., San Francisco and Washington, 1965-70; also dir.; dir. architecture Giffels Assos. Inc., Detroit, 1971-74; lectr. in architecture Columbia U., 1951-52, U. Calif., Berkeley, 1954-60; mem. faculty U. for Pres's., Young Pres's. Orgn., 1967; adj. prof. U. Detroit, 1971-72; mem. adv. bd. Nat. Clearing House for Criminal Justice Planning and Architecture, 1974-76. Works include Mus. West of Am. Craftsmen's Council, San Francisco, 1964 (Archtl. Record award for interior design 1971), Wells Hydrocombine Dam and Power Generating Facility, Columbia River, Wash., 1965, Boundary Dam, Pend Orielle River, Wash., 1965 (Am. Public Power Assn. honor award 1975), Detroit Automobile Inter-Ins. Exchange Corp. Hdqrs, Dearborn, Mich., 1972 (Detroit chpt. AIA honor award 1975), PPG Industries Research Center, Allison Park, Pa., 1973 (Detroit chpt. AIA honor award 1975, Am. Inst. Steel Constrn. Archtl. award of excellence 1975, Mich. Soc. Architects honor award 1976), Gen. Electric Research Center, Twinsburg, Ohio, 1973 (Detroit chpt. AIA honor award 1977), Appliance Buyers Credit Corp. Hdqrs. Office, Benton Harbor, Mich., 1974 (Engring. Soc. Detroit Design award 1976), Standard Tng. Bldg. Commonwealth Edison, 1989-90, Strybing Arboretum, San Francisco, 1990; contbr. articles to profl. jours.; originator various techniques for analysis of human factors in the working environment. Chmn. bd. Mus. West of Am. Crafts Coun., San Francisco, 1966-68; vice chmn. Franklin (Mich.) Hist. Dist. Commn., 1973-74; trustee So. Marin Land Trust. With U.S. Mcht. Marine, 1942-46. Recipient Hirsh Meml. prize Columbia U., 1950, 1st prize (with Miriam Leefe) Dow Chem. Co. Competition for Interior Design, 1960. Fellow AIA; hon. mem. Internat. Union Architects Working Group Habitat, trustee, So. Marin Land Trust. Home and Office: James Leefe FAIA Architect 131 Spencer Ave Sausalito CA 94965-2022 *I think of architecture as a celebration of life, of the buildings we make for ourselves as stepping stones on the path of history. This forces me to be an optimist, always searching to find a manifestation of the joy of being in my work.*

LEEGE, DAVID CALHOUN, political scientist, educator; b. Elkhart, Ind., May 18, 1937; s. Harold Martin and Nellie Josephine (Bliss) L.; m. Patricia Ann Schad, June 8, 1963; children—David McChesney, Lissa Maria, Kurt Johannes. B.A., Valparaiso U., 1959; postgrad., U. Chgo., 1959-60; Ph.D., Ind. U., 1965. Instr. social sci. Concordia Coll., River Forest, Ill., 1962-64; asst. prof. polit. sci., dir. pub. opinion survey unit U. Mo., Columbia, 1964-68; assoc. prof., dir. survey research center SUNY, Buffalo, 1968-70; assoc. prof. U. Ill., Chgo., 1970-72; prof. U. Ill., 1972-76, head dept., 1972-73; prof. govt. and internat. studies U. Notre Dame, Ind., 1976—; dir. center for study of contemporary society U. Notre Dame, 1976-85, dir. London program, 1982, dir. program for research on religion, church and society, 1984—; dir. Hesburgh Program in Pub. Service, 1987-92; program dir. for polit. sci. NSF, 1974-76; vis. prof. York U., Toronto, Ont., Can., 1970, U. Mich., 1971, 73, U. Leuven, Belgium, 1980, Cath. U. Am., 1985-86. Author: (with Wayne Francis) Political Research, 1974, (with Lyman Kellstedt) Rediscovering the Religious Factor in American Politics, 1993; editor: The Missouri Poll, 1965-68, (with Joseph Gremillion) The Notre Dame Study of Catholic Parish Life Report Series, 1984-89; contbr. articles to profl. jours. Mem. bd. overseers Am. Nat. Election Studies, 1990—, chair, 1994—; del. ICORE, 1993—; mem. coun. ICPSR, 1966-69. Mem. Am. Polit. Sci. Assn. (sect officer, program com., chmn. task force), Midwest Polit. Sci. Assn. (chair nominating com., coun., program co-chair). Lutheran. Home: 51971 S Shoreham Ct South Bend IN 46637-1358 Office: U Notre Dame Dept Govt Notre Dame IN 46556

LEEHEY, PATRICK, mechanical and ocean engineering educator; b. Waterloo, Iowa, Oct. 27, 1921; s. Florance Patrick and Monica (White) L.; m. Dorothy Feltus, Feb. 3, 1944; children—Patrick M., David J., Christopher M., Jonathan R., Susan E., Jennifer A. B.S., U.S. Naval Acad., 1942; postgrad., U.S. Naval Postgrad. Sch., 1946-47; Ph.D., Brown U., 1950. Commd. ensign USN, 1942, advanced through grades to capt., 1962; hydrofoil project officer, 1951-53; design supt. Puget Sound Naval Shipyard, 1956-58; head ship silencing br. USN Bur. Ships, 1958-63; head acoustics lab. David Taylor Model Basin, 1963-64; ret., 1964; assoc. prof. naval architecture MIT, 1964-66, prof., 1966-71, prof. mech. and ocean engring., 1971—; liaison scientist ONR, London, 1984-85; cons. Bath Iron Works, Rand Corp., Litton Industries, Office Naval Research. Mem. Am. Math. Soc., Acoustical Soc. Am., Am. Soc. Naval Engrs. Patentee in field. Home: 48 Bellevue Rd Swampscott MA 01907-1517 Office: MIT Rm 3-262 Cambridge MA 02139

LEEKLEY, JOHN ROBERT, lawyer; b. Phila., Aug. 27, 1943; s. Thomas Briggs and Dorothy (O'Hora) L.; m. Karen Kristin Myers, Aug. 28, 1965; children: John Thomas, Michael Dennis. BA, Boston Coll., 1965; LLB, Columbia U., 1968. Bar: N.Y. 1968, Mich. 1976. Assoc. Curtis, Mallet-Prevost, Colt & Mosle, N.Y.C., 1968-69, Davis Polk & Wardwell, N.Y.C., 1969-76; asst. corp. counsel Masco Corp., Taylor, Mich., 1976-77, corp. counsel, 1977-79, v.p., corp. counsel, 1979-88, v.p., gen. counsel, 1988—. Bd. visitors Columbia U. Law Sch., N.Y.C., 1994-96; mem. Freedom Twp. Bd. Tax Appeals, 1984-85. Mem. ABA (com. long range issues affecting bus. practice 1976-96), Mich. State Bar Assn. Democrat. Roman Catholic. Avocations: Percheron horse breeding, hunting, fishing, outdoor activities. Office: Masco Corp 21001 Van Born Rd Taylor MI 48180-1340

LEEMAN, CAVIN PHILIP, psychiatrist, educator; b. N.Y.C., Jan. 16, 1932; s. Stephen and May (Cavin) L.; m. Susan Epstein, Aug. 11, 1957 (div. 1983); children: Eve, Jennifer, Raphael; m. Diane Leenheer Zimmerman, Feb. 18, 1984. AB, Harvard U., 1952, MD, 1959. Diplomate Am. Bd. Psychiatry and Neurology. Intern in medicine Mass. Gen. Hosp., Boston, 1959-60; resident in psychiatry Mass. Mental Health Ctr., Boston, 1960-62; resident in psychiatry Beth Israel Hosp., Boston, 1962-64, asst. in psychiatry, 1964-66; instr. in psychiatry Harvard Med. Sch., Boston, 1966-75; chief of psychiatry Framingham (Mass.) Union Hosp., 1973-83; lectr. Harvard Med. Sch., 1975-83; chief of psychiatry VA Med. Ctr., Bklyn., 1983-85; clin. dir. psychiatry Univ. Hosp., Bklyn., 1985-96; clin. prof. psychiatry SUNY Health Sci. Ctr., Bklyn., 1984-96, clin. prof. psychiatry emeritus, 1996—; assoc. clin. prof. Boston U. Sch. Medicine, 1974-83; clin. prof. psychiatry SUNY Health Sci. Ctr., Bklyn., 1984—, faculty assoc., divsn. humanities in medicine, 1994—; mem. active med. staff Univ. Hosp., Bklyn., 1985—. Contbr. articles to profl. publs. Fellow Am. Psychiat. Assn. (life); mem. Assn. for Acad. Psychiatry, Am. Assn. Gen. Hosp. Psychiatrists, Acad. Psychosomatic Medicine, N.Y. Acad. Medicine, Physicians for Social Responsibility, Physicians for Human Rights, Soc. Bioethics Cons. Office: 344 W 23rd St Ste 1B New York NY 10011 Office: 344 W 23d St # 1B New York NY 10011

LEEMANS, WIM PIETER, physicist; b. Gent, Belgium, June 7, 1963. BS in Elec. Engring., Free U. Brussels, 1985; MS in Elec. Engring., UCLA, 1987, Ph.D. in Elec. Engring., 1991. Teaching asst. UCLA, 1986-87, rsch. asst., 1987-91; staff scientist Lawrence Berkeley Lab., Berkeley, Calif., 1991—; group leader expt. beam physics group, 1994—; presenter numerous seminars. Contbr. articles to profl. jours. Recipient Simon Ramo awd., Am. Physical Soc., 1992; grad. scholar IEEE Nuclear and Plasma Soc., 1987. Fellow Belgian Am. Ednl. Found., Francqui Found.; mem. IEEE (Nuclear and Plasma scis. soc. grad. scholar 1987), Soc. Photo-Optical Instrument Engrs., Am. Phys. Soc., Royal Flemish Engrs. Soc. Achievements include research in high intensity laser-plasma interaction, interaction of relativistic electrons with lasers and plasmas, novel radiation sources, advanced accelerator concepts, non-linear dynamics of free electron lasers. Office: Lawrence Berkeley Lab Divsn Accelerator Fusion Rsch 1 Cyclotron Road MS 71-259 Berkeley CA 94720

LEENER, JACK JOSEPH, advertising executive; b. Sierra Madre, Calif., Apr. 18, 1926; s. Edward I. and Gertrude (Krushen) L.; m. Anne Gertrude Frank, Sept. 12, 1948; children: Kathy Ellen, Craig Ellis, Douglas Scott. B.A., UCLA. Publicity dir. Los Angeles Jaycees, 1947-49; account exec. West Marquis, Inc., Los Angeles, 1949-54; account supr. Stromberger, LaVene, McKenzie, Los Angeles, 1954-59; adv. dir. Tidewater (Getty) Oil Co., Los Angeles, 1959-64; exec. v.p. Eisaman, Johns & Laws, Los Angeles, 1964—. Bd. dirs. UCLA Bruin Bench, Los Angeles, 1950—, pres., 1962; bd. dirs. Sherman Oaks Little League, Los Angeles, 1964-77, pres., 1968; bd. dirs. Hollywood YMCA, Los Angeles, 1980-81, Hollywood Human Services Project, 1983. Served with U.S. Army, 1944-45. Clubs: Western Advt. Golfers (pres. 1958); Milline Club of So. Calif. (Los Angeles) (bd. dirs. 1962-70), So. Calif. Advt. Tennis Soc. (pres. 1988-89). Office: Eisaman Johns & Laws Inc 5700 Wilshire Blvd # 600 Los Angeles CA 90036-3659

LEENEY, ROBERT JOSEPH, newspaper editor; b. New Haven, May 10, 1916; s. Patrick Joseph and Mary Alice (Ross) L.; m. Anne King Coyne, June 28, 1941; children: Robert Joseph, David Coyne, Anne Patricia. Student pub. and pvt. schs.; L.H.D. (hon.), U. New Haven, 1983, Albertus Magnus Coll., 1985. Reporter, book page editor, drama critic New Haven Register, 1940-47, editorial writer, 1947-55; editor editorial page New Haven Jour.-Courier, New Haven Register, 1956-61, exec. editor, 1961-72, editor, 1972-81, editor emeritus, 1981, v.p., dir., 1970—; sec. Register Pub. Co.; dir. Conn. Savs. Bank.; examiner adminstrv. reports, editor Ofcl. Digest State Reports, Conn., 1951-52. Columnist. Conn. pub. info. chmn. Am. Cancer Soc.; v.p. Arts Council Greater New Haven; mem. Conn. Edn. Council, Edn. Commn. of States, Conn. Commn. on Freedom of Info., 1981—; bd. dirs. St. Raphael's Hosp. Found., Long Wharf Theatre, New Haven, 1990; trustee Albertus Magnus Coll., 1984, Conn. Found. Open Govt. Served with USAAF, World War II. Named to New Eng. Journalism Hall of Fame, 1977; recipient Seal of the City award for disting. cmty. svc., 1994. Mem. Nat. Conf. Editl. Writers, Am. Soc. Newspaper Editors, New Eng. Soc. Newspaper Editors (pres. 1961), New Eng. AP News Execs. Assn. (pres. 1977), Conn. Editl. Assn., Conn. Cir. AP (pres.), New Haven C. of C. (v.p., dir., Disting. Svc. award), Outer Circle, N.H. Colony Hist. Soc., Kiwanis, Woodbridge Club, Mory's Club, Quinnipiak Club, Sigma Delta Chi (pres. Conn. chpt. 1963-69). Home: R 69 424 Carrington Hill Rd Bethany CT 06525 Office: New Haven Register 40 Sargent Dr New Haven CT 06511-5918

LEEPA, ALLEN, artist, educator; b. N.Y.C., Jan. 9, 1919; s. Harvey and Esther (Gentle) L. Student (scholar), The New Bauhaus Sch., 1937-38; scholar, Hans Hofmann Sch., 1938-39; B.S., Columbia U., 1942, M.A. (scholar), 1948, Ed.D., 1960. Art instr. Hull Sch., Chgo., 1937-38, Bklyn. Art Center, 1939-40, Met. Mus., N.Y.C., 1940-41, St. Marks Center, N.Y.C., 1941-42; draftsman Acrotorque Co., Conn., 1942, Glen Martin Aircraft, N.Y.C., 1942-44; prof. art Mich. State U., 1945-84, ret. prof. emeritus; mem. Leepa Gallery of Fine Art, Tarpon Springs, Fla., 1987-90. Author: The Challenge of Modern Art, 1949, 95, Abraham Rattner, 1974; contbr.: (anthologies) The New Art, 1966, 68, The Humanitites in Contemporary Life, 1960, Minimal Art; art editor: The Centennial Rev. Arts and Scis. Jour., 1959-62; one man shows Artists Gallery, N.Y.C., 1953, La Cours D'Ingres, Paris, 1961, Artists Mart, Detroit, 1969, Duke U., 1981; group shows include Mus. Modern Art, N.Y.C., 1953, VII Bienal, São Paulo, Brazil, 1963, Prado Mus., Madrid, Spain, 1956, Detroit Inst. Arts, 1948, 50, 56, 80, Pa. Acad. Fine Arts, 1951, 63; represented in permanent collections Mich. State U., Grand Rapids (Mich.) Mus., South Bend (Ind.) Mus.; lifetime work Tampa Mus. Fine Art. Fulbright award to Paris, 1950-51; Ford Found. grantee Brazil, 1970; recipient numerous prizes for paintings including: 1st prize statewide mural competition, Mich., 1983; 1st prize abstract painting Guld Hall Mus., East Hampton, N.Y., 1985. Mem. Mich. Acad. Arts, Scis., Letters. Office: Mich State U Art Dept East Lansing MI 48823

LEEPER, DORIS MARIE, sculptor, painter; b. Charlotte, N.C., Apr. 4, 1929; d. Ernest R. Leeper and Pauline A. (Fry) Leeper Harrison. B.A., Duke U., 1951. With graphic arts dept. Charlotte Engraving, 1951-55; artist, salesperson, designer So. Engraving, Atlanta, 1955-61; mem. adv. panels Fla. Arts Council, 1975-93. One-woman shows include Hunter Mus. Art, Chattanooga, 1968, 75, 79, Jacksonville Art Mus., Fla., 1968, 76, Mint Mus. Art, Charlotte, 1968, 76, Duke U. Mus., Durham, N.C., 1969, High Mus. Art, Atlanta, 1975, Greenville County Mus. Art, S.C., 1976, Columbia Mus. Art, S.C., 1976, Ringling Mus. Art, Sarasota, Fla., 1976, Miss. Mus. Art, Jackson, 1979, Mus. Arts and Scis., Daytona Beach, Fla., 1980, LeMoyne Art Found., Tallahassee, 1980, Anniston Mus., Natural History, Ala., 1980, G. McKenna Gallery, Charlotte, 1983, Foster Harmon Galleries, Sarasota, 1984, Atlantic Ctr. for the Arts, New Smyrna Beach, 1984, Albertson Peterson Gallery, Winter Park, 1993, Cornell Fine Arts Mus., Winter Park, 1995; group shows include Jacksonville Art Mus., 1971-72, 72, Albright-Knox Gallery, Buffalo, 1972-73, Miss. Mus. Art, 1978, Am. Acad. and Inst. Arts and Letters, N.Y.C., 1979, N. Miami Mus., Fla., 1984, Ctr. Arts, Vero Beach, Fla., 1986, Sampson Art Gallery, Stetson U., DeLand, 1990, Cornell Fine Arts Mus., Rollins Coll., Winter Park, 1990, Appalachian State U., Boone, N.C., 1990, 91, 2d Internat. Ephemeral Sculptures Exhbn., Fortaleza, Brazil, 1991, Duncan Gallery of Art, DeLand, 1991, Cummer Gallery of Art, Jacksonville, 1992, Cornell Fine Arts Mus., Rollins Coll., Winter Park, 1992, Samuel P. Harn Mus. of Art, Gainesville, 1993; commns. include Fla. State Legis. Bldg., IBM, Atlanta, Orlando Internat. Airport, Fla., others; represented in permanent collections Hunter Mus. Art, Chattanooga, Jacksonville Art Mus., Columbus Mus. Art, Ohio, Duke U., Durham, Greenville County Mus. Art, Ill. Wesleyan U., Mint Mus. Art, Miss. Mus. Art, Mus. Arts and Scis., Daytona Beach, Nat. Mus. Am. Art, Washington, Stetson U., Deland, Fla., U. S. Fla., Tampa, Wadsworth Athenaeum, Hartford, Conn., others. Founder Atlantic Ctr. for Arts, New Smyrna Beach, Fla., 1977-78, trustee, 1979-86, adv. coun. 1986-92; trustee Mus. Arts and Scis., Daytona Beach, 1977-78, Fla. Conservation Found., 1981-85; mem. adv. commn. Canaveral Nat. Seashore, 1975-85; bd. dirs. Coastal Ednl. Broadcasters, Inc., New Smyrna Beach, 1983-90; mem. internat. adv. bd. La Napoule Art Found., France, 1987-94. Nat. Endowment Arts fellow, 1972; Fla. Fine Arts Council fellow, 1977; Rockefeller Found. fellow, 1977; recipient Humanist Arts award Am. Humanist Assn., 1990, Fla. Arts Recognition award 1993, Outstanding Alumnae award Zeta Tau Alpha, 1994. Avocations: reading; tennis; environmental affairs. Home: 806 N Peninsula Ave New Smyrna Beach FL 32169-2318

LEEPER, HAROLD HARRIS, arbitrator; b. Kansas City, Mo., July 29, 1916; s. Truman Elmer and Bess Mayburn (Harris) L.; m. Maribelle Potts, Sept. 21, 1941; children: Robert Chester, Marilyn Anne. BSBA, U. Mo., 1937; JD, Oklahoma City U., 1956. Bar: Okla. 1957, U.S. Supreme Ct. 1969. Regional pers. officer VA, Oklahoma City, 1946-52; state adminstrv. officer IRS, Oklahoma City, 1952-56; pers. officer FAA, Oklahoma City, 1956-63; from hearing officer to chief hearing officer FAA, Washington, 1963-71; adminstrv. law judge Social Security Adminstrn., Dallas, 1971-73; freelance labor mgmt. arbitrator Dallas, 1974—. Pres., bd. dirs. Way Back House, Inc., Dallas, 1975-77; chmn. pers. com. Wesley Rankin Community Ctr., Dallas, 1989-95. 1st lt. U.S. Army, 1943-46, lt. col. Res. ret. Mem. Fed. Bar Assn. (pres. Dallas chpt. 1982-83), Nat. Acad. Arbitrators (regional chmn. 1990-92), Mil. Order World Wars (comdr. D.C. chpt. 1969-70), Mason, Shriner. Democrat. Methodist. Avocations: golf, sailing, flying, church activities. Home and Office: 6256 Glennox Ln Dallas TX 75214-2144

LEEPER, MICHAEL EDWARD, retired army officer, retired corporation executive; b. Republic, Pa., Jan. 28, 1917; s. Samuel and Elizabeth (Augustine) L.; m. Betty Jane Marshall, June 5, 1943 (dec.); children: Michael E., Richard A., James R.; m. Mary Hoke Austin, July 20, 1974. B.S., U. Pitts., 1940; M.B.A., Stanford U., 1949; grad., Indsl. Coll. Armed Forces, 1961. Credit mgr. finance div. Ford Motor Co., Uniontown, Pa., 1940-41; commd. 2d lt. U.S. Army, 1942, advanced through grades to brig. gen., 1969; ret., 1971, staff positions as comptroller, procurement and mil. logistics, 1942-71; G-4 8th U.S. Army, Korea, 1970-71; chmn. bd. Aloha Corp., Honolulu, 1973—; pres. DRC of Hawaii, Inc., Honolulu, 1974-78; asst. to pres. Lucky Devel. Co. Ltd., 1978-84; ret., 1984. Decorated D.S.M., Legion of Merit, Army Commendation medal (U.S.); Order of Merit (Korea). Mem. Beta Gamma Sigma, Lambda Chi Alpha. Clubs: Lion, Rotarian. Home: 7400 Crestway Dr Apt 620 San Antonio TX 78239-3091

LEER, STEVEN F., mining executive. Pres., ceo Arch Mineral Corp., St. Louis. Office: Arch Mineral Corp City Place One Saint Louis MO 63141*

LEERABHANDH, MARJORIE BRAVO, chemist, educator; b. Negros Occidental, Philippines; came to U.S., 1982.; d. Rustico Ginese and Monica Tolosa (Tolosa) Bravo; m. Sunai Leerabhandh, Oct. 2, 1986. BS in chemistry cum laude, U. Santo Tomas, 1979; PhD in chemistry, U. So. Calif., 1990. Rsch. teaching asst. chem. dept. U. So. Calif., L.A., 1984-89; faculty mem. chem. dept. Moorpark (Calif.) Coll., 1992—; project mgr. Med. Analysis Sys., Inc., Camarillo, Calif., 1989-93, rsch. team leader, 1993-94, mgr. rsch. and devel., 1994—. Author: Nitrogen Tixation Research Progress, 1985, Nitrogen Fixation: 100 Years After, 1988; contbr. articles to profl. jours. Mem. Am. Chem. Soc., Am. Assn. for Clinical Chem., Chem. Soc. U. Santo Tomas Manils (pres., 1979). Achievements include patents for Fructosamine Reagent and Calibrator Systems, Stabilization of Functional Proteins. Office: Med Analysis Sys Inc 542 Flynn Rd Camarillo CA 93012

LEES, BENJAMIN, composer; b. Harbin, China, Jan. 8, 1924; came to U.S., 1925; Studied piano, with K.I. Rodetsky, 1931, Marguerite Bitter, 1945-48; compostion, with Halsey Stevens at U. So. Calif., 1945-48, with George Antheil, 1949-54. Prof. composition Peabody Conservatory, Queen's Coll., Manhattan Sch. Music. Composer: Profile, 1952, Declamations for piano and strings, 1953, Symphony Number 1, 1953, Number 2, 1958, Piano Concerto Number 1, 1955, Divertimento Burlesca, 1957, Songs of the Night for Soprano and Orch, 1952, Violin Concerto, 1958, Prologue, Capriccio and Epilogue, 1958, Concerto for Orch, 1959, Concertante Breve, 1959, Interlude for Strings, 1957, Visions of Poets for Soprano and Tenor Solo; Chorus and Orch., 1961; The Gilded Cage; chamber music String Quartet Number 1, 1952; Evocation for Solo Flute, 1953, Violin Sonata Number 1, 1953, Movement da Camera for Flute, Clarinet, Cello and Piano, 1954, String Quartet Number 2, 1955, Three Variables for Winds and Piano, 1956; piano Sonata for Two Pianos, 1951; Toccata, 1953, Fantasia, 1954, Kaleidoscopes, 1959, Sonata Breve, 1956, Six Ornamental Etudes, 1957; songs Cyprian Songs for baritone, 1961; Concerto for Oboe and Orch, 1964, Piano Sonata 4, 1965, Piano Concerto 2, 1966, Symphony No. 3, 1968; opera Medea in Corinth, 1970; Study for Solo Cello, 1972, Sonata No. 2 for Violin and Piano, 1973, Etudes for Piano and Orch., 1974, Labyrinths for Symphonic Band, 1975, Variations for Piano and Orch., 1975, Passacaglia for Orch., 1976, Concerto for Woodwind Quintet and Orch., 1976, Staves soprano and piano, 1977; Scarlatti Portfolio; transcriptions for orch., 1978; Dialogue for Cello and Piano, 1977, Paumanok for mezzo-soprano with piano, 1980; Omen for soprano with piano, 1981; Sonata for cello and piano, 1981, String Quartet No. 3, 1982, Double Concerto for piano, cello and orch., 1982, Concerto for brass choir and orch., 1983, Portrait of Rodin (orch.), 1984, Symphony No. 4 (Memorial Candles), 1985, Odyssey II for solo piano, 1986,

Symphony # 5, 1988, String Quartet No. 4, 1989, Sonata for Violin and Piano # 3, 1989, Concerto for Horn and Orch., 1991, Mirrors for solo piano, 1992, Borealis for orch., 1993, Echoes of Normandy, 1994. Recipient Fromm Found. award, 1953; William and Noma Copley Found. award, 1955; UNESCO award, 1958; Sir Arnold Bax medal, 1958; Composers award Lancaster Symphony Orch., 1985; Guggenheim fellow, 1954, 66; Fulbright fellow, 1956. Address: 46 Grace Ave #2F Great Neck NY 11021

LEES, BRIAN PAUL, state senator; b. Amesbury, Mass., July 25, 1953; Phillip and Patricia (Wenzel) L.; m. Nancy Ward, Aug. 2, 1980. BSBA, Salem State Coll., 1975. Staff asst. U.S. Senator Edward Brooke, Washington, 1976-79; product devel. mgr. Westvaco Corp., Springfield, Mass., 1980-89; state senator Mass. Senate, Boston, 1989—, asst. minority leader, 1991-92; minority leader, 1993—. Corporator Springfield YMCA, Springfield Libr. and Mus. Assn., Brightside Children's Ctr.; bd. trustees Willie Ross Sch. for Deaf; mem. Internat. Trade Adv. Bd. Recipient Leadership award Greater Springfield chpt. NOW, 1989, Pub. Svc. award Springfield Pomona Grange, 1992, Legislator of Yr. award Western Mass. Orgn. Nursing Execs., 1994, Appreciation award Mass. Dept. Mental Health, 1995; named Headliner of Yr. Valley Press Club, 1988, Hampden County Am. Legion Legislator of Yr. 1992, Alumnus of Yr. Salem State Coll., 1995. Office: 527 Main St Springfield MA 01151-1219

LEES, MARJORIE BERMAN, biochemist, neuroscientist; b. N.Y.C., Mar. 17, 1923; d. Isadore I. and Ruth (Rogalsky) Berman; m. Sidney Lees, Sept. 17, 1946; children: David E., Andrew, Eliot. BA, Hunter Coll., 1943; MS, U. Chgo., 1945; PhD, Harvard U., Radcliffe Coll., 1951. Assoc. biochemist, asst. biochemist McLean Hosp., Belmont, Mass., 1953-62; rsch. assoc. Darmouth Med. Sch., Hanover, N.H., 1962-66; assoc. biochemist McLean Hosp., Belmont, 1966-76; prin. and sr. rsch. assoc. Harvard Med. Sch., Boston, 1966-85; biochemist E.K. Shriver Ctr., Waltham, Mass., 1976—; prof. biochemistry (neurology) Harvard Med. Sch., Boston, 1985—; biochemist Mass. Gen. Hosp., Boston, 1976—; assoc. dir. biochemistry E.K. Shriver Ctr., Waltham, 1982-90, dir. biochemistry, 1990-93, assoc. dir. mental retardation rsch. ctr., 1994—; mem. adv. com. biomed. and behavioral rsch. NASA/NIH, 1993—; mem. sci. adv. com. Nat. Multiple Sclerosis Soc., 1988-93. Chief editor Jour. of Neurochemistry, 1986-90; author (with others) books; contbr. articles to profl. jours. Mem. adv. coun. Nat. Inst. Neurological Disorders, Bethesda, Md., 1979-82; chmn. Radcliffe Grad. Soc., Cambridge, Mass., 1978-80. Predoctoral fellow USPHS, 1947-50, postdoctoral fellow Am. Cancer Soc., 1951-53; Javits Neurosci. grantee NIH, 1983-90, 91-97, prin. grantee NIH, 1962—; named to Hunter Coll. Hall of Fame, 1982. Mem. Am. Soc. Biochemistry and Molecular Biology, Internat. Soc. Neurochemistry, Am. Soc. Neurochemistry (treas. 1975-81, pres. 1983-85), Soc. for Neurosci., Am. Assn. Neuropathology (assoc.), Internat. Soc. Neuroimmunology, N.Y. Acad. Scis., Am. Women in Sci., Phi Beta Kappa. Office: E K Shriver Ctr 200 Trapelo Rd Waltham MA 02154-6332

LEES, MARTIN HENRY, pediatrician, educator; b. London, May 11, 1929; came to U.S., 1958; s. David William and Lilian Thomson (White) L.; m. Elizabeth McMahon, Sept. 5, 1959; children: Deborah Ann, Jacqueline Mary, Christina Beth. MBBS, London U., 1955, MD, 1962. Diplomate: Am. Bd. Pediatrics, Am. Bd. Pediatric Cardiology, Am. Bd. Fetal/Neonatal Medicine. Intern South Devon Hosp., Plymouth, Eng., 1955-57; resident in pediatrics Hosp. Sick Children, 1957; sr. resident, fellow in pediatric cardiology Boston Children's Hosp., 1958-61; asst. prof. McGill U., Montreal, Que., Can., 1961-62; prof. pediatrics U. Oreg. Health Ctr., Portland, 1963-95. Fellow Royal Coll. Physicians (London); mem. Am. Heart Assn., Am. Pediatric Soc., Soc. Pediatric Rsch. Home: 17 Abelard St Lake Oswego OR 97035-2340 Office: Pediatric Cardiology 501 N Graham St Ste 330 Portland OR 97227

LEES, SIDNEY, research facility administrator, bioengineering educator; b. Phila., Apr. 17, 1917; s. Charles K. and Bess Rose (Segal) L.; m. Marjorie Berman, Sept. 17, 1947; children—David E.B., P. Andrew, Eliot Jay. A.B., Coll. City N.Y., 1938; S.M., Mass. Inst. Tech., 1948, Sc.D., 1950. Observer U.S. Weather Bur., 1938-40; meteorol. instrument engr. U.S. Signal Corps, 1940-43; research asso. Mass. Inst. Tech., 1947-50, asst. prof. aero. dept., 1950-57; cons. engr., 1957-62; prof. engring. Thayer Sch., Dartmouth, 1962-66; head bioengring. dept., sr. mem. staff Forsyth Inst. Research and Advanced Study, Boston, 1966—; hon. rsch. assoc. dept. med. biophysics U. Manchester, England, 1990—; adj. prof. Northeastern U., 1980; vis. scientist U. Amsterdam, 1975; chmn. Joint Automatic Control Conf., 1965, Rsch. Conf. on Instrumentation Sci., 1971, Conf. on Ultrasonics in Bioengring. and Biophysics, 1978, Internat. Symposium on Acoustical Imaging, 1997. Coauthor: Instrument Engineering, 3 vols, 1952-55; Editor: Air, Space and Instruments, Draper Anniversary vol, 1963; Contbr. articles to profl. jours. Served with AUS, 1943-46. Mem. Am. Phys. Soc., ASME, IEEE, Engring. in Medicine and Biology Soc. IEEE (chmn. region I 1980—), Sigma Xi (pres. Dartmouth chpt. 1964-65). Home: 50 Eliot Memorial Rd Newton MA 02158-2704 Office: Forsyth Dental Center 140 Fenway Boston MA 02115-3782

LEESER, DAVID O., materials engineer, metallurgist; b. El Paso, Tex., Aug. 3, 1917; s. Oscar D. and Rose R. (Goodman) L.; m. Marilyn Bachman Kalina, Mar. 18, 1945; children: Barbara H., Joyce N. BSc in Mining, U. Tex., El Paso, 1943; MSc in Materials Sci., Ohio State U., 1950; postgrad., U. Fla., 1962, U. Mich., 1985. Registered profl. engr., Ohio, Calif., Ariz. Mining engr. Bradley Mining Co., Stibnite, Idaho, 1943-44; rsch. engr. Battelle Meml. Inst., Columbus, Ohio, 1944-50; assoc. metallurgist Argonne Nat. Lab., Lemont, Ill., 1950-54; mgr., staff metallurgist Atomic Power Devel. Assn., Detroit, 1954-61; chief scientist, materials Chrysler Corp./Missiles, Cape Canaveral, Fla., 1961-68; chief metallurgist Chrysler Corp., Amplex div., Detroit, 1968-75; sr. staff engr. Burroughs Corp. (Unisys), Plymouth, Mich., 1975-86; prin., materials cons., forensic engr. D.O. Leeser, Profl. Egnr., Scottsdale, Ariz., 1987—; materials cons. fgn. tech. divsn. Wright-Patterson AFB, Dayton, Ohio, 1958-80; charter mem. Missile, Space and Range Pioneers, Cape Canaveral, 1967—; organizer Fla. Indsl. Exhbn., Orlando, 1968; U.S. del. 2d World Metall. Congress, Chgo., 1957, Internat. Conf. on Peaceful Uses of Atom, Geneva, 1958, Internat. Atomic Energy Agy. Conf., Vienna, Austria, 1961. Contbr. articles on nuclear radiation effects on structural materials, flame deflector materials for rockets, forensic investigations to profl. publs. Vice-pres. Manzanita Villas Home Owners Assn., Scottsdale, 1990—. Recipient citation War Manpower Commn., 1945, U.S. Sci. R&D Office, 1946, Appreciation award State of Fla., 1968; Engr. of Yr. Fla. Engring. Soc.-Canaveral Coun. Tech. Socs., 1967, Outstanding Alumnus of Yr., U. Tex. at El Paso, 1969; recipient Apollo Achievement award NASA, 1969, Exemplary Action award Burroughs Corp., 1986. Mem. Am. Soc. materials Internat., Sigma Xi. Achievements include collaboration on development of atomic bomb, Apollo space program, first nuclear-powered naval vessel; pioneering studies on effects of nuclear radiation on materials. Home: 11515 N 91st St Unit 151 Scottsdale AZ 85260-6899 Office: DO Leeser Profl Engr 11515 N 91st St Unit 151 Scottsdale AZ 85260-6899

LEE-SMITH, HUGHIE, artist, educator; b. Eustis, Fla., Sept. 20, 1915; s. Luther and Alice (Williams) Smith; m. Mabel Louise Everett, 1940 (div. 1953); 1 child, Christina; m. Helen Nebraska, 1965 (div. 1974); m. Patricia Thomas-Ferry, 1978. Student, Art Sch. of Detroit Soc. Arts and Crafts, 1934-35; grad., Cleve. Inst. Art, 1938; B.S., Wayne State U., 1953; DFA (hon.), Md. Inst. Coll. Art, 1995. Instr. painting Grosse Pointe War Meml., Mich., 1956-66, Studio-on-the-Canal, Princeton, N.J., 1959-64; art tchr. Princeton Country Day Sch., 1964-65; artist-in-residence Howard U., 1969-71; instr. painting Art Students League, N.Y.C., 1972-87, ret., 1987; adj. prof. Trenton State Coll., 1972-73. One-man shows include Detroit Artists Market, Howard U. Gallery, Washington, Grand Central Art Galleries, N.Y.C., Janet Nessler Gallery, N.Y.C., U. Chgo., June Kelly Gallery, N.Y.C., Butler Inst. Am. Art, Youngstown, Ohio, Chgo. Cultural Ctr., Greenville (S.C.) Mus. Art, others; exhibited group shows Cleve. Mus. Art, Detroit Inst. Arts, Butler Inst. Am. Art, Youngstown, Bklyn. Mus., Wadsworth Atheneum, Boston Mus., San Francisco Mus., Mus. Modern Art, Whitney Mus., Am. Acad. and Inst. Arts and Letters, N.Y.; represented in permanent collections Met. Mus., Phila. Mus., Detroit Inst. Arts, Parrish Mus., Southampton, L.I., N.J. State Mus., Standard Oil of Ohio, AT&T, Wadsworth Atheneum, U. Mich., Wayne State U., Schomburg Coll., N.Y.C., Howard U., Nat. Mus. Am Art, U.S. Navy Art Ctr., Chase Manhattan Bank, N.Y.C., Forbes Mag. Collection, N.Y.C., Kidder & Peabody Co., N.Y.C., Mus. Internat. Art, Sofia, Bulgaria, Century Assn., N.Y.C., Lagos (Nigeria) Mus. With USN, 1944-45. Recipient Thomas B. Clark prize NAD, 1959, prize Allied Artists Am., 1958, Emily Lowe award, 1957, Founders prize Detroit Inst. Arts, 1953, cert. of commendation USN, 1974, Art Achievement award Wayne State U., Key to the City of Hartford (Conn.) award, Ranger Fund purchase award NAD, 1977, Audubon Artist prizes, 1982, 83, 85, 86; named Mich. Painter of Yr. Detroit News, 1953. Mem. Artists Equity Assn. (bd. dirs.), Allied Artists Am., Princeton Art Assn., Mich. Acad. Sci., Arts and Letters, NAD (mem. coun., awards juries), Audubon Artists (pres. 1980-82, exhbn. coord.), Artists Fellowship (trustee, v.p. 1985-88), Century Assn., Lotos Club (N.Y.C.). Home: 152A Chatham Dr Cranbury NJ 08512-3824

LEET, MILDRED ROBBINS, corporate executive, consultant; b. N.Y.C., Aug. 9, 1922; d. Samuel Milton and Isabella (Zeitz) Elowsky; m. Louis J. Robbins, Feb. 23, 1941 (dec. 1970); children: Jane, Aileen; m. Glen Leet, Aug. 9, 1974. BA, NYU, 1942; LHD (hon.), Coll. Human Svcs., 1988, Conn. Coll., 1996; LLD honoris causa, Marymount Coll., Tarrytown, N.Y., 1991; HHD, Lynn U., 1993; D Humanitarian Svc. (hon.), Norwich U., 1994; DHL, Conn. Coll., 1996. Pres. women's div. United Cerebral Palsy, N.Y.C., 1951-52; bd. dirs. United Cerebral Palsy, 1953-55; rep. Nat. Coun. Women U.S. at UN, 1957-64, 1st v.p., 1959-64, pres., 1964-68, hon. pres., 1968-70; sec., v.p. conf. group U.S. Nat. Orgns. at UN, 1961-64, 76-78, vice chmn., sec., 1962-64, mem. exec. com., 1961-65, 75—, chmn. hospitality info. svc., 1960-66; vice chmn. exec. com. NGO's UN Office Public Info., 1976-78, chmn. ann. conf., 1977; chmn. com. on water, desertification, habitat and environment Conf. NGO's with consultative status with UN/ECOSOC, 1976—; mem. exec. com. Internat. Coun. Women, 1960-73, v.p., 1970-73; chmn. program planning com., women's com. OEO, 1967-72; chmn. com. on natural disasters N.Am. Com. on Environment, 1973-77; N.Y. State chmn. UN Day, 1975; ptnr. Leet & Leet (cons. women in devel.), 1978—; cofounder Trickle Up Program, 1979—, co-pres., 1991—; mem. task force on Africa UN, 1995—. Contbr. articles to profl. jours.; editor UN Calendar & Digest, 1959-64, Measure of Mankind, 1963; editorial bd.: Peace & Change. Co-chmn. Vols. for Stevenson, N.Y.C., 1956; vice chmn. task force Nat. Dem. Com., 1969-72; commr. N.Y. State Commn. on Powers Local Govt., 1970-73; chmn. Coll. for Human Svcs. Audrey Colten Coll., 1985—; former mem. bd. dirs. Am. Arbitration Assn., New Directions, Inst. for Mediation and Conflict Resolution, Spirit of Stockholm; bd. dirs. Hotline Internat.; v.p. Save the Children Fedn., 1986-93; rep. Internat. Peace Acad. at UN, 1974-77, Internat. Soc. Cmty. Devel., 1977—; del. at large 1st Nat. Women's Conf., Houston, 1977; chmn. task force on internat. interdependence N.Y. State Women's Meeting, 1977; mem. Task Force on Poverty, 1977—; chmn. Task Force on Women, Sci. and Tech. for Devel., 1978; U.S. del. UN Status of Women Commn., 1978, UN Conf. Sci. and Tech. for Devel., 1979, co-dir. Trickle Up Program, Inc., 1979—; Brazzaville Centennial Celebration, 1980; mem. global adv. bd. Internat. Expn. Rural Devel., 1981—; mem. Coun. Internat. Fellows U. Bridgeport, 1982-88; trustee overseas edn. fund LWV, 1983-91; v.p. U.S. Com. UN Devel. Fund for Women, 1983—; mem. Nat. Consultative Com. Planning for Nairobi, 1984-85; co-chmn. women in devel. com. Interaction, 1985-91; mem. com. of cooperation Interam. Commn. of Women, 1986; bd. dirs. Internat. Devel. Conf., 1991—; mem. UN task force informal sector devel Africa,1995—. Recipient Crystal award Coll. Human Svcs., 1983, Ann. award Inst. Mediation and Conflict Resolution, 1985, Woman of Conscience award Nat. Coun. Women, 1986, Temple award Inst. Noetic Scis., 1987, Presdl. Edn Hunger award, 1987, Giraffe award Giraffe Project, 1987, Woman of the World award Eng.'s Women Aid, 1989, Mildred Robbins Left award Interaction, 1995; co-recipient Rose award World Media Inst., 1987, Human Rights award UN Devel. Fund for Women, 1987, (with Glen Leet) Pres.'s medal Marymount Manhattan Coll., 1988, Leadership award U.S. Peace Corps, Woman of Vision award N.Y.C. NOW, 1990, Matrix award Women in Comm., Inc., Spirit of Enterprise award Rolex Industries, 1990, Ann. award Interaction, 1990, Citation, Pres. Bush's Ann. Points of Light Award, 1992, Internat. Humanity award ARC Overseas Assn., 1992, Excellence award U.S. Com. for UNIFEM, 1992, Champion of Enterprise award Avon, 1994, Achievement award NYU-Washington Square Coll. Alumni Assn., 1995, Lizette H. Sarnoff Vol. Svc. award Yeshiva U, 1996, Disting. Svc. award N.Y. African Studies Assn., 1996. Mem. AAAS, Women's Nat. Dem. Club, Women's Forum Inc., Cosmopolitan Club, PriHome and Office: 54 Riverside Dr New York NY 10024-6509

LEET, RICHARD HALE, oil company executive; b. Maryville, Mo., Oct. 11, 1926; s. Theron Hale and Helen Eloise (Rutledge) L.; m. Phyllis Jean Combs, June 14, 1949; children: Richard Hale II, Alan Combs, Dana Ellen. B.S. in Chemistry, N.W. Mo. State Coll., 1948; Ph.D. in Phys. Chemistry, Ohio State U., 1952. Rsch. chemist Standard Oil Co., Whiting, Ind., 1953-64; dir. long-range and capital planning, mktg. dept. Am. Oil Co., Chgo., 1964-68; mgr. ops. planning, mfg. dept. Am. Oil Co., 1968-70; regional v.p. Am. Oil Co., Atlanta, 1970-71; v.p. supply Am. Oil Co., Chgo., 1971-74; v.p. planning and adminstrn. Amoco Chems. Corp., Chgo., 1974-75; v.p. mktg. Amoco Chems. Corp., 1975-77, exec. v.p., 1977-78, pres., 1978-83; dir. Amoco Corp., Chgo., 1983-91, vice chmn., 1991-92; retired, 1992; bd. dirs. Gt. Lakes Chem., Vulcan Materials Corp., ITW, Landauer, Inc. Former chmn. bd. mgrs. Met. YMCA, Chgo.; former pres. Boy Scouts Am.; former chmn. bd. Am. Indsl. Health Coun.; former bd. visitors Emory U., 1970-71; vice chmn. found. bd. Ohio State U; trustee Brenau U. With USNR, 1944-46. Mem. Am. Chem. Soc., Soc. Chem. Industry (exec. com.), Am. Petroleum Inst. (bd. dirs.), Société Industrielle de Chemie, Chem. Mfrs. Assn. (dir.), Phi Sigma Epsilon, Gamma Alpha. Office: Lighthouse Acres PO Box 1686 Gainesville GA 30503-1686

LEETCH, BRIAN JOSEPH, hockey player; b. Corpus Christi, Tex., Mar. 3, 1968. Student, Boston Coll. With N.Y. Rangers, 1986—; mem. U.S. Olympic hockey team, 1988, Team USA for 1991 Can. Cup Tournament, Stanley Cup championship team, 1994. Named mem. U.S. Coll. first-team All-Am. team, 1987, Sporting News NHL Rookie of Yr., 1989, Player of the Year, Hockey East, 1986-87, Rookie of the Year, 1986-87, Sporting News All-Star team, 1991-92; recipient Calder Meml. trophy for NHL Rookie of Yr.,1988, 1989, James Norris Meml. trophy for best defenseman, 1991, 92, Conn Smythe trophy, 1993-94. Office: NY Rangers Madison Sq Garden 4 Pennsylvania Plz New York NY 10001*

LEETE, WILLIAM WHITE, artist; b. Portsmouth, Ohio, June 12, 1929; s. Bernard Emerson and Lois Trowbridge (Denison) L.; m. Doris Louise Knight, Sept. 19, 1952; children: Amy MacDonald, Robin Schodt. B.A., Yale U., 1951, B.F.A., 1955, M.F.A., 1957. Mem. faculty dept. art U. R.I., Kingston, 1957-95, prof. emeritus, 1995; acting dept. chmn. U. R.I., 1968, 69-70, 76. Represented in permanent collections, De Cordova Mus., Lincoln, Mass., Cleve. Mus., Worcester Mus., R.I. Hosp., Trust Bank, also various pvt. collections. Served with USMC, 1951-53. Mem. AAUP, Coll. Art Assn., Siggraph, Boston Computer Soc. Home: 202 Silver Lake Ave Wakefield RI 02879-4231 Office: U RI Dept Art Kingston RI 02881

LEETS, PETER JOHN, outplacement consulting firm executive; b. London, Mar. 12, 1946; came to U.S., 1948; s. Earl Edward and Doris Eileen L.; m. Anne E. Shahinian, May 15, 1982. BS in Mktg., Ind. U., 1969. Salesman Ortho Pharm. Corp., Raritan, N.J., 1969-74; account mgr. Revlon Inc., Indpls., 1974-76; regional dir. Revlon Inc., Cleve., 1976-79; field sales mgr. Revlon Inc., Bay Village, Ohio, 1979-83; nat. field sales mgr. Binney & Smith, Bethlehem, Pa., 1983-85; v.p., dir. sales Dell Pub. Co., Inc., N.Y.C., 1985-87; exec. v.p. Geneva Corp., Irvine, Calif., 1987-88; pres. Geneva Cos., Costa Mesa, Calif., 1988-90; exec. v.p. Exec. Assets Corp., Irvine, Calif., 1990-91; pres. Exec. Assets Corp., 1992-94; mng. prin. Right Assocs., Irvine, Calif., 1994—; bd. dirs. Career Beginnings, Career Transition Ptnrs., Constl. Rights Found. Chairperson Orange County Econ. Outlook Conf.; bd. dirs. Forum for Corp. Dirs., PIHRA Found. Mem. Assn. for Corp. Growth, Internat. Assn. Career Mgmt. Profls. (bd. dirs.), Ind. U. Alumni (life), U. Calif. Irvine Chancellor's Club (bd. dirs.), Delta Chi. Office: Right Assocs 3333 Michelson Dr Ste 400 Irvine CA 92715-1684

LEEVER, HAROLD, chemical company executive; b. Detroit, May 21, 1914; s. Guy Harold and Mary (MacGregor) L.; m. Ruth Ann Salter, Oct. 5, 1935; children: Suzanne Hart, Thomas, John, Daniel, Andrew. BSChemE, Mich. State U., 1936; PhD (hon.), Post Coll., 1947. From chief chemist to v.p. McDermid Inc., Waterbury, Conn., 1938-54, pres., 1954-77, chmn. bd., 1977—. Patentee in field. Chmn. bd. Post Coll., Waterbury, 1965—; chmn. United Way, Waterbury, 1959, 81. Recipient Hiram Hayden award Boy Scouts Am., Silver Beaver award Boy Scouts Am.; named Industrialist of Yr., Conn. chpt. United Ch. of Christ, Man of the Yr. Waterbury United Way, 1989, Outstanding Fund Raiser of Conn. Nat. Soc. Fund Raising Execs., 1988. Lodge: Rotary. Home: 366 Guilds Hollow Rd Bethlehem CT 06751-1607 Office: MacDermid Inc 245 Freight St Waterbury CT 06702-1802

LEEVY, CARROLL MOTON, medical educator, hepatology researcher; b. Columbia, S.C., Oct. 13, 1920; s. Isaac S. and Mary (Kirkl) L.; m. Ruth S. Barboza, Feb. 4, 1956; children: Carroll Barboza, Maria Secora. AB, Fisk U., 1941; MD, U. Mich., 1944; ScD (hon.), N.J. Inst. Tech., 1973, U. Nebr., 1989; HHD (hon.), Fisk U., 1981; M, Am. Coll. Physicians, 1991. Intern Jersey City Med. Ctr., 1944-45, resident, 1945-48, dir. clin. investigation, 1947-57; fellow Banting-Best Inst., U. Toronto, Ont., Can., 1953; research assoc. Harvard U. Med. Sch., Cambridge, Mass., 1959; assoc. prof. U. Medicine and Dentistry of N.J., 1960-64, prof., 1964, Disting. prof., 1990—; physician in chief Univ. Hosp., 1975-91; dir. Liver Ctr. U. Medicine and Dentistry N.J., 1983-85; dir. div. hepatology and nutrition N.J. Med. Sch., 1959-75, acting chmn. dept. medicine, 1966-68, chief of medicine, 1968-71, chmn. dept. medicine, 1975-91; disting. prof. medicine Univ. Hosp., physician in chief, 1975-91; acting chmn. Sammy Davis Jr. Nat. Liver Inst., 1984-86, pres., sci. dir., 1989—; dir. N.J. Med. Sch. Liver Ctr., 1991—; chief medicine VA Hosp., East Orange, N.J., 1966-71; cons. NIH, 1965—, FDA, 1970-80, VA, 1971—, Alcohol and Nutrition Found., 1970-80, Am. Liver Found., 1979-84; cons. Health Care Fin. Adminstrn., 1990—, mem. adv. com. on liver transplantation, 1991—; mem. Nat. Commn. on Digestive Disease, 1975-78; mem. expert com. on chronic liver disease WHO, 1978; mem. nat. adv. com. digestive disease HHS, 1989-93; chmn. monitoring com. VA Coop. Study on Alcoholic Hepatitis, 1989-94—, VA Rsch. Study on Colchicine Alcoholic Cirrhosis, 1994—. Author: Practical Diagnosis and Treatment of Liver Disease, 1957, Evaluation of Liver Function in Clinical Practice, 1965, 2d edit., 1974, Liver Regeneration in Man, 1973, The Liver and Its Diseases, 1973, Diseases of the Liver and Biliary Tract, 1977, Guidelines for Detection of Drug and Chemical-Induced Hepatotoxicity, 1979, Alcohol and the Digestive Tract, 1981, Standardization of Nomenclature, Diagnostic Criteria and Prognosis for Diseases of the Liver and Biliary Tract, 1994; contbr. numerous articles to med., sci. jours.; patentee in field. Bd. dirs. U. Cape Town, South Africa, 1984—; active Cmty. Congl. Ch. Cmdr. USNR, 1954-59. E.V. Gabriel scholar, 1938, Kellog Med. scholar, 1942; recipient Modern Med. award, 1972, Edward Ill award, 1973, United Negro Coll. Fund award, 1980, Key to City of Newark, 1981, Key to City of Columbia, S.C., 1987, Key to City of Secaucus, N.J., 1981, 50th N.J. Achievement award U. Medicine and Dentistry N.J., 1995; 40th Anniversary Faculty Honoree, U. Medicine and Dentistry N.J., 1995. Mem. NAACP, ACP (publs. com. 1969-74, master), AMA (vice-chmn., chmn. program com. sect. on gastroenterology 1971-74), AAAS, Am. Assn. for Study Liver Diseases (pres. 1967-68, chmn. steering com. 1968-74, Disting. Svc. award 1991), Internat. Assn. for Study Liver (pres. 1970-74, chmn. criteria com. 1972—), Am. Gastroenterol. Assn. (edn. and tng. com. 1967-71), Assn. Profs. Medicine (Robert Williams Disting. Chmn. award 1991), Assn. Am. Physicians, Soc. Exptl. Biology and Medicine, Am. Soc. Clin. Nutrition, Am. Inst. Nutrition, Nat. Med. Assn. (award 1987, Centenial award 1995), Am. Fedn. Clin. Rsch., Assn. Acad. Minority Physicians (pres. 1986-88, chmn. bd. trustees 1988—, Disting. Achievement award 1995), Internat. Com. on Informatics in Hepatology (chmn. 1986—), Internal Hepatology Informatics Group (chmn. 1984-93), N.J. Acad. Medicine, Phi Beta Kappa, Alpha Omega Alpha, Sigma Pi Phi. Home: 35 Robert Dr Short Hills NJ 07078-1525 Office: U Medicine and Dentistry NJ Med Sch 100 Bergen St Newark NJ 07103-2407 *My goal has been to help improve quality of life of all people, the disadvantaged and advantaged. Efforts have been made through medical education and research to decrease the incidence and untoward effects of disease, as well as improve communication and the social environment.*

LE FAUVE, RICHARD ALLEN, investment company executive, marketing consultant; b. Buffalo, Nov. 19, 1950; s. George Julien and Edith Elenor (Gowan) Le F.; m. Lynn Carol Rosenzweig, Oct. 7, 1978; children: Ari Julien, Justin Charles. BS in Edn., SUNY, Brockport, 1973; master's cert. in edn., SUNY, Buffalo, 1975. Cert. permanent tchr., in phys. edn. and health sci., N.Y. Tchr., coach Sweet Home Ctrl. Schs., Amherst, N.Y., 1973-77; stock broker, br. mgr. 1st Jersey Securities, Buffalo, 1977-84; v.p., bd. dirs. Anodyne Energy Corp., Buffalo, 1984-86, mem. adv. bd., 1986-87; regional mgr., dir. tng. and broker devel. Thomas-James Assocs., Buffalo, 1986—, mktg. cons., 1993—; recruitment cons. Reliance Fin. Group, Williamsville, N.Y., 1990. Author, editor: (manuals) New Broker Training, 1991, Recruitment, 1993; editor: (manuals) Merit Advisors—Asset Allocation, 1992, Marketing, 1993. Scholarship fundraiser Sweet Home Ctrl. Schs., 1988—, mem. adv. bd. scholarship investment com., 1988—. Named Vol. of Yr., Sweet Home Ctrl. Schs., 1994. Mem. Securities Industry Assn., Nat. Assn. Securities Dealers (registered rep. series 7, prin. series series 24), N.Y. State Life Ins. Agts., Albright-Knox Art Gallery, Loch Lee Homeowners Assn. Avocations: weight training, cycling, martial arts. Home: 5574 Hidden Pines Ct Williamsville NY 14221-2844

LEFCO, KATHY NAN, law librarian; b. Bethesda, Md., Feb. 24, 1949; d. Ted Lefco and Dorothy Rose (Fox) Harris; m. Stephen Gary Katz, Sept. 2, 1973 (div. May 1984); m. John Alfred Price, Nov. 24, 1984 (dec. Jan. 1989). BA, U. Wis., 1971; MLS, U. Wis., Milw., 1975. Rsch. asst. Ctr. Auto Safety, Washington, 1971-73; asst. to dir. Ctr. Consumer Affairs, Milw., 1973-74; legis. librarian Morgan, Lewis & Bockius, Washington, 1976-78; dir. library Mulcahy & Wherry, Milw., 1978; paralegal Land of Lincoln Legal Assistance, Springfield, Ill., 1979-80; reference and interlibrary loan librarian Sch. Medicine So. Ill. U., Springfield, 1980; reader svcs. librarian Wis. State Law Library, Madison, 1981-83; ref. librarian Mudge Rose Guthrie Alexander & Ferdon, N.Y.C., 1983-85; sr. legal info. specialist Cravath, Swaine & Moore, N.Y.C., 1985-86; asst. librarian Kaye, Scholer, Fierman, Hays & Handler, N.Y.C., 1986-89; head libr. Parker Chapin Flattau & Klimpl, N.Y.C., 1989-94; dir. library svcs. Winston & Strawn, Chgo., 1994—. Author: (with others) Mobile Homes: The Low-Cost Housing Hoax, 1973. Mem. Law Libr. Assn. Greater N.Y. (sec. 1989-91), Chgo. Assn. Law Librs., Am. Assn. Law Librs. Democrat. Jewish. Avocations: biking, backgammon, politics. Home: Apt 2504 474 N Lake Shore Dr Chicago IL 60611 Office: Winston & Strawn 35 W Wacker Dr Chicago IL 60601

LEFEBVRE, ALAN J., lawyer; b. Akron, Colo., Mar. 17, 1953; s. Vern L. and Adeline V. (Molacek) L.; m. Eileen Helen Buhmann, Feb. 26, 1987. BA in Polit. Sci. with high honors and departmental distinction, U. Calif., Santa Barbara, 1975; JD, U. San Francisco, 1978. Bar: Calif. 1978, Nev. 1979, U.S. Dist. Ct. Nev. 1979, U.S. Ct. Appeals (9th cir.) 1979, U.S. Supreme Ct. 1992, U.S. Dist. Ct. (cen. dist.) Calif. 1994. Law clk. 8th Jud. Dist. Ct., Las Vegas, Nev., 1978-79; assoc. Jolly, Urga & Wirth, Las Vegas, 1979-80; assoc., ptnr. Beckley, Singleton, DeLanoy Jemison & List, Las Vegas, 1980-89; sr. ptnr. Lefebvre & Barron, Las Vegas, 1989—. Mem. Nev. Commn. on Jud. Discipline, Carson City, 1991—. Mem. Internat. Assn. Def. Counsel. Republican. Roman Catholic. Avocations: boating, fishing, classical music. Office: 301 Clark Ave Ste 600 Las Vegas NV 89101-6537

LEFEBVRE, GABRIEL FELICIEN, retired chemical company executive; b. N.Y.C., Feb. 29, 1932; s. Gabriel F. and Harriett Blanche (Terrill) L.; m. Doris Jeanette Germain, Oct. 26, 1952; children: David Marshall, Richard Terrill, Kathryn Louise. B.S., Webb Inst. Naval Arch., 1952. Registered profl. engr., Ky., Ohio. Ptnr. Leco, Inc., Paducah, Ky., 1962-63; engring. supr. B.F. Goodrich Chem. Group, Calvert City, Ky., 1963-76; plant mgr. B.F. Goodrich Chem. Group, Louisville, 1977-78; gen. mgr. Chlor-Alkali B.F. Goodrich Chem. Group, Cleve., 1978-82, v.p PVC intermediates, 1982-83, gen. mgr. PVC intermediates, 1982-83, v.p. facilities mgmt., 1983-85, pres. Convent Chem Corp., 1978-83, dir., 1978-83; v.p. LaPorte Chem. Corp. B.F. Goodrich Chem. Group, 1982-83; v.p. ops. Geon Vinyl div., 1985-87, v.p. regulatory affairs, 1987-91; tech. mgr. Abadan Petrochem Co., Tehran, Iran, 1976-77. Served to lt. USNR, 1952-56. Mem. ASME, Nat. Soc. Profl. Engrs. Episcopalian. Home: 5195 Hilltop Ln Cleveland OH 44131-1136

LEFEBVRE, PEGGY ANDERSON, advertising executive; b. Springfield, Mo., Dec. 2, 1951; d. Paul William and Norma Jean (Turk) Anderson; m.

Donald E. Lefebvre, July 25, 1980. BA in Graphic Arts cum laude, U. Ill., 1974; MBA, Pacific Western U., 1993. Coord. advt. and trade show Bell & Howell, Salt Lake City, 1971-74; designer, prodn. asst. Sta. KUTV, Salt Lake City, 1974; art dir. Associated Advt., Salt Lake City, 1977-80; owner, creative dir. Lefebvre Advt., Anaheim, Calif., 1980—; freelance designer various advt. agys., Chgo.; bd. dirs. Delmark Corp.; past guest lectr. advt. copywriting and bus. devel. Nat. U., Inc. Mag., Orange Coast Coll. One woman shows Ward Gallery, Chgo., 1974, Atrium Gallery, Salt Lake City, 1976. Past bd. dirs. MADD, Orange County Sexual Assault Network; mem. Anaheim Area Visitor and Conv. Bd., Western States Advt. Agy. Assn. Recipient Excellence in Creative Direction award, Bus. and Profl. Advt. Assn., 1989, 94, Outstanding Achievement in Advt. award Western Assn. Conv. & Visitor Burs, Award of Merit Bus. Comms. and Mktg. Assn. L.A., 1991, 95, Award of Excellence, 1995. Mem. DAR. Republican. Office: Lefebvre Advt 1547 E La Palma Ave Anaheim CA 92805-1614

LEFELHOCZ, IRENE HANZAK, nurse, business owner; b. Cleve., Nov. 10, 1926; d. Joseph J. and Gisella Elizabeth (Biro) Hanzak; m. Joseph R. Lefelhocz, Aug. 7, 1948; 1 child, Joseph R. III. RN, St. Luke's Hosp. Sch. Nursing, 1948; BSN, Case Western Res. U., 1963; MEd, John Carroll U., 1971; MSN, Case Western Reserve U., 1973. RN, Ohio, Ala. Pres., mgr. The Joseph House, Gadsen, Ala.; adminstrv. cons. The Episcopal Kyle Home, Gadsen; nurse cons. Ala. Dept. Health, Montgomery, Ala.; supr. Riverview Med. Ctr., Moragne Park, Gadsden; psychology therapist, counselor to inpatient population Mountain View Hosp., Gadsden; counselor Sch. Nursing, Holy Name of Jesus Med. Ctr. Mem. allocations com. United Way, Etowah County; active numerous other community orgns.; bd. dirs., vice chmn. Etowah County chpt. ARC. Mem. NEA, Ohio Edn. Assn., ARC (past pres.). Home: 173 Lake Shore Dr Gadsden AL 35906-8570 Office: Mountain View Hosp 3001 Scenic Dr Gadsden AL 35902

LEFER, ALLAN MARK, physiologist; b. N.Y.C., Feb. 1, 1936; s. I. Judah and Lillian G. (Gastwirth) L.; m. Mary E. Indoe, Aug. 23, 1959; children—Debra Lynn, David Joseph, Barry Lee and Leslie Ann (twins). BA, Adelphi Coll., 1957, Western Res. U., 1959; PhD (NSF fellow), U. Ill., Urbana, 1962. Instr. physiology, USPHS-NIH fellow Western Res. U., 1962-64; asst. prof. physiology U. Va., 1964-69, asso. prof., 1969-71, prof., 1972-74; vis. prof. Hadassah Med. Sch., Jerusalem, 1971-72; prof., chmn. dept. physiology Jefferson Med. Coll., Thomas Jefferson U., Phila., 1974—; dir. Ischemia-Shock Research Inst., 1980-95; cons. Merck & Co., Upjohn Co., Genentech Inc., Syntex, Inc., Ciba-Geigy, NIH, Nitromed, Bristol-Myers Squibb, Cytel Corp.; Wellcome Found.; vis. prof. 1985-86, Pfizer vis. prof. cardiovascular medicine, 1995; Nat. Bd. of Med. Examiners, Step 1, 1993-95. Author: Pathophysiology and Therapeutics of Myocardial Ischemia, 1977, Prostaglandins in Cardiovascular and Renal Function, 1979, Cellular and Molecular Aspects of Shock and Trauma, 1983; Leukotrienes in Cardiovascular and Pulmonary Function, 1985; mng. editor: Eicosanoids, 1988-93; cons. editor Circulatory Shock, 1973-80; field editor Jour. of Pharmacology and Exptl. Therapeutics Cardiovascular, 1994—; mem. editl. bd. Critical Care Medicine, Shock Am. Jour. Physiology, Endothelium, Drug News and Perspectives; contbr. to World Book Ency. Sci. Yearbook, 1979; contbr. over 500 sci. articles to profl. jours. Active Acad. Com. on Soviet Jewry, 1970—; chmn. United Jewish Appeal, 1973-74; coach basketball and baseball Huntingdon Valley Athletic Assn., 1975-78. Recipient Pres. and Visitor's prize in rsch. U. Va., 1970, Disting. Alumnus award U. Ill., 1996. Fellow Am. Coll. Cardiology; mem. AAAS, Am. Physiol. Soc., Am. Soc. Pharmacology and Exptl. Therapeutics, Internat. Heart Rsch. Soc., Am. Heart Assn. (established investigator 1968-73, fellow circulation coun., nat. grant rev. com. 1993-95), Pa. Heart Assn. (rsch. com.), Shock Soc. (chmn. membership com., pres. 1983-84, chmn. devel. com. 1985-89, chmn. internat. rels. com. 1993), Internat. Fed. Shock Socs. (coun. 1994—, pres. 4th internat. shock congress 1996—), Soc. Exptl. Biology and Medicine, Israel Soc. Physiology and Pharmacology, Phila. Physiol. Soc. (pres. 1978-79), Sierra Club, B'nai B'rith (Charlottesville chpt., v.p. 1967-68, chmn. Va. Hillel 1970-71), Sigma Xi. Democrat. Home: 3590 Walsh Ln Huntingdon Valley PA 19006-3226 Office: Thomas Jefferson Univ 1020 Locust St Philadelphia PA 19107-6731

LEFEVER, MICHAEL GRANT, state agency administrator; b. Lancaster, Pa., Sept. 12, 1947; s. Norwood Grant and Frances (Gillespie) LeF.; m. M. Malissa Burnette, 1989; 1 child, Grant Burnette. BA in English, Presbyn. Coll., 1969; MPA, U. S.C., 1976. Claims rep. Underwriters Adjusting Co., Columbia, S.C., 1972-73; project adminstr. CATAYTIC, Inc., Charlotte, N.C., 1973-75; dep. dir. S.C. Dept. Juvenile Placement and Aftercare, Columbia, 1977-81, dir., 1981; asst. commr. for adminstrn. S.C. Dept. Youth Svcs., Columbia, 1981-82, dep. commr., 1982-86; exec. dir. S.C. Worker's Compensation Commn., 1986—; interim commr. S.C. Dept. of Juvenile Justice, 1993; chmn. Serious and Violent Offender Study Com., Columbia, 1981-86; bd. dirs. State Agy. Dirs. Orgn., 1991-96, v.p. 1992, pres. 1993-95; bd. dirs. Ctr. for Cancer Treatment and Rsch. Richland Meml. Hosp., 1992, exec. com. 1994—, vice chmn., 1995—, S.C. State Quality Network, 1992-95; cons. Gov.'s Children Coordinating Cabinet, Columbia, 1981-86. Pres. Palmetto State Alumni chpt. Theta Chi, Columbia, 1973-83, Columbia Area Alumni Assn., Presbyn. Coll., Columbia, 1979, Windcrest Villas Homeowners Assn., North Myrtle Beach, S.C., 1989-90; treas. Planned Parenthood Cen. S.C., 1988-91, Bd. Assocs., 1991—; mem. adv. com. on pub. adminstrn., exec. com. U. S.C., 1988—; mem. bd. dirs. Presbyn. Coll., 1996—. Served with U.S. Army, 1970-71. Named Outstanding Pub. Adminstr., 1986. Mem. Nat. Youth Work Alliance (chmn. 1982-83), Am. Soc. for Pub. Adminstrn. (treas. S.C. chpt. 1987—), Mental Health Assn. Midlands, So. Assn. of Worker's Compensation Adminstrs. (exec. com. 1986—), Internat. Assn. Indsl. Accident Bds. and Commns. (chmn. adminstrn. and proc. com. 1989-93, exec. com. 1993—, sec. 1995—), S.C. Youth Workers Assn. (bd. dirs. 1979-83), Presbyn. Coll. Alumni Assn. (bd. dirs. 1986—, pres. 1988-89, Outstanding Young Alumnus award 1981). Home: 2721 Wheat St Columbia SC 29205-2538

LEFEVRE, DAVID E., lawyer, professional sports team executive; b. Cleve., Oct. 25, 1944; s. Fay A. and Mary (Eaton) LeF. B.A., Yale U., 1966; J.D., U. Mich., 1971. Bar: N.Y., U.S. Dist. Ct. (so. and ea. dists.) N.Y. Assoc. Reid & Priest, N.Y.C., 1971-78, ptnr., 1979—; owner Houston Astros Baseball Club, 1979-84, Cleve. Indians Baseball Club, 1984-86; gov., dir. Tampa Bay Lightning Tampa Bay Lightning, NHL; bd. dirs. lghtning Arena, Inc., TDC (USA), Inc., NHL Pension Soc.; chmn. bd. dirs. Chertsey Corp.; bd. govs. NHL, 1992—. Bd. dirs. Tampa Downtown Partnership; vol. Peace Corps, Uruguay, 1966-68. Recipient Spl. award Tampa Sports Club.; named Hon. Alumnus, Cleve. State U., 1985. Mem. ABA, Canyon Club (pres. Armonk, N.Y. 1986—), Nippon Club, Japan Soc., Alexis de Tocqueville Soc., Univ. Club of Tampa. Office: Tampa Bay Lightning 501 E Kennedy Blvd Tampa FL 33602 also: Reid & Priest 40 W 57th St New York NY 10019-4001

LEFEVRE, ELBERT WALTER, JR., civil engineering educator; b. Eden, Tex., July 29, 1932; s. Elbert Walter Sr. and Hazie (Davis) LeF.; m. Joyce Ann Terry, Nov. 28, 1957; children: Terry Ann, Charmaine Rene, George Walter, John Philip. BS in Civil Engring, Tex. A&M U., 1957, MS in Civil Engring, 1961; PhD, Okla. State U., 1966. Registered profl. engr., Ark., Tex. Faculty Tex. A&M U., Bryan, 1958, Tex. Technol. Coll., Lubbock, 1959-63, Okla. State U., Stillwater, 1963-66, U. Ark., Fayetteville, 1966—; head dept. civil engring. U. Ark., 1971-82, dean engring., 1982-83; sr. v.p. Engring. Svcs., Inc., Springdale, Ark., 1973—; dir. Nat. Rural Transp. Study Ctr., 1992—; mem. Ark. State Bd. Registration for Profl. Engrs. and Land Surveyors, 1984—, pres., 1989, 94; mem. Nat. Coun. Examiners for Engring. and Surveying, 1984—, v.p. So. zone, 1991-93, mem. accreditation bd. engring. and tech., 1985-91. Served to 1st lt. AUS, 1953-56. Fellow ASCE (pres. Mid-South sect. 1972, chmn. dist. 14 1977-80, dir. dist. 14 1983-86), Inst. Engrs. of Ireland; mem. NSPE (v.p. profl. engrs. in edn. 1982, v.p. S.W. region 1984-86, pres. 1989-90), Transp. Rsch. Bd., Am. Soc. Engring. Edn. (pres. midwest sect. 1976-77), Ark. Soc. Profl. Engrs. (pres. 1979-80, Outstanding Ark. Engr. 1980) Masons, Rotary (pres. 1973), Sigma Xi, Chi Epsilon, Tau Beta Pi, Phi Beta Delta. Home: 300 Paradise Ln Springdale AR 72762-3832 Office: Univ Ark Dept Civil Engring Fayetteville AR 72701
I owe a great debt to those whose efforts have provided me the opportunity to accomplish these things. Personal relationships dwarf the honors I have received.

LEFEVRE, GREG, bureau chief; b. Los Angeles, Jan. 28, 1947; s. Robert Bazille and Anna Marie (Violé) L.; m. Mary Deborah Bottoms, July 10, 1971. AA, Valley Coll., 1970; BS, San Diego State U., 1972, postgrad. Asst. news dir. Sta. KDEO, San Diego, 1971-73; reporter Sta. KFMB-TV, San Diego, 1973-75; sr. reporter Sta. KDFW-TV, Dallas, 1976-81; news dir. Sta. KSEE-TV, Fresno, Calif., 1981-83; corr. Cable News Network, San Francisco, 1983-89, bur. chief, 1989—. Mem. AP Broadcasters (bd. dirs. 1981-90), Soc. Profl. Journalists (pres. 1979-81), Radio and TV News Dirs. Assn. (bd. dirs. 1988-90). Club: Dallas Press (v.p. 1978-81). Office: CNN Am Inc 50 California St Ste 950 San Francisco CA 94111-4606

LEFEVRE, PERRY DEYO, minister, theology educator; b. Kingston, N.Y., July 12, 1921; s. Johannes and Faye (McFerran) LeF.; m. Carol Baumann, Sept. 14, 1946; children: Susan Faye, Judith Ann, Peter Gerret. AB, Harvard U., 1943; BD, Chgo. Theol. Sem., 1946, DD, 1992; PhD, U. Chgo., 1951. Ordained to ministry Congl. Ch., 1946. Instr. religion Franklin and Marshall Coll., 1948-49; asst., then assoc. prof. religion Knox Coll., 1949-53, Fed. Theol. Sem., U. Chgo., 1953-61; prof. constructive theology Chgo. Theol. Sem., 1961-92, dean of faculty, 1961-81, acting dean, 1990-91. Author: The Prayers of Kierkegaard, 1956, The Christian Teacher, 1958, Introduction to Religious Existentialism, 1963, Understandings of Man, 1966, Philosophical Resources for Christian Thought, 1968, Conflict in a Voluntary Association, 1975, Understandings of Prayer, 1981, Aging and the Human Spirit, 1981, Radical Prayer, 1982; editor: Paul Tillich: The Meaning of Health, 1984, Spiritual Nurture and Congregational Development, 1984, Daniel Day Williams Essays in Process Theology, 1985, Pastoral Care and Liberation Praxis, 1986, Bernard Meland Essays in Constructive Theology, 1988, Creative Ministries in Contemporary Christianity, 1991, Modern Theologies of Prayer, 1995. Mem. Phi Beta Kappa. Address: 5757 S University Ave Chicago IL 60637-1507

LEFEVRE, THOMAS VERNON, retired utility company executive, lawyer; b. Dallas, Dec. 5, 1918; s. Eugene H. and Callie E. (Powell) L.; m. Lillian Herndon Bourne, Oct. 12, 1946; children: Eugene B., Nicholas R., Sharon A., Margot P. BA, U. Fla., 1939, LLB, 1942; LLM, Harvard U., 1946. Bar: Fla. 1945, N.Y. 1947, D.C. 1951, Pa. 1955, U.S. Supreme Ct. 1953. Atty. IRS and various firms, N.Y.C., Washington, and Phila., 1946-55; ptnr. Morgan, Lewis & Bockius, Phila., 1956-79; pres., chief exec. officer UGI Corp., Valley Forge, Pa., 1979-85, chmn., 1983-89; chmn. G.P. Hospitality, Inc., 1981—; mem. Commr.'s Adv. Group IRS, 1976-77. Bd. dirs. Zool. Soc. Phila., 1982-91, WHYY Inc., 1982—; chmn. U. Arts, 1986-89; trustee Franklin Inst., 1980-89, Fox Chase Cancer Ctr., 1979-88. With USMC, 1942-46. Fellow ABA (vice chmn. govt. rels. sect. of taxation 1976-79), Am. Bar Found.; mem. Pa. Bar Assn., Phila. Club, Merion Cricket Club, Merion Golf Club, Sankaty Head Golf Club, Nantucket Yacht Club. Episcopalian. Office: Fidelity Ct Bldg Ste 145 259 Radnor Chester Rd Wayne PA 19087-5240

LE FEVRE, WILLIAM MATHIAS, JR., brokerage company executive; b. Muskegon, Mich., Dec. 22, 1927; s. William Mathias and Crystal (Atkinson) LeF.; m. Ada Marie Cannon, 1949 (div. 1973); children—Marie L. Keidel, Jeanne L. Van Vlandren, William Mathias III, Suzanne C.; m. Mathilda Bock Maguire, 1976. Grad., Phillips Exeter Acad., 1946; student, U. Mich., 1946-48. Floor ptnr. Arthur Wiesenberger & Co., N.Y.C., 1956-60; assoc. oddlot broker DeCoppet & Doremus, N.Y.C., 1961-64; v.p. Carter, Walker & Co. Inc., N.Y.C., 1964-68, Bruns, Nordeman & Co., N.Y.C., 1969-71; dir. research Sade & Co., Washington, 1972-73, Mack Bushnell & Edelman, N.Y.C., 1973-74; v.p. investment strategy Granger & Co., N.Y.C., 1974-80, Purcell, Graham & Co., N.Y.C., 1980-86; sr. v.p. market strategy Advest Inc., N.Y.C., 1986-91, Tucker Anthony Inc., N.Y.C., 1991-93, Sutro & Co., San Francisco, 1991-93; sr. market analyst Ehrenkrantz King Nussbaum Inc., N.Y.C., 1993—; mem. N.Y. Stock Exchange, 1958-64; assoc. mem. Am. Stock Exchange, 1960-62; speaker various colls., univs. and indsl. assns., 1977—. Editor: Monday Morning Market Memo, 1973—; contbr. market commentary radio and TV, 1980—. Mem. Assn. for Investment Mgmt. and Rsch., N.Y. Soc. Security Analysts. Home: 132 E 35th St New York NY 10016-3892 also: 78 Grassy Hill Rd Old Lyme CT 06371-1352 Office: Ehrenkrantz King Nussbaum Inc 598 Madison Ave New York NY 10022

LEFF, ALAN RICHARD, medical educator, researcher; b. Pitts., May 23, 1945; s. Maurice D. and Grace Ruth (Schwartz) L.; m. Donna Rae Rosene, Feb. 14, 1975; children: Marni, Karen, Alison. AB cum laude, Oberlin Coll., 1967; MD, U. Rochester, 1971. Diplomate Am. Bd. Internal Medicine, Am. Bd. Pulmonary Disease. Intern U. Mich. Hosp., Ann Arbor, 1971-72, resident, 1974-76; fellow U. Calif.-San Francisco, 1976-77, postdoctoral fellow, 1977-79; asst. prof. medicine U. Chgo., 1979-85, assoc. prof.medicine and clin. pharm., 1985-89, prof. medicine, anesthesia and critical care and clin. pharm., 1989—, prof. cell physiology, 1992—, prof. pediatrics, 1993—, prof. pharm. and physical scis., 1993—, dir. pulmonary medicine service, 1984-87, dir. Pulmonary Function Lab., 1979-87, chief sect. pulmonary and critical care medicine, 1987—; dir. NIAID Asthma and Allergic Dis. Coop. Rsch. Ctr., Chgo., 1993—; advisor San Francisco Dept. Pub. Health, 1977-79, Chgo. Dept. Health, 1979—; bd. dirs. Chgo. Lung Assn., 1984-93. Cons. editor Jour. Clin. Invest., editorial bd. Am. Jour. Physiology, Jour. Applied Physiology; editor Am. Jour. Respir. Critical Care Medicine, 1994—; assoc. editor Am. Rev. Respiratory Disease, 1989-94, Pulmonary Pharm., 1987; contbr. articles to profl. jours. Served with USPHS, 1972-74. Recipient Citation of merit Chgo. Lung Assn., 1974; Leopold Schepp Found. fellow, 1967-69. Fellow Am. Coll. Chest Physicians; mem. Am. Fedn. Clin. Research (councilor 1983-86), Am. Soc. Clin. Investigation, Am. Physiological Soc., Cent. Soc. for Clin. Investigation, Assn. Am. Physicians, Sigma Xi. Avocation: music. Home: 5730 S Kimbark Ave Chicago IL 60637-1615 Office: U Chgo Pritzker Sch Medicine Div Biological Scis MC 6076 5841 S Maryland Ave Chicago IL 60637-1463

LEFF, ILENE J(OAN), management consultant, corporate and government executive,; b. N.Y.C., Mar. 29, 1942; d. Abraham and Rose (Levy) L.; BA cum laude, U. Pa., 1964; MA with honors, Columbia U., 1969. Statis./computer analyst McKinsey & Co., N.Y.C., 1969-70, rsch. cons., 1971-74, mgmt. cons., N.Y.C. and Europe, 1974-78; dir. exec. resources Revlon, Inc., N.Y.C., 1978-81, dir. human resources, 1981-83, dir. personnel, 1983-86; cons. APM Inc., 1986-88, ind. mgmt. cons., 1988-93, 95—; dep. asst. sec. for mgmt. HUD, Washington, 1993-94; rsch. asst. U. Pa., Phila., 1964-65; employment counselor State of N.J., Newark, 1965-66; tchr., Newark, 1966-69; lectr. Grad. Program in Pub. Policy, New Sch. for Social Rsch., Wharton Sch., Duke U.; chmn. com. on employment and unemployment, mem. exec. com. Bus. Rsch. Adv. Coun., U.S. Bur. Labor Stats., 1980; sr. del. econ. rels. and trade Sino-U.S. Conf., 1986. Ops. coun. Jr. Achievement Greater N.Y., 1975-78; cons. Com. for Econ. Devel., N.Y. Hosp., Regional Plan Assn., Am. Cancer Soc.; vol. for dep. mayor for ops. N.Y.C., 1977-78. Mem. N.Y. Human Resource Planners (treas. 1984), Fin. Women's Assn. N.Y. (exec. bd., 1977-78, 83-84), The Fashion Group (treas. 1989). Contbr. issue papers and program recommendations to candidates for U.S. Pres., U.S. Senate and Congress, N.Y. State Gov., mayor N.Y.C. Office: 767 5th Ave New York NY 10153

LEFF, JOSEPH NORMAN, yarn manufacturing company executive; b. N.Y.C., Dec. 17, 1923; s. Phillip and Lillian (Wiesen) L.; m. Joyce Hochberg, June 12, 1954 (div. 1958); 1 child, Julie; m. Juanita Hughey, Dec. 17, 1967; 1 child, Valerie. BS, Columbia U., 1944, AB, 1946. Treas. Nat. Spinning Co. Inc., N.Y.C., 1949-63, pres., chief exec. officer, 1963-83, chmn., chief exec. officer, 1983—. Mem. bd. visitors Columbia Coll., N.Y.C., 1987-92; trustee Park Ave. Synagogue, N.Y.C., 1987-95; bd. dirs., pres. 92nd St. YM/YWHA, N.Y.C., 1994—; bd. dirs. Inst. Textile Tech., Va., 1982—. With U.S. Army, 1944-45. Mem. Woolknit Assocs. (bd. dirs.), Acrylic Coun. (pres. 1988—). Jewish. Clubs: Harmonie (pres. 1974-75) (N.Y.C.); Quaker Ridge Golf (Scarsdale, N.Y.).

LEFF, SANDRA H., gallery director, consultant; b. N.Y.C., Dec. 24, 1939; d. I. Bernard and Rose (Kupfer) L. BA, Cornell U., 1960; MA, Inst. Fine Arts, N.Y.C., 1969. Editorial asst. Indsl. Design Mag., N.Y.C., 1960-61; instr., asst. Mus. of City of N.Y., 1962-65; assoc. print dept. Sotheby Parke Bernet, N.Y.C., 1969-73; rsch. asst. Daniel Chester French Exhibit, Washington, 1975-77; dir. Am. painting Graham Gallery, N.Y.C., 1977-93. Author: (exhbn. catalogs) Thomas Anshutz: Paintings, Watercolors and Pastels, 1979, Guy Pène du Bois: Painter, Draftsman and Critic, 1979, Helen Torr, 1980, John White Alexander: Fin-de-Siècle American, 1980, Jan Matulka & Vaclav Vytlacil, 1992. Ford Found. fellow, 1967. Mem. Phi Beta Kappa. Avocations: reading, traveling, jogging, film, photography.

LEFF, SHERWIN ALLEN, sales and advertising executive; b. Chgo., Sept. 1, 1942; s. Herman Nathan and Ethel (Rosenberg) Lefkovitz; m. Jill Lee Lampert, May 21, 1967; children: Peter Joshua, Megan Sydney. BSBA, Roosevelt U., 1969; MBA, DePaul U., 1971. Br. mgr. Alberto-Culver, Melrose Park, Ill., 1968-70; account supr. Needham, Harper & Steers, Chgo., 1970-73; account dir. Frankel & Co., Chgo., 1973-76, dir. client svcs., 1979-82; pres. Marcus-Leff Inc., Chgo., 1976-79; exec. v.p., dir. client svcs. Foote, Cone & Belding/Impact, Chgo., 1982—. Bd. mem. B'nai Jehoshua Beth Elohim Synagogue, Glenview, Ill., 1984-88. 3d class petty officer USN, 1959-63. Jewish. Home: 2061 Glen Lake Dr Glenview IL 60025 Office: Foote Cone & Belding/IMPACT 101 E Erie Chicago IL 60611

LEFFALL, LASALLE D(OHENY), JR., surgeon; b. Tallahassee, May 22, 1930; s. LaSalle Doheny Sr. and Martha (Jordan) L.; m. Ruth McWilliams; 1 child, LaSalle Doheny III. BS, Fla. A&M U., 1948; MD, Howard U., 1952. Intern Homer G. Phillips Hosp., St. Louis, 1952-53; resident Freedmen's Hosp., Washington, 1953-57; fellow Meml. Sloan Kettering Cancer Ctr., N.Y.C., 1957-70; chmn. dept. surgery Howard U. Coll. Medicine, Washington, 1970-95, acting dean, 1970, Charles R. Drew prof. surgery, 1992—. Contbr. articles on cancer to profl. publs. Pres. Soc. Surg. Oncology, 1978-79, Am. Cancer Soc., 1978-79, ACS, 1995-96. Capt. U.S. Army, 1960-61. Recipient St. George medal and citation Am. Cancer Soc., 1977, Nat. Achievement award Black Caucus Dem. Nat. Com., 1982, Exceptional Black Scientist award CIBA-Geigy, 1984. Mem. Internat. Fedn. Surg. Colls. (assoc.), Med. Edn. for South African Blacks (bd. dirs. 1988—). Avocations: tennis, modern jazz, fgn. langs. Office: Howard Univ Coll Med 2400 6th St NW Washington DC 20059-0001

LEFFEK, KENNETH THOMAS, chemist, educator; b. Nottingham, Eng., Oct. 15, 1934; emigrated to Can., 1959, naturalized, 1966; s. Thomas and Ivy Louise (Pye) L.; m. Janet Marilyn Wallace, Sept. 26, 1958; children: Katharine, Geoffrey. B.S., Univ. Coll., London, 1956, Ph.D., 1959. Asst. prof. chemistry Dalhousie U., Halifax, N.S., 1961-67; assoc. prof. Dalhousie U., 1967-72, prof., 1972-94, dean grad. studies, 1972-90, prof. chemistry, 1990-94, ret., 1994; chmn. Atlantic Provinces Interuniv. Com. on Scis., 1975-77. Author: Sir Christopher Ingold, a Biography; contbr. articles on phys.-organic chemistry to profl. jours. Leverhulme fellow U. Kent (Eng.), 1967-68. Fellow Chem. Inst. Can., Royal Soc. Arts (London; chmn. Atlantic Can. chpt. 1987-91); mem. Chem. Soc. London, Chem. Inst. Can. (nat. dir. tech. and sci. affairs 1980-83, nat. v.p. 1985-86, pres. 1986-87). Home: 980 Kentwood Ter, Victoria, BC Canada V8Y 1A6

LEFFELL, DAVID JOEL, surgeon, dermatologist, educator, researcher; b. Montreal, Feb. 28, 1956; came to U.S., 1973; s. Allen Bernard and Freda (Deckelbaum) L. BS, Yale U., 1977; MD, McGill U., Montreal, 1981. Diplomate Am. Bd. Dermatology, Am. Bd. Internal Medicine. Resident in internal medicine Meml. Sloan-Kettering Cancer Ctr., N.Y.C., 1981-84; instr. medicine Cornell U. Sch. Medicine, N.Y.C., 1983-84; lectr., fellow dermatologic surgery U. Mich., Ann Arbor, 1987-88; resident in dermatology Yale U. Sch. Medicine, New Haven, 1984-86, assoc. prof. dermatology, plastic surgery and otolaryngology, 1988—, chief Mohs micrographic surgery and laser surgery, 1988—, dir. Yale skin cancer detection program, 1988—, med. dir. faculty practice plan, 1996—; sci. advisor Nat. Hereditary Hemorrhagic Telangiectasia Found., New Haven, 1991—. Contbg. editor: Jour. Dermatologic Surgery and Oncology; assoc. editor Med. and Surg. Dermatology; mem. editl. bd. Archives of Dermatology; assoc. editor: Geriatric Dermatology; inventor laser fluorescence device to measure photoaging. Recipient Frederic Mohs award Skin Cancer Found., 1988, 91. Mem. Conn. Dermatology Soc. (sec.-treas.). Home: 69 Mumford Rd New Haven CT 06515-2431 Office: Yale Sch Medicine 333 Cedar St New Haven CT 06510-3206

LEFFERTS, GEORGE, writer, producer, director; b. Paterson, N.J.. B.A. in Engring. (Nat. Merit scholar, William Rose scholar), Drew U., 1940; B.A. in English, U. Mich., 1942. Exec. producer, writer, dir. NBC, 1947-57; pres. George Lefferts Assocs., 1968—; exec. prodr. ABC, 1966-67, Time-Life Films, 1980-81; tchr. John Hopkins U., Balt., 1989-90, Rutgers U., 1992—; prodr., writer, dir. Network for Continuing Med. Edn., 1990—; program cons. ABC, 1981. Exhibited sculpture, Sculpture Gallery, N.Y.C., 1960; producer: series Report from America, U.S. Dept. State, Tactic, Am. Cancer Soc., others; (Recipient Nat. Media award 1961, Fame award 1962, Fgn. Press award 1963, Golden Globe award 1967, Plaudit award Producers Guild 1968, 69, Cine Golden Eagle award 1974, Peabody award 1970, 75, 1st prize San Francisco Film Festival 1970; nominee Humanitas Prize 1988); author: plays Nantucket Legend, 1960, The Boat, 1968, Hey Everybody, 1969; columnist N.Y. Observer, Litchfield County Times, 1984-87 (1st prize New England Journalism award, 1984, 85); also author mag. articles, works on piano method, syndicated columns, others; prodns. include Biographies in Sound (Peabody award 1956), NBC Theatre, (Ohio State award 1955), Kraft Theatre, Armstrong Circle Theatre, Studio One, Lights Out, Frank Sinatra Show; spl. program Pain, 1971, Bravo Picasso!, 1972, What Price Health; program NBC Investigative Reports, 1972 (Albert Lasker award), CBS, Ben Franklin Series (Peabody award 1975, Emmy award 1975), Ryan's Hope, 1977 (Emmy award 1977), Purex Specials, 1966 (Emmy award 1966), The People vs. Jean Harris, 1981; exec. producer, writer, dir., NBC, Spls. for Women (2 Emmy awards 1965); series (Emmy award 1962), 1961 (Golden Globe award 1961); exec. producer: series Breaking Point, 1962-64 (Producers Guild Plaudit award 1963), CBS, Smithsonian Spls., 1974-75, ABC, Wide World of Entertainment, 1973-74, Bing Crosby Prodns., 1962-64; exec. producer: Wolper Prodns., 1974-75, Time/Life Films, 1978-79; original films produced include: series The Living End, 1959, The Stake, 1960, The Teenager, 1965, The Harness, 1972, The Night They Took Miss Beautiful, 1977, Bud & Lou, 1978, Mean Dog Blues, 1979, The Search for Alexander the Great, 1981, Dressed to Kill, 1980; producer: series Hallmark Hall of Fame, 1969-70, Never Say Goodbye, 1987 (Emmy award 1988, Humanitas award nomination 1988), TV play Teacher, Teacher, 1974 (Emmy award 1974). Served with AUS, 1942-45. Mem. Nat. Acad. TV Arts and Scis., Am. Acad. Motion Picture Arts and Scis., Christopher Morley Knothole Assn. Club: South Bay Cruising (Babylon, (N.Y.).

LEFFERTS, GILLET, JR., architect; b. N.Y.C., May 6, 1923; s. Gillet and Helen Willets (Lambert) L.; m. Lucia Beverly Hollerith, Apr. 21, 1951; children: Helena Gillet (dec.), Robert Beverly, John Willets, Sarah Fox, David Hollerith. A.B., Williams Coll., 1947; M.F.A., Princeton, 1950. Apprentice Moore & Hutchins, N.Y.C., 1947-48, 50-55; assoc. Moore & Hutchins, 1955-66, ptnr., 1967-72; partner Hutchins, Evans & Lefferts, N.Y.C., 1972-89; mem. William A. Hall Partnership, Architecture and Planning, N.Y.C., 1990—; instr. Mechanics Inst., N.Y.C., 1955-58. Architect: master plan and ednl. facilities SUNY-Binghampton, 1956—, Buffalo, 1981-85; master plan Coll. Agr., Malaya, 1970, St. Johnland Nursing Home, L.I., N.Y., 1976, Clark Gymnasium, Cooperstown, N.Y., 1986, Nat. Baseball Hall of Fame and Mus. Expansion, Cooperstown, 1988-89, 93-94, Scholes Libr. Coll. Ceramics, Alfred U., 1992. Mem. zoning bd. appeals Town of Darien, Conn., 1961-69, mem. planning and zoning commn., 1969-77, chmn., 1973-77, mem. bd. selectmen, 1983-89; pres. Darien Hist. Soc., 1982-83; mem. bd. trustees Darien Pub. Libr., 1991—. With USAAF, 1943-46. Decorated Air medal with oak leaf cluster. Fellow AIA; mem. Fairfield County Alumni Assn. Williams Coll. (v.p. 1965-67), Nat. Inst. Archtl. Edn. (chmn. bd. trustees 1963-65, treas. 1970-73), Delta Psi. Episcopalian. Clubs: Century Assn. (N.Y.C.), Williams (N.Y.C.); Norwalk (Conn.); Yacht. Office: 42 E 21st St New York NY 10010-7201

LEFFERTS, WILLIAM GEOFFREY, physician, educator; b. Towanda, Pa., Mar. 24, 1943; s. William LeRoy and Beatrice (Smith) L.; m. Susan Lynn Hiles, Oct. 31, 1970. B.A., Hamilton Coll., 1965; M.D., Hahnemann Med. Coll., 1969. Intern Hahnemann Hosp., 1969-70; resident in internal medicine Cleve. Clinic Hosp., 1970-73, chief med. resident, 1972-73; asst. prof. internal medicine Hahnemann Med. Coll., 1973-77; assoc. prof. Med. Coll. Pa., 1978-82, dir. primary care unit, 1978-82, dir. div. gen. internal medicine, 1979-82; staff physician Cleve. Clinic Found., 1982—. Fellow ACP. Office: 9500 Euclid Ave Cleveland OH 44195-0001

LEFFLER, MELVYN P., history educator; b. N.Y.C., May 31, 1945; s. Louis and Mollie (Fuchs) L.; m. Phyllis Koran, Sept. 1, 1968; children: Sarah Ann, Elliot. BS, Cornell U., 1966; PhD, Ohio State U., 1972. Asst. prof. Vanderbilt U., Nashville, 1972-77, assoc. prof., 1977-86; internat. affairs fellow Coun. Fgn. Rels. Dept. Def., Washington, 1979-80; prof. U. Va., Charlottesville, 1986-94, Edward R. Stettinius prof. history, 1994—, chmn. hist. dept., 1990—. Author: The Elusive Quest, 1979, A Preponderance of Power, 1992 (Bancroft, Ferrell & Hoover prizes 1993), The Specter of Communism, 1994; contbr. articles to profl. jours. Fellow Woodrow Wilson Internat. Ctr., 1979, Am. Coun. Learned Socs., 1984, Nobel Peace Inst., 1994. Mem. Am. Hist. Assn., Orgn. Am. Hists., Soc. Hists. Am. Fgn. Rels. (v.p. 1993, future pres., Bernath Article prize 1984). Jewish. Home: 1612 Concord Dr Charlottesville VA 22901-3135 Office: U Va History Dept Randall Hall Charlottesville VA 22903

LEFFLER, STACY BRENT, government employee; b. Quincy, Ill., May 22, 1944; s. Burl William and Eva Elaine (Wood) L.; m. Shirley Mazer, Oct. 6, 1970; children: Sean Alisha, Bar-El Haim. BS in Math., N.Mex. Inst. Mining & Tech., 1974; MA in Internat. Rels., N.Mex. State U., 1982. Ops. rsch. analyst Dept. of the Navy, China Lake, Calif., 1974-76; ops. rsch. analyst Dept. of the Army, White Sands Missile Range, N.Mex., 1976-89, Ft. Bliss, Tex., 1989-94; chmn. Joint Svcs. Command and Control Decision Aids Working Group, 1991-92. With U.S. Army, 1963-67. Mem. NRA (life), Mil. Ops. Rsch. Soc., Assn. of the U.S. Army, Jewish War Vets., Mensa, Intertel, Pi Sigma Alpha. Jewish. Avocations: shooting sports, scuba diving, computers, reading. Home: PO Box 742 Santa Teresa NM 88008-0742

LEFKO, JEFFREY JAY, hospital planner; b. St. Paul, July 15, 1945; s Morris and Dorothy (Mindell) L.; m. Philomena M. Corno, Mar. 6, 1970 (div. Dec. 1984); children: Melissa Ann, Benjamin Scott, Ellen Rachael; m. Mary Wilson, Jan. 10, 1986 (div. June 1989); m. Susan H. Shockley, Jan. 5, 1990. BSBA with distinction, U. Nebr., 1967; M in Hosp. Adminstrn., Washington U., St. Louis, 1969. Adminstrv. resident St. John's Mercy Hosp., St. Louis, 1968-69; nat. fellow Health Services Adminstrn. Am. Hosp. Assn.-Blue Cross Assn., Chgo., 1969-70; v.p. planning/ops. Meth. Hosp. of Ind., Indpls., 1970-75; v.p. Jewish Hosp., St. Louis, 1975-78; v.p. planning Greenville (S.C.) Hosp. System, 1979-88; exec. cons. The Lash Group, Greenville, 1988-90; v.p. planning Union Meml. Hosp., Balt., 1990-93; v.p. planning and mktg. St. Joseph Med. Ctr., Balt., 1993—; adj. instr. Washington U., 1976-78; guest lectr. Duke U., Univ. S.C., Clemson U., Ind. U.; instr. Furman U., Greenville, 1982-84, Med. Univ. of S.C. 1989. Contbr. articles to profl. jours.; contbr. to (book) Guide to Strategic Plannin g for Hosps., 1981; mem. edit. bd. Health Care Strategic Mgmt., 1984—. Mem. Am. Hosp. Ass. (pres. Soc. for Hosp. Planning and Mktg. 1984-85), Am. Coll. of Health Care Execs., Carolinas Soc. of Hosp. Planning (founding mem.), Innocents Soc., Beta Gamma Sigma. Lodge: Rotary. Avocations: coaching boys' baseball, basketball clubs, reading, tennis, baseball card collecting. Office: St Joseph Med Ctr 7620 York Rd Baltimore MD 21204-7508

LEFKOWITZ, HOWARD N., lawyer; b. Utica, N.Y., Oct. 28, 1936; s. Samuel I. and Sarah Lefkowitz; m. Martha Yelon, June 16, 1958; children: Sarah, David. BA, Cornell U., 1958; LLB, Columbia U., 1963. Bar: N.Y. 1963, Fla. 1979, D.C. 1981. Ptnr. Proskauer Rose Goetz & Mendelsohn LLP, N.Y.C., 1963—; mem. tri-bar opinion com., editl. subcom. Editor Columbia Law Rev., 1963; author New York LLC Forms and Practice Manual, 1994. Served to lt. (j.g.) USN, 1958-61. Kent scholar Columbia U. Law Sch. Fellow Am. Coll. Investment Counsel; mem. ABA (mem. ltd. liability entity subcom. of bus. sect. 1993—), Assn. of Bar of City of N.Y. (chmn. com. on corp. law 1990-93), N.Y. County Lawyers Assn. (chmn. com. on comm. entertainment and arts-related law 1983-86). Office: Proskauer Rose Goetz & Mendelsohn LLP 1585 Broadway New York NY 10036-8299

LEFKOWITZ, JERRY, lawyer, accountant; b. N.Y.C., Jan. 3, 1945; s. Seymour Arthur and Edna (Mann) L.; children: David Scott, Deborah Lynn. BS in Econs., U. Pa., 1966; JD, Boston U., 1969. Bar: N.Y. 1970; CPA, N.Y., 1971. Tax mgr. Arthur Andersen & Co., N.Y.C., 1969-77, KMG Peat, Marwick, N.Y.C., 1977-82; sr. tax ptnr. Rosenblatt, Slavet & Radezky, CPA's, N.Y.C., 1982—; atty. Slavet & Lefkowitz, P.C., N.Y.C., 1982—. Avocations: tennis, golf. Home: 80 Arthur Ct Port Chester NY 10573-3124 Office: 292 Madison Ave New York NY 10017-6307

LEFKOWITZ, LAWRENCE, lawyer; b. Bklyn., Feb. 5, 1938; s. Mortimer and Sylvia Lefkowitz; m. Janet Goldblatt, Sept. 3, 1961; children: James, Karen, Diane. AB, Franklin and Marshall Coll., 1959; JD, Columbia U., N.Y.C., 1962. Bar: N.Y. 1962. Atty., examiner SEC, Washington, 1962-64; assoc., ptnr. Guzik and Boukstein, N.Y.C., 1964-73; ptnr. Reavis and McGrath, N.Y.C., 1973-77; v.p. legal, sec. Ampal-Am. Israel Corp., N.Y.C., 1977-90, pres., 1990—; counsel Bank Hapoalim, B.M., 1990—. Commr. Hartsdale (N.Y.) Pub. Parking Dist., 1973-92. Mem. ABA. Democrat. Jewish. Avocations: fishing, tennis.

LEFKOWITZ, MARY ROSENTHAL, Greek literature educator; b. N.Y.C., Apr. 30, 1935; d. Harold L. and Mena (Weil) Rosenthal; m. Alan L. Lefkowitz, July 1, 1956 (div.); children: Rachel, Hannah; m. Hugh Lloyd-Jones, Mar. 26, 1982. BA, Wellesley Coll., 1957; AM, Radcliffe Coll., 1959, PhD, 1961; LHD (honoris causa), Trinity Coll., Hartford, Conn., 1996. Instr. Greek Wellesley (Mass.) Coll., 1960-63, asst. prof. Greek and Latin, 1964-69, assoc. prof. Greek and Latin, 1969-75, prof. Greek and Latin, 1975-79; Andrew W. Mellon prof. in the humanities Wellesley (Mass.) Coll, 1979—; vis. prof. U. Calif., Berkeley, 1978; vis. fellow St. Hilda's Coll., 1979-80, Corpus Christi Coll., 1991. Author: Heroines and Hysterics, 1981, Lives of the Greek Poets, 1981, Women in Greek Myth, 1986, First Person Fictions, 1991, Not Out of Africa, 1996; co-editor: Women's Life in Greece and Rome, 1982, 2d edit., 1992, Black Athena Revisited, 1996. Fellow NEH, 1979-80, 91, ACLS, 1972-73, Hon. fellow St. Hilda's Coll., Oxford, 1994—. Mem. Am. Philol. Assn. (bd. dirs. 1974-77), Class Assn. New Eng. (pres. 1972-73). Home: 15 W Riding St Wellesley MA 02181-6914 Office: Wellesley Coll 106 Central St Wellesley MA 02181-8209

LEFKOWITZ, ROBERT JOSEPH, physician, educator; b. N.Y.C., Apr. 15, 1943; s. Max and Rose (Levine) L.; children: David, Larry, Cheryl, Mara, Joshua; m. Lynn Tilley, May 26, 1991. B.A., Columbia U., 1962, M.D., 1966. Diplomate: Am. Bd. Internal Medicine. Assoc. prof medicine Duke U., Durham, N.C., 1973-77, prof. medicine, 1977—, James B. Duke prof. medicine, 1982—, prof. biochemistry, 1985—; investigator Howard Hughes Med. Inst., Durham, 1976—. Author: Receptor Binding Studies in Adrenergic Pharmacology, 1978, Receptor Regulation, 1981, Principles of Biochemistry, 1983. Am. Heart Assn. established investigator, 1973-76, Basic Rsch. prize, 1990; recipient Young Scientist award Passano Found., 1978, George Thorn award Howard Hughes Med. Inst., 1979, Oppenheimer award, 1982, Gordon Wilson medal Am. Clin. and Climatol. Assn., 1982, Lita Annenberg Hazen award, 1983, outstanding rsch. award Internat. Soc. for Heart Rsch., 1985, H.B. van Dyke award Coll. Physicians and Surgeons Columbia U., 1986, Steven C. Beering award Ind. U. Sch. Medicine, 1986, N.C. award in Sci., 1987, Internat. award Gairdner Found., 1988, Novo Nordsk Biotech. award, 1990, Biomed. Rsch.award Assn. Am. Med. Colls., 1990, City of Medecin award, N.C., 1991, Columbia U. Coll. of Physicians and Surgeons Alumnus award for Disting. achievements in medicine, 1992, Bristol-Meyers Squibb award for Disting. achievement in Cardiovascular rsch., 1992, The Giovani Lorenzini Prize for Basic Biomedical Rsch., 1992, Columbia U. coll. of Physicians and Surgeons Joseph Mather Smith Prize, 1993, The Endocrine Soc. Gerald D. Aurbach Lectr. award Inst. of Medicine NAS, 1995, J. David Gladstone Insts. Disting. Lecture award, 1996, Bio/Tech. Winter Symposia Feodor Lynen award. Mem. Am. Soc. Biol. Chemists, Am. Soc. Clin. Investigation (counselor, 1982-85, pres.-elect 1986-87, pres. 1987-88), Assn. Am. Physicians (treas. 1989-94), Am. Soc. Pharmacology and Exptl. Therapeutics (John J. Abel award 1978, Goodman and Gilman award 1986), Endocrine Soc., Am. Fedn. Clin. Research (sec.-treas. 1980-83, mem. nat. council 1978-83), NAS, Am. Acad. Arts and Scis., Japanese Biochem.soc. (hon.), Am. Heart Assn. Basic Rsch. Soc. Office: Duke Univ Med Ctr PO Box 3821 Durham NC 27710-0001

LEFLER, LISA JANE, anthropologist and social sciences educator; b. Gastonia, N.C., Jan. 21, 1959; d. Buddy Allen and Jean (Nations) L. AA in Liberal Arts, Montreat-Anderson Coll., 1979; BA in Psychology, Appalachian State U., 1981; MA in Edn., Western Carolina U., 1988, EDS, 1991; postgrad., U. Tenn. Instr. social scis. Southwestern C.C., Sylva, N.C., 1988-93, Haywood C.C., Clyde, N.C., 1990—; instr. history Western Carolina U., Cullowhee, N.C., 1989, 93, vis. instr. anthropology Dept. Continuing Edn., 1990, instr. dept. anthropology, continuing edn. instr., 1990—, instr. regional history, 1990—, lectr. new beginning program, 1989-92, instr. anthropology, 1991—; also counselor asst. upward bound program Western Carolina U., 1989, lectr. new beginning program, 1989-92; chem. dependency curriculum writer, grant writer, lectr. Unity Regional Treatment Ctr./Indian Health Svc., Cherokee, N.C., 1990, 93—; mem. subcom. Project Healthy Cherokee. Chair Mountain Heritage Ctr. Mus. Vols.; former bd. dirs. Catch the Spirit of Appalachia, Inc. Tennis scholar Montreat-Anderson Coll., 1977-79. Mem. Am. Anthrop. Assn., Southeastern Anthrop. Soc., Appalachian Studies Assn. Mem. Worldwide Ch. of God. Avocations: tennis, walking, camping reading. Home: RR 1 Box 204C Whittier NC 28789-9626

LEFLER, WADE HAMPTON, JR., ophthalmologist; b. Statesville, N.C., Feb. 27, 1937; s. Wade Hampton and Eunice Trudye (Chilcoat) L.; AB, U. N.C., Chapel Hill, 1959; MD, Bowman Gray Sch. Medicine, 1963; m. Katherine Webb Davis, Apr. 1, 1961; children: Elizabeth Ashley Wilson, Rosemary Kirsten, Ririe. Med. intern N.Y. Hosp., Cornell Med. Center, 1963-64; resident in ophthalmology Duke U. Med. Center, 1966-69; practice medicine specializing in ophthalmology, Hickory, N.C., 1969—; partner Graystone Eye, Ear, Nose, Throat Center, Hickory, 1974—; clin. assoc. prof. ophthalmology Duke Med. Center, 1969—; mem. staff Catawba Meml. Hosp., Hickory, Frye Regional Med. Ctr., Hickory, Western Carolina Center, Morganton, N.C., Duke Eye Center, Durham, N.C., Oteen VA Hosp., Asheville, N.C. Trustee Catawba Meml. Hosp., 1990-94. Served to capt. M.C., U.S. Army, 1964-66. Duke U. Med. Center grantee, 1968-70; diplomate Am. Acad. Ophthalmology. Mem. AMA, N.C. Med. Soc., Catawba County Med. Soc., Med. Alumni Assn. Bowman Gray Sch. Medicine (pres. 1993, Disting. Svc. award 1995), Phi Beta Kappa, Alpha Omega Alpha. Presbyterian. Club: Lake Hickory Country. Home: 1260 6th St NW Hickory NC 28601-2408 Office: PO Box 2588 Hickory NC 28603

LEFLY, DIANNE LOUISE, research psychologist; b. Denver, July 17, 1946; d. Gordon Eugene Boen and Elizabeth (Welsh) Tuveson. AB, U. No. Colo., 1968; MA, U. Colo., 1980; PhD, U. Denver, 1994. Classroom tchr. Adam County Sch. Dist. #12, Thornton, Colo., 1968-77; rschr. John F. Kennedy Child Devel. Ctr., Denver, 1979-81, U. Colo. Health Scis. Ctr., 1981-89, U. Denver, 1989—. Contbr. articles to profl. jours. Mem. Colo. Rep. Party, Denver, 1968—. Scholarship U. No. Colo., 1964-68; fellowship U. Denver, 1989. Mem. Mensa. Republican. Avocations: computer activities, dancing, hiking, reading. Home: 8650 W 79th Ave Arvada CO 80005-4321 Office: U Denver 2155 S Race St Denver CO 80210-4633

LEFRAK, SAMUEL J., housing and building corporation executive; b. N.Y.C., Feb. 12, 1918; s. Harry and Sarah (Schwarz) LeF.; m. Ethel Stone, May 14, 1941; children: Denise, Richard, Francine, Jacqueline. Grad., U. Md., 1940; postgrad., Columbia U., Harvard U.; LLD (hon.), U. of Studies, Rome, 1971, N.Y. Law Sch., 1974, Colgate U., 1979; HHD (hon.), Pratt Inst., 1988, U. Md., 1990, Queens Coll., 1994, Mich. State U., 1995. Pres. Lefrak Orgn., 1948—, chmn. bd., 1975—; creator, sponsor, builder Lefrak City, Battery Park City, Gateway Pla., Newport Complex; mem. adv. bd. Sta. WHLI, 1955; commr. Landmarks Preservation Commn., N.Y.C., 1966; commr. pub. works Borough Manhattan, 1956-58; commr. Interstate Sanitation Commn., 1958; Saratoga Springs Commn., 1962—; mem. adv. bd. Chem Bank.; guest lectr. Harvard Grad. Sch. Bus. Adminstrn., 1971, Yale, 1975, NYU, 1977; guest speaker Fin. Women's Assn., N.Y., 1975; guest lectr. Princeton U., U. Haifa, 1983, Oxford U., 1984, Pratt Inst., 1987, Harvard U., 1987, Columbia Sch. Bus., 1988, Wharton Sch. Bus., 1989, Sch. Bus. NYU, 1989; speaker UN, 1988; featured speaker Instl. Investment Real Estate Conf., 1975, Fed. Home Loan Bank Conf., 1990; guest lctr. Japanese Govt., Finnish Govt., Switzerland, 1967; U.S. del. Internat. Conf. Housing and Urban Devel., Switzerland, 1967; dir. N.Y. World's Fair Corp., 1964-65, N.Y. Indsl. Devel. Corp., 1975—, chmn. bd. L.I. Post; pres. N.Y.C. Comml. Devel. Corp., 1967-71, chmn., 1971—; founding mem. World Business Coun., Inc., 1970; mem. Pres.'s Com. Employment Handicapped; spl. cons. urban affairs State Dept., 1969; mem. adv. coun. Real Estate Inst., N.Y. U., 1970—; mem. gov. fin. Pres.'s Club U. Md., 1971, com. N.Y. State Traffic Safety Council, 1966; bd. visitors Sch. Law, Columbia U., 1983; commr. Saratoga-Capital dist. N.Y. State Park and Recreation Commn., 1973; mem. real estate coun. exec. com. Met. Mus. Art, 1982; mem. N.Y.C. Pub. Devel. Corp., Nat. Energy Coun., U.S. Dept. Commerce, Mayor's Com. on Housing Devel., N.Y.C., 1974—; mem. exec. com. Citizen's Budget Com. for N.Y.C., Inc., 1975—; mem. Gov. Cuomo's Adv. Coun., 1983, N.Y. State Gov.'s Task Force on Housing, 1974; establish Lefrak Lecture Series, U. Md., 1982; creator, developer residential and business property. Vice chmn.-at-large ARC, N.Y.; mem. U.S. com. UN Orgn., 1957; chmn. nat. bd. Histadrut, 1967—; mem. Israel Bonds Prime Minister Com., 1980; dir. Ronald McDonald House, 1986; chmn. bldg. com. Saratoga Performing Arts Ctr.; mem. Fifth Ave. Assn.; dir., chmn. real estate div. Greater N.Y. Fund; hon. com. AAU; Queens chmn. United Greek Orthodox Charities, 1973; chmn. Celebrity Sports Night-Human Resources Ctr., 1973-74, Sports Assn. Hebrew U. of Jerusalem, 1979; patron Met. Mus. Art; sponsor Israel Philharm. Orch., Jan Groth Exhibit, Guggenheim Mus.; trustee, dir. Beth-El Hosp.; bd. dirs. USO, Citizens Housing and Planning Council, N.Y., 1957—, Interfaith Movement, Diabetics Found., Queens Cultural Assn., Consumer Credit Counseling Svc. Greater N.Y., Astoria Motion Picture and TV Ctr. Found.; trustee N.Y. Law Sch., Queens Art and Cultural Ctr., Jewish Hosp. at Denver, N.Y Civic Budget Com.; trustee, med. adv. bd. Brookdale Hosp. Med. Ctr., Pace U.; mem. exec. bd. Greater N.Y. couns. Boy Scouts Am.; founder Albert Einstein Sch. Medicine; mem. Bretton Woods Com.; bd. govs. Invest-in-Am. Nat. Coun.; mem. task force on energy conservation Div. Community Housing, 1981—; mem. com. N.Y. State Traffic Safety Coun., 1966; chmn. Scandinavia Today, 1981—; bd. visitors Sch. Law Columbia U., 1983; mem. adv. bd. The Explorer's Club, 1984; mem. Nat. Com. on U.S.-China Rels. Inc.; bd. dirs. Inst. Nautical Archaeology; trustee Queens Coll., 1989; adv. dir. Met. Opera, 1990; conf. bd. Keynote Address-Annual Fin. Seminar, 1987; mem. Lambda Alpha Internat. bd. trustees Guggenheim Mus., 1993; mem. bd. trustees Dana Farker Cancer Inst. Harvard Med. Sch., 1992. Decorated officer Order of Lion of Finland, 1980, Medment, 1988; officer Order St. John of Jerusalem Knights of Malta, 1982; Order of the North Star of Sweden, 1982; comdr. Royal Norwegian Order of Merit, 1987; recipient Mayor N.Y.C. award outstanding citizenship, 1960; Nat. Boys Club award, 1960; Citizen of Year award B'nai Brith, 1963; Am. Achievement award, 1984; Disting. Achievement award, 1967; Man of Year award VFW, 1963; Brotherhood award NCCJ, 1964; Chief Rabbi Herzog gold medal; Torah Fellowship citation Religious Zionist Am., 1966; John F. Kennedy Peace award, 1966; Man of Year award Bklyn. Community Hosp., 1967; Builder of Excellence award Brandeis U., 1968; Master Builder award N.Y. Cardiac Ctr., 1968; Disting. Citizen award M Club Found. U. Md., 1970; Disting. Alumnus award U. Md. Alumni Assn., 1970; Disting. Citizen and Outstanding Community Svc. award United Way, 1986; Am. Achievement award Ency. Britannica, 1984; Am. Eagle award nat. coun. Invest-in Am., 1972; Exec. Sportsman award Human Resources Ctr., 1973; Archtl. award Fifth Av. Assn., 1974; Excellence in Design award Queens C. of C., 1974; Flame Truth award Fund Higher Edn., 1986; elected hon. citizen Md., 1970; Citizen of Yr. award Bklyn. Philharm. Orch., 1983; dedication of Samuel J. LeFrak Hall U. Md., 1982, LeFrak Gymnasium, Amherst Coll., 1986, LeFrak Moot Ct., N.Y. Law Sch., 1990, LeFrak Meadow, N.Y.C., 1991, LeFrak Coun. Hall, Queens Coll., LeFrak Gallery and Sculpture Terrace, Guggenheim Mus.; LeFrak Lecture Series at U. Md. established, 1982; Comdr. of the Royal Norwegian Order of Merit, presented by King Olav V, 1987; Rough Riders award Boy Scouts Am., 1987; Torch of Progress Assoc. Builders and Owners Greater N.Y.; award Soc. Fgn. Consuls, 1988, Gold medal and Man of Yr. award Israel Bonds Found., 1990, Developer of the Yr. Associated Builders and Owners of Greater N.Y., 1990; award Assn. Graphics Arts, 1990, Disting. Citizen of World award UN, 1994, Alumni Hall of Fame award U. Md., 1995; named to Nat. Sales Club Hall of Fame, 1990. Mem. Sales Execs. Club N.Y. (dir.), United Hunts Racing Assn., Philharm. Symphony Soc. N.Y., Explorers Club (dir.), Newcomen Soc. U.S., Phi Kappa Phi, Tau Epsilon Phi (established Samuel J. LeFrak scholarship award 1975). Clubs: U. Md. Pres.'s (mem. Gov. N.Y. fin.), Lotos (bd. dirs. 1975—, Merit award 1973), Grand Street Boys, Friars (dir. Found.), Advertising, Economic, Downtown Athletic (N.Y.C.); Town, Turf and Field; Cat Cay (Nassau, Bahamas); Xanadu Yacht (Freeport, Grand Bahamas); Palm Bay (Miami Beach, Fla.); Seawane; Ocean Reef (Key Largo); Sag Harbor Yacht (L.I.). Lodges: Masons (32d degree), Shriners. Office: Lefrak Orgn Inc 97-77 Queens Blvd Rego Park NY 11374-3317

LEFRANC, MARGARET (MARGARET SCHOONOVER), artist, illustrator, editor, writer; b. N.Y.C., Mar. 15, 1907; d. Abraham and Sophie (Teplitz) Frankel; m. Raymond Schoonover, 1942 (div. 1945). Student, Art Students League, N.Y.C., Kunstschule des Westerns, Berlin, NYU Grad. Sch., Andre L'Hote, Paris, Acad. Grande Chaumiere, Paris. Tchr. art Adult Edn., Los Alamos, 1946, Miami (Fla.) Mus. Modern Art, 1975-76. Exhibited in one-person shows at Mus. N.Mex., Santa Fe, 1948, 51, 53, Phlbrook Art Ctr., Tulsa, 1949, 51,, Okla. Art Ctr., 1950, Recorder WOrkshop, Miami, 1958, St. John's Coll., Santa Fe, 1993, A Lifetime of Imaging, 1921-95; group shows include Salon de Tuileries, Paris, 1928, 29, 30, Art Inst. Chgo., 1936, El Paso Mus. Art, 1964, Mus. Modern Art, 1974, North Miami Mus. Contemporary Art, 1984, Miami Collects, 1989, Women's Caucus Invitational, 1990, Gov.'s Gallery, Santa Fe, 1992, Gene Autry Western Heritage Mus, 1995, Gilcrease Mus., Tulsa, 1996, Mus. N.Mex. Santa Fe, 1996, Brigham Young U., Provo, Utah, 1996; in collections at Beiles Artes, Mexico City, Mus. Fine Arts, Santa Fe, St. John's Coll. Santa Fe, N.Mex., 1997 works on paper, others. Bd. dirs., pres. Artist Equity of Fla., 1964-68; v.p. Miami Art Assn., 1958-60; founder, bd. dirs. Guild Art Gallery, N.Y.C., 1935-37. Recipient Illustration award Fifty Best Books of Yr., Libr. of Congress; Honorable Mention award Rodeo of Santa Fe, Mus. N.Mex., others.

LEFSTEIN, NORMAN, lawyer, educator; b. Rock Island, Ill., July 16, 1937; s. George M. and Rose Lefstein; m. Leah M. Lefstein, Apr. 15, 1962 (div.); children: Lisa, Adam, Susan. Student, Augustana Coll., 1955-58; LL.B., U. Ill., 1961; LL.M., Georgetown U., 1964. Bar: Ill. 1961, D.C. 1963. Asst. U.S. atty. Washington, 1964-65; project dir. Nat. Council Juvenile Ct. Judges, Chgo., 1965-68; staff mem. Dept. Justice, Washington, 1968-69; dep. dir. Pub. Defender Service for D.C., 1969-72, dir., 1972-75; assoc. prof. law U. N.C., Chapel Hill, 1975-79, prof., 1979-87; dean, prof. Ind. U. Sch. Law, Indpls., 1988—; vis. prof. Duke U., 1976-77, fall 1978; chmn. Ind. Pub. Defender Commn., 1990—. Bd. editors U. Ill. Law Forum, 1959-61. Mem. ABA (council criminal justice sect. 1979-88 , chmn. 1986-87, reporter Project to Update ABA Criminal Justice Standards 1977-85), Nat. Legal Aid and Defender Assn. (bd. dirs., mem. exec. com. 1975-80), Order of Coif. Home: 3405 Bay Point Dr Indianapolis IN 46240-2442 Office: Ind U Sch Law 735 W New York St Indianapolis IN 46202-5222

LEFTON, HARVEY BENNETT, gastroenterologist, educator, author; b. Cleve., May 17, 1944; s. Nat L. and Edith (Waintrup) L.; m. Paulette Lipkowitz, Aug. 24, 1968; children: Allison Rachel, Daniel Adam. BS, U. Pitts., 1966; MD, Jefferson Med. Coll., Phila., 1970. Cert. Nat. Bd. Med. Examiners, Am. Bd. Internal Medicine, Am. Bd. Gastroenterology. Intern medicine Cleve. Clinic, 1970-71, resident internal medicine, 1971-72, fellow gastroenterology, 1972-74; chief gastroenterology Scott AFB, Belleville, Ill., 1974-76; asst. clin. prof. medicine Med. Coll. Pa., Phila., 1976-78, assoc. clin. prof. medicine, 1978-81, clin. prof. medicine, 1981—; cons. gastroenterology Friends Hosp., Belmont Psychiat. Hosp., Pa., 1980—. Contbr. articles to profl. jours. Maj. USAF, 1974-76. Named Outstanding Vol. Physician, Med. Coll. Pa., 1994. Fellow ACP, Am. Coll. Gastroenterology, Coll. Physicians Phila.; mem. Am. Soc. Gastrointestinal Endoscopy, Pa. Soc. Gastroenterology, Omicron Delta Kappa. Home: 559 Long Ln Huntingdon Valley PA 19006-2935 Office: 2 Bala Plz Ste IL 22 Bala Cynwyd PA 19004

LEFTWICH, HAL WEST, health facility administrator; b. Richmond, Va., Oct. 21, 1955; Louis J. Jr. and R. Arvella (Donahoe) L. AA, Fla. Tech. U., 1977; BBA, Ea. Ky. U., 1978; MHA, Xavier U., Cin., 1980. Asst. adminstr. Greenville (S.C.) Hosp. System, 1980-82; v.p. med. svcs. Kissimmee (Fla.) Meml. Hosp., 1982-84; v.p. adminstrn. Parrish Med. Ctr., Titusville, Fla., 1984-91; chmn. planning, zoning commn. City of Titusville, Fla., 1990; COO Brooksville (Fla.) Regional Hosp., 1991—, Spring Hill Regional Hosp., 1991—; cons. Sunbelt Emergency Med. Svcs., Orlando, Fla., 1985-86; pres. Brevard County CPR, Inc., Melbourne, Fla., 1986-90; bd. mem. North Ctrl. Fla. Health Planning Coun. Bd. dirs., chmn. multisvc. agencies budget task group United Way, 1989-91. Recipient achievement award United Way of Osceola County, 1985. Fellow Am. Coll. Health Care Execs.; mem. Am. Hosp. Assn., Fla. Hosp. Assn., U. Ctrl. Fla. Alumni Assn. (bd. dirs. 1988-91), Aircraft Owners and Pilots Assn., Mensa, Rotary. Republican. Methodist. Home: 24050 Martin Dr Brooksville FL 34601-5237 Office: Brooksville Regional Hosp Quorum Health Resources 55 Ponce De Leon Blvd Brooksville FL 34601-3222

LEFTWICH, JAMES STEPHEN, management consultant; b. Stevenage, Eng., Nov. 30, 1956; came to U.S., 1957; s. James Wright and Del Maureen (Thomson) L.; m. Carol Petersen, Nov. 7, 1980 (div. Jan. 1982). AA in Criminal Justice, Butte Coll., Oroville, Calif., 1981; BA, S.W. U., 1993. Lic. internat. accredited safety auditor; cert. hazardous material specialist. Prodn. mgr. Artistic Dyers Inc., El Monte, Calif., 1976-80; mgr. loss control and risk mgmt. Mervyn's Dept. Stores, Hayward, Calif., 1982-91; dir. risk mgmt. Save Mart Corp., Modesto, Calif., 1991-93; v.p. ops. I.C.S. Corp., San Ramon, Calif., 1993-94; pres. I.C.S. Corp., Irvine, Calif., 1994-95; v.p. Health Systems of Am. Internat., 1995—; cons. R.I.M. Assocs., Walnut Creek, Calif., 1989—; instructor Claims Mgmt., 1993; speaker in field. Scriptwriter, tech. advisor 12 safety videos; contbr. articles on safety and risk mgmt. to profl. publs. Res. police officer Cotati (Calif.) Police Dept., 1983-85; fundraiser United Way, Hayward, 1986, Am. Found. for AIDS Rsch., L.A., 1990; bd. dirs. Bay Area Safety Coun., Oakland, Calif., 1987-88; trustee Calif. Safety Ctr., Sacramento, 1990-91, dir., 1991—. Mem. Am. Soc. for Safety Engrs., Nat. Safety Mgmt. Soc., Nat. Fire Protection Assn., Risk and Ins. Mgmt. Soc., Nat. Assn. Chiefs Police, Nat. Environ. Tng. Assn. Avocations: snow skiing, swimming, running, biking. Office: ICS Corp San Ramon CA 94583

LEFTWICH, ROBERT EUGENE, oncological nursing educator; b. Lubbock, Tex., July 2, 1940; s. Eugene L. and Georgia (Kirkpatrick) L. BSN, Baylor U., 1963; MS, Northern Ill. U., 1970; PhD, Clayton U., 1977. Head nurse Baylor U. Med. Ctr., Dallas, 1963-64; supr. U.S. Air Force Nurse Corps, Fla., Tex., 1964-67; instr. nursing Cameron State Coll., Lawton, Okla., 1967-68, Rock Valley Coll., Rockford, Ill., 1968-70; dir. ADN program Kankakee (Ill.) Community Coll., 1970-71, dean health edn., 1971-72; chmn. dept. adult nursing Med. Coll. Ga., Augusta, 1972-75; asst. prof. U. Louisville, 1975-77; prof. nursing Governors State U., University Park, Ill., 1977—; bd. mem. Community Health Planning Bd., Kankakee, 1970-72; curriculum cons. Purdue U., Westville, Ind., 1983; oncology nursing cons. Ingalls Hosp., Harvey, Ill., 1979-85; grievance chairperson Univ. Profls. of Ill., University Park, 1981-83. Author: Nursing, Nutrition and the Adult Client, 1974, Humanistic Teaching Strategies and Nursing Students' Attitudes about Death and Dying, 1977, Self-Care Guide for the Cancer Patient, 1989; primary rschr.: Acuity Levels on an Adult Oncology Unit, 1981, Sexual Harrassment in Nursing Education, 1995; contbr. articles to profl. jours. Organist Trinity United Meth. Ch., Chgo., 1985-87; organist, choirmaster Bethel Covenant Ch., Flossmoor, Ill., 1987—. 1st lt. U.S. Air Force, 1963-67. Mem. Univ. Profls. Ill., Am. Guild Organists, Sigma Theta Tau. Avocations: ch. organist, choirmaster, concert organist, pianist, tenor soloist. Office: Governors State U Dept Nursing University Park IL 60466

LÉGARÉ, HENRI FRANCIS, archbishop; b. Willow-Bunch, Sask., Can., Feb. 20, 1918; s. Phillippe and Amanda (Douville) L. B.A., U. Ottawa, 1940; theol. student, Lebret, Sask., 1940-44; M.A., Laval U., 1946; Dr. Social Sci., Cath. U. Lille, France, 1950; LL.D. (hon.), Carleton U., Ottawa, 1959, Windsor (Ont.) U., 1960, Queens U., Kingston, Ont., 1961, U. Sask., 1963, Waterloo (Ont.) Luth. U., 1965, U. Ottawa, Can., 1984; Doctor of Univ., U. of Ottawa. Ordained priest Roman Cath. Ch., 1943; prof. sociology Laval U., 1947, U. Ottawa, 1951; exec. dir. Cath. Hosp. Assn. Can., 1952-57; dean faculty social scis. U. Ottawa, 1954-58, pres., 1958-64; provincial Oblate Fathers, Winnipeg, Man., 1966-67; bishop of Labrador, 1967-72; archbishop Grouard-McLennan, Alta., 1972—. Contbr. articles to profl. jours. Chmn. Canadian Univs. Found., 1960- 62. Decorated grand cross merit Order Malta, 1964; order merit French Lang. Assn. Ont., 1965. Mem. Assn. Canadian Univs. (pres. 1960-62), Can. Conf. Cath. Bishops (pres. 1981-83), Internat. Assn. Polit. Sci. Address: Archbishop's House, CP 388, McLennan, AB Canada T0H 2L0

LEGASPI, JESUSA CRISOSTOMO, agricultural scientist, entomologist; b. Pasay, Manila, Philippines, Oct. 26, 1958; came to U.S., 1987; d. Benjamin Buencamino and Rosalinda Nieto (Manikis) Crisostomo; m. Benjamin Antonio Legaspi Jr., Jan. 2, 1987; 1 child, Michelle Elaine. BS, U. Philippines, Los Banos, 1978; MSc, U. Newcastle-Upon-Tyne, Eng., 1984; PhD, Purdue U., 1991. Rsch. asst. Philippine Coun. for Agr., Los Banos, 1980-82, Internat. Rice Rsch. Inst., Los Banos, 1985-86; grad. rsch. asst. Purdue U., West Lafayette, Ind., 1987-91; rsch. assoc. USDA, Weslaco, Tex., 1992-95; asst. prof. Tex. Agrl. Experiment Sta., Weslaco, 1995—. Contbr. articles to profl. jours. Sci. judge Jackson Elem. Sch., McAllen, Tex., 1992; vol. Ind. State Fair, Indpls., 1990; mem. Fil-Am Assn., Rio Grande Valley, Tex., 1993. David Ross fellow Purdue U., 1987; Colombo Plan scholar Brit. Coun., 1982. Mem. Entomol. Soc. Am., Philippine Assn. of Entomologists, Sigma Xi, Gamma Sigma Delta. Roman Catholic. Avocations: swimming, scuba diving, bowling, reading, travel. Office: Tex Agrl Experiment Sta 2415 E Hwy 83 Weslaco TX 78596-8344

LEGATE, STEPHEN, ballet dancer; b. Portland, Oreg.. Student, Marylynn's Ballet Arts, Riverside, Calif., Nat. Ballet Sch. With Nat. Ballet Can.; soloist San Francisco Ballet, 1991-92, prin. dancer, 1992—. Appeared in ballets Nanna's Lied, Rubies, The Concert, La Pavane Rouge, Seeing Stars, Handel- a Celebration, Beads of Memory, The Four Seasons, Nutcracker, La Fille mal gardee, Connotations, The End, Don Quixote, Nutcracker, La Ronde, Voluntaries, Daphnis and Chloe, Sphinx, Tagore, Swan Lake, Pastorale, Forgotten Land, Transfigured Night, Blue Snake, The Second Detail, Le Corsaire, Onegin; appeared in TV prodns. The Merry Widow, Alice. Named Best Male Dancer, Internat. Competition for Erik Bruhn Award, 1989. Office: San Francisco Ballet 455 Franklin St San Francisco CA 94102-4438

LEGATES, JOHN CREWS BOULTON, information scientist; b. Boston, Nov. 19, 1940; s. Eber Thomson and Sybil Rowe (Crews) LeG.; m. Nancy Elizabeth Boulton, Apr. 28, 1993. BA in Math., Harvard U., 1962. Edn. svcs. mgr. Telcomp Dept. Bolt Beranek & Newman, Cambridge, Mass., 1966-67; v.p. Washington Engring. Svcs., Cambridge, 1967-69; v.p., co-founder Cambridge Info. Systems, 1968-69; v.p., founder Computer Adv. Svc. to Edn., Wayland, Mass., 1966-72; exec. dir. Educom Interuniversity Communications Coun., Boston, 1969-72; founder, mng. dir. Program on Info. Resources Policy Harvard U., 1973—, founder, pres. Ctr. Info. Policy Rsch., 1978—; cons. in field. Contbr. articles to profl. jours. Bd. dirs. Nat. Telecommunications Conf., Washington, 1979. Kent fellow, 1964. Mem. NAS/NRC (telecommunications privacy, reliability and integrity panel), IEEE, Nat. Sci. Found., Soc. for Values in Higher Edn. Episcopalian. Club: Nashuba Valley Hunt (Pepperell, Mass.) (pres. 1974-80). Avocations: sailing, fox-hunting, mountaineering, classical music. Home: PO Box 6331 Lincoln Center MA 01773-6331

LEGENDRE, LOUIS, biological oceanography educator, researcher; b. Montreal, Que., Can., Feb. 16, 1945; s. Vianney and Marguerite (Venne) L. BA, U. Montreal, 1964, BSc, 1967; PhD, Dalhousie U., Halifax, 1971. Postdoctoral fellow U. Paris VI, Villefranche-sur-Mer, 1971-73; rsch. assoc. U. Laval, Quebec City, Que., 1973, asst. prof., 1974-77; assoc. prof. U. Laval, Quebec City, 1977-81, prof., 1981—; v.p. Groupe interuniversitaire de recherches océanographiques du Que., 1989—; group chmn. Natural Scis. and Engring. Rsch. Coun. Can., Ottawa, 1989-92. Co-author: (with P. Legendre) Numerical Ecology, 1983; contbr. articles to profl. jours. Vice-pres. Model Environ., Liege, Belgium, 1993—. Decorated Knight of Malta; recipient Léo-Pariseau award Assn. canadienne-française pour l'avancement des sciences, 1985, Michel-Jurdant award, 1986. Fellow Royal Soc. of Can., mem. Am. Soc. Limnology and Oceanography, Environment & Policy Soc. (bd. dirs. 1990-92). Office: U Laval, Dept Biology, Sainte Foy, PQ Canada G1K 7P4

LEGERE, LAURENCE JOSEPH, government official; b. Fitchburg, Mass., Jan. 2, 1919; s. Laurence Joseph and Aurore Hermine (Bean) L.; m. Mary Yesley Keville, Oct. 25, 1973. B.S., U.S. Mil. Acad., 1940; M.P.A., Harvard, 1948, A.M. (Littauer fellow), 1949, Ph.D., 1951. Commd. 2d lt. U.S. Army, 1940, advanced through grades to col., 1959; asst. prof. internat. relations U.S. Mil. Acad., 1945-47; student Nat. War Coll., 1960-61; asst. to mil. rep. of Pres. U.S., Washington, 1961-62; sr. staff mem. NSC, Washington, 1962-63; ret., 1966; sr. staff mem. Center for Internat. Studies, M.I.T., Cambridge, 1966-67; dir. office nat. security studies Bendix Corp., Ann Arbor, 1967-68; dir. internat. and social studies div. Inst. Def. Analyses, Arlington, Va., 1968-74; def. advisor U.S. Mission to NATO, Brussels, 1974-89, ret., 1989; mem. policy panel on Europe UN Assn., 1967-69. Contbg. author, editor: The President and the Management of National Security, 1969; Contbr. numerous articles on foreign and def. policies to profl. jours. Decorated Silver Star, Legion of Merit, Bronze Star, Purple Heart, Disting. Civilian Service medal; recipient Presdl. Service Badge, 1956-57, 61-63, medal Outstanding Pub. Service, 1976, medal Disting. Pub. Service, 1978, 81, 87, Presdl. award for Disting. Fed. Civilian Svc., 1989. Mem. Internat. Inst. Strategic Studies. Clubs: Army-Navy (Washington). Office: 1073 Riverbend Dr Advance NC 27006

LEGERTON, CLARENCE WILLIAM, JR., gastroenterologist, educator; b. Charleston, S.C., July 8, 1922; s. Clarence William and Winnie Davis (McMaster) L.; m. Mitzi Foster Herrin, May 31, 1958; children: Clarence William, Mary Pringle, Gregg McMaster. Student, Davidson Coll., 1939-43, BS, 1982; MD, Med. Coll. S.C., 1946. Intern Univ. Hosp., Balt., 1946-47, med. resident, 1947-48; med. resident Duke U. Sch. Medicine, 1951-52, fellow in gastroenterology, 1952-53, instr. medicine, 1950-53; practice medicine specializing in gastroenterology Conway, S.C., 1953-56, Charleston, 1956-66; prof. medicine, dir. div. gastroenterology Med. U. S.C., Charleston, 1966-92; asst. to pres. Med. U. S.C., 1975-80, prof. Emeritus, 1992; vis. prof. Royal United Hosp., Bath, Eng., 1987; cons. Cambridge U. Sch. Medicine (Eng.), 1978; trustee Nat. Found. for Ileitis and Colitis, 1976—; bd. dirs. Coalition Digestive Disease Orgns., 1982—; mem. nat. digestive diseases adv. bd. NIH, Washington; chmn. com. on digestive diseases rsch. ctrs. Nat. Inst. Digestive Diseases, Diabetes, and Kidney Diseases, Washington. Med. dir. Nat. Miss U.S.A. Pageant, 1977-79; dir. Citizens and So. Nat. Bank, Charleston; chmn. Charleston bd., 1974—; bd. dirs. Nations Bank, Charleston, 1992—; vice chmn. Charleston Commn. Public Works, 1959-76; chmn. water supply City of Charleston; pres. Charleston Symphony Orch. Assn., 1967-68; chmn. bd. dirs. Legerton & Co., Inc.; Mem. City Council Charleston, 1959-76, mayor pro-tem, 1960; pres. Charleston County Democratic Conv., 1960; trustee Montreat-Anderson Coll., vice chmn., 1962-74, chmn., 1974-78; trustee Queens Coll., 1965—; bd. visitors Davidson (N.C.) Coll., 1979—, trustee, 1982-84; bd. visitors Warren Wilson Coll., Swannanoa, N.C., 1993—; chmn. bd. Charleston Mcpl. Auditorium; chmn. adv. bd. Comprehensive Health Planning Council, Charleston, Berkeley and Dorchester Counties. Served to capt. AUS, 1948-50. Named Disting. Alumnus, Med. U. of S.C., 1986; recipient Alumni Svc. award Davidson Coll., 1988. Master ACP (gov. S.C. 1978-82); fellow Am. Coll. Gastroenterology (gov. for S.C. 1978-82), Am. Gastroenterology Assn. (chmn. com. on pub. policy and govt. rels. 1982—, governing bd. 1985); mem. S.C. Soc., New Eng. Soc. (pres. 1992—), Coun. Med. socs. (rep. 1980-84), Nat. Alumni Assn. Davidson Coll. (pres. 1983-84), Alpha Omega Alpha, Sigma Phi Epsilon, Alpha Kappa Alpha. Presbyterian (ruling elder 1956—, pres. corp. 1965—, moderator 1963). Clubs: Carolina Yacht (Charleston); Biltmore Forest Country (Asheville, N.C.); The Club at Seabrook Island. Home: 2 1/2 Atlantic St Charleston SC 29401-2746 *I believe life confers upon each individual a responsibility to his Creator, his community, his family, and his own person. This responsibility is discharged by the demonstration of religious faith through both precept and example, by involvement in various forms of community service for the betterment of society, by faithfulness to the family unit, and by a concern for the avoidance of those things which impair personal health, whether mental or physical.*

LEGG, BENSON EVERETT, federal judge; b. Balt., June 8, 1947; s. William Mercer Legg and Beverly Bladen (Mann) Mason; m. Kyle Prechtl Legg; children: Jennifer, Charles, Matthew. AB magna cum laude, Princeton U., 1970; JD, U. Va., 1973. Bar: Md. 1973. Law clk. to Hon. Frank A. Kaufman, Balt., 1973-74; assoc. Venable, Baetjer & Howard, Balt., 1975-81, ptnr., 1982-91; judge U.S. Dist. Ct., Dist. Md., Balt., 1991—; spl. reporter appeals com. and standing com. on rules of practice and procedure Ct. Appeals Md., 1983-85; faculty mem. nine day intensive trial advocacy program Md. Inst. Continuing Profl. Edn. for Lawyers, Inc., 1987—, program on appellate advocacy, 1988; lectr. and panelist in field. Mem. Va. Law Rev.; contbr. articles to profl. jours. Bd. dirs. Ctrl. Md. chpt. ARC, 1979-88, past chpt. gen. counsel; mem. adv. bd. Nat. Aquarium in Balt., 1987—; trustee Balt. Zoo. Mem. ABA (bus. torst litigation com. 1987), Md. State Bar Assn., Inc. (chmn. econs. of litigation com. 1981-82), Bar Assn. Balt. City (vice chmn. CLE com. 1986-87, chmn. 1987-88, exec. coun. 1987-88, judiciary com. 1989-90), The Serjeant's Inn Law Club, Order of Coif. Office: US Dist Ct 101 W Lombard St Ste 340 Baltimore MD 21201-2605

LEGG, WILLIAM JEFFERSON, lawyer; b. Enid, Okla., Aug. 20, 1925; s. Garl Paul and Mabel (Gensman) L.; m. Eva Imogene Hill, Dec. 16, 1950; children: Melissa Lou, Eva Diane, Janet Sue. Grad., Enid Bus. Coll., 1943; student, Pittsburg State U., 1944; BBA, U. Tex., Austin, 1946; JD, U. Tulsa, 1954. Bar: Okla. 1954, U.S. Supreme Ct., U.S. Ct. Appeals (10th cir.), U.S. Dist. Ct. (we. dist.) Okla. With aviation sales Phillips Petroleum Co., 1946-48; atty. Marathon Oil Co., 1954-61; pvt. practice Oklahoma City, 1962—; ptnr. Andrews Davis Legg Bixler Milsten & Price, Inc. and predecessor firms, Oklahoma City, 1962—, pres., 83-86, also dir., 1973-77, 80-81, 83-86, 90, sec., 1975-80, 82-83, 90, now sr. counsel and adv. dir., 1991—; adj. prof. law Oklahoma City U., 1975-80; lectr. Okla. U. Law Sch., 1986; bd. dirs., v.p. internat. oil cos., Turkey, Australia, Brunei; bd. dirs., gen. counsel N.J. Natural Resources Co., 1986-91; dir. Skillpath Seminars, Kansas City, Mo., 1995—; lectr. energy seminars. Contbr. articles to profl. jours. Ordained Reorganized Ch. of Jesus Christ of Latter Day Saints, 1964, dist. pres., 1975-80, br. pres., 1986-91, evangelist, 1993—; mem. com. Okla. Gov.'s Energy Adv. Council, 1973, Okla. Blue Ribbon Com. on natural gas well allowables, 1983; trustee Am. Inst. Discussion, 1962-88, chmn., 1969-72, now mem. exec. com., counsel; trustee Jenkins Found. Research, sec., 1975-81; trustee Restoration Trails Found., 1975; trustee Graceland Coll., Lamoni, Iowa, 1986—, mem. exec. com., chmn. bus. affairs com., 1988—; trustee Met. Library Endowment Trust, 1986—, treas. 1988—, chmn. investment com.; rsch. fellow Southwestern Legal Found., Dallas, 1989—. With USN, 1943-46, lt. (j.g.) USNR, 1946-66. Mem. ABA, Internat. Bar Assn., Okla. Bar Assn. (past com. chmn.), Oklahoma County Bar Assn. (past com. chmn.), Internat. Assn. Energy Econs., Econ. Club Okla., Men's Dinner Club, Petroleum Club. Home: 3017 Brush Creek Rd Oklahoma City OK 73120-1855 Office: Andrews Davis Legg Bixler Milsten & Price Inc 500 W Main St Oklahoma City OK 73102-2220

LEGGE, CHARLES ALEXANDER, federal judge; b. San Francisco, Aug. 24, 1930; s. Roy Alexander and Wilda (Rampton) L.; m. Janice Meredith Sleeper, June 27, 1952; children: Jeffrey, Nancy, Laura. AB with distinction, Stanford U., 1952, JD, 1954. Bar: Calif. 1955. Assoc. Bronson, Bronson & McKinnin, San Francisco, 1956-64, ptnr., 1964-84, chmn., 1978-84; judge U.S. Dist. Ct. (no. dist.) Calif., San Francisco, 1984—. Served with U.S. Army, 1954-56. Fellow Am. Coll. Trial Lawyers; mem. Calif. Bar Assn. (past chmn. adminstrn. justice com.). Republican. Clubs: Bohemian, World Trade (San Francisco); Orinda (Calif.) Country. Office: US Dist Ct 450 Golden Gate Ave San Francisco CA 94102*

LEGGE KEMP, DIANE, architect, landscape architect; b. Englewood, N.J., Dec. 4, 1949; d. Richard Claude and Patricia (Roney) L.; m. Kevin A. Kemp; children: Alloy Hudson, McClelland Beebe, Logan Roney. BA, Stanford U., 1972; M in Architecture, Princeton U., 1975. Architect Northrop, Kaelber & Kopf, Rochester, N.Y., 1971, Michael Graves, Architect, Princeton, 1972-75, The Ehrenkrantz Group, N.Y.C., 1975-77; ptnr. Skidmore Owings & Merrill, Chgo., 1977-89; prin. Diane Legge Kemp Architecture and Landscape Consulting, Riverside, Ill., 1989-93, pres., 1993—; pres. DLK Architecture, 1993—; chair Princeton U. adv. bd. Sch. Architecture, 1991—; dir. Newhouse Archtl. Found., Chgo., 1991—. Designer, architect: Boston Globe Satellite Printing Plant, 1984, Mfrs. Hanover Plaza, Wilmington, 1987, Herman Miller Showroom, Chgo., 1988, Arlington Internat. Racecourse, 1989, Phila. Newspapers Expansion and Retrofit, 1989, Navy Pier R constrn., 1990, McCormick Place Retrofit and Expansion, 1991, L.A. Times Master Plan, 1992, CRSS capital project mgmt. Chgo. Park Dist., 1993, Chgo. Hist. Blvds. Restoration, 1993, Roosevelt Rd. Reconstruction, Chgo., 1993, Field, Shedd, Adler Mus. Campus, Goodman Theater, Chgo., 1995, Job Corps Tng. Campus, 1995, Chgo. area Circulator Urban Design, 1995, Cook County Hosp., 1996, Chgo. Sun Times, 1996. Mem. bd. govs. Sch. of Art Inst., Chgo., 1991—; dir., past pres. Soc. for Contemporary Art, Chgo., 1991—. Recipient 40 under 40 award N.Y. Archtl. League, 1986; Urban Design award Progressive Architecture, 1984; named one of 100 Most Influential Women in Chgo., Crain's, 1996. Fellow AIA (Disting. Bldg. award 1983, Interiors award 1988, Nat. Urban Design award 1996); mem. NCARB, Am. Soc. Landscape Architects, Urban Land. Inst. Avocations: piano, flute, skiing, sailing, gardens. Office: DLK Architecture 410 S Michigan Ave Chicago IL 60605-1302

LEGGETT, DONALD YATES, academic administrator; b. Windsor, N.C., Oct. 31, 1935; s. Turner Carter Leggett and Ruby (Harden) Lanier; m. Nancy Lou Porter, Aug. 17, 1980; 1 stepson, Clayton Porter Johnston. BS in Phys. Edn., Social Studies, East Carolina U., 1958, MA in Edn., 1962; postgrad., N.C. State U., 1966-67. Tchr., coach Benhaven (N.C.) High Sch., 1958-59, Buies Creek (N.C.) High Sch., 1959-64; coach, tchr., Needham B. Broughton High Sch., Raleigh, N.C., 1964-66; asst. prin. Needham B. Broughton High Sch., Raleigh, 1966-70; dir. alumni affairs East Carolina U., Greenville, N.C., 1970-73; dir. alumni affairs and founds. East Carolina U., Greenville, 1973-79, dir. alumni rels., 1979-85, asst. to vice chancellor for instl. advancement, 1985-92, assoc. vice chancellor for alumni rels., 1992—, acting dir. Regional Devel. Inst., 1993; driver tng. coord. Raleigh City Sch. System, 1964-66; mem. numerous coms. at East Carolina U., 1970—. Editor East Carolina U. Alumni pubs. 1979-85; contbr. articles to alumni pubs. Past mem. bd. dirs. Pitt County Boys Club, Pitt-Greenville Arts Coun. (past mem. steering com.); former bd. dirs. Ea. N.C. village of Yesteryear; vice chmn. Pitt-Greenville Conv. and Visitors Authority. Named Boss of Yr. Greenville Jaycees, 1976. Mem. Coun. for Advancement and Support of Edn., East Carolina U. Pirate Club, Pitt-Greenville C. of C., Kiwanis Club (charter mem., past bd. dirs. Univ. City), Greenville Golf and Country Club, Phi Kappa Phi, Phi Delta Kappa. Baptist. Avocations: wood working, gardening. Home: 113 Belle St Greenville NC 27858

LEGGETT, GLENN, former English language educator, academic administrator; b. Ashtabula, Ohio, Mar. 29, 1918; s. Glenn H. and Celinda (Sheldon) L.; m. Doris Ruth James, June 14, 1941 (dec.); children: Leslie Ann Leggett Leonard, Susan Cady Leggett Jones, Celinda Sheldon Leggett Conrad, Joanna Ruth Leggett Sinnwell; m. Russelle Seeberger Jones, Mar. 11, 1973; children: Brian Edward Jones, Sarah Lorene Jones Krumm. A.B., Middlebury (Vt.) Coll., 1940, LL.D., 1971; M.A., Ohio State U., 1941, Ph.D., 1949; L.H.D., Rockford Coll., 1967, Ripon Coll., 1968, Coll. Idaho, 1974, Grinnell Coll., 1975; LL.D., Morningside Coll., 1975; Litt.D., Lawrence U., 1968. Instr. in English Mass. Inst. Tech., 1942-44; instr., then asst. prof. English Ohio State U., 1946-52; asso. prof. English U. Wash., 1952-58, asst. to pres., 1958-61, vice provost, 1961-63, provost, 1963-65; prof. English, pres. Grinnell Coll., 1965-75, pres. emeritus, 1979—; v.p. corporate communications Deere & Co., 1975-79; Mem. commn. English Coll. Entrance Exam. Bd., 1957-65, trustee, 1965-76, vice chmn., 1970-72, chmn., 1972-74; pres. Mayflower Retirement Homes, Inc., 1986-88. Author: (with Mead and Kramer) Handbook for Writers, 12th edit., 1995, A Conservative View, The New Professors, 1960; editor: Twelve Poets, 1959, (with Daniel and Beardsley) Theme and Form: An Introduction to Literature, 4th edit., 1975, (with Daniel) The Written Word, 1960, (with Steiner) Twelve Poets, alt. edit., 1967, Years of Turmoil: Years of Change, 1978, Teacher to Teacher: Selected Papers on Teaching, Writing, and Higher Education, 1979. Chmn. Ill.-Iowa Assn. Children with Learning Disabilities, 1976-79; bd. dirs. Quad-Cities Grad. Study Center, 1975-79, chmn., 1977-79; chmn. Conf. Coll. Composition, 1959, Iowa Coll. Found., pres., 1974-75; trustee Marycrest Coll., 1975-80; curator Stephens Coll., 1976-83; mem. exec. com. Iowa Natural Heritage Found., 1979-93; mem. Iowa Natural Resources Commn., 1982-83; bd. dirs. Stewart Library, pres., 1987-88. Served with USNR, 1944-46. Danforth grantee, 1971; recipient Edward S. Noyes award Coll. Bd., 1979. Mem. MLA, Nat. Council Tchrs. English (chmn. coll. sect. 1963-65, chmn. survey undergrad. curriculum in English 1964-67, task force career edn. 1978-79), Iowa Assn. Pvt. Colls. (pres. 1969-71), Assoc. Colls. Midwest (chmn. 1971-73), Chi Psi. Conglist. Home: 6 College Park Rd Grinnell IA 50112-1207

LEGGETT, JAMES DANIEL, church administrator; b. Williamston, N.C., Oct. 21, 1939; s. James S. and Hazel Louise (Wynn) L.; m. Clara Faye Watts, June 25, 1961; children: James Jr., Joseph Talmadge, Cynthia Faye, John David. BA, Pembroke State U.; ThB, Holmes Coll. of the Bible, hon. doctorate, 1988. Ordained to ministry Pentecostal Holiness Ch., 1960. Pastor Swan Quarter Pentecostal Holiness Ch., 1962-64, Pinetown Pentecostal Holiness Ch., 1962-64, Mt. Olive Pentecostal Holiness Ch., Pembroke, 1964-70, Culbreth Meml. Pentecostal Holiness Ch., Falcon, 1970-86; asst. gen. supt. Internat. Pentecostal Holiness Ch., Bethany, Okla., 1989-93, vice chmn., 1993—; exec. dir. Evangelism USA; pres. Extension Loan Fund; supr. N.C. Conf., 1986-89; mem. Evangelical Curriculum Commn., writer Sunday Sch. lit., instr. extension classes Holmes Coll. of the Bible, Emmanuel Coll. Sec. bd. trustees Holmes Coll. of the Bible, past bd. dirs. Office: Pentecostal Holiness Ch 7300 NW 39th Expy Bethany OK 73008-2340

LEGGETT, JOHN CARL, sociology educator; b. Detroit, Sept. 18, 1930; s. Norval John and Eileen Elizabeth (McVeigh) L.; m. Iris Leja Leggett (div. Feb. 1989); children: Britt Erika, Shannon Kelley. BA, U. Mich., 1954, MA in Polit. Sci., 1956, MA in Sociology, 1958, PhD in Sociology, 1962. Various positions U. Mich., Ann Arbor, 1954-62, lectr. dept. sociology, rsch. assoc. Sch. Social Work, 1961-62; instr. sociology U. Calif., Berkeley, 1962-63, asst. prof., 1963-66, rsch. assoc., 1964-65; asst. prof. Simon Fraser U., Berkeley, 1966-67; assoc. prof. Simon Fraser U., 1967-70; lectr. sociology U. Calif., Davis, 1968, lectr. black studies, 1971; assoc. prof. sociology Rutgers U., New Brunswick, N.J., 1971—; vis. assoc. prof. Sacramento State Coll., 1967-68; prof. U. Conn., 1968-69; vis. lectr. U. B.C. (Can.), Vancouver, 1970; cons. to labor union, including United Farm Union, AFL-CIO. Author: Class, Race and Labor: Working Class Consciousness in Detroit, 1968, paperback edit., 1971, Race, Class and Political Consciousness, 1973, Taking State Power, 1973, (with others) Allende, His Exit and Our Times, 1978, Whither Black Studies, 1971, The American Working Class, 1979, Mining the Field, A Photo History of American Farm Worker Struggles, 1991; co-author (with Suzanne Malm) The Eighteen Stages of Love, 1995; contbr. numerous articles and book revs. prof. publ. Active Free Speech Movement, Berkeley, 1964, Farm Labor Support Com., Berkeley and Delano, Calif., 1965, Vietnam Day Com., Berkeley, 1965-66, Rainbow Coalition Cen. N.J., 1984—; officer, organizer Socialist Youth League, 1951-54; mem. Socialist Party, 1958-64, New Democratic Party, 1967-70, United Farm Workers; candidate for local polit. offices; union ofcl.; chmn. Raritan Inst. With USN, 1949-50. Recipient Disting. Faculty Person award Livingston Coll. Assn. Grads., 1987, Alfred McClung Lee award Sociological Abstracts, Inc./Internat. Sociological Assn., 1994; Ford Found. fellow, 1954-55; grantee Social Sci. Rsch. Coun., 1960-61, 64, Can. Coun., 1968-70, Trans-Action Rsch. grantee, 1984-85. Mem. AAUP (officer, grievance counselor Rutgers U.), Am. Sociol. Soc., So. Sociol. Soc., Midwestern Sociol. Soc., North Cen. Sociol. Soc., Assn. for Humanist Sociology (pres. 1995—), Soc. for Study Social Problems, Students for Dem. Soc. (charter Ann Arbor chpt. 1960). Avocations: white water canoeing, mountain hiking. Home: 320 Lawrence Ave Highland Park NJ 08904-1840 Office: Rutgers U Dept Sociology New Brunswick NJ 08904

LEGGETT, ROBERTA JEAN (BOBBI LEGGETT), social services administrator; b. Kankakee, Ill., Nov. 30, 1926; d. Clyde H. and Sybil D. (Billings) Karns; m. George T. Leggett, Aug. 25, 1956. Sec. Cardov div. Chemetron Corp., Chgo., 1951-60; sec., asst. mgr. Ravisloe Country Club, Homewood, Ill., 1961-65; sec. Nationwide Paper Co., Chgo., 1966-68; exec. dir. Am. Bd. Oral and Maxillofacial Surgery, Chgo., 1969-87. Mem. Chgo. Soc. Assn. Execs., Conf. Med. Soc. Execs. of Greater Chgo., Profl. Secs. Internat. Methodist.

LEGGETT, WILLIAM C., biology educator, academic administrator; b. Orangeville, Ont., Can., June 25, 1939; s. Frank William and Edna Irene (Wheeler) L.; m. Claire Holman, May 9, 1964; children: David, John. BA, Waterloo U. Coll., 1962; MSc, U. Waterloo, 1965; PhD, McGill U., 1969; DSc, U. Waterloo, 1992; LLD, Wilfred Laurier U., 1994. Research scientist Essex (Conn.) Marine Lab., 1965-70, rsch. assoc., 1970-73; asst. prof. McGill U., Montreal, Que., Can., 1970-72, assoc. prof., 1972-79, prof., 1979—, chmn. dept. biology, 1981-85, dean of sci., 1986-91, acad. v.p., 1991-94; prin., vice chancellor Queen's U., Kingston, Ont., Can., 1994—; chmn. bd. Huntsman Marine Lab., 1980-89; pres. Groupe Interuniversitaire de Recherche Oceanographique du Que., 1986-91; chmn. grant selection com. for population biology Natural Scis. and Engring. Research Council Can., 1980-81, chmn. grant selection com. for oceans, 1986-87. Mem. editorial bd.: Can. Jour. Fisheries and Aquatic Sciences, 1980-85, Le Naturaliste Canadien, 1980-91, Can. Jour. Zoology, 1982-86; contbr. in field. Recipient Dwight D. Webster award Am. Fisheries Soc., 1989, Award for Excellence for Fisheries Edn., 1990, Fry medal Can. Soc. Zoologists, 1990, Outstanding Biologist award Can. Coun. Biol. Chmn., 1993; grantee in field. Fellow Rawson Acad., Royal Soc. Can.; mem. Am. Fisheries Soc. (pres. North-East div. 1977-78), Can. Com. for Fishery Research, Can. Soc. Zoologists, Am. Soc. Limnology and Oceanography, Am. Soc. Naturalists. Office: Queen's U, Sci Dept, Kingston, ON Canada K7L 3N6

LEGINGTON, GLORIA R., middle school educator. BS, Tex. So. U, Houston, 1967; MS, U. So. Calif., L.A., 1973. Cert. adminstr. (life). Tchr., mentor L.A. Unified Sch. Dist., 1991-93; grade level chair L.A. Unified Schs., 1975-78, faculty chairperson, 1978, 80, 84, Black history/Martin Luther King program chair, 1978, 80, 83, 86, 88, 90-92, social chair, bus. coord., svc. club sponsor, 1978-80, Indian edn. chair, 1980-84, opportunity chair, 1976-78, grade level chair, 1984; Black edn. commn. liaison, 1989-90, impact tchr., 1991-92, human rels. sponsor, 1991-92, coun. Black adminstrs. student conf. facilitator, 1992, tchr. inservice classes for area colloquium, parents, tchrs., faculty shared decision making coun., 1993-94, mem. faculty senate, 1992-93, mem. sch. improvement, 1993-94, mem. discipline com., 1993-94; del. U.S.-Spain Joint. Conf. on Edn., Barcelona, 1995. Chair United Way, 1988, 90; sponsor, 8th Grade, 1994-96; del. US/Spain Joint Conf. on Edn., Barcelona, 1995. Mem. NEA, Internat. Reading Assn., United Tchrs. L.A., Calif. League of Mid. Schs. Avocations: painting, writing, collecting black memorabilia, reading, traveling.

LEGLER, BOB, publishing company executive. Chmn. bd. First Mktg. Bd., Pompano Beach, Fla. Office: First Mktg Co 3300 Gateway Dr Pompano Beach FL 33069*

LEGLER, MITCHELL WOOTEN, lawyer; b. Alexandria, Va., June 3, 1942; s. John Clarke and Doris (Wooten) L.; m. Harriette Dodson; children: John Clarke, Dorothy Trumbull, Harriette Holland. BA in Polit. Sci. with honors, U. N.C., 1964; JD, U. Va., 1967. Bar: Va. 1967, Fla. 1967. Pres. Commander, Legler, Werber, Dawes, Sadler & Howell, Jacksonville, Fla., 1976-91; mng. ptnr. Foley & Lardner, Jacksonville, 1991-95; chmn. Fla. Bar Consumer Protection Law Com. Editorial bd. Va. Law Rev., 1966-67. Mem. Va. Bar Assn., Fla. Bar Assn. (letr. continuing legal edn.), Order of Coif, Phi Beta Kappa, Phi Eta Sigma, Delta Upsilon, Delta Theta Phi. Office: Mitchell W Legler PA One Independent Dr Ste 3104 Jacksonville FL 32202

LEGO, PAUL EDWARD, retired corporation executive; b. Centre County, Pa., May 16, 1930; s. Paul Irwin and Sarah Elizabeth (Montgomery) L.; m. Ann Sepety, July 7, 1956; children: Paul Gregory, Debra Ann, Douglas Edward, Michael John. B.S. in Elec. Engring, U. Pitts., 1956, M.S., 1958. With Westinghouse Electric Corp., 1956—; gen. mgr. Westinghouse semiconductor div. Westinghouse Electric Corp., Pitts., 1970-74; gen. mgr. electronic tube div. Westinghouse Electric Corp., Elmira, N.Y., 1974-75; bus. unit gen. mgr. electronic components divs. Westinghouse Electric Corp., Pitts., 1975-77; v.p., gen. mgr. lamp divs. Westinghouse Electric Corp., Bloomfield, N.J., 1977-80; exec. v.p. electronics and control group Westinghouse Electric Corp., Pitts., 1980-83, exec. v.p. control equipment, 1983-85, sr. exec. v.p. corp. resources, 1985-87, pres., COO, 1988-90, chmn., CEO, 1990-93, also bd. dirs.; ret., 1993; pres. Intelligent Enterprises, Pitts., 1993—; chmn. bd. Commonwealth Aluminum Corp., Louisville, 1995—; bd. dirs. PNC Bank Realty Holding Co., USX Corp., Consol. Natural Gas Co., Lincoln Electric Co. Trustee U. Pitts.; chmn. bd. visitors U. Pitts. Sch. Engring.; bd. overseers N.J. Inst. Tech., Newark, 1979—. With AUS, 1948-52. Recipient Westinghouse Order of Merit 1975, Disting. Alumni award U. Pitts. Sch. Engring., 1986, Bicentennial Medallion of Distinction award U.

Pitts., 1987. Mem. Am. Soc. Corp. Execs., Valley Brook Country Club, Duquesne Club, The Club Pelican Bay (Naples, Fla.), Laurel Valley Golf Club, Rolling Rock Club (Ligonier, Pa.). Republican. Roman Catholic. Office: Exec Assocs 1 Ppg Pl Ste 2210 Pittsburgh PA 15222-5401 *I believe that every individual in an organization should take ownership of his or her job and have the authority and responsibility to make continuous improvements in the processes by which the objectives of that job are accomplished. This approach will produce the lowest possible cost for that job and, collectively, for the company, with the highest level of quality and customer service.*

LEGOFFIC, FRANCOIS, biotechnology educator; b. Pluzunet, France, Nov. 10, 1936; s. Jacques and Marie LeGoffic; m. Marie-Thérèse Castel, Nov. 28, 1957; 1 child, Marc. Dr 3e Cycle, U. Paris, 1962, Dr Sci., 1963. Various positions Nat. Ctr. Sci. Rsch., France, 1962-74; prof. Ecole Nationale Supérieure de Chimie de Paris, 1975—; bd. dirs. UA 1389 du Centre Nat. de la Recherche Scientifique; vis. prof. Rolla U., 1975. Contbr. over 350 articles to Organic Chemistry, Biochemistry, Biotechnology and Microbiology; holder 20 patents. Recipient award Chem. Soc. France, 1968, Acad. Pharmacy, 1971, Acad. Scis., 1993; named Officier palmes academiques, 1994. Achievements include rsch. on total synthesis of natural compounds of therapeutic value, mechanism of resistance of bacteria to antibiotics, mechanism of action of antibiotics, enzyme inhibitors as drugs in antibacterial, antifungal and anticancer area, biotechnology, such as new membranes, immobilized enzymes and cells, enzymes in organic synthesis, valorization of molecules from marine origin and the use of antibodies in environmental analytical chemistry and biosensors design as well as the devel. of new bioprocesses for enzymes production and their use in environmental depollution. Home: 42 rue Jean Georget, 92140 Clamart France Office: ENSCP, 11 rue Pierre Marie Curie, 75231 Paris France

LE GRAND, CLAY, former state justice; b. St. Louis, Feb. 26, 1911; s. Nicholas and Mary Margaret (Leifield) Le G.; m. Suzanne Wilcox, Dec. 30, 1935, (wid.); children: Mary Suzanne Le Grand Murray, Julie A. Le Grand Ekstrand, Nicholas W.; m. Margaret Morris Burrows, Dec. 11, 1993. Student, St. Ambrose Coll., Davenport, Iowa, 1928-31; LL.B., Catholic U. Am., 1934. Bar: Iowa 1934. Practice law Davenport, 1934-57; judge Dist. Ct., 1957-67; justice Supreme Ct. Iowa, Davenport, 1967-83; of counsel Stanley, Rehling, Lande & Van Der Kamp, Davenport, 1983-92, Noyes, O'Brien, Gosma and Brooke, Davenport, 1992-95; Noyes & Gosma, Davenport, 1995—; lectr. St. Ambrose Coll., 1957-67. Recipient award for outstanding achievement in field of law and the cts. Cath. U. Am., 1969; award of merit for profl. achievement St. Ambrose Coll., 1976. Mem. Am., Iowa, Scott County bar assns., Am. Judicature Soc., Inst. Jud. Adminstrn. Home: 4130 Northwest Blvd Apt 32 Davenport IA 52806-4234 Office: Noyes & Gosma 400 N Main St Ste 106 Davenport IA 52801-1424

LEGRAND, MICHEL JEAN, composer; b. Paris, Feb. 24, 1932; came to U.S., 1955; s. Raymond and Marcelle Legrand; children: Hervé, Benjamin, Eugénie. Diploma, Conservatoire Nationale Superieur de Musique, Paris, 1951. Composer, condr., pianist, 1965—. Composer (score, song, adaptation) I Will Wait for You, 1965 (3 Acad. award nominations), Windmills of Your Mind, 1968 (Acad. award 1968), film scores include Summer of 42, 1970 (Acad. award 1970), Brian's Song, 1971, Land Sings the Blues, 1972, The Three Muscateers, 1973, Ode to Billy Joe, 1975, The Other Side of Midnight, 1977, Atlantic City, 1980, The Mountain Men, 1980, Never Say Never Again, 1983, Yentl, 1984 (Acad. award 1984), The Pickle, 1993, Ready to Wear, 1994, also over 100 albums; arranger (album) I Love Paris, 1954; contbr. jazz pianist with numerous orchs. including Pitts. Symphony, Minn. Orch., Buffalo Philharm.; collaborated with various artists including Barbra Streisand, Sarah Vaughan, Jack Jones, Lena Horne, Dame Kiri Te Kanawa, Ray Charles, Miles Davis; dir. (film) 5 Days in June, 1989. Mem. Dramatists Guild, Songwriters Guild of Am., Am. Fedn. Musicians, AFTRA, ASCAP, Acad. Motion Picture Arts and Scis. (Oscar award 1967, 70, 83). Avocations: boating, airplane pilot, tennis, horseback riding. Office: c/o Jim DiGiovanni 157 W 57th St PH-B New York NY 10019

LEGRICE, STEPHEN, magazine editor. Exec. editor Star Mag., Tarrytown, N.Y. Office: Star Mag 660 White Plains Rd Tarrytown NY 10591*

LEGTERS, LYMAN HOWARD, historian; b. Jamestown, N.Y., Feb. 15, 1928; s. Lyman H. and Nettie (Saunders) L.; m. Marie Bird; children: Lyman, Matthew, Nettie, Douglas. AB, U. Mich., 1949; MA, Boston U., 1956; PhD, Free U. Berlin, 1958. Assoc. dir. U. Pitts., 1958-59; assoc. prof. Am. U., Washington, 1959-62; specialist, chief U.S. Office Edn., Washington, 1962-65; prof. George Washington U., Washington, 1965-66; prof. emeritus history of Russia and Ea. Europe U. Wash., Seattle, 1966—; project dir. States and Socs. in E.-Cen. Europe, 1988—; vis. prof. Columbia U., N.Y.C., 1973, U. Warsaw, Poland, 1982; bd. dirs. Hist. Abstracts, Santa Barbara, Calif., 1970-78. Author: Eastern Europe: Transformation and Revolution, 1945-91, 1992; co-author, editor: German Democratic Republic, 1978, Marxism and Good Society, 1981, Western Society After the Holocaust, 1983, Native Americans and Public Policy, 1992, American Indian Policy, 1994, Critical Perspectives on Democracy, 1994. Served as sgt. U.S. Army, 1951-53. Sr. fellow William O. Douglas Inst., 1977—, Kennan Inst., 1978; recipient Arts and Humanities award U. Wash. Grad. Sch., 1986. Democrat. Avocations: gardening, woodcraft. Office: William O Douglas Inst 5410 S Mapleglen Rd Langley WA 98260-8210

LEGUE, LAURA ELIZABETH, resort and recreational facility executive; b. Towanda, Pa., Oct. 11, 1954; d. William Frederick and Frances Lorraine (Cease) Goeckel; m. Stephen Wheeler, Nov. 9, 1974 (div. June 1989); m. Brian E. Legue, Mar. 17, 1990. AA, Mt. Ida Jr. Coll., Newton Ctr., Mass., 1974. Lic. community assn. mgr. Gen. mgr. Towanda Motel & Restaurant, Inc., 1974-82; mgr. Wilson's Suede & Leather, Lawrenceville, N.J., 1982-83; front office mgr. Park Shore Resort Hotel, Naples, Fla., 1985-87; property mgr. World Tennis Ctr. and Resort, Naples, 1987—; pres. World Tennis Club, Inc., Naples, 1991-95, World Tennis Cmty. Assn., Inc., 1994—; notary pub. State of Fla., 1987—. Mem. Collier County Hotel Assn. (sec. 1988, v.p. 1989), Fla. Vacation Rental Mgrs. Assn., Naples Area Accomodations Assn., Hospitality Sales and Mktg. Assn. Internat. Avocations: weight lifting, interior design. Office: World Tennis Ctr. 4800 Airport Rd Naples FL 33942

LE GUIN, URSULA KROEBER, author; b. Berkeley, Calif., Oct. 21, 1929; d. Alfred Louis and Theodora (Kracaw) Kroeber; m. Charles A. Le Guin, Dec. 22, 1953; children: Elisabeth, Caroline, Theodore. B.A., Radcliffe Coll., 1951; M.A., Columbia, 1952. Vis. lectr. or writer in residence numerous workshops and univs., U.S. and abroad. Author: Rocannon's World, 1966, Planet of Exile, 1966, City of Illusion, 1967, The Word For World is Forest, 1967, A Wizard of Earthsea, 1968, The Left Hand of Darkness, 1969, The Tombs of Atuan, 1971, The Lathe of Heaven, 1971, The Farthest Shore, 1972, The Dispossessed, 1974, The Wind's Twelve Quarters, 1975, A Very Long Way from Anywhere Else, 1976, Orsinian Tales, 1976, The Language of the Night, 1979, Leese Webster, 1979, Malafrena, 1979, The Beginning Place, 1980, Hard Words, 1981, The Eye of the Heron, 1982, The Compass Rose, 1982, King Dog, 1985, Always Coming Home, 1985, Buffalo Gals, 1987, Wild Oats and Fireweed, 1988, A Visit from Dr. Katz, 1988, Catwings, 1988, Solomon Leviathan, 1988, Fire and Stone, 1989, Catwings Return, 1989, Dancing at the Edge of the World, 1989, Tehanu, 1990, Searoad, 1991, Blue Moon Over Thurman Street, 1993, Wonderful Alexander and the Catwings, 1994, Going Out With Peacocks, 1994, A Fisherman of the Inland Sea, 1994, Four Ways to Forgiveness, 1995, Unlocking the Air, 1996; also numerous short stories, poems, criticism, screenplays. Recipient Howard D. Vursell award Am. Acad. Arts and Letters, 1991, Pushcart prize, 1991, Boston Globe-Hornbook award for excellence in juvenile fiction, 1968, Nebula award (novel) 1969, (novel and story) 1975, (story) 1975, (novel) 1990, Hugo award (novel) 1969, (story) 1973, (novella) 1973, (novelette) 1988, Gandalf award, 1979, Kafka award, 1986, Newbery honor medal, 1972, Nat. Book award, 1972, H.L. Davis award Oreg. Inst. Literary Arts, 1992, Hubbub annual poetry award, 1995, Asimov's Reader's award, 1995. Mem. Sci. Fiction Research Assn., Sci. Fiction Writers Assn., Authors League, PEN, Writers Guild West, NOW, NARAL, Phi Beta Kappa. Office: c/o Virginia Kidd PO Box 278 Milford PA 18337-0278 also: c/o Matthew Bialer William Morris Agy 1350 Avenue Of The Americas New York NY 10019-4702

LEGUM, JEFFREY ALFRED, automobile company executive; b. Balt., Dec. 16, 1941; s. Leslie and Naomi (Hendler) L.; m. Harriet Cohn, Nov. 10, 1968; children: Laurie Hope, Michael Neil. BS in Econs. Wharton Sch., U. Pa., 1963; grad. Chevrolet Sch. Merchandising and Mgmt., 1966. With Park Circle Motor Co., Balt., 1963—, exec. v.p., 1966-77, pres. 1977—; pres. Legum Chevrolet-Nissan, 1977-89, also dir.; ptnr. Pkwy. Indsl. Ctr., Dorsey, Md., 1965-91; ltd. ptnr. Circle Ltd. Partnership, Glen Burnie, Md., 1991; v.p., dir. P.C. Parts Co., 1967—, pres., 1995—; v.p. Westminster Motor Co. (Md.), 1967-72, pres., dir., 1972—; pres. One Forty Corp., Westminster, 1972—; dir., exec. com. United Consol. Industries, 1970-73; dist. chmn. Chevrolet Dealers Council, 1975-77, chmn. Washington zone, 1982-83. Chmn. transp. div. Associated Jewish Charities, Balt., 1966-69; mem. Md. Svc. Acad. Review Bd., 1975-77, Bus. Adv. Bd. to Atty. Gen., 1985-87; trustee The Legum Found., Balt., 1967—; trustee Balt. Mus. Art, 1992—, mem. fine arts accessions com., 1992—, mem. investment com., 1992—, chmn., 1995—, mem. exec. com., 1993, fin. com., 1995—, contr., 1994—; trustee The Park Sch. Balt., 1979-94, chmn. investment com., 1980-96, mem. exec. com., chmn. fin. com., treas., 1981-91, mem. sr. adv. bd. 1994—; pres.'s com. U. Toronto, 1983—; bd. dirs. Assoc. Placement Bur. (Jewish Vocat. Svc.), Balt., 1964-76, v.p., 1972-76; adv. bd. The Competitive Edge, Albuquerque, 1977-81; mem. investment com. Balt. Hebrew Congregation, 1980—, bd. electors, 1990-93; bd. dirs. Preakness Celebration, Inc., 1988-89, Associated Jewish Community Fedn. Balt., 1992-96; mem. adv. coun., exec. com. Wilmer Eye Inst., The Johns Hopkins Hosp., 1991; mem. instl. rev. bd. for human subjects rsch. Johns Hopkins Bayview Med. Ctr., 1992—; mem. steering com. Govt. House Trust, 1996—. Recipient award of honor Assoc. Jewish Charities of Balt., 1967, 68; Cadillac Master Dealer award, 1980-88, 91; Cadillac Pinnacle of Excellence award, 1986; Young Pres.'s Orgn. Cert. Appreciation, 1984; Nissan Nat. Merit Master award, 1982-88; Chevrolet Nat. Svc. Supremacy award, annually 1979-89, Sales Giant award Automotive News, 1987, Minute of Gratitude The Park Sch. Bd. Trustees, 1994. Mem. Md. New Car and Truck Assn., Young Pres. Orgn. (pres.'s forum 1977-92), World Pres.' Orgn., Benjamin Franklin Assocs., Johns Hopkins Assocs., Carroll County C. of C., Md. Hist. Soc. (exec. com. Library of Md. History 1981-90), Chesapeake Pres.' Orgn., Suburban Club (Baltimore County), U. of Pa., Center Club, U. Toronto Faculty Club (hon.). Home: 10 Stone Hollow Ct Baltimore MD 21208-1860 Office: 1829 Reisterstown Rd Baltimore MD 21208-6301

LEHAN, RICHARD D'AUBIN, English language educator, writer; b. Brockton, Mass., Dec. 23, 1930; s. Ralph A. and Mildred L.; m. Ann Evans, June 11, 1960; 1 son, Edward Scott. B.A., Stonehill Coll., 1952; M.A., Boston Coll., 1953; Ph.D., U. Wis., 1958. Mem. faculty U. Wis.-Madison, 1953-57, U. Tex.-Austin, 1958-62; mem. faculty dept. English UCLA, 1962—, prof. English, 1969—, chmn. dept. English, 1971-73; Fulbright exchange prof. Moscow State U., USSR, 1974-75. Author: F. Scott Fitzgerald, 1966, Theodore Dreiser, 1969, Literary Existentialism, 1973, The Great Gatsby: The Limits of Wonder, 1990. Recipient Disting. Teaching award U. Tex., 1961, UCLA, 1970; Fulbright award, 1975; Guggenheim fellow, 1978-79, Pres.'s Rsch. fellow U. Calif., 1988-89. Home: 333 S Oakhurst Dr Beverly Hills CA 90212-3505 Office: UCLA Dept English Los Angeles CA 90024-1530

LEHISTE, ILSE, language educator; b. Tallinn, Estonia, Jan. 31, 1922; came to U.S., 1949, naturalized, 1956; d. Aleksander and Julie M. (Sikka) L. Dr.Phil., U. Hamburg (Ger.), 1948; Ph.D., U. Mich., 1959; D.Univ. (hon.), U. Essex (Eng.), 1977; Dr. Phil. (hon.), U. Lund (Sweden), 1982, U. Tartu, Estonia, 1989. Lectr. U. Hamburg, 1948-49; assoc. prof. modern langs. Kans. Wesleyan U., 1950-51, Detroit Inst. Tech., 1951-56; rsch. assoc. U. Mich., 1957-63; faculty Ohio State U., Columbus, 1963-87, prof. linguistics, 1965-87, prof. emeritus, 1987—, chmn. dept., 1965-71, 85-87; dir. Linguistic Inst. Ohio State U., 1970; vis. prof. U. Cologne, Germany, 1965, UCLA, 1966, U. Vienna, 1974, U. Tokyo, 1980. Author 11 books; latest being Lectures on Language Contact, 1988; contbr. articles to profl. jours., book revs. Guggenheim fellow, 1969, 75; grantee Am. Council Learned Socs., 1971; fellow Center for Advanced Study in Behavioral Scis., 1975-76. Fellow AAAS, Am. Acad. Arts and Scis., Acoustical Soc. Am.; mem. MLA, Linguistic Soc. Am. (exec. com. 1971-73, pres. 1980), Internat. Soc. Phonetic Scis., Societas Linguistica Europaea. Home: 985 Kennington Ave Columbus OH 43220-4018

LEHMAN, ARNOLD LESTER, museum official, art historian; b. N.Y.C., July 18, 1944; s. Sidney and Henrietta F. L.; m. Pamela Gimbel, June 21, 1969; children—Nicholas Richard, Zachary Gimbel. B.A., Johns Hopkins, 1965, M.A., 1966; M.A., Yale U., 1968, Ph.D., 1973. Chester Dale fellow Met. Mus. Art, N.Y.C., 1969-70; lectr. art history Cooper Union and Hunter Coll., 1969-72; dir. Urban Improvements Program, N.Y.C., 1970-72, Parks Council of N.Y.C., 1972-74, Met. Mus. and Art Centers, Miami, Fla., 1974-79, Balt. Mus. Art, 1979—; adj. prof. dept. art history Johns Hopkins U., 1986-93, 1995—; dir. or trustee several corps. and non-profit orgns. Author: The Architecture of Worlds Fairs 1900-1939, 1972, The New York Skyscraper: A History of its Development 1870-1939, 1974; editor: Oskar Schlemmer, 1986; also various mus. catalogs. Trustee several non-profit orgns. Mem. Assn. Art Mus. Dirs. (trustee 1987-93, pres. 1990-91), Harmonie Club (N.Y.C.). Office: Baltimore Mus Art Art Museum Dr Baltimore MD 21218-3898

LEHMAN, BRUCE ARTHUR, patent lawyer; b. Beloit, Wis., Sept. 19, 1945; s. Dean A. Lehman and Wanda R. (Westbrook) Watson. BS, U. Wis., 1967, JD, 1970. Bar: D.C. 1976, U.S. Ct. Appeals (D.C. cir.). Atty. Wis. Legislature, Madison, 1970-71, U.S. Dept. Justice, Washington, 1973-74, Swidler & Berlin, Chtd., Washington, 1983-93; counsel com. judiciary U.S. Ho. Reps., Washington, 1974-83, chief counsel subcom. civil cts., 1978-83; asst. sec. commerce, commr. patents and trademarks Dept. Commerce/U.S. Patent Trademark Office, Washington, 1993—. adv. bd. BNA Patent, Trademark and Copyright Law Jour., 1991-93. mem. Clinton/Gore Transition Team, Washington, 1992-93; vice chmn. D.C. Gen. Hosp. Commn., 1987-93, chmn. D.C. Gen. Hosp. Found., 1989-93. 1st lt. U.S. Army, 1971-73. Named Lawyer of Yr. Nat. Law Jour., 1994. Democrat. Office: US Dept Commerce US Patent & Trademark Office CPK 2 2121 Crystal Drive Arlington VA 22202

LEHMAN, CHRISTOPHER M., international business consultant; b. Phila., Dec. 15, 1948; s. John F. and Constance (Cruice) L.; m. Maureen Daly, Oct. 1971; children: Brian Thomas, Robert Francis, Christopher M. BA, St. Joseph's Coll., 1971; MA in Law and Diplomacy, Fletcher Sch., 1974, MA in Internat. Rels., 1974, PhD in Internat. Rels., 1993. Research assoc. Fgn. Policy Research Inst., Phila., 1974-76; legis. asst. Senator Harry Byrd, Washington, 1976-78, Senator John Warner, Washington, 1979-81; office dir. Dept. State, Washington, 1981-83; spl. asst. to Pres. The White House, Washington, 1983-85; sr. v.p. Black, Manafort, Stone & Kelly, Alexandria, Va., 1985-87; pres. Commonwealth Cons. Corp., Washington, 1987—; bd. dirs. Handheld Computer Systems, Inc. Bd. advisors KIDS Found.; chmn. bd. Northern Va. Scholarship Trust. Served with USNR, 1969-71. H.B. Earhart fellow, 1971, 72, 73.

LEHMAN, DAVID R., children's entertainer. Record prodr., v.p., songwriter Someday Baby Inc., Nashville. Recipient Grammy award for "The Rock-A-Bye Collection, Volume One", 1990, Best Musical Album for Children "Sleepy Time Lullabyes", 1996. Office: Someday Baby Inc 1508 16th Ave S Nashville TN 37212*

LEHMAN, DENNIS DALE, chemistry educator; b. Youngstown, Ohio, July 15, 1945; s. Dale Vern and Coryn Eleanor (Neff) L.; m. Maureen Victoria Tierney, July 19, 1969 (div. Mar. 1981); children—Chris, Hillary; m. Kathleen Kim Kuchta, May 15, 1983. B.S., Ohio State U. 1967; M.S., Northwestern U., 1968, Ph.D., 1972. Prof. chemistry Chgo. City Colls., 1968—, Northwestern U., Evanston, Ill., 1974-94; lectr. biochemistry Northwestern U. Med. Sch., Chgo., 1979-90; cons. Chgo. Bd. Edn. Mem. Am. Chem. Soc., AAAS, Sigma Xi. Author: Chemistry for the Health Sciences, 1981, 7th edit., 1993; Laboratory Chemistry for the Health Sciences, 1981, 7th edit., 1993. Home: 13780 W Elm Ln Wadsworth IL 60083-9410 Office: Chgo City Colls 30 E Lake St Chicago IL 60601-2420

LEHMAN, DONALD RAY, chemical company executive; b. Chickasha, Okla., Apr. 19, 1947; s. Theodore and Elva (Walker) L.; m. Laura Elizabeth Decker, Aug. 30, 1968; children: Shelby Lynn, Shana Beth, John David. B-SChemE, Okla. State U., 1969. Prodn. supt. Celanese Chem. Co., Pampa, Tex., 1976-79; process engr. supt. Celanese Chem. Co., Houston, 1979-81; mgr. internat. planning Celanese Chem. Co., Dallas, 1981-82, mgr. new bus. devel., 1982-83; tech. mgr. Celanese Chem. Co., Bishop, Tex., 1983-85; plant mgr. Celanese Chem. Co., Pampa, 1985-87; dir. bus. svcs. and ops. Hoechst-Celanese Corp., Portsmouth, Va., 1987-88; dir. methyl chems. Hoechst-Celanese Corp., Dallas, 1988-89, v.p., gen. mgr. methyl and oxo chemicals, 1989-90, v.p., gen. mgr. monomers and acetyl chems., 1990-94; pres. N. Amer textile polyester dept. Hoechst-Celanese Corp., Charlotte, NC, 1994; bd. dirs. Nat. Methanol Co., Al-Jabail, Saudi Arabia. Pres. Richardson (Tex.) Girls Soccer Assn., 1988, Pampa Indsl. Found., 1986; bd. dirs. Coronado Community Hosp., Pampa, 1986, Horas Alegras Presch. Mem. Rotary, Lions (v.p.). Republican. Methodist. Office: Hoechst Celanese PO Box 32414 Charlotte NC 28232-2414*

LEHMAN, DOYLE, superintendent. Supt. South Adams Schs., South Berne, Ind. Recipient State Finalist for Nat. Supt. of Yr. award, 1992. Office: South Adams Schs 1027 Us Highway 27 S Berne IN 46711-2352

LEHMAN, EDWARD WILLIAM, sociology educator, researcher; b. Regensburg, Germany, Feb. 7, 1936; came to U.S., 1939; s. William and Kate (Hoffman) L.; m. Ethna V. O'Flannery, May 26, 1962; 1 child, Robert. B.S., Fordham U., 1956, M.A., 1959; Ph.D., Columbia U., 1966. Lectr. Fordham U., 1958-59; vis. research sociologist dept. psychiatry Montefiore Hosp., Bronx, N.Y., 1959-61; lectr. Sch. Nursing, Columbia U., N.Y.C., 1964-67; research sociologist Cornell U. Med. Coll., N.Y.C., 1961-67; asst. prof., then assoc. prof. sociology NYU, 1967-78; prof., 1978—, chmn. dept., 1978-84, 93—; assoc. dir. Ctr. Policy Research, N.Y.C., 1976-85, sr. research assoc., 1969-89; mem. minority adv. com. N.Y. State Dept. Mental Hygiene, 1981-90. Author: Political Society: A Macrosociology of Politics, 1977, Coordinating Health Care: Explorations in Interorganizational Relations, 1975, The Viable Polity, 1992; editor: (with others) A Sociological Reader in Complex Organizations, 1980. Served to capt. U.S. Army, 1957. Mem. Am. Sociol. Assn., Am. Polit. Sci. Assn. Democrat. Roman Catholic. Home: 1 Washington Square Vlg New York NY 10012-1606

LEHMAN, EDWIN, minister, head of religious organization. Pres. Luth. Ch. Can., Winnipeg, Man.

LEHMAN, HARRY JAC, lawyer; b. Dayton, Ohio, Aug. 29, 1935; s. H. Jacques and Mildred (Benas) L.; m. Linda L. Rocker, June 7, 1964 (div. Mar. 1977); children: Sara Beth, Adam Henry, Matthew Daniel; m. Patricia L. Steele, Aug. 30, 1980; 1 child, Alexandra Steele. BA, Amherst Coll., 1957; JD, Harvard U., 1960. Bar: Ohio 1960. Assoc. Burke, Haber & Berick, Cleve., 1960-61; assoc. Falsgraf, Kundtz, Reidy & Shoup, Cleve., 1961-66, ptnr., 1967-70; of counsel Benesch, Friedlander, Coplan & Aronoff, Cleve., 1971-80; ptnr. Jones, Day, Reavis & Pogue, Columbus, 1980—; adj. prof. law Ohio State U., Columbus, 1980-84, 86-87; mem. Bd. Bar Examiners, State of Ohio, Columbus, 1983-85. Contbr. articles to profl. jours. Mem. Ohio Ho. of Reps., Columbus, 1971-80; chmn. House Judiciary Com., 1975-80; mem. Ohio Elections Com., Columbus, 1983-88, State Underground Parking Com., Columbus, 1983-87, chmn., 1984-86. Served with USAR, 1960-66. Named one of Ten Outstanding Young Men, Cleve. Jaycees, 1968-69; recipient Disting. Service award NAACP, 1968, Outstanding Freshman Legislator award Ohio Legis. Correspondents Assn., 1971-72, Disting. Service award Ohio Edn. Assn., 1972, Most Effective Legislator award Ohio Legis. Correspondents Assn., 1973-74, Pub. Service award Ohio Pub. Defender Assn., 1974, Outstanding Pub. Service award Ohio Pub. Transit Assn., 1978, Disting. Service award ACLU Ohio Found., 1978, Most Effective Legislator 112th Gen. Assembly Ohio award Columbus Monthly Mag., 1980, Most Effective Legislator 113th Gen. Assembly Ohio award Columbus Monthly Mag. Mem. ABA, Ohio Bar Assn., Columbus Bar Assn., Cleve. Bar Assn., Columbus Athletic Club, New Albany Country Club. Democrat. Jewish. Avocations: reading, golf, family. Home: 2642 Charing Rd Columbus OH 43221-3628 Office: Jones Day Reavis & Pogue 41 S High St Ste 1900 Columbus OH 43215-6103

LEHMAN, JAMES ALDEN, economist, educator; b. St. Charles, Ill., Oct. 20, 1947; s. Harold Richard and Elsie (Landis) L.; m. Kay Laura Behrens, Sept. 25, 1973; children: Max Behrens, Sophie Behrens. BA, Davidson Coll., 1973, MA, Duke U., 1976, PhD, 1981. Lectr. Kobe (Japan) U., 1977-80; asst. prof. Pitzer Coll., Claremont, Calif., 1981-87, assoc. prof., 1987-93, prof., 1993—; exec. dir. Thomas J. Watson Found., 1993-95; vis. asst. prof. UCLA. 1982. Contbr. articles to profl. jours. Recipient fellowship Thomas J. Watson Found., 1973, Durfee Found., 1987. Mem. Am. Econ. Assn., Western Econ. Assn. (assoc. editor Econ. Inquiry 1985—). Democrat. Presbyterian. Avocations: tennis, hiking, cycling, singing. Office: 1050 N Mills Ave Claremont CA 91711

LEHMAN, JOHN F., JR., industrialist; b. Phila., Sept. 14, 1942; s. John F. and Constance (Cruice) L.; m. Barbara Wieland, 1975; children: John F., Alexandra, Grace. B.S. in Internat. Relations, St. Joseph's Coll., 1964; B.A. in Law with honors, MA in Internat. Law and Diplomacy, Cambridge U., 1967; Ph.D. in Internat. Relations, U. Pa., 1974. Sr. staff mem. Nat. Security Council, 1969-74; dep. dir. U.S. Arms Control and Disarmament Agy., 1975-77; pres. Abingdon Corp., 1977-81; sec. of Navy Washington, 1981-87; mng. dir. Paine Webber, 1988-91; chmn. J.F. Lehman & Co., N.Y.C., 1991—, Sperry Marine Inc., N.Y.C., 1993—; bd. dirs. Ball Corp., Sedgwick Group, plc, ISO, Inc. Author: Command of the Seas, 1989, Making War, 1992. Capt. USNR, 1968—.

LEHMAN, KARL FRANKLYN, accountant; b. Lowville, N.Y., Aug. 15, 1942; s. Addison E. and Mary L. (Zehr) L.; m. Elaine K. Hartsough, Aug. 2, 1964; children: Karleia Janel, Regan Scott, Anjanette Joy. BA, Goshen Coll., 1963; MBA, Columbia U., 1965. CPA, Ind., N.Y.; cert. real estate broker, Ind. Staff acct., CPA Arthur Andersen & Co., CPA's, N.Y.C., 1965-68; mgr., CPA McGladrey & Co., CPA's, Davenport, Iowa, 1968-71; v.p., sec.-treas. ADM Industries, Inc., Elkhart, Ind., 1971-74; treas., contr. Globestar Industries, Inc., Elkhart, 1974-80; assoc. prof. acctg. Goshen (Ind.) Coll., 1980-83; pres. Karl F. Lehman & Assocs., PC CPA's, Goshen, 1980—, also bd. dirs.; mem. Creation Design and Mfg., Inc., Elkhart, Pioneer Homes, Inc., Goshen, Creation Design, Inc., Goshen. Mem. AICPA, N.Y. State Soc. CPA's. Home: 3500 Calumet Ave Elkhart IN 46514-4408 Office: Karl F Lehman & Assocs PC 316 S 3rd St Goshen IN 46526-3710 also: Karl F Lehman and Assocs PC 615 W Bristol St Elkhart IN 46514-2900 also: Karl F Lehman & Assocs PC 445 S Van Buren St Shipshewana IN 46565-9176 also: Karl F Lehman & Assocs PC 1001 N Main St Nappanee IN 46550-1016

LEHMAN, LAWRENCE HERBERT, consulting engineering executive; b. N.Y.C., Apr. 30, 1929; s. Samuel and Shirley (Freiberg) L.; m. Susan E. Green, June 29, 1957; children: Scott Jeffrey, Christopher Adam. BCE, NYU, 1949; MBA, Iona Coll., 1978. Registered profl. engr., N.Y., N.J., Ky., Ill., Mass., Conn., Ind., Pa. Project engr. Andrews & Clark (Cons. Engrs.), N.Y.C., 1951-57; project mgr. Barstow, Mulligan & Vollmer (Cons. Engrs.), N.Y.C., 1957-59; chief engr., ptnr. Vollmer Assos. (Cons. Engrs.), N.Y.C., 1959-67; chief exec. officer, dir. Berger, Lehman Assos. (P.C.), Rye, N.Y., 1967—. Recipient Third award U.S. Steel Corp., 1966, Bridge award Pre-stressed Concrete Inst., 1975, Honor award Nat. ACEC, 1995, others. Fellow ASCE (life); mem. NSPE, Am. Cons. Engrs. Coun., Soc. Am. Mil. Engrs., Transp. Rsch. Bd., Am. Ry. Engring. Assn., Internat. Assn. Bridge and Structural Engrs., Am. Rd. and Transp. Builders Assn., Am. Arbitration Assn. (nat. panel arbitrators), N.Y. Assn. Cons. Engrs. (Engring. Excellence awards 1975, 79, 90, 95), Conn. Engrs. in Pvt. Practice, West County Profl. Engrs. Soc. (Engr. of Yr. award 1991), The Moles, High Speed Rail Assn. Home: 10 Chester Dr Rye NY 10580-2204 Office: 411 Theodore Fremd Ave Rye NY 10580-1410

LEHMAN, LOIS JOAN, medical librarian; b. Danville, Pa., Apr. 25, 1932; d. Harold M. and Leona (Shuey) L. B.A., Pa. State U., University Park, 1954; M.S., Columbia U., 1959. Librarian Lankenau Hosp., Phila., 1959-66; reference librarian Sch. Medicine, U. Pa., Phila., 1966-68; asst. librarian head pub. services Coll. Medicine, Pa. State U., Hershey, 1968-71, acting librarian, 1971-72, librarian, 1972—. Mem. Med. Libr. Assn., Assn. Acad. Health Scis. Libr. Dirs., Health Scis. Librs. Consortium (bd. dirs.), Interlibr. Delivery Svc. of Pa. (bd. dirs.), Quentin Riding Club. Avocation: owner of thoroughbred race horse. Office: Pa State U Coll Medicine George T Harrell Libr The Hershey Med Ctr Hershey PA 17033

LEHMAN, ORIN, retired state official; b. N.Y.C., Jan. 14, 1922; s. Allan S. and Evelyn (Schiffer) L.; children: Susan, Brooke, Sage. BA, Princeton U., 1942; MA, NYU, 1956, PhD, 1961; LHD (hon.), Hartwick Coll., 1962, Marist Coll., 1993; LLD (hon.), Manhattan Coll., 1985. Economist Lehman Bros., N.Y.C., 1947-52; pub. and chmn. Colgreene Pub., Inc., Hudson, N.Y., 1951-59; chmn. Colgreene Broadcasting Co., Catskill, N.Y., 1958-75, Picket Prodn., Inc., N.Y.C., 1968-75; commr. N.Y. State Office of Parks, Recreation and Hist. Preservation, Albany, 1975-94; chmn. N.Y. State Commn. for Restoration of the Capitol, 1979; adv. U.S. del. UN Conf. Trade and Devel., 1964-68; chmn. N.Y. State Gov.'s Com. on Employment of Handicapped, 1956-65; mem. public adv. bd. Econ. Cooperation Adminstrn., 1950-52; mem. U.S. Nat. Commn. for UNESCO, 1968-71; chmn. N.Y.C. Bd. Corrections, 1974-75; mem. exec. com. N.Y.C. Criminal Justice Coordinating Com., 1974-75. Trustee, past chmn. New Sch. Social Research, N.Y.C., Parsons Sch. Design; trustee, chmn. Just-One-Break, Inc.; trustee, past exec. dir. Eleanor Roosevelt Meml. Found.; bd. dirs. Ednl. Broadcasting Corp., 1965-74; pres. N.Y. Citizens Com. Public Higher Edn., 1964-68. Served to capt. U.S. Army, 1942-47. Decorated D.F.C., Bronze Star, Purple Heart; recipient Disting. Svc. award Nat. Govs. Assn, 1992, citations Anti-Defamation League, citations N.Y.C. Jaycees, citations N.Y. State Jaycees, citations Pres.'s Com. on Employment of Handicapped, citations CSC U.S., citations CCNY, citations Marist Coll., citations Taft Sch., Pres.'s Pub. Svc. award Nature Conservancy, Pugsley medal Nat. Park Found., 1989. Office: 20 E 69th St Apt 4C New York NY 10021-4960

LEHMAN, PAUL V., minister. Dir. Haitian Ministy Dist. of the Christian and Missionary Alliance. Office: 211 College Ave Nyack NY 10960

LEHMAN, RICHARD LEROY, lawyer; b. Johnstown, Pa., Feb. 4, 1930; s. John S. and Deliah E. (Chase) L.; m. Lucia M. Ragnone; children: Ann Laurie, Leslie Ann, Lucia Marie. AB in Social Work, U. Ky., 1957; LLB, U. Detroit, 1960. Bar: Mich. 1961, U.S. Dist. Ct. (ea. dist.) Mich. 1961, U.S. Ct. Appeals (6th cir.) 1961. Pvt. practice Detroit; ptnr. Garan, Lucow, Miller, Lehman, Seward & Cooper, 1961-79; pres. Home Bldg. Plan Svc., Inc., Portland, Oreg., 1979-82; pres., gen. counsel Matvest Inc., Farmington Hills, Mich., 1980-86; pres. Xi Industries, Flint, Mich., 1982-86; ptnr. Lehman & Valentino, P.C., Bloomfield Hills, Mich., 1986-95; pres. Premiere Packaging, Inc., Flint, 1987-91, chmn., CEO, 1990—; vis. lectr. U. Detroit Law Sch., 1970-74, also Inst. Continuing Legal Edn. Mem. exec. com. pres.'s cabinet U. Detroit, 1975-79; mem. Old Newsboys Goodfellow Fund Detroit, 1969—, bd. dirs., 1975-78. 1st lt. AUS, 1947-53. Recipient Algernon Sydney Sullivan Medallion U. Ky., 1957. Mem. ABA, Mich. Bar Assn., Fed. Bar Assn., Genesee County Bar Assn. (bench and bar com. 1975-78), Am. Judicature Soc., Am. Arbitration Assn., Assn. Def. Trial Counsel, Def. Rsch. Inst., U. Ky. Alumni Assn., U. Detroit Law Sch. Alumni Assn. (dir. 1970-77, pres. 1974-75), U. Detroit Alumni Assn., 6th Cir. Jud. Conf. (life), Pine Lake Country Club (bd. dirs. 1991—, pres. 1994-95). Roman Catholic. Avocations: golf, downhill skiing, carpentry. Home: 4052 Waterwheel Ln Bloomfield Hills MI 48302-1870 Office: Premiere Packaging 6220 Lehman Dr Flint MI 48507-4678

LEHMAN, (ISRAEL) ROBERT, biochemistry educator, consultant; b. Tauroggen, Lithuania, Oct. 5, 1924; came to U.S., 1927; s. Herman Bernard and Anne (Kahn) L.; m. Sandra Lee Teper, July 5, 1959; children: Ellen, Deborah, Samuel. AB, Johns Hopkins U., 1950, PhD, 1954; MD (hon.), U. Gothenberg, Sweden, 1987; DSc (hon.), U. Pierre et Marie Curie, Paris, 1992. Instr. biochemistry Washington U., St. Louis, 1957-59; asst. prof. Stanford (Calif.) U., 1959-61, assoc. prof., 1961-66, prof., 1966—; sci. adv. bd., dirs. U.S. Biochem. Corp., Cleve., 1984—; sci. adv. RPI, Boulder. Author: Principles of Biochemistry, 6th edit., 1978, 7th edit., 1984. Sgt. U.S. Army, 1943-46, ETO. Recipient ASBMB-Merk award Am. Soc. for Biochemistry, 1995. Mem. NAS, Am. Acad. Arts and Scis., Am. Soc. Biol. Chemistry and Molecular Biology (Merck award 1995). Democrat. Jewish. Home: 895 Cedro Way Palo Alto CA 94305-1002 Office: Stanford U Dept Biochemistry Beckman Ctr Stanford CA 94305

LEHMAN, ROBERT NATHAN, ophthalmologist, educator; b. Lancaster, Pa., Oct. 22, 1911; s. Harry Nathan and Mable May (Shenk) L.; m. Clara May Hileman, Apr. 24, 1938; 1 dau., Mary Dorcas. B.S., Franklin and Marshall Coll., 1933; M.D., Temple U., 1937. Intern Temple U. Hosp., 1937-39, resident, 1947-48; resident Walter Reed Hosp., Washington, 1948-50, Armed Forces Inst. Pathology, Washington, 1950-51; chief ophthalmology VA Hosp., Pitts., 1954-78; prof. ophthalmology U. Pitts. Med. Sch., 1954—, lectr. pathology, 1966—. Contbr. articles to profl. jours. Served with AUS, 1939-54. Decorated Bronze Star; Croix de Guerre (2) France). Mem. ACS, Am. Acad. Ophthalmology, Pitts. Ophthal. Soc., Ea. Ophthal. Pathology Soc., Univ. Club (Pitts.). Home: 1240 S Corning St Apt 101 Los Angeles CA 90035-2478

LEHMAN, RUTH GILLESPIE, newspaper executive; b. Denver, Feb. 28, 1924; d. Dean Milton and Lillie Mae (Baldwin) Gillespie; m. Edward Lehman, Apr. 22, 1949; children: Lauren Lehman Kivimaki, Dean G. Student, U. Colo., 1941-44; LLB, Columbia U., 1947. Bar: Colo., 1947. Lawyer Denious & Denious, Denver, 1947-51, Burnett, Lehman & Lehman, Denver, 1951-57; pres. Colo. Century Corp., Denver, 1953-80; editl. page editor Longmont (Colo.) Daily Times Call, Loveland (Colo.) Daily Reporter-Herald, Canon City (Colo.) Daily Record, 1965—; v.p., treas. Lehman Comm. Corp., Longmont, 1987—; bd. mem., pres. Colo. Press Assn., Denver, 1976-82; bd. mem., treas. Inland Press Assn., Chgo., 1982-86; bd. mem. Mountain States Employers Coun., Denver, 1989—. Bd. dirs. Colo. Legal Aid Found., Denver, 1984-91, Colo. Coun. Econ. Edn., Denver, 1988—, Longmont Art in Pub. Places, 1989-92, Colo. Hist. Soc., 1996—. Named Woman of Achievement, Colo. Press Women, 1982. Mem. Internat. Newspaper Fin. Exec., Am. Soc. Newspaper Editors, Nat. Conf. Editl. Writers, Colo. Bar Assn. Office: Lehman Comm Corp 350 Terry St Longmont CO 80501-5440

LEHMANN, DORIS ELIZABETH, elementary education educator; b. Ramsey, N.J., Aug. 17, 1933; d. Alfred Harrison and Anna Elizabeth (Gerhold) Rockefeller; m. Victor S. Lehmann, June 25, 1955; children: Joanne E. Cathy Lynn, Victor A., Kristie Sue. BS in Edn. magna cum laude, Wagner Coll., 1955; student in edn., Columbia U., summers 1988-91, Jersey City State, 1990—, William Paterson, 1971. Elem. tchr. Sch. St. Sch., Ramsey, 1955-56; bedside instr. N. Bergen County schs., N.J., 1966-71; elem. tchr. Edith A. Bogert Sch., Upper Saddle River, N.J., 1971—. Author numerous poems; author: (with others) Curriculum for Values Education in New Jersey, 1991. Indian cons. Bergen County Mus. of Art and Sci., Paramus, N.J., 1983—. Recipient Fellowship of Life award Luth. Layman's Movement, 1955. Fellow Upper Saddle River Edn. Assn. (social sec. 1972-73, v.p. 1974-75, 84-85, liaison to USR hist. soc. 1986—) N.J. Edn. Assn., N.J. North Edn. Assn., Alpha Omicron Pi (life, treas. 1954, v.p. 1955). Republican. Lutheran. Office: Edith A Bogert Sch 395 W Saddle River Rd Saddle River NJ 07458-1622

LEHMANN, ERICH LEO, statistics educator; b. Strasbourg, France, Nov. 20, 1917; came to U.S., 1940, naturalized, 1945; s. Julius and Alma Rosa (Schuster) L.; m. Juliet Popper Shaffer; children: Stephen, Barbara, Fia. M.A., U. Calif. at Berkeley, 1943, Ph.D., 1946; D.Sc. (hon.), U. Leiden, 1985, U. Chgo., 1991. Asst. dept. math. U. Calif. at Berkeley, 1942-43, asso., 1943-46, instr., 1946-47, asst. prof., 1947-51, asso. prof., 1951-54, prof., 1954-55, prof. dept. statistics, 1955-88, emeritus, 1988—, chmn. dept. statistics, 1973-76; vis. assoc. prof. Columbia, 1950-51, Stanford, 1951-52; vis. lectr. Princeton, 1951. Author: Testing Statistical Hypotheses, 1959, 2d edit., 1986, (with J.L. Hodges, Jr.) Basic Concepts of Probability and Statistics, 1964, 2d edit, 1970, Nonparametrics: Statistical Methods Based on Ranks, 1975, Theory of Point Estimation, 1983. Recipient Fisher award Coms. of Pres. Stats. Socs. in N.Am., 1988; Guggenheim fellow, 1955, 66, 79; Miller research prof., 1962-63, 72-73. Fellow Inst. Math. Statistics, Am. Statis. Assn., Royal Statis. Soc. (hon.); mem. Internat. Statis. Inst., Am. Acad. Arts and Scis., Nat. Acad. Scis. Office: Educational Testing Service Mail Stop 02-T Princeton NJ 08541

LEHMANN, HEINZ EDGAR, psychiatrist, consultant, researcher; b. Berlin, July 17, 1911; came to Can., 1937, naturalized, 1948; s. Richard and Emmy (Grönke) L.; m. Annette Joyal, July 28, 1940; 1 child, François. Abiturium, Mommsen Gymnasium, Berlin, 1929; M.D., U. Berlin, 1935; LL.D. (hon.), U. Calgary, Can., 1980. Clin. dir. Douglas Hosp., Montreal, Que., Can., 1947-66; dir. research Douglas Hosp., 1966-67; prof. psychiatry McGill U., Montreal, 1965—; emeritus prof. McGill U., 1981—, chmn. dept. psychiatry, 1970-74; cons. 4 Montreal hosps., 1976—; dep. commr. research N.Y. State Office Mental Health, Albany, 1980—. Contbr. over 300 articles to profl. jours., chpts. to books. Decorated officer Order of Can., 1975; recipient Albert Lasker award Lasker Found., 1957, Heinz Lehmann Rsch. award N.Y. State Office of Mental Health, 1990. Fellow Internat. Coll. Neuropsychopharmacology (pres. 1970-72), Can. Coll. Neuropsychopharmacology (Heinz Lehmann ann. award 1983), Que. Psychiat. Assn. (Heinz Lehmann ann. award 1986); mem. Am. Coll. Neuropsychopharmacology (pres. 1965-66, life), Am. Psychiat. Assn. (life), Royal Soc. Can. Avocations: gemology; astronomy; magic; skiing; scuba diving. Office: 1033 Pine Ave W, Montreal, PQ Canada H3A 1A1

LEHMANN, MICHAEL STEPHEN, film director; b. San Francisco, Mar. 30, 1957; s. Herbert and Minette L.; m. Holland Sutton; children: Alexander, Natalie. BA, Columbia U., 1978; MFA, U. So. Calif., 1985. Mgr. electronic cinema div. Zoetrope, Hollywood, Calif., 1981-83. Dir. (films) Heathers, 1989 (Best First Feature award Ind. Feature Project 1990), Meet the Applegates, 1991, Hudson Hawk, 1991, Airheads, 1994; exec. prodr. (film) Ed Wood, 1994.

LEHMANN, PHYLLIS WILLIAMS, archaeologist, educator; b. Bklyn., Nov. 30, 1912; d. James Barnes and Florence Lourene (Richmond) Williams; m. Karl Lehmann, Sept. 14, 1944 (dec. Dec. 1960). B.A., Wellesley Coll., 1934, L.H.D., 1976; Ph.D., NYU, 1943; Litt.D., Mt. Holyoke Coll., 1971; D.F.A., Coll. Holy Cross, 1973. Asst. charge classical collection Bklyn. Museum, 1934-36; part-time instr. history art Bennett Jr. Coll., 1936-39; mem. faculty Smith Coll., 1946—, prof. art, 1955-67, Jessie Wells Post prof. art, 1967-72, William R. Kenan, Jr. prof. art, 1972-78, prof. emeritus, 1978—, dean, 1965-70; asst. field dir. excavations conducted by Archaeol. Research Fund of NYU at Samothrace, 1948-60, acting dir., 1960-62, adv. dir., 1962—; research prof. Inst. Fine Arts, NYU, 1961-62; adj. prof. Inst. Fine Arts, N.Y. U., 1965—; Flexner lectr. Bryn Mawr Coll., 1977; Baldwin lectr. Oberlin Coll., 1982. Author: Statues on Coins of Southern Italy and Sicily in the Classical Period, 1946, Roman Wall Paintings from Boscoreale in the Metropolitan Museum of Art, 1953, The Pedimental Sculptures of the Hieron in Samothrace, 1962, Samothrace, vol. 3, 1969, (with Karl Lehmann) Samothracian Reflections. Aspects of the Revival of the Antique, 1973, Skopas in Samothrace, 1973, Cyriacus of Ancona's Egyptian Visit and Its Reflections in Gentile Bellini and Hieronymus Bosch, 1977, Samothrace, Vol. 5, 1982, contbr. Vol. 7, 1992; also articles in profl. jours.; Editor: (with Karl Lehmann) Samothrace, 1961—; asst. editor: Art Bull., 1945-47; book rev. editor, 1949-52. Named hon. citizen of Samothrace, 1968; recipient Wellesley Coll. Alumnae Assn. Achievement award, 1976; Gold medal Pan Samothracian Hearth of Athens, 1981; hon. mem. Pan Samothracian Hearth of Athens, 1979; Fulbright research grantee Italy, 1952-53; Guggenheim fellow, 1952-53; Bollingen fellow, 1960. Fellow Am. Acad. Arts and Scis.; mem. Archaeol. Inst. Am. (trustee 1970-73), Coll. Art Assn. Am., Am. Numis. Soc., Soc. Archtl. Historians (Alice D. Hitchcock award 1969), AAUW, Renaissance Soc. Am., Am. Sch. Classical Studies in Athens (research fellow fall 1970, 76, exec. com. 1970-75, publ. com. 1975-80, chmn. 1977-80), Williamsburg Hist. Soc., Phi Beta Kappa. Club: Cosmopolitan. Home: 127 Main St Haydenville MA 01039-9713 Office: Smith Coll Hillyer Hall Northampton MA 01063

LEHMANN, RUTH PRESTON MILLER, literature educator; b. Ithaca, N.Y., Feb. 18, 1912; d. Ernest Allen and Lillian Allen (Phillips) Miller; m. Winfred P. Lehmann, Oct. 12, 1940; children—Terry Jon, Sandra Lehmann Hargis. B.A., Cornell U., 1932, M.A., 1934; postgrad., Bryn Mawr Coll., 1935-36; Ph.D., U. Wis.-Madison, 1942. Teaching asst. U. Wis., Madison, 1938-42; editor lang. texts U.S. Armed Forces Inst., Washington, 1943-44; instr. George Washington U., Washington, 1944-46; lectr. Washington U., St. Louis, 1946-47; instr. Georgetown U. English Lang. Program, Ankara, Turkey, 1955-56; asso. prof. English Huston Tillotson Coll., Austin, Tex., 1956-58; lectr. English U. Tex., Austin, 1960-67; asso. prof. U. Tex., 1967-72, prof., 1972-80, prof. emeritus, 1980—; delivered Rudolf Thurneysen Meml. lecture, U. Bonn., Fed. Rep. of Germany, 1985. Contbg. author: The Origins of Writing, 1989; editor: Fled Duin na nGed, 1964, (with W.P. Lehmann) Introduction to Old Irish, 1975, Early Irish Verse, 1982, Beowulf: Am Imitative Translation, 1988. Mem. MLA, Medieval Acad. Am., Early English Texts. Soc., Phi Beta Kappa (pres. Austin chpt. 1978-79), Phi Kappa Phi, Pi Lambda Theta. Democrat. Home: 3800 Eck Ln Austin TX 78734-1613 Office: U Tex Dept English Austin TX 78712 *Happiness is a state of mind and more fun than boredom.*

LEHMANN, WINFRED PHILIPP, linguistics educator; b. Surprise, Nebr., June 23, 1916; s. Phillip Ludwig and Elenore Friederike (Grosnick) L.; m. Ruth Preston Miller, Oct. 12, 1940; children: Terry Jon, Sandra Jean. BA, Northwestern Coll., Watertown, Wis., 1936; MA, U. Wis., 1938, PhD, 1941; LittD (hon.), SUNY, Binghamton, 1985; DHL (hon.), U. Wis., 1995. From instr. to asst. prof. Wash. U., 1946-49; from assoc. prof. to prof. U. Tex., 1949-63, Ashbel Smith prof. linguistics, 1963-83, Louann and Larry Temple prof. humanities, 1983-86, prof. emeritus, 1986—, chmn. dept. Germanic langs., 1953-65, chmn. dept. linguistics, 1965-72, dir. Linguistics Research Center, 1961—; Jawaharlal Nehru Meml. lectr., New Delhi, 1981; dir. Georgetown English lang. program, Ankara, Turkey, 1955-56; chmn. linguistics del. People's Republic of China, 1974, co-chmn. Social Sci./Humanities Planning Commn., 1981. Author: (with L. Faust) A Grammar of Formal Written Japanese, 1951, Proto-Indo-European Phonology, 1952, The Alliteration of Old Saxon Poetry, 1953, The Development of Germanic Verse Form, 1956, Historical Linguistics: An Introduction, 1962, 3d edit., 1992, Descriptive Linguistics: An Introduction, 1972, 2d edit., 1976, Proto-Indo-European Syntax, 1974, Linguistische Theorien der Moderne, 1981, Language: An Introduction, 1982, Gothic Etymological Dictionary, 1986, Die Gegenwartige Richtung der Indogermanistischen Forschung, 1992, Theoretical Bases of Indo-European Linguistics, 1993, Residues of Pre-Indo-European Active Structure and Their Implications for the Relationships among the Dialects, 1995; editor: Language and Linguistics in the People's Republic of China, 1974, (with R.P.M. Lehmann) An Introduction to Old Irish, 1975, Syntactic Typology, 1978, (with Yakov Malkiel) Perspectives on Historical Linguistics, 1982, Language Typology, 1985, Language Typology: Systematic Balance in Language, 1987, (with H.J.J. Hewitt) Typological Models in Reconstruction, 1988; contbr. articles to profl. jours. Chmn. bd. dirs. Center for Applied Linguistics, 1973-78. 1st lt. Signal Corps AUS, 1942-46. Decorated Comdr.'s Cross, Order Merit Fed. Republic Germany, 1987; recipient Jakob Grimm prize, 1975, Pro bene Meritis award, U. Tex., 1987; fellow Fulbright Found., Norway, 1950-51, Guggenheim Found., 1972-73. Mem. MLA (exec. coun. 1977-80, pres. 1987), Linguistic Soc. Am. (pres. 1973), Am. Coun. Learned Socs. (sec. bd. 1977-86, Harry H. Ransom award teaching excellence 1989), Danish Acad. Scis. Lutheran. Home: 3800 Eck Ln Austin TX 78734-1613

LEHMANN-HAUPT, CHRISTOPHER CHARLES HERBERT, book reviewer; b. Edinburgh, Scotland, June 14, 1934; came to U.S., 1934; s. Hellmut Otto Emil and Letitia Jane H. (Grierson) Lehmann-H.; m. Natalie S. Robins, Oct. 3, 1965; children: Rachel Louise, Noah Christopher. B.A., Swarthmore Coll., 1956; M.F.A., Yale U., 1959. Editor A.S. Barnes & Co., Inc., N.Y.C., 1961-62, Holt, Rinehart & Winston, 1962-63; sr. editor Dial Press, 1963-65; mem. staff N.Y. Times Book Review, 1965-69; sr. book reviewer N.Y. Times, 1969—; asst. prof. lit. CUNY, 1973-75. Author: Me and Di Maggio, 1986, A Crooked Man, 1995. Club: Century. Office: New York Times 229 W 43rd St New York NY 10036-3913

LEHMBERG, ROBERT HENRY, research physicist; b. Phila., Dec. 4, 1937; s. Henry and Marguerite Elenore (Schock) L.; m. Norma Geder, Dec. 29, 1966; 1 child, Karl Robert. BSc, Pa. State U., 1959; MSc, U. Ariz., 1961; PhD, Brandeis U., 1968. Rsch. physicist Naval Air Devel. Ctr., Warminster, Pa., 1966-72, Naval Rsch. Lab., Washington, 1972—; chmn. program com. Conf. on Lasers and Electro-Optics, Washington, 1991. Contbr. articles to profl. jours.; patentee in field. Fellow Am. Phys. Soc. (Excellence in Plasma Physics Rsch. award 1993); mem. AAAS, IEEE, Sigma Xi. Achievements include development of optical beam smoothing techniques for laser fusion, optical design of the Naval Research Laboratory's Nike laser facility, and research in nonlinear optics and laser-plasma interaction physics. Office: Naval Rsch Lab Plasma Physics Div 4555 Overlook Ave SW Washington DC 20375-0001

LEHMBERG, STANFORD EUGENE, historian, educator; b. McPherson, Kans., Sept. 23, 1931; s. Willard Eugene and Helen (Stanford) L.; m. Phyllis Barton, July 23, 1962; 1 son, Derek Grantham. BA, U. Kans., 1953, MA, 1954; PhD, Cambridge (Eng.) U., 1956, DLitt, 1990. Mem. faculty U. Tex., Austin, 1956-69; mem. faculty U. Minn., 1969—, prof. history, 1967—, chmn. dept., 1979-85. Author: Sir Thomas Elyot, Tudor Humanist, 1960, Sir Walter Mildmay and Tudor Government, 1966, The Reformation Parliament, 1970, The Later Parliaments of Henry VIII, 1977, The Reformation of Cathedrals, 1988, The People of the British Isles to 1688, 1991, Cathedrals Under Siege, 1996; also articles, revs. Fulbright scholar, 1954-56; Guggenheim fellow, 1965-66, 85-86. Fellow Royal Hist. Soc.; mem. Am. Hist. Assn., Midwest Conf. Brit. Studies (pres. 1982-84), Renaissance Soc. Am., Am. Soc. Reformation Research. Episcopalian. Home: 2300 Willow Ln S Minneapolis MN 55416-3863 Office: U Minn Dept History Minneapolis MN 55455

LEHNE, PASCAL HORST, chemistry educator, consultant; b. Hamburg, Germany, Apr. 17, 1915; s. Richard Wilhelm and Clarita (Voigt) L.; m. Julita Tapang Dawat, Aug. 4, 1972; 1 child, Rowena. Diploma in chemistry, U. Heidelberg, Germany, 1944. Asst. master Gewerbeschule Hansestadt Hamburg, 1956-65, sr. asst. master, 1966-80, ret., 1980, temporary appointed tutor, 1981-83; hon. co-worker Mus. für Hamburgische Geschichte, Hamburg, 1994—; vice dir. evening sch. English Inst., Heidelberg, 1950-52; subdir., tutor Inst. für Lernsysteme, Hamburg, 1980-86. Author: The Normal Gauge Electric Light Railway Altrahlstedt-Volksdorf-Wohldorf, 4 edits., 1954-86; co-author: Lead and Silver, 1966, 2nd edit., 1975, About the Mariana Islands, 1972; calculator of orbital elements of comet Paraskevopoulos (1941c) from pvt. observations; author numerous edits. Periodic Chart of Elements, 1938-52; contbr. articles to profl. jours. Mem. Gesellschaft Deutscher Chemiker, Bund für Deutsche Schrift, The Planetary Soc. Avocations: preparing Tagalog-German dictionary, compilation of comprehensive collections of elements and inorganic compounds. Home: Hamburger Strasse 110b, 22949 Ammersbek Germany Office: Staatliche Gewerbeschule für Chemie, Billwerder Billdeich 614, 21033 Hamburg Germany

LEHNER, GEORGE ALEXANDER, JR., lawyer; b. Cleve., Aug. 13, 1948; s. George Alexander and Phyllis More (Holbrook) L.; m. Diana Hill Day, May 29, 1971; children: Kristin, Alison. BA, Wesleyan U., Middletown, Conn., 1971; JD, U. Mich., 1976, M in Urban Planning, 1977. Bar: Mich. 1977, D.C. 1979, U.S. Dist. Ct. D.C. 1987, U.S. Ct. Appeals (4th cir.) 1987, U.S. Ct. Appeals (D.C. cir.) 1988, U.S. Ct. Appeals (9th cir.) 1993. Atty., advisor U.S. Dept. State, Washington, 1977-80; assoc. Arent, Fox, Kintner, Plotkin & Kahn, Washington, 1981-87; ptnr. Sloan, Lehner & Ruiz, Washington, 1987-89, Pepper, Hamilton & Scheetz, Washington, 1989—; adj. prof. Georgetown U. Law Ctr., 1990-93; gen. counsel Internat. Women's Media Found., 1990—. Co-author: Europe Without Frontiers: A Lawyer's Guide, 1989. Advisor foreign policy Mondale for Pres., 1984; Watson Fellow. Mem. ABA, Phi Beta Kappa. Avocations: sailing, photography. Home: 508 Woodland Ter Alexandria VA 22302-3317 Office: Pepper Hamilton & Scheetz 1300 19th St NW Washington DC 20036-1609

LEHNER, MARK, archaeologist, educator; b. Fargo, N.D., Apr. 2, 1950; s. Paul William and Ethel Lois (Davy) L.; m. Suzanne Ayad Massoud, July 12, 1975 (div. 1985); children: Ramsi, Luke; m. Julia Cort, July 2, 1995. BA in Anthropology, Am. U., Cairo, 1975; PhD in Egyptology, Yale U., 1990. Field dir. Sphinx and Isis Temple project Am. Rsch. Ctr., Egypt, 1979-83, co-dir. Pyramids radiocarbon dating project, 1984; dir. Giza Plateau mapping project Am. Rsch. Ctr./Oriental Inst. U. Chgo., Egypt, 1984—; dir. Koch-Ludwig Giza Plateau project U. Chgo., 1988—, instr. Egyptian Archaeology Oriental Inst., 1990-91, asst. prof., 1991—; bd. dirs. Ancient Egypt Rsch. Assocs., Inc; archtl. surveyor, draughtsman, area supervisor Nag Hammadi, Faw Qibli Expeditions Claremont Inst. Antiquity and Christianity, 1976-78; surveyor and dir. clearing ops. Sci. and Archaeology project, 1978; supr. mapping, photographer, draughtsman, various excavations in the Sphinx area, 1978; mapper Bayt al-Razzaz project Am. Rsch. Ctr., 1978; surveyor, object restorer, artist, photographer various salvage excavations, 1979; area supr., mapper, photographer, Tell el-Amarna expedition, Egypt Exploration Soc., 1979-80, archtl. surveyor Tomb of Akhenaten epigraphic survey, 1980;surveyor Deir el-Ballas expedition, Mus. Fine arts, Boston, 1983; archtl. surveyor Tombe of Aperia project, Saqqara Ctr. National de Recherches Scientifiques, 1983-85, Abdyos Regional Site Survey, U. Pa., 1983, Nasr. Mohammed Mosque Restoration, The German Archaelogical Inst., 1985; cons. Time-Life Books, 1986-87, Field Mus. Nat. History, Chgo., 1987-88, NAS Com. Sphinx conservation study, 1989, Getty Conservation Inst., 1989-90, The Jerde Partnership, 1989-90, Egyptian Antiquities Orgn. Symposium on Sphinx restoration, 1992, materials adv bd. Nat. Rsch. Coun. conservation Egyptian monuments study steering com., 1992; lectr. in field. TV appearnaces include PM Mag., 1982, LBS Mysteries of the Pyramids, 1988, National Geographic Explorer, 1992, Nova: Building a Pyramid, 1992; contbr. articles to profl. jours. Sterling Prize fellow Yale U., 1986; recipient William J. Horowitz prize Near Eastern Langs. and Civilizations, Yale U. 1991. Office: Harvard Semitic Mus 6 Divinity Ave Cambridge MA 02138

LEHNER, URBAN CHARLES, journalist; b. Grand Rapids, Mich., May 10, 1947; s. Urban Edward and Angeline Grace (Marcy) L.; m. Anne Marie Eding, May 2, 1969 (div. 1976); m. Nancy Ellen Leonard, June 28, 1980; 1 child, Alicia Ann. AB in history, U. Mich., 1969; JD, Georgetown U., 1979. Staff reporter The Wall Street Jour., N.Y.C., Phila., Chgo., Washington, 1969-80; bur. chief. The Wall Street Jour., Tokyo, 1980-83, Detroit, 1983-85; mng. editor The Wall Street Jour. Europe, Brussels, 1985-87; bur. chief The Wall Street Jour., The Asian Wall Street Jour., Tokyo, 1988-92; editor The Asian Wall Street Jour., Hong Kong, 1992—. Lt. (j.g.) USNR, 1970-72. Recipient Citation for Excellence with Alan Murray for Strained Alliance Overseas Press Club, 1991. Mem. Fgn. Corrs. Club Japan. Office: The Asian Wall St Jour, 2/F AIA Bldg CPO Box 9825, Hong Kong Hong Kong

LEHNERT, HERBERT HERMANN, foreign language educator; b. Luebeck, Germany, Jan. 19, 1925; came to U.S., 1958, naturalized, 1971; s. Bernhard Alfred and Elisabeth (Doemel) L.; m. Ingeborg Poth, Aug. 13, 1952; children—Bernard (dec.), Brigitte, Bettina. Ph.D., U. Kiel, Germany, 1952. Lectr. U. Western Ont., Can., 1957; faculty Rice U., 1958-68, prof. German, 1966-68; prof. German U. Kans., 1968-69; prof. German U. Calif., Irvine, 1969—, chmn. dept., 1974-76; vis. prof. Harvard, fall 1970. Author: Thomas Mann: Fiktion, Mythos, Religion, 1965, Struktur und Sprachmagie, 1966, Thomas Mann Forschung, 1969, Geschichte der deutschen Literatur: Vom Jugendstil zum Expressionismus, 1978, Nihilismus der Menschenfreundlichkeit: Thomas Manns Wandlung (with Eva Wessell), 1991; editor: Doctor Faustus: A Novel at the Margin of Modernism (with Peter C. Pfeiffer) 1991; contbr. articles to profl. jours. Nat. Endowment for Humanities fellow, 1973, 78; Guggenheim fellow, 1978-79. Mem. MLA, Am. Assn. Tchrs. German. Home: 8 Harvey Ct Irvine CA 92612-4033 Office: U Calif Dept German Irvine CA 92697-3150

LEHOCZKY, JOHN PAUL, statistics educator; b. Columbus, Ohio, June 29, 1943; s. Paul Nicholas and Thelma Marie (Heisterkamp) L.; m. Mary Louise Zimmerman, Sept. 10, 1966; children: Jennifer Lynne, Jessica Augusta. BA, Oberlin Coll., 1965; MS, Stanford U., 1967, PhD, 1969. Asst. prof. stats. Carnegie Mellon U., Pitts., 1969-73, assoc. prof., 1973-81, prof., 1981—, head dept., 1984-95; assoc. editor IEEE Transactions on Computers, 1995—; cons. in legal stats., statis. anlysis, math. fin. and real-time computing. Dept. editor Mgmt. Sci., 1981-86; assoc. editor Jour. Real-Time Systems, 1989—; contbr. over 90 rsch. papers in various diciplines. Fellow Am. Statis. Assn. (statistician of yr. Pitts. chpt. 1987), Inst. Math. Stats.; mem. IEEE, AAAS, Assn. for Computing Machinery, Internat. Statis. Inst., Informs. Office: Carnegie Mellon Univ Dept Stat Pittsburgh PA 15213

LEHOVEC, KURT, electrical engineering educator; b. Ladowitz, Czechoslovakia, June 12, 1918; came to U.S., 1947, naturalized, 1952; married,

1952. BS, Charles U., Prague, Czechoslovakia, 1938, MS, 1940; PhD in Physics, U. Prague, 1951. Head rsch. lab. physics inst. Prague U., 1942-45, rsch. fellow, 1945-46; rsch. fellow U.S. Signal Corps, Ft. Monmouth, N.J., 1947-52; dir. semicondr. R&D Sprague Elec. Co., 1952-66; pres. Inventors & Investors, 1967—; prof. electronics U. So. Calif., L.A., 1971-881971-197, emeritus prof. engring. and material sci., 1988—; adj. prof. Williams Coll., 1967, U. Calif., Irvine, 1980; cons. in field. Fellow IEEE, Am. Phys. Soc. Office: 202 S Juanita Ave # 2214 Los Angeles CA 90005

LEHR, DENNIS JAMES, lawyer; b. N.Y.C., Feb. 7, 1932; s. Irwin Allen and Teeny (Scofield) L.; m. Enid J. Auerbach, June 10, 1956; children—Austin Windsor, Bryant Paul, Amy Lynn. BA, NYU, 1954, LLM, 1961; LLB, Yale U., 1957. Bar: N.Y. 1959, D.C. 1967. Atty. Allstate Ins. Co., N.Y.C., 1958-59; atty. Regional Office SEC, N.Y.C., 1959-61; assoc. Borden and Ball, N.Y.C., 1961-63; atty. Office Spl Counsel Investment Co. Act Matters SEC, Washington, 1963-64; assoc. chief counsel Office Comptroller Currency U.S. Treasury Dept., Washington, 1964-67; assoc. Hogan & Hartson, Washington, 1967-69, ptnr., 1969-94, of counsel, 1994—; bd. advs. So. Meth. U. Grad. Sch. Banking; adj. prof. Georgetown Law Sch., 1964-68; legal adv. com. Nat. Ctr. on Fin. Svcs., U. Calif.; lectr. Practicing Law Inst.; adv. coun. Banking Law Inst.; pub. mem. Adminstrv. Conf. of the U.S. Bd. contbrs. Fin. Services Law Report. Contbr. articles to profl. jours. Mem. ABA (coun. mem. sect. bus. law, former chmn. com. on Long Range Issues Affecting Bus. Law Practice, former chmn., com. on devels. in investment svcs.). Office: Hogan and Hartson 555 13th St NW Washington DC 20004-1109

LEHR, JANET, art dealer, publisher, author; b. N.Y.C., June 7, 1937; d. Herbert Davis and Florence (Lustig) Cooperman; m. Lewis Lehr, Feb. 22, 1959 (div. 1984); children: Florence Rachel, Michael William, Samuel Joseph. BA, NYU, 1955; JD, Bklyn. Law Sch., 1958. Pvt. practice art dealer 20th century Am. paintings N.Y.C., 1962-72; dir. Janet Lehr Inc., 19th and 20th Century Photographs, N.Y.C., 1972—; ptnr. Vered Gallery, paintings and sculptures by modern Am. masters, emerging artists and Am. rediscovery 1920-70, East Hampton, N.Y., 1988—; co-dir. Gallery 6M, N.Y.C., 1964-72; curator Landscape Photography, State Mus. Munich, 1979. Author: William Henry Jackson, Picture Maker of the American West, William Henry Fox Talbot and the Art of Photo Mechanical Illustration, 1978; exhbns. include Horatio Ross: Scottish Photographs 1850s Yale University, British Ctr. for the Arts, 1993, Masterworks of Photography, Art Gallery of New South Wales, Sydney, Australia, 1994; also 33 quar. issues on history photography, 1976-86. Mem. Assn. Internat. Photography Art Dealers (founding), Antiquarian Book Dealers Am., Internat. Book Dealers Assn. Home and Office: 891 Park Ave New York NY 10021-0326

LEHR, LEWIS WYLIE, diversified manufacturing company executive; b. Elgin, Nebr., Feb. 21, 1921; s. Lewis H. and Nancy (Wylie) L.; m. Doris Stauder, Oct. 13, 1944; children—Mary A. Lehr Makin, William L., Donald D., John M. B.S. in Chem. Engring, U. Nebr., 1947, Sc.D. (hon.), 1977. With 3M Co., St. Paul, 1947—; v.p. med. products div. 3M Co., 1960-72, health care products group, 1972-74, tape and allied products group, 1974-75, pres. U.S. ops., 1975-79, vice chmn., 1979-80, chmn., chief exec. officer, 1980-86; bd. dirs. Jack Eckerd corp., Tampa, Fla., Sci., Inc., Bloomington, Minn., Peregrine, Inc. Trustee U. Nebr. Found. Served with AUS, 1943-46, ETO. Recipient Alumni Achievement award U. Nebr. Alumni Assn., 1976, State of Nebr. Wagon Master award, 1995. Mem. Am. Chem. Soc. Clubs: North Oaks Golf, White Bear Yacht, Minnesota. Address: Minn World Trade Ctr 30 7th St E Ste 3050 Saint Paul MN 55101-4901

LEHRER, JAMES CHARLES, television journalist; b. Wichita, Kans., May 19, 1934; s. Harry Frederick and Lois Catherine (Chapman) L.; m. Kate Staples, June 4, 1960; children: Jamie, Lucy, Amanda. A.A., Victoria Coll., 1954; B.J., U. Mo., 1956. Reporter Dallas Morning News, 1959-61; reporter, columnist, city editor Dallas Times Herald, 1961-70; exec. producer, corr. Sta. KERA-TV, Dallas, 1970-72; pub. affairs coordinator Public Broadcasting Service, Washington, 1972-73; corr. NPACT-WETA-TV, Washington, 1973—; exec. editor, anchor The NewsHour with Jim Lehrer, 1995—; instr. creative writing Dallas Coll., So. Meth. U., 1967-68. Author: (fiction) Viva Max, 1966, We Were Dreamers, 1975, Kick the Can, 1988, Crown Oklahoma, 1980, The Sooner Spy, 1990, Lost and Found, 1991, Short List, 1992, A Bus of My Own, 1992, Blue Hearts, 1993, Fine Lines, 1994, The Last Debate, 1995, (plays) Chili Queen, 1986, Church Key Charlies Blue, 1987, The Will and Bart Show, 1992. Served with USMC, 1956-59. Recipient Columbia-Dupont award; George Polk award; Peabody award; Emmy award. Mem. Am. Acad. Arts and Scis., Dramatists Guild, Authors Guild, Tex. Inst. Letters, Coun. on Fgn. Rels. Office: Sta WETA-TV PO Box 2626 Washington DC 20013-2626

LEHRER, KENNETH EUGENE, real estate advisor, consultant, developer; b. N.Y.C., Apr. 17, 1946; s. Charles Carlton and Evelyn Estelle (Rosenfeld) L.; m. Myrna Sue Newman, Apr. 4, 1981 (div. 1988); m. Geraldine Trudy Fishman, Mar. 18, 1994. BS, NYU, 1967, MBA, 1969, MA, 1972, D in Pub. Adminstrn., 1980. Registered investment advisor; cert. real estate appraiser; cert. review appraiser; lic. real estate broker. Asst. treas. Bankers Trust Co., N.Y.C., 1970-73; dir. devel. Coventry Devel. Corp., N.Y.C., 1974-77; asst. v.p. Affiliated Capital Corp., Houston, 1977-80; dir. fin. Allison/Walker Interests, Houston, 1980-82; mng. dir. Lehrer Fin. and Econ. Adv. Svcs., 1982—; prof. real estate fin. U. Houston Grad. Sch. Bus. Adminstrn., 1985—; chmn. bd. dirs. Acadia Savs. and Loan Assn., Crowley, La., French Market Homestead Savs. Assn., Metairie, La., Twin City Savs. Bank, West Monroe, La., 1st Savs. La., LaPlace, Integrated Resource Techs. Inc., 1992-95. Pres. Cornerstone Mcpl. Utilities Dist., 1978-85; bd. dirs. Ft. Bend County Mcpl. Utility Dist. #106, Houston Caliber Fin. Group, chmn., 1994—. Mem. Am. Horse Show Assn. (life), Nat. Steeplechase and Hunt Assn. (life), U.S. Tennis Assn. (life), Am. Real Estate and Urban Econs. Assn., Am. Real Estate Soc., Nat. Assn. Bus. Economists, NYU Money Marketeers, Nat. Forensic Ctr., Nat. Assn. Corp. Dirs., Am. Acad. Econ. and Fin. Experts, Internat. Coll. Real Estate Cons. Profls., Internat. Assn. Corp. Real Estate Execs., Nat. Assn. Forensic Economists, Am. Arbitration Assn., Houston Bus. Economists, Western Econ. Assn., Internat. Real Estate Inst. Fin. Club. NYC., Real Estate Educators Assn., Am. Econ. Assn., N.Am. Econs. and Fin. Assn., So. Econ. Assn., NYU Alumni Fedn. (bd. dirs. 1974-77), Tex. Rep. Assn., Rep. Senatorial Inner Cir. (life, Medal of Freedom 1994), Houston C. of C. (mem. govtl. relations com.), Atrium Club, NYU Club, Princeton Club N.Y., Jockey Club (Miami, Fla.), Capitol Hill Club (Washington). Episcopalian. Home: 5555 Del Monte Dr Apt 802 Houston TX 77056-4117 Office: Lehrer Fin and Econ Adv Svcs 1775 Saint James Pl Ste 150 Houston TX 77056-3403

LEHRER, LEONARD, artist, educator; b. Phila., Mar. 23, 1935; s. Abraham and Bessie Lehrer; m. Marilyn Bigard, May 29, 1977; 1 child, Anna-Katrina Picard; stepchildren: Tracy Peel, Janna Peel, John Peel, Jamye Pawlak. BFA, Phila. Coll. Art, 1956; MFA, U. Pa., 1960. Mem. faculty Phila. Coll. Art, 1956-70, co-dir. found. program, 1965-70; prof. art U. N.Mex., 1970-74, chmn. dept., 1970-73; prof. U. Tex., San Antonio, 1974-77; dir. divsn. art and design U. Tex., 1974-75; prof., dir. Sch. Art, Ariz. State U., Tempe, 1977-90; dir. Visual Art Rsch. Studios, 1984-91; prof., chair dept. art and art professions NYU, 1991—. One-man shows include Utah Mus. Fine Arts, Salt Lake City, 1973, 82, Marian Locks Gallery, Phila., 1974-77, 84, McNay Art Mus., San Antonio, 1975, Galerie Kühl, Hannover, Germany, 1976, 79, 82, 91, Bomann Mus., Celle, Germany, 1980, Marilyn Butler Fine Art, Scottsdale, Ariz., 1980, Assoc. Am. Artists, Phila., 1984, Am. Cultural Affairs Ctr., Madrid, 1984, numerous others; exhibited in group shows including 14th Ljubljana Internat. Print Biennial, 1981, 4th Graphic Arts Biennial of Ams., Cali, Colombia, 1981, 7th Brit. Internat. Print Biennial, Bradford, Eng., 1982, Internat. Printmaking Invitational, San Bernardino, Calif., 1983, XXXV Art Fair, Munich, 1992, XXIV Art Fair, Hannover, 1993; represented in permanent collections Met. Mus. Art, N.Y.C., Mus. Modern Art, N.Y.C., Phila. Mus. Art, Nat. Gallery Art, Fed. Res. Bd., Corcoran Gallery, Libr. of Congress, Washington, Spengel Mus. Art, Hannover; curator Large Scale Am. Prints in Art Multiple Dusseldorf, Germany, 1992; author: (introductory essay) The Art of the Book; works featured in The Art of Leonard Lehrer, 1986; contbr. articles to profl. jours. Mem. bd. trustees, v.p. Internat. Print Ctr., N.Y., Inc. Recipient 1st prize 4th Miami Internat. Print Biennial, 1980; recipient Western States Art Found. Printmaking Fellowship award, 1979, Heitland Found. prize, Celle, 1980, Gold Medal award Ariz. chpt. Nat. Soc. Arts and Letters, 1981. Office: NYU Dept Art and Art Professions New York NY 10003

LEHRER, SANDER, lawyer; b. Bronx, N.Y., Aug. 21, 1942; s. Sigmund and Rose (Sand) L.; m. Maryanne Leon, Apr. 17, 1961; children: Jon, Risë, Marc. BA, U. Mich., 1963; LLB, Harvard U., 1966. Bar: N.Y. 1967, U.S. Dist. Ct. (so., ea. dists.) N.Y., 1968. Law clerk to Hon. Dudley B. Bonsal Dist. Ct. (so. dist.) N.Y., N.Y.C., 1966-68; assoc. Webster & Sheffield, N.Y.C., 1968-73, ptnr., 1974-76, counsel, ptnr., 1978-91; gen. counsel N.Y.C. Dept. Housing and Preservation Devel., N.Y.C., 1976, commr., 1977; ptnr. McDermott, Will & Emery, N.Y.C., 1991—; adj. assoc. prof. NYU Sch. Law, 1979-81. Sec., bd. dirs. Citizens Housing and Planning Coun. N.Y.C., 1978—. Mem. Bar Assn. City N.Y., N.Y. State Bar Assn. Office: McDermott Will & Emery 1211 Avenue Of The Americas New York NY 10036-8701*

LEHRER, STANLEY, magazine publisher, editorial director, corporate executive; b. Bklyn., Mar. 18, 1929; s. Martin and Rose L.; m. Laurel Francine Zang, June 8, 1952; children: Merrill Clark, Randee Hope. BS in Journalism, N.Y. U., 1950; postgrad. in edn, San Antonio Coll., 1952. Editor and pub. Crossroads mag., Valley Stream, N.Y., 1949-50; youth service editor Open Road mag., N.Y.C., 1950-51; mng. editor School & Society, N.Y.C., 1953-68, v.p., 1956-68; pub. School & Society Books, N.Y.C., 1963-86; pres., pub. School & Society mag., N.Y.C., 1968-72; pres., pub. Intellect mag., N.Y.C., 1972-78, editorial dir., 1974-78; founder, pres., pub., editl. dir. USA Today mag., Valley Stream, N.Y., 1978—; pres., pub., editorial dir. Newsview newsletter, 1979—, Your Health newsletter, 1980—, The World of Sci. newsletter, 1980—; cons. Child Care Publs., N.Y.C., 1955. Producer: (WBAI-FM radio program) Report on Eucation, N.Y.C., 1960-61; author: John Dewey: Master Educator, 1959, Countdown on Segregated Education, 1960, Religion, Government, and Education, 1961, A Century of Higher Education: Classical Citadel to Collegiate Colossus, 1962, Automation, Education, and Human Values, 1966, Conflict and Change on the Campus: The Response to Student Hyperactivism, 1970, Leaders, Teachers, and Learners in Academe: Partners in the Educational Process, 1970, Education and the Many Faces of the Disadvantaged: Cultural and Historical Perspectives, 1972; contbr. articles to nat. mags., newspapers and profl. jours.; exhibited Stanley Lehrer memorabilia collection as part of the Ocean Liner Mus. presentation of ship memorabilia at N.Y. Yacht Club, 1983, on Cunard Line's 150th anniversary at Forbes Mag. Galleries, N.Y.C., 1989-90, on French Line's Normandie at French Embassy, N.Y.C., 1992, and Bass Mus. Art, Miami, Fla., 1993, on Ships of State: The Great Transatlantic Liners, PaineWebber Art Gallery, N.Y.C., 1994-95, S.O.S Safety on Ship: Learning from New York's Maritime Tragedies, Water Street Gellery, Seamen's Church Institute, N.Y.C., 1996—, on the Wreck of the Titanic, Nat. Maritime Mus., London, 1994-95. V.p. Garden City Park (N.Y.) Civic Assn., 1961-63; treas. Citizens' Com. Edn., Garden City Park, 1962; mem. nat. jr. book awards com. Boys' Clubs Am., 1954; mem. nat. hon. com. for Richard H. Heindel Meml. Fund, Pa. State U., 1979-80. With Signal Corps, U.S. Army, 1951-53. Recipient non-fiction awards Midwestern Writers Conf., Chgo., 1948. Mem. New Hyde Park (N.Y.) C. of C. (dir. 1961-62), Titanic Hist. Soc., S.S. Hist. Soc. Am., Soc. Advancement of Edn. (treas. 1953—, trustee 1963—, pres. 1968—), Ocean Liner Mus. (N.Y.C.), Psi Chi Omega. Home: 82 Shelbourne Ln New Hyde Park NY 11040-1044 Office: USA Today 99 W Hawthorne Ave Valley Stream NY 11580-6101

LEHRER, WILLIAM PETER, JR., animal scientist; b. Bklyn., Feb. 6, 1916; s. William Peter and Frances Reif (Muser) L.; m. Lois Lee Meister, Sept. 13, 1945; 1 child, Sharon Elizabeth. BS, Pa. State U., 1941; MS in Agr., MS in Range Mgmt., U. Idaho, 1946, 55; PhD in Nutrition and Biochemistry, Wash. State U., 1951; LLB, U. Chgo., 1972, JD, 1974; MBA, Pepperdine U., 1975. Mgmt. trainee Swift & Co., Charleston, W.Va., 1941-42; farm mgr. Maple Springs Farm, Middletown, N.Y., 1944-45; rsch. fellow U. Idaho, Moscow, 1945; asst. prof. to prof. U. Idaho, 1945-60; dir. nutrition Albers Milling Co., L.A., 1960-62; dir. nutrition and rsch. Albers Milling Co., 1962-74, Albers Milling Co. & John W. Eshelman & Sons, L.A., 1974-76, Carnation Co., L.A., 1976-81; ret.; cons. in field; speaker, lectr. more than 40 univs. in U.S. and abroad. Contbr. 115 articles to profl. jours.; co-author: The Livestock Industry, 1950, Dog Nutrition, 1972; author weekly column Dessert News, Salt Lake City. Mem. rsch. adv. co. U.S. Brewers Assn., 1969-81; mem. com. on dog nutrition, com. animal nutrition Nat. Rsch. Coun. NAS, 1970-76. With U.S. Army Air Corps, 1942-43. Named Disting. Alumnus, Pa. State U., 1963, 83, Key Alumnus, 1985; named to U. Idaho Alumni Hall of Fame, 1985; recipient Alumni Achievement award Wash. State U., 1993. Fellow AAAS, Am. Soc. Animal Sci.; mem. Am. Inst. Nutrition, Coun. for Agrl. Sci. & Tech., Am. Registry of Profl. Animal Scientists, Am. Inst. Food Technologists, Animal Nutrition Rsch. Coun., Am. Dairy Sci. Assn., Am. Soc. Agrl. Engrs., Am. Feed Mfrs. Assn. (life, nutrition coun. 1962-81, chmn. 1969-70), Calif. State Poly. U. (adv. coun. 1965-81, Meritorious Svc. award), The Nutrition Today Soc., Am. Soc. Animal Sci., Poultry Sci. Assn., Nat. Block & Bridle Club, Hayden Lake Country Club, Alpha Zeta, Sigma Xi, Gamma Sigma Delta (Alumni Award of Merit), Xi Sigma Pi. Republican. Avocations: river running, hunting, fishing, gardening, restoring furniture. Home: Rocking L Ranch 12180 Rimrock Rd Hayden Lake ID 83835

LEHRMAN, IRVING, rabbi; b. Tiktin, Poland, June 15, 1911; came to U.S. 1916; s. Abraham and Rachel Minnie (Dinowitz) L.; m. Bella Goldfarb, May 21, 1935; children: David Lehrman, Rosalind Lehrman. DHL, Jewish Theol. Sem. of Am., N.Y.C., 1948, DD, 1969; DHL, St. Thomas U., Miami, Fla., 1989; DL, Barry U., Miami, 1992; DHL, Fla. Internat. U., 1992. Ordained rabbi, 1943. Student rabbi Temple Shomrei Emunah, Montclair, N.J., 1939-43; rabbi Temple Emanu-El of Greater Miami, Miami Beach, Fla., 1943-93; founding rabbi, dean Lehrman Day Sch., 1993—; vis. prof. Homiletics Jewish Theol. Sem. Am.; nat. pres. Synagogue Coun. Am.; chmn. United Jewish Appeal Nat. Rabbinic Cabinet; chmn. Greater Miami Combined Jewish Appeal; chmn. bd. govs. Greater Miami State of Israel Bonds; found. chmn. Jewish Nat. Fund; hon. pres. S.E. region Rabbinical Assembly of Am. Author: In the Name of God, collection of sermons, articles, 1979, L'Chaim, thoughts for Jewish living, 1985, Portraits in Charcoal, 1980. Mem. White House Commn. on Obscenity and Pornography, Aging, and Food, Nutrition and Health (co-chmn. religious task force); bd. dirs. Miami Jewish Home and Hosp. for Aged, Internat. Synagogue at JFK Airport, N.Y.C.; nat. v.p. Zionist Orgn. Am.; adv. bd. St. Thomas U., Nat. Conf. Christians and Jews; former mem. exec. com. UNESCO, Greater Miami Community Rels. Bd. Recipient silver medal NCCJ, Prime Min.'s medal State of Israel, Albert Einstein Brotherhood award Technion U., Golda Meir Leadership award State of Israel Bonds, also others; Lehrman St. named in his honor, Miami Beach, 1986; Rabbi Irving Lehrman Park established in his honor by Miami Friends of Tel Aviv Found., Tel Aviv, 1988; Rabbi Irving & Belle Lehrman Recreation and Picnic Area established Jabotinsky Park, Shuni, Israel, 1992. Mem. Rabbinical Assn. Greater Miami (past pres.). Office: Temple Emanu-El 1701 Washington Ave Miami FL 33139-7541 *There is one principle that has guided my life and I always share it with others: "No matter how difficult it may seem, you will never be sorry for doing the right thing."*

LEHRMAN, MARGARET MCBRIDE, television news executive, producer; b. Spokane, Wash., Sept. 25, 1944; d. John P. and Ruth A. (Score) McBride; m. Michael Lloyd Lehrman, June 27, 1970. BA, U. Oreg., 1966; MS, Columbia U., 1970. Dir. coll. desk Peace Corps, Washington, 1966-69; asst. to exec. editor The Morning News Co., Washington, 1970-72; reporter Albright Communications, Washington, 1973-74; tv assignment editor ABC News, Washington, 1974; press asst. Senator Robert P. Griffin, Washington, 1975-79; researcher Today Show, NBC News, Washington, 1979, assoc. producer, 1979-83, Washington producer, 1983-89, dep. bur. chief, 1989-95, Washington producer, spec. coverage and events, 1995—. Trustee U. Oreg. Found., 1990—. Recipient Edwin M. Hood award for diplomatic reporting (China) adv. bd. Internat. Women's Media Found., Women's Fgn. Policy Group. Office: NBC News 4001 Nebraska Ave NW Washington DC 20016-2733

LEHRMAN, NAT, magazine editor; b. Bklyn., Aug. 5, 1929; s. Louis and Lena (Goldfarb) L.; m. Kazuko Miyajima, Nov. 13, 1956; children: Jerome M., Cynthia H. B.A., Bklyn. Coll., 1953; M.A., NYU, 1961. Travel editor internat. travel dept. Am. Automobile Assn., 1955-57; editor Relax mag., 1958, Dude, also Gent mags., 1959-61; assoc. to sr. editor Playboy mag., Chgo., 1966-71; editor new publs. Playboy Enterprises, 1972; editor, then assoc. pub. Oui mag., 1973-75; sr. v.p., assoc. pub. Playboy mag., 1976-85, dir. mag. divsn., 1980-85, pres. pub. div., 1982-85; pub.'s cons., 1985-87; dir. Essence mag.; tchr. fiction Columbia Coll., Chgo., 1967, chmn. journalism dept., 1987—. Author: Masters and Johnson Explained, 1970. Bd. dirs. Chgo. Chamber Musicians. With U.S. Army, 1953-55. Mem. Chgo. Classical Guitar Soc. (bd. dirs.). Club: Lincoln Park Tennis (pres.). Office: 600 S Michigan Ave Chicago IL 60605-1901

LEHTIHALME, LARRY (LAURI) K., financial planner; b. Montreal, Que., Can., Feb. 26, 1937; came to U.S., 1964; s. Lauri Johann and Selma Maire (Piispanen) L.; m. Elizabeth Speed Smith, Sept. 9, 1961; children: Tina Beth, Shauna Lyn. Student, Sir George Williams U., Montreal, 1960-64, Mission Coll., San Fernando, Calif., 1978-80, Pierce Coll., Woodland Hills, Calif., 1990-92. Lic. in variable annuity, life and disability ins., Calif.; lic. securities series 7 SEC, series 63. Acct., customer svc. cons. No. Electric, Montreal, 1957-64; salesman Remington Rand Systems, Wilmington, Del., 1964-67; account exec., comm. cons. Pacific Tel. & Telegraph Co., L.A., 1968-84; tech. customer support specialist AT&T, L.A., 1984-85; fin. adv., registered rep. Am. Express Fin. Advisors, L.A., 1987—. Mem. ctrl. com. Calif. 39th Assembly Dist. Rep. Com., 1976-81, City of L.A., 12th dist.; pres. North Hills Jaycees, 1969-70; sec.-treas. Com. Ind. Valley City and County Govt., 1978-82; subchmn. allocations United Way, Van Nuys, Calif., 1990; fundraiser North Valley YMCA, 1986—; formerly active numerous comty. and polit. orgns. in San Fernando Valley. Named Jaycee of Yr., Newark (Del.) Jaycees, 1966, Granada Hills Jaycees, 1971; recipient cert. of merit U.S. Ho. of Reps., 1973, cert. appreciation City of L.A., 1980, 84, State of Calif., 20th senate dist., 1983, Comty. Spirit award, 1990. Mem. L.A. Olympic Organizing Com. Alumni Assn., Jr. Chamber Internat. (life, senator 1973), U.S. Jaycees (life, Jaycee of Yr. 1965, Outstanding Local Jaycee 1965-66, Presdl. award Honor 1967, Jaycee of Month 1966-67, asst. gen. chmn. 1970-71, state dir. N. Hollywood chpt. 1970-71, Cert. Merit 1971, state gen. chmn., 1971-72, 72-73, Outstanding State Chmn. Calif. dist. 22 1973-74), Granada Hills C. of C. (bd. dirs. 1976-83, Man of Yr. award 1973), Granada Hills Jr. C. of C. Episcopalian. Avocation: community service. Home: 11408 Haskell Ave Granada Hills CA 91344-3959 Office: Am Express Fin Advisors 11145 Tampa Ave Ste 20A Northridge CA 91326-2255

LEHTINEN, MERJA HELEN, journalist, researcher, publisher; b. N.Y., Feb. 25, 1954; d. Osmo Ilmari and Hilkka Annikki (Kokkonen-Lind) L. AB in American Studies, Mount Holyoke, 1976; student, Dartmouth, 1975; cert. in Finnish and Scandinavian, U. Helsinki, 1978. Assoc. tech. writer The Travelers Ins. Co., Hartford, 1976-78; mng. editor Am. Soc. Heating, Refrigerating and Air Conditioning Engrs., N.Y., 1979-81; internat. editor Am. Soc. Civil Engrs., N.Y., 1981-83; dir. publs. Am. Assn. Engring., N.Y., 1983-84; mng. editor Bill Comms., Inc., N.Y., 1984; news editor McGraw Hill Co., N.Y., 1984-85; exec. editor Mng. Automation Mag., N.Y., 1986-87; editor-in-chief, publisher Indsl. Computing Mag. Kruger, McCarthy & Lehtinen, N.Y., 1987-93; pres. Westisle Pub. Co., Westford, Mass., 1993; owner, pub. Discover Connecticut Magazine and The Connecticut Chronicles, 1993—; intern for Sen. Strom Thurmond U.S. Senate, Washington, 1973; dir. career guidance Am. Assn. Engring. Scis., N.Y., 1983-84; commr. Econ. Devel. Commn. of Colchester, Conn., 1992-96, hearing officer, 1994—; bd. dirs. Indsl. Computing Soc., Rsch. Triangle Park, N.C., 1993-95. Author (book) Quality Control, 1977 (recipient award of excellence Soc. Tech. Comms., 1977); contbr. articles to profl. jours. and mags. Vice chmn. Rep. Town Com., 1993-96; Rep. candidate for nomination to U.S. Congress 2d dist., 1992; bd. incorporators Eliza Huntington Meml. Home, Inc., 1993—. Recipient rsch. fellow Rep. National Com., Washington, 1975. Mem. Instrument Soc. Am., Indsl. Computing Soc. (founder, mem. bd. dirs. 1993-95). Republican. Avocations: skiing, water & oil painting, gardening.

LEIBACH, DALE W., public relations executive. Reporter Kansas City Star; mgr. pub. affairs Ford Motor Co., Washington; asst. press sec. White House, 1977-81; press sec. to U.S. senator Tom Harkin; sr. v.p., mng. dir. Powell Adams & Rinehart (Ogilvy & Mather), Washington; sr. v.p., chief oper. officer Powell Tate, Washington. Office: Powell Tate 700 13th St NW Ste 1000 Washington DC 20005-3960

LEIBACHER, JOHN WILLIAM, astronomer; b. Chgo., May 28, 1941; s. George W. and Irene (Novotney) L.; m. Lise H. Ouvarard, Dec. 21, 1976. AB, Harvard U., 1963, PhD, 1971. Postdoctoral fellow U. Colo., Boulder, 1970-71; scientist Laboratoire de Physique Stellaire et Planetaire, Paris, 1972-74, Lockheed Rsch. Lab., Palo Alto, Calif., 1975-81; astronomer Nat. Solar Obs., Tucson, 1982—, dir., 1988-93; dir. Global Oscillation Network Group Project, Tucson, 1984—. Address: PO Box 26732 Tucson AZ 85726

LEIBER, GERSON AUGUST, artist; b. Bklyn., Nov. 12, 1921; s. William and Rebecca (Margulis) L.; m. Judith Maria Peto, Feb. 5, 1946. Student art, Art Students League, N.Y., 1947-52, Bklyn. Mus. Art Sch., 1952-53; DFA (hon.), Bar Ilan U., Israel, 1993. Instr. Newark Sch. Fine and Indsl. Arts; v.p. Judith Leiber, Inc., N.Y.C., 1963—. One-man shows, Oakland (Calif.) Mus., 1960, N.Y.C., 1961, 62, 63, 64, 68, 69, 72, 76, 85, 95, 96, Fine Arts Mus. L.I. (N.Y.), 1991; exhibited in numerous nat. and internat. group shows, prints and paintings represented in pvt. and permanent collections. With AUS, 1942-47. Recipient numerous prizes including Bklyn. Mus. Purchase awards, 1953-66, 2d prize of $1,000, Assoc. Am. Artists Nat. Print Exhbn., 1959, Soc. Washington Printmakers prize, 1962, purchase award Hunterdon County Art Center 6th nat. print exhbn., 1962, Audubon medals of Honor for Graphics, 1963, 65, Sonia Watter award Am. Color Print Soc., 1968, 1000 Purchase award Assn. Am. Artists, 1968, John Taylor Arms Meml. prize NAD, 1971; Tiffany fellow, 1957, 60. Mem. NAD, Soc. Am. Graphic Artists (past pres.), Art Students League N.Y. Home: 7 Park Ave New York NY 10016-4330 Studio: 27 E 31st St New York NY 10016-6810

LEIBER, JERRY, songwriter; b. 1933. Songwriter: (with Mike Stoller) Hound Dog, Loving You, Jailhouse Rock, Searchin', Young Blood, Yakety Yak, Charlie Brown, Along Came Jones, Poison Ivy, Little Egypt, Down in Mexico, D.W. Washburn, Shoppin' for Clothes, That Is Rock & Roll, Smokey Joe's Cafe, Framed, Riot in Cell Block #9, Stand By Me, Spanish Harlem, I (Who Have Nothing), On Broadway, Dance With Me, Drip Drop, Saved, Lucky Lips, Love Potion #9, Only in America, I Keep Forgettin', Kansas City, Ruby Baby, Fools Fall in Love, I'm a Woman, Black Denim Trousers and Motorcycle Boots, Treat Me Nice, (You're So Square) Baby, I Don't Care, Bossa Nova Baby, Santa Claus is Back in Town, She's Not You, Trouble. Recipient Founders' award ASCAP, 1991, Best Musical Show Album Grammy award, 1996; inducted into Songwriters' Hall of Fame, 1985, Record Producers' Hall of Fame, 1986, Rock & Roll Hall of Fame, 1987. Office: Atlantic Records 75 Rockefeller Plz New York NY 10019*

LEIBER, JUDITH MARIA, designer, manufacturer; b. Budapest, Hungary, Jan. 11, 1921; came to U.S., 1947, naturalized, 1949; d. Emil and Helen (Spitzer) Peto; m. Gerson Leiber, Feb. 6, 1946. Student pvt. schs., Hungary and Eng.; DFA (hon.), Internat. Fine Arts Coll., 1993; PhD (hon.), Bar Ilan U., Israel, 1993, Internat. Fine Arts Coll., Miami, Fla., 1993. Master handbag maker Hungary, 1942; pattern maker, designer Nettie Rosenstein, N.Y.C., 1947-60, Koret, N.Y.C., 1960-61; owner, mgr. Judith Leiber, Inc., N.Y.C., 1963—. Author: Judith Leiber, The Artful Handbag, 1995; designs represented in 30-yr. retrospective F.I.T. Mus., N.Y., 1993-94. Recipient Swarovski award and Am. Handbag Designer award Leather Industries Am., 1970, Coty award Am. Fashion Critics, 1973, Neiman-Marcus award, 1980, Women Who Made a Difference award Fashion Group, 1986, Lifetime Achievement award Dallas Mart, 1991, Am. Acad. Achievement award, 1992, FAAB Lifetime Achievement award, 1992, Ellis Island Medal Honor, 1993, Lifetime Achievement award Coun. Fashion Designers Am., 1993, Fashion Hall of Fame award Shannon Rodgers & Jerry Silverman Sch. Fashion Design and Merchandising, Kent State U., 1995; featured Retrospective of Work New Orleans Mus. Mem. Nat. Handbag Authority (dir. 1972—). Pioneering woman master handbag maker, Hungary; first woman patternmaker Am. handbag industry. Office: 20 W 33rd St New York NY 10001-3305

LEIBERT, RICHARD WILLIAM, special events producer; b. N.Y.C., Nov. 11, 1948; s. Richard William and Rosemarie Martha (Bruns) L. BS,

Boston U., 1966-70; student, Northwestern U., 1971. Producer Sta. WBZ AM/FM, Boston, 1968-70; prodn. dir. Sta. WMMR-FM, Phila., 1970; exec. producer Sta. WIND-AM, Chgo., 1970-72; program dir. Sta. KGB AM-FM, San Diego, 1972-80; pres. Events Mktg., Inc., L.A., 1980—; dir. Nat. Fireworks Ensemble, Los Angeles, Calif., 1985—. Creator (mascot, publicity stunts) Sta. KGB Chicken, 1974; creator, producer (radio fireworks show) Sta. KGB Sky Show, 1976; writer, producer (network radio show) New Music News, 1983; creator, dir. (touring co.) Nat. Fireworks Ensemble, 1985. Recipient Emmy award, 1978; named Program Dir. of Yr. Billboard Mag., 1976, Radio Program of Yr. Billboard Mag., 1976. Avocations: sailing, baseball. Office: Events Mktg Inc PO Box 65694 Los Angeles CA 90065-0694

LEIBHOLZ, STEPHEN WOLFGANG, physicist, engineering company executive, entrepreneur; b. Berlin, Jan. 28, 1932; came to U.S., 1936; s. Ernest S. and Louise (Stern) L.; m. Ann Esther Greenberg, May 29, 1958; children: Judith, Robert, Daniel. BA in Physics, NYU, 1952. Prin. engr. Repub. Fairchild Co., Farmingdale, N.Y., 1957-60; mgr. systems design and analysis Auerbach Corp., Phila., 1960-67; founder, chmn. Analytics, Inc., Willow Grove, Pa., 1967-91; advisor, cons. scientist U.S. govt. agys., Washington, 1970—, Chesapeake Tech Labs Inc., 1986—, ACS, Inc., 1987—; founder, CEO TechLabs Inc., 1990—, Inst. for Global Intelligence, 1995—. Author and editor 7 books; contbr. articles to profl. publs. Bd. dirs. Jenkintown Music Sch., 1970-74, advisor Kansas City Camerata Chamber Orch. Cons. U. of Arts, Pa. Conv. Ctr.; mem. adv. bd. Inst. for Adv. Psychology. Sr. fellow Fgn. Policy Rsch. Inst. Mem. AAAS, IEEE, Mil. Ops. Rsch. Soc. (past bd. dirs.), Cosmos Club (Washington). Office: 2333 Huntingdon Pike Huntingdon Valley PA 19006

LEIBLER, KENNETH ROBERT, financial service executive; b. N.Y.C., Feb. 21, 1949; s. Max and Martha (Dales) L.; m. Marcia Kate Reiss, July 15, 1973; children: Jessica Hope, Andrew Ethan. B.A. magna cum laude, Syracuse U., 1971; postgrad., U. Pa., 1972. Mgr. options Lehman Bros., 1972-75; v.p. options Am. Stock Exchange, N.Y.C., 1975-79; sr. v.p. adminstrn. and fin. Am. Stock Exchange, 1979-81, exec. v.p. adminstrn. and fin., 1981-85, sr. exec. v.p., 1985-86, pres., 1986-90; pres. Liberty Fin. Cos., Boston, 1990—; instr. N.Y. Inst. Fin.; dir. Securities Industry Automation Corp.; chmn. Amex Commodities Corp. Contbg. author: Handbook of Financial Markets: Securities, Options Futures, 1981. Trustee Beth Israel Med. Ctr., Dr.'s Hosp.; bd. dirs. Am. Forum for Global Edn. Mem. Fin. Execs. Inst., Securities Industry Assn., Boston Stock Exchange (bd. dir.), Phi Beta Kappa, Phi Kappa Phi. Office: Liberty Fin Cos 600 Atlanta Ave Boston MA 02110

LEIBMAN, RON, actor; b. N.Y.C., Oct. 11, 1937; s. Murray and Grace (Marks) L.; m. Linda Lavin, Sept. 7, 1969 (div.); m. Jessica Walter, June 26, 1983. Student, Ohio Wesleyan U., Actors Studio, N.Y.C. mem. Yale Repertory Co., 1967-68; acting tchr. Yale U. Sch. Drama, New Haven, 1967-68. Appearances include (theatre) debut in A View from the Bridge, 1959, Legend of Lovers, 1959, Dear Me, the Sky is Falling, 1963, We Bombed In New Haven (Theatre World award), Room Service, I Ought To Be in Pictures, 1981, Don Pasquale, 1983, Doubles, 1985, Rumors, 1988, Angels in America: Millenium Approaches, 1993 (Best Actor Tony award 1993), Angels in America: Peristroika, 1993, The Merchant of Venice, 1995; (films) Where's Poppa, 1970, Hot Rock, 1972, Slaughterhouse Five, 1972, Your Three Minutes Are Up, 1973, The Super Cops, 1974, Won Ton Ton, 1976, Norma Rae, 1979, Up the Academy, 1980, Zorro the Gay Blade, 1982, Romantic Comedy, 1983, Phar Lap, 1983, Rhinestone, 1984, Door to Door, 1984, Seven Hours to Judgment, 1988; (TV movies) Martinelli: Outside Man, Rivkin-Bounty Hunter, Christmas Eve, 1986 (Golden Globe nominee), Terrorist on Trial: The United States vs. Salim Ajami, 1988; (TV series) star in Kaz, 1978-79 (Emmy award). Recipient Drama Desk award for role in We Bombed in New Haven, Transfers, Obie award for role in Transfers. Office: Gersh Agency 232 N Canon Dr Beverly Hills CA 90210*

LEIBOLD, ARTHUR WILLIAM, JR., lawyer; b. Ottawa, Ill., June 13, 1931; s. Arthur William and Helen (Cull) L.; m. Nora Collins, Nov. 30, 1957; children: Arthur William III, Alison Aubry, Peter Collins. AB, Haverford Coll., 1953; JD, U. Pa., 1956. Bar: Pa. 1957. With Dechert, Price & Rhoads, Phila., 1956-69, ptnr., 1965-69; ptnr. Dechert, Price & Rhoads, Washington, 1972—; gen. counsel Fed. Home Loan Bank Bd. and Fed. Savs. & Loan Ins. Corp., Washington, 1969-72, Fed. Home Loan Mortgage Corp., 1970-72; lectr. English St. Joseph's Coll., Phila., 1957-59. Contbr. articles to profl. publs. Mem. Pres. Kennedy's Lawyers Com. Civil Rights, 1963, Adminstrv. Conf. U.S., 1969-72; bd. dirs. Marymount Coll. Va., 1974-75; Mem. Phila. Com. 70, 1965-74, Fellowship Commn. Mem. ABA (mem. ho. dels. 1967-69, 79-88, treas. 1979-83, mem. fin. com., mem. bd. govs. 1977-83), Fed. Bar Assn. (mem. nat. coun. 1971-80), D.C. Bar Assn., Phila. Bar Assn., Am. Bar Found. (treas. 1979-83), Am. Bar Ret. Assn. (dir. 1978-83), Am. Bar Endowment (bd. dirs. 1984—, pres. 1995—), Internat. Bar Assn., Phila. Country Club (Gladwyne, Pa.), Chester River Yacht & Country Club (Chestertown, Md.), Skating Club Phila., Orpheus Club (Phila.), Order of the Coif, Phi Beta Kappa. Republican. Roman Catholic. Home: 2014 N Kenmore St Arlington VA 22207-3711 Office: Dechert Price & Rhoads 1500 K St NW Ste 500 Washington DC 20005-1209

LEIBOVICH, SIDNEY, engineering educator; b. Memphis, Apr. 2, 1939; s. Harry and Rebecca (Palant) L.; m. Gail Barbara Colin, Nov. 24, 1962; children: Bradley Colin, Adam Keith. BS, Calif. Inst. Tech., Pasadena, 1961; PhD, Cornell U., 1965. NATO postdoctoral fellow U. Coll., London, 1965-66; asst. prof. thermal engring. Cornell U., Ithaca, N.Y., 1966-70, assoc. prof. thermal engring., 1970-78, prof. mech. and aerospace engring., 1978-89, Samuel B. Eckert prof. mech. and aerospace engring., 1989—. Editor: Nonlinear Waves, 1974; assoc. editor: Jour. Fluid Mechanics, 1982-93; co-editor: Acta Mechanica, 1986-92; mem. editorial bd. Ann. Revs. of Fluid Mechanics, 1989-93; gen. editor Cambridge U. Press Monographs on Mechanics, 1994—. Disting. lectr. Naval Ocean Rsch. Devel. Activity, 1983. Recipient MacPherson prize Calif. Inst. Tech., 1961. Fellow ASME (chmn. applied mechanics div. 1987-88), Am. Phys. Soc. (chmn. div. fluid dynamics 1987-88), Am. Acad. Arts and Scis., U.S. Nat. Com. for Theoretical and Applied Mechanics (chair 1990-92.), Nat. Acad. Engring. Office: Cornell U Upson Hall Ithaca NY 14853

LEIBOVITZ, ANNIE, photographer; b. Conn., Oct. 2, 1949. Student, San Francisco Art Inst. Chief photographer Rolling Stone, from 1973, photographer, 1970-83; photographer Vanity Fair, 1983—; photographer for advertisements, 1987—; proprietor Ann Leibovitz Studio, N.Y.C. Works exhibited various galleries; author: Photographs 1970-90, 1992. Recipient Innovation in Photography award Am. Soc. Mag. Photographers, 1987. Office: Annie Leibovitz Studio 55 Vandam St New York NY 10013-1104 also: Annie Leibovitz Studio 101 W 18th St New York NY 10013-4124*

LEIBOVITZ, MITCHELL G., retail executive; b. Phila., May 11, 1945; s. Jacob A. and Doris (Schultz) L.; m. Joanne Lippman, Aug. 24, 1969; 2 children. B.A., Temple U., 1966, M.Ed., 1971, M.B.A., 1974. C.P.A., Pa. Audit sr., acct. Arthur Young & Co., Phila., 1973-76; audit prin. Seidman & Seidman, Phila., 1976-78; various positions Pep Boys-Manny Moe & Jack, Phila., 1978-90, bd. dirs., 1985—; pres., chief oper. officer Pep Boys, 1986, chief exec. officer, 1990; chmn. bd. dirs., 1994—; bd. trustees Temple U., 1987-91, 95—. Bd. dirs. Police Athletic League, Phila., 1983—. Mem. Locust Club, Atlantic City Country Club, Green Valley Country Club (Lafayette Hill, Pa.), Squires Golf Club (Ambler, Pa.). Avocations: golf, sport fishing. Office: Pep Boys-Manny 3111 W Allegheny Ave Philadelphia PA 19132-1116

LEIBOW, LOIS MAY, secondary education educator; b. Newark, Jan. 4, 1937; d. Samuel and Sada (Rothman) Applebaum; m. Sheldon G. Leibow, Aug. 11, 1963; children: Philip, Frances, Brian. BA, Douglass Coll., 1959; MA in Sociology, CCNY, 1962. Substitute tchr. Monmouth County Registry, N.J., 1983—; telemarketer Target Teleconcepts, Inc., Hazlet, N.J., 1991—, Prudential Ins. Co., Red Bnnk, N.J., 1991—. Newspaper columnist Atlanticville, Long Branch, N.J., 1984—; contbr. Am. String Tchr., 1979. Mem. Hadassah (life, program v.p. Woodbridge, N.J. chpt. 1972-74), Sisterhood of Temple Beth El (bd. dirs.), Jewish War Vets., Woman's Club Perth Amboy N.J. Republican. Avocations: aerobics, ballroom dancing, studying languages, gardening. Office: Target Teleconcepts Village Ct Hazlet NJ 07730

LEIBOW, RONALD LOUIS, lawyer; b. Santa Monica, Calif., Oct. 4, 1939; s. Norman and Jessica (Kellner) L.; m. Linda Bengelsdorf, June 11, 1961 (div. Dec. 1974); children: Jocelyn Elise, Jeffrey David, Joshua Aaron; m. Jacqueline Blatt, Apr. 6, 1986. AB, Calif. State U., Northridge, 1962; JD, UCLA, 1965. Bar: Calif. 1966, U.S. Dist. Ct. (cen. dist.) Calif. 1966, U.S. Dist. Ct. (no., so. and ea. dists.) Calif. 1971. Spl. asst. city atty. City of Burbank, Calif., 1966-67; assoc., then ptnr. Meyers, Stevens & Walters, L.A., 1967-71; ptnr. Karpf, Leibow & Warner, Beverly Hills, Calif., 1971-74, Volk, Newman Gralla & Karp, L.A., 1979-81, Spector & Leibow, L.A., 1982-84, Stroock & Stroock & Lavan, L.A., 1984-94; ptnr. Kaye, Scholer, Fierman, Hays & Handler, L.A., 1994—, mng. ptnr., 1996—; lectr. law UCLA, 1968-69; asst. prof. Calif. State U., Northridge, 1969-71. Contbr. articles to profl. jours. Pres. Jewish Community Ctr., Greater L.A., 1983-86; v.p. Jewish Community Ctr. Assn. N.Am., N.Y.C., 1988—, Jewish Fedn. Community, Greater L.A., 1988—. Mem. ABA (bus. bankruptcy com.), Phi Alpha Delta. Avocations: writing, tennis, skiing, travel. Office: Kaye Scholer Fierman Hays & Handler 1999 Avenue Of The Stars Fl 16 Los Angeles CA 90067-6022

LEIBOWITZ, ANN GALPERIN, lawyer; b. Balt., Oct. 11, 1940; d. Harold Marcy and Dorothy Rebecca (Trivas) Galperin; m. Howard Marvin Leibowitz, July 3, 1960; children: Ellen Ann, Katherine Leibowitz Kotkin. AB, Goucher Coll., 1960; LLB, U. Md., 1964. Bar: Mass. 1964, U.S. Ct. Appeals (1st cir.) 1984. Patent agt. W.R. Grace & Co., Clarkesville, Md., 1960-63; patent atty. Polaroid Corp., Cambridge, Mass., 1963-72, corporate atty., 1972-77, sr. corporate atty. and labor counsel, 1977-95; prin., founder AGL Assocs., Weston, Mass., 1995—; lectr. Coun. Edn. in Mgmt., Walnut Creek, Calif., 1987—; mem. faculty Mass. Continuing Legal Edn., Boston, 1991—. Bd. trustees Goucher Coll., Towson, Md., 1983-89; chmn. fin. com. Town of Weston, 1989-91, active, 1984-91, chmn. bd. selectmen, 1993—, active, 1991—; mem. exec. adv. bd. Ctr. House, Boston, 1990—; exec. com. bd. trustees Deaconess Waltham Hosp., 1995—. Mem. ABA, Am. Corporate Counsel Assn. (bd. dirs. N.E. chpt. 1988-91), Mass. Bar Assn. (lectr. 1987—), Boston Bar Assn., Indsl. Rels. Rsch. Assn.

LEIBOWITZ, HERBERT AKIBA, English language educator, author; b. Staten Island, N.Y., Apr. 26, 1935; s. Morris and Rose (Rabinowitz) L.; m. Susan Yankowitz, May 3, 1978; 1 son, Gabriel. B.A., Bklyn. Coll., 1956; M.A., Brown U., 1958; Ph.D., Columbia U., 1966. Asst. prof. English Columbia U., 1967-70; asst. prof. humanities Richmond Coll., Staten Island, N.Y., 1971-73, assoc. prof., 1973-76; assoc. prof. English Coll. S.I., 1976-81; prof. English Coll. Staten Island, CUNY and Grad. Ctr., CUNY, 1981—; prof. English emeritus, 1991—; Fannie Hurot vis. prof. Washington U., St. Louis, 1995. Author: Hart Crane: An Introduction to the Poetry, 1968, Fabricating Lives, 1989; editor: Selected Music Criticism of Paul Rosenfeld, 1970, Parnassus: Poetry in Review, 1972, Parnassus: Twenty Years of Poetry in Review, 1994, Asphodel, That Greeny Flower and Other William Carlos Williams Love Poems, 1994. Recipient Fels award for editorial distinction Coordinating Coun. Lit. Mags., 1975; postdoctoral fellow U. Ill. Ctr. Advanced Study, 1968-69, Chamberlain fellow Columbia U., 1970, fellow N.Y. Inst. Humanities, 1987—, Mellon Seminar fellow NYU, 1988, Guggenheim fellow, 1991-92. Mem. PEN (Nora Magid award for disting. editing of lit. mag. 1995), Nat. Book Critics Circle (bd. dirs. 1988-94, pres. 1992-94). Jewish. Home: 205 W 89th St New York NY 10024-1828 Office: Poetry Rev Found 205 W 89th St 8F New York NY 10024

LEIBOWITZ, JACK RICHARD, physicist, educator; b. Bridgeport, Conn., July 21, 1929; BA, NYU, MS, 1955; PhD in Physics, Brown U., 1962. Rsch. physicist MIT Lincoln Lab., 1956-61, Westinghouse Rsch. Labs., Pitts., 1961-64; asst. prof. U. Md., College Park, 1964-69; assoc. prof. physics Cath. U. Am., Washington, 1969-73, prof. physics, 1974-95, prof. physics emeritus, 1995—, assoc. dean for grad. studies, 1988-93, chmn. art dept., 1882-86, acad. senate; sci. cons. govt. agys., NBC-TV. Fellow Am. Phys. Soc., Washington Acad. Scis.; mem. Sigma Xi. Contbr. numerous rsch. articles to sci. jours. and books. Research in condensed matter physics: superconductivity, electron-phonon interaction, band structure. Home: P O Box 256 Ashton MD 20861 Office: Cath U of Am Dept Physics Washington DC 20064

LEIBOWITZ, MARVIN, lawyer; b. Phila., Jan. 24, 1950; s. Aaron and Ethel (Kashoff) L.; m. Faye Rebecca Liepack, Nov. 12, 1983; 1 child, Cheryl Renée. BA, Temple U., 1971, postgrad., 1971-72; JD, Widener U., 1976. Bar: Pa. 1977, N.J. 1977, U.S. Dist. Ct. N.J. 1977, U.S. Dist. Ct. (we. dist.) Pa. 1980. Atty.-advisor HHS, Pitts., 1977—; pvt. practice law, Pitts., 1979—. Committeeman Phila. Dem. Com., 1973-77. Pa. State Scholar Pa. Higher Edn. Assistance Agy., Harrisburg, 1967-71. Recipient U.S. Dep. Health and Human Svcs. citation, 1994. Mem. Nat. Treasury Employees Union (regional steward 1982—), Pa. Bar Assn., Allegheny County Bar Assn. Democrat. Jewish. Home: 6501 Landview St Pittsburgh PA 15217-3000

LEIBRECHT, JOHN JOSEPH, bishop; b. Overland, Mo., Aug. 8, 1930. PhD, Cath. U., Washington. Ordained priest, Roman Cath. Ch., 1956. Supt. schs. St. Louis Archdiocese, 1962-81; bishop Springfield-Cape Girardeau, Mo., 1984—. Address: The Catholic Ctr 601 S Jefferson Ave Springfield MO 65806-3107*

LEIBSLA, MELVIN DONALD, data processing executive; b. Cleve., Mar. 27, 1953; s. Melvin Donald and Marguerite (Scribbner) L.; m. Barbara A. Stasko, July 4, 1981; children: Michael, Jason. BS in Applied Sci., Miami U., 1975; grad., Sch. Bank Mgmt., Madison, Wis., 1990. Programmer/analyst Fed. Res. Bank Cleve., 1975-80; system analyst Olympia Brewing, Tumwater, Wash., 1980-82; system analyst/auditor N.W. Pipeline, Salt Lake City, 1982-84; EDP audit mgr. Zions Bancorp, Salt Lake City, 1984—; speaker in field. Contbr. articles to profl. jours. Active local ch. parish coun., Salt Lake City, 1989—. Mem. EDP Auditors Assn. (pres., v.p. 1989-91, bd. dirs. 1989—), Data Processing Mgmt. Assn. Republican. Roman Catholic. Avocations: marathons, coaching and refereeing soccer, church activities. Office: Zions Bancorp 2200 S 3270 W West Valley City UT 84119

LEIBSON, IRVING, industrial executive; b. Wilkes Barre, Pa., Sept. 28, 1926; s. Henry and Sonia (Rose) L.; m. Lola Pavalow, Feb. 16, 1950; children: Russell, Sandra Eve. B.Chem. Engring. cum laude, U. Fla., 1945, M.S., 1947; M.S. Carnegie Inst. Tech., 1949; D.Sc., Carnegie Inst. Tech., 1952. Registered profl. engr., Calif., Tex. Chem. engr. to supr. Humble Oil and Refining Co., Baytown, Tex., 1952-61, mgr. process engring., 1961-63, tech. mgr., 1963-65, dir. R & D, 1965-67; gen. mgr. ABS div., 1967-68; v.p. Dart Industries Chem. Group, Paramus, N.J., 1969-74; asst. to sr. v.p., investment dept. Bechtel Corp., San Francisco, 1974-75; mgr. process and environment, v.p. C & I/Girdler Inc. (a Bechtel Co.), 1976-78; v.p., mgr. rsch. and engring. Bechtel Nat. Inc., 1978-79; sr. v.p. Bechtel Inc., 1979-81; sr. v.p., mgr. mktg. Bechtel Group Inc., 1981-85, sr. v.p., sr. tech. officer, 1985-87, exec. cons., 1987-94; founder, pres. Bold Techs., 1987—; part-time prof. Rice U., 1957, U. Md., 1954. Contbr. articles to profl. jours. Dist. commr. E. Harris County dist. Boy Scouts Am., 1958-61; vice-chmn. Intersoc. Task Force Energy, 1973; assoc. World Coal Study, 1979-80; assoc. coal industry adv. bd. Internat. Energy Agy., 1980-95; treas., vice chmn., chmn. mem. exec. com. Coun. Alternate Fuels, 1982-87; mem. Nat. Coal Coun., 1985-94, chmn. Coal Policy Commn., 1987-91; mem. exec. com., 1987-95; mem. adv. bd. Ctr. Chem. Process Safety Tech., 1985-88; mem. liquid fuels com. NRC, 1989-90. With AUS, 1953-54. Recipient Disting. Alumnus award U. Fla., 1988. Fellow Am. Inst. Chem. Engrs. (dir. 1967-69, v.p. 1973, pres. 1974, Publ. award S. Tex. chpt. 1957, Founders award 1976, Disting. Svc. award 1996); mem. Am. Chem. Soc., Engrs. Joint Coun. (dir. 1969-78), Engrs. Manpower Commn., Coal and Slurry Tech Assn. (chmn. 1986-89), Round Hill Golf and Country Club (San Francisco), World Trade Club (San Francisco), Sailfish Point Golf Club (Stuart, Fla.), Ary Club (Stuart), Villa Taverna Club (San Francisco). Patentee in field. Home: 2920 S E Dune Dr Stuart FL 34996

LEIBY, LARRY RAYMOND, lawyer; b. Phila., Nov. 3, 1947; s. Leo R. and Virginia (Danter) L.; m. Cheryll Wadsworth, Jan. 20, 1968; children—Connie Marie, Bradley Ward. Mus. B., U. Miami, 1969, J.D., 1973. Bar: Fla. 1973, U.S. Dist. Ct. (so. dist.) Fla. 1974, U.S. Dist. Ct. (mid. dist.) Fla. 1984, U.S. Ct. Claims 1981, U.S. Ct. Appeals (11th cir.) 1981, U.S. Supreme Ct. 1980. Assoc. Law Office Daniel A. Kavanaugh, Miami, Fla., 1973-74; sole practice, Ft. Lauderdale, Fla., 1974-75; ptnr. Kavanaugh & Leiby, Miami, 1975-81, Leiby & Elder, Miami, Fla., 1981-90, Leiby, Ferencik and Libanoff, P.A., 1990-92, Leiby, Ferencik, Libanoff & Brandt, P.A., 1991—; adj. prof. Dept. Constrn. Mgmt. Fla. Internat. U., 1991—. Author: Subcontractor's Guide to Florida Mechanics Lien Law, 1976; Florida Construction Law Manual, 1981, 3d edit., 1994; Nova Law Review, Construction Law Survey, 1992, 94; contbg. author: Comparative Studies in Construction Law: The Sweet Lectures, 1996. Mem. Comml. Law League Am., Fla. Bar Assn. (constrn. law com. chmn. 1976-93), ABA (forum com. on constrn. industry, So. Fla. chmn. pub. contract law sect. 1986-95), Am. Arbitration Assn. (cert. civil mediator, complex case panel). Democrat. Presbyterian. Office: Leiby Ferencik Libanoff & Brandt PA 150 S Pine Island Rd Ste 400 Plantation FL 33324-2667

LEICHTER, FRANZ S., state senator; b. Vienna, Austria, Aug. 19, 1930; s. Otto and Kathe (Pick) L.; m. Nina Williams, July 3, 1958 (dec. Feb. 1995); children: Katherine, Joshua. BA, Swarthmore Coll., 1952; JD, Harvard U., 1957. Bar: N.Y. 1957, U.S. Dist. Ct. (so. and ea. dists.) N.Y. 1959, U.S. Ct. Appeals (2d cir.) 1961. Mem. N.Y. State Assembly, Albany, 1969-74; mem. N.Y. State Senate, Albany, 1975—, ranking mem. environ. conservation com., 1986—, ranking mem. judiciary com., 1991—; ptnr. Wachtell, Manheim & Grouf, N.Y.C., 1974-88; of counsel Walter, Conston, Alexander & Green, N.Y.C., 1988—; chair N.Y. State Senate Dem. Policy Com., 1983-90. Author various reports, 1979—. Del. Dem. Nat. Convention, 1964, 84, 88. Cpl. U.S. Army, 1953-55. Recipient award Austrian Govt., 1984. Mem. ACLU, Assn. of Bar of City of N.Y., N.Y. State Bar Assn., Am. Jewish Congress. Democrat. Jewish. Avocations: hiking, skiing, tennis, reading history works. Home: 448 Riverside Dr New York NY 10027-6818 Office: NY State Senate Albany NY 12247

LEICHTLING, MICHAEL ALFRED, lawyer; b. N.Y.C., Mar. 30, 1943; s. Stanley Arthur and Roslyn Priscilla (Fuhr) L.; m. Arlene Dorf, July 30, 1966; children: Julie Karen, Nina Anastasia, Noah James. BA, SUNY, Binghamton, 1963; JD, Northwestern U., 1966; postgrad., Columbia U., 1968. Bar: N.Y. 1969, U.S. Ct. Appeals (2d cir.) 1969. Assoc. Aranow Brodsky Bohlinger Einhorn & Dann, N.Y.C., 1966, Parker Chapin & Flattau, N.Y.C., 1969-77; ptnr. Parker Chapin Flattau & Klimpl, LLP, N.Y.C., 1977—; mem. exec. com. Parker Chapin Flattau & Klimpl, N.Y.C., 1987-92; bd. dirs. H. Warshow & Sons Inc., N.Y.C. Editor Northwestern U. Law Rev., 1965-66, Equipment Leasing Jour., 1986—, Computer Leasing Today, 1989—. Bd. dirs. Friends of Israel Disabled War Vets., N.Y.C., 1986—. With U.S. Army, 1966-68; Vietnam. Decorated Bronze Star; Regents scholar, 1963, Newman scholar, 1963-66. Mem. N.Y. State Bar Assn. (corp. law sect.), N.Y. County Lawyers Assn. (banking law com., secured lending com.), Equipment Leasing (state legis. com.), Ea. Assn. Equipment Lessors (chmn. legal com., gen. counsel 1986—). Avocations: reading, painting, swimming, golf. Home: 148 Quinn Rd Briarcliff Manor NY 10510-2133 Office: Parker Chapin Flattau & Klimpl LLP 1211 6th Ave New York NY 10036-8701

LEIDEN, CARL, political scientist, educator; b. Boone, Iowa, Feb. 6, 1922; s. Carl Eric and Christine Olivia (Bergstrom) L.; m. Mary Katherine Rood, Sept. 5, 1945; children: Lisa Ingrid, Derek Stefan. B.S., Iowa State Coll., 1945; M.P.A., Wayne U., 1947; Ph.D., State U. Iowa, 1949. Instr. State U. Iowa, Iowa City, 1946-49; asst. prof. to assoc. prof. Marshall Coll., Huntington, W.Va., 1949-59; assoc. prof. Am. U., Cairo, Egypt, 1959-61; assoc. prof. to prof. polit. sci. U. Tex., Austin, 1961-87, prof. emeritus, 1987—; Fulbright lectr. Peshawar U., Pakistan, 1952-53; vis. assoc. prof. U. Calif.-Berkeley, 1957; prof. Nat. War Coll., Washington, 1972-73. Author or co-author eight books on polit. sci. Volker Found. fellow, 1945-46; Fulbright teaching grantee, 1952-53, 1966; Earhart Found. grantee, 1970. Republican. Home: 3301 Stoneridge Rd Austin TX 78746-7715 Office: Univ Texas Polit Sci Dept Austin TX 78712

LEIDER, GERALD J., motion picture and television company executive; b. Camden, N.J., May 28, 1931; s. Myer and Minnie Leider; m. Susan Trustman, Dec. 21, 1968; children: Matthew Trustman, Kenneth Harold. B.A., Syracuse U., 1953. Theater producer in N.Y.C., London, 1956-59; dir. spl. programs CBS-TV, 1960-61, dir. program sales, 1961-62; v.p. TV ops. Ashley Famous Agy., Inc., N.Y.C., 1962-69; pres. Warner Bros. TV, Burbank, Calif., 1969-74; exec. v.p. fgn. prodn. Warner Bros. Pictures, Rome, 1975-76; ind. producer motion pictures and TV GJL Prodns., Inc., Los Angeles, 1977-82; pres. ITC Prodns., Inc., Los Angeles, 1982-87; pres., chief exec. officer ITC Entertainment Group, Studio City, Calif., 1987—. Producer: Gielgud's Ages of Man, 1958-59; feature motion pictures include The Jazz Singer (with Neil Diamond), 1980, Trenchcoat, 1983; TV films include And I Alone Survived, 1978, Willa, 1979, The Hostage Tower, 1980, The Scarlet and the Black, Secrets of a Married Man, The Haunting Passion, Letting Go, A Time to Live, The Girl Who Spelled Freedom, Unnatural Causes, Poor Little Rich Girl. Mem. bd. Visitors Coll. Visual and Performing Arts, Syracuse U. Recipient Arents Alumni medal Syracuse U., 1977; Fulbright fellow U. Bristol (Eng.), 1954. Mem. Acad. Motion Picture Arts and Scis., Acad. TV Arts and Scis., Am. Film Inst. (second decade council), Hollywood Radio and TV Soc. (pres. 1975-76); mem. steering com. The Caucus for Producers, Writers & Dirs. Office: ITC Entertainment Group Ste 702 11661 San Vicente Blvd Los Angeles CA 90049

LEIDHEISER, HENRY, JR., retired chemistry educator, consultant; b. Union City, N.J., Apr. 18, 1920; s. Henry and Margaret Marie (Steinel) L.; m. Virginia Townsend, Feb. 21, 1944; children: Margaret Frances, Henry III. BS in Chemistry, U. Va., 1941, MS in Phys. Chemistry, 1943, PhD in Phys. Chemistry, 1946. Research associate U. Va., Charlottesville, 1946-49; research chemist, dir. Va. Inst. for Sci. Research, Richmond, 1949-68; prof. chemistry Lehigh U., Bethlehem, Pa., 1968-90, prof. emeritus, 1990—; cons. space science NASA, 1972-84; cons. numerous indsl. orgns. Author or editor of 8 books; 275 publs. in tech. lit.; 7 patents on crystal growth and metal surface treatment. NATO fellow to Cambridge U., England, 1969; recipient J. Shelton Horsley Rsch. award Va. Acad. Sci., 1948, Oak Ridge Inst. Nuclear Studies Rsch. award, 1949, Westinghouse Signal and Brake Award of Inst. Metal Finishing, 1954, Silver medal Am. Electroplaters' Soc., 1978, Arch T. Colwell award Soc. Automotive Engrs., 1979, Humboldt Sr. Scientist award, 1985, Tambour award 11th Congress Metal Finishing, 1984, Silver medal South African Corrosion Inst., 1986, Libsch Rsch. award Lehigh U., 1987, Mattiello Rsch. award Fedn. Soc. Coatings Tech., 1990. Fellow AAAS; mem. Am. Chem. Soc., Electrochem. Soc. (Young Author's award 1948, Rsch. award 1986, 91), Nat. Assn. Corrosion Engrs. (Whitney award 1983), Rotary. Republican. Presbyterian. Avocations: bridge, golf, collecting ceramics. Home: 822 Carnoustie Dr Venice FL 34293-4343

LEIDINGER, WILLIAM JOHN, clinic administrator; b. Chgo., Feb. 1, 1940; s. Arthur George and Anna (Choisek) L.; m. Karen Aldinger, Sept. 1, 1962; children: Michael, Steven. B.A., Loras Coll., Dubuque, Iowa, 1962; M.A., State U. Iowa, 1963. Adminstrv. asst. to city mgr. Park Forest, Ill., 1963-65; asst. to city mgr. Alexandria, Va., 1965-71; asst. city mgr. Richmond, Va., 1971-72; city mgr., 1972-78; v.p. Rolm/Atlantic Corp., 1979-81; exec. dir. McGuire Clinic, Richmond, 1981-86; exec.v.p., chief lending officer Security Federal Savings, Richmond, Va., 1986-91; county executive Fairfax County, Fairfax, Va., 1992—; instr. Purdue U., No. Va. Community Coll.; guest lectr. U. Richmond, mem. bd. assos., Va. Commonwealth U. Bd. dirs., pres. Greater Richmond Transit Co., 1973-78; mem. Richmond City Planning Commn., 1971-78; bd. dirs. Richmond Eye Hosp., 1979—, St. Luke's Hosp, Richmond Cerebral Palsy Ctr; mem. Richmond City Council, 1980—; bd. dirs. Port of Richmond. Mem. Internat. City Mgmt. Assn. (chmn. labor/mgmt. relations com. 1974-75), Nat. League Cities, Va. Municipal League, Am. Soc. Pub. Adminstrn. Roman Catholic. Office: Office of the County Exec 12000 Government Center Pky Fairfax VA 22035-0001*

LEIDNER, HAROLD EDWARD, lawyer; b. Cleve., Aug. 23, 1937; s. Nathan Nelson and Therese Loretta (Burdine) L.; children—Kenneth Jason, Andrew Mitchell. A.B., Cornell U., 1959; LL.B., Western Res. U., 1963. Bar: Ohio 1963. Since practiced in Cleve.; prin. Fuerst, Leidner, Dougherty & Kasdan Co., 1968-79; ptnr. firm Benesch, Friedlander, Coplan & Aronoff, 1984—. Law editor: Webster's New World Dictionary of the American

Language, 1970. Mem. Am., Ohio, Cleve. bar assns.; Am. Arbitration Assn. Republican. Clubs: Cornell; Commerce (Cleve.); Curzon House (London, Eng.). Home: 2112 Acacia Park Dr Lyndhurst OH 44124-3852 Office: Benesch Friedlander Coplan 2300 BP America Bldg 200 Public Sq Cleveland OH 44114-2378

LEIER, CARL VICTOR, internist, cardiologist; b. Bismarck, N.D., Oct. 20, 1944; married; 3 children. BA, Creighton U., 1965, MD cum laude, 1969. Diplomate Am. Bd. Internal Medicine, Cardiovascular Medicine, Critical Care Medicine, Geriatric Medicine, Nat. Bd. Med. Examiners; lic. med., surgical Nebr., med. Ohio. Intern Ohio State U. Coll. Medicine, Columbus, 1969-70, med. resident (instr.) dept. medicine, 1971-73, chief resident (instr.), 1973-74, fellowship divsn. cardiology, 1974-76; pathology resident dept. pathology St. Vincent Hosp., Worcester, Mass., 1970-71; trainee NIH Tng. Grant, 1974-75; asst. prof. medicine cardiology dept., Ohio State U. Coll. Medicine, Columbus, 1976-80, asst. prof. pharmacology, 1976-80, assoc. prof., 1980-84, faculty mem. grad. sch., 1980—, dir. rsch. divsn. cardiology, 1980-83, James W. Overstreet prof. of medicine, 1983—, prof. of medicine divsn. cardiology, 1984—, prof. pharmacology, dept. pharmacology, 1984—, dir. divsn. cardiology, 1986—; internship selection com. dept. medicine, Ohio State U., 1973-74, hosp. procedures com. Ohio State U. Hosps., 1973-74; mem. pharmacology and therapeutics com. Ohio State U. Hosps., 1976-80; mem. rsch. com. ctrl. Ohio chpt. Am. Heart Assn., 1977-84, bd. trustees, 1979-88, exec. rsch. com., 1979-84, vice chmn. rsch. com., 1980-82, chmn. rsch. peer rev. com., 1982-84, v.p., 1984-86, pres. elect, 1986-88; numerous other coms.; cons. cardiorenal adv. bd. Smith-Kline Labs., 1982-85, com. on cardio-vascular rsch. and devel., 1982-85., AMA on Drugs and Tech., 1985—, Lilly-Elanco devel. ractopamine, 1989; mem. ad hoc adv. com. on carvedilol in congestive heart failure, Smith, Kline and Beacham Pharms., 1991, ad hoc adv. com. on PDEI devel., McNeil Pharms., 1991, ad hoc adv. com. for clin. trials on Ibopamine, Zambon Pharms., 1993, sci. adv. com. Ohio State Univ. Brain Tumor Rsch. Ctr., 1993—, data safety monitoring bd., Otsuka Vesnarinone Trials, 1993— mem. chmn. Annual Sci. Sessions Planning Com. of the Am. Coll. of Cardiolog, 1996-97; vis. prof., lectr. and presenter at numerous sci. confs., insts. in U.S. and internationally. Editor: (book) Cardiotonic Drugs, 1986, 2d rev. edit., 1991; co-author: (with H. Boudoulas) CardioRenal Disorders and Diseases, 1986, 2d edit., 1992 (with J. Vincent) Critical Care Medicine: Recent Advances in Cardiovascular Medicine, 1990; contbr. more than 40 chpts. to other medical books and almost 200 articles to peer reviewed jours. including: Vascular Surgery, Archives of Internal Medicine, Circulation, Brit. Heart Jour., Jour. Electrocardiology, Clinical Pharmacologic Therapy, Chest, Am. Jour. Medicine, Jour. Cardiovascular Pharmacology, Am. Heart Jour., Geriatrics, Annals of Internal Medicine and others; editor in chief Congestive Heart Failure: Index and Revs., 1988—; mem. editorial bds. of ten medical jours. concerned with heart diseases, the review bds. of others including New Eng. Jour. Medicine, Internat. Jour. Cardiology, Jour. of Lab. and Clin. Medicine. Recipient Upjohn award, 1969, Lange Scholar award, 1969, Golden Apple Student Tchg. award, 1973, 75, Young Investigator award Ctrl. Ohio Heart Chpt., Am. Heart Assn., 1976-78, Rsch. Recognition award, 1978; named One of Best Doctors of Columbus, Columbus Monthly, 1992. Fellow Am. Coll. Clin. Pharmacology, Coun. on Clin. Pharmacology, Am. Heart Assn., Am. Coll. Cardiology, Am. Coll. Physicians, Coun. on Geriatric Cardiology; mem. AAAS, Ohio State Med. Assn., Am. Fedn. for Clin. Rsch., Ctrl. Soc. for Clin. Rsch., Am. Soc. Clin. Investigation, Assn. Univ. Cardiologists, Internat. Soc. for Heart Rsch., Internat. Soc. Cardiovascular Pharmacotherapy, Assn. Profs. of Cardiology. Office: Ohio State Univ Med Ctr Divsn Cardiology Columbus OH 43210

LEIES, JOHN ALEX, academic administrator, educator, clergyman; b. Chgo., Apr. 24, 1926; cre; BS in Edn., U. Dayton, 1948; STB, U. Friborg, Switzerland, 1954, STL, 1956, STD, 1958. Asst. to provincial Soc. of Mary, St. Louis, 1961-64; regional superior Marianist Missions, Peru, 1964-68; prof. theology, dir. campus ministry St. Mary's U., San Antonio, 1974-81, chmn. grad. theology dept., 1980-81, acad. v.p., 1981-85, pres., 1985-88; grad. advisor theology dept. St. Mary's U., 1977-81, dir. Ctr. for Profl. Ethics, 1991—; dir. Cath. Charismatic Bible Inst., 1977-86, 91—; theologian mem. ethics com. Santa Rosa Hosp., 1978-81, 89-94; mem. gen. chpt. Soc. of Mary, 1966-67, 71, 76, 81, 86, 91; rsch. fellow cons. Pope John Med. Moral Rsch. Ctr., Braintree, Mass., 1988—; bd. trustees Tex. Ctr. for Legal Ethics and Professionalism, 1994-95. Mem. Lambda Chi Alpha, Rotary, Univ. Faculty for Life, Fellowship of Cath. Scholars. Avocation: reading. Address: St Mary's Univ of San Antonio 1 Camino Santa Maria St San Antonio TX 78228-5433

LEIGH, HOYLE, psychiatrist, educator, writer; b. Seoul, Korea, Mar. 25, 1942; came to U.S., 1965; m. Vincenta Masciandaro, Sept. 16, 1967; 1 child, Alexander Hoyle. MA, Yale U., 1982; MD, Yonsei U., Seoul, 1965. Diplomate Am. Bd. Psychiatry and Neurology. Asst. prof. Yale U., New Haven, 1971-75, assoc. prof., 1975-80, prof., 1980-89, lectr. in psychiatry, 1989—; dir. Behavioral Medicine Clinic, Yale U., 1980-89; dir. psychiat. cons. svc. Yale-New Haven Hosp., 1971-89; chief psychiatry VA Med Ctr., Fresno, Calif., 1989—; prof., vice chmn. dept. psychiatry U. Calif., San Francisco, 1989—, head dept. psychiatry, 1989—; cons. Am. Jour. Psychiatry, Archives Internal Medicine, Psychosomatic Medicine. Author: The Patient, 1980, 2d edit., 1985, 3d edit., 1992; editor: Psychiatry in the Practice of Medicine, 1983, Consultation-Liaison Psychiatry: 1990's & Beyond, 1994. Fellow ACP, Internat. Coll. Psychosomatic Medicine (v.p.), Am. Acad. Psychosomatic Medicine; mem. AMA, AAUP, World Psychiat. Assn. Avocations: reading, music, skiing. Office: U Calif Dept Psychiat 2615 E Clinton Ave Fresno CA 93703-2223

LEIGH, JANET (JEANETTE HELEN MORRISON), actress; b. Merced, Calif., July 6, 1927; m. Tony Curtis, June 4, 1951 (div. 1962); children: Jamie Lee, Kelly; m. Robert Brandt, 1962. Student, Coll. Pacific. Actress: (films) Romance of Rosy Ridge, 1947, If Winter Comes, 1947, Hills of Home, 1948, Words and Music, 1948, Act of Violence, 1948, Little Women, 1949, That Forsythe Woman, 1949, The Red Danube, 1949, The Doctor and the Girl, 1949, Holiday Affair, 1949, Two Tickets to Broadway, 1951, Strictly Dishonorable, 1951, Angels in the Outfield, 1951, It's a Big Country, 1952, Scaramouche, 1952, Fearless Fagan, 1952, The Naked Spur, 1953, Houdini, 1953, Walking My Baby Back Home, 1953, Confidentially Connie, 1953, Prince Valiant, 1954, The Black Shield of Falworth, 1954, Rogue Cop, 1954, Living It Up!, 1954, My Sister Eileen, 1955, Pete Kelly's Blues, 1955, Just This Once, 1955, Touch of Evil, 1958, The Vikings, 1958, The Perfect Furlough, 1958, Psycho, 1960, Who Was That Lady?, 1960, The Manchurian Candidate, 1962, Bye Bye Birdie, 1963, Wives and Lovers, 1963, Grand Slam, Harper, 1966, Kid Rodello, 1966, Hello Down There, 1968, The Deadly Dream, 1971, One Is a Lonely Number, 1972, Night of the Lepus, 1972, Boardwalk, 1979, Fog, 1980, Other Realms, (TV movies) numerous including The World Series Murders, Death's Head, The Monk, 1969, Honeymoon with a Stranger, 1969, The House on Green Apple Road, 1970, The Chairman, Murdock's Gang, 1973, Telethon, 1977, Mirror, Mirror, 1979, Murder at the World Series, Murder She Wrote, Love Letters, 1991; author: (autobiography) There Really Was a Hollywood, 1984, (novel) House of Destiny, 1995, (stage) Murder Among Friends, 1976, Love Letters, 1991, (non-fiction) Psycho Revisited, Psycho: Behind the Scenes of the Classic Thriller, 1995; rec. (album) Bye Bye, Birdie. Office: Ansel Eisenstadt & Frazier 6310 San Vicente Blvd Ste 401 Los Angeles CA 90048

LEIGH, JENNIFER JASON (JENNIFER LEIGH MORROW), actress; b. L.A., Feb. 5, 1962; d. Barbara Turner and Vic Morrow. Student, Lee Strasberg Inst. Appearances include (films) Eyes of a Stranger, 1980, Fast Times at Ridgemont High, 1982, Wrong is Right, 1982, Easy Money, 1983, Grandview U.S.A., 1984, Flesh + Blood, 1985, The Hitcher, 1986, The Men's Club, 1986, Sister, Sister, 1987, Under Cover, 1987, Heart of Midnight, 1988, The Big Picture, 1989, Last Exit to Brooklyn, 1989, Miami Blues, 1990, Crooked Hearts, 1991, Backdraft, 1991, Rush, 1992, Single White Female, 1992, Short Cuts, 1993, The Hudsucker Proxy, 1994, Mrs. Parker and the Vicious Circle, 1994, Dolores Claiborne, 1994; (TV movies) Angel City, 1980, The Killing of Randy Webster, 1981, The Best Little Girl in the World, 1981, The First Time, 1982, Girls of the White Orchid, 1983, Buried Alive, 1990. Office: ICM c/o Tracey Jacobs 8942 Wilshire Blvd Beverly Hills CA 90211 also: care Elaine Rich 2400 Whitman Pl Los Angeles CA 90068-2464*

LEIGH, MONROE, lawyer; b. South Boston, Va., July 15, 1919; s. Leander Faulkner and Elizabeth Edmunds (Monroe) L.; m. Mary Gallaher Leigh, Apr. 15, 1951; children: Edward Monroe, Parker McCollester, Elizabeth Faulkner. B.A., Hampden-Sydney Coll., 1940; LL.B., U. Va., 1947. Bar: Va. 1947, D.C. 1948, U.S. Supreme Ct 1950. Assoc. firm Covington, Burling, Rublee, Acheson & Shorb, 1947-51; mem. U.S. del. N. Atlantic Council, London and Paris, 1951-53; dep. asst. gen. counsel Dept. Def., 1953-55, asst. gen. counsel internat. affairs, 1955-59; ptnr. Steptoe and Johnson, Washington, 1961-75, 77—; legal adviser Dept. State, 1975-77; lectr. U. Va. Law Sch., 1964-75, 78-88; mem. Permanent Ctr. of Arbitration, The Hague, 1975-80; mem. adv. Com. Internat. Investment U.S. Trade Rep., 1984-95; mem. Legal Adviser's Adv. Com. on Pub. Internat. Law, 1993—; mem. adv. com. Am. Law Inst. on Fgn. Rels. Law; mem. chmn.'s list of panels of conciliators and arbitrators Internat. Ctr. for Settlement of Investment Disputes. Co-editor: National Treaty Law and Practice, 1995; contbr. articles to profl. jours. Trustee U. Va. Law Sch. Found., 1988-95. Capt. USAAF, 1943-46. Recipient Superior Honor award Sec. of State, 1977. Mem. ABA (Theberge award 1989, chmn. task force on war crimes in Bosnia 1993—), Internat. Law Assn., Am. Soc. Internat. Law (pres. 1981-82, hon. pres. 1990-92), Coun. Fgn. Rels., Washington Inst. Fgn. Affairs, Am. Law Inst., Colonnade Club, Cosmos Club, Met. Club, Chevy Chase Club. Episcopalian. Home: 5205 Westwood Dr Bethesda MD 20816-1838 Office: 1330 Connecticut Ave NW Washington DC 20036-1704

LEIGH, SHARI GREER, software consulting firm executive; b. Reading, Pa., Mar. 1, 1959; d. Martin and Francine Rita (Gross) Rothenstein; m. Martin Brad Greer, Dec. 31, 1979; children: Shannon Leigh, Krista Heather. BA in Biochemistry, Wellesley Coll.-MIT, 1980; postgrad. in bus. adminstrn., Colo. State U., 1982-83. Lead thermal engr. Rockwell Internat. Space div., Downey, Calif., 1980-81; systems engr. Martin Marietta Aerospace, Denver, 1981-82, aerospace new bus. analyst, 1982-84; v.p. Miaco Corp. (Micro Automation Cons.), Englewood, Colo., 1984-87, pres., CEO, 1987—. Co-designer life systems monitor for Sudden Infant Death Syndrome, 1980. Exec. bd. dirs. Mile High chpt. ARC, 1991—. Recipient Recognition award for 500 fastest growing cos. Inc. Mag., 1990, 91, Blue Chip Enterprise award Am.'s Best Small Bus., U.S. C. of C., 1991; named Bus. Leader to Watch in the 90's Corp. Connection; finalist Colo. Small Bus. of the Yr. award C. of C., 1992-93, Person of Yr., U.S. Small Bus. Bus. Adminstrn., South Metro Small Bus. Person of Yr., 1992-93. Mem. Greater Denver Chamber (coun. mem. small bus. bd. 1991-93), So. Met. C. of C. (bd. dirs. 1994—). Office: Miaco Corp 6300 S Syracuse Way Ste 415 Englewood CO 80111-6724

LEIGH, SHERREN, communications executive, editor, publisher; b. Cleve., Dec. 22, 1942; d. Walter Carl Maurushat and Treva Eldora (Burke) Morris; m. Norman J. Hickey Jr., Aug. 23, 1969 (div. 1985). BS, Ohio U., 1965. Communications dir. Metal Lath Assn., Cleve., 1965-67; creative dir. O'Toole Inc., Chgo., 1967-69; sr. v.p. RLC Inc., Chgo., 1969-77; pres. Leigh Communications Inc., Chgo., 1978—; chmn. Today's Chgo. Woman mag., 1982—; pres. Ill. Ambassadors, Chgo., 1985-86; bd. dirs. Chgo. Fin. Exchange, 1985-87. Author: How to Write a Winning Resume, How to Negotiate for Top Dollar, How to Find, Get and Keep the Job You Want. Bd. dirs. Midwest Women's Ctr., Chgo., 1984-86, Girl Scouts Chgo., 1985-87, Black Women's Hall of Fame Found., Chgo., 1986—, Apparel Industry Bd., Chgo., 1988, Auditorium Theater of Roosevelt U. Recipient Corp. Leadership award YWCA Met. Chgo., 1979, Entrepreneurship award, 1988, Media Advocate of Yr. award U.S. SBA, 1994; named one of 10 Women of Achievement Midwest Women's Ctr., Chgo., 1987, Advt. Woman of Yr. Women's Advt. Club, Chgo., 1988; inducted City of Chgo. Women's Hall of Fame, 1988. Mem. Chgo. Network, Econ. Club Chgo., Execs. Club Chgo., Com. of 200 (founding mem.). Office: Leigh Communications, Inc 150 E Huron St # 1225 Chicago IL 60611

LEIGH, STEPHEN, industrial designer; b. N.Y.C., May 21, 1931; s. Herman Lerner and Rhea (Drinkhouse) L.; m. Barbara Lynn Haim, Feb. 14, 1984; children: Harvey Alan, Madeleine Beth. BFA, Cooper Union, 1951. Interior designer Robert Gruen Assocs., N.Y.C., 1951-55; designer, project dir. Michael Saphier Assocs., N.Y.C., 1955-59; pres. Stephen Leigh & Assocs. Inc., N.Y.C., 1959—; interior designers, cons. specializing in comml. usage, United Jewish Appeal, 1963, U.S. Pavilion, Venezuelan Pavilion, N.Y. World's Fair, 1964-65, Random House, 1969, Mitsubishi Internat. Corp., 1980, Rapid Am. Corp., 1982, Bowery Savs. Bank, 1986; lectr. NYU. Columnist Real Estate Weekly, 1963-65, The Office Mag., 1985—; one-man shows of sculpture at Cartier and East River Savings Bank; recent prin. works include Union Chelsea Nat. Bank, Faberge, Fino Restaurant, Il Menestrello Restaurant, Schenley, redesign of landmark facade at 111 8th Ave., 1989; sculpted permanent team trophy for Eisenhower Golf Tournament. Recipient AIA design award for Venezuelan Pavilion N.Y. World's Fair, 1964-65, Excellence award The Archtl. Woodwork Inst., 1988. Mem. Am. Soc. of Interior Designers (N.Y. chpt.), Charge des Missions of the Confrerie de la Chaine des Rotisseurs (Bronze Star of Excellence), Brotherhood of the Knights of the Vine. Avocations: sculpture, painting, cooking, travel, collecting Americana and American flags. Office: 157 E 57th St New York NY 10022-2115

LEIGHNINGER, DAVID SCOTT, cardiovascular surgeon; b. Youngstown, Ohio, Jan. 16, 1920; s. Jesse Harrison and Marjorie (Lightner) L.; m. Margaret Jane Malony, May 24, 1942; children: David Allan, Jenny. BA, Oberlin Coll., 1942; MD, Case Western Res. U., 1945. Intern Univ. Hosps. of Cleve., 1945-46, resident, 1949-51, asst. surgeon, 1951-68; rsch. fellow in cardiovascular surgery rsch. lab. Case Western Res. U. Sch. Medicine, Cleve., 1948-49, 51-55, 57-67, instr. surgery, 1951-55, sr. instr., 1957-64, asst. prof., 1964-68, asst. clin. prof., 1968-70; resident Cin. Gen. Hosp., 1955-57; practice medicine specializing in cardiovascular surgery, Cleve., 1957-70; pvt. practice medicine specializing in cardiovascular and gen. surgery Edgewater Hosp., Chgo., 1970-82, staff surgeon, also dir. emergency surg. services, 1970-82; staff surgeon, also dir. emergency surg. svcs. Mazel Med. Ctr., Chgo., 1970-82; emergency physician Miner's Hosp., Raton, N.Mex., 1982-83, 84-85, No. Colfax County Hosp., Raton, 1983-84, Mt. San Rafael Hosp., Trinidad, Colo., 1984-85; assoc., courtesy, or cons. staff Marymount Hosp., Cleve., Mt. Sinai Hosp., Cleve., Geauga Community Hosp., Chardon, Ohio, Bedford Community Hosp (Ohio), 1957-70. Tchr. tng. courses in CPR for med. personnel, police, fire and vol. rescue workers, numerous cities, 1950-70. Served to capt., M.C., AUS, 1946-48. Recipient Chris award Columbus Internat. Film Festival, 1964, numerous other award for sci. exhibits from various nat. and state med. socs., 1953-70; USPHS grantee, 1949-68. Fellow Am. Coll. Cardiology, Am. Coll. Chest Physicians; mem. AMA, N.Mex. Med. Assn., Colfax County Med. Assn., Ill. Med. Assn., Chgo. Med. Assn., U. Cin. Grad. Sch. Surg. Soc. Contbr. numerous articles to med. jours., chpts. to med. texts; spl. pioneer research (with Claude S. Beck) in physiopathology of coronary artery disease and CPR; developed surg. treatment of coronary artery disease; achieved 1st successful defibrillation of human heart, 1st successful reversal of fatal heart attack; provided 1st intensive care of coronary patients. Home: HC 68 Box 77 Fort Garland CO 81133-9708

LEIGHTEN, EDWARD HENRY, publisher, consultant; b. Montclair, N.J., June 22, 1914; s. Jack and Mariette G. (Ackerman) L.; m. Alice Celia Bowne, Aug. 31, 1940; children: Judith (Mrs. Harvey L. Slade), Jeanne Elizabeth (Mrs. T.E. Card). B.S. in Optics, U. Rochester, 1937. Engr. Universal Camera Corp., N.Y.C., 1938-39; mem. editorial staff Photo Technique and Product Engring. mags. McGraw-Hill Pub. Co., N.Y.C., 1939-42; tech. editor U.S. Camera mag., N.Y.C., 1946-47; editor, pub. Photo Devels. (now Photo Mktg.) mag. Master Photo Dealers Assn.), Jackson, Mich., 1947-52; editor Flow mag., Flow Quar. mag. and Flow Directory, Indsl. Pub. Co., Cleve., 1952-56; exec. editor Flow mag., Flow Quar. mag. and Flow Directory, Indsl. Pub. Co., 1956-60; with Cahners Pub. Co., Boston, 1960-82; pub. Modern Materials Handling mag., 1960-81, v.p., 1966-80; v.p., group pub. Modern Materials Handling and Traffic Mgmt. mags., 1974-80; staff v.p. Modern Materials Handling and Traffic Mgmt. mags. (Boston div. corp.), 1981-82; pres. Cons. Services Group (communications, mktg., pub. relations); asso. prof. mktg. Cape Cod Community Coll. Mem. Westlake (Ohio) Sch. Bd., 1958-60, Westlake Libr. Bd., 1958-60; vol. J.N. (Ding) Darling Nat. Wildlife Refuge, Sanibel, Fla., 1984—. Lt. USNR, 1942-46. Recipient Honor award for contbns. to materials handling edn. Internat. Material Mgmt. Soc. Mem. Material Handling Inst., Caster and Floor Truck Mfrs. Assn., Nat. Wooden Pallet and Container Assn., Internat. Material Mgmt. Soc. (cert. profl. in material handling and material mgmt.), Material Handling Equipment Dealers Assn., Nat. Council Phys. Distbn. Mgmt., Bus./Profl. Advt. Assn. (cert. bus. communicator), Theta Chi. Home and Office: 531 Riverview Dr Chatham MA 02633-1117 *Full, clear, and honest communication among people—in social, industrial, professional and commercial endeavors—is essential to our social, economic, and political growth, nationally and internationally. To be a good communicator is to be a catalyst for progress in all aspects of life. Opportunities for good communicators abound, but relatively few persons are aware of them early enough in their careers. Too many who have writing abilities or aspirations think only in terms of news or literary careers. Whatever profession, trade or technology a person may choose, training in communications will enhance his development and speed his progress.*

LEIGHTON, CHARLES MILTON, specialty consumer products executive; b. Portland, Maine, June 4, 1935; s. Wilbur F. and Elizabeth (Loveland) L.; AB, Bowdoin Coll., 1957, LLD (hon.), 1989; M.BA, Harvard U., 1960; children: Julia Loveland, Anne Throop; m. Roxanne Brooks McCormick, May 23, 1992. Product line mgr. Mine Safety Appliances Co., Pitts., 1960-64; instr. Harvard Bus. Sch., 1964-65; group v.p. Bangor Punta Corp., Boston, 1965-69; chmn., CEO CML Group, Inc., Acton, Mass., 1969—; bd. dirs. New England Investment Co., Boston, New Eng. Mut. Life Ins. Co., Boston. Past pres. Alumni Coun. Harvard Bus. Sch., Cambridge, Mass.; past pres. of trustees Concord (Mass.) Acad. Republican. Episcopalian. Clubs: New York Yacht (commodore 1993-94); Chatham (Mass.) Yacht (vice commodore 1957); Harvard of N.Y.C. and Boston, Harvard Faculty Club, Tarratine, Internat. Golf Club, Ocean Forest Golf Club. Home: PO Box 247 Bolton MA 01740-0247 Office: CML Group Inc 524 Main St Acton MA 01720-3933

LEIGHTON, FRANCES SPATZ, writer, journalist; b. Geauga County, Ohio; m. Kendall King Hoyt, Feb. 1, 1984. Student, Ohio State U. Washington corr. Am. Weekly; corr. and Washington editor This Week Mag.; Washington corr. Met. Group Sunday Mags.; contbg. editor Family Weekly; free-lance journalist Metro Sunday Group, Washington; lectr. summer confs. Dellbrook-Shenandoah Coll., Georgetown U., Washington. Author over 30 books on hist. figures, celebrities, Hollywood, psychiatry, the White House and Capitol Hill, 1957—; (with Louise Pfister) I Married a Psychiatrist, 1961, (with Francois Rysovy) A Treasury of White House Cooking, 1968, (with Frank S. Caprio) How to Avoid a Nervous Breakdown, 1969, (with Mary B. Gallagher) My Life with Jacqueline Kennedy, 1969, (with Traphes Bryant) Dog Days at the White House, 1975, (with William Fishbait Miller) Fishbait—the Memoirs of the Congressional Doorkeeper, 1977, (with Lillian Rogers Parks) My 30 Years Backstairs at the White House (made into TV mini-series), 1979, (with Hugh Carter) Cousin Beedie, Cousin Hot--, My Life with the Carter Family of Plains, Georgia, 1978, (with Jerry Cammarata) The Fun Book of Fatherhood-or How the Animal Kingdom is Helping to Raise the Wild Kids at Our House, 1978, (with Natalie Golos) Coping with Your Allergies, 1979, (with Ken Hoyt) Drunk Before Noon—The Behind the Scenes Story of the Washington Press Corps, 1979, (with Louis Hurst) The Sweetest Little Club in the World, The Memoirs of the Senate Restaurateur, 1980, (with John M. Szostak) In the Footsteps of Pope John Paul II, 1980, (with Lillian Rogers Parks) The Roosevelts, a Family in Turmoil, 1981, (with June Allyson) June Allyson, 1982, (with Beverly Slater) Stranger in My Bed, 1985 (made into TV movie, 1987), (with Oscar Collier) How to Write and Sell Your First Novel, 1986, The Search for the Real Nancy Reagan, 1987, (with Oscar Collier) How To Write and Sell Your First Nonfiction Book, 1990, (with Stephen M. Bauer) At Ease at the White House, 1991; contbr. numerous feature stories on polit., social and govtl. personalities to various publs. Bd. dirs. Nat. Found., from 1963. Recipient Edgar award, 1961. Mem. Senate Periodical Corr. Assn., White House Corr. Assn., Am. News Women's Club, The Writers Club, Nat. Press Club, Writers League of Washington (pres.), Washington League Am. Pen Women (pres.), Washington Ind. Writers, Smithsonian Assocs., Nat. Trust Historic Preservation, Lake Barcroft Women's Club, Delta Phi Delta, Sigma Delta Chi. Unitarian. Office: Lake Barcroft Lake Barcroft 6336 Lakeview Dr Falls Church VA 22041-1331

LEIGHTON, GEORGE NEVES, retired federal judge; b. New Bedford, Mass., Oct. 22, 1912; s. Antonio N. and Anna Sylvia (Garcia) Leitao; m. Virginia Berry Quivers, June 21, 1942; children: Virginia Anne, Barbara Elaine. AB, Howard U., 1940; LLB, Harvard U., 1946; LLD, Elmhurst Coll., 1964; LL.D., John Marshall Law Sch., 1973, Southeastern Mass. U., 1975, New Eng. U. Sch. Law, 1978; LLD, Loyola U., Chgo., 1989, R.I. Coll., 1992. Bar: Mass. 1946, Ill. 1947, U.S. Supreme Ct. 1958. Ptnr. Moore, Ming & Leighton, Chgo., 1951-59, McCoy, Ming & Leighton, Chgo., 1959-64; judge Circuit Ct. Cook County Ill., 1964-69, Appellate Ct. 1st Dist., 1969-76; U.S. dist. judge No. Dist. Ill., 1976-86; sr. dist. judge U.S. Dist. Ct., No. Dist. Ill., 1986-87; of counsel Earl L. Neal & Assocs., 1987—; adj. prof. John Marshall Law Sch., Chgo., 1965—; commr., mem. character and fitness com. for 1st Appellate Dist., Supreme Ct. Ill., 1955-63, chmn. character and fitness com., 1961-62; joint com. for revision Ill. Criminal Code, 1959-63; chmn. Ill. adv. com. U.S. Commn. on Civil Rights, 1964; mem. pub. rev. bd. UAW, AFL-CIO, 1961-70; Asst. atty. gen. State of Ill., 1950-51; pres. 3d Ward Regular Democratic Orgn., Cook County, Ill., 1951-53; v.p. 21st Ward, 1964. Contbr. articles to legal jours. Bd. dirs. United Ch. Bd. for Homeland Ministries, United Ch. of Christ, Grant Hosp., Chgo.; trustee U. Notre Dame, 1979-83, trustee emeritus, 1983—; bd. overseers Harvard Coll., 1983-89. Capt., inf. AUS, 1942-45. Decorated Bronze Star.; Recipient Civil Liberties award Ill. div. ACLU, 1961; named Chicagoan of Year in Law and Judiciary Jr. Assn. Commerce and Industry, 1964. Fellow ABA (chmn. coun. 1976, mem. coun. sect. legal edn. and admissions to bar); mem. NAACP (chmn. legal redress com. Chgo. br.), Am. Coll. Trial Lawyers, John Howard Assn. (bd. dirs.), Chgo. Bar Assn., Ill. Bar Assn. (joint com. mem. for revision jud. article 1959-62), Nat. Harvard Law Sch. Assn. (mem. coun.), Howard U. Chgo. Alumni Club (chmn. bd. dirs.), Phi Beta Kappa. Office: Earl L Neal & Assocs 111 W Washington St Ste 1700 Chicago IL 60602-2711

LEIGHTON, HENRY ALEXANDER, physician, consultant; b. Manila, Nov. 12, 1929; (parents U.S. citizens).; s. Raymond Harry and Theola Marie (Alexander) L.; m. Helga Maria Hell, Jan. 17, 1970; children: Alan Raymond, Henry Alexander, Michael Ballinger, John, Marni, Tammy Ballinger. BA in History, U. Calif., Berkeley, 1952, MPH, 1971; MD, U. Calif., San Francisco, 1956. Diplomate Am. Bd. Preventive Medicine. Intern So. Pacific Gen. Hosp., San Francisco, 1956-57; resident in surgery Brooke Gen. Hosp., Ft. Sam Houston, Tex., 1960-62; commd. 2d. lt. U.S. Army, 1957, advanced through grades to col., 1971; div. surgeon 8th Inf. div. U.S. Army, Germany, 1964-66; comdr. 15th Med. Bn. U.S. Army, Vietnam, 1966-67; instr. Med. Field Service Sch. U.S. Army, San Antonio, 1968-70; resident preventive medicine U.S. Army, Ft. Ord, Calif., 1971-72, chief preventive medicine, 1973-76; chief preventive medicine U.S. Army-Europe, 1976-79, ret., 1979; chief occupational health MEDDAC U.S. Army, Ft. Ord, 1981-89; pvt. practice Salinas, Calif., 1990—. Neighborhood commr. Boy Scouts Am., 1964-66; bd. dirs. Am. Lung Assn. of Calif., 1982-84, and of affiliate, 1980-86, The Calif. Acad. Preventive Medicine, 1994-96; pres. The Bluffs Homeowners Assn., 1986. Decorated Air medal with oak leaf cluster, Bronze Star, Legion of Merit, Meritorious Service medal. Fellow Am. Coll. Preventive Medicine; mem. Am. Pub. Health Assn., Am. Coll. Occupational Medicine, Assn. Mil. Surgeons, Ret. Officers Assn., Assn. U.S. Army, Theta Xi. Lodges: Masons, Shriners. Office: 14096 Reservation Rd Salinas CA 93908-9208

LEIGHTON, JOSEPH, pathologist; b. N.Y.C., Dec. 13, 1921; m. Rosalind Weinberger, Dec. 15, 1946; children—Daniel A., Edith R. AB, Columbia U., 1942; MD, L.I. Coll. Medicine, Bklyn., 1946. Intern Mt. Sinai Hosp., N.Y.C., 1946-47; resident in pathology Mass. Gen. Hosp., Boston, 1948-49, USPHS Hosp., Balt., 1950; research pathologist Nat. Cancer Inst., Bethesda, Md., 1951-56; mem. faculty dept. pathology U. Pitts. Sch. Medicine, 1956-70; prof. pathology Med. Coll. Pa., Phila., 1971-89, chmn. dept. pathology, 1971-87; pathologist Peralta Cancer Rsch. Inst., 1989-92, Aeron Biotech. Inc., San Leandro, Calif., 1994—. Author: The Spread of Cancer, 1967; inventor radial histophysiologic gradient culture chamber. Served with USPHS, 1948-56. Eleanor Roosevelt Cancer Research fellow, 1970-71. Mem. Am. Assn. Cancer Research, Tissue Culture Assn., Am. Assn. Pathologists, Internat. Acad. Pathology. Home: 2324 Lakeshore Ave Apt 2 Oakland CA 94606-1056 Office: Aeron Biotech Inc 1933 Davis St San Leandro CA 94577-1260

LEIGHTON, LAWRENCE WARD, investment banker; b. N.Y.C., July 1, 1934; s. Sidney and Florence (Ward) L.; m. Mariana Stroock, June 21, 1959; children: Sandra L. Galvin, Michelle Stroock. BSE, Princeton U., 1956; MBA, Harvard U., 1962. V.p. Kuhn Loeb & Co., N.Y.C., 1962-69, Clark, Dodge & Co., Inc., 1970-74; dir. Norton-Simon, Inc., 1974-78; ltd. ptnr. Bear, Stearns & Co., 1978-82; mng. dir. Chase Investment Bank, 1983-88; pres., CEO Union d'Etudes et d'Investissements Mcht. Bank of Credit Agricole, 1989-93; vice chmn. 2I, Inc., 1993-94, mng dir. LM Capital Corp., 1994-96; mng. dir. Windward Ptnrs., 1996—; dir. Corp. Renaissance Group, 1994—; chmn. Princeton Schs. Com. of N.Y., 1965-85. Mem. exec. com. Princeton U. Alumni Coun., 1975-80; vice chmn. nat. schs. com. Princeton U., 1980—; chmn. Harvard Bus. Sch. Fund of N.Y., 1964-65; mem. nat. fin. com. Pete DuPont for Pres., 1986-88; trustee Waterford Inst., 1985—. Served to lt. (j.g.) USN, 1957-60. Clubs: Stanwich (Greenwich, Conn.), Princeton Club of N.Y. (scholarship com. 1970—, bd. govs. 1989-96), Coral Beach and Tennis (Bermuda). Avocations: flying, golf. Home: 1088 Park Ave New York NY 10128-1132

LEIGHTON, PAUL JOE, lawyer; b. Manhattan, Kans., June 7, 1953; s. Paulson and Deloris (Salero) L.; m. Beverly B. Albright; children: Steven P., David R., Mark W., Michael B. BS, U. Nebr., 1975, JD, 1978; MBA, U. S.D., 1980. Bar: Iowa 1978. Gen. atty. Midwest Energy Co., Sioux City, Iowa, 1978-85, asst. sec., gen. atty., 1985-86, asst. sec., sr. atty., 1986-88, corp. sec., sr. atty., 1988-90; sec., asst. treas. Midwest Resources Inc., Des Moines, 1990-92, sec., asst. treas., mgr. corp. legal svcs., audit and ins., 1992-94; v.p., sec., asst. treas., mgr. corp. legal svcs. Mid America Energy Co. (formerly Midwest Resources Inc.), Des Moines, 1994—; instr. Internat. Right-of-Way Assn., L.A., 1984-85. Solicitor United Way of Siouxland, 1985-86; bd. dirs., treas. Iowa Hist. Found.; mem. Des Moines Contbns. Consortium. Mem. ABA, Iowa Bar Assn., Polk County Bar Assn., Am. Soc. Corp. Secs., Clive C. of C. (bd. dirs., pres.). Republican. Presbyterian. Office: Midwest Resources Inc 666 Grand Ave PO Box 657 Des Moines IA 50303-0657*

LEIGHTON, RICHARD F., dean. BA, Western Md. Coll., 1951; MD, U. Md., 1955. Diplomate Am. Bd. Internal Medicine (Specialty Cardiovascular Disease). Intern U. Hosp., Balt., 1955-56; flight surgeon USN, 1956-58; resident Ohio State U. Hosp., 1959-61, resident, cardiology fellow, 1961-64; from asst. prof. to assoc. prof. medicine Coll. Medicine Ohio State U., 1965-74, dir. coronary care unit, 1968-69, dir. cardiac catheterization labs., 1970-74; prof. medicine, chief cardiology Med. Coll. Ohio, 1974-90, acting chmn. dept. medicine, 1988, vice chmn., 1988-90, v.p. acad. affairs, dean Sch. Medicine, 1990-95, sr. v.p. acad. affairs, dean Sch. Medicine, 1995—. Editl. bd. La Lettre du Cardiologue, 1985—; contbr. numerous articles to profl. jours. Fellow ACP, Am. Coll. Cardiology (gov. Ohio chpt. 1985-88), Am. Heart Assn (coun. circulation, epidemiology, clinical cardiology, coun. rep. Ohio 1977-80), Royal Soc. Medicine; mem. Ctrl. Soc. Clin. Rsch., Societe Francaise Cardiologies (corr.), Alpha Omega Alpha. Office: Med Coll Ohio Off Dean Sch Med Toledo OH 43699

LEIGHTON, ROBERT, film editor. Editor: (films) Delusion, 1981, (with Peter Thornton) Kill and Kill Again, 1981, Blood Tide, 1982, The House Where Death Lives, 1982, The Being, 1983, (with Mark Goldblatt) Wavelength, 1983, This Is Spinal Tap, 1984, The Sure Thing, 1985, Stand By Me, 1986, The Princess Bride, 1987, (with Adam Weiss) Bull Durham, 1988, When Harry Met Sally..., 1989, Blaze, 1989, Misery, 1990, (with Richard Chew) Late for Dinner, 1991, A Few Good Men, 1992, Life With Mikey, 1993, North, 1994, The American President, 1995. Office: care Motion Picture Editors 7715 W Sunset Blvd Ste 220 Los Angeles CA 90046-3912

LEIJONHUFVUD, AXEL STIG BENGT, economics educator; b. Stockholm, Sweden, Sept. 6, 1933; came to U.S., 1960; s. Erik Gabriel and Helene Adelheid (Neovius) L.; m. Marta Elisabeth Ising, June 10, 1955 (div. 1977); m. Earlene Joyce Craver, June 18, 1977; children—Carl Axel, Gabriella Helene, Christina Elisabeth. Fil. kand., U. Lund, Sweden, 1960; M.A., U. Pitts., Pa., 1961; Ph.D., Northwestern U., 1967; Fil. Dr. (hon.), U. Lund, Sweden, 1983; Dr. (hon.), U. Nice, Sophia-Antipolis, France, 1995. Acting asst. prof. econs. UCLA, 1964-67, assoc. prof. econs., 1967-71, prof. econs., 1971—, chair dept. econs., 1980-83, 90-92; dir. Ctr. for Computable Econs., 1992—; prof. monetary theory and policy U. Trento, Italy, 1995—; co-dir. summer workshops Siena Internat. Sch. Econ. Rsch., 1987-91; participant numerous profl. confs.; cons., lectr., vis. prof. econs. various colls. and univs.; cons. Republic of Tatarstan, 1994. Author: On Keynesian Economics and the Economics of Keynes: A Study in Monetary Theory, 1968, Keynes and the Classics: Two Lectures, 1969, Information and Coordination: Essays in Macroeconomic Theory, 1981, (with D. Heymann) High Inflation, 1995. Mem. econ. expert com. of pres. Kazakhstan, 1991-92. Brookings Instn. fellow, 1963-64; Marshall lectr. Cambridge U., Eng., 1974; Overseas fellow Churchill Coll., Cambridge, 1974; Inst. Advanced Study fellow, 1983-84. Mem. Am. Econ. Assn., Western Econ. Assn., History of Econs. Soc. Office: UCLA Dept Econs Los Angeles CA 90024

LEIKAM, DALE FRANCIS, agronomist; b. Hays, Kans., Dec. 28, 1951; s. Robert and Louise (Gross) L.; m. Patricia D. Gilmore, July 14, 1973; children Michelle, Marianne, Melissa. BS in Argl. Edn., Kans. State U., 1973, MS in Agronomy, 1977, PhD in Agronomy, 1980. Cert. profl. agronomist, profl. soil scientist, profl. crop scientist; cert. crop adviser, Kans., Mo. Agriculturist Nat. Fertilizer Devel. Ctr. TVA, Muscle Shoals, Ala., 1980-81; area dir. TVA, Urbana, Ill., 1981-82; agronomist agri-prodn. svcs. dept. CENEX, St. Paul, 1982-84; agronomist tech. svcs. dept. Farmland Industries, Inc., Kansas City, Mo., 1984—; numerous invited lectures; presenter in field to seminars, symposia, assns., and confs.; bd. dirs. Kans. Fertilizer and Chem. Inst., 1985-88; bd. dirs. Kans. Agrl. Edn. Found., 1988—, mem. sci. rev. bd., 1990—; mem. planning com. Gt. Plains Soil Fertility Workshop, 1984-92, chmn.-elect, 1992, chmn., 1994; mem. exam. and fin. coms. Kans. Cert. Crop Advisor Bd., 1992—, chmn. continuing edn., 1993—; mem. Nat. Cert. Crop Advisor Coord. Coun., 1993; past proposal reviewer Kans. Fertilizer Rsch. Fund. Contbr. numerous articles to profl. jours. and popular publs. Mem. Am. Soc. Agronomy (reviewer, presenter, Werner L. Nelson award for diagnosis of yield limiting factors 1993), Soil Sci. Soc. Am. (reviewer), Kans. Fertilizer and Chem. Assn. (bd. dirs. 1985—, dealer edn. com., pub. edn. com., program planning com., awards com., scholarship com., expn. planning com., conservation plan for pesticides and wildlife task force, agrl. speakers bur.), Gamma Sigma Delta, Alpha Tau Alpha. Avocations: fishing, hunting, camping. Home: 159 S Dartmouth Dr Manhattan KS 66502-3023 Office: Farmland Industries Inc PO Box 7305 Kansas City MO 64116-0005

LEIKEN, EARL MURRAY, lawyer; b. Cleve., Jan. 19, 1942; s. Manny and Betty G. L.; m. Ellen Kay Miner, Mar. 26, 1970; children: Jonathan, Brian. BA magna cum laude, Harvard U., 1964, JD cum laude, 1967. Asst. dean, assoc. prof. law Case Western Res. U., Cleve., 1967-71; ptnr. Hahn, Loeser, Freedheim, Dean & Wellman, Cleve., 1971-86, Baker & Hostetler, Cleve., 1986—; adj. faculty, lectr. law Case Western Res. U., 1971-86. Pres. Shaker Heights (Ohio) Bd. Edn., 1986-88, Jewish Community Ctr., Cleve., 1988-91, Shaker Heights Family Ctr., 1994—. Named one of Greater Cleve.'s 10 Outstanding Young Leaders, Cleve. Jaycees, 1972; recipient Kane award Cleve. Jewish Community Fedn., 1982. Mem. ABA, Greater Cleve. Bar Assn. (chmn. labor law sect. 1978). Home: 20815 Colby Rd Cleveland OH 44122-1903 Office: Baker & Hostetler 3200 Nat City Ctr 1900 E 9th St Cleveland OH 44114-3401

LEIMKUHLER, FERDINAND FRANCIS, industrial engineering educator; b. Balt., Dec. 31, 1928; s. Ferdinand Frank and Louise (Kimmel) L.; m. Natalie Therese Morin, July 4, 1956; children: Kristin, Margaret, Jeanne, Benedict, Thomas, Ernest. B.S. cum laude, Loyola Coll., Balt., 1950; B.Engring., Johns Hopkins U., 1952, D.Engring. with distinction, 1962. Mgmt. engr. E.I. DuPont de Nemours & Co., Inc., 1950-57; research engr. Johns Hopkins U., 1957-61; prof. indsl. engring. Purdue U., 1961—, head Sch. Indsl. Engring., 1969-74, 81-93, dir. tech. assistance program, 1993-96; vis. prof. U. Calif., Berkeley, 1968-69, 90; vis. prof. (Fulbright-Hayes sr. lectr.), U. Ljubljana, Slovenia, 1974-75; cons. in field. Served with AUS, 1952-54. Fellow Inst. Indsl. Engrs.; mem. Ops. Rsch. Soc. Am., Inst. Mgmt. Scis., Am. Soc. Engring. Edn., Sigma Xi, Alpha Sigma Nu, Tau Beta Pi. Office: Dept Indsl Engring Purdue U West Lafayette IN 47907-1286

LEIN, MALCOLM EMIL, architect; b. Havre, Mont., July 19, 1913; s. Emil A. and Ruth (Fredeen) L.; m. Miriam Balliet Bend, Apr. 13, 1939; children: Eric Manning, Kristin Anker, R. Kurt Harrison. Student, U. Wis., 1930; BArch, U. Minn., 1936; student, U.S. Army C.I. Sch., 1943, Command & Gen. Staff Sch., U.S. Army, 1943, Nat. War Coll., 1963. Asst. head constrn. dept. F.W. Woolworth Co., Dist. Office, Mpls., 1936-41; pvt. practice architecture and design St. Paul, 1946—; instr. Macalester Coll., St. Paul, 1947-50; dir. Minn. Mus. of Art, St. Paul, 1947-77, pres., 1973-79; pres., founder Design Cons., Inc., St. Paul, 1949—, Mid-West Credit Corp., St. Paul, 1959—, Desconi Corp.; founder, dir. Gallery St. Paul, The Commodore, St. Paul, 1981-85; founder, pres. Madeline Island Art Ctr., La Pointe, Wis., 1991—. Trustee, founder Benlei Found., Scottsdale, Ariz., 1988—; bd. dirs. Phoenix Chamber Music Soc. Col. C.E., AUS, 1935-66, WWII CBI. Mem. Am. Assn. Mus., Am. Fedn. Art, Archives Am. Art, Res. Officers Assn., Air Force Assn., Japan Am. Soc. Minn. (v.p. bd. dirs.), Smithsonian Assocs., Phoenix Art Mus., Asian Art Coun. of Mpls. Art Inst., Planned Parenthood of Cen. & No. Ariz. (chmn. endowment and planned giving com.). Club: University (St. Paul). Home: 6200 E Hummingbird Ln Paradise Vly AZ 85253-3651 Office: 361 Summit Ave Saint Paul MN 55102-2168 *Goals: Find challenging creative work without sacrificing principles. Acknowledge the help and guidance from so many and do as much for others. Appreciate beauty. Live in harmony with nature, God and neighbors. Learn throughout life, Keep an open mind. Acquire wisdom. Remain a free spirit. And "be prepared" to live forever or die tomorrow.*

LEINBACH, PHILIP EATON, librarian; b. Winston-Salem, N.C., Sept. 17, 1935; s. Gray Newton and Martha Elizabeth (Eaton) L.; m. Nancy Lee Yocom, July 27, 1957; children—Jonathan Eaton, David Timothy. A.B., Duke U., 1956; M.A. in History, Ind. U., 1963, M.L.S., 1964. Adminstrv. asst. Harvard U. Library, Cambridge, Mass., 1964-66; asst. librarian for acquisitions Harvard U., Cambridge, 1966-67, specialist in book selection, 1967-71, asst. univ. librarian, 1972-82; univ. librarian Tulane U., New Orleans, 1982—; acting chief libr. Harvard U. Div. Sch., Cambridge, 1978-79; dep. libr. Queen Mary Coll., London, 1970-71. Author: Handbook for Librarians, 1977, Personnel Administration in an Automated Environment, 1990. Served with USNR, 1957-61. Fellow Ind. U., 1963-64; UCLA Grad. Sch. Library and Info. Sci., 1982; NDEA modern lang. fellow, 1962-63. Mem. ALA (council 1984-88), La. Library Assn., Omicron Delta Kappa, Beta Phi Mu, Pi Sigma Alpha. Home: 7530 Saint Charles Ave New Orleans LA 70118-3878 Office: Tulane U Howard-Tilton Memorial Library New Orleans LA 70118-5682

LEINEN, MARGARET SANDRA, oceanographic researcher; b. Chgo., Sept. 20, 1946; d. Earl John and Ester (Louis) Leinen; m. Denzel Earl Gleason, 1984; 1 child, Daniel Glenn Whaley. BS, U. Ill., 1969; MS, Oreg. State U., 1975; PhD, U. R.I., Kingston, 1980. Marine scientist U. R.I., Kingston, 1980-82, asst. rsch. prof., 1982-86, assoc. prof., 1986-88, prof., 1988—, assoc. dean, 1988-92, dean and vice provost, 1992—. Office: U RI Grad Sch Oceanography Narragansett RI 02882-1197

LEINENWEBER, HARRY D., federal judge; b. Joliet, Ill., June 3, 1937; s. Harry Dean and Emily (Lennon) L.; m. Lynn Morley Martin, Jan. 7, 1987; 5 children; 2 stepchildren. AB cum laude, U. Notre Dame, 1959; JD, U. Chgo., 1962. Bar: Ill. 1962, U.S. Dist. Ct. (no. dist.) Ill. 1967. Assoc. Dunn, Stefanich, McGarry & Kennedy, Joliet, Ill., 1962-65, ptnr., 1965-79; city atty. City of Joliet, 1963-67; spl. counsel Village of Park Forest, Ill., 1967-74; spl. prosecutor County of Will, Ill., 1968-70; spl. counsel Village of Bolingbrook, Ill., 1975-77, Will County Forest Preserve, 1977; mem. Ill. Ho. of Reps., Springfield, 1973-83, chmn. judiciary I com., 1981-83; ptnr. Dunn, Leinenweber & Dunn, Joliet, 1979-86; fed. judge U.S. Dist. Ct. (no. dist.) Ill., Chgo., 1986—; bd. dirs. Will County Bar Assn., 1984-86, State Jud. Adv. Coun., 1973-85, sec. 1975-76. Bd. dirs. Will County Legal Assistance Found., 1982-86, Good Shepard Manor, 1981—, Am. Cancer Soc., 1981-85, Joliet (Ill.) Montessori Sch., 1966-74; del. Rep. Nat. Conv., 1980; precinct committeeman, 1966-86. Recipient Environ. Legislator Golden award. Mem. Will County Bar Assn. (mem. jud. adv. coun., 1973-85, sec. 1975-76, bd. dirs. 1984-86), Nat. Conf. Commrs. on Uniform State Laws (exec. com. 1991-93). Roman Catholic. Office: US Dist Ct 219 S Dearborn St Rm 1946 Chicago IL 60604-1706

LEINIEKS, VALDIS, classicist, educator; b. Liepaja, Latvia, Apr. 15, 1932; came to U.S., 1949, naturalized, 1954; s. Arvid Ansis and Valia Leontine (Brunaus) L. BA, Cornell U., 1955, MA, 1956; PhD, Princeton U., 1962. Instr. classics Cornell Coll., Mount Vernon, Iowa, 1959-62, asst. prof. classics, 1962-64; assoc. prof. classics Ohio State U., 1964-66; assoc. prof. classics U. Nebr., Lincoln, 1966-71, prof. classics, 1971—, chmn. dept. classics, 1967-95, chmn. program comparative lit., 1970-86, interim chmn. dept. modern langs., 1982-83. Author: Morphosyntax of the Homeric Greek Verb, 1964; The Structure of Latin, 1975; Index Nepotianus, 1976; The Plays of Sophokles, 1982. Contbr. articles to profl. jours. Mem. AAUP, Am. Classical League, Classical Assn. Middle West and South, Am. Philol. Assn. Republican. Home: 2505 A St Lincoln NE 68502-1841 Office: U Nebr Dept Classics Lincoln NE 68588-0337

LEININGER, MADELEINE MONICA, nurse, anthropologist, administrator, consultant, editor; b. Sutton, Nebr., July 13, 1925; d. George M. S. and Irene (Sheedy) L. BS in Biology, Scholastic Coll., 1950, LHD, 1976; MS in Nursing, Cath. U. Am., 1953; PhD in Anthropology, U. Wash., 1965; DSc (hon., U. Indpls., 1990; PhDN (hon.), Ind. State U., 1990, U. Kuopio, Finland, 1991. RN; cert. transcultural nurse. Instr., mem. staff, head nurse med.-surg. unit, supr. psychiat. unit St. Joseph's Hosp., Omaha, 1950-54; assoc. prof. nursing, dir. grad. program in psychiat. nursing U. Cin. Coll. Nursing, 1954-60; research fellow Nat. League Nursing, Eastern Highlands of New Guinea, 1960-62, 78, 92; research assoc. U. Wash. Dept. Anthropology, Seattle, 1964-65; prof. nursing and anthropology, dir. nurse-scientist PhD program U. Colo., Boulder and Denver, 1966-69; dean sch. nursing, prof. nursing, lectr. anthropology U. Wash., Seattle, 1969-74; dean coll. nursing, prof. nursing and anthropology U. Utah, Salt Lake City, 1974-80; Anise J. Sorell prof. nursing Troy (Ala.) State U., 1981; prof. nursing, adj. prof. anthropology, dir. Ctr. for Health Research, dir. transcultural nursing offerings Wayne State U., Detroit, 1981-95, prof. emeritus, 1995—; adj. prof. anthropology U. Utah, 1974-81; disting. vis. prof. at 75 univs., U.S. and overseas, 1970—; cons. Saudi Arabia, Brazil, Europe, Japan, Thailand, Indonesia, Australia, South Africa, Finland, Sweden, The Netherlands, New Guinea, Australia, Jordan, Iran, Africa, 58 health instn.'s in U.S. Author: 28 books including Nursing and Anthropology: Two Worlds to Blend, 1970, Contemporary Issues in Mental Health Nursing, 1973, Caring: An Essential Human Need, 1981, Reference Sources for Transcultural Health and Nursing, 1984, Basic Psychiatric Concepts in Nursing, 1960, Care: The Essence of Nursing and Health, 1984, Qualitative Research Methods in Nursing, 1985, Care: Discovery and Clinical-Community Uses, 1988, Ethical and Moral Dimensions of Caring, 1990, Culture Care, Diversity and Universality: A Theory of Nursing, 1991, Care: The Compassionate Healer, 1991, Caring Imperative for Nursing Education, 1991, Transcultural Nursing, 1995; editor Jour. of Transcultural Nursing, 1989—; mem. editl. bd. 10 nat. and internat. jours.; editor or contbr. over 200 articles to profl. jours., 47 chpts. to books; lectr. in field. Disting. vis. scholar at 80 univs., U.S. and overseas; recipient Outstanding Alumni award Cath. U. Am., 1969, Recognition award Am. Assn. Colls. of Nursing, 1976, Nurse of Yr. award Dist. 1 Utah Nurses Assn., 1976, Lit. award Utah Nurses Assn., 1978, Trotter Disting. Pub. Lectr. award U. Tex., 1985, Disting. Faculty Tchg. Recognition award Wayne State U., 1985, Outstanding Faculty Rsch. scholar award Wayne State U. and Gerontology Inst., 1985, Gershenson Rsch. award Wayne State U., 1985, Pace Inst. Rsch. award, 1992, Hewlett Packard Rsch. award, 1992, award for Acad. Excellence AAUW-Detroit, 1986, Disting. award Bd. Govs., 1987, Pres. Excellence in Tchg. award, 1988, Women of Sci. award U. Calif. at Fullerton, 1990, Outstanding Univ. Grad. Mentor award Wayne State U., 1995, Nightingale Rsch. award Oakland U., 1995, outstanding nursing leader Russell Sage Coll, Sigma Theta Tau Intl. Disting. scholar award Russell Sage Coll., 1995. Fellow ANA, Am. Anthropol. Soc. for Applied Anthropology (exec. com. 1980-84), Am. Acad. Nursing; mem. Am. Assn. Humanities, Am. Applied Anthropol. Soc., Mich. Nurses Assn. (Bertha Culp Human Rights award 1994), Ctrl. States Anthropology, Amnesty Internat., Transcultural Nursing Soc. (founder, bd. dirs., pres. 1974-80), Cultural Cmty. Group Assn. (ethics, humanities heritage study group), Nat. Rsch. Care Confs. (leader human care rsch.), Internat. Assn. Human Caring (founder, pres., bd. dirs.), Nordic Caring Soc. Sweden (hon.), Sigma Xi, Pi Gamma Mu, Sigma Theta Tau (Lectr. of Yr. 1987—), Delta Kappa Gamma, Alpha Tau Delta. Office: 11211 Woolworth Plz Omaha NE 68144

LEIPER, ROBERT DUNCAN, protective services official; b. Houston, July 22, 1953; s. William Harper Leiper and Frances Ann (Wright) Freeman; m. Glynna Dell Wilson, May 18, 1985; children: Kelsey Allison, Chad Wilson. AAS in Fire Protection, San Jacinto Coll., 1983; BA in Pub. Mgmt., U. Houston, 1988. Master fire fighter, Tex. Lt. Spring Br. Fire Dept., Houston, 1973-75; asst. svc. mgr. Archer Motor Sales, Houston, 1975-77; fire fighter Baytown (Tex.) Fire & Rescue, 1977-80, driver, 1980-83, lt., 1983-88, capt., 1988-92, fire chief, 1992—; instr. Tex. A & M U., College Station, 1988-92, Lamar U., Beaumont, Tex., 1990-92. Chmn. bd. Baycoast Med. Ctr., Baytown, Tex., 1994-95. Named Exec. Fire Officer, Nat. Fire Acad.; recipient Fire Fighter of Yr. award VFW, 1987, 90. Mem. Nat. Fire Protection Assn., Baytown Profl. Fire Fighters (v.p. 1982), Hispanic C. of C., Baytown C. of C., Kiwanis Club (pres. 1994, Rookie of Yr. award 1989). Avocations: wood working, camping, photography. Office: Baytown Fire and Rescue Svcs 201 Wye Dr Baytown TX 77521-4121

LEIPPER, DALE FREDERICK, physical oceanographer, educator; b. Salem, Ohio, Sept. 8, 1914; s. Robert and Myrtle (Cost) L.; m. Virginia Alma Harrison, May 14, 1942; children: Diane Louise, Janet Elizabeth, Bryan Robert, Anita Dale. BS in Edn., Wittenberg Coll., 1937, DSc (hon.), 1968; MA, Ohio State U., 1939; postgrad., UCLA, 1939-40; Ph.D., Scripps Instn. Oceanography, 1950. Tchr. city schs. San Diego, 1940-41; research oceanographer, tchr. Scripps Instn. Oceanography, U. Calif., 1945-49; mem. faculty dept. oceanography and meteorology Tex. A&M U., 1949-68, head dept., 1949-64, prof., 1964-68; prof., chmn. dept. oceanography Naval Postgrad. Sch., 1968-79; supr. rsch. program NSF, Internat. Geophys. Year, Office Naval Rsch.; mem. tech. panel oceanography, exec. vice chmn. meteorology panel U.S. Nat. Com. Internat. Geophys. Year; chmn. com. marine scis. Soc. Regional Edn. Bd., 1952-56; assoc. dir. Tex. A&M Rsch. Found., 1953-54. Contbr. articles on West Coast fog, oceanography, hurricane-ocean interaction, ocean currents to jours. in field. Served as maj. USAAF, 1941-45; weather officer, oceanographer. Mem. Am. Meteorol. Soc., Am. Geophys. Union, Am. Soc. Limnology and Oceanography (pres. 1957-58), Tex. Acad. Sci. (pres. 1955), Nat. Acad. Sci. (panel chmn. 1959-64), Marine Tech. Soc., Am. Soc. Oceanography (pres. 1967-68), U. Corp. for Atmospheric Rsch. (founding mem., bd. dirs.), The Oceanography Soc., Sigma Xi, Phi Kappa Phi. Club: Rotary (pres. Bryan, Tex. 1965-66). Home and Office: 716 Terra Ct Reno NV 89506-9606

LEIPZIG, ARTHUR, photographer, educator emeritus; b. Bklyn., Oct. 25, 1918; s. Julius M. and Esther Pearl (Rubin) L.; m. Mildred Levin, Mar. 21, 1942; children: Joel Myron, Judith Anne. Student, Photo League, 1942-43, Paul Strand Photo Workshop, 1946. Staff photographer PM newspaper, N.Y.C., 1942-46, Internat. News Photos, N.Y.C., 1946; freelance photographer East Meadow, N.Y., 1946—; prof. art, dir. photography C.W. Post Sch. of Arts, L.I. U., Greenvale, N.Y., 1968—. Contbr. photographs to Fortune, Look, Parade, Life, Natural History, Sunday Times, also indsl. mags.; guest editor Infinity Mag., N.Y.C., 1970, mem. editorial bd., 1973-75; interview and photographs included Life Documentary Photo Book, N.Y.C., 1972, 83; exhibited works Mus. Modern Art, 1946-51, 55-58, Met. Mus. Art, 1961, 62, Nassau Mus. Art, 1975, Queens Mus. Art, 1982, Transco Gallery, Houston, 1985, Daniel Wolf Gallery, N.Y.C., Houston Foto Fest, 1986, Photo Find Gallery, Woodstock, Coll. Art Gallery, New Paltz, N.Y., Smithsonian Mus., Washington, 1987, Mus. of the City of N.Y., Children's Games, 1988, Photofind Gallery, N.Y.C., 1990 Salena Gallery, Bklyn., JCP, 1992; one-man shows include Midtown Y Gallery, 1978, Henry St. Settlement, Arts for Living Ctr., 1986, Frumkin Adams Gallery, N.Y.C., 1990, 92, Photofind Gallery, 1990, Howard Greenberg Gallery, 1991, Salena Gallery, Bklyn., 1992, Port Washington Libr., 1994, Mus. of the City of N.Y., 1995, 96; represented in permanent collections Mus. Modern Art, Bklyn. Mus., Eastman House, Nat. Gallery Art, Nassau Mus. Art, Houston Mus. Fine Arts, Midtown Y Gallery, Visual Studies Workshop, Pablo Casals Mus., Internat. Ctr. Photography, Nat. Mus. Am. Art, Washington, Consol. Freightways, San Francisco, Bank of Am. Art Program, San Francisco, Bibliotheque Nationale, Paris, The Jewish Mus., N.Y.C., Mus. Folkwang, Essen, Germany, The Nat. Portrait Gallery, Washington, The Gilman Paper Co., Queens Coll., N.Y., Dreyfus, N.Y.C.; retrospective exhbn. Hillwood Gallery, Brookville, N.Y., 1989, Musée De La Civilisation, Quebec City, 1990; featured on World of Photography, Sta. WABC-TV; pub. Classic Photographs from the Brooklyn Museum Collection, 1987, Sarah's Daughters, 1988, Master Photographs Photography in Fine Arts Exhbt. Internat. Ctr. Photography, 1988, 92, The Nat. Portrait Gallery, 1992, High Mus., Altlanta, 1992, Growing up in N.Y., 1995. Adv. bd. Midtown Y Gallery, 1983; bd. dirs. Nassau Mus. Fine Art, 1973-75. Recipient Nat. Urban League award, 1962, ORT award, 1976, Nassau County Office Cultural Devel. award, 1982, David Newton Excellence in Teaching award, 1989, Award for Scholarly Achievement, L.I. U. Trustees, 1983, 89. Mem. Am. Soc. Mag. Photographers (bd. govs., trustee 1960-65, treas. 1965). Office: LI Univ CW Post Coll Art Dept Northern Blvd Greenvale NY 11548-1207 *For me, the most important thing is loving what I do. I love photography and I love to teach photography. Both photography and teaching came into my life by chance. My success in both areas is due to may passion for my work.*

LEIS, HENRY PATRICK, JR., surgeon, educator; b. Saranac Lake, N.Y., Aug. 12, 1914; s. Henry P. and Mary A. (Disco) L.; m. Winogene Barnette, Jan. 8, 1944; children: Henry Patrick III, Thomas Frederick. BS cum laude, Fordham U., 1936; MD, N.Y. Med. Coll., 1941. Diplomate Am. Bd. Surgery. Intern Flower and Fifth Ave Hosps., N.Y.C., 1941-42, resident, 1943-44, 46-49, attending surgeon, chief breast service, 1960-81; resident in surgery Kanawa Valley Hosp., Charleston, W.Va., 1942-43; attending surgeon, chief breast service Met. Hosp., N.Y.C., 1960-81, emeritus chief breast service, 1982—; attending surgeon Coler Meml. Hosp., N.Y.C., 1960-76; chief breast surgery Cabrini Hosp. Med. Ctr., 1978-85, cons. breast surgery, 1985—; emeritus surgeon Lenox Hill Hosp.,, N.Y.C., 1980-83, hon. surg. staff, 1984—; hon. surg. staff Drs. Hosp., N.Y.C., Grand Strand Gen. Hosp., Myrtle Beach, S.C., 1985—; liason officer Am. Coll. Surgeons Commn. on Cancer; attending surgeon Westchester County Med. Ctr., 1977-81, emeritus surgeon, 1982—; clin. prof. surgery U. S.C. Sch. Medicine, Breast Surg. Oncology, Columbia, 1985—; hon. dir. breast cancer ctr., cons. in breast surgery Winthrop Univ. Hosp., Mineola, 1971—; cons. in breast surgery VA Hosp., Columbia, S.C., 1985—; cons. in breast surgery St. Claires Hosp., N.Y.C., 1979; attending surg. staff Richland Meml. Hosp., Columbia, 1986-90; clin. prof. surgery, 1960-81, prof. emeritus, 1982—, co-dir. Inst. Breast Diseases, 1978-82, emeritus, 1982—, chief breast svc. N.Y. Med. Coll., 1960-81, emeritus, 1982—; cons. in breast surgery SUNY Div. Rehab., 1965—, Med. and Surg. Specialists Plan N.Y.; mem. Am. Joint Com. on Breast Cancer Staging and End Results; v.p. N.Y. Met. Breast Cancer Group, 1975-76, pres., 1977-79; cons. Med. Advs. Selective Svc. System, N.Y.C. Alumni trustee N.Y. Med. Coll., 1971-76; adv. coun. Fordham Coll. Pharmacy, 1968; bd. dirs. Hall Fame and Mus. Surg. History and Related Scis. Author: Diagnosis and Treatment of Breast Lesions: The Breast, 1970, Management of Breast Lesions, 1978, Breast Cancer: Conservative and Reconstructive Surgery, 1989, Breast Lesions: Diagnosis and Treatment, 1988; co-editor: Breast; hon. editor Internat. Surgery Jour.; mem. editorial bd. jour. Senolgia, 1982—, Breast: An Internat. Jour.; contbr. articles to profl. jours. Mem. Women's Cancer Task Force of S.C. Capt. M.C., AUS, 1944-46, PTO. Decorated knight Grand Cross Equestrian Order Holy Sepulchre Jerusalem, knight Mil., Order of Malta, Knight Noble Co. of the Rose; recipient award of Merit Am. Cancer Soc., 1969, 87, cert. and award for outstanding and devoted services to indigent sick City N.Y., 1965, Dr. George Hohman Meml. medal, 1936, N.Y. Apothecaries medal, 1936, Internat. cert. merit for disting. service to surgery, 1970, award of merit N.Y. Met. Breast Cancer Group, 1976, medal of Ambrogino (Italy), 1977, Service award of Honor N.Y. Med. Coll., 1969, medaille d'Honneur (France), medal of City of Paris, 1979. Fellow ACS (cancer liaison physician Surgeons commn. on Cancer 1987—, Peruvian Acad. Surgery (hon.), Am. Acad. Compensation Medicine, Am. Soc. Clin. Oncology, Am. Assn. Cancer Rsch., Am. Geriatrics Soc., Indsl. Med. Assn., Internat. Coll. Surgeons (1st v.p. 1973-74, pres. 1977-78, v.p., chmn. coun. examiners U.S. sect. 1962-68, pres. 1971, Svc. award of honor 1971), Internat. Paleopathology Assn. (founder), N.Y. Acad. Medicine, N.Y. Coun. Surgeons, Royal Soc. Health (Eng.); mem. AMA, AAAS, AAUP, Am. Cancer Soc. (com. breast cancer),

Am. Med. Writers Assn., Am. Profl. Practice Assn., Assn. Am. Med. Colls., Am. Coll. Radiology (com. mammography and breast cancer), Assn. Mil. Surgeons U.S., Cath. Physicians Guild (pres. N.Y. 1970-78), Gerontol. Soc., Internat. Platform Assn., N.Y. Cancer Soc., N.Y. County Med. Soc., N.Y. Surg. Soc., Pan Am Med. Assn. (v.p. N.Am. sect. on cancer 1967—), Pan Pacific Surg. Assn. (v.p. 1980, Res. Officers Assn. U.S., Soc. Acad. Achievement (editorial bd. 1969—), Nat. Consum Breast Ctrs. (bd. dris. 1991—), Soc. Med. Jurisprudence, Soc. Nuclear Medicine Surg. Soc. N.Y. Med. Coll., WHO, World Med. Assn., Alumni Assn. N.Y. Med. Coll. (gov. 1960—, pres. 1971), Assn. Mil. Surgeons U.S., Catholic War Vets Assn., VFW, Hollywood Acad. Medicine (hon.), Alpha Omega Alpha, Phi Chi; hon. mem. Argentine Soc. Mammary Pathology, Argentina Cardiac and Thoracic Surg. Soc., Ecuador Med. Assn., Mo. Surg. Soc., Venezuela Surg. Soc., Italian Surg. Soc., S.C. Oncology Soc., So. Med. Assn. Club: Ocean Dunes, Surf. Lodge: K.C. (4th deg.).

LEISER, BURTON MYRON, philosophy and law educator; b. Denver, Dec. 12, 1930; s. Nathan and Eva Mae (Newman) L.; m. Janet A. Johnson, Aug. 12, 1984; children: Shoshana, Illana, Phillip, stepdaughter Sheri Johnson. BA, U. Chgo., 1951; MHL, Yeshiva U., 1956; PhD, Brown U., 1968; JD, Drake U., 1981. Bar: Iowa 1982, N.Y. 1985, U.S. Dist. Ct. (so. dist.) N.Y. 1986, U.S. Supreme Ct. 1986. Instr. Fort Lewis Coll., Durango, Colo., 1963-65; asst. prof. SUNY, Buffalo, 1965-68, assoc. prof., 1968-70; assoc. prof. Sir George Williams U., Montreal, Can., 1969-72; prof., chmn. Drake U., Des Moines, 1972-83; E.J. Mortola prof. philosophy, adj. prof. law Pace U., N.Y.C., 1983-88, disting. prof. philosophy, 1988—; del. UN for Am. Profs. for Peace in the Middle East, 1988-91. Author: Custom, Law and Morality, 1969, Values in Conflict, 1981, Liberty, Justice and Morals, 1986. Chmn. bd. trustees Congregation Bet Am Shalom, White Plains, N.Y., 1990-92; chmn. regional bd. Anti-Defamation League, Westchester-Putnam-Rockland Counties, 1995—. Brown U. fellow 1959-62, NYU fellow 1955-57; grantee NEH, Exxon Ednl. Found. Mem. Am. Profs. for Peace in the Middle East (nat. sec. 1983-89), Am. Soc. Value Inquiry (pres. 1978-80). Republican. Jewish. Avocations: bird watching, music. Office: Pace Univ Philosophy Dept Briarcliff Manor NY 10510 *If God hadn't wanted us to stick our necks out, he wouldn't have given us necks.*

LEISER, ERNEST STERN, journalist; b. Phila., Feb. 26, 1921; s. Monroe Felsenthal and Gertrude (Stern) L.; m. Caroline Thomas Camp, Oct. 26, 1946; children: Nancy, Shelley, Nicholas. AB, U. Chgo., 1941. Reporter City News Bur. Chgo., 1941; asst. picture editor Chgo. Herald-Am., 1941-42, 46; corr. Overseas News Agy., 1947-52; successively corr., producer, dir. TV news, exec. producer CBS News, N.Y.C., 1953-72; sr. producer, producer bicentennial coverage, spl. reports CBS News, 1975-79, v.p. spl. events and polit. coverage, 1979-81, v.p., dep. dir. news, 1981-85; exec. producer ABC News, N.Y.C., 1972-75; sr. fellow Gannett Ctr. for Media Studies, 1987-88. Author: This is Germany, 1950; contbr. articles to mags. Served with AUS, 1942-46. Decorated Bronze Star, Croix de Guerre; recipient Sigma Delta Chi award for TV reporting, 1956, Peabody awards for TV reporting and producing, 1956, 77, Ohio State awards, 1969, 77, Nat. Acad. TV Arts and Scis. award, 1968-71. Home: 15 College Ave Nyack NY 10960

LEISH, KENNETH WILLIAM, publishing company executive; b. Cambridge, Mass., Dec. 31, 1936; s. Frank and Lillian (Kargir) L.; m. Barbara Lynn Ackerman, Nov. 27, 1966; children: Matthew, Emily, Adam. A.B. magna cum laude, Harvard U., 1958; M.S. in Journalism, Columbia U., 1959. Interviewer Oral History Office, Columbia, 1960; free lance drama reviewer Variety, 1961-66; editor Am. Heritage Pub. Co., Inc., N.Y.C., 1961-69; v.p., gen. mgr. book div. Am. Heritage Pub. Co., Inc., 1971-77; editor-in-chief Am. Heritage Press, 1970-71; mgr. large-format paperbacks Bantam Books Inc., N.Y.C., 1977-81; editor-in-chief Grolier Inc. Project Editorial Group, 1981-87; v.p., dir. product devel. Grolier Internat., Inc., Danbury, Conn., 1988-91; v.p. new product devel. Grolier Inc., Danbury, Conn., 1992—. Author: The White House, 1972, A History of the Cinema, 1974. Served with AUS, 1959-60. Home: 3 Vermont Ave White Plains NY 10606-3507 Office: Grolier Inc Sherman Turnpike PO Box 1788 Danbury CT 06816-1788

LEISHMAN, HELEN TERESA, elementary school educator; b. Jersey City, July 16, 1965; d. Donald B. and Barbara A. (Kopilok) L. BS in Math. and Sci. Edn., West Ga. Coll., 1988; MEd in Math. and Social Studies Edn., Ga. State U., 1992. Cert. mid. sch. tchr., Ga. Math. lab. paraprofl. Gresham Park Elem. Sch. DeKalb County, Atlanta, 1985-86; 5th and 7th grade tchr. Terry Mill Elem. Sch., DeKalb County, 1988-94, grade chairperson, 1989-91, supervising tchr. for student tchrs., 1990-92, mem. exec. com. Future Tchrs., 1990-91, acad. bowl coach, 1990-94, student/tchr. support team, 1990-93; 5th grade tchr. Norcross (Ga.) Elem. Sch., 1994—, grade level mgr., 1995—; curriculum writer Atlanta Com. for the Olympic Games, 1992. Sch. sponsor ARC, Atlanta, 1991-94; mem. Friends of Fernbank, 1994. Gender Equity Mentor Program at Ga. Tech., 1994-95. Mem. Nat. Coun. Tchrs. Math., Ga. Assn. Educators, Ga. Indsl. Fellowship for Tchrs., Chi Omega (Greek Woman of Yr. 1988). Democrat. Roman Catholic. Avocations: tennis, aerobics, travelling, reading, decorating. Home: 3230-320 Mercer Univ Dr Chamblee GA 30341 Office: Norcross Elem Sch 150 Hunt St Norcross GA 30071-3939

LEISSA, ARTHUR WILLIAM, mechanical engineering educator; b. Wilmington, Del., Nov. 16, 1931; s. Arthur Max and Marcella E. (Smith) L.; m. Gertrud E. Achenbach, Apr. 11, 1974; children: Celia Lynn, Bradley Glenn. BME, Ohio State U., 1954, MS, 1954, PhD, 1958. Engr., Sperry Gyroscope Co., Great Neck, N.Y., 1954-55; rsch. assoc. Ohio State U., 1955-56, instr. engring. mechanics, 1956-58, asst. prof., 1958-61, assoc. prof., 1961-64, prof., 1964—; vis. prof. Eidgenossische Technische Hochschule, Zurich, Switzerland, 1972-73, USAF Acad., Colorado Springs, Colo., 1985-86; Plenary lectr. 2nd Internat. Conf. on Recent Advances in Structural Dynamics, Southampton, Eng., 1984, 4th Internat. Conf. on Composite Structures, Paisley, Scotland, 1987, Dynamics and Design Conf., Japan Soc. Mech. Engrs., Kawasaki, 1990, Energy Sources and Tech. Conf., ASME, Houston, 1992; cons. in field. Author: Vibration of Plates, 1969, Vibration of Shells, 1973, Buckling of Laminated Composite Plates and Shell Panels, 1985; assoc. editor Applied Mechanics Revs., 1985-93, editor-in-chief, 1993—; assoc. editor Jour. Vibration and Acoustics, 1990-93; mem. editl. bd. Jour. Sound and Vibration, 1971—, Internat. Jour. Mech. Sci., 1972—, Composite Structures, 1982—, Applied Mechanics Revs., 1988-93, Jour. Vibration and Control, 1994—; contbr. over 150 articles to profl. jours. Performer Columbus Symphony Orch. Operas, 1971-79; gen. chmn. Pan Am. Congress Applied Mechanics, Rio de Janeiro, 1989; leader Ohio State U. Mt. McKinley Expdn., 1978. Recipient Recognition plaque Inst. de Mecanica Applicada, Argentina, 1977, Centennial cert., Am. Soc. Engring. Edn., 1993. Fellow ASME, Am. Acad. Mechanics (pres. 1987-88), Japan Soc. for Promotion Sci.; mem. Am. Soc. for Engring. Edn., Am. Alpine Club. Home: 1294 Fountaine Dr Columbus OH 43221-1520 Office: 155 W Woodruff Ave Columbus OH 43210-1117

LEISURE, GEORGE STANLEY, JR., lawyer; b. N.Y.C., Sept. 16, 1924; s. George S. and Lucille E. (Pelouze) L.; m. Joan Casey, June 22, 1949; children: Constance, Timothy, Matthew, George III. B.A., Yale U., 1948; LL.B., Harvard U., 1951. Bar: N.Y. 1953, U.S. Supreme Ct. 1966. Asst. U.S. atty. So. Dist. N.Y., 1954-56; trial atty. antitrust div. Dept. Justice, N.Y.C., 1956-57; partner firm Donovan Leisure Newton & Irvine, N.Y.C., 1957—; spl. counsel to Gen. William Westmoreland in Westmoreland vs. CBS, 1984-85. Served with USN, 1943-46; served to lt. USNR, 1951-53. Fellow Am. Coll. Trial Lawyers (chmn. N.Y. downstate com. 1975-77); mem. Fed. Bar Council (pres. 1976-78), Assn. Bar City N.Y. (exec. com. 1962-66), Fed. Bar Assn., ABA, N.Y. State Bar Assn., N.Y. County Lawyers Assn. Home: Cottage 467 PO Box 30221 Sea Island GA 31561 Office: Donovan Leisure et al 30 Rockefeller Plz New York NY 10112

LEISURE, PETER KEETON, federal judge; b. N.Y.C., Mar. 21, 1929; s. George S. and Lucille E. (Pelouze) L.; m. Kathleen Blair; Feb. 27, 1960; children: Lucille K. (dec.), Mary Blair, Kathleen K. B.A., Yale U., 1952; LL.B., U. Va., 1958. Bar: N.Y. 1959, U.S. Supreme Ct. 1966, D.C. 1979, U.S. Dist. Ct. Conn. 1981. Assoc. Breed, Abbott & Morgan, 1958-61; asst. U.S. atty. So. Dist. N.Y., 1962-66; partner firm Curtis, Mallet-Prevost, Colt & Mosle, 1967-78; ptnr. Whitman & Ransom, N.Y.C., 1978-84; judge U.S. District Court Southern New York, New York, NY, 1984—. Bd. dirs. Retarded Infants Svcs., 1968-78, pres., 1971-75; bd. dirs. Community Coun. of Greater N.Y., 1972-79, Youth Consultation Svcs., 1971-78; trustee Ch. Club of N.Y., 1973-81, 87-90; mem. jud. ethics com. Jud. Conf., 1990-93, fin disclosure com. Fellow Am. Bar Found., Am. Coll. Trial Lawyers; mem. ABA, Am. Law Inst., Am. Judges Assn., D.C. Bar Assn., Fed. Bar Coun. (trustee, v.p. 1973-78), Assn. Bar. City of N.Y., Nat. Lawyers Club (hon.). Office: US Dist Ct 1910 US Courthouse 500 Pearl St New York NY 10007-1312

LEITCH, VINCENT BARRY, literary studies educator; b. Hempstead, N.Y., Sept. 18, 1944; s. Eugene Vincent and Lucile Jean (Amplo) L.; m. Jill Robin Berman, May 20, 1970 (div. May 1987); children: Kristin M., Rory G. BA, Hofstra U., 1966; MA, Villanova U., 1967; PhD, U. Fla., 1972. Postdoctoral fellow Sch. Criticism and Theory, U. Calif., Irvine, 1978; interim asst. prof. U. Fla., Gainesville, 1972-73; from asst. prof. to prof. English Mercer U., Macon, Ga., 1973-86; prof. English Purdue U., West Lafayette, Ind., 1986—, co-dir. English and philosophy doctoral program, 1986-93; sr. Fulbright lectr. U. Tampere, Finland, 1979; reviewer NEH, 1985-88; bd. dirs. Purdue U. Press, 1988-90; Moss chair of excellence U. Memphis, 1991; mem. adv. bd. Modern Fiction Studies, 1992—, Symploke, 1995—. Author: Deconstructive Criticism, 1983, American Literary Criticism from the 1930s to the 1980s, 1988, Cultural Criticism, Literary Theory, Poststructuralism, 1992, Postmodernism: Local Effects, Global Flows, 1996; mem. editl. bd. lit. and film series Fla. State U. Press, 1983—, Purdue Univ. Press, 1988-90; mem. staff Abstracts of English Studies, 1972-75; mem. editl. bd. South Atlantic Rev., 1985-87. Recipient Outstanding Acad. Book award Assn. Coll. and Rsch. Librs., 1988; Am. Philos. Soc. grantee, 1974; fellow NEH, 1980, Mellon Found., 1981, Am. Coun. Learned Socs., 1985-86, Ctr. for Humanistic Studies, Purdue U., 1989, 96. Mem. MLA (publs. com. 1990-93, assembly del. 1990-92, 93-95, chair organizing com. 1995, chair ad hoc com. on governance issues 1995, mem. 1996, exec. com. lit. criticism divsn. 1994—), Soc. for Critical Exch. (bd. dirs. 1978-83), PEN Am. Ctr., Internat. Assn. for Philosophy and Lit. Office: Purdue U Dept English West Lafayette IN 47907

LEITE, CARLOS ALBERTO, physician, medical educator; b. Rio de Janeiro, Feb. 2, 1939; s. Indayassu and Munira (Raed) L. BSc, Coleg. Ext. Sao Jose, Rio de Janeiro, 1956; MD, U. Brazil, Rio de Janeiro, 1962, PhD, 1972. Intern Rochester (N.Y.) Gen. Hosp., 1963-64; resident Henry Ford Hosp., Detroit, 1964-65; resident, fellow, researcher Jackson Meml. Hosp. and U. Miami, Fla., 1965-68; ltd. practice Nanticoke Meml. Hosp., Seaford, Del., 1968; prof. medicine U. Fed. de Rio de Janeiro, 1972—; emeritus prof. medicine Faculty Medicine Soc. Ens. Sup. Nova Iguacu, Rio de Janeiro, 1986—; dir. Hosp. de Nova Iguacu-Posse, Rio de Janeiro, 1991; instr. medicine Fac. Nac. Med., U. Fed. Rio de Janeiro, 1963-72; chief in-patient ward Santa Casa da Misericordia Hosp., Rio de Janeiro, 1968-72, chief outpatient dept., 1968-76, cons. physician surg. unit, 1969—; chercheur visitant temporaire Inst. Pasteur, Paris, 1988; prof. U. Fed. Rio de Janeiro, Brazil, 1993; prof. medicine Univ. Fed. Fluminense, 1994; expert cons. for EMBRATEL. Med. writer Today's Medicine/Jour. Commerce, 1975—; editor: Metabolic Aspects of 95% Pancreatic Resection, 1971, Medicine, Logique and Reasoning, 1992, Limited Abduction of the Thumb-A New Physical Sign, 1992, Signs and Manoevers in Physical Diagnosis, 1992; editor: Crural Hernias, 1993; contbr. articles to profl. jours. 2d lt. Brazilian Army, 1961-62. Recipient Carlos Chagas medal State of Guanabara, 1972, medal Tiradentes, 1992, Pedro Americo medal, 1993; prize Argentine Meeting of Gastroenterology, 1971. Fellow ACP, Colegio Interamericano de Medicos y Cirurjanos; mem. N.Y. Acad. Scis., Am. Venereal Disease. Brazilian Coll. Surgeons, Clube Monte Libano (counsel mem. 1972—). Home: 70 Rua Redentor Apt 101, Ipanema, 22421-030 Rio de Janeiro Brazil Office: Ste 302, 595 Rua Visconde de Piraja, 22410-003 Rio de Janeiro Brazil

LEITER, ELLIOT, urologist; b. Bklyn., May 24, 1933; s. David and Freda (Pearlman) L.; m. Renee Anita Epstein, June 9, 1963; children: Ariane L., Karen R., Michael E. AB, Columbia U., 1954; MD, NYU, 1957. Diplomate Nat. Bd. Med. Examiners, Am. Bd. Urology. Intern Johns Hopkins Hosp., Balt., 1957-58, resident in surgery, 1958-59; resident in surgery NYU Hosp., 1959-60; resident in urology Bellevue Hosp., N.Y.C., 1960-63; asst. in urology Johns Hopkins Hosp., Balt., 1958-59; asst. in urology NYU, N.Y.C., 1960-63, instr. in urology, 1963; instr. in urology Columbia U., N.Y.C., 1966-67; asst. prof. Mt. Sinai Sch. Medicine, N.Y.C., 1966-69, assoc. prof., 1969-78, prof., 1978-89; clin. prof. urology, 1989—; acting chmn. urology Mt. Sinai Sch. Medicine, N.Y.C., 1982-84; dir. urology Beth Israel Med. Ctr., N.Y.C., 1978-85; attending urologist, dir. pediatric urology Mt. Sinai Hosp., 1976-78; pres. Metro-Litho, Inc., N.Y.C., 1988-91, bd. dirs., 1991—. Contbr. articles to profl. publs., chpts. to books. Pres. Emerald Marine Ltd., Wilmington, Del., 1981; bd. dirs. Brith Milah Bd., 1970. Fellow Am. Urolog. Assn. (com. mem., 1st prize N.Y. sect. 1963, 64, pres. 1985-86), N.Y. Acad. Medicine (chmn. judicial com. urolog. sect. 1976, ACS; mem. Soc. Univ. Urologists, Royal Soc. Health, Soc. Pediatric Urology, Am. Acad. Pediatrics, Internat. Coll. Surgeons, N.Y. Met. Lithotriptor Assn. (pres. 1987), N.Y. Met. Biliary Lithotriptor Assn. (pres. 1989), Saugatuck Harbor Yacht Club, Seven Ses Cruising Assn. Republican. Jewish. Avocations: sailing, skiing, reading, music. Home: 181 Hawks Way Sequim WA 98382-3862 Office: 109 E 38th St New York NY 10016-2601

LEITER, RICHARD ALLEN, law educator, law librarian; b. Sacramento, Mar. 21, 1952; s. Lionel and Lois Rose Leiter; m. Wendy Ellin Werges, Dec. 30, 1978; children: Madeline Rose, Anna Joy, Rebecca Hope. BA in Anthropology and Religious Studies with honors, U. Calif., Santa Cruz, 1976; JD, Southwestern U., 1981; M of Libr. and Info. Sci., U. Tex., 1986. Libr. asst. Irell & Manella, L.A., 1977-78; libr. Hopkins, Mitchell & Carley, San Jose, Calif., 1982-84; head of reference Law Sch., U. Tex., Austin, 1984-86; pub. svcs. libr. Law Sch., U. Nebr., Lincoln, 1986-88; head libr. Littler, Mendelson, Fastiff & Tichy, San Francisco, 1988-91; dir. law libr., assoc. prof. law Regent U. Sch. Law, Virginia Beach, Va., 1991-94, Howard U. Sch. Law, A.M. Daniels Law Libr., Washington, 1994—; mem. Westlaw Acad. Adv. Bd., 1990-93; sec. bd. dirs. StoneBridge Sch., 1993-94; mem. adv. bd. Oceana Publs., Inc., 1994—. Editor: (book sect.) Yellow Pads to Computers, 1986, 91; author: (bibliography) New Frontiers of Forensic & Demonstrative Evidence, 1985; editor: Automatome, 1987-89, The Spirit of Law Librarianship, 1991, National Survey of State Laws, 1993; editor Southwestern U. Law Review; contbr. articles to profl. jours. Mem. adv. com. StoneBridge Ednl. Found. Mem. ABA, Am. Assn. Law Librs. (so. chpt., automation and sci. devel. spl. interest sect. 1986—, chair 1989-90, indexing of periodical lit. adv. com. 1990-91, chair 1990-91, mem. spl. com. to promote development of resources for legal info. cmty. 1994—), San Francisco Pvt. Law Librs. (steering com. 1989), Consortium Southeast Law Librs. (vice chair), Scribes. Avocations: bicycling, reading, backpacking. Home: 2830 Woodlawn Ave Falls Church VA 22042-2011 Office: Howard U Daniel Law Libr 2900 Van Ness St NW Washington DC 20008-1106

LEITER, ROBERT ALLEN, journalist, magazine editor; b. Phila., Apr. 21, 1949; s. Samuel Simon and Beverly (Agins) L.; m. Barbara Ann Field, May 6, 1973; children: Lauren, James, Rebecca. BA in English and Creative Writing with honors, U. Iowa, 1970. Freelance writer short stories, book revs., feature articles The Nation, The New Republic, Redbook, Am. Scholar, N.Y. Times, Partisan Rev., The Forward, others, 1973—; mng. editor, book columnist Inside mag., Phila., 1983-87; gen. reporter, book editor Jewish Exponent, Phila., 1987—; co-editor Friday, lit. supplement newspaper Jewish Exponent, Phila., 1983-87, mgn. editor Jewish Exponent 100th Anniversary edit., 1987, editor Extra Extra, weekly mag. sect., 1987-94; news editor Jewish Exponent, 1994-95, literary supplement editor, 1995—; contbr. editor Am. Poetry Rev., Phila., 1987—; instr. writing Am. lit., theater Cheltenham (Pa.) Adult Sch., 1983-87. Author: (with others) Jewish Profiles, 1992. Asst. to vice chmn. U.S. Commn. on Civil Rights, Washington, 1987-88. Recipient Smolar award for excellence in N.Am. Jewish journalism for articles series, 1989, 2 Simon Rockower awards, 1990, Rockower award, 1993, Keystone Press award, 1994. Mem. Phi Beta Kappa. Republican. Jewish. Avocation: collecting books, antique furniture and paintings. Home: 1002 Prospect Ave Elkins Park PA 19027-3058 Office: Phila Jewish Exponent 226 S 16th St Philadelphia PA 19102-3348

LEITH, CECIL ELDON, JR., retired physicist; b. Boston, Jan. 31, 1923; s. Cecil Eldon and Elizabeth (Benedict) L.; m. Mary Louise Henry, July 18, 1942; children: Ann, John, Paul. A.B., U. Calif. at, Berkeley, 1943, Ph.D., 1957. Exptl. physicist Lawrence Radiation Lab., Berkeley, 1946-52; theoretical physicist Lawrence Radiation Lab., Livermore, Calif., 1952-68; sr. scientist Nat. Center for Atmospheric Research, Boulder, Colo., 1968-83; div. dir. Nat. Center for Atmospheric Research, 1977-81; physicist Lawrence Livermore Nat. Lab. (Calif.), 1983-90; Symons Meml. lectr. Royal Meteorol. Soc., London, 1978; chmn. com. on atmospheric scis. NRC, 1978-80, sci. program evaluation com. Univ. Corp. for Atmospheric Rsch., 1991—; mem. joint sci. com. world climate research program World Meteorol. Organ. and Internat. Council Sci. Unions, 1976-83; mem. program adv. com. Office Advanced Sci. Computing, NSF, 1984-85. Served with AUS, 1944-46. Fellow Am. Phys. Soc., Am. Meteorol. Soc. (Meisinger award 1967, Rossby research medal 1982). Home: 627 Carla St Livermore CA 94550-2316 Office: Lawrence Livermore Nat Lab PO Box 808 Livermore CA 94551-0808

LEITH, EMMETT NORMAN, electrical engineer, educator; b. Detroit, Mar. 12, 1927; s. Albert Donald and Dorothy Marie (Emmett) L.; m. Lois June Neswold, Feb. 17, 1956; children: Kim Ellen, Pam Elizabeth. B.S., Wayne State U., 1950, M.S., 1952, Ph.D., 1978; DSc (hon.), U. Aberdeen, Scotland, 1996. Mem. research staff U. Mich., 1952—, prof. elec. engring., 1968—; cons. several indsl. corps. Contbr. articles to profl. jours. Served with USNR, 1945-46. Recipient Gordon Meml. award S.P.I.E., 1965; citation Am. Soc. Mag. Photographers, 1966; Achievement award U.S. Camera and Travel mag., 1967; Excellence of Paper award Soc. Motion Picture and TV Engrs., 1967; Daedalion award, 1968; Stuart Ballantine medal Franklin Inst., 1969; Distinguished Faculty Achievement award U. Mich., 1973; Alumni award Wayne State U., 1974; cited by Nobel Prize Commn. for contbns. to holography, 1971; Holley medal ASME, 1976; named Man of Year Indsl. Research mag., 1966; Nat. medal of Sci., 1979; Russel lecture award U. Mich., 1981; recipient Dennis Gabor medal Soc. Photo-Instrumentation Engrs., 1983, Gold medal, 1990; Mich. Sci. Trailblazer award, 1986. Fellow Optical Soc. Am. (Wood medal 1975, Herbert Ives medal 1985), IEEE (Liebmann award 1967, Inventor of Year award 1976), Enging. Soc. Detroit (hon.); mem. Nat. Acad. Enging., Sigma Xi, Sigma Pi Sigma. Patentee in field. First demonstrated (with colleague) capability of holography to form high-quality 3-dimensional image. Home: 51325 Murray Hill Dr Canton MI 48187-1030 Office: Univ Mich Inst Sci and Tech PO Box 618 Ann Arbor MI 48106-0618

LEITH, JAMES CLARK, economics educator; b. Brandon, Man., Can., Dec. 9, 1937; s. James Scott and Bertha Miriam (Clark) L.; m. Carole Ann Mason, Aug. 29, 1964; children: James Douglas, Deborah Ann, Jonathan Gregory. B.A., U. Toronto, 1959; M.S., U. Wis., 1960, Ph.D., 1967. Fgn. service officer Trade Commn. Service-Govt. of Can., 1960-67, Santo Domingo, Dominican Republic, 1961-64, Chgo., 1965; asst. prof. econs. U. Western Ont., 1967-71, assoc. prof., 1971-78, prof., 1978—, chmn. dept. econs., 1972-76, v.p. acad. provost, 1980-86; econ. cons. Ministry Fin. and Devel. Planning, Gaborone, Botswana, 1986-88; dir. rsch. Bank of Botswana, 1993-95, sr. policy advisor, 1995—; vis. lectr. U. Ghana, Legon, 1969-71; sr. research assoc. Nat. Bur. Econ. Research, 1971-75; vis. researcher Inst. Internat. Econ. Studies, Stockholm, 1976-77; vis. prof. Catholic U., Lima, Peru, 1979; vis. scholar Harvard Inst. Internat. Devel., Cambridge, Mass., 1992-93. Author: Foreign Trade Regimes..., Ghana, 1974, Ghana: Structural Adjustment Experience, 1996; co-author: (with P.T. Ellsworth) The International Economy, 1975, 84; co-editor: (with D. Patinkin) Keynes, Cambridge and the General Theory, 1977; contbr. articles to econ. jours. Mem. United Ch. of Can.

LEITH, JOHN HADDON, clergyman, theology educator; b. Due West, S.C., Sept. 10, 1919; s. William H. and Lucy Ann (Haddon) L.; m. Ann Caroline White, Sept. 2, 1943; children—Henry White, Caroline Haddon. A.B., Erskine Coll., 1940, D.D. (hon.), 1972; B.D., Columbia Theol. Sem., 1943; M.A., Vanderbilt U., 1946; Ph.D., Yale U., 1949; D.D. (hon.), Davidson Coll., 1978; D.Litt. (hon.), Presbyn. Coll., 1990. Ordained to ministry Presbyterian Ch. 1943. Pastor chs. in Nashville and Auburn, Ala., 1944-59; Pemberton prof. theology Union Theol. Sem., Richmond, Va., 1959-90; vis. prof. Columbia Theol. Sem., Eckerd Coll., New Coll. at U. Edinburgh; adj. prof. Va. Commonwealth U.; mem. ad interim com. to revise book of ch. order Presbyn. Ch. U.S., 1955-61, mem. com. to write brief statement of faith, 1960-62, mem. com. to prepare brief statement of reformed faith, 1984-91; chmn. com. revision of chpt. 3 of Confession of Faith, 1959-60, mem. permanent nominating com. gen. assembly, 1972-75; chmn. bd. Presbyn. Survey, 1961-70; bd. dirs. Presbyn. Outlook Mag., 1962—; moderator Presbyn. Synod N.C., 1977-78; mem. Gov.'s Commn. on Seasonal and Migrant Farm Workers, 1982-94; mem. adv. coun. Ctr. of Theol. Inquiry, Princeton, N.J., 1989-94. Author: Creeds of the Churches, 1963, 3d. rev. edit., 1982, The Church, A Believing Fellowship, 1965, rev., 1980, Assembly at Westminster, 1973, Greenville Church, The Story of a People, 1973, The Reformed Tradition, A Way of Being the Christian Community, 2d edit., 1981, John Calvin, the Christian Life, 1984, The Reformed Imperative, 1988, John Calvin's Doctrine of the Christian Life, 1989; editor: Guides to Reformed Theology, The Reformed Imperative, 1988, From Generation to Generation, 1990, Basic Christian Doctrine, 1993; editor (with Stacy Johnson) A Reformed Reader, A Source Book for Christian Theology, 1993. Trustee Erskine Coll.; bd. dirs. Inst. Religion and Democracy, 1985-93; mem. Richmond City com. Dem. Party, 1973-93. Kent fellow, 1946-48; Folger Library fellow, 1964; grantee Advanced Religious Studies Found., 1974. Mem. Calvin Studies Soc. (pres. 1980-83). Home: 3311 Suffolk Rd Richmond VA 23227-4724

LEITMANN, GEORGE, mechanical engineering educator; b. Vienna, Austria, May 24, 1925; s. Josef and Stella (Fischer) L.; m. Nancy Lloyd, Jan. 28, 1955; children: Josef Lloyd, Elaine Michèle. BS, Columbia U., 1949, MA, 1950; PhD, U. Calif., Berkeley, 1956; D Engring. honoris causa, Tech. U. Vienna, 1988; D honoris causa, U. Paris, 1989, Tech. U. Darmstadt, 1990. Physicist, head aeroballistics sect. U.S. Naval Ordnance Sta., China Lake, 1950-57; mem. faculty U. Calif., Berkeley, 1957—, prof. engring. sci., 1963—, prof. grad. sch., 1995—, assoc. dean acad. affairs, 1981-90, assoc. dean rsch., 1990-94, acting dean, 1988, chair of the faculty, 1994—; cons. to aerospace industry and govt. Author: An Introduction to Optimal Control, 1966, Quantitative and Qualitative Games, 1969, The Calculus of Variations and Optimal Control, 1981, others; contbr. articles to profl. jours. Served with AUS, 1944-46, ETO. Decorated Croix de Guerre France, Fourragere Belgium; recipient Pendray Aerospace Lit. award AIAA, 1979, Von Humboldt U.S. Sr. Scientist award Von Humboldt Found., 1980, Levy medal Franklin Inst., 1981, Mechanics and Control of Flight award AIAA, 1984, Berkeley citation U. Calif.-Berkeley, 1991, von Humboldt medal Von Humboldt Found., 1991, Rufus Oldenburger medal ASME, 1995, Bellman Continuum Soc. award, 1995; named Miller Rsch. prof., 1966. Mem. NAE, Acad. Sci. Bologna, Internat. Acad. Astronautics, Argentine Nat. Acad. Engring., Russian Acad. Natural Sci., Georgian Acad. Engring., Bavarian Acad. Sci., A.V. Humboldt Assn. Am. (pres. 1994). Office: U Calif Coll Engring Berkeley CA 94720

LEITNER, ALFRED, mathematical physicist, educator, educational film producer; b. Vienna, Austria, Nov. 3, 1921; came to U.S., 1938, naturalized, 1944; s. Philipp and Lona (Machlup) L.; m. Marzia O'Neil, Nov. 24, 1948; children: Kathleen Adams, Deborah Matulis, David. B.A., U. Buffalo, 1944; M.S., Yale U., 1945, Ph.D., 1948. Research assoc. Courant Inst. Math. Scis., N.Y. U., 1947-51; from asst. prof. to prof. physics Mich. State U., 1951-67; prof. physics Rensselaer Poly. Inst., 1967-88, prof. emeritus, 1988—; research assoc. Harvard U., 1965-66; cons. Harvard project physics, 1966-68; vis. prof. U.S. Mil. Acad., West Point, 1983-85. Author papers on theory spl. functions, boundary value problems, antennas, history of sci., teaching.; Films Liquid Helium, 1963, Superconductivity, 1966, Project Physics, 1965-68; Dispersion, 1973, Fraunhofer (2 films), 1974, A Story of Research, 1981; (videotapes) Our Favorite Physics Demonstrations, 1987. Guggenheim fellow, 1958-59; Deutscher Akademischer Austauschdienst fellow, 1977. Fellow Am. Phys. Soc.; mem. Assn. Physics Tchrs., Am. Assn. Univ. Profs., Phi Beta Kappa, Sigma Xi. Home: 1201 8th Ter N Naples FL 33940-5411

LEITNER, PAUL R., lawyer; b. Winnsboro, S.C., Nov. 11, 1928; s. W. Walker and Irene (Lewis) L.; m. Jeannette C. Card, Mar. 16, 1985; children by previous marriage: David, Douglas, Gregory, Reid, Cheryl. AB, Duke U., 1950; LLB, McKenzie Coll., 1954. Bar: Tenn. 1954; cert. civil trial specialist Nat. Bd. Trial Advocacy and Tenn. Commn. on Continuing Legal Edn. and Specialization. Pvt. practice law Chattanooga, 1954; assoc. firm

Leitner, Warner, Moffitt, Williams, Dooley, Carpenter & Napolitan and predecessor firms, 1952-57, ptnr., 1957—; Tenn. chmn. Def. Rsch. Inst., 1978-89. Bd. dirs. Family Service Agy., 1957-63, Chattanooga Symphony and Opera Assn., 1986-89, sec., 1987-89; mem. Chattanooga-Hamilton County Community Action Bd.; mem. Juvenile Ct. Commn., Hamilton County, 1955-61, chmn., 1958-59; chmn. Citizens Com. for Better Schs.; mem. Met. Govt. Charter Commn. Served with U.S. Army, 1946-47. Named Young Man of Yr. Chattanooga Area, 1957. Fellow Am. Coll. Trial Lawyers, Tenn. Bar. Found, Chattanooga Bar Found. (founding); mem. ABA, Tenn. Bar Assn., Jaycees (Chattanooga, pres. 1956-57), Fed. Ins. Corp. Counsel, Internat. Assn. Def. Coun., Trial Attys. Am., Tenn. Def. Lawyers Assn. (pres. 1975-76), Am. Bd. Trial Advs. (advocate), U.S. Sixth Cir. Jud. Conf. (life). Methodist. Home: Augusta Dr Lookout Mountain TN 37350

LEITZELL, TERRY LEE, lawyer; b. Williamsport, Pa., Apr. 15, 1942; s. Ernest Richard and Inez Mae (Taylor) L.; m. Lucy Acker Emmerich, June 18, 1966; children: Thomas Addison, Charles Taylor, Robert Davies. A.B., Cornell U., 1964; J.D., U. Pa., 1967. Bar: D.C. bar 1967. Consular officer Dept. State, Bombay, India, 1968-70; atty.-adv. for oceans affairs Dept. State, Washington, 1970-77; chief U.S. negotiator UN law of sea negotiations Dept. State, Geneva, also N.Y.C., 1974-77; asst. adminstr. for fisheries and dir. Nat. Marine Fisheries Service, NOAA, Dept. Commerce, Washington, 1978-81; practice law Washington, 1981-92, Seattle, 1992—. Mem ABA, Mem. D.C. Bar Assn., Am. Soc. Internat. Law. Democrat. Home: 3150 W Laurelhurst Dr NE Seattle WA 98105-5346 Office: Bogle & Gates 2 Union St Seattle WA 98101-2023

LEITZKE, JACQUE HERBERT, psychologist, corporate executive; b. Watertown, Wis., Dec. 25, 1929; s. Herbert Wilbert and Ruth Valberg (Stavenow) L.; m. Mary Annis Lacey, June 20, 1950 (div. Nov. 1963); children: Keith Alan, Sari Dawn, Thora Jacquelynne. BS, U. Wis., Madison, 1955; MA, Kent State U., 1958. Lic. psychologist, Wis., Ill., N.Y. Sch. psychologist Bur. Child Guidance, N.Y.C., 1959-61; clin. psychologist, psychotherapist Winnebago County Guidance Ctr., Neenah, Wis., 1961-64; sch. psychologist Waukegan City (Ill.) Sch. Dist. 61, 1965-66; clin. psychologist Wis., Ill., 1967-78; corp. pres., CEO Psychometrics Internat. Corp., Watertown, 1979—. Author: Definitively Incorporeal Human Intelligence Itself; originator intelligence test Abecedarian Measure of Human Intelligence, 1979. Trustee Human Intelligence Rsch. Found. Served with USAF, 1948-51. Mem. APA, Mensa. Avocation: painting. Home: 1153 Boughton St Apt 807 Watertown WI 53094-3106 Office: Psychometrics Internat Corp PO Box 247 Watertown WI 53094-0247

LEIWEKE, TIMOTHY, sales executive, marketing professional; b. St. Louis, Apr. 21, 1957; s. John Robert and Helen (Caicuey) L.; m. Pamela Leiweke, Nov. 1, 1984. Grad. high sch., St. Louis. Salesperson New Eng. Mut. Life Ins. Co., St. Louis, 1976-79; asst. gen. mgr. St. Louis Steamers/MISL, 1979-80; gen. mgr. Balt. Blast/MISL, 1980-81; v.p., gen. mgr. Kansas City (Mo.) Comets/MISL, 1981-84; v.p. Leiweke and Co., Kansas City, 1984-85; pres. Kansas City Comets/MISL, 1986-88; v.p. sales and mktg. div. Minn. Timberwolves, Mpls., 1988-91; sr. v.p. of bus. ops. Denver Nuggets, Denver, 1991-92; pres. Denver Nuggets, Denver, CO, 1992-96; pres., CEO LA Kings, Los Angeles, 1996—. Bd. dirs. Kidney Found., Minn., 1989—, Spl. Olympics, Minn., 1989—, Timberwolves Community Found., Minn., 1989—. Named Rookie of the Yr., Mo. Life Underwriters, 1976, Kansas Citian of the Yr., Kansas City Press Club, 1983; recipient William Brownfield award U.S. Jaycees, 1978, William Brownfield award Mo. Jaycees, 1978, Excalibur award Am. Cancer Soc., 1987. Mem. Kansas City Mktg. and Sales Execs., Mpls. Club. Avocations: running, golf, cross-country skiing, soccer, basketball. Home: 1635 Clay St Denver CO 80204-1799*

LEIZEAR, CHARLES WILLIAM, retired information services executive; b. Balt., Dec. 15, 1922; s. Charles R. and Nellie Beyer L.; m. Jean Smith, Nov. 26, 1947; children: Robin DeBarry, Kathy King. Charles R. II. B.S. cum laude, Loyola Coll., Balt., 1949. With Burroughs Co., 1949-71; v.p. mktg. data systems Singer Co., N.Y.C., 1972-76; group v.p. cash mgmt. services Nat. Data Corp., Atlanta, 1976-81, exec. v.p. fin. service and systems, 1981-83, exec. v.p. ops., 1983-85, exec. v.p. retail systems, 1984, sr. v.p., 1985-88; mktg. and quality process cons. Charles Assocs., Atlanta, 1989—. Served with U.S. Army, 1942-45. Recipient Susan Anthony award for highest acad. achievement Loyola U., 1947.

LEJEUNE, DENNIS EDWARD, investment counsel; b. Chgo., Feb. 25, 1942; s. Edward George and Eileen Marie (Donnellan) L.; m. Barbara Katharine Benson, July 24, 1965; children: Angela Marie, Katharine Kelly, Amy Eileen. B.B.A., U. Notre Dame; postgrad., Northwestern U. Internat. banking officer Provident Nat. Bank, Phila., 1971-73; fgn. exch. trader Harris Trust & Savs. Bank, Chgo., 1966-71, asst. v.p., 1973-74, v.p., mgr. IMM div., 1974-80, sr. v.p., mgr. investment dept., 1980-81, exec. v.p., 1981-86; dir. internat. fin. svcs. Stotler & Co., Chgo., 1986-88; pvt. investment counsel Traverse City, Mich., 1988—. Tchr. St. Faith, Hope & Chairty Ch., Winnetka, Ill., 1977-81; trustee Glen Arbor Twp., 1992; pres. Glen Lake Assn., 1992-93, bd. dirs., 1989-95. Mem. Forex Assn. N.Am. (sec. 1976-80), Pub. Securities Assn. (dir. 1983-85), Bond Club Chgo. (dir., pres. 1988), Rotary. Republican. Roman Catholic. Clubs: Univ. (Chgo.), Glen Lake Yacht, Traverse City Golf and Country. Avocations: sailing, golf, swimming, ancestry. Home: 7366 S Glen Lake Rd Glen Arbor MI 49636 Office: Investment Counsel 12935 S West Bay Shore Dr Traverse City MI 49684-5453

LE JEUNE, FRANCIS ERNEST, JR., otolaryngologist; b. New Orleans, Jan. 3, 1929; s. Francis Ernest and Anna Lynne (Dodds) LeJ.; m. Ena Kay Hudson, Dec. 21, 1963; children: Francis III, Baltzer, Katherine, Ann. B.S., Tulane U., 1950, M.D., 1953. Intern Charity Hosp., La., New Orleans, 1953-54; resident U. Iowa Hosps., Iowa City, 1954-57; mem. staff dept. otolaryngology Ochsner Clinic, New Orleans, 1959—, chmn. dept. otolaryngology, 1963-89; clin. prof. dept. otolaryngology Tulane U. Sch. Medicine, New Orleans, 1977—. Served with USAF, 1957-59. Mem. ACS, Am. Laryngol. Assn., Am. Laryngol., Rhinol. and Otol. Soc., Am. Broncho-Esophagol. Soc., Am. Soc. Head and Neck Surgery, Am. Acad. Otolaryngology, Head and Neck Surgery, La.-Miss. Ophthalmol. and Otolaryngol. Soc. (pres. 1993-94), So. Yacht Club, Boston Club. Home: 334 Garden Rd New Orleans LA 70123-2004 Office: 1514 Jefferson Hwy New Orleans LA 70121-2429

LEJINS, PETER PIERRE, criminologist, sociologist, educator; b. Moscow, Jan. 20, 1909; came to U.S., 1940, naturalized, 1944; s. Peter P. and Olga (Makarova) L.; m. Nora Muller, June 6, 1937. M. Philosophy, U. Latvia, 1930, LL.M., 1933; postgrad., U. Paris, 1934; Ph.D. (Rockefeller fellow), U. Chgo., 1938; LLD (hon.), Eastern Ky. U., 1986. Chair criminal law U. Latvia, 1938-40; prof. sociology U. Md., College Park, 1941-79, prof. emeritus, 1979—; acting dept. chmn. U. Md., 1944-46, 61; dir. Inst. Criminal Justice and Criminology, 1969-79; chmn. bd. dirs. Nat. Criminal Justice Ednl. Devel. Consortium, 1975-76; prof. Sch. Criminology, Fla. State U., 1982-84; cons. area human resources USAF, 1951-55; lectr. delinquency and crime Frederick A. Moran Meml. Inst., summers 1956, 57, 63; Mem. exec. com. Correctional Service Assos., 1947-50, Com. for Am. Participation in 2d Internat. Congress Criminology, Paris, 1950; mem. U.S. delegation 12th Internat. Penal and Penitentiary Congress, The Hague, 1950, 1st UN Congress for Prevention Crime and Treatment Delinquents, Geneva, 1955, 2d Congress, London, Eng., 1960; mem. U.S. delegation 3d UN Congress for Prevention Crime and Treatment of Offenders, Stockholm, 1965, 4th Congress, Kyoto, 1970, 5th Congress, Geneva, 1975; ofl. del. various assns. 7th UN Congress on Prevention of Crime and Treatment of Offenders, Milan, 1985; U.S. corr. to UN in social def. matters, 1965-76; vice chmn. bd. Joint Commn. on Manpower and Tng. in Corrections, 1964-70; U.S. rep. Internat. Penal and Penitentiary Found., 1974—, v.p., 1981-90; mem. Task Force Commd. to Study Correctional System, Joint Commn. on Mental Illness and Health, 1956-57; chmn. cons. com. Uniform Crime Reporting, FBI, 1957-58; mem. bd. Criminal Justice Assn., Washington; pres. bd. Md. Prisoners Aid Assn., 1957-60; chmn. Joint Baltic Am. Com., 1961-62, 66; exec. com. corrections sect. United Community Services, Washington; mem. Md. Gov.'s Commn. Prevention and Treatment Juvenile Offenders; mem. exec. bd. profl. coun., counc. rsch., trustee Nat. Coun. Crime and Delinquency, 1968-71; also mem. Md. Coun.; chmn. adv. bd. Md. Children's Ctr., 1959-65; chmn. rsch. com., adv. coun. Inst. Criminological Rsch., Dept. Corrections, D.C.; chmn. adv. bd., mem. governing bd. Patuxent Inst. Defective Delinquents; chmn. subcom. on instns. task force on correction Gov.'s Crime Commn., 1968-70; mem. rsch. and devel. task force Nat. Adv. Commn. Criminal Justice Standards and Goals, Law Enforcement Assistance Adminstrn., 1972-74, Phase II, 1974-76, chmn., 1974-76; vis. prof. Kuwait U., 1973; pres. Am. Assn. Doctoral Programs in Criminal Justice and Criminology, 1976—; mem. Md. Gov.'s Task Force on Alternative Sanctions to Incarceration, 1991. Chief editor: Jour. Rsch. in Crime and Delinquency, 1968-69, bd. editors, 1969-89; contbr. articles to profl. jours. and encys. Chmn. Social Survey Com., Prince Georges County, 1946-47 Community Chest Planning Coun., Prince Georges County, 1949-57; bd. dirs. Health and Welfare Coun. Nat. Capitol Area; 1st v.p. Prince Georges County Regional Com., bd. dirs. Washington Action for Youth, United Planning Orgn., Bok Tower Gardens Found., 1977—; chmn. D.C. Commrs. Com. on Youth Opportunity; pres. bd. dirs. Oscar Freire Inst., Sao Paolo, Brazil, 1974-77. Recipient Alumni Profl. Achievement award U. Chgo., 1973; establishment of annual Peter P. Lejins award for outstanding research in corrections, Am. Correctional Assn., 1987; decorated three stars govt. Republic of Latvia, 1995. Fellow Washington Acad. Sci., Am. Soc. Criminology, Internat. Centre Comparative Criminology; mem. AAUP, Am. Correctional Assn. (dir., mem. exec. com., chmn. com. on research and planning, pres. 1962-63, chmn. research council, E.R. Cass correctional achievement award 1980), Am. Sociol. Soc. (past pres. D.C.), Eastern Sociol. Soc., So. Sociol. Soc., Soc. Advancement Criminology, Nat. Probation Assn., Internat. Soc. Criminology (pres. sci. commn. 1973-80, hon. pres. 1981—, v.p. 1981-90), Latvian Frat. Assn. (past pres.), Am. Latvian Assn. (pres. 1951-70, now hon. pres.), Acad. Sci. Ind. Republic of Latvia (hon. mem. 1990), Free World Latvian Fedn. (pres. 1956-70), Phi Kappa Phi (disting. mem. on nat. level) Omicron Delta Kappa, Alpha Kappa Delta. Clubs: Cosmos (Washington); Faculty (U. Md.) (College Park and Baltimore); Pres. Club (U. Md., U. Chgo.); Colonnade Soc. (U.MD. Coll. Pk.), Lettonia (past pres.). Lodge: Rotary.

LELAND, HENRY, psychology educator; b. N.Y.C., Feb. 13, 1923; s. Ida (Miller) L.; m. Helen D. Faitos (div. 1979); children: Colombe, David Jean, Daniel Louis; m. Sherrie Lynn Ireland, Dec. 7, 1980. AB, San Jose State Coll., 1948; PhD, Université de Paris (Sorbonne), 1952. Lic. psychologist, Ohio. Clin. psychologist with Dr. Jean Biro, Paris, 1949-52; sr. clin. psychologist N.Y. State Mental Health Commn., Syracuse, 1952-54; dir. dept. psychol. svc. Muscatatuck State Sch., Butlerville, Ind., 1954-57; chief clin. psychologist Parsons (Kans.) State Hosp. and Tng. Ctr., 1957-63; coord. profl. tng., edn. and demonstration Parsons (Kans.) State Hosp. and Tng. Ctg., 1963-70; assoc. in child rsch. Kansas U. Bur. child Rsch., Lawrence, 1963-70; assoc. prof. psychology Ohio State U., Columbus, 1970-72; prof. Ohio State U., 1972-93, prof. emeritus, 1993—; chief psychology Herschel W. Nisonger Ctr., Columbus, 1970-93; tchg. asst. Ind. U. Extension Svc., 1956-57; assoc. prof. Kansas State Coll., 1958-70; dist. vis. lectr. U. So. Calif., L.A., 1969; prin. investigator Adaptive Behavior Project, Ohio Dept. Mental Health and Mental Retardation, 1972-75, cons., 1972-75; bd. examiners State Bd. Psychology Ohio, 1987-88, 93-94, sec., 1988-89, pres., 1989-90, 94-95, active, 1986-95; cons. Cen. Ohio Psychiat. Hosp., 1986-93; com. on acad. misconduct Ohio State U., 1990-93. Author: (wih D. Smith) Play Therapy with Mentally Subnormal Children, 1965, (with others) Brain Damage and Mental Retardation, 1967, (with others) Handbuch der Kinderpsychotherapie, Vol. II, Germany, 1968, (with others) Social Perceptual Training Kit for Community Living, 1968, Impairment in Adaptive Behavior: A Community Dimension, Tracks, Vols. II, 12, 1960-67, (with others) Social Inference Training of Retarded Adolescents at the Pre-Vocational Level, 1968, (with others) Mental Health Services for the Mentally Retarded, 1972, (with others) Sociobehavioral Studies in Mental Retardation, 1973, (with others) Mental Retardation: Current and Future Perspectives, 1974, (with others) Research to Practice in Mental Retardation and Education and Training, II, 1977, (with others) International Encyclopedia of Psychiatry, Psychology, Psychoanalysis and Neurology, II, 1977, (wth others) Psychological Management of Pediatric Problems, 1978, (with Deutsch)Abnormal Behavior, 1980, (with others) Pscychoeducational Assessment of Preschool and Primary Age Children, 1982, (with others) Comprehensive Handbook of Mental Retardation, 1983, (with others) The Foundations of Clinical Neuropsychology, 1983, (with others) Institutions for the Mentally Retarded: A Changing Role in Changing Times, 1986; cons. editor Am. Jour. Mental Deficiency, 1965-70, Profl. Psychology, 1977-95, Mental Retardation, 1980-84; contbr. articles to profl. jours. Sgt. U.S. Army, 1942-45, ETO. Recipient Disting. Svc. in Mental Deficiency award, Am. Assn. on Mental Deficiency, 1985. Fellow AAAS, APA (councilor 1986-90 , Edgar A. Doll Meml. award div. 33 1990), Am. Assn. on Mental Retardation (councilor 1964-68), Ohio Psychol. Assn., Soc. for Pediatric Psychology. Democrat. Jewish. Avocations: stamp collecting, gourmet cooking. Home: 2120 Iuka Ave Columbus OH 43201-1322

LELAND, JOY HANSON, anthropologist, alcohol research specialist; b. Glendale, Calif., July 29, 1927; d. David Emmett and Florence (Sockerson) Hanson; m. David A. Riegert, Nov. 14, 1993. B.A. in English Lit., Pomona Coll., Claremont, Calif., 1949; M.B.A., Stanford U., 1960; M.A. in Anthropology, U. Nev., 1972; Ph.D. in Anthropology, U. Calif., Irvine, 1975. With Desert Research Inst., U. Nev., 1961—, asst. research prof., 1975-77, assoc. research prof., 1977-79, rsch. prof., 1979-89, rsch. prof. emerita, 1990—. Author: monograph Firewater Myths, Frederick West Lander-A Biographical Sketch; contbg. author: Smithsonian Handbook of North American Indians; also articles, book chpts. Bd. dirs. Desert Rsch. Inst. Found. NIMH grantee, 1972-73; Nat. Inst. Alcohol Abuse and Alcoholism grantee, 1974-75, 79-81. Mem. Am. Anthrop. Assn., Southwestern Anthrop. Assn., Soc. Applied Anthropology, Soc. Med. Anthropology, Gt. Basin Anthrop. Conf., Phi Kappa Phi. Office: Desert Rsch Inst U Nev System PO Box 60220 7010 Dandini Blvd Reno NV 89512-3901

LELAND, LAWRENCE, insurance executive; b. C., Can., Nov. 13, 1915. A.B., Earlham Coll. C.L.U. Asst. supt. agys. Am. United Life Ins. Co., 1948-58, agy. v.p., 1958-67, dir., 1962-67; sr. v.p., mem. operating com. Nat. Life Ins. Co., Montpelier, Vt., 1967-72; exec. v.p. Nat. Life Ins. Co., 1972-80, ret., 1980; dir. Nat. Life Investment Mgmt. Co., Inc.; pres., dir. Equity Service, Inc., Adminstrv. Services, Inc.; exec. com. Audit Na'. Life Ins. Co. Trustee Earlham Coll., 1958-67, acting pres., 1984-85, hon. life trustee, 1985—; mem. Vt. Employment Security Bd.; bd. visitors Guilford Coll., 1980-85. Mem. Gen. Agts. and Mgrs. Assn., Central Vt. Life Underwriters Assn., Lafayette (Ind.) Life Underwriters Assn. (past pres.), Ind. Leaders Club. Club: Meridian Hills Country. Lodge: Masons. Home: 12 Westwood Dr Montpelier VT 05602-4211

LELAND, MARC ERNEST, trust advisor, lawyer; b. San Francisco, Apr. 20, 1938; s. Herbert and Sarah Betty (Robinson) L.; m. Elisabeth Gustava De Rothschild, July 7, 1970 (div. Sept. 1980); children: Natasha Hanna, Olivia Mitzi; m. Jacqueline de Botton, 1989. AB in Govt., Harvard U., 1959; MA in Law, St. John's Coll.-Oxford U., Eng., 1961; JD, U. Calif.-Berkeley, 1963. Ford Found. fellow Inst. Comparative Law-U., Paris, 1963-64; assoc. Cerf Robinson & Leland, San Francisco, 1964-68, ptnr., 1972-76; faculty fellow Harvard U. Law Sch., Boston, 1968-70; gen. counsel Peace Corps, Washington, 1970-71, ACTION, Washington, 1971-72; ACDA rep. Force Reduction Talks, Vienna, Austria, 1976-78; resident ptnr. Proskauer Rose Goetz & Mendelsohn, London, 1978-81; asst. sec. internat. affairs Dept. Treasury, Washington, 1981-84; pres. Marc E. Leland & Assocs., Washington, 1984—. Republican. Jewish. Office: 1001 19th St N Ste 1700 Arlington VA 22209-1722

LELAND, PAULA SUSAN, educational administrator, educator; b. Duluth, Minn., Feb. 10, 1953; d. Clarence Henry and Agnes Gudrun (Feiring) L. BS in Elem. Edn. and Music with honors, U. Minn., Duluth, 1975, BS in English, Lang. Arts and Sec. Edn. with honors, 1979; MS in Edn. Adminstrn. and Edn. summa cum laude, U. Wis., Superior, 1982, MEd in Profl. Devel., English and Language Arts summa cum laude, 1984, Spl. degree in Edn. Adminstrn. summa cum laude, 1988, postgrad., 1988—; postgrad., U. St. Thomas, 1989, U. Minn., Mpls., 1996—. Tchr. elem. gifted children U. Minn., Mpls., 1980; tchr. Hermantown (Minn.) Cmty. Schs. Dist. 700, 1975—, substitute adminstr., 1982-92; mem. staff devel. com. Hermantown (Minn.) Cmty. Schs. Dist. 700, Hermantown, 1987—; dist. coord. and chairperson, planning, evaluating and reporting com., adminstrv. rep. State Dept. of Edn. for Minn. #700, Hermantown, 1984-86; supr. student tchrs. U. Wis., Superior, 1977—, adminstr. practicum, 1981-82; supr. student tchrs. U. Minn., Duluth, 1977—; mem. faculty community adv. com. for student tchrs., 1985—; Coll. St. Scholastica, 1977—; supr. tchr. aides, parent vols., and interpreters, 1980—; fgn. exch. tchr. host, 1982-83; profl. edn. tutor, 1989-90; mem. textbook com. Hermantown Schs., 1977—; writer, reporter Hermantown Star, 1978. Curriculum writer Hermantown Community Schs.; music arranger, composer, lyricist. Mem. Dem. Nat. Conv. supporter, Dem. Party Local Affiliation, Duluth, 1972—, Lake Superior Ctr. Non-Profit Orgn.; choir dir., dir. music Zion Luth. Ch., 1980—, dir./coord. music and handbell, 1983—, asst. dir. 1976-79, co-chair music and co-author music tape for Centennial Celebration, 1988, mem. nominating and worship coms. chairperson, 1992-94, recorder, sec. and choir sec., pastor-selected com. for assoc. in ministry, 1980—, vocalist, 1967—, Sunday Sch. tchr., Bible sch. tchr. 1968-75, substitute asst. dir., 1976-80, coun. mem. 1992—, v.p. 1993-94, pres. 1994—, chair call com. pastor-elect, 1994—, found. bd. dirs., 1994—; supporter Reading is Fundamental, 1975—, United Way of Greater Duluth, 1975—; mem. Dairy Coun., Hermantown Arts Coun.; active Goodwill Industries, Salvation Army, Clean Water Action, Minn. Dept. Natural Resource-Wildlife, U. Minn. Legis. Network, 1992—; Archtl. Planner Ednl. Facilities and Creative Activity, 1984; bd. dirs. Duluth Fed. Employees Credit Union, 1994-95. Named to The Nat. Women's Hall of Fame, 1995; Alworth scholar, 1971-75, Denfeld scholar, 1968-71. Mem. AAUW, NAFE, Am. Mus. Nat. Hist., Assn. Lutheran Ch. Musicians (invited), Future Tchrs. Orgn., Red Cross Club (pres, former v.p., svc. award), Sons of Norway (Viking Ship Project), N.Am. Assn. for Environ. Edn., Norwegian Am. Heritage Fund, Minn. Valley Nat. Wildlife Refuge, N.D. Parks and Recreation, Friends of Deep Portage, Arrowhead Reading Coun., Minn. Reading Assn., Hermantown Fedn. Tchrs., Hermantown Sch. Dist. Cont. Edn. (co-chair, former sec., cert. of appreciation 1990), Hermantown Fedn. Tchrs., Minn. Hist. Soc., Midwest Fed. Banking Consortium, U. Minn.-Duluth Alumni Assn., U. Wis.-Superior Alumni Assn., Minn. Naturalists Assn., Tweed Mus. Art, Mpls. Soc. of the Arts, Mpls. Soc. of Fine Arts, Minn. Inst. Art, Internat. Platform Assn., Smithsonian Nat. Assocs., Smithsonian Inst., Charles F. Menninger Soc., Laura Ingalls Wilder Meml. Soc., Midwesterners Club, Alpine Club, Zoofari Club, Queen Mary and Spruce Goose Voyager Club, Kappa Delta Pi, Sigma Alpha Iota, Phi Kappa Phi, Phi Delta Kappa, Delta Kappa Gamma, Beta Sigma Phi, Alpha Delta Kappa. Home: 2237 W 11th St Duluth MN 55806 Office: 4289 Ugstad Rd Hermantown MN 55811-3615

LELAND, SARA, ballet dancer; b. Melrose, Mass., Sept. 2, 1941; m. Arthur Kevorkian. Student with, E. Virginia Williams, Melrose, Mass. Dancer New England Civic Ballet, Joffrey Ballet, 1959-60; dancer N.Y.C. Ballet, 1960-83, asst. ballet mistress, 1983—. Dancer: (ballets) Les Biches, 1960, Don Quixote, Jewels, 1967, Symphony in Three Movements, 1972, Union Jack, 1976, Vienna Waltzers, Dances at a Gathering, 1969, The Golberg Variations, 1971, Illuminations, The Concert, 1971, Gaspard de la Nuit, 1973, Lost Sonata, 1972, Choral Variations on Bach's Von Himmel Hoch, 1972, Scherzo Fantastique, 1972; ballet master staged works for the Joffrey Ballet, Boston Ballet, the Dance Theater of Harlem. Office: NYC Ballet Inc NY State Theater Lincoln Ctr Plz New York NY 10023

LELAND, TIMOTHY, newspaper executive; b. Boston, Sept. 24, 1937; s. Oliver Stevens and Frances Chamberlain (Ayres) L.; m. Natasha Bourso, Sept. 26, 1964 (div. 1981); children: Christian Bourso, London Chamberlain; m. Julie S. Hatfield, Nov. 23, 1984. A.B. cum laude, Harvard U., 1960; M.S. with honors, Columbia Sch. Journalism, 1961. Med. editor Boston Herald, 1963-64; sci. editor Boston Globe, 1965-66, State House bur. chief, 1966-67, asst. city editor, 1968-69, investigative reporter, 1970-71, asst. mng. editor, 1972, mng. editor (Sunday), 1976-81, mng. editor (daily), 1981-82, asst. to pub., 1984—, v.p., 1990—. Bd. dirs. Boys and Girls Clubs of Boston, World Affairs Coun. of Boston. Recipient Am. Polit. Sci. award, 1968; Pulitzer Prize for investigative reporting, 1972; Sigma Delta Chi award for civic service (reporting), 1972; award for pub. service A.P. Mng. Editors, 1974; Sevellon Brown award, 1974; U.S.-South African Leader Exchange Program traveling grantee, 1969; Internat. fellow Columbia, 1961. Mem. Am. Assn. Sunday and Feature Editors (past pres.), Harvard Club. Office: Boston Globe 135 Morrissey Blvd Dorchester MA 02107

LELCHUK, ALAN, author, educator; b. Bklyn., Sept. 15, 1938; s. Harry and Belle (Simon) L.; married; 2 children. B.A., Bklyn. Coll., 1960; M.A., Stanford, 1963; Ph.D., Stanford U., 1965; student, U. London, 1963-64. Writer-in-residence Brandeis U., 1966-81; vis. writer Amherst Coll., 1982-84; guest Mishkenot Sha'Ananim, Jerusalem, 1976-77; adj. prof. Dartmouth Coll., 1985—; writer-in-residence Haifa U., Israel, 1986-87; vis. writer CCNY, fall 1991; vis. prof. U. Rome Torvergata, Apr., 1996. Author: American Mischief, 1973, Miriam at Thirty-four, 1974, Shrinking, 1978, Miriam in Her Forties, 1985, (young adult novel) On Home Ground, 1987, Brooklyn Boy, 1990, Playing the Game, 1995; assoc. editor Modern Occasions, 1970-72; editor: Eight Great Hebrew Short Novels, 1983, co-founder Steerforth Press, 1993; manuscript collection Mugar Meml. Libr., Boston U.; contbr. fiction, criticism to lit. mags. Yaddo and MacDowell Colony fellow, 1968-69; Guggenheim fellow, 1976-77; Fulbright grantee, 1986-87. Mem. Authors Guild, P.E.N. Home: RR 2 Canaan NH 03741-9802 Office: care Georges Borchardt 136 E 57th St New York NY 10022-2707

LELE, PADMAKAR PRATAP, physician, educator; b. Chanda, India, Nov. 9, 1927; came to U.S., 1958; s. Pratap Vasudev and Indira (Prabhudesai) L.; m. Carla Maria Tophoff, Jan. 23, 1959; children: Martin, Malcolm. M.D., Seth G.S. Med. Coll., 1950; D.Phil., Oxford (Eng.) U., 1955. Intern K.E.M. Hosp., Bombay, India, 1950-51; resident K.E.M. Hosp., 1951-52; lectr. Oxford U., 1952-57; vis. scientist NIH, Bethesda, Md., 1958-59; tech. dir. med. acoustics research group and asst. neurophysiologist Mass. Gen. Hosp., Boston, 1959-69; assoc. in neurosurgery Harvard Med. Sch.; assoc. prof. medicine MIT, Cambridge, 1969-71; prof. MIT, 1972-94, prof. emeritus, sr. lectr., 1994—; prof. Harvard-MIT Div. Health Scis. and Tech, also prof. exptl. medicine and dir. Hyperthermia Ctr.; cons. NIH. Mem. editl. bd. Ultrasound in Medicine and Biology, 1973-94, In Vivo, 1985—; contbr. articles to med. jours. Recipient History Med. Ultrasound Pioneer award World Fedn. Ultrasound in Medicine and Biology, 1988. Fellow Acoustical Soc. Am., Am. Inst. Ultrasound in Medicine (governing bd. 1973-76, Joseph H. Holmes Pioneer award 1988); mem. IEEE, Am. Soc. Clin. Hyperthermic Oncology, European Soc. for Hyperthermic Oncology, N.Am. Hyperthermia Group, Am. Assn. Physicists in Medicine, Bioelectromagnetics Soc. (charter). Home: 5820 Ravenswood Rd La Jolla CA 92037-7419

LELYVELD, JOSEPH SALEM, newspaper executive editor, correspondent; b. Cin., Apr. 5, 1937; s. Arthur Joseph and Toby (Bookholz) L.; m. Carolyn Fox, June 14, 1959; children: Amy, Nita. BA summa cum laude, Harvard U., 1958, MA, 1959; MS in Journalism, Columbia U., 1960. Reporter, editor N.Y. Times, 1963—, fgn. corr., Johannesburg, New Delhi, Hong Kong, London, 1965-86, columnist mag., staff writer, 1977, 84-85, fgn. editor, 1987-89, mng. editor, 1990-94; exec. editor, 1994—. Author: Move Your Shadow, 1985 (Pulitzer prize, L.A. Times Book prize, Sidney Hillman award, Cornelius P. Ryan award, all 1986). Recipient George Polk Meml. award, 1972, 84; Guggenheim fellow, 1984. Mem. The Century Assn. Office: The NY Times 229 W 43rd St New York NY 10036-3913

LEM, RICHARD DOUGLAS, painter; b. L.A., Nov. 24, 1933; s. Walter Wing and Betty (Wong) L.; B.A., UCLA, 1958; M.A., Calif. State U.-Los Angeles, 1963; m. Patricia Ann Soohoo, May 10, 1958; 1 son, Stephen Vincent. Exhibited in one-man shows at Gallery 818, Los Angeles, 1965; group shows at Lynn Kottler Galleries, N.Y.C., 1973, Palos Verdes Art Gallery, 1968, Galerie Mouffe, Paris, France, 1976, Le Salon des Nations, Paris, 1984, numerous others; represented in permanent collections; writer, illustrator: Mile's Journey, 1983, 2nd edit., 1995; cover illustrator: The Hermit, 1990, The Hermit's Journey, 1993. Served with AUS, 1958-60. Mem. UCLA Alumni Assn. Address: 1861 Webster Ave Los Angeles CA 90026-1229 *Personal philosophy: It requires a great deal of inner strength to pursue your personal vision with single mindedness - it's a challenge that justifies my existence.*

LEMAIRE, JACQUES, professional hockey coach; b. Lasalle, Que., Can., Sept. 7, 1945. Player Montreal Canadiens, 1967-79, head coach, 1983-85; head coach, player Sierre Hockey Club, Switzerland, 1979-81; asst. coach

SUNY Coll., Plattsburgh, 1981-82; coach Longueuil Chevaliers, maj. jr. league, Que., 1982-83; dir. of hockey pers. Montreal Canadiens, 1985-87, asst. to mng. dir., 1987-93; head coach N.J. Devils, 1993—; mem. Stanley Cup Championship teams, 1968, 69, 71, 73, 76-79. Named NHL Coach of Yr., Sporting News, 1993, 94. Office: NJ Devils PO Box 504 East Rutherford NJ 07073-0504*

LE MAISTRE, CHARLES AUBREY, internist, epidemiologist; b. Lockhart, Ala., Feb. 10, 1924; s. John Wesley and Edith (McLeod) LeM.; m. Joyce Trapp, June 3, 1952; children: Charles Frederick, William Sidney, Joyce Anne, Helen Jean. BA, U. Ala., 1943, LLD (hon.), 1971; MD, Cornell U., 1947; LLD (hon.), Austin Coll., 1970; DSc (hon.), U. Dallas, 1978, Southwestern U., 1981; D honoris causa, U. Guadalajara (Mex.), 1989. Intern, then resident medicine N.Y. Hosp., 1947-49; research fellow infectious diseases Cornell U. Med. Coll., 1949-51, mem. faculty, 1951-54, asst. prof. medicine, 1953-54; mem. faculty Emory U. Sch. Medicine, 1954-59, prof. preventive medicine, chmn. dept., 1957-59; prof. medicine U. Tex. Southwestern Med. Sch., 1959-78, assoc. dean, 1965-66; vice chancellor health affairs U. Tex. System, Austin, 1966-68; exec. vice chancellor U. Tex. System, 1968-69, dep. chancellor, 1969-70, chancellor, 1971-78, prof. medicine, 1978—; pres., internist U. Tex. M.D. Anderson Cancer Ctr., 1978—; cons. epidemiology Communicable Disease Center, USPHS, 1953—; cons. medicine VA, 1954-59; area med. cons. VA (Atlanta area), 1958-59; vis. staff physician Grady Meml. Hosp., Atlanta, 1954-59, Emory U. Hosp., 1954-59; sr. attending staff mem. Parkland Meml. Hosp., Dallas, 1959-66; med. dir. chest div. Woodlawn Hosp., Dallas, 1959-65; mem. Surgeon Gen.'s Adv. Com. Smoking and Health, 1963-64, AMA-Edn. Research Found. com. research tobacco and health, 1964-66; chmn. Gov. Tex. Com. Tb Eradication, 1963-64; cons. internal medicine Baylor U. Med. Center, Dallas, 1962-66, St. Paul Hosp., Dallas, 1966; cons. div. hosp. and med. facilities USPHS, 1966; mem. N.Y.C. Task Force on Tb, 1967; cons. Bur. Physician, HEW, 1967-70; mem. grad. med. edn. nat. adv. com. Health Resources Adminstrn., 1977-80; mem. Tex. Legislature Dept. Health, Edn. and Welfare, 1967, Tex. Legislature Com. on Organ Transplantation, 1968, Carnegie Commn. on Non-Traditional Study, 1971-73; mem. bd. commrs. Nat. Commn. on Accrediting, 1973-76; mem. joint task force on continuing competence in pharmacy Am. Pharm. Assn.-Am. Assn. Coll. in Pharmacy, 1973-74; mem. exec. com. Legis. Task Force on Cancer in Tex., 1984-86; adv. bd. 6th World Conf. on Smoking and Health. Contbr. med. jours.; contbg. author: A Textbook of Medicine, 10 and 11th edits, 1963, Pharmacology in Medicine, 1958; Translating author: The Tubercle Bacillus, 1955; mem. editorial bd. Am. Rev. Respiratory Diseases, 1955-58. Mem. President's Commn. White House Fellows, 1971; chmn. subcom. on diversity and pluralism Nat. Council on Ednl. Research, 1973-75; bd. dirs. Assn. Tex. Colls. and Univs., 1974-75; mem. devel. council United Negro Coll. Fund, 1974-78; mem. nat. adv. council Inst. for Services to Edn., 1974-78; mem. exec. com. Assn. Am. Univs., 1975-77; mem. Project HOPE com. on Health Policy, 1977; chmn. steering com. Presbyn. Physicians for Fgn. Missions, 1960-62; mem. Ministers Cons. Clinic, Dallas, 1960-62; trustee Austin Coll., 1979-83, Stillman Coll., 1978-84; bd. dirs. Ga. Tb Assn., 1955-59; bd. dirs. Damon Runyon-Walter Winchell Cancer Fund, 1976-85, chmn. exec. com., v.p., 1978, pres., 1979-83; trustee Biol. Humanics Found., Dallas, 1973-82; chmn. health manpower com. Assn. Am. Univs., 1975-78; sec. Council So. Univs., Inc., 1976-78, pres., 1977-78; hon. life trustee Menninger Found.; Host com. Houston Econ. Summit, 1990. Recipient Cornell Univ. Alumni of Distinction award, 1978, Disting. Alumnus award U. Alabama Sch. Medicine, 1982, Pres.' award Am. Lung Assn., 1987, Gibson D. Lewis award for Excellence in Cancer Control Tex. Cancer Coun., 1988, award of Honor Am. Soc. Hosp. Pharmacists, 1988, Svc. to Mankind award Leukemia Soc. Am. Tex. Gulf Coast chpt., 1991, People of Vision award Tex. Soc. to Prevent Blindness, 1991, Outstanding Tex. Leader award 7th Ann. John Ben Sheppard Pub. Leadership Forum, 1991; Inst. Religion's Caring Spirit Tribute, 1993, AMA Disting. Svc. award, 1995; named Houstonian of Yr. Houston Sch. for Deaf Children, 1987. Mem. AMA, (Disting. Svc. award 1995), NASA, NIH (chair joint adv. com. behavioral rsch. 1992), Am. Thoracic Soc. (past v.p.), So. Thoracic Soc. (past pres.), Nat. TB Assn., Tex. Med. Assn., Ga. Med. Assn., Soc. Assn. Oncology (bd. dirs.), Am. Cancer Soc. (tex. bd. dirs. 1977-89, med. and sci. com. 1974, chmn. study com. on tobacco and cancer 1976—, pub. edn. com. 1976-87, chmn., mem. various nat. coms., v.p., pres. 1986, med. dir.-at-large 1977-89), Houston C. of C. (dir. 1979-89), Philos. Soc. Tex. (pres. 1980-81), Greater Houston Ptnrship (bd. dirs. 1989—), Alpha Omega Alpha. Presbyterian. Home: 5316 Grand Lake St Bellaire TX 77401-4928 Office: U Tex M D Anderson Cancer Ctr 1515 Holcombe Blvd Houston TX 77030-4009

LE MAISTRE, CHRISTOPHER WILLIAM, educational director; b. Moradabad, India, Aug. 20, 1938; came to U.S., 1978; s. Archibald William and Kathleen Mary (Minas) L.; m. Patricia Margaret Briggs, May 18, 1963; children: Anne Louise, Nicole Marie. B of Applied Sci. in Metallurgy, U. Adelaide, Australia, 1962; PhD, Rensselaer Poly. Inst., 1971. Cert. materials engr. Trainee in metallurgy A. Simpson & Son., Ltd., Adelaide, 1957-60; cadet def. sci. Australian Dept. Supply, Adelaide, 1961-64; exptl. officer Weapons Rsch. Establishment, Adelaide, 1964-68, sr. rsch. scientist, 1971-74; R&D attache Australian High Commn., London, Eng., 1974-77; acting head lab. program Australian Def. Dept., Canberra, 1977-78; assoc. dir. mfg. ctr. Rensselaer Poly. Inst., Troy, N.Y., 1978-84, dir. ctr. for indsl. innovation, 1984—; cons. Xerox Corp., Nortons, Exxon, Bendix Corp., U. Ariz., N.J. State U., 1975—; chmn. peer rev. panel N.J Commn. on Sci. and Tech., Newark, 1987; bd. dirs. tech. adv. com. Hudson Valley Community Coll., Troy, 1988. Author: Computer Integrated Manufacturing, 1987, Technical Innovations and Economic Growth, 1987; editor: Industrial Innovation Productivity and Employment, 1986. Mem. Am. Soc. Metals (chmn. 1983), Am. Ceramic Soc. (chmn. 1984), Am. Soc. Engring. Edn. (chmn. St. Lawrence sect. 1991-92). Avocation: photography. Home: Joseph St Troy NY 12180 Office: Rensselaer Poly Inst Ctr for Indsl Innovation Troy NY 12180

LEMAITRE, LOUIS ANTOINE, secondary education educator; b. Monagas, Venezuela, May 27, 1946; came to U.S., 1964; s. Leon A. and Teodosia M. (Urbaez) Aumaitre. BA, Don Bosco Coll., 1973; MA, St. John's U., 1974; MS in Secondary Edn., CUNY, 1978, MS in Supervision and Adminstrn., 1984; PhD in Edn., NYU, 1980. Cert. adminstr., N.Y. Instr. bilingual/ESL N.Y.C. Sch. System, 1975—; adj. prof. NYU, Adelhi U. Author: Between Flight and Longing, a Life of Teresa de la Parra, 1988, Mujer Ingeniosa, a Life of Teresa de la Parra, 1992, Venezolana y Universal, Rosario Blanco, 1993 (Spl. Commendation 1993). Mem. MLA Assn. Republican. Roman Catholic. Avocations: golf, tennis. Home: 31 43 Steinway St 3 F Long Island City NY 11103

LEMAN, LOREN DWIGHT, civil engineer; b. Pomona, Calif., Dec. 2, 1950; s. Nick and Marian (Broady) L.; m. Carolyn Rae Bratvold, June 17, 1978; children: Joseph, Rachel, Nicole. BSCE, Oreg. State U., 1972; MS in Civil, Environ. Engring., Stanford U., 1973. Registered profl. engr., Alaska. Project mgr. CH2M Hill, San Francisco, 1973, Reston, Va., 1973-74, Ketchikan, Alaska, 1974-75, Anchorage, 1975-87; state rep. State of Alaska, 1989-93, state senator, 1993—; owner Loren Leman, P.E., Anchorage, 1987—; mem. Anchorage Hazardous Materials Commn., Local Emergency Planning Com., 1989-93. Contbr. articles to profl. jours. Mem. Breakthrough Com., Anchorage, 1978; del. to conv. Rep. Party of Alaska, 1976-90; basketball coach Grace Christian Sch., Anchorage, 1985-88; commr. Pacific States Marine Fisheries Commn.; chmn. Pacific Fisheries Legis. Task Force. Mem. ASCE, Alaska Water Mgmt. Assn., Am. Legis. Exch. Coun., Water Environment Fedn., Toastmasters (pres.). Republican. Avocations: reading, fishing, biking, music, basketball. Home: 2699 Nathaniel Ct Anchorage AK 99517-1016 Office: Alaska State Legis 716 W 4th Ave # 520 Anchorage AK 99501-2107

LEMANN, THOMAS BERTHELOT, lawyer; b. New Orleans, Jan. 3, 1926; s. Monte M. and Nettie E. (Hyman) L.; m. Barbara M. London, Apr. 14, 1951; children: Nicholas B., Nancy E. A.B. summa cum laude, Harvard U., 1949, LL.B., 1952; M.C.L., Tulane U., 1953. Bar: La. 1953. Since practiced in New Orleans; assoc. Monroe & Lemann, New Orleans, 1953-58, ptnr., 1958—; bd. dirs. B. Lemann & Bro., Mermentau Mineral and Land Co., So. States Land & Timber Corp., Avrico Inc. Contbr. articles to profl. publs. Mem. council La. State Law Inst., sec. trust adv. com.; chmn. Mayor's Cultural Resources Com., 1970-75; pres. Arts Coun. Greater New Orleans, 1975-80, bd. dirs.; mem. vis. com. art museums Harvard U., 1974-80; trustee Metairie Park Country Day Sch., 1956-71, pres., 1967-70, New Orleans Philharmonic Symphony Soc., 1956-78, Flint-Goodridge Hosp., 1960-70, La. Civil Service League, pres., 1974-76, New Orleans Mus. Art, 1986-92; bd. dirs. Zemurray Found., Hever Found., Parkside Found., Azby Fund, Greater New Orleans Found., Musica da Camera. Served with AUS, 1944-46, PTO. Mem. ABA, La. Bar Assn. (bd. govs. 1977-78), New Orleans Bar Assn., Assn. Bar City N.Y., Am. Law Inst., Soc. Bartolus, Phi Beta Kappa. Jewish. Clubs: New Orleans Country, Wyvern (New Orleans); Harvard (N.Y.C.). Home: 6020 Garfield St New Orleans LA 70118 Office: Monroe & Lemann 201 St Charles Ave New Orleans LA 70170-3300

LEMANSKE, ROBERT F., JR., allergist, immunologist; b. Milw., 1948. MD, U. Wis., 1975. Diplomate Am. Bd. Pediats., Am. Bd. Allergy and Immunology. Intern U. Wis. Hosp., Madison, 1975-76, resident in pediats., 1976-78, asst. prof. medicine. Fellow Am. Acad. Pediats., Am. Acad. Allergy and Immunology. Office: Clin Sci Ctr 600 Highland Ave Madison WI 53792-0002*

LEMANSKI, LARRY FREDRICK, medical educator; b. Madison, Wis., June 5, 1943; s. Fredrick Everett and Marjery Ulila (Hill) L.; m. Sharon Lee Wulf, Aug. 6, 1966; children: Scott Fredrick, Jennifer Lee. BS, U. Wis., Platteville, 1966; MS, Ariz. State U., 1968, PhD, 1971. Asst. prof. U. Calif., San Francisco, 1975-77; assoc. prof. U. Wis., Madison, 1977-79, prof., 1979-83; prof., chmn. dept. anatomy and cell biology SUNY, Syracuse, 1983—, dir. cell and molecular biology doctoral tng. program and consortium, 1987—; rsch. prof. biology Syracuse U., 1988—; mem. ad hoc rev. panel NIH. Adult leader for Boy Scouts Am., mem. nat. staff Boy Scout Jamboree 1989, coun. tng. chmn., 1992—. Officer USAR, 1965-69. Recipient Pres'. award Rsch. SUNY HSC, 1987, Disting. Alumnus award U. Wis., 1990, Profl. Excellence award N.Y. State/United Univ. Professions, 1990; NIH fellow, 1968-71, 71-73, Muscular Dystrophy fellow, 1973-75; grantee NIH, 1975—. Mem. AAAS, Am. Heart Assn. (Wis. affiliate rsch. com. 1982-83, Louis N. Katz Rsch. prize 1978, Outstanding Rsch. award 1982, Established Investigator award 1976-81), Electron Microscopy Soc. Am., Am. Assn. Anatomists, Am. Soc. Cell Biology (congrl. liaison com. 1993—), Soc. Devel. Biology, Am. Assn. Anatomy Chmn., N.Y. Acad. Scis., Masons (3d degree master), Sigma Xi, Beta Beta Beta. Methodist. Avocations: gardening, fishing, boating, camping, music. Home: 4163 Coye Rd Jamesville NY 13078-9780 Office: SUNY Coll Medicine Dept Anatomy Cell Biol Syracuse NY 13210

LEMARI, KUNIO DAVID, federal official; b. Jabor, Jaluit, Marshall Islands, Nov. 29, 1942; s. David Lemari and Tujo Lebje; m. Helisa A. Kaious, June 21, 1967 (div. Feb. 1985); children: Wesley, Ranny, Hearlds, Evangeline, Diane, Kimberlynn, Dickson; m. Christina Maryrose Myazoe, Apr. 24, 1987; 1 child, Lyla. Degree in Theology, Bethel Bible Inst., Manila, 1967. Gen. supt. Micronesian Assemblies, Marshall Islands, 1976-80; coord. food svcs. Ministry of Social Svc., Marshall Islands, 1980-82; asst. hosp. adminstr. Ministry of Health Svc., Marshall Islands, 1982-83; officer pub. works adminstrn. Ministry of Pub. Works, Marshall Islands, 1983-84; senator Parliament of Marshall Islands, 1984-86; min. justice Govt. of Marshall Islands, 1986-87, min. transp. and comm., 1987—. Avocations: reading, fishing, baseball, bowling. Home: PO Box 648 Majuro MH 96960-0648

LE MASTER, DENNIS CLYDE, forest economics and policy educator; b. Startup, Wash., Apr. 22, 1939; s. Franklin Clyde and Delores Ilene (Schwartz) Le M.; m. Kathleen Ruth Dennis, Apr. 4, 1961; children: Paul, Matthew. BA, Wash. State U., 1961, MA, 1970, PhD, 1974. Asst. prof. dept. forestry and range mgmt. Wash. State U., Pullman, 1972-74, assoc. prof., 1978-80, prof., chair dept., 1980-88; prof., head dept. forestry and natural resources Purdue U., West Lafayette, Ind., 1988—; dir. resource policy Soc. Am. Foresters, Bethesda, Md., 1974-76; staff counsel subcom. on forests Ho. of Reps., Washington, 1977-78; cons. USDA Forest Svc., Washington, 1978, Com. on Agr., Ho. of Reps., 1979-80, Forest History Soc., Durham, N.C., 1979-83, The Conservation Found., 1989-90, Office Tech. Assessment, Washington, 1989-91, Consultative Group on Biol. Diversity, 1991. Author: Decade of Change, 1984; co-editor 8 books; contbr. articles to profl. jours. Bd. dirs. Pinchot Inst. for Conservation. Mem. AAAS, Soc. Am. Foresters (coun. 1988, chair house of soc. dels. 1982), Inland Empire Soc. of Soc. Am. Foresters (chair 1980-81, Forester of Yr. award 1982), Soc. for Range Mgmt., Forest Products Soc., Omicron Delta Epsilon, Beta Gamma Sigma, Xi Sigma Pi. Democrat. Episcopalian. Avocation: fishing. Home: 824 Lazy Ln Lafayette IN 47904-2722 Office: Purdue U Dept Foresty & Natural Resources West Lafayette IN 47907

LEMAY, JACQUES, lawyer; b. Quebec City, Can., July 10, 1940; s. Gerard and Jacqueline (Lachance) LeM. B.A., Que. Sem., 1959; LL.L., Laval U., 1962; postgrad., U. Toronto, 1964; D.E.S., 1965. Bar: Que. 1963. Practice in Quebec City, 1964—; mem. firm Prevost, Gagne, Flynn, Chouinard & Jacques, 1964-67; ptnr. Flynn, Rivard, Jacques, Cimon, Lessard & LeMay, 1968-86, Flynn, Rivard, 1986—; legal adviser Societe des Ajusteurs d'Assurance, 1969; bd. dirs. Can. 88 Energy Corp. Mem. Societe des Etudes Juridiques (pres. 1969). Club: Cercle de la Garnison (Que.). Home: 2342 Marie-Victorin, Sillery, PQ Canada G1T 2W5 Office: 70 Dalhousie, Bureau 500, Quebec, PQ Canada G1K 7A6

LEMBERG, LOUIS, cardiologist, educator; b. Chgo., Dec. 27, 1916; s. Morris and Frances Lemberg; m. Dorothy Feinstein, 1940 (dec. 1969); children: Gerald, Laura Bott, Paula Saltzman; m. Miriam Mayer, Jan. 29, 1971. B.S., U. Ill.-Chgo., 1938, M.D., 1940. Intern Mt. Sinai Hosp., Chgo., 1940-41, resident, 1945-48; asst. prof. med. 1955-58; assoc. prof. med. 1958-70; prof. clin. cardiology U. Miami Sch. Medicine (Fla.), 1970—, dir. coronary care unit, 1965-75; chief cardiology Mercy Hosp., 1974-79; chief staff Nat. Children's Cardiac Hosp., 1959-66; cons. cardiology VA Hosp., Miami, 1953-64; dir. Cardiology Dade County Hosp., 1953-64, dir. Heart Sta. and Electrocardiography, U. Miami Jackson Meml. Med. Ctr., 1952-75, program dir. Courses in Coronary Care for Practicing Physician, 1970—, Master Approach to Cardiovascular Problems, 1972-82, Cardiology Update for Intensive Care Nurses, 1978-92, Cardiology Update, 1987—. Served to maj. AUS, 1941-55; ETO. Recipient U. St. Torres (Phillippines) Luis Guerrero hon. lectr. award, 1977; Recognition award U. Miami Sch. Medicine; Key to City of Miami Beach, Fla. Fellow ACP, Am. Coll. Cardiology (editorial bd. jour.); mem. Heart Assn. Greater Miami (pres.), Fla. Heart Assn. (pres.), Am. Heart Assn. (fellow Council Clin. Cardiology), AMA (Physician's Recognition award 1970-86, 1986-94, 95—). Democrat. Jewish. Clubs: Palm Bay (Miami), Williams Island. Author: Vectorcardiography, 1969, (1975 2d edit.); Electrophysiology of Pacing and Cardioversion, 1969. Editor-in-chief Current Concepts in Cardiovascular Disorders, 1984-86. Contbr. to med. publs. Pioneer in devel. Demand Pacemaker, 1964, A chair in Cardiology established at the U. Miami Sch. of Medicine entitled The Louis Lemberg Professor of Cardiology, 1990. Home: 720 NE 69th St Apt 18 South Miami FL 33138-5738 Office: Mercy Hosp Professional Office Bldg 3661 S Miami Ave Ste 606 Miami FL 33133-4214

LEMBERGER, AUGUST PAUL, university dean, pharmacy educator; b. Milw., Jan. 25, 1926; s. Max N. and Celia (Gehl) L.; m. Charlyne A. Young, June 30, 1947; children: Michael, Mary, Thomas, Terrence, Ann, Kathryn, Peter. BS, U. Wis., 1948, PhD, 1952. Sr. chemist Merck & Co., Inc., Rahway, N.J., 1952-53; asst. prof. U. Wis. Sch. Pharmacy, 1953-57, asso. prof., 1957-63, prof. pharmacy, 1963-69; prof. pharmacy, dean U. Ill. Coll. Pharmacy, Chgo., 1969-80; prof. pharmacy, dean U. Wis.-Madison Sch. Pharmacy, 1980-91, ret., 1991; sec. Wis. Pharmacy Internship Bd., 1965-69; conf. dir. Nat. Indsl. Pharm. Research Conf., 1966-69; mem. Am. Council on Pharm. Edn., 1978-84, v.p., 1980-84. Served to 1st lt. AUS, 1944-46. Recipient Kiekhofer Meml. Teaching award U. Wis., 1957, citation of merit, 1977, Disting. Pharmacist award Wis. Pharm. Assn., 1969, Higuchi Lecture award Acad. Pharm. Sci. and Tech., Japan, 1989, Pres.' award Wis. Soc. Hosp. Pharmacists, 1991, Alumnus of Yr. award Pharmacy Alumni Assn., 1991. Fellow AAAS, Am. Found. for Pharm. Edn. (Disting. Svc. Profile award 1990), Acad. Pharm. Scis., Am. Assn. Pharm. Scientists; mem. Am. Soc. Hosp. Pharmacists, Am. Assn. Colls. Pharmacy (past com. chmn., exec. com. 1971-74, chmn. coun. deans 1975-77, chmn. sect. tchrs. of pharmacy Conf. Tchrs., hon. pres. 1993-94), Acad. Pharm. Scis. (v.p. 1976-77, pres. 1983-84), Am. Pharm. Assn. (mem. jud. bd. 1976-79, trustee 1985-88, treas. 1989-90, hon. pres. 1996-97), Wis. Pharm. Assn., Sigma Xi, Rho Chi (v.p. 1979-81, pres. 1981-83). Home: 7439 Cedar Creek Trl Madison WI 53717-1538 Office: 425 N Charter St Madison WI 53706-1508

LEMBERGER, LOUIS, pharmacologist, physician; b. Monticello, N.Y., May 8, 1937; s. Max and Ida (Siegal) L.; m. Myrna Sue Diamond, 1959; children: Harriet Felice Schor, Margo Beth. B.S. magna cum laude, Bklyn. Coll. Pharmacy, L.I. U., 1960; Ph.D. in Pharmacology, Albert Einstein Coll. Medicine, 1964, M.D., 1968; Doctorate (hon.), L.I. U., 1994. Pharmacy intern VA Regional Office, Newark, summer 1960; postdoctoral fellow Albert Einstein Coll. Medicine, 1964-68; intern in medicine Met. Hosp. Center, N.Y. Med. Coll., N.Y.C., 1968-69; rsch. assoc. NIH, Bethesda, Md., 1969-71; clin. pharmacologist Lilly Lab. for Clin. Rsch., Eli Lilly & Co., Indpls., 1971-75; chief clin. pharmacology Lilly Lab. for Clin. Rsch., Eli Lilly & Co., 1975-78, dir. clin. pharmacology, 1978-89, clin. rsch. fellow, 1982-93; asst. prof. pharmacology Ind. U., 1972-73, asst. prof. medicine, 1972-73, assoc. prof. pharmacology, 1973-77, assoc. prof. medicine, 1973-77, prof. pharmacology, 1977—, prof. medicine, prof. psychiatry, 1977—, mem. grad. faculty, 1975—; adj. prof. clin. pharmacology Ohio State U., 1975-86; physician Wishard Meml. Hosp., 1976—; cons. U.S. Nat. Commn. on Marijuana and Drug Abuse, 1971-73, Can. Commn. Inquiry into Non-Med. Use of Drugs, 1971-73; mem. Pharm. Mfrs. Assn. Commn. on Medicines for Drug Dependence and Abuse, 1990-93, Ind. Optometric Legend Drug Adv. Com., 1991—; guest lectr. various univs., 1968—; lectr. U. Minn., 1993—; mem. adv. com. Faseb Life Scis. Rsch. Office, 1993—. Author: (with A. Rubin) Physiologic Disposition of Drugs of Abuse, 1976; contbr. numerous articles on biochemistry and pharmacology to sci. jours.; editorial bd.; Excerpta Medica, 1972—, Clin. Pharmacology and Therapeutics, 1976—, Communications in Psychopharmacology, 1975-91, Pharmacology, Interant. Jour. Exptl. and Clin. Pharmacology, 1978-94, Drug and Alcohol Abuse Rsch., 1979-86, Drug Devel. Rsch., 1980-87, Trends in Pharmcol. Scis., 1980-85. Post adviser Crossroads of Am. council Boy Scouts Am., 1972-77. Served with USPHS, 1969-71. Recipient Disting. Alumnus award Albert Einstein Coll. Medicine, 1989, Disting. Alumnus award L.I. U., 1990. Fellow ACP, AAAS, Am. Coll. Neuropsychopharmacology (chmn. credentials com. 1993), Am. Coll. Clin. Pharmacology; mem. Am. Soc. Pharmacology and Exptl. Therapeutics (com. div. clin. pharmacology 1972-78, chmn. com. 1978-83, coun. 1980-83, chmn. long-range planning com. 1984-86, pres. 1987-88, ASPET award in Therapeutics, 1985, Harry Gold award for rsch. and teaching excellence in clin. pharmacology 1993), Am. Soc. Clin. Pharmacology and Therapeutics (chmn. sect. neuropsychopharmacology 1973-80, chmn. fin. com. 1976-83, 89-92, v.p. 1981-82, pres. 1983-84, dir. 1975-81, 84-87, Rawls-Palmer award 1986, Henry Elliot Disting. Svc. award 1992), Am. Soc. Clin. Investigation, Collegium Internat. Neuro-Psychopharmacologicum, Am. Fedn. Clin. Rsch. Ctrl. Soc. Clin. Rsch., Soc. Neurosci., Sigma Xi, Alpha Omega Alpha, Rho Chi. Jewish. Home: 3315 Walnut Creek Dr N Carmel IN 46032-9038 Office: Ind Univ Sch Medicine Dept Pharmacology and Medicine Indianapolis IN 46202

LEMBERIS, THEODORE THOMAS, international law and law educator; b. LaPorte, Ind., Sept. 15, 1948; s. Thomas Theodore and Helen N. (Pappas) L.; m. Renna T. Theodorakas, Nov. 13, 1978; children: Eleni, Stephanie. BA, Purdue U., 1972; MPA, Roosevelt U., 1978; JD, John Marshall Law Sch., Chgo., 1982. Bar: Ill. 1982, U.S. Dist. Ct. (no. dist.) Ill. 1982. Systems analysis Metro. Reclamation, Chgo., 1979-82; pub. defender Cook County, Chgo., 1982-85; assoc. Hinshaw & Culberson, Chgo., 1985-86; ptnr. Keck, Mahin & Cate, Chgo., 1986-94; prof. law Chgo.-Kent Law Sch., 1994-95; ptnr. Arstein & Lehr, Chgo., 1995—; adj. prof. Chgo.-Kent Law Sch., 1995—. Contbr. articles to profl. jours. Mem. Ill. Bar Assn. (sect. counsil mem.). Greek Orthodox. Avocations: tennis, horse-back riding. Office: Arstein & Lehr Ste 1200 120 S Riverside Plz Chicago IL 60606-3193

LE MEHAUTE, BERNARD JEAN, marine physics educator; b. St. Brieuc, Bretagne, France, Mar. 29, 1927; m. Marie-Josseline Roy; children by previous marriage: Anne, Patrick. Licence es Scis., U. Toulouse, France, 1951, D in Engring., 1951; D in Advanced Study, U. Paris, 1953; PhD, U. Grenoble, France, 1957. Hydraulic engr. Sogreah, Grenoble, 1953-57; asst. prof. Ecole Polytechnique, Montreal, Can., 1957-61; dir. geomarine div. Nat. Engring. Sch. Cy., Pasadena, Calif., 1963-66; v.p., sr. v.p., corp. chief engr. TeTraTech. Inc., Pasadena, 1966-78, bd. dirs., 1966-81; chmn. ocean engring dept. Rosenstiel Sch. Marine and Atmospheric Scis., Miami, Fla., 1978-85; prof. applied marine physics U. Miami, 1985-92, prof. emeritus, 1992—. Author: Hydrodynamic and Water Waves, 1976, Ocean Engineering Science, 2 vols., 1990, Water Waves Generated by Explosion. Mem. nat. sea grant adv. bd. NOAA, 1971-78; mem. Coastal Engring. Rsch. Bd., C.E., U.S. Army, 1982-88. Mem. ASCE, NAE, Am. Shore and Beach Preservation Assn. (bd. dirs. 1966-93, dir. emeritus 1993—), Nat. AC Eng. Republican. Roman Catholic. Office: Univ of Miami Dept of Ocean Engring 4600 Rickenbacker Cswy Miami FL 33149-1031

LE MENAGER, LOIS M., incentive merchandise and travel company executive; b. Cleve., Apr. 25, 1934; d. Lawrence M. and Lillian C. (Simicek) Stanek; m. Charles J. Blabolil (dec. 1982); children—Sherry L., Richard A.; m. Spencer H. Le Menager, Mar. 23, 1984. Grad. high sch., Cleve. Bank teller, sec. to v.p., Peoples Savs. and Loan, Cleve., 1951-56; travel counselor Mktg. Innovators, Rosemont, Ill., 1978-80, mktg. dir., 1980-82, chmn., chief exec. officer, owner, 1982—; dir. Northwest Commerce Bank, Rosemont. Mem. Am. Inst. Entrepreneurs (Entrepreneur of Yr. 1988), Am. Mktg. Assn., Internat. Soc. Mktg. Planners, Mktg. Planners Internat., Soc. Incentive Travel Execs., Am. Soc. Travel Agents, Nat. Fedn. Ind. Bus., Nat. Assn. Women Bus. Owners, Nat. Assn. Female Execs., Des Plaines C. of C., Rosemont C. of C., Czechoslovak Soc. Am. Republican. Congregationalist. Club: Executive (Chgo). Office: Mktg Innovators Internat Inc 9701 W Higgins Rd Des Plaines IL 60018-4703

LE MENER, GEORGES PHILIPPE, hotel executive; b. Paris, Feb. 7, 1948; came to U.S., 1983; m. Annie Desmont, 1972; children: Sophie, Loic. BA in Hotel Mgmt., Paris, 1966. Gen. mgr. Novotel Siem, Eury, France, 1969-72, regional mgr., 1972-77, exec. v.p. ops. and human rels., 1977-83; pres. Accor N.Am. and Pacific, Scarsdale, N.Y., 1983-1992. Home: 2 Overhill Rd # 420 Scarsdale NY 10583-5316 Office: Accor N Am Corp 1500 Broadway New York NY 10036-4015*

LEMER, ANDREW CHARLES, engineer, economist; b. Maxwell Field, Ala., Dec. 25, 1944; s. Samuel Theodore and Carol (Oppenheimer) L.; m. Patricia Spear, Aug. 1967 (div. Dec. 1981); m. Jane Felsten, Aug. 1992; children: Elizabeth Catherine, Daniel Evan. SB, MIT, 1967, SM, 1968, PhD, 1971. Assoc. Alan M. Voorhees & Assoc., Inc., McLean, Va., 1971-76; sr. assoc. PRC Planning & Econs., Inc., McLean, 1976-80; chief planner PRC (Nigeria) Ltd., Lagos, 1980-82; div. v.p. PRC Engring., Inc., McLean, 1982-85; pres. Matrix Group, Inc., Washington, 1985—; dir. bldg. rsch. bd. Nat. Acad. Scis., Washington, 1988-94; cons. Fed. Rail Adminstrn., Washington, 1975, FAA, Washington, 1986—, World Bank, Washington, 1980—, Abell Found., Balt., 1993—, Transp. Rsch. Bd., Washington, 1993—; vis. prof. civil engring. Purdue U., West Lafayette, Ind., 1995—. Prin. author: In Our Own Back Yard: Principles for Improving the Nation's Infrastructure, 1993, Toward Infrastructure Improvement: A Research Agenda, 1994, Solving the Innovation Puzzle: Challenges Facing the U.S. Design and Construction Industry, 1996; contbr. articles to profl. jours.; editl. adv. bd. Jour. Infrastructure Sys., Constrn. Bus. Rev., Constrn. Mgmt. and Econs. Mem. ednl. coun. MIT, Washington, 1974—. Loeb fellow Harvard U., 1992-93. Mem. ASCE, Am. Inst. Cert. Planners, Engring. Soc. Balt., Cosmos Club (Washington). Office: 4701 Keswick Rd Baltimore MD 21210-2322

LEMERT, JAMES BOLTON, journalist, educator; b. Sangerfield, N.Y., Nov. 5, 1935; s. Jesse Raymond and Caroline Elizabeth (Brown) L.; m. Rosalie Martha Bassett, Mar. 23, 1972. AB, U. Calif., Berkeley, 1957, M in Journalism, 1959; PhD, Mich. State U., 1964. Newspaper reporter Oakland (Calif.) Tribune, 1955-56, Chico (Calif.) Enterprise-Record, 1957, 58-60; asst. prof. journalism So. Ill. U., Carbondale, 1964-67; asst. prof. U. Oreg., Eugene, 1967-69, assoc. prof., 1969-76, prof., 1976—, dir. divsn. comm. rsch., 1967—, dir. grad. program Sch. Journalism, 1983-86, 88-93; chmairperson task force to revise faculty governance U. Oreg., 1983-84, mem. senate, 1981-83, 86-88, 93-94, mem. pres.'s adv. coun., 1990-91, chairperson pres.'s adv. coun., 1991-92, mem. grad. coun., 1984-86, 89-90, 94—, chairperson grad. coun., 1993-94, chairperson task force on rsch. and grad. edn., 1990-91. Prodr., on-air host Old Grooves show Sta. KWAX-FM,

1977-80, 82-84; author: Does Mass Communication Change Public Opinion After All? A New Approach to Effects Analysis, 1981, Criticizing the Media: Empirical Approaches, 1989, News Verdicts, The Debates and Presidential Campaigns, 1991, Politics of Disenchantment: Bush, Clinton, Perot and the Press, 1996; editor Daily Californian, 1957; contbr. articles to profl. jours. Mem. Oreg. Alcohol and Drug Edn. Adv. Com., 1968-69; pres. South Hills Neighborhood Assn., 1976-77, bd. dirs., 1982-84, 86-88; bd. dirs. Traditional Jazz Soc. Oreg., 1981-83, 87; v.p. Met. Cable Access Corp., 1983-84; mem. exec. bd. AAUP, 1975-76, 91-94; mem. state exec. com., head chpt. Assn. Oreg. Faculties, 1981-83, 85-87, state v.p., 1987-89, del. to Oreg. Faculties Polit. Action Com., 1986-89. Recipient Outstanding Journalist award Sigma Delta Chi, 1957, Donald M. McGammon Communication Rsch. Ctr. critical rsch. grantee, 1988-89, Allen Family Found. grantee; NSF fellow, 1963, 64; Calif. Newspaper Pubs. fellow, 1957; Butte County Alumni scholar, 1953-54. Mem. Assn. Edn. in Journalism (vice chairperson civic journalism interest group 1995-96), Am. Assn. Pub. Opinion Rsch., Am. Polit. Sci. Assn., Speech Comm. Assn., Phi Beta Kappa (membership chmn. 1985-86, v.p., pres. 1989-91). Home: 10 E 40th Ave Eugene OR 97405-3487 *Journalism is one of the more tradition-bound crafts. A constant underlying theme in the research and writing I do is that the research might help journalism redefine itself. There certainly is much need for change in long-held journalistic practices. Habit and "we've always done it this way" are no longer good enough reasons— if they ever were.*

LEMESANY, LOWELL RICHARD, financial planner; b. Colorado Springs, Colo., Apr. 20, 1947; s. Richard Ernest and Marcella Lois (Mcclaskey) L.; m. Ursula Josephine Lipp, Nov. 20, 1971 (div. Feb. 1988); children: Richard, Aaron, Andrew, Sara, Verena; m. Cynthia Lynette Hester, July 13, 1989; children: Zachary, Mara. BA, U. No. Colo., 1969; cert., Coll. for Fin. Planning, Denver, 1981. CFP. Account exec. Waddell & Reed Inc., Colorado Springs, 1976-78; asst. v.p. E. F. Hutton & Co., Colorado Springs, 1978-88; 1st v.p. Prudential Securities, Colorado Springs, 1988-94; v.p. Stifel Nicolaus & Co. Inc., Colorado Springs, 1994—; instr. in fin. planning U. Colo., Colorado Springs, 1978-89, Denver, 1980-83; mem. adv. coun. Keystone Mut. Funds, Boston, 1994, Alliance Mut. Funds, N.Y.C., 1993; mem. Golden Scale coun. Putnam Mut. Funds, Boston, 1984-88. Scoutmaster Boy Scouts Am., Calhan, Colo., 1985-86, troop com. chmn., Colorado Springs, 1987-88; br. pres. LDS Ch., Calhan, 1985-87. Capt. U.S. Army, 1969-76. Mem. Internat. Assn. Fin. Planners, Inst. CFPs, Toastmasters (area gov. 1987-88, Able Toastmaster 1987). Republican. Avocations: jogging, skiing. Office: Stifel Nicolaus & Co Inc 111 S Tejon St Ste 705 Colorado Springs CO 80903-2286

LEMESH, NICHOLAS THOMAS, designer, filmmaker; b. McKees Rocks, Pa., May 21, 1946; s. Nicholas and Sophie (Nowak) L. B.F.A. with honors, Carnegie-Mellon U., 1968; M.F.A., NYU, 1971. Asst. program dir. Kingsley Assn., Pitts., 1968-70; art dir. William Sloane House YMCA, N.Y.C., 1969-71; graphic designer Kahn Assos., N.Y.C., 1971; adminstrv. asst. Grad. Inst. Film and TV, NYU, 1971-72; v.p., film producer Grey Advt., N.Y.C., 1972—. Youth rep. League of Red Cross Socs. to UN; nat. gov. Nat. ARC, 1970-77, chmn. hist. resources com., Washington, bd. dirs. N.Y. chpt.; U.S. rep. Internat. Red Cross Conf., Geneva, 1969. Recipient Internat. Disting. Service award for humanitarian service Macalester Coll., 1970; CLIO award for comml. excellence, 1984, 86; Andy One Show Houston Film Festival award. Mem. Nat. Inst. Social Scis., Broadcast Advt. Producers Soc. Am. Democrat. Mem. Byzantine Cath. Ch. Home: 240 E 35th St New York NY 10016-4282 Office: 777 3rd Ave New York NY 10017

LEMIEUX, CLAUDE, professional hockey player; b. Buckingham, Que., July 16, 1965. Right wing Montreal Canadiens, 1983-90, N.J. Devils, 1990-95, Colo. Avalanche, 1995—; mem. Stanley Cup Championship teams, 1986, 95, 96. Named to Que. Major Jr. Hockey League All-Star second team, 1983-83, first team, 1984-85; recipient Guy Lafleur trophy, 1985, Conn Smythe trophy for most valuable player in playoffs, 1995. Office: Colo Avalanche McNichols Arena 1635 Clay St Denver CO 80204*

LEMIEUX, JEROME ANTHONY, JR., electrical and computer engineer; b. Fond du Lac, Wis., July 9, 1957; s. Jerome Anthony and Janet Ann (Lehman) L.; m. Cynthia Maureen Hahn, Nov. 29, 1980; children: Angela Kay, Jerome Anthony III. BSEE, U. Wis., 1980; MSEE, Miss. State U., 1984, PhD in Elec. Engring., 1987. Commd. 2d lt. USAF, 1980, advanced through grades to maj.; squadron officer sch. residence program USAF, Maxwell AFB, Ala., 1985; T-38 instr. pilot 50th Flying Tng. Squadron USAF, Columbus AFB, Miss., 1982-86; fighter lead in tng. capt. 434th Tactical Fighter Squadron USAF, Hollomon AFB, N.Mex., 1986; fighter pilot capt. 21st and 562nd Tactical Fighter Squadron USAF, George AFB, Calif., 1986-87; F-16C/F-46 combat ready fighter pilot, flight comdr., instr. pilot, capt. USAF, Spangdahlem Air Base, Germany, 1987-90; ret.; tech. staff mem., sys. and signal processing engr. MIT Lincoln Lab., Lexington, Mass., 1990-94, cons. engr., 1994—; airline pilot Delta Air Lines/Atlanta Internat. Airport, Boston, 1991—; R&D engr. MITRE Corp., Bedford, Mass., 1994—; adj. prof. elec. engring. Boston U., 1988-91, U. Md., 1987-88; cons. engr. USAF, Hanscom AFB, Mass., 1994—; chmn. 1995 IEEE Internat. Radar Conf., Washington, com. mem., 1993, 94. Editor: Fourier Analysis Textbook, 1994; contbr. numerous articles to profl. jours. Maj. USAFR, 1990—. Decorated Air Force Commendation medal with oak leaf cluster. Mem. IEEE, IEEE Aerospace and Electronics Sys. Soc., IEEE Signal Processing Soc., Alpha Delta Phi, Tau Beta Pi, Eta Kappa Nu, Kappa Mu Epsilon. Avocations: running, weightlifting, reading, computer programming, flying. Home: 6 Unicorn Way Nashua NH 03063 Office: USAF Hanscom AFB/FMXS 9 Eglin St Lexington MA 01731

LEMIEUX, JOSEPH HENRY, manufacturing company executive; b. Providence, Mar. 2, 1931; s. Mildred L. Lemieux; m. Frances Joanne Schmidt, Aug. 11, 1956; children: Gerald Joseph, Craig Joseph, Kimberly Mae Lemieux Wolff, Allison Jo. Student, Stonehill Coll., 1949-50, U. R.I., 1950-51; BBA summa cum laude, Bryant Coll., 1957. With Owens-Ill., Toledo, 1957—, various positions with glass container div. and closure and metal container group; exec. v.p. Owens-Ill. Owens-Ill., Inc., Toledo, 1984, pres. pkg. ops., 1984, pres., chief oper. officer, 1986-90, pres., chief exec. officer, 1990-91, chmn. bd., chief exec. officer, 1991—, also bd. dirs.; bd. dirs. Ohio Citizens Bank, Toledo, Nat. City Corp., Cleve. Vice chmn. bd. govs. Edison Indsl. Systems Ctr. U. Toledo, 1986. Served to staff sgt. USAF, 1951-55. Named one of Outstanding Young Men Am., Jaycees, 1965. Mem. Glass Packaging Inst. (chmn. 1984-86), Inverness Club (Toledo). Roman Catholic. Avocations: golf, tennis. Office: Owens-Illinois Inc 1 Seagate Toledo OH 43666-1000*

LEMIEUX, LINDA DAILEY, museum director; b. Cleve., Sept. 6, 1953; d. Leslie Leo LeMieux Jr. and Mildred Edna (Dailey) Tutt. BA, Beloit Coll., 1975; MA, U. Mich., 1979; assoc. cert., Mus. Mgmt. Program, Boulder, Colo., 1987. Asst. curator Old Salem, Inc., Winston-Salem, N.C., 1979-82; curator Clarke House, Chgo., 1982-84; curator Western Mus. Mining and Industry, Colorado Springs, Colo., 1985-86, dir., 1987—. Author: Prairie Avenue Guidebook, 1985; editor: The Golden Years--Mines in the Cripple Creek District, 1987; contbr. articles to mags. and newspapers. Fellow Hist. Deerfield, Mass., 1974—. Research grantee Early Am. Industries Assn., 1978. Mem. Am. Assn. Mus., Am. Assn. State and Local History, Colo.-Wyo. Mus. Assn., Colo. Mining Assn., Nev. Mining Assn., Mountain Plains Assn. Mus., Women in Mining. Republican. Presbyterian. Home: 1337 Hermosa Way Colorado Springs CO 80906-3050 Office: Western Mus of Mining & Industry 1025 N Gate Rd Colorado Springs CO 80921-3018

LEMIEUX, MARIO, professional hockey player; b. Montreal, P.Q., Can., Oct. 5, 1965; m. Nathalie Asselin, June 26, 1993; 1 child, Lauren. With Pitts. Penguins, 1984—; mem. NHL All-Star team, 1987-88, 88-89, 92-93, Stanley Cup Championship team, 1991, 92; player NHL All-Star game, 1992-93. Recipient Hart Meml. trophy for most valuable player, 1988, 89, Conn Smythe trophy for most valuable player in playoff, 1991, Art Ross Meml. trophy, 1987-88, 88-89, 91-92, 92-93, Dodge Performance of the Year award, 1987-88, 88-89, Dodge Ram Tough award, 1988-89, Michel Briere trophy, 1983-84, Jean Beliveau trophy, 1983-84, Michael Bossy trophy, 1983-84, Guy LaFleur trophy, 1983-84, Calder Meml. trophy, 1984-85, Lester B. Pearson award, 1985-86, 87-88, 92-93, Pro Set NHL Player of the Year, 1991-92, Bill Masterson Meml. trophy, 1992-93; named Sporting News All-Star team, 1987-88, 88-89, 92-93, Player of the Year Canadian hockey League, 1983-84, All-Star game MVP, 1985, 88, 90, Player of the Year NHL, 1992-93. Office: Pittsburgh Penguins Civic Arena Gate # 9 Pittsburgh PA 15219*

LEMIEUX, RAYMOND URGEL, chemistry educator; b. Lac La Biche, Alta., Can., June 16, 1920; s. Octave L.; m. Virginia Marie McConaghie, 1948; children: 1 son, 5 daus. BS with honors, U. Alta., 1943; PhD in Chemistry, McGill U., 1946; DSc (hon.), U. N.B., 1967, Laval U., Quebec, 1970, U. Ottawa, 1975, U. Waterloo, 1980, Meml. U., Nfld., 1981, Université du Quebec, 1982, Queen's U., Kingston, 1983, McGill U., Montreal, 1984; Dr. honoris causa, Université de Provence, Marseille, France, 1972; LLD (hon.), U. Calgary, 1979, U. Sask., 1993; DSc (hon.), Université de Sherbrooke, 1986, McMaster U., 1986, U. Alta., 1991; PhD (hon.), U. Stockholm, 1988. Postdoctoral fellow Ohio State U., Columbus, 1946-47; asst. prof. U. Sask., Saskatoon, Can., 1947-49; sr. rsch. officer NRC of Can., Saskatoon, 1949-54; prof., chmn. chemistry dept. U. Ottawa, Can., 1954-61; vice dean, faculty of pure and applied sci. U. Ottawa, 1954-61; prof. organic chemistry U. Alta., Edmonton, Can., 1961-81, Univ. prof., 1981-85, prof. emeritus, 1985—. Author 243 published articles in sci. field. Decorated companion Order of Can.; recipient Louis Pariseau medal, Association Canadienne Francaise pour l'Advancement des Sciences, 1961, Centennial of Can. medal, 1968, award of achievement Province of Alta., 1980, diplome d'Honneur Le Groupe Francais des Glucides, Lyon, France, 1981, Izaak Walton Killam award The Can. Coun., 1981, rsch. prize U. Alta., 1982, Sir Frederick Haultain prize, Govt. Alta., 1982, Tishler award lectr. Harvard U., 1983, Gairdner Foun. Internat. award, 1985, Rhone-Poulenc award Royal Soc. Chemistry, Eng., 1989, King Faisal Internat. prize in sci., 1990, Gold medal Nat. Scis. and Engring. Rsch. Coun. Can., 1991, Manning award of distinction, 1992, PMAC Health Rsch. Found. Medal of Honor, 1992, Albert Einstein award World Cultural Coun., 1992, Gt. Can. award, 1993, Alta. Pioneer award Alta. Sci. and Tech. Found., 1993; inauguration of The Lemieux Lectures, U. Ottawa, 1972; inauguration of The Raymond U. Lemieux Lectures on Biotechnology, U. Alta., 1987; inauguration of The R.U. Lemieux Award for Organic Chemistry, Can. Soc. for Chemistry, 1992; inducted into Alta. Order of Excellence, 1990. Fellow Chem. Inst. Can. (hon., 1st div. award div. organic chemistry 1954, Palladium medal, 1964) Royal Soc. Can., Royal Soc. London, Am. Chem. Soc. (C.S. Hudson award 1966), The Chem. Soc. (Haworth medal 1978), medal of hon. Can. Med. Assn., 1985). Home: 7602 119th St, Edmonton, AB Canada T6G 1W3 Office: U Alta, Dept Chemistry, Edmonton, AB Canada T6G 2G2

LEMKE, JAMES UNDERWOOD, physicist; b. Grand Rapids, Mich., Dec. 26, 1929; s. Andrew Bertram and Frances (Underwood) L.; m. Ann Stickley, Aug. 1, 1953; children: Catherine, Susan, Michael. BS in Physics, Ill. Inst. Tech., 1959; MS in Physics, Northwestern U., 1960; PhD in Physics, U. Calif., Santa Barbara, 1966. From assoc. to tech. v.p. Armour Rsch. Found., Chgo., 1957-60; dir. Bell & Howell Rsch. Labs., Pasadena, Calif., 1960-68; pres. Spin Physics, Inc. subs. Eastman Kodak, San Diego, 1968-82; fellow rsch. labs. Eastman Kodak, Rochester, N.Y., 1982-86; pres. Rec. Physics, Inc., San Diego, 1986—; founder, dir. Visqus Corp., 1989; adj. prof. U. Calif. at San Diego, LaJolla, 1982—. Contbr. numerous sci. and tech. articles to phys. jours.; patentee in field. Bd. dirs. San Diego Aero-Space Mus., 1982—. Recipient Revelle medal U. Calif. San Diego. Mem. NAE, AAAS, Am. Phys. Soc., Magnetic Soc. (IEEE (Reynold Johnson medal 1995). Democrat. Avocation: airplane pilot.

LEMKE, JUDITH A., lawyer; b. New Rochelle, N.Y., Sept. 28, 1952; d. Thomas Francis and Sara Jane (Blish) Fanelli; m. W. Frederick Lemke, Apr. 1, 1980; 1 child, Morgan Frederick. Student, Manhattanville Coll., Purchase, N.Y., 1970-72; BA, Case Western Res. U., Cleve., 1974, MA, 1975, JD, 1978. Sr. cert. pub. acct. Price Waterhouse, Cleve., 1978-81; assoc. Benesch Friedlander Coplan & Aronoff, Cleve., 1981-85; adjunct faculty Cleve. Marshall Coll. Law, 1982-86; ptnr. Benesch Friedlander Coplan & Aronoff, Cleve., 1986-94; prin. Kahn Kleinman Yanowitz & Arnson Co., Cleve., 1994-95; tax mgr. ops. Chiquita Brands Internat., Cin., 1995—; adj. faculty Case Western Res. U. Sch. of Law, 1993-95. Recipient Elijah Watt Sells award for highest distinction AICPA, N.Y.C. 1979. Mem. ABA, Ohio State Bar Assn., Cleve. Bar Assn., Cleve. Tax Club, Internat. Fiscal Assn., Case Western Res. U. Undergrad. Alumni Assn. (exec. com. 1987-95, trustee 1987-95, chmn. spl. events com. 1989-90, pres. 1990-92, v.p. 1993-94). Avocations: kayaking, wilderness canoe camping, guitar. Home: 7119 St Edmunds Dr Cincinnati OH 45230 Office: Chiquita Brands Internat 250 E 5th St Cincinnati OH 45202

LEMKE, LAURA ANN, assistant principal, foreign language educator; b. Hollis, L.I., N.Y., May 4, 1964; d. Ronald Louis Zarobinski and Donna Jean (Strayer) Williams; m. David Michael Lemke, Aug. 25, 1984; 1 child, Kelsey Marie. BA in French and Bus. with honors, Mich. State U., 1987, M in Edn. Adminstrn., 1993. Cert. secondary tchr., vocat. and adminstrn. Teaching asst. East Lansing (Mich.) Pub. Schs., 1985-87, French and bus. tchr. comty. edn., 1985-87; tchr. French and bus. Grand Blanc (Mich.) Comty. Schs., 1987&, coord. elem. fgn. lang., 1990-91, coord. K-12 fgn. lang., 1991—; chair North Cen. accreditation Grand Blanc Mid. Sch., 1990—. Vol. Flint Internat. Inst., 1987-91, United Way, Flint, 1992. Mem. Nat. Bus. Edn. Assn. (Award of Merit 1987), Am. Assn. of Tchrs. of French, Mich. Fgn. Lang. Assn. (presider's chair 1994-95), Mich. Bus. Edn. Assn. (Outstanding Bus. Educator award 1986-87), Phi Kappa Phi. Avocations: reading mysteries, camping, traveling. Home: 6057 E Maple Ave Grand Blanc MI 48439-9003 Office: Grand Blanc Comty Schs 11920 S Saginaw St Grand Blanc MI 48439-1402

LEMLE, ROBERT SPENCER, lawyer; b. N.Y.C., Mar. 6, 1953; s. Leo Karl and Gertrude (Bander) L.; m. Roni Sue Kohen, Sept. 5, 1976; children: Zachary, Joanna. AB, Oberlin Coll., 1975; JD, NYU, 1978. Bar: N.Y. 1979. Assoc. Cravath, Swaine & Moore, N.Y.C., 1978-82; assoc. gen. counsel Cablevision Systems Corp., Woodbury, N.Y., 1982-84, v.p., gen. counsel, 1984-86, sr. v.p., gen. counsel, sec., 1986-94, exec. v.p., gen. counsel, sec., 1994—; bd. editors Cable TV and New Media Law and Fin., N.Y.C., 1983—, bd. dirs. Cablevision Systems Corp., 1988—. Bd. trustees L.I. Children's Mus., 1990—; bd. trustees Oberlin Coll., 1996—. Mem. ABA, N.Y. State Bar Assn. Avocation: real estate. Home: 7 Grace Dr Old Westbury NY 11568-1228 Office: Cablevision Systems Corp 1 Media Crossway Dr Woodbury NY 11797

LEMLEY, STEVEN SMITH, academic administrator; b. Oakland, Calif., Jan. 7, 1945; married, 1967; 3 children. BA, Pepperdine U., 1966, MA, 1970; PhD in speech, communication, Ohio State U., 1972. Asst. prof. communication Pepperdine U., L.A., 1972-78, assoc. dean student life, 1972-76, dean student life, 1976-78; assoc. prof. speech, dean Lubbock (Tex.) Christian U., 1978-82, now pres. Office: Lubbock Christian U Office of Pres 5601 19th St Lubbock TX 79407-2031

LEMMON, GEORGE COLBORNE, bishop; b. St. John, N.B., Can., Mar. 20, 1932; m. Lois Jean Foster, June 7, 1957; children: Paul, Marilu, Robert. BA, U. N.B., 1959; Licentiate in Theology, Wycliffe Coll., Toronto, Can., 1962, BD, 1964, DD (hon.), 1991; DD (hon.), King's Coll., Halifax, N.S., Can., 1990. Ordained deacon Anglican Ch. Can., 1962, priest, 1963. Consecrated bishop Diocese of Fredericton (N.B.), Anglican Ch. Can., 1989—; linotype operator, 10 yrs.; mem. nat. exec. com., nat. stewardship com. Anglican Ch. Can. Columnist The Daily Gleaner, 1986—. Active Mayor's Adv. Com. on Econ. Devel., Fredericton, 1991; sec. Crake Found. Inc.; founding mem. Cons for Christ, Fredericton. Mem. Irenaeus Fellowship. Office: Diocese of Fredericton, 115 Church St, Fredericton, NB Canada E3B 4C8 Home: 791 Brunswick St, Fredericton NB Canada E3B 1H8

LEMMON, JACK (JOHN UHLER LEMMON, III), actor; b. Boston, Feb. 8, 1925; s. John Uhler, Jr. and Mildred LaRue (Noel) L.; m. Cynthia Boyd Stone, May 7, 1950; 1 child, Christopher; m. Felicia Farr, Aug. 17, 1962; 1 child, Courtney. Grad., Phillips Andover Acad., 1943; B.S., B.A., Harvard U., 1947. Pres. Jalem Prodns., N.Y.C., 1952—. Appeared in summer stock, 1940-48, radio, TV shows, 1948-52; including TV series That Wonderful Guy, 1950; summer replacement: Toni Twin Time, 1950; appeared in TV series: The Adlibbers, 1951, Couple Next Door, 1951-52, Heaven for Betsy, 1952; appeared on Broadway in: Room Service, 1953, Face of A Hero, 1960, Tribute, 1979 (Broadway Drama Guild award); other stage appearances Idiot's Delight, 1970, Juno and the Paycock, 1975, Long Day's Journey Into Night, 1986; appeared in films: Mister Roberts (Acad. award best supporting actor), It Happened to Jane, You Can't Run Away From It, Fire Down Below, Cowboy, Operation Madball, Bell Book and Candle, Miss Casy Jones, Some Like It Hot, The Apartment, The Wackiest Ship in the Army, Notorious Landlady, Irma La Douce, Under The Yum Yum Tree, Days of Wine and Roses, Good Neighbor Sam, How to Murder Your Wife, The Great Race, The Fortune Cookie, Luv, The Odd Couple, The April Fools, The Out-of-Towners, The War Between Men and Women, 1972, Avanti, 1972, Save the Tiger, 1973 (Acad. award best actor), The Front Page, 1974, The Prisoner of 2d Avenue, 1975, Alex & the Gypsy, 1976, Airport, 1977, The Gentleman Tramp, 1977, The China Syndrome, 1978 (Best Actor Cannes Film Festival), Tribute, 1980, Buddy Buddy, 1981, Missing, 1981 (Best Actor Cannes Film Festival), Mass Appeal, 1984, Macaroni, 1985, That's Life, 1986, Dad, 1989, JFK, 1990, The Player, 1992, Glengarry Glen Ross, 1992, Short Cuts, 1993, Grumpy Old Men, 1993, Getting Away with Murder, 1995, The Grass Harp, 1995; TV appearances include: The Entertainer, 1975 (Emmy award nomination), 'S Wonderful, 'S Marvelous, 'S Gershwin, 1972 (Emmyaward), The Murder of Mary Phagan, 1988, A Life in the Theatre, 1993, For Richer, For Poorer, 1992. Served as ensign USNR, 1945-46. Recipient Lifetime Achievement award, Am. Film Inst., 1988, D.W. Griffith award, 1987. Clubs: Hasty Pudding (pres. 1945-46), Delphic (v.p. 1945-46), Dramatic (v.p. 1945) (Harvard U.); Players (N.Y.C.). Office: Creative Artists Agy 9830 Wilshire Blvd Beverly Hills CA 90212-1804*

LEMMON, JEAN MARIE, editor-in-chief; b. Duluth, Minn., Nov. 11, 1932; d. Lawrence Howard and Marie Julien (Gunderson) H.; m. Richard LuVerne LemMon, Apr. 17, 1965 (div. 1976); 1 child, Rebecca Jean. BA, U. Minn., 1954. Editor Better Homes and Gardens Mag., Des Moines, 1961-63, dept. head crafts, 1985-86, editor-in-chief, 1993—; women's editor Successful Farming, Des Moines, 1963-68; pres. Jean LemMon & Assocs., Des Moines, 1968-84; project editor Meredith Pub. Svcs., Des Moines, 1984-85; editor-in-chief Country Home Mag., Des Moines, 1986-93; adv. bd. Drake U. Journalism Sch., 1991—. Mem. ASCAP, Mensa Internat., Am. Soc. Interior Designers. Office: Better Homes and Gardens 1716 Locust St Des Moines IA 50309-3023*

LEMMOND, JOSEPH SHAWN, state legislator, insurance agent; b. Ft. Thomas-Kentfield, Ky., May 4, 1958; s. David Rea and Joyce Francis (Kinard) L.; m. Karen Alicia Flynt, May 9, 1987; stepchildren: Jason Anthony Mullis, Kenneth Allen Mullis. Degree in econs., U. N.C. Inside salesperson Robert E. Mason Assocs., Charlotte, N.C.; mayor Town of Matthews, 1987-91; ins. agt. Dean, Heckle, Hill, Inc., Matthews, N.C.; rep. N.C. State Ho. of Reps., 1992—. Mem. city coun., police com. Town of Matthews, 1983-87. With USN, 1976-82. Republican. Roman Catholic. Avocations: sailing, backpacking. Office: NC State Ho of Reps Legislative Blvd Rm 1317 Raleigh NC 27603

LEMNIOS, ANDREW ZACHERY, aerospace engineer, educator, researcher; b. Newburyport, Mass., Nov. 23, 1931; s. Zaharias Vasilios and Evangelia (Malamoglou) L.; m. Aspasia Soula Hanos, Sept. 26, 1954; children: Karen Eve, Keith Harold. SB, MIT, 1953, SM, 1954; PhD, U. Conn., 1967; grad. advanced mgmt. program, Harvard U., 1983. Rsch. engr. United Techs. Rsch., East Hartford, Conn., 1954-60; sr. analytical engr. Kaman Aerospace Corp., Bloomfield, Conn., 1961-63, chief of fluid mechanics, 1963-68, chief rsch. engr., 1969-76, dir. rsch. and tech., 1976-89, asst. v.p. rsch. and tech. programs, 1989-93; adj. prof. Western New Eng. Coll., Springfield, Mass., 1956-76, U. Mass., Amherst, 1976-78; mem. aeronautics adv. com. NASA, Washington, 1979-84; mem. rotorcraft adv. com. Rensselaer Poly. Inst., Troy, N.Y., 1985-92, rsch. prof., dir., 1993—; mem. rotorcraft adv. com. U. Md., College Park, 1985-92. Patentee controllable twist rotor, rotor trim tab. Fellow AIAA (assoc.); mem. Am. Helicopter Soc. Republican. Greek Orthodox. Avocations: carpentry, gardening, music, reading. Home: 144 Primrose Dr Longmeadow MA 01106 Office: Rensselaer Polytechnic Inst Rotorcraft Tech Ctr Jonsson Engring Ctr Troy NY 12180

LEMOLE, GERALD MICHAEL, surgeon; b. S.I., N.Y., Dec. 17, 1936; s. Joseph Michael and Mary (Boylan) L.; B.S. in Biology, Villanova U., 1958; M.D., Temple U., 1962; m. Emily Jane Asplundh, Dec. 8, 1962; children—Lisa Jane, Laura Leigh, Emily Anne, Gerald Michael, Samantha Mary, Christopher Robin. Intern, S.I. Hosp., 1962-63; resident in gen. surgery Temple U., Phila., 1963-67; resident in thoracic surgery Baylor Affiliated Hosps., Houston, 1967-69; practice medicine specializing in cardio thoracic surgery, Phila., 1969—, Browns Mills, N.J., 1972-84; chief sect. cardiac and thoracic surgery Temple U. Hosp., Phila., 1970-77; prof. surgery Temple U. Health Scis. Ctr., 1975-77; chmn. dept. surgery Deborah Heart and Lung Ctr., Phila., 1972-84; chief sect. cardiovascular surgery Med. Ctr. Del.; vis. prof. cardiac surgery U. Dublin (Ireland), 1974, U. Istanbul, Turkey, 1982, Mil. Med. Coll., Ankara, Turkey, 1985, Beijing Heart Inst., 1991; clin. prof. surgery U. Pa., 1979, Rutgers Med. Sch. Diplomate Am. Bd. Surgery, Am. Bd. Thoracic Surgery. Recipient Disting. Alumnus award VIllanova U., 1987. Fellow ACS, Am. Coll. Cardiology, Am. Coll. Chest Physicians (cardiovascular com. 1974—); mem. Phila. Coll. Physicians, Am. Assn. Thoracic Surgery, Am. Fedn. Clin. Research, Am., Pan Am. thoracic socs., Internat., Cardiovascular Soc., Denton A. Cooley Cardiovascular Surg. Soc., Am. Coll. Angiology, Pa., Phila. County med. socs., Phila. Acad. Surgery, Phila. Acad. Cardiology (pres. 1976-79, chmn. exec. com. 1976—), Assn. Acad. Surgeons, Soc. Vascular Surgery, Pa. Assn. Thoracic Surgeons, AMA, Am. Heart Assn. (cardiovascular council 1973—, pres. Del. chpt. 1991, chmn. bd. dirs. 1992), Pa. Assn. Thoracic Surgery (program chmn. 1975—). Contbr. numerous articles on cardiovascular surgery and disease to med. jours.; research in cardiovascular physiology. Home: 404 Tomlinson Rd Huntingdon Valley PA 19006-4818 Office: Med Ctr Del 4745 Ogletown Stanton Rd # 20 Newark DE 19713-2070

LEMON, HENRY MARTYN, physician, educator; b. Chgo., Dec. 23, 1915; s. Harvey Brace and Louise (Birkhoff) L.; m. Harriet Tuxbury Qua, May 3, 1941 (dec. Jan. 1976); children—Elizabeth Anne Lemon Carr, Harvey Brace, Stanley Moncrief, David Tuxbury, Jennifer Jane Lemon Dewitt; m. Dorothy Campbell, May 28, 1976. B.S., U. Chgo., 1938; M.D. cum laude, Harvard U., 1940. Diplomate: Am. Bd. Internal Medicine, Am. Bd. Med. Oncology. Intern Billings Hosp., Chgo., 1940-41; asst. resident medicine Billings Hosp., 1941-42; asst. dept. medicine U. Chgo., 1942-43; chief med. resident Univ. Hosp., Boston, 1946-48; instr. medicine Boston U., 1946-48, asst. prof. medicine, 1948-54, assoc. prof., 1954-61; dir. Eugene C. Eppley Cancer Inst. U. Nebr. Coll. Medicine, Omaha, 1961-68, prof. internal Medicine, 1961-86, emeritus prof., 1986—; cons. internal medicine VA, Boston, Omaha, 1950-86; bd. dirs. Mass., Nebr. divs. Am. Cancer Soc. Served to capt. M.C. U.S. Army, 1943-46; col. USAR; ret. Recipient Disting. Service award U. Chgo. Med. Alumni, 1952, awards of merit AMA Sci. Exhibits, 1957, 1962, 1965, Disting. Teaching award U. Nebr. Med. Center, 1976, Meritorious Service award, 1980, Margaret Hay Edwards medal Am. Assn. Cancer Edn., 1989. Fellow ACP; mem. AMA, Am. Assn. Cancer Research, Am. Soc. Clin. Oncology, Endocrine Soc., Soc. Surg. Oncology, Central Soc. Clin. Research, Planned Parenthood Omaha and Council Bluffs (pres. 1990), Res. Officers Assn., Phi Beta Kappa, Phi Beta Kappa Assocs. Omaha (pres. 1985-87), Sigma Xi (Disting. Research award U. Nebr. chpt. 1985), Alpha Omega Alpha. Unitarian. Club: Rotary. Rsch. in air-borne infection, Cytodiagnosis Pancreatic cancer, transplantation human cancer to hamsters, estrogen imbalance in breast cancer, endocrine and chemotherapy cancer, reduction toxicity in cancer chemotherapy, estriol prevention breast cancer, carcinogenesis breast, leukemia and lymphoma. Home: 10805 Poppleton Ave Omaha NE 68144-1843 Office: U Nebr Dept Internal Medicine Omaha NE 68198-3330 *My medical life in service, education and research has taken place during the golden age of American medicine, a period of unprecedented growth in our ability to diagnose and treat most diseases. My work has received inestimable benefit from those who were my teachers, and I have found my own greatest reward in attempting to illuminate the paths of my students; this fact and the privilege of serving my patients have been my chief professional guides along the way.*

LEMON, LESLIE GENE, consumer products and services company executive, lawyer; b. Davenport, Iowa, June 14, 1940. BS, U. Ill., 1962, LLB, 1964. Bar: Ill. 1964, Ariz. 1972. Asst. gen. counsel Am. Farm Bur. Fedn., Chgo., 1964-69; sr. atty. Armour and Co., Chgo., 1969-71; with The Dial

Corp (formerly Greyhound Corp.), Phoenix, 1971—, sr. asst. gen. counsel, 1975-77, gen. counsel, 1977—, v.p., 1979—; bd. dirs. FINOVA Group. Vestryman All Saints Episcopal Ch., Phoenix, 1975-81; trustee Phoenix Art Mus., 1985—; bd. dirs. Phoenix Children's Hosp., 1985—; bd. visitors U. Calif. Med. Sch., Davis, 1983—. Mem. ABA, Assn. Gen. Counsel, Maricopa County Bar Assn., State Bar Ariz., Phoenix C. of C. (bd. dirs. 1989-95). Home: 1136 W Butler Dr Phoenix AZ 85021-4428 Office: The Dial Corp Dial Tower 1850 N Central Ave Phoenix AZ 85077-0001

LEMOND, GREGORY JAMES, former professional bicycle racer; b. L.A., June 26, 1961; m. Kathy Morris, 1980; children: Geoffrey James, Scott, Simone. Mem. Renault Team, 1980-83, La Vie Claire Team, 1983-89, Team Z, 1989-95; ptnr. Tour de France restaurant, Edina, Minn., 1990—. Winner Tour de France, 1986, 89, 90, profl. road racing championships, Altershein, Switzerland, 1983, 89; named Sportsman of Yr., 1989; winner Tour Du Pont, 1992. Office: care Pat Stahl Cycle Goods 2801 Hennepin Ave Minneapolis MN 55408-1907*

LE MONE, ARCHIE, religious organization administrator; b. N.Y.C., Sept. 30, 1938; s. Archie and Christine (Webb) Le M.; m. Anita Joyce Colvin, June 18, 1966; children: Adae Ronald, Amani Philip (dec.). AB in History, Morgan State U., 1962; MDiv, Crozer Theol. Sem., 1965. Asst. pastor White Rock Bapt., Phila., 1962-66; divsn. asst. Am. Bapt. Convn., Valley Forge, Pa., 1965-66; mem. exec. staff World Coun. Chs., Geneva, 1966-75, Caribbean Conf. Chs., West Indies, 1975-80, Cleve. Coun. Chs., 1981-83; exec. dir. Home Mission Bd. Progressive Bapt. Conv., Washington, 1983—; bd. dirs. Nat. Coun. Chs., N.Y.C., 1983—, Washington Office on Africa, 1983—. Editor: RISK Study Series, 1973; contbr. articles to profl. jours. Mem. monitoring com. Montgomery County (Md.) Pub. Schs., 1994. Mem. Alpha Phi Alpha (chaplain 1993—). Avocations: foreign languages, reading, swimming. Office: Prog Nat Baptist Conv Inc 601 50th St NE Washington DC 20019-5499

LEMONICK, AARON, physicist, educator; b. Phila., Feb. 2, 1923; s. Samuel and Mary (Ferman) L.; m. Eleanor Leah Drutt, Feb. 12, 1950; children—Michael Drutt, David Morris. B.A., U. Pa., 1950; M.A., Princeton U., 1952, Ph.D., 1954. Asst. prof. physics Haverford Coll., Pa., 1954-57, assoc. prof., 1957-61; assoc. prof. Princeton U., N.J., 1961-64, prof., 1964-94, assoc. chmn. dept. physics, 1967-69, dean grad. sch., 1969-73, dean faculty, 1973-89, dean of faculty emeritus, 1989—; assoc. dir. Princeton-Pa. Accelerator, 1961-67; prof. emeritus Princeton U., N.J., 1994—; v.p. Princeton U. Press, 1973—; dep. dir. Princeton Plasma Physics Lab., 1989-90. Trustee Bryn Mawr Coll., 1988—. Fellow AAAS, Am. Phys. Soc.; mem. AAUP, Am. Assn. Physics Tchrs., Phi Beta Kappa, Sigma Xi. Office: Princeton U Dept Physics Princeton NJ 08544

LE MONS, KATHLEEN ANN, portfolio manager, investment broker; b. Trenton, N.J., Apr. 6, 1952; d. Albert Martin and Veronica Grace (Kerr) LeM.; m. Walter Everett Faircloth, Apr. 15, 1978 (div. Dec. 1988); m. Jeffery West Benedict, June 29, 1991. Attended, Rollins Coll., 1970-71, Fla. State U., 1971-76; BSBA magna cum laude, Christopher Newport U., 1995; post-grad., Coll. William and Mary, 1995—. Registered rep. NASD/NYSE, investment advisor; cert. portfolio mgr. Sci. rsch. assoc. NASA, Hampton, Va., 1973-76; fin. cons. Merrill Lynch Pierce Fenner Smith, Hampton, 1985-88; cert. portfolio mgr. Wheat First Butcher Singer, Newport News, Va., 1988—; curriculum chair Grad. Sch. Bus. Coll. William and Mary, 1995—. Pres. James Landing Assn., 1991-95; life mem. Capital Dist. Found., 1992; mem. exec. panel fund distbn. Va. Peninsula United Way, 1996—. George F. Hixson fellow, 1996. Mem. Am. Mktg. Assn., Va. Peninsula C. of C. (transp. task force 1993—, govtl. affairs task force 1993—), MBA Assn. (charter, chair curriculum com., v.p. 1996—), Oyster Point Kiwanis Club (charter), James River Country Club (9-hole golf group), Alpha Chi. Republican. Avocations: golf, snowskiing. Home: 61 Queens Ct Newport News VA 23606-2034 Office: Wheat First Butcher Singer 11817 Canon Blvd Newport News VA 23606-2569

LEMOS, RAMON MARCELINO, philosophy educator; b. Mobile, Ala., July 7, 1927; s. Marcelino and Marie Louise (Moore) L.; m. Mamie Lou McCrory, Dec. 26, 1951 (dec. Apr. 1990); children: Noah Marcelino, William Ramon, Christopher Tait, John Paul; m. Anne Craft, Aug. 7, 1994. B.A., U. Ala., 1951; M.A., Duke, 1953, Ph.D., 1955; Fulbright scholar, U. London, Eng., 1955-56. Mem. faculty U. Miami, 1956—, prof. philosophy, 1967—, chmn. dept., 1971-84. Author: Experience, Mind and Value, 1969, Rousseau's Political Philosophy, 1977, Hobbes and Locke: Power and Consent, 1978, Rights, Goods, and Democracy, 1986, Metaphysical Investigations, 1988, The Nature of Value: Axiological Investigations, 1995. Served with USMC, 1945-49. Named Outstanding Tchr. U. Miami, 1968. Mem. Am. Philos. Assn. (program chmn. Eastern div. meeting 1983), Fla. Philos. Assn. (pres. 1963), Phi Beta Kappa, Phi Kappa Phi, Omicron Delta Kappa. Home: 6960 SW 82nd Ct Miami FL 33143-2509 Office: U Miami Dept Philosophy Coral Gables FL 33124

LEMOYNE, IRVE CHARLES, career officer; b. Brownsville, Tex., June 28, 1939; s. McPherson and Doris (Grimm) LeM.; m. Elizabeth Gzeckowicz, June 11, 1961; children: Irve Charles Jr., Elizabeth Christian. BS in Indsl. Mgmt., Ga. Inst. Tech., 1961; MS in Mgmt., Naval Postgrad Sch., Monterey, Calif., 1972. Commd. ensign USN, 1961, advanced through grades to rear adm., 1991; div. officer USS Massey (DD 778), Mayport, Fla., 1961-62; student underwater demolition team tng. U.S. Naval Amphibious Base, Little Creek, Va., 1962-66, ops. officer Underwater Demolition Team 22, 1963 -66; exec. officer Seal Team 1 U.S. Naval Amphibious Base, Coronado, Calif., 1966-69; commdg. officer Underwater Demolition Team 11, Coronado, Calif., 1969-71; student Naval Postgrad. Sch., Monterey, 1971-72; spl. warfare project officer Naval Sea Systems Command, Washington, 1972-75; asst. to spl. warfare mission and resource officer OPNAV Staff, The Pentagon, Washington, 1975-77; student Nat. War Coll., Washington, 1977-78; commdg. officer Inshore Undersea Warfare Group One, Coronado, 1978-79; chief staff officer Naval Spl. Warfare Group 1, Coronado, 1979-81; spl. asst. Dep. chief Naval Material for Resources Mgmt., Arlington, Va., 1981-82, chief ops. div., 1982-83; comdr Naval Sp. Warfare Group 1, Coronado, 1983-85; fellow Chief Naval Ops. Strategic Study Group, Naval War Coll., Newport, R.I., 1985-86; br. head Naval Spl. Warfare Plans and Policy Dep. Chief Naval Ops. for Plans, Policy and Ops., Washington, 1986-87; comdr. Naval Spl. Warfare Command, Naval Amphibious Base, Coronado, 1987-89; dir. resources U.S. Spl. Ops. Command, MacDill AFB, Fla., 1989-93, dep. commander-in-chief, 1993-96. Decorated Legion of Merit with two gold stars, Bronze Star with gold star and Combat V, Meritorious Svc. medal with two gold stars. Mem. U.S. Naval Inst. Episcopalian. Avocations: beekeeping, windsurfing. Office: US Spl Ops Command Dep Comdr in Chief Tampa FL 33621

LEMP, JOHN, JR., telecommunications engineer; b. Trenton, N.J., Dec. 10, 1936; s. John and Helena M. (Braddock) L.; BS in Elec. Engring., Princeton U., 1959; MS in Elec. Engring., Poly. Inst. Bklyn., 1968; MBA, Colo. State U., 1973; grad. Air Command and Staff Coll., 1974; grad. Indsl. Coll. Armed Forces, 1981; m. Susan N. Rose, 1955; children: John, Thomas K., Carl A., Adam F.H. Project engr. Gen. Devices, Inc., Princeton, N.J., 1959-60; with Bell Telephone Labs., N.J. and Colo., 1962-74; mgr. bus. planning Aeronutronic Ford Corp., Willow Grove, Pa., 1974-76; mgr. R & D ITT, Corinth, Miss., 1976-78; lectr. Sch. Bus., Temple U., Phila., 1976, Sch. Bus., U. Colo., 1982—; project leader Nat. Telecommunication and Info. Adminstrn., U.S. Dept. Commerce, Boulder, Colo., 1978-82; dir. Info. Access Systems, Inc., 1981-84. Lemp Devel. Co., Inc., 1975—; mgr. Swinerton & Walberg Property Svcs., Inc., 1995. Mem. CAP, 1970—; pres. Carolyn Heights Civic Assn., 1972-73; treas. Frazier Woods Civic Assn., 1975-76; treas. Light Fantastic, 1990-91, pres., 1991-92. Served with USAF, 1960-63; served to col. USAFR, ret. Decorated Air Force Commendation medal, Meritorious Svc. medal, Legion of Merit; named Outstanding Elec. Engr., Armed Forces Communications & Electronics Assn., 1959; cert. instrument flight instr., FAA. Mem. IEEE (sr.), Am. Statis. Assn., Inst. Ops. Rsch. & Mgmt. Sci., Am. Armed Forces Communications and Electronics Assn., Assn. Computing Machinery, Air Force Assn. Patentee in field; contbr. articles to profl. jours. Home: 3745 23rd St Boulder CO 80304-1611 Office: U Colo PO Box 419 Boulder CO 80309-0419

LEMPERT, PHILIP, advertising executive, author, syndicated columnist; b. East Orange, N.J., Apr. 17, 1953; s. Sol and Lillian E. L.; married Laura Gray; 1 son. BS in Mktg., Drexel U., 1974; degree in Package Design, Pratt Inst., 1978. With Lempert Co., Belleville, N.J., 1974-89; pres. Consumer Insight, Inc., 1990—; sr. v.p., sr. ptnr. AGE Wave Inc., 1991-93; columnist Chgo. Tribune, 1993—; correspondent Today Show, WGN-TV, KTLA-TV, WGNX-TV, Tribune TV; Columnist, Supermarket News, founder, CEO Supermarket Alliance, 1993—; adj. prof. Fairleigh Dickinson U., Seton Hall U. Pub., editor newsletter The Lempert Report. Mem. Am. Assn. Advt. Agencies (bd. govs. 1986-88, legis. liason 1988-90, legis. coord. 1987-90), Nat. Food Brokers Assn. (chmn. food svcs. com.). Republican. Jewish. Office: Consumer Insight PO Box 207 Tiburon CA 94920

LEMPERT, RICHARD OWEN, lawyer, educator; b. Hartford, Conn., June 2, 1942; s. Philip Leonard and Mary (Steinberg) L.; m. Cynthia Ruth Willey, Sept. 10, 1967; 1 child, Leah Rose. A.B., Oberlin Coll., 1964; J.D., U. Mich., 1968, Ph.D. in Sociology, 1971. Bar: Mich. 1978. Asst. prof. law U. Mich., Ann Arbor, 1968-72, assoc. prof., 1972-74, prof. law, 1974—, prof. sociology, 1985—, Francis A. Allen collegiate prof. law, 1990—, acting chair dept. sociology, 1993-94, chair dept. sociology, 1995—; Mason Ladd disting. vis. prof. U. Iowa Law Sch., 1981; vis. fellow Centre for Socio-Legal Rsch., Wolfson Coll., Oxford (Eng.) U., 1982; mem. adv. panel for law and social sci. div. NSF, 1976-79, mem. exec. com. adv. com. for social sci., 1979; mem. com. law enforcement and adminstrn. of justice NRC, vice chmn., 1984-87, chmn., 1987-89; mem. adv. panel NSF program on Human Dimensions of Global Change, 1989, 92—; mem. com. on DNA technology in forensic sci. NRC, 1989-92, com. on drug testing in workplace, 1991-93. Author: (with Stepehn Saltzburg) A Modern Approach to Evidence, 1977, 2d edit., 1983; (with Joseph Sanders) An Invitation to Law and Social Science, 1986, Under the Influence, 1993; editor: (with Jacques Normand and Charles O'Brien) Under the Influence? Drugs and the American Work Force, 1994; editorial bd. Law and Soc. Rev., 1972-77, 89-92, editor, 1982-85; editorial bd. Evaluation Rev., 1979-82, Violence and Victims, 1985—, Jour. Law and Human Behavior, 1980-82; contbr. articles to profl. jours. Fellow Ctr. for Advanced Study in Behavioral Scis., 1994-95. Fellow Am. Acad. Arts and Scis.; mem. Am. Sociol. Assn. (chair sect. sociology of law 1995-96), Law and Society Assn. (trustee 1977-80, 90-93, exec. com. 1979-80, 82-87), Soc. Am. Law Tchrs., Order of Coif, Phi Beta Kappa, Phi Kappa Phi. Office: U Mich Law Sch 625 S State St Ann Arbor MI 48109-1215

LENAHAN, WALTER CLAIR, retired foreign service officer; b. Everett, Wash., Apr. 20, 1934; s. James Harold and Doris Anne (Larson) L.; m. Patricia Anne Casey, July 6, 1957; children—Karen Diane, Desiree, Lorelei, Casey James. B.A., U. Oreg., 1960. Commd. fgn. service officer Dept. State, 1961; officer Dept. State, Washington, 1961-72, U.S. Embassy, Beijing, People's Republic of China, 1979-81, Dept. Commerce, Washington, 1981-86; dep. asst. sec. for textiles and apparel Dept. Commerce, 1982-86; v.p. Am.-Philippine Fiber Industry, Inc., Manila, 1972-76; pres. Internat. Bus. and Econ. Research Corp., Washington, 1986-95; retired, 1995. Served to sgt. U.S. Army, 1953-56. Recipient Sr. Fgn. Service Presdl. award Dept. State, 1984. Lutheran. Avocations: tennis; contract bridge.

LENARD, GEORGE DEAN, lawyer; b. Joliet, Ill., Aug. 26, 1957; s. Louis George and Jennie (Helopoulos) L.; m. Nancy Ilene Sundquist, Nov. 11, 1989. BS, Ill. State U., 1979; JD, Thomas Cooley Law Sch., 1984. Bar: Ill. 1984, U.S. Dist. Ct. (no. dist.) Ill. 1984, U.S. Supreme Ct. 1990. Asst. states atty. Will County States Attys. Office, Joliet, 1984-88; asst. pub. defender Will County Pub. Defenders Office, Joliet, 1988-95; pvt. practice law Joliet, 1988—. Mem. ABA, ATLA, Nat. Assn. Criminal Def. Lawyers, Ill. State Bar Assn., Chgo. Bar Assn., Phi Alpha Delta (Isaac P. Christiancy chpt.). Avocations: target shooting, golf, baseball. Office: Ste 206 81 N Chicago St Joliet IL 60432

LENARD, MARY JANE, accounting and information systems educator; b. York, Pa., July 8, 1955; d. Martin and Anne Ruth (Zimmerman) Kondor; m. Robert Louis Lenard; children: Kevin, Kelsey. BS in Econ. and Adminstrv. Sci., Carnegie Mellon U., 1977; MBA in Fin., U. Akron, 1982; PhD in Bus. Adminstrn., Kent State U., 1995. Cert. mgmt. acct. Mgmt. trainee Equibank, N.A., Pitts., 1977-78; acct., auditor The Goodyear Tire & Rubber Co., Akron, Ohio, 1978-86; instr. U. Akron, 1986-93; mem. adj. faculty Cleve. State U., 1994—. Pres. Hillcrest Elem. PTA, 1992-93; v.p. Summit County PTA, 1994—; active Revere Schs. Computer Curriculum Com., 1994-95. Mem. Am. Acctg. Assn., Inst. Mgmt. Accts. (dir. mem. retention 1994—), Inst. Ops. Rsch. and the Mgmt. Scis., Decision Scis. Inst., Akron Women's Network. Office: Cleveland State Univ Cleveland OH 44115

LENARD, MICHAEL BARRY, merchant banker, lawyer; b. Chgo., May 20, 1955; s. Henry Madart and Jacqueline Jo Anne (Silver) L.; m. Amy Jeanne Rifenbergh, Oct. 10, 1987; children: Madeline M., Nicholas X. BBA, U. Wis., 1977; postgrad., NYU, 1981-82; JD, U. So. Calif., 1982. Assoc. Whitman & Ransom, N.Y.C., 1982-83; assoc. Latham & Watkins, L.A., 1984-91, ptnr., 1992-93; mng. dir., counsellor William E. Simon & Sons, L.A., 1993—; bd. dirs. William E. Simon & Sons (Asia), Hong Kong, Wallem Simon Asian Shipping Investments, Ltd., Hong Kong, Wyle Labs., L.A., Creative Optics, Phoenix, Internat. Logistics, Ltd., Chgo., Pacific Precision Metals, L.A. With So. Calif. Law Rev. mag., 1980-81. V.p. U.S. Olympic Com., 1989—, mem. exec. com., bd. dirs., 1985—, mem. athletes' adv. coun., 1981-89, vice chmn. athletes' adv. coun., 1985-89; named to Internat. Coun. for Arbitration of Sport, Internat. Olympic Com., 1994—; bd. dirs. L.A. Sports Coun., 1988—, Atlanta Com. for Olympic Games, 1990—. Named semi-finalist Outstanding Undergrad. Achievement award, 1977, USA Team Handball Athlete of Yr., 1985, USOC Olympian Mag. Team Handball SportsMan of Yr., 1985, Nat. Champion in Team Handball, 1975, 77, 79, 80, 82, 87, 95; recipient Harry A. Bullis scholarship, 1977; mem. 1984 Olympic Team, U.S. Nat. Team, 1977-85 (capt. 1985). Mem. Order of the Coif, Phi Kappa Phi, Beta Gamma Sigma, Beta Alpha Psi, Phi Eta Sigma. Home: 1433 El Bosque Ct Pacific Palisades CA 90272-1915 Office: William E Simon & Sons 10990 Wilshire Blvd Ste 1750 Los Angeles CA 90024-3913

LENARDON, ROBERT JOSEPH, classics educator; b. Fort William, Ont., Can., Sept. 8, 1928; came to U.S., 1949; s. Louis and Nina (Boffa) L. BA with honors in Latin, U. B.C., Can., 1949; MA in Classics, U. Cin., 1950, PhD, 1954. Instr. Greek and Latin Columbia, 1954-57; asst. prof. classics U. Wash., Seattle, 1957-59; mem. faculty dept. classics Ohio State U., Columbus, 1959—; assoc. prof. Ohio State U., 1963-69, prof., dir. grad. studies, 1969-84, prof. emeritus, 1984-92; prof., head dept. classics Siena Coll., 1992-95; vis. prof. U. B.C., summers 1960-61, 66, NYU, 1973, 91-92. Author: (with Mark P.O. Morford) Classical Mythology, 1971, 5th edit., 1995, The Saga of Themistocles, 1977; book rev. editor Classical Jour., 1961-68. Taft scholar and fellow, 1950-54; vis. fellow Corpus Christi Coll., Cambridge (Eng.) U., 1971. Mem. Am. Philol. Assn., Archeol. Inst. Am., Classical Assn. Atlantic States. Home: 62 Willett St Albany NY 12210-1140

LENCEK, RADO L., Slavic languages educator; b. Mirna, Slovenia, Oct. 3, 1921; came to U.S., 1956; s. Ludovik Ivan and Kati (Jaksa) L.; m. Nina A. Lovrencic, May 4, 1946; children: Bibi-Alice, Lena-Maria. Studied Slavic philology, U. Ljubljana, Slovenia, 1940-45, U. Padova, Italy, 1946-47; teaching diploma, Istituto Magistrale, Gorizia, Italy, 1947; MA in Linguistics, U. Chgo., 1959; PhD in Slavic Langs., Harvard U., 1962. Asst. prof. Istituto Magistrale Sloveno, Gorizia-Trieste, Italy, 1944-55; editor USIS-Trieste, Italy, 1951-54; asst. prof. U. Ill., Urbana, 1962-65; asst. prof. Slavic langs. Columbia U., N.Y.C., 1965-69, assoc. prof., 1969-74, prof., 1974-92, prof. emeritus, 1992—; assoc. Averell Harriman Inst. for Advanced Study of the Soviet Union; mem. Inst. on East Cen. Europe; vis. assoc. prof. NYU, 1969-72; vis. prof. Yale U., 1974, U. Ill., Urbana, 1977; coord. Nat. Com. Serbo-Croatian Teaching Materials, 1982—; U.S. coord. for Cooperation Project on Slavistics, 1983—; active U.S.-USSR Commn. on the Humanities and Social Scis., Inst. East Ctrl. Europe; participant Internat. Congs. of Slavists Prague, 1968, Warsaw, 1973, Zagreb-Ljubljana, 1978, Kiev, 1983, Sofia, 1988, Bratislava, 1993; coord. Columbia U. Program in Slavic Cultures, organized symposia Columbia U., 1974, 84, Prato di Resia, Italy, 1979, Northwestern U., 1980, U. Chgo., 1984, Acad. of Scis. USSR, Moscow, 1987, Am. Assn. Tchrs. of Slavic and East European Langs. Annual Convention, San Francisco, 1991, Toronto, Can., 1993; mem. adv. bd. Slovenski jezik-Slovene Linguistic Studies, 1994—. Author: Ob Jadranu, Ethnographic Studies, 1947, The Verb Pattern of Contemporary Slovene, 1966, A Bibliographical Guide to Slavic Civilizations, 1966, An Outline of the Course on Slavic Civilizations, 1970, 2d edit., 1978, The Structure and History of Slovene Language, 1982, Slovenes, The Eastern Alpine Slavs, and Their Cultural Heritage, 1989, The Correspondence Between Jan Baudouin de Courtenay (1845-1929) and Vatroslav Oblak (1864-96), 1992, Izbrane Razprave in Eseji (selected papers and essays), 1996; editor: (with others): Xenia Slavica, Gojko Ruzicic Festschrift, 1975, The Dilemma of the Melting Pot: The Case of the South Slavic Languages, 1976, To Honor Jernej Kopitar, 1780-1980, 1982, A Bibliography of Recent Literature on Macedonian, Serbo-Croatian and Slovene Languages, 1990; co-editor: Who's Who of Slovene Descent in the United States, 1992, 2d edit. 1995; editor U.S. Info. Svcs. Bull., Trieste, Italy, 1951-54; editor (series) Papers in Slovene Studies, 1975-76, editl. com., editor book revs. Slovene Studies, 1979—; editl. com. Folia Slavica, 1976-89, Nationalities Papers, 1979—, Geschichte, Kultur und Geisteswelt der Slowenen, Munich, 1982-91, Beiträge zur Kenntnis Südosteuropas, Munich, 1983-91, Münchner Zeitschrift für Balkankunde, 1983-91, Geschichte, Kultur und Geisteswelt der Südslaven, Munich, 1990; mem. coun. jours. Slavisticna revija, 1991—; contbr. articles in field of Slavic linguistics and cultures to scholarly jours. and proceedings of internat. confs., symposiums. Fulbright fellow, 1986; named Amb. of Rep. of Slovenia for Sci. Ministry for Sci. and Tech. of Rep. of Slovenia, 1995; grantee NSF, 1974, 79, Japan Soc. for Promotion Sci., 1989, Internat. Rsch. Exchs. Bd., 1971, 72, 83, 85, 94; recipient Lit. prize for publ. of Who's Who of Slovene Descent in U.S. 1995 Soc. Slovene Intellectuals of Trieste (Italy), 1996. Fellow Am. Coun. Learned Socs., Bulgarian Acad. Scis.; mem. Slovenska Kulturna Akcija (Buenos Aires), Slavists' Assn. Slovenia (hon. Ljubljana chpt. 1989—), Linguistic Soc. Am., Linguistic Cirle N.Y., Am. Assn. Advancement Slavic Studies, Am. Assn. Tchrs. Slavic and East European Langs. (Disting. Scholarly Career award 1994), Soc. Slovene Studies (founder, pres. 1973-83, editor newsletter 1973-77, editor Letter 1978-83, dir. Ctr. for Rsch. and Documentation 1988—), Inst. on East Ctrl. Europe, N.Y. Acad. Scis., Slovene Acad. Scis. and Arts, Fulbright Assn., Am. Slovene Cong. (orgnl. com. 1993-94, acad. advisor to coun. on acad. activities 1994—). Home: 560 Riverside Dr New York NY 10027-3202 Office: Columbia U 420 W 118th St New York NY 10027-7213

LENDARIS, GEORGE GREGORY, systems science educator; b. Helper, Utah, Apr. 2, 1935; s. Gregory George and Argie (Xenakis) L.; m. Irene Kokinos, June 26, 1958 (dec. July 1988); children: Miriam, Dorothy. BSEE cum laude., U. Calif., Berkeley, 1957, MSEE, 1958; PhD in Electrical Engring., 1961. Registered profl. engr., Calif., Oreg. Sr. rsch. engr., program mgr. Gen. Motors Corp., Defense Rsch. Labs., Santa Barbara, Calif., 1961-69; assoc. prof. systems sci., chmn. faculty Oreg. Grad. Ctr. for Rsch., Beaverton, 1969-71; prof. systems sci., electrical engring. Portland State U. Systems Sci. PhD Program, Oregon, 1971—; with Accurate Automation Corp., Chattanooga, 1993—, also bd. dirs.; cons. various bus.; editorial bd. Internat. Jour. of Gen. Systems (Gordon & Breach), 1974—, Systems Rsch. Jour. 1985—, IEEE Transactions on Neural Networks, 1991—; chmn. gen. Internat. Joint Conf. on Neural Networks, Oreg., 1991-93; presiding officer Faculty Senate Portland State U., 1995-96. Author jour. article Diffraction Pattern Sampling, 1970, selected reprints book IEEE, 1978, chpt. in book Conceptual Graphs & Neural Networks, 1992, numerous conf. articles. Choir dir. local chs. Greek Orthodox Ch., Santa Barbara, Portland, 1962-73, pres., chmn. various coms., 1962—, mem. justice and human rights com. local ch., Portland, 1974—; mem. Gov.'s Tech. Adv. Com., Oreg., 1970-72, oreg. State Senate Task Force on Econ. Devel., 1972-73; mem. adv. panel Portland Energy Commn., 1980. NAS fellow, 1974. Fellow IEEE; mem. AAAS, Systems, Man and Cybernetics Soc., Internat. Neural Network Soc. (bd. govs. 1996—), Internat. Soc. Knowledge Engrs., Am. Helenic Edn. Progressive Assn., Sigma Xi, Tau Beta Pi, Eta Kappa Nu. Avocations: woodworking, Greek folk dancing instructor, church choir singing. Office: Portland State U Sys Sci PhD Program PO Box 751 Portland OR 97207-0751 *People often consider the statement, "Peace on Earth, good will toward men," as descriptive of some future time. I consider it a dictum—for today.*

LENDER, ADAM, electrical engineer; b. Gleiwitz, Germany, Sept. 15, 1921; s. Joseph and Regina (Waksberg) L.; m. Lilia Sadowski, Aug. 10, 1945; children: James, Richard. BSEE, Columbia U., 1954, MSEE, 1956; PhDEE, Stanford U., 1972. Mem. tech. staff Bell Telephone Labs., Murray Hill, N.J., 1954-60; project engr. Internat. Tel. & Tel. Labs., Nutley, N.J., 1960-61; head advanced devel. GTE Lenkurt, Inc., San. Carlos, Calif., 1961-84; sr. cons. scientist, sr. mem. Lockheed Rsch. Labs., Palo Alto, Calif., 1984-93; adj. prof. grad. sch. elec. engring. U. Santa Clara (Calif.), 1976-87. Author: (with others) Digital Communications, 1981; contbr. articles to profl. jours.; inventor correlative techniques applied in digital communications and magnetic tape recordings, patentee in field. Recipient Stuart Ballantine medal Franklin Inst., 1984. Fellow IEEE (editor-in-chief Transactions in Comm. 1978-84, sr. tech. editor IEEE Comm. Mag. 1987-94, Donald J. McLellan award 1983, Centennial medal 1984), AIAA (assoc.); mem. Comm. Soc. IEEE (bd. govs. 1977-79, 82-84, Edwin Armstrong Achievement award 1995), Columbia U. Alumni Assn. (N.Y.C.), Stanford U. Aumni Assn., Ta Beta Pi, Eta Kappa Nu. Avocations: music, history. Home: 4124 Briarwood Way Palo Alto CA 94306-4609

LENDER, HERMAN JOSEPH, reinsurance company executive; b. Irvington, N.J., Sept. 2, 1923; s. Herman Joseph and Monica (Martesteck) L.; m. Janet Harriet Van Wert, June 15, 1945; children: Mark, Jonathan, David, Paul. Student, NYU, 1941-43, Rutgers U., 1943-45. Underwriter, br. office Am. Surety Co., Newark, 1940-49; supervising underwriter Fidelity & Casualty Co., N.Y.C., 1949-58; v.p. bonding Excess and Treaty Mgmt. Co., N.Y.C., 1958-67; v.p. mktg. Gen. Reins. Corp., Greenwich, Conn., 1967-85; reins. cons., 1986—; instr. Coll. Ins., N.Y.C., 1949-55. Pres., trustee Mt. Tabor Free Library Assn., N.J., 1962-71; lay leader United Meth. Ch., 1955-71, chmn. edn. com., New Canaan, 1971-85; chmn. council of ministries United Meth. Ch., Mt. Tabor, N.J. Mem. Soc. C.P.C.U.s (chmn. edn. com. H.Y. chpt. 1951-53). Home and Office: 39 Strowbridge Ave Mount Tabor NJ 07878

LENEHAN, ART, newspaper editor. Grad., Columbia U., 1971. Asst. mng. editor electronic news The Star-Ledger, Newark. Office: Newark Morning Ledger Co One Star Ledger Plz Newark NJ 07102-1200

LENERTZ, MARY LEE, women's health nurse, nursing supervisor; b. Galveston, Tex., Feb. 16, 1942; d. Carlos Wilson and Muta Mary (Yeager) Van Dyke; m. Robert Deane Lenertz, Nov. 3, 1959 (dec. June 1979); children: Robert D. Jr., Daniel Steven, Thomas Wayne. AS, Alvin Jr. Coll., 1968; BSN, U. Tex., 1972, advanced nurse practitioner, 1988. RN, Tex.; cert. women's health nurse practitioner. Charge nurse U. Tex. Med. Br., Galveston, 1972-73; nursing supr. Big Bend Meml. Hosp., Alpine, Tex., 1974-75, DON, 1975-76; field office nurse mgr. Tex. Dept. Health, Ft. Davis, 1976-88; advanced nurse practitioner Tex. Dept. Health, San Angelo, 1988—, nursing supr. Concho Valley, 1991—; nurse cons. Bethphage Found., Marfa, Tex., 1986-88. Mem. Tex. Rural Health Assn., Am. Cancer Soc. (Quality of Life award 1985, 87, Lifesaver award 1985). Avocations: oil painting, travel. Home: 3714 High Meadow Dr San Angelo TX 76904-5958

LENESS, GEORGE CRAWFORD, lawyer; b. N.Y.C., Oct. 10, 1936; s. George John and Christine (Gibbs) L. AB magna cum laude, Harvard U., 1958; LLB, Columbia U., 1961. Bar: N.Y. 1962, D.C. 1972. Assoc. Simpson Thacher & Bartlett, N.Y.C., 1961-66; assoc. Hale Russell & Gray, N.Y.C., 1966-69, ptnr., 1969-85; ptnr. Winthrop, Stimson, Putnam & Roberts, N.Y.C., 1985-92, sr. counsel, 1992—. Sgt. USAR, 1954-60. Mem. N.Y.C. Bar Assn., Harvard Club N.Y.C., Westchester Country Club (Harrison, N.Y.). Republican. Office: Winthrop Stimson Putnam et al 1 Battery Park Plz New York NY 10004-1405

LENFANT, CLAUDE JEAN-MARIE, physician; b. Paris, Oct. 12, 1928; came to U.S., 1960, naturalized, 1965; s. Robert and Jeanine (Leclerc) L.; children: Philipe, Bernard, Martine Lenfant Wayman, Brigitte Lenfant Martin, Christine. B.S., U. Rennes, France, 1948; M.D., U. Paris, 1956; D.Sc. (hon.), SUNY, 1988. Asst. prof. physiology U. Lille, France, 1959-60; from clin. instr. to prof. medicine physiology and biophysics U. Wash. Med. Sch., 1961-72; asso. dir. lung programs Nat. Heart, Lung and Blood Inst. NIH, Bethesda, Md., 1970-72; dir. div. lung diseases Nat. Heart, Lung and Blood Inst. NIH, 1972-80; dir. Fogarty Internat. Center NIH, 1980-82, assoc. dir. internat. research, 1980-82; dir. Nat. Heart, Lung and Blood Inst., 1982—. Assoc. editor: Jour. Applied Physiology, 1976-82, Am. Jour. Medicine, 1979-91 ; mem. editorial bd.: Undersea Biomed. Research, 1973-75, Respiration Physiology, 1971-78, Am. Jour. Physiology and Jour. Applied Physiology, 1970-76, Am. Rev. Respiratory Disease, 1973-79; editor-in-chief: Lung Biology in Health and Disease. Fellow Royal Coll. Physicians; mem. Assn. Am. Physicians, Am. Soc. Clin. Investigation, French Physiol. Soc., Am. Physiol. Soc., N.Y. Acad. Scis., Undersea Med. Soc., Inst. of Medicine of Nat. Acad. Sci., USSR Acad. Med. Scis., French Nat. Acad. Medicine. Home: 13201 Glen Rd Gaithersburg MD 20878-8855 Office: Nat Heart Lung & Blood Inst Bldg 31A Rm 5A52 Bethesda MD 20892

LENFEST, HAROLD FITZ GERALD, cable television executive, lawyer; b. Jacksonville, Fla., May 29, 1930; s. Harold Churchill and Rena (FitzGerald) L.; m. Marguerite Brooks, July 9, 1955; children: Diane, H. Chase, Brook. AB, Washington and Lee U., 1953; LLB, Columbia U., 1958. Bar: N.Y. 1959. Assoc. Davis Polk & Wardwell, N.Y.C., 1958-65; assoc. counsel Triangle Publs., Phila., 1965-70; mng. dir. communications div. Triangle Publs., N.Y.C., 1970-74; editorial dir., pub. Seventeen mag., N.Y.C., 1970-74; pres. Suburban Cable TV Co., 1970—, Empire State Cable TV Co., 1970-74, Lenfest Communications, Inc., 1974—; bd. dirs. TCI West, Inc., Seattle, Liberty Media Corp., Cable Advt. Bur., Videopole (France), Australis Media Ltd. (Australia), Voice FX, Inc., C-Span; chmn. Video JukeBox, Inc.; chief exec. officer Cable AdNet, Inc., 1981-92, StarNet, Inc., 1989—, TelVue, Inc., 1990—. Bd. dirs., v.p. Columbia U. Sch. Law, N.Y.C., 1960-65, 74-78, mem. bd. visitors, 1992—; trustee Walter Kaitz Found., Oakland, Calif., 1986-88; trustee, nat. campaign chmn. Washington and Lee U., 1990-95; mem. bd. regents Mercersburg Acad., 1989—, pres., 1994—; mem. James Madison Coun. Libr. of Congress, 1989—; bd. dirs. Phila. Mus. Art, 1993—, C-SPAN, 1995—; trustee, exec. com. Chesapeake Bay Found., 1995—. Capt. USNR, 1953-76, active duty, 1953-56, 62, ret. Named Man of Yr. Phila. Area Easter Seal Soc., 1992. Mem. Pa. Cable TV Assn. (bd. dirs., officer 1976-79), Assn. of Bar of City of N.Y., The Mayflower Soc., Soc. of Colonial Wars. Home: 2445 Oaks Cir Huntingdon Valley PA 19006-5621 Office: The Lenfest Group 202 Shoemaker Rd Pottstown PA 19464-6420

LENG, SHAO CHUAN, political science educator; b. Chengtu, China, Feb. 14, 1921; came to U.S., 1945, naturalized, 1953; s. Yin Tung and Nan (Chen) L.; m. Alice Li, Dec. 12, 1944 (dec. 1968); 1 child, David; m. Nora Yen, June 14, 1970. B.A., Nat. Central U. China, 1943; M.A., Yale, 1948; Ph.D., U. Pa., 1950. Lectr. U. Pa., 1949-50; from lectr. to prof. U. Va., Charlottesville, 1950-72; Doherty Found. prof. U. Va., 1972-85, D. Compton prof. gvt. and fgn. affairs, 1985-92, Compton prof. emeritus, chmn. com. Asian studies, 1965-68, 74-92; Fulbright lectr. Doshisha (Japan) U., 1956-57; adviser Union Research Inst., Hong Kong, 1961; vis. scholar Harvard, 1962; research asso. Duke U. Rule of Law Research Center, 1964-66; Cons. Research Analysis Corp., 1968-71, HEW, 1978; research asso. Harvard Law Sch., 1968-69. Author: Japan and Communist China, 1959, (with Norman D. Palmer) Sun Yat-sen and Communism, 1961, (with others) Sovereignty within the Law, 1965, Justice in Communist China, 1968, Criminal Justice System in Post-Mao China, 1985. Editor: (with Hungdah Chiu) Law in Chinese Foreign Policy, 1972, Post-Mao China and U.S.-China Trade, 1977, (with Hungdah Chiu) China: 70 Years After the 1911 Revolution, 1984, Changes in China: Party, State, and Society, 1989, Coping with Crisis: How Governments Deal with Emergencies, 1990, Chiang Ching-Kuo's Leadership in the Development of the Republic of China on Taiwan, 1992, Reform and Development in Deng's China, 1994; cons. editor: Asian Forum, 1974-81, Asian Affairs, 1983—, Asia Pacific Rev., 1989—, Jour. Chinese Studies, 1984—, World Affairs, 1975-84. Social Sci. Research Council grantee, 1956; research fellow Social Sci. Research Council-Am. Council Learned Socs., 1961-62, 68-69; Fulbright Research scholar Hong Kong and Taiwan, 1977; vis. scholar Wilson Center, 1980; research fellow Inst. for Study of World Politics, 1984; chmn. bd. dirs. U.S.-Asia Research Inst., 1983—. Mem. Am. Polit. Sci. Assn., Am. Soc. Internat. Law, Assn. Asian Studies, Assn. Chinese Social Scientists in N.Am. (pres. 1989-91). Home: 217 Highview Ln Charlottesville VA 22901-1017

LENGA, J. THOMAS, lawyer; b. Toledo, Dec. 16, 1942; s. Casimir M. and Rose C. (Sturniolo) L.; children by previous marriage: Christina M., John Thomas Jr., Peter M. BA, U. Toledo, 1965, JD, 1968. Bar: Mich. 1968, Ohio 1968. Assoc. Clark Hill, Plc., Detroit, 1972—; mem. com. on std. jury instrns. Mich. Supreme Ct.; adv. Am. Bd. of Trial Advs. Capt. JAGC, U.S. Army, 1968-72. Named Disting. Alumnus, Coll. Law, U. Toledo, 1987. Fellow Am. Coll. Trial Lawyers; mem. ABA, Detroit Bar Assn. (pres. 1989-90), State Bar Mich. (bd. commrs. 1992—, treas. 1995-96), Internat. Assn. Def. Counsel. Office: Clark Hill Plc 1600 1st Fed Bldg Detroit MI 48226-1962

LENGEMANN, FREDERICK WILLIAM, physiology educator, scientist; b. N.Y.C., Apr. 8, 1925; s. Peter and Dorathea Johanna (Wolter) L.; m. J. Joan Doremus, Dec. 23, 1950; children—Frederick William Jr., David Munson. Student, N.Y. State Sch. Agr., Farmingdale, 1942-43; B.S. with distinction, Cornell U., 1950, M.Nutrition Sci., 1951; Ph.D., U. Wis., 1954. Research asso. U. Tenn.-AEC Agrl. Research Program, Oak Ridge, 1954-55; asst. prof. dept. chemistry U. Tenn. Med. Sch., Memphis, 1955-59; prof. dept. physiology N.Y. State Coll. Vet. Medicine, Cornell U., 1959-88, prof. physiology emeritus, 1988—; biochemist div. biology and medicine AEC, 1962-63; cons. FAO-IAEA, Vienna, Austria, 1966-67, 76-77, Fed. Radiation Council, 1964-65, NRC, 1970-73, Nat. Com. on Radiation Protection, 1970-73, 79, 82; IAEA expert U. Nacional Agraria, Peru, 1978; lectr., dir. tng. courses. Contbr. articles to profl. jours. Mem. planning bd. Town of Dryden, N.Y., 1963-68. Served with USNR, 1943-46. Decorated Air medal with 3 stars. Fellow AAAS; mem. Council Agrl. Sci. and Tech., Am. Dairy Sci. Assn., Am. Nutrition Soc., Fed. Am. Socs. for Exptl. Biology, Nat., N.Y. State Christmas tree growers assns., Sigma Xi, Phi Kappa Phi. Home: PO Box 161 Rome PA 18837-0161 Office: Cornell U NY State Coll Vet Medicine Dept Physiology Ithaca NY 14853

L'ENGLE, MADELEINE (MRS. HUGH FRANKLIN), author; b. N.Y.C., Nov. 29, 1918; d. Charles Wadsworth and Madeleine (Barnett) Camp; m. Hugh Franklin, Jan. 26, 1946; children: Josephine Franklin Jones, Maria Franklin Rooney, Bion. A.B., Smith Coll., 1941; postgrad., New Sch., 1941-42, Columbia U., 1960-61; holder 19 hon. degrees. Tchr. St. Hilda's and St. Hugh's Sch., 1960—; mem. faculty U. Ind., 1965-66, 71; writer-in-residence Ohio State U., 1970, U. Rochester, 1972, Wheaton Coll., 1976—, Cathedral St. John the Divine, N.Y.C., 1965—. Author: The Small Rain, 1945, Ilsa, 1946, Camilla Dickinson, 1951, A Winter's Love, 1957, And Both Were Young, 1949, Meet the Austins, 1960, A Wrinkle in Time, 1962, The Moon by Night, 1963, The 24 Days Before Christmas, 1964, The Arm of the Starfish, 1965, The Love Letters, 1966, The Journey with Jonah, 1968, The Young Unicorns, 1968, Dance in the Desert, 1969, Lines Scribbled on an Envelope, 1969, The Other Side of the Sun, 1971, A Circle of Quiet, 1972, A Wind in the Door, 1973, The Summer of the Great-Grandmother, 1974, Dragons in the Waters, 1976, The Irrational Season, 1977, A Swiftly Tilting Planet, 1978, The Weather of the Heart, 1978, Ladder of Angels, 1980, A Ring of Endless Light, 1980, Walking on Water, 1980, A Severed Wasp, 1982, And It Was Good, 1983, A House Like a Lotus, 1984, Trailing Clouds of Glory, 1985, A Stone for a Pillow, 1986, Many Waters, 1986, Two-Part Invention, 1988, A Cry Like a Bell, 1987, Sole Into Egypt, 1989, From This Day Forward, 1988, An Acceptable Time, 1989, The Glorious Impossible, 1990, Certain Women, 1992, The Rock That Is Higher: Story As Truth, 1993, Anytime Prayers, 1994, Troubling a Star, 1994, Penguins and Golden Calves, 1996, A Live Coal in the Sea, 1996. Pres. Crosswicks Found. Recipient Newbery medal, 1963, Sequoyah award, 1965, runner-up Hans Christian Andersen Internat. award, 1964, Lewis Carroll Shelf award, 1965, Austrian State Lit. award, 1969, Bishop's Cross, 1970, U. South Miss. medal, 1978, Regina medal, 1985, Alan award Nat. Coun. Tchrs. English, 1986, Kerlan award, 1990; collection of papers at Wheaton Coll. Mem. Authors Guild (pres., mem. council, mem. membership com.), Authors League (mem. council), Writers Guild Am., Colonial Dames. Episcopalian. Home: 924 W End Ave Apt 95 New York NY 10025-3534 Office: care Cath St John the Divine 1047 Amsterdam Ave New York NY 10025 *Over the years I've worked out a philosophy of failure which I find extraordinarily liberating. If I'm not free to fail, I'm not free to take risks, and everything in life that's worth doing involves a willingness to take a risk and involves the risk of failure. Each time I start a new book I am risking failure. Although I have had over 40 books published, there are at least 6 full unpublished books which have failed, but which have been necessary for the book which then gets published. The same thing is true in all human relationships. Unless I'm willing to open myself up to risk and to being hurt, then I'm closing myself off to love and friendship.*

LENGYEL, ALFONZ, art history, archeology and museology educator; b. Godollo, Hungary, Oct. 21, 1921; came to U.S., 1957; s. Aurel and Margit (Furedy) L.; m. Hongying Liu. Terminal degree in Law and Polit. Sci., Miskolc Law Acad., Budapest, Hungary, 1944; M.A., San Jose State Coll., 1959; Ph.D., U. Paris, 1964; LL.D., London Inst. Applied Research, 1973. Asst. prof. San Jose State Coll. (Calif.), 1961-63; faculty U. Md. European Div., Paris and Heidelberg, Germany, 1963-68; intern museology Ecole du Louvre, Paris, 1965-66; prof. Wayne State U., Detroit, 1968-72, No. Ky. U., Highland Heights, 1972-77; dean, prof. Inst. Mediterranean Art and Archaeology, Cin., 1977-82; coord. art history Rosemont Coll. (Pa.), 1982-86; research prof. art history, dir. Goebel's Print Collection, 1986-88; pres. Fudan Mus. Found., 1988—; adj. curator Detroit Inst. Arts, 1968-72; cons. Paris Am. Acad., 1963—; dir. UPAO, Washington, 1983—; adv. prof. Fudan U., Shanghai, Peoples Republic of China; cons. prof. Xian Jiaotong U., Xian, Peoples Republic of China, founder Sino-Am. Summer Field Sch. Archaeology. Author: Archaeology for Museologists, 1993, Chinese Chronological History, 1993; co-author: The Archaeology of Roman Pannonia, 1983; contbr. numerous articles to profl. jours. Bd. dirs. Hungarian-Am. Fedn., Cleve., 1983-91, exec. v.p., Ft. Laudedale, Fla., 1951—; mem. Republican Presdl. Task Force, Washington, 1982—; mem. adv. bd. U.S. Dept. Interior Nat. Park Service, 1987-91. Rockefeller Found. grantee U. Vienna, 1957; Govt. of France grantee U. Paris, 1962-63; S. H. Kress Found. lectureship Denison U. (Ohio), 1967-68; Smithsonian Instn. grantee, 1968; NEH grantee, 1971, 76. Fellow Internat. Acad. Sci. and Lettres, Arpad Acad. (pres. 1982—), Szechenyi Acad, Am. Assn. Swiss, German, Austrian Profs.; mem. Internat. Coun. Mus., Renaissance Soc Am., Coll. Art Assn. Am., Archaeol. Inst. Am., Nat. Fedn. Hungarian-Ams., Soc. Architectural Historians, N.Y. Acad. Scis., Mich. Acad. Scis. and Letters, Soc. Profl. Archaeologists, Christopher Giest Hist. Soc., Detroit Classical Assn. Republican. Roman Catholic. Home: 1522 School House Rd Ambler PA 19002-1939 Office: Fudan Mus Found Ambler PA 19002

LENGYEL, CORNEL ADAM (CORNEL ADAM), author; b. Fairfield, Conn., Jan. 1, 1915; s. Elmer Alexander and Mary Elizabeth (Bismarck) L.; m. Teresa Delaney Murphy, July 10, 1933; children: Jerome Benedict, Paul Joel, Michael Sebastian, Cornelia (Mrs. Charles Burke). LittD (hon.), World Acad. of Arts and Culture, Taiwan, 1991. Editor, supr. Fed. Research Project, San Francisco, 1938-41; music critic The Coast, San Francisco, 1937-41; shipwright, personnel officer Kaiser Shipyard, Richmond, Calif., 1942-44; mgr. Forty-Nine Theatre, Georgetown, Calif., 1946-50; editor W.H. Freeman Co., San Francisco, 1952-54; founder, exec. editor Dragon's Teeth Press, Georgetown, 1969—; vis. prof., lectr. English lit. Sacramento State Coll., 1962-63; writer-in-residence Hamline U., St. Paul, 1968-69; guest lectr. MIT, 1969; transl. from Hungarian; editorial cons. HEW; ednl. dir. ILGWU. Author: (history) American Testament: The Story of the Promised Land, 1956, Four Days in July, 1958, I, Benedict Arnold: The Anatomy of Treason, 1960, Presidents of the U.S.A., 1961, Ethan Allen and the Green Mountain Boys, 1961, Jesus the Galileean, 1966, The Declaration of Independence, 1969; (poetry) Thirty Pieces, 1933, First Psalms, 1950, Fifty Poems, 1965, Four Dozen Songs, 1970, The Lookout's Letter, 1971, Late News from Adam's Acres, 1983, El Dorado Forest: Selected Poems, 1986; (plays) The World's My Village, 1935, Jonah Fugitive, 1936, The Giant's Trap, 1938, The Atom Clock, 1951, Eden, Inc., 1954, rev. edit. Omega, 1963, Will of Stratford, 1964, Three Plays, 1964, The Case of Benedict Arnold, 1975, Doctor Franklin, 1976, The Shadow Trap, 1977, The Second Coming, 1985, Mengele's Passover, 1987, A Clockmaker's Boy: Part One, 1987; (novel) Malunkyaputta: His Quest for Edification, 1996; (essay) The Creative Self, 1971, contbr. to anthologies, The Golden Year, 1960, Interpretation for Our Time, 1966, The Britannica Library of Great American Writing, 1961, The Menorah Treasury, 1964, The Courage to Grow Old, 1988, From These Hills, 1990, Blood to Remember, 1991, Anthology of Contemporary Poets, 1992, World Poetry, 1993, We Speak for Peace, 1993, also Poet Lore, The Coast, The Argonaut, Saturday Rev., Menorah Jour., others. Served with U.S. Merchant Marine, 1944-45. Recipient Albert M. Bender award in lit., 1945; recipient 1st prize Maritime Poetry Awards, 1945, 1st prize Poetry Soc. Va., 1951, Maxwell Anderson award drama, 1950, Di Castagnola award Poetry Soc. Am., 1971, Internat. Who's Who in Poetry award, 1972; Huntington Hartford Found. resident fellow, 1951, 64; MacDowell Colony resident fellow, 1967; Ossabaw Island Found. fellow, 1968; Nat. Endowment for Arts fellow, 1976-77. Mem. MLA, AAUP, PEN, Poetry Soc. Am., Poetry Soc. Eng., Authors Guild. Address: Adam's Acres Georgetown CA 95634 *What would a writer convey through his work? His vision of life, his response to the oddity, terror, humor, beauty, pathos, or grandeur of experience. He would renew our original sense of wonder at the mystery of things and speak in a human voice fittingly of man's mortal adventures amid the immortal dance of the elements . . . To endure, a book must stir a variety of men in any generation. Though all that we do may prove perishable, we must proceed as if . . . Do one thing well enough to endure, we tell ourselves. A thing done well is well done for all time.*

LENGYEL, ISTVÁN, chemist, educator; b. Kaposvar, Hungary, July 12, 1931; came to the U.S., 1958; s. István and Margit (Palásthy) L. Diploma in chemistry, Eotvos Lorand U., 1955; PhD in Organic Chemistry, MIT, 1964. Rsch. chemist G. Richter Pharm. Works Inc., Budapest, 1953-55; chemist State Geophys. Inst., Budapest, 1955-56; rsch. chemist Biochemie GmbH, Kundl, Austria, 1957-58; rsch. asst. Johns Hopkins Med. Sch., Balt., 1958-59; predoctoral fellow MIT, Cambridge, 1959-63, postdoctoral fellow, 1964; NIH postdoctoral fellow Techn. U., Munich, 1964-65; rsch. assoc. MIT, Cambridge, 1965-67; prof. chemistry St. John's U., Jamaica, N.Y., 1967—, chmn. dept. chemistry, 1985-91; vis. scholar U.S. Nat. Acad. Sci. and Hungarian Acad. Scis., 1973. Recipient award Alexander von Humboldt Found., 1973-74. Avocations: swimming, travel. Home: 84-01 169th St Jamaica NY 11432-2033 Office: Saint Johns U 8000 Utopia Pky Jamaica NY 11439

LENHART, CYNTHIA RAE, conservation organization executive; b. Cheverly, Md., Nov. 3, 1957; d. Donald Edward and Vesta Jean (Morris) L.; m. John Charles Doyle Jr., Oct. 24, 1987. BS in Environ. Studies, Coll. William & Mary, 1979; MS in Environ. Sci., SUNY, Syracuse, 1983. Asst. to pres. Environ. Policy Inst., Washington, 1979-81; wildlife policy analyst Nat. Audubon Soc., Washington, 1984-90; exec. dir. Hawk Mountain Sanctuary, Kempton, Pa., 1990—; bd. dirs. Am. Bird Conservancy, Washington. Contbr. chpts. to Audubon Wildlife Report, 1985, 87, 88, 89. Chair Everglades Coalition, Washington, 1986-88. Mem. NAFE. Office: Hawk Mountain Sanctuary RR 2 Box 191 Kempton PA 19529

LENHART, JAMES THOMAS, lawyer; b. Cambridge, Mass., Nov. 3, 1946; s. James Wills and Martha Agnes (Everly) L.; m. Lynn Dexter Stevens, June 21, 1969; children—Amanda Brooks, James Edward, Abigail Ames. Cert. in History, U. Edinburgh, Scotland, 1967; A.B., Columbia U., 1968, J.D., 1972. Bar: N.Y. 1973, D.C. 1974. Clk. to judge U.S. Dist. Ct. (so. dist.) N.Y., 1972-73; assoc. Shaw, Pittman, Potts & Trowbridge, Washington, 1973-79, ptnr., 1980—; adj. prof. Cornell Law Sch., 1992-93; instr. Washington Coll. Law of Am. U., Washington, 1976-78. Chair exec. com. Westmoreland Congregational Ch., Washington, 1989, bd. dirs. 1978-79, 83-84. Harlan Fiske Stone scholar Columbia U., 1968-69, 71-72. Mem. Am. Law Inst., D.C. Def. Lawyers Assn., ABA, D.C. Bar Assn., Fed. City Club, The Barristers. Democrat. Mem. United Ch. of Christ. Office: Shaw Pittman Potts & Trowbridge 2300 N St NW Washington DC 20037-1122

LENHART, LOWELL CORDELL, hospital administrator, consultant; b. Oklahoma City, Jan. 19, 1940; s. Herbert William and Helen Nancy Lenhart; m. Sharen Annette Gambill, Jan. 21, 1961; 1 child, Lance Christian. B.S., Central State U., 1963; M.S., Okla. State U., 1967; Ph.D., Okla. U., 1976. Tech. dir. service outcome measurement project Div. Rehab. Services, Oklahoma City, 1968-70; research utilization supr. Dept. Pub. Welfare, Oklahoma City, 1970-72; program evaluation supr. Dept. Instns., Oklahoma City, 1972-74; coordinator dept. mgmt. services Dept. Human Services, Oklahoma City, 1974-79; dep. adminstr. O'Donoghue Rehab. Inst., Oklahoma City, 1979-81, adminstr., 1981—; cons. in field. Contbr. articles to profl. jours. Pres. Okla. Ptnrs. of Americas, 1981-82; mem. Oklahoma City Alliance for Safer Cities, 1975-76; cons. Community Workshop, 1978-79. Mem. Am. Coll. Hosp. Adminstrs., Am. Hosp. Assn., Okla. Hosp. Assn., Nat. Rehab. Assn. Okla. Rehab. Assn. (bd. dirs.). Democrat. Lodge: Rotary. Avocations: renovation of historic homes; snow skiing; gardening; writing. Office: Chisholm Trail Counseling Svcs PO Box 851290 Yukon OK 73085-1290

LENHERR, FREDERICK KEITH, neurophysiologist, computer scientist; b. N.Y.C., Feb. 4, 1943; s. Frederick Joseph and Thelma Frances (DeFrehn) L. A.B., Harvard U., 1965; M.S., U. Mass., 1973, Ph.D., 1975. Instr. biology and physics Taft Sch., Watertown, Conn., 1965-66; rsch. and devel. engr. No. Rsch. & Engring., Cambridge, Mass., 1966-69; turbine engr. Gen. Electric Co., Lynn, Mass., 1969-70; neurophysiologist, computer scientist Ctr. Systems Neurosci., U. Mass., Amherst, 1974-77; dir. Berkeley Brain Ctr., 1977-80; pres. New Salem (Mass.) Rsch., 1981—; sr. engr. Visual Intelligence, Amherst, Mass., 1982-85; project scientist Harvard U., Cambridge, Mass., 1986-87; microcomputer faculty Holyoke Community Coll., 1991-92; sr. engr. App. Comp. Sys. Inst. Mass., 1993—. Founding editor: Brain Theory Newsletter, 1975-77. Democrat. Lutheran. Home and Office: W Main St New Salem MA 01355

LENHOFF, HOWARD MAER, biological sciences educator, academic administrator, activist; b. North Adams, Mass., Jan. 27, 1929; s. Charles and Goldie Sarah (Rubin) L.; m. Sylvia Grossman, June 20, 1954; children: Gloria, Bernard. B.A., Coe Coll., 1950, D.Sc. (hon.), 1976; Ph.D., Johns Hopkins U., 1955. USPHS fellow Loomis Lab., Greenwich, Conn., 1954-56; vis. lectr. Howard U., Washington, 1957-58; rsch. assoc. George Washington U., Washington, 1957-58; postdoctoral fellow Carnegie Instn., Washington, 1958; investigator Howard Hughes Med. Inst., Miami, 1958-63; prof. biology, dir. Lab. for Quantitative Biology U. Miami, Coral Gables, 1963-69; prof. biol. scis. U. Calif., Irvine, 1969-92, prof. polit. sci., 1986-92, assoc. dean biol. scis., 1969-71, dean grad. div., 1971-73, faculty asst. to vice chancellor of student affairs, 1986-88, 90—, chair faculty senate, 1988-90, 96—, prof. emeritus, rsch. prof., 1993—, faculty asst. to dir. fin. aid; vis. scientist, Louis Lipsky fellow Weizmann Inst. Sci., Rehovot, Israel, 1968-69; vis. prof. chem. engring., Rothschild fellow Israel Inst. Tech., 1973-74; vis. prof. Hebrew U., Jerusalem, spring 1970, fall 1971, 77-78; Hubert Humphrey Inst. fellow Ben Gurion U., Beersheva, Israel, 1981; sr. rsch. fellow Jesus Coll., U. Oxford, 1988; dir. Nelson Rsch. & Devel. Co., Irvine, 1971-73; bd. dirs. BioProbe Internat., Inc., Tustin, Calif., 1983-89, chmn. bd., 1983-86. Editor/author: Biology of Hydra, 1961, Hydra, 1969, Experimental Coelenterate Biology, 1972, Coelenterate Biology—Review and Perspectives, 1974, Hydra: Research Methods, 1983, Enzyme Immunoassay, 1985, From Trembley's Polyps to New Directions in Research on Hydra, 1985, Hydra and the Birth of Experimental Biology, 1986, Biology of Nematocysts, Conception to Birth, 1988; mem. editorial bd. Jour. Solid Phase Biochemistry, 1976-80. Vice chmn. So. Calif. div. Am. Assn. Profs. for Peace in Middle East, 1972-80; bd. dirs. Am. Assn. for Ethiopian Jews, 1974-93, pres., 1978-82; bd. govs. Israel Bonds Orange County, Calif., 1974-80, Dade County Heart Assn., Miami, 1958-61, So. Calif. Technion Soc., 1976; pres. Hillel Coun. of Orange County, 1976-78; nat. chmn. faculty div. State of Israel Bonds, 1976; mem. sci. adv. bd. Am. Friends of Weizman Inst. Sci., 1980-84; bd. dirs. Hi Hopes Identity Discovery Found., Anaheim, Calif., 1982-87, pres. bd. govs., 1983-85, William Syndrome Found., trustee, 1992, pres., bd. dirs., 1993-95, exec. v.p., 1995—; v.p. edn. Williams Syndrome Assn., 1994, bd. dirs., 1993-94. 1st lt. USAF, 1956-58. Recipient Career Development award USPHS, 1965-69; Disting. fellow Iowa Acad. Sci., 1986. Fellow AAAS; mem. Soc. Physics and Natural History of Swiss Acad. Scis. (hon.), Am. Chem. Soc., Am. Biophys. Soc., Am. Soc. Zoologists, History of Sci. Soc., Am. Soc. Cell Biologists, Am. Soc. Biol. Chemists, Biophysics Soc., Soc. Gen. Physiologists, Soc. Growth and Devel. Office: U Calif Sch Biol Scis Mesa Office Bldg Irvine CA 92717 Address: 304 Robin Hood Ln Costa Mesa CA 92627-2134

LENKE, JOANNE MARIE, publishing executive; b. Chgo., Aug. 27, 1938; d. August Julian and Dorothy Anna (Gold) L.; B.S., Purdue U., 1960; M.S., Syracuse U., 1964, Ph.D., 1968. Tchr. pub. schs., Evanston, Ill., 1960-63; editor Test Dept., Harcourt, Brace & World, Inc., N.Y.C., 1967-70; research psychologist Harcourt Brace Jovanovich, Inc., N.Y.C., 1970-73, exec. editor, 1973-75; asst. dir. ednl. measurement div. The Psychol. Corp., N.Y.C., 1975-83, dir. ednl. measurement and psychometrics, Cleve., 1983-85, San Antonio, 1986, v.p., dir. Measurement div., 1986-88, sr. v.p., 1988-91, exec. v.p., 1991—; field reader U.S. Office Edn., 1972, NSF grantee, 1963-64. Mem. Nat. Council on Measurement in Edn., Am. Psychol. Assn., Am. Ednl. Research Assn. Adv. editor Jour. of Ednl. Measurement, 1974-78. Home: 1311 Vista Del Monte San Antonio TX 78216-2229 Office: The Psychol Corp 555 Academic Ct San Antonio TX 78204-2455

LENKER, MAX V., consumer products company executive; b. 1946. Pres. Racetrac Petroleum Inc., Smyrna, Ga., 1975—. Office: Racetrac Petroleum Inc 300 Technology Ct Smyrna GA 30082-5235*

LENKOSKI, LEO DOUGLAS, psychiatrist, educator; b. Northampton, Mass., May 13, 1925; s. Leo L. and Mary Agnes (Lee) L.; m. Jeannette Teare, July 12, 1952; children—Jan Ellen, Mark Teare, Lisa Marie, Joanne Lee. A.B., Harvard, 1948, spl. student, 1948-49; M.D., Western Res. U., 1953; grad., Cleve. Psychoanalytic Inst., 1964. Intern Univ. Hosps., Cleve., 1953-54, resident in psychiatry, 1956-57, dir. psychiatry, 1970-86, chief of staff, 1982-90; dir. profl. services Horizon Ctr. Hosp., 1980; asst. resident in psychiatry Yale U., New Haven, 1954-56; teaching fellow Case Western Res. U., Cleve., 1957-60, from instr. to prof. psychiatry, 1960-93; prof. emeritus, 1993—; assoc. dean Sch. Medicine Case Western Res. U., Cleve., 1982-93, dir. Substance Abuse Ctr., 1990-93; cons. Cleve. Ctr. on Alcoholism, DePaul Maternity and Infant Home, St. Ann's Hosp., Def. Dept., Cleve. VA Hosp., Psychiat. Edn. br. NIMH; mem. Cuyahoga County Mental Health and Retardation Bd., 1967-73, 94—, Health Planning and Devel. Commn., 1967-73, Ohio Mental Health and Retardation Commn., 1976-78. Contbr. articles to profl. jours. Bd. dirs. Hough-Norwood Health Ctr., Hitchcock Ctr., Hopewell Inn. 1st lt. USAAF, 1943-46. Decorated D.F.C., Air medal with oak leaf cluster.; Career Tchr. grantee NIMH, 1958-60. Fellow Am. Psychiat. Assn. (life), Am. Coll. Psychiatrists, Am. Coll. Psychoanalysts (pres. 1988-89); mem. AMA, AAAS, Ohio Psychiat. Assn. (pres. 1974—), Am. Psychoanalytic Assn., Assn. Am. Med. Colls., Cleve. Acad. Medicine (bd. dirs. 1987-90), Ohio Med. Assn., Pasteur Club, Am. Assn. Chairmen Depts. Psychiatry (pres. 1978-79), Alpha Omega Alpha. Home: 1 Bratenahl Pl Apt 1010 Cleveland OH 44108-1155 Office: 11000 Euclid Ave Cleveland OH 44106-1714

LENMAN, BRUCE PHILIP, historian, educator; b. Aberdeen, Scotland, Apr. 9, 1938; s. Jacob Philip and May (Wishart) L. MA in History with 1st class honors, Aberdeen U., 1960; MLitt, U. Cambridge, 1965, LittD, 1986. Asst. prof. U. Victoria, B.C., Can., 1963; lectr. Queen's Coll., Dundee, Scotland, 1963-67, U. Dundee, 1967-72; lectr. U. St. Andrews, Scotland, 1972-78, sr. lectr., 1978-83, reader, 1983-92, prof. of modern history, 1992—; James Pinckney Harrison prof. history Coll. William and Mary, Williamsburg, Va., 1988-89; mem. econs. and bus. studies panel Scottish Edn. Dept., Ediburgh, 1979-81, humanities sub.-com. Council for Nat. Acad. Awards, London, 1985-87. Author: From Esk to Tweed, 1975, Economic History of Modern Scotland, 1977 (Scottish Arts Coun. award 1977), The Jacobite Risings 1689-1746, 1980 (Scottish Arts Coun. award 1980), Scotland 1746-1832, 1981, The Jacobite Clans of the Great Glen, 1984, The Jacobite Clause, 1986, The Eclipse of Parliament, 1992; co-author: (with John S. Gibson) The Jacobite Threat, 1990; editor: Chambers Dictionary of World History, 1993. Brit. Acad.-Newberry Library fellow, 1982, John Carter Brown Library fellow, 1984, Mellon fellow Va. Hist. Soc., 1990. Fellow Royal Hist. Soc.; mem. Am. Soc. for 18th Century Scottish Studies, Am. Soc. for 18th Century Studies, Soc. for History of Discoveries, Hakluyt Soc. Clubs: Royal Commonwealth (London); New Golf (St. Andrews). Avocations: golf, hill walking, squash, badminton, swimming. Office: U St Andrews Dept Modern History, St Katharine's Lodge, Saint Andrews KY16 9AL, Scotland

LENN, STEPHEN ANDREW, lawyer; b. Ft. Lauderdale, Fla., Jan. 6, 1946; s. Joseph A. and Ruth (Kreis) L.; 1 child, Daniel Lenn. BA, Tufts U., 1967; JD, Columbia U., 1970. Assoc. Kronish, Lieb, Shainswit, Weiner & Hellman, N.Y.C., 1970-72, Shereff, Friedman, Hoffman & Goodman, N.Y.C., 1972-75; exec. v.p., gen. counsel Union Commerce Bank, Union Commerce Corp., Cleve., 1975-83; ptnr., mng. ptnr. Porter, Wright, Morris

& Arthur, Cleve., 1983-88; ptnr. Baker & Hostetler, Cleve., 1988—. Trustee Gt. Lakes Mus. Mem. ABA (com. on devel. in investment svcs. 1980—), Ohio Bar Assn., Cleve. Bar Assn., N.Y.C. Bar Assn., Calif. Bar Assn., Oakwood Club. Office: Baker & Hostetler 3200 Nat City Ctr 1900 E 9th St Cleveland OH 44114-3401

LENNARZ, WILLIAM JOSEPH, research biologist, educator; b. N.Y.C., Sept. 28, 1934; s. William and Louise (Richter) L.; m. Roberta S. Lozensky, June 16, 1956 (div. June 1973); children: William, Matthew, David; m. Sheila Jackson, July 13, 1973. B.S., Pa. State U., 1956; Ph.D., U. Ill., 1959; research fellow, Harvard, 1959-62. Mem. faculty Johns Hopkins Sch. Medicine, 1962-83, assoc. prof. biochemistry, 1966-70, prof., 1971-83; R.A. Welch prof. and chmn. dept. biochemistry and molecular biology U. Tex. Cancer Ctr., M.D. Anderson Hosp., Houston, 1983-89; leading prof., chmn. dept. biochemistry and cell biology SUNY, Stony Brook, 1989—; cons. NIH. Editorial bd.: Biochem. Biophys. Research Commn., Biosci. Reports. Clayton Found. scholar, 1962-64; Lederle Faculty awardee, 1965-67; recipient Distinguished Young Scientist award Md., 1967. Mem. NAS, Am. Chem. Soc., Am. Soc. Biol. Chemists and Molecular Biologists (pres. 1989-90), Am. Soc. Microbiology, Am. Soc. Cell Biology (pub. affairs com.), Assn. Med. Grad. Sch. Dept. Biochemistry (pres. 1993), Internat. Union Biochemists and Molecular Biologists (exec. com.), Worcester Found. (mem. scientific adv. bd.), Soc. Glycobiology (pres. 1993), Sigma Xi, Phi Kappa Phi, Alpha Chi Sigma. Rsch. biochemistry of cell surface molecules and of fertilization. Home: 43 Erland Rd Stony Brook NY 11790-1124 Office: SUNY at Stony Brook 450 Life Scis Stony Brook NY 11790

LENNERS, COLLEEN RENEE, secondary education educator; b. Beatrice, Nebr., Aug. 31, 1956; d. Virgil M. and Edith B. (Fritzen) L. BS in Bus. Edn., U. Nebr., 1978, MEd in Bus. Edn., 1982. Tchr. bus. edn. Council Bluffs (Iowa) Pub. Schs., 1978-89; tchr. trainer Tchr. Effectiveness Tng. II Program, Council Bluffs, 1988-89; instr. bus.-vocat. edn., supr. student tchrs., project dir. U. Nebr., Omaha, 1990-91; tchr. bus. edn. Omaha Pub. Schs., 1991—. Tchr. sunday sch. Kountze Meml. Luth. Ch., Omaha, 1983—, mem. ch. coun., 1987-90, mem. youth com., 1987-94, mem. edn. com., 1994—; vol. Honey Sunday Greater Omaha Assn. for Retarded Citizens and Madonna Sch., 1991—; vol. Toys for Tots, USMCR, Omaha, 1992—; vol. Camp Quality HEartland, 1995. Recipient Belong Excel Study Travel in Nebr. award Nebr. Dept. Edn., 1994, 95. Mem. NEA, Nebr. Edn. Assn., Omaha Edn. Assn., Nat. Bus. Edn. Assn., Nebr. Bus. Edn. Assn. (co-coord. fall conf. 1993), Delta Pi Epsilon (past newsletter editor, corr. sec., v.p., pres., editor Tchg. Tips for Classroom 1985). Republican. Avocations: cooking, travel, reading. Home: 5110 Grover St Apt 8 Omaha NE 68106-3852 Office: Central HS 124 N 20th St Omaha NE 68102-4896

LENNES, GREGORY, manufacturing and financing company executive; b. Chgo., Aug. 5, 1947; s. Lawrence Dominic and Genevieve (Karoll) L.; m. Maryann Meskers, July 27, 1968; children: Robert, Sandra, Ryan. BA, U. Ill., 1969, MA, 1971, postgrad., 1971-73. Corp. archivist Navistar Internat. Corp. (formerly Internat. Harvester Co.), Chgo., 1973-80, records mgr., 1980—, asst. sec., 1980—; sec. Navistar Fin. Corp., Schaumburg, Ill., 1980—, Navistar Internat. Transportation Corp., 1987—. Editor: Historical Records in the Farm Equipment Industry, 1977. Mem. Am. Soc. Corp Secs., Assn. Records Mgrs. and Adminstrs., Soc. Am. Archivists, Midwest Archives Conf., Assn. Info. and Image Mgmt. Home: 19641 S Schoolhouse Rd Mokena IL 60448-1700 Office: Navistar Internat Corp 455 N Cityfront Plaza Dr Chicago IL 60611-5503

LENNON, A. MAX, food products company executive; b. Columbus County, N.C., Sept. 27, 1940; m. Ruth Carter; children—Daniel Ray, Robin LuRay. AA, Mars Hill Coll., 1960; BS, N.C. State U., 1962, PhD, 1970. Owner, operator crop and livestock farm, 1962-66; grad. asst. N.C. State U., Raleigh, 1966-70; asst. prof. animal sci. Tex. Tech U., Lubbock, 1970-72, assoc. prof., 1972, prof., chmn. dept. animal sci., 1974-77; asst. dean, dir. rsch. Coll. Agrl. Scis., Tex. Tech U., 1977-79, assoc. dean, dir. rsch., 1979; sr. swine nutritionist Central Soya Co., Decatur, Ind., 1973; dir. swine feeds rsch. Cen. Soya Co., Decatur, Ind., 1974; chairperson dept. animal husbandry U. Mo.-Columbia, 1980, dir. agrl. experiment sta., dean coll. agr., 1980-83; v.p. for agrl. adminstrn., exec. dean for agr., home econs. and natural resources Ohio State U., Columbus, 1983-86; pres. Clemson (S.C.) U., 1986-94; pres., CEO Ea. Foods Inc., Atlanta, 1994—; Seaman A. Knapp lectr. Dallas, 1988; past co-chmn. Ohio Gov.'s Commn. on Agr.; past chmn. N. Cen. region Coun. of Adminstrv. Heads of Agr.; bd. dirs. First Union Corp., Delta Woodside Industries, Inc., Duke Power Co., Escuela Agricola de la Region Tropical Humeda, Baptist Med. Ctr. Found.; past bd. govs. Am. Royal; E.T. York Disting. lectr. Auburn U., 1991. Contbr. articles to profl. jour. Mem. S.E. regional adv. bd. Inst. Internat. Edn.; adv. com. for task force on agriculture devel. and cooperation, Internat. Devel. Agy.; co-chair policy adv. com. Competitive Rsch. Grants; bd. dirs. Farm Found., Nat. Dropout Prevention Fund Devel. Coun., Greenville Tech. Coll. Fed. Devel. Coun., Fellowship Christian Farmers Internat. State Panel, S.C. Women in Higher Edn.; mem. Dept. Def. Clothing & Textile Bd., Adv. Com. for Task Force on Agrl. Devel. and Cooperation; trustee Palmetto Partnership, Found. for Drug Abuse Prevention, adv. bd. McDonald's Initiative , So. Assn. Coll. and Schs. Com. on Intercollegiate Athletics, Internat. Assn. of Agribus; mem. Congl. Office Tech. Assessment Coun., So. Assn. Colls. and Schs., Commn. on Colls. Class of 1994, rep. S.C.'s Exec. Coun.; bd. dirs. Bapt. Med. Ctr. Found. Recipient Disting. Alumnus award Coll. Agr. and Life Scis., N.C. State U., 1989, Nat. 4-H Alumni award, 1989, Thomas Green Clemson medallion Clemson U., 1991. Mem. AAAS, Am. Soc. Animal Sci., Internat. Assn. Agribus., Coun. for Agrl. Sci. and Tech., Farm House Assn., Internat. Devel. Agy., Alpha Zeta, Phi Sigma, Phi Kappa Phi, Gamma Sigma Delta. Office: Eastern Foods Inc 1000 Naturally Fresh Blvd Atlanta GA 30349

LENNON, DONALD RAY, archivist, historian; b. Brunswick County, N.C., Oct. 6, 1938; s. George William and Eula Lee (Rowell) L.; m. Billie Mae Royall, Dec. 20, 1969; children: William Christopher, Mark Whitfield. BS, East Carolina U., 1960, MA, 1962. Cert. archivist Am. Soc. Cert. Archivists. Archivist II N.C. Divsn. Archives and History, Raleigh, 1964-67; dir. manuscript collection East Carolina U., Greenville, N.C., 1967—; coord. spl. collections East Carolina U., Greenville, 1987—; mem. state hist. records adv. bd., Raleigh, 1975-85; mem. Hist. Bath (N.C.) Commn., 1982-88. Co-author: A Quest for Glory, 1991 (Society Cup award 1992); co-editor: The Wilmington Town Book, 1743-1778 (Clarendon Cup award 1974), Harnett, Hooper and Howe, 1979, Politics, Bar and Bench, 1980. Bd. dirs. N.C. Preservation Consortium, Durham, 1989-93. With U.S. Army, 1962-64. Mem. Soc. Am. Archivists, Hist. Soc. N.C. (pres. 1992-93), Soc. N.C. Archivists. Democrat. Baptist. Home: 201 Cherrywood Dr Greenville NC 27858-8611 Office: East Carolina U Joyner Libr Special Collections Department Greenville NC 27858

LENNON, ELIZABETH M., retired educator; b. Chgo., Apr. 29; d. John Joseph and Johanna Amelia (Pfaff) L. AB, Ind. U., 1941; postgrad., Butler U., 1946, N.C. State U., 1956, San Francisco State U., 1960; MA in Edn. of Physically Handicapped, Columbia U., 1947. Elem. tchr., typing tchr. Ind. Sch. for the Blind, 1944-51; lower sch. tchr. Perkins Sch. for the Blind, 1951-53; tchr., insvc. coord. Gov. Morehead Sch., Raleigh, N.C., 1953-54; staff devel. specialist N.C. Commn. for the Blind, 1964-67; asst. prof. blind rehab. Western Mich. State U., Kalamazoo, 1967-78, part-time asst. prof. blind rehab., 1978-81, 88. Author publs. in field. Bd. dirs. Nat. Accreditation Coun. for Agys. Serving the Blind and Visually Impaired, 1976-83; vice chair Mich. Commn. for the Blind, 1978-84; vice chair bd. dirs Shepherd's Ctr. of Greater Kalamazoo, 1989-90, chmn., 1990—; sec. Affiliated Leadership League of and for the Blind of Am., 1978-91; bd. dirs. Southcentral Mich. Commn. on Aging, 1978-91, sec., 1986-88; sec. Am. Coun. of the Blind, 1988-90; bd. dirs. Voluntary Action Ctr. of Greater Kalamazoo, 1986—; bd. dirs., mem. com., founder Kalamazoo Ctr. for Ind. Living, 1980—; pres. Coun. of Citizens with Low Vision, 1985-88. Recipient Robert D. Mahoney award for Outstanding Svc. to Visually Impaired of Mich., Mich. Assn. of Blind and Visually Impaired, 1978, Clare Lynch award Kalamazoo Coun. of the Blind, 1981, George Card award for Outstanding Svc. to Visually Imparied Nationwide, Am. Coun. of the Blind, 1983, Spl. Tribute, State of Mich., 1984, Lifetime Achievement award Kalamazoo Ctr. for Ind. Living, 1987, Outstanding Svc. to the Older Citizens of S.W. Mich., Mich. Legislature, 1990, Jim Neubacher Lifetime Achievement award Kalamazoo Ctr. for Ind. Living, 1991, Golden Bell award J.C. Penney, 1992. Mem. Assn. for Edn. and Rehab. of the Blind and Visually Impaired (mem. various coms. on state and nat. levels), Coun. for Exceptional Children, Mich. Assn. of Transcribers for the Visually Impaired (past pres., editor newletter, bd. dirs., founding mem.). Avocations: reading, music, travel. Home: 1400 N Drake Rd # 218 Kalamazoo MI 49006

LENNON, GERARD PATRICK, civil engineering educator, researcher; b. N.Y.C., Nov. 15, 1951; s. Eugene Francis and Monica (Burghardt) L.; m. Linda More, June 5, 1976; children: Elizabeth, Brian, Marianne. BS, Drexel U., 1975; MS, Cornell U., 1977, PhD, 1980. Rsch. assoc. Cornell U., Ithaca, N.Y., 1978-80; asst. prof. Lehigh U., Bethlehem, Pa., 1980-86, assoc. prof., 1986-95; prof., 1995—; acting dir. Environ. Studies Ctr. Lehigh U., Bethlehem, Pa., 1989-91; cons. Woodward-Clyde Cons., Plymouth Meeting, Pa., 1985—. Editor Symposium on Groundwater, 1991; contbr. articles to profl. jours. including Jour. Hydraulic Engring., Marine Geology. Consistory 1st United Ch. of Christ, Hellertown, Pa., 1988-93, budget chmn., 1990-93. Mem. ASCE (tech. com. 1983-91). Republican. Achievements include design of (with Richard Weisman) fluidization systems for coastal applications; research in boundary element method for solving groundwater flow problems. Office: Lehigh U 13 E Packer Ave Bethlehem PA 18015-3101

LENNON, JOSEPH LUKE, college official, priest; b. Providence, Sept. 21, 1919; s. John Joseph and Marjorie (McCabe) L. AB, Providence Coll., 1940; STB, Immaculate Conception Coll., 1946; MA, U. Notre Dame, 1950, PhD, 1953; LLD, Bradford Durfee Coll. Tech., 1963; LittD (hon.), U. Southeastern Mass., 1975; DHL (hon.), Roger Williams Coll., 1980. Ordained priest Roman Cath. Ch., 1947; instr. U. Notre Dame, 1948-50; mem. edn. dept. Providence Coll., 1950-51, 53-56, asst. dean men, 1953, dean of men, 1954-56, dean of coll., 1956-68, v.p. community affairs, 1968-88, ret., 1988; dir. Tchrs. Guild of Thomistic Inst., 1953-56, Pennywise Shop; bd. trustees So. New Eng. Sch. of Law, 1994—. Author: The Role of Experience in the Acquisition of Scientific Knowledge, 1952, The Dean Speaks, 1958, College is for Knowledge, 1959; rev. as 30 Ways to Get Ahead at College, 1964. Mem. adv. council Citizens Ednl. Freedom; adv. bd. Perceptional Edn. and Research Center; co-chmn. Easter Seals, 1968; arbitrator R.I. Bd. Labor; adv. com. Mental Retardation, R.I.; chmn. Nat. Library Week, 1962; mem. R.I. Adv. Com. Vocational Edn.; ann. lectr. Psychology and Everyday Life, WJAR-TV, 1960-75; mem. Gov. R.I. Com. to Study R.I. State Inst. at Howard; chmn. speaker's bur. United Fund Campaign, 1971; coordinator Civil Rights Affirmative Action Program, 1970-78; mem. Com. Future Jurisprudence in, R.I; com. clergy renewal Diocese Providence; mem. Com. for CROP-Community Hunger Appeal of Ch. World Service, 1974-75; mem. subcom. on family law Gov.'s Commn. on Jurisprudence of Future; mem. membership com. Cancer Control Bd., R.I., 1977; mem. Gov.'s Commn. on Consumer's Council, 1977, Gov.'s Leadership Conf. on Citizen Participation.; bd. dirs. Blue Cross and Blue Shield, Progress for Providence, R.I. Legal Services, Fed. Hill House, Pawtucket YMCA, The Samaritans, Handgun Alert, Vols. in R.I. Schs., Meeting St. Sch., Big Sisters, Big Bros. Assn. R.I., R.I. Easter Seal, Blackstone Valley Surgicare, R.I. Heart Assn.; chmn. 1975 Heart Fund campaign; trustee R.I. chpt. Leukemia Soc. Am.; adv. bd. Parents Without Partners; bd. govs. John E. Fogarty Found., Irish Scholarship Found.; bd. dirs., trustee Big Sisters Assn., R.I.; bd. dirs. Diabetes Assn.; adv. bd. St. Joseph's Merged Hosps.; mem. corp. R.I. Hosp.; trustee Emma Pendleton Bradley Hosp., 1984—, Southern New Eng. Sch. Law, 1994—; chmn. Laborer's Internat. Union North Am. Scholarship Program, 1995—; mem. adv. council Quirk Inst.; mem. Spl. Legis. Commn. Created on Catastrophic Health Ins., 1979-82, Gov.'s Screening Com. for the Judiciary, 1980-89; mem. Save the Bay, 1986-88; bd. dirs. John Burke Scholarship Found., 1973— Scholarship Funds of the Luturers' International Union of North America. Recipient Seal of Approval R.I. Automobile Dealers Assn., 1978. Mem. Nat. Cath. Edn. Assn., Am. Cath. Sociol. Soc., Nat. Soc. Study Edn., Am. Philosophers Edn. Assn., New Eng. Ednl. Assn., New Eng. Guidance and Personnel Assn., Greater Providence Epilepsy Assn., Nat. Soc. Study Edn., Am. Arbitration Assn., Alpha Epsilon Delta, Delta Epsilon Sigma (pres. 1966-69).

LENNOX, ANNIE, rock musician; b. Aberdeen, Scotland, Dec. 25, 1954; m. Radha Raman, Mar. 1984 (div. 1985). Student, Royal Acad. Music, London. Mem. musical group Catch, Tourists, 1977-80; founding mem. Eurythmics. Albums: (with Eurythmics) In The Garden, 1980, Sweet Dreams, 1983, Touch, 1984, 1984 (For the Love of Big Brother), 1984, Be Yourself Tonight, 1985, Revenge, 1986, Savage, 1988, We Too Are One, 1989, Greatest Hits, 1991, Eurythmics Live, 1993; (solo) Diva, 1992, Medusa, 1994; actress (film) Revolution. Office: c/o Simon Fuller Mgmt Unit 32, 35-37 Parkgate Rd, London England SW11 4NP

LENNOX, DONALD D(UANE), automotive and housing components company executive; b. Pitts., Dec. 3, 1918; s. Edward George and Sarah B. (Knight) L.; m. Jane Armstrong, June 11, 1949; children: Donald D., J. Gordon. BS with honors, U. Pitts., 1947. CPA, Pa. With Ford Motor Co., 1950-69, Xerox Corp., 1969-80; corp. v.p. and sr. v.p. info. tech. group Xerox Corp., Rochester, N.Y., 1969-73, group v.p. and pres. info. tech. group, 1973-75, group v.p., pres. info. systems group, 1975-80; sr. v.p., sr. staff officer Xerox Corp., Stamford, Conn., 1973-74; sr. v.p. ops. staff Navistar Internat. Corp., Chgo., 1980-81, exec. v.p., 1981-82, pres., chief operating officer, 1982, chmn., chief exec. officer, 1983-87, also bd. dirs.; chmn., chief exec. officer Schlegel Corp., Rochester, N.Y., 1987-89; chmn. Internat. Imaging Materials, Inc., Amherst, N.Y., 1990—; also bd. dirs. Internat. Imaging Materials, Inc., Amherst; bd. dirs. Prudential-Securities Mut. Funds, Gleason Corp. Served with AC USN, 1942-45. Decorated D.F.C. with 2 gold stars, Air medal with 4 gold stars. Mem. Rochester Area C. of C. (pres. 1979), Country Club of Rochester, Genesee Valley Econ. Club, Chgo. Club, Order of Artus, Beta Gamma Sigma. Republican. *What modest success I have enjoyed is the result of hard work and dedication to the success of the organization public or private. Rarely is one's contribution to the success of the organization not recognized or rewarded.*

LENNOX, EDWARD NEWMAN, holding company executive; b. New Orleans, July 27, 1925; s. Joseph Andrew and May Alice (Newman) L.; B.B.A., Tulane U., 1949; m. Joan Marie Landry, Sept. 3, 1949; children: Katherine Sarah, Anne Victoria, Mary Elizabeth, Laura Joan. Mktg. service clk. Shell Oil Co., New Orleans, 1949; with W.M. Chambers Truck Line, Inc., 1950-60, exec. v.p., 1954-60; v.p., gen. mgr. Radcliff Materials, Inc., New Orleans, 1961-71; v.p. Office Pub. Affairs, So. Industries Corp., 1971-88; v.p. Dravo Natural Resources Co., 1982-91, Dravo Corp., 1989-91; pres. Tidelands Industries, Inc., 1982-85; bd. dir. Home Savings & Loan Assn., 1979-89 , pres., 1982-88, chmn., 1984-89; cons. Martin-Marietta Aggregates, 1995—. Pres., La. Tank Truck Carriers, 1954-55; mem. La. Bd. Hwys., 1965-67; chmn. New Orleans Aviation Bd., 1965-66; bd. dirs. Travelers Aid Soc., 1966-68, Met. Area Com., 1967-80, Constrn. Industry Legis. Council, 1968-85, Miss. Valley Assn., 1969-72; pres. bd. levee commrs. Orleans Levee Dist., 1969-72; pres. Met. New Orleans Safety Council, 1969-71; bus. and fin. adviser Congregation Sisters of Immaculate Conception; vice chmn. transp. task force Goals for La., 1969-72; mem. New Orleans Bd. Trade, 1971-89; mem. Ala. Gov.'s Adv. Coun. on Econs., 1971-72, Gov.'s Adv. Com. River Area Transp. and Planning Study, 1971-72; area v.p. Pub. Affairs Rsch. Coun. La., 1972-73; mem. exec. com. La. Good Roads Assn., 1972-74; industry del. La. Constl. Conv., 1973; mem. exec. com. Miss. Valley World Trade Coun., 1973-74; bd. dirs., exec. com. Pendleton Meml. Meth. Hosp., 1963-81, dir. emeritus, 1981—; bd. dirs. Boys' Clubs Greater New Orleans, 1973-79; bd. dirs., mem. exec. bd. Goodwill Industries Greater New Orleans, Inc., 1975-79, 81—, treas., 1984-85, first v.p., 1987-88, chmn. 1989-90; bd. dirs. Americanism Forum, 1975—, Tragedy Fund, Inc., 1976—; bd. govs. La. Civil Svc. League, 1974—, pres., 1977-78; dir. chmn. bd. trustees La. Found. Pvt. Colls., 1980-83. Capt. AUS, 1943-46. Recipient Industry Svc. award Assoc. Gen. Contractors Am., 1967, Cert. of Appreciation Constrn. Industry Assn. New Orleans, 1972, New Orleans Jaycees award, 1960, Cert. of Merit Mayoralty of New Orleans, 1964, 67, Monte M. Lemann award La. Civil Svc. League, 1976; named Hon. Life Chmn., 1980, hon. Citizen and Amb. at Large City of Jacksonville, 1966. Mem. NAM (pub. affairs steering com. So. div. 1979—), La. Motor Transport Assn. (pres. 1963-64), Ala. Trucking Assn. (v.p. 1956-60), So. Concrete Masonry Assn. (pres. 1963-68), Greater New Orleans Ready Mixed Concrete Assn. (pres. 1966-68), La. Shell Producers Assn. (pres. 1966-68), C. of C. New Orleans Area (bd. dir. 1968-73, 75-77, pres. elect 1973), Internat. House (bd. dir. 1977-79), Traffic Club New Orleans, Lakeshore Property Owners Assn. (bd. dir. 1974-86 , pres. 1976-77, 79-80), Tulane Alumni Assn., Mobile Area C. of C. Club: Metairie Country (bd. govs. 1976-82, 89-92, pres. 1980-81). Home: 862 Topaz St New Orleans LA 70124-3626 Office: 120 Mallard St Ste 150 Saint Rose LA 70087-9452

LENO, JAY (JAMES DOUGLAS MUIR LENO), television personality, comedian, writer; b. New Rochelle, N.Y., Apr. 28, 1950; s. Angelo and Cathryn Leno; m. Mavis Nicholson, 1980. Grad., Emerson Coll., 1973. Worked as Rolls-Royce auto mechanic and deliveryman. Stand-up comedian playing Carnegie Hall, Caesar's Palace, others; numerous appearances on Late Night with David Letterman; exclusive guest host The Tonight Show, NBC-TV, 1987-92, host, 1992— (Emmy award, 1995); host, prodr. Show-time Spl. Jay Leno and the American Dream, 1986, Saturday Night Live, 1986, Jay Leno's Family Comedy Hour (Writers Guild Am. nomination), 1987, Our Planet Tonight; film appearances include: The Silver Bears, Fun with Dick and Jane, 1977, American Hot Wax, 1978, Americathon, 1979, Collision Course, 1988, Dave, 1993. Avocations: antique motorcycles and automobiles. Office: PO Box 7885 Burbank CA 91510-7885*

LENON, RICHARD ALLEN, chemical corporation executive; b. Lansing, Mich., Aug. 4, 1920; s. Theo and Elizabeth (Amon) L.; m. Helen Johnson, Sept. 13, 1941; children: Richard Allen, Pamela A., Lisa A. BA, Western Mich. Coll., 1941; postgrad., Northwestern U., 1941-42. Mgr. fin. div. Montgomery Ward & Co., Chgo., 1947-56; v.p. fin. Westinghouse Air Brake Co., 1963-67, treas., 1965-67; v.p., treas. Internat. Minerals & Chem. Corp., Skokie, Ill., 1956-63; group v.p. fin. and adminstrn. Internat. Minerals & Chem. Corp., 1967-68, exec. v.p., 1968-70, pres., 1970-78, chmn., 1977-86, chmn. exec. com., 1986-88; chmn. exec. com. IMC Global Inc., 1989—; bd. dirs. IMC Global Inc. Lt. comdr. USNR, 1942-47. Clubs: University (Chgo.); Glen View (Ill.). Home: 803 Solar Ln Glenview IL 60025-4464 Office: IMC Global Inc 2100 Sanders Rd Northbrook IL 60062-6139

LENOX, ANGELA COUSINEAU, healthcare consultant; b. Vergennes, Vt., Dec. 12, 1946; d. Romeo Joseph and Colombe Mary (Gevry) C.; m. Donald Allen Lenox, Oct. 5, 1969 (div.); 1 child, Tiffanie Jae. RN diploma, Albany Med. Ctr. Sch. Nursing, 1969; BS, Barry U., 1982; M of Health Mgmt., St. Thomas U., 1990. Cert. in profl. healthcare quality. Intravenous therapist Holy Cross Hosp., Ft. Lauderdale, Fla., 1979-91; utilization review coord. North Borward Hosp., Pompano Beach, Fla., 1984-89; med. staff quality mgr. Humana Bennett, Plantation, Fla., 1990-91; med. resource analyst Hermann Hosp., Houston, 1991-93; assoc. mgr. quality improvement The Prudential, Sugarland, Tex., 1993-95; cons. ACL Cons., Houston, 1995—. Contbr. articles to profl. jours. 1st lt. U.S. Army res., 1991—. Mem. Tex. Gold Coast Assn. Healthcare Quality, Tex. Soc. Quality Assurance, Nat. Assn. Healthcare Quality. Avocations: skiing, running, reading, writing. Home: 8523 Dawnridge Dr Houston TX 77071-2441 Office: 8523 Dawnridge Dr Houston TX 77071

LENOX, ROGER SHAWN, lawyer; b. Prescott, Ark., June 27, 1961; s. Ollie and Mae (Simpson) L.; m. Patricia Mickens; 1 child, Mariah. BSN cum laude, U. Ala., Huntsville, 1987; JD, U. Mich., 1991. Bar: Tex. 1992, D.C. 1993, U.S. Ct. Appeals (D.C. cir.) 1993, U.S. Dist. Ct. (no., so., ea. and we. dists.) Tex. 1994, U.S. Ct. Appeals (5th cir.) 1995; RN, Ala. Summer assoc. Dykema Gossett, Detroit, 1989-90; assoc. Fulbright & Jaworski, L.L.P., Dallas, 1991-95; pvt. practice Dallas, 1995—; firm rep. Dallas Black C. of C., 1992—, The Sci. Place, Dallas, 1993—; speaker Greater Tex. chpt. Nat. Assn. Pediat. Nurse Assn., 1995. Atty. mentor for Criminal Cts. Day, Youth Leadership Dallas, 1994; career day spkr. Dallas Bus. Magnet H.S., 1993. Lt. (j.g.) USN, 1987-91. Recipient Faculty Award for Clin. Excellence, U. Ala., Huntsville, 1987, Nat. Collegiate Nursing award U.S. Achievement Acad., 1987; U. Mich. Law Sch. Clarence Darrow scholar, 1988-91. Mem. ABA, Am. Assn. Nurse Attys., Tex. Bar, No. Tex. Soc. for Healthcare Risk Mgmt., D.C. Bar, Dallas Bar Assn., J.L. Turner Legal Assn., Sigma Theta Tau. Avocations: travel, water skiing, biking, automotive mechanics. Home: 842 Clear Fork Dr Dallas TX 75232 Office: PO Box 222128 Dallas TX 75222

LENT, JAMES A., analytical equipment company executive. Ceo Boehringer Mannheim Corp, Indpls., 1993—. Office: Boehringer Mannheim Corp 700 Orthopaedic Dr PO Box 988 Warsaw IN 46521-0988*

LENT, JOHN ANTHONY, journalist, educator; b. East Millsboro, Pa., Sept. 8, 1936; s. John and Rose (Marano) L.; remarried Rose Kueny, 1988; children: Laura, Andrea, John, Lisa, Shahnon. B.S., Ohio U., 1958, M.S., 1960; Ph.D., U. Iowa, 1972; cert., Press Inst. of India, Sophia U., Tokyo, Japan, U. Oslo, Guadalajara, Mex., Summer Sch. Dir. public relations, instr. English W.Va. Tech., Montgomery, 1960-62; Newhouse research asst. and asst. to dir. communications research Syracuse (N.Y.) U., 1962-64; lectr. De La Salle Coll., Manila, 1964-65; asst. prof. W.Va. Tech., 1965-66; asst. prof. journalism U. Wis., Eau Claire, 1966-67; asst. prof. journalism, head tchrs.' journalism sequence Marshall U., Huntington, W.Va., 1967-69; vis. assoc. prof. U. Wyo., Laramie, 1969-70; asst. editor Internat. Comm. Bull., Iowa City, 1970-72; coord. mass comm. U. Sains Malaysia, Penang, 1972-74; assoc. prof. comm. Temple U., Phila., 1974-76, prof. comm., 1976-95, prof. broadcasting, telecomm., and mass media, 1995—, Benedum vis. disting. prof., 1987. Author: Asian Newspapers Reluctant Revolution, 1971, Asian Mass Communications: A Comprehensive Bibliography, 1975, 78, Third World Mass Media and Their Search for Modernity, 1977, Broadcasting in Asia and Pacific, 1978, Topics in Third World Mass Media, 1979, Caribbean Mass Commmunications: A Comprehensive Bibliography, 1981, Asian Newspapers: Contemporary Trends and Problems, 1982, Videocassettes in the Third World, 1989, Asian Film Industry, 1990, Caribbean Popular Culture, 1990, Caribbena Mass Communications, 1990, Transnational Communications, 1991, Women and Mass Communications: An International Annotated Bibliography, 1991, Bibliographic Guide to Caribbean Mass Communications, 1992, Bibliography of Cuban Mass Communications, 1992, Cartoonmeter, 1994, Animation, Caricature, and Gag and Political Cartoons in the U.S. and Canada: An International Bibliography, 1994, Comic Art of Europe: An International, Comprehensive Bibliography, 1994, Comic Books and Comic Strips in the United States: An International Bibliography, 1994, Asian Popular Culture, 1995, A Different Road Taken, 1995, Comic Art in Africa, Asia, Australia and Latin America: A Comprehensive, International Bibliography, 1996, others; founding editor: Berita, 1975—; founding mng. editor: WittyWorld, 1987—; editor: Westview Press Internat. Comm. series, 1992-95. Anchor Hocking scholar, 1954-59, U. Oslo scholar, 1962, Fulbright scholar, The Philippines, 1964-65; recipient Benedum award, 1968, Broadcast Preceptor award (2), 1979, Paul Eberman Outstanding Rsch. award, 1988, Ray and Pat Browne Nat. Book award, 1995, Temple U. Exceptional award, 1995; decorated Chapel of Four Chaplains' Legion of Honor. Mem. Malaysia/Singapore/Brunei Studies Group (founding chmn. 1975-82), L.Am. Studies Assn., Caribbean Studies Assn., Assn. Asian Studies, Internat. Assn. Mass Comm. Rsch. (visual and comic art organizer, chair 1984—), Asian Cinema Studies Soc. (chmn. 1994—), Sigma Delta Chi, Sigma Tau Delta, Kappa Tau Alpha, Phi Alpha Theta. Home: 669 Ferne Blvd Drexel Hill PA 19026-3110 Office: Temple Univ Journalism Dept Philadelphia PA 19122 *I have cherished the principles of hard work over long hours, accuracy, comprehensiveness, and honesty in my intellectual and scholarly endeavors. I have considered it important to set and meet goals, to share my work with others, to remain untainted by organizations or individuals who, I feel, are not working for the good of mankind. I also cherish, and protect and use, my right to speak out on those issues which I feel are offensive to the public; the result has been that my writings have incurred the wrath of government ministers in at least two countries.*

LENT, NORMAN FREDERICK, JR., former congressman; b. Oceanside, N.Y., Mar. 23, 1931; s. Norman Frederick and Ellen (Bain) L.; m. Barbara Ann Morris, Aug. 4, 1979; children from previous marriage: Norman Frederick 3d, Barbara Anne, Thomas Benjamin. BA, Hofstra U., 1952; LLB, Cornell U., 1957; LLD (hon.), Kyung Hee U., Seoul, Republic of Korea, 1975, Molloy Coll., 1985, Hofstra Coll., 1988. Bar: N.Y. 1957, Fla. 1976. Assoc. police judge East Rockaway, N.Y., 1958-60; confidential law sec. to N.Y. State Supreme Ct., 1960-62; mem. N.Y. State Senate, 1963-70, chmn. joint legislative com. public health, 1966-70; mem. 92nd Congress 5th Dist. N.Y., 1971-73; mem. 93rd-102d Congresses 4th Dist. N.Y., 1973-93; vice chmn. Energy and Commerce com. 100th-102nd Congresses U.S. Ho. Reps., 1986-93, vice chmn. Mcht. Marine subcom., 1987-93; cons. Lent &

Scrivner, Washington, 1993—; Rep. exec. leader, East Rockaway, N.Y., 1968-70. Mem. bd. visitors U.S. Mcht. Marine Acad., Kings Point, N.Y. With USNR, 1952-54. Recipient George Estabrook Disting. Service award Hofstra U., 1967, Israeli Prime Minister's medal, 1977, Disting. Achievement medal N.Y.C. Holland Soc., 1987, Tree of Life award Jewish Nat. Fund., 1987, Anatoly Sharansky Freedom award L.I. Com. for Soviet Jewry, 1983. Mem. ABA, Nassau County Bar Assn., Fla. Bar Assn. Office: Lent & Scrivner 555 13th St NW Ste 305 E Washington DC 20004-1109

LENTON, ROBERTO LEONARDO, research facility and environmental administrator; b. Buenos Aires, Feb. 28, 1947; s. Leonard Gersham and Katie (McCulloch) L.; m. Julia Anne Frend, June 11, 1971; children: Alexandra, James, Christopher, Jessica. Civil Engr., U. Buenos Aires, 1971; SM in Civil Engring., MIT, 1973, PhD in Water Resources Systems, 1974. Planning asst. Ministry Pub. Works, Buenos Aires, 1970-71; vis. rsch. engr. MIT, Cambridge, 1971-72, rsch. asst., 1972-74, asst. prof., 1974-77; project specialist Ford Found., New Delhi, 1977-80, program officer, 1980-83; program officer Ford Found., N.Y.C., 1983-86; dep. dir. gen. Internat. Irrigation Mgmt. Inst., Kandy, Sri Lanka, 1986-87; dir. gen. Internat. Irrigation Mgmt. Inst., Colombo, Sri Lanka, 1987-94; dir. sustainable energy and environ. divsn. UN Devel. Programme, N.Y.C., 1995—. Co-author: Applied Water Resources Systems Planning, 1979. Bd. dirs., treas. Am. Embassy Sch., New Delhi, 1981-83; bd. dirs. Overseas Children's Sch., Colombo, 1989-93. Mem. ASCE, Am. Geophys. Union, Centro Argentino Ingenieros. Avocations: windsurfing, tennis, running. Home: 48 Rye Rd Rye NY 10580 Office: UN Devel Programme One UN Plz New York NY 10017

LENTS, DON GLAUDE, lawyer; b. Kansas City, Mo., Nov. 4, 1949; s. Donald Victor and Helen Maxine (Draper) L.; m. Peggy Lynn Iglauer, Aug. 27, 1972; children: Stacie Lee, Kelsey Lynn. BA magna cum laude, Harvard U., 1971, JD magna cum laude, 1974. Bar: Mo. 1974, U.S. Dist. Ct. (ea. dist.) Mo. 1975, U.S. Ct. Appeals (8th cir.) 1975. Jr. ptnr. Bryan Cave, St. Louis, 1974-81, ptnr., 1982, 84—; ptnr. Bryan Cave, London, 1982-84; mgr. internat. dept. Bryan Cave, St. Louis, 1984-88, mgr. corp. and bus. dept., 1988-95, chair exec. com., 1988—, chair corp. and bus. dept., 1995-96, head transactions group, 1996—; instr. law Washington U., 1979-80. Co-author: Missouri Corporate Law and Practice, 1989, 91 and ann. supplements. Bd. dirs. Leadership St. Louis, Inc., 1978-81, 86-91, pres., 1989-91; bd. dirs. Coro Found., St. Louis, Inc., 1986-91, gen. counsel, sec., 1988-90; vol. St. Louis Lawyers and Accts. for Arts, 1988-93, v.p., 1990-92, pres., 1992-93; vol. Brit. Am. Project, 1989-94, pres., 1993-94; bd. dirs., exec. com. Confluence St. Louis, 1995—. Sheldon fellow Harvard U., 1974-75. Mem. ABA, Mo. Bar Assn. (coun. corp. and bus. law sect. 1987-93, vice chmn. 1988-92), Met. St. Louis Bar Assn. (sec. bus. law sect. 1980-81), Harvard Alumni Assn. (regional dir. 1993-96), Hasty Pudding Club, Harvard Club (exec. com. St. Louis Club 1978-82, v.p. 1987-92, pres. 1992-93). Office: Bryan Cave 1 Metropolitan Sq 211 S Broadway Saint Louis MO 63102-1705

LENTZ, CONSTANCE MARCHAND, accountant; b. Tampa, Fla., May 6, 1948; d. George Ray and Allie Mae (Renner) L. BSBA, Calif. State U., Northridge, 1970, MSBA, 1974. CPA, Nev. Staff acct. Laventhol & Horwath CPA, Las Vegas, Nev., 1981-84; sr. mgr., acct. Deloitte, Haskins & Sells, Las Vegas, 1984-90; acct., pres. Constance M. Lentz, CPA, Ltd., Las Vegas, 1990—. Treas., bd. dirs. Warm Springs Res. Homeowners Assn., Henderson, Nev., 1990-94; trustee New Vista Ranch, Las Vegas, 1990—; treas. bd. trustees Las Vegas Natural History Mus., 1989-94; treas., bd. dirs. Clark County unit/Nev. divsn. Am. Cancer Soc., Las Vegas, 1978-85; treas. New Vista Ranch, Las Vegas, 1995—. Mem. AICPA, Nev. Soc. CPAs, Las Vegas C. of C. (Leadership Las Vegas grad. 1991), Leadership Las Vegas Alumni Assn. Avocations: reading, running, working out, sailing. Office: 930 S 3rd St Ste 100A Las Vegas NV 89101-6843

LENTZ, DEBORAH LYNN, telemetry, thoracic surgery nurse; b. Greenport, N.Y., Oct. 24, 1971; d. Stanley Antone Jr. and Linda Ann (Bernhard) C.; m. Stephen C. Lentz III, Dec. 1993; 1 child, Stephen C. Lentz IV. Cert. LPN, Harry Ward Tech. Ctr., Riverhead, N.Y., 1989; ADN, SUNY, Alfred, 1991. RN, N.Y.; cert. BLS, ACLS. LPN San Simeon By the Sound, Greenport, 1989-91; RN Meml. Sloan Kettering Cancer Ctr., Manhattan, N.Y., 1991-92, L.I. Jewish Hosp., New Hyde Park, N.Y., 1992-94, Ctrl. Suffolk Hosp., 1994—. Mem. N.Y. State Nurses Assn. Roman Catholic. Avocations: music, animal and nature lover. Home: 68750 Route 48 Greenport NY 11944-2217

LENTZ, HAROLD JAMES, lawyer; b. Hackensack, N.J., Feb. 22, 1947; s. Harold John and Winifred (Fallon) L.; m. Susan Pope, June 22, 1974; 1 son, Miles. BArch, U. Nebr., 1971; M in Bldg. Constrn., U. Fla., 1974; JD, Stetson U., 1983. Bar: Fla. 1984; lic. architect, Fla., Ga., Colo., Tex.; cert. gen. contractor, Fla. Atty. Pilot Corp., Palm Harbor, Fla., 1983-88; prin. H. James Lentz & Assocs., P.A., Palm Harbor, 1988-94; shareholder Lentz & Fair P.A., Palm Harbor, 1994—. Mem. ABA, Fla. Bar Assn., Colo. Bar, D.C. Bar, Am. Arbitration Assn. (mem. panel 1987—), Am. Inst. Constructors, AIA, Trial Advocacy Soc., Nat. Coun. Archtl. Registration Bds., Gargoyle, Phi Kappa Phi, Sigma Lambda Chi. Roman Catholic. Avocations: golf, snow skiing. Office: Lentz & Fair PA 35111 US Hwy 19 N Ste 302 Palm Harbor FL 34684-1934

LENTZ, THOMAS LAWRENCE, biomedical educator, dean, researcher; b. Toledo, Mar. 25, 1939; s. Lawrence Raymond and Kathryn (Heath) L.; m. Judith Ellen Pernaa, June 17, 1961; children: Stephen, Christopher, Sarah. Student, Cornell U., 1957-60; MD, Yale U., 1964. Instr. in anatomy Yale U. Sch. Medicine, New Haven, 1964-66, asst. prof. of anatomy, 1966-69, assoc. prof. of cytology, 1969-74, assoc. prof. of cell biology, 1974-85, prof. of cell biology, 1985—, asst. dean for admissions, 1976—, vice chmn. cell biology, 1992—; mem. cellular and molecular neurobiology panel NSF, 1987-88, mem. cellular neurosci. panel, 1988-90; mem. neurology B-1 study sect. Nat. Inst. Neurol. Disorders and Stroke, NIH, 1996. Author: The Cell Biology of Hydra, 1966, Primitive Nervous Systems, 1968, Cell Fine Structure, 1971; contbr. over 90 articles to sci. publs. Vice chmn., chmn. Planning and Zoning Commn., Killingworth, Conn., 1979—; active Killingworth Hist. Soc. Recipient Conn. Fedn. Planning and Zoning Agys. award, 1995, Citizen of Yr. award Killingworth Lions Club, 1993; fellow Trumbull Coll., Yale U.; grantee NSF, 1968-92, Dept. Army, 1986, NIH, 1987—. Mem. AAAS, Am. Soc. Cell Biology, Soc. for Neurosci., N.Y. Acad. Scis., Appalachian Mountain Club (trails com.), Appalachian Trail Conf., Mt. Washington Obs., Wonalancet Out Door Club, Alpha Omega Alpha. Republican. Mem. United Ch. of Christ. Achievements include study of primitive nervous systems, identification of neurotoxin binding site on the acetylcholine receptor, identification of cellular receptor for rabies virus. Office: Yale U Sch Medicine Dept Cell Biol 333 Cedar St PO Box 208002 New Haven CT 06520-8002

LENZ, CHARLES ELDON, electrical engineering consultant, author; b. Omaha, Apr. 13, 1926; s. Charles Julius and Hattie Susan (Wageck) L. SB, MIT, 1951; MS, U. Calif., Irvine, 1971; SM, MIT, 1953; PhD, Cornell U., 1957. Registered profl. engr., Mass. Elec. engr. GE, Pittsfield, West Lynn, Mass., Syracuse, Ithaca, N.Y., 1949-56; sr. staff engr. Avco Corp., Wilmington, Mass., 1958-60; mem. tech. staff Armour Rsch. Found., Chgo., 1960-62; sr. staff engr. North Am. Aviation, Inc., Anaheim, Calif., 1962-69; prof. U. Hawaii, Honolulu, 1966-68, U. Nebr., Omaha, 1973-78; sr. engr. Control Data Corp., Omaha, 1978-80; elec. engr. USAF, Offutt AFB, Nebr., 1980-84; sr. rsch. engr. Union Pacific Railroad, Omaha, 1984-87; engring. cons., author, 1987—; guest lectr. Coll. of Aeronautics, Cranfield, Eng., 1969, Cornell U., Ithaca, N.Y., UCLA, U. Minn., Mpls. Contbr. articles to profl. jours. including IEEE Internat. Conv. Record, ISA Conf. Procs., ISA Transactions, Procs. of the IEEE Electronics Conf., Procs. of Internat. Aerospace Instrumentation Symposium, Procs. of Modeling and Simulation Conf., Procs. of IEEE Electronics Conf., Procs. of Nat. Aerospace Electronics Conf., Procs. of Nat. Congress of Applied Mechanics. Program com. mem. N.E. Rsch. and Engring. Meeting, Boston, 1959. With USNR, 1944-46. Recipient 1st prize for tech. papers Am. Inst. Elec. Engrs., 1949; tuition scholar MIT, 1948-51, John McMullen Grad. scholar Cornell U., 1955-56; Charles Bull Earl Meml. fellow Cornell U., 1956-57, postgrad. fellow, U. Calif., Irvine, 1971. Mem. ASCE, IEEE (sr., life, nat. feedback control com., nat. control subcom. on computers), Sci. Rsch. Soc. Am. (life), N.Y. Acad. Scis. (life), Inst. Soc. Am. (sr.), Tau Beta Pi (life), Eta Kappa Nu (life), Sigma Xi (life). Achievements include protoprogramming and patents in the fields of computer safety, storage and testing, phase-angle measurement, radar-signal processing, and ultraprecise control. Home: 5016 Western Ave Omaha NE 68132-1466

LENZ, EDWARD ARNOLD, trade association executive, lawyer; b. White Plains, N.Y., Sept. 28, 1942; s. Frederick and Hildegarde (Bunzel) L.; m. Anna Maria Bartusiak, Mar. 21, 1987; children: Scott, Eric. BA, Bucknell U., 1964; JD, Boston Coll., 1967; LLM, NYU, 1968. Bar: N.Y. 1968, D.C. 1973, Mich. 1982. Trial atty. U.S. Dept. Justice, Washington, 1970-72; assoc. gen. counsel U.S. Cost of Living Coun., Washington, 1973; assoc. Miller & Chevalier, Washington, 1973-80; counsel Health Ins. Assn. Am., Washington, 1980-82; v.p., asst. gen. counsel Kelly Svcs. Inc., Troy, Mich., 1982-89; chmn. legis. com. Nat. Assn. Temp. & Staffing Svcs., Alexandria, Va., 1985-89; sr. v.p., gen. counsel Nat. Assn. Temp. Svcs., Alexandria, Va., 1989-93, sr. v.p. legal and govt. affairs, 1993—. Author: Co-employment--Employer Liability Issues in Staffing Services Arrangements, 1994. Capt. U.S. Army, 1968-70, Vietnam. Decorated Bronze Star. Mem. ABA, N.Y. Bar Assn., D.C. Bar Assn., Am. Corp. Counsel Assn., Pi Sigma Alpha, Sigma Alpha Epsilon. Home: 818 S Lee St Alexandria VA 22314-4334 Office: Nat Assn Temp & Staffing Svcs 119 S St Asaph St Alexandria VA 22314-3119

LENZ, HENRY PAUL, management consultant; b. N.Y.C., Nov. 24, 1925; s. Ernest and Margaret (Schick) L.; m. Norma M. Kull, Jan. 25, 1958; children: Susan, Scott, Theresa. A.B., U. N.C., 1946; M.B.A., Coll. Ins., 1974. Underwriter U.S. Casualty Co., N.Y.C., 1948-55; underwriting mgr. Mass. Bonding & Ins. Co., N.Y.C., 1955-60; with Home Ins. Co., N.Y.C., 1960-85; sr. v.p. Home Ins. Co., 1972-75, exec. v.p., dir., 1975-85; chmn. bd. Lenz Enterprises Ltd., Chatham, NJ, 1985—; former pres., dir. Home Indemnity Co.; pres., dir. Home Ins. Co. Ind., Home Ins. Co. Ill., City Ins. Co., Home Group Risk Mgmt.; chmn. bd. Home Reins. Co., Scott Wetzel Services Inc.; chmn., pres. Cityvest Reins. Ltd., City Ins. Co. (U.K.) Ltd.; trustee Am. Inst. Property and Liability Underwriters, Ins. Inst. Am. Served with USNR, 1944-47, 52-53. Decorated Army Commendation medal. Mem. Soc. CPCU's, Phi Beta Kappa, Sigma Nu. Office: Lenz Enterprises Ltd 42 Edgehill Ave Chatham NJ 07928-1937

LENZ, PHILIP JOSEPH, municipal administrator; b. Monterey Park, Calif., Sept. 15, 1940; s. Philip George and Irene Mary (Bowers) L.; m. Mary Lou Antista, July 16, 1966; children: Brian Joseph, Jonathan Thomas. BA, Calif. State U., L.A., 1966; MS, Pepperdine U., 1974. Dir. West Valley div. San Bernardino County (Calif.) Probation Dept., 1977-79, dir. juvenile div., 1979-82, dir. adminstrv. services, 1982-88, dir. dist. services, 1988-90; dep. chief probation officer, 1990—; instr. dept. bus. Calif. State U., San Bernardino; instr. dept. social rels. Loma Linda U., 1988. Sec. bd. trustees Upland (Calif.) Sch. Dist., 1986—, pres. sch. bd., 1989-90, 94-96; mgr., coach Upland Am. Little League, 1981-90, bd. dirs., 1982-90; pres. Fontana (Calif.) Family Svc. Agy., 1972-74; mem. adv. com. corrections Chaffey Coll., Alta Loma, Calif., 1977—; mem. Upland Parks and Recreation Com., 1986—, chmn., 1989-91; bd. dirs. Highlander Ednl. Found., v.p., 1991—; mem. Calif. Youth Authority CADRE of Cons. Recipient Tim Fitzharris award Chief Probation Officers of Calif., 1987. Mem. Calif. Probation, Parole and Correctional Assn. (liaison, regional v.p. 1981-83, 2d v.p. 1985-86, 1st v.p. 1986—, pres. 1987—), Probation Bus. Mgr.'s Assn. (regional chmn. 1984-86, v.p. 1987), Western Correctional Assn., Assn. for Criminal Justice Rsch. (bd. dirs.), Probation Adminstrs. Assn. (regional chair 1992-93). Democrat. Roman Catholic. Avocations: baseball, bicycle riding, hiking. Home: 1375 Stanford Ave Upland CA 91786-3147 Office: San Bernardino County Dept Probation 175 W 5th St San Bernardino CA 92401-1401

LENZ, ROBERT WILLIAM, polymer chemistry educator; b. N.Y.C., Apr. 28, 1926; s. Henry B. and Olga A. (Grote) L.; m. Madeleine Leblanc, June 6, 1953; children: Kathleen, Douglas, Cynthia, Suzanne. BSChemE, Lehigh U., 1949; PhD, SUNY, Syracuse, 1956. Rsch. chemist Chicopee Mfg. Co., Chicopee Falls, Mass., 1951-53; rsch. chemist Dow Chem. Co., Midland, Mich., 1955-61, Framingham, Mass., 1961-63; asst. dir. FRL Inc., Dedham, Mass., 1963-66; prof. U. Mass., Amherst, 1996-95, prof. emeritus, 1995—; cons. many cos. in the chem. industry, 1966—; dist. faculty lectr. U. Mass., 1994. Author: Organic Chemistry of Synthetic High Polymers, 1967; assoc. editor Macromolecules, 1982-94, editor-in-chief, 1995—; contbr. over 375 articles to publs. Mem. adv. bd. Petroleum Rsch. Fund, 1989-93, Greve Found., N.Y.C., 1988-94; bd. dirs. Cult Awareness Network, Chgo., 1989-91. Recipient Sr. Humboldt prize, Humboldt Found., Bonn, Fed. Republic of Germany, 1979, Polymer Chemistry award Am. Chem. Soc., 1992, Outstanding Contbns. to Polymer Chemistry award Soc. of Polymer Sci. Japan, 1995; faculty fellow U. Mass., 1984. Achievements include 16 patents in field. Home: 43 Aubinwood Rd Amherst MA 01002-1623 Office: U Mass Polymer Sci Engring Dept Amherst MA 01003

LENZEN, CONNIE LOU, genealogist; b. Portland, Oreg., Feb. 1, 1939; d. Grayland Dudley and Agnes Cecilia (Stariha) Miller; m. Gerald Sylvester Lenzen, Sept. 19, 1959; children: Daniel Mark, Jennifer Anne. BS in Edn., Portland State Coll., 1960; MS in Edn., Portland State U., 1981. Cert. geneal. record specialist, 1983. Elem. tchr. Pleasant Valley Sch., Portland, Oreg., 1960-63, Portland Pub. Schs., 1969-94; profl. genealogist Portland, 1983—. Author: Huiras Family in America (8 vols.), 1986-89, Oregon Guide to Genealogical Resources, 1991, St. Mary's Cemetery, Portland, Oregon, 1987, How to Find Naturalization Records in Oregon, 1989; contbr. articles to geneal. mags. Mem. Assn. Profl. Genealogists (trustee 1992-94), Nat. Geneal. Soc. (conf. author 1991, Excellence award, 1995), Geneal. Coun. Oreg. (membership chair), Geneal. Forum Oreg. (1st. v.p., 1994—), Oreg. Hist. Soc., Oreg. Hist. Cemeteries Assn. Democrat. Roman Catholic. Home and Office: 10411 SW 41st Ave Portland OR 97219-6984

LENZEN, LAURA ELAINE, civil engineer; b. Lincoln, Nebr., Apr. 6, 1947; d. George Harry and Esther Ruth (Gies) DeBus; children: Timothy A., Amy L.; m. Louis W. Lenzen, Feb. 15, 1980. Registered profl. engr., Nebr.; cert. profl. mgr. From sec. to traffic engr. supr. Nebr. Dept. Rds., Lincoln, 1969-89, wetlands engr. unit head, 1989—. Recipient Environ. award Fed. Hwy. Adminstrn., 1995, Environ. Excellence award U.S. Dept. Transp., 1995. Mem. Nebr. Mgrs. Assn., Engrs. Club Lincoln (bd. dirs., sec.-treas.). Avocations: books, classical music, piano, computers, travel. Home: 2017 N 57th St Lincoln NE 68505-1107 Office: Nebr Dept Roads PO Box 94759 Lincoln NE 68509-4759

LENZI, MARK, Olympic athlete, springboard diver. Olympic springboard diver Barcelona, Spain, 1992; nat. spokesperson Learn To Fly program Nat. Air Transp. Assn. Recipient Gold medal springboard diving Olympics, Barcelona, 1992, 17 internat. titles, 7 nat. titles, 2 World Cups. Achievements include first person to score over 100 points on a single dive; first American to complete a forward 4 1/2 somersault in national competition. Office: c/o US Olympic Com 1750 E Boulder St Colorado Springs CO 80909-5724*

LENZING, HARRY F., electrical engineer; b. Jersey City, June 5, 1934. BS in Physics, Stevens Inst. Tech., MS in Physics. Disting. mem. tech. staff AT&T Bell Labs. Fellow IEEE. Office: AT&T Bell Labs Crawfords Corner Rd Room Crb 21200 Holmdel NJ 07733*

LEO, JACQUELINE M., TV executive. Feature writer Singapore Herald, AP; sr. editor Modern Bride; co-founder Child, N.Y.C., 1986, editor-in-chief, 1987-88; editor-in-chief Family Circle, N.Y.C., 1988-94; editl. dir. women's mags. group N.Y. Times Co., N.Y.C., 1994, dir. mag. and media devel., 1994—; editorial dir. Good Morning America ABC-TV News, N.Y.C., 1994—. Author: New Woman's Guide To Getting Married; mem. editl. bd. The Scis., NAS. Bd. dirs. Nat. Com. To Prevent Child Abuse, Women's Commn. for Refugee Women and Children, Child Care Action Campaign. Recipient Matrix award Women in Comm., 1993. Mem. Am. Soc. Mag. Editors (bd. dirs.). Office: ABC News/Good Morning Am 147 Columbus Ave New York NY 10023

LEO, JOHN P., columnist; b. Hoboken, N.J., June 16, 1935; s. Maurice M. and Maria M. (Trincellita) L.; m. Stephanie Wolf, Dec. 30, 1967 (div.); children: Kristin, Karen; m. Jacqueline Jasous, Jan. 21, 1978; 1 child, Alexandra. BA, U. Toronto, 1957; LittD (hon.), Marietta Coll., 1996. Reporter Bergen Record, Hackensack, N.J., 1957-60; editor Cath. Messenger, Davenport, Iowa, 1960-63; assoc. editor Commonweal mag., N.Y.C., 1963-67; reporter The New York Times, N.Y.C., 1967-69; dep. adminstr. N.Y.C. Dept. Environ. Protection, 1970-73; press columnist Village Voice, N.Y.C., 1973-74; assoc. editor, sr. writer Time mag., N.Y.C., 1974-88; columnist U.S. News & World Report, N.Y.C., 1988—. Author: How the Russians Invented Baseball, 1989, Two Steps Ahead of the Thought Police, 1994. Mem. ch.-state com. ACLU, 1964-66; bd. advisors Columbia Journalism Rev., 1994—. Office: US News & World Report 1290 6th Ave Ste 600 New York NY 10104

LEO, PETER ANDREW, newspaper columnist; b. Teaneck, N.J., Aug. 3, 1943; s. Maurice Matthew and Mary (Trincellita) L.; m. Sylvia Weed, July 26, 1970; children—Steven, Jane. A.B., U. Toronto, 1966; M.A., NYU, 1967. High sch. tchr. Peace Corps, Nairobi, Kenya, 1968-69; reporter AP, N.Y.C., 1970, Greensboro Record (N.C.), 1971-72, Wilmington News-Jour. (Del.), 1973-78; reporter, asst. city editor, columnist Pitts. Post-Gazette, 1978—. Recipient Headliners award Atlantic City Press Club, 1972, Golden Quill award Pitts. Press Club, 1980, Keystone award Pa. Newspaper Pubs. and Editors Assn., 1984. Home: 5266 Beelermont Pl Pittsburgh PA 15217-1010 Office: PG Pub Co 34 Blvd Of The Allies Pittsburgh PA 15222-1204

LEOGRANDE, WILLIAM MARK, political science educator, writer; b. Utica, N.Y., July 1, 1949; s. John James and Patricia Ann (Ryan) LeoG; m. Martha J. Langelan. AB, Syracuse U., 1971, MA, 1973, PhD, 1976. Asst. prof. Hamilton Coll., Clinton, N.Y., 1976-78; dir. polit. sci. Am. U., Washington, 1980-82, asst. prof. polit. sci., 1978-83, assoc. prof., 1984-89, prof., 1989—; chair dept. govt. U. Washington, Washington, 1992-96; mem. profl. staff U.S. Senate, 1982-83, cons., 1984-85. Author: Cuba's Policy in Africa, 1980; editor: (with Morris Blachman) Confronting Revolution; Security Through Diplomacy in Central America, 1986, (with Louis Goodman) Political Parties and Democracy in Central America; dir. Latin Am. Rsch. Rev., 1982-86, World Policy Jour., 1983-93. Dir. svc. com. Unitarian-Universalist Ch., Boston, 1983-86; mem. staff John Anderson Presdl. Campaign, 1980, Michael Dukakis Presdl. Campaign, 1988. Council Fgn. Relation Internat. Affairs fellow, 1982-83. Mem. Coun. Fgn. Rels., Am. Polit. Sci. Assn., Latin Am. Studies Assn. (exec. council 1984-87). Democrat. Home: 7215 Chestnut St Bethesda MD 20815-4051 Office: Am U Sch Pub Affairs Ward Cir Washington DC 20016

LEON, ARTHUR SOL, research cardiologist, exercise physiologist; b. Bklyn., Apr. 26, 1931; s. Alex and Anne (Schrek) L.; m. Gloria Rakita, Dec. 23, 1956; children: Denise, Harmon, Michelle. BS in Chemistry with high honors, U. Fla., 1952; MS in Biochemistry, U. Wis., 1954, MD, 1957. Intern Henry Ford Hosp., Detroit, 1957-58; fellow in internal medicine Lahey Clinic, Boston, 1958-60; fellow in cardiology Jackson Meml. Hosp.-U. Miami (Fla.) Med. Sch., 1960-61; dir. clin. pharmacology research unit Hoffmann-La Roche Inc.-Newark Beth Israel Med. Ctr., 1969-73; from instr. to assoc. prof. medicine Coll. Medicine and Dentistry N.J., Newark, 1967-73; from assoc. prof. to prof. div. epidemiology U. Minn., Mpls., 1973—, H.L. Taylor prof. exercise sci. and health enhancement, dir. lab. physiol. hygiene and exercise sci., div. kinesiology, Coll. Edn., 1991—, dir. applied physiology and nutrition, 1973-91; mem. med. eval. team Gemini and Apollo projects NASA, 1964-67. Assoc. editor Surgeon Gen.'s Report on Health Benefits of Exercise, 1994-96; contbr. numerous articles to profl. publs. Trustee Vinland Nat. Sports Health Ctr. for Disabled, 1978—; mem. gov.'s coun. physical fitness sports, 1979—. Served as officer M.C. U.S. Army, 1961-67, 90-91, col. Res. 1978-92, ret. Recipient Anderson award AAHPER, 1981; Am. Heart Assn. fellow, 1960-61. Fellow Am. Coll. Cardiology, Am. Coll. Chest Physicians, Am. Coll. Clin. Pharmacology, N.Y. Acad. Scis., Am. Coll. Sports Medicine (trustee 1976-78, 82-83, v.p. 1977-79, pres. Northland chpt. 1975-76, Citation award 1995), Am. Assn. Cardiovasc. and Pulmonary Rehab. (trustee 1989-90), Am. Acad. Kinesiology and Phys. Edn.; mem. Am. Physiol. Soc., Am. Soc. Pharmacology and Exptl. Therapeutics, Am. Inst. Nutrition, Am. Heart Assn. (v.p. Hennepin County divsn. 1980-81, pres. 1982-83), Am. Coll. Nutrition, Am. Fedn. Clin. Rsch., Minn. Lung Assn. (trustee 1978-81), Phi Beta Kappa, Phi Kappa Phi. Jewish. Home: 5628 Glen Ave Hopkins MN 55345-6610 Office: U Minn Sch Kinesiology & Leisure Studies 110 Cooke Hall Minneapolis MN 55455-0136

LEON, BENJAMIN JOSEPH, electrical engineering educator; b. Austin, Tex., Mar. 20, 1932; s. Harry Joshua and Ernestine (Franklin) L.; m. Maxine Murphy, Jan. 26, 1954; children: Nathaniel J., Victoria R., Jennifer A., Theresa S. BS, U. Tex., 1954; SM, MIT, 1957, ScD, 1959. Registered profl. engr., Ky., La. Mem. tech. staff Lincoln Lab. MIT, Lexington, 1954-59; mem. tech staff Hughes Rsch. Labs., Malibu, Calif., 1959-62; assoc. prof. Purdue U., West Lafayette, Ind., 1962-64; prof. Purdue U., West Lafayette, 1964-80; chmn. dept. elec. engring U. Ky., Lexington, 1980-84, prof. elec. engring., 1980-88; sr. staff officer NRC, Washington, 1988-90; prof., coord. grad. telecommunications studies, dept. elect. and computer engring. U. Southwestern La., Lafayette, 1990—; vis. prof. Cornell U., Ithaca, N.Y., 1968-69; electronics engr. Def. Commn. Agy., Reston, Va., 1975-76; communications cons. Westinghouse Corp., Pitts., 1980; vis. prof. So. Meth. U., Dallas, 1986-87. Author: Lumped Systems, 1968, Basic linear Networks, 1970; editor IEEE Trans on Circuits, 1967-68, IEEE Impact, 1980-85, IEEE Profl. Perspective, 1985; patentee in field. Pres. Meml. Soc., Lafayette, 1963-68; sec. Wabash Vol. Fire Fighters, West Lafayette, 1978-79. Fellow IEEE (v.p. 1979-80), IEEE Cirs. and Sys. Soc. (pres. 1970-71), AAAS (coun. del. 1994-96); mem. NSPE. Unitarian. Home: 200 Cherry St Lafayette LA 70506-3626 Office: Univ Southwestern La Dept Elec and Computer Engring USL Box 43890 Lafayette LA 70504-3890

LEON, BRUNO, architect, educator; b. Van Houten, N.Mex., Feb. 18, 1924; s. Giovanni and Rose (Cunico) L.; m. Louise Dal-Bo, Sept. 4, 1948 (dec. 1974); m. Bonnie Bertram, Sept. 12, 1976; children: Mark Jon, John Anthony, Lisa Rose. Student, Wayne State U., 1942, U. Detroit, 1945-48; LHD (hon.), U. Detroit, 1984; BArch, N.C. State Univ., 1953. Registered architect, Mich., N.C., Mass., N.Y., N.Mex., Fla. Head design staff Fuller Research Found., Raleigh, N.C., 1954-55; archtl. designer I.M. Pei & Assos., N.Y.C., 1955-56; instr. Mass. Inst. Tech., 1956-59; designer Catalano & Belluschi (architects), Cambridge, Mass., 1958-59; asst. prof. U. Ill. at Urbana, 1959-61; dean Sch. Architecture, U. Detroit, 1961-93, dean emeritus, 1993; pvt. practice architecture, 1956—. Served with USAAF, 1942-45. Fellow AIA (dir. Detroit 1963-64); mem. Alpha Sigma Nu (hon.), Phi Kappa Phi. Home: 9 Redonda Ct Santa Fe NM 87505-8308 *I believe the integral quality of the human spirit to be the ability to dream rather than to rationalize.*

LEON, DONALD FRANCIS, university dean, medical educator; b. Washington, Aug. 19, 1932; s. Frank A. and Madeline (Wildman) L.; children: Anne, James, John, Sharon. AB, Georgetown U., 1953, MD, 1957. Diplomate Am. Bd. Internal Medicine, Subspeciality Bds. in Cardiovascular Diseases. Instr. medicine U. Pitts., 1965-67, asst. prof. medicine, 1967-70, assoc. prof., 1971-75, vice chmn. medicine, 1971-75, assoc. prof., 1975-77, exec. assoc. dean, 1975-79, prof. medicine, 1977—, pres. Univ. Health Ctr., 1979-83, dean Sch. Medicine, 1979-84; dean clin. affairs Georgetown U. Hosp., Washington, 1989-94, prof. medicine divsn. cardiology, 1994—; bd. dirs. Blue Cross Western Pa. Co-editor: Pericardial Disease, 1982, Am. Heart Assn. Monograph, 1975. Served to capt. USAF, 1961-63. Am. Heart Assn. scholar, 1968-73. Fellow ACP, Council on Clin. Cardiology, Am. Heart Assn. (fellow Coun. on Circulation), Am. Coll. Cardiology (bd. dirs.); mem. Am. Fedn. for Clin. Rsch., Cen. Soc. for Clin. Rsch. Office: Georgetown Univ Hosp 3800 Reservoir Rd NW Washington DC 20007-2196

LEÓN, EDUARDO A., diplomat, business executive; b. Santiago de los Caballero, Dominican Republic, Oct. 13, 1920; s. Eduardo and Maria León Jimenes; m. Ana Tavares, Feb. 16, 1946. Student, O'Sullivan Bus. Coll., Montreal, Can., 1937; BBA, McGill U., 1939. Under sec. of state Industry and Commerce Ministry, Santo Domingo, Dominican Republic, 1953, Fgn. Affairs Ministry, Santo Domingo, Dominican Republic, 1954; minister of comml. affairs Embassy of Dominican Republic, Washington, 1955; envoy extraordinary and minister Plenipotenciary of Dominican Republic, London, 1956, Otawa, Can., 1957; pres. E. León Jimenes, C. por A., Santiago de Caballeros, 1939—; ambassador extraordinary Plenipotenciary of Dominican Republic, Washington, 1986-89, Plenipotenciary at Large, Dominican

Republic, 1989—. Named to Order of Duarte, Sánchez and Mell in the Grade of Grand Cross, Order of Christopher Columbus in the Grade of Comdr., Order of Cuban Red Cross in Grade of Grand Cross, Decoration of Christopher Columbus in Grade of Grand Cross Silver Plate, 1995; recipient Paul Harris medal Rotary Internat., Gold Ring Philip Mo rris Inc. Mem. Nat. Coun. Businessmen, Assn Industries of Dominican Republic, Ctrl. Bank Dominican Republic, Bank of Agriculture and Industry, State Coun. of Sugar, Rotary, Met. Club N.Y., Union League Club, Internat. Golf Club, Centro Espanol Club. Roman Catholic. Avocations: tennis, golf, shooting, collector of wines, travel. Office: EPS Esp No B 101 PO Box 02 5360 Miami FL 33102

LEON, RICHARD J., lawyer, former government official; b. South Natick, Mass., Dec. 3, 1949; s. Silvano B. and Rita (O'Rorke) L.; m. M-Christine Costa; Nicholas Cavanagh. AB, Holy Cross Coll., 1971; JD cum laude, Suffolk Law Sch., 1974; LLM, Harvard U., 1981. Bar: R.I. 1975, U.S. Ct. Appeals (2d cir.) 1977, U.S. Dist. Ct. R.I. 1976, U.S. Supreme Ct. 1984, D.C. 1991, U.S. Dist. Ct. D.C. 1991, U.S. Ct. Appeals (D.C. cir.) 1991. Law clk. to justices Superior Ct. Mass., 1974-75, to justice R.I. Supreme Ct., 1975-76; spl. asst. U.S. atty. U.S. Attys. Office (so. dist.) N.Y., 1977-78; asst. prof. law St. John's U. Law Sch., 1979-83; sr. trial atty., criminal sect., tax div. U.S. Dept. Justice, Washington, 1983-87, dep. asst. atty. gen. environment and natural resources divsn., 1988-89; ptnr. Baker & Hostetler, Washington, 1989—; dep. chief minority counsel House Select Iran-Contra Com., 1987; active Jud. Conf. D.C. cir., 1991—, Pres. Commn. on White House Fellowships, 1990-93; chief minority counsel House Fgn. Affairs Com. 'October Surprise' Task Force, 1992; mem. admissions and grievances com. U.S. Ct. Appeals D.C. cir., 1994—; spl. counsel house banking com. Whitewater investigation, 1994. Author: (chpt.) Environmental Crime, Lawyers' Desk Book on White Collar Crime, 1991; contbr. articles to legal jours. Bd. trustees Suffolk U., 1990—. Mem. ABA, Order of Barristers, R.I. Bar Assn., Fed. Bar Council, Suffolk Law Sch. Assn. Met. N.Y. (past pres.), Suffolk Law Sch. Assn. Met. Washington (past pres.). Clubs: Harvard of N.Y.C., Harvard of Boston, University (Washington). Republican. Roman Catholic. Office: Baker & Hostetler 1050 Connecticut Ave NW Washington DC 20036-5303

LEON, ROBERT LEONARD, psychiatrist, educator; b. Denver, Jan. 18, 1925; s. Louis and Rae (Brown) L.; m. Willena Lee, Sept. 14, 1947; children: Alexis Kay, Mark Robert, Jeffrey Clayton, Stacy Lee. MD, U. Colo., 1948. Diplomate Am. Bd. Psychiatry and Neurology. Intern U. Mich. Hosp., Ann Arbor, 1948-49; resident in psychiatry U. Colo. Med. Ctr., Denver, 1949-52, child psychiatry fellow, 1951-52; child psychiatry fellow Bur. Mental Hygiene, New Haven, Conn. Dept. Health/Student Health Svc., Yale U., 1952-53; asst. dir., acting dir. child psychiatry Greater Kansas City Mental Health Found., 1953-54; instr. psychiatry U. Kans. Sch. Medicine, Kansas City, 1956-57; asst. prof. psychiatry U. Tex. Health Sci. Ctr. at Dallas, Southwestern Med. Sch., 1957-61, assoc. prof., 1961-65, prof., 1965-67; prof., chmn. dept. psychiatry Sch. Medicine U. Tex. Health Sci. Ctr., San Antonio, 1967-95, interim chmn., 1995-96; Ashbel Smith prof. U. Tex. Health Sci. Ctr., San Antonio, 1990—; chief psychiatry U. Health Sys., Bexar County, San Antonio, 1967-96; cons. psychiatry Audie Murphy Vet.'s Hosp., 1973—; cons. Mental Health Orgn., region IV, HEW, 1957-73; mem. Psychiat. Tng. Rev. NIMH, Rockville, Md., 1970-74. Author: Psychiatric Interviewing: A Primer, 1982, 2d edit., 1989; contbr. articles to profl. jours. Sr. surgeon USPHS, 1954-57. Fellow ACP (pres. 1987-88), Am. Psychiat. Assn. (life), Am. Orthopsychiat. Assn. (life), Am. Acad. Child and Adolescent Psychiatry (life), Am. Assn. Social Psychiatry (pres. 1990-92); mem. Am. Assn. Chmn. Depts. Psychiatry (pres. 1982-83), Benjamin Rush Soc., World Assn. for Social Psychiatry. Home: 6866 Stonykirk St San Antonio TX 78240-2743 Office: U Tex Health Sci Ctr 7703 Floyd Curl Dr San Antonio TX 78284-7792

LEÓN, TANIA JUSTINA, composer, music director, pianist; b. Havana, Cuba, May 14, 1943; came to U.S., 1967; d. Oscar and Dora (Ferran) L. BA in Piano and Theory, Peyrellade Conservatory Music, Havana, 1963; MA in Music Edn., Nat. Conservatory Music, Havana, 1965; BA in Acctg., U. Havana, 1965; BS Music Edn., NYU, 1973, BS in Music Edn., 1973, MA in Composition, 1975. Prof. Bklyn. Coll. Conservatory of Music, 1994—; vis. prof. Yale U., New Haven, 1993; vis. lectr. Harvard U., Cambridge, Mass., 1994; resident composer Lincoln Ctr. Inst., 1985, teaching artist, 1982-88; composer in residence Nat. Black Music Festival, 1990, Cabrillo Music Festival, 1990, Yaddo, 1991, Ravinia Festival, 1991, Cleve. Inst., 1992, Bellagio Ctr., Italy, 1992, Cornish Coll., Seattle, 1993, Billings Symphony, 1993, Carnegie Mellon U., Pitts., 1993, Harvard Coll., Cambridge, Mass., 1993, Voices of Change, Dallas, 1993; panelist N.Y. State Council on the Arts, 1980, 81, 86, NEA composing program, 1980-82, recording program, 1985-87; mem. adv. bd. Bklyn. Coll. Conservatory, 1982-84, Meet the Composer, 1983—, Children TV Workshop; artistic dir. Composers Forum Inc., N.Y.C., 1987—; assoc. prof. composition Bklyn. Coll., 1987—; bd. dirs. Am. Music Ctr., N.Y. Found. for Arts; with Cin. Symphony Orch., 1991—, Revson Composer fellow N.Y. Philharmonic, 1993—; U.S. rep. U.S.-Mex. Fund for Culture, 1994. Piano soloist, Cuba, 1964-67; piano soloist, N.Y. Coll. of Music Orch., N.Y.C., 1967, NYU Orch., N.Y.C., 1969, Buffalo Symphony Orch., 1973; staff pianist, condr., Dance Theatre of Harlem, N.Y.C., 1968—, assoc. condr., 1983—, music dir., 1968-79; founder, Dance Theatre of Harlem Orch., 1975; concert series Meet the Performer, 1977; music dir. concert series Dance in Am. Spl., Sta. WNET-TV; guest condr. concert series, Genova (Italy) Symphony Orch., 1972, Juilliard Orch., Festival Two Worlds, Spoleto, Italy, Symphony New World, 1974, Royal Ballet Orch., 1974, 76, BBC Orch., 1974, 76, Halle Orch., 1974, Buffalo Philharm. Orch., 1975, Concert Orch. of L.I., 1979, Sadler's Wells Orch., 1979, London Universal Symphony, 1979, Composer's Forum, 1979, Lincoln Ctr. Outdoor Festival, 1980, Bklyn. Coll. Symphony, 1981, J. F. Kennedy Ctr. Opera House Orch., 1981, 82, Radio City Music Hall, 1982, Spoleto Festival, Charleston, 1983, Orch. of Our Time, N.Y., N.Y. Grand Opera, Colonne Orch., Paris, Mich. Opera, Human Comedy, Royale Theatre, Broadway, Pasadena Orch., P.R. Symphony, Met. Opera Orch., Phoenix Symphony, Columbus Symphony Orch., Fund. Latinoamericana Musica Contemporanea P.R., Am. Women Condr./Composer Symposium, Eugene, Oreg., New Music Am., Houston, New Music in Am., 1989 and Concert in the Pk., 1990 both with Bklyn. Philharm., Cabrillo Festival, 1990, Nat. Black Arts Festival, Atlanta, 1990, La Crosse Symphony, Wis., 1991, Dance Theatre of Harlem, 1991, 92, 93, 25th Anniversary Season-94, Celebrate Bklyn. Festival, 1991, Bklyn. Philharm., 1991, New World Symphony, Miami, Fla., 1991, 94, Cosmopolitan Symphony Orch., N.Y.C., 1991, Beethovenhalle Symphony Orch., Bonn, Germany, 1992, Opera Orch. of Johannesburg, 1992, Nat. Symphony Orch., Johannesburg, 1992, Louisville Symphony, 1992, RIAS Orch., Berlin, 1992, Billings Symphony, 1993, Dance Theater of Harlem, 1993, 94, Carnegie Mellon Orch., 1993, Alvin Ailey 35th Anniversary Season, 1993, Am. Composers Orch. Chamber Ensemble, 1994, Munich Biennale, 1994, others; royal command performer concert series, London Palladium, 1974, 76, Concert Orch. L.I., 1976, concert pianist, Sta. WNYC-FM, 1968-70; conductor coord.: concert series Music by Black Composers Series, Bklyn. Philharmonia, 1978-79; music dir., condr., Bklyn. Philharm. Community Concert Series, 1977—; mus. dir., condr. The Wiz, Broadway Theatre, 1978; music dir. Death, Destruction and Detroit, 1979, Alvin Ailey Am. Dance Theatre, 1983—, Whitney Mus. Contemporary Music Concert Series, 1986, 87; mus. dir., composer: Maggie Magalita, J.F. Kennedy Ctr. Performing Arts, 1980, TWindows, 1982; apptd. music dir. concert series, Intar Theatre, N.Y.C.; condr., mus. dir. concert series Godspell, NYU, 1978, Carmencita, 1978; composer (ballet music) Haiku, 1974, (piano concerto) Tones, 1970, Sailor's Boat, (score for musical) Dougla, 1974, (African ballet) La Ramera de la Cueva, 1974, (score for musical) Namiac Poems, 1974, (for voice, chorus and orch.) Spiritual Suite, 1975, (2 sopranos, chorus and mixed ensemble with narrator), Concerto Criollo, 1976, (concerto for piano, 8 timpanies and orch.) Pet's Suite, 1979, (for flute and piano) I Got Ovah, 1980, (for soprano, piano and percussion, based on poems by Carolyn M. Rodgers) Concerto Criollo, 1980, Four Pieces for Cello, 1981, De-Orishas, 1982, Ascend, Fanfare for Brass and Percussion, 1983, (for solo piano) Momentum, 1984, Bata, 1985, Permutation Seven, 1985, A La Par, 1986, Ritual, 1987, Pueblo Mulato, 1987, Heart of Ours, a piece, 1988, Parajota Delaté, 1988, Kabiosile, 1988, Latin File, 1988, Indigena for instrumental ensemble, 1991, Solisti Chamber Orch N.Y., 1991, Carabali for orch., 1992, Crossings for brass ensemble, 1992, Arenas d'un Tempo for clarinet, cello and piano, 1992, Son Sonora for flute and guitar, 1993, Scourge of Hyacinths: chamber opera, 1994, Para Viola y Orquesta for viola and orch., 1994, Sin Normas Ajenas for chamber orch., 1994; records on CRI, WesternWind, Albany Records, Newport Classics, Leonarda Records. Bd. dirs. Am. Composers Orch. Recipient Young Composers prize Nat. Council Arts, Havana, 1966, Alvin Johnson award Am. Council Emigres in the Profession, 1971, Cintas award in composition, 1974-75, 78-79, Achievement award Nat. Council Women of U.S., 1980, Byrd Hoffman Found. award, 1981, Key to City of Detroit, 1982, Queens Council on Arts award, 1983, Meet The Composer awards, 1978-94, Manhattan Arts award, 1985, Dean Dixon Achievement award, 1985, N.Y. State Coun. on Arts award, 1988, Mayor's citation, City of N.Y., 1989, Celebrate Bklyn. Achievement award, 1990, award in music Am. Acad. and Inst. of Arts and Letters, 1991; Nat. Endowment for Arts fellow, 1975. Mem. ASCAP (Composers award 1978-94), French Soc. Composers, Am. Acad. Poets (bd. dirs.), Am. Composers Orch. (bd. dirs.), Am. Fedn. Musicians, Ctr. New Music, Am. Music Ctr. (bd. dirs. 1985—), Internat. Artists Alliance, Am. Women Composers, AFL-CIO.

LEON, TOMAS CARLOS, foreign exchange broker; b. Mexico City, July 20, 1951; came to U.S., 1983; s. Richard C. and Manuela (Santacruz) de Leon; m. Maria Sofia Cardenas, Nov. 1, 1979; children: Sofia, Tomas. BBA, Anahuac U., Mexico City, 1973; MBA, U. Tex., 1978. Account exec. Securities Banco Nacional de Mex., S.A., Mexico City, 1973-77; retail div. mgr. Casa de Bolsa Banamex, S.A. de C.V., Mexico City, 1979-80, mgr. securities rsch., 1981-82; dir. capital markets group Valores Finamex, S.A. de C.V., Mexico City, 1982-83; vice chmn., dir. Trans-Tex. Holdings Corp., Austin, 1983—; chief operating officer, dir. PSI Techs. Corp., Austin, 1986-87; chmn., chief exec. officer Impex Trading Corp., Austin, 1987-89; chmn., chief exec. officer, dir. Internat. Forex Corp., Austin, 1989—, Tex. Paymaster Corp., Austin, 1991—. Patentee investment and loan instruments indexed to inflation. Mem. Univ. Club de Mex. A.C., Austin Internat. Club, KC, U. Tex. Ex-Students Assn., Asociacion de Ex-Alumnos de la Universidad Anahuac. Roman Catholic. Office: Internat Forex Corp Ste 202 1001 Capital Of Tex Hwy S Austin TX 78746*

LEONARD, SISTER ANNE C., superintendent, education director; b. N.Y.C., Dec. 22, 1936; d. Patrick A. and Mary T. (McAlpin) L. BS in Edn. and Social Sci., Fordham U., 1962, MA, 1965; CAGS, Boston U., 1972; postgrad., Hunter Coll., U. San Francisco, U. Northern Ill., Notre Dame U. Cert. tchr. K-12, adminstr. N.Y. Tchr., asst. prin., prin. Notre Dame Acad., Staten Island, N.Y., 1957-68; prin. Maternity B.V.M. Sch., Bourbonnais, Ill., 1968-69, St. Jude the Apostle Sch., South Holland, Ill., 1969-78; dir. Cath. Elem. Schs. Archdiocese of Chgo., 1978-83, dir. ednl. svcs., mem. Cardinal Bernadin's cabinet, 1983-90, exec. officer commn. ednl. svcs., 1983-90; supt. schs., dir. edn. Archdiocese of Okla. City, 1990—; chair edn. divisn. Cath. Conf. Ill., 1988-90; del. gen. chpt. Congregation Notre Dame, mem. provincial coun.; mem. edn. com. U.S. Cath. Conf. Bishops, Washington, 1985-88; speaker in field; lectr., presenter workshops; mem. Fortune 500 panel edn. and bus.; devel. mission statement, just principles compensation, new models compensation for prins., 1987-91; initiated, organized Dirs. Edn. Wis., Ill., Ind., Ohio, Mich.; attended symposia in field; mem. com. prep. Office of Cath. Edn. Conciliation Process; exec. officer local sch. bds.; initiated individually guided edn. program St. Jude Sch. Cons. textbooks William H. Sadlier, Inc.; contbr. articles to profl. jours. Trustee DePaul U., 1986—, bd. dirs., chair acad. affairs com.; bd. dirs. Jr. Achievement, Chgo., 1984-90, Okla. City, 1991—; mem. NCCJ, 1992—, Gov. Ill. adv. com. on non-pub. schs., Springfield, 1978-82, planning com. Big Shoulders Project. Mem. ASCD, Nat. Cath. Ednl. Assn. (pres. chief adminstrs. Cath. edn. 1991-94, v.p. 1989-91, vice chair bd. 1991—, task force 1990-91, supervision, pers., curriculum, Educator or Yr. award 1990), Archdiocesan Prins. Assn. (pres. 1973-78), Chgo. Coun. Fgn. Rels., Phi Delta Kappa (Educator of Yr. 1984). Avocations: reading, swimming, traveling. Home: 10804 Greystone Ave Oklahoma City OK 73120-3218 Office: Archdiocese Okla City PO Box 32180 Oklahoma City OK 73123-0384

LEONARD, BARBARA M, former secretary of state, federal agency administrator, state agency administrator. Grad., Brown U.; PhD (hon.), Johnson & Wales U. Cert. tchr. R.I., Ohio. Owner, CEO H & H Screw Products Mfg. Co., Lincoln, R.I.; regional adminstr. region 1 Gen. Svcs. Adminstrn. New England; dir. of devel. for child care ctrs. for federal employees throughout U.S.; sec. of state R.I., 1993-94. Pres. R.I. Philharmonic Orch.; trustee emerita Brown U., Bryant Coll.; bd. dirs., sec. United Way; bd. dirs. Nat. Conf. Christians and Jews. Recipient R.I. Woman Bus. Advocate of Yr. award, 1983, Nat. Humanitarian award, 1983, Rhode Islander of Yr. award, 1984. Republican. Baptist. Office: State House Rm 218 Providence RI 02903*

LEONARD, CLAIRE OFFUTT, pediatric geneticist educator; b. Rochester, N.Y., Apr. 1, 1945; d. Edward Preble and Virginia Leoma (Williams) Offutt; divorced; children: Christopher Edward, Kathleen. BA, Mount Holyoke Coll., 1967; MD, John Hopkins U., 1971. Diplomate Am. Bd. Pediatrics, Am. Bd. Genetics. Intern and resident in pediat. U. Colo., 1971-74, fellow in genetics and birth defects, 1974-75; fellow in genetics Johns Hopkins Hosp., Balt., 1978-80; asst. prof. pediatrics John Hopkins U., Balt., 1980-81; asst. prof. pediatrics U. Utah, Salt Lake City, 1981-87, assoc. prof. pediatrics, 1987—. Mem. Am. Soc. Human Genetics, Am. Acad. Pediatrics, Am. Coll. Human Genetics, Soc. Inherited Metabolic Disorders. Mem. Soc. of Friends. Avocations hiking, cooking, camping. Office: U Utah Dept Peds 50 N Medical Dr Salt Lake City UT 84112-1122

LEONARD, DAVID ARTHUR, hospital executive emeritus; b. Red Oak, Iowa, June 3, 1928; s. Morris Condit and Wynona Loveland (Farquhar) L.; m. Elizabeth Harvey Berry; children: Deborah Anne Leonard Kotarski, Thomas Berry, Jane Elizabeth Leonard Shellum. AB, Grinnell Coll., 1949; MA, U. Minn., 1950. Pers. assoc. Mayo Clinic, Rochester, Minn., 1950-61, adminstrv. asst., 1962-75, chmn. div. pers. svcs., 1976-81, chmn. div. adminstrv. svcs., 1982-86; adminstr. St. Marys Hosp., Rochester, 1987-90, pres., trustee, 1974-82. Trustee Mayo Found., Rochester, 1988-90, Rochester Meth. Hosp., 1987-90; bd. dirs. Minn. Conf. Cath. Healthcare Facilities, St. Paul, 1988-90; chmn. adv. com. City Coun. Orgn., Rochester, 1978-80, Total Community Devel. Project, Rochester, 1966-68; councilman City of Rochester, 1961-64. Recipient Outstanding Young Man award Rochester Jaycees, 1962. Republican. Episcopalian. Office: Mayo Clinic Emeritus Office 200 1st St SW Rochester MN 55905-0001

LEONARD, DAVID MORSE, lawyer; b. Akron, Ohio, Dec. 4, 1949; s. Frank O. and Barbara J. (Morse) L.; m. Sharon Elaine Quati, May 7, 1977; children: Michael Morse, Lindsey Marie. BS in Chem. Engring., Purdue U., 1972; JD, Emory U., 1975. Bar: Ga. 1975, U.S. Ct. Appeals (4th, 5th and 11th cirs.), U.S. Dist. Ct. (no., mid. and so. dists.) Ga., U.S. Dist. Ct. (so. dist.) Ala., U.S. Dist. Ct. (we. dist.) La.; cert. mediator, cert. mediation tng. Assoc. Montet & Smith, Atlanta, 1975-79; assoc. Hurt, Richardson, Garner, Todd & Cadenhead, Atlanta, 1979-83, ptnr., 1983-85; of counsel Lord, Bissell & Brook, Atlanta, 1985-87, ptnr., 1987—; mem. panel of arbitrators Am. Arbitration Assn., 1995—. Mem. ABA (litigation sect., tort and ins. practice sect.), Profl. Liability Underwriting Soc., Atlanta Lawyers Club, Atlanta C. of C., Am. Arbitration Assn. (panel of arbitrators). Home: 4152 Club Dr NE Atlanta GA 30319-1116 Office: Lord Bissell & Brook Ste 3700 1201 W Peachtree St NW Atlanta GA 30309-3421

LEONARD, EDWARD PAUL, naval officer, dentist, educator; b. Greenfield, Mass., Dec. 29, 1935; s. Laurence Francis and Hilda Mae (Coutu) L.; m. Lola Jeanne Ahern, Sept. 6, 1958; children: Lisa Ann, Jeffrey Torbert, Julie Marie, Laurence Edward. Student, St. Joseph's Sem., 1953-56, St. Anselm's Coll., 1956, U. Mass., 1956-58; DDS, Georgetown U., 1962; MS, U. Md., 1968, PhD, 1970; attended, Marymount U., 1990-92. Commd. lt. USN, 1962, advanced through grades to capt., 1979; asst. dental officer Subic Bay Naval Sta. USN, The Philippines, 1970-72; assoc. histopathologist dental rsch. inst. USN, Great Lakes Naval Base, Ill., 1972-76, chief histopathologist dental rsch. inst., 1976-80; program mgr. Naval Med. R & D USN, Bethesda, Md., 1980-83; quality assurance officer Office Dir. Naval Med. USN, Washington, 1983-84, dental care analyst Office Dir. Naval Med., 1984-86; exec. officer Naval. Dental Clin. USN, Parris Island, S.C., 1986-88; comdg. officer Naval Dental Clin. USN, Charleston, S.C., 1988—; mem. exec. coun. Mgmt. Devel. Adv. Bd. Navy Surgeon Gen., Washington, 1983-86; grant reviewer div. rsch. grants NIH, Washington, 1981-83; tchr. biology, ecology Hargrave Mil. Acad., asst. basketball coach, sailing club sponsor, astronomy club sponsor; evaluator Va. Ind. Schs. Assn. Contbr. articles to profl. jours. Vol. coach Vienna (Va.) Youth League, 1983-84; coach McLean (Va.) Youth League, 1984. Recipient Carl A. Schlack Rsch. award Assn. Mil. Surgeons of U.S., 1989. Fellow Internat. Coll. Dentists, Am. Coll. Dentists; mem. Internat. Assn. Dental Rsch., Am. Assn. Dental Rsch., Am. Assn. Pub. Health Dentistry, Nat. Assn. Biology Tchrs. Democrat. Roman Catholic. Avocations: sailing, astronomy, historic preservation. Home: 9085 Wexford Dr Vienna VA 22182-2152

LEONARD, EDWIN DEANE, lawyer; b. Oakland, Calif., Apr. 22, 1929; s. Edwin Stanley and Gladys Eugenia (Lee) L.; m. Judith Swatland, July 10, 1954; children: Garrick Hillman, Susanna Leonard Hill, Rebecca, Ethan York. BA, The Principia, 1950; LLB, Harvard U., 1953; LLM, George Washington U., 1956. Bar: D.C. 1953, Ill. 1953, N.Y. 1957. Assoc. Davis Polk Wardwell Sunderland & Kiendl, N.Y.C., 1956-61; ptnr. Davis Polk & Wardwell, N.Y.C., 1961—. Trustee the Brearley Sch., N.Y.C., 1980-90. Served to 1st lt. JAGC, 1953-56. Mem. ABA, N.Y. Bar Assn., N.Y. County Bar Assn., Assn. of Bar of City of N.Y. (chmn. various coms.), Millbrook Equestrian Ctr. (pres.). Home: 1148 Fifth Ave New York NY 10128-0807 Office: Davis Polk & Wardwell 450 Lexington Ave New York NY 10017-3911

LEONARD, ELMORE JOHN, novelist, screenwriter; b. New Orleans, Oct. 11, 1925; s. Elmore John and Flora Amelia (Rivé) L.; m. Beverly Claire Cline, Aug. 30, 1949 (div. 1977); children: Jane, Peter, Christopher, William, Katherine; m. Joan Leanne Lancaster, Sept. 15, 1979 (dec. 1993); m. Christine Kent, Aug. 19, 1993. PhB, U. Detroit, 1950. Author over 30 novels including Hombre, 1961, City Primeval, 1980, Split Images, 1982, Cat Chaser, 1982, La Brava, 1983, Stick, 1983, Glitz, 1985, Bandits, 1987, Touch, 1987, Freaky Deaky, 1988, Killshot, 1989, Get Shorty, 1990, Maximum Bob, 1991, Rum Punch, 1992, Pronto, 1993, Riding the Rap, 1995, Out of Sight, 1996. With USN, 1943-46. Recipient Mystery Writers of Am. Grand Master award, 1992. Mem. Writers Guild of Am., Authors Guild, Mystery Writers of Am., Western Writers of Am. Roman Catholic. Address: Creative Artists Agy c/o Michael Siegel Beverly Hills CA 90212

LEONARD, EUGENE ALBERT, banker; b. St. Louis, Aug. 27, 1935; s. Albert Hiram and Mary (Crowson) L.; m. Mary Ann Sampson, Aug. 31, 1956 (div. 1994); children: Charles, James, Susan; m. Constance Anne Deschamps, June 3, 1995. BS, U. Mo., 1957, MS, 1958, PhD, 1962; postgrad., Stonier Grad. Sch. Banking, Rutgers U., 1964-66. Instr. agrl. econs. U. Mo. at Columbia, 1959-60; with Fed. Res. Bank St. Louis, 1961-77; v.p., mgr. Fed. Res. Bank St. Louis (Memphis br.), 1967-70, sr. v.p., 1970-71, 1st v.p., 1971-77; on loan to bd. govs. FRS as asst. sec., Washington, 1970-71; sr. v.p. Merc. Bancorp. Inc., St. Louis, 1977-87; pres. Corp. for Fin. Risk Mgmt., St. Louis, 1987—; instr. econs. Central States Sch. Banking, 1962-69, Ill. Bankers Sch., 1962-74, Sch. Banking South, 1970-83, Stonier Grad. Sch. Banking, 1975-80, bd. regents, 1978-81; adj. assoc. prof. econs. Memphis State U., 1969-70. Bd. dirs. Logos Sch., St. Louis, 1977-85, chmn., 1985; bd. dirs. Repertory Theater of St. Louis, 1981-87. Mem. Mo. Bankers Assn. (treas. 1984-85, pres. 1986-87), U. Mo. Columbia Alumni Assn. (nat. pres. 1980-81, bd. dirs. devel. fund 1981-89, Faculty Alumni award 1986), Gamma Sigma Delta, Kappa Sigma. Unitarian. Home: 30 Portland Pl Saint Louis MO 63108-1204 Office: Corp for Fin Risk Mgmt 8675 Olive Blvd Saint Louis MO 63132-2503

LEONARD, GEORGE EDMUND, real estate, bank, and consulting executive; b. Phoenix, Nov. 20, 1940; s. George Edmund and Marion Elizabeth (Fink) L.; m. Gloria Jean Henry, Mar. 26, 1965 (div. Feb. 1981); children: Tracy Lynn, Amy Theresa, Kristin Jean; m. Mary C. Short, Sept. 22, 1990. Student, Ariz. State U., 1958-60; BS, U.S. Naval Acad., 1964; postgrad., Pa. State U., 1969-70; MBA, U. Chgo., 1973. Commd. ensign, USN, 1964, advanced through grades to lt. comdr., 1975; v.p. 1st Nat. Bank Chgo., 1970-75; exec. v.p., chief banking, chief fin. and chief lending officer Mera Bank, Phoenix, 1975-90, also bd. dirs., 1982-90; pres., chief exec. officer Cen. Savs., San Diego, 1985-87; chmn., CEO AmBank Holding Co. of Colo., Scottsdale, Ariz., 1990-91, Consumer Guarantee Corp., Phoenix, 1996—; pres., CEO Diversified Mgmt. Svcs., Inc., Phoenix, 1991—, GEL Mgmt. Inc., Phoenix, 1991—; bd. dirs. Beverly Hills (Calif.) Savs., Am. Nat. Bank of Scottsdale, Bank of Santa Fe, 1990-91, 1st Am. Bank of Colo. Springs. Active Phoenix Thunderbirds, 1979—; bd. dirs. Maricopa Community Colls. Found., treas., 2d v.p., 1991-93, 1st v.p., 1993-94, pres. 1994-95, Camelback Charitable Trust, 1991-92, The Samaritan Found., 1993—, chmn. fin. com., 1994—, vice chmn., 1996—. Mem. Phoenix Met. C. of C. (bd. dirs. 1975-82), Inst. Fin. Edn. (bd. dirs. 1980-87, nat. chmn. 1985-86), Ariz. State U. Coll. of Bus. Deans Coun. of 100, Paradise Valley Country Club (bd. dirs. 1991—, treas. 1992-95, pres. 1995—), Univ. Club (San Diego), Kiwanis. Republican. Roman Catholic. Home: 3064 E Stella Ln Phoenix AZ 85016-2244 Office: Consumer Guarantee Corp 221 E Indianola Phoenix AZ 85012

LEONARD, GLEN M., museum administrator; b. Salt Lake City, Nov. 12, 1938; s. Burnham J. and Allene (Green) L.; m. Karen Wright, Mar. 15, 1968; children: Cory, Kyle, Keith. BA, U. Utah, 1964, MA, 1966, PhD, 1970. Mng. editor Utah State Hist. Soc., Salt Lake City, 1970-73; sr. rsch. assoc. history div. Ch. of Jesus Christ of Latter-day Saints, Salt Lake City, 1973-78; dir. Mus. Ch. History and Art, Salt Lake City, 1979—; mem. adv. bd. editors Utah Hist. Quarterly, Salt Lake City, 1973-88; assoc. editor Jour. Mormon History, Provo, Utah, 1974-80; bd. dirs. Western Studies Ctr., Brigham Young U., Provo. Co-author: The Story of the Latter-day Saints, 1976; contbr. articles to profl. publs. Mem. Hist. Preservation Commn., Farmington, Utah, 1986-92; mem. adv. coun. Mormon Pioneer Nat. Hist. Trail, Nat. Pk. Svc., 1980-86; mem. Utah Pioneer Sesquicentennial Celebration Coordinating Coun., 1995—. Recipient Dale Morgan Article award Utah State Hist. Soc., 1973. Mem. Orgn. Am. Historians, Western History Assn., Am. Assn. Mus. (mus. assessment program cons.), Western Mus. Assn., Utah Mus. Assn. (bd. dirs. 1980-83), Am. Assn. State and Local History. Avocations: photography, music, gardening. Office: Mus Ch History and Art 45 N West Temple Salt Lake City UT 84150-1003

LEONARD, GUY MEYERS, JR., international holding company executive; b. Bluefield, W.Va., Sept. 22, 1926; s. Guy Meyers and Mabel (Bonham) L.; A.B., BS, Morris Harvey Coll., 1949; B.Div., Southwestern Bapt. Sem., 1952; S.T.M., Harvard U., 1957; m. Pat Kirby, June 28, 1949; children—Calvin David, Dinah Lynn. Commd. ensign U.S. Navy, 1952, advanced through grades to capt., 1968, ret., 1972; dir. R & D Ency. Britannica Ednl. Corp., Chgo., 1972-76; pres. Communication Programming Svcs., Inc., Charleston, S.C., 1976—; pres., CEO First Don Trading Co., 1982—; chmn., chief exec. officer Transocean Ltd., internat. holding co., 1982-86; pres. GHL, Inc., Pacific rim, Africa, 1991—; cons. drug control programs for schs., cons. Ency. Britannica, Home Mission Bd. and Brotherhood Commn. So. Bapt. Conv. Sec., U.S. Power Squadron, Charleston, 1969; chmn. Spl. Commn. on Drug Abuse for Armed Forces, 1970-72; active Conn. coun. Boy Scouts Am., 1959-62; chmn. stewardship com. Episc. Dioces of S.C. Served with USN, 1943-72. Decorated Legion of Merit, Meritorious Svc. medal, Navy Commendation medal, Disting. Svc. Medal; recipient Disting. Svc. award City of Louisville, 1963. Mem. Harvard Club S.C., C. of C., Trident Chamber (Charleston), Navy League U.S., Ret. Officers Assn. Club: Kiwanis (spl. projects chmn., 1964-65). Designer, produced with Harvard U. and sta. WGBH, Boston, mediated coll. curriculum leading to B.S. degree for use by naval personel.

LEONARD, HERMAN BEUKEMA (DUTCH LEONARD), public finance and management educator; b. Carlisle Barracks, Pa., Dec. 26, 1952; s. Charles Frederick and Margery Alden (Beukema) L.; m. Kathryn Anne Angell, Oct. 9, 1983; children: Whitney Angell, Dana Angell. AB summa cum laude, Harvard U., 1974, AM, 1976, PhD, 1979. Asst. prof. pub. policy John F. Kennedy Sch. Govt., Harvard U., Cambridge, Mass., 1979-83, assoc. prof., 1983-86, George F. Baker prof. pub. mgmt., 1986—, acad. dean for teaching programs, 1992—; mem. Gov.'s Coun. Econ. Policy, Alaska, 1980-82; chmn. Gov.'s Task Force on Coll. Opportunity, Mass., 1987-88; bd. dirs. Mass. Health and Ednl. Facilities Authority, 1988—; mem. adv. bd. N.Y.C. Debt Mgmt., 1990-94. Co-author: Discrimination in Rural Housing, 1976; author: Checks Unbalanced: The Quiet Side of Public Spending, 1986, By Choice or By Chance? Tracking the Values in Massachusetts Public Spending, 1992; contbr. numerous articles on pub. fin. and mgmt. to jours. in field. Recipient grad. fellowship NSF, 1974; jr. fellow Soc. Fellows,

Harvard U., 1976-79; Presdl. scholar, 1970. Mem. Phi Beta Kappa. Office: Harvard U John F Kennedy Sch Govt 79 Jfk St Cambridge MA 02138-5801

LEONARD, HUGH (JOHN KEYES BYRNE), playwright; b. Dublin, Ireland, Nov. 9, 1926; s. Nicholas Keyes and Margaret (Doyle) Byrne; m. Paule Jacquet, 1955; 1 child. Student, Presentation Coll., Ireland, 1941-45. Civil servant Dublin, 1945-59; TV script editor Granada TV, Manchester, Eng., 1961-63; freelance writer London, 1963-70; lit. editor Abbey Theatre, Dublin, 1976-77. Author: (plays) The Italian Road, 1954, The Big Birthday, 1956, A Leap in the Dark, 1957, Madigan's Lock, 1958, A Walk on the Water, 1960, The Passion of Peter McGinty, 1961, Stephen D, 1962, Dublin One, 1963, The Poker Session, 1963, The Family Way, 1964, The Saints Go Cycling In, 1965, Mick and Nick, 1966, The Quick, and the Dead, 1967, The Late Arrival of the Incoming Aircraft, 1968, The Au Pair Man, 1968, The Barracks, 1969, The Patrick Pearce Motel, 1971, Da, 1973 (Tony award for best play 1978, N.Y. Drama Critics' Circle award for best play 1978, Drama Desk award for outstanding new play 1978, Outer Critics Circle award for outstanding play 1978), Thieves, 1973, Summer, 1974, Irishmen, 1975, Time Was, 1976, Some of My Best Friends Are Husbands, 1976, Liam Liar, 1976, A Life, 1979 (Harvey award), Moving Days, 1981, Kill, 1982, Pizzazz, 1982, Good Behaviour, 1983, O'Neill, 1983, The Mask of Moriarty, 1985, Moving, 1991, Senna for Sonny, 1994, The Lily Lally Show, 1994; (autobiographies) Home Before Night, 1979, Out After Dark, 1987; (essays) Leonard's Last Book, 1978, A Peculiar People and Other Foibles, 1979, Rover and Other Cats, 1992; (novels) Parnell and the Englishwoman, 1990, The Off-Off-Shore Island, 1993; (screenplays) Great Catherine, 1968, Interlude, 1968, Whirligig, 1970, Percy, 1971, Our Miss Fred, 1972, Herself Surprised, 1977, Da, 1988, Widow's Peak, 1994; (teleplays) The Irish Boys, 1962, A King of Kingdom, 1963, The Second Wall, 1964, A Triple Irish, 1964, Realm of Error, 1964, My One True Love, 1964, The Late Arrival of the Incoming Aircraft, 1964, Second Childhood, 1964, Do You Play Requests?, 1964, The View From the Obelisk, 1965, I Loved You Last Summer, 1965, Great Big Blond, 1965, The Lodger, 1966, The Judge, 1966, Insurrection, 1966, The Retreat, 1966, Silent Song, 1966 (Italia prize Internat. Concourse for Radio and TV 1967, Merit award Writers Guild of Gt. Britain 1967), A Time of Wolves and Tigers, 1967, Love Life, 1967, Great Expectations (Dickens), 1967, Wuthering Heights (Bronte), 1967, No Such Thing as a Vampire, 1968, The Egg on the Face of the Tiger, 1968, The Corpse Can't Play, 1968, A Man and His Mother-in-Law, 1968, Assassin, 1968, Nicholas Nickleby (Dickens), 1968, A Study in Scarlet, 1968, The Hound of the Baskerville (Doyle), 1968, Hunt the Peacock, 1969, Talk of Angels, 1969, The Possessed (Dostoevsky), 1969, Dombey and Son (Dickens), 1969, P and O (Maugham), 1969, Jane (Maugham), 1970, A Sentimental Education (Flaubert), 1970, White Walls and Olive Green Carpets, 1971, The Removal Person, 1971, Pandora, 1971, The Virgins, 1972, The Ghost of Christmas Present, 1972, The Trugh Game, 1972, The Moonstone (Collins), The Sullen Sisters, 1972, The Watercress Girl (Bates), 1972, The Higgler, 1973, High Kampf, 1973, Milo O'Shea, 1973, Stone Cold Sober, 1973, The Bitter Pill, 1973, Another Fine Mess, 1973, Judgement Day, 1973, The Travelling Woman, 1973, The Hammer of God, 1974, The Actor and the Alibi, 1974, The Eye of Apollo, 1974, The Forbidden Garden, 1974, The Three Tools of Death, 1974, The Quick One, 1974, London Belongs to Me, 1977, The Last Campaign, 1978, The Ring and the Rose, 1978, Strumpet City, 1979, The Little World of Don Camillo, 1980, Kill, 1982, Good Behaviour, 1982, O'Neill, 1983, Beyond the Pale, 1984, The Irish RM, 1985, Troubles, 1987, Hunted Down, 1989, Parnell and the Englishwoman, 1991, The Celadon Cup, 1993; (TV series) Saki, 1962, Jezebel Ex-UK, 1963, The Hidden Truth, 1964, Undermine, 1964, Blackmail, 1965, Public Eye, 1965, The Liars, 1966, The Informer, 1966, Out of the Unknown, 1966-67, The Sinners, 1970-71, Me Mammy, 1970-71, Tales from the Lazy Acre, 1972, Father Brown, 1974. Office: 6 Rossaun, Pilot View, Dalkey County Dublin, Ireland

LEONARD, IRVIN ALAN, lawyer; b. Phila., Feb. 7, 1944; s. Sidney K. and Anne (Barmack) L.; m. Elin Leslie Fleischer, Aug. 19, 1967; children: Ethan Gabriel, Jessica Silver, Matthew David. BA, U. Pitts., 1964; JD, NYU, 1967. Bar: N.Y. 1967, Ohio 1969. Law clk. to judge U.S Dist. Ct. (so. Dist.) N.Y., N.Y.C., 1967, 68; assoc. Jones, Day, Reavis & Pogue, Cleve., 1969-75, ptnr., 1975—; alt. gov. San Jose Sharks', NHL, 1991—, dir., 1991—, San Jose Arena Mgmt. Corp., 1991—. Trustee Jewish Community Fedn., Cleve., 1976—, Bur. Jewish Edn., 1977—, Agnon Sch., Cleve., 1986—; bd. trustees Convention and Visitors Bur. of Greater Cleve., 1988—. Recipient Kane award Jewish Community Fedn., Cleve., 1976—. Mem. ABA, Cleve. Bar Assn., Nat. Health Lawyers Assn., Am. Hosp. Assn., Order of Coif. Democrat. Office: Jones Day Reavis & Pogue N Point 901 Lakeside Ave Cleveland OH 44114

LEONARD, JAMES EDWARD, accountant; b. Binghamton, N.Y., Oct. 14, 1951; s. Ray Monty and Beatrice Mary (Williams) L.; m. Michelle Louise Montgomery, Aug. 3, 1985; 1 child, Celeste. Student, U. Hawaii, 1971-72, U. Md., Okinawa, Japan, 1973-74; AS in Bus., Broome C.C., Binghamton, N.Y., 1976; BS in Acctg. magna cum laude, U. Albany, 1978. CPA, N.Y. Staff acct. Peat, Marwick, Mitchell, White Plains, N.Y., 1978-80; exec. v.p. Richardson & Co., PC, Endicott, N.Y., 1980-85; owner James E. Leonard, CPA, Endicott, 1986—. Founder, chmn. Susquehanna River Walk Com., Endicott, 1992—; dir., treas. Broome County Pub. Libr., Binghamton, N.Y., 1993—; dir., officer Boys & Girls Club Western Broome, Endicott, 1993—. Petty officer 2d class USN, 1970-74. Mem. AICPA, N.Y. State Soc. CPA's, United Health Svcs. Found. (dir. 1994), Ideal Sr. Living Ctr. (dir. 1994), Endicott Rotary Club (past pres. 1982—), Endicott Rotary Found. (dir. 1992—). Avocations: reading, live steam engines, home winemaking, cooking. Office: James E Leonard CPA 1310 North St Endicott NY 13760-5424

LEONARD, JAMES JOSEPH, physician, educator; b. Schenectady, June 17, 1924; s. James Joseph and Helena (Flood) L.; m. Helen Louise Mitchell, Oct. 24, 1953; children: James Joseph, W. Jeffrey, Paul Mitchell, Kathleen Marie. M.D., Georgetown U., 1950. Intern medicine Georgetown U. Hosp., 1950-51, jr. asst. resident, 1951-52, fellow cardiology, 1953-54; asst. resident medicine Boston City Hosp., 1952-53; resident pulmonary diseases D.C. Gen. Hosp., 1954-55, med. officer, 1955-56; instr. medicine Georgetown U. Med. Sch., 1955-56, Duke Med. Center, 1956-57; asst. prof. medicine, dir. div. cardiology Georgetown U. service D.C. Gen. Hosp., 1957-59; asst. prof. medicine U. Tex. Med. Br., Galveston, 1959-62; asso. prof. medicine Ohio State U. Med. Sch., 1962-63; dir. div. cardiology U. Pitts. Med. Sch., 1963-70, asso. prof. medicine, 1963-67, prof. medicine, 1967-77, acting chmn. dept., 1970, chmn. dept., 1971-77; prof., chmn. dept. medicine Uniformed Services U. of Health Scis., 1977—. Mem. So. Soc. Clin. Investigation, Am. Clin. and Climatol. Assn., Central Soc. Clin. Research, Assn. Am. Physicians, Assn. Profs. Medicine, Assn. U. Cardiologists. Home: 3200 Farmington Dr Chevy Chase MD 20815-4827 Office: 4301 Jones Bridge Rd Bethesda MD 20814-4712

LEONARD, JEFFREY S., lawyer; b. Bklyn., Sept. 14, 1945; m. Maxine L. Bortnick, Dec. 28, 1967; children: Deborah, Jennifer. AB in History, U. Rochester, 1967; JD, U. Ariz., 1974. Bar: Ariz. 1974; U.S. Dist. Ct. Ariz. 1974, U.S. Ct. Appeals (9th cir.) 1974, U.S. Supreme Ct. 1985. Law clk. to judge U.S. Dist. Ct. Ariz., 1974-75. Mem. editorial bd. Ariz. Law Rev., 1973-74. Mem. Order of Coif. Office: Leonard Collins & Kelly PC Two Renaissance Sq 40 N Central Ave Ste 2500 Phoenix AZ 85004

LEONARD, JOANNE, photographer, educator; b. Los Angeles, Sept. 8, 1940; 1 child, Julia Marjorie. BA, U. Calif., Berkeley, 1962; postgrad., San Francisco State U., 1963-64; Minor White workshop, 1973. Prof. women's studies, 1995—; official photographer U.S. Olympic team Sapporo, Japan, 1972; instr. photography San Francisco Art Inst., 1973-75, Mills Coll., Oakland, Calif., 1975-78; lectr., asst. prof. various colls. and art schs., 1970-78; asst. prof. Sch. Art & Design U. Mich., Ann Arbor, 1978-80, assoc. prof., 1980-84, prof., 1985—, faculty assoc. Am. culture program, 1993—, mem. women's studies faculty, 1995—. One-person shows include de Young Mus., San Francisco, 1968, Hopkins Ctr. Dartmouth Coll., 1968, Seligman Gallery, Seattle, 1969, Wall St. Gallery, Spokane, Wash., 1973, San Francisco Art Inst., 1974, Bristol (Eng.) Poly. Art Gallery, 1975, Laguna Gloria Art Mus., Austin, Tex., 1980, U. Mich. Mus. Art, 1980, Orange Coast Coll. Gallery, Costa Mesa, Calif., 1984, Jeremy Stone Gallery, San Francisco, 1985, 88, Art Mus. of U. Mich., Ann Arbor, 1992, Schlesinger Libr., Archive the History of Women., Radcliffe Coll., Cambridge, Mass., 1995; 2-person show San Francisco Mus. Modern Art, 1981; group shows include Focus Gallery, San Francisco, 1967-74, George Eastman House, Rochester, N.Y., 1969-70, Oakland Mus., 1971, Pasadena Art Mus., 1970, Smith Anderson Gallery, Palo Alto, Calif., 1971, Mus. Contemporary Crafts, N.Y.C., 1971-72, San Francisco Mus. Art, 1971 and 1975, Light Gallery, N.Y.C., 1972, Laguna Beach (Calif.) Mus. Art, 1973, Boston U., 1973, Hansen Fuller Gallery, San Francisco, 1974, Woods-Gerry Gallery, Providence, R.I., 1975, Neikrug Gallery, N.Y.C., 1975-76, Stanford U. Mus., 1976, 112 Green St. Gallery, N.Y.C., 1977, Gallery 115, Santa Cruz, Calif., 1977, downtown br. Whitney Mus. Art, N.Y.C., 1978, MIT, 1978, San Francisco Mus. Modern Art. 1981, 85, Franklin Inst., Phila., 1983, Gallery of Art and Sci., IBM, N.Y.C., 1984, Calif. Mus. of Photography, Riverside, 1984, Santa Barbara (Calif.) Mus. Art, 1986 (3 person) Detroit Inst. Art, 1989, Bard Coll., Annondale on Hudson, N.Y., 1995, Hood Mus., Hanover, N.H., 1996; represented in permanent collections, U.S. State Dept., Am. Arts Documentation Centre, Exeter, Eng., The Oakland Mus., San Francisco Mus. Art, Internat. Mus. Photography, Rochester, N.Y., U. Mass. Art Mus. Stanford U. Mus., Crocker Art Mus., Sacramento, Calif., also numerous pvt. Am. collections; represented in various mus. catalogs and books including Contemporary Photographers, 1983, Photography in California 1945-80, 1984, Janson's History of Art, 1986, American Women Artists, Past and Present, 1990, Gardner's Art Through the Ages, 9th edit., 1991. Recipient Phelan Prix award, 1971, Josephine Nevins Keal award U. Mich., 1981; photosurvey grantee Nat. Endowment for Arts, 1977; fellow Humanities Inst., U. Mich., 1993-94. Pioneering mem. of women and first photographers to be included in textbook Janson's History of Art, 3d edit., 1986, also in Gardner's Art Through the Ages, 9th edit., 1991. Office: U Mich Sch Art Ann Arbor MI 48109

LEONARD, JOHN HARRY, advertising executive; b. N.Y.C., June 28, 1922; s. Frederick H. and Florence (Kiechlin) L.; m. Marjorie Jane Haslun, Oct. 19, 1946; children—John Kiechlin, Janet Ann. B.S., N.Y. U., 1942, M.B.A., 1951. Advt. mgr. Autographic Register Co., 1946-47; promotion mgr. Macfadden Pub. Co., 1947-50; successively copywriter, account exec., v.p. and account supr. Batten, Barton, Durstine & Osborn, 1950-64; with DDB Needham Worldwide (formerly Doyle Dane Bernbach, Inc.), N.Y.C., 1964-87, group sr. v.p., 1972-87; lectr. Grad. Sch. Bus., N.Y. U., 1959-61. Bd. dirs., past exec. com. Am. Bible Soc.; past chmn. bd. dirs. Wartburg Home, Mt. Vernon, N.Y.; trustee NYU, 1978-84. With USAAF, 1943-46. Recipient Alumni Meritorious Service award N.Y. U., 1969. Mem. NYU Grad. Sch. Bus. Alumni Assn. (pres.), NYU Commerce Alumni Assn. (pres. 1979-80), Alpha Delta Sigma. Home: 310A Heritage Vlg Southbury CT 06488-1752

LEONARD, JOHN WIRTH, English educator, retailer; b. Balt., July 23, 1946; s. John William and Margaret Mary (Wirth) L.; m. Ellen Louise Brooks, June 21, 1969 (div.); children—Cora Lee, John Joseph. B.S., Loyola Coll., 1968; M. equivalent Towson State U., 1977. Licensed pyrotechnist, Md. Instr. English, Baltimore County Bd. Edn., Towson, Md., 1968—; pres. Pyrotechnics Guild Inc., White Marsh, Md., 1973-76; owner, operator Sparkler City, U.S.A., Perry Hall, Md., 1983—; pyrotechnic operator Zambelli Fireworks, New Castle, Pa., 1979—. Designer fireworks ground display (Plaque for best display), 1975. Mem. Pyrotechnics Guild Internat., Inc. (pres. 1975-77). Republican. Roman Catholic. Clubs: Crackerjacks; Fireworks (Wood Bridge, Va.) (pres. 1982—). Lodge: K.C. (warden 1978-79). Home: 221 Spring Ave Lutherville MD 21093 Office: Baltimore County Bd Edn 1000 S Marilyn Ave Baltimore MD 21221

LEONARD, KURT JOHN, plant pathologist, university program director; b. Holstein, Iowa, Dec. 6, 1939; s. Elvin Elsworth and Irene Marie (Helkenn) L.; m. Maren Jane Simonsen, May 28, 1961; children: Maria Catherine, Mary Alice, Benjamin Andrew. BS, Iowa State U., 1962; PhD, Cornell U., 1968. Plant pathologist Agrl. Rsch. Svc. USDA, Raleigh, N.C., 1968-88; dir. Cereal Rust Lab. U. Minn. USDA, St. Paul, 1988—. Author (with others) Annual Review of Phytopathology, 1980; co-editor: Plant Disease Epidemiology, vol. 1, 1986, vol. 2, 1989; editor-in-chief Phytopathology, 1981-84, Am. Phytopathol. Soc. Press, 1994-96; contbr. 85 articles to profl. jours. Fellow Am. Phytopathol. Soc. (coun. 1981-84, 94—); mem. Am. Mycol. Soc., Internat. Soc. Plant Pathology (councilor 1982-93), Brit. Soc. Plant Pathology, Phi Kappa Phi, Sigma Xi, Gamma Sigma Delta. Achievements include description of new species and genera of plant pathogenic fungi; research on spread of disease through crop mixtures, on relationships between virulence and fitness in plant pathogenic fungi. Office: U Minn USDA Ars Cereal Lab Saint Paul MN 55108

LEONARD, MICHAEL A., automotive executive; b. Cadillac, Mich., Aug. 3, 1937; s. Hugel A. and Mildred (Johnson) L.; m. Frances Erickson, June 18, 1960; children: Kristin, Anne. MA, Alma Coll., 1959; MBA, Wayne State U., 1964; MS, MIT, 1971. Exec. Chrysler Corp., Highland Park, Mich., 1959-75; group v.p. Bendix Corp., Southfield, Mich., 1975-83; v.p., group exec. Allied Signal Automotive, Bloomfield Hills, Mich., 1983-91; pres. Harman, Inc., Southfield, Mich., 1991-94; mng. ptnr. Exec. Resources Inc., Bloomfield Hills, Mich., 1994—; bd. dirs. Kalyani Brake Co., Pune, India, Bendix France, Paris, Bendix Italy, and fgn. subs. Trustee Alma (Mich.) Coll.; bd. dirs. Presbyn. Villages of Mich. Sloan fellow, MIT. Mem. Soc. Automotive Engrs., Delta Sigma Phi (pres. 1958-59). Presbyterian. Avocations: swimming, golf, boating. Home: 4375 Barchester Dr Bloomfield Hills MI 48302-2116 Office: Executive Resources Inc PO Box 625 Bloomfield Hills MI 48303-9999

LEONARD, MICHAEL STEVEN, industrial engineering educator; b. Salisbury, N.C., Feb. 2, 1947; s. Charles Thomas and Dorothy Francis (Loflin) L.; m. Mary Elizabeth Stewart, June 21, 1969; children: Dorothy Elizabeth, Amanda Brooke, Gabrielle Francis. B in Engring., U. Fla., 1970, M in Engring., 1972, PhD, 1973. Registered profl. engr., Mo., S.C. Asst. prof. health systems rsch. ctr. Georgia Tech, Atlanta, 1973-75; asst. prof. indsl. engring. U. Mo., Columbia, 1975-79, assoc. prof. indsl. engring., 1979-82, prof. indsl. engring., 1982-90, dept. chmn. indsl. engring., 1985-90; dept. head indsl. engring. Clemson (S.C.) U., 1990-95; engring. accreditation commn. bd. engring. and tech., Balt., 1994—. Editor Jour. Soc. for Health Systems, 1989-91; contbr. articles to profl. jours. evaluation adv. com. Am. Blood Commn., Washington, 1977-80; bd. dirs. Am. Cancer Soc. Boone County Mo. unit, Columbia, 1978-90. Mem. Soc. Health Systems (bd. dirs. 1989-94, pres. elect 1991-92, pres. 1992-93), Inst. Indsl. Engrs. (nat. dir. career guidance 1987—), Mo. Soc. Profl. Engrs. (cen. chpt. treas. 1988-89, v.p. 1989-90). Office: Clemson U Dept Indsl Engring Clemson SC 29634

LEONARD, NELSON JORDAN, chemistry educator; b. Newark, Sept. 1, 1916; s. Harvey Nelson and Olga Pauline (Jordan) L.; m. Louise Cornelie Vermey, May 10, 1947 (dec. 1987); children: Kenneth Jan, Marcia Louise, James Nelson, David Anthony; m. Margaret Taylor Phelps, Nov. 14, 1992. B.S. in Chemistry, Lehigh U., 1937, Sc.D., 1963; B.Sc., Oxford (Eng.) U., 1940, D.Sc., 1983; Ph.D., Columbia U., 1942; D.h.c., Adam Mickiewicz U., Poland, 1980; D.Sc. (hon.), U. Ill., 1988. Fellow and rsch. asst. chemistry U. Ill., Urbana, 1942-43, instr., 1943-44, assoc., 1944-45, 46-47, asst. prof., 1947-49, assoc. prof., 1949-52, prof. organic chemistry, 1952-73, head div. organic chemistry, 1954-63, prof. biochemistry, 1973-86, R.C. Fuson prof. chemistry, mem. Ctr. for Advanced Study, 1981-86, R.C. Fuson prof. emeritus, 1986—; investigator antimalarial program Com. Med. Research, OSRD, 1944-46; sci. cons. and spl. investigator Field Intelligence Agy. Tech., U.S. Army and Dept. Commerce, 1945-46; mem. Can. NRC, summer 1950; Swiss-Am. Found. lectr., 1953, 70; vis. lectr. UCLA, summer 1953; Reilly lectr. U. Notre Dame, 1962; Stieglitz lectr. Chgo. sect. Am. Chem. Soc., 1962; Robert A. Welch Found. lectr., 1964, 83; Disting. vis. lectr. U. Calif.-Davis, 1975; vis. lectr. Polish Acad. Scis., 1976; B.R. Baker Meml. lectr. U. Calif., Santa Barbara, 1976; Ritter Meml. lectr. Miami U., Oxford, Ohio; Werner E. Bachman Meml. lectr. U. Mich., Ann Arbor, 1977; vis. prof. Japan Soc. Promotion of Sci., 1978; Arapahoe lectr. U. Colo., 1979; Tanabe rsch. lectr. Scripps Rsch. Inst., La Jolla, Calif., 1993; mem. program com. in basic scis. Arthur P. Sloan, Jr. Found., 1961-66; Philips lectr. Haverford Coll., 1971; Backer lectr., Groningen, Netherlands, 1972; FMC lectr. Princeton U., 1973; plenary lectr. Laaxer Chemistry Conf., Laax, Switzerland, 1980, 82, 84, 88, 90, 92; Calbiochem-Behring Corp. U. Calif.-San Diego Found. lectr., 1981; Watkins vis. prof. Wichita State U. (Kans.), 1982; Ida Beam Disting. vis. prof. U. Iowa, 1983; Fogarty scholar-in-residence NIH, Bethesda, Md., 1989-90; Sherman Fairchild Disting. scholar Calif. Inst. Tech., 1991; Syntex. disting. lectr. U. Colo., 1992; faculty assoc. Calif. Inst. Tech., 1992—; mem. adv. com. Searle Scholars program Chgo. Community Trust, 1982-85; ednl. adv. bd. Guggenheim Found., 1969-88, mem. com. of selection, 1977-88. Editor: Organic Syntheses, 1951-58, mem. adv. bd., 1959—, bd. dirs., 1969—, v.p., 1976-80, pres., 1980-88; editorial bd. Jour. Organic Chemistry, 1957-61, Jour. Am. Chem. Soc., 1960-72; adv. bd. Biochemistry, 1973-78, Chemistry International, 1984-91, Pure and Applied Chemistry, 1984-91; contbr. articles to profl. jours. Recipient medal Synthetic Organic Chem. Mfrs., 1970, Wheland award U. Chgo., 1991, creativity award U. Oreg., 1994, Arthur C. Cope Scholar award Am. Chem Soc., 1995; named to Mt. Vernon (N.Y.) H.S. Hall of Fame, 1985; fellow Rockefeller Found., 1950, Guggenheim fellow, 1959, 67. Fellow Am. Acad. Arts and Scis. (v.p. 1991-93); mem. NAS, AAAS, Polish Acad. Scis. (fgn.), Ill. Acad. Sci. (hon.), Am. Chem. Soc. (award for creative work in synthetic organic chemistry 1963, Edgar Fahs Smith award and lectureship Phila. sect. 1975, Centennial lectr. 1976, Roger Adams award 1981, Paul G. Gassman Disting. Svc. award divsn. organic chemistry 1994, A.C. Cope rsch. scholar award 1995), Am. Soc. Biol. Chemists, Chem. Soc. London, Swiss Chem. Soc., Internat. Union Pure and Applied Chemistry (sec. organic chemistry divsn. 1989, v.p. 1989-91, pres. 1991-93), Pharm. Soc. Japan (hon.), Phi Beta Kappa, Phi Lambda Upsilon (hon.), Tau Beta Pi, Alpha Chi Sigma. Achievements include patents on synthesis of sparteine; esters of pyridine dicarboxylic acid as insect repellents; fluorescent derivatives of adenine- and cytosine-containing compounds. Home: 389 California Ter Pasadena CA 91105-2463

LEONARD, PAUL HARALSON, retired lawyer; b. Houston, Mar. 4, 1925; s. Paul Haralson and Dovie Lore (Shuler) L.; m. Barbara Ann Underwood, Nov. 26, 1948; children: Leslie Ann, Scott Paul. BA, Rice U., 1948; JD, South Tex. Coll. of Law, 1957. Bar: Tex. 1957, U.S. Patent and Trademark Office 1960, U.S. Ct. Appeals (10th cir.) 1963, U.S. Ct. Mil. Appeals 1965, U.S. Supreme Ct. 1965, U.S. Ct. Appeals (5th cir.) 1981, U.S. Ct. Appeals (Fed. cir.) 1982. Acct. Highland Oil Co., Houston, 1948-50; statis. acct. Union Oil and Gas Corp. of La., Houston, 1953-59; assoc. Hayden & Pravel, Houston, 1959-61; patent atty. Halliburton Co., Duncan, Okla., 1961-69; div. patent atty. Ethyl Corp., Baton Rouge, 1969-87; v.p. Cen. Foods, Inc., Baton Rouge, 1979-90, bd. dirs. V.p. Plato Dependent Sch. Dist., Duncan, Okla., 1966-67, pres., 1968. Served to lt. comdr., USNR, 1942-67. Me. Tex. Bar Assn, Masons. Republican. Avocations: U.S. coins, stamp collecting. Home and Office: 10639 Rondo Ave Baton Rouge LA 70815-4847

LEONARD, R. MICHAEL, lawyer; b. Atlanta, Feb. 27, 1953; s. Charles C. and Catherine (Martin) L.; m. Margaret Ellen Mead, June 29, 1985 (div. 1993); 1 child, Sarah Marie. AB, U. N.C., 1975, JD with honors, 1978. Bar: Ala. 1978, N.C. 1987. Assoc. Cabaniss, Johnston, Gardner, Dumas & O'Neal, Birmingham, Ala., 1978-85, ptnr., 1985-86; assoc. Womble Carlyle Sandridge & Rice, Winston-Salem, N.C., 1986-88, ptnr., 1988—. Author: Trail and Naturalist's Guide to Oak Mountain State Park, Alabama, 1982. bd. dirs. Ala. Conservancy, Birmingham, 1981-85, Piedmont Land Conservancy, Greensboro, N.C., 1989-91; bd. dirs. Ala. Trails Assn., Birmingham, 1985—, founder, pres., 1985-87; trustee N.C. Nat. Heritage Found., Raleigh, 1989-92, Nature Sci. Ctr., Winston-Salem, 1994-95; gov.'s appointee bd. trustees N.C. Natural Heritage Trust Fund, 1994—; nat. adv. coun. Trust for Pub. Land, San Francisco, 1991—; mem. adv. coun. N.Y. Yr. of the Mtns., 1995-96; pres. Bethania (N.C.) Hist. Property Owners Assn., Inc., 1996—; founding chmn. Ga. Pinhoti Trail Assn., Rome, 1996—. Recipient Oak Leaf award Nature Conservancy, Washington, 1991, Sol Feinstone Environ. award Coll. Environ. Sci. & Forestry, SUNY, Rochester, 1991, Chpt. Svc. award N.C. Chpt. Sierra Club, 1990, Malcolm Stewart Conservationist of Yr. award Ala. Conservancy, Birmingham, 1983. Mem. Ala. Bar Assn., N.C. Bar Assn., Birmingham Bar Assn., Forsyth County Bar Assn., Carolina Club, Black Bear Club, Order of Coif, Phi Beta Kappa, Phi Eta Sigma. Democrat. Avocations: writing, hiking, mountain climbing, camping, turkey hunting. Office: Womble Carlyle Sandridge & Rice 200 W 2nd St Ste 1600 BB&T Winston Salem NC 27101-4036

LEONARD, RICHARD ALAN, newspaper editor; b. Beverly, Mass., Aug. 8, 1952; s. Philip E. and Cecilia M. (Sikora) Boynton; m. Laura Jean Nowicki, Sept. 17, 1983; children: Matthew, Susan, Audrey. BA in History and Sociology, Holy Cross Coll., 1974; MS in Journalism, Columbia U., 1976. Reporter Westchester-Rockland Newspapers, White Plains, N.Y., 1977-80, metro editor, 1980-83; mng. editor The Journal News, West Nyack, N.Y., 1983-87; exec. editor Gannett Co. Inc., Arlington, Va., 1987-95. Mem. Am. Soc. Newspaper Editors. Office: Valley News Dispatch 210 4th Ave Tarentum PA 15084

LEONARD, RICHARD HART, journalist; b. N.Y.C., May 23, 1921; s. Richard Barstow and Stella Burnham (Hart) L.; m. Barbara Klausner, July 11, 1948; children: Laurie, Lisa. BA, U. Wis., 1947. Reporter Milw. Jour., 1947, picture editor, 1948, with Madison (Wis.) bur., 1949-50, state desk, 1951-52, state editor, 1953-62, mng. editor, 1962-66; editor, v.p. Milw. Jour. Co., 1967-85, v.p., 1967-77, sr. v.p., 1977-85, ret., 1986; editor-in-residence East-West Ctr., Honolulu, 1987; sr. fellow East-West Ctr., 1988-89; mem. Pulitzer Prize Bd., 1976-86; prof. jouralism Marquette U., 1989—. With AUS, 1942-46. Recipient Carr Van Anda award Ohio U., 1972, East-West Ctr. Disting. Svc. award, Disting. Svc. award U. Wis. Mem. Am. Soc. Newspaper Editors, Internat. Press Inst. (chmn. 1984-86), Milw. Press Club (pres. 1965, elected Hall of Fame), Sigma Delta Chi (nat. pres. 1976), Phi Kappa Phi. Presbyterian. Home: 330 E Beaumont Ave Milwaukee WI 53217-4867

LEONARD, ROBERT SEAN, actor; b. N.J., Feb. 28, 1969; s. Robert Howard and Joyce (Peterson) L. Stage debut in Oliver; stage appearences include Coming of Age in Soho, Sally's Gone, She's Left Her Name, 1985, The Beach House, Brighton Beach Memoirs, 1986, Breaking the Code, 1987, When She Danced, Biloxi Blues (tour), Romeo and Juliet, The Speed of Darkness, Our Town, Candida, Arcadia; film appearences include The Manhattan Project, 1986, My Best Friend Is A Vampire, 1988, Dead Poets Society, 1989, Mr. & Mrs. Bridge, 1990, Married to It, 1993, Swing Kids, 1993, Much Ado About Nothing, 1993, The Age of Innocence, 1993, Safe Passage, 1994; TV movies include My Two Loves, 1986, Bluffing It, 1987. Office: William Morris Agency 151 S El Camino Dr Beverly Hills CA 90212-2704*

LEONARD, ROY JUNIOR, civil engineering educator; b. Central Square, N.Y., Aug. 17, 1929; s. Roy Jackson and Margaret Elizabeth (Keller) L.; m. Edith Campbell Gilmore; children: Robert J., Constance J. BS, Clarkson Coll. Tech., 1952; MS, U. Conn., 1954; postgrad., Mich. State U., 1954-55; PhD, Iowa State U., 1958. Registered profl. engr., N.Y., Pa., Kans., Mo., Colo.; registered profl. geologist, Mo. Asst. prof. civil engring. U. Del., 1957-59; assoc. prof. Lehigh U., 1959-65; spl. projects engr. Dames and Moore (geotech. cons.), N.Y.C., 1965; prof. civil engring. U. Kans., Lawrence, 1965-95; pres. Alpha-Omega Geotech., Inc., Kansas City, Kans. NSF fellow, 1963-65. Fellow ASCE; mem. NSPE, ASTM (chair com. vitrified clay pipe), Assn. Engring. Geologists, U.S. Com. Large Dams, Soc. Mining Engrs., Nat. Soc. Forensic Engrs., Am. Concrete Inst., Am. Pub. Works Assn., Chi Epsilon. Episcopalian. Home: 25003 Mackey Rd Lawrence KS 66044-7340

LEONARD, SAMUEL WALLACE, oil company and bank executive; b. Cumberland, R.I., Sept. 29, 1922; s. Samuel James and Hazel Della (Flagg) L.; m. Dorothy Wilma Carpenter, Oct. 15, 1949. BS in Acctg. and Fin., Bryant Coll., 1941; BA in Econs., Brown U., 1948; AMP, Harvard Bus. Sch., Soldiers Field, Mass., 1968. Internal auditor Conoco Inc., Ponca City, Okla., 1948-51; asst. dir. employee benefits Conoco Inc., Houston, 1952-54; pres., gen. mgr. Sahara Petroleum Co., Alexandria, Egypt, 1954-60; v.p., treas. Pasa Petroquimica Argentina, Buenos Aires, 1961-66; pres. Conoco Libya, Tripoli, 1966-71, Conoco Española, Madrid, Spain, 1971-72; exec. asst. pres. Conoco Inc., Stamford, Conn., 1972-76; v.p., gen. mgr. Dubai (United Arab Emirates) Petroleum, 1976-82; ret.; chmn. bd. dirs. Security Bank & Trust Co. (merger 4th Fin. Corp. 1993), Ponca city, 1992-93; bd. dirs. Bank IV Okla., Ponca City. Chmn. Little League, Tripoli, Libya, 1966-71; bd. dirs. Ponca City Libr., 1988-94. Staff sgt. U.S. Army, 1942-45, U.S. and Europe. Decorated Purple Heart, Bronze Star Valor. Mem. VFW, Am. Legion, Ponca City Country Club, Elks. Republican. Episcopal. Avocations: hunting, fishing, travel, gardening. Home and Office: PO Box 667 Ponca City OK 74602-0667

LEONARD, SHELDON, television producer, director; b. N.Y.C., Feb. 22, 1907; s. Frank and Anna (Levitt) Bershad; m. Frances Bober, June 28, 1931; children: Andrea, Stephen W. BA, Syracuse U., 1929. Pres. T. & L. Prodns.; ptnr. Mayberry Prodns.; ptnr., officer Calvada Prodns., Sheldon Leonard Enterprises; guest prof. Syracuse U. Screenwriter: Checkmate, others, 1948-57; actor numerous Broadway plays, 1930-39; numerous motion picture appearances; radio roles with Jack Benny, Bob Hope, Phil Harris, others; producer, dir. TV shows: I Spy, Dick Van Dyke, Andy Griffith, Danny Thomas, others; star TV series: Big Eddie, 1975 (Emmy award 1957, 61, Best Comedy Producer, 1970, 74, Christopher award 1955, Golden Globe award 1972, Sylvania award 1973). Trustee Motion Picture Home. Recipient Man of Yr. awards Nat. Assn. Radio Announcers, Profl. Mgrs. Guild, B'nai B'rith; Arents medal Syracuse U., Spl. Achievement award NAACP, Spl. Tribute award Nat. Collegiate Athletic Assn., Letterman of Distinction award Varsity Club Syracuse U., Govs. award Cinematographers Guild; inducted TV Hall of Fame, 1992. Mem. Dirs. Guild (hon. life, nat. trustee, bd. govds., v.p., Aldrich award). Home: 1141 Loma Vista Dr Beverly Hills CA 90210-2622 Office: Sheldon Leonard Prodns 1875 Century Park E # 2250 Los Angeles CA 90067-5010 *A man must be at peace with himself.*

LEONARD, SUGAR RAY (RAY CHARLES LEONARD), retired professional boxer; b. Wilmington, N.C., May 17, 1956; s. Cicero and Getha L.; m. Juanita Wilkinson, Jan. 19, 1980 (div. 1990); children: Ray Charles, Jr., Jarrell Giulio. Profl. boxer, 1977-82, 84, 1987-91; pres. SRL Mgmt., Inc.; with Franklin Sports Industries, Inc. Commentator boxing broadcasts; exercise video: Boxout with Sugar Ray Leonard, 1993. Recipient Gold medal Olympic Games, 1976; winner World Boxing Coun. Welterweight Championship, 1979, World Boxing Assn. Championship Jr. Middleweight div., 1981, World Boxing Coun. Championship and World Boxing Assn. Welterweight Championship, 1981, World Boxing Coun. Middleweight Championship, 1987, World Boxing Coun. Light Heavyweight and Super Middleweight Championship, 1988. Office: care Mike Trainer 4922 Fairmont Ave Bethesda MD 20814-6020*

LEONARD, THOMAS ALOYSIUS, lawyer; b. Phila., Sept. 5, 1946; s. Thomas Aloysius and Mary Teresa (Kelly) L.; m. Kathleen Mary Duffy; children: Sarah, Mary Kate, Tom. BS, Drexel U., 1968; JD, Temple U., 1971. Bar: Pa., U.S. Supreme Ct., U.S. Ct. Appeals (3d cir.), U.S. Dist. Ct. (ea., mid., we. dists.) Pa., U.S. Dist. Ct. (so. dist.) N.J., U.S. Dist. Ct. Utah, U.S. Dist. Ct. (so. dist.) N.Y. Assoc. Dilworth, Paxson, Kalish & Kauffman, Phila., 1972-76, ptnr., 1976-79, 83-87, sr. ptnr., mem. exec. com., 1987—; controller City of Phila., 1987-91; chmn. litigation dept., sr. ptnr., permanent mem. mgmt. com. Obermayer, Rebmann, Maxwell and Hippel, Phila., 1991—; bd. dirs. Fed. Nat. Mortgage Assn., Independence Blue Cross; vice chmn. Phila. Gas Commn., 1979-83; register of wills City of Phila., 1976-79; mem. disciplinary bd. Supreme Ct., Pa., 1991-95, vice chmn., 1995-96, chmn., 1996—. Mem. editorial bd. Amran's Pa. Practice, 1972; contbr. articles to profl. publs. Mem. Dem. Nat. Com., Washington, 1976-83, mem. fin. com., 1988, vice chair fin., 1993, Pa. fin. chair, 1993—, bd. dirs.; del. Dem. Nat. Conv., 1976, 80, 92; chmn. Pa. fin. com. Clinton for Pres., 1992, 96; co-chair Rendell for Mayor, 1991, 95; mem. coun. Phila. Orch., 1981-86; bd. dirs. Acad. Scis., Phila., 1981-85; pres. Pa. chpt. Irish Am. Partnership. Capt. U.S. Army, 1971-77. Recipient Man of Yr. award Emerald Soc., 1979, Korean-Am. Friendship Soc., 1982, Carmel Humanitarian award Haifa U., 1981, Merit award Chapel of Four Chaplains, 1983. Mem. ABA, Pa. Bar Assn., Phila. Bar Assn. (bd. govs. 1979-82), Union League, Phila. Racquet Club, Serra Club (past pres.). Roman Catholic. Office: Obermayer Rebmann Maxwell and Hippel Packard Building Fl 14 Philadelphia PA 19102-2625

LEONARD, TIMOTHY DWIGHT, judge; b. Jan. 22, 1940; s. Dwight and Mary Evelyn Leonard; m. Nancy Louise Laughlin, July 15, 1967; children: Kirstin Dione, Ryan Timothy, Tyler Dwight. BA, U. Okla., 1962; JD, 1965; student Mil. Naval Justice Sch., 1966. Bar: Okla. 1965, U.S. Dist. Ct. (no. and we. dists) Okla. 1969, U.S. Ct. Appeals (10th cir.) 1969, U.S. Supreme Ct. 1970. Asst. atty. gen. State of Okla., 1968-70, senator, 1979-88; ptnr. Blankenship, Herrold, Russell et al, Oklahoma City, 1970-71, Trippet, Leonard & Kee, Beaver, 1971-88; of counsel Huckaby, Fleming, et al., Oklahoma City, 1988-89; U.S. atty. Western Dist. Okla., 1989-92; judge U.S. Dist. Ct. (we. dist.) Okla., 1992—; guest lectr., tchr. Oklahoma City U., 1988-89. Mem. U.S. Atty. Gen.'s Adv. Com., 1990-92, chmn. office mgmt. and budget subcom., 1990-92. Co-author: 4 Days, 40 Hours, 1970. Rep. lt. gov. candidate Okla.; minority leader Okla. State Senate, 1985-86; white ho. mil. aide, Washington, 1966-67. Lt. USN, 1965-68, Washington. Named Outstanding Legislator Okla. Sch. Bd. Assn., 1988. Mem. ABA, Okla. Bar Assn., Phi Alpha Delta, Beta Theta Pi. Republican. Methodist. Avocations: basketball, running, reading. Home: PO Box 54587 Oklahoma City OK 73154-1587 Office: 200 NW 4th St Ste 5102 Oklahoma City OK 73102-3031

LEONARD, WALTER RAYMOND, retired biology educator; b. Scott County, Va., July 5, 1923; s. Homer Stanley and Minnie Eunice (Neal) L.; m. Alice Ann McCaskill, Sept. 1, 1951; children—Leslie Ann, Walter Raymond. B.A., Tusculum Coll., Greeneville, Tenn., 1946; M.A., Vanderbilt U., 1947, Ph.D., 1949. Mem. faculty Wofford Coll., Spartanburg, S.C., 1949-93; John M. Reeves prof. biology Wofford Coll., 1954-87, William R. Kenan Jr. prof. biology, 1987-93, William R. Kenan Jr. prof. emeritus, 1993—; instl. rev. bd. mem. Spartanburg Regional Med. Ctr., 1994—; faculty athletic rep. NCAA. Served with USAAF, 1942-43. Named to Sports Hall of Fame, Tusculum Coll., 1983; Walter Raymond Leonard scholarship created Wofford Coll., 1973; W. Ray Leonard award established Beta Beta Beta, 1993; W. Ray Leonard Retirement Fund established Former Students Wofford Coll., 1993. Mem. AAAS, S.C. Acad. Sci., Letterman's Club (hon.), Scabbard and Blade (hon.), Lambda Chi Alpha (Hall of Fame 1996). Methodist. Rsch. on cell metabolism. Home: 110 Pinetree Cir Spartanburg SC 29307-2938 Office: Wofford Coll N Church St Spartanburg SC 29301

LEONARD, WILL ERNEST, JR., lawyer; b. Shreveport, La., Jan. 18, 1935; s. Will Ernest and Nellie (Kenner) L.; m. Maureen Laniak; children—Will Ernest III, Sherry Elizabeth, Robert Scott, Stephen Michael, Christopher Anthony, Colleen Mary, Leigh Alison. B.A., Tulane U., 1956, LL.B., 1958; LL.M., Harvard U., 1966. Bar: La. 1958, D.C. 1963, U.S. Supreme Ct. 1963. Announcer sta. WVUE-TV, New Orleans, 1958-60; legislative asst. to U.S. Senator Russell B. Long, 1960-65; profl. staff mem. com. fin. U.S. Senate, 1966-68; mem. Internat. Trade Commn. (formerly U.S. Tariff Commn.), 1968-77, chmn., 1975-76; ptnr. Ablondi, Foster, Sobin & Davidow, Washington, 1996—; Congl. staff fellow Am. Polit. Sci. Assn., 1965-66. Home: 7324 Bradley Blvd Bethesda MD 20817-2130 Office: Ablondi Foster Sobin & Davidow Ste 500 1130 Connecticut Ave NW Washington DC 20036

LEONBERGER, FREDERICK JOHN, electrical engineer, photonics manager; b. Washington, Sept. 25, 1947; s. Melvin Fred and Mary Dorothy (Burchell) L.; m. Janet Marie Bueche, Aug. 8, 1970; children—Gregory, Katharine. B.S.E., U. Mich., 1969; S.M., MIT, 1971, E.E., 1972, Ph.D., 1975. Mem. staff MIT Lincoln Lab., Lexington, 1975-81; group leader MIT Lincoln Lab., 1981-84; mgr. photonics and applied physics United Tech. Rsch. Ctr., East Hartford, Conn., 1984-91; gen. mgr. United Tech. Photonics, Bloomfield, 1991-95; v.p., chief tech. officer UTP, Inc., Bloomfield, 1995—. Contbr. articles to profl. jours.; patentee in field. Fellow IEEE (tech. program com. 1979—, assoc. editor Jour. Quantum Electronics 1983-87), Optical Soc. Am. (tech. program com. 1979—, assoc. editor Optics Letters 1988-91); mem. IEEE Lasers and Electrooptics Soc. (adminstrv. com. 1984-86, pres. 1988, Quantum Electronics award 1993), Sigma Xi, Tau Beta Pi, Eta Kappa Nu. Avocations: tennis; golf; hiking; classical music. Office: UTP 1289 Blue Hills Ave Bloomfield CT 06002-1302

LEONDES, CORNELIUS T., systems engineer, educator; b. Phila., July 21, 1927. BSEE, U. Pa., 1949, MSEE, 1951, PhD, 1954. Prof. Engring. Sys. Divsn. Guggenheim fellow, 1962-63, Fulbright Rsch. scholar, 1962-63. Fellow IEEE (Baker prize award 1970, Barry Carlton Honorable Mention award 1973. Office: Engineering Systems Div 1801 Starling Ct Carlsbad CA 92009*

LEONE, GEORGE FRANK, pharmaceutical executive; b. Astoria, N.Y., Aug. 1, 1926; s. George and Fannie K. (Teano) L.); m. Mary Louise Potts, Dec. 14, 1945; children: Pamela Ann, George Frank. BS, Wesleyan U., 1949; postgrad., NYU, 1951; grad. Advanced Mgmt. Program,, Harvard Bus. Sch., 1959; postgrad., U. Tex., 1977; DSc (hon.), Tex. Wesleyan U., 1990. Chemist, Lederle Labs., Pearl River, N.Y., 1949-50; with Alcon Labs., Inc., Ft. Worth, 1950—; med. sales rep. Alcon Labs., Inc., 1950-54, dist. sales mgr., 1954-58, regional sales mgr., 1958-63, nat. sales mgr., 1963-66, dir. mktg., 1966-69, gen. mgr. domestic, 1969-70, v.p. sci., tech., 1971-81, sr. v.p., 1981—, also dir.; Pres. Laksmi Corp., Fort Worth, 1989—; pres. Avicon, Inc., 1972-79; exec. com. trustee Alcon Rsch. Inst., 1980—; trustee C.V. Whitney Lab., U. Fla., St. Augustine, 1996—. Pres., commr. Earth County Water Control and Improvement, Dist. 1, 1976-80; trustee Tex. Wesleyan U., fin. com., exec. com., 1985—; bd. dirs. Tex. Christian U. Rsch. Found., 1976-82; chmn. athletic com. Dan Danciger Jewish Community Ctr.; pres. Peninsula Pecan Growers Assn., 1980-85; mem. fin. com. Fort Worth Acad., 1984-88, bd. dirs., 1986-88. With USN, 1944-46. Named Disting. Alumnus, Tex. Wesleyan U., 1979. Mem. Yoga Soc. N.Y. (pres., bd. dirs. 1978—), Am. Radio Relay League, Alpha Chi. Club: Fort Worth. Home: 4100 Hildring Dr E Fort Worth TX 76109-4714 also: 321 Monika Pl Saint Augustine FL 32084-6441 Office: Laksmi Corp 6201 S Freeway PO Box 1959 Fort Worth TX 76134-2099 also: 4100 Hildring Dr E Fort Worth TX 76109-4714

LEONE, LUCILE P., retired health administrator; b. Ohio, 1902; m. Nicholas C. Leone, 1952. BA, U. Del., 1924; BS, Johns Hopkins U., 1927; MS, Columbia U., 19929; 9 hon degrees. Staff nurse Johns Hopkins Hosp., Balt., 1927-29; instr., prof. U. Minn., Mpls., 1929-41; comdt. Student Nursing Svc. USPHS, 1941-42, dir. Cadet Corps Program, 1942-48, chief nurse officer, asst. surgeon gen., 1948-66; assoc. dean nursing Tex. Woman's Coll., 1977-82; advisor internat. students Sch. Nursing U. Calif., San Francisco, 1978-83. Mem. Inst. Medicine/Nat. Acad. Sci. Address: 1400 Geary Blvd San Francisco CA 94109

LEONE, STEPHEN ROBERT, chemical physicist, educator; b. N.Y.C., May 19, 1948; s. Dominic and Annie Frances (Sappa) L. BA, Northwestern U., 1970; PhD, U. Calif., Berkeley, 1974. Asst. prof. U. So. Calif., L.A., 1974-76; physicist/fellow Nat. Inst. Standards and Tech., Boulder, Colo., 1976-94, acting chief Quantum Physics divsn., 1994—; adj. prof. U. Colo., Boulder, 1976—. Contbr. over 200 articles to profl. publs.; mem. editorial bd. Optics Letters, Jour. Chem. Physics, Chem. Revs., Jour. Phys. Chemistry, Molecular Physics, Chem. Physics Letters, Progress in Reaction Kinetics; patentee in field. Recipient silver and gold medals Dept. Commerce, 1980, 85, Coblentz award Coblentz Soc., 1984, Arthur S. Flemming award U.S. Govt., 1986, Samuel Wesley Stratton award Nat. Inst. Standards and Tech., 1992; Alfred P. Sloan fellow Sloan Found., 1977-81, Guggenheim fellow, 1988. Fellow AAAS, Optical Soc. Am., Am. Phys. Soc. (chair div. chem. physics 1987-88, Herbert P. Broida prize 1989); mem. NAS, Am. Chem. Soc. (pure chemistry award 1982, nobel laureate signature award 1983). Office: JILA Univ of Colo Campus Box 440 Boulder CO 80309

LEONE, WILLIAM CHARLES, retired manufacturing executive; b. Pitts., May 3, 1924; s. Joseph and Fortuna (Sammarco) L.; m. Sara Jane Hollenback, Aug. 26, 1950; children: William Charles, David M., Patricia Ann, Mary Jane. BS, Carnegie Inst. Tech., 1944, MS, 1948, DSc, 1952. Asst. prof. engring. Carnegie Inst. Tech., Pitts., 1946-53; mgr. Indsl. Sys. divsn. Hughes Aircraft, L.A., 1953-59; v.p., gen. mgr., dir. Rheem Califone, L.A., 1960, Rheem Electronics, L.A., 1960-68; group v.p. Rheem Mfg. Co., 1968-71; exec. v.p. Rheem Mfg. Co., N.Y.C., 1971-72, pres., 1972-76; also dir. Rheem Mfg. Co.; pres. City Investing Co. Internat., Inc., 1972-76; pres., dir. Farah Mfg. Co., El Paso, Tex., 1976-77; bus. cons., 1977-79; acting vice chmn. McCulloch Oil Corp. (MCO), L.A., 1979-80, also bd. dirs.; pres., dir. MAXXAM Inc. (formerly MCO Holdings, Inc.), 1980-90; vice chmn. MAXXAM Inc., 1990-92; chmn., CEO, dir. Pacific Lumber Co., 1986-90, Horizon Corp., 1984-89. Trustee Carnegie Mellon U., 1984-92. Mem. ASME, IEEE, Am. Inst. Aerospace and Aeronautics, Sigma Xi, Tau Beta Pi, Pi Tau Sigma, Theta Tau, Pi Mu Epsilon. Home: 2209 Chelsea Rd Palos Verdes Peninsula CA 90274-2603

LEONETT, ANTHONY ARTHUR, banker; b. Summit, N.J., Jan. 4, 1929; s. Joseph J. and Margaret (DiGuglielmo) L.; m. Ann Marino, Oct. 6, 1974; 1 son by previous marriage, Anthony Arthur. B.S., Seton Hall U., 1950; certificate, Am. Inst. Banking, 1956; postgrad., U. Wis., 1962. Mgr. First Nat. Bank & Trust Co., Summit, 1950-56; sr. v.p., auditor Nat. State Bank, Elizabeth, N.J., 1956—; instr. principles of auditing and bank operations Am. Inst. Banking; faculty N.J. Data Processing Sch., Princeton, Bank Adminstrn. Sch. of U. Wis. Bd. dirs. N.J. affiliate Am. Heart Assn. Served with U.S. Army, 1951-53. Recipient Irving Grabiel award for outstanding leadership in banking, 1979. Mem. Am. Inst. Banking (dir. chpt.), Bank Adminstrn. Inst. (N.J. state dir. 1977-79, pres. N.J. chpt., dist. dir. 1979-81). Republican. Roman Catholic. Clubs: K.C., Minisink (Chatham). Home: 102 N Hillside Ave Chatham NJ 07928-2825 Office: 68 Broad St Elizabeth NJ 07201-2206

LEONETTI, MATTHEW FRANK, cinematographer. Films include: The Bat People, 1974, Mr. Billion, 1977, The Chicken Chronicle, 1977, Breaking Away, 1979, Raise the Titanic, 1980, Eyewitness, 1981, Poltergeist, 1982, Fast Times at Ridgemont High, 1982, The Buddy System, 1984, The Ice Pirates, 1984, Songwriter, 1984, Fast Forward, 1985, Weird Science, 1985, Jagged Edge, 1985, Commando, 1985, Jumpin' Jack Flash, 1986, Extreme Prejudice, 1987, Dragnet, 1987, Action Jackson, 1988, Red Heat, 1988, Johnny Handsome, 1989, Hard to Kill, 1990, Another 48 Hrs., 1990, Dead Again, 1991, Leap of Faith, 1992, Hot Shots! Part Deux, 1993, Angels in the Outfield, 1994. Address: 1626 Chaston Pkwy Pacific Palisades CA 90272

LEONG, LAM-PO (LANBO LIANG), artist, educator; b. Canton, Guangdong, China, July 3, 1961; came to U.S., 1983; BFA in Chinese Brush Painting, Canton Fine Arts Inst., 1983; MFA in Painting with high distinction, Calif. Coll. Arts & Crafts, 1988. Instr. art Calif. Coll. Arts & Crafts, Oakland, 1986-87, U. Calif. Ext. & ASUC, Berkeley, 1989, 90—, San Jose (Calif.) State U. Ext., 1989-91; lectr. San Francisco State U., 1988—; instr. art Chabot Coll., Hayward, Calif., 1989—; artistic dir. Oakland Asian Cultural Ctr., Calif., 1990-92; lectr./speaker in field. One-man shows include Markings Gallery, Berkeley, 1984, Sumitomo Bank, Albany, Calif., 1985, Calif. Coll. Arts & Crafts, 1985, Rosicrucian Egyptian Mus., San Jose, 1986, U. Utah, Salt Lake City, 1986, Patrick Gallery, Regina, Sask., Can., 1986, Mus. Macao Luis De Camoes, Macao, 1986, Kai Ping County Mus., Guangdong, 1987, Chinatown Gallery, San Francisco, 1987, Guangzhou Fine Arts Mus., Canton, 1988, The Arlington Gallery, Oakland, 1989, Moy Ying Ming Gallery, Chgo., 1990, Chinese Culture Ctr., San Francisco, 1991, Stanwood Gallery, San Francisco, 1992, Sanuk Fine Asian Collectables, San Francisco, 1992, The Univ. Gallery, San Francisco, 1994, Michael Thompson Gallery, San Francisco, 1995, China Art Expo '95, Guangzhou, China, 1995, Chinese Art Gallery, San Leandro, Calif., 1996, MTC Gallery, Oakland, Calif., 1996; exhibited in group shows at Hong Kong Arts Ctr., 1980, Chinese Painting Exhibit Guangdong Province, 1981 (3d Prize award 1981), Macao Artists Assn. Exhbn., 1982, 96, Mus. Canton Fine Arts Inst., 1983, Nat. Mus. Art, Beijing, 1985, Macao Young Artist Exhbn. (Excellence award, 1st prize 1985), Pacific Art Ctr., Seattle, 1985, Chinese Culture Ctr., 1986, Faculty & MFA Show Calif. Coll. Arts & Crafts, San Francisco Campus, 1986, Chinese-Am. Artist Exhbn., Taipei, Taizhong, Taiwan, 1986, Sullivan Galleries, Salt Lake City, 1987, Oriental Gallery, N.Y., 1987, Santa Cruz Art League (Spl. award 1988, 1st prize 1990), Asian Resource Gallery, Oakland, 1988, Nat. Mus. Fine Arts, Beijing, 1988, 90, Chinese Art Gallery, San Leandro, Calif., 1989, Stanwood Gallery, 1989, Gallery Imago, San Francisco, 1990, Sun Gallery, Hayward, 1990, N.Y. Art Expo, N.Y.C., 1991, Gallery 5, Santa Monica, Calif., 1991, Butterfield & Butterfield Auction, San Francisco, 1992, 95-96, Asian Art Mus., San Francisco, 1992, Ke Shan Art Gallery, Taipei, 1993, Wan Fung Art Gallery, Hong Kong, 1993, Gallery On The Rim, San Francisco, 1994, Resource for Art, 1995, Ginsberg Collection, 1995, Macao Art Expo, 1988-96, World Assn. Chinese Artists Exhibition, Tokyo, 1996, Acad. Art Coll., San Francisco, 1996; work represented in various mus., corp. and pvt. collections including Guangzhou Arts Mus., Macao Camoes Mus., Mus. Canton Fine Arts Inst., Asian Art Mus. San Francisco, United Savs. Bank, Calif., Hotel East 21, Tokyo, The Tokyo Westin Hotel, Comml. Bank, San Francisco, Westin Surabaya, Indonesia; author: Brush Paintings of Lam-Po Leong, 1986, Journey of the Heart, 1994; illustrator: Brushstrokes-Styles and Techniques of Chinese Painting, 1993, The Tao of Power, 1986; designer (granite courtyard) New Chinatown Pk., San Francisco, 1993; (multi-image projection) Ctr. Arts Yerba Buena Gardens, San Francisco, 1996. Recipient Outstanding Merit award Young Art Now Competition, 1980, Decade of Achievement award Asian/Pacific Heritage Week, 1988, 2d prize Zunyi Internat. Brush Painting Competition, 1989; inductee Pan-Pacific Asian Hall of Fame at San Francisco Internat. Expo., 1987; grantee City of Oakland Cultural Arts Divsn., 1994-96. Mem. Asian Artists Assn. Am., Oriental Art Assn., U.S.A. (v.p.), Macao Soc. Social Scis., Hai-Ri Artists Assn. (China), Nat. Modern Delicate Painting Soc. (China), Chinese Am. Culture Exch. Assn. (co-founder, dir. 1992—). Avocations: film, ballroom dance, travel, photography. Office: Brushwork Gallery 166 Palisades Dr Daly City CA 94015-4517

LEONG, SUE, retired community health and pediatrics nurse; b. Alameda, Calif., Feb. 15, 1930; d. Leong Dai Sun and Leong San See. BS, U. Calif., San Francisco, 1953; MPH, U. Mich., 1963; MA, San Francisco Theol. Sem., 1958. Cert. sch. nurse, sch. nurse practitioner, nurse specialist. Head nurse Lafayette Clinic, Detroit; pub. health nurse San Francisco Health Dept.; assoc. dir. Ecumenical Campus Ctr., Ann Arbor, Mich.; sch. nurse practitioner Ann Arbor Pub. Schs.; adj. asst. prof. U. Mich. Contbr. articles to profl. jours. Mem. NEA, Mich. Assn. Sch. Nurses (Disting. Svc. award 1990, Dorothy Christy award 1993). Home: 1506 Golden Ave Ann Arbor MI 48104-4327

LEONHARDT, FREDERICK WAYNE, lawyer; b. Daytona Beach, Fla., Oct. 26, 1949; s. Frederick Walter and Gaetane Laura L.; m. Victoria Ann Cook, Dec. 27, 1975; children: Ashley Victoria, Frederick Whitaker. BA, U. Fla. 1971, JD, 1974. Bar: Fla. 1974, N.C. 1984, D.C. 1985; cert. real estate lawyer, Fla., 1987. Gen. counsel Fla. House of Reps., 1974-75; ptnr. Cobb, Cole and Bell, Daytona Beach, 1975-79; pres. Leonhardt & Upchurch, 1979-87; ptnr. Holland & Knight, Orlando, Fla., 1987-93; ptnr. Gray, Harris & Robinson, P.A., Orlando and Cocoa Beach, 1993—. Chmn. bd. dirs. Orlando/Orange County Compact, 1989-90; founder Leadership Daytona Beach; grad. participant Leadership Fla., Leadership Orlando, 1992, Leadership Ctrl. Fla., 1995; bd. dirs. Orlando Regional Med. Ctr. Found., 1992—; past chmn. Orlando Area Sports Commn. Mem. ABA (state and local govt. law sect. vice-chmn., past editor sect. newsletter 1991-94), Orange and Volusia Counties Bar Assn., Greater Orlando C. of C. (chmn. 1991-92), Daytona Beach Area C. of C. (pres. 1985), Fla. C. of C. (bd. dirs. 1984-90, 93—), Phi Alpha Delta, Delta Chi. Office: Gray Harris & Robinson PA PO Box 3068 201 E Pine St Ste 1200 Orlando FL 32802

LEONHARDT, THOMAS WILBURN, librarian, technical services director; b. Wilmington, N.C., Feb. 7, 1943; s. Thomas Beauregard and Rachel Virginia (Callicutt) L.; m. Margaret Ann Pullen, Sept. 19, 1966; children: Hilary, Thomas, Rebecca, Benjamin. AA, Pasadena (Calif.) City Coll., 1968; AB, U. Calif., Berkeley, 1970, MLS, 1973. Head gift and exch. div. Stanford (Calif.) U. Librs., 1973-76; head acquisition dept. Boise (Idaho) State U. Libr., 1976-79, Duke U. Librs., Durham, N.C., 1980-82; asst. univ. libr. U. Oreg., Eugene, 1982-87; dean librs. U. of the Pacific, Stockton, Calif., 1987-92; dir. tech. svcs. U. Okla. Librs., Norman, 1992—; editor RTSD Newsletter, Chgo., 1986-89, Info. Tech. & Librs., Chgo., 1990-95. Editor Advances in Collection Development and Resource Management, JAI Press, 1994—; publisher, editor Callicutt Family Chronicle; contbr. articles to profl. jours. Bd. dirs. No. Regional Libr. Facility, Richmond, Calif., 1988-92, Feather River Inst. for Libr. Acquisitions, Blairsden, Calif. With U.S. Army, 1963-66. Mem. ALA, Assn. Coll. Rsch. Librs. (v.p./pres.-elect 1995—), Libr. and Info. Tech. Assn., Assn. for Libr. Collections and Tech. Svcs., Ctrl. Assn. Librs. (bd. dirs. Stockton chpt. 1987-92). Democrat. Avocations: trumpet, guitar. Home: 204 Terra Ct Norman OK 73069-8641

LEONIS, JOHN MICHAEL, aerospace executive; b. Whittier, Calif., Oct. 21, 1933; s. Michael Arthur and Minnie Augusta (Peterson) L.; m. Edith Ann Pattison, Aug. 30, 1958; children: Susan Elizabeth, Carolyn Ann, Linda Maria. BEE, U. Ariz., 1959. Past pres. Litton Guidance and Control Systems, Woodland Hills, Calif.; chmn., CEO Litton Industries, Inc., Woodland Hills, Calif., 1995—. Mem. AIAA, Inst. Navigation, Air Force Assn., Assn. U.S. Army, Assn. Naval Aviation, Naval Helicopter Assn., Am. Electronics Assn. Office: Litton Industries Inc 21240 Burbank Blvd Woodland Hills CA 91367

LEONSIS, TED, communications company executive, publishing company executive; b. Vero Beach, Fla., Jan. 8, 1956. BA magna cum laude, Georgetown U., 1976; postgrad. Suffolk U. Law Sch., 1980. Copywriter, advt. mgr. Wang Labs., Inc., 1976-78, corp. publicity/pub. relations dir., 1978-81; dir. mktg. communications Harris Corp., Melbourne, Fla., 1981-83; exec. v.p. Redgate Pub. Co., Vero Beach, Fla., 1983—, also dir.; pres. Redgate Communications Corp., 1986—; founder Collegiate Entrepreneurs Fund; dir. Preview Media Inc., Brevard Venture Fund. Chmn. United Fund campaign, Wang Labs. Inc., 1980; bd. dirs. Big Bros. Brevard County, 1981. Brevard Art Ctr. and Mus., Brevard Council of Arts, 1981, Juvenile Employment Project, Lowell, Mass., Merrimack Regional Theatre. Mem. Pub. Relations Soc. Am. (cert.), Publicity Club Boston, Bus. Profl. Advt. Adminstrs., Am. Mktg. Assn. Author: Software Master for the IBM PC, Mastering The IBM Assistant Series, Software Master for PFS, Blue Magic; pub. The Macintosh Buyer's Guide, Apple II Rev., The Apple IIGS Buyer's Guide, COMPAQ, FYI; The Harris Mag. for Info. Mgmt.; contbr. articles to profl. jours. Office: America Online Svcs Co 8619 Westwood Ctr Dr Vienna VA 22182

LEONTIEF, WASSILY, economist, educator; b. Leningrad, Russia, Aug. 5, 1906; s. Wassily and Eugenia (Bekker) L.; m. Estelle Helena Marks, Dec. 25, 1932; 1 child, Svetlana Eugenia Alpers. Student, U. Leningrad, 1921-25; grad. Learned Economist; PhD, U. Berlin, 1928; PhD honoris causa, U. Bruxelles, Belgium, 1962, U. York, Eng., 1967, U. Louvain, 1971, U. Paris, 1972, U. Pa., 1976, U. Lancaster, Eng., 1976; D honoris causa, Adelphi Coll., 1988; LHD (hon.), Rensselaer Poly. Inst., 1988; D honoris causa, U. Cordoba, 1990, Humboldt U. of Berlin, 1995. Rsch. economist Inst. Weltwirtschaft U. Kiel, Germany, 1927-28, 30; econ. adviser to Chinese govt. Nanking, 1929; with Nat. Bur. Econ. Rsch., N.Y.C., 1931; instr. econs. Harvard U., Cambridge, Mass., 1932-33; asst. prof. Harvard U., Cambridge, 1933-39, assoc. prof., 1939-46, prof., 1946-75, dir. econ. project, 1948-72, Henry Lee prof. econs., 1953-75; prof. econs. NYU, 1975—, univ. prof., 1983—, founder Inst. Econ. Analysis, 1978-85, mem. rsch. staff, 1986; cons. Dept. Labor, 1941-47, OSS, 1943-45, UN, 1961-62, Dept. Commerce, 1966-82, EPA, 1975-80 , UN, 1980—. Author: The Structure of the American Economy, 1919-29, 2d edit., 1976, Studies in the Structure of the American Economy, 1953, 2d edit., 1977, Input-Output Economics, 1966, 2d edit., 1986, Collected Essays, 1966, Theories, Facts and Policies, 1977, The Future of the World Economy, 1977, (with Faye Duchin) The Future Impact of Automation on Workers, 1986; Contbr. articles to sci. jours. and periodicals U.S. and abroad. Mem. Commn. to Study Orgn. of Peace, 1978; trustee N.C. Sch. Sci. and Math., 1978; mem. issues com. Progressive Alliance, 1979; mem. Com. for Nat. Security, 1980. Decorated officer Order Cherubim U. Pisa; comdr. Order Arts and Letters, Legion of Honor (France); Order of Rising Sun (Japan); recipient Bernhard-Harms prize econs. Fed. Republic of Germany, 1970, Nobel prize in econs., 1973, Takemi Meml. award Inst. Seizon and Life Scis., Japan, 1991; Guggenheim fellow, 1940, 50. Fellow Soc. Fellows Harvard (sr. fellow, chmn. 1964-75), Econometric Soc., Royal Statis. Assn. (hon.), Inst. de France (corr.), N.Y. Acad. Scis.; mem. NAS, AAAS, Am. Philos. Soc., Internat. Statis. Inst., Am. Econ. Assn., Am. Statis. Assn., USSR Acad. Scis. (fgn.), Royal Econ. Soc., Japan Econ. Rsch. Ctr. (hon.), Brit. Acad. (corr.), French Acad. Scis. (corr.), Royal Irish Acad. (hon.), World Acad. for Progress of Planning Sci. (hon. pres. 1993), Academie Universelle des Cultures, Brit. Assn. Advancement of Sci. (pres. Sect. F 1976), USSR Acad. Scis. (fgn.), Soc. of Optimate Italian Culture Inst., Century Club. Mem. Greek Orthodox Church. Office: NYU Dept Econs 269 Mercer St New York NY 10003-6633

LEOPOLD, GEORGE ROBERT, radiologist; b. Lewistown, Pa., 1937. MD, U. Pitts., 1962. Intern York Hosp., 1962-63; resident U. Pitts., 1965-68; chmn., prof. dept. radiology U. Calif., San Diego. Mem. Am. Coll. Radiology, AIUM, ARRS, AUR, RSNA. Office: U Calif San Diego Med Ctr Med Ctr 8756 200 W Arbor Dr San Diego CA 92103-8756*

LEOPOLD, LUNA BERGERE, geology educator; b. Albuquerque, Oct. 8, 1915; s. Aldo and Estella (Bergere) L.; m. Barbara Beck Nelson, 1973; children: Bruce Carl, Madelyn Dennette. BS, U. Wis., 1936, DSc (hon.), 1980; M.S., UCLA, 1944; Ph.D., Harvard, 1950; D Geography (hon.), U. Ottawa, 1969; DSc (hon.), Iowa Wesleyan Coll., 1971, St. Andrews U., 1981, U. Murcia, Spain. With Soil Conservation Service, 1938-41, U.S. Engrs. Office, 1941-42, U.S. Bur. Reclamation, 1946; head meteorologist Pineapple Research Inst. of Hawaii, 1946-49; hydraulic engr. U.S. Geol. Survey, 1950-71, chief hydrologist, 1957-66, sr. research hydrologist, 1966-71; prof. geology U. Calif. at Berkeley, 1973—. Author: (with Thomas Maddock, Jr.) The Flood Control Controversy, 1954, Fluvial Processes in Geomorphology, 1964, Water, 1974, (with Thomas Dunne) Water in Environmental Planning, 1978; also tech. papers. Served as capt. air weather service USAAF, 1942-46. Recipient Disting. Svc. award Dept. of Interior, 1958, Veth medal Royal Netherlands Geog. Soc., 1963, Cullum Geog. medal Am. Geog. Soc., 1968, Rockefeller Pub. Service award, 1971, Busk medal Royal Geog. Soc., 1983, Berkeley citation U. Calif., David Linton award British Geomorphol. Rsch. Group, 1986, Linsley award Am. Inst. Hydrology, 1989, Caulfield medal Am. Water Resources Assn., 1991, Nat. Medal Sci. NSF, 1991, Palladium medal Nat. Audubon Soc., 1994, Joan Hodges Queneau Palladium medal Am. Assn. Engrng. Socs., 1994. Mem. NAS (Warren prize), ASCE (Julian Hinds award), Geol. Soc. Am. (Kirk Bryan award 1958, pres. 1972, Disting. Career award geomorphological group 1991, Penrose medal 1994), Am. Geophys. Union (Robert E. Horton medal 1993), Am. Acad. Arts and Scis., Am. Philos. Soc., Sigma Xi, Tau Beta Pi, Phi Kappa Phi, Chi Epsilon. Club: Cosmos (Washington). Home: 400 Vermont Ave Berkeley CA 94707-1722 Office: U Calif Dept Geology Berkeley CA 94720

LEOPOLD, MARK F., lawyer; b. Chgo., Jan. 23, 1950; s. Paul F. and Corinne (Shapira) L.; m. Jacqueline Rood, June 9, 1974; children: Jonathan, David. BA, Am. U., Washington, 1972; JD, Loyola U., Chgo., 1975. Bar: Ill. 1975, U.S. Dist. Ct. (no. dist.) Ill. 1975, Fla. 1976, U.S. Ct. Appeals (7th cir.) 1976, U.S. Ct. Appeals (8th cir.) 1979. Assoc. McConnell & Campbell, Chgo., 1975-79; atty. U.S. Gypsum Co., Chgo., 1979-82, sr. litigation atty., 1982-84; sr. litigation atty. USG Corp., 1985-87, corp. counsel, 1987, sr. corp. counsel, 1987-89; asst. gen. counsel G.D. Searle & Co., 1989-93; asst. gen. counsel Household Internat., Inc., Prospect Heights, Ill., 1993—; adv. bd. Roosevelt U. Legal Asst. Program, 1994—; legal writing instr. Loyola U. Sch. Law, Chgo., 1978-79; pres., bd. dirs. Internat. Policyholders Assn., 1992-93; del. candidate Rep. Nat. Conv., 1996. Mem. Lake County Study Commn. II, Waukegan, Ill, 1989-90; commr. Lake County, Waukegan, Ill., 1982-84, Forest Preserve, Libertyville, Ill., 1982-84, Pub. Bldg. Commn., Waukegan, Ill., 1980-82; chmn. Deerfield Twp. Rep. Cen. Com., Highland Park, Ill., 1984-86, officer, 1981-89; vice chmn. Lake County Rep. Cen. Com., Waukegan, Ill., 1982-84; bd. dirs. Am. Jewish Com., Chgo., 1988-91. Recipient Disting. Svc. award Jaycees, Highland Park, 1983. Mem. ABA (antitrust com. 1976—, litigation com. 1980—, torts and ins. practice com. 1989—), Pi Sigma Alpha, Omicron Delta Kappa. Republican. Office: Household Internat 2700 Sanders Rd Prospect Heights IL 60070-2701

LEPAGE, CANDYCE RUTH, school psychologist; b. Springfield, Mass., Aug. 5, 1951; d. Stephen Edward and Ina Ruth (Melenek) LeP. BS in Edn., Am. Internat. Coll., 1973; MEd, CAGS, Springfield Coll., 1974. Cert. sch. psychologist; NCSP., lic. ednl. psychologist. Home tchr. Springfield (Mass.) Pub. Schs., 1975; substitute tchr. Springfield and Chicopee (Mass.) Pub. Schs., 1975-77; substitute sch. psychologist Chicopee Pub. Schs., 1975, counselor-examiner, 1977-78, counselor, examiner, chair chpt. 766, 1978-80; sch. psychologist Ralph C. Mahar Regional Sch., Orange, Mass., 1980—. Bd. dirs. membership Human Resource Ctr. for Rural Communities, Athol, Mass., 1985-86. Mem. Nat. Sch. Psychologists Assn., Mass. Sch. Psychologists Assn., We. Mass. Sch. Psychologists Assn., Franklin/Hampshire Guidance Assn., Athol-Orange Health and Human Svcs. Coalition, Athol-Orange Community Devel. Corp., Psi Chi. Avocation: reading.

LEPAGE, EILEEN MCCULLOUGH, financial consultant, educator; b. Phila., Oct. 16, 1946; d. Charles Norman and Marie Teresa (Inglesby) McCullough; m. Clifford Bennett LePage Jr., May 17, 1969; children: Clifford Bennett III, Alexander Pierce. BA in English and Secondary Edn., George Washington U., 1969; MEd, Temple U., 1972. Cert. secondary sch. tchr.; registered securities rep. Record-keeper child growth and devel. program Children's Hosp. of Phila., 1965; with advt. dept. Phil. Inquirer, 1966-67; with ops. control U.S. Civil Svc. Commn., Washington, 1967-69; mgr. N.J. Bell Telephone, Trenton, 1969; researcher Temple U., Phila., 1969-71; tchr. Wyomissing (Pa.), 1972-77; fin. cons. various orgns., 1984-93; cons. EML Consulting, Reading, 1994—; adj. instr. Reading (Pa.) Area Community Coll., 1978-81; lectr. English Albright Coll., Reading, 1981-84; founding mem. Common Cents Investment Club, 1983-93. Author: The Clue in the Snow, 1957; editor: 1st Complete Pocket Guide to Atlantic City Casinos, 1984, The Autobiography of Capt. Michael Kevolic, 1986. Bd. dirs. Nat. Found. March of Dimes, Reading, 1969-75, chmn., 1974-75; bd. sch. dirs. Wyomissing Area Sch. Dist., 1984-92; bd. dirs. Wyomissing Pub. Libr., Reading, 1980-85; asst. chmn Region 8 Pa. Sch. Bds. Assn., 1989-91; dir. Saturday Morning Sch., Assn. for Children with Learning Disabilities, Reading, 1970; acting sec. Berks County Commn. for Women, Reading, 1993; active Reading Community Players, 1980. Mem. AAUW (topic chmn.), Am. Assn. Individual Investors (life). Avocations: swimming, hiking, photography, computing. Home and Office: EML Cons 10 Phoebe Dr Reading PA 19610-2857

LEPAGE, ROBERT, actor, director, playwright; b. Quebec City, Canada, 1957. Degree in drama, Conservatoire d'Art Dramatique, Quebec, 1978. Actor Ligue Nationale d'Improvisation, 1980-82; actor, dir. Le Théâtre Rep'40re, 1982—; artistic dir. French theatre Nat. Arts Ctr., Ottawa, Can, 1990-92. Prodsn. include (TV) Needles and Opium, 1991, Tectonic Plates, 1990, A Midsummer Night's Dream, 1992, Coriolanus, 1993, Seven Streams of the River Ofa, 1994, (TV series) The Dragon's Trilogy; in theatre: dir., co-writer Circulations, 1984; dir., writer, actor Vinci, 1986; dir. Le Polygraphe, 1988, Echo, 1989, Macbeth, 1993, The Tempest, 1993; actor (film) Jesus of Montreal, 1988. Recipient Gov. Gen.'s Performing Arts award, 1994. Office: c/o Union des Artistes, 1290 rue St-Denis, Montreal, PQ Canada H2X 3J7

LEPENE, GLENN MAYNARD, banker; b. Rochester, N.H., Nov. 27, 1950; s. Richard Lawrence and Joyce Marlene (Freeman) L.; m. Ronda Frances Piro, Oct. 1, 1978; children: Elisa Joyce, Bethany Ann. BS in Bus. Adminstrn., U. N.H., 1972; MBA, N.H. Coll., 1982; diploma Grad. Sch. Fin. & Mgmt., Fairfield U., 1987. CFP. Mgmt. trainee First Nat. Bank, Rochester, 1972-74; v.p. retail lending Bankeast Savs. Bank & Trust Co., Rochester, 1974-86; pres., CEO, dir. Farmington (N.H.) Nat. Bank, 1986-95; fin. planner GML Fin. Adv. Svcs., Rochester, N.H., 1995—; trustee N.H. Bankers Ins. Benefit Trust, Concord, 1992-95, No. New Eng. Credit Ins. Trust, Concord, 1989-95; dir. Farmington Bus. Devel. Group, 1992-95; mem. cmty. bank adv. coun. Office of Comptr. of Currency, Boston, 1993-95. Corporator Frisbie Meml. Hosp., Rochester, 1993—; trustee of trust funds City of Rochester, 1991—; past dir. Stafford County YMCA, Rochester. Staff sgt. N.H. Nat. Guard, USAF, 1972-76. Mem. Greate Rochester C. of C. (dir. 1988-95). Home: 37 Blue Hills Dr Rochester NH 03839-4909 Office: GML Fin Adv Svcs PO Box 1498 Rochester NH 03867

LEPERI, KARIN A., government official; b. St. Louis, May 12, 1952; d. Edwin Oral and Alice Louise Reed; m. Dominic Thomas Leperi, Jr., Nov. 1, 1990; children: Karson Troy, Kosette Dominique. BA in Polit. Sci., Calif. State U., L.A., 1973, MS in Pub. Adminstrn., 1974; postgrad., U. Md., 1980-85. Registered profl. flight engr.; CFP. Presidential intern Dept. Navy, Washington, 1973-74; sr. budget analyst Dept. Energy, Germantown, Md., 1974-83; chief fin. control br. USDA, Washington, 1983-84; systems acct. Nat. Fin. Ctr., New Orleans, 1987; dept. fin. adv. Office Internat. Cooperation and Devel., Washington, 1987-88; chief fin. mgmt. branch U.S. Dept. Agriculture, Washington, 1984-88, dep. dir. budget and acctg. div., 1988-91; asst. dep. adminstr. for resource mgmt. support Internat. Svcs., U.S. Dept. Agr., 1991—; flight engr. U.S. Naval Air Res., Washington, 1983-86; advisor/mentor Women's Exec. Leadership Program, Washington, 1991-92. Mem. Naval Res. Assn., Am. Coun. of Exercise (cert. personal trainer, aerobics instr., lifestyle and weight mgmt. counselor), Internat. Dance and Exercise Assn. (master), Carpathia Soc., Taipan, Oxford Club. Republican. Avocations: aviation, aerobics, fitness tng., doll collecting, internat. finance. Home: 6006 Greenbelt Rd Ste 329 Greenbelt MD 20770-1019

LEPIE, ALBERT HELMUT, chemist, reseacher; b. Malapane, Silesia, Germany, Aug. 6, 1923; came to U.S., 1963; s. Albert and Emilia (Zachlod) L.; m. Claire Kortz, 1956 (div. 1964); 1 child, Karin. Degree in chem. engring., Staatliche Ing. Schule, Essen, Germany, 1953; diploma in chemistry, Tech. Hochschule, Aachen, Germany, 1959; D in Natural Scis., Tech. Hochschule, Munich, Germany, 1961. Chem. engr. Pahl'sche Gummi & Asbest, Düsseldorf, 1953-59; chemist Deutsche Versuchanstalt für Luftfahrt, Munich, 1961-63; rsch. chemist U.S. Naval Propellant Plant, Indian Head, Md., 1963-64; rsch. chemist Naval Weapons Ctr., China Lake, Calif., 1964-95, ret., 1995; chmn. mech. properties panel Joint Army, Navy, NASA, and Air Force Interagy. Rocket Propulsion, 1977-84. Inventor air curtain incinerator for energetic materials and fiber peal force measurement device, flywheel high rate tensile tester for viscoelastic materials. Recipient Joint Army, Navy, NASA, and Air Force award, 1984, William B. McLean award Naval Weapons Ctr. Mem. AAAS, Am. Chem. Soc. (sec. China Lake chpt. 1968, 69), China Lake Astron. Soc., Sigma Xi. Roman Catholic. Avocations: astronomy, computer programming, motorcycling. Home: 121 S Desert Candles St Ridgecrest CA 93555-4218

LEPINE, JEAN, cinematographer. Dir. photography: (films) Les Amazones, 1990, On a Marche Sur la Lune, 1990, Vincent & Theo, 1990, Montreal Vu Par, 1991, The Player, 1992, Bob Roberts, 1992, A Home of Our Own, 1993, Ready to Wear (Pret-a-Porter), 1994, Habitat, 1995; (TV movies) Tanner 88, 1988, J.F.K. Reckless Youth, 1993, Talking With, 1994, Beyond the Call, 1995. Office: Doug Apatow Agency 10559 Blythe Ave Los Angeles CA 90064

LEPKOWSKI, WIL (WILBERT CHARLES LEPKOWSKI), journalist; b. Salem, Mass., Sept. 3, 1934; s. Charles J. and Alice (Bartnicki) L.; m. Jane Littlefield, Oct. 28, 1961 (div. May 1975); children: David E., Rebecca A., Thomas M.C.; m. Helene Kay Hollander, Feb. 4, 1984; 1 child, Katherine Angela. BS in Chemistry, U. Mass., 1956; MS in Biochemistry, Ohio State U., 1961. Asst. chemist Doeskin Products Inc., Easthampton, Mass., 1956; asst. editor Chem. Abstracts Svcs., Columbus, Ohio, 1956-58; reporter UP Internat., Columbus, 1960, Providence Jour.-Bull., Westerly, R.I., 1961; sci. writer Johns Hopkins Med. Instns., Balt., 1961-63, Newhouse Newspapers, Washington, 1963-65; bur. head, S.E. Chem. & Engring. News, Washington, 1965-69, sr. corr., 1977—; sci. corr. Bus. Week, Washington, 1969-75; free-lance writer, cons., 1975-77. Contbr. articles to jours. in field. Sloan/Rockefeller fellow Advanced Sci. Writing Prgram, Columbia U. Grad. Sch. Journalism, 1959-60. Mem. Nat. Press Club, Nat. Assn. Sci. Writers, Am. Sci. Affiliation, Latin Am. Parents Assn., U.S. Assn. for Club of Rome. Roman Catholic. Avocations: natural history, geography, poetry, spiritual reading. Office: Chem & Engring News 1155 16th St NW Washington DC 20036-4800 *Tell the truth.*

L'EPLATTENIER, NORA SWEENY HICKEY, nursing educator; b. N.Y.C., Mar. 16, 1945; 1 child, Brendan Sweeny Hickey. Diploma, Bellevue Mills Sch. Nursing, 1965; BS in Health Sci. summa cum laude, Bklyn. Coll., 1978; MS in Psychiat.-Mental Health Nursing, Adelphi U., 1982, PhD, 1988. RN, N.Y., N.J.; cert. specialist in adult mental health; cert. group therapist. Dir. psychiat. staff devel. Bellevue Hosp. Ctr., N.Y.C., 1980-82; group psychotherapist Jewish Inst. Geriatric Care, New Hyde Park, N.Y., 1983; staff psychotherapist New Hope Guild, N.Y.C., 1984; assoc. prof. grad. and undergrad. L.I. U. Bklyn., N.Y.C., 1986—; nurse rschr. Englewood (N.J.) Hosp. and Med. Ctr., N.Y.; pvt. practice N.Y., 1982—. Maj. USAR, 1977—. Isabel McIsaac scholar, 1983, Am. Legion scholar, 1962. Mem. Ea. Group Psychotherapy Soc., Sigma Theta Tau.

LEPLEY, CHARMAINE GUNNOE, special education educator; b. Charleston, W.Va., Dec. 20, 1939; d. Arnold Leo and Ruth Louise (Fleck) Thomas; m. William Delano Lepley; children: Timothy, Pamela. BA, Glenville State Coll., 1961; MA, W.Va. U., 1970, DEd, 1993. Cert. spl. edn., reading, coop. learning tchr. Educator Kanawha County Schs., Charleston, 1961-92; adj. instr. Coll. of Grad. Studies U. W.Va., Institute, 1985-92; assoc. prof. U. Rio Grande, Ohio, 1992—; curriculum cons. W.Va. Dept. Edn., Charleston, summer 1985-87; session speaker W.Va. Reading Assn., White Sulphur Springs, 1988-92; workshop cons., speaker U. W.Va. Coll. of Grad. Studies, Institute, 1989-92, U. Rio Grande, 1992—. Co-author (class text) Ideophobia, 1990; guest editor newspaper articles, 1991; contbr. articles to newsletters and jours. Pres. Pilot Club, St. Albans, W.Va., 1994; spl. events speaker United Meth. Ch., St. Albans, 1985—. Mem. ASCD, Internat. Reading Assn. (session speaker 1988, 94), Coun. for Exceptional Children (co-founder student chpt. 1994), Ohio Assn. Tchr. Edn., Ohio Early Childhood Spl. Edn. Higher Edn. Consortium, Phi Delta Kappa. Democrat. Avocations: reading, volunteer work, cooking, gardening. Home: 105 Cedar Ln Saint Albans WV 25177-3401 Office: Univ Rio Grande 210 N College Rio Grande OH 45674

LEPORE, MARIE ANN, home care nurse; b. Bronx, N.Y., Aug. 21, 1946; d. John Paul and Lillian Josephine (Lucenta) LePore; 1 child, Marie Ann Bank. Student, Cambridge Acad., 1982, S.I., N.Y., 1983, Barton Sch., 1986, Laurel Sch., 1986; A. Specialized Bus., I.C.S., Scranton, Pa., 1995, A in Computer Specialist in Sci., 1996. Home care nurse Dept. Social Svcs., N.Y.C., 1975-78; home health care worker Massive Home Health Svcs., Bronx, N.Y., 1978-82; home careworker Puerto Rican Home Care Svcs., Bronx, N.Y., 1982-84; home care nurse Entea Home Care, Bronx, N.Y., 1986-89, Montefiore Hosp., Bronx, 1989—; dental asst. Recipient numerous professional awards. Home: 3304 White Plains Rd Bronx NY 10467-5703

LEPOW, LESLIE HUGH, lawyer; b. N.Y.C., Sept. 16, 1949; s. Harold Irving and Lillian (Lakin) L.; m. Susan Helen Geggel, June 2, 1974. AB, Columbia U., 1971; JD, Georgetown U., 1974. Bar: U.S. Ct. Appeals (D.C. cir.) 1975, U.S. Ct. Appeals (fed. cir.) 1983. Assoc. Lobel Novins and Lamont, Washington, 1974-75, Nicholson and Carter, Washington, 1975-78; assoc. Squire Sanders and Dempsey, Washington, 1979-82, ptnr., 1982-90; ptnr. Jenner & Block, Washington, 1991—. Office: Jenner & Block 601 13th St NW Washington DC 20005-3807

LEPPARD, RAYMOND JOHN, conductor, harpsichordist; b. London, Aug. 11, 1927; came to U.S., 1976; s. Albert Victor and Bertha May (Beck) L. MA, U. Cambridge, Eng., 1955; DLitt (hon.), U. Bath, Eng., 1973; hon. doctorate, U. Indpls., 1991, Purdue U., 1992; hon. degree, Butler U., 1994, Wabash Coll., 1995. Fellow Trinity Coll., Cambridge; univ. lectr. in music U. Cambridge, 1958-68. Mus. dir. English Chamber Orch., London, 1959-77; prin. condr. BBC Philharm., Manchester, Eng., 1972-80; condr. symphony orchs. in Am. and Europe, Met. Opera, N.Y.C., Santa Fe Opera, San Francisco Opera, Covent Garden, Blyndebourne, Paris Opera; prin. guest condr. St. Louis Symphony Orch., 1984-90, music dir. Indpls. Symphony Orch., 1987—, European Tour, 1993; rec. artist, composer numerous film scores; author: (books) Authenticity in Music, 1989, Raymond Leppard on Music/An Anthology of Critical and Personal Writings, 1993. Decorated Commendatore Della Republica Italiana; comdr. Order Brit. Empire. Office: M L Falcone Pub Rels 155 W 68th St Apt 1114 New York NY 10023-5817 also: Indpls Symphony Orch 45 Monument Cir Indianapolis IN 46204-2907

LEPPER, MARK ROGER, psychology educator; b. Washington, Dec. 5, 1944; s. Mark H. and Joyce M. (Sullivan) L.; m. Jeanne E. Wallace, Dec. 22, 1966; 1 child, Geoffrey William. BA, Stanford U., 1966; PhD, Yale U., 1970. Asst. prof. psychology Stanford (Calif.) U., 1971-76, assoc. prof., 1976-82, prof., 1982—; chmn., 1990-94; fellow Ctr. Advanced Study in Behavioral Scis., 1979-80; chmn. mental health behavioral scis. research rev. com. NIMH, 1982-84, mem. basic sociocultural research rev. com., 1980-82. Co-editor: The Hidden Costs of Reward, 1978; cons. editor Jour. Personality and Social Psychology, 1977-85, Child Devel., 1977-86, Jour. Ednl. Computing Research, 1983—, Social Cognition, 1981-84; contbr. articles to profl. jours. Recipient Hoagland prize Stanford U., 1990; Woodrow Wilson fellow, 1966-67, NSF fellow, 1966-69, Sterling fellow, 1969-70, Mellon fellow, 1975, fellow Stanford U., 1988-90; grantee NSF, 1978-82, 86-88, NIMH, 1978-86, 88—, Nat. Inst. Child Health and Human Devel., 1975-88, 90—, U.S. Office Edn., 1972-73. Fellow APA, Am. Psychol. Soc., Soc. Personality and Social Psychology, Soc. Psychol. Study Social Issues; mem. Am. Ednl. Rsch. Assn., Soc. Exptl. Social Psychology, Soc. Rsch. in Child Devel. Home: 1544 Dana Ave Palo Alto CA 94303-2813 Office: Stanford U Dept Psychology Stanford CA 94305

LEPPERT, RICHARD DAVID, humanities educator; b. Fargo, N.D., Aug. 28, 1943; s. Frederick W. and Eunice I. (Conlon) L. B.A., Moorhead State U., 1966, B.S., B.A., 1966; M.M., Ind. U., 1969, Ph.D., 1973. Asst. prof. humanities U. Minn.-Mpls., 1973-78, assoc. prof., 1978-82, prof., 1982—, chmn. humanities program, 1980-86, chmn. dept. cultural studies & comparative lit., 1993—. Author: Theme of Music in Flemish Paintings of 17th Century, 1977, Arcadia at Versailles, 1978; editor (with others): Music and Society: The Politics of Composition, Performance and Reception, 1987, Music and Image, 1988, The Sight and Sound: Music Representation and the History of the Body, 1993, Art and the Committed Eye: The Cultural Functions of Imagery, 1996. Woodrow Wilson fellow, 1970-71; Fulbright fellow, 1970-72; Guggenheim fellow, 1979-80; Nat. Endowment Humanities sr. fellow, 1986-87. Office: U Minn Dept Cultural Studies & Comp Lit Folwell Hall # 350 Minneapolis MN 55455-0194

LEPPIK, MARGARET WHITE, state legislator; b. Newark, N.J., June 5, 1943; d. John Underhill and Laura Schaefer White; m. Ilo Elmar Leppik, June 18, 1967; children: Peter, David, Karina. BA, Smith Coll., 1965. Rsch. asst. Wistar Inst., U. Pa., Phila., 1967-68, U. Wis., Madison, 1968-69; mem. Minn. Ho. Reps., St. Paul, 1990, 92, 94. Commr. Golden Valley (Minn.) Planning Com., 1982-90; mem. Golden Valley Bd. Zoning Appeals, 1985-87. Recipient Citizen of Distinction award Hennepin County Human Svcs. Planning Bd. 1992; named Legislator of Yr., U. Minn. Alumni Assn., 1995. Mem. LWV (v.p., dir. 1984-90), Minn. Opera Assn. (pres. 1986-88), Rotary Internat., Optimists Internat. Republican. Avocations: gardening, hiking. Home: 7500 Western Ave Golden Valley MN 55427-4849 Office: 393 State Office Bldg Saint Paul MN 55155

LEPRI, DANIEL B., light manufacturing executive; b. 1953. BA, Coll. of the Holy Cross, 1975; MBA, Rutgers, 1976. Sr. auditor Coopers & Lybrand, N.Y.C., 1976-79; v.p., contr. Thico Plan, Inc., N.Y.C., 1979-82; asst. contr. Rheem Mfg. Co., N.Y.C., 1982-84, v.p., contr., 1984, now v.p., CFO. Office: Rheem Mfg Co 405 Lexington Ave New York NY 10174*

LEPRINO, JAMES G., food products executive; b. 1937. With Leprino Foods Co., Denver, 1955—, now chmn. bd. Office: Leprino Foods Co 1830 W 38th Ave Denver CO 80211-2225*

LEPS, THOMAS MACMASTER, civil engineer, consultant; b. Keyser, W.Va., Dec. 3, 1914; s. Thomas Davis and Grace (King) L.; m. Catherine Mary Sacksteder, June 22, 1940; 1 son, Timothy. B.A., Stanford U., 1936; M.S., MIT, 1939. Jr. and asst. civil engr. Calif. Divsn. Hwys., U.S. C.E., Bur. of Reclamation, 1936-41; Chief civil engr. So. Calif. Edison Co., Los Angeles, 1946-61; chief engr. Shannon & Wilson Co., Seattle, 1961-63; cons. civil engr. U.S. and abroad, Dinuba, Calif., 1963—; mem. over 90 bds. of cons. on hydro, steam and nuclear power projects. Contbr. articles to profl. jours., chpts. to engring books. Served to comdr. USN, 1943-46, with USNR, ret. Recipient certificate of Appreciation Calif. Dept. Water Resources, 1971. Mem. NAE (life mem., nominations com. for officers 1991), ASCE (life mem., cert. of appreciation 1961), U.S. Com. on Large Dams (life mem. vice-chmn. exec. com. 1980-81), Phi Beta Kappa, Tau Beta Pi. Presbyterian. Address: PO Box 217 Dinuba CA 93618-0217

LEPSELTER, MARTIN P., engineering educator; b. N.Y.C., Nov. 24, 1929. BME, CUNY, 1951. Dir. advanced very large scale integration devel. lab. AT&T Bell Labs., Murray Hill, N.J., 1957-86; chmn., pres., CEO Lepton Inc., 1986-93; pres. Bell Telephone Labs. Fellows, Inc., 1993—. Fellow IEEE; mem. Nat. Acad. Engring. Office: Lepton Inc 25 Sweetbriar Rd Summit NJ 07901*

LE QUESNE, PHILIP WILLIAM, chemistry educator, researcher; b. Auckland, New Zealand, Jan. 6, 1939; came to U.S., 1967; s. Ernest W. B. and Bettie A. (Colwill) Le Q.; m. Mary E. Kinloch, 1965 (dec. 1988); children: Elizabeth Ruth, Martin James. B.S., U. Auckland, 1960, M.S., 1961, Ph.D., 1964, D.Sc. (hon.), 1979. Asst. prof. U. Mich., Ann Arbor, 1967-72; assoc. prof. Northeastern U., Boston, 1973-78, prof., 1978—, chmn. dept. chemistry, 1979-87; assoc. dir. Barnett Inst. for Chem. analysis and Materials Sci., 1993—. Contbr. articles on chemistry to profl. jours. Sr. warden Ch. of the Advent, Boston, 1990-96. Home: 17 Stafford Rd Newton Center MA 02159-1818 Office: Northeastern U Chemistry Dept 360 Huntington Ave Boston MA 02115-5005

LERACH, WILLIAM S., lawyer; b. Pitts., Mar. 14, 1946. BA, U. Pitts., 1967, JD magna cum laude, 1970. Bar: Pa. 1970, Calif. 1976. presenter numerous seminars, confs. Contbr. articles to profl. jours. Mem. ABA, Assn. Trial Lawyers Am., Pa. Bar Assn., State Bar Calif., Calif. Trial Lawyers Assn., San Diego Bar Assn., San Diego County Trial Lawyers Assn., Order of Coif. Office: Milberg Weiss Bershad Hynes & Lerach Ste 1800 One Am Plz Blvd 600 W Broadway San Diego CA 92101-3311*

LERCH, RICHARD HEAPHY, lawyer; b. Balt., Oct. 8, 1924; s. Charles Sebastian and Marguerite Mary (Mullen) L.; m. Marie Therese Logan, Feb. 11, 1950; children—Marie L., Elizabeth L., Ellen C. A.B. magna cum laude, Loyola Coll., Balt., 1947; LL.B., U. Md., 1949. Bar: Md. bar 1948. Since practiced in Balt.; partner Lerch & Huesman, 1959—; Pres. Jr. Bar Assn., 1960. Served with AUS, 1944-46, 51-52. Mem. Am., Md., Balt. bar assns., Internat. Assn. Ins. Counsel. Democrat. Roman Catholic. Home: 5906 Meadowood Rd Baltimore MD 21212-2435 Office: 102 W Pennsylvania Ave Baltimore MD 21204-4526

LERITZ, LAWRENCE, choreographer, singer, dancer, producer, director, songwriter; b. Alton, Ill., Sept. 26, 1952; s. Leonard Henry and Marcella Rose (Fravle) L. Student Harkness Ballet Sch., 1973-74; Sch. Am. Ballet, 1975-76. Debut: State Fair, St. Louis Muny Opera, 1969, appeared in Can Can, 1983; TV appearances include: Capitol, 1982, All My Children, 1981-85, Home Sweet, Homeless; Rodney Dangerfield: It's Lonely at the Top, HBO, 1992, various commls.; guest expert on various talk shows including Rolanda, Charles Perez, Sally Jesse Raphael, American Muscle Mag.; film debut: Stardust Memories, 1979; appeared in Easy Money, 1982; star Leritz and His Girls, 1983-85; Broadway appearances include: Fiddler On the Roof, 1981, Fonteyn and Nureyev on Broadway, 1975; appeared Met. Opera telecast of Manon Lescaut, 1980; choreographer feature film musical The Last Dragon, 1984; choreographer, co-star home video Treehouse Trolls Birthday Day, 1993; dancer with Harkness Ballet, Paris Opera, Hamburg Ballet, Chgo. Ballet, world wide guest star; dir., choreographer own co. Dance Celebration which represented U.S. at Internat. Choreographic Competitions, Paris, 1979; dir. mus. numbers for Shields and Yarnell; creator mus. indsls. for Lily of France, Bausch & Lomb, Christian Dior; pres. Leritz Prodns., Ltd., N.Y.C. and L.A., 1983—; star exercise cruise on Queen Elizabeth II, 1995; rec. artist: It Takes Two to Tango, 1984, Crank It Up, 1989, Bright Light, 1992; song lyricist, composer; east coast co-prodr. Day of Compassion, 1995. Full scholar Sch. Am. Ballet, Harkness Ballet Sch.; Lawrence R. Leritz Day declared, recipient Key to City, Wood River, Ill., 1983, Alton, Ill., 1987; appeared on cover Dance Pages mag., fall 1987, spring 1989; writer Muscular Devel. mag., Ironman mag., Men's Fitness mag., Muscle & Fitness mag.; creator, star of video Total Stretch! with Lawrence Leritz, 1992. Mem. AFTRA, ASCAP (Pop Music awards for songwriting 1985—), SAG (mem. film nominating com. 1996), Actors Equity Assn., Am. Guild of Musical Artists (bd. govs. 1979-92, 94—, prodn. supr./choreographer 50th Anniversary Gala 1986, Life Membership award for disting. svc. 1991); choreographer, guest dancer Placido Domingo's L.A. Music Ctr. Opera, 1987. Office: 318 W 45th St Apt 3 New York NY 10036-3343

LERMAN, EILEEN R., lawyer; b. N.Y.C., May 6, 1947; d. Alex and Beatrice (Kline) L. BA, Syracuse U., 1969; JD, Rutgers U., 1972; MBA, U. Denver, 1983. Bar: N.Y. 1973, Colo. 1976. atty. FTC, N.Y.C., 1972-74; corp. atty. RCA, N.Y.C., 1974-76; corp. atty. Samsonite Corp. and consumer products div. Beatrice Foods Co., Denver, 1976-78, assoc. gen. counsel, 1978-85, asst. sec., 1979-85; ptnr. Davis, Lerman, & Weinstein, Denver, 1985-92, Eileen R. Lerman & Assocs., 1993—; bd. dir. Legal Aid Soc. of Met. Denver, 1979-80. Bd. dirs., vice chmn. Colo. Postsecondary Ednl.

Facilities Authority, 1981-89; bd. dirs., pres. Am. Jewish Com., 1989-92; mem. Leadership Denver, 1983. Mem. ABA, Colo. Women's Bar Assn. (bd. dir. 1980-81), Colo. Bar Assn. (bd. govs.), Denver Bar Assn. (trustee), N.Y. State Bar Assn., Rhone Brackett Inn (pres.-elect 1996), Denver Law Club, Rutgers U. Alumni Assn., University Club. Home: 1018 Fillmore St Denver CO 80206-3332 Office: Eileen R Lerman & Assocs 50 S Steele St Ste 420 Denver CO 80209-2809

LERMAN, LEONARD SOLOMON, science educator, scientist; b. Pitts., June 27, 1925; s. Meyer Louis and Freamah (Hoffman) L.; m. Claire Carol Lindegren, July 14, 1952 (div. Sept. 1973); children: Averil, Lisa, Alexander; m. Elizabeth Knox Taylor, May 11, 1974 (div. 1996). BS, Carnegie Inst. Tech., 1945; PhD, Calif. Inst. Tech., 1950. Postdoctoral fellow U. Chgo., 1949-51; from asst. to assoc. prof. U. Colo., Denver, 1951-63, prof. biophysics, 1963-65; prof. molecular biology Vanderbilt U., Nashville, 1965-76; prof., chmn. biology SUNY, Albany, 1976-84; dir. diagnostics Genetics Inst., Cambridge, Mass., 1984-87; sr. lectr. MIT, Cambridge, 1987—; mem. panel Dept. Energy, Washington, 1986-93; mem. Health and Environ. Rsch. Adv. Com. Bd., Bd. Radiation Effects Rsch., NRC, 1988-96. Editor: Molecular and Gen. Genetics jour., 1976-82; mem. editorial bd. Genomics; contbr. articles to profl. jours. Guggenheim Found. fellow, 1971-72. Mem. NAS, AAAS, Am. Acad. Arts & Scis., Am. Soc. Biol. Chemists, Human Genome Orgn., Am. Soc. Human Genetics. Home: 100 Memorial Dr Apt 11-6A Cambridge MA 02142-1332 Office: MIT Dept Biology Bldg 68 Rm 630 Cambridge MA 02139

LERMAN, MILES, federal agency administrator; m. Chris Lerman. Mem. U.S. Holocaust Meml. Coun., Washington, 1980-93, chmn., 1993—; chmn. Internat. Rels. Com., Campaign to Remember; nat. vice chmn. Israel Bond Orgn. Office: US Holocaust Meml Coun 100 Raoul Wallenberg Pl SW Washington DC 20024-2150

LERNER, AARON BUNSEN, dermatologist, biochemist, educator; b. Mpls., Sept. 21, 1920; m. 1945; 4 children. BA, U. Minn., 1941, MS, 1942; M of Medicine, PhD in Physiology Chem., 1945, MD, 1945. Diplomate Am. Bd. Dermatologists. Asst. physiol chemist U. Minn., 1941-45; asst. prof. dermatology U. Mich. Med. Sch., 1959-52; assoc. prof. U. Oreg., 1952-55; assoc. prof. dermatology and biochemistry Yale U. Med. Sch., 1955-57, prof. dept. dermatology, 1958-95, prof. emeritus, 1995—; chmn. dermatology dept. Yale U. Sch. Med., 1958-85. Recipient Myron-Gordon award, 1969, Stephen Rothman award, 1971, Li Annenberg Hazen award, 1981; named Dome Lectr., 1980. Office: Yale U Sch of Med Dept of Dermatology 333 Cedar St New Haven CT 06510-3206*

LERNER, ABRAM, retired museum director, artist; b. N.Y.C., Apr. 11, 1913; s. Hyman and Sarah (Becker) L.; m. Pauline Hanenberg, Oct. 7, 1940; 1 child, Aline. B.A., NYU, 1935; student, Ednl. Alliance, Art Students League, Bklyn. Mus.; pvt. studies, Florence, Italy. Asso. dir. A.C.A. Gallery and Artist's Gallery, N.Y.C., 1945-57; curator Joseph H. Hirshhorn Collection, N.Y.C., 1957-66; dir. Hirshhorn Mus. and Sculpture Garden, Washington, 1967-85; founding dir. emeritus, ret. Joseph H. Hirshhorn Mus. and Sculpture Garden, Smithsonian Instn., Washington, 1985; Adv. bd. Archives Am. Art, 1970—. Author: Hirshhorn Museum and Sculpture Garden - Inaugural Book, 1974, Gregory Gillespie, 1977; contbr. to mags., mus. catalogues.; one man show, Davis Gallery, N.Y.C., 1958, group shows include, A.C.A. Gallery, Peridot Gallery, Bklyn.-Mus., Pa. Acad., Davis Gallery, represented in pvt. collections. Decorated commandeur in de Orde Van Oranje-Nassau (The Netherlands); chevalier des L'Ordre des Arts et des Lettres (France). Home: 98 Lewis St Southampton NY 11968-5006

LERNER, ALAN BURTON, financial service executive, lawyer; b. N.Y.C., Nov. 17, 1930; s. Samuel A. and Helen (Zisfein) L.; m. Elisabeth Waltraud Bruttel, July 5, 1959; children: Raissa, Anthony, Jessica, James. BBA, CCNY, 1951; LLB, Yale U., 1954. Bar: N.Y. 1954, D.C. 1973. Assoc. Chadbourne, Parke, Whiteside & Wolff, N.Y.C., 1956-60; with legal dept. C.I.T. Fin. Corp., N.Y.C., 1960-81; gen. counsel, sec. C.I.T. Fin. Corp., 1976-81, v.p., 1977-81; sr. exec. v.p. Assocs. Corp. of N.Am., Dallas, 1981-93, ret., 1993; cons. Fed. Res. Bd., 1973, Nat. Conf. Commrs. on Uniform State Laws, 1966-68. Mem. adv. coun. Sch. Mgmt. and Adminstrn., U. Tex., Dallas, 1981-87; mem. Fin. Commn. of State of Tex., 1983-89; mem. adv. bd. Salvation Army Dallas County, 1991-95. Mem. ABA, D.C. Bar Assn., Assn. Bar City N.Y., Am. Fin. Svcs. Assn. (bd. dirs. 1983-88, 90-95, vice chmn. 1991-92, chmn. 1992-93, chmn. exec. com. 1993-94).

LERNER, ALFRED, real estate and financial executive; b. N.Y.C., May 8, 1933; s. Abraham and Clara (Abrahmson) L.; m. Norma Wokloff, Aug. 7, 1955; children: Nancy Faith, Randolph David. BA, Columbia U., 1955. Chmn. bd., chief exec. officer Multi-Amp Corp., Dallas, 1970-80, Realty Refund Trust, Cleve., 1971-90; pres., chief exec. officer Refund Advisers, Inc., 1971—, Town & Country Mgmt. Corp., 1979-93; chmn., dir. Equitable Bancorp., Balt., 1981-90; chmn., bd. dirs. Prog. Corp., Cleve., 1988-93; chmn., CEO MBNA Corp., Newark, 1991—, Town & Country Trust, 1993—; chmn., bd. dirs. MNC Corp., Balt., 1991-93. Trustee Columbia U., Cleve. Clinic, Case Western Res. U. 1st lt. USMCR, 1955-57. Mem. Young Pres. Orgn., Beechmont Club (Cleve.), Harmonie Club (N.Y.C.). Jewish. Home: 19000 S Park Blvd Cleveland OH 44122-1853 Office: 25875 Science Park Dr Beachwood OH 44122-7304

LERNER, ARNOLD STANLEY, radio station executive; b. Phila., Feb. 17, 1930; s. Joseph C. and Rose L. (Friedmann) L.; m. Maureen Ann Ireland, Aug. 7, 1972; children: Hilary R., Joseph C. BS in Econs., U. Pa., 1951; M in Liberal Studies, Boston U., 1974. Ptnr. Sta. KOMA, Oklahoma City, 1956-58, Sta. KITO, San Bernadino, Calif., 1959, Sta. WORC, Worcester, Mass., 1984-89, Sta. WNVE, Rochester, N.Y., 1986—, Sta. WJMN, Boston, 1987-94, Sta. WZOU, Gorham, Maine, 1988—, Sta. WQSS, Camden, Maine, 1988—, WTHT, Portland, Maine, 1994—; pres. Sta. WADK, Newport, R.I., 1960-77, Comm. Mgmt., Inc., Hollis, N.H., 1978-87; chmn., gen. mgr. Sta. WSSH, Lowell, Mass., 1963-86, Sta. WLLH, Lowell, 1963—; treas. Stas. WLAM/WKZS, Lewiston, Maine, 1977—; dir. Sta. WKSZ, Media-Phila., 1984—; bd. dirs., exec. com. First Bank, Chelmsford, Mass., 1977-88; vice chmn. Enterprise Bank and Trust, Lowell, 1988—; bd. dirs. Courier Corp. Trustee St. Joseph's Hosp., Lowell, 1976-87, Applewild Sch., Fitchburg, Mass., 1979-92, pres., 1985-89; bd. dirs.. Merrimack Valley Goodwill Industries, Lowell, 1972-86, chmn., 1976-78; bd. dirs. Merrimack Repertory Theatre, Lowell, 1988—, v.p., 1989-91, treas. 1992-94. Recipient Meritorious Svc. award Nat. Rehab. Assn., 1975. Mem. Nat. Assn. Broadcasters (bd. dir. 1977-81, chmn. radio bd. 1979-81), Mass. Broadcasters Assn. (bd. dir. 1968-87, pres. 1969-70), Vesper Country Club (Tyngsboro, Mass.), Kiwanis (pres. 1968, Citizen of Yr. award 1979, Lowell). Jewish. Home and Office: 155 Pine Hill Rd Hollis NH 03049-5939

LERNER, DANIEL MERRIL, broadcasting company executive; b. Phila., Nov. 26, 1932; s. Joseph C. and Rose L. (Friedmann) L.; m. Elaine Gomberg, Sept. 11, 1954; children: Ann, Paul, Julie. A.B., U. Pa., 1954, M.A. in Communications, 1961. Personnel officer City of Phila., 1954-60; account exec. Sta. WADK, Newport, R.I., 1961-62, Sta. WFIL-AM/TV, Phila., 1962-63; v.p. Sta. WLLH/WSSH-FM, Boston, 1963-82; chmn. Sta. WPLY-FM, Phila., 1982—; owner, cons. Daniel Lerner Co., Merion, Pa., 1974—; gen. ptnr. Cloverleaf Real Estate Partnership, Media, Pa., 1985—; co-owner Sta. WZOU-FM, Boston, 1987-94, Sta. WQSS-FM, Camden, Maine, 1988—. Bd. dirs. Delaware County ARC, Pa., 1985-88, Delaware County YMCA, 1994—. Mem. Broadcast Pioneers, Pa. Assn. Broadcasters, Del. County C. of C. (bd. dirs.). Avocations: boating; tennis. Office: Sta WPLY-FM 1003 Baltimore Pike Media PA 19063

LERNER, EDWARD MICHAEL, hospital administrator, lawyer; b. N.Y.C., Oct. 28, 1942; s. Gabriel and Dorothy (Sigoda) L.; m. Susan Katz, 1965 (div. 1975); children: Mindy, Stacey; m. Carol Sarashon, June 12, 1975; 1 child, David. Student, N.Y.C. Community Coll., 1968; AA with honors, Dade (Fla.) Community Coll., 1972; BS in Health Sci. with honors, Fla. Internat. U., 1974, MS in Pub. Adminstrn., 1975, MS in Health Svcs. Adminstrn., 1982; JD, U. Miami, 1987. Bar: Fla. 1988, U.S. Supreme Ct., U.S. Ct. Appeals (11th cir.). Mng. optician T.S. Budd Opticians, Miami, Fla., 1972-73, Jack Eckerd Corp., Miami, 1973-75; pres. Vogue Opticians, Pompano Beach, Fla., 1975-82; asst. adminstr. profl. svcs. Fla. Med. Ctr., Fort Lauderdale, 1982-86, assoc. adminstr., gen. counsel, 1987-93; sr. atty. State of Fla. Agy. for Health Care Adminstrn., Miami, 1994—; cons. Fla. Inst. Health, Broward and Coral Springs Diagnostic Ctrs.; bd. dirs. Aesculapious Ins. Trust. Recipient Award of Merit, N.Y. City Police Dept., 1968. Mem. ABA, Am. Hosp. Assn., Am. Soc. Hosp. Risk Mgrs., Am. Coll. Hosp. Attys., So. Fla. Adminstrv. Forum, Am. Coll. Health Care Execs., Fla. Hosp. Assn., Fla. Soc. Hosp. Risk Mgrs., Fla. Bar Assn. (health law sect., adminstrv. and govt. law sect.), Broward County Quality Assurance Profls., Nat. Acad. Opticianry, Lions, Rotary, Phi Alpha Delta, Phi Theta Kappa. Home: 9306 Chelsea Dr N Fort Lauderdale FL 33324-6204 Office: Agy for Health Care Adminst Office of Gen Counsel 3810 Inverrary Blvd #405 Lauderhill FL 33319

LERNER, HARRY JONAS, publishing company executive; b. Mpls., Mar. 5, 1932; s. Morris and Lena (Liederschneider) L.; m. Sharon Ruth Goldman, June 25, 1961 (dec. 1982); children: Adam Morris, Mia Carol, Daniel Aryeh, Leah Anne. Student, U. Mich., 1952, Hebrew U., Jerusalem, 1953-54; B.A., U. Minn., 1957. Founder Lerner Publs. Co., Mpls., 1959; pres., chief exec. officer, pub. Lerner Publs. Co., 1959—; founder Muscle Bound Bindery, Inc., 1967, chief exec. officer, 1967—; founder Carolrhoda Books, Inc., 1969; pres., gen. mgr. Interface Graphics Inc., 1969—, CEO, 1993—; bd. visitors U. Minn. Press; del. White House Conf. on Libr. and Info. Svcs., 1979; chmn. North Loop Bus. Assn., Mpls., 1972-79, Minn. Book Pubs. Roundtable, 1974; bd. overseers Hill Monastic Manuscript Libr., St. John's U., Collegeville, Minn., 1986-89; bd. dirs., libr. dir. Jewish Community Ctr. Pres. Twin City chpt. Am. Jewish Com., 1980-85; bd. dirs. Fgn. Policy Assn. Minn., 1970-71; bd. dirs. Children's Book Coun., N.Y.C., 1991-94; bd. advisors Books for Africa, 1996. Recipient Brotherhood award NCCJ, 1961, also numerous graphic arts awards. Mem. ACLU, Mpls. Inst. Art, Walker Art Ctr, St. Paul-Mpls. Com. on Fgn. Affairs, Ampersand Club, Daybreakers Breakfast Club (Mpls.). Home: 2215 Willow Ln N Minneapolis MN 55416-3862 Office: Lerner Pub Co 241 1st Ave N Minneapolis MN 55401-1607

LERNER, HERBERT J., accountant; b. Newark, Aug. 19, 1938; s. Morris David Lerner and Evelyn L. (Shapiro) Kaplan; m. Dianne Joan Prag, Aug. 23, 1959; children—Joy Ellen, Mark Allen. B.S., Rutgers U., 1959; LL.B., Georgetown U., 1963. Bar: D.C. 1964; C.P.A., D.C. With Ernst & Young, Washington, 1963—; ptnr. Ernst & Young, 1970-83, 83-89; vice chmn. tax Ernst & Young, Washington, 1990—; nat. dir. tax policy and standards Ernst & Young, now CPA; mem. IRS Commrs. Adv. Group, 1982-83, CCH Tax Adv. Bd., 1983—; treas., trustee Am. Tax Policy Inst., 1990—; bd. dirs. Tax Coun., 1984—, Internat. Tax and Investment Ctr., 1993—; mem. tax adv. coun. United Jewish Appeal Fedn., Washington, 1982—. Author: (with others) Federal Income Taxation of Corporations Filing Consolidated Returns, 4 vols., 1975, with ann. supplement; contbr., editor pvt. letter rulings column Jour. Taxation. Mem. AICPA (exec. com. tax divsn. 1979-82, 85, 89, past chmn., bd. dirs., co-chmn. nat. conf. lawyers and CPAs), ABA, Internat. Fiscal Assn., George Town Club. *

LERNER, JULIUS, mechanical engineer; b. Phila., July 27, 1919; s. Joseph and Gertrude (Leather) L.; children: Nina, Leon. Diploma in mech. engring., Drexel Inst. Tech., 1943, BS, 1953. Registered profl. engr., Calif., Pa. Machinist apprentice U.S. Navy Yard, Phila., 1940-41; lead machinist Baldwin Locomotive, Eddystone, Pa., 1941-44; sr. staff engr. Sun Oil Co., Newtown Square, Pa., 1946-83; pres. J. Lerner, Inc., Broomall, Pa., 1983—; speaker in field. Contbr. articles to profl. jours. Bd. dirs. Merci Haverford Hosp., Havertown, Pa., 1990—, Congregation Beth El Suburban; leader sr. group Broomall, 1991—; math tutor Chester H.S.; guest spkr. Marple-Newtown H.S.; mem. Marple Planning Commn. Sgt. U.S. Army, 1944-46, ETO. Mem. Am. Soc. Safety Engrs., Instrument Soc. Am., NSPE, Pa. Soc. Profl. Engrs. (bd. dirs. Delaware County br., chmn. selection com. for Delaware County Engr. of Yr.), ASME (life), IEEE, Am. Petroleum Inst. (com. on dynamic measurement), Am. Acad. Forensic Scis. Achievements include 21 U.S. patents, several patents pending. Home and Office: 2516 Parke Ln Broomall PA 19008-2204

LERNER, MARTIN, museum curator; b. N.Y.C., Nov. 14, 1936; s. Joseph and Rose (Kolberg) L.; m. Roberta M. Rubenstein, Feb. 26, 1968; children: Benjamin Louis, Seth Laurence, Jocelyn Ann. BA, Bklyn. Coll., 1959; postgrad., Inst. Fine Arts, NYU, 1961-65. Asst. prof. U. Calif., Santa Barbara, 1965-66; asst. curator Oriental art Cleve. Mus. Art, 1966-72; asst. prof. Case Western Res. U., 1968-72; vice chmn. charge Far Eastern art Met. Mus. Art, N.Y.C., 1972-75; curator Indian and S.E. Asian art Met. Mus. Art, 1978—; cons. in field; internat. lectr. Author: Bronze Sculptures from Asia, 1975, Blue and White: Early Japanese Export Ware, 1978, The Flame and the Lotus, 1984, (with W. Felten) Cambodian and Thai Sculpture: From the 6th to the 14th Century, 1989, Entdeckungen: Skulpturen der Khmer und Thai, 1989, (with S. Kossak), The Lotus Transcendent, 1991, Ancient Khmer Sculpture, 1994; contbr. articles to profl. jours. Served with U.S. Army, 1959-61. Clubs: East India; Devonshire (London). Home: Giglio Ct Croton-on-Hudson NY 10520 Office: Met Mus Art Fifth Ave at 82d St New York NY 10028

LERNER, MICHAEL ALBERS, health and environmental educator; b. N.Y.C., Oct. 22, 1943; s. Max and Genevieve Edna (Albers) L.; m. Leslie Acoca, 1974 (div. 1981); 1 child, Joshua Hawkes; m. Sharyle Martiel Patton, July 10, 1983. BA, Harvard U., 1965; PhD, Yale U., 1971. Asst. prof. Yale U., New Haven, 1971-72; assoc. Carnegie Coun. on Children, New Haven, 1971-72; exec. dir. Full Circle Sch., Bolinas, Calif., 1973-75; pres. Commonweal, Bolinas, 1975—; dir. Commonweal Cancer Help Program, Bolinas, 1985—; chief cons. Office of Tech. Assessment, U.S. Congress, Unconventional Cancer Treatments, 1989-91; chmn. bd. Hale Fund, San Francisco, 1991—; pres. Jenifer Altwaer Found., 1992—. Author: Choice in Cancer, 1992; co-editor: A Reader in Personality and Politics, 1970; contbr. articles to jours. in field. Coord. Californians for Juvenile Justice Reform, 1988—. Fulbright fellow, Brazil, 1965-66; Woodrow Wilson fellow Yale U., 1971; MacArthur Found. prize fellow, 1983-88; Gerrude Enelow Found. prize Assn. for Humanistic Medicine, 1987; Fetzer Sr. Advisor, Kalamazoo, 1992. Mem. Ctr. for Advancement Health (bd. dirs., sci. adv. coun. 1983—, Japan Soc. (U.S.-Japan leadership program 1990). Avocations: yoga, hiking. Office: Commonweal PO Box 316 Bolinas CA 94924-0316

LERNER, MILDRED SHERWOOD, clinical psychologist, psychoanalyst, psychotherapist; b. N.Y.C., Mar. 29, 1929; d. Samuel Jerome and Rose (Malina) Sherwood; children—Andrew Roy, Julie Sue. B.A. with honors, CCNY, 1951, M.A., 1952; Ph.D., NYU, 1957. Pvt. practice psychology N.Y.C., 1962—; supr. N.Y. Clinic Mental Health, N.Y.C.; instr. adult edn. CCNY, N.Y.C., 1952-54; chief psychologist High Point Hosp., Port Chester, N.Y., 1954-61; bd. dirs., tng. analyst, tchr. Nat. Psychol. Assn. for Psychoanalysis, N.Y.C., 1968—; dean student tng. Nat. Psychol. Assn. for Psychoanalysis, 1968-72, pres., 1972-74, v.p., 1986—; prof. Womanschool, N.Y.C., 1974-76; dir. grad. program in psychoanalysis Internat. Grad. U. Leysin, Switzerland, 1975-76; therapy cons. Canyon Ranch, 1989—. Contbr. articles to profl. jours. Trustee Chamber Ballet U.S.A. Alvin Johnson scholar, 1951; Psychology fellow, CCNY, 1952-54. Fellow Am. Psychol. Assn.; mem. AAUW, N.Y. State Psychol. Assn., N.Y. Soc. Clin. Psychologists, Am. Assn. Psychotherapy, Psychotherapists in Pvt. Practice, Am. Humanistic Psychol. Assn., Am. Group Psychol. Assn., Mcpl. Art Soc., NY. Acad. Sci.; Nat. Arts Club (music chmn.), Psi Chi. Address: 2 5th Ave New York NY 10011-8856 also: 2 5th Ave Apt 19A New York NY 10011-8842 also: Canyon Ranch 8600 E Rockcliff Rd Tucson AZ 85715-9733

LERNER, NATHAN BERNARD, artist; b. Chgo., Mar. 15, 1913; s. Louis Alexander and Ida Lerner; m. Kiyoko Asai, July 1, 1968; children: Michael John, Amy Elizabeth. Student, Nat. Acad. Art, Chgo., 1931, Art Inst. Chgo., 1933-34; B.S., Sch. Design in Chgo., 1941. Head of photo workshop Sch. of Design in Chgo., 1941-43; head of product design workshop, dean of faculty and students Inst. of Design, Chgo., 1945-49; ednl. dir. Inst. of Design, 1946-47; prof. U. Ill., Chgo., 1967-72; pres. Lerner Design Assos., 1949-72. One man shows include Chgo. Mus. Sci. and Industry, 1974, Bauhaus Archives, Berlin, 1975, Pentax Gallery, Osaka, Japan, 1976, Harry Lunn Gallery, Washington, 1977, Frumkin Gallery, Chgo., 1977, G.R. Hawkins Gallery, Los Angeles, 1977, Chgo. Hist. Soc., 1983, Photog. Gallery Internat., Tokyo, 1984, Ill. State Mus., Springfield, Chgo. Cultural Ctr., Ind. State U., Terre Haute, 1974, Bradley U., Peoria, Ill., 1973, Frumkin Gallery, Chgo., 1975, New York, 1976, Inst. of Contemporary Art, Boston, 1978, Augustana Mus., Rockford, Ill., 1987, The Photographers Gallery, London, 1988, Valparaiso U. Mus., 1989, U. Iowa Mus., 1993, Milw. Mus. Fine Art, 1995; represented in permanent collections Art Inst. Chgo., Mus. Modern Art, N.Y.C., Met. Mus. Art, N.Y.C., Mus. Fine Arts, Houston, Mus. Modern Art, Paris, Bibliotheque National, Paris, Eastman House, Rochester, Bauhaus Archive, Berlin, Mpls. Art Inst., Mus. Contemporary Art, Chgo., Nihon U., Tokyo, Seattle Mus. Art, Monterey (Calif.), Inst. Art, Amon Carter Mus., Fort Worth Israel Mus., Jerusalem, Kyoto Mus. Art, Japan, San Francisco Mus. Art, Ill. State Mus. Art, Internat. Ctr. Photography, N.Y.C., Ctr. for Creative Photography, Tucson, Santa Fe Mus. Fine Arts, Milw. Art Mus., Smart Gallery, Chgo., Les Recontres D'Arles, France. Ill. Arts Council grantee 1977-78. Mem. Artists Guild Chgo., Art Inst. Chgo. Alumni Assn. Patentee in field. Address: 849 W Webster Ave Chicago IL 60614-3615

LERNER, RALPH, architect, university dean; b. N.Y.C., Oct. 17, 1949; s. Irvin Louis and Sonia (Levine) L.; m. Lisa Diana Fischetti, June 20, 1982; children: Sigmund Michael, Esther Diana. BArch, Cooper Union, 1974; MArch, Harvard U., 1975. Registered architect, N.Y., N.J., Mass. Asst. prof. U. Va., Charlottesville, 1975-79; sr. lectr. Poly. Cen. London, 1979-80; assoc. prof. Harvard U., Cambridge, Mass., 1980-83; lectr. Princeton (N.J.) U., 1983-87, assoc. prof., 1987-89, prof., dean Sch. Architecture, 1989—, George Dutton '27 prof. of architecture, 1994—; pvt. practice, Princeton, 1980—. Prin. works include Villa Vasone (Progressive Architechture award 1981), Indira Gandhi Nat. Centre for The Arts, New Delhi, 1986 (1st prize design competition 1986). Recipient 1st prize internat. design competition Epping Town Coun., Essex, Eng., 1984, 1st award Progressive Architecture, 1987, 1st prize Eva's Kitchen and Sheltering Svcs., 1994. Mem. AIA, N.J. Soc. Architects. Office: 306 Alexander St Princeton NJ 08540-7124

LERNER, RALPH E., lawyer; b. N.Y.C., Apr. 12, 1943. BS, Bucknell U., 1964; JD, Boston U., 1967; LLM, NYU, 1969. Bar: N.Y. 1968, U.S. Tax Ct. 1969, Fla. 1975. Ptnr. Sidley & Austin, N.Y.C.; adj. asst. prof. paralegal studies NYU, 1975—. Co-author: Art Law: The Guide for Collectors, Investors, Dealers and Artists, 1989. Mem. ABA (mem. sect. taxation), Internat. Bar Assn., Assn. Bar City N.Y., N.Y. State Bar Assn. (mem. sect. taxation). Office: Sidley & Austin 875 3rd Ave New York NY 10022-6225

LERNER, STEPHEN ALEXANDER, microbiologist, physician, educator; b. Chgo., Oct. 4, 1938; s. David G. and Florence (Trace) L.; m. June 6, 1963 (div. 1990); children: Deborah, Daniel, Susan; m. Aug. 18, 1991. AB magna cum laude, Harvard U., 1959, MD magna cum laude, 1963. Intern, then resident Peter Bent Brigham Hosp., 1963-65; rsch. assoc. NIH, 1965-68; postdoctoral fellow Stanford (Calif.) U., 1968-71; asst. prof. then assoc. prof. U. Chgo., 1971-86; prof. of medicine Wayne State U., Detroit, 1986—; convenor Soviet-Am. Symposium Antibiotics and Chemotherapy, Moscow, 1988. Editor: Aminoglycoside Ototoxicity, 1981; mem. editl. bd. Antimicrobial Agts. and Chemotherapy, 1981—, European Jour. Clin. Microbiology and Infectious Diseases, 1992—; contbr. articles to profl. jours. With USPHS, 1965-67. Recipient Borden Rsch. award, 1963. Fellow Infectious Disease Soc. Am., Am. Acad. Microbiology (mem. com. on awards); mem. Am. Soc. Microbiology (chmn. antimicrobial chemotherapy 1987-88, divsn. group rep. 1990-92, councillor 1990-92, chmn. confs. com. 1993—, internat. coord. com. 1993—), Inter-Am. Soc. for Chemotherapy (pres. 1986-88, bd. dirs. 1988—, chmn. 1988-93), Internat. Soc. Chemotherapy (exec. com. 1987-93), Phi Beta Kappa, Sigma Xi, Alpha Omega Alpha. Democrat. Jewish. Avocations: travel photography, Russian language, collecting antique maps. Office: Harper Hosp Div Infectious Diseases 3990 John Rst Detroit MI 48201-2018

LERNER, STEVEN JAY, communications executive, educator; b. N.Y.C., Oct. 14, 1954; s. Bernard and Sandra (Herman) L.; m. Sharon Van Horn; children: Sarah, Rachel. BA, SUNY, Buffalo, 1977; MA, U. N.C., 1980, PhD, 1983. Pres. FGI, Chapel Hill, N.C., 1982-88, chmn., dir., 1989—; adj. prof. U. N.C., Chapel Hill, N.C. 1983—; dir. Sterling Cellular, Atlanta, 1991—, Sloan Comm., Durham, N.C., 1995—, PCS Devel. Corp., Greenville, S.C., 1995; chmn. CMS, Chapel Hill. Assoc. editor: Jour. Social Methods and Rsch. Dir. Real Enterprises, Durham, 1993, Independent Publs., Durham, 1994-95. Home: 110 Sandy Creek Trail Chapel Hill NC 27514 Office: FGI 206 W Franklin St Chapel Hill GA 27514

LERNER, STEVEN PAUL, lawyer; b. Bklyn., Nov. 9, 1958; s. Lloyd J. and Arline May (Solomon) L.; m. Donna Lynn Borges, Sept. 9, 1984; children: Kaitlin Olga, Colin Lane, Cody Layton. BA, L.I. U., 1980; JD, Syracuse U., 1983. Bar: N.Y. 1984, U.S. Dist. Ct. (ea. and so. dists.) N.Y. 1984, U.S. Ct. Appeals (2d cir.) 1984. Assoc. Robert & Schneider, Hempstead, N.Y., 1983-86; ptnr. Robert, Lerner & Robert, Rockville Centre, N.Y., 1986—. Advisor, sponsor Nassau County Rep. Com., Mineola, N.Y., 1990—; sponsor Suffolk County Rep. Com., Riverhead, N.Y., 1992—; vice chmn. budget com. Baldwin (N.Y.) Ednl. Assembly and Baldwin Bd. Edn., 1994; mem., lectr. Nassau/Suffolk Health Sys. Agy., N.Y., 1994. Mem. ABA, Nassau Bar Assn., Suffolk Bar Assn., Kings Bar Assn., Nassau Acad. Law (lectr. 1987—), Nat. Acad. Elder Care Attys. Jewish. Avocations: golf, all sports, my children. Home: 1854 Longfellow St Baldwin NY 11510-2336 Office: Robert Lerner & Robert 100 Merrick Rd Ste 508W Rockville Centre NY 11570-4801

LERNER, VLADIMIR SEMION, computer scientist, educator; b. Odessa, Ukraine, Sept. 12, 1931; came to U.S., 1990; s. Semion N. and Manya G. (Grosman) L.; m. Sanna K. Gleyzer, Sept. 28, 1954; children: Alex, Tatyana, Olga. BSEE, Odessa Poly. Inst., 1954; MEE, Inst. Problem's Controls, Moscow, 1959; PhD in Elec. Engring., Moscow Power Inst., 1961; D Sci. in Systems Analysis, Leningrad State U., 1974. Prof. elec. engring. Kishinev (Moldova) State U., 1962-64; prof. elec. engring. and control systems Kishinev Poly. Inst., 1964-79; sr. scientist in applied math. Acad. Sci., Kishinev, 1964-79; dir. math. modeling and computer sci. lab. Rsch. Inst., Odessa, 1979-89; sr. lectr. UCLA, 1991-93, rschr., 1993—; chmn. computer sci. dept. West Coast U., L.A., 1993—; mem. adv. bds. Acad. Sci., Kishinev, 1964-79, Poly. Inst., Kishinev, 1964-79; vis. prof. Leningrad State U., 1971-73; cons., mem. adv. bd. Poly. Inst., Odessa, 1979-89; mem. hon. editl. adv. bd. Encyclopedia of Life Support Sysss, Informational Macrodynamics. Author: Physical Approach to Control Systems, 1969, Superimposing Processes in Control Problems, 1973, Dynamic Models in Decision Making, 1974, Special Course in Optimal and Self Control Systems, 1977, Lectures in Mathematical Modelling and Optimization, 1995; contbr. 150 articles to scientific jours.; holder 23 patents; founder new sci. discipline Informational Macrodynamics. Recipient Silver medal for rsch. achievements, Moscow, 1961, outstanding achievements in edn., Kishinev, 1975. Avocations: bicycling, travel. Office: West Coast U 440 Shatto Pl Los Angeles CA 90020-1704

LERNER, WARREN, historian; b. Boston, July 16, 1929; s. Max and Rebecca (Rudnick) L.; m. Francine Sandra Pickow, Aug. 16, 1959; children: Suzanne Rachel, Amy Florence, Daniel Joseph. B.S., Boston U., 1952; M.A. and cert. of Russian, Inst. Columbia U., 1954, Ph.D. (Am. Council Learned Socs.-Social Service Research Council fgn. area fellow), 1961. Asst. prof. history Roosevelt U., 1959-61; asst. prof. Duke U., 1961-65, assoc. prof., 1965-72, prof., 1972—, chmn. dept., 1985-90; cons. NEH, 1974-80. Author: Karl Radek: The Last Internationalist, 1970, A History of Socialism and Communism in Modern Times, 1982, rev. edit., 1993; editor: The Development of Soviet Foreign Policy, 1973, (with Clifford M. Foust) The Soviet World in Flux, 1967; contbr. articles to profl. jours.; mem. internat. editorial bd. Studies in Comparative Communism, 1973-91. Served with U.S. Army, 1954-56. Am. Philos. Soc. fellow, 1972, 82; NEH, 1974-75. Mem. Conf. Slavic and East European History (exec. council 1978-80, pres. 1986-87), Am. Assn. Advancement Slavic Studies, Am. Hist. Assn., So. Conf. Slavic Studies. Jewish. Office: Duke U Dept History PO Box 90719 Durham NC 27708-0719

LEROUX, BETTY M., elementary education educator; b. Rockingham County, N.C., Oct. 18, 1938; d. J. Melvin and Callie M. (Edens) Moore; m. Daneel Leon leRoux, July 25, 1959; 1 child, Anna Elizabeth. Student, Appalachian State U., 1957-59, Longwood Coll., 1959-61, U. N.C., Greensboro, 1962; BS, East Carolina U., 1966. English tchr. Appomattox (Va.) County Schs., 1959-61; middle sch. tchr. Madison (N.C.)-Mayodan City, 1961-65; tchr. Pitt County Schs., Greenville, N.C., 1966—; chmn. Middle Sch.

Comm., Greenville, 1986—; com. mem. Pitt County Middle Sch. Task Force, Greenville, 1992-93, Pitt County Writing Handbook, Greenville; chmn. Chicod Sch. So. Assn., Greenville. Treas. Rockingham County (N.C.) Dem. Women's Orgn., 1961-65; mem. Jr. Svc. League, Madison, N.C., 1961-65; corr. sec. Bus. and Profl. Women, Greenville, 1972-80. Named Outstanding Young Women of Am., Bus. and Profl. Women's Club, Greenville, 1972. Mem. ASCD, Delta Kappa Gamma Internat. (membership chmn.), Women's Ministries (pres. 1978-81). Avocations: traveling, piano, gardening, antiquing, reading.

LE ROY, BRUCE MURDOCK, historian; b. Hornell, N.Y., June 9, 1920; s. Leland Bruce and Nina Boyce (Murdock) Le R.; m. Esther Buschman, Nov. 7, 1947; children: Philip Alden, Carolyn Sue (dec.). Student, Syracuse U., 1938-40, Transylvania U., 1941-42, Harvard Sch. Overseas Adminstrn., 1943-44; A.B., U. Calif., Berkeley, 1950. Mgr. coll. dept. Found. Press, N.Y.C., 1950; rep. Houghton Mifflin Co., 1950-58; dir. Wash. State Hist. Soc., Tacoma, 1959-84, dir. emeritus, 1985—; vis. lectr. Ft. Steilacoom Coll., 1985-86, U. Puget Sound, 1974-76; cons. U. Wash. Press, 1956-58; chmn. Gov. Wash. Boundary Survey Coun., 1960-61, Wash. Civil War Centennial Commn., 1960-65, Pacific N.W. Hist. Conf., 1960, 63, 78, Wash. Am. Revolution Bicentennial Commn., 1970-76. Author: H.M. Chittenden: A Western Epic, 1961, series Northwest History in Art, 1963-69, Lairds, Bards and Mariners: The Scot in Northwest America, 1978; gen. editor: Pacific Northwest Ethnic History Series, 1975-81; mem. editorial bd. Pacific N.W. Quar., 1958-84, N.W. Today, 1961-70, The American West, 1965-75, Manuscripts, 1978-94. Trustee Tacoma Art Mus., 1960-62, Allied Arts, 1962-65; pres. Tacoma Community Coll. Friends of the Library, 1981-83. Served with USAAF, 1943-46. Recipient award Calif. Writers Club, 1950, Nat. Archives and Record Services, 1958; Wash. Diamond Jubilee award, 1964; Disting. Service award Tacoma Public Library, 1977; John Binns award, 1976. Mem. Manuscript Soc., Am. Assn. State and Local History, Bibliog. Soc. Am., Western History Assn., Am. Studies Assn. (sec.-treas. 1961-64), Coun. Regional Rsch. (sec. 1959-84), Am. Folklore Soc., Am. Antiquarian Soc., SR. Presbyterian. Clubs: Univ. Union (trustee 1966-70), Tacoma, Clan Donald. Home: 10511 Sunnybrook Ln SW Tacoma WA 98498-3743

LEROY, DAVID HENRY, lawyer, state and federal official; b. Seattle, Aug. 16, 1947; s. Harold David and Lela Fay (Palmer) L.; 2 children. B.S., U. Idaho, 1969, J.D., 1971; LL.M., NYU, 1972; JD (hon.), Lincoln Coll., 1993. Bar: Idaho 1971, N.Y. State 1973, U.S. Supreme Ct. 1976. Law clk. Idaho 4th Dist. Ct., Boise, 1969; legal asst. Boise Cascade Corp., 1970; asso. firm Rothblatt, Rothblatt, Seijas & Peskin, N.Y.C., 1971-73; dep. prosecutor Ada County Prosecutor's Office, Boise, 1973-74; pros. atty. Ada County Prosecutor's Office, 1974-78; atty. gen. State of Idaho, Boise, 1978-82, lt. gov., 1983-87; ptnr. Runft, Leroy Coffin & Matthews, 1983-88, Leroy Law Offices, 1988—; candidate for Gov. of Idaho, 1986, U.S. Congress, 1994; U.S. nuclear waste negotiator, 1990-93; U.S. Presdl. elector, 1992; lectr., cons. in field. Mem. State Task Force on Child Abuse, 1975; mem. Ada County Coun. on Alcoholism, 1976; del. Rep. Nat. Conv., 1976, 80, 84; chmn. Nat. Rep. Lt. Gov.'s Caucus, 1983-86; bd. dirs. United Fund, 1975-81; del. Am. Coun. Young Polit. Leaders, USSR, 1979, Am. Coun. for Free Asia, Taiwan, 1980, U.S./Taiwan Investment Forum, 1983; del. leader Friendship Force Tour USSR, 1984; legal counsel Young Reps., 1974-81; candidate for Gov. Idaho, 1986; presdl. elector, 1992; candidate U.S. Ho. Reps. 1st Dist, Idaho, 1994. Mem. Nat. Dist. Attys. Assn., Idaho Prosecutors Assn., Am. Trial Lawyers Assn., Idaho Trial Lawyers Assn., Nat. Assn. Attys. Gen. (chmn. energy subcom., exec. com., del to China 1981), Western Attys. Gen. Assn. (vice chmn. 1980-83, chmn. 1981), Nat. Lt. Govs. Assn. (exec. bd. 1983), Idaho Bar Assn., Sigma Alpha Epsilon. Presbyterian. Office: The Leroy Offices PO Box 193 Boise ID 83701-0193

LEROY, G. PALMER, art dealer; b. N.Y.C., July 15, 1929; s. John Minturn and Georgiana Kip (Palmer) LeR.; m. Kyra Hawkins, June 18, 1955; children: Kyra, Nina, Pamela. BA, Harvard U., 1951. With N.Y. Times, 1951-52, Frank Best & Co., N.Y.C., 1952-53, Kenyon & Eckhardt, Inc., N.Y.C., 1953-55, Inmont Corp., U.S. and Europe, 1955-83; v.p. sales Inmont Internat., Inc., N.Y.C., 1974-83; ptnr. Clinton R. Howell, Inc. Antiques, Pound Ridge, N.Y., 1984-85; mng. dir. Met. Opera Guild, Inc., N.Y.C., 1985-94; pub. Opera News, N.Y.C., 1985-94; dealer 19th and 20th Century Am. Art Palmer LeRoy Fine Art, Bedford, N.Y., 1994—; mem. industry sector adv. com. chem. industry U.S. Commerce Dept., 1976-83. Pres. Friends of John Jay Homestead, Inc., Katonah, N.Y., 1977-95, chmn., 1995—; bd. dirs. The Bedford Assn., 1972-85, pres., 1975-80, bd. dirs. emeritus, 1986—; bd. dirs. Wildlife Preservation Trust Internat., Inc., Phila., 1983-94, pres., 1990-93, emeritus coun., 1994—; bd. dirs. N.Y. br. English Speaking Union, 1993—, chmn., 1994—; sr. warden St. Matthew's Ch., Bedford, 1985-89.

LEROY, JOY, model, designer; b. Riverdale, Ill., Sept. 8, 1927; d. Gerald and Dorothea (Wingebach) Reasor. BS, Purdue U., 1949. Model, sales rep. Jacques, Lafayette, Ind., 1950; book dept. sales rep. Loebs, Lafayette, 1951-52; window trimmer Marshall Fields and Co., Evanston, Ill., 1952-53; sales and display rep. Emerald Ho., Evanston, 1954-55; model, narrator, designer J.L. Hudson Co., GM Corp., Coca Cola Co., Hoover Vacuum Co., Jam Handy Orgn., Am. Motors Corp., Speedway Petroleum Corp., Ford Motors Tractor & Implement Divsn.-The Sykes Co., Detroit, 1958-61; tour guide, model The Christian Sci. Publ. Soc., spl. events coord. Prudential Ins. Co., model Copley 7, Boston, 1962-70. Author: Puzz-its, 1986-96. Founding angel Asolo Theatre, Sarasota, 1960s; mem. Ft. Lauderdale Internat. Film Festival, 1990, Mus. of Art, 1978, Fla. Conservation Assn., Rep. Senatorial Com. Inner Cir., 1990, Congrl. Com., 1990, Nat. Trust for Hist. Preservation, 1987, Fla. Trust for Hist. Preservation, 1987, Nat. Wildflower Rsch. Ctr., 1992; one of founding friends 1000 Friends of Fla., 1991; mem. Rep. Presdl. Task Froce, 1993. Mem. Nat. Wildlife Fedn., Internat. Wildlife Fedn., Purdue U. Golf Coast Club, Stratford Shakespearean Festival of Am., USS Constn. Mus. (charter mem. 1993), Purdue Alumni Assn., Walt Disney's Magic Kingdom Club, Wilderness Soc., Magic Kingdom Enterntainment Club, Maupin Alumni, Fla. Wildlife Fedn., Ducks Unltd., Paddelwheel Steamboatin' Soc. Am., Internat. Marine Animal Trainers Assn., The Cyrstal Soc., The Cousteau Soc., Corvette Club, Coastal Conservation Assn., Captain's Cir., Intravler Club, Am. Queen Inaugural Soc., Zeta Tau Alpha. Avocation: travel. Home: 2100 S Ocean Ln Apt 2104 Fort Lauderdale FL 33316-3827

LE ROY, L. DAVID, journalist; b. Tignall, Ga., Jan. 2, 1920; s. Lansing Burrows and Glennie (David) LeR.; m. Mary Margaret Pridgeon, Sept. 2, 1945 (div.); children: David Charles, Gregory Alan; m. Ydoine B. Marholec, Apr. 30, 1988 (div.). A.B., U. Ga., 1941; student, Va. C. C., Shenandoah Coll., 1980. Mng. editor Air Force Times, 1950-53; with U.S. News & World Report, 1953-70, news editor, 1953-64; mem. Capitol Hill staff, 1964-70; publs. dir. Republican Congl. Com., 1970-74, pub. relations dir., 1974-76; exec. dir. Nat. Press Found., 1977-80. Author: Gerald Ford--Untold Story, 1974, The Outdoorsman's Guide to Government Surplus, 1978, World War II As I Knew It, 1994. Active local Boy Scouts Am. Served with AUS, 1941-46. Decorated Purple Heart. Mem. Nat. Press Club (pres. 1967, bd. govs., chmn. bd. govs.), Nat. Rifle Assn., Sigma Delta Chi. Lutheran. Home: PO Box 145 New Market VA 22844-0145

LERSCH, DELYNDEN RIFE, computer engineering executive; b. Grundy, Va., Mar. 22, 1949; d. Woodrow and Eunice Louise (Atwell) Rife; m. John Robert Lersch, May 9, 1976; children: Desmond, Kristofer. BSEE, Va. Poly. Inst. and State U., 1970; postgrad. Boston U., 1975—. With Stone & Webster Engring. Corp., 1970-91, elec. engr., supr. computer applications, Boston, 1978-80, mgr. computer graphics, 1980-84, mgr. engring. systems and computer graphics, 1984-87, div. chief info. techs., 1987-90, v.p., 1990-91; chief A.D.P. officer Univ. Rsch. Assocs., 1991-94; CARE Sys. Corp. account mgr. Perot Sys. Corp., Dallas, 1994—; acct. mgr. PMI, 1995—. Named Stone and Webster's Woman Engr. of Yr., 1976, 79; Mass. Solar Energy Research grantee, 1978; honored by Engring. News Record mag. for contbns. to constrn. industry, 1983. Mem. IEEE (sr.), Assn. Women in Sci., Soc. Women Engrs. (sr.), Women in Sci. and Engring., Energy Communicators, Nat. Computer Graphics Assn., Profl. Council New Eng., Women in Energy (dir. Mass. chpt. 1978, New Eng. region 1979), LWV, Rotary (Rotarian of Yr. 1993-94). Congregationalist. Club: Boston Bus. and Profl. Women's. Author: Cable Schedule Information Systems As Used in Power Plant Construction, 1973, 2d edit., 1975; Information Systems Available for Use by Electrical Engineers, 1976; contbr. articles in field of computer aided design and engring. Home: 1106 Bristol Cir De Soto TX 75115-2818 Office: Perot Sys Corp 12377 Merit Dr Ste 1100 Dallas TX 75251-3233

LERUD, JOANNE VAN ORNUM, library administrator; b. Jamestown, N.D., Nov. 21, 1949; d. Elbert Hiel and Dorothy Arlene (Littrick) Van Ornum; m. Gerald Henry Groenewold, Jan. 15, 1971 (div. Nov. 1978); 1 child, Gerd Heil Groenewold; m. Jeffrey Craig Lerud, Aug. 30, 1980; 1 child, Jesse Currier. BS in Geology, U. N.D., 1971, MS in Geology, 1979; MA in Librarianship and Info. Mgmt., U. Denver, 1979. Assoc. tech. info. specialist Marathon Oil Co., Littleton, Colo., 1980-86; libr. dir. Mont. Coll. Mineral Sci. and Tech., Butte, 1986-89, Colo. Sch. Mines, Golden, 1989—; report investigator in field. NSF grantee, 1970. Mem. Geosci. Info. Soc. (v.p. 1988, pres. 1989). Avocations: reading, needlework, antiques. Office: Colo Sch Mines Arthur Lakes Libr Golden CO 80401

LERUDE, WARREN LESLIE, journalism educator; b. Reno, Oct. 29, 1937; s. Leslie Raymond and Ione (Lundy) L.; m. Janet Lagomarsino, Aug. 24, 1961; children: Eric Warren, Christopher Mario Leslie, Leslie Ann. BA in Journalism, U. Nev., 1961. Reporter, editor, correspondent The AP, Las Vegas, Reno, Nev., 1960-63; reporter, editor, pub., pres. Reno Evening Gazette, Nev. State Jour., 1963-81; prof. journalism U. Nev., Reno, 1981—; bd. dirs. Oakland (Calif.) Tribune; lectr. Am. Press Inst.; cons. ABA, NBC, Nat. Jud. Coll.; mem. nat. adv. com. The Freedom Forum's Mus. Co-author: American Commander in Spain, Robert Hale Merriman and the Abraham Lincoln Brigade, 1986; mem. editorial bd. USA Today, 1982—. Trustee U. Nev.-Reno Found.; trustee, mem. cmty. adv. bd. Sta. KNPB-TV, Reno; mem. legis. com. Greater Reno C. of C.; mem. bd. dirs. Squaw Valley Ski Corp. Served with USNR, 1957-59. Co-recipient Pulitzer prize, 1977. Mem. Nev. State Press Assn. (past pres.), Calif.-Nev. News Execs. Council of the AP, Calif. Newspaper Pub. Assn. (editors conf.), Sigma Delta Chi. Club: Rotary. Avocations: skiing, sailing, traveling, reading. Home: 3825 N Folsom Dr Reno NV 89509-3015 Office: U Nev Reynolds Sch Journalism Reno NV 89557

LERUP, LARS G., architecture educator, college dean. Civil engring. diploma, Helsingborg Tech. Coll., Sweden, 1960; BArch, U. Calif., Berkeley, 1968; MArch in Urban Design, Harvard U., 1970. Asst. prof. architecture U. Calif., Berkeley, 1970-77, assoc. prof. architecture, 1977-87, prof. architecture, 1987-93; Harry K. and Albert K. Smith prof. and chair in architecture Rice U., Houston, 1993—, dean Sch. of Architecture, 1993—; counselor Assn. Collegiate Schs. Architecture, Western Region, 1972-73, 76-77, 77-78; teaching cons. CCNY Sch. of Architecture, 1974; assoc. dean, chair environ. design program U. Calif., Berkeley, 1978-79; vis. fellow Inst. Architecture and Urban Studies, N.Y.C., 1979-81, dir. ednl. programs, 1981; Andrew Carnegie vis. prof. Cooper Union, N.Y.C., 1980-81; vis. prof. Rice U. Sch. Architecture, Houston, 1983, Caudill vis. prof., 1987; vis. prof. Architecture Assn., London, 1985, So. Calif. Inst. Architecture, L.A. and Vico Morcote, Switzerland, 1985, 91-93, ednl. dir., 1990-93; vis. prof. architecture U. Grenoble, France, 1990; mem. numerous coms. U. Calif., Berkeley, So. Calif. Inst. Architecture, Rice U.; supr. grad. students; lectr., rschr., guest critic in field. Author: Building the Unfinished: Architecture and Human Action, 1977, 3rd edit., 1983, Planned Assaults: Nofamily Hous. Love/House, Texas Zero, 1987, (with others) Fires and Human Behavior, 1980, Designer's Own Homes: Private Residences of Thirty of America's Leading Interior Designers, 1984, Architecture and Body, 1988, Architect's People, 1989, Visionary San Francisco, 1990; contbr. articles to profl. jours. and catalogs; prin. works include Folksam Ins. Co. Hdqrs., Farsta, Sweden, Ecole Maritime, La Rochelle, Bretagne, France, Cmty. Ctr., Eskilstuna, Sweden, Ch., Stora Tuna, Sweden, Bldg. Sci. Rm., U. Calif., also furniture design. Regents Tuition scholar U. Calif., 1966-67, 67-68; Arthur Lehman grantee Harvard U., 1969-70, Gulf Oil grantee, 1969-70; recipient citation for excellence Progressive Architecture Awards Program, 1976, citation Assn. Collegiate Schs. Architecture, 1986. Office: Rice U Sch of Architecture 6100 Main St Houston TX 77005*

LESAR, HIRAM HENRY, lawyer, educator; b. Thebes, Ill., May 8, 1912; s. Jacob L. and Missouri Mabel (Keith) L.; m. Rosalee Berry, July 11, 1937 (dec. Oct. 1985); children: James Hiram, Albert Keith, Byron Lee; m. Barbara Thomas, Feb. 12, 1987. AB, U. Ill., 1934, JD, 1936; JSD, Yale U., 1938. Bar: Ill. 1936, Mo. 1954, U.S. Supreme Ct. 1960. Asst. prof. law U. Kans., 1937-40, assoc. prof., 1940-42; sr., prin. atty. bd. legal examiners U.S. CSC, 1942-44; assoc. prof. law U. Mo., 1946-48, prof., 1948-57; prof. law Washington U., St. Louis, 1957-72, dean Sch. Law, 1960-72; founding dean, prof. law So. Ill. U., Carbondale, 1972-80, interim pres. univ., 1974, acting pres., 1979-80, disting. service prof., 1980-82, prof. emeritus, 1982—, vis. disting. svc. prof., 1983—; disting. vis. prof. McGeorge Sch. Law, 1982-83; vis. prof. law U. Ill., summer 1947, Ind. U., summer 1952, U. So. Calif., summer 1959, U. N.C., summer 1961, NYU, summer 1965. Author: Landlord and Tenant, 1957; Contbr. to: Am. Law of Property, 1952, supplement, 1977, also, Dictionary Am. History, Ency. Brit. Bd. dirs. Legal Aid Soc., St. Louis and St. Louis County, 1960-72, pres. 1966-67; mem. Human Rels. Commn., University City, Mo., 1966-71, chmn., 1966, 67; bd. dirs. Land of Lincoln Legal Assistance Found., 1972-82, pres., 1982, vice chmn., 1988—; mem. Fed. Mediation and Conciliation Svc., other arbitration panels; bd. dirs. Bacone Coll., 1981-87; trustee Lincoln Acad. Ill., 1987—. Lt. comdr. USNR, 1944-46. Recipient Pres.' award Mo. Bar, 1968; named Laureate Lincoln Acad. of Ill., 1985. Fellow Am. Bar Found., Ill. Bar Found.; mem. ABA, AAUP, FBA, Am. Arbitration Assn., Am. Law Inst., Ill. Bar Assn., Mo. Bar Assn., St. Louis Bar Assn., Am. Judicature Soc., Univ. Club St. Louis, Yale Club Chgo., Rotary Internat., Jackson Country Club, Masons, K.T., Shriners, Order of Coif, Phi Beta Kappa, Phi Kappa Phi, Phi Delta Phi (hon.). Baptist. Home: 11 Hillcrest Dr Carbondale IL 62901-2444

LESCAZE, LEE ADRIEN, editor; b. N.Y.C., Dec. 8, 1938; s. William Edmond and Mary (Hughes) L.; m. Rebecca Giraud Hughes, Mar. 25, 1967; children: Alexandra Hughes, Miranda Mary, Adrien William. A.B., Harvard, 1960. With Washington Post, 1963—, asst. fgn. editor, 1965-67, Saigon corr., 1967-68, Hong Kong corr., 1970-73, fgn. editor, 1973-74, nat. editor, 1975-77, N.Y. corr., 1977-80, White House corr., 1980-82, asst. mng. editor, 1982-92; weekend editor The Wall Street Jour., 1995—. Office: The Wall St Jour 200 Liberty St New York NY 10281

LESCH, ANN MOSELY, political scientist, educator; b. Washington, Feb. 1, 1944; d. Philip Edward and Ruth (Bissell) Mosely; BA, Swarthmore Coll., 1966; PhD, Columbia U., 1973. Rsch. assoc. Fgn. Policy Rsch. Inst., Phila., 1972-74; assoc. Middle East rep. Am. Friends Svc. Com, Jerusalem, 1974-77; Middle East program officer Ford Found., N.Y.C., 1977-80, program officer, Cairo, 1980-84; assoc. Univs. Field Staff Internat., 1984-87; prof. Villanova U., 1987—, assoc. dir. ctr. Arab and Islamic studies, 1992-95. Author: The Politics of Palestinian Nationalism, 1973, Arab Politics in Palestine, 1979, Political Perceptions of the Palestinians on the West Bank and Gaza, 1980, (with Mark Tessler) Israel, Egypt and the Palestinians, 1989, Transition to Palestinian Self-Government, 1992; contbr. articles to profl. jours. Bd. dirs. Am. Near East Refugee Aid, 1980-86, Middle East Report, 1989-93, Mid. East Watch, 1989—; co-chair middle East Program Com., Am. Friends Svc. Com., 1989-94; mem. Quaker UN Com., 1979-80, U.S. adv. com. Interns for Peace, 1978-82. Fellow Catherwood Found., 1965; NDFL fellow, 1967-71; Am. Rsch. Ctr. grant Egypt, 1988, U.S. Inst. of Peace Rsch. grant, 1990-91; Wilson Ctr. Guest scholar Smithsonian, 1990, Rockefeller Fdn. Bellagio Ctr., 1996. Mem. Middle East Studies Assn. (bd. dirs. 1988-91, pres. 1993-96), Middle East Inst., Am. Polit. Sci. Assn., Sudan Studies Assn. (sec. 1993-96), Coun. Fgn. Rels. Unitarian. Office: Villanova U Dept Polit Sci Villanova PA 19085

LESCH, MICHAEL, cardiologist; b. N.Y.C., June 30, 1939; s. Maurice and Rose (Linn) L.; m. H. Bella Samuels, June 25, 1961; children—Leah Deura, Ian Samuel. A.B., Columbia U., 1960; M.D., Johns Hopkins U., 1964. Diplomate: Am. Bd. Internal Medicine, Am. Bd. Cardiology. Intern, then resident in medicine Johns Hopkins Hosp., 1964-66; physician USPHS, 1966-68; chief resident physician, fellow cardiology, asst. prof., then asso. prof. medicine Harvard U. Med. Sch.-Peter Bent Brigham Hosp., 1968-76; Magerstadt prof. medicine Northwestern U. Med. Sch., 1976-89; clin. prof. medicine, chmn. dept. medicine, Henry Ford Hosp. U. Mich., Detroit, 1989—; prof. Medicine Case Western U., Cleve., 1994—; mem. life scis. adv. com. NASA, 1980. Editor: Progress in Cardiovascular Diseases, 1971—; editorial bd. profl. jours. Fellow A.C.P., Am. Coll. Cardiology; mem. Am. Soc. Clin. Investigation, Am. Heart Assn. (gov. 1978-81), Chgo. Heart Assn. (pres. 1982-83). Office: Henry Ford Hosp 2799 W Grand Blvd Detroit MI 48202-2608

LESCH, MICHAEL OSCAR, lawyer; b. Berlin, May 28, 1938; came to U.S., 1940, naturalized, 1946; s. Adolf F. and Maria E. Leschnitzer; m. Judith Willis, Aug. 31, 1965; children—Sara, Benjamin. A.B., Columbia U., 1958; LL.B., Harvard U., 1961. Bar: N.Y. 1961, U.S. Dist. Ct. (so. dist.) N.Y. 1963, U.S. Dist. Ct. (ea. dist.) N.Y. 1965, U.S. Ct. Appeals (2d cir.) 1968, U.S. Supreme Ct. 1975, U.S. Ct. Appeals (3d cir.) 1979, U.S. Ct. Appeals (7th cir.) 1979. Assoc. Shea & Gould and predecessors, N.Y.C., 1961-69; ptnr. Shea & Gould and predecessors, 1970-94, LeBoeuf, Lamb, Greene & MacRae, N.Y.C., 1994—. Contbr. articles to profl. jours. Mem. ABA, N.Y. State Bar Assn., Assn. Bar City N.Y., Fed. Bar Council, Am. Arbitration Assn. (panel of arbitrators). Office: LeBoeuf Lamb Greene & MacRae 125 W 55th St New York NY 10019-5369

LESER, LAWRENCE A., broadcasting company executive; b. Cin., 1935; married. BS, Xavier U., 1957. With Haskins & Sells, 1957-68; with Scripps Howard, Cin., 1968—, former sec., treas., former v.p. fin., dir. corp. devel., now pres., chief exec. officer, also bd. dirs.; mem. nat. adv. bd. Chem. Bank; bd. dirs. Newspaper Advt. Bur., Union Cen. Life Ins. Co., Heekin Can. Inc. Office: Scripps Howard 1100 Central Trust Towers Cincinnati OH 45202

LESESNE, JOAB MAULDIN, JR., college president; b. Greenville, S.C., June 21, 1937; s. Joab Mauldin and Henrietta (Fennell) L.; m. Ruth Osborne, Feb. 1, 1958; children: Julia Ruth, Maryrose Lyle, Joab Mauldin III, Henry Herbert. B.A., Erskine Coll., 1959; M.A., U. S.C., 1961, Ph.D., 1967; hon. degree, Lander Coll., 1991. Instr. U. S.C.-Coastal Carolina br., Conway, 1960-62; mem. faculty Wofford Coll., 1964—, dean coll., 1970-72, pres., 1972—; past pres. S.C. Assn. Colls. and Univs.; past chmn. S.C. Tuition Grants Commn., 1972; mem. S.C. Commn. on Archives and History.; pres. So. Univ. Conf.; bd. dirs. Am. Coun. on Edn.; chmn. bd. dirs. NationsBank, N.C. and S.C. Author: History of Erskine College, 1967. Bd. dirs. Spartanburg County Found., United Way, chmn., 1991. Mem. S.C. Hist. Assn. (past pres.), Nat. Assn. Ind. Colls. and Univs. (chmn. 1985-86). Methodist. Office: Wofford Coll Office of Pres 429 N Church St Spartanburg SC 29303

LESH, PHILIP CHAPMAN, musician, composer; b. Berkley, Calif., Mar. 15, 1940; s. Frank Hamilton and Barbara Jewel (Chapman) L.; m. Jill Winifred Johnson, Sept. 12, 1984; children: Graham Hamilton, Brian James. Student, Coll. San Mateo, 1958-61, Mills Coll., 1962. Co-founder, bass and vocals group Grateful Dead, 1965—. Albums include American Beauty, Grateful Dead, 1967, Anthem of the Sun, Aoxomoxoa, 1969, Live Dead, 1970, Workingman's Dead, 1970, The Grateful Dead, 1971, Bear's Choice: History of the Grateful Dead, Vol. 1, 1973, Skeletons From the Closet, 1974, What A Long Strange Trip It's Been: The Best of the Grateful Dead, 1977, Wake Of the Flood, 1973, From Mars Hotel, 1974, Blues for Allah, 1975, Steal Your Face, 1976, Terrapin Station, 1977, Shakedown Street, 1978, Built to Last, 1989, Dead Set, Europe, 1972, Reckoning, 1986, Go To Heaven, In the Dark, 1987, Without a Net, 1990, One From the Vault, Two From the Vault, and others; songwriter (with Robert Hunter) Box of Rain, 1970, (with Robert M. Petersen) New Potato Caboose, 1967, Unbroken Chain, 1974, Pride of Cucamonga, 1974; composer Foci for 4 orchs., 1963. Office: care Grateful Dead Prodns. PO Box 1073 San Rafael CA 94915-1073

LE SHANA, DAVID CHARLES, seminary president; b. Lucknow, India, Nov. 15, 1932; came to U.S., 1949; naturalized, 1958; s. Newman John and Gwendolyn Beatrice (White) Le S.; m. Rebecca Ann Swander, June 8, 1951; children: Deborah Lynn, James David, Catherine Ann, Christine Joy. AB, Taylor U., Upland, Ind., 1953; AM in Edn, Ball State U., 1959; PhD, U. So. Calif., 1967; LHD (hon.), George Fox Coll., 1982. Ordained to ministry Friends Ch., 1953; pastor Ypsilanti (Mich.) Friends Ch., 1953-54; dir. pub. relations, chaplain Taylor U., 1954-61; pastor 1st Friends Ch., Long Beach, Calif., 1961-67; mem. staff George Fox Coll., Newberg, Oreg., from 1967, pres., 1969-82; pres. Seattle Pacific U., 1982-91, pres. emeritus, 1991—; pres. Western Evang. Sem., Portland, Oreg., 1992—; min. Pacific N.W. Conf. of Free Meth. Ch.; bd. dirs. Coun. Ind. Colls., 1971-80, chmn., 1976-78; chmn. commn. higher edn. Nat. Assn. Evangelicals, 1973-75; chmn. Oreg. Ind. Colls. Assn., 1971-72, 81-82; mem. So. Calif. Radio and TV Commn., 1963-67; bd. dirs. Christian Coll. Consortium, chmn., 1984-86; mem. fact-finding group to Bangladesh, 1972; mem. adv. bd. Oriental Missionary Soc.; bd. advs. Latin Am. Mission, Friends Ctr., Azusa Pacific U. Author: Quakers in California, 1969; Rec.: album Songs of Discipleship, 1965. Bd. dirs. Oreg. Ind. Coll. Found., 1969-82, 92—, George Fox Coll. Found., 1971-82, Herbert Hoover Found., Oreg., 1975-82, Ind. Colls. of Wash., 1982-91, Wash. Friends of Higher Edn., 1982-91; bd. assocs. Pacific Sci. Ctr.; mem. Wash. Gives Leadership Coun., 1989-92, mem. edn. commn. States Task Force on State Policy and Ind. Higher Edn., 1986-89; trustee CRISTA Ministries, 1982-88, 90—, bd. dirs., 1982—; chmn. bd. Christian Coll. Coalition, 1991. Recipient Alumni Service award Taylor U., 1961, Chamber of Achievement award, 1978; Tchr. of Yr. award Ball State U., 1978. Mem. Nat. Assn. Evangs. (bd. adminstrn., chmn. theology com. 1992—), Portland Rotary Club. Address: 5737 Charles Cir Lake Oswego OR 97035-8714

LESHER, DONALD MILES, lawyer; b. Middleport, Ohio, May 29, 1915; s. Miles Mosser and Edith Katherine (McMaster) L.; m. Josephine Kirkmeyer, May 31, 1942; children: Donna J. Lesher Pinder, Karen A. Lesher Mariea, Lorraine C. Lesher Boyd; m. Barbara Jean Johnson, Feb. 20, 1963; m. Jimmie H. Queen, Mar. 22, 1981. BA, Colo. U., 1937; LLB, Okla. U., 1940. Bar: Colo. 1941. Since practiced in Denver; ptnr. Knight & Lesher, 1953-58, Lesher, Schmidt & Van Cise, 1958-64, Lesher & Gregg, 1964-72, Knight & Lesher, P.C., 1981-87; pvt. practice Donald M. Lesher P.C., 1972-81, 87—; bd. dirs. First S & L Shares, Inc., Majestic Savs. & Loan Assn.; instr. real estate law Westminster Law Sch., Denver U., 1955-59. Mem. Colo. Gen. Assembly, 1943-47. With USN, 1940-41. Mem. ABA, Colo. Bar Assn. (trustee 1948-51, v.p. 1954-55, award of merit 1958, chmn. real estate sect. 1962-64), Denver Bar Assn. (hon. life), Denver Athletic Club, Sigma Chi. Republican. Roman Catholic. Home: 7017 E Girard Ave Denver CO 80224-2903

LESHER, JOHN LEE, JR., consulting services company executive; b. Harrisburg, Pa., Feb. 7, 1934; s. John Lee and Mary Alice (Watkeys) L.; m. Nancy Smith, July 11, 1970; children by previous marriage: John David, James Elam, Andrew Gwynne. BA cum laude, Williams Coll., 1956; MBA, Harvard U., 1958. Budget dir., asst. sec. The Barden Corp., Danbury, Conn., 1958-61; cons. Booz, Allen & Hamilton Inc., N.Y.C., 1961-64, assoc., 1964-66, v.p., 1966-76, pres., 1976-85; pres. Mars & Co. Cons. Inc., Greenwich, Conn., 1985-87, Home Group Fin. Services, N.Y.C., 1987-88; v.p. Cresap, McCormick & Paget, N.Y.C., 1988-89; mng. dir. Korn/Ferry Internat., N.Y.C., 1989-93; pres. Jack Lesher & Assocs., Greenwich, Conn., 1993—. Clubs: Harvard Bus. Sch., Watch Hill Yacht, Misquamicut (Watch Hill, R.I.), Round Hill (Greenwich, Conn.), River (N.Y.C.), Coral Beach (Bermuda).

LESHER, MARGARET LISCO, newspaper publisher, songwriter; b. San Antonio, Tex., May 4, 1932; d. Lloyd Elmo Lisco and Dovie Deona (Maynard) Lisco Welch; m. William Jarvis Ryan (dec.); children: Patricia Ryan Simmonds, Wendi Ryan Alves, Jill Ryan Heidt, Roxanne Ryan Gibson; m. Dean Stanley Lesher, Sr., Apr. 2, 1973 (dec.). Student Coalinga (Calif.) Jr. Coll. Dir. sales Chatmar, Inc., Concord, Calif., 1970-73; dir. cmty. svcs. Contra Costa Times Newspaper, Walnut Creek, Calif., 1973-94; chmn. bd. Lesher Comm., Inc., Walnut Creek, 1974—, Calif. Delta Newspapers, Inc., Antioch, 1975—, No. Calif. Publs., Inc., Telegraph.-News Publs., Inc.; pres., ceo, dean Margaret Lesher Found. Composer, lyricist gospel song Margaret Lesher Album, 1976 (So. Calif. Motion Picture Coun. Bronze Halo award 1982); author 14 published poems. Pres., exec. dir. Dean and Margaret Lesher Found.; regent Holy Names Coll., Oakland, Calif., 1979-86; chief of protocol Contra Costa County, 1980—; dir. Bay Area Sports Hall of Fame, San Francisco, 1982—; bd. overseers U. Calif., San Francisco, 1983-90; bd. dirs. Yosemite Fund; mem. San Francisco Host

Com., 1983—, Internat. Host Com. of Calif., 1983-86, Nat. Reading Initiative Coordinating Coun., 1988—; dir. emeritus Alameda-Contra Costa Regional Parks Found.; developed Contra Costa County Citizen Recognition Awards Program with County Police Chiefs Assn.; founded Contra Costa Literacy Alliance; commr. Port of Richmond, Calif., 1983-86; chmn. adv. bd. Crisis Nursery of Bay Area, Concord, 1983-86; adv. bd. Oakland A's Baseball Team, 1984-85, Battered Women, 1983—; pres. bd. dirs. Mt. Diablo Hosp. Found., 1980-81; bd. dirs. Contra Costa Council, 1980-90; mem. adv. bd. Las Trampas Sch. Mentally Retarded, chmn., 1984-90; trustee Oakland Symphony Orch., 1985-86; host Informed Viewer pub. svc. program Sta. KFCB-TV. Recipient Spl. Merit award State of Calif., 1982, Charles E. Scripps award Outstanding Contbn. in the Promotion of Literacy, 1988, 2 Internat. Silver Angel awards, 1st pl. for lit. program Calif. Newspaper Pub.'s Assn., 1988; named Calif. Assembly Woman of Yr. Mem. Am. Newspaper Pub. Assn. (ednl. svcs. com. 1988—), Gospel Music Assn., ASCAP, Nat. TV Acad. Arts & Scis., Calif. Cattlemen's Assn., Cancer of the Prostate Cure, Walnut Creek Rotary, Blackhawk Country Club. Republican. Christian. Avocation: horses. Office: Contra Costa Times Lesher Comm Inc 2640 Shadelands Dr Walnut Creek CA 94598-2513

LESHER, RICHARD LEE, professional society administrator; b. Doylesburg, Pa., Oct. 28, 1933; s. Richard E. Lesher and Rosalie Orabelle (Meredith) Lesher Ehrhart; m. Agnes Marie Plocki, June 13, 1981; children by previous marriage: Douglas Allen, Laurie Lynn, Betsy Lee, Craig Collin. BBA, U. Pitts., 1958; MS, Pa. State U., 1960; DBA, Ind. U., 1963, LLD (hon.), 1979; D of Pub. Service (hon.), Ferris State Coll., 1981; DBA (hon.), Lawrence Inst. Tech., 1985. Asst. prof. Coll. Commerce and Adminstrn., Ohio State U., Columbus, 1963-64; cons. NASA, Washington, 1964-65; dep. asst. adminstr. NASA, 1965-66, asst. adminstr., 1966-69; bus. and mgmt. cons. Washington, 1969-71; pres. Nat. Ctr. for Resource Recovery, Washington, 1971-75, U.S. C. of C., Washington, 1975—; bd. dirs. G&L Realty Corp.; mem. bd. advs. CORDECOM, Norfolk So. Corp. Author: Economic Progres...It's Everybody's Business, 1980, Meltdown on Main Street: How Small Business is Leading the Revolution Against Big Government, 1996; syndicated newspaper columnist; participant (syndicated weekly TV show) It's Your Business. Mem. bd. visitors Coll. Bus. Adminstrn. Pa. State U.; mem. Sch. Bus. Dean's Adv. Coun. Ind. U. With U.S. Army, 1954-56. Recipient Superior Achievement award NASA, 1968, Exceptional Svc. award, 1968, Alumni Achievement award Pa. State U., 1976, Acad. of Alumni Fellows award Ind. U., 1977, Disting. Alumni Svc. award, 1995, Religious Heritage award, 1978, Horatio Alger award, 1980, Bicentennial medal of distinction U. Pitts., 1987, Golden Exec. medal Gen. C. of C. of Taiwan, 1988, Disting. Alumni fellow Pa. State U., 1990, Assn. of Yr. award Assn. Trends, 1994, Disting. Alumni Svc. award Ind. U., 1995. Mem. Am. Soc. Assn. Execs. (Spl. Key award 1992), Washington Soc. Assn. Execs., Am. C. of C. Execs. (bd. dirs.), Congl. Country Club, Met. Club, Phi Alpha Kappa, Beta Gamma Sigma (dir.'s table, nat. award 1977). Avocations: golfing, fishing, horseback riding, tennis. Office: C of C of the USA 1615 H St NW Washington DC 20062-0001

LESHER, ROBERT OVERTON, lawyer; b. Phoenix, Apr. 6, 1921; s. Charles Zaner and Alice Marguerite (Heckman) L.; children: Stephen Harrison, Janet Kay. BA, U. Ariz., 1942, LLB, 1949. Bar: Ariz. 1949, Ill. 1949. Atty. A. T. & Santa Fe Ry., 1949-54; pvt. practice law Tucson, 1954—; ptnr. Lesher & Williams, Tucson, 1960—; adj. prof. Law Sch., U. Ariz., 1954-84; mem. Supreme Ct. Ariz., 1960. With AUS, 1942-46, 50-52. Fellow Am. Coll. Trial Lawyers; mem. Am. Law Inst., Am. Bd. Trial Advs. (diplomate), Internat. Assn. Ins. Counsel, Tucson Country Club. Home: 659 N Richey Tucson AZ 85716-5102 Office: 3773 E Broadway Blvd Tucson AZ 85716-5409

LESHER, WILLIAM RICHARD, retired academic administrator; b. Carlisle, Pa., Nov. 14, 1924; s. David Luther and Carrie LaVerne (Adams) L.; m. Veda E. Van Etten, June 16, 1946; children—Eileen Fern, Martha Zoe Lesher Keough. Th.B., Atlantic Union Coll., South Lancaster, Mass., 1946; M.A., Andrews U., 1964; Ph.D., NYU, 1970. Ordained to ministry Seventh-day Adventist Ch., 1951. Pastor No. New Eng. Conf. Seventh-day Adventists, 1946-56; pastor, mission dir. Delta sect. Nile Union Seventh-day Adventists, Alexandria, Egypt, 1957-58; prin. Nile Union Acad., Cairo, Egypt, 1959-61; sec. Middle East Div. Seventh-day Adventists Beirut, Lebanon, 1962-64; assoc. prof. religion, dir. summer sch., asst. to pres. Atlantic Union Coll., 1964-71; assoc. dir. Sabbath sch. dept. Gen. Conf. Seventh-day Adventists, Washington, 1971-79; dir. Bibl. Research Inst., Gen. Conf. Seventh-day Adventists, Washington, 1979-84; gen. v.p. Gen. Conf. Seventh-day Adventists, Washington, 1981-84; pres. Andrews U., Berrien Springs, Mich., 1984-94; ret., 1994. Author: Tips for Teachers, 1979; editor adult Sabbath Sch. lessons, 1971-79, studies in sanctuary and atonement, 1980-81; contbr. articles to religious jours. Recipient Founders Day award NYU, 1970. Home: 4703 Greenfield Dr Berrien Springs MI 49103-9566

LESHY, JOHN D., lawyer, legal educator; b. Winchester, Ohio, Oct. 7, 1944; s. John and Dolores (King) L.; m. Helen M. Sandalls, Dec. 15, 1973; 1 child, David Alexander. AB cum laude, Harvard U., 1966, JD magna cum laude, 1969. Trial atty. Civil Rights Divsn. Dept. Justice, Washington, 1969-72; atty. Natural Resources Def. Coun., Palo Alto, Calif., 1972-77; assoc. solicitor energy and resources Dept. Interior, Washington, 1977-80; prof. law Ariz. State U., Tempe, 1980—; spl. counsel to chair Natural Resources Com. U.S. Ho. Reps., Washington, 1992-93; solicitor Dept. Interior, 1993—; cons. Calif. State Land Commn., N.Mex. Atty. Gen., Western Govs. Assn., Congl. Rsch. Svc., Ford Found.; mem. com. Onshore Oil & Gas Leasing, NAS Nat. Rsch. Coun., 1989-90; vis. prof. Sch. Law U. San Diego, 1990. Author: The Mining Law: A Study in Perpetual Motion, 1987, The Arizona State Constitution, 1993; co-author Federal Public Land and Resources Law, 3d edit., 1992; contbr. articles, book chpts. to profl. jours., environ. jours. Bd. dirs. Ariz. Ctr. Law in Pub. Interest, 1981-86; mem. Gov.'s Task Force Recreation on Fed. Lands, 1985-86, Gov.'s Task Force Environ. Impact Assessment, 1990, City of Phoenix Environ. Quality Commn., 1987-90. Robinson Cox vis. fellow U. Western Australia Law Sch., Perth, 1985, rsch. fellow U. Southampton, Eng., 1986; Ford Found. grantee, Resources for the Future grantee. Democrat. Avocations: piano, hiking, whitewater rafting, photography. Office: Department of the Interior Solicitor 1849 C St NW Washington DC 20240-0001

LESIKAR, RAYMOND VINCENT, business administration educator; b. Rogers, Tex., June 29, 1922; s. Vince E. and Albina J. (Stanislaw) L.; m. Lu Clay Allen, July 7, 1945 (dec. July 1993); children: Patricia Lesikar King, Raymond Vincent. B.B.A., U. Tex., 1947, M.B.A., 1948, Ph.D., 1954. With Douglas Aircraft Co., 1941-42, Sears, Roebuck & Co., 1947; instr. Tex. Christian U., 1948-49; asst. prof. U. Tex., 1949-54; faculty La. State U., Baton Rouge, 1954-77; prof. bus. adminstrn. La. State U., 1959—, chmn. dept. mgmt., 1959-77; dean La. State U. (Coll. Bus. Adminstrn.), 1963-64, 72-73, prof. emeritus, 1977—; adj. prof. U. Tex., Austin, 1977-79; prof., chmn. dept. mgmt. U. North Tex., Denton, 1979-88; guest prof. univs., People's Republic China, spring 1982, 83, 84; cons. in field. Author: Business Communication: Theory and Application, 1968, 7th edit. 1993, Report Writing for Business, 9th edit., 1994, Introduction to Business: A Societal Approach, 1972, 3d rev. edit., 1979, Productive Business Writing, 1959, Business Report Writing, 1957, How to Write Reports, 1974, 2d rev. edit., 1984, Basic Business Communication, 1979, 7th rev. edit., 1996; contbr. articles to profl. jours. Served with AUS, 1943-46. Fellow Am. Bus. Communication Assn. (pres. 1961); mem. S.W. Social Sci. Assn. (pres. 1967), Acad. Mgmt., Internat. Communication Assn., Internat. Soc. Gen. Semantics, Horseshoe Bay Country Club, Beta Gamma Sigma, Phi Kappa Phi, Sigma Iota Epsilon. Home and Office: PO Box 7912 Horseshoe Bay TX 78657-9203

LESK, I. ARNOLD, electrical engineer; b. Regina, Sask., Can., Jan. 26, 1927. BSc, U. Alta., 1948; MS, U. Ill., 1949, PhD, 1951. V.p. tech. staff Motorola Inc. Fellow IEEE; mem. Am. Phys. Soc., Electrochem. Soc., Sigma Xi, Eta Kappa Nu, Phi Kappa Phi, Pi Mu Epsilon. Office: Motorola Inc 5005 E McDowell Rd MS A102 Phoenix AZ 85008*

LESKO, HARRY JOSEPH, transportation company executive; b. Cleve., Dec. 6, 1920; s. Theodore Prokop and Bertha Barbara (Trojack) L.; m. Evelyn Martha Culley, Feb. 3, 1945; children—Harry Richard, Larry J., Garry E., Mark J., John M. B.B.A., Cleve. State U., 1956. Schedule analyst Cleve. Ry. System, 1938-40; pres., dir. Greyhound Lines, Inc., Phoenix, 1940—; pres. Atlantic Greyhound Lines of Va., Inc.; v.p. Gelco Bus Leasing Co., 1979—; pres. Trailways Lines Inc., Dallas, 1979—; pres., dir. The Trailways Corp., Trailways, Inc.; dir. Trailways Lines Inc. (25 subs.), Southeastern Stages, Inc., Atlanta, N.Mex. Transp. Co., Roswell, KG Lines, Tulsa, Okla. Transp. Co., Lubbock, Tex., Jefferson Lines Inc., Mpls., Kerrville Bus. Co., Tex., Continental Lines, Amarillo, Tex., Service Coach Co., Jacksonville, Fla., Gen. Fire and Casualty Co. Served to capt. USMC, 1942-46. Mem. Am. Bus. Assn. (dir.). Republican. Roman Catholic. Club: Brookhaven Country.

LESKO, LEONARD HENRY, Egyptologist, educator; b. Chgo., Aug. 14, 1938; s. Matthew Edward and Josephine Bernice (Jaszczak) L.; m. Barbara Jadwiga Switalski, Dec. 29, 1966. B.A., Loyola U., Chgo., 1961, M.A., 1964; Ph.D., U. Chgo., 1969; M.A. ad eundem, Brown U., 1983. Tchr. Quigley Prep. Sem. South, Chgo., 1961-64; Egyptologist, epigrapher, epigraphic survey Oriental Inst., U. Chgo., Luxor, Egypt, 1964-65; acting instr. U. Calif. at Berkeley, 1966-67, acting asst. prof., 1967-68, asst. prof., 1968-72, asso. prof., 1972-77, prof. Egyptology, 1977-82, dir. Center Nr. Eastern Studies, 1973-75, chmn. dept., 1975-77, 79-81, chmn. grad. program in ancient history and archeology, 1978-79, chmn. humanities council, 1980-81; dir. Seila project, 1981; C.E. Wilbour prof. Egyptology, chmn. dept. Brown U., 1982—; chmn. faculty, faculty exec. com., 1992-93. Author: The Ancient Egyptian Book of Two Ways, 1972, Glossary of the Late Ramesside Letters, 1975, King Tut's Wine Cellar, 1977, Index of the Spells on Egyptian Middle Kingdom Coffins and Related Documents, 1979; co-author: Religion in Ancient Egypt, 1991, Pharoah's Workers: The Villagers of Deir el-Medina, 1994; editor: A Dictionary of Late Egyptian, vol. I, 1982, vol. II, 1984, vol. III, 1987, vol. IV, 1989, vol. V, 1990, Egyptological Studies in Honor of Richard A. Parker, 1986; contbr. articles to profl. publs. and encys. Recipient award computer oriented rsch. in humanities Am. Coun. Learned Socs., 1973; NEH fellow, 1970-71, grantee, 1975-79, co-dir. Summer Inst., 1995; FIAT faculty fellow U. Torino, 1990. Mem. Am. Rsch. Ctr. in Egypt (gov. 1973-75), Am. Oriental Soc., Archeol. Inst. Am. (pres. San Francisco chpt. 1976-78, pres. Narragansett chpt. 1994-95), Internat. Assn. Egyptologists, Egypt Exploration Soc., Found. Egyptologique Rein Elisabeth, Soc. Francaise d'Egyptologie, U.S. Lighthouse Soc., Lighthouse Preservation Soc., Explorers Club. Office: Brown U Dept Egyptology PO Box 1899 Providence RI 02912-1899

LESKOVAR, BRANKO, electrical engineeer, researcher; b. Zagreb, Croatia, July 2, 1930. Diplom-ingenieur, U. Zagreb, 1954, DSc in Electronics and Elec. Comm., 1963. Sect. leader, electronics rschr. Lawrence Berkeley Lab. Fellow IEEE (guest editor IEEE Transactions on Nuclear Sci. 1982, vice chmn. edn. and continued profl. devel. com. Nuclear and Plasma Scis. Soc. 1981—, tech. program com. mem. IEEE Nuclear Sci. Symposia 1980-86, vice chmn. NPSS San Francisco Bay Area Coun. 1978-83); mem. AAAS, N.Y. Acad. Scis., Croatian Acad. Scis. and Arts (corr.), Sigma Xi (sr.). Office: Univ California Lawrence Berkeley Lab Electronics Rsch Berkeley CA 94720*

LESLIE, GERRIE ALLEN, immunologist; b. Red Deer, Alta., Can., Nov. 19, 1941; s. John Allen and Lily Elizabeth (von Hollen) L.; m. Anna Magdalene Madsen Ladefoged, July 31, 1965; children: Kirsten, John Gerrie. BS in Pharmacy, U. Alta., 1962, MS in Microbiology, 1965; PhD, U. Hawaii, 1968. Postdoctoral fellow U. Fla., Gainesville, 1968-70; prof. Tulane U. Med. Sch., New Orleans, 1970-74, Oreg. Health Scis. U., Portland, 1974-86; pres., chief exec. officer Immunology Cons. Lab., Lake Oswego, Oreg., 1979—; sci. adviser Epitope Inc., Beaverton, Oreg., 1987-91, Ultra Diagnostics, Seattle, 1987-91; cons. to biotech. cos. S.Am., Thailand, U.S. Author and co-author 110 sci. articles. Grantee NIH,1968-86, NSF, 1970-85, Kroc Found., 1970-86, Cancer Found., Med. Rsch. Found., John Hartford Found., others. Mem. Am. Assn. Immunology, Oreg. Polled Hereford Assn. (bd. dirs. 1991—, pres. 1996—). Lutheran. Avocations: stamp collection, coin collecting, fishing, farming.

LESLIE, HENRY ARTHUR, lawyer, retired banker; b. Troy, Ala., Oct. 15, 1921; s. James B. and Alice (Minchener) L.; m. Anita Doyle, Apr. 5, 1943; children: Anita Lucinda Leslie Bagby, Henry Arthur Jr. B.S., U. Ala., 1942, J.D., 1948; J.S.D., Yale U., 1959; grad., Sch. Banking, Rutgers U., 1964. Bar: Ala. 1948. Asst. prof. bus. law U. Ala., 1948-50, 52-54; prof. law, asst. dean U. Ala. (Sch. Law), 1954-59; v.p. trust officer Birmingham Trust Nat. Bank, Ala., 1959-64; sr. v.p., trust officer Union Bank & Trust Co., Montgomery, Ala., 1964-73; sr. v.p., sr. loan officer Union Bank & Trust Co., 1973-76, exec. v.p., 1976-78, pres., chief exec. officer, 1978-91, also bd. dirs.; ret., 1991; sole practice Montgomery, Ala., 1991—; mem. Ala. Oil and Gas Bd., 1984-85; dir. First Fin. Mgmt. Corp., 1981—. Pres. Downtown Unltd., 1983-84; mem. Ala. Bd. Bar Examiners, 1973-78, Bus. Com. for Arts, Inc.; bd. dirs. YMCA, 1992—; chmn. bd. Ala. Bankers Found., 1971-77; trustee Ala. Assn. Ind. Colls. Decorated Bronze Star. Mem. ABA, Ala. Bar Assn., Montgomery Bar Assn. (Liberty Bell award 1989), Ala. Ind. Bankers (chmn. 1983-84), Ala. Bankers Assn. (trust div. pres. 1963-65), Ind. Bankers Assn. Am. (dir. 1983-90), Farrah Order Jurisprudence (pres. 1973), Order of Coif Alumni, Newcomen Soc. N.Am., Montgomery C. of C. (dir. 1983-84, pres. 1987-88), Maxwell Officers Club, Montgomery Country Club, Kiwanis, Delta Sigma Pi, Phi Delta Phi, Omicron Delta Kappa, Pi Kappa Phi. Episcopalian (past sr. warden). Home: 3332 Boxwood Dr Montgomery AL 36111-1702 Office: 456 S Court St Montgomery AL 36104-4102

LESLIE, JACQUES ROBERT, JR., journalist; b. L.A., Mar. 12, 1947; s. Jacques Robert and Aleen (Wetstein) L.; m. Leslie Wernick, June 21, 1980; 1 child, Sarah Alexandra. BA, Yale U., 1968. Tchr. New Asia Coll., Chinese U., Hong Kong, 1968-70; free-lance journalist Washington, 1970-71; fgn. corr. L.A. Times, Saigon, 1972-73, Phnom Penh, 1973, Washington, 1974; chief New Delhi (India) bur. L.A. Times, 1974-75, Madrid, 1975-76; chief Hong Kong bur. L.A. Times, 1976-77; freelance journalist, 1977—. Author: The Mark: A War Correspondent's Memoir of Vietnam and Cambodia. Recipient Best Fgn. Corr. award Sigma Delta Chi, 1973, citation reporting Overseas Press Club, 1973. Home: 124 Reed St Mill Valley CA 94941-3448

LESLIE, JOHN WALTER, development consultant; b. Norfolk, Va., Sept. 18, 1929; s. John Walter and Ella Arden (Squires) L.; m. Audrey May Munford, Apr. 9, 1957. B.A., Coll. William and Mary, 1952; student, Mich. State U., 1957-58, U. Oreg., 1962-64; M.A., Am. U., 1968. From copy boy to sports reporter Norfolk Virginian-Pilot, 1944-49; sports reporter Newport News (Va.) Daily Press, 1950-52, asst. sports editor, 1956-57; asst. news editor Mich. State U., 1957-58; asso. dir. Ketchum, Inc., 1958-60; dir. devel. and pub. relations Lewis and Clark Coll., 1960-63; exec. v.p. Am. Coll. Pub. Relations Assn., 1963-74; pres. Instl. Advancement Consultants, Inc., N.Y.C., 1974-80; sr. v.p. Brakeley, John Price Jones, Inc., N.Y.C., 1974-80; v.p. devel. U. Houston System, 1981-85; pres. John W. Leslie Inc., Potomac, Md., 1986—. Author: Focus on Understanding and Support: A Study in College Management, 1969, Seeking the Competitive Dollar, 1971; contbr. articles to profl. jours. Served to 1st lt. USAF, 1952-56. Home: 8004 Grand Teton Dr Rockville MD 20854-4074

LESLIE, JOHN WEBSTER, JR., communications company executive; b. Milw., July 20, 1954; s. John and Joanne Marie (Chamberlain) L.; m. Laura Elizabeth Bafford, June 7, 1986; children: Finn Elizabeth, John Webster III. BS in Fgn. Service, Georgetown U., 1976. Legis. asst. Senator Edward Kennedy, Washington, 1976-80; campaign dir. northeast region Kennedy for Pres., Washington, 1980-81; polit. dir. Senator Edward Kennedy for U.S. Senate, Washington, 1981-82; exec. dir. Fund for Dem. Majority, Washington, 1982-83; pres. Sawyer/Miller Group, N.Y.C., 1983-93; ptnr. Robinson Lerer Sawyer Miller, N.Y.C., 1993—; Bd. dirs. Internat. Policy Research, Inc., N.Y.C., Creative Media, Inc., N.Y.C. Contbr. articles to profl. jours.; speaker in field. Bd. dirs. Nat. Student Edn. Fund, Washington, 1977-79. Fellow Circumnavigators Found., Am. Assn. Polit. Cons. Roman Catholic. Club: N.Y. Athletic. Office: Robinson Lerer Sawyer Mille 75 Rockefeller Plz Fl 5 New York NY 10019-6908

LESLIE, JOHN WILLIAM, public relations and advertising executive; b. Indpls., Nov. 22, 1923; s. John Edward and Catherine (Harris) L.; m. Joan Williams, Dec. 26, 1970; 1 dau. by previous marriage, Catherine Alexandra. Student, U.S. Naval Acad., 1943-44, George Washington U., 1949, Indsl. Coll. Armed Forces, 1956. Dep. excise adminstr. Ind., 1946-47; pvt. pub. relations bus., 1947-49; dir. pub. relations Ind. Democratic State Central Com., 1948-49, Ind. Dept. Vets. Affairs, 1949; press officer Dept. Labor, 1949-51, acting asst. dir. info., 1951-52, asst. dir., 1952-56, dep. dir., 1956-59, dir., 1959-81; sr. assoc. Kamber Group, Washington, 1981-84; counselor Kamber Group, 1984-88, exec. v.p., COO, 1988—, also bd. dirs.; mem., dir. pub. D.C. Com. Employment Physically Handicapped, 1952-53; charter mem. U.S. Sr. Exec. Svc., 1979—. Author numerous articles in field. Advt. cons. Pres.'s Com. on Youth Employment, 1964-80; U.S. del Internat. Graphic Design Coun., Japan, 1973; trustee Washington chpt. Leukemia Soc. Am., 1976-82; chmn. Pub. Printers Adv. Com. on Printing and Publs, 1977-79. Served with USN and USNR, 1941-46. Recipient commendation President's Com. Employment Physically Handicapped, 1954; Disting. Service award Dept. Labor, 1962; citation outstanding service Navy Dept., 1964; Presdl. citation, 1966; Merit award Internat. Labor Press Assn., 1969; Disting. Career Service award Dept. Labor, 1973; Communications award Ga. chpt. Pub. Relations Soc. Am., 1972; Sec. Labor's Recognition award, 1974; Communicator of Yr. award Nat. Assn. Govt. Communicators, 1981. Mem. Am. Assn. Polit. Cons., Am. League Lobbyists, Nat. Press Club, English Speaking Union. Episcopalian. Home: 4290 Massachusetts Ave NW Washington DC 20016-5558 Office: Kamber Group 1920 L St NW # 700 Washington DC 20036-5004

LESLIE, LYNN MARIE, secondary education educator; b. Lake City, Fla., Nov. 17, 1948; d. Billy Verlyn Spooner and Dorothy Marie (Odom) Loomis; m. Roy Hamner Leslie, Nov. 25, 1967; children: Kim Ball, Billy Leslie, Dodi Leslie. BS in Edn., Trevecca U., 1970; ME in Spl. Edn., Tenn. State U., 1987. Cert. career ladder III, Tenn. Tchr. Leesburg (Fla.) Elem. Sch., 1970-71, Wessington Pl. Elem. Sch., Hendersonville, Tenn., 1974-87, Knox Doss Mid. Sch., Hendersonville, 1987—; mem. Sumner County Ins. Trust, Gallatin, Tenn., 1991-96. Mem. Sumner County Edn. Assn. (pres. 1991-92, 95-96, sec. 1992-95). Mem. Ch. of Nazarene. Avocations: reading, cross stitch. Home: 1032 Carriage Hill Pl Hendersonville TN 37075

LESLIE, NAN S., nursing educator, womens' health nurse; b. Pitts.; d. Peter E. and Verda S. (Sill) Scolere; m. David C. Leslie, Aug. 13, 1966; children: Erin Lyn, Scott David. Nursing diploma, Presbyn. U. Hosp. Sch. Nursing, 1965; BSN summa cum laude, U. Pitts., 1971, MN, 1973, PhD, 1989. RN, Pa., W.Va.; registered nurse practitioner. Staff nurse ICU Presbyn. U. Hosp., Pitts., 1965-66; staff nurse ICU Temple U. Hosp., Phila., 1966-68, asst. head nurse ICU, 1968-69; staff nurse ICU Montefiore Hosp., Pitts., 1971; founder, bd. dirs., various positions Circle Cmty. Food Pantry, Wash., Pa., 1978-83; grad. rsch. asst. U. Pitts., 1985-86; lectr. nursing rsch. Carlow Coll., Pitts., 1987-89; asst. prof. Sch. Nursing W.Va. U., Morgantown, 1990—. Mem. rev. bd. Perspectives in Psychol. Care, 1989-91. Bd. dirs. Family Svcs., Wash., 1979-82; dist. coord. U.S. Pony Club, Brush Run, Pa., 1989-90. NIMH trainee U. Pitts., 1971-73; rsch. grantee W.Va. U., 1992-93, CDC Cancer Screening grantee, 1991-93. Mem. ANA, AWHONN (cert. registered nurse practitioner), So. Nursing Rsch. Soc., Oncology Nursing Soc., Presbyn. Univ. Hosp. Nurses Alumnae Assn., Sigma Theta Tau. Avocations: painting, horses, classical music. Home: 2262 N Main St Washington PA 15301-6150 Office: WVa U Sch Nursing Byrd Health Scis Ctr Morgantown WV 26506

LESLIE, ROBERT LORNE, lawyer; b. Adak, Alaska, Feb. 24, 1947; s. J. Lornie and L. Jean (Conelly) L.; children—Lorna Jean, Elizabeth Allen. B.S., U.S. Mil. Acad., 1969; J.D., Hastings Coll. Law, U. Calif.-San Francisco, 1974. Bar: Calif. 1974, D.C. 1979, U.S. Dist. Ct. (no. dist.) Calif. 1974, U.S. Ct. Claims 1975, U.S. Tax Ct. 1975, U.S. Ct. Appeals (9th and D.C. cirs.), U.S. Ct. Mil. Appeals 1980, U.S. Supreme Ct. 1980. Commd. 2d lt. U.S. Army, 1969, advanced through grades to maj., 1980; govt. trial atty. West Coast Field Office, Contract Appeals, Litigation Div. and Regulatory Law Div., Office JAG, Dept. Army, San Francisco, 1974-77; sr. trial atty. and team chief Office of Chief Trial Atty., Dept. Army, Washington, 1977-80; ptnr. McInerney & Dillon, Oakland, Calif., 1980—; lectr. on govt. contracts CSC, Continuing Legal Edn. Program; lectr. in govt. procurement U.S. Army Materiel Command. Col. USAR. Decorated Silver Star, Purple Heart. Mem. ABA, Fed. Bar Assn., Associated Gen. Contractors, The Beavers. Office: Ordway Building Fl 18 Oakland CA 94612-3610

LESLIE, SEAVER, artist; b. Boston, Aug. 22, 1946; s. John Frederick and Joan (Warland) L.; m. Anne Cleland Rogers; children: Genevieve, Marion, Frances. BFA, RISD, 1969, MEd, 1970. Exhibited in shows at Hirschl & Adler Gallery, N.Y.C., 1981, Tatistcheff Gallery, N.Y.C., 1982, Decordova Mus., Lincoln, Mass., 1989, Maine Coast Artists, Rockport, 1993, Portland (Maine) Mus. of Art, 1993. Author: 12 Points: Putting the Case for Customary Measure, 1979, Why America Should Not Go Metric, 1993. Founder Ams. for Customary Weight and Measure, N.Y.C., The Morris Farm Trust; co-founder Maine Trans. Coalition, Wicasset. Office: Old Stone Farm Wiscasset ME 04578

LESLIE, SEYMOUR MARVIN, communications executive; b. N.Y.C., Dec. 16, 1922; s. Harry and Fay (Goldstein) L.; m. Barbara Miller, Mar. 30, 1947; children: Ellen, Jane, Carol. EE, Syracuse U., 1945; grad., Advanced Mgmt. Program, Harvard U., 1971; DHL, Hofstra U., 1974. Sales mgr. Voco, Inc., N.Y.C., 1946-52; founder Pickwick Internat., Inc., Woodbury, N.Y., 1953, chmn. bd., pres., 1953-77; chmn. Leslie Group, Inc., 1977—; pres. CBS Video Enterprises div. CBS, Inc., N.Y.C., 1980-82; chmn., pres., chief exec. officer MGM/UA Home Entertainment Group, Inc., 1982-87; co-chmn. Leslie/Linton Entertainment Corp., 1993—; bd. dirs. Shorewood Packaging Corp., Gametek Corp., Allied Digital Corp., Songwriters Hall of Fame; vis. disting. prof. Syracuse U. Sch. Music, 1984. Active Boy Scouts Am., 1947-50; mem. corp. adv. coun. Syracuse U.; mem. coun. Hofstra U.; bd. govs. Anti Defamation League, 1960—; v.p., dir. T.J. Martell Found.; v.p. Friars Found. Sgt. U.S. Army, 1942-46, PTO. Recipient Presdl. award Nat. Assn. Record Merchandisers, 1976, Disting. Svc. award, 1977, Outstanding Arents Alumnus award Syracuse U., 1978; named Man of Yr. Time Mag., 1987; named to Video Hall of Fame, 1987. Mem. ASCAP, N.Y. Coun. for Humanities, Record Industry Assn. Am. (profl. group), B'nai B'rith, Friars Club, Harvard Club, Harvard Bus. Club. Office: Leslie Group Inc 1370 Ave Of The Americas New York NY 10019-4602

LESLIE, (ROBERT) TIM, state legislator; b. Ashland, Oreg., Feb. 4, 1942; s. Robert Tabor Leslie and Virginia (Hall) P.; m. Clydene Ann Fisher, June 15, 1962; children: Debbie, Scott. BA in Political Sci., Calif. State U., Long Beach, 1963; MPA, U. Southern Calif., L.A., 1969. Prin. analyst Sacramento County Exec. Office, Calif., 1965-69; cons. Assm. W. & M. Commn., Sacramento, 1965-72; prin. legis. rep. County Sups. Assn., Sacramento, 1972-80; founder bd. dirs. Comm. Act. Against Drg., Sacramento, 1975-83; v.p. Moss & Thompson, Inc., Sacramento, 1980-84; exec. v.p. Kuhl. Corp., Sacramento, 1984-86; assemblyman Calif. State Legislature, Sacramento, 1986-91, senator, 1991—; vice chmn. Appropriations Com., Judiciary Com.; mem. Health Com., Natural Resources Com. Recipient Hang Tough award Nat. Tax Limitation Com., Calif., 1987; named Legislator of Yr., Sacramento County Taxpayers League and Osteo. Surgeons of Calif., 1990, Calif. Rife and Pistol Assn., 1993, Women in Timber, 1994, Safari Club Internat., 1994. Republican. Presbyterian. Capital office: 4081 State Capital Sacramento CA 95814 District office: 1200 Melody Ln Ste 110 Roseville CA 95678-5189

LESLIE, WILLIAM BRUCE, history educator; b. Orange, N.Y., July 21, 1944; s. William and Annette (Riedell) L.; children: William Andrew, Sarah Acton; 1 step-child, Dorothy Kaul. BA, Princeton U., 1966; PhD, Johns Hopkins U., 1971. Asst. prof. history SUNY, Brockport, 1970-79, assoc. prof., 1979-76, prof., 1996—; vis. prof. Jordanhill Coll., 1972, dir. MA in History program, 1984-90; co-dir. SUNY Social Sci. Program, London, 1978-79, 82-83, 89; mem. editorial bd. Hist. of Higher Edn. Ann., 1991—. Author: Gentlemen and Scholars, 1993; contbr. articles and revs. to profl jours. Fulbright fellow to Denmark, 1996-97. Mem. Orgn. Am. Historians, Am. Hist. Assn., History of Edn. Soc., Adirondack Mountain Club, Western Monroe Hist. Soc., Amnesty Internat., Princeton Club N.Y., Phi Alpha Theta. Democrat. Avocations: camping, travel, gardening. Office: SUNY History Dept Brockport NY 14420-2956

LESLIE, WILLIAM CAIRNS, metallurgical engineering educator; b. Dundee, Scotland, Jan. 6, 1920; came to U.S., 1925, naturalized, 1940; m. Florence M. Hall, 1948; 1 dau. B.Metall. Engring., Ohio State U., 1947, M.Sc., 1948, Ph.D., 1949. Metallurgist U.S. Steel Research Lab., Kearny,

N.J., 1949-53; assoc. dir. staff research and devel. Thompson Products, Inc., Cleve., 1953-54; with U.S. Steel Corp., Monroeville, Pa., 1954-73; mgr. phys. metallurgy E.C. Bain Lab. for Fundamental Research, 1963-73; prof. materials engrng. U. Mich., 1973-85, prof. emeritus, 1985—; adj. prof. metallurgy Bklyn. Poly. Inst., 1952-53; Battelle vis. prof. metallurgy Ohio State U., 1964-65; vis. prof. U. Melbourne, Australia, 1979; Am. Soc. Metals and AIME rep. to EJC Metric Council and Am. Nat. Metric Council, 1971-80; mem. ship research com. NRC, 1978-81; Garofalo lectr. Northwestern U., 1977; U.S. rep. Internat. Conf. Strength of Metals and Alloys, 1970-82; mem. Charles Hatchett award panel Metals Soc. Gt. Britain, 1978-81; cons. in field; mem. adv. com. div. metals and ceramics Oak Ridge Nat. Lab., 1974-75; mem. com. on basic research, advisor to Army Research Office, Durham, N.C., 1973-78; mem. ad hoc com. on non-magnetic structural steels Nat. Materials Adv. Bd., 1973-74. Author: The Physical Metallurgy of Steels, 1981; Contbr. articles to profl. jours. Served to 1st lt. C.E. U.S. Army, 1943-46. Named Disting. Alumnus Ohio State U. Coll. Engring., 1967, Disting. Alumnus lectr., 1984. Fellow Am. Soc. Metals Internat. (chmn. publs. com. 1966-68, mem. metals sci. divsn. coun. 1970-75, Pitts. chpt. Andrew Carnegie lectr. 1970, Edward DeMille Campbell lectr. 1971, Phila. chpt. Albert Sauveur lectr. 1975, Cleve. chpt. Zay Jeffried lectr. 1975, hon. mem. 1986, Barrett medal Rocky Mtn. chpt. 1992, Gold medal 1995), Inst. Materials of Gt. Britain (fellow 1984), Metall. Soc. (chmn. Inst. Metals divsn. 1971-72, bd. dirs. 1971-72, sr. fellow), Internat. Metallographic Soc. (Henry Clifton Sorby award 1991); mem. AIME (v.p., dir. 1975), Krumb lectr. 1967), Henry Marion Howe lectr. 1982), AAAS, Sigma Xi, Tau Beta Pi. Patentee in field. Home and Office: RR 7 Box 7416 Palmyra VA 22963-9510

LESLY, PHILIP, public relations counsel; b. Chgo., May 29, 1918; m. Ruth Edwards, Oct. 17, 1940 (div. 1971); 1 son, Craig.; m. Virginia Barnes, May 11, 1984. BS magna cum laude, Northwestern U., 1940. Asst. to news editor Chgo. Herald & Examiner, 1935-37; copywriter advt. dept. Sears, Roebuck & Co., Chgo., 1940-41; asst. dir. publicity Northwestern U., 1941-42; account exec. Theodore R. Sills & Co. (pub. rels.), Chgo., 1942; v.p. Theodore R. Sills & Co. (pub. rels.), 1943, exec. v.p., 1945; dir. pub. rels. Ziff-Davis Pub. Co., 1945-46; exec. v.p. Harry Coleman & Co. (pub. rels.), 1947-49; pres. Philip Lesly Co. (pub. rels.), Chgo., 1949—; lectr. pub. rels., pub. opinion to bus. and sch. groups. Co-author: Public Relations: Principles and Procedures, 1945, Everything and the Kitchen Sink, 1955; author: The People Factor, 1974, Selections from Managing the Human Climate, 1979, How We Discommunicate, 1979, Overcoming Opposition, 1984, Bonanzas and Fool's Gold, 1987; bimonthly Managing the Human Climate; editor: Public Relations in Action, 1974, Public Relations Handbook, 3d rev. edit., 1967, Lesly's Public Relations Handbook, 1971, rev. edit., 1978, 83, Lesly's Handbook of Public Relations and Communications, 1991, 96; contbr. articles to bus. publs. Recipient Gold Anvil award Pub. Relations Soc. Am., 1979; voted leading active practitioner Pub. Relations Reporter Survey, 1978. Mem. Pub. Rels. Soc. Am., Phi Beta Kappa. Home and Office: 155 N Harbor Dr Apt 5311 Chicago IL 60601-7326 *One should stand out by focusing on those talents and skills that others cannot demonstrate, rather than by competing with the crowd.*

LESONSKY, RIEVA, editor-in-chief; b. N.Y.C., June 20, 1952; d. Gerald and Muriel (Cash) L. BJ, U. Mo., 1974. Researcher Doubleday & Co., N.Y.C., 1975-78; researcher Entrepreneur Mag., L.A., 1978-80, rsch. dir., 1983-84, mng. editor, 1985-86, exec. editor, 1986-87; editor Entrepreneur Mag., Irvine, Calif., 1987-90; editor-in-chief Entrepreneur Mag. Bus. Start-Ups Entrepreneur Group, Irvine, Calif., 1990—; rsch. dir. LFP Inc., L.A., 1980-82; speaker, lect. in field. Editor: 184 Businesses Anyone Can Start, 1990, Complete Guide to Owning a Home-based Business, 1990, 168 More Businesses Anyone Can Start, 1991, 111 Businesses You Can Start for Under $10,000, 1991; contbr. articles to mags. Apptd. SBA Nat. Adv. Coun., 1994-96. Named Dist. Media Advocate of Yr., Small Bus. Adminstrn., 1993, Dist. Women in Bus. Advocate, Small Bus. Adminstrn., 1995. Mem. Women's Network for Entrepreneurial Tng. (bd. dirs., advisor, nat. steering com.), Nat. Assn. Women's Bus. Advocates (bd. dirs.). Avocations: books, magazines, baseball. Office: Entrepreneur Mag Group 2392 Morse Ave Irvine CA 92714-6234

LESS, ANTHONY ALBERT, retired naval officer; b. Salem, Ohio, Aug. 31, 1937; s. Joseph Anthony and Mildred Gertrude (Bair) L.; m. Leanne Carol Kuhl, Mar. 3, 1962; children: Robyn, Pamela, Theresa, Christina. BS in Chemistry, Heidelberg Coll., 1959. Designated naval aviator. Commd. ensign USN, 1960, advanced through grades to vice adm., 1991, ret., 1994; commdg. officer USS Wichita (AOR-1), 1979-81; chief of staff Commdr. 7th Fleet, Yokosuka, Japan, 1983-84; dir. Polit. Mil Br. JCS, Washington, 1985-87; commdr. Carrier Group One, Pacific, 1987-88, Mid. East Force, Manama, Bahrain, 1988-89; dir. Plans and Policy Navy Staff, Washington, 1989-91; comdr. Naval Air Force Atlantic Fleet, Norfolk, Va., 1991-94; pres. Assn. Naval Aviation, Washington, 1994—; cons. Kaman Aerospace, Bloomfield, Conn., 1994—. Mem. Assn. Naval Aviation (pres. 1994), Soc. Naval Engrs. Roman Catholic. Avocations: racquetball, farming, reading. Office: Assn of Naval Aviation 5205 Leesburg Pike Ste 200 Falls Church VA 22041-3802

LESSARD, MICHEL M., finance company executive; b. Quebec City, Can., Aug. 31, 1939; s. Maurice and Jacqueline (Lacasse) L.; m. Doris Lamoureux; children: Eric, Christine. BA, Laval U., Quebec, 1958, B in Commerce, 1961, M in Commerce, 1962; MBA, Harvard U., 1967. With Can. Ingersoll Rand, Allied Chem. Can., DomGlass Ltd., Montreal, Que., Can.; with Credit Foncier, Montreal, 1970-86, asst. gen. mgr., treas., 1978-79, sr. asst. gen. mgr., 1979-80, exec. v.p., 1980-81, pres., dir., mem. exec. com., 1981-86, pres., chief exec. officer, 1984-86; pres. Sogexfi Inc., 1986—; pres. and CEO Immobiliere Natgen Inc., 1993-95; chmn. Mildev Real Estate Svcs.; v.p., bd. dirs. Sucana Investments Inc., Montreal; bd. dirs. Jonergin Inc., Kree Tech., Inc., Montreal, Overseas Med. Ventures N.V. Mem. Pride Can. Inc. Fellow Trust Cos. Inst., Winchester Club, Club de Golf de la Vallee du Richelieu. Home: 11 O'Reilly Apt 1503, Verdun, PQ Canada H3E 1T6

LESSARD, RAYMOND W., bishop; b. Grafton, N.D., Dec. 21, 1930. Student, St. Paul Sem., Am. Coll., Rome. Ordained priest Roman Cath. Ch. Mem. staff Congregation for Bishops, Roman Curia, 1964-73; consecrated bishop, 1973; bishop Diocese of Savannah Diocese of Savannah, Ga., 1973-95. Office: Catholic Pastoral Ctr 601 E Liberty St Savannah GA 31401-5118

LESSEM, JAN NORBERT, medical director; b. Malmo, Sweden, Apr. 7, 1948; s. Slom and Frida (Marcus) L.; m. Eva K. Löfquist, July 11, 1976; children: Martin A., Sarah E. MD, U. Lund, 1974, PhD, 1982. Med. diplomate. Intern, then resident in cardiology; assoc. prof. U. Lund, Sweden, 1981-82; med. dir. Merck, Sharp & Dohme, Rahway, N.J., 1982-83, Bristol-Myers, Evansville, Ind., 1983-85; sect. head cardiology div. Syntex Research, Palo Alto, Calif., 1986-87, sr. dept. head cardiology div., 1987-90; dir. clin. investigation SB Pharma., Phila., 1991-95; med. dir. Takeda Am., Princeton, N.J., 1995—. Contbr. over 150 articles to profl. jours. Bd. dirs. Am. Swedish Hist. Mus., Phila., 1992—. Fellow Am. Coll. Cardiology, Coll. of Physicians Phila., Swedish Soc. Cardiology, Royal Swedish Coll. Med. Jewish Youth. Club: Jewish (Malmo) (pres. 1966-73). Avocations: opera, art, books, tennis, travelling. Office: Takeda am Ste 207 101 Carnegie Ctr Princeton NJ 08540

LESSEN, LARRY LEE, federal judge; b. Lincoln, Ill., Dec. 25, 1939; s. William G. and Grace L. (Plunkett) L.; m. Susan Marian Vaughn, Dec. 5, 1964; children: Laura, Lynn, William. BA, U. Ill., 1960, JD, 1962. Bar: U.S. Bankruptcy Ct. 1964, U.S. Tax Ct. 1982, U.S. Ct. Appeals (7th cir.) 1981, U.S. Supreme Ct. 1981. Law clk. to presiding justice U.S. Dist. Ct., 1962-64; asst. state's atty. State of Ill., Danville, 1964-67; mng. ptnr. Sebat, Swanson, Banks and Lessen, Danville, 1967-85; judge U.S. Bankruptcy Ct., Danville, 1973-85, U.S. Magistrate, Danville, 1973-84; chief judge U.S. Bankruptcy Ct., Springfield, Ill., 1985-93; U.S. bankruptcy judge Springfield divsn., 1993—. Mem. ABA, Fed. Bar Assn., Sangamon County Bar Assn., Vermilion County Bar Assn., Nat. Conf. Bankruptcy Judges, Am. Bankruptcy Inst., Lincoln-Douglas Inn of Cts. Office: US Bankruptcy Ct 235 US Courthouse 600 E Monroe Springfield IL 62701

LESSEN, MARTIN, engineering educator, consulting engineer; b. N.Y.C., Sept. 6, 1920; s. Philip and Lena (Sukornik) L.; m. Elizabeth Scher, Aug. 27, 1948; children: Margot, Deborah, David. B.S.M.E., CCNY, 1940; M.M.E., NYU, 1942; Sc.D., MIT, 1948. Registered profl. engr. Mech. engr. Bklyn. Navy Yard, 1940-46; aero. research scientist NACA Cleve., 1948-49; prof. aero. engring. Pa. State U., State College, 1949-53; prof. and chmn. applied mechanics U. Pa., Phila., 1953-60; prof., chmn. dept. mech. engring U. Rochester, N.Y., 1960-70; Yates Meml. prof. engring. U. Rochester, 1967-83, Yates Meml. prof. engring. emeritus, 1983—; liaison scientist Office Naval Research, London, 1976-79; cons. Gen. Electric Co., 1954-58, RCA Co., 1957-64, Bausch & Lomb, 1965-75, Eastman Kodak Co., 1964—, Energy div. ORNL, 1984—; advisory com. Oak Ridge Nat. Lab., 1984-87. Author numerous papers in field; patentee in field. Sr. postdoctoral fellow NSF, Cambridge, Eng., 1966; Vollmer Fries hon. fellow Rensselaer Poly. Inst., Troy, N.Y., 1978; exchange lectr. Nat. Acad. Sci., USSR, 1967. Fellow ASME (founding chmn. energetics 1964), Am. Phys. Soc., AAAS. Club: Cosmos (Washington). Home and Office: 12 Country Club Dr Rochester NY 14618-3720

LESSENCO, GILBERT BARRY, lawyer; b. Balt., June 19, 1929; s. Jacob David and Sarah (Bank) L.; B.S., Johns Hopkins U., 1950; LL.B., Harvard U., 1953; m. Elaine Beitler, Sept. 3, 1952; children: Susan Donna, Amy Gail, Robert Howard. Admitted to D.C. bar, 1953; since practiced in Washington; with Wilner and Bergson, 1955-60; ptnr. Wilner & Scheiner, 1960-90, Semmes, Bowen & Semmes, 1990-95, mng. ptnr., Washington, 1992-95; of counsel Thompson, Hine and Flory, 1995—. Mem., treas. Democratic Central Com., Montgomery County, Md., 1970-74; chmn. Internat. Visitors Service Council, 1962; bd. dirs. Jewish Social Service Agy. of Greater Washington, 1978—, pres., 1984-86; bd. dirs. Mental Health Assn. of Montgomery County, 1980-84, pres., 1981-82; trustee Meridian House Found.; commr. Washington Suburban San. Commn., 1987-93, chmn., 1989-90; co-chmn., fundraiser St. Luke's House, 1989. Served to lt. USAF, 1953-55. Named Outstanding Young Lawyer of Yr., D.C. Jr. Bar, 1965. Mem. Phi Sigma Delta (v.p.). Home: 10731 Gloxinia Dr Rockville MD 20852-3442 Office: 1920 N St NW Washington DC 20036

LESSER, GERSHON MELVIN, physician, lawyer, medical and legal media commentator; b. N.Y.C., Apr. 3, 1933; s. Herman and Dora (Kronfeld) L.; m. Michelle Elyse Lesser; children: Hadrian, Aaron, Jason. BA, UCLA, 1954; MD, U. So. Calif., 1958; JD, UWLA, 1977. Atty. in pvt. practice L.A., 1977-82; med. dir. Westside Hosp., Am. Med. Inc., Beverly Hills, 1964-75; pvt. practice cardiology L.A., 1963-92; mem. pres.'s coun. Salk Inst., La Jolla, Calif.; broadcaster KGIL Radio, San Fernando Valley, 1984-92, KCRW-Nat. Pub. Radio, Santa Monica, Calif., 1980-94; med. broadcaster KTTV, Hollywood, Calif., 1984-86; med. dir. CD, L.A., 1978-89; adj. prof. law U. West L.A. Sch. Law, 1980-87; instr. internal medicine and med. malpractice, U. So. Calif. Sch. Medicine, L.A., 1963-80. Author: Growing Younger, 1987, When You Have Chest Pain, 1989; TV commentator Alive and Well, USA Cable, L.A., 1984-95. Fellow Am. Coll. Legal Medicine, Royal Soc. Health, Am. Coll. Angiology, Am. Coll. Geriatrics; mem. Am. Acad. Preventive Medicine, Am. Coll. Thoracic Medicine, Am. Soc. Internal Medicine, Sacerni Collegium, Phi Delta Epsilon. Office: 8230 Beverly Blvd Los Angeles CA 90048

LESSER, JOAN L., lawyer; b. L.A.. BA, Brandeis U., 1969; JD, U. So. Calif., 1973. Bar: Calif. 1973, U.S. Dist. Ct. (cen. dist.) Calif. 1974. Assoc. Irell and Manella, L.A., 1973-80, ptnr., 1980—; mem. planning com. Ann. Real Property Inst., Continuing Edn. of Bar, Berkeley, 1990—; speaker at profl. confs. Trustee Windward Sch.; grad. Leadership L.A., 1992. Mem. Orgn. Women Execs., Order of Coif. Office: Irell and Manella 1800 Avenue of the Stars Ste 900 Los Angeles CA 90067-4211

LESSER, JOSEPH M., retired business executive, retail store executive; b. N.Y.C., July 27, 1928; s. Jacob and Sonia (Gustow) L.; m. Sonia Rabinowitz, Nov. 26, 1948; children: Brett Paul, Peter John. BS in Social Sci., CCNY, 1949; JD, Bklyn. Law Sch., 1953. With Allied Stores Corp., 1955—, personnel and labor relations advisor, 1955-58, dir. cen. services, 1960-68; asst. to pres., 1958-60; coordinator control and ops. divs. Allied Stores Corp., 1963-65, v.p. control and ops., electronic data processing divs., 1967-80, v.p. food services div., 1967-80, pres. Alcomp Electronic Data Systems div., 1968-75; sr. v.p., exec. group mgr. Allied Stores Corp., N.Y.C., 1980—; dir., sr. v.p. Allied Stores-Penn. Ohio-Inc., N.Y.C., 1981—, Allied Cen. Stores, Inc., N.Y.C., 1984-88; sr. v.p. Allied Stores III, Inc., N.Y.C., 1985-88; dir., exec. v.p. Allied Stores-East, Inc., N.Y.C., 1986-88, ret.; exec. v.p. Internat. Collectibles Inc., 1989-92; ret.; bd. govs. Allied Stores Assocs., 1991—. Pres. Briarcliff Schs., Briarcliff Manor, N.Y., 1973; bd. dirs. North-East Council Schs., N.Y.C., 1967; life trustee Indpls. Mus. Art. Mem. Nat. Retail Mchts. Assn. (bd. dirs. 1977-79), Marco Island Art League, U.S. Power Squadrons (lt.-cruise comdr.) USCG Aux. Flotilla, Marco Island Civic Assn., Princeton Club (N.Y.C.) Calif. Yacht Club, Island Country Club, Hideaway Club (chmn. archtl. rev. com. 1991-93). Office: 2000 Royal Marco Way #603 Marco Island FL 33937

LESSER, LAURENCE, academic administrator, musician, educator; b. Los Angeles, Oct. 28, 1938; s. Moses Aaron and Rosalyne Anne (Asner) L.; m. Masuko Ushioda, Dec. 23, 1971; children—Erika, Adam. AB, Harvard U., 1961; student of Gaspar Cassadó, Germany, 1961-62; student of Gregor Piatigorsky, 1963-66. Mem. faculty U. So. Calif., Los Angeles, 1963-70, Peabody Inst., Balt., 1970-74; mem. faculty New Eng. Conservatory Music, Boston, 1974—, pres., 1983—; former vis. prof. Eastman Sch. Music, Rochester, N.Y.; vis. prof. Toho Gakuen Sch. Music, Tokyo, 1973—; performed with New Japan Philharm., Boston Symphony, London Philharm., L.A. Philharm. and Marlboro, Spoleto, Casals, Santa Fe and Banff festivals; rec. artist; overseer Boston Symphony Orch. Trustee WGBH Ednl. Found.; mem. adv. coun. Chamber Music Am. Recipient prize Tchaikovsky Competition, Moscow, 1966; Fulbright scholar, 1961-62; Ford Found. grantee, 1972. Mem. Am. Acad. Arts and Scis., Harvard Mus. Assn., Tavern Club, Phi Beta Kappa, Pi Kappa Lambda, Sigma Alpha Iota. Jewish. Home: 65 Bellevue St Newton MA 02158-1918 Office: New Eng Conservatory Music 290 Huntington Ave Boston MA 02115-5018

LESSER, LAWRENCE J., advertising agency executive; b. Bklyn., June 1, 1939; m. Joanna Savarese, Aug. 26, 1962; children: Eileen, Kristin. AAS, N.Y.C. Community Coll., 1959. Asst. acct. exec. Friend Reiss Advt., 1959-63; v.p., acct. supr. sr. v.p. L.W. Frohlich, 1963-72; sr. v.p Medicus Comm. Inc., N.Y.C., 1972-76; pres., ceo, chmn. Medicus Group Internat., N.Y.C., 1976-95; exec. v.p. D'Arcy Masius Benton & Bowles, Inc., N.Y.C., 1996—, also bd. dirs., mem. exec. com. Office: D'Arcy Masius Benton & Bowles Inc 1675 Broadway New York NY 10019-5820

LESSER, WENDY, literary magazine editor, writer, consultant; b. Santa Monica, Calif., Mar. 20, 1952; d. Murray Leon Lesser and Millicent (Gerson) Dillon; m. Richard Rizzo, Jan. 18, 1985; 1 stepchild, Dov Antonio; 1 child, Nicholas. BA, Harvard U., 1973; MA, Cambridge (Eng.) U., 1975; PhD, U. Calif., Berkeley, 1982. Founding ptnr. Lesser & Ogden Assocs., Berkeley, 1977-81; founding editor The Threepenny Rev., Berkeley, 1980—; Bellagio resident Rockefeller Found, Italy, 1984. Author: The Life Below the Ground, 1987, His Other Half, 1991, Pictures at an Execution, 1994; editor: Hiding in Plain Sight, 1993. Fellow NEH, 1983, 92, Guggenheim fellow, 1988. Fellow NEH, 1983, 92, Guggenheim Found, 1988, ACLS, 1996. Democrat. Office: The Threepenny Rev PO Box 9131 Berkeley CA 94709-0131

LESSER, WILLIAM HENRI, marketing educator; b. N.Y.C., Dec. 19, 1946; s. Arthur and Ethel (Boissevain) L.; m. Susan Elizabeth Bailey, Dec. 27, 1975; children: Andrew, Jordan. BA in Geography, U. Wash., 1968; MS in Resource Econs., U. R.I., 1974; PhD in Agrl. Econ., U. Wis., 1978., 1993-94; From asst. to assoc. prof. mktg. Cornell U, Ithaca, N.Y., 1978-91, prof., 1991—; acting exec. dir. Internat. Svc. for Acquisition of Bio-tech Applications, 1994-95; with Internat. Acad. Environ., Geneva, 1993-94; grad. field rep. Dept. Agrl. Econs., Ithaca, 1985-88; dir. Cornell Western Socs. Program, 1991-93; cons. World Bank, Washington, US/AID, Winrock Internat., Morrilton, Ark. Editor: Animal Patents: The Legal Economic and Social Issues, 1990; author: Equitable Patent Protection in the Developing World, 1991, Marketing Livestock and Meat, 1993. Zone capt. Dem. com. Town of Ithaca, 1985-90, mem. planning bd., 1987-93. Nat. fellow Kellogg Found., 1988-91. Mem. Am. Agrl. Econ. Assn., Patent & Trademark Office Soc. Avocations: gardening, painting, antique cars. Home: 406 Coddington Rd Ithaca NY 14850-6012 Office: Cornell U Dept Argl Econs 405 Warren Hall Ithaca NY 14853-7801

LESSIN, LAWRENCE STEPHEN, hematologist, oncologist, educator; b. Washington, Oct. 14, 1937; s. Maurice and Anna (Brodsky) L.; m. Judith Ann Lustok, Dec. 23, 1961; children: Jennifer Lynn, Jonathan Lustok, Martine Rose. Student, U. Mich., 1955-58; M.D., U. Chgo., 1962. Diplomate Am. Bd. Internal Medicine (assoc. mem. 1976-82). Intern, resident in internal medicine, chief resident, fellow in hematology Hosp. U. Pa., 1962-67; spl. fellow Nat. Heart Inst., Inst. for Cell Pathology, Paris, 1967-68; asst. prof. medicine Duke U., 1968-70; assoc. prof. medicine and pathology George Washington U., 1970-74, prof. medicine and pathology, dir. div. hematology and oncology, 1974—; dir. George Washington U. Cancer Ctr., Washington, 1991-93; med. dir. Washington Cancer Inst. Washington Hosp. Ctr., 1993—; vis. physician medicine br. Nat. Cancer Inst., 1971-74; cons. hematology Washington VA Hosp., 1971—; cons. ARC Blood Bank, 1972—, Nat. Naval Med. Ctr., Bethesda, Md., 1974—, Nat. Heart, Lung and Blood Inst., 1974; Walter Reed Army Med. Ctr., 1978—; ad hoc cons. Nat. Heart, Lung and Blood Inst., Study Sect. Program-Project Grants, 1977; mem. NASA Biomed. Rev. Panel, 1981-88; chmn. div. blood diseases and resources adv. com. Nat. Heart, Blood and Lung Inst., NIH, 1985-86; chmn., program dir. Assn. Hematology-Oncology, 1983-87. editorial reviewer: Annals of Internal Medicine, 1969—, Nouvelle Revue de Hematologie, 1970—, Blood, Jour. Hematology, 1971—, Archives of Internal Medicine, 1972—, Nature, 1973, Jour. Clin. Investigation, 1973—, New Eng. Jour. Medicine; mem. editorial Blood Cells, 1979—, Hematologic Pathology, 1985—; contbr. articles to profl. jours., chpts. to books. Served to capt. M.C. USAR, 1963-69. Named Intern of Year U. Pa. Hosp., 1963; nominee for Golden Apple award, 1975; Nat. Heart Inst. spl. fellow Paris, 1967-68. Fellow ACP, Internat. Soc. Hematology; mem. Am. Coll. Physicians (chair Hematology Med. Knowledge Self-Assessment program, 1992—), Am. Soc. Hematology, Am. Fedn. Clin. Research, Am. Soc. Clin. Oncology, Am. Blood Commn., Am. Soc. Internal Medicine, D.C. Med. Soc., Internat. Blood Cells Club, Am. Soc. Clin. Oncology, Sigma Xi, Alpha Omega Alpha. Club: Cosmos (Washington). Office: 2150 Pennsylvania Ave NW Washington DC 20037-2396

LESSING, BRIAN REID, actuary; b. Miami, Fla., Feb. 2, 1954; s. Kenneth Oliver Ralph and Margaret (Takash) L. AB magna cum laude, Princeton (N.J.) U., 1976; MS, N.Y.U., 1979. Cert. FSA, Soc. Actuaries, 1989, CLU, Am. Coll., 1992. Tech. asst. Mutual of N.Y., 1980-84; actuarial asst. Equitable Life Assurance, N.Y.C., 1984-87; asst. actuary, 1987-89, assoc. actuary, 1989-91, actuary, 1991-93, asst. v.p., 1993—; adj. instr. N.Y. Inst. Tech., 1979, Pace U., N.Y.C., 1979, 80; adj. asst. prof. The Coll. of Ins., N.Y.C., 1989-91. Mem. ch. coun. exec. com. Community Ch. of N.Y., 1984-87, fin. com., 1989—. Recipient Rsch. assistantship N.Y.U., 1976-80. Fellow Soc. of Actuaries; mem. Am. Soc. CLU and ChFC, Am. Acad. Actuaries, Phi Beta Kappa. Unitarian Universalist. Home: 433 W 24th St Apt 5F New York NY 10011-1203 Office: Equitable Life Assurance 2 Penn Plz # 21H New York NY 10121

LESSING, DORIS (MAY), writer; b. Kermanshah, Persia, Oct. 22, 1919; d. Alfred Cook Taylor and Emily Maude McVeach; m. Frank Charles Wisdom, 1939 (div. 1943); m. Gottfried Anton Nicholas Lessing, 1945 (div. 1949); children: John W. (dec.), Jean W., Peter L. Educated in, So. Rhodesia; DLitt (hon.), Princeton U., 1979, Durham U., 1980; D Fellow in Lit., Sch., Eng. Am. Studies, U. East Anglia, 1991; DLitt (hon.), Warwick U., 1994; LittD (hon.), Bard Coll., 1994, Harvard U., 1995. Author: (novels) The Grass is Singing, 1950, Five Short Novels, 1955, Retreat to Innocence, 1959, The Golden Notebook, 1962 (Prix Medicis Award for work translated into French, 1976), Children of Violence, 5 vols., 1964-69, Briefing For a Descent Into Hell, 1971, The Summer Before the Dark, 1973, The Memoirs of a Survivor, 1975, Shikasta, 1979, Marriages Between Zones Three, Four and Five, 1980, The Sirian Experiments, 1981 (Booker McConnell Prize nominee, 1981), The Making of the Representative for Planet 8, 1982, Documents Relating to the Sentimental Agents in the Volyen Empire, 1983, The Diaries of Jane Somers (Diary of a Good Neighbour, 1983, and If the Old Could..., 1984, pub. under pseudonym Jane Somers), The Good Terrorist, 1985 (W.H. Smith Lit. Award, 1976; Palermo Prize, 1987; Premio Internazionale Monello, 1987), The Fifth Child, 1988, The Libretto of the Making of the Representative for Planet 8, 1988, The Fifth Child, 1988, Playing the Game, 1995, Love, Again, 1996; (nonfiction) Going Home, 1957, In Pursuit of the English, 1961, Particularly Cats, 1967, Prisons We Choose to Live Inside, 1986, The Wind Blows Away Our Words...and Other Documents Relating to the Afghan Resistance, 1987, Particularly Cats and More Cats, 1989, African Laughter: Four Visits to Zimbabwe, 1992; (autobiography) Under My Skin: Volume One of My Autobiography, to 1949, 1994; (short stories) This Was the Old Chief's Country, 1952, The Habit of Loving, 1958, A Man and Two Women, 1963, African Stories, 1965, The Temptation of Jack Orkney and Other Stories, 1972, The Story of a Non-Marrying Man, 1972, Collected African Stories, 1973, London Observed: Stories and Sketches (U.K.)/The Real Thing (U.S.), 1992; (collections) To Room 19 (Collected Stories Vols. 1 and 2), 1978, The Doris Lessing Reader, 1990; (plays) Each in His Own Wilderness, 1958, Play with a Tiger, 1962, The Singing Door, 1973; (essays) A Small Personal Voice, 1974; (poetry) Fourteen Poems, 1959; (libretto for opera with music by Philip Glass) The Making of the Representative for Planet 8, 1988; also newspaper reports. Recipient Somerset Maugham award Soc. of Authors, 1954, Austrian State prize for European Lit., 1981, Shakespeare prize, Hamburg, 1982, Grinzane Cavour award, Italy, 1989; named Woman of Yr. Norway, 1995. Fellow MLA (hon.); mem. Nat. Inst. Arts and Letters., Am. Acad. Arts & Letters (assoc. mem. 1974), Inst. Cultural Research. Office: care Jonathan Clowes Ltd. 10 Iron Bridge House, Bridge Approach, London NW1 8BD, England

LESSITER, FRANK DONALD, magazine editor; b. Pontiac, Mich., Oct. 5, 1939; s. Milon John and Donalda Belle (Taylor) L.; m. Pamela Ann Fuzak, Nov. 23, 1963; children—Deborah, Susan, Michael, Kelly. B.S. in Dairy Sci, Mich. State U., 1961, postgrad. in Advt., 1962-65. Info. specialist Mich. Coop. Extension Service, East Lansing, 1962-65; exec. editor Agrl. Pubs., Milw., 1965-68; editor Nat. Livestock Producer mag., Chgo., 1969-72, No-Till Farmer, 1972—; v.p., editor Nat. Livestock Producer, 1974-78; editor Rural Builder, 1977-89; exec. v.p. Reiman Assocs., 1977-81; editor Farmer's Digest, 1988—; pres. Am. Farm Bldg. Services, Inc., 1981-89, No-Till Farmer, Inc., 1981—, Lessiter Pubs., Brookfield, Wis., 1989—; editor Ridge Till Hotline, 1991—, Am. Farrier's Jour., 1992—. Author: (with Pamela Ann Fuzak Lessiter) Agricultural Travel Guide, 1971, Horsepower, 1977, 100 Most Common No-Tillage Questions, 1981; editor, pub. Am. Farriers Jour., 1992—; contbg. author: (with Pamela Ann Fuzak Lessiter) Commodity Yearbook, 1972, 75. Named Farm Mag. Editor of Year Dekalb AgResearch Program, 1972, Newsletter Editor of Year Newsletter Clearing House, 1973, Best Farm Mktg. Writer CIBA-Ceigy Awards Program, 1976, Farm Mag. Writer of Yr., 1977. Mem. Nat. Press Photographers Assn., Nat. Agrl. Mktg. Assn., Am. Agrl. Editors Assn. (Photographer of Year 1975). Home: 16000 Choctaw Trl Brookfield WI 53005-5504 Office: PO Box 624 Brookfield WI 53008-0624

LESSLER, RICHARD SIGMUND, advertising executive; b. Lynbrook, N.Y., Aug. 26, 1924; s. William S. and Minnie (Gold) L.; m. Evelyn Sobotka, Aug. 31, 1952; children: Michael Jay, Jonathan Peter, Daniel Stephen. B.A. in Exptl. Psychology, U. N.C., 1943; M.B.A., Columbia U., 1948; postgrad., NYU, 1948-52. Research assoc. CBS, 1948-49; with Dancer-Fitzgerald-Sample, Inc., 1949-55; with Grey Advt., Inc., 1955-72, chmn. bd., 1967-72; also dir., mem. exec. com., chmn. mgmt. com.; vice chmn. bd., chief operating officer U.S., chmn. exec. com. McCann-Erickson, Inc., N.Y.C., 1972-79; vice chmn. bd., chmn. ops. com. The Interpublic Group Cos., Inc., N.Y.C., 1979-80; exec. cons. The Interpublic Group Cos., Inc., 1980-82; mktg., communications cons. Carpinteria, Calif., 1990—; mgr. Western region Canter, Achenbaum, Assocs., Inc., 1980-89; exclusive cons. Bozell, Inc., Dallas, 1989-93; cons. Temerlen McClain, Dallas, 1993-94; mktg. cons., prof. mktg. and advt. U. Ariz., 1980-83. Author: (with Brown and Weilbacher) Advertising Media, 1957, (with Nugent Wedding) Advertising Management, 1962. Served to lt. USNR, World War II. Mem. Phi Beta Kappa, Beta Gamma Sigma. Home: 1946 Paquita Dr Carpinteria CA 93013-3026

LESSY, ROY PAUL, JR., lawyer; b. Wallingford, Pa., Feb. 27, 1944; s. Roy Paul and Ruth W. Lessy; m. Ellen Mauck, Jan. 24, 1970 (dec. Dec. 1994); children: Rose-Ellen, Anne, Page. BA, Franklin and Marshall U., 1966; JD, George Washington U., 1969; postgrad., Harvard U., 1979. Bar: D.C. Atty.-advisor Office of Sec. U.S. Treasury Dept., Washington, 1969-72; dep. chief hearing counsel U.S. Nuclear Regulatory Commn., Washington, 1972-82; atty. and counsel Morgan, Lewis & Bockius, Washington, 1983-86; ptnr. Akin, Gump, Strauss, Hauer & Feld, Washington, 1986—; mem. lawyers steering com. Atomic Indsl. Forum, Washington, 1984—. Author: Casenote on Federal Jurisdiction, 1969. Mem. ABA (lectr. Am. Law Inst. 1984—), Fed. Energy Bar Assn., Phi Delta Phi. Home: 8605 Fenway Dr Bethesda MD 20817-2709 Office: Akin Gump Strauss Hauer & Feld Ste 400 1333 New Hampshire Ave NW Washington DC 20036-1511

LESTAGE, DANIEL BARFIELD, retired naval officer, physician; b. Jennings, La., July 7, 1939; s. Henry Oscar Jr. and Juliet Xavier (Barfield) L.; m. Helen Newcomer, Mar. 9, 1963; children: Juliet Lestage Hirsch, Diane Lestage Davis, Daniel B. Jr. Grad., La. State U., 1959, MD, 1963; grad., Naval Sch. Aviation, 1964; MPH, Tulane U., 1969; diploma, Indsl. Coll. Armed Forces, 1978. Diplomate Am. Bd. Preventive Medicine (trustee 1988-94), Am. Bd. Family Practice. Commd. ensign USN, 1962, advanced through grades to rear adm., 1986; rotating intern Charity Hosp., New Orleans, 1963-64; resident in family practice Lafayette (La.) Charity Hosp., 1964; student flight surgeon Naval Sch. Aviation Medicine, Pensacola, Fla., 1964; staff flight surgeon/med. officer Carrier Air Wing 16 USS Oriskany, NAS Lemoore, Calif., 1965-67; sr. med. officer Naval Med. Clinic, NAS New Orleans, 1967-68, USS John F. Kennedy, Norfolk, Va., 1971-73; resident in aerospace medicine Naval Aerospace Med. Inst., Pensacola, 1969-71; sr. med. officer Br. Clinic, Jacksonville NAS, 1973-77; chief preventive medicine dept. Naval Regional Med. Ctrs., Jacksonville, 1973-77; spl. asst. to surgeon gen. Navy Bur. Medicine and Surgery Dept. Navy, Washington, 1978-81; head operational medicine br., aeromed. advisor Office of Chief Naval Ops., Washington, 1978-81; dir. clin. svcs., dir. med. edn., exec. officer Naval Regional Med. Ctr., Portsmouth, Va., 1981-83; commanding officer Naval Hosp., Millington, Tenn., 1983-84; comdr. U.S. Naval Med. Command, London, 1984-86; fleet med. officer U.S. Naval Forces Europe, 1984-86; fleet surgeon U.S. Atlantic Fleet, Norfolk, 1986-88; command surgeon U.S. Atlantic Command U.S. Atlantic Command/Supreme Allied Comdr., Norfolk, 1986-89; asst. dir. naval medicine Office of Chief Naval Ops., 1989; insp. gen. Navy Bur. of Medicine and Surgery, 1989-90; comdr. Naval Med. Ctr., Portsmouth, Va., 1990-92; corp. med. dir. Blue Cross/Blue Shield of Fla., Jacksonville, 1992-95; v.p., med. ops. Blue Cross/Blue Shield of Fla., 1995—; asst. dean Ea. Va. Med. Sch., Norfolk, 1981-83, assoc. dean, 1990-92; del. AMA ho. of dels from Aerospace Med. Assn., 1993—; del. Fla. Med. Assn. ho. of dels. from Fla Soc. Preventative Medicine, 1995—. Dir. Blood Bank, Jacksonville, 1973-77; bd. dirs. Cath. Family Svcs., Portsmouth, 1981-83, Fraser-Millington Mental Health Ctr., Memphis, 1983-84. Decorated Legion of Merit with four oak leaf clusters, Meritorious Svc. medal, Air medal with oak leaf cluster, Navy Commendation medal; recipient Physician's Recognition award AMA, 1972, 75, 78, 81, 85, 88, 91, 94, 97. Fellow Am. Coll. Physicians, Am. Coll. Preventive Medicine, Am. Acad. Family Physicians, Aerospace Med. Assn. (pres. 1988-89); mem. AMA (del. 1993—), Fla. Acad. Family Physicians (bd. dirs. 1995-98), Fla. Soc. for Preventive Medicine (pres. 1995-96), Fla. Med. Assn. (del. 1995—), VFW, Am. Legion, Internat. Acad. Aviation and Space Medicine, Am./Fla. Coll. of Occupl. and Environ. Medicine, Rotary, Elks. Roman Catholic. Avocations: travel, cooking. Home: 1782 Long Slough Walk Orange Park FL 32073-7033 Office: Blue Cross/Blue Shield Fla 8057 Baypine Rd Jacksonville FL 32256-7513

LESTER, ANDREW WILLIAM, lawyer; b. Mpls., Feb. 17, 1956; s. Richard G. and Marion Louise (Kurtz) L.; m. Barbara Regina Schmitt, Nov. 22, 1978; 1 child, Susan Erika. Student, Ludwig-Maximilians Univ., Munich, 1975-76; BA, Duke U., 1977; MS in Fgn. Service, JD, Georgetown U., 1981. Bar: Okla. 1981, D.C. 1985, Tex. 1990, U.S. Supreme Ct. 1992, Colo. 1995. Cons. Dresser Industries, Inc., Washington, 1979-81; assoc. Conner & Winters, Tulsa, 1981-82; asst. atty. City of Enid, Okla., 1982-84; ptnr. Lester & Bryant, P.L.L.C. and predecessor firms, Oklahoma City, Tulsa and Enid, 1984—, Denver, 1984—; adj. prof. Okla. City Univ. Sch. of Law; lectr. in field; U.S. magistrate judge Western Dist. Okla., 1988—; constl. law specialist Ctrl. and East European Law Initiative, ABA, Ukraine and Moldova, 1993. Author: Constitutional Law and Democracy, 1994; contbr. book revs. and articles to profl. jours. Intern Office of Senator Bob Dole, Washington, 1977-78; mem. transition team EEOC Office Pres.-Elect Reagan, Washington, 1980-81; chmn. Enid Police Civil Service Commn., 1985-87; bd. dirs. Enid Habitat for Humanity, 1986-88, Booker T. Washington Community Ctr., Enid, 1987-90; mem. Martin Luther King, Jr. Holiday Commn. of Enid, 1988-91. Fellow Okla. Bar Found.; mem. Okla. Bar Assn., D.C. Bar Assn., Tex. Bar Assn., Colo. Bar Assn., Okla. Assn. Mcpl. Attys. (bd. dirs. 1987-91, 94—, gen. counsel 1987-88, pres. 1988-90, 94—), Oklahoma County Bar Assn., Def. Rsch. Inst. (govt. liability com.), Federalist Soc. Republican. Baptist. Avocations: German language, cartography. Office: Lester & Bryant PLLC Ste 820 119 N Robinson Ave Oklahoma City OK 73102-4625

LESTER, BARNETT BENJAMIN, editor, foreign affairs officer; b. Toronto, Can., Aug. 7, 1912; came to U.S., 1917; s. Louis and Lena (Rubenstein) L.; m. Rita Constance Hatcher, May 31, 1943 (dec.); m. Claudette Yvonne Gionet, Apr. 19, 1970. Student, Cleve. Coll., Western Res. U., 1933; AB (Miller Scholar), Oberlin Coll., 1934, (grad. scholar), 1934-35; grad. scholar, Nat. Inst. Pub. Affairs, Washington, 1935-36; scholar, Syracuse U., 1935-36, Acad. Internat. Law, The Hague, 1936; student, fellow, Fletcher Sch. Law and Diplomacy, 1935-36; student, Fgn. Service Inst., 1952, 56, Dep. Chiefs Mission Seminar, Dept. State, 1981. Mem. staff, corr. Cleve. Plain Dealer and Cleve. News, 1928-33; feature writer Boston Sunday Post, 1935-38; mng. editor, later editor Exclusive Features Syndicate, Boston, 1936-38; assoc. editor The Writer mag., Boston, 1936-38; info. officer Dept. Justice, 1938-41; asst. dir. feature div. Office Inter-Am. Affairs, 1941-45; info. publicist Dept. State, 1945; pub. relations exec. Al Paul Lefton Co., Inc., Phila., 1945-46; info. specialist, chief motion pictures, acting chief audio-visual sect. USPHS, Office Surgeon Gen., 1947-48; info. specialist Fed. Security Agy., 1948-49; chief editorial and prodn. sect. Nat. Heart Inst. (info. specialist, sci. reports br. NIH), 1949-52; pub. info. chief NIH, 1950; review officer Dept. State, 1952-61, supervisory publs. editor, 1961-63, editor-writer, 1963-73, pub. info. officer, 1973-85; assoc. editor Newsletter, 1977-81; assoc. editor State Mag., 1981-86, sr. editor, 1986-89, on contract, 1989; pub. affairs specialist, 1985-89; fgn. svc. res. officer, 1965-73, assigned to policy and pub. info. affairs program, 1962-67; assigned to policy and pub. info affairs program Newsletter and Info. Office, Office Dir. Gen. Fgn. Svc., 1967-81, Office Pub. Affairs and State Mag., Office Dir. Gen. Fgn. Svc., 1981-89, Career counselor Oberlin Coll., 1940—; rep. Office Surg. Gen., USPHS, on Interdepartmental com. med. tng. aids, 1947-48; invited participant U.S. Commr. Edn. Conf. Audio-Visual Aids to Edn., 1948; mem. info. staff Pres.'s Midcentury White House Conf. on Children and Youth, 1950; mem. spl. survey audio-visual tchg. and tng. aids Nat. Heart Inst., USPHS and Assn. Am. Med. Colls., 1951; invited participant symposium The White House: The First 200 Yrs., White House Hist. Assn., 1992. Author: (with others) The Writer's Handbook, 1936. Recipient War Service award Coord. Inter-Am. Affairs, 1945, Meritorious Honor Group award Dept. State, 1967, 40 Year Service award, 1979, Spl. Achievement award, 1979, Superior Honor award, 1983, Superior Honor Group award, 1984; Loy W. Henderson—Joseph C. Satterthwaite award for pub. service, 1987; Bicentennial award Am. Revolution Bicentennial Adminstrn., 1977; award for excellence Soc. Tech. Communications, 1982; award for achievement Soc. Tech. Communication, 1985; 50 Yr. Pin, Fletcher Sch. Law and Diplomacy, 1986; 50 Yr. Svc. award, bronze plaque for 51 yrs. U.S. Govt. Svc., 1989; John Jacob Rogers award for outstanding career achievement, Dept. State, 1989; cert. commendation Dept. State, 1989. Mem. Am. Fgn. Svc. Assn., Am. Polit. Sci. Assn., Am. Acad. Polit. and Social Sci., Acad. Polit. Sci., Diplomatic and Consular Officers Ret., Fed. Editors Assn. (Blue Pencil award 19750, Nat. Assn. Govt. Communicators (Blue Pencil Publs. award 1983), Consular Officers Assn., Marquis Libr. Assn. (adv. mem.), U.S. Diplomatic Courier Assn. (hon., Silver Diplomatic Courier medal and cert. appreciation 1990), Nat. Press Found. (charter), Nat. Trust for Hist. Preservation, U.S. Capitol Hist. Soc. Civil War Trust (charter), Assn. for Diplomatic Studies and Tng., Internat. Club (charter honored as founding mem.) (Washington), Nat. Press Club, Silver Owl Club (Washington), Am. Fgn. Svc. (Washington). Two suggestions adopted by U.S. Postal Service resulted in issuing Treaty of Paris stamp and Great Seal of U.S. embossed stamped envelope. Home: 2507 N Lincoln St Arlington VA 22207-53

LESTER, CHARLES TURNER, JR., lawyer; b. Plainfield, N.J., Jan. 31, 1942; s. Charles Turner and Marlyn Elizabeth (Tate) L.; m. Nancy Hudmon Simmons, Aug. 19, 1967; children: Susan Hopson, Mary Elizabeth. B.A., Emory U., 1964, J.D., 1967. Bar: Ga. 1966, U.S. Dist. Ct. (no. dist.) Ga. 1967, D.C. 1970, U.S. Ct. Appeals (5th cir.) 1967, U.S. Ct. Appeals (11th cir.) 1982, U.S. Ct. Appeals (10th cir.) 1984. Assoc. Sutherland, Asbill & Brennan, Atlanta, 1970-77, ptnr., 1977—. Mem. Leadership Atlanta, 1980-81; pres. Atlanta Legal Aid Soc., 1979-80. Lt. JAGC, USNR, 1967-70. Fellow Am. Bar Found; mem. ABA, State Bar of Ga. (pres. young lawyers sect. 1977-78, bd. govs. 1977-78, 80-93, chmn. formal adv. opinion bd. 1987-90, exec. com. 1977-78, 1987-93, pres. 1991-92), Atlanta Bar Assn., Am. Judicature Soc., Lawyers Club Atlanta (treas. 1982-83, exec. com. 1982-90, 2d v.p. 1986-87, 1st v.p. 1987-88, pres. 1988-89), D.C. Bar Assn., Ga. C. of C. (bd. dirs. 1994—). Democrat. Methodist. Home: 1955 Musket Ct Stone Mountain GA 30087-1703 Office: Sutherland Asbill & Brennan 999 Peachtree St NE Atlanta GA 30309-3996

LESTER, GEORGE N., electrical engineer; b. Atlanta, Apr. 7, 1928. BEE, Ga. Inst. Tech., 1950. Prin. engr. Boston Edison Co. Fellow IEEE (sec. 1979-80, vice-chmn. 1981-82, chmn. 1983-84, PES Switchgear com., adminstrv. subcom. PES Switchgear com. 1975—, sec. 1974, chmn. 1975-79, high voltage cir. breaker subcom., mem. working group on capacitance current switching 1960-85, chmn. working group on capacitance current switching 1960-68, mem. working group on revisions of cir. breaker stds. 1968—, chmn. working group on revisions of cir. breaker stds. 1974, mem. working group on quality and reliability 1973—, others). Office: Boston Edison Co 800 Boylston St/P234 Boston MA 02199-8001*

LESTER, JAMES DUDLEY, classicist, educator; b. Fort Smith, Ark., Mar. 5, 1935; s. Kenneth R. and Essie Fae (Bailey) L.; m. Martha B. Lester, 1958; children: Jim, Mark. BA, East Cen. Okla. State U., 1957; MA, Okla. State U., 1963; PhD, Tulsa U., 1970. Dir. pub. rels. East Cen. Okla. U., Ada, 1957; aide to Sen. Robert S. Kerr U.S. Senate, Washington, 1958-59; tchr. Fort Smith (Ark.) High Sch., 1959-63; from instr. to asst. prof. Emporia (Kans.) State U., 1963-67; grad. asst. Tulsa U., 1967-70; from asst. prof. to prof. Austin Peay State U., Clarksville, Tenn., 1970—. Pub., editor: Cumberland Mag., 1976-80, Tenn. Monthly, 1980-82. F.B. Parriott scholar U. Tulsa, 1969-70. Mem. MLA, South Ctrl. MLA, Nat. Coun. Tchrs. English, Conf. Coll. Comm. and Composition. Democrat. Methodist. Home: 489 Pond Apple Rd Clarksville TN 37043-2208 Office: Austin Peay State U Dept Classics Clarksville TN 37044

LESTER, JULIUS B., author; b. St. Louis, Jan. 27, 1939; s. W.D. and Julia (Smith) L.; m. Milan Sabatini; children: Jody Simone, Malcolm Coltrane, Elena Milad, David Julius, Lian Brennan. BA, Fisk U., 1960. Prof. Judaic studies U. Mass., Amherst, 1971—. Profl. musician and singer, recording for Vanguard Records, folklorist and writer, dir., Newport Folk Festival, 1966-68; author: (with Pete Seeger) The 12-String Guitar as Played by Leadbelly, 1965, Look Out, Whitey, Black Power's Gon' Get Your Mama, 1968, To Be a Slave, 1968 (Newberry Honor book 1968), Black Folktales, 1969, Revolutionary Notes, 1969, Search for the New Land, 1970, The Knee-High Man and Other Tales, 1972, Long Journey Home: Stories from Black History, 1972 (Nat. Book Award finalist 1972), Two Love Stories, 1972, Who I Am, 1974, All Is Well, 1976, This Strange New Feeling, 1982, Do Lord Remember Me, 1985, The Tales of Uncle Remus: The Adventures of Brer Rabbit, 1987, The Tales of Uncle Remus, The Further Adventures of Brer Rabbit, 1988, Lovesong: Becoming a Jew, 1988, How Many Spots Does A Leopard Have?, 1989, Further Tales of Uncle Remus, 1990, Falling Pieces of the Broken Sky, 1990, Last Tales of Uncle Remus, 1994, And All Our Wounds Forgiven, 1994, The Man Who Knew Too Much, 1994, John Henry, 1994, Othello: A Novel, 1995; editor: Seventh Son: The Thoughts and Writings of W.E.B. DuBois, vol. 1 and 2, 1971; assoc. editor: Sing Out, 1964-69; contbg. editor: Broadside of New York, 1964-70. Address: PO Box 9634 North Amherst MA 01059-9634 *The older I become, the greater the mystery of my life. I think I see my life as journey into mystery, in awe and fear, with joy and apprehension. Whatever my accomplishments, my life is more than and other than, and finally, best expressed by the silence of winter snow, prairie skies, or a feathered serpent. To be as true and eloquent as a drop of water hanging from a twig—that is my ideal.*

LESTER, JUNE, library-information studies educator; b. Sandersville, Ga., Aug. 25, 1942; d. Charles DuBose and Frances Irene (Cheney) L.; 1 child, Anna Elisabeth Engle. B.A., Emory U., 1963, M.Librarianship, 1971; D in Library Sci., Columbia U., 1987; cert. in advanced librarianship Columbia U., 1982. Asst. prof., cataloger U. Tenn. Library, Knoxville, 1971-73; librarian div. library and info. mgmt. Emory U., Atlanta, 1973-81, asst. prof. div. library and info. mgmt., 1976-80, assoc. prof., 1980-87; accreditation officer Am. Library Assn., 1987-91; assoc. dean, assoc. prof. Sch. Libr. and Info. Scis., U. North Tex., Denton, 1991-93; dir., prof. Sch. Libr. and Info. Studies, U. Okla., Norman, 1993—. UCLA sr. fellow, 1987. Mem. ALA (council mem. 1987), Assn. for Libr. and Info. Sci. Edn. (bd. dirs. 1985-87, pres. 1995-96), Am. Soc. Info. Sci., Ga. Library Assn., Phi Beta Kappa, Beta Phi Mu. Unitarian. Home: 2006 Trailview Ct Norman OK 73072-6654 Office: U Okla Sch Libr and Info Studies 401 W Brooks Norman OK 73019-0528

LESTER, LANCE GARY, education educator, researcher; b. Wausau, Wis., Sept. 12, 1943; s. Lawrence Harold and Joanna Susan (Martin) L.; m. Rochelle Damson McDermott, Sept. 25, 1973 (div.); stepchildren: Barbara Ann Brady, John Patrick McDermott. BA in English, St. John's U., 1965, MS in Secondary Edn., 1967; MA in Cinematography, NYU, 1969. Prof. football player N.Y. Jets/Titans, N.Y.C., 1960-61; educator Newtown High Sch., Elmhurst, N.Y., 1965—; mgr. B. S. Klein Real Estate, Bayside, N.Y., 1974—, track coach, 1973—; prof. film St. John's U., Jamaica, N.Y., 1981—; prof. White Magic Moving Pictures & Video, Glendale, N.Y., 1986—; lectr. N.Y. Jet Parking & Chowder Soc., N.Y.C., 1986, Queensborough Coll. Film Forum, Bayside, 1988—. Named N.Y.C. Track Coach of Yr., 1986. Mem. United Fedn. of Tchrs., N.Y.C. Coun. of English, Cinephiles. Roman Catholic. Avocations: Karate, track, travel agent. Office: Newtown High Sch 48-01 90th St Elmhurst NY 11373

LESTER, MALCOLM, historian, educator; b. Georgetown, Ga., Dec. 9, 1924; s. Malcolm Nicholson and Emmie (Bledsoe) L.; m. Pauline Hardeman Domingos, July 7, 1956; 1 dau., Pauline Malcolm (dec.). A.B., Mercer U., 1945; M.A., U. Va., 1946, Ph.D., 1954; Fulbright scholar, U. London (King's Coll.), 1949-50. Instr. history Mercer U., Macon, Ga., 1946-47, asst. prof., 1947-50, assoc. prof., 1950-54, prof., 1954-59, dean Coll. Liberal Arts, 1955-59; prof. history Davidson (N.C.) Coll., 1959-89, Charles A. Dana prof. history, 1977-89, prof. emeritus, 1989—, chmn. history dept., 1962-87; dir. Davidson summer program at Cambridge U., 1981-87. Author: Anthony Merry Redivivus: A Reappraisal of the British Minister to the United States, 1803-6, 1978; contbr. to American National Biography, Dictionary of National Biography; contbr. book revs. to various hist. jours. Elder Presbyn. Ch., 1964—, moderator Mecklenburg Presbytery, 1974; mem. internat. adv. coun. U. Buckingham, England, 1980—. Recipient Algernon Sydney Sullivan award Mercer U., 1945, Thomas Jefferson award Davidson Coll., 1982. Fellow Royal Hist. Soc. (Eng.); mem. Am. So. Hist. Assns., Orgn. Am. Historians, Nat. Trust (Eng.), Hist. Assn. (Eng.), Conf. Brit. Studies, AAUP, Nat. Assn. Scholars, Soc. Nautical Rsch. (Eng.), English Speaking Union, Raven Soc., Sons Confederate Vets., Colonnade Club (U. Va.), Phi Beta Kappa (sen. United chpts. 1976-82, com. qualifications 1978-82), Omicron Delta Kappa. Republican. Presbyterian. Home: 228 Roundway Down PO Box 548 Davidson NC 28036-0548

LESTER, RICHARD, film director; b. Phila., Jan. 19, 1932; s. Elliott and Ella (Young) L.; m. Deirdre Vivian Smith, 1956; 2 children. B.S., U. Pa. TV dir., CBS, 1951-54, dir., TV Goon Shows, 1956; directed: Running, Jumping and Standing Still Film (Acad. award nomination, 1st prize San Francisco Festival 1960); dir.: feature films It's Trad, Dad, 1962, Mouse on the Moon, 1963, A Hard Day's Night, 1964, The Knack, 1964 (Grand Prix, Cannes Film Festival), Help, 1965 (Best Film award, Best Dir. award Rio de Janeiro Festival), A Funny Thing Happened on the Way to the Forum, 1966, How I Won the War, 1967, Petulia, 1968, The Bed-Sitting Room, 1969 (Ghandi Peace prize, Berlin Festival 1969), The Three Musketeers, 1973, Juggernaut, 1974 (Best Dir., Teheran Festival), The Four Musketeers, 1975, Royal Flash, 1975, Robin and Marian, 1976, The Ritz, 1976, Butch and Sundance—The Early Days, 1978, Cuba, 1979, Superman II, 1980, Superman III, 1982, Finders Keepers, 1984, Return of the Musketeers, 1989, Get Back, 1991. Office: Twickenham Film Studios, St Margarets, Middlesex England

LESTER, RICHARD ALLEN, economist, educator; b. Blasdell, N.Y., Mar. 1, 1908; s. Garra Kimble and Jessie Isabel (Holmes) L.; m. Doris Margaret Newhouse; children: Margaret Wing, Harriet Tarver, Robert A. PhB, Yale U., 1929; AM, Princeton (N.J.) U., 1930, PhD, 1936. With Princeton U., 1931-32, 34-38, prof., 1945-74, prof. emeritus, 1974—; assoc. dean Woodrow Wilson Sch., 1966-68; dean faculty Princeton U., 1968-73, rsch. assoc. Indsl. Rels. sect., 1973—; asst. prof. U. Wash., Seattle, 1938-40; from asst. to assoc. prof. Duke U., Durham, N.C., 1940-45; br. chief War Prodn. Bd. and War Manpower Commn., Washington, 1941-42; manpower cons. Office of Sec. of War, Washington, 1943-44; chmn. N.J. Employment Security Coun., Trenton, 1954-64; N.J. chmn. Pub. Employer-Employee Rels. Study Commn., Trenton, 1974-75; trustee Tchrs. Ins. and Annuity Assn., N.Y.C., 1959-63; v.p. Princeton U. Press, 1969-72. Author: Monetary Experiments, 1939, As Unions Mature, 1958, Economics of Labor, 2d edit., 1964, Labor Arbitration, 1984, Wages, Benefits and Company Employment Systems, 1988. Elected mem. Princeton Borough Coun., 1958-61; trustee Ctr. for Analysis Pub. Issues, Princeton, 1970-83; vice chmn. Pres.'s Commn. on Status of Women, Washington, 1961-63. U.S. Dept. Labor Merit award, 1968. Mem. Indls. Rels. Rsch. Assn. (pres. 1956), Am. Econ. Assn. (exec. com. 1951-53, v.p. 1961), Nat. Acad. Social Ins. Democrat. Avocations: swimming, fishing. Home: Meadow Lakes Meadow Lks Apt 46-03U Hightstown NJ 08520-3332 Office: Princeton U Indsl Rels Sect Firestone Libr Princeton NJ 08544

LESTER, RICHARD GARRISON, radiologist, educator; b. N.Y.C., Oct. 24, 1925; s. L. I. and Pauline (Smolan) L.; m. Marion Louise Kurtz, Jan. 17, 1949; children: Elizabeth P., Andrew W. A.B., Princeton U., 1946; M.D., Columbia U., 1948. Intern N.Y.C. Hosp., 1948-49; asst. resident radiology Stanford Hosp., 1950-51, 53-54; from instr. to asso. prof. radiology U. Minn., 1954-61; prof. radiology, chmn. dept. Med. Coll. Va., 1961-65, Duke Sch. Medicine, 1965-76; prof. radiology U. Tex. Med. Sch., Houston, 1976-84; chmn. dept. U. Tex. Med. Sch., 1977-81; interim pres. Meharry Med. Coll., Nashville, 1981-82; dean Eastern Va. Med. Sch., Norfolk, 1984-89, prof. radiology, 1984-93, chmn. dept., 1989-91; prof. emeritus, 1993—; v.p. acad. affairs Med. Coll. of Hampton Roads, formerly Eastern Va. Med. Authority, Norfolk, 1984-89; trustee Meharry Med. Coll., 1975—. Author: (with others) Congenital Heart Disease, 1965, Exposure of the Pregnant Patient to Diagnostic Radiations, 1985; also numerous articles. Deacon Freemason St. Bapt. Ch. Capt. USAF, 1951-53. Fellow Am. Coll. Radiology, Am. Coll. Chest Physicians; mem. Assn. Univ. Radiologists, Am. Roentgen Ray Soc., Soc. Pediatric Radiology, Radiol. Soc. N.Am. (dir. 1976—, chmn. bd. 1981, pres. 1983). Home: 1362 De Bree Ave Norfolk VA 23517-2131 Office: Ea Va Med Sch PO Box 1980 Norfolk VA 23501-1980

LESTER, ROBERT CARLTON, religious studies educator; b. Lead, S.D., Feb. 1, 1933; s. Odell and Mary Olivia (Martin) L.; m. Donna Helene Larson, Apr. 15, 1954; children: Paul E., Charles F., R. Timothy. BA, U. Mont., 1955; BD, Yale U., 1958, MA, 1959, PhD, 1963. From asst. prof. to assoc. prof. Am. U., 1962-70; mem. faculty U. Colo., Boulder, 1970—, prof. religious studies, 1972—; vis. prof. Cornell U., 1968-69; vis. lectr. Dept. State., monthly, 1963-70; mem. faculty Humanities Inst, NEH, 1979. Author: Theravada Buddhism in Southeast Asia, 1973, Ramanuja on the Yoga, 1975, Srivacana Bhushana of Pillai Lokacharya, 1979, Buddhism: The Path to Nirvana, 1987. Ford. Found. fellow, 1960-62, Fulbright Hays fellow, 1967, 74-75, faculty fellow U. Colo., 1974-75, Am. Inst. of Indian Studies fellow, 1982-83, 88. Mem. Am. Acad. Religion, Assn. Asian Studies, Soc. Values in Higher Edn., Phi Kappa Phi. Office: U Colo Dept Religious Studies Boulder CO 80309

LESTER, ROBIN DALE, educator, author, former headmaster; b. Holdrege, Nebr., Mar. 1, 1939; s. Earl L. and Evelyn Grace (Robinson) L.; m. Helen Sargent Doughty, Aug. 26, 1967; children: Robin Debevoise, James Robinson. Student, St. Andrews U., Scotland, 1958-61; BA, Pepperdine U., 1962, MA, 1963; MAT, U. Chgo., 1966, PhD, 1971. Resident head, dean students office U. Chgo., 1964-72, Ferdinand Schevill fellow dept. history, 1966-68; asst. prof. history Columbia Coll., Chgo., 1966-70; chmn. social scis. dept. Columbia Coll., 1970-72; chmn. history dept. Collegiate Sch., N.Y.C., 1972-75; headmaster Trinity Sch., N.Y.C., 1975-86, San Francisco U. Sch., 1986-88, Latin Sch. of Chgo., 1989-93; tchr. Francis W. Parker Sch., Chgo., 1994—; adj. prof. Columbia Coll., Chgo., 1992—. Author: Stagg's University, 1995, Wuzzy Takes Off, 1995; contbr. to N.Y. Times, 1979, 80, 81, Jour. Am. History, 1980, 95, Chgo. Tribune, 1989, Jour. Sports History, 1991, History of Edn. Quar., 1995, U. Chgo. mag., 1995. Mem. Manhattan Borough Dem. Com., N.Y.C., 1977-86; commr. Commn. on Ednl. Issues, 1980-86; mem. edn. com. Chgo. Hist. Soc., 1991-95; mem. Chgo.-Prague Sister Cities Com., 1991; trustee, treas. St. Andrews U. Am. Found., 1985—; precinct capt. Dem. Party, Chgo., 1964. Lauder fellow Aspen Inst., 1985. Mem. Am. Hist. Assn., Am. Studies Assn., N.Am. Soc. Sport Historians, Orgn. Am. Historians, Headmaster's Assn., Country Day Sch. Headmaster's Assn., University Club (N.Y.), Quadrangle Club. Episcopalian. Home: 2230 N Lincoln Park W Chicago IL 60614-3814 Office: Francis W Parker Sch 330 W Webster Ave Chicago IL 60614-3811

LESTER, VIRGINIA LAUDANO, advocate civil rights consumer protection; b. Phila., Jan. 5, 1931; d. Edmund Francis and Emily Beatrice (Downes) Laudano; children: Pamela Lester Golde, Valerie Lester. BA, Pa. State U., 1952; MEd, Temple U., 1955; PhD, Union Grad. Sch., 1972; JD, Stanford U. Law Sch., 1988. Tchr. pub. schs. Abington, Pa., 1952-55, Greenfield Center, N.Y., 1956; instr. edn. dept. Skidmore Coll., Saratoga Springs, N.Y., 1962-64; dir. ednl. research Skidmore Coll., 1967-72, asst. to the pres., 1968-72; asst. dir. Capitol Dist. Regional Supplementary Edn. Center, Albany, N.Y., 1966-67; assoc. dean, asst. prof. state-wide programs Empire State Coll., State U. N.Y., Saratoga Springs, 1973-75; sr. assoc. dean, assoc. prof. Empire State Coll., State U. N.Y., 1975-76, acting dean statewide programs, 1976; pres., prof. interdisciplinary studies Mary Baldwin Coll., Staunton, Va., 1976-85; cons. to bd. trustees Mary Baldwin Coll., 1985-88; assoc. Hunton & Williams, Richmond, Va., 1988-90; interim pres. Friends World Coll., Huntington, N.Y., 1990-91; dir. presdl. search consultation svc. Assn. of Governing Bds. of Univs. and Colls., 1991-94; sr. mgmt. advisor office of exec. dir. Am. Assn. Retired Persons, 1994—; mem. cons. core faculty Union Grad. Sch., Union for Experimenting Colls. and Univs., Cin., 1975-82; vis. faculty fellow Harvard U. Grad. Sch. Edn., 1976; cons. in field; bd. dirs. So. Bankshares, So. Bank; bd. dirs. Council Advancement of Small Colls., 1977-81, Am. Council Edn., 1983-85. Mem. com. on criminal sexual assault Va. State Crime Commn., 1976; v.p. Costume Collection, Inc., 1971-73; v.p. Warren, Washington, Saratoga Counties Planned Parenthood, 1972-74, bd. dirs., 1970-74; mem. Saratoga Springs Housing Bd. Appeals, 1966-76, Commn. on Future of Va., 1982-84; bd. dirs. Nat. Urban League, 1979-86; pres. commn. NCAA, 1984-85. Mem. Am. Acad. Polit. and Social Scis., Va. Found. Ind. Colls. (trustee, exec. com.), Va. Council Ind. Colls., Am. Council on Edn. (commn. on women in higher edn. 1977-80), Nat. Assn. Ind. Colls. and Univs. (dir.), Assn. Va. Colls. (sec.-treas. 1978-79, pres. 1980-81, dir.), Assn. Ch. Related Colls. and Univs. of South (pres. 1983), Pi Lambda Theta, Pi Gamma Mu, Chimes. Mem. Soc. of Friends. *I believe, not unlike many successful women in my generation, that I accepted each new opportunity as a gift of which to make the most. Now, three decades later, I aspire to create my own opportunities.*

LESTER, WILLIAM ALEXANDER, JR., chemist, educator; b. Chgo., Apr. 24, 1937; s. William Alexander and Elizabeth Frances (Clark) L.; m. Rochelle Diane Reed, Dec. 27, 1959; children: William Alexander III, Allison Kimberleigh. B.S., U. Chgo., 1958, M.S., 1959; postgrad., Washington U., St. Louis, 1959-60; Ph.D., Cath. U. Am., 1964. Phys. chemist Nat. Bur. Standards, Washington, 1961-64; asst. dir. Theoretical Chemistry Inst. of U. Wis.-Madison, 1965-68; research staff mem. IBM Research Lab., San Jose, Calif., 1968-75; mgr., 1976-78; mem. tech. planning staff IBM T.J. Watson Research Center, Yorktown Heights, N.Y., 1975-76; dir. Nat. Resource for

Computation in Chemistry, Lawrence Berkeley (Calif.) Lab., 1978-81, also assoc. dir., staff sr. scientist, 1978-81, faculty sr. scientist, 1981—; prof. chemistry U. Calif., Berkeley, 1981—, assoc. dean Coll. Chemistry, 1991-95; lectr. chemistry U. Wis., 1966-68; cons. NSF, 1976-77, mem. chem. divsn. adv. panel, 1980-83, adv. com. Office Advanced Sci. Computing program, 1985-87, chmn., 1987, sr. fellow for sci. and engring., asst. to dir. for human resource devel., 1995—; mem. U.S. nat. com. Internat. Union Pure and Applied Chemistry, 1976-79; mem. com. on recommendations for U.S. Army Basic Sci. Rsch. NRC, 1984-87, mem. steering com., 1987-88; chemistry rsch. evaluation panel AF Office Sci. Rsch., 1974-78; chmn. Gordon Conf. Atomic and Molecular Interactions, 1978; mem. NRC panel on chem. physics Nat. Bur. Stds., 1980-83; mem. com. to survey chem. scis. RRC, 1982-84, Fed. Networking Coun. Adv. Com., 1991—; mem. blue ribbon panel on high performance computing NSF, 1993; mem. com. on high performance computing and comm.: status of a major initiative NRC, 1994-95, mem. com. on math. challenges from computational chemistry, 1994-95. Editor: Procs. of Conf. on Potential Energy Surfaces in Chemistry, 1971; author: (with Brian L. Hammond and Peter J. Reynolds) Monte Carlo Methods in Ab Initio Quantum Chemistry, 1994; mem. editl. bd. Jour. Phys. Chemistry, 1979-87, Jour. Computational Chemistry, 1980-87, Computer Physics Comm., 1981-86; mem. adv. bd. Sci. Yr., 1989-93. Recipient Alumni award in sci. Cath. U. Am., 1983. Fellow AAAS (com. on nominations 1988-91, nat. bd. dirs. 1993—), Am. Phys. Soc. (chmn. div. chem. physics 1986); mem. Am. Chem. Soc. (sec.-treas. Wis. sect. 1967-68, chmn. div. phys. chemistry 1979, treas. div. computers in chemistry 1974-77), Nat. Orgn. Black Chemists and Chem. Engrs. (Percy L. Julian award 1979, Outstanding Tchr. award 1986, exec. bd. 1984-87). Home: 4433 Briar Cliff Rd Oakland CA 94605-4624 Office: U Calif Dept Chemistry Berkeley CA 94720 *Perseverance is the watchword-the will to hold on.*

LESTINA, GERALD F., wholesale grocery executive. Pres., CEO Roundy's Inc., Pewaukee, Wis. Office: Roundy's Inc 23000 Roundy Dr Pewaukee WI 53072*

LESTON, PATRICK JOHN, judge; b. Maywood, Ill., May 2, 1948; s. John R. and Lorraine (McQueen) L.; m. Kristine Brzezinski; children: Alison, Adam. BS in Communications, U. Ill., 1970; JD cum laude, Northwestern U., Chgo., 1973. Bar: Ill. 1973, U.S. Dist. Ct. (no. dist.) Ill. 1973, U.S. Ct. Appeals (7th cir.) 1973. Ptnr. Jacobs & Leston, Villa Park, Ill., 1973-79; pvt. practice Glen Ellyn, Ill., 1979-89; ptnr. Keck, Mahin & Cate, Oakbrook Terrace, Ill., 1989-95; judge 18th Cir. Ct., DuPage County, Ill., 1995—; presenter at profl. confs. Editor Ill. State Bar Assn./Young Lawyers Divsn. Jour., 1983-85. Class rep. Northwestern U. Law Sch. Fund, 1982-88; organizer DuPage County (Ill.) Law Explorers. Fellow ABA (Ill. del. to ABA/Young Lawyers divsn. assembly 1982-85), Ill. State Bar Assn. (chmn. fellows 1991-92, mem. bd. govs. 1990—, chmn. young lawyers divsn. 1985, chmn. agenda com. 1986, del. to 18th jud. cir. assembly 1982-88), Ill. Bar Found. (charter), Am. Bar Found.; mem. Chgo. Bar Assn., DuPage County Bar Assn. (pres. 1987, bd. dirs. 1979-84, chmn. judiciary com. 1988, gen. counsel 1989), Lions Club, Chi Psi. Avocations: volleyball, skiing, scuba diving, travel. Office: 18th Jud Cir Ct 505 N County Farm Rd Wheaton IL 60183-3907

LESZCZYNSKI, JERZY RYSZARD, chemistry educator, researcher; b. Tomaszow, Poland, May 26, 1949; cam to U.S., 1986; s. Leslaw and Hanna (Kaptur) L.; m. Danuta, June 25, 1972; children: Rafal, Magda. MS, Tech. U. Wroclaw (Poland), 1972, PhD, 1975. Lectr. chemistry Tech. U. Wroclaw, 1976-86; vis. sci. U. Fla., Gainesville, 1986-88; rsch. assoc. U. Ala., Birmingham, 1988-90; from asst. to assoc. prof. Jackson (Miss.) State U., 1990-95, prof., 1995—; conf. chmn. organizing com. Current Trends in Computational Chemistry, 1992-96; presenter in field. Author chpts. in books; editor: Computational Chemistry, Revs. of Current Trends, 1995, Electronic Jour. Theoretical Chemistry; co-author Computational Quantum Chemistry, 1988, Combustion Efficiency and Air Quality, 1995; guest editor: Structural Chemistry, 1995, Theochem, 1996; referee Jour. Am. Chem. Soc., Internat. Jour. Quantum Chemistry, Chem. Physics Letters, Structural Chemistry, Jour. Phys. Chemistry, Jour. Molecular Structure, Jour. Computational Chemistry, Jour. Biomolecular Structure and Dynamics; mem. editl. bd. Structural Chemistry; contbr. articles to profl. jours. Recipient Outstanding Faculty award AT&T, 1992, Higher Edn. Appreciation Day, Working for Acad. Excellence award Legislature of Miss., 1995. Mem. Am. Chem. Soc. (exec. com. 1995—), Internat. Soc. Quantum Biiology and Pharm., Miss. Acad. Sci. Office: Jackson State U Dept Chemistry 1400 Lynch St Jackson MS 39217-0510

LETAW, HARRY, JR., technology corporation executive; b. Miami, Fla., Aug. 7, 1926; s. Harry and Ninda (Cook) L.; m. Joyce Winston Brown, June 4, 1947; children: Anne Winston, Kaye Lynn, John Robert, Mary Jane, Amelia Elizabeth, James Brown. BS in Chemistry with high honors, U. Fla., 1949, MS, 1951, PhD, 1952. Rsch. asst. prof. Elec. Engring. dept., U. Ill., Urbana, 1952-55; mktg. mgr. Raytheon Co., Wayland, Mass., 1955-61; dir. advanced programs Elec. div. Martin Marietta, Middle River, Md., 1961-64; v.p., gen. mgr. Ea. Tech. Ctr., Inc., Bunker-Ramo Corp., 1964-65; pres. Severn Comms. Corp., Millersville, Md., 1965—, Logos Ltd., Arlington, Va., 1968-72; chmn., pres. Radiation Systems, Inc., McLean, Va., 1974-78; pres. Intellinet Corp., Millersville, 1983—; chmn., pres., CEO Essex Corp., Columbia, Md., 1988—, also bd. dirs.; adj. assoc. prof. bus. adminstrn. Drexel Inst., 1963-64; cons. Compagnie Internat. Pour L'Informatique, St. German-en-Laye, France, 1966-68. Contbr. articles to profl. jours; patentee in field. Bd. dirs. Econ. Opportunity Com., Anne Arundel County, 1969-71; chmn. adv. com. on ednl. aspects of contemporary issues Md. State Dept. Edn., 1969-73; pres. Greater Severna Park Coun., 1972-73; participant DOD Joint Civilian Orientation Conf. 58, 1995. Sgt. U.S. Army, 1944-47; 2d lt. USAR, 1948-50. Emory U. Alumni scholar, 1943-44; U. Fla. rsch. corp. fellow, 1950; U.S. AEC predoctoral fellow Oak Ridge Inst. for Nuclear Studies, 1950-52. Mem. IEEE (sr.), Am. Phys. Soc., Security Affairs Support Assn. (bd. dirs. 1992-95), Phi Beta Kappa, Sigma Xi. Avocations: hiking, reading, public affairs. Office: Essex Corp 9150 Guilford Rd Columbia MD 21046-1891

LETENDRE, JACQUELYN LEE, special education consultant; b. Charlottesville, Va., Apr. 8, 1941; d. Jesse Francis and Elizabeth Constance (Campbell) Richardson; m. Charles Richard Letendre, July 13, 1960; children: Constance Allyn, Brian Richard. BS, Westfield State Coll., 1975, MEd, 1977. Cert. tchr. elem. edn., spl. edn.; adminstr. spl. edn. Clin. tchr. nursery sch. State Dept. Mental Health, Boston, 1973-75; tchr., coord. So. Worcester County Edn. Collaborative, Southbridge, Mass., 1975-83; pvt. practice various orgns., Wales, Mass., 1985—. Author: (series) Circus Approach to Parenting, 1993; columnist Southridge News, 1985-94; editor: (newsletter) Drug Concerns Program, 1972-86, AARP, 1987-89. Mem. Coun. Exceptional Children, Coun. Learning Disabilities. Avocations: oil painting, gardening, piano playing. Home and Office: 116 Union Rd Wales MA 01081-9793

LETEY, JOHN JOSEPH, JR., soil scientist, educator; b. Carbondale, Colo., June 13, 1933; s. John Joseph and Rosine (Tisseur) L.; m. Patricia Kaye Fitzgerald, Sept. 19, 1992; children: Laura, Donald, Lisa. BS in Agronomy, Colo. State U., 1955; PhD in Soil Physics, U. Ill., 1959. Asst. prof. soil physics UCLA, 1959-61; asst. prof., assoc. prof., prof. U. Calif., Riverside, 1961—, chmn. dept. soil and environ. scis., 1975-80; assoc. dir. water and wetlands resources, 1993—; FAO cons. Bulgaria, 1973, Cen. Soil Salinity Rsch. Inst., Karnal, India, 1989; dir. Kearney Found., U. Calif., 1980-85; mem. Soil Sci. Delegation to People's Republic of China, 1983; keynote speaker Internat. Conf. Soil Salinity Under Irrigation-Processes and Mgmt., Israel, 1984; researcher in field. Author: (with Stahrl Edmunds) Environmental Administration, 1973; contbr. numerous chpts. to books, articles to profl. jours. Mem. Soil Sci. Soc. Am. (fellow 1972, past chmn. soil physics div., assoc. editor proceedings 1967-73), Am. Soc. Agronomy (soil sci. award 1970). Mormon. Avocation: oil painting. Home: 435 W Campus View Dr Riverside CA 92507-4028 Office: U Calif Dept Soil & Environ Scis Riverside CA 92521

LETHBRIDGE, FRANCIS DONALD, architect; b. Hackensack, N.J., Oct. 5, 1920; s. Berry B. and Florence A. (Lapham) L.; m. Mary Jane Christopher, June 21, 1947; children: Catherine B. (Mrs. Robert A. Grove), Mary P. (Mrs. Christopher G. Cromwell), Christopher B., Margaret F. (Mrs. Arsim Cejku). Student, Stevens Inst. Tech., 1937-40, Yale Sch. Architecture, 1945-46. Ptnr. archtl. firm Keyes, Smith, Satterlee & Lethbridge, Washington, 1951-55, Keyes, Lethbridge & Condon, Washington, 1956-75, Francis D. Lethbridge & Assocs., Washington, 1975-90; mem. fgn. bldgs. archtl. rev. panel U.S. State Dept., 1977-80; mem. archtl. adv. panel Fed. Res. Bd., 1979-83; mem. Potomac Planning Task Force, 1965-67; bd. advisers Nat. Trust for Hist. Preservation, 1969-71; mem. Joint Com. Landmarks Nat. Capital, 1964-79, chmn., 1964-73. Co-author: Guide to the Architecture of Washington, D.C; prin. works include Pine Spring Community, Fairfax County, Va., 1951-54, Potomac Overlook, 1955-58, U.S. Chancery, Lima, Peru, 1957, Forest Industries Bldg., Washington, 1961, Carderock Springs Community, Montgomery County, Md., 1963-65, Unitarian Ch, River Road, Md., 1964, master plan Arlington Nat. Cemetery, 1966-68, Ft. Lincoln New Town, 1968, Visitors Ctr., Arlington Nat. Cemetery, 1988. Trustee Nantucket Atheneum; advisor Nantucket Hist. Assn. Officer, pilot USNR, 1942-45. Decorated D.F.C., Air medal; recipient Design Merit award AIA, 1955, 66, 1st honor award, 1966, Potomac Valley Chpt. archtl. award, 1956, 58, 60, 62, 64, 66, 68, 70, 72, 74, 76, joint award of honor AIA-Nat. Assn. Home Builders, 1960; award in architecture Washington Bd. Trade, 1953, 55, 61, 63, 65, 67, 69, 71, 73; Renchard prize for historic preservation, 1983. Fellow AIA (pres. Washington Met. chpt. 1964, v.p. 1969-70, pres. AIA found. 1971-73); mem. Cosmos Club (Washington). Home and Office: 48 Orange St Nantucket MA 02554-3937

LETICHE, JOHN MARION, economist, educator; b. Uman, Kiev, Russia, Nov. 11, 1918; came to U.S., 1941, naturalized, 1949; s. Leon and Mary (Grossman) L.; m. Emily Kuyper, Nov. 17, 1945; 1 son, Hugo K. BA, McGill U., 1940, MA, 1941; PhD in Econs, U. Chgo., 1951. Rockefeller fellow Council Fgn. Relations, N.Y.C., 1945-46; Smith-Mundt vis. prof. U. Aarhus and U. Copenhagen, Denmark, 1951-52; spl. tech. econ. adv. UN ECA, Africa, 1961-62; prof. U. Calif. at Berkeley, 1960—; cons. AID, U.S. Depts. State, Labor, HUD and Treasury, 1962—; emissary to Japan and Korea, Dept. State, 1971; cons. Econ. Coun. Can., 1972—, World Bank, 1981—, Bank of Eng., London, Bundesbank, Frankfurt, Fed. Republic of Germany; lectr. Stockholm, Paris, Uppsala, Hamburg, Kiel, Oxford (Eng.), 1973—, Vancouver, Toronto, Montreal, Zagreb, 1983, Frankfurt, Bonn, Moscow and Nakhodka Acad. Scis. USSR, 1986, Hong Kong, Shanghai, Wuhan, Beijing, London, Bonn, Frankfurt, De Hague, 1987, Bundesbank, 1992, 93, Peoples Republic China, Beijing, Shanghai, 1988, 90, 94, New Delhi, 1996, Acad. Scis., Taipei, 1989, joint session Calif. legis., 1975; ext. examiner adv. degrees U. Hong Kong, U. Calcutta, India. Author: Reciprocal Trade Agreements in the World Economy, 1948, in Japanese, 1951, System or Theory of the Trade of the World, 2d edit., 1957, Balance of Payments and Economic Growth, 2d edit., 1976, A History of Russian Economic Thought, 2d edit., 1977, The Key Problems of Economic Reconstruction and Development in Nigeria, 1970, Dependent Monetary Systems and Economic Development, 1974, Lessons of the Oil Crisis, 1977, Gains from Trade, 1979, Controlling Inflation, Recession, Federal Deficits and the Balance of Payments, 1980, The New Inflation and Its Urban Impact, 1980, Monetary Systems of Africa in the 1980s, 1981, International Economic Policies and Their Theoretical Foundations, 1982, 2d edit., 1992; Russian Statecraft: An Analysis and Translation of Iuril Krizhanich's Politika, 1985, Economics of the Pacific Rim, 1989; editor Royer Lectures, 1980-90, Toward a Market Economy in China, 1992, China's Emerging Monetary and Financial Markets, 1995; contbr. articles to encys., congl. coms. and profl. jours. Supervisory bd. Sch. Econs., St. Petersburg, Russia, 1994—. Recipient certificate merit Ency. Brit., certificate merit Inst. World Affairs, certificate merit Internat. Legal Center, U. Mich., U.S. Office Personnel Mgmt. Sr. Fed. Govt. Execs. and Mgrs., U. Calif.-Berkeley; Adam Smith medal U. Verona, 1977; Guggenheim fellow, 1956-57. Mem. Am. Econ. Assn. (nominating com. 1968-69), Econometric Soc., Royal Econ. Soc., U.S.-Asian Econ. Com. (bd. dirs. 1983—), African Studies Assn., Am. Soc. Internat. Law (bd. 1969-72). Home: 968 Grizzly Peak Blvd Berkeley CA 94708-1549

LETKI, ARLEEN, secondary school educator; b. Pitts., Sept. 30, 1949; d. Henry S. and Monica (Kocinski) K. BS, Lambuth Coll., 1971; MA, Glassboro State Coll., 1989; postgrad., Widener U., 1991—. Cert. social studies, English, elem., spl. edn., pupil pers. svcs., supr., prin., N.J., elem. and secondary prin., Pa. 3d, 5th and 6th grade tchr. St. Mary Sch., Camden, N.J., 1971-72; 7th grade tchr. Annunciation Sch., Belmawr, N.J., 1972-74; 7th and 8th grade tchr. St. Rose Sch., Haddon Heights, N.J., 1974-84; spl. edn. tchr. Glassboro (N.J.) Intermediate Sch., 1984-87, lang. arts tchr., 1987-89; social studies tchr. Glassboro H.S., 1989—; prin. adult H.S., alternative evening sch., cmty. sch. Mem. ASCD, AAUW, Nat. Coun. for Social Studies. Republican. Roman Catholic. Avocations: calligraphy, gardening, reading, walking. Home: 18 Bells Lake Dr Turnersville NJ 08012-1532 Office: Glassboro HS Bowe Blvd Glassboro NJ 08028

LETOURNEAU, DUANE JOHN, biochemist, educator; b. Stillwater, Minn., July 12, 1926; s. John Peter and Olga Margaret (Lange) LeTourneau; m. Phyllis Jean Kaercher, June 22, 1947; children: Bruce Duane, Diane Elaine, Keith George. B.S., U. Minn., 1948, M.S., 1951, Ph.D., 1954. Asst. prof., asst. agrl. chemist U. Idaho, Moscow, 1953-58; assoc. prof., assoc. agrl. chemist U. Idaho, 1958-63, prof., biochemist, 1963-91, asst. dept. head, 1988-89, sec. faculty, 1990-91, sec. faculty, prof. biochemistry emeritus, 1992—; vis. prof. botany U. Sheffield (Eng.), 1973; vis. scientist Nat. Research Council Can., Saskatoon, 1981; Bd. dirs. Idaho Inst. Christian Edn., 1958-62, 73-75, v.p., 1959-62. Author research publs. on plant biochemistry. Bd. dirs. U. Idaho Luth. Campus Coun., 1962-64, 73-75, chmn., 1963-64; trustee FarmHouse Internat. Found., 1974-80, chmn., 1976-80; trustee Gritman Meml. Hosp., 1969-82, v.p., 1977-80; bd. dirs. Gritman Med. Ctr., 1991—, Palouse Regional Health Corp., 1992—; bd. dirs. Latah County Hist. Soc., 1982-89, 92—, pres. bd. dirs., 1984-87; trustee Idaho Hist. Soc., 1992—. With USAAF, 1945. Recipient Outstanding Faculty award Asso. Students U. Idaho, 1960-62, 87, Coll. Agr. Outstanding Instr. award, 1962, R.M. Wade Excellence in Teaching award, 1968, 78, Disting. Faculty award, 1982, Prof. of Yr. award, 1983; Citation for Disting. Achievement, U. Idaho, 1984; Nat. Acad. Scis.-NRC sr. postdoctoral fellow, 1964-65. Fellow AAAS, Am. Inst. Chemists; mem. AAUP (v.p. U. Idaho chpt. 1959-60, sec. 1984-87), Am. Chem. Soc., Am. Soc. Plant Physiologists, Am. Inst. Biol. Scis., Am. Phytopath. Soc., Idaho Acad. Sci. (v.p. 1985-86, pres. 1986-87, editor jour. 1983-89), Mycol. Soc. Am., Phytochem. Soc. N.Am., Am. Soc. Plant Physiologists, Iron Wedge, FarmHouse (dir. Idaho chpt. 1957-62, 72-75, 82-90, pres. 1957-62, 74, 82-85, 90; nat. dir. 1960-64, nat. v.p. 1962-64), Lions (bd. dirs. Moscow Central club 1971-74, 90-91, pres. 1973-74), Sigma Xi, Alpha Zeta, Gamma Alpha, Gamma Sigma Delta (pres. U. Idaho chpt. 1979-80), Phi Kappa Phi (v.p. U. Idaho chpt., pres. 1990-91), Phi Sigma (regional v.p. 1993—). Lutheran (chmn. ch. council and congregation, 1966-69). Home: 479 Ridge Rd Moscow ID 83843-2521

LETOURNEAU, GILLES, judge; b. Que., Can., July 14, 1945; s. romeo and Marguerite (Thibault) L.; m. Claudette tremblay, July 1, 1971; children: Simon, christian, Marie-Eve. BA in Arts, Levis (Que.) Coll., 1965; LLL, Laval U., Que., 1968; LLM, London sch. Econs./Polit. Sci., 1972, PhD, 1975. Bar: Que. 1969. Pvt. practice Que., 1969-71, 75-77; faculty law, vice dean Laval U., 1975-77; dir. policy making and legis. drafting Que. Dept. Justice, 1977-84; assoc. gen. sec. Govt. Que., 1984-85; v.p., pres. Law Reform Commn. of Can., Ottawa, Ont., 1985-90, 90-92; judge Fed. Ct. of Can., Ottawa, 1992—. contbr. articles to profl. jours. Recipient Merit award Levis Coll., 1992, Que. Bar, 1992. Avocations: fishing, outdoor activities. Office: Federal Court of Canada, Supreme Ct of Canada Bldg, Wellington St, Ottawa, ON Canada K1A 0H9

LETOURNEAU, JEAN-PAUL, business association executive and consultant; b. St.-Hyacinthe, Que., Can., May 4, 1930; s. Eugene and Annette (Deslandes) L.; m. Claire Paquin, Sept. 26, 1956. Counsellor in Indsl. Relations, U. Montreal, Que., 1953; cert. c. of c. adminstrn., U. Syracuse, 1962; cert. advanced mgmt. U.S. C. of C, 1965. Mcpl. sec. Mont St.-Hilaire, Que., 1950-53; personnel mgr. Dupuis Freres (mail order house), 1953; editor Jeune Commerce, weekly tabloid Fedn. Que. Jr. C's. of C., 1953; sec. gen. Montreal Jr. C. of C., 1953-56; asst. gen. mgr. Province Que. C. of C., Montreal, 1956-59, gen. mgr., 1959-71, exec. v.p., 1971-90. Author: Quebec, The Price of Independence, 1969, Report on Corporate Social Responsibilities, 1982. Mem. C. of C. Execs. Can. (pres. 1982-83, mem. coun. excellence 1986), Corp. Consellors in Indsl Rels. of Que., Am. C. of C. Execs. (bd. dirs. 1982-83), Can. Exec. Svc. Orgns. (bd. dirs. 1991-95, vice chair 1993-95), Office Persons Handicapped of Que. (bd. dirs. 1992—, exec. com. 1994—), St.-Denis Club. Roman Catholic. Office: 165 Cote Ste-Catherine #202, Outremont, PQ Canada H2V 2A7 *Liberty is priceless; but liberty imposes responsibility, and if one is not responsible he will lose his liberty.*

LETOURNEAU, JOCELYN, history educator; b. Lauzon, PQ, Canada, Oct. 26, 1956; d. Robert and Jacqueline (Roy) L.; m. Esther Ross; children: Lavinia, Gaultier, Saskia, Nathaniel. BA, Laval U., Quebec City, 1978; MA, U. Toronto, Can., 1979; PhD, Laval U., 1985. Asst. prof. dept. history Laval U., Quebec City, 1985-90, assoc. prof., 1990-94, dir. Célat, Faculty of Letters, 1990-94, prof. Faculty of Letters, 1994—; fellow Zentrum Für Interdisziplinare Forschung U. Bielefeld, Germany, 1994-95; mem. editl. bd. (periodical) Social Discourse, Montreal, 1994—. Author: (book) Le Coffre à Outils du Chercheur Débutant, 1989; editor: (book) La Question Identitaire au Canada Français: Recits, Parcours, enjeux, Hors-Lieux, 1994, La Condition du Québec Enjeux et Horizons d'une Societe en Devenir, 1994. Office: Laval U (CELAT), Pavillon Charles De Koninck, Quebec, PQ Canada G1K 7P4 also: U Bielefeld, Wellenberg 1, Bielefeld, PQ Canada D-33615

LETOURNEAU, RICHARD HOWARD, retired college president; b. Stockton, Calif., Jan. 3, 1925; s. Robert G. and Evelyn (Peterson) LeT.; m. Louise Marion Jensen, Feb. 8, 1947; children: Robert Gilmore, Caleb Roy, Linda Louise, Liela Lynn. Student, Wheaton Coll., 1946, LeTourneau Coll., 1956; B.S., Tex. A&M U., 1958, M.S., 1961; Ph.D., Okla. State U., 1970. Gen. mgr. Miss. div. R.G. LeTourneau, Inc., Longview, Tex., 1949-52; v.p. prodn. R.G. LeTourneau, Inc., 1952-57, exec. v.p., 1966, pres., 1966-71; sr. v.p. Marathon Mfg. Co., Houston, 1971-72; dir. Marathon Mfg. Co., 1971-76; pres. Mosley Machinery Co., Waco, Tex., 1972-73; v.p. LeTourneau Found., 1973-75; prof. bus. mgmt. Belhaven Coll., Jackson, Miss., 1993—; mem. Tex. Indsl. Commn., 1959-66; adminstrv. v.p. LeTourneau Coll., 1958-62, pres., 1962-68, 75-85, chancellor, 1985-86, pres. emeritus, 1986—, chmn. bd. trustees, 1968-75; cons. to higher edn., 1986-93. Author: Management Plus, 1973, Keeping Your Cool in a World of Tension, 1975, Success Without Succeeding, 1976, Success Without Compromise, 1977, Democracy in Trouble, 1985, More Than Knowledge, 1985, Laws of Success for Christians, 1985, Finding Your Niche in Life, 1985. Past pres. LeTourneau Found. Served with C.E. AUS, 1944-46, PTO. Mem. Sigma Xi, Phi Kappa Phi, Tau Beta Pi, Alpha Pi Mu. Home and Office: 2724 Timberwood Trl Longview TX 75605-2140 *As a successful industrialist, educator and author, I have found that life is more than mind and body. Everyone, to have a joyous and truly successful life must also trust Jesus Christ as Lord for a spiritual dimension and overall balance in life. With this element missing, regardless of the profession followed, life will be hollow and meaningless, and an eternity of regret is certain.*

LETSINGER, ROBERT LEWIS, chemistry educator; b. Bloomfield, Ind., July 31, 1921; s. Reed A. and Etna (Phillips) L.; m. Dorothy C. Thompson, Feb. 6, 1943; children: Louise, Reed, Sue. Student, Ind. U., 1939-41; B.S., Mass. Inst. Tech., 1943, Ph.D., 1945; DSc (hon.), Acadia U., Can., 1993. Research assoc. MIT, 1945-46; research chemist Tenn. Eastman Corp., 1946; faculty Northwestern U., 1946—, prof. chemistry, 1959—, chmn. dept., 1972-75, joint prof. biochemistry and molecular biology, 1974—, Clare Hamilton Hall prof. chemistry, 1986-92, Clare Hamilton Hall prof. emeritus chemistry, 1992—; Mem. med. and organic chemistry fellowship panel NIH, 1966-69, medicinal chem. A study sect., 1971-75; bd. on chem. scis. and tech. Nat. Research Council, 1987-90. Mem. bd. editors Nucleic Acids Research, 1974-80; contbr. articles to profl. jours. Guggenheim fellow, 1956; JSPS fellow Japan, 1978; recipient Rosenstiel Medallion, 1985, Humboldt Sr. US Scientist award, 1988, NIH merit award, 1988, Arthur C. Cope scholar award, 1993. Fellow Am. Acad. Arts and Scis., Nat. Acad. Scis., Am. Assn. Arts and Scis.; mem. Am. Chem. Soc. (bd. editors 1969-72, bioconjugate chemistry 1992—, Arthur C. Cope scholar award 1993), Internat. Union Pure and Applied Chemistry, Sigma Xi, Phi Lambda Upsilon (hon. mem.). Home: 316 3rd St Wilmette IL 60091-3461 Office: Northwestern U Chemistry Dept 2145 Sheridan Rd Evanston IL 60208-0834

LETSOU, GEORGE VASILIOS, cardiothoracic surgeon; b. Boston, 1958; s. Vasilios George and Helen (Valacellis) L.; m. Jane Elizabeth Carter, June 1, 1985; children: Christopher George, Philip Taylor, John Carter. AB magna cum laude, Harvard U., 1979; MD, Columbia U., 1983. Diplomate Am. Bd. Surgery, Am. Bd. Thoracic Surgery. Resident in gen. surgery Yale-New Haven Hosp., 1983-88, chief resident, instr. surgery, 1987-88, clin. fellow in cardiothoracic surgery, 1988-89, Cystic Fibrosis Found. fellow in cardiopulmonary transplantation, 1988-89, Winchester scholar in cardiothoracic surg. rsch., 1989-90, resident in cardiothoracic surgery, 1990-91; chief resident in cardiothoracic surgery, 1991-92; instr. surgery Yale U., New Haven, 1987-88, 91-92; attending surgeon Yale-New Haven Med. Ctr., 1992-95; Meth. Hosp., Ben Taub Hosp., Houston, 1995—; asst. prof. surgery Yale U., 1992-95; assoc. prof. surgery Baylor Coll. Medicine, Houston, 1995—. Mem. AMA, ACS, Am. Coll. Cardiology, Am. Coll. Chest Physicians, Soc. Thoracic Surgeons. Office: Dept Surgery One Baylor Plaza Ste 4040 Houston TX 77030

LETT, LEON, professional football player; b. Mobile, Ala., Oct. 12, 1968. Student, Hinds Jr. Coll., Emporia (Kans.) State U. Defensive lineman Dallas Cowboys, 1991—. Selected to Pro Bowl, 1994. Mem. Dallas Cowboys Super Bowl Champions, Super Bowl XXVII, 1992, XXVIII, 1993. Office: Dallas Cowboys 1 Cowboys Pky Irving TX 75063

LETT, PHILIP WOOD, JR., defense consultant; b. Newton, Ala., May 4, 1922; s. Philip Wood Sr. and Lily Octavia (Kennedy) L.; m. Katy Lee Howell, June 26, 1948; children: Kathy, Warren, Lisa. B MechE, Ala. Poly. Inst., 1943; MS in Engring., U. Ala., 1947; PhD MechE, U. Mich., 1950; MS in Indsl. Mgmt., MIT, 1960. Registered profl. engr., Mich. Lab. engr., engring. div. Chrysler Corp., 1950-52, project engr., def. engring. div., 1952-54, chief engr., def. engring. div., 1954-61, operating mgr., def. engring. div., 1961-73; head XM1 Tank task force Chrysler Corp., Sterling Heights, Mich., 1973-76; gen. mgr. Sterling Def. div. Chrysler Corp., 1976-79; v.p. engring. Chrysler Def. Inc., Center Line, Mich., 1980-82; v.p. research & engring. Gen. Dynamics Land Systems Div., Center Line, 1982-86, v.p., asst. to gen. mgr., 1986-87; pres. PWL Inc., 1995; mem. U.S. delegation to NATO Indsl. Adv. Group. Contbr. articles to tech. jours. and to Internat. Def. Rev. Trustee Judson Ctr., 1989—. Capt. U.S. Army, 1943-46. Decorated Cheonsu medal Republic of Korea; awarded membership U.S. NAE, 1984; recipient Outstanding Engr. award Auburn U., 1984, Ben S. Gilmer award, 1991, Silver medal Am. Def. Preparedness Assn., 1989; named Disting. Engring. fellow U. Ala. Coll. Engring., 1992; named to Ala. Engring. Hall of Fame, 1992; Sloan fellow MIT, 1960-61. Mem. Orchard Lake Country Club. Baptist. Home: 1330 Oxford Rd Bloomfield Hills MI 48304-3952 Office: PO Box 2074 Warren MI 48090-2074

LETTERMAN, DAVID, television personality, comedian, writer; b. Indpls., Apr. 12, 1947; s. Joseph and Dorothy L.; m. Michelle Cook, 1969 (div. 1977). Grad., Ball State U., 1969. Radio and TV announcer, Indpls.; performer The Comedy Store, Los Angeles, 1975—; appearances on TV include (variety series) Mary, CBS; frequent guest host The Tonight Show; host (morning comedy/variety program) David Letterman Show, NBC, 1980, Late Night with David Letterman, NBC, 1982-1993, The Late Show with David Letterman, CBS, 1993— (also writer); host, Academy Awards, 1995; writer for TV including Bob Hope Special, Good Times, Paul Lynde Comedy Hour, John Denver Special; author: (with others) The Late Night with David Letterman Book of Top Ten Lists, 1990, An Altogether New Book of Top Ten Lists, 1991; film appearances include: Cabin Boy, 1994. Recipient 6 Emmy awards, 1981-88. Avocations: baseball, basketball, auto racing, running. Office: Late Show with David Letterman Ed Sullivan Theater 1697 Broadway New York NY 10019-2902*

LETTMANN, JOHN WILLIAM, cereal manufacturing company executive; b. St. Louis, July 5, 1942; s. Henry William and Josephine (Randazzo) L.; m. Vicky Hodges; children: Susan, Jason, Michael. BSBA, U. Kans., 1964; MBA, Ind. U., 1968. Sr. auditor Gen. Mills, Inc., Mpls., 1964-66, with product mgmt. dept., 1968-71; v.p. mktg. and sales Malt-O-Meal Co., Mpls., 1971-85, pres., chief exec. officer, 1985—; bd. dirs. Horton Mfg., Mrs. Clark's Foods Co., Liberty Mut. Adv. Bd., Am. Mgmt. Assoc. Bd. Gov. Cos. Recipient Leadership award Bush Found., 1969. Mem. Am. Mgmt. Assn. (council 1987—), Grocery Mfrs. Assn., Mpls. Athletic Club, Interlachen Country Club. Avocations: handball, golf, skiing, tennis. Office: Malt-O-Meal Co 80 S 8th St Ste 2600 Minneapolis MN 55402-2100

LETTON, ALVA HAMBLIN, surgeon, educator; b. Tampa, Fla., May 23, 1916; s. James Hervey and Minerva (Hamblin) L.; m. Roberta Rogers, Oct. 7, 1938; children: Robert Hamblin (dec.), Alice Roberta. Student, U. Tampa, 1933-35, U. Fla., 1935-37; MD, Emory U., 1941. Diplomate Am. Bd. Surgery. Intern Ga. Baptist Hosp., Atlanta, 1941-42; resident Ga. Baptist Hosp., 1942-43; pvt. practice medicine specializing gen. surgery (oncology) Atlanta, 1946—; chief staff, attending surgeon Ga. Bapt. Hosp., 1965-73; sr. mem. Letton and Maron Surgery, Atlanta, 1980-95; dir. breast cancer demonstration project Bapt. Med. Ctr., 1972-78; chmn. exec. com. oncology dept. Bapt. Med. Ctr., 1972-78; clin. prof. surgery Med. Coll. Ga.; A. Hamblin Letton chair surg. oncology Ga. Bapt. Med. Ctr., 1990—; assoc. dir. Harris Cancer Ctr., Ga.; vis. prof. Egypt Cancer Inst., 1985, Med. and Dental Sch. N.J., 1986, Coll. Medicine U. Ill., Peoria, 1990; cons. Cobb. Gen. Grady Meml., Scottish Rite hosps.; chmn. cancer task force Ga. Regional Med. Program, 1966-71; mem. Ga. Sci. and Tech. Com., 1964-70; active Am. Cancer Soc., 1949—, nat. chmn. pub. edn., 1965-68, nat. chmn. svc. com. 1968-69, nat. chmn. med. and sci. com., 1969-70, v.p., nat. pres. elect, 1970-71, nat. pres. 1971-72, hon. bd. dirs. life, 1979—; pres. Atlanta Med. Ctr., 1965—, Atlanta Health Evaluation Ctr. 1973-82; mem. Gov.'s Sci. Adv. Coun., 1972-75, U.S. nat. com. Nat. Acad. Scis., 1976-79; Roswell Park Meml. lectr., 1983; A. Hamblin Letton ann. lectr. Southeastern Surg. Congress, 1985—; bd. judges Criss Award; mem. Ethicon Gen. Surg. Adv. Panel, 1975-85; mem. cancer control adv. com. Nat. Cancer Inst., 1975-79; chmn. first cancer postgrad. course USA/USSR/ Union Internat. Contre Cancer, Leningrad, USSR, 1989, mem. profl. edn. com. Union Internat. Contre Cancer, 1966-78, cons., Budapest, Hungary, 1986, cons. to exec. sec., 1972; Consultant to forming Russian cancer Society, 1991-93—. Mem. editorial bd. Internat. Advances in Surg. Oncology, Jour. Cancer Prevention and Detection, 1985—; chmn. editorial bd. Oncology Times, 1979-90; guest editor Seminars in Surg. Oncology; contbr. articles to profl. jours., films. Deacon Bapt. ch. With M.C. USNR, 1943-46. Recipient Presdl. citation, 1944, Aven Citizenship award Fulton County Med. Soc., 1960, Honor Alumnus award Emory U., 1973, Hardman award Med. Assn. Ga., 1973, highest award John Muir Med. Film Festival, 1978, Disting. Svc. award Am. Cancer Soc., 1980, Nat. Div. award Am. Cancer Soc., 1986, Vaughn award Ga. div. Am. Cancer Soc.1987. Fellow ACS, Southeastern Surg. Congress (hon. 1986—, sec.-dir. 1960-86, Disting. Svc. award 1982); mem. Soc. Surg. Oncology, So. Surg. Assn., Soc. Nuclear Medicine, Am. Thyroid Assn., Soc. Internat. de Chirugie, Capital City Club (Atlanta), Univ. Yacht Club (Flowery Branch, Ga.). Baptist. Home: 3384 Rilman Rd NW Atlanta GA 30327-1508 Office: 315 Boulevard NE Atlanta GA 30312-1200

LETTOW, CHARLES FREDERICK, lawyer; b. Iowa Falls, Iowa, Feb. 10, 1941; s. Carl Frederick and Catherine (Reisinger) L.; m. Sue Lettow, Apr. 20, 1963; children: Renee, Carl II, John, Paul. BS in Chem. Engring., Iowa State U., 1962; LLB, Stanford U., 1968. Bar: Calif. 1969, Iowa 1969, D.C. 1972, Md. 1991. Law clk. to Hon. Ben C. Duniway U.S. Ct. Appeals (9th cir.), San Francisco, 1968-69; law clk. to Hon. Warren E. Burger U.S. Supreme Ct., Washington, 1969-70; counsel Council on Environ. Quality, Washington, 1970-73; assoc. Cleary, Gottlieb, Steen & Hamilton, Washington, 1973-76, ptnr., 1976—; pres. Busy Way Farms, Inc., 1989—. Contbr. articles to profl. jours. Trustee Potomac Sch., McLean, Va., 1983-90, chmn. bd. trustees, 1985-88. 1st lt. U.S. Army, 1963-65. mem. ABA, Am. Law Inst., D.C. Bar Assn., Iowa Bar Assn., Order of Coif. Club: University. Office: 1752 N St NW Washington DC 20036-2806

LETTS, J. SPENCER, federal judge; b. 1934. BA, Yale U., 1956; LLB, Harvard U., 1960. Commd. U.S. Army, 1956, advanced through grades to capt., resigned, 1965; pvt. practice law Fulbright & Jaworski, Houston, 1960-66, Troy, Malin, Loveland & Letts, L.A., 1973-74, Hedlund, Hunter & Lynch, L.A., 1978-82, Latham & Watkins, L.A., 1982-85; gen. counsel Teledyne, Inc., 1966-73, 75-78, legal cons., 1978-82; judge U.S. Dist. Ct. (cen. dist.) Calif., L.A., 1986—. Contbr. articles to profl. jours. Mem. ABA, Calif. State Bar, Tex. State Bar, L.A. Bar Assn., Houston Bar Assn. Office: US Dist Ct 312 N Spring St Los Angeles CA 90012-4701*

LETTVIN, THEODORE, concert pianist; b. Chgo., Oct. 29, 1926; s. Solomon and Fannie (Naktin) L.; m. Joan Rorimer; children: Rory, Ellen, David. Mus. B., Curtis Inst. Music, 1949; postgrad., U. Pa. Head piano dept. Cleve. Music Sch. Settlement, 1957-68; prof. piano New Eng. Conservatory Music, Boston, 1968-77; prof., dir., doctoral program in piano performance U. Mich. Sch. Music, Ann Arbor, 1977-87; disting. prof. dept. music Rutgers U., New Brunswick, N.J., 1987—, dir. doctor of mus. arts and artist's diploma program, 1987-92, studio tchr., coach chamber music, 1992—; vis. lectr. U. Colo., 1956-57; tchr. master classes U. S.E. Mass., summer 1973, U. Calif., San Jose, 1992, 93; mem. faculty Chamber Music Sch., U. Maine, Orono. First appeared as concert pianist, 1931, solo debut with Chgo. Symphony Orch., 1939, solo, orchestral appearances include Boston Symphony Orch., N.Y. Philharm., Phila. Orch., Cleve. Orch., Chgo. Orch., Washington Nat. Symphony, Pitts. Symphony, Seattle Symphony, Mpls. Symphony, Atlanta Symphony, other Am. and European orchs.; radio appearance Bell Telephone Hour, 1948, debut Ravinia Festival, 1951, apprentice condr. William Steinberg, Buffalo Symphony Orch., 1950-51, concertized throughout U.S., Can., Europe, Africa, 1952-85; concert appearances Pitts., Cin., Atlanta, Boston, N.Y.C., Phila., Chgo., Cleve., Mpls. and Chautauqua, Ravinia, Interlochen and New Coll., Town Hall, Alice Tully Hall concerts, in N.Y.C., Boston Symphony Orch.; performances in concert with Bernard Greenhouse, cellist; concert tours, Europe, 1952, 55, 58, 60, 62-85, Israel, 1973, Africa and Japan, 1974; also numerous performances with European orchs., summer festivals, TV; asst. artist: Africa and Japan, Marlboro Music Festival, 1963. Recipient award Soc. Am. Musicians, 1933, Naumberg award, 1948, Michaels Meml. award, 1949, Laureate internat. piano competition Queen Elisabeth of Belgium. Mem. Am. Fedn. Musicians, Am. Guild Mus. Artists, AAUP (exec. com.), Music Tchrs. Nat. Assn., Am. Liszt Soc., Curtis Inst. Music Alumnae Assn. (bd. dirs.). Home: 12 Bernard Rd East Brunswick NJ 08816-1306 Office: Rutgers U Marryott Music Bldg Douglass Campus New Brunswick NJ 08903 also: 463 Rowe Mountain Rd Bradford NH 03221-9116

LETWIN, LEON, legal educator; b. Milw., Dec. 29, 1929; s. Lazar and Bessie (Rosenthal) L.; m. Alita Zurav, July 11, 1952; children—Michael, Daniel, David. Ph.B., U. Chgo., 1950; LL.B., U. Wis., 1952; LL.M., Harvard U., 1964. Bar: Wis. 1952, Calif. 1969. Teaching fellow Harvard Law Sch., Boston, 1963-64; faculty Law Sch. UCLA, 1964—, prof., 1968—. Contbr. articles to profl. jours. Active ACLU. Mem. Conf. Critical Legal Studies, Nat. Lawyers Guild, State Bar Calif. Home: 2226 Manning Ave Los Angeles CA 90064-2002 Office: UCLA Law Sch 405 Hilgard Ave Los Angeles CA 90024-1301

LETZIG, BETTY JEAN, association executive; b. Hardin, Mo., Feb. 18, 1926; d. Robert H. and Alina Violet (Mayes) L. BA, Scarritt Coll., 1950, MA, 1968. Ednl. staff The Methodist Ch., Ark., Okla. Tex., 1953-60; with Internat. Deaconess Exchange Program, London, 1961-62; staff exec. Nat. Div. United Meth. Ch., N.Y.C., 1962-95, ret. 1995; coord. Mission Pers. Support Svcs., 1984-88; exec. sec. Deaconess Program Office, 1989-95. Contbr. articles to profl. jours. Bd. dirs. Internat. Svcs. Assn. for Health, Inc., Atlanta, 1974-88, Vellore Christian Med. Coll., N.Y.C., 1984-94; mem. U.S. com. Internat. Coun. Social Welfare, Washington, 1983-89; active Nat. Interfaith Coalition on Aging, Athens, Ga. and Washington, 1972—, pres., 1981-85. Recipient Deaconess Exch. award Commn. Deaconess Work, 1961-62. Mem. Nat. Coun. Aging, Nat. Voluntary Orgns. Ind. Living for Aging (exec. com. 1978-84), Nat. Coun. Social Welfare, Older Women's League. United Methodist. Avocations: travel, beachcombing, photography, needlework. Home: 235 E 22nd St Apt 1U New York NY 10010-4630 Office: Nat Program Divsn Gen Bd Global Ministries 475 Riverside Dr Ste 300 New York NY 10115-0122

LEUBERT, ALFRED OTTO PAUL, international business consultant, investor; b. N.Y.C., Dec. 7, 1922; s. Paul T. and Josephine (Haaga) L.; m. Celestine Capka, July 22, 1944 (div. 1977); children: Eloise Ann (Mrs. Kevin B. Cronin), Susan Beth; m. Hope Sherman Drapkin, June 4, 1978 (div. 1982). Student, Dartmouth Coll., 1943; BS, Fordham U., 1946; MBA, NYU, 1950. Account mgr. J.K. Lasser & Co., N.Y.C., 1948-52; controller Vision, Inc., N.Y.C., 1952-53; controller Old Town Corp., 1953-54, sec., controller, 1954-56, sec.-treas., 1956-57, v.p., treas., 1957-58; dir. subsidiaries Old Town Corp. (Old Town Internat. Corp., Old Town Ribbon & Carbon Co., Inc.), Mass. and Calif., 1955-58; v.p., controller Willcox & Gibbs, Inc., N.Y.C., 1958-59; v.p., treas. Willcox & Gibbs, Inc., 1959-65, pres., dir., chief exec. officer, 1966-76; founder, pub., pres. Leubert's Compendium of Bus. (Fin. and Econ. Barometers), 1978-82; pres. Alfred O.P. Leubert Ltd., 1981-82, chmn. CEO, 1993—; chmn., CEO Solidyne, Inc., 1982; chmn. bd., pres., CEO, dir. Chyron Corp., 1983-91; dir. K & E Real Estate Ltd., China, 1994—; chmn. bd. CEO Leubert & Co. (H.K.) Ltd., 1994—; dir. Laser-Pacific Media Corp., 1995—; chmn. bd., CEO, bd. dirs. Chyron Group (U.K.) Ltd., 1985-89; dir. Isis Interactive Inc., 1996—; chmn. bd., CEO, bd. dirs. CMX Corp.; bd. dirs. Aurora Systems, 1988-91; CEO, dir. CGS Units, Inc., 1988-90, chmn. bd., 1989-90; bd. dirs. Digital Svcs. Corp.; vice chmn. bd. dirs. CMX Laser Sys., Inc., 1988-93; instr. accountancy Pace Coll., 1955-57. Bd. dirs. United Fund of Manhasset, 1963-69, pres., 1964-65; bd. dirs. Actor's Studio, 1972-76; adv. bd. St. Anthony's Guidance Clinic, 1967-69. Served to 1st lt., inf. USMCR, 1943-46. Decorated Bronze Star; recipient Humanitarian award Hebrew Acad., N.Y.C., 1971. Mem. AICPA, N.Y. State Soc. CPAs, Fordham U. Alumni Assn. Roman Catholic. Club: N.Y. Athletic (N.Y.C.). Home and Office: 1 Lincoln Plz New York NY 10023-7129

LEUBSDORF, CARL PHILIPP, newspaper executive; b. N.Y.C., Mar. 17, 1938; s. Karl and Bertha (Boschwitz) L.; m. Carolyn Cleveland Stockmeyer, Mar. 26, 1963 (div. 1978); 1 child: Carl Philipp Jr.; stepchildren: Lorna Stockmeyer, E. William Stockmeyer Jr., C. Cleveland Stockmeyer, Claire C. Stockmeyer; m. Susan Page, May 23, 1982; children: Benjamin Page, William Page. BA in Govt., Cornell U., 1959; MS in Jour., Columbia U., 1960. Staff writer AP, New Orleans, 1960-63, Washington, 1963-75; corr. Balt. Sun, Washington, 1976-81; AME Washington bur. chief Dallas Morning News, Washington, 1981—. Mem. White House Corrs. Assn. (pres. 1995-96), Gridiron Club, National Press Club (Washington). Office: Dallas Morning News 1012 National Press Building Washington DC 20045-2001

LEUKART, RICHARD HENRY, II, lawyer; b. Detroit, Mar. 15, 1942; s. Richard Henry and Marjorie Ruth (Smith) L.; m. Barbara Joan Gottfried, Oct. 7, 1977; children: Elisabeth, Jennifer, Kathleen, Richard Henry III, Brian. AB, Dartmouth Coll., 1964; AB, Amos Tuck Sch. Bus., 1964; JD, U. Mich., 1967. Bar: Ohio 1967. Ptnr. Baker & Hostetler, Cleve., 1967—, Firmwide Employment Law and Employee Benefits Group (Chair 1995—). Bd. Trustees Hudson Heritage Assn., 1984-88. Alfred P. Sloan Found. scholar, 1960-62; Daniel Webster scholar, 1963-64. Mem. ABA, Ohio Bar Assn., Cleve. Bar Assn., County Club of Hudson (trustee 1996—), Union Club of Cleve. Republican. Presbyterian. Office: Baker & Hostetler 3200 Nat City Ctr 1900 E 9th St Cleveland OH 44114-3401

LEUNG, FRANKIE FOOK-LUN, lawyer; b. Guangzhou, China, 1949; married; 1 child. BA in Psychology with honors, Hong Kong U., 1972; MS in Psychology, Birmingham U., Eng., 1974; BA, MA in Jurisprudence, Oxford U., Eng., 1976; JD, Coll. of Law, London, 1977. Bar: Calif. 1987. Barrister Eng. and Hong Kong, 1977—; lectr. Chinese law for businessmen Hong Kong U., 1984-85, 85-86; vis. scholar Harvard U. Law Sch., 1983; barrister, solicitor Supreme Ct. of Victoria, Australia, 1983—, Calif. Bar, 1987—; cons. prof. Chinese Law Diploma Program, U. East Asia, 1986-87; adj. prof. Loyola Law Sch., L.A., 1988—, Pepperdine U. Law Sch., 1989-90; lectr. Stanford U. Law Sch., 1995—. Author 3 books; contbr. numerous articles to profl. jours., chpts. to 4 books. Bd. advisors Hong Kong Archives Hoover Instn.-Stanford U., 1988—. Mem. Calif. State Bar (mem. exec. coun. internat. sect. 1989-92, Wiley W. Manuel award 1993), Hong Kong Bar Assn., European Assn. for Chinese Law (mem. exec. coun. 1986—, country corr. 1985—), Am. C. of C. (chmn. subcom. on Chinese intellectual property law 1985-86), Am. Soc. Internat. Law (judge moot ct. 1984-86). Office: Lewis D'Amato 221 N Figueroa St Ste 1200 Los Angeles CA 90012-2601

LEUPP, EDYTHE PETERSON, retired education educator, administrator; b. Mpls., Nov. 27, 1921; d. Reynold H. and Lillian (Aldridge) Peterson; m. Thomas A. Leupp, Jan. 29, 1944 (dec.); children: DeEtte (dec.), Patrice, Stacia, Roderick, Braden. BS, U. Oreg., 1947, MS, 1951, EdD, 1972. Tchr. various pub. schs. Idaho, 1941-45, Portland, Oreg., 1945-55; dir. tchr. edn. Northwest Nazarene Coll., Nampa, Idaho, 1955-61; sch. adminstr. Portland Pub. Schs., 1963-84; dir. tchr. edn. George Fox Coll., Newberg, Oreg., 1984-87; ret., 1987; vis. prof. So. Nazarene U., Bethany, Okla., 1988-95; pres. Portland Assn. Pub. Sch. Adminstrs., 1973-75; dir.-at-large Nat. Coun. Adminstrv. Women in Edn., Washington, 1973-76; state chmn. Oreg. Sch. Prins. Spl. Project, 1978-79; chair Confdn. Oreg. Sch. Adminstrs. Ann. Conf.; rschr. 40 tchr. edn. programs in colls. and univs.; designer tchr. edn. program George Fox Coll. Author tchr. edn. materials. Pres. Idaho State Aux. Mcpl. League, 1957, Nampa PTA, 1958, Nampa unit AAUW, 1956; bd. dirs. Portland Fedn. Women's Clubs, 1963. Idea fellow Charles Kettering Found., 1978, 80, 87, 91, 92, 93, 94. Mem. ASCD, Am. Assn. Colls. Tchr. Edn., Delta Kappa Gamma (state pres. 1986-88, Golden Gift award 1984), Phi Delta Kappa, Pi Lambda Theta. Republican. Nazarene. Avocations: travel, crafts, photography. Home: 8100 SW 2nd Ave Portland OR 97219-4602

LEUTHOLD, RAYMOND MARTIN, agricultural economics educator; b. Billings, Mont., Oct. 13, 1940; s. John Henry and Grace Irene L.; m. Jane Hornaday, Aug. 20, 1966; children—Kevin, Gregory. Student, Colo. U., 1958-59; B.S., Mont. State U., 1962; M.S., U. Wis., 1966, Ph.D., 1968. Faculty U. Ill., Urbana-Champaign, 1967—; now prof. dept. agrl. econs. U. Ill., T.A. Hieronymus disting. prof., dir. office futures and options rsch.; vis. scholar Stanford U., 1974, Chgo. Mercantile Exch., 1990, 91. Co-author: The Theory and Practice of Futures Markets, 1989; editor: Commodity Markets and Futures Prices, 1979; co-editor: Livestock Futures Research Symposium, 1980. Served with U.S. Army, 1962-64. Fulbright research scholar Institute de Gestion Internationale Agro-Alimentaire, Cergy, France, 1981. Mem. Am. Econ. Assn., Am. Agrl. Econs. Assn. (Disting. Policy award 1980, Outstanding Instr. award 1986, 88, 90, 92, College Funk award 1993). Office: 305 Mumford Hall 1301 W Gregory Dr Urbana IL 61801-3608

LEUTZE, JAMES RICHARD, academic administrator, television producer and host; b. Charleston, S.C., Dec. 24, 1935; w. Willard Parker and Magdalene Mae (Seith) L.; m. Kathleen Shirley Erskine, Feb. 13, 1960; children—Magdalene Leigh, Jay Erskine, James Parker. B.A., U. Md., 1957; M.A., U. Miami, 1959; Ph.D., Duke U., 1968. Legis. asst. U.S. Senator Hubert Humphrey, Washington, 1963-64; prof. history U. N.C., Chapel Hill, 1968-87, chmn. curriculum peace, war, and def., 1979-87, Bowman and Gordon Gray prof., 1982, Dowd prof. Peace and War, 1986; TV host-producer N.C. Ctr. for Pub. TV, Chapel Hill, 1984—; pres. Hampden-Sydney (Va.) Coll., 1987-90; chancellor U. N.C. at Wilmington, 1990—. Author: Bargaining for Supremacy: Anglo-American Naval Collaboration, 1937-41, 1977 (Bernath prize 1978), A Different Kind of Victory: The Biography of Admiral Thomas C. Hart, 1981 (John Lyman Book award 1981); editor: London Journal Gen. Raymond E. Lee, 1972, The Role of the Military in a Democracy, 1974; contbr. articles to profl. jours. Served to capt. USAF, 1960-63. Recipient Standard Oil award for teaching U. N.C., 1971, Tanner award for teaching, 1978, Order of Golden Fleece award, 1983. Mem. Orgn. Am. Historians, Royal U.S. Inst. (London), Am. Hist. Assn., Univ. Club (N.D.), George C. Marshall Found., Phi Beta Kappa. Democrat. Episcopalian. Avocations: sportsman; hunting; fishing. Office: U NC 601 S College Rd Wilmington NC 28403-3201

LEUVER, ROBERT JOSEPH, former government official, association executive; b. Chgo., Feb. 2, 1927; s. Joseph Anthony and Helen Yolanda (Fornaciari) L.; m. Hilda Sanjuana Ortiz, July 29, 1950; 1 dau., Mary Ellen. AB, Loyola U., L.A., 1950; MA, Cath. U. Am., 1954. Exec. v.p., treas. Claretians, Inc., Chgo., 1959-72; chief mgmt. analysis divsn. ACTION, Washington, 1972-74; chief treas. payroll divsn. U.S. Dept. Treasury, Washington, 1974-79; asst. dir. Bur. Engraving and Printing, Washington, 1979-82, dep. dir., 1982, dir., 1983-88; now exec. dir. Am. Numismatic Assn., Colorado Springs, Colo.; mem. Citizens Stamp Adv. Com. to Postmaster Gen., U.S. Postal Service, 1983-88. Bd. dirs. Cath. Journalism Scholarship Fund, N.Y.C., 1967-72; v.p., dir. Southampton Assn., Arlington, Va., 1979-86. Recipient Best Editorial award Cath. Press Assn., 1964, Sr. Exec. award, 1980, 84, 85, Presdl. Meritorious Svc. award U.S. Pres., Washington, 1983, Presdl. Disting. Svc. award, 1986. Mem. Fed. Exec. Inst. (grad.), Sr. Exec. Assn. Roman Catholic. Office: Am Numismatic Assn 818 N Cascade Ave Colorado Springs CO 80903-3208

LEV, ALEXANDER SHULIM, mechanical engineer; b. Tselinograd, USSR, May 4, 1945; came to U.S., 1979; s. Borukh and Golda (Kopitman) L.; m. Polina Zhdanovskaja, Aug. 31, 1968; 1 child, Victoria. MSME, Lvov Polytech Inst., 1968. Project mgr. Glavspetsavtotrans, Lvov, USSR, 1968-78; sr. engr. Machine Plant, Lvov, USSR, 1978-79; metalurgist Ronson Metals Corp., Newark, N.J., 1980-82, foundry quality control mgr., 1982-83, reduction dept. mgr., 1986; project mgr. FMB Systems Inc., Harrison, N.J., 1986-94; v.p. Internat. Fair Share Inc., Rockaway, N.J., 1994—. Patentee in field. Mem. Am. Metals Soc., Metallurgical Soc. Avocations: reading, art, metal work, tennis. Home: 16 Princeton St Maplewood NJ 07040-3517

LEV, ALLEN P., lawyer; b. Chgo., Nov. 24, 1947. BA, U. Ill., 1968, JD with honors, 1971. Bar: Ill. 1971. Mng. ptnr. Holleb & Coff, Chgo., 1989—. V.p. bd. edn. Northbrook (Ill.) Sch. Dist., 1983-89. Mem. Chgo. Bar Assn. Office: Holleb & Coff 55 E Monroe St Ste 4100 Chicago IL 60603-5803

LEVA, JAMES ROBERT, electric utility company executive; b. Boonton, N.J., May 10, 1932; s. James and Rose (Cocci) L.; m. Marie Marinaro, Dec. 19, 1950; children: James, Daniel, Linda, Michael, Christopher. BSEE, magna cum laude, Fairleigh Dickinson U., 1960; JD, Seton Hall Law Sch., 1980. Lineman Jersey Central Power and Light Co., Morristown, N.J., 1952-60, elec. engring. and operating depts., 1960-62, personnel rep., 1962-68, mgr. employee relations, 1968-69, v.p. personnel and services, 1969-79, v.p. consumer affairs, 1979-82, dir., 1976-82; pres., COO, dir. Pa. Electric Co., Johnstown, 1982-86; pres., COO Jersey Cen. Power & Light Co., Morristown, N.J., 1986-92; chmn., pres., CEO Gen. Pub. Utilities, 1992—, also bd. dirs.; chmn., pres., CEO, bd. dirs. GPU Service Corp., Parsippany, N.J.; chmn. bd. dirs. GPU Nuc. Corp., Parsippany, N.J.; chmn. CEO, bd. dirs. Met. Edison Co., Reading, Pa., Pa. Electric Co., Johnstown, Pa., Utilities Mut. Ins. Co., N.J. Utilities Assn.; chmn. St. Clares Health Care Found.; bd. overseers N.J. Inst. Tech.; trustee Tri-County Scholarship Fund, Fairleigh Dickinson U.; chmn. Sch. Planning & Pub. Policy Rutgers U. Served with USMC, 1949-51, Korea. Mem. N.J. Bar, N.J. Bar Assn. Roman Catholic. Club: Mendham (N.J.) Golf & Tennis. Office: Gen Pub Utilities 100 Interpace Pky Parsippany NJ 07054-1149

LEVA, MARX, lawyer; b. Selma, Ala., Apr. 4, 1915; s. Leo and Fannie Rose (Gusdorf) L.; m. Shirley Pearlman, Oct. 31, 1942; children: Leo Marx, Lloyd Leva Plaine. B.S., U. Ala., 1937, LL.D., 1978; LL.B., Harvard U., 1940. Bar: Ala. 1940, U.S. Supreme Ct. 1946, D.C. 1950. Law clk. to Justice Hugo Black, U.S. Supreme Ct., 1940; sr. atty. O.P.A., 1941; acting regional atty. for Mich. and Ohio WPB, 1942; counsel to fiscal dir. of Navy, 1946, spl. asst. to sec. of navy, 1947; spl. asst. and gen. counsel to Sec. Def., 1947-49; asst. sec of def. (legal and legis.), 1949-51; ptnr. Fowler, Leva, Hawes & Symington, 1951-67, Leva, Hawes, Symington, Martin & Oppenheimer, 1967-85, Leva, Hawes, Mason & Martin, 1985-90; of counsel Robins, Kaplan, Miller & Ciresi, 1990-93; Chmn. civilian-mil. review panel for spl. com. U.S. Senate, 1957; mem. Pres.'s Commn. to Rev. Fgn. Aid, 1958-59, Pres.'s Com. on Def. Establishment, 1960-61. Note editor: Harvard Law Rev, 1939-40; overseer, 1950-55. Served with amphibious forces USNR, 1943-44, ETO. Decorated Bronze Star with combat disting. device; named Outstanding Young Man In Govt., Washington Jr. C. of C., 1949. Home: 7115 Bradley Blvd Bethesda MD 20817-2125 Office: 1801 K St NW Washington DC 20006-1301

LEVACK, ARTHUR PAUL, history educator emeritus; b. Boston, Dec. 16, 1909; s. Arthur Joseph and Marie Agnes (St Onge) L.; m. Helen Gertrude O'Brien, Aug. 28, 1939; children—Ann Marie, Brian Paul. B.A. magna cum laude, Harvard, 1932, M.A., 1934, Ph.D., 1941. Teaching fellow Amherst Coll., 1935-36; instr. Fordham U., 1936-42, asst. prof., 1942-47, assoc. prof., 1947-67, prof., 1967-79, emeritus, 1979—, chmn. dept. history, 1950-65, dean summer session, 1965-78. Author: (with R.J.S. Hoffman) Burke's Politics, 1949, (with A.I. Abell) A History of the United States, 1951; Contbr. to Ency. Americana also articles to profl. jours. Mem. Am. Hist. Assn., Am. Cath. Hist. Assn. (pres. 1951), U.S. Cath. Hist. Soc. (pres. 1952-53). Democrat. Roman Catholic.

LEVADA, WILLIAM JOSEPH, archbishop; b. Long Beach, Calif., June 15, 1936; s. Joseph and Lorraine (Nunez) L. B.A., St. John's Coll., Camarillo, Calif., 1958; S.T.L., Gregorian U., Rome, 1962, S.T.D., 1971. Ordained priest Roman Cath. Ch., 1961, consecrated bishop, 1983. Assoc. pastor Archdiocese of L.A., 1962-67; prof. theology St. John's Sem., Camarillo, Calif., 1970-76; ofcl. Doctrinal Congregation, Vatican City, Italy, 1976-82; exec. dir. Calif. Cath. Conf., Sacramento, 1982-84; aux. bishop Archdiocese of L.A., 1983-86; archbishop Archdiocese of Portland, Oreg., 1986-95; Archbishop of San Francisco, 1995—. Trustee Cath. U. Am.; chmn. bd. dirs. Pope John XXIII Med.-Moral Rsch. and Edn. Ctr. Mem. Nat. Conf. Cath. Bishops (com. on doctrine), U.S. Cath. Conf., Cath. Theol. Soc. Am., Canon Law Soc. Am. Office: Archbishop of San Francisco 445 Church St San Francisco CA 94114-1799

LEVAL, PIERRE NELSON, federal judge; b. N.Y.C., Sept. 4, 1936; s. Fernand and Beatrice (Reiter) L. B.A. cum laude, Harvard U., 1959, J.D. magna cum laude, 1963. Bar: N.Y. 1964, U.S. Ct. Appeals 2d Circuit 1964, U.S. Dist. Ct. So. Dist. N.Y 1966. Law clk. to Hon. Henry J. Friendly, U.S. Ct. Appeals, 1963-64; asst. U.S. atty. So. Dist. N.Y., 1964-68, chief appellate atty., 1967-68; assoc. firm Cleary, Gottlieb, Steen & Hamilton, N.Y.C., 1969-74; ptnr. firm, 1973-75; 1st asst. dist. atty. Office of Dist. Atty., N.Y. County, 1975-76; chief asst. dist. atty. Office of Dist. Atty., 1976-77; U.S. dist. judge So. Dist. N.Y., N.Y.C., 1977-93; judge U.S. Ct. of Appeals (2d cir.), N.Y.C., 1993—. Contbr. articles to profl. jours. Served with U.S. Army, 1959. Mem. Am. Law Inst. (council), Assn. Bar City N.Y., N.Y. County Lawyers Assn. Office: US Courthouse Foley Square New York NY 10007-1501*

LEVALIER, DOTIAN, harpist; b. Salem, Mass., June 2, 1943; d. Curtis Levitt and Audrey Lois (Sargent) Bushby; m. William Daniel Carter, Sept. 3, 1965 (div. 1986); children: Lisa Dianne, Janice Elizabeth. Diploma, Curtis Inst., Phila., 1964. Prin. harpist Phila. Lyric Opera, 1964-69, Phila. Chamber Orch., 1965-68, Pa. Ballet, Phila., 1965-69, Nat. Symphony Orch., Washington, 1969—; solo harpist Stern & Levalier, Flute and Harp Duo, Washington, 1982—. Episcopalian. Avocations: camping, sewing, gardening, hiking, travel. Office: Nat Symphony Orch JFK Ctr Performing Arts Washington DC 20566

LEVALLEY, JOAN CATHERINE, accountant; b. Decatur, Ill., Nov. 27, 1931; d. Clarence and Pearl Mae (McClure) Krall; m. Charles R. LeValley, Apr. 13, 1958 (div.); children: Curtis Ray, Cara Marie. BA in Bus., Manchester Coll., 1957. Accredited tax advisor, Ill. Acct. with various firms, 1960-76; pvt. practice acctg., Park Ridge, Ill., 1964-79; pres., dir. LeValley & Assocs., Inc., Park Ridge, 1979—; mem. tax adv. com. Chgo. IRS Dirs.; mem. com. United Way of Park Ridge, 1991, co-chmn., 1992. Mem. Nat. Assn. Pub. Accts., Ind. Acct. Assn. Ill. (2d woman pres. 1987-88, Person of Yr. award 1990), Bus. and Profl. Women Park Ridge (pres. 1974-75, Bus. Woman of Yr. 1983), Park Ridge C. of C. (treas. 1985-87). Baptist. Avocations: baking; sewing; gardening. Home: 2200 Bouterse St Apt 101 Park Ridge IL 60068-2367 Office: LeValley & Assocs Inc 6215 S 44th St Lincoln NE 68516-5506

LE VAN, DANIEL HAYDEN, gas industry executive; b. Savannah, Ga., Mar. 29, 1924; s. Daniel Hayden and Ruth (Harner) LeV. Grad., Middlesex Sch., 1943; BA, Harvard U., 1950; postgrad., Babson Inst., 1950-51. Underwriter Zurich Ins. Co., N.Y.C., 1951-52; co-owner, dir. Overseas Properties, Ltd., N.Y.C., 1970—; dir. Colonial Gas Co., Lowell, Mass., 1973—. With AUS, 1943-46. Mem. Harvard Club (N.Y.C. and Boston).

LEVANT, BRIAN, film director. films include: Problem Child II, 1991, Beethoven, 1992, The Flintstones, 1994. Office: Telvan Prodns 9528

Dalegrove Dr Beverly Hills CA 90210-1711 also: United Talent Agy 9560 Wilshire Blvd Fl 5 Beverly Hills CA 90212-2401

LEVASSEUR, SUSAN LEE SALISBURY, secondary education educator; b. Wyandotte, Mich., Nov. 20, 1967; d. David Henry and Lynda Lee (Macaulay) Salisbury; m. John Peter LeVasseur, Dec. 19, 1992. BS in Edn., Ctrl. Mich. U., 1990; postgrad., Wayne State U., 1991—. Cert. secondary tchr., Mich. Substitute tchr. Dearborn (Mich.) Schs., 1991, Allen Park (Mich.) Schs., 1991; tchr. sci. Berkley (Mich.) Schs., 1991—. Instr. Mich. Red Cross, Detroit, 1983—; deacon Allen Park Presbyn. Ch., 1991-93. Mem. ASCD, AAUW, Nat. Counseling Assn., Am. Kennel Club, Nat. Sci. Tchrs. Assn., Mich. Sci. Tchrs. Assn., Mich. Counseling Assn., Mich. Edn. Assn., Mich. Sci. Tchrs. Assn., Kappa Delta Pi, Alpha Phi Omega. Presbyterian. Avocations: figure skating, swimming, dog training. Home: 22436 Cobb Dearborn MI 48128

LEVASSEUR, WILLIAM RYAN, lawyer; b. Fredericksburg, Va., June 10, 1935; s. George B. and Martha F. (Callegary) L.; m. Joanne Bowers, May 30, 1958; children: William Ryan Jr., John M., Michele Henzi. AA, U. Balt., 1958, JD, 1961. Bar: Md. 1962, U.S. Dist. Ct. Md. 1962, U.S. Supreme Ct. 1972, D.C. 1979, U.S. Ct. Appeals (4th cir.) 1979. Pvt. practice Balt., 1962-69; asst. atty. gen. Md. Atty. Gen.'s Office, Balt., 1969-71; assoc. Semmes, Bowen & Semmes, Balt., 1971-73, ptnr., 1974-94; ptnr. Howell, Gately, Whitney & Carter, Towson, Md., 1994—. Mem. adv. bd. Villa Julie Coll., 1982—, U. Balt. Sch. Law, 1985-91, trustee; trustee Md. Law Rev. With USAFR, 1955-59. Named Alumnus of the Yr. U. Balt. Alumni Assn., 1989. Mem. ABA (tort and ins. practice sect., litigation sect., elected to sect. coun., 1996, mem. Balto. adv. com., 1996, minority women and gen. mem. involvement com. 1992-95, women and minority involvement 1995-96, chmn. arrangements com., 1995-96, co-chmn. family life com. 1991-93, mem. pub. rels. com. 1990-93, chmn. liaison jud. adminstrv. divsn. 1986-89, chmn. Profl. Issues, 1987-88, chmn. Scope and Correlation, 1988-89, chmn. workers' compensation and employers' liability commn. and chmn. nat. inst. 1985-86, program chmn. 1983-84, sr. vice chmn. 1987—), Fed. Bar Assn. (pres. Md. chpt. 1987-88, chair select com. bench bar 1993-94, cir. officer 4th cir. 1988-92, chair nat. mem., com. 1991-93, mem. 1993-94, nat. mem. svcs. com. 1988-89, nat. nominating com. 1988, ops. rev. com., advisor found. 1991-93, bd. dirs., pres. 1994—), Md. State Bar Assn. (sect. adminstrn., law, litigation, negligence and compensation, mem. fed. dist. ct. com.), D.C. Bar Assn. (litigation divsn.), Assn. Def. Trial Counsel (workers compensation com.), Assn. Compensation Inst. Attys. (pres. 1982), Bar Assn. Balt. City (sec. 1993-94, v.p. 1990, 94-95, treas. 1992, chmn. law sch. activities/funding com. 1983-90, jud. com. 1989-94, chmn. 1991-92, chair legis. com. joint task, force for injured workers rehab. 1987—, pres.-elect 1995-96, pres. 1996—), Balt. City Bar Found., Md. Inst. for Continuing Profl. Edn. Lawyers (trustee), U. Balt. Alumni Assn. (pres. 1983-85, sch. law adv. bd. 1985-91), KC. Democrat. Roman Catholic. Home: 1917 Knollton Rd Lutherville Timonium MD 21093-5248 Office: Howell Gately Whitney & Carter 401 Washington Ave 12th Fl Towson MD 21204

LEVE, ALAN DONALD, electronic materials manufacturing company owner, executive; b. Los Angeles, Dec. 15, 1927; s. Milton Lewis and Etta L.; m. Annette Einhorn, Sept. 3, 1962; children—Laura Michelle, Elise Deanne. BS, UCLA, 1951. CPA, Calif. Staff acct., mgr. Joseph S. Herbert & Co. (C.P.A.s), Los Angeles, 1951-57; ptnr. Joseph S. Herbert & Co. (C.P.A.s), 1957-63; fin. and adminstrv. v.p., sec./treas. Mica Corp., Culver City, Calif., 1963-82, also bd. dirs., 1963-82, chmn. bd., chief exec. officer, 1982-83; v.p., bd. dirs. Micaply Internat. Inc., 1968-1982; v.p. Micaply AG, Switzerland, 1972-83, also bd. dirs., chief exec. officer, also bd. dirs., 1982-83; v.p., bd. dirs. Micaply Internat., Ltd., U.K., 1971-82; chmn. bd., mng. dir., chief exec. officer Micaply Internat. Ltd., U.K., 1982-83; v.p., bd. dirs. Titan Chem. Corp., Edgecraft Corp., Culver Hydro-Press, Inc., L.A., 1963-75; chmn. bd., pres., chief exec. officer Ohmega Techs., Inc., Culver City, Calif., 1983—, Ohmega Electronics, Inc., Culver City, 1986—. Served with USAAF, 1946-47. Home: 16430 Dorado Dr Encino CA 91436-4118 Office: 4031 Elenda St Culver City CA 90232-3723

LEVE, SAMUEL, scenic designer; b. USSR, Dec. 1, 1910; 1 child, Teri. Student, various art schs., N.Y.C, Yale U., Jewish Theol. Sem. Am. instr., lectr. CCNY, Baylor U., Waco, Tex., Yale U., NYU, Fla. State U., Tallahassee, YMHA. Designer over 100 Broadway prodns. for Shurberts, George Abbott, Theatre Guild, Rodgers and Hammerstein, Orson Welles, David Merrick, Saroyan, Met. Opera, Maurice Schwartz (Yiddish Theatre), Habimah, others; design Chanukah Festivals at Madison Square Garden, N.Y.C., McCormick Place, Chgo.; designer two synagogues N.Y.C., St. John the Divine Cathedral, and for five presidents. Address: 277 W End Ave New York NY 10023-2604

LEVEE, JOHN HARRISON, artist, designer; b. Los Angeles, Apr. 10, 1924; s. Michael Charles and Roze L.; m. Claude Marie, Dec. 19, 1964. B.A., UCLA, 1948; postgrad., New Sch. Social Research, N.Y.C., 1949, Acad. Julian, 1950. vis. prof. art U. Ill., 1965, N.Y. U., 1967-68, U. So. Calif., 1971. One-man shows include Konig Galerie, Geneva, 1971, Andre Emmerich Gallery, N.Y.C., 1957-59, 62, 66, Gimpel Fils, London, 1958, 60, 66, Galerie de France, 1961, 62, 64, 69, Nora Gallery, Jerusalem, Haira (Israel) Mus. Art, Moose Gallery, Toronto, 1963, Phoenix Mus. Art, 1964, U. Ill. Krannert Art Mus., 1965, Tel Aviv (Israel) Mus., 1969, Margo Leavin Gallery, L.A., 1970, Galerie la Toabis, Paris, 1975, Palm Springs (Calif.) Mus., 1978, Mus. Nice, France, 1980, Galerie La Closerie des Lilacs, Paris, 1983, 86, Galerie 1900-2000, Paris, Galerie de Poche, Paris, 1990; oneman retrospective Galerie Le Gall, Paris, 1986, retrospective of the 1950's, Gallerie Callu, Paris, 1989, retrospective of the 1960's, 1989, retrospective 1953-93 Toulouse Mus., France; group shows, Salon de Mai, Paris, 1954-79, 96, Salon des Realités Nouvelles, 1954-96, Salon Comparison, 1978-92, Paris, Carnegie Internat., 1955-58, Washington's Corcoran Gallery of Art, 1956, 58, Mus. Modern Art N.Y.C., 1957, Whitney Mus., 1957-59, 65, Arts Club Chgo., 1958, Guggenheim Mus., 1966, others, many archtl. projects, France, U.S.A. Served with USAAF, 1944-46. Recipient prizes including Watercolor Assn. Ann. 1955, 56, Commonwealth of Va. Biann. Purchase award 1966, grand prix Woolmark Found. 1974-75, gran prix Biennale de Paris 1969; Ford grantee, 1969; Tamarind fellow Los Angeles, 1969. Jewish. Home: 119 rue Notre Dame des, Champs, 6 Paris France *Most thinkers and artists are not historical geniuses who have broken with previous tradition, perceived relationships hitherto unnoticed, or even invented new relationships or had new visions thus transforming the categories in terms of which human beings think of their place in the universe. But for each historical period there are these men of genius and it is the moral imperative of us all to strive, to reach out in our own way and within our own limits, toward this end.*

LEVEILLE, GILBERT ANTONIO, food products executive; b. Fall River, Mass., June 3, 1934; s. Isidore and Rose (Caron) L.; divorced; children: Michael, Kathleen, Edward; m. Carol A. Phillips, Aug. 7, 1981. B in Vocat. Agriculture, U. Mass, 1956; MS, Rutgers U., 1958, PhD, 1960. Prof. nutritional biochemistry U. Ill., Urbana, 1965-71; chmn. dept. food sci. and human nutrition Mich. State U., East Lansing, 1971-80; dir. nutrition and health sci. Gen. Foods Corp., Tarrytown, N.Y., 1980-86; v.p. for rsch. and tech. svcs. Nabisco Inc., East Hanover, N.J., 1986—. Author: The Set Point Diet, 1985 (N.Y. Times nonfiction bestseller); also over 300 articles. Served to 1st lt. U.S. Army, 1960-62. Recipient rsch. award Poultry Sci. Assn., 1965, Disting. Faculty award Mich. State U., 1980. Mem. AAAS, Am. Chem. Soc., Am. Inst. Nutrition (pres. 1988-89, Mead Johnson rsch. award 1971), Am. Soc. for Clin. Nutrition, Inst. Food Technologists (pres. 1983-84, fellow 1983, Carl Fellers award 1992). Office: Nabisco Inc PO Box 1944 East Hanover NJ 07936-1944

LEVEL, LEON JULES, information services executive; b. Detroit, Dec. 30, 1940; s. Leon and Madeline G. (Mayea) L.; m. Constance Kramer, June 25, 1966; children—Andrea, Aileen. B.B.A., U. Mich., 1962, M.B.A., 1963. CPA, Mich. Asst. accountant Deloitte Haskins & Sells, Detroit, 1963-66, sr. accountant, 1966-69, prin., 1969-71; asst. corp. controller Bendix Corp., Southfield, Mich., 1971-81; v.p. fin. planning Burroughs Corp., Detroit, 1981-82, v.p., treas., 1982-86; v.p., treas. Unisys Corp., Blue Bell, Pa., 1986-89; v.p., chief fin. officer Computer Scis. Corp., El Segundo, Calif., 1989—; mem. U. Mich. adv. bd., Ann Arbor, 1984-90, Providence Hosp. Adv. Bd., Southfield, Mich., 1984-86, Allendale Ins. Adv. Bd., Cleve., 1985-89, 96—. Trustee Walnut St. Theatre, Phila., 1988-89. Mem. Fin. Execs. Inst. (sec. Detroit chpt. 1983-85, v.p. 1985-86, pres. 1986-87), Am. Inst. C.P.A.s, Mich. Assn. C.P.A.s, Inst. Mgmt. Accts. Office: Computer Scis Corp 2100 E Grand Ave El Segundo CA 90245-5024

LEVELL, EDWARD, JR., city official; b. Jacksonville, Ala., Apr. 2, 1931; m. Rosa M. (Casellas) L, Aug. 3, 1951; children: Edward III (dec.), Ruben C., Kenneth W., Randy C., Raymond C., Cheryl D. Levell Rivera, Michael K. BS, Tuskegee Inst., 1953; MA in Urban Sociology, U. No. Colo., 1972; M in Mgmt., Indsl. Coll./Air War Coll., 1974. Commd. 2d lt. USAF, 1953, advanced through grades to col., 1978, various flight tng., air ops. and command positions, 1953-69; comdr. cadet group, then dep. commandant cadet wing USAF Acad., 1969-73; dep. comdr., wing comdr., vice comdr. 1st spl. ops. wing USAF, 1973-77, wing comdr. 58th tactical air command tng. wing, 1977-78, col., vice comdr., comdr. 20th air divsn., 1978-83, ret., 1983; dep. commr. aviation City of Chgo. Dept. Aviation, 1983-89; dep. dir. aviation, fin. and adminstrn. City of New Orleans Dept. Aviation, 1989-90, dep. dir. aviation, ops. and maintenance, 1990-92, dir. aviation, 1992—. bd. dirs. Tourist & Conv. Commn., New Orleans; trustee Dryades YMCA, New Orleans; mem. transp. com. World Trade Ctr. Decorated Legion of Merit, D.F.C. (2), Meritorious Svc. Medal (2), Air Medal (8), Air Force Commendation Medal; recipient Disting. Svc. award Jacksonville, Ala., 1974, State of Fla. Commn. Human Rels. award for spl. recognition, 1977, Air Force Assn. Spl. Citation of Merit, 1977, Disting. Svc. award City of Chgo. Dept. Aviation, 1986, 87, 88; inducted in Tuskegee Univ. Hall of Fame, 1991. Mem. Airport Ops. Coun. Internat. (task force chmn. ann. conf. New Orleans 1991), Am. Assn. Airport Execs., Gulf Coast Internat. Hispanic C. of C. Home: 1500 W Esplanade Ave Apt 46F Kenner LA 70065-5346 Office: New Orleans Aviation Bd New Orleans Intl Airport Box 20007 New Orleans LA 70141

LEVELT SENGERS, JOHANNA MARIA HENRICA, research physicist; b. Amsterdam, The Netherlands, Mar. 4, 1929; came to U.S., 1963; d. Wilhelmus Henricus and Maria Antonia Josephine (Berger) Levelt; m. Jan V. Sengers, Feb. 21, 1963; children: Rachel Teresa, Adriaan Jan, Maarten Willem, Phoebe Josephine. BS, Municipal U., Amsterdam, 1950, MS, 1954, PhD in Physics, 1958; hon. doctorate, Delft U. Tech., 1992. Rsch. asst. Municipal U., Amsterdam, 1954-63; postdoctoral assoc. U. Wis., Madison, 1958-59; rsch. physicist Nat. Bur. Standards, Gaithersburg, Md., 1963-95, group leader, 1978-88, scientist emeritus, 1995—; vis. prof. U. Louvain, Belgium, 1971; vis. scientist Mcpl. U., Amsterdam, 1974-75; Regents prof. UCLA, 1982; sr. fellow Nat. Inst. Standards and Tech., Gaithersburg, 1983-95. Contbr. 12 chpts. to books and over 100 articles to profl. jours. Recipient DOC silver medal, 1972, DOC gold medal, 1978, WISE award U.S. Interagy. Com., Women in Sci. and Engring., Washington, 1985, A.V. Humboldt Rsch. award Ruhr-U., Bochum, Germany, 1991. Fellow Am. Phys. Soc.; mem. ASME (nat. del. rsch. com. water and steam 1988—), AIChE, AAAS, NAE, Royal Netherlands Acad. Scis. (corr.), Internat. Assn. Properties Water and Steam (v.p. 1988-90, pres. 1990-91, hon. fellow 1994), European Phys. Soc., Am. Chem. Soc. (divsn. phys. chemistry), Sigma Xi. Democrat. Avocations: gardening, hiking, swimming, traveling, reading. Home: 110 N Van Buren St Rockville MD 20850-1861 Office: Nat Inst Standards & Tech Gaithersburg MD 20899

LEVEN, ANN RUTH, arts administrator; b. Canton, Ohio, Nov. 1, 1940; d. Joseph J. and Bessie (Scharff) L. AB, Brown U., 1962; cert. with distinction in program in bus. adminstrn., Harvard-Radcliffe Univs., 1963; MBA, Harvard U., 1964. Product mgr. household products div. Colgate-Palmolive, N.Y.C., 1964-66; account exec. Grey Advt., N.Y.C., 1966-67; fin. asst. Met. Mus. Art, N.Y.C., 1967-69; asst. treas. Met. Mus. Art, 1970-72, treas., 1972-79; v.p., sr. corp. planning officer Chase Manhattan Bank, N.Y.C., 1979-83; pres. ARL Assocs., N.Y.C., 1983—; treas. Smithsonian Instn., 1984-90; dep. treas. Nat. Gallery Art, Washington, 1990-94, treas., 1994—; adj. asst. prof. Grad. Sch. Bus., Columbia U., 1975-77, adj. assoc. prof., 1977-79, adj. prof., 1980-93; exec.-in-residence Amos Tuck Sch., Dartmouth Coll., winter 1976, spring, 1984; dir. Alliance Capital Res., Inc., 1978-79, Short Term Asset Res., 1985-93, Oreg. Tax Free Trust, 1986—, Churchill Tax-Free Fund of Ky., 1987—, Churchill Cash Res. Trust, 1995—, Cascades Cash Fund, 1989-94, Del. Group, 1989—. Artist (awarded prizes for painting and graphic arts); author articles on grad. bus. edn., mgmt. studies on the arts. Mem. exec. bd. new leadership div. Fedn. Jewish Philanthropies, 1968-70; mem. council N.Y. Public Library, mem. exec. com., 1976-79; mem. mus. adv. panel N.Y. State Council on Arts, 1977-79; bd. dirs. Camp Rainbow, 1970-84, v.p., 1976-78, treas., 1982-84; bd. overseers Amos Tuck Sch., 1978-84, chmn. ednl. affairs com., 1979-84; trustee Brown U., 1976—, also mem. fin. and budget com., student life com., devel. com., adv. and exec. coms.; bd. mem. Ctr. for Fgn. Policy Devel., 1989-94; trustee Artists' Choice Mus., 1979-87; bd. dirs. Reading Is Fundamental, 1987-91, adv. coun., 1991-94; mem. vis. com. Harvard U. Bus. Sch., 1979-84; trustee ARC Endowment Fund, 1985-90; bd. dirs. Am. Arts Alliance, 1990-92; bd. dirs. Twyla Tharp Dance Found., 1982-87; bd. overseers Hood Mus.-Hopkins Ctr. Dartmouth Coll., 1984-91, chmn., 1988-91; mem. staff Presdl. Task Force on Arts and Humanities, 1981. Recipient Young Leadership award Council Jewish Fedns. and Welfare Funds, 1968; named N.Y. State's Outstanding Young Woman, 1976. Mem. Harvard Bus. Sch. Alumni Assn. (exec. coun. 1976-79, v.p. 1978-79), Women's Fin. Assn., Women's Forum, Econ. Club of Washington, Cosmopolitan Club, Harvard Bus. Sch. Club, Radcliffe Club, Brown Club, Art Table. Home: 785 Park Ave New York NY 10021-3552 Office: Nat Gallery Art Washington DC 20565

LEVEN, CHARLES LOUIS, economics educator; b. Chgo., May 2, 1928; s. Elie H. and Ruth (Reinach) R.; m. Judith Danoff, 1950 (div. 1970); m. Dorothy Wish, 1970; children: Ronald L., Robert M., Carol E., Philip W., Alice S. Student, Ill. Inst. Tech., 1945-46, U. Ill., 1947; B.S., Northwestern U., 1950, M.A., 1957, Ph.D., 1958. Economist Fed. Res. Bank of Chgo., 1950-56; asst. prof. Iowa State U., 1957-59, U. Pa., 1959-62; asso. prof. U. Pitts., 1962-65; prof. econs. Washington U., St. Louis, 1965-91, chmn. dept. econs., 1975-80, prof. emeritus, 1991—; dir. Inst. Urban and Regional Studies, 1965-85; disting. prof. U. Mo., St. Louis, 1991—; cons. EEC, Ill. Auditor Gen., Polish Ministry of Planning and Constrn., St. Louis Sch. Bd., Ukrainian Ctr. for Markets and Entrepreneurship, European Inst. Comparative Urban Rsch. Author: Theory and Method of Income and Product Accounts for Metropolitan Areas, 1963, Development Benefits of Water Resource Investment, 1969, An Analytical Framework for Regional Development Policy, 1970, Neighborhood Change, 1976, The Mature Metropolis, 1978. Served with USNR, 1945-46. Ford Found. fellow, 1956; grantee Social Sci. Rsch. Coun., 1960; grantee Com. Urban Econ., 1965; grantee NSF, 1968, 73, Merc. Bancorp., 1976, HUD, 1978, NIH, 1985. Mem. Am. Econ. Assn., Regional Sci. Assn. (pres. 1964-65, Walter Izard award for distig. scholarship 1995), Western Regional Sci. Assn. (pres. 1974-75), So. Regional Sci. Assn. (disting. fellow 1991). Home: 7042 Delmar Blvd Saint Louis MO 63130-4301 Office: Washington U Box 1208 1 Brookings Dr Saint Louis MO 63130-4862 also: U Mo 8001 Natural Bridge Rd Saint Louis MO 63121 *Achievement is satisfying, but especially so when one can win without others losing. At the same time, it appears unnecessary to be a failure to prove one's sincerity.*

LEVENDUSKY, PHILIP GEORGE, clinical psychologist, administrator; b. Lowell, Mass., Oct. 21, 1946; s. Harry George and Phyllis Mary (Gowgill) L.; m. Cynthia Ann Becton; 1 child, Jason Philip. BA magna cum laude, U. Mass, 1968; MS, Wash. State U., 1971, Wash. State U., 1973. Diplomate Am. Bd. Profl. Psychology. Asst. to dir. Human Rels. Ctr., Wash. State U., Pullman, 1971-73; asst. psychologist McLean Hosp., Belmont, Mass., 1974-82; assoc. psychologist McLean Hosp., Belmont, 1982-92, psychologist, 1992—, dir. cognitive behavior therapy unit, 1974-94, dir. ambulatory care, 1991-93, asst. gen. dir., 1993-95, dir. ambulatory care svcs., 1994-95, v.p. network devel., 1995—; instr. psychiatry Harvard Med. Sch., 1974-88, asst. prof., 1989—; dir. Levendusky and Assocs., Arlington, Mass., 1980—; bd. dirs. Pullman Mgmt., Manchester, Mass., 1976-80, Feeding Ourselves, 1980, Anorexia Bulemia Care, 1991-93; dir. Bain & Co., Employee Consultation, Boston, 1987—; cons. Va Hosp., Boston, 1977-85, Boston Cardiovascular Health, 1983-85, Mass. Dept. Mental Health, 1987—; mem. Mass. Bd. Psychology, Boston, 1988-93. Contbr. articles to profl. jours., mags., newspapers; author book chpts.; guest numerous TV and Radio programs, Boston. Mem. Am. Psychol. Assn., Assn. Advancement Behavior Therapy, New Eng. Soc. of Behavior Analysis and Therapy (bd. dirs. 1991), Phi Beta Kappa. Republican. Roman Catholic. Avocations: skiing, jogging. Home: Manchester by the Sea MA 01944-1405 Office: McLean Hosp 115 Mill St Belmont MA 02178-1041

LEVENFELD, MILTON ARTHUR, lawyer; b. Chgo., Mar. 18, 1927; s. Mitchell A. and Florence B. (Berman) L.; m. Iona R. Wishner, Dec. 18, 1949; children—Barry, David, Judith. Ph.B., U. Chgo., 1947, J.D., 1950. Bar: Ill. 1950. Ptnr. Altman, Levenfeld & Kanter, Chgo., 1961-64, Levenfeld and Kanter, Chgo., 1964-80, Levenfeld, Eisenberg, Janger & Glassberg, Chgo., 1980—; former dir. Bank of Chgo., Garfield Ridge Trust & Savs. Bank; lectr. in fed. taxation. Contbr. articles to profl. jours. Bd. dirs. Spertus Coll. Judaica, Jewish Fedn. Chgo., 1975-84, Am. Israel C. of C., 1st nat. v.p.; chmn. legacies and endowments com., 1982-84; co-gen. chmn. Chgo. Jewish United Fund, 1977, vice chmn. campaign, 1979; gov. mem. Orchestral Assn. Chgo. Symphony Orch.; vis. com. U. Chgo. Law Sch., 1989-91; pres. Am. Israel C. of C. of Met. Chgo., 1993-95. With USNR, 1944-45. Recipient Keter Shem Tov award Jewish Nat. Fund, 1978. Mem. ABA, Ill. Bar Assn., Chgo. Bar Assn. Home: 866 Stonegate Dr Highland Park IL 60035-5145 Office: 33 W Monroe St Chicago IL 60603-5302

LEVENSON, ALAN BRADLEY, lawyer; b. Long Beach, N.Y., Dec. 13, 1935; s. Cyrus O. and Jean (Kotler) L.; m. Joan Marlene Levenson, Aug. 19, 1956; children: Scott Keith, Julie Jo. AB, Dartmouth Coll., 1956; BA, Oxford U., Eng., 1958, MA, 1962; LLB, Yale U., 1961. Bar: N.Y. 1962, U.S. Dist. Ct. D.C. 1964, U.S. Ct. Appeals (D.C. cir.) 1965, U.S. Supreme Ct. 1965. Law clk., trainee div. corp. fin. SEC, Washington, 1961-62, gen. atty., 1962, trial atty., 1963, br. chief, 1963-65, asst. dir., 1965-68, exec. asst. dir., 1968, dir., 1970-76; v.p. Shareholders Mgmt. Co., L.A., 1969, sr. v.p., 1969-70, exec. v.p., 1970; ptnr. Fulbright & Jaworski, Washington, 1976—; lectr. Cath. U. Am., 1964-68, Columbia U., 1973; adj. prof. Georgetown U., 1964, 77, 79-81, U.S. rep. working party OECD, Paris, 1974-75; adv. com. SEC, 1976-77; mem. adv. bd. Securities Regulation Inst., U. Calif., San Diego, 1973—, vice chmn. exec. com., 1979-83, chmn., 1983-87, emeritus chmn., 1988—; mem. adv. coun. SEC Inst., U. So. Calif., L.A., Sch. Acctg., 1981-85; mem. adv. com. Nat. Ctr. Fin. Svcs., U. Calif.-Berkeley, 1985-89; mem. planning com. Ray Garrett Ann. Securities Regulation Inst. Northwestern U. Law Sch.; mem. adv. panel to U.S. compt.-gen. on stock market decline, 1987, panel of cons., 1989—; mem. audit adv. com. GAO, 1992—. Mem. bd. editl. advisors U. Iowa Jour. Corp. Law, 1978—; Bur. Nat. Affairs adv. bd. Securities Regulation and Law Report, 1976—; bd. editors N.Y. Law Jour., 1976—; bd. advisors, corp. and securities law advisor Prentice Hall Law & Bus., 1991-95; contbr. articles to profl. jours.; mem. adv. bd. Banking Policy Report. Recipient Disting. Service award SEC, 1972; James B. Richardson fellow Oxford U., 1956. Mem. ABA (adv. com., fed. regulation securities com., task force rev. fed. securities laws, former chair subcom. on securities activities banks), Fed. Bar Assn. (emeritus mem. exec. com. securities law com.), Am. Law Inst., Practicing Law Inst. (nat. adv. com. 1974, adv. com. ann. securities reg. inst.), AICPA (pub. dir., bd. dirs. 1983-90, fin. com. 1984-90, chmn. adv. coun. auditing standards bd. 1979-80, future issues com. 1982-85), Nat. Assn. Securities Dealers (corp. fin. com. 1981-87, nat. arbitration com. 1983-87, gov.-at-large, bd. govs. 1984-87, exec. com. 1986-87, long range planning com. 1987-90, chmn. legal adv. bd. 1988-93, spl. com. governance and structure 1989-90, numerous adv. coms.). Home: 12512 Exchange Ct S Potomac MD 20854-2431 Office: Fulbright & Jaworski LLP 801 Pennsylvania Ave NW Washington DC 20004-2615

LEVENSON, ALAN IRA, psychiatrist, physician, educator; b. Boston, July 25, 1935; s. Jacob Maurice and Frances Ethel (Biller) L.; m. Myra Beatrice Katzen, June 12, 1960 (div. 1993); children: Jonathan, Nancy; m. Linda Ann Nadell, Jan. 30, 1994. AB, Harvard U., 1957, MD, 1961, MPH, 1965. Diplomate: Am. Bd. Psychiatry and Neurology. Intern U. Hosp., Ann Arbor, Mich., 1961-62; resident psychiatry Mass. Mental Health Center, Boston, 1962-65; staff psychiatrist NIMH, Chevy Chase, Md., 1965-66; dir. div. mental health service programs NIMH, 1967-69; prof. psychiatry U. Ariz. Coll. Medicine, Tucson, 1969—, head dept. psychiatry, 1969-89; chief exec. officer Palo Verde Mental Health Svcs., Tucson, 1971-91, chief med. officer, med. dir., 1991-93; chmn. bd. dirs., CEO Psychiatrists' Purchasing Group, 1991—; chmn. bd. dirs. Psychiatrists' Risk Retention Group, 1991—; mem. staff Tucson Med. Ctr., U. Med. Ctr., Tucson. Author: The Community Mental Health Center: Strategies and Programs, 1972; Contbr. papers and articles to psychiat. jours. Bd. dirs. Tucson Urban League, 1971-78, Pima Council on Aging, 1976-83. Served with USPHS, 1965-69. Fellow Am. Psychiat. Assn. (treas. 1986-90), Am. Coll. Psychiatrists (regent 1980-83, v.p. 1983-85, pres.-elect 1985-86, pres. 1986-87), Am. Coll. Mental Health Adminstrn. (v.p. 1980-82, pres. 1982-83); mem. Group for Advancement Psychiatry, Harvard Alumni Assn. (bd. dirs. 1988-91). Office: 75 N Calle Resplendor Tucson AZ 85716-4937

LEVENSON, HARVEY STUART, manufacturing company executive; b. N.Y.C., May 1, 1940; s. Abraham and Lucile (Lichtenstein) L.; m. Merrilee Borenstein, Aug. 28, 1960; children: Lee Alan, Gary Scott. BA, Drake U., 1962, JD, 1963; LLM, Georgetown U., 1966. Bar: Iowa 1963, N.Y. 1964, Conn. 1968. Atty. IRS, Washington, 1964-68; assoc. Murtha, Cullina, Richter & Pinney, Hartford, Conn., 1968-69; ptnr. Murtha, Cullina, Richter & Pinney, Hartford, 1970-82; sr. v.p., chief fin. officer Kaman Corp., Bloomfield, Conn., 1982-90; pres., chief oper. officer Kaman Corp., Bloomfield, 1990—, bd. dirs.; lectr. U. Conn. Law Sch., Hartford, 1972-76; bd. dirs. Conn. Natural Gas Corp., and Security Conn. Corp.; adv. bd. dirs. Shawmut Bank; corporator St. Francis Hosp., Hartford Hosp., Inst. of Living. Co-author: Depreciation & The Investment Tax Credit, 1983; contbr. various articles on taxation to profl. jours.

LEVENSON, JACOB CLAVNER, English language educator; b. Boston, Oct. 1, 1922; s. Joseph Mayer and Frances (Hahn) L.; m. Charlotte Elizabeth Getz, June 6, 1946; children: Anne Berthe, Jill Mayer, Paul Getz. AB, Harvard U., 1943, PhD, 1951. Tutor in history and lit. Harvard, 1946-50, vis. lectr. English and gen. edn., 1951-52; instr. English U. Conn., 1950-54; asst. prof. to prof. English U. Minn., 1954-67; Edgar Allan Poe prof. English U. Va., Charlottesville, 1967—; chmn. dept. U. Va., 1971-74; faculty Salzburg (Austria) Seminar in Am. Studies, 1947, 49; Mem. Com. of Cons., Notable Am. Women, 1607-1950, 63-72. Author: The Mind and Art of Henry Adams, 1957, Hist. and Critical Introductions The Works of Stephen Crane, II-V, VII, 1969-76; editor: Stephen Crane: Prose and Poetry, 1984, Mark Twain Life on the Mississippi, 1967, Discussions of Hamlet, 1960, The Letters of Henry Adams I-III, 1982, IV-VI, 1988; mem. editorial bd.: Am. Quar., 1964-70, Va. Quar. Rev., 1968—, New Literary History, 1969—, Am. Lit., 1988-91; contbr. articles to profl. jours. Served with AUS, 1943-45. Decorated Bronze Star medal; Guggenheim fellow, 1958-59; Am. Council Learned Socs. fellow, 1961-62; Am. Philos. Soc. Penrose grantee, 1956; recipient E. Harris Harbison award for disting. teaching Danforth Found., 1966. Mem. MLA, Am. Studies Assn., Signet Soc., Phi Beta Kappa. Home: 1100 Free State Rd Charlottesville VA 22901-1819

LEVENSON, MARC DAVID, optics and lasers specialist, scientist; b. Phila., May 28, 1945; s. Donald William and Ethyl Jean Levenson; m. Naomi Francis Matsuda, Oct. 24, 1971. SB, MIT, 1967; MS, Stanford U., 1968, PhD, 1971. Rsch. fellow Harvard U., Cambridge, Mass., 1971-74; asst. prof. physics U. So. Calif., L.A., 1974-77, assoc. prof., 1977-79; mem. rsch. staff IBM Rsch. div., San Jose, Calif., 1979-93, head mgr. OSC, 1987, mgr. quantum metrology, 1990; v.p. Focused Rsch., Inc., Sunnyvale, Calif., 1993-95; propr., cons. Marc D. Levenson Optics, Saratoga, 1993-95; vis. fellow Joint Inst. for Lab. Astrophysics, U. Colo., Boulder, 1995-96. Author: Introduction to Nonlinear Laser Spectroscopy, 1988; editor: Lasers, Spectroscopy, New Ideas, 1987, Resonances, 1991; West Coast editor Solid State Tech. mag., 1993—; editor-in-chief Microlithography World Mag., 1995—; contbr. articles to profl. jours. Alfred Sloan rsch. fellow, 1975. Fellow IEEE, Optical Soc. Am. (Adolph Lomb medal 1976), Am. Phys. Soc., Bay Area Chrome Users Soc./Soc. Photog. and Instrumentation Engrs. (award 1991). Avocations: gardening, reading.

LEVENSON, STANLEY RICHARD, public relations and advertising executive; b. Cin., Dec. 28, 1933; s. Irven Philip and Dorothy (Aftel) L.; m. Barbara Lind, July 23, 1962; children: Laura, Amy. B.A., U. Mich., 1956; postgrad., Am. U. S.W. sales and promotion mgr. DOT Records, Hollywood, Calif., 1959-62; S.W. sales and mktg. rep. Pickwick Internat. Co., 1963-65; pres., chmn. bd. Stan Levenson Assos., Dallas, 1966-76; exec. v.p., gen. mgr. public relations div. S.W., Bozell & Jacobs, Dallas, 1976-81; pres.,

CEO Levenson & Levenson, Dallas, 1981-83; CEO Levenson Pub. Rels., 1984—; dir. Fidelity Nat. Bank, Dallas; Trustee TACA, 1980, Dallas Alliance, 1988; adj. prof. in pub. relations mgmt. So. Meth. U., 1987-88, mem. adv. bd. Pub. Rels. sequence studies. Group leader comm. task force Dallas Police Dept.; assoc. mem. Dallas Assembly; bd. dirs. Dallas Arboretum, Vis. Nurses Assn., Family Place; mem. adv. bd. Crystal Charity Ball; co-chmn. Dallas Mayor's Task Force on Mktg.; mem. exec. com., bd. dirs. Ctrl. Downtown Assn., Dallas, 1993-94. With U.S. Army, 1956-58. Mem. Pub. Rels. Soc. Am. (accredited, North Tex. Teich award), Soc. Profl. Journalists. Home: 4545 Mill Run Rd Dallas TX 75244-6432 Office: Plz Ams S Tower 600 N Pearl St Ste 910 Dallas TX 75201-2872

LEVENSTEIN, ALAN PETER, advertising executive; b. N.Y.C, May 25, 1936; s. Jules David and Mollie Jarvis Levenstein; m. Gail Susan Berman, Sept. 15, 1963; children: Miranda, Jessica, Antony. AB magna cum laude, Amherst Coll., 1956. Copywriter J. Walter Thompson Co., N.Y.C., 1959-60, The Marschalk Co., N.Y.C., 1961-62; with Kenyon & Eckhardt Advt. Inc., N.Y.C., 1964-79, v.p., 1967-79; freelance journalist and advt. cons. N.Y.C, 1979-85; with Bozell, Jacobs, Kenyon & Eckhardt (now Bozell Worldwide), N.Y.C., 1985—; vice chmn. Bozell Worldwide, 1991—. Bd. dirs. Planned Parenthood, N.Y.C., 1988—; mem. coun. Nat. Acad. Design, 1993—. Mem. Phi Beta Kappa, Century Assn. Club (N.Y.). Democrat. Jewish. Office: Bozell Worldwide Inc 40 W 23 St New York NY 10010

LEVENSTEIN, ROSLYN M., advertising consultant, writer; b. N.Y.C., Mar. 26, 1920; d. Leo Rapoport and Stella Schimmel Rosenberg; m. Justin Seides, June 7, 1943 (div. 1948); 1 child, Leland Seides.; m. Lawrence Levenstein, June 25, 1961. BA in Advt., NYU, 1940. Sr. v.p., assoc. creative dir. Young and Rubicam, Inc., N.Y.C., 1962-79; cons. Young and Rubicam, Inc., Los Angeles and San Diego, 1979-83; advt. cons., writer mag. articles La Jolla, Calif., 1979—. Author: (poetry) I Have to Kill My Husband, 1996; creator Excedrin headache commls. (Andy awards 1967, 68, 69), I'm Only Here for the Beer (Cannes award 1970, Clio jury award 1970). Recipient: Silver Lion award Cannes Film Festival, 1968, multiple advt. awards U.S. and Eng.; named one of YWCA Women of Yr., 1978. Mem. Charter 100, Women's Com. Brandies U., Nat. Pen Women, San Dieto Writers & Editors Guild. Home: 5802 Corral Way La Jolla CA 92037-7423

LEVENTHAL, BENNETT LEE, psychiatry and pediatrics educator, administrator; b. Chgo., July 6, 1949; s. Howard Leonard and Florence Ruth (Albert) L.; m. Celia G. Goodman, June 11, 1972; children: Matthew G., Andrew G., Julia G. Student, Emory U., 1967-68, La. State U., 1968-70; BS, La. State U., 1972, postgrad., 1970-74, MD, 1974. Diplomate Am. Bd. Psychiatry and Neurology in Psychiatry, Am. Bd. Psychiatry and Neurology, Child Psychiatry; lic. physician N.C., La., Ill., Va. Undergrad. rsch. assoc. Lab. Prof. William A. Pryor dept. chemistry, La. State U., 1968-70; house officer I Charity Hosp. at New Orleans, 1974; resident in psychiatry Duke U. Med. Ctr., Durham, N.C., 1974-78, chief fellow divsn. dept. psychiatry, 1976-77, chief resident dept. psychiatry, 1977-78, clin. assoc. dept. psychiatry, 1978-80; staff psychiatrist, head psychiatry dept. Joel T. Boone Clinic, Virginia Beach, Va., 1978-80; staff psychiatrist, faculty mem. dept. psychiatry Naval Regional Med. Ctr., Portsmouth, Va., 1978-80; asst. prof. psychiatry and pediats. U. Chgo., 1978-85, dir. Child Psychiatry Clinic, 1978-85, dir. Child and Adolescent Psychiatry Fellowship tng. program, 1979-88; psychiat. cons. Caledonia State Prision/Halifax Mental Health Ctr., Tillery, N.C., 1976-77, Fed. Correctional Inst., Butner, N.C., 1977-78; cons. Norfolk Cmty. Mental health Ctr., 1978-80; adj. prof. psychology, biopsychology, and devel. psychology U. Chgo., 1990, adj. assoc. prof. dept. psychology and com. on biopsychology, 1987-90; meed. dir. Child Life and Family Edn. program Wyler Children's Hosp. of U. Chgo., 1983-95; dir. child and adolescent programs Chgo. Lakeshore Hosp., 1986—; Pfizer vis. prof. dept. psychiatry U. P.R., 1992; examiner Am. Bd. Psychiatry and Neurology in Gen. Psychiatry and Child Psychiatry, 1982—; mem. steering com. Harris Ctr. for Devel. Studies, U. Chgo., 1983—; mem. com. on evaluation of GAPS project AMA, 1993—; treas. Chgo. Consortium for Psychiat. Rsch., 1994; pres. Ill. Coun. Child and Adolescent Psychiatry, 1992-94; vis. scholar Hunter Inst. Mental Health and U. New Castle, NSW, Australia, 1995; mem. Gov.'s Panel on Health Svcs., 1993-94; prof. psychiatry & pediats. U. Chgo., 1990—, chmn. dept. psychiatry, 1991—; presenter in field. Mem. editl. bd. Univ. Chgo. Better Health Letter, 1994—; cons. editor: Jour. Emotional and Behavioral Disorders, 1992-96; reviewer: Archives of Gen. Psychiatry, 1983—, Biol. Psychiatry, 1983—, Am. Jour. Psychiatry, 1983—, Jour. AMA, 1983—, Jour. Am. Acad. Child and Adolescent Psychiatry, 1983—, Sci., 1983—; book rev. editor Jour. Neuropsychiatry and Clin. Neuroscis., 1989-92, mem. editl. bd., 1989-92; contbr. articles to profl. jours. Lt. comdr. M.C., USNR, 1978-80. Recipient Crystal Plate award Little Friends, 1994, Individual Achievement award Autism Soc. Am., 1991, Merit award Duke U. Psychiat. Resident's Assn., 1976, Bick award La. Psychiat. Assn., 1974; Andrew W. Mellon Found. faculty fellow U. Chgo., 1983-84; John Dewey lectr. U. Chgo., 1982. Fellow Am. Acad. Child and Adolescent Psychiatry (Outstanding Mentor 1988, dep. chmn. program com. 1979—, chmn. arrangements com. 1979—, new rsch. subcom. for ann. meeting 1986—, mem. work group on rsch. 1989—), Am. Psychiat. Assn. (Falk fellow, mem. Ittleson Award Bd. 1994-97, mem. Am. Psychiat. Assn./Wisniewski Young Psychiatrists Rsch. Award Panel 1994—), Am. Acad. Pediats., Am. Orthopsychiat. Assn.; mem. AAAS, Am. Coll. Psychiatrists, Brain Rsch. Inst., Ill. Coun. Child and Adolescent Psychiatry, Ill. Psychiat. Soc., Soc. for Rsch. in Child Devel., Soc. of Profs. of Child and Adolescent Psychiatry, Soc. Biol. Psychiatry, Nat. Bd. Med. Examiners, Mental Health Assn. Ill. (profl. adv. bd. 1991—), Sigma Xi. Office: U of Chgo Pritzker Sch of Medicine 5841 S Maryland Ave Chicago IL 60637-1463

LEVENTHAL, CARL M., neurologist, government official; b. N.Y.C., July 28, 1933; s. Isidor and Anna (Semmel) L.; m. Brigid Penelope Gray, Feb. 4, 1962 (wid. Feb. 1994); children: George Leon, Sarah Elizabeth Roark, Dinah Susan, James Gray. A.B. cum laude, Harvard U., 1954; M.D., U. Rochester (N.Y.), 1959. Diplomate: Am. Bd. Psychiatry and Neurology. Fellow in anatomy U. Rochester, 1956-57; intern, then asst. resident in medicine Johns Hopkins Hosp., 1959-61; asst. resident, then resident in neurology Mass. Gen. Hosp., Boston, 1961-64; commd. officer USPHS, 1963—, asst. surgeon gen., 1979-83; asso. neuropathologist Nat. Inst. Neurol. Diseases and Blindness, 1964-66; neurologist Nat. Cancer Inst., 1966-68; asst. to dep. dir. sci., 1968-73; acting dep. dir. sci. NIH, 1973-74; dep. dir. bur. drugs FDA, Rockville, Md., 1974-77; dep. dir. Nat. Inst. Arthritis, Diabetes and Digestive and Kidney Diseases, 1977-81; div. dir. Nat. Inst. Neurol. Disorders and Stroke, 1981—; sr. policy analyst for life scis. Office of Sci. and Tech. Policy, Exec. Office of Pres., 1983; asst. clin. prof. neurology Georgetown U. Med. Sch., 1966-76. Recipient Commendation medal USPHS, 1970, Meritorious Svc. medal, 1974, 77, 91, Outstanding Svc. medal, 1988, dir's. award NIH, 1992. Fellow Am. Acad. Neurology; mem. Am. Assn. Neuropathologists, Am. Neurol. Assn., Soc. for Exptl. Neuropathology (councillor), Alpha Omega Alpha. Home: 9254 Old Annapolis Rd Columbia MD 21045-1832 Office: Nat Inst Neur Disorders & Stroke Fed Building Rm 810 Bethesda MD 20892-9150

LEVENTHAL, KATHY NEISLOSS, magazine publisher. Pub. Vanity Fair, N.Y.C. Office: Vanity Fair 350 Madison Ave New York NY 10017-3704*

LEVENTHAL, KENNETH, real estate company director. BS in Acctg., UCLA. CPA, Calif. Founder, acct., CEO Kenneth Leventhal & Co., L.A., 1949-95; chmn. E&Y Kenneth Leventhal Real Estate Group, L.A., 1995-96, chmn. emeritus, 1996—; leader, speaker at acctg. and real estate symposia and seminars. Columnist Profl. Builder. Trustee U. So. Calif. Office: Kenneth Leventhal & Co 2049 Century Park E Los Angeles CA 90067-3101*

LEVENTHAL, NATHAN, performing arts executive, lawyer; b. N.Y.C., Feb. 19, 1943; s. Harry and Fay (Bronstein) L.; m. Gretchen Dykstra, Feb. 12, 1993. B.A. in Pub. Affairs, Queens Coll., 1963; J.D. cum laude, Columbia U., 1966. Bar: N.Y. 1967. Commr. Rent and Housing Maintenance, N.Y.C., 1972-73; chief counsel U.S. Senate Subcom. Adminstrv. Practice and Procedure, Washington, 1973-74; assoc. and ptnr. Poletti, Freidin, Prashker, Feldman & Gartner, N.Y.C., 1974-78; commr. Housing Preservation and Devel., N.Y.C., 1978-79; dep. mayor ops. City of N.Y., 1979-84; pres. Lincoln Ctr. for Performing Arts, N.Y.C., 1984—; lectr. govt. housing policy New Sch. Social Research, N.Y.C., 1979; lectr. health care and pub. policy Columbia Law Sch., N.Y.C., 1971. Editor-in-chief: Columbia Law Rev., 1965-66. Bd. visitors City Univ. Law Sch., N.Y.C., 1983—, Columbia Law Sch., 1989—, The New Sch., N.Y.C., 1992—; chmn. Citizens Union, 1994—; active Council on Jud. Adminstrn., Bar Assn. N.Y. City, 1983-90; dir. Nat. Youth Service Corp. for N.Y.C., 1983-85; commr. N.Y.C. Charter Revision Commn., 1986-89, N.Y. State Commn. on Constl. Revision, 1993—; dir. Queen's Coll. Found., 1988—; chair David M. Dinkins Mayoral Transition Com., 1989-90. Harlan Fiske Stone scholar Columbia Law Sch., 1963-65, Jerome Michael scholar, 1965-66; Disting. Service award Citizens Housing and Planning Council, N.Y.C., 1984, Am. Soc. Pub. Adminstrn. outstanding pub. adminstr. award 1982, Columbia Univ. Medal for Excellence, 1985.

LEVENTHAL, ROBERT STANLEY, academic administrator; b. Cambridge, Mass., Jan. 8, 1927; s. Harold A. and Matilda (Goldwyn) L.; children by previous marriage: Jeffrey Nelson, Daniel Philip; m. Jean B. Viereck, Feb. 14, 1994. A.B., Harvard U., 1948, M.B.A., 1956. Commd. ensign USN, 1948, advanced through grades to comdr., 1964; supply officer Naval Support Activity, Da Nang, Vietnam, 1965-66; with Office of Sec. of Def., Washington, 1966-68; ret., 1968; exec. asst. to chmn., dir. supply and distbn. Amerada Hess Corp., Woodbridge, N.J., 1968-71; exec. v.p. Engelhard Industries, Murray Hill, N.J.; sr. v.p. Engelhard Minerals and Chems. Corp., N.Y.C., 1971-75, Beker Industries Corp., Greenwich, Conn., 1975-77; pres., chief exec. officer Publicker Industries Inc., Phila., 1977-81; also. dir. Publicker Industries Inc.; pres. Tele-Total, Inc., 1981-83; pres., chief exec. officer Communications Products Corp., 1983-84; chmn., pres. Western Union Corp., Upper Saddle River, N.J., 1984-87, chief exec. officer, 1984-88, chmn., 1987-88; cons. Western Union Corp., Upper Saddle River, 1988-89; dean Sch. Bus. Administrn. U. Wash., Seattle, 1989-94. Decorated Legion of Merit with gold star.

LEVENTHAL, SHEILA SMITH, secondary education educator; b. Raymondville, Tex., May 4, 1941; d. M. C. and Jessie Mae (Sansom) Smith; m. Ira Yale Leventhal, Aug. 5, 1966; 1 child, Adam Yale. BS, N. Tex. State U., 1963, MEd, 1965; postgrad. Nova U., 1972, MIT, 1979. Elem. tchr. Grapevine Pub. Schs. (Tex.), 1963-65; tchr., team leader Lamplighter Sch., Dallas, 1965—, mem. steering com., computer staff, 1979-84, sci. com., 1990—, chair, 1993, 94. Staff mem. Episcopal Sch. of Spirituality, Dallas, 1983, dir., 1989—; presenter Internat. Conf. Tech. in Edn., U. London, 1994, pub. Interat. Conf. Tech. in Edn. Procs., 1993, 94; staff Ind. Sch. Assn. of the SW, Beginning Tchr. Inst., 1993, 94; presenter Internat. Coop. Learning Conf., Columbus, Ohio, 1996, pub. Procs.; pub. Dallas Opera Instrl. Series. Mem. Women of St. Francis (v.p. Dallas 1983), Phi Delta Kappa. Home: 2947 Talisman Dr Dallas TX 75229-3702 Office: Lamplighter Sch 11611 Inwood Rd Dallas TX 75229

LEVER, ALVIN, health science association administrator; b. St. Louis, Jan. 27, 1939; s. Jack I. and Sabina (Vogel) L.; m. Norine Sue Schwedt, Jan. 27, 1963; children: Daniel Jay, Michael Leonard. BS in Archtl. Scis., Washington U., St. Louis, 1961, B in Architecture, 1963; MA in Applied Psychology, U. Santa Monica, 1992. Registered architect, Mo., Ill. Project designer Sir Basil Spence, Architects, Edinburgh, Scotland, 1963-65; sr. project designer Hellmuth, Obata & Kassabaum, St. Louis, 1965-68, v.p., project mgr., 1968-72; v.p. facility devel. Michael Reese Med. Ctr., Chgo., 1972-74; v.p., gen. mgr. Apelco Internat., Ltd., Northbrook, Ill., 1974-90; dir. membership and fin. Am. Coll. Chest Physicians, Northbrook, 1990-92, exec. dir., 1992-95, exec. v.p., CEO, 1995—; pub. jour. Chest. Pub. Chest. V.p. Congregation B'nai Tikvah, 1987-91, pres., 1993-95. Mem. Profl. Conv. Mgmt. Assn., Am. Soc. Med. Soc. Execs., Am. Soc. Assn. Execs., Chgo. Soc. Assn. Execs., Alliance for Continuing Med. Edn. Avocations: scuba diving, bicycling, travel., golf. Office: Am Coll Chest Physicians 3300 Dundee Rd Northbrook IL 60062-2303

LEVERE, RICHARD DAVID, physician, academic administrator, educator; b. Bklyn., Dec. 13, 1931; s. Samuel and Mae (Fain) L.; m. Diane L. Gonchar, Jan. 15, 1978; children: Elyssa C., Corinne G., Scott M. Student, NYU, 1949-52; MD, SUNY, N.Y.C., 1956. Intern Bellevue Hosp., N.Y.C., 1956-57, resident, 1957-58; resident Kings County Hosp., 1960-61; asst. prof. medicine SUNY Downstate Med. Center, 1965-69, assoc. prof., 1969-73, prof., 1973-77, vice-chmn. dept. medicine, 1975-77, chief hematology/oncology div., 1970-77; asst. prof. Rockefeller U., 1964-65; prof., chmn. dept. medicine N.Y. Med. Coll., 1977-93, vice dean, 1991-93; med. dir. Westchester County Med. Ctr., 1991-92; v.p. med. affairs St. Agnes Hosp., 1991-93; sr. v.p. The Bklyn. Hosp. Ctr., 1994—; assoc. dean, prof. medicine NYU Sch. Medicine, 1994—; adj. prof. Rockefeller U., 1973—. Contbr. articles to profl. jours. Bd. dirs. Leukemia Soc. Am., 1970-85, Am. Heart Assn., 1978-94; trustee Our Lady of Mercy Med. Ctr., 1993-96. NIH grantee, 1971-76, 65-86. Fellow ACP (gov. N.Y. State 1990-94, pres. N.Y. State chpt. 1992-93, Physician Recognition award 1986), N.Y. Acad. Medicine; mem. Harvey Soc., Am. Soc. Clin. Investigation, Soc. Study of Blood (pres. 1973-74), Soc. Devel. Biology, Am. Soc. Pharm. Exptl. Therapeutics (William Dock Teaching award, Tinsley Harrison Rsch. award), Den Tiroler Adler-Ordern of Austria, Alpha Omega Alpha. Home: 5 Seymour Pl W Armonk NY 10504-2516 Office: Bklyn Hosp Ctr 121 Dekalb Ave Brooklyn NY 11201-5425

LEVERT, JOHN BERTELS, JR., investment executive; b. Birmingham, Ala., Apr. 16, 1931; s. John Bertels Sr. and Jacqueline (Tutwiler) L.; m. Anne Barrington King, Dec. 27, 1954; children: John Bertels III, Anne Lee. BA, Tulane U., 1954. Salesperson Carl E. Woodward Constrn. Co., New Orleans, 1956-58; from salesperson to exec. v.p. Metal Bldg. Product Co., Inc., New Orleans, 1958-70; stockbroker Howard Weil LaBouisse Friedrichs, New Orleans, 1970-75, pres., chief exec. officer, 1975-86, chmn., chief exec. officer, 1986—. Pres. United Way of Greater New Orleans, 1979-80; chmn. Archbishops Community Appeal, New Orleans, 1984; chmn. bd. trustees Loyola U., New Orleans, 1986—; chmn. fin. svc. survey com. New Orleans New Bus. Initiative, 1989—. 1st lt. U.S. Army, 1954-56. Recipient Humanitarian award Arthritis Found., 1989. Mem. N.Y. Stock Exch. (allied, regional firms adv. com. 1983-86), So. Yacht (commodore 1987-89). Republican. Roman Catholic. Avocations: sailing, flying. Office: Howard Weil LaBouisse Friedrichs 1100 Poydras St Ste 900 New Orleans LA 70163-1100

LEVERTOV, DENISE, poet; b. Ilford, Essex, Eng., Oct. 24, 1923; came to U.S., 1948, naturalized, 1955; d. Paul Philip and Beatrice A. (Spooner-Jones) Levertoff m. Mitchell Goodman, Dec. 2, 1947 (div. 1975); 1 child, Nikolai. Ed. privately; Litt.D. (hon.), Colby Coll., 1970, U. Cin., 1973, St. Lawrence U., 1984, Bates Coll., 1984, Allegheny Coll., 1987, St. Michael's Coll., 1987, Mass. Coll. of Art, 1989, U. Santa Clara, 1993. Tchr. YMCA-YWCA Poetry Ctr., N.Y.C., 1964; vis. lectr. Drew U., Madison, N.J., 1965, CCNY, 1965, Vassar Coll., Poughkeepsie, N.Y., 1966-67, U. Calif., Berkeley, 1969; vis. prof. MIT, Cambridge, 1969-70; scholar Radcliffe Inst. Ind. Study, 1964-65, 66-67; artist-in-residence Kirkland Coll., Clinton, N.Y., 1970-71; Elliston lectr. U. Cin., spring 1973; prof. Tufts U., Medford, Mass., 1973-79, Stanford U., Calif., 1981-93; prof. emeritus, 1993—; poet-in-residence Brandeis U., Waltham, Mass., 1981-83; A.D. White Prof. at Large Cornell U., Ithaca, N.Y., 1993—. Author: The Double Image, 1946, Here and Now, 1957, Overland to the Islands, 1958, Five Poems, 1958, With Eyes at the Back of Our Heads, 1959, The Jacob's Ladder, 1961, O Taste and See, 1964, City Psalm, 1964, Psalm Concerning the Castle, 1966, The Sorrow Dance, 1967, A Tree Telling of Orpheus, 1968, A Marigold from North Vietnam, 1968, Three Poems, 1968, In the Night: A Story, 1968, The Cold Spring and Other Poems, 1969, Embroideries, 1969, Relearning the Alphabet, 1970, Summer Poems, 1969, A New Year's Garland for My Students, 1970, To Stay Alive, 1971, Footprints, 1972, The Poet in the World, 1974, The Freeing of the Dust, 1975, Chekov on the West Heath, 1977, Modulations for Solo Voice, 1977, Life in the Forest, 1978, Collected Earlier Poems 1940-60, 1979, Pig Dreams: Scenes from the Life of Sylvia, 1981, Wanderer's Daysong, 1981, Light Up the Cave, 1981, Candles in Babylon, 1982, Poems 1960-1967, 1983, Oblique Prayers, 1984, El Salvador: Requiem and Invocation, 1984, The Menaced World, 1984, Selected Poems, 1986, Poems 1968-1972, 1987, Breathing the Water, 1987, A Door in the Hive, 1989, Evening Train, 1992, New and Selected Essays, 1992, Tesserae, 1995; translator: Selected Poems of Guillevic, 1969, Black Iris: Selected Poems of Jean Joubert, 1988; translator, editor: (with Edward C. Dimock, Jr.) In Praise of Krishna: Songs from the Bengali, 1967; editor: Out of the War Shadow: An Anthology of Current Poetry, 1967. Recipient Bess Hokin prize Poetry mag. 1959, Longview award 1961, Harriet Monroe Meml. prize 1964, Inez Boulton prize Poetry mag. 1964, Morton Dauwen Zabel Meml. prize Poetry mag., 1965, Lenore Marshall Poetry prize 1976, Elmer Holmes Bobst award in poetry 1983, Shelley Meml. award Poetry Soc. of Am., 1984, Robert Frost medal, 1990, Lannan award, 1993; Am. Acad. and Inst. of Arts and Letters grantee, 1965; Guggenheim fellow, 1962; NEA Sr. Fellowship, 1990. Mem. Am. Inst. Arts and Letters, Academie Mallarmé (corr.). Office: care New Directions 80 8th Ave New York NY 10011-5126

LEVESON, IRVING FREDERICK, economist; b. N.Y.C., June 28, 1939; s. Hyman Wolf and Minnie L.; m. Barbara Diane Wurtzelman, Jan. 28, 1961; children: Stephen Martin, Scott Owen. BA (N.Y. State Regents scholar), CCNY, 1960, MBA, 1963; PhD, Columbia U., 1968. Rsch. analyst, rsch. asst. Nat. Bur. Econ. Rsch., 1963-67; rsch. economist N.Y.C. Health Svcs. Adminstrn., 1967-68; economist RAND Corp., 1968-69; dir. rsch. Office Comprehensive Planning, N.Y.C., Planning Commn., 1969-71; asst. adminstr. health systems planning N.Y.C. Health Services Adminstrn., 1971-74; sr. profl. staff, dir. econ. studies Hudson Inst., Croton-on-Hudson, N.Y., 1974-84; sr. v.p., dir. rsch. Hudson Strategy Group, N.Y.C., 1984-90; pres. Leveson Cons., Marlboro, N.J., 1990—; mem. Gov. N.Y. health adv. coun., 1975-78, mem. adv. commn. on budget rels. for the 80s, 1983-84; lectr., cons. in field. Author: The Future of the Financial Services Industry, 1982, American Challenges: Business and Government in the World of the 1990s, 1991; editor: Quantitative Explorations in Drug Abuse Policy, 1980; co-editor: Analysis of Urban Health Problems, 1976, Western Economies in Transition, 1980. Trustee Monmouth Heights Civic Assn., 1971-77. Mem. Bronx County Com. (1961); Mem. Am. Econ. Assn., Nat. Assn. Bus. Economists, Met. Econ. Assn., Assn. Social Scis. in Health (exec. council 1973-82). Jewish. Home and Office: 23 Prescott Dr Marlboro NJ 07746-1351 *Keep learning and striving for self-improvement and quality. Both the striving and the cumulative benefits over time can be greatly rewarding.*

LEVESQUE, LOUIS, bishop; b. Amqui, Que., Can., May 27, 1908; s. Philippe and Catherine (Beaulieu) L. B.A., Laval U., 1928, Ph.L., 1930, Th.D., 1932; S.S.L., Bib. Inst., Rome and Jerusalem, 1935. Ordained priest Roman Cath. Ch., 1932; tchr. holy scripture Rimouski, Que., 1936-51; bishop of Hearst, Ont., 1952-64; archbishop of Rimouski, 1964-73, retired archbishop, 1973—; Chmn. Canadian Cath. Conf., 1965-67; mem. Congregation Bishops, Rome, 1968-73. Mem. Cath. Bibl. Assn. Am. Home: 300 Ave du Rosaire, Rimouski, PQ Canada G5L 3E3

LEVESQUE, RENE JULES ALBERT, retired physicist; b. St. Alexis, Que., Can., Oct. 30, 1926; s. Albert and Elmina Louisa (Veuilleux) L.; m. Alice Farnsworth, Apr. 6, 1956 (div.); children: Marc, Michel, Andre; m. Michèle Robert, Feb., 1992. B.Sc., Sir George Williams U., 1952; Ph.D., Northwestern U., 1957. Research assoc. U. Md., 1957-59; asst. prof. U. Montreal, 1959-64, assoc. prof., 1964-67, prof., 1967-87, dir. nuclear physics lab., 1965-69, chmn. dept. physics, 1968-73, vice dean arts and scis., 1973-75, dean, 1975-78, v.p. research, 1978-85, v.p. research and planning, 1985-87, prof. emeritus, 1987; mem. Atomic Energy Control Bd., Ottawa, Can., 1985-87, pres., 1987-93; ret., 1993; mem. adv. com. ING project Atomic Energy of Can. Ltd., 1966-69; mem. adv. bd. physics NRC Can., 1972-74, pres. nuclear physics grant selection, 1973; mem. adv. bd. on TRIUMF, 1979-87; v.p. Commn. Higher Studies Que. Ministry Edn., 1976-77, Natural Scis. and Engring. Research Council Can., 1981-87; v.p. bd. dirs. Can.-France-Hawaii Telescope Corp., 1979-80, pres., 1980-81; pres. permanent research com. Conf. Rectors and Prins. Que. Univs., 1979-80; pres. Mouvement Laïc de Langue française, 1961. Mem. Can. Assn. Physicists (pres. 1976-77), U. Montreal Faculty Assn. (pres. 1971), Fedn. Que. Faculty Assn. (pres. 1971-72), Interciencia Assn. (v.p. bd. dirs. 1979-80), Assn. Sci., Engring. and Technol. Community Can. (v.p. 1979-80, pres. 1980-81). Home: 190 Willowdale PH 1, Outremont, PQ Canada H3T 1G2

LEVETON, IAN SINCLAIR, civil engineer; b. Birmingham, Eng., Nov. 27, 1942; came to U.S., 1953; s. Eric Karl and Zena (Altman) L. BA in Physics and Econs., NYU, 1965; cert. of achievement, Orange Coast Coll., Costa Mesa, Calif., 1990. Computer programmer trainee Bklyn. Union Gas Co., 1969; computer programmer Elizabeth Arden Sales Corp., N.Y.C., 1970; electronics expeditor Bendix Navigation & Controls, Teterboro, N.J., 1971; inventory control supr. Roman Products Inc., South Hackensack, N.J., 1972; nuclear mech. engr. Pub. Svc. N.J., Newark, 1973; mech. engr. Chemplant Designs divsn. DuPont, N.Y.C., 1974-78, Holmes and Narver, Inc., Orange, Calif., 1978-82; tech. writer nuclear safety So. Calif. Edison, Rosemead, Calif., 1983-85; civil engr. tech. City of Santa Ana, Calif., 1985—; cons. Islian Assocs., Teaneck, N.J., 1970-71. Mem. Teaneck Bicentennial Com., 1976; coord. United Way, City Pub. Works Agy., Santa Ana, 1992. Mem. KP (sec. 1974-76). Avocations: tennis, boating, reading, music, traveling. Home: 19302 Steven Ln Huntington Beach CA 92646-2711

LEVETOWN, ROBERT ALEXANDER, lawyer; b. Bklyn., July 20, 1935; s. Alfred A. and Corinne L. (Cohen) L.; m. Roberta S. Slobodkin, Oct. 18, 1959. Student, U. Munich, Fed. Republic Germany, 1954-55; AB, Princeton U., 1956; LLB, Harvard U., 1959. Bar: D.C. 1960, N.Y. 1982, Va. 1984, Pa. 1985. Assoc. Pierson, Ball & Dowd, Washington, 1960-62; asst. U.S. atty. Washington, 1962-63; atty. Chesapeake & Potomac Telephone Cos., Washington, 1963-66, gen. atty., 1966-68, gen. solicitor, 1968-73, v.p., gen. counsel, 1975-83; exec. v.p., gen. counsel Bell Atlantic, 1983-91, vice chmn., 1991-92, also bd. dirs., 1989-92; bd. dirs. Telecom NZ. Mem. ABA (vice chmn. comm. com., pub. utility law sect. 1986-93), Washington Met. Corp. Counsels' Assn. (bd. dirs. 1981-83), Nat. Legal Ctr. (legal adv. coun. 1986-92). Republican. Jewish.

LEVEY, GERALD SAUL, physician, educator; b. Jersey City, N.J., Jan. 9, 1937; s. Jacob and Gertrude (Kantoff) L.; m. Barbara Ann Cohen, June 4, 1961; children: John, Robin. AB, Cornell U., 1957; MD, N.J. Coll. Medicine, 1961. Diplomate: Am. Bd. Internal Medicine. Med. intern Jersey City Med. Ctr., 1961-62, asst. med. resident, 1962-63; postdoctoral fellow dept. biol. chemistry Harvard U. Med. Sch., 1963-65; med. resident Mass. Gen. Hosp., Boston, 1965-66; clin. assoc. clin. endocrinology br. Nat. Inst. Arthritis and Metabolic Diseases NIH, Bethesda, Md., 1966-68, clin. assoc. Nat. Heart and lung Inst., 1968-69, sr. investigator Nat. heart and Lung Inst., 1969-70; assoc. prof. medicine U. Miami Sch. Medicine, Fla., 1970-73, prof. medicine, 1973-79; prof., chmn. dept. medicine U. Pitts. Sch. Medicine, 1979-91; physician-in-chief Presbyn.-Univ. Hosp., Pitts., 1979-91; sr. v.p. for med. and sci. affairs Merck and Co., Inc., Whitehouse Sta., N.J., 1991-94; provost med. scis., dean Sch. of Medicine UCLA, 1994—; Harold Jeghers lectr. N.J. Coll. Medicine, 1977; Marian Blankenhorn lectr. Cin. Soc. Internal Medicine, 1982; co-prin. investigator Nat. Study of Internal Medicine Manpower, 1984—. Mem. editorial bd.: Endocrinology, 1972-76, Am. Jour. Physiology, 1972-76, Jour. Applied Physiology, 1972-76, Annals of Internal Medicine, 1981-84; cons. editor: Hosp. Medicine, 1981-91; contbr. articles to profl. jours. Bd. dirs. Am. Jewish Com., Miami, 1975-79; mem. United Jewish Fedn. Pitts. Leadership Devel., 1981-82; bd. dirs. Jewish Family and Children's Services, 1982-83. NIH grantee, 1971-91; Fla. Heart Assn. grantee, 1971-74. Fellow ACP; mem. AMA, Am. Thyroid Assn. (mem. membership com. 1977-80), Am. Fedn. Clin. Rsch. (councillor so. sect. 1973-76, pres. so. sect. 1977-78), Am. Soc. Clin. Investigation, Endocrine Soc., Assn. Profs. Medicine (chmn. ad hoc com. for use of animals in rsch., 1982-85, chmn. task force on internalmedicine manpower 1983-90, nat. pres. 1990-91), So. Soc. Clin. Investigation, Soc. Gen. Internal Medicine, Assn. Am. Physicians, Alpha Omega Alpha. Home: 1132 Laurel Way Beverly Hills CA 90210-2221 Office: UCLA Merck and Co Inc 10883 Le Conte Ave Los Angeles CA 90024-3010*

LEVEY, ROBERT FRANK, newspaper columnist; b. N.Y.C., June 2, 1945; s. Stanley Victor and Sylvia Rose (Frank) L.; m. Jane Ellen Freundel, May 17, 1980; children: Emily Susanna, Alexander Freundel. B.A., U. Chgo., 1966. Reporter Albuquerque Tribune, 1966-67; reporter, editor Washington Post, 1967-81, columnist, 1981—; vis lectr. Duke U., Durham, N.C., 1979—; adviser journalism Cath. U. Am., Washington, 1979-81. Talk show host Sta. WRC-AM, 1981-83, Sta. WTTG-TV, Washington, 1982-87, Sta. WBAL, 1988-92, Sta. WMAL, 1993—; commentator Sta. WASH-FM, 1983-84, Sta. WJLA-TV, 1984-86, Sta. WETA-FM, 1985-90. Woodrow Wilson fellow. Mem. Reporters Com. for Freedom of the Press, Newspaper Guild (chmn. Washington Post unit 1972-75), AFTRA, U. Chgo. Alumni Assn. (bd. govs.

1992—), Sigma Delta Chi. Jewish. Office: Washington Post 1150 15th St NW Washington DC 20071-0001

LEVEY, SAMUEL, health care administration educator; b. Cape Town, South Africa, July 11, 1932; came to U.S., 1949, naturalized, 1954; s. Harry and Esther (Turecka) L.; m. Linda Anne Madison, Dec. 26, 1965; children: Eric B., Andrea E., Sara B. A.B., Bowdoin Coll., 1955; A.M., Columbia U., 1956; M.A., U. Iowa, 1959, Ph.D., 1961; M.S., Harvard U., 1963. Adminstrv. assoc. U. Iowa hosps. and Clinics, Iowa City, 1958-60; instr. U. Iowa, 1960-61, asst. prof., 1961-62; dir. div. Mass. Dept. Public Health, Boston, 1963-67; asst. dir. med. care planning Harvard Med. Sch., Boston, 1967-68; lectr. health service adminstrn. Harvard Sch. Public Health, 1967-69; asst. commr. Mass. Dept. Public Welfare, Boston, 1968-69; prof., chmn. grad. program in health care adminstrn. CUNY, 1969-77; prof., adminstr. medicine Mt. Sinai Sch. Medicine, N.Y.C., 1973-77; G. Hartman prof. and head of grad. program in hosp. and health adminstrn. Ctr. for Health Services Research Coll. Medicine and Grad. Coll., U. Iowa, Iowa City, 1977-91; G. Hartman prof. Coll. Medicine and Grad. Coll., U. Iowa, 1991—; hosp. and health cons. Author: (with N.P. Loomba) Health Care Administration: A Managerial Perspective, 1973, 2d edit., 1984, Health Care Administration: A Selected Bibliography, 1973, (with H. Rosen and J. Metsch) The Consumer and the Health Care System, 1977, (with N.P. Loomba) Long Term Care Administration, vols. 1, 11, 1977, (with T. McCarthy) Health Management for Tomorrow, 1980, Hospital Leadership and Accountability, 1992; sr. editor: Spectrum series on Heath Systems Management, 1974-86; editor: Hosp. and Health Services Adminstrn., 1987-92. Named Otho Ball fellow Am. Coll. Hosp. Adminstrs., 1958-59; Faculty fellow Found. Econ. Edn., 1962; HHS trainee, 1962-63. Mem. Assn. Univ. Programs in Health Adminstrn. (dir. 1979-80, chmn. bd. 1980-81), Am. Pub. Health Assn., Internat. Hosp. Fedn., Am. Coll. Healthcare Execs., Am. Hosp. Assn. Home: 336 Macbride Dr Iowa City IA 52246-1716 Office: U Iowa Steindler Bldg Iowa City IA 52242

LEVI, DAVID F., federal judge; b. 1951. BA, Harvard U., MA, 1973; JD, Stanford U. Bar: Calif. 1983. U.S. atty. ea. dist. State of Calif., Sacramento, 1986-90; judge U.S. Dist. Ct. (ea. dist.) Calif., 1990—; chmn. task force on race, religious and ethnic fairness U.S. Ct. Appeals (9th cir.), 1994—, mem. jury com., 1993-95. Adv. com. on Civil Rules, 1994—; vis. com. U. Chgo. Law Sch., 1995—. Mem. Am. Law Inst., Milton L. Schwartz Inn of Ct. (pres. 1992-95). Office: 2504 Fed Bldg 650 Capitol Mall Sacramento CA 95814-4708

LEVI, EDWARD HIRSCH, former attorney general, university president emeritus; b. Chgo., June 26, 1911; s. Gerson B. and Elsa B. (Hirsch) L.; m. Kate Sulzberger, June 4, 1946; children: John, David, Michael. PhB, U. Chgo., 1932, JD, 1935; JSD, Yale U., 1938; LLD, U. Mich., 1959, U. Calif., Santa Cruz, 1968, Jewish Theol. Sem. Am., 1968, U. Iowa, 1968, Brandeis U., 1968, Lake Forest Coll., 1968, Dropsie U., 1968, Columbia U., 1968, Yeshiva U., 1968, U. Rochester, 1969, U. Toronto, Ont., Can., 1971, Yale U., 1973, U. Notre Dame, 1974, Denison U., 1974, U. Pa., 1976, U. Nebr., U. Miami, Boston Coll., Brigham Young U., Duke U., Ripon Coll., Georgetown U., Benjamin N. Cardozo Sch. Law, Claremont Ctr. and Grad. Sch., Ind. U.; LHD, Hebrew Union Coll., 1968, Loyola U., 1970, U. Chgo., Bard Coll., 1985, Beloit Coll., DePaul U., 1978; DCL, NYU. Bar: Ill., U.S. Supreme Ct. 1945. Asst. prof. U. Chgo. Law Sch., 1936-40, prof. law, 1945-75, dean, 1950-62; provost U. Chgo., 1962-68, univ. pres., 1968-75, pres. emeritus, 1975—; Karl Llewellyn Disting. Svc. prof. U. Chgo. Law Sch., 1975—, Glen A. Lloyd Disting. Svc. prof., 1977-85, Glen A. Lloyd Disting. Svc. prof. emeritus, 1985—; atty. gen. U.S., 1975-77; Thomas Guest prof. U. Colo., summer 1960; Herman Phleger vis. prof. Stanford Law Sch., 1978; lectr. Salzburg (Austria) Seminar in Am. Studies, 1980; spl. asst. to atty. gen. U.S., Washington, 1940-45; 1st asst. war div. Dept. Justice, 1943, 1st asst. antitrust div., 1944-45; chmn. interdeptl. com. on monopolies and cartels, 1944; counsel Fedn. Atomic Scientists with respect to Atomic Energy Act, 1946; counsel subcom. on monopoly power Judiciary Com., 81st Congress, 1950; trustee Aerospace Corp., 1978-80; Mem. rsch. adv. bd. Com. Econ. Devel., 1951-54; bd. Social Sci. Rsch. Coun., 1959-62, Coun. Legal Edn. and Profl. Responsibility, 1968-74; chmn. 1969-73; mem. Citizens Commn. Grad. Med. Edn., 1963-66, Commn. Founds. and Pvt. Philanthropy, 1969-70, Pres.'s Task Force Priorities in Higher Edn., 1969-70, Sloan Commn. Cable Comm., 1970, Nat. Commn. on Productivity, 1970-75, Nat. Council on Humanities, 1974-75, Nat. Coun. on Legal clinics, 1960-65; chmn. Coun. on Edn. in Profl. Responsibility, 1965-69. Author: Introduction to Legal Reasoning, 1949, Four Talks on Legal Education, 1952, Point of View, 1969; editor: (with J.W. Moore) Gilbert's Collier on Bankruptcy, 1936, Elements of the Law, (with R.S. Steffen), 1950. Hon. trustee U. Chgo.; trustee Internat. Legal Ctr., 1966-75, Woodrow Wilson Nat. Fellowship Found., 1972-75, 77-79, Inst. Psychoanalysis Chgo., 1961-75, Urban Inst., 1968-75, Mus. Sci. and Industry, 1971-75, Russell Sage Found., 1971-75, Aspen Inst. Humanistic Studies, 1970-75, 77-79, Inst. Internat. Edn. (hon.), 1969; public dir. Chgo. Bd. Trade, 1977-80; bd. overseers U. Pa., 1978-82; chmn. bd. Nat. Humanities Ctr., 1979-83, life trustee, 1978—; bd. dirs. MacArthur Found., 1979-84, William Benton Found., 1980-92, Martin Luther King Jr. Fed. Holiday Commn., 1986; bd. of govs. U. Calif. Humanities Rsch. Inst., 1988-91; mem. bd. trustees Skadden Fellowship Found., 1988—. Decorated Legion of Honor (France); recipient Learned Hand medal Fed. Bar Coun. 2nd Cir., 1976, Fordham Stein prize Fordham U., 1977, Louis Dembitz Brandeis medal Brandeis U., 1979; Sterling fellow Yale U., 1935-36; named laureate of Lincoln Acad. Ill., 1976. Mem. ABA, FBA (Honor award 1975), Am. Bar Found., Am. Philos. Soc. (v.p. 1991-94), Ill. Bar Assn. (award of honor 1983), Ill Bar Found. (Disting. Svc. award 1990), Am. Law Inst., Am. Judicature Soc., Chgo. Bar Assn. (Centennial award 1975), Supreme Ct. Hist. Soc., Constl. Rights Found. (Disting. Svc. award 1992), Chgo. Comml. Club, Quadrangle Club, Columbia Yacht Club, Order of Coif, Phi Beta Kappa. Office: U Chgo 1116 E 59th St Chicago IL 60637-1513

LEVI, HERBERT WALTER, biologist, educator; b. Frankfurt, Germany, Jan. 3, 1921; came to U.S., 1938, naturalized, 1945; s. Ludwig and Irma (Hochschild) L.; m. Lorna Rose, June 13, 1949; 1 child, Frances. Student, Art Students League, N.Y.C., 1938-39; B.S., U. Conn., 1946; M.S., U. Wis., 1947, Ph.D., 1949; MA (hon.), Harvard U., 1970. Instr., then asst. prof. to asso. prof. zoology, extension div. U. Wis., 1949-56; asst. curator arachnology Mus. Comparative Zoology Harvard U., 1956-57, assoc. curator, 1957-66, curator, 1966-91, prof. biology, 1970-91, Agassiz prof. zoology, 1972-91, prof. emeritus, 1991—; sec. Rocky Mountain Biol. Lab., 1959-65; vis. prof. Hebrew U., Jerusalem, 1975; bd. govs. Nature Conservancy, 1956-62; taxonomic cons. Smithsonian projects, 1979; cons. Syntax, Cambridge, Mass., 1986. Author: (with L.R. Levi) Spiders and Their Kin, 1968, 69, Aranas y especies afines, 1971; also numerous articles; translator, editor: Invertebrate Zoology (Kaestner), 3 vols.; bd. reviewers Pacific Insects, 1980-85; bd. editors Psyche, 1957-92, Zoomorphology, 1980-85, Sci. Bull. de Mus., Paris, 1980—, (internat.) Annales Zoologici Warszawa Poland, 1993—, Memorias do Instituto Butantan, São Paulo, Brazil, 1994—. Fellow AAAS; mem. Am. Soc. Zoologists, Soc. Study Evolution, Soc. Systematic Zoology (councillor 1967-69), Am. Micros. Soc. (bd. reviewers 1973-94), Am. Arachnol. Soc. (hon. mem., bd. editors 1974—, dir. 1975-83, pres. 1979-81), Am. Ecol. Soc., Am. Inst. Biological Scis., Wildlife Soc., Am. Ornithol. Union, Assn. Systematics Collections (council nat. systematic collections and resources 1975), British Arachnological Soc., Cambridge Entomology Club, Centre International de Documentation Arachnologique (v.p. 1965-68, pres. 1980-83), Japanese Arachnological Soc. (hon.), Soc. Systematic Biologists, Spider Club So. Africa (hon.), Wilson Ornithological Soc., Wilderness Soc. Home: 45 Wheeler Rd Pepperell MA 01463-1025 Office: Harvard U Mus Comparative Zoolog Cambridge MA 02138

LEVI, ILAN MOSCHE, computer and communications company executive; b. Haifa, Israel, July 17, 1943; came to U.S., 1956; s. Seligman P. and Ruth (Bril) L.; m. Barbara Goss, Sept. 10, 1966; children: Daniel Steven, Sharon Ruth. BSME, The Cooper Union, 1965; MS in Aeros. and Astronautics, Stanford U., 1966, PhD in Structural Mechanics, 1968. Research assoc. Dept. Aeros. and Astronautics, Stanford U., Calif., 1968-69; mem. tech. staff engrng. mechanics and physics dept. Bell Labs., Whippany, N.J., 1969-71, supr., 1971-80, dept. head, 1980-85; dir. Bell Labs., Holmdel, N.J., 1985—; dir. bus. terminals devel. lab AT&T Labs., Holmdel, 1985-88; dir. customer systems devel. lab. AT&T Bell Labs., Middletown, N.J., 1988-94; cons. dir., product devel. AT&T Global Bus. Comm. Systems, 1994-95, retired, 1996; cons. Lawrence Radiation Lab., Livermore, Calif., 1968-69, N.J. Com. on Sci. and Industry, Trenton, 1985-86. Contbr. articles to profl. jours., chpts. to books. NSF fellow, 1965. Jewish. Avocations: tennis, backpacking, bicycling, photography. Home: 1616 La Vista Del Oceano Santa Barbara CA 93109-1790 Office: Lucent Techs Bell Labs 200 S Laurel Ave Middletown NJ 07748-1914

LEVI, ISAAC, philosophy educator; b. N.Y.C., June 30, 1930; s. Eliezer Asher and Eva (Lunenfeld) L.; m. Judith S. Rubins, Dec. 25, 1951; children: Jonathan Abram, David Isser. B.A., NYU, 1951; student, Jewish Theol. Sem., 1947-52; M.A., Columbia, 1953, Ph.D., 1957; PhD honoris causa, Lund U., 1988. Part-time instr. Rutgers U., 1954-56; lectr. CCNY, 1956-57, asst. prof. philosophy, 1962-64; asst. prof. philosophy Western Res. U., 1957-62, assoc. prof., 1964-67, prof., 1967-70, chmn. dept., 1968-70; prof. philosophy Columbia U., 1970—, chmn. dept., 1973-76, 89-91; vis. scholar Corpus Christi Coll., Cambridge (Eng.) U. 1973, vis. fellow Darwin Coll., 1980, 93; vis. rsch. fellow Australian Nat. U., 1987; vis. fellow All Souls Coll., Oxford (Eng.) U., 1988; vis. fellow Inst. Advanced Study, Hebrew U. Jerusalem, 1994. Author: Gambling With Truth, 1967, The Enterprise of Knowledge, 1980 Decisions and Revisions, 1984, Hard Choices, 1986, The Fixation of Belief and Its Undoing, 1991, For the Sake of the Argument, 1996; contbr. articles to profl. jours. Fulbright scholar, 1966-67; Guggenheim fellow, 1966-67; NEH fellow, 1979-80. Fellow Am. Acad. Arts and Scis.; mem. AAUP, Am. Philos.Assn., Philosophy of Sci. Assn., Brit. Soc. Philosophy of Sci., Phi Beta Kappa, Pi Mu Epsilon. Democrat. Home: 25 Claremont Ave New York NY 10027-6827

LEVI, JAMES HARRY, real estate executive, investment banker; b. Boston, Oct. 28, 1939; s. Robert Emmett and Doris (Cohen) L.; m. Constance Jo Adler, Dec. 30, 1967; children: James H. II, Andrew R., Deanne D., Constance Jo. AB, Harvard U., 1961, MBA, 1964. Past pres. Value Properties Inc., N.Y.C.; now pres. Levi Co., Larchmont, N.Y.; chmn. bd. dirs. New Millenium Energies, Inc., St. Louis; pres. Gt. Train Store co., Dallas, others; prof. Bus. Sch. Columbia U., N.Y.C.; past pres. Oppenheimer Properties, Inc., N.Y.C.; exec. v.p., mem. exec. com. Oppenheimer & Co., Inc.; pres., chmn. bd. dirs. numerous affiliated cos. Mem. Bus. Sch. coun. Tulane U., N.Y.; mem. bd. govs. Hebrew Union Coll./Jewish Inst. Religion; mem. bd. overseers Sch. Architecture, Ill. Inst. Tech.; mem. exec. bd. Westchester Putnam coun. Boy Scouts Am.; mem. traffic commn. Village of Larchmont, N.Y.; mem. joint planning commn. Villages of Larchmont and Mamaroneck; trustee Larchmont Hist. Soc. Ensign USN, 1961-62. Named Man of Yr., St. Louis Rabbinical Coll., 1986. Mem. Real Estate Securities and Syndication Inst. (former gov.), Nat. Assn. Realtors, Nat. Assn. Rev. Appraisers (cert.), Soc. for Indsl. Archeology, Soc. Archtl. Historians, Nat. Assn. Security Dealers (registered prin.), Sheldrake Yacht Club (past treas.). Avocations: boating and sailing, collecting antiques, travelling, opera, kinetic sculpture. Home: 85 Larchmont Ave Larchmont NY 10538-3748 Office: Levi Co 85 Larchmont Ave Larchmont NY 10538-3748

LEVI, JOHN G., lawyer; b. Chgo., Oct. 9, 1948; s. Edward H. and Kate (Sulzberger) L.; m. Jill Felsenthal, Oct. 7, 1979; children: Benjamin E., Daniel F., Sarah H. AB, U. Rochester, 1969; JD, Harvard U., 1972, LLM, 1973. Bar: Ill. 1973. Ptnr. Sidley & Austin, Chgo. Vice chmn. bd. Weiss Mem. Hosp., Chgo.; v.p. trustee Francis W. Parker Sch., Chgo.; bd. dirs. Chgo. Child Care Sco.; vis. com. U. Chgo. Coll.; mem. Citizens Com. Juvenile Ct., Chgo. Mem. ABA, Ill. Bar Assn., Chgo. Bar Assn., Law Club Chgo. Office: Sidley & Austin 1 1st Nat Plz Chicago IL 60603

LEVI, JOSEF ALAN, artist; b. New York, Feb. 17, 1938; s. Jacob and Evelyn D. (Speizer) L. B.A., U. Conn., 1959; postgrad., Columbia U., 1960. Artist in residence Appalachian State U., N.C., 1969, vis. prof. art, Pa. State U., 1976. One-man shows of paintings include Stable include N.Y.C., 1966, 67, 68, 69, 70, Arts Club of Chgo., 1967, J.B. Speed Art Mus., Louisville, Ky., 1968, Appalachian State U., Boone, N.C., 1969, Lambert Gallery, Los Angeles, 1971, Gertrude Kasle Gallery, Detroit, 1971, Jacobs Ladder Gallery, Washington, 1972, Images Gallery, Toledo, Ohio, 1972, A.M. Sachs Gallery, N.Y.C., 1975, 76, 78, O.K. Harris Gallery, N.Y.C., 1983, 85, 87, 90, 92, 94, 96, Adams-Middleton Gallery, Dallas, 1986, Harmon Meek Gallery, Naples, Fla., 1996; numerous group shows, 1965—, latest being, Balt. Mus. Art, 1975, Mus. Art, R.I. Sch. Design, 1976, Art Mus., U. N.C., Greensboro, 1977, Russell Sage Coll., Troy, N.Y., 1977, Washington U., St. Louis, 1977, Whitney Mus., N.Y.C., 1978-79, Meml. Art Gallery, U. Rochester, N.Y., 1979, Aldrich Mus. Contemporary Art, Ridgefield, Conn., 1980, Western Assn. Art Museums, 1981, Worcester (Mass.) Art Mus., 1981, Palace Theatre of Arts Gallery, Stamford, Conn., 1984, Randolph Macon Coll., Ashland, Va., 1985, Robert I. Kidd Galleries, Birmingham, Mich., 1985, Elaine Benson Gallery, Bridgehampton, N.Y., 1985; others; represented in numerous permanent collections including, Aldrich Mus. Contemporary Art, Albright-Knox Gallery, Buffalo, N.Y., Mus. Modern Art, N.Y.C., Krannert Art Mus., U. Ill., Urbana, Va. Mus. Fine Arts, Richmond, AT&T, N.Y.C., Corcoran Gallery, Washington, U. Md., College City, Chrysler Corp., Detroit., Spellman Coll., Atlanta, Exxon Corp., N.Y.C., Minolta Corp., N.Y.C., Des Moines Art Ctr., Newark Mus., Dartmouth Coll., Hanover, N.H., Storm King Art Ctr., Mountainville, N.Y., U. Notre Dame Art Gallery, South Bend, Ind., J. B. Speed Art Mus., Louisville, Bank of N.Y., N.Y.C., Lewis and Clark Coll., Portland, Oreg., Technimetrics Inc., N.Y.C., Best Products Corp., Ashland, Va., Southland Corp., Dallas, TRW Corp., Cleve., Bklyn. Mus. Art, Worcester (Mass.) Art. Mus., Albion (Mich.) Coll., Prudential Ins. Co. Am., Newark. Served to 1st. lt. Adj. Gen. Corps U.S. Army, 1959-60. Mem. N.Y. Artist Equity Assn.

LEVI, JULIAN HIRSCH, lawyer, educator; b. Chgo., July 25, 1909; s. Gerson Baruch and Elsa (Hirsch) L.; m. Marjorie Reynolds, Sept. 16, 1938; children: William Gerson, Kay Levi Pick. Ph.B. with honors, U. Chgo., 1929, J.D. cum laude, 1931; LL.D. (hon.), John Marshall Law Sch., Chgo., Lake Forest (Ill.) Coll., 1967. Bar: Ill. 1931. Ptnr. Wilhartz & Hirsch, Chgo., 1931-46; officer Reynolds Pen Co., also Reynolds Printasign Co., Chgo., 1946-52; exec. dir. S.E. Chgo. Commn., 1952-80; prof. urban studies U. Chgo., 1962-80; vis. prof. Hastings Coll. Law, U. Calif., San Francisco, 1978-79, 79-80; prof. Hastings Coll. Law, U. Calif., 1981—; founder, chmn. Pub. Law Rsch. Inst., 1984—; dir. Hyatt Corp., 1977-79, Elsinor Corp., 1979—; chmn. Chgo. Plan Commn., 1973-79; sec. Am. Council Edn., 1971-72; vice chmn. White House Task Force Cities, 1967; adv. to architect of Capitol, Washington, 1976—. Author: Municipal and Institution Relations in Boston, 1964, Financing Education and the Effect of Tax Laws, 1975; chmn. editorial adv. bd.: Urban Affairs Reporter, 1972-82. Trustee Michael Reese Hosp., Chgo., 1967-80, Calif. State Libr. Found., 1992—. Recipient Rockefeller Public Service award Princeton U., 1977, Alumni Svc. medal U. Chgo., 1989. Mem. ABA, Am. Law Inst., Am. Soc. Planning Ofcls., Chgo. Bar Assn., Order of Coif, Phi Beta Kappa. Jewish. Clubs: Tavern, Arts, Quadrangle (Chgo.). Office: U Calif Hastings Coll Law 200 Mcallister St San Francisco CA 94102-4707

LEVI, KURT, retired banker; b. Wiesbaden, Germany, May 20, 1910; came to U.S., 1937, naturalized, 1942; s. Josef and Martha (Kahn) L.; m. Ruth Neumann, Feb. 17, 1938; 1 son, Peter. LL.B., U. Frankfurt, Germany, 1931. Mdse. mgr. Consol. Retail Stores, Kansas City, Mo., 1937-55; with United Mo. Bank, Kansas City, 1956-80; sr. v.p. United Mo. Bank, 1971-80, Traders Bank, Kansas City, 1980-85; adj. prof. Park Coll., Parkville, Mo., 1984-85. Gen. and area chmn. Kansas City (Mo.) United campaign, 1962; chmn. finance com. Camp Fire Girls Am., 1964; chmn. Kansas City Mayor's Prayer Breakfast Club, 1968; gen. chmn. Greater Kansas City Bonds for Israel, 1959; chmn. Greater Kansas City Conf. Soviet Jewry, 1966; vice chmn., mem. exec. bd. Community Relations Bur., 1972; pres. Heart Am. chpt., Religious Zionists Am., 1971; bd. govs. Jewish Fedn. and Council Kansas City, 1972-88, div. chmn. Fedn. campaign, 1986; bd. govs. Kansas City chpt. Am. Jewish Com., nat. bd. dirs.; pres., chmn. bd. Kehilath Israel Synagogue, lifetime hon. Gabbi; bd. govs., ombudsman Temple Sholom, Pompano Beach, Fla., 1988-94. Mem. Kansas City C. of C., B'nai B'rith (pres. Kansas City lodge 1984 1965, Greater Kansas City Coun. 1966, pres. Dist. II 1975-76, exec. v.p., bd. dirs., pres. Ft. Lauderdale 1990-92, pres. Kol Haverim lodge 1990-95), Kiwanis (v.p. Kansas City 1955), Legion of Honor, Playa del Sol Social Club (pres. 1989-90). Home: Playa del Sol 3500 Galt Ocean Dr Apt 2405 Fort Lauderdale FL 33308-6809 also: 121 W 48th St Kansas City MO 64112

LEVI, MAURICE DAVID, economics educator; b. London, Sept. 28, 1945; came to U.S., 1967; s. Karl and Louisa Hannah (Magson) L.; m. Kathleen Birkinshaw, Jan. 14, 1979; children—Adam Julian, Naomi Anne, Jonathan Karl. B.A. in Econs. with 1st class honors, U. Manchester, Eng., 1967; M.A., U. Chgo., 1968, Ph.D., 1972. Vis. prof. Hebrew U., Jerusalem, 1978; vis. assoc. prof. U. Calif.-Berkeley, 1979; vis. scholar MIT, Cambridge, 1980; prof. business U. B.C., Vancouver, Can., 1972—; vis. prof. London Bus. Sch., 1985. Author: Economics Deciphered, 1981, Thinking Economically, 1985, International Finance, 3rd edit., 1996, Economics and the Modern World, 1994; contbr. articles to profl. jours. Mem. Vancouver Mayor's Econ. Adv. Commn., 1983-84, Fed. Provincial Initiative, 1987-90. Recipient Seagram award, 1978; grantee Ford Found., 1969-70, Can. Coun., 1978, 80, 85; Nomura fellow U. Exeter, 1990. Jewish. Avocations: astronomy; salmon fishing.

LEVI, PETER STEVEN, chamber of commerce executive, lawyer; b. Washington, June 3, 1944; s. Kurt and Ruth (Neumann) L.; m. Enid Goldberg, Jan. 26, 1969; children: Joshua, Jeff. BA, Northwestern U., 1966; JD, U. Mo., Kansas City, 1969, LLM in Urban Legal Affairs, 1971. Bar: Mo. 1969. Gen. counsel Mid Am. Regional Coun., Kansas City, 1971-77, exec. dir., 1977-90; pres. Greater Kansas City C. of C., 1990—; participant internat. local govt. mgmt. exch. program with Israel, Internat. City Mgmt. Assn., 1985-86. Author: Model Subdivision Regulations, 1975; contbr. numerous articles to legal and pub. adminstrn. jours. Bd. dirs. Starlight Theatre, Kansas City Area Devel. Coun., Downtown Coun., Kansas City region NCCJ, Full Employment Coun., City of Fountains, Project NEIGHBOR-H.O.O.D., Am. Royal Assn., Edn. Inc.; mem. policy adv. group Bus.-Edn. Expectations; cmty. advisor Jr. League; past pres. Kehilath Israel Synagogue. Recipient Pub. Adminstr. of Yr. award Am. Soc. Pub. Adminstrn., 1985, L.P. Cookingham Pub. Adminstrn. award, 1989; Walter Scheiber Regional Leadership award Nat. Assn. Regional Couns., 1990; fellow U.S. Dept. Transp., 1975. Mem. Assn. C.C. Execs., Rotary. Home: 3720 W 119th Ter Leawood KS 66209-1046 Office: Greater Kans City C of C 911 Main St Ste 2600 Kansas City MO 64105-2009

LEVI, YOEL, orchestra conductor; b. Sotmar, Rumania, Israeli, Aug. 16, 1950; naturalized U.S. citizen, 1987; m. Jacqueline; 3 children. MA in Violin and Percussion, U. Tel Aviv, 1975; grad. degree, Jerusalem Acad. Music, 1976; studied with, Mendi Rodan; Diploma, Guildhall Sch. Music and Drama, London, 1978; studied with Franco Ferrara, Siena, Acad. Santa Cecilia, Rome and Kiril Kondrashin, Hilversum. Percussionist Israel Philharmonic Orch., 1975, conducting asst., 1978-80; resident condr. Cleve. Orch., 1980-84; music dir. Atlanta Symphony Orch., 1988—; guest condr. N.Am. and European orchs. Albums include The Artistry of Yoel Levi: The Telarc Collection, Vol. 8; recs. with Angel-EMI, Schwann, Telarc. Recipient 1st prize Condrs. Internat. Competition, Besancon, 1978. Office: Atlanta Symphony Orch 1293 Peachtree St NE Ste 300 Atlanta GA 30309-3527 also: Columbia Artists Mgmt Foster Divsn 165 W 57th St New York NY 10019

LEVIE, HOWARD S(IDNEY), lawyer, educator, author; b. Wolverine, Mich., Dec. 19, 1907; s. J. Walter and Mina (Goldfarb) L.; m. S. Blanche Krim, July 24, 1934. A.B., Cornell U., 1928, J.D., 1930; LL.M., George Washington U., 1957. Bar: N.Y. 1931, Mo. 1965, U.S. Dist. Ct. (ea. dist.) N.Y. 1934, U.S. Dist. Ct. (so. dist.) N.Y. 1935, U.S. Supreme Ct. 1947, U.S. Ct. Appeals (D.C. cir.) 1949, U.S. Ct. Mil. Appeals 1953. Assoc. Weit & Goldman, N.Y.C., 1931-42; with JAGC, U.S. Army, 1942, advanced through grades to col., 1954; staff officer UN Command Armistice Del., Korea, 1951-52; chief internat. affairs div. Office of JAG, 1954-58; legal adviser U.S. European Command, Paris, 1959-61; ret. 1963; prof. law St. Louis U., 1963-77, prof. emeritus, 1977—; prof. U.S. Naval War Coll., Newport, R.I., 1971-72, Charles H. Stockton prof. internat. law, 1971-72; instr. internat. law Salve Regina Coll., Newport, R.I., 1984-88; adj. prof. Naval War Coll., 1991—. Author: Prisoners of War in International Armed Conflict (Internat. Soc. for Mil. Law and the Law of War Ciardi prize 1982), 1979, Documents on Prisoners of War, 1980, Protection of War Victims, 4 vols., 1979-81, The Status of Gibraltar, 1983, The Code of International Armed Conflict, 1986, The Law of Non-International Armed Conflict, 1987, The Law of War and Neutrality: A Selected English-Language Bibliography, 1988, Mine Warfare at Sea, 1992, Terrorism in War: The Law of War Crimes, 1993. Decorated Legion of Merit, Bronze Star; grantee Ctr. for Advanced Rsch., Naval War Coll., 1980-82, U.S. Inst. Peace, 1991; Howard S. Levie Mil. Chair of Operational Law established by U.S. Naval War Coll., 1994; recipient Outstanding Civilian Svc. medal Dept. of the Army, 1995; named Disting. Mem. of Judge Advocate Gen.'s Corps Regiment, 1995. Mem. ABA, Am. Soc. Internat. Law (exec. coun. 1969-70), Internat. Law Assn., Ret. Army Judge Advs. Assn., Internat. Soc. for Mil. Law and Law of War, Phi Beta Kappa. Democrat. Home and Office: 41 Sherman St Newport RI 02840-2959

LEVIE, JOSEPH HENRY, lawyer; b. N.Y.C.; s. Mortimer Joseph and Pearl (Seelig) L.; m. Hallie Ratzkin, Jan. 26, 1963; children: Matthew Benjamin, Jessica Ruth. AB, Columbia U., 1949, LLB, 1951. Bar: N.Y. 1952, U.S. Supreme Ct. 1954. Assoc. Laporte & Meyers, N.Y.C., 1955-59; asst. gen. counsel Loew Theatres Inc., N.Y.C., 1959-63; from assoc. to ptnr. Rathheim, Hoffman, Kassel & Levie, N.Y.C., 1964-81; ptnr. Rogers & Wells, N.Y.C., 1982-94, sr. counsel, 1995—; lectr. banking and related subjects to various profl. groups. Contbr. articles to profl. jours. With JAGC, U.S. Army, 1952-55. Fellow Am. Coll. Comml. Fin. Attys.; mem. Columbia Coll. Alumni (pres. class of 1949). Home: 131 Riverside Dr New York NY 10024-3713 Office: Roger & Wells 200 Park Ave New York NY 10166-0005

LE VIEN, JOHN DOUGLAS (JACK LE VIEN), motion picture and television producer, director; b. N.Y.C., July 18, 1918; s. Christopher Luke and Rose Jeanette Le V. Chmn. bd. TCA Travel Corp. Am., 1979—; chmn. bd. Electronic Pub. Co., London. Div. News editor Pathé News, 1946-57; ind. motion picture and TV dir. and producer, 1958—; producer: (TV series) Valiant Years, 1959-60; exec. producer: (film) Black Fox, 1962 (Acad. award); producer and dir.: (films) Finest Hours, 1963-64, A King's Story, 1965, Churchill Centenary, 1974; (TV shows) Other World of Winston Churchill, 1964, The Gathering Storm, 1973, The Amazing Voyage of Daffodil and Daisy, 1974, Cicero, 1975, Where the Lotus Fell, 1976, Flames Over the Sahara, 1977, Children of the Lotus, 1978, Churchill and The Generals, 1980; pres., exec. producer TV movies, Le Vien Internat. Prodns. Ltd., N.Y.C., 1958—; chmn. bd., exec. producer TV shows, Le Vien Films Ltd., London, Eng., 1963—; author: The Valiant Years, 1961, The Finest Hours, 1964, (with Lady Mosley) The Duchess of Windsor, 1979, (with Barrie Pitt) Churchill and The Generals. Served to col. AUS, World War II, ETO; col. Res. Decorated Legion of Merit, Bronze Star; Legion of Honor; Croix de Guerre France). Mem. Brit. Acad. Film & Television Arts. Club: Overseas Press (N.Y.C.). Home: 15 Chesterfield Hill, London W1, England

LE VIEUX, JANE STUART, pediatrics nurse; b. Washington, May 1, 1956; d. Richard Stuart and Jane Marie (O'Connell) Le V.; m. Gary B. Elliott, Sept. 4, 1982; children: Julianne, Aimée. BSN, U. South Ala., 1979; MS in Child Devel., U. North Tex., 1989, MEd in Counseling and Play Therapy, 1991. Lic. profl. counselor; registered play therapist, Tex. Staff nurse ICU Children's Med. Ctr., Dallas, 1979-81, RN cardiac cath lab., 1981-84, bone marrow transplant child life specialist, 1991—; supr. cardiac cath lab. Humana Hosp.-Medical City, Dallas, 1984-86, pediatric clin. nurse educator, 1986-87; child and family therapist The Caring Ctr., Dallas, 1992—; children's grief therapist and cons. Family Hospice, 1993—; clin. instr. Tex. Woman's U. Coll. Nursing, 1995—; therapist Grief Camp El Tesoro De La Vida, First Tex. coun. Camp Fire Girls, 1995. Active Weekend to Wipe Out Cancer, Dallas, Children's Cancer Fund, Jr. League of Dallas; bd. dirs. Trinity Ministry to the Poor. Author: (with others) A Handbook for Practitioners, 1993. Mem. Assn. for Play Therapy, ANA, Tex. Nurses Assn., Child Life Coun., Assn. for Care of Children's Health, Phi Delta Kappa. Roman Catholic. Avocations: windsurfing, running, tennis, needlepoint. Home: 4815 Royal Ln Dallas TX 75229-4208 Office: The Caring Ctr 8222 Douglas Ave Ste 777 Dallas TX 75225-5938

LEVIN, A. LEO, law educator, retired government official; b. N.Y.C., Jan. 9, 1919; s. Isaachar and Minerva Hilda (Shapiro) L.; m. Doris Feder, Dec. 28, 1947; children—Allan, Jay Michael. BA, Yeshiva Coll., 1939; JD, U. Pa., 1942; LLD (hon.), Yeshiva U., 1960, NY Law Sch., 1980, Quinnipiac Coll., 1995; PhD (hon.), Bar-Ilan U., Israel, 1990. Bar: N.Y. 1947, U.S.

Supreme Ct. 1982. Instr., then asst. prof. law U. Iowa, 1947-49; law faculty U. Pa., Phila., 1949-69, 70-89, Meltzer prof. law, 1987-89, Meltzer prof. emeritus, 1989—, vice provost, 1965-68; v.p. for acad. affairs Yeshiva U., N.Y.C., 1969-70; dir. Fed. Jud. Ctr., Washington, 1977-87; chmn. Pa. State Legis. Reapportionment Commn., 1971-73; founding dir. Nat. Inst. Trial Advocacy, 1971-73; conf. coord. Nat. Conf. on Causes of Popular Dissatisfaction with Adminstrn. of Justice (Pound Conf.); chmn. bd. cert. Circuit Execs., 1977-87; mem. adv. bd. Nat. Inst. Corrections, 1977-87. Author: (with Woolley) Dispatch and Delay: A Field Study of Judicial Administration in Pennsylvania, 1961; (with Cramer) Problems on Trial Advocacy, 1968; editor: (with Schuchman and Yablon) Cases on Civil Procedure, 1992, Supplement, 1994. Hon. trustee Bar Ilan U., Ramat Gan, Israel, 1967—; hon. pres. (former pres.) Jewish Publ. Soc. Am. Served to 1st lt. USAF, 1942-46, ETO. Recipient Mordecai Ben David award Yeshiva U., 1967, Disting. Svc. award U. Pa. Law Sch. Alumni, 1974, Bernard Revel award Yeshiva Coll., 1963, Justice award Am. Judicature Soc., 1995; White lectr. La. U., 1970, Jeffords lectr., N.Y. Law Sch., 1980, Murrah Lectr. U. Pa. Law Sch., 1989. Fellow Am. Acad. Arts and Scis.; mem. Am. Law Inst., Am. Judicature Soc. (pres. 1987-89), Order of Coif (nat. pres. 1967-70). Jewish. Office: U Pa Law Sch 3400 Chestnut St Philadelphia PA 19104-6204

LEVIN, AARON REUBEN, pediatrician, educator; b. Johannesburg, Transvaal, Republic of South Africa, Mar. 19, 1929; came to U.S., 1964; s. Louis and Fanny (Galgut) L.; m. Lenore Zhita Gladstone, Dec. 6, 1955; children: Sheryl Rina, Terry Larice, Serle Kevin. BS, Witwatersrand U., 1948, MB, BCh, 1953, MD, 1969. Diplomate Am. Bd. Pediatrics, Pediatric Cardiology. Intern Edenvale Hosp., Johannesburg, 1954-55; sr. med. officer Fever Hosp., Johannesburg, 1955-56; registrar in pediatrics Coronation Hosp., Johannesburg, 1956-61, Charing Cross Hosp., London, 1961-62; attending pediatrician Edenvale Hosp., Johannesburg, 1962-64; instr. in pediatrics Duke Univ. Med. Sch., Durham, N.C., 1964-66; asst.-assoc. prof. pediatrics Cornell Univ. Med. Coll., N.Y.C., 1966-73, prof. pediatrics, 1973-94; prof. pediatrics N.Y. Med. Coll., 1994—; attending pediatrician N.Y. Hosp. Cornell Med. Ctr., 1966-94, also dir. pediatric catheterization labs. 1966-94; cons. cardiologist Englewood (N.J.) Hosp., 1980—; assoc. attending pediatric cardiologist Westchester County Med. Ctr., 1994—. Contbr. articles and papers to profl. jours. Pres. Beth Emeth Synagogue, Larchmont, N.Y., 1973, Pediatric Cardiology Soc. Greater N.Y., 1978. Fellow Am. Heart Assn., Am. Coll. Cardiology, N.Y. Heart Assn., Am. Angiology Soc., Royal Coll. Physicians (Edinburgh, Scotland). Avocations: stamp collecting, reading, gardening.. Home: 10 Hall Ave Larchmont NY 10538-2929 Office: New York Medical College 601 Munger Pavilion Valhalla NY 10595

LEVIN, ALAN M., television journalist; b. Bklyn., Feb. 28, 1926; s. Herman and Shirley (Levinstein) L.; m. Hannah Alexander, Oct. 30, 1948; children: Marc, Nicole, Danielle, Juliet. B.A., Wesleyan U., Middletown, Conn., 1946. Reporter, columnist Plainfield (N.J.) Courier News, 1957-60; statehouse corr. AP, Trenton, N.J., 1960-61; writer N.Y. Post, 1961-63; press sec. Sen. Harrison Williams, Washington, 1963-64; news producer, writer WABC-TV, N.Y.C., 1965-67; owner Levin Mediaworks Inc., producers documentaries for comml. and pub. TV, N.Y.C. Documentary film maker, NET, N.Y.C., 1968-69, documentary film maker, pub. affairs, news writer, dir., producer, WNET-TV, N.Y.C., 1969-82. Served with AUS, 1944-46. Recipient numerous awards including George Polk Meml. award, Dupont Columbia award, Emmy awards. Home: 88 Claremont Ave Maplewood NJ 07040-2024 Office: Levin Mediaworks Inc 142 W 26th St New York NY 10001-6814

LEVIN, ALAN SCOTT, pathologist, allergist, immunologist, lawyer; b. Chgo., Jan. 12, 1938; s. John Bernhard and Betty Ruth (Margulis) L.; m. Vera S. Byers, June 15, 1971. BS in Chemistry, U. Ill., Champaign-Urbana, 1960; MS in Biochemistry, U. Ill., Chgo., 1963, MD, 1964; JD, Golden Gate U., 1995. Diplomate Am. Bd. Allergy and Immunology, Am. Bd. Pathology; bar: Calif. 1995. Intern Children's Hosp. Med. Ctr., Boston, 1964-65; adj. instr. pediatrics U. Calif., San Francisco, 1971-72, asst. prof. immunology dept. dermatology, 1972-78, adj. assoc. prof., 1978-88; dir. lab. immunology U. Calif. & Kaiser Found. Rsch. Inst. Joint Program Project, San Francisco, 1971-74; attending physician dept. medicine Mt. Zion/U. Calif. San Francisco Hosps., 1971—; dir. div. immunology Western Labs., Oakland, Calif., 1974-77; med. dir. MML/Solano Labs. Div. Chemed-W.R. Grace, Inc., Berkeley, Calif., 1977-79; med. dir. Levin Clin. Labs., Inc., San Francisco, 1979-81; pvt. practice San Francisco, 1981—. Contbr. articles to profl. jours., chpts. to books. Lt. USN, 1966-69, Vietnam. Decorated Bronze Star, Silver Star, 4 Air medals; Harvard Med. Sch. traineeship grantee, 1964, USPHS hematology tng. grantee U. Calif., San Francisco Med. Ctr., 1969-71; recipient Faculty Rsch. award Am. Cancer Soc., 1970-74. Fellow Coll. Am. Pathologists, Am. Coll. Emergency Physicians, Am. Soc. Clin. Pathologists; mem. AMA, Am. Acad. Allergy and Immunology, Am. Coll. Allergy and Immunology, Am. Assn. Clin. Chemists, Am. Acad. Environ. Medicine, Calif. Med. Assn., San Francisco Med. Soc. Jewish. Office: Immunology Inc 500 Sutter St Ste 512 San Francisco CA 94102-1114

LEVIN, ALVIN IRVING, composer, educator; b. N.Y.C., Dec. 22, 1921; s. David and Frances (Schloss) L.; m. Beatrice Van Loon, June 5, 1976 (div. 1981). BMus in Edn., U. Miami (Fla.), 1941; MA, Calif. State U., L.A., 1955; EdD with honors, UCLA, 1968. Composer, arranger for movies, TV, theater Allied Artists, Eagle-Lion Studios, Los Angeles, 1945-65; tng. and supervising tchr. Los Angeles City Schs., 1957-65, adult edn. instr., 1962-63; research specialist Los Angeles Office Supt. Edn., 1965-67; asst. prof. ednl. research Calif. State U., Los Angeles, 1968; asst. prof. elem. edn. Calif. State U., Northridge, 1969-73; self-employed, Northridge, 1973—; founder, pres. Alvin Irving Levin Philanthropic Found., 1973—; ordained to ministry Ch. of Mind Sci., 1975; founder, pres. Divine Love Ch.-An Internat. Metaphys. Ch., 1977—, Meet Your New Personality, A Mind Expansion Program, 1975-77. Bd. overseers Calif. Sch. Profl. Psychology, 1974—; gen. chmn., producer Fiftieth Anniversary Pageant of North Hollywood Park, 1977. Author: My Ivory Tower, 1950, Symposium: Values in Kaleidoscope, 1973, (TV series) America, America!, 1978-79, (docudrama) One World, 1980; composer: Symphony for Strings, 1984, Tone Poem for Male Chorus and Brass, 1984, Hymn to the United Nations for chorus and symphony orch., 1991, Hiawatha Suite for Chorus and Symphony Orch., 1994, (music-drama) Happy Land, 1971, (musical plays) A Tale of Two Planets, 1988, Blueprint for a New World Model, 1991; producer UN Festival Calif. State U., Northridge, 1991; compiler, contbr. U.S. Dept. Edn. reports Adult Counseling and Guidance, 1967, Parent Child Preschool Program, 1967, English Classes for Foreign Speaking Adult Professionals, 1967, Blueprint for New World Order, 1991. Recipient plaque State of Calif., 1977, Golden Merit medal Rep. Presdl. Task Force, 1985. Named to Rep. Task Force Presdl. Commn., 1986. Mem. Nat. Soc. for Study Edn., AAUP, Am. Statis. Assn., Internat. Council Edn. for Teaching, Los Angeles World Affairs Council, Internat. Platform Assn., World Federalist Assn. (pres. San Fernando Valley chpt. 1991—), North Hollywood C. of C. (dir. 1976—), Phi Delta Kappa. Home and Office: 5407 Colfax Ave Apt 223 North Hollywood CA 91601-5209 *Personal philosophy: Always dream the impossible dream; then make it come true, with every possible action!.*

LEVIN, BERNARD, physician; b. Johannesburg, Republic of South Africa, Apr. 1, 1942; came to U.S. 1966, naturalized 1972; m. Ronelle DuBrow; children: Adam, Katherine. MD, U. Witwatersrand, 1964. Resident Presbyn. St. Lukes Hosp., Chgo., 1966-68; rsch. fellow U. Chgo., 1968-71; NIH fellow U. Chgo., 1971-72; instr. medicine U. Chgo., 1971-73, asst. prof. medicine, 1973-78, assoc. prof., 1979-84; prof. med., chmn. dept gastrointestinal oncology and digestive diseases, U. Tex. Med. Ctr. M.D. Anderson Hosp., Houston, 1984-94, Robert R. Herring prof., 1986-91, Ellen F. Knisely chair, 1991-94, v.p. for Cancer Prevention (ad interim), 1992-94, v.p. for Cancer Prevention, 1994—, Betty Marcus chair 1994—; mem. large bowel cancer working group Nat. Cancer Inst., 1984-85; cons. spl. study sect. Nat. Cancer Inst., 1976-84, chair nat. adv. com. on colorectal cancer, 1990—. Contbr. articles to profl. jours.; mem. editorial bd. Pancreas, Jour. Nat. Cancer Inst. J. Clin. Oncology USPHS grantee, 1976-80; Melamid Found. Gift, U. Chgo., 1978-83; NCI grantee, 1980-84, others. Fellow ACP, Am. Coll. Gastroenterology; mem. AAAS, Am. Assn. Cancer Rsch., Am. Gastroenterol. Assn., Am. Soc. Gastrointestinal Endoscopy, Am. Pancreatic Assn, Am. Soc. Preventive Oncology, Internat. Assn. Pancreatology, Am. Soc. Clin. Oncology, Am. Cancer Soc. (chair nat. adv. com. on colorectal cancer), Sigma Xi. Jewish. Office: UT M D Anderson Cancer Ctr 1515 Holcombe Blvd 203 Houston TX 77030-4095

LEVIN, BETSY, lawyer, educator, university dean; b. Balt., Dec. 25, 1935; d. M. Jastrow and Alexandra (Lee) L. AB, Bryn Mawr (Pa.) Coll., 1956; LLB, Yale U., 1966. Bar: D.C. 1967, Colo. 1982. Research geologist U.S. Geol. Survey, Washington, 1956-63; law clk. to judge U.S. Ct. Appeals (4th cir.), Balt., 1966-67; spl. asst. to U.S. Amb. to UN, Arthur J. Goldberg N.Y.C., 1967-68; dir. edn. studies Urban Inst., Washington, 1968-73; prof. law Duke U., Durham, N.C., 1973-80; gen. counsel U.S. Dept. Edn., Washington, 1980-81; dean, prof. law U. Colo., Boulder, 1981-87; exec. v.p. Assn. Am. Law Schs., Washington, 1987-92; Arch T. Allen vis. disting. prof. law U. N.C. Sch. Law, Chapel Hill, 1993; vis. prof. law Am. U. Washington Coll. Law, 1994, Georgetown U. Law Ctr., Washington, 1994; disting. vis. prof. sch. law U. Balt., 1995-96; mem. Nat. Coun. Ednl. Rsch., 1978-79; mem. civil rights reviewing authority HEW, 1979-80. Co-author: Educational Policy and the Law, 2d edit., 1982, 3d edit., 1991; editor: Future Directions for School Finance Reform, 1975; co-editor: The Courts, Social Science and School Desegregation, 1977, School Desegregation: Lessons of the First 25 Years, 1979. White House fellow, 1967-68. Fellow Am. Bar Found., Colo. Bar Found.; mem. ABA, Nat. Assn. Women Judges (program com. 1985-92), Am. Law Inst. (coun.), Order of Coif. Office: U Balt Sch Law 1420 N Charles St Baltimore MD 21201-5720

LEVIN, BURTON, diplomat; b. N.Y.C., Sept. 28, 1930; s. Benjamin and Ida (Geller) L.; m. Lily Lee, Jan. 4, 1960; children: Clifton, Alicia. BA, CUNY, 1952; M Internat. Affairs, Columbia U., 1954; postgrad., Harvard U., 1964; LLD (hon.), Carleton Coll., 1993. Commd. fgn. service officer Dept. State, 1954; counselor/econ. officer Am. Embassy, Taipei, Taiwan, 1954-56, polit. officer, 1969-74; intelligence research specialist Dept. State, Washington, 1956-58, dir. Republic China affairs, 1974-77; polit. officer Am. Embassy, Jakarta, Indonesia, 1959-63; polit. officer Am. Consulate Gen. Hong Kong, 1965-69, dep. chief mission, 1977-78, consul gen., 1981-86; dep. chief mission Am. Embassy, Bangkok, Thailand, 1978-81; amb. to Burma, 1987-90; dir. Asia Soc. Hong Kong Ctr., 1990-95; vis. prof. Carleton Coll., 1995; vis. fellow Stanford U., 1974; vis. lectr. Harvard U., 1986, Carleton Coll., 1994; bd. dirs. Mansfield Found., China Fund, Yaohan Food Processing and Trading Co. Ltd.; mem. coun. Nanjing U. Ctr. for Chinese and Am. Studies Johns Hopkins U. Mem. Am. Fgn. Service Assn. Clubs: Am., Hong Kong Country. Home: 314 2d St E Northfield MN 55057

LEVIN, CARL, senator; b. Detroit, June 28, 1934; m. Barbara Halpern, 1961; children: Kate, Laura, Erica. BA, Swarthmore Coll., 1956; JD, Harvard U., 1959. Ptnr. Grossman, Hyman & Grossman, Detroit, 1959-64; asst. atty. gen., gen. counsel Mich. CRC, 1964-67; chief appellate defender City of Detroit, 1968-69, mem. coun., 1970-73, pres. coun., 1974-77; ptnr. Schlussel, Lifton, Simon, Rands & Kaufman, 1971-73, Jaffe, Snider, Raitt, Garratt & Heuer, 1978-79; U.S. senator from Mich., 1979—; past instr. Wayne State U., U. Detroit; mem. Armed Svcs. Com., Govtl. Affairs Com., Com. on Small Bus., Senate Dem. Steering & Coordination Com. Mem. Mich. Bar Assn., D.C. Bar. Democrat. Office: US Senate 459 Russell Senate Off Washington DC 20510*

LEVIN, CARL, public and government relations consultant; b. Ringgold, La.; m. Doris Wechsler; m. Sonia Atlas, Oct. 13, 1958; children: Judith Friedman, Richard (dec.), Virginia Vinick, Alan Schwartzbach. Student, CCNY, 1930-33. Corr. CCNY N.Y. Herald Tribune, 1930-34, staff reporter, 1934-43, Washington corr., 1943-45, 46-50; war and fgn. corr. N.Y. Herald Tribune, Europe, 1945-46; free lance mag. writer, 1942-50; Washington mgr. William H. Weintraub & Co. (advt. and pub. relations), 1950-52; charge Washington activities Schenley Industries, Inc., 1952-62, v.p., 1955-62; dir. pub. support Trade Expansion Act, White House, 1962; pres. Carl Levin Assos., Inc., 1962-68; v.p., gen. mgr. Burson-Marsteller, Washington, 1968-72; v.p., sr. cons. Burson-Marsteller, 1972-83, sr. v.p., 1983-87; mem. Nat. Small Bus. Adv. Coun., 1964-68; cons. in field. Collaborator books on journalism, postwar security investigations; contbr. to nat. mags. Active in founding Am.-Israel Pub. Affairs Soc.; bd. dirs. Interracial Coun. Bus. Opportunity, 1972-75; mem. bd. Com. Accuracy on Middle East Reporting in Am., 1985-91, Am. Gas Index Fund, 1990—; trustee Opera Soc. Washington, 1963-70, Fords Theater Soc., Washington, 1975-81; co-chmn. Citizens Com. Opera, 1963. Mem. Soc. Profl. Journalists, Lotos Club (N.Y.C.). Home: 5450 Whitley Park Ter Bethesda MD 20814-2057

LEVIN, CHARLES EDWARD, lawyer; b. Chgo., Oct. 6, 1946; m. Barbara Serwer, Dec. 28, 1975. BA with high honor, DePaul U., 1968; JD cum laude, Northwestern U., Chgo., 1971. Bar: Ill. 1971. Asst. instr. legal writing and rsch. Northwestern U. Law Sch., 1970-71; assoc. D'Ancona & Pflaum, Chgo., 1971-76, ptnr., 1977-90; ptnr. Jenner & Block, Chgo., 1990—; mem. governing bd. Comml. Fin. Assn. Edn. Found., 1990—; asst. instr. legal writing, rsch. Northwestern U., 1970-71. Mem. bd. editors Northwestern U. Law Rev., 1970-71. Mem. aux. bd. Chgo. Architecture Found., 1989—; mem. governing bd. Comml. Fin. Assn. Edn. Found., N.Y. Mem. ABA (bus. sect. 1992—), Chgo. Bar Assn. (vice chmn. architecture and law com. 1974-75, vice chmn. divsn. D, mem. exec. com. fed. tax com. 1983-84, comml. fin. and trans. com. 1990—, Article 9 drafting subcom.), Assn. for Corp. Growth, East Bank Club Chgo., 410 Club. Avocations: acquisition fine arts, support arts organizations, jogging. Office: Jenner & Block 1 E IBM Plz Fl 4400 Chicago IL 60611-3586

LEVIN, CHARLES LEONARD, state supreme court justice; b. Detroit, Apr. 28, 1926; s. Theodore and Rhoda (Katzin) L.; children: Arthur, Amy, Fredrick. B.A., U. Mich., 1946, LL.B., 1947; LL.D. (hon.), Detroit Coll. of Law, 1980. Bar: Mich. 1947, N.Y. 1949, U.S. Supreme Ct. 1953, D.C. 1954. Pvt. practice law N.Y.C., 1948-50, Detroit, 1950-66; ptnr. Levin, Levin, Garvett & Dill, Detroit, 1951-66; judge Mich. Ct. Appeals, Detroit, 1966-73; assoc. justice Mich. Supreme Ct., 1973—; mem. Mich. Law Revision Commn., 1966. Trustee Marygrove Coll., 1971-77, chmn., 1971-74; mem. vis. coms. to Law Schs., U. Mich., U. Chgo., 1977-80, Wayne State U. Mem. Am. Law Inst. Office: Mich Supreme Ct 500 Woodward Ave 20th Fl Detroit MI 48226-3435*

LEVIN, DAVID ALAN, lawyer; b. Cheverly, Md., Nov. 16, 1947; s. Jacob Solomon and Elaine (Astrin) L.; m. Pamela Evelyn Ruff, Sept. 18, 1976; 1 child, Michael Brian. BS, U. Md., 1968, JD, 1972. Bar: Md. 1972, U.S. Ct. Appeals (4th cir.) 1975. Ptnr. Levin & Levin, Langley Park, Md., 1972-75, O'Malley, Miles, Largo, Md., 1975-84, Wharton, Levin, Ehrmantraut, Klein & Nash, Annapolis, Md., 1984—. Fellow Am. Coll. Trial Lawyers. Office: Wharton Levin et al PO Box 551 104 West St Annapolis MD 21404-0551

LEVIN, EDWARD JESSE, lawyer; b. Balt., Oct. 31, 1951; s. Cyril and Virginia Lee (Kremer) L.; m. Cheri Wyron, Feb. 18, 1973; children: Paul Clifford, Benjamin Lawrence. BA, Johns Hopkins U., 1973; JD, U. Va., 1976. Bar: Md. 1976, U.S. Supreme Ct. 1980. Assoc. Piper & Marbury LLP, Balt., 1976-84; ptnr. Piper & Marbury, Balt., 1984—. Co-author: Maryland Real Estate Leasing Forms and Practice, 1988. 1st v.p. Balt. Bd. of Jewish Edn., 1987-89, pres., 1989-91. Fellow Am. Coll. Real Estate Lawyers (chmn. attys.' opinions com. 1992—); mem. Md. State Bar Assn. (chmn. sect. real property, planning and zoning 1988-90. co-chmn. spl. joint com. lawyers' opinions comml. transactions 1989—), Balt. City Bar Assn. (co-chmn. spl. joint com. lawyers' opinions comml. transactions 1989—). Democrat. Jewish. Office: Piper & Marbury LLP 36 S Charles St Baltimore MD 21201-3018

LEVIN, EDWARD M., lawyer, government administrator; b. Chgo., Oct. 16, 1934; s. Edward M. and Anne Meriam (Fantl) L.; children from previous marriage: Daniel Andrew, John Davis; m. Margot Aronson, Apr. 4, 1993. BS, U. Ill., 1955; LLB, Harvard U., 1958. Bar: Ill. 1958, U.S. Supreme Ct. 1968. Mem. firm Ancel, Stonesifer, Glink & Levin and predecessors, Chgo., 1958, 61-68; draftsman Ill. Legis. Reference Bur., Springfield, 1961; spl. asst. to regional adminstr. HUD, Chgo., 1968-71, asst. regional adminstr. community planning and mgmt., 1971-73; asst. dir. Ill. Dept. Local Govt. Affairs, Chgo., 1973-77; of counsel Holleb, Gerstein & Glass, Ltd., Chgo., 1977-79; chief counsel Econ. Devel. Adminstrn., U.S. Dept. Commerce, Washington, 1979-85; sr. fellow Nat. Gov's. Assn., 1985-86; sr. counsel U.S. Dept. Commerce, Washington, 1987—; lectr. U. Ill., 1972-73, adj. assoc. prof. urban scis., 1973-79; lectr. Loyola U., 1976-79, No. Va. law Sch., 1988. Assoc. editor Assistance Mgmt. Jour., 1990-95; contbr. articles to profl. jours. Mem. Ill. Nature Preserves Com., 1963-68, Northeastern Ill. Planning Commn., 1974-77, Ill.-Ind. Bi-State Commn., 1974-77; bd. dirs. Cook County Legal Assistance Found., 1978-79, D.C. Appleseed Ctr., 1994—; mem. Ill. divsn. ACLU, 1965-68, 77-79, v.p., 1977-78. With AUS, 1958-60. Mem. ABA (chmn. fed. assistance com. 1995—), Fed. Bar Assn. (chmn. fed. grants com. 1991-95), Ill. Bar Assn. (Lincoln award 1977), Nat. Grants Mgmt. Assn. (bd. dirs. 1988-92, pres.'s award 1994), Appleseed Found. (bd. dirs., exec. com. 1994—). Home: 3201 Porter St NW Washington DC 20008-3212 Office: 14th & Constitution Ave NW Washington DC 20230-0002

LEVIN, FRANK S., physicist, educator; b. N.Y.C., Apr. 14, 1933; s. James J. and Celia (Aronovitch) L.; m. Madeline Carol McMurrough, Apr. 1973; 4 children. B.A., Johns Hopkins U., 1955; Ph.D., U. Md., 1961. Research assoc. Rice U., Houston, 1961-63, Brookhaven Nat. Lab., Upton, N.Y., 1963-66, U.K. Atomic Energy Authority, Harwell, Eng., 1965-67; mem. faculty Brown U., Providence, 1967—; prof. physics Brown U., 1977—. Fellow Am. Phys. Soc. (founder, 1st chmn. topical group on few body systems and multiparticle dynamics). Office: Brown U Physics Dept PO Box 1843 Providence RI 02912-1843

LEVIN, GEOFFREY ARTHUR, botanist; b. Los Alamos, N.Mex., Dec. 7, 1955; s. Jules Samuel and Jane Walden (Settle) L.; m. Renée Patricia Papini, May 24, 1981; children: Tobias, Madeline. BA, Pomona Coll., 1977; MS, U. Calif., Davis, 1980, PhD, 1984. Asst. prof. Ripon (Wis.) Coll., 1982-84; curator, chmn. botany dept. San Diego Natural History Mus., 1984-93; lectr. U. San Diego, 1984-90; asst. profl. scientist Ill. Natural History Survey, Champaign, 1994—; adj. asst. prof. dept. plant biology U. Ill., 1995—, adj. asst. prof. dept. natural resources and environ. studies, 1995—; rsch. assoc. Mo. Bot. Garden, 1994—. Contbr. articles to jours. in field. Bd. dirs. Fond du Lac Audubon Soc., 1983-84, San Diego Audubon Soc., 1986-87; pres. Summit Unitarian Universalist Fellowship, El Cajon, Calif., 1989-91. Recipient Jesse M. Greenman award. Mo. Bot. Garden, 1987; NSF grad. fellow, 1977-81. Mem. Am. Inst. Biol. Scis., Am. Soc. Plant Taxonomists, Bot. Soc. Am., Calif. Bot. Soc. (bd. editors 1992-95), Phi Beta Kappa, Sigma Xi. Democrat. Office: Ill Natural History Survey Ctr for Biodiversity 607 E Peabody Dr Champaign IL 61820-6917

LEVIN, GERALD MANUEL, media and entertainment company executive; b. Phila., May 6, 1939; s. David and Pauline (Schantzer) L.; m. Carol S. Needleman, Aug. 30, 1959 (div. Aug. 1970); children: Laura, Leon, Jonathan; m. Barbara J. Riley, Oct. 11, 1970; children: Michael, Anna. BA, Haverford Coll., 1960; LLB, U. Pa., 1963; LLD (hon.), Tex. Coll., 1985; LLD (hon.), Middlebury Coll., 1994; LHD (hon.), U. Denver, 1995. Assoc. Simpson, Thacher & Bartlett, N.Y.C., 1963-67; gen. mgr., chief operating officer Devel. and Resources Corp., N.Y.C., 1967-71; rep. Internat. Basic Economy Corp., Tehran, Iran, 1971-72; v.p. programming Home Box Office, N.Y.C., 1972-73, pres., chief exec. officer, 1973-76, chmn., chief exec. officer, 1976-79; group v.p. video Time, Inc., N.Y.C., 1979-84, exec. v.p., 1984-88, vice chmn., dir., 1988-90; vice chmn., dir. Time Warner Inc., N.Y.C., 1990—, chief oper. officer, 1991-92, pres., co-chief exec. officer to chmn. and CEO, 1992—; bd. dirs. Turner Broadcasting System, Inc. Trustee Haverford Coll., 1983-95, chmn. bd. dirs., 1990-95; bd. dirs., treas. N.Y. Philharm., 1989. Mem. Ctr. for Comm. (bd. dirs.), The Aspen Inst., N.Y. City Partnership, Nat. Cable TV Ctr. and Mus. (coun. on fgn. rels.), The Trilateral Commn., Corp. Governance Task Force of the Bus. Roundtable, Phi Beta Kappa. Avocations: reading, jogging. Office: Time Warner Inc 75 Rockefeller Plz New York NY 10019-6908

LEVIN, GILBERT VICTOR, health information, services and products; b. Balt., Apr. 23, 1924; s. Henry I. and Lillian R. (Richman) L.; m. Karen Salisbury, Oct. 25, 1953; children: Ron L., Henry L., Carol Y. BE, Johns Hopkins U., 1947, MS, 1948, PhD, 1963. Registered profl. engr., D.C., Md. With Md. State Dept. Health, 1948-50, Calif. Dept. Health, 1950-51, D.C. Dept. Pub. Health, 1951-55; v.p. Resources Research, Inc., Washington, 1955-63; dir. life systems div. Hazleton Labs., Inc., Reston, Va., 1963-67; chief exec. officer, chmn. bd. Biospherics Inc., Beltsville, Md., 1967—. Contbr. 100 articles to profl. jours.; mem. editorial bd. BioScience, 1960-63. Trustee John Hopkins U., 1982-85. Merchant Marine USCG, 1944-46. Recipient Pub. Svc. medal NASA, 1977. Fellow Am. Pub. Health Assn.; mem. ASCE, AAAS (Newcomb Cleveland prize 1977), Am. Water Works Assn., Water Pollution Control Fedn., Am. Soc. Microbiology, N.Y. Acad. Scis. Club: Cosmos. NASA experimenter Mariner 9 mission, 1971, Viking Mission Labeled Release Life Detection expt.; 1976; mem. team Mars oxident expt. for Russian Mars lander, 1996; patentee in field; inventor PhoStrip process for wastewater nutrient removal, microbial radiorespirometry, nonfattening sweeteners use of D-Tagatose as antihyperglycemic agent and in diabetes treatment; application of firefly bioluminescent assay for adenosine triphosphate bioassays to biomass determination and to microbial enumeration. Home: 3180 Harness Creek Rd Annapolis MD 21403-1614 Office: Biospherics Inc 12051 Indian Creek Ct Beltsville MD 20705-1261 *Man's ability to accumulate information through learning and to pass it on to his descendents frees his generations from endless repetition. He may hope to understand the universe and his place in it.*

LEVIN, HAL ALAN, psychiatrist; b. Bklyn., Feb. 13, 1935; s. David and Rose M. (Rosen) L.; children of former marriage: Julie Levin Keith, Susan Levin Davis, Mark D. Levin; m. Sharon Greenleaf, Feb. 9, 1973; children: Anne Levin Warrick, Julie Elizabeth, Alisa M., Kimberly L. Grimes, Christopher Lenk. BS, Roosevelt U., 1958; MD, Tulane Med. Sch., New Orleans, 1967. Diplomate Am. Bd. Psychiatry and Neurology, Am. Bd. Forensic Examiners, Am. Bd. Forensic Medicine. Intern Norfolk (Va.) Gen. Hosp., 1967-68; resident in psychiatry Sheppard & Enoch Pratt Hosp., Towson, Md., 1968-70, Crownsville (Md.) Hosp., 1970-71; fellow in forensic psychiatry U. So. Calif., L.A., 1983-84; staff psychiatrist Atascadero (Calif.) State Hosp., 1971-72; pvt. practice psychiatry San Bernardino, Calif., 1972-85; asst. prof. clin. psychiatry Mich. State U., East Lansing, 1985-86; asst. dir. mental health State of Mich., Lansing, 1985-86; dir. mental health State of Ariz., Phoenix, 1986-87; pvt. practice psychiatry Tempe, Ariz., 1987—; cons. psychiatrist San Bernardino County Hosp., 1972-85, San Bernardino Superior Ct., 1972-85; dir. Desert Valley Clinic, Apple Valley, Calif., 1973-80; med. dir. Big Bear (Calif.) Psychiat. Clinic, 1980-84; med. dir. Ctr. for Behavioral Health, Tempe, 1989—. cons. Jewish Family Svcs., Tempe, 1990—, Interfaith Counseling, Mesa, Ariz., 1991—. Mem. AMA, Am. Psychiat. Assn., Ariz. Med. Assn., Am. Acad. Psychiatry & the Law, Am. Bd. Forensic Examiners, Friends of Phoenix Symphony. Democrat. Avocations: computers, film, reading, swimming, music. Office: 5410 S Lakeshore Dr # 103 Tempe AZ 85283-2171

LEVIN, HARVEY JAY, financial institutions design and construction specialist, developer, auctioneer; b. Fitchburg, Mass., Apr. 27, 1936; s. Abe and Ila L.; children: Kimberly, Tara, Robin, Vanessa. Student Brandeis U., Boston U., U. Md., Ind. U.; BBA in Fin., U. Mass., 1960; MA in Econs., U. N.H., 1970; PhD LaSalle U. Lic. real estate broker, Mass., N.H.; lic. comml. pilot; lic. auctioneer, Maine, Mass., N.H., Vt., Accredited Auctioneer Real Estate, CAI. Pres. Central Tool Warehouse, Leominster, Mass., 1959-66; dir. mktg. and sales Spacemakers, Canton, Mass., 1970-72, New Eng. Homes, Biddeford, Maine, 1973-74; gen. mgr. Great No. Homes, Boston, 1966-70; cons. service mgr. Bank Bldg. Corp., St. Louis, 1974-80; v.p. Shelter Resources, Birmingham, Ala., 1972-73; v.p. Fin. Concepts, Natick, Mass., 1980-85; pres. Am. Bank Design, Inc., and Credit Union Bldg. Corp., Portsmouth, N.H., Harv Levin, Inc., Auctioneers, 1986—; cons. Republic Homes, Truro, Can., 1974. Author, lectr. personal and profl. seminars. Chmn. sch. bldg. com. Kensington, N.H., 1985; pres. Pheasant Run Condominium Assn., 1993—; chairperson Parents Fund, U. N.H., 1993-95, pres.- elect Parents Coun., 1995—. Served with U.S. Army, 1955-57. Recipient Award of Honor, Bank Bldg. Corp. of Am., 1976, 1st Place Design award Bank Bldg. Corp. of Am., 1977, Best Mktg. and Sales Plan award Automation in Housing Assn., 1972, FMHA award for Best Elderly Housing Project (Hazel Dell Apts., Alfred, Maine); named Hon. Lt. Col. Aide-de-Camp by Gov. of Ala., 1978. Mem. Aircraft Owners and Pilots Assn., Phi Sigma Kappa. Clubs: The River (Kennebunkport, Maine); Hampton River Boat, Portsmouth Power Squadron. Lodge: Masons. Office: Am Bank Design Inc and Harv Levin Inc 6 Greenleaf Woods Dr Ste 102 Portsmouth NH 03801-5443

LEVIN, HENRY MORDECAI, economist, educator; b. N.Y.C., Dec. 7, 1938. B.S. cum laude, NYU, 1960; M.A., Rutgers U., 1962, Ph.D., 1967.

assoc. research scientist, Grad. Sch. Pub. Adminstrn., NYU, 1965-66; research assoc. social econs. Econ. Studies div. Brookings Inst., Washington, 1966-68; asst. prof. edn. and econs. Stanford U., Calif., 1968-69, assoc. prof. econs., 1969-75, prof. econs. and edn., 1975—, David Jacks Prof. of Higher Edn. and Econs., 1992—, fellow Ctr. for Advanced Studies in Behavioral Scis., 1976-77, dir. Inst. Research on Ednl. Fin. and Governance, 1978-84. Office: Stanford U Ctr Edn Rsch CERAS Bldg 109 Stanford CA 94305

LEVIN, IRA, author, playwright; b. N.Y.C., Aug. 27, 1929; s. Charles and Beatrice (Schlansky) L.; m. Gabrielle Aronsohn, Aug. 20, 1960 (div. 1968); children: Adam, Jared, Nicholas; m. Phyllis Finkel, Aug. 26, 1979 (div. 1982). Student, Drake U., Des Moines, 1946-48; A.B., N.Y. U., 1950. Freelance writer, 1950—; author: A Kiss Before Dying, 1953, Rosemary's Baby, 1967, This Perfect Day, 1970, The Stepford Wives, 1972, The Boys from Brazil, 1976, Sliver, 1991; playwright: No Time for Sergeants, 1955, Interlock, 1958, Critic's Choice, 1960, General Seeger, 1962, Drat! the Cat, 1965, Dr. Cook's Garden, 1967, Veronica's Room, 1973, Deathtrap, 1978, Break a Leg, 1979, Cantorial, 1989. Served with U.S. Army, 1953-55. Recipient Edgar Allan Poe award, 1953, 80. Mem. Dramatists Guild (council mem. 1980—). Office: care Harold Ober Assocs 425 Madison Ave New York NY 10017-1110

LEVIN, JACK S., lawyer; b. Chgo., May 1, 1936; s. Frank J. and Judy G. (Skerball) L.; m. Sandra Sternberg, Aug. 24, 1958; children: Lisa, Laura, Leslie, Linda. B.S. summa cum laude, Northwestern U., 1958; LL.B. summa cum laude, Harvard U., 1961. Bar: Ill. 1961; C.P.A. (gold medalist), Ill., 1958. Law clk. to chief judge U.S. Ct. of Appeals 2d Circuit, N.Y.C., 1961-62; asst. for tax matters to Solicitor Gen. of U.S., Washington, 1965-67; assoc. law firm Kirkland & Ellis, Chgo., 1962-65, ptnr., 1967—; frequent lectr. on legal aspects of venture capital transactions, mergers, acquisitions, buyouts, and workouts, fed. income tax matters; vis. com. Harvard Law Sch., 1987-93; lectr. Law Sch. U. Chgo., 1988—. Author book on structuring venture capital, pvt. equity and entrepreneurial transactions; co-author multi-volume work on mergers, acquisitions and buyouts; case editor Harvard Law Rev., 1959-61; contbr. numerous articles to legal jours. and chpts. to law books. Parliamentarian Winnetka (Ill.) Town Meetings, 1974-83, 89, 93-96; chmn. nat. fundraising drive Harvard Law Sch., 1985-86, 90-91, 96, chmn. lawyer's divsn. Jewish United Fund Chgo., 1993-95. Mem. ABA (chmn. subcom. 1968-79), Fed. Bar Assn., Chgo. Bar Assn. (exec. com. 1985—), Am. Coll. Tax Counsel. Clubs: Mid-Am. (bd. dirs. 1985-88), Birchwood (Highland Park, Ill.) (pres. 1980-82). Home: 1220 Sunset Rd Winnetka IL 60093-3628 Office: Kirkland & Ellis 200 E Randolph St Chicago IL 60601-6436

LEVIN, JACOB JOSEPH, mathematician, educator; b. N.Y.C., Dec. 21, 1926; s. David and Rose (Kaplan) L.; m. Avis Harriet Ofstrock, Sept. 7, 1952; children—Debra F., Kenneth E., Claire B. B.E.E., Coll. City N.Y., 1949; Ph.D., Mass. Inst. Tech., 1953. Instr. math. Purdue U., 1953-55; lectr. Mass. Inst. Tech., 1955-56; staff mem. Lincoln Lab. of Mass. Inst. Tech., 1956-63; prof. math. U. Wis., 1963—; vis. prof. U. B.C., Vancouver, Can., 1977-78. Contbr. articles to profl. jours. Served with AUS, 1945-46. NSF sr. postdoctoral fellow, 1970-71. Mem. Am. Math. Soc., Soc. Indsl. and Applied Math., Sigma Xi. Home: 1110 Frisch Rd Madison WI 53711-3120

LEVIN, JERRY WAYNE, cosmetics executive; b. San Antonio, Tex., Apr. 18, 1944; s. Bernard H. and Marion (Bromberg) L.; m. Carol Lee Motel, Dec. 18, 1966; children—Joshua, Abby. B.S.E.E., U. Mich., 1966, B.S.E. in Math., 1966; M.B.A., U. Chgo., 1968. With Tex. Instruments, Dallas, 1966-72; with Marsh & McLennan, Chgo., 1972-74; with The Pillsbury Co., Mpls., from 1974, exec. v.p. corporate devel., treas., from 1985, exec. v.p. corp. devel., chmn. Haagen-Dazs div., 1987-88; exec. v.p. corp. devel. and chmn. S&A Restaurant Corp., from 1988; chmn. Burger King Corp., 1988-89; exec. v.p. MacAndrews Forbes, N.Y.; chmn., CEO, Revlon Inc., N.Y.C., 1995—; bd. dirs. Apogee Enterprises, Inc., Coleman, Ecolabs, First Bank Sys., Paradise Kitchens, Meridian. Bd. dirs. United Way, N.Y.C., N.Y. Hillel, N.Y. Fedn., N.Y. Philharm., U. Mich. Engring. Sch. Mem. U. Chgo. Alumni Bd., Oak Ridge Country Club, Ventana Canyon Country Club, Minneapolis Club. Home: 15 E 70th St New York NY 10021-4907 Office: Revlon Inc 625 Madison Ave New York NY 10022-1801

LEVIN, LAUREN (LO LEVIN), artist, teacher, designer; b. Framingham, Mass., June 8, 1949; d. Abraham and Ida Rena (Cohen) L. Grad., Art Inst. Boston, 1971; postgrad., Sch. Fashion Design, Boston, 1976, Parsons Sch. Design, N.Y.C., 1979. Owner, creator Struck of Loke (improvisational theater and cafe), Worcester, Mass., 1971-75; designer, 'Lo'Scapes Fashion Art, Honolulu, 1983—; artist portraits and impressions Faces by 'Lo', Honolulu, 1969—, Cape Cod, 1969—, Ibiza, Spain, 1969—; owner, operator, artist Artspace Gallery, Honolulu, 1990-91; tchr. Very Spl. Arts, Hawaii, 1983—. Mem. Pacific Handcrafters Guild (bd. dirs.), Hawaii Handcrafters Ednl. Found. (bd. dirs. 1992—). Avocations: portraits, fabric art and design, teaching art with disabled, costuming. Home: PO Box 61820 Honolulu HI 96839-1820

LEVIN, LINDA ROSE, mental health counselor; b. Des Moines, June 29, 1951; d. Morris Sam and Betty Francis (Burns) Nemirovski; m. Michael Arthur Levin, Feb. 25, 1971; children: David Bradley, Shane Michael. Student, Grandview Jr. Coll., 1969-70; BS in Psychology, Ottawa Univ., 1992, MA in Counseling, 1994. Cert. hypnotherapist, advanced hypnotherapist. Asst. dir. trade practice Better Bus. Bur., Phoenix, 1980-83; program coord. Carnation Health and Nutrition Ctr., Phoenix, 1983-85; v.p. AAA Telephone Answering Svc., Phoenix, 1985-90; past state of Ariz. rep. Toughlove, Phoenix, 1988-90; counselor level II, resident advisor Wayland Family Ctrs., Phoenix, 1990-91; case mgr. for the serious mentally ill Community Care Network, Phoenix, 1991-92; pvt. practice in hypnotherapy Counseling Ctr. for Personal Growth, Phoenix, 1992—. Vol. arbitrator Better Bus. Bur., 1983—. Mem. Am. Arbitration Assn. Democrat. Jewish. Avocations: swimming, reading, karate (brown belt), aerobics. Office: Counseling Ctr for Personal Growth 13231 N 35th Ave A-10 Phoenix AZ 85029-1233

LEVIN, MARK JAY, lighting designer, director of photography, cinematographer, writer; b. Mpls., July 30, 1957; s. Myron Yale and Phyllis (Goodman) L. BA, U. Wis., 1979. Lighting dir., cameraman Sta. WHA-TV, Madison, Wis., 1978-79, NBC, 1980, ABC, Hollywood, 1982-89; dir. photography Columbia Pictures TV, 1989-93; dir. photography comedy, dramatic, music, variety, news and talk format prodns. Numen Lumen Prodns., Burbank, 1991—, IFA West, 1994—, Disney TV, 1994—; lighting dir. Bob Booker/Universal TV, 1984, Platypus Prodn., 1983-85, Dick Clark Prodn., 1982-83, Sta. KABC-TV, 1984-86; dir. photography Amos Prodn., 1982; pres. Numen Lumen Prodns., Burbank, Calif.; agt. IFA West, Glendale, Calif., 1994—. Lighting designer, dir. photography numerous TV series spls. and CD Rom games including The New Love American Style, 1985, Charmed Lives, 1986, Sweet Surrender, 1986, The Charmings, 1986-87, Facts of Life, 1987, Women in Prison, 1987-88, Who's the Boss, 1985-92 (6 Emmy award nominations 1986-91, Emmy award 1989), Hanging with Mr Cooper, 1993, The Martin Short Show, 1994, Treasure Quest CD Rom 1995, Who Makes You Laugh, 1995, Kelsey Crammer's Look at Parenthood, 1995, Unhappy Ever After 1994-96, Cleghorne, 1994-95, High School USA, 1996, General Hospital, 1984-89, 91, 92, Living Dolls, 1989, Faerie Tale Theater, 1983-85 (Ace award 1983), American Bandstand, 1983-86, The Love Boat Spl., 1984, Home Movies, 1982, The Love Connection, 1984-85, ABC's World News Tonight, 1984-86, Married With Children, Nat. Cerebral Palsey Telethon, 1985, 87, 89, One of the Boys, 1989, numerous local prodns.; dir. of photography Married People, 1990, Guys Next Door, 1990; lighting designer Up With People, 1990, Countdown, 1990; dir. of photography Rap Tap, 1991, Vinnie and Bobby, 1992, Hangin' with Mr. Cooper, 1992, The Hannigans, 1992; (pilot) Country Comfort, (pilot) Beakmans World, 1992, Letting Go, 1992, Hangin' With Mr. Cooper, 1992-93, George, 1993, (pilot) Family, 1993, Who Makes You Laugh?, 1994, The Martin Short Show, 1994, The Jerry Springer Show, 1994, The Dirs. Round Table, 1994, Romance Theatre, 1994, Bill Cosby-In Concert, 1994, Unhappily Ever After, 1994-95, Kelsey Grammers Affectionate Look at Fatherhood, 1995, Cleghorne!, (CD rom game) Treasure Quest, Christmas from the Los Angeles Music Ctr., The Iceman Cocketh (pilot), It Ain't Easy (pilot); contbg. editor Lighting Dimensions mag., 1980-85; author: Cosmos the Space Ship; contbr. articles to profl. jours. Active Big Bros. of Greater L.A., 1984-91. Recipient ACE award for Lighting Design in a Dramatic Presentation, 1983, Patriotic Svc. award U.S. Dept. of the Treasury, 1984, Outstanding Excellence award Am. Soc. Lighting Designers, 1988-91, Outstanding Artistic Achievement (4), 1989, Emmy award Outstanding Lighting Dir., 1989. Mem. Am. Soc. of Lighting Designers, Internat. Assn. Theatrical Stage Employees, World Underwater Fedn., Nat. Assn. Broadcast Employees and Technicians, Soc. Operating Cameramen, Profl. Assn. Diving Instrs. (divemaster), Underwater Photographic Soc., Internat. Photographers Guild (I.A.T.S.E. local 659), Soc. TV Lighting Dirs. (Can.), Nat. Assn. Underwater Instrs. (divemaster), Soc. Motion Picture and TV Engrs. Home: 9318 Via Ferrara Burbank CA 91504-1509 also: Numen Lumen Prodns 859 N Hollywood Way Ste 172 Burbank CA 91505-2833 also: IFA West 229 N Central Ave Ste 333 Glendale CA 91203-2537

LEVIN, MARSHALL ABBOTT, judge, educator; b. Balt., Nov. 22, 1920; s. Harry Oscar and Rose (DeLaviez) L.; m. Beverly Edelman, Aug. 6, 1948; children: Robert B., Susan R. Lieman, Burton H. BA, U. Va., 1941; JD, Harvard Law Sch., 1947. Bar: Md. 1947, U.S. Dist. Ct. Md. 1947, U.S. Ct. Appeals (4th cir.) 1950, U.S. Supreme Ct. 1953. Bill drafter, legis. asst. Dept. Legis. Reference, Annapolis, Md., 1948-49; rsch. asst. Workers Compensation Commn., 1951, police magistrate, 1951-55, magistrate housing ct., 1955-58; ptnr. Levin & Levin, Balt., 1947-66; pvt. practice Balt., 1966-68; ptnr. Edelman, Levin, Levy & Rubenstein, Balt., 1968-71; judge cir. ct. City of Balt., 1971-87, judge for asbestos litigation, 1987—; lectr. nationally on toxic torts, complex litigation, asbestos, death penalty; lectr. Nat. Conf. on Child Abuse, 1976; dir. Legal Aid Soc., Balt., 1979-81; chmn. jud. bd. sentencing State of Md., 1979-83, chmn. sentencing guidelines bd., 1983-87; instituted One Trial/One Day jury system, Balt., 1983; adj. prof. mass torts, legal & ethical studies grad. sch. U. Balt., 1979—; charter mem. faculty coun., coord. and faculty general jurisdiction current issues in civil litigation Nat. Jud. Coll., 1980—; mem. vis. faculty trial advocacy workshop Harvard Law Sch. Contbr. articles to law revs. Mem. Jud. Disability Commn., 1980-87; chmn. Mass Tort Litigation Com. NEH fellow, 1976. Mem. ABA (vice chmn. mass tort and litigation com.), Md. State Bar Assn. (Leadership award 1984), Balt. City Bar Assn. (commendation 1982). Home: 6106 Ivydene Ter Baltimore MD 21209-3522 Office: 245 Courthouse Ct Baltimore MD 21204-4702

LEVIN, MARTIN P., publishing executive, lawyer; b. Phila., Dec. 20, 1918; s. Harry and Sarah (Haimovitz) L.; m. Marcia Obrasky, Apr. 2, 1939; children: Jeremy Carl, Wendy, Hugh Lauter. B.S., Temple U., 1950, post-grad. (personnel Council fellow), 1950; J.D., N.Y. Law Sch., 1983. Adminstrv. officer U.S. War Dept., 1940-44, VA, 1945-50; sr. v.p. Grosset & Dunlap, Inc., N.Y.C., 1950-66; pres. book pub. div. Times Mirror Co., N.Y.C., 1966-83; cons. Times Mirror; counsel Cowan, Leibowitz and Latman, P.C.; adj. prof. Benjamin N. Cardozo Law Sch., N.Y. Law Sch., Stetson Law Sch., Pace U. Grad. Sch.; resident fellow pub. course Stanford U.; cons. Ford Found., India, 1957-58; mem. Pres.'s Working Com. on Books and Publs. Abroad; mem. exec. com. Ctr. for the Book, Libr. of Congress; trustee Harvard U. Press; mem. Assn. Am. Pubs. delegation to USSR, 1976, to People Republic of China, 1979; former chmn. Franklin Book Programs. Author: Be Your Own Literary Agent, 1995; contbr. articles to profl. jours. Trustee William Alanson White Inst.; chmn. Assn. Am. Book Pubs., 1982. With AUS, 1944-45. Recipient Pub. of Yr. award ADL, 1980, Friend of Jerusalem award, 1985. Mem. Assn. Am. Pubs. (chmn., dir. exec. com.), Pubs. Lunch Club (past pres.), Friars Club. Home: 221 Kirby Ln Rye NY 10580-4321 also: 9150 Blind Pass Rd Sarasota FL 34242-2978 Office: Cowan Leibowitz & Latman 1133 Ave of Americas New York NY 10036

LEVIN, MARVIN EDGAR, physician; b. Terre Haute, Ind., Aug. 11, 1924; s. Benjamin A. and Bertha Levin; m. Barbara Yvonne Symes; 3 children. BA, Washington U., St. Louis, 1947, MD, 1951. Diplomate Am. Bd. Internal Medicine. Intern Barnes Hosp., St. Louis, 1951-52, asst. resident in internal medicine, 1952-53; Nat. Polio Found. fellow in metabolism and endocrinology Sch. Medicine, Washington U., St. Louis, 1953-55; prof. clin. medicine, assoc. dir. Endocrine, Diabetes and Metabolism Clinic, Washington U., St. Louis; attending physician Barnes Hosp., Jewish Hosp. St. Louis; vis. prof. endocrinology and diabetes Internat. Sino-Am. Exch. Program, People's Republic China, 1982, Jakarta, Indonesia, Taipei, 1994; cons. endocrine panel U.S. Pharmacopeia: med. dir. Harry and Flora D. Freund Meml. Found. Co-editor: (with L.W. O'Neal and J. Bowker) The Diabetic Foot, 1973, 5th edit., 1993; contbr. numerous articles to profl. jours., book chpts. Fellow ACP, Soc. Vascular Medicine and Biology; mem. AMA, Am. Diabetes Assn. (nat. bd. dirs. 1984-86, chmn. publ. com. 1986-87, bd. dirs. Mo. chpt. 1987-93, editor Clin. Diabetes 1988-93, co-editor Diabetes Spectrum 1988-93), St. Louis Clin. Diabetes Assn. (pres. 1965-66), Am. Thyroid Assn., Endocrine Soc., Am. Fedn. for Clin. Rsch. (emeritus), St. Louis Soc. Internal Medicine, St. Louis Internist Club (pres. 1972), Sigma Xi, Alpha Omega Alpha. Avocations: golf, collecting Belle Epoque French prints. Office: 732 Fairfield Lake Dr Chesterfield MO 63017-5928

LEVIN, MICHAEL STUART, steel company executive; b. N.Y.C., Aug. 2, 1950; s. Morton Sheldon and Ruth Jean (Leff) L.; m. Laurence Diane deBardon deSegonzac, Dec. 13, 1984; children: Alex Rene-Philippe, Max-André Simon, Sebastien Pierre. B.A. with honors, U. Wis., 1972; M.B.A., Harvard U., 1974. Asst. trader Titan Indsl. Corp., N.Y.C., 1974-75, trader, 1975-76, export mgr., 1976-78, v.p., 1978-80, sr. v.p., 1980-82, pres., 1982—, mem. coun. on fgn. rels.; dir. Aiesec USA, Inc. Chmn. Erick Hawkins Dance Found. Clubs: Gulfstream Polo, N.Y. Yacht, Mashomack Fish and Game Preserve, Millbrook G & T. Avocations: polo, sailing, skiing, shooting. Office: Titan Industrial 555 Madison Ave10th Fl New York NY 10022-3301*

LEVIN, MORTON D(AVID), artist, printmaker, educator; b. N.Y.C., Oct. 7, 1923; s. Louis and Martha (Berusch) L. B.S. in Art Edn, CCNY, 1948; student in painting, Andre LHote, Paris, 1950; in sculpture, Ossip Zadkine, 1950; etching and engraving, Federico Castellon, N.Y.C., 1948, Stanley W. Hayter, Paris, 1951; student in lithography, Pratt Graphic Art Center, N.Y.C., 1966. Founder, dir., instr. printmaking, painting Morton Levin Graphics Workshop, San Francisco, 1972-91. Once-man shows include Galerie Breteau, Paris, 1952, Winston Gallery, San Francisco, 1972, 80, 83, 85-96; exhibited in group shows at Seattle Art Mus., 1946-49, Libr. of Congress, Washington, 1946, 49, Pa. Acad. Fine Arts, 1948, Mus. Modern Art, Paris, 1951, Pallazzo del Academia, Genoa, Italy, 1951; represented in permanent collections at N.Y. Pub. Libr., Libr. of Congress, History of Medicine Div. Nat. Libr. Medicine; work featured in Jour. Erotic Arts, Yellow Silk #34, 1990. Served with inf. U.S. Army, 1943-45. Recipient Bryan Meml. prize Villager Travel Exhbn., N.Y.C., 1964, 3d prize Washington Sq. Art Exhbn., 1964. *My goal has been to define our world and the primal forces of desire, love, procreation, death, and rebirth. To this end, I have created a universe in my art inhabited by the natural and fantastic. Humans, birds, and beasts, male and female, interact and strive on an elemental level. In a romantic expressionistic style, I have attempted to illuminate the human condition.*

LEVIN, MURRAY SIMON, lawyer; b. Phila., Feb. 8, 1943; s. Sidney Michael and Eva (Goldstein) L.; m. Jalond Marie Robinson, June 9, 1968; children—Adrianne Lesley, Alexandra Amber-Rose. BA, Haverford Coll., 1964; MA, Harvard U., 1968, LLB, 1968; cert., Hague Internat. Acad. Law, 1967. Bar: Pa. 1968, U.S. Dist. Ct. (ea. dist.) Pa. 1970, U.S. Ct. Appeals (3d cir.) 1970, U.S. Supreme Ct. 1979. Instr. English Harvard U., 1965-68; law clk. to U.S. Dist. Ct. Judge, 1968-70; instr. govt. Haverford Coll., 1970-71; litigation ptnr. Pepper, Hamilton & Scheetz, Phila., 1970—, mem. firm exec. com., 1993-95; overseas lectr., U.K., Sweden, Germany, Senegal, Kenya, Cameroon, Morocco, Israel, 1988-95; law seminar speaker. Weekly commentator radio Sta. WCAU Dick Clayton Show, TV program Morningside, 1973-76; weekly host, interviewer Sta. WHYY, 1974-79; TV commentator O.J. Simpson trial, 1995; contbr. articles to profl. jours. Chmn. Phila. Coun. Expt. in Internat. Living, 1967-70; mem. Phila. Urban Coalition Housing Task Force, 1968-80; chmn. coll. divsn. Allied Jewish Appeal, 1968-70; pres. Ctrl. Phila. Reform Dems., 1973-74; bd. dirs. Grad. Hosp. Phila., 1975—, Friends Ctrl. Sch., 1988—, divsn. Fgn. Policy Rsch. Com. Mid. East Coun., 1992-94, Mid. East Forum, 1994—. Root-Tilden fellow, 1964. Mem. ABA, Pa. Bar Assn. (ho. of dels.), Phila. Bar Assn. (young lawyers exec. bd. 1973, bd. govs. 1985-88, zone del. 1988—, chmn. profl. guidance com. 1989-92, co-chmn. internat. human rights com. 1990-91), Phila. Trial Lawyers Assn., Assn. Internat. des Jeunes Avocats Brussels (bd. dirs. 1981-85, 1st Am. pres. 1985-88), Union Internationale des Avocats Paris (advisor to pres., mem. exec. com. 1993—, pres. Am. chpt. 1995—), Am. Law Inst., Am. Judicature Soc., Phi Beta Kappa. Office: Pepper Hamilton & Scheetz 3000 2 Logan Sq 18th & Arch Sts Philadelphia PA 19103-2799

LEVIN, PAUL JOSEPH, evangelist; b. Rock Island, Ill., Oct. 13, 1914; s. Peter and Hulda (Vromberg) L.; m. Dorothy Hayslip, Mar. 17, 1936 (dec. Oct. 1994). DD (hon.), San Francisco Bapt. Sem., 1969. Radio evangelist 41 stas., throughout U.S., 1957—; pres., founder Bible Tracts, Inc., Carlock, Ill., 1938—; bd. dirs. Bill Rice Ranch, Murfreesboro, Tenn., 1956-89. Author: Pre Wedding Days, 1935, One Step at a Time, 1976, and numerous tracts; recorded albums with Bob Findley, 1933-1975. Republican. Avocation: baseball. Home: PO Box 144 205 E Franklin Carlock IL 61725 Office: Bible Tracts Inc P O Box 188 1925 S Main St Bloomington IL 61702

LEVIN, PETER J., hospital administrator, public health professor; b. N.Y.C., Apr. 25, 1939; s. Sol and Kate (Gottlieb) L.; m. Judith S. Bolton, June 3, 1967; children: Edward, Gael, Karen. B.A., Harvard U., 1961; M.P.H., Yale U., 1965; Sc.D., Johns Hopkins U., 1969. Asso. exec. dir. Bronx (N.Y.) Municipal Hosp. Center, 1970-72; exec. dir. New Haven Health Care, Inc., 1972-74; assoc. commr. Dept. Health, N.Y.C., 1974-77; assoc. v.p. med. affairs, exec. dir. Stanford U. Hosp., 1977-81; asst. clin. prof. dept. epidemiology and pub. health Yale Med. Sch., 1973-75; assoc. clin. prof. dept. community health Albert Einstein Coll. Medicine, 1976-77; clin. assoc. prof. dept. family, community and preventive medicine Stanford U., 1978-81; dean Coll. Pub. Health, prof. health adminstrn. U. Okla., Oklahoma City, 1982-84; dean Coll. Pub. Health U. South Fla., Tampa, 1984-94, prof. pub. health, 1984—; vis. scholar Hoover Inst., Stanford U., 1994-95. Chmn. Hosp. Cost Containment Bd., State of Fla., 1985-88, Fla. HMO Quality Care Interagy. Task Force, 1987, Hillsborough County Health Care Adv. Bd., 1990-92; Served with USPHS, 1965-67. Fellow Health Care Office of Senator Connie Mack, 1994. Fellow APHA, Am. Coll. Healthcare Execs.

LEVIN, RICHARD C., lawyer; b. Dallas, June 15, 1945; s. Paul Michael and Yetta Gail (Caplan) L.; m. Kay Robins, June 18, 1982; children: Edward C., Henry A. BA, Tulane U., 1967; JD, Georgetown U., 1970. Bar: Tex. 1975. Law clerk 5th cir. U.S. Ct. Appeals, 1970-71; assoc. Sulivan & Cromwell, N.Y.C., 1971-74; assoc. Akin, Gump, Strauss, Hauer & Feld L.L.P., Dallas, 1974-77, ptnr., 1978—; with Dallas Mgmt. com., 1989—; co-head litigation sect. Akin, Gump, Strauss, Hauer & Feld, head antitrust sect., internat. litigation sect.; spkr. in field. Contbr. articles to profl. jours. Former mem. exec. bd. Dallas Opera; former mem. bd. govs. Dallas Symphony; corp. com. Dallas Mus. Fine Arts; former mem., v.p. bd. trustees Hist. Preservation League; former mem. Landmark Com. City Dallas, bd. trustees Arts Magnet Sch.; former mem., dep. vice chmn., mgmt. com. Arts Dist. in Dallas; former chmn. Task Force Multi-Purpose Performing Arts Hall Dallas Opera, Dallas Ballet; bd. dirs. Dallas Opera, Salzburg Music Festival. Mem. Dallas Bar Assn. (coun. mem. Antitrust, Trade Regulation sect. 1987—, internat. law sect. 1990—). Jewish. Avocations: classical music, art, sports. Home: 4408 Saint Johns Dr Dallas TX 75205-3825 Office: Akin Gump Strauss Hauer & Feld 1700 Pacific Ave Ste 4100 Dallas TX 75201-7322*

LEVIN, RICHARD CHARLES, academic administrator, economist; b. San Francisco, Apr. 7, 1947; s. D. Derek and Phylys M. (Goldstein) L.; m. Jane Ellen Aries, June 24, 1968; children: Jon, Daniel, Sarah, Rebecca. BA, Stanford (Calif.) U., 1968; LittB, Oxford (Eng.) U., 1971; PhD, Yale U., 1974; LLD (hon.), Princeton U., 1993, Harvard U., 1994. With Yale U., New Haven, 1974—, pres., 1993—, chmn. econs. dept., 1987-92, Frederick William Beinecke prof. econs., 1992—, dean Grad. Sch., 1992-93; rsch. assoc. Nat. Bur. Econ. Rsch., Cambridge, Mass., 1985-90; program dir. Internat. Inst. Applied Sys. Analysis, Vienna, 1990-92; mem. exec. com. Consortium on Financing Higher Edn.; trustee Tanner Lectures on Human Values; cons. numerous law and bus. firms. Trustee Hopkins Sch., New Haven, 1988-95. Yale-New Haven Hosp., 1993—, Univs. Rsch. Assn., 1994—; bd. dirs. Yale-New Haven Health Svcs. Corp., Inc., 1993—. Mem. Am. Econ. Assn., Econometric Soc. Democrat. Jewish. Office: Yale U 105 Wall St New Haven CT 06511-6608

LEVIN, RICHARD LOUIS, English language educator; b. Buffalo, Aug. 31, 1922; s. Bernard and Meta (Block) L.; m. Muriel Abrams, June 22, 1952; children: David, Daniel. B.A., U. Chgo., 1943, M.A., 1947, Ph.D., 1957. Mem. faculty U. Chgo., 1949-57, asst. prof. English., 1953-57; prof. English, SUNY at Stony Brook, 1957—, acting chmn. English dept., 1960-63, 65-66; mem. adv. bd. World Center for Shakespeare Studies.; mem. acad. adv. council Shakespeare Globe Ctr.; Fulbright lectr., 1984-85. Author, cons. in field.; Editor: Tragedy: Plays, Theory and Criticism, 1960, The Question of Socrates, 1961, Tragedy Alternate, 1965, (by Thomas Middleton) Michaelmas Term, 1966, The Multiple Plot in English Renaissance Drama, 1971, New Readings vs. Old Plays: Recent Trends in the Reinterpretation of English Renaissance Drama, 1979. Served to lt. (j.g.) USNR, 1943-46, ETO. Recipient Explicator award, 1971; Am. Council Learned Socs. fellow, 1963-64; research fellow State U. N.Y., 1961, 65-68, 71, 73; NEH sr. fellow, 1974; Guggenheim fellow, 1978-79, Nat. Humanities Ctr. fellow, 1987-88; SUNY faculty exchange scholar. Mem. MLA (mem. adv. com. publs., mem. del. assembly), Internat. Shakespeare Assn., Shakespeare Assn. Am. (trustee), N.Y. Shakespeare Soc., Malone Soc., Joseph Crabtree Found., Marlowe Soc. Am., Medieval and Renaissance Drama Soc. (mem. council), AAUP, Inst. for Renaissance Interdisciplinary Studies. Democrat. Jewish. Home: 26 Sparks St Melville NY 11747-1727 Office: SUNY Humanities Bldg Stony Brook NY 11794

LEVIN, ROBERT JOSEPH, retail grocery chain store executive; b. Everett, Mass., Mar. 19, 1928; s. Edward A. and Rose E. L.; m. Carrol Silverman, June 21, 1948; children: Richard J., Cathy Levin Shuman. B.A. cum laude, U. Wis., 1948. From dir. store ops. and purchasing to pres., treas. C.B. Perkins Tobacco Co., Boston, 1948-73; from dir. store ops. and purchasing to pres., treas. C.B. Perkins Tobacco Co. (co. merged with Stop & Shop), Boston, 1970; v.p., then pres. Medi Mart div. Stop & Shop, 1971-75; group v.p. Stop & Shop Cos., Inc., Boston, 1975-79; sr. v.p. Stop & Shop Cos., Inc., 1979-82, vice. chmn., 1982—, also dir.; bd. dirs. S.A.Y. Industries, Sterling Inc.; chmn. bd. S.A.Y. Packaging, 1988—. Bd. dirs. U. Wis. Found. Mem. Nat. Mass Retailing Inst. (dir.). Jewish. Home: 65 Grove St Apt 343 Wellesley MA 02181-7806 Office: 1776 Heritage Dr Quincy MA 02171-2101 also: PO Box 369 Boston MA 02101-0369

LEVIN, RONALD MARK, law educator; b. St. Louis, May 11, 1950; s. Marvin S. and Lois (Cohn) L.; m. Anne Carol Goldberg, July 29, 1989. BA magna cum laude, Yale U., 1972; JD, U. Chgo., 1975. Bar: Mo. 1975, D.C. 1977. Law clk. to Hon. John C. Godbold U.S. Ct. Appeals, 5th cir., 1975-76; assoc. Sutherland, Asbill & Brennan, Washington, 1976-79; asst. prof. law Washington U., St. Louis, 1979-80, assoc. prof. law, 1980-85, prof. law, 1985—, assoc. dean, 1990-93; cons. Adminstrv. Conf. U.S., 1979-81, 93-95. Co-author: Administrative Law and Process, 3d edit., 1990; mem. adv. bd. Adminstrv. Law Rev., 1985—. Chair senate coun. Washington U., 1988-90. Mem. ABA (coun. sect. adminstrv. law and regulatory practice 1986-89), Assn. Am. Law Sch. (chair sect. adminstrv. law 1993, chair sect. legis. 1995). Home: 7352 Kingsbury Blvd Saint Louis MO 63130-4142 Office: Wash Univ Sch Law Campus Box 1120 Saint Louis MO 63130

LEVIN, SANDER M., congressman; b. Detroit, Sept. 6, 1931; s. Saul R. and Bess (Levinson) L.; m. Victoria Schlafer, 1957. B.A., U. Chgo., 1952; M.A., Columbia U., 1954; LL.B., Harvard U., 1957. Supr. Oakland County Bd. Suprs., Mich., 1961-64; mem. Mich. Senate, 1965-70; fellow Kennedy Sch. Govt., Inst. Politics, Harvard U., Cambridge, Mass., 1975; asst. administr. AID, Washington, 1977-81; mem. 98th-104th Congresses from 17th (now 12th) Mich dist., 1983—; mem. ways and means com., subcoms. oversight and human resources; adj. prof. law Wayne State U., Detroit, 1971-74. Chmn. Mich. Dem. Com., 1968-69; Dem. Candidate for Gov., 1970, 74. Office: US Ho of Reps 2230 Rayburn HOB Washington DC 20515-2212*

LEVIN, SIMON, lawyer; b. Newark, Aug. 4, 1942; m. Barbara Leslie Lasky, Dec. 21, 1989; children: David, Jennifer Menken, Yale, Michael,

Jacob. BS cum laude, Lehigh U., 1964; JD, NYU, 1967, LLM in Taxation, 1974. Bar: N.J. 1967, U.S. Tax Ct. 1971, U.S. Ct. Claims 1972, N.Y. 1980. Assoc. Shanley & Fisher, Newark, 1970, Hannoch Weisman, Newark, 1970-73; ptnr. Robinson, Wayne, Levin, Riccio & La Sala, Newark, 1973-88; mem., co-chmn. tax dept. Sills Cummis Zuckerman Radin Tischman Epstein & Gross, Newark, 1988—; civillian aide to Sec. Army for N.J., 1992-95; mem. N.J. Dept. Treasury Transition Team for Gov. Christine Todd Whitman, 1993-94; mem. treas. adv. group N.J. Dept. of Treasury, 1995—; lectr., panelist numerous orgns. Co-author: Taxation Investors in Securities and Commodities, 1983, 2d edit., 1984, supplement, 1986, Estate Planning and Administration in New Jersey, 1987; contbr. articles to profl. jours. Trustee, mem. exec. com. Jewish Comty. Found., MetroWest, Whippany, N.J., pres., 1979-83; trustee, mem. exec. com. Israel Bond Campaign MetroWest, Livingston, N.J., 1988—, chmn., 1988-89; commr. N.J. Vietnam Vets. Meml. Commn., Princeton, 1994—. Capt. U.S. Army, 1968-69, Vietnam. Recipient Cohn Leadership award Jewish Fedn. MetroWest, 1982, Endowment Achievement award Coun. Jewish Fedns., 1986, N.J. Meritorious Svc. medal, 1995. Fellow Am. Coll. Tax Counsel; mem. ABA, N.J. Bar Assn. (chmn. commodities sect. 1982-86), Essex County Bar Assn. (chmn. sect. taxation 1974-76), Monmouth County Bar Assn., Phi Delta Phi. Avocations: tennis, skiing, politics, opera, charitable activities. Office: Sills Cummis Zuckerman Radin Tischman Epstein & Gross 1 Riverfront Plz Newark NJ 07102-5401

LEVIN, SIMON ASHER, mathematician, ecologist, educator; b. Balt., Apr. 22, 1941; s. Theodore S. and Clara G. L.; m. Carole Lotte Leiffer, Aug. 4, 1964; children: Jacob, Rachel. BA in Math., Johns Hopkins U., 1961; PhD in Math. (NSF fellow), U. Md., 1964; DSc (hon.), Ea. Mich. U., 1990. Teaching asst. U. Md., 1961-62, research assoc., 1964, visitor, 1968; NSF fellow U. Calif., Berkeley, 1964-65; asst. prof. math. Cornell U., 1965-70, assoc. prof. applied math., ecology, theoretical and applied math., 1971-77, prof. applied math. and ecology, 1977-92, Charles A. Alexander prof. biology, 1985-92, adj. prof., 1992—, chmn. sect. ecology and systematics div. biol. scis., 1974-79, dir. Ecosystems Rsch. Ctr., 1980-87, dir. Ctr. for Environ. Rsch., 1987-90; George Moffett prof. biology Princeton U., 1992—, associated faculty applied math., 1992—; dir. Princeton Environ. Inst., 1993—; vis. scholar U. Wash., 1973-74; vis. scientist Weizmann Inst., Rehovot, Israel, 1977, 80; hon. prof. U. B.C., 1979-80; Lansdowne lectr. U. Victoria, 1981; disting. vis. scientist SUNY, Stony Brook, 1984; vis. fellow All Souls Coll., U. Oxford, 1988; Ostrom lectr. Washington State U., Pullman, 1994; co-chmn. Gordon Conf. on Theoretical Biology, 1970, chmn. Gordon Conf. on Theoretical Biology and Biomath., 1971; chmn. Am. Math. Soc./Soc. Indsl. and Applied Maths. Com. on Maths. in Life Scis., 1973-79; mem. core panel on math. in biol. scis., program com. Internat. Congress Mathematicians, 1977-78; co-convenor Biomath. Conf., Oberwolfach, W. Ger., 1978; co-dir. Internat. Ctr. for Theoretical Physics Autumn Course on Math. Ecology, Trieste, Italy, 1988, 92, 96; mem. adv. com. divsn. environ. scis. Oak Ridge Nat. Lab., 1978-81; vice chmn. math. Com. Concerned Scientists, N.Y.C., 1979—; mem. sci. panel Hudson River Found., 1982-86, chmn., 1985-86, bd. dirs., 1986—; mem. Commn. on Life Scis., NRC, 1983-89, mem. com. ecosys. mgmt. of sustainable marine fisheries ocean studies bd., 1995—; mem. Health and Environ. Rsch. Adv. Com. Dept. of Energy, 1986-90; prin. lectr. Conf. Bd. on Math. Scis. course on math. ecology, 1985; mem. oversight rev. bd. U.S. Nat. Acid Precipitation Assessment Program; spkr. commencement address Ea. Mich. U., 1990; sci. bd. Sante Fe Inst., 1991—; bd. dirs. Beijer Inst., 1994—; bd. dirs. The H. John Heinz III Ctr. for Sci., Econs. and the Environment, 1994—. Editor: Lectures on Mathematics in Life Sciences, vols. 7-12, 1974-79, Ecosystem Analysis and Prediction, 1974, (with R.H. Whittaker) Niche: Theory and Application, 1975, Studies in Mathematical Biology, 2 vols., 1978, New Perspectives in Ecotoxicology, 1983, Mathematical Population Biology, 1984, Mathematical Ecology, 1984, Math Ecology: An Introduction, 1986, (with others) Mathematical Ecology, 1988, Ecotoxicology: Problems and Approaches, 1989, Perspectives in Theoretical Ecology, 1989, (with T. Hallam and L. Gross) Applied Mathematical Ecology, 1989, (with T. Powell and J.H. Steele) Patch Dynamics, 1993, Frontiers in Mathematical Biology, 1994; editor-in-chief Ecological Applications, 1988-95; editor: Ecology and Ecol. Monographs, 1975-77; editor Jour. Math. Biology, 1976-79, mng. editor, 1979-95; mng. editor Biomath., 1976-95, Lecture Notes in Biomath., 1973-95; mng. editor Princeton U. Press, Monographs in Population Biology, 1992—; assoc. editor Theoretical Population Biology, 1976-84; mem. editl. bd. Evolution Theory, 1976—, Ecol. Issues, 1995—, Discrete Applied Math., 1978-87, Internat. Jour. Math. and computer Modelling, 1979—; mem. editl. bd. Princeton U. Press, Complexity series, 1992—; mem. adv. bd. Jour. Theoretical Biology, 1977—; also various other editl. positions. Bd. dirs. N.J. chpt. Nature Conservancy, 1995—. Guggenheim fellow, 1979-80, Japanese Soc. for Promotion of Sci. fellow, 1983-84; recipient Disting. Statis. Ecologist award Internat. Assn. Ecology, 1994. Fellow AAAS (bd. dirs. 1994—), Am. Acad. Arts and Scis.; mem. Ecol. Soc. Am. (chmn. Mercer awards subcn. 1975-77, ad hoc com. to evaluate ecol. consequences of nuclear war 1982-83, pres.-elect 1989-90, pres. 1990-91, MacArthur award 1988), Soc. and Indsl. and Applied Math. (mem. coun. 1977-79, coun. exec. com. 1978-79, coun. rep. to bd. trustees 1978-79, chmn. human rights com. 1980-83, mng. editor Jour. Applied Math. 1975-79), Am. Inst. Biol. Scis., Am. Math. Soc. (dir. short course on math. population biology 1983), Am. Soc. Naturalists, Soc. Math. Biology (pres. 1987-89), Brit. Ecol. Soc., Soc. Study Evolution, U.S. Com. for Israel Environ., Sigma Xi. Jewish. Home: 11 Beechtree Ln Princeton NJ 08540 Office: Princeton U Dept Ecology & Evolutionary Biology Eno Hall Princeton NJ 08544-1003

LEVIN, WILLIAM COHN, hematologist, former university president; b. Waco, Tex., Mar. 2, 1917; s. Samuel P. and Jeanette (Cohn) L.; m. Edna Seinsheimer, June 23, 1941; children: Gerry Lee Levin Hornstein, Carol Lynn Levin Cantini. B.A., U. Tex., 1938, M.D., 1941; M.D. (hon.), U. Montpellier, 1980. Diplomate: Am. Bd. Internal Medicine. Intern Michael Reese Hosp., Chgo., 1941-42; resident John Sealy Hosp., Galveston, Tex., 1942-44; mem. staff U. Tex. Med. Br. Hosps., Galveston, 1944—, assoc. prof. internal medicine, 1948-65, prof., 1965—; Warmoth prof. hematology U. Tex. Med. Br., 1968-86, Ashbel Smith prof., 1986—, pres., 1974-87; past chmn., past mem. cancer clin. investigation rev. com. Nat. Cancer Inst., past. mem. Bd. Sci. Counselors. Exec. com., mem. nat. bd. Union Am. Hebrew Congregations; trustee Houston-Galveston Psychoanalytic Found., 1975-78, Menil Found., 1976-83. Recipient Nicholas and Katherine Leone award for adminstrv. excellence, 1977; decorated Palmes Académiques France. Fellow ACP, Internat. Soc. Hematology; mem. Am. Fedn. Clin. Research, Central Soc. Clin. Research, Am. Soc. Hematology, Phi Beta Kappa, Sigma Xi, Alpha Omega Alpha. Office: Am Indemnity Co PO Box 1259 Galveston TX 77553-1259

LEVINE, ALAN J., entertainment company executive; b. L.A., Mar. 8, 1947; s. Phil and Shirley Ann (Lauber) L.; m. Judy B. Birnbaum, July 18, 1973; children: Andrea, Jay. BS in Bus., U. So. Calif., L.A., 1968, JD, 1971. Bar: Calif. 1972, U.S. Dist. Ct. (so. dist.) Calif. 1972. Ptnr. Pacht, Ross, Warne, Bernhard & Sears, L.A., 1971-78, Schiff, Hirsch & Schreiber, Beverly Hills, Calif., 1978-80, Armstrong, Hirsch & Levine, L.A., 1980-89; pres., COO, SONY Pictures Entertainment, Inc., Culver, Calif., 1989—; v.p. cinema circulus dept. cinema and TV, U. So. Calif., L.A., 1988-90, bd. councilors of dept., 1991—; bd. dirs. UCLA Entertainment Symposium, 1986-89. Chmn. cabinet entertainment div. United Jewish Fedn., L.A., 1990-93; bd. govs. Cedars-Sinai Med. Ctr., L.A., 1989—. Mem. Calif. State Bar Assn., L.A. County Bar Assn., Beverly Hills Bar Assn., Acad. Motion Picture Arts and Scis., Acad. TV Arts and Scis. Democrat. Office: SONY Pictures Entertainment Inc 10202 Washington Blvd Culver City CA 90232-3119*

LEVINE, ARTHUR ELLIOTT, academic administrator, educator; b. N.Y.C., June 16, 1948; s. Meyer and Katherine (Kalman) L.; m. Linda Christine Fentiman, Aug. 18, 1974; children: Jamie Sloan Fentiman, Rachel Elizabeth Fentiman. B.A. in Biology, Brandeis U., 1970; Ph.D., SUNY-Buffalo, 1976; LHD (hon.), U. Puget Sound, 1981, U. New Eng, Biddeford, Maine, 1983, Unity Coll., Maine, 1984, Greensboro Coll., N.C., 1988, Bradford Coll., 1989, Capital U., 1991, Taitung Tchrs. Coll., Taiwan, 1991, Albright Coll., 1993, William Jewell Coll., 1995, U. N.H., 1995. Sr. fellow Carnegie Council on Policy Studies in Higher Edn., Berkeley, Calif., 1975-80, Carnegie Found., Washington, 1980-82; pres. Bradford Coll., Mass., 1982-89; chmn. Inst. for Edn. Mgmt. Harvard U., Cambridge, Mass., 1989-94; pres. Tchrs. Coll., Columbia U., N.Y.C., 1994—; cons. to numerous colls., univs., U.S. Co-author: Reform of Undergraduate Education, 1973 (Am. Coun. on Edn. Book of Yr. award 1974), Quest for Common Learning, 1982, Opportunity in Adversity, 1985, Shaping Higher Education's Future, 1989, Higher Learning in America, 1993; author: Handbook on Undergraduate Curriculum, 1978, Why Innovation Fails, 1980, When Dreams and Heroes Died, 1980. Recipient Edn. Press Assn. Am. award, 1981, 89, 90, 93, 94; book named Book of Yr., Am. Coun. on Edn., 1974; Spencer fellow, 1979, 89, Guggenheim fellow, 1982. Office: Tchrs Coll Columbia U 525 W 120th St New York NY 10027-6625

LEVINE, ARTHUR SAMUEL, physician, scientist; b. Cleve., Nov. 1, 1936; s. David Alvin and Sarah Ethel (Rubinstein) L.; m. Ruth Eleanor Rubin, Oct. 14, 1959; children: Amy Elizabeth, Raleigh Hannah, Jennifer Leah. AB, Columbia U., 1958; MD, Chgo. Med. Sch., 1964. Diplomate Am. Bd. Pediatrics, Am. Bd. Pediatric Hematology-Oncology. Intern in pediatrics U. Minn., Mpls., 1964-65, resident in pediatrics, 1965-66, USPHS fellow in hematology and genetics, 1966-67; capt. USPHS, 1967-92, rear adm., asst. surgeon gen., 1992—; clin. assoc. div. cancer treatment Nat. Cancer Inst., Bethesda, Md., 1967-69, sr. staff fellow, 1969-70, sr. investigator, 1970-73, head sect. infectious disease, pediatric oncology br., 1973-75, chief pediatric oncology br., 1975-82; sci. dir. Nat. Inst. Child Health and Human Devel., Bethesda, 1982—; clin. prof. medicine and pediatrics Georgetown U., Washington, 1975—; clin. prof. pediatrics Uniformed Svcs. U. Health Scis., Bethesda, 1983—; vis. prof. Cold Harbor Spring Lab., N.Y., 1973, Benares Hindu U., India, 1975, U. Minn., 1974, Hebrew U., Israel, 1981, U. Bologna, 1989, Northwestern U., 1992, Moscow State U., 1996; Karon meml. lectr. U. So. Calif., 1983; Seham lectr. U. Minn., 1983; Harris lectr. Va. Commonwealth U., 1995. Author: Cancer in the Young, 1982; editor-in-chief The New Biologist, 1989-92; contbr. articles to profl. jours. Recipient Disting. Alumnus award Chgo. Med. Sch., 1972, NIH Dir.'s award, 1984, Meritorious Svc. award USPHS, 1987, Disting. Svc. award, 1991, Surgeon Gen.'s Exemplary Svc. award, 1993. Mem. Am. Soc. Clin. Investigation, Soc. Pediatric Research, Am. Assn. Cancer Research, Am. Soc. Hematology, Am. Soc. Clin. Oncology, Am. Fedn. Clin. Research, AAAS, Am. Soc. Microbiology, Am. Soc. Pediatric Hematology/Oncology. Office: NIH Bldg 31 Room 2A-50 Nat Inst Child Health and Human Devel 9000 Rockville Pike Bethesda MD 20892-0001

LEVINE, CARL MORTON, motion picture exhibition, real estate executive; b. Bklyn., Sept. 24, 1931; s. Joseph M. and Frances Pearl (Smith) L.; m. Judith Ann Pollack, June 12, 1955 (div.); m. Miriam Scott Zeldman Duberstein, June 24, 1973; children: Jonathan Mark, Suzanne Beth; stepchildren: Debra Wiley-Hart, Douglas Reed Duberstein. BA, Bklyn. Coll., 1953; M in Dramatic Arts, Columbia U., 1955. Unit mgr., fl. and stage mgr., asst. dir., assoc. producer Sta. WRCA-TV NBC, N.Y.C., 1952-57; theatre mgr., asst. mgr. Forty Second St. Co. Lawbin Theatre Corp., Inc., N.Y.C., 1958-62, supr., 1963-65, gen. mgr., 1965-74; owner, mgr. Double L. Ranch, Adirondack Mountains, 1958-62; v.p., gen. mgr. Midtown Theatre Corp. Brandt Theatres, N.Y.C., 1974-86; gen. mgr., dir. theatre ops. Sameric Mgmt. Corp., Phila., 1986; comml. ops. mgr. Newmark & Co. Real Estate, Inc., N.Y.C., 1987-88; mng. dir. Loews 84th St. Sixplex Theater, N.Y.C., 1988-89; dir. ops. Eugene M. Grant & Co., N.Y.C., 1989-96; founder, producer, v.p., treas. Mirca Prodns. Ltd., N.Y.C., 1981-88; bd. dirs. Variety Club, N.Y.C., 1981-86, entertainment div. UJA-Fedn., N.Y.C., 1985; mem. Nat. Commn. Anti-Defamation League, 1965-86; v.p. Queens Coun. on Arts, 1977-80, pres., 1980-81. Chmn. producer Vets. Com. Variety Shows, VA Hosp., 1968-71; mem. adv. bd. Nassau County Fine Arts Mus., 1981-83. Mem. Acad. TV Arts and Scis., Variety Internat., Motion Picture Pioneer (life), Ind. Theatre Owner's Assn. (v.p. 1967-85), League N.Y. Theatres and Producers (labor negotiation com. 1980-83), Cinema B'nai B'rith (pres. 1970-72). Republican. Jewish. Office: 277 Park Ave New York NY 10172-0099

LEVINE, CHARLES MICHAEL, publishing company executive, consultant; b. Buffalo, Dec. 19, 1942; s. Abraham and Rose (Ackman) L.; 1 child, Gabriel Lee. B.A., Columbia U., 1963; M.A., Ind. U., 1966. With Peace Corps, 1967-69; editor McGraw Hill F.E.P., Singapore, 1972-75; mng. dir. APA Publs., Singapore, 1976-78; former dir. gen. ref. and sci. Macmillan Pub. Co. Inc., N.Y.C., from 1978; formerly with Simon & Schuster; v.p., exec. pub. John Wiley & Sons, to 1994; with Random House Inc., N.Y.C., 1994—. Mem. Phi Beta Kappa. Office: Random House Reference/Info Mail Drop 3-2 201 E 50th St New York NY 10022-7703

LEVINE, DANIEL BLANK, classical studies educator; b. Cin., July 22, 1953; s. Joseph and Elizabeth (Blank) L.; m. Judith Robinson, Aug. 14, 1984; children: Sarah Ruth, Amy Elizabeth. Student, Am. Sch. Classical Studies, Athens, 1974, 78-89; BA in Greek and Latin magna cum laude, U. Minn., 1975; PhD in Classics, U. Cin., 1980. Seymour fellow Am. Sch. Classical Studies, 1978-79; asst. prof. U. Ark., 1980-84, assoc. prof., 1984—; dir. Summer Session Am. Sch. Classical Studies, Athens, 1987, 95; dir. study tour in Greece Vergilian Soc., 1990; referee Classical Jour., 1984-88, Helios, 1984-88, Cornell U. Press, 1988-89, 91—, Classical Outlook, 1988-89; panelist NEH, Washington, 1986; co-dir., instr. gifted and talented H.S. students summer program State of Ark. Dept. Edn. Grant, 1988; mem. mng. com. Am. Sch. Classical Studies Athens, 1991—. Contbr. articles to profl. jours. Grantee NEH 1981, 82, 83, 84, 92; recipient Outstanding Tchr. award Mortar Bd. Sr. Honor Soc., U. Ark., 1991, Master Tchr. award Fulbright Coll., 1995. Mem. Am. Philological Assn. (Excellence in Teaching Classics award 1992), Am. Classical League, Classical Assn. Mid. West and South (Ovatio 1996, v.p. com. promotion Latin in Ark. 1980-86, 91—, chmn. regional rep. com. for promotion Latin, Outstanding State V.P. for 1982-83), U. Ark. Teaching Acad., Phi Beta Kappa. Home: 904 Park Ave Fayetteville AR 72701-2027 Office: U Ark Dept Fgn Langs 425 Kimpel Hall Fayetteville AR 72701

LEVINE, DAVID LAWRENCE, social work educator; b. N.Y.C., Aug. 30, 1919; s. Harold D. and Caroline (Leibowitz) L.; m. Laura Ann Kaplan, June 5, 1942; children: Edwin Alfred, Deborah Janet, Elizabeth Phylis, Helen Dorothy. B.S. in Social Scis., CCNY, 1941; M.S.W., U. Pa., 1943; Ph.D., U. Minn., 1953. Lic. clin. social worker, Ga. Visitor, intake worker Assn. Jewish Children, Phila., 1943-45; asst. to dir. Bklyn. Jewish Child Care Council, 1945-47; supr. children's services Jewish Family and Children's Services, Mpls., 1947-51; instr. family life edn. U. Minn., 1949-53, instr. Sch. Social Work, 1952-53; from asst. prof. to prof. Sch. Social Welfare, Fla. State U., 1953-67, chmn. dept. social work, 1965-67; asso. dean Sch. Social Work, Syracuse U., 1967-69; prof. social work Faculty Gerontology, U. Ga., Athens, 1968-90, prof. emeritus, 1990—; clin. prof. Dept. Psychiatry and Health Behavior Med. Coll. Ga., 1987—; rsch. assoc. cmty. mental health, Harvard Sch. Pub. Health, 1959-60; cons. Operation Headstart, 1965-67, Geriatric Clinic, U. Miami, Fla., 1955; chmn. NE Ga. Cmty. Svc., Mental Health Bd. Mental Retardation; hon. bd. dirs. Athens Cmty. Coun. Aging, 1995; del. White House Conf. on Aging, 1995. Pres. Leon County (Fla.) Mental Health Assn., 1961-63; chmn. Leon County Community Action Com., 1966; mem. bd. Fla. Assn. Mental Health, 1965-67; chmn. Twin Cities group Vocat. Guidance Assn., 1951; chmn. community planning and devel. com. Athens Community Council on Aging, 1969-86, pres. bd. dirs. 1992-93; cons. Ga. State Commn. on Aging, 1969-70; chmn. Univ. Council on Gerontology, 1970-74; Ga. del. White House Conf. on Aging, 1971; v.p. Nat. Inter-Faith Coalition on Aging, 1972-73; chmn. edn. and research com., mem. research team Social Work Manpower Study; pres. Athens-Clarke County Community Coordinated Child Care, 1973; cons. Inst. for Creative Devel., Union Am. Hebrew Congregations, 1974-77; chmn. com. on licensing Ga. State Conf. on Social Welfare, 1975-76; chmn. Title XX Planning Council, Dist. 10, Ga. Dept. Human Resources, 1976-85 , State 1st v.p., 1979-80; co-dir. Livingston Found. Seminars on Humanistic Mgmt. in Health Care, U. Ga.; mem. univ. council U. Ga., 1981-82; mem. tech. com., nat. del. White House Conf. on Aging, 1981; mem. Ga. Council Aging, 1982—, chmn. (1985-87). Fellow Am. Orthopsychiat. Assn., Gerontol. Soc. (Elsie Alvis Disting. Svc. award Ga. chpt. 1981); mem. Acad. Cert. Social Workers, Nat. Assn. Social Workers (Ga. coun. 1975-76, Frankie V. Adams disting. career award 1981), Nat. Assn. Social Workers (diplomate in Clinical Work), 1993. Address: 189 Colonial Dr Athens GA 30606-4015

LEVINE, DAVID M., newspaper editor; b. Newark, Oct. 2, 1949; s. Seymour I. and Fay D. Levine; m. Arleen Weintraub, Apr. 5, 1987. BA, Montclair State Coll., 1971; MS, Columbia U., 1973. Reporter, state house corr. Herald-News, Passaic, N.J., 1971-74; editorial writer Phila. Bull., 1974-79; night mng. editor Trenton (N.J.) Times, 1979-83; exec. fin. editor Washington Times, 1983-85; exec. editor Lebhar-Friedman Co., N.Y.C., 1985-86; editor Daily Jour., Elizabeth, N.J., 1986-87, Hudson Dispatch, Union City, N.J., 1987-91, The Daily Jour., Elizabeth, N.J., 1990-92; editor, v.p. The Herald-News, Passaic, N.J., 1992-94; editor-in-chief Mariner Cmty. Newspapers, 1995—; adj. instr. English dept. Rutgers U., Newark, 1987—; prin. Jour. Publs., Trenton, 1971—, Levine Publs., Trenton, 1974—. Author: Editorial Style, 1974.

LEVINE, DONALD NATHAN, sociologist, educator; b. New Castle, Pa., June 16, 1931; s. Abe and Rose (Gusky) L.; m. Joanna Bull, Nov. 6, 1955 (div. 1967); children: Theodore, William; m. Ruth Weinstein, Aug. 26, 1967; 1 child, Rachel. AB, U. Chgo., 1950, MA, 1954, PhD, 1957; postgrad., U. Frankfurt, Germany, 1952-53. Asst. prof. sociology U. Chgo., 1962-65, assoc. prof., 1965-73, prof., 1973-86, dean of Coll., 1982-87, Peter B. Ritzma prof., 1986—. Author: Wax and Gold: Tradition and Innovation in Ethiopian Culture, 1965, Georg Simmel on Individuality and Social Forms, 1971, Greater Ethiopia: The Evolution of a Multiethnic Society, 1974, Simmel and Parsons: Two Approaches to the Study of Society, 1980, The Flight from Ambiguity: Essays in Social and Cultural Theory, 1985, Visions of the Sociological Tradition, 1995; editor: The Heritage of Sociology series, 1988—. Recipient Quantrell award U. Chgo., 1971; Guggenheim fellow, 1980; fellow Center for Advanced Study in Behavioral Scis., 1980-81. Mem. Internat. Soc. Comparative Study Civilization, Am. Sociol. Assn. Jewish. Office: U Chgo 1126 E 59th St Chicago IL 60637-1580

LEVINE, DOUGLAS GARY, music industry executive; b. N.Y.C., Sept. 1, 1954; s. Edward Charles and Rhoda Evelyn (Polstein) L.; m. Susan Levitin, June 5, 1982; children: Zachary, Valorie. BS in Acctg., N.Y.U., 1976. Licensed prin. Nat. Assn. Securities Dealers. Jr. acct. J.K. Lasser & Co., N.Y.C., 1976; sec. OCG Tech. Inc., N.Y.C., 1977—; pres. Masterdisk Corp., N.Y.C., 1978—; chmn. bd. Masterdisk Corp., N.Y.C., 1984—. Chapter chief NSA, 1975—. Democratic. Nichiren Shoshu Buddhist. Club: Hampshire Country (Mamaroneck, N.Y.).

LE VINE, DUANE GILBERT, petroleum company executive; b. Balt., July 5, 1933; s. Harry B. and Frances Annette (Culleton) LeV.; m. Patricia J. Allman, Aug. 10, 1957; children: Duane Gilbert, Michele P., William A., James D., Erin A., Megan K. B.S. in Chem. Engring., Johns Hopkins U., 1956, M.S., 1958. With Exxon Research & Engring. Co., 1959—; dir. fuels products research lab. Exxon Research & Engring. Co., Linden, N.J., 1971-74; mgr. gasoline and lube processes div. Exxon Research & Engring. Co., Florham Park, N.J., 1974-76; gen. mgr. Baytown (Tex.) research and devel. site, 1976-78, exec. dir. corp. research sci. labs., 1979-84; mgr. worldwide environ. affairs Exxon Corp., N.Y.C., 1984-90; mgr. sci. and strategy devel. Exxon Corp., Dallas, 1990—; mem. Nat. Air Pollution Rsch. Adv. Com., 1971-74, Tex. Energy and Natural Resources Adv. Coun., 1976-78; mem. com. energy tech. assessment NASA, 1974; participant UN/industry-sponsored conf. on environ. mgmt., Versailles, France, 1984; chmn. Rene Dubos Internat. Forum on Mng. Hazardous Materials, N.Y.C., 1988, Rene Dubos Internat. Forum on Global Urbanization, N.Y.C., 1989; mem. adv. com. Calif. Inst. Tech., Johns Hopkins U., Rene Dubos Ctr.; chmn. Internat. Petroleum Industry Global Climate Change Symposium, Rome, 1992. Author: (with Upton) Management of Hazardous Agents, 1992, The City as a Human Environment, 1994; patentee, author combustion, electrochemistry, environ. petroleum/synthetic fuels. Fellow Am. Inst. Chemists; mem. AIChE, AAAS, Internat. Combustion Inst., Am. Chem. Soc., Am. Petroleum Inst., N.Y. Acad. Scis., Internat. Petroleum Industry Environ. Conservation Assn. (exec. com. 1984—, vice chmn. 1994-95, chmn. and chief officer 1996—), Sigma Xi, Tau Beta Pi, Phi Lambda Upsilon. Achievements include research on automotive emission control catalyst systems, on evaporative loss control devices, on exhaust recycle systems for NOx control, on catalytic coal gasification, on donor solvent coal liquifaction, and on direct synthesis of hydrocarbon liquids from CO/H2. Office: Exxon Corp Rm 3314 5959 Las Colinas Blvd Irving TX 75062-2298

LEVINE, EDWARD LESLIE, lawyer; b. Sheboygan, Wis., June 11, 1927; s. Joseph and Rose (Nemschoff) L.; m. Rosalie Bernstein, July 5, 1953; children: Carol Lovseth, Alex H., James L. BS, U. Wis., 1950, LLB, 1952. Counsel Comptroller of the Currency, Washington, 1952-56; assoc. Cole & Deitz, N.Y.C., 1956-62; ptnr. Winston & Strawn and predecessor firms, N.Y.C., 1962—; counsel N.Y. Legislature, Com. to Revise Banking Law, Albany, 1967-68; cons. UN Devel. Program to Draft Banking Law for Federated States of Micronesia; mem. com. on counsel N.Y. Clearing House Assn. Bd. visitors U. Wis. Law Sch., Madison, 1989—; mem. Gov.'s Coun. on Fin. Svcs., N.Y., 1986-88. With USAF, 1945-47. Mem. ABA (banking law com.), Assn. of Bar of City of N.Y. (banking law com. 1987-90). Democrat. Jewish. Avocations: tennis, bridge. Office: Winston & Strawn 200 Park Ave New York NY 10166-4193

LEVINE, EDWIN BURTON, retired classics educator; b. Chgo., Nov. 11, 1920; s. Benjamin and Bertha (Kauffman) L.; m. Myra Estrin, Apr. 22, 1944; children—William Alan, Patricia Ann. A.B., U. Chgo., 1949, A.M., 1950, Ph.D., 1953. Instr. classics U. Nebr., 1951-52; instr., then asst. prof. Wayne State U., Detroit, 1955-60; instr. Detroit Bd. Edn., 1960-61, New Trier High Sch., Winnetka, Ill., 1962-64; vis. lectr. U. Ill. at Chgo. Circle, 1964-65, mem. faculty, 1965—, prof. classics, 1968-87, prof. emeritus, 1987—, founder and 1st head dept., 1969-74. Author: Introduction to Classical Greek, 1968; prin. compiler: Follett World-Wide Latin-English Dictionary, 1968, Hippocrates, 1971, Landor's Latin Poetry, 1968. Served with AUS, 1943-46. Fellow AAAS; mem. Am. Philol. Assn., Soc. for History of Medicine, Archaeol. Inst. Am., Chgo. Classical Club (pres. 1967-69). Home: 701 Forum Sq Apt 509 Glenview IL 60025-3866

LEVINE, ELLEN R., magazine editor; b. N.Y.C., Feb. 19, 1943; d. Eugene Jack and Jean (Zuckman) Jacobson; m. Richard U. Levine, Dec. 21, 1964; children: Daniel, Peter. Student, Wellesley Coll. Reporter The Record, Hackensack, N.J., 1964-70; editor Cosmopolitan mag., N.Y.C., 1976-82; editor in chief Cosmopolitan Living mag., N.Y.C., 1980-81, Woman's Day mag., N.Y.C., 1982-91, Redbook mag., N.Y.C., 1991-94, Good Housekeeping, N.Y.C., 1994—; dir. N.J. Bell, Newark; commr. U.S. Atty. Gen.'s Commn. on Pornography, 1985-86. Author: Planning Your Wedding, Waiting for Baby, Rooms That Grow With Your Child. Mem. exec. com. Senator Bill Bradley, 1984—. Named to Writers Hall of Fame, 1981, Acad. Women Achievers, YWCA, 1982; recipient Outstanding Profl. Achievement award N.J. coun. Girl Scouts U.S., 1984, Woman of Achievement award N.J. Fedn. Women's Clubs, 1984, Matrix award N.Y. Women in Communications, Inc., 1989, honor award Birmigham So. Coll., 1991. Office: Good Housekeeping 959 8th Ave New York NY 10019-3767*

LEVINE, GEORGE LEWIS, English language educator, literature critic; b. N.Y.C., Aug. 27, 1931; s. Harris Julius and Dorothy Sara (Podolsky) L.; m. Margaret Bloom, Aug. 19, 1956; children: David Michael, Rachel Susan. B.A., NYU, 1952; M.A., U. Minn., 1953, Ph.D., 1958. Instr. Ind. U., Bloomington, 1959-62, asst. prof., 1962-65, assoc. prof., 1965-68; prof. English Rutgers U., New Brunswick, N.J., 1968—, chmn. dept., 1979-83; Kenneth Burke prof. Rutgers U., New Brunswick, 1985—; vis. prof. U. Calif.-Berkeley, 1968, Stanford U., Calif., 1974-75; vis. research fellow Girton Coll., Cambridge U., Eng., 1983; dir. Ctr. for Critical Analysis of Contemp. Culture. Author: Boundaries of Fiction, 1968, The Endurance of Frankenstein, 1975, The Realistic Imagination, 1981, One Culture, 1987, Darwin and the Novelists, 1988, Lifebirds, 1995; author, editor: The Art of Victorian Prose, 1968, Mindful Pleasures, 1975, Constructions of the Self, 1992, Realism and Representation, 1993, Aesthetics and Ideology, 1994; editor: Victorian Studies, 1959-68. Served with U.S. Army, 1953-55. Guggenheim Found. fellow, 1971-72; NEH fellow, 1978-79; Rockefeller Found. fellow, 1983. Mem. MLA, AAUP. Democrat. Jewish. Home: 419 Lincoln Ave Highland Park NJ 08904-2728 Office: Rutgers U Ctr Critical Analysis Cont New Brunswick NJ 08903

LEVINE, GEORGE RICHARD, English language educator; b. Boston, Aug. 5, 1929; s. Jacob U. and Rose Lillian (Margolis) L.; m. Joan Adler, June 8, 1958 (div. 1977); children—David, Michael; m. Linda Rashman, Apr. 17, 1977. B.A., Tufts Coll., Medford, Mass., 1951; M.A., Columbia, 1952, Ph.D., 1961. Lectr. English Columbia, 1956-58; instr. Northwestern U., 1959-63; mem. faculty State U. N.Y., Buffalo, 1963—; prof. English State

U. N.Y., 1970—, dean faculty arts and letters, 1975-81. Author: Henry Fielding and The Dry Mock, 1967; editor: Harp on the Shore: Thoreau and the Sea, 1985, Jonathan Swift: A Modest Proposal and Other Satires, 1995; contbr. articles to profl. jours. Chmn. bd. dirs. Youth Orch. Found., Buffalo, 1974-75; trustee Buffalo Chamber Music Soc., Arts Devel. Svcs.; bd. dirs. Buffalo Philharm. Orch. With AUS, 1952-54. Univ. fellow Columbia U., 1958-59; Faculty Research fellow SUNY, 1966, 67; Fulbright lectr. W. Ger., 1969-70; recipient Chancellor's award excellence in teaching SUNY, Buffalo, 1973-74. Mem. MLA, Am. Soc. 18th Century Studies, Internat. Assn. Univ. Profs. English. Jewish. Clubs: Adirondack Mountain. Home: 388 Parker Ave Buffalo NY 14216-2146 Office: SUNY Dept English 306 Clemens Hall Buffalo NY 14260

LEVINE, GERALD RICHARD, investment and merchant banker, financial advisor; b. N.Y.C., Nov. 7, 1936; s. Irving Arthur and Lillian (Kronstadt) L.; m. Linda L. Paige, May 17, 1991.; children from previous marriage: Jodi Levine Avergun, Debby Levine Rifkin, James H. AB, Brown U., 1958; MBA, GM Inst. Tech., Flint, Mich., 1960; postgrad., Pohs Inst. Ins., N.Y.C., 1978, Securities Tng. Inst., N.Y.C., 1981; postgrad. real estate, NYU, 1993. Pres. Town and Country Motors (Div. KLZ Corp.), Woodmere, N.Y., 1959-78, TAR Brokerage Corp., 1977—; nat. mktg. dir. Performance Dynamics Inc., N.Y.C., 1978-81; v.p. Oppenheimer & Co., N.Y.C., 1981-84; sr. v.p. Twenty-First Securities Corp., N.Y.C., 1984-89; assoc. nat. dir. corp. and instl. investment programs Devel. Corp. for Israel, N.Y.C., 1989-91; assoc. dir. estate planning div. Prudential Securities/Ins., N.Y.C., 1991-92; dir. corp. philanthropy Anti-Defamation League, N.Y.C., 1992-93; dir. Sealy Hoffman & Sheehan Inc., 1993-94; sr. mng. dir. Investment Adv. Group, N.Y.C., 1994—. Pres. 5 Towns div. Salvation Army, Woodmere, 1968-85; mem. exec. com., adv. bd. commerce and industry div. State of Israel Bonds, N.Y.C., 1988-89; mem. exec. com. Brown Ann. Fund, Providence, 1987-89, 92-94, Brown Corp. Com. on Devel., 1987-89, 92-94, major gifts chmn. 30th Reunion, 1988, 35th Reunion, 1993, N.Y.C. Brown Reg. Devel. Com., 1988-93; advisor Brown U. Sports Found., 1987—; bd. dirs. Brown U. Football Assn., Providence, 1988-92; bd. dir. Head Marshall Alumni Divsn. 1983-84, 88-89, head class agt. 1978-88, treas. class of 1958, 1988-93, pres. class of '58, 1993—, Alumni Marshall, 1993. Recipient Disting. Alumni Svc. award Brown U., 1988. Mem. Brown U. Alumni Assn. (exec. bd. assn. class officers 1994—), Brown U. Club N.Y. (pres. 1990-92, v.p., exec. dir. 1989-90), K.P. (mem. at large), Princeton Club, Nat. Arts Club. Republican. Jewish. Avocations: golf, fishing, antique car restorations, woodworking, chess. Office: Investment Adv Group Ste 1700 317 Madison Ave New York NY 10017

LEVINE, GUILLERMO, computer scientist, educator; b. Guadalajara, Mex., Apr. 27, 1953; s. Leo and Aurora (Gutierrez) L. Electronic Engr., U. Guadalajara, 1975; MSc in Computer Sci., Nat. U. Mex., 1979. Prof. U. Guadalajara, 1973-75, Met. U., Mexico City, 1976-86, Nat. U., Mexico City, 1980-89; rsch. dir. Micrologica, Mexico City, 1982-90, gen. dir., 1991; founder, 1st dir. computer sci. faculty U. Guadalajara, 1991-95; cons. Internat. Ctr. of Social Security Studies, OAS, UN, Mexico City, 1983-85; acad. cons. Red Uno, Mex., 1994—. Author: Introduction to Computer Science, 1984, Introduction to Programming, 1989, Elements Computing, 1993; coord. nat. report Computer Sci. Edn., 1988, 95. Mem. IEEE, Assn. Computing Machinery. Jewish. Avocations: reading, classical music. Home and Office: PO Box 1-953 Centro, 44100 Guadalajara Mexico

LEVINE, HAROLD, lawyer; b. Newark, Apr. 30, 1931; s. Rubin and Gussie (Lifshitz) L.; children: Brenda Sue, Linda Ellen Levine Gersen, Louise Abby, Jill Anne Levine Zuvanich, Charles A., Cristina Gussie, Harold Rubin II; m: Cristina Cervera, Aug. 29, 1980. B.S. in Engring., Purdue U., 1954; J.D. with distinction, George Washington U., 1958. Bar: D.C. 1958, Va., 1958, Mass. 1960, Tex. 1972, U.S. Patent Office, 1958. Naval architect, marine engr. U.S. Navy Dept., 1954-55; patent examiner U.S. Patent Office, 1955-58; with Tex. Instruments Inc., Attleboro, Mass., 1959-77, asst. sec., Dallas, 1969-72, asst. v.p. and gen. patent counsel, 1972-77; ptnr. Sigalos & Levine, Dallas, 1977-93; prin. Levine & Majorie LLP, 1994—; chmn. bd. Vanguard Security, Inc., Houston, 1977—; chmn. Tex. Am. Realty, Dallas, 1977—; lectr. assns., socs.; del. Geneva and Lausanne (Switzerland) Intergovtl. Conf. on Revision, Paris Pat. Conv., 1975-76. Mem. U.S. State Dept. Adv. Panel on Internat. Tech. Transfer, 1977. Mem. ABA (chmn. com. 407 taxation pats. and trdmks. 1971-72), Am. Patent Law Assn., Dallas Bar Assn., Assn. Corp. Pat. Csl. (sec.-treas. 1971-73), Dallas-Fort Worth Patent Law Assn., Pacific Indsl. Property Assn. (pres. 1975-77), Electronic Industries Assn. (pres. pat. com. 1972), NAM, Southwestern Legal Inst. on Patent Law (planning com. 1971-74), U.S. C. of C., Dallas C. of C., Alpha Epsilon Pi, Phi Alpha Delta. Republican. Jewish. Club: Kiwanis. Contbr. chpt. to book, articles to profl. jours. Editor: George Washington U. Law Rev., 1956-57; mem. adv. bd. editors Bur. Nat. Affairs, Pat., Trdmk. and Copyright Jour., 1979-87. Office: Levine and Majorie LLP 12750 Merit Dr Ste 1000 Dallas TX 75251-1243

LEVINE, HENRY DAVID, lawyer; b. N.Y.C., June 7, 1951; s. Harold Abraham and Joan Sarah (Price) L.; m. Barbara Wolgel, Aug. 28, 1976; children: David, Rachel, Daniel. AB, Yale U., 1972; JD, M in Pub. Policy, Harvard U., 1976. Bar: N.Y. 1977, D.C. 1978, U.S. Supreme Ct. 1980. Assoc. Wilmer, Cutler & Pickering, Washington, 1976-80; assoc. Morrison & Foerster, Washington, 1981-83, ptnr., 1983-92; ptnr. Levine, Blaszak, Block & Boothby, Washington, 1993—; cons. to GSA on FTS2000 Successor System, 1994—. Editor Telematics, 1984-89. Mem. Nat. Rsch. Coun. Com on High Tech. Bldgs., 1985-88. Named one of the twenty-five most powerful people in networking Network World, 1996. Mem. ABA, Fed. Communication Bar Assn. Home: 5208 Edgemoor Ln Bethesda MD 20814-2342 Office: Levine Blaszak Block & Boothby 1300 Connecticut Ave NW # 500 Washington DC 20036

LEVINE, HOWARD HARRIS, health facility executive; b. Bklyn., Sept. 30, 1949; s. Roy and Lucille Levine. MPH in Hosp. Administrn., UCLA, 1974; BBA in Mktg., Baruch Coll., 1972. Adminstrv. resident Inter-Community Hosp., Covina, Calif., 1973-74; adminstrv. asst. to exec. dir. John F. Kennedy Med. Ctr., Edison, N.J., 1974-75; assoc. exec. dir. John F. Kennedy Med. Ctr., Edison, 1975-78; adminstr. Robert Wood Johnson Jr. Rehab. Inst., Edison, 1975-78; asst. dir. Beth Israel Med. Ctr., N.Y.C., 1978-81, assoc. dir., 1981-84, sr. assoc. dir. for ops., 1984-87; v.p. Staten Island Univ. Hosp., 1988, sr. v.p., chief oper. officer, 1988-91; CEO Chapman Med. Ctr., Orange, Calif., 1992—; v.p. OrNda Health Corp., 1994-95; adj. lectr. dept. health care adminstrn. Bernard M. Baruch Coll./Mt. Sinai Sch. Medicine, N.Y.C., 1982-93; Health Profl. adv. com. March of Dimes, 1992—; joint com. patient svcs. Calif. Hosp. Assn., 1992—; guest lectr. svcs. Calif. Hosp. Assn., 1992—; guest lectr. NYU Grad. Sch. Pub. Adminstrn., 1984-86; mem. mental health and substance abuse com. Greater N.Y. Health Adminstrn., 1988-91, profl. affairs and hosp. ops. com., 1989-91, chmn. com. on utilization rev., 1988-91; exec. and planning com. Hosp. Coun. So. Calif., 1992—, coun. on profl. practices N.J. Hosp. Assn., Princeton, 1977-78, dist. bd. Health Svcs. Adminstrn., N.Y.C., 1979-80. Mem. editorial adv. bd. The Malpractice Reporter, N.Y.C., 1980-88. Mem. ins. profl. adv. com. Fedn. Jewish Philanthropies Ins., 1981-87; mem. tech. adv. panel N.J. State Health Coordinating Coun., Princeton, 1976-78; bd. dirs. Meals-on-Wheels Program, Metuchen, Edison and Woodbridge, N.J., 1974-76; mem. budget com. United Crusade L.A., 1973-74. Fellow Am. Coll. Healthcare Execs.; mem. Coun. Hosp. Adminstrs. (pres. 1986-87), Met. Health Adminstrs. Assn. (pres. 1980-82), Am. Coll. Healthcare Mktg., Hosp. Adminstrs. Discussion Group. Home: 309 Bay Hill Dr Newport Beach CA 92660-5235 Office: Chapman Med Ctr 2601 E Chapman Ave Orange CA 92669-3206

LEVINE, IRVING RASKIN, news commentator, university dean, author, lecturer; b. Pawtucket, R.I.; s. Joseph and Emma (Raskin) L.; m. Nancy Cartmell Jones, July 12, 1957; children—Jeffrey Claybourne Bond, Daniel Rome, Jennifer Jones. BS, Brown U., 1944, LHD (hon.), 1969; MS, Columbia, 1947; LHd (hon.), Bryant Coll., 1974; D.Journalism (hon.), Roger Williams Coll., 1985; LLD (hon.), U. R.I., 1988; LHD (hon.), Lynn U., 1992; LLD (hon.), Northeastern U., 1993; D in Journalism (hon.), R.I. Coll., 1996. Writer obits. Providence Jour., 1940-43; fgn. news editor Internat. News Service, 1947-48; chief Vienna (Austria) bur., 1948-50; with NBC, 1950-95; war corr. NBC, Korea, 1950-52; radio anchor World News Roundup, Moscow, 1953-54; chief corr. NBC, Moscow, Rome, 1968-71, London, 1967-68; chief econs. corr. NBC, Washington, 1971-95; dean Sch. Internat. Studies, Lynn U., Boca Raton, Fla., 1995—; commentator Consumer News and Bus. Channel Cable TV affiliate svc. NBC TV News, 1990—; spl. writer London Times, 1995-59; covered assignments in Can., China, Czechoslovakia, Bulgaria, Poland, Japan, Vietnam, Formosa, Thailand, Eng., France, Germany, Switzerland, Algeria, Congo, Israel, Turkey, Tunisia, Greece, Yugoslavia, Union of South Africa, Denmark, Sweden, Ireland; press group with pres. Ford, Carter, Reagan, Bush, Clinton; attended G-7 Econ. Summits, 1975-95; lectr. univs., bus. groups, cruise ships. Author: Main Street, USSR, 1959, Travel Guide to Russia, 1960, Main Street, Italy, 1963, The New Worker in Soviet Russia, 1973; contbr. articles to nat. mags.; guest on numerous TV shows including Murphy Brown, 1989, David Letterman Show, 1990, Jay Leno Show, 1990. With Signal Corps, U.S. Army, 1944-47, Philippines, Japan. Recipient award for best radio-TV reporting from abroad Overseas Press Club, 1956, award for outstanding radio network broadcasting Nat. Headliners Club, 1957, 50th Anniversary award Columbia Sch. Journalism, 1963, Emmy citation 1966, Martin R. Gainsbrugh award for best econ. reporting, 1978, William Rogers award Brown U., 1988, Silver Circle award Nat. Acad. TV Arts and Scis., 1990, 93; named one of 10 Outstanding Young Men, U.S. Jaycees, 1956; named to R.I. Hall of Fame, 1972, Pawtucket Hall of Fame, 1986, Nat. Broadcasters Hall of Fame Lifetime Achievement award, 1995; honoree Loyola Coll.'s Beta Gamma Sigma, 1994,. Mem. Coun. on Fgn. Rels. (fellowship 1952-53), Cosmos, Phi Beta Kappa, Beta Gamma Sigma. Office: Lynn U 3601 N Military Trail Boca Raton FL 33431-5598

LEVINE, ISRAEL E., writer; b. N.Y.C., Aug. 30, 1923; s. Albert Ely and Sonia (Silver) L.; m. Joy Elaine Michael, June 23, 1946; children: David, Carol. BS, CCNY, 1946. Asst. dir. pub. rels. CCNY, 1946-54, dir., 1954-77, editor Alumnus Mag., 1952-74, 87-89; editor Health Care Week, 1977-79, William H. White Publs., 1979-81; dir. communications Am. Jewish Congress, 1981-87; COO Richard Cohen Assocs., N.Y.C., 1987—. Author: (with A. Lateiner) The Techniques of Supervision, 1954; The Discoverer of Insulin: Dr. Frederick G. Banting, 1959, Conqueror of Smallpox: Dr. Edward Jenner, 1960, Behind the Silken Curtain: The Story of Townsend Harris, 1961, Inventive Wizard: George Westinghouse, 1962, Champion of World Peace: Dag Hammarskjold, 1962, Miracle Man of Printing: Ottmar Mergenthaler, 1963, Electronics Pioneer: Lee DeForest, 1964, Young Man in the White House: John Fitzgerald Kennedy, 1964, 91, Oliver Cromwell, 1966, Spokesman for the Free World: Adlai Stevenson, 1967, Lenin: The Man Who Made a Revolution, 1969, The Many Faces of Slavery, 1975; contbr. over 200 articles to mags. Mem. exec. com. Com. for Pub. Higher Edn., N.Y.C., 1987—. 2d lt., navigator USAAF, 1943-45, ETO. Decorated Air medal with 3 oak leaf clusters, 3 battle stars USAAF; recipient 125th Anniversary medal; CCNY, 1972, Svc. medal CCNY Alumni Assn., 1974. Mem. The Authors Guild, Authors' League Am., Soc. of Silurians, 2d Air Divsn. Assn. Jewish. Avocation: gardening. Address: Richard Cohen Assocs 40 W 55th St Ste 503 New York NY 10019

LEVINE, JACK, artist; b. Boston, Jan. 3, 1915; s. Samuel Mayer and Mary (Grinker) L.; widowed; 1 child, Susanna Levine Fisher. AFD, Colby Coll., Waterville, Maine, 1956. One-man shows include Downtown Gallery, N.Y.C., 1938, Artists, 1942, Mus. Modern Art, N.Y.C., 1943; exhibited in group shows at Jeu de Paume, Paris, 1938, Carnegie Internat. exhbns., 1938-40, Artists for Victory, Met. Mus., N.Y.C., 1942, retrospective at Jewish Mus., N.Y.C., 1978-79; represented in permanent collections Mus. Modern Art, Met. Mus. Art, N.Y.C., William Hayes Foggs Mus., Harvard U., Addison Gallery, Andover, Mass., Mus. Vatican, Midtown Payson Galleries, N.Y.C. With AUS, 1942-45. Mem. Am. Acad. Arts and Letters (pres., chancellor), Inst. Arts and Letters (pres. 1993), Nat. Acad. Design, Century Club.

LEVINE, JACK ANTON, lawyer; b. Monticello, N.Y., Dec. 23, 1946; s. Milton and Sara (Sacks) L.; m. Eileen A. Garsh, Sept. 7, 1974; children: Matthew Aaron, Dara Esther. BS with honors, SUNY, Binghamton, 1968; JD with honors, U. Fla., 1975, LLM in Taxation, 1976. Bar: Fla. 1975, U.S. Ct. Appeals (11th cir.) 1981, U.S. Tax Ct., 1982. Tax atty. legis. and regulations divsn. Office chief counsel IRS, Washington, 1977-81; assoc. Holland & Knight, Tampa, Fla., 1981-83, ptnr., 1984—; lectr. in field. Contbr. articles to profl. jours. Mem. ABA, Fla. Bar Assn. (sect. taxation exec. coun. 1984—, chmn. ptnrship. com. 1985-88, chmn. taxation regulated public utilities com. 1988-92, co-chmn. corps. and tax-exempt orgns. com. 1992—, bd. cert. in tax law 1984—), Harbour Island Athletic Club. Democrat. Jewish. Avocations: golf, reading, traveling. Home: 10905 Carrollwood Dr Tampa FL 33618-3903 Office: Holland & Knight 400 N Ashley Dr Ste 2300 Tampa FL 33602-4317

LEVINE, JAMES, conductor, pianist, artistic director; b. Cin., June 23, 1943; s. Lawrence M. and Helen (Goldstein) L. Studied piano with Rosina Lhevinne and Rudolf Serkin, studied conducting with Jean Morel, Fausto Cleva and Max Rudolf, studied theory and interpretation with Walter Levin; student, Juilliard Sch. Music; hon. degree, U. Cin., New Eng. Cons., Northwestern U. Music dir. Ravinia Festival, 1973-93; artistic dir. Met. Opera, 1986—; guest lectr. Sarah Lawrence Coll., Harvard U., Yale U. Piano debut with Cin. Symphony, 1953; conducting debut at Aspen Music Festival, 1961; Met. Opera debut, 1971; Chgo. Symphony debut at Ravinia Festival, 1971; regularly appears throughout U.S. and Europe as condr. and pianist, including Vienna Philharm., Berlin Philharm., Chgo. Symphony, Phila. Orch., Boston Symphony, N.Y. Philharm., Dresden Staatskapelle, Philharmonia Orch., Israel Philharmonic, Wagner Festival at Bayreuth; made Bayreuth debut in new prodn. of Parsifal, 1982; condr. Salzburg Festival, 1975-93; Salzburg premieres include Schönberg's Moses und Aron, 1987, Offenbach's Tales of Hoffmann, Mahler's Seventh Symphony, Mendelssohn's Elijah; condr. Met. premiere prodns. of Verdi's I Vespri Siciliani, Stifelio, I Lombardi, Weill's The Rise and Fall of the City of Mahogonny, Stravinsky's Oedipus Rex, Berg's Lulu, Mozart's Idomeneo and La Clemenza di Tito, Gershwin's Progy and Bess, world premiere Corigliano/Hoffman The Ghosts of Versailles; subject of documentary for PBS; artistic dir. Met. Opera. Recipient Smetana medal, 1987, 8 Grammy awards. Office: Met Opera Assn Inc Met Opera House Lincoln Ctr New York NY 10023

LEVINE, JEFFREY BARRY, lawyer; b. Detroit, Jan. 13, 1949; s. Jack Morris and Blanche (Kaufman) L. BA, Wayne State U., 1971, JD cum laude, 1974; LLM in Taxation, NYU, 1975. Bar: Mich. 1974, U.S. Dist. Ct. (ea. dist.) Mich. 1977, U.S. Ct. of Appeals (6th cir. 1979), U.S. Tax Ct. 1981. Assoc. Thomas W. Kimmeryl P.C., Bloomfield Hills, Mich., 1974-78; chief counsel DeLoren Motor Co., Bloomfield Hills, 1978; assoc. Rubenstein, Isaacs, Lax & Bordman, Southfield, Mich., 1978-82; ptnr. Hyman, Gurwin, Nachman, Friedman & Winkelman, Southfield, 1982-88; assoc. Carson, Fischer & Potts, Birmingham, Mich., 1988-91; of counsel Rubenstiein, Isaacs, Haroutunian & Sobel, Southfield, 1991-92; shareholder Rubenstein, Plotkin P.C., Southfield, 1992—; spkr. orgns. of attys. and pub. accts. on taxation and bus. law. issues. Office: Rubenstein Plotkin PC 2000 Town Ctr Ste 2700 Southfield MI 48075

LEVINE, JEROME, psychiatrist, educator; b. N.Y.C., July 10, 1934; s. Abraham and Sadie (Glowatz) L.; children: Ross W., Lynn R., Andrew R. BA, U. Buffalo, 1954, MD, 1958. Intern, then psychiat. resident E.J. Meyer Meml. Hosp., Buffalo, 1958-61; sr. psychiat. resident St. Elizabeth's Hosp., Washington, 1961-62; staff psychiatrist USPHS Hosp., Lexington, Ky., 1962-64; research psychiatrist, asst. chief psychopharmacology research br. NIMH, 1964-67, chief of br., 1967-81, chief pharmacologic and somatic treatments research br., 1981-84; research prof. psychiatry U. Md. Sch. Medicine, Balt., 1985-94; dep. dir. Nathan Kline Inst. for Psychiat. Rsch., Orangeburg, N.Y., 1994—; rsch. prof. psychiatry NYU, 1994—; instr. psychiatry Johns Hopkins Med. Sch., 1964-72; vis. prof. U. Pisa, Italy, 1977. Author books and papers on psychopharmacology, clin. trial methodology, somatic treatment assessment for psychiat. disorders. Mem. Soc. Clin. Trials, Am. Psychiat. Assn. (Hofheimer Research prize 1970), Am. Coll. Neuropsychopharmacology, Collegium Internationale Neuropsychopharmacologicum, Am. Soc. Clin. Pharmacology and Therapeutics. Home: 15 Stony Hollow Chappaqua NY 10514-2014 Office: Nathan Kline Inst Bldg 37 140 Old Orangeburg Rd Orangeburg NY 10962

LE VINE, JEROME EDWARD, retired ophthalmologist, educator; b. Pitts., Mar. 23, 1923; s. Harry Robert and Marian Dorothy (Finesilver) L.; m. Marilyn Tobey Hiedovitz, Apr. 14, 1957; children: Loren Robert, Beau Jay, Janice Lynn. B.S., U. Pitts., 1944; M.D., Hahnemann Med. Sch., Phila., 1949; postgrad. in ophthalmology U. Pa., 1951-52. Diplomate Am. Bd. Disability Cons., Am. Bd. Quality Assurance & Utilization Rev. Intern, St. Francis Hosp., Pitts., 1949-50; resident in ophthalmology Jefferson U. Med. Sch. Hosp., Phila., 1952-54; ophthalmologist Leech Farm VA Hosp., Pitts., 1955-59; chief eye dept. Stanocola Clinic, Baton Rouge, 1959-64; sole practice medicine specializing in ophthalmology, Baton Rouge, 1959-86; cons. La. State U., East La. State Hosp. Infirmary, Villa Feliciana Geriatric Hosp., disability dept. Social Security Adminstrn., div. blind La. State Pub. Welfare dept.; mem. staff Our Lady of the Lake Hosp., Baton Rouge Gen. Hosp., Women's Hosp.; instr. spl. edn. U. Southeastern La., 1971. Mem. Am. Bd. Quality Assurance and Utilization Rev., 1990. Served with MC, AUS, 1942-44. Fellow Am. Geriatric Soc., Royal Soc. Health; mem. AMA, La. State Med. Soc., East Baton Rouge Parish Med. Soc., 6th Dist. Med. Soc., New Orleans Acad. Ophthalmology, So. Med. Assn., La. Med. Soc., Baton Rouge Parish Med. Soc., Pi Lambda Phi, Phi Delta Epsilon. Democrat. Jewish. Office: PO Box 66787 Baton Rouge LA 70896-6787

LEVINE, JOHN DAVID, lawyer; b. Winona, Minn., June 9, 1936; s. Jerry R. and Marian S. (Shoresman) L.; m. Marcia Weinstein, June 24, 1962; children: James Scott, Karen Sue. BA, Carleton Coll., 1958; JD, Yale U., 1961. Assoc. Dorsey & Whitney, Mpls., 1961-67, ptnr., 1967-93, of counsel, 1994—, chair trial dept., 1978-86, group head trial and adminstrn. group, 1986-93; mem. Legal Advice Clinics, Ltd., Mpls., 1965—; vice chmn., 1981-86, chmn. Lawyers Profl. Responsibility Bd., St. Paul, 1986-89. Chmn. St. Louis Park (Minn.) Referendum Com., 1979; vice chmn. bd. visitors U. Minn. Law Sch., 1987-89, chmn., 1989-91; trustee Carleton Coll., Northfield, Minn., 1979-92; bd. dirs. Walker Art Ctr., Mpls., 1983-89. Leadership scholar Edward John Noble Found., N.Y., 1958; recipient Disting. Svc. award Carleton Coll., 1978. Fellow Am. Coll. Trial Lawyers, Am. Bar Found.; mem. ABA, Minn. Bar Assn. (chmn. ad hoc com. on ct. unification 1983-84), Minn. State Bar Found. (past bd. dirs., past pres.), Minn. State Bar Assn. (chmn. long range planning com. 1979-82), Hennepin County Bar Found. (past bd. dirs., past officer 1970-72, Outstanding Svc. award 1986, Disting. Svc. award 1995). Office: Dorsey & Whitney 220 S 6th St Minneapolis MN 55402-4502

LEVINE, JOSEPH MANNEY, lawyer; b. Bklyn., Jan. 6, 1948; s. Albert A. and Frances D. (Toorock) L.; m. Sheila R. Gluck, July 31, 1969; children: Adam J., Matthew J. BA, Syracuse U., 1968; JD, Columbia U., 1972. Bar: N.Y. 1972. Assoc. Norton, Sacks, Mollineaux & Pastore, N.Y.C., 1972; atty. advisor Office of Gen. Counsel, U.S. Dept. Commerce, Washington, 1972-79, dep. asst. gen. counsel for adminstrn., 1979-84; chief counsel MBDA, Washington, 1984-88, EDA, Washington, 1988-94; sr. counsel Office Gen. Counsel, 1994—; 1st vice chairperson, bd. dirs. Dept. of Commerce, Fed. Credit Union, Washington, 1981—. Pres. Aspen Hill Park Community Assn., Rockville, Md., 1976-77, bd. dirs. 1975-78. Office: Office Gen Counsel Rm 6087B US Dept Commerce Washington DC 20230

LEVINE, JULES D., materials engineer; b. N.Y.C., June 24, 1937; married; 2 children. BS, Columbia U., 1959; PhD in Physics and Nuclear Engring., MIT, 1963. Mem. tech. staff surface and material rsch. David Sarnoff Rsch. Ctr., RCA Labs., 1963-73, project mgr. flat panel TV, 1973-76, project mgr. cathode R&D, 1976-79; br. mgr. solar cell devel. Tex. Instruments, Dallas, 1979—; vis. lectr. elec. engring. Princeton U., 1971-72, 74-75. Fellow IEEE; mem. Vacuum Soc. (sr.). Office: Texas Instruments Co Mgr Flat Panel Display Project PO Box 655303/MS 8207 Dallas TX 75265*

LEVINE, LAINIE See KAZAN, LAINIE

LEVINE, LAURENCE BRANDT, investment banker; b. N.Y.C., Dec. 17, 1941; s. Martin and Beulah (Brandt) L.; m. Laura Lynn Vitale; 1 child, Blair Brandt. BA (Francis Biddle prize 1961), Princeton U., 1964; LLB, Stanford U., 1967. V.p., voting shareholder Drexel Burnham Lambert, N.Y.C., 1968-71; corp. planning officer Office of Chmn., Ogden Corp., N.Y.C., 1971-73; pres. Investment Research Assos., West Chester, Pa., 1973-80; sr. v.p., dir. investment banking Kramer Capital Cons., Inc., N.Y.C., 1981; exec. v.p. Henry Ansbacher Inc., N.Y. and London, 1982-84; sr. v.p. Rothschild Inc., N.Y., 1984-86; exec. v.p. and dir. corp. fin. Smith New Ct. Inc., N.Y. and London, 1986-90; chmn. Blair Corp., N.Y. and London, 1990—, dir. First Internat. Fin. Group, Hamburg, London and Bermuda, Landmark Funds Svcs., Inc., N.Y.C.; dir., vice chmn. Signature Fin. Group, Boston; Bd. visitors Stanford U. Law Sch., 1968-71, exec. com., 1970; dir. Musica Sacra, N.Y., 1981-86, Concert Artists Guild, N.Y., 1989-92, Ballet Fla., 1992—, Palm Beach Performing Arts Sch., 1992—; adv. bd. Kravis Ctr., 1991—. With USMCR, 1961-65. Mem. City Athletic Club, Harmonie Club, St. James Club (London), Princeton Club (N.Y.), Gentlemen of the Garden (Palm Beach), Soc. Four Arts (Palm Beach), Mar-a-Lago (Palm Beach), Old Oaks Country Club (Purchase, N.Y.), Loch Lomond Club (Scotland). Office: 250 Royal Palm Way Ste 205 Palm Beach FL 33480-4309

LEVINE, LAURENCE HARVEY, lawyer; b. Cleve., Aug. 23, 1946; s. Theodore and Celia (Chaikin) Levine; m. Mary M. Conway, May 13, 1978; children: Abigail, Adam, Sarah. BA cum laude, Case Western Res. U., 1968; JD, Northwestern U., 1971. Bar: Ill. 1971, U.S. Dist. Ct. (no. dist.) Ill. 1972, U.S. Ct. Appeals (6th, 7th, 10th and D.C. cirs.). Law clk. to presiding judge U.S. Ct. Appeals (6th cir.), Detroit, 1971-72; assoc. Kirkland & Ellis, Chgo., 1972-76; ptnr. Latham & Watkins, Chgo., 1976—. Bd. editors Northwestern Law Rev., 1968-71. Mem. ABA, Chgo. Bar Assn., Mid-Am. Club. Office: Latham & Watkins Sears Tower Ste 5800 Chicago IL 60606

LEVINE, LAURENCE WILLIAM, lawyer; b. N.Y.C., Apr. 9, 1931; s. Robert L. and Molly (Brunner) L. B.A., Union Coll., 1952; LL.B., Harvard U., 1955. Bar: N.Y. 1958. Teaching fellow Def. Studies Program, Harvard U., 1955-56; aide to Adlai Stevenson N.Y.C., 1956-57; office mgr. N.Y. com. Stevenson, Kefauver, Wagner, 1956; sec. N.Y. com. for Dem. Voters, 1962-66; ptnr. Walsh & Levine (merged with Bigham Englar Jones & Houston 1990), N.Y.C., 1958—; sec.-treas. Kabuki Japanese Restaurant, N.Y.C., 1958-80; counsel Northeast Airlines, N.Y.C., 1958-67, Brit. Eagle Airlines, 1963-69, Aerolineas Argentinas, 1960—, Banco de la Nacion Argentina, N.Y.C., 1972-79, Banco de Intercambio Regional Argentina, 1977-80; ptnr. San Francisco Mdse. Mart, 1964-84, Holiday Inn-Union Sq., 1969-89, Kaanapoli Hotel, Hawaii, Hilton Hotel, Pasadena, Calif., 1969-88, Gray Lines, Inc., San Francisco, 1980—, Investco Mortgage Co. of Boston, 1975—, Southern Cone Pub. Co., 1980-86, Arion Press, San Francisco, 1979—, Calix and Corolla; dir. Alaska Airline, 1966-68, Stanley Aviation Corp., 1966-73, Foothill Group, 1972-80, Security Nat. Bank, 1983-84, Pan Australian Fund, 1972-74, N.Y. Venture Fund., Venture Income Plus, R.P. F. Funds of Am., 1984—; liquidator Transcontinental Airlines, 1960-63; chmn. creditors com. Am. Hydrofoil Co., 1965-68, Imperial 400 Motels, 1967-74, Harvard Industries; treas., co-owner Games Mag., 1980-81; sec., dir. Games Mag., 1978-80; pub. mem. Blue Cross/Blue Shield, Downtown Eye and Ear Hosp. N.Y.C., 1978-93; sec. Sale Tilney (N.A.), Inc., 1987-90. Author: Gullibles Travels Thru Harvard, 1955, U.S.-China Relations, 1972; contbr. to: East-Europe mag., 1969, Cambio Mag., Argentina, Harvard Law Sch. Bull, N.Y. Times; Argentine newspapers Rev. of River Plate. Treas. Citizens for McCarthy, 1968; mem. Coun. on State Priorities State N.Y., 1982; trustee Bklyn. Poly. Prep. Country Day Sch., 1992. Mem. Assn. of Bar of City of N.Y., N.Y. County Lawyers Assn., Argentine-Am. C. of C. (pres. 1985-87, bd. dirs. 1972-94), Downtown Assn., Goergetown Club, Harvard Club. Home: 245 Everglades Ave Palm Beach FL 33480-3719 Office: Bigham Englar Jones et al 22d Fl 14 Wall St New York NY 10005-2101

LEVINE, LAWRENCE STEVEN, lawyer; b. Bklyn., Mar. 30, 1934; s. Harry and Bess (Feiner) L.; m. Linda Robbins, June 16, 1957; children: Lauren Victoria, Audrey Elizabeth, Hilary Anne. AB, Colgate U., 1955; LLB, Yale U., 1958. Bar: N.Y. 1958, U.S. Supreme Ct. 1973. Asst. U.S. Atty. Ea. Dist. N.Y. U.S. Dept. Justice, N.Y.C., 1958-62; assoc. firm Kronish & Lieb, N.Y.C., 1962-63; ptnr. Beldock Levine & Hoffman, N.Y.C., 1964—; vis. instr. Harvard Law Sch., 1991. Bd. dirs. Jewish Fund for Justice, 1984—, chair, 1988—; mem. nat. bd. New Jewish Agenda, 1980-89, New Outlook Mag., 1982-90; trustee YM-YWHA's Greater N.Y., Harry Levine Meml. Found., 1965—, Riverdale Coutnry Sch., 1979-89. Mem. Fed. Bar Assn., N.Y. County Lawyers Assn., N.Y. State Dist. Attys. Assn., N.Y.

Civil Liberties Union (cooperating counsel), Yale Club. Democrat. Home: 122 E 76th St New York NY 10021-2833 Office: Beldock Levine & Hoffman 99 Park Ave New York NY 10016

LEVINE, LEON, retail executive; b. 1937; married. Student, Wingate Coll., U. Miami. V.p. Hub Dept. Store Inc., Rockingham, N.C., 1954-57; pres. Union Craft Co. Inc., Wingate, N.C., 1957-59; with Family Dollar Stores, Matthews, N.C., 1959—, pres., chief exec. officer, now chmn., treas., also bd. dirs. Office: Family Dollar Stores Inc PO Box 1017 Charlotte NC 28201-1017*

LEVINE, LEWIS E., retail executive; b. 1933; married. Student, U. N.C., Wake Forest U. Pres. Super Discount Stores Inc., 1962-70; with Family Dollar Store, Matthews, N.C., 1970-74, 75—, chief operating officer, exec. v.p., pres., 1977-87, also bd. dirs.; with Rite-Aid Co., Harrisburg, Pa., 1974. Served with USAR, 1954-74. Lodge: Masons. Office: Family Dollar Stores Inc PO Box 25800 Charlotte NC 28229-5800

LEVINE, LOUIS DAVID, museum director, archaeologist; b. N.Y.C., June 4, 1940; s. Moe Wolf and Jeanne (Greenwald) L.; m. Dorothy Abrams, Dec. 30, 1962 (div. 1991); children: Sarra L., Samuel E. Student, Brandeis U., 1960; BA with honours, U. Pa., 1962, PhD with distinction, 1969. Instr. of Hebrew U. Pa., Phila., 1966-69; asst. curator Royal Ont. Mus., Toronto, Can., 1969-75, assoc. curator, 1975-80, curator, 1981, assoc. dir., 1987-90; asst. commr., dir. N.Y. State Mus., Albany, 1990—; vis. sr. lectr. Hebrew U., Jerusalem, 1975-76; vis. prof. U. Copenhagen, 1985; asst. prof. U. Toronto, 1969-74, assoc. prof. U. Toronto, 1974-81, prof., 1981-90; dir. Seh Gabi Expdn., western Iran, 1971-73, dir. Mahidasht Project, western Iran, 1975-79. Author: Two Stelae from Iran, 1972, The Neo-Assyrian Zagros, 1974; editor: Mountains and Lowlands, 1977; contbr. articles to profl. jours. NDEA fellow U. Pa., 1962-65, Fulbright fellow, 1965, W.F. Albright fellow, Am. Schs. of Oriental Rsch., 1966, fellow Inst. for Advanced Studies, Hebrew U. Mem. Brit. Inst. of Persian Studies, Brit. Sch. of Archaeology in Iraq, Am. Assn. Mus., Am. Oriental Soc. Jewish. Avocations: woodworking, music. Office: NY State Mus Cultural Edn Ctr Rm 3099 Albany NY 12230

LEVINE, MADELINE GELTMAN, Slavic literatures educator, translator; b. N.Y.C., Feb. 23, 1942; d. Herman and Nettie (Kritman) Geltman; m. Steven I. Levine; children: Elaine, Daniel. B.A., Brandeis U., 1962; M.A., Harvard U., 1964, Ph.D., 1971. Asst. prof. Grad Sch. CUNY, N.Y.C., 1971-74; assoc. prof. U. N.C., Chapel Hill, 1974-80, prof., 1980-94, Kenan prof. Slavic lits., 1994—, chmn. dept. Slavic langs., 1979-87, 94—; chmn. joint com. on Ea. Europe, Am. Coun. Learned Socs.-Social Sci. Rsch. Coun., 1989-92. Translator: A Memoir of the Warsaw Uprising (Miron Bialoszewski), 1977, 2d edit. 1991, The Poetry of Osip Mandelstam: God's Grateful Guest (Ryszard Przybylski), 1987, Beginning With My Streets: Essays and Recollections (Czeslaw Milosz), 1992, A Year of the Hunter (Czeslaw Milosz), 1994; translator with Francine Prose: A Scrap of Time and Other Stories (Ida Fink), 1986, 2d edit., 1995; author: Contemporary Polish Poetry, 1925-75, 1981. NEH fellow, 1984; recipient (with Francine Prose) award for lit. translation PEN-America, 1988. Mem. Am. Assn. for Advancement of Slavic Studies, Polish Inst. of Arts and Scis. Am., Am. Assn. Tchrs. of Slavic and East European Langs., Am. Literary Translators Assn., Pen-Am. Home: 5001 Whitehorse Rd Hillsborough NC 27278-9399 Office: U NC 421 Dey Hall CB # 3165 Chapel Hill NC 27599

LEVINE, MARK LEONARD, lawyer; b. Bath, Maine, Mar. 6, 1945; s. Saul and Sophie Gertrude (Greenblatt) L.; m. Stephanie M. von Hirschberg, Nov. 9, 1989. AB, Columbia U., 1966, MS in Journalism, 1979; JD, NYU, 1969. Bar: N.Y. 1969, U.S. Dist. Ct. (so. and ea. dists.) N.Y. 1971. Assoc. White & Case, N.Y.C., 1969-78; pub. Scarf Press, N.Y.C., 1979-85; pvt. practice law N.Y.C., 1981-85; of counsel Sullivan & Worcester, N.Y.C., 1985-88, ptnr., 1988—. Author: Negotiating a Book Contract: A Guide for Authors, Agents and Lawyers, 1988; co-editor: The Tales of Hoffman, 1970, The Complete Book of Bible Quotations, 1986; contbg. editor Small Press Mag., 1986; contbr. articles to profl. jours. Campaign coord. McCarthy for Pres., Marshfield, Wis., 1968; dep. campaign mgr. Perrotta for Comptr./Com. to Re-elect John Lindsay Mayor, N.Y.C., 1969; cons. McGovern for Pres. Com., Albany, N.Y., 1972. Recipient Citation of Appreciation Laymen's Nat. Bible Com., 1979. Mem. Assn. of Bar of City N.Y., Authors Guild, Am. Book Producers Assn. (bd. dirs. 1984-87, v.p. 1986-87), B'nai B'rith Youth Orgn. (internat. v.p. 1963-64). Democrat. Jewish. Avocations: reading, chess, movies. Office: Sullivan & Worcester 767 3rd Ave New York NY 10017-2023

LEVINE, MELDON EDISES, lawyer, former congressman; b. Los Angeles, June 7, 1943; s. Sid B. and Shirley B. (Blum) L.; children: Adam Paul, Jacob Caplan, Cara Emily. AB, U. Calif., Berkeley, 1964; MPA, Princeton U., 1966; JD, Harvard U., 1969. Bar: Calif. 1970, D.C. 1972. Assoc. Wyman, Bautzer, Rothman & Kuchel, 1969-71; legis. asst. U.S. Senate, Washington, 1971-73; ptnr. Levine Krom & Unger, Beverly Hills, Calif., 1973-77; mem. Calif. Assembly, Sacramento, 1977-82, 98th-102d Congresses from 27th Calif. dist., Washington, 1983-93; ptnr. Gibson, Dunn & Crutcher, L.A., 1993—. Author: The Private Sector and the Common Market, 1968; contbr. articles to various publs. Co-pres. Builders for Peace; mem. governing bd. U.S.-Israel Sci. and Tech. Commn., So. Calif. chpt. Anti-Defamation League, So. Calif. chpt. Am. Jewish Com., So. Calif. chpt. Am. Jewish Congress, So. Calif. chpt. NAACP Legal Def. Fund, U. Judaism, City of Hope, U. Calif. Alumni Coun.; mem. amateur baseball team Hollywood Stars, 1971—. Mem. Calif. Bar Assn., Los Angeles Bar Assn.

LEVINE, MELVIN CHARLES, lawyer; b. Bklyn., Nov. 12, 1930; s. Barnet and Jennie (Iser) L. BCS, NYU, 1952; LLB, Harvard U., 1955. Bar: N.Y. 1956, U.S. Supreme Ct. 1964. Assoc., Kriger & Haber, Bklyn., 1956-58, Black, Varian & Simons, N.Y.C., 1959; sole practice, N.Y.C., 1959—; devel. multiple dwelling housing. Mem. N.Y. County Lawyers Assn. (civil ct. com., housing ct. com., uniform housing ct. rules com., liaison to Assn. Bar City of N.Y. on selection of housing and civil ct. judges, com. on judiciary task force on tort reform). Democrat. Jewish. Home: 146 Waverly Pl New York NY 10014-3848 Office: 271 Madison Ave Ste 1404 New York NY 10016-1001

LEVINE, MICHAEL, public relations executive, author; b. N.Y.C., Apr. 17, 1954; s. Arthur and Virginia (Gaylor) L. Student, Rutgers U., 1978. Owner, operator TV News Mag., Los Angeles, 1977-83; owner Levine/Schneider Pub. Rels., now Levine Comms. Office, Inc., Los Angeles, 1982—; mem. Gov.'s adv. bd. State Calif., Sacramento, 1980-82; pres., owner Aurora Pub., L.A., 1986—; moderator Thought Forum; lectr. in field. Author: The Address Book: How to Reach Anyone Who's Anyone, 1984, The New Address Book, 1986, The Corporate Address Book, 1987, The Music Address Book, 1989, Environmental Address Book, 1991, Kid's Address Book, 1991, Guerrilla P.R., Lessons at Halfway Point, Take It From Me; pub., writer For Consideration newsletter. Mem. Ronald Reagan Pres.'s Libr.; founder The Actor's Conf., Aurora Charity, 1987; bd. dirs. Felice Found., Micah Ctr.; adv. bd. Dare America. Mem. TV Acad. Arts and Scis., Entertainment Industries Coun., Musician's Assistance Program, West Hollywood C. of C. (bd. dirs. 1980-82). Jewish. Office: 433 N Camden Dr 4th Flr Beverly Hills CA 90210

LEVINE, MURRAY, psychology educator; b. Bklyn., Feb. 24, 1928; s. Israel and Birdie (Cutler) L.; m. Adeline Gordon, June 15, 1952; children: David Israel, Zachary Howard. BS, CCNY, 1949; MA in Psychology, U. Pa., 1951, PhD in Psychology, 1954; JD, SUNY, Buffalo, 1983. Bar: N.Y. 1984; lic. psychologist, N.Y.; diplomate in clin. psychology Am. Bd. Profl. Psychology. Psychologist VA, Phila., 1949-57, Deveraux Schs., Devon, Pa., 1957-63; from asst. to assoc. prof. psychology Yale U., New Haven, 1963-68; prof. SUNY, Buffalo, 1968—, Disting. Svc. prof., 1995—. Author: Community Psychology, 1987, 2d edit., 1996, Helping Children, 1992; contbr. articles to profl. jours. Chmn. bd. dirs. Citizens Cleaning House Hazardous Wastes, Falls Church, Va., 1983—; U.S. adv. bd. Child Abuse and Neglect. Mem. APA (fellow sects. 12, 27, 41, disting. contbns. award 1987, teaching and mentoring award 1992), APLS. Home: 74 Colonial Cir Buffalo NY 14213-1467

LEVINE, NAOMI BRONHEIM, university administrator; b. N.Y.C., Apr. 15, 1923; d. Nathan and Malvina (Mermelstein) Bronheim; m. Leonard Levine, Apr. 11, 1948; 1 dau., Joan. B.A., Hunter Coll., 1944; LL.B., Columbia, 1946, J.D., 1970. Bar: N.Y. bar 1946. With firm Scaadrett, Tuttle & Chalaire, N.Y.C., 1946-48, Charles Gottleib, N.Y.C., 1948-50; with Am. Jewish Congress, 1950-78, exec. dir., 1972-78; v.p. to sr. v.p. external affairs NYU, 1978—; asst. prof. law and police sci. John Jay Coll., N.Y.C., 1969-73, L.I. U., 1965-69. Author: Schools in Crisis, 1969, The Jewish Poor-an American Awakening, 1974, Politics, Religion and Love, 1990; mem. editorial staff Columbia Law Rev., 1945-46. Bd. dirs. Interracial Council Bus. Opportunities, Am. Women's Econ. Devel. Council; trustee N.Y. UJA-Fedn. Recipient Constl. Law prize Hunter Coll., 1944; named to Hall of Fame, 1972. Office: 70 Washington Sq S New York NY 10012-1019

LEVINE, NORMAN GENE, insurance company executive; b. N.Y.C., Sept. 14, 1926; s. Harris J. and Dorothy S. (Podolsky) L.; m. Sandra Leibow, Dec. 11, 1969; children—Linda, Daniel, Donald. Student, U. Wis.-Madison, 1943-48. Agt. Aetna Life Ins. Co., N.Y.C., 1948-56; supr. Aetna Life Ins. Co., 1956-59, gen. agt., 1959-75; mng. gen. agt. Mut. Benefit Life Ins. Co. in No. Calif., San Francisco, 1975-91; br. mgr. Sun Life of Can., 1991—; pres. Levine Fin. Group, 1975—; internat. speaker in field; past div. v.p. Million Dollar Round Table; nat. chmn. Life Underwriters Tng. Council, 1983-84; nat. pres. Gen. Agts. and Mgrs. Conf., 1986-87. Author: How to Build a $100,000,000 Aggency in Five Years or Less, Yes You can, Life Insurance to Diversification, Field Guide to World Class Selling; editor: bi-weekly news report Probe; contbr. numerous articles to profl. jours.; author tapes on ins., mgmt., photography, Americanism. Past mem. bd. dirs. Calif. Law Enforcement Needs Com. Served with AUS, 1944-46, ETO. Recipient Julian Myrick award, 1969, John Newton Russell Meml. award, 1986; named to Hall of Fame Gen. Agts. and Mgrs. Conf., 1982. Mem. N.Y.C. Assn. Life Underwriters (pres. 1967-68), N.Y. State Assn. Life Underwriters (pres. 1968-69), Nat. Assn. Life Underwriters (pres. 1974-75, dir. polit. action com. 1967-69), N.Y.C. Life Mgrs. Assn. (pres. 1974-75), Assn. Advanced Life Underwriters, Am. Soc. C.L.U.s, San Francisco Gen. Agts. and Mgrs. Assn. (pres. 1983), Golden Key Soc., Linnaean Soc., San Francisco C. of C., Audubon Soc., Am. Israel Friendship League (trustee). Mem. Order B'nai Zion (pres. 1964-67). Home: 251 Crest Rd Woodside CA 94062-2310 Office: 1 California St San Francisco CA 94111-5401 *Profit and concern for people are not mutually exclusive and, in fact, people working in a synergistic relationship produce greater profit and general well-being. Democracy with all its problems is still clearly the best of all available methods of government; capitalism and free enterprise create the competition and reward that best challenge the human mind and body; and freedom to "stand tall" with faith, integrity and dignity are the basis for one's conscience and a guide for society's morality.*

LEVINE, PAMELA GAIL, business owner; b. Alameda, Calif., Nov. 20, 1942; d. Carl B. and Lucille N. (Lua) Leverenz; m. George David Barth (div. 1974); children, Claudia Anne, Shanette Michelle; m. Leonard Stuart Levine; children: Leslie, Julie, Susan, Stuart Carl. BA in Archtl. Design/Fine Arts, U. Calif., Berkeley, 1965. Designer Trude of Calif., San Francisco, 1965-66; tchr. TWA, Kansas City, Mo., 1966-69; ptnr., owner, archtl. designer Leverenz of N.Y., 1970—; owner, designer Ressco, Katonah, N.Y., 1974—; cons. archtl. design and real estate devel.; founder, owner Sintec-Internat. Bus. Opportunities, 1989—. Designer of Sets/Costumes, Chappaqua Drama Group, 1973—. Devel. com. Mount Holyoke Coll., S. Hadley, Mass., 1987—; co-founder Looking Glass Players, Mt. Kisco, N.Y., 1985—; active Jr. League, Caramoor, Katonah Mus. Mem. No. Westchester Ctr. for the Arts (exec. com., v.p. bd. dirs., bd. dirs. devel. com., co-chmn. bldg. com.), Chappaqua Drama Group (bd. dirs.). Republican. Avocations: painter, costume design, set design, doll design, artist. Home: RR 6 Katonah NY 10536-9806 Office: Real Estate Support Svcs PO Box 574 Katonah NY 10536-0574

LEVINE, PAUL MICHAEL, paper industry executive, consultant; b. Bklyn., Apr. 15, 1934; s. Isaac Bert and Jessie Sue (Palevsky) L.; m. Lois Jaffin, June 11, 1954 (div.); children: Daniella Sarah, Julie Ann, Carl Joseph; m. 2d Noelle Tenedou, July 14, 1974; children: Simone Allana, Alexander Owen. A.B. in Econs., Harvard Coll., 1954; A.M. in Internat. Econs., Fletcher Sch. Internat. Law and Diplomacy, 1955. Sales mgr. U.S. Industries, Stamford, Conn., 1956-61; chief exec. officer subs. cos. Parsons and Whittemore-Black Clawson, N.Y.C., 1962-69; dep. adminstr. City of N.Y., 1970-72; v.p. S&S Corrugated Paper Machinery Co., Bklyn., 1973-76, Continental Group, Stamford, Conn., 1977-83; chmn. New Lehigh Corrugated Products, Farmingdale, N.Y., United Container Corp., Phila.; lectr., fellow Yale U., U. Conn., Fordham U., 1979-90; bd. dirs. Seidman, Friant, Levine Ltd., N.Y.C.; chmn. Windsor Mktg., Inc., Tulsa, Internat. Creative Data Industries, Inc., Bethel, Conn., Neeltran Inc., New Milford, Conn., Shulz Electric Corp., New Haven, Conn. Author: Proceedings 6th World Forestry Congress, 1966; editor: Study of Peoria County Model Program, 1970, Practical Exporting, 1962, The Role of Venture Capital in Europe and the World. Trustee Hartman Regional Theatre, Stamford, 1981-82; bd. dirs. Ridgefield Orch., 1978-83, Bklyn. Arts and Culture Assn., 1973-92. Mem. Turnaround Mgmt. Assn., Explorers Club. Democrat. Jewish. Office: Paul M Levine & Assocs 466 Ridgebury Rd Ridgefield CT 06877-1228 *Creativity, innovation and laughter are the glories of the world.*

LEVINE, PETER HUGHES, physician, health facility administrator; b. Everett, Mass., Nov. 13, 1938; s. Louis and Helen (Hughes) L.; m. Catherine Brooks Holst, Aug. 26, 1962; children: Thomas H., William H., James L. BS, Tufts U., 1960; MD, Tufts U., Boston, 1964. Diplomate Am. Bd. Internal Medicine, Am. Bd. Hematology. Hematology fellow Tufts - N.E. Med. Ctr., Boston, 1967-69; hematologist Andrews AFB Referral Hosp., Washington, 1969-71; dir. blood coagulation lab. and hemophilia ctr. Tufts - N.E. Med. Ctr., Boston, 1971-75; chmn. dept. medicine Worcester (Mass.) Meml. Hosp., 1975-90, dir. Blood Rsch. Lab., 1975—; pres., chief exec. officer Med. Ctr. of Cen. Mass., Worcester, 1990—; asst. prof. medicine Tufts U. Sch. Medicine, Boston, 1971-75; prof. medicine U. Mass. Med. Sch., Worcester, 1975—. Contbr. 164 articles to med. jours., 131 published abstracts in area of hematology. Med. dir. Nat. Hemophilia Found., N.Y.C., 1983-87; pres. Worcester County Music Assn., 1989-92; trustee Worcester Poly. Inst., 1990—, Mass. Biotech. Rsch. Inst., 1990—, Worcester Bus. Devel. Com., 1992—, United Way Ctrl. Mass., 1993—; trustee and exec. com. mem. Mass. Hosp. Assn., 1992—. Maj. USAF, 1969-71. Recipient Disting. Tchr. award Tufts U. Sch. Medicine, Boston, 1973, 75, Outstanding Med. Educator, U. Mass. Med. Sch., Worcester, 1981, 85, 86, 88, 89, 91, House Staff Disting. Tchr., Worcester Meml. Hosp., 1980, 87, 88, Murray Thelin Award for Rsch. Nat. Hemophilia Found., 1987. Fellow ACP; mem. Am. Soc. Hematology, Am. Fedn. Clin. Rsch. Achievements include patent pending on cure of hemophilia by gene therapy; development of model program for home therapy of hemophilia; research on production and effects of leukocyte-generated oxidants, on omega-3 fatty acids, prostanoids, and platelet and leukocyte function. Office: Med Ctr Ctrl Mass 119 Belmont St Worcester MA 01605-2903

LEVINE, PHILIP, poet, educator; b. Detroit, Jan. 10, 1928; s. A. Harry and Esther Gertrude (Priscol) L.; m. Frances Artley, July 12, 1954; children: Mark, John, Teddy. B.A., Wayne State U., 1950, A.M., 1955; M.F.A., U. Iowa, 1957, studied with John Berryman, 1954. Instr. U. Iowa, 1955-57; instr. Calif. State U., Fresno, 1958—; prof. English Calif. State U., 1969-92, Tufts U.; tchr. Princeton U., Columbia U., U. Calif., Berkeley.; Elliston lectr. poetry U. Cin.; poet-in-residence Vassar Coll., Nat. U. Australia; chmn. lit. panel Nat. Endowment Arts, 1985; adj. prof. NYU, Spring, 1984; Univ. prof. Brown U., spring 1985; tchr. NYU, U. Iowa, Vanderbilt U. Author: On the Edge, 1961, Silent in America: Vivas for Those Who Failed, 1965, Not This Pig, 1968, 5 Detroits, 1970, Thistles, 1970, Pili's Wall, 1971, Red Dust, 1971, They Feed They Lion, 1972, 1933, 1974, On The Edge & Over, 1976, The Names of the Lost, 1976 (Lenore Marshall award Best Am. Book Poems 1976), 7 Years from Somewhere, 1979 (Nat. Book Critics Circle prize 1979, Notable Book award Am. Libr. Assn. 1979), Ashes, 1979 (Nat. Book Critics Circle prize 1979, Nat. Book award 1979), Don't Ask, 1979, One for the Rose, 1981, Selected Poems, 1984, Sweet Will, 1985, A Walk with Tom Jefferson, 1988 (Bay Area Book Reviewers award), What Work Is, 1991 (L.A. Times Book Prize 1991, Nat. Book award for poetry, 1991), New Selected Poems, 1991, Earth, Stars, and Writers, 1992, The Bread of Time: Toward an Autobiography, 1994, Simple Truth, 1994 (Pulitzer Prize for poetry 1995); editor: (with Henri Coulette) Character and Crisis, 1966, (with E. Trejo) The Selected Poems of Jaime Sabines, (with Ada Long) Off the Map, The Selected Poems of Gloria Fuertes, 1984, (with D. Wojahn and B. Henderson) The Pushcart Prize XI, 1986, The Essential Keats, 1987. Active anti-Vietnam war movement. Recipient Joseph Henry Jackson award San Francisco Found., 1961, The Chaplebrook Found. award, 1968, Frank O'Hara Meml. prize, 1973; Amer. Academy of Arts and Letters Award of Merit, 1974; Levinson Prize, 1974; Harriet Monroe Meml. prize for poetry, 1976; Golden Rose award New Eng. Poetry Soc., 1985, Ruth Lilly Poetry Prize, Modern Poetry Assn. and Am. Council Arts, 1987, Elmer Bobst award NYU, 1990, Lit. Lion New York Public Library 1993; named outstanding lectr. Calif. State U., Fresno, 1971, outstanding prof. Calif. State U. System, 1972; Stanford U. poetry fellow, 1957, Nat. Inst. Arts and Letters grantee, 1973, Guggenheim fellow, 1973-74, 80; Nat. Endowment for Arts grantee, 1969, 70 (refused), 76, 81, 87. Home: 4549 N Van Ness Blvd Fresno CA 93704-3727 *My hope is to write poetry for people for whom there are no poems.*

LEVINE, PHILIP, classics educator; b. Lawrence, Mass., Sept. 8, 1922; s. Samuel and Jennie (Derdak) L.; m. Dinnie Moseson, June 19, 1955; children—Jared Elliott, Harlan Alcon. A.B., Harvard, 1946, A.M., 1948, Ph.D., 1952; DHL (hon.), U. Judaism, 1986. Instr., asst. prof. classics Harvard, 1952-59; assoc. prof. classical langs. U. Tex. at Austin, 1959-61; assoc prof., prof. classics UCLA, 1961-91, prof. emeritus, 1991—; dean div. humanities U. Calif. at Los Angeles, 1965-83; Biggs resident lectr. Washington U., 1993; info. officer Coun. U. Calif. Emeriti Assn. Author: Lo Scriptorium Vercellese da S. Eusueblo ad Attone, 1958, St. Augustine, City of God, Books 12-15, 1966; editor: Latin lt. sect. Twayne World Author Series, 1964—; adv. editor, U. Calif. Publs. in Classical Studies, 1963-72; assoc. editor, contbr. to U. Calif. Studies in Classical Antiquity, 1967-75, sr. co-editor, 1975-78; mem. editorial bd. Classical Antiquity, 1986-93. Mem. rev. com., sr. fellowship program Nat. Endowment for Humanities, 1966-70; bd. govs. U. Judaism, 1968-90, coun. visitors, 1990-94, acad. adv. coun., 1994—. With AUS, 1943-46. Sheldon fellow Italy; Guggenheim fellow; Fulbright Research grantee; recipient Bromberg Humanities award; decorated Cavaliere dell' Ordine al Merito della Repubblica Italiana. Mem. Am. Philol. Assn. (dir. 1968-70), Mediaeval Acad. Am. (exec. council 1969-72), Renaissance Soc., Am. Philol. Assn., Pacific Coast (chmn. gen. lit. 1964-65), Phi Beta Kappa. Home: 224 S Almont Dr Beverly Hills CA 90211-2507 Office: U Calif Dept Classics Los Angeles CA 90095

LEVINE, RACHMIEL, physician; b. Poland, Aug. 26, 1910; came to U.S., 1936, naturalized, 1944; s. Solomon and Bessie (Benzion) L.; m. Anne Gussack, Mar. 4, 1943; children—Judith Ann, Daniel Saul. B.A., McGill U., 1932, M.D., 1936. Intern, then resident Michael Reese Hosp., Chgo., 1936-38; research fellow Michael Reese Hosp., 1939, dir. dept. metabolism, 1942-60, chmn. dept. madicine, 1952-60, dir. med. edn., 1952-60; professorial lectr. physiology U. Chgo., 1945-60; prof., chmn. dept. medicine N.Y. Med. Coll., 1960-71; exec. med. dir. City of Hope Med. Center, Duarte, Calif., 1971-78; dir. research City of Hope Med. Center, 1978—; Active United Jewish Appeal, Chgo., 1959-60; Cons. NSF, 1956-59, mem. bd. found. fund psychiat. research, 1958-61; Jakobaeus lectr. Karolinska Inst., Stockholm, 1963. Contbr. numerous articles to profl. jours. Fellow Am. Acad. Arts and Scis.; mem. Am. Physiol. Soc., Nat. Acad. Scis., Endocrine Soc. (Upjohn award 1957), A.C.P., Assn. Am. Physicians, N.Y. Acad. Medicine, Chgo. Inst. Medicine, Am. Diabetes Assn. (Banting medal 1961, council 1958, pres. 1964-65), Internat. Diabetes Assn. (pres. 1967-70, hon. pres. 1970—), Harvey Soc. (pres. 1967-68, Gairdner award 1971, Joslin medal 1972). Home: 2024 Canyon Rd Arcadia CA 91006-1503 Office: City of Hope Med Ctr Duarte CA 91010

LEVINE, RHEA JOY COTTLER, anatomy educator; b. N.Y.C., Nov. 26, 1939; d. Zachary Robert Cottler and Hildreth (Abramson) Cottler Rosenfeld; m. Stephen Maxwell Levine, June 16, 1960; children: Elizabeth, Michael Gordon, Zachary Thomas. AB summa cum laude, Smith Coll., 1960; MS, NYU, 1963, PhD, 1966. Lab. instr. NYU Sch. Commerce, N.Y.C., 1963-64; postdoctoral fellow, instr. histology Yale U. Sch. Medicine, New Haven, 1966-68; rsch. assoc. U. Pa. Sch. Medicine, Phila., 1968-69; asst. prof. anatomy Med. Coll. Pa., Phila., 1969-74, assoc. prof. anatomy, 1974-80, prof. anatomy, 1980—, vice chmn., 1988-89; manuscript reviewer numerous sci. journals, Washington and N.Y.C., 1975—; reviewer grant proposals NSF, Washington, 1975—, mem. NIH Study Sect., 1980-84. Contbr. sci. articles to profl. jours. Trustee Richard Stockton Coll. N.J., Pomona, 1983—, chmn. bd. trustees, 1991-94; trustee Smith Coll., 1996—; bd. dirs. Hollybush Festival, Glassboro, N.J., 1987-91, Smith Coll. Friends of Libr., Northampton, Mass., 1968-72. NYU Sch. Medicine summer rsch. fellow, 1960, NSF grad. fellow, 1960-65, A.H. Robins rsch. fellow, 1966, USPHS fellow, 1966-68; grantee Women's and Program project NIH, NSF, 1973—; recipient Founder's Day award NYU, 1966, Smith Coll. medal, 1994. Mem. AAAS, Coalition Jewish Profl. Women South N.J. (steering com.), Am. Assn. Anatomists, Am Soc. Cell Biology, Biophys. Soc. (coun. 1991-94, chair pub. sci. policy com. 1992-94), Histochem. Soc., Soc. Gen. Physiology, Wilderness Med. Soc., N.Y. Acad. Scis., Smith Coll. Club, Woodcrest Country Club (house chair 1983-84), Phi Beta Kappa, Sigma Xi. Jewish. Office: Med Coll Pa/Hahnemann Univ Dept Neurobiology/Anatomy 3200 Henry Ave Philadelphia PA 19129-1137

LEVINE, RICHARD E., lawyer; b. Flushing, N.Y., Aug. 6, 1950; s. Sol and Betty (Broad) L.; m. Lori A. Balter, Oct. 28, 1979; 1 child, Jamie Balter. BS in Mech. Engring., Bucknell U., 1972; JD, U. Md., 1975; LL.M. in Taxation, Georgetown U., 1978. Bar: Md. 1975, U.S. Tax Ct. 1979, D.C. 1980, U.S. Supreme Ct. 1983, U.S. Ct. Appeals (4th cir.) 1984. Assoc. Miles & Stockbridge, Balt., 1978-83, prin., 1983—; adj. prof. U. Md. Law Sch., Balt., 1988. Contbr. articles to profl. jours. Bd. dirs. Har Sinai West Sr. Citizens Housing, Balt., 1983-92. Fellow Am. Coll. Tax Counsel; mem. ABA (tax sect., chair partnerships 1990-92), Md. State Bar Assn. (tax sect. coun. 1983-86), The Center Club (house com. 1990—). Avocations: golf, music. Office: Miles & Stockbridge 10 Light St Baltimore MD 21202-1435

LEVINE, RICHARD JAMES, publishing executive; b. N.Y.C., Jan. 24, 1942; s. Irving Joseph and Dorothy Joyce (Thome) L.; m. Neil Ann Stuckey, June 1, 1963; children: Jonathan Donald, Russell Neilan. BS, Cornell U., 1962; MS with high honors, Columbia U., 1963. Gen. assignment reporter Wall St. Jour., Washington, 1966-67, labor corr., 1967-70, mil. writer, 1970-75, chief econ. writer, outlook columnist, 1975-80; editl. dir./data base pub. Dow Jones & Co., Princeton, N.J., 1980-87, v.p. info. svcs. group, 1987-89, v.p. and editl. dir. info. svcs. group, mem. mgmt. com., 1989-92, v.p., mng. editor info. svcs. segment, mem. mgmt. com., Dow Jones & Co., N.Y.C., 1992-95; v.p. fin. info. svcs. group, mng. editor Dow Jones News Svcs., Dow Jones & Co., N.Y.C., 1995—; pres. Dow Jones AER Co., Inc., 1994—; pres. Econ. Rsch. Co. Inc., 1994—; dep. chmn. UWD GmbH; bd. dirs. Internat. Electronic Pub. Rsch. Ctr. Author: (with others) The Wall Street Journal Views America Tomorrow, 1977. 1st lt. U.S. Army, 1964-66. Columbia U. Pulitzer fellow, 1963-64. Mem. Cornell U. Tower Club, Cornell Mag. Com., Soc. Profl. Journalists, Cornell Club (N.Y.C.), Princeton Indoor Tennis Ctr. Home: 108 Parkside Dr Princeton NJ 08540-4815 Office: Harborside Fin Ctr 600 Plaza Two Jersey City NJ 07311

LEVINE, ROBERT A., cardiologist; b. N.Y.C., Jan. 29, 1953; s. Jules and Shirley (Krupnick) L. AB summa cum laude, Harvard Coll., 1974; MD, Harvard Med. Sch., 1978. Diplomate Am. Bd. Internal Medicine. Intern, resident in medicine Beth Israel Hosp., Boston, 1978-81; fellow in cardiology Mt. Sinai Hosp., N.Y.C., 1981-83; clinical & rsch. fellow Mass. Gen. Hosp., Boston, 1983-85; instr. in medicine Harvard Med. Sch., Boston, 1985-87; asst. prof. medicine Harvard Med. Sch., 1987-94, assoc. prof. medicine, 1994—; staff physician cardiac unit Mass. Gen. Hosp., Boston, 1985—, dir. cardiac ultrasound labs., 1995—; sci. session abstract chmn. Am. Soc. Echocardiography, 1993-95, program chmn., 1996—. Recipient awards NIH, 1985, 87, 95; clinician-scientist, est. investigator Am. Heart Assn., 1986, 91. Office: Mass Gen Hosp Cardiac Ultrasound VBK523 Boston MA 02114

LEVINE, ROBERT ARTHUR, economist, policy analyst; b. Bklyn., July 7, 1930; s. Isaac Bert and Jessie Sue (Palevsky) L.; m. Esther Carol Knudsen, Mar. 2, 1953; children: David Knudsen, Peter Kemmerer, Joseph Karl. BA, Harvard U., 1950, MA, 1951; PhD, Yale U., 1957. Economist Rand Corp., 1957-61, sr. economist, 1962-65, 69-73, 87—; research assoc. Harvard U.

Center Internat. Affairs, 1961-62; asst. dir. for research, plans, programs and evaluation OEO, Washington, 1966-69; pres. N.Y.C.-Rand Inst., 1973-75; dep. dir. Congl. Budget Office, Washington, 1975-79; v.p. System Devel. Corp., Santa Monica, Calif., 1979-85; pres. Canyon Analysts, 1985—; sr. fellow Nat. Security Studies Program, UCLA, 1964-65; vis. prof. public policy Stanford U. Grad. Sch. Bus., 1972; adj. prof. econs. Pepperdine U. Sch. Bus. and Mgmt., 1984. Author: The Arms Debate, 1963, The Poor Ye Need Not Have With You, 1971, Public Planning: Failure and Redirection, 1972, Evaluation Research and Practice, 1981, Still the Arms Debate, 1990, Turmoil and Transition in the Atlantic Alliance, 1991. With USN, 1951-54. Ford Found. grantee, 1969, 85; German Marshall Fund grantee, 1979; Carnegie Corp. grantee, 1986. Mem. Am. Econ. Assn., Inst. Strategic Studies. Club: Beverly Glen Democratic. Home and Office: 10321 Chrysanthemum Ln Los Angeles CA 90077-2812

LEVINE, ROBERT JAY, lawyer; b. Hackensack, N.J., Aug. 7, 1950; s. Nathan R. and Naomi (Bendel) L.; m. Joan Beth Mirviss, Aug. 10, 1975. AB, Brown U., 1972; JD, U. Pa., 1975. Bar: N.Y. 1976, U.S. Dist. (so. and ea. dist.) N.Y. 1976. Assoc. Davis Polk & Wardwell, N.Y.C., 1975-82, ptnr., 1983—; pres. and dir. Sylvan Winds, Inc. Mem. ABA, N.Y. State Bar Assn., Assn. of Bar of City of N.Y., Phi Beta Kappa. Democrat. Jewish. Club: Brown of N.Y.C. Avocations: golf, travel, cooking, film. Home: 115 Central Park W New York NY 10023-4153 Office: Davis Polk & Wardwell 450 Lexington Ave New York NY 10017-3911

LEVINE, ROBERT JOHN, physician, educator; b. N.Y.C., Dec. 29, 1934; s. Benjamin Bernard and Ruth Florence (Schwartz) L.; m. Jeralea Fooshee Hesse, Nov. 28, 1987; children from previous marriage: John Graham, Elizabeth Hurt Braun. Student, Duke U., 1951-54; MD with distinction, George Washington U., 1958. Diplomate Am. Bd. Internal Medicine. Med. house officer Peter Bent Brigham Hosp., Boston, 1958-59, asst. resident in medicine, 1959-60; clin. assoc. Nat. Heart Inst., Bethesda, Md., 1960-62, investigator, 1963-64; chief med. resident VA Hosp., West Haven, Conn., 1962-63; mem. faculty depts. medicine and pharmacology Yale U., New Haven, 1964-73, chief sect. clin. pharmacology, 1966-74, prof. medicine, lectr. pharmacology, 1973—; mem. med. staff Yale-New Haven Med. Ctr., 1964-68, attending physician, 1968—; mem. Conn. Adv. Com. on Foods and Drugs, 1967-82, sec. 1969-71, chmn., 1971-73; mem. adv. com. AIDS program U.S. HHS, 1989-95; cons. Nat. Commn. Protection of Human Subjects of Biomed. and Behavioral Rsch., 1974-78; bd. dirs. Medicine in the Pub. Interest, Inc., 1976—, sec., 1983—. Author: Ethics and Regulation of Clinical Research, 1981, 2d edit., 1986; co-editor: Ethics and Research on Human Subjects: International Guidelines, 1993; editor Clin. Rsch., 1971-76, IRB: Rev. Human Subjects Rsch., 1978—; contbr. numerous articles to profl. jours. Mem. Conn. Humanities Coun., 1983-89, chmn. 1988-89, Coun. Internat. Orgn. Med. Scis., co-chmn. steering com. revision internat. ethical guidelines for biomed.rsch. involving human subjects, 1991-93. Multiple rsch. grantee. Fellow ACP, Am. Coll. Cardiology, The Hastings Ctr.; mem. AAAS (coun. del. 1987-91), Am. Soc. Clin. Investigation, Am. Soc. Clin. Pharmacology and Therapeutics (bd. dirs. 1981-85), Am. Fedn. Clin. Rsch. (nat. coun. 1967-76, exec. com. 1971-76), Am. Soc. Pharmacology and Exptl. Therapeutics (exec. com. 1974-77), Am. Soc. Law, Medicine and Ethics (bd. dirs. 1986—, pres. 1989-90, 94-95), Pub. Responsibility in Medicine and Rsch. (bd. dirs. 1986—), Soc. for Bioethics Consultation (bd. dirs. 1988-94), Sigma Xi, Alpha Omega Alpha. Office: Yale U Sch Medicine 333 Cedar St New Haven CT 06520-8010

LEVINE, ROBERT JOSEPH, secondary school administrator; b. Bklyn., Jan. 7, 1945; s. Robert J. Sr. and Thelma Lillian (Myatt-Coates) L.; m. Marilyn Barbara Sokol, Dec. 24, 1965 (div. Apr. 1970); m. Martha Klein Levine, May 24, 1981; children: Justin David, Ryan Michael. BA in Anthropology, U. Ariz., 1967; MS in Edn., CUNY, 1974, advanced cert. edn. adminstrn./super., 1976. Cert. adv. prof., Md.; supr. and prin., guidance, social studies, N.Y.; supr., prin. Tchr. social studies Intermediate Sch. 128M, N.Y.C., 1968-70, Prospect Heights H.S., Bklyn., 1970-71; tchr. social studies, English, Spanish, TESOL John Jay H.S., Bklyn., 1971-76; guidance counselor Lake Clifton H.S., Balt., 1976-79, Ea. H.S., Balt., 1980-83, Francis M. Wood Alternative H.S., Balt., 1983-85; guidance counselor Balt. Poly. Inst., 1988-92, asst. prin., 1992—; dir. summer opportunity program Friends Sch. of Balt., 1978-86; chmn. guidance adv. panel Balt. City Pub. Schs., 1981-85; chmn. Balt. Nat. Coll. Fair, 1989—. Author: (curriculum document) The History of Brooklyn, 1975. Mem. exec. bd. Hist. Balt. Soc., 1989-92; parent com. Cub Scout Pack 18, Balt., 1990-92. Mem. Nat. Assn. Secondary Sch. Prins., Nat. Assn. Coll. Admission Counselors, Soc. for Applied Anthropology, Pipe Club of Gt. Britain (life). Avocations: bicycling, music, chess. Home: 14 Strongwood Rd Owings Mills MD 21117-2442 Office: Balt Poly Inst 1400 W Cold Spring Ln Baltimore MD 21209

LEVINE, ROBERT SIDNEY, chemical engineer; b. Des Moines, June 4, 1921; s. George Julius and Betty (Dennen) L.; m. Sharon Lorraine White; children: George, Gail, Tamara, Michelle, James. B.S. in Chem. Engring, Iowa State U., 1943; S.M. (Standard Oil Co. Ohio fellow 1947-48), M.I.T., 1946, Sc.D., 1949. With Rocketdyne div. Rockwell Internat. Co., 1948-66; assoc. research dir. NASA, 1966-74; chief liquid rocket tech. Nat. Bur. Standards, Washington, 1974—; chief fire dynamics Nat. Bur. Standards (now Nat. Inst. Standards and Tech.), Washington, 1975—; mem. faculty UCLA, 1962-64, George Washington U., 1977; pres. Combustion Inst., 1974-78; chmn. Am. and Soviet Com. on Fire Rsch. in Housing, 1977-82. Author papers in field; mem. Washington editl. rev. bd. NIST, 1976—. Named Engr. of Year Los Angeles sect. Am. Inst. Chem. Engrs., 1961. Mem. Am. Chem. Soc., AIAA, Nat. Fire Prevention Assn., Soc. Fire Protection Engrs. Home: 19017 Threshing Pl Gaithersburg MD 20879-2150 Office: Nat Inst Standards & Tech Gaithersburg MD 20899

LEVINE, RONALD H., physician, state official; b. N.Y.C., Mar. 30, 1935; m. Elizabeth P. Kanof; children—Mitchell, Rebecca Ann. BS, Union Coll., Schenectady, N.Y., 1955, DSc (hon.), 1990, MD, SUNY-Bklyn., 1959; MPH, U. N.C., 1967. Officer USPHS, Raleigh, N.C., 1963-65; chief communicable disease br. N.C. State Bd. Health, Raleigh, 1965-67, chief community health sect., 1968-73; asst. dir., dep. dir. N.C. Div. Health Services, Raleigh, 1974-81, state health dir., 1981—. Recipient Stevens award N.C. Assn. Local Health Dirs., 1982. Fellow Am. Acad. Pediatrics, Am. Pub. Health Assn., Am. Coll. Preventive Medicine, mem. N.C. Pub. Health Assn. (pres. 1974-75, Reynolds award 1973), Wake County Med. Soc. (pres. 1978), N.C. Med. Soc. Office: Dept Environ Health & Natural Resources PO box 27687 512 N Salisbury St Raleigh NC 27604-1118

LEVINE, RONALD JAY, lawyer; b. Bklyn., June 23, 1953; s. Louis Leon and Marilyn Priscilla (Markovich) L.; m. Cindy Beth Israel, Nov. 18, 1979; children: Merisa, Alisha. BA summa cum laude, Princeton U., 1974; JD cum laude, Harvard U., 1977. Bar: N.Y. 1978, U.S. Dist. Ct. (so. and ea. dists.) N.Y. 1978, D.C. 1980, N.J. 1987, U.S. Supreme Ct. 1982, U.S. Ct. Apeals (2d cir.) 1983, N.J. 1987, U.S. Dist. Ct. N.J. 1987, U.S. Dist. Ct. (we. dist.) N.Y. 1991, U.S. Ct. Appeals (3d cir.) 1991, Pa. 1995. Assoc. Phillips, Nizer, Benjamin, Krim & Ballon, N.Y.C., 1977-80, Debevoise & Plimpton, N.Y.C., 1980-84; assoc. Herrick, Feinstein, N.Y.C., 1984-85, ptnr., 1985—; gen. counsel Greater N.Y. Safety Council, N.Y.C., 1979-81; arbitrator Small Claims Ct. of Civil Ct. of City of N.Y., 1983-85. Mem. Site Plan Rev. Adv. Bd., West Windsor, N.J., 1986, planning bd., 1987. Mem. ABA (litigation sect.), N.Y. State Bar Assn. (chmn. com. on legal edn. and bar admission 1982-92, com. on profl. discipline 1989-90), N.J. State Bar Assn. (product liability com. 1991—, profl. responsibility com. 1992—), Assn. of Bar of City of N.Y. (coun. jud. adminstrn. 1994—, com. on profl. responsibility 1980-83, com. on legal assistance 1983-86, product liability com. 1987-91, trustee career devel. awards 1989-90), Phi Beta Kappa. Home: 6 Arnold Dr Princeton Junction NJ 08550-1521 Office: Herrick Feinstein 2 Park Ave New York NY 10016-5603

LEVINE, RUTH ROTHENBERG, biomedical science educator; b. N.Y.C.; d. Jacob and Jeannette (Bandel) Rothenberg; m. Martin J. Levine, June 21, 1953. B.A. magna cum laude, Hunter Coll., 1938; M.A., Columbia U., 1939; Ph.D., Tufts U., 1955. Asst. prof. sch. medicine Tufts U., 1955-58; asst. prof. pharmacology sch. medicine Boston U., 1958-61, assoc. prof. sch. medicine, 1961-65, prof. sch. medicine, 1965—, univ. prof., 1972—; chmn. grad. div. med. and dental scis. Boston U. Sch. Medicine, 1964-89, assoc. dean grad. biomed. scis., 1981-89, assoc. dean emeritus, 1989—; mem. sci. adv. bd. U.S. EPA, 1976-82, Internat. Joint Commn., State Dept., 1983-89. Author: Pharmacology, Drug Actions and Reactions, 1973, 4th edit., 1990; coord. internat. symposia of subtypes of muscarinic receptors. Fellow AAAS; mem. Am. Soc. Pharmacology and Exptl. Therapeutics (sec.-treas. 1975-76), Biophys. Soc., Am. Chem. Soc., Am. Pharm. Assn., Acad. Scis., Phi Beta Kappa, Sigma Xi. Home: 212 Crafts Rd Chestnut Hill MA 02167-1452 Office: Boston U Sch Medicine Div Med and Dental Scis Boston MA 02118

LEVINE, SANFORD HAROLD, lawyer; b. Troy, N.Y., Mar. 13, 1938; s. Louis and Reba (Semegren) L.; m. Margaret R. Appelbaum, Oct. 29, 1967; children—Jessica Sara, Abby Miriam. A.B., Syracuse U., 1959, J.D., 1961. Bar: N.Y. 1961, U.S. Dist. Ct. (no. dist.) N.Y. 1961, U.S. Dist. Ct. (we. dist.) N.Y. 1979, U.S. Dist. Ct. (ea. and so. dists.) N.Y. 1980, U.S. Ct. Appeals (2d cir.) 1962, U.S. Supreme Ct. 1967. Law asst. to assoc. judge N.Y. Ct. Appeals, Albany and to justice N.Y. Supreme Ct., 1962-66; law asst. to assoc. judge N.Y. Ct. Appeals, Albany, 1964; asst. counsel N.Y. State Temporary Commn. on Constl. Conv., N.Y.C., 1966-67; assoc. counsel SUNY System, Albany, 1967-70, dep. univ. counsel, 1970-78, acting counsel, 1970-71, acting univ. counsel, 1978-79, univ. counsel and vice chancellor legal affairs, 1979—; adj. prof. Sch. of Edn. State U. N.Y., Albany, 1992—; mem. paralegal curriculum adv. com. Schenectady County Community Coll., 1975—. Fellow Am. Bar Found., N.Y. Bar Found.; mem. ABA (ho. dels. 1987-89), N.Y. State Bar Assn., Albany County Bar Assn., Nat. Assn. Coll. and Univ. Attys. (exec. bd. 1979-82, pres. 1986-87), Am. Soc. Pub. Adminstrn., Am. Acad. Healthcare Attys., Nat. Health Lawyers Assn. Editorial bd. Syracuse U. Law Rev., 1960-61; editorial adv. bd. Jour. Coll. and Univ. Law, 1977-81. Home: 1106 Godfrey Ln Schenectady NY 12309-2712 Office: State University Plz Albany NY 12246

LEVINE, SEYMOUR, lawyer; b. Bklyn., Jan. 29, 1924; s. Abraham and Lena (Gitlin) L.; m. Anna Baron, Sept. 6, 1952; children: Ronnie Livia, Alison M. BBA, CCNY, 1949; JD, Harvard U., 1952. Bar: N.Y. 1952, Fla. 1974. Tax lawyer S.D. Leidesdorf and Co., N.Y.C., 1952-58; assoc. Parker, Chapin, Flattau and Klimpl, N.Y.C., 1958-1967, ptnr., 1967-92, of counsel, 1993—; adj. assoc. prof. Inst. of Paralegal Studies, NYU, 1978-86, mem. adv. com.; chmn. of faculty, lectr. Practicing Law Inst., N.Y., Chgo., San Francisco, 1981-85; lectr. on estate planning, N.Y.C., San Francisco, Chgo. Contbr. articles to profl. jours. Pres., bd. dirs. Met. Jewish Geriatric Ctr., Bkyn., 1969—; active Vols. of Legal Svcs., Inc., N.Y.C., 1988—. Sgt. USMC, 1943-46. Fellow Am. Coll. Trust and Estates Counsel; mem. ABA, Fla. Bar Assn., N.Y. State Bar Assn., Assn. of Bar of City of N.Y., Harvard Club of N.Y. Avocation: tennis. Office: Parker Chapin Flattau & Klimpl 1211 Avenue Of The Americas New York NY 10036-8701

LEVINE, SOL, sociologist; b. Greenwood, Miss., Apr. 3, 1922; s. Samuel and Gussie (Kozlove) L.; m. Alice S. Gordon, July 15, 1963; children: Andrea, Pamela, Joshua. BA, Queens Coll., CUNY, 1942; MA, NYU, 1948, PhD, 1953. Instr. dept. sociology Univ. Heights Coll., NYU, 1951-53; from asst. to assoc. prof. social psychology Harvard U. Sch. Pub. Health, Cambridge, Mass., 1956-63, dir. social sci. program, 1963-66; prof. social rels. Johns Hopkins U., 1966-67; prof., dir. div. behavioral scis. Johns Hopkins U. Sch. Hygiene and Pub. Health, 1966-67, prof., chmn. dept. behavioral scis., 1967-72; univ. prof., prof. sociology, prof. pub. health Boston U., 1973-88, dir. univ. profs. program, 1973-76, chmn. dept. sociology, 1976-79, adj. univ. prof., 1988-93, fellow of univ. profs., 1993—; v.p. Henry J. Kaiser Family Found., Palo Alto, Calif., 1988-90; prof. health and social behavior, prof. health policy Harvard Sch. Pub. Health, 1990—, interim chair dept. health & social behavior, 1993-95; sr. scientist New Eng. Med. Ctr., Boston, 1990—; dir. joint program in society and health New England Med. Ctr., Boston, 1990-95; nat. program dir. awards health policy rsch. Robert Wood Johnson Found., 1994—; mem. study vol. agys. Rockefeller Found., 1957; mem. health services research study sect. NIH, 1964-68; mem. Sec.'s adv. com. on health protection and disease prevention HEW, 1969; chmn. alcohol research rev. com. Nat. Inst. on Alcohol Abuse and Alcoholism, 1976-77, mem., 1973-77; bd. dirs. Robert Wood Johnson Clin. Scholars Program, 1978-89. Author: (with others) Ency. Sociology, 1991; co-author: (with Odin Anderson and Gerald Gordon) Non-Group Enrollment for Health Insurance: A Study of Adminstrative Approaches of Blue Cross Plans, 1957, (with Sydney H. Croog) The Heart Patient Recovers, 1978, Life After a Heart Attack, 1982; co-editor: (with Howard E. Freeman and Leo G. Reeder) Handbook of Medical Sociology, 1963, 2d edit., 1972, 3d edit., 1978, (with Howard E. Freeman) 4th edit., 1989, (with Freeman, Orville Brim and Norman Scotch) The Dying Patient, 1970, (with Scotch) Social Stress, 1970, (with Abraham Lilienfeld) Epidemiology and Health Policy, 1986, (with Benjamin Amick, Alvin Tarlov, Diana Chapman Walsh) Society and Health, 1995. Mem. research com. Nat. Edni. TV, 1973-77, mem. nat. adv. council. Mem. Am. Pub. Health Assn., Am. Sociol. Assn. (chmn. med. soc. sect. 1968-69, Leo G. Reeder award 1986), Inst. Medicine-Nat. Acad. Scis. Home: 30 Powell St Brookline MA 02146-3921 Office: The Health Inst New Eng Med Ctr 750 Washington St # 345 Boston MA 02111-1533

LEVINE, SOLOMON BERNARD, business and economics educator; b. Boston, Aug. 10, 1920; s. Isaac William and Sybil (Mannis) L.; m. Elizabeth Jane Billett, Dec. 24, 1943; children: Janet Ruth Levine Thal, Michael Alan, Samuel Billett, Elliott Mannis. AB magna cum laude, Harvard Coll., 1942; cert. Japanese Lang., U. Colo., 1944; MBA with honors, Sch. Bus. Adminstrn., Harvard U., 1947; postgrad., MIT, 1947-49, Ph.D. in Indsl. Econs., 1951. Teaching asst. dept. econs. and social sci. MIT, 1947-49; faculty U. Ill., 1949-69, prof. labor and indsl. relations and Asian studies, 1964-69; prof. bus. and econs. U. Wis.-Madison, 1969-89, prof. emeritus, 1989—, mem. East Asian Studies Program, chmn., 1968-77, co-chmn., 1982-88, dir. Nat. Resource Ctr. for East Asian Studies, 1985-87, participating faculty mem. Indsl. Relations Research Inst.; Fulbright prof. Keio U., Tokyo, 1959; vis. prof. dept. econs. Pa. State U., 1960; vis. prof. labor relations dept. econs. MIT, 1962-63; vis. prof. econs. U. Singapore, 1968; vis. lectr. and research scholar various univs., Indonesia, 1973, Australia, 1973, N.Z., 1973, vis. scholar univs., Japan, 1978, Australia, 1978, N.Z., 1978, Singapore, 1978, South Korea, 1978; vis. prof., sr. scholar Monash U., Australia and Japan, 1981-82, vis. research scholar Macquarie U., Australia, 1985; vis. prof. Internat. U. Japan, 1984; vis. prof. Nanzan U., Nagoya, Japan, 1989-91, U. Hawaii, Manoa, 1991; vis. fellow Swinburne Inst. Tech., Australia, 1992; vis. scholar Japan Ctr. for Mich. Univ., Japan, 1994. labor arbitrator. Author: Industrial Relations in Postwar Japan, 1958, Japanese transl., 1959, (with Hishashi Kawada) Human Resources in Japanese Industrial Development, 1980; co-editor, co-author: chpts. and preface Workers and Employers in Japan: The Japanese Employment Relations System, 1973, (with Koji Taika) Japan's External Economic Relations: Japanese Perspectives, 1991; contbr. to sect. Ency. Americana; chpts. to books, articles to publs. Treas. Stevenson for Pres. Campaign, Champaign-Urbana, Ill., 1952; mem. Community Integration Council, 1965-69. Sheldon traveling fellow Harvard U., Mex., 1942; Social Sci. Rsch. Coun. tng. fellow, 1948-49; Fulbright rsch. scholar and Ford Found. rsch. fellow Hitotsubashi U., Tokyo, 1953-54; Social Sci. rsch. Coun. fellow Carnegie Inst. Tech., 1957; life fellow Found. Keio U., 1961; Fulbright-Hays faculty rsch. scholar Japan, 1968, 73, 78, Singapore, 1968, 78, Australia, 1978; Fulbright-Hays faculty scholar N.Z., 1978; Japan Found. scholar, 1978; hon. Fulbright sr. scholar Australia, 1981. Mem. Indsl. Rels. Rsch. Assn., Am. Econ. Assn., Assn. for Asian Studies, Midwest Conf. of Asian Affairs (pres. 1961), Japan Soc., Internat. House of Japan, Internat. Indls. Rels. Assn., Japan Illini Club (hon. life), Wis. Alumni Assn. Japan (pres. 1990), Phi Beta Kappa, Beta Gamma Sigma. Home: 916 Van Buren St Madison WI 53711-2167

LEVINE, STUART GEORGE, editor, English literature educator, author; b. N.Y.C., May 25, 1932; s. Max and Jean (Berens) L.; m. Susan F. Matthews, June 6, 1962; children: Rebecca, Aaron, Allen. A.B., Harvard U., 1954; M.A., Brown U., 1956, Ph.D., 1958. Teaching fellow Brown U., 1956-57; instr. in English U. Kans., Lawrence, 1958-61; asst. prof. U. Kans., 1961-64, assoc. prof. Am. studies, 1964-66, prof., 1966—, founder, chmn. dept. Am. Studies, 1963-70, prof. English, 1976-92, Exxon intra-univ. vis. prof. dept. music history, 1981-82, prof. emeritus, 1992—; Fulbright disting. lectr., Naples chair U. Naples, Italy, 1994-95; Fulbright prof. U. La Plata (Argentina), 1962, U. Costa Rica, 1965, 67, Nat. Autonomous U. Mexico, 1973, several univs. in Chile, 1985; exch. professorship U. West Indies, 1988; scholar-in-residence U. Ariz., 1972-73; profl. concert musician, 1955-58, 73—, also artist; dir. NEH Summer Seminar for Coll. Tchrs., 1978; also cons. panels; vis. prof. various univs. Author: (with N.O. Lurie) The American Indian Today, 1968, Caffin's The Story of American Painting, 1970, Edgar Poe: Seer and Craftsman, 1972, (fiction) The Monday-Wednesday-Friday Girl and Other Stories (Gross-Woodley competition winner 1994); also author short stories pub. in various mags.; editor in chief Am. Studies, 1960-89, founding editor, 1989—; editor (with Susan F. Levine) The Short Fiction of Edgar Allan Poe: An Annotated Edition, 1976, 90; one-man shows include Regents Ctr. Gallery, Kansas City, 1983, Lawrence Arts Ctr., 1984; French horn player Lawrence Woodwind Quartet, Lawrence Symphony Orch., Lawrence Mcpl. Band, CottonWood Winds. Recipient Anisfield Wolf award (with others) Saturday Rev., 1968, citation NCCJ, 1969; grantee Kans. Com. for Humanities, 1982-83, 83-84. Mem. Am. Studies Assn. (exec. com. nat. meeting 1965-66, publs. com. nat. meeting 1965-66, Gabriel and Bode prize coms. 1983, chmn. both coms. 1984-85), Mid-Am. Am. Studies Assn. (exec. and editorial bds. 1960—), MLA, Am. Fedn. Musicians. Home: 1644 University Dr Lawrence KS 66044-3150 *Open exchange of great ideas and of decent people were as important as economic failure in toppling the Iron Curtain. We cannot yet know whether humane ideals and rational discourse can trump ancient fears and old hatreds. Looked to for leadership, our nation is uncertain of its course. I worry that at this critical time we allow deterioration in the quality of our ideas, perhaps even in our ability to reason. The dangerous irrationality of our contemporary political life may reflect failure to insist on highest standards early in our citizens' education-our poorest citizens' especially. Schoolteachers themselves clumsy of thought, ignorant of history and culture, frightened of science and mathematics, cannot train the bright creators of ideas which our country and the interlocked world need. Our best people, our best effort, should be engaged in doing better.*

LEVINE, SUMNER NORTON, industrial engineer, educator, editor, author, financial consultant; b. Boston, Sept. 5, 1923; s. Frank and Lillian (Gold) L.; m. Caroline Gassner, Nov. 27, 1952; 1 dau., Joanne. B.S., Brown U., 1946; Ph.D., U. Wis., 1949; postgrad., M.I.T., 1956. Instr. U. Chgo., 1949-50; sr. research fellow Columbia, 1950-54; dir. research labs. VA, East Orange, N.J., 1954-56; adv. scientist comml. atom power div. Westinghouse Electric Co., Pitts., 1956; dir. chemistry Metallurgy and Materials Labs.; also staff adv. engr. Gen. Engring. Labs., Am. Machine & Foundry Co., Greenwich, Conn., 1956-58; sect. head, materials and advanced electronic devices RCA, 1958-61; chmn. materials scis. dept., prof. engring., also prof., dir. grad. program in indsl. adminstrn. SUNY, Stony Brook, 1961-91; dir. urban research, vis. prof. CUNY Grad. Center, 1967-68; Danforth vis. lectr., 1968-69; vis. prof. Yale Sch. Orgn. and Mgmt., 1976; prof. fin. Coll. Urban and Policy Scis., SUNY, Stony Brook, 1978—; cons. to industry; bd. dirs. Norteck Assocs.; editorial adviser Ocean Engring. Author textbooks, profl. articles; editor: Financial Analysts Handbook, 1975, 2d edit., 1987, Investment Manager's Handbook, Dow Jones-Irwin Bus.and Investment Almanac, 1976—, Acquisition Manual, 1990, Turnaround and Bankruptcy Investing, 1991, Handbook of Global Investing, 1992, Internat. Bus. and Investment Almanac, 1992—; editor-in-chief Jour. Biomed. Materials Rsch., 1966-78, Jour. Socio-Econ. Planning Scis., 1966, Advances in Biomed. Engring. and Med. Physics, 1966. Recipient award for distinguished contbn. to biomed. materials research, 1973. Mem. IEEE, World Conf. Planning Scis., Am. Chem. Soc., Am. Soc. Metals, Electrochem. Soc., Ops. Research Soc. Am., Inst. Mgmt. Scis., Fgn. Policy Assn., N.Y. Acad. Scis. (chmn. conf. materials in biomed. engring. 1966, chmn. colloquia socioecon. planning 1966-68), Soc. for Biomaterials (dir. 1974-76), N.Y. Soc. Security Analysts (chmn. edn. and seminar com., Vols. award 1984), Mus. Modern Art, Met. Mus. of Art, Princeton Club N.Y., Brown U. Club, Sigma Xi. Office: PO Box 2118 Setauket NY 11733-0883

LEVINE, SUZANNE BRAUN, magazine editor; b. N.Y.C., June 21, 1941; d. Imre and Esther (Bernson) Braun; m. Robert F. Levine, Apr. 2, 1967; children: Joshua, Joanna. BA with honors, Radcliffe Coll., 1963. Reporter Seattle mag., 1963-65; reporter, researcher Time/Life Books, N.Y.C., 1965-67; features editor Mademoiselle, N.Y.C., 1967-68, McCalls mag., N.Y.C., 1968-69; free-lance writer, 1970; mng. editor Sexual Behavior mag., 1971-72, MS. mag., N.Y.C., 1972-88; editor Columbia Journalism Rev., N.Y.C., 1989—; adj. prof. Columbia Grad. Sch. Journalism. Co-editor: The Decade of Women, A Ms History of the Seventies, 1980; exec. producer: Ms. HBO TV spl., 1981, She's Nobody's Baby, TV documentary, 1981 (Peabody award). Woodrow Wilson guest lectr. coord. Chautauqua Conf. on Families. Mem. Am. Soc. Mag. Editors (v.p.), Women's Media Group. Office: Columbia U Columbia Journalism Rev 700 Journalism Bldg New York NY 10027

LE VINE, VICTOR THEODORE, political science educator; b. Berlin, Dec. 6, 1928; came to U.S., 1938; s. Maurice and Hildegard (Hirschberg) LeV.; m. Nathalie Jeanne Christian, July 19, 1958; children: Theodore, Nicole. BA, UCLA, 1950, MA, 1958, PhD, 1961. Research assoc. UCLA, 1958-60; prof., head dept. polit. sci. U. Ghana, Legon, 1969-71; vis. prof. Hebrew U., Jerusalem, 1978, U. Tex., Austin, 1980; Fulbright prof. U. Yaounde, Cameroon, 1981-82; prof. polit. sci. Washington U., St. Louis, 1961—; cons. U.S. Dept. State, Dept. Def., 1971—; lectr. USIA, 1981—; mem. U.S. Nat. Cmemn. UNESCO, 1964; dir. Office Internat. Studies, Washington U., 1975-76; vis. lectr. Fudan U., U. Nanjing (China), 1987, Ibn Saud and King Abdulazziz Univs., Saudi Arabia, 1990; mem. Carter Ctr. Internat. monitoring team to Ghana nat. elections, 1992. Author: Cameroons: Mandate to Independence, 1964, 70, Cameroon Federal Republic, 1971, Political Corruption: Ghana, 1975, (with Timothy Luke) Arab-African Connection, 1979; (with Heidenheimer and Johnston) Political Corruption: A Handbook, 1990. Mem., dir. UN Assn., St. Louis, 1964-74; mem. Coun. on World Affairs, 1969—; pres. Ctr. for Internat. Understanding, 1988—. With U.S. Army, 1951-54. Ford. Found. fellow Cameroon, 1960-61; Hoover Instn. fellow, 1974; Lester Martin fellow Truman Instn., Jerusalem, 1978; Fulbright lectr. U.S. Fulbright Commn., Yaounde, Cameroon, 1981-82. Mem. Am. Polit. Sci. Assn., African Studies Assn., Mideast Studies Assn., Midwest Polit. Sci. Assn., Mo. Polit. Sci. Assn. Office: Washington U Dept Polit Sci Saint Louis MO 63130

LEVINE, WILLIAM SILVER, electrical engineering educator; b. Bklyn., Nov. 19, 1941; s. Louis Nathan and Gertrude (Silver) L.; m. Shirley Johannesen, Feb. 14, 1963; children: Bruce Jonathan, Eleanor Joan. BEE, MIT, 1962, MEE, 1965, PhD in Elec. Engring., 1969. Project engr. Data Tech. Inc., Cambridge, Mass., 1962-64; grad. asst. MIT, Cambridge, 1964-69; asst. prof. U. Md., College Park, 1969-73, assoc. prof., 1973-81, prof., 1981—; cons. IBM Fed. System Div., Gaithersburg, Md., 1972-75, Computational Engring. Inc., Laurel, Md., 1980-90. Co-author: Using MATLAB to Analyze and Design Control Systems, 1992, 2d edit., 1995; editor: The Control Handbook, 1996; contbr. articles to profl. jours. Recipiet numerous rsch. grants, 1969—. Fellow IEEE, IEEE Control Systems Soc. (pres. 1990, disting. mem. 1990); mem. IEEE Medicine and Biology Soc. (disting. lectr. 1991), Soc. for Indsl. and Applied Math. Office: U Md Dept Elec Engring College Park MD 20742

LEVINGER, BERYL BETH, development specialist, organization administrator; b. N.Y.C., July 31, 1947; d. Adolph Seymour Schapira and Beatrice Glickman Lemeshnik; m. Samuel Levinger, June 17, 1967; children: Lisa, Andrea. BS, Cornell U., 1968; MA, U. Ala., 1974, PhD, 1977. Vol. U.S. Peace Corps, Colombia, 1967-69; assoc. dir U.S. Peace Corps, Bogota, Colombia, 1974-75; tchr., adminstr. Am. Schs. Abroad, Honduras and Colombia, 1970-74; edn. advisor AID, Bogota, 1975-77; spl. asst. to pres. Save the Children, Westport, Conn., 1977-79; dep. dir. tech. svcs. unit World Edn., N.Y.C., 1979-81; sr. rsch. assoc., adj. asst. prof. Columbia U., N.Y.C., 1981-84; sr. v.p. CARE, N.Y.C., 1984-89; pres. AFS Intercultural Programs, N.Y.C., 1989-93; disting. prof. nonprofit mgmt. Monterey (Calif.) Inst. Internat. Studies, 1992—; sr. dir. for internat. programs Edn. Devel. Ctr., Newton, Mass., 1992—; cons. in field. Mem. Cornell Club. Democrat. Jewish. Avocations: hiking, boating, cross-country skiing, music. Home: 17 Woods Grove Rd Westport CT 06880-2427

LEVINGER, JOSEPH SOLOMON, physicist, educator; b. N.Y.C., Nov. 14, 1921; s. Lee J. and Elma (Ehrlich) L.; m. Gloria Edwards, Aug. 14, 1943; children—Sam, Laurie, Louis, Joe. B.S., U. Chgo., 1941, M.S., 1944; Ph.D., Cornell U., 1948. Physicist Metall. Lab., U. Chgo., 1942-44, Franklin Inst., Phila., 1945; instr. Cornell U., 1948-51, vis. prof., 1961-64; from asst. prof. to prof. La. State U., 1951-61; prof. physics Rensselaer Poly. Inst., 1964-92, prof. emeritus, 1992—; Fulbright fellow, asso. prof. U. Paris—Sud, 1972-73.

Author: Nuclear Photo-disintegration, 1961, Secrets of the Nucleus, 1967, The Two and Three Body Problem, 1974. Guggenheim fellow, 1957-58. Fellow Am. Phys. Soc. Home: Red Mill Rd Rensselaer NY 12144-3010 Office: Rensselaer Poly Inst Physics Dept Troy NY 12180

LEVINS, JOHN RAYMOND, investment advisor, management consultant, educator; b. Jersey City, Aug. 4, 1944; s. Raymond Thomas and Catherine (Kelly) L. BS in Acctg., U. N.H., 1973; MBA, U. N.H., Plymouth, 1976. Registered investment advisor; cert. mgmt. cons., enrolled to practice IRS; cert. licensing instr., real estate and multiple lines ins. broker, comml. arbitration panelist; accredited tax advisor. Mgmt. risk analyst Express Treaty Mgmt. Corp., N.Y.C., 1962-67; asst. risk mgr. Bigelow-Sanford, Inc., N.Y.C., 1967-71; cons., broker BYSE, Inc., Laconia, N.Y., 1971-74; asst. prof. Nathaniel Hawthorne Coll., Antrim, N.H., 1975-82, Keene (N.H.) State Coll., 1982—; prin. Levins & Assocs., Concord, N.H., 1986—; investment advisor Reality Techs., Internat. Fin., Concord, 1991—; dir. Small Bus. Inst. Keene State Coll., 1982-86; exec. seminar leader Strategic Mgmt. Group, Inc., 1986—, Boston U., 1986—, Worcester Poly. Tech. Inst., 1992; gen. securities rep. H.D. Vest Fin. Svcs., 1990; mem. bd. advisors Am. Biog. Inst.; pvt. practice real estate, ins. cons., Concord, 1981; panelist securities arbitration Nat. Assn. Security Dealers, Am. Stock Exch.; consumer affair mediator Dept. Justice, Office of Atty. Gen., N.H.; mortgage banker; comml. financing broker; mem. SEC, spkr., seminar leader in field. Author: Finance and Accounting, 1979 (Excellence award 1980), Financial Analysis, 1981 (Excellence award 1980), Managing Cash Flow, 1988 (Excellence award 1988), Finance and Management, 1989. Incorporator Spaulding Youth Ctr., Tilton, N.H., 1990; colleague Found. for Acctg. Edn., assoc., profl. standing, 1988; mem. Nat. Consortium Edn. and Tng., Madison, Wis., 1989. With USN, 1969-71, S.E. Asia. Named Outstanding Support Leader U.S. Small Bus. Adminstrn., Concord, 1985, Oustanding Svc. Leader Community Leaders Am., N.H., 1990, One of Outstanding Young Men Am. U.S. Jaycees Bd. Adv.'s, 1983. Mem. AICPA (mem. Profl. Devel. Inst., sponsor trainer 1988-89), Investment Co. Inst. (assoc., nat. standing 1987), Inst. Mgmt. Cons. (assoc., nat. standing 1985), Nat. Soc. Pub. Accts. (del., profl. standing 1985), Nat. Soc. Non-Profit Orgns. (svc. provider 1989, colleague), Accreditation Coun. for Accountancy (fed. taxation accreditation 1987, colleague). Avocations: boating, teaching, community service, athletics. Home and Office: Levins & Assocs PO Box 442 624 Alton Woods Dr Concord NH 03302-0442

LEVINS, RICHARD, science educator; b. N.Y.C., June 1, 1930; s. Ruben and Ruth (Sackman) L.; m. Rosario Morales, June 10, 1950; children: Aurora, Ricardo, Alejandro. A.B., Cornell U., 1951; Ph.D., Columbia U., 1965. Farmer, P.R., 1951-56; research assoc. U. Rochester, N.Y., 1960-61; assoc. prof. biology U. P.R., 1961-66; assoc. prof. biology and math. biology U. Chgo., 1967-68, prof., 1969-75; John Rock prof. population sci. Harvard Sch. Pub. Health, 1975—; mem. sci. adv. council natural resources P.R. Dept. Pub. Works, 1970-72; mem. adv. bd. N.Y. Marxist Sch. Author: Evolution in Changing Environments, 1968; co-author: (with R.C. Lewontin) The Dialectical Biologist, (with C. Puccia) Qualitative Modeling of Complex Systems, (with Yrjo Haila) Humanity and Nature, 1992; editorial bd.: La Escalera, 1965-72, Am. Naturalist, 1968-71, Theoretical Population Biology, 1970—. Coffee region organizer P.R. Communist Party, 1952-54; mem. Partido Socialista Puertorriqueño; bd. dirs. Concilo Hispano, 1986-94, Oxfam Am., 1988-95. Recipient Arthur Felberbaum award Brech Forum, 1995; Edinburgh medal The Wider Soc., 1996. Mem. Am. Acad. Arts and Sci., New World Agr. and Ecol. Group, Sci. for Vietnam, Nat. Organic Farmers Assn., Cuban Botanical Assn. (corr. mem.). Home: 107 Amory St Cambridge MA 02139-1229 *Understand the world in order to change it, and in changing it get to understand it better.*

LEVINSKY, NORMAN GEORGE, physician, educator; b. Boston, Apr. 27, 1929; s. Harry and Gertrude (Kipperman) L.; m. Elena Sartori, June 17, 1956; children—Harold, Andrew, Nancy. A.B. summa cum laude, Harvard U., 1950, M.D. cum laude, 1954. Diplomate Am. Bd. Internal Medicine. Intern Beth Israel Hosp., Boston, 1954-55; resident Beth Israel Hosp., 1955-56; commd. med. officer USPHS., 1956; clin. assoc. Nat. Heart Inst., Bethesda, Md., 1956-58; NIH fellow Boston U. Med. Center, 1958-60; practice medicine, specializing in internal medicine and nephrology Boston, 1960—; chief of medicine Boston City Hosp., 1968-72, 93—; physician-in-chief, dir. Boston U. Med. Ctr. Hosp., Boston, 1972—; asst. prof., then assoc. prof. medicine Boston U., 1960-68, Wesselhoeft prof., 1968-72, Wade prof. medicine, 1972—, chmn. dept. medicine, 1972—; mem. drug efficacy panel NRC; mem. nephrology test com.-Am. Bd. Internal Medicine, 1971-76: mem. gen. medicine B rev. group NIH; mem. comprehensive test com. Nat. Bd. Med. Examiners, 1986-89; chmn. com. to study end-stage renal disease program Nat. Acad. Scis./Inst. Medicine, 1988-90, chmn. com. on Xenografts, 1995. Editor (with R.W. Wilkins) Medicine: Essentials of Clinical Practice, 3d edit., 1983, (with R. Rettig) Kidney Disease and the Federal Government, 1991; contbr. chpts. to books, sci. articles to med. jours. Recipient Distinguished Teacher awd., Am. Coll. of Physicians, 1992. Master ACP; mem. AAAS, Am. Fedn. Clin. Rsch., Am. Soc. Clin. Investigation, Am. Heart Assn., Assn. Am. Physicians, Am. Physiol. Soc., Assn. Profs. Medicine (sec., treas. 1984-87, pres.-elect 1987-88, pres. 1988-89), Am. Soc. Nephrology, Inst. Medicine NAS, Interurban Clin. Club (pres. 1985-86), Phi Beta Kappa, Alpha Omega Alpha. Home: 20 Kenwood Ave Newton MA 02159-1439 Office: Boston U Med Ctr 75 E Newton St Boston MA 02118-2340

LEVINSON, ARNOLD IRVING, allergist, immunologist; b. Balt., 1944. MD, U. Md. Sch. Medicine, 1969. Intern Balt. City Hosps., 1969-70, resident internal medicine, 1970-71; fellow U. Pa., Phila., 1973-75, assoc. prof. neurology, 1987—. Mem. AAI, AFCR, AFEB, ASCI, Brit. Soc. Immunology. Office: U Pa Hospital 3400 Spruce St Philadelphia PA 19104-4219*

LEVINSON, BARRY L., film director; b. Balt., Apr. 6, 1942. Ed., Am. U., Washington. film writer, actor: Silent Movie, 1976, High Anxiety, 1978; writer: ...And Justice for All, 1979, Inside Moves, 1980, Best Friends, 1982, Unfaithfully Yours, 1984; dir.: The Natural, 1984, Young Sherlock Holmes, 1985, Good Morning Vietnam, 1987, Rain Man, 1988 (Academy award 1989, Dirs. Guild Am. award 1989); screenwriter, dir.: Diner, 1982, Tin Men, 1987, Avalon, 1990 (Writers Guild Am. award 1990); co-prodr., dir. Bugsy, 1991, Disclosure, 1994; co-writer, dir., prodr. Toys, 1992, Jimmy Hollywood, 1994 (also actor); actor: Quiz Show, 1994; dir. (TV) Homicide: Life on the Street, 1993 (Emmy award, Outstanding Individual Achievement in Directing in a Drama Series, 1993, Peabody award 1993). Mem. Dirs. Guild Am., Writers Guild Am. Address: c/o CAA 9830 Wilshire Blvd Beverly Hills CA 90212

LEVINSON, DANIEL RONALD, lawyer; b. Bklyn., Mar. 24, 1949; s. Gerald Sam and Risha Rose (Waxer) L.; m. Luna Frances Lambert, Sept. 13, 1980; children: Luna Claire, Hannah Louise. AB, U. So. Calif., 1971; JD, Georgetown U., 1974; LLM, George Washington U., 1977. Bar: N.Y. 1975, Calif. 1976, D.C. 1976, U.S. Supreme Ct. 1978. Law clk. appellate divsn. N.Y. Supreme Ct., Bklyn., 1974-76; assoc. McGuiness & Williams, Washington, 1977-81, ptnr., 1982-83; dep. gen. counsel U.S. Office Personnel Mgmt., Washington, 1983-85; gen. counsel U.S. Consumer Product Safety Commn., Washington, 1985-86; chmn. U.S. Merit Sys. Protection Bd., Washington, 1986-93; of counsel Shaw Branstord & O'Rourke, Washington, 1993-94; chief of staff U.S. Rep. from Ga. Bob Barr, Washington, 1995—; adj. lectr. Am. U., Washington, 1981-82, Cath. U. Am., Washington, 1982. Notes and comments editor Am. Criminal Law Rev., 1973-74; contbr. articles to profl. jours. Bd. dirs. Washington Hebrew Congregation; prin. Coun. for Excellence in Govt., 1993-94. Mem. ABA, Adminstrv. Conf. U.S. (govt. mem. 1984-93), Phi Beta Kappa. Republican. Home: 3529 Woodbine St Chevy Chase MD 20815-4047 Office: 1607 Longworth Ho Offc Bldg Washington DC 20515

LEVINSON, GARY HOWARD, real estate investor; b. Mpls., May 30, 1945; s. Sidney B. and Ruth F. L.; m. Susan Lynn Austrian, Dec. 15, 1968 (div. 1982); children: Bradley Ross, Todd Matthew. BA, U. Minn., 1967, JD cum laude, 1970. Bar: Minn., U.S. Ct. Appeals (8th cir.), U.S. Dist. Ct. Minn., Minn. Supreme Ct. Ptnr. Robins, Davis & Lyons, Mpls., 1970-81; prin. Bradley Todd Group, Mpls., 1981-84; mng. ptnr., sr. v.p. Phila. region Lincoln Property Co., Dallas, 1985-92; investor, 1992—; CEO Togar Property Co., Phila., 1995—. Mem. Mayor's Non-Partisan Coord. Com. Criminal Justice Ctr., Phila., 1990-91; exec. com., dir. Friends of Rittenhouse Square, Phila., 1986—, chmn., 1991-92, pres., 1987-90; bd. govs. mid. east coun. Fgn. Policy Rsch. Inst., 1993-95; steering com. Phila. Ctr. City Concerned Citizens, 1989-93; exec. com., dir. Anti-Defamation League, 1992—. Recipient award for Excellence Pa. Soc. Cons. Engrs., 1991. Mem. Nat. Apt. Assn., Nat. Home Builders Assn., Pa. Apt. Assn. (Planet Earth award 1992), Nat. Multi Housing Coun. (fin. com. 1993-94), Pa. Builders Assn., Order of Coif. Avocations: music, travel, ballet, film. Office: 580 W Germantown Pike Ste 202 Plymouth Meeting PA 19462

LEVINSON, HARRY, psychologist, educator; b. Port Jervis, N.Y., Jan. 16, 1922; s. David and Gussie (Nudell) L.; m. Roberta Freiman, Jan. 11, 1946 (div. June 1972); children—Marc Richard, Kathy, Anne, Brian Thomas; m. Miriam Lewis, Nov. 23, 1990. BS, Emporia (Kans.) State U., 1943, MS, 1946; PhD, U. Kans., 1952. Coordinator profl. edn. Topeka State Hosp., 1950-53, psychologist, 1954-55; dir. div. indsl. mental health Menninger Found., Topeka, 1955-68; visiting prof. MIT, 1961-62, U. Kans. Bus. Sch., 1967, Texas A&M U., 1976; Thomas Henry Carroll-Ford Found. distinguished vis. prof. Harvard Grad. Sch. Bus., Boston, 1968-72; adj. prof. Coll. Bus. Adminstrn., Boston U., 1972-74; lectr. Harvard Med. Sch., 1972-85; adj. prof. Pace U., 1972-83; clin. prof. psychology Harvard Med. Sch., 1985-92, emeritus prof., 1992—; head sect. orgnl. mental health Mass. Mental Health Ctr., 1983-92; pres. The Levinson Inst., 1968-91, chmn. bd., 1991—; mem. Am. Bd. Profl. Psychology, 1972-80, chmn., 1978-80; Ford Found. prof. Mathur Inst., Jaipur India, 1974; conducted internat. course on social psychiatry Finnish Govt. Inst., 1979. Author: Emotional Health In the World of Work, 1964, Executive Stress, 1970, The Exceptional Executive (McKinsey Found. and Acad. Mgmt. awards), 1968 (James A. Hamilton Hosp. Adminstrs. Book award), Organizational Diagnosis, 1971, The Great Jackass Fallacy, 1973, Psychological Man, 1976, Casebook for Psychological Man; (with S. Rosenthal) CEO: Corporate Leadership in Action (Am. Coll. Health Care Adminstrs. Book award 1986), 1984, Ready, Fire, Aim, 1986, Designing and Managing Your Career, 1989, Career Mastery, 1992. Chmn. Kans. adv. com. U.S. Civil Rights Commn., 1962-68; chmn. Topeka Human Relations Commn., 1967-68. Served with F.A. AUS, 1944-46. Recipient Perry Rohrer Cons. Psychology Practice award, 1984, Career award Mass. Psychol. Assn., 1985, First award Soc. Psychologists in Mgmt.; Eminent scholar in bus. Fla. Atlantic U., 1995. Fellow APA (award for disting. profl. contbn. to knowledge 1992); mem. AAAS, Acad. Mgmt., Authors Guild. Home: 225 Brattle St Cambridge MA 02138-4623

LEVINSON, JOHN MILTON, obstetrician-gynecologist; b. Atlantic City, Aug. 17, 1927; m. Elizabeth Carl Bell; children: Patricia Anne, John Carl, Mark Jay. BA, Lafayette Coll., Easton, Pa., 1949; MD, Thomas Jefferson U., 1953. Diplomate Am. Bd. Ob-Gyn. Intern Atlantic City Hosp., 1953-54; Am. Cancer Soc. clin. fellow Jefferson Med. Coll. Hosp., Phila., 1954-55; resident in ob-gyn. Del. Hosp., Wilmington, 1955-57; pvt. practice ob-gyn. Wilmington, 1957-85; prof. dept. ob-gyn. Jefferson Med. Coll., Thomas Jefferson U., Phila., hon. clin. prof., 1990—; sr. attending physician emeritus Med. Ctr. Del., Wilmington, 1986—; attending chief dept. ob-gyn. St. Francis Hosp., Wilmington, chief emeritus, 1986-92; founder, pres. Aid for Internat. Medicine, Inc., 1966—; med. dir., chief surgeon Quark Expeditions, 1991-95; cons. Riverside Hosp., 1972-86, Wilmington Pa. Blue Shield, 1982—: cons. gynecology U.S. VA, 1974-85; founding mem., treas., bd. dirs. Physicians Health Svcs., Del., Ltd., 1985-87; vis. prof., cons., ship's surgeons, practicing physician various orgns. in Africa, Antarctica, Arctic regions, Ctrl. Am., Europe, S.E. Asia,, S.W. Asia, 1963—; lectr. in field; internat. med. cons. to Sen. Edward M. Kennedy, 1967—; chmn. Antarctic expdns. study group to advise NSF, 1992-93; co-chmn. Com. for Safety in Arctic and Antarctic Frontier Expeditions, 1992-93. Author: Shorebirds: The Birds, the Hunters, the Decoys, 1991; contbr. articles to profl. jours., book chpts. Bd. dirs. Del. com. Project H.O.P.E., 1965-75, ARC, 1968-70, Charles A. Lindbergh Fund, Inc., 1985-90; trustee Blue Cross/ Blue Shield Del., Inc., 1968-86, Brandywine Coll., 1972-77; bd. dirs. Nat. Assn. Blue Shield Plans, 1971-77; mem adv. com. Trinity Alcohol and Drug Program, 1978-85; mem. Del. Gov.'s Commn. on Health Care Cost Mgmt., 1985-87; bd. dirs. founding mem. World Affairs Coun. Wilmington Inc, v.p., 1981-86; pres. Rockland Mills Cmty. Assn., 1992-94. With USN, 1945-47; col. M.C., USAFR, 1984-87. Recipient Brandywine award Brandywine Coll., 1968, cert. of appreciation for med. svcs. Ministry of Health, Republic of Vietnam, 1963-66, commendation Pres. of U.S., 1971, The Eisenhower award People to People Internat., 1986, Commemorative medal Charles A. Lindbergh Fund, 1987, Phila. Explorers award 1987, Citation for Outstanding Contbn. to People of Del., Med. Soc. Del., 1992. Fellow Am. Assn. Ob.-Gyns., Royal Geog. Soc. London; mem. AMA, Am. Assn. Gyn. Laparoscopists (founding, bd. dirs.), Del. Obstetric Soc. (pres. 1980-82), Phila. Obstetric Soc., Med. Soc. Del. (Citation of Merit award 1992), New Castle County Med. Soc., Soc. Ob-Gyn. Vietnam (hon.), Ducks Unltd. (sponsor, mem. Del. com. 1980-92), Explorers Club (fellow 1966—, chmn. Phila. chpt. 1983-85, bd. dirs. 1981-88, pres. N.Y.C. 1985-87), Univ. and Whist Club Wilmington (life, bd. govs. 1961-64), Rotary (bd. dirs. local club 1991-93), Theta Chi (pres. 1945) Phi Beta Pi (pres. 1952), Kappa Beta Phi (pres. 1952). Avocations: hunting, polar history, sailing, collecting, bird decoys. Home: 55 Millstone Ln Rockland DE 19732

LEVINSON, JOSEPH, computer company executive, marketing and sales consultant; m. Carolyn Ophelia Price; children: Sandra Lynn Nall, Scott Joseph, Gary David, Cherilyn Carole Schutze, Barry Drew. Student, Northwestern U.; attended, U. Colo., Troy State U.; MS in Mil. Sci. and Tactics, U.S. Army Command and Gen. Staff Coll., 1961. With USN, 1942-46; aviation radioman, gunner, radar operator Patrol Wings Atlantic Fleet, WWII; enlisted U.S. Army, 1950, advanced through grades to col.; arty. liaison, liaison pilot, arty. adjustment pilot, forward observer pilot, asst. ops. officer 45th Inf. Divsn. Aviation Sec., 189th Field Arty. Bn., Korea; officer in charge Armed Forces Courier Svc.; dep. chief of staff 2d USA Missile Command, Ft. Carson, Colo.; ops. officer 16th Sky Cav.; dep. chief of staff G3 Ops., Programs and Budgets U.S. Army Aviation Ctr., Ft. Rucker, Ala.; chief advanced studies for Army Aviation U.S. Army Combat Devels. Command, Ft. Rucker, Ala.; commdg. officer 121st Aviation Co. Air Mobile Light Delta Bn and 13th Aviation Bn., Vietnam; air field comdr. Mekong Delta Airfield, Vietnam; ret. U.S. Army, 1967; v.p. southwestern sales Alden Press, Inc.; sales assoc. Am. Printers and Lithographers , Inc.; pres., CEO Ad Am., Inc.; pres. Internat. Web Graphics divsn., Lexcom, Inc.; v.p. advt. and mktg. Percom Data Corp.; pres., cons. Access Unlimited divsn. With USN, 1942-46, U.S. Army, 1950-67. Decorated Legion of Merit, 2 Bronze Stars, 13 Air medals (one with valor device), Army and Air Force Commendation medals, Korean Army Aviator Wings, Vietnamese Cross of Gallantry with Gold Palm, Vietnamese Cross of Gallantry with Bronze Palm. Mem. Army Aviation Assn. Am., Vietnam Helicopter Pilots Assn., Am. Legion China Post 1, VFW, DAV, Ret. Officers Assn. Ctrl. Tex. (legis. liaison officer), Quarter Century Wireless Assn., Family Motor Coach Assn., Nat. Head Injury Found., Elks. Address: 5292 Dacy Lane Buda TX 78610

LEVINSON, KENNETH S., lawyer, corporate executive; b. Mineola, N.Y., Oct. 27, 1947; s. Max Leonard and Eva (Klamen) L.; m. Laura R. Levinson, Sept. 14, 1969 (div. 1981); 1 child, Barbara Ann Schmidt; m. Jerelyn E. Jarmacz, Feb. 6, 1982; children: Alexander T., Brianna F., Joshua K. BA in Polit. Sci. with distinction, U. Wis., 1969; JD with honors, George Washington U., 1975; LLM in Taxation, Georgetown U., 1978. Bar: D.C. 1975, Va. 1975, U.S. Ct. Claims 1976, U.S. Dist. Ct. (D.C. dist.) 1976, U.S. Tax Ct. 1976, U.S. Ct. Appeals (D.C. cir.) 1976, U.S. Supreme Ct. 1979. Atty., advisor Office Chief Counsel Interpretative div. IRS, Washington, 1975-78, reviewer, asst. br. chief Office Chief Counsel, 1978-79; sr. tax atty. Pepper, Hamilton & Scheetz, Washington, 1979-81; v.p., mng. tax dir. Marriott Corp., Bethesda, Md., 1981-85, v.p. internat. project fin., 1985-90; v.p. tax NW Airlines, Inc., Eagan, Minn., 1990-92, v.p. tax, risk mgmt., ins., 1992-94; v.p. fin. and planning cargo/charter divsn., 1994—; adj. prof. Georgetown U. Law Ctr., Washington, 1978-86; asst. sec., v.p. various Marriott Corp. subs., Bethesda, 1981-90; v.p. Wings Holdings, Inc./N.W. Airlines Corp., 1990—; v.p. tax N.W. Airlines, Inc., 1990—, v.p. various subs.; cons., pres. The Chechhi Group, Beverly Hills, Calif., 1990—; bd. dirs. City Harbour Hotel, Ltd., London. Contbr. articles to profl. jours. Bd. dirs. Minn. Taxpayers Assn., Mpls. Lt. USN, 1969-72. Mem. ABA (subcom. chair 1978-84), D.C. Bar, Va. State Bar, Tax Execs. Inst., Washington Tax Group, Air Transport Assn., Internat. Air Transport Assn. (chair taxation com. 1991, chair ins. com. 1994, elected chair risk mgrs. forum 1995). Avocations: golf, sports, art appreciation/collection, boating. Home: 401 Peavey Ln Wayzata MN 55391-1534 Office: NW Airlines Inc Dept C 5610 5101 Northwest Dr Saint Paul MN 55111-3027

LEVINSON, LAWRENCE EDWARD, lawyer, corporation executive; b. N.Y.C., Aug. 25, 1930; s. Samuel Keever and Sara Lee (Tarvin) L.; m. Margaret Ann Bishop, Aug. 20, 1989; children: Elizabeth, Suzanne, Lucia. B.A. magna cum laude, Syracuse U., 1952; LL.B., Harvard U., 1955. Bar: N.Y. 1957, U.S. Supreme Ct. 1958. Atty. Office Sec. Air Force, Washington, 1957-63; spl. assignments Office Sec. Def., Washington, 1963-65; dep. counsel to Pres. U.S., Washington, 1965-69; sr. v.p. Paramount Communications, Inc., N.Y.C., 1969-94; sr. Washington counsel VIACOM Internat., 1994-95; ptnr. Verner, Liipfert, Bernhard, McPherson and Hand, Washington, 1995—; mem. Nat. Council on Health Planning and Devel., Washington, 1978-84; host pub. affairs TV program Capital Notebook, 1991—. Mem. bd. visitors Syracuse U. Coll. Arts and Scis., 1981—. Served with Judge Adv. div. U.S. Army, 1955-57. Mem. Assn. Am. Pubs. (bd. dirs. 1989-95). Home: 5715 Little Falls Rd Arlington VA 22207-1554

LEVINSON, L(ESLIE) HAROLD, lawyer, educator; b. Bournemouth, Eng., Oct. 17, 1929; s. Abraham and Ada (Bloomberg) L.; m. Joan Gluck, Mar. 28, 1965; children: Andrea, Lara. BBA, 1957, LLB, U. Miami, 1962; LLM, NYU, 1964; JSD, Columbia U., 1974. Bar: Fla. 1962, N.Y. 1964; CPA. Ptnr. acctg. firm Miami, Fla., 1958-62; instr. acctg. NYU, 1962-64; lectr. on devel. financing UN, N.Y.C. and Geneva, summers 1963-65; asst. to legal dir. ACLU, N.Y.C., summers 1964-65; asst. prof. U. Fla., 1966-67, assoc. prof., 1967-70, prof., 1970-73; vis. prof. Vanderbilt U. Sch. Law, Nashville, 1973-74, prof., 1974—; mem. Fla. Law Rev. Coun., 1972-74; cons. Adminstrv. Conf. U.S. 1976-86; reporter 1981 Revision Model State Adminstrv. Proc. Act., Nat. Conf. Commrs. Uniform State Laws, 1978-81; vis. prof. NYU Sch. Law, 1994. Mem. ABA, Am. Law Inst., Am. Inst. CPA's. Office: Vanderbilt U Sch Law 21st Ave S Nashville TN 37240

LEVINSON, PETER JOSEPH, lawyer; b. Washington, June 11, 1943; s. Bernard Hirsh and Carlyn Virginia (Krupp) L.; m. Nanette Susan Segal, Mar. 30, 1968; children: Sharman Risa, Justin David. AB in History cum laude, Brandeis U., Waltham, Mass., 1965; JD, Harvard U., 1968. Bar: Hawaii 1971, U.S. Supreme Ct. 1975. Summer supr. Harvard Legal Aid Bur., Cambridge, Mass., 1968; research asst. Harvard Law Sch., 1968-69; teaching fellow Osgoode Hall Law Sch., York U. (Can.), 1969-70, research assoc., 1969-70, asst. prof., 1970-71; dep. atty. gen. State of Hawaii, 1971-75; vis. fellow Harvard U., 1976-77; ptnr. Levinson and Levinson, Honolulu, 1977-79; spl. asst. to dir. Office Program Support, Legal Services Corp., Washington, 1979; cons. Select Commn. on Immigration and Refugee Policy, Washington, 1980-81; minority counsel subcom. on immigration, refugees and internat. law com. on judiciary, U.S. Ho. of Reps., Washington, 1981-85, minority counsel subcom. monopolies and comml. law, 1985-89, minority counsel subcom. econ. and comml. law, 1989-95, counsel com. on judiciary, 1995—. Trustee, Hawaii Jewish Welfare Fund, 1972-75, chmn. fund drive, 1972; trustee Temple Emanu-El, Honolulu, 1973-75; mem. alumni admissions council Brandeis U., 1978-82. Recipient award of merit United Jewish Appeal, 1974. Mem. Hawaii State Bar Assn. (chmn. standing com. on continuing legal edn. 1972, chmn. standing com. on jud. adminstrn. 1979), ABA, Am. Judicature Soc. Contbr. articles to profl. jours. Office: B353 Rayburn House Office Bldg Washington DC 20515

LEVINSON, RASCHA, psychotherapist; b. N.Y.C., Nov. 27, 1930; d. Frank Alfred and Goldye Dena (Preiser) Cohen; m. Monroe Louis Levinson, Oct. 6, 1955 (div. 1973); 1 child, Nadia Levinson Fogel. BA, NYU, 1960; MSW, Columbia U., 1962; Tng. in Hypnosis, Milton Erickson Soc., N.Y.C., 1992-93. Lic. social worker, N.Y. Pvt. practice N.Y.C., 1970—; psychotherapist Wasington Sq. Inst., N.Y.C., 1973-74; intake therapist Women's Psychotherapy Referral Svcs., N.Y.C., 1973-76; supr. psychotherapy Mid-Hudson Cons. Ctr., Wappinger Falls, N.Y., 1974-83; workshop leader New Sch. Social Rsch., N.Y.C., 1980-87. Fellow Soc. Clin. Social Workers (pres. Westchester chpt. 1986-88); mem. Assn. for Women in Psychology, N.Y.C. Coalition for Women's Mental Health (bd. dirs. 1986-89), Advanced Feminist Therapy Inst. (editor newsletter 1990-92). Avocations: writing, motorcycle riding, reading, movies. Office: 55 Central Park W # 1B New York NY 10023-6003

LEVINSON, ROBERT ALAN, textile company executive; b. Balt., July 26, 1925; s. Louis and Frieda (Kellert) L.; m. Patricia S. Schulte, Apr. 23, 1954; children: Margot, Andrew, John. AB, Dartmouth Coll., 1946, MBA, 1946; postgrad., London Sch. Econs., 1946-47. With Burlington Industries, N.Y.C., 1949-51; v.p., dir. Bangor Punta, Inc., N.Y.C., 1964-68; chmn. bd. Duplan Corp., N.Y.C., 1968-79; chmn. Andrex Industries Corp., N.Y.C.; cons. Dillon Yarn Corp.; chmn., pres. Levcor Internat.; dir., chmn., mem. exec. com. Belding Heminway Corp. Trustee Bklyn. Mus., chmn., 1972-84; chmn. Harlem Sch. of Arts, Nat. Dance Inst.; bd. dirs., exec. com., vice chmn. Nat. Commn. on U.S.-China Relations. With USNR, 1943-45, 52-54. Home: 1035 5th Ave New York NY 10028-0135 Office: 1071 6th Ave New York NY 10018-3704

LEVINSON, SANFORD VICTOR, legal educator; b. Hendersonville, N.C., June 17, 1941; s. Meyer Mayer and Shirley (Achler) L.; m. Cynthia Yenkin, June 8, 1966; children: Meira, Rachel. BA, Duke U., 1962; PhD, Harvard U., 1969; JD, Stanford U., 1973. Bar: Calif. 1973, U.S. Supreme Ct. 1981. Asst. prof. dept. polit. sci. Ohio State U., 1968-70; law clk. to judge U.S. Dist. Ct., Charlotte, N.C., 1973-74; staff atty. Children's Def. Fund., Cambridge, Mass., 1974-75; asst. prof. dept. politics Princeton (N.J.) U., 1975-79; prof. Dept. Govt. and Law Sch. U. Tex., Austin; vis. prof. Hebrew U., 1984, Harvard Law Sch., 1991-92; mem. Inst. Advanced Studies, Princeton, 1986-87; fellow program in ethics and the professions Harvard U., 1991-92. Author: Constitutional Faith, 1988; co-editor: Power and Community, 1971, Processes of Constitutional Decisionmaking, 1983, 92, Interpreting Law and Literature: A Hermeneutic Reader, 1988. Woodrow Wilson fellow, 1962, Kent fellow, 1966, Russell Sage fellow, 1970. Mem. Am. Law Inst., Conf. on Critical Legal Studies, Phi Beta Kappa. Democrat. Jewish. Home: 3410 Windsor Rd Austin TX 78703-2248 Office: U Tex Law Sch 727 E 26th St Austin TX 78705-3224*

LEVINSON, SHAUNA TITUS, bank and financial services marketing executive; b. Denver, Aug. 1, 1954; d. Charles and Geraldine D. Titus; m. Kenneth L. Levinson, Dec. 21, 1986. BA cum laude, U. Puget Sound, 1976; M Bank Mktg. with honors, U. Colo., 1986. Cert. fin. planner. Fin. planning analyst Swift and Co., Chgo., 1977-79; from credit analyst to asst. v.p. Ctrl. Bank of Denver, 1979-84; v.p. fin. svcs. First Nat. Bank S.E. Denver, 1984-94; dir. mktg. First Nat. Bank, 1991-94; pres., CEO Fin. Directions, Inc., Denver, 1994—; mem. bankers edn. com. Colo. Bankers Assn., Denver, 1992-94. Chmn. human resources com., mem. adminstrv. coun. Jr. League of Denver, 1983—; mem. cmty. assistance fund, placement adv. com., fundraiser Women's Libr. Assn. U. Denver, 1990-94, 96—; fundraiser Good Shepherd Cath. Sch., 1986—, Jewish Cmty. Ctr., Denver, 1990-95, St. Mary's Acad., 1995—. Recipient Gold Peak award Am. Bankers Assn.-Bank Mktg. Assn., 1987; named Businessperson of Week Denver Bus. Jour., 1995. Mem. AAUW, Internat. Assn. Fin. Planners, Colo. Bankers Assn., Jr. League Denver, U. Denver Pioneer Hockey Club, Denver Athletic Club, Kappa Alpha Theta (program chair Northwest Chgo. alumnae 1977-79), Phi Kappa Phi. Office: 1624 Market St # 475 Denver CO 80202

LEVINSON, WARREN MITCHELL, broadcast journalist; b. Bklyn., Feb. 23, 1953; s. Abraham and Roslyn Anne (Bell) L.; m. Debra Lynn Galant, Sept. 1, 1985; children: Margot, Noah. BA, Duke U., 1975. Reporter Sta. WCHL Radio, Chapel Hill, N.C., 1974-77; news dir. Sta. WBLG/WKQQ Radio, Lexington, Ky., 1977-78; newswriter AP, N.Y.C., 1979-82; corr. AP Radio, N.Y.C., 1982—. Co-host (radio talk program) Newsweek on Air, 1985—. Recipient Silver medal for News Mag. Internat. Radio T.V. Soc., 1989. Avocations: bicycling, poetry. Office: AP 50 Rockefeller Plz New York NY 10020-1605

LEVINTHAL, ELLIOTT CHARLES, physicist, educator; b. Bklyn., Apr. 13, 1922; s. Fred and Rose (Raiben) L.; m. Rhoda Arons, June 4, 1944; children—David, Judith, Michael, Daniel. B.A., Columbia Coll., 1942; M.S., Mass. Inst. Tech., 1943; Ph.D., Stanford U., 1949. Project engr. Sperry Gyroscope Co., N.Y.C., 1943-46; research assoc. nuclear physics

Stanford (Calif.) U., 1946-48, sr. scientist dept. genetics Sch. Medicine, 1961-74, dir. Instrumentation Research Lab., 1961-80, assoc. dean for research affairs, 1970-73, adj. prof. genetics Sch. Medicine, 1974-80, research prof. mech. engring., dir. Inst. Mfg. and Automation Sch. Engring., 1983-90, assoc. dean for research Sch. Engring., 1986-90, assoc. dean spl. programs, 1990-91, prof. emeritus, 1991—; research physicist Varian Assocs., Palo Alto, Calif., 1949-50, dir. research, 1950-52; chief engr. Century Electronics, Palo Alto, 1952-53; pres. Levinthal Electronics, Palo Alto, 1953-61; dir. def. scis. office Def. Advanced Projects Agy., Dept. Def., Arlington, Va., 1980-83; mem. NASA Adv. Coun., 1980-84, space studies bd., NRC, 1989-91, mem. human exploration, 1991-92, army sci. bd., 1989-91; cons. HEW. Recipient NASA Public Service medal, 1977. Mem. AAAS, IEEE, Am. Phys. Soc., Optical Soc. Am., Biomed. Engring. Soc., Sigma Xi. Democrat. Jewish. Home: 59 Sutherland Dr Atherton CA 94027-6430 Office: Stanford U Sch of Engring 530 Duena St Rm 104 Stanford CA 94305-3030

LEVINTON, JEFFREY S., biology educator, oceanographer; b. N.Y.C., Mar. 20, 1946; s. Nathan and Lillian (Moshman) L.; m. Joan Miyeko Miyazaki, Mar. 30, 1979; children: Nathan Toshi, Andrew Koji. BS, CCNY, 1966; M in Philosophy, Yale U., 1969, PhD, 1971. Asst. prof. biology SUNY, Stony Brook, 1970-75, assoc. prof., 1975-83, prof., 1983—, head dept., 1984-90, 91-93; vis. prof. U. Arhus, Denmark, 1966-67, Uppsala (Sweden) U., 1981, U. Cambridge, England, 1983; chmn. panel Hudson River Found, 1986-90. Author: Marine Ecology, 1982, Genetics, Paleontology, and Macroevolution, 1988, Marine Biology, 1995; reviewer, contbr. over 100 articles to profl. jours. Mem. Environ. Policy Com. Conn., 1969. NSF fellow, 1969, Sterling hon. fellow, 1969, John Simon Guggenheim fellow, 1983. Mem. Ecol. Soc. Am. (editor 1986-93), Am. Soc. Naturalists (editor 1974-79). Democrat. Office: SUNY Ecology and Evolution Dept Stony Brook NY 11794-5245

LEVIS, DONALD JAMES, psychologist, educator; b. Cleve., Sept. 19, 1936; s. William and Antoinette (Stejskal) L.; children: Brian, Katie. Ph.D., Emory U., 1964. Postdoctoral fellow clin. psychology Lafayette Clinic, Detroit, 1964-65; asst. prof. psychology U. Iowa, Iowa City, 1966-70, assoc. prof., dir. research and tng. clinic, 1970-72; prof. SUNY-Binghamton, 1972—. Author: Learning Approaches to Therapeutic Behavior Modification, 1970, Implosive Therapy, 1973; cons. editor: Jour. Abnormal Psychology, 1974-80, Jour. Exptl. Psychology, 1976-77, Behavior Moedifications, 1977-81, Behavior Therapy, 1974-76, Clin. Behavior Therapy Rev., 1978—; contbr. articles to profl. jours. Served to capt. AUSR, 1958-66. Fellow Behavior and Therapy Research Soc. (charter, clin.), Am. Psychol. Assn.; mem. Assn. Advancement Behavior Therapy (publ. bd. 1979-82), AAAS, Psychonomic Soc., N.Y. State Psychol. Assn., Sigma Xi. Home: 48 Riverside Dr Binghamton NY 13905-4402 Office: SUNY Dept Psychology Binghamton NY 13901

LEVIT, EDITHE JUDITH, physician, medical association administrator; b. Wilkes-Barre, Pa., Nov. 29, 1926; m. Samuel M. Levit, Mar. 2, 1952; children: Harry M., David B. BS in Biology, Bucknell U., 1946; MD, Woman's Med. Coll. of Pa., 1951; DMS (hon.), Med. Coll. Pa., 1978; DSc (hon.), Wilkes U., 1990. Grad. asst. in psychology Bucknell U., 1946-47; intern Phila. Gen. Hosp., 1951-52, fellow in endocrinology, 1952-53, clin. instr., assoc. in endocrinology, 1953-57, dir. med. edn., 1957-61, cons. med. edn., 1961-65; asst. dir. Nat. Bd. Med. Examiners, Phila., 1961-67; assoc. dir., sec. bd. Nat. Bd. Med. Examiners, 1967-75, v.p., sec. bd., 1975-77, pres., chief exec. officer, 1977-86, pres. emeritus, life mem. bd., 1987—; cons. in field, 1964—; mem. coun. Coll. Physicians of Phila., 1986—; mem. adv. coun. Inst. for Nuclear Power Ops., Atlanta, 1988-93; bd. dir. Phila. Electric Co. Contbr. articles to profl. jours. Bd. dirs. Phila. Gen. Hosp. Found., 1964-70; bd. dirs. Phila. Council for Internat. Visitors, 1966-72; bd. sci. counselors Nat. Library Medicine, 1981-85. Recipient award for outstanding contbns. in field of med. edn. Commonwealth Com. of Woman's Med. Coll., 1970; Alumni award Bucknell U., 1978; Disting. Dau. of Pa. award, 1981; Spl. Recognition award Assn. Am. Med. Colls., 1986; Disting. Service award Fedn. State Med. Bds., 1987; Master A.C.P. Fellow Coll. Physicians of Phila.; mem. Inst. Medicine of Nat. Acad. Scis., AMA, Pa., Phila. County med. socs., Assn. Am. Med. Colls., Phi Beta Kappa, Alpha Omega Alpha, Phi Sigma. Home: The Rittenhouse 210 W Rittenhouse Sq Philadelphia PA 19103-5726

LEVIT, HELOISE B. (GINGER LEVIT), arts administrator, fine arts and media consultant; b. Phila., Apr. 2, 1937; d. Elmer and Claire Frances (Schwartz) Bertman; m. Jay Joseph Levit, July 14, 1962; children: Richard Bertman, Robert Edward, Darcy Francine. BA in French Literature, U. Pa., 1959; MA in French Literature, U. Richmond, 1975; Cert., Alliance Française, Paris, 1991, Chambre de Commerce et d'Industrie de Paris, 1991, La Sorbonne, Paris, 1994, Instituto Lorenzo di Medici Firenze, Italy, 1996; postgrad., Va. Commonwealth U., Richmond. Arts broadcaster Richmond, Va., 1976-82; dir. Fine Arts Am., Inc., Richmond, 1982-84; tchr. Henrico County Pub. Schs., Richmond, 1984-88; dir. devel. Sta. WVST-FM Va. State U., Petersburg, 1987-88; mgr., dir. devel. Richmond Philharm. Orch., 1988-94; fine arts and media cons. Art-I-Facts, Richmond, 1988—. Author: Moments, Monuments & Monarchs, 1986 (Star award 1986); arts writer Richmond Rev., 1989-90; anchor, producer (syndicated radio series) Va. Arts Report, 1978-83, Va. Women, 1984 (Va. Press Women award 1986). V.p. Va. Mus. Collector's Cir., Richmond, 1986-91, mem. steering com.; pres. Richmond Area Dem. Women's Club, 1992-93; mem. Va. Mus. Coun., Richmond; mem. Richmond Symphony Orch. League. Mem. Am. Assn. Tchrs. of French, Va. Capitol Corrs. Assn., Va. Press Women, U. Pa. Alumni Club (v.p. 1980-90, Ben Franklin award 1990), Am. Symphony Orch. League, Amicale Francaise, Alliance Francaise (cert. 1989, 91), La Table Francaise (pres. 1996), Va. Writers Club. Avocations include tennis, art collecting, classical music, foreign travel. Home and Office: Art-I-Facts 1608 Harborough Rd Richmond VA 23233-4720

LEVIT, JAY J(OSEPH), lawyer; b. Phila., Feb. 20, 1934; s. Albert and Mary Levit; m. Heloise Bertman, July 14, 1962; children: Richard Bertman, Robert Edward, Darcy Francine. AB, Case Western Res. U., 1955; JD, U. Richmond, 1958; LLM, Harvard U., 1959. Bar: Va. 1958, D.C. 1961, U.S. Supreme Ct. 1961. Trial atty. U.S. Dept. Justice, Washington, 1960-64; sr. atty. Gen. Dynamics Corp., Rochester, N.Y., 1965-67; ptnr. Stallard & Levit, Richmond, Va., 1968-77, Levit & Mann, Richmond, 1978—; instr. U. Mich. Law Sch., Ann Arbor, 1964-65; adj. assoc. prof. U. Richmond Law Sch., 1974-77; adj. lectr. Va. Commonwealth U., Richmond, 1970-85; lectr. in field. Contbg. editor The Developing Labor Law-Bur. Nat. Affairs, 1974—. Mem. ABA (labor com.), Va. Bar Assn. (labor com.), Fed. Bar Assn. (labor com.). Avocations: art collecting, jogging, swimming, travel. Home: 1608 Harborough Rd Richmond VA 23233-4720 Office: Levit & Mann Hamilton Pl Ste 100 1301 N Hamilton St Richmond VA 23230

LEVIT, LOUIS WILLIAM, lawyer; b. Chgo., Aug. 31, 1923; m. Ellen Goodyear Levit; children: Alan, Robert. BS, U. Chgo., 1943, JD, 1946. Bar: Ill. 1947, Supreme Ct. Ill. 1947, U.S. Dist. Ct. (no. dist.) Ill. 1948, U.S. Supreme Ct., 1965, U.S. Ct. Appeals (7th cir.) 1969, U.S. Dist. Ct. (ea. dist.) Wis. 1991; CPA. With Legis. Reference Bur., Springfield, Ill., 1947-48; pvt. practice Chgo., 1948-71; founder, prin. Levit & Mason Ltd., Chgo., 1971-89; atty. Ross & Hardies, Chgo., 1990—; lectr. in field. Author in field. Active Ill. Inst. Continuing Legal Edn. Fellow Am. Coll. Bankruptcy (bd. regents 1993—); mem. ABA (sect. corp. banking and bus. law, com. bus. bankruptcy, chmn. subcom. sects. 1985-89), Insol Internat. (exec. coun. 1990-94), Chgo. Bar Assn. (treas. 1985-87, bd. mgrs. 1978-80, com. bankruptcy and reorgn. 1959—, chmn. 1966-67), Chgo. Bar Found. (dir. 1987-90, comml. code com. 1964-74, chmn. 1972-73, com. assn. mtgs. 1975-85, chmn. 1976-78, com. evaluation candidates 1980-83, profl. responsibility 1983-88, fin. 1984-88, chmn. 1985-87, 88-89, com. judiciary 1987—, long-range planning com. 1987-89), Ill. State Bar Assn. (coun. sect. comml. banking and bankruptcy law 1965-72, sec. 1968-70, chmn. 1970-71, chmn. com. corp. bankruptcy 1969-70), Ill. Bankers Assn. (com. bank counsel 1988-90), Comml. Law League Am. (chmn. bankruptcy com. 1973-75, chmn. spl. jud. com. 1975-77, edn. com. 1970-71, assoc. editor comml. law jour. 1967-85, 94—, chmn. bankruptcy and insolvency sect. 1988-89), Bar Assn. Seventh Fed. Cir. (chmn. com. bankruptcy and insolvency 1982—). Office: Ross & Hardies 150 N Michigan Ave Chicago IL 60601

LEVIT, MAX, food service executive. V.p., 1958-1993; pres. Grocers Supply Co., Houston, 1993—. Office: Grocers Supply Co 3131 E Holcombe Blvd Houston TX 77021-2116*

LEVIT, MILTON, grocery supply company executive; b. 1924; married. Grad., U. Tex., 1946. With Grocers Supply Co. Inc., Houston, 1946—, v.p., 1947-75, pres., 1975—, also chmn. bd., dir. Served with USN. Office: Grocers Supply Co Inc 3131 Holcombe Blvd Houston TX 77021-2116*

LEVIT, VICTOR BERT, lawyer, foreign representative, civic worker; b. Singapore, Apr. 21, 1930; s. Bert W. and Thelma (Clumeck) L.; m. Sherry Lynn Chamove, Feb. 25, 1962; children: Carson, Victoria. A.B. in Polit. Sci. with great distinction, Stanford, 1950; LL.B., Stanford U., 1952. Bar: Calif. 1953. Assoc. Long & Levit, San Francisco and Los Angeles, 1953-55, ptnr., 1955-83; mng. ptnr. Long & Levit, San Francisco and L.A., 1971-83; ptnr. Barger & Wolen, San Francisco, L.A. and Newport Beach, 1983—; assoc. and gen. legal counsel U.S. Jaycees, 1959-61; legal counsel for consul gen. Ethiopia for San Francisco, 1964-71; hon. consul for Ethiopia for San Francisco, Ethiopia, 1971-76; guest lectr. Stanford U. Law Sch., 1958—, Haile Selassie I Univ. Law Sch., 1972-76; mem. com. group ins. programs State Bar Calif., 1980—; Mem. Los Angeles Consular Corps, 1971-77; mem. San Francisco Consular Corps, 1971-77, vice dean, 1975-76; Grader Calif. Bar Exam., 1956-61; del. San Francisco Mcpl. Conf., 1955-63, vice chmn., 1960, chmn., 1961-63. Author: Legal Malpractice in California, 1974, Legal Malpractice, 1977, 2d edit., 1983; Note editor: Stanford Law Rev, 1952-53; legal editor: Underwriters' Report, 1963—; Contbr. articles to legal jours. Campaign chmn. San Francisco Aid Retarded Children, 1960; mem. nat. com. Stanford Law Sch. Fund, 1959—; mem. Mayor's Osaka-San Francisco Affiliation Com., 1959-65, Mayor's Com. for Mcpl. Mgmt., 1961-64; mem. San Francisco Rep. Country Cen. Com., 1956-63; assoc. mem. Calif. Rep. Cen. Com., 1956-63, 70-72; campaign chmn. San Francisco Assemblyman John Busterud, 1960; bd. dirs. San Francisco Comml. Club, 1967-70, San Francisco Planning and Urban Renewal Assn., 1959-60, San Francisco Planning and Urban Renewal Assn. Nat. Found. Infantile Paralysis, 1958, Red Shield Youth Assn., Salvation Army, San Francisco, 1960-70, bd. dirs. NCCJ, San Francisco, 1959—, chmn., No. Calif., 1962-64, 68-70; mem. nat. bd. dirs., 1964-75; bd. dirs. San Francisco Tb and Health Assn., 1962-70, treas., 1964, pres., 1965-67; bd. dirs. San Francisco Assn. Mental Health, 1964-73, pres., 1968-71; mem. com. Nat. Assn. Mental Health, 1969-71; trustee United Bay Area Crusade, 1966-74, Ins. Forum San Francisco; bd. visitors Stanford Law Sch., 1969-75; mem. adv. bd. Jr. League San Francisco, 1971-75. Named Outstanding Young Man San Francisco mng. editors San Francisco newspapers, 1960, One of Five Outstanding Young Men Calif., 1961. Fellow ABA (chmn. profl. liability com. for gen. practice sect. 1979-81, council gen. practice sect. 1982-86, sec.-treas. gen. practice sect. 1986-87); mem. San Francisco Bar Assn. (chmn. ins. com. 1962, 73, chmn. charter flight com. 1962-66), State Bar Calif. (chmn. or group ins. programs 1980—, chmn. gen. practice sect. 1988—), Consular Law Soc., Am. Arbitration Assn. (arbitrator), World Assn. Lawyers (chmn. parliamentary law com. 1976—), Am. Law Inst. (adviser restatement of law governing lawyers 1985—), Internat. Bar Assn., San Francisco Jr. C. of C. (dir. 1959, pres. 1958), U.S. Jaycees (exec. com. 1959-61), Jaycees Internat. (life, senator), Calif. Scholarship Fedn., U.S. C. of C. (labor com. 1974-76), San Francisco C. of C. (dir.), Phi Beta Kappa, Order of Coif, Pi Sigma Alpha. Clubs: Commercial (San Francisco) (dir.); Commonwealth (quar. chmn.), California Tennis; World Trade; Bankers. Home: 59 Lupine # 303 San Francisco CA 94418 Office: Barger & Wolen 101 California St Ste 4725 San Francisco CA 94111-5802

LEVIT, WILLIAM HAROLD, JR., lawyer; b. San Francisco, Feb. 8, 1938; s. William Harold and Barbara Janis (Kaiser) L.; m. Mary Elizabeth Webster, Feb. 13, 1971; children: Alison Jones, Alexandra Bradley, Laura Elizabeth Fletcher, Amalia Elizabeth Webster, William Harold, III. B.A. magna cum laude, Yale U., 1960; M.A. in Internat. Rels., U. Calif., Berkeley, 1962; LL.B., Harvard U., 1967. Bar: N.Y. 1968, Calif. 1974, Wis. 1979. Fgn. service officer Dept. State, 1962-64; assoc. firm Davis Polk & Wardwell, N.Y.C., 1967-73; assoc., then ptnr. firm Hughes Hubbard & Reed, N.Y.C. and Los Angeles, 1973-79; sec. and gen. counsel Rexnord Inc., Milw., 1979-83; ptnr., dir., chair internat. practice group Godfrey & Kahn, Milw., 1983—; substitute arbitrator Iran-U.S. Claims Tribunal, The Hague, 1984-88; lectr. Practicing Law Inst., ABA, Calif. Continuing Edn. of Bar, State Bar of Wis. Contbr. to: Mergers and the Private Antitrust Suit: The Private Enforcement of Section 7 of the Clayton Act, 1977. Bd. dirs. Wis. Humane Soc., 1980-90, pres., 1986-88; bd. dirs. Vis. Nurse Corp., Milw., 1980-90, chmn., 1985-87; bd. dirs. Vis. Nurse Found., 1986-95, chmn., 1989-91; bd. dirs. Aurora Health Care Inc., 1988-93, Wis. Soc. to Prevent Blindness, 1981-91, Columbia Coll. Nursing, 1992—, Aurora Health Care Ventures, 1993—; rep. Assn. Yale Alumni, 1976-79, 81-84, 90-93; pres. Yale Club So. Calif., 1977-79; mem. neutral advisor panel CPR Inst. for Dispute Resolution. Ford Found. fellow U. Pa., 1961-62, NDEA fellow U. Calif., Berkeley, 1962. Mem. ABA (com. on corp. counsel litigation sect.), Am. Soc. Corp. Secs. (pres. Wis. chpt. 1982-83, dir. 1981-92), Am. Arbitration Assn. (panel arbitrators 1977—), Assn. of Bar of City of N.Y., State Bar Calif. (com. on continuing edn. of bar 1977-79), L.A. County Bar Assn. (ethics com. 1976-79), State Bar Wis. (dir. internat. bus. transactions sect. 1985-92, dist. 2 bd. attys. profl. responsibility com. 1985-94, chmn. 1993-94), Bar Assn. 7th Cir. (gen. chair com. on rules and practice 1995—), Am. Br. Internat. Law Assn., Nat. Assn. Security Dealers (bd. arbitrators 1988—), Chartered Inst. Arbitrators (assoc., London), N.Y. Stock Exch. (panel arbitrators 1988—), N.Am. Coun. London Ct. of Internat. Arbitration, Am. Soc. Internat. Law, Inst. Jud. Adminstrn., Milw. Club, Milw. Athletic Club, Town Club, Phi Beta Kappa. Office: 780 N Water St Ste 1500 Milwaukee WI 53202-3512

LEVITAN, DAN, investment banker; b. N.Y.C., May 13, 1957; s. Milton B. and Minna (Osinoff) L. BA magna cum laude, Duke U., 1979; MBA, Harvard U., 1983. Jr. exec. trainee Merrill Lynch & Co., N.Y.C., 1979-81; assoc. Wertheim Schroder & Co., Inc., N.Y.C., 1983-86, v.p., 1987-88, 1st v.p., 1989, assoc. mng. dir., 1989-90; dir. corp. fin. west coast Wertheim Schroder & Co., Inc., L.A., 1990-91, mng. dir., head investment banking West Coast, 1991-93; head bus. devel. Wertheim Schroder & Co., Inc., N.Y.C., 1993-94, mgr. dir., head fin. sponsor group, 1994—; head restaurant industry group investment banking Schroder Wertheim & Co. Inc., N.Y.C., 1994—; bd. dirs. Marmot Mountain Ltd. Bd. trustees Pilchuck Glass Sch.; mem. Duke Univ. N.Y.C. Exec. Leadership Bd. Mem. Harvard Club of N.Y., Beta Theta Pi. Office: Schroder-Wertheim & Co Inc 787 7th Ave New York NY 10019-6018

LEVITAN, DAVID M(AURICE), lawyer, educator; b. Tver, Lithuania, Dec. 25, 1915; (parents Am. citizens); m. Judith Morley; children: Barbara Lane Levitan, Stuart Dean Levitan. B.S., Northwestern U., 1936, M.A., 1937; Ph.D., U. Chgo., 1940; J.D., Columbia U., 1948. Bar: N.Y. 1948, U.S. Supreme Ct. 1953. Various U.S. Govt. adminstrv. and advisory positions with Nat. Youth Adminstrn., Office Price Adminstrn., War Prodn. Bd., Fgn. Econ. Adminstrn. Supreme Hdqrs. Allied Expeditionary Force, and Cen. European div. Dept. State, 1940-46; cons., sec. joint-com. of 5th and 6th coms., 2d Gen. Assembly, dir. com. of experts for establishing adminstrv. tribunal UN, 1946-47; cons. pub. affairs dept., producer series of pub. affairs programs on TV and radio ABC, 1946-53; pvt. practice N.Y.C., 1948-66; ptnr. Hahn & Hessen, N.Y.C., 1966-86, counsel, 1986-95; instr. U. Chgo., 1938-41; adj. prof. public law Columbia U., 1946-65; adj. prof. John Jay Coll. Criminal Justice, CUNY, 1966-75; adj. prof. polit. sci. Post Coll., 1964-66; adj. prof. law Cardozo Sch. Law, 1978-82; pvt. practice, 1995—; asst. to Ill. state adminstr. Nat. Youth Adminstrn., chief budget sect., Washington, 1940-41; mgmt. analyst Office of Price Adminstrn., 1941; spl. asst. to chmn. War Prodn. Bd., 1942-43; chief property control divsn. Fgn. Econ. Adminstrn., Washington, 1944-45; with U.S. Group of Control Coun. for Germany at SHAEF, London, 1944; advisor Ctrl. European divsn. U.S. Dept. State, 1945; cons. UN, 1946-47, Sect. Joint Com. 5th and 6th Coms., 1946-47, 2d session of 1st Gen. Assembly, 1946-47; dir. Com. of Experts on Establishment of Adminstrn. Tribunal, 1946-47; cons. pub. affairs dept. ABC, 1946-53. Contbr. articles to legal jours. Mem. Nassau County (N.Y.) Welfare Bd., 1965-69; chmn. Planning Bd., Village of Roslyn Harbor, N.Y., 1965-66; chmn. Bd. of Zoning Appeals, Village Roslyn Harbor, 1967—. Recipient Demobilization award Social Sci. Rsch. Coun., 1946-48. Fellow Am. Coll. Trust and Estate Counsel; mem. ABA, Am. Polit. Sci. Assn., Am. Soc. Internat. Law, Am. Law Inst., Assn. Bar City N.Y. Home and Office: 250 Scudders Ln Roslyn NY 11576-1038 Office: 350 Fifth Ave New York NY 10118

LEVITAN, IRWIN BARRY, neuroscience educator, academic administrator; b. Jan. 13, 1947; came to U.S., permanent resident; married; two children. BSc in Biochemistry with first class honors, McGill U., Montreal, 1967, MSc in Biochemistry, 1968, PhD in Biochemistry, 1970. Rschr. in lab. of Dr. T. E. Webb, cancer rsch. unit McGill U., 1967-70; rschr. in lab of prof. H. Hyden, Inst. Neurobiology U. Goteborg, Sweden, 1970-72; rschr. in lab. of Dr. S. H. Barondes, dept. psychiatry U. Calif. San Diego, 1972-74; permanent staff and group leader Friedrich Miescher Institut, Basel, Switzerland, 1974-82; assoc. prof. biochemistry Brandeis U., Waltham, Mass., 1982-85, prof. biochemistry, 1985—, Nancy Lurie Marks Prof. neuroscience, 1992—; dir. biochem. seminar McGill U., 1969-70; instr. neurochemistry U. Calif. San Diego, 1972-73; coord. and instr. introductory neurobiology Friedrich Miescher Institut, 1975-77, mem. exec. com., 1975-78; instr. introductory neurobiology Biozentrum, U. Basel, 1975-82; instr. introductory and advanced neurobiology Brandeis U., 1983—, coord. and dir. neurosci. program, 1983—, dir. ctr. complex sys., 199—; vis. prof. cellular neurology MIT, 1987-93; co-dir. summer course in neurobiology Marine Biolog. Lab., Woods Hole, Mass., 1990-94; chmn. Gordon Conf. on Ion Channels, 1986; mem. adv. bd. Whitney Lab. Marine Biology-U. Fla., nominating com. Bristol Myers Squibb award for disting. achievement in neurosci.; disting. vis. prof. Duke U., Durham, N.C., 1993, Dana Alliance for Brain Initiatives Charles A. Dana Found., 1994. Author: (with L. K. Kaczmarek) Neuromodulation: the Biochemical Control of Neuronal Excitability, 1987, (with L. K. Kaczmarek) The Neuron: Cell and Molecular Biology, 1991; editor (with P. D. Evans) Ion Channels and Receptors, 1986; mem. editorial bd. Jour. Neuroscience, Jour. Molecular Biology, Jour. Exptl. Biology, Neuron; contbr. numerous articles to profl. jours. and chapters to books. Mem. adv. bd. Cystic Fibrosis Rsch. Ctr.-U. Ala. Woodrow Wilson fellow 1967; Centennial fellow Med. Rsch. Coun. Can., 1970-73; Quebec scholar, 1968, 69; scholar McGill U., 1963, 66, 67; bursar Nat. Rsch. Coun. Can., 1967, studentship, 1968, 69; named Helen Wendler Deane Disting. lectr. Wellesley Coll., 1988, J. H. Quastel Disting. Vis. prof. McGill U., 1989, Rushton lectr. Fla. State U., 1991, Cooper lectr. Yale U., 1992, Disting. Vis. prof. in Pharmacology and Neurobiology, Duke U., 1993; recipient Jacob Javits Neuroscience Investigator award NIH, 1985, 1992. Office: Brandeis Univ Volen Cte Complex Sys 415 South St Waltham MA 02254-9110

LEVITAN, JAMES A., lawyer; b. N.Y.C., Mar. 24, 1925; s. Leo and Della (Brody) L.; m. Ruth Terry White, Jan. 30, 1951; children—Deborah A., Judith T., Susan J. B.S. in Chem. Engring, M.I.T., 1948; LL.B. (mem. bd. Law Rev. 1950-51), Columbia U., 1951. Bar: N.Y. bar 1951. Since practiced in N.Y.C.; ptnr. Skadden, Arps, Slate, Meagher & Flom, 1965-95, of counsel, 1995—; life mem. MIT Corp., Cambridge, Mass., 1995—, chmn. audit com., 1994—; regional chmn. N.Y.C. MIT Ednl. Coun., 1974-90; lectr. in field of tax. Served with USNR, 1944-46. Stone scholar, 1948-51; Kent scholar, 1950. Mem. N.Y. State Bar Assn., Assn. Bar City N.Y., Tau Beta Pi. Home: 26 Wake Robin Ln Stamford CT 06903-4611 Office: Skadden Arps Slate Meagher & Flom 919 Third Ave New York NY 10022-3903

LEVITAN, LAURENCE, lawyer, former state senator; b. Washington, Oct. 22, 1933; s. Maurice Land Nathlie (Rosenthal) L.; BS, Washington and Lee U., 1955; JD, George Washington U., 1958; m. Barbara E. Levin, 1957; children: Jennifer, Michelle, Lisa. Admitted to Md. bar, 1964; with Levitan, Cramer & Weinstein, 1959-72, Levitan Ezrin, West & Kenxton, 1973-85, Beckett Cromwell & Myers, 1985-90, Frank Bernstein Conaway & Goldman, 1990-92; of counsel Baker & Hostetler, 1992-95; ptnr. Rifkin, Livingston, Levitan and Silver, LLC, Annapolis, Md., 1995—; mem. Md. Ho. of Dels., 1971-74; mem. Md. Senate, 1975-94, chmn. budget and taxation com., policy com., spending affordability com., mem. joint com. on mgmt. pub. funds., legis. com. on budget and audit, gov.'s commn. to rev. state taxes & taxes structure, joint legis. com. on tax reform, govtl. commn. to revise annotated code of Md., joint subcom. on program open space, chmn. drunk and drugged driving task force, chmn. joint com. on ins. tax reform; mem. Montgomery County Exec.'s Commn. for Higher Edn. in High Tech.; past mem. Gov.'s Commn. To Study Unification of Circuit Ct., Gov.'s Commn. to Study Condominium Laws, Gov.'s Commn. Law Enforcement and Adminstrn. Justice, Gov.'s Subcom. on Revenue Structure of Task Force to Study State-Local Relationships; mem. Gov.'s Commn. To Study Feasibility of Biennial Budget, Gov.'s Task Force on Real Property Closing Costs, Task Force To Study Md. Tax Ct., Gov.'s Commn. Sch. Funding, Joint Task Force on Md.'s Procurement Law; apptd. co-chmn. transition team on budget review Gov. Glendening. Mem. ABA, D.C. Bar Assn., Md. Bar Assn., Nat. Conf. State Legislatures (mem. subcom. on fed. budget and taxation com., fiscal affairs govt. oversight com.), So. Legis. Conf. (chmn. fiscal affairs and govt. ops. steering com. 1992-93), Am. Legis. Exch. Coun. (tax task force). Democrat. Jewish. Office: 163 Conduit St Annapolis MD 21401-2512 also: 11426 Georgetowne Dr Potomac MD 20854-3722

LEVITAN, VALERIE FASSLER, fraternal organization executive; b. Phila., Aug. 18, 1932; d. Joseph Lionel and Regina (Sekler) Fassler; m. Peter Wallfield Levitan, Dec. 20, 1950 (div. Nov. 1972); children: Daniel, Regine. BEd, U. Pa., 1954, postgrad, 1954, 65-66. Co-owner, adminstr. Levitan Sch., Phila., 1950-69; exec. dir. Soroptimist Internat. Am., Phila., 1970-79, Zonta Internat., Chgo., 1979-95; dir. pubs. various orgn. manuals; author, presenter Category I status application Econ. and Social Org. UN, 1985. Pres. Cong. Kol Ami, Chgo., 1986-87, pres., 1987. Recipient Merit award Alumnae Assn. Phila. High Sch. for Girls, 1970, Achievement award, Zonta Internat., 1985, Am.'s Citizen Vol. award, U.S. Savs. Bond, 1982. Mem. AAUW, Am. Soc. Assn. Execs., Am. Assn. World Health (bd. dirs. 1986—), UN Assn. (bd. dirs. 1986—, pres. USA Ill., 1988, sec. greater Chgo. area), Nat. Vol. Orgn. for Ind. Living of Aging (grantee 1976-77, chmn. 1986-86), Nat. Council Aging (bd. dirs. 1984-86), League of Women Voters. Democrat. Jewish. Avocations: reading, painting, cooking, visiting museums.

LEVITAS, MITCHEL RAMSEY, editor; b. N.Y.C., Dec. 1, 1929; s. Samuel M. and Fira (Zilboorg) L.; m. Gloria Barach, Dec. 24, 1950; children: Anthony, Daniel. AB, Bklyn. Coll., 1951. With Dept. State, 1951-53; reporter N.Y. Post, 1953-60; asst. editor Time mag., 1960-64; editor, writer N.Y. Times Mag., 1965-70; editor Metropolitan, 1976; editor Week in Rev. N.Y. Times, from 1977; editor Sunday Book Rev., 1983-89; sr. editor weekends N.Y. Times, 1989—; editor Op-Ed page N. Y. Times, 1990-95; editl. dir. N.Y. Times Book Devel., 1995—; vis. scholar Woodrow Wilson Found., 1979—. Author: America in Crisis. Recipient George Polk award investigative reporting, 1957; Woodrow Wilson fellow, 1951, Nieman fellow, 1958. Mem. Century Assn., Coun. Fgn. Rels., Phi Beta Kappa. Office: NY Times Co 229 W 43rd St New York NY 10036-3913

LEVITCH, JOSEPH See LEWIS, JERRY

LEVITETZ, JEFF, food wholesaler. CEO Purity Wholesale Grocers, Boca Raton, Fla. Office: Purity Wholesale Grocers 6413 Congress Ave Ste 250 Boca Raton FL 33487

LEVITIN, LEV BEROVICH, scientist, educator; b. Moscow, Sept. 25, 1935; U.S., 1981; s. Ber L. and Tzetzilia (Gushansky) L.; m. Yulia Shmukler, 1959 (div. 1970); 1 son, Boris. M.Sc., Moscow U., 1960; Ph.D., Acad. Scis. of USSR, 1969. Sr. research scientist Inst. Info. Transmission Problems, USSR Acad. Scis., 1961-73; sr. lectr. Tel-Aviv U., 1974-80; vis. prof. Bielefeld U., W. Ger., 1980-81, Syracuse (N.Y.) U., 1981-82; prof. engring. Boston U., 1982-86; disting. prof. engring. sci., 1986—; vis. scientist Heinrich-Hertz Inst., Berlin, 1980, Institut fü r Optoelektronik, Oberpfaffenhofen, W.Ger., 1981; cons. Vishay Israel, Ltd., Tel-Aviv, 1979. Editor: Principles of Cybernetics (in Russian), 1967; contbr. articles sci. jours. Fellow IEEE; mem. AAUP, Am. Math. Soc., Assn. Computing Machinery, Soc. Indsl. and Applied Math., N.Y. Acad. Scis., Am. Soc. for Engring. Edn., Math. Assn. Am., AAAS, Memento, Resistance Internat., Amnesty Internat. Office: Boston U Coll Engring 44 Cummington St Boston MA 02215-2407

LEVITON, ALAN EDWARD, museum curator; b. N.Y.C., Jan. 11, 1930; s. David and Charlotte (Weber) L.; m. Gladys Ann Robertson, June 30, 1952; children: David A., Charlotte A. AB, Stanford U., 1949, MA, 1953, PhD,

1960; student, Columbia U., summers 1947, 48, 53, NYU, 1948, U. Nebr., 1954. Asst. curator herpetology Calif. Acad. Scis., San Francisco, 1957-60, assoc. curator, 1960-61, chmn., curator, 1962-82, 89-92, curator, 1983-88, 93—; chmn. computer svcs. Calif. Acad. Scis., 1983-92; editor Sci. Publs., 1994—; assoc. curator zool. collections Stanford, 1962-63; lectr. biol. sci., 1963-70; professorial lectr. Golden Gate U., 1953-63; adj. prof. biol. sci. San Francisco State U., 1967—. Author: North American Amphibians, 1970, Reptiles of the Middle East, 1992, T.H. Hittel's California Academy of Sciences, 196; contbr. numerous articles to sci. and profl. jours. Am. Philos. Soc. grantee, 1960, NSF grantee, 1960-61, 77-79, 80, 83-86, 86-89, 91-93, Belvedere Sci. Fund grantee, 1958-59, 62. Fellow AAAS (mem. coun. 1976—, mem. com. coun. affairs 1983-85, sec.-treas. Pacific divsn. 1975-79, exec. dir. 1980—), Calif. Acad. Scis., Geol. Soc. Am. (vice chmn. history geology divsn. 1989-90, chmn. 1990-91); mem. Am. Soc. Ichthyologists and Herpetologists (mem. bd. govs. 1960-84), Soc. Systematic Zoology (sec.-treas. Pacific sect. 1970-72), Forum Historians of Sci. Am. (coord. com. 1986-88, sec.-treas. 1988-90), Herpetologists League (pres. 1961-62), History of Sci. Soc. Home: 571 Kingsley Ave Palo Alto CA 94301-3225 Office: Calif Acad Scis Golden Gate Park San Francisco CA 94118

LEVITSKY, LARRY, publishing executive; b. N.Y.C., May 7, 1952; s. Joseph and Rose (Mandelblit) L. BA in Russian Lang., Ohio U., 1975. Dir. mktg. Grove Press, N.Y.C., 1981-83, Microsoft Press, Redmond, Wash., 1983-87; v.p. sales & opers. Ventana Communications, Chapel Hill, N.C., 1990-93; gen. mgr., publisher Osnorne McGraw-Hill, Berkeley, Calif., 1993—. Office: Osborne McGraw-Hill 2600 10th St Berkeley CA 94710-2522

LEVITSKY, MELVYN, ambassador; b. Sioux City, Iowa, Mar. 19, 1938; s. David and Mollie (Schwartz) L.; m. Joan Daskovsky, Aug. 12, 1962; children: Adam, Ross Josh. BA, U. Mich., 1960; MA, U. Iowa, 1963. Polit. officer U.S. Embassy, Moscow, 1972-75; officer-in-charge Soviet-U.S. bilateral relations Dept. State, Washington, 1975-78, dep. dir. UN polit. affairs, 1978-80, dir. UN polit. affairs, 1980-82, dep. asst. sec. for human rights and humanitarian affairs, 1982-83; dep. dir. Voice of Am., Washington, 1983-84; dep. assoc. dir. broadcasting USIA, Washington, 1983-84; U.S. amb. to Bulgaria, 1984-87; exec. sec., spl. asst. to sec. Dept. State, Washington, 1987-89, asst. sec. state internat. narcotics matters, 1989-94; U.S. amb. to Brazil, 1994—. Recipient Meritorious Honor award Dept. State, 1968, Superior Honor award Dept. State, 1975, 82, Presdl. Meritorious Svc. awards, 1986-91. Mem. Am. Fgn. Service Assn.

LEVITT, ARTHUR, JR., federal agency administrator, securities and publishing executive; b. Bklyn., Feb. 3, 1931; s. Arthur and Dorothy (Wolff) L.; m. Marylin Blauner, June 12, 1955; children: Arthur III, Lauri. BA, Williams Coll., 1952, LLD (hon.), 1980; LLD (hon.), Pace U., 1980, Hamilton Coll., 1981, L.I. U., 1984, Hofstra U., 1985. Asst. promotion dir. Time, Inc., N.Y.C., 1954-59; exec. v.p., dir. Oppenheimer Industries, Inc., Kansas City, Mo., 1959-62; with Shearson Hayden Stone Inc. (now Shearson Lehman Bros., Inc.), N.Y.C., 1962-78, pres., 1969-78; chmn., chief exec. officer, dir. Am. Stock Exchange, N.Y.C., 1978-89; chmn. Levitt Media Co., N.Y.C., 1989-93, N.Y.C. Econ. Devel. Corp., 1990-93, SEC, Washington, 1993—. Chmn. President's Pvt. Sector Survey on Cost Control, 1982-84, President's Task Force on Pvt. Sector Initiatives, 1981-82, White House Small Bus. Conf. Commn., 1978-80; mem. N.Y. State Coun. on Arts, 1969—; chmn. bd. dirs. Spl. Adv. Task Force on Future Devel. West Side Manhattan, President's Base Closure and Realignment Commn.; trustee Williams Coll.; bd. dirs. Revson Found. With USAF, 1952-54, maj. Res. Recipient Medal of Excellence Bd. Regents State of N.Y. Mem. Am. Bus. Conf. (chmn. 1980-89), Phi Beta Kappa. Office: SEC 450 5th St NW Washington DC 20549-0002

LEVITT, B. BLAKE, medical and science writer; b. Bridgeport, Conn., Mar. 25, 1948; d. John Joseph and Beatrice Dolores (Rozanski) Blake; m. Andrew Levitt, Dec. 20, 1968 (div. May 1977); m. Jon P. Garvey, Nov. 19, 1983. BA in English magna cum laude, BA in History summa cum laude, Quinnipiac Coll., 1972; postgrad., Yale U., 1988. Instr. English as fgn. lang. U. Khon Kaen, Thailand, 1968-69; market researcher Lyons Bakeries Ltd., London, summer 1971; traffic mgr., copywriter Provocatives Advt. Agy., Danbury, Conn., 1976-78; tech. writer tng. divsn. Jack Morton Prodns., N.Y.C., 1978-82; freelance feature and med. writer Litchfield County Times, New Milford, Conn., 1982-85, N.Y. Times, N.Y.C., 1985-89; freelance writer med. and sci. books, 1989—. Author: Electromagnetic Fields: A Consumer's Guide to the Issues and How to Protect Ourselves, 1995, 50 Essential Things to do When the Doctor Says It's Infertility, 1995; co-author: (with John R. Sussman) Before You Conceive, The Complete Pre-Pregnancy Guide, 1989 (Will Solimene Book Award of Excellence 1991); contbr. articles to N.W. Hills mag., New Eng. Monthly, Conn. Mag. Founding mem., bd. dirs. Warren (Conn.) Land Trust, 1989-91; mem. Dem. Town Com., Warren, 1993—; vice-chmn. zoning bd. appeals Town of Warren, 1993-95. Mem. Nat. Assn. Sci. Writers, Am. Med. Writers Assn., Author's Guild, Author's League. Avocations: architectural design and renovation, reading, hiking, gardening.

LEVITT, BRIAN MICHAEL, consumer products and services company executive, lawyer; b. Montreal, Que., Can., July 26, 1947; s. Eric and Rya Levitt; m. Claire Gohier, Jan. 25, 1992; children: Marie-Anne, Katherine. BASc, U. Toronto, Ont., Can., 1969, LLB, 1973. Spl. asst. to provost U. Toronto, 1969-73; dir. interpretation Anti-Inflation Bd. Govt. Can., Ottawa, 1975-76; assoc. Osler, Hoskins & Harcourt, Toronto, 1976-79, ptnr., 1979-91; pres. Imasco Ltd., Montreal, 1991—, COO, 1993—, CEO, 1995—, also bd. dirs.; bd. dirs. First Fed. Savs. & Loan Assn., Rochester, N.Y., CT Fin. Svcs., Inc., Westbury Can. Life Ins. Co.; mem. adv. bd. faculty of mgmt. McGill U., Montreal. Contbr. articles to profl. jours. Bd. dirs. Montcrest Schs.; mem. adv. coun. Soc. Ednl. Visits and Exchanges in Can. Mem. ABA (bus. law subsect.), Can. Bar Assn., Law Soc. Upper Can., Caledon Ski, Toronto Club, Mt. Royal Club, Donalda Club, Mt. Bruno Country Club. Avocation: skiing, riding, sailing. Office: Imasco Ltd #1900, 600 Boul De Maisonneuve O, Montreal, PQ Canada H3A 3K7*

LEVITT, GEORGE, retired chemist; b. Newburg, N.Y., Feb. 19, 1925; m. Julie Zeto; children: Barbara Klein, Jeffery, David, Gregory. BS, Duquesne U., 1950, MS, 1952; PhD, Mich. State U., 1957. Rsch. chemist Exptl. Sta. E.I. du Pont de Nemours & Co., Inc., 1956-63, rsch. chemist Stine Lab., 1963-66, rsch. chemist Exptl. Sta., 1966-68, sr. rsch. chemist, 1968-80, rsch. assoc., 1981-86; instr. Del. Tech. and C.C., 1975-80. Pres. We Care in Del., 1986-87, bd. dirs., 1986-94. Recipient pesticide rsch. award Swiss Soc. Chem. Industries, 1982, Chesapeake chpt. Nat. Agrl. Mktg. Assn., 1987, Disting. Alumnus of Yr. award Duquesne U. Coll. Arts and Sci., 1988, Nat. Medal of Tech., 1993. Mem. AAAS, Am. Chem. Soc. (Creative Invention award 1989, Kenneth Spencer award 1991), Internat. Union Pure & Applied Chemistry, Sigma Xi. Achievements include research in organic syntheses, herbicides, fungicides, medicinals, pesticides; synthesis of heterocyclic compounds; characterization and identification of novel organic compounds for biological evaluation; defined and optimized chemical structure-biological activity relationships and sulfonylurea herbicides. Home: 110 Downs Dr Greenville DE 19807-2556

LEVITT, GERALD STEVEN, natural gas company executive; b. Bronx, N.Y., Mar. 21, 1944; s. Charles and Beatrice (Janet) L.; m. Natalie Lillian Hoppen; children: Mark, Roy. B in Mgmt. Engring., Rensselaer Poly. Inst., 1965; MBA, DePaul U., 1972. Registered profl. engr., Ill. Tech. rep. Worthington Air Conditioning Co., Ampere, N.J., 1965-67; indsl. sales engr. Peoples Gas Light & Coke Co., Chgo., 1967-71; planning specialist Peoples Gas Co., Chgo., 1971-72; v.p. Stone & Webster Mgmt. Cons., Inc., N.Y.C., 1972-82; exec. v.p., chief staff officer South Jersey Gas Co., Folsom, N.J., 1982—; v.p., CFO South Jersey Industries, Inc., Folsom, N.J., 1987—. Bd. dirs. Camden County coun. Boy Scouts Am., West Collingswood, N.J., Rowan Coll. Found. Mem. Am. Gas Assn., Greater Atlantic City C. of C. (past bd. dirs.), N.J. State C. of C. (bd. dirs.). Office: S Jersey Gas Co 1 S Jersey Plz Rte 54 Hammonton NJ 08037

LEVITT, GREGORY ALAN, education educator; b. Memphis, Jan. 12, 1952; s. Robert Riley and Martha Lorraine (Swincher) L.; m. Billie Diane Tomblin (div. June 1985); 1 child, Joshua Paul; m. Yueping Guo, June 3, 1994; 1 child, Maya Guo. BA, Capital U., Columbus, Ohio, 1975; MA, Ohio State U., 1988, PhD, 1990. Cert. secondary sch. tchr., adminstr.; cert. tchr. Chinese lang. Tchr. Wehrle High Sch., Columbus, 1975-85; grad. teaching assoc. Ohio State U., Columbus, 1985-90; cons./rschr. CBS News, Beijing, China, 1989; dir. fgn. tchrs. Beijing U. of Aero. and Astro. Engring., 1988-90; assoc. prof. U. New Orleans, 1990—; assoc. dir. Ctr. for the Pacific Rim, New Orleans, 1990—; dir. A World of Difference Inst., New Orleans, 1994—. Contbr. articles to profl. jours., chpts. to books; editl. rev. bd. Teaching About Asia Jour., 1993—. Bd. dirs. Tyomey Ctr. for Peace Through Justice, New Orleans, 1994—; mem. cmty. bd. Success Dropout Prevention, New Orleans, 1990—; coll. organizer AIDS Walk, U. New Orleans, 1993-94. Grantee U.S. Dept. Edn., 1994, East-West Ctr., Honolulu, 1994, La. Endowment for Humanities, 1993. Mem. ASCD, Nat. Coun. for the Social Studies, Assn. for Asian Studies, Nat. Assn. for Multicultural Edn., La. Coun. for the Social Studies, La. Ednl. Rsch. Assn., Phi Beta Delta, Phi Delta Kappa (advisor 1994—). Avocations: golf, racquetball, tennis, snorkeling, swimming. Home: 5820 Hurst St New Orleans LA 70115-4260 Office: Univ of New Orleans Coll of Edn Dept of C&I New Orleans LA 70148

LEVITT, IRVING FRANCIS, investment company executive; b. Braddock, Pa., July 3, 1915; s. Charles and Frances (Goretsky) L.; m. Florence Chaikin, Oct. 10, 1937; children: Robert Bruce, Linda Ann (Mrs. Stanley L. Ehrenpreis). B.S. (hon.) in journalism, U. Mich., 1936. Advt. mgr. feature writer Braddock (Pa.) Free Press, 1936-37; advt. mgr. Levitt Bros. Furniture Stores, 1936-38; partner, exec. adminstr. stores in Levitt Bros. Furniture Stores, Braddock, Vandergrift and New Kensington, Pa., 1938-55; exec. asst., v.p. Levinson Steel Co., Pitts., 1942-44; real estate, indsl. devel., 1938-82; pres. Lepar, Inc., 1950-80; pres., chmn. bd. Union Screw & Mfg. Co., Pitts.; chmn. bd. Investment Capital Corp., Pitts., 1955—, Radix Orgn., Inc., N.Y., Radix Real Estate, Inc., RRE Enterprises, Inc.; pres. Kirwan Heights Land Co., King Land Co., Ind., Blawnox Realty Co.; chmn. bd. Apollo Industries, Inc., 1959-68; chmn. bd., dir. Apollo Internat. Corp.; pres., dir. Apollo-Peru S.A., Oakland Investment Corp., Pitts.; v.p., dir. Apollo Indsl., Inc., Apollo Investment Co., Pitts.; sr. v.p. Parker-Levitt Corp., Sarasota, Fla., Marble Island, Inc., Vt.; ptnr. Oliver-Smithfield Venture, Pitts., Nineteen Hundred Group Ltd., Sarasota, Fla.; bd. dirs. Comml. Bank & Trust Co., Pitts., Nuclear Materials & Equipment Corp., Ednl. Audio Visual, Inc., N.Y., London, Radix Ventures, N.C., N.Y.; chmn. bd., dir. Lido Beach Devel. Co., Inc., Sarasota, Fla.; partner One Hundred Kennedy Ltd., Tampa, Fla., SMP, Ltd., Pine Run Devel., Inc., Sarasota; mem. Pitts. Bd. Realtors, New Kensington Indsl. Devel. Corp., Smaller Mfrs. Coun. Bd. dirs. Massanutten Mil. Acad., Woodstock, Va., United Jewish Fedn. Finance, Pitts., Irene Kaufman Settlement Bd.; trustee Levitt Found. Pitts., Rodef Shalom Temple, Pitts. Mem. Nat. Sales Execs. Club (dir. 1952-82), Am. Jewish Com., Chautauqua Soc., Am. Arbitration Assn. (panel of arbitrators), Nat. Assn. Securities Dealers (bd. arbitration). Clubs: Westmoreland Country (Export, Pa.) (v.p. 1948-83); Metropolis Country (White Plains, N.Y.); Longboat Key Country; Marco Polo (N.Y.C.); Standard (Pitts.) (dir.), Pitts. Athletic Assn. (Pitts.); Belfry New Century (London); Univ. (Sarasota). Office: Investment Capital Corp 595 Bay Isles Rd Ste 120-G Longboat Key FL 34228-3102 also: 230 Park Ave Rm 630 New York NY 10169-0699

LEVITT, ISRAEL MONROE, astronomer; b. Phila., Dec. 19, 1908; s. Joseph and Jennie (Marriner) L.; m. Alice Gross, July 3, 1937; children: Peter Leighton, Nancy Bambino. BSME, Drexel U., 1932, DSc, 1958; MA, U. Pa., 1937, PhD, 1948; DSc, Temple U., 1958, Phila. Coll. Pharmacy and Sci., 1963. Astronomer, Fels Planetarium of The Franklin Inst., Phila., 1934-39; asst. asso. dir. Fels Planetarium of The Franklin Inst., 1939-49, dir., 1949-72, v.p. inst., 1970-72; exec. dir. Phila. Mayor's Sci. and Tech. Adv. Council, 1972-93; sr. lectr. astronomy U. Pa., 1977; astronomer The Flower Obs., 1946-48; dir. (Sci. Council), 1953—; sci. cons. to City of Phila., 1956-63; chmn. Air Pollution Control Bd. Phila., 1965—. Author: Precision Laboratory Manual, 1932, (with Roy K. Marshall) Star Maps for Beginners, 1942, Space Traveler's Guide to Mars, 1956, Target for Tomorrow, 1959, Exploring The Secrets of Space, 1963, (with Dandridge M. Cole) Beyond the Known Universe, 1974; developer NASA Spacemobile; inventor oxygen mask, pulse counting photoelectric photometer (with William Blitzstein); contbr. articles in jours., mags. on sci. subjects; author: internationally syndicated Space column for Gen. Features. Recipient USN Ordnance Devel. award, 1945; Henry Grier Bryant gold medal Geog. Soc. Phila., 1962; Joseph Priestley award Spring Garden Inst., Phila., 1963; Writing award Aviation/Space Writers Assn., 1965; Samuel S. Fels Medal award, 1970; cert. of recognition NASA, 1977. Fellow AAAS, Am. Astronautical Soc., Brit. Interplanetary Soc.; mem. AIAA, Am. Astron. Soc., Rittenhouse Astron. Soc. (past pres.), Acad. Scis. Phila. (v.p. 1993), Nat. Assn. Sci. Writers, Aviation Writers Assn., Explorers Club, Pi Tau Sigma. Home: 3900 Ford Rd Apt 19D Philadelphia PA 19131 Office: 1515 Market St Fl 17 Philadelphia PA 19102-1921

LEVITT, JERRY DAVID, medical educator; b. Phila., Apr. 11, 1941; s. Abraham and Nettie (Dash) L.; m. Julie Meranze,k June 2, 1967; children: Rachel, Daniel, Gabriel. BA, U. Pa., 1962, MD, 1966. Diplomate Am. Bd. Anesthesiology; lic. physician, Pa., Maine. Intern Mt. Sinai Hosp., N.Y.C., 1966-67; resident in anesthesia U. Pa. Hosp., Phila., 1967-69, rsch. fellow, 1971-72; instr. anesthesia U. Pa., phila., 1972-73, asst. prof. anesthesia, 1973-82; assoc. prof. anesthesiology Med. Coll. Pa. and Hahnemann U., Phila., 1982—. Author: (with others) Basic Pharmacology in Medicine, 1990; contbr. articles to profl. jours. With USPHS, 1969-71. Avocations: photography, hiking, music. Office: Hahnemann Univ Hosp Broad & Vine Sts Philadelphia PA 19102

LEVITT, LEROY PAUL, psychiatrist, psychoanalyst; b. Wilkes-Barre, Pa., Jan. 8, 1918; s. Samuel and Paula (Goldstein) L.; divorced; children: Steven C., Susan M., Jeremy W., Sara H.; m. Jane A. Glaim, Apr. 7, 1971. B.S., Pa. State U., 1939; M.D., Chgo. Med. Sch., 1943; postgrad., Inst. Psychoanalysis, Chgo., 1950-59. Diplomate: Am. Bd. Psychiatry and Neurology. Intern Beth David Hosp., N.Y.C., 1943; resident Elgin (Ill.) State Hosp., 1947-49; pvt. practice, specializing in psychiatry and psychoanalysis Chgo., 1949—; prof. psychiatry Chgo. Med. Sch., 1949-76, dean, 1966-73; dir. Ill. Dept. Mental Health, 1973-76; v.p. Mt. Sinai Hosp. Med. Ctr., Chgo., 1976-82, chmn. dept. psychiatry, 1982-87, dir. med. edn., 1987-88; prof. psychiatry Rush Med. Coll., 1977-89, prof. emeritus, 1989—; mem. staff Naples Community Hosp., 1989—; cons. Blue Cross-Blue Shield, 1977-80, Nat. Council Aging, Ill. Psychiat. Inst.; mem. Mayor's Commn. on Aging, 1955-60. Pres. Chgo. Bd. Health, 1979-83; bd. dirs. Med. Ctr. YMCA, Med. Careers Council; bd. govs. Inst. of Medicine of Chgo. Med. Soc. Served to capt. M.C. AUS, 1944-46. Named Prof. of Year Chgo. Med. Sch., 1964, Tchr. of Year Ill. Psychiat. Inst., 1966, Chicagoan of Yr. in Medicine, 1970; WHO fellow Europe, 1970; recipient Sinai Health Service award, 1986. Fellow Am. Psychiat. Assn. (life), Am. Acad. Psychoanalysis, Am., Internat. psychoanalytic assns., Ill. Psychiat. Soc. (pres.), Chgo. Inst. Medicine, Am. Coll. Psychiatrists, Am. Coll. Psychoanalysts (pres. 1983, Laughlin award 1985), Sigma Xi, Alpha Omega Alpha, Phi Lambda Kappa (Gold medal sci. award). Home: 222 Harbour Dr Naples FL 33940-4022

LEVITT, MIRIAM, pediatrician; b. Lampertheim, Germany, June 10, 1946; came to U.S., 1948; d. Eli and Esther (Kingston) L.; m. Harvey Flisser, June 25, 1967; children: Adam, Elizabeth, Eric. AB, NYU, 1967; MD, Albert Einstein Coll. Medicine, Yeshiva U., 1971. Diplomate Am. Bd. Pediatrics. Intern Montefiore Med. Ctr., Bronx, N.Y., 1970-71, resident in pediatrics, 1971-73, attending pediatrician, 1975—; dir. outpatient svcs. pediatrics Bronx-Lebanon Hosp., N.Y.C., 1973-77; instr. pediatrics Albert Einstein Coll. Medicine, N.Y.C., 1973-76, asst. prof. clin., 1976—; med. staff Lawrence Hosp., Bronxville, N.Y., 1978—, dir. pediatrics, 1988—; sch. physician Bronxville Bd. Edn., 1983—. Fellow Am. Acad. Pediatrics; mem. Westchester County Med. Soc. Office: 1 Pondfield Rd Bronxville NY 10708-3706

LEVITT, MITCHELL ALAN, management consultant; b. N.Y.C., June 20, 1944; s. Ben and Rhea (Brody) L. BA, CUNY, 1967; MA, Temple U., 1969. Sr. ptnr., pres. Klein Consultants, N.Y.C., 1979—; bd. dirs. Hyde Products, Cleve. Mem. Am. Psychol. Assn., Inst. Mgmt. Cons. Home: 1675 York Ave New York NY 10128-6752 Office: Klein Cons 305 Madson New York NY 10165

LEVITT, RAYMOND ELLIOT, civil engineering educator; b. Johannesburg, Republic of South Africa, Aug. 7, 1949; came to U.S., 1972; s. Barnard and Riva Eleanor (Lazarus) L.; m. Kathleen Adele Sullivan, Nov. 26, 1976; children: Benjamin John, Joanna Maurine, Zoë Ellen. BSCE, U. Witwatersrand, Johannesburg, 1971; MSCE, Stanford U., 1973, PhDCE, 1975. Project engr. Christiani & Neilsen, Cape Town, Republic of South Africa, 1971-72; asst. prof. civil engring. MIT, Cambridge, 1975-79, assoc. prof., 1979-80; assoc. prof. Stanford (Calif.) U., 1980-88, prof., 1988—; assoc. dir. Ctr. for Integrated Facility Engring.; chmn. bd. Design Power, Inc., Cupertino, Calif.; advisor U.S. Dept. Labor, Washington, 1976-77, Calif. Pub. Utilities Commn., San Francisco, 1982-84. Co-author: Union and Open-Shop Construction, 1978, Construction Safety Management, 1987, 2d edit., 1993, Knowledge-Based Systems in Engineering, 1990. Pres. Stanford Homeowners Assn., 1981-83. Recipient Marksman award Engring. News Record, N.Y.C., 1985, Commitment to Life award Nat. Safe Workplace Inst., 1987. Mem. ASCE (Huber Prize award 1982), Am. Assn. Artificial Intelligence, Project Mgmt. Inst. Unitarian. Avocations: swimming, trout fishing, tennis, music. Office: Stanford U Dept Civil Engring # 4020 Stanford CA 94305

LEVITT, ROBERT E., gastroenterologist; b. Phila., Oct. 22, 1948; s. Martin E. and Miriam G. (Elson) L.; m. Linda Levitt, Mar. 13, 1976; children: Adam, Ashley. BA summa cum laude, Temple U., 1970, MD, 1974. Diplomate Am. Bd. Internal Medicine, Am. Bd. Gastroenterology. Chief hepatology and gastrointestinal rsch. Presbyn. U. of Pa. Med. Ctr., Phila., 1979-88, staff gastroenterologist, 1979—, assoc. dir. Inst. Gastroenterology, 1981-89; chief svc. gastroenterology Bryn Mawr (Pa.) Hosp., 1985—, chief gastrointestinal sect. dept. medicine, 1988—, dir. endoscopy ste., 1988—; asst. prof. medicine U. Pa. Sch. Medicine, 1979—; dir. endoscopy suite Bryn Mawr Hosp., 1988—. Contbr. articles to med. jours., chpts. to med. books; mem. editorial adv. bd. Post-Grad. Medicine. Fellow ACP; mem. AMA (Physicians Recognition award 1978, others), Am. Gastroenterol. Assn., Am. Coll. Gastroenterology, Am. Soc. for Gastrointestinal Endoscopy, Pa. Soc. Gastroenterology, Med. Club Phila., Phi Eta Sigma, Alpha Omega Alpha. Office: 933 E Haverford Rd Bryn Mawr PA 19010-3819

LEVITT, SEYMOUR HERBERT, physician, radiology educator; b. Chgo., July 18, 1928; s. Nathan E. Levitt and Margaret (Chizever) D.; m. Phillis Jeanne Martin, Oct. 31, 1952 (div. Oct. 1981); children: Mary Jeanne, Jennifer Gaye, Scott Hayden; m. Solveig I. Ostberg, Feb. 6, 1983. B.A., U. Colo., 1950, M.D., 1954. Diplomate: Am. Bd. Radiology (trustee). Intern Phila. Gen. Hosp., 1954-55; resident in radiology U. Calif. at San Francisco Med. Center, 1957-61; instr. radiation therapy U. Mich., Ann Arbor, 1961-62, U. Rochester, N.Y., 1962-63; asso. prof. radiology U. Okla., Oklahoma City, 1963-66; prof. radiology, chmn. div. radiotherapy Med. Coll. Va., Richmond, 1966-70; prof., head dept. therapeutic radiology U. Minn., Mpls., 1970—; cons. in field. Exec. bd. Am. Joint Com. for End Result Reporting and Cancer Staging; com. radiation oncology studies Nat. Cancer Inst. Bd. dirs., mem. exec. com. Am. Cancer Soc., 1990-95. With M.C., AUS, 1955-57. Recipient Disting. Svc. award U. Colo., 1988. Fellow Am. Coll. Radiology (bd. chancellors, Gold medal 1995), Royal Coll. Radiology (hon.); mem. Am. Radium Soc. (sec. 1981-83, pres. 1983-84, Janeway medal 1989), Radiol. Soc. N.Am. (bd. dirs. 1991—), Am. Assn. Cancer Rsch., Am. Cancer Soc. (pres. Minn. divsn. 1979-80, nat. bd., exec. com.), Am. Roentgen Ray Soc., Soc. Chairmen of Acad. Radiation Oncology Programs (pres. 1974-76), Internat. Soc. Radiation Oncology (pres. 1981-85), Soc. Nuclear Medicine, Am. Soc. Clin. Oncology, Am. Soc. Therapeutic Radiologists (exec. bd. 1974-78, pres. 1978-79, chmn. bd. 1979-80, Gold medal 1991), Deutsche Rontgengesellschaft Gesellschaft fur Medizinische Radiologie E.V. (hon.), Phi Beta Kappa, Sigma Xi., Alpha Omega Alpha. Home: 7233 Lewis Ridge Pkwy Minneapolis MN 55439-1106 Office: U Minn PO Box 436 Minneapolis MN 55455

LEVITZ, PAUL ELLIOT, publishing executive; b. Bklyn., Oct. 21, 1956; s. Alfred Lazarus and Hannah (Brenner) L.; m. Jeanette Francine Cusimano, Nov. 2, 1980; children: Nicole, Philip, Garret. Student, N.Y. U., 1973-76. Editor, pub. The Comic Reader, Bklyn., 1971-73; writer, asst. editor Nat. Periodical Publs., Inc., N.Y.C., 1973-76; editor, editorial coordinator, writer DC Comics, N.Y.C., 1976-80, mgr. bus. affairs, 1980-82, v.p. ops., 1982-84, exec. v.p., 1984-89, exec. v.p., pub., 1989—; exec. v.p., pub. MAD mag., 1993—. Jewish. Home: 23 Stony Hollow Chappaqua NY 10514 Office: DC Comics 1700 Broadway New York NY 10019

LEVMORE, SAUL, law educator; b. 1953. BA, Columbia Coll., 1973, PhD, 1978; JD, Yale U., 1980. Bar: Va. 1983. Dean Jonathan Edwards Coll. Yale U., 1979-80; asst. prof. U. Va., Charlottesville, 1980-84, prof., 1984—; Brokaw prof. of law; lectr. econs. Yale U., 1976-80, vis. prof., 1986-87; vis. prof. Harvard U., 1990-91, U. Chgo., 1993. Office: U Va Law Sch 580 Massie Rd Charlottesville VA 22903-1789

LEVOVITZ, PESACH ZECHARIAH, rabbi; b. Poland, Sept. 15, 1922; came to U.S., 1923; s. Reuben and Leah Zlate (Kustanowitz) L.; m. Bluma D. Feder, Feb. 5, 1945 (dec. 1970); children: Sivya, Yaakov; m. Eleanore Herman Klugmann, 1972 (dec. Nov. 1980); children: Maurice, Danny, Renee, Jackie; m. Frayde Twersky Perlow, Dec. 18, 1989; stepchildren: Yitzchok, Faige, Joseph. B.A., Yeshivah U., 1942. Rabbi Mesivtha Tifereth Jerusalem Rabbinical Sem., 1943, Congregation Sons of Israel, Lakewood, N.J., 1944—; founder, 1945; since dean Bezalel Day Sch.; Pres. Rabbinical Council Am., 1966-68, chmn. commn. on internat. affairs, 1972; asso. chmn. Soviet Jewry commn., 1980; mem. exec. com. Synagogue Council Am., 1953—; standing com. Conf. European Rabbis and Asso. Rabbis, 1964—; steering com. World Conf. Ashkenazi and Sephardi Synagogues; Co chmn. rabbinic cabinet Bonds for Israel, 1972; chaplain Lakewood Police Dept., 1950—; vis. chaplain Naval Air Sta., Lakehurst, N.J., 1945—; nat. chmn. an. conv. Rabbinical Council of Am., 1971; v.p. Religious Zionists Am., 1974; nat. chmn. Vaad Haroshi Religious Zionists Am., 1975; pres. Beth Din of Am., 1986. Mem. adv. bd. Lakewood Housing Council, Nat. Community Relations Adv. Council, United Jewish Appeal; chmn. bd. Sons of Israel Sr. Citizens Housing Inc., 1980; mem. N.J. Drug Utilization Council.; chmn. adv. council on protection kosher legislation to Atty. Gen., State of N.J.; mem. exec. Ocean County Jewish Fedn., 1988; co-chmn. BLue Ribbon Panel Lakewood Twp., 1992—. Recipient Revel Meml. award in religion and religious edn. Yeshivah Coll. Alumni Assn., 1967; award for outstanding rabbinic leadership Union of Orthodox Jewish Congregations Am., 1969; Nat. Assn. Hebrew Day Schs., 1980; chief Rabbi Issas Halevi Herzog Torah Fellowship award Religious Zionists Am., 1972; chmn. nat. conv., 1974; named Rabbi of Yr., Israel Bond Orgn., 1991. Mem. Conf. Presidents Nat. Jewish Orgns., Am. Conf. Soviet Jewry. Home: 403 6th St Lakewood NJ 08701-2609 Office: Congregation Sons of Israel Madison Ave Lakewood NJ 08701

LEVOY, MYRON, author; b. N.Y.C., Jan. 30, 1930; s. Bernard and Elsie (Schwartz) L.; m. Beatrice Fleischer, Jan. 27, 1952; children: David, Deborah. BS in Chem. Engring., CCNY, 1952; MS in Chem. Engring., Purdue U., 1953. Engr. Pratt & Whitney Aircraft Co., East Hartford, Conn., 1953-56; project engr. Reaction Motors Inc., Rockaway, N.J., 1956-67; engr. specialist Polytech. Design, Livingston, N.J., 1973-81; writer, 1955—. Author: (novel) A Necktie in Greenwich Village, 1968; Penny Tunes and Princesses, 1972, The Witch of Fourth Street and Other Stories, 1972 (Book World Honor Book 1972), Children's Book Showcase award 1973), Alan and Naomi, 1977 (Boston Globe-Horn Book award, Honor Book 1978, Jane Addams Honor Book award 1978, Am. Book award finalist 1980, Silver Pencil award The Netherlands 1981, Austrian State prize for children's lit 1981, German State prize for young adult lit. 1982, Buxtehuder Bulle award Fed. Republic Germany 1982), A Shadow Like a Leopard, 1981 (ALA Best Book for Young Adults 1981), Three Friends, 1984, The Hanukkah of Great-Uncle Otto, 1984, Pictures of Adam, 1986 (ALA Best Book for young adults 1986, Internat. Reading Assn. young adult choice 1986), The Magic Hat of Mortimer Wintergreen, 1988 (Jr. Lit. Guild selection 1988), Kelly 'N' Me, 1992, also poetry and plays; contbr. articles to profl. jours. Mem. PEN, The Authors Guild, The Dramatists Guild. Jewish. Avocations: tennis, cross-country skiing, swimming, museums, films. Office: Writers House Inc 21 W 26th St New York NY 10010-1003

LEVY, ALAIN M., record company executive; b. France, Dec. 19, 1946. Grad., Ecole des Mines, France; MBA, U. Pa. Asst. to the pres. CBS Internat., N.Y.C., 1972-73; v.p. mktg. for Europe CBS Internat., Paris, 1973, v.p. of creative ops. for Europe; also mgr. CBS/Italy, 1978; mng. dir. CBS Disques, France, 1979; chief exec. officer PolyGram France, 1984; exec. v.p. PolyGram group, France and Fed. Republic of Germany, 1988; mgr. U.S. ops. PolyGram group, 1990—; pres., chief exec. officer, mem. bd. mgrs. PolyGram USA, 1991—; apptd. to group mgmt. com. Phillips Electronics, majority shareholder of PolyGram USA, 1991—. Office: PolyGram Records Inc 825 8th Ave New York NY 10019-7416 also: 30 Berkeley Sq, London W1X 5HA, England*

LEVY, ALAN DAVID, real estate executive; b. St. Louis, July 19, 1938; s. I. Jack and Natalie (Yawitz) L.; grad. Sch. Real Estate, Washington U., 1960; m. Abby Jane Markowitz, May 12, 1968; children: Jennifer Lynn, Jacqueline Claire. Property mgr. Solon Gershman Inc., Realtors, Clayton, Mo., 1958-61; gen. mgr. Kodner Constrn. Co., St. Louis, 1961-63; regional mgr. Tishman Realty & Constrn. Co., Inc., N.Y.C., 1963-69, v.p., Los Angeles, 1969-77; exec. v.p., dir. Tishman West Mgmt. Corp., 1977-88; pres. Tishman West Cos., 1988-92, chmn. Tishman Internat. Cos., 1993—; guest lectr. on real estate mgmt. to various forums. Mem. L.A. County Mus. Art; chmn. Am. Art Coun.; trustee Archives Am. Art, Harvard-Westlake Sch.; bd. govs. W.L.A. coun. Boy Scouts Am. Mem. Bldg. Owners and Mgrs. Assn. L.A. (dir.), N.J. (co-founder, hon. dir.), Inst. Real Estate Mgmt. (cert. property mgr.), Urban Land Inst., Internat. Council Shopping Centers. Contbr. articles on property mgmt. to trade jours. Office: 10900 Wilshire Blvd Ste 510 Los Angeles CA 90024-6525

LEVY, ALAN JOSEPH, editor, journalist, writer; b. N.Y.C., Feb. 10, 1932; s. Meyer and Frances (Shield) L.; m. Valerie Wladaver, Aug. 7, 1956; children: Monica, Erika. A.B., Brown U., 1952; M.S. in Journalism, Columbia U., 1953. Reporter Louisville Courier-Jour., 1953-60; free-lance contbr. Life, Sat. Eve. Post, N.Y. Times, others, 1960-91; investigator Carnegie Commn. Ednl. TV, Boston, 1966-67; fgn. corr. Life, N.Y. Times mags., Prague, Czechoslovakia, 1967-71; dramaturg Vienna's English Theatre, Austria, 1977-82; free-lance author, dramatist, corr. Vienna, 1971-90; founding editor in chief The Prague Post (Eng. language weekly newspaper), 1991—; lectr. on theatre Salzburg Seminar in Am. Studies, Austria, 1981; adj. prof. lit. and jounralism Webster U., Vienna, 1983—; lectr.-in-residence Gritti Palace, Venice, Italy, 1987; prof. non-fiction Ctrl. European U. Summer Writers' Workshop, 1994, Charles U. Summer Writers' Workshop, Pargue, 1996. Author: Draftee's Confidential Guide, 1957, 2d edit., 1966, Operation Elvis, 1960, The Elizabeth Taylor Story, 1961, Wanted: Nazi Criminals at Large, 1962, Interpret Your Dreams, 1962, 2d edit., 1975, Kind-Hearted Tiger, 1964, The Culture Vultures, 1968, God Bless You Real Good, 1969, Rowboat to Prague, 1972, 2d edit. titled So Many Heroes, 1980, Good Men Still Live, 1974, The Bluebird of Happiness, 1976, Forever, Sophia, 1979, 2d edit., 1986, Treasures of the Vatican Collections, 1983, Ezra Pound: the Voice of Silence, 1983, W.H. Auden: In the Autumn of the Age of Anxiety, 1983, Vladimir Nabokov: The Velvet Butterfly, 1984, Ezra Pound: A Jewish View, 1988, The Wiesenthal File, U.K. edit. 1993, U.S. edit. 1994 (U.S. Author of the Year Am. Soc. of Journ. and Authors, 1995); dramatist The World of Ruth Draper, 1982; librettist Just an Accident?, 1983 (Ernst Krenek prize City of Vienna, 1986). Trustee Thomas Nast Found., Landau, Germany, 1978—, Saving Our Heritage Assn., Oberdorf, Switzerland, 1994—. Served with U.S. Army, 1953-55. Recipient New Republic Younger Writer award, 1958, Bets Enterprise Reporting award Sigma Delta Chi, 1959, golden Johan Strauss medal City of Vienna, 1981, travel writing awards Pacific Area Travel Assn., 1978, Govt. of Malta, 1985, Franz Kafka medal European Franz Kafka Circle, Prague, 1996; Bernard De Voto fellow Middlebury Coll., 1963. mem. Am. Soc. Journalists and Authors, Authors Guild and Dramatists Guild of Authors League of Am., Overseas Press Club Am., PEN, Fgn. Press assns. Vienna, Prague, Austrian Soc. Authors, Composers and Music Pubs., Czech Union Journalists. Democrat. Jewish. Office: Wallace Literary Agency 177 E 70 St New York NY 10021 Address: The Prague Post, Na Porici 12, CZ-11530 Prague 1, Czech Republic

LEVY, ARNOLD S(TUART), real estate company executive; b. Chgo., Mar. 15, 1941; s. Roy and Esther (Scheff) L.; m. Eva Cichosz, Aug. 8, 1976; children: Adam, Rachel, Deborah. BS, U. Wis., 1963; MPA, Roosevelt U., 1970. Dir. Neighborhood Youth Corps, Chgo., 1966-68; v.p. Social Planning Assn., Chgo., 1968-70; planning dir. Office of Mayor Chgo., 1970-74; dep. dir. Mayor's Office Manpower, Chgo., 1974-75; sr. v.p. Urban Investment & Devel. Co., Chgo., 1975-93; pres., CEO Stone-Levy, LLC, Chgo., 1994—; mem. S-L Hospitality Group, LLC, 1995—; pres. JMB/Urban Hotels, Hotel and Resort Devel. Group, JMB/Urban Devel. Co., 1985-93; ptnr. Pierce and Co., 1994—; bd. dirs. Hostmark Mgmt. Group, Inc.; mem. Urban Land Inst. Pres. Ark, Chgo., 1970-72, Parental Stress Svcs., Chgo., 1978-79; past lectr. DePaul U., Roosevelt U., Loyola U.; v.p. Inst. Urban Life, Chgo., 1983—. Co-editor: The Professionals' Guide to Commercial Property Development, 1988. Bd. dirs. Mus. Broadcast Communications, Chgo. Coun. of Urban Affairs, Am Shalom, pres. Ill. Humane Soc. ; steering com. Radio Hall of Fame; chmn. Spertus Inst. Jewish Studies, Glencoe Plan Commn., Carlton Club (Chgo.), Twin Orchard Club. Home: 535 Park Ave Glencoe IL 60022-1501 Office: Stone-Levy & Co LLC 8700 W Bryn Mawr Ave Ste 900 Chicago IL 60631-3507

LEVY, ARTHUR JAMES, public relations executive, writer; b. Bklyn., Dec. 23, 1947; s. Bernard and Bernice (Lipner) L.; m. Andrea Susan Hall, May 11, 1980; children: Zoe Jess, Jake Benjamin. BA, Brandeis U., 1969. Account exec., disc jockey Sta. WBUS-FM, Miami Beach, Fla., 1971; pop music critic Magic Bus Newspaper, Miami Beach, 1971; sr. editor, writer Zoo World mag., Ft. Lauderdale, Fla., 1971-74; chief writer Atlantic Records, N.Y.C., 1975-78; assoc. dir. Press and Pub. Info. dept. Columbia Records, N.Y.C., 1978-88, nat. dir. media services, publicity dept., 1988-93; v.p. Sony Music Entertainment Comms. Dept., N.Y.C., 1993-95; so. regional v.p. Rock Writers of the World, 1973-74; seminar panelist United Jazz Coalition, N.Y.C., 1983—, CMJ Folk, 1987—, New Music Seminar Folk, 1989—. Writer, researcher album and video liner notes for Rolling Stones, Blue Öyster Cult, Eric Andersen, Johnny Cash, Herbie Mann, Taj Mahal, Al Kooper, Robert Johnson, Jan Hammer, Julio Iglesias, Boomtown Rats, Jimmy Webb, Pete Seeger, Montreux Festival '77, Elvis Presley: Golden Celebration, 1985 (Grammy nomination), Songs of the Civil War; appeared on album session (Finnadar Records) Idil Biret's New Line Piano, 1978, (Columbia) Jaroslav Jakubovic's Checkin' In, 1978. Named Publicist of Yr. Columbia Records, 1982, 87, Media Man of Yr. Record World mag., N.Y.C., 1981. Mem. NARAS (gov. N.Y. chpt., Grammy voting com., crafts com.), Rock and Roll Hall of Fame (nominating com., mus. experts com.), Nat. Acad. Popular Music. Avocation: record collecting.

LEVY, BERNARD C., electrical engineer, educator; b. Princeton, N.J., July 31, 1951. Ingenieur civil des mines, Paris, 1974; PhD in Elec. Engring., Stanford U., 1979. Prof. dept. elec. and computer engr. U. Calif. Fellow IEEE (image and multidimensional signal processing tech. com. 1992—). Office: Univ of California Davis Dept Electrical & Computer Eng Davis CA 95616*

LEVY, BURTON See LANE, BURTON

LEVY, DALE PENNEYS, lawyer; b. Phila., Sept. 10, 1940; d. Harry M. and Rosalind (Fried) Penneys; m. Richard D. Levy, Dec. 20, 1970; children: Jonathan D., Michael Z. BA, Wellesley Coll., 1962; JD, U. Pa., 1967. Bar: Pa. 1967, U.S. Ct. Appeals (3d cir.) 1971. Assoc. Blank, Rome, Comisky & McCauley, Phila., 1967-76, ptnr., 1976—; bd. dirs. Phila. Sch., Phila. Indsl. Devel. Corp. Contbr. articles to profl. jours. Bd. dirs., chair Women in Transition, 1983-85, active adv. bd., 1985—; chair Women's Rights Com., 1978; bd. dirs. Phila. Sr. Ctr., 1994—, Phila. Theatre. Co., 195—. Mem. ABA, Pa. Bar Assn., Phila. Bar Assn. (past chair women's rights com.). Mem. ABA (real property, probate and trust law sect., vice chairperson com. on pub.-pvt. ventures/privatization internat. law and practice sect.), Phila. Bar Assn. (real estate, corp., banking and bus. law sect., mem. women's rights com.). Office: Blank Rome Comisky & McCauley 4 Penn Center Plz Philadelphia PA 19103-2521

LEVY, DAVID, lawyer, insurance company executive; b. Bridgeport, Conn., Aug. 3, 1932; s. Aaron and Rachel (Goldman) L. BS in Econs., U. Pa., 1954; JD, Yale U., 1957. Bar: Conn. 1958, U.S. Supreme Ct. 1963, D.C. 1964, Mass. 1965, N.Y. 1971, Pa. 1972; CPA, Conn. Acct. Arthur Andersen & Co., N.Y.C., 1957-59; sole practice Bridgeport, 1959-60; specialist tax law IRS, Washington, 1960-64; counsel State Mut. Life Ins. Co., Worcester, Mass., 1964-70; assoc. gen. counsel taxation Penn Mut. Life Ins. Co., Phila., 1971-81; sole practice Washington, 1982-87; v.p., tax counsel Pacific Mut. Life Ins. Co., Newport Beach, Calif., 1987—. Author: (with others) Life Insurance Company Tax Series, Bureau National Affairs Tax Management Income Tax, 1970-71. Mem. adv. bd. Tax Mgmt., Washington, 1975-90, Hartford Inst. on Ins. Taxation, 1990—; bd. dirs. Citizens Plan E Orgn., Worcester, 1966-70. With AUS, 1957. Mem. ABA (vice-chmn. employee benefits com. 1980-86, ins. cos. com. 1984-86, torts and ins. practice sect., subcom. chair ins. cos. com. tax sect. 1994—), Assn. Life Ins. Counsel, AICPA, Beta Alpha Psi. Jewish.

LEVY, DAVID, broadcasting executive; b. Phila.; s. Benjamin and Lillian (Potash) L.; m. Lucile Alva Wilds, July 25, 1941 (div. 1970); children: Lance, Linda; m. Victoria Robertson, Apr. 23, 1987; 1 stepchild, Kate Jolson. BS in Econs., U. Pa., 1934, MBA, 1935. With Young & Rubicam, Inc., N.Y.C., 1938-59, v.p., assoc. dir. radio-TV dept.; v.p. charge network programs and talent NBC, N.Y.C., 1959-61; exec. producer Filmways, L.A., 1964-68, Goodson-Todman Prodns., West Coast, 1968-69; exec. v.p., dir. Golden Orange Broadcasting Co., Anaheim, Calif., 1969-88, bd. dirs.; exec. v.p. charge TV activities Four Star Internat., Inc., Beverly Hills, Calif., 1970-72; pres. Wilshire Prodns. Inc., Beverly Hills, 1972—; mem. faculty Calif. State U., Northridge, 1973-77; TV advisor Citizens for Eisenhower, 1952, 56, Haig for Pres., 1988; dir. radio and TV for Citizens for Eisenhower-Nixon, 1956; prodr., writer 3-network program for closing Rep. campaign broadcast Four More Years, 1956; writer, co-prodr. closing program election eve behalf of Wendell Willkie, 1940; cons. Sec. Treasury, 1944-46; chief radio sect. war fin. divsn. Treasury Dept. Exec. prodr. Double Life of Henry Phyffe, 1965; exec. prodr., creator TV series Addams Family, 1964-66, The Pruitts of Southampton ABC-TV, 1966-67; prodr. world premier Sarge, also exec. prodr., creator TV series Universal Studios NBC, 1971-72; creator Holywood Screen Test, Bat Masterson, Appointment with Adventure, Outlaws, The Americans, Real West, The Kate Smith Daytime Hour, others; launched Maverick, Shirley Temple, National Velvet, Father Knows Best, Godfrey's Talent Scouts, People's Choice, I Married Joan, Life of Riley, Dr. Kildare, Bonanza, Hitchcock Presents, Thriller, Saturday Night at the Movies, Walt Disney's Wonderful World of Color, Robert Taylor and the Detectives, The Deputy, Car 54, 1st Bob Newhart Show, 1st Phil Silvers Show, Goodyear TV Playhouse, Peter Pan (starring Mary Martin), What's My Line, Make the Connection, Say When, others; prodr. Paramount TV, 1972-73, Hanna Barbera Prodns. NBC, 1973-74; creative cons. Name That Tune, Ralph Edwards Prodns. and Sandy Frank Prodns., 1974-81; creative cons. You Asked For It, Battle of the Planets; TV cons. Mark Goodson Prodns., 1989—; co-creator, exec. prodr. Face the Music TV series, 1980-81; author: (novels) The Chameleons, 1964, The Network Jungle, 1976, The Gods of Foxcroft, 1970, Potomac Jungle, 1990; contbr. short stories to popular mags. Lt. USN, 1944-46. Lt. USN, 1944-46. Recipient Treasury medal and disting. svc. citation U.S. Treasury Dept., 1946. Mem. ASCAP, TV Acad., Writers Guild Am., Prodrs. Guild Am. (past sec., bd. dirs.), Hollywood Radio-TV Soc. (pres. 1969-70, award 1970), Caucus for Prodrs., Writers and Dirs. (sec., steering com., exec. dir. 1974—, Disting. Svc. award 1985, Spl. award of merit for 20 yrs. svc. 1994). Republican. Jewish. Avocation: writing. Office: 210 S Spalding Dr Beverly Hills CA 90212-3608

LEVY, DAVID ALFRED, immunology educator, physician, scientist; b. Washington, Aug. 27, 1930; s. Stanley A. and Blanche B. (Berman) L.; m. Annette Levy-Badoux; children: Jill, William, Stanley. BS, U. Md., 1952, MD, 1954. Diplomate Am. Bd. Internal Medicine, Am. Bd. Allergy and Immunology. Intern, resident in medicine U. Hosp., Balt., 1954-59; physician VA Hosp., Balt., 1961-62; fellow dept. microbiology Sch. Medicine Johns Hopkins U., 1962-66, asst. prof. radiol. sci. Sch. Hygiene and Pub. Health, Sch. Medicine, 1966-68, assoc. prof. Sch. Hgiene and Pub. Health, Sch. Medicine, 1968-71, prof. radiol. sci. and epidemiology Sch. Hygiene and Pub. Health, Sch. Medicine, 1972-73, prof. biochemistry Sch. Hygiene and Pub. Health, Sch. Medicine, 1973-82, with joint appointments in epidemiology and medicine Sch. Medicine, 1973-82, in pathobiology Sch. Medicine, 1980-82, prof. immunology and infectious diseases Sch. Medicine, 1982-86; mem. FDA Panel on Rev. of Allergenic Extracts, 1975-83; mem. allergy and immunology rev. com. Nat. Inst. Allergy and Infectious Diseases, 1975-77; adj. dir. Centre d'Immunologie et de Biologie, Pierre Fabre, S.A., 1985-90; cons. to pharm. industry, 1990—. Editorial bd. Clin. Immunology and Immunopathology, 1971-76, Revue d'Allergologie Française; contbr. articles to med. jours. and books. Sci. dir. Centre d'Allergie, Hopital Rothschild, Paris, 1991—. With U.S. Army, 1959-61. Fellow Am. Acad. Allergy and Immunology; mem. Internat. Union Immunol. Socs. (vice chmn. allergen standardization subcom. 1980-83), Am. Assn. Immunologists, French Soc. Allergology, Sigma Xi. Home and Office: 11 Quai St Michel, 75005 Paris France

LEVY, DAVID CORCOS, museum director; b. N.Y.C., Apr. 10, 1938; s. Edgar Wolf and Lucille (Corcos) L.; m. Janet Meyer, June 7, 1959 (div.); children: Jessica Anne, Thomas William; m. Carole L. Feld, May 19, 1992; 1 child, Alexander Wolf. BA, Columbia U., 1960; MA, NYU, 1969, PhD, 1979; DFA (hon.), New Sch. for Social Rsch., 1989. Asst. dir. admissions Parson Sch. Design, N.Y.C., 1961-62, dir. admissions, 1962-67, v.p., 1967-70, dean, chief adminstrv. officer, 1970-79, exec. dean, chief adminstrv. officer, 1979-89; chancellor New Sch. for Social Rsch., N.Y.C., 1989-90; pres., dir. The Corcoran Gallery of Art, Washington, D.C., 1991—. Photographer of works exhibited in Guggenheim Mus., Mus. Modern Art; art dir. jours., books, posters; contbr. articles to jours. and newspapers. Decorated Chevalier des Arts et des Lettres (France). Home: 2556 Massachusetts Ave NW Washington DC 20008-2822 Office: Corcoran Gallery of Art 500 17th St NW Washington DC 20006-4804

LEVY, DAVID FRANKLIN, sales and marketing executive; b. Sao Paulo, Brazil, Apr. 12, 1945; came to U.S., 1975; s. Benjamin Teodoro and Lydia (Defez) L.; m. Luciene Souhami, Feb. 15, 1973; 1 child, Tatiana Souhami. BS in Mech. Engring., Pontifical U. Catolica, Rio de Janeiro, 1969; MBA, John F. Kennedy U., 1979. Prodn. mgr. Bloch Pub., Rio de Janeiro, 1969-71; v.p. ops. Sedegra, Inc., Rio de Janeiro, 1971-75; mfg. mgr. Signetics Corp., Sunnyvale, Calif., 1978-82; v.p. sales and mktg. Micro Air Systems, Sunnyvale, 1982-85, Dexon, Inc., Mpls., 1985-88; pres., chief exec. officer SubMicron Systems Inc., Mpls., 1988—. Avocations: tennis, racquetball, skiing, bicycling. Office: 11728 Welters Way Eden Prairie MN 55347-2837*

LEVY, DAVID MATTHEW, lawyer; b. Boston, Feb. 13, 1954; s. Harold and Lillian (Kruger) L.; m. Keily Downey, June 14, 1986. BA, Cornell U., 1975; JD, U. Mich., 1979. Bar: D.C. 1979, U.S. Ct. Appeals (D.C. and 10th cirs.) 1980, U.S. Ct. Appeals (3rd cir.) 1982, U.S. Ct. Appeals (9th cir.) 1986, U.S. Supreme Ct. 1989. Assoc. Sidley & Austin, Washington, 1979-86, ptnr., 1986—. Contbr. articles to profl. jours. Mem. ABA (vice-chair postal matters com. adminstrv. law sect. 1991-92, chair 1992-95). Office: Sidley & Austin 1722 I St NW Washington DC 20006-3704

LEVY, DAVID STEVEN, college administrator; b. L.A., Mar. 9, 1955; s. Henry and Gloria Grace (Barouh) L. BA, Occidental Coll., 1977; MA, 1979. Asst. dir. fin. aid Calif. State Coll., San Bernardino, 1978-79; fin. aid counselor Calif. State U.-Northridge, 1979-80; assoc. dir. student fin. aid Calif. State U.-Dominguez Hills, 1980-82; dir. fin. aid Occidental Coll., L.A., 1982-88; dir. fin. aid Calif. Inst. Tech., Pasadena, Calif., 1988—, assoc. dean of students, 1991—; mem. Title IA Adv. Com. Calif., 1977—; negotiator U.S. Dept Edn. Mem. life-long learning com. Calif. Postsecondary Edn. Commn., 1980—, mem. student fin. aid issues com., 1984—. Richter fellow Princeton U., 1976; Calif. State U. adminstrv. fellow, 1981—. Mem. Nat. Assn. Student Fin. Aid. Adminstrs. (Meritorious Achievement award 1988, bd. dirs. 1991—, commn. dir. 1994-95), Mortar Board Alumni Assn. (pres. 1977—), Calif. Assn. Student Fin. Aid Adminstrs. (ind. segmental rep. 1984, sec. 1985, treas. 1986-88, Pres.'s award 1986, 93, Meritorious Svc. award 1994, Segmental Leadership award 1992, Creative Leadership award 1990), Western Assn. Student Fin. Aid Adminstrs. (Disting. Svc. award 1990, Pres. Disting. Svc. award 1992), Nat. Assn. Student Fin. Aid Adminstrs., Phi Beta Kappa, Delta Phi Epsilon, Psi Chi, Phi Alpha Theta, Sigma Alpha Epsilon. Jewish. Co-editor Calif. Student Aid Commn. Student Aid Workbook, 1977—; co-author, contbr. Playing the Selective College Admissions Game, 1994. Home: 368 Mount Carmel Dr Glendale CA 91206 Office: CalTech 515 S Wilson Ave Pasadena CA 91106-3212

LEVY, EDWARD CHARLES, JR., manufacturing company executive; b. Detroit, Nov. 14, 1931; s. Edward Charles and Pauline (Birndorf) L.; m. Julie Ruth Honigman, July 11, 1955; 2 children. S.B., MIT, 1952. With Edward C. Levy Co., Detroit, 1952—; v.p. ops. and engring. Edward C. Levy Co., 1957-63, exec. v.p., 1963-70, pres., 1970—. Bd. dirs. Edward C. Levy Found., Karmanos Cancer Inst., Detroit, Round Table of Christians and Jews; trustee Children's Hosp. of Mich., Citizens Rsch. Coun. Mich., Washington Inst. for Near East Policy; officer Am. Israel Pub. Affairs Com. Mem. Am. Concrete Inst., ASTM, Engring. Soc. Detroit. Jewish. Clubs: Detroit, Renaissance (Detroit); Franklin Hills Country (Franklin, Mich.). Office: Edward C Levy Co Inc 8800 Dix St Detroit MI 48209-1093

LEVY, EDWARD K., mechanical engineering educator. BS, U. Md., 1963; MS, MIT, 1964, ScD, 1967. Prof. mech. engring. Lehigh U., 1967—; assoc. prof. NAE. Mem. AIChE, ASME, Am. Nuclear Soc. Achievements include research in fluid mechanics, heat transfer and applied thermodynamic aspects of energy with emphasis on power generation systems. Office: Lehigh U Energy Rsch Ctr 117 Atlss St Bethlehem PA 18015-4728

LEVY, ETIENNE PAUL LOUIS, surgical department administrator; b. Paris, Feb. 17, 1922; s. Pierre-Paul and Jeanne (Dreyfus) L.; m. Suzanne Binvignat, Nov. 20, 1965; 1 child, Anne Cécile. Baccalaureat, Janson Sailly, Paris, 1935; engr., French Nat. Agronomic Inst., Paris, 1947; PhD in Engring., U., Paris, 1949, MD, 1956. Chief lab., dept. surgery Salpetriere Hosp., Paris, 1956-61; attaché rsch. INSERM, Paris, 1956-61, chief rsch., 1961-67, master rsch, 1967-87, dir. rsch., 1981-91; head dept. surg. gastrointestinal ICU Hosp. St. Antoine, Paris, 1960—; assoc. prof. Faculty Medicine, Paris, 1967—; cons. in field. Contbr. articles to profl. jours. Maj. French Mil., 1943-45, 56-57. Decorated officer Legion of Honour. Mem. N.Y. Acad. Scis., French Alpine Club. Home: 106 Ave Villiers, 75017 Paris France Office: Hosp St Antoine, 184 rue fb St Antoine, 75012 Paris France

LEVY, EUGENE, actor, director, screenwriter; b. Hamilton, Ont., Can.. Appearences include (films) Cannibal Girls, 1972, Running, 1979, Nothing Personal, 1980, Heavy Metal, 1981, Strange Brew, 1983, Going Berserk, 1983, National Lampoon's Vacation, 1983, Splash, 1984, Armed and Dangerous, 1986, The Canadian Conspiracy, 1986, Club Paradise, 1986, Speed Zone, 1989, Father of the Bride, 1991, Once Upon A Crime, 1992, Stay Tuned, 1992, I Love Trouble, 1994; (TV) The Lovebirds, 1979, From Cleveland, 1980, George Burn's Comedy Week, 1985, Dave Thomas: The Incredible Time Travels of Henry Osgood, 1986, Billy Crystal-Don't Get Me Started, 1986, Bride of Boogedy, 1987, Ray Bradbury Theatre, 1988; actor, dir.: (TV) Second City TV, 1977-81, SCTV Network, 1981-83, The Last Polka, 1985, Autobiographies: The Enigma of Bobby Bittman, 1988; dir.: (TV) Second City's 50th Anniversary Special, 1988, Partners in Love, 1992, Sodbusters, 1994. Office: William Morris Agy 151 S El Camino Dr Beverly Hills CA 90212-2704*

LEVY, EUGENE HOWARD, planetary sciences educator, researcher; b. N.Y.C., May 6, 1944; s. Isaac Philip and Anita Harriet (Guttman) L.; children: Roger P., Jonathan S., Benjamin H. AB in Physics with high honors, Rutgers U., 1966; PhD in Physics, U. Chgo., 1971. Teaching asst. dept. physics U. Chgo., 1966-69, rsch. asst. Enrico Fermi Inst., 1969-71; postdoctoral fellow dept. physics and astronomy U. Md., 1971-73; asst. prof. physics and astrophysics Bartol Rsch. Found., Franklin Inst., Swarthmore, Pa., 1973-75; asst., then assoc. prof. U. Ariz., Tucson, 1975-83, prof. planetary scis., 1983-95, mem. faculty applied math. program, 1981—, head dept. planetary scis., dir. lunar and planetary lab., 1983-94, mem. theoretical astrophysics program, 1985—; dean coll. of sci. U. Ariz., 1993—; dir. NASA-Ariz. Spacegrant Coll. Consortium U. Ariz., Tucson, 1989—, prof. physics, 1996—; mem. com. on planetary and lunar exploration of space sci. bd., Nat. Acad. Scis., 1976-79, chmn., 1979-82, co-chair Space Sci. Bd. Study on Exploration Primitive Solar-System Bodies, 1978, mem. Space Sci. Bd., 1979-82, head U.S. del., co-chair Nat. Acad. Scis.-European Sci. Found. Joint Working Group on Cooperation in Planetary Exploration, 1982-84, mem. steering group com. on major directions for space sci. 1995-2015, 1984-86, chair adv. com. on internat. cooperation for Mars sample return, 1986-88; mem. Comet Halley Sci. Working Group, NASA, 1977, mem. spacelab phys. sci. rev. panel space sci. steering com., 1979, mem. rev. panel on origin plasmas in Earth's neighborhood, 1980, mem. solar system exploration com. of Adv. Coun., 1980-83, mem. Ames Rsch. Ctr. Planetary Detection Study, 1983, Solar System Exploration Mgmt. Coun., 1983-87, mem. com. on future space-sta. sci. projects, 1985, mem. Space Sta. Sci. Users' Working Group, 1985-86, Space and Earth Sci. Adv. Com., 1985-88, chair Comet Rendevous and Asteroid Flyby Rev. Panel, 1986, mem. Mars Exploration Strategy Adv. Group, 1986, Mars Rover Sample Return Sci. Working Group, 1987—; sci. cons. Rockwell Internat. Corp., 1980; mem. COSPAR Internat. Tech. Panel on Comets, 1980-82; U.S.-NASA del. to discussions on internat. cooperation investigations of Comet Halley, Padua, Italy, 1981, to U.S.-USSR Joint Working Group on Near-Earth Space, the Moon and Planets, 1981; mem. program adv. bd. Internat. Conf. on Cometary Exploration, Budapest, Hungary, 1982; mem. exec. com. univs.' space sci. working group Assn. Am. Univs., 1982-86; study panel U.S.-Soviet cooperation in space sci. U.S. Cong. Office of Tech. Assessment, 1984; chair planetary exploration panel Pacific Rim Nations Internat. Space Yr. Conf., Kona, Hawaii, 1987; mem. working group planetary systems sci. NASA, 1988—, rev. panel lunar and planetary, 1988-90, rev. panel origins solar systems programs, 1990-91; chair formation/detection group, 1993-95; mem. astronomy and astrophysics survey com., sci. opportunities panel NAS, 1989-90; mem. study panel on robotic exploration of Moon and Mars, U.S. Cong. Office Tech. Assessment, 1991; chmn. coun. of instns., bd. dirs. U.S. Space Rsch. Assn., 1991—, vice-chmn. bd. dirs. 1993—; chmn. NASA Origins of Solar Syss. Planet Formation and Defection Rev. Panel, 1993-95, Internat. Sci Found. Astronomy Rev. Panel, 1993-94, NASA Origins of Solar Syss. Mgmt. Ops. Working Group, 1994—, Am. Astron. Soc. Com. on Pub. Edn., 1994; cons. and lectr. in field. Editor: Protostars and Planets III, 1993; contbr., author articles for gen. pub., adv. reports for Congl. Record, abstracts, book revs., others. Recipient Disting. Pub. Svc. medal NASA, 1983, Alexander von Humboldt-Stiftung Sr. Scientist award Fed. Republic Germany, 1989; Disting. vis. scientist Jet Propulsion Lab., Calif. Inst. Tech., 1985-91; NASA predoctoral fellow U. Chgo., 1966-69, fellow Ctr. for Theoretical Physics, U. Md., 1971-73; rsch. grantee NASA, NSF. Mem. AAAS, Am. Astron. Soc. (com. on pub. edn., 1994-95), Am. Geophys. Union, Am. Phys. Soc., Internat. Astron. Union,ace Rsch. Assn. (bd. dirs. 1991—), Coun. Instns. (pres. 1991-92, vice chmn. bd. dirs. 1993-94), NASA Origins of Solar Syss. Mgmt. Working Group (chair 1993—), Phi Beta Kappa, Sigma Xi. Achievements include research in theoretical cosmical physics, planetary geophysics, magnetohydrodynamics, space and solar physics, magnetic field generation, physical processes associated with the formation of stars and planetary systems. Office: U Ariz Lunar and Planetary Lab Tucson AZ 85721-4090

LEVY, EUGENE PFEIFER, architect; b. Little Rock, Dec. 14, 1936; s. Emmanuel Gabe and Elizabeth (Pfeifer) L.; m. Gertrude Watkins Cromwell, June 24, 1959; children: Edwin Cromwell, Andrew Stewart, Charles Pfeifer. B.Arch., U. Va., 1959. Registered architect, Ark., Calif., Ga., Tex. Apprentice Erhart, Eichenbaum, Rauch & Blass, Little Rock, 1959-60; architect, pres. Cromwell, Truemper, Levy, Thompson & Woodsmall, Inc., Little Rock, 1962—. Bd. dirs. Little Rock Boys' Club, 1973—; bd. dirs. Temple B'nai Israel, Little Rock, 1975-78, Little Rock chpt. NCCJ, 1984, Ark. chpt. ARC, 1989. Capt. U.S. Army, 1960-62. Recipient numerous awards including: U.S. Corps. of Engrs. 1985 Design award for Resident Office and Visitors Ctr., Greers Ferry Lake, Ark., USAG 1985 First Honor award for commissary, Camp Foster, Okinawa, Japan, AIA 1980 Design award for Master Plan and First Phase Design for Multi Agy. Office Bldg., State of Ark. Capitol Ground, Little Rock, AIA Honorable Mention award for Systematics, Inc., Corp. Hdqrs., 1982, AIA Design award for Winthrop Rockefeller Meml. Gallery Ark. Arts Ctr., Little Rock, 1982, AIA Design for Commissary, USAF Acad., Colo., 1983, Little Rock Riverfront Belvedere, AIA Design award, 1987, AIA Design award for Itzkowitz residence, Little Rock, 1991. Fellow AIA (Design award Commissary USAF; mem. Greater Little Rock C. of C. (com. 1983-84). Clubs: Little Rock

Country, Little Rock Athletic. Home: 5415 Sherwood Rd Little Rock AR 72207-5333 Office: Cromwell Truemper Levy Thompson Woodsall Inc 101 S Spring St Little Rock AR 72201-2428

LEVY, EZRA CESAR, aerospace scientist, real estate broker; b. Habana, Cuba, Sept. 22, 1924; s. Mayer D. and Rachel Levy; m. Gaynor D. Popejoy, 1980; children from previous marriage: Daniel M., Diana M. Levy Friedman, Linda R. Levy Brenden. MS, UCLA, 1951. Sect. head Douglas Aircraft Co., Santa Monica, Calif., 1951-54; dept. head Lockheed Aircraft Co., Van Nuys, Calif., 1954-56, Librascope, Glendale, Calif., 1956-57, Radioplane, Van Nuys, 1957-58; asst. dept. mgr. Space Tech. Labs., Redondo Beach, Calif., 1958-60; asst. divsn. dir. TRW, Redondo Beach, Calif., 1960-74; now real estate broker Regency Realty Corp., Temple City, Calif. Author: Laplace Transform Tables, 1958; contbr. articles to profl. jours. Cpl. U.S. Army, 1944-46. Mem. Temple City C. of C. (bd. dirs. 1992—), Masons (past master and sec.). Democrat. Jewish. Avocations: art, music, philately.

LEVY, GERARD G., industrial gases executive; b. 1939. With L'Air Liquide, SA, Paris, France, 1961—; chrm. bd. Bigg Three Industries Inc., Houston, 1988—. Office: Big Three Industries Inc 3535 W 12th St Houston TX 77008-6005*

LEVY, GERHARD, pharmacologist; b. Wollin, Germany, Feb. 12, 1928; came to U.S., 1948, naturalized, 1953; s. Gotthold and Eliesabeth (Luebeck) L.; m. Rosalyn Mincer, June 8, 1958; children: David, Marc, Sharon. B.S., U. Calif. at San Francisco, 1955, Pharm.D., 1958; Dr. honoris causa, Uppsala (Sweden) U., 1975, Phila. Coll. Pharmacy and Sci., 1979, L.I. U., 1981, U. Ill., 1986, Hoshi U., Japan, 1996. Asst. prof. pharmacy U. Buffalo, 1958-60; asso. prof. pharmacy State U. N.Y. at Buffalo, 1960-64, prof. biopharmaceutics, 1964-72, distinguished prof. pharmaceutics, 1972-75, chmn. dept. pharmaceutics, 1966-70, univ. disting. prof. emeritus, 1995; vis. prof. Hebrew U., Jerusalem; cons. WHO, 1966, Bur. Drugs Adv. Panel System, FDA, 1971-74; mem. com. on problems of drug safety NRC, 1971-75; mem. pharmacol.-toxicol. com. NIH, 1971-75. Mem. editorial bd. Jour. Pharm. Sci, 1970-75, Clin. Pharmacology and Therapeutics, 1969—, Internat. Jour. Clin. Pharmacology, 1968-78, Drug Metabolism and Disposition, 1973-78, Jour. Pharmacokin Biopharm, 1972—, Internat. Jour. Pharm., 1977-95, Jour. Pharmacobi-Dynamics, 1979-93, Pharm. Res., 1983-95; contbr. articles to profl. jours. Served with AUS, 1950-51. Recipient Ebert prize, 1969, Am. Pharm. Assn. Research Achievement award, 1969, McKeen Cattell award Am. Coll. Clin. Pharmacology, 1978, Host-Madsen medal Internat. Pharm. Fedn., 1978, Oscar B. Hunter award in exptl. therapeutics Am. Soc. Clin. Pharmacology and Therapeutics, 1982, Volwiler Research Achievement award Am. Assn. Colls. Pharmacy, 1982, Scheele award Swedish Acad. Pharmaceutical Scis., 1992, 1st Lifetime Achievement in the Pharm. Scis. award Internat. Pharm. Assn., 1994; named Alumnus of Year U. Calif. Sch. Pharmacy Alumni Assn., 1970. Fellow Am. Pharm. Assn., Acad. Pharm. Scis. (Takeru Higuchi Research prize 1983), AAAS; mem. Inst. Medicine of Nat. Acad. Scis., Am. Assn. Pharm. Scientists (Dale E. Wurster Rsch. award 1992), Am. Soc. Exptl. Pharmacology and Therapeutics. Home: 169 Surrey Run Buffalo NY 14221-3321 Office: SUNY Sch Pharmacy Amherst NY 14260

LEVY, H. RICHARD, biochemistry educator; b. Leipzig, Germany, Oct. 22, 1929; came to U.S., 1946; s. Berthold and Charlotte Agnes Hedwig (Frank) L.; m. Betty Louise Samuels, June 12, 1960; 1 child, Karen. BSc in Chemistry, Rutgers U., 1950; PhD in Biochemistry, U. Chgo., 1956. Instr. Ben May Lab. for Cancer Rsch., U. Chgo., 1959-61, asst. prof., 1961-63; asst. prof. dept. bacteriology and botany Syracuse (N.Y.) U., 1963-66, assoc. prof. dept. bacteriology and botany, 1966-70, assoc. prof. dept. biology, 1970-71, prof. of biochemistry, 1971—; chmn. dept. biology, 1993—. Contbr. articles and revs. to profl. publs. Grantee NIH, NSF, 1963—. Mem. AAAS, AAUP, Am. Chem. Soc., Am. Soc. for Biochemistry and Molecular Biology, Protein Soc. Home: 144 Lewis Ave Syracuse NY 13224-2232 Office: Syracuse U Biology Dept 130 College Pl Syracuse NY 13244-1220

LEVY, HERBERT MONTE, lawyer; b. N.Y.C., Jan. 14, 1923; s. Samuel M. and Hetty D. L.; m. Marilyn Wohl, Aug. 30, 1953; children: Harlan A., Matthew D., Alison Jill. A.B., Columbia U., 1943, LL.B., 1946. Bar: N.Y. 1946, U.S. Dist. Ct. (so. dist.) N.Y. 1946, U.S. Ct. Appeals (2d cir.) 1949, U.S. Dist. Ct. (ea. dist.) N.Y. 1949, U.S. Supreme Ct. 1951, U.S. Ct. Appeals (10th cir.) 1956, U.S. Tax Ct. 1973, U.S. Ct. Appeals (4th cir.) 1988. Assoc. Rosenman, Goldmark, Colin & Kaye, 1946-47, Javits & Javits, 1947-48; staff counsel ACLU, 1949-56; sole practice, 1956-64; ptnr. Hoffman, Gartlir, Hoffheimer, Gottleib & Gross, 1965-69; sole practice, N.Y.C., 1969—; bd. dirs. Music Outreach; faculty N.Y. County Lawyers Assn.; former lectr. Practising Law Inst. Exec. com. on law and social action Am. Jewish Congress, 1961-66; trustee Congregation B'nai Jeshurun, 1987—, chmn. bd. trustees 1988-91, gen. counsel bd. trustees, 1991-92. Mem. Fed. Bar Coun. (past trustee), Bar Assn. City N.Y., N.Y. County Lawyers Assn., 1st Amendment Lawyers Assn. Democrat. Author: How to Handle an Appeal (Practising Law Inst.), 1968, rev. edit. 1982, 2d rev. edit., 1990; also legal articles. Home: 285 Central Park W Apt 12W New York NY 10024-3006 Office: 60 E 42nd St Rm 4210 New York NY 10165-4299

LEVY, IRVIN L., diversified company executive; b. Dallas, 1929. BBA, So. Meth. U., 1950. With NCH Corp. (formerly Nat. Chemsearch Corp.), Irving, Tex., 1950—, now pres., CEO, 1965—, also bd. dirs. Office: NCH Corp 2727 Chemsearch Blvd Irving TX 75062-6454*

LEVY, JACQUES, educator, theater director, lyricist, writer; b. N.Y.C., July 29, 1935; s. Milton and Jean (Brandler) L.; m. Claudia Carr, Apr. 27, 1980; children: Maya, Julien. BA, CCNY, 1956; MA, Mich. State U., 1958, PhD, 1961. Moderator dirs./playwrights unit The Actors Studio; co-dir. Open Theater Workshop, N.Y.C.; tchr. play analysis, lyric writing New Sch. Social Rsch.; tchr. acting, directing, playwriting Hunter Coll., N.Y.C.; tchr. directing Tisch Sch Arts NYU, Grad. Dept. Theater Columbia U., Sch. Drama Yale U.; head univ. theater program Colgate U., Hamilton, N.Y., prof. Eng. Dir.: (Broadway plays) Oh! Calcutta!, Almost an Eagle, Doonesbury; dir., writer: (off-Broadway, regional, European plays) Turtlenecks, Back Country, Miami Lights; dir.: (off-Broadway, regional, European plays) America Hurrah, Scuba Duba, Red Cross (Obie award for disting. direction), La Turista, Geography of a Horse Dreamer, Rock Garden, Where Has Tommy Flowers Gone?, American Days, Sleep, Mensch Meyer, The Golden Land, The Potsdam Quartet, The Bed Was Full, Green Pants, K2, The Glass Menagerie, Exact Change, Blood Wedding, A Chekhov Concert, The Beggar's Opera, The Rolling Thunder Review; playwright, lyricist: Miami Lights, Berchtesgaden, Back Country, Just a Season, (adaptation) Alcestis, Eyes in the Heat, Tell the Rain; lyricist: (Byrds'albums) Byrdmaniax, Untitled, (Roger McGuinn's solo album) Thunderbyrd, (Bob Dylan's album) Desire, Fame...the Musical, The Golden Land. Recipient Obie award disting. direction, Obie award group achievement as co-dir. Open Theater, Drama Desk directing award nominations, Outer Critics Circle directing award nominations, Grammy award lyricist nominations; BMI grantee (5). Office: Colgate U Univ Theater 13 Oak Dr Hamilton NY 13346-1338

LEVY, JAMES PETER, publishing company executive; b. Oak Park, Ill., June 17, 1940; s. Andrew and Anna (Solsrud) L.; m. Loretta Constance Puglia; children: Elyssa, Andrew, Adam, Gina. Ed.B., U. Ill., 1962, B.A. in Edn., 1963. Sales rep. Prentice-Hall Pubs., Englewood Cliffs, N.J., 1963-66; engring. editor Prentice-Hall Pubs., Englewood, N.J., 1966-67; co-founder, exec. v.p. Goodyear Pub., Santa Monica, Calif., 1967-78; sr. v.p., gen. mgr. Scott, Foresman & Co., Glenview, Ill., 1978-88, bd. dirs.; pres. Higher Edn. Div. McGraw-Hill, N.Y.C., 1988-89; pres., CEO Merrill Pub. Co., Columbus, Ohio, 1989-90, Macmillan/McGraw-Hill, N.Y.C., 1990-92, Harcourt Brace Ednl. Pub., Chestnut Hill, Mass., 1992—, Harcourt General, Chestnut Hill, MA. Mem. Assn. Am. Pubs. (chmn. higher edn. div. 1982-84). Home: 65 Essex Rd Chestnut Hill MA 02167-1316 Office: Harcourt General 27 Boylston St Chestnut Hill MA 02167*

LEVY, JOSEPH, lawyer; b. N.Y.C., June 9, 1928; s. Morris Joseph and Dora (Cohen) L.; m. Gertrud C. Roeder, Jan. 20, 1967; children—Diana N., Susan R. BBA cum laude, Coll. City N.Y., 1950; JD cum laude, N.Y. U., 1954. Bar: N.Y. 1955, D.C. 1968. Asso. Parker, Chapin and Flattau, N.Y.C., 1954-62; ptnr. firm Rivkin, Sherman & Levy (and predecessors), N.Y.C., 1962-84, Schnader, Harrison, Segal & Lewis, 1984-93; v.p., sec., dir. Trecom Bus. Sys., Inc., Edison, N.J., 1993—; sec., dir. Horizons Comms. Corp., 1970-78, Quad Typographers, Inc., 1965-79; sec. Savin Bus. Machines Corp., 1959-84, On-Line Systems, Inc., 1968-78, Lambda Tech., Inc., 1970-78, Programming Methods, Inc., 1969-72, Kreisler Mfg. Cor., 1969-72, Peck & Peck, 1970-73, v.p., sec., dir. Trecom Bus. Systems, Inc., 1985—. Served to capt. AUS, 1951-53. Home: 254 University Way Paramus NJ 07652-5516 Office: Trecom Bus Sys Inc 333 Thornall St Edison NJ 08837

LEVY, JOSEPH LOUIS, publishing company executive; b. Bklyn., June 21, 1947; s. Myron M. and Miriam M. (Glick) L.; m. Carol A. Arschin, July 3, 1973; children: Darren Ross, Marissa Darcel. BBA, Pace U., 1970. Dir. mktg. Frost & Sullivan Inc., N.Y.C., 1966-71; v.p. Internat. Data Corp., Waltham, Mass., 1972-80, v.p. mktg., Framingham, Mass, 1980-86; pres. Pub. and Communications Group, 1986-87, group pres. Internat. Data Corp., 1987; pres., pub. CIO mag., 1988—. Contbr. spl. reports on computer industry and tech. to Fortune mag., 1975-86, Industry Week mag., 1984-85, US News and World Report, 1986, Forbes mag, 1987—. Named Young Exec. of Yr., Internat. Data Corp., 1972-76. Mem. Am. Mktg. Assn. (Mktg. Man of Yr. 1970), Am. Mgmt. Assn., Soc. Mgmt. Info. Systems, Sales Execs. Club. Republican. Office: 492 Old Connecticut Path Framingham MA 01701-4584

LEVY, JOSEPH WILLIAM, department stores executive; b. Fresno, Calif., 1932; m. Sharon Sorokin; children: Felicia, Jody, Bret. BS, U. So. Calif., 1954. Asst. merchandising mgr., then mgr. Gottschalks, Inc., Fresno, 1956-72, exec. v.p., 1972-82, chmn., chief exec. officer, 1982—; chmn. exec. com. Frederick Atkins Inc., N.Y.C., 1992—, also bd. dirs. Chmn. Fresno Econ. Devel. Corp., 1982-83; mem. Calif. Transp. Commn., 1983-91, chmn., 1986-87; sec. City of Fresno Equipment Corp.; mem. bus. adv. coun. Sch. Bus. and Adminstrv. Scis., Calif. State U., Fresno; trustee Community Hosps. Cen. Calif. With USNR, 1950-58. Mem. Calif. C. of C. (bd. dirs.), Fresno County and City C. of C. (transp. com.), U. So. Calif. Sch. Bus. Alumni Assn., San Joaquin Country Club, U. Sequoia-Sunnyside Country Club, Downtown Club (Fresno). Home: 6475 N Sequoia Dr Fresno CA 93711-1232 Office: Gottschalks Inc PO Box 28920 Fresno CA 93729-8920

LEVY, KENNETH, music educator; b. N.Y.C., Feb. 26, 1927; s. Meyer and Sylvia (Licht) L.; m. Clara Brooks Emmons, Jan. 25, 1956; children: Robert Brooks, Helen Gardner. A.B., Queens Coll., 1947; M.F.A., Princeton U., 1949, Ph.D., 1956. Instr. music Princeton (N.J.) U., 1952-54; from asst. prof. to Fredrick R. Mann. prof. Brandeis U., Waltham, Mass., 1954-66; prof. music Princeton U., 1966—, chmn. dept. music., 1967-70, 88, Scheide prof. music history, 1988-95. Author: Music: A Listener's Introduction, 1983; assoc. editor: Anthologie de la Chanson Parisienne au Seizieme Siecle, 1953; mem. editorial bd. Monumenta Musicae Byzantinae, 1968—, Grove's Dictionary, 6th edit, Early Music History, 1980—; contbr. articles to profl. jours. With USNR, 1945-46. Recipient Fulbright award Italy, 1962-63, Howard T. Behrman award for disting. achievements in humanities, 1983, Deems Taylor award ASCAP, 1989; Guggenheim fellow, 1955-56, Am. Coun. Learned Socs. fellow, 1970-71, sr. fellow Dumbarton Oaks, Harvard U., 1992—; vis. fellow Cambridge U., 1995. Fellow Medieval Acad. Am.; mem. Am. Philos. Soc. Office: Princeton U Dept Music Woolworth Ctr Mus Studies Princeton NJ 08544

LEVY, KENNETH JAMES, advertising executive; b. Cleve., June 15, 1949; s. Morton Leonard and Joan (Beitman) L.; m. Carol Wallisa, Sept. 7, 1974; children: Michael, Allison. BSBA, Ohio State U., 1971, MBA, 1973. Asst. account exec. Ketchum Advt., Pitts., 1973-75, account exec., 1975-77, account supr., 1977-78; account exec. Grey Advt., N.Y.C., 1978-79, account supr., 1979-80, v.p., mgmt. supr., 1980-84, v.p., group mgmt. supr., 1984-87, sr. v.p., 1987-94; exec. v.p., 1994—. Advisor Jr. Achievement Pitts., 1979. Mem. Ohio State U. Alumni Assn., Whippoorwill Country Club (Armonk, N.Y.). Avocations: golf, physical fitness, biographical reading. Home: 3 Carolyn Pl Armonk NY 10504-1101

LEVY, KENNETH JAY, psychology educator, academic administrator; b. Dallas, Sept. 18, 1946; s. Reuben and Ruth (Okon) L.; children: Ryan S., Scott D. BA, U. Tex., 1968, MA, 1969; PhD, Purdue, 1972. Asst. prof. psychology SUNY, Buffalo, 1972-75, assoc. prof., 1976-78, prof., 1979—, chmn. dept. psychology, 1976-78, dean social scis., 1978-82, various adminstrv. positions, 1985—, assoc. provost, 1987—. Contbr. numerous articles to profl. jours.; editorial cons. Psychometrika. Home: 39 Shire Dr S East Amherst NY 14051-1816 Office: SUNY Capen Hall Buffalo NY 14260

LEVY, LEAH GARRIGAN, federal official; b. Miami, Fla., Apr. 29, 1947; d. Thomas Leo and Mary (Flaherty) Garrigan; m. Roger N. Levy, May 2, 1977; children: Philip, Aaron. Student, George Mason U. Mem. legis. staff U.S. Ho. Reps., 1973-75; mem. scheduling staff U.S. Senate, 1975-77, mem. administrv. scheduling staff, 1977-81; staff asst. pub. liaison The White House, 1982-84; spl. asst. U.S Dept. Transport, Washington, 1984-89, U.S. Dept. Housing, Washington, 1989—; scheduling asst. Empower Am., Washington, 1993-94; scheduler majority leader Dick Armey U.S. Ho. of Reps., Washington, 1995—. Contbr. to Rep. Nat. Com., Washington. Contbr. Rep. Nat. Conv. Va. Rep. Party, Washington; del. Va. State GOP Conv., Richmond, 1994. Roman Catholic. Avocations: tennis, golf, reading (nonfiction).

LEVY, LEON, investment company executive; b. N.Y.C., Sept. 13, 1925; s. Jerome and Sadie (Samuelson) L.; m. Roxanne Wruble, Dec. 13, 1959 (div.); m. Shelby White, Aug. 12, 1983. BSS, City Coll., 1948. Security analyst Hirsch & Co., N.Y.C., 1948-51; gen. ptnr. Odyssey Ptnrs. (formerly Oppenheimer & Co.), N.Y.C., 1951—; chmn. bd. dirs. Oppenheimer Mutual Funds; chmn. bd. dirs. Avatar Holdings, Inc.; bd. dirs. United Kingdom Fund, Electra Investment Trust P.L.C., Mercury Assets Mgmt., Ltd.; lectr. CCNY, 1952-59. Trustee Bard Coll., Inst. Fine Arts, NYU, Inst. Advanced Studies, Rockefeller U.; pres. Jerome Levy Inst. for Econ. Rsch., N.Y.C.; bd. dirs. Internat. Found. Art Rsch., John Simon Guggenheim Found. Office: Odyssey Ptnrs LP 31 W 52d St New York NY 10019

LEVY, LEONARD WILLIAMS, history educator, author; b. Toronto, Ont., Can., Apr. 9, 1923; s. Albert and Rae (Williams) L.; m. Elyse Gitlow, Oct. 21, 1944; children: Wendy Ellen, Leslie Anne. BS, Columbia U., 1947, MA, 1948, PhD (Univ. fellow), 1951; LHD, Brandeis U., 1987; DHL (hon.), Claremont Grad. Sch., 1991. Research asst. Columbia U., 1950-51; instr., asst. prof., asso. prof., prof. Brandeis U., Waltham, Mass., 1951-70, first incumbent Earl Warren chair constl. history, 1957-70, dean Grad. Sch. Arts and Scis., 1958-63, dean faculty arts and scis., 1963-66; Andrew W. Mellon prof. humanities, history, chmn. grad. faculty history Claremont (Calif.) Grad. Sch., 1970-90, prof. emeritus, 1990—; Disting. scholar in residence So. Oreg. State Coll., 1990—; Reiser lectr. U. Chgo. Law Sch., 1964; Gaspar Bacon lectr. Boston U., 1972; Elliott lectr. U. So. Calif. Law Sch., 1972; Hugo Black lectr. U. Ala., 1976; Bicentennial lectr., City of St. Louis, 1976; disting. lectr. U. Cin., 1978. Author: The Law of the Commonwealth and Chief Justice Shaw, 1957, Legacy of Suppression; Freedom of Speech and Press in Early American History, 1960, Jefferson and Civil Liberties; The Darker Side, 1963, Origins of the Fifth Amendment, 1968 (Pulitzer Prize in history 1969), Judgments: Essays on American Constitutional History, 1972, Against The Law: The Nixon Court and Criminal Justice, 1974, Treason Against God: History of the Offense of Blasphemy, 1981, Emergence of a Free Press, 1985, Constitutional Opinions, 1986, The Establishment Clause, 1986, Original Intent and the Framers' Constitution, 1988, Blasphemy: Verbal Offense Against the Sacred, 1993, Seasoned Judgments, 1994, A License to Steal: The Forfeiture of Property, 1995; editor: Major Crises in American History, 1962, The American Political Process, 1963, The Presidency, 1964, The Congress, 1964, The Judiciary, 1964, Parties and Pressure Groups, 1964, Freedom of the Press from Zenger to Jefferson, 1966, American Constitutional Law, 1966, Judicial Review and the Supreme Court, 1967, Freedom and Reform, 1967, Essays on The Making of the Constitution, 1969, rev. edit. 1987, The Fourteenth Amendment and the Bill of Rights, 1970, The Supreme Court Under Earl Warren, 1972, Jim Crow in Boston, 1974, Essays on the Early Republic, 1974, Blasphemy in Massachusetts, 1974, The Framing and Ratification of the Constitution, 1987, The American Founding, 1988, American Constitutional History, 1989; co-editor: Ency. Am. Presidency, 4 vols., 1993; gen. editor: Am. Heritage Series, 60 vols., Harper Documentary History of Western Civilization, 40 vols.; editor-in-chief Ency. Am. Constn., 4 vols., 1986, supplement, 1991; gen. editor: Bicentennial History of the American Revolution; adv. bd.: Revs. in Am. History, John Marshall Papers, Salmon P. Chase Papers; contbr. articles to profl. jours. Mem. nat. bd. Commn. on Law and Social Action, Am. Jewish Congress; mem. U.S. Bicentennial Commn. Am. Revolution, 1966-68; mem. exec. council Inst. for Early Am. History and Culture; mem. nat. adv. council ACLU, Pulitzer prize juror, chmn. biog. jury, 1974, history jury, 1976. With AUS, 1943-46. Recipient Sigma Delta Chi prize for journalism history, 1961, 86; Frank Luther Mott prize Kappa Tau Alpha, 1961; Pulitzer prize for history, 1969; Commonwealth Club prize for nonfiction, 1975; Oboler Meml. Prize of Am. Library Assn. for Intellectual Freedom, 1986; Cert. Merit ABA, 1986; Henry L. Mencken award Free Press Assn., 1986; Dartmouth Medal Am. Library Assn., 1987, 95; Guggenheim fellow, 1957-58; Center For Study Liberty in Am. fellow Harvard, 1961-62; Am. Bar Found. sr. merit fellow, 1973-74; Am. Coun. Learned Socs. fellow, 1973; NEH sr. fellow, 1974. Mem. Am. Hist. Assn. (Littleton-Griswold com. legal history), Orgn. Am. Historians, Am. Soc. Legal History (dir.), Am. Antiquarian Soc., Soc. Am. Historians, Inst. Early Am. History and Culture (exec. coun.), Mass. Hist. Soc., Kappa Delta Pi. Democrat. Home: 1025 Timberline Ter Ashland OR 975-3436

LEVY, LESTER A., sanitation company executive; b. Dallas, 1922; married. Grad. in law, U. Tex., 1945. With NCH Corp. (formerly Nat. Chemsearch Corp.), Irving, Tex., 1946—, now chmn., also bd. dirs. Office: NCH Corp 2727 Chemsearch Blvd Irving TX 75062-6454*

LEVY, LOUIS EDWARD, retired accounting firm executive; b. Cleve., Nov. 16, 1932; s. Jerome and Bessie (Goldberg) L.; m. Sandra Harris, Mar. 4, 1956; children: Jerold, Richard, Lawrence. BBA, Case Western Res. U., 1956. CPA, N.Y. Agt. IRS, Cleve., 1956; ptnr., vice chmn. KPMG Peat Marwick, N.Y.C., 1958-90; bd. dirs. Household Internat. Inc., Kimberly-Clark Corp., Alex Brown Group Mutual Funds; former mem. emerging issues task force Fin. Acctg. Standards Bd.; mem. bd. advisors Morin Ctr. for Banking Law Studies, Boston U. Sch. Law. Chmn. emeritus Nat. Multiple Sclerosis Soc., N.Y.C., 1978—; fellow Brandeis U., Boston, 1981—. Recipient Braden award Weatherhead Sch. Mgmt. Case Western Res. U., 1984, Community Svc. award Brandeis U., 1980. Mem. AICPA, Ohio Soc. CPA's, Maplewood Country Club (N.J.), Sky Club. Republican. Jewish. Avocations: tennis, boating.

LEVY, MARIAN MULLER, transportation executive; b. N.Y.C., Mar. 10, 1942; d. Arthur Russ and Diana Elise (Ornstein) Muller; m. Richard Dennis Levy, Nov. 16, 1962; children: Dawn, Nicole, Jason, Adam. Student, Bklyn. Coll., 1959-61, 68-70. Sec. ASCAP, N.Y.C., 1959-61; tchr. spl. edn Garden Park Sch., Phoenix, 1974-76; v.p. Pac Expediters, Ltd., Scottsdale, Ariz., 1976—. Bd. dirs. Outreach, Phoenix, 1982-92; co-chmn. Council Jews Spl. Needs, Phoenix, 1987-88; chairperson Hospice of the Valley Art Com. Recipient Paul D. Mahoney Outstanding Svc. award Hospice of the Valley, 1991. Mem. Scottsdale Ctr. for Arts, Fine Art for Fine Causes, Phoenix Art Mus., The Heard Mus. Avocations: travel, art, theater, music. Home: 7850 E Camelback Rd Unit 602 Scottsdale AZ 85251-2291 Office: Pac Expediters Ltd 3020B N Scottsdale Rd Scottsdale AZ 85251-7210

LEVY, MARK IRVING, lawyer; b. Chgo., June 28, 1949; s. Kenneth Warren and Arleen (Langhaus) L.; m. Judith Jarrell Levy, Sept. 8, 1979; children: Elizabeth Sara, Mitchell Bennett. BA summa cum laude/hons. ex. distinction, Yale U., 1971, JD, 1975. Bar: D.C. 1976, U.S. Dist. Ct. D.C. 1977, U.S. Supreme Ct. 1980, Ill. 1986, U.S. Ct. Appeals (D.C. cir.) 1990, U.S. Ct. Appeals (6th, 7th and 8th cirs.) 1990, U.S. Tax Ct. 1990, U.S. Ct. Appeals (9th cir.) 1993, U.S. Ct. Appeals (2d, 4th and 10th cirs.) 1994. Law clk. Judge Gerhard A. Gesell, Washington, 1975-76; assoc. Covington & Burling, Washington, 1976-79, 81-83; asst. to solicitor gen. U.S. Dept. Justice, Washington, 1979-81, 83-86; ptnr. Mayer, Brown & Platt, Chgo., 1987-93; dep. asst. atty. gen. Civil Div. U.S. Dept. Justice, Washington, 1993-95; ptnr. Howrey & Simon, Washington, 1995—. Exec. editor Yale Law Jour., 1974-75. Recipient Israel H. Peres prize Yale Law Sch., 1975. Mem. Law Club of Chgo., Mich. Shores Club, Yale Law Sch. Alumni Assn. (former treas., exec. com. mem. 1987-90), Phi Beta Kappa. Home: 7609 Winterberry Pl Bethesda MD 20817-4847 Office: Howrey & Simon 1299 Pennsylvania Ave NW Washington DC 20004

LEVY, MARK RAY, lawyer; b. Denver, Mar. 2, 1946; s. Richard C. and Hilde (Lindauer) L.; m. Patricia Loeb, June 13, 1971; children: Betsy, Robert. BA, U. Colo., 1968, JD, 1972. Bar: Colo. 1972, U.S. Dist. Ct. Colo. 1972. Assoc. Holland & Hart, Denver, 1972-78; ptnr. Holland & Hart, 1978—; adj. prof. the lawyering process U. Denver Law Sch., 1990-93. Author: (with others) Colorado Corporations Manual, 1987, Colorado Corporation Law and Practice, 1990. Trustee Congregation Emanuel, Denver, 1984-90, mem. legal com., 1989-93; chmn. Denver Alumni Phonathon U. Colo. Law Sch., 1989-90, mem. alumni bd., 1992-96, chmn. alumni bd., 1994-95; trustee Nat. Repertory Orch., 1995—. Mem. ABA, Colo. Bar Assn. (mem. Blue Sky Law task force 1980-81, co-chmn. Colo. securities law rev. com. 1988-91), Denver Bar Assn., Rockies Venture Club. Office: Holland and Hart 555 17th St Ste 3200 Denver CO 80202

LEVY, MARVIN DANIEL, professional football coach, sports team executive; b. Chgo., Aug. 3, 1929. BA, Coe Coll., 1950; MA, Harvard U., 1951. High sch. coach St. Louis, 1951-52; asst. football coach Coe Coll., Cedar Rapids, Iowa, 1953-55; asst. coach, then head coach U. N.Mex., 1956-59; head coach U. Calif., Berkeley, 1960-63, Coll. William & Mary, Williamsburg, Va., 1964-68; asst. coach Phila. Eagles, NFL, 1969, Los Angeles Rams, NFL, 1970, Washington Redskins, NFL, 1971-72; head coach Montreal (Que., Can.) Alouettes, Can. Football League, 1973-77, Kansas City (Mo.) Chiefs, NFL, 1978-82, Chgo. Blitz, U.S. Football League, 1984; head coach Buffalo Bills, NFL, 1986—, v.p., 1995—. Office: Buffalo Bills 1 Bills Dr Orchard Park NY 14127-2237*

LEVY, MARVIN DAVID, composer; b. Passaic, N.J., Aug. 2, 1932; s. Benjamin and Bertha (Tramberg) L. B.A., N.Y. U., 1954; M.A., Columbia U., 1956; pupil, Philip James, Otto Luening. Asst. dir. Am. Opera Soc., 1952-61; music critic Mus. Am. Herald Tribune, 1952-58; assoc. prof. of music Bklyn. Coll., 1974-76. Composer: orchestral Caramoor Festival Overture, 1958, Symphony, 1960, Kyros, 1961, One Person, 1962, Piano Concerto, 1970, Trialogus, 1972, In Memoriam: W.H. Auden, 1974, Canto de los Maranos, 1978, Pascua Florida, 1987, Arrows of Time, 1988; oratorios For The Time Being, 1959, Sacred Service, 1964, Masada (Nat. Symphony commn.); operas Mourning Becomes Electra (Met. Opera commn.), 1967, Escorial, 1958, Sotoba Komachi, 1957, The Tower, 1956; musical The Grand Balcony, 1990, 95; film theater scores; chamber music; artistic dir. Ft. Lauderdale Opera, 1989-94. Recipient Prix de Rome, 1962, 65, N.Y.C. Scroll award for Disting. and Exceptional Svc., 1967; Guggenheim grantee, 1960, 64, Ford Found. grantee, 1965, Damrosch grantee, 1961, NEA grantee, 1974, 78. Mem. ASCAP. Office: care Sheldon Soffer Mgmt 130 W 56th St New York NY 10019-3818

LEVY, MICHAEL B., business educator; b. Balt., July 12, 1947; m. Bonny B. Wolf; 1 child. BA, Brown U., 1969; PhD, Rutgers U., 1979. Tchr. social studies, coach Loyola High Sch., Balt., Md., 1973-76; teaching asst. Rutgers U., New Brunswick, N.J., 1977-78, instr., 1978-84; asst. prof. Tex. A&M Univ., College Sta., 1978-84, assoc. prof. polit. sci., 1984-85; economist joint econ. com. U.S. Congress, Washington, 1985-87; adminstrv. asst. to Sen. Lloyd Bentsen U.S. Senate, Washington, 1987-93; asst. sec. legis. affairs U.S. Dept. Treasury, Washington, 1993-95; adj. instr. Georgetown U., Washington, 1986-93, disting. vis. prof., 1995—; legis. cons. Brownstein, Hyatt, Farber and Strickland, Denver and Washington, 1995—. Editor: Political Thought in America, 1981, 87, (with Philip Abbot) The Liberal Future in America: Essays in Renewal, 1985, (with Edward Portis) Handbook of Political Theory and Policy Sciences, 1989; contbr. articles to profl. jours. Bevier fellow Rutgers U., 1979; R.J. Reynolds fellow for So. High Sch. Tchrs. Office: Georgetown U Sch Bus 37th & O NW Washington DC 20057

LEVY, MICHAEL RICHARD, publishing executive; b. Dallas, May 17, 1946; s. Harry Aaron and Florence (Friedman) L.; m. Rebecca Gloria Schulman, Jan. 19, 1969 (div. 1993); children: Anne Rachel, Tobin Janel and Mara Elizabeth (twins). BS, U. Pa., 1968; JD, U. Tex., 1972. Bar: Tex.

1972. Pres. Mediatex Communications Corp., Austin, Tex., 1972—; founder, pub. Tex. Monthly mag., 1973—. Mem. bd. dirs. M.D. Anderson Hosp.; trustee Capital of Tex. Pub. Telecomms. Coun., Austin; mem. cmty. adv. bd. Jr. League of Austin; mem. Austin EMS Quality Assurance Com.; trustee Tex. Med. Assn. Found., Rice U. Pub. Program Adv. Coun., 1996. Named One of Outstanding Amss. under 40, Esquire mag., 1984; recipient Excellence in Media award Susan G. Komen Found., 1989, Disting. Alumnus award St. Mark's Sch. Tex., 1994. Mem. State Bar Tex., Young Pres.' Orgn., Mag. Pubs. Am. (bd. dirs.), World Pres.' Orgn., Ex-Students' Assn. U. Tex. (life), Met. Club, Rockefeller Ctr. Club, Crescent Club, Westwood Country Club, Headliners Club. Home: PO Box 146 Austin TX 78767-0146 Office: Texas Monthly PO Box 1569 Austin TX 78767-1569

LEVY, NELSON LOUIS, physician, scientist, corporate executive; b. Somerville, N.J., June 19, 1941; s. Myron L. and Sylvia (Cohen) L.; m. Joanne Barnett, Dec. 21, 1963 (div. 1972); children: Scott, Erik, Jonathan; m. Louisa Douglas Stiles, Dec. 21, 1974; children: Michael, Andrew, David. BA/BS summa cum laude, Yale U., 1963; MD, Columbia U., 1967; PhD, Duke U., 1972. Diplomate Am. Bd. Allergy and Immunology. Intern, U. Colo. Med. Ctr., Denver, 1967-68; resident Duke U. Med Ctr., Durham, N.C., 1970-73; rsch. assoc. NIH, Bethesda, Md., 1968-70; asst. prof. immunology Duke U. Med. Ctr., 1972-75, assoc. prof. immunology and neurology, 1975-80, prof., 1980-81; dir. biol. rsch. Abbott Labs., Abbott Park, Ill., 1981, v.p. rsch., 1981-84; pres. Nelson L. Levy Assocs., Inc., 1984-87; chief exec. officer The CoreTechs Corp., Lake Forest, Ill., 1987-92; pres., Fujisawa Pharm., Deerfield, Ill., 1992-93; CEO Ill. Tech. Devel. Corp., 1993—; cons. Upjohn Co., Inc., Kalamazoo, 1976-77, G.D. Searle Inc., Skokie, Ill., 1984-87, Erbamont Inc., Stamford, Conn., 1984-90, Eastman Kodak, Rochester, N.Y., LyphoMed, Inc., Rosemont, Ill., 1985-89, The Nutrasweet Co., Skokie, Ill., 1985-88, Bayer AG, 1987-89, Fujisawa Pharm. Co., 1988-92, Alcide Corp., 1991—, Ameritech, 1993—, several venture cos.; bd. dirs. Intek Diagnostics, Inc., Helis, Inc., Bionica Pty, Ltd., Software Care Mgmt. Systems, Inc., Heybach Enterprises, Inc., Saniguard Products Corp., MedVac, Inc., Anthra Pharms., Inc., Myotech Corp., ChemBridge Corp. Editor several books; contbr. articles to profl. publs., chpts. to books. Coach Little League, Am. Youth Soccer Orgn.; corp. adv. bd. Family Svc. of South Lake County, 1991—. Surgeon USPHS, 1968-70. Grantee Am. Cancer Soc., 1970-75, NIH, 1971-81, Nat. Multiple Sclerosis Soc., 1974-81, Ill. Dept. Commerce and Cmty. Affairs, 1993—. Mem. Am. Assn. Immunologists, Am. Assn. Cancer Rsch., Licensing Execs. Soc., Rotary, Phi Beta Kappa, Sigma Xi, Alpha Omega Alpha, Phi Gamma Delta. Avocations: triathlons, tennis, biking, sailing. Office: 1391 Concord Rd Lake Forest IL 60045-1506

LEVY, NORMAN, motion picture company executive; b. Bronx, N.Y., Jan. 3, 1935; s. Irving and Helen (Saunders) L.; m. Hirsch, Nov. 11, 1962; children—Jordan, Brian, Matthew. BA, CCNY. Salesman Universal Pictures, 1957-67, Nat. Gen. Pictures, 1967-74; gen. sales mgr. Columbia Pictures, Burbank, Calif., 1974-75; exec. v.p. in charge domestic sales Columbia Pictures, 1975-77, exec. v.p. mktg., 1977-78, pres. domestic distbn., 1978-80, pres. Twentieth Century Fox Entertainment Group, 1980-81, vice chmn., 1981-85; mktg., distbn. cons., 1985—; chmn. New Century/Vista Film Co. L.A., 1985-91; chmn., chief exec. officer Domino Entertainment, L.A., 1991-92; pres., CEO Creative Film Enterprises, L.A., 1992—. Served with U.S. Army, 1955-57. Office: Creative Film Enterprises Ste 1201 1801 Avenue of the Stars Los Angeles CA 90067

LEVY, NORMAN B., psychiatrist, educator; b. N.Y.C., 1931; s. Barnett Theodore and Lena (Gulnick) L.; m. Lya Weiss (dec.); children: Karen, Susan, Joanne; m. Carol Lois Spiegel, 1 son, Robert Barnett. B.A. cum laude, NYU, 1952; M.D., SUNY. Diplomate: Am. Bd. Psychiatry and Neurology (examiner). Intern Maimonides Med. Center, Bklyn.; resident physician in medicine U. Pitts.-Presbyn. Hosp.; resident in psychiatry Kings County Hosp. Center, Bklyn.; instr. psychiatry State U. N.Y. Downstate Med. Center Coll. Medicine, Bklyn.; asst. prof. State U. N.Y. Downstate Med. Center Coll. Medicine, asso. prof., prof.; presiding officer faculty State U. N.Y. Downstate Med. Center Coll. Medicine (Coll. Medicine), assoc. dir. med-psychiat. liaison service; prof. psychiatry, medicine, surgery and coordinator psychiat. liaison services N.Y. Med. Coll.; clin. prof. psychiatry, adj. prof. of medicine Health Science Ctr. SUNY, Bklyn., 1992—; dir. liaison psychiatry divsn. Westchester County Med. Ctr., 1980-95, mem. exec. com. med. staff, 1981-85, 89-92; dir., consultation-liaison and emergency psychiatry Coney Island Hosp., Bklyn., 1996—; clin. prof. psychiatry and adj. prof. medicine SUNY, Health Sci. Ctr. at Bklyn., 1996—; vis. prof. psychiatry and medicine So. Ill. U. Sch. Medicine; vis. prof. psychiatry John A. Burns Sch. Medicine, U. Hawaii, 1981; coord. 1st Internat. Conf. Psychol. Factors in Hemodialysis and Transplantation, 1978, 2d-10th Internat. Confs. on Psychonephrology; cons. NIMH; chief med. svcs. USAF Hosp., Ashiya, Japan. Author: (with others), editor: Living or Dying: Adaptation to Hemodialysis, 1974, Psychonephrology I: Psychological Factors in Hemodialysis and Transplantation, 1981, Men in Transition: Theory and Therapy, 1982, Psychonephrology II: Psychological Problems in Kidney Failure and their Treatment, 1983; contbr. articles to jours., chpts. to textbooks in field.; assoc. editor: Gen. Hosp. Psychiatry, 1978-82, sect. editor, 1982—; sect. editor: Internat. Jour. Psychiatry in Medicine, 1977-78; mem. editorial bd., book rev. editor Jour. Dialysis and Transplantation, 1979—; mem. editorial bd. Resident and Staff Physician, 1981-91, Internat. Jour. Artificial Internal. Organs, 1983-93, Geriatric Nephrology and Urology, 1990—, Kidney: A Current Survey of World Literature, 1990—. Served to capt. M.C., USAF. Served to capt. M.C., USAF. Recipient Willaim A. Console Master Tchr. award, SUNY, Brooklyn, 1991; Thomas P. Hackett award Acad. Psychosomatic med., 1993. Fellow ACP, Am. Coll. Psychiatrists, Am. Psychiat. Assn. (pres. Kings County dist. br. 1981-82), Internat. Coll. Psychosomatic Medicine, Acad. Psychosomatic Medicine; mem. AAAS, Am. Psychosomatic Soc. (coun. 1994—), N.Y. Acad. Scis., Psychonephrology Found. (pres. 1978—), Assn. Acad. Psychiatry, Internat. Soc. Nephrology, Am. Soc. Nephrology, Am. Assn. Artificial Internal Organs, Soc. Liaison Psychiatry (bd. dirs. 1979-80, sec. 1980-81, pres.-elect 1991-92, pres. 1992-94, bd. dirs. 1995—), Phi Beta Kappa, Sigma Xi. Home: 169 Westminster Rd Brooklyn NY 11218-3445 Office: Coney Island Hosp Dept Psychiatry Brooklyn NY 11235

LEVY, NORMAN JAY, investment banker, financial consultant; b. N.Y.C., Aug. 14, 1942; s. Benjamin and Sophie (London) L.; m. Rene S. Cohen; children—Ellen, David. B.B.A., U. Cin., 1964; M.B.A., Columbia U., 1966. Assoc., v.p. Salomon Bros., N.Y.C., 1966-77, spl. ptnr., 1977-79, gen. ptnr., 1979-81; sr. v.p. Wertheim & Co., N.Y.C., 1982; mng. dir. L.F. Rothschild, Unterberg, Towbin, N.Y.C., 1983-84; private practice investment cons. Tenafly, N.J., 1985—. Mem. Securities Industry Assn. (com. on acctg. 1977-79). Home: 40 Mayflower Dr Tenafly NJ 07670-3130

LEVY, PETER, cinematographer. Cinematographer: (films) A Nightmare on Elm Street Part 5: The Dream Child, 1989, Dangerous Game, 1989, Predator 2, 1990, Ricochet, 1992, Judgment Night, 1993, Blown Away, 1994. Office: The Gersh Agency 232 N Canon Dr Beverly Hills CA 90210-5302

LEVY, RALPH, engineering executive, consultant; b. London, Apr. 12, 1932; came to U.S., 1967, naturalized, 1978; s. Alfred and Esther L.; m. Barbara Dent, Dec. 12, 1959; children: Sharon E., Mark S. B.A., Cambridge U., 1953, M.A., 1957; Ph.D., Queen Mary Coll. U. London, 1966. Mem. sci. staff GEC, Stanmore, Middlesex, Eng., 1953-59; mem. sci. staff Mullard Research Labs., Redhill, Eng., 1959-64; lectr. dept. elec. and electronic engring. U. Leeds, 1964-67; v.p. research Microwave Devel. Labs., Inc., Natick, Mass., 1967-84; v.p. engring. KW Engring., San Diego, 1984-88; v.p. research Remec Inc., San Diego, 1988-89; R. Levy Assocs., 1989—. Author: (with J.O. Scanlan) Circuit Theory, 1970, 2d vol., 1973; contbr. articles in field. Fellow IEEE (editor Transactions on Microwave Theory and Techniques 1986-88); mem. Instn. Elec. Engrs. (London). Patentee in field. Office: 1897 Caminito Velasco La Jolla CA 92037-5725

LEVY, RICHARD HERBERT, lawyer; b. Chgo., Sept. 15, 1943; s. Milton David and Sophie (Lippert) L.; m. Ilyse Powell; children: Joshua, Rachel, Stacey. BS, So. Ill. U., 1966; JD magna cum laude, DePaul U., 1976. Bar: Ill. 1976, Colo. 1994. Ptnr. Felwell, Galper & Lasky, Chgo., 1976, Rudnick & Wolfe, Chgo., 1983-88, Vedder, Price, Kaufman & Kammholz, Chgo., 1992—; counsel to exec. bd. Home Builders Chgo., Oak Brook, Ill., 1986—. Mem. ABA, Chgo. Vol. Lawyers Soc., Practising Law Inst. (real estate law adv. com.). Home: 1205 Wincanton Deerfield IL 60035 Office: Vedder Price Kaufman & Kammholz 222 N La Salle St Chicago IL 60601-1003

LEVY, RICHARD PHILIP, physician, educator; b. Hempstead, N.Y., Nov. 3, 1923; s. Edward I. and Elma (Nathan) L.; m. Barbara Quint, Sept. 15, 1945; children: Donald Martin, Ellen Susan, Charles Edward. B.S., Yale U., 1944, M.D., 1947. Intern, resident Univ. Hosps. of Cleve., 1947-53; faculty Case Western Res. Med. Sch., Cleve., 1953—, prof. medicine, 1977-78, clin. prof. medicine, 1978—, prof. internal medicine, 1978—, chmn. dept. internal medicine, 1983-89; prof. internal medicine endocrinology Coll. Medicine Northeastern Ohio U., Akron, Ohio, 1978—; svc. chief endocrinology St. Thomas Med. Ctr., Akron, 1985-92; med. editor Webster's New World Dictionary, 1970. Contbr. articles to profl. jours. Served with USNR, 1949-51. Fellow ACP; mem. Thyroid Assn., Endocrine Soc., Am. Diabetes Assn., Am. Coll. Clin. Endocrinology, Ohio Med. Assn., Summit County Med. Soc., Sigma Xi. Office: 444 N Main St Akron OH 44310-3110

LEVY, ROBERT EDWARD, biotechnology company executive; b. Cin., May 23, 1939; s. Aaron F. and Elizabeth W. (Hirsch) L.; m. Candace Ann Wolfe, June 20, 1970; children: Brian D., Jessica A. BChemE, Cornell U., 1962; PhDChemE, U. Calif. at Berkeley, 1967. Various positions, including mgr. synthetic fuels devel., rsch. and engring. Exxon Co., Florham Park, N.J., 1967-80, 84-86; mgr. tech. dept. Lago Oil & Transport Co., Esso Interam. div. Exxon Co., Aruba, Netherlands Antilles, 1980-84; v.p., dir. tech. devel. M.W. Kellogg Co., Houston, 1987-93; v.p. govt. and regulatory affairs Energy Biosystems Corp., The Woodlands, Tex., 1993—; cons. in field. Patentee in field. Indsl. mem. Comm. for Prevention of Shoreline Pollution by Oil, Aruba, 1982-84. Mem. AIChE (long range planning com.), Indsl. Rsch. Inst. (bd. editors 1992-95, pre-coll. edn. com. 1995—), Sigma Xi (pres. Kellogg chpt. 1991-92). Avocations: tennis, jogging, sailing. Office: Energy Biosystems Corp 4200 Rsch Forest Dr The Woodlands TX 77381

LEVY, ROBERT ISAAC, physician, educator, research director; b. Bronx, N.Y., May 3, 1937; s. George Gerson and Sarah (Levinson) L.; m. Ellen Marie Feis, 1958; children: Andrew, Joanne, Karen, Patricia. B.A. with high honors and distinction, Cornell U., 1957; M.D. cum laude, Yale U., 1961. Intern, then asst. resident in medicine Yale-New Haven Med. Ctr., 1961-63; clin. assoc. molecular diseases Nat. Heart, Lung and Blood Inst., Bethesda, Md., 1963-66, chief resident, 1965-66, attending physician molecular disease br., 1965-80, head sect. lipoproteins, 1966-80, dep. clin. dir. inst., 1968-69, chief clin. services molecular diseases br., 1969-73, chief lipid metabolism br., 1970-74, dir. div. heart and vascular diseases, 1973-75, dir. inst., 1975-81; v.p. health scis., dean Sch. Medicine Tufts U., Boston, 1981-83, prof. medicine, 1981-83; v.p. health scis. Columbia U., N.Y.C., 1983-84, prof., 1983-88, sr. asst. v.p. health scis., 1985-87; pres. Sandoz Research Inst., East Hanover, N.J., 1988-92; pres. Wyeth-Ayerst Rsch. Wyeth-Ayerst Labs div. Am. Home Products, Phila., 1992—; attending physician Georgetown U. med. div. D.C. Gen. Hosp., 1966-68; spl. cons. anti-lipid drugs FDA. Editor: Jour. Lipid Rsch., 1972-80, Circulation, 1974-76, Am. Heart Jour., 1980-90; contbr. articles to profl. jours. Served as surgeon USPHS, 1963-66. Recipient Kees Thesis prize Yale U., 1961; Arthur S. Flemming award, 1975; Superior Service award HEW, 1975; Rsch. award and Van Slyke award Am. Soc. Clin. Chemists, 1980; Roger J. Williams award, 1985; award Humana Heart Found., 1988. Mem. Am. Heart Assn. (mem. coun. on atherosclerosis), Am. Inst. Nutrition, Am. Fedn. Clin. Rsch., N.Y. Acad. Scis., Am. Soc. Clin. Nutrition, Am. Soc. Clin. Investigation, Am. Coll. Cardiology, Inst. Medicine of Nat. Acad. Scis., Am. Soc. Clin. Pharmacology and Therapeutics, Assn. Am. Physicians, Phi Beta Kappa, Sigma Xi, Alpha Omega Alpha, Alpha Epsilon Delta, Phi Kappa Phi. Office: Wyeth-Ayerst Rsch PO Box 8299 Philadelphia PA 19101-0082

LEVY, ROBERT MICHAEL, neurosurgeon, researcher; b. Tyndall AFB, Fla., Oct. 22, 1954; s. Ira Mortimer and Rheda Bertha (Fisch) L. BA summa cum laude, Northwestern U., 1976, MS, 1976; PhD, Stanford U., 1980; MD, Stanford Medical Sch., 1981. Diplomate Am. Bd. Neurological Surgery, Nat. Bd. Medical Examiners. Intern general surgery Stanford U Medical Ctr., Stanford, Calif., 1981-82; postgrad. rsch. surgeon dept. neurological surgery U. Calif., San Francisco, 1982-87, resident dept. neurosurgery, 1982-87; chief resident San Francisco Gen. Hosp., 1984; chief resident neurological surgery VA Medical Ctr., San Francisco, 1986, U. Calif., San Francisco, 1987; acting chief div. neurological surgery Northwestern U. Medical Sch., Chgo.; cons. Medtronics, Mpls.; asst. prof. dept. surgery, Northwestern U. Medical Sch., 1987-90, asst. prof. dept. physiology, 1987-90, charter mem. Inst. Neuroscience, 1988—, dir. Northwestern Comprehensive Pain Clinic Northwestern Medical Faculty Found., 1987—; head sect. of stereotactic/functional neurosurgery, 1987—; assoc. prof. dept. surgery, 1990—, assoc. prof. dept. physiology, 1990—; deputy chief div. neurosurgery, 1991-93, rsch. dir. dept. surgery, 1992-94, dir. residency training program div. neurosurgery, 1993-95. Co-author: AIDS and Nervous System, 1988, The Neurosurgery of Chronic Pain, 1996, AIDS and the Nervous System 2d edit., 1996; contbr. numerous articles to profl. jours. Recipient Rsch. award Nat Inst. Health, 1974, Henry B. Newman award San Francisco Neurological Soc., 1983, First Annual Clinical Neuroscience Trainee award L.A. Soc. Neurology & Psychiatry, 1987, William H. Sweet Young Investigators award, Am. Assn. Neurological Surgeons, 1993; recipient numerous rsch. grants. Mem. Am. Assn. Neurological Surgeons, Am. Coll. Surgeons, Am. Epilepsy Soc., AMA, Am. Pain Soc., Am. Soc. Stereotactic and Functional Neurosurgery, Calif. Medical Assn., Chgo. Neurological Soc., Congress Neurological Surgeons, Internat AIDS Soc., Internat. Narcotics Rsch. Congress, Internat. Assn. Study of Pain, Am. Assn. of Neurological Surgeons and Congress of Neurological Surgeons, Soc. Magnetic Resonance in Medicine, World Soc. Stereotactic and Functional Neurosurgery, Internat. Coll. Surgeons. Office: Northwestern U Medical Sch 250 E Superior St Ste 928 Chicago IL 60611

LEVY, ROBIN CAROLE, elementary guidance counselor; b. Berlin, Apr. 13, 1964; parents Am. citizens; d. Kenneth and Henrietta Nan (Weithorn) Kaplan; m. Guy Glickson Levy, July 27, 1986; 1 chld, Clare Sydney. BS, Fla. State U., 1986; MEd, Coll. William and Mary, 1991. Cert. tchr. Presch. tchr. Talent House Pvt. Sch., Fairfax, Va., 1986-87; 4th grade tchr. Mt. Vernon Elem., Tabb, Va., 1987-92; elem. counselor Bethel Manor Elem., LAFB, Va., 1992-95; family mediator Dispute Settlement Ctr., Norfolk, Va., 1993—, Dispute Resolution Ctr., Richmond, Va., 1994—. Past pres., v.p. Denbigh Jaycees, Va., 1987-94 (Project Mgr. of Yr. 1991, 93, Outstanding Local Pres. 1994), sec., treas. Mem. ASCD, ACA, Va. Counselors Assn., Va. Sch. Counselors Assn., Peninsula Counselors Assn. Democrat. Jewish. Avocations: jogging, swimming, reading. Home: 463 Cheshire Ct Newport News VA 23602-6404

LEVY, ROCHELLE FELDMAN, artist; b. N.Y.C., Aug. 4, 1937; d. S. Harry and Eva (Krause) Feldman; m. Robert Paley Levy, June 4, 1955; children: Kathryn Tracey, Wendy Paige, Robert Paley, Angela Brooke, Michael Tyler. Student Barnard Coll., 1954-55, U. Pa., 1955-56; BFA, Moore Coll. Art, 1979. Mgmt. cons. Woodlyne Sch., Rosemont, Pa., 1983-84; sr. ptnr. DRT Interiors, Phila., 1983—; ptnr. Phila. Phillies, 1981-94. One-woman shows: Watson Gallery, Wheaton Coll., Norton, Mass., 1977, U. Pa., 1977, Med. Coll. Pa., Phila., 1982, Aqueduct Race Track, Long Island, N.Y., 1982, 68, Phila. Art Alliance, 1983, Moore Coll. Art, Phila., 1984, Phila. Art Alliance, 1994. Pres., League of Children's Hosp., Phila., 1969-70; bd. overseers Ctr. for Judaic Studies U. Pa., 1993-96. Recipient G. Allen Smith Prize, Woodmere Art Gallery, Chestnut Hill, Pa., 1979; Woman honoree Samuel Paley Day Care Ctr., Phila., 1990, Jefferson Bank Declaration award, 1991, Nat. Philanthropy honoree The Nat. Soc. of Fund Raising Execs. Greater Phila. chpt., 1994. Trustee Moore Coll. Art, 1979—, chmn. bd. trustees, 1988—; mem. selections and acquisitions com. Pa. Acad. Fine Arts, 1979—; bd. mgrs., 1975—, chmn. exec. com., 1982—, bd. trustees, 1990—. Mem. Allied Artists Am., Artist's Equity, Phila. Art Alliance, Phila. Print Club. Office: 2 Logan Sq Ste 2525 Philadelphia PA 19103

LEVY, S. WILLIAM, dermatologist; b. San Francisco, Sept. 28, 1920; s. Joseph and Dora (Taylor) L.; m. Elisabeth Rellstab, Mar. 17, 1974; children: David Lewis, Ann Louise. BS, U. Calif., San Francisco, 1943, MD, 1949. Practice medicine specializing in dermatology San Francisco; research dermatologist Biomechanics Lab., U. Calif., San Francisco; mem. staff Children's Hosp., Mt. Zion Hosp. and Med. Center; cons. to Letterman Army Hosp.; central med. adv. Calif. Blue Shield, San Francisco; clin. prof. dermatology U. Calif.; cons. in field. Author: Skin Problems of the Amputee, 1983; co-author: The Skin in Diabetes, 1986, Dermatology, 3rd edit., 1992, Dermatology in General Medicine, 4th edit., 1993, Atlas of Limb Prosthetics, 2d edit., 1992, Cutis, 1995. Served with USN, 1943-46. Recipient Lehn and Fink Gold Medal award. Fellow Am. Acad. Dermatology (Gold medal); mem. San Francisco Dermatol. Soc. (pres.), Pacific Dermatologic Assn. (v.p.), AMA, Calif. Med. Assn. (sci. council 1977-84), San Francisco Med. Soc. Office: Ste 203 599 Sir Francis Drake Blvd Greenbrae CA 94904

LEVY, SAM, consumer products company executive. Pres. Schwegmann Giant Super Markets, New Orleans, La., 1962—. Office: Schwegmann Giant Super Markets 5300 Gentilly Rd New Orleans LA 70126-5007

LEVY, SAM MALCOLM, advertising executive; b. Henderson, Ky., Nov. 26, 1901; s. Mike Meyer and Hattie Belle (Wile) L.; m. Isabel Helen Cone, Apr. 22, 1929; 1 child, Sue Levy Klau. Student, U. Mo., 1919-21; PhB, U. Chgo., 1921-23; postgrad., Harvard Coll., 1926. Exec. McCann Erickson, N.Y.C., 1923-30; adv. dir. News & Record, Greensborough, N.C., 1930-31; v.p. dir. Keelor & Stites, Cin., 1931-46; lectr. speech U. Cin., 1940-44; pres. Assoc. Adv. Agy., Cin., 1946-71; sr. v.p. Sive Inc. - A Div. Young & Rubicam, 1971-89; ret. Sive Inc.-A Div. Young & Rubicam, 1989; life trustee Clean Cin. Inc., bd. govs. Big Bros. Assn., Glen Manor Home for Aged, 1963—; instr. advt. evening coll. U. Cin., 1945-48. Editor: Socony Monthly Mag., 1925-27. Active Friend of Serengeti Aftrica; mem. Cin. Art Mus. Named to Hon. Order of Ky. Cols., 1984; donated Glass Gallery to Cin. Art Mus., 1980, Floral Clock to Cin. Park Bd., 1988; recipient Key to the City of Cin., 1988, Emerald award, 1993. Mem. Advts. Club Cin., Black Friars Club Chgo., Bankers Club, Losanti Ville Country Club Cin., Founders Soc., Cin. Symphony Orch., Thomas Schippers Soc., Zeta Beta Tau (pres., grad club). Republican. Home: 2444 Madison Rd Cincinnati OH 45208-1256

LEVY, STANLEY HERBERT, lawyer; b. Phila., Apr. 11, 1922; s. Max and Rose (Cohen) L.; m. Gloria Kamber, Dec. 20, 1953; children: Steven M., Peter B. B.A., Cornell U., 1943; LL.B., Harvard U., 1949, J.D., 1968. Bar: N.Y. 1949, U.S. Dist. Ct. (ea. and so. dists.) N.Y., U.S. Treasury 1949, U.S. Supreme Ct. 1949. Practiced in N.Y.C., 1949—. Mem. Republican Town Com., Scarsdale, 1963-65, Temple Emanu-el, Westchester, N.Y. Served to 1st lt. F.A., AUS, 1943-47. Mem. Assn. Bar City N.Y., Confrérie des Chevaliers du Tastevin (officier commandeur), Commanderie de Boreaux (comdr.), Harvard Club, Yale Club, Century Country Club (Purchase, N.Y.), Westchester Flying Club (White Plains, N.Y.), Mashomack Fish and Game Preserve (Pine Plains, N.Y.). Home: 3 Richbell Rd Scarsdale NY 10583-4421 Office: 521 5th Ave New York NY 10175

LEVY, STEPHEN RAYMOND, diversified high technology company executive; b. Everett, Mass., May 4, 1940; s. Robert George and Lillian (Berfield) L.; m. Sandra Helen Rosen, Aug. 26, 1961; children: Phillip, Susan. B.B.A., U. Mass., 1961. Chmn. emeritus, dir. Bolt Beranek and Newman Inc., Cambridge, Mass.; mem. policy adv. com. on trade U.S. Dept. Def. Mem. Gov.'s Coun. Econ. Growth and Tech. (chmn. com. telecomms. devel.); bd. dirs. Mass. Telecomms. Coun., Mass. High Tech. Coun.; bd. overseer Boston Symphony Orch. With AUS, 1963-66. Decorated Army Commendation medal. Mem. Am. Bus. Conf., Am. Electronics Assn. (chmn. 1986), Mass. High Tech. Coun. (chmn. 1987-89). Home: 300 Boylston St Apt 1204 Boston MA 02116-3923 Office: Bolt Beranek & Newman Inc 150 Cambridgepark Dr Cambridge MA 02140-2322

LEVY, (ALEXANDRA) SUSAN, construction company executive; b. Rockville Centre, N.Y., Apr. 26, 1949; d. Alexander Stanley and Anna Charlotte (Galasieski) Jankoski; m. William Mack Levy, Aug. 12, 1977. Student, Suffolk Community Coll., Brentwood, N.Y., 1976. Cert. constrn. assoc. Supr. N.Y. Telephone Co., Babylon, 1970-74; v.p. Aabbacco Equipment Leasing Corp., Lindenhurst, N.Y., 1974-81; pres., owner Femi-9 Contracting Corp., Lindenhurst, 1981—. Mem. affirmative action adv. coun. N.Y. State Dept. Transp., Albany, 1984-88, human resources adv. panel Long Island Project 2000; mem. Presdl. Task Force, Washington, 1982—; mem. Leadership Am., 1994-95. With U.S. Army, 1967-69. Recipient Henri Dunant Corp. award ARC Suffolk County, 1986, Race to the Top award Bridgestone Tire Corp., 1992, Nawbo award Nat. Assn. Women Bus. Owners, 1993; named honoree Women on the Job, 1989. Mem. Nat. Assn. Women in Constrn. (founder L.I. chpt., pres. 1983-85, regional chmn. woman-owned bus. enterprise com., nat. chmn. pub. rels. and mktg. com., nat. dir. Region 1 1988-89, Mem. of Yr. L.I. chpt. 1987, Exec. of Yr. L.I. chpt., nat. dir., 1988-89, nat. treas. 1991-93, nat. v.p. 1993-94, nat. pres.-elect 1994-95, pres. 1995-96), Nassau Suffolk Contractors Assn. (sec. 1984-87, sec.-treas. 1987-96, bd. dirs.), Nat. Assn. Women Bus. Owners (charter, Top Woman Bus. Owner award 1993), Am. Plat form Assn. Republican. Roman Catholic. Avocations: reading, writing, golf. Home: 133 Hollins Ln East Islip NY 11730-3006 Office: Femi-9 Contracting Corp 305 E Sunrise Hwy Lindenhurst NY 11757-2521

LEVY, WALTER JAMES, oil consultant; b. Hamburg, Germany, Mar. 21, 1911; s. Moses and Bertha (Lindenberger) L.; m. Augusta Sondheimer, Apr. 11, 1942 (dec.); children: Robert Alan (dec.), Susan Clementine. Student, U. Heidelberg, 1929-30, U. Berlin, 1930-31, U. Kiel, 1931-32. Asst. to editor Petroleum Press Bur., London, Eng., 1936-41; free lance economist N.Y.C., 1941-42; chief petroleum sect. OSS, Washington, 1942-45; asst. office intelligence research Dept. State, 1945-48, cons., also Pres. com. fgn. aid, 1948; chief oil br. ECA, 1948-49, cons., 1949-51; econ. cons., 1949—, NSRB, 1950; pres. Materials Policy Commn., 1951; cons. policy planning staff Dept. State, 1952-53, ICA, 1956-57; cons. office Under Sec. and Asst. Secs., 1960-80, Office Civil and Def. Moblzn., 1960, European Econ. Community, 1970; fgn. econ. adviser Socony-Vacuum Oil Co., 1948; adviser to Mr. Harriman on mission to Iran, 1951; Petroleum adviser U.S. del. Council Fgn. Ministers meeting, 1947; mem. U.S. del. of Austrian Treaty Commn., 1947, State Dept. del. for oil discussions with U.K., 1946, U.S. del. trade discussion with Sweden, 1945, U.S. world programming group on petroleum, 1945; mem. enemy oil com. Joint Chiefs Staff, 1943-45; oil adviser to spl. emissary of Pres. Kennedy to Pres. of Indonesia, 1963; Mem. adv. council to Sch. Advanced Internat. Studies Johns Hopkins U. Author (Oil Strategy and Politics, 1941-81 1982); Contbr. articles to profl. publs. Recipient spl. plaque in grateful appreciation for invaluable contbr. to welfare U.S., Sec. State, 1968; decorated Dato Setia haila Jasa Sultan Brunei, 1968; Order of Taj Iran, 1969; hon. companion Order St. Michael and St. George, Eng.; insignia of comdr.'s cross Order of Merit Fed. Republic of Ger., 1979; President's certificate of merit. Mem. Council on Fgn. Relations. Home: 300 Central Park W New York NY 10024-1513

LEVY, WALTER KAHN, management consultant executive; s. Benn Barnet and Beatrice (Kahn) L.; m. Anita von Bachelle, July 23, 1955; children: Gregg W., Evonne A. BA, Washington & Jefferson Coll., 1952; MS in Retail, NYU, 1966. Cert. mgmt. cons. Mgmt. trainee Burlington Mills, N.Y.C., 1952; buyer, merchandiser Bloomindale Bros., N.Y.C., 1953-65; cons. Cresap, McCormack & Padget, N.Y.C., 1965-68; v.p. ops. Bonwit Teller, N.Y.C., 1968-71; cons., chmn. Walter K. Levy & Robert E. Kerson Assocs., Inc., N.Y.C., 1971-95; cons. Goldman Sachs, N.Y.C. Trustee Washington & Jefferson Coll., Washington, Pa., 1980—; bd. dirs. Sch. Bd. Selection Com., Larchmont, N.Y., 1973-76. Sgt. USAR, 1954-62. Mem. Japan Soc., Larchmont Yacht Club. Avocations: history, reading, travel, tennis. Home: 35 Ellsworth Rd Larchmont NY 10538-1414

LEW, JOYCELYNE MAE, actress; b. Santa Monica, Calif., Feb. 25, 1962; d. George and Mabel Florence (Lum) L. BA in Theatre Arts, UCLA, 1981, teaching credential, 1982; MA in Urban Edn., Pepperdine U., 1984; bilingual cert., U. So. Calif., 1983; postgrad., Stella Adler Acad., 1988; studied with, The Groundlings Improv Group, 1987. Appeared in films Tai-Pan, 1987, Fatal Beauty, 1989, The Royal Affair, 1993, Shattered Image, 1993, Dr. Boris and Mrs. Duluth, 1994, Hindsight, 1996, Fire in My Heart, 1996, TV programs The Young and the Restless, 1990, Phil Donahue Show, 1993, Hard Copy, 1994, Current Affair, 1995, Gordon Elliott, 1995; voice over artist, mag. model, body double, dancer; appeared in comml. Good Seasons, 1996, Pillsbury Doughboy, 1996, Pacific Bell, 1996; co-writer film script They Still Call Me Bruce, 1986 (award); song lyricist Nighttime Blues. Mem. judging com. for film grants Nat. Endowment for Arts, 1986; mem.

L.A. Beautiful, 1993. Mem. AFTRA, SAG, NATAS (blue ribbon com. for Emmy awards 1986-90), Assn. Asian Pacific Am. Artists (treas. 1983-89), Nat. Asian Am. Telecomms. Assn., Am. Film Inst. Conservatory Workshop, Calif. PTA (life). Avocations: calligraphy, makeup art and hair, charcoals, fashion and interior design. Home and Office: 1958 N Van Ness Ave Los Angeles CA 90068-3625

LEW, ROGER ALAN, manufacturing company executive; b. N.Y.C., Mar. 16, 1941; s. Louis Arthur and Estelle Bebe (Marcus) L.; m. Marilyn Drourr, May 29, 1962; children—William, Jeffrey, Richard. B.S. in Fin, NYU, 1963. With Franklin Nat. Bank, N.Y.C., 1963-66; sr. v.p. Security Nat. Bank, N.Y.C., 1966-75; v.p. NVF Co., N.Y.C., 1975-78; sr. v.p. NVF Co., 1978-81, treas., 1979-81; pres., dir. Wormuth Bros. Foundry, Inc., Athens, N.Y., 1981—; pres., bd. dirs. Mirage Fin., Inc., 1985—, transmission Gear Sales, Inc., 1985—, Hudson Valley Buyers, Inc., 1985—; former sr. v.p., treas. Sharon Steel Corp., Pa. Engrng. Corp., DWG Co., Southeastern Pub. Svc. Co.; former sr. v.p., treas., bd. dirs. Wilson Bros.; former mem. small bus. and agr. adv. coun. to N.Y. Fed. Res. Bank. Trustee, former exec. v.p. Universal Housing & Devel. Co.; former v.p. Security Mgmt. Corp. Served with U.S. Army, 1959-60. Mem. Am. Iron and Steel Inst. Clubs: Colonie Country (Voorhees, N.Y.); Sag Harbor (N.Y.) Yacht. Office: Howard Hall Rd PO Box 171 Athens NY 12015

LEW, RONALD S. W., federal judge; b. L.A., 1941; m. Mamie Wong; 4 children. BA in Polit. Sci., Loyola U., L.A., 1964; JD, Southwestern U., 1971. Bar: Calif. 1972. Dep. city atty. L.A. City Atty's. Office, 1972-74; ptnr. Avans & Lew, L.A., 1974-82; commr. fire and police pension City of L.A., 1976-82; mcpl. ct. judge County of L.A., 1982-84, superior ct. judge, 1984-87; judge U.S. Dist. Ct. (cen. dist.) Calif., L.A., 1987—; Bar: Calif. 1971. Mem. World Affairs Council of L.A., 1976—, Christian Businessmen's Com. of L.A., 1982—. 1st lt. U.S. Army, 1967-69. Recipient Vol. award United Way of L.A., 1979, cert. of merit L.A. Human Relations Commn., 1977, 82. Mem. Am. Judicature Soc., Calif. Assn. of Judges, So. Calif. Chinese Lawyer's Assn. (charter mem. 1976, pres. 1979), Chinese Am. Citizens Alliance, San Fernando Valley Chinese Cultural Assn., Delta Theta Phi. Office: US Dist Ct 312 N Spring St Los Angeles CA 90012-4701

LEW, SALVADOR, radio station executive; b. Camajuani, Las Villas, Cuba, Mar. 6, 1929; came to U.S., 1961; s. Berko and Clara (Lewinowicz) L.; m. Laura F. Lew; 1 child, Esther Maria. JD magna cum laude, U. Havana, 1952. Editor Sch. Mural Newspaper, Camajuani, Cuba, 1941-43; pres. youth sect. and nat. sec. Cuban People's Party, Cuba, 1948-53; Latin Am. cons. Walters, Moore & Costanzo, Miami, Fla., 1961-72; news dir. Sta. WMIE and Sta. WQBA, Miami, 1961-70; gen. mgr., news dir. Sta. WRHC, Miami, 1973-89; host talk show, 1989—; pres. adv. bd. Cuba Broadcasting, 1992.Trustee, dir. United Way, 1985—. Recipient Lincoln Marti award Sec. HEW, 1964; FBI Award for Community Svcs., 1983; community svc. awards various orgns., 1973-84. Mem. Cuban Lawyers Assn. Exile. Jewish. Home: 2863 SW 23rd St Miami FL 33145-3309

LEWCOCK, RONALD BENTLEY, architect, educator; b. Brisbane, Australia, Sept. 27, 1929; s. Harry Kingsley and Ena (Orrock) L.; m. Barbara Sansoni, Aug. 8, 1981. Student, U. Queensland, 1947-49; BArch, Capetown U., South Africa, 1951; PhD, U. Cape Town, South Africa, 1961; MA, Cambridge U., Eng., 1970; Eliza Howard vis. fellowship, Columbia U., 1963. Pvt. practice architecture, 1951—; Whitehead research fellow Clare Hall, Cambridge U., Eng., 1970-72, ofcl. fellow, 1976-84; research officer Middle East Centre, Cambridge, 1973-80; Aga Khan prof. architecture for Islamic culture, dir. program in architecture for Islamic socs. MIT, Cambridge, 1984-91; chmn. Aga Khan program for Islamic architecture MIT and Harvard U., 1985-87; prof. architecture Ga. Inst. Tech., Atlanta, 1991—; cons. UNESCO, Habitat, World Bank, British Coun., Am. Rsch. Cen., Egypt, 1976—; lectr. U. Natal, 1952-57, sr. lectr., 1958-69; lectr., examiner Cambridge U., 1973-85; unit leader design in developing world Archtl. Assn., London, 1977-81; lectr. Archtl. Assocs. Sch., London, 1971-82; vis. prof. grad. sch. architecture Ga. Inst. Tech., 1979-84, Harvard, 1984, Louvain U., 1984; vis. Aga Khan prof., MIT, 1991-93. Author: Early 19th Century Architecture in South Africa, 1963, Traditional Architecture in Kuwait and the Northern Gulf, 1978, 2d edit. 81, Wadi Hadramawt and the Walled City of Shibam, 1986, The Old World City of San'a', 1986; editor: (with R.B. Serjeant) San'a' an Arabian Islamic City, 1983; contbr. articles to profl. jours., Architecture in the Islamic World, 1976, New Grove Dictionary of Music and Musicians, 1980. Mem. coun. Inst. History and Archaeology East Africa, London, 1976-86, Middle East Centre, Cambridge, Eng., 1981-88, British Sch. Archaeology in Jerusalem, London, 1981—; tech. coord. Internat. Campaign for the Conservation of Sana'a in Yemen Arab Rep. and Shibam and Wadi Hadramaut in Peoples Dem. Rep. of Yemen, 1978-93, UNESCO/UNDP Campaign for Conservation of Monuments and Cities in Uzbekistan, 1994—; steering com. mem. Aga Khan award, 1990-93, Aga Khan Trust for Culture, Geneva, 1993—. Mem. Royal Inst. British Architects (assoc.). Office: Georgia Institute of Technology Atlanta GA 30332

LEWELL, PETER A., international technology executive, researcher; b. St. John, N.B., Can.. Exec. dir. N.B. Rsch. and Productivity Coun., Fredericton, N.B., Can.; bd. dirs. Brunswick Ltd., N.B. Mfg. Tech. Ctr., Ctr. Nuclear Energy Rsch. Office: NB Rsch & Productivity Coun, 921 ch College Hill Rd, Fredericton, NB Canada E3B 6Z9

LEWELLEN, WILBUR GARRETT, management educator, consultant; b. Charleroi, Pa., Jan. 21, 1938; s. Anthony Garrett and Cozie Harriett (Watson) L.; m. Jean Carolyn Vanderlip, Dec. 8, 1962 (div. 1982); children—Stephen G., Jocelyn A., Jonathan W., Robyn E.; m. Eloise Evelyn Vincent, Mar. 5, 1983. B.S., Pa. State U., University Park, 1959; M.S., MIT, Cambridge, 1961, Ph.D., 1967. Asst. prof. mgmt. Purdue U., West Lafayette, Ind., 1964-68, assoc. prof. mgmt., 1968-72, prof., 1972-83, Loeb prof. mgmt., 1983-88; Krannert disting. prof. mgmt. Purdue U., 1988—; dir. exec. edn. programs Purdue U., West Lafayette, Ind., 1985—; cons. Bank Am., San Francisco, 1975—, Ind. Bell tel. Co., Indpls., 1976—, Am. Water Works Co., Wilmington, Del., 1978—, Indpls. Power and Light Co., 1993—; bd. dirs. USF & G Corp. Author: Executive Compensation in Large Industrial Corporations, 1968, Ownership Income of Management, 1971, The Cost of Capital, 1981. Recipient Salgo-Noren award as Outstanding Tchr. in Grad. Profl. Programs, Salgo-Noren Found., 1973, 77, 79, 84. Mem. Fin. Mgmt. Assn. (v.p. 1973-74), Am. Fin. Assn., Strategic Mgmt. Soc., AAUP, Western Fin. Assn., Lafayette Country Club, Ford's Colony Country Club. Methodist. Home: 3809 W Capilano Dr West Lafayette IN 47906-8881 Office: Purdue Univ Grad Sch Mgmt West Lafayette IN 47907

LEWENT, JUDY CAROL, pharmaceutical executive; b. Jan. 13, 1949. BA, Goucher Coll., 1970; MS in Mgmt., MIT, 1972. With corp. fin. dept. E.F. Hutton & Co., Inc., 1972-74; asst. v.p. for strategic planning Bankers Trust Co., 1974-75; sr. fin. analyst corp. planning Norton Simon, 1975-76; div. contr. Pfizer, Inc., 1976-80; dir. acquisitions and capital analysis Merck & Co., Inc., Whitehouse Station, N.J., 1980-83, asst. contr., 1983-85, exec. dir. fin. evaluation and analysis, 1985-87, v.p., treas., 1987-90, v.p. fin., CFO, 1990-92, sr. v.p., CFO, 1993—. Office: Merck & Co Inc PO Box 100 One Merck Dr Whitehouse Station NJ 08889-0100

LEWIN, ANN WHITE, museum director, educator; b. Boston, Dec. 19, 1939; d. Albert and Florence (Levy) White; m. Robert S. Benham; 1 child, Daniel Lewin. AB, Bryn Mawr Coll., 1960. Tchr., adminstr. Montessori Sch., Annandale, Va., 1965-69; dir. staff devel. Nat. Child Research Ctr., Washington, 1969-70; founder, adminstr. Parkmont Sch., Washington, 1970-75; exec. dir., founder Capital Children's Mus., Washington, 1975-95; founder, pres. The Nat. Learning Ctr., Wasington, 1983-95; cons. Arlington County Pub. Schs., Va., 1970-75, Edufax, Washington, 1969-70, George Washington U., Washington, 1970-71. Contbr. articles to profl. jours. Named Washingtonian of Yr., Washingtonian mag., 1979, Women of Dist. award Nat. Conf. for Coll. Women Student Leaders, 1990, Creative Peron of the Year award Odyssey of the Mind, 1991. Mem. Am. Assn. Mus., Cultural Alliance, Assn. Sci. and Tech. Ctrs. (bd. dirs. 1982), Nat. Assn. Edn. Young Children, Assn. Childhood Edn. Internat. Home: 1577 Cherry Park Dr Memphis TN 38120-4322

LEWIN, DAVID, management educator; b. Nov. 9, 1943. BS in Acctg., Calif. State U., L.A., 1965; MBA, UCLA, 1967, PhD in Bus. Adminstrn., 1971. Staff acct. Alexander Grant & Co., L.A., 1965-66; assoc. in bus. Columbia U., N.Y.C., 1970-71, asst. prof., 1971-74, assoc. prof., 1974-80, prof., 1980-90; prof. mgmt. UCLA, 1990—, dir. Inst. Indsl. Rels., 1990-94, vice dean, faculty dir. MBA program Anderson Grad. Sch. Mgmt.; vis. prof. UCLA, 1988; mem. adv. coun. N.Y. State Sch. Indsl. and Labor Rels. Cornell U., 1987-91; active U.S. Dept. Labor Com on Labor-Mgmt. Cooperation, 1988—, Econ. Policy Coun. Com. on Labor-Mgmt. Cooperation, 1989—; mediator, factfinder labor disputes N.Y. State, 1977-90; participant IBM Human Resources Forum, Armonk, N.Y., 1993; cons. U.S. Dept. Labor, State of Ill., County of L.A., City of L.A., U.S. Office Personnel Mgmt., N.Y. State Gov. Office Employee Rels., U. Calif., numerous others; prin. investigator, co-investigator numerous grants; attendee numerous confs. on human resources and cmty. rels.; lectr. in field. Author: (with others) The Urban Labor Market: Institutions, Information, Linkages, 1974, Collective Bargaining and Manpower Utilization in Big City Governments, 1979, The Labor Sector, 1980, Advances in Industrial and Labor Relations, vol. 3, 1986, vol. 4, 1987, vol. 5, 1991, vol. 6, 1994, vol. 7, 1996, Public Sector Labor Relations: Analysis and Readings, 1988, The Modern Grievance Procedure in the United States, 1988 (Outstanding Book in Indsl. Rels., Princeton U. 1988), Research Frontiers in Industrial Relations and Human Resources, 1992 (Outstanding Book in Indsl. Rels., Princeton U. 1993), International Perspectives and Challenges in Human Resource Management, 1994, Human Resource Management: An Economic Approach, 1995, The Human Resource Management Handbook, 1996; contbr. chpts. to books; sr. editor: Advances in Indsl. and Labor Rels., 1986—; mem. editl. bd. Indsl. Rels., 1988-92, 94—, Calif. Mgmt. Rev., 1990—; referee numerous profl. jours. Ford Found. grantee, 1982. Fellow Nat. Acad. Human Resource Mgmt. (founding dir. 1992-94); mem. AAAS, Am. Econ. Assn., Indsl. Rels. Rsch. Assn. (chmn. subcom. on rels. with other scholarly and profl. orgns. 1985-89, mem. program com. 1986-88, mem. exec. bd. 1987-90, mem. task force on programs and ann. and semiann. meetings 1987-88, mem. task force on rsch. and pubs. 1987-88, So. Calif. chpt. exec. bd. 1990—), Acad. Mgmt., Internat. Indsl. Rels. Assn., Inst. Indsl. Rels. Assn. (mem. exec. bd. 1990—), Univ. Coun. Indsl. Rels. and Human Resource Programs (pres. 1994-95), Beta Gamma Sigma. Appeared on local and nat. television and radio news and spl. reports on human resource mgmt., labor and employee rels. Office: UCLA A 423 110 Westwood Plz Anderson Grad Sch Mgmt Los Angeles CA 90095-1481

LEWIN, GEORGE FOREST, former insurance company executive; b. Plainfield, N.H., Oct. 25, 1916; s. George Forest and Maude (Welch) L.; m. Barbara DeFord, May 26, 1943. A.B., Middlebury Coll., 1940; LL.B., J.D., Georgetown U., 1951. Claims adjuster Liberty Mut. Ins. Co., 1940-41; exec. trainee Provident Mut. Life Ins. Co., 1941-43; asst. Washington rep. Anthracite Coal Industry, 1943-45; asst. traffic mgr. Aircraft Industries Assn., 1945-47; with Govt. Employees Ins. Co., Washington, 1947-73; v.p., sec. Govt. Employees Ins. Co., 1963-70, sr. v.p., 1970-73; v.p. Govt. Employees Life Ins. Co., Govt. Employees Ins. Co., Govt. Employees Financial Corp., 1974-76; sec. Criterion Ins. Co., 1964-70, exec. v.p., 1973-74, pres., 1974-81, also former dir.; ret., 1981. Trustee Kimball Union Acad., Meriden, N.H., 1977-82. Mem. Am., Va. bar assns., Newcomen Soc., Phi Alpha Delta, Kappa Delta Rho. Republican. Methodist. Home: 5225 Connecticut Ave NW Washington DC 20015-1845

LEWIN, JOSEPH, mechanical engineer, retired; b. Petrograd, Russia, Feb. 9, 1921; came to U.S., 1928; s. Samuel Markovich and Anna Osipovna (Pliner) L.; m. Suzanne Mellan O'Rorke, Sept. 18, 1944; children: Leonore, Elaine, David, Myra, William. BSME, Cooper Union, N.Y., 1951. Prof. engr., Tenn. Draftsman Cox & Stevens Co., N.Y.C., 1941-42; draftsman, designer EDO Aircraft Co., Flushing, N.Y., 1946-49, ELO Devel. Co., Long Island City, N.Y., 1951-55; engr. East Coast Aeronautics, Mt. Vernon, N.Y., 1949-51, Republic Aviation, Farmingdale, N.Y., 1950, Martin Aircraft Co., Balt., 1955-58, O.R.N.L. Union Carbide, Oak Ridge, Tenn., 1958-85; interpreter A.C.D.A., Geneva, Switzerland, 1986-88; contract interpreter U.S. Dept. State Office of Lang. Svcs., Washington, 1959-95; interpreter, engr. for nuclear reactor and scis. exch. visits with Russian Ministries on Peaceful Uses of Nuclear Energy, 1959-94, U.S. Atomic Energy Commn., U.C. NRC and State of Alaska. Contbr. articles to profl. jours. Pres. Friends of Oak Ridge Libr., 1993; reader Recording for the Blind, Oak Ridge, 1970-79. Sgt. USAAF, 1942-45. Mem. Elks Lodge, Sigma Xi. Avocations: private pilot, history, writing.

LEWIN, K(ATHERINE) TAMAR, reporter; b. Cleve., Dec. 6, 1949; d. David Victor and Doris (Shapiro) L.; m. Robert L. Krulwich, June 29, 1980; children: Nora, Jesse. BA, Barnard Coll., 1971; JD, Columbia U., 1974. Bar: N.Y. 1975, D.C. 1978. Reporter, Bergen Record, Hackensack, N.J., 1975-77; investigative researcher Common Cause, Washington, 1977-78; Washington Bur. chief Nat. Law Jour., 1978-80, mng. editor, N.Y.C., 1980-82; legal affairs reporter, nat. corr. N.Y. Times, N.Y.C., 1982—.

LEWIN, KLAUS J., pathologist, educator; b. Jerusalem, Israel, Aug. 10, 1936; came to U.S., 1968; s. Bruno and Charlotte (Nawratzki L.; m. Patricia Coutts Milne, Sept. 25, 1964; children: David, Nicola, Bruno. Attended, King's Coll. U. London, 1954-55; MB, BS, Westminster Med. Sch. London, Eng., 1959; MD, U. London, 1966. Diplomate Am. Bd. Pathology, Royal Coll. Pathologists (London), lic. Calif. Casualty officer Westminster Med. Hosp., 1960; resident Westminster Hosp. Med. Sch., London, 1960-68; pediatric house physician Westminster Hosp. Med. Sch., Westminster Children's Hosp., 1961; house physician St. James Hosp., Balham, London, 1961; asst. prof. pathology Stanford (Calif.) U., 1970-76; assoc. prof. pathology UCLA, L.A., 1977-80; attending physician Dept. Medicine Gastroenterology divsn. UCLA, Wadsworth, Va., 1978—; prof. pathology UCLA Med. Sch., L.A., 1980—, prof. dept. medicine divsn. gastroenterology, 1986—; divsn. surg. pathology UCLA Ctr. Health Scis.; resident pathologist clinical chemistry, bacteriology, hematology, blood transfusion, serology, Westminster Hosp. Med. Sch., 1961-62, registrar dept. morbid anatomy, 1962-64, rotating sr. registrar morbid anatomy, Royal Devon, Exeter Hosp., 1964-68; vis. asst. prof. pathology, Stanford U. Med. Sch., 1968-70; vice chmn. pathology UCLA, L.A., 1979-86; pres. L.A. Soc. Pathologists Inc., 1985-86; mem. curriculum com. U. Calif. Riverside, 1977-84; cons. Wadsworth VA Hosp., L.A., carcinoma of esophagus intervention study, Polyp Prevention study, Nat. Cancer Inst., Cancer Preservation Studies br., Bethesda, Md., Sepulveda VA Hosp.; mem. various coms. UCLA in field; rschr. structure, function, pathologic disorders of gastrointestinal tract and liver. Author: (with Riddel R., Weinstein W.) Gastrointestinal Pathology and Its Clinical Implications, 1992; edit. bd. Human Pathology, 1986—, Am. Jour. Surg. Pathology, 1990—; reviewer Gastroenterology and Archives of Pathology; contbr. papers, abstracts, review articles to profl. jours., chpts. in books; lectr., presenter in field. Dir. diagnostic Immonuhistochenistry Lab.; mem. diagnostic surg. Pathology svc. Recipient Chesterfield medal Inst. Dermatology, London, 1966; named Arris and Gale lectr. Royal Coll. Surgeons, London, 1968; Welcome Trust Rsch. grantee, 1968; fellow Found. Promotion Cancer Rsch., Tokyo, 1992. Fellow Royal Coll. Pathologists (Eng.); mem. Pathological Soc. Great Britain, Am. Gastroenterology Soc., Gastrointestinal Pathology Soc. (founder, pres. 1985-86, exec. com., edn. com. 1990—), U.S. Acad. Pathology, Can. Acad. Pathology, Assn. Clin. Pathologists, Pathological and Bacteriological Soc. Great Britain, Internat. Acad. Pathology, L.A. Pathology Soc. (bd. dirs.), Calif. Soc. Pathology (edn. com. 1983—), So. Calif. Soc. Gastrointestinal Endoscopy, Arthur Purdy Stout Soc., Gastrointestinal Pathology Soc. (pres., by-laws com., chmn. edn. com., exec. com.). Avocations: internat. travel, geographic pathology, hiking, swimming. Home: 333 N Las Casas Ave Pacific Palisades CA 90272-3307 Office: UCLA Sch Medicine Dept Pathology 10833 Le Conte Ave Los Angeles CA 90095-1732

LEWIN, MARTIN J., lawyer; b. Trenton, N.J., Apr. 18, 1949. BS in Econs., U. Pa., 1970, JD, 1973. Bar: D.C. 1973, U.S. Ct. Internat. Trade, U.S. Ct. Customs and Patent Appeals. Atty. advisor U.S. Gen. Acctg. Office, Washington, 1974-78; investigator subcom. on internat. orgns. U.S. House Reps., Washington, 1978-79; legal advisor U.S. Internat. Trade Commr., Washington, 1979-80; assoc. Daniels Houlihan & Palmeter, Washington, 1980-82; prin. Daniels Houlihan & Palmeter, 1983-84; ptnr. Mudge Rose Guthrie Alexander, Washington, 1984-93, Aitken, Irvin, Lewin, Berlin, Vrooman & Cohn, Washington, 1993—; bd. dirs., gen. counsel Am. Import Shippers Assn., 1988—; mem. trade counsel Fashion Accessories Shippers Assn., 1993—. Office: Aitken Irvin Lewin et al 1709 N St NW Washington DC 20036-2801

LEWIN, MOSHE, historian, educator; b. Wilno, Poland, Nov. 6, 1921; came to U.S., 1978; s. Leo J. and Fima L. (Koltunova) L. B.A., Tel Aviv U., 1961; Ph.D., Sorbonne, Paris, 1964. Dir. study Ecole des Hautes Etudes, Paris, 1965-66; sr. fellow Columbia U., N.Y.C., 1967-68; research prof. Birmingham U., Eng., 1968-78; prof. history U. Pa., Phila., 1978—; mem. acad. council Kennan Inst. for Russian Studies, Washington, 1981-84. Author: Russian Peasant and Soviet Power, 1968, Lenin's Last Struggle, 1968, Political Undercurrents in Soviet Economic Debates, 1974, 2d edit., The Making of the Soviet System, 1985, The Gorbachev Phenomenon, 1988, expanded edit., 1991, Stalinism and the Roots of Reform, 1991, Russia-USSR-Russia, 1995, (with Ian Kershaw) Dictators Unleashed, 1996. Fellow Inst. for Advanced Studies, Princeton, N.J., 1972-73, Wilson Kennan Ctr., Washington, 1976-77, John Simon Guggenheim Found., 1995. Mem. AAUP, AAAS, Am. Hist. Assn., Inst. d'Etudes Slaves (Paris), The Authors' Guild, Inc. Home: 309 S 25th St Philadelphia PA 19103-6403

LEWIN, PETER A., electrical engineer, educator; b. Oct. 27, 1945. BSc and MSc, U. Denmark, 1969, PhD, 1979. Prof. dept. elec. and computer engr. Drexel U. Fellow IEEE (mem. tech. com. IEEE Ultrasonics Symposium 1985, mem. stds. subcom. on ultrasonics, sensors, session chmn. IEEE Ultrasonics Symposia, session chmn./organizer, Lithotripsy, EMBS conf. 1990, co-chmn. med. ultrasound track EMBS conf. 1990, co-chmn. indsl. exhibits com. EMBS conf. 1990, co-editor IEEE Med. Ultrasound Parameter Measurement Guide 1984-88, reviewer IEEE Transactions, co-editor spl. issue IEEE Transactions on Ultrasonics, Frequency and Frequency Control 1988). Office: Drexel University Dept Electrical & Computer Eng Philadelphia PA 19104*

LEWIN, RALPH ARNOLD, biologist; b. London, Apr. 30, 1921; came to U.S., 1947; s. Maurice and Ethel Lewin; m. Joyce Mary Chismore, June, 1950 (div. 1965); m. Cheng Lanna, June 3, 1969. BA, Cambridge U., Eng., 1942, MA, 1946; PhD, Yale U., 1950; ScD, Cambridge U., Eng., 1973. Instr. Yale U., New Haven, Conn., 1951-52; sci. officer Nat. Research Council, Halifax, N.S., Can., 1952-55; ind. investigator NIH, Woods Hole, Mass., 1956-59; assoc. prof., now prof. U. Calif., La Jolla, 1960—. Editor: Physiology and Biochemistry of Algae, 1962, Genetics of Algae, 1976, Biology of Algae, 1979, Biology of Women, 1981, Origins of Plastids, 1993; co-editor: Prochloron, a microbial enigma, 1989; transl. Winnie-La-Pu (Esperanto), 1972, La Dektri Horlogoj, 1993. Served with British Army, 1943-46. Mem. Phycological Soc. Am. (pres. 1970-71, Darbaker prize 1963). Avocations: Esperanto, recorders, badminton. Home: 8481 Paseo Del Ocaso La Jolla CA 92037-3024 Office: U Calif San Diego Scripps Inst Oceanogra # 0202 La Jolla CA 92093

LEWIN, SEYMOUR ZALMAN, chemistry educator, consultant; b. N.Y.C., Aug. 16, 1921; s. Charles and Ida (Lazaroff) L.; m. Pearl Goldman, Oct. 17, 1943; children: David, Jonathan. BS, CCNY, 1941; MS, U. Mich., 1942, PhD, 1950; Prof. (hon.), Instituto Quimico de Sarria, Spain, 1961. Lectr. U. Mich., Ann Arbor, 1947-48, rsch. fellow, 1948-50; instr. NYU, N.Y.C., 1950-51, asst. prof., 1951-54, assoc. prof., 1954-59, prof. chemistry, 1959-91, emeritus, 1991—; cons. in field; vis. prof. Internat. Ctr. Conservation, Venice, Italy, 1974—. Author: Earth, Air, Fire, Water and DNA, 1970; Editor: Chemists' Dictionary, 1963; Funk & Wagnall Ency., 1972-77. Patentee in field. With U.S. Army, 1943-45. Recipient K. Fajans prize U. Mich., 1954, Golden Dozen Teaching Excellence awards NYU, 1960, 89, Oscar Foster prize N.Y. Chemistry Tchrs. Soc., 1973; Belgian-Am. Found. fellow, 1962. Fellow N.Y. Acad. Scis. (Cressy Morisson prize 1958), Am. Inst. Chemists; mem. Am. Chem. Soc. (chmn. analytical group N.Y. sect. 1973-74, tour speaker of yr. 1970-71), Am. Assn. Cereal Chemists, Sigma Xi (pres. NYU chpt. 1965-66), Inst. Food Technologists. Home: 4231 N Walnut Ave Arlington Heights IL 60004-1302

LEWIN, TED BERT, writer, illustrator; b. Buffalo, N.Y., May 6, 1935; s. Sidney Walter and Berenece (Klehn) L.; m. Betsy Reilly, 1963. BFA, Pratt Inst., 1956. Author: I Was a Teenage Professional Wrestler, 1993 (ALA Notable award 1993); illustrator: Island of the Blue Dolphins, 1990, Bird Watch, 1990 (ALA Notable award), Herds of Thunder Manes of Gold, 1989, National Velvet, 1985, The Day of Ahmed's Secret, 1990 (ALA Notable award), I Wonder if I'll See a Whale?, 1991, The Potato Man, 1991, Faithful Elephants, 1988, Brother Francis and the Friendly Beasts, 1991, Sami and the Time of the Troubles, 1992, Matthew's Meadow, 1992, Matthew Wheelock's Wall, 1992, The Great Pumpkin Switch, 1992, Cowboy Country, 1993, The Always Prayer Shawl, 1993, Pepe the Lamplighter, 1993 (Caldecott Honor award 1994), Just in Time for Christmas, 1994, Lost Moose, 1994; author, illustrator: Tiger Trek, 1990, When the Rivers Go Home, 1992, Amazon Boy, 1993, The Reindeer People, 1994, Sacred River, 1995, Market!, 1996, Seawatch, 1996, American Too, 1996. Home and Office: 152 Willoughby Ave Brooklyn NY 11205-3729

LEWINE, ROBERT F., broadcasting company executive; b. N.Y.C., Apr. 16, 1913; s. Irving I. and Jane (Weinberg) L.; m. Lucille Litwin, May 18, 1938; 1 child, Robert W. B.A., Swarthmore Coll., 1934; L.H.D., Columbia Coll., 1975. V.p. ops. Cine-TV Studios, Inc., 1945-47; dir. radio and TV Hirshon-Garfield, Inc., 1949-52; dir. programs Ea. div. ABC, 1953-54, nat. dir. programs, 1954-55, v.p. programming and talent, 1955-56; v.p. night time programs NBC, N.Y.C., 1957; v.p. nat. programs NBC, 1958-59; v.p. in charge programs CBS Films, Inc., 1959-62; v.p. programs Hollywood, CBS TV Network, 1962-64; exec. v.p. Creative Mgmt. Assocs., Ltd., 1964-65; v.p. charge Warner Bros. TV, Burbank, Calif., 1965-68; pres., chief exec. officer Nat. Acad. TV Arts and Scis., Beverly Hills, Calif., 1970-76; sr. cons. NBC-TV Network, Burbank, 1977—; chmn. bd. Riverside Broadcasting Co., Los Angeles, 1977—; vis. prof. Calif. State U.-Northridge, 1979—, U. So. Calif., 1979—, UCLA, 1979—; mktg. cons. A.M.E. & Co., 1988—. Trustee Am. Women in Radio and TV Soc. Found., Columbia Coll., Los Angeles; pres. Acad. TV Arts and Scis. Found., 1965-85, Film and TV Study Center, Los Angeles; bd. dirs. Paw Soc.; mem. internat. adv. council Population Inst. Served as lt. USNR, 1942-45. Recipient Nat. Acad. of Television Arts & Scis. Founders award, 1992. Mem. Nat. Acad. TV Arts and Scis. (pres. N.Y. chpt. 1958-59, 1st nat. v.p. 1958-59, gov. 1954-62, pres. 1961-63, pres. 1970-77, chmn. membership com. 1960). Clubs: Quaker Ridge (N.Y.); Golf (dir. 1953-55). Home: 9360 Readcrest Dr Beverly Hills CA 90210-2533

LEWINS, STEVEN, security analyst, investment advisor, corporate officer; b. N.Y.C., Jan. 22, 1943; s. Bruno and Kaethe (Czhoeck) L.; m. Rayna Lee Kornreich, July 4, 1968 (div. 1991); children: Shani Nicole, Scott Asher. BA, Queens Coll., CUNY 1964, MA in Diplomatic-Econ. History, 1966, postgrad. in bus. adminstrn., 1969-72; postgrad. cert. in public adminstrn. NYCSC, SUNY, 1967. Park ranger-historian Nat. Park Svc., Statue of Liberty, N.Y.C., 1964-66; traffic asst. AT&T, White Plains, N.Y., 1966; adminstrv. intern N.Y. State, Albany, 1966-67; asst. to commr. N.Y. State Narcotics Addiction Control Commn., N.Y.C., 1967-69; security analyst Value Line Investment Survey, N.Y.C., 1969-71, assoc. rsch. dir., 1971-74, rsch. dir., directing editor Value Line Investment Survey, 1974-80, v.p. Value Line Data Svcs., 1975-80 (created Value Line Financial Data Base, 1974); v.p. Arnold Bernhard & Co., 1975-80, dir., 1976-80, mem. exec. com., 1977-80; ptnr. Ray-Lux Products, 1978-80; pres. RayLux Assocs., 1980-81, dir., 1980-86; founder RayLux Fin. Svc., 1980 (1st SEC-registered electonic investment adv. svc.); v.p., unit head investment div. Citibank N.A., 1981-86, v.p. Citicorp Investment Mgmt., Inc., 1986-88; v.p. transp. and aerospace investment mgmt. Chancellor Capital Mgmt., 1988-92; mng. dir., rsch. dir., head of equity First Capital Advisers/F.C. Fin. Svcs., N.Y.C., 1992-93; v.p. Investment Rsch. Gruntal & Co., Inc., 1994—; adv. corp. disclosure com. SEC, 1977-78, ICC, 1982-92, Dept. Transp., 1982-92, Dept. Justice, 1982-92, Dept. State, 1986-92. Participant U.S.-USSR Emigration/Jackson Vanek, 1984-91, U.S.-USSR Pan Am-Aeroflot Aviation Agreement, 1985, USSR Student Exchg., 1985-86, U.S.-USSR Anti-Internat. Terrorism, 1985-91, U.S.-USSR Rights of Terrorists, 1985, U.S.-USSR Trans-Siberian-CSX Corp. Initiative, 1989, TRW, Inc-Energia N.P.O. Look Down Satellite Agreement, 1989-90, U.S.-USSR Orbital Space Coop., 1989-90, U.S.- USSR Def. Conv. Projects, 1990-93, Reagan-Gorbachev Summit Preparations, 1986, 87, 88, Bush-Gorbachev Summit Preparation, 1990, U.S.-USSR AMR Corp.-Aeroflot Bilateral Discussion, 1989, U.S.-USSR Spl. Mission /Secure Info. Negotiation, 1983-92; sponsor U.S.-USSR Pace U., rsch. exch., 1990; Citicorp liaison USSR mission to UN, 1982-88, Inst. U.S. and Can., Acad. Scis. USSR, 1985-88, econs. dept. Acad. Scis. USSR, 1988; liaison Chancellor Capital Mgmt., USSR, 1988-92; overseas fact-finding visits include Saudi

Arabia, Egypt, Jordan, Israel, 1979, Peoples Republic of China, Japan, Hong Kong, 1981, USSR, 1985, 86, 89, 90, Georgia SSR, 1985, Uzbekistan SSR, 1986, Baykhal, Irkutsk, Olha, Siberia, 1989, Kazakhstan SSR, Republic of Georgia, Baykonour-Soyuz Launch Ctr., 1990. Acting col. S.I.N., USAF, M.A.C., 1990. Recipient Commendation award U.S. Dept. of Justice for spl. assistance in pursuit of U.S.-USSR rels., 1990, U.S. Commendation citation for Gulf War, 1992. Mem. Croton-on-Hudson Narcotics Guidance Coun., 1972-75, Cortland Indsl. Com., 1975-77; dist. leader Dem. Party, 1979-83; founding mem. Challenger Found., 1987. Fellow Fin. Analyst Fedn. Mem. N.Y. Soc. Security Analysts (sr. security analyst, membership com., computer applications symposium, airline splinter group, motor carrier splinter group, aerospace splinter group), Bus. Economists Coun., Washington Transp. Roundtable, Assn. Computer Users, Internat. Platform Assn., N.Y. Assn. Bus. Economists, Nat. Assn Bus. Economists, Nat. Planetary Soc., Nat. Space Soc., Nat. Air and Space Mus., Tau Delta Phi (pres. 1963, 64, undergrad. of yr. 1963, spl. student senate recognition 1964, Coll. Distinction medal French 1964). Democrat. Author: Fashoda Crisis of 1898, 1966, Knowing Your Common Stocks, 1979, The Social Overhaul of the USSR, 1986, Economics Can Bind U.S.-USSR, 1986, Ecomonic Reform in the U.S.S.R., 1990, USA: 21st Century World Transportation Crossroads, 1994, U.S. Needs World-Class Transportation System, 1994; co-author: (with Bogdanov) US-USSR Anti-International Terrrist Protocol, 1989, (with Bogdanov) Rights of Terrorist, 1990, (with Bogdanov, Semenov) U.S.-USSR Space Cooperation, 1990; editor: Megatrends, 1980, Witch Doctor of Wall Street, 1990. Speaker security analysis, econs., transp., aerospace, def., corp. disclosure, deregulation, air traffic control and safety, fin. data svcs., U.S. megatrends, USSR Glastnost and Perestroika. Home: 66 Grand St Croton On Hudson NY 10520-2519 Office: Gruntal & Co Inc 14 Wall St Fl 15 New York NY 10005-2101

LEWINTON, CHRISTOPHER L., business executive; b. London, Jan. 6, 1932; came to U.S., 1960; s. Joseph and Elizabeth (Gee) L.; m. Jennifer A. Alcock, 1957 (div. 1973); children: Stephen, Peter; m. Louise H. Tidd, July 26, 1978. Grad. in mech. engring., London U., 1958. Sr. devel. engr. Wilkinson Sword Ltd., London, 1955-58; mktg. dir. Graviner Ltd., London, 1958-60; pres., chief exec. officer Wilkinson Sword Inc., N.J., 1960-70; mng. dir. Wilkinson Sword Ltd., London, 1970-78; exec. v.p., dir. Allegheny Internat., Pitts., 1978—; chmn. internat. group Allegheny Internat., London, 1978—; dir. Rowenta, Frankfort, W. Ger., Wilkinson Sword Group, London, Sunbeam Internat., London. Mem. council World Wildlife Fund, London. Served to capt. Brit. Army, 1953-55, Egypt. Fellow Inst. Mech. Engrs. (charter mem.). Office: TI Group Inc 375 Park Ave 2nd Fl New York NY 10152*

LEWIS, A. DUFF, JR., investment executive; b. Pitts., May 3, 1939; s. A. Duff and Helen Raley (Woolford) L.; m. Nancy Bastian, May 3, 1969; children: Amie D., Jennifer E., Katherine E., Jonathan K. BSME, Grove City Coll., 1962; MS, Purdue U., 1965. Chartered fin. analyst. Project engr. Bailey Meter Co., Wickliffe, Ohio, 1962-64; from fin. analyst mfg. to fin. analyst corp. Eastman Kodak Co., Rochester, N.Y., 1965-82, pension investment coord., 1982-91; mng. dir. Rogers, Casey & Assocs., Darien, Conn., 1992-96; investment officer U. Rochester, N.Y., 1996—. Mem. Inst. Chartered Fin. Analysts, Fin. Analysts Fed., Rochester Soc. Security Analysts, Mill Creek Community Club, Inc. (co-founder, treas.). Republican. Lutheran. Home: 1231 Stockbridge Rd Webster NY 14580-9145 Office: U Rochester Treasurer's Office Adminstrn Bldg Rm 263 Rochester NY 14627

LEWIS, ALAN JAMES, pharmaceutical executive, pharmacologist; b. Newport Gwent, UK. BSc, Southampton U., Hampshire, 1967; PhD in Pharmacology, U. Wales, Cardiff, 1970. Postdoctoral fellow biomedical sci. U. Guelph, Ont., Can., 1970-72; rsch. assoc. lung rsch. ctr. Yale U., 1972-73; sr. pharmacologist Organon Labs., Ltd., Lanarkshire, Scotland, 1973-79; rsch. mgr. immunoinflammation Am. home products Wyeth-Ayerst Rsch., Princeton, N.J., 1979-82, assoc. dir. exptl. therapeutics, 1982-85, dir., 1985-87, asst. v.p., 1987-89, v.p. rsch., 1989-93; pres. Signal Pharms. Inc., San Diego, 1994—. Editor allergy sect. Agents & Actions & Internat. Archives Pharmacodynamics Therapy; reviewer Jour. Pharmacology Exptl. Therapy, Biochemical Pharmacology, Can. Jour. Physiol. Pharmacology, European Jour. Pharmacology, Jour. Pharm. Sci. Mem. Am. Soc. Pharmacological and Exptl. Therapeutics, Am. Pheumatism Assn., Mid-Atlantic Pharmacology Soc. (v.p. 1991-93, pres. 1993-94), Pulmonary Rsch. Assn., Inflammation Rsch. Assn. (pres. 1986-88), Pharm. Mfrs. Assn., Internat. Assn. Inflammation Socs. (pres. 1990-95). Achievements include research in mechanisms and treatment of inflammatory diseases including arthritis and asthma cardiovascular diseases, metabolic disorders, central nervous system diseases, osteoporosis and viral diseases. Office: Signal Pharms Inc 5555 Oberlin Dr Ste 100 San Diego CA 92121-3746

LEWIS, ALEXANDER, JR., oil company executive; b. Danville, Pa., July 21, 1916; s. Alexander and Elizabeth (Mason) L.; m. Alice Kabakjian, May 1, 1942; children—Alexander III, Dennis James, Brady Mason. B.S., Ursinus Coll., 1938; M.S., U. Pa., 1940; Ph.D., U. Pitts., 1951. Chemist refinery tech. div. Gulf Oil Corp., Phila., 1938-42; chief product devel. engr. Gulf Oil Corp., Pitts., 1951-54; mgr. chem. mktg. Gulf Oil Corp., 1954-58, mgr. petrochems. dept., 1958—, v.p., 1960-64, sr. v.p., 1964-78; pres. Internat. Trade and Tech., 1978—; dir. Tri Century Ins. Corp., 1985—; mem. Pa. Gov.'s Sci. Adv. Com., 1965-75, Pa. State Com. for Nuclear Energy Devel. and Radiation Control, 1969-79, Pa. State Bd. Edn., 1969-77; pres. Gulf Oil Found., 1973-78; v.p. World Petroleum Congresses, London, 1975-79. Trustee Ursinus Coll., 1972, Point Park Coll., 1973; bd. regents Georgetown U.; bd. dirs. St. Clair Meml. Hosp., Pitts., Internat. Mgmt. and Devel. Inst., Washington. Served to lt. USNR, 1942-46. Fellow Mellon Inst. Indsl. Research, 1946-51. Mem. Am. Chem. Soc., Am. Petroleum Inst., Soc. Automotive Engrs., AAAS, Pitts. Chemists Club, Explorers Club, Duquesne Club, Univ. Club (Pitts.), Downtown Club (Pitts.), Longue Vue Club, Frosty Valley Country Club (Danville, Pa.), Sigma Psi, Phi Lambda Upsilon.

LEWIS, ALEXANDER INGERSOLL, III, lawyer; b. Detroit, Apr. 10, 1946; s. Alexander Ingersoll Jr. and Marie T. (Fuger) L.; m. Gretchen Elsa Lundgren, Aug. 8, 1970; children: Jennifer L., Katherine F., Elisabeth M., Alexander Ingersoll IV. BA with honors, Johns Hopkins U., 1968; JD cum laude, U. Pa., 1971. Bar: Md. 1972, U.S. Dist. Ct. Md. 1972, U.S. Ct. Appeals (4th cir.) 1975, U.S. Supreme Ct. 1976, D.C. 1982. Assoc. Venable, Baetjer & Howard, LLP, Balt., 1972-75, 78-80, ptnr., 1981—; head estate and trust practice group Venable, Baetjer & Howard LLP, Balt., 1993—; asst. atty. gen. State of Md., Balt., 1975-77; cons. subcom. on probate rules, standing com. on rules and procedures Md. Ct. Appeals, 1976—; mem. Md. Gov.'s Task Force to Study Revision of Inheritance and Estate Tax Laws, 1987-88; lectr. Md. Inst. Continuing Profl. Edn. Lawyers, 1978—, Nat. Bus. Inst., 1986-87, 92—, Cambridge Inst., 1986-90, Nat. Law Found., 1988—. Contbr. articles to legal jours. Vice chmn. Md. Gov.'s Task Force on Long-Term Fin. Planning for Disabled Individuals, 1990-94. 1st lt. U.S. Army, 1972. Fellow Am. Coll. Trust and Estate Counsel; mem. ABA, Md. Bar Assn. (chmn. probate reform and simplification com. estates and trusts coun. 1984-86, sec. 1987-88, chmn. 1989-90, com. on laws 1994—), D.C. Bar Assn., Bar Assn. City Balt., Immigration Lawyers Assn., Balt. Estate Planning Coun., Johns Hopkins Club. Republican. Roman Catholic. Avocations: canoeing, camping, tennis. Home: 922 Army Rd Ruxton MD 21204-6703 Office: Venable Baetjer & Howard LLP 1800 Two Hopkins Plz Baltimore MD 21201

LEWIS, ALLAN, conductor, ballet company music director. Former asst. artistic dir. The Joffrey Ballet, N.Y.C.; now music dir. The Joffrey Ballet. Office: Joffrey Ballet 130 W 56th St New York NY 10019-3818

LEWIS, ANDRE LEON, artistic director; b. Hull, Que., Can., Jan. 16, 1955; s. Raymond Lincoln and Theresa L. Student, Classical Ballet Studio, Ottawa, Royal Winnipeg (Man.) Ballet Sch., 1975; studies with David Moroni, Arnold Spohr, Rudi van Dantzig, Jiri Kylian, Peter Wright, Hans van Manen, and Alicia Markova, among others. Mem. corps de ballet Royal Winnipeg (Man.) Ballet, 1979-82, soloist, artistic coord., 1984-89, interim artistic dir., 1989-90, assoc. artistic dir., 1990-95, artistic dir., 1995—; staged Danzig's Romeo and Juliet, Teatro Comunale, Florence, Italy, Greek Nat. Opera, Athens. Dancer, soloist (ballets) Song of a Wayfarer, Fall River Legend, Nuages Pas de deux, Lento A Tempo E Appassionatto, Nutcracker, Four Last Songs, Romeo and Juliet, Belong Pas de deux, Ectasy of Rita Joe, (TV and films) Fall River Legend, Giselle, Heartland, Romeo and Juliet, The Big Top, Firebird, Belong Pas De Deux; performed at many events including the opening Gala performance of the Internat. Ballet competition in Jackson, Miss., Le Don Des Etoiles, Montreal, a spl. gala honoring Queen Beatrix of Holland and at a Gala performance in Tchaikovsky Hall, Moscow; appeared as a guest artist throughout N.Am., the Orient and USSR. Avocation: listening to opera. Office: Royal Winnipeg Ballet, 380 Graham Ave, Winnipeg, MB Canada R3C 4K2

LEWIS, ANDREW LINDSAY, JR. (DREW LEWIS), transportation and natural resources executive; b. Phila., Nov. 3, 1931; s. Andrew Lindsay and Lucille (Bricker) L.; m. Marilyn S. Stoughton, June 1, 1950; children: Karen Lewis Sacks, Russell Shepherd, Andrew Lindsay IV. BS, Haverford (Pa.) Coll., 1953; MBA, Harvard U., 1955; postgrad., MIT, 1968. With Henkels & McCoy, Inc., Blue Bell, Pa., 1955-60, Am. Olean Tile Co., Inc., Lansdale, Pa., 1960-68, Nat. Gypsum Co., Buffalo, 1960-70; chmn. Simplex Wire & Cable Co., Boston, 1970-74, chief exec. officer, 1972-74; pres., chief exec. officer Snelling & Snelling, Inc., Boston, 1972-74; fin. and mgmt. cons. Lewis & Assocs., Plymouth Meeting, Pa., 1974-81; sec. U.S. Dept. Transp., Washington, 1981-83; chmn. Warner Amex Cable Communications Inc., N.Y.C., 1983-86; chmn., chief exec. officer Union Pacific R.R., Omaha, 1986; pres. Union Pacific Corp., N.Y.C., 1986-87; chmn., CEO Union Pacific Corp., Bethlehem, Pa., 1987—; bd. dirs. Am. Express, Ford Motor Co., AT&T FPL Group Inc., Gannett Co., Inc., Gulfstream Aerospace Corp.; trustee Com. for Econ. Devel. Rep. candidate for gov., Pa., 1974; mem. Rep. Nat. Com., 1976-90, dep. chmn., 1980; dep. polit. dir. Reagan-Bush Campaign Com., 1980; co-chmn. Nat. Econ. Commn., 1988-89; chmn. The Bus. Roundtable, 1990-92; mem. nat. exec. bd. Boy Scouts of Am. Mem. Phila. Club, Sunnybrook Golf Club (Plymouth Meeting, Pa.), Saucon Valley Country Club (Bethlehem, Pa.), Bohemian Club (San Francisco). Office: Union Pacific Corp Martin Tower 8th & Eaton Ave Bethlehem PA 18018

LEWIS, ANNE, federal agency administrator; b. Boston, Aug. 4, 1960. BA cum laude, Smith Coll., 1982; MPA, Harvard U., 1985. Legis. asst. U.S. Sen. Carl Levin, 1989, chief of staff, 1990-91; legis. dir. U.S. Senator Hanis Wofford, 1991; dir. Great Am. Media (Clinton for Pres./Paid Media Ops.), 1991-92; mem. Presdl. Transition Team, Washington, 1992; dep. asst. sec. for pub. affairs U.D. Dept. HHS, Washington, 1993; asst. sec. for pub. affairs U.S. Dept. of Labor, 1993-95, asst. sec. for policy, 1995—. Office: Dept Labor Office Policy and Budget 200 Constitution Ave NW Washington DC 20210

LEWIS, ANTHONY, newspaper columnist; b. N.Y.C., Mar. 27, 1927; s. Kassel and Sylvia (Surut) L.; m. Linda Rannells, July 8, 1951 (div.); children: Eliza, David, Mia; m. Margaret H. Marshall, Sept. 23, 1984. A.B., Harvard U., 1948. Deskman Sunday dept. N.Y. Times, 1948-52; staff Democratic Nat. Com., 1952; reporter Washington Daily News, 1952-55, Washington bur. N.Y. Times, 1955-64; chief London bur. N.Y. Times, 1965-72; editorial columnist, 1969—; lectr. on law Harvard U., 1974-89; James Madison vis. prof. Columbia U., 1983—. Author: Gideon's Trumpet, 1964 (award as best fact-crime book Mystery Writers Am.), Portrait of a Decade: The Second American Revolution, 1964, Make No Law: The Sullivan Case and the First Amendment, 1991; contbr. articles to profl. jours. Recipient Heywood Broun award, 1955, Pulitzer prize for nat. reporting, 1955, 63; Nieman fellow, 1956-57. Mem. Am. Acad. Arts and Scis., Tavern Club. Office: NY Times 2 Faneuil Hall Marketplace Boston MA 02109

LEWIS, ARTHUR DEE, corporation executive; b. Greenville, Tex., Sept. 13, 1918; s. Carl Hamilton and Maxie (Curtis) L.; m. Hildegard Bair, Dec. 7, 1946; children: Gregory Scott, Kimberly Kealani. Student, U. Tex., 1935-41, Advanced Mgmt. Program, Harvard, 1952; Sc.D., Clarkson Coll. Tech. With Am. Airlines, 1941-55, beginning as cargo research analyst, successively supr. spl. projects, mgr. econ. analysis br., dir. econ. planning div., 1941-54, asst. v.p. planning, 1954-55; exec. v.p. Hawaiian Airlines, 1955, pres., dir., chief exec. officer, 1955-64; sr. v.p., gen. mgr., dir. Eastern Air Lines, 1964-67, pres., chief operating officer, dir., 1967-69; gen. partner F. S. Smithers & Co., 1969—; chmn., pres., chief exec. officer F. Smithers & Co., 1969-73; chmn., chief exec. officer U.S. Ry. Assn., 1974-77; pres., dir., chief exec. officer Am. Bus Assn., 1977-82; chmn., chief exec. officer U.S. Africa Airways, 1990-94, bd. dirs., chmn. emeritus, cons.; chmn. bd. Airline Media Assocs., Inc.; organizer Consol. Ry. Corp.; organizer Nat. Ry. Passenger Corp.; dir. Riegel Paper Corp., Rexham Corp., Bankers Security Life Ins. Soc., Bank of Commerce, Iroquois Brands Ltd., C. Brewer & Co., Bishop Trust Co., Internat. Bank; chmn. Mid Pacific Airlines, Honolulu; cons. airline moblzn., transp. div. Nat. Security Resources Bd., Korean War; cons. Def. Air Transp. Adminstrn., 1951-55, Dept. Transp., 1969. Bd. regents U. Hawaii; bd. govs. Pacific and Asian Affairs Council, Iolani Sch. Boys; bd. dirs. Hawaii Visitors Bur.; trustee, chmn. emeritus Clarkson Coll. Tech. Mem. Am. Mgmt. Assn. (dir., mem. exec. com.), Honolulu C. of C. (dir. 1958-59), Young Pres. Orgn., World Bus. Coun. (pres., dir. 1973-74), Conquistadores del Cielo (dir.), Burning Tree Club (Bethesda, Md.).

LEWIS, AUDREY GERSH, financial marketing consultant; b. Phila., Dec. 1, 1933; d. Benjamin and Augusta (Fine) Gersh; divorced; children: Jamie Lewis Keith, Ruth-Ellen. Student, Temple U., 1951-53. Asst. mgr. accounts payable/receivable Turner Constrn. Co., Louisville, 1953-55; rep. sales, mktg., fin. depts. Benjamin Gersh Wholesaler Jeweler, Wyncote, Pa., 1955-69; registered rep. Seaboard Planning Corp. (formerly B.C. Morton Broker Del.), Greenwich, Conn. and Wyncote, 1969-72; placement counselor sales and mktg. dept. Greyhound Permanent Pers. subs. Greyhound Corp., Stamford, Conn., 1974-77; asst. v.p. Am. Investors Corp., Greenwich, 1977-85; founder, pres. Audrey Gersh Lewis Cons. Ltd., Greenwich, 1985—. Chair Cancer Fund, Wyncote, United Fund Leadership Award, Wyncote; asst. treas. Republican Town Com., Greenwich, 1981-82; mem. Greenwich Town Alarm Appeals Bd., 1985—. Mem. Assn. Corp. Growth (bd. dirs., v.p. mktg. and pub. rels. N.Y. chpt. 1989-92, mem. nat. ann. meeting planning com. 1992, 93, 94), Fin. Women's Assn., Women's Econ. Round Table, Greenwich C. of C. (mem. pub. rels. com. 1990—, corp. devel. com. 1991—), Centre for the Study of the Presidency (nat. adv. coun.), N.Y. Hong Kong Assn., Am. C. of C. in Hong Kong, World Trade Centres in Can. Avocations: antiquing, walking, reading. Office: Audrey Gersh Lewis Cons Ltd PO Box 4644 Greenwich CT 06830-8644

LEWIS, BERNARD, Near Eastern studies educator; b. London, May 31, 1916; s. H. Lewis; m. Ruth Helene Oppenhejm, 1947 (div. 1974); 2 children. BA, U. London, PhD; postgrad., univs. of London and Paris; hon. doctorate, Hebrew U., Jerusalem, 1974, Tel Aviv U., 1979, SUNY, Binghamton, 1987, U. Pa., 1987, Hebrew Union Coll., 1987, Yeshiva U., 1991; Haifa U., 1991, Bar-Ilan U., 1992, Brandeis U., 1993. Asst. lectr. in Islamic history Sch. Oriental Studies U. London, 1938, prof. history Near and Middle East, Sch. Oriental and African Studies, 1949-74, hon. fellow, 1986; Cleveland E. Dodge prof. nr. ea. studies Princeton U., 1974-86, prof. emeritus, 1986—; A.D. White prof. at large Cornell U., 1984-90; dir. Annenberg Rsch. Inst., Phila., 1986-90; Ataturk prof. (hon.) Princeton (N.J.) U., 1992-93; vis. prof. history UCLA, 1955-56, Columbia U., 1960, Ind. U., 1963; vis. prof. College de France, 1980, Ecole des Hautes Etudes, Paris, 1983-86; Class of 1932 lectr. Princeton U., 1964; vis. mem. Inst. for Advanced Study, Princeton, N.J., 1969, long-term mem., 1974-86; Gottesman lectr. Yeshiva U., 1974; Jefferson lectr. NEH, 1990; Tanner lectr. Oxford U., 1990; Weizmann lectr. in Humanities, 1991; Henry M. Jackson meml. lectr., 1992; Siemens Stiftung lectr., Munich, 1993; Merle-Curti lectr., Madison, Wis., 1993; lectr. N.Y. Pub. Libr., 1993. Author: The Origins of Ismailism, 1940, Turkey Today, 1940, British Contributions to Arabic Studies, 1941, Handbook of Diplomatic and Political Arabic, 1947, The Arabs in History, 1950, new edit., 1993, Notes and Documents from the Turkish Archives, 1952, The Emergence of Modern Turkey, 1961, rev. edit., 1968, (transl. from Ibn Gabirol) The Kingly Crown, 1961, Istanbul and the Civilization of the Ottoman Empire, 1963, The Middle East and the West, 1964, The Assassins, 1967, Race and Color in Islam, 1971, Islam in History, 1973, new edit., 1993, Islam from the Prophet Muhammad to the Capture of Constantinople, 2 vols., 1974, History Remembered, Recovered, Invented, 1975, Studies in Classical and Ottoman Islam, 7th-16th centuries, 1976, The Muslim Discovery of Europe, 1982, The Jews of Islam, 1984, Semites and Anti-Semites, 1986, The Political Language of Islam, 1988, Race and Slavery in Islam, 1990, Islam and the West, 1993, The Shaping of the Modern Middle East, 1994, Cultures in Conflict: Christians, Muslims and Jews in the Age of Discovery, 1995; (with Amnon Cohen) Population and Revenue in the Towns of Palestine in the Sixteenth Century, 1978; author, editor: Land of Enchanters, 1948, The World of Islam: Faith, People, Culture, 1976; author, co-editor: Historians of the Middle East, 1962, Ency. of Islam, 1956-87; editor: (with others) The Cambridge History of Islam, vols. 1-11, 1971; co-editor: Muslims in Europe, 19942, Religionsgespräche im Mittelalter, 1992; also articles. Served with Royal Armoured Corps and Intelligence Corps, Brit. Army, 1940-41; with dept. Fgn. Office, 1941-45. Recipient Cert. of Merit for svcs. to Turkish culture, Turkish Govt., 1973, Harvey prize, 1978; Univ. Coll. of London fellow, 1976. Fellow Brit. Acad., Royal Hist. Soc., Turkish Hist. Soc. (hon.), Sch. of Oriental and African Studies (hon.); mem. Am. Acad. Arts and Scis., Am. Philos. Soc., Am. Hist. Assn., Soc. Asiatique (hon.), Inst. d'Egypte (Cairo, assoc.), Inst. de France (corr.). Office: Near East Studies Dept Princeton Univ Princeton NJ 08544

LEWIS, BERNARD LEROY, electronic scientist, consultant; b. Storm Lake, Iowa, Dec. 19, 1923; s. Leo Leroy and Francis Mae (Cutchael) L.; m. Dorothy Louise Simonezux, Feb. 16, 1946 (dec. Feb. 1985); children: David Leroy, Michael Peter, Patrick Daniel, Timothy Mark; m. Marilyn W. McCullum, Oct. 10, 1990. BS in Physics, Tulane U., 1947, MS in Physics, 1948; postgrad., U. Md., 1953-56. Sect. head Naval Rsch. Lab., Washington, 1948-57; cons. Systems Inc., Orlando, Fla., 1957-60; prin. engr. Radiation Inc., Orlando, 1960-61; design engr. Martin Marietta Co., Orlando, 1961; chief engr. Airtronics, Washington, 1961-63; prin. engr. Harris Intertype, Melbourne, Fla., 1963-69; bus. ptnr. McDowell Assocs., Melbourne, 1969-72; sr. scientist Naval Rsch. Lab., Washington, 1972-84; radar cons. Bernard L. Lewis Assocs., Melbourne, Fla., 1984—; cons. Sperry Rand, Great Neck, N.Y., 1984-87, Naval Rsch. Lab., Washington, 1987-88; adj. prof. Fla. Inst. Tech., Melbourne, Fla., 1984-89. Author: Aspects of Radar Signal Processing; contbr. over 72 tech. papers to profl. jours.; patentee in field. Lt. USN, 1957. Recipient Disting. Civilian Svc. award USN Rsch. Lab., 1981, 5 times Best Paper of the Yr. award Naval Rsch. Lab., 1972-82, Outstanding Alumnus award Tulane U., 1984. Fellow IEEE. Democrat. Roman Catholic. Avocations: physics theory, bridge, golf, dancing. Home and Office: 817 Villa Dr Melbourne FL 32940-7037

LEWIS, BOYD DE WOLF, publisher,editor, writer; b. Boston, Aug. 18, 1905; s. Harry Braddock and Margaret De Wolf (Wade) L.; m. Hazel Reviere Bestick, Sept. 1, 1929; children: David De Wolf, Patricia Ann. Student, Boston U., 1923-27. Reporter, editor and bur. mgr. UP Assns., 1927-45; war corr. with Canadian, Brit. and Am. forces, 1944-45; 1 of 3 Am. press reps. at German surrender Rheims, France, 1945; European news mgr. UP, 1945; exec. editor Newspaper Enterprise Assn., N.Y.C., 1945—; v.p. Newspaper Enterprise Assn., 1949-63, pres., 1963-72; v.p. pub. info. Nat. Safety Council, 1949-57; pub. The World Almanac, 1966-72; Sec. bd. Wolf Trap Found., 1975-76; trustee Cooper Inst., Naples, Fla.; cons. editor and columnist Maturity News Service, 1987—. Author: autobiography Not Always a Spectator, 1981. Mem. Mayflower Descs. Am. Address: 9319 Old Courthouse Rd Vienna VA 22182-2015

LEWIS, BRIAN KREGLOW, computer consultant; b. Durban, Republic of South Africa, Sept. 2, 1932; s. Arthur Armington and Isabel (Kreglow) L.; m. Mary Helen Kidwell, July 14, 1953; children: Brian E., James A., Charles A., Carol J., Robert E., Sharon H. BS, Ohio State U., 1954; PhD, Tufts U., 1971. Biology tchr. Lincoln-Sudbury (Mass.) Regional High Sch., 1965-66; rsch. assoc. May Inst. for Med. Rsch., Cin., 1971-75; from asst. to assoc. prof. health sci. Grand Valley State U., Allendale, Mich., 1975-81; prin. Lewis Assocs., Sarasota, Fla., 1984—; adj. asst. prof. physiology Cin. Coll. Medicine, 1972-75; assoc. prof. Ponce (P.R.) Sch. Medicine, 1981-84, prof., chmn. physiology, 1987-91; instr. Macintosh computer for beginners Sarasota County Tech. Inst., 1995—. Contbr. revs. and articles to Computer Shopper, Proceedings Soc. Exptl. Biology Medicine, Am. Heart Jour., Atherosclerosis; developer business and ednl. software. Cubmaster, scoutmaster Boy Scouts Am., 1963-78; mem. fin. com., ch. choir St. Andrew Ch., Sarasota, 1984—; bd. dirs. Sarasota chpt. Soc. Promotion and Encouragement Barbershop Quartet Singing in Am., 1994, sec., 1995—; active Village Voices, Greenhills, Ohio, 1972-75. Lt. Supply Corps USN, 1954-62. NIH fellow, 1965-71. Mem. Endocrine Soc., Soc. for Study Reproduction, Soc. for Study Fertility, Sarasota IBM PC Users Group (spreadsheet SIG leader 1993-94, software reviewer 1992—). Office: 6423 Caracara St Sarasota FL 34241-9104

LEWIS, BROCK, investment company executive; b. New Bedford, Mass., July 16, 1930; s. Frank Edward and Mary (Brock) L.; m. Susan Wahl, Sept. 4, 1954; children: Juliana D., Christopher B., Josiah E., Victoria D. BA, Dartmouth Coll., 1952; LLB, Boston U., 1955; postgrad., NYU, 1959-61. Asst. v.p. Fidelity Union Trust Co., Newark, 1955-64; v.p., trust officer County Nat. Bank, Poughkeepsie, N.Y., 1964-67, Capital Nat. Bank, Houston, 1967-69; v.p. Lionel D. Edie & Co., Houston, 1969-72, Dominick Mgmt. Co., N.Y.C., 1972-75, Marine Midland Bank, N.Y.C., 1975-80; 1st v.p. Lehman Mgmt. Co., N.Y.C., 1980-82; owner, pres. Brock Lewis Assocs. Ltd., Trenton, N.J., 1982—; chmn., CEO Skandii Group, Inc., Princeton, N.J., 1991—; pres. SGI Internat., Inc., Princeton, N.J., 1991—; cons. State of N.J. Adminstrn. Office of Cts., Trenton, 1993—; dir. Inst. Social and Econ. Policy Middle East, Cambridge, Mass., 1993—. Pres. Greater Trenton Symphony, 1993—; dir. Steinway Soc., Princeton, 1990. Mem. Assn. Bus. Economists (chmn. internat. Bus. Rish Mgmt., Danish Am. C. of C., Swedish Am. C. of C., Finnish Am.C. of C., European Am. C. of C., Princeton C. of C., Mercer County C. of C., Nat. U.S.-Arab C. of C., Global Bus. Assn., The Americas Soc., Tabor Acad. Alumni Assn. (chmn. 1995—, trustee 1995—), Nassau Club, Pacific Club, Dartmouth Clubs of N.Y. and Princeton, Dartmouth Rowing Club, Union Boat Club Boston. Office: Univ Park Plz, PO Box 7057 743 Alexander Rd Princeton NJ 08543-7057

LEWIS, C. A., church administrator. Exec. sec. Ch. of the Living God Exec. Bd.

LEWIS, CALVIN FRED, architect, educator; b. Chgo., Mar. 27, 1946; s. Howard George and Fern Teresa (Voelsch) L.; m. L. Diane Johnson, Aug. 24, 1968; children: Nathan, Miller, Cooper, Wilson. B of Architecture, Iowa State U., 1969. Architect Charles Herbert and Assocs., Des Moines, 1970-86; prin. Herbert Lewis Kruse Blunck Architecture, Des Moines, 1987—; arch., lectr. Inter Market Sq., Mpls., 1985, Nat. Tile Conf., L.A., 1987, Am. Soc. Landscape Archs., 1988, Iowa State U., 1985, 89; awards juror Dallas AIA, Kans. AIA, Nebr. AIA. Projects published in profl. jours. Chmn. profl. adv. bd. Iowa State U. Recipient Best in Design award Time Mag., 1982; named one of Top Young Architects in Country, Met. Home mag., 1983. Mem. AIA (50 design awards 1972—, nat. fellowship 1995—), FAIA. Avocations: sports, photography. Office: Herbert Lewis Kruse Blunk Architecture 202 Fleming Building Bldg Des Moines IA 50309-4081

LEWIS, CARL, Olympic track and field athlete; b. Birmingham, Ala., July 1, 1961; s. Bill and Evelyn (Lawler) L. Student, U. Houston. Competed in Europe and U.S.; track meets include: Nat. Collegiate Athletic Assn. indoor championships, Baton Rouge, La., 1981, Nat. Outdoor Championships, Knoxville, Tenn., 1982, Nat. Sports Festival, 1982, Athletic Congress Outdoor Championships, Indpls., World Championships, Helsinki, 1983, Millrose Games, N.Y., 1984, Summer Olympics, L.A., 1984; recorded album Break it Up, 1986. Recipient James E. Sullivan award best amateur athlete, 1981, Jesse Ownes award, 1982, Athlete of Yr. award Assoc. Press Sports, 1983; winner 3 Gold medals World Championships, 1983, 4 Gold medals Olympics, 1984, Long Jump competition IAAF World Track and Field Championships, 1987, 100 Meter Dash Olympic Games, 1988; named to U.S. Olympic Hall of Fame, 1985; Gold medal, Long Jump competition, Olympics, 1992. Office: care Tom Tellez U Houston Athletic Dept 4800 Calhoun Rd Houston TX 77004-2610*

LEWIS, CEYLON SMITH, JR., internist, educator; b. Muskogee, Okla., July 19, 1920. Dir. internat. studies internal medicine Med. Coll., U. Okla., Tulsa. Mem. Inst. Med.-Nat. Acad. Sci. Office: Dept Internal Med U Okla Medical Coll Tulsa OK 74129

LEWIS, CHARLES A., investment company executive; b. Orange, N.J., Oct. 23, 1942; s. F. Donald and Edna H. L.; m. Gretchen Smith, July 1967 (div.); m. Penny Bender Sebring, June 9, 1984. BA, Amherst Coll., 1964;

MBA, U. Pa., 1966. Asst. to pres. Computer Tech., Inc., Skokie, Ill., 1969-70; 1st v.p. White, Weld, & Co., 1970-78; vice chmn. investment banking Merrill Lynch & Co., Chgo., 1978—. Trustee Amherst Coll., 1989—, Chgo. Symphony Orch., 1989—, Ravinia Festival, 1995—; assoc. Northwestern U., 1989—; life dir. Juvenile Diabetes Found., Met. Chgo. Mem. Chgo.Club, Glen View Club, Econ. Club Chgo. Office: Merrill Lynch & Co 5500 Sears Tower Chicago IL 60606

LEWIS, CHARLES ARLEN, financial services company executive; b. Columbus, Ga., Nov. 7, 1943; s. Harlin B. and Dorothy A. (Elliott) L.; m. Linda L. McDowell, Dec. 5,1964; 1 child, Bryan C. Security trader White & Co. Investments, St. Louis, 1964-67; dist. sales mgr. Horizon Corp., Overland Park, Kans., 1967-73; mgr. U.S. Realty & Investment Co., St. Louis, 1973-75; fin. cons. Profesco, Inc., St. Louis, 1975-77; pres., CEO Am. Econ. Svcs., Ltd., St. Louis, 1977-82, Nat. Investment Corp., St. Louis, 1982-88; pres., CEO Le Bryan Corp., Washington, 1988-93, bd. dirs.; pres., CEO Integrated Mgmt. Sys., Inc., Lancaster, Calif., 1994—, also chmn. bd., 1994—; bd. dirs. Grimm Fin. Resources Inc., McLean, Va., Elliott, McDowell & Davis, Ltd., St. Louis. Adv. bd. mem. Child Find Internat., St. Louis, 1987-88; chmn. bd. World Practical Taekwondo Fedn., Hong Kong, 1986—. 2d lt. U.S. Army, 1961-64. Recipient Disting. Svc. award Hong Kong Taekwondo Assn., 1982, Outstanding Svc. award World Practical Taekwondo Fedn., 1984, 87. Avocations: flying, golf.

LEWIS, CHARLES D., insurance executive, rancher; b. Denver, June 22, 1936; s. Harry Thompson and Margretta (Borrmann) L.; m. Penelope Hall, June 18, 1956; children: C. Randel, Christina, Vanda H. Student, Dartmouth Coll., 1954-55; BSBA, U. Denver, 1959, MBA, 1961. Tax mgr. Arthur Andersen & Co., Denver, 1959-64; exec. v.p., treas. Vail (Colo.) Assocs., Inc., 1964-67, Writer Constrn. Corp., Denver, 1967-69; pres., chief exec. officer, founder Copper Mountain (Colo.), Inc., 1969-82; gen. ptnr. W.F.R. Ltd., Kremmling, Colo., 1979—; gen. ptnr., dir. Boettcher & Co., Denver, 1982-85; pres. L.W.P. Svcs., Inc., Golden, Colo., 1985-95; pres., dir. Arlberg Holding Co., 1990—; pres. Arlberg Ins. Co., 1990—; mng. mem. Eldora Enterprises L.L.C., 1990—; bd. dirs. Eire County Investment Co. Chmn. Copper Mountain Water & Sanitation Dist., 1972-82, Copper Mountain Met. Dist., 1972-82; mem. Colo. Passenger Tramway Bd., 1974-82, chmn., 1976-82. Recipient Industry and Environ. award Rocky Mountain Ctr. on Environment, 1974; named Outstanding Design, Ski Mag., 1975, Colo. Ski Hall of Fame, 1989. Mem. AICPA, Am. Arbitration Assn., Colo. Soc. CPAs, Nat. Ski Areas Assn. (chmn. 1981-83), Colo. Ski Country USA (chmn. 1978-79), Am. Ski Fedn. (vice chmn. 1980-82), Colo. Wildlife Commn., Denver Club. Republican. Episcopalian. Avocations: climbing, fishing. Home: 19752 US Hwy 40 Kremmling CO 80459-9603 Office: LWP Svcs Inc 575 Union Blvd Ste 310 Lakewood CO 80228

LEWIS, CHARLES EDWIN, physician, educator; b. Kansas City, Dec. 28, 1928; s. Claude Herbert and Maudie Friels (Holaday) L.; m. Mary Ann Gurera, Dec. 27, 1963; children—Kevin Neil, David Bradford, Matthew Clinton, Karen Carleen. Student, U. Kans., 1948-49; M.D., Harvard, 1953; M.S., U. Cin., 1957, Sc.D., 1959. Diplomate Am. Bd. Preventive Medicine (Occupl. Medicine). Intern, resident U. Kans. Hosp., 1953-54; trainee USPHS, 1956-58; fellow occupational health Eastman Kodak Co., 1958-59; asst. clin. prof. epidemiology Baylor U. Sch. Medicine, 1960-61; asso. prof. medicine U. Kans. Med. Sch., 1961-62, prof., chmn. dept. preventive medicine, 1962-69; coordinator Kan. Regional Med. Program, 1967-69; prof. social medicine Harvard Med. Sch., 1969-70; prof. pub. health, head div. health adminstrn. UCLA Med. Sch., 1970-72, prof. medicine, div. head, 1972-90; prof., 1972-89; prof. nursing Sch. Nursing UCLA Med. Sch., 1973—, head div. preventive and occupational medicine, 1991-93; dir. Health Svcs. Rsch. Ctr., 1991-93, UCLA Ctr. Health Promotion and Disease Prevention, 1991—; chair acad. senate UCLA, 1995-96; chmn. acad. senate UCLA, 1995-96; cons. Getty Trust, Walt Disney Prodns.; mem. Nat. Bd. Med. Examiners, 1964-68, 8-83, Jt. Commn. on Accreditaiton Health Care Orgns., 1989-95; mem. health svcs. rsch. study sect. USPHS, 1968-76; vis. scholar Annenberg Sch. Comm., U. So. Calif., 1980-81; mem. adv. bd. Hosp. Rsch. and Edn. Trust, 1972-75. Contbr. articles to profl. Jours. Served to capt. USAF, 1954-56. Recipient Ginsberg prize medicine U. Kans., 1954, Glasier award Soc. Gen. Internal Medicine, 1988. Fellow APHA, Acad. Occupl. Medicine; mem. ACP (regent 1988-94, Rosenthal award 1980, Laureate award So. Calif. III 1994, mastership, 1996), Internat. Epidemiology Soc., Assn. Tchrs. Preventive Medicine (pres. coun. 1977-80), Am. Assn. Physicians. Home: 221 S Burlingame Ave Los Angeles CA 90049-3702

LEWIS, CHARLES JOSEPH, journalist; b. Bozeman, Mont., July 10, 1940; s. Vern Edward James and Mary (Brooke) L.; m. Sarah Withers; children: Peter, Patrick, Barbara. BS in Humanities with Honors, Loyola U., Chgo., 1962; JD, Columbia U., 1965. Bar: Ill. 1965. Atty. McDermott, Will & Emery, Chgo., 1965-67; reporter City News Bur., Chgo., 1967-68; reporter, editor Chgo. Sun-Times, 1968-73; with AP, 1974-89, reporter, editor, Washington, 1974-78, reporter, editor, L.A., 1978-80, personnel mgr., N.Y.C., 1981-83, bur. chief, Hartford, Conn., 1980-81, bur. chief, Washington, 1984-89; bur. chief Hearst Newspapers, Washington, 1989—. Bd. dirs. Nat. Press Found., Washington, 1985—, treas., 1987-88, vice chmn., 1988-90, chmn., 1990-92; dir. Reporters Com. for Freedom of the Press, 1993—, SDX Found. Washington, 1996—. Lance cpl. USMCR, 1963-67. Mem. Gridiron Club, Sigma Delta Chi (v.p. Washington chpt. 1988-89). Office: Hearst Newspapers 1701 Pennsylvania Ave NW Washington DC 20006-5805

LEWIS, CHARLES LEONARD, psychologist; b. Wellsville, Ohio, Jan. 6, 1926; s. Cleo L. and Charlotte (Hahn) L.; m. Charlotte J. Wynn, Sept. 8, 1948 (dec. Mar. 1987); children: Stephen C., Janet J., Judith A.; m. Jane E. McCormick, Oct. 1, 1988. B.S. in Edn. with honors, Ohio U., 1949; M.A., U. Minn., 1953, Ph.D., 1955. Assoc. dir. activities U. Minn., 1950-55; dean student affairs, assoc. prof. psychology U. N.D., 1955-62; exec. dean, assoc. prof. ednl. psychology U. Tenn., 1962-67; v.p. student affairs Pa. State U., 1967-72; exec. dir. Am. Personnel and Guidance Assn., Washington, 1972-74, exec. v.p., 1974-83, exec. v.p. emeritus, 1984—; pres. Charles L. Lewis & Assocs., Annandale, Va., 1983-85, Chuck Lewis et al, Lancaster, Pa., 1985—; guest prof. U. Md., 1973; mem. Nat. Adv. Com. for Devel. Guidance Components-Career Edn., 1972-76. Founding editor Jour. Coll. Students Pers., 1958-64; mem. editl. bd. Pers. and Guidance Jour., 1954-57. Mem. Pres.'s Com. for Handicapped, 1972-80; bd. dirs. Ctr. Cmty. Hosps., Bellefonte, Pa. With U.S. Army, 1944-47. Recipient George Hill Disting. Alumni award Ohio U., 1981, Outstanding Alumnus Coll. Edn. Ohio U., 1988. Mem. APA, AAUP, Am. Assn. Higher Edn., Am. Coll. Pers. Assn. (pres. 1968-69), Nat. Assn. Student Pers. Adminstrs., Nat. Assn. Woman Deans and Counselors, Am. Pers. and Guidance Assn. (dir. 1967-70), Am. Assn. Univ. Adminstrs. (dir. 1973), Coun. Advancement of Stds. (bd. dirs.), Ohio U. Alumni Soc. and Friends Coll. Edn. (coun. 1985-92, bd. dirs. 1986-92), Psi Chi, Kappa Delta Pi, Beta Theta Pi, Chi Sigma Iota (founding dir. 1984-90). Episcopalian.

LEWIS, CHRISTINA LYNN, educational administrator; b. Brook Park, Ohio, June 19, 1963; d. Albert Joseph and Gail Ann (Kohler) Urbas; m. Timothy Allen Lewis, Aug. 3, 1989; 1 child, Cherie Ann. AA, Pasco Hernando C.C., Brooksville, Fla., 1996; student, Thomas Edison State Coll., 1996—. Owner, operator Spl. Touch Day Care, Olmsted Twp., Ohio, 1986-89, Spring Hill, Fla., 1989-94; dir., tng. coord. United Cerebral Palsy, Brooksville, 1994-96; area supr. childhood devel. svcs. Head Start, Inverness, Fla., 1996—; mentor, tng. advisor child care outreach program United Cerebral Palsy, Brooksville, 1993—; advisor, instr. Child Devel. Assoc. Credential Program, Brooksville, 1991—; coun. mem. Pre-K Interagy. Coun., Brooksville, 1994—; com. mem. Collaborative Partnership Grant, Brooksville, 1994-95. Author (tng. packet) CDA: Everything You Need to Know to Get Started, 1992. Dep. registrar Supr. Elections, Hernando County, 1994; vol. instr. ARC. Recipient Resolution 91-70 award Hernando County Commr., Brooksville, 1991. Mem. Nat. Assn. for the Edn. Young Children, Assn. for Better Child Care (founding mem., newsletter editor 1990, sec., resource and referral 1989-93, Tchr. of Yr. 1990), Phi Theta Kappa. Republican. Avocations: snorkeling, pottery, camping. Home: 9063 Spring Hill Dr Spring Hill FL 34608-6241 Office: Childhood Devel Svcs 613 S US Hwy 41 Inverness FL 34450

LEWIS, CHRISTOPHER ALAN, lawyer; b. Phila., Sept. 16, 1955; s. Charles Edward and Florence (Scott) L.; m. Sheilah Diane Vance, Oct. 18, 1986. BA magna cum laude, Harvard U., 1975; JD magna cum laude, U. Mich., 1978. Bar: Pa. 1979, U.S. Dist. Ct. (ea. dist.) Pa. 1979, U.S. Ct. Appeals (3d cir.) 1979. Law clk. to judge U.S. Dist. Ct. (ea. dist) Pa., Phila., 1978-80; assoc. Dilworth, Paxson, Kalish & Kauffman, Phila., 1980-85, ptnr., 1986-87; exec. dep. gen. counsel Commonwealth of Pa., Harrisburg, 1987-89, sec., 1989-91; ptnr. firm Blank, Rome, Comisky & McCauley, Phila., 1991—. Mem. steering com. 21st Century Inst. for Polit. Action, 1985—, Com. on Seventy; bd. dirs. Pub. Interest Law Ctr. of Phila., 1984-87, Crime Prevention Assn., 1986-87. Mem. ABA, Fed. Bar Assn., Phila. Bar Assn., Barristers' Assn. Phila., Kappa Alpha Psi (treas. alumni chapt. 1981-83), Sigma Pi Phi. Democrat. Episcopalian. Avocation: sailing. Home: 520 Sugartown Rd Devon PA 19333-1716 Office: Blank Rome Comisky McCauley 1200 Four Penn Ctr Plz Philadelphia PA 19103*

LEWIS, CLAUDE AUBREY, columnist; b. N.Y.C., Dec. 14, 1936; s. Robert George Lewis and Hazel (Perkinson) Gray; m. Beverly McKelvey, Oct. 18, 1953; children: Pamela, Bryan, Craig, Beverley. AB in English, CCNY, 1958; LHD (hon.), Thomas Jefferson U., 1986. From editorial asst. to asst. editor Newsweek, N.Y.C., 1953-64; reporter N.Y. Herald Tribune, N.Y.C., 1964-65, NBC, Phila., 1965-67; assoc. editor, columnist Phila. Bull., 1967-82; editor, pub. Nat. Leader, Phila., 1982-84; columnist, mem. editorial bd. Phila. Inquirer, 1984—. Author: Muhammad Ali, 1962, Adam Clayton Powell, 1965, Benjamin Banneker, 1968; co-author: New York City in Crisis, 1966. Bd. dirs. Valley Forge Med. Ctr., Phila., Met. Hosp., Phila., Djonge McNair Health Fund, Phila. Recipient Gold Typewriter award Schaefer, 1964, 67; 1st pl. award Phila. Med. Soc., 1967, Martin Luther King Jr. award Nat. Orgn. of Unions, 1967. Mem. Nat. Assn. Black Journalists (founder). Avocations: photography, reading. Office: Phila Inquirer 400 N Broad St Philadelphia PA 19130-4015

LEWIS, CLEOTRICE O. NEY TILLIS, retired elementary education educator; b. Dallas, Oct. 2, 1933; d. Christopher Columbus and Ida Bell (Knox) Tillis; divorced; 1 child, Glenn Eric. BS in Elem. Edn., Prairie View A&M U., 1955; MEd, Tex. so. U., 1964; postgrad., U. Nebr., 1978, U. Houston, 1988. Cert. tchr., Tex. Tchr. Drew Elem. Sch.-Crosby (Tex.) Ind. Sch. Dist., 1955-57, Wesley Elem. Sch.-Houston Ind. Sch. Dist., 1958-60; tchr. Osborne Elem. Sch.-Houston Ind. Sch. Dist., 1960-84, chpt. coord., 1985-93; substitute tchr. Houston Ind. Sch. Dist., 1993—; presenter in field. Mem. Foster Pl. Civic Club, Houston, 1990—, YWCA, Houston, 1991—, Greater Houston Area Writing Project; sponsor writing lab., Osborne Elem. Sch., Houston, 1991—, life mem. Nat. Congress PTA. Mem. Greater Houston Area Reading Assn., Tex. Tchrs. Assn., Houston Assn. Childhood Edn. Internat., Assn. Tex. Profl. Educators, Internat. Reading Assn. Methodist. Avocations: reading, weaving, bowling, writing, knitting. Home: 6504 Sherwood Dr Houston TX 77021-4032

LEWIS, CLYDE A., lawyer; b. Hoquiam, Wash., June 20, 1913; s. J.D. Clyde and Loretta C. (Adelsperger) L.; A.B., U. Notre Dame, 1934; J.D., Harvard U., 1939; m. Helen M. Judge, Sept. 22, 1936 (dec. Sept. 1985); m. Patricia Davis Judge, Oct. 1, 1988; children: Clyde A., John E. Admitted to N.Y. bar, 1940, U.S. Supreme Ct. bar, 1959; mem. Lewis & Rogers, and predecessor firms, Plattsburgh, N.Y. Comdr. in chief VFW, 1949-50, also served as sr. and jr. vice comdr. in chief, mem. nat. legis. com. Served to maj. USAAF, 1942-45. Decorated D.F.C. with 2 oak leaf clusters, Air medal with 4 oak leaf clusters; USAF Exceptional Svc. award; Croix de Guerre (France); invested Knight of Malta. Mem. Am. Legion, Am., N.Y. State bar assns., Notre Dame, Harvard alumni assns., U.S. Strategic Inst., Def. Orientation Conf. Assn. Republican. Roman Catholic. Clubs: Capitol Hill, K.C., Elks. Home: 93 Lighthouse Rd Plattsburgh NY 12901-7018 Office: 53 Court St Plattsburgh NY 12901-2834

LEWIS, DALE KENTON, retired lawyer, mediator; b. Goodland, Kans., June 20, 1937; s. W. Homer and L. (Fern) L.; m. Constance L. Coover, Dec. 27, 1958; children—James W., Bari Lynn, Brad Kenton. B.A., State U. Iowa, 1959; J.D., Colo. U., 1962. Bar: Colo. 1962, Ind. 1968. Mem. firm Lewis & Ausenhus, Loveland, Colo., 1962-67; with Eli Lilly and Co., 1967-90; counsel Elanco Products Co., 1969-77; gen. counsel, sec. Elizabeth Arden, Inc., 1977-81, corp. asst. sec. and asso. gen. counsel, 1981-83, corp. asst. sec., dep. gen. counsel, 1983-86, sec., dep. gen. counsel, 1986-89; v.p., sec., gen. counsel DowElanco, Indpls., 1989-95; ret., 1995. Mem. Am. Corp. Counsel Assn., Order of Coif. Episcopalian. Office: 9330 Zionsville Rd Indianapolis IN 46268-1053

LEWIS, DAN ALBERT, education educator; b. Chgo., Feb. 14, 1946; s. Milton and Diane (Sabath) L.; m. Stephanie Riger, Jan. 3, 1982; children: Matthew, Jake. BA cum laude, Stanford U., 1968; PhD, U. Calif., Santa Cruz, 1980. Rsch. assoc. Arthur Bolton Assocs., Sacramento, 1969-70; survey contr. Sci. Analysis Corp., San Francisco, 1971; dir. Stanford Workshops on Polit. and Social Issues Stanford (Calif.) U., 1971-74; projects adminstr. Ctr. Urban Affairs and Policy Rsch., Northwestern U., Evanston, Ill., 1975-80, asst. prof. edn., 1980-86, assoc. prof. edn., 1986-90, assoc. dir., chair grad. program human devel./social policy, 1987-90, prof. edn., 1990—; vis. scholar Sch. Edn., Stanford U., 1990-91; mem. task force on restructuring mental health svcs. Chgo. Dept. Health, 1982; mem. human rights authority Ill. Guardianship and Advocacy Commn., 1980-82; adv. mem. com. on planning and inter-agy. coordination Commn. Mental Health and Devel. Disabilities, 1979; interim adv. com. on mental health City of Chgo., 1978; adv. mem. Gov.'s Commn. to Revise Mental Health Code Ill., 1975-77; presenter at profl. confs.; presenter workshops. Editor: Reactions to Crime, 1981; co-author: Fear of Crime: Incivility and the Production of a Social Problem, 1986, The Social Construction of Reform: Crime Prevention and Community Organizations, 1988, The Worlds of the Mentally Ill, 1991, The State Mental Patient in Urban Life, 1994, Race and Educational Reform, 1995; contbr. articles, book revs. to profl. publs. Bd. dirs. Designs for Change, Ill. Mental Health Assn.; rsch. adv. com. Chgo. Urban League, Chgo. Panel Pub. Sch. Finances, 1989-91; needs assessment tech. com. United Way Chgo., 1989-90; ednl. coun. Francis W. Parker Sch., Chgo., 1988-90; task force on restructuring mental health svcs. Chgo. Dept. Health, 1982; com. on mentally disabled Ill. State Bar Assn., 1983-89; rsch. policy com. Ill. Dept. Mental Health, 1978; bd. dirs. Mental Health Assn. Greater Chgo., 1977-84, v.p. pub. policy, 1979-83. Office: Northwestern Univ 2040 Sheridan Rd Evanston IL 60208-0855

LEWIS, DANA KENNETH, trading company executive, consultant; b. L.A., Aug. 24, 1945; s. Kenneth Robert and Ouida Jo (Norris) L.; m. Yoko Koshio, Sept. 12, 1969; 1 child, Michelle Cynthia. BA, Friends World Coll., Huntington, N.Y., 1976; MA, Goddard Coll., Plainfield, Vt., 1980. Cons. to pres. Emile, Inc., Osaka, Japan, 1976-77; residential houseparent Bethany Children's Home, Womelsdorf, Pa., 1977-78, cottage life supr., 1978-86, dir. home life, adminstr., 1986-94; co-founder, pres. Lewis Mktg., Inc. (formerly Pacific Rim Enterprises, Inc.), Fleetwood, Pa., 1989—; founder The Metalog Group, Fleetwood, Pa., 1993—; instr. Pa. State U., 1981-83, Family Life Devel., Cornell U., 1982-85; presenter Treischman Conf., Boston, 1989. Author: Working with Children, 1981; author, speaker, audio cassettes Child Care and Communications, 1979—; mem. editorial bd. Jour. 1984; book reviewer, 1988; contbr. articles to profl. jours. Lectr. various local facilities, 1978—. Served as staff sgt., USAF. Mem. Child Care Assn. of Pa. (trainer, presenter 1979-87, keynote speaker Regional Confs. 1986, Dedicated Service award 1986). Avocations: computers, reading, poetry, writing, travelling. Home: 22 Bick Rd Fleetwood PA 19522-9611 Office: Lewis Mktg Inc 22 Bick Rd Fleetwood PA 19522-9611

LEWIS, DARRELL L., retail executive; b. Mason City, Iowa, Nov. 20, 1931; s. Milton Loren and Blanche Ione (Wilson) L.; m. Mary Jo Bahnsen, Oct. 22, 1950; children—John L., Lonnette Ann, Sherri Jo. MBA, Stanford U., 1970. With Osco Drug, Inc. subsidiary Jewel Cos., Inc., 1949-62; with Jewel Turn-Style, 1962; pres. Turn-Style Family Centers, Franklin Park, Ill., 1967-74; head Jewel Hypermarket Turn-Style Family Centers, 1974; pres. Osco Drug, Inc., 1974-75, v.p. store and sales devel., 1976-77; pres. D.L. Lewis Drug Co. Inc., Bensenville, Ill., 1978—, chmn. bd., 1987—. Home: 12338 Sunset Dr Three Rivers MI 49093-9580 Office: DL Lewis Drug Co 1325 W Irving Park Rd Bensenville IL 60106-1764

LEWIS, DAVID, foundation administrator; b. Carmel, Calif., Aug. 18, 1944; s. Chester Allen and Harriet E. (Minster) L. BA, Calif. State U., Sacramento, 1967. Cert. Assn. Exec., FAAO. Assoc. dir. Jr. Statesman Found., Palo Alto, 1970; dir., govt. affairs Calif. Optometric Assn., Sacramento, 1971-75; various positions Am. Optometric Assn., Washington, 1975-86; exec. dir. Am. Acad. Optometry, Bethesda, Md., 1986—, Am. Soc. Adolescent Psychiatry, Bethesda, Md., 1987-93; sr. acct. exec. PAI Mgmt., Bethesda, Md., 1986—; 1st vice chmn. Nat. Vol. Orgns. for Ind. Living for Aging, Washington, 1986-89, chmn., 1989-90; cons. Internat. Coun. Prison Med. Svcs., Washington and Paris, 1987-92. Co-author: Community and Public Health Optometry, 1989. Officer, trustee Jr. Statesmen Found., Palo Alto, 1967-70, 71-76, hon. trustee, 1976; sr. warden St. Paul's Episc. Ch., Washington, 1991-92. Sgt. U.S. Army, 1968-70, Vietnam. Recipient Bronze star, Air medal, U.S Army, Vietnam, 1969. Fellow Am. Acad. Optometry; mem. Am. Soc. Assn. Execs., Internat. Assn. Optometric Execs., Calif. Optometric Assn. (hon.). Office: PAI Mgmt 4330 E West Hwy Ste 1117 Bethesda MD 20814-4408

LEWIS, DAVID CARLETON, medical educator, university center director; b. Hartford, Conn., May 19, 1935; s. Theodore and Lillian (Levin) L.; m. Eleanor Grace Levinson, Aug. 23, 1959; children: Deborah, Steven. AB magna cum laude, Brown U., 1957; MD, Harvard U., 1961. Intern Beth Israel Hosp., Boston, 1961-62, jr. resident, 1962-63, chief med. resident, 1966-67, dir. emergency unit and med. outpatient dept., 1969-71; sr. resident U. Hosps. Cleve., 1963-64, Parkland Meml. Hosp., Dallas, 1964-66; fellow U. Tex. Southwestern Med. Hosp., Dallas, 1964-66; Sloan Found. fellow Harvard Med. Sch., Boston, 1971-72; med. dir. Washingtonian Ctr. for Addictions, Boston, 1972-77; dir. div. alcohol and substance abuse Roger Williams Gen. Hosp., Providence, 1976—; dir. program in alcoholism and drug abuse Brown U., Providence, 1976-82, prof. medicine and community health, 1982—, Donald G. Millar prof. alcohol and addiction studies, 1987—, chmn. dept. community health, 1981-86, dir. Ctr. Alcohol and Addiction Studies, 1982—; mem. nat. adv. coun. Nat. Alcohol Inst., Rockville, Md., 1981-85, cons. to dir., 1985—; mem. sci. adv. bd. Children of dir., 1985—; cons. WHO,, 1986—, mem. WHO cocaine global adv. com., 1992-95; chair Physician Consortium on Substance Abuse Edn., 1989—; mem. Carnegie Substance Abuse Adv. com., 1989-92; scholar-in-residence Nat. Inst. Med., 1991-92; mem. adv. panel to U.S. Pharmacopoeia, 1995—; mem. Drug Strategies Nat. Adv. Panel, 1994—; mem. nat. adv. com. Robert Wood Johnson Found. Fighting Back program, 1996—. Author: The Drug Experience: Data for Decision Making, 1970; editor: Providing Care for Children of Alcoholics, 1986; editor Brown U. Digest of Addiction Theory and Application, 1986—; exec. editor Substance Abuse jour., 1984—; contbr. numerous articles to profl. jours. Med. dir. Beacon Hill Free Clinic, Boston, 1968-71; chmn. Mayor's Coun. on Drug Abuse, Boston, 1972-80. Grantee Nat. Alcohol and Drug Insts., 1986—, Edward John Noble fellow Harvard U. Med. Sch., 1957-91. Fellow ACP; mem. NAS, Inst. Medicine Study on Treatment Alcohol Problems, Assn. Med. Edn. and Rsch. in Substance Abuse (pres. 1983-88, Excellence in Medicine award 1986), Am. Soc. Addiction Medicine (chair core curriculum com. 1989-96, chair sect. on internal medicine 1990—, bd. dirs. 1995—), U.S. Pharmacopea (mem. adv. panel), Brown Med. Alumni Assn. (pres. 1974-76), Phi Beta Kappa, Sigma Xi. Avocations: choral singing, sailing, photography. Office: Brown Univ Ctr Alcohol & Addiction Studies Box G Providence RI 02912

LEWIS, DAVID ELDRIDGE, airport development executive; b. Washington, Mar. 10, 1924; s. S. Lawrence and Ruth (Eldridge) L.; m. Anne Hutchison Reppert, Aug. 19, 1949; children: David Eldridge, Charles Adams, Laura Peter. B.A., Yale U., 1945; postgrad., Harvard U., 1946-47. Sales rep. J.W. Valentine Co., Inc., N.Y.C., 1948-53; asst. to sales mgr. Wellington Sears Co., N.Y.C., 1953-58; mgr. converted fabrics div. Wellington Sears Co., 1958-59, mgr. converted apparel fabrics, 1959-60, v.p., 1960-66; v.p. mktg. West Point Pepperell, N.Y.C., 1966-70; v.p., gen. mgr. Nonwoven Fabrics div. Internat. Paper Co., N.Y.C., 1970-75; with Blessings Corp., N.Y.C., 1975-89, exec. v.p., 1976-77, pres., dir., mem. exec. com., 1975-76, 76-89, chief exec. officer, 1978-87, vice chmn., 1988; asst. sec. U.S. Dept Vets. Affairs, 1989-92; mng. dir. KACI Internat., 1992—; dir. J.L. Prescott Co., Internat. Barrier Corp. Bd. dirs. Inst. Infant Svcs., 1982-84, coun. mem. Decatur House, 1993—. Served to ensign U.S. Navy, 1944-46; lt. 1950-51. Mem. Nat. Policy Forum (mem. policy coun. on entrepreneurial and small bus. 1994—), Coral Beach and Tennis Club (Bermuda), Army and Navy Club (Washington), Chevy Chase (Md.) Club. Republican. Presbyterian. Home: 4994 Glenbrook Rd NW Washington DC 20016-3223 Office: 4005 64th St Bethesda MD 20816-2617

LEWIS, DAVID JOHN, lawyer; b. Zanesville, Ohio, Feb. 4, 1948; s. David Griff and Barbara Ann (Hoy) L.; m. Susan G. Smith; 1 child, Ann Elizabeth. BS in Fin., U. Ill., 1970, JD, 1973. Bar: Ill. 1973, D.C. 1974. Law clk. to Judge Philip W. Tone U.S. Dist. Ct. For North Dist. Ill., Chgo., 1973-74; assoc. Sidley & Austin, Washington, 1974-80, ptnr., 1980—. Mem. ABA. Office: Sidley & Austin 1722 I St NW Washington DC 20006-3705

LEWIS, DAVID KELLOGG, philosopher, educator; b. Oberlin, Ohio, Sept. 28, 1941; s. John Donald and Ewart (Kellogg) L.; m. Stephanie Robinson, Sept. 5, 1965. BA, Swarthmore Coll., 1962; MA, Harvard U., 1964, PhD, 1967; DLitt (hon.), U. Melbourne, 1995. Asst. prof. philosophy UCLA, 1966-70; mem. faculty Princeton U., 1970—, prof. philosophy, 1973—; cons. Hudson Inst., 1962-75; Fulbright lectr., Australia, 1971; Locke lectr. Oxford U., 1984.; Kant lectr. Stanford U., 1988. Author: Convention: A Philosophical Study, 1969, Counterfactuals, 1973; On the Plurality of Worlds, 1986, Philosophical Papers, vol. I, 1983, vol. II, 1986, Parts of Classes, 1991. Fulbright rsch. fellow N.Z., 1976, Santayana fellow Harvard U., 1988; Recipient Matchette prize for philos. writing, 1972. Mem. AAAS, AAUP, NAS, Brit. Acad., Australian Acad. Humanities. Office: Princeton U Dept Philosophy Princeton NJ 08544

LEWIS, DAVID LEVERING, history educator; b. Little Rock, May 25, 1936; s. John Henry and Alice Urnestine (Bell) L.; m. Sharon Lynn Siskind, 1965 (div. Oct. 1988); children: Eric, Allison, Jason; m. Ruth Ann Stewart, Apr. 15, 1994; 1 child, Allegra. BA in History/Philosophy, Fisk U., 1956; MA in U.S. History, Columbia U., 1959; PhD in Modern Europe/France, London Sch. Econs. & Polit. Sci., 1962. Lectr. European history U. Ghana, Legon, 1963-64; lectr. history Howard U., Washington, 1964-65; from asst. to assoc. prof. Morgan State U., Balt., 1966-70; from assoc. prof. to prof. U. D.C., 1970-80; prof. U. Calif. San Diego, La Jolla, 1981-85; M.L. King, Jr. Univ. prof. Rutgers U., New Brunswick, N.J., 1985—; commr. Nat. Portrait Gallery, Smithsonian Instn., Washington, 1989-94; mem. selection com. Rsch. Triangle Park, N.C., 1994; bd. dirs. Nat. Humanities Ctr. 1993-97. Author: King: A Biography, 1970, Prisoners of Honor: The Dreyfus Affair, 1974, District of Columbia: A Bicentennial History, 1976, When Harlem Was in Vogue, 1981, The Race to Fashoda: European Colonialism and African Resistance in the Scramble for Africa, 1988, W.E. DuBois: Biography of a Race, 1868-1919, Vol. I, 1993 (Pulitzer prize 1994), The Civil Rights Movement in America, 1986, Harlem Renaissance: Black Art of America, 1987, Bridges and Boundaries: African Americans and American Jews, 1992. With U.S. Army, 1962-63. Recipient Bancroft prize Columbia U., 1994, Francis Parkman prize Soc. Am. Historians, 1994; fellow Drug Abuse Coun., Inc., Ford Found., 1972-73, Woodrow Wilson Internat. Ctr. Scholars, Smithsonian Instn., 1977-78, 90-91, Ctr. Advanced Study Behavioral Scis., 1980-81, Nat. Humanities Ctr., 1983-84, Guggenheim Meml. Found., 1986-87,. Mem. AAUP, Am. Hist. Assn., African Studies Assn., Orgn. Am. Historians, Soc. French Hist. Studies, So. Hist. Assn., Century Club, Phi Beta Kappa (chmn. Am. scholar com., 1991-93, senator united chpts. 1991—). Avocations: traveling, cycling. Office: Rutgers U Dept History Van Dyck Hall New Brunswick NJ 08903

LEWIS, DELANO EUGENE, broadcast executive; b. Arkansas City, Kans., Nov. 12, 1938; s. Raymond Ernest and Enna (Wordlow) L.; m. Gayle Carolyn Jones; children: Delano Jr., Brian, Geoffrey, Phillip. BA, U. Kansas, 1960; JD, Washburn U., 1963; LHD (hon.), Marymount U., 1988; D of Humane Letters, Bowie State U., 1992; D of Pub. Svc., George Washington U., 1991. Staff atty. U.S. Dept. of Justice, Washington, 1963-65, EEOC, Washington, 1965-66; assoc. dir., country dir. U.S. Peace Corps, Nigeria, Uganda, 1966-69; legis. asst. Sen. Edward Brooke Mass., Washington, 1969-71; adminstrv. asst. Congressman Walter Fauntroy, Washington, 1971-73; mgr. pub. affairs Chesapeake & Potomac Telephone Co.,

Washington, 1973-76, asst. v.p., 1976-83, v.p., 1983-88, pres., 1988-93; pres., CEO Nat. Public Radio, Washington, 1994—; bd. dirs. Eugene & Agnes Meyer Found., Psychiat. Inst., Chase Manhattan Corp., Apple Computer, Guest Svcs., Inc., Black Entertainment TV, Colgate-Palmolive. Pres. Greater Washington Bd. Trade, 1988; chmn. Mayor's Transition Com., 1978, D.C. Youth Employment Adv. Coun., 1992; co-chair D.C. Vocational Edn. and Career Opportunities Com., 1991, NPR Found.; mem. emeritus bd. Washington Performing Arts Soc., 1990—, Nat. Bd. AFRICARE, 1990—; bd. dirs. Lincoln Theatre. Named Washingtonian of Yr. Washingtonian mag., 1978, Man of Yr., Greater Washington bd. trustees, 1992; recipient Pres. medal Cath. U., Washington, 1978, Tree of Life award NCCJ, 1989, Social Responsibility award George Washington U. Sch. Bus., 1990, Spl. award Women of Washington, Disting. Alumni Citation U. Kans. Mem. Kans. Bar Assn., D.C. Bar Assn., Georgetown Club. Democrat. Roman Catholic. Avocations: jogging, tennis, racquetball. Office: Nat Public Radio 635 Massachusetts Ave NW Washington DC 20001-3752

LEWIS, DELBERT O'NEAL, disability consultant, former state official; b. Searcy, Ark., Oct. 15, 1947; s. Scott and Viola Marie (Hodges) L. BA in Psychology and Sociology, Harding U., 1969; 2M Rehab. Counseling, Ark. State U., 1972. Cert. rehab. counselor. With divsn. rehab. svcs. Ark. Dept. Human Svcs., Little Rock, 1972-90, planning specialist, 1978-90; ret., 1990, cons. on disability issues to govt., legal, ednl., and pvt. orgns., 1990—; former staff and advisor Ark. Com. on Equal Access for Handicapped, Interdeptl. Task Force on Rights of Handicapped; former rehab. specialist Disability Determination Svcs. Social Security Adminstrn., Little Rock; former mem. planning coun. CETA, Little Rock and Pulaski County; guest lectr. on disability issues U. Ark., Little Rock; founding mem., past pres. Ark. Environ. Barriers Coun.; mem. Ark. Adv. Com. to U.S. Commn. on Civil Rights; cons. Emerging Issues Project Inst. for Info. Studies, Washington. Contbr. articles to profl. publs. First Pub. Mem. Ark. Bd. Archs.; former mem. Nat. Ctr. for Barrier-Free Environ., Washington, OurWay, Inc., Little Rock; active Ark. Child Find to Implement Edn. for Handicapped Children Act., others. Recipient plaque of appreciation for svcs. as pres. Ark. br. Nat. Rehab. Counseling Assn., 1976, certs. City of Little Rock, 1975-85, Mover and Shaker award Ark. Gov.'s Commn. on People with Disabilities, 1978, recognition of svc. plaque Ark. Rehab. Assn., 1990, dedicated svc. plaque Ark. Divsn. Rehab. Svcs. Consumer Adv. Coun., 1990, pub. svc. plaque ARKLA Gas Co., 1991, Cert. of Svc. award U.S. Commn. on Civil Rights, Washington, 1995. Fellow Internat. Biog. Assn.; mem. Found. for Sci. and Disability, Gazette Internat. Networking Inst.-Internat. Polio Network, Drug Policy Found., Alliance for Cannabis Therapeutics, Rehab. Tech. Assn. Avocations: disability rights and access advocate, writing, anti war on drugs. Home and Office: 2400 Riverfront Dr Apt 12-f Little Rock AR 72202

LEWIS, DONALD EMERSON, banker; b. Orange, N.J., Apr. 3, 1950; s. Donald Emerson Lewis and Marie (Gannon) Slaght; m. Suzanne Kimm, Oct. 12, 1974; children: Andrew Gannon, Meredith Marie, Carolyn Ann. AB, Villanova U., 1972; MBA, Boston Coll., 1974. V.p. Citibank N.A., N.Y.C., 1974-85, Boston Safe Deposit & Trust Co., N.Y.C., 1985-87; sr. v.p. United Jersey Banks, Princeton, N.J., 1987-91; v.p. Fleet Bank, N.A., Glen Rock, N.J., 1991—. Republican. Roman Catholic. Club: Canoe Brook Country. Avocations: golf, platform tennis. Office: Fleet Bank NA 208 Harristown Rd Glen Rock NJ 07452

LEWIS, DOUGLAS, art historian; b. Centreville, Miss., Apr. 30, 1938; s. Charles Douglas and Beatrice Fenwick (Stewart) L. B.A. in History; B.A. in History of Art, Yale U., 1960, M.A., 1963, Ph.D., 1967; B.A. in Fine Arts, Clare Coll., Cambridge (Eng.) U., 1962, M.A., 1966. Asst. in instrn. Yale U., 1962-64; asst. prof. art Bryn Mawr Coll., 1967-68; vis. lectr. U. Calif., Berkeley, spring 1970, fall 1979; adj. prof. Johns Hopkins U., 1973-77; curator sculpture and decorative arts Nat. Gallery Art, Washington, 1968—; professorial lectr. Georgetown U., 1980-93; adj. prof. U. Md., 1989-91, 93—; mem. art adv. coms. Mt. Holyoke Coll. Art Mus., Lawrenceville Sch.; vice-chmn. nat. citizens stamp adv. com. U.S. Postal Svc.; adv. bd. Centro Palladiano, Vicenza, Italy. Author: The Late Baroque Churches of Venice, 1979, The Drawings of Andrea Palladio, 1981, intro. to Renaissance Master Bronzes, 1986. Mem. Am. fellowship com. Belgian-Am. Ednl. Found. Recipient Copley medal Nat. Portrait Gallery, 1981; Chester Dale fellow; David E. Finley fellow Nat. Gallery Art, 1964-67; Rome Prize fellow Am. Acad. Rome, 1964-66. Mem. Coll. Art Assn. Am., Soc. Archtl. Historians, Nat. Trust Historic Preservation, Washington Collegium for the Humanities (adv. bd.), Manuscript Soc. Episcopalian. Clubs: Yale (N.Y.C.); Falcons (Cambridge U.). Office: Nat Gallery Art Washington DC 20565-0001

LEWIS, E. GREY, lawyer; b. Altlantic City, N.J., Sept. 27, 1937; s. John Connell and Ella P. (Grey) L.; m. Carolyn Groves; children: Amy, Leslie, Peter, Sarah. AB, Princeton U., 1959; LLB, U. Pa., 1963. Pa. 1964, D.C. 1964, U.S. Supreme Ct. 1968. Asst. atty. U.S. Atty.'s Office, Washington, 1966-68; dept. asst. atty. gen. civil div. U.S. Dept. Justice, Washington, 1971-73; gen. counsel USN, Washington, 1973-77; ptnr. McDermott, Will & Emery, Washington, 1977—. Recipient Disting. Civilian Scv. award, U.S. Navy, 1977. Office: McDermott Will & Emery 1850 K St NW Ste 500 Washington DC 20006-2213

LEWIS, EDWARD ALAN, religious organization adminstrator; b. Brazil, Ind., July 22, 1946; s. Edward and Ruth Margaret (Eberwein) L. B in Music Edn., Grace Coll., 1969; M in Divinity, Grace Sem., 1973. Asst. to pastor, youth dir. Grace Brethren Ch., Winona Lake, Ind., 1969-73; nat. dir. youth ministries Grace Brethren Ch. Christian Edn., Winona Lake, 1973-85; dir. candidate personnel Grace Brethren Fgn. Missions, Winona Lake, 1982-88; exec. dir. Grace Brethren Ch. Christian Edn., Winona Lake, 1985—. Mem. Grace Brethren Ch., Winona Lake, 1969—, exec. mem. denominational youth com., 1984—; moderator Nat. Fellowship of Grace Brethren Chs., 1994-95. Mem. Grace Sem. Alumni Assn. (pres. 1984-85), Ind. Dist. Ministerium, Nat. Ministerium Assn. Avocations: music, piano, singing, jogging, travel. Home and Office: PO Box 365 Winona Lake IN 46590-0365

LEWIS, EDWARD B., biology educator; b. Wilkes-Barre, Pa., May 20, 1918; s. Edward B. and Laura (Histed) L.; m. Pamela Harrah, Sept. 26, 1946; children: Hugh, Glenn (dec.), Keith. B.A., U. Minn., 1939; Ph.D., Calif. Inst. Tech., 1942; Phil.D., U. Umea, Sweden, 1982; DSc, U. Minn., 1993. Instr. biology Calif. Inst. Tech., Pasadena, 1946-48, asst. prof., 1949-56, prof., 1956-66, Thomas Hunt Morgan prof., 1966-88, prof. emeritus, 1988—; Rockefeller Found. fellow Sch. Botany, Cambridge U., Eng., 1948-49; mem. Nat. Adv. Com. Radiation, 1958-61; vis. prof. U. Copenhagen, 1975-76, 82; researcher in developmental genetics, somatic effects of radiation. Editor: Genetics and Evolution, 1961. Served to capt. USAAF, 1942-46. Recipient Gairdner Found. Internat. award, 1987, Wolf Found. prize in medicine, 1989, Rosenstiel award, 1990, Nat. Medal of Sci. NSF, 1990, Albert Lasker Basic Med. Rsch. award, 1991, Louisa Gross Horowitz prize Columbia U., 1992, Nobel Prize in Medicine, 1995. Fellow AAAS; mem. NAS, Genetics Soc. Am. (sec. 1962-64, pres. 1967-69, Thomas Hunt Morgan medal), Am. Acad. Arts and Scis., Royal Soc. (London) (fgn. mem.), Am. Philos. Soc., Genetical Soc. Great Britian (hon.). Home: 805 Winthrop Rd San Marino CA 91108-1709 Office: Calif Inst Tech Div Biology 1201 E California Blvd Pasadena CA 91125-0001

LEWIS, EDWARD SHELDON, chemistry educator; b. Berkeley, Calif., May 7, 1920; s. Gilbert Newton and Mary (Sheldon) L.; m. Fofo Catsinas, Dec. 21, 1955; children—Richard Peter, Gregory Gilbert. B.S., U. Calif., Berkeley, 1940; M.A., Harvard U., 1947, Ph.D., 1947. NRC postdoctoral fellow UCLA, 1947-48; from asst. prof. to prof. chemistry Rice U., Houston, 1948-90, prof. emeritus, 1990—, chmn. dept. chemistry, 1963-67, 80-85; Vis. prof. U. Southampton, Eng., 1957, Phys. Chem. Lab., Oxford (Eng.) U., 1967-68, U. Kent, Canterbury, Eng., 1977, H.C. Ørsted Inst. , U. Copenhagen, 1980. Contbr. articles to profl. jours.; Editor: Investigation of Rates and Mechanisms of Reactions, 1974. Served with USNR, 1944-46. Guggenheim fellow, 1968. Fellow AAAS, Royal Irish Acad.; mem. Am. Chem. Soc. (S.W. regional award 1987), Royal Soc. of Chemistry, Phi Beta Kappa, Sigma Xi, Phi Lambda Upsilon. Home: 5651 Chevy Chase Dr Houston TX 77056-4004

LEWIS, EDWIN REYNOLDS, biomedical engineering educator; b. Los Angeles, July 14, 1934; s. Edwin McMurtry and Sally Newman (Reynolds) L.; m. Elizabeth Louise McLean, June 11, 1960; children: Edwin McLean, Sarah Elizabeth. AB in Biol. Sci., Stanford U., 1956, MSEE, 1957, Engr., 1959, PhD in Elec. Engring., 1962. With research staff Librascope div. Gen. Precision Inc., Glendale, Calif., 1961-67; mem. faculty dept. elec. engring. and computer sci. U. Calif., Berkeley, 1967—, dir. bioengring. tng. program, 1969-77, prof. elec. engring. and computer sci., 1971-94, prof. grad. sch., 1994—, assoc. dean grad. div., 1977-82, assoc. dean interdisciplinary studies coll. engring., 1988-96; chair joint program bioengring. U. Calif., Berkeley and San Francisco, 1988-91. Author: Network Models in Population Biology, 1977, (with others) Neural Modeling, 1977, The Vertebrate Inner Ear, 1985, also numerous articles. Grantee NSF, NASA, 1984, 87, Office Naval Rsch., 1990-93, NIH, 1975—; Neurosci. Rsch. Program fellow, 1966, 69; recipient Disting. Teaching Citation U. Calif., 1972; Jacob Javits neurosci. investigator NIH, 1984-91. Fellow IEEE, Acoustical Soc. Am.; mem. AAAS, Assn. Rsch. in Otolaryngology, Soc. Neurosci., Toastmasters (area lt. gov. 1966-67), Sigma Xi. Office: Dept Elec Engring & Computer Scis U Calif Berkeley CA 94720

LEWIS, ELENA DAWN, programmer analyst; b. South Bend, Ind., July 13, 1964; d. Joseph Paul Lewis and Helen Paulette (King) Pyles; 1 child, Jocelyn Janelle. BBA, Ohio U., 1986. Jr. programmer Centerior Energy, Cleve., 1987-89; tech. cons. Datronics Inc./Alcoa Aluminum, N.Y., Tenn., 1989-91; sr. programmer, analyst Allen Bradley Co., Cleve., 1992—. Career beginnings mentor Urban League, Cleve., 1993; career beginnings tutor Urban League/Allen Bradley, Cleve., 1993-94. Mem. Black Data Processing Assn., Approve Workman Are Not Ashamed. Baptist. Avocations: traveling, skiing, swimming, Bible study. Office: Allen Bradley Co 747 Alpha Dr Cleveland OH 44143-2124

LEWIS, ELISAH B., university official; b. Coral Gables, Fla., Feb. 14, 1961; d. Jean Sara (Mechlouitz) L. BFA, EdB, U. Miami, 1983, MEd, 1985, PhD, 1990. Art tchr. U. Miami, Coral Gables, Fla., 1979-89, Lowe Art Mus.; grad. asst. fin. assistance dept. U. Miami, Coral Gables, 1983-88, grad. asst. to acad. advisor, 1985-88, master tutor coord., 1988-89, testing examiner, 1988—, coord. transfer, jr. acad. advisor, 1989—. Mem. Fairchild Tropical Garden, Parrot Jungle and Garden, Lowe Art Mus. Recipient Silver Knight award in Art, 1979, Hibiscus award Fairchild Tropical Garden, 1993, Rose award, 1994; named Outstanding Young Women in Am., 1988. Mem. Nat. Acad. Adv. Assn. (grantee 1990, award 1991), Winterthur Mus., Nat. Geog. Soc., Audubon Soc., Omicron Delta Kappa, Rho Lamda, Alpha Epsilon Phi (officer 1980-83, award 1983). Avocations: painting, tennis, gardening. Office: U Miami Coll Arts & Scis PO Box 248004 Coral Gables FL 33124-8004

LEWIS, ELLEN CLANCY, assistant principal; b. Hartford, Conn., Feb. 18, 1945; d. Thomas Gerard and Hedwig Ann (Kondrasiewicz) Clancy. BA, Barry U., Miami, Fla., 1967; EdM, U. S.C., 1988, EdS, 1992, PhD, 1995. Cert. adminstr./supr. elem. grades, English, middle grades, data collection. Tchr. math. Bayvale Elem. Sch., Augusta, Ga., 1967-70; tchr. sci./math. Terrace Manor Elem. Sch., Augusta, 1970-72; tchr. sci. Wheeless Rd. Elem. Sch., Augusta, 1972-74; tchr. social studies/sci./math. Grovetown (Ga.) Elem. Sch., 1974-88; JTPA coord./tchr. Harlem (Ga.) H.S., 1988-92, asst. prin., 1992—. Editor: HHS At-Risk Manual, 1991. Commr. Profl. Stds. Com., Atlanta, 1991-95. Named Columbia County Tchr. of Yr. Columbia County Bd. Edn., 1988, Augusta C. of C. Tchr. of Yr., 1988; grantee Job Tng. Partnership Act, 1989-96. Mem. Profl. Assn. Ga. Educators. Avocations: horse breeding, reading, stamp collecting. Home: 3994 Evans To Lock Rd Evans GA 30809-9561 Office: Columbia County Bd of Edn Harlem High Sch PO Box 699 Harlem GA 30814

LEWIS, EMANUEL RAYMOND, retired librarian, historian, psychologist; b. Oakland, Calif., Nov. 30, 1928; s. Jacob A. and Rose (Grossman) L.; m. Joan R. Wilson, Feb. 7, 1954; 1 son, Joseph J.; m. Eleanor M. Gamarsh, Aug. 24, 1967. B.A., U. Calif., Berkeley, 1951, M.A., 1953; Ph.D., U. Oreg., 1962. Asst. prof. psychology Oreg. Coll. Edn., 1961-62, Oreg. State U., 1962-67; project mgr. System Devel. Corp., Falls Church, Va., 1968-69; vis. postdoctoral research asso. in Am. history Smithsonian Instn., Washington, 1969-70; chief historian, dir. research Contract Archeology, Alexandria, Va., 1971-73; librarian U.S. Ho. of Reps., Washington, 1973-95, libr. emeritus, 1995—. Author: Seacoast Fortifications of the United States, 1970, 2d edit. 1979, 3d edit. 1993; editor: The Educational Information Center, 1969. Served with M.I. U.S. Army, 1954-56. NIMH research fellow, 1960.

LEWIS, FLORA, journalist; b. Los Angeles; d. Benjamin and Pauline (Kallin) L.; m. Sydney Gruson, Aug. 17, 1945 (div.); children—Kerry, Sheila, Lindsey. B.A., UCLA, 1941; M.S., Columbia U., 1942, LHD (hon.), 1984; LL.D., Princeton U., 1981; hon. doctorate, Mt. Holyoke Coll., Bucknell U., Muhlenberg Coll., Manhattan Marymount. Reporter Los Angeles Times, 1941, A.P., N.Y., Washington, London, 1942-46; free lance or contract for Observer, Economist, Financial Times, France-soir, Time Mag.; free lance or contract for N.Y. Times Mag., London, Warsaw, Berlin, Hague, Mexico City, Tel Aviv, 1946-54, Prague, Warsaw, 1956-58; editor McGraw-Hill, N.Y.C., 1955; bur. chief Washington Post, Bonn, London, N.Y.C., 1958-66; syndicated columnist Newsday, Paris, N.Y.C., 1967-72; bur. chief N.Y. Times, Paris, 1972-80; European diplomatic corr. N.Y. Times, 1976-80, fgn. affairs columnist, 1980-90, sr. columnist, 1990—. Author: Case History of Hope, 1958, Red Pawn, 1964, One of Our H-Bombs is Missing, 1967, Europe: A Tapestry of Nations, 1987, Europe: A Road to Unity, 1992; contbr. to anthologies, books, mags. Arthur D. Morse fellow in communications and society Aspen Inst. for Humanistic Studies, 1977; decorated chevalier Legion d'Honneur; recipient awards for best interpretation fgn. affairs, 1956, best reporting fgn. affairs, 1960; Overseas Press Club award; Columbia Journalism Sch. 50th Anniversary Honor award, 1963; award for disting. diplomatic reporting George Washington U. Sch. Fgn. Service, 1978, Carr Van Anda award Ohio State U. Sch. Communications, 1982, Fourth Estate award Nat. Press Club, 1985, Matrix award for Newspapers N.Y. Women in Communications Inc., 1985, Elmer Holmes Bobst award in Arts and Letters NYU, 1987, Internat. House award, 1990; named hon. fellow UCLA Coll. Arts and Scis. Mem. Coun. on Fgn. Rels., Internat. Inst. for Strategic Studies (coun.), Inst. for East-West Security Studies, Phi Beta Kappa. Office: Am University in Paris, 34 Ave de New York, 75014 Paris 75116, France

LEWIS, FLOYD WALLACE, former electric utility executive; b. Lincoln County, Miss., Sept. 23, 1925; s. Thomas Cassidy and Lizzie (Lofton) L.; m. Jimmie Etoile Slawson, Dec. 27, 1949; children: Floyd Wallace, Gail, Julie, Ann, Carol, Michael Paul. B.B.A., Tulane U., 1945, LL.B., 1949. Bar: La. 1949. With New Orleans Pub. Service Inc., 1949-62, v.p., chief fin. officer, 1960-62; v.p. Ark. Power & Light Co., Little Rock, 1962-63; sr. v.p. Ark. Power & Light Co., 1963-67; exec. v.p., dir. La. Power & Light Co., New Orleans, 1967-68; pres. La. Power & Light Co., 1968-70, chief exec. officer, 1968-71, chmn. bd., 1970-72; pres. Middle South Utilities, Inc., 1970-79, 80-85, chmn. bd., 1979-85, also dir., chief exec. officer, 1972-85; pres., dir. Middle South Services, Inc., New Orleans, 1970-75, chmn., 1975-85, chief exec. officer, 1972-79; pres., dir. Middle South Energy, Inc., 1974-85; chmn. bd. System Fuels, Inc., 1972-85; dir. New Orleans br. Fed. Res. Bank, 1974-75, chmn., 1975; past dir. Fed. Res. Bank of Atlanta, Breeder Reactor Corp., Ark. Power and Light Co., La. Power & Light Co., La. Power & Light Co., New Orleans Pub. Service Inc., Ark. Power and Light Co., La. Power & Light Co., Miss. Power and Light Co., U.S. Chamber Commerce; mem. adv. com. Elec. Cos. Advt. Program, 1969-72, chmn., 1970-71; mem. electric utility adv. com. to Fed. Energy Adminstrn., 1975-76; chmn. Edison Electric Inst., 1976-77, mem. exec. com., 1974-78; mem. exec. com. Assn. Edison Illuminating Cos., 1973-80; dir. Electric Power Research Inst., 1977-82, chmn., 1979-81; dir. Am. Nuclear Energy Council, 1982-86. Mem. exec. bd. New Orleans area council Boy Scouts Am., 1967-80, v.p., 1970-74, pres., 1975-76, mem. regional exec. com., 1968-80; v.p. Com. for a Better La., 1975-76, sr. v.p., 1976-77, pres., 1977-78; bd. dirs. La. World Expn. Inc., 1976-89, chmn., 1980-81, 83-89, pres., 1981-83; chmn. Utility Nuclear Power Oversight Com., 1979-81; vice chmn. campaign United Fund, New Orleans, 1970, chmn., 1971; bd. dirs. New Orleans Symphony Soc., 1974-75, Atomic Indsl. Forum, 1982-86, vice chmn., 1985-86; bd. dirs. Pub. Affairs Research Council of La.; pres. New Orleans Bapt. Sem. Found., 1973-76, 91-92; trustee La. Coll., 1984-90; New Orleans Baptist Theol. Sem., 1954-62, 1968-78, v.p., 1970-78; bd. adminstrs. Tulane U., 1973-88, bd. visitors, 1968-71; bd. govs. Med. Center, 1969-73, vice chmn., 1969-71; chmn. alumni adv. council Grad. Sch. Bus., 1970-73; bd. dirs. U.S. Com. Energy Awareness, 1982-85, vice-chmn., 1983-84, chmn., 1985; v.p. Internat. House, 1970; trustee Com. Econ. Devel., 1972-87; mem. bd. Ochsner Med. Found., 1976-96, mem. exec. com., 1977-96; 1st chmn. Parents Council, Furman U.; mem. Parents Council, Wake Forest U., 1980-81. Served to ensign USNR, 1945-46. Recipient Silver Beaver, Silver Antelope Boy Scouts Am.; Oliver Townsend medal Atomic Indsl. Forum; Outstanding Alumni award Grad. Sch. Bus., 1970; Disting. Alumnus award Tulane U., 1983. Mem. Tulane Alumni Assn. (exec. com., treas. 1970), Order of Coif, Beta Gamma Sigma, Omicron Delta Kappa, Beta Theta Pi, Phi Delta Phi. Baptist (deacon).

LEWIS, FRANK HARLAN, botanist, educator; b. Redlands, Calif., Jan. 8, 1919; s. Frank Hooker and Mary Elizabeth (Smith) L.; m. Margaret Ruth Ensign, Aug. 2, 1945 and Aug. 2, 1984; children: Donald Austin, Frank Murray; m. Ann Gibbons, Dec. 23, 1968 (dec. 1983). AA, San Bernardino Valley Coll., 1939; BA, UCLA, 1941, MA, 1942, PhD, 1946; postgrad., Calif. Inst. Tech., 1942-44. Mem. faculty UCLA, 1946-82, prof. botany, 1956-82, prof. emeritus, 1982—, systematist expt. sta., 1956-62, chmn. dept., 1959-62, dean of life scis., 1962-82, dean emeritus, 1982—; Cons. genetics NSF, 1958-61, specialized biol. facilities, 1963-68. Bd. editors: Evolution, 1951-53; editor, 1972-74; bd. editors: Am. Jour. Botany, 1964-66, Am. Naturalist, 1965-67, 77-79; chmn. bd. editors U. Calif. publs. in botany, 1958-62. Trustee Graeme Joseph Revolving Scholarship Fund, 1968-86. NRC fellow John Innes Hort. Instn., London, 1947-48; Guggenheim fellow, 1954-55. Fellow AAAS (council mem. 1974-76), Calif. Acad. Sci.; mem. Bot. Soc. Am. (pres. Pacific div. 1959, Merit award 1972), Soc. Study Evolution (pres. 1961), Internat. Orgn. Plant Biosystematists (exec. com. 1961-81, v.p. 1964-69, pres. 1969-75), Am. Soc. Naturalists (pres. 1971), Am. Soc. Plant Taxonomists (pres. 1969), Internat. Soc. Plant Taxonomists, Phi Beta Kappa, Sigma Xi. Home: 14280 W Sunset Blvd Pacific Palisades CA 90272-3933

LEWIS, GARY, trucking executive; b. 1953. Pres. Schneider National Carriers, Green Bay, Wis., 1979—; now gen. mgr. Schneider Nat. Logistics, Green Bay, WI. Address: Schneider National PO Box 2545 Green Bay WI 54306-2545*

LEWIS, GENE DALE, historian, educator; b. Globe, Ariz., Feb. 20, 1931; s. Abner E. and May J. (Hyatt) L.; m. Dottie Ladd Bidlingmeyer, Aug. 3, 1963. BA, Ariz. State U., 1951, MA, 1952; PhD, U. Ill., 1957. Lectr. Ariz. State U., 1953, So. Ill. U., 1957-58; vis. assoc. prof. history U. Ill., Urbana, 1965, Case Western Res. U., Cleve., 1966; prof. history U. Cin., 1958—, acting head dept., 1981-82, dir. grad. studies, 1989, head dept., 1989—; sr. v.p., provost, 1973-76. Author: Charles Ellet Jr., Engineer as Individualist, 1968; editor: New Historical Perspectives: Essays on the Black Experience in Antebellum America, 1984; co-editor Greater Cincinnati Bicentennial History Series, 1988—. Recipient Barbour award for excellence U. Cin., 1969, Nat. award Omicron Delta Kappa, 1968. Mem. AAUP, So. Hist. Assn., Am. Hist. Assn., Orgn. Am. Historians. Home: 444 Rawson Woods Ln Cincinnati OH 45220-1142 Office: U Cin Dept History Cincinnati OH 45221

LEWIS, GENE EVANS, retired medical equipment company executive; b. Terrell, Tex., May 17, 1928; s. John Evans and Helen Elizabeth (Paterson) L.; m. Sonya Dolishny, Jan. 21, 1950; children: Robert, Melissa. BSEE, Tex. A&M U., 1949. Sales, mktg. and engring. mgr. GE, Schenectady, Dallas, Pittsfield, Holyoke, Lynn, 1950-68; gen. mgr. various bus. GE, Milw., 1970-77; group product mgr. Picker X-Ray, Cleve., 1968-70; pres. sci. instruments div. Am. Optical Corp., Southbridge, Mass., 1977-78; pres. internat. div. Am. Optical Corp., 1978-79, pres., 1979-84; pres. Baker Instruments Corp., Allentown, Pa., 1985-88; chmn., CEO Novecon Technologies, 1994—; bd. dirs. EDITEK, Inc., Alpine Group, Inc.; exec. mem. The Holly Inn; sr. adv. bd. Novecon Corp. With Signal Corps U.S. Army, 1949. Mem. Calibogue Club, Sea Pines Country Club. Home: 25 Spartina Cres Hilton Head Island SC 29928-2925 Office: Novecon Technologies 12030 Sunrise Valley Dr Ste 300 Reston VA 22091-3409

LEWIS, GEORGE RAYMOND, state agency administrator, clinical social worker; b. Bridgeton, N.J., July 7, 1944; s. Raymond and Evelyn Rhoda (Mitchell) L.; m. Tenelia Kay Boykin, Sept. 3, 1966. BA, U. N.Mex., 1966; MSW, Our Lady of the Lake Coll., 1971. Cert. social worker; lic. ind. social worker. With N.Mex. Health and Social Services Dept., 1971-92; dist. tng. officer N.Mex. Health and Social Services Dept., Roswell, 1972-73, field office mgr., 1973-75, social worker cons., 1975-84, dist. ops. mgr., 1984-92; clin. dir. Assurance Home Inc., 1992—; behavioral sci. specialist Cmty. Guidance Ctr., San Antonio, 1971; ajd. instr. N.Mex. State U., Las Cruces, 1971, 83, 85, 94, 95, Ea. N.Mex. U., Roswell, 1973-76, 92; clin. dir. Chaves County 1st Offender Program, Roswell, 1974-77; field instr. Tex. Tech. U., Lubbock, 1981; bd. dirs. Assurance Home Inc., Roswell; mem. N.Mex. Bd. Social Work Examiners, 1989-91; N.Mex. del. to Am. Assn. State Social Work Bd., 1990-93. Bd. dirs. Chaves County Home Health Agy. Inc., Roswell, 1973-76, Parents Anonymous of N.Mex. Inc., 1978-79; mem. State N.Mex. Acupuncture Bd., 1994-95. Named an Outstanding Young Man of Am., U.S. Jaycees, 1978, 81. Mem. Nat. Assn. Social Workers (New Mexico Rose Praisner award, 1992), Acad. Cert. Social Workers, Order of the Arrow, Blue Key. Democrat. Baptist. Avocations: greenhouse gardening, camping, fishing, hunting. Home: 1018 N Plains Park Dr Roswell NM 88201-2516 Office: Assurance Home Inc 100 E 18th St Roswell NM 88201

LEWIS, GEORGE WITHROW, business executive; b. Berwyn, Ill., May 13, 1929; s. George Edward and Katherine (Withrow) L.; m. Ellen Freer Baker, Sept. 14, 1963 (div. Apr. 1987); children: George Baker, Martha Freer; m. Elizabeth Morgan Williams, Dec. 26, 1992. A.B., Princeton, 1951; M.B.A., Harvard, 1955. With Ford Motor Co., 1955-62; cons. McKinsey & Co., N.Y.C., 1962-64; mng. dir. Rolls-Royce Motors Internat. Div., 1964-83. Vice-pres. fin. Eisenhower Exchange Fellowships, 1985-92. 1st lt., arty. AUS, 1952-53, Korea. Mem. Harvard Bus. Sch. Club of Phila. (past pres.). Episcopalian (vestryman). Home: 1325 Lombard St Philadelphia PA 19147-1003

LEWIS, GERALD JORGENSEN, judge; b. Perth Amboy, N.J., Sept. 9, 1933; s. Norman Francis and Blanche M. (Jorgensen) L.; m. Laura Susan McDonald, Dec. 15, 1973; children by previous marriage: Michael, Marc. AB magna cum laude, Tufts Coll., 1954; JD, Harvard U., 1957. Bar: D.C. 1957, N.J. 1961, Calif. 1962, U.S. Supreme Ct. 1968. Atty. Gen. Atomic, LaJolla, Calif., 1961-63; ptnr. Haskins, Lewis, Nugent & Newnham, San Diego, 1963-77; judge Mcpl. Ct., El Cajon, Calif., 1977-79; judge Superior Ct., San Diego, 1979-84; assoc. justice, Calif. Ct. of Appeal, San Diego, 1984-87; dir. Fisher Scientific Group, Inc., 1987—, Bolsa Chica Corp., 1991-93, Gen. Chemical Group, Inc., 1996—; of counsel Latham & Watkins, 1987—; dir. Wheelabrator Techs., Inc., 1987-93, Henley Mfg., Inc., 1987-89; adj. prof. evidence Western State U. Sch. Law, San Diego, 1977-85, exec. bd., 1977-89; faculty San Diego Inn of Ct., 1979—, Am. Inn of Ct., 1984—. Cons. editor: California Civil Jury Instructions, 1984. City atty. Del Mar, Calif., 1963-74, Coronado, Calif., 1972-77; counsel Comprehensive Planning Orgn., San Diego, 1972-73; trustee San Diego Mus. Art., 1986-89; bd. dirs. Air Pollution Control Dist., San Diego County, 1972-76. Served to lt. comdr. USNR, 1957-61. Named Trial Judge of Yr., San Diego Trial Lawyers Assn., 1984. Mem. Am. Judicature Soc., Soc. Inns of Ct. in Calif., La Jolla Wine and Food Soc., Confrerie des Chevaliers du Tastevin, Order of St. Hubert (Knight Commdr.), Friendly Sons of St. Patrick. Republican. Episcopalian. Clubs: Bohemian; LaJolla Country (dir. 1980-83); Venice Island Hunt Club; Prophets. Home: 6505 Caminito Blythefield La Jolla CA 92037-5806 Office: Latham & Watkins 701 B St Ste 2100 San Diego CA 92101-8116

LEWIS, GLADYS SHERMAN, nurse, educator; b. Wynnewood, Okla., Mar. 20, 1933; d. Andrew and Minnie Elva (Halsey) Sherman; R.N., St. Anthony's Sch. Nursing, 1953; student Okla. Bapt. U., 1953-55; AB, Tex. Christian U., 1956; postgrad. Southwestern Bapt. Theol. Sem., 1959-60, Escuela de Idiomas, San Jose, Costa Rica, 1960-61; MA in Creative Writing, Central (Okla.) State U., 1985; PhD in English Okla. State U. 1992; m. Wilbur Curtis Lewis, Jan. 28, 1955; children: Karen, David, Leanne, Cristen. Mem. nursing staff various facilities, Okla., 1953-57; instr. nursing, med. missionary Bapt. mission and hosp., Paraguay, 1961-70; vice-chmn. edn. commn. Paraguay Bapt. Conv., 1962-65; sec. bd. trustees Bapt. Hosp., Paraguay, 1962-65; chmn. personnel com., handbook and policy book officer Bapt. Mission in Paraguay, 1967-70; trustee Southwestern Bapt. Theol. Sem., 1974-84, chmn. student affairs com., 1976-78, vice-chmn. bd. 1978-80; ptnr.

Las Amigas Tours, 1978-80; writer, conference leader, campus lectr., 1959—; adj. prof. English Cen. State U., Okla. (name changed to U. Cen. Okla.), 1990-91; faculty mem., asst. prof. English U. Cen. Okla., 1991-95, assoc. prof., 1996—. Active Dem. com., Evang. Women's Caucus, 1979-80; leader Girl Scouts U.S.A., 1965-75; Okla. co-chmn. Nat. Religious Com. for Equal Rights Amendment, 1977-79; tour host Meier Internat. Study League, 1978-81. Mem. AAUW, Internat. and Am. colls. surgeons women's auxiliaries, Okla. State, Okla. County med. auxiliaries, Am. Nurse Assn., Nat. Women's Polit. Caucus, 1979-80. Author: On Earth As It Is, 1983; Two Dreams and a Promise, 1984, Message, Messenger and Response, 1994; also religious instructional texts in English and Spanish; editor Sooner Physician's Heartbeat, 1979-82; contbr. articles to So. Bapt. and secular periodicals. Home: 14501 N Western Ave Edmond OK 73013-1828

LEWIS, GOLDY SARAH, real estate developer, corporation executive; b. West Selkirk, Man., Can., June 15, 1921; d. David and Rose (Dwor) Kimmel; m. Ralph Milton Lewis, June 12, 1941; children: Richard Alan, Robert Edward, Roger Gordon, Randall Wayne. B.S., UCLA, 1943; postgrad., U. So. Calif., 1944-45. Pvt. practice acctg. L.A., 1945-57, law office mgr., 1953-55; dir., exec. v.p. Lewis Homes, Upland, Calif., 1955—, Lewis Construction Co. Inc., Upland, 1959—, Lewis Bldg. Co., Inc., Las Vegas, 1960—, Republic Sales Co., Inc., 1956—, Kimmel Enterprises, Inc., 1959—; mng. partner Lewis Homes of Calif., 1973—; mng. ptnr. Lewis Homes of Nev., 1972—, Western Properties, 1972—, Foothill Investment Co., 1971—, Republic Mgmt. Co., 1978—. Contbr. articles to mags., jours. Mem. Dean's Coun. UCLA Grad. Sch. Architecture and Urban Planning; mem. UCLA Found., Chancellor's Assocs.; endowed Ralph and Goldy Lewis Ctr. for Regional Policy at UCLA, 1989, Ralph and Goldy Lewis Hall of Planning and Devel. at U. S.C., 1989, others. Recipient 1st award of distinction Am. Builder mag., 1963, Homer Briggs Svc. to Youth award West End YMCA, 1990, Spirit of Life award City of Hope, 1993; co-recipient Builder of Yr. award Profl. Builder Mag., 1988, Housing Person of Yr. award Nat. Housing Conf., 1990, Entrepreneur of Yr. award Inland Empire, 1990; Ralph and Goldy Lewis Sports Ctr. named in their honor City of Rancho Cucamonga, 1988, also several other parks and sports fields including Lewis Park in Claremont.; named one of Woman of Yr. Calif. 25th Senate Dist., 1989, (with husband Ralph M. Lewis) Disting. Chief Exec. Officer, Calif. State U., San Bernadino, 1991, Mgmt. Leaders of the Yr. Univ. Calif., Riverside, 1993. Mem. Nat. Assn. Home Builders, Bldg. Industry Assn. So. Calif. (Builder of Yr. award Baldy View chpt. 1988), Internat. Coun. Shopping Ctrs., Urban Land Inst. Office: Lewis Homes PO Box 670 Upland CA 91785-0670

LEWIS, GORDON GILMER, golf course architect; b. Shawnee, Okla., Sept. 7, 1950; s. Ted Eugene and Janet Garvin (Panner) L.; m. Karen Louise McKenzie, June 2, 1973 (div. Dec. 1981); children: Melanie Marie Lewis-Lehr, Katie McKenzie Lewis-Lehr; m. Susette Mamie London, June 11, 1988; children: London Marshall, Sarah June Victoria. B of Landscape Architecture, Kans. State U., 1974. Registered landscape architect, Ala., Kans., Fla. Golf course architect David Gill, St. Charles, Ill., 1974-75, Charles M. Graves Orgn., Atlanta, 1975-78, Gordon G. Lewis, Naples, Fla., 1978—. Prin. works include Meadowbrook Links, Rapid City, S.D. (Top 50 Pub. Courses in U.S.), The Hulman Links at Los Creek, Terre Haute, Ind. (Top 50 Pub. Courses in U.S.), Lagoon Park, Montgomery, Ala. (Top 75 Pub. Courses in U.S.), The Forest, Ft. Myers, Fla. (Top 50 Courses in Fla.), The Vines, Estero, Fla. (Golf Digest One of Top New Courses 1986), Worthington, Bonita Springs, Fla., Tsai-Hsing, Taipei, Taiwan, others. Republican. Presbyterian. Avocation: golf. Home: 5098 2nd Ave SW Naples FL 33999-2528

LEWIS, GREGORY WILLIAMS, scientist; b. Seattle, Mar. 3, 1940; s. Delbert Srofe and Eileen Julianne (Williams) L.; m. Stephanie Marie Schwab, Sept. 18, 1966; children: Jeffrey Williams, Garrick Peterson. BS, Wash. State U., 1962, MA, 1965, PhD, 1970. Tchr., rsch. asst. Wash. State U., Pullman, 1965-69; prin. investigator U.S. Army Med. Rsch. Lab., Ft. Knox, Ky., 1970-74; prin. investigator USN Pers. R & D Ctr., San Diego, 1974—, head neurosci. lab., 1980-95, leader security systems, 1981-83, head neurosci. projects office, 1987-89, div. head neurosci., 1989-95, sr. prin. scientist, 1995—; cons. in field. Contbr. articles to profl. jours. Bd. dirs., pres. Mesa View Homeowners Assn., Calif., 1980-82; bd. dirs. Santa Fe Assn., Calif., 1994-96. Capt. U.S. Army, 1967-74. Fellow Internat. Orgn. Psychophysiology; mem. AAAS, Soc. Neurosci., Internat. Brain Rsch. Orgn., N.Y. Acad. Scis., Soc. Psychophysiol. Rsch., Sigma Xi, Alpha Kappa Delta, Delta Chi, Psi Chi. Achievements include research in ophthalmic ultrasonography, neuroelectric research and development of brain activity and variability for improving the evaluation of education and training materials, personnel assessment, and prediction of job performance; physiological correlates of performance; psychophysiology of individual differences; neuromagnetic research directed toward individual differences and personnel performance; neuroelectric and neuromagnetic data acquisition and analysis; patent for development of neuroelectric and neuromagnetic method and system for individual identification and impairment of function using artificial neural network analyses; developing personnel performance models for use in preliminary design and rapid prototyping of ship systems. Avocations: music, electronics, working on timber land and vacation log home. Home: 410 Santa Cecelia Solana Beach CA 92075-1505 Office: US Navy Pers R&D Ctr 53335 Ryne Rd San Diego CA 92152-7250

LEWIS, HAROLD ALEXANDER, insurance company executive; b. Kingston, Jamaica, Feb. 25, 1953; came to U.S., 1980; s. Frankie Lewis and Kathlene (Smith) Benjamin. Student, Mt. St. Benedict, Trinidad, W.I., 1978-80, Don Bosco Coll., Newton, N.J., 1980-82. With Brit. Caribbean Inc., Kingston, 1972-74, 76-78; substitute tchr. St. Philip Neri Elem. Sch., Houston, 1982-83; licensing examiner Nat. Benefit Life Ins. Co., N.Y.C., 1983-89, mgr. microsystems and records retention, 1989-92; licensing adminstr., 1992-95; pres. Consulting Mgmt., Bronx, N.Y., 1995—. Vice chmn. Health Ins. Plan-HMO Consumer Coun., Bronx, 1984—; sec. Bronx Regional Coun., 1986-89; mem. Scout Assn. of Jamaica (W.I.), 1976-78; bd. dirs. Health Ins. Plan of Greater N.Y., mem. coun., 1990—. Named Consumer of Yr., HIP, 1987. Mem. NAFE, Assn. of Records Mgrs. and Adminstrs. Avocations: playing guitar and organ, reading, tennis, charitable work. Home: 1210 Sherman Ave Apt 6C Bronx NY 10456-3044 Office: Consulting Mgmt P O Box 31 Bronx NY 10456

LEWIS, HENRY RAFALSKY, manufacturing company executive; b. Yonkers, N.Y., Nov. 19, 1925; s. Jasper R. and Freda (Rafalsky) L.; m. Barbara Connolly, June 15, 1957; children—Peter, Susan, Abigail. AB, Harvard U., 1949, MA, 1951, PhD, 1957. Group head Ops. Evaluation Group, Washington, 1955-57; mem. staff Electronic Rsch. Lab. RCA, Princeton, N.J., 1957-66, dir., 1966-70; v.p. rsch./devel. Itek Corp., Lexington, Mass., 1970-74; pres. Optel Corp., Princeton, N.J., 1974; sr. v.p. Dennison Mfg. Co., Waltham, Mass., 1974-85, vice chmn., 1986-91, also bd. dirs.; chmn., CEO Celadon Scis. Inc., Boston, 1991—; chmn. bd. dirs. Delphax Sys., Randolph, Mass.; bd. dirs. Cenzyme Corp., Cambridge, Mass., Dyax Corp., Cambridge. Contbr. articles to profl. jours. Chmn. investment com. Powers (Mass.) Music Sch., 1978-90; mem. Harvard Grad. Soc. Coun., 1992-95. With U.S. Army, 1944-46. Mem. IEEE, Am. Phys. Soc., Phi Beta Kappa, Sigma Xi. Club: Harvard. Home: 35 Clover St Belmont MA 02178-2410 Office: Delphax Systems Canton Tech Ctr 5 Campanelli Cir Canton MA 02021-2480

LEWIS, HENRY WILKINS, university administrator, lawyer, educator; b. Jackson, N.C., Nov. 7, 1916; s. Edmund Wilkins and Jane Crichton (Williams) L. A.B., U. N.C., 1937; J.D., Harvard, 1940. Bar: N.C. bar 1940. Practice in Jackson, 1940-41; mem. staff Inst. of Govt., U. N.C., 1946-51, research prof. pub. law and govt., 1951-57, prof., 1957-73; acting v.p. U. N.C., 1968-69; dir. Inst. Govt., 1973-78, Kenan prof. pub. law and govt., 1975-78, emeritus, 1978—; v.p., bd. dirs. Wilkins Texas Corp., 1967-92. Author: Property Tax Collection in North Carolina, 1951, rev. edit., 1957, The General Assembly of North Carolina: Organization and Procedure, 1952, Legislative Committees in North Carolina, 1952, Basic Legal Problems in the Taxation of Property, 1958, (with Robert G. Byrd) In Rem Property Tax Foreclosure, 1959, An Introduction to County Government, 1963, rev. edit., 1968, Primary and General Election Law and Procedure, 11 edits., latest, 1968, Property Tax Exemptions and Classifications, 1970, The Property Tax: An Introduction, 1972, rev. edits., 1975, 78, Northampton Parishes, 1951, The Doctor and Mrs. Lewis, 1980, More Taste Than Prudence: A Study of John Evans Johnson (1815-1870), 1983, Compelled to Wander, 1987; contbr. articles to profl. jours. Counsel N.C. Elections Laws Commn., 1967; counsel N.C. Commn. for Study Local and Ad Valorem Tax Structure, 1970, N.C. Commn. for Study Property Tax Exemptions and Classifications, 1973; mem. N.C. Criminal Justice Tng. and Standards Council, 1973-78, N.C. Criminal Justice Edn. and Tng. System Council, 1973-78, N.C. Commn. on Productivity in State Govt., 1976-77; Mem. adv. bd. N.C. State Art Soc., 1962-63; mem. Com. for Restoration St. John's Ch., Williamsboro, N.C., 1950-79; mem. adv. bd. Ackland Art Center, U. N.C., 1957-78, mem. vis. com. 1987—; trustee Va. Episcopal Sch., 1974-80, U. N.C. Center for Public TV, 1980-88; bd. dirs. N.C. Pub. TV Found., 1987-88. Served to capt. AUS, 1941-46. Mem. Lincoln's Inn Soc., N.C. Bar Assn., N.C. Lit. and Hist. Assn. (v.p. 1972-75), N.C. Collectors (pres. 1965-66), N.C. Soc. (dir.), Roanoke-Chowan Group (convenor 1962-65), Nat. Sporting Libr. (hon. life), Va. Hist. Soc., Jamestowne Soc., Order of Gimghouls, Phi Beta Kappa, Alpha Tau Omega. Episcopalian (parish conv. del. intermittently 1948—, mem. diocesan standing com. intermittently 1957-91, com. on constitution and canons 1973—, dep. Gen. Conv. 1967, 69, 70, 76, 79, 82, 85). Home: 386 Fearrington Post Pittsboro NC 27312-8518

LEWIS, HERBERT SAMUEL, anthropologist, educator; b. Jersey City, May 8, 1934; s. Frederic and Estelle (Sachs) L.; m. Marcia Barbash, June 23, 1957; children—Tamar Anne, Paula Miriam, Joshua Daniel. A.B., Brandeis U., 1955; Ph.D., Columbia U., 1963. Instr. Northwestern U., Evanston, Ill., 1961-63; lectr. anthropology Columbia U., N.Y.C., 1961; from asst. to full prof. anthropology U. Wis., Madison, 1963-73, prof., 1973—, dir. African studies program, 1993-95; vis. prof. Hebrew U., Jerusalem, 1969-70; cons. AID, Africare, 1981-84. Author: A Galla Monarchy, 1965, After the Eagles Landed: The Yemenite Jews of Israel, 1989, (monograph) Leaders and Followers: Anthropological Perspectives, 1974, The Origins of the Galla and Somali; contbr. articles to profl. jours. Research grantee Ford Found., Ethiopia, 1958-60, NSF, Ethiopia, 1965-66, Israel, 1975-77; Fulbright research grantee, 1987. Fellow Am. Anthropol. Assn., Royal Anthropol. Inst. of Gt. Britain and Ireland, African Studies Assn. Home: 1009 Tumalo Trl Madison WI 53711-3024 Office: U Wis Dept Anthropology Social Sci Bldg Madison WI 53706

LEWIS, HUEY (HUGH ANTHONY CREGG, III), singer, composer, bandleader; b. N.Y.C., July 5, 1951; s. Hugh Anthony II and Magda Cregg; m. Sidney Conroy, 1983; children: Kelly, Austin. Student, Cornell U. Mem. Clover, 1972-77; singer, composer leader Huey Lewis and the News, 1978—. Rec. artist: (with Clover) Clover, 1977, Unavailable, 1977, Love on the Wire, 1977, (with Huey Lewis and the News) Huey Lewis and the News, 1980, Picture This, 1982, Sports, 1983, Fore, 1986, Small World, 1988, Hard at Play, 1991, Best of Huey Lewis and the News, 1992, Four Chords and Several Years Ago, 1994; hit singles include Do You Believe in Love?, Workin' for a Living, I Want a New Drug, The Heart of Rock 'n' Roll, Heart and Soul, Walking on a Thin Line, Hip To Be Square, I Know What I Like, (single from Back to the Future soundtrack) The Power of Love; contbr. (single and video) We Are the World, 1984; appeared in films: Back to the Future, 1985, Short Cuts, 1993. Office: care Capito-EMI Records 1750 Vine St Hollywood CA 90028-5247

LEWIS, HUNTER, financial advisor, publisher; b. Dayton, Ohio, Oct. 13, 1947; s. Welbourne Walker and Emily (Spivey) L.; m. Elizabeth Sidamon-Eristoff, July 3, 1993. AB magna cum laude, Harvard U., 1969. Asst. to office of pres. Boston Co., 1970, v.p., 1972-73; pres. Boston Co. Fin. Strategies, Inc., 1971-72; co-founder Cambridge Assocs. Inc. and Cambridge Capital Advisors, Inc., Washington, 1973—; former dir., chmn. bd. Shelburne Farms Inc. Former trustee, chmn. fin. com. Groton Sch.; former chmn. adv. bd. Dumbarton Oaks, affiliate of Harvard U.; pres., trustee Am. Sch. Classical Studies at Athens; former mem. pension fin. com. World Bank; bd. dirs., treas. World Wildlife Fund; former dir. Worldwide Fund for Nature; chmn. bd. dirs. Worldwatch Inst.; chmn. fin. com., trustee Pierpont Morgan Libr., N.Y.C.; former trustee Thomas Jefferson Found., Monticello; chmn., bd. dirs. Trearne Found. With USMC, 1969-70. Author: The Real World War, 1982, A Question of Values, 1990; contbr. articles to N.Y. Times, Atlantic Monthly, Washington Post, other mags. and newspapers; author monographs on specialized fin. subjects. Mem. Univ. Club (N.Y.C.), Knickerbocker Club (N.Y.C.), Union Boat Club (Boston), Met. Club (Washington). Office: 1110 N Glebe Rd Ste 1100 Arlington VA 22201

LEWIS, HYLAN GARNET, sociologist, educator; b. Washington, Apr. 4, 1911; s. Harry Wythe and Ella (Wells) L.; A.B., Va. Union U., 1932; A.M. (Social Sci. Research Council fellow 1932, Rosenwald Found. fellow 1939-41), U. Chgo., 1936, Ph.D., 1951; m. Leighla Whipper, Oct. 4, 1935 (div. May 1945); 1 dau., Carole Ione Lewis Bovoso; m. Audrey Carter, Nov. 2, 1946; 1 son, Guy Edward. Instr. sociology Howard U., Washington, 1934-41, prof. sociology, 1964-67; prof. social sci. Talladega (Ala.) Coll., 1941-42; info. specialist OWI, 1942-45; asso. prof. Hampton Inst., 1945-48; asso. prof. sociology Atlanta U., 1948-55, prof., 1955-57; asso. dir. community services Unitarian Service Com., Inc., Boston, 1957-59; dir. child rearing study Health and Welfare Council, Washington, 1959-64; mem. delinquency grants rev. com. NIMH, 1963-67, mem. social problems research rev. com., 1969-73; mem. devel. behavioral scis. study sect. NIH, 1974-76; prof. sociology Bklyn. Coll. 1967-77, prof. emeritus, 1977—; vis. prof. Grad. Center, CUNY, 1977—; Michael Harrington prof. Queens Coll. CUNY, 1990-91, vis. prof. sociology, 1991-92; sr. cons. Clark, Phipps, Clark & Harris, Inc., 1975-85; sr. assoc. Kenneth B. Clark & Assocs., 1985—; sr. v.p. Met. Applied Research Center, Inc., 1967-75; vis. scholar Russell Sage Found., 1974-75. Research asso. Inst. for Research in Social Sci., U. N.C., 1947-48; cons. Volta River Project Preparatory Commn., Gold Coast, 1954; Ashmore project Fund for Advancement Edn., 1953, So. Regional Council, 1954-58, Commn. on Race and Housing, 1956-57; cons. disaster study com. NRC, 1955-56; mem. adv. com. grants program U.S. Children's Bur., 1962-66; mem. adv. panel small grants program U.S. Dept. Labor, 1963-83; chief cons. family panel White House Conf. Civil Rights Planning, 1965; mem. rev. panel U.S. Office Edn., 1965-67; mem. Head Start research adv. com. Office Econ. Opportunity, 1965-67; mem. grants adv. com. Nat. Endowment for the Humanities, Nat. Found. Arts and Humanities, 1967-68, others. Fund for Advancement Edn. fellow, 1955-56. Fellow AAAS; mem. Am. Sociol. Assn. (DuBois-Johnson-Frazier award 1976), Soc. Rsch. Assn., Eastern Sociol. Soc. (merit award 1979), Alpha Phi Alpha. Author: Blackways of Kent, 1955. Home: 372 Central Park W New York NY 10025-8240

LEWIS, IRVING JAMES, community health educator, health policy analyst, public administrator; b. Boston, Mass., July 9, 1918; s. Harry and Sarah (Bloomberg) L.; m. Rose Helen Greenwald, June 15, 1941; children—Deborah Ann, Amy Rebecca, William David. AB, Harvard U., 1939; AM, U. Chgo., 1940. With U.S. Govt., 1942-70; dep. chief internat. div. Bur. Budget, 1959-65; dept. head Intergovtl. Com. European Migration, Geneva, 1957-59; chief health and welfare div. Bur. Budget, 1965-67; dep. asst. dir. Bur., 1967-68; dep. adminstr. health services and mental health adminstrn. HEW, 1968-70; prof. community health Albert Einstein Coll. Medicine, Bronx, N.Y., 1970-86, prof. emeritus, 1986; cons. to fed. and state govts. Co-author: The Sick Citadel, A Study of Academic Medicine, 1983; author articles on health policy and fin. Served with CIC AUS, 1 943-46. Recipient Exceptional Svc. award Bur. Budget, 1964; Ann. Career Svc. award Nat. Civil Svc. League, 1969; Brookings Instn. rsch. fellow, 1941; Who summer fellow, 1977. Assoc. fellow N.Y. Acad. Medicine (com. on medicine and society, chmn. ann. health conf. 1985); mem. APHA, Med. Health and Rsch. Assn., Assn. Am. Med. Colls., Am. Vets. Com. (pres. Washington 1949), Inst. Medicine/NAS, Harvard Club (Washington). Jewish (pres. temple). Home: Apt 623 3310 N Leisure World Blvd Silver Spring MD 20906-5664 Office: Albert Einstein Coll Medicine Bronx NY 10461

LEWIS, JACK (CECIL PAUL LEWIS), publishing executive, editor; b. North English, Iowa, Nov. 13, 1924; s. Cecil Howell and Winifred (Warner) L.; children—Dana Claudia, Brandon Paul, Scott Jay, Suzanne Marie. B.A., State U. Iowa, 1949. Publicist savs. bonds U.S. Treasury Dept., Des Moines, 1948-49; reporter Santa Ana (Calif.) Register, 1949-50; motion picture writer Monogram Pictures, 1950; reporter Daily Pilot, Costa Mesa, Calif., 1956-57; editor Challenge Pub., North Hollywood, Calif., 1957-60; pres. Gallant/Charger Publs. Inc, Capistrano Beach, Calif., 1960—; editor, pub. Gun World, 1960—. Author 8 novels, 25 other books, 11 TV shows, 7 motion pictures; pub. mags. Bow and Arrow Hunting, Horse and Horseman; editor 25 books; contbr. articles to mags. Served to lt. col. USMCR, 1942-46, 50-56, 58, 70. Decorated Bronze Star, Air medal (3), Meritorious Service medal, Navy Commendation medal. Mem. Writers Guild Am., U.S. Marine Corps Combat Corrs. Assn. (pres. 1970-71, 73-74, 80-81, chmn. bd. 1972-78), Sigma Nu, Sigma Delta Chi. Republican. Home: 405 Avenida Teresa San Clemente CA 92672-2234 Office: Gallant Charger Publs 34249 Camino Capistrano Capistrano Beach CA 92624

LEWIS, JAMES EARL, investment banker; b. Chgo., Aug. 1, 1939; s. J. Earl and Elsie L. (Danneberg) L.; m. Patricia Ann Martin, Jan. 19, 1980. BA, DePauw U., 1961; MBA, U. Chgo., 1966. Analyst Harris Trust & Savs. Bank, Chgo., 1966-68; v.p. Paine, Webber, Jackson & Curtis, Boston, 1968-70; mgr. corp. loan component Gen. Electric Credit Corp., Stamford, Conn., 1971-77; v.p. Rauscher Pierce Refsnes Inc., Dallas, 1978-82; sr. v.p., mgr. corp. fin. dept. First Oklahoma Bancorp. Inc., Dallas and Oklahoma City, 1982-84; v.p., mgr. corp. fin. group PNC Mcht. Banking Co., Phila., 1984-87; v.p., dir. corp. fin. Ferris & Co., Inc., Washington, 1987-88; v.p. Washington Sq. Capital Markets Inc., Bala Cynwyd, Pa., 1988-90; pres., founder Mid. Atlantic Capital, Wayne, Pa., 1990-94; founder, dir. Phila. Factors, Inc., 1993—; bd. dirs. Phila. Factors. With U.S. Army, 1962-64. Mem. Phila. Fin. Assn., Delaware Valley Venture Group, Orpheus Club. Home: 852 Briarwood Rd Newtown Square PA 19073-2620 Office: 175 Strafford Ave Ste 1 Wayne PA 19087-3317

LEWIS, JAMES ELDON, health care executive; b. Pontiac, Mich., Jan. 5, 1938; s. Wilbur Arthur and Mary Helen (Eatwell) L.; m. Anita L. Koplan, Sept. 28, 1988; children from previous marriage: James Eldon, Sara Ann. BA in Geography, Ea. Mich. U., 1961; MS in Urban and Econ. Geography, U. Ga., 1963, PhD in Urban and Econ. Geography, 1966. Urban geographer Gulf South Rsch. Inst., Baton Rouge, 1966-69; asst. prof. La. State U., 1966-69, U. Va., 1969-73; v.p., dir. Enviro-Med Inc., Washington, 1973-74; sr. profl. assoc. Inst. Medicine, NAS, 1974-77; interim dean, then dean Med. Coll. U. Okla., Tulsa, 1977-78; dir. Health Sci. Ctr. U. Okla., Washington, 1978-89; v.p., then sr. v.p. CDP Assocs. Inc., Rockville, Md., 1979-83; pres. Health Resources Devel. Group, 1979-83; sr. exec. officer, prof. dept. medicine, U. Ala., Birmingham, 1983-95, spl. asst. to pres., 1994—; cons. in field. Pres. Lupus Found. Am., 1987-88. Alumni Found. fellow U. Ga., 1964-66. Mem. Adminstrs. Internal Medicine (pres. 1990-91). Office: Office of Pres U Ala Birmingham AL 35294

LEWIS, JAMES HISTED, retired foreign service officer; b. Carbondale, Pa., Dec. 18, 1912; s. Edward Butts and Laura (Histed) L.; m. Betty Prater, Dec. 12, 1943; children—Jane, Marie, David, Jon. AB., George Washington U., 1935, A.M., 1939. Asst. in polit. sci. George Washington U., Washington, 1934-36; mem. staff div. trade agreements U.S. Dept. State, Washington, 1936-42; fgn. service aux. officer, spl. asst. amb. Am. Embassy, London, 1942-44; economist div. comml. policy U.S. Dept. State, Washington, 1944-45, sec. Sec. State's Staff Com., 1945-46, advisor econs. U.S. Del. of Paris Peace Conf. and Council Fgn. Ministers, 1946, chief Brit. Commonwealth br. div. comml. policy, 1947-49, with Office Brit. Commonwealth and No. European Affairs, 1949-54; mem. U.S. del. GATT trade negotiations, Annecy, France, 1949; head negotiator GATT trade negotiations, Torquay, England, 1950-51, Geneva, 1956, 61; commd. fgn. service officer U.S. Dept. State, Washington, 1954, 1st sec. Am. embassy and consul in London, 1954-57, counselor econ. affairs Am. embassy in Copenhagen, 1957-61, chief div. trade agreements, 1961-62, chief div. comml. policy and treaties, 1962-63, dep. dir. Office Internat. Trade, 1963-65, minister-counselor for econ. affairs U.S. mission to Geneva, also dep. head U.S. del. Kennedy round trade negotiations, 1965-67, dep. dir. gen. with personal rank of ambassador GATT Secretariat in Geneva, 1967-69, counselor Am. embassy in Bonn, Fed. Republic Germany, 1969-70, dep. amb. Am. embassy in Helsinki, 1970-73, ret., 1973; cons. multilateral trade matters, 1975—. Mem. Am. Fgn. Service Assn., Pi Gamma Mu, Delta Phi Epsilon. Presbyterian. Home: 8800 Clifford Ave Bethesda MD 20815-4745

LEWIS, JAMES LEE, JR., actuary; b. Toungoo, Burma, June 11, 1930; s. James Lee and Lilly (Ryden) L.; m. Tamra Dell Johns, June 30, 1954; children: James Lee III, David Alexander, Stephen John, Susan Kim, Michael Ryden. BA, U. Mich., 1952, MA, 1956. Actuary Lincoln Nat. Life Ins. Co., Ft. Wayne, Ind., 1956-74; sr. v.p. Mutual Security Life Ins. Co., Ft. Wayne, 1974-83; v.p., actuary Montlife Corp., Itaska, Ill., 1983-84; v.p., sr. actuary Covenant Life Ins. Co., Phila., 1984-94; actuary provident Mut. Life Ins. Co., Phila., 1994—. Pres. Associated Chs., Ft. Wayne., 1982; chmn. Project Commitment, Ft. Wayne, 1969. With U.S. Army, 1952-54. Fellow Soc. of Actuaries (com. chair 1988-91); mem. Am. Acad. of Actuaries (charter), Phila. Actuaries Club. Baptist. Avocations: racquetball, barbershop singing.

LEWIS, JEROME A., petroleum company executive, investment banker; b. Wichita, Kans., 1927; married. BA in Engring., U. Okla. Geologist Shell Oil Co., 1950-51; pres. Lewmont Drilling, Inc., 1951-65, Border Exploration Co., 1965-68; pres., chmn. bd., chief exec. officer Petro-Lewis Corp., 1968-87; pres. Princeps Ptnrs., Inc., 1987—; also dir. DenverAmerican Petrol. 1991—. Bd. dirs. Denver Leadership Found., Trinity Forum, Downing St. Found. Mem. Ind. Petroleum Assn. Am., Oil Investment Inst. (founding gov.), World Pres.' Orgn., Am. Assn. Petroleum Geologists, Am. Petroleum Inst., Chief Execs. Orgn. Office: Princeps Ptnrs Inc 1775 Sherman St #1450 Denver CO 80203-1100

LEWIS, JERROLD See **BOCK, JERRY**

LEWIS, JERRY, congressman; b. Oct. 21, 1934. BA, UCLA, 1956. Former underwriter life ins. underwriter; field rep. for former U.S. Rep. Jerry Pettis; mem. Calif. State Assembly, 1968-78; vice chmn. rules com., chmn. subcom. on air quality; mem. 96th-103rd Congresses from 35th (now 40th) Calif. dist., 1979—; chmn. appropriation com. Va.-HUD subscom., mem. defense subcom., select com. on intelligence, chmn. subcom. on human intelligence. Presbyterian. Office: 2112 Rayburn Bldg Washington DC 20515

LEWIS, JERRY (JOSEPH LEVITCH), comedian; b. Newark, Mar. 16, 1926; s. Danny and Mona Levitch; m. Patti Palmer, 1944 (div.); children: Gary, Ron, Scott, Chris, Anthony, Joseph; m. Sandra Pitnick, 1983. Edn., Irvington (N.J.) High Sch.; DHL (hon.), Mercy Coll., 1987. Prof. cinema U. So. Calif.; pres. JAS Prodns., Inc., P.J. Prodns., Inc. Began as entertainer with record routine at Catskill (N.Y.) hotel; formed comedy team with Dean Martin, 1946-56; performed as a single, 1956—; formed Jerry Lewis Prodns. Inc., prod., dir., writer, star, 1956; films include: My Friend Irma, 1949, My Friend Irma Goes West, 1950, At War with the Army, 1950, That's My Boy, 1950, Sailor Beware, 1951, The Stooge, 1952, Jumping Jacks, 1952, Scared Stiff, 1953, The Caddy, 1953, Money From Home, 1953, Three Ring Circus, 1954, Living it Up, 1954, You're Never Too Young, 1955, Artists and Models, 1955, Partners, 1956, Hollywood or Bust, 1956, The Delicate Delinquent, 1957, The Sad Sack, 1957, The Geisha Boy, 1958, Rockabye Baby, 1958, Don't Give Up the Ship, 1959, Li'l Abner, 1959, Visit to a Small Planet, 1960, The Bellboy, 1960, Cinderfella, 1960, The Ladies Man, 1961, It's Only Money, 1962, The Errand Boy, 1962, It's a Mad, Mad, Mad, Mad World, 1963, The Nutty Professor, 1963, Who's Minding The Store, 1963, The Patsy, 1964, The Disorderly Orderly, 1964, The Family Jewels, 1965, Boeing-Boeing, 1965, Three On A Couch, 1965, Way ... Way ... Out, 1966, The Big Mouth, 1967, Don't Raise the Bridge, Lower the Water, 1968, Hook, Line and Sinker, 1969, One More Time, 1969, Which Way To the Front?, 1970, Hardly Working, 1981, King of Comedy, 1983, Smorgasbord, 1983, Slapstick, 1984, To Catch A Cop, 1984, How Did You Get In?, 1985, Cookie, 1989, Arrowtooth Waltz, 1991, Mr. Saturday Night, 1992; appeared on Broadway in Damn Yankees, 1995, on tour, 1995—; author: The Total Film-Maker, 1971, Jerry Lewis in Person, 1982; principal TV appearances include master of ceremonies ann. Labor Day Muscular Dystrophy Telethon, 1966—. Comdr. Order of Arts & Letters, France, 1984; nat. chmn. Muscular Dystrophy Assn. Recipient most promising male star in TV award Motion Picture Daily's 2nd Ann. TV poll, 1950, (as team), one of TV's 10 money making stars award Motion Picture Herald - Fame poll, 1951, 53-54, 57, best comedy team award Motion Picture Daily's 16th annual radio poll, 1951-53, Nobel Peace Prize nomination, 1978. Mem. Screen Producers Guild, Screen Dirs. Guild, Screen Writers Guild. Office: Jerry Lewis Films

Inc 3160 W Sahara Ave # 16C Las Vegas NV 89102-6003 also: William Morris Agy Inc 151 S El Camino Dr Beverly Hills CA 90212-2704

LEWIS, JERRY LEE, country-rock singer, musician; b. Ferriday, La., Sept. 29, 1935; s. Elmo and Mary Ethel L.; m. Kerrie Lee; children: Phoebe, Jerry Lee Jr. Student, Waxahachie (Tex.) Bible Inst. Rock and roll performer, recs. on Sun Records label, Whole Lotta Shakin' Goin' On, 1957, Great Balls of Fire, Mercury/Phonogram, 1963-78, Elektra Records, 1978-81; shifted to country and rock repertoire: recs. include Golden Hits, Odd Man In, Country Class, Roll Over Beethoven, High Heel Sneakers, Jerry Lee Lewis, Southern Roots, Good Rockin' Tonight, Taste of Country, Sunday After Church, Rural Route #1, Drinkin Wine Spo Dee O Dee, Golden Cream of Country, Monsters, Old Tyme Country Music, Rockin with From the Vaults of Sun; appeared in films American Hot Wax, Disc Jockey Jamboree, High School Confidential; albums include Sold Gold, 1986, The Killer Rocks On, 1987, Rocket, 1988, 1992, Killer: The Mercury Years Vol. One, Vol. Two, Vol. Three, 1989, Great Balls of Fire, 1989, Whole Lotta Shakin' Goin' On, 1992, Rockin' My Life Away, 1992, Heartbreak, 1992, All Killer, No Filler: The Anthology, 1993. Named to Rock and Roll Hall of Fame, 1986.

LEWIS, JERRY M., psychiatrist, educator; b. Utica, N.Y., Aug. 18, 1924; s. Jerry M. and Margaret (Miller) L.; m. Patsy Ruth Price, Sept. 24, 1949; children: Jerry M., Cynthia Lewis-Reynolds, Nancy Minns, Tom. MD, Southwestern Med. Sch., Dallas, 1951. Diplomate Am. Bd. Psychiatry and Neurology. Staff psychiatrist Timberlawn Psychiat. Hosp., Dallas, 1957-63, chief women's svc., 1963-66, chief adolescent svcs., 1966-70, dir. profl. edn., 1970-79, psychiatrist-in-chief, 1979-88, dir. rsch., 1988-93; dir. rsch. and tng. Timberlawn Psychiat. Rsch. Found., Dallas, 1967-88, sr. rsch. psychiatrist, 1988—; clin. prof. psychiatry, family practice and cmty. medicine Southwestern Med. Sch.; cons. in psychiatry Baylor U. Med. Ctr., Dallas. Author: No Single Thread, 1976, How's Your Family, 1978, To Be a Therapist, 1979, The Long Struggle, 1983, Swimming Upstream: Teaching Psychotherapy in a Biological Era, 1991, The Monkey-Rope, 1995. Served with USN, 1943-45. Fellow Am. Coll. Psychiatrists (pres. 1985), Am. Psychiat. Assn., So. Psychiat. Assn. (pres. 1979); mem. Group for Advancement of Psychiatry (pres. 1987), Benjamin Rush Soc. (pres. 1994-95), AMA, Tex. Med. Assn. Home: PO Box 270789 Dallas TX 75227-0789

LEWIS, JESSICA HELEN (MRS. JACK D. MYERS), physician, educator; b. Harpswell, Maine, Oct. 26, 1917; d. Warren Harmon and Margaret (Reed) L.; m. Jack D. Myers, Aug. 31, 1946; children: Judith Duane (dec.), John Lewis, Jessica Reed, Elizabeth Reed, Margaret Anne. A.B., Goucher Coll., 1938; M.D., Johns Hopkins U., 1942. USPHS Research fellow U. N.C., 1947-48, research assoc. dept. physiology, 1948-55; assoc. dept. medicine Duke Med. Sch., 1951-55; research assoc. dept. medicine U. Pitts., 1955-58, faculty, 1958-92, research assoc. prof., 1965-70, prof. medicine, 1970-92, prof. medicine emeritus, 1992—; dir. research Central Blood Bank Pitts., 1969-74, v.p., 1974-85, med. dir. and sr. v.p., 1985-89, sci. dir., sr. v.p., 1985-92, sr. v.p., med. and sci. dir. emeritus, 1992—; dir. Hemophilia Center Western Pa., 1973-81. Author: Comparative Hemostasis in Vertebrates, also more than 250 sci. papers. Mem. Am. Physiol. Soc., Am. Soc. Clin. Investigation, Am. Fedn. Clin. Research, Soc. for Exptl. Biol. Medicine, Internat. Soc. Hematology, Am. Soc. Hematology, Sigma Xi. Rsch. on mechanism blood coagulation, fibrinolysis, hemorrhagic and thrombotic diseases and comparative vertebrate coagulation. Home: Dithridge House 220 N Dithridge St Apt 900 Pittsburgh PA 15213-1424 Office: Central Blood Bank Pitts 812 Fifth Ave Pittsburgh PA 15219

LEWIS, JOHN BRUCE, lawyer; b. Poplar Bluff, Mo., Aug. 12, 1947; s. Evan Bruce and Hilda Kathryn (Kassebaum) L.; m. Diane F. Grossman, July 23, 1977; children: Samantha Brooking, Ashley Denning. BA, U. Mo., 1969, JD, 1972; LLM in Labor and Employment Law, Columbia U., 1978; diploma, Nat. Inst. Trial Advocacy, 1982. Bar: Mo. 1972, U.S. Ct. Appeals (8th cir.) 1973, U.S. Dist. Ct. (ea. dist.) Mo. 1974, U.S. Dist. Ct. (no. dist.) Ohio 1979, Ohio 1980, U.S. Ct. Appeals (6th cir.) 1982, U.S. Dist. Ct. (ea. dist.) Mich. 1983, U.S. Ct. Appeals (3d cir.) 1987, U.S. Supreme Ct. 1987, U.S. Dist. Ct. (no. dist.) Calif. 1987, U.S. Ct. Appeals (7th cir.) 1990. Assoc. Millar, Schaefer & Ebling, St. Louis, 1972-77, Squire, Sanders & Dempsey, Cleve., 1979-85; ptnr. Arter & Hadden, Cleve., 1985—; chair Labor and Employment Law Practice Group, 1987—; lectr. in field. Contbr. articles to legal jours. Mem. Cleve. Council on World Affairs. Mem. ABA (sec. labor and employment law, com. EEO law, comm. law forum), Ohio State Bar Assn. (sec. labor and employment law), Greater Cleve. Bar Assn. (sec. labor law), St. Louis Met. Bar Assn., Am. Law Inst., Def. Rsch. Inst., Selden Soc., Ohio C. of C. (labor adv. com.). Office: Arter & Hadden 925 Euclid Ave Cleveland OH 44115

LEWIS, JOHN CLARK, JR., manufacturing company executive; b. Livingston, Mont., Oct. 15, 1935; s. John Clark and Louise A. (Anderson) L.; m. Carolyn Jean Keesling, Sept. 4, 1960; children: Robert, Anne, James. BS, Fresno (Calif.) State U., 1957. With Service Bur. Corp., El Segundo, Calif., 1960-70, Computer Scis. Corp., 1970; with Xerox Corp., El Segundo, 1970-77, pres. bus. systems div., 1977; pres. Amdahl Corp., Sunnyvale, Calif., 1983-87, chief exec. officer, 1983—, chmn., 1987—. Served with USNR, 1957-60. Roman Catholic. Office: Amdahl Corp PO Box 3470 1250 E Arques Ave Sunnyvale CA 94808-4730*

LEWIS, JOHN D., financial services company executive; b. 1941. Mng. ptnr. Arthur Anderson and Co., N.C., S.C., 1978-90; mng. ptnr., CFO Arthur Anderson and Co., 1990-93; mng. ptnr. Arthur Anderson and Co. Societe Coop., 1993—. Office: Arthur Anderson & Co 69 W Washington St Chicago IL 60602-3004*

LEWIS, JOHN FRANCIS, lawyer; b. Oberlin, Ohio, Oct. 25, 1932; s. Ben W. and Gertrude D. Lewis; m. Catharine Monroe, June 15, 1957; children: Ben M., Ian A., Catharine G., William H. B.A., Amherst Coll., 1955; J.D., U. Mich., 1958. Bar: Ohio 1958, U.S. Dist. Ct. (no dist.) Ohio 1959, U.S. Supreme Ct. 1973. Assoc. firm Squire, Sanders & Dempsey, Cleve., 1958-67; ptnr. Squire, Sanders & Dempsey, 1967—, mng. ptnr. Cleve. office, 1985—. Co-author: Baldwin's Ohio School Law, 1980-91, Ohio Collective Bargaining Law, 1983. Trustee, chmn. Case Western Res. U.; trustee Playhouse Sq. Found., chmn., 1980-85; mem. Cleve. Tomorrow; mem. exec. com. Greater Cleve. Growth Assn., Univ. Circle, Inc., New Cleve. Campaign; trustee Cleve. Commn. on Higher Edn., Musical Arts Assn.; hon. chmn. Found. for Sch. Bus. Mgmt., Leadership Cleve., 1977-78. Recipient Malcolm Daisley Labor-Mgmt. Rels. award, 1991, Tree of Life award Jewish Nat. Fund, 1993, Nat. Conf. award, 1995. Mem. Cleve. Bar Assn., Ohio Bar Assn., ABA (com. pub. edn.), Nat. Sch. Bd. Assn., Nat. Orgn. Legal Problems (past pres.), Ohio Assn. Sch. Bus. Ofcls. (hon. life), Fifty Club of Cleve., Ohio Council Sch. Bd. Attys. Episcopalian. Home: 2001 Chestnut Hills Dr Cleveland OH 44106-4601 Office: Squire Sanders & Dempsey 4900 Society Tower 127 Public Sq Cleveland OH 44114-1216

LEWIS, JOHN FURMAN, lawyer, oil company executive; b. Fort Worth, Apr. 24, 1934; s. Ben B. and Minnie W. (Field) L.; children from previous marriage: Joyce Ann, George Field, William Patrick; m. Virginia Edmonds Kingsley. Student, Tex. Christian U., summer 1955; B.A. in Econs., Rice U., 1956; J.D. with honors, U. Tex., 1962; postgrad., Princeton U., 1965-66; M.B.A., Bowling Green State U., 1971. Bar: Tex. 1962, U.S. Dist. Ct. 1965, U.S. Supreme Ct. 1967, Ohio 1968, U.S. Ct. Mil. Appeals 1971, Okla. 1987. Atty. Atlantic Richfield Co., 1962-67; with Marathon Oil Co., Findlay, Ohio, 1967-86, gen. atty., 1978, sr. atty., 1978-81, assoc. gen. counsel, 1981-83, v.p., gen. counsel, 1983-84, v.p., gen. counsel sec., 1985-86; sr. v.p., gen. counsel The Williams Cos., Tulsa, 1986—; mem. adv. bd. Internat. Oil and Gas Ednl. Ctr. of Southwestern Legal Found. Contbr. articles to profl. jours. Mem. exec. com., trustee United Way of Hancock County, Findlay, Ohio, 1984-86; bd. dirs. No-We-Oh coun. Camp Fire, Inc., Findlay, 1974-86, Okla. Green Country coun., Tulsa, 1987-89; mem. Arts and Humanities Coun., Tulsa, 1991-95. Lt. (j.g.) USN, 1956-59. Mem. ABA (subcom. chmn. 1984-85), Tex. Bar Assn., Am. Petroleum Inst. (lawyer-adviser mktg. com. 1982-84, gen. law com. 1983—), Ohio Bar Assn., Okla. Bar Assn., Tulsa County Bar Assn., U. Tex. Law Sch. Alumni Assn. (bd. dirs. 1994—). Republican. Avocations: jogging, tennis, golf. Office: Williams Cos 1 Williams Ctr PO Box 2400 Tulsa OK 74172-2400

LEWIS, JOHN HARDY, JR., lawyer; b. East Orange, N.J., Oct. 31, 1936; s. John Hardy and Sarah (Ripley) L.; m. Mary Ann Spurgeon, June 25, 1960; children: Peter, David, Mark. AB magna cum laude, Princeton U., 1958; JD cum laude, Harvard U., 1961. Bar: Pa. 1962. Assoc. Morgan, Lewis & Bockius, Phila., 1965-69, ptnr., 1969—. trustee Blair Acad., Blairstown, N.J.; rector's warden All Saints' Ch., Wynnewood, Pa. Served to major USAF, 1962-65. Fellow Am. Coll. Trial Lawyers. Home: 1000 Green Valley Rd Bryn Mawr PA 19010-1912 Office: Morgan Lewis & Bockius 2000 One Logan Sq Philadelphia PA 19103

LEWIS, JOHN LEEMAN, JR., obstetrician, gynecologist; b. San Antonio, June 5, 1929; s. John Leeman and Lois Black (Perry) L.; student U. Tex. at Austin, spring, 1948; B.A., Harvard, 1952, M.D. (Frederick Sheldon Traveling fellow 1952-53, Nat. scholar 1953-57), 1957; m. Jane Darling Davis, July 30, 1955 (div. 1976); children—Anne Darling, Elizabeth Perry, Katherine Folsom; m. Susan Vere Paris, Oct. 16, 1976 (div. 1981); m. Patricia Ann Mazzola, May 8, 1984 (div. 1994). Diplomate Am. Bd. Ob-Gyn (dir. 1971—, cert. spl. competence gynecologic oncology). Intern Mass. Gen. Hosp., Boston, 1957-58, resident, 1958-59, 61-62; clin. asso. endocrinology Nat. Cancer Inst., Bethesda, Md., 1959-61; resident Boston Lying-in Hosp., 1962-65, Free Hosp. for Women, Brookline, 1962-65; sr. investigator surgery br. Nat. Cancer Inst., Bethesda, Md., 1965-67; assoc. attending obstetrician and gynecologist Presbyn. Hosp., N.Y.C., July-Dec. 1967, also asso. prof. obstetrics and gynecology Coll. Phys. and Surgs. Columbia; pvt. practice medicine, specializing in obstetrics and gynecology, N.Y.C., 1967—; chief gynecology service Meml. Hosp. for Cancer and Allied Diseases, N.Y.C., 1968-90, attending surgeon, 1990—; chmn. instl. rev. bd., 1984—; assoc. prof. Cornell U. Med. Coll. at N.Y.C., 1968-71, prof., 1971—; assoc. attending obstetrician and gynecology N.Y. Lying-in Hosp., N.Y.C., 1968-71, attending obstetrician and gynecologist, 1971—; mem. Sloan Kettering Inst. Cancer Rsch., 1971—; v.p. Internat. Gynecologic Cancer Soc., 1993—; chmn. Gynecologic Cancer Found., 1994—; mem. editorial bd. Jour. Am. Coll. Surgeons, 1994—. Served with USPHS, 1959-67. Recipient Alumni award Harvard Med. Sch., 1957. Mem. Harvard Med. Alumni Assn. (councilor 1969-70). Democrat. Episcopalian. Clubs: Griffis Faculty (N.Y.C.), Englewood Field Club (N.J.); Harvard (N.Y.C.). Assoc. editor Obstetrical and Gynecological Survey. Contbr. articles to profl. jours. Home: 1175 York Ave New York NY 10021-7169 Office: 1275 York Ave New York NY 10021-6007

LEWIS, JOHN MILTON, cable television company executive; b. nr. Slocomb, Ala., Mar. 29, 1931; s. Phil Truman and Vermell Beatrice (Avery) L.; grad. high sch.; m. Mary Lee Robledo, June 9, 1951; children: Janet Lee, Lee Michael. With Gulf Power Co., Panama City, Fla., 1949-56; self employed vehicle svc. co., Panama City, 1956-58; v.p., bd. dir., Burnup & Sims of Fla., Inc., West Palm Beach, 1958-70; pres., bd. dir. Wometco Cable Corp., Miami, Fla., 1970-94; pres., CEO SPI Holding, Inc., Richardson, Tex., 1988-89, also bd. dirs.; CEO Spectradyne, Inc., Richardson, 1988-89; pres. Key Capital Group, Inc., Miami, 1995—; bd. dirs. Allied Waste Mgmt., Phoenix; cons. in field. Recipient Tower Club award So. TV Assn. Mem. Cable TV Pioneers, Masons. Republican. Office: Key Capital Group Inc PO Box 561009 9500 S Dadeland Blvd Ste 603 Miami FL 33156

LEWIS, JOHN P., bank executive; b. 1936. With Interfirst Bank, Dallas; mng. dir. Mason-Best Co., Dallas, 1985-87; with Ameri Serv, Dallas, 1987—, now CEO; pres., CEO Lewis Partners, Dallas, TX, 1992—. Office: Lewis Partners 13355 Noel Rd Ste 2225 Dallas TX 75240-6657*

LEWIS, JOHN R., congressman; b. Pike County, Ala., Feb. 21, 1940; m. Lillian Miles, 1968; 1 child, John-Miles. BA, Am. Bapt. Theol. Sem., Nashville, 1961, Fisk U., 1963. Mem. City Coun., Atlanta, 1982-86, 100th-104th Congresses from 5th Ga. dist., Washington, 1986—; former chief dep. majority whip. Civil rights leader; mem. Martin Luther King Ctr. for Social Change, African Am. Inst., Robert F. Kennedy Meml. Office: US Ho of Reps 229 Cannon Bldg Washington DC 20515-0003*

LEWIS, JOHN ROBERT, zoo administrator; b. Ironton, Mo., Aug. 17, 1952; s. Bob G. Lewis and Joan (Burlingame) Shank; m. Deborah June Holley, Jan. 15, 1972; children: Jill Elizabeth, Ian James, Robert Thomas. BS in Animal Sci., NE La. U., 1974, postgrad., 1974-77; postgrad., St. Thomas Coll., 1981-84. Primate supr. La. Purchase Garden and Zoo, Monroe, 1974-76, zoo supr., 1976-77; curator Minn. Zoo, Apple Valley, 1977-80, sr. curator, 1980-83, asst. dir., 1983-86; dir. John Ball Zoo, Grand Rapids, Mich., 1986—. Author: Clouded Leopard Studbook, 1982, vol. II, 1987; several TV appearances. Mem. Internat. Union for Conservation Nature and Natural Resources (cat specialist group 1984—). Avocations: photography, fly-tying and fishing, gardening. also: John Ball Zoological Garden 1300 W Fulton St Grand Rapids MI 49504-6100

LEWIS, JOHN WILSON, political science educator; b. King County, Wash., Nov. 16, 1930; s. Albert Lloyd and Clara (Lewis) Seeman; m. Jacquelyn Clark, June 19, 1954; children: Cynthia, Stephen, Amy. Student, Deep Springs Coll., 1947-49; AB with highest honors, UCLA, 1953, MA, 1958, PhD, 1962; hon. degree, Morningside Coll., 1969, Lawrence U., 1986. Asst. prof. govt. Cornell U., 1961-64, assoc. prof., 1964-68; prof. polit. sci. Stanford U., 1968—, William Haas prof. Chinese politics, 1972—, co-dir. arms control and disarmament program, 1971-83, co-dir. NE Asia U.S. Forum on Internat. Policy, 1980-90, co-dir. Ctr. for Internat. Security and Arms Control, 1983-91, sr. fellow, 1991—, dir. Project on Peace and Cooperation in the Asian-Pacific Region; chmn. Internat. Strategic Inst., 1983-89; chmn. joint com. on contemporary China Social Sci. Rsch. Coun.-Am. Coun. Learned Socs., 1976-79; mng. dir. Generation Ventures, 1994—; former vice chmn., bd. dirs. Nat. Com. on U.S.-China Rels.; cons. Senate Select Com. on Intelligence, 1977-81, Los Alamos Nat. Lab., Lawrence Livermore Nat. Lab., Dept. of Def., 1994-96; mem. Def. Policy Bd., 1994-96; chmn. com. advanced study in China Com. Scholarly Comm. with People's Republic of China, 1979-82; mem. com. on internat. security and arms control Nat. acad. Scis., 1980-83; organizer first univ. discussion arms control and internat. security matters Chinese People's Inst. Fgn. Affairs, 1978, first academic exch. agreement Dem. People's Repb. of Korea, 1988; negotiator first univ. tng. and exch. agreement People's Rep. of China, 1978. Author: Leadership in Communist China, 1963, Major Doctrines of Communist China, 1964, Policy Networks and the Chinese Policy Process, 1986; co-author: The United States in Vietnam, 1967, Modernization by Design, 1969, China Builds the Bomb, 1988, Uncertain Partners: Stalin, Mao, and the Korean War, 1993, China's Strategic Seapower: The Policits of Force Modernization in the Nuclear Era, 1994; editor: The City in Communist China, 1971, Party Leadership and Revolutionary Power in China, 1970, Peasant Rebellion and Communist Revolution in Asia, 1974; contbr.: Congress and Arms Control, 1978, China's Quest for Independence, 1979, others; mem. editl. bd. Chinese Law and Govt., China Quar., Survey, The Pacific Rev. Served with USN, 1954-57. Mem. Assn. Asian Studies, Am. Polit. Sci. Assn., Coun. Fgn. Rels. Home: 541 San Juan St Stanford CA 94305-8432 Office: Stanford U 320 Galvez St Stanford CA 94305-6105

LEWIS, JORDAN DAVID, management consultant, author, international speaker, educator; b. Chgo., Aug. 9, 1937; s. Murray Robert and Ruth (Weinstein) L.; m. Lynn Lopata, Sept. 20, 1964; children: Matthew Michael, Katherine Anne. B.S.Engring. in Physics., U. Mich., 1960, B.S. Engring. in Math, 1960, M.S. Engring. in Instrumentation (fellow), 1963, M.S. Engring. in Nuclear Engring., 1963, Ph.D. in Thermonuclear Physics, 1966. Instr. physics U. Mich. at Dearborn, 1962-64, research asst., 1964-66; with Battelle Devel. Corp., Columbus, Ohio, 1966-72; asst. mgr. devel. dept. Battelle Devel. Corp., 1968-70, mgr. gen. operations, 1970-72; dir. applied tech. programs Batelle Columbus Labs., Columbus, 1972; dir. presdl. tech. and econ. policy program Nat. Bur. Standards, Washington, 1973-77; exec. dir. A.T. Internat., Washington, 1977-79; mgmt. cons., 1979—; sr. lectr. Wharton Sch., U. Pa.; U.S. del. to OECD, Paris; advisor strategic alliance to nat. govts. and internat. corps.; fellow World Econ. Forum, Geneva, 1993; chmn. Fed. Task Force on Energy Intensive Products, 1975. Author: Partnerships for Profit: Structuring and Managing Strategic Alliances, 1990, The Connected Corporation: How Leading Firms Win Through Customer-Supplier Alliances, 1995; editor: (with Lynn L. Lewis) Industrial Approaches to Urban Problems, 1972; guest columnist Wall St. Jour., N.Y. Times; contbr. articles to newspapers and profl. jours. Co-chmn. Columbus Outdoor Summer Concerts, 1968-70; chmn. bd. dirs. Columbus Inner-City Econ. Devel. Corp., 1969-71. AEC fellow, 1964-66. Fellow AAAS (mem. council; chmn. indsl. sci. sect. 1975); mem. Am. Econs. Assn., Sigma Xi. Home: 3707 33rd Pl NW Washington DC 20008-3201

LEWIS, JULIETTE, actress; b. Fernando Valley, Calif., June 21, 1973; d. Geoffrey and Glenis Batley L. TV appearences include Homefires (Showtime miniseries), I Married Dora, 1988, A Family For Joe, 1990; TV Movies include Too Young To Die, 1989; films include My Stepmother is an Alien, 1988, Meet the Hollowheads, 1989, National Lampoons Christmas Vacation, 1989, Cape Fear, 1991 (Academy Award nomination best supporting actress 1991), Crooked Hearts, 1991, Husbands and Wives, 1992, Kalifornia, 1993, That Night, 1993, What's Eating Gilbert Grape, 1993, Romeo is Bleeding, 1994, Natural Born Killers, 1994, Mixed Nuts, 1994, Strange Days, 1995. Office: William Morris Agy 151 S El Camino Dr Beverly Hills CA 90212-2704*

LEWIS, JULIUS, lawyer; b. Omaha, Nov. 29, 1931; s. Aaron and Dorothy (Gendler) L. B.A., U. Chgo., 1950, M.A., 1954; LL.B., Yale U., 1957. Bar: Ill. 1957. Assoc. Sonnenschein Nath & Rosenthal, Chgo., 1957-65, ptnr., 1965—; bd. dirs. Juno Lighting, Inc., Des Plaines, Ill., The Fremont Found., O.L. and Hazel Rhoades Fund. Trustee Art Inst. Chgo.; pres., bd. dirs. Alliance Française de Chgo., 1983—. Mem. Chgo. Bar Assn., Legal Club of Chgo., Law Club of Chgo., Casino Club, Racquet Club, Yale Club N.Y. Democrat. Office: Sonnenschein Nath & Rosenthal 233 S Wacker Dr Ste 8000 Chicago IL 60606

LEWIS, KATHRYN HUXTABLE, pediatrician; b. Lakewood, Ohio, July 23, 1934; d. Harold Stafford and Otillie Louise (May) H.; m. Samuel T. Lewis III, Apr. 8, 1967 (dec. Sept. 1994); children: Samuel T. IV, Stephen A., Anne E. Student, Cornell U., 1952-55; MD, Yale U., 1959; MPH, Johns Hopkins U., 1964. Diplomate Nat. Bd. Med. Examiners, Am. Bd. Pediatrics. Intern Univ. Hosps., Cleve., 1959-60, resident in pediatrics, 1961-62, chief resident in pediatrice, 1962-63; resident in pediatrict Children's Hosp. of Phila., 1960-61, Cleve. Met. Gen. Hosp., 1961-62; tchg. fellow in pediatrics Western Res. U., Cleve., 1962-63, sr. instr. dept. pediatrics, 1965-67, sr. clin. instr. dept. preventive medicine, 1965-66, sr. instr. dept. preventive medicine, 1966-67; tchg. fellow in pediatrics Johns Hopkins U., Balt., 1963-64; rsch. assoc. Sch. Hygiene and Pub. Health Johns Hopkins U., Lahore, Pakistan, 1964-65; tchg. assoc. Ford Found., Lahore, 1964-65; clin. asst. prof. dept. pediatrics/dept. preventive medicine U. Pitts. Sch. Medicine, 1967-75; asst. dir. out-patient dept. Children's Hosp. of Pitts., 1967-75; dir. pediatric clinics ambulatory svcs. Cleve. Met. Gen. Hosp., 1966-67; cons. in field.; sch. physician Tyrone Area Bd. Edn., 1976—; dir. Pediatric Outpatient Ctr. Tyrone Hosp., 1975-92, Pediatric Outpatient Ctr. Geisinger Tyrone divsn., 1992—. Contbr. articles to profl. jours. Recipient Disting. Alumni award in sci. Lakewood H.S., 1993. Fellow Am. Acad. Pediatrics, APHA ; mem. Pa. Med. Soc., Assn. for Ambulatory Pediatric Svcs., Phi Beta Kappa. Office: Geisinger Med Group 1 Hospital Dr Tyrone PA 16686

LEWIS, KIRK MCARTHUR, lawyer; b. Schenectady, N.Y., Jan. 3, 1957; s. David MacArthur and Eleanor Burrows (Smith) L.; m. Barbara Jean Lewis, June 12, 1982; children: John Christopher, Kerry Elizabeth. BS, Cornell U., 1979; JD, Syracuse U., 1985. Bar: N.Y. 1986, U.S. Dist. Ct. (no. dist.) N.Y. 1988, U.S. Dist. Ct. (ea. dist.) N.Y. 1991, U.S. Ct. Appeals (2d cir.) 1989. Jud. clk to Hon. Conrad K. Cyr U.S. Dist. Ct. Maine, Bangor, 1985-87; assoc. DeGraff, Foy, Holt, Harris, Mealey & Kunz, Albany, N.Y., 1987-93, ptnr., 1993—. Bd. dirs., v.p., pres. Schenectady (N.Y.) Assn. for Retarded Citizens, 1990—. Mem. ABA, N.Y. State Bar Assn. Home: 30 Washington Rd Scotia NY 12302 Office: DeGraff Foy Holt Harris Mealey & Kunz 90 State St Albany NY 12207

LEWIS, LANIGHTA WEST, rehabilitation nurse; b. Johnson, Vt., Feb. 9, 1932; d. Trefley W. and Emma (Wildes) West; m. Donald E. Lewis, Nov. 9, 1955; children: Eric Patrick, Paula Lewis Hegner, Anita Lewis Carlsson, Scott Christopher. Diploma, Gifford Meml. Hosp., Randolph, Vt., 1955; cert. in drug/alcohol rehab., St. Louis U.; student, Orlando (Fla.) Tech. Coll.; cert. in profl. counseling, Internat. Loss Control Inst., St. Paul. Lic. risk mgr., Fla.; cert. ins. rehab. specialist, Fla.; cert. case mgr., ins. rehab. specialist. With Gifford Meml. Hosp., 1955-63; house supr. Holiday Hosp., Orlando, 1964-68; nurse Ctr. for Nursing, 1968-73; with Mid Fla. Ctr. Alcoholism, Orlando, 1971-73; asst. adminstr. Extendicare Subacute Facility, 1971-73; with Orlando Regional Hosp. and Kissimee (Fla.) Meml. Hosp., 1973-75; health care risk mgmt./rehab. specialist St. Paul Fire & Marine Ins. Co., Maitland, Fla., 1975-88; founder, pres., CEO, rehab. specialist Caduceus Cons., Inc., Orlando, 1988—. Author: (with others) Nursing Skills Text Book, 1975; contbr. articles to nursing jours. Mem. adv. bd. Lucerne Spinal Cord Ctr. Named to Nat. Disting. Svc. Registry, 1989. Mem. ANA, Rehab. Nurses Assn., Women for Responsible Legislation, Fla. Nursing Assn. (ho. of dels.), Case Mgmt. Soc., Fla. Nurses Assn., Ctrl. Fla. Rehab. Nurses Assn. (mem. govtl. affairs com.), Physician Nurses Assn. Home: 410 Bywater Dr Orlando FL 32839-2961

LEWIS, LARRY L., human resources specialist company executive; b. 1945. With Homefinders Inc., Jackson, Miss., 1970-90; pres. People Lease Inc., Jackson, Miss., 1984—. With U.S. Army, 1968-70. Office: People Lease Inc 4735 Old Canton Rd Jackson MS 39236*

LEWIS, LARRY LYNN, college official, minister, denominational official; b. Mexico, Mo., Jan. 27, 1935; s. Artie Francis and Mary Lue (Whiteside) L.; m. Betty Jo Cockerell, Feb. 28, 1964; children—Janet Lynn, Christy Ann, Mark Ray. A.A., Hannibal-LaGrange Coll., 1954; B.A., U. Mo., 1956; B.D., Southwestern Bapt. Sem., 1960, M.R.E., 1960; D.Ministry, Luther Rice Sem., 1978. Ordained to ministry Southern Bapt. Conv., 1954; pastor Parsons Bapt. Ch., Columbus, Ohio, 1961-66, Delaware Valley Bapt. Ch., Willingboro, N.J., 1966-71; dir. religious edn. Bapt. Conv. Pa./South Jersey, Harrisburg, Pa., 1971-74; pastor Tower Grove Bapt. Ch., St. Louis, 1974-81; pres. Hannibal-LaGrange Coll., Hannibal, Mo., 1981-87, pres. Home Mission Bd. off So. Bapt. Conv., 1987—; minister edn., youth Tri-Village Bapt. Ch., Columbus, 1961-62; pub. sch. tchr. Columbus Pub. Sch., 1962-63; ch. growth cons. Bapt. Sunday Sch. Bd., Nashville, 1971-74; pres. Tower Grove Christian Sch., 1978-81; pres. Mo. Bapt. Pastors Conf., 1979; v.p. Southern Bapt. Pastors Conf., Southern Bapt. Conv., 1980. Bd. dirs. Hannibal YMCA. Author: The Bus Ministry, 1971, The Church Planter's Handbook, 1992; (with others) Outreach with Church Buses, 1973; Organize to Evangelize, 1980. Editor: Walking with God, 1972. Contbr. articles to various ch. mags. Mem. Mo. Edn. Assn., Hist. Hannibal Assn., Hannibal C. of C. (pres. 1985). Lodge: Hannibal Rotary. Avocation: farming. Home: 319 Nimblewill Way SW Lilburn GA 30247-6517 Office: So Bapt Home Mission Bd 1350 Spring St NW Atlanta GA 30309-2844

LEWIS, LOIDA NICOLAS, food products holding company executive; b. The Philippines, 1942; m. Reginald Lewis, 1968; children: Leslie, Christina. BA, St. Theresa's Coll., 1963; LLB, U. Philippines, 1967. Immigration atty. N.Y.C.; with Immigration and Naturalization Svc.; chmn., CEO TLC Beatrice Internat. L.P., N.Y.C., 1994—. Author: How the Filipino Veteran of World War II Can Become a U.S. Citizen (According to the Immigration Act of 1990), 1991, One Hundred One Legal Ways to Stay in the U.S.A.: or, How to Get a Green Card According to the Immigration Act of 1990, 1992, How to Get a Green Card: Legal Ways to Stay in the U.S.A., 1993. Office: TLC Beatrice Internat LP 9 W 57th St 39th Fl New York NY 10019

LEWIS, LOIS A., health services administrator; b. Tuskegee, Ala.; d. Arthur J. and Katie (Cephus) Long; m. Charles Lewis; children: Robin Jordan, Michelle Allen. BSN, U. Conn., 1959, MS, 1974; PhD, Columbia Pacific, 1989. CNAA. Community health nurse Hartford VNA, Conn., 1967-68, 70-71; sch. nurse Clark County Schs., Las Vegas, 1968-70; dir. job corps. Community Renewal Team, Hartford, 1971-72; sr. nurse Cap. Reg. Mental Health, Hartford, 1974-75; exec. dir. Manchester (Conn.) VNA, 1975-87; br. dir. Vis. Nurse and Home Care, Inc., Hartford, 1987-88; dir. community nursing and home health State Dept. Health, Hartford, 1988-96; ret., 1996; chairperson Cedarcrest Hosp., Newington, Conn., 1980-95; mem. adv. bd. dirs. U. Ct. Health Ctr., Farmington, 1982—, Hartford Hosp., 1992-96. Contbr. articles to profl. jours. Bd. dirs. ARC, Farmington, Conn., 1989—; mentor Career Beginnings, Hartford, 1989, 90. With USN, 1959-61. Mem. Nat. Assn. for Home Care (bd. dirs. 1980-83, 85-88), Conn. League for Nursing, Conn. Pub. Health Assn., Am. Pub. Health Assn.,

Sigma Theta Tau, Chi Eta Phi. Democrat. Methodist. Avocations: swimming, reading, knitting.

LEWIS, LUCINDA, musician; b. Kansas City, Mo., May 8, 1953; d. William Merle and Beverly (Hampton) L. MusB, Manhattan Sch. Music, N.Y.C., 1970, MusM, 1974. Prin. horn N.J. Symphony, Newark, 1977—. Office: NJ Symphony 213 Washington St Newark NJ 07102-2917

LEWIS, MARGARET M., marketing professional; b. Bridgeport, Conn., Sept. 27, 1959; d. Raymond Phillip and Catherine Helen (Gayda) Palovchak; m. William A. Lewis Jr., Oct. 4, 1980. BS summa cum laude, Sacred Heart U., 1986; postgrad., U. Bridgeport; AS, Katharine Gibbs Sch., 1980. Program mgr. sales svc. group Newspaper Coop. Couponing, Inc., Westport, Conn., 1985-87; sales adminstr. Supermarket Communication Systems, Inc., Norwalk, Conn., 1987-88, mgr. mktg. support, 1988-89; asst. project mgr. sales promotion Mktg. Corp. Am., Westport, 1989-91, account exec., 1991-92; mgr. program svcs. Ryan Partnership, Westport, 1992-93, sr. program mgr., 1993-95, mng. dir., 1995-96; account dir. Creative Alliance, Westport, Conn., 1996—. Mem. NAFE, Direct Mktg. Assn., Am. Mgmt. Assn. Democrat. Roman Catholic. Home: 16 Nickel Pl Monroe CT 06468-3005 Office: 55 Post Rd W Westport CT 06880-4205

LEWIS, MARILYN WARE, water company executive; b. 1943. Former pres. Solanco Pub. Co.; vice chmn. Am. Water Works Co., Inc., Voorhees, N.J., now chmn., also bd. dirs.; bd. dirs. Penn Fuel Gas Co., Cigna Corp. Office: Am Water Works Co Inc 2 East Main St Strasburg PA 17579

LEWIS, MARTIN EDWARD, shipping company executive, foreign government concessionary; b. Chgo., Dec. 27, 1958; s. Martin Luther and Anna Adlene (Gaines) L. BA, Johns Hopkins U., 1981; postgrad., Rush Med. Coll., 1983-85. Chmn. bd., chief exec. officer Internat. Financier Inc., Chgo., 1987—; co. rep. Assn. S.E. Asia Nations Secretariat Gen., Jakarta, Indonesia, 1995—; co. rep. OPEC, Vienna, 1988—, Supreme Coun. States of Cooperation Coun., Summit Confs. Countries of Cooperation Coun. for Arab States of Gulf, Secretariat Gen., Riyadh, Saudi Arabia, 1989—; corp. amb. plenipotentiary GM Overseas Ops., N.Y.C., 1977, Adam Opel, Russelsheim, Fed. Republic Germany, 1977. Mem. Asia Soc., Japan Soc. Republican. Avocations: golf, tennis, yachting, scuba diving.

LEWIS, MARTIN R., paper company executive; b. N.Y.C., Feb. 14, 1929; s. William and Ida (Goldman) L.; m. Renee Raines, Aug. 13, 1950 (div.); children: Jeffrey, Wendy, Lisa; m. Diane Carol Brandt, July 4, 1975. BA, NYU, 1949, LLB, 1951; LLM, U. Mich., 1952. CEO Williamhouse-Regency, Inc., N.Y.C., 1955-95. Bd. dirs. McBurney br. YMCA, N.Y.C. Mem. Envelope Mfg. Assn., Paper Club N.Y., N.Y. Jewish.

LEWIS, MELVIN, psychiatrist, pediatrician, psychoanalyst; b. London, May 18, 1926; came to U.S., 1956; s. Abraham George and Kitty (Merrick) L.; m. Dorothy S. Otnow, May 30, 1963; children: Gillian Io, Eric Anthony. M.B., B.S., Guy's Hosp. Med. Sch., London, 1950; D.C.H., 1954; M.A. (hon.), Yale U., 1972. Diplomate Am. Bd. Psychology and Neurology, Am. Bd. Child Psychiatry; cert. in psychoanalysis, child and adolescent psychoanalysis. Intern Lambeth Hosp., 1950, Fulham Hosp., 1951 (both Eng); resident in pediatrics Yale U. Sch. Medicine, 1956-57, resident in psychiatry and child psychiatry, 1957-61; instr. psychiatry Yale U. Child Study Center, New Haven, 1961-63; asst. prof. pediatrics and psychiatry Yale U. Child Study Center, 1963-67, assoc. prof., 1967-70, prof., 1971—, dir. med. studies, 1970—. Author: Clinical Aspects of Child and Adolescent Development, 1971, 3d edit. (with Fred Volkmar), 1991; editor: Jour. Am. Acad. Child & Adolescent Psychiatry, 1975-87, Child and Adolescent Psychiatry, A Comprehensive Textbook, 1991, 92; cons. editor: Child and Adolescent Psychiatric Clinics of North America, 1991—. Served with M.C. Royal Army, 1951-53. Fellow Am. Acad. Child and Adolescent Psychiatry, Am. Psychiat. Assn., Royal Coll. Psychiatrists; mem. Royal Soc. Medicine, Am. Pediatric Soc., Am. Psychoanalytic Assn. Home: 10 St Ronan Ter New Haven CT 06511-2315 Office: Yale U Child Study Ctr 333 Cedar St New Haven CT 06510-3206

LEWIS, MICHAEL, small business owner; b. St. Thomas, Ont., Can., Dec. 18, 1950; m. Krystyna Katherine Ballantyne; 2 children: Shannon, Jessica. BS, Queen's U., Kingston, Ont., Can., 1973; MBA, York (Can.) U., 1977. Sr. cons. CLC Can. Mktg. Assn. Ltd, Toronto, Ont., Can., 1981-85; v.p. No Frills Divsn. Loblaws Supermarkets Ltd., 1985-89; pres. Willson Stationers, Mississauga, Ont., Can., 1989-92, Manchu Wok, Harkham, Ont., Can., 1993—; bd. dirs. Kennedy Marchant Shields Inc., Toronto, 1991—. Mem. Young Pres.'s Orgn., Toronto Cricket and Skating Club. Home: 115 Melrose Ave, Toronto, ON Canada M5M 1Y8 Office: Manchu Wok, 500 Hood Rd, Markham, ON Canada L3R 0P6

LEWIS, MO, professional football player; b. Atlanta, Ga., Oct. 21, 1969. Student, U. Georgia. With N.Y. Jets, 1991—. Office: New York Jets 1000 Fulton Ave Hempstead NY 11550-1030

LEWIS, NATHAN SAUL, chemistry educator; b. L.A., Oct. 20, 1955. BS in Chemistry with highest honors, MS in Chemistry, Calif. Inst. Tech., 1977; PhD in Chemistry, MIT, 1981. Asst. prof. chemistry Stanford (Calif.) U., 1981-86, assoc. prof., 1986-88; assoc. prof. Calif. Inst. Tech., 1988-90, prof., 1990—; cons. Lawrence Livermore (Calif.) Nat. Lab., 1977-81, 84-88, Solar Energy Rsch. Assocs., Santa Clara, Calif., 1981-85, Am. Hosp. Supply, Irvine, Calif., 1983-85, Molecular Devices, Palo Alto, Calif., 1983-88; mem. U.S. Japan Joint Conf. Photochemistry and Photoconversion, 1983, Chem. Revs. Adv. Bd., 1989-92, long range planning com. Electrochem. Soc., 1991-94, Adv. Bd. Progress Inorganic Chemistry, 1992-94, vis. com. dept. applied sci. Brookhaven Nat. Lab., 1993—. Divisional editor Jour. Electrochemical Soc., 1984-90; mem. editorial adv. bd. Accounts Chem. Rsch., 1993—. Recipient Presdl. Young Investigator award, 1984-88, Fresenius award Phi Lambda Upsilon, 1990, Pure Chemistry award Am. Chem. Soc., 1991; Achievement Rewards Coll. Scientists Found. scholar Calif. Inst. Tech., 1975-77, Calif. State scholar, 1976-77, Carnation Co. Acad. Merit scholar, 1976-77, Camille and Henry Dreyfus Tchr. scholar, 1985-90; Fannie and John Hertz Found. fellow MIT, 1977-81, Alfred P. Sloan Rsch. fellow, 1985-87. Office: Calif Inst Tech Dept Chem 127-72 Pasadena CA 91125

LEWIS, NORMAN, English language educator, writer; b. N.Y.C., Dec. 30, 1912; s. Herman and Deborah (Nevins) L.; m. Mary Goldstein, July 28, 1934; children—Margery, Debra. B.A., CUNY, 1939; M.A., Columbia U., 1941. Instr., lectr CUNY, N.Y.C., 1943-52; assoc. prof. English NYU, N.Y.C., 1955-64; instr. Compton Coll., Calif., summers 1962-64, UCLA, 1962-69; prof. English Rio Hondo Coll., Whittier, Calif., 1964-91, chmn. communications dept., 1964-75. Author: (with others) Journeys Through Wordland, 1941, Lessons in Vocabulary and Spelling, 1941, (with Wilfred Funk) Thirty Days to a More Powerful Vocabulary, 1942, rev. edit., 1970, Power with Words, 1943, How to Read Better and Faster, 1944, rev. edit., 1978, The Lewis English Refresher and Vocabulary Builder, 1945, How to Speak Better English, 1948, Word Power Made Easy, 1949, rev. edit., 1978, The Rapid Vocabulary Builder, 1951, rev. edit., 1980, 3d edit., 1988, How to Get More Out of Your Reading, 1951, Twenty Days to Better Spelling, 1953, The Comprehensive Word Guide, 1958, Dictionary of Correct Spelling, 1962, Correct Spelling Made Easy, 1963, rev. edit. 1987, Dictionary of Modern Pronunciation, 1963, New Guide to Word Power, 1963, The New Power with Words, 1964, Thirty Days to Better English, 1964, The Modern Thesaurus of Synonyms, 1965, RSVP-Reading, Spelling, Vocabulary, Pronunciation (books I-III), 1966, 77, See, Say, and Write! (books I and II), 1973, Instant Spelling Power, 1976, R.S.V.P. for College English Power (books I-III), 1977-79, R.S.V.P. with Etymology (books I and II), 1980-81, Instant Word Power, 1980, New American Dictionary of Good English, 1987; editor: New Roget's Thesaurus of the English Language in Dictionary Form, 1961; also numerous articles in nat. mags.

LEWIS, NORMAN G., academic administrator, researcher, consultant; b. Irvine, Ayrshire, Scotland, Sept. 16, 1949; Came to U.S., 1985; s. William F. and Agnes H. O. L.; m. Christine I. (div. Oct. 1994); children: Fiona, Kathryn. BSc in Chemistry with honors, U. Strathclyde, Scotland, 1973; PhD in Chemistry 1st class, U. B.C., 1977. NRC postdoctoral fellow U. Cambridge, Eng., 1978-80; rsch. assoc. chemistry dept. Nat. Rsch. Coun., Can., 1980; asst. scientist fundamental rsch. divsn. Pulp and Paper Rsch. Inst. Can., Montreal, 1980-82, group leader chemistry and biochemistry of woody plants, grad. rsch. chemistry divsn., 1982-85; assoc. prof. wood sci. and biochemistry Va. Poly. Inst. and State U., Blacksburg, 1985-90; dir. Inst. Biol. Chemistry, Wash. State U., Pullman, 1990—; Eisig-Tode disting. prof.; cons. NASA, DOE, USDA, NIH, NSF, Am. Inst. Biol. Scis., other industries, 1985—. Mem. editl. bd. Holzforschung, 1986, TAPPI, 1986, 89, Jour. Wood Chemistry and Tech., 1987—, Polyphenols Actualities, 1992—; mem. editl. bd., N.Am. assoc. editor Phytochemistry, 1992—; author or co-author more than 94 publs., books, articles to profl. jours. Hon. mem. Russian Assn. Space and Mankind. Recipient ICI Merit awards Imperial Chem. Industries, 1968-69, 69-70, 70-71, 71-72, ICI scholar, 1971-73, Chemistry awards Kilmarnock Coll., 1969-70, 70-71; NATO/SRC scholar U. B.C., 1974-77; named Arthur M. and Kate E. Tode Disting. Prof. Mem. Am. Chem. Soc. (at-large cellulose divsn., organizer symposia, programme subcom. cellulose, paper and textile divsn. 1987-90, editorial bd.), Am. Soc. Plant Physiologists, Am. Soc. Gravitational and Space Biology, Phytochemical Soc. N.A. (phytochemical bank com. 1989—), Chem. Inst. Can. (treas. Montreal divsn. 1982-84, Am. Inst. Chemists and Chem. Inst. Can. Montreal conf. 1982-84), Can. Pulp and Paper Assn., Tech. Assn. of Pulp and Paper Industry, Societe de Groupe Polyphenole, Gordon Rsch. Conf. (vice-chmn. raenewable resources com. 1993—). Presbyterian. Achievements include 2 patents in field. Home: 1710 NE Upper Dr Pullman WA 99163-4624 Office: Washington State U Inst Biol Chemistry Clark Hall Pullman WA 99164

LEWIS, ORME, JR., investment company executive, land use advisor; b. Phoenix, Apr. 26, 1935; s. Orme and Barbara (Smith) L.; m. Elizabeth Bruening, Oct. 17, 1964; children: Joseph Orme, Elizabeth Blaise. BS, U. Ariz., 1958. Assoc. Coldwell Banker, Phoenix, 1959-64; v.p. Braggiotti Constrn., Phoenix, 1964-65; pvt. practice investment brokerage Phoenix, 1966-69; dep. asst. sec. Dept. Interior, Washington, 1969-73; dir. devel. Ariz. Biltmore Estates, 1973-76; exec. World Resources Co., Phoenix and McLean, Va., 1978-91; mng. mem. Applewhite Laflin & Lewis, Phoenix, 1979-96; gen. ptnr. Equity Interests, Phoenix, 1982—; mng. dir. Select Investments, Phoenix, 1996—; bd. dirs. Biofoam Corp., Phoenix; co-chmn. U.S. Adv. Com. on Mining and Mineral Rsch., Washington, 1982-94; mem. U.S. Emergency Minerals Adminstrn., 1987—, Disease Control Rsch. Commn., 1995—, Gov.'s Regulatory Rev. Coun., 1992-95, State Plant Site Transmission Line Com., Phoenix, 1974-85. Mem. Ariz. Senate, 1955-59; chmn. Phoenix Children's Hosp., 1981—; mem. governing bd. Polycystic Kidney Rsch. Found., Kansas City, Mo., 1983—, Ariz. Cmty. Found., 1986-91, Ariz. Parks and Conservation Coun., 1985—, Ariz. State U. Found., Tempe, 1981—, Ariz. Hist. Found., 1984—, Desert Bot. Garden, 1987-89, Men's Art Coun., 1983-85. Mem. Ariz. C. of C., Met. Club (Washington), Ariz. Valley Field Riding and Polo Club, Paradise Valley Country Club, Rotary. Republican. Home: 4325 E Palo Verde Dr Phoenix AZ 85018-1127 Office: Select Investments Ste 260-E 4350 E Camelback Rd Phoenix AZ 85018-2757

LEWIS, PAUL LE ROY, pathology educator; b. Tamaqua, Pa., Aug. 30, 1925; s. Harry Earl and Rose Estella (Brobst) L.; m. Betty Jane Bixby, June 2, 1953; 1 child, Robert Harry. AB magna cum laude, Syracuse U., 1950; MD, SUNY, Syracuse, 1953. Diplomate Am. Bd. Pathology. Intern Temple U. Hosp., Phila., 1953-54; resident in pathology Hosp. of U. Pa., Phila., 1954-58, asst. instr., 1957-58; instr. pathology Thomas Jefferson U. Coll. Medicine, Phila., 1958-62, asst. prof., 1962-65, assoc. prof., 1965-75, prof., 1975-93, prof. emeritus, 1993—; pathologist Thomas Jefferson U. Hosp., 1958-91; attending pathologist Meth. Hosp., Phila., 1975-93, dir. clin. labs., chmn. dept. pathology, 1975-92, consulting pathologist, 1993—; pathologist pvt. practice Phila., 1993—; pres. Penndel Labs. Inc., Ardmore, Pa., 1974-85; cons. VA Hosp., Coatesville, Pa., 1976-85; mem. med. adv. com. ARC Blood Bank, Phila., 1978—. Contbg. author: Atlas of Gastrointestinal Cytology, 1983; contbr. articles to med. jours. 2d lt. USAAF, 1943-46. Fellow Am. Soc. Clin. Pathologists, Coll. Am. Pathologists; mem. AMA, Pa. Med. Soc., Philadelphia County Med. Soc., Internat. Acad. Pathology, Am. Soc. Cytology, Masons, Phi Beta Kappa, Alpha Omega Alpha, Nu Sigma Nu. Republican. Methodist. Avocations: photography, hiking. Home and Office: 521 Baird Rd Merion Station PA 19066-1301

LEWIS, PEIRCE FEE, geographer, educator; b. Detroit, Oct. 26, 1927; s. Peirce and Amy Lois (Fee) L.; m. Felicia Louise Stegeman, Feb. 2, 1952; 1 child, Hugh Gilchrist. BA summa cum laude, Albion Coll., 1950; MA, U. Mich., 1953, PhD, 1957. Geographer, U.S. Army Forces, Tokyo, 1953-55; lectr. U. Mich., Ann Arbor, 1958; NSF fellow, U. Wash., Seattle, 1957-58; vis. prof. U. Calif., Berkeley, 1976-77; asst. prof. Pa. State U., University Park, 1958-62, prof. geography, 1962—, prof. emeritus, 1995—; John Hannah prof. Integrative Studies, Mich. State U., E. Lansing, 1992; cons., author Smithsonian Instn., Washington, 1974-77, Smithsonian Instn. Books, 1989-90, Ency. Britannica, Chgo., 1973-74, 81-83, 89-90, Pa. Pub. TV, 1982-83; cons. Nat. Geog. Soc., 1981—, Nat. Mus. Am. History, Washington, 1990—, Nat. Rural Studies Com., 1991, So. Living Mag.; cons. Strong Mus., Rochester, N.Y., Newberry Libr., Chgo.; mem. steering com. Pioneer Am. Soc. vols. on Nat. Rd. Author: New Orleans: Making An Urban Landscape, 1976; editor: Visual Blight in America, 1973; contbr. articles to profl. jours. Mem. Borough Planning Commn., State College, Pa., 1967-76, mem. traffic commn., 1968-70; bd. dirs. Pa. Roadside Council, 1969-74. Served with U.S. Army, 1945-47. Recipient First Prize essay Internat. Geog. Congress, Stockholm, 1960; Lindback Teaching award Pa. State U., 1981; Disting. Teaching award Nat. Council for Geog. Edn., 1982; Nat. Honors award Assn. Am. Geographers, 1977, Trustee of Am. award Ctr. for Hist. Preservation, Mary Washington Coll., 1987, Disting. Geographer award Pa. Geog. Soc., 1991; rsch. assoc. U. Calif., Berkeley, 1986; John Simon Guggenheim Fellow, 1986-87, Woodrow Wilson fellow Woodrow Wilson Internat. Ctr. for Scholars, Smithsonian Inst., 1988, John Bracken fellow Pa. State U., 1993—. Mem. Assn. Am. Geographers (pres. 1983-84, nat. councillor 1981-82, 84-85, vis. geog. scientist, chmn. J.B. Jackson prize com.), Am. Geog. Soc., Nat. Council for Geog. Edn., Phi Beta Kappa. Democrat. Club: State College Literary. Avocation: travel. Home: 1377 Penfield Rd State College PA 16801-6420 Office: Pa State Univ Dept Geography 302 Walker Bldg University Park PA 16802

LEWIS, PERRY JOSHUA, investment banker; b. San Antonio, Feb. 11, 1938; s. Perry Joshua and Zelime L. L.; m. Memrie Taylor Mosier, May 12, 1962 (div. 1994); children—Perry Joshua, IV, Memrie Fraser. B.A., Princeton U., 1959. Registered rep. Lee Higginson Corp., N.Y.C., 1960-63; comml. project mgr. Parsons & Whittemore, Inc., N.Y.C., 1964-67; sr. v.p., mgr. corp. fin. div. Smith Barney, Harris Upham & Co. Inc., N.Y.C., 1967-79; pres. MacKay-Lewis Inc., N.Y.C., 1980-81; ptnr. Morgan Lewis Githens & Ahn, Conn., N.Y.C., 1982—; bd. dirs. Aon Corp., Chgo., Tyler Corp., Dallas, Evergreen Media Corp., Haynes Internat., Quaker Fabric Corp., ITI Techs., Inc., North St. Paul, Stuart Entertainment, Inc., The Gradall Co., New Philadelphia, Ohio. With U.S. Army, 1959-60, 61-62. Clubs: Knickerbocker of N.Y., Doubles N.Y., Field (Greenwich, Conn.). Office: Morgan Lewis Githens & Ahn 2 Greenwich Plz Greenwich CT 06830-6353

LEWIS, PETER BENJAMIN, insurance company executive; b. Cleve., Nov. 11, 1933; s. Joseph M. and Helen (Rosenfeld) L.; married, June 19, 1955 (div. 1980); children: Ivy, Jonathan, Adam. A.B., Princeton U., 1955. With Progressive Ins. Cos., 1955—; pres., CEO Progressive Casualty Ins. Co., The Progressive Corp., Ohio, 1965—, Mayfield Village, 1965-94; chmn. bd., pres., CEO Progressive Corp., 1993—. Mem. Soc. C.P.C.U. Clubs: Ceve. Racquet, Oakwood, Union. Office: Progressive Corp 6300 Wilson Mills Rd Mayfield OH 44143*

LEWIS, PHILIP, educational and technical consultant; b. Chgo., Oct. 23, 1913; s. Solomon and Fannie (Margolis) L.; m. Geraldine Gisela Lawenda, Sept. 1, 1947; 1 child, Linda Susan. BS, DePaul U., Chgo., 1937, MA, 1939; EdD, Columbia Tchrs. Coll., 1951. Chmn. dept. edn. Chgo. Tchrs. Coll.; also asst. prin., tchr. South Shore High Sch., Chgo., 1940-51; prin. Herman Felsenthal Elementary Sch., Chgo., 1955-57; dir. Bur. Instructional Materials, Chgo. Pub. Schs., 1957-63, Bur. Research Devel. and Spl. Projects, 1963-67; pres. Instructional Dynamics Inc., Chgo., 1967-89, ret., 1989; ednl. and tech. cons., 1991—; nat. cons. TV and instructional techniques, 1955—; ednl. cons. to accrediting bur. Health Edn. Schs., 1971-89; chmn. adv. com. U.S. Office Edn., Title VII, 1964-67. Author: Educational Television Guidebook for Electronics Industries Association, 1961, also numerous articles.; mem. editorial bd. Nation's Schs. and Colls; multimedia tech. editor: Tech. Horizons in Edn; cons.: Jour. Ednl. Tech. and Communications; producer ednl., multimedia, tng. and mental health and human devel. materials. Served to lt. comdr. USNR, 1942-45. Mem. Soc. Programmed and Automated Learning (pres. 1960-65), NEA (v.p. dept. audiovisual instrn., chmn. commn. on tech. standards dept. audiovisual instrn. 1965-85), Nat. Assn. Ednl. Broadcasters, Am. Legion, Council for Ednl. Facilities Planners (editorial adv. bd. 1972-80) Ill. C. of C. (edn. com. 1970-77), Chgo. Assn. Commerce and Industry (chmn. edn. com. 1970-80), Nat. Audio-Visual Assn. (profl. devel. bd. 1969-76, chmn), Chgo. Press Club, Masons, Shriners, Rotary, Phi Delta Kappa. Home: 2 E Oak St Apt 3201 Chicago IL 60611-1216

LEWIS, PHILLIP HAROLD, museum curator; b. Chgo., July 31, 1922; s. Bernard and Sonia (Pimstein) L.; m. Sally Leah Rappaport, Aug. 25, 1949; children—David Bernard, Betty Alice and Emily Ruth (twins). B.F.A., Art Inst. Chgo., 1947; M.A., U. Chgo., 1953, Ph.D., 1966; postgrad. (Fulbright ednl. grant), Australian Nat. U., Canberra, 1953-54. Conducted field research projects on art and soc. of New Ireland, 1953-54, 70, 81; asst. curator primitive art Field Mus. Natural History, Chgo., 1957-59; asso. curator Field Mus. Natural History, 1960, curator, 1961-67, curator primitive art and Melanesian ethnology, 1968-92, ret., 1992, chmn. dept. anthropology, 1975-79, co-chmn. dept., 1980-81, acting chmn. dept., 1987; curator emeritus, 1994—. Served with USAAF, 1942-45. Fellow Royal Anthrop. Inst. Gt. Britain and Ireland, Am. Anthrop. Assn. Home: 1118 Main St Evanston IL 60202-1649 Office: Field Mus Natural History Roosevelt Dr Chicago IL 60607

LEWIS, RALPH JAY, III, management and human resources educator; b. Balt., Sept. 25, 1942; s. Ralph Jay and Ruth Elizabeth (Schmeltz) L. BS in Engring., Northwestern U., 1966; MS in Adminstrn., U. Calif., Irvine, 1968; PhD in Mgmt., UCLA, 1974. Rsch. analyst Chgo. Area Expressway Surveillance Project, 1963-64, Gen. Am. Transp. Co., Chgo., 1965-66; assoc. prof. mgmt. and human resources mgmt. Calif. State U., Long Beach, 1972—; cons. Rand Corp., Santa Monica, Calif., 1966-74, Air Can., Montreal, Que., 1972-73, Los Angeles Times, 1973;. Co-author: Studies in the Quality of LIfe, 1972; author instructional programs, monographs; co-designer freeway traffic control system. Bd. dirs. Project Quest, Los Angeles, 1969-71. Mem. AAAS, APA, The World Future Soc., Soc. of Mayflower Descendants, SAR (Ill. Soc.), Beta Gamma Sigma. Democrat. Office: Calif State U Dept Human Resources Mgmt Long Beach CA 90840

LEWIS, RALPH MILTON, real estate developer; b. Johnstown, Pa., Nov. 9, 1919; s. Morris and Sarah (Galfond) L.; m. Goldy Sarah Kimmel, June 12, 1941; children: Richard Alan, Robert Edward, Roger Gordon, Randall Wayne. AA, Los Angeles City Coll., 1939; BS, UCLA, 1941; postgrad., U. So. Calif., 1945-48. Bar: Calif. 1952. Pvt. practice acctg. Los Angeles, 1945-55, pvt. practice law, 1953-55; founder Lewis Homes, 1957; chmn. bd. Lewis Construction Co., Inc., Upland, Calif., 1959—, Lewis Bldg. Co., Inc., Las Vegas, 1960—, Republic Sales Co. Inc.; dir., v.p. Kimmel Enterprises, Inc., 1959—; mng. partner Lewis Homes of Calif., 1973—, Lewis Homes of Nev., 1972—, Western Properties, Upland, 1972—, Foothill Investment Co., Las Vegas, 1971—, Republic Mgmt. Co., Upland, 1978-86; dir. Gen. Telephone Co. Calif., 1981-86; mem. adv. bd. Inland divsn. Bank of Am.; instr. U. So. Calif., UCLA, L.A. City Coll., 1948-54, Dooley Law Rev. Course, 1953-54; guest lectr. numerous colls., univs. Author: Land Buying Checklist, 1981, 85, 88, 90; contbr. articles to mags., jours. Mem., com. chmn. Calif. Commn. of Housing and Community Devel., 1965-67; mem. Calif. Gov.'s Task Force on the Home Bldg. and Construction Industry, 1967; pres. Bd. of Edn. Citrus Community Coll. Dist., Azusa, Calif., 1969, 73, mem., 1967-73; mem. Citizens Planning Council, Los Angeles County Regional Planning Commn., 1972-73, UCLA Found., Chancellor's Assoc.; mem. dean's council UCLA Grad. Sch. Architecture and Urban Planning; trustee U. Calif. Riverside Found.; bd. dirs. Regional Research Inst. So. Calif., 1983-84; chmn. land use and planning com. Citizens' Adv. Council, Calif. Senate Housing Com., 1983-84; founding mem. Rancho Cucamonga Community Found., 1987-88; donated $5 million to Lewis Ctr. for Regional Policy Studies Grad. Sch. UCLA, 1989, $5 million to the Ralph and Goldy Lewis Hall of Planning and Devel. Sch. Urban and Regional Planning U. So. Calif., 1989; funded Goldy & Ralph Lewis Edn. Ctr. Temple Beth Israel, Pomona, Calif.; land donor to City of Claremont, Calif., City of Rancho Cucamonga, Calif., City of Ontario, Calif.; bd. dirs. Calif. Community Colls., 1992—. Recipient Profl. Achievement commendation Calif. State Assembly, 1977, Humanitarian award NCCJ, 1979, Builder of Year award Bldg. Industry Assn. So. Calif., 1970; named as U. So. Calif.'s 1st Developer in Residence, 1988 at Lusk Ctr. for Real Estate Devel., (with wife Goldy) Entrepreneur of Yr., Inland Empire, 1990, 92, Housing Person of Yr. Nat. Housing Conf., 1990; recipient Good Scout award Old Baldy council Boy Scouts Am., 1984, (with wife) Builder of Yr. award Profl. Builder mag., 1987, Disting. chief exec. officer award Calif. State U., San Bernardino, 1991, Calif. State Legis. recognition Outstanding Leadership in the Bus. World, 1991, Spirit of Life award City of Hope, 1993, Mgmt. Leaders of Yr. award U. Calif., Riverside, 1993; inducted Nat. Housing Ctr.'s Hall of Fame, Washington, 1988; named Builder of Century, U. Calif., Irvine and Sumigarden Group, 1991. Mem. Am. Bar Assn., Calif. Soc. C.P.A.'s, Nat. Assn. Home Builders (dir.), Calif. Bldg. Industry Assn. (dir., chmn. affordable housing task force 1978-80, named to Hall of Fame 1987), Bldg. Industry Assn. So. Calif. (past treas., pres., dir., Bldg. Industry Assn. Medal of Honor, 1986, Builder of Yr. 1988).). Office: Lewis Homes 1156 N Mountain Ave Upland CA 91786-3633

LEWIS, RAMSEY EMANUEL, JR., pianist, composer; b. Chgo., May 27, 1935; s. Ramsey Emanuel and Pauline (Richards) L.; m. Geraldine Taylor, Apr. 7, 1954 (div. Mar. 1989); children—Vita Denise, Ramsey Emanuel III, Marcus Kevin, Dawn, Kendall, Frayne, Robert; m. Janet Tamillow, June 10, 1990. Student, Chgo. Music Coll., 1947-54, U. Ill., 1953-54, De Paul U., 1954-55; DHL (hon.), De Paul U., 1993, U. Ill., Chgo., 1995; hon. degree, DePaul U., Chgo., 1993, U. Ill., 1995. Mgr. record dept. Hudson-Ross, Inc., Chgo., 1954-56. Organizer Ramsey Lewis Trio, 1956; now solo artist; 1st profl. appearance, Chgo. 1957, appeared N.Y.C., 1958—, San Francisco, 1962, played Randall's Island Jazz Festival, N.Y.C., 1959, Saugatuck (Mich.) Jazz Festival, 1960, Newport (R.I.) Jazz Festival, 1961, 63, numerous jazz concerts at various festivals and univs. since 1961; toured with New Sounds of 1963; appeared in film Save the Children, 1973; recipient Grammy awards for The In Crowd 1965, Hold It Right There 1966, Hang on Sloopy 1973); albums include Another Voyage, 1970, The Piano Player, 1970, Them Changes, 1970, Back To The Roots, 1971, Upendo Ni Pamoja, 1972, Funky Serenity, 1973, Legacy, 1978, Best of Ramsey Lewis, 1981, Salongo, 1976, Sun Goddess, 1974, Tequila Mockingbird, 1977, Ramsey, 1979, Routes, 1980, (with Nancy Wilson) The Two of Us, 1984, Fantasy, 1985, Keys to the City, 1987, A Classic Encounter (with London Philharm. Orch.), 1988, Urban Renewal, 1989, We Meet Again (with Billy Taylor), 1989, The Electric Collection, 1991, Ivory Pyramid, 1992, Sky Island, 1993, Maiden Voyage, 1994, Urban Knights, 1995; composer: Sound of Spring, Fantasia for Drums, Look-a-Here, Sound of Christmas; organizer, Rams' L Prodns., Inc., Chgo., 1966, Ramsel Pub. Co., Chgo., 1966, Ivory Pyramid Prodns., Inc., 1995; host weekly jazz TV show, Sta. B.E.T. (cable TV) Ramsey Lewis on Jazz Ctrl., 1990—; host weekly jazz radio show The Ramsey Lewis Show, 1990—, Sta. WNUA, Chgo., syndicated in various cities throughout the U.S.; artistic dir. Jazz series at Ravinia Festival Chgo., 1993—; numerous TV appearances; lectr. various univs.; performance at White House, 1995. Named Person of Week ABC Nightly News, 1995. Address: 180 N La Salle St Ste 2200 Chicago IL 60601-2702

LEWIS, RICHARD, actor, comedian; b. Bklyn., June 29, 1948; s. Bill and Blanche L. Student, Ohio State U., 1970. Head copywriter N.J. advt. agency, 1970-71; appearances include Greenwich Village club, The Improv, The Tonight Show. Co-writer: (TV special) Diary of a Young Comic; actor (TV series) Harry, 1987, King of the Building, 1987, Anything But Love, 1990-92, Daddy Dearest, 1993, over 40 appearances on Late Night With David Letterman, 1982; appeared in (cable special) I'm In Pain, 1985, I'm Exhausted, 1988 (ACE award nomination 1988), All-Star Toast to the Improv, 1988, I'm Doomed, 1990; films include The Wrong Guys, 1988, That's Adequate, 1989, Once Upon a Crime, 1992, Robin Hood: Men in Tights, 1993, Wagons East, 1994. also: ICM 8942 Wilshire Blvd Beverly Hills CA 90211-1934 Office: 1999 Ave of the Stars Ste 2850 Los Angeles CA 90067*

LEWIS, RICHARD, SR., securities broker, consultant; b. Macon, Ga., Jan. 18, 1930; s. William Chapman and Florida (Zelius) L.; m. Iris Joy Clements, Sept. 10, 1949; children: Richard Jr., Linda Lee. Cert. investments securities broker, pistol and rifle instr. State trooper Fla. Hwy. Patrol, various cities, 1951-72; pres. Gateway Shooters Supply, Inc., Jacksonville, Fla., 1972-82; broker Global Investments Securities Inc., Miami, 1985-86, Investacorp, Inc., Miami Lakes, Fla., 1986-89. Lobbyist Fla. Assn. of State Troopers, Tallahassee, 1988-89. With U.S. Army, 1952-54. Recipient cert. of appreciation, State of Fla., Tallahassee, 1972; Demolay Cross of Honor, Internat. Coun., Kansas City, Mo., 1973; cert. of commendation, State of Fla., 1972. Mem. NRA (life), Fla. Assn. State Troopers (legis. chmn. retirees 1987), V.F.W., Jacksonville Pistol Club (pres. 1968-72), Marion Dunn Masonic Lodge, Elks, Sons Am. Revolution, Sons Confederate Vets., Mil. Order Stars and Bars, Fraternal Order Police, Scottish Rite, Nobles Mistic Shrine (Ambassador-at-large). Republican. Methodist. Avocations: fishing, photography, competitive pistol shooting. Home: 461 High Meadow Tr Cleveland GA 30528

LEWIS, RICHARD ALLAN, financial planner, business consultant; b. Pitts., Feb. 25, 1952; s. Harry C. and Vera E. (Williams) L. BS in Econs., Allegheny Coll., 1974; MBA in Fin., U. Pitts., 1978. CFP. Trainee Mellon Bank, Pitts., 1974-75, various positions with, 1975-84, v.p. N.Am. ops., 1984-86; pres., COO WorkWell, Pitts., 1987-89; sr. fin. planner The Acacia Group, Pitts., 1989—. Mem. Nat. Automated Clearing House Assn. (bd. dirs. 1981-86), Tri-State Automated Clearing House Assn. (pres. 1984-86, treas. 1980-83, v.p. 1984-85), Masons, Blue Lodge, Phi Beta Kappa, Delta Tau Delta (pres. house corp. 1976—). Republican. Methodist. Avocations: skiing, jogging, travel, gourmet cooking. Home: 106 Fairway Landings Dr Canonsburg PA 15317-9567 Office: Acacia Group Acacia Bldg Pittsburgh PA 15220

LEWIS, RICHARD HAYES, lawyer, former state legislator; b. Hopkinsville, Ky., Dec. 3, 1937; s. Fred Theodore and Nola Angeline (Hayes) L.; m. Martha Jane Cunningham, June 24, 1961; children: Laura Elizabeth, Cynthia Jane, Katherine Hayes. BS, Murray (Ky.) State U., 1960; JD, U. Ky., 1965. Bar: Ky. 1965, U.S. Dist. Ct. (we. dist.) Ky. 1965, U.S. Ct. Appeals (6th cir.) 1983, U.S. Ct. Appeals (fed. cir.) 1986, U.S. Supreme Ct. 1983, Tenn. 1995. Assoc. Lovett & Lovett, Benton, Ky., 1965-69, Lovett & Lewis, Benton, 1969-76; CEO to Gov. Julian Carroll State of Ky., Frankfort, 1975-76, mem. worker's compensation bd., 1976-78; prin. Law Office of Richard Lewis, Benton, 1976-93; ptnr. Lewis & Telle P.S.C., Benton, 1993—; mem. Ky. Ho. of Reps., Frankfort, 1970-75, 89-94, commr. Ky. alcoholic beverage control com., 1980-82. Sec. Marshall County C. of C., 1974; pres. Lions, Benton, 1974; bd. regents Murray State U., 1995. Capt. U.S. Army, 1960-62. Mem. Marshall County Bar Assn. (pres.), Ky. Bar Assn., Assn. Trial Lawyers Am., Ky. Trial Lawyers Assn., Nat. Bd. Trial Advocacy (cert. civil trial advocate 1994), Murray State Alumni Assn. (pres. 1977). Democrat. Baptist. Home: RR 8 Box 508 Benton KY 42025-9808 Office: Lewis & Telle PSC PO Box 430 1100 Main St Benton KY 42025-1450

LEWIS, RICHARD JAY, marketing educator, university dean; b. Marion, Ohio, July 14, 1933; s. Harley Franklin and Christina Mary (Anderson) L.; m. Patricia Ruth Montgomery, Sept. 17, 1955; children: Pamela Kay, Gregory Carl, Scott Alan. BS, Miami U., Oxford, Ohio, 1957, MBA, 1959; DBA, Mich. State U., 1964. Mem. faculty Mich. State U., East Lansing, 1964-93, prof. mktg., 1970-93, dean Coll. Bus., 1975-93; dean Faculty of Bus. U. Nigeria, Enugu, 1966-67; mem. faculty, dean Coll. Mgmt., N.C. State U., Raleigh, 1993—; bd. dirs. First of Mich. Corp., Detroit, First of Mich. Capital Corp., Am. Assembly Collegiate Schs. Bus. Author: Logistical Information System for Marketing Analysis, 1970, (with B. von H. Gilmer) Industrial and Organizational Psychology, 1971. Bd. dirs. Edward W. Sparrow Hosp., 1985—. Served with U.S. Army, 1953-55. Decorated Commendation medal. Mem. Am. Mktg. Assn., Lansing Regional C. of C. (bd. dirs. 1980-83), Am. Assembly Collegiate Schs. Bus. (pres. elect 1990, pres. 1991), Golden Key, Sigma Xi, Beta Gamma Sigma (bd. govs. 1976-82, nat. pres. 1980-82), Sigma Beta Delta (exec. coun.), Omicron Delta Epsilon. Home: 6100 Heatherstone Dr Raleigh NC 27606-8701 Office: NC State U Coll Mgmt Raleigh NC 27606-8614

LEWIS, RICHARD KNOX, city official; b. Auburn, N.Y., June 25, 1946; s. Harry C. and Jean E. (Knox) L.; m. Barbara, Dec. 28, 1968; children: Wendy, Adam. AA, Auburn Community Coll., 1968; BA, U. Miss., 1970, MA, 1972. Project planner Mo. Dept. Community Affairs, Jefferson City, Mo., 1971-73; planning dir. City of Ocala, Fla., 1973-79; asst. city mgr., airport mgr. City of Ocala, 1979-96; dep. city mgr. City of Ocala, Fla., 1996—. Past pres. Vol. Svc. Bur. Bd., Ocala, 1991, United Way of Marion County, Ocala, 1984-85, past campaign chmn., 1981-82; chmn. United Way Fla., 1995-96. Recipient Community Svc. award Marion County Jaycees, 1986. Mem. Am. Planning Assn., Am. Inst. Cert. Planners, Assn. Urban Planners, Fla. Airport Mgrs. Assn. (bd. dirs.), Am. Assn. Airport Execs., Statewide Continuing Fla. Divsn. Sys. Plan Com. Episcopalian. Office: City of Ocala 151 SE Osceola Ave Ocala FL 34471-2148

LEWIS, RICHARD M., lawyer; b. Gallipolis, Ohio, Dec. 11, 1957; s. Denver E. and Mary Esther (Mobley) L.; m. Cheryl F. Hickman (div.); m. Diane K. Williams, Apr. 26, 1986. BA in Polit. Sci., Ohio State U., 1979; JD, Capital U., 1982. Bar: Ohio 1982, U.S. Dist. Ct. (so. dist.) Ohio 1984, U.S. Supreme Ct. 1986; cert. civil trial advocacy Nat. Bd. Trial Advocacy. Pvt. practice law, 1982-83; assoc. Mary Bone Kunze, Jackson, Ohio, 1983-85; pvt. practice law Jackson, 1985-86; ptnr. Ochsenbein, Cole & Lewis, Jackson, 1986—; lectr. in field. Mem. ABA, ATLA, Ohio State Bar Assn., Jackson County Bar Assn. (past pres.), Ohio Acad. Trial Lawyers (bd. trustees 1993-94, 94-95, budget com. 1993-94, supreme ct. screening com. 1994, vice-chairperson family law com. 1994-95, chairperson-elect family law com. 1995—, chairperson family law com. 1995-96). Home: 603 Reservoir Rd Jackson OH 45640-8714 Office: Ochsenbein Cole and Lewis 295 Pearl St Jackson OH 45640-1748

LEWIS, RICHARD PHELPS, physician, educator; b. Portland, Oreg., Oct. 26, 1936; s. Howard Phelps and Wava Irene (Brown) L.; m. Penny A. Brown, Oct. 12, 1982; children: richard Phelps, Heather Brown. BA, Yale U., 1957; MD, U. Oreg., 1961. Intern Peter Bent Brigham Hosp., Boston, 1961-62, resident, 1962-63; Howard Irwin fellow in cardiology U. Oreg., Portland, 1963-65; sr. resident Stanford U., 1965-66, instr. dept. medicine, 1968-69; asst. chief cardiology Madigan Gen. Hosp., Tacoma, 1966-68; asst. prof. medicine div. cardiology Ohio State U., 1969-71, assoc. prof., 1971-75, prof., 1975—, dir. Divsn. Cardiology, 1972-86, dir., 1972-86, assoc. chmn. for hosp. and clin. affairs, 1980-86; mem. cardiovascular sect. Am. Bd. Internal Medicine, 1981-87, critical care medicine, 1988-92. Contbr. articles to profl. jours. Served with M.C. U.S. Army, 1966-68, col. res. Decorated Army Commendation medal. Fellow ACP (gov. Ohio chpt. 1976-80, chmn. MKSAP cardiovascular sect. 1989-82), Am. Heart Assn. (coun. on clin. cardiology), Am. Coll. Cardiology (Ohio gov. 1988-91, chmn. bd. govs. 1990-91, trustee 1991—, chmn. self assessment program, v.p. 1994-95, pres.-elect 1995-96, pres. 1996-97), Am. Clin. and Climatological Assn.; mem. Am. Fedn. Clin. Rsch., Ctrl. Soc. Clin. Rsch., Laennec Soc., Am. Heart Assn., Assn. U. Cardiologists, Alpha Omega Alpha. Republican. Episcopalian. Home: 5088 Stratford Ave Powell OH 43065-8771 Office: 466 W 10th Ave Columbus OH 43210-1240

LEWIS, RICHARD STANLEY, author, former editor; b. Pitts., Jan. 8, 1916; s. S. Morton and Mary L. (Lefstein) L.; m. Louise G. Silberstein, June 8, 1938; children: Jonathan, David. B.A., Pa. State U., 1937. Reporter Cleve. Press, 1937-38; rewrite man, drama critic Indpls. Times, 1938-43, reporter, city editor, 1946-49; reporter St. Louis Star-Times, 1949-51; mem. staff Chgo. Sun-Times, 1951-68, sci. editor, 1967-68; mng. editor Bull. Atomic Scientists, Chgo., 1968-70; editor Bull. Atomic Scientists, 1971-74; writing cons. earth sci. curriculum project NSF, summers 1964-65. Author: The Other Child, 1951, (rev. edit, 1960), A Continent for Science, 1965, Appointment on The Moon, 1968, rev. edit., 1969, The Nuclear Power Rebellion, 1972, The Voyages of Apollo, 1974, From Vinland to Mars: 1000 Years of Exploration, 1976, The Other Child Grows Up, 1977, The Voyages of Columbia, 1984, Challenger: The Final Voyage, 1987, Space in the 21st Century, 1990; prin. author: The New Illustrated Encyclopedia of Space Exploration; editor: Man on the Moon, 1969, Alamogordo Plus 25 Years, 1970, Frozen Future, 1972, The Energy Crisis, 1972, The Environmental Revolution, 1973. Mem. Indialantic Town Council, 1980-82, apptd. dep. mayor, 1980. Served with AUS, 1943-46, ETO. Fellow Brit. Interplanetary Soc. (London); Mem. Authors Guild, Authors League Am. Club: Nat. Press (Washington); Canaveral Press (Cocoa Beach, Fla.) (pres. 1985). Home: 1401 S Magnolia Ave Indialantic FL 32903-3510

LEWIS, RICHARD WARREN, advertising executive; b. N.Y.C., June 8, 1951; s. Stanley and Janet (Sweet) L.; m. Isabel Ellen Abrams, Mar. 19, 1977; children: Ariane, Amanda, Sam. BA, Hofstra U., 1973; MBA, NYU, 1978. Advt. exec., pres. GGK New York, 1978-84; mgmt. supr. Lois/GGK, N.Y.C., 1985-86; exec. v.p., mgmt. supr. TBWA Chiat/Day, N.Y.C., 1987—. Author: Absolutbook: The Absolut Vodka Advertising Story, 1996. Coach Dobbs Ferry (N.Y.) Baseball League, 1990—. Recipient Clio award, 1989, Andy award Advt. Club N.Y., 1989, Kelly award Mag. Pubs. Am., 1989. Mem. Am. Advt. Fedn. (speaker). Home: 256 Clinton Ave Dobbs Ferry NY 10522-3007 Office: TBWA Advt Inc 292 Madison Ave New York NY 10017-6307

LEWIS, RICHARD WARRINGTON BALDWIN, language professional, educator; b. Chgo., Nov. 1, 1917; s. Leicester Crosby and Beatrix Elizabeth (Baldwin) L.; m. Nancy Lindau, June 28, 1950; children: Nathaniel Lindau, Sophia Baldwin. A.B., Harvard U., 1939; M.A., U. Chgo., 1941, Ph.D., 1953; Litt.D., Wesleyan U., Middletown, Conn., 1961. Tchr. Bennington Coll., 1948-50; dean Salzburg Seminar Am. Studies, 1950-51; vis. lectr. English Smith Coll., 1951-52; assoc. prof., then prof. English Newark Coll., Rutgers U., 1954-59; vis. lectr. English Yale U., 1959-60, prof. English and Am. studies, from 1960; Fulbright lectr. Am. lit. U. Munich, 1957-58; lit. cons. Universal Pictures, 1966—. Author: The American Adam, 1955, The Picaresque Saint, 1959, Trials of the World, 1965, Edith Wharton: A Biography, 1975; Editor: Herman Melville (A Reader), 1962, The Presence of Walt Whitman, 1962, Malraux: A Collection of Critical Essays, 1964, Short Stories of Edith Wharton, 1910-1937; contbg. editor: Major Writers of America, 1962. Served to maj. AUS, 1942-46. Decorated Legion of Merit; recipient award Nat. Inst. Arts and Letters, 1958; Pulitzer prize for biography, 1976; Hodder fellow in humanities Princeton, 1952-53; resident fellow creative writing, 1953-54; Kenyon Rev. fellow criticism, 1954-55; Am. Council Learned Socs. fellow, 1962-63; fellow Sch. Letters Ind. U., 1957—; sr. fellow, 1964—; chmn. English Inst., 1965; fellow Calhoun Coll. Office: Yale University Dept Am Studies New Haven CT 06520

LEWIS, RITA HOFFMAN, plastic products manufacturing company executive; b. Phila., Aug. 6, 1947; d. Robert John and Helen Anna (Dugan) Hoffman; 1 child, Stephanie Blake. Student Jefferson Med. Coll. Sch. Nursing, 1965-67, Gloucester County Coll., 1993—; Gen. mgr. Sheets & Co., Inc. (now Flower World, Inc.), Woodbury, N.J., 1968-72; dir., exec. v.p., treas. Hoffman Precision Plastics, Inc., Blackwood, N.J., 1973—; ptnr. Timber Assocs.; commr. N.J. Expressway Authority, 1990—, sec., 1990-91, treas., 1991—, chmn. pers., 1991—; apptd. mem. N.J. Senate Forum on Budget and Revenue Alternatives, 1991; guest speaker various civic groups, 1974; poetry editor SPOTLIGHTER Innovative Singles Mag. Author: That Part of Me I Never Really Meant to Share, 1979; In Retrospect: Caught Between Running and Loving; columnist Innovative Singles mag., 1989—. Mem. Com. for Citizens of Glen Oaks (N.J.), 1979—, Gloucester Twp. Econ. Devel. Com., 1981—, Gloucester Twp. Day Scholarship Com., 1984—; mem. adv. coun. Gloucester Twp. Econ. Devel., 1995—; chairperson Gloucester Twp. Day Scholarship Found., 1985—; bd. dirs. Diane Hull Dance Co. Recipient Winning Edge award, 1982, Mayor's award for Womens' Achievement, 1987, Outstanding Cmty. Svc. award Mayor, Coun. and Com., 1987. Mem. NAFE, Sales Assn. Chem. Industry, Blackwood Businessmen's Assn., Soc. Plastic Engrs. Roman Catholic.

LEWIS, ROBERT, periodical editor, journalist; b. Montreal, Que., Can., Aug. 19, 1943; s. Leon R. and Margaret (Horan) L.; m. Sara Lewis, May 27, 1967; children: Christopher Robert, Timothy O'Neill. BA, Loyola Coll., 1964. Gen. reporter Montreal Star, 1964-65, Ottawa corr., 1965-66; chief Montreal bur. Time mag., 1967-68, Ottawa corr., 1968-70, Boston corr., 1970-72, chief Toronto bur., 1972-74; chief Ottawa bur. Maclean's Mag., 1975-82, mng. editor, 1982-93, editor, 1993—. Home: 31 Brooke Ave, Toronto, ON Canada M5M 2J5 Office: Maclean's Mag, 777 Bay St, Toronto, ON Canada M5W 1A7

LEWIS, ROBERT ALAN, physiologist, environmental toxicologist; b. Chillicothe, Ohio, Apr. 23, 1933; s. Clarence Albert and Ethel (Hamm) L.; m. Carolyn Jane Weber, Dec. 22, 1960; 1 child, Cynthia Anne. B.Sc., Ohio State U., 1959; M.Sc., Rutgers U., 1963; Ph.D., U. Wash., 1971. Asst. curator vertebrate collections Ohio Hist. Mus., Columbus, 1958-60; field rep. for vet. pub. health N.J. Dept. Health, Trenton, 1960-61; acting chmn. dept. biology Monroe Coll., Rochester, N.Y., 1963; zoologist Avian Physiology Lab., U. Wash., Seattle, 1966-73, research assoc. dept. zoology, 1973-74, sr. research assoc. dept. zoology, 1974-77; sr. scientist, environ. physiologist Nat. Ecol. Research Lab., Corvallis, Oreg., 1973-77; gen. ecologist, program mgr. Office Health and Environ. Research U.S. Dept. Energy, Washington, 1977-81; prof., dir. Inst. Biogeography U. Saarland, Saarbruecken, Fed. Republic Germany, 1982, prof. Sch. Biogeography, 1982-91; adj. prof. Grad. Sch., Hood Coll., Frederick, Md., 1978-93; cons. toxicology, environmental and biol. monitoring, biotech., risk mgmt., 1991-93; sr. scientist, program dir. Waste Policy Inst., Washington; mem. Pres.'s Water Policy Study; mem. Interagy. Com. on Health and Environ. Effects of Advanced Energy Tech.; mem. Working Group on Western Range Mgmt. of Commn. on Food and Renewable Resources, Fed. Coordinating Council for Sci., Engring. and Tech.; bd. examiners Banares U., India; dir. Mont. Coal-fired power Plant Study, 1973-77; lectr. in field; advisor to govts., facilitator coop. activities between U.S. and West German agys.; ofcl. liaison between Man and the Biosphere Program of U.S. Dept. State and Fed. Republic Germany, 1986—; evaluated and recommended system of Nat. Ecol. Research Parks which were then established by Fed. Republic Germany; dir. programs of rsch. on geomedicine, biol. monitoring, and health and environ. effects of toxic chemicals, pesticides, and air pollutants; mem. sci. adv. coun. environ. assessment program Christian-Albrechts U., Kiel, Fed. Republic Germany; participant Expert Colloquium on Integrated Environ. Assessment, Berlin; chmn. cost efficient acquisition and utilization of data in mgmt. of hazardous waste sites Internat. Conf., Herndon, Va., 1994; participant White House Conf. Tech. for Sustainable Future, 1994; chmn. Internat. Conf. Challenge and Innovation in Mgmt of Hazardous Waste, Washington, 1995. Author, editor: Guidelines for the Establishment of an Environmental Specimen Bank in the Federal Republic of Germany: Ecological Foundations, 1985; editor: Environmental Specimen Banking and Monitoring as Related to Banking, 1984, Cost Efficient Acquisition and Utilization of Data in the Management of Hazardous Waste Sites, 1994, Challenge and Innovations in the Management of Hazardous Waste, 1995; mem. editl. bd. Toxicology and Environmental Chemistry; contbr. chpts. to books and numerous articles to profl. jours.; co-inventor zonal air pollution system. Served with U.S. Army, 1955-58. Grantee in field. Mem. AAAS, Air and Waste Mgmt. Assn., Delattinia, Internat. Statis. Program, Soc. Environ. Toxicology and Chem., Wheaton Club of Ohio, Sigma Xi. Republican. Avocations: hiking; bicycling; camping; natural history. Established research field station; co-designer remote, computerized air quality monitoring and micrometeorological network; tested and applied state-of-the-art controlled environment system; developed new remote sensing application in assessment of chronic pollution effects; active in development environmentally safe energy techs., environ. toxicology, risk assessment. Led the team that selected the Nat. Ecological Rsch. Parks for Fed. Republic Germany.

LEWIS, ROBERT DAVID GILMORE, editor; b. Chgo., Jan. 16, 1932; s. James Lee and Betty (Ryden) L.; m. Georgia Demopoulos, Aug. 4, 1956 (div. July 1988); children: Peter, Sarah, Mary, John, Elizabeth, Daniel, Susan; m. Jacqueline Mc Gregor, July 15, 1988. BA, Mich. State U., 1955. Reporter, city editor Galesburg (Ill.) Register-Mail, 1955-59; reporter, bus. editor Kalamazoo Gazette, 1960-64; state capitol corres. Booth Newspapers, Lansing, Mich., 1964-66; Washington corres. Booth Newspapers, Washington, 1966-87, Newhouse Newspapers, Washington, 1987-91; sr. editor Am. Assn. Retired Persons Bull., Washington, 1991—. Mem. Soc. Profl. Journalists (chmn. freedom info. com. 1978-83, sec.-treas., pres.-elect then pres., 1983-86, Wells Meml. Key award 1980), White House Corres. Assn., Nat. Press Club (chmn. bd. govs. 1975-77), Sigma Delta Chi Found. (bd. dirs. 1986-88). Avocations: antique furniture collecting, fishing. Home: 301 Maryland Ave NE Washington DC 20002-5711 Office: AARP Bulletin 601 E St NW Washington DC 20049

LEWIS, ROBERT EDWIN, JR., pathology immunology educator, researcher; b. Meridian, Miss., Mar. 11, 1947. BA in Biology and Chemistry, U. Miss., 1969, MS in Microbiology, 1973, PhD in Pathology, 1976; specialty tng., Barnes Hosp., U. Miami Med. Ctr., U. Tenn. Ctr. for Health Scis., City of Memphis Hosps., St. Jude Children's Research Hosp. Instr. pathology, anesthesiology U. Miss. Med. Ctr., Jackson, 1976-77, asst. prof. pathology, 1977-84, asst. prof. anesthesiology, 1977-85, asst. dir. clin. immnuopathology lab., 1978-81, assoc. dir. tissue typing lab., 1980-84, dir. paternity testing lab., 1981—, assoc. dir. clin. immunopathology lab., 1981-84, asst. prof. nurse anesthesiology, 1981-85, assoc. prof. pathology, 1984-91, prof., 1991—, co-dir. clin. immunology, tissue typing lab., 1984—, mem. grad. council, 1981—, prof., 1991—. Co-author: Illustrated Dictionary of Immunology, 1995; editor: (with J.M. Cruse) Concepts in Immunopathology, Vols. 1-8, 1985-91, The Year in Immunology-1984-85, 1985, The Year in Immunology-1986-87, 1987, The Year in Immunology-1988, 1989, The Year in Immunology-1989-90, 1990, Progress in Experimental Tumor Research, Vol. 32, 1987, Contributions to Microbiology and Immunology, Vol. 8, 1986, Vol. 9, 1987, Vol. 10, 1989, Vol. 11, 1989, The Year in Immunopathology, 1987, Complement Profiles, Vol. 1, 1992; sr. editor Pathology and Immunopathology Research, 1982-90, Immunologic Research, 1981—, Transgenics, 1993; series editor Concepts in Immunopathology, The Year in Immunology, Contributions to Microbiology and Immunology; vol. editor Progress in Experimental Tumor Research; immunology editor Dorland's Illustrated Medical Dictionary, 26th and 27th edits.; dep. editor-in-chief Pathobiology, 1990—; contbr. chpts. to books. Am. Cancer Soc. grantee, NIH grantee, Wilson Found. grantee, 1990-95. Fellow Royal Soc. Health; mem. AAAS, Am. Assn. Pathologists, Am. Assn. Immunologists, Clin. Immunology Soc., Can. Soc. Immunology, Reticuloendothelial Soc., Am. Soc. Microbiology, Am. Soc. Histocompatibility and Immunogenetics (co-chmn. publs. com., co-chmn. 1987-95), Exptl. Biology and Medicine, N.Y. Acad. Scis., Miss. Acad. Scis., Sigma Xi. Office: U Miss Med Ctr Pathology Dept 2500 N State St Jackson MS 39216-4500

LEWIS, ROBERT ENZER, lexicographer, educator; b. Windber, Pa., Aug. 12, 1934; s. Robert Enzer and Katharine Torrence (Blair) L.; m. Julie Fatt Cureton, May 14, 1977; children: Perrin Lewis Rubin, Torrence Evans Lewis; stepchildren: Sarah Cureton Kaufman, James S. Cureton. BA, Princeton U., 1959; MA, U. Pa., 1962, PhD, 1964. Tchr. English Mercersburg (Pa.) Acad., 1959-60; teaching fellow U. Pa., Phila., 1961-63; lectr. Ind. U., Bloomington, 1963-64, asst. prof., 1964-68, assoc. prof., 1968-75, prof. English, 1975-82; prof. English U. Mich., Ann Arbor, 1982—. Author: (with A. McIntosh) Descriptive Guide to the Manuscripts of the Prick of Conscience, 1982, (with others) Index of Printed Middle English Prose, 1985; editor: De Miseria Condicionis Humane (Lotario dei Segni), 1978; co-editor: Middle English Dictionary, 1982-83, editor-in-chief: vols. 8, 9, 10, 11, 1983—; gen. editor: Chaucer Libr., 1970—, chmn. editl. com., 1978-89; mem. editl. bd. New Oxford English Dictionary, 1984—. Bd. regents Mercersburg Acad., 1975-87. U.S. Army, 1954-56. Vis. rsch. fellow Inst. Advanced Studies in the Humanities, U. Edinburgh, 1973-74; Am. Coun. Learned Socs. fellow, 1979-80. Mem. Medieval Acad. Am. (mem. publs. com. 1987-92), Dictionary Soc. N.Am., New Chaucer Soc. Episcopalian. Office: Middle English Dictionary 555 S Forest Ave Ann Arbor MI 48104-2531

LEWIS, ROBERT J., secondary education educator. Tchr. sci. Downers Grove (Ill.) High Sch. North. Recipient James Bryant Conant award Am. Chem. Soc., 1995. Office: Downers Grove High School N 4436 Main St Downers Grove IL 60515

LEWIS, ROBERT LAWRENCE, lawyer, educator; b. N.Y.C., Sept. 25, 1919; s. Isador and Sadie (Holzinger) L.; m. Frieda Friedman, Nov. 24, 1940 (dec. 1961); children—Brian S., Paul E., David N.; m. Joanne Marcia Waxman, June 16, 1963; children—Pavia S., Eraclea S. A.B., Hamilton Coll., 1940; LL.B., Case Western Res. U., 1948. With firm Ulmer & Berne, Cleve., 1948-64, ptnr., 1956-64; ret., 1964; prof. law, dir. grad. div. Cleve.-Marshall Law Sch. (now Cleve. State U.), 1948-53; bd. dirs. Banner Industries, Inc., Cleve.; scholar-in-residence, prof. classics Cuayhoga C.C.; adj. prof. nonprofit governance Case Western Res. U., Cleve. Author: Five Angry Women, 1990, Agatharcus, 1993. Cons., evaluator North Central Assn. Colls. and Schs., Middle States Assn. Mem. Cleve. Area Arts Council, 1971-73; pres. Fairmount Center for Creative and Performing Arts, 1973-75; trustee, chmn. bd. Cuyahoga Community Coll.; trustee Cuyahoga Community Coll. Found., Playhouse Sq. Found., Cleve., Cleve. Commn. Higher Edn., Lake Erie Coll., Council for Interinstnl. Leadership, Pace Assn., New Orgn. for Visual Arts; bd. dirs. Assn. Governing Bds. Univs. and Colls.; bd. advisers Cleve. Ballet; trustee, v.p. New Cleve. Opera Co. Served to 1st lt., arty. and ordnance corps AUS, 1942-46, NATOUSA. Decorated Legion of Merit, Purple Heart. Mem. Exec. Order Ohio Commodore, Phi Beta Kappa. Home: 2425 N Park Blvd Apt 4 Cleveland OH 44106-3154 Office: 900 Bond Ct Bldg Cleveland OH 44114 *There is neither a standard nor a uniform set of qualities which best fits one to be a member of society, and anyone who contends to the contrary, may be equated with the infamous and mythical Procrustes. I for one prefer the preservation of individuality. No one of us should be fitted to the bed of Procrustes. I prefer that we shall all survive; and each of us shall then be the richer for the survival of the other.*

LEWIS, ROBERT LEE, lawyer; b. Oxford, Miss., Feb. 26, 1944; s. Ernest Elmo and Johnice Georgia (Thirkield) L.; children: Yolanda Sherice, Robert Lee Jr., Dion Terrell, Viron Lamar, William Lovell. BA, Ind. U., 1970, JD, 1973; M in Pub. Service, West Ky. U., 1980. Bar: Ind. 1973, Ky. 1979, U.S. Ct. Claims, U.S. Ct. Internat. Trade, U.S. Tax. Ct., U.S. Ct. Mil. Appeals, U.S. Ct. Appeals (fed. cir.), U.S. Supreme Ct. Sole practice Evansville, Ind., 1973-75, Gary, Ind., 1980—; atty., army officer U.S. Army, Ft. Knox, Ky., 1975-78; appellate referee Ind. Employment Security Div., Indpls., 1978-80. Mem. adv. com. Vincennes (Ind.) U., 1983—; bd. dirs. Opportunities Industrialization Ctr., Evansville, 1973-75. Served to sgt. JAGC, USMC, 1962-66, Vietnam, sgt. U.S. Army, 1975-78, lt. col. USAR. Named Ky. Col. Mem. ABA, Ind. Bar Assn., Ky. Bar Assn., Nat. Bar Assn., Ind. Bd. Realtors, Ind. U. Alumni Assn., Phi Alpha Delta. Methodist. Home and Office: 2148 W 11th Ave Gary IN 46404-2306

LEWIS, ROGER KUTNOW, architect, educator, author; b. Houston, Jan. 9, 1941; s. Nathan D. and Betty (Kutnow) L.; m. Eleanor Draper Roberts, June 24, 1967; 1 child, Kevin Michael. BArch, MIT, 1964, MArch, 1967. Registered architect, D.C., Va., Md. Vol. architect Peace Corps, Nabeul, Tunisia, 1964-66; designer Wilkes & Faulkner, Washington, 1967-68; ptnr. Chavarria/Lewis Assocs., Washington, 1968-71; prin. Roger K. Lewis AIA & Assocs., Washington, 1971-80; pres. Pecla Corp., Washington, 1971-81; ptnr. Chesapeake Design Group, Balt., 1980-81; prin. Roger K. Lewis FAIA, Architect & Planner, Washington, 1981—; prof. U. Md. Sch. Arch., 1968—; mem. D.C. Com. on Design Arts, Washington, 1988-92. Author: Architect? A Candid Guide to the Profession, 1985, Shaping the City, 1987; co-author Growth Management Handbook, 1989; author articles in jours.and periodicals, chpts. in books, encys.; columnist The Washington Post, 1984—. Recipient Fed. Design Achievement award Nat. Endowment for the Arts, Washington, 1988, numerous awards Am. Planning Assn., AAUW, 1985—. Fellow AIA (numerous design awards 1973—); mem. Washington Area Architecture Group (co-founder), Faberge Arts Found. (bd. advs.), Cosmos Club, Lambda Alpha. Home: 5034 1/2 Dana Pl NW Washington DC 20016-3441 Office: Univ Md Sch Architecture College Park MD 20742

LEWIS, ROLLAND WILTON, real estate manager; b. Chgo., Oct. 13, 1930; s. Chester Chalmers and Lillian A. Florence (Fair) L.; m. Sally Louise Watts; children: John, Jeffrey, James Brian, Robert. Student, U. Ill., Chgo. Broker John W. Watts Jr. Seedsman Co., Mt. Vernon, Ill., 1959-75; real estate contractor Lewis & Farley Constrn. Co., Mt. Vernon, 1960-65; pres., gen. mgr. House de Lions, Ltd., Mt. Vernon, 1962-69; v.p., CEO Mr. Ice of Ill., Inc., Mt. Vernon, 1977-89; mgr. Rolland and Sally Lewis, A Co., Mt. Vernon, 1984—; chmn. bd. rev. dept. employment securities State of Ill., 1993—; bd. dirs. Risk Mgmt. Assn., IML; mem. Greater Egypt Planning Commn.; past mem. Gov.'s Adv. Bd. Ill.; chmn. bd. review Dept. Employment Securities, State Ill., 1993—. Mayor City of Mt. Vernon, 1969-77, 85—; participant USEPA Pub.-Pvt. Parternship Program, Washington, 1988—; bd. dirs. Fed. Environ. Fin. Adv. Bd., Washington, 1989—, Ill.

Econ. Bd., 1990—, Ill. Commn. on the Future of Pub. Svc., 1990—; pres., exec. com. Ill. Mcpl. League; past pres. Mt. Vernon YMCA; past v.p. So. Ill. YMCA; past drive chmn. United Fund, Jefferson County, Ill.; lt. col. de camp State of Ala.; active VFW, Amvets, Am. Legion. Gunnery sgt. USMC, 1957-59. Recipient Nat. Fellowship award YMCA; named to Hon. Ky. Cols. Mem. Mt. Vernon Jaycees (hon. life mem.), So. Ill. Mayors Assn. (organizer, 1st pres., bd. dirs.). Republican. Avocations: history, armed and edged weapons.

LEWIS, RON, congressman; b. Greenup County, Ky., Sept. 14, 1946; m. Kayi Gambill, 1966; children: Ronald Brent, Allison Faye. Student, Morehead State U.; BA in History and Polit. Sci., U. Ky., 1969; MA in Higher Edn., Morehead State U., 1981; student, USN Officer Candidate Sch. Ordained to ministry Bapt. Ch. With Ky. Hwy. Dept., Ea. State Hosp.; with sales various cos.; tchr. Watterson Coll., 1980-85; pastor White Mills Bapt. Ch.; owner small bus. Elizabethtown, Ky.; mem. 103d-104th Congresses from 2d Ky. Dist., 1994—; mem. mil. procurement and mil. pers. subcoms., nat. security com., mem. risk mgmt. and splty. crops and resource conservation, rsch. and forestry subcoms., agr. com. Past pres. Hardin and Larue County Jail Ministry. Named Guardian of Srs.' Rights, Tax Fairness Srs.; honoree U.S. Term Limits, League Pvt. Property Rights, Coun. Citizens Against Govt. Waste, Nat. Fed. Ind. Bus. Mem. Severus Valley Ministerial Assn., Elizabethtown C. of C. Office: US House Representatives 412 Cannon House Office Bldg Washington DC 20515-1702

LEWIS, RUSSELL CARL, JR., family nurse practitioner; b. Charlotte, N.C., Nov. 8, 1946. AS, Cen. Piedmont Community Coll., Charlotte, 1972. Cert. family nurse practitioner, BCLS, ACLS. Adminstr., healthcare provider, owner Downtown Med. Ctr., Charlotte; staff nurse, mem. emergency room computer com. Carolinas Med. Ctr., Charlotte; prin. in design of downtown med. ctr. With USNR, 1964-70.

LEWIS, RUSSELL T., newspaper publishing executive. Pres., gen. mgr. The N.Y. Times, N.Y.C., 1993—. Office: NY Times 229 W 43rd St New York NY 10036-3913

LEWIS, SAMUEL WINFIELD, retired government official, former ambassador; b. Houston, Oct. 1, 1930; s. Samuel Winfield and Sue Roselle (Hurley) L.; m. Sallie Kate Smoot, June 20, 1953; children: Pamela Gracelle, Richard Winfield. BA magna cum laude, Yale U., 1952; MA, Johns Hopkins U., 1954; PhD (hon.), Tel Aviv U., 1985, Hebrew U. Jerusalem, 1985, Weizman Inst. Sci., 1985; DHL (hon.), Hebrew Union Coll., 1986, Balt. Hebrew U., 1988; LLD (hon.), Salem-Teikyo U., 1991. Exec. asst. Am. Trucking Assn., Washington., 1953-54; fgn. svc. officer Dept. State, Washington, 1954-85; consular officer Naples, Italy, 1954-55; consul Florence, Italy, 1955-59; officer-in-charge Italian affairs Washington, 1959-61, spl. asst. to undersec. state, 1961, spl. asst. to spl. rep. of pres., 1961-63; dep. asst. dir. US AID Mission to Brazil, Rio de Janeiro, 1964-65; exec. officer embassy, Rio de Janeiro, 1965-67; dep. dir. Office Brazil Affairs, Washington, 1967-68; sr. staff mem. for Latin Am. Affairs Nat. Security Council, White House, Washington, 1968-69; spl. asst. for policy planning Bur. Inter-Am. Affairs, Washington, 1969; spl. asst. to dir. gen. Fgn. Svc., 1970-71; dep. chief mission and counselor embassy Kabul, Afghanistan, 1971-74; dep. dir. policy planning staff Dept. State, 1974-75, asst. sec. state for internat. orgn., 1975-77; U.S. ambassador to Israel, 1977-85; lectr., diplomat-in-residence Johns Hopkins Fgn. Policy Inst., Washington, 1985-86; pres. U.S. Inst. of Peace, Washington, 1987-93; dir. policy planning staff U.S. Dept. State, Washington, 1993-94; cons. U.S. Dept. State, 1994-95; sr. internat. fellow The Dayan Ctr., Tel Aviv U., 1986-87; chmn. bd. overseers Harry S. Truman Rsch. Inst. for Advancement of Peace and Hebrew U., 1986-91; guest scholar The Brookings Inst., Washington, 1987; mem. bd. advisors Washington Inst. Near East Policy, 1986-93, counselor, 1995—; adv. com. Initiative for Peace and Cooperation on the Mid. East, Washington, 1994—; vis. prof. Hamilton Coll., spring 1995, adj. prof. Sch. Fgn. Svc., Georgetown U., 1996. Author: Making Peace Among Arabs and Israelis, 1991; contbg. author: The Middle East: Ten Years After Camp David, 1988, Soviet-American Competition in the Middle East, 1988, Israel: The Peres Era, 1987; contbr. articles to profl. jours., also N.Y. Times, Washington Post. Bd. dirs. Inst. for Study Diplomacy, Georgetown U., 1994—; vice chmn. Ctr. Preventive Action, Coun. Fgn. Rels., 1994—. Recipient William A. Jump award for outstanding service in pub. adminstrn., 1967, Meritorious Honor award Dept. State, 1967, Meritorious Honor award AID, 1967, Pres.' Mgmt. Improvement cert., 1971, Distinguished Honor award Dept. State, 1977, 85, Disting. Alumnus award Johns Hopkins U., 1980, Wilbur J. Carr award Dept. State, 1985; vis. fellow Princeton U., 1963-64. Mem. Am. Acad. Diplomacy (vice chmn. bd. dirs. 1995—), Am. Fgn. Svc. Assn., UN Assn., Coun. Fgn. Rels., Middle East Inst., Assn. Diplomatic Studies and Tng. (bd. dirs. 1995—), Cousteau Soc., Sierra Club, Phi Beta Kappa. Episcopalian.

LEWIS, SHARI, puppeteer, entertainer; b. N.Y.C., Jan. 17, 1934; d. Abraham B. and Ann (Ritz) Hurwitz; m. Jeremy Tarcher, Mar. 15, 1958; 1 child, Mallory. Star weekly NBC-TV show The Shari Lewis Show, 1960-63, weekly syndicated series Lambchop's Play-Along (named TV Guide's Best of Best for Children), 1975-77, weekly TV show BBC, London, 1969-75, weekly TV show for ind. network in Gt. Britain, 1970, daily TV show PBS, 1992—; writer, producer, star NBC spl. A Picture of Us, 1971; performer or condr. with over 100 symphonies in U.S., Can., Japan, 1977—; command performances, London, 1970, 73, 78; author 60 pub. books including 15 One Minute Bedtime Stories (bestselling series); 24 home video cassettes: including 101 Things for Kids to do Shari's Christmas Concert, Don't Wake Your Mom, 1992, Let's Make Music, 1994; appeared in shows including Bye Bye Birdie, Funny Girl. Past mem. nat. bd. dirs. Girl Scouts U.S.; past internat. bd. dirs. Boy Scouts Am.; past pres. Am. Ctr. Films for Children; past hon. chmn. bd. trustees Internat. Reading Found.; trustee Greater L.A. Zoo Assn. Recipient 11 Emmy awards, including award for best program and outstanding female personality, 1989, for outstanding performer in a children's program, 1992, outstanding writing in children's series, 1993, outstanding performer in a children's series, 1993, 94, 95, daytime Emmy for performer in a children's series; Peabody award, 1960, 50th Anniversary Dir.'s award Ohio State Award Com., 1988, Monte Carlo Internat. TV award, 1963, Radio-TV Mirror award, 1960, Kennedy Ctr. award for excellence in arts for young people, 1986, Video Choice award, 1988, Parents Choice award, 1992, Calif. Media award, 1992, Dir. Choice Recognition award, 1992, Assn. Visual Communicators Gold Cindy award, 1992, Parents Mag. prize, 1993, Gemini award for LambChop's Play Along, 1994; TV Guide Top Ten Children's Shows, 1993. Office: care Jim Golden 3128 Cavendish Dr Los Angeles CA 90064-4743

LEWIS, SHEILA MURIEL O'NEIL, retired communications management specialist; b. Glendive, Mont., Sept. 23, 1937; d. John Edward and Muriel Christine (Johnson) O'Neil; m. Lyndell W. Lewis, Dec. 14, 1957 (div. 1973); children: Sheri Lynne, Debra Lynne, Linda Marie, Valerie Jean. AA, Colo. Women's Coll., 1957; BS, U. No. Colo., 1976; postgrad., Stanford U. Adminstrv. asst. DAFC/Dept. Defense DOT/FAA, Denver, 1956-64; substitute tchr. Portland (Oreg.) Public Schs., 1964-72; communications operator Denver Air Rt. Traffic Control Ctr., 1972-78, communications specialist, 1978-80, computer programmer, 1980-82, air traffic controller, 1982-86; communications specialist Air Force Space Command, Falcon AFB, Colo., 1986-95, retired, 1995. Troop leader Campfire Girls, Las Vagas, 1964-72, pres. PTA, Las Vagas, 1964-72. ,. Mem. AAUW, Armed Forces Communications and Electronics Assn., Aviation Space Edn. Assn., Civil Air Patrol, Univ. Aviation Assn., Order of Eastern Star, Order of White Shrine Jerusalem, Chi Omega. Democrat. Lutheran. Avocations: pilot, travel, history, archeology, anthropology. Home: 4934 Daybreak Cir Colorado Springs CO 80917-2657

LEWIS, SHELDON NOAH, technology consultant; b. Chgo., July 1, 1934; s. Jacob Joseph and Evelyn (Mendelsohn) Iglowitz; m. Suzanne Joyce Goldberg, June 17, 1957; children: Sara Lynn, Matthew David, Rachel Ann. BA with honors, Northwestern U., 1956, MS (Univ. fellow), 1956; PhD (Eastman Kodak fellow), UCLA, 1959; postgrad. (NSF fellow), U. Basel, Switzerland, 1959-60; postgrad. cert. in research mgmt, Indsl. Research Inst., Harvard U., 1973. With Rohm & Haas Co., 1960-78, head lab., 1963-68, research supr., 1968-73, dir. splty. chem. research, 1973-74; gen. mgr. DCL Lab. AG subs., Zurich, Switzerland, 1974-75; dir. European Labs. Valbonne, France, 1975-76; corp. dir. research and devel. worldwide for polymers, resins and monomers Spring House, Pa., 1976-78; with The Clorox Co., Oakland, Calif., 1978-91, v.p. R&D, 1978, group v.p., 1978-84, exec. v.p., 1984-91, also bd. dirs.; pres. SNL Inc., Lafayette, Calif., 1991—; mem. indsl. panel on sci. and tech. NSF. Referee: Jour. Organic Chemistry; patentee in field; contbr. articles to profl. publs. Mem. Calif. Inst. Adv. Bd., World Affairs Council, UCLA Chemistry Adv. Council, Bay Area Sci. Fair Adv. Bd., Mills Coll. Adv. Council for Sci. and Math. Recipient cert. in patent law Phila. Patent Law Assn., 1962, Roon award for coatings research Fedn. Socs. Coatings Tech., 1966, cert. of service Wayne State U. Polymer Conf. Series, 1967, cert. in mgmt. by objectives Am. Mgmt. Research, Inc., 1972. Mem. Soap and Detergent Assn. (bd. dirs.), Chem. Ind. Inst. of Toxicology (bd. dirs.), Indsl. Rsch. Inst., Am. Chem. Soc. (chmn. Phila. polymer sect. 1970-71), Soc. Chem. Industry London, Sigma Xi. Jewish. Office: SNL Inc 3711 Rose Ct Lafayette CA 94549-3030

LEWIS, SHERMAN RICHARD, JR., investment banker; b. Ottawa, Ill., Dec. 11, 1936; s. Sherman Richard and Julia Audrey (Rusteen) L.; m. Dorothy Marie Downie, Sept. 9, 1967; children: Thomas, Catherine, Elizabeth, Michael. AB, Northwestern U., 1958; MBA, U. Chgo., 1964. With investment dept. Am. Nat. Bank & Trust Co., Chgo., 1961-64; v.p. Halsey, Stuart & Co., N.Y.C., 1964-70, v.p. in charge corp. fin. dept., 1970-73; v.p. C.J. Lawrence & Sons, N.Y.C., 1970; ptnr. Loeb, Rhoades & Co., N.Y.C., 1973-76, ptnr. in charge corp. fin. dept., 1975-76, exec. v.p., bd. dirs., 1976-77, pres., co-chief exec. officer, 1977-78; vice chmn., co-chief exec. officer Loeb Rhoades, Hornblower & Co., N.Y.C., 1978-79; pres. Shearson/Am. Express Inc., N.Y.C., 1979-82, vice chmn., 1983-84; vice chmn. Shearson Lehman/Am. Express Inc., 1984-85, Shearson Lehman Bros. Inc., 1985-87, Shearson Lehman Hutton Inc., 1988-89; co-chief exec. officer, vice chmn., chmn. exec. com. Lehman Bros., 1990; vice chmn. Shearson Lehman Bros. Holdings, Inc., N.Y.C., 1990-93, Lehman Bros. Holdings, Inc., Lehman Bros., Inc., 1993—. Mem. Pres.'s Commn. on Housing, 1981-82, Pres.'s Coun. on Internat. Youth Exch., 1982-88; trustee Northwestern U., 1992—, regent, 1990—; mem. vis. com. Coll. Arts and Scis., Northwestern U., 1981—, chmn., 1990—; mem. coun. Grad. Sch. Bus., U. Chgo., 1991—; bd. dirs. The Korea Soc., U.S.-Greek Bus. Coun. Commd. officer USMC, 1958-61. Mem. N.Y. Soc. Security Analysts, The Pilgrims, Bond Club, Ridgewood Country Club, Univ. Club, Quogue Field Club. Office: Lehman Bros Inc 3 World Financial Ctr New York NY 10285-1800

LEWIS, STEPHEN RICHMOND, JR., economist, academic administrator; b. Englewood, N.J., Feb. 11, 1939; s. Stephen Richmond and Esther (Magan) L.; children: Virginia, Deborah, Mark. BA, Williams Coll., 1960, LLD, 1987; MA, Stanford U., 1962, PhD, 1963; LHD, Doshisha U., 1993. Instr. Stanford U., 1962-63; research advisor Pakistan Inst. Devel. Econs., Karachi, 1963-65; asst. prof. econs. Harvard U., 1965-66; asst. prof. econs. Williams Coll., 1966-68, assoc. prof., 1968-73, prof., 1973-76, Herbert H. Lehman prof., 1976-87, provost of coll., 1968-71, 73-77, spl. asst. to pres., 1979-80, dir. Williams-Botswana Project, 1982-88, chmn. dept. econs., 1984-86; vis. sr. research fellow Inst. Devel. Studies, Nairobi, Kenya, 1971-73; econ. cons. to Ministry of Finance and Devel. Planning, Govt. of Botswana, 1977—; vis. fellow Inst. Devel. Studies, Sussex, Eng., 1986-87; pres., prof. econs. Carleton Coll., Northfield, Minn., 1987—; cons. econs. Ford Found., Edna McConnell Clark Found., World Bank, Orgn. Econ. Coop. and Devel., Govts. of Kenya, Philippines, Botswana; trustee Carnegie Endowment for Internat. Peace, 1988—. Author: (with others) Relative Price Changes and Industrialization in Pakistan, 1969, Economic Policy and Industrial Growth in Pakistan, 1969, Pakistan: Industrialization and Trade Policy, 1970, Williams in the Eighties, 1980, Taxation for Development, 1983, South Africa: Has Time Run Out?, 1986, Policy Choice and Development Performance in Botswana, 1989, The Economics of Apartheid, 1989; editorial bd. Jour. Econ. Lit., 1985-87. Contbr. chpts. to books, articles to profl. jours. Exec. com. Indianhead coun. Boy Scouts Am., 1989—. Decorated Presdl. Order of Meritorious Svc. (Botswana), 1983; Danforth Found. fellow, 1960-63; Ford Found. dissertation fellow, 1962-63; recipient Disting. Eagle Scout award, 1993. Mem. Council on Fgn. Relations, Nat. Tax Assn., Am. Econ. Assn., Phi Beta Kappa. Office: Carleton Coll Office Pres 1 N College St Northfield MN 55057-4001*

LEWIS, STEVE, Olympic athlete, track and field. Olympic track and field participant Seoul, Korea, 1988, Barcelona, Spain, 1992. Recipient 400m Track and Field Gold medal Olympics, Seoul, 1988, 400m Track and Field Silver medal Olympics, Barcelona, 1992, 4x400m relay Gold medal Olympics, Seoul, 1988, Barcelona, 1992. Office: US Olympic Com 1750 E Boulder St Colorado Springs CO 80909-5724*

LEWIS, SYLVIA GAIL, journalist; b. N.Y.C., Apr. 8, 1945; d. Ben and Clara Lewis. BA, Cornell U., 1967; MA, U. Wash., Seattle, 1968; MS in Journalism, Northwestern U., 1974. Reporter Seattle-Post Intelligencer, 1968-69; asst. editor Cowles Book Co., N.Y.C., 1969-70; with Am. Planning Assn., Chgo., 1974—, mng. editor Planning mag., 1975-77, dir. pubs., editor, assoc. pub. Planning mag., 1977—. Contbr. articles to profl. jours. Bd. dirs. Bright New City, 1995—. Mem. Soc. Profl. Journalists, Chgo. Headline Club (pres. 1992-93), Soc. Nat. Assn. Publs. (pres. Chgo. chpt. 1986-87, nat. bd. dirs. 1989-91), Northwestern U. Alumni Assn., Cornell Club of Chgo., Phi Beta Kappa. Office: Am Planning Assn 1313 E 60th St Chicago IL 60637-2830

LEWIS, THOMAS B., specialty chemical company executive; b. Cleve.; s. Bryn H. and Margaret (Connaughton) L.; m. Mary C. Lewis. B.S., John Carroll U., M.S.; Ph.D., MIT; postdoctoral fellow, Cornell U.; postgrad. Exec. Program, Stanford U., 1983. With Monsanto Co., St. Louis, 1966-88, sr. rsch. chemist, rsch. group leader, project mgr., mgr. comml. devel., dir. corp. rsch. labs. & R&D, gen. mgr. Rubber Chem. divsn.; corp. v.p. Celgene Corp., Warren, N.J., 1988-92; pres., CEO Chiral Techs. Inc., Exton, Pa., 1992—; pres. Akron Polymer Lecture Group, 1977-78. Mem. AAAS, Am. Chem. Soc., Am. Phys. Soc., Soc. Chem. Industries, N.Y. Acad. Sci., Sigma Xi. Roman Catholic. Office: Chiral Techs Inc PO Box 564 Exton PA 19341-0564

LEWIS, THOMAS JOHN, III, hospital administrator; b. Pitts., Mar. 26, 1952; s. Thomas John and Nancy (Hoser) L.; m. Kathleen Dalrymple, Sept. 4, 1983; children: Benjamin Stephen, Jeffrey Thomas. BA in Biology, Bucknell U., 1974; MHA, Duke U., 1976. Adminstrv. resident Thomas Jefferson U. Hosp., Phila., 1976-77, acting dir. quality assurance and MR, 1977-79, mgr. care program, 1979-82, asst. exec. dir., 1982-85, dir., 1984-85, assoc. exec. dir., 1985-89, exec. dir., chief oper. officer, 1989-90, sr. v.p., chief exec. officer, 1990—; now pres., CEO Thomas Jefferson Univ. Hospital, Philadelphia, PA. Bd. dirs. Phila. Healthh Acad., 1989—, Welcon of Delaware Valley, Phila., 1990—. Mem. Am. Coll. Health Care Execs. (nominee), Delaware Valley Hosp. Coun., Hosp. Assn. Pa. Home: 123 W End Ave Haddonfield NJ 08033-2617 Office: Thomas Jefferson U Hosp Walnut 11th St Philadelphia PA 19107*

LEWIS, THOMAS PROCTOR, law educator; b. Ashland, Ky., Mar. 26, 1930; s. Blaine and Hallie Maud (Heal) L.; m. Nancy Ann Magruder, Sept. 27, 1949; children: Jean, Catherine, Jennifer, Blaine. A.B., U. Ky., 1959, LL.B., 1954; S.J.D., Harvard U., 1964. Asst. prof. law U. Ky., 1957-59, assoc. prof., 1959-60, prof., 1961-65, acad. asst. to pres., 1964-65, dean Coll. of Law, 1976-82, prof., 1982—; prof. law U. Minn., 1965-72, Boston U., 1972-76; of counsel Wyatt, Tarrant & Combs, 1982-86 ; vis. prof. U. Chgo., 1962, U. Wash., 1963-64; labor arbitrator, 1965—; spl. justice Ky. Supreme Ct., 1995. Author: (with R. Levy, P. Martin) Social Welfare and the Individual, 1971; contbr. articles to law jours. Served with USNR, 1954-57. Mem. Ky., Mass. bar assns., Nat. Acad. Arbitrators, Am. Law Inst., Am. Arbitration Assn. Office: U Ky Coll of Law Lexington KY 40506

LEWIS, TIMOTHY K., federal judge; b. 1954. BA, Tufts U., 1976; JD, Duquesne U., 1980. Asst. dist. atty. Allegheny County Dist. Attys. Office, Pa., 1980-83; asst. U.S. atty. U.S. Attys. Office (we. dist.) Pa., 1983-91; fed. judge U.S. Dist. Ct. (we. dist.) Pa., 1991-92, U.S. Ct. Appeals (3d cir.), Pitts., 1992—; vis. com. mem. U. Chgo. Law Sch., 1993-96. Former bd. dirs. Ctr. Victims Violent Crime; former mem. Aid Citizen Enterprise. Mem. Pa. Bar Assn. (del. to PBA ho. of dels. 1989-91), Allegheny County Bar Assn. (mem. jud. com. 1988-90, mem. profl. ethics com., mem. planning com., chmn. subcom. minorities in law of planning com., mem. nominating com., mem. fin. com., mem. minorities mentor program, mem. women in law com., fed. ct. sect.), Homer S. Brown Bar Assn., The Boule, Alpha House (former bd. dirs.). Office: US Ct of Appeals 3rd Cir 1014 US Courthouse 7th Ave And Grant St Pittsburgh PA 15219*

LEWIS, TOLA ETHRIDGE, JR., state agency administrator, martial arts instructor; b. Columbia, S.C., July 7, 1945; s. Tola Ethridge and Hettie (Willets) L.; m. Frances Rebecca Coggins, July 10, 1965 (div. Jan., 1978); m. Martha E. Cartwright, Mar. 24, 1978: children: Toby Isaac, Charles Andrew. AB, East Carolina U., 1972. Dist. vets. svc. officer N.C. Div. Vets. Affairs, Elizabeth City, 1972—; instr. karate. Contbr. articles to martial arts jours. With USN, 1964-66, retired USNR, 1989. Mem. Am. Legion (comdr. dist., chmn. oratorical contest), Nat. Karate and Jujitsu Union (dir. 1989—). Republican. Baptist. Avocations: karate (9th degree black belt). Home: PO Box 1331 Elizabeth City NC 27906-1331 Office: NC Div Vets Affairs 1023 Us Highway 17 S Ste 2 Elizabeth City NC 27909-9666

LEWIS, WALTER DAVID, historian; b. Towanda, Pa., June 24, 1931; s. Gordon Cleon and Eleanor Esther (Tobias) L.; m. Carolyn Wyatt Brown, June 12, 1954 (div. 1980); children: Daniel Kent, Virginia Lorraine, Nancy Ellyn; m. Patricia L. Freeman, Apr. 26, 1986. BA cum laude, Pa. State U., 1952, MA, 1954; PhD, Cornell U., 1961. Instr. pub. speaking Hamilton Coll., Clinton, N.Y., 1954-57; fellowship coordinator Eleutherian Mills-Hagley Found., Wilmington, Del.; also lectr. history U. Del., 1959-65; assoc. prof. history SUNY, Buffalo, 1965-71, prof., 1971; Hudson prof. history and engring. Auburn (Ala.) U., 1971-95, disting. Univ. prof., 1994—; dir. univ. project tech., human values and so. future, 1974-79; sr. fellow in Am. civilization Cornell U., 1958-59; vis. prof. history U. Tex.-Dallas, summer 1982, 83, 84; pres., dir. conf. on history of civil and comml. aviation (ICCA 92), Swiss Transport Mus., Lucerne, Switzerland, 1992; Charles A. Lindbergh prof. of aerospace history Nat. Air and Space Mus., 1993-94. Exec. co-prodr. (documentary film): About Us: A Deep South Portrait, 1977; author: From Newgate to Dannemora: The Rise of the Penitentiary in New York, 1965, Iron and Steel in America, 1976, Sloss Furnaces and The Rise of the Birmingham District: An Industrial Epic, 1994; co-author: Delta: The History of an Airline, 1979, Hopewell Furnace, 1983, The Airway to Everywhere: A History of All American Aviation, 1937-53, 1988; contbg. author: The Professions in America, 1965, Technology in Western Civilization, 1967, The Development of an American Culture, 1969, Notable American Women, 1971, Great Engineers and Pioneers in Technology, 1981, Technology in America, 2d edit., 1990, Science-Technology Relationships, 1993; co-editor: Economic Change in the Civil War Era, 1965, The Southern Mystique: Technology and Human Values in Changing Region, 1977; gen. editor Procs. of the Internat. Conf. on the History of Civil and Commercial Aviation, 1995; contbr. articles to profl. jours. Grantee NEH, 1973-79, 80—, Delta Airlines Found. 1973-79, Eleutherian Mills Hist. Libr., 1970-73, 80; postdoctoral fellow Nat. Humanities Inst., U. Chgo., 1978-79, Mellon fellow Va. Hist. Soc., 1988, 89, 92; recipient Leonardo da Vinci medal, (Soc. for the Hist. of Tech., 1993). Mem. Soc. History Tech., Ala. Hist. Assn., Lexington Group Transp. Historians, Phi Beta Kappa. Episcopalian. Home: 210 Lee Dr Auburn AL 36830-6722 Office: Auburn U Dept History 310 Thach Hall Auburn AL 36849-5207

LEWIS, WAYNE H., investment company executive; b. N.Y.C., July 3, 1931; s. Harry Wayne and Eleanor (Diegoli) L.; m. Mary Jane Durnford, June 18, 1956; 1 child, Laura Alane. AB, Harvard U., 1953. Sales, instr. Exxon Corp., Boston, 1956-59; sales Conn. Gen. Life Ins. Co., Hartford, Conn., 1959-62; mgr. Mass. Gen. Life Ins. Co., Boston, 1962-67; v.p. sales Integon Corp., Winston-Salem, N.C., 1967-69; v.p. Lionel D. Edie & Co., N.Y.C., 1969-72; v.p. fin. planning 1st Pa. Bank, Phila., 1970-72; pres., owner Investor Svcs. Ltd., Villanova, Pa., 1972—. Chmn., bd. trustees Anthony Wayne Found., Paoli, 1991—; pres. Wayne Family Orgn., Paoli, 1988—; mem., oper. com. Wayne Mus., Paoli, 1984—. Mem. Union League Pa. (life), Merion Cricket Club, Desert Mountain Club, The Estancia Club, Chaine des Rotisseurs (officer exec. com. 1982—). Avocations: aerobics, off road driving & hiking, exploring nat. and state parks. Home: 200 S Ithan Ave Villanova PA 19085-1432 Office: Investor Svcs Ltd PO Box 310 Villanova PA 19085-0310

LEWIS, WELBOURNE WALKER, JR., lawyer; b. Lewisburg, Tenn., Jan. 11, 1915; s. Welbourne Walker and Jessie (Culbertson) L.; m. Esther Phillips, July 26, 1975; children by previous marriage—Welbourne Walker III, H. Hunter, Berton B. A.B., Dartmouth, 1936; J.D., Harvard U., 1939. Bar: Ohio 1939. Since practiced in Dayton; asso. Smith, Schnacke & Compton, 1939-45; mem. Smith & Schnacke, 1945-75; chmn. Master Consol., Inc., 1950-67; sec. Mead Corp., Dayton, 1952-64, gen. counsel, 1958-75, dir., 1959-75. Former mem. bd. dirs. Dayton dept. ARC; former trustee Dayton Pvt. Sch. Found. Mem. Phi Beta Kappa, Delta Tau Delta, Delta Sigma Rho. Episcopalian (former trustee, mem. planning com. Diocese So. Ohio, former mem. diocesan standing com., former sr. warden). Club: Dartmouth (Dayton). Home: 3720 Ridgeleigh Rd Dayton OH 45429-1252

LEWIS, WILBUR CURTIS, surgeon; b. Okmulgee, Okla., Sept. 10, 1930; s. Charles D. and Eula Alice (Cole) L.; m. Gladys Sherman, Jan. 28, 1955; children: Karen Kay, Mark David, Leanne Gwynneth, Cristen Sue. BS, Okla. Bapt. U., 1952; MD, Okla. U., 1955. Diplomate Am. Bd. Family Practice (charter); ordained to ministry Bapt. Ch. as pastor, 1953. Intern Harris Hosp., Ft. Worth, 1955-56; resident in surgery VA Hosp., Dallas, 1956-57, Univ. Hosp., Oklahoma City, 1965-67; med. missionary So. Bapt. Conv., Costa Rica and Paraguay, 1959-70; pvt. practice medicine specializing in surgery, Oklahoma City, 1970—; leader med. disaster relief team, Honduras, 1975, Guatemala, 1976, Dominican Republic, 1977; surgeon, lectr. Maraciabo, Venezuela, 1989, Taxila, Pakistan, 1990, Bangalore, India, 1990, Guito, Ecuador, 1991, Signatepeque and Teguigalpa, Honduras, 1993; mem. staff Bapt. Hosp., Deaconess Hosp., Mercy Hosp., St. Anthony Hosp., Oklahoma City Hosp.; deacon, mem. meml. trust com. 1st Bapt. Ch., Oklahoma City; former chmn. deacons and social ministries com.; former pastor various chs., Okla. and Paraguay; co-founder, former pres. Baptist Med. Dental Fellowship; lectr. on surgery and burn care topics in Venezuela, Pakistan, India and Equador and Honduras. Past pres. Midwest City C. of C. Capt. USAF, 1957-59. Decorated knight Knights of Malta. Fellow ACS, Internat. Coll. Surgeons; mem. AMA, Internat. Fedn. Surgical Colls., Okla. State Med. Assn. (former del. and alt. del.), Christian Med. and Dental Soc. (former del.), Oklahoma City Surg. Soc., Am. Burn Assn., Internat. Soc. Burn Injuries (burn care com.), Oklahoma City Clin. Soc. Democrat. Home: 14501 N Western Ave Edmond OK 73013-1828 Office: 3141 NW Expressway St Oklahoma City OK 73112-4143

LEWIS, WILBUR H., educational management consultant; b. Belmont, Ohio, Sept. 16, 1930; s. Charles W. and Lily B. (Dunfee) L.; m. Jean E. Lewis, Aug. 23, 1958; children—David, Deretta, Denise, Dawn, Darrin. Student, Miami U., Oxford, Ohio, 1948-51; B.S.B.A., Ohio State U., 1953; M.Ed., Ohio U., 1961, Ph.D., 1964. Tchr. pub. schs. Scioto County, Ohio, 1957; tchr., adminstr. public schs. Belmont County, Ohio, 1958-60; grad. asst. Ohio U., 1960-61; prin. high sch., adminstrv. asst. to supt. public schs. Athens, Ohio, 1961-64; asst. prof., adviser to Govt. of Nigeria, 1964-66; asst. supt. pub. schs. Athens, Ohio, 1966-67; prin. high sch. public schs. Wilmington, Ohio, 1967-68; with Parma (Ohio) City Schs., 1968-77, asst. to supt., 1968-70, asst. supt., 1970-72, assoc. supt., 1972-75, supt., 1975-77; supt. Tucson Unified Sch. Dist., 1977-79; cons. ednl. mgmt. Tucson, 1979—; vice chmn. nat. adv. coun. Edn. Disadvantaged Children, 1972-80; interim supt. Ariz. State Schs. for Deaf and Blind, 1994-95. Planning divsn. United Way, Tucson, 1978-80; bd. dirs. Jr. Achievement, 1978-80. With U.S. Army, 1954-56. Recipient numerous civic awards for community service; Kettering Found. fellow, 1970. Mem. Am. Assn. Sch. Adminstrs., Buckeye Assn. Sch. Adminstrs., Masons, Shriners, Rotary Internat. (v.p. Tucson 1987—, past pres., dist. gov.'s rep. group study exch. dist. 9120 Nigeria, dist. 550 1990, chmn. group study exch. dist. 5490 1991-93), Phi Delta Kappa, Lambda Chi Alpha, Sigma Phi Epsilon. Rsch. in orgnl. devel., adminstrv. behavior patterns, tchr. job satisfaction, student achievement. Home: PO Box 31690 Tucson AZ 85751-1690 *To achieve one must aspire. To aspire one must dream. But if dreams and aspirations are to become achievements one must persevere. The perseverance necessary to turn dreams and aspirations into achievements has always been made easier for me knowing that children and youth were the benefactors of my efforts.*

LEWIS, WILLIAM HEADLEY, JR., manufacturing company executive; b. Washington, Sept. 29, 1934; s. William Headley and Lois Maude (Bradshaw) L.; BS in Metall. Engring., Va. Poly. Inst., 1956; postgrad. Grad. Sch. Bus. Adminstrn., Emory U., 1978; m. Carol Elizabeth Cheek, Apr. 22, 1967; children: Teresa Lynne, Bret Cameron, Charles William, Kevin Marcus. Various positions Lockheed Corp., Marietta, Ga. 1956-1987; mgr. engring. tech. services, 1979-83, dir. engring. Getex div., 1983-86; gen. mgr. Inspection Systems div. Lockheed Air Terminal, Inc., 1986-87; pres., CEO Measurement Systems Inc., Atlanta, 1987—; chmn. Lockheed Corp. Task Force on NDE, 1980-86; mem. Com. to Study Role of Advanced Tech. in Improving Reliability and Maintainability of Future Weapon Systems, Office of Sec. of Def., 1984-85; co-founder, dir., exec. v.p. Applied Tech. Svcs., Inc., 1967—; pres. CEO Applied Tech. Fin. Corp., Atlanta, 1993—; mng. ptnr. Tech. Fin. Co., LLC; lectr. grad. studies and continuing edn. Union Coll., Schenectady, 1977-82. Served to 1st lt. USAF, 1957-60. Registered profl. engr., Calif. Fellow Am. Soc. for Non-destructive Testing (nat. dir. 1976-78, chmn. nat. tech. council 1977-78, chmn. aerospace com. 1972-74, nat. nominating com. 1982-83, 1984-85); mem. Am. Inst. Aeronautics and Astronics, Am. Soc. for Metals, Nat. Mgmt. Assn., NAS (mem. com. on compressive fracture 1981-83), Brotherhood of the Knights of the Vine, St. Ives Country Club, Country Club Sapphire Valley. Editor: Prevention of Structural Failures: The Role of Fracture Mechanics, Failure Analysis, and NDT, 1978; patentee detection apparatus for structural failure in aircraft. Home: 3127 St Ives Country Club Pky Duluth GA 30155-2038 Office: 2262 Northwest Pky Ste B Marietta GA 30067-9306

LEWIS, WILLIAM HENRY, JR., lawyer; b. Durham, N.C., Nov. 12, 1942; s. William Henry Sr. and Phyllis Lucille (Phillips) L.; m. Jo Ann Whitsett, Apr. 17, 1965 (div. Sept. 1982); 1 child, Kimberly N.; m. Peyton Cockrill Davis, Nov. 28, 1987. Student, N.C. State U., 1960-63; AB in Polit. Sci., U. N.C., 1965, JD with honors, 1969. Bar: Calif., D.C., U.S. Dist. Ct. (cen. dist.) Calif., U.S. Ct. Appeals (D.C. cir., 2nd and 5th cirs.), U.S. Supreme Ct. Assoc. Latham & Watkins, Los Angeles, 1969-74; exec. officer Calif. Air Resources Bd., Los Angeles and Sacramento, Calif., 1975-78; dir. Nat. Com. on Air Quality, Washington, 1978-81; counsel Wilmer, Cutler & Pickering, Washington, 1981-84; ptnr. Morgan, Lewis & Bockius LLP, Washington, 1984—; spl. advisor on environ. policy State of Calif., L.A. and Sacramento, 1975; lectr. Law Sch. U. Va., 1993—. Bd. dirs. For Love of Children, Inc., Washington, 1985-95, pres., 1987-91; bd. dirs. Advs. for Families, Washington, 1985-87, Hillandale Homeowners Assn., Washignton, 1986-87, Thurgood Marshall Ctr. Trust, Washington, 1989-95; mem. EPA Clean Air Act Adv. Com., 1994—. Mem. ABA. Home: 3900 Georgetown Ct NW Washington DC 20007-2127 Office: Morgan Lewis & Bockius LLP 1800 M St NW Washington DC 20036-5802

LEWIS, WILLIAM LEONARD, food products executive; b. Providence, Apr. 8, 1946; s. George Dawson and Margaret Eleanor (Cuddigan) L.; m. Barbara Jane Fournier, July 20, 1968; children: Hillary, Megan. BBA, Gonzaga U., 1973; MBA, Dartmouth Coll., 1975. With product mgmt. dept. Frito-Lay div. Pepsico, Dallas, 1975-80; product mgr. grocery products div. Ralston-Purina Co., St. Louis, 1981-83, brand dir., 1983-84, group dir., 1985-86, dir. mktg., 1986-87; exec. v.p. grocery products div. Ralston-Purina Can., Inc., Mississauga, Ont., 1987-89, pres. grocery products div., 1989-90, pres. parent co., 1990—. With U.S. Army, 1968-71. Office: Ralston Purina Can Inc, 2500 Royal Windsor Ave, Mississauga, ON Canada L5J 1K8

LEWIS, WILLIAM WALKER, management consultant; b. Roanoke, Va., Mar. 29, 1942; s. William Walker and Nancy Katherine (Phipps) L.; m. Jutta Maria Schwarzkopf, Dec. 27, 1966; children: Christopher William, Monica Gisela. BS in Physics with honors, Va. Poly. Inst. and State U., 1963; PhD in Theoretical Physics, Oxford U., 1966. Mem. staff Office of Asst. Sec. for Systems Analysis, Dept. Def., Washington, 1966-69; asso. provost for resource planning, lectr. public and internat. affairs Princeton U., 1969-71; dir. office of analytical studies U. Calif., Berkeley, 1971-73; sr. ops. officer World Bank, 1973-77; prin. dep. asst. sec. for program analysis and evaluation Dept. Def., Washington, 1977-79; asst. sec. policy and evaluation Dept. Energy, Washington, 1979-81; pres. Dist. Heat and Power, Inc., Washington, 1981-82; ptnr. McKinsey & Co., Inc., Washington, 1982—; dir. McKinsey Global Inst., Washington, 1990—. Trustee George C. Marshall Found. Rhodes scholar, 1963-66. Office: 1101 Pennsylvania Ave NW Washington DC 20004-2514

LEWIS, WILMA A., federal agency administrator. BA with distinction, Swarthmore Coll., 1978; JD, Harvard U., 1981. Assoc. Steptoe & Johnson, Washington, 1981-1985; asst. U.S. atty. civil divsn. U.S. Atty.'s Office, Washington, 1986-1993; assoc. solicitor divsn. gen. law U.S. Dept. Interior, 1993-95, inspector gen., 1995—; mem. civil justice reform act adv. group U.S. Dist. Ct. D.C., mem. adv. com. on local rules; lectr., instr. George Washington U. Nat. Law Ctr.; mem. faculty Coll. Trial Advocacy. Mem. Phi Beta Kappa. Office: US Dept Interior Office Inspector Gen 1849 C St NW Washington DC 20240

LEWISON, EDWARD FREDERICK, surgeon; b. Chgo., Feb. 11, 1913; s. Maurice and Julia (Trockey) L.; m. Elizabeth Oppenheim, July 24, 1938 (wid. 1947); 1 child, John Edward; m. Betty Fleischmann, Mar. 21, 1948; children: Edward M., Robert S., Richard J. BS, U. Chgo., 1932; MD, Johns Hopkins U., 1936. Lic. MD Ill., Md., Fla.; diplomate Am. Bd. Surgery. Chief, Breast Clin. Johns Hopkins Hosp., Balt., 1948-72; asst. prof. surgery Johns Hopkins U. Sch. Med., Balt., 1954-69, assoc. prof. surgery, 1969-80, assoc. prof. surgery, emeritus, 1980—; vice-chmn. breast cancer comm., WHO, Geneva, 1968-70; chmn. nat. conf. breast cancer, Am. Cancer Soc., Washington, 1969, Swiss Cancer League, Lucerne, 1976; mem. H.S. Nat. Comm. of the Nat. Rsch. Coun., Washington, 1983-87. Author: Breast Cancer and Its Diagnosis and Treatment, 1955; editor: Breast Cancer, 1977, Conference on Spontaneous Regression of Cancer, 1974; co-author: Diagnosis and Treatment of Breast Cancer, 1981. Bd. dirs. United Way of Md., Balt., 1986-94. Named Humanitarian of Yr., Wyman Guild, Balt., 1990, Disting. Citizen, Gov. State Md., 1980; recipient Cert. of Merit award European Theater Ops., 1945. Fellow AMA, Royal Soc. Medicine, Am. Coll. Surgeons; mem. Am. Cancer Soc. (hon. life, Vol. Leadership award 1984, Premier award 1995), N.Y. Acad. Scis. Achievements include invention of rayable gauze for surgery. Home: 4100 N Charles St Baltimore MD 21218

LEWITT, SOL, artist; b. Hartford, Conn., 1928. B.F.A., Syracuse U., 1949. Instr. Mus. Modern Art Sch., 1964-67, Cooper Union, 1967, Sch. Visual Arts, N.Y.C., 1969-70, NYU, 1970. Contbr. articles on sculpture, drawing, conceptual art to jours., mags.; one-man shows include Guggenheim Mus., 1971, Mus. Modern Art, N.Y.C., 1971, Walker Art Center, Mpls., 1972, Mus. Modern Art, Oxford, Eng., 1973, Stedelijk Mus., Amsterdam, The Netherlands, 1974, Visual Arts Mus., N.Y.C., 1976, San Francisco Mus. Art, 1975, Wadsworth Atheneum, Hartford, Conn., 1981, Musee d'Art Contemporain, Bordeaux, France, 1983, retrospective travelling exhbn., Mus. Modern Art, N.Y.C., 1990-95, Mus. Contemporary Art, Montreal, Krannert Mus., Champaign, Ill., Mus. Contemporary Art, Chgo., La Jolla (Calif.) Mus., 1978-79, Stedelijk Mus., Amsterdam, 1984, Stedelijk Van Abbe Mus., Eindhoven, 1984, Musee d'Art Moderne de la ville de Paris, 1987, Tate Gallery, 1986, Walker Art Ctr., Mpls., 1988, Kunstlalle Bern, Switzerland, 1989, Touko Mus., 1990, Porticus, Frankfort, Fed. Republic Germany, 1990, Drawings 1958-92 Haags Gemeentemus., The Hague and tour, Structures 1962-93 Mus. Modern Art, Oxford and tour, 25 Years of Wall Drawings 1968-93 Addison Gallery, Phillips Acad., Andover, Mass., Mus. Modern Art, N.Y.C.; group exhbns. include Sculpture Ann, Whitney Mus. Am. Art, N.Y.C., 1967, Minimal Art, The Hague, 1968, Documenta, Kassel, W. Ger., 1968, 72, 77, 82, Prospect, 1968, Dusseldorf, 1968, Stadtische Kuntshalle, Dusseldorf, 1969, La Jolla Mus. Contemp. Art, 1970, Tokyo Biennale, 1970, Guggenheim Internat., N.Y.C., 1971, Whitney Biennial, Whitney Mus. Am. Art, N.Y.C., 1979, Hayward Gallery, London, 1980, Internat. Sculpture exhbn., Basel, Switzerland, 1980, Westkunst, Cologne, Fed. Republic Germany, 1981, Musee Nat. d'Art Moderne, Paris, 1981, Art Inst. Chgo., 1982, Mus. Modern Art, N.Y.C., 1983, Mus. Contemporary Art, Los Angeles, 1986, Whitney Biennial, 1987, Skultitur Projekk, Münster, Fed. Republic Germany, 1987, Venice (Italy) Biennale, 1988, Zeitlos, Hamburg, Fed. Republic Germany; represented in permanent collections, Stedelijk Mus., Albright-Knox Art Gallery, Buffalo, Art Gallery Ont., Toronto, Los Angeles County Mus. Art, Los Angeles, Mus. Modern Art, N.Y.C., Tate Gallery, London, Centre Georges Pompidou, Paris, Whitney Mus. Am. Art, N.Y.C., Met. Mus. Art, N.Y.C., Art Inst. Chgo.; work also in German, Swiss, Australian, Dutch, Belgian and Am. mus. Office: care Susanna Singer 50 Riverside Dr New York NY 10024-6555

LEWITZKY, BELLA, choreographer; b. Los Angeles, Jan. 13, 1916; d. Joseph and Nina (Ossman) L.; m. Newell Taylor Reynolds, June 22, 1940; 1 child, Nora Elizabeth. Student, San Bernardino Valley (Calif.) Jr. Coll., 1933-34; hon. doctorate, Calif. Inst. Arts, 1981; PhD (hon.), Occidental Coll., 1984, Otis Parsons Coll., 1989, Juilliard Sch., 1993; DFA, Santa Clara U., 1995. Chmn. dance dept., chmn. adv. panel U. So. Calif., Idyllwild, 1956-74; founder Sch. Dance, Calif. Inst. Arts, 1969, dean, 1969-74; vice chmn. dance adv. panel Nat. Endowment Arts, 1974-77, mem. artists-in-schs. adv. panel, 1974-75; mem. Nat. Adv. Bd. Young Audiences, 1974—, Joint Commn. Dance and Theater Accreditation, 1979; com. mem. Am. chpt. Internat. Dance Coun. of UNESCO, 1974—; trustee Calif. Assn. Dance Cos., 1976—, Idyllwild Sch. Music and Arts, 1986-95, Dance/USA, 1988-95, Calif. State Summer Sch. of Arts, 1988—; cons. the dance project WNET, 1987—. Co-founder, co-dir. Dance Dance Assocs., L.A., 1951-55; founder, 1966; artistic dir. Lewitzky Dance Co., L.A.; choreographer, 1948—; founder, former artistic dir. The Dance Gallery, L.A.; contbr. articles in field; choreographed works include Trio for Saki, 1967, Orrenda, 1969, Kinaesonata, 1971, Pietas, 1971, Ceremony for Three, 1972, Game Plan, 1973, Five, 1974, Spaces Between, 1975, Jigsaw, 1975, Inscape, 1976, Pas de Bach, 1977, Suite Satie, 1980, Changes and Choices, 1981, Confines, 1982, Continuum, 1982, The Song of the Woman, 1983, Nos Duraturi, 1984, 8 Dancers/8 Lights, 1985, Facets, 1986, Impressions #1, 1987, Impressions #3, 1988, Agitime, 1989, Impressions #3, 1989, Episode #1, 1990, Glass Canyons, 1991, Episode #2, 1992, Episode #3, 1992, Episode #4, 1993, Meta 4, 1994, Four Women in Time, 1996. Mem. adv. com. Actors' Fund of Am., 1986—, Women's Bldg. Adv. Council, 1985-91, Calif. Arts Council, 1983-86, City of Los Angeles Task Force on the Arts, 1986—; mem. artistic adv. bd. Interlochen Ctr. for Arts, 1988—. Recipient Mayoral Proclamation, City of L.A., 1976, 1982, ann. award Dance mag., 1978, Dir.'s award Calif. Dance Educators Assn., 1978, Plaudit Award, Nat. Dance Assn., 1979, Labor's Award of Honor for Community Svc., L.A. County AFL-CIO, 1979, L.A. Area Dance Alliance and L.A. Junior C. of C. Honoree, 1980, City of L.A. Resolution, 1980, Distguished Artist Award, City of L.A. and Music Ctr., 1982, Silver Achievement award YWCA, 1982, California State Senate Resolution, 1982, 1984, Award of Recognition, Olympic Black Dance Festival, 1984, Distinguished Women's Award, Northwood Inst., 1984, California State U. Distinguished Artist, 1984, Vesta Award, Woman's Bldg, L.A., 1985, L.A. City Council Honors for Outstanding Contributions, 1985, Woman of the Year, Palm Springs Desert Museum, Women's Committee, 1986, Disting. Svc. award Western Alliance Arts Adminstrs., 1987, Woman of Achievement award, 1988, Am. Dance Guild Ann. award, 1989, So. Calif. Libr. for Social Studies & Rsch. award, 1990, Am. Soc. Journalists & Authors Open Book award, 1990, Internat. Soc. Performing Arts Adminstrs. Tiffany award, 1990, Burning Bush award U. of Judaism, 1991, 1st recipient Calif. Gov.'s award in arts for individual lifetime achievement, 1989; honoree L.A. Arts Coun., 1989, Heritage honoree, Nat. Dance Assn., 1991, Vaslav Nijinsky award, 1991, Hugh M. Hefner First Amendment award, 1991, Artistic Excellence award Ctr. Performing Arts U. Calif., 1992, Lester Horton Lifetime Achievement award Dance Resource Ctr. of L.A., 1992, Occidental Coll. Founders' award, 1992, Dance/USA honor, 1992, Visual Arts Freedom of Expression award Andy Warhol Found., 1993, Artist of Yr. award L.A. County High Sch. Arts, 1993, Freedom of Expression honor Andy Warhol Found. Visual Arts, 1993, Calif. Alliance Edn. award, 1994, Lester Horton Sustained Achievement award, 1995 Danie Resource Ctr. of L.A.; grantee Mellon Found., 1975, 81, 86, Guggenheim Found., 1977-78, NEA, 1969-94; honoree Women's Internat. League Peace and Freedom, 1995.Am. Arts Alliance (bd. dirs. 1977), Internat. Dance Alliance (adv. council 1984—), Dance/USA (bd. dirs. 1988). Office: Lewitzky Dance Co 1055 Wilshire Blvd Ste 1140 Los Angeles CA 90017-2498 *Dance is communicative of personal, emotive knowledge-- of sensory information common to all. The feel of the wind, the exhilaration of clear space, the headiness of an enormous height, the marvel of human power, one's personal worth-- can take shape and be illuminated in dance. How wonderful to work at something you love! How remarkable to be given the opportunity to utilize one's whole being, one's physical knowledge, intellectual capacity, imagination and creativity in a single persuit. How good to practice dance and know that it will not engage you in mass murders of warfare; it will not destroy our environment. It is capable of healing, celebrating, and sharing human resources. My philosophy is predicated on the belief that choreography is the taskmaster of us all. In each work, I attempt to discover again the truth of that statement.*

LEWKOWITZ, KAREN HELENE, orthodontist; b. Bklyn., Dec. 26, 1956; d. William A. and Janet B. (Kagan) L.; m. Robert Louis Shpuntoff, Dec. 18, 1983; children: Hilana Megan, Ariana Elizabeth. BA magna cum laude, CUNY, 1978; DDS, Columbia U., 1982; cert. in orthodontics, NYU, 1984. Researcher W. M. Krogman Ctr., Children's Hosp. Phila., Pa., 1976; ptnr. Bayside (N.Y.) Orthodontic Assocs., 1984—; pres. med. awareness com. Queens Coll.-CUNY, 1977-78; attending orthodontist, lectr. Jamaica (N.Y.) Hosp., 1984—. Mem. Temple Torah, Little Neck, N.Y., 1988-94, Temple Israel, Great Neck, N.Y., 1994—, Hadassah, Great Neck, 1990—; v.p. of programming Orgn. Rehab. Thru Tng., Lake Success, N.Y., 1991. Mem. ADA, Acad. Gen. Dentistry, Am. Assn. Women Dentists, Am. Assn. Orthodontists, Queens County Dental Soc. (trustee 1985—, historian 1990, treas. 1991, sec. 1992, v.p. 1993, pres.-elect 1994, pres. 1995), Alpha Omega (pres. Columbia U. chpt. 1980-82, pres. Queens-Nassau chpt. 1984-87, Presdl. citation 1986, regent N.Y. met. area 1990, 91). Avocations: piano, tennis. Office: Bayside Orthodontic Assocs 59-01 Springfield Blvd Bayside NY 11364

LEWTER, HELEN CLARK, elementary education educator; b. Millis, Mass., Jan. 14, 1936; d. Waldimar Kenville and Ida Mills (Currier) Clark; m. Alvin Council Lewter, June 18, 1966; children: Lois Ida, David Paul, Jonathan Clark. BA, U. Mass., 1958; MS, Old Dominion U., 1978. Postgrad. profl. cert. reading specialist, sociology, elem. grades 1-7. Tchr. Juniper Hill Sch., Framingham, Mass., 1960-63, Aragona Elem. Sch., Virginia Beach, Va., 1963-65, Park Elem., Chesapeake, Va., 1965-67; edn. specialist Riverview Sch., Portsmouth, Va., 1977-78; reading tchr. Truitt Jr. H.S., Chesapeake, 1979-83; reading resource tchr. Southeastern Elem., Chesapeake, 1983-86; tchr. Deep Creek Elem. Sch., Chesapeake, 1986—; pers. task force Chesapeake (Va.) Pub. Schs., 1984-85, textbook adoption com., 1984-85, employee handbook com., 1986-87, K-6 writing curriculum com., 1988-89. Tchr., workshop leader, dir., mem. various coms. Fairview Heights Bapt. Ch., Deep Creek Bapt. Ch., Va. So. Bapt. Retreats, 1968—; mem. mayor's adv. coun. City of Chesapeake, Va., 1988-89; mem. summer missionary Va. So. Bapts., 1993; active PTA. Mem. NEA, Va. Edn. Assn., Chesapeake Edn. Assn., Chesapeake Reading Assn. (v.p., pres., honor and merit coun., chmn. various coms.), Internat. Reading Assn., Va. Reading Assn., Delta Kappa Gamma (legis. chmn.), Kappa Delta Pi, Phi Kappa Phi. Republican. Avocations: church related activities, reading. Home: 428 Plummer Dr Chesapeake VA 23323-3116 Office: Deep Creek Elem Sch 2809 Forehand Dr Chesapeake VA 23323-2005

LEWY, RALPH I., hotel executive; b. Leiwen, Trier, Germany, May 28, 1931; s. Rudolf Reuben and Isabella (Haas) L.; m. Doris J. Laser, Apr. 12, 1964; children: Reuben Mark, Gary Daniel. B.S. in Commerce, Roosevelt U., 1953. C.P.A., Ill. Partner, Katz, Wagner & Co. (C.P.A.s), Chgo.; Partner Grant Thornton (C.P.A.s), Chgo., 1970-76; sr. v.p. Americana Hotels Corp., Chgo., 1976-87; pres. Ralph Lewy Ltd., Chgo., 1987—. Sec., treas., bd. dirs. Albert Pick Jr. Fund; trustee Emanuel Congregation, Chgo.; v.p., bd. dirs. Lois and Leonard Laser Charitable Found. Mem. AICPA. Jewish. Office: 180 N La Salle St Ste 2401 Chicago IL 60601-2704

LEWYN, THOMAS MARK, lawyer; b. N.Y.C., July 2, 1930; s. Oswald and Agnes (Maas) L.; m. Ann Salfeld, July 15, 1955; children—Alfred Thomas, Mark Henry. B.A., Stanford, 1952, postgrad., 1952-54; LL.B., Columbia, 1955. Bar: N.Y. 1957. Since practiced in N.Y.C.; assoc. Simpson, Thacher & Bartlett, N.Y.C., 1957-64, ptnr., 1965-75, sr. ptnr., 1976-90, of counsel, 1991—; bd. dirs. Metro-Goldwyn-Mayer, Inc. Contbr. articles to profl. jours. Served to 1st lt., F.A. AUS, 1955-57. Mem. ABA, Assn. of Bar of City of N.Y., N.Y. State Bar Assn. Home: 911 Park Ave New York NY 10021-0337 Office: Simpson Thacher & Bartlett 425 Lexington Ave New York NY 10017-3903

LEY, HERBERT LEONARD, JR., retired epidemiologist; b. Columbus, Ohio, Sept. 7, 1923; s. Herbert Leonard and Laura (Spencer) L. M.D., Harvard U., 1946, M.P.H., 1951. Commd. 1st lt. M.C., U.S. Army, 1947, advanced through grades to lt. col., 1955; resigned, 1958; ret. col. USAR, 1983; prof. microbiology George Washington U. Sch. Medicine, 1958-61; civil service with U.S. Army Research Office, 1961-63; asso. prof. epidemiology and microbiology Harvard Sch. Pub. Health, 1963-66; dir. Bur. Medicine, FDA, 1966-68, commr. food and drugs, 1968-69; cons. to food and drug industry, 1969-93. Contbr. sci. articles to profl. jours., chpts to med. texts. Decorated Bronze Star. Fellow Am. Coll. Preventive Medicine; mem. Am. Acad. Microbiology. Office: 4816 Camelot St Rockville MD 20853-3018

LEY, LINDA SUE, employee benefits company executive; b. Franklin, Ind., Nov. 27, 1949; d. Jiles Rex and Naomi Katherine (Van Horn) Riggs; m. Thomas Alan Ley, Feb. 28, 1987. BS in Edn. with distinction, Ind. U.-Purdue U., 1971, MS in Edn. with highest distinction, 1975. Cert. paralegal; lic. life, accident, health, property and casualty ins. agt., Ind. Elem. tchr. Indpls. Pub. Schs., 1972-74, Center Grove Community Schs., Greenwood, Ind., 1974-81; dir. adminstrn. Brougher Agy., Inc., Greenwood, 1981-84; mgr. claims/customer svc. The Associated Group, Inc., Indpls., 1984-89; v.p. team ops. Key Benefit Adminstrs., Inc., Indpls., 1989-92; regional mgr. ops. rev. Anthem Benefit Svcs. Corp., Indpls., 1992—. Mem. cotillion com. Humane Soc. Indpls., 1991; vol. Riley Run for Children, Indpls., 1985-92. Recipient Good Girl Citizenship award Women's Aux. of Am. Legion, 1968. Mem. Am. Mgmt. Assn., Nat. Assn. Life Underwriters, Nat. Assn. Health Underwriters, Inst. Internal Auditors, Indpls. Paralegal Assn., Toastmasters Internat. Republican. Episcopalian. Home: 6358 Bluff Acres Dr Greenwood IN 46143-9037 Office: Anthem Health Cos 4040 Vincennes Cir Indianapolis IN 46268

LEY, RONALD, psychologist, educator; b. Buffalo, N.Y., Oct. 19, 1929; s. August Andreas and Marie (Jerge) L.; m. Carmen De Brito, Jan. 16, 1965; 1 child, Jessica Elizabeth. BA, U. Buffalo, 1951; PhD, Syracuse U., 1963. Rsch. dir. Madison Area Project, Syracuse, 1962-63; asst. prof. psychology No. Ill. U., DeKalb, 1963-64, Grad. Faculty, New Sch. for Social Rsch., N.Y.C., 1964-66; prof. psychology and stats. SUNY, Albany, 1966—; cons. Nat. Inst. for Occupational Safety and Health; vis. prof. psychology U. P.R., 1969, cardiac dept., Charing Cross Hosp., London, 1988. Author: A Whisper of Espionage, 1990, Rumores de Espionaje: Wolfgang Köhler y los Monos en Tenerife, 1995; editor: Behavioral and Psychological Approaches to Breathing Disorders, 1994; editl. bd. Jour. Behavior Therapy and Exptl. Psychiatry, 1993—; guest editor: Biofeedback and Self-Regulation, 1994; contbr. numerous articles to profl. jours. Bd. dirs. Father's Assn. of the Albany Acad. for Girls, 1981-84. SUNY rsch. fellow, 1967, 68, 70, 74, 76, 78, 91; SUNY rsch. grantee, 1967-68, 69-70, 71-72, 74-75, 76, 78, 87-88, 91-92, 95-96, Nat. Inst. Occupl. Safety and Health grantee, 1982-83, 87, 88, others. Fellow Behavior Therapy and Rsch. Soc.; mem. APA, Am. Psychol. Soc., Am. Statis. Assn., Assn. Advancement Behavior Therapy, Assn. Applied Psychophysiology and Biofeedback, Author's Guild, Author's League Am., Ea. Psychol. Assn., Internat. Soc. Advancement Respiratory Psychophysiology (pres. 1993-96), New Eng. Soc. Behavior Analysis and Therapy, Psychol. Assn. Northeastern N.Y. (sec. 1967-68, pres. 1983-84), N.Y. Acad. Scis., Soc. Psychophysiol. Rsch., Psychonomic Soc., Sigma Xi. Home: 22 Marion Ave Albany NY 12203-1823 Office: SUNY 1400 Washington Ave Albany NY 12222-0100

LEYDEN, DONALD ELLIOTT, chemist, researcher; b. Gadsden, Ala., June 26, 1938; s. Elliott Hampton and Vivian Ione (Buckner) L.; m. Alice Jane Trowbridge, June 10, 1961; children: Mary Dawn, Sean Michael. BS, Kent State U., Ohio, 1960; MS, Emory U., 1961, Ph.D., 1964. Faculty U. Ga., Athens, 1965-76; Phillipson prof. environ. and mining chemistry U. Denver, 1976-81; prof. chemistry Colo. State U., Ft. Collins, 1981-88; assoc. prin. scientist Philip Morris USA, Richmond, Va., 1988—. Mem. editorial adv. bd. Analytica Chimica Acta, 1977-89, Internat. Jour. Environ. Analytical Chemistry, 1977-91, Mikrochimica Atca, X-Ray Spectrom, 1987-91; editor Chemically Modified Surfaces, 1985-90; contbr. articles to profl. jours. NIH grantee, 1965-68; NSF grantee, 1970-88; Philip Morris Tobacco Co. grantee, 1973-74. Mem. Am. Chem. Soc., Soc. for Applied Spectroscopy. Home: 502 Rivers Bend Cir Chester VA 23831-2570 Office: Philip Morris USA PO Box 26583 Richmond VA 23261-6583

LEYDEN, EDWARD E., secondary school principal. Prin. Bishop Lynch High Sch., Dallas. Recipient Blue Ribbon Sch. award U.S. Dept. Edn., 1990-91. Office: Bishop Lynch High Sch 9750 Ferguson Rd Dallas TX 75228-3818

LEYDEN, NORMAN, conductor; m. Alice Leyden; children: Robert, Constance. Grad., Yale U., 1938; MA, Columbia U., PhD, 1970. Bass clarinetist New Haven Symphony; arranger Glenn Miller Air Force Band, Eng., France; chief arranger Glenn Miller Orch., 1946-49; freelance arranger N.Y.C.; mus. dir. RCA Victor Records, Arthur Godfrey, 1956-59; with Oreg. Symphony, 1970—, assoc. conductor, 1974—; music dir. Seattle Symphony Pops, 1975-93; tchr. Columbia U.; guest condr. over 30 Am. symphony orchs. including Boston Pops, Minn. Orch., Pitts. Symphony, St. Louis Symphony, San Diego Symphony, San Francisco Symphony, Nat. Symphony, Utah Symphony; condr. Army Air Force. Author: The Big Band Style: A Guide for Performers. Office: Oreg Symphony Orch 711 SW Alder St Ste 200 Portland OR 97205

LEYDET, FRANÇOIS GUILLAUME, writer; b. Neuilly-sur-Seine, France, Aug. 26, 1927; came to U.S., 1940, naturalized, 1956; s. Bruno and Dorothy (Lindsey) L. AB, Harvard, 1947, postgrad. Bus. Sch., 1952; postgrad. Johns Hopkins Sch. Advanced Internat. Studies, 1952-53; Bachelier-es-lettres-philosophie, U. Paris (France), 1945; m. Patience Abbe, June 17, 1955 (div.); step-children: Catherine Abbe Geissler, Lisa Amanda O'Mahony; m. Roslyn Carney, June 14, 1970; step-children: Walter E. Robb IV, Rachel R. Avery, Holly H. Prunty, Mary-Peck Peters. Past dir. Marin County Planned Parenthood Assn., Planned Parenthood Center Tucson; docent Ariz.-Sonora Desert Mus. 1st lt. French Army, 1947-48. Mem. Nat. Parks Assn., Wilderness Soc., Sierra Club, Nat. Audubon Soc., World Wildlife Fund, Am. Mus. Natural History, Environ. Def. Fund, Ariz.-Sonora Desert Mus., Ariz. Hist. Soc., LWV, Ariz. Opera League, Commonwealth Club. Author: The Last Redwoods, 1963, Time and the River Flowing: Grand Canyon, 1964, The Coyote: Defiant Songdog of the West, 1977; editor: Tomorrow's Wilderness, 1963; editor Noticias; contbr. to Nat. Geog. mag. Home: 5165 N Camino Real Tucson AZ 85718-5026

LEYDON, JOSEPH PATRICK, film critic, journalist; b. New Orleans, Aug. 22, 1952; s. Michael and Beverly (Garvey) L.; 1 child, George Michael. Student, U. New Orleans, 1969-72; BA in Journalism, Loyola U., New Orleans, 1974. Staff writer Dallas Morning News, 1979-82; contbg. editor Dallas Observer, 1982-91; film critic Houston Post, 1982-95, Houston Press, 1995—, Sta. KPRC-TV (NBC), 1995—; corr. Variety, N.Y.C., 1990—; film critic New Orleans Mag., 1980-83; film series advisor Media Ctr. Rice U., Houston, 1984—, film class instr. div. continuing studies, 1987-89; selection com. advisor Houston Internat. Film Festival, 1984-91. Recipient Critical Rev. award New Orleans Press Club, 1976, 81, 82, Newspaper Commentary award Houston Press Club, 1985, 86, Mag. Feature award, 1988, Comment and Criticism award AP Mng. Editors of Tex., 1986, 90, 93, 95. Democrat. Roman Catholic. Address: PO Box 1916 Bellaire TX 77402-1916

LEYDORF, FREDERICK LEROY, lawyer; b. Toledo, June 13, 1930; s. Loftin Herman and Dorothy DeRoyal (Cramer) L.; m. Mary MacKenzie Malcolm, Mar. 28, 1953; children—Robert Malcolm, William Frederick, Katherine Ann, Thomas Richard, Deborah Mary. Student, U. Toledo, 1948-49; B.B.A., U. Mich., 1953; J.D., UCLA, 1958. Bar: Calif. 1959. Assoc. Hammack & Pugh, L.A., 1959-61; ptnr. Willis, Butler, Scheifly, Leydorf & Grant, L.A., 1961-81, Pepper, Hamilton & Scheetz, L.A., 1981-83, Hufstedler & Kaus, L.A., 1983-95; lectr., cons. Calif. Continuing Edn. of Bar, 1965-92; mem. planning com. Probate and Trust Conf., U. So. Calif., 1984-92. Contbg. author: California Non-Profit Corporations, 1969; contbr.

articles to profl. jours. Chmn. pub. adminstr.-pub. guardian adv. commn. Los Angeles County Bd. Suprs., 1972-73; bd. dirs. J.W. and Ida M. Jameson Found., 1967—, Western Ctr. on Law and Poverty, Inc., 1980-82, L.A. Heart Inst., 1988-90; mem. legal com. Music Ctr. Found., 1980-95; mem. lawyers adv. coun. Constl. Rights Found., 1982-85; mem. devel. adv. bd. U. Mich. Sch. Bus. Adminstrn., 1984-90; mem. adv. bd. UCLA-CEB Estate Planning Inst., 1979-92; Lt. USNR, 1953-55. Mem. ABA, L.A. County Bar Assn. (bd. trustees 1973-75), State Bar Calif. (chmn. conf. dels. 1977, Alumnus of Yr. award, conf. of dels. 1983, mem. exec. com. estate planning, trust and probate law sect. 1979-80), L.A. County Bar Found. (pres. 1977-79, bd. dirs. 1975-87), Am. Coll. Trust and Estate Counsel, Internat. Acad. Estate and Trust Law (v.p. N.Am. 1978-82), Life Ins. and Trust Coun. L.A. (pres. 1983-84), UCLA Law Alumni Assn. (pres. 1982), L.A. World Affairs Coun., Chancery Club (pres. 1991-92), Jonathan Club, Laguna Hills Golf Club, Phi Delta Phi, Phi Delta Theta. Republican. Lutheran. Home: 3078-D Via Serena S Laguna Hills CA 92653-2771

LEYH, GEORGE FRANCIS, trade association administrator; b. Utica, N.Y., Oct. 1, 1931; s. George Robert and Mary Kathleen (Haley) L.; m. Mary Alice Mosher, Sept. 17, 1955; children—Timothy George, Kristin Ann. B.C.E., Cornell U., 1954; M.S. (Univ. fellow), 1956. Structural engr. Eckerlin and Klepper, Syracuse, N.Y., 1956-59; asso. dir. engring. Martin Marietta Corp., Chgo., 1959-63; structural engr. Portland Cement Assn., Chgo., 1963-67; dir. mktg. Concrete Reinforcing Steel Inst., Chgo., 1967-75; exec. v.p. Am. Concrete Inst., Detroit, 1975—; editor jour. Am. Concrete Inst., 1975—. Mem. Planning Commn., Streamwood, Ill., 1960-68; chmn. Lake Bluff (Ill.) Citizens Com. for Conservation, 1972. Recipient Bloem Disting. Service award Am. Concrete Inst., 1972. Mem. ASCE, Am. Soc. Assn. Execs. (chmn. key profl. assns. com. 1989-90), Nat. Inst. Bldg. Scis., Am. Ry. Engring. Assn., Am. Nat. Standards Inst. (bd. dirs. 1986—), Am. Soc. for Concrete Constrn. (bd. dirs. 1984—), Phi Kappa Phi. Clubs: North Cape Yacht, Lake Bluff Yacht (dir. 1969-74, commodore 1973). Home: 1327 Lone Pine Rd Bloomfield Hills MI 48302-2756 Office: Am Concrete Inst PO Box 9094 Farmington Hills MI 48333

LEYH, RICHARD EDMUND, SR., retired investment executive; b. Union City, N.J., Mar. 25, 1930; s. Louis Anthony and Grace Agnes (Barringer) L.; m. Patricia Ann Ryan, Apr. 18, 1949; children: Gail, Gloria, Anne, Teresa, Richard, Elizabeth, David. Student, Rutgers U., 1948-49. Sr. clk. Jersey Cen. Power and Light Co., Asbury Park, N.J., 1949-52; dist. mgr. N.J. Natural Gas Co., Asbury Park, 1952-56; methods analyst Univac, Newark, 1957-60; adv. systems engr. IBM, N.Y.C., 1960-65; mgr. real time systems N.Y. Stock Exchange, N.Y.C., 1965-66; dir. ops. Carlisle DeCoppet and Co., N.Y.C., 1967-76; exec. v.p., chief ops. officer Securities Industry Automation Corp., N.Y.C., 1976-91. Mem. Am. Mgmt. Assn., Inst. for Certification Computer Profls. Democrat. Roman Catholic. Avocations: bridge, golf, swimming. Home: 149 Ocean Hollow Ln Saint Augustine FL 32095 Office: Securities Industry Automation Corp Two MetroTech Ctr Brooklyn NY 11201

LEYHANE, FRANCIS JOHN, III, lawyer; b. Chgo., Mar. 29, 1957; s. Francis J. and Mary Elizabeth (Crowley) L.; m. Diana M. Urizarri, May 8, 1982; children: Katherine, Francis J. IV, Joseph, Brigid Rose, James Matthew. BA, Loyola U., Chgo., 1977, JD, 1980. Bar: Ill. 1980, U.S. Dist. Ct. (no. dist.) Ill. 1980, U.S. Ct. Appeals (7th cir.) 1986. Assoc. Condon, Cook & Roche, Chgo., 1980-87; ptnr. Condon & Cook, Chgo., 1988—. Contbr. articles to profl. jours. Mem. Sch. bd. Immaculate Conception Parish, Chgo., 1993-96. Fellow Ill. Bar Found.; mem. Appellate Lawyers Assn. Ill., Ill. State Bar Assn. (mem. assembly 1987-90), Chgo. Bar Assn., Blue Key. Office: Condon & Cook 745 N Dearborn St Chicago IL 60610-3826

LEYLAND, JAMES RICHARD, professional baseball team manager; b. Toledo, Dec. 15, 1944; m. Katie Leyland. Player various minor league teams Detroit Tigers, 1964-69, coach minor league system, 1970-71, mgr. minor league system, 1971-81; coach Chgo. White Sox, 1981-85; mgr. Pitts. Pirates, 1985—. Christmas chmn. Salvation Army, 1990-91. Named Nat. League Mgr. of Yr. Baseball Writers' Assn. Am., 1988, 90, Sporting News, 1990, Man of Yr. Arthritis Found., 1989, Epilepsy Found., 1991. Office: Pitts Pirates 600 Stadium Cir Pittsburgh PA 15212-5731*

LEYLEGIAN, JACK H., II, investment management company executive; b. Providence, Oct. 26, 1935; m. Dorothy Patricia Aprahamian, July 21, 1957; children: George A., Debra A. BSBA, Boston U., 1957; MBA, U. So. Calif., 1960. Vice pres. No. Trust Co., Chgo., 1966-71; pres. Dreyfus Mgmt. Inc., N.Y.C., 1971-77, Bank Am. Investment Mgmt. Co., San Francisco, 1977-81, Leylegian Investment Mgmt. Inc., Menlo Park, Calif., 1981--; bd. dirs. Imperial Bank, Los Angeles. Mem. Chartered Fin. Analysts Soc., San Francisco Security Analysts Soc. Office: Leylegian Investment Mgmt 601 Gateway Blvd Ste 700 South San Francisco CA 94080-7007

LEYMASTER, GLEN R., former medical association executive; b. Aurora, Nebr., Aug. 17, 1915; s. Leslie and Frances (Wertman) L.; m. Margaret Hendricks, June 20, 1942; children: Mark H., Mary Beth, Lynn F. A.B., U. Nebr., 1938; M.D., Harvard, 1942; M.P.H., Johns Hopkins U., 1950. Intern, asst. resident, resident Harvard Med. Service, Boston City Hosp., 1942-44; mem. faculty Johns Hopkins Med. Sch., 1944-48; instr., asst. prof. bacteriology Sch. Pub. Health and Hygiene, 1946-48; asso. prof. pub. health, instr. medicine U. Utah Sch. Medicine, 1948-50, prof., head dept., preventive medicine, asst. prof. medicine, also dir. univ. health service, 1950-60; adviser med. edn.- preventive medicine ICA, Bangkok, Thailand, 1956-58; asso. sec. council med. edn. and hosps. AMA, Chgo., 1960-63; pres., dean Women's Med. Coll. Pa., 1964-70; dir. dept. undergrad. med. edn. AMA, 1970-75; exec. dir. Am. Bd. Med. Spltys., Evanston, Ill., 1975-81; ret. exec. dir., 1981. Contbr. articles to profl. jours. Mem. AMA, Ill. Med. Assn., Inst. Medicine Chgo., Phi Beta Kappa, Sigma Xi, Alpha Omega Alpha. Home: 154 Kendal at Longwood Kennett Square PA 19348

L'HEUREUX, JOHN CLARKE, English language educator; b. South Hadley, Mass., Oct. 26, 1934; s. Wilfred Joseph and Mildred (Clarke) L'H.; m. Joan Ann Polston, June 26, 1971. AB, Weston Coll., 1959, Licentiate in Philosophy, 1960; MA, Boston Coll., 1963; Licentiate in Sacred Theology, Woodstock Coll., 1967; postgrad., Harvard U., 1967-68. Ordained priest Roman Catholic Ch., 1966, laicized, 1971; writer in residence Georgetown U., 1964-65, Regis Coll., 1968-69; staff editor The Atlantic, 1968-69, contbg. editor, 1969-83; vis. prof. Am. lit. Hamline U., 1971, Tufts Coll., 1971-72; vis. asst. prof. Harvard U., 1973; asst. prof. Stanford U., 1973-79, assoc. prof., 1979-81, prof., 1981—, Lane prof. humanities, 1985-90, dir. creative writing program, 1976-89. Author: Quick as Dandelions, 1964, Rubrics for a Revolution, 1967, Picnic in Babylon, 1967, One Eye and a Measuring Rod, 1968, No Place for Hiding, 1971, Tight White Collar, 1972, The Clang Birds, 1972, Family Affairs, 1974, Jessica Fayer, 1976, Desires, 1981, A Woman Run Mad, 1988, Comedians, 1990, An Honorable Profession, 1991, The Shrine at Altamira, 1992, The Handmark of Desire, 1996. Office: Stanford U Dept English Stanford CA 94305

L'HEUREUX, WILLARD JOHN, real estate lawyer, diversified company executive; b. Ottawa, Ont., Can., May 25, 1947; s. Willard Joseph and Viola L'Heureux; m. Janet Elizabeth Button, 1973; children: Willard John, Jocelyn Marie, Robert Malcolm. BA, U. Western Ont., 1968; LLB, U. Toronto, 1971. Bar: Ont. 1973; called to Queen's Counsel 1983. Read law with Tory, Tory, DesLauriers & Binnington, 1972-73, assoc., 1973-79, ptnr., 1979-83; mng. ptnr. fin. svcs. Hees Internat. Bancorp., Toronto, 1983-88, pres., mng. ptnr., 1988-93; pres., CEO Carena-Bancorp Inc., Toronto, 1985-88, Trizec Corp. Ltd., Calgary, Alta., Can., 1993—; bd. dirs. Astral Comm., Trizec Corp. Ltd. Dir., past chmn. Can. Spl. Olympics; hon. chmn. Intercollegiate Hockey Championships, Univ. Cup, 1994; mem. governing coun. U. Toronto; mem. adv. coun. Can. Canoe Mus. Mem. Royal Can. Yacht Club, Queen's Tennis Club, Calgary C. of C. (mem. pres. coun.). Office: 181 Bay St, BCE Place 39th fl, Toronto, ON Canada M5J 2T3

L'HEUREUX-DUBÉ, CLAIRE, judge; b. Quebec City, Que., Can., Sept. 7, 1927; d. Paul H. and Marguerite (Dion) L'H.; m. Arthur Dubé (dec. 197u); children: Louise, Pierre (dec. 1994). BA magna cum laude, Coll. Notre-Dame de Bellevue, Que., 1946; LLL cum laude, Laval U., Que., 1951, LLD (hon.), 1984; LLD (hon.), Dalhousie U., 1981, Montreal U., 1983, Ottawa U., 1988, U. Que., 1989, U. Toronto, 1994. Bar: Que. 1952. Ptnr. Bard, L'Heureux & Philippon, 1952-73; sr. ptnr. L'Heureux, Philippon, Garneau, Tourigny, St.Arnaud & Assocs., from 1969; Puisne judge Superior Ct. Que., 1973-79, Ct. Appeal of Que., 1979-87, Supreme Ct. Can., Ottawa, 1987—; commr. Part II Inquiries Act Dept. Manpower and Immigration, Montreal, 1973-76; del. Gen. Coun. Bar of Que., 1968-70, com. on adminstrn. justice, 1968-73, others; pres. family law com. Family Ct. com. Que Civil Code Rev. Office, 1972-76; pres. Can. sect. Internat. Commn. Jurists, 1981-83, v.p., 1992—. Editor: (with Rosalie S. Abella) Family Law - Dimensions of Justice, 1983; chmn. editorial bd. Can. Bar Rev., 1985-88; author articles, conf. proc., book chpt. Bd. dirs. YWCA, Que., 1969-73, Ctr. des Loisirs St. Sacrement, 1969-73, Ctr. Jeunesse de Tilly-Ctr. des Jeunes, 1971-77; v.p. Can. Consumers Coun., 1970-73; v.p. Vanier Inst. of the Family, 1972-73; lifetime gov. Found. Univ. Laval, 1980, bd. dirs., 1984-85; mem. Comité des grandes orientations de l'Univ. Laval, 1971-72; mem. nat. coun. Can. Human Rights Found., 1980-82, 82-84; mem. Can. del. to Peoples Republic China on Status of Women, 1981; pres. Can. sect. Internat. Commn. Jurists, 1981-83, v.p. internat. bd., 1992—. Apptd. Queen's Counsel, 1969; recipient Medal of the Alumni, U. Laval, 1986, Médaille du Barreau de Que., 1987. Mem. Can. Bar Assn. Can. Inst. Adminstrn. Justice, Internat. Soc. Family Law (bd. dirs. 1977-88, v.p. 1981-88), Internat. Fedn. Women Lawyers, Fedn. Internat. des Femmes Juristes, L'Assn. des Femmes Diplômées d'Univ., Assn. Québécoise pour l'Étude Comparative du Droit (pres. 1984-90), Am. Coll. Trial Lawyers (hon.), Am. Law Inst., Phi Delta Phi. Roman Catholic. Office: Supreme Ct Can, Wellington St, Ottawa, ON Canada K1A 0J1

LHEVINE, DAVE BERNARD, radiologist, educator; b. Tulsa, May 20, 1922; s. Morris Boise and Sarah Fannie (Piatt) L.; m. Mary Helen Orr, Dec. 19, 1963 (div. July 1986); children: Rhonda Dean, Paul Morris; m. Catherine Marie Garvey, Mar. 28, 1992. BA, Okla. U., 1943, MD, 1945. Diplomate Am. Bd. Radiology. Intern U.S. Naval Hosp., Bklyn., 1945-46; resident in radiology St. Louis City Hosp., Bklyn., 1948-51, 1948-51; dir. dept. radiology Hillcrest Med. Ctr., Tulsa, 1951-83, dir. dept. radiation therapy, 1983-86; clin. prof. dept. radiation oncology Okla. U., Oklahoma City, 1987-95; vice chmn. dept. radiology Okla. U. Sch. Medicine Tulsa Med. Coll., 1978—; corp. sec. Sterling Oil Co. of Okla., Tulsa, 1987-94. Active Tulsa County Dem. politics. Elected chmn. Tulsa County Dem. Com., 1995. Lt. (j.g.) USN, 1942-47. Fellow Am. Coll. Radiology (hon., emeritus); mem. AMA, Radiol. Soc. of N.Am., Okla. State Radiol. Soc. (pres. 1958). Democrat. Avocations: sailing, painting, photography, computers. Home: 2716 E 26th Pl Tulsa OK 74114-4308 Office: Tulsa Co Dem Party 3930 E 31st St Tulsa OK 74135

LHOTKA, SIDNEY BRUNO, tax accountant; b. Sevetin, Bohemia, Czechsolvakia, Apr. 4, 1926; came to U.S., 1956; s. Vaclav Vojtech and Helena (Valkova) L.; m. Jana M. Lhotka, Mar. 29, 1958. A in Acctg., U. Queensland, Australia, 1958, B in Comm., 1959. Acct., acctg. mgr. Bechtel Corp., San Francisco, 1956-61, product svcs. mgr., 1964-66, 68-83; asst. svcs. mgr. Transport Co. of Tex., Kwajalein, Mich., 1962-64; office mgr. systems and procedures RMK-BRJ Vietnam, Saigon, 1966-68; prin. Fin. and Tax Svcs., Concord, Calif., 1983—. Fellow Australian Soc. of Cert. Practicing Accts.; mem. Nat. Soc. of Pub. Accts., Nat. Assn. of Enrolled Agts., Internat. Assn. of Fin. Planning. Avocations: bicycle riding, swimming, walking. Home: 1314 Corte De Los Vecinos Walnut Creek CA 94598-2902 Office: Fin and Tax Svcs Concord CA 94520

L'HUILLIER, PETER (PETER), archbishop; b. Paris, Dec. 3, 1926; came to U.S., 1980; s. Eugene Henry and Emilienne (Haslin) L'H. Diploma, Inst. St. Denys, Paris, 1949; License of Theology, Moscow Theol. Acad., 1962, D of Canon Law, 1985. Ordained priest Russian Orthodox Ch. in Western Europe, 1954. Lectr. St. Denys Inst., Paris, 1949-50, Three Hierarchs Sem., Villemoisson, France, 1952-62; priest Russian Ch., Paris, 1954-68; prof. Cath. U., Paris, 1966-78; bishop of Chersonese, Diocese of France Russian Ch., Paris, 1968-79, archbishop of Chersonese, 1979; aux. bishop of Bklyn. Orthodox Ch. in Am., N.Y.C., 1979-81; bishop N.Y. and N.J. Orthodox Ch. in Am., 1981-89; archbishop of N.Y. and N.J. Orthodox Ch. in Am., N.Y.C., 1990—; chmn. dept. external affairs Orthodox Ch. in Am., Syosset, N.Y., 1990—; adj. prof. St. Vladimir's Orthodox Sem., Crestwood, N.Y., 1980—; canonical advisor, chmn. theol. edn. commn. Standing Conf. Canonical Orthodox Bishops in Am., N.Y.C. Author: The Church of the Ancient Councils, 1996. Office: Orthodox Ch in Am 33 Hewitt Ave Bronxville NY 10708-2333

LI, CHAOYING, biomedical researcher; b. Jingshan, Hubei, China, July 20, 1958; came to U.S., 1990; s. Yi Li and Yulan Liu; m. Chuli Yi, June 10, 1985; 1 child, Shu. MD, Tongji Med. U., Wuhan, Hubei, China, 1983, MS in Neurobiology, 1989. Asst. Tongji Med. U., Wuhan, 1983-89, lectr., 1989-90; vis. fellow NIH, Rockville, Md., 1990-94, intramural rsch. training award fellow, 1994-95, sr. staff fellow, 1995—. Author: Alcohol, Cell Membranes and Signal Transolution, 1993; contbr. articles to profl. jours. Mem. Soc. Neurosci. Achievements include demonstrating for the first time that alcohols affect the function of a neuronal membrane receptor by a direct interaction with the receptor protein, demonstrating for the first time that Zn potentiates excitatory action of ATP on mammalian neurons. Home: 110 Apple Blossom Way Gaithersburg MD 20878 Office: NIH/NIAAA/LMCN 12501 Washington Ave Rockville MD 20852

LI, CHIAYANG, environmental engineer; b. Taipei, Taiwan, Rep. of China, May 11, 1963; came to the U.S., 1988; s. Kao-Kon and Chin-Chi (Hsu) L.; m. Yi-Ju Wu, Dec. 24, 1994. BS in Environ. Sci., Feng-Chia U., 1985; MS in Environ. Engring., Ga. Inst. Tech., 1990. Rsch. asst. Ga. Inst. Tech., Atlanta, 1988-90; environ. engr. Holton and Dycus, Inc., Knoxville, Tenn., 1991-93, Indsl. Compliance, Knoxville, 1993—. Contbr. articles to profl. jours. Mem. Am. Chem. Soc., Am. Water Works Assn. Achievements include research in effect of soil organic carbon on sorption of benzene vapor, retardation factors of benzene and jet fuel vapors in unsaturated soil. Office: Indsl Compliance 308 N Peters Rd Ste 110 Knoxville TN 37922-2327

LI, CHING-CHUNG, electrical engineering, computer science educator; b. Changshu, Kiangsu, China, Mar. 30, 1932; came to U.S., 1954, naturalized, 1972; s. Lung-Han and Lien-Tseng (Hwa) L.; m. Hanna Wu, June 10, 1961; children: William Wei-Lin, Vincent Wei-Tsin. B.S.E.E., Nat. Taiwan U., 1954; M.S.E.E., Northwestern U., 1956, Ph.D., 1961. Jr. engr. analytical dept. Westinghouse Electric Corp., East Pittsburgh, Pa., 1957; inst. fellow Northwestern U., Evanston, Ill., 1957-59; asst. prof. elec. engring. U. Pitts., 1959-62, assoc. prof., 1962-67; vis. assoc. prof. elec. engring. U. Calif.-Berkeley, 1964; vis. prin. scientist Alza Corp., Palo Alto, Calif., 1970; faculty rsch. participant Pitts. Energy Tech. Ctr., Dept. Energy, Pitts., 1982, 83, 85, 88, 89; prof. elec. engring. U. Pitts., 1967—, prof. computer sci., 1977—; mem. Ctr. Multivariate Analysis, 1982-87, Ctr. for Parallel and Distributed Intelligent Systems, 1986—; sabbatical leave Lab. for Info. and Decision Systems, MIT, 1988; mem. sci. adv. com. Horus Therapeutics, Inc., 1995—. Guest editor Jour. Cybernetics and Info. Sci., 1979, Computerized Med. Imaging and Graphics, 1991; assoc. editor Pattern Recognition, 1985—; contbr. articles to profl. jours. Co-recipient cert. of merit Radiol. Soc. N.Am., 1979; rsch. grantee NSF, 1975-81, 85-87, Pa. Dept. Health, 1977-79, We. Pa. Advanced Tech. Ctr., 1983-84, 86-88, Health Rsch. and Svc. Found., 1985-86, Air Force Office Sci. Rsch., 1990-93. Fellow IEEE (tech. com., com. chmn. 1967—); mem. Biomed. Engring. Soc., AAAS, N.Y. Acad. Sci., Pattern Recognition Soc., Sigma Xi, Eta Kappa Nu. Home: 2130 Garrick Dr Pittsburgh PA 15235-5033 Office: U Pitts Dept Elec Engring Pittsburgh PA 15261

LI, CHU-TSING, art history educator; b. Canton, China, 1920; came to U.S., 1947; m. Yao-wen; children: Ulysses, Amy. B.A., U. Nanking, 1943; M.A. in English Lit., U. Iowa, 1949, Ph.D. in Art History, 1955. Instr. U. Iowa, 1954-55, 56-58, asst. prof., 1958-62, assoc. prof., 1962-65, prof., 1965-66; prof. art history U. Kans., Lawrence, 1966-78, dept. chmn., 1972-78, Judith Harris Murphy Disting. prof., 1978-90, prof. emeritus, 1990—, dir. NEH summer seminar on Chinese art history, 1975, 78, coordinator Mellon faculty seminar, 1979; acting asst. prof. Oberlin Coll., 1955-56; asst. prof. Ind. U., summer 1956; coordinator N.Y. state faculty seminar on Chineses Art History, SUNY, 1965; research curator Nelson Gallery of Art, Kansas City, 1966—; vis. prof. fine arts Chinese U., Hong Kong, 1972-73, summer 1971, leader China visit group, 1973; vis. prof. Grad. Inst. Art History, Nat Taiwan U., 1990; vis. Andrew W. Mellon prof. U. Pitts., 1995; dir. NEH Summer Inst. Modern Chinese Art and Culture, 1991; participant Internat. Symposiums on Chinese Painting, Nat. Palace Mus., Taipei, 1970, Cleve. Mus. Art, 1981, Huangshan Sch. Painters, Hefei, Ahnui, Rep. China, 1984, on Words and Images in Chinese Painting, Met. Mus. Art, N.Y.C., 1985, on the Elegant Brush: Chinese Painting under the Qianlong Emperor, Phoenix Art Mus., 1985, to celebrate 60th anniversary Nat. Palace Mus., Taipei, Taiwan, 1985, on History of Yuan Dynasty, Nanjing U., China, 1986, on art of Badashanren (Chu Tua), Nanchang, China, 1986; on Dunhuang Grottoes, China, 1987; on the Four Monk Painters, Shanghai Mus., 1987; on art of Chang Dai-chien, Nat. Mus. History, Taipei, 1988; Symposium on Contemporary Artistic Development, Nanjing, 1988; Symposium on Chinese Painting of Ming Dynasty Chinese U. Hong Kong, 1988; Symposium on Chinese Painting of the Ming and Qing Dynasties from the Forbidden City, Cleve. Mus. Art, 1989, Symposium on Hist. Studies, since 1911, Nat. Taiwan U., 1989, Symposium on 40th Anniversary of Founding of Liaoning Provincial Mus., Shenyang, China, 1989, Symposium on Painting of Wu Sch., Palace Mus., Beijing, 1990; Internat. Colloquium on Chinese Art History, Nat. Palace Mus. Taipei, 1991, Internat. Symposium on Art of Four Wangs, Shanghai, 1992, VIIeme Colloque Internat. de Sinologie, Chantilly, France, 1992, Symposium Painting at Close Qing Empire, Phoenix, 1992, Symposium on Ming & Qing Painting, Beijing, Symposium on Art of Zhao Meng-fu, Shanghai, 1995, Symposium on 20th Century Chinese Painting, Hong Kong Mus. Art, 1995; spl. cons. Chinese U., Hong Kong, 1971, Symposium on Painting and Calligraphy by Ming Loyalists, Early Ch'ing Period, 1975. Author: books and exhbn. catalogues including The Autumn Colors on the Ch'iao and Hua Mountains, A Painting by Chao Meng-fu, 1254-1322, 1965, Liu Kuo-sung: The Development of a Modern Chinese Artist, 1970, A Thousand Peaks and Myriad Ravines: Chinese Paintings in the Charles A. Drenowatz Collection, 2 vols., 1974, Trends in Modern Chinese Painting, 1979; co-editor, contbr. Chinese Scholar's Studio: Artistic Life in Late Ming, Asia Soc., N.Y.C., 1987; editor, contbr.: Artists and Patrons: Some Social and Economic Aspects of Chinese Painting, 1990; contbr. articles to books and catalogues. Ford Found. Fgn. Area Tng. fellow, 1959-60; grantee Am. Council Learned Socs. and Social Sci. Research Council, 1963-64, NEH, 1975, 78, 91, Com. for Scholarly Communication with People's Republic of China Nat. Acad. Scis., 1979, Am. Council Learned Socs., 1980, Asian Cultural Council, N.Y., 1981, Kans. U., summers 1966-80; U. Iowa research prof., 1963-64; Fulbright-Hayes faculty fellow, 1968-69. Mem. Coll. Art Assn. Am., Assn. for Asian Studies, Midwest Art History Soc., Internat. House of Japan, Min-chiu Soc. Hong Kong, Phi Tau Phi, Phi Beta Kappa (hon.), Phi Beta Delta. Home: 1108 Avalon Rd Lawrence KS 66044-2506 Office: Univ Kans Kress Found Dept Art History Lawrence KS 66045

LI, DAVID WAN-CHENG, cell biologist; b. Heng Shan, Peoples Republic of China, Sept. 2, 1960; came to the U.S., 1986; s. Xi-Lin and Xin-Tao (Guo) L.; m. Lily Liu, June 17, 1986; children: Flora, Jesse. BS, Hunan Normal U., 1982, MS, 1985; PhD, U. Wash., 1992. Lectr. in biology Hunan Normal U., Chang Sha, Peoples Republic of China, 1987-94, adj. prof. biology, 1995—; teaching asst. U. Alta., Edmonton, Can., 1986; teaching and rsch. asst. U. Wash., Seattle, 1986-92; rsch. scientist Columbia U., N.Y.C., 1992-95, asst. prof. ophthalmology, 1996—. Contbr. articles to profl. jours. Exec. pres. June 4th Found., Seattle, 1990-92, bd. dirs., 1989—. Mem. AAAS, Am. Soc. Cell Biology, Am. Soc. Biochemistry and Molecular Biology, Assn. for Rsch. in Vision and Ophthalmology. Achievements include devel. of a set of biol. stds. for the hybrid yue carp and its parents; identification of pair of duplicated genes coding for two different isoelectric forms of insect pigment protein and cloning of these genes; discovery of a potential cellular mechanism for non-congenital cataract formation in humans and animals. Home: PO Box 263 Audubon Sta New York NY 10032 also: 441 Lawn Ave Palisades Park NJ 07650 Office: Columbia U Dept Ophthalmology 630 W 168th St New York NY 10032

LI, FU, electrical engineering educator, editor; b. Chengdu, Sichuan, China, Sept. 12, 1958; came to U.S., 1985; s. Zhi and Xiu-Juan (Ding) L.; m. Grace Hui Fang, Mar. 18, 1984; children: Susan J., Karen M. BS in Physics, Sichuan U., 1982, MS in Physics, 1985; PhD in Elec. Engring., U. R.I., 1990. Profl. engr., Oreg. Rsch./teaching asst. U. R.I., Kingston, 1986-89; rsch. staff Philips Labs., Briarcliff Manor, N.Y., summer 1987; tech. staff Prime Computer, Inc., Bedford, Mass., 1989-90; asst. prof. elec. engring. Portland (Oreg.) State U., 1990-94, assoc. prof. elec. engring., 1994—; session chair Internat. Conf. on Acoustics, Speech and Signal Processing, 1993-96. Author chpts. to 4 books, 1991-94; contbr. articles to profl. jours. Recipient Faculty Devel. award Portland State U., 1991, Pew Teaching Leadership award 2d Nat. Conf. on Teaching Assts., 1989, Excellent Paper award Chinese Assn. Sci. and Tech., 1986. Mem. IEEE (sr., assoc. editor Transactions on Signal Processing 1993—, organizer Oreg. chpt. 1993, chair 1993-95, exec. com. 1993—, session chair statis. signals and array processing workshop 1992, 94, tech. com. on statis. signals and array processing 1992—, chair tech. subcom. power spectrum estimation 1992—, chair 1994—, recognition award 1993, chpt. chmn. award 1994, outstanding counselor award 1995), Eta Kappa Nu. Avocations: thinking, reading, playing computer, swimming, investing. Office: Portland State Univ Dept Elec Engring 1800 SW 6th Ave Portland OR 97201-5204

LI, GERALD, architect, film producer and director; b. Washington, Mar. 4, 1942; s. Chen Sheng and Gloria (Mark) L.; m. Annemarie van Kersen, Oct. 31, 1972 (div. 1990); children: Alexis, Madison. BS, Rensselaer Poly. Inst., 1963, BArch, 1965. Architect Edward Larabee Barnes, N.Y.C., 1965-67; with Romaldo Guirgola, N.Y.C., 1967-68, Brown-Daltas, Rome, 1969-70, Conklin-Rossant, N.Y.C., 1970-72; chief designer Odell Assocs., Charlotte, N.C., 1972-73; prin. Clark Tribble Harris and Li, Charlotte, N.C., 1973-86; chmn., CEO Tribble Harris Li, Inc., Charlotte, N.C., 1986-90; dir. Young Pres'. Orgn., N.Y.C., L.A., 1988-90, Covell Matthews Wheatley, PLC, London, 1987-90, THL, Inc., Delaware, 1986-90. Prin. works include Saatchi-Saatchi World Hdgrs., Georgetown Park Shopping Mall, N.W. Mut. Office Bldg., Milw., Ritz Carlton Hotel, Aspen, Bank of Spain, N.Y.C.; dir. short film Cafe Argentina, 1995. Recipient Young Profls. Design award Building Design Construction Mag., 1980. Fellow AIA (Honor award for Discovery Place Mus. 1984); mem. Nat. Coun. Archtl. Registration Bds. Home: 929 E 2nd St Ste 202 Los Angeles CA 90012-4337

LI, GRACE CHIA-CHIAN, accountant, strategic management consultant; b. Taipei, Taiwan, Republic of China, Aug. 7, 1963; came to U.S., 1987; d. Chuan-Chun and Yu-Lin (Hsueh) L.; m. Michael H. Chang, Dec. 21, 1993. BA, Nat. Cheng Chi U., Taipei, 1985; MBA, Wash. U., 1989. Acct. Cosa Libermann LTD, Taipei, 1985-86; cost acctg. supr. Johnson & Johnson, Taipei, 1988; planning and control specialist IBM Corp., Taipei, 1986-87; fin. analyst Ameritech Cellular, St. Louis, 1989-92; mgr. market planning Ameritech Internat., Hoffman Estates, Ill., 1992-94; internat. mktg. mgr. Pactel Internat., Walnut Creek, Calif., 1994; bus. cons. Decision Consulting, San Ramon, Calif., 1994-95; bus. planning mgr. Mitsubishi Wireless Comm. Inc., Sunnyvale, Calif., 1995—; guest spkr. on China telecom. industry devel. Nat. Comm. Forum, Chgo., 1993. Mem. Am. Inst. CPAs, CPA Soc. Ill. Avocations: reading, traveling, listening to music. Office: Mitsubishi Wireless Comm Inc 1050 E Arques Ave Sunnyvale CA 94086

LI, JIANKE, astronomer; b. Yuhang County, Zhejiang, People's Republic of China, Oct. 23, 1957; s. Xiqing Li and Xiufang Jin; m. Ling Zhao, Mar. 18, 1984; 1 child, Ge. BS in Physics, Zhejiang Tchrs. Coll., 1982; MS in Astronomy, Shaanxi Astron. Obs., People's Republic of China, 1985; PhD in Astronomy, U. Sussex, Brighton, Eng., 1992. Rsch. asst. Shaanxi Astron. Obs., Shaanxi Province, People's Republic of China, 1985-88; postdoctoral fellow Rsch. Ctr. for Theoretical Astrophysics U. Sydney, NSW, Australia, 1992-93; postdoctoral fellow High Altitude Obs. Nat. Ctr. Atmospheric Rsch., Boulder, Colo., 1993—. Contbr. rsch. papers to profl. publs. Vis. fellow Astrophysics Inst. Potsdam, Germany, 1995, Astrophysics Theory Ctr., Australian Nat. U., 1994; scholar Sino-Brit. Friendship Scholarship, 1988. Achievements include research in astrophysics in area of magnetohydrodynamics; magnetic binary stars; pulsar wind; late-type stars; accretion discs. Avocations: music, sports, reading.

LI, NORMAN N., chemicals executive; b. Shanghai, China, Jan. 14, 1933; came to U.S.; naturalized, 1969.; s. Lieh-wen and Amy H. Li; m. Jane C. Li, Aug. 17, 1963; children: Rebecca H., David H. BSin Chem. Engring., Nat. Taiwan U., Taipei, 1955; MS, Wayne State U., 1957; PhD, Stevens Inst.

Tech., 1963. Sr. scientist Exxon Rsch. and Engring. Co., Linden, N.J., 1963-81; dir. separation sci. and tech. UOP, Des Plaines, Ill., 1981-88; dir. engineered products and process tech. Allied-Signal Inc., Des Plaines, Ill., 1988-92, dir. rsch. and tech., 1993-95; pres., CEO NL Chem. Technology, Inc., 1995—; mem. NRC, 1985-89; lectr. Am. Inst. Chem. Engrs., 1975-86. Editor 13 books on separation sci. and tech.; contbr. articles to jours. in field; patentee in field. Fellow AICE (dir. divsn. food, pharms. and bioengring. 1988-91, Alpha Chi Sigma rsch. award 1988, bd dirs 1992-94, Ernest Thiele award 1995); mem. NAE, Am. Chem. soc. (Seperation Sci. and Tech. award 1988), N.Am. Membrane Soc. (pres. 1991-93). Home: 620 Rolling Ln Arlington Heights IL 60004-5820

LI, PEARL NEI-CHIEN CHU, information specialist, executive; b. Jiangsu, China, June 17, 1946; came to U.S., 1968; d. Ping-Yung and Yao-Hwa (Li) Chu; m. Terry Teng-Fang Li, Sept. 20, 1969; children: Ina Ying, Ping Li. BA, Nat. Taiwan U., Taipei, 1968; MA, W.Va. U., 1971; cert. advanced study in info. studies, Drexel U., 1983. Cert. sr. libr., N.J. Instr. Nat. Tchr.'s Coll., Chang-Hua, Taiwan, 1977-78; reference libr. Camden County Libr., Voorhees, N.J., 1981-82; libr. Kulzer and Dipadova, P.A., Haddonfield, N.J., 1982-87; libr. dir. Am. Law Inst., Phila., 1987-92; gen. mgr., info. specialist Unitek Internat. Corp. (Am.), Mt. Laurel, N.J., 1992—; tchr. South Jersey Chinese Sch., Cherry Hill, N.J., 1978-82. Editor: CLE Around the Cuontry (annually), 1988-92; contbr. articles to profl. jours. Bus. mgr. Chinese Community Ctr., Voorhees, 1981. Mem. NAFE, N.J. Entrepreneurial Network, Inc., Spl. Librs. Assn., Soc. Competitive Intelligence Profls. Home: 1132 Sea Gull Ln Cherry Hill NJ 08003-3113 Office: Unitek Internat Corp 131A Gaither Dr Mount Laurel NJ 08054

LI, PUI-PUI, interior and graphic designer; b. Hong Kong, Nov. 22, 1954; came to U.S., 1975; d. Hung Tong and Choi Gee Lee; m. Eric M. Jones, July 8, 1979. BFA, Art Ctr. Coll. Design, Pasadena, Calif., 1979. Creative dir. Atelier Internat. Ltd., L.I., N.Y., 1987-92; prin. Jones Studio Ltd., 1980—; v.p. design Internat. Contract Furnishings, N.Y.C., 1994—; creative dir. Cassina USA, Inc., Flos Inc., 1995—. Prin. art works exhibited at Artists and Poets of Hong Kong, Art Ctr. Coll. of Design Gallery, Sundance Film Festival, 1987, Design Industry Found. for AIDS, Sotheby's, N.Y., 1989, Murray Feldman Gallery, L.A., 1990, Cooper-Hewitt Gallery, L.A., 1990, Nat. Bldg. Mus., Washington, 1991, (design) Atelier Internat. Showroom, Chgo., 1992, ICF Showroom, Seattle, 1994, (film) Notes from Underground, 1995. Recipient Creativity award Art Direction mag., 1985, 87, 89, Product Lit. award Interiors Mag., 1988, Showroom award Am. Soc. Interior Designers, 1988, 92, Neocon Product Display award AIA, 1988, Strathmore Cert. of Silver, 1993, Packaging Design award I.D. mag., 1993, Interplan Gold award, 1995, Graphis Brochure 2, 1996. Office: Jones Studio Ltd PO Box 140402 Staten Island NY 10314-0402

LI, TINGYE, electrical engineer; b. Nanking, China, July 7, 1931; came to U.S., 1953, naturalized, 1963; s. Chao and Lily Wei-peng (Sie) L.; m. Edith Hsiu-hwei Wu, June 9, 1956; children: Deborah Chunroh, Kathryn Dairoh. BSEE, U. Witwatersrand, South Africa, 1953; MS, Northwestern U., Evanston, Ill., 1955, PhD, 1958; DEng (hon.), Nat. Chiao Tung U., Hsinchu, Republic of China, 1991. Mem. tech. staff AT&T Bell Labs., Holmdel, N.J., 1957-67; dept. head repeater techniques research dept. Bell Labs., 1967-76, lightwave media research dept., 1976-84, lightwave systems research dept., 1984-96; dept. head lightwave networks rsch. dept. AT&T Bell Labs., Holmdel, N.J., 1996—; hon. prof. Tsinghua U., Shanghai Jiao Tong U., Beijing U. Posts and Telecomms., U. Electronic Sci. and Tech. of China, Qufu Normal U., No. Jiao Tong U., Tianjin U., Nankai U., Fudan U. Assoc. editor Optics Letters, 1977-78, topical editor, 1989-91; assoc. editor Jour. of Lightwave Tech., 1983-86; editor book series: Optical Fiber Communications; mem. editorial bd. Procs. IEEE, 1974-83, Microwave and Optical Tech. Letters, 1987—, Internat. Jour. High Speed Electronics, 1990—; contbr. articles on microwave antennas and propagation, lasers, coherent optics, optical communications, optical-fiber transmission to sci. jours., chpts. in books. Recipient Alumni Merit award Northwestern U. Fellow IEEE (W.R.G. Baker prize 1975, David Sarnoff award 1979), AAAS, Photonics Soc. Chinese-Ams., Optical Soc. Am. (chmn. optical comms. tech. group 1979-80, bd. dirs. 1985-87, chmn. internat. activities com. 1988-90, chmn. photonics divsn. 1991-92, pres. 1995, John Tyndall award 1995); mem. NAE, Chinese Inst. Engrs. U.S.A. (bd. dirs. 1974-78, Achievement award 1978), Academia Sinica (Taiwan), Chinese Am. Acad. and Profl. Assn. (bd. dirs. 1985-89, Achievement award 1983), Electromagnetics Acad., F.F. Fraternity Club, Sigma Xi, Eta Kappa Nu, Phi Tau Phi (pres. East Am. chpt. 1991-93). Club: F.F. Fraternity. Patentee in field. Office: AT&T Bell Labs PO Box 400 Holmdel NJ 07733

LI, TZE-CHUNG, lawyer, educator; b. Shanghai, China, Feb. 17, 1927; came to U.S., 1956; s. Ken-hsiang Li and Yun-hsien (Chang) Li; m. Dorothy In-lan Wang, Oct. 21, 1961; children—Lily, Rose. LL.B., Soochow U., Shanghai, 1948; Diploma, Nat. Chengchi U., Nanking, 1949, China Research Inst. of Land Econs., Taipei, 1952; M.C.L., So. Meth. U., Dallas, 1956; LL.M., Harvard U., Cambridge, 1958; M.S., Columbia U., N.Y.C., 1965; Ph.D., New Sch. for Social Research, N.Y.C., 1963. Judge Hwa-lien Dist. Ct., Hwa-lien, Taiwan, Republic of China, 1949-51; dist. atty. Ministry of Justice, Tapei, 1951-52; chief law sect. Ministry of Nat. Def., Tapei, 1952-56; asst. prof. library sci. Ill. State U., Normal, 1965-66; asst. prof. polit. sci., library sci. Rosary Coll., River Forest, Ill., 1966-69, assoc. prof. library sci., 1969-70, 72-74, prof. library sci., 1974-82, dean, prof. Grad. Sch. Library and Info. Sci., 1982-88, prof., 1988—; vis. assoc. prof. law Nat. Taiwan U., 1969; vis. assoc. prof. polit. sci. Soochow U., Taipei, 1969; dir. Nat. Central Library, Taipei, 1970-72; chmn. Grad. Inst. Library Sci., Nat. Central Library, Taipei, 1971-72; commr. Ministry of Examination, Examination Yuan, Taipei, 1971; chmn. com. on library standards, Ministry of Edn., Taipei, 1972; library cons. Soochow U., Nat. Chengchi U., Dr. Sun Yat-sen Meml. Library; mem. library adv. com. Ency. Britannica, 1982—; hon. prof. library and info. sci. Jiangxi U., People's Republic of China, 1985—; vis. prof. law Suzhou U., Peking U., 1991, Nat. Taiwan U., 1991; hon. cons. univ. library, 1985—; hon. cons. Jiangxi Med. Coll., 1985—; adv. prof. East China Normal U., 1987—; cons. Nova U., 1987-88; mem. ad hoc adv. com. Chgo. Pub. Library Bldg. Planning, 1987-88. Author books including: Social Science Reference Sources, 1980, 2d edit., 1990, Mah Jong, 1982, 2d edit., 1991, An Introduction to Online Searching, 1985; also numerous articles in profl., scholarly jours.; founding editor Jour. Library and Info. Sci., 1975-80, mem. editorial bd. 1986-90; founding chmn., mem. editorial bd. Internat. Jour. of Revs., 1984-89. Pres. Chinese Am. Ednl. Found., Chgo., 1968-70; chmn. Com. for Chinatown Library, Chgo., 1966-67; advisor Friends of Soochow, Los Angeles, 1974-87; bd. dirs. Asian Human Services, Inc., Chgo., 1978; co-chmn. Com. for Expansion of Chinatown Library, Chgo., 1984-86; pres. China Council on Cultural Renaissance, Midwest chpt., 1974-85. Recipient Govt. Citation Republic of China, 1956, 1972, Philip D. Sang Excellence in Teaching award Rosary Coll., 1971, Disting. Service award Phi Tau Phi, Chgo., 1982, Service award HUD, Chgo. region, 1985, Disting. Service award Chinese Am. Librarians Assn., 1988. Mem. ALA1 Am. Soc. Info. Sci., Assn. for Asian Studies, Assn. Coll. and Research Libraries, Assn. Library ad Info. Sci. Edn., Chinese Am. Librarians Assn. (founding pres. 1976-80), Library Assn. China (Taipei), Spl. Library Assn., Phi Tau Phi (pres. 1985-87). Republican. Roman Catholic. Home: PO Box 444 Oak Park IL 60303-0444 Office: Rosary Coll 7900 Division St River Forest IL 60305-1066

LI, WEIYE, ophthalmologist, biochemist, educator; b. Zhejiang, China, Oct. 10, 1946; came to U.S., 1990; s. Zhao-ji Li and Qin Yue; m. Xinru Liu, Apr. 12, 1986; 1 child, Yafeng. MD, Peking Second Med. Coll., China, 1970; postgrad., Acad. Med. Scis., China, 1978-80; PhD, U. Pa., 1984. Intern Chao Young Hosp., Peking, 1970-71, resident ophthalmology, 1971-78; rsch. fellow dept. ophthalmology and biochem. grad. sch. Sch. Medicine U. Pa., Phila., 1981-84, postdoctor, asst. prof. dept. ophthalmology Scheie Eye Inst. Sch. Medicine, 1984-85; asst. prof., attending physician ophthalmology Peking Union Med. Coll. Hosp., 1985-86, assoc. prof. ophthalmology, 1986-88, prof. ophthalmology, 1988-93, chmn. dept. ophthalmology, 1989-93; prof. ophthalmology, dir. rsch. dept. ophthalmology, prof. pathology, mem. faculty interdepartmental program molecular biology and biotech. Hahnemann U., Phila., 1990—. Recipient Rsch. award Internat. Juvenile Diabetes Found., 1984-86, 1st Class Sci. and Tech. Advances prize Chinese Ministry Pub. Health, 1988; grantee NIH, 1981-82, 86—, Fight for Sight, Inc., 1982-83, Am. Diabetes Assn., 1990—, Frank E. Snider Trust Fund, 1990—; Postdoctoral fellow Internat. Juvenile Diabetes Found., 1982-84. Mem. Assn. Rsch. in Vision and Ophthalmology, Assn. Chinese Ophthal. Soc. Avocations: table tennis, bicycling, classical music. Office: Hahnemann U Dept Ophthalmology MS 209 Broad and Vine Sts Philadelphia PA 19102-1192

LI, YONGJI, chemistry educator; b. Beijing, Sept. 5, 1933; came to U.S., 1981; s. Zhi-Ping and Zhi-Zhang (Chen) L.; m. Zhihua Yu, June 30, 1956; children: Zidan, Lisa. BS in Physics, Beijing U., 1955; PhD in Chemistry, SUNY, Buffalo, 1985. Instr., lectr. physics Jilin U., Changchun, Jiling, China, 1955-81; rsch. asst., teaching asst. SUNY, Buffalo, 1981-85; postdoctoral rsch. assoc. U. New Orleans, 1985-89; assoc. prof. chemistry U. P.R., San Juan, 1989-93, dir. X-Ray Lab., 1989-93; adj. assoc. prof. chemistry N.Y. Inst. Tech., L.I., 1994—. Contbr. articles to profl. jours. Grantee High Edn. Ministry, China, 1979, NSF, 1992. Mem. Am. Chem. Soc., Am. Crystallographic Assn. Achievements include construction of first Chinese ultra-high pressure mini-generator (diamond anvil cell, 300kb without a gasket); x-ray crystallographic studies on inorganic and/or biologically active compounds; accurate measurements of electron density distribution on organometallics and biologically active compounds; avocations: sports, music, dancing, bridge, travel. Home: 12 Osage Ct Coram NY 11727 Office: NY Inst Tech Old Westbury NY 11568-8000

LIACOS, PAUL JULIAN, state supreme judicial court chief justice; b. Peabody, Mass., Nov. 20, 1929; s. James A. and Pitsa K. (Karis) L.; m. Maureen G. McKean, Oct. 6, 1954; children: James P., Diana M., Mark C., Gregory A. AB magna cum laude, Boston U. Coll. Liberal Arts, 1950; LLB magna cum laude, Boston U., 1952; LLM, Harvard U., 1953; diploma, Air Command and Staff Sch., 1954; LLD (hon.), Suffolk U., 1984, New Eng. Sch. Law, 1985; LHD (hon.), Salem State Coll., 1988; LLD (hon.), Northeastern U., 1991. Bar: Mass. 1952, U.S. Dist. Ct. Mass. 1954, U.S. Ct. Mil. Appeals 1955, U.S. Ct. Appeals (1st cir.) 1971, U.S. Supreme Ct. 1980. Ptnr. firm Liacos and Liacos, Peabody, Mass., 1952-76; prof. law Boston U., 1952-76, adj. prof. law, 1976-89; assoc. justice Mass. Supreme Jud. Ct., 1976-89, chief justice, 1989—; Distinguished lectr. on law U.S. Mil. Acad., West Point, N.Y., 1972; lectr. Suffolk U. Sch. Law, 1978-79; U.S. Constn. Bicentennial lectr. Boston Pub. Library, 1987; cons. to atty. gen. Mass. on staffing and personnel, 1974-75; lectr. on criminal evidence Boston Police Acad., 1963-64; reporter New Eng. Conf. on Def. of the Indigent, Harvard Law Sch., 1963; reader and cons. on legal manuscripts Little, Brown & Co., Boston, 1968-76; editorial cons. Warren, Gorham & Lamont, 1968-69; mem. steering com. Lawyers Com. for Civil Rights under Law, Boston, 1969-72; chmn. com. on discrimination in the cts. Conf. of Chief Justices, 1993—. Author: Handbook of Massachusetts Evidence, 6th edit., 1994, supplement, 1995; contbr. articles in field to legal jours.; book rev. editor Boston U. law Rev., 1952. Trustee Suffolk U., Boston, 1993—; trustee, mem. exec. com. Chamberlayne Sch. and Jr. Coll., Boston, 1982-84; trustee Anatolia Coll., Salonika, Greece, 1980—, exec. com., 1986-89; hon. trustee Deree-Pierce Colls., Athens, 1976—; corp. mem. MIT, 1989. With JAG, USAF, 1953-56. Named Man of Yr. Boston Law Sch., 1952, Man of Yr. Alpha Omega, 1977, Mem. Colleguum Disting. Alumni Boston U. Coll. Liberal Arts, 1974; recipient Disting. Pub. Svc. award Boston U. Alumni, 1980, Aooied Profl. award Mass. Psychol. Assn., 1987, Man of Vision award Nat. Soc. to Prevent Blindness, 1988, State Bill of Rights award Nat. Assn. Criminal Def. Lawyers, 1988, Good Neighbor award Mishkan Tefila Brotherhood, 1990, Founders' award Lawyers Com. for Civil Rights Under the Law, Boston Bar Assn., 1993, citation of jud. excellence Boston Bar Assn., 1995. Mem. ABA (jud. cert. of appreciation 1994), ATLA (editor 1968-73, Outstanding State Appellate Judge 1982), Mass. Bar Assn. (criminal law com. 1964-66), Essex County Bar Assn., Peabody Bar Assn., Greater Lowell Bar Assn. (hon.), Harvard Law Sch. Assn., Boston U. Law Sch. Alumni Assn. (Silver Shingle award 1977), Phi Beta Kappa. Democrat. Mem. Greek Orthodox Ch. Office: Mass Supreme Jud Ct Pemberton Sq 1300 New Courthouse Boston MA 02108

LIAKOS, JAMES CHRIST, business manager; b. Washington, Feb. 10, 1933; s. Christ and Xantippe (Franks) L.; m. Alexandra Avayanos, Jan. 1, 1956 (div. Jan. 1960); 1 child, Stephanie; m. Roberta Sue Katzman, May 31, 1963. B Comml. Scis., Benjamin Franklin U., 1956. Supr. acctg. dept. Bakery & Confectionery Union Industry Internat. Welfare and Pension Funds, Washington, 1955-66; adminstrv. asst. Am. Physiol. Soc., Bethesda, Md., 1966-76, asst. bus. mgr., bus. mgr., 1985—. With U.S. Army, 1953-54, ETO. Mem. Nat. Soc. Pub. Acctg., Am. Soc. Assn. Execs. Greek Orthodox. Home: 11001 Lopa Ln North Potomac MD 20878-2542 Office: Am Physiol Soc 9650 Rockville Pike Bethesda MD 20814-3998

LIANG, EDISON PARKTAK, astrophysicist, educator, researcher; b. Canton, Republic of China, July 22, 1947; came to U.S., 1964; s. Chi-Sen and Siu-Fong (Law) L.; m. Lily K. Yuen, Aug. 7, 1971; children: Olivia, James, Justin. BA, U. Calif., Berkeley, 1967, PhD, 1971. Rsch. scientist U. Tex., Austin, 1971-73; assoc. instr. U. Utah, Salt Lake City, 1973-75; asst. prof. Mich. State U., East Lansing, Mich., 1975-76, Stanford (Calif.) U., 1976-79; physicist, group leader Lawrence Livermore Nat. Lab., Livermore, Calif., 1980-88; assoc. div. leader Lawrence Livermore Nat. Lab., Livermore, 1988-91; prof. Rice U., Houston, Tex., 1991—; mem. NASA Rev. Panels, Washington, 1988—. Editor: (book) Gamma Ray Bursts, 1986. Named Sci. fellow and Anthony scholar U. Calif., Berkeley, 1967-69. Fellow Am. Physical Soc.; mem. Am. Astron. Soc., Internat. Astron. Union, Phi Beta Kappa, Sigma Xi. Office: Rice U MS 108 PO Box 1892 Houston TX 77251-1892

LIANG, JEFFREY DER-SHING, retired electrical engineer, civil worker, diplomat; b. Chungking, China, Oct. 25, 1915; came to U.S., 1944, naturalized, 1971; s. Tze-hsiang and Sou-yi (Wang) L.; m. Eva Yin Hwa Tang, Jan. 2, 1940; 1 child, Shouyu. BA, Nat. Chengchih U., Chungking, 1940; BAS, U. B.C., Vancouver, 1960. Office asst. Ministry of Fgn. Affairs, Chungking, 1940-43; vice consul, Chinese consulate Ministry of Fgn. Affairs, Seattle, 1944-50; consulate-gen. Ministry of Fgn. Affairs, San Francisco, 1950-53; consul, Chinese consulate-gen. Ministry of Fgn. Affairs, Vancouver, 1953-56; engr.-in-tng. Can. Broadcasting Corp., Vancouver, 1960-65; assoc. engr. Boeing Co., Seattle, 1965-67, rsch. engr., 1967-70, engr., 1970-73, sr. engr., 1973-75, specialist engr., 1975-78; cons. Seattle, 1979-81. Mem. chancelor's cir. Wesbrook Soc. U. B.C., Vancouver, 1986—, Seattle-King County Adv. Coun. on Aging, 1984-88, Gov.'s State Coun. on Aging, Olympia, 1986-88, Pres. Coun., Rep. Nat. Com.; permanent mem. Rep. Nat. Senatorial Com., Washington State Rep. Party, Seattle Art Mus.; life mem. Am. Assn. Individual Investors, Rep. Presdl. Task Force; sustaining mem. Rep. Nat. Congl. Com., Rep. Presdl. Adv. Com.,. Mem. IEEE (life), Heritage Found., Nat. Trust Hist. Preservation, Hwa Sheng Chinese Music Club (v.p. 1978-79, chmn. nomination com. 1981-88, 90-94). Republican. Mem. Christian Ch. Avocations: Chinese calligraphy, opera, poetry, physical fitness. Home: 1750 152d Ave NE Apt 302 Bellevue WA 98007-4270 *Always try to do one's best since that is a sure way to go through life without regrets.*

LIANG, JEROME ZHENGRONG, radiology educator; b. Chongging, Sichuan, China, June 23, 1958; came to U.S., 1981; BS, Lanzhou U., China, 1982; PhD, CUNY, 1987. Rsch. instr. Albert Einstein Coll. Medicine, Bronx, N.Y., 1986-87; rsch. assoc. Duke U. Med. Ctr., Durham, N.C., 1987-89; asst. med. rsch. prof. Duke U. Med. Ctr., 1990-92; asst. prof. SUNY, Stony Brook, 1992—. Contbr. articles to profl. jours. Grantee Soc. Thoracic Radiology, 1994-95, ADAC Rsch. Lab., 1995-96; recipient NIH awards, 1990-94, 95—, AHA award, 1996—. Mem. Assn. Chinese-Am. Sr. Profls., Inc. (trustee 1994—). Achievements include devel. of Bayesian image processing, quantitative emission computed tomography, tissue segmentation from magnetic resonance images. Avocations: swimming, fitness, tennis. Office: Dept Radiology SUNY Stony Brook 4th Fl Rm 092 Stony Brook NY 11794

LIANG, JUNXIANG, aeronautics and astronautics engineer, educator; b. Hangzhou, Zhejiang, China, Aug. 17, 1932; s. Yigao and Yunruo (Yu) L.; m. Junxian Sun, Jan. 27, 1960; 1 child, Song Liang. Grad., Harbin Inst. Tech., 1960. Head control dept. Shenyang (Liaoning, China) Jet Engine R&D Inst., 1960-70, China Gas Turbine Establishment, Jiangyou, Sichuan, China, 1970-78; assoc. chief engr. China Gas Turbine Establishment, Jiangyou, 1978-83; vis. scientist MIT, Cambridge, Mass., 1984-86; prof. China Aerospace Inst. Systems Engring., Beijing, China, 1986—; grads. supr. Beijing U. Aero-Astronautics, Beijing, 1986—; chief engr. Full Authority Digital Elec. Engine Control China Aerospace Industry Ministry, Beijing, 1986-93; mem. China Aerospace Sci. and Tech. Com., Beijing, 1983-94, Aero-engine R&D Adv. Bd., Beijing, 1991-95; bd. dirs. China Aviation Ency. Editl. Bd., Beijing, 1991-95; tech. support supr., mgmt. info. svc. mgr. Am. PC, Inc., Union City, Calif., 1993—. Author: Nonlinear Control System Oscillation, 1964; contbr. articles to Jour. Aeronautics and Astronautics, Jour. Propulsion Tech., Internat. Aviation, Acta Aeronautica et Astronautica Sinica. Recipient Nat. Sci. and Tech. 2d award, China Nat. Sci. and Tech. Com., Beijing, 1965, Sic. and Tech. Progress award, China Aerospace Industry Ministry, 1991, Nat. Outstanding Sci. and Tech. Contbn. award, 1992. Mem. AIAA, Chinese Soc. of Aeronautical, Astronautical Engine Control (mem. commn. 1987—). Achievements include solution of oscillation problem on nonlinear control system; formulation of aircraft overall strategy, study and control of High Thrust/Weight Engine Rsch. Program. Home: 2973 Carmel St Oakland CA 94602-3410 Office: China Aerospace Inst Sys Engring, Beiyuan-Dayuan # 2 An-Wai, Beijing 100012, China

LIANG, QINGJIAN JIM, petroleum engineer; b. Dalian, China, Apr. 18, 1957; came to U.S., 1988; s. Jishun Liang and Shuzhen Sui; m. Huang Xiaozhong, Apr. 14, 1983; 1 child, Zheng Liang. BS, Daqing (China) Petroleum Inst., 1982; MS, Mont. Coll. Mineral Sci./Tech., 1989; DEng, La. Tech. U., 1993. Drilling engr. Daqing No. 3 Drilling Co., Daqing, 1982-87; rsch. asst. La. Tech. U., Ruston, 1989-93; divsn. engr. Sonat Offshore Drilling Inc., Morgan City, La., 1993—. Assoc. mem. SPE. Achievements include development of new experimental methodology of transport coefficients measurement for two-phase flow in porous media; derived analytical model of two-phase immiscible fluids flow in capillary tube model porous media, discovered evidence of coupling effect. Avocations: fishing, painting, playing volleyball. Office: Sonat Offshore Drilling Inc 3850 N Causeway Blvd Ste 500 Metairie LA 70002

LIAO, HSIANG PENG, chemist; b. Nanping, China, May 4, 1924; came to U.S., 1948, naturalized, 1953; s. Samuel and Chung (Chang) L.; B.S., Fukien Christian U., 1945; Ph.D., Northwestern U., 1952; m. Chen Hansing, Jan. 6, 1950; children—Jacob, Wesla Mildred, Michael Lawrence. Chemist, Standard Oil Co., Ind., 1952-60; research chemist FMC Corp., Balt., 1960—, research asso., Princeton, N.J., 1980—; lectr. Fukien Christian U., 1945-47; grad. seminar lectr. Johns Hopkins, W.Va. U., 1961. Mem. AAAS, Am. Chem. Soc. Sigma Xi, Alpha Chi Sigma, Phi Lamda Upsilon. Methodist. Patentee in field. Home: 260 Fisher Pl Princeton NJ 08540-6444 Office: FMC Corp PO Box 8 Princeton NJ 08540

LIAO, MEI-JUNE, biopharmaceutical company executive; came to U.S., 1974; BS, Nat. Tsing-Hua U. Taiwan, 1973; MPh, Yale U., 1977, PhD, 1980. Tchg. asst. Nat. Taiwan U., 1973-74, Temple U., Phila., 1974-75; tchg. asst. Yale U., New Haven, 1975-76, rsch. asst., 1976-79; postdoctoral assoc. MIT, Cambridge, 1980-83; sr. scientist Interferon Scis., Inc., New Brunswick, N.J., 1983-84; group leader Interferon Scis. Inc., New Brunswick, N.J., 1984-85, dir. cell biology, 1985-87; dir. R&D Interferon Scis., Inc., New Brunswick, N.J., 1987-94, v.p. rsch. & deve., 1995—. Contbr. articles to profl. jours.; inventor in field. Mem. Am. Soc. Biochemistry and Molecular Biology, Internat. Soc. Interferon and Cytokine Rsch., Soc. Chinese Bioscientists in Am. Office: Interferon Sci Inc 783 Jersey Ave New Brunswick NJ 08901-3605

LIAO, PAUL FOO-HUNG, communications research company executive, physicist; b. Phila., Nov. 10, 1944; s. Tseng Wu and Tung Mei (Lin) L.; m. Karen Ann Pravetz, Aug. 31, 1968; children: Teresa S., Joanna S. BS, MIT, 1966; PhD, Columbia U., 1973. Rsch. assoc. Columbia U., N.Y.C., 1972-73; mem. tech. staff Bell Labs., Holmdel, N.J., 1973-80, dept. head., 1980-83; div. mgr. Bell Communications Rsch., Red Bank, N.J., 1984-89, asst. v.p., 1989-93, gen. mgr., 1993-95, v.p., 1996—. Co-editor: Academic Press Quantum Electronics Book Series; contbr. over 75 articles to profl. jours.; holder over 12 patents in field. Bd. trustees Brookdale C.C. Fellow IEEE, Optical Soc. Am. (editor jour.), Am. Phys. Soc.; mem. Lasers and Electro Optic Soc. of IEEE (pres. 1987). Office: Bell Communications Rsch Rm 1A209A 331 Newman Springs Rd Red Bank NJ 07701-5657

LIAO, SHUTSUNG, biochemist, oncologist; b. Tainan, Taiwan, Jan. 1, 1931; s. Chi-Chun Liao and Chin-Shen Lin; m. Shuching Liao, Mar. 19, 1960; children: Jane, Tzufen, Tzuming, May. BS in Agrl. Chemistry, Nat. Taiwan U., 1953, MS in Biochemistry, 1956; PhD in Biochemistry, U. Chgo., 1961. Rsch. assoc., 1960-63; asst. prof. U. Chgo., 1964-69; assoc. prof. dept. biochemistry Ben May Lab. Cancer Rsch., U. Chgo., 1969-71; prof. depts. biochemistry and cancer biology Ben May Inst., 1972—; cons. various nat. and internat. confs., agys., founds., and workshops. Mem. editorial bd. Jour. Steroid Biochemistry and Molecular Biology, The Prostate, and Receptors; assoc. editor Cancer Research, 1982-89; contbr. over 200 articles to profl jours. V.p. Chgo. Formosan Fed. Credit Union, 1977-79; trustee Taiwanese United Fund in U.S., 1981—; mem. adv. com. Taiwan-U.S. Cultural Exch. Ctr., 1984—. Recipient Sci-Tech. Achievement prize Taiwanese-Am. Found., 1983, Pfizer Lecture fellow award Clin. Rsch. Inst. Montreal, 1972, Gregory Pincus medal and award Worcester Found. for Exptl. Biology, 1992, Tzongming Tu award Formosan Med. Assn., 1993, C.H. Li Meml. Lecture award, 1994; NIH grantee, 1962—; Am. Cancer Soc. grantee, 1971-81. Mem. Am. Soc. Biochemistry and Molecular Biology, Am. Assn. Cancer Rsch., Endocrine Soc., N.Am.-Taiwanese Profs. Assn. (pres. 1980-81, exec. dir. 1981—), Academia Sinica. Achievements include discovery of androgen activation mechanism and androgen receptors; cloning and structural determination of androgen receptors and other novel nuclear receptors, and their genes, and receptor gene mutation in hereditary abnormalities and cancers; rsch. on regulation of hormone-dependent gene expression and cell growth, molecular bases of cancer cell growth and progression, chemoprevention, and therapeutic treatment of hormone-sensitive and insensitive cancers and diseases. Home: 5632 S Woodlawn Ave Chicago IL 60637-1623 Office: U Chgo Ben May Inst 5841 S Maryland Ave Chicago IL 60637-1463

LIAU, GENE, medical educator; b. Hsing-Chu, Taiwan, Nov. 28, 1954; came to U.S., 1965; BS in Biology, U. N.C., 1977; DPhil, Vanderbilt U., 1982. Postdoctoral fellow Lab. Molecular Biology Nat. Cancer Inst. NIH, Bethesda, Md., 1982-85; assoc. mem. Dept. Cell Biology Revlon Biotech. Rsch. Ctr., Rockville, Md., 1985-87; scientist I Dept. Molecular Biology Am. Red Cross Jerome H. Holland Lab., Rockville, 1987-90, scientist II, 1990—; assoc. prof. Dept. Anatomy George Washington U. Med. Ctr., Washington, 1995—; mem. AHA Vascular Wall Biology Rsch. Study Com., 1992-96, Pathology A Study Sect. NIH, 1994—; invited spkr. in field. Contbr. articles to profl. jours. Arthritis Found. fellow, 1982-85; pub. health svc. grantee, 1988—; recipient Nat. Rsch. Svc. award NIH, 1977-81, Rsch. Career Devel. award, 1990-95. Mem. AAAS, Am. Soc. Cell Biology, Am. Heart Assn. Coun. Basic Sci. (Established Investigator 1990, Grant-in-Aid 1992-95, 95—), Soc. Chinese Bioscientists, Sigma Xi. Home: 14900 Kelley Farm Dr Darnestown MD 20874 Office: Dept Molecular Biology Holland Lab 15601 Crabbs Branch Way Rockville MD 20855

LIBA, PETER MICHAEL, communications executive; b. Winnipeg, Man., Can., May 10, 1940; s. Theodore and Rose Liba; m. Shirley Ann Collett, May 4, 1963; children: Jennifer, Jeffrey, Christopher. Reporter, news editor The Daily Graphic, Portage la Prairie, Man., 1957-59; reporter The Winnipeg Tribune, 1959-67, city editor, 1967-68; ind. communications cons. Winnipeg, 1968-73; v.p. pub. affairs CanWest Broadcasting Ltd., Winnipeg, 1974-75, exec. v.p., 1979—; asst. gen. mgr. Sta. CKND-TV, Winnipeg, 1975-79, mgr., 1980-87, gen. mgr., 1987-92; pres., CEO CKND TV Inc./SaskWest TV Inc., Winnipeg, 1988-94; exec. v.p. CanWest Global Comm. Corp., Winnipeg, 1993—; bd. dirs. CanWest Comm. Corp., Winnipeg, Global Comm. Ltd., Toronto, CanWest Boradcasting Ltd., Winnipeg, CanWest TV, Inc., Winnipeg, CanWest Prodns., Ltd., Winnipeg, CanWest Properties Ltd., Winnipeg, CanWest Maritime TV, Inc., Halifax, LaRed Network, Chile, TV 3 Network, New Xealand, Network Ten, Australia; pres. Peli Ventures, Inc., 1975—, Peli Mgmt. Inc., 1982—. Trustee Transcona-Springfield Sch. div., Winnipeg, 1964-67; bd. dirs. Conv. Ctr. Corp., Winnipeg, 1976-86, Atomic Energy of Can., Ltd., Ottawa, Ont., Can., 1981-86, St. Boniface Gen. Hosp., Winnipeg, 1987—, chmn. bd., 1992—. Decorated Order of Can.; recipient Presdl. citation Variety Clubs Internat., 1983, Internat. Media award Variety Clubs Internat., 1986, commemorative medal 125th Anniversary Can., 1992; named Manitoban of Month, Mid-Can. Commerce mag., 1982. Mem.

Broadcasters Assn. Man. (pres. 1981-82), Western Assn. Broadcasters (pres. 1984-85, Broadcaster of Yr. award 1991, Broadcaster of Decade award 1994), Can. Assn. Broadcasters (chmn. bd. 1990-92), St. Charles Cluntry Club, Man. Club, Variety Club Man. (chief barker 1984-85). Office: CanWest Global Comm Corp. 31st Fl TD Centre, 201 Portage Ave, Winnipeg, MB Canada R3B 3L7

LIBASSI, FRANK PETER, lawyer, dean; b. N.Y.C., Apr. 20, 1930; s. Frank G. and Mary (Marino) L.; m. Mary Frances Steen, July 10, 1954; children: Thomas, Timothy, Jennifer. B.A. cum laude with honors in Polit. Sci, Colgate U., 1951; LL.B., Yale U., 1954. Bar: N.Y. 1955, Conn. 1980. Enforcement atty. N.Y. State Housing and Rent Commn., 1954-56; regional dir. N.Y. State Commn. on Human Rights, Albany, 1956-62; dep. staff dir. U.S. Commn. on Civil Rights, 1962-66; spl. asst. to sec., dir. office for civil rights HEW, Washington, 1966-68; exec. v.p. The Urban Coalition, Washington, 1968-71; v.p. Am. City Corp., Columbia, Md., 1971-72; pres., chief exec. officer Greater Hartford Process Inc. (Greater Hartford Community Devel. Corp.), 1971-77; gen. counsel HEW, Washington, 1977-79; partner firm Verner, Liipfert, Bernhard and McPherson, Washington, 1979-82; sr. v.p. Travelers Corp., Hartford, Conn., 1982-93; of counsel Verner, Liipfert, Bernhard & McPherson, Washington, 1993—; dean Barney Sch. of Bus. and Pub. Adminstrn., U. Hartford, West Hartford, Conn., 1993—; mem. Urban Land Inst., 1971-77; adv. bd. Bur. Nat. Affairs Housing and Cmty. Devel. Reporter, 1972-77; vis. lectr. Anderson Coll., Chatham Coll., Goddard Coll., Ohio Wesleyan U., 1974-76; adj. faculty Grad. Sch. Bus. and Pub. Adminstrn. U. Hartford, 1976-77; chmn. bd. dirs. Forstmann Corp., 1994—. Author: The Negro in the Armed Forces, 1963, Family Housing and the Negro Serviceman, 1963, Equal Opportunity in Farm Programs, 1965, Revitalizing Central City Investment, 1977. Bd. dirs. legis. com. Am. Coun. Life Ins., 1987-90; bd. dirs., exec. com. Ins. Inst. of Hwy. Safety, 1984-88; mem. pub. relations policy com. Health Ins. Assn. Am., 1988-93; incorporator Inst. Living, 1973—, Hartford Hosp., 1973—, St. Francis Hosp., 1990—, Hartford Seminary, 1993-95; mem. adv. com. Dem. Nat. Com., 1974-77; chmn. Ct. Community Care, Inc., 1980-86; mem. Mt. Sinai Hosp., 1982-90; mem. com. on an aging soc. Nat. Acad. Scis., 1982-86; mem. exec. com. Downtown Council Hartford, 1983-86, Greater Hartford Arts Council, 1985-86; chmn. Gov.'s Commn. on Financing Long Term Care, 1986-87; mem. nat. consumer adv. com. Am. Health Care Assn., 1985-86; mem. com. on elderly people living alone The Commonwealth Fund, 1985-91; mem. Sec. Bowen's Task Force on Long-term Health Care Policies of Health Care Financing Adminstrn., 1986-87; bd. dirs. Alliance for Aging Research, 1986-91; mem. Nat. Retirees Vol. Ctr., 1988-90; mem. Pew Commn. on future of health profls., 1990-93; mem. pub. affairs rsch. coun. conf. bd., 1990-93; mem. United Srs. Health Cooperative, 1990-91; mem. health adv. coun. Johns Hopkins U., 1990-96— , mem. com. predicting future diseases Inst. Medicine, 1991-93, bd. advisors Nat. Acad. on Aging, 1992-95; trustee Conn. Pub. Expenditure Coun., 1991-95; mem. adv. com. on health care reform The Commonwealth Fund, 1993—; mem. Children's Fund of Conn., 1993—, Duncaster Cmty., 1993—. Recipient Superior Performance award U.S. Commn. on Civil Rights, 1963, Meritorious Svc. award, 1965; Sec.'s spl. citation, 1967; Disting. Svc. award HEW, 1968, Friend of La Casa de Puerto Rico, Hartford, award, 1992; Woodrow Wilson sr. fellow, 1973-77. Mem. ABA, Fed. Bar Assn., N.Y. State Bar Assn., Conn. Bar Assn., Am. Assn. Retired Persons (nat. steering com. for new roles in soc. 1987-90), Greater Hartford C. of C. (bd. dirs. 1985-93, exec. com.). Club: Hartford. Home: 580 Mountain Rd Apt J West Hartford CT 06117-1827 Office: Barney Sch Bus/Pub Adminstn U Hartford 200 Bloomfield Ave West Hartford CT 06117-1545

LIBBEY, DARLENE HENSLEY, artist, educator; b. La Follette, Tenn., Jan. 9, 1952; d. Charles Franklin and Geneva (Chitwood) Hensley; children: Michael Damon McLaughlin, Marina Auston. BFA in Painting, San Francisco Art Inst., 1989; MFA in Painting/Drawing, U. Tenn., 1994. Grad. asst. Alliance of Ind. Colls., N.Y.C., 1989; gallery asst. Holley Solomon Gallery, N.Y.C., 1989; teaching assoc., instr. U. Tenn., Knoxville, 1991-94; lectr., instr. U. Tex.-Pan Am., 1994—, South Tex. Cmty. Coll., 1995—; curator Belleza Salon, Knoxville, 1993—; invitational rep. San Francisco Art Inst., N.Y. Studio Program, Alliance Ind. Colls., 1989; organizer Multi-Media Group Exhbn.; lectr., instr. South Tex. C.C., McAllen. One-woman shows include U. Tex.-Pan Am., 1995, 96; exhibited in group shows at San Francisco Art Inst., 1985, 86, 87, 88, 89, Pacific Ctr., San Francisco, 1988, alliance of Ind. Colls., N.Y.C., 1989, San Francisco Mus. Modern Art, 1990, Bluxom Studios, San Francisco, 1991, Gallery 1010, Knoxville, 1991, 92, Ewing Gallery, U. Tenn., Knoxville, 1991, 92, 93, 94, SUNY, Syracuse, 1992, Printers Mark, Knoxville, 1993, Unitarian Ch., Knoxville, 1993, Tomato Head, Knoxville, 1994, Belleza Salon, Knoxville, 1994, U. Pan Am., 1995, 96; group show Museo Historico de Reynosa, Tamalipus, Mex., 1996. Vol. San Francisco Mus. Modern Art, 1990-91; founding mem. Grad. Student Union, U. Tenn., Knoxville, 1993; vol. instr. Knox County Schs., Knoxville, 1992-93; vis. artist Marin County Schs., San Anselmo, Calif., 1989. Tuition scholar San Francisco Art Inst., 1987; materials grantee U. Tenn., 1993, grantee Buck Found., 1987-89. Mem. Coll. Art Assn. Democrat. Unitarian. Avocations: cooking, reading. Home: 1118 W Upas Ave Mcallen TX 78501 Office: U Tex-Pan Am Art Dept 1201 W University Dr Edinburg TX 78539-2909

LIBBEY, ROBERT DAVID, television producer; b. Bangor, Maine, Feb. 28, 1962; s. Fred Harold and Alice Virginia (Keirstead) L.; m. Denise Marie O'Connel, Oct. 8, 1988. BA in Theatre and Broadcasting, U. Maine, 1984. Videographer Community Broadcasting Svc., Bangor, 1985-87; TV producer Maine Pub. Broadcasting Network, Bangor, 1987—; bd. dirs. Bangor Community Theatre, 1988—. Producer TV shows Painting in Maine, 1989-90, The Air We Breathe, 1990. Democrat. Avocations: tennis, dance, acting. Office: Maine Pub Broadcasting 65 Texas Ave Bangor ME 04401-4324

LIBBIN, ANNE EDNA, lawyer; b. Phila., Aug. 25, 1950; d. Edwin M. and Marianne (Herz) L.; m. Christopher J. Cannon, July 20, 1985; children: Abigail Libbin Cannon, Rebecca Libbin Cannon. AB, Radcliffe Coll., 1971; JD, Harvard U., 1975. Bar: Calif. 1975, U.S. Dist. Ct. (cen. dist.) Calif. 1977, U.S. Dist. Ct. (no. dist.) Calif. 1979, U.S. Dist. Ct. (ea. dist.) Calif. 1985, U.S. Ct. Appeals (2d cir.) 1977, U.S. Ct. Appeals (5th cir.) 1982, U.S. Ct. Appeals (7th cir.) 1976, U.S. Ct. Appeals (9th cir.) 1976, U.S. Ct. Appeals (D.C. cir.) 1978. Appellate atty. NLRB, Washington, 1975-78; assoc. Pillsbury Madison & Sutro LLP, San Francisco, 1978-83, ptnr., 1984—; dir. Alumnae Resources, San Francisco. Mem. ABA (labor and employment sect.), State Bar Calif. (labor law sect.), Bar Assn. San Francisco (labor law sect.), Nat. Women's Health Network, Anti-Defamation League (ctrl. Pacific regional adv. bd.), Radcliffe Club (San Francisco). Office: Pillsbury Madison & Sutro 235 Montgomery St San Francisco CA 94104-2902

LIBBY, GARY RUSSELL, museum director; b. Boston, June 7, 1944; s. Charles W. and Sylvia P. L. BA, U. Fla., 1967, MA (NDEA fellow), 1968; MA, Tulane U., 1972. Instr. English Tulane U., 1968-71; asst. prof. Stetson U., Deland, Fla., 1972-77, vis. prof., 1977-86; dir. Mus. Arts and Scis., Daytona Beach, Fla., 1977—; reviewer Inst. Mus. Svcs., mem. panel Mus. Assessment Program; reviewer Accreditation Commn. of Am. Assn. of Mus. Author: Two Centuries of Cuban Art, 1985; editor: Archipenko: Themes and Variations, 1989, Chihuly: Form From Fire, 1994 (Southeastern Mus. Conf. award 1994), A Century of Jewelry and Gems, 1995, Celebrating Florida, 1995. Trustee Cuban Found.; mem. visual arts panel, youth and children's mus. panel, sci. mus. panel A.D.A. statewide panel Fla. Arts Coun.; panelist Challenge Grant Program; panelist Cultural Instns. Program; mem. hist. mus. grants panel Fla. Divsn. History. Mem. Fla. Art Mus. Dirs. Assn. (govt. liaison 1990, pres. 1995-96), Fla. Assn. Mus. (bd. dirs. 1992—, sec. 1995-96), Fla. Cultural and Ednl. Alliance (bd. dirs. 1995), Am. Assn. Mus. (accreditation commn. 1994—). Home: 419 Jessamine Blvd Daytona Beach FL 32118-3740 Office: Mus of Arts & Scis 1040 Museum Blvd Daytona Beach FL 32114-4510

LIBBY, JOHN KELWAY, financial services company executive; b. Washington, June 13, 1926; s. John H.and Violet K. (Bamber) L.; m. Mary Seymour Kindel, Dec. 30, 1960; children: Carolyn K., Anne K., Virginia K. BA, Haverford Coll., 1945; postgrad., Harvard U., 1946. With U.S. Dept. State, Washington, 1947-48, Capital Airlines Inc., 1949-51, S.G. Warburg & Co., London, 1954; assoc. and v.p. Kuhn Loeb & Co., N.Y.C., 1955-66, gen. ptnr., 1967-77; mng. dir. Lehman Bros. Kuhn Loeb, Inc., N.Y.C., 1977-80, adv. dir., 1981-84; gen. ptnr. K.L. Assocs., N.Y.C., 1985—; adviser Cen. Bank Venezuela, 1974-75; bd. dirs. various corps. Trustee Brearley Sch., N.Y.C., 1977-85. Lt. USN, 1944-46, PTO, 1951-53. Office: K L Assocs 450 Park Ave New York NY 10022-2605

LIBBY, LAUREN DEAN, foundation executive; b. Smith Center, Kans., Jan. 9, 1951; s. Dean L. and Elizabeth V. (Hansen) L.; m. June Ellen Hofer, Apr. 29, 1979; 1 child, Grant Lauren. BS in Agrl. Econs., Kans. State U., 1973; MBA, Regis U., 1988. Radio sta. employee, 1968-72; asst. program dir. info. br. Kans. State Extension Svc., Manhattan, 1969-73; economist Howard Houk Assocs., Chgo., 1973-75; asst. to pres. The Navigators, Colorado Springs, Colo., 1975-78, ministry devel. coord., 1979-86, dir. min. advancement, 1986-90, v.p., 1990—; pres. New Horizons Found., Colorado Springs, 1990—; bd. dirs. Navigators, Colorado Springs, 1993—; founding bd. dirs. Sta. KTLF-FM/Ednl. Comms. of Colorado Springs, 1987—; cons. 15 listener-supported radio stas., 1989—. Contbr. articles to mags. Bd. dirs. Christian Stewardship Assn., 1995—. Mem. Nat. Soc. Fundraising Execs., Ctrl. States VHF Soc. (pres.). Avocation: amateur radio. Home: 6166 Del Paz Dr Colorado Springs CO 80918-3004 Office: The Navigators 3820 N 30th St Colorado Springs CO 80904-5001

LIBBY, PETER, cardiologist, medical researcher; b. Berkeley, Calif., Feb. 13, 1947; s. Henry and Vivian (Green) L; m. Beryl Rica Benacerraf, Nov. 22, 1975; children: Oliver, Brigitte. BA, U. Calif., Berkeley, 1969; MD, U. Calif., San Diego, 1973. Diplomate Am. Bd. Internal Medicine and Cardiovascular Disease. Intern Peter Bent Brigham Hosp., Boston, 1973-74, resident, 1974-76; fellow Harvard Med. Sch., Boston, 1976-79, Brigham & Women's Hosp., Boston, 1979-80; asst. Prof. Tufts U. Sch. Sch. Medicine, Boston, 1980-86, assoc., 1986-90; asst. physician New Eng. Med. Ctr., Boston, 1980-87, physician, 1987-90; dir. vascular medicine and atherosclerosis unit Brigham and Women's Hosp., Boston, 1990—, physician, 1992—; assoc. prof. medicine Harvard Med. Sch., Boston, 1990-96, prof. medicine, 1996—; mem. ad hoc peer rev. com. NIH, Bethesda, Md., mem. pathology A study sect., 1988-92; mem. advisor W.W. Smith Charitable Trust, Phila., 1985-88; mem. peer rev. com. Am. Heart Assn., Mass., 1982-88, chmn., 1992-94, chmn. rsch. com., 1994—. Recipient Established Investigator award Am. Heart Assn., 1986-91; MERIT award Nat. Heart, Lung, Blood Inst., 1993—; S.A. Levine fellow Am. Heart Assn., Mass., 1976-77, Med. Found., Inc. fellow, Boston, 1980-82, fellow Council Arteriosclerosis, Am. Heart Assn. and Coun. on Circulation. Fellow Am. Coll. Cardiology; mem. Am. Soc. Clin. Investigation, Am. Physiol. Soc., Assn. Am. Physicians, Am. Soc. Cell Biology. Home: 111 Perkins St Jamaica Plain MA 02130-4313 Office: Brigham & Women's Hosp 221 Longwood Ave Boston MA 02115-5817

LIBBY, RONALD THEODORE, political science educator, consultant, researcher; b. L.A., Nov. 20, 1941; s. Theodore Harold and Patricia Mildred (Griswold) L.; m. Kathleen Christina Jacobson, June 3, 1982; children: Kathleen Elizabeth Libby, Erin Kristin Jenne. BA, Wash. State U., 1965; MA, U. Wash., 1966, PhD, 1975. Lectr. U. Bostwana, Lesotho and Swaziland, 1973-75, U. Malawi, Zomba, 1975-76, U. Zambia, Lusaka, 1976-79; asst. prof. U. Notre Dame, South Bend, Ind., 1981-83; sr. lectr. U. West Indies, Kingston, Jamaica, 1983-85; assoc. prof. Northwestern U., Evanston, Ill., 1985-86; sr. rsch. fellow Australian Nat. U., Darwin, 1986-87; sr. lectr. Victoria U., Wellington, New Zealand, 1987-89; prof. S.W. State U., Marshall, Minn., 1989-96; prof., chair St. Joseph's U., Phila., 1996—; treas. New Zealand Polit. Sci. Assn., Wellington, 1988-89. Author: Towards an Africanized U.S. Policy for Southern Africa, 1980, The Politics of Economic Power in Southern Africa, 1987, Hawke's Law, 1989 (Choice award 1991), Protecting Markets: U.S. Policy and the World Grain Trade, 1992; contbr. articles to profl. jours. With U.S. Army, 1962-64. Rsch. grantee Carnegie Endowment, 1971. Mem. Am. Polit. Sci. Assn., Internat. Studies Assn., Australian Polit. Sci. Assn. Roman Catholic. Avocations: tennis, handball, piano, singing. Office: Polit Sci St Joseph's U Philadelphia PA 19131-1395 *Through the many travails of life the one abiding principle that has guided me is intellectual honesty and integrity.*

LIBBY, SANDRA CHIAVARAS, special education educator; b. Clinton, Mass., Apr. 8, 1949; B.S. in Spl. Edn., Fitchburg (Mass.) State Coll., 1970, M.Ed. in Reading, 1976; postgrad. (fellow) Clark U., 1981-83; 2 children. Tchr. spl. class Webster (Mass.) Schs., 1970-73, asst. coord. program materials, resource room, 1974, tchr./coord. primary spl. needs program, 1975-78 , tchr. jr. high English, 1978-79, reading tchr. jr. high, 1979-80 adminstrv. asst. intern Shepherd Hill Regional Sch., Dudley, Mass., 1980-81; dir., owner Teddy Bear Day Care Ctr., Dudley, Mass., 1983-85; devel. specialist Ft. Devens Post Learning Ctr., Shirley, Mass., 1985-86; resource room tchr. Murdock High Sch., Winchendon, Mass., 1986; tchr. behavioral modification Middle Sch., Winchendon, 1986-87; coord., tchr. gifted and talented Lancaster Pub. Schs., 1987-90; tchr. learning disabilities Leominster Pub. Sch., 1990-91, tchr. primary level behavior modification, 1991—. V.p. Samoset Sch. PTO, Leominister, Mass., 1995—; mem. Edn. Reform Change Team, 1996—. Mem. Nat. Edn. Assn., Mass. Tchrs. Assn., Leonminster Tchrs. Assn. (bldg. rep. 1992-95, negotiating com. 1993—, sec. 1995—), Internat. Reading Assn. (v.p. 1994-95, chairperson celebrate literacy award 1994-95), Mass. Reading Assn. (mem. North Worcester County coun. 1994-95), Webster Emblem Club (pres. 1984-85), Phi Delta Kappa (Horace Mann grant 1989-90). Cert. in elem. and spl. edn., reading, reading supervision, learning disabilities, English (secondary), Mass. Home: 166 Chapman Pl Leominster MA 01453

LIBCHABER, ALBERT JOSEPH, physics educator; b. Paris, Oct. 23, 1934; came to U.S., 1983; s. Charles and Cyrla (Markowska) L.; m. Irene Gelman, Sept. 11, 1955; children—Jacques, Remy, David. B.S., U. Paris, 1956; M.S., U. Ill., 1959; Ph.D., Ecole Normale Superieure, Paris, 1965. Matre de Recherche CNRS, Ecole Normale, Paris, 1967-74, dir. research, 1974-83; prof. physics U. Chgo., 1983-91, Paul Snowden Disting. Svc. prof., 1987—; prof. dpet. physics Princeton (N.J.) U., 1991-94; prof. Rockefeller U., N.Y.C., 1994—, Detlev W. Bronk prof., 1995—. Served as officer French Army, 1959-61. Recipient Wolf prize Wolf Found., Herzlia, Israel, 1986, MacArthur Found. Fellow, 1986-91. Fellow NEC Rsch. Inst. Princeton; mem. Am. Phys. Soc., French Phys. Soc. (Silver medal 1971, prix Ricard 1979), Am. Acad. Arts and Scis. Jewish. Home: 1161 York Ave New York NY 10021

LIBERATI, MARIA THERESA, fashion production company executive; b. Phila., July 16, 1965; d. Edward Michael and Anna Maria Liberati. Student, Laval U., Que., Can., 1984; BS in Fgn. Lang. Edn., Temple U., 1986. Pres., bd. dirs. Sierra Ctr., Feasterville, Pa., 1988—; pres. M.T.L. Prodns., Phila., 1989—; spokesperson Compassion for Animals, Phila., 1988—. Author: Fashion, Fun and Fitness, 1989; editor mab. Better Nutrition for Today's Living, 1990—. Named Miss Pa., 1985, Miss World, 1986; recipient Merit award Actors and Artists Assn., Rome. Mem. AFTRA, NAFE (adv. bd. 1988—). Avocations: reading, cooking. Office: Sierra Ctr divsn MTL Prodns PO Box 52193 Philadelphia PA 19115

LIBERATORE, NICHOLAS ALFRED, business consultant; b. N.Y.C., June 19, 1916; s. Alexander and Angelina (Laspagnoletta) L.; m. Jean Talbot MacAdam, June 6, 1943 (dec.); children: Virginia, George, Nicholas, Elliott, Mark; m. Marianne Westpalm van Hoorn Jewett, Feb. 10, 1973. Student, NYU; MA, Fairfield U., 1975. Vice pres. Ebasco Internat. Co., N.Y.C., 1956-58; pres. Raymond Concrete Pile Co. Am., N.Y.C., 1958-59; chmn. operating com. Brown-Raymond-Walsh, Madrid, Spain, 1959-62; v.p. Raymond Internat. Inc., N.Y.C., 1962-65; sr. v.p., pres. internat. Group Lone Star Industries, Inc., Greenwich, Conn., 1965-74; sr. v.p. Ebasco Services Inc., N.Y.C., 1974-77; exec. v.p. Genstar Ltd., San Francisco, 1977-83; cons. Royal Bank of Can., Toronto, 1983-90; bd. dirs. Internat. Mining Corp. Bd. dirs. Fgn. Trade Coun. Served to capt. C.E., AUS, 1943-46. Decorated Bronze Star medal, Army Commendation medal; Cross of Isabel the Catholic, (Spain). Mem. Internat. Coun. (conf. bd.), Brazilian-Am. C. of C. (founder), Pan. Am. Soc. (pres.), Argentine-Am. C. of C. (pres.), Chile-U.S. C. of C. (pres.), St. Francis Yacht Club, Econ. Club N.Y., Bankers' Club San Francisco, Recess Club. Home: 4 Mayflower Ln Weston CT 06883-2632

LIBERMAN, ALEXANDER, artist, editor; b. Kiev, Russia, Sept. 4, 1912; came to U.S., 1941, naturalized, 1946; s. Simon and Henriette (Pascar) L.; m. Tatiana Yacovleff Du Plessix, Nov. 4, 1942 (dec. Apr. 1991); 1 stepdau., Francine Du Plessix Gray; m. Melinda Pechangco, Dec., 1992. Student in architecture, Ecole des Beaux Arts, Paris, 1930; DFA (hon.), R.I. Sch. Design, 1980. Art dir., mng. editor Vu Paris, 1931-36, Vogue mag., Conde Nast Publs., N.Y.C., 1941-43; art dir. Vogue mag., Conde Nast Publs., 1943-62; editorial dir. Conde Nast Publs., 1962-94; deputy chmn.-editorial Conde Nast Pbls., 1994—. Exhibited photographs Mus. Modern Art, N.Y.C., 1959, retrospective painting and sculpture exhibit, Corcoran Gallery Art, Washington, 1970; scuptor works: Covenant, U. Pa., 1975, Symbol, Rockford, Ill., 1978, On High, New Haven, 1979, Windward, Miami, 1983, Stargazer, San Diego, 1983, Olympic Iliad, Seattle, 1984, Galaxy, Oklahoma City, 1984, Venture, Dallas, 1985, Beyond, Cleve., 1985, Aura, Palm Beach, 1986, Faith, Jerusalem, 1987, Ulysses, L.A., 1988, Vice-Versa-Korea I, Kyongju, 1991, Lightweb, N.Y., 1991; painting and sculpture in permanent collection Mus. Modern Art; author: The Artist in His Studio, 1960, 2nd edit., 1968, rev. and expanded edit., 1988, Greece, Gods and Art, 1968, Marlene: An Intimate Photographic Memoir, 1992, Campidoglio: Michelangelo's Roman Capitol, 1994, then: Alexander Liberman Photographs 1925-95, 1995. Decorated chevalier Legion of Honor, France; recipient Henry Johnson Fisher award, 1994, 95. Subject of book Alexander Liberman (Barbara Rose), 1981, Alex: The Life of Alexander Liberman (Dodie Kazanjian and Calvin Tomkins), 1993. Office: Conde Nast Publs Inc 350 Madison Ave New York NY 10017-3704 Gallery: Andre Emmerich 41 E 57th St New York NY 10022-1908

LIBERMAN, ALVIN MEYER, psychology educator; b. St. Joseph, Mo., May 10, 1917; s. Max and Lotte (Korbholz) L.; m. Isabelle Yoffe, June 1, 1941; children—Mark Yoffe, Michael Charles, Sarah Ivy. A.B., U. Mo., 1938, M.A., 1939; Ph.D., Yale U., 1942. Prof. emeritus Psychology U. Conn., Storrs, 1949—; prof. emeritus Linguistics Yale U., Storrs, 1950-87; Alumni Assn. Disting. prof. U. Conn., Storrs, 1979—; pres., dir. rsch. Haskins Labs., New Haven, 1975-86, sr. v.p., 1986—. Contbr. articles to profl. jours. Guggenheim fellow, 1964-65. Fellow Am. Acad. Arts and Scis.; mem. Nat. Acad. Scis., Soc. Exptl. Psychologists (Warren medal 1975), Acoustical Soc. Am., Am. Psychol. Assn. (Disting. Sci. Contbn. award 1980, F.O. Schmitt medal and prize in neuroscience 1988). Address: 614 Storrs Rd Mansfield Center CT 06250-1225

LIBERMAN, GAIL JEANNE, editor; b. Neptune, N.J., Feb. 26, 1951; d. Si and Dorothy (Gold) L.; m. Alan Lavine, Dec. 20, 1991. BA, Rutgers U., 1972. Youth editor AP, N.Y.C., 1972-73; writer United Feature Syndicate, N.Y.C., 1973; reporter, broadcast editor UPI, Phila. and Hartford, Conn., 1973-75; reporter Courier-Post, Camden, N.J., 1976-80, Bank Advt. News, North Palm Beach, Fla., 1981-82; editor Bank Rate Monitor, North Palm Beach, 1982—. Author: Improving Your Credit and Reducing Your Debt, 1994 (endorsed Inst. CFPs), The Complete Idiot's Guide to Making Money With Mutual Funds, 1996; columnist: Boston Herald, 1994—, America Online, 1996—.

LIBERMAN, IRA L., real estate broker; b. Richmond, Va., June 21, 1926; s. Morris Joseph and Dora (Sharove) L.; m. Frances Sour, Sept. 26, 1953; children—Barbara Janet, Lynn Dora, Leslie Ann. B.S., U. Va., 1949. With Richmond Tomato Repacking Co., Va., 1949; with Duke City Lumber Co., Inc., Albuquerque, 1949-85; pres., chmn., chief exec. officer Duke City Lumber Co., Inc., 1974-85; assoc. real estate broker Vaughan and Co., 1985-91, Berger Briggs Real Estate & Ins., Albuquerque, 1991—; nat. chmn. Western Wood Products Assn., 1985-86. Bd. dirs. Albuquerque Indsl. Devel., Albuquerque Symphony Orch., State Girl Scout Council. Served with USAF, 1944-46. Mem. Albuquerque Bd. Realtors, S.W. Pine Assn. (past pres.), Fed. Timber Purchasers Assn. (past pres.), Nat. Forest Products Assn. (dir.). Clubs: Four Hills Country, Crossroads Flying. Lodge: Masons. Home: 2601 Schell Ct NE Albuquerque NM 87106-2532 Office: Berger Briggs Real Estate & Ins Inc 275 3rd St SW Albuquerque NM 87102-3311 also: PO Box 27754 Albuquerque NM 87125-7754

LIBERMAN, ROBERT PAUL, psychiatry educator, researcher, writer; b. Newark, Aug. 16, 1937; s. Harry and Gertrude (Galowitz) L.; m. Janet Marilyn Brown, Feb. 16, 1973; children: Peter, Sarah, Danica, Nathaniel, Annalisa. AB summa cum laude, Dartmouth Coll., 1959, diploma in medicine with honors, 1960; MS in Pharmacology, U. Calif.-San Francisco, 1961; MD, Johns Hopkins U., 1963. Diplomate Nat. Bd. Med. Examiners, Am. Bd. Psychiatry and Neurology. Intern Bronx (N.Y.) Mcpl. Hosp.-Einstein Coll. Medicine, 1963-64; resident in psychiatry Mass. Mental Health Ctr., Boston, 1964-68; postdoctoral fellow in social psychiatry Harvard U., 1966-68, teaching fellow in psychiatry, 1964-68; mem. faculty group psychotherapy tng. program Washington Sch. Psychiatry, 1968-70; with Nat. Ctr. Mental Health Svc., Tng. and Rsch., St. Elizabeths Hosp., also mem. NIMH Clin. and Rsch. Assocs. Tng. Program, Washington, 1968-70; asst. clin. prof. psychiatry UCLA, 1970-72, assoc. clin. prof., 1972-73, assoc. rsch. psychiatrist, 1973-76, rsch. prof. psychiatry, 1976-77, prof. psychiatry, 1977—; dir. Camarillo-UCLA Clin. Rsch. Unit, 1970—, dir. Clin. Rsch. Ctr. Schizophrenia and Psychiat. Rehab., 1977—; chief Rehab. Medicine Svc., West L.A. VA Med. Ctr., Brentwood divsn., 1980-92; cons. div. mental health and behavioral scis. edn. Sepulveda (Calif.) VA Hosp., 1975-80; practice medicine specializing in psychiatry, Reston, Va., 1968-70, Thousand Oaks, Calif., 1977—; staff psychiatrist Ventura County Mental Health Dept., 1970-75; staff psychiatrist Ventura County Gen. Hosp.; mem. med. staff UCLA Neuropsychiatric Inst. and Hosp., Ventura Gen. Hosp., Camarillo State Hosp., West Los Angeles VA Med. Ctr.; dir. Rehab. Rsch. and Tng. Ctr. Mental Illness, 1980-85. Bd. dirs. Lake Sherwood Community Assn., 1978—, pres., 1979-81, 90-92, v.p., 1992-95; mem. Conejo Valley Citizens Adv. Bd., 1979-81. Served as surgeon USPHS, 1964-68. Recipient Noyes award for Rsch. in Schizophrenia, 1992, Kolb award in Schizophrenia, 1994. Research grantee NIMH, SSA, NIDA, VA, 1972—. Mem. Assn. Advancement Behavior Therapy (exec. com. 1970-72, dir. 1972-79), Am. Psychiat. Assn. (Hibbs and Van Ameringen awards), Assn. Clin. Psychosocial Research (exec. com. 1985—), Phi Beta Kappa. Author: (with King, DeRisi and McCann) Personal Effectiveness: Guiding People to Assert Their Feelings and Improve Their Social Skills, 1975; A Guide to Behavioral Analysis and Therapy, 1972; (with Wheeler, DeVisser, Kuehnel and Kuehnel) Handbook of Marital Therapy: An Educational Approach to Treating Troubled Relationships, 1980, Psychiatric Rehabilitation of Chronic Mental Patients, 1987, (with De Risi and Mueser) Social Skills Training for Psychiatric Patients, 1989, (with Kuehnel, Rose and Storzbach) Resource Book for Psychiatric Rehabilitation, 1990, Handbook of Psychiatric Rehabilitation, 1992, (with Yager) Stress in Psychiatric Disorders, 1993, (with Corrigan) Behavior Therapy in Psychiatric Hospitals, 1994; mem. editorial bd. Jour. Applied Behavior Analysis, 1972-78, Jour. Marriage and Family Counseling, 1974-78, Jour. Behavior Therapy and Exptl. Psychiatry, 1975—, Behavior Therapy, 1979-84, Assessment and Invervention in Devel. Disabilities, 1980-85; assoc. editor Jour. Applied Behavior Analysis, 1976-78, Schizophrenia Bull., 1981-87; Internat. Rev. Jour. Psychiatry, 1988—, Psychiatry, 1993—; contbr. over 300 articles to profl. jours., chpts. to books. Home: 528 Lake Sherwood Dr Thousand Oaks CA 91361-5120 Office: Cmty & Rehab W LA Psychiatry VA Med Ctr (116 AR) 11301 Wilshire Blvd Los Angeles CA 90073

LIBERT, DONALD JOSEPH, lawyer; b. Sioux Falls, S.D., Mar. 23, 1928; s. Bernard Joseph and Eleanor Monica (Sutton) L.; m. Jo Anne Murray, May 16, 1953; children: Cathleen, Thomas, Kevin, Richard, Stephanie. B.S. magna cum laude in Social Scis., Georgetown U., 1950, LL.B., 1956. Bar: Ohio. From assoc. to ptnr. Manchester, Bennett, Powers & Ullman, Youngstown, Ohio, 1956-65; various positions to v.p., gen. counsel and sec. Youngstown Sheet & Tube Co., 1965-78; assoc. group counsel LTV Corp., Youngstown and Pitts., 1979; v.p. and gen. counsel Anchor Hocking Corp., Lancaster, Ohio, 1979-87. Served to lt. (j.g.) USN, 1951-54. Mem. Ohio Bar Assn. (chmn. sr. lawyers com.), Columbus Bar Assn., Fairfield County Bar Assn., Lancaster Country Club, Rotary. Republican. Roman Catholic. Office: 127 W Wheeling St Lancaster OH 43130-3737

LIBERTH, RICHARD FRANCIS, lawyer; b. Bklyn., Mar. 1, 1950; s. S. Richard and Frances J. (Falconer) L.; m. Lisa M. Feenick, June 8, 1974; children: Andrew R., Erica M. BS in Bus. Adminstrn., U. Denver, 1972; JD, Bklyn. Law Sch., 1976. Bar: N.Y. 1977, U.S. Dist. Ct. (so. and ea. dists.) N.Y. 1981, U.S. Dist. Ct. (no. dist.) N.Y. 1991. Staff atty. Mental Health Legal Svcs., Poughkeepsie, N.Y., 1976-78; sr. asst. dist. atty. Rockland County Dist. Attys. Office, N.Y.C., 1978-81; prin. Drake, Sommers, Loeb, Tarshis & Catania, Newburgh, N.Y., 1981—. Dir. Legal Aid Soc. Orange County, Goshen, N.Y., 1982-84, Orange County Cerebral Palsy Assn., Goshen, 1986-89; mem. Rep. Nat. Com., Washington, 1990—. Mem. N.Y. Bar Assn., Newburgh Bar Assn. (pres. 1991), Orange County Bar Assn. (v.p. 1995), Woodbury Lions Club (Central Valley, N.Y.) (past pres.). Avocations: golf, tennis, reading, collecting. Home: 75 Buena Vista Terr Central Valley NY 10917 Office: Drake Sommers Loeb Tarshis & Catania One Corwin Ct Newburgh NY 12550

LIBERTI, PAUL ALFONSO, biotechnology executive, inventor, entrepreneur, consultant; b. Lyndhurst, N.J., Mar. 18, 1936; s. Paul Frank and Rose (Pollara) L.; m. Rae Francis, July 1, 1961 (div. Jan. 1996); children: Paul P., Theodore L., Roseanne, Joseph F. AB, Columbia U., 1959; postgrad., Loyola U., Chgo., 1959-61; PhD, Stevens Inst. Tech., Hoboken, N.J., 1966. Prof. biotechnology, immunology Jefferson Med. Coll., Phila., 1968-83, adj. prof., 1984—; pres., founder Immunochem. Assocs., 1981—; pres., founder Immunicon Corp., Huntingdon Valley, Pa., 1984-91, dir. R & D, 1991-95; vis. scientist Inst. for Med. Rsch., London, 1976-77; mem. adv. bd. Ben Franklin Partnership; mem. study sect. NIH/NSF U.S. Army Breast Cancer Program. Mem. adv. bd. Jour. Immunology, Molecular Immunology; contbr. more than 60 articles to profl. jours. Founder, speaker Anti-Drug Program, Bucks County, Pa., 1981-83. Recipient Rsch. Career award NIH, 1971-77. Mem. Am. Assn. Immunologists, Am. Soc. Hematologists, Internat. Soc. Hematopoetic Graft Engring. Achievements include 16 patents for biotechnology, which include high gradient magnetic separation technology, several new classes of highly magnetic biocompatible magnetic liquids and their use in medically relevent applications such as contrast agents for magnetic resonance imaging, liver tumor agents and blood pool agents; automated immunossays; in purging bone marrow of tumor cells (oncology therapy); in the isolation of stem cells for bone marrow therapy; in the analysis of rare cells for diagnostic purposes (genetic disorders, viral insertions, circulating tumor cells, isolation of fetal cells from maternal blood); discovery of ferrofluid phasing, magnetic chaining in magnetic colloids and its role in magnetic separation of cell alignment principles on micron sized magnetic wires and its adaptation to hematologic analysis; of Immunoglobulin - Clq structure, function relationship, of antigenicity and conformation of calcium binding polypeptides. Home: 1503 Grasshopper Rd Huntingdon Valley PA 19006-5807 Office: Immunicon Corp 1310 Masons Mill Business Park Huntingdon Valley PA 19006-3515

LIBERTO, JOSEPH SALVATORE, banker; b. Balt., Apr. 26, 1929; s. Cosimo and Anna (Serio) L.; m. Mary Jane Colandro, May 20, 1962; children—Joseph C., Grace Ann. Student, Balt. City Coll., 1945-47; certificate accounting, Balt. Coll. Commerce, 1949; grad., Nat. Assn. Bank Auditors, and Comptrollers Sch. Banking, U. Wis., 1968. With Signet Bank, Md., Balt., 1954—; auditor Union Trust Co. Md., 1963—, asst. v.p., security officer, 1979—. Served with AUS, 1951-53, Japan. Mem. Bank Adminstrn. Inst. (pres. Balt. 1968—), Inst. Internal Auditors. Home: 5609 Biddison Ave Baltimore MD 21206-3442 Office: Signet Bank Baltimore St Baltimore MD 21202-1603

LIBIN, PAUL, theatre executive, producer; b. Chgo., Dec. 12, 1930; m. Florence Rowe, Sept. 25, 1956; children: Charles, Claire, Andrea. Student, U. Ill.; B.F.A., Columbia U., 1956. Producing dir., v.p. Jujamcyn Theaters, N.Y.C., 1990—. Producer (plays) including The Crucible, 1958, Six Characters in Search of an Author, 1963, Royal Hunt of the Sun, 1965, Circle in the Sq. Theatre, N.Y.C., 1965-90; co-producer (plays) Uncle Vanya, 1973, The Iceman Cometh, 1973, Death of a Salesman, 1975, The Lady from the Sea, 1976, The Night of the Iguana, 1976, The Club, 1976, Tartuffe, 1977, The Inspector General, Man and Superman, Spokesong, Loose Ends, 1978, Major Barbara, Past Tense, The Man Who Came to Dinner, 1979, The Bacchae, John Gabriel Borkman, The Father, Scenes and Revelations, 1980, Candida, MacBeth, Eminent Domain, 1981, Present Laughter, The Queen and the Rebels, The Misanthrope, 1982, The Caine Mutiny Court-Martial, Heartbreak House, Awake and Sing, 1983, Design for Living, 1984, Arms and the Man, Marriage of Figaro, 1985, You Never Can Tell, 1986, Coastal Disturbances, 1987, A Streetcar Named Desire, Juno and the Paycock, 1988, The Night of the Iguana, 1988, The Devil's Disciple, 1988, Ghetto, 1989, Sweeney Todd, 1989, Zoya's Apartment, 1990, The Miser, 1990; producing dir. plays I Hate Hamlet, 1991, Secret Garden, 1991, La Bete, 1991, Two Trains Running, 1992, Jelly's Last Jam, 1992, Tommy, 1993, Angels in America, 1993, My Fair Lady, 1993, Grease, 1994, Love! Valour! Compassion!, 1995, Smokey Joe's Cafe, 1995, My Thing of Love, 1995, Moon Over Buffalo, 1995, Patti LuPone on Broadway, 1995, Seven Guitars, 1996, A Funny Thing Happened on the Way to the Forum, 1996. Served with U.S. Army, 1953-55. Recipient Obie award The Club, Village Voice, 1977, Tony award, 1976, 92, 93, 94, 95. Mem. 2d League Off Broadway Theatres and Producers (pres. emeritus), 1st League Am. Theatres and Producers (officer, exec. com., bd. govs.). Office: Jujamcyn Theatres St James Theatre 246 W 44th St New York NY 10036-3910 also: Circle in the Sq Theatre 1633 Broadway New York NY 10019-6708

LIBKA, ROBERT JOHN, educational director, consultant; b. Pigeon, Mich., Sept. 19, 1951; s. Neil August and Joan Lois (Frank) L.; m. Bonnie Rae Borcher, June 16, 1973; children: Michelle, Kimberly, Jennifer. Cadet, U.S. Coast Guard Acad., 1969-71; BA in Edn., Concordia U., River Forest, Ill., 1975, MA in Edn., 1978. Cert. tchr. elem. & secondary schs., Ill., spl. guidance cert. Dir. residence hall Concordia U., River Forest, Ill., 1975-79; dir. student activities Concordia U., River Forest, 1975-87; dir. student ctr. dir. Koehneke Community Ctr., River Forest, 1975-88; project coord. Khusrau translation Harvard U. and Smithsonian Instn., Boston, Washington, 1988-89; pres. Attitudinal Dynamics Internat., Inc., Maywood, Ill., 1970—; dir. guidance Walther Lutheran High Sch., Maywood, Ill., 1989—; exec. dir. Luth. HS Assn. Kane and DuPage Counties, St. Charles, Ill., 1993—; cons. Harvard U., Smithsonian Instn., Century Insur., Cook Cty. Sheriff's Officeand others, 1970—. Author: (Book) India: Price of Adventure, 1990; producer: Many videos of Internat. Religions and Cultures, 1988—; contbr. numerous articles to profl. and religious jours. Leader ARC, Chgo., 1975-85; mem. N. Maywood (Ill.) Community Orgn., 1975-85; pres. St. Paul Luth. Ch., 1987-88. Recipient Rsch. grant Smithsonian Instn., New Delhi, India, 1988. Mem. Am. Mgmt. Assn., Am. Personnel & Guidance Assn., Ill. Assn. Coll. Admissions Counselors, Luth. Edn. Assn. (life mem.), Gospel Music Assn., Nat. Assn. Campus Activities (bd. dirs. 1985-87). Avocations: travel, video production, distance running, photography. Home: 805 N 6th Ave Maywood IL 60153-1046 Office: Fox Valley Luth Acad Exec Dir 2400 E Main St Saint Charles IL 60174-2415

LIBMAN, STEVEN BRADLEY, performing arts administrator; b. Providence, Oct. 5, 1959; s. Herman and Marilyn Kayla (Zettel) L.; m. Keitha Ann Grace, Aug. 17, 1980; 1 child, Tracy. B.A. magna cum laude, R.I. Coll., 1980; asst. mng. dir. R.I. Coll., Providence, 1978-80; box office mgr. Trinity Sq. Repertory Co., Providence, 1980-81; mng. dir. Auburn Civic Theatre, N.Y., 1981-83, Fulton Opera House, Lancaster, Pa., 1983-86; devel. dir. Pitts. Ballet Theatre, 1987-91, exec. dir., 1991—; guest lectr. Non-Profit Mgmt. U., Pitts. Trustee Citizens for Arts in Pa., Harrisburg, 1984—, Regent Theatre, 1993—, Dance/USA, (co-chmn. mgr's. coun. 1994—); mem. theatre panel Pa. Council on the Arts, 1986-88; mem. adv. com. arts mgmt. program Carnegie Mellon U., Pitts., 1993— . Recipient Theatre Mgmt. award R.I. Coll., 1979. Jewish. Home: 716 Kewanna Ave Pittsburgh PA 15234-1205 Office: Pitts Ballet Theatre 2900 Liberty Ave Pittsburgh PA 15201-1511

LIBOFF, RICHARD LAWRENCE, physicist, educator; b. N.Y.C., Dec. 30, 1931; s. William and Sarah (Mell) L.; m. Myra Blatt, July 4, 1954; children: David, Lisa. A.B., Bklyn. Coll., 1953; Ph.D., NYU, 1961. Asst. prof. physics NYU, 1961-63; prof. applied physics, applied math. and elec. engring. Cornell U., 1964—; prin. investigator Air Force Office Sci. Research, 1978-83, Army Research Office, 1984—; cons. Batelle Columbus Lab. Author: Introduction to the Theory of Kinetic Equations, 1969, 79, Russian edit., 1974, Introductory Quantum Mechanics, 1980, 2d edit., 1991, Korean edit., 1993, Waveguides, Transmission Lines and Smith Charts, 1984, Kinetic Theory: Classical, Quantum and Relativistic Descriptions, 1990. Served with Chem. Corps U.S. Army, 1953-55. Recipient Founders Day cert. N.Y. U., 1961; Solvay fellow, 1972; Fulbright scholar, 1984. Fellow Am. Phys. Soc.; mem. IEEE (sr.), Sigma Xi. Office: Cornell U Phillips Hall Ithaca NY 14853

LIBONATI, MICHAEL ERNEST, lawyer, educator, writer; b. Chgo., May 25, 1944; s. Roland V. and Jeannette K. Libonati; m. Yvonne M. Barber, Sept. 30, 1967; children: Michael, Emma. LLB, Yale U., 1967, LLM, 1969. Bar: D.C. 1968, Ill. 1975, Pa. 1976. Prof. law Temple U., Phila., 1972-90, Carnell prof. law, 1990—; cons. U.S. Adv. Commn. Intergovernmental Rels.; vis. prof. law U. Ala., Tuscaloosa, summer 1976, Cornell U., Ithaca, N.Y., spring 1977, Coll. William and Mary, Williamsburg, Va., fall 1987. Author: (with Sands and Martinez) Local Government Law, 4 vols., 1981-82, (with Hetzel and Williams) Legislative Law and Process, 2d edit., 1993, Local Government Autonomy, 1993; asst. editor articles Am. Jour. Legal History, 1971-82. Recipient Williams prize for Excellence in Teaching, 1985, 90; named Hon. Editor Temple U. Law Quarterly, vol. 59, 1986. Mem. NAS (nat. rsch. bd., highway law project adv. commn.), ABA (coun. urban state and local govt. law sect. 1979-83), Am. Law Inst., Nat. Assn. Atty.'s Gen. (state constitution law project adv. bd.). Office: Temple U Sch Law 1719 N Broad St Philadelphia PA 19122-6098

LIBOUS, THOMAS WILLIAM, state senator; b. Binghamton, N.Y., Apr. 16, 1953; s. William Abraham and Kathrine (Haddad) L.; m. Frances Pianella, Sept. 27, 1975; children: Matthew, Nicholas. AAS in Mktg., Broome Community Coll., 1973; BS in Mktg. and Fin., SUNY, Utica, 1975. Dir. mktg. Chase Lincoln First Bank, Binghamton, 1975-83; v.p. mktg. Johnson City Pub. Co., Binghamton, 1983-88; senator N.Y. State Legislature, Albany, 1989—. Minority leader Binghamton City Coun., 1985-88; del. Rep. Nat. Conv., 1992, 96. Mem. Rotary, KC. Republican. Roman Catholic. Office: 1607 State Office Bldg 44 Hawley St Binghamton NY 13901-4400

LIBOVE, CHARLES, mechanical and aerospace engineering educator; b. N.Y.C., Nov. 7, 1923; s. Meyer and Anna (Steinberg) L.; m. Rosa Greenspan, July 12, 1951; children: Joel, Fred. BCE, CCNY, 1944; M in Applied Mechanics, U. Va., 1952; PhD in ME, Syracuse (N.Y.) U., 1962. Aero. rsch. scientist Nat. Adv. Com. for Aeronautics, Hampton, Va., 1944-53; assoc. prof. aero. engring. Tri-State Coll., Angola, Ind., 1955-58; applied mathematician Brush Labs. Co., Cleve., 1953-55; from instr. to prof. mech. and aerospace engring. Syracuse U., 1958—; pvt. practice cons., Syracuse, 1958—. Contbr. numerous articles to profl. jours. Recipient Outstanding Tchr. awards Syracuse U., 1967-89, numerous grants. Fellow ASME, AIAA (assoc. fellow); mem. ASCE, AAUP, Am. Acad. Mechs., Structural Stability Rsch. Coun. (mem.-at-large). Home: 209 Locksley Rd Syracuse NY 13224-1826 Office: Syracuse U Dept Mech Aerospace and Mfg Engring Syracuse NY 13244

LIBRIZZI, ROSE MARIE MEOLA, library administrator, counselor; b. Newark, Apr. 15, 1940; d. Salvatore J. and Marie (Consoli) Meola; m. Vincent F. LiBrizzi, June 25, 1965 (div. 1983); children: Vincent, Steve. BA in History and Pre-law magna cum laude, Bloomfield (N.J.) Coll., 1965; MLS, Rutgers U., 1967; JD, Seton Hall U., 1989; MA in Counseling, MontclairState U., 1992. Cert. tchr., N.J.; cert. sch. libr.; profl libr. cert. Acting children's libr. Newark Pub. Libr., 1965-66; head children's svcs. Belleville (N.J.) Pub. Libr., 1966-68; asst. dir. Kearny (N.J.) Pub. Libr., 1969; mem. adj. faculty Kean Coll., Union, N.J., 1969-73; supr. children's svcs. Jersey City Pub. Libr., 1973-87, asst. dir., 1987-90, 91—, libr. dir., 1990-91. Mem. ABA, ALA, N.J. Libr. Assn. (v.p. 1988, mem.-at-large 1982, sec. 1981, pres. and founder adminstr. sect. 1978, chairperson pers. adminstrn. com., chairperson resolutions, nominations and honor and awards coms., chairperson NJLA Centennial Celebration com. 1984-89, Adminstrn. section award), Hudson County Libr. Dirs. Assn. (pres. 1990—), Exxex-Hudson Region Exec. Bd. (mem-at-large, sec. 1990-93, chairperson continuing edn. com. 1986-88), Rutgers Alumni Assn. (pres., senator, mem. alumni fedn. bd. 1990—), Infolink (mem-at-large). Home: 5 Squier Ct Livingston NJ 07039-2506 Office: Jersey City Pub Libr 472 Jersey Ave Jersey City NJ 07302-3499

LIBURD, ALMANDO LEANDO, senator; b. Cruz Bay, St. John, V.I., Jan. 12, 1953; s. Hugo O. and Catherine M. Liburd; m. Faye Liburd, Oct. 31, 1985; 1 child, Alana. BA in Spanish, Inter-Am. U., Hato Rey, P.R., 1978, postgrad.; postgrad., U. V.I. Tchr. Dept. Edn., St. Thomas, V.I., 1974-90; senator V.I. Legislature, St. John and St. Thomas, 1991—. V.p. Coral Bay Community Orgn., St. John, 1987-90; bd. dirs. representing St. John, Pvt. Industry Coun., 1979-84. Mem. Ind. Citizens Movement Party. Office: VI Legislature PO Box 1690 Saint Thomas VI 00804-1690

LICATA, ARTHUR FRANK, lawyer; b. N.Y.C., June 16, 1947. BA in English, Le Moyne Coll., 1969; postgrad., SUNY, Binghampton, 1969-71; JD cum laude, Suffolk U., 1976. Bar: Mass. 1977, N.Y. 1985, U.S. Ct. Appeals (1st cir.) 1977, U.S. Dist. Ct. Mass. 1977, admitted Frank B. Murray, Jr. Inns of Ct. 1990-92. Assoc. Parker, Coulter, Daley & White, Boston, 1977-82; pvt. practice Arthur F. Licata P.C., Boston, 1982—; prin. Ardlee Internat. Trading Co., Ea. Europe and Russia, 1989—; lectr. Mass. Continuing Legal Edn., Boston, 1982-90, mem. trial adv. com., 1984-88; mem. working group on drinking and drunk driving Harvard Sch. Pub. Health Ctr. for Health Comms., 1986; spkr. Conv. Nat. Fedn. Paralegal Assns., Boston, 1987; del. U.S.-People's Republic of China Joint Session on Trade, Investment and Econ. Law, Beijing, 1987; co-sponsor Estonian legal del. visit to Mass. and N.H. correctional instns., 1990; Boston host former Soviet legal del. visit, 1989; legal advisor Czech Anglo-Am. Bus. Inst., Prague, Czech Republic, 1989—, Russian Children's Fund, 1992-94, Estonia Acad. for Pub. Safety, 1992-94, Estonia Acad. for Pub. Safety, 1992-94; del. White House Conf. on Trade and Investment on Cen. Europe, Cleve., 1995; mem. Ford Found.'s Legal Resource Ctr, Czech Republic, 1994—, Soviet Children's Fund, 1992-93. Panel mem. sta. WBZ TV, Boston; contbr. articles to profl. jours. U.S. Del. 6th People to People Juvenile Justice Program to USSR, Moscow, 1989; legal advisor Plymouth County (Mass.) chpt., 1984-87; mem. State Adv. Com. Med. Malpractice, Boston, 1985; bd. dirs. Boston Ctr. for the Arts, 1990-94; mem. profl. adv. bd. Mass. Epilepsy Assn., 1986-93; Boston host to former Soviet Legal Del., People to People Orgn., 1989; counsel state coord. commn. MADD, Mass., 1984-86. Recipient Outstanding Citizen award Mothers Against Drunk Driving, 1986. Fellow Mass. Bar Found.; mem. ABA, ATLA, Mass. Bar Assn. (bd. dirs., young lawyers sect. 1979-80, 21st Century Club 1984), Nat. Bd. Trial Advocacy (bd. cert. civil trial advocate 1992—), Mass. Acad. Trial Attys. (bd. dirs. 1991—). Avocation: travel. Office: Fed Res Plz 600 Atlantic Ave Boston MA 02210

LICH, GLEN ERNST, writer, government, business, and higher education consultant; b. Fredericksburg, Tex., Nov. 5, 1948; s. Ernst Perry and Thelma Olive (Woolfley) L.; m. Lera Patrick Tyler, Sept. 5, 1970; children: James Ernst Lich-Tyler (dec.), Stephen Woolfley Lich-Tyler, Elizabeth Erin Lich-Tyler. Student, U. Vienna, Austria, 1969-70; BA, Southwestern U., 1971; MA, U. Tex., 1976; MA, S.W. Tex. State U., 1978; PhD, Tex. Christian U., 1984; grad., U.S. Army Command and Gen. Staff Coll., 1984. Instr. U. New Orleans, 1979-80; asst. prof. Schreiner Coll., 1980-87; assoc. prof. and dir. regional studies Baylor U., 1987-90; prof. and chair U. of Winnipeg, 1990-93; exec. dir. Hill Country Inst., 1992—; dir. World Heritage Tours, 1978—; adj. faculty U.S. Army Command and Gen. Staff Coll., 1987—; vis. fellow Yale U., 1987, German Fgn. Ministry, 1983; rsch. fellow Mosher Inst. Internat. Policy Studies, Tex. A & M U., 1988-93; sr. rsch. fellow Ctr. Socioeconomic Rsch. U. Coahuila, Mexico, 1990-95; coord. Standing Conf. Ethnic Chairs and Professorships in Can., 1991-92; chmn. bd. dirs. Picacho Operating Mining Co., Mexico, 1996—; cons. in field. Author: The German Texans, 1981, The Humanities and Public Issues, 1990, Fred Gipson at Work, 1990, The Women of Viscri, 1996; editor: (with Dona Reeves-Marquardt) Retrospect and Retrieval: The German Element in Review: Essays on Cultural Preservation, 1978, German Culture in Texas: A Free Earth, 1980, The Cabin Book, 1985, (with Dona Reeves-Marquardt) Texas Country: The Changing Rural Scene, 1986, (with Joseph A. McKinney) Region North America: Canada, United States, Mexico, 1990, Regional Studies: The Interplay of Land and People, 1992; assoc. editor Jour. German-Am. Studies, 1977-80, Yearbook of German-Am. Studies, 1981-93; editor: Jour. Am. Studies Assn. Tex., 1988-90; contbr. articles to profl. publs. Served with U.S. Army, 1972-75, lt. col. USAR, asst. attache to Portugal, 1987-92, asst. attache to Germany, 1992-94; project officer U.S. Embassy, Bucharest, Romania, 1993, Ljubljana, Slovenia, 1993-94; dir. internat. programs Adj. Gen.'s Dept. of State of Tex., 1994-95. Recipient Gold Def. medal Republic of Slovenia, 1994; NEH rsch. grantee, 1978, 86-87; Fed. Republic Germany, 1983, 87; Swiss Humanities Acad., 1988; Tex. Com. Humanities, 1988, 89; Am. Coun. of Learned Socs., 1988; Embassy of Can., 1988; Max Kade Found., 1989-92; Joint Econ. Com. of U.S. Congress, 1989-91; Ministry of Multiculturalism and Citizenship of Can., 1991-92; Soc. Scis. and Humanities Rsch. Coun. Can., 1991-92, Interactivity Found., 1996—; Mem. MLA, Am. Studies Assn., Assn. Am. Geographers, Am. Folklore Assn., Am. Assn. Tchrs. German, Nat. Coun. Tchrs. English, Soc. for Romanian Studies, Assn. for Can. Studies in U. S., Can. Ethnic Studies Assn., Oral History Assn., Tex. Folklore Soc., Tex. State Hist. Assn., German Studies Assn., Pi Kappa Alpha. Office: Hill Country Inst PO Box 1850 Kerrville TX 78029-1850

LICHT, PAUL, zoologist, educator; b. St. Louis, Mar. 12, 1938; s. Harry and Betty L.; m. Barbara Margaret Morrison, June 30, 1963; children: Andrew Stephen, Rachael Margaret, Carolyn Ann. BA, Washington U., St. Louis, 1959; PhD, U. Mich., 1964. Asst. prof. zoology U. Calif., Berkeley, 1964-68; asso. prof. U. Calif., 1968-72, prof., 1972—, chmn. dept. zoology, 1977-82; dean divsn. biol. scis. U. Calif., Berkeley, 1994—. Numerous publs. in field, 1961—; editor McGraw Hill Book Series, 1976-78; mem. editorial bds. Gen. Comparative Endocrinology, 1978—, Jour. Exptl. Zoology, 1990—; author/owner microcomputer bibliographic program REFMENU. Recipient Grace Pickford medal Soc. Comparative Endocrinology, 1980. Fellow AAAS, Calif. Acad. Sci.; mem. Am. Soc. Zoology (chmn. divsn. comparative endocrinology 1992-93). Office: U Calif Dept Zoology Berkeley CA 94720

LICHT, RICHARD A., lawyer; b. Providence, Mar. 25, 1948; s. Julius M. Licht and Irene (Lash) Olson; m. Roanne Sragow; children: Jordan David, Jeremy Michael, Jaclyn Rose. AB cum laude, Harvard U., 1968, JD cum laude, 1972; LLM in Taxation, Boston U., 1975. Law clk. to chief justice R.I. Supreme Ct., Providence, 1973-74; ptnr. Letts, Quinn & Licht, Providence, 1974-84; mem. R.I. Senate, Providence, 1975-84, chmn. judiciary com. and rules com., 1984; lt. gov. State of R.I., Providence, 1985-89; ptnr. Licht & Semonoff, Providence, 1989—; former chmn. R.I. Commn. on Racial, Religious and Ethnic Harrassment, Dr. Martin Luther King Jr. Holiday Commn., State Energy and Tech. Study Commn. rules com.; chmn. Coun. of State Govt., Intergovtl. Affairs Com., Nat. Focus Team, Bd. Gov. Higher Edn.; bd. regents Elem. and Secondary Edn.; mem. Pub. Telecom. Authority R.I., Univ. R.I. Found., Community Coll. R.I. Found. Bd. dirs. Roger Williams Hosp.; advisor Community Prep. Sch.; corporator Roger Williams Hosp.; trustee Save the Bay, Inc., Emma Pendleton Bradley Hosp.; bd. dirs. Temple Emanuel, Providence, Jewish Fedn. R.I., Samaritans; chmn. Small Bus. Adv. Council, Task Force on Teenage Suicide Prevention, CD Civil Preparedness Adv. Council, Urban League R.I., 1980-82, John Hope Settlement House, 1976-81; chair Am. Cancer Soc. Ball, 1989, Jewish Fedn. R.I. Passage to Freedom, 1989; chair R.I. chpt. Anti-Defamation League; mem. Meeting St. Sch. steering com. for capital fund drive, 1989-92; mem. Women and Infants Corp., Dorcas Place, PARI, UNITAM, NCLG task force of Youth Suicide Prevention, Jewish Home for the Aged of R.I., bd. govs. for the handicapped; active YWCA of Greater R.I., Vols. in Action, Inc., Big Sister Assn. of R.I., Big Bros. R.I.; coordinator vols. gubernatorial campaigns Frank Licht, 1968, 70; active Jewish Community Ctr., Providence, 1975-83, E. Side Sr. Citizens Ctr., 1975-76, R.I. Youth Guidance Ctr., Inc., 1987, Block Island Conservancy, Inc., Notre Dame Health Care Corp., 1987; Dem. candidate for U.S. Senate, 1988; ann. campaign chair Meeting St. Sch., 1990-91. Named an Outstanding Young Man of R.I., R.I. Jaycees, 1979; recipient David Ben Gurion award State of Israel Bonds, 1977, Outstanding Pub. Service award Temple Torat Yisrael, 1985, Disting. Services to the Hispanic Community award Casa Puerto Rico, 1985, Hon. Pub. Service award Meeting St. Sch., 1986, Recognition award R.I. Day Care Dirs. Assn., 1986, award of Appreciation Child Care/Human Services, 1986, Govtl. Services award Ocean State Residences for the Retarded, 1987. Mem. R.I. Bar Assn., Corp. Womens' and Infants' Hosp., Corp. Roger Williams Hosp., Vols. in Action, Inc. Democrat. Office: Licht & Semonoff One Park Row Providence RI 02903

LICHTBLAU, JOHN H., economist; b. Vienna, Austria, June 26, 1921; came to U.S., 1939; s. Ernst and Alice (Fischer) Lichtblau-Lind; m. Charlotte M. Adelberg, Apr. 12, 1944; 1 child, Claudia L. Payne. B in Social Sci., CCNY, 1949; postgrad., NYU, 1950-53. Economist U.S. Dept. Labor, Washington, 1951-53, Conf. Bd., N.Y.C., 1953-54, Walter J. Levy Assocs., N.Y.C., 1955-56; research dir. Petroleum Ind. Research Found. Inc., N.Y.C., 1956-61, exec. dir., 1961-72, chmn., 1972—; chmn. Petroleum Ind. Research Assocs. Inc., N.Y.C., 1977—. Mem. editorial bd. Energy Policy (London), 1987—; contbr. articles to profl. jours., book chpts. Served with U.S. Army, 1944-47, ETO. Mem. Am. Petroleum Inst., Nat. Petroleum Council, Am. Econ. Assn., Internat. Assn. Energy Economists (5th Ann. award for outstanding contbns. 1986), Council on Fgn. Relations. Office: Petroleum Industry Rsch Found 122 E 42nd St New York NY 10168-0002

LICHTBLAU, MYRON IVOR, language educator; b. N.Y.C., Oct. 10, 1925; s. Samuel and Sadonia (Weinberg) L.; m. Bernice Glanz, June 23, 1956; children: Mark (dec.), Anita, Eric. BA, CCNY, 1947; MA, U. Nacional Mex., 1948; PhD, Columbia U., 1957; diploma (hon.), U. de Nuevo Leon, Mex., 1964. Tchr. spanish secondary schs., N.Y.C., 1948-57; instr. Ind. U., Bloomington, 1957-59; prof. Syracuse U., N.Y., 1959—, chmn. dept. fgn. langs., 1967-74, 86-88; vis. prof. Colgate U., Hamilton, N.Y., 1970, SUNY-Binghamton, 1975; coordinator language program Peace Corps, 1966. Author: The Argentine Novel in the Nineteenth Century, 1959, El Arte estilistico de Eduardo Mallea, 1967, Manuel Galvez, 1972, A Practical Reference Guide to Reading Spanish, 1977, Rayuela y la creatividad artistica, 1989; editor: Manuel Galvez: Las dos vidas del Pobre Napoleon, 1963, E. Caballero Calderon: Manuel Pacho, 1980, Eduardo Mallea Ante La Critica, 1985, Emigration and Exile in Twentieth-Century Hispanic Literature, 1988, Mario Vargas Llosa: A Writer's Reality, 1990, Manuel Galvez: La maestra normal, 1991; editor Symposium, 1995—; translator: Eduardo Mallea: History of an Argentine Passion, 1983; book rev. editor Symposium, 1966-94, Hispania, 1974-83; mem. editorial bd. Critica Hispánica, 1985—. Bd. dirs. Syracuse Jewish Community Ctr., 1973; pres. Rabbi Jacob Epstein Sch. Jewish Studies, 1981-83; trustee Temple Beth Sholom, 1987-88. With U.S. Army, 1944-46. Mem. AAUP, MLA, Am. Assn. Tchrs. of Spanish and Portuguese (assoc. editor 1974-83), Inst. Internat. de Lit. Iberoamericana (exec. sec. 1959-63), Internat. Assn. Hispanistas. Jewish. Avocation: tennis. Office: Syracuse U Dept Lang and Lit Syracuse NY 13244

LICHTENBERG, BYRON K., futurist, manufacturing executive, space flight consultant; b. Stroudsburg, Pa., Feb. 19, 1948; s. Glenn John and Georgianna (Bierei) L.; m. Lee Lombard, July 25, 1970 (divorced); children—Kristin, Kimberly. Sc.B., Brown U., 1969; M.S., MIT, 1975, Sc.D., 1979. Rsch. scientist MIT, Cambridge, 1978-84; pres. Payload Systems, Inc., Cambridge, 1984-89, chief scientist, 1989-91; pres., chief exec. officer Omega Aerospace Inc., Virginia Beach, Va., 1991—. Contbg. author NASA Payload Specialist, 1979-92, Flew on Space Shuttle Mission #9, #45; contbr. articles to profl. jours. Served to lt. col. USAF, Mass. Air N.G., 1969-93. Recipient NASA Space Flight award, 1983, 92, Spaceflight award VFW, 1983, Haley Spaceflight award AIAA, 1983. Mem. Tau Beta Pi, Sigma Xi. Avocations: golf; racquetball; windsurfing; skiing. Office: Omega Aerospace Inc 728 Wolfsnare Cres Virginia Beach VA 23454-2748

LICHTENBERG, JUDITH A., philosophy educator; b. N.Y.C., Apr. 19, 1948; d. Al and Friedel (Rothschild) L.; m. David J. Luban, Mar. 5, 1983; children: Daniel, Rachel. BA, U. Wis., 1968, MA, 1971; PhD, CUNY, 1978. Asst. prof. philosophy U. N.C., Chapel Hill, 1978-81; rsch. scholar Inst. Philosophy and Pub. Policy U. Md., College Park, 1981—, assoc. prof., 1991—. Editor: Democracy and the Mass Media, 1990; contbr. articles to profl. jours. Mem. Am. Philos. Assn., Am. Soc. Polit. and Legal Philosophy. Office: U Md Dept Philosophy College Park MD 20742

LICHTENBERG, MARGARET KLEE, publishing company executive; b. N.Y.C., Nov. 19, 1941; d. Lawrence and Shirley Jane (Wicksman) Klee; m. James Lester Lichtenberg, Mar. 31, 1963 (div. 1982); children: Gregory Lawrence, Amanda Zoe. BA, U. Mich., 1963; postgrad., Harvard U., 1963. Book rev. editor New Woman mag., 1972-73; assoc. editor children's books Parents Mag. Press, 1974; editor, rights dir. Books for Young People, Frederick Warne & Co., N.Y.C., 1975-78; sr. editor Simon & Schuster, N.Y.C., 1979-80; dir. sales promotion Grosset & Dunlap, N.Y.C., 1980-81; ednl. sales mgr. Bantam Books, N.Y.C., 1982-84; dir. mktg. and sales Grove

Press, N.Y.C., 1984-86; dir. of sales Grove Press, 1986-87; dir. sales Weidenfeld & Nicolson, N.Y.C., 1986-87; mktg. dir. Beacon Press, Boston, 1988-95; book mktg. coach, 1995—; writer, freelance critic, 1961—. Contbr. articles, essays, stories, poetry, revs. to mags., newspapers and anthologies. Bd. dirs. Children's Book Council, 1978. Recipient 2 Avery Hopwood awards in drama and fiction, 1962, 2 in drama and poetry, 1963; coll. fiction contest award Mademoiselle mag., 1963; Woodrow Wilson fellow, 1963. Mem. Women's Nat. Book Assn. (past pres. N.Y. chpt.). Home and Office: PO Box 268 Santa Fe NM 87504

LICHTENBERGER, HORST WILLIAM, chemical company executive; b. Yugoslavia, Nov. 5, 1935; came to U.S., 1950, naturalized, 1955; s. Andrew W. and Hella L.; m. Patricia Ann Thomas, June 15, 1957; children: Erich, Lisa. B.A., U. Iowa, 1957, B.S. in Chem. Engring., 1959; M.B.A., SUNY, Buffalo, 1962. With Union Carbide Corp., 1959-1992; bus. mgr. Union Carbide Corp., N.Y.C., 1972-75; v.p., gen. mgr. Linde div. Union Carbide Corp., Geneva, 1975-80; v.p. mktg. Union Carbide Corp., N.Y.C., 1980-82; v.p., gen. mgr. gas products Union Carbide Corp., 1982-85, pres. Solvents and Coatings div., 1985-1992, pres. Chemicals and Plastics group, 1986-92; pres., CEO Praxair Inc., 1992—; also chmn. Praxair Inc., Danbury, C.T. Mem. Iowa N.G., 1954-62. Mem. Am. Iron and Steel Inst., Chem. Mfg. Assn., Soc. of Chem. Industry. Republican. Achievements include patentee storage cryogenic fluids. Office: Praxair Inc 39 Old Ridgebury Rd Danbury CT 06810 *Progress is best achieved by encouraging people to innovate and to take prudent risks.**

LICHTENSTEIN, ELISSA CHARLENE, legal association executive; b. Trenton, N.J., Oct. 23, 1954; d. Mark and Rita (Field) L. AB cum laude, Smith Coll., Northampton, Mass., 1976; JD, George Washington U., 1979. Bar: D.C. 1980, U.S. Dist. Ct. (D.C. dist.) 1980, U.S. Ct. Appeals (D.C. cir.) 1980. Law clk. U.S. EPA, Washington, 1978-79; staff dir. ABA, Washington, 1979—, assoc. dir. pub. svcs. div., 1981-85, dir., 1985—. Editor, contbr.: Common Boundary/Common Problems: The Environmental Consequences of Energy Production, 1982, Exit Polls and Early Election Projections, 1984, The Global Environment: Challenges, Choices and Will, 1986, (newsletter) Environ. Law; co-editor, contbr. The Environ. Network; co-editor: Determining Competency in Guardianship Proceedings, 1990, Due Process Protections for Juveniles in Civil Commitment Proceedings, 1991, Environmental Regulation in Pacific Rim Nations, 1993, The Role of Law in the 1992 UN Conference on Environment and Development, 1992, Trade and the Environment in Pacific Rim Nations, 1994, Public Participation in Environmental Decisionmaking, 1995, Endangered Species Act Reauthorization: A Biocentric Approach. Mem. Nat. Trust for Hist. Preservation. Named Outstanding Young Woman of Am., 1982. Mem. ABA, NAFE, Am. Soc. Assn. Execs., Washington Coun. Lawyers, Women in Communications, Inc., Environ. Law Inst. (assoc.), Met. Washington Environ. Profls. (pres. 1986-96), D.C. Bar Assn. Democrat. Jewish. Office: ABA Div Pub Svcs 740 15th St NW Washington DC 20005

LICHTENSTEIN, HARVEY, performing arts executive; b. Bklyn., Apr. 9, 1929; s. Samuel and Jennie (Meiner) L.; m. Phyllis Holbrook, Nov. 14, 1971; children: Saul, John. BA, Bklyn. Coll., 1951, LHD (hon.), 1986; postgrad., Bennington (Vt.) Coll., 1953; ArtsD (hon.), L.I. U., 1989; MusD (hon.), Mannes Coll. Music, 1989; LHD (hon.), Pratt Inst., 1993. Subscription and group sales mgr. N.Y.C. Ballet, also N.Y.C. Opera, 1965-67; pres., exec. producer Bklyn. Acad. Music, 1967—; exec. producer Bklyn. Philharm. Symphonic Orch., 1989—; Am. dir. Spoleto (Italy) Festival, 1971-73. Mem. Century Assn. (N.Y.C.). Office: Bklyn Acad Music 30 Lafayette Ave Brooklyn NY 11217-1430

LICHTENSTEIN, LAWRENCE JAY, lawyer; b. Phila., June 22, 1929; s. Leo and Harriet (Herbach) L.; m. Barbara Eberhardt, June 13, 1987. AB, Dickinson Coll., 1951; LLB, U. Pa., 1954. Bar: Pa. 1954, U.S. Dist. Ct. Pa. 1954, U.S. Ct. Appeals (3d cir.) 1991. Ptnr., chair bankruptcy dept. Mesirov, Gelman, Jaffe, Cramer & Jamieson, Phila., 1983-91; shareholder Buchanan Ingersoll P.C., Phila., 1991—. Mem. ABA (bus. bankruptcy com., comml. fin. svcs. com., co-chair chpt. II subcom. task force on mediation in bankruptcy), Phila. Bar Assn. (chair bus. law sect. bd. govs., pres. consumer bankruptcy assistance project eastern dist. bankruptcy conf.). Office: Buchanan Ingersoll PC 1200 Two Logan Sq Philadelphia PA 19103

LICHTENSTEIN, LAWRENCE MARK, allergy, immunology educator, physician; b. Washington, May 31, 1934; s. Samuel and Lillian (Colodny) L.; m. Carolyn Eggert, June 15, 1956; children: Elizabeth, Joshua, Rebekah. MD, U. Chgo., 1960; PhD, Johns Hopkins U., 1965. Diplomate: Am. Bd. Allergy and Immunology. Intern, Johns Hopkins Hosp., 1960-61, resident in medicine, 1965-66; asst. prof. medicine Johns Hopkins U. Sch. Medicine, 1966-70, assoc. prof., 1970-75, prof., 1975—, dir. Johns Hopkins Asthma and Allergy Ctr.; mem. Nat. Adv. Allergy and Infectious Diseases Coun. Mem. editorial bd.: Clin. Immunology and Pathology, Immunology, Pulmonary, Allergy; editor 11 books; contbr. articles to profl. jours. Fellow ACP; mem. Am. Soc. Pharmacology and Exptl. Therapeutics, Am. Assn. Immunology (sec., treas.), Am. Fedn. Clin. Rsch., Am. Soc. Clin. Investigation, Am. Acad. Allergy and Immunology (past pres.), Am. Soc. Exptl. Pathology, Collegium Internat. Allergologicum (pres.), Assn. Am. Physicians. Democrat. Jewish. Home: 1600 The Terraces Baltimore MD 21209-3637 Office: John Hopkins Asthma & Allergy Ctr 5501 Hopkins Bayview Cir Baltimore MD 21224-6821

LICHTENSTEIN, ROBERT JAY, lawyer; b. Phila., Jan. 23, 1948; s. Irving M. and Marjorie J. (Weiss) L.; m. Sandra Paley, Aug. 14, 1971; children: David P., Kate. BS in Econs., U. Pa., 1969; JD, U. Pitts., 1973; LLM in Taxation, NYU, 1974. Bar: Pa. 1974, U.S. Tax Ct. 1978, U.S. Dist. Ct. (ea. dist.) Pa. 1979, U.S. Ct. Appeals (3rd cir.) 1982, U.S. Ct. Appeals (4th cir.) 1987. Ptnr. Saul, Ewing, Remick & Saul, 1978-88; assoc. Morgan, Lewis & Bockius, Phila., 1974-78, ptnr., 1988—; dir. Maritrans Inc.; instr. Main Line Paralegal Inst., Wayne, Pa., 1984-87, Paralegal Inst., Phila., 1987-90; adj. prof. law Villanova U. Sch. Law, 1991—. Trustee Temple Brith Achim, King of Prussia, Pa., 1986-91. Mem. ABA, Pa. Bar Assn., Phila. Assn., Locust Club. Democrat. Avocations: skiing, tennis, reading. Office: Morgan Lewis Bockius LLP 2000 One Logan Sq Philadelphia PA 19103

LICHTENSTEIN, ROY, artist; b. N.Y.C., Oct. 27, 1923; s. Milton and Beatrice (Werner) L.; m. Isabel Wilson, June 12, 1949 (div.); children: David, Mitchell; m. Dorothy Herzka, Nov. 1, 1968. BFA, Ohio State U., 1946, MFA, 1949; DFA (hon.), Calif. Inst. Arts., 1977, Ohio State U., 1988, Bard Coll., 1989. Instr. Ohio State U., 1946-51; asst. prof. SUNY-Oswego, 1957-60, Douglass Coll., Rutgers U., 1960-63. Pop art and other themes derived from comic strip techniques; one-man shows include Leo Castelli Gallery, N.Y.C., 1962, 63, 65, 67, 71, 72, 73, 74, 75, 77, 79, 81, 83, 85, 86, 87, 89, 92, Galerie Ileana Sonnabend, Paris, 1963, 65, 70, 75, Pasadena (Calif.) Art Mus., 1967, Walker Art Ctr., Mpls., 1967, Stedelijk Mus., Amsterdam, 1967, Tate Gallery, London, 1968, Guggenheim Mus., N.Y.C., 1969, Nelson Gallery, Kansas City, Mo., 1969, Mus. Contemporary Art, Chgo., 1970, Centre National D'Arte Contemporain, Paris, 1975, and traveling to: Nationalgalerie Staatliche Museum Kulterbesitz, Berlin, Seattle Art Mus., 1976, Inst. Contemporary Art, Boston, 1979, Portland Ctr. for Visual Arts, 1980, St. Louis Art Mus., 1981, Fundacion Juan March, Madrid, 1982, Walker Art Ctr., Mpls., 1986, 'The Drawings of Roy Lichtenstein', Mus. Modern Art, N.Y.C., 1987, and traveling to: Mus. Overholland, Amsterdam, 1987, Tel Aviv Mus., Israel, 1987, Schirn Kunsthalle, Frankfurt, 1988, Mus. Modern Art, Oxford, Eng., 1988, Corcoran Gallery of Art, Washington, 1988; group shows include Whitney Mus. Am. Art, N.Y.C., 1966, 67, 68, 70, 72, 73, 74, 75 (Downtown), 77, 78, 80, 82, 83, 84, 85, 87, Mus. Modern Art, N.Y.C., 1966, 67, 68, 74, 76, 80, 85, 88, Solomon R. Guggenheim Mus., N.Y.C., 1965,76, Venice Biennale, 1966, Corcoran Gallery Art 36th Biennale, Washington, D.C., 1978, Solomon R. Guggenheim MUs., N.Y.C., 1965, 76, Hirschorn Mus., Washington, 1980, Bklyn. Mus. Art, N.Y.C., 1981, Nat. Mus. Am. Art, Smithsonian Inst., Washington, 1984, Palacio Velazquez, Madrid, Spain, 1991, Galerie Martine Queval, Paris, 1992, Galerie Joachim Becker, Paris, 1992; represented in permanent collections: Mus. Modern Art, N.Y.C., Whitney Mus. Am. Art, N.Y.C., Corcoran Gallery Art, Washington, Hirschorn Mus. and Sculpture Garden, Washington, Libr. Congress, Washington, Nat. Gallery Art, Washington, Chgo. Art Inst., Smithsonian Inst., Washington, Victoria and Albert Mus., London, Seibu Art Mus., Tokyo, Ludwig Mus., Cologne, Stedelijk Mus., Amsterdam, Norton Simon Mus., Pasadena, Yale U., New Haven, Walker Art Ctr., Mpls., San Francisco Mus. Modern Art, Albright Knox Gallery, Buffalo; created outside wall for Circarama, N.Y. State Pavillion, N.Y. State World's Fair, 1963, large Painting for Expo '67, Montreal, 1967, Brushstroke Murals for Dusseldorf U. Med. Ctr., 1970, 'Mermaid' (NEA grantee), pub. sculpture for Theatre Performing Arts in Miami Beach, Fla., 1979, 'Brushstrokes in Flight', Port Columbus Airport, Columbus, Ohio, 1984, 'Mural with Blue Brushstroke', Equitable Life Assurance Bldg. with Whitney Mus. Art, 1985, 'Coups de Pinceau', Caisse des Depots and Consignations, Paris, 1988, Tel Aviv Mus. Art, Tel Aviv, 1989. With AUS, 1943-46. Recipient Skowhegan medal for painting, 1977. Mem. Am. Acad. and Inst. Arts and Letters. Office: care Leo Castelli Gallery 420 West Broadway New York NY 10012*

LICHTER, EDWARD ARTHUR, physician, educator; b. Chgo., June 5, 1928; s. Joseph and Eva (Wise) L.; m. Charlotte Sells, Sept. 7, 1952; children: Michael, Jay. PhB, U. Chgo., 1947; BS, Roosevelt U., 1949; MS, U. Ill., 1951, MD, 1955. Intern Fitzsimons Army Hosp., Denver, 1955-56; resident internal medicine U. Ill., Chgo., 1958-61, assoc. prof. preventive medicine and community health Med. Ctr., 1966-69, prof., dept. head preventive medicine and community health, 1969-86, prof., dept. head health care svcs., 1972-79, prof. community health scis., 1979—, prof. internal medicine, assoc. chief Sect. of Gen. Internal Medicine, 1986—, mem. exec. com., 1990—; mem. exec. com. Univ. Senates Conf., 1992-95; practice medicine specializing in internal medicine and preventive medicine Chgo., 1966—; fellow in immunology NIH, 1961-63, USPHS officer, mem. staff immunology, 1963-66. Served with AUS, 1955-58. Fellow ACP, APHA, Am. Coll. Preventive Medicine; mem. Am. Coll. Epidemiology, Cen. Soc. for Clin. Rsch., Assn. Tchrs. Preventive Medicine, Chgo. Heart Assn., Alpha Omega Alpha. Home: 1310 Maple Ave Evanston IL 60201-4325 Office: 840 S Wood St Chicago IL 60612-7317

LICHTER, PAUL RICHARD, ophthalmology educator; b. Detroit, Mar. 7, 1939; s. Max D. and Buena (Epstein) L.; m. Carolyn Goode, 1960; children: Laurie, Susan. BA, U. Mich., 1960, MD, 1964, MS, 1968. Diplomate Am. Bd. Ophthalmology. Asst. to assoc. prof. ophthalmology U. Mich., Ann Arbor, 1971-78, prof., chmn. dept. ophthalmology, 1978—; chmn. Am. Bd. Ophthalmology, 1987. Editor-in-chief Ophthalmology jour., 1986-94. Served to lt. comdr. USN, 1969-71. Fellow Am. Acad. Opthalmology (bd. dirs. 1981—, pres. 1996, sr. honor award 1986); mem. AMA, Pan Am. assn. Opthalmology (bd. dirs. 1988—, sec.-treas. English speaking countries 1991-95), Mich. State Med. Soc., Washtenaw County Med. Soc., Mich. Opthalmol. Soc. (pres. 1993-95), Assn. Univ. Profs. Opthalmology (trustee 1986-93, pres. 1991-92), Alpha Omega Alpha. Office: U Mich Med Sch Kellogg Eye Ctr 1000 Wall St Ann Arbor MI 48105-1912

LICHTERMAN, MARTIN, history educator; b. N.Y.C., July 18, 1918; s. Joseph Aaron and Esther S. (Schacknowitz) L.; m. Charlotte Rottenberg, Oct. 7, 1945; children: Joshua David, Andrew Marc. B.S., Harvard U., 1939, A.M., 1947; Ph.D., Columbia U., 1952. Instr. Rutgers U., Newark, 1948-51; instr., lectr. Princeton U., 1953-55; mem. research staff Princeton U. (Center for Research on World Polit. Instns.), 1951-53; asst. prof. M.I.T., 1955-60; dir. research to gov. Mass., 1959-60; exec. sec., dir. New Eng. Bd. Higher Edn., Winchester, Mass., 1961-66; dean Center Humanities and Social Scis. Union Coll., Schenectady, 1966-71; acting dean faculty Union Coll., 1971-72, dean faculty, 1972-76; prof. history Center Humanities and Social Scis. Union Coll., 1966-76, distinguished prof. history and higher edn., 1976-78; dean Empire State Coll., 1978-82, prof. history, 1982-83, prof. emeritus, 1983—; pres. Alternative Lifelong Learning, Berkeley, Calif., 1989-91; cons. 20th Century Fund, N.Y.C., 1955-57, Friends World Coll., 1984-86; mem. Mass. Bd. Collegiate Authority, 1961-66. Author: To the Yalu and Back, 1963; co-author: Political Community in the North Atlantic Area, 1957; contbr. articles to profl. jours. Vice chmn. bd. Mass. Com. Children and Youth, 1963-66, mem. exec. bd., 1961-66; adv. bd. Civil Liberties Mass., 1963-66; chmn. bd. New Eng. Council Advancement Sch. Adminstrn., 1961-63; vice chmn. Capital Dist. Civil Liberties Union, 1966-67; chmn. Freedom Forum, Inc., 1970-71, Schenectady Renewals, Inc., 1972-76; bd. dirs. Suffolk County chpt. N.Y. Civil Liberties Union, 1981-87; bd. dirs. Della Corte Internat., Inc., 1983-88. Mem. Am. Hist. Assn., Orgn. Am. Historians. Home: 2587 Hilgard Ave Berkeley CA 94709-1104

LICHTIN, (JUDAH) LEON, pharmacist; b. Phila., Mar. 5, 1924; s. Aaron and Rosa (Rosenberg) L.; m. Beverly I. Cohen, Aug. 6, 1950; children—Benjamin Lloyd, Alan Eli. B.S. in Pharmacy, Phila. Coll. Pharmacy and Sci., 1944, M.S. in Pharmacy, 1947; Ph.D. in Pharmacy, Ohio State U., 1950. Asst. prof. pharmacy U. Cin., 1950-51, assoc. prof., 1951-64, prof., 1964—, Andrew Jergens prof. pharmacy, 1971-91, Andrew Jergens prof. pharmacy emeritus, 1991—; cons. in cosmetic sci. Contbr. articles to pharm. jours.; composer string music, vocal music. Past pres. No. Hills Synagogue, Cin. Fellow AAAS, Soc. Cosmetic Chemists; mem. Sigma Xi, Rho Chi. Achievements include patents in field. Home: 801 Cloverview Ave Cincinnati OH 45231-6017

LICHTIN, NORMAN NAHUM, chemistry educator; b. Newark, Aug. 10, 1922; s. James Jechiel and Clara (Greenspan) L.; m. Phyllis Selma Wasserman, May 30, 1947; children—Harold Hirsh, Sara Marjorie, Daniel Albert. B.S., Antioch Coll., 1944; M.S., Purdue U., 1945; Ph.D., Harvard U., 1948. Faculty Boston U., 1947-93, prof. chemistry, 1961-93, prof. emeritus, 1993—, Univ. prof., 1973-93, chmn. dept. chemistry, 1973-84, dir. Div. Engring. and Applied Sci., 1983-87; chief scientist Synlize, Inc., 1987-90, Project Sunrise Inc., 1990-92, ClearFlow Inc., 1993-94, Photox Corp., Boston, 1993—; vis. chemist Brookhaven Nat. Lab., Upton, N.Y., 1957-58, research collaborator, 1958-70; guest scientist Weizmann Inst. Sci., Rehovoth, Israel, 1962-63; vis. prof. Inst. Phys. and Chem. Research, Wako, Japan, 1980, Hebrew U., Jerusalem, 1962-63, 70-71, 75, 76, 80; Coochbehar lectr. Indian Assn. Cultivation of Sci., Calcutta, 1980. Assoc. editor Solar Energy, 1976-93; rsch. and publs. on mechanisms of chem. reactions including reaction of atomic nitrogen with organic compounds, influence of high energy radiation on organic compounds and photoredox reactions of dyes; photochem. conversion solar energy, ionization processes and ionic reactions in solutions in liquid sulfur dioxide, photo assisted solid-catalysis; catalytic and photocatalytic decomposition of organic and inorganic pollutants of air and water. NSF fellow, 1962-63. Fellow AAAS; mem. Am. Chem. Soc., Inter-Am. Photochem. Soc., Internat. Solar Energy Soc., Sigma Xi, Phi Beta Kappa (hon.). Home: 195 Morton St Newton MA 02159-1522 Office: 590 Commonwealth Ave Boston MA 02215-2407

LICHTMAN, DAVID MICHAEL, military officer, health care administrator, orthopedist, educator; b. Bkyln., Jan. 14, 1942; s. Harry S. and Frances (Rubin) L.; m. Frances Lubin; children: James Matthew, Elisabeth Jill. Student, Tufts Coll., 1962; MD, SUNY, Bklyn., 1966. Diplomate: Am. Bd. Orthopaedic Surgery. Intern U. Minn. Hosp., 1966-67, Naval Aerospace Med. Inst., Pensacola, Fla., 1967; commd. lt. USN, 1967, advanced through grades to rear adm., 1988, flight surgeon Air Wing 3, 1968-69; mem. staff orthopaedic svc. Nat. Naval Med. Ctr., Bethesda, Md., 1974-77, chmn. dept. orthopaedic surgery, head, hand surgery svc., 1984-87; dir. orthopaedic residency program Nat. Naval Med. Ctr., Bethesda, Md., 1984-87; asst. chmn. dept. orthopaedic surgery Nat. Naval. Med. Ctr., Bethesda, Md., 1975-77, chmn. dept. orthopaedic surgery, head hand surgery svc., dir. orthopaedic residency program, 1984-87; chmn. dept. orthopaedic surgery and rehab. Naval Hosp., Oakland, Calif., 1977-83, dir. orthopaedic residency program/dir. navy hand fellowship, 1977-83, head hand and microsurgery svc., 1977-83; mem. staff orthopaedic surgery, sr. hand/microsurgery cons., 1988-91, commanding officer, 1989-91; comdr. San Francisco Med. Command, Oakland, 1988-91; promoted to Rear Adm. (lower half), 1989, Rear Adm. (upper half), 1991; retired USN, 1994; John Dunn prof. orthopaedic hand surgery Baylor Coll. Medicine, Houston, 1994—; cons. orthopaedic surgery asst. sec. def. for health affairs Dept. Def., Washington, 1988-94; specialty advisor naval surgeon gen. for orthopaedic surgery and hand surgery Bur. Medicine and Surgery Dept. Navy, Washington, 1983-86; prof. surgery and head divsn. orthopaedic surgery Uniformed Svcs. U. of Health Scis., Bethesda, 1984-94, ex-officio mem. bd. regents, 1991-94. Editor: The Wrist and Its Disorders, 1988, Hand and Wrist Sect. Current Opinion in Orthopaedics.; contbr. articles to profl. jours. Mem. ACS (bd. govs.), Am. Acad. Orthopaedic Surgeons, Am. Soc. for Surgery of the Hand Assn., Am. Orthopaedic Assn. (hon.), Mil. Surgeons U.S. (Philip Hench award 1982), Soc. Naval Flight Surgeons, Soc. Mil. Orthopaedic Surgeons (bd. dirs.). Home: 45 Briar Hollow #11 Houston TX 77027 Office: Dept Orthopedic Surgery Baylor Coll Medicine 6550 Fannin Ste 2525 Houston TX 77030

LICHTMAN, MARSHALL ALBERT, medical educator, physician, scientist; b. N.Y.C., June 23, 1934; s. Samuel and Vera L.; m. Alice Jo Maisel, June 23, 1957; children—Susan, Joanne, Pamela. AB, Cornell U., 1955; MD, U. Buffalo, 1960. Diplomate Am. Bd. Internal Medicine. Resident in medicine Strong Meml. Hosp., 1960-63; surgeon USPHS and postdoctoral research assoc. Sch. Pub. Health, U. N.C., 1963-65; chief resident and instr. medicine Strong Meml. Hosp., 1965-66; sr. instr. medicine, research trainee in hematology U. Rochester Sch. Medicine, N.Y., 1966-67, asst. prof. medicine, spl. postdoctoral research fellow in hematology, 1968-70, assoc. prof. medicine and radiation biology and biophysics, 1971-74, prof. medicine and radiation biology and biophysics, 1974—, chief hematology unit dept. medicine, 1975-77, co. chief, 1977-89; sr. assoc. dean for acad. affairs and research, 1979-90, dean Sch. of Medicine and Dentistry, 1990-95; vis. prof. univs.; lectr. in field. Leukemia Soc. Am. scholar, 1969-74; recipient contracts U.S. Army Research, 1972-78, U.S. Dept. Energy, 1972-80; USPHS grantee, 1971-95. Editor: Abnormalities of Granulocytes and Monocytes, 1975, Hematology for Practitioners, 1978, Hematology and Oncology, 1980, (with W.J. William, E. Beutler, A.J. Erslev) Hematology, 3d edit., 1983, 4th edit., 1990, (with E. Beutler, B. Coller, T.J. Kipps) 5th edit., 1995; (with H.J. Meiselman and P.L. LaCelle) White Cell Mechanics: Basic Science and Clinical Aspects, 1984. Contbr. articles to profl. jours. Master ACP; mem. NIH (hematology study sect., 1982-86), Am. Fedn. Clin. Research, AAAS, Am. Soc. Hematology (pres. 1989), Internat. Soc. Hematology, N.Y. Acad. Scis., Am. Soc. Clin. Investigation, Assn. Am. Physicians, Am. Assn. for Cancer Research, Am. Physiol. Soc., Reticuloendothelial Soc., Soc. Exptl. Biology and Medicine, Am. Soc. Cell Biology. Home: 64 Woodbury Pl Rochester NY 14618-3445 Office: U Rochester Sch Medicine/Dentistry Box 610 601 Elmwood Ave Rochester NY 14642-9999

LICHTWARD, FRED, headmaster; b. St. Paul, Apr. 27, 1950; s. Fred Whitmore and Violet (Hunter) L.; m. Deborah Ann Schultz, Jan. 13, 1973; 1 child, Fred. BS, Mercy Coll., Dobbs Ferry, N.Y., 1973; MA, U. North Fla., Jacksonville, 1974; EdS, U. Fla., 1979; EdD, U. Sarasota, 1981. Cert. in spl. edn., elem. edn., ednl. adminstrn., Fla. Tchr. Nassau County Schs., Fernandina Beach, Fla., 1974-79; headmaster St. Andrew's Episc. Sch., Jacksonville, 1979-82, Assumption Sch., Jacksonville, 1982-87; exec. dir. Hope Haven Children's Clinic, Jacksonville, 1987-90; headmaster Arlington Country Day Sch., Jacksonville, 1990—. Author ednl. games Games for Remediation, 1975; contbr. articles to ednl. jours. Bd. dirs. YMCA, Jacksonville, 1984-86; pres., bd. dirs., umpire Assumption Athletic Assn., Jacksonville, 1988-90; bd. dirs. Southside Youth Athletic Assn., Jacksonville, 1984-87, Arlington Child Devel. Ctr., Jacksonville, 1990-92; vol. coach YMCA, Arlington, 1984—. Named Tchr. of Yr., West Jacksonville Jaycees, 1974, Vol. of Yr., YMCA, Jacksonville, 1984; U. North Fla. grad. fellow, 1973. Avocations: reading, walking, tutoring. Office: Arlington County Day Sch 5725 Fort Caroline Rd Jacksonville FL 32277-1752

LICHTWARDT, ROBERT WILLIAM, mycologist; b. Rio de Janeiro, Nov. 27, 1924; s. Henry Herman and Ruth Moyer Lichtwardt; m. Elizabeth Thomas, Jan. 27, 1951; children: Ruth Elizabeth, Robert Thomas. AB, Oberlin Coll., 1949; MS, U. Ill., 1951, PhD, 1954. Postdoctoral fellow NSF, Panama, Brazil, 1954-55; postdoctoral rsch. assoc. Iowa State U., Ames, 1955-57; asst. prof. U. Kans., Lawrence, 1957-60, assoc. prof., 1960-65; sr. postdoctoral fellow NSF, Hawaii, Japan, 1963-64; prof. U. Kans., Lawrence, 1965-94, prof. emeritus, 1994—. Author: The Trichomycetes, Fungal Associates of Arthropods, 1986; contbr. 95 articles to profl. jours. Mem. Mycological Soc. Am. (life, pres. 1971-72, editor-in-chief 1965-70, William H. Weston award for tchg. excellence in mycology 1982, Disting. Mycologist award 1991), Brit. Mycological Soc., Japan Mycological Soc. (hon.). Office: U Kans Dept Of Botany Lawrence KS 66045

LICK, DALE WESLEY, academic administrator; b. Marlette, Mich., Jan. 7, 1938; s. John R. and Florence M. (Baxter) L.; m. Marilyn Kay Foster, Sept. 15, 1956; children: Lynette (dec.), Kitty, Diana, Ronald. BS with honors, Mich. State U., 1958, MS in Math, 1959; PhD in Math, U. Calif., Riverside, 1965. Research asst. physics Mich. State U., East Lansing, 1958; teaching asst. math. Mich. State U., 1959; instr., chmn. dept. math. Port Huron (Mich.) Jr. Coll., 1959-60; asst. to comptroller Mich. Bell Telephone Co., Detroit, 1961; instr. U. Redlands, 1961-63; teaching asst. math. U. Calif., Riverside, 1964-65; asst. prof. math. U. Tenn., Knoxville, 1965-67; postdoctoral fellow Brookhaven Nat. Lab., Upton, N.Y., 1967-68; assoc. prof. U. Tenn., 1968-69; assoc. prof., head dept. math. Drexel U., Phila., 1969-72; adj. assoc. prof. dept. pharmacology Med. Sch., Temple U., Phila., 1969-72; v.p. acad. affairs Russell Sage Coll., Troy, N.Y., 1972-74; prof. math. and computing scis. Old Dominion U., Norfolk, Va., 1974-78; also dean Old Dominion U. (Sch. Scis. and Health Professions); pres., prof. math. and computer sci. Ga. So. Coll., Statesboro, 1978-86; pres., prof. math. U. Maine, Orono, 1986-91; pres., prof. math. Fla. State U., Tallahassee, 1991-93, univ. prof., 1993—; Cert. in tng., mng. orgnl. change. Author: Fundamentals of Algebra, 1970; contbr. articles to profl. jours. Bd. dirs. Statesboro/Coll. Symphony, 1978-86, Statewide Health Coordinating Coun. Va., 1976-78; chmn. higher edn. adv. bd. Reorganized Ch. of Jesus Christ of Latter Day Sts., 1986—; mem. planning com. Bulloch Meml. Hosp., 1979-86; active Coastal Empire coun. Boy Scouts Am., 1982-86, Katalidin coun., 1986-91; bd. dirs. Health Care Ctrs. Am., Virginia Beach, Va., 1978, Ea. Va. Health Systems Agy., 1976-78; chmn., bd. dirs. Assembly Against Hunger and Malnutrition, 1977-78, pres., 1977-78. Mem. AAUP, AAAS, Am. Math. Soc., Math. Assn. Am., Am. Assn. Univ. Adminstrs., Am. Soc. Allied Health Professions, Am. Assn. State Colls. and Univs. (chmn. com. agr. resources and rural devel. 1981-86), Am. Assn. Higher Edn., Sigma Xi, Phi Kappa Phi, Pi Mu Epsilon (governing coun. 1972-77), Beta Gamma Sigma, Pi Sigma Epsilon. Mem., high priest Reorganized LDS Ch. Office: Learning Systems Inst 205 Dodd Hall Tallahassee FL 32306-4041

LICK, WILBERT JAMES, mechanical engineering educator; b. Cleve., June 12, 1933; s. Fred and Hulda (Sunntag) L.; children—James, Sarah. B.A.E., Rensselaer Poly. Inst., 1955, M.A.E., 1957, Ph.D., 1958. Asst. prof. Harvard, 1959-66; sr. research fellow Calif. Inst. Tech., 1966-67; mem. faculty Case Western Res. U., 1967-79, prof. earth scis., 1970-79, chmn. dept., 1973-76; prof. mech. engring. U. Calif.-Santa Barbara, 1979—, chmn. dept., 1982-84. Home: 1236 Camino Meleno Santa Barbara CA 93111-1007 Office: U Calif Dept Mech & Environ Engring Santa Barbara CA 93106

LICKHALTER, MERLIN EUGENE, architect; b. St. Louis, May 4, 1934; s. Frank E. and Sophia (Geller) L.; m. Harriet Braen, June 9, 1957; children: Debra, Barbara. BArch, MIT, 1957. Registered arch., Mo., Ill., Calif., Fla., Mich., Wis., Nev., Tex., Ala., Okla., Va. Ptnr. Drake Partnership, Architects, St. Louis, 1961-77; pres. JRB Architects, Inc., St. Louis, 1977-81; sr. v.p., mng. dir. Stone, Marraccini & Patterson, St. Louis, 1981-93; sr. v.p., dir. Cannon, 1993—; owner, pres. mgmt. program Harvard U. Bus. Sch., 1992; cons. Dept. Def., Washington, 1977-78; lectr. Washington U. Sch. Medicine, 1989—. Trustee United Hebrew Cong., St. Louis, 1980-88, 93—; exec. com. bd. dirs. Arts & Edn. Coun. St. Louis, 1991—. Capt. U.S. Army, 1957-59. Recipient Renovation Design award St. Louis Producers Coun., 1976, USAF Europe Design Award, 1990. Mem. AIA (nat. acad. architect for health, chmn. 1993), Am. Hosp. Assn., Am. Assn. for Health Planning, St. Louis Regional Growth Assn., Hawthorn Found., St. Louis Club, St. Louis Ambs., Frontenac Racquet Club, Masons. Jewish. Home: 2 Warson Ln Ladue MO 63124-1251 Office: Cannon One City Ctr Saint Louis MO 63101

LICKLE, WILLIAM CAUFFIEL, banker; b. Wilmington, Del., Aug. 2, 1929; m. Renee Carpenter Kitchell, Nov. 24, 1950; children: Sydney Cauffiel Lindley, Garrison duPont, Ashley L. O'Neil, Kemble L. O'Donnell. BA, U. Va., 1951, LLB, 1953. Bar: Va. 1953. Chmn., CEO Laird, Bissell & Meeds, Inc., 1952-73; sr. v.p. Dean Witter & Co. Inc., 1973-77; chmn., CEO Del. Trust Co., Wilmington, 1977-88, J.P. Morgan Fla., 1989-93; chmn., J.P. Morgan Internat. Holdings, 1989-92; vice chmn. M.P. Morgan Del., 1989-92; chmn. Register Transfer Co., 1963-65; bd. dirs. Bessemer Trust Co., 1974-88, Gen. Recreation Corp., 1974-78, Marvin Palmer Assoc., 1993—, Ashbridge Investment Mgmt. Del. Blue Cross-Blue Shield, 1963-68, Med. Ctr., 1965—, Better Bus. Bur., 1966-72; trustee Thomas Jefferson U., Phila., 1971-78, Winterthur Mus., 1989-94; bd. dirs. Boys' Club Wilmington, 1963—,

Breeder's Cup Ltd., Lexington, Ky., 1984-95; commr. New Castle County (Del.) Airport, 1964-67, New Castle County Transp. Commn., 1967-69; pres. U. Va. Alumni Assn., 1987-94; spl. asst. Gov.'s Econ. Devel. for State of Del., 1987-91; bd. dirs. Raymond F. Kravis Ctr., Palm Beach, Fl., 1990-95. Clubs: Vicmead Hunt (del.); Wilmington Country (del.), Everglades, Bath and Tennis (Palm Beach); Saratoga Golf and Polo, Reading Room (Saratoga, N.Y.); Springdale Hall (Camden, S.C.); Coral Beach (Paget, Bermuda). Home: 568 Island Dr Palm Beach FL 33480-4747

LIDDELL, JANE HAWLEY HAWKES, civic worker; b. Newark, Dec. 8, 1907; d. Edward Zeh and Mary Everett (Hawley) Hawkes; AB, Smith Coll., 1931; postgrad. in art history, Harvard U., 1933-35; MA, Columbia U., 1940; Carnegie fellow Sorbonne, Paris, 1937; m. Donald M. Liddell, Jr., Mar. 30, 1940; children: Jane Boyer, D. Roger Brooke. Pres., Planned Parenthood Essex County (N.J.), 1947-50; trustee Prospect Hill Sch. Girls, Newark, 1946-50; mem. adv. bd., publicity and public relations chmn. N.J. State Mus., Trenton, 1952-60; sec., then v.p. women's br. N.J. Hist. Soc.; women's aux. prodn. chmn. Englewood (N.J.) Hosp., 1959-61; pres. Dwight Sch. Girls Parents Assn., 1955-57; v.p. Englewood Sch. Boys Parents Assn., 1958-60; mem. Altar Guild, women's aux. bd., rector's adv. council St. Paul's Episcopal Ch., Englewood, 1954-59; bd. dir. N.Y. State Soc. of Nat. Soc. Colonial Dames, 1961-67, rep. conf. Patriotic and Hist. Socs., 1964—; bd. dirs. Huguenot Soc. Am., 1979-86, regional v.p., 1979-82, historian, 1983-84, co-chmn. Tercentennial Book, 1983-85; bd. dirs. Soc. Daus. Holland Dames, 1965-82; nat. jr. v.p. Dames of Loyal Legion, USA; bd. dirs., mem. publs. com. Daus. Cin., 1966-72; bd. dirs. Ch. Women's League Patriotic Service, 1962—, pres., 1968-70, 72-74; bd. dirs., chmn. grants com. Youth Found., N.Y.C., 1974—; chmn. for Newark, Smith Coll. 75th Ann. Fund, 1948-50; pres. North N.J. Smith Club, 1956-58; pres. Smith Coll. Class 1931, 1946-51, 76-81, editor 50th anniversary book, 1980-81. Author: (with others) Huguenot Refugees in the Settling of Colonial America, 1982-85; contbr. The Dutch Contribution to the Development of Early Manhattan, 1969. Recipient various commendation awards. Republican. Mem. Colonial Dames Am. (N.Y.C. chpt.). Clubs: Colony, City Gardens, Church (N.Y.C.); Jr. League N.Y.; N.Y. Jr. League; Needle and Bobbin, Nat. Farm and Garden . Editor: Maine Echoes, 1961; research and editor asst., Wartime Writings of American Revolution Officers, 1972-75.

LIDDELL, W. KIRK, specialty contracting and distribution company executive, lawyer; b. Lancaster, Pa., July 24, 1949; m. Pamela E. Trow; four children. AB in Econs. magna cum laude, Princeton U., 1971; MBA, U. Chgo., 1976, JD, 1976. Assoc. Covington & Burling, Washington, 1976-80; gen. counsel, v.p. AC and S Inc/Irex Corp., Lancaster, 1980-83; pres., chief exec. officer Irex Corp., 1984—; bd. dirs. High Industries Inc.; Chmn. Lancaster City Ptnrship., 1986; chmn. Lancaster County C. of C. & Industry, 1991; bd. dirs., fin. com. Pa. C. of C. & Industry; bd. dirs. The Lancaster Alliance; bd. dirs., v.p. Econ. Devel. Co. Lancaster County; chmn. United Way of Lancaster County, 1995; Nat. Football Found. Served as lt. USAR, 1971-73. Leon Carol Marshall scholar U. Chgo. Grad. Sch. Bus., 1974-76. Office: Irex Corp 120 N Lime St Lancaster PA 17602-2951

LIDDICOAT, RICHARD THOMAS, JR., professional society administrator; b. Kearsarge, Mich., Mar. 2, 1918; s. Richard Thomas and Carmen (Williams) L.; m. Mary Imogene Hibbard, Sept. 21, 1939. BS in Geology, U. Mich., 1939, MS in Mineralogy, 1940; grad. gemologist, Gemological Inst. Am., 1941; MS in Meteorology, Calif. Inst. Tech., 1944. Cert. gemologist (hon.) Am. Gem Soc. With Gemological Inst. Am., L.A., 1940-42, 46-76, Santa Monica, Calif., 1976—; dir. edn. Gemological Inst. Am., 1942, 46-49, asst. dir., 1950-52, exec. dir., 1952-83, pres., 1970-83, chmn. bd., 1983—, also author courses; editor Gem and Gemology, 1952—; hon. mem. rsch. staff L.A. Mus. Natural History, 1968—; U.S. dep. to Internat. Gem Conf., 1960, 64, 66, 68, 70, 72, 75, 77, 79, 81, 83, 85, 89; del. Pres.'d Conf. on Small Bus., 1957. Author: Handbook of Gem Identification, 12th edit, 1987, (with others) The Diamond Dictionary, 1960, 2d edit., 1977, (with Copeland) Jewelers Manual, 2d edit, 1967; numerous articles.; contbr. to Ency. Britannica Jr., Ency. Americana, McGraw-Hill Ency. of Sci. and Tech. Trustee Nat. Home Study Coun., 1988-88. Recipient Lifetime Achievement award Modern Jeweler's mag., 1985, award Internat. Soc. Appraisers, 1985, Spl. award Internat. Colored Stone Assn., 1984, Lifetime Achievement award Morris B. Zale, 1987; named Man of Yr., Consol. Jewelers Assn. Greater N.Y., 1984; named to Nat. Home Study Coun. Hall of Fame, 1991; Liddicoatite species of tourmaline group named for him. Fellow Mineral. Soc. Am., Geol. Soc. Am., Gem Assn. Gt. Britain (hon.); mem. AAAS, Am. Gem Soc. (supr. ednl. sessions ann. conclaves 1948-83, Shipley award 1976), Am. Gem Trade Assn. (hon.), Gem Assn. Australia (hon. v.p.), Gem Testing Lab. Gt. Britain (1st hon. life mem.), Bel Air Country Club (bd. dirs. 1980-83, Twenty-Four Karat Club (N.Y.C. and So. Calif.), Sigma Xi, Sigma Gamma Epsilon. Developer system of diamond grading. Home: 1484 Allenford Ave Los Angeles CA 90049-3614 Office: Gemological Inst Am 1660 Stewart St Santa Monica CA 90404-4020

LIDDLE, ALAN CURTIS, architect; b. Tacoma, Mar. 10, 1922; s. Abram Dix and Myrtle (Maytum) L. B.Arch., U. Wash., 1948; postgrad., Eidgenoissche Technische Hochschule, Zurich, Switzerland, 1950-51. Asst. prof. architecture U. Wash., 1954-55; prin. Liddle & Jones, Tacoma, 1957-67, Alan Liddle (architects), Tacoma, 1967-90, Liddle & Jacklin, Tacoma, 1990—. Architect oceanography bldgs, U. Wash., 1967, Tacoma Art Mus., 1971, Charles Wright Acad., Tacoma, 1962, Pacific Nat. Bank Wash., Auburn, 1965. Pres. bd. Allied Arts Tacoma, 1963-64, Civic Arts Commn. Tacoma-Pierce County, 1969; commr. Wash. Arts Commn., 1971; Bd. dirs. Tacoma Art Mus., Tacoma Zool. Soc., Tacoma Philharmonic, Inc. Served with AUS, 1943-46. Fellow A.I.A. (pres. S.W. Wash. chpt. 1967-68); mem. Wash. Hist. Soc., U. Wash. Alumni Assn. (all life). Home: 12735 Gravelly Lake Dr SW Tacoma WA 98499-1459 Office: 703 Pacific Ave Tacoma WA 98402-5207

LIDDY, RICHARD A., insurance company executive; b. 1935. BS, Iowa State U., 1957. V.p. ops. Conn. Gen. Life, Hartford, 1957-82; exec. v.p. Continental Corp., 1982-88; pres., COO, now pres., CEO Gen. Am. Life Ins. Co., St. Louis, 1988—. Office: Gen Am Life Ins Co 700 Market St Saint Louis MO 63101-1829 also: Repertory Theatre St Louis PO Box 191730 Saint Louis MO 63119-7730*

LIDE, DAVID REYNOLDS, science editor; b. Gainesville, Ga., May 25, 1928; s. David Reynolds and Laura Kate (Simmons) L.; m. Mary Ruth Lomer, Nov. 5, 1955 (div. Dec. 1988); children: David Alston, Vanessa Grace, James Hugh, Quentin Robert; m. Bettijoyce Breen, 1988. BS, Carnegie Inst. Tech., 1949; PhD, Harvard U., 1952, AM, 1951. Physicist Nat. Bur. Standards, Washington, 1954-63, chief molecular spectroscopy sect., 1963-69; dir. standard reference data Nat. Bur. Standards, Gaithersburg, Md., 1969-88; editor-in-chief Handbook of Chemistry and Physics, CRC Press, 1988—; pres. Com. on Data for Sci. and Tech., Paris, 1986-90. Editor: Jour. Phys. and Chem. Reference Data, 1972-92; author: Basic Laboratory and Industrial Chemicals, 1993, Handbook of Organic Solvents, 1995, (with G.W.A. Milne) Handbook of Data on Organic Compounds, 3rd edit., 1993, (with H.V. Kehiaian) Handbook of Thermophysical and Thermochemical Data, 1994, (with G.W.A. Milne) Names, Synonyms, and Structures of Organic Compounds, 1995, (with G.W.A. Milne) Handbook of Data on Common Organic Compounds, 1995. Recipient Skolnik award for Chem. Info., Am. Chem. Soc., 1988, Patterson-Crane award, 1991, Presdl. Rank award in sr. exec. svc., 1986. Mem. Internat. Union Pure and Applied Chemistry (pres. phys. chemistry div. 1983-87). Achievements include use of microwave spectroscopy for studying hindered internal rotation, explanation of HCN laser. Home and Office: 13901 Riding Loop Dr North Potomac MD 20878-3879

LIDICKER, WILLIAM ZANDER, JR., zoologist, educator; b. Evanston, Ill., Aug. 19, 1932; s. William Zander and Frida (Schroeter) L.; m. Naomi Ishino, Aug. 18, 1956 (div. Oct., 1982); children: Jeffrey Roger, Kenneth Paul; m. Louise N. DeLonzor, June 5, 1989. B.S., Cornell U., 1953; M.S., U. Ill., 1954, Ph.D., 1957. Instr. zoology, asst. curator mammals U. Calif., Berkeley, 1957-59; asst. prof., asst. curator U. Calif., 1959-65, assoc. prof., assoc. curator, 1965-69; assoc. dir. Mus. Vertebrate Zoology, 1968-81, acting dir., 1974-75, prof. zoology, curator mammals, 1969-89, prof. integrative biology, curator of mammals, 1989-94, prof., curator emeritus, 1994—. Contbr. articles to profl. jours. Bd. dirs. No. Calif. Com. for Environ. Info., 1971-77; bd. trustees BIOSIS, 1987-92, chmn., 1992; N.Am. rep. steering com., sect. Mammalogy IUBS, UNESCO, 1978-89; chmn. rodent specialist group Species Survival Commn., IUCN, 1980-89; mem. sci. adv. bd. Marine World Found. at Marine World Africa USA, 1987—; pres. Dehnel-Petrusewicz Meml. Fund, 1985—. Fellow AAAS, Calif. Acad. Scis.; mem. Am. Soc. Mammalogists (dir., 2d v.p. 1974-76, pres. 1976-78, C.H. Merriam award 1986, elected hon. mem. 1995), Am. Soc. Naturalists, Berkeley Folk Dancers Club (pres. 1969, tchr. 1984—), Westwind Internat. Folk Ensemble (dancer 1994—), others. Office: U Calif Mus Vertebrate Zoology Berkeley CA 94720

LIDOW, ERIC, electrical parts manufacturing company executive; b. Vilnius, Lithuania, Dec. 22, 1912; came to U.S., 1937, naturalized, 1941; s. Leon and Rachel (Schwartz) L.; m. Judith Margolis, July 2, 1939 (div. 1952); 1 son, Alan; m. Elizabeth Hay, Oct. 1952; children: Derek Balfour, Alexander. M. Elec. Engring., Technische Hochschule, Berlin, Germany, 1937. Elec. engr. Super Electric Co., Berlin, Germany, 1937; elec. devel. engr. Emby Products Cal., 1939-41; co-founder, v.p. Selenium Corp. Am., 1941-46; with Internat. Rectifier Corp., El Segundo, Calif., 1946—, now pres., chmn. bd., also dir. corp. and domestic and fgn. subsidiaries.; Mem. Assos. Calif. Inst. Tech. Bd. dirs. Lidow Found.; trustee City of Hope, Los Angeles County Mus. Art. Sr. mem. IEEE; mem. Am. Technion Soc. (v.p.). Achievements include patents in semiconductors. Home: 454 Cuesta Way Los Angeles CA 90077-3434 Office: Internat Rectifier Corp 233 Kansas St El Segundo CA 90245-4316*

LIDTKE, DORIS KEEFE, computer science educator; b. Bottineau County, N.D., Dec. 6, 1929; d. Michael J. and Josephine (McDaniels) Keefe; m. Vernon L. Lidtke, Apr. 21, 1951. BS, U. Oreg., 1952; MEd cum laude, Johns Hopkins U., 1974; PhD, U. Oreg., 1979. Programmer analyst Shell Devel. Co., Emeryville, Calif., 1955-59, U. Calif., Berkeley, 1960-62; asst. prof. Lansing (Mich.) Community Coll., 1963-68; ednl. specialist Johns Hopkins U., Balt., 1968; assoc. program mgr. NSF, Washington, 1984-85; program dir., 1992-93; sr. mem. tech. staff Software Productivity Consortium, Reston, Va., 1987-88; asst. prof. Towson State U., Balt., 1968-80, assoc. prof., 1980-90, prof. computer sci., 1990—. Named Outstanding Educator, Assn. for Ednl. Data Systems, 1986. Mem. Assn. for Computing Machinery (edn. bd. 1980—, coun. 1984-86, 94—, spl. interest group bd. 1985—, chair 1994—, Recognition Svc. award 1978, 83, 85, 86, 90, 91, Outstanding Contbn. award 1995), Computer Soc. of IEEE (Outstanding Contbn. award 1986, 92), Nat. Ednl. Computer Conf. (steering com., vice chmn. 1983-85, chmn. 1985-89, Recognition award 1988, 92, 95), Computing Scis. Accreditation Bd. (v.p. 1993-95, pres. 1995—). Home: 4806 Wilmslow Rd Baltimore MD 21210-2328 Office: Towson State U Computer & Info Scis Baltimore MD 21204

LIDTKE, VERNON LEROY, history educator; b. Avon, S.D., May 4, 1930; s. Albert William and Aganeta (Boese) L.; m. Doris Eileen Keefe, Apr. 21, 1951. B.A., U. Oreg., 1952, M.A., 1955; Ph.D., U. Calif., Berkeley, 1962. Tchr. high sch. Riddle, Oreg., 1953-55; instr. social sci. U. Calif., Berkeley, 1960-62; asst. prof. history Mich. State U., 1962-66, asso. prof., 1966-68; vis. asst. prof. U. Calif., Berkeley, 1963; asso. prof. Johns Hopkins U., 1968-73, prof., 1973—, chmn. dept. history, 1975-79; chair Friends of the German Historical Inst., Washington, 1991-94; chair Modern European Sect., Am. Hist. Assn., 1992. Author: The Outlawed Party: Social Democracy in Germany, 1878-1890, 1966, The Alternative Culture: Socialist Labor in Imperial Germany, 1985; editorial bd.: Jour. Modern History, 1973-76, Central European History, 1982-89, Internat. Labor and Working Class History, 1984-89; contbr. articles to profl. jours. Fulbright research fellow, 1959-60, 66-67; Nat. Endowment Humanities fellow, 1969-70; fellow Wissenschaftekolleg zu Berlin, 1987-88. Mem. AAUP, Am. Hist. Assn., Conf. Group for Cen. European History (v.p. 1985, pres. 1986), Conf. Group German Politics (officer 1975-83), Johns Hopkins Club. Home: 4806 Wilmslow Rd Baltimore MD 21210-2328 Office: Johns Hopkins U Dept History Baltimore MD 21218

LIDZ, CHARLES WILMANNS, sociologist; b. Balt., Feb. 1, 1946; s. Theodore and Ruth (Wilmanns) L.; m. Christine MacDougall, June 18, 1967 (div. 1978); m. Lynn C. Brown, May 26, 1979; children: James H. Carwile, Heather M. Carwile, Molly E.M. Lidz. BA, Yale U., 1967; MA, Harvard U., 1968, PhD, 1974. Asst. prof. psychiatry and sociology U. Pitts., 1974-80, assoc. prof., 1980-86, prof., 1986—, assoc. dir. rsch. Ctr. for Med. Ethics, 1987—. Editor, Qualitative Sociology, 1987-91; co-author: Connections: Notes from the Heroin World, 1974, Heroin, Deviance and Morality, 1980, Informed Consent: A Study..., 1984, Informed Consent: Legal Theory and Clinical Practice, 1987, The Erosion of Autonomy in Long-Term Care, 1992. Co-founder New Haven Half-Way House, 1967; bd. dirs. Am. Chronic Pain Assn., Rocklin, Calif., 1982—, pres., 1987, 89; bd. dirs. Transitional Svcs., Inc., Pitts., 1986-93, 95—, v.p., 1991-92. Grantee NIMH, 1976-79, 85-94, Pres. Commn. on Bioethics, 1981-82, Retirement Rsch. Found., 1987-89, MacArthur Found., 1990—. Mem. Soc. for Study of Social Problems, Am. Sociol. Assn. Office: WPIC/U of Pitts 3811 Ohara St Pittsburgh PA 15213-2593

LIEB, ELLIOTT HERSHEL, physicist, mathematician, educator; b. Boston, July 31, 1932; s. Sinclair M. and Clara (Rosenstein) L.; m. Christiane Fellbaum; children: Alexander, Gregory. BSc, MIT, 1953; PhD, U. Birmingham, Eng., 1956; DSc (hon.), U. Copenhagen, 1979; Dr. (hon.), Ecole Poly. Fed. Lausanne, Switzerland, 1995. With IBM Corp., 1960-63; sr. lectr. Fourah Bay Coll., Sierra Leone, 1961; mem. faculty Yeshiva U., 1963-66, Northeastern U., 1966-68; mem. faculty MIT, Cambridge, 1968-75, prof. physics, 1963-68, prof. math., 1968-73, prof. math. and physics, 1973—; prof. math. and physics Princeton (N.J.) U., 1975—. Author: (with D.C. Mattis) Mathematical Physics in One Dimension, 1966, (with B. Simon and A. Wightman) Studies in Mathematical Physics; also articles. Recipient Boris Pregel award chem. physics N.Y. Acad. Scis., 1970; Dannie Heineman prize for mathematical physics Am. Inst. Physics and Am. Phys. Soc., 1978; Prix Scientifique, Union des Assurances de Paris, 1985; Birkhoff prize Am. Math. Soc. and Soc. Indsl. Applied Math., 1988; Max-Planck medal German Phys. Soc., 1992; Guggenheim Found. fellow, 1972, 78. Fellow Am. Phys. Soc.; mem. NAS, Austrian Acad. Scis., Danish Royal Acad., Am. Acad. Arts and Scis., Internat. Assn. Math. Physics (pres. 1982-84). Office: Princeton U Jadwin Hall-Physics Dept PO Box 708 Princeton NJ 08544-0708

LIEB, MICHAEL, English educator, humanities educator. AB in Eng. Lit., Rutgers U., 1962, AM in Eng. Lit., 1964, PhD in Eng. Lit., 1967; student, U. Iowa, 1962-63, U. Chgo. Divinity Sch., 1974-75, Spertus Coll. of Judaica, 1987-92. Asst. prof. Eng. Coll. of William and Mary, Williamsburg, Va., 1967-70; assoc. prof. Eng. U. Ill., Chgo., 1970-75, prof. Eng., 1975-88, rsch. prof. humanities, prof. Eng., 1988—; vis. professorial lectr. U. Chgo. Divinity Sch., 1979; bd. dirs. Friends of Milton's Cottage; mem. exec. com. U. Chgo. Renaissance Seminar, 1977—; mem. exec. com. Divsn. 17th Century Eng. Lit. MLA, 1982-86, Divsn. Religious Approaches to Lit., 1987-91; mem. exec. com. Ctr. Renaissance Studies Newberry Libr., 1979—, mem. com. Brit. Acad. Fellowships, 1982-83, mem. search com. for dir., 1984; mem. adv. com. 2d Internat. Milton Symposium, 1983, 4th, 1990; campus rep. Woodrow Wilson Found., 1982-83; mem. numerous coms. U. Ill. Author: The Dialectics of Creation: Patterns of Birth and Regeneration in Paradise Lost, 1970, Poetics of the Holy: A Reading of Paradise Lost, 1981 (James Holly Hanford award Milton Soc. Am.), The Sinews of Ulysses: Form and Convention in Milton's Works, 1989, The Visionary Mode: Biblical Prophecy, Hermeneutics and Cultural Change, 1991, Milton and the Culture of Violence, 1994; co-editor, contbg. author: Achievements of the Left hand: Essays on the Prose of John Milton, 1974, Eyes Fast Fixt: Current Perspectives in Milton Methodology, 1975, Literary Milton: Text, Pretext, Context, 1994, The Miltonic Samson, 1996; contbr. articles to profl. jours.; symposia speaker in field; panelist; invited speaker; cons. edit. bds., univ. presses, profl. jours., librs., depts. Eng., Comparative Lit., Divinity. Pres., co-founder Oak Park Housing Ctr., 1971-73, Advocate award 1992; mem. hon. com. Ill. Humanities Coun., 1986; mem. Am. Jewish Com. Academicians Seminar, Israel, 1986. NEH U. Tchrs. fellow, 1991-92, John Simon Guggenheim Meml. Found. fellow 1987-88, U. Ill. Chgo. Inst. for Humanities sr. fellow 1983, Newberry Libr. Nat. Endowment for Humanities sr. fellow 1981-82, NEH Younger Humanist Study fellow 1974-75; recipient Am. Coun. Learned Societies Grant-in-Aid, 1985, Am. Philosophical Soc. Grant-in-Aid, 1983, Folger Shakespeare Libr. fellow, 1970, 74; Honors Coll. U. Ill. Chgo. fellow 1986—; others. Mem. Milton Soc. Am. (chair James Holly Hanford awards com. 1991-93, treas. 1973-77, v.p. 1980, pres. 1981, honored scholar 1992), Modern Lang. Assn., Milton Soc. of Japan, Southeastern Renaissance Conf., Renaissance Soc. of Am., Calif. Renaissance Conf., Northeastern Modern Lang. Assn., Newberry Libr. Milton Seminar (co-founder, co-chair 1986—), Newberry Libr. Dante Lectures. Home: 212 S Ridgeland Ave Oak Park IL 60302-3226 Office: U Ill Chgo Dept Eng M/c 162 Chicago IL 60607

LIEBE, HANS J., electrical and communications engineer; b. Insterburg, Germany, Jan. 21, 1934. BSEE, Tech. U. West Berlin, 1957, MSEE, 1959, PhD in Elec. Engring., 1964. Sr. rsch. engr. Ntia-Inst. Tel. Sci. Recipient Humboldt award Fed. Rep. Germany, 1976, 77, Silver medal awards U.S. Dept. Commerce, 1984, 91. Fellow IEEE (Boulder-Denver local chpt. seminar talks 1966, 71, 76, 77). Office: Ntia Inst Tele Sci/S3 325 Broadway Boulder CO 80303*

LIEBELER, SUSAN WITTENBERG, lawyer; b. New Castle, Pa., July 3, 1942; d. Sherman K. and Eleanor (Klivans) Levine; BA, U. Mich., 1963, postgrad. U. Mich., 1963-64; LLB (Stein scholar), UCLA, 1966; m. Wesley J. Liebeler, Oct. 21, 1971; 1 child, Jennifer. Bar: Calif. 1967, Vt. 1972, D.C. 1988. Law clk. Calif. Ct. of Appeals, 1966-67; assoc. Gang, Tyre & Brown, 1967-68, Greenberg, Bernhard, Weiss & Karma, L.A., 1968-70; assoc. gen. counsel Rep. Corp., L.A., 1970-72; gen. counsel Verit Industries, L.A., 1972-73; prof. of law law sch. Loyola U., L.A., 1973-84; spl. counsel, chmn. John S. R. Shad, SEC, Washington, 1981-82; commr. U.S. Internat. Trade Commn. Washington, 1984-88, vice chmn., 1984-86, chmn., 1986-88; ptnr. Irell & Manella, L.A., 1988-94; sr. v.p. Legal Rsch. Network, Inc., L.A., 1994-95; pres. Lexpert Rsch. Svcs., L.A., 1995—; vis. prof. U. Tex., summer 1982; cons. Office of Policy Coordination, office of Pres.-elect, 1981-82; cons. U.S. Ry. Assn., 1975, U.S. EPA, 1974, U.S. Price Commn., 1972; mem. Adminstrv. Conf. U.S., 1986-88. Mem. editorial adv. bd. Regulation mag. CATO Inst. Mem. ABA, State Bar Calif. (treas., vice chair, chair exec. com. internat. law sect.), L.A. County Bar Assn., Practicing Law Inst. (internat. law adv. com.), ITC Trial Lawyers Assn., Washington Legal Found. (acad. adv. bd.), bd. dirs. Century City Hosp., adv. bd. U. Calif. Orientation in U.S.A. Law, Order of Coif. Jewish. Sr. editor UCLA Law Review, 1965-66; contbr. articles to legal publ.

LIEBENSON, HERBERT, economist, trade association executive; b. Chgo., July 26, 1920; s. Michael and Evelyn (Zimmerman) L.; m. Gloria Rachel Krasnow, Mar. 11, 1944; children: Lauren Ward, Lynn Green. B.A., Roosevelt U., 1948; postgrad., U. Chgo., 1948, Am. U., 1949-52. Research assoc. United Mineworkers Pension and Welfare Fund, Washington, 1948-52; employee benefit/labor relations analyst C. of C. U.S., Washington, 1952-58; with Nat. Small Bus. Assn., Washington, 1958—; v.p. Nat. Small Bus. Assn., 1958-80, pres., 1980-86, sr. cons., 1986—; exec. dir. Small Bus. Legis. Council, 1980-86, chmn. tech. for new products and jobs, 1986—; mem. exec. com., chmn. com. on taxation SBA Nat. Adv. Council, 1982-86; pres. del. White House Conf. on Small Bus., 1986; mem. Sec. Labor's mgmt. adv. com. on Landrum-Griffin Act, U.S. Employment Service Adv. Com.; mem. adv. com. on jobs Dept. Commerce Com. on Product Standards; alt. mem. Presdl. Pay Bd., 1973-74; mem. steering com. Nat. Com. to Preserve Family Bus., 1981; mem. nat. com. Am. Energy Week, 1981. Served with USAAF, 1942-46. Mem. Indsl. Relations Research Assn. (pres. chpt. 1961-62), Bus. Adv. Council Fed. Reports (bd. govs. 1970-85), Am. Soc. Assn. Execs. Jewish. Club: Internat. Home: 2703 Unicorn Ln NW Washington DC 20015-2233

LIEBER, CHARLES DONALD, publisher; b. Scheveningen, The Netherlands, Jan. 30, 1921; came to U.S., 1941, naturalized, 1944; s. Edmund Z. and Gabrielle (Lifczis) L.; m. Miriam Levin, July 17, 1960; children: John Nathan, James Edmund, George Theodore, Anne Gabrielle. Student, U. Brussels, 1938-40; B.A., New Sch. for Social Research, 1948. With H. Bittner & Co. (Pubs.), N.Y.C., 1947-49; with Alfred A. Knopf, Inc., 1949-52; dir. coll. dept. Random House, N.Y.C., 1952-64; pub. Atherton Press, N.Y.C., 1964-67; pres. Atherton Press, Inc., N.Y.C., 1967-70; v.p. Aldine-Atherton, Inc., N.Y.C., Chgo., 1971-72; pres. Lieber-Atherton, Inc., N.Y.C., 1972—; gen. mgr. Hebrew Pub. Co., 1980-85, pres., 1985—; pres. Lieber Publs., Inc., N.Y.C., 1981—. Author: (with A.D. Murphy) Great Events of World History, 1964; chmn. publ. com., mem. editl. bd. Reconstructionist mag., 1983-93. Chmn. West Side Jewish Cmty. Coun., Manhattan, 1978-82, mem.-at-large, 1974—; exec. bd. Jewish Reconstrn. Found., 1979-83, vice chmn., 1979-80, chmn., 1980-83, nat. bd. dirs., 1983-92; trustee St. Ann's Sch., 1983-89, Soc. for Advancement Judaism, 1974-90, treas., 1976-79, co-chmn., 1979-81; bd. dirs. Hebrew Arts Sch., 1974-82, Fedn. Reconstructionist Congregations, 1983-91; founding mem. Lenox Hill Club, 1957. Lt. AUS, 1942-46, CBI. Recipient Mordecai M. Kaplan award Jewish Reconstructionist Found., 1988. Mem. Coll. Pubs. Group (chmn. 1965-66), Assn. Jewish Book Pubs. (pres. 1988-90). Office: Hebrew Publishing Co PO Box 222 Spencertown NY 12165-0222

LIEBER, CHARLES SAUL, physician, educator; b. Antwerp, Belgium, Feb. 13, 1931; came to U.S., 1958, naturalized, 1966; s. Isaac and Lea (Maj) L.; m. M. A. Leo; children: Colette, Daniel, Leah, Samuel, Sarah. Candidate in natural and med. sci., U. Brussels, 1951, M.D., 1955. Intern, resident U. Hosp., Brugmann, Brussels, Belgium, 1954-56; research fellow med. found. Queen Elizabeth, 1956-58; research fellow Thorndike Meml. Lab., Harvard Med. Sch., 1958-60, instr., 1961; assoc. Harvard U., 1962; assoc. prof. medicine Cornell U., 1963-68; dir. liver disease and nutrition unit Bellevue Hosp., N.Y.C., 1963-68; chief sect. liver disease, nutrition and GI-Liver Tng. Program VA Hosp., Bronx, N.Y., 1968—; prof. medicine Mt. Sinai Sch. Medicine, 1969—, prof. pathology, 1976—, dir. Alcohol Research and Treatment Ctr., 1977—; assoc. vis. physician Cornell Med. div. Bellevue, Meml., James Ewing hosps., 1964-69; Am. Coll. Gastroenterology disting. lectr., 1978, Henry Baker lectr., 1979. Recipient award of Belgian Govt. for rsch. on gastric secretion, 1956, Rsch. Career Devel. award NIH, USPHS, 1964-68, E.M. Jellinek Meml. award, 1976, A. Boudreau award Laval U., 1977, W.S. Middleton award, 1977, Leahy Rsch. award, highest honor for med. rsch. Dept. Vets. Affairs, 1994. Fellow AAAS; mem. Assn. Am. Physicians, N.Y. Gastroent. Assn. (pres. 1974-75), Am. Soc. Biochemistry and Molecular Biology, ACP, Am. Inst. Nutrition, Am. Soc. Addictive Medicine (pres. 1974-77, Sci. Achievement award 1989), Assn. Clin. Biochemists (Kone award 1994), Am. Soc. Clin. Nutrition (McCollum award 1973, pres. 1975-76, Robert H. Herman Memorial award 1993), Am. Coll. Nutrition (Outstanding Achievement award, 1990), Am. Soc. Clin. Investigation, Am. Soc. Pharmacol. Exptl. Therapy, Am. Gastroent. Assn. (Disting. Achievement award 1973, Hugh R. Butt award for liver/nutrition 1992), Research Soc. on Alcoholism (pres. 1977-79, Sci. Excellence award 1980, Disting. Svc. award 1992), Am. Coll. Nutrition (Outstanding Achievement award 1990, Am. Assn. Study Liver Diseases. Home: 6 Johnson Ave Englewd Clfs NJ 07632-2107 Office: 130 W Kingsbridge Rd Bronx NY 10468-3992

LIEBER, DAVID LEO, university president; b. Stryj, Poland, Feb. 20, 1925; came to U.S., 1927, naturalized, 1936; s. Max and Gussie (Jarmush) L.; m. Esther Kobre, June 10, 1945; children—Michael, Daniel, Deborah, Susan. B.A., CCNY, 1944; B.Hebrew Lit., Jewish Theol. Sem. Am., 1944, M.Hebrew Lit., 1948, D. Hebrew Lit., 1951; M.A., Columbia, 1947; postgrad., U. Wash., 1954-55, UCLA, 1961-63; L.D.H. hon., Hebrew Union Coll., 1982—. Ordained rabbi, 1948. Rabbi, 1948, Sinai Temple, Los Angeles, 1950-54; dir. (B'nai B'rith Hillel), Seattle, Cambridge, 1954-56; dean students U. Judaism, Los Angeles, 1956-63; Samuel A. Fryer prof. Bible, pres. U. Judaism, 1963-92, Skovron Disting. Svc. prof. Bibl. lit., 1990—, pres. emeritus, 1992—; pres. emeritus U. Judaism, L.A., 1992—; lectr. Hebrew UCLA, 1957-90; vice chancellor Jewish Theol. Sem., 1972-92; mem. exec. coun. Rabbinical Assembly, 1966-69, v.p., 1994-96, pres., 1996—; vice chmn. Am. Jewish Com., L.A., 1972-75; bd. dirs. Jewish Fedn. Coun., L.A., 1980-86, bd. govs., 1986—. Mem. editorial bd.: Conservative Judaism, 1968-70. Served as chaplain USAF, 1951-53. Recipient Torch of Learning award Hebrew U., 1984. Mem. Assn. Profs. Jewish Studies (dir. 1970-71), Phi Beta Kappa. Office: U Judaism 15600 Mulholland Dr Los Angeles CA 90077-1519

LIEBER, DAVID LESLIE, journalist; b. Gastonia, N.C., June 26, 1957; s. Stanley J. and Denise (Berwald) L.; m. Karen Pasciutti, Feb. 18, 1995;

stepchildren: Desiree Lauren, Jonathan Lawrence. BA in Am. Civilization, U. Pa., 1979. Feature writer, media columnist Ft. Myers (Fla.) News-Press, 1980-81; statehouse reporter Charleston (W.Va.) Gazette, 1981-83; staff writer Phila. Inquirer, 1983-93; metro columnist, mem. editl. bd. Ft. Worth (Tex.) Star-Telegram, 1993—. Named Outstanding Journalist W.Va. Trial Lawyers Assn., 1982-83; recipient Smolar award Coun. Jewish Fedns., 1989, Best Commentary award Assn. Black Communicators, 1995. Mem. Investigative Reporters and Editors, Soc. Profl. Journalists, Pen and Pencil, Nat. Soc. Newspaper Columnists (1st prize writing contest 1995; sec./newsletter editor), Lonesome Dove Cemetery Assn. Avocation: political memorabilia collector. Office: Ft Worth Star-Telegram 3201 Airport Fwy Bedford TX 76021-6036

LIEBER, ROBERT JAMES, political science educator, writer; b. Chgo., Sept. 29, 1941; m. Nancy Isaksen; 2 children. BA in Polit. Sci. with high honors, U. Wis., 1963; postgrad. in Polit. Sci., U. Chgo., 1963-64; PhD in Govt., Harvard U., 1968; postgrad. St. Antony's Coll., Oxford (Eng.) U., 1969-70. Asst. prof. Polit. Sci. U. Calif., Davis, 1968-72, assoc. prof., 1972-77, chmn. dept. Polit. Sci., 1975-76, 77-80, prof., 1977-81; prof. Georgetown U., Washington, 1982—, chmn. dept. govt., 1990-96; vis. prof. Oxford U., 1969, Fudan U., Shanghai, 1988; rsch. assoc. Ctr. Internat. Affairs, Harvard U., 1974-75; cons. U.S. Dept. State and Dept. Def., 1975—. Author: British Politics and European Unity, 1970, Theory and World Politics, 1972, Oil and the Middle East War: Europe in the Energy Crisis, 1976, The Oil Decade: Conflict and Cooperation in the West, 1983, No Common Power: Understanding International Relations, 1988, 3rd edit., 1995; co-author: Contemporary Politics: Europe, 1976; editor, contbg. author: Eagle Entangled: U.S. Foreign Policy in a Complex World, 1979, Eagle Defiant: U.S. Foreign Policy in the 1980s, 1983, Will Europe Fight for Oil?, 1983, Eagle Resurgent? The Reagan Era in American Foreign Policy, 1987; co-editor, contbg. author: Eagle in a New World: American Grand Strategy in the Post-Cold War Era, 1992; contbr. articles to Harper's, Politique, Etrangere, N.Y. Times, Washington Post, Christian Sci. Monitor, others, and profl. jours. Advanceman nat. campaign staff McCarthy for Pres., 1968; fgn. policy advisor presdl. campaigns of Sen. Edward Kennedy, 1979-80, Walter Mondale. 1984, Bill Clinton, 1991-92; coord. Mid. East Issues presdl. campaign Michael Dukakis, 1988. Woodrow Wilson fellow, 1963, fellow NDEA, 1963-64, Harvard U., 1964-68, Social Sci. Rsch. Coun., 1969-70, Coun. Fgn. Rels., 1972-73, Guggenheim Found., 1973-74, Rockefeller Found., 1978-79, Wilson Ctr. Smithsonian Inst., 1980-81, Ford Found., 1981; vis. fellow Atlantic Inst. Internat. Affairs, Paris, 1978-79; guest scholar Brookings Inst., 1981. Mem. Coun. on Fgn. Rels., Internat. Inst. for Strategic Studies, Phi Beta Kappa. Office: Georgetown U Dept of Government Washington DC 20057

LIEBER, ROBERT M., lawyer, vineyard owner; b. Bklyn., Jan. 29, 1942; s. Milton D. and Hermene L. (Dryer) L.; m. Betty Lue Fisher, June 30, 1963 (div.); children: Terry Ellen, Hilarie Anne. AB in History, Antioch Coll., 1963; LLB, U. Calif., Berkeley, 1966. Bar: Calif. 1967, U.S. Ct. Appeals (6th cir.) 1967, U.S. Ct. Appeals (9th, 10th and D.C. cirs.) 1968, U.S. Supreme Ct. 1972. Atty. Nat. Labor Rels. Bd., Washington, 1966-69; assoc. Littler, Mendelson & Fastiff, San Francisco, 1969-70; ptnr. Littler, Mendelson, Fastiff, Tichy & Mathiasen, San Francisco, 1971—. Contbg. author: McGraw Hill Construction Business Handbook, 1985, Investigation of Substance Abuse in the Workplace, 1990. Mem. Meadowwood Country Club. Avocation: grape grower, wine prodr. Office: Littler Mendelson Fastiff Tichy & Mathiasen 650 California St San Francisco CA 94108-2702

LIEBER, STANLEY MARTIN See LEE, STAN

LIEBERGOTT, JACQUELINE W., academic administrator; b. Balt., Mar. 17, 1942; d. Mendel Stiebel and Jeane (Levin) Weis; m. Harvey Liebergott, June 20, 1965; children: Jessica Liebergott Hamblen, Cory. BA in Hearing and Speech Sci., U. Md., 1963; MS in Speech-Lang. Pathology, U. Pitts., 1966, PhD in Speech-Lang. Pathology, 1973. Lic. in speech-lang. pathology Commonwealth of Mass. Lectr. dept. speech and hearing U. Md., College Park, 1969-70; asst. prof. dept. comm. disorders Emerson Coll., Boston, 1970-73, assoc. prof. divsn. comm. disorders, 1973-79, prof. divsn. comm. disorders, 1979—, dean grad. studies, 1984-87, v.p., acad. dean, 1987-92, interim pres., 1992-93, pres., 1993—; manuscript reviewer in speech and hearing Grune and Stratton Pub. Co., 1972-73; manuscript reviewer in lang. Little Brown and Co., 1977; vis. assoc. prof. dept. comm. disorders Memphis (Tenn.) State U., summer 1974; co-chairperson conv. program com. Mass. Speech and Hearing Assn., 1978; cons. to ABT Assocs., Evaluating the Health Impact of Head Start, 1978-80; proposal reviewer Boston Univ. Lang. Conf., 1978, 84, 86; cons. on spl. edn. tng. in P.R., U.S. Office of Edn., Bur. Edn. of the Handicapped, 1979, cons. and proposal reviewer divsn. pers. preparation, 1978, 79, 80, 84-88; study sect. reviewer Divsn. Communicative Diseases and Stroke, NIH, 1979, 80, 83, 84, 85; cons. in lang. Brookline Early Edn. Project, 1979-83; project cons. TADS, Chapel Hill, N.C., 1980; program evaluator Pre-Sch. Program, Chepecket, R.I., 1980; editl. advisor in speech and lang. Little Brown and Co., 1980-88; associated sci. staff Children's Hosp. Med. Ctr., Harvard Med. Sch., 1984—; program chairperson and responder Session on Lang. Disabilities, Boston U. Lang. Conf., 1984-85; proposal reviewer minority participation in higher edn. U.S. Dept. Edn., Office of Post-Secondary Edn., 1990-92; accreditation vis. team New Eng. Assn. Schs. and Colls., 1992; presenter and cons. in field. Mem. editl. bd. ACTA Symbolica, 1973-80, Applied Health and Behavioral Scis. Jour., 1977-80, Jour. Speech and Hearing Disorders, 1977-81, Jour. Speech and Hearing Rsch., 1981-85, Am. Speech and Hearing Assn., 1985-90; contbr. articles to profl. jours. chair staff com. Children's Ctr. Brookline, 1970-75; founding parent, mem. staff com. Newton After-Sch. Program, 1978-81; v.p., trustee Autism Soc., 1984—; trustee, mem. programming com. Boston Cable Access Bd., 1991—; trustee New Eng. Bus. Coun., 1992—, bd. mem., 1993—; bd. mem. Downtown Crossing Assn., 1994—, The Cambridge Partnership for Pub. Edn., 1994—; active Friends of the Pub. Garden and Boston Common, 1994—. Fellow Am. Coun. Edn. (fellowship selection com. 1991-92); mem. Am. Speech-Lang. and Hearing Assn. (com. on lang., subcom. on speech-lang. pathology svc. delivery with infants and toddlers 1987-90), Am. Assn. Higher Edn., Assn. Ind. Colls. and Univs. Mass., Mass. ACE/NIP, New Eng. Assn. Schs. and Coll. Inc. (liaison), New Eng. Coun., Mass. Women's Forum, Boston C. of C. Office: Emerson Coll Office of the Pres 100 Beacon St Boston MA 02116-1511

LIEBERMAN, ARCHIE, photographer, writer; b. Chgo., July 17, 1926; s. Sol and Rose (Schiff) L.; m. Esther Kraus, Jan. 11, 1948; children: Eric Joseph, Robert Charles Vories, Kurt Murrow. Student, Inst. Design, Chgo., 1946-48. Contract photographer Time Mag., Chgo., 1950-51; staff photographer Black Star Pub. Co., N.Y.C., 1951-61; adj. prof. Chgo. Theol. Sem., 1976-74; instr. Columbia Coll., Chgo., 1968-74. One man shows include Presbyn.-St. Luke's Hosp., Chgo., Chapel Hill Shopping Ctr., Akron, Ohio Mchts. Assn., Flint, Mich., Arie Crown Theater, Chgo., Carson Pirie Scott & Co., Chgo., Prudential Bldg., Chgo., Agr. U.S.A., Soviet Union, U. Ill., Lake Forest Coll., Kodak Gallery, Grand Central Sta., N.Y.C., Rizzoli Gallery, Chgo., U. Dubuque (retrospective), 1987, Dubuque Mus. Art, Lands End Gallery, Dodgeville, Wis., 1991, Ford Ctr. Fine Art-Knox Coll., 1993, Elveahjem Mus., Madison, Wis., 1994, Freeport Art Mus., 1994, Lake Forest Coll., 1995; group shows include Jewish Mus., N.Y.C., Tower Gallery, Chgo., Garrett Bible Inst., Evanston, Met. Mus. Art, N.Y.C., Expo '67, Montreal, Art Inst. Chgo., 1986, Photography in Fine Arts, N.Y.C., San Diego Mus. Photographic Arts, 1986, Mitchell Mus., Mt. Vernon, Ill., 1987, 88, The Art Inst. of Chgo., 1986, 92, numerous others; author, photographer: The Israelis, 1965 (One of Best 50 Books award), Farm Boy (Friends of Lit. award), Neighbors, 1993; photographer books: Shalom, A Solitary Life, The Future of Religions, The Eternal Life, Holy Holy Land, The Story of Israel, Chicago In Color, Chicago, God Make Me Brave For Life, (with Ray Bradbury) The Mummies of Guanajuato, Chicago: A Celebration, 1990; photojournalist for mags. including: Look, Life, Saturday Evening Post, Collier's, Ladies Home Jour., Fortune, London Illustrated, Redbook, Farm Jour., Pageant, Parade, Bus. Week, Am. Weekly, Venture, U.S. News & World Report, Newsweek, Paris Match, Chgo. Mag.; indsl. photographer for corps. including Inland Steel, Acme Steel, Lands' End, Harvester, Gould Inc., McDonald's, Motorola, Grumman Corp., Internat. Minerals & Chem. Corp.; advt. photographs for: Allstate Ins., Phillip Morris, Schlitz, United Airlines, Jack Daniel, others. Recipient Peter Lisagor award Headline Club of Sigma Delta Chi, 1980; Sinai Health Service award Mt. Sinai Hosp. Med. ctr., Chgo., 1985; various award U. Mo. Sch. Journalism. Clubs: Arts of Chgo., Chgo. Press, Tavern Club, Galena Artists Guild. Office: PO Box 61 Scales Mound IL 61075-0061 *People are not creative. There was only one creative act-The making of somethingout of a void-The creation itself. What people do is to discover that which hasalways been and position it in a new way. Therefore we must be discoverers to invent new things.*

LIEBERMAN, CAROL, healthcare marketing communications consultant, city planning administrator; b. St. Louis, June 14, 1938; d. Norman Leonard and Ethel (Silver) Mistachkin; m. Malcolm P. Cooper, Aug. 25, 1962 (div. June 1977); children: Lawrence, Edward, Marcus; m. Edward Lieberman, Apr. 1992. BS, U. Wis., 1959; MA, N.Y. Inst. Tech., 1992. Media buyer Lennen and Newell, Los Angeles, 1959-61; advt. mgr. Hartfield-Zodys, Los Angeles, 1961-62, Haggarty's, L.A., 1962-63; sales rep. Abbott Labs., Bklyn., 1974-75; edn. dir. N.Y. and N.J. Regional Transp. Program, N.Y.C., 1975-78; account exec. Med. Edn. Dynamics, Woodbridge, N.J., 1978-79; dir. program devel. Kallir, Phillips & Ross Info. Media, N.Y.C., 1979-81; exec. v.p. sales and mktg. Audio Visual Med. Mktg., N.Y.C., 1981-85; exec. v.p. Park Row Pubs./John Wiley & Sons Med. Div., N.Y.C., 1985-88; pres., prin. Park Row Pubs., N.Y.C., 1988-91; healthcare mktg. communications cons., Southampton, N.Y., 1991—; cons., prof. comms. and speech N.Y. Inst. Tech., 1991—; exec. dir. Bus. Improvement Dist., Riverhead, N.Y., 1994-95; exec. sec. Cardiopulmonary Bypass Consensus Panel, 1994—; cons. Am. Acad. Physician Assts., Washington, 1986-87, Am. Soc. Anesthesiologists, Chgo., 1986-88, Am. Acad. Family Physicians, 1987-91, Am. Psychiat. Assn., 1988, Am. Coll. Gen. Practitioners, 1988, N.Am. Soc. pacing and Electrophysiology, 1988-91, Cardiopulmonary Bypass Consensus Panel, 1993—. Editor pub. med. papers, med. films, med. jours. for pharmaceutical cos. Mem. Am. Women in Radio and TV, Soc. Tchrs. Family Medicine (cons.), Pharm. Advt. Council, Nat. Council Jewish Women, Hadassah. Avocations: tennis, writing fiction, classical piano. Home and Office: 41 Barkers Island Rd Southampton NY 11968-2702

LIEBERMAN, CHARLES, economist; b. Landsburg, Bavaria, Germany, July 25, 1948; s. Leo and Tola (Melcer) L.; m. Anne Rosenberg, Aug. 26, 1972; children: David, Michael, Jeremy. BS, MIT, 1970; AM in Econs., U. Pa., 1972, PhD in Econs., 1974. Asst. prof. U. Md., College Park, 1974-79; vis. assoc. prof. Northwestern U., Evanston, Ill., 1978-79; economist Fed. Res. Bank N.Y., N.Y.C., 1979-81; sr. economist Morgan Stanley, N.Y.C., 1981-83; v.p., sr. economist Shearson Lehman Bros., N.Y.C., 1983-86; mng. dir., dir. fin. market rsch. Chem. Securities Inc./Mfrs. Hanover Securities Corp., N.Y.C., 1986-96; chief economist The Global Bank, Chase Manhattan Bank, 1996—; econs. commentator CNBC. Author: (newsletter) Market Commentary; contbr. articles to profl. jours. Sgt. U.S. Army Res., 1970-76. Stonier fellow, 1973, Fellow NSF, 1971. Mem. Forecasters Club N.Y. (treas. 1987-89, v.p. 1990-91, pres. 1991-92), Money Marketeers NYU (bd. govs., v.p., pres. 1992-93). Jewish. Avocations: tennis, skiing, classical music. Office: Chase Securities 270 Park Ave New York NY 10017-2014 *Work hard, play hard, and enjoy life.*

LIEBERMAN, DAVID, law educator; b. Canton, Ohio, May 21, 1953; s. George Bernard and Sylvia (Klein) L.; m. Carol Louise Brownstein, Dec. 20, 1987; children: George, Hannah. BA with honors, Cambridge U., Eng., 1974, MA, 1978; PhD, U. London, Eng., 1980. Rsch. fellow St. Catharines Coll., Cambridge, Eng., 1978-82; fellow, lectr. Christ's Coll., Cambridge, Eng., 1982-83; acting prof. U. Calif., Berkeley, 1984-89, prof. law sch., 1989—. Author: Province of Legislation Determined, 1989. Rsch. fellow Am. Bar Found., 1978-79, Inst. Hist. Rsch., 1977-78; hon. rsch. fellow U. Coll., London U., 1986. Mem. Am. Soc. for Legal History, Internat. Soc. for Utilitarian Studies. Office: JSP Program 2240 Piedmont Ave Berkeley CA 94720*

LIEBERMAN, FREDRIC, ethnomusicologist, educator; b. N.Y.C., Mar. 1, 1940; s. Stanley and Bryna (Mason L.). MusB, U. Rochester, 1962; MA in Ethnomusicology, U. Hawaii, 1965; PhD in Music, UCLA, 1977; diploma in Electronics, Cleve. Inst. Electronics, 1973; cert. Inst. for Ednl. Mgmt., Harvard U., 1984. Asst. prof. music Brown U., Providence, 1968-75; assoc. prof. U. Wash., Seattle, 1975-83, chmn. dir. ethnomusicology, 1977-80, dir. sch. music, 1981-83; prof. U. Calif., Santa Cruz, 1983—, dir. dept. arts, 1983-85, provost Porter Coll., 1983-85; chmn. Bd. of Studies in Music, 1988-92; expert witness and musicology cons. Virgin Records, 1991—; fieldworker, Taiwan and Japan, 1963-64, Sikkim, winter 1970, Madras, India, winters 1977, 78, 82, 83; mem. folk arts panel Nat. Endowment for Arts, 1977-80, internat. panel, 1979-80; panelist basic rsch. divsn. NEH, 1982-84, Calif. Arts Coun., 1993, Mass. Cultural Coun., 1995; fieldworker, presenter Smithsonian Instn. Festival Am. Folklife, 1978-82; reviewer Ctr. for Scholarly Comm. with People's Republic China, 1979—; exch. lectr. U. Warsaw, Poland, spring 1980; co-dir. summer seminar for coll. tchrs. NEH, 1977; dir. Am. Mus. Heritage Found., 1991—. Author: Chinese Music: An Annotated Bibliography, 1970, 2d edit, 1979, A Chinese Zither Tutor: The Mei-An Chin-P'u, 1983, (with Mickey Hart) Drumming at the Edge of Magic, 1990, Planet Drum: A Celebration of Percussion and Rhythm, 1991; editor: (with Fritz A Kuttner) Perspectives on Asian Music: Essays in Honor of Lawrence Picken, 1975; gen. editor Garland Bibliographies in Ethnomusicology, 1980-86; mem. editl. bd. Musica Asiatica, 1984—; contbr. numerous articles and revs. to profl. publs.; composer: Suite for Piano, 1964, Sonatina for Piano, 1964, Two Short String Quartets, 1966, Leaves of Brass (for brass quartet), 1967, Psalm 136: By the Rivers of Babylon (for chorus), 1971; records include China I: String Instruments, 1969, China II: Amoy Music, 1971, Music of Sikkim, 1975; ethnomusicology cons. 360 Degrees Prodns., 1988—; filmer, editor (with Michael Moore) Traditional Music and Dance of Sikkim, Parts I and II, 1976; prodr., dir., editor videotape Documenting Traditional Performance, 1978, South Indian Classical Music House Concert, 1994. Mem. exec. bd. Pub. Radio Sta. KRAB-FM, Seattle, 1977-78; mem. King County Arts Commn., Seattle, 1977-80. Grantee Nat. Endowment for the Arts, 1978, NEH, 1978, 80, 95-97, N.Y. State Regents fellow, 1958-62, East-West Ctr. fellow and travel grantee, 1962-65, UCLA Chancellor's tchg. fellow, 1965-69, John D. Rockefeller 3d Fund rsch. fellow, 1970-71. Mem. NARAS, Soc. for Ethnomusicology (editor Ethnomusicology 1977-81, nat. coun. 1970-72, 74-76, 78-81, 83-86), Soc. for Asian Music (editorial bd. Asian Music 1968-77, editor publs. series 1968—), Coll. Music Soc. (nat. coun. 1973-75, exec. bd. 1974-75, 76-77), Conf. on Chinese Oral and Performing Lit. (exec. bd. 1971-74, 78-80), ASCAP, Internat. Coun. Traditional Music, Am. Musical Heritage Found. (treas. 1991—), Phi Mu Alpha Sinfonia. Avocations: amateur radio, photography. Office: U Calif Porter Coll Santa Cruz CA 95064

LIEBERMAN, GAIL FORMAN, financial executive; b. Phila., May 26, 1943; d. Joseph and Rita (Groder) Forman. BA in Physics and Math., Temple U., 1964, MBA in Fin., 1977. Dir. internat. fin. Standard Brands Inc., N.Y.C., 1977-79; staff v.p. fin. and capital planning RCA Corp., 1979-82; CFO, exec. v.p. Scali McCabe Sloves, Inc., 1982-93; v.p. finance, CFO, mng. dir. Moody's Investors Svc., N.Y.C., 1994—; bd. dirs. Allied Devices, Inc. Bd. dirs. Vineyard Theater Group, N.Y.C. Mem. Fin. Execs. Inst. Office: Moody's Investor Svcs 99 Church St New York NY 10007-2701

LIEBERMAN, GERALD J., statistics educator; b. N.Y.C., Dec. 31, 1925; s. Joseph and Ida (Margolis) L.; m. Helen Herbert, Oct. 27, 1950; children—Janet, Joanne, Michael, Diana. B.S. in Mech. Engring., Cooper Union, 1948; A.M. in Math. Stats., Columbia U., 1949; Ph.D., Stanford U., 1953. Math. statistician Nat. Bur. Standards, 1949-50; mem. faculty Stanford U., 1953—, prof. statistics and indsl. engring., 1959-67, prof. statistics and operations research, 1967—, chmn. dept. operations research, 1967-75, assoc. dean Sch. Humanities and Scis., 1975-77, acting v.p. and provost, 1979, vice provost, 1977-85, dean research, 1977-80, dean grad. studies and research, 1980-85, provost, 1992-93; cons. to govt. and industry, 1953—. Author: (with A.H. Bowker) Engineering Statistics, 1959, 2d edit., 1972, (with F.S. Hillier) Introduction to Operations Research, 1967, 6th edit., 1995. Ctr. Advanced Studies in Behavioral Scis. fellow, 1985-86. Fellow Am. Statis. Assn., Inst. Math. Statistics, Am. Soc. Quality Control (Shewhart medal 1972), AAAS; mem. Nat. Acad. Engring., Inst. Mgmt. Sci. (pres. 1980-81), Ops. Research Soc. Am., Sigma Xi, Pi Tau Sigma. Home: 811 San Francisco Ter Stanford CA 94305-1021

LIEBERMAN, JAMES, federal agency administrator; b. Providence, Nov. 24, 1945. BSME, U. R.I., 1967; MS in Thermal Engring., Cornell U., 1969; JD with honors, George Washington U., 1974. Bar: Va. 1974, D.C. 1976. Engr. Combustion Engring. Co., Windsor, Conn., 1967; devel. engr. Eastman Kodak Co., Rochester, N.Y., 1968-71; legal asst. Berlin, Roisman & Kessler, Washington, 1973; law clk. McKean, Whitehead & Wilson, Washington, 1973-74; atty. Office of Exec. Legal Dir. NRC, Washington, 1974-81, dir. enforcement staff Office Inspection and Enforcement, 1982, chief counsel for regional ops. and enforcement, 1982-86, asst. gen. for enforcement, chief counsel regional ops., 1986-87, dir. Office of Enforcement, 1987—. Contbr. articles to profl. publs. John McMullen fellow, 1967-69. Office: NRC Office of Enforcement Washington DC 20555

LIEBERMAN, JOSEPH I., senator; b. Stamford, Conn., Feb. 24, 1942; s. Henry and Marcia (Manger) L.; m. Hadassah Freilich, Mar. 20, 1983; children: Matthew, Rebecca, Ethan, Hana. B.A., Yale U., 1964, J.D., 1967. Bar: Conn. 1967. Mem. Conn. Senate, 1971-81, Senate majority leader, 1975-81; ptnr. Lieberman, Segaloff & Wolfson, New Haven, 1972-83; atty. gen. State of Conn., Hartford, 1983-89; U.S. Senator from Conn., 1989—. Author: The Power Broker, 1966, The Scorpion and the Tarantula, 1970, The Legacy, 1981, Child Support in America, 1986. Democrat. Jewish. Office: 316 Hart Senate Office Bldg Washington DC 20510*

LIEBERMAN, LAURENCE, poet, educator; b. Detroit, Feb. 16, 1935; s. Nathan and Anita (Cohen) L.; m. Bernice Clair Braun, June 17, 1956; children—Carla, Deborah, Isaac. BA, U. Mich., 1956, MA in English, 1958; postgrad., U. Calif.-Berkeley. Prof. English Coll. V.I., 1964-68; prof. English and creative writing U. Ill., Urbana, 1968—; U. Ill. Ctr. for Advanced Study Creative Writing fellow, Japan, 1971-72. Author: The Unblinding, 1968, The Achievement of James Dickey, 1969, The Osprey Suicides, 1973, Unassigned Frequencies: American Poetry in Review (1964-77), 1977, God's Measurements, (1979-82), 1983, The Mural of Wakeful Sleep, 1985, (poems) The Creole Mephistopheles, 1989, The Best American Poetry, 1991 (award), New and Selected Poems (1962-92), 1993, (poems) The St. Kitts. Monkey Feuds, 1995, Beyond the Muse of Memory: Essays on Contemporary Poets, 1995, Dark Songs: Slave House and Synagogue, 1996; poetry editor poetry books program U. Ill. Press, 1970—; contbr. poetry to lit. jours., popular mags. Recipient award for Best Poems of 1968, Nat. Endowment for Arts, 1969, Jerome P. Shestack award Am. Poetry Rev., 1986; creative writing fellow U. Ill. Ctr. for Advanced Study, Nat. Endowment Arts, 1986-87. Office: U Ill English Dept 608 S Wright St Urbana IL 61801

LIEBERMAN, LEONARD, retired supermarket executive; b. Elizabeth, N.J., Jan. 23, 1929; s. Joseph Harry and Bessie (Bernstein) L.; m. Arlene Ginsberg; children: Elizabeth Susan, Nancy Ellen, Anne Judith. B.A., Yale U., 1950; J.D., Columbia U., 1953; grad., Advanced Mgmt. Program, Harvard U., 1970. Bar: N.J. bar 1954. Assoc., then partner firms in Newark and Orange, 1954-65; v.p., gen. counsel, dir. Supermarkets Operating Co., Union, N.J., 1963-66; v.p., gen. counsel Supermarkets Gen. Corp., Woodbridge, N.J., 1966-69, sr. v.p., 1969-81, chmn. Pathmark div., 1977-79, exec. asst. to pres., 1979-80, chief adminstrv. and fin. officer, 1980-82, exec. v.p., 1981-82, pres., 1982-87, chief exec. officer, 1983-87, chmn., 1986-87; bd. dirs. Outlet Comm., Inc., chmn., CEO, 1991; bd. dirs. Celestial Seasonings, Inc., Republic N.Y. Corp., La Petite Acad., Inc., Sonic Industries; instr. Am. Inst. Banking, 1954-55; co-chmn. joint industry com. on uniform comm. sys. for the grocery industry, 1978-81, com. to improve shipping container design, 1984-86; co-chmn. Gov. Florio's task force on local partnerships, 1991-92. Trustee Jewish Counseling and Svc. Agy. Essex County, 1968-73, Fund for N.J., 1987—, Ctr. for Analysis of Pub. Issues, 1987—, chmn. 1990-92; trustee Newark Beth Israel Med. Ctr., Newark, 1971-82, treas., 1972-73, pres., 1973-78, hon. pres., 1982—; bd. dirs. Newark Performing Arts Corp., 1987-91; commr. N.J. Pub. Broadcasting Authority, 1982-86, 1st v.p., 1983-86; chmn. N.J. Acad. for Aquatic Scis., Inc., 1989-92; mem. coun. for N.J. affairs, Princeton U., 1988—; bd. regents Seton Hall U., 1989-90; trustee, mem. exec. com., treas. N.J. Ctr. for Performing Arts, 1989—; mem. N.J. com. Regional Plan Assn., 1982—; task force chmn. Gov.'s Mgmt. Improvement Program, 1982-83; mem. Partnership for N.J., 1983—; assoc. gov. Hebrew U., 1983-84, bd. govs., 1984-90; bd. dirs. Ctr. Excellence in Govt., 1981-83; trustee Victim Svc. Agy., 1986—; mem. N.J. State Planning Commn., 1986-90. Recipient Justice Louis D. Brandeis Humanitarian award N.J. region Zionist Orgn. Am., 1977. Mem. Food Mktg. Inst. (dir. exec. com. 1983-87), Regional Plan Assn. (dir. 1985-95). Office: One Gateway Ctr Ste 532 One Gateway Ctr Ste 106 Newark NJ 07102

LIEBERMAN, LESTER ZANE, engineering company executive; b. Newark, July 4, 1930; s. Herman P. and Cecile A. (Ashenfeld) L.; m. Judith Mazor, Aug. 11, 1957; children—Susan, Jane. BS in Mech. Engring., Newark Coll. Engring., 1951, postgrad., 1953-58; DHL (hon.), Clarkson U., 1991. Registered profl. engr., N.J., Pa. Pres. Crest Engring. Inc., Newark, 1955-60; chmn., pres. Atmos Engring. Co. Inc., Kenilworth, N.J., 1960-78; pres., chief exec. officer Clarkson Industries, Inc., N.Y.C., 1978-90; bd. dirs. Lazard Fund, Cives Steel Corp. Trustee Clarkson U., Potsdam, N.Y.; chmn. Beth Israel Med. Ctr., Newark, 1970—, Irvington Gen. Hosp., 1991—. With USCG, 1951-53. Named Alumnus of Yr., Newark Coll. Engring., 1980. Mem. ASHRAE (pres. 1964-65), Nat. Soc. Profl. Engrs., N.J. Soc. Profl. Engrs., Assn. Energy Engrs., Am. Acad. Environ. Engrs. (diplomate), Mason., Mountain Ridge Country Club (N.J.), Stockbridge Country Club (Mass.), Cornell Club (N.Y.), Tau Beta Pi (Key award 1982). Jewish. Lodge: Masons. Avocations: skiing, sailing, tennis, golf. Home: Spring Valley Rd Morristown NJ 07960-7011 Office: 25 Vreeland Rd Florham Park NJ 07932-1902

LIEBERMAN, LOUIS (KARL LIEBERMAN), artist; b. Bklyn., May 7, 1944; s. Abraham and Jeannette (Feinberg) L. BFA, R.I. Sch. Design, 1969; cert., Bklyn. Mus. Art Sch., 1964; BA, Bklyn. Coll., 1966. Adj. lectr. Bklyn. Coll., 1971-78, Lehman Coll., Bronx, N.Y., 1972-75; vis. artist Ill. State U., Normal, 1978, Hamilton Coll., Clinton, N.Y., 1982. One-man shows include Vancouver Art Gallery, B.C., Can., 1969, James Yu Gallery, N.Y.C., 1973, 74, Nina Freudenheim Gallery, Buffalo, 1976, Root Art Ctr., Hamilton Coll., Clinton, N.Y., 1980, Harm Bouckaert Gallery, N.Y.C., 1981, John Davis Gallery, Akron, Ohio, 1983, 85, Columbus Mus. Art, Ohio, 1983, John Davis Gallery, N.Y.C., 1986; group shows include Aldrich Mus. Contemporary Art, Ridgefield, Conn., 1973, 74, Johnson Mus. Art, Ithaca, N.Y., 1981, Fine Arts Mus. L.I., Hempstead, N.Y., 1982, Cleve. Inst. Art, 1982, Met. Mus. Art, N.Y.C., 1983, Byer Mus. Art, Evanston, Ill., 1982, Visual Arts Ctr., Beer-Sheva, Israel, 1985, Kunsthauses, Zurich, Switzerland, McNay Art Mus., San Antonio, Phila. Mus. of Art, 1988, Erie (Pa.) Art Mus., 1988, Art Mus. of Santa Cruz, Calif., 1988, Hunter Mus., Chattanooga, 1989, others; represented in permanent collections including Kenan Ctr., Lockport, N.Y., Aldridge Mus. Contemporary Art, Ridgefield, Conn., Met. Mus. Art, N.Y.C., Phila. Mus. Art, Stamford (Conn.) Mus., Bklyn. Mus., Mus. Fine Arts, Budapest, Hungary, Istvan Kiraly Mus., Budapest, Ackland Art Mus., Chapel Hill, N.C.; art critic N.Y. Arts Jour., 1978-79. Recipient Sculpture award Creative Artist Pub. Service Found., 1971-72, Graphics award Creative Artist Pub. Svc. Found., 1980-81, Graphics award N.Y. Found. Arts, 1984-85; visual arts fellow Nat. Endowment for Arts, 1979-80; Pollack-Krasner Found. fellow, 1987; Adolf and Esther Gottlieb Found. grantee, 1989.

LIEBERMAN, MARK JOEL, lawyer; b. Chgo., Apr. 12, 1949; s. Eugene and Pearl Naomi (Feldman) L.; m. Gail Sue Garfinkel, Aug. 3, 1975; children: Amy, Kevin. BA, DePaul U., 1971, JD, 1974. Bar: Ill. 1974, Calif. 1980, Tex. 1989. House counsel Mercantile Fin. Corp., Chgo., 1974-80; sr. atty. Assocs. Comml. Corp., Chgo., 1981-84; v.p., asst. gen. counsel Assocs. Comml. Corp., Dallas, 1984—. Mem. ABA, Calif. State Bar Assn. Republican. Jewish. Avocation: woodcarving. Office: Assocs Comml Corp 300 E Carpenter Fwy Irving TX 75062

LIEBERMAN, MELVYN, biology educator; b. Bklyn., Feb. 4, 1938; married; 2 children. BA in Zoology, Cornell U., 1959; PhD in Physiology, SUNY Downstate Med. Ctr., 1965. Lectr., lab in instr., dept. biology Queens Coll., CUNY, 1960, 63-64; teaching asst. dept. physiology SUNY Downstate Med. Ctr., Bklyn., 1960-64; postdoctoral fellow dept. embryology Carnegie Inst. Washington, Balt., 1964-65, Inst. de Biofisica, U. Federal do Rio de Janeiro, Brazil, 1965-67; postdoctoral fellow div. biomed. engring. Duke U., Durham, N.C., 1967, rsch. assoc. dept. physiology and pharmacology, 1967-68; asst. prof. Duke U. Med. Ctr., Durham, N.C., 1968-73, assoc. prof., 1973-78, prof. dept. physiology, 1978-88, dir. dept. grad. studies, 1977-80, prof. dept. cell biology, 1988—, dir. grad. studies, 1988-90;

assoc. prof. medicine, mem. integrated toxicology program, 1989—; spl. asst. to exec. v.p. Duke U. Med. Ctr., Durham, N.C., 1990-95, spl. asst. to sr. v.p. rsch. adminstr., 1995-96, mem. Heart Ctr., 1988—, mem. Comprehensive Cancer Ctr., 1992—, dir. univ. assocs. program, 1992—; prof. dept. biomed. engring., 1993—; Internat. Affairs Commn., 1994—; coordinator U.S.-Japan Coop. Sci. Program Conf., Tokyo, 1974, 88, U.S.-Brazil Coop. Sci. Program Conf., Rio de Janeiro, 1980, Gordon Conf.-Muscle, 1979; vis. investigator Jan Seammerdam Inst., U. Amsterdam, Netherlands, 1975; cons. Macy Found., 1970, NIH, 1972—, physiology study sect., 1980-84, Rsch. Tng. Rev. Comm., 1990-94, NSF, 1974—, others; mem. rsch. rev. com. N.Y. Heart Assn., 1980-85; mem. cardiovascular rsch. study com. Am. Heart Assn., 1987-90; Howard Hughes Predoctorate Fellowship Evaluation, 1994—; participant numerous sci. symposia; mem. basic Sci. coun. Am. Heart Assn., 1963, established investigator, 1971-76, pub. rev. com., 1989-93, Rsch. Program and Evaluation Commn., 1995—; rsch. rev. subcom. N.C. Heart Assn., 1972-75, chmn., 1975-76, pub. affairs com., 1988-91, rsch. com., 1993—; microstructure com., N.C. Bd. Sci. and Tech., 1989-93, Task Force on Intellectual property and licensing govt. univ. industry rsch. roundtable, 1991-93, Indsl. Liaison program, Rsch. Triangle Univs., 1991-93; acad. adv. coun. Indsl. Rsch. Inst., 1994—, Pres.'s adv. coun., Houston Advanced Rsch. Ctr., 1995—. Co-editor: Development and Physiological Correlates of Cardiac Muscle, 1975, Excitable Cells in Tissue Culture, 1981, Normal and Abnormal Conduction of the Heart, 1982, Electrogenic Transport: Fundamental Principles and Physiological Implications, 1984; assoc. editor Am. Jour. Physiology, Cell, 1981—; mem. editorial adv. bd. Experientia, 1982-90, Physiol. Revs., 1985-91, Molecular Cell Biochemistry, 1991—; editorial cons. contbr. numerous articles to profl. jours. Recipient founders award, 1975, achievement award N.C. Heart Assn., 1984, Cecil Hall award Electron Microscopy Soc. Am., 1989. Mem. AAAS, AAUP, Am. Heart Assn., Am. Physiol. Soc. (Porter devel. com. 1974-77, ednl. materials rev. bd. 1975-77, internat. physiol. com. 1993, chmn. 1994-95, councillor cell and gen. physiol. sect. 1984-87, chmn. 1987-88, 91-95, sect. adv. com. 1992-95), Am. Soc. Cell Biology, Biophys. Soc., Cardiac Muscle Soc., Internat. Soc. Heart Rsch. (councillor 1993—), N.Y. Acad. Sci., N.C. Heart Assn., Physiol. Soc., Soc. Gen. Physiologists (sec. 1969-71, rep. NRS 1971-74, pres. 1981-82, publs. com. 1982-85), Physiol. Soc. (U.K.), Sigma Xi. Home: 1110 Woodburn Rd Durham NC 27705-5738 Office: Duke U Med Ctr Dept Cell Biology Box 3709 Div Physiology Durham NC 27710

LIEBERMAN, MICHAEL A., electrical engineer, educator; b. N.Y.C., Oct. 3, 1940; married; two children. BS, MS, MIT, Cambridge, 1962; PhD, MIT, 1966. Prof. Electronic Rsch. Labs. U. Calif., Berkeley, 1977-80; asst. prof. biochem. dept. nutrition Harvard Sch. Pub. Health, Boston, 1981-83; assoc. prof. molecular genetics, biochemistry & microbiology Coll. Medicine U. Cin., 1983—; mem. study sect. cellular biology & physiology NIH, 1986-89. Fellow IEEE (award for contbns. to rsch. in plasma-assisted materials processing, nonlinear dynamics and controlled fusion). Office: Univ California Berkeley Electronics Rsch Lab 253 Cory Hall Berkeley CA 94720*

LIEBERMAN, PHILLIP LOUIS, allergist, educator; b. Memphis, Mar. 20, 1940; m. Barbara; children: Ryan, Lee, Jay. Student, London Sch. Econs., 1961; BA in Sociology, Tulane U., 1962; MD, U. Tenn., 1965. Intern City of Memphis Hosp. U. Tenn., 1965-66, asst. resident internal medicine, 1966-67, assoc. resident internal medicine, 1967-68, chief resident, 1968-69; fellow in allergy, immunology Northwestern U., Evanston, Ill., 1969-71; asst. prof., chief div. allergy, immunology U. Tenn., 1971-74, assoc. prof., chief div. allergy, immunology, 1974-79, prof., chief div. allergy, immunology, 1979—; instr. internal medicine U. Tenn., 1968-69; mem. exec. bd. Joint Coun. of Allergy & Immunology, 1985-90, AAAI rep., 1990; AAAI rep. Mothers for Asthmatics, 1990. Co-editor: Asthma Edition: Abstract-a-Card System, 1991—; contbr. numerous articles, abstracts to profl. publs.; author numerous presentations in field, book chpts., revs. Exec. bd. dirs. Asthma and Allergy Found. of Am., 1990—, mem. med. scientific coun., 1987, chmn., 1990—. Served to cpt. USAR, 1965-71. Mem. Am. Acad. Allergy (com. on alternative forms of therapy, 1980—), Am. Acad. Allergy and Immunology (exec. com. 1983-91, constitution and by-laws com. 1984-87, also chmn. 1985, undergraduate com. 1985, pres.-elect. 1987-88, pres. 1988-89, nominating com. 1987, also chmn. 1989, program com. 1987), Am. Coll. Allergists, Am. Assn. Allergists (sec. 1985), Am. Assn. Certified Allergists (2d v.p. 1986-87, pres. 1989-90), Am. Bd. Allergy and Immunology. Office: U Tenn 300 S Walnut Bend Rd Cordova TN 38018-7293 also: Allergy Assocs 920 Madison Ave Ste 909N Memphis TN 38103-3451

LIEBERMAN, SEYMOUR, biochemistry educator emeritus; b. N.Y.C., Dec. 1, 1916; s. Samuel D. and Sadie (Levin) L.; m. Sandra Spar, June 5, 1944; 1 child, Paul B. B.S., Bklyn. Coll., 1936; M.S., U. Ill., 1937; Ph.D. (Rockefeller scholar 1939-41), Stanford U., 1941; Traveling fellow, U. Basle, Switzerland, Eidgenoess. Tech. Hochschule, Zurich, Switzerland, 1946-47. Chemist Schering Corp., 1938-39; spl. research asso. Harvard U., 1941-45; assoc. mem. Sloan-Kettering Inst., 1945-50; mem. faculty Columbia Coll. Physicians and Surgeons, N.Y.C., 1950—; prof. biochemistry Columbia Coll. Physicians and Surgeons, 1950-87, prof. emeritus, 1987—; assoc. dean Inst. Health Scis., St. Luke's Roosevelt Hosp. Center, 1984-90, pres., 1981—, vice provost, 1991; assoc. dir. office sci. and tech. Columbia U., N.Y.C., 1991—; Pfizer traveling fellow McGill U., 1968; Syntex lectr. Mexican Endocrine Soc., 1970; mem. Am. Cancer Soc. panel steroids, 1945-49, hormones, 1949-50, mem. com. pathogenesis of cancer, 1957-60; mem. endocrine study sect. NIH, 1959-63, chmn., 1963-65, mem. gen. clin. research centers, 1967-71; mem. med. adv. com. Population Council, 1961-73; mem. endocrinology panel Cancer Chemotherapy Nat. Service Center, 1958-62; cons. WHO human reprodn. unit, 1972-74, Ford Found., 1974-77. Editor Jour. Clin. Endocrinology and Metabolism, 1963-67, editorial bd., 1958-63, 68-70, Jour. Biol. Chemistry, 1975-80; contbr. articles to profl. jours. Recipient Disting. Alumnus award Bklyn. Coll., 1971, Disting. Svc. award Columbus U., 1991. Fellow N.Y. Acad. Scis., NAS; mem. Am. Soc. Biol. Chemists, Am. Chem. Soc., Internat. Soc. Endocrinology (U.S. del. central com.), Endocrine Soc. (Ciba award 1952, Koch award 1970, council 1970-73, pres. 1974-75, Roussel prize 1984, Dale medal 1986, Boehringer-Mannheim award lectr. 1992), Harvey Soc. Home: 515 E 72nd St New York NY 10021-4032 Office: 432 W 58th St New York NY 10019-1102

LIEBERMANN, LOWELL, composer, pianist, conductor; b. N.Y.C., Feb. 22, 1961. D in Musical Arts, Juilliard Sch.; studied with David Diamond, Vincent Persichetti, Jacob Lateiner, Laszlo Halasz. Composer (orchestra) War Songs for Bass Voice and Orch. Op. 7, 1981, Concertino for Cello and Chamber Orch. Op. 8, 1982, Symphony No. 1 Op. 9 (BMI award, 1st prize Juilliard Orch. Competition 1987), 1982, Three Poems of Stephen Crane Op. 11 for baritone, string orch., two horns, harp (Devora Nadworney award Nat. Fed. Music Clubs 1986) 1983, Concerto No. 1 for Piano and Orch. Op. 12, 1983, Sechs Gesaenge Nach Gedichten Von Nelly Sachs Op. 18 for soprano and orch., 1986, The Domain of Arnheim Op. 33, 1990, Concerto No. 2 for Piano and Orch. Op. 36, 1992, Flute Concerto Op. 39, 1992, Revelry for Orch. Op. 47, 1995, Concerto for Flute, Harp, and Orch. Op. 48, 1995; (opera) The Picture of Dorian Gray Op. 45, 1995, (chorus) Two Choral Elegies Op. 2 for SATB a capella (Fred Waring Choral award Nat. Fed. Music 1978), 1977, Missa Brevis Op. 15 for SATB chorus, tenor and baritone solos, organ (3d prize Ch. and Artist Composers Competition 1987), 1985; (piano solo) Piano Sonata Op. 1 (Outstanding Composition award Yamaha Music Found. 1982, 1st prize Nat. Composition Contest Music Tchrs. Nat. Assn. 1978), 1977, Piano Sonata No. 2 Sonata Notturna Op. 10, 1983, Variations on a Theme by Anton Bruckner Op. 19, 1987, Nocturne No. 1 Op. 20, 1987, Four Apparitions Op. 17, 1987, others; (chamber music) Sonata for Violoncello and Piano Op. 3, 1978, Two Pieces for Violin and Viola Op. 4, 1978, Sonata for Viola and Piano Op. 13 (1st Place Victor Herbert/ASCAP awards Nat. Fed. Music Clubs 1986, Brian Israel prize Soc. for New Music 1986), 1984, Sonata for Contrabass and Piano Op. 24, 1987, Fantasy on a Fugue by J.S. Bach Op. 27 for flute, oboe, clarinet, horn, bassoon, piano, 1989, Quintet for Piano and Strings Op. 34 for piano and string quartet, 1989, others; also organ music, voice and piano. Mem. ASCAP, Corp. Yaddo (dir.). Democrat. Office: 155 W 68th St Apt 315 New York NY 10023-5809

LIEBERSON, STANLEY, sociologist, educator; b. Montreal, Que., Can., Apr. 20, 1933; s. Jack and Ida (Cohen) L.; m. Patricia Ellen Beard, 1960; children—Rebecca, David, Miriam, Rachel. Student, Bklyn. Coll., 1950-52; MA, U. Chgo., 1958, PhD, 1960; MA (hon.), Harvard U., 1988; LHD (hon.), U. Ariz., 1993. Asso. dir. Iowa Urban Community Research Center, U. Iowa, 1959-61, instr., asst. prof. sociology, 1959-61; asst. prof. sociology U. Wis., 1961-63, asso. prof., 1963-66, prof., 1966-67; prof. sociology U. Wash., 1967-71, dir. Center Studies Demography and Ecology, 1968-71; prof. sociology U. Chgo., 1971-74, assoc. dir. Population Research Center, 1971-74; prof. sociology U. Ariz., Tucson, 1974-83, head dept., 1976-79; prof. sociology U. Calif., Berkeley, 1983-88; prof. sociology Harvard U., 1988-91, Abbott Lawrence Lowell prof. sociology, 1991—; vis. prof. Stanford U., summer 1970; Claude Bissell disting. vis. prof. U. Toronto, 1979-80; mem. com. on sociolinguistics Social Sci. Research Council, 1964-70; mem. sociology panel NSF, 1978-81. Author: (with others) Metropolis and Region, 1960, Ethnic Patterns in American Cities, 1963; editor: Explorations in Sociolinguistics, 1967, (with Beverly Duncan) Metropolis and Region in Transition, 1970, Language and Ethnic Relations in Canada, 1970, A Piece of the Pie, 1980, Language Diversity and Language Contact, 1981, Making It Count, 1985, (with Mary C. Waters) From Many Strands, 1988; assoc. editor Social Problems, 1965-67, Sociol. Methods and Research, 1971—; editorial cons. Sociol. Inquiry, 1965-67; adv. editor: Am. Jour. Sociology, 1969-74; editorial bd. Lang. in Society, 1972-74, Internat. Jour. Sociology of Lang, 1974—, Canadian Jour. Sociology, 1975—, Social Forces, 1980-83; adv. council Sociol. Abstracts, 1972-73, Language Problems and Language Planning, 1984-87; mem. editorial com. Ann. Rev. Sociology, 1992—. Recipient Colver Rosenberger Ednl. prize, 1960; Guggenheim fellow, 1972-73, fellow Ctr. for Advanced Study in Behavioral Scis., 1995-96. Fellow NAS, Am. Acad. Arts and Scis.; mem. Am. Sociol. Assn. (coun. mem. 1985-87, pres. 1990-91, Disting. Contbn. to Scholarship award 1982), Am. Sociol. Found. (trustee 1992—), Population Assn. Am. (dir. 1969-72), Internat. Population Union, Pacific Sociol. Assn. (v.p. 1984-85, pres. 1986-87), Sociol. Rsch. Assn. (exec. com. 1976-81, pres. 1981), Am. Name Soc., Oakland Sch. Sociology. Home: 5 Mystic Lake Dr Arlington MA 02174-2305 Office: Harvard U Dept Sociology William James Hall Cambridge MA 02138

LIEBERT, ARTHUR EDGAR, retired hospital administrator; b. Milw., Nov. 18, 1930; married. B, Lake Forest Coll; MHA, Northwestern U. Adminstrv. resident Rochester (N.Y.) Gen. Hosp., 1953-54, adminstrv. asst., 1954, asst. adminstr., 1957-65, assoc. dir., 1965-70, admitting dir., 1970-73, pres., 1973-93; co-pres. Greater Rochester Health Sys., 1994-96, Greater Rochester Health Sys. Inc., Rochester, 1994-96. Mem. Am. Hosp. Assn. (del.), Hosp. Assn. N.Y. (del.). Home: 611 Dewitt Rd Webster NY 14580-1333

LIEBERT, LARRY STEVEN, journalist; b. St. Louis, Apr. 30, 1950; s. Charles Bernard and Tobie Lee (Londe) L.; m. Evelyn Ann Hsu, Mar. 26, 1983; children: Rachel Hsu, Emily Hsu. BA in Polit. Sci., Stanford U., 1972. Reporter San Francisco Chronicle, 1972-73, urban affairs reporter, 1973-75, Sacramento bur. chief, 1975-78, polit. writer, 1978-79, chief polit. writer, 1979-87, Washington bur. chief, 1987-90; news editor, weekly reporter Congl. Quar., Washington, 1990-94, editor, congl. monitor, 1994—; Washington columnist Calif. Jour., Sacramento, 1987-94. Office: Congl Quar 1414 22d St NW Washington DC 20037-1003

LIEBES, RAQUEL, import/export company executive, educator; b. San Salvador, El Salvador, Aug. 28, 1938; came to the U.S., 1952, naturalized, 1964; d. Ernesto Martin and Alice (Philip) L.; m. Richard Paisley Kinkade, June 2, 1962 (div. 1977); children: Kathleen Paisley, Richard Paisley Jr., Scott Philip. BA, Sarah Lawrence Coll., 1960; MEd, Harvard U., 1961; MA, Yale U., 1963, postgrad., 1963-65; PhD in English, Oxford (Eng.) U., 1994. Teaching fellow in Spanish Sarah Lawrence Coll., Bronxville, N.Y., 1958-60; econ. teaching fellow Yale U., New Haven, 1964-65, instr. Spanish, 1964-66; exec. stockholder Import Export Co., San Salvador, 1968-89, also bd. dirs.; adj. prof. Am. U., Washington, 1989-91, dept. fgn. lang. and linguistics dept. fgn. studies Georgetown U., Washington, 1989-93. Contbr. glossary of Spanish med. terms. Hon. consul Govt. of El Salvador, 1977-80; docent High Mus. of Art, Atlanta, 1972-77; vol. Grady Hosp., Atlanta, 1966-71; instr. Spanish for med. drs. Tucson Med. Ctr., 1966-71; chmn. Atlanta Coun. for Internat. Visitors, 1966-71; mem. Outreach Group on Latin Am., Washington, 1982-86; founding mem. John Kennedy Ctr. for Performing Arts, 1980—; mem. Folger/Shakespeare Libr., Smithsonian Inst., Agape, El Salvador. Econ. fellow Yale U., 1964-65; Corcoran Mus. Art fellow, 1984-85; Smithsonian Mus. awardee, 1981-96. Mem. MLA, Am. Biog. Inst. Rsch. Assn. (hon. consul of El Salvador, dep. gov. 1978-80, bd. advisors 1994), Jr. League of Washington, Harvard Club, Yale Club. Republican. Avocations: comparative literature, languages, international business, English literature, Shakespeare. Home: 700 New Hampshire Ave NW Washington DC 20037-2406 *Throughout my life, I have applied the tradition of ethics in each and everyone of my activities and have expected. The self-same principle in each and everyone of those with whom I have surrounded myself. The persons I know, as well as writers which I have admired.*

LIEBHABER, JACK MITCHELL, lawyer; b. Great Neck, N.Y., Apr. 6, 1958; s. Leslie and Lois Betty (Peiser) L.; 1 child, Brandon Matthew. BA, SUNY, Binghamton, 1980; JD, Pepperdine U., 1983. Bar: Calif. 1984. Pvt. practice, 1983-86; assoc. Spray, Gould & Bowers, L.A., 1986-93; shareholder Robinson, Di Lando & Whitaker, L.A., 1993—. Avocations: running, reading, theater, basketball, golf. Home: 10577 Cheviot Dr Los Angeles CA 90064 Office: Robinson DiLando & Whitaker 800 Wilshire Blvd Ste 1300 Los Angeles CA 90017

LIEBIG, RICHARD ARTHUR, retired manufacturing company executive; b. Quincy, Ill., Sept. 2, 1923; s. Arthur William and Florence Ann (Parrott) L.; m. Peggy O. Shiley, Aug. 4, 1946; children: Lynn Margaret, Ann Kay. BS, U. Ill., 1949; LLD (hon.), Culver-Stockton Coll., 1989. With Moorman Mfg. Co., Quincy, 1949-88, credit mgr., 1958-60, mgr. fin. adminstrn., 1960-64, treas., 1960-76, bd. dirs., 1960-93, v.p. fin. adminstrn., 1964-75, sec., mem. exec. com., 1971-75, exec. v.p. fin., 1975-76, pres., COO, 1976-77, pres., CEO, 1977-84, chmn. bd., CEO, 1984-87, chmn. bd., 1987-88; bd. dirs. Quincy Soybean Co., 1960-93, sec., 1961-76, v.p., 1968-76, mem. exec. com., 1963-93; v.p. Moorman Co. Fund, 1960-75; mem. exec. com. Moorman Found., 1969-90, 1st v.p., 1972-80, pres., 1980-90; pres., mem. exec. com. CFM Found., 1990—, also bd. dirs.; mem. St. Louis adv. bd. Liberty Mut. Ins. Co., 1980, 93; mem. adv. coun. Coll. Commerce and Bus. Adminstrn. U. Ill., Urbana, 1974—; mem. exec. com. Convocom, 1983—, sec., 1990—, also bd. dirs. Mem. adv. coun. Culver-Stockton Coll., Canton, Mo., 1971-82, trustee, 1983—, mem. exec. com., chmn. bd. trustees, 1989—; vice chmn. Profit Sharing Coun. Am., 1979, bd. dirs., 1972-82; mem. Sch. Dist. 172 Bd. Edn., 1963-69, pres., 1969; trustee Quincy Found. for Quality Edn., 1989—; bd. dirs., treas. ednl. revolving fund Blessing Hosp., Quincy, 1963-85; mem. adv. bd. YWCA, 1984—; bd. dirs. Inst. Human Studies, 1985—. With AUS, 1943-47. Paul Harris fellow, 1987. Mem. Fin. Execs. Inst., Ill. MFrs. Assn. (bd. dirs. 1982-88), Ill. State C. of C. (bd. dirs. 1980-86), Indsl. Assn. Quincy (2nd v.p., mem. exec. com. 1969-71, 75-88, trustee Profit Sharing Rsch. Found. 1986-92), Rotary (bd. dirs. Quincy chpt.). Methodist. Home: 2311 Vermont St Quincy IL 62301-3163

LIEBLING, JEROME, photographer, educator; b. N.Y.C., Apr. 16, 1924; s. Maurice and Sarah (Goodman) L.; married, Nov. 11, 1949 (div. 1969); children: Madeline, Tina, Adam, Daniella, Rachel Jane. Student, Bklyn. Coll., 1942, 46, 48, New Sch. for Social Research, N.Y.C., 1948-49; LLD (hon.), Portland (Maine) Sch. Art, 1989. Prof. photography U. Minn., Mpls., 1949-69; prof. SUNY-New Paltz, 1957-58, Yale U., New Haven, 1976-77, Hampshire Coll., Amherst, Mass., 1970—. Author, photographer: Jerome Liebling Photographs (Best of Yr. 1982), Aperture, N.Y.C., 1988, The People Yes, The Photographs of Jerome Liebling, Aperture, 1995; editor: Photography-Current Perspective, 1977. Served with U.S. Army, 1942-45, ETO, Africa. Fellow Mass. Arts Found., 1975; fellow Nat. Endowman Arts, 1979, Guggenheim, 1977, 81. Mem. Soc. Photog. Edn. Home: 39 Dana St Amherst MA 01002-2208 Office: Hampshire Coll West St Amherst MA 01002-2954

LIEBMAN, HOWARD MARK, lawyer; b. L.A., Dec. 20, 1952; s. Martin Irving and Frances (Weiner) L.; m. Alena Bekova, Aug. 16, 1975 (div. Dec. 17, 1990); 1 child, Peter. AB, Colgate U., 1974, AM, 1975; JD, Harvard Law Sch., 1977. Cons. Office of Tax Analysis, U.S. Treasury Dept., Washington, 1975; assoc. Paul, Weiss, Rifkind, Wharton & Garrison, N.Y.C., 1976, Covington & Burling, Washington, 1977-79; ptnr. Oppenheimer, Wolff & Donnelly, Brussels, 1979-94; mng. ptnr. Morgan, Lewis & Bockius, Brussels, 1994—; mem. div. coun. on fin. and banking Mgmt. Ctr. Europe, Brussels, 1984—; adv. mem. N.Am. Free Trade & Investment Rep., 1988—. Co-author: Business Operations in the European Union; contbg. editor Tax Planning Internat. Rev., 1982—, Jour. Strategy in Internat. Taxation, 1984-86. Bd. dirs. Harvard Club of Belgium, Brussels, 1989—, pres., 1993-95; co-chmn. Dukakis for Pres. Belgian Campaign. Recipient Fulbright fellowship Fulbright Commn., 1979. Mem. ABA, Am. C. of C. in Belgium asbl. Democrat. Home: 30 Ave de Boetendael, 1180 Brussels Belgium Office: Morgan Lewis & Bockius, rue Guimard 7, 1040 Brussels Belgium

LIEBMAN, LANCE MALCOLM, dean, lawyer; b. Newark, Sept. 11, 1941; s. Roy and Barbara (Trilinsky) L.; m. Carol Bensinger, June 28, 1964; children: Jeffrey, Benjamin. B.A., Yale U., 1962; M.A., Cambridge U., 1964; LL.B., Harvard U., 1967. Bar: D.C. 1968, Mass. 1976. Asst. to Mayor Lindsay, N.Y.C., 1968-70; asst. prof. law Harvard U., 1970-76, prof., 1976-91, assoc. dean, 1981-84; dean, Lucy G. Moses prof. law Columbia U. Sch. Law, N.Y.C., 1991—. Successor trustee Yale Corp., 1971-83. Office: Columbia U Sch Law 435 W 116th St New York NY 10027-7201

LIEBMAN, NINA R., economic developer; b. Toledo, Ohio, May 27, 1941; d. Jules Jay and Phyllis Gertrude (Kasle) Roskin; m. Theodore Liebman, Oct. 27, 1968; children: Sophie, Hanna, Tessa. Student, U. Marseilles, Aix-en-Provence, France, 1959-60, Skidmore Coll., 1960-61, NYU, 1961-63; cert. labor negotiator, Cornell U., 1993. Pub. info. officer Young Adult Inst., N.Y.C., 1978-81; U.S.A. dir. Rhone-Alps Econ. Devel. Assn., N.Y.C. and Lyon, France, 1981-85; internat. mktg. specialist N.Y. State Dept. Econ. Devel., N.Y.C., 1985-89, chief internat. programs, 1989-95; cons. Russian Fedn. Housing Project-The World Bank, N.Y.C., 1995—. Co-author: Biz Speak: A Dictionary of Business Terms, Slang and Jargon, 1986. Vol., trained mediator Bklyn. Mediation Ctr.; mem. internat. adv. coun. Eisenhower Found.; mem. internat. adv. bd. Nat. Minority Bus. Coun. Fellow Eisenhower Exch. Fellowship Program, 1993. Mem. Alliance Am. and Russian Women, U.S. Com. for UN Devel. Fund for Women, Minority Internat. Network for Trade, Bklyn. C. of C. (bd. dirs., internat. advisor), Bklyn. Heights Assn., Mcpl. Arts Soc., Grace Choral Soc. (bd. dirs. 1993—). Democrat. Jewish. Avocation: choral singing.

LIEBMAN, PAUL ARNO, biophysicist, educator; b. Pitts., Aug. 1, 1933; s. Arno Jack and M. Josephine (Schurr) L.; m. Elizabeth Loeffler, Nov. 6, 1982; 1 child, Erica. BS in Chemistry, U. Pitts., 1954; MD, Johns Hopkins U., 1958. Intern in medicine Barnes Hosp., St. Louis, 1958-59; postdoctoral fellow Johnson Rsch. Found., Phila., 1959-63; asst. prof. physiology U. Pa. Sch. Medicine, Phila., 1963-67, assoc. prof. anatomy, 1967-76, prof. anatomy, 1976-92, prof. ophthalmology, 1982—, prof. neurosci., prof. biophysics/biochemistry, 1992—; dir. U. Pa. Vision Rsch. Ctr., Phila., 1976—. Contbr. numerous articles to Jour. Biol. Chemistry, Science, Nature, others. Winner numerous U.S. and world whitewater kayak championship medals, 1969-75; grantee NIH, 1962—. Mem. Biophys., Soc. for Neurosci., Assn. for Rsch. in Vision and Ophthalmology, Phila. Canoe Club (hon., life mem., founder). Achievements include invention of UV-VIS microspectrophotometers, ultrasensitive pH recording instruments; discovered color vision pigments, biochemical mechanism of visual transduction, membrane protein lateral diffusion. Office: U Pa Vision Rsch Ctr Sch of Medicine 143 Anatomy Chem 36th & Hamilton Walk Philadelphia PA 19104-6058

LIEBMAN, RONALD STANLEY, lawyer; b. Balt., Oct. 11, 1943; s. Harry Martin and Martha (Altgenug) L.; m. Simma Liebman, Jan. 8, 1972; children: Shana, Margot. BA, Western Md. Coll., Westminster, 1966; JD, U. Md., 1969. Bar: Md. 1969, D.C. 1977, U.S. Dist. Ct. (ea. dist.) Va. 1970, U.S. Dist. Ct. Md. 1970, U.S. Dist. Ct. D.C. 1982, U.S. Dist. Ct. (no. dist.) Calif. 1994, U.S. Ct. Appeals (4th cir.) 1972, U.S. Ct. Appeals (D.C. cir.) 1982, U.S. Ct. Appeals (5th cir.) 1985, U.S. Supreme Ct. 1995. Law clk. to chief judge U.S. Dist. Ct. Md., 1969-70; assoc. Melnicove, Kaufman & Weiner, Balt., 1970-72; asst. U.S. atty. Office of U.S. Atty., Dept. Justice, Balt., 1972-78; ptnr. Sachs, Greenebaum & Tayler, Washington, 1978-82, Patton Boggs, L.L.P., Washington, 1982—. Author: Grand Jury, 1983; co-editor: Testimonial Privileges, 1983. Recipient spl. commendation award U.S. Dept. Justice, 1978. Mem. ABA, D.C. Bar Assn., Md. Bar Assn. Club: Sergeants Inn (Balt.). Office: Patton Boggs LLP 2550 M St NW Washington DC 20037-1301

LIEBMAN, THEODORE, architect; b. Newark, May 7, 1939; s. Edward and Miriam (Applebaum) L.; m. Nina Roskin, Oct. 27, 1968; children—Sophie, Hanna, Tessa. B.Arch., Pratt Inst., 1962; M.Arch., Harvard U., 1963. Registered architect, Mass., N.Y., Colo., Ind. Fla. Project design officer Boston Redevel. Authority, Mass., 1963-64; project dir. David A. Crane, Architect, Phila., 1966-69; chief architect N.Y. State Urban Devel. Corp., N.Y.C., 1969-75; prin. urban design and archtl. adviser Harvard Inst. Internat. Devel., Tehran, Iran, 1975-77; pres. HAUS Internat., Inc., N.Y.C., 1977-79, The Liebman Melting Partnership, Architects and Planners, N.Y.C., 1979—, land devel. mgr. Russian Fed. Housing Project, Moscow, 1995-96; bd. advisers Inst. Urban Design, N.Y.C., 1980-84; assoc. prof. urban design Pratt Inst., Bklyn., 1983-88. Mem. editorial bd. Metropolis, N.Y.C., 1981-88. Contbr. articles to mags. Fellow Am. Acad. in Rome, 1966; Wheelwright travelling fellow Harvard U., 1971. Fellow AIA (pres. N.Y. chpt. 1983-84); mem. Urban Land Inst., Urban Land Inst. Internat. Coun. Home: 105 Montague St Brooklyn NY 11201-3459 Office: The Liebman Melting Partnership 330 W 42nd St New York NY 10036-6902

LIEBMANN, GEORGE WILLIAM, lawyer; b. N.Y.C., June 20, 1939; s. William Liebmann and Margaret (Hirschman) Cook; m. Anne-Lise Grimstad, Apr. 29, 1967; children: Pamela Dione, George William, Franklin Alexander. AB, Dartmouth Coll., 1960; JD, U. Chgo., 1963. Bar: Md. 1964, Ill. 1964. With Chaucer Head Book Shop, Inc., N.Y.C., 1958-59; law clk. to chief judge Ct. Appeals Md., 1963-64; with Frank, Bernstein, Conaway and Goldman, Balt., 1964-79; asst. atty. gen. State of Md., Balt., 1967-69; exec. asst. to Gov. Md., Annapolis, 1979-80; sole practice Balt., 1980—; lectr. U. Md. Law Sch., 1977-78, Johns Hopkins U., 1991-92; asst. reporter Md. Commn. on Criminal Law and Procedure, 1965-70; mem. Gov.'s Commn. to Revise Annotated Code Md., 1974-83; alt. mem. State Planning Coun. on Radioactive Waste Mgmt., 1980-82; chmn. Gov.'s Task Force on Local Govt. Antitrust Liability, 1982-83, Gov.'s Commn. Health Care Providers' Profl. Liability Ins., 1983-84; gen. coun. Md. Econs. Devel. Corp., 1985—; vis. fellow U. Salford, Eng., 1996. Author: Maryland District Court Law and Practice, 2 vols., 1976, Maryland Civil Practice Forms, 2 vols., 1984, The Little Platoons: Sub-Local Governments in Modern History, 1995; mng. editor U. Chgo. Law Rev., 1962-63; mem. adv. bd. Accessory Housing, 1990—; contbr. articles to law jours. Sec. Coalition Against the SST, Washington, 1969; trustee Hist. Annapolis Found., 1991—. Simon indsl. and profl. fellow U. Manchester, Eng., 1993-94. Mem. Am. Law Inst., Fed. Jud. Conf. 4th Cir., Libr. Co. Balt. Bar (bd. dirs. 1967—, pres. 1975-77), Engring. Soc. Md. (assoc.). Office: 8 W Hamilton St Baltimore MD 21201-5031

LIEBMANN, MARTHA, psychotherapist; b. Bklyn., Apr. 13, 1938; d. Edward M. and Elsa (Henner) Heyman; m. Jordan C. Schreiber, Dec. 25, 1958 (div. Dec. 1971); children: Eric, Nancy; m. Richard O. Liebmann, Aug. 25, 1990. BA, Queens Coll., 1957; MSW, Columbia U., 1959; PhD, Union Inst., Cin., 1989. Cert. social worker, N.Y.; lic. marriage and family counselor, N.J. Staff therapist group and indivdual therapy Washington Square Inst., N.Y.C., 1968—, dir. psychiat. social svcs., sr. supr., mem. faculty, 1980—; pvt. practice, 1974—. Mem. Am. Group Psychotherapy Assn., Nat. Assn. for Advancement Psychoanalysis, Coun. Psychoanalytic Psychotherapists. Jewish. Home: 229 Franklin St Haworth NJ 07641-1411 : Washington Square Inst 41 E 11th St Fl 4 New York NY 10003-4602 Office: Psychotherapy Assocs 253 S Washington Ave Bergenfield NJ 07621-3707

LIEBMANN, SEYMOUR W., construction consultant; b. N.Y.C., Nov. 1, 1928; s. Isidor W. and Etta (Waltzer) L.; m. Hinda Adam, Sept. 20, 1959; children: Peter Adam, David W. BSME, Clarkson U. (formerly Clarkson Coll. Tech.), 1948; grad. Indsl. Coll. Armed Forces, 1963, U.S. Army Command and Gen. Staff Coll., 1966, U.S. Army War Coll., 1971. Registered profl. engr., N.Y., Mass., Ga. Area engr. constrn. div. E.I. DuPont de Nemours & Co., Inc., 1952-54; constrn. planner Lummus Co., 1954-56; prin.

mech. engr. Perini Corp., 1956-62; v.p. Boston Based Contractors, 1962-66; v.p. A.R. Abrams, Inc., Atlanta, 1967-74, pres., 1974-78, also bd. dirs.; founder Liebmann Assocs., Inc., Atlanta, 1979—; mem. nat. adv. bd. Am. Security Council. Author: Military Engineer Field Notes, 1953, Prestressing Miter Gate Diagonals, 1960; contbr. articles to publs. Mem. USO Council, Atlanta, 1968—, v.p., 1978, mem. exec. com., 1975-79; mem. Nat. UN Day Com., 1975; sr. army coord., judge Sci. Fair, Atlanta Pub. Schs., annually 1979-88, 92-96; asst. scoutmaster troop 298 Atlanta area council Boy Scouts Am., 1980-87, Explorer advisor, 1982-86, unit commr., 1985, dist. commr. North Atlanta Dist., Atlanta Area Council, 1988-90, asst. coun. commr., 1990-95, mem. faculty Commrs. Coll., 1985-88, 92, North Atlanta Dist. com. BSA, 1996—; mem. alumni adv. com. Clarkson Coll. Tech., 1981—, alumni bd. govs., 1983-94, Disting. Alumni Golden Knight award, 1983; mem. exec. com., zoning chmn. neighbor planning unit City of Atlanta, 1982—, chmn., 1988, 95, 96, vice-chmn., 1989; pres. West Paces/Northside Neighborhood Assn., 1991—; apptd. civil engr. mem. to City of Atlanta Water and Sewer Appeals Bd., 1992—; apptd. mem. to Mayor's Bond Oversight Com. City of Atlanta, 1995—. Col. AUS Ret. Corps Engrs., 1948-52, Korea, Germany. Decorated Legion of Merit, Meritorious Service medal, U.S. Army Res. medal, 1975; elected to Old Guard of Gate City Guard, 1979; recipient cert. of Achievement Dept. Army, 1978, USO Recognition award, 1979, Order of Arrow award Boy Scouts Am., 1983, 87, Scouters Key Boy Scouts Am., 1988, North Atlanta Dist. Merit award Boy Scouts Am., 1989, Silver Beaver award, 1991, Disting. Commn. award, 1991, Engring. Profl. award Am. Inst. Plant Engrs., 1987; named Met. Atlanta Engr. of Yr. in Pvt. Practice Ga., 1991, Engr. of Yr. in Pvt. Practice, 1991. Fellow Soc. Am. Mil. Engrs. (bd. dirs. 1986—, chmn. readiness com. 1986-88, program chmn. Atlanta post 1980-81, v.p. 1982, pres. 1983, program chmn. 1988 nat. meeting, asst. regional v.p. for readiness So. region 1991—, Nat. award of Merit 1982-83, Atlanta post Leadership award 1988, life dir. Atlanta Post, 1994, elected nat. dir. 1994—, James Lucas Chair Atlanta Post, 1994, life mem.); mem. ASTM, NSPE, Am. Cons. Engrs. Coun. (state and nat. pub. rels. coms., nat. ethics com., state legis. liaison com.), Am. Concrete Inst., Soc. 1st U.S. Inf., Res. Officers Assn. (life mem.), U.S. Army War Coll. Found. (life mem.), Nat. Def. Univ. Found., U.S. Army War Coll. Alumni Assn. (life), Ga. Soc. Profl. Engrs. (bd. dirs. Buckhead chpt., state ethics com.), Engrs. Club Boston, Assn. U.S. Army, Def. Preparedness Assn., Am. Arbitration Assn. (panel arbitrators 1979—, constrn. adv. com. 1984—), Cobb C. of C., Downtown Atlanta Kiwanis, Mil. Order World Wars, Order of Engr., Army Engr. Assn. (life), Appalachian Trail Conf., Benyton Mackaye Trail Assn., Ga. Conservancy, Atlanta Hist. Soc., NRA. Republican. Jewish. Clubs: Ft. McPherson Officers; Ga. Appalachian Trail. Lodges: Masons (32 deg.), Shriners, Nat. Sojourners, Heros of '76, Elks, Civitan. Home: 3260 Rilman Dr NW Atlanta GA 30327-2224 Office: Ste 700 210 Interstate North Pky NW Atlanta GA 30339-2120

LIEBOW, JOANNE ELISABETH, marketing communication coordinator; b. Cleve., May 15, 1926; d. Arnold S. and Rhea Eunice (Levy) King; m. Irving M. Liebow, June 30, 1947 (div. Jan. 1972); children: Katherine Ann Liebow Frank, Peter. Student, Smith Coll., 1944-47; BA, Case Western Res. U., 1948. Cleve. reporter Fairchild Publs., N.Y.C., 1950-51; freelance pub. rels., Cleve., 1972-78; pub. info. specialist Cuyahoga Community Coll., Cleve., 1979—. Founder, pres. Mt. Sinai Hosp. Jr. Women's Aux., Cleve., 1948-50; pres. PTA, Bryden Elem. Sch., Beachwood, Ohio, 1964; mem. bd., pres. Beachwood Bd. Edn., 1968-76. Recipient Exceptional Achievement award Coun. for Advance Edn., 1982, Citation award, 1982, Grand Prize, 1983; Sophia Smith scholar Smith Coll., 1946, Cleve. Communicator's award Women in Communications, Inc., 1982. Home: 23511 Chagrin Blvd Apt 211 Cleveland OH 44122-5538 Office: Cuyahoga Community Coll Ea Campus 4250 Richmond Rd Cleveland OH 44122-6104

LIEBOW, PHOEBE AUGUSTA RECHT, nursing educator, school nurse; b. Pitts., Aug. 1, 1925; d. Nathan and Frieda (Laufe) Recht; m. Ely Milton Liebow, June 27, 1948; children: Wendy Faith Liebow Burson, Cynthia Hope Liebow, Franette Liebow. RN, Garfield Meml. Hosp., Washington, 1946; BA, Northeastern Ill. U., Chgo., 1972; MA, 1981. Asst. night supr. Garfield Meml. Hosp., Washington, 1946-47; head nurse, med./surg., 1947-48; vis. nurse Chgo., 1948-49, VNA of Ea. Union County, Elizabeth, N.J., 1948-51; clinic nurse North End Clinic, Detroit, 1951-52; substitute sch. nurse Dist. # 113, Highland Park, Deerfield, Ill., 1968-73; cert. sch. nurse Dist. # 39, Wilmette, Ill., 1973-91; mem. adj. faculty Nat. Louis U., Wheeling, Ill., 1992—; coord. and facilitator for anorexia nervosa peer support group northeastern Ill. U., Project Hope, Chgo., 1977-84; mem. health and safety curriculum com. Sch. Dist. 39, Wilmette, Ill., 1988-91. Co-author: (1 chpt.) Nursing Care Plan Workbook, 1985; contbr. articles to profl. jours. Vol. crisis line North Shore Help Line, Deerfield, Ill., 1970-71. Recipient Nursing on the Move plaque, ANA, 1990; grantee Creative Nutrition Edn. Tng., Ill., 1988. Fellow Am. Orthopsychiatric Assn.; mem. Ill. Assn. Sch. Nurses, Cert. Health Edn. Specialist, Garfield Meml. Hosp. Alumnae Assn., Nat. Found. for Osteoprorosis, Congregation Solel. Avocations: reading, travel, swimming, attending conferences on Sherlock Holmes and Conan Doyle and popular culture. Home: 1694 Elmwood Dr Highland Park IL 60035-2320

LIEBOWITZ, HAROLD, federal agency administrator, aeronautical engineering educator, dean emeritus; b. Bklyn., June 25, 1924; s. Samuel and Sarah (Kaplan) L.; m. Marilyn Iris Lampert, June 24, 1951; children: Alisa Lynn, Jay, Jill Denice. B. in Aero. Engring., Poly. Inst. Bklyn., 1944, M. in Aero. Engring., 1946, D. in Aero. Engring., 1948. With Office Naval Research, 1948-60; asst. dean Grad. Sch., exec. dir. engring. expt. sta. U. Colo., Boulder, 1960-61; also vis. prof. aero. engring. U. Colo.; head structural mechs. br. Office Naval Research, 1961-68, dir. Navy programs in solid propellant mechanics, 1962-68; dean Sch. Engring. and Applied Sci., George Washington U., Washington, 1968-90; L. Stanley Crane endowed prof., 1990—; rsch. prof., endowed prof. Cath. U., Washington, 1962-68; pres. NAE, Washington, 1995; cons. AERDCO, 1960—, Office Naval Rsch., 1970—, Pratt & Whitney Aircraft Co., 1981-82, Pergamon Press, 1968—, Acad. Press, 1968—; mem. Israeli-Am. Materials Adv. Group, 1970—; sci. adviser Congl. Ad Hoc Com. on Environ. Quality, 1969—; co-dir. Joint Inst. for Advancement Flight Scis. NASA-Langley Rsch. Ctr., Hampton, Va., 1971—. Editor: Advanced Treatise on Fracture, 7 vols., 1969-72; founder, editor-in-chief Internat. Jour. Computers and Structures, 1971—; founder, editor Internat. Jour. Engring. Fracture Mechanics, 1968—; founder computer series jours., 1968—; contbr. articles to profl. jours. Bd. govs. U. Denver, 1987—. Recipient Outstanding award Office Naval Research, 1961, Research Accomplishment Superior award, 1961; Superior Civilian Service award USN, 1965, 67; Commendation Outstanding Contbns. sec. navy, 1966; Wash. Soc. Engrs. award, Ednl. Service award, Wash. Soc. Engrs., Fundacion Gran Mariscal de Avacucho, Service cert. Tech. Contbns. to Structures and Materials Panel, NATO, Disting. Alumnus award Polytechnic Inst. Bklyn., Tech. Achievement cert. Washington sect. ASME, Civilian Service award USN, Albert Einstein prize, 1991, Washington Acad. of Scis. award for Disting. career in Sci., 1990. Fellow AAAS, AIAA, Am. Soc. Metals; mem. Soc. Engring. Scis. (past pres.), Sci. Rsch. Soc. Am., Am. Technion Soc. (dir.), Am. Acad. Mechanics (founder, pres.), Internat. Coop. Fracture Inst. (founder, v.p.), Engrs. Coun. for Profl. Devel., nat. Acad. Engring. (home sec.), Engring. Acad. Japan, Argentina NAS, Hungarian Acad. Scis., Sigma Xi, Tau Beta Pi, Sigma Gamma Tau, Omega Rho, Pi Tau Sigma, Sigma Tau. Office: National Academy of Engineering Office of the President 2101 Constitution Ave NW Washington DC 20418-0007

LIEBOWITZ, LEO, oil company executive; b. 1926. Former pres. Leemilts Petroleum Inc., L.I., N.Y., from 1961; now pres., chief exec. officer Getty Petroleum Co., Jericho, N.Y. Served with U.S. Army, 1943-46. Office: Getty Petroleum Corp 125 Jericho Tpke Jericho NY 11753-1016*

LIEBTAG, BENFORD GUSTAV, III (BEN LIEBTAG), engineer, consultant; b. Pitts., Sept. 20, 1941; s. Benford Gustav and Alice Mildred (Hunt) L.; children: Cindy, Ben. BSEE, U. Pitts., 1964. Sr. heating and air-conditioning engr. Duquesne Light Co., Pitts., 1964-79; dir. energy mgmt. Van Wagenen and Searcy, Inc., Jacksonville, Fla., 1979-80, v.p., 1980-81; pres. Liebtag, Robinson, and Wingfield, Inc., Jacksonville and Gainesville, Fla., 1981. Mem. ASHRAE (Merit award, Disting. Service award), Assn. Energy Engrs., Soc. Am. Mil. Engrs. Methodist. Lodges: Masons, Kiwanis. Home: 4084 Big Hollow Ln Jacksonville FL 32277 Office: 4201 Baymeadows Rd Ste 1 Jacksonville FL 32217

LIECHTY, ERIC, church administrator. Youth dir. The Missionary Church, Fort Wayne, Ind. Office: The Missionary Ch PO Box 9127 3811 Vanguard Dr Fort Wayne IN 46809-3304

LIEDERMAN, DAVID SAMUEL, child welfare administrator; b. Malden, Mass., Apr. 26, 1935; s. Harry A. Liederman; married; children: Wendy, Keith, Larry. BA, U. Mass., 1957; MEd, Springfield Coll., 1958; MSW, U. Pitts., 1962. Teenage supr. Youngstown (Ohio) Jewish Community Ctr., 1958-62; dir. extension services Roxbury (Mass.) Neighborhood House, 1962-64; asst. dir. Roxbury Fedn. Neighborhood Ctrs., 1964-66; dir. family relocation United South End Settlements, Boston, 1966-69; state rep. Mass. Ho. Reps., Boston, 1969-73; dir. Mass. State Office for Children, Boston, 1973-75; chief of staff Mass. Gov. Michael S. Dukakis, Boston, 1975-79; exec. dir. pub. affairs Fedn. Jewish Philanthropies, N.Y.C., 1979-84; exec. dir. Child Welfare League Am., Washington, Boston, Chgo., and L.A., 1984—. Contbr. numerous articles to profl. jours. Bd. dirs. Nat. Assembly, Washington, 1984—; mem. United Way Am. Leadership 18, Alexandria, Va., 1984—; chair Nat. Collaboration for Youth, 1990-94; co-chair Generations United, 1987—. Recipient Disting. Alumni award U. Pitts., 1975. Office: Child Welfare League Am 440 1st St NW Washington DC 20001-2028

LIEDMAN, JULIE, magazine editor; b. Phila., Mar. 16, 1947; d. Samuel and Tybie (Marder) Moshinsky; m. John Liedman, Nov. 23, 1969; children: Eli Andrew, Gabriel Ethan, Amy Elizabeth. BA, Pa. State U., 1968. Reporter Evening & Sunday Bull., Phila., 1967-79; prin. Liedman Enterprises, Phila., 1979-89; sr. editor Bus. Phila. Mag., 1990-93, exec. editor, 1993-95, editor-in-chief, 1995—. Office: Business Phila Magazine 260 S Broad St Philadelphia PA 19102

LIEF, HAROLD ISAIAH, psychiatrist; b. N.Y.C., Dec. 29, 1917; s. Jacob F. and Mollie (Filler) L.; m. Myrtis A. Brumfield, Mar. 3, 1961; Caleb B., Frederick V., Oliver F.; children from previous marriage: Polly Lief Goldberg, Jonathan F. BA, U. Mich., 1938; MD, NYU, 1942; cert. in psychoanalysis, Columbia Coll. Physicians and Surgeons, 1950; MA (hon.), U. Pa., 1971. Intern Queens Gen. Hosp., Jamaica, N.Y., 1942-43; resident psychiatry L.I. Coll. Medicine, 1946-48; pvt. practice psychiatry N.Y.C., 1948-51; asst. physician Presbyn. Hosp., N.Y.C., 1949-51; asst. prof. Tulane U., New Orleans, 1951-54, asso. prof., 1954-60, prof. psychiatry, 1960-67; prof. psychiatry U. Pa., Phila., 1967-82, prof. emeritus, 1982—; dir. div. family study U. Pa., 1967-81; dir. Marriage Council of Phila., 1969-81, Ctr. for Study of Sex. Edn. in Medicine, 1968-82; mem. staff U. Pa. Hosp., 1967-81, Pa. Hosp., 1981—; clin. prof. psychiatry Jefferson Med. U., 1994—. Author: (with Daniel and William Thompson) The Eighth Generation, 1960; Editor: (with Victor and Nina Lief) Psychological Basis of Medical Practice, 1963, Medical Aspects of Human Sexuality, 1976, (with Arno Karlen) Sex Education in Medicine, 1976, Sexual Problems in Medical Practice, 1981, (with Zwi Hoch) Sexology: Sexual Biology, Behavior and Therapy, 1982, (with Zwi Hoch) International Research in Sexology, 1983, Human Sexuality With Respect to AIDS and HIV Infection, 1989; contbr. numerous articles to publs. Bd. dirs. Ctr. for Sexuality and Religion; mem. La. State Commn. Civil Rights, 1958-67. Maj. M.C. U.S. Army, 1943-46. Commonwealth Fund fellow, 1963-64; recipient Gold Medal award Mt. Airy Hosp., 1977, Lifetime Achievement award Phila. Psychiat. Soc., 1992. Fellow Phila. Coll. Physicians, Am. Psychiat. Assn. (life), N.Y. Acad. Scis., AAAS, Am. Acad. Psychoanalysis (charter, past pres.), Am. Coll. Psychiatrists (founding), Am. Coll. Psychoanalysts (charter); mem. Am. Assn. Marriage and Family Therapists, Sex Info. and Edn. Council U.S. (past pres.), Group Advancement Psychiatry (life), Am. Soc. Adolescent Psychiatry, Am. Psychosomatic Soc., Assn. Psychoanalytic Medicine (life), Internat. Acad. Sex Rsch., Soc. Sci. Study of Sex, Am. Soc. Sex Educators, Counselors and Therapists, Soc. Sex Therapists and Researchers, World Assn. Sexology (past v.p.), Soc. Exploration of Psychotherapy Integration (adv. bd.), Columbia Club, Mich. Club of Greater Phila., Penn Club of N.Y., Sigma Xi, Alpha Omega Alpha, Phi Eta Sigma, Phi Kappa Phi. Home: 101 S Buck Ln Haverford PA 19041-1104 Office: Ste 719 987 Old Eagle School Rd Wayne PA 19087 *The conflict between individual gratification and the needs of society, between competition and cooperation, appears to me to be the most fundamental issue confronting mankind. My goal in life has been to steer a course that fosters service to others and to society without undue sacrifice of individual aspirations.*

LIEF, THOMAS PARRISH, sociologist, educator; b. N.Y.C., Oct. 4, 1931; s. Alfred and Zola Nina (Vogel) L. BA, U. N.Mex., 1955, MA, 1961; PhD, Tulane U., 1970. Bd. cert. substance abuse counselor, La.; case presentation evaluator. Counselor, archaeology asst. U. N.Mex., Albuquerque, 1959-60, 60-61; tchg. asst. dept. sociology Tulane U., New Orleans, 1961-64; instr. to asst. prof. dept. sociology Loyola U., New Orleans, 1964-69; assoc. prof. to prof. dept. sociology So. U., New Orleans, 1968—; cons. on curriculum devel. Tuskegee Inst. Drug Abuse Human Svcs. Manpower Devel. Tng., 1973-78; adj. prof. sociology, assoc. grad. faculty mem. U. New Orleans, 1975-76; cons. various orgns., 1981-82; vis. prof. dept. sociology Tulane U., New Orleans, 1986; rev. com. mem. Alcohol, Drug Abuse & Mental Health Adminstrn. Office, 1987—; bd. dirs. Nat. Assn. Alcoholism and Drug Abuse Counselors, 1990-91; pres. La. Assn. Substance Abuse Counselor and Trainers, 1990-91; adv. bd. Michael Halbrook Recovery Ctr. East Lake Hosp., 1990-92; mem. La. State Bd. Certification for Substance Abuse Counselors, 1988-92, Adv. Com. for Historically Black Colls. and Univs. Program for Substance Abuse Tng., 1987-89; tng. cons. Am. Indian Tng. Inst., Sacramento, Calif., 1985—; mem. La. Commn. on Alcohol and Drug Abuse, 1984-91; mem. L.A. Drug Control and Violent Crime Policy Bd., 1993—; contract cons. Ctr. for Substance Abuse Treatment, 1994—; founder, bd. dirs. Accreditation Coun.: Alcohol and Drug Counselor Program in Higher Edn.; cons. in field. Contbr. numerous articles to profl. jours.; mem. editl. rev. com. Counselor, 1986-92; co-author: Academic Linkages Resource Manual. Co-chair La. State-Wide Taskforce Counselor Manpower, 1984-90; pres., founder Nat. Assn. Substance Abuse Trainers and Educators, 1983—; bd. dirs. Nat. Commn. on Accreditation of Alcoholism and Drug Abuse Counselors, 1982-90, Certification Reciprocity Consortium/Alcohol and Other Drug Abuse, Inc., 1981-82; pres., founder La. Cert. Examining Bd. of La. Assn. Substance Abuse Counselor & Trainers, 1978-82; mem. Child Abuse Com. Dist. Atty.'s Office, 1976-80; co-dir. Insight House Adv. Bd., 1976-80. Mem. Am. Sociol. Assn., Am. Acad. Polit. and Social Scis., La. Assn. Substance Abuse Counselors and Trianers, La. Alcohol and Drug Abuse Assn., Nat. Assn. Alcoholism and Substance Abuse Counselors, Nat. Assn. Substance Abuse Trainers and Educators, Soc. for Applied Anthropology, Soc. for Study of Social Problems, So. Sociol. Soc., Substance Abuse Counselor Orgn., Nat. Commn. on Accreditation of Alcoholism and Drug Abuse Counselors Credentialing Bodies. Office: 6400 Press Dr New Orleans LA 70126-1009

LIEGL, JOSEPH LESLIE, lawyer; b. Fond du Lac, Wis., Jan. 20, 1948; s. Melvin Theodore and Verna Lavinia (Jagdfeld) L.; m. Janet L. Meyer, Feb. 1, 1969; children: Matthew, Jeremy. BA with distinction, U. Wis., 1970, JD cum laude, 1973. Bar: Wis. 1973, U.S. Supreme Ct. 1976, Ohio 1978, U.S. Dist. Ct. (no. dist.) Ohio 1978, U.S. Ct. Claims 1978, U.S. Tax Ct. 1978. Assoc. Muchin & Muchin S.C., Manitowoc, Wis., 1973-74; trial atty. U.S. Dept. Justice, Washington, 1974-78; assoc. Jones, Day, Reavis & Pogue, Cleve., 1978-83, ptnr., 1984-96; ptnr. Coopers & Lybrand LLP, Detroit, 1996—. Mem. ABA (taxation sect.), Cleve. Bar Assn. (chmn. tax sect. 1987-88), Cleve. Tax Club (v.p. 1993-95, pres. 1995-96, past bd. dirs.), Order of Coif, Phi Eta Sigma, Phi Kappa Phi. Avocation: music. Home: 16824 Holbrook Rd Cleveland OH 44120-3446 Office: Jones Day Reavis & Pogue 983 Cold Spring Dr Northville MI 48167 also: Coopers & Lybrand LLP 400 Renaissance Ctr Detroit MI 48243-1507

LIEN, BRUCE HAWKINS, minerals and oil company executive; b. Waubay, S.D., Apr. 7, 1927; s. Peter Calmer and LaRece Catherine (Holm) L.; m. Deanna Jean Browning, May 4, 1978. BS in Bus., Wyo. U., 1953; D of Bus. (hon.), S.D. Sch. Mines & Tech., 1996. Chmn. bd. Pete Lien & Sons, Inc., Rapid City, S.D., 1944-84, bd. chmn., 1984—; chmn. Concorde Gaming Corp., 1990—, Browning Resources U.S., 1989—. Chmn. Community Chest, Rapid City, S.D., 1956; pres., nat. council Boys Club Am., Rapid City, S.D., N.Y.C., 1968; commr. Presdl. Scholars Commn., Washington, 1982; pres. U. Wyo, Found., 1989-90; life bd. dirs. Salvation Army. Served to 1st lt. U.S. Army, 1945-47, 50-52. Recipient Disting. Service award S.D. Sch. Mines, Rapid City, 1972, Disting. Service award Cosmopolitan Internat., Rapid City, 1983; named Disting. Alumnus, Wyo. U., Laramie, 1982. Mem. Internat. Lime Assn. (pres. 1973-75), Nat. Lime Assn. (pres. 1973-75, Merit award 1973, bd. dirs.), VFW, Am. Legion. Republican. Lutheran. Club: Cosmopolitan (Rapid City, S.D.). Lodges: Masons, Elks. Home: PO Box 440 Rapid City SD 57709-0440 Office: Pete Lien & Sons Inc I 90 & Deadwood Ave PO Box 440 Rapid City SD 57709-0440

LIEN, ERIC JUNG-CHI, pharmacist, educator; b. Kaohsiung, Taiwan, Nov. 30, 1937; came to U.S., 1963, naturalized, 1973; m. Linda L. Chen, Oct. 2, 1965; children: Raymond, Andrew. B.S. in Pharmacy (Frank Shu China Sci. scholar), Nat. Taiwan U., 1960; PhD in Pharm. Chemistry, U. Calif., San Francisco, 1966; postdoctoral fellow in bio-organic chemistry, Pomona Coll., Claremont, Calif., 1967-68. Hosp. pharmacist 862 Hosp. of Republic of China, 1960-61; asst. prof. pharmaceutics and biomedicinal chemistry U. So. Calif., L.A., 1968-72; assoc. prof. U. So. Calif., 1972-76, prof., 1976—, coord. sects. biomedicinal chemistry and pharms., 1975-78, coord. sect. biomedicinal chemistry, 1975-84; cons. Internat. Medication Sys., Ltd., 1978, NIH, 1971, 82-87, 92, 94, Inst. Drug Design, Inc., Calif., 1971-73, Allergan Pharms., Inc., 1971-72, EPA, 1985, 89, Ariz. Disease Control Rsch. Commn., 1986—; sci. adv. nat. labs. Dept. Health, Foods and Drugs, Exec., Yuan, China, Dept. Health Taipei, Taiwan, 1992-94; referee Jour. Pharmacokinetics and Biopharmaceutics, Jour. Medicinal Chemistry, Jour. Food Agr. Chemistry, Jour. Pharm. Sci., Pesticide Biochemistry and Physiology, Chem. Resv., Jour. Organic Chemistry, Pharm. Rsch., Jour. Drug Target, Internat. Jour. Oriental Medicine, Am. Jour. Pharm. Edn. Author 3 books; mem. editorial bd. Jour. Clin. Pharmacy and Therapeutics, 1979—, Internat. Jour. Oriental Medicine, Med. Chem. Rsch., 1991—, Chinese Pharm. Jour., 1991-93, Acta Pharmaceutica, 1992—; contbr. numerous articles to profl. jours. Grantee Merck, 1970, Abbott, 1971-72, NSF, 1972-74, 76-77, IMS, 1979, H & L Found., 1989-96. Fellow AAPS, AAAS, Louis Pasteur Found.; mem. Am. Assn. Cancer Rsch., Acad. Pharm. Scis., Am. Chem. Soc., Am. Assn. Pharm. Scientists, Internat. Union Pure and Applied Chemistry, Sigma Xi, Rho Chi, Phi Kappa Phi. Office: U So Calif Sch Pharmacy 1985 Zonal Ave Los Angeles CA 90033-1058

LIENHARD, JOHN HENRY, mechanical engineering educator; b. St. Paul, Aug. 17, 1930; s. John Henry and Catherine Edith Lienhard; m. Carol Ann Bratton, June 20, 1959; children: John Henry V, Andrew Joseph. A.S., Multnomah Jr. Coll., 1949; BS, Oreg. State Coll., 1951; MS in M.E., U. Wash.-Seattle, 1953; PhD in Mech. Engring., U. Calif.-Berkeley, 1961. Assoc. prof. mech. engring. Wash. State U., Pullman, 1961-67; prof. mech. engring. dept. U. Ky., Lexington, 1967-80; Clyde chair prof. U. Utah, Salt Lake City, summer 1981; prof. mech. engring. U. Houston, 1980-89; M.D. Anderson prof. mech. engring. and history, 1989—. Recipient Portrait award Am. Women in Radio and TV, 1990. Mem. ASME (hon., heat transfer meml. award, Charles Russ Richards award, Ralph Coats Roe medal), Am. Soc. Engring. Edn. (Ralph Coates Roe Teaching medal). Episcopalian. Author 4 books; author/host of program on Pub. Radio, The Engines of Our Ingenuity, also numerous articles in profl. jours. Home: 3719 Durhill St Houston TX 77025 Office: U Houston Dept Mech Engring Houston TX 77204-4792

LIENHART, DAVID ARTHUR, geologist, consultant, laboratory director; b. Cin., Sept. 28, 1939; s. Arthur C. and Grace H.J. (Burger) L.; m. Donna Paula Klosterman, June 12, 1964; children—Devin Scott, Dana Ann. B.A., U. Cin., 1961, M.S., 1964. Cert. profl. geologist, Ind.; registered geologist, Del.; lic. profl. geologist, N.C. Petrographer Ohio River Div. Lab., Cin., 1964-70, geologist, 1970-76; geologist, lab. dir. Ohio River Div. Lab., 1976-90; hydrologist geotech. HTRW div. U.S. Army Corps Engrs., 1990-95; cons. constrn. rock properties and evaluation of rock for erosion control, 1995—; ptnr. Rock Products Cons.; agy. chmn. Combined Fed. Campaign, 1982-84, 89; guest spkr. internat. tech. seminars. Contbr. articles to profl. jours.; author and editor tech. publs. U. Cin. Dept. Army fellow, 1986-87; recipient Outstanding Pub. Svc. award, City of Cin., 1994. Fellow Geol. Soc. Am., Geol. Soc. London; mem. ASCE, ASTM (Excellence in Symposium and Publ. Mgmt. 1995), Assn. Engring. Geologists, Nat. Ground Water Assn., Geol. Soc. Ky., Internat. Soc. Engring. Geologists, Sigma Xi. Methodist. Avocations: fishing, music. Office: 7229 Longfield Dr Cincinnati OH 45243-2209

LIEPMANN, HANS WOLFGANG, physicist, educator; b. Berlin, Germany, July 3, 1914; came to U.S. 1939, naturalized, 1945.; s. Wilhelm and Emma (Leser) L.; m. Kate Kaschinsky, June 19, 1939 (div.); m. Dietlind Wegener Goldschmidt, 1954; 2 children. Student, U. Istanbul, 1933-35, U. Prague, 1935; Ph.D., U. Zurich, 1938; Dr. Engring. (hon.), Tech. U. Aachen, 1985. Research fellow U. Zurich, 1938-39; mem. faculty Calif. Inst. Tech., Pasadena, 1939, prof. aeronautics, 1949—, dir. Grad. Aeronautical Labs., 1972-85, Charles Lee Powell prof. fluid mechanics and thermodynamics, 1976-83, Theodore von Kármán prof. aeronautics, 1983-85, Theodore von Kármán prof. aeronautics emeritus, 1985—; mem. research and tech. adv. com. on basic research NASA. Co-author: (with A.E. Puckett) Aerodynamics of a Compressible Fluid, 1947; (with A. Roshko) Elements of Gas-dynamics, 1957. Contbr. articles to profl. jours. Recipient Physics prize U. Zurich, 1939, Pradtl Ring, German Soc. Aeros. and Astronautics, 1968, Worcester Reed Warner medal ASME, 1969, Michelson-Morley award Case Inst. Tech., 1979, Nat. Medal of Sci., U.S. Dept. Commerce, 1986, Guggenheim Med, Daniel Guggenheim Med. Bd. of Award, 1986, Nat. Medal of Tech., U.S. Dept. Commerce, 1993. Address: Calif Inst Tech Dept Aeronautics Pasadena CA 91125

LIETZ, JEREMY JON, educational administrator, writer; b. Milw., Oct. 4, 1933; s. John Norman and Dorothy B. (Drew) L.; m. Cora Fernandez, Feb. 24, 1983; children: Cheryl, Brian, Angela, Andrew, Christopher. BS, U. Wis., Milw., 1961; MS, U. Wis., Madison, 1971; EdD, Marquette U., 1980. Tchr. Milw. Pub. Schs., 1961-63, diagnostic counselor, 1968-71; sch. adminstr., 1971-95; Tchr. Madison (Wis.) Pub. Schs., 1964-65; rsch. assoc. U. Wis., Madison, 1965-67; instr. Marquette U., Milw., 1980-82; lectr. HEW Conf. on Reading, Greeley, Colo., 1973, NAESP Conf. on Reading, St. Louis, 1974, various state and nat. orgns.; co-founder, bd. dirs., cons. Ednl. Leadership Inst., Shorewood, Wis., 1980—; dir. Religious Edn. Program, Cath. Elem. East, Milw., 1985-86. Author: The Elementary School Principal's Role in Special Education, 1982; contbr. numerous articles, chpts., tests, revs. to profl. jours. V.p. PTA, 1961-62. With U.S. Army, 1954-56, ETO. Recipient Cert. of Achievement award NAESP, 1974. Mem. AAAS, Assn. Wis. Sch. Adminstrs. (mem. state planning com. 1977-79, lectr. 1982), Adminstrs. and Suprs. Coun. (mem. exec. bd. dist. 1977-79, mem. contract negotiations com. 1991-95), Filipino Am. Assn. Wis., U. Wis. Alumni Assn. (Madison), Milw. Mcpl. Chess Assn., U.S. Chess Fedn., Phi Delta Kappa. Home: 2205 N Summit Ave Milwaukee WI 53202-1213 Office: Ednl Leadership Inst PO Box 11411 Milwaukee WI 53211-0411

LIETZKE, MILTON HENRY, chemistry educator; b. Syracuse, N.Y., Nov. 23, 1920; s. Henry Robert and Emma (Gutknecht) L.; m. Marjorie Helen Padrutt, May 31, 1943; children: Kathryn Ann, Milton Henry, Carol Lynn; m. Eleanor Jean Hawkins, May 29, 1965; adopted children: Susan Lucinda, Mary Lindl. B.A., Colgate U., 1942; M.S., U. Wis., 1944, Ph.D., 1949. Lab. supr. Tenn. Eastman Corp., Oak Ridge, 1944-47; group leader chemistry div. Oak Ridge Nat. Lab., 1949-74, sr. scientist, 1978-83; prof. chemistry U. Tenn., Knoxville, 1964-90, prof. emeritus, 1990—. Contbr. numerous articles and reports to profl. jours. Bd. dirs. Oak Rige Festival, 1962-64. Fellow Am. Inst. Chemists, N.Y. Acad. Scis.; mem. Am. Chem. Soc. (D.A. Shirley award East Tenn. sect. 1991), Sci. Research Soc. Am., Tenn. Acad. Sci., Alpha Chi Sigma. Home: 7600 Twining Dr Knoxville TN 37919-7127 Office: U Tenn Dept Chemistry Knoxville TN 37916

LIFFERS, WILLIAM ALBERT, retired chemical company executive; b. Union City, N.J., Jan. 12, 1929; s. William F. and Gertrude (Wildemann) L.; m. Mary Rafferty, Sept. 5, 1953; children—Steven, Linda, Wendy. B.S. in Bus. Adminstrn, Seton Hall U., 1953. With Am. Cyanamid Co., Wayne, N.J., 1953—; v.p. Cyanamid Internat., 1972-74; pres. Cyanamid Internat. (Cyanamid Americas/Far East), 1974-76, corp. v.p., 1976-77, sr. v.p., dir., 1977-78, vice chmn., 1978-93; ret., 1993; sr. advisor UN Devel. Programme, 1994. Bd. dirs. Nat. Planning Assn., N.J. Inst. Tech., Coun. U.S. and Italy. Served with Finance Corps U.S. Army, 1951-53.

LIFFLANDER, MATTHEW L., lawyer; b. N.Y.C., Sept. 18, 1932; s. Ben and May (Galowitz) L.; m. Barbara Bukowska, June 10, 1961; children: Clay, Justin. B.A., NYU, 1954; J.D., Cornell U., 1957. Bar: N.Y. 1958. Asst. counsel to N.Y. Gov. Averell Harriman; v.p., chief internat. counsel Hertz Internat. Ltd.; chmn. bd. Uniworld, 1969-72; ptnr. Townley and Updike, N.Y.C.; dir., chief counsel Med. Practice Task Force, N.Y. State Assembly, 1977-78; counsel Select Com. on Election Law Reform, N.Y. State Legislature, 1973-74; dir. Ralph Lauren Footwear, Inc. Author: Final Treatment, 1976. Mem. Gov.'s Task Force on Tourism in N.Y. State, 1975; trustee Hudson River Mus., 1986—, chmn. bd. dirs., 1991—; mem. Nat. Adv. Council SBA, 1967-68; fin. chmn. N.Y. State Democratic Party, 1973-74. Mem. Assn. Bar City N.Y., N.Y. State Magistrates Assn. Clubs: Nat. Democratic, Wings, University (N.Y.C.). Office: 405 Lexington Ave New York NY 10174

LIFLAND, JOHN C., federal judge; b. 1933. BA, Yale U., 1954; LLB, Harvard U., 1957. Pvt. practice law, 1957-59; law sec. to Hon. Thomas F. Meaney U.S. Dist. Ct. N.J., 1959-61; mem. firm Stryker, Tams & Dill, 1961-88; dist. judge U.S. Dist. Ct. N.J., Newark, 1988—; mem. N.J. State Bd. Bar Examiners, 1968-77. 1st lt. U.S. Army, 1958. Fellow Am. Bar Found., Assn. Fed. Bar (v.p. 1986—), N.J. State Bar Assn., Essex County Bar Assn.; mem. ABA (antitrust sect. publs. com., books editor/co-editor Antitrust Law Jour. 1981-87), Clearwater Seim Club, Essex Club, Harvard Law Sch. Assn. Office: US Dist Ct M L King Fed Bldg & Cthouse PO Box 999 Newark NJ 07101-0999*

LIFLAND, WILLIAM THOMAS, lawyer; b. Jersey City, Nov. 15, 1928; s. Charles and Carolyn (Francks) L.; m. Nancy Moffat, May 29, 1954; children—Carol M., Charles C., J. Kerin, David T. B.S., Yale U., 1949; J.D., Harvard U., 1952. Bar: D.C. 1954, N.Y. 1955, N.J. 1965. Law clk. to Justice John M. Harlan U.S. Supreme Ct., 1954-55; assoc. Cahill Gordon & Reindel, N.Y.C., 1955-58, Paris, 1958-60; ptnr. Cahill Gordon & Reindel, N.Y.C., 1965—; adj. prof. Fordham Law Sch., N.Y.C. Served as lt. USAF, 1952-54. Mem. ABA, N.Y. State Bar Assn., N.J. Bar Assn., D.C. Bar Assn., N.Y. County Lawyers Assn., Assn. Bar City N.Y. Clubs: India House (N.Y.C.), Nassau Club (Princeton, N.J.). Office: Cahill Gordon & Reindel 80 Pine St New York NY 10005-1702

LIFSCHULTZ, PHILLIP, financial and tax consultant, lawyer; b. Oak Park, Ill., Mar. 5, 1927; s. Abraham Albert and Frances Rhoda (Siegel) L.; m. Edith Louise Leavitt, June 27, 1948; children: Gregory, Bonnie, Jodie. BS in Acctg., U. Ill., 1949; JD, John Marshall Law Sch., 1956. Bar: Ill. 1956; CPA, Ill. Tax mgr. Arthur Andersen & Co., Chgo., 1957-63; v.p. taxes Montgomery Ward & Co., Chgo., 1963-78; fin. v.p., contr. Henry Crown & Co., Chgo., 1978-81; prin. Phillip Lifschultz & Assocs., Chgo., 1981—; exec. dir. Dodi Orgn., 1987-90. Mem. adv. coun. Coll. Commerce and Bus. Adminstrn. U. Ill., Urbana-Champaign, 1977-78; chmn., Civic Fedn. Chgo., 1980-82; chmn. adv. bd. to Auditor Gen. of Ill., 1965-73; project dir. Exec. Service Corps of Chgo., Chgo. Bd. Edn. and State of Ill. projects, 1980-87. With U.S. Army, 1945-46. Mem. Ill. Bar Assn., Chgo. Bar Assn., Am. Inst. CPA's, Ill. CPA Soc., Am. Arbitration Assn. (comml. panel 1983-94), Nat. Retail Merchants Assn. (chmn. tax com. 1975-78), Am. Retail Fedn. (chmn. taxation com. 1971), Standard Club. Home and Office: 976 Oak Dr Glencoe IL 60022-1427

LIFSON, KALMAN ALAN, management consultant, retail executive; b. Mpls., Oct. 15, 1926; s. Maurice Kalman and Gertrude (Shulkin) L.; m. Irene Londer, June 17, 1950 (dec. July 1968); m. Judith Abrams, Sept. 3, 1969; children: Valerie Leftwich, Kipp, Ione Spear, Stacey Dorfman, Grant Dorfman. BS in Naval Tech., U. Minn., 1946, MABA, 1949; PhD in Psychology, Purdue U., 1951. Commd. ensign USN, 1945, lt. (j.g), 1952; engrng. officer Panama Canal Zone, 1945-46; supr. indsl. engrng. Temco Aircraft, Dallas, 1951-52; mgmt. engrng. officer USN, Washington, 1953-54, resigned; prin. Lifson, Wilson, Ferguson & Winick, Dallas, 1954-94, Pers. Decisions, Inc., Dallas, 1995—; chmn. Harris'Dept. Stores, San Bernadino, Calif., 1980-94, Tex. Rsch. and Electronic Corp. and successors, Dallas, 1962-94, Electronic Mgmt. Info. Sys., 1970-94; chmn. emeritus B.R. Blackmarr & Assocs., Dallas, 1986—; chmn. Fed. Home Loan Bank of 9th Dist., Little Rock, 1979-80; bd. dirs. Bioseparations Inc., Tucson, Ariz., Century Univ., Albuquerque; speaker in fields of psychology, retailing, banking, ops. rsch. Contbr. articles to profl. jours. Chmn. Congl. Commn. on Guaranteed Student Loans, Washington, 1975, Commn. on Orgn. of U.S. Dept. Labor, Washington, 1976; mem. Tex. Commn. on State Employee Productivity, Austin, Tex., 1985. Mem. Am. Psychol. Assn., World Pres. Orgn., Columbian Club (treas. 1950—), Crescent Club, Sigma Xi. Jewish. Office: Pers Decisions Inc Ste 1700 600 E Las Colinas Blvd Irving TX 75039 *"Winners" are those who can make the big play, who can turn the game around, who can conceive and institute dramatic changes. Those few of us who have been so endowed and developed must use our winnership to effect significant improvements to the well-being of those within our spheres of influence.*

LIFTIN, JOHN MATTHEW, lawyer; b. Washington, June 25, 1943; children: Eric, Hilary. AB, U. Pa., 1964; LLB, Columbia U., 1967. Bar: N.Y.. 1967, D.C. 1974, U.S. Dist. Ct. D.C. 1975, U.S. Ct. Appeals (D.C. cir.) 1975, U.S. Supreme Ct. 1980. Assoc. Sullivan & Cromwell, N.Y.C., 1967-71; spl. counsel to chmn. SEC, Washington, 1971-72, assoc. dir. market reg. div., 1972-74; ptnr. Rogers & Wells, Washington, 1974-85; pres. Quadrex Securities Corp., N.Y.C., 1985-87; sr. v.p., gen. counsel Kidder, Peabody Group Inc., N.Y.C., 1987—; mem. adv. bd. securities regulation and law reports Bur. Nat. Affairs, Inc., Washington, 1979—. Contbr. articles on securities law to profl. jours. Mem. ABA (chmn. com. on fed. regulation securities), Univ. Club. Office: Kidder Peabody & Co Inc 60 Broad St 3rd Fl New York NY 10004

LIFTON, ROBERT JAY, psychiatrist, author; b. N.Y.C., May 16, 1926; s. Harold A. and Ciel (Roth) L.; m. Betty Jean Kirschner, Mar. 1, 1952; children: Kenneth Jay, Natasha Karen. Student, Cornell U., 1942-44; MD, N.Y. Med. Coll., 1948, DHL, 1977; DSc (hon.), Lawrence U., 1971, Merrimack Coll., 1973; DHL (hon.), Wilmington Coll., 1975, N.Y. Med. Coll., 1977, Marlboro Coll., 1983, Maryville Coll., 1983, Iona Coll., 1984; DSc (hon.), U. Vt., 1984, Amerika Institut Der Universitat, Munich, 1989; DHL (hon.), U. New Haven, 1986. Intern Jewish Hosp., Bklyn., 1948-49; resident psychiatry State U. N.Y. Downstate Med. Center, 1949-51; mem. faculty Washington Sch. Psychiatry, 1954-55; research assoc. psychiatry, also assoc. East Asian studies Harvard U., 1956-61; Found.'s Fund for research psychiatry assoc. prof. Yale Med. Sch., 1961-67, research prof., 1967—; disting. prof. psychiatry and psychology, dir. Ctr. on Violence and Human Survival John Jay Coll. Criminal Justice, the Grad Sch. and Univ. Ctr. and Mt. Sinai Sch. Medicine, CUNY, 1985—; cons. behavioral scis. study sect. NIMH, 1962-64; com. invasion of privacy N.Y. State Bar Assn., 1963-64, various law firms, Columbia seminars modern Japan and Oriental thought and religion, 1965-70; Peter B. Lewis lectr., Princeton U., 1988; Gay lectr. Harvard Med. Sch., 1976, Messenger lectr. Cornell U., 1980. Author: Thought Reform and the Psychology of Totalism: A Study of Brainwashing in China, 1961, 1989, Revolutionary Immorality: Mao Tse-Tung and the Chinese Cultural Revolution, 1968, Death in Life: Survivors of Hiroshima (Nat. Book award), 1969, 1991, (Van Wyck Brooks award), History and Human Survival, 1970, Boundaries: Psychological Man in Revolution, 1970, Home from the War: Vietnam Veterans—Neither Victims Nor Executioners, 1973 (Nat. Book award nominee), (with Eric Olson) Living and Dying, 1974, The Life of the Self, 1976, (with Shuichi Kato and Michael Reich) Six Lives/Six Deaths: Portraits from Modern Japan, 1979, The Broken Connection: On Death and the Continuity of Life, 1979, (with Richard A. Falk) Indefensible Weapons: The Political and Psychological Case Against Nuclearism, 1982, 1991; humorous cartoons Birds, 1969, PsychoBirds, 1979, (with Nicholas Humphrey) In a Dark Time, 1984 (Brit. edit. selected Top Twenty Nat. Peace Book Week, Martin Luther King award, Eng.), The Nazi Doctors: Medical Killing and Psychology of Genocide, 1986 (Nat. Jewish Book award, Los Angeles Times Book prize for history 1987, Lisl and Leo Eitinger award, Oslo, Norway, 1988), German edit. 1988, The Future of Immortality and Other Essays for a Nuclear Age, 1987; (with Eric Markusen) The Genocidal Mentality: Nazi Holocaust and Nuclear Threat, 1990, The Protean Self: Human Resilience in an Age of Fragmentation, 1993, (with G. Mitchell) Hiroshima in America: Fifty Years of Denial, 1995; editor: Woman in America, 1965, America and the Asian Revolutions, 1970, (with R.A. Falk and G. Kolko) Crimes of War, 1971, (with Eric Olson) Explorations in Psychohistory: The Wellfleet Papers, 1975, (with Eric Chivian, Suzanna Chivian, John E. Mack) Last Aid: Medical Dimensions of Nuclear War, 1982, The Genocidal Mentality: Nazi Doctor and Nuclear Threat, 1990. Organizer redress group opposing Vietnam War IAEA, Vienna, 1975. Served to capt. USAF, 1951-53. Recipient Pub. Svc. award N.Y. Soc. Clin. Psychologists, Alumni medal N.Y. Med. Coll., 1970, Karen Horney lectr. award, 1972, Disting. Svc. award Soc. Adolescent Psychiatry, 1972, Mt. Airy Found. Gold medal, 1973, Hiroshima Gold medal, 1975, Gandhi Peace award, 1984, Bertrand Russell Soc. award, 1985, Holocaust Meml. award, 1986, 1st Ann. Nuc. Psychology Rsch. award Harvard U., 1986, Brit Hadorot Convenant of Generations award, 1987, Max A. Hayman award Am. Orthopsychiat. Assn., 1992, Nat. Living Treasure award Psychiat. Inst., 1994, Outstanding Achievement award Armenian Am. Soc. for Studies on Stress and Genocide, 1996. Fellow Am. Acad. Arts and Scis., Am. Psychiat. Assn. (Oskar Pfister award 1987); mem. Assn. Asian Studies, AAAS, Group Study Psychohist. Process (coordinator), Fedn. Am. Scientists, Soc. Psychol. Study of Social Issues. Office: John Jay Coll Criminal Justice 899 10th Ave New York NY 10019-1029

LIFTON, ROBERT KENNETH, diversified companies executive; b. N.Y.C., Jan. 9, 1928; s. Benjamin and Anna (Pike) L.; m. Loretta J. Silver, Sept. 5, 1954; children: Elizabeth Gail Lifton Hooper, Karen Grace Lifton Healy. BBA magna cum laude, CCNY, 1948; LLB, Yale U., 1951; doctorate (hon.), Bar Ilan U., Israel, 1993. Bar: N.Y. 1952. Assoc. Kaye, Scholer, Fierman, Hays & Handler, N.Y.C., 1955-56; asst. to pres. Glickman Corp., N.Y.C., 1956-57; pres. Robert K. Lifton, Inc., N.Y.C., 1957-61; chmn. bd. Terminal Tower Co., Inc., Cleve., 1959-63; pres. Transcontinental Investing Corp., N.Y.C., 1961-72, chmn. bd., 1969-72; ptnr. Venture Assocs., 1972-89; pres. Preferred Health Care Ltd., 1983-88; chmn. bd. dirs. Marcade Group, Inc., 1986-91, Medis El, 1993—, Cell Diagnostics, Inc., 1992—, Medis Inc., 1992—; treas. Consol. Accessories Corp., 1980-88, Caron's Connection, Inc., 1985-89; bd. dirs. Bank Leumi Trust co., N.Y.C.; mem. faculty Columbia U. Law Sch., 1973-78, Yale U. Law Sch., 1972-75; guest lectr. Practicing Law Inst., Yale Law Sch., Pace Inst., NYU; founder Nat. Exec. Conf., Washington, Inc.; chmn. oversight com. for Masters Degree, NYU Real Estate Inst., 1987-88. Author: Practical Real Estate: Legal Tax and Business Strategies, 1978; contbr. articles to profl. jours. and handbooks. Mem. McGovern econ. adv. com., 1972-73; chmn. parents com. Barnard Coll., 1976-78; mem. com. of the collection Whitney Mus., 1976-79; trustee Yale U. Sch. Fund, 1974-77, NYU Real Estate Inst., 1983-89; chmn., bd. dirs. Fund for Religious Liberty, 1987-88; pres. Am. Jewish Congress, 1988-94; chmn. Internat. Bd. U.S. Mid. East Project coun. fgn. rels., 1994—; pres. Israel Policy Forum, 1994—; bd. dirs. Builders for Peace, 1993—; vice-chmn. NJCRAC, 1994—; exec. com. AIPAC, 1993—. Lt. (j.g.) USN, 1952-55. Recipient Achievement award Sch. Bus. Alumni Soc. CCNY, James Madison award Fund for Religious Liberty, 1987, Stephen S. Wise award Am. Jewish Congress, 1993. Mem. Order of Coif. Home: 983 Park Ave New York NY 10028-0808 Office: 805 3rd Ave New York NY 10022-7513

LIFTON, WALTER M., psychology and education consultant; b. Bklyn., Nov. 2, 1918; s. Samuel S. and Sarah G. (Berman) L.; m. Ruth S. Knoppow, Oct. 1, 1940; children: Hazel Miriam Kroesser Palmer, Robert William. B.A., Bklyn. Coll., 1942; M.A., NYU, 1947, Ph.D., 1950. Sr. vocat. appraiser Vets. Guidance Center, Hunter Coll., 1946-48; psychologist, research div. NYU, 1948-50; assoc. prof. edn., guidance and counseling U. Ill., 1950-59; dir. guidance publs. and services Sci. Research Assocs., Chgo., 1959-63; coordinator pupil personnel services Rochester City Sch. Dist., N.Y., 1964-70; prof. edn. dept. counseling psychology and student devel. SUNY-Albany, 1970-82, prof. emeritus, 1982—; edn. and psychology cons., 1982—; disting. vis. prof. Coll. Grad. Studies, W.Va., 1985-86; vis. prof., lectr. guidance and counseling 34 colls. and univs.; cons. in field. Author: Keys to Vocational Decisions, 1964, Working With Groups, 2d edit, 1966, Educating for Tomorrow—The Role of Media, Career Devel. and Society, 1970, Groups—Facilitating Individual Growth and Societal Change, 1972; film Just Like a Family, 1979; contbr. articles to profl. jours. Mem. White House Conf. on Children and Youth, 1969-70; cons. Title III ESEA project, Knox County, Tenn., 1967; interim dir. Action for a Better Community, Rochester, 1964-65, Center for Coop. Action in Urban Edn., 1966; apptd. to Durham County Youth Svcs. Bd., 1994. Served with AUS, 1942-46. Fellow Assn. for Specialists in Group Work (sec. 1976—, pres. 1980-81, Eminent Career award 1986); mem. Nat. Assn. Pupil Personnel Adminstrs. (pres. 1970), Nat. Vocat. Guidance Assn. Home and Office: 2701 Pickett Rd Apt 3036 Durham NC 27705-5651 *As a person in the mental health field my focus has been increasingly concerned with prevention rather than remediation, and with helping people shape their environments not just adjust to the status quo.*

LIGETT, WALDO BUFORD, chemist; b. Middletown, Ohio, Nov. 2, 1916; s. Waldo Buford and Mabel Louise (Berkley) L.; m. Ann Elizabeth Hartwell, Aug. 29, 1940; children: Robert A., John D., Michael T., Steven D., Daniel L. B.S., Antioch Coll., 1939; M.S., Purdue U., 1941, Ph.D., 1944, D.Sc. (hon.), 1965; grad., Advanced Mgmt. Program, Harvard U., 1967. Chemist Eastman Kodak Co., Rochester, N.Y., 1935-38; research supr. Ethyl Corp., Detroit, 1944-51; asst. dir. chem. Ethyl Corp., 1951-52, asso. dir. chem., 1952-62, dir. research and devel., 1962-63; v.p. Celanese Chem. Co., Corpus Christi, Tex., 1963-64; v.p. tech. and mfg. Celanese Chem. Co., 1964-66; tech. dir. Celanese Corp., N.Y.C., 1966-67; v.p. Celanese Corp., 1967-72, Franklin Inst., Phila., 1973-81; pres. Franklin Inst. Research Labs., 1975-81; dir. Franklin-Hahnemann Inst., 1974-81. Fellow Am. Inst. Chemists; mem. Am. Chem. Soc., AAAS, Indsl. Research Inst., Research Soc. Am., N.Y. Assn. Research Dirs., Am. Nuclear Soc., Atomic Indsl. Forum. Patentee in field. Home: 377 Carolina Meadows Villa Chapel Hill NC 27514-7521

LIGGETT, HIRAM SHAW, JR., retired diversified industry financial executive; b. St. Louis, Jan. 12, 1932; s. Hiram Shaw and Lucille (Gardner) L.; m. Margaret McGinness, Jan. 21, 1961; children: Lucille Gardner, Frances Shelby. BA, Colo. Coll., 1953; LLD (hon.), Maryville U., 1991. Cashier Brown Group, Inc., St. Louis, 1957-64, asst. treas., 1964-68, treas., 1968—, v.p., 1983—; bd. dirs. Roosevelt Fed. Savs. and Loan, St. Louis. Past trustee, vice chmn. bd. dirs. McKendree Coll., Lebanon, Ill., 1980-88; trustee, past chmn. bd. trustees Maryville U., St. Louis, 1982-91; past chmn. Provident Counseling, 1983; past v.p., bd. dirs. Jr. Achievement Miss. Valley, 1983; past dir. bi-state chpt. ARC, 1983; bd. dirs., pres. Cardinal Ritter Inst.; bd. dirs., chmn. devel. bd. Paraquad. Capt. USNR, 1953-79. Mem. Fin. Execs. Inst. (pres., dir. 1983—), St. Louis Coun. Navy League (bd. councilors 1982), Univ. Club (St. Louis, chmn. house com. 1975-78), Strathalbyn Farms Club (chmn. house com, bd. mem.), Alpha Kappa Psi, Tau Kappa Alpha. Republican. Presbyterian. Home: 64 Chesterfield Lakes Rd Chesterfield MO 63005-5400

LIGGETT, LAWRENCE MELVIN, vacuum equipment manufacturing company executive; b. Denver, June 22, 1917; s. Thomas Harrison and Mary Deacon (Taylor) L.; m. Edith Irene Harris, June 20, 1943; children: Pamela Jane Liggett Schwartz, Betty Sue Liggett Brooks El Gammal. A.B., Central Coll., Pella, Iowa, 1938; Ph.D. in Chemistry, Iowa State Coll., 1943. Research chemist NDRC, Iowa State Coll., 1941-43; plant mgr. Cardox Corp., Claremore, Okla., 1943-48; dir. inorganic research Wyandotte Chems. Corp., 1948-55; dir. research, v.p. tech. dir. Airco Speer div. Airco, Inc., 1955-70, pres. Airco Electronics div., 1970-75; pres. Airco Temescal div. BOC Group, Berkeley, Calif., 1975-82; cons. bus. and tech., 1982—. Author. Mem. Am. Chem. Soc., Electronic Industries Assn. Republican. Patentee in field. Home: 1856 Piedras Cir Danville CA 94526-1329

LIGGETT, THOMAS JACKSON, retired seminary president; b. Nashville, May 27, 1919; s. Thomas Jackson and Lola Cleveland (Ballentine) L.; m. Virginia Corrine Moore, Aug. 12, 1941; children: Thomas Milton, Margaret Ann Liggett Herod. A.B., Transylvania U., 1940; M.Div., Lexington Theol. Sem., 1944; postgrad., Union Theol. Sem. and Columbia U., 1950-52; LL.D., Interam. U., 1965, Culver-Stockton Coll., 1959, Butler U., 1975; D.H.L., Transylvania U., 1969; D.D., Eureka Coll., 1971, Phillips U., 1989. Ordained to ministry Christian Ch., 1940; pastor in Danville, Ky., 1943-45; missionary Argentina, 1946-57; prof. Union Theol. Sem., Buenos Aires, 1948-57; pres. Evang. Sem. of P.R., 1957-65; exec. sec. for Latin Am. Christian Ch., 1965-67, chmn. div. world mission, 1967-68; pres. United Christian Missionary Soc., 1968-74; pres. Christian Theol. Sem., Indpls., 1974-86, ret., 1986; del. World Council Chs. assembly in Uppsala, 1968, adviser assembly, Nairobi, Kenya, 1975; mem. governing bd. Nat. Council Chs., 1969-75, 85-87; moderator Disciples of Christ, 1985-87. Author: Where Tomorrow Struggles to be Born, 1970; Editor: Cuadernos Teologicos, 1954-55. Co-chmn. McGovern Task Force on Fgn. Policy in Latin Am., 1972, Democratic precinct committeeman, 1970-72. Mem. Disciples of Christ Hist. Soc. (life), Theta Phi. Home: 647 W Harrison Ave Claremont CA 91711-4537

LIGGETT, TWILA MARIE CHRISTENSEN, academic administrator, public television company executive; b. Pipestone, Minn., Mar. 25, 1944; d. Donald L. Christensen and Irene E. (Zweigle) Christensen Flesher. BS, Union Coll., Lincoln, Nebr., 1966; MA, U. Nebr., 1971, PhD, 1977. Dir. vocal and instrumental music Sprague (Nebr.)-Martell Pub. Sch., 1966-67; tchr. vocal music, pub. schs., Syracuse, Nebr., 1967-69; tchr. Norris Pub. Sch., Firth, Nebr., 1969-71; cons. fed. reading project, pub. schs., Lincoln, 1971-72; curriculum coord. Westside Community Schs., Omaha, 1972-74; dir. State program Right-to-Read, Nebr. Dept. Edn., 1974-76; asst. dir. Nebr. Commn. on Status of Women, 1976-80; asst. dir. project adminstrn./devel. Great Plains Nat. Instructional TV Libr., U. Nebr., Lincoln, 1980—; exec. prodr. Reading Rainbow, PBS nat. children's series, 1980— (9 Emmy awards 1990-96); cons. U.S. Dept. Edn., 1981; Far West Regional Lab., San Francisco, 1978-79; panelist, presenter AAAS, NEA, NEH, NSF, Corp. Pub. Broadcasting, Internat. Reading Assn., Blue Ribbon panelist, Acad. TV Arts & Scis., 1991-96, final judge Nat. Cable Programming Awards, 1991-92. Author: Reading Rainbow's Guide to Children's Books: The 101 Best Titles, 1994. Bd. dirs. Planned Parenthood, Lincoln, 1979-81. Recipient Grand award N.Y., 1993, Gold medal award Internat. Film and TV Festival, 1996, World Gold medal N.Y. Internat. Film & TV, 1995, Coun. on Internat. Nontheatrical Events Golden Eagle award, 1995, 2 Golden Eagle awards Coun. on Internat. Nontheatrical Events. Mem. NATAS, Internat. Reading Assn. (Spl. award Contbns. Worldwide Literacy 1992), Am. Women in Film and TV,Phi Delta Kappa. Presbyterian. Home: 649 S 18th St Lincoln NE 68508-2681 also: 301 E 79th St Apt 23P New York NY 10021-0944 Office: PO Box 80669 Lincoln NE 68501-0669

LIGGIO, CARL DONALD, lawyer; b. N.Y.C., Sept. 5, 1943. AB, Georgetown U., 1963; JD, NYU, 1967. Bar: N.Y. 1967, D.C. 1967, Wis. 1983. Cons. Arent, Fox, Kintner, Plotkin & Kahn, Washington, 1968-69; assoc. White & Case, N.Y.C., 1969-72; gen. counsel Arthur Young & Co., N.Y.C., 1972-89, Ernst & Young, N.Y.C., 1989-94; ptnr. Dickinson, Wright, Moon, Van Dusen & Freeman, Chgo., 1995—. Contbr. articles to legal and bus. jours. Trustee Fordham Prep. Sch. Mem. ABA, N.Y. State Bar Assn., D.C. Bar Assn., Assn. of Bar of City of N.Y., Am. Corp. Counsel Assn. (chmn. bd. dirs. 1984, mem. exec. com. 1982-95), Am. Judicature Soc. (bd. dirs. 1988-92), Coll. Law Mgmt. Home: 233 E Walton Pl Chicago IL 60611 Office: 225 W Washington St Chicago IL 60606-3418

LIGGIO, JEAN VINCENZA, adult education educator, artist; b. N.Y.C., Nov. 5, 1927; d. Vincenzo and Bernada (Terrusa) Verro; m. John Liggio, June 6, 1948; children: Jean Constance, Joan Bernadette. Student, N.Y. Inst. Photography, 1965, Elizabeth Seton Coll., 1984, Parsons Sch. of Design, 1985. Hairdresser Beauty Shoppe, N.Y.C., 1947-65; freelance oil colors and portraits N.Y.C., 1958-75; instr. watercolor N.Y. Dept. Pks., Recreation and Conservation, Yonkers, 1985-89, Bronxville (N.Y.) Adult Sch., 1989—; substitute tchr. cosmetology Yonkers Bd. Edn., 1988-89. Paintings pub. by Donald Art Co., C.R. Gibson Greeting Card Co.; 12 watercolor paintins for Avon Calendar, Avon Cosmetics Co., 1994, 96; 12 florals for Avon-Can. Publ., 1996, 97; 12 floral paintings published by Enesco Corp., 1996; 2 floral greeting cards published by C.R. Gibson Co. Publ., 1996. Recipient numerous awards. Mem. Mt. Vernon Art Assn. (pres. membership com. 1983—), Mamaroneck Artist's Guild, Hudson River Contemporary Artist's, Scarsdale Art Assn. (publicity chmn. 1984-89), New Rochelle (N.Y.) Art Assn. Avocation: collect antiques. Home and Office: 166 Helena Ave Yonkers NY 10710-2524

LIGHT, ALFRED ROBERT, lawyer, political scientist, educator; b. Atlanta, Dec. 14, 1949; s. Alfred M. Jr. and Margaret Francis (Asbury) L.; m. Mollie Sue Hall, May 25, 1977; children: Joseph Robert, Gregory Andrew. Student Ga. Inst. Tech., 1967-69; BA with highest honors, Johns Hopkins U., 1971; PhD, U. N.C., 1976; JD cum laude, Harvard U., 1981. Bar: D.C. 1981, Va. 1982. Tax clk. IRS, 1967; lab. technician Custom Farm Services Soils Testing Lab., 1968; warehouse asst. State of Ga. Mines, Mining and Geology, 1970; clk.-typist systems mgmt. div., def. contract adminstrv. services region Def. Supply Agy., Atlanta, 1971, research and teaching asst. dept. polit. sci. U. N.C., Chapel Hill, 1971-74; research asst. Inst. Research in Social Sci., 1975-77; program analyst Office of Sec. Def., 1974; asst. prof. polit. sci., research scientist Ctr. Energy Research, Tex. Tech U., Lubbock, 1977-78; research asst. grad. sch. edn., Harvard U., 1978-79; assoc. Butler, Binion, Rice, Cook & Knapp, Houston, summer 1980, Bracewell & Patterson, Washington, summer 1980, Hunton & Williams, Richmond, Va., 1981-89, of counsel, 1989-93, 95—; assoc. prof. St. Thomas U. Sch. Law, Miami, Fla., 1989-93, prof., 1993—, interim dean, 1993-94. Bd. advisors Toxics Law Reporter, Bur. Nat. Affairs, Washington, 1987—; contbr. articles to profl. jours. Charter mem. West Broward Community Ch. Capt. USAR, 1971-85. Grantee NSF, Inst. Evaluation Research, U. Mass., Ctr. Energy Research, Tex. Tech U., 1977-78; recipient Julius Turner award Johns Hopkins U., 1971, William Anderson award Am. Polit. Sci. Assn., 1977. Mem. ABA (vice-chmn. tort and ins. practice sect. 1988—, nat. res. and environ. sect. 1993—), Fed. Bar Assn., Va. Bar Assn., Richmond Bar Assn., Phi Beta Kappa, Phi Eta Sigma. Democrat. Home: 1042 Woodfall Ct Fort Lauderdale FL 33326-2832 Office: St Thomas U Sch Law 16400 NE 32nd Ave Miami FL 33054

LIGHT, ARTHUR HEATH, bishop; s. Alexander Heath and Mary Watkins (Nelson) L.; m. Sarah Ann Jones, June 12, 1954; children: William Alexander, Philip Nelson, John Page, Sarah Heath. BA, Hampden-Sydney Coll., 1951, DD, 1987; M.Div., Va. Theol. Sem., 1954, DD, 1970; DD, St. Paul's Coll., 1979. Ordained priest Episcopal Ch., 1955. Rector West Mecklenburg Cure, Boydton, Va., 1954-58, Christ Ch., Elizabeth City, N.C., 1958-63, St. Marys Ch., Kinston, N.C., 1963-67, Christ and St. Luke's Ch., Norfolk, Va., 1967-79; bishop Diocese of Southwestern Va., Roanoke, 1979—; pres. Province III Espiscopal Ch., 1984-93; mem. adv. coun. to presiding bishop, 1985-93; nominating com. 25th presiding bishop of the Episcopal Ch., 1994-97. Author: God, The Gift, The Giver, 1984. Bd. dirs. United Communities Fund, 1969-79, Norfolk Seamen's Friends Soc., 1969-79, Tidewater Assembly on Family Life, 1970-79, Friends of Juvenile Ct., 1975-79, Va. Inst. Pastoral Care, 1971-72; bd. dirs., mem. exec. com. Va. Coun. Chs., 1979—; bd. dirs. Roanoke Valley Coun. of Community Svcs., 1980-83, Virginians Organized for Informed Community Effort (VOICE), 1981—; bd. dirs. Appalachian People's Svc. Orgn., 1981-91, pres., 1981-85, v.p., 1989-91; mem. bio-med. ethics com. Ea. Va. Med. Sch., 1973-79, Lewis Gale Hosp., Salem, 1988—, Community Hosp. Roanoke Valley, 1990-94; trustee Va. Episc. Sch., Lynchburg, 1979—, Episc. High Sch., Alexandria, 1979—, Boys' Home, Covington, 1979—, Stuart Hall Sch., Staunton, 1979—, St. Paul's Coll., Lawrenceville, 1979-88; chmn. com. on continuing edn. Va. Theol. Sem., Alexandria, 1985—, v.p. bd. trustees, 1987—; bd. dirs., co-chair rural residency program Appalachian Ministries Ednl. Resource Ctr., Berea, Ky., 1985-87; mem. coordinating cabinet, Va. Counc. Churches, 1988—, chair com. on church and society, 1989-92; mem. Am. com. Kiyosato Ednl. Experiment Project, 1990—, v.p., 1991—; mem. Gen. Conv. Standing Com. on World Mission, 1988-94, chair, 1991-94; trustee Kanuga Conf. Ctr., 1991—. Named Young Man of Yr., Jaycees, 1961, 63; fellow St. George's Coll., Jerusalem, 1978, 89, fellow in biomed. ethics U. Va., 1989. Democrat. Office: PO Box 2068 1000 1st St SW Roanoke VA 24009

LIGHT, BETTY JENSEN PRITCHETT, former college dean; b. Omaha, Sept. 14, 1924; d. Lars Peter and Ruth (Norby) Jensen; m. Morgan S. Pritchett, June 27, 1944 (dec. 1982); children: Randall Wayne, Robin Kay Pritchett Church, Royce Marie Pritchett Creech; m. Kenneth F. Light, Nov. 23, 1985. B.S., Portland State U., 1965; M.B.A., U. Oreg., 1966; Ed.D., Oreg. State U., 1973. Buyer Rodgers Stores, Inc., Portland, Oreg., 1947-62; chmn. bus. div. Mt. Hood Community Coll., Gresham, Oreg., 1966-70, dir. evening coll., 1970-71, assoc. dean instn., 1972-77, dean humanities and behavioral scis., 1977-79, dean devel. and spl. programs, 1979-83; dean communication arts, humanities and social scis. Mt. Hood Community Coll.,

1983-86; mem. state com. for articulation between cmty. colls. and higher edn., 1976-78; mem. Gov.'s Coun. on Career and Vocat. Edn., 1977-86; owner Effective Real Estate Mgmt., 1982—. Author: Values and Perceptions of Community College Professional Staff in Oregon, 1973; contbg. author: (case study) The Pritchett Study in Retailing, An Economic View, 1969. Mem. Gresham City Council, 1983-86. Mem. Oreg. Bus. Edn. Assn., Am. Assn. Higher Edn., Nat. Assn. Staff and Oreg. Devel., Oreg. Women's Polit. Caucus, Am. Vocat. Assn., Oreg. Vocat Assn., Danish Heritage Soc. Club: Soroptimist (pres. 1974-75, 81-82). Home: 1635 NE Country Club Ave Gresham OR 97030-4432

LIGHT, CHRISTOPHER UPJOHN, writer, computer musician; b. Kalamazoo, Jan. 4, 1937; s. Richard and Rachel Mary (Upjohn) L.; m. Lilykate Victoria Wenner, June 22, 1963 (div. 1986); children: Victoria Mary, Christopher Upjohn Jr.; m. Margo Ruth Bosker, Jan. 2, 1994. AB, Carleton Coll., 1958; MS, Columbia U., 1962; MBA, We. Mich. U., 1967; PhD, Washington U., 1971. Editor, pub. The Kalamazoo mag., 1963-66; pres. Mich. Outdoor Pub. Co., Kalamazoo, 1965-68; product planner The Upjohn Co., Kalamazoo, 1967-68; asst. prof. U. Utah, Salt Lake City, 1971-72; assoc. prof., chmn. fin. dept. Roosevelt U., Chgo., 1975-78; vis. prof. fin. No. Ill. U., 1978-79; freelance writer, computer musician, 1979—; editor Charles Dickens' Village Coquettes, 1992; mgr. spl. projects Sarasota Music Archive, 1992—. Trustee Harold and Grace Upjohn Found., 1965-85, 94—, pres. 6 yrs.; trustee Kalamazoo Symphony Orch. Assn., 1990—, Sarasota Music Archive, 1990-95, Kalamazoo Coll., 1991-93, Am. Symphony Orch. League, 1992—. Recipient ann. press award Mich. Welfare League, 1967. Mem. ASCAP, NARAS (voting com.), Fin. Mgmt. Assn., Soc. Profl. Journalists. Contbr. articles to profl. and microcomputer jours.; music compositions include Ten Polyrhythmic Etudes 1991, Piano Sonata # 1, 1992, record albums include Apple Compote, 1983, One-Man Band, 1985, Ultimate Music Box, Vol. I, 1988, Vol. II, 1993. Mem. U. Club Chicago, Gull Lake Country Club. Office: 136 E Michigan Ave Kalamazoo MI 49007

LIGHT, HAROLD L., health care facility executive; b. Perth Amboy, N.J., Apr. 21, 1929; s. Samuel and Augustia (Schmeir) L.; m. Marilyn Weintraub, Aug. 19, 1951; children: Julie, Jeffrey. BA, Brooklyn Coll., 1950; MSS, NYU, 1959. Adminstr. Gouverneur Ambulary Care Program, N.Y.C., 1962-67; spl. asst. ambulatory care planning N.Y.C. Dept. of Health, 1967-87; asst. adminstr. St. Vincent Hosp., N.Y.C., 1968-70; sr. v.p. adminstrn. L.I. Jewish Med. Ctr., North Hyde Park, N.Y., 1970-77; pres. L.I. Coll. Hosp., Bklyn., 1977—. Trustee Bklyn. Botanic Garden, 1983—. With U.S. Army 1951-53. Fellow Am. Coll. Health Care Execs., Am. Pub. Health Assn.; mem. Greater N.Y. Hosp. Assn. (bd. govs. 1977—, chmn.), Hosp. Assn. N.Y.C. (chmn.), League of Voluntary Hosps. (bd. trustees 1979—). Home: 18442 Tudor Rd Jamaica NY 11432-1512 Office: L I Coll Hosp 340 Henry St Brooklyn NY 11201-5525*

LIGHT, JAMES FOREST, English educator; b. Memphis, Nov. 5, 1921; s. Luther and Lois Ginevra (Billings) L.; m. Norma Rowena Neal, Mar. 8, 1948 (dec. 1959); children—Sheldon Neal, Matthew Forest, Jama Rowena; m. Amy Marcella Wolf, Dec. 20, 1959. B.A., U. Chgo., 1945, M.A., 1947; Ph.D., Syracuse U., 1953. Instr. U. Ky., 1947-48, Syracuse U., 1948-53; assoc. Radford Coll., 1953-56; asst. prof. Ind. State U., 1956-59, assoc., 1959-61, prof., 1961-65; Bernhard prof., chmn. dept. English U. Bridgeport, 1965-71; dean Sch. of Humanities of Calif. State U.-Fresno, 1971-72; dean of faculties Lehman Coll., CUNY, 1972-73, provost, 1973-79; dean Coll. Liberal Arts So. Ill. U., Carbondale, 1979-85, prof. English, 1979-88, prof. emeritus, 1988—; Fulbright prof. Keele U., Eng., 1963-64; vis. prof. CUNY, summers 1966-69; Fulbright prof. Canterbury U., N.Z., 1986. Author: Nathanael West: an Interpretive Study, rev. edit, 1971, John William DeForest, 1965, J.D. Salinger, 1967; editor The Modern Age, 4th rev. edit, 1981, Studies in All the Kings Men, 1971; contbr. articles to profl. jours. Fellow Found. Econ. Edn., Yaddo Writers and Artists Colony.; mem. MLA, AAUP, Nat. Council Tchrs. English, Ind. Coll. English Assn. (pres. 1962-63), New Eng. Coll. English Assn. (dir. 1969-71). Democrat. Office: 47 Dogwood Dr Apt 301 Nashua NH 03062-4413

LIGHT, JO KNIGHT, stockbroker; b. DeQueen, Ark., Mar. 15, 1936; d. Donald R. and Auda (Waltrip) Knight; m. Jerry T. Light, June 21, 1958 (dec. 1979); m. Victor E. Menefee Jr., Nov. 18, 1981; 1 child, Jerry T. BA cum laude, U. Ark., 1958. Cert. fin. planner. Travel cons. Comml. Nat. Bank, Little Rock, 1971-76; dist. mgr. Am. Express Co., N.Y.C., 1976-82; account exec. Dean Witter Reynolds, N.Y.C., 1982—, v.p. investments, 1987—. Mem. Jr. League of Little Rock; vol. Happiness Singers. Mem. Inst. Cert. Fin. Planners, Internat. Assn. Fin. Planners (bd. dirs. 1972—, pres. bd. dirs. 1995-96), U. Ark. Alumni Assn. (bd. dirs. 1974-77), Little Rock Country Club, Razorback Club, Phi Beta Kappa, Kappa Kappa Gamma. Avocations: music, tennis, sailing, snow skiing. Office: Dean Witter Reynolds 401 W Capitol Ave Ste 101 Little Rock AR 72201-3437

LIGHT, JOHN CALDWELL, chemistry educator; b. Mt. Vernon, N.Y., Nov. 24, 1934; s. Robert Fredrich and Alice (Caldwell) L.; m. Phyllis M. Kittel, Dec. 17, 1978; children: David C., Robert S., Erik G. B.A., Oberlin Coll., 1956; Ph.D., Harvard U., 1960. Postdoctoral rsch. assoc. U. Libre de Bruxelles, 1959-61; instr. U. Chgo., 1962-63, asst. prof., 1963-66, assoc. prof., 1966-70, prof. chemistry, 1970—, chmn. dept. chemistry, 1980-82; mem. adv. bd. Petroleum Rsch. Fund, 1981-86; cons. Inst. Def. Analyses, 1962-65, IBM Rsch Labs., San Jose, 1975, Lawrence Livermore Lab., 1979—; adv. com. Army Rsch. Office, Durham, N.C., 1966-72; vis. prof. Yale U., New Haven, 1968; vice chmn. Theoretical Chemistry Conf., Boulder, 1978, chmn., 1981; vis. scientist JILA, U. Colo., Boulder, 1976-77, others. Editor: Jour. Chem. Physics, 1983—. NSF predoctoral/postdoctoral fellow, 1956-61; Alfred P. Sloan Found. fellow. Fellow AAAS, Am. Phys. Soc., Am. Chem. Soc.; mem. Internat. Acad. Quantum Molecular Sci. Home: 1034 E 49th St Chicago IL 60615-1814 Office: 5640 S Ellis Ave Chicago IL 60637-1433

LIGHT, JOHN ROBERT, lawyer; b. Kansas City, Mo., Feb. 13, 1941; s. Robert Ralph and Marcia Ruth (Springer) L.; m. Sharon Dietrich Koch, Dec. 27, 1966; children: Allison, Robert. BA, U. Kans., 1963, JD with highest distinction, 1967. Bar: Calif., U.S. Dist. Ct. (cen. , no., so., ea. dists.) Calif., U.S. Ct. Appeals (9th cir.). Assoc. Latham & Watkins, L.A., 1967-73, ptnr., 1973—. Mem. Soc. of Fellows of Huntington Mus. Mem. ABA (chmn. Sherman Act com. antitrust sect. 1982-84), Calif. Bar Assn., U. Kans. Chancellor's Club. Republican. Episcopalian. Avocations: golf, swimming, art collecting. Office: Latham & Watkins 633 W 5th St Ste 4000 Los Angeles CA 90071-2005

LIGHT, KEN, photojournalist, educator; b. N.Y.C., Mar. 16, 1951; s. Stanley and Dorothea (Gottfried) L.; m. Carmen Lising, June 1976 (div. Aug. 1985); children: Stephen, Allison Rose; m. Melanie Hastings, Aug. 1, 1992. BGS, Ohio U., 1973. Instr. Contra. Costa Coll., San Pablo, Calif., 1974-84; photographer Labor Occ. Health Program, Berkeley, Calif., 1975-81; mem. staff Alameda Neighborhood Arts Program, Oakland, Calif., 1975-81; instr. Grad. Sch. Journalism U. Calif., Berkeley, 1986-89; cons. photographer Libr. Congress Folklife Ctr., 1989-90; faculty San Francisco Acad. Art Coll, 1977-96; lectr. Berkeley Grad. Sch. Journalism, 1983—; founder fund Documentary Photography, 1988—. Author: To the Promised Land, 1988, With These Hands, 1986, In the Fields, 1984, Delta Time, 1994. Recipient Meritorious Achievement award Media Alliance, 1990, Thomas More Storke Internat. Journalism award World Affairs Coun., 1989; nominee Pulitzer Prize Feature Photography, 1993; grantee Am. Film Inst., 1979; NEA fellow, 1982, 86, Dorothea Lange fellow. Mem. Soc. Photog. Edn., ASMP, fellow Erna and Victor Hasselblad Found. Home: 3107 Deakin St Berkeley CA 94705-1950

LIGHT, KENNETH B., manufacturing company executive; b. N.Y.C., June 2, 1932; s. Max and Mollie (Schein) Lichtenholtz; m. Judith Klein, May 28, 1961; children: Corey, Randi Beth, Allison. B.S., NYU, 1954, LL.B. cum laude, 1957; M.B.A., U. Chgo., 1976. Bar: N.Y. 1957. Partner firm Light & Light, Bklyn., 1958-61; asst. sec. Gen. Bronze Corp., Garden City, N.Y., 1961-69; sec., gen. counsel Allied Products Corp., Chgo., 1969-76; v.p., gen. counsel Allied Products Corp., 1976-79, sr. v.p., 1979-83, exec. v.p., 1983-93; dir. Allied Products Corp., Chgo., 1993—; exec. v.p., CFO Allied Products Corp., 1995—; pres. Midwest Steel Processing, Inc., 1982-84; dir. Aurora Corp. Ill., Chgo.; vice chmn. Family Res. Ctr., Chgo., 1989-94, chmn., 1994—; v.p., dir. Verson Corp., Bush Hog Corp. Mem. Chgo. Bar Assn., N.Y.C. Subcontractors Assn. (v.p. 1967-69), Am. Subcontractors Assn. (dir. 1967-68), Chgo. Assn. Commerce and Industry. Home: 1825 Cavell Ave Highland Park IL 60035-2202 Office: Allied Products Corp 10 S Riverside Plz Chicago IL 60606-3708

LIGHT, KENNETH FREEMAN, college administrator; b. Detroit, Jan. 22, 1922; s. Delbert Bertram and Hilma (Stolt) L.; m. Shirley Claire Bower, Jan. 7, 1944 (dec. 1984); children—Karen Christine, Kevin Harold, Brian Curtis; m. Betty Jensen Pritchett, Nov. 23, 1985. B.S., U. Ill., 1949; M.A., Mich. State U., 1952, Ph.D., 1967. Instr. mech. engring. dept. Mich. Tech. U., 1956-60, assoc. prof., coord. for tech. edn., 1960-65; vice chancellor for acad. affairs, v.p. for acad. affairs Lake Superior State Coll., Sault Ste. Marie, Mich., 1965-76; pres. Lake Superior State Coll., 1982-86, Oreg. Inst. Tech., Klamath Falls, 1976-82. Pres. Upper Peninsula Health Edn. Corp., 1975-76; mem. Mich. Manpower Commn., 1973-74, Vocat. Edn. Adv. Council, 1973-76, Oreg. Career and Vocat. Adv. Council, 1977-82, Oreg. Manpower Commn., 1978-80; mem. Econ. Devel. Corp. Chippewa County, 1982-86. Served with USAF, 1942-45, to maj., USAFR. Mem. AAUP, Am. Soc. Engring. Edn., Am. Soc. Mil. Engrs., Air Force Assn., Phi Delta Kappa. Home (summer): 6 Partridge Ave Kincheloe MI 49788

LIGHT, MURRAY BENJAMIN, newspaper editor; b. Bklyn., Oct. 14, 1926; s. Paul and Rose (Liatsk) L.; m. Joan M. Cottrell; children: Lee Light Monier, Laura Light Arbogast, Jeffrey Eugene. B.S., Bklyn. Coll., 1948; M.S. in Journalism, Northwestern U., 1949. Copy editor New York Wold-Telegram, 1949; with Buffalo Evening News, 1949—, news editor, 1962-69, mng. editor for news, 1969-79, editor, v.p., 1979—, sr. v.p., 1983—; mem. temporary State Commn. on Constl. Revision, 1993-95; mem. arts adv. coun. SUNY, Buffalo, 1987-94, N.Y. State Jud. Screening Com. for 4th Dept., 1983-93; mem. nominating jury for journalism Pulitzer Prize, 1990, 01. Mem. adv. coun. to pres. on journalism St. Bonaventure U., 1980—; mem. cmty. adv. coun. SUNY, Buffalo, 1979—; steering com. State Citizen Bee, 1990—. Wiht AUS, WWII. Mem. N.Y. State Soc. Newspaper Editors (pres. 1977), Am. Soc. Newspaper Editors, A.P. Mng. Editors Assn., N.Y. Fair Trial Free Press Conf. (past chmn.). Office: Buffalo News PO Box 100 1 News Plz Buffalo NY 14203-2994

LIGHT, RICHARD JAY, statistician, education educator; b. N.Y.C., Sept. 10, 1942; s. Solomon Julius and Muriel (Szwarcman) L.; m. Patricia Kahn, June 27, 1965; children: Jennifer Susan, Sarah Elizabeth. BS, U. Pa., 1962, AM, 1964; PhD, Harvard U., 1969; LLD (hon.), U. Winnipeg, Can., 1991. Mem. faculty Harvard U., Cambridge, Mass., 1969—, prof. stats., 1975—; dir. faculty studies John F. Kennedy Inst. Politics, 1971-76; mem. panel children's and family policy Nat. Acad. Scis., 1977—, chmn. panel on evaluation, 1982; panel program evaluation Social Sci. Research Council, 1977—; bd. dirs Huron Inst., Cambridge, Mass., 1971—; cons. World Bank, 1975—; dir. Harvard Assessment Seminar, Cambridge, 1986—. Co-author: Data for Decisions, 1982, Summing Up, 1984, By Design, 1990, Meta-analysis for Explanation, 1992; editor: Learning from Experience, 1982, Evaluation Studies Rev., 1983. Trustee Buckingham, Browne and Nichols Sch., Cambridge, 1977—; mem. policy adv. group Mass. Office of Children, 1977—; bd. dirs. Fund for Improvement Post-Secondary Edn., 1992-95. N.Y. State Advanced Coll. Teaching fellow, 1965; vis. fellow Ctr. Analysis Health Practices, Harvard U. Sch. Pub. Health, 1977-78; Sr. Research award Spencer Found., Chgo., 1978-84; research fellow Ford Found., N.Y.C., 1981; recipient Paul Lazarsfeld award for contbns. to sci., 1992. Mem. Am. Assn. Higher Edn. Assn., Am. Ednl. Rsch. Assn., Am. Sociol. Assn., Am. Evaluation Assn. (pres. 1986), Coun. Applied Social Rsch., Evaluation Rsch. Soc. (Paul Lazarsfeld award 1991), Am. Assn. for Higher Edn. (nat. bd.), Fund for Improvement Postsecondary Edn. (nat. bd.). Home: 31 Dunbarton Rd Belmont MA 02178-2458 Office: John F Kennedy Sch Govt Harvard U Cambridge MA 02138

LIGHT, ROBERT M., broadcasting association executive; b. Denver, June 23, 1911; s. Louis and Sally (Conn) L.; m. Margaret Colville Dodgson, Oct. 2, 1943; 1 child, Robert Louis; m. Julie Fraser Giguere, Dec. 10, 1953; children: Jonathan Fraser, Lisa Light Piscitelli. Student, pub. schs., Denver and N.Y.C. Actor theater, radio, TV NBC, N.Y.C., 1934-39; contract player Warner Studios, Hollywood, Calif., 1935-37; writer, dir., radio programs ABC, NBC, Los Angeles, 1939-42; tchr., exec. dir. refresher course AFRA, Los Angeles, 1946-49; writer Alan Ladd Radio Show Abbott Kimbal Co. Advt., Los Angeles, 1949-53; dir. promotion and advt. western div. RKO Gen., Los Angeles, 1953-59; pres. So. Calif. Broadcasters Assn., Hollywood, 1959-89; pres. emeritus, 1989—; lectr., tchr. UCLA, U. So. Calif., Los Angeles City Coll., London U. Mem. Los Angeles County Hwy. Safety Commn.; mem. adv. council So. Calif. Assn. Govts.; bd. dirs. Pacific Pioneer Broadcasters, mem. PPB Diamond Circle. Lt. col. Armed Forces Radio, 1942-46, ETO. Decorated Bronze Star; recipient honor Los Angeles County Bd. Suprs., Los Angeles City Council. Mem. So. Calif. Theater Assn. (v.p.). Home: 3272 Longridge Ave Sherman Oaks CA 91423-4910

LIGHT, TERRY RICHARD, orthopedic hand surgeon; b. Chgo., June 22, 1947. BA, Yale U.; MD, Chgo. Med. Sch. Asst. prof. Yale U., New Haven, 1977-80; asst. prof. Loyola U., Maywood, Ill., 1980-82, assoc. prof., 1982-88, prof., 1988-90, Dr. William M. Scholl prof., chmn. dept. orthopaedic surgery, 1991—; attending surgeon Hines (Ill.) VA Hosp., 1980—, Shriner's Hosp., Chgo. and Tampa, Fla., 1981—, Foster McGaw Hosp., Maywood, Ill., 1981—; hand cons., mem. med. adv. bd. DuPage Easter Seal, Villa Park, Ill., 1980—. V.p. Frank Lloyd Wright Home and Studio Found., Oak Park, Ill., 1985-88, pres., 1988-90. Fellow ACS, Am. Acad. Orthopaedic Surgeons; mem. Am. Soc. for Surgery of the Hand, Am. Assn. Hand Surgery (bd. dirs. 1989-91), Chgo. Soc. for Surgery of the Hand (sec. 1985-87, pres.-elect 1987-88, pres. 1988-89), Twenty-First Century Orthopaedic Assn. (pres. 1979—). Avocations: collecting American arts and crafts. Office: Loyola U Med Ctr 2160 S 1st Ave Maywood IL 60153-3304

LIGHTBURN, ANITA LOUISE, dean, social work educator; b. San Diego, Jan. 2, 1946; d. Kenneth E. and Ann Lorraine (Rosepiler) Schimp; m. Kenneth Dale Lightburn, Aug. 25, 1973; children: Tiffany, Kara. BA, Wheaton Coll., 1968; MS, Columbia U., 1972, MEd, 1988, EdD, 1989. Social worker Mass. Divsn. Child Guardianship, Boston, 1968-70; supr. psychiat. social work McMahon Meml. Shelter, N.Y.C., 1972-73; lectr. Flinders U., Adelaide, Australia, 1973-85; asst., then assoc. prof. Columbia U., N.Y.C., 1989-94; dean, prof. Sch. Social Work Smith Coll., Northampton, Mass., 1994—; vis. prof. U. Conn., West Hartford, 1985, Columbia U., N.Y.C., 1986-88; cons., clinician, therapist in field. Author chpts. to books; contbr. articles to profl. jours. Mem. NASW. Home: 22 Main St Hatfield MA 01038 Office: Smith Coll Sch Social Work Northampton MA 01063

LIGHTFOOT, DAVID WILLIAM, linguistics educator; b. Looe, Eng., Feb. 10, 1945; s. William Richard and Peggy May (Stevens) L.; m. Sarah Elizabeth Hairs, Feb. 7, 1946 (div. 1980); children: Kirsten, Heidi; m. Sari Ruth Hornstein, Nov. 24, 1955; children: Eric, Alexander. BA with honors, U. London, 1966; MA, U. Mich., 1968, PhD, 1971. Asst. prof. McGill U., Montreal, Que., Can., 1970-75; assoc. prof. McGill U., Montreal, Que., 1975-78; prof. U. Utrecht, The Netherlands, 1978-83, U. Md., College Park, 1983—. Author: Natural Logic and Greek Moods, 1975, Principles of Diachronic Syntax, 1979, Explanation in Linguistics, 1981, The Language Lottery, 1982, How to Set Parameters, 1991, Verb Movement, 1994. Mem. Linguistic Soc. Am., Linguistic Assn. Gt. Britain. Home: 7208 Heatherhill Rd Bethesda MD 20817-4657 Office: Univ Md Dept Linguistics College Park MD 20472

LIGHTFOOT, GORDON MEREDITH, singer, songwriter; b. Orillia, Ont., Can., Nov. 17, 1938; s. Gordon Meredith and Jessie Vick (Trill) L.; divorced; children: Fred, Ingrid; m. Elizabeth Moon; children: Eric, Miles. Student, Westlake Coll. Music, Los Angeles, 1958. Singer, songwriter, 1959—; compositions include Early Morning Rain, 1965, Canadian Railroad Trilogy, 1967, If You Could Read My Mind, 1970, Sundown, 1974, Carefree Highway, 1974, The Wreck of the Edmund Fitzgerald, 1976, Race Among the Ruins, 1976; album Lightfoot, 1966, Way I Feel, 1967, Did She Mention My Name, 1968, Back Here On Earth, 1969, Early Lightfoot, 1969, Sunday Concert, 1969, Summerside of Life, 1971, Don Quixote, 1972, Old Dan's Records, 1972, Cold On Shoulder, 1975, Gord's Gold, 1975, Summertime Dream, 1976, Endless Wire, 1978, Dream Street Rose, 1980, Salute, 1983, Gord's Gold, Vol. II, 1989, East of Midnight, Songbook, 1986, Best of Gordon Lightfoot, 1991, The United Artists Collection, 1993, Waiting For You, 1993. Decorated Order Can., 1970; recipient Vanier award Canadian Jaycees, 1977, Juno Hall of Fame award, 1986, Juno Gold Leaf awards, 1965-66, 68-69, 73-77, Pop Record of Yr. award Music Operators Am., 1974; named Top Folksinger, 1965-66, 68-69, 73-77, Top Male Vocalist, 1967, 70-72, 74, Composer of Yr., 1972, 76, Can. Male Rec. Artist of Decade, 1980; recipient awards for songs ASCAP, 1971, 74, 76, 77; numerous Gold albums in Can., U.S., Australia; numerous Platinum albums including Sundown, Summertime Dream, Gord's Gold. Mem. Order of Ont. Address: care ICM 40 W 57th St New York NY 10019-4001

LIGHTFOOT, JAMES ROSS, congressman; b. Sioux City, Iowa, Sept. 27, 1938; s. Elmer and Altha Lightfoot; m. Nancy Lightfoot; children: Terri, Jamie, Allison, James. Police officer City of Tulsa, 1959-61; broadcaster, 1961-70; Mgr. farm equipment plant Corsicana, Tex., 1970-76; small bus. owner Shenandoah, Iowa, 1981—; mem. 99th-104th Congress from 5th (now 3rd) Iowa dist., 1985—, appropriations com., chmn. treas., postal svc. and gen. govt. subcom., fgn. ops. appropriations subcom., sub. appropriations, trans. Farm editor Sta. KMA-Radio, Shenandoah, Iowa, 1976-84. Served with U.S. Army, then USAR, 1956-64. Mem. FAA (outstanding service award, vol. safety counselor), Farm Bur., U.S. Feed Grains Council, Soybean Assn., Nat. Agr. Mktng. Assn. (agr. spokesman of the year award), Iowa Park Prodrs. Assn., Iowa Cattleman's Assn. (broadcasting award); participant numerous world confs. to promote agr. Office: US House of Reps 2161 Rayburn Bldg Washington DC 20515-0005

LIGHTHIZER, ROBERT E., lawyer; b. Ashtabula, Ohio, 1947. BA, Georgetown U., 1969, JD, 1973. Bar: D.C. 1973. Ptnr. Skadden, Arps, Slate, Meagher & Flom, N.Y.C.; chief of staff U.S. Senate Com. Fin., 1981-83; dep. U.S. Trade Rep. rank of amb. Mem. Internat. Bar Assn. Office: Skadden Arps Slate Meagher & Flom 1440 New York Ave NW Washington DC 20005-2111*

LIGHTMAN, ALAN PAIGE, physicist, writer; b. Memphis, Nov. 28, 1948; s. Richard Lovis and Jeanne (Garretson) L.; m. Jean Greenblatt, Nov. 28, 1976; children: Elyse, Kara. AB, Princeton U., 1970; PhD in Physics, Calif. Inst. Tech., 1974. Postdoctoral fellow Cornell U., Ithaca, N.Y., 1974-76; asst. prof. Harvard U., Cambridge, Mass., 1976-79; staff scientist Smithsonian Astrophys. Obs., Cambridge, 1979-88; prof. sci. and writing MIT, Cambridge, 1988-95; John E. Burchard prof., 1995—. Author: Problem Book in Relativity and Gravitation, 1974, Radiative Processes in Astrophysics, 1976, Time Travel and Papa Joe's Pipe, 1984, A Modern Day Yankee in Connecticut Court, 1986, Origins: The Lives and Worlds of Modern Cosmologists, 1990 (Most Outstanding Sci. Book in Phys. Sci. award Assn. Am. Pubs.), Ancient Time for the Stars, 1992, Einstein's Dreams, 1993, Good Benito, 1995, Dance for Two, 1996. Fellow AAAS, Am. Acad. Arts and Scis., Am. Phys. Soc.; mem. Am. Astron. Soc. (chmn. high energy astrophysics divsn. 1991). Achievements include proof of Schiff Conjecture for relativistic gravitation theories; discovery of secular instabilities in accretion disks; pioneering development of theory of relativistic plasmas in astrophysics. Office: MIT 77 Massachusetts Ave Cambridge MA 02139-4301

LIGHTMAN, HAROLD ALLEN, marketing executive; b. Gloucester, Mass., Oct. 23, 1925; s. Abraham and Gertrude (Chait) L.; m. Irma Shorell, Feb. 19, 1954; children: Timothy, Harold, Jr., Stacey. Student, Norwich U., 1943; student, Cambridge U., Eng., 1946; BBA, U. Miami, 1949. Acct. exec. Grant Advt., Miami, Fla., 1948-50; advt. dir. Sears Roebuck & Co., Tampa, Fla., 1950-51; account exec. Robert Otto Internat., N.Y.C., 1952-53; account exec., field supr. Amos Parish & Co., N.Y.C., 1954-56; acct. exec. Dowd, Redfield & Johnstone, N.Y.C., 1957-59; chmn. bd. dirs. H. Allen Lightman Inc., N.Y.C., 1959—; bd. dirs. Irma Shorell Inc., N.Y.C.; pres., bd. dirs. Ind. Cosmetic Mfg. and Distbrs. U.S.A., v.p. nat. legis. affairs, 1974—; exec. v.p. Alfin Fragrances, Inc., 1985-87; pres. I.S. Labs. Inc., 1987—. Author newspaper column: Seen & Heard, 1965-83; producer: Cable TV program Seen & Heard, 1978—. Sgt. U.S. Army, 1943-46, ETO. Decorated Purple Heart, Bronze Star (2), Combat Infantry Badge; recipient Pub. Rels. Gold Key award, 1987. Fellow Winston Churchill Meml. Libr., Harry S. Truman Meml. Libr.; mem. Nat. Fedn. Ind. Bus. (del. 1979), Internat. Platform Assn., Alpha Delta Sigma (founder, 1st pres. 1947-48), DAV, Am. Legion (vice comdr. 1948-49), Vets. of the Battle of the Bulge, The Jockey Club. Office: 75 E End Ave New York NY 10028-7918

LIGHTSTONE, RONALD, lawyer; b. N.Y.C., Oct. 4, 1938; s. Charles and Pearl (Weisberg) L.; m. Nancy Lehrer, May 17, 1973; 1 child, Dana. AB, Columbia U., 1959; JD, NYU, 1962. Atty. CBS, N.Y.C., 1967-69; assoc. dir. bus. affairs CBS News, N.Y.C., 1969-70; atty. NBC, N.Y.C., 1970; assoc. gen. counsel Viacom Internat. Inc., N.Y.C., 1970-75; v.p., gen. counsel, sec. Viacom Internat. Inc., 1976-80; v.p. bus. affairs Viacom Entertainment Group Viacom Internat., Inc., 1980-82, v.p. corp. affairs, 1982-84, sr. v.p. corp. and legal affairs, 1984-87; exec. v.p. Spelling Entertainment Inc., L.A., 1988-91, COO, 1991-93; chmn. Multimedia Labs. Inc., 1994—; bd. dirs. Starsight Telecast, Inc.; chmn. Prodrs. Entertainment Group, Ltd., 1995—. Served to lt. USN, 1962-66. Mem. ABA (chmn. TV, cable and radio com.), Assn. Bar City N.Y., Fed. Communications Bar Assn.

LIGOMENIDES, PANOS ARISTIDES, electrical and computer engineering educator, consultant; b. Pireaus, Greece, Apr. 3, 1928; came to U.S., 1955; s. Aristides P. and Sonia (Akritides) L.; m. Danae J. Tsarmaklis, Dec. 29, 1973;children: Katerina, Christina. BSc in Physics with high honors, U. Athens, 1951, MSc in Radio Engring, 1952; MSc in Elec. Engring., Stanford U., 1956, PhD in Elec. Engring. and Physics, 1958. Registered profl. engr. Research engr. IBM, Poughkeepsie, N.Y., 1958-59, San Jose, Calif., 1959-64; asst. prof. elec. engring. UCLA, 1964-69; adj. prof. elec. engring. Stanford U., Calif., 1969-71, Fulbright prof., 1970-71; disting. vis. prof. U. Md., College Park, 1971-72, prof. elec. engring., 1971-93, prof. emeritus, 1993—, chmn. computer engring., elec. engring. dept., 1972-76; prof. U. Patras, Greece, 1993—; pres., Computer Engring. Cons., Lanham, Md., 1976-80; dir. Cybernetics Rsch. Lab., 1982—; v.p. Caelum Rsch. Corp., 1988-93; cons. to various industries and govt. orgns.; elected chair of informatics, Acad. of Athens, Greece, 1993; pres. Acad.'s Applied Sci. Divsn., Greece, 1995. Author: Information Processing Machines, 1969, Notions, Measures of Probability, 1978, Axiomatic Probability Theory, 1979, Computer Application in Industry and Management, 1981, Management and Office Information Systems, 1984, Visual Languages, 1986, Uncertainty in Knowledge-Based Systems, 1987; assoc. editor sci. jours.; contbr. over 160 articles to sci. and engring. books, jours., conf. proceedings; patentee pathfinder algorithm. Lt. Greek Navy, 1952-54. OECD fellow, 1965, 74; Ford Found. fellow, 1966-68; Salzburg Seminar fellow, 1971; recipient grants and contracts for rsch. in computers and artificial intelligence. Mem. IEEE (life, sr.), N.Y. Acad. Sci. Home: 39 Bakoyianni St, 15235 Athens Greece Office: Acad Athens, 28 Panepistimiou Ave, 10679 Athens Greece

LIGUORI, FRANK NICKOLAS, temporary personnel company executive; b. Bklyn., July 2, 1946; s. August and Mary (Perotto) L.; m. JoAnn Scioscia, July 7, 1968; children: Frank Jr., Mark. BS in Acctg., St. Francis Coll., Bklyn., 1964. CPA, N.Y. Sr. auditor Coopers & Lybrand, N.Y.C., 1964-71; successively controller, treas., sr. v.p., exec. v.p., pres., CEO, chmn. Olsten Corp., Westbury, N.Y., 1971—, also bd. dirs.; bd. dirs. WLIW 21, Plainview, N.Y. Mem. Am. Inst. CPAs, N.Y. State Soc. CPAs, Nat. Assn. Temporary Services (bd. dirs.). Home: 2 Talisman Ct Huntington Station NY 11746-5320*

LIJINSKY, WILLIAM, biochemist; b. Dublin, Ireland, Oct. 19, 1928; came to U.S., 1951; s. Morris and Rebecca (Hershman) L.; m. Rosalie K. Elespuru, June 10, 1973; 1 dau., Catherine Elizabeth; 1 dau. by previous marriage, Sharon Anne. B.Sc. with honours, U. Liverpool, Eng., 1949, Ph.D., 1951. Asst. prof., then asso. prof. Chgo. Med. Sch., 1955-68; prof. biochemistry U. Nebr. Med. Sch., Omaha, 1968-71; group leader carcinogenesis program Oak Ridge Nat. Lab., 1971-76; dir. chem. carcinogenesis program Frederick (Md.) Cancer Research Facility, 1976-91; expert Nat. Inst. Environ. Health Scis., N.C., 1991-92. Author research papers, revs. Mem. Biochem. Soc., Am. Chem. Soc., Am. Assn. Cancer Research, Am. Soc. Biol. Chemists, Environmental Mutagen Soc., Soc. Occupational and

Environ. Health, Sigma Xi. Home: 11398 High Hay Dr Columbia MD 21044-1029

LIJOI, PETER BRUNO, lawyer; b. Suffern, N.Y., Sept. 2, 1953; s. Salvatore and Josephine (Gentile) L.; m. Christine Louise Confroy, Aug. 19, 1978; children: Jonathan Peter, Christopher Andrew. BA in History and Econs., Montclair State Coll., 1975; postgrad. in urban planning, Rutgers U., 1975-76; JD, Pace U., 1979; postgrad., Harvard U., 1992. Bar: N.J. 1981, N.Y. 1988. Rsch. intern N.J. Dept. Edn., Trenton, 1976; intern Office U.S. Atty., N.Y.C., 1977-78; energy coord. Rockland County, 1979-80; dep. dir., of counsel Pvt. Industry Coun., Pearl River, N.Y., 1980-91; pvt. practice law Summit, N.J., 1981—; dir., counsel County of Rockland Indsl. Devel. Agy., 1981-95; v.p., gen. counsel Rockland Econ. Devel. Corp., Pearl River, 1990-91; cons. U.S. Dept. Energy, Washington, 1980; mem. program of instrn. for lawyers Law Sch., Harvard U., 1992; legal counsel K. Hovnanian Cos. North Jersey, Inc., 1993—. Guest writer The Bond Buyer. Bd. dirs. Rockland County coun. Girl Scouts U.S., 1982-92; pres. Washington Elem. Sch. PTA, Summit, 1986—; mem. Summit Planning Bd., desegregation grant adv. com. Summit Bd. Edn., 1992—. Mem. ABA, N.J. Bar Assn., N.Y. Bar Assn., Union County Bar Assn., Assn. Trial Lawyers Am., Nat. Assn. Bond Lawyers. Roman Catholic. Avocations: running, coaching youth soccer. Home: 124 Canoe Brook Pky Summit NJ 07901-1436 Office: 110 Fieldcrest Ave Edison NJ 08837

LIKENS, GENE ELDEN, biology and ecology educator, administrator; b. Pierceton, Ind., Jan. 6, 1935; s. Colonel Benjamin and Josephine (Garner) L.; m. Phyllis Craig; children: Kathy, Gregory, Leslie. BS, Manchester (Ind.) Coll., 1957, DSc (hon.), 1979; MS, U. Wis., 1959, PhD, 1962; DSc (hon.), Rutgers U., 1985, Plymouth State Coll., U. N.H., 1989, Miami U., 1990; LHD (hon.), Union Coll., 1991; DSc (hon.), U. Bodenkultur, Vienna, Austria, 1993, Marist Coll., 1993. Asst. zoology Manchester Coll., 1955-57; grad. teaching asst. U. Wis., 1957-59, vis. lectr., 1963; instr. zoology Dartmouth Coll., 1961, instr. biol. scis., 1963, asst. prof., then assoc. prof., 1963-69; mem. faculty Cornell U., 1969-83, prof. ecology, 1972-83, Charles A. Alexander prof. biol. scis., 1983, adj. prof., 1983—; v.p. N.Y. Botanical Garden, 1983-93; dir. Inst. Ecosystem Studies, Millbrook, N.Y., 1983—, pres., 1993—; dir. Mary Flagler Cary Arboretum, 1983—; prof. biology Yale U., 1984—; prof. grad. field of ecology Rutgers U., 1985—; vis. prof. Ctr. Advanced Rsch., also dept. environ scis. U. Va., Charlottesville, 1978-79; lectr. Williams Summer Inst. Coll. Tchrs., 1966, 67, Drew Summer Inst. Coll. Tchrs., 1968, Cornell U. Alumni Assn., 1978; Paul C. Lemon ecology lectr. SUNY, Albany, 1978; chmn. New Eng. div. task force conservation aquatic ecosystems U.S. Internat. Biol. Program, 1966-67; vis. assoc. ecologist Brookhaven Nat. Lab., 1968; C.P. Snow lectr. Ithaca Coll., 1979, 89; Robert S. Campbell lectr. U. Mo., 1980; A.E. Waller lectr. Ohio State U., 1990; Disting. Ecologist lectr. N.C. State U., 1980; Henry J. Oosting lectr. Duke U., 1985; Rilett vis. scholar Ill. State U., 1985; vis. scholar James Madison U., 1988; Class of 1960 vis. scholar, Williams Coll., Williamstown, Mass., 1988; Jack R. Hargis lectr. U. Minn., Duluth, 1988; Robert H. Woodworth lectr. in sci. Bennington (Vt.) Coll., 1988; mem. Nat. Commn. on Environment, 1991; Olin lectr. Environ. Fairfield U., 1990; lectr. Golden Series, Universität für Bodenkultur, 1991; William V. Kaesar Meml. scholar U. Wis., Madison, 1991; disting. scientist lecture series Bard Coll., 1991; Donnell Foster Hewett Lecture series Lehigh U., 1992; Miles C. Horton spl. lect. Va. Polytech. Inst., State U., 1993, Marine Biological Lab. Fri. evening lecture series Woods Hole, 1993; Granville Sewell disting. lectr. Columbia U., 1994; vis. disting. ecologist, Colo. State U., 1994; Raymond Lindeman Meml. lectr. U. Minn., 1994; lectr. in field; cons. in field; mem. numerous govt. and sci. panels, participant numerous confs. Author 12 books and more than 335 sci. jour. publs. Recipient Conservation award Am. Motors Corp., 1969, 75th Anniversary award U.S. Forest Svc., 1980, Disting. Achievement award Lab. Biomed. and Environ. Studies, UCLA, 1982, Regents medal of excellence SUNY, 1984, award N.Y. Acad. Scis., 1986, Internat. ECI prize for Limnetic Ecology, 1989, Disting. Svc. award N.Y. Bot. Garden, 1989, Disting. Svc. award Am. Inst. Biol. Scis., 1990, The Garden Club Am. Spl. Citation, 1992, The Tyler World Environment prize U. So. Calif., 1993, Australia Prize, 1994; NATO sr. fellow, 1969, Guggenheim fellow, 1972-73; grantee NSF, EPA, Dept. Energy, USDA Forest Svc., NOAA. Fellow AAAS; mem. NAS (chmn. sect. 27 1986-89), Ecol. Soc. Am. (chmn. study com. 1971-74, v.p. 1978-79, pres. 1981-82, eminent ecologist award 1995), Am. Soc. Limnology and Oceanography (pres. 1976-77, 1st G.E. Hutchinson award for excellence in rsch. 1982), Internat. Assn. Theoretical and Applied Limnology (nat. rep., Naumann-Thienemann medal 1995), Royal Swedish Acad. Scis., Am. Polar Soc., Explorers Club, Freshwater Biol. Assn., Internat. Assn. Gt. Lakes Rsch., Internat. Water Resources Assn. (charter), Australian Soc. Limnology, Am. Water Resources Assn. (hon.), Br. Ecol. Soc. (hon.), Am. Inst. Biol. Scis., Royal Danish Acad. Sci., Sigma Xi, Gamma Alpha, Phi Sigma. Methodist. Office: Inst Ecosys Studies Box AB Millbrook NY 12545

LIKENS, JAMES DEAN, economics educator; b. Bakersfield, Calif., Sept. 12, 1937; s. Ernest LeRoy and Monnie Jewel (Thomas) L.; m. Janet Sue Pelton, Dec. 18, 1965 (div.); m. Karel Carnohan, June 4, 1988 (div.); children: John David, Janet Elizabeth. BA in Econs., U. Calif., Berkeley, 1960, MBA, 1961; PhD in Econs., U. Minn., 1970. Analyst Del Monte Corp., San Francisco, 1963; economist 3M Co., Mpls., 1968-71; asst. prof. econs. Pomona Coll., 1969-75, assoc. prof. econs., 1975-83, prof. econs., 1983-85, Morris B. Pendleton prof. econs., 1989—; vis. asst. prof. econs. U. Minn., 1970, 71, vis. assoc. prof., 1976-77; pres., dean Western CUNA Mgmt. Sch., Pomona Coll., 1975—; chmn. bd. 1st City Savs. Fed. Credit Union, 1978—; coord. So. Calif. Rsch. Coun., L.A., 1980-81, 84-85; mem. adv. coun. Western Corp. Fed. Credit Union, 1993—; cons. in field. Author: (with Joseph LaDou) Medicine and Money, 1976, Mexico and Southern California: Toward A New Partnership, 1981, Financing Quality Education in Southern California, 1985; contbr. articles to profl. jours. Served with USCG, 1961-67. Rsch. grantee HUD-DOT, Haynes Found., Filene Rsch. Inst. Mem. ABA, Am. Econ. Assn., Western Econ. Assn. Home: 725 W 10th St Claremont CA 91711-3719 Office: Pomona Coll Dept Econs Claremont CA 91711

LIKINS, PETER WILLIAM, academic administrator; b. Tracy, Calif., July 4, 1936; s. Ennis Blaine and Dorothy Louise (Medlin) L.; m. Patricia Ruth Kitsmiller, Dec. 18, 1955; children: Teresa, Lora, Paul, Linda, Krista, John. BCE, Stanford U., 1957, PhD in Engring. Mechanics, 1965; MCE, MIT, 1958; hon. doctorates, Lafayette Coll., 1983, Moravian Coll., 1984, Med. Coll. Pa., 1990, Lehigh U., 1991, Allentown St. Francis de Sales, 1993; hon. doctorate, Czech Tech U., 1993. Devel. engr. Jet Propulsion Lab., Pasadena, Calif., 1958-60; asst. prof. engring. UCLA, 1964-69, assoc. prof., 1969-72, prof., 1972-76, asst. dean, 1974-75, assoc. dean, 1975-76; dean engring. and applied sci. Columbia U., N.Y.C., 1976-80, provost, 1980-82; Lehigh U., Bethlehem, Pa., 1982—; engring. cons. U.S. and fgn. corps. and govt. agys., 1965—. Author: Elements of Engineering Mechanics, 1973, Spacecraft Dynamics, 1982; Contbr. articles to profl. jours. Mem. U.S. Pres.'s Coun. Advisers Sci. and Tech., 1990-93. Ford Found. fellow, 1970-72; named to Nat. Wrestling Hall of Fame. Fellow AIAA; mem. Nat. Acad. Engring., Phi Beta Kappa, Sigma Xi, Tau Beta Pi. Office: Lehigh U 27 Memorial Dr W Bethlehem PA 18015-3089

LILEY, PETER EDWARD, mechanical engineering educator; b. Barnstaple, North Devon, Eng., Apr. 22, 1927; came to U.S., 1957; s. Stanley E. and Rosa (Ellery) L.; m. Elaine Elizabeth Kull, Aug. 16, 1963; children: Elizabeth Ellen, Rebecca Ann. B.Sc., Imperial Coll., U. London, 1951, Ph.D. in Physics, 1957, D.I.C., 1957. With Brit. Oxygen Engring., London, 1955-57; asst. prof. mech. engring. Purdue U., West Lafayette, Ind., 1957-61, assoc. prof., 1961-72; assoc. sr. researcher Thermophys. Properties Research Ctr., Purdue U., West Lafayette, Ind., 1961-72, prof. mech. engring., 1972—; sr. rschr. Ctr. for Info. and Numerical Data Analysis and Synthesis, Purdue U., West Lafayette, Ind., 1972-92; cons. in field. Author: Sect. 3 Perry's Chemical Engineers Handbook, 4th edit., 1963, 5th edit., 1972, 6th edit., 1985; (with Hartnett et al.) Handbook of Heat Transfer Fundamentals, 2nd edit., 1985; (with others) Marks Mechanical Engineers Handbook, 9th edit., 1987, Schaums 2000 Solved Problems in Mechanical Engineering Thermodynamics, 1988, Tables and Charts for Thermodynamics, 1995, Kutz Mechanical Engineers Handbook, 1986; co-author: Steam and Gas Tables with Computer Equations, 1985, Thermal Conductivity of Nonmetallic Liquids and Gases, 1970, Properties of Nonmetallic Fluid Elements, 1981, Properties of Inorganic and Organic Fluids, 1988; editor, mem. editl. bd. Internat. Jour. Thermophysics, 1980-86; contbr. chpts. to handbooks in field; contbr. articles to profl. jours.; reviewer profl. jours. Served with Royal Corps Signals, Brit. Army, 1945-48. Lutheran. Home: 3608 Mulberry Dr Lafayette IN 47905-3937 Office: Purdue U Dept Mech Engring West Lafayette IN 47907

LILIEN, ELLIOT STEPHEN, secondary education educator; b. Maplewood, N.J.; s. Bernard Banner and Judith Batson (Mulally) L.; m. Louise Anne Hoehl, Jan. 29, 1965 (div. July 1968); m. Nancy Goddard Pierce, July 21, 1985. BA, U. Chgo., 1961; JD, Columbia U., 1964; MAT, Harvard U., 1965. Tchr. Concord (Mass.)-Carlisle H.S., 1965—, head coach fencing, 1965-85, head coach tennis, 1989—; head coach fencing Brown U., Providence, 1987-93; dir. Concord-Acad. Fencing Camp, 1975-94. Author: German History 1815-1945, 1972, History of Greece and Rome, 1979, Competition Experiment, 1986. Commr. Northeast Fencing Conf., Boxboro, Mass., 1993—. Grantee Coun. for Basic Edn., 1983. Mem. Four Sch. Consortium (founder, pres. 1987), Concord-Carlisle Tchrs. (pres. 1972-94). Avocations: tennis, WWI poster collecting, swords, beer steins, autographs. Home: 62 Chester Rd Boxboro MA 01719-1808 Office: Concord-Carlisle H S 500 Walden St Concord MA 01742-3617

LILIEN, MARK IRA, publishing, retailing and systems executive; b. Kew Gardens, N.Y., Sept. 7, 1953; s. Robert Samuel and Annette Audrey (London) L. BS in Labor Relations, Cornell U., 1974; MBA in Entrepreneurial Mktg., U. Pa., 1976. Buyer, mdse. controller Korvettes Dept. Stores, N.Y.C., 1976-79; dir. mdse. adminstrn. Walden Books, Stamford, Conn., 1979-84, U.S. Retail div. Genesco, Nashville, 1984-85; sr. assoc. Booz Allen & Hamilton, N.Y.C., 1985-86; v.p. Penguin USA, N.Y.C., 1986-89, Barnes & Noble Bookstores, N.Y.C., 1989-92, Lechters, 1992-94, McGraw-Hill, N.Y.C., 1994—. Mem. editorial bd. Retail Systems Alert Newsletter, 1991-94. Schirer fellow Wharton Sch. Bus. U. Pa., 1975-76. Mem. Book Industry Systems Adv. Com. (vice chmn. 1983-84, chmn. 1988-89), Book Industry Study Group, Assn. Am. Pubs. (bus. mgrs. com., Pubnet com. 1986-89), Nat. Retail Fedn. (chmn. SpecNet com. 1990-92). Avocations: theatre, films. Home: 350 Bleecker St Apt 3E New York NY 10014-2631

LILIENFIELD, LAWRENCE SPENCER, physiology and biophysics educator; b. Bklyn., May 5, 1927; s. Henry Jacob and Lee (Markman) L.; m. Eleanor Marion Russ, Oct. 22, 1950; children: Jan, Adele, Lisa. BS, Villanova (Pa.) U., 1945; MD, Georgetown U., 1949, MS, 1954, PhD, 1956. Diplomate Nat. Bd. Med. Examiners, Am. Bd. Internal Medicine. Intern Georgetown U. Hosp., Washington, 1949-59, 1949-50, resident in internal medicine, 1950, 52-54, rsch. fellow, 1954-55; instr. medicine Sch. Medicine Georgetown U., Washington, 1955-56, asst. chief cardiovascular rsch. lab., dept. medicine, 1956-63, asst. chief cardiovascular rsch. lab. dept. medicine, 1956-63, assoc. prof. physiology, biophysics and medicine Sch. Medicine, 1961-64, prof. physiology and biophysics Sch. Medicine, 1964-95, prof., chmn. dept. physiology and biophysics Sch. Medicine, 1963-93; attending physician VA Hosp., Washington, 1956-70; cons. USPHS, 1964-69, NASA, 1964-70, U.S. Dept. State, 1967-74; established investigator Am. Heart Assn., 1958; vis. prof. faculty of medicine U. Saigon, Republic of Korea, 1965-74. Contbr. numerous articles to profl. jours. Bd. dirs. Washington Heart Assn., 1962-67, chmn., 1966. With USN, 1945; capt. USAF, 1950-52. Recipient Established Investigator award Am. Heart Assn., 1958; Rsch. Career Devel. award USPHS, 1963, Rsch. Career award, 1963, Kaiser-Permanente Teaching award, 1987; USPHS rsch. and rsch. tng. grantee, 1987. Fellow ACP; mem. Am. Soc. for Clin. Investigation, Am. Physiol. Soc., Soc. for Exptl. Biology and Medicine, Am. Fedn. for Clin. Rsch. (chair ea. sect. 1965-66). Avocations: computers in education. Office: Georgetown U Sch Medicine 3900 Reservoir Rd NW Washington DC 20007-2187

LILIENTHAL, ALFRED M(ORTON), author, historian, editor; b. N.Y.C., Dec. 25, 1913; s. Herbert and Lottye (Kohn) L. BA, Cornell U., Ithaca, N.Y., 1934; LLB, Columbia U., 1938, JD, 1969. Bar: N.Y. 1938. With Bennett, House & Couts, N.Y.C., 1939-41, State Dept., 1942-43, 45-48; cons. U.S. del. UN San Francisco Conf., 1945; adminstrv. practice, 1947-50; counsel Am.-Arab Assn. Commerce & Industry, 1960-65; editor, pub. Middle East Perspective (monthly newsletter), 1967-85; lectr. on Middle East at numerous colls. and clubs throughout U.S. and fgn. countries, 1951-94, frequent guest TV and radio news commentator on Middle East devels., 1951-91; lectr. cultural symposium United Arab Emirates, Libya, Lebanon, Vienna, Baghdad, Prague; polit. columnist daily Al Qabas, Kuwait, 1976-77; accredited corr. to UN; chmn. Am. Coun. on the Middle East; cons. UN Internat. Conf. on Question Palestine, Geneva, 1983; participant Model Internat. Conf. on Middle East, Prague, 1988, 27 Middle East trips including West Bank and Gaza, 1953-94; guest of UN Sec.-Gen. at 50th Commemorative meeting, San Francisco, 1995. Author: Which Way to World Government, 1949, What Price Israel?, 1954, There Goes the Middle East, 1957, Studies in Twentieth Century Diplomacy, 1959, The Other Side of the Coin, 1965, The Zionist Connection, 1978, The Zionist Connection II, 1982, rev. Czechoslovakian edit., 1989, Japanese edit., 1991, This I Do Believe, 1994; contbr. to: book Zionism-The Dream and the Reality, 1974; monthly commentaries Washington Report on Middle East Affairs, 1988—; also numerous mag. articles and syndicated newspieces. Pres. Rep. First Voters League, 1940; Fusion Party candidate for N.Y.C. Coun., 1941; leader fight against Communist controlled Am. Youth Congress, 1941. With AUS, 1943-45. Papers housed in archives of Hoover Instn., Stanford, Calif. Mem. Nat. Rep. Club, Univ. Club, Capitol Hill Club, Nat. Press Club, Cornell Club Washington. Home and Office: 800-25th St NW Washington DC 20037

LILJA, SVEN INGVAR, marine industry executive; b. Helsingborg, Sweden, May 4, 1936; s. Claes Emil and Syster Ella (Tengvall) L.; divorced; children: Kristin, Asa, Bo, Ollegard, Karin; m. Maria Helena, Aug. 16, 1986; children: Rebecca, Alexandra. Master Mariner, Marine Acad., Malmoe, Sweden, 1958; LLM, U. Lund, Sweden, 1963. Asst. judge Sweden, 1964-66; co. atty. Port Authority of Gothenburg, Sweden, 1966-67, Grangesberg Co., Stockholm, 1968-73; co. atty. Salen Shipping Co., Stockholm, 1973-74, gen. mgr. Tanker div., 1975-79; v.p. Det Norske Veritas, Oslo, 1980-84; sr. v.p. DNV East Med. & BS, Greece, 1986-96; with bus. devel. DNV Divsn. Americas, N.J., 1996—. Mem. The Marine Club (Piraeus), The Yacht Club of Greece, Ekali Club, Stockholm Shipping Lodge. Mem. The Conservative Party. Christian Protestant. Avocations: architectural design, yachting. Office: DNV Divsn Americas RNCA 70 Gr Ave River Edge NJ 07661

LILJEBECK, ROY C., transportation company executive; b. 1937; married. BA, U. Puget Sound, 1961. Acct. Touche Ross Bailey and Smart, 1961-67; with Pacific Air Freight Inc., 1967-68; treas. Airborne Freight Corp., Seattle, 1968-88, v.p., 1968-73, sr. v.p., 1973-79, exec. v.p., 1979—, chief fin. officer, 1984—. Office: Airborne Freight Corp PO Box 662 Seattle WA 98111-0662

LILJEGREN, FRANK SIGFRID, artist, art association official; b. N.Y.C., Feb. 23, 1930; s. Josef Sigfrid and Ester (Davidsson) L.; m. Donna Kathryn Hallam, Oct. 12, 1957. Student, Art Students League, N.Y.C., 1950-55. Instr. painting, drawing, composition Westchester County Center, White Plains, N.Y., 1967-77, Art Students League, 1974-75, Wassenberg Art Center, Van Wert, Ohio, 1978-80, Wright State U. Br. Western Ohio Campus, Celina, Ohio, 1981—; corr. sec. Allied Artists Am., N.Y.C., 1967, exhbn. chmn., 1968—, pres., 1970-72, also dir. Exhibited at Suffolk Mus., Stonybrook, N.Y., Springfield (Mass.) Mus., Marion Kugler McNay Art Inst., San Antonio, Philbrook Mus., Tulsa, N.A.D., N.Y.C., New Britain (Conn.) Mus. Art, Ft. Wayne (Ind.) Mus. Art; represented in permanent collections Art Students League, Univ. Mus., S.E. Mo. State U., Manhattan Savs. Bank, N.Y.C., Am. Ednl. Pubs. Inst., N.Y.C., New Britain Mus. Am. Art, Cape Girardeau, Mo. Served with AUS, 1951. Recipient numerous awards for still life oil paintings. Mem. Fine Arts fedn. N.Y, Art Students League (life), Acad. Artists Assn., Coun. Am. Artists Socs., Artists Fellowship, Salmagundi. Office: Liljegren Galleries 203 S Cherry St Van Wert OH 45891-2006 *The best advice I could give young artists is to first learn their craft to the fullest so that they can then be free to express themselves in what ever style and medium they then choose to work. Last but not least, they should have self-respect and great love for what they are doing.*

LILLARD, JOHN FRANKLIN, III, lawyer; b. Cheverly, Md., Aug. 2, 1947; s. John Franklin, Jr. and Madeline Virginia (Berg) L.; m. Shannon Leslie Oliver, June 1, 1991; 1 child, John F. Lillard IV. B.A., Washington and Lee U., 1969, J.D., 1971. Bar: N.Y. 1972, D.C. 1974, Md. 1975. Assoc. Donovan, Leisure, Newton & Irvine, N.Y.C., 1971-74, Pierson, Ball & Dowd (merged into Reed, Smith, Shaw & McClay), Washington, 1974-76; trial atty. civil div. Dept. Justice, Washington, 1976-77; ptnr. Lillard & Lillard, Washington, 1977—. Vice chair Village Council of Friendship Heights, Chevy Chase, Md., 1975-77; candidate U.S. Congress from 5th dist. Md., 1981; chair Am. Solar Energy Assn.; founding mem. Nat. Adv. Coun. Ctr. for the Study of The Presidency, 1970—, Md. State Adv. Bd. on Spl. Tax Dists., 1976-77, alcoholic beverage adv. bd. Montgomery County, 1977-79; chair Eisenhower Centennial Meml. Com., 1990—. Served to 1st lt. USAF Aux., 1973-77. Recipient Eastman award Am. Arbitration Assn., 1971. Mem. Md. Bar Assn., Prince George's County Bar Assn., Anne Arundel County Bar Assn. Republican. Episcopalian. Clubs: Metropolitan (Washington); Tred Avon Yacht (Oxford, Md.); Marlborough Hunt (Upper Marlboro, Md.). Office: Lillard & Lillard 124 South St Annapolis MD 21401

LILLARD, MARK HILL, III, computer consulting executive, former air force officer; b. Jacksonville, Fla., Sept. 1, 1943; s. Mark Hill Jr. and Cornelia Kingman (Callaway) L.; m. Marie-Jacques Le Guyader, June 3, 1972; children: Mark Hill IV, Michael Robert. BA, Bowling Green U., 1965, MS, St. Mary's U., San Antonio, 1976; MBA, Auburn U., 1977. Commd. 2d lt. USAF, 1965, advanced through grades to brig. gen., 1991; dir. spl. actions Combined Forces Command, Republic of Korea, 1980-83; comdr. 596 BMS, Barksdale AFB, La., 1983-85; dep. comdr. OPS, 2 BMS, Barksdale AFB, La., 1985; chief force mgmt. Strategic Air Command Hdqrs, Offutt, Nebr., 1985-87; comdr. 64 ABG, Reese AFB, Tex., 1987, 64 FTW, Reese AFB, Tex., 1987-88; exec. to chief of staff SHAPE (NATO), Mons, Belgium, 1988-91; comdr. 57th Air Div., Minot AFB, N.D., 1991; ret., 1991; exec. v.p. Pilot Rsch. Assocs., Inc., Vienna, Va., 1991—, also bd. dirs. Author: Simulation, 1976. Decorated Legion of Merit, Def. Superior Svc. medal, Def. Meritorious Svc. medal; Samil medal (Republic of Korea). Mem. Air Force Assn., Lions, Kiwanis, Phi Delta Theta. Republican. Avocations: tennis, golf. Home: 9516 Locust Hill Dr Great Falls VA 22066-2021 Office: Pilot Rsch Assocs Inc 1953 Gallows Rd Ste 350 Vienna VA 22182-3934

LILLEHEI, C. WALTON, surgeon; b. Mpls., Oct. 23, 1918; s. Clarence Ingewald and Elizabeth Lillian (Walton) L.; m. Katherine Ruth Lindberg, Dec. 31, 1946; children—Kimberle Rae (Mrs. Allen Loken), Craig Walton, Kevin Owen, Clark William. B.S., U. Minn., 1939, M.D., 1942, M.S. in Physiology, 1951, Ph.D. in Surgery, 1951; Dr. Medicinae h.c., U. Oslo, 1976; hon. degree, Faculte De Medecinae De Montpellier, France, 1977; Dr. honoris causa, Sorbonne U., Paris, 1986, U. Rome, 1991; LHD (hon.), Oklahoma City U., 1987; DSc, W.Va. U., 1993. Diplomate: Am. Bd. Surgery, 1951, Am. Bd. Thoracic Surgery, 1954. Pvt. practice medicine, 1942—, specializing gen., thoracic and cardiovascular surgery, 1945—; instr. dept. surgery U. Minn. Med. Sch., 1949-51, asso. prof. surgery, 1951-56, prof. surgery, 1956-67, clin. prof. surgery, 1967—; dir. med. affairs St. Jude Med. Sch., St. Paul, 1979—; chmn. dept. surgery Cornell U. Med. Center, N.Y.C., 1967-74, Lewis Atterbury Stimson prof. surgery Med. Coll., 1967-74; surgeon-in chief N.Y. Hosp., N.Y.C., 1967-70; bd. dirs. Getz Bros. Med., Tokyo. Served lt. col. M.C., AUS, 1942-46. Decorated Bronze Star; officer Order of Leopold (Belgium); recipient Theobald-Smith award AAAS, 1951, Ida. B. Gould award, 1957; 1st prize Am. Coll. Coll. Chest Physicians, 1952; Lasker award, 1955; Hektoen Gold medal AMA, 1957; Oscar B. Hunter award Am. Therapeutic Soc., 1958; Purdue Frederick Med. Achievement Travel award Internat. Consul for Health, 1958; Malcom F. Rogers Meml. award Wis. Heart Assn., 1962; Cummings Humanitarian award Am. Coll. Cardiology, 1963; Gairdner Found. Internat. award, 1963; Honor award Stevens Inst. Tech., 1967; Gold Plate award Am. Acad. Achievement, 1968; Bio-Med. Tech. Innovative Contbn. award Congl. Inst. for Space, Sci., and Tech., 1985; Outstanding Achievement award Bd. of Regents, U. Minn., 1991, Markowitz award Acad. Surgical Rsch., 1994; Lillehei Endowed Chair in thoracic and cardiovascular surgery named in his honor U. Minn. Med. Sch., 1988, Lillehei Libr. named in his honor, 1991; named to Minn. Inventors Hall of Fame, 1993. Fellow A.C.S., Am. Coll. Chest Physicians, Am. Coll. Cardiology (pres. 1966-67), Am. Coll. Angiology, Am. Heart Assn., Halsted Soc., Internat. Soc. Surgery, Allen O. Whipple Surg. Soc., Pan Am. Med. Soc., Royal Soc. Medicine (Gt. Britain), Soc. Thoracic Surgery; mem. AMA (Billings silver medal 1972), Am. Surg. Assn., Acad. Surg. Rsch., Am. Assn. Thoracic Surgery, Soc. U. Surgeons, Soc. Exptl. Biology and Medicine, AAAS, Internat. Cardiovascular Soc., Soc. Vascular Surgery, Sigma Xi. Home: 73 Otis Ln Saint Paul MN 55104-5645

LILLESTOL, JANE BRUSH, career development company executive; b. Jamestown, N.D., July 20, 1936; d. Harper J. and Doris (Mikkelson) Brush; m. Harvey Lillestol, Sept. 29, 1956; children: Kim, Kevin, Erik. BS, U. Minn., 1969, MS, 1973, PhD, 1977; grad. Inst. Ednl. Mgmt., Harvard U., 1984. Dir. placement, asst. to dean U. Minn., St. Paul, 1975-77; assoc. dean, dir. student acad. affairs N.D. State U., Fargo, 1977-80; dean Coll. Human Devel. Syracuse (N.Y.) U., 1980-89, v.p. for alumni rels., 1989-95, project dir. IBM Computer Aided Design Lab., 1989-92; prin. Lillestol Assocs.; charter mem. Mayor's Commn. on Women, 1986-90; NAFTA White House Conf. for Women Leaders, 1993. Bd. dirs. Univ. Hill Corp. Syracuse, 1983-93; mem. steering com. Consortium for Cultural Founds. of Medicine, 1980-89; trustee Pebble Hill Sch., 1990-94, Archbold Theatre, 1990-95, N.D. State U., 1992—. Recipient award U.S. Consumer Product Safety Commn., 1983, Woman of Yr. award AAUW, 1984, svc. award Syracuse U., 1992. Roman Catholic.

LILLEVANG, OMAR JOHANSEN, civil engineer; b. Los Angeles, Sept. 8, 1914; s. Gunnar Johansen and Nina (Christiansen) L.; m. D. Miriam Guest, Sept. 10, 1939 (dec. Sept. 1990); children—Ralph Glen, Carol Ellen. A.A., Los Angeles Jr. Coll., 1935; B.S., U. Calif., Berkeley, 1937, postgrad., 1950-51. Registered profl. engr., Alaska, Calif., Hawaii, N.J., Oreg., Utah, Wash., Wis. Topographic surveyor Calif. Hwy. Commn., 1937; asst. engr. Coachella Valley County (Calif.) Water and Stormwater Dist., 1938; harbor constrn. engr., 1939-40, cantonment design and constrn. engr., 1941, constrn. engr. dams, aqueduct, tunnel, pump plants, 1942, water resources analyst, 1943; with Leeds, Hill, Barnard and Jewett (Cons. Engrs., and successors), Los Angeles, 1938-43, 46-61; supervising engr. Leeds, Hill, Barnard and Jewett (Cons. Engrs., and successors), 1950-61; v.p., dir. Leeds, Hill & Jewett Inc. (Cons. Engrs.), Los Angeles, 1961-64; cons. civil engring., especially for harbors, rivers, lakes, seas, coastal processes L.A., Whittier, 1964—; mem. advisory panel for shore erosion protection U.S. Army Chief Engrs. Contbr.: articles to profl. jours. including Shore & Beach mag. Trustee, chmn. bldg. com. Plymouth Congregational Ch. of Whittier, Calif. Served with USN, 1943-46. Fellow ASCE (mem. task groups, John G. Moffatt-Frank E. Nichol Meml. award 1981); mem. Am. Shore Beach Preservation Assn., Permanent Internat. Assn. Navigation Congresses, U.S. Power Squadrons. Club: Rotary Internat. Home: 14318 Eastridge Dr Whittier CA 90602-2721 Office: PO Box 4382 Whittier CA 90607-4382

LILLEY, ALBERT FREDERICK, lawyer; b. Harrisburg, Pa., Dec. 21, 1932; s. Frederick Anthony and Jane Sander (Ingham) L.; m. Judith Carter Pennock, Sept. 1, 1956; children: Kirk Anthony, Kristin Sander, James Alexander. A.B., Bowdoin Coll., 1954; LL.B., U. Va., 1959. Assoc. Milbank, Tweed, Hadley & McCloy, N.Y.C., 1959-67, ptnr., 1967—. Trustee No. Highlands Regional H.S., Allendale, N.J., 1964-65; mem. Allendale Bd. Zoning Adjustment, 1965-66; bd. overseers Bowdoin Coll., 1976-88, overseer emeritus, 1988—; trustee Valley Hosp., Ridgewood, N.J., 1978-92, vice chmn. bd., 1985-89, chmn. bd., 1989-92; bd. dirs. Valley Care Corp., 1992—, Valley Home and Cmty. Health Care, Inc., 1992—; mem. alumni coun. U. Va. Law Sch., 1991-94, U.S. Can. Law Project Adv. Bd. 1st lt. U.S. Army, 1954-56. Mem. ABA, Am. Law Inst., N.Y. State Bar Assn., Assn. of Bar of City of N.Y., U. Va. Law Sch. Alumni Assn. (fund class mgr.). Home: 180 Lincoln Ave Ridgewood NJ 07450-4106 Office: Milbank Tweed Hadley & McCloy 1 Chase Manhattan Plz New York NY 10005-1401

LILLEY, JAMES RODERICK, foreign relations expert, former federal government official; b. Tsingtao, China, Jan. 15, 1928; s. Frank Walder and Inez (Bush) L.; m. Sally Booth, May 1, 1954; children: Douglas, Michael, Jeffrey. BA, Yale U., 1951; MA, George Washington U., 1972. Fgn. affairs officer U.S. State Dept., various East Asian posts, 1958-75; dep. asst. sec. of state U.S. State Dept., Washington, 1985-86; nat. intelligence officer CIA, Washington, 1975-78; sr. East Asian specialist NSC, Washington, 1981; dir. Am. Inst. in Taiwan, Taipei, 1982-84; ambassador U.S. Embassy, Seoul, Korea, 1986-89, Beijing, People's Republic of China, 1989-91; asst. sec. Dept. Defense, Washington, 1991-93; resident fellow Am. Enterprise Inst., Washington, 1993—; cons. Hunt/Sedco Oil Co., Dallas, 1979-81, United Techs., Hartford, Ct., 1979-80, Otis Elevator, Farmington, Ct., 1984-85, Westinghouse, Balt., 1984. Author: Beyond MFN, 1994. With U.S. Army, 1946-47; 1st lt. USAFR, 1950-67. Recipient Disting. Intelligence medal, CIA, 1979, Kang Hua medal Republic of Korea. Mem. Met. Club (Washington), Royal Bangkok Sports Club. Republican. Home: 7301 Maple Ave Chevy Chase MD 20815-5107 Office: 1150 17th St NW Fl 11 Washington DC 20036-4603

LILLEY, JOHN MARK, academic administrator, dean; b. Converse, La., Mar. 24, 1939; s. Ernest Franklin and Sibyl Arrena (Geoghagan) L.; children: Sibyl Elizabeth, Myles Durham; m. Geraldine Murphy; stepchildren: Benjamin Murphy, Jason Murphy. B in Music Edn., Baylor U., 1961, MusB, 1962, MusM, 1964; D of Musical Arts, U. So. Calif., 1971. Mem. faculty Claremont McKenna, Harvey Mudd, Pitzer and Scripps Colls., Claremont, Calif., 1966-76; asst. dean faculty Scripps Coll., 1973-76; asst. dean arts and scis. Kans. State U., Manhattan, 1976-80; provost, dean Pa. State U., Erie, 1980—; bd. dirs. Erie Conf., 1980—, Erie Plastics Corp., 1994—; mem. N.W. Pa. Indsl. Resource Ctr., 1987—. Condr. 1st performances Kubik, 1972, 76, Ives, 1974, (recording) Kubik, 1974. Bd. dirs., v.p. So. Calif. Choral Music Assn., L.A., 1971-76; mem. Archtl. Commn., Claremont, 1974-76; bd. dirs. Erie Philharm., 1980-86, United Way, Erie County, 1981—, Sta. WQLN Pub. Broadcasting of N.W. Pa., 1992—; mem. Regents Commn. on Nursing Edn., Kansas City, Kans., 1978-79; pres. Pacific S.W. Intercollegiate Choral Assn., L.A., 1969-70. NEH grantee, 1978. Mem. Am. Assn. Higher Edn., Coll. Music Soc., Am. Choral Dirs. Assn., Am. Assn. State Colls. and Univs. (vice chair confs. and profl. devel. com. 1989, chair 1990, bd. dirs. 1995—, govs. tuition account program adv. bd. 1996—), Erie Club, Kahkwa Club, Rotary (bd. dirs. Manhattan club 1979-80, Erie club 1981-88), Phi Mu Alpha Sinfonia, Omicron Delta Kappa. Republican. Presbyterian. Avocation: golf. Home: 601 Pasadena Dr Erie PA 16505-1038 Office: Pa State U Behrend Coll Station Rd Erie PA 16563

LILLEY, THEODORE ROBERT, financial executive; b. Paterson, N.J., Jan. 11, 1923; s. Ernest Raymond and Antoinette Eleanor (Hartmann) L.; m. Marguerite Anne Gallman, Jan. 27, 1951; children—Cheryl Anne, Wayne Robert, Ross Warren. B.A. cum laude, N.Y. U., 1946; M.B.A., Columbia U., 1948. Chartered financial analyst. With Standard Oil Co., N.J., 1948-64; investment mgr. Standard Oil Co., 1956-62, fin. mgr., 1962-64; asst. treas. Esso Internat. Inc., 1964-69; v.p. Tchr. Ins. and Annuity Assn. and Coll. Retirement Equities Fund, 1969-72; exec. dir. Fin. Analysts Fedn., N.Y.C., 1972-73; pres. Fin. Analysts Fedn., 1973-81, T.R. Lilley Assocs., 1981—; mem. advisory council Fin. Acctg. Standards Bd., 1976-80. Mem. bd. nat. missions United Presbyn. Ch. U.S.A., 1966-72; mem. United Presbyn. Found., 1972-81; trustee Englewood Hosp., 1979-85; bd. dirs. Near East Found., 1970—; trustee Ramapo Coll., 1977-95, chmn. bd., 1980-82. 1st lt. inf. AUS, 1943-46, ETO. Decorated Bronze Star, Purple Heart. Mem. Phi Beta Kappa, Phi Lambda Upsilon, Beta Gamma Sigma. Office: TR Lilley Assos PO Box 426 Tenafly NJ 07670-0426

LILLEY, WILLIAM, III, communications business consultant; b. Phila., Jan. 14, 1938; s. William, Jr. and Ida Weaver (Macklin) L.; m. Eve Auchincloss, Mar. 12, 1977; children—Buchanan Morgan, Brooke Carole, Whitman Elisa, Justin Weaver. B.A. magna cum laude, U. Pa., 1959; M.A., Yale U., 1961, Ph.D., 1965. Asst. prof. history Yale U., New Haven, 1962-69; prof. govt. U. Va., Charlottesville, 1977; co-founder, editor Nat. Jour., Washington, 1969-73; dep. asst. sec. HUD, Washington, 1973-75; dep., then dir. Council Wage and Price Stability, Washington, 1975-77; staff dir. Com. on Budget, Ho. of Reps., Washington, 1977-78; v.p. CBS, Inc., Washington, 1980-81; v.p. corporate affairs CBS, Inc., N.Y.C., 1981-84, sr. v.p. corporate affairs, 1985-86; pres. Am. Bus. Conf., 1986-88, Policy Communications Inc., Washington, 1988—; chmn., chief exec. officer InContext, Inc., Washington, 1992—; bd. dirs. Ply Gem Industries, Inc., Econ. and Social Rsch. Inst., Madison Ctr. for Ednl. Affairs. Co-author: New Technologies Affecting Broadcasting, 1981, Economic and Social Impacts of Media Advertising, 1989, Impact of Advertising on the Competetive Structure of the Media, 1990, Impact of Media Advertising on International Competetiveness, 1991, Geographic Distribution of U.S. Businesses Which Advertise Heavily, 1991, Almanac of State Legislatures, 1994, State Atlas of Political and Cultural Diversity, 1996, State Legislative Elections: Voting Patterns and Demographics, 1996; contbr. articles to profl. jours. Recipient U.S. Govt. Disting. Svc. award 1975, 76; Samuel F.B. Morse Rsch. fellowship, 1967-68; George Washington Eggleston prize; Most Disting. PhD Dissertation, humanities divsn., Yale U., 1965; Woodrow Wilson Fellowship, 1959-61. Mem. Yale Club, Merion Cricket, Cosmos, River Club, Chevy Chase, Met. Club. Clubs: Yale, Merion Cricket, Cosmos, River, Chevy Chase. Office: Policy Communications Inc 1615 L St NW Washington DC 20036-5610

LILLIBRIDGE, JOHN LEE, retired airline executive; b. Dover, Okla., Nov. 3, 1924; s. John Lee and Myra Ina (Munger) L.; m. Audrey Rae Hart, Aug. 22, 1948; 1 son, John Lee III. B.S. in Mech. Engring., Okla. A&M Coll., 1950; B.S. in Civil Engring., Tex. A&M Coll., 1956. Enlisted in U.S. Army, 1943, advanced through grades to col., 1970, ret., 1973—; officer Corps of Engrs., 1950-73; v.p. Eastern Airlines, Miami, Fla., 1973-86. Democrat.

LILLICH, RICHARD B., law educator; b. 1933. AB, Oberlin Coll., 1954; LLB, Cornell U., 1957; LLM, JSD, NYU, 1960. Bar: N.Y. 1957, D.C. 1980. Pvt. practice N.Y.C., 1957-60; vis. asst. prof. Ind. U., 1960; asst. prof. Syracuse U., 1960-63, assoc. prof., 1963-67, prof., 1967-69; prof. U. Va., 1969—, Fla. State U., 1996—; legal cons. U.S. Naval War Coll., 1964-78, chair internat. law, 1968-69; vis. prof. NYU, 1977, Fla. State U., 1992, Ga. U., 1994, St. Louis U., 1995. Ford fellow, Eng., 1963, Guggenheim fellow, Eng., 1966-67, Sr. fellow NEH, Eng., 1974-75, Thomas Jefferson vis. fellow Downing Coll., Eng., 1980-81, vis. fellow All Souls Coll., Eng., 1987, vis. fellow Max Planck Inst., Heidelberg, 1993. Mem. Internat. Law Assn. (exec. coun., chmn. internat. com. on human rights law and practice), Am. Soc. Internat. Law (exec. coun. 1966-72, 73-76, 82-85), Procedural Aspects of Internat. Law Inst. (pres.). Office: U Va Sch Law Charlottesville VA 22903 Office: florida State Univ College of Law Tallahassee FL 32306

LILLIE, CHARISSE RANIELLE, lawyer, educator; b. Houston, Apr. 7, 1952; d. Richard Lysander and Vernell Audrey (Watson) L.; m. Thomas L. McGill, Jr., Dec. 4, 1982. B.A. cum laude, Conn. Wesleyan U., 1973; J.D., Temple U., 1976; LL.M., Yale U., 1982. Bar: Pa. 1976, U.S. Dist. Ct. (ea. dist.) Pa. 1977, U.S. Ct. Appeals (3d cir.) 1980. Law clk. U.S. Dist. Ct. (ea. dist.) Pa., Phila., 1976-78; trial atty., honors program, civil rights div. Dept. Justice, Washington, 1978-80; dep. dir. Community Legal Services, Phila., 1980-81; asst. prof. law Villanova U. Law Sch., Pa., 1982-83, assoc. prof., 1983-84, prof., 1984-85; asst. U.S. atty. U.S. Dist. Ct. (ea. dist.) Pa., 1985-88; gen. counsel Redevel. Authority City of Phila., 1988-90; city solicitor Law Dept. City of Phila., 1990-92; ptnr. litigation dept. Ballard, Spahr, Andrew and Ingersoll, 1992—, exec. com. bd. dirs., 1994—; mem. 3d Cir. Lawyers Adv. Com., 1982-85, legal counsel Pa. Coalition of 100 Black Women, Phila., 1983-88; bd. dirs. Juvenile Law Center, Phila., 1982—, Pa. Intergovernmental Coop. Authority, 1992—, Fed. Res. Bank Phila., 1996—; commr. Phila. Ind. City Charter Commn., 1991-94; trustee Women's Law Project, Phila., 1984—; mem. Mayor's Commn. on May 13 MOVE Incident, 1985—. Bd. dirs. Women's Way, Phila. Davenport fellow, 1973; Yale Law Sch. fellow, 1981; recipient Equal Justice award Community Legal Svcs., Inc, 1991, J. Austin Norris award Barristers Assn., 1991, Outstanding Alumna award Wesleyan U., 1993, Elizabeth Dole Glass Ceiling award ARC, Phila. chpt., 1994; named One of the Top Three Phila. Labor Mgmt. Attys. Phila. Mag., 1994. Mem. ABA, Nat. Bar Assn., Fed. Bar Assn. (1st v.p. Phila. chpt. 1982-84, pres. Phila. chpt.1984-86, 3rd cir. rep. 1991—), Nat. Conf. Black Lawyers (pres. 1976-78, Outstanding Service award 1978), Am. Law Inst., Phila. Bar Assn. (vice chair bd. govs. 1994, chair, bd. of govs., 1995—), Hist. Soc. U.S. Dist. Ct. (ea. dist.) Pa. (dir. 1983—), Barristers Assn. (J. Austin Norris award 1991). Home: 7000 Emlen St Philadelphia PA 19119-2556 Office: Ballard Spahr Andrews Ingersoll 1735 Market St Ste 51 Philadelphia PA 19103-7501

LILLIE, HELEN, journalist, novelist; b. Glasgow, Scotland, Sept. 13, 1915; came to U.S., 1938; d. Thomas and Helen Barbara (Lillie) L.; m. Charles S. Marwick, Sept. 20, 1956. MA, U. Glasgow, 1938; postgrad., Yale U., 1938-40. Rsch. asst. info. divsn. Brit. Info. Svcs., N.Y.C., 1942-45, Brit. Security Coord., N.Y.C., 1945-46; asst. U.S. mgr., writer Media Reps., Inc., N.Y.C., 1947-54; with advt. dept. Family Cir. Mag., N.Y.C., 1955-56; Am. corr. The Glasgow Herald (name now The Herald), 1956-94; freelance feature writer, book reviewer Detroit Free Press, 1965-66. Author: The Listening Silence, 1970, Call Down the Sky, 1973, Home to Strathblane, 1993, (columns) Inside USA, Helen Lillie's Washington Letter. V.p., acting pres. Cosmopolitan B PM Club of DC, 1972-73. Mem. Am. News Women's Club D.C., Soc. Women Geographers, Advt. Women of N.Y. (various coms.). Presbyterian. Avocations: music, politic watching, travel, theater, reading. Home and Office: 3219 Volta Pl NW Washington DC 20007-2732

LILLIE, JAMES WOODRUFF, JR., lawyer; b. Toms River, N.J., Oct. 10, 1931; s. James Woodruff and Madeleine (Pendergast) L.; m. Barbara markoe Scott, Jan. 10, 1953 (div. Oct. 1983); children: Lydia, Christopher, James III, Derek; m. Inger Irene Andersson, June 27, 1987. BA, U. Pa., 1953, JD, 1959. Bar: N.Y., U.S. Dist. Ct., U.S. Ct. Appeals. Ptnr. N.Y.C., 1959-85; ptnr. sr. resident Bryan, Cave, McPheeters & McRoberts, N.Y.C., 1985—. mem. mgmt. bd. Internat. Tennis Fedn., London, 1978—. Served to lt. USNR, 1953-56. Mem. ABA, N.Y. State Bar Assn., Assn. of the Bar of the City of N.Y., Internat. Bar Assn., Order of Barrister. Clubs: Quail Ridge Golf Country (N.Y.C.), Board Room, Rockefeller Ctr. (N.Y.C.). Avocations: ocean racing, golf. Office: Morgan Lewis & Bockus 101 Park Ave New York NY 10178*

LILLY, EDWARD GUERRANT, JR., retired utility company executive; b. Lexington, Ky., Oct. 29, 1925; s. Edward Guerrant and Elisabeth Read (Frazer) L.; m. Nancy Estes Cobb, Nov. 25, 1961; children: Penelope Read, Edward Guerrant III, Collier Cobb (dec.), Steven Clay. B.S., Davidson Coll., 1948; M.B.A., U. Pa., 1949. Credit analyst Citizens and So. Nat. Bank, Charleston, S.C., 1949-50; asst. v.p. Wachovia Bank and Trust Co., Charlotte, 1952-55, v.p., 1956; v.p., loan adminstrv. officer Wachovia Bank and Trust Co., Wilmington, N.C., 1956-60; sr. v.p., area exec. Wachovia Bank and Trust Co., Kinston, N.C., 1961-62, Durham, N.C., 1963-70; sr. v.p., mgr. trust investment svcs. dept. Wachovia Bank and Trust Co., Winston-Salem, N.C., 1970-71, also bd. dirs., 1971-88; sr. v.p., group exec. Carolina Power and Light Co., Raleigh, N.C., 1971-76, sr. v.p., chief fin. officer, 1976-81; exec. v.p., chief fin. officer Carolina Power and Light Co., Raleigh, 1981-90; also bd. dirs. Carolina Power and Light Co., Raleigh, N.C.; bd. dirs. CSC Industries, N.C. Enterprise Corp. Mem. U. N.C. bd. visitors, 1974-87; bd. dirs. Rsch. Triangle Found., Research Triangle Park; trustee Davidson Coll., 1976-88, Union Theol. Seminary. Served to Lt. USNR, 1950-52,. Mem. Edison Electric Inst. (chmn. fin. group 1979). Presbyterian. Lodge: Rotary (Raleigh).

LILLY, ELIZABETH GILES, mobile park executive; b. Bozeman, Mont., Aug. 5, 1916; d. Samuel John and Luella Elizabeth (Reed) Abegg; m. William Lilly, July 1, 1976; children: Samuel Colborn Giles, Elizabeth Giles. RN, Good Samaritan Hosp., Portland, Oreg., 1941; student, Walla Walla Coll., Lewis and Clark Coll. Bus., Portland. ARC nurse area high schs., Portland; owner Welton Studio Interior Design, Portland; in pub. rels. Chas. Eckelman, Portland, Fairview Farms-Dairy Industry; owner, builder Mobile Park Plaza, Inc., Portland. Del. platform planning com. Rep. Party; mem. Sunnyside Seventh Day Adventist Ch. Recipient Svc. award Multnomah County Commrs., 1984. Mem. Soroptimist Internat. (local bd. dirs., bd. dirs. Women in Transition), Rep. Women's Club (pres.), C. of C., World Affairs Coun., Toastmistress (pres.), Oreg. Logging Assn. (pres. bd. dirs.), Rep. Inner Circle (life). Address: 19825 SE Stark St Portland OR 97233-6039

LILLY, GLADYS DORRIS, nurse; b. Montrose, Ark., Nov. 17, 1935; d. Henry Kilpatrick (dec.) and Leonia E. (Simmons) Jackson; m. Moses Lilly, Nov. 14, 1955 (dec. Jan. 1986); children: Glen, Dorris, Moses Jr. Lic. Vocat. Nurse, Delta Coll., 1958. Unit coord. Lic. vocat. nurse cancer ward Dameron Hosp., Stockton, Calif., 1967-81, Lic. vocat. nurse new born baby nursery, 1981—; ret., 1993; Lic. vocat. nurse coronary care unit, Stockton, 1970; exec. bd. Calif. Lic. Vocat. Nurses Assn. Nursing State Bd., Sacramento; hosp. nursing P.P.C., mem. negotiation com. Dameron Hosp., 1969-89; part-time nurse Del Monte Corp., summers 1993—. Treas., stewardess, mem. St. Matthews Christian Meth. Episcopal Ch., Stockton, 1955—. Democrat. Avocations: traveling, meeting people, writing letters. Home: 8122 N El Dorado St Stockton CA 95210-2308

LILLY, JOHN RICHARD, II, lawyer; b. Phila., July 20, 1962; s. John Richard Sr. and Elizabeth Anne (Brown) L.; children: John Richard III, Cameron Ludwig. BA, Geoge Washington U., 1987; JD, U. Balt., 1991. Bar: Md. 1992, U.S. Dist. Ct. Md. 1995, U.S. Ct. Mil. Appeals 1994. Law clk. 7th Jud. Cir. Md., Upper Marlboro, 1991-92; asst. state's atty. State's Atty.'s Office Prince George's County Md., Upper Marlboro, 1992—; chmn., co-founder Prince George's County Task Force on Environ. Crimes, Upper Marlboro, 1994—. Comments editor U. Balt. Jour. Environ. Law. Chmn. Oakland Mills Village Bd., Columbia, Md., 1990-92; pres. St. Stephen's Area Civic Assn., Crownsville, Md., 1994-95. Ensign USNR, 1988—. Mem. ABA, Md. Bar Assn., Prince George's County Bar Assn., Anne Arundel Bar Assn. Avocations: tennis, sailing, woodworking, biking, racquetball. Home: 1306 Eva Gude Dr Crownsville MD 21032 Office: State's Atty's Office Ct House Upper Marlboro MD 20772

LILLY, MARTIN STEPHEN, university dean; b. New Albany, Ind., Aug. 31, 1944; s. Raymond John and Amy Elizabeth (Peake) L.; m. Marilyn Ann MacDougall, Jan. 8, 1966; children—Matthew William, Mark Christopher, Rachel Marie, Martin Stephen, Jason Wood. B.A., Bellarmine Coll., Louisville, 1966; M.A., Peabody Coll., Nashville, 1967, Ed.D., 1969. Instr. dept. spl. edn. Peabody Coll., 1967-69; asst. prof. edn. U. Oreg., 1969-71; research coordinator N.W. Regional Spl. Edn. Instructional Materials Center, 1969-71; research coordinator div. research Bur. Edn. for Handicapped U.S. Office Edn., 1971-72; assoc. prof. dept. spl. edn. U. Minn., Duluth, 1972-75; assoc. prof., chmn. dept. spl. edn. U. Ill., Urbana-Champaign, 1975-79, prof., chmn., 1979-81, assoc. dean grad. studies Coll. Edn., 1981-84; dean Coll. Edn. Wash. State U., Pullman, 1984-90, Calif. State U., San Marcos, 1990—; cons. in field. U.S. Office Edn. fellow, 1966-69. Author: Children with Exceptional Needs: A Survey of Special Education, 1979, (with C.S. Blankenship) Mainstreaming Students With Learning and Behavior Problems, 1981; assoc. editor: Exceptional Children, 1969-79; cons. editor: Edn. Unltd, 1979-81; reviewer: Jour. Tchr. Edn, 1980—; mem. editorial bd. Tchr. Edn. and Spl. Edn, 1980-83, co-editor, 1983-84; contbr. chpts. to books, articles to profl. jours. Mem. Coun. for Exceptional Children, Assn. Tchr. Educators, Am. Assn. Colls. Tchr. Edn., Phi Delta Kappa. Democrat. Roman Catholic. Office: Calif State U San Marcos CA 92096-0001

LILLY, MICHAEL ALEXANDER, lawyer; b. Honolulu, May 21, 1946; s. Percy Anthony Jr. and Virginia (Craig) L.; m. Kathryn I. Collins, Aug. 10, 1991; children: Michael Jr., Cary J., Laura B., Claire F., Winston W. AA, Menlo Coll., Menlo Park, Calif., 1966; BA, U. Calif., Santa Cruz, 1968; JD with honors, U. of Pacific, 1974. Bar: Calif. 1974, U.S. Dist. Ct. (no., so. and ea. dists.) Calif. 1974, U.S. Ct. Appeals (9th cir.) 1974, Hawaii 1975, U.S. Dist. Ct. Hawaii 1975, U.S. Ct. Appeals (D.C. cir.) 1975, U.S. Supreme Ct. 1978, U.S. Ct. Appeals (7th cir.) 1979. Atty. Pacific Legal Found., Sacramento, 1974-75; dep. atty. gen. State of Hawaii, Honolulu, 1975-79, 1st dep. atty. gen., 1981-84, atty. gen., 1984-85; ptnr. Feeley & Lilly, San Jose, Calif., 1979-81, Ning, Lilly & Jones, Honolulu, 1985—. Author: If You Die Tomorrow-A Layman's Guide to Estate Planning. Bd. dirs. Diamond Head Theatre; Lt. USN, 1968-71, Vietnam; capt. USNR. Named hon. Ky. col. Mem. Nat. Assn. Attys. Gen., Hawaii Law Enforcement Ofcls. Assn., Navy Res. Assn. (pres. 14th dist. 1986-89), Navy League (nat. dir., contbg. editor Fore 'N Aft mag., pres., dept. judge adv. to bd. Honolulu coun.), Outrigger Canoe Club. Home: 2769 Laniloa Rd Honolulu HI 96813-1041 Office: Ning Lilly & Jones 707 Richards St Ste 700 Honolulu HI 96813-4623 *Personal philosophy: Always do what you are afraid to do. Never give up. Forgive your enemies.*

LILLY, PETER BYRON, coal company executive; b. Beckley, W.Va., Sept. 26, 1948; s. Wallace Byron and Mabel Elizabeth (Dodson) L.; m. Brenda Jean Ernst, June 20, 1970; children: Lauren E., Peter E. BS in Engring., U.S. Mil. Acad., 1970; MBA, Harvard U., 1977. Commd. 2d lt. U.S. Army, 1970, advanced through grades to capt., served in Vietnam, resigned, 1975; mgmt. cons. Emory Ayers Assocs., N.Y.C., 1977-80; mgr. maintenance Kerr-McGee Coal Corp., Okla. City, 1980-81, dir. adminstrn., 1981-83; gen. mgr. Galatia Mine Kerr-McGee Coal Corp., Galatia, Ill., 1983-88; v.p. mktg. and planning Kerr-McGee Coal Corp., Oklahoma City, 1988-89, pres., 1989-91; sr. v.p. Kerr-McGee Coal Corp., Oklahoma City, 1989-91; pres. Ea. Associated Coal Corp., Charleston, W.Va., 1991-95; pres., CEO Peabody Holding Co., St. Louis, 1995—. Decorated Bronze Star, Purple Heart; Cross of Gallantry (South Vietnam). Mem. Nat. Coal Assn. (bd. dirs. 1989—), Am. Mining Congress (bd. dirs. 1989-91), Nat. Coal Coun. Office: Peabody Holding Co 701 Market St Ste 700 Saint Louis MO 63101*

LILLY, SHANNON JEANNE, dancer; b. Alexandria, Va., Feb. 18, 1966; d. John Howard Lilly and Barbara Lynn (Root) Graham. Student, Contra Costa Ballet Centre, San Francisco Ballet Sch. Dancer Phoenix Ballet Co., 1985-86; mem. of Corps de Ballet San Francisco Ballet, 1986-88, soloist, 1988-91, prin. dancer, 1991-94; prin. dancer Northern Ballet Theatre, Birmingham, England, 1994—; Performed with San Francisco Opera, 1993; performed at the Reykjavik Arts Festival, Iceland, 1990. Performed with Jean Charles Gil and Friends, Paris, 1988, Tanantella, 1989, In the Middle Somewhat Elevated, 1990, Rubies, 1991, Bagaku, 1991, Sleeping Beauty, 1991; ballets include New Sleep, Connotations, Narcisse, Interplay, The Concert, Handel-a Celebration, Ballet d'Isoline, Menuetto, Giuliani: Variations on a Theme, Contredanses, Concerto in d: Poulenc, Con Brio, Intimate Voices, Calcium Light Night, Krazy Kat, Serenade, Swan Lake, Flower Festival at Genzano, Dark Elegies, Who Cares?, Theme and Variations, Airs de Ballet, Pulcinella, The Wanderer Fantasy, The Sons of Horus, Ballo Della Regina, The Theme Variations, Dreams of Harmony, Nutcracker, La Fille mal gardee, Rodeo, La Sylphide, The Sleeping Beauty, Meistens Mozart, Bugaju, Rubies, Symphony in C, The Four Temperaments, Star and Stripes, In the middle, somewhat elevated, Seeing Stars, Company B, La Pavane Rouge, Job, Harvest Moon, Tagore, Romeo and Juliet, Il Distratto, Divertissement d'Auber, Sinfonia, Scarlatti, Portfolio, The Comfort Zone, Dreams of Harmony, The End, Forgotten Land, Napoli. Episcopalian. Avocations: swimming, reading, movies, family, cooking. Office: Northern Ballet Company, Spring Hall Huddersfield Rd, Halifax HX3 0AQ, England

LILLY, THOMAS GERALD, lawyer; b. Belzoni, Miss., Sept. 17, 1933; s. Sale Trice and Margaret Evelyn (Butt) L.; m. Constance Ray Holland, Dec. 29, 1962; children: Thomas Gerald Jr., William Holland, Carolyn Ray. BBA, Tulane U., 1955; LLB, U. Miss., 1960, JD, 1968. Bar: Miss. 1960. Assoc. firm Stovall & Price, Corinth, Miss., 1960-62; asst. U.S. atty. No. Dist. Miss., Oxford, 1962-66; assoc. firm Wise Carter Child & Caraway (and predecessor), Jackson, Miss., 1966-67; ptnr. Wise Carter Child & Caraway (and predecessor), 1967-94, Lilly & Wise, Jackson, 1994—. Served with USNR, 1955-58; rear adm. Res. ret. Decorated Legion of Merit, Navy Commendation medal. Mem. ABA, Fed. Bar Assn. (nat. coun. 1972—, rec. sec. 1975-76, gen. sec. 1976-77, 2d v.p. 1977-78, pres.-elect 1978-79, pres. 1979-80), Hinds County Bar Assn., Miss. State Bar, Miss. Bar Found., Miss. Def. Lawyers Assn., Inter-Am. Bar Assn., Internat. Bar Assn., Am. counsel Assn., Democracy Devel. Initiative (bd. dirs. 1995—), Internat. Trade Club Miss. (bd. dirs. 1995—), Res. Officers Assn. (pres. Miss. dept. 1982-83), Naval Res. Assn., Naval Order of U.S., Navy Supply Corps Assn., Navy League (pres. Ctrl. Miss. Coun. 1993), Mil. Order World Wars, Southeastern Legal Found. (legal adv. bd. 1988-95), Lamar Order, Newcomen Soc., English-Speaking Union, Omicron Delta Kappa, Phi Delta Phi, Sigma Nu. Office: Lilly & Wise 2180 Deposit Guaranty Plz 210 E Capitol St Jackson MS 39201-2306

LILLY, WILLIAM ELDRIDGE, government official; b. Liberty, Tex., Aug. 25, 1921; s. Lawrence C. and Maude (McKinney) L.; m. Blanche Elizabeth Bromert, Jan. 18, 1944; children—Lizbeth Kristine, William Michael. A.B., U. Calif. at Berkeley, 1950, grad. student, 1950-51. Program analyst Naval Ordnance Test Sta., China Lake, Calif., 1950-52; head estimates and analysis Naval Bur. Ordnance, Washington, 1952-54; dep. budget officer Nat. Bur. Standards, 1954-56; asst. dir. plans and programs Navy Polaris program, 1956-60; with NASA, 1960—, asst. adminstr. for adminstrn., 1967-72, comptroller, 1972-82, cons., 1982—. Pres. Arlington County (Va.) Youth Orgn., 1966-69. Served with USN, 1940-46. Recipient Exceptional Service medal NASA, 1966, 69, Disting. Service medal, 1973, 81; Career Service award Nat. Civil Service League, 1978; presdl. rank of Disting. Exec., 1980. Mem. Phi Beta Kappa, Pi Sigma Alpha. Home: PO Box 2028 Arlington VA 22202-0028 Office: P100 L'Enfant Plz N SW Washington DC 20024

LILLYA, CLIFFORD PETER, musician, educator; b. Joliet, Ill., Jan. 20, 1910; s. Arthur Henning and Anna Wilhelmina (Lindstrum) L.; m. Helen Tait Keltie, Dec. 27, 1931; children: Clifford Peter, Sarah Ann. MusB, VanderCook Coll. Music, 1931; MusM, Northwestern U., 1944; MusD (hon.), VanderCook Coll. Music, 1990. Instrumental music tchr. Chgo. Public Schs., 1931-47; faculty U. Mich., Ann Arbor, 1947-80; prof. music (trumpet) U. Mich., 1947-80, chmn. wind and percussion dept., 1970-80, Earl V. Moore prof. music (trumpet), 1974-80, Earl V. Moore prof. emeritus, 1980—; prof. trumpet U. Kans., summer 1936; instr. trumpet U. Mich., summers 1937-40, Nat. Music Camp, Interlochen, Mich., summers 1945-50. Freelance musician trumpet, 1928-33; author: Lillya Method for Cornet and Trumpet, vol. I, 1937, vol. II, 1940, Trumpet Technic, 1952; composer: (with Merle J. Isaac) Concert Overture in G minor, 1942; for symphonic band A Childhood Fantasy, 1935, A Christmas Fantasy, 1937; transcription for band (choral prelude by J.S. Bach) A Mighty Fortress Is Our God, 1948; (with Harold Bachman) edition for band Ariane Overture by Louis Boyer, 1935; editor: Thirty Trios for 3 cornets (by Wilhelm Wurm), 1985. Recipient Edwin Franko Goldman Meml. citation Am. Bandmaster's Assn., 1989. Mem. Internat. Trumpet Guild (dir. 1977-81, v.p. 1975-77), Mich. Sch. Band and Orch. Assn., Kappa Kappa Psi, Pi Kappa Lambda. Internationally known authority on trumpet pedagogy. Address: 1212 Henry St Ann Arbor MI 48104-4341

LILLY-HERSLEY, JANE ANNE FEELEY, nursing researcher; b. Palo Alto, Calif., May 31, 1947; d. Daniel Morris Sr. and Suzanne (Agnew) Feeley; children: Cary Jane, Laura Blachree, Claire Foale; m. Dennis C. Hersley, Jan. 16, 1993. BS, U. Oreg., 1968; student, U. Hawaii, 1970; BSN, Sacramento City Coll., 1975. Cert. ACLS, BCLS. Staff and charge nurse, acute rehab. Santa Clara Valley Med. Ctr., San Jose, Calif., staff nurse, surg. ICU and trauma unit; clin. project leader mycophenolate mofetil program team Syntex Rsch., Palo Alto. Co-founder, CFO and dir. scientific rsch. Citizens United Responsible Environmentalism, Inc. Mem. AACN.

LILLYMAN, WILLIAM JOHN, German language educator; b. Sydney, Australia, Apr. 17, 1937; came to U.S., 1963, naturalized, 1974; s. John and Christina Mary (Munro) L.; m. Ingeborg Wolz, Sept. 14, 1962; children: Gregory, Christina. AB, U. Sydney, 1959; PhD, Stanford U., 1964. Asst. prof. Stanford (Calif.) U., 1964-67; assoc. prof. U. Calif., Santa Cruz, 1967-72; prof. German U. Calif., Irvine, 1972—, dean humanities, 1973-81, vice chancellor acad. affairs, 1981-82, exec. vice chancellor, 1982-88. Author: Otto Ludwig's Zwischen Himmel und Erde, 1967, Otto Ludwig: Romane und Romanstudien, 1977, Reality's Dark Dream The Narrative Fiction of Ludwig Tieck, 1979, Goethe's Narrative Fiction, 1983; co-editor: Probleme der Moderne, 1983, Horizonte Festschrift für H. Lehnert, 1990, Critical Architecture and Contemporary Culture, 1994. Mem. MLA, Am. Assn. Tchrs. German. Office: U Calif Dept German Irvine CA 92717

LIM, ALEXANDER RUFASTA, neurologist, clinical investigator, educator; b. Manila, Philippines, Feb. 20, 1942; s. Benito P. and Maria Lourdes (Cuyegkeng) L.; m. Norma Sue Hanks, June 1, 1968; children: Jeffrey Allen, Gregory Brian, Kevin Alexander, Melissa Gail. AA, U. Santo Tomas, Manila, Philippines, 1959, MD, 1964. Intern Bon Secours Hosp., Balt., 1964-65; resident internal medicine Scott and White Clinic, Temple, Tex., 1965-67; resident in neurology Cleve. Clinic, 1967-69, chief resident in neurology, 1969-70, fellow clin. neurophysiology, 1970-71, clin. assoc. neurologist, 1971-72; neurologist, co-founder, co-mng. ptnr. Neurol. Clinic, Corpus Christi, Tex., 1972—; pres., CEO Neurology, P.A., Corpus Christi, 1972-92; chief neurology Meml. Med. Ctr., Corpus Christi, 1975-90, Spohn

Hosp., Corpus Christi, 1974-90, Reynolds Army Hosp., Ft. Sill, Okla., 1990-91; clin. assoc. prof. Sch. Medicine U. Tex. Health Sci. Ctr., San Antonio. Mem. editorial bd. Coastal Bend Medicine, 1988—. Lt. col. Med. Corps, 1990-91. Recipient Army Commendation medal, 1991, Nat. Def. medal U.S. Army, 1991. Mem. AMA, Tex. Med. Assn. (chmn. neurology 1985-86), Tex. Neurol. Soc. (sec. 1986-88, pres. 1989-90), Am. Acad. Neurology, Am. Epilepsy Soc., Am. Acad. Clin. Neurophysiology, Am. Electroencephalographic Soc., So. Electroencephalographic Soc., Am. Acad. Pain Mgmt., Physician Com. Responsible Medicine, Am. Legion, Internat. Platform Assn., KC. Republican. Roman Catholic. Avocations: tennis, philately, travel, snow skiing, bonsai. Home: 4821 Augusta Cir Corpus Christi TX 78413-2711 Office: The Neurological Clinic 3006 S Alameda St Corpus Christi TX 78404-2601

LIM, DANIEL VAN, microbiology educator; b. Houston, Apr. 15, 1948; s. Don H. and Lucy (Toy) L.; m. Carol Lee, Sept. 2, 1973. BA in Biology, Rice U., 1970; PhD in Microbiology, Tex. A&M U., 1973. Postdoctoral fellow Baylor Coll. Medicine, 1973-76; asst. prof. U South Fla., Tampa, 1976-81, assoc. prof. microbiology, 1981-87, chmn. dept. biology, 1983-85, prof. 1987—; pres. Micro Concepts Rsch. Corp; dir. Inst. Biomolecular Sci., 1988-93; cons. in field. Author: Microbiology, 1989, Introduction to Microbiology, 1995; inventor bacteriological broth. Recipient Outstanding Ph.D. Dissertation in U.S. award Phi Sigma, 1974, Outstanding Contbn. in Sci. and Tech. award Fla. Gov. Fellow Am. Acad. Microbiology; mem. Inter-Am. Soc. Chemotherapy (v.p. 1983-88), Am. Soc. Microbiology (pres. southeastern br. 1990-91, Carski award com. 1983-86, Margaret Green Outstanding Tchr. award). Office: U South Fla 4202 E Fowler Ave LIF136 Tampa FL 33620-5150

LIM, DAVID JONG-JAI, otolaryngology educator, researcher; b. Seoul, Republic of Korea, Nov. 27, 1935; came to U.S., 1964; s. Yang Sup Lim and Cha Nang Yoo; m. Young Sook Hahn, May 14, 1966; children: Michael, Robert. AB, Yonsei U., Seoul, 1955, MD, 1960. Research fellow in otolaryngology Mass. Eye & Ear Infirmary, Boston, 1965-66; research assoc. dept. otolaryngology Ohio State U. Coll. Medicine, Columbus, 1966-67, asst. prof., 1967-71, assoc. prof., 1971-76, prof. dept. otolaryngology, 1976-91, dir. otological research labs., 1967-91, prof. cell biology, neurobiology and anatomy, 1977-91, prof. emeritus, 1992—; rsch. prof. cell and neurobiology U. So. Calif., 1996—; dir. intramural rsch. program Nat. Inst. on Deaf and Other Communication Disorders, NIH, Bethesda, Md., 1992-94, chief lab cellular biology, 1993-95; exec. v.p. House Ear Inst., L.A., 1995—; mem. nat. adv. neurol. and communicative disorders and stroke coun. NIH, Bethesda, Md., 1979-83; mem. adv. bd. Nat. Inst. Deafness and Other Communication Disorders, 1989-91; cons., bd. dirs. Rsch. Fund Am. Otol. Soc., 1982-87; mem. adv. bd. Cen. Inst. for Deaf, 1989-91. Contbr. articles to profl. jours., chpts. to textbooks. Pres. Korean Assn. in Columbus, 1970; chmn. bd. dirs. Cen. Ohio Korean Lang. Sch., Columbus, 1986; bd. dirs. Deafness Rsch. Found., N.Y.C., 1980—. Fogarty Internat. fellow Karolinska Inst., Stockholm, 1982; recipient Disting. Scholar award Ohio State U., 1985, Javits award NIH, 1985, Guyot prize U. Groningen, 1994; grantee various orgns., 1969-91. Fellow Am. Acad. Otolaryngology (Gold award 1972); mem. Assn. for Research in Otolaryngology (sec./treas. 1973-75, pres. 1976-77, editor-historian 1980-93, historian, 1993—, Merit award 1993), Am. Laryngol. Rhinol. and Otol. Soc., Collegium Oto-rhino-laryngologicum Amicitiae Sacrum (Shambaugh prize 1993), Am. Otol. Soc., Soc. Neurosci., Am. Soc. Cell Biology, Histochem. Soc., Soc. for Mucosal Immunology, Aspen Hill Racquet and Fitness Club (Silver Spring, Md.). Methodist. Avocations: tennis, skiing. Home: 775 Panorama Pl Pasadena CA 91105-1020 Office: House Ear Inst 2100 W Third St Los Angeles CA 90057

LIM, JAE SOO, engineering educator, information systems; b. Taegu, Korea, Dec. 2, 1950. SB, 1974, SM, 1975, ScD, 1978. Prof. elec. engring. and computer sci. MIT. Recipient Sr. award ASSP Soc., 1984. Fellow IEEE (sec. 1979-83, chmn. 1983-85, tech. com. on digital signal processing, session chmn. 1980-83, registration chmn. 1981-83, internat. conf. on acoustics, speech and signal processing, tech. program co-chmn. workshop on M-D signal processing 1982-83, registration chmn. 1983, session chmn. 1984, tech. program co-chmn. 1985 Internat. Conf. on Acoustics, Speech and Signal Processing, chmn. workshop on digital signal processing 1983-85, tech. com. on multidimensional signal processing 1983-86, sec./treas. 1986-87). Office: MIT 77 Massachusetts Ave Cambridge MA 02139*

LIM, JOHN K., state senator, business executive; b. Yeoju, South Korea, Dec. 23, 1935; came to U.S., 1966, naturalized, 1976; s. Eun Kyu and Seu Nyu (Chung) L.; m. Grace Young-Hee Park, Dec. 9, 1963; children: Peter, Billy, Gloria. BA in Religion, Seoul Theol. Coll., 1964; MDiv, Western Evang. Sem., Portland, Oreg., 1970. Founder, chmn. Am. Royal Jelly Co., 1972—; founder, pres. ARJ Co., 1973—; pres. Realty Resources, 1981-91; mem. Oreg. State Senate, 1993—; chair Senate Trade and Econ. Devel. Com., 1995; vice chair Senate Bus. and Consumer Affairs Com., 1995; mem. Govs. Adv. Com. on DUII, 1993—; mem. sheriffs forum Multnomah County, Oreg., 1994; asst. majority leader Oreg. State Senate, 1995. Pub.: World Korean Conference Journal, 1989; editor, pub.: (directory) World Korean C. of C., 1990, The World Korean Soc. Directory, 1989. Oreg. Gubernatorial Candidate, 1990; nat. chair Asian Am. Voters Coalition, 1990-91; bd. dirs. Rep. Nat. Com. Asian Adv., 1992; mem. exec. com. Billy Graham Crusade, Portland, Oreg., 1992; mem. Oreg.-Korea Econ. Coop., 1986-88; mem. Cmty. Bd. Mt. Hood Med. Ctr., 1993—; bd. mem. Western Evang. Sem., 1995—. Mem. Oreg. Royal Rosarian Soc., Portland Rose Soc. Republican. Avocations: golf, fishing, skiing. Office: 3630 SE Division St Portland OR 97202-1546

LIM, ROBERT CHEONG, JR., surgeon, educator; b. San Francisco, Aug. 27, 1933; s. Robert Cheong and Helen (Ho) L.; m. Carolee Yee, Aug. 23, 1959; children: Gregory Matthew, Jonathan Robert. A.B., U. Calif., Berkeley, 1956; M.D., U. Calif., San Francisco, 1960. Diplomate: Am. Bd. Surgery. Intern U. Calif., San Francisco, 1960-61; asst. resident in surgery U. Calif., 1963-64, VA Hosp., San Francisco, 1961-63; chief resident VA Hosp., 1964-65, NIH fellow in vascular surgery, 1965-66; practice medicine specializing in gen. trauma and vascular surgery San Francisco; asst. prof. U. Calif., San Francisco, 1968-74; asso. prof. U. Calif., 1974-78, prof., 1978—; mem. staffs U. Calif. Hosps., San Francisco Gen. Hosp. Contbr. articles on surgery to profl. jours. Mem. ACS (gov.), Am. Burn Assn., Am. Assn. Surgery of Trauma (v.p. 1996), Am. Surg. Assn., Am. Trauma Soc., Internat. Cardiovascular Soc., Calif. Med. Assn., Assn. Acad. Surgery, Howard C. Naffziger Surg. Soc. (pres. 1995), Pacific Coast Surg. Assn., Pan Pacific Surg. Assn., San Francisco Surg. Soc. (past pres.), Soc. Univ. Surgeons, Soc. Vascular Surgery, Western Surg. Assn., Western Vascular Soc., Alpha Omega Alpha. Presbyterian. Office: U Calif PO Box 780 # U San Francisco CA 94143

LIM, SONIA YII, minister; b. China, Jan. 1, 1924; arrived in The Philippines; d. Edward C. C. and King Hua (Co) Yii; m. Teddy T. Lim, Jan. 3, 1943; children: Dorothy, DoraMay Cantada, Sally Jane, Teddy Jr., Nellie Ann L. Tan, Raymond, Roger. AB, Am. Bordner Sch., Manila, 1944; postgrad., St. Thomas U., Manila, 1948, Cornell U., 1972; DD (hon.), Am. Fellowship Ch., Monterey, Calif., 1982; D of Prayer Tech., World Inst., Manila, 1989. Ordained to ministry Full Gospel Ch., 1981. Min. Internat. Fellowship of Clergy, Alta Vista, Calif., 1980-84; founder, pres. Dove Found. Internat. Inc., 1982—; min. Gospel Crusade Ministerial Fellowship Inc., Bradenton, Fla., 1983—; underwriter Insular Life Ins., Pasay, The Philippines, 1991—; Bishop, first lady in Asia, Christian Ch. Fellowship Internat., amb. of goodwill to all nations; conductor ann. Nat. Week of Prayer, Philippines, 25th Ann. World Prayer Congress for Peace, Unity and Progress; chmn. Golden Mother's Day and Golden Father's Day celebrations; group dir. Giorelli Internat., 1992; condr. tng. seminars. V.p., award chmn. Consumers Union of The Philippines, 1944—, bd. dirs. 1971—; chaplain, chmn. internat. rels. Mother's Day and Father's Day Coun., Manila, 1988—; ann. awards chmn. Ann. Grand Tribute to Achievers Parangal ng Bayan, 1995, 96; chmn. Young Achievers Awards, Golden Scroll Awards, Top Entertainers Awards, Golden Heart Awards, Internat. Citation Awards, Grand Achievement Awards, Golden Parents Awards, Celebrity Parents Awards, Family and Parents Week Celebration. Recipient Angel award Religion in Media, 1984, Golden Leadership award Humanitarian Ctr. The Philippines, 1988, award Internat. Cops for Christ Inc., 1990, Grand Achievement award Young Achiever's Found., 1994, 95, Top Prodr.'s award CAP, 1994, Trophy of Distinction award and Century Club Qualifier award IL Assurance Co. Ltd., 1995, Grand Achievement award Parangal ng Bayan, 1995, Asian Mother award Gintong Ina Found., 1996, Key to City of Detroit, Flint, Mich., Jacksonville, Fla., Covina, Calif., Wilson, N.C., Las Vegas, Ft. Worth, Corsicana, Tex., Manila, Mandaluyong, Baguio, Davao, Quezon City, Olongapo, Subic Bay, Cavite; named Mother of Yr., Gintong Ina Found., 1988, hon. mayor Oklahoma City. Mem. Philippine Bible Soc. (life), Info. and Referral Svcs. The Philippines (life), Makati C. of C. and Industry (bd. dirs. 1968-72), Manila Bay Breakfast Club (bd. dirs. 1976—), Makati Breakfast Club (chaplain 1988—), Manila Overseas Press Club (assoc.), Nat. Prestige Club. Mem. Movers Party. Office: Dove Found Internat Sunset View Towers, 2230 Roxas Blvd Ste 402, Pasay Metro Manila, The Philippines

LIMA, LUIS EDUARDO, tenor; b. Cordoba, Argentina, Sept. 12, 1950; s. Horacio and Yayi (Junyent) L.; m. Caterin de Virgilio, Feb. 18, 1979; children: Rodrigo, Camila, Martin-Geronimo Leandro. B.A. in Music, Teatro Colon, Argentina, 1971; student voice, Carlo Guichandut, Buenos Aires, Gina Cigna, Italy. Am. debut Carnegie Hall, 1976; appeared in maj. opera houses throughout the world, including La Scala, Milan, Italy, 1978, N.Y.C. Opera, 1978-79, Met. Opera, N.Y.C., 1978, 84-85, San Francisco Opera, 1980, 83-91, Covent Garden, London, 1984-91, Vienna State Opera, 1988-93; performances at maj. festivals; author: Poems, 1982; recs.: Donizetti: Gemma di Vergy, Le Roi de Laohr, La Traviata, Requiem; appeared in films: Cossi fan Tutte, Carmen, Don Carlo. Mem. Am. Guild Musicians. Roman Catholic. Avocations: painting; horseback riding. Office: 1950 Redondela Dr Palos Verdes Peninsula CA 90275 also: ICM Artists Inc 40 W 57th St New York NY 10019-4001

LIMA, ROBERT, Hispanic studies and comparative literature educator; b. Havana, Cuba, Nov. 7, 1935; came to U.S., 1945; BA in English and Philosophy, Villanova U., 1957, MA in Theatre Arts and Drama, 1961; PhD in Romance Lits., NYU, 1968. Prof. Spanish and comparative lits. Pa. State U., University Park, 1965—; fellow Inst. for Arts and Humanistic Studies Pa. State U., 1986—; vis. prof. comparative lit. Pontificia Universidad Católica del Peru; poet-in-residence Universidad Nacional Mayor de San Marcos, Peru, 1976-77; lectr. Romance langs. and lits. Hunter Coll. CUNY, 1962-65, USIA lectr., Peru, Cameroon, Equatorial Guinea. Author: The Theatre of Garcia Lorca, 1963, An Annotated Bibliography of Ramon del Valle-Inclan, 1972, (poetry) Fathoms, 1981, The Olde Ground, 1985, Mayaland, 1992, Dark Prisms Occultism in Hispanic Drama, 1995, The International Annotated Bibliography of Ramon del Valle-Inclan, Valle-Inclan El Teatro de Su Vida, 1995, (biography) Valle-Inclan, 1976, The Theatre of His Life, 1988; co-author: Dos Ensayos Sobre Teatro Español de los viente, 1984; editor, translator: Borges the Labyrinth Maker (A.M. Barrenechea), 1965, Valle-Inclan: Autobiography, Aesthetics, Aphorism, 1966; editor, contbr. Borges and the Esoteric, 1993; translator: The Lamp of Marvels, Aesthetic Meditations (Ramon del Valle-Inclan), 1986, Savage Acts: Four Plays (Valle-Inclan), 1993; co-editor Readers Ency. Am. Lit., 1962; contbr. numerous articles, essays, book revs., poetry, plays, and poetry translations to profl. jours.; prodr., cons., TV and radio programs Centro de Estudios de Television de la Univ. Catolica, Lima, Peru, 1976-77, Voice of Am., N.Y.C., 1961-62, Pendulum Prodns., 1960-61. Bd. dirs. Pa. Ctr. for Book. Recipient Founders Day award NYU, 1968, Play Translation prize Modern Internat. Drama, cert. of merit Writer's Digest Mag., 1982; Rsch. grantee Fund for Rsch. Pa. State U., Inst. for Arts and Humanistic Studies; Cintas Found. fellow in poetry Inst. Internat. Edn., 1971-72, fellow Commonwealth Speakers Program Pa. Humanities Coun., Sr. Fulbright fellow Coun. Internat. Exch. Scholars, 1976-77; others. Fellow Inst. for Arts and Humanistic Studies, Phi Kappa Phi (hon.), Phi Sigma Iota (hon.); mem. Internat. PEN, Poetry Soc. Am., Am. Assn. Tchrs. Spanish and Portuguese, Archaeol. Inst. Am., Am. Comparative Lit. Assn., Internat. Comparative Lit. Assn., Galician Studies Assn., Internat. Assn. Valleinclanistas, Am. Name Soc., Am. Soc. Sephardic Studies, Poets and Writers, Hermetic Text Soc., Beast Fable Soc., Pa. Humanities Coun., N.Am. Acad. Spanish Lang., Fulbright Alumni Assn., Alpha Psi Omega. Home: 485 Orlando Ave State College PA 16803-3477 Office: Pa State U N-346 Burrowes Bldg University Park PA 16802

LIMAN, ARTHUR LAWRENCE, lawyer; b. N.Y.C., Nov. 5, 1932; s. Harry K. and Celia L.; m. Ellen Fogelson, Sept. 20, 1959; children: Lewis, Emily, Douglas. A.B., Harvard U., 1954; LL.B., Yale U., 1957. Bar: N.Y. bar 1958. Asst. U.S. atty. So. Dist. N.Y., 1961-63, spl. asst. U.S. atty., 1965; with firm Paul, Weiss, Rifkind, Wharton & Garrison, N.Y.C., 1957-61, 63—; ptnr. Paul, Weiss, Rifkind, Wharton & Garrison, 1966—; chief counsel N.Y. State Spl. Commn. on Attica, 1972; chmn. Legal Action Center, N.Y.C., 1975; v.p. Legal Aid Soc., N.Y.C., 1973; pres. Legal Aid Soc., 1983-85; chmn. Gov. N.Y. Adv. Commn. Adminstrn. Justice in N.Y. State, 1981-83; mem. N.Y. State Exec. Adv. Com. Sentencing, 1977; mem. adv. com. civil rules U.S. Jud. Conf., 1980-85; mem. commn. on reduction costs and delay U.S. 2d Cir., 1976-80; bd. dirs. Continental Grain Co., Equitable Life Assurance Soc. U.S.; chmn. bd. dirs. Capital Defenders Office, 1995—; chmn. mayor's com. on appointments, 1990-93; chief counsel U.S. Senate select com. on secret mil. assistance to Iran and tne Nicaraguan Opposition, Washington, 1987. Contbr. articles to legal jours.; bd. editors: Nat. Law Jour, 1979—. Bd. overseers Harvard U., 1988-94. Fellow Am. Coll. Trial Lawyers, Am. Bar Found.; mem. ABA, N.Y. State Bar Assn., Bar Assn. City N.Y. (exec. com., Lawyers Com. Civil Rights Under Bd. Overseers, Harvard U., 1988-94). Home: 1060 Fifth Ave New York NY 10128-0104 Office: Paul Weiss Rifkind Wharton & Garrison 1285 Avenue Of The Americas New York NY 10019-6064

LIMARZI, JOSEPH, artist; b. Chgo., Sept. 15, 1907; s. Joseph and Mary Della (Guardia) LiM. With Mus. Fine Arts, Springfield, Mass.; instr. painting High Sch. Art & Design, N.Y., 1952-73. Commn. works include HIst. Fed. Govt., Fed. Bldg., Wapokeneta, Ohio, 1937, Fed. Govt., Staten Island, N.Y., 1942; Royal Scarlet Foods, N.Y., 1951; Gen. Cables, Inc., N.Y., 1952; exhibits include Art Inst. Chgo., Bklyn. Mus. Nat., Pa. Acad. Fine Arts; one man shows include Comtemporary Arts, N.Y., Simon's Rock, Mass. & Lehman Gallery, Red Rock, N.Y., 1975; Cleve. Art Inst., Mus. Modern Art, N.Y.; liberal Arts Ctr., Newport, N.H., Berkshire Mus., Pittsfield, Mass., Spencertown Acad., N.Y. Recipient Hon. award Fed. Govt., 1937. Mem. Painters and Sculptors Soc. N.J., Audubon Artists of N.Y., Am. Soc. Contemporary Artists. Avocations: classical, jazz and folk music, history Jefferson and Lincoln. Home: PO Box 144 East Chatham NY 12060-0144 Office: Ella Lerner Gallery 17 Franklin St Lenox MA 01240-2303

LIMATO, EDWARD FRANK, talent agent; b. Mt. Vernon, N.Y., July 10, 1936; s. Frank and Angelina (Lacerra) L. Grad. high sch., Mt. Vernon. With Ashley Famous, 1966, I.F.A., N.Y.C., William Morris Agy., L.A.; talent agt. Internat. Creative Mgmt., N.Y.C., L.A. Mem. Acad. Motion Picture Arts & Scis. (assoc.). Republican. Roman Catholic. Office: Internat Creative Mgmt 8942 Wilshire Blvd Beverly Hills CA 90211

LIMB, BEN QUINCY, lawyer; b. Taejon, Korea, Nov. 28, 1936; came to U.S., 1964; s. Tong-shik and San-jong (Lee) L.; m. Mary Shinkawa, Feb. 4, 1968; children: Amy, Lisa. BA, Korea U., 1961; MA, Seton Hall U., 1969; JD, N.Y. Law Sch., 1984; PhD, St. John's U., 1979. Bar: N.Y. 1985, U.S. Ct. Appeals (fed. cir.) 1988, U.S. Ct. Internat. Trade 1988, U.S. Supreme Ct. 1991. Pvt. practice N.Y.C., 1985—; speaker nationality law and human rights The Law of the World Conf., 1987; lectr. Sta. KBC-Radio Legal Edn. Program, 1990; anniversary lectr. Han Nam U., Taejon, Republic of Korea, 1991. Mem. Mayor Dinkin's Fact Finding Com. on Racial Conflicts in Bklyn., 1990, Nelson Mandela N.Y. Welcoming Com., N.Y.C., 1990; pres. Korean Inst. for Human Rights, Washington, 1989—; chair Asian Pacific Am. Com. for Dem. Nat. Conv., 1992. Recipient Appreciation award Assn. of Korean Christian Scholars in North Am., L.A., 1988. Mem. ABA, Fed. Bar Assn., N.Y. State Bar Assn., N.Y. County Lawyers Assn. (com. minorities and law 1989—), Korean-Am. Lawyers Assn. of N.Y. (pres. 1989-91), N.Y. Law Sch. Alumni Assn. (bd. dirs. 1987—), Am. Immigration Lawyers Assn. (co-chmn. N.Y. chpt. ethics 1988-89), Korea Bar assn. (lectr. annual seminar, Seoul 1988), Asian Am. Bar Assn. of N.Y. (bd. dirs. 1994—, pres. 1996). Office: Abram & Silver 500 5th Ave Ste 1610 New York NY 10110-1699

LIMB, JOHN O., electrical engineer; b. Pinjarra, Australia, Aug. 19, 1939. BEE, U. Western Australia, 1963, PhD in Elec. Engring., 1967. Engr. rsch. labs. Australia Post Office, 1966-67; mem. tech. staff Bell Tel. Labs., 1967-71, dept. head comm., 1971-83; divsn. mgr. Bell Comm. Rsch., 1983-85; lab. dir. Hewlett-Packard Labs., 1986—. Fellow IEEE (Leonard G. Abraham paper prize award Comm. Soc. 1973, Donald G. Fink prize award 1982, Donald W. McLellan Meritorious Svc. award Comm. Soc. 1988, Alexander Graham Bell medal 1991, bd. govs. Comm. Soc. 1983-85, editor-in-chief IEEE Transactions on Comm. 1984, editor-in-chief IEEE Jour. on Selected Areas in Comm. 1984-88, mem. awards bd. Comm. Soc. 1990-92, chmn. awards bd. Comm. Soc. 1993—); mem. Optical Soc. Am., Assn. Computing Machinery. Office: Hewlett Packard 1501 Page Mill Rd/MS 1U-19 San Luis Obispo CA 93403*

LIMBACH, WALTER F., construction company executive; b. Pitts., June 17, 1924; s. Emil and Sarah (Zuckerman) L.; m. Sarah Z. Minard, June 16, 1976; children by previous marriage: Elsa, Kurt. B.S., Lehigh U., 1947. With Limbach Co., Pitts., 1947-80; v.p. Limbach Co., 1955-57, pres., 1957-81, dir., 1955-84; chmn., chief exec. officer, dir. Limbach Inc., Pitts., 1980-86; chmn., chief-exec.-officer, dir. Limbach Holdings, Inc., Pitts., 1986-88; dir. Contractors Mut. Assn., Washington, 1971-84; vice chmn. Contractors Mut. Assn., 1973-78, chmn., 1978-84. Bd. dirs. Hill House Assn., Pitts., v.p., 1968-73, 75-80; bd. dirs. Vocat. Rehab. Ctr., Pitts., 1975—, chmn. 1991-93; bd. dirs. Nat. Constrn. Employers Coun., Washington, 1979-84; bd. dirs. Neighborhood Ctrs. Assn., Pitts., 1989—, treas., 1990—. Served with USNR, 1943-46. Mem. Sheet Metal and Air Conditioning Contractors Nat. Assn. (pres. 1958-59), ASME. Home: 123 Beechmont Rd Pittsburgh PA 15206-4513

LIMBACK, E(DNA) REBECCA, vocational education educator; b. Higginsville, Mo., Mar. 23, 1945; d. Henry Shobe and Martha Pauline Rebecca (Willard) Ernstmeyer; m. Duane Paul Limback, Nov. 9, 1963; children: Lisa Christine, Derek Duane. BE, Cen. Mo. State U., 1968, MEd, 1969, EdS, 1976; EdD, U. Mo., 1981. Cert. bus., English and vocat. tchr. Supervising tchr. Lab. Sch. Cen. Mo. State U., Warrensburg, 1969-76, asst. to grad. dean, 1977-79, asst. prof., asst. to bus. dean, 1981-83, assoc. prof. computer and office info. systems, 1984—; prof. computer and office info. systems, 1996—; mem. manual editing/revision staff State of Mo., Jefferson City, 1989-90; textbook reviewer Prentice-Hall, Englewood Cliffs, N.J., 1990-91. Author various curriculum guides; mem. editl. bd. Cen. Mo. State U. Rsch., 1982-92. Active Warrensburg Band Aides, 1989-93. Grantee RightSoft Corp., 1988. Mem. DAR, Nat. Bus. Edn. Assn. (mem. conf. profl. opportunities com. 1989, info. processing editor Bus. Edn. Forum 1991), Am. Vocat. Assn., North Cen. Bus. Edn. Assn. (Mo. rep., Collegiate Disting. Svc. award 1993), Mo. Bus. Edn. Assn. (all-chpt. pres. 1988-89, Postsecondary Tchr. of Yr. 1992), Assn. Bus. Comms., Warrensburg Athletic Booster Club, Phi Delta Kappa (all-chpt. pres. 1985), Delta Pi Epsilon (rsch. rep. 1989-92, nat. publs. com. 1993—). Lutheran. Avocations: archaeology, oil painting. Home: 1102 Tyler Ave Warrensburg MO 64093-2049 Office: Dockery 200-1/COIS Dept Cen Mo State U Warrensburg MO 64093

LIMBAUGH, RONALD HADLEY, history educator, history center director; b. Emmett, Idaho, Jan. 22, 1938; s. John Hadley and Evelyn E. (Mortimore) L.; m. Marilyn Kay Rice, June 16, 1963; 1 child, Sally Ann. BA, Coll. Idaho, 1960; MA, U. Idaho, 1962, PhD, 1967. Hist. libr. Idaho State Hist. Soc., Boise, 1963-66; instr. Boise Coll., 1964-66; asst. prof. history U. of the Pacific, Stockton, Calif., 1966-71; archivist, curator U. of the Pacific, Stockton, 1968-87, prof. history, 1977—, Rockwell Hunt chair of Calif. history, 1989—; dir. Holt-Atherton Ctr., U. of the Pacific, Stockton, 1984-87; exec. dir. Conf. of Calif. Hist. Socs., Stockton, 1973-76, 77-78, 82-86, 90—; dir. John Muir Ctr. for Regional Studies, U. of Pacific, Stockton, 1989—; cons., evaluator NEH, 1983, 86. Author: Rocky Mountain Carpetbaggers, 1982, John Muir's Stickeen and the Lessons of Nature, 1996; co-editor: (microform) John Muir Papers, 1986, (book) Guide to Muir Papers, 1986; contbr. articles to profl. jours. With U.S. Army, 1955-56. NDEA fellow, 1960; grantee Calif. Coun. Humanities, 1976, Nat. Hist. Publs. and Records Commn., 1980-82, NEH, 1983, Inst. European Studies, 1989. Mem. AAUP, Western History Assn., Orgn. Am. Historians, Phi Kappa Phi (pres. UOP chpt. 1988), Mining History Assn. Christian Humanist. Avocations: hiking, golf. Office: Univ Pacific 3601 Pacific Cir Stockton CA 95211-0110

LIMBAUGH, RUSH HUDSON, radio and talk show host; b. Cape Girardeau, Mo., 1951; s. Rush Hudson Jr. and Millie Limbaugh; m. Marta Fitzgerald, May 27, 1994. Various disc jockey positions, 1960-88; host The Rush Limbaugh Show on 480 radio stations nationwide, 1988—. Author: The Way Things Ought To Be, 1992, See, I Told You So, 1993; TV syndicated show The Rush Limbaugh Show, 1992—; publisher, monthly newsletter, The Limbaugh Letter, 1995—. Office: Sta WABC 125 W End Ave # 6 New York NY 10023-6345

LIMBAUGH, STEPHEN NATHANIEL, federal judge; b. Cape Girardeau, Mo., Nov. 17, 1927; s. Rush Hudson and Bea (Seabaugh) L.; m. DeVaughn Anne Mesplay, Dec. 27, 1950; children—Stephen Nathaniel Jr., James Pennington, Andrew Thomas. B.A., S.E. Mo. State U., Cape Girardeau, 1950; J.D., U. Mo., Columbia, 1951. Bar: Mo. Prosecuting atty. Cape Girardeau County, Mo., 1954-58; judge U.S. Dist. Ct. (ea. and we. dists.) Mo., St. Louis, 1983—. Served with USN, 1945-46. Recipient Citation of Merit for Outstanding Achievement and Meritorious Service in Law, U. Mo., 1982. Fellow Am. Coll. Probate Counsel, Am. Bar Found.; mem. ABA (ho. of dels. 1987-90), Mo. Bar Assn. (pres. 1982-83). Republican. Methodist. Office: US Dist Ct 1114 Market St Rm 315 Saint Louis MO 63101-2038

LIMBAUGH, STEPHEN NATHANIEL, JR., judge; b. Cape Girardeau, Mo., Jan. 25, 1952; s. Stephen N. and Anne (Mesplay) L.; m. Marsha Dee Moore, July 21, 1973; children: Stephen III, Christopher K. BA, So. Meth. U., 1973, JD, 1976. Bar: Tex. 1977, Mo. 1977. Assoc. Limbaugh, Limbaugh & Russell, Cape Girardeau, 1977-78; pros. atty. Cape Girardeau County, Cape Girardeau, 1979-82; shareholder, ptnr. Limbaugh, Limbaugh, Russell & Syler, Cape Girardeau, 1983-87; cir. judge 32d Jud. Cir., Cape Girardeau, 1987-92; judge Supreme Ct. Mo., Jefferson City, 1992—. Mem. ABA, State Bar Tex., Mo. Bar. Office: Supreme Ct Mo 207 W High St Jefferson City MO 65101-1516

LIMERICK, PATRICIA NELSON, history educator; b. Banning, Calif., May 17, 1951. BA, U. Calif., Santa Cruz, 1972; PhD, Yale, 1980. Prof. history dept. U. Colo., Boulder; chmn. bd. dirs. Ctr. Am. West. Author: (books) Desert Passages: Encounters With the American Deserts, 1985, The Legacy of Conquest: The Unbroken Past of the American West, 1987. MacArthur fellow, 1995. Office: Univ CO Boulder Dept History Box 234 Boulder CO 80309

LIMON, LAVINIA, social services administrator; b. Compton, Calif., Mar. 5, 1950; d. Peter T. and Marie W. Limon; m. Mohamad Hanon. BA in Sociology, U. Calif., Berkeley, 1972. Asst. dir., office mgr. Ch. World Svc., Camp Pendleton, Calif., 1975-77; chief Vietnamese refugee sect. Internat. Rescue Com., Bangkok, 1977-79; dir. Internat. Rescue Com., L.A., 1983-86, 1983-86; asst. dir. ops. Am. Coun. for Nationalities Svcs., L.A., 1979-83; exec. dir. Internat. Inst., L.A., 1986-93; dir. office refugee resettlement and office family assistance Adminstrn. for Children and Families Dept. HHS, Washington, 1993—; bd. dirs. Am. Coun. for Nationalities Svc., 1992, chair standing com. of profl. coun., 1992; organizer U.S. refugee conf. Am. Coun. Vol. Agys., Manila, 1982; cons. Dept. of State, 1979, 80. Mem. bd. human rels. hate violence response alliance City of L.A., 1992; chair corp. coun. execs. United Way of L.A., 1992, mem. task force fund on devel., 1990; mem. citizen's adv. com. Eastside Neighborhoods Revitilazation Study, 1992; mem. steering com. Coalition for Humane Immigration Rights of L.A., 1992; mem. steering com. Jerusalem Coop. Cities Project, 1991; chair Refugee Forum L.A. County, 1984-85, chair vol. agy. com., 1983-84; treas. Calif. Refugee Forum, 1985-86. Democrat. Home: 4508 Flintstone Rd Alexandria VA 22306-1204 Office: Refugee Resettlement Office 370 Lenfant Plz SW Washington DC 20447-0001

LIMÓN ROJAS, MIGUEL, Mexican government official; b. Veracruz, Mex., Dec. 17, 1943. BA in Law, Nat. Autonomous U., 1967. Lawyer, 1968—; dep. dir. demographics, population Ministry of Govt. of Mex., 1971, dir. demographics, population, 1973; pvt. sec. to undersec. to pres., prof. constl. law Govt. Mex., 1970, advisor to sec. edn., negotiator nat. ednl. plan, 1982-88; dir. Inst. Indigenous Peoples, 1983-88, undersec. population and migration, 1988-93, sec. agrarian reform, 1993-94, sec. pub. edn., 1995—; dir. dept. humanities, Autonomous U.; acad. sec. U. Pedagógica Nat. Mem. Instl. Revolutionary Party. Office: Embassy of Mexico 1911 Pennsylvania Ave NW Washington DC 20006*

LIMPITLAW, JOHN DONALD, retired publishing executive, clergyman; b. N.Y.C., Jan. 4, 1935; s. Robert and Olga (Lang) L.; m. Susan Elizabeth Glover, May 21, 1960; children: Alison, Amy Elizabeth. BA, Trinity Coll., Hartford, Conn., 1956; MA in Religion, Yale U., 1992. With Marine Midland Bank Trust Co. N.Y., N.Y.C., 1956-61, Celanese Corp., N.Y.C., 1961-63; mgr. personnel Westvaco Corp., N.Y.C., 1963-69; v.p. Warnaco Inc., Bridgeport, Conn., 1969-77, Macmillan Inc., N.Y.C., 1977-89; vicar Parish of Christ's Ch., Easton, Conn., 1992—; dir. St. Mark's Day Care Ctr., Easton, 1995—; seminarian Yale Divinity Sch., New Haven, Conn., 1989-92; trustee Episcopal Investment Funds; bd. dirs. Inter-Ch. Residences, Inc., 3030 Park, Inc. Democrat. Episcopalian. Avocations: sailing; skiing. Home: 120 Chelsea St Fairfield CT 06430-4941

LIN, ALICE LEE LAN, physicist, researcher, educator; b. Shanghai, China, Oct. 28, 1937; came to U.S., 1960, naturalized, 1974; m. A. Marcus, Dec. 19, 1962 (div. Feb. 1972); 1 child, Peter A. AB in Physics, U. Calif., Berkeley, 1963; MA in Physics, George Washington U., 1974. Statis. asst. dept. math. U. Calif., Berkeley, 1962-63; rsch. asst. in radiation damage Cavendish Lab. Cambridge (Eng.) U., 1965-66; info. analysis specialist Nat. Acad. Scis., Washington, 1970-71; teaching fellow, rsch. asst. George Washington U., Catholic U. Am., Washington, 1971-75; physicist NASA/Goddard Space Flight Ctr., Greenbelt, Md., 1975-80, Army Materials Tech. Lab., Watertown, Mass., 1980—. Contbr. articles to profl. jours. Mencius Ednl. Found. grantee, 1959-60. Mem. AAAS, N.Y. Acad. Scis., Am. Phys. Soc., Am. Ceramics Soc., Am. Acoustical Soc., Am. Men and Women of Sci., Optical Soc. Am. Democrat. Avocations: rare stamp and coin collecting, art collectibles, home computers, opera, ballet. Home: 28 Hallett Hill Rd Weston MA 02193-1753 Office: Army Materials Tech Lab Bldg 39 Watertown MA 02172

LIN, CHIN-CHU, physician, educator, researcher; b. Taichung, Taiwan, Oct. 24, 1935; came to U.S., 1969; naturalized, 1977; s. Kung Yen and Nung (Chiang) L.; m. Sue S. Hsu; children: Jim, John, Juliet. BS, Nat. Taiwan U., 1956, MD, 1961. Diplomate Am. Bd. Ob-Gyn., Am. Bd. Maternal-Fetal Medicine (bd. examiners 1986-89). Rsch. fellow SUNY Downstate Med. Ctr., N.Y.C., 1969-71; resident in ob-gyn Columbia U., N.Y.C., 1972-74; fellow in maternal-fetal medicine Albert Einstein Med. Coll., 1974-76; lectr., staff Nat. Taiwan U. Hosp., Taipei, 1966-69, 1971-72; staff, asst. prof. U. Chgo., 1976-80, assoc. prof., 1980-87, prof., 1987—; maternal-child health adv. com. Dept. of Health, Chgo., 1985-88; frequent keynote spkr. numerous internat. confs. including 12th Asian and Oceanic Congress on Ob-Gyn., 1989, 8th Congress of Fedn. Asian Oceanic Perinatal Soc., Taiwan, 1994, 5th World Congress Ultrasound in Ob-Gyn., Japan, 1995; vis. prof. univs. in U.S., Japan, People's Republic of China, Republic of China, 1981—; keynote spkr., prof. S.J. Chiu Meml. lectures, Taiwan, 1989. Author: Interauterine Growth Retardation, 1984, The High Risk Fetus, 1993; editor in chief Taiwan Tribune Med. Issues, 1986-89; contbr. over 80 articles to profl. jours., 17 chpts. to books; reviewer for Am. Jour. Ob-Gyn., Jour. Perinatal Medicine, Obstetrics and Gynecology, Jour. Maternal-Fetal Medicine, Jour. Formosan Med. Assn.; pres. 10th ann. meeting N.Am. Taiwanese Profs. Assn., Taiwan, 1990. People to People Ob-Gyn del. to USSR, 1987; bd. dirs. Taiwanese United Fund, 1980—, pres. 1984-85. Selected candidate semifinalist dean of med. sch. Nat. Taiwan U., 1993; disting. scholar lectr. award Formosa Med. Assn., 1981, Kenote Speaker award Asia-Oceanic Congress Perinatology, 1986, 94, 2d Internat. Symposium on Obstetrics and Perinatal Medicine, Beijing, 1988, 28th Sci. Meeting Assn. Ob-gyn., Taiwan, 1988, 12th Asian Oceanic Congress on Obstetrics and Gynecology, 1989, 33d Ann. Meeting Assn. Ob-gyn., Taiwan, 1993, 5th World Congress Ultrasound in Ob-gyn., Japan, 1995. Mem. Am. Coll. Ob.-Gyn. (jour. reviewer 1982—, Purdue Frederick award 1978), N.Am. Taiwanese Profs. Assn. (bd. dirs. 1988-91, bull. editor 1980—, v.p. 1988-89, pres. 1989-90, pres. 10th ann. meeting Taiwan 1990), N.Am. Taiwanese Med. Assn. (chmn. ednl. com. 1984-88, bd. dirs. 1991-93, chmn. scientific program 1994), Taiwanese United Fund (bd. dirs. 1980—, pres. 1984-85), Cen. Assn. Ob.-Gyn., Soc. Perinatal Obstetricians, Internat. Soc. Study Hypertension in Pregnancy, Am. Inst. Ultrasound in Medicine, Chgo. Gynecol. Soc. Avocations: tennis, swimming. Home: 500 Devon Dr Burr Ridge IL 60521-8319 Office: U Chgo Dept Ob-Gyn 5841 S Maryland Ave Chicago IL 60637-1463

LIN, EDWARD DANIEL, anesthesiologist; b. Apr. 19, 1953; s. Henry and Ruth Lin. BS magna cum laude, SUNY, Fredonia, 1973; Woodburn fellow, Roswell Park Cancer Inst., Buffalo, 1974-76; DO, U. Osteopathic Medicine and Health Scis., Des Moines, 1980. Intern. in gen. medicine Millard Fillmore Hosp., Buffalo, 1980-81, emergency physician, 1981-82; resident in anesthesiology Yale-New Haven Med. Ctr., Yale U. Sch. Medicine, 1982-84; attending anesthesiologist Doctors Hosp., Massillon, Ohio, 1984-89; chmn. dept. anesthesiology Massillon Cmty. Hosp., 1991; dep. coroner Stark County, Ohio, 1984-90; assoc. prof. anesthesiology Ohio U. Coll. Osteopathic Medicine, Athens, 1984—; guest lectr. on spinal opiates and pain therapy nat. profl. meetings; founder, pres. Ingenious Techs. Corp, 1991—. Achievements include numerous inventions and patents in medical, telecommunications and consumer fields. Office: Ingenious Techs Corp 556 Roxbury Ave NW Massillon OH 44646-3281

LIN, FRANK CHIWEN, computer science educator; b. Shanghai, China, Aug. 28, 1936; came to U.S., 1953; s. Elmer C. and Virginia (Chang) Ling; m. Margareta Lundgren, Mar. 8, 1968 (div. Aug. 1979); children: Ulrika Lin, Sigrid Lin; m. Helen M. Baldado, Mar. 17, 1987. BECE, Yale U., 1957; postgrad., U. Goettingen (Germany), 1958; PhD in Theoretical Physics, Yale U., 1965; grad. studies in computer sci., Polytech. U. N.Y., 1980, 81, 82. Rsch. assoc. dept. theoretical physics Chalmers Tech. U., Goeteborg, Sweden, 1965-70; vis. prof. physics Nat. Taiwan U., Taipei, 1970; asst. to pres. Biomed. Scis. Inc., Fairfield, N.J., 1971-75; instr. physics, engring., and computer sci. L.B. Wallace State Jr. Coll., Andalusia, Ala., 1976-84; assoc. prof. computer sci. Western Conn. State U., Danbury, 1984-85; from asst. to assoc. prof. computer sci. U. Md., Princess Anne, Md., 1986—. Author: Elementary FORTRAN with Scientific and Business Applications, 1983, Structured BASIC for Mini- and Micro-Computers, 1985; contbr. numerous articles to profl. jours. Prin. investigator numerous grants, 1981-93. Mem. IEEE (treas./sec. local chpt. 1989-90, vice-chmn. local chpt. 1990-91), Assn. Computing Machinery, Yale Sci. and Engring. Assn., N.Y. Acad. Scis., Am. Assn. for Artificial Intelligence, Internat. Neural Network Soc., Am. Med. Informatics Assn., Tau Beta Pi. Avocation: classical music. Home: 711 Riverside Pines Ct Salisbury MD 21801 Home: 1692 S Ocean Ln #166 Fort Lauderdale FL 33316

LIN, HUNG C., electrical engineer educator; b. Shanghai, China, Aug. 8, 1919. BSEE, Chiao Tung U., 1941; MSE, U. Mich., 1948; D in Engring., Poly. Inst. Bklyn., 1956. Engr. Ctrl. Radio Works of China, 1941-44, Ctrl. Broadcasting Adminstrn. China, 1944-47; rsch. engr. RCA, 1948-56; mgr. appliance CBS Semiconductor Ops., 1956-59; lectr. U. Md., College Park, 1966-69, vis. prof. elec. engring., 1969-71, prof. elec. engring., 1971—; adv. engr. Rsch. Lab., Westinghouse Corp., Balt., 1959-63; adj. prof. U. Pitts., 1959-63; vis. lectr. U. Calif., Berkeley, 1965-66. Achievements include research in semiconductor and integrated circuits. Fellow IEEE (Ebers award Electron Device Soc. 1978), Sigma Xi. Office: Univ Maryland Electrical Eng Dept College Park MD 20742*

LIN, JAMES CHIH-I, biomedical and electrical engineer, educator; b. Dec. 29, 1942; m. Mei Fei, Mar. 21, 1970; children: Janet, Theodore, Erik. BS, U. Wash., 1966, MS, 1968, PhD, 1971. Asst. prof. U. Wash., Seattle, 1971-74; prof. Wayne State U., Detroit, 1974-80; prof. U. Ill.-Chgo., 1980—, head dept. bioengring., 1980-92, dir. robotics and automation lab., 1982-89, dir. spl. projects Coll. Engring., 1992-94, NSC chair prof., 1993-94; vis. prof. in Beijing, Rome, Shan Dong, Taiwan Univs.; lectr. of short courses, 1974—; cons. Battelle Meml. Inst., Columbus, Ohio, 1973-75, SRI Internat., Palo Alto, Calif., 1978-79, Arthur D. Little, Inc., Cambridge, Mass., 1980-83, Ga. Tech. Rsch. Inst., Atlanta, 1984-86, Walter Reed Army Inst. Rsch., 1973, 87, 88, Naval Aerospace Med. Rsch. Labs., Pensacola, 1982-83, U.R.S. Corp., San Francisco, 1985-87, CBS, Inc., N.Y., 1988, U. Va., 1991-92, ACS, Inc., Santa Clara, Calif., 1989-90, Luxtron Corp, Mountainview, Calif., 1991-92, Commonwealth Edison, Chgo., 1991-95; program chmn. Frontiers of Engring. and Computing Conf., Chgo., 1985; chmn., convener URSI Joint Symposium Electromagnetic Waves in Biol. Systems, Tel-Aviv, 1987, Internat. Conf. on Sci. and Tech., 1989-91; chmn. Chinese-Am. Acad. and Profl. Conv., 1993; mem Congrl. Health Care Adv. Coun., 13th dist. Ill., 1987—; mem. citizen's adv. coun. Hinsdale Cen. High Sch., 1988-93. Author: Microwave Auditory Effects and Applications, 1978, Biological Effects and Health Implications of Radiofrequency Radiation, 1987, Electromagnetic Interaction with Biological Systems, 1989; assoc. editor Jour. Microwave Power and Electromagnetic Energy, 1988-90; editor Advances in Electromagnetic Fields in Living Systems; also numerous papers. Panelist NSF Presdl. Young Investigator award com., Washington, 1984, 89, mem. NIH diagnostic radiology, 1981-85, chmn. SBIR study sect., 1986-94; mem. U.S. Nat. Commn. for URSI, NAS, 1980-82, 90—, chair Commn. K, 1990—; mem. Pres. Com. Nat. Medal of Sci., 1992-93; mem. Nat. Coun. Radiation Protection and Measurement, 1992—, chmn. radio frequency scientific com., 1995—; mem. NAS Extremely Low Frequency Field Monitoring com., 1995—. Recipient IEEE Transaction Best Paper award, 1975; Nat. Rsch. Svcs. award, 1982, Disting. Svc. award, Outstanding Leadership award Chinese Am. Acad. and Profl. Assn. MidAm., 1989 (pres. 1991-92). Fellow AAAS, AIMBE, IEEE (tech. policy coun. 1990-91, chmn. com. on man and radiation 1990-91, assoc. and guest editor transactions on biomed. engring., guest editor transactions on microwave theory and techniques, disting. lectr. engring. in medicine and biology 1991-93); mem. NSPE, Biomed. Engring. Soc. (sr. mem.), Robotics Internat. (sr. mem.), Am. Soc. Engring. Edn., Bioelectromagnetics Soc. (charter, pres.-elect 1993-94, pres. 1994-95, chmn. ann. meeting 1994), Electromagnetics Acad., Golden Key, Sigma Xi, Phi Tau Phi (v.p.), Tau Beta Pi. Office: U Ill Coll Engring 1030 SEO MC/154 851 S Morgan St Chicago IL 60607

LIN, JOSEPH PEN-TZE, neuroradiologist, clinical administrator, educator; b. Foochow, China, Nov. 25, 1932; came to U.S., 1959, naturalized, 1974; s. Tai Shui and Chin Sien Lin; m. Lillian Y. Hsu, Dec. 23, 1959; children: James S., Carol W., Julia W. MD, Nat. Taiwan U., 1957. Diplomate Am. Bd. Radiology. Rotating intern Robert B. Green Meml. Hosp., San Antonio, 1959-60; resident in radiology Santa Rosa Med. Center, San Antonio, 1960-61, Bellevue Hosp. Center, N.Y.C., 1961-63; fellow in neuroradiology NYU Med. Ctr., N.Y.C., 1963-65; instr. radiology NYU Med. Ctr., 1965-67, asst. prof., 1967-70, assoc. prof., 1970-74, prof., 1974—; dir. neuroradiology sect. Univ. Hosp., N.Y.C., 1974—; cons. Manhattan VA Hosp., N.Y.C., 1974—, Booth Meml. Hosp., N.Y.C., 1978-84, St. Vincent's Hosp., S.I., N.Y., 1978-85, New Rochelle (N.Y.) Hosp., 1978-85. Contbr. articles on neuroradiology to med. jours. Fellow Am. Coll. Radiology, Am. Heart Assn. (stroke coun.); mem. Am. Chinese Med. Soc. (pres. 1978), Am. Soc. Neuroradiology, Radiol. Soc. N.Am., Assn. Univ. Radiologists. Home: 15 Oxford Rd New Rochelle NY 10804-3712 Office: NYU Med Ctr 550 1st Ave New York NY 10016-6481

LIN, MING SHEK, allergist, immunologist; b. Taipei, Taiwan, Oct. 11, 1937; came to U.S., 1965; s. Joseph and Tong-Kai (Chan) Lynn; m. Mary Liao, Nov. 22, 1969; children: Jerry, Michael. MD, Nat. Taiwan U., 1964; PhD, U. Pitts., 1974. Diplomate Am. Acad. Allergy and Immunology, Am. Bd. Pediatrics. Asst. prof. U. Pitts. Grad. Sch. Pub. Health, 1976-80; asst. and assoc. prof. dept. pediatrics U. Pitts. Sch. Medicine, 1981—; chief sect. of allergy and immunology Forbes Health System, Pitts., 1987—; pres. Pitts. Allergy Soc., 1994—. Contbr. articles to Jour. Allery and Immunology, Internat. Congress of Immunology, Jour. Allergy, Jour. Pediatrics, Jour. Cellular Immunology. Named Winklestan lectr., 1976. Fellow Am. Soc. for Microbiology; mem. AMA. Home: 81 Locksley Dr Pittsburgh PA 15235-5117 Office: 4099 William Penn Hwy Ste 805 Monroeville PA 15146-2518

LIN, MING-CHANG, physical chemistry educator, researcher; b. Hsinpu, Hsinchu, Taiwan, Oct. 24, 1936; came to U.S., 1967, naturalized, 1975; s. Fushin and Tao May (Hsu) L.; m. Juh-Huey Chern, June 26, 1965; children: Karen, Linus H., Ellena J. BSc, Taiwan Normal U., Taipei, 1959; PhD, U. Ottawa, Ont., Can., 1966. Postdoctoral rsch. fellow U. Ottawa, 1965-67; postdoctoral rsch. assoc. Cornell U., Ithaca, N.Y., 1967-69; rsch. chemist Naval Rsch. Lab., Washington, 1970-74, supervisory rsch. chemist, head chem. kinetics sect., 1974-82, sr. scientist for chem. kinetics, 1982-88; Robert W. Woodruff prof. phys. chemistry Emory U., Atlanta, 1988—; mem. adv. bd. Internat. Jour. Chem. Kinetics, 1990-93, Chemistry, World Sci. Pub. Co., Singapore, 1991—, Inst. Atomic and Molecular Sci., Taipei, 1991—; mem. young presdl. award com. NSF, Washington, 1990. Contbr. over 300 articles to profl. jours. 2d lt. Taiwan ROTC, 1960-62. Recipient Civilian Meritorious award USN, 1979, Humboldt award Humboldt Found., 1982, prize in sci. tech. Taiwanese-Am. Found., 1989; Guggenheim fellow, 1982. Mem. Am. Chem. Soc. (Hillebrand prize 1975), Combustion Inst., Am. Vacuum Soc., Materials Rsch. Soc., N.Am. Taiwanese Profs. Assn., Sigma Xi (Pure Sci. award 1976 Naval Rsch. Lab. chpt.). Achievements include discovery of numerous chemical lasers, use of lasers to elucidate mechanisms of combustion, propulsion and gas-surface reactions; first use of lasers to ionize nonfluorescing radicals and to probe for radicals formed in heterogeneous catalytic reactions. Office: Emory Univ Dept Of Chemistry Atlanta GA 30322

LIN, PEN-MIN, electrical engineer, educator; b. Liaoning, China, Oct. 17, 1928; came to U.S., 1954; s. Tai-sui and Tse-san (Tang) L.; m. Louise Shou Yuen Lee, Dec. 29, 1962; children: Marian, Margaret, Janice. B.S.E.E., Taiwan U., 1950; M.S.E.E., N.C. State U., 1956; Ph.D. in Elec. Engring., Purdue U., 1960. Asst. prof. Purdue U., West Lafayette, Ind., 1961-66, assoc. prof., 1966-74, prof. elec. engring., 1974-94, prof. emeritus, 1994—. Author: (with L.O. Chua) Computer Aided Analysis of Electronic Circuits, 1975, Symbolic Network Analysis, 1991, (with R.A. DeCarlo) Linear Circuit Analysis, 1995. Fellow IEEE. Home: 3029 Covington St West Lafayette IN 47906-1107 Office: Purdue Univ Sch Of Elec Engring West Lafayette IN 47907

LIN, PING-WHA, university educator; b. Canton, China, July 11, 1925; m. Sylvia Lin; children: Karl, Karen. BS, Jiao-Tong U., Shanghai, China, 1947; PhD, Purdue U., 1951. Engr. various, 1951-61; cons., engr. WHO, Geneva, 1962-66, 84, project mgr., 1980-82; Laurence L. Dresser chair, prof. Tri-State U., Angola, Ind., 1966-95, prof. emeritus, 1995—, pres., 1966-95, prof. emeritus, 1995—; pres. Lin Techs Inc., Angola, Ind., 1989—. Contbr. articles to profl. jours., including articles on or related to Lin's Theory of Flux. Grantee Dept. of Energy, 1983-84. Fellow ASCE (past pres. Ind. chpt.); mem. Am. Chem. Soc., Am. Water Works Assn. (life), Sigma Xi. Achievements include patents in the fields. Home: 506 S Darling St Angola IN 46703-1707

LIN, SHU-FANG HSIA, librarian; b. Kweiling, China, Jan. 7, 1939; came to U.S., 1962; d. Chien-cheng and Yu-chia (Sun) Hsia; m. George Chwen-Chen Lin; children: Michael, Lawrence. BA, Tunghai U., 1961; MA, Vanderbilt U., 1963, St. John's U., 1981. Internat. law diplomate. Contbr. articles to profl. jours. Mem. AAUP, ALA, Cath. Libr. Assn., Chinese Am. Librs. Assn., Metro Govt. Docs. Interest Group. Avocations: travel, movies, opera, reading. Office: St John's U Libr 8000 Utopia Pky Jamaica NY 11432-1335

LIN, TUNG HUA, civil engineering educator; b. Chungkin, China, May 26, 1911; s. Yao-Ching and Yue (Kuo) L.; m. Susan Z. Chiang, Mar. 15, 1939; childern: Rita P., Lin Chiou, Robert P., James P. B.S., Tangshan Coll., Chiaotung U., 1933; S.M., MIT, 1936; D.Sc., U. Mich., 1953. Prof. Tsing Hua U., China, 1937-39; chief engr. Chinese 2d Aircraft Co., Nancheun, Szechuan, 1939-44; prodn. mgr. Mfg. Factory, China, 1940-44; mem. tech. mission in charge of jet aircraft design, 1945-49; prof. aero. engring. U. Detroit, 1949-55; prof. engring. and applied scis. UCLA, 1955-78, prof. emeritus, 1978—; cons.N.Am. Aviation, N.Am. Rockwell, L.A., 1964-74, Atomic Internat., Canoga Park, Calif., 1965-68, ARA Inc., Industry City, Calif., 1964-94. Author: Theory of Inelastic Structure, 1968; contbr. articles to profl. jours.; mem. editorial bd.: Jour. Composite Materials, 1966-75; patentee in field. Chinese Nat. fellow Tsing-Hua U., 1933; recipient medal for Design of 1st Chinese twin-engine airplane, 1944, Disting. Svc. award Applied Mechanics Rev. ASME, 1966, NSF grantee, 1954-78; named prin. investigator Office Naval Rsch., 1985-93, Air Force Office of Sci. Rsch., 1988—. Fellow ASME, Am. Acad. Mechanics; mem. ASCE (life, gen. chmn. engring. mechanics conf. 1965, Theodore von Karman award 1988); mem. NAE. Home: 906 Las Pulgas Rd Pacific Palisades CA 90272-2441 Office: UCLA Dept Civil Engring 405 Hilgard Ave Los Angeles CA 90024-1301

LIN, TUNG YEN, civil engineer, educator; b. Foochow, China, Nov. 14, 1911; came to U.S., 1946, naturalized, 1951; s. Ting Chang and Feng Yi (Kuo) L.; m. Margaret Kao, July 20, 1941; children: Paul, Verna. BS in Civil Engring., Chiaotung U., Tangshan, Republic of China, 1931; MS, U. Calif., Berkeley, 1933; LLD, Chinese U. Hong Kong, 1972, Golden Gate U., San Francisco, 1982, Tongji U., Shanghai, 1987, Chiaotung U., Taiwan, 1987. Chief bridge engr., chief design engr. Chinese Govt. Rys., 1933-46; asst., then assoc. prof. U. Calif., 1946-55, prof., 1955-76, chmn. div. structural engring., 1960-63, dir. structural lab., 1960-63; chmn. bd. T.Y. Lin Internat., 1953-87, hon. chmn. bd., 1987-92; pres. Inter-Continental Peace Bridge, Inc., 1968—; cons. to State of Calif., Def. Dept., also to industry; chmn. World Conf. Prestressed Concrete, 1957, Western Conf. Prestressed Concrete Bldgs., 1960; chmn. bd. Lin Tung Yen, China, 1993—. Author: Design of Prestressed Concrete Structures, 1955, rev. edit., 1963, 3d edit. (with N.H. Burns), 1981, (with B. Bresler, Jack Scalzi) Design of Steel Structures, rev. edit., 1968, (with S.D. Statesbury) Structural Concepts and Systems, 1981, 2d edit., 1988; contbr. articles to profl. jours. Recipient Berkeley citation award, 1976, NRC Quarter Century award, 1977, AIA Honor award, 1984, Pres.'s Nat. Med. of Sci., 1986, Merit award Am. Cons. Engrs., Coun., 1987, John A. Roebling medal Bridge Engring., 1990, Am. Segmental Bridge Inst. Leadership award, 1992, Outstanding Paper of Yr. award Internat. Assn. Bridge and Structural Engring., 1993, Lifetime Achievement award Asian Am. Archs. and Engring. Assn., 1993, Outstanding Achievement award AAAE Assn. of So. Calif., Prix Albert Caquot award Assn. Française pour Construction, 1995; fellow U. Calif. at Berkeley. Mem. ASCE (hon., life, Wellington award, Howard medal), Nat. Acad. Engring., Academia Sinica, Internat. Fedn. Prestressing (Freyssinet medal), Am. Concrete Inst. (hon.), Prestressed Concrete Inst. (medal of honor). Home: 8701 Don Carol Dr El Cerrito CA 94530-2734 Office: 315 Bay St San Francisco CA 94133-1923 *Fear incites fear; complex breeds complex. If one learns to control one's own fear and complex, and at the same time understands those of others, one will have gone a long way toward success and happiness.*

LIN, WILLIAM WEN-RONG, economist; b. Pintung, Taiwan, Sept. 5, 1942; came to U.S., 1967; naturalized, 1976; s. Ming-Lay and Shyr-Mey (Chow) L.; m. Kimy Kuei-mei Juan, Oct. 5, 1964; children: Susan, George, Roger. BS, Chung-Hsing U., Taichung, Taiwan, 1964; MS, U. Calif.-Davis, 1969, PhD, 1973. Economist Oak Ridge Nat. Labs., Tenn., 1974-76; agrl. economist U.S. Dept. Agriculture, Washington, 1976-80, sect. head Econ. Rsch. Svc., 1982-92; sr. agrl. economist, 1992—; economist U.S. Dept. Energy, Washington, 1980-81, U.S. Dept. Interior, 1981-82; leader livestock feed del. to China, 1991, OECD, 1991; cons. in field. Contbr. articles to profl. jours. Mem. Taiwanese Am. Assn., 1976-86; legis. affairs com. Saratoga Cmty. Assn., Springfield, Va., 1983; pres. Chinese-Am. Profl. Assn. Met. Washington, 1995. U. Calif. fellow, 1967-68, Disting. scholar, 1969-71; Merit award U.S. Dept. Agr., 1979, 85, 90, 92. Mem. Am. Agrl. Econ. Assn. (productivity com. 1978-80, lectr. 1977), Am. Econs. Assn., Chinese-Am. Profls. Assn. (bd. dirs. 1994), Western Agrl. Econ. Assn. (lectr. 1979), Southern Agrl. Econ. Assn. Home: 9404 Crosstimber Ct Fairfax Station VA 22039-3175 Office: USDA Econ Rsch Svc 1301 New York Ave NW Rm 832 Washington DC 20005-4788

LIN, Y. K., engineer, educator; b. Foochow, Fukien, China, Oct. 30, 1923; came to U.S., 1954, naturalized, 1964; s. Fa Been and Chi Ying (Cheng) L.; m. Ying-yuh June Wang, Mar. 29, 1952; children: Jane, Della, Lucia, Winifred. BS, Amoy U., 1946; MS, Stanford U., 1955, PhD, 1957; Dr. Engring. honoris causa, U. Waterloo, Can., 1994. Tchr. Amoy U., China, 1946-48, Imperial Coll. Engring., Ethiopia, 1957-58; engr. Vertol Aircraft Corp., Morton, Pa., 1956-57; research engr. Boeing Co., Renton, Wash., 1958-60; asst. prof. U. Ill., Urbana, 1960-62, assoc. prof., 1962-65, prof. aero. and astron. engring., 1965-83; Charles E. Schmidt Eminent scholar chair Coll. Engring., dir. Ctr. for Applied Stochastics Rsch. Fla. Atlantic U., Boca Raton, 1984—; vis. prof. mech. engring. M.I.T., 1967-68; sr. vis. fellow Inst. Sound and Vibration Research, U. Southampton, Eng., 1976; cons. Gen. Motors Corp., Boeing Co., Gen. Dynamics Corp., TRW Corp., Brookhaven Nat. Lab. Author: Probabilistic Theory of Structural Dynamics, 1967, Stochastic Structural Mechanics, 1987, Stochastic Approaches in Earthquake Engineering, 1987, Stochastic Structural Dynamics, 1990, Probabilistic Structural Dynamics: Advanced Theory and Applications, 1995; contbr. articles to profl. jours. Sr. postdoctoral fellow NSF, 1967-68. Fellow ASCE (Alfred M. Freudenthal medal 1984), Am. Acad. Mechs., Acoustical Soc. Am., AIAA (assoc.); mem. Sigma Xi, Internat. Assn. for Structural Safety and Reliability (stochastic dynamics rsch. award 1993). Home: 2684 NW 27th Ter Boca Raton FL 33434-6001 Office: Fla Atlantic U Coll Engring Boca Raton FL 33431

LINANE, WILLIAM EDWARD, corporate real estate executive; b. Chgo., Apr. 15, 1928; s. Francis John and Eva (Knott) L.; m. Elaine Ruth Linstead, Oct. 22, 1948 (div. Jan. 1957); children: James Richard, Judith Linane Healey. AA, N. Park Coll., 1948; BS, Northwestern U., 1952; MBA, U. Chgo., 1964. Various positions Eastern Weighing & Insp. Bur., Chgo., 1948-52; with freight sales div. Matson Navigation Co., Chgo., 1952-55, Ill. Calif. Express, Chgo., 1955-61; exec. dir. Am. Soc. Traffic & Transp., Chgo., 1961-69; v.p. William Kritt & Co., Chgo., 1969-74; pres. Linane & Co., Inc., Rosemont, Ill., 1974—; midwest regional advisor N.Am. Property Assn., Coeur D Alene, Idaho, 1988—. Author: Encyclopedia of Professional Management, 1979. Mem. Coun. of Logistics Mgmt. (pres. Ill. chpt. 1984-85). Avocations: aviation, golf, skiing, scuba diving, reading.

LINCE, JOHN ALAN, pharmacist; b. Cleve., Sept. 15, 1940; s. John Alexander and Isabelle Stella (Wirbalas) Lincewicz; m. Katherine Ann Hudson, Sept. 9, 1961 (div. Aug., 1984); children: John Jr., Karen, Mark; m. Shirley Ann Baker, Jan. 18, 1985. BS in Pharmacy, Ohio State U., 1964. Registered pharmacist, Ohio. Pharmacist, owner Hill & Dale Pharmacy, Columbus, Ohio, 1964-75, Franklin Park Med. Pharmacy, Columbus, 1975—. Pharmacy Mktg. award Johnson & Johnson, N.J., 1964. Mem. Coop. of Ohio Pharmacies (charter mem., pres. 1991—), Am. Pharm. Assn., Nat. Assn. Retail Druggists, Ohio Pharmacists Assn., Acad. Pharmacy Ctrl. Ohio (trustee 1994-95, pres. 1995-97), Ohio State Alumni Assn., Ohio State U. Coll. Pharmacy Alumni Assn. (charter), Mid-Ohio Combat Shooters Assn. (pres. 1985-88), Rho Chi. Avocations: photography, woodworking, target shooting. Home: 4645 Meekison Dr Columbus OH 43220-3038 Office: Franklin Park Med Pharmacy 1829 E Long St Columbus OH 43203-2066

LINCHITZ, RICHARD MICHAEL, psychiatrist, pain medicine specialist, physician; b. Bklyn., Mar. 29, 1947; m. Rita A. Colao, Sept. 22, 1973; children: Elise Ann, Michael Benjamin, Jonathan Adam. BA cum laude in Psychology, Cornell U., 1967, MD, 1973; student L.I. Univ., 1967-68, U. Lausanne Med. Sch., 1968-71. Diplomate Am. Bd. Psychiatry and Neurology, Am. Acad. Pain Mgmt., AM. Bd. Pain Medicine. Intern, Moffit Hosp., San Francisco, 1973-74; resident in psychiatry Langley Porter Neuropsychiat. Inst., San Francisco, 1974-77; practice medicine specializing in treatment of chronic pain conditions and psychiatry, Carle Place, N.Y., 1978—; med. dir. Roslyn Mental Health Ctr. (N.Y.), 1978—, Pain Alleviation Center, Carle Place, 1978-93. Recipient letter of commendation White House, 1977; Nathan Seligman award Cornell U. Med. Coll., 1973; Nat. Psychiat. Endowment Fund award Langley Porter Neuropsychiat. Inst., 1977; Langley Porter Youth Service award, 1977. Fellow Am. Coll. Pain Medicine; mem. Am. Psychiat. Assn., Acad. Pain Research, Am. Pain Soc., Nassau Psychiat. Soc., Am. Acad. of Pain Medicine (bd. dirs.), Am. Acad. Pain Mgmt. (cert.), Alpha Omega Alpha. Author: Life Without Pain, 1987. Office: 179 Westbury Ave Carle Place NY 11514-1227

LINCICOME, BERNARD WESLEY, journalist; b. Zanesville, Ohio, Sept. 13, 1941; s. Robert Parr and Mary Edith Lincicome; m. Jaye Slaughter, Sept. 21, 1963; children: Romey, David. B.S. in Edn., Ohio State U., 1963. Staff writer Sun-Sentinel, Ft. Lauderdale, Fla., 1968-70, sports editor, 1970-73; sports editor Ft. Lauderdale News, 1973-83; columnist Chgo. Tribune, 1983—. Served with USAF, 1958-61. Recipient Best Sports Column award

Fla. Press Club, 1981; Column writing award AP Sports Editors, 1982, 85, 88; Best Sports Column award AP, 1984; Peter Lisagor award, 1985, 87. Mem. Fla. Sportswriters Assn. (pres. 1977, Sportswriter of Yr. award 1973, 75, 79, 81).

LINCICOME, DAVID RICHARD, biomedical and animal scientist; b. Champaign, Ill., Jan. 17, 1914; s. David Rosebery and Olive Iola (Casper) L.; m. Dorothy Lucile Van Cleave, Sept. 1, 1941 (dec. Nov. 1952); children: David Van Cleave, Judith Ann; m. Margaret Stirewalt, Dec. 29, 1953. BS, MS with high honors, U. Ill., 1937; PhD in Tropical Medicine, Tulane U., 1941. Diplomate (emeritus) Am. Bd. Microbiology; diplomate Am. Coll. Animal Physiology; cert. animal scientist Am. Registry Profl. Animal Scientists. Asst. instr. U. Ill., 1937; asst. instr. tropical medicine Tulane U. Med. Sch., 1937-41; asst. prof. parasitology U. Ky., 1941-47; sr. rsch. parasitologist Du Pont Co., 1949-53; from asst. prof. to full prof. biol. Scis. Howard U., 1953-70; vis. sci. NIH, 1965-66; registrar, Jacob Sheep Conservancy, 1989-96, bd. dirs., 1990—, pres., 1996; vis. scholar Nat. Agrl. Libr. USDA, 1990-92; guest scientist USDA Exp. Sta., Beltsville, Md., 1978—, Naval Med. Rsch. Inst., 1954-62. Founder, editor Exptl. Parasitology, 1949-76; editor Transactions of the Ky. Acad. Sci., 1946-49, Transactions of the Am. Microscopical Soc., 1970-71, Internat. Rev. Tropical Medicine, 1953-63; founder Virology, 1950, Advances in Vet. Sci., 1952. Lt. col. Med. Svc. Corps, U.S. Army, World War II, PTO. Recipient Anniversary award Helminthological Soc., 1975; rsch. grantee NIH, 1958-68. Fellow AAAS, Explorers Club (nat., N.Y.); mem. Helminthological Soc. (pres. 1958, emeritus), Am. Physiol. Soc. (emeritus), Soc. Invertebrate Zoology (emeritus), Am. Soc. Zoologists (emeritus), Am. Soc. Parasitologists, Am. Soc. Cell Biology, Am. Microscopical Soc. (emeritus), Royal Soc. Tropical Medicine (emeritus), Am. Soc. Tropical Medicine (emeritus), Am. Goat Soc. (bd. dirs. 1992—), Am. Dairy Goat Assn. (founder., 1st sec. rsch. found. 1979, bd. dirs. 1972-87), Nat. Pygmy Goat Assn. (bd. dirs. 1976-92, pres. 1979), Natural Colored Wool Growers Assn. (bd. dirs. 1988-94), Jacob Sheep Breeders Assn., Jacob Sheep Soc. (Eng.), Nat. Tunis Sheep Registry (bd. dirs. 1991-93, sec. 1991-92), Soft-coated Wheaten Terrier Club of Am. (mem rescue com. 1993—), Greater Washington D.C. Area Soft-Coated Wheaten Terrier Club (founder, pres. 1991-92), Am. Livestock Breeds Conservancy (bd. dirs. 1994—), Va. State Dairy Goat Assn. (founder, pres. 1976), Midwestern Conf. Parasitologists (founder, 1st sec. 1949), Soc. Exptl. Biology & Medicine (sec. D.C. chpt. 1996, emeritus), Phi Beta Kappa, Sigma Xi (assoc. mem. 1936, mem. 1941, pres. Howard U. chpt. 1962). Achievements include breeding of two rare and endangered breeds of sheep, Jacob and Tunis and a rare dog the soft coated Whesten Terrier; founder and first sec. The Rsch. Found. of the Am. Dairy Goat Assn.; founder Midwestern Conf. of Parasitologists. Home: Frogmoor Farm 3032 Courtney Sch House Rd Midland VA 22728-9748 Office & Home: PO Box 13 4419 Cambria Ave Garrett Park MD 20896 also Office: USDA BARC East Rm 207 Bldg 467 Beltsville MD 20705

LINCOLN, ABBEY (ANNA MARIE WOOLRIDGE, GABY LEE, AMINATA MOSEKA), jazz singer, actress; b. Chicago, IL, Aug. 6, 1930; m. Max Roach, 1962 (div. 1970). Albums include: Affair: A Story of a Girl in Love, 1956, That's Him, 1957, It's Magic, 1958, Abbey is Blue, 1959, We Insist: Freedom Now Suite, 1960, Straight Ahead, 1961, It's Time, 1962, People in Me, 1979, Golden Lady, 1981, Talking to the Sun, 1984, Abbey Sings Billie, 1987, The World is Falling Down (with Stan Getz), 1990, You Gotta Pay the Band, 1991, Abbey Sings Billie, Volume 2, 1992, Devil's Got Your Tongue, 1993, Talking To The Sun, 1993, Lincoln on Paris, 1993, When There Is Love (with Hank Jones), 1994; film appearances include: The Girl Can't Help It, 1956, Nothing But a Man, 1964, For the Love of Ivy, 1968, A Short Walk to Daylight, 1972, Mo' Better Blues, 1990; wrote, directed and produced play, A Pig in a Poke, 1975. inducted into Black Filmakers Hall of Fame, 1975. Office: care Verve 825 8th Ave New York NY 10019-7416

LINCOLN, EDMOND LYNCH, investment banker; b. Wilmington, Del., Aug. 3, 1949; s. Edmond Earl and Mary Margaret (Lynch) L.; B.A. magna cum laude, Harvard U., 1971, M.B.A., with distinction, 1974; m. Pamela Wick, Sept. 3, 1977; children: Lucy Arms, Emily Lord. Acting rare book librarian Henry Francis duPont Winterthur Mus. (Del.), 1971-72; with Kidder Peabody & Co., Inc., N.Y.C., 1974-94, asst. v.p., 1977-79, v.p. 1979-91, sr. v.p., 1991-94, mgr. govt. agy. fin., 1984-86, transp. group, 1986-94; mng. dir. PaineWebber Inc., N.Y.C., 1994—; pub. interest dir. Fed. Home Loan Bank of N.Y., 1987-89. Recipient Washburn History prize, Harvard U., 1971. Treas., Fed. Hall Meml. Assocs., 1981-87; mem. vis. com. Harvard Coll. Library, 1981-86, 88-94; exec. com. Friends of Harvard U. Track, 1972—, sec., 1976-87. Mem. Investment Assn. N.Y., Friends of Winterthur (trustee 1976-81, 87-93, sec. 1978-81, Winterthur Mus. acad. affairs com. 1992—), Assn. Internationale de Bibliophilie, Assn. of Fellows, The Pierpont Morgan Library, Club of Odd Volumes, Bond Club of N.Y., Grolier Club, Harvard Club (N.Y.C.), India House, Wilmington Club, Wilmington Country Club, Phi Beta Kappa. Republican. Roman Catholic. Home: 161 E 79th St New York NY 10021-0421 Office: PaineWebber Inc 1285 Ave of the Americas New York NY 10019

LINCOLN, LARRY W., automotive executive; b. 1944. BS in psychology, Mich. Univ., 1965, MA in psychology, bus., 1980. Gen. superintendent Truck and Bus/Chevrolet, Chevrolet Bay City, 1965-86; gen. superintendent Pontiac West Assembly Truck and Bus General Motors Corp., Pontiac, Mich., 1986-93; CEO Mark III Industries, Ocala, Fla., 1993—. Office: PO Box 1868 Ocala FL 34478

LINCOLN, ROSAMOND HADLEY, modern painter, photographer; b. Worcester, Mass., June 27, 1924; d. Ralph Gorham and Grace (Wardwell) Hadley; m. Brayton Lincoln, Jan. 15, 1949; children: Rosamond, Christopher, Daniel, Dorothy. BA, Radcliffe Coll., 1946; postgrad., Assumption Coll., 1975-76. Interior display trainee G. Fox & Co. Dept. Store, Hartford, Conn., 1944; advt. mgr. So. New Eng. Ice and Oil Co., Hartford, Conn., 1945-46; head instr. Worcester (Mass.) Art Mus., 1946-48, 70-76; dir. continuing edn. Swain Sch. Design, New Bedford, Mass., 1980-83; artist self-employed South Dartmouth, Mass., 1983—; bd. dirs. The Arts Ctr., New Bedford, 1977-80; pres. The Bierstadt Art Soc., New Bedford, 1982-84; chmn. Dartmouth Arts Lottery Coun., 1984-86. Mem. League of Women Voters, New Bedford, 1980-86; mem. The Women's Ctr., New Bedford, 1986—. Recipient First prize Bierstadt Art Gallery, 1989, Middleboro Art Assn., 1988. Mem. AAUW, Westport Art Group, Waterfront Hist. Area League, Rotch-Jones-Duff House and Garden Mus., The Whaling Mus., The Marion Art Ctr., Gallery X, The Worcester Art Mus. Unitarian. Home: 43 Pleasant St South Dartmouth MA 02748-3441

LINCOLN, SANDRA ELEANOR, chemistry educator; b. Holyoke, Mass., Mar. 11, 1939; d. Edwin Stanley and Evelyn Ida (Mackie) L. BA magna cum laude, Smith Coll., 1960; MSChem, Marquette U., 1970; PhD in Inorganic Chemistry, SUNY, Stony Brook, 1982. Tchr., prin. Oak Knoll Sch., Summit, N.J., 1964-74; tchr. Holy Child High Sch., Waukegan, Ill., 1974-76; lectr. chemistry, dir. fin. aid Rosemont (Pa.) Coll., 1976-78; teaching asst. SUNY, Stony Brook, 1978-82; assoc. prof. chemistry U. Portland, Oreg., 1982—; researcher Oreg. Grad. Ctr., Beaverton, 1982—. Contbr. articles to profl. jours. Cath. sister Soc. Holy Child Jesus, 1963—. Recipient Pres.'s award for Teaching, SUNY, Stony Brook, 1981; Burlington No. Outstanding scholar, 1987. Mem. Am. Chem. Soc., Phi Beta Kappa, Sigma Xi. Democrat. Home: 5431 N Strong St Portland OR 97203-5711 Office: U Portland 5000 N Willamette Blvd Portland OR 97203-5743

LINCOLN, WALTER BUTLER, JR., marine engineer, educator; b. Phila., July 15, 1941; s. Walter Butler and Virginia Ruth (Callahan) L.; m. Sharon Platner, Oct. 13, 1979; children: Amelia Adams, Caleb Platner. BS in Math., U. N.C., 1963; Ocean Engr., MIT, 1975; MBA, Rensselaer Poly. Inst., 1982; MA, Naval War Coll., 1994. Registered profl. engr., N.H., Conn.; chartered engr., U.K. Ops. rsch. analyst Applied Physics Lab. Johns Hopkins U., Silver Spring, Md., 1968-70; grad. asst. MIT, Cambridge, 1971-75; ocean engr. USCG R&D Ctr., Groton, Conn., 1976-78, chief marine syss. & environ. tech. divsn., 1983—; prin. engr. Sanders Assocs., Nashua, N.H., 1978-83; lectr. U. Conn., Avery Point, 1986—; master, U.S. Mcht. Marine. Contbr. articles to profl. jours. Comdr. USNR, 1963—. Fellow MIT, 1971. Mem. SAR, Am. Soc. Naval Engrs., Am. Geophys. Union, N.Y. Acad. Scis., Nat. Assn. Underwater Instrs. (instr. 1971—), Royal Inst. Naval Architects, Soc. Naval Architects & Marine Engrs. (chmn. New Eng. sect. 1996—), Marine Tech. Soc. (exec. bd. New Eng. sect. 1980), Navy Sailing Assn. (ocean master), Pi Mu Epsilon. Achievements include rsch. in integrated systems modeling and engring. of deep ocean systems; devel. of algorithms for simulation of hydromechs. of ocean systems and ships; engring. mgmt. of ship and marine and environmental system rsch., devel., test and evaluation. Office: USCG R&D Ctr 1082 Shennecossett Rd Groton CT 06340

LIND, CARL BRADLEY, retired museum director; b. Bethel, Vt., Apr. 22, 1929; s. Carl Olaf and Signe Alfield (Anderson) L.; m. Barbara Ann Eskridge, Oct. 22, 1951; children: Carl Garrett, Susan Ann, Craig Ira. BA, Norwich U., 1951; cert., Command and Gen. Staff Coll., Fort Leavenworth, Kans., 1960; MA, Columbia U., 1963; cert., NATO Def. Coll., Rome, 1976. Commd. 2d lt. U.S. Army, advanced through grades to col., 1968; asst. prof. U.S. Mil. Acad., West Point, N.Y., 1961-64; comdr. 1st Squadron 3d Armored Cavalry Rgt. U.S. Army, Fed. Republic Germany, 1965-67; sr. advisor Vietnamese Nat. Mil. Acad. U.S. Army, Dalat, Vietnam, 1967-68; chief Congl. Inquiry Div., Office Sec. of the Army U.S. Army, Washington, 1968-71; area comdr. 2d ROTC Region U.S. Army, Fort Knox, Ky., 1973-75; exec. for interoperability to SACEUR, SHAPE NATO, Mons, Belgium, 1977-79; exec. v.p. Evans Llewellyn Securities, Bellevue, Wash., 1979-81; dep. dir. Mus. of History and Industry, Seattle, 1984-88, exec. dir., 1988-91; bd. dirs. Museum of History and Industry, Seattle, Coast Guard Mus. of Northwest, Seattle. Contbr. articles to jours. in field. Neighborhood commr. Boys Scouts Am., Baumholder, Fed. Rep. Germany, 1965-66; pres. PTA, Baumholder, 1965-66; commr. King County (Wash.) Landmarks & Heritage Commn., 1992—, Wash. State Heritage Caucus, 1990—; bd. dirs. Hydroplane and Antique Race Boat Mus., Seattle, 1993—; exec. bd. Bigelow House Preservation Assn., Olympia, Wash., 1993—. Decorated Bronze star, Dept. Def. Superior Svc. medal. Legion of Merit, Meritorious Svc. medal. Mem. VFW (comdr. Mercer Island, Wash. post 5760 1984-85), Assn. of U.S. Army, U.S. Armor Assn., Ret. Officer Assn., Am. Assn. State and Local History, Lions, Rotary. Home: 3023 Country Club Rd NW Olympia WA 98502-3738

LIND, JAMES FOREST, surgeon, educator; b. Fillmore, Sask., Can., Nov. 22, 1925; s. James Forest and Isabella (Pringle) L.; m. Dorothy Anne Berlette, Aug. 23, 1950; children: Heather, James, Scott, Robert, Gregory. M.D., C.M., Queen's U., 1951. Intern Hamilton (Ont.) Gen. Hosp., 1951-52, resident in pathology, 1952-53; fellow in anatomy Queen's U., 1953-54, fellow in medicine, 1954-55; fellow in surgery, 1955-56; registrar in surgery Liverpool, 1956-58; fellow in physiology Mayo Found., 1958-60; lectr. in surgery U. Man., 1960-62, asst. prof. surgery, 1962-64, assoc. prof., 1964-66, prof., 1966-72, head dept. surgery, 1969-72; prof., chmn. dept. surgery McMaster U., 1972-79, Eastern Va. Med. Sch., 1979-94;*retired, 1994; dir. surgery Med. Center Hosps., Norfolk, Va., 1979—; chief surgery Sentara Hosps., 1995—; hon. cons. attending staff Norfolk Gen. Hosp., Leigh Meml. Hosp., Norfolk, De Paul Hosp., Norfolk; practice medicine specializing in surgery Norfolk, 1979-95; vis. prof. U. B.C., 1966, U. Alta., 1967, U. Sask., 1968, Royal Victoria Hosp., 1969, McGill U., 1969, U. Calgary, 1969, Meml. U., Newfoundland, 1973, Harvard U., 1972, numerous others. Contbr. numerous articles to med. jours. Served with RCAF, 1943-45; lt. comdr. RCN(R), 1948—. John S. McEashern fellow Can. Cancer Soc., 1956-57; recipient George Christian Hoffman award Queen's U., 1957-58; John and Mary Markle scholar, 1960; other honors. Mem. Royal Coll. Phys. and Surg. Can., Can. Assn. Clin. Surgeons, Can. Assn Gastroenterology (pres. 1972), Can. Soc. Clin. Investigation, Am. Surg. Assn., Central Surg. Assn., Mayo Alumni Assn., Soc. Surg. Chmn., Soc. Univ. Surgeons, Soc. Surgery Alimentary Tract, A.C.S., AMA, Va. Med. Soc., Va. Surg. Soc., Southeastern Surg. Congress, Soc. Am. Gastrointestinal Endoscopic Surgeons (pres. 1986), Am. Motility Soc., Assn. Acad. Surgery, Norfolk Medicine Acad., Esophageal Club. Home: 4044 Sherwood Ln Virginia Beach VA 23455-5613 Office: 825 Fairfax Ave Norfolk VA 23507-1912

LIND, JON ROBERT, lawyer; b. Evanston, Ill., July 4, 1935; s. Robert A. and Ruth (Anderson) L.; m. Jane Langfitt, Aug. 29, 1959; children: Jon Robert Jr., Elizabeth Neal, Susan Porter. AB, Harvard U., 1957, LLB, 1960; diploma in comparative law, Cambridge (Eng.) U., 1961. Bar: Ill. 1961. Assoc. Isham, Lincoln & Beale, Chgo., 1961-68, ptnr., 1968-88; ptnr. McDermott, Will & Emery, Chgo., 1988—. Atty. Winnetka (Ill.) Park Dist., 1973-78; bd. dirs. Swedish-Am. Mus. Ctr., 1988—. Mem. ABA, Chgo. Bar Assn., Harvard U. Alumni Assn. (sec. 1970-73), Econ. Club of Chgo., Legal Club of Chgo. Home: 644 Walden Rd Winnetka IL 60093-2035 Office: McDermott Will & Emery 227 W Monroe St Chicago IL 60606-5016

LIND, MARSHALL L., academic administrator. Dean Sch. Extended and Grad. Studies U. Alaska, Juneau, until 1987, chancellor, 1987—. Office: U of Alaska Southeast Office of Chancellor 11120 Glacier Hwy Juneau AK 99801-8625

LIND, NIELS CHRISTIAN, civil engineering educator; b. Copenhagen, Mar. 10, 1930; s. Axel Holger and Karen (Larsen) L.; m. Veronica Claire Hummel, Nov. 29, 1957 (div. 1979); children: Julie Wilhelmina, Peter Christian, Adam Conrad; m. Viriginia Patricia Cano Reynoso, Jan. 26, 1985 (div. 1996); 1 child, Andreas. MSc, Tech. U. Denmark, 1953; PhD, U. Ill., 1959. Design engr. Dominia Ltd., Copenhagen, 1953-54; engr. I Bell Telephone Co., Montreal, 1954-55; field engr. Drake-Merritt, Labrador, Nfld., 1955; asst. prof. U. Ill., Urbana, 1959-60; assoc. prof. civil engring. U. Waterloo, Ont., 1960-62, prof., 1962-91, disting. prof. emeritus, 1992, dir. Inst. Risk Research, 1982-88; adj. prof. U. Victoria, B.C., 1993-95. Recipient Ostenfeld gold medal, 1978; recipient Cancam award Can. Congress Applied Mechanics, 1981. Fellow Royal Soc. Can., Am. Acad. Mechanics (pres. 1972-73). Home: 504-640 Montreal St, Victoria, BC Canada V8V 1Z8

LIND, THOMAS OTTO, barge transportation company executive; b. New Orleans, Apr. 24, 1937; s. Henry Carl Lind and Elinor (Rooney) Messersmith; m. Eugenia Niehaus, June 8, 1963; children: Elinor Ashley, Elizabeth Kelly. BS in MechE, Tulane U., 1959, LLB, 1965. Cert. mech. engr., 1959. Assoc. Jones, Walker, Waechter, Poitevent, Carrere and Denegre, New Orleans, 1965-66; v.p., sec., counsel Ingram Corp., New Orleans, 1966-84; v.p. Gulf Fleet Marine Corp., New Orleans, 1984-85; v.p., regulatory counsel, sec. and asst. treas. New Orleans Pub. Svc., Inc and La. Power and Light Co., 1985-92; regional counsel for La. Entergy Svcs., Inc., 1993-94; risk mgr., sec. Canal Barge Co., Inc., New Orleans, 1994—. Trustee Metairie Park Country Day Sch., 1991-95; mem. bd. govs. Trinity Sch., New Orleans. 1982-85; vestryman Trinity Ch., New Orleans, 1987-91; active Family of Cmty. and Utility Supporters, New Orleans, 1987-94. Lt. (j.g.) USN, 1959-62; comdr. USNR, 1962-79. Mem. ABA, La. State Bar Assn. (bd. dirs. corp. law sect. 1973-75), New Orleans Bar Assn. (exec. com. 1989—, 2d v.p. 1989-90, sec. 1992-93, 1st v.p. 1993-94, pres.-elect 1994-95, pres. 1995—, bd. dirs. New Orleans B-Pro Bono project 1994-96), La. Orgn. for Jud. Excellence (bd. dirs.), New Orleans Lawn Tennis Club (pres. 1986-88). Republican. Episcopalian. Avocations: tennis, jogging, numismatics. Home: 1126 Octavia St New Orleans LA 70115-3129 Office: Canal Barge Co Inc 835 Union St New Orleans LA 70112-1401

LINDA, GERALD, advertising and marketing executive; b. Boston, Nov. 25, 1946; s. Edward Linda and Anne Beatrice (Lipofsky) Coburn; m. Claudia Wollack, Sept. 24, 1978; children—Jonathan Daniel Rezny, Jessica Simone. BS in Bus. Adminstrn., Northeastern U., 1969, MBA, 1971; postgrad., U. Mich., 1971-75. Faculty U. Ky., Lexington, 1975-77; ptnr. Tatham-Laird & Kudner, Chgo., 1977-80; v.p. Marsteller, Chgo., 1980-84; sr. v.p. HCM, Chgo., 1984-86; pres. Gerald Linda & Assocs., Chgo., 1986-89; prin. Kurtzman/Slavin/Linda, Inc., Chgo., 1990-93, Kapuler Mkgt. Rsch., Chgo., 1993-94; pres. Gerald Linda & Assocs., Glenview, Ill., 1994—. Mem. editorial review bd. Jour. Current Issues and Rsch. in Advt., 1984—. Mem. Am. Mktg. Assn. (exec.), Assn. for Consumer Rsch.

LINDAHL, CHARLES BLIGHE, research chemist, chemical company executive; b. North Platte, Nebr., Feb. 4, 1939; m. Jeanne Moore, 1959; children: David, Laura. BS, Iowa State U., 1960; PhD in Chemistry, U. Calif., Berkeley, 1964. Chemist Ames Lab, 1960; rsch. asst. Lawrence Berkeley Lab, 1961-64; sr. chemist Eastman Kodak, 1964-65; mem. tech. staff Rocketdyne divsn. Rockwell Internat., 1965-70; sr. chemist Reheis Chem., 1970-71; head new product devel. Ozark-Mahoning Co., Tulsa, Okla., 1971-72, tech. dir., 1973-90; gen. mgr., tech. dir. Ozark-Mahoning Co., Tulsa, 1990—. Mem. Am. Chem. Soc., Am. Assn. Dental Rsch., Internat. Assn. Dental Rsch., Sigma Xi. Office: Elf Atochem N Am 2000 Market St Philadelphia PA 19103-3231*

LINDAHL, THOMAS JEFFERSON, university dean; b. Norwalk, Wis., July 4, 1937; s. Gust Adolf and Mabel Louise (Zietlow) L.; m. Lee Ann Snowberry, Dec. 22, 1962; children: Gary, Mark. BS, U. Wis., 1960; MEd, U. Ill., 1970; PhD, Iowa State U., 1977. Instr. Stockton (Ill.) Community High Sch., 1968-74, Highland Community Coll., Freeport, Ill., 1968-74; instr. Iowa State U., Ames, 1974-75; chmn. dept. Area I Vocat.-Tech. Sch., Calmar, Iowa, 1975-77; assoc. prof., chmn. agrl. bus. dept. U. Minn., Waseca, 1977-83, vice chancellor, 1983-90, acting chancellor, 1990-91; dean Coll. Agriculture U. Wis., Platteville, 1991-94, dean Coll. Bus. Industry, Life Sci. and Agr., 1994—; cons., evaluator North Ctrl. Assn. Commn. on Instns. Higher Edn., Chgo., 1985—; numerous presentations in field. Author: (with Bennie L. Byler) Professional Education In-Service Needs of Agriculture Instructors in Iowa Post Secondry Area Vocational Schools, 1977, (with Wayne Robinson and N.J. Guderon) Cooperative College of Kenya Feasibility Study for Expansion, 1980, (with Myron A. Eighmy) An Individualized Course in Getting Started, 1980, (with James L. Gibson) Associate Instructor Handbook, 1980; also articles and corr. courses. Lay speaker United Meth. Ch., 1980—; v.p. Am. Assn. Colls. & Schs. Agr., 1995-96; pres. Wis. Rural Leadership Program Bd., 1995—. Recipient hon. state degree Wis. Future Farmers Am., 1993. Fellow Nat. Assn. Coll. Tchrs. Agr. (exec. com., v.p. 1991-92, pres. 1992-93); mem. NEA, Nat. Vocat. Agrl. Tchrs. Assn., Am. Vocat. Assn., Wis. Vocat. Assn., Minn. Vocat. Agrl. Tchrs. Assn. (25-yr. Tchg. award 1985), Iowa Vocat. Agrl. Tchrs. Assn. (15-yr. Membership award), Wis. Assn. Inst. Agr., Phi Delta Kappa, Kappa Delta Pi, Phi Kappa Phi. Home: 295 Flower Ct Platteville WI 53818-1915 Office: U Wis Coll Agr University Plz Platteville WI 53818

LINDARS, LAURENCE EDWARD, retired health care products executive; b. N.Y.C., Oct. 14, 1922; s. Arthur John and Florence Vera (Cunard) L.; m. Mary Gibson Grandy, Jan. 22, 1972; children—John L., William A., Nancy E. Student, Dartmouth Coll., 1943-44; B.S., Columbia U., 1947. Sr. auditor Arthur Young & Co., N.Y.C., 1947-51; chief acct. Deering, Milliken & Co., 1951-53; treas., dir. Poloron Products, Inc., New Rochelle, N.Y., 1953-58; controller Atlas Gen., Inc., N.Y.C., 1958-59; controller, treas., dir. fin. planning Pepperidge Farm, Inc., Norwalk, Conn., 1959-67; with C.R. Bard, Inc., Murray Hill, N.J., 1967-88; dir. C.R. Bard, Inc., 1972-92, vice chmn., 1983-88; mem. adv. bd. of Summit Trust Co., 1970-84. Trustee Overlook Hosp., 1973-79, Found., 1988-91, treas., 1989-90; trustee Epilepsy Found. N.J., 1985-90, pres., 1986-87, chmn., 1988-90. Lt. (j.g.) USNR, 1943-46. Mem. Fin. Execs. Inst., Canoe Brook Country Club, Harbour Ridge Yacht and Country Club, Delta Upsilon. Presbyterian.

LINDAU, JAMES H., grain exchange executive; b. Red Wing, Minn., May 21, 1933; s. Gottfrid and Stasia J. (Holmstrom) L.; m. Barbara Ann Marie Braaten, June 12, 1955; 1 child, James H. Jr. BA, Grinnell Coll., 1955. Mgmt. trainee The Glidden Co., Indpls., 1955-56; adminstrv. asst. Honeywell, Mpls., 1959-60; commodity merchandising v.p. The Pillsbury Co., Fresno, Mpls., 1960-83; mayor City of Bloomington, Minn., 1977-88; pres. Mpls. Grain Exch., 1988—; bd. dirs. Nat. Futures Assn., Chgo., 1988—, mem. exec. com., 1996—; bd. dirs. Nat. Grain Trade Coun., Washington, 1988—, vice chmn., 1996; owner franchise Burger King Restaurant, Burnsville, 1983—; mem. agrl. tech. adv. com. Depts. of Agriculture and Trade, 1990-94. Mem. Bloomington Bd. Edn., 1972-75, chmn., 1973-75; mem. Hennepin County Vo-Tech. Sch. Bd., Mpls., 1972-75, Hennepin Parks Found., 1990-92; candidate for lt. gov. Minn. (Rep., primary), 1982; candidate for gov. Minn. (Rep., primary), 1986; pres. Bloomington Minn. Port Authority, 1982-87. Capt. USAF, 1956-59. George F. Baker scholar Grinnell Coll., 1951-55; recipient Outstanding Leader award City of Bloomington, 1986, Good Neighbor award WCCO Radio, Mpls., 1987. Mem. Am. Swedish Inst., Svenska Sallskapet, Swedish Am. C. of C. (pres. Minn. chpg. 1990-94), Grand Nat. Quail Club (treas. 1986). Lutheran. Avocations: hunting, fishing, golfing, cooking, politics. Office: Mpls Grain Exch 400 Grain Exchange Minneapolis MN 55415-1411

LINDBERG, CHARLES DAVID, lawyer; b. Moline, Ill., Sept. 11, 1928; s. Victor Samuel and Alice Christine (Johnson) L.; m. Marian J. Wagner, June 14, 1953; children: Christine, Breta, John, Eric. AB, Augustana Coll., Rock Island, Ill., 1950; LLB, Yale U., 1953. Bar: Ohio 1954. Assoc. Taft, Stettinius & Hollister, Cin., 1953-61, ptnr., 1961-85; mng. ptnr. Taft, Stettinius & Hollister, 1985—; dir. Cin. Bengals Profl. Football Team, Gibson Greetings, Inc., Arga Co., Schonstedt Instrument Co. Editor Nat. Law Jour., 1979-90. Sec. Good Samaritan Hosp., Cin.; bd. dirs. Taft Broadcasting Co., Cin., 1973-87, Dayton Walther Corp., 1986-87; bd. dirs. Augustana Coll., 1978-87, 91—, sec., 1981-82, vice-chmn., 1982-83, chmn., 1983-86; pres. Cin. Bd. Edn., 1971, 74, Zion Luth. Ch., Cin., 1966-69; chmn. policy com. Hamilton County Rep. Com., 1981-90; mem. exec. com. Ohio Rep. Fin. Com., 1989-90; trustee Greater Cin. Ctr. Econ. Edn., 1976-91, pres., 1987-89, chmn., 1989-91; chmn. law firm divsn. Fine Arts Fund, 1985; trustee Pub. Libr. Cin. and Hamilton County, 1982—, pres., 1989-96. Mem. Ohio Bar Assn., Cin. Bar Assn., Greater Cin. C. of C. (trustee 1985, exec. com., vice chmn. govt. and cmty. affairs com. 1989-91), Ohio Libr. Trustees Assn. (bd. dirs. 1986-87), Ohio C. of C. (bd. dirs. 1988-89), Queen City Club (sec. 1989-91), Commonwealth Club, Comml. Club (sec. 1994-96), Cin. Country Club, Optimists. Office: 1800 Star Bank Ctr 425 Walnut St Cincinnati OH 45202-3904

LINDBERG, DONALD ALLAN BROR, library administrator, pathologist, educator; b. N.Y.C., Sept. 21, 1933; s. Harry B. and Frances Seeley (Little) L.; m. Mary Musick, June 8, 1957; children: Donald Allan Bror, Christopher Charles Seeley, Jonathan Edward Moyer. AB, Amherst Coll., 1954, ScD (hon.), 1979; MD, Columbia U., 1958; ScD (hon.), SUNY, 1987; LLD (hon.), U. Mo., Columbia, 1990. Diplomate Am. Bd. Pathology, Am. Bd. Med. Examiners (exec. bd. 1987-91). Rsch. asst. Amherst Coll., 1954-55; intern in pathology Columbia-Presbyn. Med. Ctr., 1958-59, asst. resident in pathology, 1959-60; asst. in pathology Coll. Physician and Surgeons Columbia U., N.Y.C., 1958-60; instr. pathology Sch. of Medicine U. Mo., 1962-63, asst. prof. Sch. of Medicine, 1963-66, assoc. prof. Sch. of Medicine, 1966-69, prof. Sch. of Medicine, 1969-84, dir. Diagnostic Microbiology Lab. Sch. of Medicine, 1960-63, dir. Med. Ctr. Computer Program Sch. of Medicine, 1962-70, staff, exec. dir. for health affairs Sch. of Medicine, 1968-70, prof., chmn. dept. info. sci. Sch. of Medicine, 1969-71; dir. Nat. Libr. of Medicine, Bethesda, Md., 1984—; adj. prof. pathology U. Md. Sch. Medicine, 1988—, clin. prof. pathology U. Va., 1992—; dir. Nat. Coord. Office for High Performance Computing and Comms., exec. office of Pres., Office Sci. & Tech. Policy, 1992-95; mem. computer sci./engring. bd. Nat. Acad. Sci., 1971-74, chmn. Nat. Adv. Com. Artificial Intelligence in Medicine, Stanford U., 1975-84; U.S. rep. to Internat. Med. Info. Assn./Internat. Fedn. Info. Processing, 1975-84; bd. dirs. Am. Med. Info. Assn., 1992—; adv. coun. Inst. Medicine, 1992—. Author: The Computer and Medical Care, 1968; The Growth of Medical Information Systems in the United States, 1979; editor: (with W. Siler) Computers in Life Science Research, 1975; (with others) Computer Applications in Medical Care, 1982; editor Methods of Info. in Medicine, 1970-83, assoc. editor, 1983—; editor Jour. Med. Systems, 1976—, Med. Informatics Jour., 1976—; chief editor procs. 3d World Conf. on Med. Informatics, 1980; editorial bd. Jour. of AMA, 1991—; contbr. articles to jours. Recipient Silver Cord award Internat. Fedn. for Info. Processing, 1980, Walter C. Alvarez award Am. Med. Writers Assn. 1989, PHS Surgeon Gen.'s medallion, 1989, Nathan Davis award AMA, 1989, Presdl. Disting. Exec. Rank award, Sr. Exec. Svc., Outstanding Svc. medal Uniformed Svcs. U. of the Health Scis., 1992, Computers in Healthcare Pioneer award, 1993; Simpson fellow Amherst Coll., 1954-55; Markle scholar in acad. medicine, 1964-69. Mem. Inst. Medicine of NAS, Coll. Am. Pathologists (commn. on computer policy and coordination 1981-84), Mo. State Med. Assn., Assn. for Computing Machines, Salutis Unitas (Am. v.p. 1981-91), Am. Assn. for Med. Systems and Informatics (internat. com. 1982-89, bd. dirs. 1982, editor conf. procs. 1983, 84), Gorgas Meml. Inst. Tropical and Preventive Medicine (bd. dirs. 1987—), Am. Med. Informatics Assn. (pres. 1988-91), Sigma Xi. Democrat. Club: Cosmos (Washington). Avocations: photography; riding. Home: 13601 Esworthy Rd Germantown MD 20874-3319 Office: Nat Libr of Medicine 8600 Rockville Pike Bethesda MD 20894-0001

LINDBERG, DUANE R., minister. Presiding pastor The Am. Assn. Luth. Chs., Waterloo, Iowa. Office: Amer Assn of Lutheran Churches PO Box 416 Waterloo IA 50704-0416

LINDBERG, GEORGE W., federal judge; b. Crystal Lake, Ill., June 21, 1932; s. Alger Victor and Rilla (Wakem) L. BS, Northwestern U., 1954, JD, 1957. V.p., legal counsel John E. Reid & Assocs., Chgo., 1955-68; ptnr. Franz, Franz, Wardell & Lindberg, Crystal Lake, 1968-73; comptr. State of Ill., Springfield, 1973-77; dep. atty. gen. State of Ill., Chgo., 1977-78; justice Ill. Appellate Ct., Elgin, 1978-89; dist. judge U.S. Dist. Ct. (no. dist.) Ill., Chgo., 1989—; chmn. Ill. House Com. on Judiciary, Com. on Ethics, Springfield, 1970-73. Holder numerous govt. offices, 1966—. Office: US Dist Ct 219 S Dearborn St Chicago IL 60604-1702

LINDBERG, LAWRENCE V., lawyer; b. Youngstown, Ohio, Dec. 21, 1947. BA, Coll. Wooster, 1970; JD, NYU, 1973. Bar: Ohio 1973. Ptnr. Baker & Hostetler, Cleve. Office: Baker & Hostetler 3200 Nat City Ctr 1900 E 9th St Cleveland OH 44114-3401*

LINDBERG, TOD MARSHALL, editor, writer; b. Syracuse, N.Y., Feb. 25, 1960; s. Robert Sheridan and Dorothy Louise (Farris) L.; m. Christine Ann Tedeschi, Apr. 29, 1989. B.A., U. Chgo., 1982. Asst. editor Pub. Interest, N.Y.C., 1982-83, mng. editor, 1983-85; exec. editor Nat. Interest, Washington, 1985-86; sr. editor Insight, Washington, 1986, exec. editor news, 1987-90, dep. mng. editor, 1990—; editorial cons. Manhattan Inst., N.Y.C., 1983, Inst. for Ednl. Affairs, N.Y.C., 1983-85, Simon & Schuster, Pubs., N.Y.C., 1985. Contbr. articles to profl. jours. Office: Insight 3600 New York Ave NE Washington DC 20002-1947

LINDBLAD, RICHARD ARTHUR, retired health services administrator, drug abuse epidemiologist; b. Atlantic, Iowa, July 15, 1937; s. Clifford Robert and Emma Ruth (Dunham) L.; children: Julie, Richard, Mark. B.S., San Jose State Coll., 1961; M.S., U. Colo., 1965; M.P.H., Johns Hopkins U., 1971, Dr.P.H., 1974. Capt. USPHS, 1961, col., 1975, ret. capt., 1961-94; various assignments including adminstrn., epidemiology, research and prevention of substance abuse disorders Fed. Drug Abuse Treatment Hosp., Ft. Worth, Denver; now dir. internat. programs Nat. Inst. on Drug Abuse, Rockville, Md.; cons. in drug abuse epidemiology WHO, UN; designed and supervised devel. of UN Internat. Drug Abuse Assessment System; cons. on drug abuse rsch. and program devel. Designed and supervised devel. of the International Visiting Scientist and Technical Exchange program of the dept. of Health and Human Svcs.; Contbr. articles to profl. jours. Mem. Am. Public Health Assn., Md. Public Health Assn., Commd. Officers Assn. USPHS, Nat. Assn. Uniformed Services. Home: PO Box 179 Libertytown MD 21762-0179

LINDBLOM, MARJORIE PRESS, lawyer; b. Chgo., Mar. 17, 1950; d. John E. and Betty (Grace) P.; m. Lance E. Lindblom, June 13, 1971; children: Derek, Ian. AB cum laude, Radcliffe Coll., 1971; JD with honors, U. Chgo., 1978. Bar: Ill. 1978, U.S. Dist. Ct. (no. dist.) Ill. 1978, U.S. Ct. Appeals (7th cir.) 1978, U.S. Ct. Appeals (10th cir.) 1983, U.S. Supreme Ct. 1983, U.S. Ct. Appeals (5th cir.) 1984, N.Y. 1995, U.S. Dist. Ct. (so. and ea. dist.) N.Y. 1995, U.S. Ct. Appeals (2d cir.) 1995. Assoc. Kirkland & Ellis, Chgo., 1978-84, ptnr., 1984-94; N.Y.C., 1994—; asst. dir. fiscal affairs Ill. Bd. Higher Edn., 1973-75; budget analyst Ill. Bur. Budget, Office of Gov., 1972-73; admissions officer Princeton U., 1971-72; adj. prof. Northwestern U., Evanston, Ill., 1994. Comment editor U. Chgo. Law Rev., 1977-78. Bd. dirs. Chgo. Lawyers Com. for Civil Rights Under Law, 1989-94, Pub. Interest Law Initiative, 1989-94. Mem. ABA, Chgo. Coun. Lawyers (bd. govs. 1987-91, legal counsel 1986-87), 7th Cir. Bar Assn., Women's Bar Assn. of Ill. Office: Kirkland & Ellis Citicorp Ctr 153 E 53rd St New York NY 10022-4602

LINDBURG, DAYTHA EILEEN, physician assistant; b. Emporia, Kans., June 24, 1952; d. Kenneth Eugene and Elsie Eileen (Smith) L. BS cum laude, Kans. State U., 1974; BS magna cum laude, Wichita State U., 1976. Registered cert. physician asst. Physician asst. in family practice Fredrickson Clinic, Lindsborg, Kans., 1976-93; physician asst. in ob/gyn. Mowery Clinic, Salina, Kans., 1993—; cons. McPherson County (Kans.) Health Dept., 1983—. Mem. adv. bd. Riverview Estates Nursing Home, 1980-86; bd. dirs. McPherson County Humane Soc., 1989-93; choir mem. Messiah Luth. Ch., Lindsborg, 1981—, liturgist, 1991—, mem. Altar Guild, 1976—, mem. music and worship com., 1981-88. Kans. Bd. Regents scholar, 1970-71, Kans. State U. scholar, 1972, 73, Smurthwaite scholar, 1970-74. Mem. Assn. of Physician Assts. in Obstetrics and Gynecology, Kans. Acad. Physician Assts., Am. Acad. Physician Asst. Avocations: crafts, floral arranging, piano, reading, drawing.

LINDE, HANS ARTHUR, state supreme court justice; b. Berlin, Germany, Apr. 15, 1924; came to U.S., 1939, naturalized, 1943; s. Bruno C. and Luise (Rosenhain) L.; m. Helen Tucker, Aug. 13, 1945; children: Lisa, David Tucker. BA, Reed Coll., 1947; JD, U. Calif., Berkeley, 1950. Bar: Oreg. 1951. Law clk. U.S. Supreme Ct. Justice William O. Douglas, 1950-51; atty. Office of Legal Adviser, Dept. State, 1951-53; pvt. practice Portland, Oreg., 1953-54; legis. asst. U.S. Sen. Richard L. Neuberger, 1955-58; from assoc. prof. to prof. U. Oreg. Law Sch., 1959-76; justice Oreg. Supreme Ct., Salem, 1977-90, sr. judge, 1990—; Fulbright lectr. Freiburg U., 1967-68, Hamburg U., 1975-76; cons. U.S. ACDA, Dept. Def., 1962-76; mem. Adminstrv. Conf. U.S., 1978-82. Author: (with George Bunn) Legislative and Administrative Processes, 1976. Mem. Oreg. Constl. Revision Commn., 1961-62, Oreg. Commn. on Pub. Broadcasting, 1990-93. With U.S. Army, 1943-46. Fellow Am. Acad. Arts and Scis.; mem. Am. Law Inst. (council), Order of Coif, Phi Beta Kappa.

LINDE, MAXINE HELEN, lawyer, business executive, private investor; b. Chgo., Sept. 2, 1939; d. Jack and Lottie (Kroll) Stern; B.A. summa cum laude, UCLA, 1961; J.D., Stanford U., 1967; m. Ronald K. Linde, June 12, 1960. Bar: Calif. 1968. Applied mathematician, reseach engr. Jet Propulsion Lab., Pasadena, Calif., 1961-64; law clk. U.S. Dist. Ct. No. Calif., 1967-68; mem. firm Long & Levit, San Francisco, 1968-69, Swerdlow, Glikbarg & Shimer, Beverly Hills, Calif., 1969-72; sec., gen. counsel Envirodyne Industries, Inc., Chgo., 1972-89; pres. The Ronald and Maxine Linde Found., 1989—; vice chmn. bd., gen. counsel Titan Fin. Group, LLC, Chgo., 1994—. Mem. bd. visitors Stanford Law Sch., 1989-92, law and bus. adv. coun., 1991-94, dean's adv. coun. 1992-94. Mem. Order of Coif, Phi Beta Kappa, Pi Mu Epsilon, Alpha Lambda Delta.

LINDE, ROBERT HERMANN, economics educator; b. Schlewecke, Germany, July 22, 1944; s. Robert and Emma (Lohmann) L.; m. Sabine Rinck, Mar. 12, 1976 (div. 1985); children: Niels Christian, Johanne Cornelia; m. Ingrid Windus, June 30, 1987. Diploma in Econs., U. Gottingen, Fed. Republic Germany, 1969, D in Polit. Sci., 1977, D in Habilitation, 1981. Asst. U. Gottingen, 1976-81, lectr., 1981-86, prof. econs., 1986-87; prof. econs. U. Luneburg, Fed. Republic Germany, 1987—. Author: Theory of Product Quality, 1977, Pay and Performance, 1984, Introduction to Microeconomics, 2d edit., 1992; co-author: Production Theory, 1976. Mem. Am. Econ. Assn., Verein für Socialpolitik, European Econ. Assn. Office: U Luneburg, Scharnhorststrasse 1 Haus 4, 21332 Luneburg Germany

LINDE, RONALD KEITH, corporate executive, private investor; b. L.A., Jan. 31, 1940; s. Morris and Sonia Doreen (Hayman) L.; m. Maxine Helen Stern, June 12, 1960. BS with honors, UCLA, 1961; MS (Inst. scholar), Calif. Inst. Tech., 1962, PhD (ARCS scholar, Rutherford scholar), 1964. Cons. Litton Industries, L.A., 1961-63, engr., 1961; materials scientist Poulter Labs., Stanford Rsch. Inst., Menlo Park, Calif., 1964; head solid state rsch. Stanford Rsch. Inst., Menlo Park, Calif., 1965-67; chmn. shock wave physics dept., mgr. tech. svcs. Poulter Labs., 1967, dir. shock and high pressure physics div., 1967-68, chief exec. labs., 1968-69; dir. phys. scis. Stanford Rsch. Inst., 1968-69; chmn. bd., CEO Envirodyne Industries, Inc., Chgo., 1969-89; chmn. bd. The Ronald and Maxine Linde Found., Chgo., 1989—; co-chmn. bd. Titan Fin. Group, LLC, Chgo., 1994—; law and bus. adv. coun. Stanford Law Sch., 1991-94, dean's adv. coun. 1992-94. Contbr. articles to various publs.; patentee in field. Mem. adv. bd. ARCS Found., Chgo., 1993—; mem. Northwestern U. Assocs., 1978—; trustee Calif. Inst. Tech., 1989—, Harvey Mudd Coll., 1989—, vice chmn., bd. trustees, 1993—. Mem. Sigma Xi, Tau Beta Pi, Phi Eta Sigma. Office: Linde Found Unit 5801 180 E Pearson St Chicago IL 60611-2115

LINDELL, EDWARD ALBERT, former college president, religious organization administrator; b. Denver, Nov. 30, 1928; s. Edward Gustaf and Estelle (Lundin) L.; m. Patricia Clare Eckert, Sept. 2, 1965; children—Edward Paul, Erik Adam. B.A., U. Denver, 1950, M.A., 1956, Ed.D., 1960, L.H.D. (hon.), 1975; Litt.D. (hon.), Tusculum Coll., 1979; D.H.L. (hon.), Roanoke Coll., 1981; Litt.D (hon.), Christ Coll., Irvine, 1992. Tchr. N. Denver High Sch., 1952-61; asst. dean Coll. Arts and Scis., U. Denver, 1961-65, dean, 1965-75; pres. Gustavus Adolphus Coll., St. Peter, Minn., 1975-80, Luth. Brotherhood Mut. Funds, Mpls., Minn., 1980—; v.p. Lutheran Brotherhood Found., 1980—, exec. dir. Mem. exec. bd. Rocky Mountain Synod Lutheran Ch. Am., 1968—, also pres. bd. coll. edn. and ch. vocations.; Trustee Midland Luth. Coll., Fremont, Nebr., Kans. Wesleyan U., Colo. Assn. Ind. Colls. and Univs., Luth. Med. Center, Wheatridge, Colo., Luth. Sch. Theology, Chgo., 1975—, St. John's U., Minn., 1978—; bd. dirs. Pacific Luth. Theol. Sem., 1978-80, Loretto Heights Coll., Colo., 1978-86, Swedish Council Am., 1978—, Gettysburg Theol. Sem., 1981-83; exec. bd. Luth. Council U.S.A., v.p., 1975—; mem. adv. bd. Royal Swedish Acad. Scis., 1980; v.p. Am.-Swedish Inst., 1980; exec. v.p. for external affairs Luth. Brotherhood, 1981—; pres. Nat. Fraternal Congress Am., 1988—; bd. dirs. Wittenberg U., 1988, Bethany Coll., 1991—, Minn. Orch., 1983—, Am. Scandinavian Found., 1982—, Fairview Hosp., 1982—, U.S. Swedish Found. Internat. Sci. Rsch., 1981— (v.p. 1986—), Habitat for Humanity Internat., 1992—. Named Outstanding Faculty Mem. Coll. Arts and Scis., U. Denver, 1964; decorated knight King of Sweden, 1976; recipient Suomi Disting. Svc. award, 1989. Mem. Swedish Pioneer Hist. Soc. (dir. 1979—), U. Denver Alumni Assn. (Career Alumni Achievement award 1994), Phi Beta Kappa. Office: Luth Brotherhood Mut Funds 625 4th Ave S Minneapolis MN 55415-1624

LINDEMANN, EDNA MEIBOHM, museum director, art consultant; b. Buffalo, N.Y., Feb. 25, 1915; d. Carl H. and Pearl (Nason) Meibohm; m. Fred H. Lindemann (dec.). BS in Art with distinction, U. Buffalo, 1936; MA in Art magna cum laude, Northwestern U., 1939; studies with Eliel Saarinen, Cranbrook Acad., 1940-42; EdD in Art, Columbia U., 1956. Instr. U. Buffalo, N.Y., 1936-47, U. Vt., Burlington, 1945-46, NYU, 1949-56; prof. design SUNY, Buffalo, 1956-66, dir. cultural affairs, 1960-66; founding dir. Burchfield Art Ctr., Buffalo, 1967-85; pvt. practice art cons., appraiser, 1985—; dir. emeritus Burchfield Art Ctr., 1985—. Organizer exhbns., including Burchfield Internat. Exhbn., 1968, Emily Dickinson Tribute Exhbn., 1977, 150 Yrs. of Portraiture in Western N.Y., 1981, Design in Buffalo, 1982, Nevelsons of Western N.Y., 1984, Niagara Falls, New Impressions, 1985, Robert N. Blair, A Soldier's Portfolio, 1985; curator exhbn., author catalog Burchfield and His Colleagues, 1989. Mem. Creative Leadership Council, Buffalo, 1969—; founding mem., bd. dirs. Maude Gordon Homes Arboretum, Buffalo, 1966-78; trustee Buffalo State Coll. Found., 1969-85. Recipient Focus award Buffalo Courier-Express, 1976, Outstanding Patron award Buffalo Soc. Artists, 1981, Achievement award AAUW, 1983; named Citizen of Yr. Buffalo News, 1985. Mem. Appraisers Assn. Am. Inc., Gallery Assn. N.Y. State (founding, chair 1969-79), Assoc. Coll. and U. Mus. (recording sec. 1980-83). Avocations: landscape and architectural design. Home and Office: 52 Behm Rd West Falls NY 14170-9741

LINDEMER, LAWRENCE BOYD, lawyer, former utility executive, former state justice; b. Syracuse, N.Y., Aug. 21, 1921; s. George F. and Altamae (Reimers) L.; children—Lawrence Boyd, David G. Student, Taft Sch., 1939, Hamilton Coll., 1939-41; A.B., U. Mich., 1943, LL.B., 1948. Bar: Mich. 1948. Asst. pros. atty. Ingham County, 1949-51; asst., commn. on orgn. Exec. Br. Govt., Hoover Comm., 1953-55; partner Foster, Lindemer, Swift & Collins (and predecessor firm), 1955-75; justice Mich. Supreme Ct., Lansing, 1975-76; sr. v.p., gen. counsel Consumers Power Co., 1977-86. Mem. Mich. Ho. of Reps., 1951-52; Republican state chmn., 1957-61; mem. Rep. Nat. Com., 1957-61; Rep. candidate atty. gen. Mich., 1966; bd. regents U. Mich., 1968-75; trustee Gerald R. Ford Found., 1985—. Served with USAAF, 1943-45. Mem. ABA, State. Bar Mich. (commr. 1963-70), Mich. State Bd. Ethics, U. Mich. Alumni Assn. (pres. 1983-85), Am. Automobile Assn. (bd. dirs. 1987-96, chmn. 1993-95), Auto Club Mich. (b.d dirs. 1977-96, chmn. bd. 1985-87). Presbyterian (elder). Home: PO Box 667 Stockbridge MI 49285-0667 Office: Foster Swift Collins & Smith PC 313 Washington Sq S Lansing MI 48933-2122

LINDEMULDER, CAROL ANN, interior designer, artist; b. San Diego, May 2, 1936; d. Franklin Geert and Leone Augusta (Oltman) L. BA in Decorative Arts, U. Calif., Berkeley, 1959; postgrad. in fine arts, San Diego State U., 1965-67. Tchr. interior design and fine arts adult edn. divsn. San Diego City Schs., 1960-67; with Milo of Calif., Inc. subs. Milo Electronics Corp., 1968-73, corp. staff asst., 1972, asst. to dir. mktg., 1972-73; with Frazee Industries, 1975-77; owner, designer-artist Call Carol, San Diego, 1976--; former instr. U. Calif. Extension, San Diego, instr. San Diego landscape painting, 1993—. One-woman show Point Loma Art Assn., 1967, Scandia Interiors, 1977, Cen. Fed. Savs. & Loan, 1978, John Duncan Interiors, 1979, Villa Montezuma Mus., 198l; exhibited in group shows Calif. Western U., 1963, Jewish Community Ctr., 1963-64, So. Calif. Expn., 1964, San Diego Mus. Art, 1966, 71, 75, San Diego State U., 1974, Spectrum Gallery, 1985, A.R.T. Beasley Gallery, 1985, Atrium Gallery, Mich., 1989, San Diego Artist Showcase, 1991. Coord. Christmas program San Diego Community Vol. Bur., 196l; a founder, treas., bd. dirs. Save Our Heritage Orgn., 1969-7l, pres., 1974-75, 79-81; mem. San Diego Hist. Sites Bd., 1985-93, vice chmn., 1985-92; founder, pres. Save the Coaster Com., 1981-83; co-founder San Diego Hist. Preservation Endowment Fund, 1990; mem. Calif. Preservation Found. Named Vol. of Month, San Diego Community Vol. Bur., 196l; recipient President's commendation Save Our Heritage Orgn., 1984. Mem. Nature Conservancy, Jr. League San Diego. Republican. Avocations: gardening, travel. Office: PO Box 81718 San Diego CA 92138-1718

LINDEN, CAROL MARIE, special education educator; b. Pitts., Dec. 24, 1953; d. Enio P. and Mary C. (Santillo) Cardone; m. Frank J. Miller Jr., Dec. 21, 1974 (div. 1989); children: Emily, Karl, Richard; m. James Anthony Linden, Dec. 9, 1989; children: Shiloh, Shane, Shasta, Shelby (dec.). BS, California (Pa.) State U., 1974; MS, Youngstown State U., 1981. Cert. moderate, severe, profoundly retarded, educable mentally retarded, learning disabled/behavior disordered, speech and hearing. Tchr. multi-handicapped Youngstown (Ohio) City Schs., 1987—; tchr. multihandicapped Trumbull County Bd. Edn., Lordstown, Ohio, 1986-87; spl. vocat. edn. coord. Trumbull County Joint Vocat. Sch., Warren, Ohio, 1985-86; lang. devel. specialist Fairhaven Sheltered Workshop, Niles and Champion, Ohio, 1976-85. Grantee N.E. Ohio Spl. Edn. Resource Ctr., 1989-92, Ohio Bell and Ameritech Impact II, 1991-92, 95, Consumer/Econ. grantee, 1989-95; Wolves Club Carapolis scholar, 1971. Mem. Ohio Speech and Hearing Assn., Coun. for Exceptional Children, Nat. Soc. for Autistic Citizens (sec. 1986-87). Roman Catholic/Baptist. Avocations: reading, crafts, camping. Home: 432 Hunter Ave Niles OH 44446-1625

LINDEN, HAL, actor, singer; b. Bronx, N.Y., Mar. 20, 1931; s. Charles and Frances (Rosen) Lipshitz; m. Frances Martin, Apr. 13, 1958; children: Amelia Christine, Jennifer Dru, Nora Kathryn, Ian Martin. BBA, CCNY, 1952; student, Am. Theatre Wing, N.Y.C., 1954-55; student acting, Paul Mann, 1956-60, Lloyd Richards, 1962-63; student voice, Lou McCollogh, 1953-56, John Mace, 1958-64. Saxophone player and singer; played with bands of Sammy Kaye, Bobby Sherwood and, Boyd Raeburn; stage debut in Wonderful Town, Cape Cod Melody Tent, Hyannis, Mass., 1955; N.Y. stage debut as understudy to Sydney Chaplain in Bells are Ringing, 1956, then took over lead; other stage appearances include The Rothschilds (Tony award 1971), Three Men on a Horse, Anything Goes, Pajama Game, I'm Not Rappaport, 1987, The Sisters Rosensweig, 1993; appeared in film Bells are Ringing, 1959, When You Comin' Back, Red Ryder?, 1979, A New Life, 1988; TV series Barney Miller, 1975-82, Blacke's Magic, 1985-86, Jack's Place, 1992-93, The Boys are Back, 1994-95; host: children's series Animals Animals Animals; informational series FYI, ABC-TV, 1980; narrator: series Saga of the Western World, 1963-64; film When You Comin' Back, Red Ryder?, 1979, A New Life, 1988; TV films include Mr. Outside, 1973, The Love Boat, 1976, How to Break a Happy Divorce, 1976, Father Figure, 1980, Starflight, the Plane That Couldn't Land, 1983, The Other Woman, 1983, My Wicked, Wicked Ways: The Legend of Errol Flynn, 1985, The O'Connors, Dream Breakers, 1989; appeared with L.A. Philharm. Orch., Hollywood Bowl, 1984. Served in U.S. Army, 1952-54. Mem. Actors Equity, Screen Actors Guild, AFTRA, AGVA, Am. Fedn. Musicians. Office: William Morris Agy 151 El Camino Beverly Hills CA 90212*

LINDEN, HENRY ROBERT, chemical engineering research executive; b. Vienna, Austria, Feb. 21, 1922; came to U.S., 1939, naturalized, 1945; s. Fred and Edith (Lermer) L.; m. Natalie Govedarica, 1967; children by previous marriage: Robert, Debra. BS, Ga. Inst. Tech., 1944; MChemE, Poly. U., 1947; PhD, Ill. Inst. Tech., 1952. Chem. engr. Socony Vacuum Labs., 1944-47; with Inst. of Gas Tech., 1947-78, various rsch. mgmt. positions, 1947-61, dir., 1961-69, exec. v.p., dir., 1969-74, pres., trustee, 1974-78; various acad. appointments Ill. Inst. Tech., Chgo, 1954-86, Frank W. Gunsaulus Disting. Prof. chem. engring., 1987-90, McGraw prof. energy and power engring. and mgmt., 1990—, interim pres., CEO, 1989-90, interim chmn., CEO Ill. Inst. Tech. Rsch. Inst., 1989-90; COO, Gas Devel. Corp. subs. Inst. Gas Tech., Chgo., 1965-73, CEO, 1973-78, also bd. dirs.; pres., dir. Gas Rsch. Inst., Chgo., 1976-87, exec. advisor, 1987—; bd. dirs. Centennial Holdings, Inc., AES Corp., Resources for the Future Inc. Author tech. articles; holder U.S. and fgn. patents in fuel tech. Recipient award of merit oper. sect. Am. Gas Assn., 1956, Disting. Svc. award, 1974, Gas Industry Rsch. award, 1982, R & D award Nat. Energy Resources Orgn., 1986, Homer H. Lowry award for excellence in fossil energy rsch. U.S. Dept. Energy, 1991, award U.S. Energy Assn., 1993, Walton Clark medala Franklin Inst., 1972, Bunsen-Pettenkofer-Ehrentafel medal Deutscher Verein des Gas und Wasserfaches, 1978, Alumni medal Ill. Inst. Tech., 1995; named to Hall of Fame, Ill. Inst. Tech., 1982. Fellow AIChE, Inst. Energy; mem. NAE, Am. Chem. Soc. (recipient H.H. Storch award, chmn. divsn. fuel chemistry 1967, councilor 1969-77), So. Gas Assn. (hon. life). Office: Ill Inst Tech PH 135 10 W 33d St Chicago IL 60616-3730 also: Gas Rsch Inst 8600 W Bryn Mawr Ave Chicago IL 60631-3505

LINDENBAUM, SANDFORD RICHARD, lawyer; b. N.Y.C., July 6, 1948; s. Sidney Lewis and Ruth Jane (Krauskopf) L.; m. Leslie Sircus, Jan. 17, 1982; children: Dara, David. BA, Franklin & Marshall Coll., 1970; JD with honors, George Washington U., 1973. Bar: N.Y. 1974, U.S. Dist. Ct. (so. dist.) N.Y. 1975, U.S. Dist. Ct. (no. dist.) N.Y. 1985. Asst. dist. atty. County of Westchester, White Plains, N.Y., 1973-78; from assoc. to ptnr. Bower & Gardner, N.Y.C., 1978-94; assoc. Garbarini & Scher, N.Y.C., 1994—. Mem. ABA, N.Y. State Bar Assn. Office: Garbarini and Scher 1114 Avenue Of The Americas New York NY 10036-7703

LINDENBAUM, S(EYMOUR) J(OSEPH), physicist; b. N.Y.C., Feb. 3, 1925; s. Morris and Anne Lindenbaum; m. Leda Isaacs, June 29, 1958. A.B., Princeton U., 1945; M.A., Columbia U., 1949, Ph.D., 1951. With Brookhaven Nat. Lab., Upton, N.Y., 1951—; sr. physicist Brookhaven Nat. Lab., 1963—, group leader high energy physics research group, 1954-89; vis. prof. U. Rochester, 1958-59; Mark W. Zemansky chair in physics CCNY, 1970—; cons. Centre de Etudes Nucleaire de Saclay, France, 1957, CERN, Geneva, 1962; head CCNY Experimental High Energy Physics Rsch. Group, 1970—; dep. for sci. affairs ERDA, 1976-77. Author: Particle Interaction Physics at High Energies, 1973. Contbr. articles to profl. jours. Fellow Am. Phys. Soc.; mem. N.Y. Acad. Scis., AAAS. Achievements include discovering nucleon isobars dominated high energy particles interactions, isobar model; inventor on line computer technique in scientific experiments; proved experimentally that Einstein's special theory of relativity was correct down to subnuclear distances one hundredth the radius of a proton; discovered the glueball states predicted by quantum chromodynamics. Office: Brookhaven Nat Lab Dept Physics Upton NY 11973 *I was always fascinated by the orderly and powerful laws of nature. Thus I decided to concentrate on one of mankind's greatest intellectual endeavours—scientific inquiry into the physical laws which govern our universe.*

LINDENBERG, STEVEN PHILLIP, counselor, consultant; b. Lancaster, Pa., Dec. 6, 1945; s. Sidney David and Ruth Lillian (Levine) L.; m. Linda Kathleen Young, Aug. 26, 1967; children: Sara Michelle, Karen Rebecca, Elisabeth Claudine. BS, Millersville U., 1968; MEd, Shippensburg State U., 1974; PhD, U. Ga., 1977. Cert. clin. mental health counselor, Nat. Acad. Cert. Clin. Health Counseling, cert. counselor Nat. Bd. Cert. Counselors, cert. sch. psychologist, Pa. Jr. high sci. tchr. Chambersburg (Pa.) Area Sch. Dist., 1972-74; grad. asst. dept. counseling edn. Univ. Ga., Athens, 1974-77; ptnr., cert. clin. mental health counselor Hershey (Pa.) Psychiat. Assocs., 1977-93; founder Lindenberg Inst. for Therapy, 1993—; co-founder, 1st vice-chair Nat. Acad. Cert. Clin. Mental Health Counselors, Falls Church, Va., 1978-80; founder Lindenberg & David, Assocs., Hershey, 1990—; bd. dirs. Ctrl. Pa. Behavioral Health Network. Mem. editorial bd.: Jour. Mental Health Counseling, 1991-94, author: Group Psychotherapy with People Who Are Dying, 1983; contbr. articles to profl. jours. Founding bd. mem. Hospice of En. Pa., Enola, 1978-87, past pres., mem. bereavement com. 1978-93; mem. profl. devel. com. Am. Cancer Soc., Harrisburg, Pa., 1986-87; past pres., mem. bd. sch. dirs. No. Lebanon Sch. Dist., Fredericksburg, Pa., 1988-93. Decorated Am. Spirit of Honor medal Citizens Com. for Army, Navy and Air Force, Inc., Lackland AFB, Tex., 1968. Mem. AACD (bd. dirs. 1979-80), Am. Mental Health Counselors Assn. (pres. 1979-80, profl. recognition awards 1981, 89, charter mem.), Pa. Mental Health Counselors Assn. (treas. 1993-95, pres. 1995—, eminent practitioner 1988), Pa. Alliance Counseling Profls. (pres.-elect 1995-96, pres. 1996—), Dauphin County Bar Assn. (task force mem. 1994—), Phi Kappa Phi, Kappa Delta Pi. Avocations: real estate investment, writing, music composition and performance, gardening. Office: Lindenberg Inst Therapy 218 W Governor Rd Hershey PA 17033-1726

LINDENBERGER, HERBERT SAMUEL, writer, literature educator; b. Los Angeles, Apr. 4, 1929; s. Hermann and Celia (Weinkrantz) L.; m. Claire Flaherty, June 14, 1961; children: Michael James, Elizabeth Celia. BA, Antioch Coll., Yellow Springs, Ohio, 1951; PhD, U. Wash., Seattle, 1955. From instr. to prof. English and comparative lit. U. Calif., Riverside, 1954-66; prof. German and English, chmn. program comparative lit. Washington U., St. Louis, 1966-69; Avalon prof. humanities Stanford U., 1969—, chmn. program comparative lit., 1969-82; dir. Stanford Humanities Ctr., 1991-92. Author: On Wordsworth's Prelude, 1963, Georg Büchner, 1964, (play) Lear and Cordelia at Home, 1968, Georg Trakl, 1971, Historical Drama: The Relation of Literature and Reality, 1975, Saul's Fall: A Critical Fiction, 1979, Opera: The Extravagant Art, 1984, The History in Literature: On Value, Genre, Institutions, 1990; contbr. articles to profl. jours. Fulbright scholar Austria, 1952-53; Guggenheim fellow, 1968-69; Nat. Endowment Humanities fellow, 1975-76, 82-83; Stanford U. Humanities Center Fellow, 1982-83. Mem. MLA (2d v.p. to pres. 1995-97), Am. Comparative Lit. Assn. Office: Stanford Univ Dept Comparative Lit Stanford CA 94305

LINDENFELD, PETER, physics educator; b. Vienna, Austria, Mar. 10, 1925; came to U.S., 1948, naturalized, 1957; s. Bela and Elda (Lachs) L.; m. Lore Kadden, May 31,1953; children: Thomas, Naomi. Student, U. Man., Can., 1942-43; B.A.Sc., U.B.C., Can., 1946, M.A. Sc., 1948; Ph.D., Columbia U., 1954. Vis. lectr. Drew U., Madison, N.J., 1952-53; instr. Rutgers U., 1953-55, asst. prof. physics, 1955-61, assoc. prof., 1961-66, prof., 1966—; cons. summer inst. AID, Tirupati, India, 1965; regional counselor N.J. Am.. Inst. Physics, 1963-71; dir. NSF In-svc. Insts. High Sch. Tchrs., 1964-66; Rutgers Rsch. Coun. fellow and guest scientist Faculte de Scis., U. Paris-Sud, Orsay, France, 1970-71; vis. scholar Kyoto U., Japan, 1982. Contbr. articles to profl. jours. Recipient Warren I. Susman award for excellence in teaching, 1988, Robert A. Millikan Lecture award and medal Am. Assn. Physics Tchrs., 1989. Fellow Am. Phys. Soc.; mem. AAUP, Am. Assn. Physics Tchrs. (hon. mem. N.J. sect.). Home: 121 Harris Rd Princeton NJ 08540-3375 Office: Rutgers U Dept Physics and Astronomy Piscataway NJ 08855-0849

LINDENLAUB, J.C., electrical engineer, educator; b. Milw., Sept. 10, 1933; m. Deborah Hart, 1957; children: Brian, Mark, Anne, David. BS, MIT, 1955, MS, 1957; PhD in Elec. Engring., Purdue U., 1961. From asst. prof. to assoc. prof. Purdue U., West Lafayette, Ind., 1961-62, dir. Ctr. instrnl. Devel. Engring., 1977-81, prof. elec. engring., 1972—; mem. tech. staff Bell Telephone Labs., 1968-69. Recipient Helen Plants award Frontiers in Edn. Conf., 1980; Danforth Found. assoc., 1966. Fellow IEEE (Edn. Soc. Achievement award 1984), Am. Soc. Engring. Edn. (Chester F. Carlson award 1988). Office: Purdue Univ Electrical Eng School Lafayette IN 47907*

LINDER, BERTRAM NORMAN, foundation administrator, horse-breeder, actor; b. N.Y.C., Nov. 24, 1915; s. Albert Aaron and Bess (Newman) L.; m. Eleanor Jones (dec.); children: Robert Allan (dec.), Denise J.; m. Mary Ellen Smith. BA, Williams Coll., 1936; postgrad., Yale U., 1937-38, Columbia U., 1938-39. V.p. Linder Bros., Inc., Scranton, Pa., 1940-65, pres., treas., 1965-80; pres., treas. Albert A. & Bertram N. Linder Found., Inc., N.Y.C., 1965—; owner Hickory Hill Farm, Dalton, Pa., 1947—. Author: Songs to the Night, 1941. Pres. Jewish Fedn., Scranton, 1949-52; pres., co-founder Child Guidance & Psychiatry Ctr., Lackawanna County, Pa.; chmn. adv. bd. Salvation Army, Scranton, 1947-50; pres. United Way, Lackawanna County, 1960-63. 1st lt. inf. U.S. Army, 1943-46, ETO. Recipient Community Svc. award Scranton C. of C., 1949, Salvation Army, 1950, Citizenship award AFL-CIO, 1962, 65, Americanism award B'nai B'rith, 1965. Mem. AFTRA, SAG, Thoroughbred Owners and Breeders Assn., Thoroughbred of Am. Club (Lexington, Ky.), N.Y. Thoroughbred Breeders, Ky. Thoroughbred Assn., Penn Horse Breeders Assn., B'nai B'rith, Phi Beta Kappa. Republican. Jewish. Avocations: fishing, travel. Home: Hickory Hill Farm W Main St Dalton PA 18414-9522 Office: Linder Found Inc 305 E 40th St New York NY 10016-2189

LINDER, JOHN E, congressman, dentist; b. Deer River, Minn., Sept. 2, 1942; s. Henry and Vera Elizabeth Davis L.; m. Lynne Leslee Peterson, 1963; children: Kristine Kerry, Matthew John. BS, U. Minn., 1963, DDS, 1967. Pvt. practice Atlanta, Ga., 1967-82; mem. Ga. Ho. of Reps., 1975-80, 82-90; pres. Linder Fin. Corp., 1977-92; mem. 103d-104th Congress from 4th Ga. Dist., 1993—; house rules com., subcom. on legis. process, Rep. steering com., NRCC exec. com. U.S. Ho. of Reps. Founder I Care, 1970. Capt. USAF, 1967-69. Mem. ADA, Ga. Dental Assn., No. Dist. Dental Soc., Rotary. Republican. Presbyterian. Office: US Ho of Reps 1318 Longworth Bldg Washington DC 20515-0004

LINDER, STU, film editor. Editor: (films) The Fortune, 1975, (with Susan Martin) First Family, 1980, My Bodyguard, 1980, Six Weeks, 1982, Diner, 1982, The Natural, 1984, Young Sherlock Holmes, 1985, Code Name: Emerald, 1985, Good Morning, Vietnam, 1987, Tin Men, 1987, Rain Man, 1988 (Academy award nomination best film editing 1988), Avalon, 1990, Bugsy, 1991, Toys, 1992, Quiz Show, 1994. Office: care Motion Picture Editors 9898 Beverly Grove Dr Beverly Hills CA 90210

LINDERS, JOHN R., engineering executive, electric engineer; b. Cleve., Sept. 30, 1908. BSEE cum laude, Lafayette Coll., 1930. Pres. Nordon Techs., Inc. Fellow IEEE (Disting. Svc. award power sys. relaying com. 1983, PES recognition award for chmn. of the noteworthy 1987 working group report, prize paper award 1990); mem. Tau Beta Pi, Eta Kappa Nu. Office: Nordon Tech Inc 1781 Independence Blvd/Ste 4 Sarasota FL 34234*

LINDGREN, A(LAN) BRUCE, church administrator; b. Grand Rapids, Mich., July 1, 1948; m. Carole Coonce; children: Stacey, Michael, David (dec.). BS in Sociology, Mich. State U., 1970; MDiv, St. Paul Sch. Theology, 1975. Ordained high priest. Campus minister Park Coll., 1975-77; dir. ministerial edn. Temple Sch., 1986-92; exec. min., World Ch. sec., exec. asst. to 1st presidency Reorganized Ch. of Jesus Christ of Latter Day Saints, 1992—; dir. devel. basic leadership curriculum Temple Sch., 1977-86. Editor: Leaders Handbook, 1985-92. Office: Reorganized Ch of Jesus Christ PO Box 1059 Independence MO 64051-0559

LINDGREN, D(ERBIN) KENNETH, JR., lawyer; b. Mpls., Aug. 25, 1932; s. Derbin Kenneth and Margaret (Anderson) L.; m. Patricia Ann Ransier, Dec. 17, 1955; children—Christian Kenneth, Carol Ann, Charles Derbin. BS, U. Minn., 1954, JD, 1958. Bar: Minn. 1958, U.S. Supreme Ct. 1968, U.S. Tax Ct. 1959, U.S. Ct. Appeals (D.C. cir.) 1981. Gen. practice law Mpls., 1958—; mem. Larkin, Hoffman, Daly & Lindgren, Ltd., Mpls., 1960-95, of counsel, 1995—. Contbr. articles to profl. jours. Active Ind. Sch. Dist. 287 Bd. Edn. (Area Vocat. Tech. Coll.), 1979-83, Ind. Sch. Dist. 274 Bd. Edn., Hopkins, Minn., 1970-76, chmn., 1972-76; trustee Mpls. Soc. Fine Arts, 1982-88; Minn. Landscape Arboretum Found., 1989—, pres., 1992-95; bd. overseers Mpls. Inst. Art, 1986-88, Mpls. Coll. Art and Design, 1980-86, vice-chmn., 1982-83, chmn., 1983-86, trustee, 1988-96; active Govs. Commn. on Reform Govt., 1983. Lt. USAF, 1955-57. Fellow Am. Coll. Trust and Estate Counsel; mem. ABA, Minn. Bar Assn., Hennepin County Bar Assn., Alpha Delta Pi, Phi Delta Phi. Congregationalist. Clubs: Mpls. Athletic; Interlachen Country. Home: 225 Hawthorne Rd Hopkins MN 55343-8511 Office: 1500 Norwest Financial Ctr 7900 Xerxes Ave S Minneapolis MN 55431-1106

LINDGREN, JENNIFER GOUX, business executive, financial planner, educator; b. L.A., Jan. 10, 1946; d. Warren Goux and Violet (Louis) Goux Knupp; m. Larry E. Lindgren, July 1, 1967; children: Todd E., Kristen E., Kurt W. BA in Psychology, UCLA, 1967. Cert. tchr., Calif.; CFP; gen. securities lec., Calif.; lic. ins. agt., Calif. Elem. tchr. L.A. City Schs., 1968-72; art tchr. Sierra Canyon Day Camp, Newhall, Calif., summer 1975,76; co-owner Lindgren's Jewelry, Porterville, Calif., 1978—; instr. Porterville Adult Sch., 1988-94; investment exec. Baraban Securities/Volker Ins., Woodland Hills, Calif., 1989-94, Fin. West Group, Tarzana, Calif., 1994, Investment Ctrs. of Am., Bank of Sierra, Porterville, 1995—. Troop co-leader Girl Scouts U.S., Porterville, 1984-86; student host family Rotary Internat., Porterville, 1990-91; sec.-treas. Porterville Edn. Found., 1988—. Mem. AAUW (pres., v.p., other offices 1987—, Named Gift honoree 1991), Inst. CFPs, Central Valley Soc. CFPs, UCLA Alumni Assn., Porterville C. of C., Zonta Club. Republican. Avocations: bicycling, boating, skiing, walking, gourmet cooking. Office: 90 N Main St Porterville CA 93257-3712

LINDGREN, JOHN RALPH, philosophy educator; b. Oak Park, Ill., Oct. 8, 1933; s. Francis L. and Leona (Toussaint) Nichols; m. Shirley Ann Tryon, Dec. 27, 1958; children: J. Thomas, Michael B., David J., Timothy P., Kathryn A. B.S. in Bus. Adminstrn., Northwestern U., 1959; M.A. in Philosophy, Marquette U., 1961, Ph.D. in Philosophy, 1963. Instr. dept. philosophy Holy Cross Coll., Worcester, Mass., 1962-64, asst. prof., 1964-65; asst. prof. Lehigh U., Bethlehem, Pa., 1965-69, assoc. prof., 1969-79, chmn. dept. philosophy, 1973-85, dir. law and legal instns. program, 1978-94, prof., 1979-95, William Wilson Selfridge prof., 1985-88, Clara H. Stewardson prof., 1989-95; vis. scholar Oxford U., 1986, U. Pa. Law Sch., Phila., 1977-78. Author: Social Philosophy of Adam Smith, 1973, Sex Discrimination in Higher Education, 1984, The Law of Sex Discrimination, 1988, 2d edit., 1993; editor: Early Writing of Adam Smith, 1967, Horizons of Justice, 1996. Mem. adv. bd. Alternatives to Violence Project University City Sci. Ctr., Phila., 1980-83. Served with U.S. Army, 1953-55. Mem. Am. Philos. Assn., Internat. Soc. for Philosophy of Law (exec. bd. dirs. 1981-83), Soc. for Philosophy and Pub. Affairs (exec. bd. 1987-95). Democrat. Office: Lehigh U Dept Philosophy 15 University Dr Bethlehem PA 18015-3057

LINDGREN, ROBERT KEMPER, securities investor, county tax collector; b. LaPorte, Ind., Sept. 25, 1939; s. Ralph Arthur and Georgia Lillian (Kemper) L.; m. Charmaine Katherine Freeman, Feb. 2, 1963; children: Scott Edward, Amber Louise, Vincent Kemper. Grad., Culver Mil. Acad., 1958; BS, Western Mich. U., 1963. Comml. printing mgr. Livingston (Mont.) Enterprise Comml. Printing, Livingston, 1968-70; prodn. mgr. Mont. Graphic Arts Ctr., div. of Lee Enterprises, Helena, 1970-71; ptnr., sales mgr. Ashton Printing Co., Butte, Mont., 1971-72; ptnr., sales mgr., corp. sec. Thurber Printing Co./Office Supplies, Helena, 1972-86; securities and investments trader Helena, 1968—; ins. agt. Am. Bankers Life Ins. Co., Helena, 1989-91, Surety Life and Continental Gen. Ins. Co., Helena, 1989-91; instr. Officer Candidate Sch., Mont. Mil. Acad., Mont. Army NG, Helena, 1974-75; adv. staff Civil Def. of the Mont. NG, Helena, 1975-76; chmn. Helena Demolition Derby of the annual Rodeo and Stampede, Helena, 1982-87. Water safety instr. ARC, 1959-62; swimming team coach Ft. Leavenworth Post, Kans., 1963-64; scout leader, Webelo Cub Scouts, Boy Scouts Am., Helena, 1973-76; bd. mem. Lewis & Clark County Planning Bd., Helena, 1977-79, Sch. Dist. No. 4 Bd. Trustees, Canyon Creek, Mont., 1981—, bd. chmn., 1984—; mem. Lewis & Clark Sheriff's Res., Helena, 1988—, Nat. High Sch. Rodeo, 1976; supply officer Sheriff's Res., 1990—; mem. coun. for Prevention Child Abuse, 1987; bd. dirs. Friends of Fairgrounds Found., 1990—; water safety instr. ARC 1959-62. Capt. (Signal Corps) U.S. Army, 1963-68. Recipient Certs. of Achievement, Boy Scouts Am., Helena, 1975, 85; Certs. of Service, County Commrs., Helena, 1977, 79. Mem. Toastmasters Internat., Am. Legion, Mont. Sheriff's and Peace Officers Assn., Lions. Republican. Avocations: big game hunting, fishing, photography, auto mechanics. Home and Office: 5200 Hidden Valley Dr Helena MT 59601-9433

LINDGREN, TIMOTHY JOSEPH, supply company executive; b. N.Y.C., Dec. 7, 1937; s. Carl Herbert and Ruth Elizabeth (Pickering) L.; m. Barbara Fiorini, Feb. 7, 1957; children: Sharon, Mark, Susan. AA, Pierce Coll., Woodland Hills, Calif., 1959; BS in Prodn. Mgmt., Calif. State U., Northridge, 1961; MBA in Indsl. Relations, UCLA, 1962. Registered profl. engr., Calif. cert. tchr., Calif. Systems analyst, methods acct. Pacific Tel. & Tel., Van Nuys, Calif., 1964-65; dir. mfg. Olga Co., Van Nuys, 1965-69; dir. prodn. Calif. Almond Orchards, Bakersfield, 1970-72, gen. mgr., 1972-73; pres. United Wholesale Lumber Co., Montebello, Calif., 1973-77; pres., chief exec. officer Fruit Growers Supply Co., Sherman Oaks, Calif., 1978—. Mem. Calif. C. of C. (chair com. on natural resources). Office: Fruit Growers Supply Co 14130 Riverside Dr Sherman Oaks CA 91423-2313

LINDGREN, WILLIAM DALE, librarian; b. Peoria, Ill., Mar. 8, 1936; s. Hugh Gottfried and Olive Kathryn (Myer) L. BA, Bradley U., 1958, MA, 1959; MSLS, U. Ill., 1967. Tchr. Limestone High Sch., Bartonville, Ill., 1960-68; asst. dir. Learning Resources Ctr. Ill. Cen. Coll., East Peoria, 1968-73, dir., 1973—; mem. transition bd. merger of four systems, 1993-94; bd. dirs. Alliance Libr. Sys., 1994—. Chmn. East Peoria Oral History Com., 1983-84, Resource Sharing Alliance West Ctrl. Ill. Adv. Coun., 1985—; v.p. Ill. Valley Libr. System, pres. bd., 1988, 90—, treas., 1989, bd. dirs., 1990—; bd. dirs. Alliance Libr. System, 1993—. Mem. ALA, Ill. Libr. Assn. (co-chair cracker barrels program ann. conf. 1989, 90, 91), Assn. Ednl. Media Tech., Assn. Ednl. Media and Tech. Ill., Coun. Libr. Tech., Creve Coeur Club (Peoria). Office: Ill Cen Coll One College Dr Peoria IL 61635-0001

LINDH, PATRICIA SULLIVAN, banker, former government official; b. Toledo, Oct. 2, 1928; d. Lawrence Walsh and Lillian Winifred (Devlin) Sullivan; m. H. Robert Lindh, Jr., Nov. 12, 1955; children: Sheila, Deborah, Robert. B.A., Trinity Coll., Washington, 1950, LL.D., 1975; LL.D., Walsh Coll., Canton, Ohio, 1975, U. Jacksonville, 1975. Editor Singapore Am. Newspaper, 1957-62; spl. asst. to counsellor to Pres., 1974, spl. asst. to Pres., 1975-76; dep. asst. sec. state for ednl. and cultural affairs Dept. State, 1976-77; v.p., dir. corp. comms. Bank Am., L.A., 1978-84; corp. pub. rels. Bank Am., San Francisco, 1985-93. Trustee La. Arts and Sci. Center, 1970-73, Calif. Hosp. Med. Ctr., 1979-84; bd. dirs. Jr. League of Baton Rouge, 1969, Children's Bur. Los Angeles, 1979, 84, USO Northern Calif.; Rep. state vice chairwoman La., 1970-74; Rep. nat. committeewoman, La., 1974; mem. pub. affairs com. San Francisco World Affairs Coun., 1985; adv. bd. Jr. League Los Angeles, 1980-84; bd. visitors Southwestern U. Sch. Law. Roman Catholic. Home: 850 Powell St San Francisco CA 94108-2051

LINDHEIM, JAMES BRUCE, public relations executive; b. Cleve., Nov. 26, 1945; s. John Arthur and Lois (Reinitz) L.; m. Barbara Levitz, June 6, 1970 (div. May 1978). BA, Williams Coll., 1967; MS in Pub. Affairs, Princeton U., 1970. Asst. dean Woodrow Wilson Sch. Pub. and Internat. Affairs Princeton (N.J.) U., 1971-73; rsch. assoc. Mathematica, Inc., Princeton, 1973-75; dir. corp. priorities svc. Yankolovich, Skelly and White, N.Y.C., 1975-80; exec. v.p., dir. pub. affairs Burson-Marsteller, N.Y.C., 1981-88; dir. corp. svcs. Europe Burson-Marsteller, London, 1989; dir. corp. svcs. Europe Burson-Marsteller, Paris, 1990—, vice-chmn., 1990-92; chmn. Burson-Marsteller, Europe, Paris, 1992-94, Burson-Marsteller, N.Y.C., 1994-95; pres. JLindheim & Co., N.Y.C., 1995—. Home and Office: 832 Broadway New York NY 10003

LINDHEIM, RICHARD DAVID, television company executive; b. N.Y.C., May 28, 1939; s. Gilbert R. and Pearl (Gruskin) L.; m. Elaine Lavis, Dec. 22, 1963; children: Susan Patricia, David Howard. B.S., U. Redlands, 1961; postgrad, U. So. Calif., 1963. Adminstrv. asst. story dept. CBS, L.A., 1962-64; project dir. entertainment testing ASI Market Rsch., L.A., 1964-69; v.p. program research NBC, L.A., 1969-78, v.p. dramatic programs, 1978-79; producer Universal TV, L.A., 1979-81, v.p. current programs, 1981-85, sr. v.p. series programming, 1986-87, exec. v.p. creative affairs, 1987-91; exec. v.p. program strategy MCA TV Group, 1991-92; exec. v.p. Paramount TV Group, 1992—; asst. prof. Calif. State U.; sr. lectr. U. So. Calif.; lectr. UCLA; reviewer NEH; bd. dirs. AFS Intercultural Program-USA. Author: (with Richard Blum) Primetime: Network Television Programming, 1987, Inside Television Producing, 1991; contbr. articles to profl. jours. Mem. Acad. TV Arts and Scis., Producers Guild Am., Writers Guild Am. Democrat. Jewish. Avocations: model railroading, photography, music, traveling. Office: Universal Studios 100 Universal City Plz Universal City CA 91608 *In this sophisticated society there are fewer and fewer opportunities for the individual. Technology has made most tasks too complex for one man. As a result the ability to work with other people and to provide leadership and management to groups of people has become vital. The key ingredients are communication, respect for others, and a feeling of belonging, while working in a relaxed, casual environment, where the leader is responsible and receptive.*

LINDHOLM, CLIFFORD FALSTROM, II, engineering executive, mayor; b. Passaic, N.J., Dec. 8, 1930; s. Albert William and Edith (Neandross) L.; m. Margery Nye (div.); children: Clifford, Elizabeth, John; m. Karen Cooper, Oct. 7, 1989. BS in Engring., Princeton U., 1953; M in Engring., Stevens Inst. Tech., 1957. Supr. prodn. GM, Linden, N.J., 1953-56; pres. Falstrom Co., Passaic, N.J., 1956—; Bd. dirs. N.J. Mfg. Ins. Co., Trenton. Mayor Twp. Montclair, N.J., 1988-92; pres. Montclair Bd. Edn., 1968-72; bd. dirs. Albert Payson Terhune Found., N.J., 1976—. Mem. N.J. Bus. and Industry Assn. (bd. dirs. 1977—), Princeton Club N.Y., Upper Montclair Golf Club, Mantoloking Yacht Club. Republican. Mem. Ch. of Christ. Home: 10 Mountainside Park Ter Montclair NJ 07043-1209 Office: Falstrom Co 3 Falstrom Ct Passaic NJ 07055

LINDHOLM, DWIGHT HENRY, lawyer; b. Blackduck, Minn., May 27, 1930; s. Henry Nathanial and Viola Eudora (Gummert) L.; m. Loretta Catherine Brown, Aug. 29, 1958; children: Douglas Dwight, Dionne Louise, Jeanne Marie, Philip Clayton, Kathleen Anne. Student, Macalester Coll., 1948-49; BBA, U. Minn., 1951, LLB, 1954; postgrad., Mexico City Coll. (now U. of Ams.), 1956-57. Bar: Minn. 1954, Calif. 1958. Sole practice Los Angeles, 1958-65, 72-81, 84—; ptnr. Lindholm & Johnson, Los Angeles, 1965-69, Cotter, Lindholm & Johnson, Los Angeles, 1969-72; sole practice Los Angeles, 1972-81; of counsel Bolton, Dunn & Moore, Los Angeles, 1981-84. Mem. Calif. Republican Central Com., 1962-63, Los Angeles Republican County Central Com., 1962-66; bd. dirs. Family Service Los Angeles, 1964-70, v.p., 1968-70; bd. dirs. Wilshire YMCA, 1976-77; trustee Westlake Girls Sch., 1978-81; hon. presenter Nat. Charity League Coronet Debutante Ball, 1984; bd. dirs. Calif. State U.-Northridge Trust Fund, 1989-93; bd. dirs. Queen of Angeles/Hollywood Presbyn. Med. Ctr., 1990—. Served as capt. JAG Corps USAF, 1954-56. Recipient Presdl. award Los Angeles Jr. C. of C., 1959. Mem. ABA, Calif. Bar Assn., L.A. County Bar Assn., Wilshire Bar Assn. (bd. govs. 1989-91), Internat. Genealogy Fellowship of Rotarians (founding pres. 1979-86), Calif. Club, Ocean Cruising Club Eng. (Newport Harbor port officer), Rotary (dir. 1975-78), Delta Sigma Pi, Delta Sigma Rho, Delta Theta Phi (state chancellor 1972-73). Presbyterian. Avocations: sailing, offshore cruising. Office: 3580 Wilshire Blvd Fl 17 Los Angeles CA 90010-2501

LINDHOLM, FREDRIK ARTHUR, electrical engineering educator; b. Tacoma, Wash., Feb. 26, 1936; s. George Fred and Evelyn Blanche (Faul) L.; m. Susanne Shroad Howry, Aug. 22, 1959 (div. July 1966); m. Merle Elizabeth Flannery, Dec. 20, 1969. BS, Stanford U., 1958, MS, 1960; PhD, U. Ariz., 1963. Sr. engr. Motorola Corp., Phoenix, 1963-66; asst. prof. U. Ariz., Tucson, 1963-64, assoc. prof., 1964-66; prof. U. Fla., Gainesville, 1966—; vis. prof. U. Leuven, Belgium, 1973-74; gen. chmn. Internat. Electron Devices Meeting Conf., Washington, 1974; program chmn. Internat. Photovoltaics Specialists Conf., Washington, 1978; cons. Jet Propulsion Lab., Pasadena, Calif., 1978-87, Los Alamos (N.Mex.) Nat. Lab., 1981-86. Author: Principles and Applications of Semiconductor Device Modeling, 1971; contbr. numerous articles to profl. jours.; patentee high-low emitter solar cell. Recipient Best Paper award Internat. Solid-State Cirs. Conf., 1963, 65, Outstanding Engring. Faculty award U. Fla., 1975, univ. tchr.-scholar, 1988. Fellow IEEE; mem. Am. Phys. Soc. Home: 4406 SW 17th Ter Gainesville FL 32608-3910 Office: Dept Elec & Computer Engr Univ Fla Gainesville FL 32611

LINDHOLM, JOHN VICTOR, business executive; b. Kane, Pa., Dec. 29, 1934; s. John Edwin and Mary (Nord) L.; m. Ann Christine Lundquist, Apr. 27, 1957; children: Scott Benjamin, Kristine Ann, John Edwin. BBA, Upsala Coll., 1956; postgrad., NYU, 1960-66. Loan officer Irving Trust Co., N.Y.C., 1960-61, coord. spl. svcs., 1969-72, exec. dir., 1972-74; pres., exec. dir. EOPI, 1974—; dir. fin. Guideposts Assocs., Inc., 1975-91, chief fin. officer, exec. dir., 1991, dir. fin. and support svcs., 1992-95; pres. Econ. Svcs., Inc., 1995; dir. fin. and support svcs. Christian Children's Fund, Richmond, Va.; bd. dirs. Naromi Land Trust, Sherman, Conn., County Bank, Carmel, N.Y.; chmn. bd. dirs. Country Bank, Carmel, 1988-93; pres., dir. Country Bank, 1993; pres. Putnam Alliance, 1980-82. Treas. Putnam Alliance, 1978-80; trustee Bethel Meth. Home, 1978-85, 87—; dir. fin. Christian Children's Fund, Inc., 1992—. Lt. USNR, 1956-59. Mem. W.O. Assn. (pres. 1994—). Home: 6400 Buckhill Rd Richmond VA 23225-1320 Office: Christian Children's Fund 2821 Emerywood Pky Richmond VA 23294-3726

LINDHOLM, RICHARD THEODORE, economics and finance educator; b. Eugene, Oreg., Oct. 5, 1960; s. Richard Wadsworth and Mary Marjorie (Trunko) L. m. Valaya Nivasananda, May 8, 1987. BA, U. Chgo., 1982, MA, 1983, PhD, 1993. Ptnr. Lindholm and Osanka, Eugene, 1986-89, Lindholm Rsch., Eugene, 1989—; guest lectr. Nat. Inst. Devel. Adminstrn., Bangkok, Thailand, 1989; pres. Rubicon Inst., Eugene, 1988—; adj. asst. prof. U. Oreg., Eugene, 1988—. Campaign co-chmn. Lane C.C. Advocates, Eugene, 1988; coord., planner numerous state Rep. Campaigns, Oreg., 1988—; campaign mgr. Jack Roberts for Oreg. State Labor Commn., 1994; mem. staff Oreg. Senate Rep. Office, 1989-90; precinct committeeperson Oreg. Rep. Party, 1987-92, 94—; bd. dirs. Rubicon Soc., Eugene, 1987—, pres., 1993—. Republican. Lutheran. Home: 3335 Bardell Ave Eugene OR 97401-8021

LINDHOLM, ULRIC SVANTE, engineering research institute executive, retired; b. Washington, Sept. 11, 1931; s. Svante Godfred and Hedwig (Krueger) L.; m. Laura Ann Carranza, July 6, 1962; children: Karl, Kirsten, Jon, Siri. BS, Mich. State U., 1953, MS, 1955, PhD, 1960. Rsch. instr. Mich. State U., East Lansing, 1959-60; sr. engr., mgr., dir., v.p. Southwest Rsch. Inst., San Antonio, 1960-94, ret., 1994; lectr. St. Mary's U., San Antonio, 1961-62. Assoc. editor Soc. Exptl. Stress Analysis Exptl. Mechanics, 1979-82; contbr. numerous articles to profl. jours.; patentee in field. Chmn. bd. dirs. Healy-Murphy Ctr., San Antonio, 1970-81. With USN, 1955-57. Fellow ASME (assoc. editor Jour. Applied Mechanics 1981-83), AAAS; mem. Am. Soc. Metals. Democrat. Avocations: woodworking, antiques. Home: 110 Honey Bee Ln San Antonio TX 78231-1205

LINDIG, BILL M., food distribution company executive; b. 1936; married. Attended, U. Tex. With Sysco Corp., Houston, 1969—, exec. v.p., from 1984, COO, 1984—, now pres., COO.; chmn. Sysco Avard Food Svcs., Inc., Union City, Calif., Santa Fe Pacific Corp., Schaumburg, Ill. Office: Sysco Corp 1390 Enclave Pky Houston TX 77077-2025*

LINDLEY, F(RANCIS) HAYNES, JR., foundation president, lawyer; b. L.A., Oct. 15, 1945; s. Francis Haynes and Grace Nelson (McCanne) L.; m. Hollinger McCloud Lindley, Apr. 1, 1977; 1 child, Anne Hollinger Lindley. BA, Claremont (Calif.) Men's Coll., 1967; MFA, Claremont (Calif.) Grad. Sch., 1972; JD, Southwestern U., L.A., 1976. Bar: Calif. 1976, U.S. Supreme Ct. 1980. Deputy pub. defender Office of Pub. Defender, L.A., 1977-79; staff atty., Dept. Trial Counsel The State Bar of Calif., L.A., 1979-81; pvt. practice, 1981-90; pres. John Randolph Haynes and Dora Haynes Found., L.A., 1987—; trustee John Randolph Haynes and Dora Haynes Found., L.A., 1978—. Mem. bd. dirs. TreePeople, L.A., 1985-87, So. Calif. Assn. Philanthropy, L.A., 1985-89; mem. bd. fellows Claremont (Calif.) U. Ctr. and Grad. Sch., 1987—; mem. bd. dirs. Marin Agrl. Land Trust, 1995—. Recipient Disting. Svc. award The Claremont (Calif.) Grad. Sch., 1994. Mem. The Calif. Club. Avocation: sailing, art history, banjo. Home: PO Box 1404 Ross CA 94957-1404 Office: John Randolph Haynes and Dora Haynes Found 888 W Sixth St Ste 1150 Los Angeles CA 90017

LINDLEY, JOHN, cinematographer. Cinematographer: (TV movies) The Demon Murder Case, 1983, Girls of the White Orchid Death Ride to Osaka, 1983, (films) The Goodbye People, 1983, Lily in Love, 1985, Home of the Brave, 1986, Killer Party, 1986, The Stepfather, 1987, In the Mood, 1987, Shakedown, 1988, The Serpent and the Rainbow, 1988, True Believer, 1989, Field of Dreams, 1989, Immediate Family, 1989, Vital Signs, 1990, Sleeping with the Enemy, 1991, Sneakers, 1992, Father of the Bride, 1992, The Good Son, 1993, I Love Trouble, 1994. Office: care Spyros Skouras Sanford Skouras Gross & Assocs 1015 Gayley Ave Fl 3 Los Angeles CA 90024-3424

LINDLEY, THOMAS ERNEST, environmental lawyer, law educator; b. Danville, Ill., July 15, 1948; s. Oscar Ernest and Helen (Milewski) L. BA, U. Ill., 1970; postgrad., U. Tex., 1970-71; JD, Vanderbilt U., 1977. Bar: Ill. 1977, U.S. Dist. Ct. (no. dist.) Ill. 1978, U.S. Dist. Ct. (cen. dist.) Ill. 1983, U.S. Ct. Appeals (7th cir.) 1978, U.S. Supreme Ct. 1982, Oreg. 1985, U.S. Dist. Ct. Oreg. 1985, Trial Bar No. Dist. Ill. 1985, U.S. Ct. Appeals (9th cir.) 1985, Wash. 1987, U.S. Dist. Ct. (we. dist.) Wash. 1987, U.S. Dist. Ct. (ea. dist.) Wash. 1988. Asst. dir. div. EMS Tenn. Dept. Health, Nashville, 1972-74; lawyer Jenner & Block, Chgo., 1977-83, Balbach, Fehr & Lindley, Urbana, Ill., 1983-84, Miller, Nash, Wiener, Hager & Carlsen, Portland, Oreg., 1985—; adj. prof. Lewis & Clark Northwestern Sch. Law, Portland, 1991—; lectr. ITT-Kent Coll. Law, Chgo., 1981-83; extern Supreme Ct. Tenn., Nashville, 1976-77; co-chair and author 7th Ann. EPA/Lewis & Clark Hazardous Waste Law & Mgmt. Conf., 1990, 8th Ann. Conf., 1991; chair Assoc. Oreg. Industries' Environ. Crimes Task Forces, 1993, 97; com. chair on internat. environ. crimes Internat. Ctr. for Criminal Reform and Justice, 1994; mem. U.S. Del. 9th Conf. of Parties of Cites, 1994; chair Assn. Oreg. Industries, Water Resources Com., 1995—. Author: Contracting for Environmental Services, 1991, Reducing Lender Liability, 1994; co-author: Oregon's Environmental Audit Privilege: Traveling the Path to Consensus: Preventive Law Reporter, 1994, Oregon Environmental Law--Crimes and Contracting, 1994, Environmental Audit Privilege: BNA, 1993; editor: Oregon Environmental Law--Insurance Coverage, 1991. Bd. dirs. Oreg. Environ. Tech. Assn., 1993—, sec., 1994—, United Way Columbia-Willamette, Oreg., 1990-91, United Cerebral Palsy, Oreg., 1987-90, 95—, mem., 1987—, Mental Health Svcs. West, Oreg., 1985, Ill. Pub. Action Coun., 19880-83; chmn. Adv. Bd. CANPAC, 1981; coord. counsel Kennedy for Pres., Ill., 1979-80; vol. Cook County Spl. Bail Project, Ill., 1978-79; candidate U.S. Congress, Ill., 1983-84. Mem. ABA (natural resource sect., litig. sect.), Wash. State Bar Assn. (land use and environ. law sect.), Oreg. State Bar (environ. law sect.). Avocations: backpacking, cross country skiing, theater, politics. Office: Miller Nash Wiener et al 3500 US Bancorp Tower 111 SW 5th Ave Portland OR 97204-3604

LINDMARK, RONALD DORANCE, retired federal agency administrator; b. Clearwater County, Minn., May 3, 1933; s. John G. and Aaste L. (Torgerson) L.; m. Lynette C. Larson, Dec. 16, 1961; children: Eric Karl, Kirstin Sigrid. BS in Forestry, U. Minn., 1961, MS, 1963; PhD in Agrl. Econs., Ohio State U., 1971. Forestry aide No. Pacific Rwy., Seattle, 1959-60; rsch. asst. U. Minn., St. Paul, 1961-63; scientist Ctrl. State Forest Experiment Sta., Columbus, Ohio, 1963-66, No. Ctrl. Forest Experiment Sta., Duluth, Minn., 1966-69; scientist, project leader No. Ctrl. Forest Experiment Sta., Carbondale, Ill., 1969-74; asst. dir. Intermountain Forest Experiment Sta., Ogden, Utah, 1974-77; staff asst., dep. chief Forest Svc. Rsch., Washington, 1977-81; dir. Forest Environ. Rsch., Washington, 1982-87, No. Ctrl. Forest Experiment Sta., St. Paul, 1987-93; ret., 1993; legis. fellow to Congressman from Ohio, 1981. Contbr. articles to profl. jours. With USN, 1952-56. Avocations: travel, photography, outdoor recreation, woodcraft. Home: 1140 Amble Dr Arden Hills MN 55112-5713

LINDNER, CARL HENRY, JR., financial holding company executive; b. Dayton, Ohio, Apr. 22, 1919; s. Carl Henry and Clara (Serrer) L.; m. Edith Bailey, Dec. 31, 1953; children: Carl Henry III, Stephen Craig, Keith Edward. Co-founder United Dairy Farmers, 1940; pres. Am. Fin. Corp., Cin., 1959-84, chmn., 1959—, chief exec. officer, 1984—; chmn., chief exec. officer, chmn. exec. com. United Brands Co. (now Chiquita Brands Internat. Inc.), N.Y.C., 1984—; chmn. Penn Cen. Corp. (now American Premier Underwriters), Cin., 1983—, chief exec. officer, 1987-1994, also bd. dirs.; chmn., chief exec. officer Gt. Am. Communications Co., Cin., 1987—; bd. dirs. Mission Ins. bd. advs. Bus. Adminstrn. Coll., U. Cin. Republican. Baptist. Office: Charter Co 1 W Charter Plz Jacksonville FL 32202-3105*

LINDNER, JOSEPH, JR., physician, medical administrator; b. Cin., Apr. 5, 1929; s. Joseph and Mary (Apger) L.; m. Doris G. Beatty, July 29, 1961; children: Laura Lynn, Karen Leslie. AB, Dartmouth Coll., 1951; MD, U. Cin., 1955; MPH, Harvard U., 1977. Intern Cin. Gen. Hosp., 1955-56, resident in medicine, 1958-60, fellow in cardiology, 1960-61; mem. faculty dept. medicine U. Cin. Coll. Medicine, 1961-79, prof., 1975-79; sr. assoc. v.p. U. Cin., 1975-79, sr. assoc. dir., 1977-79; pres., chief exec. officer St. Barnabas Med. Ctr., Livingston, N.J., 1979-85, Trimark Corp., West Orange, N.J.; ptnr. Cons. Assocs., Inc., 1991-92; pres. J. Lindner, Inc., Hilton Head, S.C., 1992—. Trustee Mt. St. Joseph Coll., 1972-76, The Asheville Sch., 1995—. With USN, 1956-58. Fellow Am. Coll. Physician Execs.; mem. N.J. Med. Soc., Commonwealth Club, Cin. Country Club, Baltusrol Golf Club, Country Club Hilton Head, Bear Creek Golf Club, Short Hills Club. Home and Office: 31 Old Fort Dr Hilton Head Island SC 29926

LINDNER, KEITH E., food company executive. Formerly sr. exec. v.p. United Brands Co., Cincinnati; now pres., chief oper. officer Chiquita Brands Internat. Inc. (formerly United Brands Co.), Cincinnati. Office: Chiquita Brands Internat Inc 250 E 5th St Cincinnati OH 45202-4103*

LINDNER, KENNETH EDWARD, academic administrator and chemistry educator emeritus; b. LaCrosse, Wis., Nov. 29, 1922; s. Henry B. and Cora (Ward) L.; m. Ila M. Jacobson, Feb. 28, 1947 (div.); children: Diane, Charles, Barbara, Nancy, John, Sara; m. Marcia A Lee, March 17, 1990. B.S., Wis. State U., 1949; M.A., U. Iowa, 1953, Ph.D., 1966; HHD (hon.), Tex. Chirpractic Coll., 1994. High sch. chemistry tchr. Black River Falls, Wis., 1949-55; prof. chemistry Wis. State U., LaCrosse, 1956-67; head acad. affairs Wis. State U. System, Madison, 1967-70; chancellor U. Wis.-LaCrosse, 1971-79, chancellor emeritus, Disting. prof., 1983—; chmn. Council Chancellors U. Wis. System, 1978-79; sec. Wis. State Dept. Adminstrn., 1979-82; chmn. bd. Digicators Systems, Inc., 1985-90; adv. bd. Deli Corp., 1980-90; v.p. adminstrn.-provost Tex. Chiropractic Coll., Pasadena, Tex., 1993-94, advisor to pres., 1994—; cons. N.Y. Chiropractic Coll., 1994-95; cons. for closure Coll. St. Teresa, Winona, Minn., 1988-90; cons.-examiner North Ctrl. Assn. Colls. and Secondary Schs., 1972-79, commr., 1976-79; cons. data processing Sentry Ins. Co., 1983, govt. relations Gateway Foods, Inc., LaCrosse, Wis.; cons. radiation chemistry Dairyland Power Coop., LaCrosse Boiling Water Reactor, 1966-67; cons. radiation safety Gunderson Clinic, Luth. Hosp., LaCrosse, 1966-67. Chmn. bd. trustees Coll. St. Teresa, Winona, Minn., 1986-88. Served with AUS, 1942-45. Mem. Internat. Radiation Protection Soc., Am. Chem. Soc., Health Physics Soc. Home: 3407 Shadow Meadows Dr Houston TX 77082

LINDNER, ROBERT DAVID, finance company executive; b. Dayton, Ohio, Aug. 5, 1920; s. Carl Henry and Clara (Serrer) L.; m. Betty Ruth Johnston, Mar. 29, 1947; children—Robert David, Jeffrey Scott, Alan Bradford, David Clark. Grad. high sch. Chmn. bd. United Dairy Farmers, Cin., 1940—; With Am. Financial Corp., Cin., 1950—, former v.p., vice chmn. bd., now vice chmn. bd. dirs. Trustee No. Bapt. Theol. Sem. Served with U.S. Army, 1942-45. Mem. Masons (33 degree). Home: 6950 Given Rd Cincinnati OH 45243-2840 Office: United Dairy Farmers 3955 Montgomery Rd Cincinnati OH 45212-3733 also: American Financial Corp 1 E 4th St Cincinnati OH 45202-3717*

LINDQUIST, CLAUDE S., electrical and computer engineering educator; b. Des Moines, Mar. 13, 1940; s. Claude R. and Eva E. (Cox) L.; children: Todd, Tad. BA, U. Redlands, 1963; BSEE, Stanford U., 1963; MSEE, Oreg. State U., 1964, PhD, 1968. Design engr. Collins Radio, Newport Beach, Calif., 1968-71; prof. Calif. State U., Long Beach, 1971-84; prof. elec. and computer engring. U. Miami, Fla., 1984—; cons. Phoenix Data, Computer Automation, Edwards Pacemaker Systems, Bournes, KVB Equipment Systems, Vega Electronics, Datanetics, 1973-81, SHAPE Tech. Ctr., 1993; pres. E&H Electronics, Long Beach, 1979-84; vis. prof. U. Calif., Irvine, 1983-84. Author: Active Network Design, 1977, Adaptive and Digital Signal Processing, 1989; contbr. over 100 tech. papers. Mem. IEEE (sr.), CAS Soc., AASP Soc., Omicron Delta Kappa, Phi Beta Delta, Alpha Epsilon Lambda. Republican. Mem. Assemblies of God Ch. Avocations: church out-reach programs, boating. Office: U Miami Elec and Computer Engring Dept PO Box 24-8294 Miami FL 33124

LINDQUIST, EVAN, artist, educator; b. Salina, Kans., May 23, 1936; s. E.L. and Linnette Rosalie (Shogren) L. B.S.E., Emporia State U., 1958; M.F.A., U. Iowa, 1963; m. Sharon Frances Huenergardt, June 8, 1958; children: Eric, Carl. One man shows include Mo. Arts Council, 1973-75, Albrecht Art Mus., St. Joseph, Mo., 1975, 89, S.E. Mo. State U., 1977, Sandzen Gallery, Lindsborg, Kans., 1978, Galerie V. Kunstverlag Wolfbrum, Vienna, 1979, Poplar Bluff, Mo., 1987, Gallery V, Kans. City, Mo., 1988, Northwest Mo. State U., 1991, U. Iowa, Iowa City, 1995; group shows include Benjamin Galleries, Chgo., 1976, City of Venice, 1977, Boston Printmakers, 1971-87, Visual Arts Ctr. of Alaska, Anchorage, 1979, Western Carolina U., 1980, Pa. State U., 1980, Kans. State U., 1980, U. N.D., 1981 & 92, Ariz. State U., 1981, 93, Barcelona, Cadaques, Girona, 1990, 93, 94, Tulsa, 1982, Jay Gallery, N.Y.C., 1983, Artists Books, German Dem. Republic, 1984, U. Tenn.-Knoxville, 1985, Memphis State U., 1985, Ark. Arts Ctr., 1983-83, Miss. State U., 1986, Hunterdon Art Ctr., Clinton, N.J., 1986-87, 94, 95, Washington, 1988, Soc. of Am. Graphic Artists/Printmakers, 1988-94, Boston, 1989-94, John Szoke Gallery, 1989, Woodstock, N.Y., 1990, 92, Silvermine Guild Galleries, New Canaan, Conn., 1992, 93, Woodstock Artists Assn., Littman Gallery, Portland State U., Galeria Brita Prinz, Madrid, Spain, 1992, U. Nebraska, 1992, Parkside National, Kenosha, Wis., 1993, 95, Minot, N.D., 1994, Fla. Community Coll., Jacksonville, Fla., 1995, Stonemetal Press, San Antonio, Tex., 1995, San Diego Art Inst., 1995, Schenectady (N.Y.) Mus., 1995; represented in permanent collections Albertina, Vienna, Art Inst. Chgo., Nelson-Atkins, Kansas City, Phoenix Art Mus., Uffizi Gallery, Florence, Municipal Gallery, Dublin, San Francisco Art Mus., Whitney Mus. Am. Art, N.Y.C., St. Louis Art Mus., Museo Reina Sofia, Madrid, others; staff artist Emporia State U., 1958-60; prof. Ark. State U., 1963—, pres.'s fellow, 1981-82, 84-85. Mem. Soc. Am. Gr. Artists, Coll. Art Assn. Am., MidAm. Coll. Art Assn., Visual Artists and Galleries Assn. Office: PO Box 2782 State University AR 72467-2782

LINDQUIST, MARY LOUISE, special education educator; b. South St. Paul, Minn., May 30, 1925; d. Henry Emanuel and Hulda Laura Margaret (Brocker) L. BS in Edn., Minot State Coll., 1962; MS, U. Wis., 1964, PhD, 1969. Cert. psychologist N.D. Missionary in Japan Augustana Luth. Bd. Fgn. Missions, Mpls., 1952-56; elem. sch. tchr. Upham (N.D.) Pub. Schs., 1958-59, Vang Sch. Dist., Ryder, N.D., 1959-61, Minot (N.D.) Pub. Schs., 1961-63; sch. psychologist Madison (Wis.) Pub. Schs., 1966-69; prof. U. N.D., Grand Forks, 1969-95, prof. emeritus, 1995—; cons. Multi-County Spl. Edn., New Rockford, N.D., 1982-85; vis. psychologist Turtle Mountain Schs., Belcourt, N.D., 1978-82; pvt. practice psychologist, Grand Forks, 1980—. Author: Sunday Sch. curriculum/Bd. of Parish Edn., Assn. Free Luth. Congregations. Grantee Office Edn., U. N.D., 1984, 87. Mem. Am. Assn. Christian Counselors, Internat. Coun. Learning Disabilities (N.D. rep. 1992-95), Internat. Platform Assn., No. Lights Coun. Learning Disabilities (pres. 1993-94). Republican. Lutheran. Avocations: singing, reading. Home and Office: 3720 Cherry G25 Grand Forks ND 58201-7696

LINDQUIST, RAYMOND IRVING, clergyman; b. Sumner, Nebr., Apr. 14, 1907; s. Rev. Elmer H. and Esther (Nyberg) L.; m. Ella Sofield, Sept. 16, 1930; children: Ray Irving, Ruth Elizabeth Lindquist McCalmont. Student, Kearney State Coll., 1925; A.B., Wheaton Coll., Ill., 1929; student, Columbia U. Law Sch., 1929-30; A.M., Princeton U., 1933; Th.B. (Hugh Davies prize homiletics; Erdman prize Bible; Zwemer fellow Comparative Religions), Princeton Sem., 1933; D.D., Cumberland U., 1939, Ursinus Coll., 1980; LL.D., Bloomfield Coll., N.J., 1957, Eastern Coll., 1977; L.H.D., Calif. Coll. Medicine, 1963. Ordained to ministry Presbyn. Ch., 1934; dir. religious edn. Third Presbyn. Ch., Newark, 1931-34; minister Old First Presbyn. Ch., Orange, N.J., 1934-53, Hollywood First Presbyn. Ch., 1953-71; vis. prof. homiletics Bloomfield Sem., N.J., 1945-53; lectr. Princeton Sem., Pittcairn-Crabbe, Pitts., U. Iowa, USAF, Israel, Germany, Johnston Island, UCLA, U. Soc. Calif., Pentagon, Northwestern U., Chgo. Sunday Evening Club, Westminster Coll., Mo., Tel Aviv, Zurich, Switzerland; pres. bd. nat. missions United Presbyn. Ch., 1955-62, gen. coun., 1955-62; v.p. Templeton Found. Author: Notes for Living. Bd. dirs. Covenant Life (formerly Presbyn. Ministers Fund), Phila., chmn. bd., 1980—; bd. dirs. Presbyn. Med. Center, Hollywood, Calif., 1954—, Met. YMCA, Los Angeles; trustee Princeton Theol. Sem., So. Calif. Presbyn. Homes., Olmstead Trust, Hollywood, Calif., 1954—. Recipient Gold medal Religious Heritage Am., 1984. Mem. Phi Kappa Delta. Clubs: Rotary (Los Angeles) (bd. dirs.), Los Angeles Country (Los Angeles); Symposium (Princeton); Glen Lake (Sparta, N.J.), Sunset Rock (Sparta, N.J.); Shadow Mountain (Palm Desert, Calif.). Home: 568 Avenida Sevilla # B Laguna Hills CA 92653-4075 *Faith is not jumping to conclusions: it is concluding to jump...The thought of God swings the world like a rock on a rope.*

LINDQUIST, ROBERT JOHN, accountant, financial investigator; b. Victoria, B.C., Can., Sept. 8, 1945; s. George Albert and Lenore Rose (Assef) L.; m. Angela Martha Janicki, June 29, 1974; children: Justin, Aimee, Scott. B of Commerce, U. Windsor (Ont., Can.), 1968. Chartered acct.; cert. fraud examiner. Acct. Touche Ross & Co., Toronto, Ont., 1968-74; sr. ptnr. Lindquist Holmes & Co., Toronto, 1975-84; nat. dir. Peat Marwick, Toronto, 1985-89; chmn. internat. forensic acctg. network KPMG Peat Marwick, Toronto, 1989-91; sr. ptnr. Lindquist Avey MacDonald Baskerville, Toronto, 1991-93; chmn., CEO Lindquist Avey MacDonald Baskerville Inc., Washington, 1993—. Co-author: Fraud Auditing & Forensic Accounting, 1987, 2d edit., 1995, Accountants Handbook of Fraud & Commercial Crime, 1992. Mem. Assn. Cert. Fraud Examiners (chmn. 1993), Can. Inst. Chartered Accts., Inst. Chartered Accts. Ont., York Down Golf and Country Club, Albany Club. Avocations: tennis, golf, travel, motorsport. Office: Lindquist Avey MacDonald Baskerville Inc 805 15th St NW Ste 1110 Washington DC 20005-2207

LINDQUIST, SUSAN PRATZNER, museum executive; b. San Francisco, Dec. 20, 1940; d. Carleton Edward Pratzner and Edith Crane (Johnson) Cox; m. Philip George Lindquist, Oct. 27, 1962; children: Tucker D., Travis C. BS in Edn., Lesley Coll., 1962; MEd, Northeastern U., Boston, 1979; postgrad., U. Calif., Berkeley, 1994. Tchr. local sch. Marshfield, Mass., 1962-63, Peabody, Mass., 1963-66; coord. early intervention Dept. Mental Health, Hyannis, Mass., 1976-79; supr. Dept. Social Svcs., Hyannis, 1981; program dir. Latham Sch., Brewster, Mass., 1982-85; vol. coord. Cape Cod Mus. Natural History, Brewster, 1986—, assoc. dir., 1987, pres., CEO, 1987—; corp. trustee Cape Cod Five Bank, 1992. Bd. dirs. Cape Cod C. of C., 1993, Mus. Inst. for Teaching Sci., Boston; trustee Cape Cod Acad., 1994; mem. Brewstr Bd. Appeals, 1977-87; founder, trustee Cape Cod Lighthouse Charter Sch., 1994—. Avocations: world travel, gardening. Office: Cape Cod Mus Natural History PO Box 1710 Rte 6A Brewster MA 02631

LINDROS, ERIC BRYAN, professional hockey player; b. London, Ont., Can., Feb. 28, 1973; s. Carl and Bonnie L. Student, York U., Toronto. With Detroit Compuware, 1989—, Phila. Flyers, 1992—; mem. Canadian Olympic Team, 1992, Cup All-Star team, 1989-90, OHL All-Star team 1990-91, NHL All-Star team, 1992-93; player NHL All-Star game, 1992-93. Recipient Plus/Minus award Canadian Hockey League, 1990-91, Red Tilson trophym 1990-91, Eddie Powers Meml. trophy, 1990-91; named Most Valuable Player World Jr. Hockey Championships, 1990, Most Valuable Player Ont. Jr. Hockey Assn., 1991, Player of the Year Canadian Hockey League, 1990-91, Hart Trophy, 1995, Lester B. Pearson Award, 1995, Nat. Hockey League. Office: care Rick Curran PO Box 735 Devon PA 19333-0735*

LINDROTH, LINDA (LINDA HAMMER), artist, curator, writer; b. Miami, Sept. 4, 1946; d. Mark Roger and Mae Lang Hammer; m. David George Lindroth, May 26, 1968 (div. Mar. 1985); m. Craig David Newick, June 6, 1987; 1 child, Zachary Eran Newick. BA in Art, Douglass Coll., 1968; MFA in Art, Rutgers U., 1979. Exhibits include Aetna Gallery, 1987, 89, 91, Bergen Cmty. Mus., Paramus, N.J., 1972, Franklin Furnace, N.Y.C., 1977, Calif. Inst. Arts, Valencia, 1980, Eye Gallery, San Francisco, 1984, Conn. Commn. Arts, Hartford, 1985, 96, Aldrich Mus. Contemporary Art, Ridgefield, Conn., 1987, 95, Downey (Calif.) Mus. Art, 1989, Zimmerli Art Mus. Rutgers U., 1989, Wesleyan U. Ctr. for the Arts, 1990, Boston Pub. Libr., 1991, John Michael Kohler Art Ctr., Sheboygan, Wis., 1992, James Bakker Gallery, Provincetown, Mass., 1993, Joseloff Gallery U. Hartford, 1994, Artspace, New Haven, 1991, 92, 93, 94, 95, DeCordova Mus., Lincoln, Mass., 1995, Urban Glass, Bklyn., 1996, others; represented in permanent collections The Mus. Modern Art, N.Y.C., The Met. Mus. of Art, N.Y.C., The Mus. City of N.Y., Polaroid Collection/Artist Program, N.J. State Mus., Trenton, The Bibliotheque Nationale, Paris, Ctr. for Creative Photography, Tucson, The Newark Mus., The Jane Voorhees Zimmerli Art Mus., New Brunswick, N.J., High Mus. Art, Atlanta, Yale U. Dir. Artspace, Inc., New Haven; mem. Mayor's Task Force on Pub. Art, New Haven. Recipient Ann. Design Rev. award ID Mag., 1990, 91, 93, Honorable Mention, Nat. Peace Garden Design Competition, 1989, Pitts. Corning Archtl. Design Competition, 1988, Individual Artist fellow N.J. State Coun. on Arts, 1974-75, 83-84; grantee Found. for Contemporary Performance Arts, Inc., 1989, 90, Fission Fusion NEA InterARts, 1989, grantee New Eng. Found. for Arts, 1992, Fairfield U., 1995; Conn. Commn. Arts fellow, 1995, New Eng. Found. Arts/NEA Regional Photography fellow, 1995-96. Studio: Lindroth & Newick 219 Livingston St New Haven CT 06511-2209

LINDSAY, BRUCE GEORGE, statistics educator; b. The Dalles, Oreg., Mar. 7, 1947; s. George Speers and Geneva Elizabeth (Davis) L.; m. Teresa Ann Goff, Aug. 23, 1969 (div. 1995); children: Dylan Brantley, Camden James. BA, U. Oreg., 1969; PhD, U. Wash., 1978. Postdoctoral fellow Imperial Coll., London, 1978-79; asst. prof. Pa. State U., University Park, 1979-85, assoc. prof., 1985-87, prof. stats., 1987-91, disting. prof. stats., 1992—. Assoc. editor Annals Stats., 1985-91, 93—, Annals Stat. Math., 1987—, Math. Methods Stats., 1992—; contbr. articles to profl. jours. Scoutmaster Boy Scouts Am., State College, Pa., 1988-89. With USCG, 1970-74. Recipient Humboldt Sr. scientist award, 1990; Guggenheim Found. fellow, 1996. Fellow Inst. Math. Stats.; mem. Am. Statis. Assn., Math. Assn. Am., Internat. Statis. Inst. Democrat. Avocations: running, hiking, reading. Office: Pa State U Dept Stats 326 Classroom Bldg University Park PA 16802

LINDSAY, CHARLES JOSEPH, banker; b. Bklyn., Mar. 21, 1922; s. George Patrick and Evelyn (Roth) L.; m. Marie A. Faraone, Jan. 19, 1947; children—George, Charles, Mary Ann. Student, U. Mo., 1943; grad., Am. Savs. and Loan Inst., 1947, Savs. and Loan Grad. Sch., Ind. U.; Profl. Studies in Bus. Adminstrn; Degree with high distinction, Pace U., 1973. With Nassau Fed. Savs. formerly Serial Fed. Savs. & Loan Assn., N.Y.C., 1947—, successively teller, supr., asst. v.p., asst. sec., sec., v.p. and sec., sr. v.p. and dir., pres., 1965—; ret. as pres. Nassau Fed. Savs., 1986, bd. dirs.; mem. faculty, bd. govs. Savs. and Loan Inst.; gov. for N.Y. State, Nat. League Savs. Assns. Mem. pres.'s adv. council Fairfield U., Pace U. Served with USAAF, World War II. Decorated Air medal with cluster; recipient Alumnus of Year award Pace U., 1975. Mem. N.Y. Fin. Advertisers, State League Savs. Assn. (dir.), Nat. League Savs. Assns. (exec. com., dir.), Alumni Assn. Pace U. (pres. 1977—, dir.). Club: Aspetuck Country (Weston, Conn.). Home: Winter Leaves 4 Lilac Ln Weston CT 06883-3008 also: 100 Worth Ave Palm Beach FL 33480-4447

LINDSAY, DALE RICHARD, research administrator; b. Bunker Hill, Kans., Aug. 9, 1913; s. Charles Edwin and Iva (Missimer) L.; m. Sybil Anne McCoy, June 6, 1937; children—Martha Lou Lindsay Cover, Judith Anne Lindsay Clapp, Patricia Dale. A.B., U. Kans., 1937, M.A., 1938; Ph.D., Iowa State Coll., 1943. Entomologist Dept. Agr., summers 1937-39; teaching fellow, instr., research asso. Iowa State Coll., 1938-43; commd. officer USPHS, 1943—, scientist dir., 1955; assigned malaria control in war areas, 1943-45; entomologist charge operations Communicable Disease Center Activies, Pharr, Tex., 1945-48; chief Thomasville (Ga.) field sta., 1948-53; chief program evaluation sect., div. research grants NIH, 1953-55, asst. chief div., 1955-60, chief div., 1960-63; dep. to gen. dir. Mass. Gen. Hosp., Boston, 1963-65; spl. asst. to chancellor health scis. U. Calif. at Davis, 1965-67, asst. chancellor research and health scis., 1968-69; asso. commr. sci. FDA, 1969-71; asso. dir. med. and allied health edn. Duke U., 1971-75; asst. dir. for sci. coordination Nat. Center for Toxicol. Research, Jefferson, Ark., 1975-76; adj. prof. medicine U. Ark. Med. Sch., 1975-76; asso. dept. family and community medicine U. Ariz., 1977-82; Agrl. bd. Nat. Acad. Sci.-NRC, 1970-73; mem. exec. com., public trustee Nutrition Found., 1972-76, Environ. and Agrl. Found., 1974-79; chmn. sci. adv. bd. Nat. Center for Toxicol. Research, 1972-74. Fellow AAAS, Am. Public Health Assn.; mem. Entomol. Soc. Am. (gov. bd. 1958-62), Commd. Officer Assn. USPHS (treas. nat. exec. com. 1959-61) , Sigma Xi, Phi Kappa Phi, Gamma Sigma Delta.

LINDSAY, DAVID BREED, JR., aircraft company executive, former editor and publisher; b. Fayetteville, N.C., Dec. 25, 1922; s. David Breed and Helen Carter (Dodson) L.; m. Elizabeth Hotchkiss Girvin, June 19, 1944; children: David G.B., Robert A., Ann C., Edward H. B.S., Purdue U., 1947. Reporter/photographer Marion (Ind.) Chronicle, 1947-48; editor, gen. mgr. Sarasota (Fla.) Herald Tribune, 1948-55, editor, pres., 1955-82; pres. Cavalier Aircraft Corp., 1955-70, Lindair, Inc., 1971—; designer, test pilot Enforcer Aircraft; cons. Piper Aircraft Corp. Founder, trustee New Coll., Sarasota, 1950-75. Served with U.S. Army, 1943-46. Decorated Army Commendation medal. Mem. Am. Newspaper Pubs. Assn. (dir.), Am. Newspaper Pubs. Assn. Found. (pres.), Inter Am. Press Assn. (dir.), Soc. Exptl. Test Pilots., Sigma Delta Chi. Episcopalian. Clubs: Met. (Washington); Old Capital (Monterey, Calif.). Inventor various aircraft systems, including Enforcer Aircraft. Office: PO Box 13367 Sarasota FL 34278-3367

LINDSAY, DIANNA MARIE, educational administrator; b. Boston, Dec. 7, 1948; d. Albert Joseph and June Hazelton (Mitchell) Raggi; m. James William Lindsay III, Feb. 14, 1981. BA in Anthropology, Ea. Nazarene Coll., 1971; MEd in Curriculum and Instrn., Wright State U., 1973, MEd in Social Studies Edn., 1974, MEd in Edn. Adminstrn., 1977; EdD in Edn. Adminstrn., Ball State U., 1976. Supr. social edn. Ohio Dept. Edn., Columbus, 1976-77; asst. prin. Orange City Schs., Pepper Pike, Ohio, 1977-79; prin. North Olmsted (Ohio) Jr. High Sch., 1979-81; dir. secondary edn. North Olmsted City SChs., 1981-82; supt. Copley (Ohio)-Fairlawn City Schs., 1982-85; prin. North Olmsted High Sch., 1985-89, New Trier High Sch., Winnetka, Ill., 1989—; bd. dirs. Harvard Prins. Ctr., Cambridge, Mass. Contbr. articles to profl. jours. Bd. dirs. Nat. PTA, Chgo., 1987-89 (Educator of Yr. 1989). Named Prin. of Yr. Ohio Art Tchrs., 1989, one of 100 Up and Coming Educators, Exec. Educator Mag., 1988; recipient John Vaughn Achievements in Edn. North Cen. Assn., 1988. Mem. AAUW, Ill. Tchrs. Fgn. Lang., Rotary Internat., Phi Delta Kappa. Methodist. Avocations: stained glass, reading, travel, biking, snorkling. Office: Worthington Kilbourne High Sch 1499 Hard Rd Columbus OH 43235

LINDSAY, DONALD PARKER, former savings bank executive; b. Spokane, Aug. 31, 1915; s. Alexander John and Alice Maude (Kelly) L.; m. Patricia Lally, Oct. 2, 1940; children: Karen, Bridget, Monica. Student, U. Wash., 1934-35. With Lincoln Mut. Savs. Bank, Spokane, 1935-85; pres. Lincoln Mut. Savs. Bank, 1962-80, chief exec. officer, 1969-80, chmn., 1978-85; past dir. First Nat. Bank, Spokane; cons. AID Mission to Iran, 1964. Chmn. United Red Feather drive, Spokane, 1952; past pres. Spokane Philharmonic; trustee Spokane Unltd.; past trustee Mcpl. League Spokane; past chmn. Champagne Ball Charities; chmn. adv. com. on bond issues Spokane Sch. Bd., 1978; mem. bus. adv. com. Wash. State U. Coll. Bus. and Econs., 1979—; mem. Spokane Arts Com., 1976-85, chmn., 1984-85. Served from pvt. to 1st lt. USAAF, 1942-46. Mem. Wash. Savs. League (pres. 1961-62), Nat. Assn. Mut. Savs. Banks (past dir.), Savs. and Loan Found. (past mem. nat. bd.), Mut. Savs. Bank Assn. Wash. (pres. 1979), U.S. League Savs. Assns. (mut. instns. com.), Nat. League Insured Savs. Assn. (mem. bd. govs. 1966-76, mem. exec. com. 1974-76), Soc. Residential Appraisers (pres. Spokane chpt. 1952), Spokane C. of C. (trustee, exec. com. 1970-72, 78-82, sec.-treas. 1979, vice chmn. 1980-81, chmn. 1981-82). Clubs: University (past pres.), Spokane Country (past pres.), Spokane, Manito Golf and Country, Empire, Prosperity, Spokane. Office: 905 W Riverside Ave Spokane WA 99201-1099

LINDSAY, FRANKLIN ANTHONY, business executive, author; b. Kenton, Ohio, Mar. 12, 1916; s. Harry Wyatt and Ruth (Andrews) L.; m. Margot Coffin, Dec. 17, 1948; children: Catherine, Alison (dec.), John Franklin. A.B., Stanford U., 1938; postgrad., Harvard U., 1946. With Columbia div. U.S. Steel Corp., 1938-39; exec. asst. to Bernard Baruch, U.S. del. UN Atomic Energy Commn., 1946; cons. Ho. of Reps. Select (Herter) Com. on Fgn. Aid, 1947-48, ECA, Paris; rep. to exec. com. OEEC, 1948-49; with CIA, 1949-53; with pub. affairs program Ford Found., 1953-56; prin. McKinsey & Co., Inc., N.Y.C., 1956-61; exec. v.p., dir. Itek Corp., Lexington, Mass., 1961-62, pres., dir., 1962-75, chmn. bd., 1975-81, chmn. exec. com., 1981-83; chmn. Engenics, Inc., Menlo Park, Calif., 1983-85; rsch. Assoc. Inst. Politics, Harvard U., 1967-71; cons. 2d Hoover Commn., 1954, The White House, 1955; mem. Rockefeller Spl. Studies Panel Econ. Policy, 1956, Gaither Com. Nat. Security Policy, 1957; asst. staff dir. President's Com. World Econ. Policy, 1958; mem. President Elect's Task Force on Disarmament, 1960; dir. Com. for Nat. Trade Policy, 1956-71; adv. coun. dept. econs. Princeton U., 1961-64; mem. Wilson Ctr. Adv. coun. Smithsonian Instn., 1980-94; trustee Bennington Coll., 1963-73; chmn. bd. trustees Edn. Devel. Ctr., 1967-73; mem. vis. com. dept. econs. Harvard U., 1976-80; mem. President's Adv. Com. on Trade Negotiations, 1976-79; bd. dirs. Nat. Bur. Econ. Rsch., 1976-93, mem. exec. com., 1980—, chmn. 1983-86; mem. adv. coun. Gas Rsch. Inst., 1977-83; vice chmn. energy and raw materials, bus. and industry adv. com. OECD, 1977-82, chmn. 1980, mem. adv. bd. Pub. Agenda Found., 1978-84; mem. NRC Commn. Engring. Systems, 1978-84, panel on balancing nat. interest NAS, 1985-87; bd. dirs. Resources for the Future, 1978-86; assoc. Ctr. for Internat. Affairs, Harvard U., 1988—; vis. scholar Woodrow Wilson Ctr. for Scholars, Washington, 1987-88, 90; adj. prof. Internat. Mgmt. Inst., Kiev, Ukraine, 1993—; mem. standing policy group on Russia and Eurasia, The Atlantic Coun. of the U.S., 1996—. Author: New Techniques of Management Decision Making, 1958, Beacons in the Night: War and Revolution in Yugoslavia 1941-45, 1993; contbg. author: Prepariong Tomorrow's Business Leaders Today, The Conscience of the City, Removing Obstacles to Economic Growth; contbr. articles on nat. and fgn. policy to profl. jours. Vis. scholar Woodrow Wilson Ctr. for Scholars, Washington, 1987-88, 90. Lt. col. AUS, 1940-45; with guerrilla forces 1944-45, Europe (OSS); chief U.S. Mil. Mission to Yugoslavia, 1945. Decorated Legion of Merit; recipient Gold Freedom medal Republic of Slovenia. Mem. Nat. Planning Assn. (vice chmn. com. arms control 1959-62), Coun. Fgn. Rels., Inst. Strategic Studies (London), Com. for Econ. Devel. (trustee 1967—, vice chmn. 1974-88, mem. rsch. and policy com. 1968—), Can.-Am. Com., Hudson Inst. (pub. mem.), Saturday Club (Boston), Century Club (N.Y.), Phi Beta Kappa, Tau Beta Pi.

LINDSAY, GEORGE CARROLL, former museum director; b. Cochranville, Pa., Sept. 28, 1928; s. J. George and M. Elizabeth (Copeland) L.; m. Mary-Edythe Shelley, June 27, 1953. BA, Franklin and Marshall Coll., 1950; student, Dickinson Sch. Law, 1950-53; M.A. (Wintherthur fellow early Am. culture 1953-55), U. Del., 1955. Asst. to dir. Henry Francis du Pont Winterthur Mus., Del., 1955-56; asst. curator ethnology Smithsonian Instn., 1956-57, asso. curator cultural history, 1957-58, curator mus. service, 1958-66; dir. mus. services N.Y. State Mus., 1966-81, dir., 1981-83, dir. planning and program devel., 1983-86; exec. dir. Vanderbilt Mus., 1986-89; lectr. early Am. decorative arts and architecture; cons. in field; v.p. Alexandria Assn., Va., 1961-62, pres., 1962-63, bd. dirs., 1963-66; bd. dirs. Greater Washington Edni. TV Assn., 1964-66, mem. programming com., 1965-66; bd. dirs. No. Va. Fine Arts Assn., 1964-66, Mus. Audio-Visual Applications Group, 1962-70; mem. com. furnishing ofcl. reception room State Dept., 1960-75. Bd. dirs. Menands (N.Y.) Pub. Libr., 1970-86, Albany Symphony Orch., 1969-72, ARC, Albany, 1977-86; active Strasburg (Pa.) Borough Coun., 1992-96, pres., 1994-95; trustee Octoraro United Presbyn. Ch., 1993—. Mem. Am. Assn. Mus. (coun. 1969-72, v.p. 1970-71, chmn. profl. rels. com. 1974-80), N.Y. State Assn. Mus. (sec. 1968-77, pres. 1977-79, coun. 1985-89), N.E. Mus. Conf. (bd. govs. 1982-85, chmn. long range planning com. 1983-85), St. Andrew's Soc. (pres. Albany 1983-85), St. Andrew's Soc. Phila. Mem. Soc. of Friends. Address: 255 Wallingford Rd Strasburg PA 17579-1448

LINDSAY, GEORGE EDMUND, museum director; b. Pomona, Calif., Aug. 17, 1916; s. Charles Wesley and Alice (Foster) L.; m. Geraldine Kendrick Morris, 1972. Student, San Diego State Coll., 1936-39; B.A., Stanford U., 1951, Ph.D., 1956. Dir. Desert Bot. Gardes, Phoenix, 1939-40, San Diego Natural History Mus., 1956-63; Dir. Calif. Acad. Scis., San Francisco, 1963-82, dir. emeritus, 1982—. Served to capt. USAAF, 1943-46. Decorated Air medal with 3 clusters, Bronze Star. Fellow San Diego Soc. Natural History, Zool. Soc. San Diego, Calif. Acad. Scis., A.A.A.S., Cactus and Succulent Soc. Spl. rsch. taxonomy desert plants, Cactaceae of Baja Calif., Mex. Home: 87 Barbaree Way Tiburon CA 94920-2223 Office: Calif Acad Scis San Francisco CA 94118

LINDSAY, GEORGE PETER, lawyer; b. Bklyn., Feb. 22, 1948; s. Charles Joseph and Marie Antionette (Faraone) L.; m. Sharon Winnett, Sept. 8, 1973; children: William Charles, Kimberly Michelle. BA, Columbia U., 1969; JD, Harvard U., 1973. Bar: N.Y. 1974, Mass. 1985, U.S. Dist. Ct. (so. dist.) N.Y. 1974, U.S. Ct. Appeals (2d cir.) 1975. Assoc. White & Case, N.Y.C., 1973-82; ptnr. Miller, Wrubel & Dubroff, N.Y.C., 1982-83, Sullivan & Worcester LLP, N.Y.C., 1983—. Mem. ABA, Assn. Bar City of N.Y., N.Y. State Bar Assn. Office: Sullivan & Worcester LLP 767 3rd Ave New York NY 10017-2023

LINDSAY, JAMES WILEY, agricultural company executive; b. Des Moines, Sept. 13, 1934; s. Worthington U. Lindsay and Marsha E. (Wiley) Asher; m. Shirley L. Shutt, July 2, 1953 (div. May 1985, dec. 1990); children: Elizabeth Lindsay Foster, James W. II, Jennifer, Lindsay; m. Jean M. Baumann, Aug. 2, 1986; 1 child, Amanda Marie. Mgr. ops. Archer, Daniels, Midland, Fredonia, Kans., 1968-70, Lincoln, Nebr., 1970-72; mgr. export Archer, Daniels, Midland, Decatur, Ill., 1972-74; v.p. western region Archer, Daniels, Midland, Lincoln, 1974-76; v.p. ops. Archer, Daniels, Midland, Cedar Rapids, Iowa, 1979-80; ops. mgr. Archer, Daniels, Midland, Decatur, 1980-83; pres. Brazil ops. T.V.P., Inc., Campinas, Brazil, 1976-79; chief exec. officer AG Processing Inc., Omaha, 1983—; bd. dirs. ABC Ins., Des Moines; mem. adv. bd. FirstBank. Mem. Nat. Soybean Processors Assn. (chmn. 1987-91), Jaycees (pres. Fredonia chpt. 1963-64, bd. dirs. Des Moines chpt. 1960). Republican. Roman Catholic. Lodge: Masons. Avocations: singing, guitar, acting. Office: AG Processing Inc PO Box 2047 Omaha NE 68103-2047

LINDSAY, JOHN VLIET, former mayor, former congressman, author, lawyer; b. N.Y.C., Nov. 24, 1921; s. George Nelson and Eleanor (Vliet) L.; m. Mary Harrison, June 18, 1949; children—Katharine, Margaret, Anne, John Vliet. Grad., St. Paul's Sch., Concord, N.H., 1940; B.A., Yale U., 1944, LL.B., 1948; LL.D. (hon.), Harvard U., 1969, Williams Coll., 1968. Bar: N.Y. State 1949, N.Y. Dist. Ct. (so. dist.) N.Y 1950, U.S. Supreme Ct. 1955, D.C. 1958. Mem. firm Webster & Sheffield, N.Y.C., 1953-60, 74-91, presiding ptnr., 1989-91; of counsel Mudge Rose Guthrie Alexander & Ferdon, N.Y.C., 1991-94, ret., 1994; exec. asst. to U.S. atty. gen., 1955-56; mem. 86th-89th Congresses from 17th Dist. N.Y.; mayor N.Y.C., 1965-73; Commentator on TV. Author: Journey Into Politics, 1966, The City, 1970, The Edge, 1976. Bd. mem. emeritus Lincoln Ctr. for Performing Arts; chmn. emeritus bd. dirs. Lincoln Ctr. Theatre Co. Lt. USNR, 1943-46. Mem. Assn. of Bar of City of N.Y. (exec. com. 1956-60), ABA, N.Y. State Bar Assn., Assn. Former Mems. Congress (pres. 1987-88). Episcopalian. Democrat.

LINDSAY, LESLIE, packaging engineer; b. Amsterdam, N.Y., Oct. 30, 1960; d. R. Gardner and Dorothy (Loucks) L. BA in Advt., Mich. State U., 1981, BS in Package Engring., 1982. Cert. profl. engr. in packaging. Constrn. inspector N.Y. State Dept. Transp., Albany, 1983; sr. package design engr. Wang Labs., Inc., Lowell, Mass., 1983-90; packaging engr. Apple Computer, Inc., Santa Clara, Calif., 1990—; conf. speaker Internat. Safe Transit Assn., 1994. N.Y. State Regents scholar, 1977; recipient Silver Ameristar award for electronics packaging, 1993. Mem. Soc. Packaging Profls., Inst. Packaging Profls. (mem. reduction, reuse, and recycling of protective packaging task group), Boston Women's Rugby Club (tour chmn. 1985), Wang Ultimate Frisbee (social chmn. 1986-89). Home: 239 Erie Way Apt 5 Campbell CA 95008-1630 Office: Apple Computer Inc 20650 Valley Green Dr Cupertino CA 95014-1704

LINDSAY, NATHAN JAMES, aerospace company executive, retired career officer; b. Monroe, Wis., May 24, 1936; s. Ralph Allen and Gertrude (Wartenweiler) L.; m. Shirley Rae Montgomery, Feb. 2, 1958; children: Lori E. Lindsay Smith, Anne, Nathan J. Jr., Susan E. BS in Mech. Engring., U.Wis., 1958, MS in Mech. Engring., 1965; MS in Systems Mgmt., U. So. Calif., L.A., 1976. Commd. 2d lt. USAF, 1958, advanced through grades to maj. gen., 1988; munitions officer USAF Weapons Ctr., Tripoli, Libya, 1959-61; weapons logistics officer USAF Europe, Wiesbaden, Germany, 1961-63; Titan III propulsion officer USAF Space Systems Divsn., L.A., 1965-69; aircraft guns devel. officer Air Force Armament Lab., Fla., 1969-70; grad. Armed Forces Staff Coll., Norfolk, Va., 1970; mgmt. auditor Air Force Systems Command, Andrews AFB, Md., 1971-73; grad. Def. Systems Mgmt. Coll., Ft. Belvoir, Va., 1973; space systems policy officer Air Force Office Special Projects, L.A., 1973-74, launch systems integration mgr., 1974-78; dir. policy and adminstrn. Air Force Office Space Systems, Pentagon, Washington, 1978-80; dir. space ops. support Air Force Space Divsn., L.A., 1980-82, program mgr. launch and control systems, 1982-84; comdr. Ea. Space and Missile Ctr., Patrick AFB, Fla., 1985-86; dep. comdr. for space launch and control systems Air Force Space Divsn., L.A., 1986-87; dir. office spl. projects Office Sec. of Air Force, L.A., 1987-92; v.p. comml. programs Lockheed Martin Astrospace; mem. investigation task force NASA Challenger Accident, Kennedy Space Ctr., 1986. Co-chmn. Brevard County, Fla. Civilian-Mil. Affairs Coun., Cocoa Beach, 1984-86; elder Presbyn. Ch. Decorated D.S.M., Def. Superior Svc. medal, Legion of Merit with one oak leaf cluster, Meritorious Svc. medal with one oak leaf cluster, Joint Svc. Commendation medal, Air Force Commendation medal with one oak leaf cluster, Def. Disting. Svc. medal, NASA Disting. Svc. medal, Gen. Thomas White USAF Space trophy, 1992, AAS Mil. Astronautics award, 1993. Mem. AIAA, Am. Astronautical Soc., Air Force Assn. (Bernard A. Shriever Space award 1989), Nat. Space Club (bd. dirs. 1992-94), U. Wis. Alumni Assn., Am. Legion. Avocations: hiking, travelling, fishing, reading. Home: 48 Madison Dr Plainsboro NJ 08536-2318

LINDSAY, PATRICIA MAE, physician, medical administrator; b. Kilbourne, Ill., Aug. 26, 1942; d. William Louden and Virginia Mae (Sutton) L. BA, Drake U., 1964; MD, U. Ill., 1971. Assoc. med. dir. Ill. State U. Med. Ctr., Normal, 1978-81; chief of hypertension City of Faith, Tulsa, 1981-86; ptnr. Glass-Nelson Med. Clinic, Tulsa, 1986-88; med. dir. Med. Missions, Tulsa, 1983—; asst. prof. U. Okla. Med. Sch.; assoc. with med. dir. various med. hosps. and clinics, St. Petersburg, Russia, 1991-96, also internat. clinics. NIH fellowship, 1968; Vsevolesk Hosp. wing named in her honor, St. Petersburg, 1994. Mem. AMA, Am. Coll. Physicians, Geriatric Med. Soc., Okla. Med. Soc., Tulsa Med. Soc. Office: Med Missions 2918 E 78th St Tulsa OK 74136-8732

LINDSAY, ROGER ALEXANDER, investment executive; b. Dundee, Scotland, Feb. 18, 1941; s. Archibald Carswell Lindsay and Edith Paterson Bissett. Student, The Morgan Acad., Dundee, Queen's Coll. U. St. Andrews, Scotland. Asst. acct., office mgr. Andrew G. Kidd Ltd., Dundee, 1964; head office acct. Associated British Foods Ltd., London, 1966; sec., treas. Wittington Investments, Ltd., Toronto, 1971-95; exec. v.p. Wittington Investments Ltd., Toronto, 1991-95; pres. Fort House Investments, Toronto, 1995—; bd. dirs. Loblaw Cos. Ltd., Intercon Security Ltd., United World Coll. Internat. Can., Inc., The W. Garfield Weston Found., Bachmann Channell Islands Ltd.; pres. Trustee Presbyn. Ch. of Can. Knight, Comdr. The Sov. Order of St. John, Serving Bro. Ven. Order Hosp. St. John. Fellow Inst. Mgmt., Inst. Dirs., Soc. Antiquaries Scotland; mem. Inst. Chartered Accts. Scotland, Royal Overseas League, The Nat. Club (1st v.p. Toronto), Coral Beach Club (Bermuda), Montes Club (London). Avocations: heraldry, antique silver. Office: Fort House Investments, 150 Heath St W Ste 1301, Toronto, ON Canada M4V 2Y4

LINDSAY, WILLIAM KERR, surgeon; b. Vancouver, B.C., Can., Sept. 3, 1920; s. James Arthur and Lottie Mary (Early) L.; m. Frances Beatrice Ferris, Feb. 15, 1945; children—William Arthur, Barbara Susanne, Katherine Mary, Anne Louise. M.D., U. Toronto, 1945, BS in Medicine, 1949, M.S., 1959. Intern Toronto Gen. Hosp., 1945-46; resident Toronto Gen. Hosp. and Hosp. Sick Children, 1948-51, Montreal Gen. Hosp., 1951-52, Baylor U. Hosp., 1952-53; practice medicine, specializing in plastic surgery Toronto, 1953—; staff surgeon to head divsn. plastic surgery Hosp. for Sick Children, 1953-86, cons., 1986—; project dir. Research Inst., 1954-85; faculty dept. surgery U. Toronto Faculty of Medicine, 1953-86, prof., 1968-86, chmn. interhospital com. for plastic surgery, 1965-86, prof. emeritus, 1986—; Chmn. med. dental staff com. Ont. Hugh MacMillan Treatment Ctr. (formerly Crippled Childrens Ctr.), 1958-63. Trustee McLaughlin Found., 1986—. With M.C., Royal Can. Army, 1943-46; surg. lt. Royal Can. Navy, 1946-47. Hon. head burn and plastic surgery dept. Gansu Provincial People's Hosp., Lanzhou City, China, 1994—. Fellow ACS, Royal Coll. Surgeons Can.; mem. Am. Assn. Plastic Surgeons (pres. 1970-71, Hon. award 1995), Can. Soc. Plastic Surgeons (pres. 1963), Easter Seal Soc. Ont. (chmn. med. adv. com. 1957-65, cons. 1952-95, mem. rsch. inst. 1979-95, Gold award 1995), Am. Soc. Plastic and Reconstructive Surgeons (Spl. Achievement award 1979), Am. Soc. Surgery of Hand, Am. Cleft Palate Assn., Brit. Soc. Surgery of Hand. Home: 77 Clarendon Ave, Toronto, ON Canada M4V 1J1 Office: 555 University Ave, Toronto, ON Canada M5G 1X8

LINDSEY, CASIMIR CHARLES, zoologist; b. Toronto, Ont., Can., Mar. 22, 1923; s. Charles Bethune and Wanda Casimira (Gzowski) L.; m. Shelagh Pauline Lindsey, May 29, 1948. B.A., U. Toronto, 1948; M.A., U. B.C., Vancouver, 1950; Ph.D., Cambridge (Eng.) U., 1952. Div. biologist B.C. Game Dept., 1952-57; with Inst. Fisheries, also dept. zoology U. B.C., 1953-66; prof. zoology U. Man., Winnipeg, 1966-79; dir. Inst. Animal Resource Ecology, U. B.C., 1980-85; mem. Fisheries and Oceans Adv. Council, 1981-86; prof. emeritus U. B.C., 1988—; bd. govs. Vancouver Public Aquarium, 1956-66, 80-95; external assessor univs. S ingapore and Nanyang, 1979-81; cons. in field. Author papers in field. Served with Can. Army, 1943-45. Recipient Publ. award Wildlife Soc., 1972; Saunderson award for excellence in teaching U. Man., 1977; Rh Inst. award, 1979; Nuffield Found. grantee, 1973; Killam sr. fellow, 1985-86. Fellow Royal Soc. Can.; mem. Can. Soc. Zoologists (pres. 1977-78), Can. Soc. Environ. Biologists (v.p. 1974-75), Am. Soc. Ichthyologists and Herpetologists (gov.). Office: U BC Dept of Zoology, 6270 University Blvd, Vancouver, BC Canada V6T 1Z4

LINDSEY, D. RUTH, physical education educator; b. Kingfisher, Okla., Oct. 26, 1926; d. Lewis Howard and Kenyon (King) L. BS, Okla. State U., 1948; MS, U. Wis., 1954; PEd, Ind. U., 1965. Registered kinesiotherapist, 1970. Instr. Okla. State U., Stillwater, 1948-50, Monticello Coll., Alton, Ill., 1951-54, DePauw U., Greencastle, Ind., 1954-56; prof. Okla. State U., Stillwater, 1956-75; vis. prof. U. Utah, Salt Lake City, 1975-76; prof. phys. edn. Calif. State U., Long Beach, 1976-88; prof. emeritus phys. edn. Calif. State U., 1988—; freelance author, cons. Westminster, Calif. Co-author: Fitness for the Health of It, 6th edit., 1989, Concepts of Physical Fitness, 8th edit., 1993, Fitness for Life, 3d edit., 1993, Concepts of Physical Fitness and Wellness, 1993, The Ultimate Fitness Book, 1984, Survival Kit for Those Who Sit, 1989, A Menu of Concepts: Physical Fitness Concepts, Toward Active Lifestyles and Fitness and Wellness Concepts, Toward Health Lifestyles, 1996; editor: Perspectives: Jour. of Western Soc. for Phys. Edn. Coll. Women, 1988-95. Amy Morris Homans scholar, 1964; recipient Disting. and Meritorious Svc. Honor award Okla. Assn. Health, Phys. Edn. and Recreation, 1970, Meritorious Performance award Calif. State U., 1987, Julian Vogel Meml. award Am. Kinesiotherapy Assn., 1988, Fellow AAHPERD, Am. Kinesiotherapy Assn., Calif. Assn. Health, Phys. Edn., Recreation and Dance, Nat. Coun. Against Health Fraud, Orange County Nutrition Coun., Tex. and Acad. Authors Assn., Western Soc. for Phys. Edn. of Coll. Women (hon. mem.), Phi Kappa Phi. Republican. Baptist. Avocations: golf, travel, writing.

LINDSEY, DAVID HOSFORD, lawyer; b. Kingsville, Tex., July 25, 1950; s. Ernest Truman and Helen Elizabeth (Hosford) L.; m. Marilyn Kay Williams, June 8, 1974; children: Seth Williams, Brooks Daniel. BS in Bus. Adminstrn., U. Mo., 1972; JD, Washburn U., 1975. Bar: Mo. 1975. With trust dept. Commerce Bank, Kansas City, Mo., 1974-75, asst. v.p., 1979-83, v.p., 1983-85, sr. v.p., 1985-94, chief credit officer, 1989—; mgr., sales dept. Pioneer Pallet, Inc., North Kansas City, Mo., 1976; asst. cashier Nat. Bank, North Kansas City, 1977, asst. v.p., 1977-78, v.p., 1978-79. Vice chmn. planning and zoning com. City of Liberty, Mo., 1981-93; bd. dirs. Kansas City Met. YMCA (treas., mem. exec. com.). Mem. Mo. Bar Assn., Lawyers Assn. Kansas City, Kansas City Met. Bar Assn., Robert Morris Assn. (bd. dirs. Kansas City chpt.), Kansas City C. of C., Kansas City Alumni Assn. (bd. dirs.), Clayview Country Club, Phi Gamma Delta, Omicron Delta Kappa. Baptist. Home: 602 Camelot Dr Liberty MO 64068-1176 Office: Commerce Bank 1000 Walnut St Kansas City MO 64106-2107

LINDSEY, DOTTYE JEAN, marketing executive; b. Temple Hill, Ky., Nov. 4, 1929; d. Jesse D. and Ethel Ellen (Bailey) Nuckols; m. Willard W. Lindsey, June 14, 1952 (div.). BS, Western Ky. U., 1953, MA, 1959. Owner, Bonanza Restaurant, Charleston, W.Va., 1965; tchr. remedial reading Alice Waller Elem. Sch., Louisville, 1967-75, tchr., 1953-67, 1975-84, contact person for remedial reading, 1968—; regional mgr. A.L. Williams Fin. Mktg. Co., 1988—; profl. model Cosmo/Casablancas Modeling Agy., Louisville, 1984-89; with Primerica Fin. Svcs. (formerly A.L. Willams Fin. Svcs.), Louisville, 1988—; model, 1984-89; regional mgr. Primerica Fin. Svcs., 1988—. Treas. Met. Louisville Women's Polit. Caucus, 1980-88, Ky. Women's Polit. Caucus, 1988-91; bd. sponsor ROTC Western Ky. U., 1950; local precinct capt., 1987—; election officer, 1984—; treas. Ky. Women's Polit. Caucus, 1988-91. Named Miss Ky., 1951. Mem. NEA, Ky. Edn. Assn., Jefferson County Tchrs. Assn., various polit. action coms., Internat. Reading Assn., Am. Childhood Edn. Assn. Democrat. Baptist.

LINDSEY, GINA MARIE, airport executive. Gen. mgr. Seattle-Tacoma Internat. Airport. Office: Seattle-Tacoma Internat. Airport PO Box 68727 Seattle WA 98168*

LINDSEY, JACK LEE, curator; b. June 7, 1958; s. Charles Edward and Ruth Jacquelyn (Hensley) L. BA in Am. Social and Cultural History with honors, BA in Studio Art with honors, Guilford Coll., 1980; MA in Am. Civilization and Curatorial Studies, U. Pa., 1986, postgrad., 1986—. Asst. curator exhibitions Guilford Coll., Greensboro, N.C., 1978-80; chmn. dept. art and history Atlantic Friends Sch., Northfield, N.J., 1981-85; field rschr., archivist U. Pa., Phila., 1986-87, instr. depts. Am. civilization and folklore and folklife, 1986-89; asst. curator Am. decorative arts Phila. Mus. Art, 1986-88, assoc. curator Am. decorative arts, 1988-89, curator Am. decorative arts, 1990—; chmn. adv. bd. Phila. Folklore Project, 1989-91; lectr. in field. Contbr. articles to profl. jours. Recipient Outstanding Educators award Friends Coun. in Edn., 1984, 85; Newlin Grad. History scholar Guilford Coll., 1980; Rotary Internat. Edn. scholar, 1980-81; rsch. grantee NEA, 1980; Edward Maverick fellow Attingham Trust, 1987. Mem. Am. Folklore Soc. (vice chmn. adv. bd. 1989-90). Office: Phila Mus Art 26th And The Pky Philadelphia PA 19130

LINDSEY, JOHN HORACE, insurance executive, museum official; b. Waxahachie, Tex., July 28, 1922; s. Harry E. and Marie (Smith) L.; m. Sara Houstoun, Aug. 30, 1946; children: Edwin (dec.), David C. BA, Tex. A&M U., 1944. Propr. Lindsey Ins. Agy., Houston, 1953—; bd. of regents Texas A&M U System. Former v.p. Houston Mus. Fine Arts; former pres. Alley Theatre; bd. dirs. South Tex. Coll. Law, Tex. A&M Rsch. Found., College Station; pres. Tex. A&M U. Alumni, 1964; vice chmn. bd. visitors U.S. Mil. Acad.; bd. dirs. George Bush Presdl. Libr. Found. Recipient Disting. Alumni award Tex. A&M U. Home: 3640 Willowick Rd Houston TX 77019-1114 Office: Tex Am Bldg 921 Main St Ste 625 Houston TX 77002-6422

LINDSEY, JONATHAN ASMEL, development executive, educator; b. Bulloch County, Ga., June 9, 1937; s. Joel Wesley and Ethel Iora (Stickland) L.; m. Edythe Annette Loewer, Apr. 3, 1965; children—Julianna Elizabeth, Jonathan Edward. A.B., George Washington U., 1961; B.D., So. Bapt. Sem., Louisville, 1964; Ph.D., So. Bapt. Sem., 1968; M.S.L.S., U. Ala., 1975. Assoc. prof., librarian Judson Coll., Marion, Ala., 1967-77; assoc. dean, librarian Meredith Coll., Raleigh, N.C., 1977-83; librarian Baylor U., Waco, Tex., 1983-89, dir. found. devel., 1989-95; dir donor info./recognition, 1995—. Author: (monographs) Free To Be, 1975, Change and Challenge, 1978, (with others) Professional Ethics and Librarians, 1985, Performance Evaluation: A Management Basic, 1986; editor: N.C. Libraries (H.W. Wilson award 1981), 1979-83, Publications in Librarianship, 1988-93; contbr. articles and book revs. to profl. publs. Mem. Waco Peace Alliance, PTA. Mem. ALA, Nat. Soc. Fund Raising Execs., Coun. for Advancement and Support of Edn., Tex. Libr. Assn. Home: 8265 Mosswood Dr Waco TX 76712-2407 Office: Baylor U PO Box 97026 Waco TX 76798-7026

LINDSEY, LAWRENCE BENJAMIN, economist, federal official; b. Peekskill, N.Y., July 18, 1954; s. Merritt Hunt and Helen Ruth (Hissam) L.; m. Susan Ann McGrath, Aug. 28, 1982; 2 children. AB magna cum laude, Bowdoin Coll., Brunswick, Maine, 1976; MA, Harvard U., 1981, PhD, 1985; JD (hon.), Bowdoin Coll., 1993. Economist Coun. Econ. Advisers, Washington, 1981-84; from asst. prof. to assoc. prof. Harvard U., Cambridge, Mass., 1984-90; faculty rsch. fellow Nat. Bur. Econ. Rsch., Cambridge, 1984-89; from assoc. dir. to spl. asst. to Pres., Office of Policy Devel., The White House, Washington, 1989-91; gov. Fed. Res. Bd., Washington, 1991—. Author: The Growth Experiment, 1990; contbr. articles to profl. jours. Recipient Walter Wriston award Manhattan Inst., 1988. Mem. Phi Beta Kappa. Office: Fed Res Bd 20th & C Sts NW Washington DC 20551*

LINDSEY, LYDIA, education educator, researcher; b. Trenton, N.J., Jan. 10, 1951; d. Charles and Ollie S. Lindsey. BA, Howard U., 1972, MA, 1974; PhD, U. N.C., 1992. Asst. prof. N.C. Ctrl. U., Durham, 1974-92; archivist N.C. Ctrl. U., 1992—; adj. prof. U. N.C., Chapel Hill, 1992—; cons. A Philip Randolph Ednl. Found., 1975-78; rsch. assoc. U. Warwick, Coventry, Engr., 1985-86; Rockefeller doctoral fellow Duke-U.N.C. Women's Studies Rsch. Ctr., 1985-886; bd. dirs. Carolina Wren Press, Durham, Stagville Plantation, 1992—; minority postdoctoral fellow U. N.C., 1994-96, participant in nat. land interaction confs. Contbr. articles to profl. jours. Campaign mgr. Beverly Jones Sch. Bd., Durham, 1991-92; active People's Alliance, Durham, 1991-92, Durham Hist. Preservation Soc., 1991-92. U. N.C. Minority Postdoctoral fellow, 1994—, N.C. Bd. Gov.'s Doctoral fellow, 1986-87, NEH fellow for coll. tchrs. of historically black colls., 1985-86, U. N.C.-Chapel Hill Reynolds Overseas Grad. fellow, 1985-86, Rockefeller fellow from Duke-U. N.C. Women's Studies Rsch. Ctr. Doctoral fellow, 1985-86; N.J. State scholar, 1968-72, Fulbright scholar, 1995; Recipient DAR History award. Mem. Assn. Black Women Historians, Assn. for Study African, Caribbean and Asian Culture in Britain, Assn. for Study of Afro-Am. Life and History, Assn. Caribbean Studies, Assn. So. Women Historians, Assn. Social and Behavioral Scis., Collegium for African Am. Studies, Am. Hist. Assn., Nat. Coun. Black Studies, Nat. Coun. Black Women, Carolina Symposium Brit. Study, So. Confs. Brit. Studies, Golden Key (hon.), Delta Sigma Theta, Pi Gamma Mu, Phi Alpha Theta. Democrat. Baptist. Avocations: reading, writing, gardening, swimming, travel. Home: 2210 Alpine Rd Durham NC 27707-3970 Office: NC Ctrl U Durham NC 27707

LINDSEY, SETH MARK, lawyer, federal agency administrator; b. L.A., Oct. 18, 1947; s. Seth Rankin and Lela Belle (Johnson) L.; m. Susan Adelaide Badger, June 29, 1968; 1 child, Samantha. BA, U. So. Calif., L.A., 1968; JD, Yale U., 1971. Bar: Calif. 1972, U.S. Supreme Ct. 1984. Honors atty. Housing and Urban Devel., Washington, 1971-72, atty., 1972-76; asst. chief counsel Fed. Railroad Adminstrn., Washington, 1976-86, chief counsel, 1986—, acting adminstr., 1993; spl. counsel for Conrail and Union Sta. Redevel. Fed. Railroad Adminstrn., 1984-86. Recipient Silver medal Dept. Transp., 1977, 83, Gold medal, 1984. Baptist. Office: Dept Transp Fed RR Adminstrn Adminstrn 400 7th St SW Ste 8201 Washington DC 20590-0001

LINDSEY, STEVEN FRANK, banker; b. Herrin, Ill., Jan. 7, 1955; s. Frank Jr. and Dorene (Pattarozzi) L.; m. Nancy Beth Lawrence, Nov. 11, 1977; children: Jill Ellen, Andrea Maria. BA in Econs. and Bus. Adminstrn., Coe Coll., 1977; student, Ill. Bankers Sch., 1984-85, Herbert V. Prochnow Sch. Bank., 1985-87. Teller Bank of West Frankfort, Ill., 1977-79; loan officer Bank of Zeigler, Ill., 1979; v.p. lending Banterra Bank of West Frankfort, 1979—. Mem., advisor task force Treas. of State of Ill., Springfield, 1992. Mem. Ill. Small Bus. Growth Corp. (chmn. bd. dirs. 1991—, Lender of Yr. for State of Ill. 1993, 94), U.S. Small Bus. Adminstrn. (cert. lending status, preferred lending status, SBA Fin. Svcs. Advocate of Yr. for Ill. 1995), Moose (lodge # 795), Franklin County Country Club. Southern Baptist. Avocations: golf, gardening. Office: Banterra Bank West Frankfort 110 E Oak St West Frankfort IL 62896-2741

LINDSEY, SUSAN LYNDAKER, zoologist; b. Valley Forge, Pa., Aug. 23, 1956; d. Howard Paul and Lillian Irene (Whitman) Lyndaker; m. Kevin Arthur Lindsey, July 17, 1982. BS in Biology, St. Lawrence U., 1978; MA in Zoology, So. Ill. U., Carbondale, 1980; PhD in Zoology, Colo. State U., 1987. Rschr. St. Lawrence U., Kenya, East Africa, 1974; tchr. Beth Jacob H.S., Denver, 1986-87; rschr. mammal dept. Dallas Zoo, 1988-93; exec. dir. Wild Canid Survival and Rsch. Ctr., Eureka, Mo., 1993—; adj. prof. Cedar Valley Coll., 1992-93; propagation group mem. Red Wolf Species Survival Plan, Tacoma, Wash., 1994—, Mexican Gray Wolf Species Survival Plan, Albuquerque, 1993—. Contbr. articles to profl. jours. Docent Denver Zool. Found., Denver Zoo, 1985-88. Mem. Am. Zoo and Aquarium Assn., Am. Behavior Soc., Am. Soc. of Mammalogists, Beta Beta Beta, Phi Beta Kappa, Psi Chi. Avocations: horseback riding, canoeing, gardening, photography, travel. Office: Wild Canid Survival Rsch Ctr Wash U PO Box 760 Eureka MO 63025

LINDSKOG, DAVID RICHARD, lawyer; b. New Haven, Aug. 4, 1936; s. Gustaf Elmer and Charlotte (Birely) L.; m. Elisabeth Lagg, Jan. 28, 1978; 1 child, Stefanie. B.A., Yale U., 1958; LL.B., U. Va., 1965. Bar: N.Y. 1966, conseil juridique France 1978, avocat 1992. Assoc., Curtis, Mallet-Prevost, Colt & Mosle, N.Y.C., 1965-72, ptnr., 1973—. Served to lt. USNR, 1958-62. Mem. Internat. Bar Assn. Episcopalian. Club: Yale (N.Y.C.). Home: 22 Shore Acre Dr Old Greenwich CT 06870-2130 Office: Curtis Mallet-Prevost Colt & Mosle 101 Park Ave New York NY 10178-0061

LINDSKOG, NORBERT F., business and health administration educator, consultant; b. St. Cloud, Minn., Aug. 2, 1932; s. Magnus Alf and Dorthey Ann (Donken) L. BS, St. Cloud State U., 1954, MS, 1957; MHA, Northwestern U., 1960; DEd, Ariz. State U., 1977. Bus. tchr. Minn. High Schs. and Santa Barbara (Calif.) City Coll., 1954-58; adminstrv. extern Louis A. Weiss Meml. Hosp., Chgo., 1958-59, exec. v.p., 1960-66; adminstrv. resident St. Luke's Hosp., St. Paul, 1959-60; mgmt. cons. in Health & Med. Adminstrn. Booz Allen & Hamilton, Inc., Chgo., 1966-68; cons. in Hosp. adminstr., assoc. for Edn. Ill. Hosp. Assoc., Chgo., 1968-71; faculty assoc. Ctr. for Health Svcs. Adminstr. Grad. Sch. Bus., Ariz. State U., Tempe, 1974-75; asst. prof. bus. Harold Washington Coll. City Colls. of Chgo., 1968-71, assoc. prof. bus., 1971-76, prof. bus., health adminstrn., 1976—, chmn. dept. bus., 1970-82; bd. dirs. Shoreline Corp., 1988—; lectr. Harold Washington Coll., 1962-68; Cen. YMCA Coll., Chgo, 1973-78, cons. 1978; adj. prof. Internat. Acad. Merchandising & Design, 1978—. Prepub. editor and reviewer for many recent bus. related texts; contbr. to profl. jours. Fellow Royal Soc. Health, Am. Assn. Health Care Execs.; mem. Nat. Assn. Mgmt. Educators, Ill. CPA Found., Am. Soc. for Health Manpower Edn. and Tng., Nat. Bus. Edn. Assn., Ill. Bus. Edn. Assn., Chgo. Bus. Edn. Assn., Am. Hosp. Assn., Northwestern U. Health Adminstrn. Alumni Assn., Ariz. State U. Alumni Assn., St. Cloud State U. Alumni Assn., Masons, Phi Delta Kappa, Delta Pi Epsilon, Alpha Delta Mu, Kappa Delta Pi, Pi Omega Pi, Pi Delta Epsilon, Apha Pi Omega. Home: 6301 N Sheridan Rd Chicago IL 60660-1728 Office: Harold Washington Coll 30 E Lake St Chicago IL 60601-2420

LINDSLEY, DONALD BENJAMIN, physiological psychologist, educator; b. Brownhelm, Ohio, Dec. 23, 1907; s. Benjamin Kent and Mattie Elizabeth (Jenne) L.; m. Ellen Ford, Aug. 16, 1933; children: David Ford, Margaret, Robert Kent, Sara Ellen. A.B., Wittenberg Coll. (now Univ.), 1929, D.Sc. (hon.), 1959; A.M., U. Iowa, 1930, Ph.D., 1932; Sc.D. (hon.), Brown U., 1958, Trinity Coll., Hartford, Conn., 1965; D.Sc. (hon.), Loyola U. Chgo., 1969; Ph.D. (hon.), Johannes Gutenberg U., Mainz, W.Ger., 1977. Instr. psychology U. Ill., 1932-33; NRC fellow Harvard U. Med. Sch., 1933-35; research assoc. Western Res. U. Med. Sch., 1935-38; asst. prof. psychology Brown U.; also dir. psychol. and neurophysiol. lab. Bradley Hosp., 1938-46; dir. war research project on radar operation Yale, OSRD, Nat. Def. Research Com., Camp Murphy and Boca Raton AFB, Fla., 1943-45; prof.

psychology Northwestern U., 1946-51; prof. psychology, physiology, psychiatry and pediatrics UCLA, 1951-77, prof. emeritus, 1977—, mem. Brain Research Inst., 1961—, chmn. dept. psychology, 1959-62; William James lectr. Harvard, 1958; Univ. Research lectr. U. Calif. at Los Angeles, 1960; Phillips lectr. Haverford Coll., 1961; Walter B. Pillsbury lectr. psychology Cornell U., 1963; vis. lectr. Kansas State U., 1966, Tex. A & M U., 1980; Mem. sci. adv. bd. USAF, 1947-49; undersea warfare com. NRC, 1951-64; cons. NSF, 1952-54; mem. mental health study sect. NIMH, 1953-57; neurol. study sect. Nat. Inst. Neurol. Diseases and Blindness, 1958-62; cons. Guggenheim Found., 1963-70, mem. ednl. adv. bd., 1970-78; chmn. behavioral scis. tng. com. Nat. Inst. Gen. Med. Scis., 1966-69; mem. behavioral biology adv. panel AIBS-NASA, 1966-71; mem. space sci. bd. NAS, 1967-70; mem. com. space medicine, 1969-71; mem. Calif. Legis. Assembly Sci. and Tech. Coun., 1970-71. Cons. editor Jour. Exptl. Psychology, 1947-68, Jour. Comparative and Physiol. Psychology, 1952-62, Jour. Personality, 1958-62; mem. editorial bd. Internat. Jour. Physiology and Behavior, 1965-77, Exptl. Brain Rsch., 1965-76, Developmental Psychobiology, 1968-82, Neurosci. and Behavioral Physiology, 1976—; contbr. numerous articles on physiol. psychology, neurosci., brain and behavior to sci. jours., also numerous chpts. in books. Trustee Grass Found., 1958-95, emeritus trustee, 1996—. Awarded Presdl. Cert. of Merit (for war work), 1948; recipient Disting. Sci. Achievement award Calif. Psychol. Assn., 1977, Disting. Sci. Contbn. award Soc. Psychophysiol. Rsch., 1984, Disting. Grad. award Dept Psychology U. Iowa, 1987, Disting. Alumnus award for Achievement U. Iowa, 1988, Gerard prize (with H.W. Magoun) Soc. Neurosci., 1988, Gold Medal award Am. Psychol. Found., 1989, Hon. Life Mem. award Dept. Psychobiology, U. Calif., Irvine, 1989; Guggenheim fellow Europe, 1959, hon. fellow UCLA Sch. Medicine, 1986. Mem. Nat. Acad. Scis. (chmn. com. long duration missions in space 1967-72, mem. space sci. board), Am. Psychol. Assn. (Distinguished Sci. Contbn. award 1959), Am. Physiol. Soc., Soc. Exptl. Psychologists, Am. Electroencephalographic Soc. (pres. 1964-65, hon. mem. 1980—, Herbert Jasper award 1994), AAAS (v.p. 1954, chmn. sect. J 1977), Midwest Psychol. Assn. (pres. 1952), Am. Acad. Cerebral Palsy, Western Soc. Electroencephalography (hon. mem. with great distinction, pres. 1957), Western Psychol. Assn. (pres. 1959-60), Am. Acad. Arts and Scis., Internat. Brain Research Orgn. (treas. 1967-71), Soc. Neuroscis. (Donald B. Lindsley prize in behavioral neurosci. established in his name), Finnish Acad. of Sci. and Letters (fgn. mem.), Sigma Xi, Alpha Omega Alpha, Gamma Alpha, Phi Gamma Delta. Conglist. Home: 471 23rd St Santa Monica CA 90402-3125

LINDSLEY, JOHN MARTIN, chemical engineer; b. Syracuse, N.Y., Sept. 4, 1914; s. Floyd Adelbert and Katherine Agusta (Birch) L.; m. Lois Dorothy Eshleman, May 6, 1939; children: Katherine Virginia Lindsley Scherer, Nancy Sarah Morris, Karen Jean Knowles. Diploma, Mechanics Inst. (now R.I.T.), 1940; certificate, John Huntington Polytech. Inst, 1940-41; student, U. Pitts., 1944-46. Registered profl. engr., N.Y. Pipe fitter, design draftsman Eastman Kodak Kodak Park, Rochester, N.Y., 1935-40; design engr. chem. plant Carbide and Carbon Chems., South Charleston, W.Va., 1940-42; engr. design Koppers Co., Pitts., 1942-46; new plant ops. Buffalo, Houston, Granite City, Ill., 1943-45; project engr. Eastman Kodak, Kodak Park, Rochester, 1947-55, dept. head construction & maintaince div., 1955-67, dept. head utilities, waste disposal solid and liquid, 1967-75; design ops. assignment Kodak Carbide Carbon, Oak Ridge, Tenn., 1951-54; chair subcom. incineration Mfg. Chemist Assn., Washington, 1968-75; vice chmn. Monroe County Sewer Agy./Pure Waters Agy, 1964-73. Mem., chair Gates, Chili Ogden Sch. Bd., Monroe County, Rochester, 1959-68; rep. dist. 21 Republican Party, St. Lucie County, Fla., 1980-85, chair exec. com., 1983-85; mem. Gates Town Planning Bd., Monroe County, 1956-62, 67-75, Monroe County Pure Waters Bd., 1973-75, St. Lucie County Water/Sewer Authority, 1986-92. Mem. AICE (cert., emeritus). Achievements include designing, built and conceived thin film climbing film evaporator single-pass for heat sensitive materials-high vacuum. 90 million Btu/hr. chemical waste incinerator for hazardous/toxic waste, liquid and solid upgraded to 120 million Btu/hr in 1986. EPA approved -no violations in 18 years of operation; conceived, designed, built and put into operation in cooperation with Dow Chem. and 3M.

LINDSTEDT-SIVA, (KAREN) JUNE, marine biologist, environmental consultant; b. Mpls., Sept. 24, 1941; d. Stanley L. and Lila (Mills) Lindstedt; m. Ernest Howard Siva, Dec. 20, 1969. Student, U. Calif.-Santa Barbara, 1959-60, U. Calif.-Davis, 1960-62; B.A., U. So. Calif., 1963, M.S., 1967, Ph.D., 1971. Asst. coordinator Office Sea Grant Programs U. So. Calif., 1971; environ. specialist So. Calif. Edison Co., Rosemead, 1971-72; asst. prof. biology Calif. Luth. U., 1972-73; sci. advisor Atlantic Richfield Co., Los Angeles, 1973-77, sr. sci. advisor, 1977-81, mgr. environ. scis., 1981-86, mgr. environ. protection, 1986-96; environ. cons., 1996—; mem. Nat. Sci. Bd., 1984-90; mem. panels on environ. issues Nat. Rsch. Coun.; mem. Polar Rsch. Bd., 1994—; mem. EPA Panel on Environ. Risk Reduction, 1992-94; mem. NAS Alaska Panel; mem. biology adv. coun. Calif. State U.-Long Beach, 1980-92; bd. dirs. So. Calif. Acad. Scis., 1983-93, pres., 1990-92; mem. Marine Scis.; adv. coun. U. So. Calif. Inst. Coastal and Marine Scis.; trustee Bermuda Biol. Sta. for Rsch.; chmn. Oil Spill Conf., San Antonio, 1989, API Oil Spills Com. Contbr. articles to profl. jours. Recipient Calif. Mus. Sci. and Industry Achievement award, 1976, Trident award for Marine Scis., 11th Ann. Rev. Underwater Activites, Italy, 1970, Achievement award for Advancing Career Opportunities for Women, Career Planning Council, 1978; research grantee; distg. scholar biology Calif. Lut. U. Colloquim Scholars, 1988. Fellow AAAS, ASTM (award of merit 1990), So. Calif. Acad. Scis., Soc. Petroleum Industry Biologists (pres. 1976-80); mem. Marine Tech. Soc., Calif. Native Plant Soc., Am. Inst. Biol. Sci., Phi Beta Kappa, Sigma Xi, Phi Kappa Phi.

LINDSTROM, CHARLES CLIFFORD, hospital administrator; b. Sauk Center, Minn., Apr. 15, 1928; married;. BA, U. Minn., 1952, MA, 1960. Asst. exec. dir. Twin City Regional Hosp. Coun., St. Paul, 1955-57; administr. rsch. St. John's Hosp., St. Paul, 1957-58, Abbott Hosp., Mpls., 1959-60; asst. adminstr. Mpls. Gen. Hosp., 1960-63; administr. Hennepin County Med. Ctr., Mpls., 1963-64, Fairview Southdale Hosp., Mpls., 1964-66; CEO, now advisor St. Luke's Health Sys., Kansas City, 1966—. Mem. ACHE (com. svc.), AHA (com. svc.), Kans. Hosp. Assn. (bd. dirs., com. svc.). Office: St Luke's Hosp PO Box 119000 Kansas City MO 64171-9000*

LINDSTROM, DONALD FREDRICK, JR., priest; b. Atlanta, July 18, 1943; s. Donald Fredrick Sr. and Elizabeth (Haynes) L.; m. Marcia Pace, Dec. 30, 1983; children: Christopher, Eric, Ashley, Ellison. ABJ, U. Ga., 1966; MDiv, Va. Theol. Sem., 1969; JD, Woodrow Wilson Coll. Law, 1977; postgrad., U. West Fla., 1984. Lic. marriage and family therapist. Broadcast journalist radio and TV Atlanta and N.Y.C., 1961-68; priest Episcopal ch., 1969—; rector Episcopal Ch. Mediator, Meridian, Miss., 1991—; pvt. practice as marriage and family therapist, Pensacola, Fla., 1983-91; ecumenical officer Diocese of Ctrl. Gulf Coast, 1989-91, Miss., 1992—; bd. visitors Kanuga Conf. Ctr., 1993—; guest chaplain U.S. Ho. of Reps., nat. prayer breakfast, 1994; mem. ecumenical staff gen. conv. Episcopal Ch., 1994. Writer, producer The Cry for Help, The Autumn Years. Chaplain Atlanta Police Dept., 1975-78, Meridian Police Dept., 1995—; pres. N.W. Fla. chpt. Nat. Kidney Found., 1987-88; mem. Leadership Atlanta, 1975; bd. dirs. Leadership Pensacola; trustee Fla. Trust for Hist. Preservation. Mem. Am. Assn. for Marriage and Family Therapy (clin.), Mental Health Assn. (life, bd. dirs. Pensacola 1986-88), Navy League, Order of Holy Cross (assoc.), Bailli (pres.), Confrerie de la Chaine des Rotisseurs, Bailliage de Meridian, Alpha Tau Omega, Sigma Delta Chi, Delta Gamma Kappa. Avocations: music, photography, traveling, gourmet, fly fishing. Office: Episcopal Ch Mediator 3825 35th Ave Meridian MS 39305-3617

LINDZEN, RICHARD SIEGMUND, meteorologist, educator; b. Webster, Mass., Feb. 8, 1940; s. Abe and Sara (Blachman) L.; m. Nadine Lucie Kalougine, Apr. 7, 1965; children: Eric, Nathaniel. A.B., Harvard U., 1960, S.M., 1961, Ph.D., 1964. Research assoc. U. Wash., Seattle, 1964-65; Research asso. U. Oslo, 1965-66; with Nat. Center Atmospheric Research, Boulder, Colo., 1966-68; mem. faculty U. Chgo., 1968-72; prof. meteorology Harvard U., 1972-83, dir. Center for Earth and Planetary Physics, 1980-83; Alfred P. Sloan prof. meteorology MIT, 1983—; Lady Davis vis. prof. Hebrew U., 1979; Sackler prof. Tel Aviv U., 1992; Vikram Sarabhai prof. Phys. Rsch. Lab., Ahmendabad, India, 1985; Lansdowne lectr. U. Victoria, 1993; cons. NASA, Jet Propulsion Lab., others; mem. bd. on atmospheric scis. and climate NRC, corr. mem. com. on human rights NAS. Author: Dynamics in Atmospheric Physics; co-author: Atmospheric Tides; contbr. to profl. jours. Recipient Macelwane award Am. Geophys. Union, 1968. Fellow NAS, AAAS, Am. Geophys. Union, Am. Meteorol. Soc. (Meisinger award 1969, councillor 1972-75, Charney award 1985), Am. Acad. Arts and Scis., Norwegian Acad. Scis. and Letters; mem. Internat. Commn. Dynamic Meteorology, Woods Hole Oceanographic Instn. (corp.), Institut Mondial des Scis. (founding mem.). Jewish. Office: MIT 54 1720 Cambridge MA 02139

LINDZEY, GARDNER, psychologist, educator; b. Wilmington, Del., Nov. 27, 1920; s. James and Marguerite (Shotwell) L.; m. Andrea Lewis, Nov. 28, 1944; children: Jeffrey, Leslie, Gardner, David, Jonathan. AB, Pa. State U., 1943, MS, 1945; PhD, Harvard U., 1949; LHD (hon.), U. Colo., 1990; DSc (hon.), Rutgers U., 1992. Research analyst OSRD, 1944-45; instr. psychology Pa. State U., 1945-46; teaching fellow Harvard U., Cambridge, Mass., 1946-47, research fellow, 1947-49, research assoc., asst. prof., 1949-53, lectr., chmn. psychol. clinic staff, 1953-56, prof., chmn. dept., 1972-73; prof. psychology Syracuse (N.Y.) U., 1956-57, U. Minn., 1957-64; prof. psychology U. Tex., 1964-72, chmn., 1964-68, v.p. acad. affairs, 1968-70, v.p. ad interim, 1971, v.p., dean Grad. Studies, prof. psychology, 1973-75; dir. Ctr. for Advanced Study in Behavioral Scis., Stanford (Calif.) U., 1975-89, dir. emeritus, 1989—; mem. psychopharmacology study sect. NIMH, 1958-62, mem. program-project com., 1963-67, mem. adv. com. on extramural research, 1968-71; mem. com. faculty research fellowships Social Sci. Research Council, 1960-63, bd. dirs., 1962-76, mem. com. problems and policy, 1963-70, 72-76, chmn., 1965-70, mem. exec. com., 1970-75, chmn., 1971-75, mem. com. genetics and behavior, 1961-67, chmn., 1961-65; mem. com. biol. bases social behavior, 1967—; mem. com. work and personality in middle years, 1972-77; mem. sociology and social psychology panel NSF, 1965-68, mem. spl. commn. social scis., 1968-69, mem. adv. com. research, 1974—, mem. Waterman award com., 1976-79; mem. exec. com., assembly behavioral and social sci. NAS-NRC, 1970—, mem. com. life sci. and pub. policy, 1968-74, mem. panel nat. needs for biomed. and behavioral research personnel, 1974—, mem. com. social sci. in NSF, 1975—, mem. Inst. Medicine, 1975—; mem. com. on drug abuse Office Sci. and Tech., 1962-63; mem. Presdl. Com. Nat. Medal Sci., 1966-69; bd. dirs. Found.'s Fund Research in Psychiatry, 1967-70; bd. dirs. Am. Psychol. Found., 1968-76, v.p., 1971-73, pres., 1974-76. Author: (with Hall) Theories of Personality, 1957, 70, 78; (with Allport and Vernon) Study of Values, 1951, 60; Projective Techniques and Cross-Cultural Research, 1961; (with J.C. Loehlin and J.N. Spuhler) Race Differences in Intelligence, 1975; (with C.S. Hall and R.F. Thompson) Psychology, 1975; also articles; editor: Handbook of Social Psychology, Vols. 1 and 2, 1954, Vols. 1-5, 1969, Assessment of Human Motives, 1958, Contemporary Psychology, 1967-73, History of Psychology in Autobiography, Vol. 6, 1974, vol. 7, 1980, vol. 8, 1989; assoc. editor Psychol. Abstracts, 1960-62, Ency. Social Scis., 1962-67; co-editor Century Psychology Series, 1960-74, Theories of Personality: Primary Sources and Research, 1965, History of Psychology in Autobiography, Vol. V, 1968, Behavioral Genetics: Methods and Research, 1969, Contributions to Behavior-Genetic Analysis, 1970. Fellow Ctr. Advanced Study Behavioral Scis., Stanford, 1955-56, 63-64, 71-72, Inst. Medicine, 1975—. Fellow Am. Psychol. Assn. (bd. dirs. 1962-68, 70-74, mem. publs. bd., 1956-59, 70-73, chmn. 1958-59, mem. council of reps. 1959-67, 68-74, pres. divsn. social and personality psychology 1963-64, mem. policy and planning 1975, 78, pres. assn. 1966-67, mem. council of editors 1968-73, chmn. com. sci. award 1968-69, pres. divsn. gen. psychology 1970-71), Am. Acad. Arts and Scis., Am. Philos. Soc., Inst. Medicine, NAS, AAAS; mem. Am. Eugenics Soc. (bd. dirs. 1962-70), Soc. Social Biology (bd. dirs. 1972—, pres. 1978—), Am. Psychol. Assn. (dir. ins. trust 1973—), Univs. Research Assn. (bd. dirs. 1973-75). Home: 109 Peter Coutts Cir Palo Alto CA 94305-2517

LINEBERGER, PETER SAALFIELD, lawyer; b. Akron, Ohio, Mar. 9, 1947; s. Walter F. Jr. and Mary Robinson (Saalfield) L.; children: Katherine Ann, Mary Elizabeth; m. Constance Meyers, Mar. 12, 1988. BA in English, Williams Coll., 1969; JD, Gonzaga U., 1976. Bar: Mont. 1976, Wash. 1994, U.S. Dist. Ct. Mont. 1977, U.S. Dist. Ct. (ea. dist.) Wash. 1994. Legal intern Witherspoon, Kelly, Davenport, O'Toole, Spokane, 1975; law clk. Mont. Supreme Ct., Helena, 1976; assoc. Landoe, Gary, Bozeman, Mont., 1977-78; ptnr. Landoe, Brown, Planalp, Komers & Lineberger, Bozeman, Mont., 1979-83, Lineberger & Davis, Bozeman, Mont., 1984-85, Lineberger & Harris, P.C., Bozeman, Mont., 1986-88, Lineberger, Walsh & McKenna, P.C., Bozeman, Mont., 1989-94; atty. sole practitioner Peter S. Lineberger, Spokane, 1994—; city atty. Town of West Yellowstone, Mont., 1978-94; chmn. Gallatin County Legal Svcs. Com., Bozeman, 1985-89, chmn. Mont. Child and Family Law Sect., 1993-94. Lt. USNR, 1969-72. Mem. ABA (mem. family law sect. 1987-95), Wash. State Bar Assn. (mem. family law sect.), Am. Acad. Matrimonial Lawyers, Wash. State Trial Lawyers Assn. (mem. family law sect. 1995), Gallatin County Bar Assn. (pres. 1992), Mont. City Attys. Assn. (pres. 1983). Avocations: fly fishing, skiing. Office: 422 W Riverside #501 Spokane WA 99201

LINEBERGER, WILLIAM CARL, chemistry educator; b. Hamlet, N.C., Dec. 5, 1939; s. Caleb Henry and Evelyn (Cooper) L.; m. Katharine Wyman Edwards, July 31, 1979. BS, Ga. Inst. Tech., 1961, MSEE, 1963, PhD, 1965. Research physicist U.S. Army Ballistic Research Labs., Aberdeen, Md., 1967-68; postdoctoral assoc. Joint Inst. for Lab. Astrophysics U. Colo., Boulder, 1968-70, from asst. prof. to prof. chemistry, 1970-83, E.U. Condon prof. chemistry, 1983—; Phi Beta Kappa nat. lectr., 1989. Served to capt. U.S. Army, 1965-67. Fellow AAAS, Joint Inst. for Lab. Physics, Am. Phys. Soc. (H.P. Broida prize 1981, Bomen Michelson prize 1987, Optical Sci. Am. Meggers prize 1988, Plyler prize 1992); mem. NAS, Am. Chem. Soc., Am. Acad. Arts and Scis., Sigma Xi. Office: U Colo Joint Inst Lab Astrophysics CB 440 Boulder CO 80309-0440

LINEBERRY, PAUL F., JR., secondary education music educator; b. Waynesville, N.C., Aug. 6, 1944; s. Paul F. and Elmorene L. Lineberry; m. Jane Bulla, Aug. 27, 1966; children: Scott Eric, Brittnay Anne. MusB Edn., East Carolina U., 1966, MusM Edn., 1967. Cert. music tchr. K-12, Pa., supvr. pub. sch. music, Pa. Adj. graduate faculty Music Dept., Trenton State Coll., N.J.; dist. coord. music edn. Coun. Rock Sch. Dist., Richboro, Pa.; instrumental music instr. Coun. Rock H.S., Newtown, Pa., 1991—, chairperson music dept., 1993—; dir. sch. bands in performance in U.S. and Western Europe; cons. pub. sch. music programs, Bucks County, Pa.; lectr. in field. Curriculum devel. com. Coun. Rock Sch. Dist., Richboro, Bucks County Int. Unit Task Force on Music Edn., 1991—; mem. Pa. State Profl. Stds. Com. in Music Edn., 1990—. Recipient graduate study grant Fed. HEW Dept. Mem. NEA, ASCD, Music Educators Nat. Conf., Pa. Music Educators Assn. (com. chmn., Citation of Excellence in Teaching award 1991), Bucks County Music Edn. Assn. (past pres. and com. chmn.), Coun. Rock Edn. Assns., Pa. Edn. Assn., Phi Mu Alpha, Phi Beta Mu. Home: 197 Fletcher Dr Morrisville PA 19067-5968

LINEHAN, PATRICK FRANCIS, JR., financial planner; b. Jefferson Heights, N.Y., July 31, 1945; s. Patrick Francis and Dorothy Frances (Rowland) L.; m. Jane Elizabeth Ufting, Nov. 18, 1967; children: Patrick Francis III, Colleen Elizabeth, Erin Kathleen. BS in Edn., St. John's U., Jamaica, N.Y., 1966, MS in Edn., 1970. CFP; registered fin. cons.; cert. investment specialist. Math tchr. Bellmore (N.Y.)-Merrick Sch. Dist., 1967-85; fin. planner Amityville, N.Y., 1984—; ocean lifeguard Jones Beach-State Park, Babylon, N.Y., 1965-86; speaker Estate Planning and Seminars, Coll. Fin. Plan Seminars, Tchr. Retirement Seminars. Editor (quar. newsletter) Think About It, 1967—. Mem. Inst. of CFP, Internat. Assn. of Fin. Planners, Internat. Assn. Profl. Fin. Cons., Elks, K.C. Roman Catholic. Avocations: reading, music, golf, swimming. Home: 142 Richmond Ave Amityville NY 11701-4209 Office: Planning for Life 142 Richmond Ave Amityville NY 11701-4209

LINEMEYER, DAVID LEE, molecular biologist; b. Denver, Apr. 19, 1949; s. Clarence Brockman and Frances Pauline (Whitlock) L. BS with highest distinction, Colo. State U., 1971; MS, U. Wash., 1973, PhD, 1977. Staff fellow Nat. Cancer Inst., Bethesda, Md., 1977-80, sr. staff fellow, 1980-81; rsch. fellow Merck Rsch. Labs., Rahway, N.J., 1981-89, assoc. dir., 1989-95; dir. Synaptic Pharm. Corp., Paramus, N.J., 1995—. Contbr. articles to sci. jours.; patentee mutant acidic fibroblast growth factor field. Scholar Colo. State U., 1967-71. Mem. AAAS, Am. Soc. for Biochemistry and Molecular Biology, Am. Soc. for Microbiology, Phi Kappa Phi. Office: Synaptic Pharm Corp 215 College Rd Paramus NJ 07652-1431

LINEVSKY, MILTON JOSHUA, physical chemist; b. Glen Cove, N.Y., Apr. 20, 1928; s. David I. and Tillie Linevsky; m. Barbara Jody Rutenberg, June 29, 1958; children: Joanne, Richard. BS in Chemistry, Rensselaer Poly. Inst., 1949; MS, Pa. State U., 1950, PhD, 1953. Phys. chemist GE, King of Prussia, Pa., 1957-79, Johns Hopkins Applied Physics Lab., Laurel, Md., 1979—; with NSF, Washington, 1993—. With U.S. Army, 1955-57. Gotshall Powel scholar, 1946. Mem. Am. Chem. Soc. Achievements include invention and development of technique for matrix isolation applied to high-temperature materials, development of first flame laser using chemical pumping reactions. Home: 700 Hermleigh Rd Silver Spring MD 20902-1647 Office: Johns Hopkins Applied Physics Lab Johns Hopkins Rd Laurel MD 20723 also: NSF 4201 Wilson Blvd Arlington VA 22230

LINFORD, RULON KESLER, physicist, engineer; b. Cambridge, Mass., Jan. 31, 1943; s. Leon Blood and Imogene (Kesler) L.; m. Cecile Tadje, Apr. 2, 1965; children: Rulon Scott, Laura, Hilary, Philip Leon. BSEE, U. Utah, 1966; MS in ElecE, Mass. Inst. Tech., 1969, PhD in ElecE, 1973. Staff CTR-7 Los Alamos (N.Mex) Nat. Lab., 1973-75, asst. group leader CTR-7, 1975-77, group leader CTR-11, 1977-79, program mgr., group leader compact toroid CTR-11, 1979-80, program mgr., asst. div. leader compact toroid CTR divsn., 1980-81, assoc. CTR divsn. leader, 1981-86, program dir. magnetic fusion energy, 1986-89, program dir., div. leader CTR div. office, 1989-91, program dir. nuclear sys., 1991-93; staff LER, 1993-94, U. Calif. coord. sci. and tech., 1994—. Contbr. articles to profl. jours. Recipient E. O. Lawrence award Dept. of Energy, Washington, 1991. Fellow Am. Physical Soc. (exec. com. 1982, 90-91, program com. 1982, 85, award selection com. 1983, 84, fellowship com. 1986); mem. Sigma Xi. Office: Los Alamos Nat Lab PO Box 1663 MS F673 Los Alamos NM 87545

LING, DAVID CHANG, international book dealer; b. Shanghai, Feb. 17, 1939; s. H.C. and Katherine (Chang) L.; m. Janine Peters, June 20, 1970 (div. Feb. 1975). BA, U. Ore., 1962; MA, U. Wis., 1964, PhD, 1971. Vis. instr. U. of the South, Sewanee, Tenn., 1964-65; asst. prof. U. Wis., Kenosha, 1969-73; owner Ling's Internat. Books, San Diego, 1974—. Mem. Phi Beta Kappa. Democrat. Home: 5012 Westminster Ter San Diego CA 92116-2103 Office: Ling's Internat Books 7531 Convoy Ct San Diego CA 92111-1113

LING, DWIGHT L., college administrator, history educator; b. Johnstown, Pa., Oct. 9, 1923; s. Leroy Victor and Nellie Grace (Cypher) L.; m. Phyllis Cooper, June 8, 1946; children—Douglas, Gregory, Angela. B.A., Pa. State U., 1948, M.A., 1949; Ph.D., U. Ill., 1955. Cert. tchr., Pa. Asst. prof. history Centre Coll., Danville, Ky., 1949-52; teaching asst. U. Ill.-Champaign-Urbana, 1952-55; prof. history DePauw U., Greencastle, Ind., 1955-72; provost Rollins Coll., Winter Park, Fla., 1972-79; dean, provost Marietta Coll., Ohio, 1979-86, prof. history, 1986—, emeritus prof. history, 1989—; counselor, examiner North Central Assn., Chgo., 1965-70. Author: Tunisia: From Protectorate to Republic, 1967; Morocco and Tunisia: A Comparative History, 1979. Mem. adv. bd. Glenridge Jr. High Sch., Winter Park, Fla., 1977-79; mem. adv. com. Marietta Pub. Schs., 1985. Served with U.S. Army, 1943-46. Rockefeller fellow, 1952-53; Tunisian Govt. fellow, 1963; Am. Philos. Soc. fellow, 1963; Fulbright scholar, Netherlands, 1976. Mem. Am. Assn. Higher Edn., Fulbright Alumni Assn. Democrat. Clubs: Marietta Reading (pres. 1985—), Econ. Roundtable. Lodge: Rotary. Avocations: tennis; traveling; reading; North African history. Home: 107 Rathbone Rd Marietta OH 45750-1438 Office: Marietta Coll Marietta OH 45750

LING, JOSEPH TSO-TI, manufacturing company executive, environmental engineer; b. Peking, China, June 10, 1919; came to U.S., 1948, naturalized, 1963; s. Ping Sun and Chong Hung (Lee) L.; m. Rose Hsu, Feb. 1, 1944; children: Lois Ling Olson, Rosa-Mai Ling Ahlgren, Louis, Lorraine Ling-LaRoy. B.C.E., Hangchow Christian Coll., Shanghai, China, 1944; M.S. in Civil Engring, U. Minn., 1950, Ph.D. in San. Engring, 1952. Registered profl. engr., Minn., Ala., N.J., Okla., W.Va., N.Y., Ill., Ind., Pa., Mich. Civil engr. Nanking-Shanghai R.R. System, 1944-47; research asst. san. engring. U. Minn., 1948-52; sr. staff san. engr. Gen. Mills, Inc., Mpls., 1953-55; dir. dept. san. engring. research Ministry Municipal Constrn., Peking, 1956-57; prof. civil engring. Bapt. U., Hong Kong, 1958-59; head dept. water and san. engring. Minn. Mining & Mfg. Co., St. Paul, 1960-66, mgr. environ. and civil engring., 1967-70, dir. environ. engring. and pollution control, 1970-74, v.p. environ. engring. and pollution control, 1975-84, community service exec., 1985—; adv. mem. on air pollution Minn. Bd. Health, 1964-66; mem. Minn. Gov.'s Adv. Com. on Air Resources, 1966-67; mem. adv. panel on environ. pollution U.S. C. of C., 1966-71; mem. chem. indsl. com., adv. to Ohio River Valley Water Sanitation Commn., 1962-76; mem. environ. quality panel Electronic Industries Assn., 1971-80; mem. environ. quality com. NAM, 1965-84; mem. Pres.'s Adv. Bd. on Air Quality, 1974-75; vice chmn. environ. com. U.S. Bus. and Industry Adv. Com. to OECD, 1975-84; mem. adv. subcom. on environ., health and safety regulations Pres.'s Domestic Policy Rev. of Indsl. Innovation, 1978-79; adv. panel indsl. innovation and health, safety and environ. regulation Office Tech. Assessment of U.S. Congress, 1978-80; exec. com. engring. assembly NRC, 1977-80; also environ. studies bd. Commn. Natural Resources, 1977-82; mem. staff svcs. subcom. of environ. com. Bus. Roundtable, 1975-84; vice chmn. environ. com. U.S. Coun., Internat. C. of C., 1978-89; adv. com. on rsch. applications policy NSF, 1976-80; mem. Sci. Adv. Bd. EPA, 1984-88, selection com. Pres.' Environment and Conservation Challenge Award, 1991-93. Contbr. articles to profl. jours. Trustee Belwin Outdoor Lab., St. Paul, 1970—; bd. dirs. Fresh Water Found., 1974—, Northwest Area Found., 1970-87, St. Paul Area YMCA, 1974-80, Midwest China Study Center, Minn. Environ. Sci. Found., 1970-78, Nat. Water Alliance, 1983-88, World Environ. Ctr., 1984—. Woodrow Wilson Sr. fellow, 1975—; recipient numerous awards, including Joan Hodges Queneau award Am. Assn. Engring. Socs., 1990; named Laureate, Global 500 Honor Role UN Environ. Program, 1990. Fellow ASCE (life): mem. NAE, Am. Acad. Environ. Engrs. (diplomate, chmn. examination update com. 1981-83), Minn. Assn. Commerce and Industry, Am. Water Works Assn. (life), Air and Waste Mgmt. Assn. (dir.), Chem. Mfg. Assn. Club: Rainbow (Mpls.). Home: 2090 Arcade St Saint Paul MN 55109-2564 *There must be a goal in any stage of one's life. It must be high enough to offer a challenge. One should not wait for the opportunity but create the opportunity to achieve that goal.*

LING, TA-YUNG, physics educator; b. Shanghai, Feb. 2, 1943; married, 1969; 3 children. BS, Tunghai U., Taiwan, 1964; MS, U. Waterloo, Ont., Can., 1966; PhD in Physics, U. Wis., 1971. Teaching asst. physics U. Waterloo, 1965-66, U. Wis., Madison, 1966-67; rsch. asst. U. Wis., 1967-71; rsch. assoc. physics U. Pa., Phila., 1972-75, asst. prof., 1975-77; from asst. prof. to assoc. prof. Ohio State U., Columbus, 1977-83, prof. physics, 1983—. Recipient Outstanding Jr. Investigator award Dept. of Energy, 1977. Mem. Am. Phys. Soc. Achievements include research in experimental high energy physics; deep inelastic neutrino-nucleon scattering, neutrino masses and mixing, neutrino oscillations, deep inelastic electron-proton scattering, high energy proton-proton collisions. Office: Ohio State U High Energy Physics Lab Physics Dept/Smith Lab 174 W 18th Ave Columbus OH 43210-1106*

LINGAFELTER, EDWARD CLAY, JR., chemistry educator; b. Toledo, Mar. 28, 1914; s. Edward Clay and Winifred (Jordan) L.; m. Roberta Crowe Kneedler, Apr. 30, 1938; children—Robert Edward, Thomas Edward, James Edward, Richard Edward, Daniel Edward. B.S., U. Calif.-Berkeley, 1935, Ph.D., 1939. Mem. faculty U. Wash., Seattle, 1939—; prof. chemistry U. Wash., 1952-84, prof. emeritus, 1984—, assoc. dean Grad. Sch., 1960-68. Contbr. articles to profl. jours. Mem. Am. Chem. Soc., Am. Crystallographic Assn. (pres. 1974), Assn. Italian Cristallografia. Rsch. on solutions, molecular structures of paraffin-chain and coordination compounds. Home: 5323 27th Ave NE Seattle WA 98105-3105 Office: U Wash Dept Chemistry Box 351700 Seattle WA 98195-1700

LINGAMNENI, JAGANMOHAN RAO, criminology educator; b. Dondapadu, India, Mar. 15, 1942; came to U.S., 1967, naturalized, 1974; s. Satyanarayana and Satyavathi Settipalli L.; m. Uma Uppaluri, Feb. 26, 1967; children: Santhisri, Pragathisri. BS, A.P. Agrl. Coll, India, 1962; MS, A.P.

Agrl. U., 1965; PhD, Mich. State U., 1972; MS in Criminal Justice, U. Ala.-Birmingham, 1979. Research asst. A.P. State Dept. Agr., 1964-65; instr. A.P. Agrl. U., 1965-66; research asst. Mich. State U., Nat. Inst. Community Devel. Diffusion Project, Hyderabad, India, 1966-67; teaching asst., grad. research asst., diffusion research fellow Mich. State U., East Lansing, 1967-70; lectr. Mich. State U.-AID Communication Workshops, 1969-75; asst. prof. sociology W. Ga. Coll, 1970-75; assoc. prof. W. Ga. Coll., 1975-80, dir. grad. program., 1973-75, 76-80; vice chmn. dept. sociology W. Ga. Coll, 1973-74; prof. human justice Governors State U., University Park, Ill., 1979-83, univ. prof. criminal justice, 1983-85, 91—, coord. criminal justice program, 1992—, univ. prof. pub. adminstrn., 1985-91, chmn. div. communications and human services, 1982-83; mem. adj. faculty Emory U., Atlanta, 1976-80, Union Inst., Cin., 1986—; sec., chmn., trustee Telugu Found. (N. Am.), 1981-90. Author: Status Inconsistency, Communication Behavior and Modernization, 1972; assoc. editor, So. Jour. Criminal Justice, 1977-81, Jour. Communication Therapy; contbr. articles to profl. jours. Diffusion research fellow Mich. State U., 1967-68. Mem. Am. Soc. Criminology (life mem., adv. internat. liason com. 1978—), Acad. Criminal Justice Scis. (life mem., com. internat. criminology and criminal justice 1978—), Internat. Communication Assn., Midwestern Criminal Justice Educators Assn., Ill. Criminal Justice Educators Assn. (v.p. 1981-83, pres. 1989—), Am. Sociol. Assn., So. Sociol Soc. (racial and ethnic minorities com. 1978-80), So. Assn. Criminal Justice Educators (sec.-treas. 1978-80), Alpha Kappa Delta, Lambda Alpha Epsilon. Hindu. Home: 77 Graymoor Ln Olympia Fields IL 60461-1215 Office: Govs State U Coll Arts and Scis Divsn Liberal Arts University Park IL 60466 *In my life, I always strove to be an ethical individual and maintained standards of excellence for myself that I and others around me could be proud of. As a naturalized citizen, I have been a true believer of the melting-pot of American ethnicity in providing equal opportunities for all to achieve success. Although my belief in the fundamental fairness of the American System has diluted somewhat, my obligation and commitment to contribute toward that broader goal continues to persist.*

LINGEMAN, RICHARD ROBERTS, editor, writer; b. Crawfordsville, Ind., Jan. 2, 1931; s. Byron Newton and Vera Frances (Spencer) L.; m. Anthea Judy Nicholson, Apr. 3, 1965; 1 child, Jenifer Kate. BA, Haverford Coll., 1953; postgrad., Yale U. Law Sch., 1956-58, Columbia U. Grad. Sch. Comparative Lit., 1958-60. Exec. editor Monocle mag., N.Y.C., 1960-69; assoc. editor, columnist N.Y. Times Book Review, 1969-78; exec. editor The Nation, N.Y.C., 1978-95, sr. editor, 1995—; cons. editor The Nation, 1996—; bd. dirs. Small Town Inst., Ctr. Middletown Studies. Author: Drugs from A to Z, 1969, Don't You Know There's A War On?, 1971, Small Town America, 1980, Theodore Dreiser: At the Gates of the City 1871-1907, 1986, Theodore Dreiser: An American Journey, 1908-1945, 1990 (Chgo. Sun-Times Book of Yr.). With U.S. Army, 1953-56. Mem. PEN, Authors Guild, Soc. Am. Historians, Nat. Book Critics Cir., N.Y. Hist. Soc., Phi Beta Kappa. Office: 72 Fifth Ave New York NY 10011-8004

LINGENFELTER, SHERWOOD GALEN, university provost, anthropology educator; b. Hollidaysburg, Pa., Nov. 18, 1941; s. Galen Miller and Kathern Margaretta (Rogers) L.; m. Judith Elaine Beaumont, Aug. 10, 1962; children: Jennifer Elaine, Joel Sherwood. BA, Wheaton Coll., 1963; PhD, U. Pitts., 1971. Dir. acad. advising U. Pitts., 1964-66; instr. SUNY, Brockport, N.Y., 1966-67; asst. prof SUNY, Brockport, 1969-74, assoc. prof., 1974-82, prof. anthropology, 1982-83; NIH predoctoral fellow U. Pitts., 1967-69; prof. Biola U., La Mirada, Calif., 1983-88, provost, sr. v.p., 1988—; cons. in anthropology Summer Inst. Linguistics, Dallas, 1977-96; tng. cons. Liebenzell Mission of Am., Schooleys Mountain, N.J., 1981-89; evaluating cons. Trust Terr. of the Pacific Islands, Saipan, Mariana Islands, 1969-74. Author: Yap: Political Leadership, 1975, The Deni of Western Brazil, 1980, Ministering Cross-Culturally, 1986, Transforming Culture, 1992, Agents of Transformation, 1996; editor: Political Development in Micronesia, 1974, Social Organization of Sabah Societies, 1990. Bd. dirs. Christian Scholars Rev., 1989-95, Grace Brethren Internat. Missions, 1994—. Recipient Disting. Teaching award Biola U., 1987-88; grantee NSF, 1967-69, 79-81, SUNY Rsch. Found., 1970. Fellow Am. Anthrop. Assn., Soc. for Applied Anthropology, Am. Ethnol. Soc.; mem. Assn. Social Anthropology Oceania, Am. Conf. Acad. Deans. Democrat. Mem. Grace Brethern Ch. Office: Biola U Office of Provost 13800 Biola Ave La Mirada CA 90639-0002

LINGERFELT, B. EUGENE, JR., minister; b. Highland Park, Mich., Dec. 18, 1955; s. Beecher Eugene and Nellie Beatrice (Sampson) L.; m. Suzanne Marie Martin, Aug. 7, 1976; children: Austin Stuart, Krystina Marie. BA, Cen. Bible Coll., Springfield, Mo., 1976; MDiv, Tex. Christian Univ., 1980; D of Ministry, Southwestern Bapt. Theol., Seminary, Ft. Worth, 1984. Ordained min. Cathedral of Praise Ch., 1984. Assoc. pastor Bethel Temple, Ft. Worth, 1978-82; missionary, guest lectr. East Africa Sch. of Theology, Nairobi, Kenya, 1982-83; marriage enrichment seminar speaker, 1983; founder and sr. pastor Cathedral of Praise, Arlington, Tex., 1984—; founder Cathedral Christian Acad., 1988—; founder Overcoming Faith TV, 1994—. Co-author: Money: A Spiritual Force, 1985, The Spirit of Excellence, 1994, Compromise in the Church, 1995; contbr. articles to religious jours. Named to Outstanding Young Men of Am., 1980. Republican. Office: Cathedral of Praise PO Box 121234 Arlington TX 76012-1234

LINGL, FRIEDRICH ALBERT, psychiatrist; b. Munich, Germany, Apr. 4, 1927; came to U.S., 1957, naturalized, 1962; s. Friedrich Hugo and Marie Luise (Lindner) L.; m. Leonore E. Trautner, Nov. 15, 1955; children—Herbert F., Angelika M. M.D., Ludwig-Maxim U., Munich, 1952. Diplomate Am. Bd. Psychiatry and Neurology, Am. Bd. Med. Psychotherapists (fellow); cert. mental health adminstr. Intern Edward W. Sparrow Hosp., 1957-58; resident internal medicine City Hosp., Augsburg, Germany, 1953-54; resident psychiatry Columbus (Ohio) State Hosp., 1958-61; supt. Hawthornden State Hosp., Northfield, Ohio, 1963-66; dir. Cleve. Psychiat. Inst., 1966-72; pvt. practice, 1972-92; med. dir. Windsor Hosp., 1976-92, med. dir. emeritus, 1992—; asst. clin. prof. Case Western Res. U., Cleve., 1970-95. Contbr. articles to med. jours. Fellow Am. Psychiat. Assn. (life); mem. AMA, Ohio Med. Assn., Ohio Psychiat. Assn., Am. Assn. Psychiat. Adminstrs., N.Y. Acad. Scis., Cleve. Psychiat. Soc. Address: 40 Farwood Dr Chagrin Falls OH 44022-6848

LINGLE, CRAIG STANLEY, glaciologist, educator; b. Carlsbad, N.Mex., Sept. 11, 1945; s. Stanley Orland and Margaret Pearl (Ewart) L.; m. Diana Lynn Duncan, Aug. 21, 1972; 1 child, Eric Glenn. BS, U. Wash., 1967; MS, U. Maine, 1978; PhD, U. Wis., 1983. Nat. rsch. coun. resident rsch. assoc. Coop. Inst. for Rsch. in Environ. Scis., U. Colo., Boulder, 1983-84, rsch. assoc., 1984-86; program mgr. polar glaciology divsn. polar programs NSF, Washington, 1986-87; cons. Jet Propulsion Lab., Pasadena, Calif., 1987-88; nat. rsch. coun. resident rsch. assoc. NASA Goddard Space Flight Ctr., Oceans and Ice Branch, Greenbelt, Md., 1988-90; rsch. assoc. prof. Geophys. Inst., U. Alaska, Fairbanks, 1990—. Contbr. articles to profl. jours. Recipient Rsch. Project of Month award Office of Health and Environ. Rsch., U.S. Dept. Energy, 1990, Group Achievement award NASA, 1992. Mem. AAAS, Internat. Glaciological Soc., Am. Geophys. Union, Sigma Xi. Avocations: downhill and cross-country skiing, canoeing. Office: Geophys Inst Univ Alaska PO Box 757320 Fairbanks AK 99775-7320

LINGLE, SARAH ELIZABETH, research scientist; b. Woodland, Calif., July 22, 1955; d. John Clayton and Dorothy Adelaide (Dubois) L.; m. Thomas Pratt Washington IV, May 20, 1989. BS, U. Calif., Davis, 1977; MS, U. Nebr., 1978; PhD, Washington State U., 1982. Lab. asst. U. Calif., Davis, 1975-77; rsch. asst. U. Nebr., Lincoln, 1977-78; rsch., teaching asst. Wash. State U., Pullman, 1979-82; rsch. assoc. Agrl. Rsch. Svc., USDA, Fargo, N.D., 1982-84; supr. plant physiologist USDA, Weslaco, Tex., 1984—, acting rsch. leader, 1991-92. Assoc. editor Crop Sci.; contbr. articles to profl. jours. Mem. AAAS, Am. Soc. of Plant Physiologists, Am. Soc. Agronomy, Crop Sci. Soc. of Am., Sigma Xi. Episcopalian. Achievements include research in biochemistry and physiology of sugar deposition in sucrose-storing plant tissues. Office: USDA Agrl Rsch Svc 2413 E Us Hwy 83 Weslaco TX 78596-8344

LINGNAU, LUTZ, pharmaceutical executive; b. 1943; came to the U.S., 1989; With Schering Berlin, Inc., Germany, 1965-89; pres., CEO Schering Berlin, Inc., Cedar Knolls, N.J., 1989—. Office: Schering Berlin Inc 110 E Hanover Ave Cedar Knolls NJ 07927-2007*

LINHARDT, ROBERT JOHN, medicinal chemistry educator; b. Passaic, N.J., Oct. 18, 1953; s. Robert J. and Barbara A. (Kelley) L.; m. Kathryn F. Burns, May 31, 1975; children: Kelley, Barbara. BS in Chemistry, Marquette U., 1975; MA in Chemistry, Johns Hopkins U., 1977, PhD in Organic Chemistry, 1979; postgrad., Mass. Inst. Tech., 1979-82. Rsch. assoc. Mass. Inst. Tech., Cambridge, 1979-82; asst. prof. U. Iowa, Iowa City, 1982-86, assoc. prof., 1986-90, prof. medicinal and natural products chemistry, 1990—, prof. chem. and biochem. engring., 1996—, F. Wendell Miller Disting. prof., 1996; cons. in field.; interacad. exchange scientist to USSR NAS, 1988. Mem. editl. bd. Applied Biochemistry and Biotech., 1985—, Carbohydrate Rsch., 1990—, Analytical Biochemistry, 1991—, Jour. Biol. Chem., 1995—; contbr. numerous articles to profl. jours. Johnson and Johnson fellow MIT, 1981; NIH grantee, 1982-95. Mem. AAAS, Am. Chem. Soc. (Horace S. Isbell award Carbohydrate Chemistry 1994), Soc. Glycobiology. Office: U Iowa Coll of Pharmacy Phar # 303A Iowa City IA 52240

LINHARES, JUDITH YVONNE, artist, educator; b. Pasadena, Calif., Nov. 2, 1940; d. Helen Evangeline (Frew) Coe.; m. Philip E. Linhares June 15, 1961 (div. July, 1971); 1 child, Amanda Linhares Mason. Student, LA Otis Art Inst., 1960, San Francisco Art Inst., 1963; BFA, Calif. Coll. Arts & Crafts, 1964, MFA, 1970. Art tchr. San Francisco State Coll., 1969-71, San Jose City Coll., 1971-72, U. Calif., Davis, Berkeley, 1979, U. San Francisco, San Francisco Art Inst. other univs., Calif., N.Y., La., 1978—, Sch. of Visual Arts, N.Y.C., 1981—, NYU, 1990—; lectr. at univs. and art insts. nationwide, 1974—. Artist: one-person exhibitions include, Berkeley Gallery, San Francisco, 1972, San Francisco Art Inst., 1976, Paule Anglim Gallery, San Francisco, 1978, 80, 82, 84, 88, 89, 94, Nancy Lurie Gallery, Chgo., 1981, 89, 90, Concord Gallery, N.Y.C., 1982, 83, Ruth Siegel Gallery, N.Y., 1985, Mo David Gallery, N.Y., 1985, L.A. Louver Gallery, Venice, Calif., 1988, Julie Sylvester Edition, N.Y., 1989, The Gaibreath Gallery, Lexington, Ky., 1993, Greenville (S.C.) County Mus. of Art, 1994, (survey exhibition 1971-93), Sonoma (Calif.) State U., 1994; selected group exhibitions San Francisco Art Inst., 1973, Indpls. Mus. of Art, 1984, Peninsula Mus., Monterey, Calif., 1987, Michael Walls Gallery, N.Y., 1987, Rosenberg Gallery, N.Y.C., 1992; represented in pub. collections including Greenville (S.C.) County Mus. of Art, Oakland (Calif.) Mus., Butler Inst. of Am. Art, Youngstown, Ohio, Crocker Art Mus., Sacramento, Calif., San Francisco Mus. of Modern Art, City of San Francisco Airport Commn.,. Recipient Adeline Kent award San Francisco Art Inst., 1976; grantee: Nat Endowment for Arts, 1979, 87, 93-94, Gottleib 1993.

LINHART, LETTY LEMON, editor; b. Pittsburg, Kans., Sept. 22, 1933; d. Robert Sheldon and Lois (Wise) Lemon; m. Robert Spayde Kennedy, June 8, 1955 (div. 1978); children: Carole Shea, Nancy Schrimpf, Nina Kennedy; m. Daniel Julian Linhart, June 9, 1986. BS, BA in English and Journalism, U.Kans., 1955; MS in Journalism, Boston U., 1975. Reporter Leavenworth (Kans.) Times, 1954; editor Human Resources Rsch. Office George Washington U., Washington, 1955-56; editor Behavior Rsch. Lab. Harvard Med. Sch., Boston, 1956-58; instr. Boston YMCA, 1960-64; freelance writer and columnist, 1975—; editor Somerville (Mass.) Times, 1975-77; pub. rels. dir. Lettermen of Lexington, Mass., 1978; instr. English Rollins Coll., Winter Park, Fla., 1978-79, Valencia Community Coll., Orlando, Fla., 1978-82, U. Cen. Fla., Orlando, 1979-82; tech. writer Kirschman Software, Altamonto Springs, Mass., 1980-81, Dynamic Control Software, Winter Park, Fla., 1981-82; editor Fla. Specifier, Winter Park, 1982-85, Mobile Home News, Maitland, Fla., 1985-86; instr. English Seminole C.C., Sanford, Fla., 1986-94; Elderhostel instr. Canterbury Rsch. Ctr., 1994—; editor Oviedo (Fla.) Voice, 1994-95, 96. Author: Are These Extravagant Promises, 1989, Clues for the Clueless, 1996; contbr. articles to profl. jours. Pres. MIT Dames Boston, 1958-59, Boston Alumnae of Delta Delta Delta, 1959-62; dist. pres Delta Delta Delta, Tex., 1962-65; mem. Friends of Cornell Mus., Winter Park, Fla. Named Outstanding Collegiate Delta Delta Delta, 1955. Mem. NAFE, Ctrl. Fla. Jazz Soc. (bd. dirs. 1983-93), Internat. Platform Soc., Soc. Women Execs., Altrusa Club (publicity com. 1980-83), Orlando Press Club (bd. dirs.), Univ. Club Winter Park, Mortar Bd., Phi Beta Kappa (Belmont, Mass. pres. 1965-78), Theta Sigma Phi, Sigma Delta Chi, Delta Sigma Rho. Avocations: swimming, singing, jazz. Home: PO Box 621131 Oviedo FL 32762-1131

LINICK, ANDREW S., marketing executive; b. 1945. PhD in Indsl. Psychology, NYU, 1972. Chmn. bd. dirs. Linick Group Inc., Middle Island, N.Y. Office: Linick Group Inc Linick Bldg PO Box 102 Middle Island NY 11953-0102*

LINK, ARTHUR STANLEY, history educator, editor; b. New Market, Va., Aug. 8, 1920; s. John William and Helen Elizabeth (Link) L.; m. Margaret McDowell Douglas, June 2, 1945; children: Arthur Stanley, James Douglas, Margaret McDowell, William Allen. A.B. with highest honors, U. N.C., 1941, Ph.D., 1945; postgrad., Columbia U., 1944-45; M.A., Oxford (Eng.) U., 1958; Litt.D., Bucknell U., 1961, Bethany Coll., 1994; U. N.C., Washington and Lee U., 1965; L.H.D., Washington Coll., 1962, Eastern Ill. U., 1983, Northwestern U., 1984, Monmouth Coll., N.J., 1993; H.H.D. (hon.), Davidson Coll., 1965; Westminster Coll. (Pa.), 1984. Instr. N.C. State Coll., 1943-44; instr. Princeton U., 1945-48, asst. prof., 1948-49; mem. (Inst. Advanced Study), Princeton, 1949, 54-55; assoc. prof. Northwestern U., 1949-54, prof., 1954-60; prof. Princeton U., 1960-65, Edwards prof. Am. history, 1965-76, George H. Davis '86 prof. Am. history, 1976-91, prof. emeritus, 1991—; disting. adj. prof. Am. history U. N.C., Greensboro, 1992—; historian Bowman Gray Sch. Medicine, 1993—; Albert Shaw lectr. Johns Hopkins, 1956; Harmsworth prof. Am. history Oxford U., 1958-59; Commonwealth Fund lectr. U. London, 1977; mem. Nat. Hist. Publs. Commn., 1968-72; pres. Nat. Commn. on Social Studies in Schs., 1987-90. Author: Wilson: The Road to the White House, 1947, (with R. W. Leopold and Stanley Coben) Problems in American History, 1972, Woodrow Wilson and the Progressive Era, 1954, 63, 88, (with William B. Catton and William A. Link) American Epoch, 2 vols., 1986, Wilson: The New Freedom, 1956, Wilson the Diplomatist, 1957, Wilson: The Struggle for Neutrality, 1914-15, 1960, La Política de los Estados Unidas en América Latina, 1960, (with D.S. Muzzey) Our American Republic, 1963, Our Country's History, 1964, Woodrow Wilson, A Brief Biography, 1963, Wilson: Confusions and Crises, 1915-1916, 1964, Wilson: Campaigns for Progressivism and Peace, 1916-17, 1965; editor: (with R.W. Patrick) Writing Southern History, 1967, The Growth of American Democracy, 1968, Woodrow Wilson, A Profile, 1968, The Impact of World War I, 1969, (with W.M. Leary, Jr.) The Diplomacy of World Power: The United States, 1889-1920, 1970, (with Stanley Coben) The Democratic Heritage: A History of the United States, 1971, The Higher Realism of Woodrow Wilson and Other Essays, 1970, (with William M. Leary, Jr.) The Progressive Era and the Great War, 1978, Woodrow Wilson: Revolution, War, and Peace, 1979, Woodrow Wilson and a Revolutionary World, 1913-1921, 1982, (with Richard L. McCormick) Progressivism, 1983, (with W.A. Link) The Twentieth Century: An American History, 1991, Brother Woodrow: A Memoir of Woodrow Wilson (Stockton Axson), 1993; editor: Papers of Woodrow Wilson, 69 vols., 1966-94; editor, sr. writer: A Concise History of the American People, 1984, The American People: A History, 1987; translator, editor: Paul Mantoux, The Deliberations of the Council of Four, 2 vols., 1992; mem. bd. editors Jour. So. History, 1955-58, 63-66, Jour. Am. History, 1967-70; contbr. articles to popular and profl. jours. Trustee Westminster (Pa.) Coll., 1971-82, Warren Wilson Coll., 1993—. Recipient Bancroft prize for biography, 1957, 61; Guggenheim fellow, 1950-51; hon. fellow Jagiellonian U., Cracow, Poland. Fellow Am. Acad. Arts and Scis., Soc. Am. Historians; mem. Am. Philos Soc. (Thomas Jefferson medal 1994), Am. Hist. Assn. (pres.-elect 1983-84, pres. 1984), So. Hist. Assn. (v.p. 1967-68, pres. 1968-69), Orgn. Am. Historians (pres.-elect 1983-84, pres. 1984-85), Nat. Coun. Chs. (v.p. 1963-66), Mass. Hist. Soc. (corr.), Assn. Documentary Editors (pres. 1978-79), Soc. Colonial Wars, Nassau Club, Cosmos Club, Phi Beta Kappa. *I have no thoughts on life that do not stem from my Christian faith. I believe that God created me to be a loving, caring person to do His work in the world. I also believe that He called me to my vocation of teacher and scholar.*

LINK, GEORGE HAMILTON, lawyer; b. Sacramento, Calif., Mar. 26, 1939; s. Hoyle and Corrie Elizabeth (Evans) L.; m. Betsy Leland; children—Thomas Hamilton, Christopher Leland. AB, U. Calif., Berkeley, 1961; LLB, Harvard U., 1964. Bar: Calif. 1965, U.S. Dist. Ct. (no., ea., ctrl. and so dists.) Calif. 1965, U.S. Ct. Appeals (9th cir.) 1965. Assoc. Brobeck, Phleger & Harrison, San Francisco, 1964-69, ptnr., 1970—; mng. ptnr. Brobeck, Phleger & Harrison, L.A., 1973-93; mng. ptnr. firmwide Brobeck Phleger & Harrison, 1993-96; chmn. Pacific Rim Adv. Coun., 1992-95. Bd. regents U. Calif., 1971-74; trustee Berkeley Found., Jr. Statesmen Am.; bd. govs. United Way, 1979-81; trustee, v.p. Calif. Hist. Soc., 1987—. Fellow Am. Bar Found.; mem. ABA, Calif. Bar Assn., L.A. Bar Assn., U. Calif. Alumni Assn. (pres. 1972-75), Calif. Club, Bohemian Club, Jonathan Club. Republican. Methodist. Home: 315 N Carmelina Ave Los Angeles CA 90049-2701 Office: Brobeck Phleger & Harrison 550 S Hope St Los Angeles CA 90071-2627

LINK, O(GLE) WINSTON, photographer; b. Bklyn., Dec. 16, 1914; s. Ernest Albert L. and Ann Winston (Jones) L.; m. Marteal Oglesby 1942 (div. 1946); 1 child, Winston Conway L.; m. Conchita Mendoza, 1983 (div. 1993). BSCE, Poly. Inst. of Bklyn., 1937. Photographer Carl Boyir and Assocs., 1937-42; engr., photographer Airborne Instruments Lab., Columbia U., 1942-45; free-lance indsl. photographer, 1945-83, railroad photographer, 1955-60. Collection of railroad photography include: Steam, Steel and Stars: America's Last Steam Railroad, 1987, The Last Steam Railroad in America, 1995. Office: c/o Thomas H Garver PO Box 3493 Madison WI 53704-0493

LINK, ROBERT ALLEN, lawyer, financial company executive; b. Detroit, July 2, 1932; s. Raymond Henry and Helen Emily (Grassley) L.; m. Cynthia Louise Krans, June 15, 1957; children: Charles Nicholas, Frederick Allen. B.S., Wayne State U., 1954; J.D., U. Mich., 1957. Bar: Mich. 1958, U.S. Dist. Ct. (ea. dist.) Mich. 1958, U.S. Ct. Appeals (6th cir.) 1960. Assoc. firm Darden & Bonk, Detroit, 1958-61; pvt. practice Detroit, 1961-63; assoc. firm Manikoff & Munde, Pontiac, Mich., 1963-64; atty. Chrysler Fin. Corp., Detroit, 1964-67; sr. atty. Chrysler Fin. Corp., Southfield, Mich., 1967-70; sec. Chrysler Fin. Corp., Troy and Southfield, Mich., 1970—. Mem. ABA, State Bar Mich., Detroit Bar Assn. Home: 945 Harmon St Birmingham MI 48009-3818 Office: Chrysler Fin Corp 27777 Franklin Rd Southfield MI 48034

LINK, ROBERT JAMES, lawyer, educator; b. Washington, May 25, 1950; s. Robert Wendell and Barbara Ann (Bullock) L.; m. Cheryl Ann Brillante, Apr. 22, 1978; children: Robert Edward, Holden James. BA, U. Miami, 1972, JD, 1975. Bar: Fla. 1975, U.S. Dist. Ct. (mid. dist.) Fla. 1980, U.S. Ct. Appeals (5th cir.) 1980, U.S. Ct. Appeals (11th cir.) 1981, U.S. Supreme Ct. 1984, U.S. Dist. Ct. (no. dist.) Fla. 1989. Asst. pub. defender City of Miami, Fla., 1975-78, City of Jacksonville, Fla., 1978-82; ptnr. Greenspan, Goodstein & Link, Jacksonville, 1982-84, Goodstein & Link, Jacksonville, 1984-85; sole practice Jacksonville, 1985-88; assoc. Howell, Liles & Milton, Jacksonville, 1988-89; ptnr. Pajcic & Pajcic P.A., 1990—; guest instr. U. Miami, 1976, U. Fla., 1979-88, Stetson Law Sch., 1984, Jacksonville U., 1987-88, U. North Fla., 1991. Atty. legal panel ACLU, Jacksonville, 1982-88; bd. dirs. Jacksonville Legal Aid, 1990-92. Mem. Fla. Bar Assn. (chmn. com. for representation of indigents criminal law sect. 1980, cert. criminal trial lawyer 1989), Jacksonville Bar Assn. (criminal law sect.), Nat. Assn. Criminal Def. Lawyers (vice-chmn. post conviction com. 1990), Fla. Pub. Defender Assn. (death penalty steering com. 1980-82, instr. 1979-89). Democrat. Methodist. Avocations: sailing, fishing, diving, softball. Home: 3535 Carlyon St Jacksonville FL 32207-5836 Office: 1900 Independent Sq Jacksonville FL 32202

LINK, WILLIAM P., insurance company executive. Exec. v. pres. Prudential Ins. of Am. Inc., Newark, 1990—. Office: Prudential Ins. of Am. Inc. 56 Livingston Ave Roseland NJ 07068*

LINK, WILLIAM THEODORE, television writer, producer; b. Phila., Dec. 15, 1933; s. William Theodore and Elsie (Roerecke) L.; m. Margery Nelson, Sept. 5, 1980. B.S., U. Pa., 1956. bd. govs. The TV Acad., 1976. Writer, creator, producer (with ptnr. Richard Levinson) TV series Columbo, Mannix, McCloud, Murder, She Wrote, also others; writer, producer: made-for-TV movies The Storyteller; My Sweet Charlie, That Certain Summer, The Execution of Private Slovik, The Gun, Crisis at Central High, The U.S. vs. Salim Ajami, The Boys, The Bill Cosby Mysteries; Author: Fineman, 1973, Stay Tuned, 1981, The Playhouse, 1985, Off-Camera, 1986. Served with SIgnal Corps U.S. Army, 1956-58. Recipient Emmy awards Acad. TV Arts and Scis., 1970, 72, Golden Globe awards Hollywood Fgn. Press Assn., 1972 (2), Peabody award, Edgar Allan Poe award Mystery Writers Am., 1980, 81, 83, 84; Paddy Chayefsky Laurel award, 1986, Ellery Queen Lifetime Achievement award, 1989, Bouchercon Performance in the Arts award, 1989; inductee TV Hall of Fame, 1995. Mem. Writers Guild Am., Dramatists Guild, Mystery Writers Am., Screen Actors Guild.

LINKE, RICHARD A., systems engineer, researcher; b. Plainfield, N.J., Feb. 15, 1946; married; 2 children. BA, Columbia U., 1968, MS, 1970, PhD in Physics, 1972. Mem. tech. staff radio physics rsch. Bell Telephone Labs., 1972-86, head lightware comm. rsch. dept., 1986-89; sr. rsch. scientist NEC Rsch. Inst., 1989—. Fellow IEEE , Optical Soc. Am. Office: Nec Rsch Inst 4 Independence Way Princeton NJ 08540*

LINKLATER, ISABELLE STANISLAWA YAROSH-GALAZKA (LEE LINKLATER), foundation executive, secondary education educator; b. Chgo., Sept. 15, 1939; d. Baron Stanislaw and Isabelle Lydia (Yarosh) Galazka. BE, Chgo. State U., 1959. Cert. tchr., Ill. Pub. rels. coord. Kelling Co., Chgo., 1955-57; tchr. Chg. Bd. Edn., 1957-89, coord. computer lab., 1989—; founder, pres., exec. dir. Assisi Animal Found. Edn. writer, coord. Elsa Internat. Wild Animal Appeal, Ill., 1985—; writer Lakeland Press, 1992. Bd. dirs. Townsquare Players, Woodstock (Ill.) Opera House, 1989-91. Recipient Outstanding Citizen award CBS Broadcasting, 1992. Mem. McHenry County Defenders (bd. dirs. 1989-91), East African Wildlife Soc. (U.S. rep.). Avocations: travel, music, theater. Office: Assisi Animal Found PO Box 143 Crystal Lake IL 60039-0143

LINKLATER, WILLIAM JOSEPH, lawyer; b. Chgo., June 3, 1942; s. William John and Jean (Connell) L.; m. Dorothea D. Ash, Apr. 4, 1986; children: Erin, Emily. BA, U. Notre Dame, 1964; JD, Loyola U., 1968. Bar: Ill. 1968, Calif. 1981, U.S. Dist. Ct. (no. dist.) Ill. 1968, U.S. Ct. Appeals (7th cir.) 1971, U.S. Supreme Ct. 1971, U.S. Ct. Appeals (6th cir.) 1990, U.S. Ct. Appeals Washington 1978, Calif. 1981, U.S. Dist. Ct. (cen. dist.) Calif. 1981, U.S. Tax Ct. 1982, U.S. Dist. Ct. (no. dist.) Calif. 1983, U.S. Dist. Ct. (ea. dist.) Mich. 1989, U.S. Dist. Ct., Colo. 1990, U.S. dist. Ct. Hawaii, 1992. Atty. Fed. Defender Project, Chgo.; assoc. Baker & McKenzie, Chgo., 1968-75, ptnr., 1975—. Contbr. articles to profl. jours. Mem. ABA (past co-chmn. com. on internat. criminal law criminal justice sect., mem. criminal practice and procedure com. antitrust sect.), FBA, Ill. Bar Assn., 7th Cir. Bar Assn., Chgo. Bar Assn. (bd. mgrs., past v.p. jud. candidates evaluation com., chmn. large law firm com., Internat. Inst.), Calif. Bar Assn., Colo. Bar Assn., Am. Coll. Trial Lawyers, Am. Bd. Criminal Lawyers, Chgo. Inn of Ct., Wong Sun Soc. San Francisco (internat. proctor), Alpha Sigma Nu. Office: Baker & McKenzie 1 Prudential Plz Ste 3000 Chicago IL 60601

LINKLETTER, ARTHUR GORDON, radio and television broadcaster; b. Moose Jaw, Sask., Can., July 17, 1912; s. Fulton John and Mary (Metzler) L.; m. Lois Foerster, Nov. 25, 1935; children: Jack, Dawn, Robert (dec.), Sharon, Diane (dec.). A.B., San Diego State Coll., 1934. Program dir. Sta. KGB, San Diego, 1934; program dir. Calif. Internat. Expn., San Diego, 1935; radio dir. Tex. Centennial Expn., Dallas, 1936; San Francisco World's Fair, 1937-39; pres. Linkletter Prodns.; ptnr., co-owner John Guedel Radio Prodns.; chmn. bd. Linkletter Enterprises; owner Art Linkletter Oil Enterprises. Author: theme spectacle Cavalcade of Golden West, 1940; author and co-producer: theme spectacle Cavalcade of Am, 1941; writer, producer, star in West Coast radio shows, 1940-55; former star, writer: People Are Funny, NBC-TV and radio, Art Linkletter's House Party, CBS-TV and radio; Author: People Are Funny, 1953, Kids Say The Darndest Things, 1957, The Secret World of Kids, 1959, Confessions of a Happy Man, 1961, Kids Still Say The Darndest Things, 1961, A Child's Garden of Misinformation, 1965, I Wish I'd Said That, 1968, Linkletter Down Under, 1969, Oops, 1969, Drugs at My Door Step, 1973, Women Are My Favorite People, 1974, How to be a Super Salesman, 1974, Yes, You Can!, 1979, I Didn't Do It Alone, 1979, Public Speaking for Private People, 1980, Linkletter on Dynamic Selling, 1982, Old Age is not for Sissies, 1988; lectr. convs. and univs. Nat. bd. dirs. Goodwill Industries; commr. gen. to U.S. Exhibit at Brisbane Expo 88, Australia, 1987; amb. to The 200th Anniversary Celebration, Australia, 1987—; bd. regents Pepperdine U.; pres. bd. advisors Ctr. on Aging, UCLA; chmn. bd. French Found. for Alzheimers Rsch. Recipient numerous awards. Address: 8484 Wilshire Blvd Ste 205 Beverly Hills CA 90211-3220

LINKONIS, SUZANNE NEWBOLD, pretrial case manager, counselor; b. Phila., Aug. 24, 1945; d. William Bartram and Kathryn (Taylor) Newbold; m. Bertram Lawrence Linkonis, May 29, 1966; children: Robert William, Deborah Anne, Richard Anthony. AA in Psychology, Albany (Ga.) Jr. Coll., 1979; BA in Psychology, Albany (Ga.) State Coll., 1981; MS in Indsl. Psychology, Va. Commonwealth U., 1986. Office mgr., media buyer Long Advt. Agy., Richmond, Va., 1981-84; media mgr. Clarke & Assocs., Richmond, Va., 1984-85; human resources asst. Continental Ins., Richmond, Va., 1985; rsch. assoc. Signet Bank, N.A., Richmond, Va., 1986-87; program coord. Med. Coll. Va., Richmond, 1988; personnel mgr. Bur. Microbiology, Richmond, 1988; personnel specialist Va. State Dept. Corrections, Richmond, 1989-90; human rights advocate Va. State Dept. Youth & Family Svcs., Richmond, 1990-92, rehab. counselor, 1992-94, sr. rehab. counselor, 1994; pre-trial case mgr./counselor Henrico County Govt., 1995-96; future dir., cons. Mary Kay Cosmetics, Springfield, Va., 1975-77. Mem. NAFE, APA. Republican. Roman Catholic. Avocations: professional jours. in psychology, networking groups, walking, tennis. Home: 401 Saybrook Dr Richmond VA 23236-3621 Office: 8600 Dixon Powers Dr Richmond VA 23228-2737

LINKOUS, WILLIAM JOSEPH, JR., lawyer; b. Roanoke, Va., July 17, 1929; s. William Joseph and Mary Virginia (Lester) L.; m. Anita Marie Stedronsky, Oct. 15, 1960; children—William Joseph III, Brian Keith. BA, Roanoke Coll., Salem, Va., 1951; MA in Econs., U. Va., 1954, JD, 1956. Bar: Va. 1956, Ga. 1957. Assoc. Powell, Goldstein, Frazer & Murphy, Atlanta, 1956-62, ptnr., 1962-79, 85—, mng. ptnr., 1979-85. Trustee Holy Innocents Episcopal Sch., Atlanta, 1974-80, Roanoke Coll., 1980-95, emeritus 1995—. Fellow Am. Coll. Trust and Estate Counsel, Am. Bar Found.; mem. State Bar Ga. (past chmn. fiduciary sect., co-chmn. Ga. trust law revision com. 1988-91, chmn. Ga. probate code revision com. 1991—), Va. State Bar, Am. Law Inst., Internat. Acad. Estate and Trust Law, Atlanta Estate Planning Coun. (pres. 1983-84). Avocation: tennis. Home: 730 Langford Ln NW Atlanta GA 30327-4732 Office: Powell Goldstein Frazer & Murphy 191 Peachtree St NE Ste 16 Atlanta GA 30303-1741

LINMAN, JAMES WILLIAM, retired physician, educator; b. Monmouth, Ill., July 20, 1924; s. Chester E. and Ruth L. (Pearson) L.; m. Frances Firth, Aug. 31, 1946; children—John, Jean, James, Jeffrey. B.S., U. Ill., 1945, M.D., 1947. Intern, resident internal medicine Med. Sch., U. Mich., Ann Arbor, 1947-51, fellow in hematology, 1951-52, 54-56, asst. prof. internal medicine, 1955-56; chief hematology sect. VA Research Hosp. Chgo.; assoc. prof. medicine Med. Sch., Northwestern U., Evanston, Ill., 1956-65; prof. internal medicine Mayo Grad. Sch. Medicine, U. Minn., Mpls.; cons. hematology and head spl. hematology sect. Mayo Clinic-Found., Rochester, Minn., 1965-72; prof. medicine, dir. Osgood Leukemia Ctr., Health Sci. Ctr., U. Oreg., Portland, 1972-79, head hematology div., 1974-78; prof. medicine John A. Burns Sch. Medicine, U. Hawaii, Honolulu, 1979-92; emeritus prof., 1992—; chmn. admissions com. John A. Burns Sch. Medicine, U. Hawaii, Honolulu, 1983-92, asst. dean for admissions, 1988-92; chmn. State of Hawaii Adv. Commn. on Drug Abuse and Controlled Substances, 1986-88; dir. med. edn. The Queen's Med. Ctr., Honolulu, 1987-88. Author: Principles of Hematology, 1966, Factors Controlling Erythropoiesis, 1960, The Leukemias, 1971, Hematology, 1975; Contbr. articles to profl. jours. Served with USAF, 1952-54. Recipient Tchr. of Year award Mayo Fellows Assn., 1970, Tchr. of Year award U. Hawaii, 1980, 81. Mem. Am. Soc. Clin. Investigation, Central Soc. Clin. Research, Am., Internat. socs. hematology, A.C.P., Western Assn. Physicians, Western Soc. Clin. Research, Pacific Interurban Clin. Club, Alpha Omega Alpha, Phi Kappa Phi. Club: Oahu Country. Home: 2130 Pililani Pl Honolulu HI 96822-2513

LINN, DIANA PATRICIA, elementary education educator; b. Perth, Australia, Dec. 31, 1943; came to U.S., 1948; d. Evan Andrew and Grace Henrietta (Springhall) Jarboe; m. Jim F. Erlandsen, July 9, 1966 (div. Mar. 1989); children: Rebecca, Tim, Jenny; m. Richard George Linn, Mar. 31, 1990; 1 stepchild, Cristal. AA, Olympic Coll., 1963; BA in Elem. Edn., Western Wash. U., 1965; MEd, U. Ariz., 1969. Cert. tchr., Wash. Tchr. 3d grade Neomi B. Willmore Elem., Westminster, Calif., 1965-66; tchr. English and sci. 7-8th grade Sunnyside Jr. H.S., Tucson, 1966-70; tchr. kindergarten All Seasons, Tucson, 1972-74; tchr. K-1st grade St. Cyril's, Tucson, 1974-77; tchr. 1st grade Grace Christian Sch., Tucson, 1977-80; tchr. K-1st grade, reading K-6th grade Ridgeview Christian Ctr., Spokane, Wash., 1983-85, Spokane Christian Schs., 1985-87; dir. Ridgeview Christian Learning Ctr., Spokane, 1987-88; tchr. kindergarten Arlington Elem., Spokane, 1988—; mem. curriculum study com. Sunnyside Sch. Dist., Tucson, 1967-68; chmn. accreditation and sch. bd. St. Cyril's Sch., Tucson, 1976-77; chair faculty involvement group, chair staff devel., chair wellness com. Arlington Elem., Spokane, 1992-93, sch. reporter, 1994-95; instr. reading readiness Family Learning Fair, Home Schooling Seminar, Spokane Falls C.C., Spokane, 1988; chair, coord. pre-sch. coop. Arlington Elem. with Spokane Falls C. C. of Spokane C.C., 1992-93; chair faculty involvement group, Arlington Elem., Spokane, 1995—; chmn. Imagination Celebration, 1994. Coord. Christian edn. Valley Foursquare Ch., Spokane, 1982-87; coord. children's ch. Victory Faith Fellowship, Spokane, 1993—; Brownie troop leader Willmore Elem., Westminster, 1965-66; ednl. restructuring rep. for Arlington Elem., Spokane Sch. Dist. # 81, 1992-93. Scholar Naval Officer's Wives Club, 1961-62; recipient Eisenhower grant, 1990, 94. Mem. ASCD, NEA, Wash. Edn. Assn., Spokane Edn. Assn. (Arlington Elem. rep. 1991-93), CPA Wives Club (sec., ball chair 1983-84), Alpha Delta Kappa (membership chair 1994-95, program planning chmn.). Republican. Avocations: collecting dolls, plates, swimming, quilt-making. Home: 2403 E Illinois Ave Spokane WA 99207-5655 Office: Arlington Elem Sch 6363 N Smith St Spokane WA 99207-7616

LINN, EDWARD ALLEN, writer; b. Boston, Nov. 14, 1922; s. Hyman and Gertrude (Ober) L.; m. Ruth Goldberg, June 12, 1949; children: Michael, David, Hildy. B.S. in Journalism, Boston U., 1950. With USIS, Washington, 1951-52; asst. editor Macfadden Publs., 1952-53; contbg. writer Sat. Eve. Post, 1964-68. Free-lance writer, 1953-63; author: The Eternal Kid, 1961, Veeck-as in Wreck, 1962, The Last Loud Roar, 1964, The Hustler's Handbook, 1965, Koufax, 1966, Masque of Honor, 1969, Thirty Tons a Day, 1972, The Adversaries, 1973, Big Julie of Vegas, 1974, Out of the Fire, 1975, Nice Guys Finish Last, 1975, Where The Money Was, 1976, Inside the Yankees, The Championship Season, 1978, Steinbrenner's Yankees, 1982, A Great Connection, 1988, The Great Rivalry, 1991, Hitter, 1993, The Life and Turmoils of Ted Williams. Named Mag. Sportswriter of Year, Nat. Sportscasters and Sportswriters Assn., 1963; recipient Oppie award, 1975. Address: 1150 Anchorage Ln San Diego CA 92106-3119

LINN, GARY DEAN, golf course architect; b. Wichita, Kans., May 11, 1955; s. Richard W. and Marilyn (Hanson) L.; m. Vicki Duncan, Aug. 6, 1977; children: Rachel, Jason, Nathan. B of Landscape Architecture, Kans. State U., 1978. Registered landscape architect Kans., 1979. Mem. Am. Soc. Landscape Architects, Am. Soc. Golf Course Architects. Avocations: family, golf, sports cards, sports. Office: 705 Forest Ave Palo Alto CA 94301-2102

LINN, JAMES HERBERT, retired banker; b. Jacksonville, Fla., Nov. 22, 1925; s. Herbert P. and Evelyn Lucile (Gore) L.; m. Betty J. Thatcher, Oct. 22, 1949; children: David, Donald, Charles, Craig, Jill. BA in Liberal Arts, U. Mo., Kansas City, 1948. With various commerce cos., 1948; vice-chmn. Commerce Bancshares, Inc., Kansas City, 1970-90; ret., 1990—; bd. dirs. Commerce Bank NA, Hays, Manhattan, El Dorado, Lenexa and Leavenworth, Kans. Dir. Eye Found. of Kansas City. Mem. Robert Morris Assos. Home: 10261 Rosewood Dr Overland Park KS 66207-3456

LINN, JUDY, photographer; b. Detroit, June 28, 1947. BFA, Pratt Inst., 1969. Staff Getty Collection, L.A., Detroit Art Inst., Dallas Mus. Fine Art; adj. asst. prof. photography Pratt Inst., Bklyn., 1974-85. Exhibited in group shows at Dallas Mus. Fine Arts, 1976; Padigione d'Arte Contemporanea, Milan, Italy, 1980, New Wave,N.Y.C., 1981, Susane Hilberry Gallery, Birmingham, 1982, Detroit Art Inst., 1985, Gallery 55, N.Y.C., 1985, Sandra Berler Gallery, Chevy Chase, Md., 1986, Feature Gallery, N.Y.C., 1995. Grantee Bob and Stephanie Scull, 1985, Line 11, 1986. Office: 252 Elizabeth St New York NY 10012*

LINN, MARCIA CYROG, education educator; b. Milw., May 27, 1943; d. George W. and Frances (Vanderhoof) Cyrog; m. Stuart Michael Linn, 1967 (div. 1979); children: Matthew, Allison; m. Curtis Bruce Tarter, 1987. BA in Psychology and Stats., Stanford U., 1965, MA in Ednl. Psychology, 1967, PhD in Ednl. Psychology, 1970. Prin. investigator Lawrence Hall Sci. U. Calif., 1970-87, prin. investigator Sch. Edn., 1985—, asst. dean Sch. Edn., 1983-85, prof., 1989—; Fulbright prof. Weizmann Inst., Israel, 1983; exec. dir. seminars U. Calif., 1985-86, dir. instnl. tech. program, 1988—; cons. Apple Computer, 1983—; mem. adv. com. on sci. edn. NSF, 1978—, Ednl. Testing Svc., 1986—, Smithsonian Instn., 1986—, Fulbright Program, 1983-86, Grad. Record Exam. Bd., 1990-94; chair Cognitive Studes Bd. McDonell Found., 1994—. Author: Education and the Challenge of Technology, 1987; co-author: The Psychology of Gender--Advances Through Meta Analysis, 1986—, Designing Pascal Solutions, 1992—, Designing Pascal Solutions with Data Structures, 1996; contbr. articles to profl. jours. Sci. advisor Parents Club, Lafayette, Calif., 1984-87; mem. Internat. Women's Forum, Women's Forum West, 1992—. Recipient fellow Ctr. for Adv. Study in Behavior. Scis. 1995—. Fellow AAAS (bd. dirs. 1996—), APA, Am. Psychol. Soc.; mem. Nat. Assn. Rsch. in Sci. and Teaching (bd. dirs. 1983-86, assoc. editor jour., Outstanding Paper award 1978, Outstanding Jour. Article award 1975, 83, Disting. Contbns. to Sci. Edn. Through Rsch. award 1994), Am. Ednl. Rsch. Assn. (chmn. rsch. on women and edn. 1983-85, Women Educators Rsch. award 1982, 88, edn. in sci. and tech. 1989-90, ann. mtg. program com. 1996, Willystine Goodsell award 1991), Nat. Sci. Tchrs. Assn. (mem. rsch. agenda com. 1987-90, task force 1993-94), Soc. for Rsch. in Child Devel. (editl. bd. 1984-89), Soc. Rsch. Adolescence, Sierra Club. Avocations: skiing, hiking. Office: U Calif Sch Edn 4611 Tolman Hall Berkeley CA 94720

LINN, RICHARD, lawyer; b. Bklyn., Apr. 13, 1944; s. Marvin and Enid (Rowe) L.; m. Patricia Madden, Aug. 8, 1966; children: Sandra Joan, Deborah Anne. BEE, Rensselaer Poly. Inst., 1965; JD, Georgetown U., 1969. Bar: Va. 1969, D.C. 1970, N.Y. 1994, U.S. Dist. Ct. (ea. dist.) Va. 1969, U.S. Dist. Ct. D.C. 1970, U.S. Ct. Appeals (4th cir.) 1970, U.S. Ct. Appeals (D.C. cir.) 1970, U.S. Ct. Appeals (fed. cir.) 1982, U.S. Supreme Ct. 1994. Patent examiner U.S. Patent and Trademark Office, Washington, 1965-68; patent agent Office Naval Rsch., Washington, 1968-69; assoc. Brenner, O'Brian, Guay & Connors, Arlington, Va., 1969-71, Stepno & Neilan, Arlington, 1971-72; ptnr. Stepno, Schwab & Linn, Arlington, 1972-74; pvt. practice Washington, 1974-77; ptnr. Wender, Murase & White (name changed to Marks & Murase), Washington, 1977—, mng. ptnr. Washington office, 1982—. Mem. ABA, Am. Intellectual Property Law Assn., Internat. Trademark Assn., Va. Bar Assn. (founding bd. govs. Intellectual Property sect. 1971), Rensselaer Washington Alumni Assn. (chmn. 1972). Avocations: flying, swimming, woodworking. Office: Marks & Murase 2001 L St NW Ste 750 Washington DC 20036-4910

LINN, STUART MICHAEL, biochemist, educator; b. Chgo., Dec. 16, 1940; s. Maurice S. and Pauline L.; m. Priscilla K. Cooper; children: Matthew S., Allison D., Meagan S. B.S. with honors in Chemistry, Calif. Inst. Tech., 1962; Ph.D. in Biochemistry, Stanford U., 1967. Asst. prof. biochemistry U. Calif., Berkeley, 1968-72, assoc. prof., 1972-75, prof., 1975-87, head div. biochemistry and molecular biology, 1987-90, 95—. Mem. editorial bd. Nucleic Acids Rsch., 1974—, Jour. Biol. Chemistry, 1975-80, Molecular and Cellular Biology, 1987-91; contbr. articles to profl. jours., chpts. to books. Helen Hay Whitney fellow, 1966-68; John Simon Guggenheim fellow, 1974-75; recipient USPHS Merit Grant award, 1988—. Mem. AAAS, Am. Soc. Biol. Chemists (coun.), Am. Soc. Microbiologists. Office: U Calif Divsn Biochem & Mo Bio Barker Hall Berkeley CA 94720

LINNA, TIMO JUHANI, immunologist, researcher, educator; b. Tavastkyro, Finland, Mar. 16, 1937; came to U.S., 1968, naturalized, 1981; foster s. Gustaf Lennart and Anne-Marie (Forsstrom) Ackell; m. Rhoda Margareta Popova, May 20, 1961; children: Alexander, Fredrik, Maria. MB, U. Uppsala, Sweden, 1959, MD, 1965, PhD, 1967. Intern, resident hosps. Sweden, pvt. practice medicine hosps. and clinic; asst. prof. histology U. Uppsala, 1967-71; asst. prof. microbiology and immunology Temple U., Phila., 1970-71; dir. lab. clin. immunology hosps. Temple U., 1970-72, adviser clin. immunology, 1972-80; assoc. prof. microbiology, immunology Temple U., Phila., 1971-78; prof. Temple U., 1978-80, research prof., 1980-90; group leader immunology central research and devel. dept. E.I. duPont de Nemours & Co., Wilmington, Del., 1980-84, research supr., 1984-85, mgr. med. research products dept., 1986-87, assoc. med. dir., 1987-90; sr. dir. cellular immunology Applied Immune Scis., Inc., Menlo Park, Calif., 1990-91; sr. assoc. med. dir. inst. clin. immunology and infectious diseases, devel. rsch., Syntex (USA) Inc., Palo Alto, Calif., 1992-94, dir. med. rsch., 1994-95; dir. med. rsch. Roche Globe Devel., Palo Alto, Calif., 1995—; immunology cons. UNDP/World Bank/WHO Spl. Program for Research and Tng. in Tropical Diseases, WHO, Geneva, 1978-79; mem. sci. adv. coun. Internat. Inst. Immunology Tng. and Research, Amsterdam, Netherlands, 1975-81. Author books; contbr. articles to profl. publs. USPHS Internat. postdoctoral research fellow, 1968-70; spl. research fellow U. Minn., 1970; Eleanor Roosevelt Am. Cancer Soc. fellow, 1976; grantee Swedish Med. Research Council, 1969-71; grantee NIH, 1972-80. Mem. Am. Assn. Cancer Research, Am. Assn. Immunologists (chmn. edn. com. 1975-80), Am. Assn. Pathologists, Am. Soc. Microbiology, Internat. Soc. Exptl. Hematology, Internat. Soc. Lymphology, N.Y. Acad. Scis., Reticuloendothelial Soc., Royal Lymphatic Soc. Uppsala, Scandinavian Soc. Immunology, Soc. Swedish Physicians, Swedish Med. Assn. Lutheran. Home: 260 Highland Ave San Carlos CA 94070-1911 Office: PO Box 10850 3401 Hillview Ave Palo Alto CA 94303

LINNAN, JUDITH ANN, psychologist; b. Pasadena, Calif., July 11, 1940; d. Robert Emmet Linnan and Jane Thomas (Shutz) H.; m. Ralph Theodore Comito, Feb. 1, 1964 (div. Mar. 1975); children: Matthew, Andrew, Kristine. BA, U. Portland, 1962; MS, Calif. State U., Long Beach, 1974; PhD, CCI Internat. U., 1982; postgrad., Newport Psychoanalytical Inst., 1984-87, 95—. Lic. MFCC pupil pers., lic. rsch. psychoanalyst. Probation officer L.A. County Probation Dept., 1962-63; social worker L.A. County Dept. Probation and Social Svcs., 1963-69; counselor Huntington Beach (Calif.) Free Clinic, 1970-73, counseling ctr., Calif. State U., Long Beach, 1973-74; psychologist Fullerton (Calif.) Union High Sch. Dist., 1975-80, Psychiat. Med. Group, Orange County, Calif., 1981-82; psychologist, dir. Berkeley Psychol. Svcs., Placentia, Calif., 1982—; pvt. practice psychotherapist Huntington Beach, 1975—; founder, dir. Pacific Acad., Fullerton, 1981-82; dir. human resources So. Calif. Coll. Optometry, Fullerton, 1986—; cons., expert witness Orange County Social Svcs., 1992—; dir. student parent program Placentia Sch. Dist., 1993—. Democrat. Roman Catholic. Avocation: horses. Office: Berkeley Psychol Svcs 101 N Kraemer Blvd Ste 125 Placentia CA 92670-5000

LINNELL, ROBERT HARTLEY, environment, safety consultant; b. Kalkaska, Mich., Aug. 15, 1922; s. Earl Dean and Constance (Hartley) L.; m. Myrle Elizabeth Talbot, June 17, 1950; children: Charlene LeGro, Lloyd Robert, Randa Ruth, Dean Maxfield. B.S., U. N.H., 1944, M.S., 1948; Ph.D., U. Rochester, 1950. Asst. instr. U. N.H., 1942-44, instr., 1947; asst. prof. chemistry Am. U., Beirut, 1950-52; assoc. prof., chmn. chemistry dept. Am. U., 1952-55; v.p. Tizon Chem. Corp., Flemington, N.J., 1955-58; assoc. prof. chemistry U. Vt., 1958-61; dir. Scott Research Labs., Plumsteadville, Pa., 1961-62; program dir. phys. chemistry NSF, 1962-65, planning assoc., 1965-67, program mgr. departmental sci. devel., 1967-69; dean Coll. Letters, Arts and Scis., U. So. Calif., Los Angeles, 1969-70; dir. Office Instl. Studies U. So. Calif., 1970-82, chmn. safety sci. dept., 1982-85, prof. emeritus, 1985—; pres. Harmony Inst., 1985-92; cons. Reheis Corp., 1958-61, Coll. Chemistry Cons. Service, 1970-76, EPA, 1971-73, Lake Erie Environment Program, 1971-73. Author: Graduate Student Support and Manpower Resources in Graduate Science Education, 1968, Air Pollution, 1973, Hydrogen Bonding, 1971, Dollars and Scholars, 1982, Meeting The Needs of The Non-Smoking Traveler, 1986, Ignition Interlock Devices: An Assessment of Their Application to Reducing DUI, 1991; contbr. articles to profl. jours. Mem. traffic adv. com. Auto Club So. Calif., 1985-93; treas. Norwich Congl. Ch., 1995-96, chair bus. com. 1996—; coord. Concord Coalition, Upper Valley, N.H. and Vt., 1995—. With USNR, 1944-46. Recipient Outstanding Achievement award Coll. Tech., U. N.H., 1969. Fellow AAAS; mem. AAUP, Am. Chem. Soc. (program chmn. Washington 1968, divsn. chem. edn. 1971), Am. Assn. Higher Edn., Assn. Instl. Rsch., Am. Soc. Safety Engrs., Nat. Safety Mgmt. Soc., Am. Assn. Univ. Adminstrs., Am. Lung Assn. (bd. dirs. 1986-92, pres. 1991-92), Upper Valley Habitat for Humanity (bd. dirs. 1993-95), Rotary. Patentee in chemistry field. Home: 255 Kings Hwy W White River Junction VT 05001-3200

LINNEMEYER-BUSCH, ANNIE, library director; b. Joplin, Mo., Jan. 6, 1947; d. George Lee and Margaret Eleanor (Williams) Chancellor; 1 child, William Andrew Keller. BA, Mo. U., 1969, MA, 1976. Br. mgr. St. Charles (Mo.) City Coun. Libr., 1977-84; br. mgr. Springfield/Greene County (Mo.) Libr., 1985-89, exec. dir., 1989—; mem. exec. bd. Mo. Libr. Network Corp., St. Louis, 1991-96. Mem. adv. bd. Springfield Pub. Sch. Found., 1992-94; pres. Ozarks Regional Info. On-Line Network, Springfield, 1993—; mem. Gov.'s Commn. on Informational Tech.; mem. exec. bd. Mo. Rsch. and Edn. Network, pres., 1996-97; bd. dirs. Ozarks Pub. TV, 1994—; mem. task force Mo. Goals 2000, 1995. Mem. ALA, Mo. Libr. Assn. (pres. 1993-94, exec. bd. 1990-94), Forum, Pub. Libr. Assn., Rotary (treas. Springfield Club 1994). Office: Springfield-Greene Cty Libr 620 W Republic Rd Springfield MO 65807-5818

LINNEY, BEVERLY See HALLAM, BEVERLY

LINNEY, ROMULUS, author, educator; b. Phila., Sept. 21, 1930; s. Romulus Zachariah Linney and Maitland (Thompson) Clabaugh; m. Laura Callanan; children: Laura, Susan. BA, Oberlin Coll., 1953, LittD (hon.), 1995; MFA, Yale U., 1958; DLitt. (hon.), Applachian State U., 1995; DLitt (hon.), Oberlin Coll., 1995. Prof. arts Sch. Arts Columbia U., N.Y.C.; lectr. U. N.C., Chapel Hill, Raleigh, U. Pa., Bklyn. Coll., Conn. Coll., Princeton U., Hunter Coll.; adj. prof. playwriting Actors Studio, New Sch. Social Rsch., N.Y.C.; dir. Corp. of Yaddo. Author: (novels) Heathen Valley, 1962, Slowly, By Thy Hand Unfurled, 1965, Jesus Tales 1980, (plays) The Sorrows of Frederick, 1968, Democracy and Esther, and the Love Suicide at Schofield Barracks, 1973, Holy Ghosts, and The Sorrows of Frederick, 1977, Old Man Joseph and His Family, 1978, The Captivity of Pixie Shedman, 1981, Tennessee, 1981 (Obie award 1992, Excellence in Playwriting 1992), Childe Byron, 1981, The Death of King Philip, 1983, Laughing Stock, 1984, Sand Mountain, 1985, A Woman Without a Name, 1986, Pops, 1987, Juliet, Yance and April Snow, 1989, Three Poets, 1989, Unchanging Love, 1990, '2', 1990, Ambrosio, 1991, Spain, 1993, True Crimes, 1995, Oscar Over Here, 1995. With U.S. Army, 1954-56. Grantee NEA, Guggenheim Found., Rockefeller Found., others; recipient Lit. award AAAL. Mem. Dramatists Guilde (coun.), Ensemble Studio Theatre, Fellowship of So. Writers, Corp of Yaddo (bd. dirs.). Address: 35 Claremont Ave # 9N New York NY 10027-6823

LINOWES, DAVID FRANCIS, political economist, educator, corporate executive; b. N.J., Mar. 16, 1917; m. Dorothy Lee Wolf, Mar. 25, 1946; children: Joanne Linowes Alinsky, Richard Gary, Susan Linowes Allen (dec.), Jonathan Scott. BS with honors, U. Ill., 1941. Founder, ptnr. Leopold & Linowes (name now BDO Siedman), Washington, 1946-62; cons. sr. ptnr. Leopold & Linowes, 1962-82; nat. founding ptnr. Laventhol & Horwath, 1965-76; chmn. bd, chief exec. officer Mickleberry Comm. Corp., 1970-73; chmn., CEO Perpetual Investment Co., Inc., 1950-88; dir. Horn & Hardart Co., 1971-77, Piper Aircraft, 1972-77, Saturday Rev./World Mag., Inc., 1972-77, Chris Craft Industries, Inc., 1958—, Work in Am. Inst., Inc.; prof. polit. economy, pub. policy, bus. adminstrn. U. Ill., Urbana, 1976—, Boeschensten prof. emeritus, 1987—; cons. DATA Internat. Assistance Corps., 1962-68, U.S. Dept. State, UN, Sec. HEW, Dept. Interior; chmn. Fed. Privacy Protection Commn., Washington, 1975-77, U.S. Commn. Fair Market Value Policy for Fed. Coal Leasing, 1983-84, Pres.'s Commn. on Fiscal Accountability of Nation's Energy Resources, 1981-82; chmn. Pres.' Commn. on Privatization, 1987-88; mem. Council on Fgn. Relations; cons. panel GAO; adj. prof. mgmt. NYU, 1965-73; Disting. Arthur Young Prof. U. Ill., 1973-74; emeritus chmn. internat. adv. com. Tel Aviv U.; headed U.S. State Dept. Mission to Turkey, 1967, to India, 1970, to Pakistan, 1968, to Greece, 1971, to Yugoslavia, 1991; U.S. rep. on privacy to Orgn. Econ. Devel. Intergovtl. Bur. for Informatics, 1977-81, cons., N.Y.C., 1977-81; U.S. State Dept. mission to Chile, Argentina and Uruguay, July, 1988, Yugoslavia, May, 1991. Author: Managing Growth Through Acquistion, Strategies for Survival, Corporate Conscience; commn. report Personal Privacy in Information Society, Fiscal Accountablility of Nation's Energy Resources, The Privacy Crisis In Our Time; editor: The Impact of the Communcation and Computer Revolution on Society, Privacy in America, 1989; contbr. articles to profl. jours. Trustee Boy's Club Greater Washington, 1955-62, Am. Inst. Found., 1962-68; assoc. YM-YWHA's Greater N.Y., 1970-76; chmn. Charities Adv. Com. of D.C., 1958-62; emeritus bd. dirs. Religion in Am. Life, Inc.; former chmn. U.S. People for UN; chmn. citizens com. Combat Charity Rackets, 1953-58. Served to 1st lt. Signal Corps, AUS, 1942-46. Recipient 1970 Human Relations award Am. Jewish Com., U.S. Pub. Service award, 1982, Alumni Achievement award U. Ill., 1989, CPA Distinguished Pub. Svc. award, Washington, 1989. Mem. AICPA (v.p. 1962-63), U. Ill. Found. (emeritus bd. dirs. 1), Coun. Fgn. Rels., Cosmos Club (Washington), Phi Kappa Phi (nat. bd. dirs.), Beta Gamma Sigma. Home: 803 Fairway Dr Champaign IL 61820-6325 Office: U Ill 308 Lincoln Hall Urbana IL 61801 also: 9 Wayside Ln Scarsdale NY 10583-2907

LINOWITZ, SOL MYRON, lawyer; b. Trenton, N.J., Dec. 7, 1913; s. Joseph and Rose (Oglenskye) L.; m. Evelyn Zimmerman, Sept. 3, 1939; children: Anne, June, Jan, Ronni. AB, Hamilton Coll., 1935; JD, Cornell U., 1938; LLD (hon.), Allegheny Coll., Amherst Coll., Bucknell U., Babson Inst., Brandeis U., Colgate U., Curry Coll., Dartmouth Coll., Elmira Coll., Georgetown U., Hamilton Coll., Hebrew Union Coll., Ithaca Coll., Marietta Coll., John Hopkins U., Oberlin Coll., St. John Fisher Coll., St. Lawrence U., Jewish Theol. Sem., Washington U., St. Louis, U. Miami, Muskingum Coll., Notre Dame U., U. Pacific, U. Pa., Rutgers U., Pratt Inst., Rider Coll., Roosevelt U., Chapman Coll., U. Mich., Govs. State U., U. Mo., Syracuse U.; LHD (hon.), Am. U., Loyola U., U. Rochester, Yeshiva U., U. Judaism, Wooster Coll.; PhD (hon.), U. Haifa. Bar: N.Y. 1938. Asst. gen. counsel OPA, Washington, 1942-44; ptnr. Sutherland, Linowitz & Williams, 1946-58, Harris, Beach, Keating, Wilcox & Linowitz, Rochester, N.Y., 1958-66; chmn. Nat. Urban Coalition, 1970-76; chmn. bd. dirs., chmn. exec. com., gen. counsel Xerox Corp., 1958-66; chmn. bd. dirs. Xerox Internat., 1966; sr. ptnr. Coudert Bros., 1969-84, sr. counsel, 1984-94; ambassador to OAS, 1966-69; hon. chmn. Acad. Ednl. Devel., Washington, 1992—; co-negotiation Panama Canal treaties, 1977-78; spl. Middle East negotiator for Pres. Carter, 1979-81; chmn. Am. Acad. of Diplomacy, 1984-89; co-chmn. Inter-Am. Dialogue, 1981-92; hon. chmn. Acad. for Ednl. Devel., 1986—; pres. Fed. City Coun., 1974-78; chmn. Pres. Commn. World Hunger, 1978-79; bd. dirs., co-founder Internat. Exec. Svc. Corps; chmn. State Dept. Adv. Com. on Internat. Orgns., 1963-66. Author: The Betrayed Profession, 1994, (memoir) The Making of a Public Man, 1985, This Troubled Urban World, 1974; contbr. articles to profl. jours. Trustee Hamilton Coll., Cornell U., Johns Hopkins U., Am. Assembly; chmn. bd. overseers, bd. dirs. Jewish Theol. Sem., 1971-79. Lt. USNR, 1944-46. Fellow Am. Acad. Arts and Scis.; mem. Am. Assn. for UN (pres. N.Y. State), Rochester Assn. for UN (pres. 1952), Rochester C. of C. (pres. 1958), ABA, N.Y. Bar Assn., Rochester Bar Assn. (v.p. 1949-50), Am. Assn. UN (bd. dirs.), Council on Fgn. Relations, Order of Coif, Phi Beta Kappa, Phi Kappa Phi. Office: Acad for Ednl Devel 1875 Connecticut Ave NW Washington DC 20009-5728

LINSCOTT, JERRY R., lawyer; b. Falls City, Nebr., July 21, 1941; s. Judd M. and Viola M. (Apel) L.; m. Dona L. Friesen (div. 1980); m. Linda S. Paintieri (div. 1985); children: Mark, Todd; m. Theresa Watkins, May 17, 1986; 1 child, Palmer Jarvis. BS, U. Nebr., 1963, LLB, 1966. Bar: Mo. 1966, U.S. Dist. Ct. (mid. dist.) Mo. 1967, Fla. 1972, U.S. Dist. Ct. (mid. dist.) Fla. 1972, U.S. Ct. Appeals (11th cir.) 1990. Mem. firm Linde, Thomson, Langworthy, Van Dyke & Kohn, Kansas City, Mo., 1966-72; ptnr. Young, Turnbull & Linscott, Orlando, Fla., 1972-79, Baker & Hostetler, Orlando, 1979—. Mem. ABA (state leader litigation sect. 1990—). Office: Baker & Hostetler PO Box 112 Orlando FL 32801*

LINSENMEYER, JOHN MICHAEL, lawyer; b. Columbus, Ohio, June 20, 1940; s. John Cyril and Ruth Theresa (Motz) L.; m. Barbara Panish, Aug. 12, 1961; children: Ann Elizabeth Linsenmeyer Nelson, Thomas More, Barbara Mary Linsenmeyer Malone. AB, Georgetown U., 1961, JD, 1964.

Bar: Va. 1964, N.Y. 1965, U.S. Supreme Ct.1967, D.C. 1975. Assoc. Cravath, Swaine & Moore, N.Y.C., 1966-75; ptnr. Forsyth, Decker, Murray & Broderick, N.Y.C., 1975-80, Morgan, Lewis & Bockius, N.Y.C., 1980—. Columnist Southern Conn. Newspapers, Greenwich, 1984—; contbr. articles to profl. jours. Police officer, sgt. Greenwich Police Dept. Special Div., 1966-87; cons. firearms Presdl. Commn. on the Causes and Prevention of Violence, 1968-69; bd. dirs. Fairfield County Fish and Game Agy., Newtown, Conn., 1973-77. Mem. N.Y. State Bar Assn., N.Y.C. Fed. Cts. Com., N.Y.C. Fed. Bar Coun., Univ. Club (N.Y.C.), Can. Club (N.Y.C.), Squadron A (N.Y.C.), Rocky Point (Old Greenwich, Conn.), Royal Can. Milit. (Toronto). Republican. Roman Catholic. Clubs: University (N.Y.C.), Squadron A (N.Y.C.), Rocky Point (Old Greenwich, Conn.), Royal Can. Mil. (Toronto), Can. Club of N.Y. Avocations: hunting, shooting, horses, military history. Home: 9 Hendrie Ave Riverside CT 06878-1808 Office: Morgan Lewis & Bockius 101 Park Ave New York NY 10178

LINSENMEYER, TODD ALAN, medical educator, physician. Student, Whittier (Calif) Coll., 1971-72; BS with honors, Stanford U, 1975; MD, U. Hawaii, 1979. Diplomate Am. Bd. Urology, Am. Bd. Phys. Medicine and Rehab. Surg. intern Queen's Hosp., Honolulu, 1979-80; resident urology Tripler Army Med. Ctr., Honolulu, 1980-84; resident physical medicine and rehab. Stanford (Calif.) Med. Ctr., 1986-89; clin. asst. prof. surgery U. Medicine and Dentistry/N.J. Sch. Medicine, Newark, 1989-95, asst. prof. rehab. medicine, 1989—, asst. prof. surgery, 1995—, assoc. prof. rehab. medicine, 1996—; asst. chief urology 98th Gen. U.S. Army Hosp., Nuremberg, Germany, 1984-86; dir. urology Kessler Inst. Rehab. Medicine, West Orange, N.J., 1989—; cons. urodynamics Dept. Vets. Affairs Med. Ctr., East Orange, 1991—; vis. prof. phys. medicine and rehab. Stanford U., 1992; reviewer Male Spinal Cord Injury Fertility Program: Miami Project for Cure of Paralysis, 1994; mem. sci. adv. bd. Paralyzed Vets. Am., 1995—; mem. grant rev. com. NIH, 1991, 92; mem. adv. com. Spinal Cord Injury Practice Consortium, 1995—, mem. steering com., 1995—; chmn. autonomic dysreflexia practice parameter guideline com. SCI Practice Parameter Consortium, 1995—; presenter various meetings, orgns., confs. Contbr. articles to profl. jours., chpts. to books. Maj. M.C. U.S. Army, 1980-87. Recipient 2nd pl. award paper competition ACS, Honolulu, 1984; grantee Sprague Dawley Rat Eastern Paralyzed VA, 1992-93, NIH, 1992-95, VA, 1995-98, Am. Paraplegia Soc., 1995-96. Mem. AMA, Am. Paraplegia Soc. (bd. dirs. 1993—, membership com. 1990, chmn. membership com. 1992-94, chmn. clin. practice parameter com. 1995—), Am. Spinal Cord Injury Assn. (mem. urology com. sexuality and disability 1991—, mem. program com., publs. com. 1994—), Am. Acad. Phys. Medicine and Rehab., Am. Congress Rehab. Medicine (mem. nat. task force on sexuality and disability 1988—), Am. Urodynamics Soc. (assoc.), Assn. Acad. Physiatrists, Am. Urol. Assn. Office: Kessler Inst Rehab 1199 Pleasant Valley Way West Orange NJ 07052

LINSEY, NATHANIEL L., bishop; b. Atlanta, July 24, 1926; s. Samuel and L. E. (Forney) L.; m. Mae Cannon Mills, June 8, 1951; children: Nathaniel Jr., Ricardo Mills, Julius Wayne, Angela Elise. BS, Paine Coll., 1948, LLD (hon.), 1990; BD, Howard U., 1951; MA in Evangelism, Scarritt Coll., 1974; DD (hon.), Miles Coll., 1975, Tex. Coll., 1985. Ordained to ministry Christian M.E.Ch., 1948. Nat. dir. youth Christian M.E.Ch., 1951-52; pastor Rock of Ages Christian M.E.Ch., 1952-53; presiding elder Columbia (S.C.) dist. Christian M.E.Ch., 1953-55; pastor Vanderhorst Christian M.E.Ch., 1955-56, Mattie E. Coleman Christian M.E.Ch., 1956-62, Thirgood Christian M.E.Ch., 1962-66; gen. sec. evangelism Christian M.E.Ch., 1966-78, chmn. bd. lay activities, 1978-82, chmn. fin. com., 1982-86, elected 39th bishop, 1978—, sr. bishop, CEO, presiding bishop 2d dist., 1994, founder Congress on Evangelism, chmn. dept. fin., 1982-86, chmn. bd. evangelism, missions and human concerns, chmn. Coll. of Bishops, 1980, 92; v.p. Interfaith Christian Coun., Washington, 1979-82; mem. presidium World Meth. Coun.; regional sec. N.Am. sect. world evangelism com. World Methodist Coun. Pres. local chpt. NAACP, Knoxville, Tenn., 1957; trustee Miles Coll., Birmingham, Ala. Recipient Disting. Alumni award Paine Coll., 1978, Presdl. citation Nat. Assn. for Equal Opportunities in Higher Edn., 1979, Disting. Svc. award Govt. D.C., 1984, Pub. Svc. award Tex. Coll., 1984, Disting. Missionary award Calif. conf. M.E.Ch., 1985; chieftancy of Obong Uwanna Ibibio Tribe, Nigeria, 1992—. Mem. World Meth. Coun., So. Calif. Ecumenical Coun. Chs. (pres. L.A. chpt. 1984). Democrat. Home: 5115 Rollman Estate Dr Cincinnati OH 45236

LINSK, MICHAEL STEPHEN, real estate executive; b. L.A., Apr. 20, 1940; s. Abe P. and Helen Linsk; BS in Bus. Adminstrn., U. So. Calif., 1965, MBA, 1969; m. Wilma M. Stahl, Aug. 11, 1979; children by previous marriage: Cari E., Steven D. CFO Larwin Group, Inc., Encino, Calif., 1970-75; v.p. fin., dir. Donald L. Bren Co., Los Angeles, 1976-78; v.p., CFO, treas., dir. Wilshire Mortgage/Wilshire Diversified, Burbank, Calif., 1980-81, pres., dir. subs. Wilshire Mortgage Corp., Burbank, 1981-84; pres., dir. Wilshire Realty Investments, Burbank, 1981-84, Glenfed Investments Inc., subs. Glendale Fed. Savs., 1982-84; pres. Eastern Pacific Fin. Group, Los Angeles, 1984-85; sr. v.p. Leisure Tech., Inc., Los Angeles, 1985-87, CEO, Investec Realty Group, Inc., Encino, Calif., 1987-88; sr. v.p. L.A. Land Co., 1988-91, dir. real estate consulting Price Waterhouse, 1992—; dir. Presdl. Savs. Bank, dir. Jewel City Ins., Glendale, Verdugo Services, Inc., Glendale. Treas. Temple Judea, Tarzana, Calif., 1982-83, trustee, 1981-83; treas., bd. dirs. Am. Theater Arts; bd. dirs. North Hollywood Cultural Ctr., Inc. Mem. Bldg. Industry Assn. (dir. Los Angeles chpt. 1981-88), AICPA, Calif. Soc. CPAs, Beta Gamma Sigma. Office: Price Waterhouse 400 S Hope St Los Angeles CA 90071-2801

LINSLEY, ROBERT MARTIN, retired geology educator; b. Chgo., Feb. 19, 1930; s. Robert Martin and Mary (Morgan) L.; m. JoAnn Hoehler (div.); children: David, Barbara, Christopher. B.S., U. Mich., 1952, M.S., 1953, Ph.D., 1960. Ford teaching intern Colgate U., Hamilton, N.Y., 1954-55; mem. faculty Colgate U., 1955—, Whitnall prof. geology, chmn. dept. geology, 1955-92, ret., 1992. Contbr. articles to profl. jours. Office: Colgate U Dept Geology Hamilton NY 13346

LINSTONE, HAROLD ADRIAN, management and systems science educator; b. Hamburg, Fed. Republic Germany, June 15, 1924; came to U.S., 1936; s. Frederic and Ellen (Seligmann) L.; m. Hedy Schubach, June 16, 1946; children: Fred A., Clark R. BS, CCNY, 1944; MA, Columbia U., 1947; PhD, U. So. Calif., 1954. Sr. scientist Hughes Aircraft Co., Culver City, Calif., 1949-61, The Rand Corp., Santa Monica, Calif., 1961-63; assoc. dir. planning Lockheed Corp., Burbank, Calif., 1963-71; prof. Portland (Oreg.) State U., 1970—; pres. Systems Forecasting, Inc., Santa Monica, 1971—; cons. 1973—. Author: Multiple Perspectives for Decision Making, 1984; co-author: The Unbounded Mind, 1993, The Challenge of the 21st Century, 1994; co-editor The Delphi Method, 1975, Technological Substitution, 1976, Futures Research, 1977; editor-in-chief Technol. Forecasting Social Change, 1969—. NSF grantee, Washington, 1976, 79, 85. Mem. Inst. Mgmt. Scis., Ops. Rsch. Soc., Internat. Soc. Systems Scis. (pres. 1993-94). Avocation: photography. Office: Portland State U PO Box 751 Portland OR 97207-0751

LINSTROTH, TOD B., lawyer; b. Racine, Wis., Feb. 19, 1947; s. Eugene and Gloria L.; m. Jane Kathryn Zedler, June 23, 1972; children: Kathryn, Krista, Kassandre, Kyle. BBA in Acctg., U. Wis., 1970, JD, 1973. Bar: Wis. Assoc. Michael, Best & Friedrich, Madison, Wis., 1973-79, ptnr., 1980—. Mem. Madison Plan Commn., 1978-82, Wis. Gov.'s Task Force Am. Motors Corp., Madison, 1986; mem. bus. alumni bd. U. Wis., Madison, 1991—; mem. Wis. Gov.'s Sci. and Tech. Coun., Madison, 1993—; bd. dirs., v.p. Madison Repertory Theatre. 1st lt. USAR, 1970-78. Mem. Madison Club (bd. dirs.). Republican. Avocation: sailing. Office: Michael Best & Friedrich 1 S Pinckney St # 900 Madison WI 53703-2808

LINTINGER, GREGORY JOHN, electrical engineer, educator; b. New Orleans, Oct. 8, 1946; s. Emile John Jr. and Lucy (Perez) L.; m. Barbara Gaudet, Mar. 14, 1965 (div. Sept. 1981); children: Gregory John Jr., Melissa Anne; m. Brenda Celeste Wambsgans, Dec. 12, 1981; 1 child, Emily Celeste. BS in Elec. Engring., U. New Orleans, 1985. Registered profl. engr., La., Tenn. Office mgr. Upper City Electric Co., New Orleans, 1967-72, elec. estimator, 1972-76, elec. designer, estimator, 1976-87, v.p. elec. design/estimating, 1987-94; mgr., elec. and instrumental engring. dept. Wink Engring., New Orleans, 1994—; instr. Associated Builders and Contractors, New Orleans, 1975-95. Pres. Young Men's Bus. Club of Greater New Orleans, 1975. Recipient Bush award Young Men's Bus. Club, New Orleans, 1973-75, Colomb award, 1975. Mem. Illuminating Engrs. Soc. (sec. 1987-88), Kiwanis (treas. 1986-87), A.B.C. (bd. dirs. New Orleans chpt. 1986-87). Republican. Roman Catholic. Avocations: piano, computers, music, philanthropy. Home: 639 Labarre Dr Metairie LA 70001-5442 Office: Wink Engineering Elect & Instrumental Engring Dept 4949 Bullard Ave New Orleans LA 70128

LINTON, FREDERICK M., strategic planning consultant; b. Stanton, Mich., 1932; m. Peggy Jensen, May 27, 1954; children: Michael, Melinda, Margaret. B.A., Mich. State U., 1959, M.A., 1960. Tchr. San Diego, 1960-66; with AMCORD, Inc., 1966-69, Peat, Marwick & Mitchell, Los Angeles, 1969-70; sr. v.p. Shareholders Capital Corp., Los Angeles, 1970-72; pres., chief exec. officer Boyden Assos. Inc., N.Y.C. and Los Angeles, 1972-74; pres., chmn. Delta Group Inc., Laguna Beach, Calif., 1974—; pres. Universal Paper Goods, 1983-85; dir Irvine Indsl. League. Bd. dirs. U. Calif. at Irvine Indsl. Assn. Mem. Calif. Council Econ. Edn. (pres., trustee), Newcomen Soc. N.Am., Town Hall Calif., World Affairs Council, World Bus. Council. Home: 26851 Salazar Dr Mission Viejo CA 92691-5011 Office: 23276 Del Lago Dr Laguna Hills CA 92653-1308

LINTON, GORDON J., federal agency administrator. BS in Econs., Lincoln U.; MS in Counseling, Antioch U. Mem. Pa. Ho. Reps., Harrisburg, 1980-93; administrator Fed. Transit Administration, Washington, 1993—; past vice chmn. Ho. Appropriations Com., Pa. Ho. of Reps., chmn. transp. com. on pub. trnsp., chmn. Pa. legis. black caucus; bd. dirs. Southeastern Pa. Transp. Authority. Mem. Conf. Minority Transp. Officials (nat. legis. dir.). Democrat. Office: Fed Transit Auth 400 7th St SW Washington DC 20590-0001*

LINTON, JACK ARTHUR, lawyer; b. N.Y.C., May 29, 1936; s. Paul Phillip and Helen (Feller) L.; m. Nancy A., Sept. 1, 1957; children: Ann Deborah Linton Wilmot, James Paul, John Michael. BA, Albright Coll., 1958; JD, NYU, 1961, LLM in Taxation, 1966. Bar: Pa. 1962, N.Y. 1963, U.S. Tax Ct. 1966, U.S. Dist. Ct. (ea. dist.) Pa. 1978, U.S. Ct. Appeals, 1984. Assoc. DeLong, Dry & Binder, Reading, Pa., 1961-63; asst. ho. counsel Bob Banner Assocs., Inc., N.Y.C., 1963-66; ptnr. DeLong, Dry, Cianci & Linton, Reading, 1967-70, Williamson, Miller, Murray & Linton, Reading, 1970-72, Gerber & Linton, P.C., Reading, 1972-88; Linton, Giannascoli, Barrett & Distasio, P.C. Linton, Giannascoli, Barrett & Distasio, P.C., Reading, 1989—; solicitor Reading Parking Authority, 1967-76, City of Reading, 1980—; bd. dirs. The Group, Inc., Small Bus. Coun. Am., Inc., chmn. polit. action com., 1988—, numerous med. profl. corps., Reading area; lectr. nat. seminars on tax problems for small bus.; co-founder, mem. Estate Planning Coun. Berks County, 1978—. Editor Tax Law Rev., 1965-67; contbr. articles to profl. jours. Pres. Berks County Mental Health Assn., 1968-69, Reading Jewish Community Ctr., 1980-82; mem. Mental Health/Mental Retardation Bd. Berks County, 1974-80; treas., bd. dirs. Reading-Berks Youth Soccer League, 1982-85; bd. dirs. Gov. Mifflin Sch. Dist., Shillington, 1985-93. Kenneson fellow NYU Sch. Law, 1965-67. Mem. ABA (mem. personal svc. orgn. com., tax sect. 1981—, chairperson task force for repeal top-heavy rules 1987-89, vice chmn. personal svc. orgn. com. 1990-92, chmn. personal svc. orgn. com. 1992-94), Pa. Bar Assn., Berks County Bar Assn. (treas. 1969-72), Berks County C. of C. (mem. nat. affairs com.). Democrat. Jewish. Avocations: sports, photography, horticulture. Office: Linton Giannascoli Barrett & Distasio PC PO Box 461 1720 Mineral Spring Rd Reading PA 19603-0461

LINTON, ROY NATHAN, graphic arts company executive; b. Jamestown, Ohio, Jan. 22, 1918; s. Lindley Vanniman and Pearl Candice (Jackson) L.; m. Joyce Sandra Phillips, Dec. 11, 1945; children—Michael, Philip. A.B., Cedarville Coll., 1938; postgrad., Ohio State U., 1938-40. Tchr. math. Blanchester (Ohio) High Sch., 1938-41; with Standard Register Co., Dayton, 1947-83; v.p. ops. Standard Register Co., 1971-72, exec. v.p., 1972-77, pres., 1977-83, chief exec. officer, 1981-83, also dir. Past trustee Miami Valley Hosp., Dayton. Maj. field arty. AUS, 1941-46. Republican. Clubs: Masons (Jamestown), Rotary (San Diego). Office: 5969 Madra Ave San Diego CA 92120-3954

LINTZ, PAUL RODGERS, physicist, engineer, patent examiner; b. Dallas, Feb. 8, 1941; s. Norman Edmund and Sarah Kathleen (Powers) L.; m. Mary Grace Caggiano, Nov. 27, 1965; children: Matthew Thomas, Eileen Sarita, Jerome Peter, Elizabeth Irene. BA cum laude, U. Dallas, 1963; MS, Cath. U. Am., 1965, PhD, 1977. Mem. tech. staff Tex. Instruments, Dallas, 1965-67; rsch. physicist Teledyne Geotech. Co., Alexandria, Va., 1967-74; scientist Planning Systems Inc., McLean, Va., 1974-76; prin. investigator Sci. Applications Internat. Corp., McLean, 1976-84; systems engr. Mitre Corp., McLean, 1984-87; ind. cons. Vienna, Va., 1987-92; patent examiner U.S. Patent and Trademark Office, Washington, 1992—. Mem. Providence Dist. Dem. Com., Vienna, 1985; com. mem. Vienna area Boy Scouts Am., 1986-90; pres. Tysons Woods Civic Assn., Vienna, 1991. Mem. IEEE, D.C. Bar, Internat. Platform Assn., Sigma Xi. Roman Catholic. Achievements include development of digital signal processing techniques for defense purposes in seismic detection of underground nuclear blasts, submarine sonar signal processing, passive bistatic radar signal processing, detection, tracking. Home: 2222 Craigo Ct Vienna VA 22182-5038 Office: US Dept Commerce Patent and Trademark Office ART Unit 2307 Box 13 Washington DC 20231 *The optimist argues the glass is half full of water. The pessimist argues it is half empty. The pragmatic, being thirsty drinks the water.*

LINTZ, ROBERT CARROLL, financial holding company executive; b. Cin., Oct. 2, 1933; s. Frank George and Carolyn Martha (Dickhaus) L.; m. Mary Agnes Mott, Feb. 1, 1964; children—Lesa, Robert, Laura, Michael. B.B.A., U. Cin., 1956. Staff accountant Alexander Grant, Cin., 1958-60; dist. mgr. Uniroyal, Memphis, 1960-65; v.p. Am. Fin. Corp., Cin., 1965—; dir. Rapid-American Corp., McGregor Corp., Faberge Inc., all N.Y.C., H.R.T. Industries Inc., Los Angeles. Fisher Foods Inc., Cleve., Am. Agronomics, Tampa, Fla. Trustee, St. Francis-St. George Hosp., Cin., 1974-81. Served to capt. U.S. Army, 1956-58, 61-62. Republican. Roman Catholic. Home: 5524 Palisades Dr Cincinnati OH 45238-5620 Office: Am Fin Corp 1 E 4th St Cincinnati OH 45202-3717

LINVILL, JOHN GRIMES, engineering educator; b. Kansas City, Mo., Aug. 8, 1919; s. Thomas G. and Emma (Crayne) L.; m. Marjorie Webber, Dec. 28, 1943; children: Gregory Thomas, Candace Sue. A.B., William Jewell Coll., 1941; S.B., Mass. Inst. Tech., 1943, S.M., 1945, Sc.D., 1949; Dr. Applied Sci., U. Louvain, Belgium, 1966; DSc, William Jewell Coll., 1992. Asst. prof. elec. engring. Mass. Inst. Tech., 1949-51; mem. tech. staff Bell Telephone Labs., 1951-55; assoc. prof. elec. engring. Stanford U., 1955-57, prof., dir. solid-state electronics lab., 1957-64, prof., chmn. dept. elec. engring., 1964-80, prof., dir. Center for Integrated Systems, 1980-90—, Canon USA prof. engring., 1988-89, prof. emeritus, 1989—; co-founder, dir., chmn. bd. Tele Sensory Corp.; dir. Read-Rite Corp. Author: Transistors and Active Circuits, 1961, Models of Transistors and Diodes, 1963; inventor Optacon reading aid for the blind. Recipient citation for achievement William Jewell Coll., 1963, John Scott award for devel. of Optacon, City of Phila., 1980, Medal of Achievement Am. Electronics Assn., 1983, Louis Braille Prize Deutscher Blindenverband, 1984. Fellow IEEE (Edn. medal 1976), AAAS; mem. Nat. Acad. of Engring., Am. Acad. of Arts and Scis. Home: 30 Holden Ct Portola Valley CA 94028-7913 Office: Stanford U Dept Elec Engring Stanford CA 94305

LINVILLE, RAY PATE, logistics analyst; b. Winston-Salem, N.C., Feb. 27, 1946; s. Clyde Burton and Nellie Pearl (Helm) L.; m. Mary Ann Slordal, July 30, 1970; children: Russell Pate, Rachel Ann. BA in Journalism, U. N.C., 1967; MS in Logistics Mgmt. with distinction, Air Force Inst. Tech., 1973. Commd. 2d lt. USAF, 1967, advanced through grades to col., 1989; materials mgr. USAF, Madrid, 1973-76; mem. staff Tactical Air Command, Hampton, Va., 1976-79; plans officer UN Command, Seoul, Korea, 1980-81; staff analyst USAF, Washington, 1981-85; rsch. fellow Harvard U., Cambridge, Mass., 1985-86; chief combat support analysis Joint Chiefs of Staff, Washington, 1986-89; dir. logistics plans Strat. Air Command, Omaha, 1989-92; chief logistics plans and programs Air Combat Command, Hampton, 1992-93; ret. USAF, 1994; analyst Logistics Mgmt. Inst., McLean, Va., 1993—; adj. prof. U. Va., Falls Church, 1986-88; grad. prof. Webster U., Washington, 1988—; adj. grad. prof. U. So. Calif., L.A., 1981. Author: (monograph) Command and Control of Forces..., 1987; asst. editor, lit. editor, mem. rev. bd. Logistics Spectrum, 1990—; contbr. articles to profl. jours. Dir., v.p., treas. Danbury Forest Com. Assn., Springfield, Va., 1982-84; youth group advisor, deacon Presbyn. Ch., Omaha and Fairfax, Va., 1986-92. Decorated Legion of Merit; recipient Outstanding Young Man of Am. award U.S. Jaycees, 1978. Mem. Soc. Logistics Engrs. (sr., life, cert. profl. logistician, chpt. chmn. 1990-91, Bronze award 1991), Air Force Assn. (life), Mil. Ops. Rsch. Soc., Retired Officers Assn., U. N.C. Gen. Alumni Assn. (life), U.S. Chess Fedn. (life), Sigma Iota Epsilon. Avocations: writing, golf, piano, chess. Home: 5231 Capon Hill Pl Burke VA 22015-1615 Office: Logistics Mgmt Inst 2000 Corporate Rdg Ste 5080 Mc Lean VA 22102-7805

LINXWILER, LOUIS MAJOR, JR., retired finance company executive; b. Blackwell, Okla., Mar. 7, 1931; s. Louis Major and Flora Mae (Horton) L.; m. Susan Buchanan, July 27, 1963; children: Louis Major III, Robert William. BS, Okla. State U., 1954. Mgr. credit dept. Valley Nat. Bank, Tucson, 1957-60; sales rep. Vega Industries, Syracuse, N.Y., 1960-62; program dir. Am. Cancer Soc., Phoenix, 1962-67; v.p., mgr. credit dept. United Bank Ariz., Phoenix, 1967-76; dean edn. Am. Inst. Banking, Phoenix, 1976-80; cons. Phoenix, 1980-81, United Student Aid Funds Inc., Phoenix, 1981-82; founder, pres., chief exec. officer Ariz. Student Loan Fin. Corp., Phoenix, 1982-88, also bd. dirs.; founder, chmn., chief exec. officer Western Loan Mktg. Assn., Phoenix, 1984-90, also bd. dirs.; pres. Precision Design and Engring., Inc., Escondido, Calif., 1993—. Editor: Money and Banking, 1978. Pres. City Commn. Sister Cities, Phoenix, 1986-87, Am. Inst. Banking, Phoenix, 1973-74, Phoenix YMCA Bd. Dirs., 1974-75; v.p. North Mountain Behavioral Inst., Phoenix, 1975-77. Served to 1st lt. U.S. Army, 1954-56. Mem. Shriners, Hiram Club, Rotary (bd. dirs. 1982-83, 93-94, 96—), Beta Theta Pi. Republican. Presbyterian. Avocations: restoring automobiles, World War II history, travel. Home: 3311 E Georgia Ave Phoenix AZ 85018-1424

LINZ, ANTHONY JAMES, osteopathic physician, consultant, educator; b. Sandusky, Ohio, June 16, 1948; s. Anthony Joseph and Margaret Jane (Ballah) Linz; m. Kathleen Ann Kovach, Aug. 18, 1973; children: Anthony Scott, Sara Elizabeth. BS, Bowling Green State U., 1971; D.O., U. Osteo. Med. and Health Scis., 1974. Diplomate Nat. Bd. Osteo. Examiners; bd. cert., diplomate Am. Osteo. Bd. Internal Medicine, Internal Medicine, Med. Diseases of Chest and Critical Care Medicine. Intern Brentwood Hosp., Cleve., 1974-75, resident in internal medicine, 1975-78; subsplty. fellow in pulmonary diseases Riverside Meth. Hosp., Columbus, Ohio, 1978-80; med. dir. pulmonary svcs. Sandusky (Ohio) Meml. Hosp., 1980-85; med. dir. cardio-pulmonary svcs. Firelands Community Hosp., Sandusky, 1985—; cons. pulmonary, critical care and internal medicine, active staff sect. internal medicine, chmn. dept. medicine, head div. pulmonary medicine Firelands Community Hosp., 1985—; cons. staff dept. medicine Good Samaritan Hosp., 1982-85, sect. internal medicine specializing pulmonary diseases; cons. pulmonary, critical care, and internal medicine Providence Hosp., Sandusky, Mercy Hosp., Willard, Ohio; clin. prof. internal medicine Ohio U. Coll. Osteo. Medicine; clin. prof. medicine Univ. Health Scis. Coll. Osteo. Medicine, Kansas City, Mo.; clin. asst. prof. med. Med. Coll. of Ohio at Toledo; adj. prof. applied scis. Bowling Green State U.; mem. respiratory tech. adv. bd. Firelands Campus, Bowling Green State U., 1983—; med. dir. Respiratory Therapy program., Bowling Green State U., 1984—. Author, contbr. articles and abstracts to profl. jours. Water safety instr. ARC, 1965—; med. dir., clin. rsch. investigator Camp Superkid Asthma Camp, 1984—; bd. trustees Stein Hospice, 1986-90. Recipient Edward Ruff Comty. Svc. award Am. Lung. Assn., 1985, Master Clinician award Ohio U. Coll. Osteopathic Medicine, 1987, Golden Rule award J.C. Penney, 1990, Disting. Alumna/Alumnus award Firelands Coll., Bowling Green State U., 1995. Fellow Am. Coll. Chest Physicians, Am. Coll. Critical Care Medicine, Am. Coll. Osteo. Internists; mem. AAAS, European Thoracic Soc., Am. Osteo. Assn., Ohio Osteo. Assn. (past pres., past v.p., past sec.-treas., acad. trustees 5th dist. acad.), Am. Heart Assn., Am. Thoracic Soc., Ohio Thoracic Soc., Am. Lung Assn. (pres., 1st v.p., med. adv. bd. chmn., exec. bd. dirs., bd. dirs. Ohio's So. Shore sect. 1984—), Nat. Assn. Med. Dirs. Respiratory Care, Ohio Soc. Respiratory Care (med. adviser/dir. 1982—), So. Critical Care Medicine, Am. Coll. Physicians (Ohio chpt.), Found. Critical Care (mem. Founder's Cir.), Sandusky Yacht Club, Sandusky chpt.), Alpha Epsilon Delta, Beta Beta Beta, Pi Kappa Alpha, Atlas Med. Fraternity. Roman Catholic.

LION, PAUL MICHEL, III, transportation engineer, executive; b. Washington, Dec. 7, 1934; s. Paul Miller and Anna Louise (Chandler) L.; m. Jane Sanford, June 16, 1956; children: David, James, Thomas, William. BS, U.S. Mil. Acad., 1956; MA, MSE in Aero. Engring., Princeton U., 1963, PhD, 1965. Engr. Applied Physics Lab., Silver Spring, Md., 1960-61; rsch. asst. Princeton (N.J.) U., 1961, postdoctoral fellow, 1965-66, asst. prof. transp., 1966-70, assoc. prof., 1970-74, prof., 1974-79; dir. ops. and cost analysis U.S. Ry. Assn., Washington, 1977-81; cons. Snavely King, Harris, Washington, 1981-83, Tech. Resource Ctr., Arthur D. Little, 1983-94; v.p. ALK, Washington, 1994—. Contbr. articles to profl. publs. With arty. U.S. Army, 1956-59. Mem. IEEE, Ops. Rsch. Soc. Am., Cosmos Club. Home: 7012 Hamel Hill Ct Mc Lean VA 22101-4307 Office: ALK 888 16th St NW Ste 700 Washington DC 20006

LIONAKIS, GEORGE, architect; b. West Hiawatha, Utah, Sept. 5, 1924; s. Pete and Andriani (Protopapadakis) L.; student Carbon Jr. Coll., 1942-43, 46-47; BArch., U. Oreg., 1951; m. Iva Oree Braddock, Dec. 30, 1951; 1 dau., Deborah Jo. With Corps Engrs., Walla Walla, Wash., 1951-54; architect Liske, Lionakis, Beaumont & Engberg, Sacramento, 1954-86, Lionakis-Beaumont Design Group, 1986—. Mem. Sacramento County Bd. Appeals, 1967—, chmn., 1969, 75, 76; pres. Sacramento Builders Exchange, 1976. Served with USAAF, 1943-46. Mem. AIA (pres. Central Valley chpt., 1972—), Constrn. Specifications Inst. (pres. Sacramento chpt., 1962; nat. awards, 1962, 63, 65), Sacramento C. of C. (code com., 1970—). Club: North Ridge Country (pres. 1987). Lodge: Rotarian (pres. East Sacramento 1978-79). Prin. works include Stockton (Calif.) Telephone Bldg., 1968, Chico (Calif.) Main Telephone Bldg., 1970, Mather AFB Exchange Complex Sacramento, 1970, Base Chapel Mather AFB, Sacramento, 1970, Woodridge Elementary Sch., Sacramento, 1970, Pacific Telephone Co. Operating Center Modesto, Calif., 1968, Sacramento, 1969, Marysville, Calif., 1970, Red Bluff, Calif., 1971, Wells Fargo Banks, Sacramento, 1968, Corning, Calif., 1969, Anderson, 1970, Beale AFB Exchange Complex, Marysville, 1971, Cosumnes River Coll., Sacramento, 1971, base exchanges at Bergstrom AFB, Austin, Tex., Sheppard AFB, Wichita Falls, Tex., Chanute AFB, Rantoul, Ill., McChord AFB, Tacoma, Wash., health center Chico State U., Sacramento County Adminstrn. Center, Sacramento Bee Newspaper Plant. Home: 160 Breckenwood Way Sacramento CA 95864-6968 Office: Lionakis Beaumont Design Group 1919 19th St Sacramento CA 95814-6714

LIOTTA, LANCE ALLEN, pathologist; b. Cleve., July 12, 1947; married; 2 children. BA in Gen. Sci. and Biology, Hiram Coll., 1969; PhD in Biomed. Engring. and Biomath., Case Western U., 1974, MD, 1976. Cert. basic life support Am. Heart Assn., advanced life support Am. Heart Assn. Instr. pathology for inhalation therapists dept. pathology St. Luke's Hosp., Cleve., 1972-74; sr. instr. pulmonary pathology Phase I and Phase II, Sch. Medicine Case Western Reserve U., 1973-74; USPHS resident physician Lab. Pathology, Nat. Cancer Inst. NIH, Bethesda, Md., 1976-78, pathologist, expert/cons. Lab. Pathophysiology, Nat. Cancer Inst., 1978-80, sr. investigator, pub. health svc. officer Lab. Pathophysiology and Pathology, Nat. Cancer Inst., 1980-82, chief tumor invasion and metastases sect. Lab. Pathology and Lab. Pathology, Nat. Cancer Inst., 1982—, dir. anatomic pathology residency program Lab. Pathology, Nat. Cancer Inst., 1982—, dep. dir. intramural rsch., 1992-93; adj. clin. prof. pathology Sch. Medicine George Wash. U.; mem. adj. faculty Sch. Medicine Georgetown U.; invited faculty mem. Rockefeller U., 1979; speaker in field. Author: (with others) Cancer Invasion and Metastasis, 1977, Pulmonary Metastasis, 1978, Metastatic Tumor Growth, 1980, Bone Metastasis, 1981, Cell Biology of Breast Cancer, 1980, New Trends in Basement Membrane Research, 1982, Tumor Invasion and Metastasis, 1982, Progress in Clinical and Biological Research, 1982, Growth of Cells in Hormonally Defined Media, 1982, Understanding Breast Cancer: Clinical and Laboratory Concepts, 1983, The Role of Extracellular Matrix in Development, 1984, Basic Mechanisms and Clinical Treatment of Tumor Metastasis, 1985, Hemostatic Mechanisms and Metastasis, 1984, Biological Responses in Cancer, vol. 4, 1985, The Cell in Contact: Adhesions and Junctions as Morphogenetic Determinants, 1985, Rheumatology, vol. 10, 1986, Progress in Neuropathology, vol. 6, 1986, Cancer Metastasis: Experimental and Clinical Strategies, 1986, Biochemistry and Molecular Genetics of Cancer Metastasis, 1986, Basement Membranes, 1985, 1986 Year Book of Cancer, New Concepts in Neoplasia as Applied to Diagnostic Pathology, 1986, Head and Neck Management of the Cancer Patient, 1986, Cancer Metastasis: Biological and Biochemical Mechanisms and Clinical Aspects, 1988, Important Advances in Oncology, 1988, Breast Cancer: Cellular and Molecular Biology, 1988, Cancer: Principles and Practice of Oncology, vol. 1, 3d edit., 1989, Molecular Mechanisms in Cellular Growth and Differentiation, 1991, Peptide Growth Factors and Their Receptors, 1990, Molecuar Genetics in Cancer Diagnosis, 1990, Cancer Surveys-Advances & Prospects in Clinical, Epidemiological and Laboratory Oncology, vol. 7, no. 4, 1988, Genetic Mechanisms in Carcinogenesis and Tumor Progression, 1990, Molecular and Cellular Biology, Host Immune Responses and Perspectives for Treatment, 1989, Origins of Human Cancer: A Comprehensive Review, 1991, Cancer and Metastasis Reviews, vol. 9, 1990, Comprehensive Textbook of Oncology, 1991, Textbook of Internal Medicine, 2d edit., vol. 2, 1992, Molecular Foundations in Oncology, 1991, Genes, Oncogenes, and Hormones: Advances in Cellular and Molecular Biology of Breast Cancer, 1991, Cell Motility Factors, 1991, Oncogenes and Tumor Suppressor Genes in Human Malignancies, 1993, Principles and Practice of Gnecologic Oncology, 1992, Cancer Medicine, 3d edit., 1993; contbr. articles to profl. jours. NIH Pre-doctoral fellow; recipient Arthur S. Flemming award, 1983, Flow award lectureship Soc. Cell Biology, 1983, Nat. award and lectureship Am. Assn. Clin. Chemistry, 1987, Rsch. award Susan G. Komen Found., 1987, Disting. Lectr. award Rush Cancer Ctr., 1987, George Hoyt Whipple award and lectureship Sch. Medicine U. Rochester, 1988, Karen Grunebaum Symposium award lectureship Hubert H. Humphrey Cancer Rsch. Ctr., 1988, Cancer Rsch. award Milken Family Med. Found., 1988, William M. Shelly Meml. award and lectureship Centennial Johns HopkinMed. Inst., 1989, Josef Steiner Cancer Found. prize, 1989, Basic Rsch. award Am. Soc. Cytology, 1989, Officer's Recognition award Equal Employment Opportunity, 1990, John W. Cline Cancer Rsch. award and lectureship U. Calif., 1990, Herman Pinkus award lectureship Am. Soc. Dermatology, 1990, Simon M. Shubitz award U. Chgo. Cancer Ctr., 1991, Stanley Gore Rsch. award, 1991, Lila Gruber Cancer Rsch. award Am. Acad. Dermatology, 1991, Am.-Italian Found. Cancer Rsch. award, 1992, Scie. Achievement medal U.S. Surgeon Gen., 1994. Mem. Am. Assn. Cancer Rsch. (bd. dirs., 6th Ann. Rhoads Meml. award 1985), Am. Assn. Pathologists (Warner-Lambert/Parke-Davis award 1984), Am. Soc. Cell Biology, Am. Soc. Clin. Investigation, Internat. Acad. Pathology, Internat. Assn. Metastasis Rsch. (pres. 1990-93), Sigma Xi, Phi Beta Kappa. Achievements include patents for method and device for determining the concentration of a material in a liquid, method for isolating bacterial colonies, test method for separating and/or isolating bacteria and tissue cells, device and method for detecting phenothiazine-type drugs in uring, in vitro assay for cell invasiveness, enzyme immunoassay with two-zoned device having bound antigens, metalloproteinase peptides, matrix receptors role in diagnosis and therapy of cancer, genetic method for predicting tumor aggressiveness, therapeutic application of an anti-invasive compound; patents for role of tumor motility factors in cancer diagnosis, role of tumor metalloproteinases in cancer diagnosis, peptide inhibitor of metalloproteinases, protein inhibitors of metalloproteinases, autotaxin motility stimulating proteins diagnosis and therapy, motility receptor protein and gene diagnosis and therapy. Office: Lab of Pathology Nat Cancer Inst 9000 Rockville Pike Bethesda MD 20892-0001

LIOTTA, RAY, actor; b. Newark, NJ, Dec. 18, 1955; s. Alfred and Mary L. Grad., U. Miami. TV appearances: Another World, NBC, 1978-80, Hardhat & Legs, CBS movie, 1980, Crazy Times, ABC pilot, 1981, Casablanca, NBC, 1983, Our Family Honor, NBC, 1985-86, Women Men = In Love There Are no Rules, 1991.; films: The Lonely Lady, 1983, Something Wild, 1986, Arena Brains, 1987, Dominick and Eugene, 1988, Field of Dreams, 1989, Goodfellas, 1990, Article 99, 1992, Unlawful Entry, 1992, No Escape, 1994, Corrina, Corrina, 1994, Operation Dumbo Drop, 1995. mem. SAG, AFTRA. Office: Creative Artists Agy Inc 9830 Wilshire Blvd Beverly Hills CA 90212-1804*

LIOU, KUO-NAN, atmospheric science educator, researcher; b. Taipei, Taiwan, Republic of China, Nov. 16, 1943; m. Agnes L.Y. Hung, Aug. 3, 1968; children: Julia C.C., Clifford T.C. BS, Taiwan U., 1965; MS, NYU, 1968, PhD, 1970. Rsch. assoc. Goddard Inst. for Space Studies, N.Y.C., 1970-72; asst. prof. atmospheric sci. U. Wash., Seattle, 1972-74; assoc. prof. U. Utah, Salt Lake City, 1975-80, prof., 1980—, dir. grad. studies in meteorology, 1981-84, dir. Ctr. for Atmospheric and Remote Sounding Studies, 1987—; rsch. prof. physics, 1992—; vis. prof. UCLA, 1981, U. Ariz., Tucson, 1995; affiliated prof. Peking U., Beijing, China, 1991—; vis. scholar HArvard U., 1985; cons. NASA Ames Rsch. Ctr., Moffett Field, Calif., 1984—, Los Alamos (N.Mex.) Nat. Lab., 1984-88. Author: An Introduction to Atmospheric Radiation, 1980, Radiation and Cloud Processes in the Atmosphere, 1992; editor: Atmospheric Radiation Progress and Prospects, 1987; contbr. articles to profl. jours. Fellow NRC, Washington, 1970, David Gardner fellow U. Utah, Salt Lake City, 1978; recipient Founders Day award NYU, 1971, NSF grant, 1974—. Fellow Optical Soc. Am., Am. Meterol. Soc. (chmn. radiation com. 1982-84); mem. AAAS, Am. Geophys. Union. Home: 4480 Adonis Dr Salt Lake City UT 84124-3923 Office: U Utah Dept Meteorology Salt Lake City UT 84112

LIOU, MING-LEI, electrical engineer; b. Tinghai, Chekiang, China, Jan. 6, 1935; came to U.S., 1958, naturalized, 1971; s. Ih-Min and Hsiao-Pao (Cheng) L.; m. Pearl B. Shen; children: Michael, Christopher, Derek. B.S.E.E., Nat. Taiwan U., 1956; M.S.E.E., Drexel U., 1961; Ph.D. E.E., Stanford U., 1964. Communications engr. Chinese Govt. Radio Adminstrn., Taiwan, 1957-58; instr. dept. elec. engring. Drexel U., Phila., 1958-61; research asst. Stanford Electronics Labs., Stanford U., 1961-63; mem. tech. staff Bell Labs., North Andover, Mass., 1963-66; supr. AT&T Bell Labs., 1966-84; dir. Bell Communications Research, Red Bank, N.J., 1984-92; prof. Hong Kong U. Sci. and Tech., 1992—; dir. Hong Kong Telecom. Inst. Info. Tech., 1993—. Contbr. chpts. to engring. books. Served to 2d lt. ROTC Chinese Air Force, 1956-57, Taiwan. Fellow IEEE, Hong Kong Inst. Engrs.; mem. IEEE Cirs. and Sys. Soc. (chmn. publs. bd. 1981-85, co-chmn. awards com. 1981-83, exec. v.p. 1986, pres. 1988, founding editor Trans. on Cirs. and Sys. for video tech. 1991-95, spl. prize paper award 1973, Darlington prize paper award 1977, Disting. Svc. award 1991, editor Trans. on Cirs. and Sys. 1979-81), Hong Kong Inst. Sci., Sigma Xi, Eta Kappa Nu. Office: The Hong Kong U Sci and Tech, Dept EEE, Clear Water Bay, Kowloon Hong Kong

LIOY, PAUL JAMES, environmental health scientist; b. Passaic, N.J., May 27, 1947; s. Nicholas Paul and Jean Elizabeth (Licurse) L.; m. Mary Jean Yonone, June 13, 1971; 1 child, Jason. BA in Physics and Edn., Montclair State Coll., 1969; MS in Physics and Applied Math., Auburn U., 1971; MS in Environ. Sci., Rutgers U., 1973, PhD in Environ. Sci., 1975. Sr. engr. air pollution Interstate Sanitation Commn., N.Y.C., 1975-78; asst. to assoc. prof. Inst. Environ. Medicine/NYU Med. Ctr., N.Y.C., 1978-85; dep. dir. lab. of aerosol rsch. Inst. Environ. Medicine/NYU Med. Ctr., 1982-85; assoc. prof. to prof. Robert Wood Johnson Med. Sch. U. Medicine and dentistry of N.J., Piscataway, N.J., 1985—; dir. exposure measurement and assessment divsn. Environ. and Occupational Health Scis. Inst. (EOHSI), Piscataway, 1986-94; dep. dir. Environ. and Occupational Health Scis. Inst. (EOHSI), 1995—; mem. grad. faculty Rutgers U., 1986—, admissions chair in environ. scis., 1993—; cons. bd. environ. studies and toxicology NRC, NAS, Washington, 1989-92, mem. numerous coms., 1984—; chmn. Clean Air Coun., N.J. Dept. Environ. Protection, Trenton, 1981—; mem. Internat. Air Quality Bd., Internat. Joint Commn. U.S.-Can., 1991—; mem. sci. adv. bd. U.S. EPA, 1991—; mem. European Cmty. Air Pollution Exposure Adv. Com., 1996—; mem. adv. com. Coll. Sci. and Math. Auburn U., Ala.; adj. asst. prof. Bklyn. Coll., 1977-78; sci. cons. on environ. health, indoor air pollution and hazardous waste investigations and remediations. Author 146 scientific publs., 1975—, chpts. in 6 books; author: (book) Toxic Air Pollution, 1987, co-editor: (with M.J. Yonone-Lioy) Air Sampling Instruments, 1985; exec. editor: Atmospheric Environment jour., 1989-94; assoc. editor: Environ. Rsch., 1995—; patentee, 1994. Chair Cranford (N.J.) Environ. Commn., 1978; treas. Cranford Little League, 1984-85. Rsch. grantee EPA, NIH, CDC, ATSDR, N.J. Dept. Environ. Protection, API, DOE, 1978—. Mem. Air Waste Mgmt. Assn. (chmn. editorial bd. 1978-80), Am. Conf. Gov. Indsl. Hygiene (chmn. air sample inst. com. 1984-87), Am. Assn. Aerosol. Rsch. (editorial bd. 1990-93), Internat. Soc. Environ. Epidemiology (bd. councilors 1988-89), Internat. Soc. Exposure Analysis (pres. 1993-94, treas. 1990-91, exec. com. 1989—); Soc. of Risk Analysis. Avocations: restoration of houses, tennis, automobiles. Office: Environ/Occupational Health Scis Inst 3d Flr 681 Frelinghuysen Rd Piscataway NJ 08855

LIOZ, LAWRENCE STEPHEN, lawyer, accountant; b. N.Y.C., Sept. 24, 1945; s. William and Irma (Berksohn) L.; m. Carol Renee Skolnik, Nov. 20, 1971; children: Adam Russell, Randall Eric. BS, SUNY, Albany, 1967; JD, SUNY, Buffalo, 1970; LLM in Taxation, NYU, 1975. Bar: N.Y.; CPA, N.Y. Mgr. Ernst & Whinney, N.Y.C., 1970-79; dir. tax affairs Azcon Corp., N.Y.C., 1979-82; mgr. Deloitte Haskins & Sells, N.Y.C., 1982-83, ptnr., 1983-84; ptnr. Deloitte Haskins & Sells, Woodbury, N.Y., 1984-87, Margolin, Winer & Evens L.L.P., Garden City, N.Y., 1987—; speaker various tax seminars, 1986—. Contbr. articles on tax to profl. jours. Pres. Rolling Wood Civic Assn., Roslyn, N.Y., 1983—; trustee Flower Hill (N.Y.) Assn., 1985-87, Village of Flower Hill, 1987-92; treas. Roslyn Sch. Dist., 1986—. Mem. ABA, AICPAs, N.Y. State Bar Assn., N.Y. State Soc. CPAs (chmn. fed. tax com. Nassau chpt. 1989-92, exec. bd. 1992—), L.I. Assn. Advancement for Commerce and Industry (dir.), L.I. Housing Partnership (dir.). Jewish. Avocations: skiing, golf. Home: 84 Knollwood W Roslyn NY 11576-1319 Office: Margolin Winer & Evens LLP 400 Garden City Plz Garden City NY 11530-3317

LIPCON, CHARLES ROY, lawyer; b. N.Y.C., Mar. 20, 1946; s. Harry H. and Rose Lipcon; m. Irmgard Adels, Dec. 1, 1974; children: Lauren, Claudia. B.A., U. Miami, 1968, J.D., 1971. Bar: Fla. 1971, U.S. Dist. Ct. (so. dist.) Fla. 1971, U.S. Ct. Appeals (5th cir.) 1972, U.S. Supreme Ct. 1976, U.S. Ct. Appeals (D.C. cir.) 1980, U.S. Dist. Ct. (so. dist.) Tex. 1982, U.S. Ct. Appeals (11th cir.) 1994. Pvt. practice, Miami, Fla., 1971—; lectr. U. Miami Sch. Law; moderator Am. On Line section on Admiralty Law. Author: Help for the Auto Accident Victim, 1984, Seaman's Rights in the United States When Involved in An Accident, 1989. Named Commodore of High Seas, Internat. Seaman's Union. Mem. Fla. Bar Assn., Am. Trial Lawyers Assn., ABA, Fla. Trial Lawyers, Dade County Bar Assn., Dade County Trial Lawyers. Club: Rotary (Key Biscayne). Contbr. articles to profl. jours. Office: 2 S Biscayne Blvd Ste 2480 Miami FL 33131-1801

LIPELES, MAXINE INA, lawyer; b. N.Y.C., Sept. 26, 1953; d. David Arthur and Pauline (Cooper) L.; m. Joel Kramer Goldstein, Aug. 31, 1980; children: Rachel, Joshua. AB, Princeton U., 1975; JD, Harvard U., 1979. Bar: Mass. 1980, Mo. 1982, U.S. Dist. Ct. (ea. dist.) Mo. 1982, U.S. Dist. Ct. Mass., U.S. Ct. Appeals (1st cir.) 1980, U.S. Ct. Appeals (8th cir.) 1982. Law clk. U.S. Dist. Ct. (no. dist.) Calif., San Francisco, 1979-80; asst. atty. gen. State of Mass., Boston, 1980-82; assoc. Husch & Eppenberger, St. Louis, 1982-86, ptnr., 1986-94, of counsel, 1995—; part-time prof. environ. regulation and policy sch. engring. Washington U., St. Louis, 1990—. Co-author: Hazardous Waste, 1992, Water Pollution, 1993. Mem. ABA, Mo. Bar Assn., Bar Assn. Met. St. Louis (chmn. environ. law com. 1986-88). Office: Husch & Eppenberger 100 N Broadway Ste 1300 Saint Louis MO 63102-2706

LIPFORD, ROCQUE EDWARD, lawyer, corporate executive; b. Monroe, Mich., Aug. 16, 1938; s. Frank G. and Mary A. (Mastromarco) L.; m. Marcia A. Griffin, Aug. 5, 1966; children: Lisa, Rocque Edward, Jennifer, Katherine. BS, U. Mich., 1960, MS, 1961, JD with distinction, 1964. Bar: Mich. 1964, Ohio 1964. Instr. mech. engring. U. Mich., 1961-63; atty. Miller, Canfield, Paddock & Stone, Detroit, 1965-66; asst. gen. counsel Monroe Auto Equipment Co., 1966-70, gen. counsel, 1970-72, v.p., gen. counsel, 1973-77; v.p., gen. counsel Tenneco Automotive, 1977-78; ptnr. firm Miller, Canfield, Paddock & Stone, Detroit, 1978—, mng. ptnr., 1988-91; bd. dirs. La-Z-Boy Chair Co., Monroe Bank & Trust, Kincaid Furniture Co., Q.E.D. Environ. Systems, Ferrous Environ. Recycling Corp. Mem. Mich. Bar Assn., Legatu·, Knights of Malta, North Cape Yacht Club, Monroe Golf and Country Club, Otsego Ski Club, Ocean Reef Club, Tau Beta Pi, Pi Tau Sigma. Home: 1065 Hollywood Dr Monroe MI 48161-3045 Office: Miller Canfield Paddock & Stone 214 E Elm Ave Monroe MI 48161-2678

LIPINSKI, ANN MARIE, newspaper editor. Assoc. mng. editor for met. news. Chgo. Tribune, now dep. mng. editor. Recipient Pulitzer prize for series on politics and conflicts of interest Chgo. City Coun., 1988. Office: Chgo Tribune PO Box 25340 435 N Michigan Ave Chicago IL 60611

LIPINSKI, BARBARA JANINA, psychotherapist, psychology educator; b. Chgo., Feb. 29, 1956; d. Janek and Alicja (Brzozkiewicz) L.; m. Bernard Joseph Burns, Feb. 14, 1976 (div. 1985). B of Social Work, U. Ill., Chgo., 1978; MFCC, MA, U. Calif., Santa Barbara, 1982; PhD, U. So. Calif., 1992. Cert. tchr., Calif., psychology tchr., Calif.; cert. adminstrn.; cert. non-pub. agt.; lic. marriage, family and child therapist; bd. cert. forensic examiner. Police svc. officer Santa Barbara (Calif.) Police Dept., 1978-79; peace officer Airport Police, Santa Barbara, 1979-80; emergency comms. Univ. Police, Santa Barbara, 1980-82; facilitator, instr. Nat. Traffic Safety Inst., San Jose, Calif., 1981-87; assoc. dir. Community Health Task Force on Alcohol and Drug Abuse, Santa Barbara, 1982-86; instr. Santa Barbara C.C., 1987-88; patients' rights adv. Santa Barbara County Calif. Mental Health Adminstrn., 1986-89; pvt. practice psychotherapist Santa Barbara, 1985—; faculty mem., clin. coord. Pacifica Grad. Inst., Carpinteria, Calif., 1989—; intern clin. psychology L.A. County Sheriff's Dept., 1991-92, cons. Devereaux Found., Santa Barbara, 1993-95, Ctr. for Law Related Edn., Santa Barbara, 1986; cons., trainer Univ. Police Dept., Santa Barbara, 1982, 89. Vol. crisis work Nat. Assn. Children of Alcoholics, L.A., 1987; crisis intervention worker Women in Crisis Can Act, Chgo., 1975-76; vol. counselor Santa Barbara Child Sexual Assault Treatment Ctr.-PACT, Santa Barbara, 1981-82. Recipient Grad. Teaching assistanship U. So. Calif., 1990-92. Mem. APA, Am. Profl. Soc. on Abuse of Children, Am. Coll. Forensic Examiners, Internat. Critical Incident Stress Found., Calif. Assn. Marriage and Family Therapists, Internat. Soc. for Traumatic Stress Studies. Avocations: writing, dancing, hiking, ecology, pottery. Home: 301 Los Cabos Ln Ventura CA 93001 Office: Pacifica Grad Inst 249 Lambert Rd Carpinteria CA 93013-3019

LIPINSKI, WILLIAM OLIVER, congressman; b. Chgo., Dec. 22, 1937; s. Oliver and Madeline (Collins) L.; m. Rose Marie Lapinski, Aug. 29, 1962; children: Laura, Daniel. Student, Loras Coll., Dubuque, Iowa, 1957-58. Various positions to area supr. Chgo. Parks, 1958-75; alderman Chgo. City Coun., 1975-83; mem. 98th-104th Congresses from 5th (now 3rd) Dist. Ill., 1983—; ranking minority mem., mem. transp. and infrastructure subcom. on railroads. Dem. ward committeeman, Chgo., 1975—; del. Dem. Nat. Midterm Conv., 1974, Dem. Nat. Conv., 1976, 84, 88; pres. Greater Midway Econ. and Community Devel. Com.; mem. Chgo. Hist. Soc., Art Inst., Chgo., pres.'s coun. St. Xavier Coll.; mem. Congl. Competitive Caucus, Congl. Caucus for Women's Issues, Congl. Hispanic Caucus, Congl. Human Rights Caucus, Congl. Populist Caucus, Dem. Study Group, Export Task Force, Inst. for Ill., Maritime Caucus, N.E.-Midwest Congl. Coalition, Urban Caucus. Named Man of Yr. Chgo. Park Dist. 4, 1983; recipient Archer Heights Civic Assn. award 1979, 23d Ward Businessmen and Mchts. award Chgo., 1977, Garfield Ridge Hebrew Congregation award Chgo., 1975-77, Installing Officer award Vittum Park Civic Assn., 23d Ward Minuteman award, Friends of Vittum Park Polish award, Nathan Hale Grand award from S.W. Liberty Soc., S.W. Am. Edn. and Recreation program award, Sentry of Yr. award Stars & Stripes Soc., Ill. State Minuteman award 1991. Mem. Polish Nat. Alliance, Kiwanis (Disting. Svc. award, pres., Peace Through Strength Leadership award 1991). Democrat. Roman Catholic. Office: US Ho of Reps 1501 Longworth House Bldg Washington DC 20515-1303 also: 5832 S Archer Ave Chicago IL 60638-1637*

LIPKA, DAVID H., food company executive; b. Bklyn., Nov. 14, 1929; s. Charles and Leonie Viola L.; m. Lillian Wissner, Feb. 14, 1954; children: Andrew, Wendy, Suzanne. B.A., Bklyn. Coll., 1954; student, N.Y. U. Sch. Bus. With DCA Food Industries, 1955—, v.p. ops., 1969-72, pres., 1972—, COO, 1978-82, 1982—; pres., CEO DCA Food Industries, N.Y.C., 1978—; dir. Allied-Lyons PLC, N. Am. Cos., J. Lyons Inc. Pres. bd. dirs. Karen Horney Clinic. Served with U.S. Army, 1951-53. Mem. Am. Baking Assn. (Privy Council), Inst. Food Technologists, Am. Inst. Baking (dir.), Am. Mgmt. Assn., Nat. Indsl. Conf. Bd. Club: Mill River (Upper Brookville, Oyster Bay, N.Y.). Patentee food processing. Home: 19 Oakwood Cir Roslyn NY 11576-1428 Office: D C A Food Industries Inc 1501 Franklin Ave Garden City NY 11530*

LIPKIN, DAVID, chemist; b. Phila., Jan. 30, 1913; s. William and Ida (Zipin) L.; m. Silvia Stantic Alvarez, Nov. 10, 1973; children—Jeffrey Alan, Edward Walter. B.S., U. Pa., 1934; Ph.D., U. Calif., Berkeley, 1939. Research chemist Atlantic Refining Co., Phila., 1934-36; research fellow U. Calif., Berkeley, 1939-42; research chemist Manhattan Project, Berkeley, 1942-43; research chemist, group leader Los Alamos Sci. Lab., 1943-46; mem. faculty Washington U., St. Louis, 1946—; prof. chemistry Washington U., 1948-66, chmn. dept., 1964-70, William Greenleaf Eliot prof., 1966-81, emeritus, 1981—; sr. vis. fellow Agrl. Research Council, Cambridge, Eng., 1960; vis. research scientist John Innes Inst., Norwich, Eng., 1971, 78; trustee Argonne Univs. Assn., 1969-71; cons. in field. Author. Guggenheim fellow, 1955-56. Mem. Am. Chem. Soc. (St. Louis award 1970), AAUP, Sigma Xi, Tau Beta Pi, Pi Mu Epsilon. Patentee in field. Office: Washington Univ Chemistry Dept Saint Louis MO 63130

LIPKIN, MARTIN, physician, scientist; b. N.Y.C., Apr. 30, 1926; s. Samuel S. and Celia (Greenfield) L.; m. Joan Schulein, Feb. 16, 1958; children—Richard Martin, Steven Monroe. A.B., NYU, 1946, M.D., 1950. Diplomate: Nat. Bd. Med. Examiners. Practice medicine specializing in internal medicine, gastroenterology and neoplastic diseases N.Y.C.; mem. staff N.Y. Hosp., Meml. Hosp. for Cancer and Allied Diseases; prof. medicine Cornell U. Med. Coll., 1978—, prof. Grad. Sch. Med. Scis., 1978—; mem. and attending physician Meml. Sloan-Kettering Cancer Ctr., 1985-96; dir. clin. rsch. Shang Cancer Prevention Ctr., N.Y.C., 1996—; vis. physician Rockefeller U. Hosp., 1981—; hon. lectr. Israel Med. Assn. and Gastroenterology Soc., 1982; nominator Nobel Prize for Physiology and Medicine, 1982; bd. dirs., officer Med. Ednl. and Sci. Found. of N.Y.; chmn. bd. Irving Weinstein Found. Mem. editorial bd. Cancer Epidemiology, Biomarkers and Prevention, Cancer Rsch., Cancer Letters, Internat. Jour. Oncology; editor: Gastrointestinal Tract Cancer, 1978, Inhibition of Tumor Induction and Development, 1981, Gastrointestinal Cancer: Endogenous Factors, 1981, Calcium, Vitamin D and Prevention of Colon Cancer, 1991, Cancer Chemoprevention, 1992; contbr. articles to profl. jours. Served as officer USN, 1953-55. Recipient NIH career devel. award, 1962-71; Albert F.R. Andresen ann. award and lectureship N.Y. State Med. Soc., 1971. Fellow ACP, Am. Coll. Gastroenterology; mem. Med. Soc. State of N.Y. (chmn. sci. program com. 1990-91, chmn. edn. com. 1991—), Digestive Diseases Soc. (founder), Internat. Soc. Investigative Gastroenterology (founder), Am. Soc. Clin. Investigation, Am. Physiol. Soc., Am. Assn. Cancer Rsch., Am. Gastroenterol. Assn., Soc. for Exptl. Biology and Medicine, Harvey Soc. Office: 1230 York Ave New York NY 10021-6007

LIPKIN, MARY CASTLEMAN DAVIS (MRS. ARTHUR BENNETT LIPKIN), retired psychiatric social worker; b. Germantown, Pa., Mar. 4, 1907; d. Henry L. and Willie (Webb) Davis; m. William F. Cavenaugh, Nov. 8, 1930 (div.); children: Molly C. (Mrs. Gary Oberbillig), William A.; m. Arthur Bennett Lipkin, Sept. 15, 1961 (dec. June 1974). Student, Pa. Acad. Fine Arts, 1924-28; postgrad., U. Wash., 1946-48. Nursery sch. tchr. Miquon (Pa.) Sch., 1940-45; caseworker Family Soc. Seattle, 1948-49, Jewish Family and Child Service, Seattle, 1951-56; psychiat. social worker Stockton (Calif.) State Hosp., 1957-58; supr. social service Mental Health Research Inst., Fort Steilacoom, Wash., 1958-59; engaged in pvt. practice, Bellevue, Wash., 1959-61. Former mem. Phila. Com. on City Policy. Former diplomate and bd. mem. Conf. Advancement of Pvt. Practice in Social Work; former mem. Chestnut Hill women's com. Phila. Orch; mem. Bellevue Art Mus., Assoc. Am. Assn. of U. Women, Wing Luke Mus. Mem. ACLU, LWV, Linus Pauling Inst. Sci. and Medicine, Inst. Noetic Scis., Menninger Found., Smithsonian Instn., Union Concerned Scientists, Physicians for Social Responsibility, Center for Sci. in Pub. Interest, Asian Art Council, Seattle Art Mus., Nature Conservancy, Wilderness Soc., Sierra Club. Home: 10022 Meydenbauer Way SE Bellevue WA 98004-6041

LIPKIN, SEYMOUR, pianist, conductor, educator; b. Detroit, May 14, 1927; s. Ezra and Leah (Vidaver) L.; m. Catherine Lee Bing, Dec. 27, 1961 (div. 1983); 1 son, Jonathan Michael. Mus. B., Curtis Inst. Music, 1947; studied piano with, David Saperton, 1938-41, Rudolf Serkin, Mieczyslaw Horszowski, 1941-47; conducting with, Serge Koussevitzky, Berkshire Music Center, 1946, 48, 49. Piano tchr. Juilliard Sch. Music, N.Y.C., 1986—; mem. faculty Manhattan Sch. Music, 1965-70, 72-86, NYU, 1980-86; mem. piano faculty Curtis Inst. Music, 1969—, New Eng. Conservatory, 1984-86, faculty music dept. Marymount Coll., Tarrytown, N.Y., 1963-72, chmn. music dept., 1968-71. Condr. Bklyn. Coll. Orch., 1973-74; Ford Found. commn. to perform concerto by Harold Shapero, 1959; debut with Detroit Civic Orch., 1937; apprentice condr. to George Szell, Cleve. Orch., 1947-48; appearances as pianist other U.S. orchs. including Boston Symphony in Tanglewood; ann. tours including soloist, Buffalo and Nat. Symphony, soloist, asst. condr. N.Y. Philharm. tour, Europe and Russia, 1959; conducting debut Detroit Symphony, 1944; recitalist, 92d St YMHA, N.Y.C., 1981, 83, soloist N.Y. Philharm., N.Y.C., 1983, participant in chamber music, Spoleto Festivals, 1982, 83, co-condr. Curtis Inst. Orch., 1952-53, asst. condr. Goldovsky Opera Co. on tour, 1953, condr. N.Y.C. Opera Co., 1958, 1 of 3 asst. condrs. New York Philharm., 1959-60; mus. dir. Teaneck Symphony, N.J., 1961-70, L.I. Symphony, 1963-79, Scarboro Chamber Orch., N.Y., 1964-65, Joffrey Ballet, N.Y. City Center, 1966-68, 1972-79, prin. guest condr., 1968-72; artistic dir. Kneisel Hall Summer Chamber Music Sch. and Festival, 1987— (performed cycle of 32 Beethoven Sonatas 1988-90, 10 Beethoven Violin Sonatas with Andrew Dawes 1995); appearances as opera condr. Curtis Inst., Teatro Petruzzelli, Bari, Italy, 1986-87; participant in chamber music Norfolk Fest., 1984-85, Marlboro Fest., 1986; recorded Stravinsky Piano Concerto with N.Y. Philharm., Grieg, Saint-Saens, Strauss sonatas with Aaron Rosand (violin), Grieg, Dohnanyi, Weiner sonatas with Oscar Shumsky (violin), Franck Sonata, Chausson Concerto with Rosand, Hindemith Sonata with Rafael Hillyer (Viola), Beethoven Sonatas op106 and 109 (solo), Schubert Works and Weber Sonatas with Arnold Steinhardt (violin); artistic dir. internat. piano festival and William Kapell competition U. Md., 1988-92. Recipient 1st prize Rachmaninoff Piano Competition, 1948. Mem. Am. Guild Mus. Artists, Am. Fedn. Musicians. Home: 420 W End Ave New York NY 10024-5708 Office: Perform Artist Internat 500 Main St Ste 700 Fort Worth TX 76102

LIPKIN, WILLIAM JOEL, controller, history educator; b. Newark, June 27, 1939; s. Jack N. and Martha (Schartoff) L.; m. Barbara B. Brooks, July 11, 1965; children: Jeffrey, Glen. BA, Rutgers U., Newark, 1960; MA, Rutgers U., 1962, PhD (equivalency), 1963; postgrad in Edn., Kean Coll., 1963-65. Controller Hagin & Koplin, Inc., Newark, 1961-72; pres., CFO Allcar Leasing Corp., Springfield, N.J., 1972-87; controller, CFO Thomas Lincoln Mercury, Westfield, N.J., 1987—; cons. Am. Internat. Rent-A-Car, Springfield, N.J., 1980-86; instr. history Kean Coll., Union, N.J., 1962-73, Union County Coll., 1989—. Recipient Teaching fellowship Rutgers U., 1961, 62. Mem. Am. Hist. Assn., Nat. Notary Assn., N.J. Auto Accts. Assn., B'nai Brith. Avocations: computers, music, sports. Home: 921 Sheridan St Union NJ 07083-6537 Office: Thomas Lincoln Mercury Inc 369 South Ave E Westfield NJ 07090-1465

LIPMAN, BERNARD, internist, cardiologist; b. St. Joseph, Mo., June 14, 1920; s. Harry and Sarah K. (Kross) L.; m. Leslie Joy Garber, Apr. 23, 1949; children: Lawrence Alan, Robert Bruce, Bradford Craig, William Lloyd. A.B., Washington U., 1941, M.D., 1944. Diplomate: Am. Bd. Internal Medicine, Am. Bd. Cardiology. Intern Barnes Hosp., St. Louis, Newington Hosp.-Yale Med. Sch.; resident in medicine Barnes Hosp., 1947-49; teaching fellow U. Wash. Med. Sch., 1949-50; mem. faculty Emory U. Sch. Medicine, Atlanta, 1950—; clin. prof. medicine Emory U. Sch. Medicine, 1978-83, clin. prof. emeritus, 1983—; mem. staff St. Joseph Hosp., Grady Hosp., Piedmont Hosp., Emory U. Hosp., West Paces Ferry Hosp.; dir. heart sta. St. Joseph Hosp.; co-dir. Giddings Heart Clinic. Co-author Lipman-Massie Clinical Electrocardiography, 8th edit., 1989, ECG Pocket Guide, 1987; contbr. articles to med. jours. Co-trustee Albert Steiner Found. Served to capt. M.C. AUS, 1945-47. Fellow A.C.P., Am. Coll. Cardiology (emeritus); mem. Am. Heart Assn. (mem. council clin. cardiology), Am. Fedn. Clin. Research, Am. Soc. Internal Medicine, Phi Beta Kappa, Sigma Xi, Alpha Omega Alpha. Home: 2652 Brookdale Dr NW Atlanta GA 30305-3504

LIPMAN, DAVID, multimedia company executive; b. Springfield, Mo., Feb. 13, 1931; s. Benjamin and Rose (Mack) L.; m. Marilyn Lee Vittert, Dec. 10, 1961; children: Gay Ilene, Benjamin Alan. BJ, U. Mo., 1953. Sports editor Jefferson City (Mo.) Post-Tribune, 1953, Springfield Daily News, 1953-54; gen. assignment reporter Springfield Leader and Press, 1956-57; reporter, copy editor Kansas City (Mo.) Star, 1957-60; sports reporter St. Louis Post-Dispatch, 1960-66, asst. sports editor, 1966-68, news editor, 1968-71, asst. mng. editor, 1971-78, mng. editor, 1979-92; chmn. Pulitzer 2000 Pulitzer Pub. Co., 1992—; bd. dirs. Pulitzer Charitable, RXL Pulitzer; chmn. oper. com. Ptnrs. Affiliated for Exploring Tech., 1994-96; guest lectr. Am. Press Inst., Columbia U. Journalism Sch., 1967-70; chmn. bd. advisors U. Mo. Sch. Journalism, chmn. bd. dirs. multi-cultural mgmt. program, 1995—; bd. dirs. Columbia Missourian. Author: Maybe I'll Pitch Forever, The Autobiography of LeRoy (Satchel) Paige, 1962, reissued, 1993, Mr. Baseball, The Story of Branch Rickey, 1966, Ken Boyer, 1967, Joe Namath, 1968; co-author: The Speed King, The Story of Bob Hayes, 1971, Bob Gibson Pitching Ace, 1975, Jim Hart Underrated Quarterback, 1977. Bd. dirs. Mid-Am. Press Inst., 1973—, chmn., 1975-77; trustee United Hebrew Congregation, 1975-77; chmn. com. 21st Century, U. Mo., 1993-94; vice chair Mo. Gov.'s Commn. on Info. Tech., 1994-95. 1st lt. USAF, 1954-56. Recipient Univ. Mo. Faculty and Alumni award, 1988, Univ. Mo. Disting. Svc. in Journalism award, 1989, St. Louis Jermiah award, 1991. Mem. Am. Soc. Newspaper Editors, Newspaper Assn. Am. (industry devel. com. 1994—), Interactive Svcs. Assn. (bd. dirs. 1968), Mo. Editors and Pubs. Assn. (pres. 1990-91), Mo. Soc. Newspaper Editors (bd. dirs. 1990—, vice chmn. 1992-93, chmn. 1993), Mo. Press Assn. (first v.p. 1996), AP Mng. Editors Assn., U. Mo. Sch. Journalism Nat. Alumni Assn. (chmn. 1980-83), Press Club of St. Louis (chmn. 1987-94), Sigma Delta Chi (pres. St. Louis chpt. 1976-77), Kappa Tau Alpha, Omicron Delta Kappa. Jewish. Office: Pulitzer Pub Co 900 N Tucker Blvd Saint Louis MO 63101-1069

LIPMAN, FREDERICK D., lawyer, writer, educator; b. Phila., Nov. 16, 1935; s. Charles S. and Beatrice (Sanderow) L.; m. Gail Heller, July 25, 1965; children—L. Keith, Darren A. AB, Temple U.; LLB, Harvard Law Sch. Bar: Pa. 1960. Sole practice Phila., 1960-62; corp. counsel AEL Industries, Inc., Colmar, Pa., 1962-69; ptnr. Blank, Rome, Comisky & McCauley, Phila., 1972—; lectr. U. Pa. Law Sch., 1989—, Temple U. Law Sch., 1989-94. Author: Going Public, 1994, Audit Committees, 1995. Bd. dirs. Phila. Ch. of Bezalel, 1989-91. Harvard Law Sch. scholar, 1957; Temple U. scholar, 1953. Mem. Phila. Bar Assn. (bd. govs. 1984-85), Greater Phila. C. of C. (bd. dirs., mem. exec. com. 1980-90, chmn. tech. council 1983-85), Harvard Law Sch. Assn. Greater Phila. (pres. 1988-89). Democrat. Jewish. Lodge: Masons. Avocation: tennis. Office: Blank Rome Comisky & McCauley 4 Penn Center Plz Philadelphia PA 19103-2521

LIPMAN, IRA ACKERMAN, security service company executive; b. Little Rock, Nov. 15, 1940; s. Mark and Belle (Ackerman) L.; m. Barbara Ellen Kelly Couch, July 5, 1970; children: Gustave K., Joshua S, M Benjamin. Student, Ohio Wesleyan U., 1958-60; LLD (hon.), John Marshall U., Atlanta, 1970. Salesman, exec. Mark Lipman Svcs. Inc., Memphis, 1960-63; v.p. Guardsmark, Inc., Memphis, 1963-66; pres. Guardsmark, Inc., 1966—, CEO, 1968—, chmn. bd., 1968—; bd. dirs. Nat. Coun. on Crime and Delinquency, 1975—, chmn. fin. com., treas., 1978-79, vice chmn. bd. dirs., 1982-86, chmn. exec. com., 1986-93, chmn. bd. dirs., 1993-94, chmn. emeritus, 1995—; bd. dirs. Greater Memphis Coun. Crime and Delinquency, 1976-78, entrepreneurial fellow Memphis State U., 1976; mem. environ. security com., pvt. security adv. coun. Law Enforcement Assistance adminstrn., 1975-76; mem. conf. planning com. 2d Nat. Law Enforcement Exploreer Conf., 1980. Author: How to Protect Yourself From Crime, 1975, 3d edit., 1989; contbr. numerous articles to profl. jours., mags. and newspapers. Bd. dirs. Memphis Jewish Cmty. Center, 1974, Memphis Shelby County unit Am. Cancer Soc., 1980-81, Memphis Orchestral Soc., 1980-81, Memphis Jewish Fedn., 1974-83; chmn. Shelby County com. U.S. Savs. Bonds, 1976; mem. president's coun. Memphis State U., 1975-79;, mem. visual arts coun., 1980-82; Memphis met. chmn. Nat. Alliance Businessmen, 1970-71; mem. task force Reform Jewish Outreach, Union Am. Hebrew Congregations, 1979-83; mem. young leadership cabinet United Jewish Appeal, 1973-78, mem. S.E. regional campaign cabinet, 1980; exec. bd. Chickasaw council Boy Scouts Am., 1978-81; bd. dirs., exec. com. Tenn. Ind. Coll. Fund, 1979; trustee Memphis Acad. Arts, 1977-81; mem. president's club Christian Bros. Coll., 1979; bd. dirs. Future Memphis, 1980-83, 83-86; nat. trustee NCCJ, 1980-92, exec. com., 1981-92, nat. Jewish co-chmn., 1985-88, nat. chmn., 1988-92, hon. chmn., past nat. chmn. nat. conf. Christians and Jews, 1992—; bd. dirs. Memphis chpt., 1980-85, life bd. dirs. Memphis chpt. 1985—; group II chmn. for 1982 campaign United Way Greater Memphis, 1981; v.p. exec. com. Internat. Coun. Christians and Jews, 1992-94; bd. govs. United Way of Am., 1992—, bd. gov.'s liaison, 1991-92, chmn. ethics com., 1992—, mem. exec. com., 1992—, co-chmn. vol. involvement com., 1992—, mem. strategic planning com., 1994—; chmn. UWLC steering com. 1995—; mem. Alexis de Tocqueville Soc. Nat. Leadership Coun., 1992—, mem. Second Century Initiative Vol. Involvement com., 1987-91; chair Task Force on Critical Markets, 1987-91, mem. exec. cabinet, 1990-91; trustee Memphis Brooks Mus. Art, 1980-83, Yeshiva U.; trustee Simon Wiesenthal Ctr., 1982—, chmn. campaign com., 1983—, mem. fin. and audit com., 1993—; bd. dirs. Nat. Alliance against Violence, 1983-85, Nat. Ctr. Learning Disabilities, 1989-94, United Way of Greater Memphis, 1984-85, gen. campaign chmn., 1985-86; founder, bd. overseers B'nai Brith, 1980; bd. dirs. Tenn. Gov.'s Jobs for High Sch. Grads. Program, 1980-83; trustee Ohio Wesleyan U., 1988—; vice chmn. spl. task force on endowment growth Ohio Wesleyan U., 1990—; mem. bd. overseers Wharton Sch., U. Pa., 1991—, devel. com., 1995—; assoc. trustee U. Pa., 1991—; mem. exec. com. Am. Israel Pub. Affairs Com., 1991—. Recipient Humanitarian of Yr. award NCCJ, 1985, Outstanding Cmty. Sales award Sales and Mktg. Execs. Memphis, 1987, Jr. Achievement Master Free Enterprise award, 1987, Alexis de Tocqueville Soc. award, 1995; one of 10 cited as Best Corp. Chief Exec. of Achievement, Gallagher Pres.'s Report, 1974. Mem. Internat. Assn. Chiefs Police, Am. Soc. Criminology, Internat. Soc. Criminology, Am. Soc. Indsl. Security (cert. protection profl.), 100 Club, B'nai B'rith, Ridgeway Country Club, Racquet Club, Summit Club, Econ. Club (bd. dirs. 1980-85, v.p. 1983-84, pres. 1984-85, chmn. exec. com. 1984-85), Internat. Club (Washington). Republican.

LIPMAN, JANE CRAWFORD, school nurse; b. Tilton, N.H., Feb. 21, 1930; d. John William and Anne Rita (Sweeney) Crawford; m. Earl Stanley, May 27, 1956; children: John, Eric Lee. BSN, Mount Saint Mary Coll., 1952; MSN, Columbia U., 1952. RN, N.Y. Head nurse, premature nursery Mt. Sinai Hosp., N.Y.C., 1952-54, substitue evening obstetric supr., 1954-56, Klingenstein Pavillion float nurse, 1954-56; sch. nurse, tchr. Spencerport (N.Y.) H.S., 1956-59; sch. nurse West Ind. Ctrl. Sch. Dist., 1988-92, Brighton Ctrl. Sch. dist., Rochester, N.Y., 1992—; co-chmn., founding parent interim Jr. H.S., Rochester City Sch. Dist., 1969-70, 71-72; commr. Gordon Ambach's exec. adv. coun. N.Y. State Gifted and Talented, 1986-90; mem. exec. bd. Rochester Magnet Sch. Found., 1986-88. Pres. Genesee Valley Gifted and Talented Edn. Team, 1986-90; dep. leader Rep. 24th Legis. Dist., 1987-92. Recipient award Greater N.Y. Mensa, 1989; scholar Belle Peabody Found., 1952; nursing fellow Columbia U., 1954-56. Mem. AAUW (edn. award 1989), N.Y. State Sch. Nurses Assn., Monroe Health Assn. (edn. com. learning disabilities chpt., cert. of appreciation), Monroe County Med. Soc. Aux., Susan B. Anthony Assn. (civic award 1987), Lakes Regional Ski Club. Avocations: skiing, ice skating, reading, politics. Home: 1100 Meigs St Rochester NY 14620-2406

LIPMAN, JONATHAN, architect, historic preservationist; b. Kenosha, Wis., Apr. 17, 1953; s. William Louis and Anna Lee (Goldstein) L.; m. Pamela Whitworth, Aug. 20, 1989. BArch, Cornell U., 1978. Lic. architect. Prin. Jonathan Lipman Design, Washington, 1983-85; archtl. historian Lipman Davis Architects, Washington, 1987-88; assoc. Lethbridge & Assocs., Washington, 1989-91; prin. Prairie Architects, Fairfield, Iowa, 1991-95, Jonathan Lipman & Assocs., Fairfield, Iowa, 1995—; vis. scholar Cornell U., 1979-82, guest lectr., 1980-82; guest curator H.F. Johnson Mus. Art, Ithaca, N.Y., 1982-86, Nat. Mus. Modern Art, Kyoto, Japan, 1989-91, Renwick Gallery/Smithsonian Instn., Washington, 1986, Wis. Acad. Arts, Scis. & Engring, 1994—; guest lectr. Harvard U., Cambridge, Mass., 1982, Yale U., 1982, Columbia U., 1982, 85, Mus. Modern Art, N.Y.C., 1994, Cath. U., 1996, So. Calif. Inst. of Architecture, 1987, Wis. chpt. AIA, 1994, Iowa chpt. AIA, 1993; outside grant evaluator J. Paul Getty Trust, Malibu, Calif., 1989-94; cons. curator Milw. Art Mus., 1991-92, Mus. Modern Art, N.Y.C., 1979-81, 94; restorer of major bldgs. designed by Frank Lloyd Wright including "Wingspread" and the Johnson Wax Adminstrn. Bldg. Author: Frank Lloyd Wright and the Johnson Wax Buildings, 1986, Frank Lloyd Wright's Pope Leighey House, 1996; essayist: A Frank Lloyd Wright Primer, 1991; archtl. cons. video documentary Uncommon Places: The Architecture of Frank Lloyd Wright, 1985 (Gold medal N.Y. Internat. Video Festival 1985). Active State Iowa Nat. Register Nominations Rev. Com., Jefferson County Hist. Pres. Com. Grantee N.Y. State Coun. on Arts, 1979, Graham Found., 1980; Eidlitz fellow Cornell U., 1981. Mem. AIA, Frank Lloyd Wright Bldg. Conservancy (pres.). Jewish. Home: 205 W Jefferson Ave Fairfield IA 52556-3411 Office: Jonathan Lipman & Assocs 205 W Jefferson Fairfield IA 52556

LIPNER, HARRY, retired physiologist, educator; b. N.Y.C., Aug. 26, 1922; s. Samuel and Sarah L.; m. Ethel Lapis, Nov. 11, 1949 (dec. Nov. 1979); children—Laura Jean, Sandra Lea, William F., Michael A.; m. Janet C.A. Mauney, July 10, 1981. B.S., L.I. U., 1942; M.S., U. Chgo., 1947; Ph.D., U. Iowa, 1952. Instr. Chgo. Med. Sch., 1954-55; asst. prof. physiology and endocrinology Fla. State U., Tallahassee, 1955-60; asso. prof. Fla. State U., 1960-67, prof., 1967-89, prof. emeritus, 1990—; potter/glazemaker Art ctr., Fla. State U., 1992—; vis. prof. Harvard U. Med. Sch., 1969-70 mem. rev. panel regulatory biology program NSF, 1984-87. Mem. editorial bd.: Endocrinology, 1968-74; contbr. chpts. to textbooks, articles to profl. jours. NIH fellow, 1952-55; Spl. postdoctoral fellow, 1969-70; Fulbright lectr. India, 1974-75. Mem. AAAS, Am. Physiol. Soc., Endocrine Soc., Sigma Xi. Office: Fla State U Dept Biol Sci Tallahassee FL 32306

LIPNER, WILLIAM E., information systems executive; b. 1947. BSEE, U. Toledo, 1968, BBA, 1971. With Honeywell Corp., 1971-74, NFO Rsch. Inc. and predecessor cos., Greenwich, Conn., 1974—; chmn., pres. NFO Rsch. Inc., Greenwich. Office: NFO Rsch Inc PO Box 315 Toledo OH 43697-0315*

LIPO, THOMAS A., electrical engineer, educator; b. Milw., Feb. 1, 1938; married; 4 children. BEE, Marquette U., 1962, MSEE, 1964; PhD, U. Wis., 1968. Grad. trainee Allis-Chalmers Mfg. Co., Milw., 1962-64, engring. analyst, 1964; instr. U. Wis., Milw., 1964-66; NRC rsch. fellow U. Manchester (Eng.) Inst. Sci. and Tech., 1968-69; elec. engr. Gen. Electric Co., Schenectady, 1969-79; prof. Purdue U., West Lafayette, Ind., 1979-80; prof. U. Wis., Madison, 1981-90, W.W. Grainger prof. pwoer electronics and elec. machines, 1990—; co-dir. Wis. Elec. Machines and Power Electronics Consortium, 1981—. Fellow IEEE, IEEE Power Engring. Soc., IEEE Indsl. Applications Soc., IEEE Power Electronics Soc. Office: U Wis Dept Elec & Comp Eng 1415 Johnson Dr Madison WI 53706*

LIPOVSKI, G. JACK, computer and electrical engineer, educator; b. Jan. 28, 1944. AB, BSEE, U. Notre Dame; MS, U. Ill., PhD. Prof. elec. engring and computer sci. U. Tex., Austin. Fellow IEEE (bd. govs. Computer Soc., chmn. tech. com. on computer arch., Honor Roll of computer Soc. 1982, Cert. of Appreciation 1986). Office: Engring Texas Univ of Austin Austin TX 78712*

LIPOWSKI, ZBIGNIEW JERZY, psychiatrist, educator; b. Warsaw, Poland, Oct. 26, 1924; emigrated to Can., 1955, naturalized, 1960; s. Jerzy Ignacy and Zofia (Szeliski) L.; m. Ingrid Thiessen, Nov. 27, 1978; children: Christopher John, Anna Christina. M.B., B.Ch., U. Coll., Dublin, 1954; Diploma in Psychiatry, McGill U., 1959; M.D. (hon.), U. Helsinki, 1981; M.A. (hon.), Dartmouth Coll., 1981. Resident in psychiatry Allan Meml. Inst., Montreal, Que., Can., 1955-58, Mass. Gen. Hosp., Boston, 1958-59; teaching fellow in psychiatry Harvard U., Boston, 1958-59; demonstrator in psychiatry McGill U., Montreal, 1959-62; lectr. McGill U., 1962-65, asst. prof., 1965-67, assoc. prof., 1967-71; dir. psychiat. cons. service Royal Victoria Hosp., Montreal, 1959-71; prof. psychiatry Dartmouth Med. Sch., Hanover, N.H., 1971-83; prof. psychiatry U. Toronto, Ont., Can., 1983-90, prof. emeritus psychiatry, 1990—; cons. psychiatrist Montreal Neurol. Inst., 1968-71; vis. prof. psychiatry Med. U. S.C., Charleston, 1977-78. Author: Delirium: Acute Brain Failure in Man, 1980, Psychosomatic Medicine and Liaison Psychiatry. Selected Papers, 1985, Delirium: Acute Confusional States, 1990; mem. editorial bd.: Gen. Hosp. Psychiatry, 1978—, Jour. Psychosomatic Research, 1981—, Advances in Psychosomatic Medicine, 1968— ; editor: Psychosocial Aspects of Physical Illness, 1973, (with D.R. Lipsitt and P.C. Whybrow) Psychosomatic Medicine: Current Trends and Clinical Applications, 1977, (with E. Kurstak and P.V. Morozov) Viruses, Immunity and Mental Disorders, 1987; contbr. numerous articles to profl. jours. Recipient Lapinlahti medal Finland, 1980; Mona Shenkman Bronfman fellow, 1958-59. Fellow Royal Coll. Physicians Can., Am. Psychiatric Assn. (life, task force on nomenclature 1975-79, Spl. Presdl. Commendation 1987), Acad. Psychosomatic Medicine; mem. Am. Psychosomatic Soc., Polish Inst. Arts and Scis. in Am. Office: 170 St George St, Toronto, ON Canada M5R 2M8

LIPP, ROBERT I., bank holding company executive; b. 1938; married. G-rad., Williams Coll.; grad. in bus., Harvard U.; JD, NYU, 1969. With Chem. Bank, N.Y.C., 1963-86, sr. trainee, 1963-65, office asst. control div., 1965-66, asst. controller, 1966-67, asst. v.p. corp. planning, 1967-69, corp. sr. v.p., dep. head ops., 1972-74, exec. v.p., head ops. div., 1974-77, exec. v.p., head met. div., 1977-79, corp. sr. exec. v.p., head met. div., 1979, sr. exec. v.p., 1979-83, pres., 1983-86; v.p. corp. planning, treas. Chem. N.Y. Corp., 1969-70, dep. mgr. ops. div., 1970-72; exec. v.p. for consumer fin. services group Comml. Credit Co., Balt., 1986-89, chmn. consumer fin. svcs., 1989—; exec. v.p. consumer fin. svcs. Primerica Corp. (parent co.), N.Y.C., 1988—; exec. v.p., chmn., ceo Travelers Aetna Property, Hartford, CT; bd. dirs. Greater N.Y. Fund; mem. mgmt. team Comml. Credit Corp., San Antonio. Trustee Jackie Robinson Found. Office: Travelers Aetna Property 1 Tower Sq Hartford CT 06183-0001*

LIPPARD, LUCY ROWLAND, writer, lecturer; b. N.Y.C., Apr. 14, 1937; d. Vernon William and Margaret Isham (Cross) L.; m. Robert Tracy Ryman, Aug. 19, 1961 (div. 1968); 1 child, Ethan Isham Ryman. BA, Smith Coll., 1958; MA in Art History, NYU, 1962; DFA, Moore Coll. Art, 1972, San Francisco Art Inst., 1984, Maine Coll. Art, 1994. Freelance writer, lectr., curator, 1964—; prof. Sch. Visual Arts, N.Y.C., Williams Coll., Queensland U., Brisbane, Australia, U. Colo., Boulder; mem. adv. bd. Franklin Furnace, N.Y.C., 1979—; bd. dirs. Printed Matter, N.Y.C., Ctr. for Study of Polit. Graphics, L.A., Time & Space Ltd., Hudson, N.Y.; co-founder W.E.B., Ad Hoc Women Artist's Com., Artists Meeting for Cultural Change, Heresies Collective and Jour., Artists Call Against U.S. Intervention in Ctrl. Am., Polit. Art Documentation/Distbn. Author: Overlay: Contemporary Art and the Art of Prehistory, 1983, Mixed Blessings: New Art in a Multicultural America, 19990, Pop Art, 1966, The Graphic work of Philip Evergood, 1966, Changing: Essays in Art Criticism, 1971, Tony Smith, 1972, Six Years: The Dematerialization of the Art Object, 1973, From the Center: Feminist Essays on Women's Art, 1976, Eva Hesse, 1976, (with Charles Simonds) Cracking (Brüchig Werden), 1979, Ad Reinhardt, 1981, Get the Message? A Decade of Art for Social Change, 1984, A Different War: Vietnam in Art, 1990, The Pink Glass Swan: Selected Feminist Essays on Art, (with Alfred Barr and James Thrall Soby) The School of Paris, 1965, (novel) I See/You Mean, 1979; author, editor: Partial Recall: Photographs of Native North Americans, 1992; editor: Surrealists on Art, 1970, Dadas on Art, 1971; contbg. editor: Art in Am.; contbr. monthly columns Village Voice, 1981-85, In These Times, Z Mag., also numerous articles to mags., anthologies, and mus. catalogs, 1964—. Mem. Dem. Socialists Am., Atlatl, Nat. Writers Union. Recipient Frederick Douglass award North Star Fund, 1994, Frank Jewett Mather award for criticism Coll. Art Assn., 1974, Claude Fuess award for pub. svc. Phillips Andover Acad., 1975, curating award Penny McCall Found., 1989, citation N.Y.C. mayor David Dinkins, 1990, Smith Coll. medal, 1992; Guggenheim fellow, 1968. Avocations: hiking, amateur archaeology, sailing. Home and Office: HC 75 Box 77 Galisteo NM 87540

LIPPARD, STEPHEN JAMES, chemist, educator; b. Pittsburgh, Pa., Oct. 12, 1940; s. Alvin I. and Ruth (Green) L.; m. Judith Ann Drezner, Aug. 16, 1964; children: Andrew (dec.), Joshua, Alexander. BA, Haverford Coll., 1962; PhD, MIT, 1965; DSc (hon.), Tex. A&M U., 1995. Postdoctoral research fellow chemistry MIT, Cambridge, 1965-66, prof. chemistry, 1983-89, Arthur Amos Noyes prof. chemistry, 1989—, head chemistry dept., 1995—; asst. prof. chemistry Columbia U., N.Y.C., 1966-69; asso. prof. Columbia U., 1969-72, prof., 1972-82; dept. head MIT, Cambridge, 1995—; mem. study sect. medicinal chemistry NIH, 1973-77. Editor: Progress in Inorganic Chemistry, 1967-92; mem. editorial bd. Inorganic Chemistry, 1981-83, 89-91, assoc. editor, 1983-88; mem. editorial bd. Account Chem. Res., 1986-88; contbr. articles to profl. jours. Coach Demarest Borough Soccer Team, 1975-82, league adminstr., 1979-82. NSF fellow, 1962-66; Alfred P. Sloan fellow, 1968-70; Guggenheim fellow, 1972; recipient Tchr.-Scholar award Camille and Henry Dreyfus Found., 1971-76, Henry J. Albert award Internat. Precious Metals Inst., 1985, Alexander von Humboldt U.S. Sr. Scientist award, 1988, Am. Chem. Soc. award for Disting. Svc. in the Advancement of Inorganic Chemistry, 1994; sr. internat. fellow John E. Fogarty Internat. Center, 1979. Fellow AAAS; mem. NAS, Am. Acad. Arts and Sci., Nat. Inst. Medicine, Am. Chem. Soc. (chmn. bioinorganic subdiv. 1987-88, Inorganic Chemistry award 1987, Remson award 1987, Mallinckrodt Disting. Svc. award 1994, William H. Nichols medal 1995, assoc. editor jour. 1989—, chmn. inorganic div., chmn. 1992), Am. Crystallographic Assn., Am. Soc. Biol. Chemists, Nat. Inst. Medicine, Chem. Soc. (London), Biophys. Soc., Phi Beta Kappa. Home: 15 Humboldt St Cambridge MA 02140 Office: MIT 77 Massachusetts Ave Cambridge MA 02139-4301

LIPPE, MELVIN KARL, lawyer; b. Chgo., Oct. 21, 1933; s. Melvin M. and Myrtle (Karlsberg) L.; children: Suzanne, Michael S., Deanna; m. Sandra M. Bauer, Jan. 5, 1974. B.S., Northwestern U., 1955, J.D., 1958; grad. cert., Grad. Sch. Banking, U. Wis., 1965; cert., Sr. Bank Officers Seminar, Harvard U., 1966. Bar: Ill. 1958; C.P.A. Assoc. D'Ancona, Pflaum, Wyatt & Riskind, Chgo., 1958-61; asst. to chmn. bd. Exchange Nat. Bank of Chgo., 1961-62, asst. v.p., 1962-64, v.p., 1964-66, sr. v.p., sec. to bd. dirs., 1966-69, exec. v.p., dir., 1969-74, vice chmn. bd., 1974-76, also dir.; dir. Am.-Israel Bank, Ltd., 1974-76; ptnr. Antonow & Fink, Chgo., 1977-88, Altheimer and Gray, Chgo., 1988—; instr. Ill. Inst. Tech., 1960-63. Bd. dirs. Jewish Cmty. Ctrs. Chgo., 1972—, pres., 1980-82; bd. dirs. Chgo. chpt. Am. Jewish Com., 1974-78; life bd. dirs. Jewish Coun. for Youth Svcs., Chgo., pres., 1971; bd. dirs. Family Focus, 1992—. With Ill. N.G., 1959. Mem. Am., Ill., Chgo. bar assns., Am. Jewish Com., Phi Epsilon Pi, Beta Gamma Sigma. Jewish. Club: Standard (Chgo.). Office: Altheimer & Gray 10 S Wacker Dr Chicago IL 60606-7407

LIPPE, PHILIPP MARIA, neurosurgeon, educator; b. Vienna, Austria, May 17, 1929; s. Philipp and Maria (Goth) L.; came to U.S., 1938, naturalized, 1945; m. Virginia M. Wiltgen, 1953 (div. 1977); children: Patricia Ann Marie, Philip Eric Andrew, Laura Lynne Elizabeth, Kenneth Anthony Ernst; m. Gail B. Busch, Nov. 26, 1977. Student Loyola U., Chgo., 1947-50; BS in Medicine, U. Ill. Coll. Medicine, 1952, MD with high honors, 1954. Rotating intern St. Francis Hosp., Evanston, Ill., 1954-55; asst. resident gen. surgery VA Hosp., Hines, Ill., 1955, 58-59; asst. resident neurology and neurol. surgery Neuropsychiat. Inst., U. Ill. Rsch. and Ednl. Hosps., Chgo., 1959-60, chief resident, 1962-63, resident neuropathology, 1962, postgrad. trainee in electroencephalography, 1963; resident neurology and neurol. surgery Presbyn.-St. Luke's Hosp., Chgo., 1960-61; practice medicine, specializing in neurol. surgery, San Jose, Calif., 1963—; instr. neurology and neurol. surgery U. Ill., 1962-63; clin. instr. surgery and neurosurgery Stanford U., 1965-69, clin. asst. prof., 1969-74, clin. assoc. prof., 1974—; staff cons. in neurosurgery O'Connor Hosp., Santa Clara Valley Med. Ctr., San Jose Hosp., Los Gatos Cmty. Hosp., El Camino Hosp. (all San Jose area); chmn. divsn. neurosugery Good Samaritan Hosp, 1989—; founder, exec. dir. Bay Area Pain Rehab. Center, San Jose, 1979—; clin. adviser to Joint Commn. on Accreditation of Hosps.; mem. dist. med. quality rev. com. Calif. Bd. Med. Quality Assurance, 1976-87, chmn., 1976-77. Served to capt. USAF, 1956-58. Diplomate Am. Bd. Neurol. Surgery, Nat. Bd. Med. Examiners, Am. Bd. Pain Medicine. Fellow ACS, Am. Coll. Pain Medicine (bd. dirs. 1991-94, v.p. 1991-92, pres. 1992-93); mem. AMA (Ho. of Dels. 1981—), Am. Coll. Physician Execs., Calif. Med. Assn. (Ho. of Dels. 1976-80, sci. bd., council 1979-87, sec. 1981-87, Outstanding Svc. award 1987), Santa Clara County Med. Soc. (coun. 1974-81, pres. 1978-79, Outstanding Contbn. award 1984, Benjamin J. Cory award 1987), Chgo. Med. Soc., Congress Neurol. Surgeons, Calif. Assn. Neurol. Surgeons (dir. 1974-82, v.p. 1975-76, pres. 1977-79), San Jose Surg. Soc., Am. Assn. Neurol. Surgeons (chm. sect. on pain 1987-90, dir. 1983-86, 87-90, Disting. Svc. award 1986, 90), Western Neurol. Soc., San Francisco Neurol. Soc., Santa Clara Valley Profl. Standards Rev. Orgn. (dir., v.p., dir. quality assurance 1975-83), Fedn. Western Socs. Neurol. Sci., Internat. Assn. for Study Pain, Am. Pain Soc. (founding mem.), Am. Acad. Pain Medicine (sec. 1983-86, pres. 1987-88, Philipp M. Lippe Disting. Svc. award 1995, past med. dir. 1996—), Am. Bd. Pain Medicine (exec. v.p., 1994—), Alpha Omega Alpha, Phi Kappa Phi. Assoc. editor Clin. Jour. of Pain; contbr. articles to profl. jours. Pioneered med. application centrifugal force using flight simulator. Office: 2100 Forest Ave Ste 106 San Jose CA 95128-1422

LIPPERT, JOHN RICHARD, magazine editor; b. Pitts., Mar. 28, 1952; s. John Jacob and Thelma Rose (Watzlaf) L.; m. Abla Mawoussi Gbedegbebou, June 29, 1977 (div. June 1987); 1 child, Brigitte Akossi; m. Jane Marie Young, Jan. 1, 1990. BA, U. Pitts., 1974, M Pub. and Internat. Affairs, 1979. Secondary sch. tchr. U.S. Peace Corps, Togo, West Africa, 1974-76; rschr. Grad. Sch. Pub. and Internat. Affairs U. Pitts., 1978; intern analyst City of Pitts., 1979; info. mgr., advisor, solar energy inquiry coord., cons. Vols. in Tech. Assistance, Arlington, Va., 1980-87; project mgr., supr., sr. writer Advanced Scis. Inc., Arlington, 1987-94; mng. editor Consumers' Checkbook mag. Ctr. for the Study of Svcs., Washington, 1994—; reviewer, advisor walls subcom. Bldg. Environ. and Thermal Envelope Coun., Washington, 1993. Contbr. articles to profl. publs. and mags. Tchr. religion class St. Bernard's Cath. Ch., Riverdale, Md., 1995—. Mem. Am. Solar Energy Soc., Md., D.C., Va. Solar Energy Industries Assn. (assoc.), Electric Vehicle Assn. of Greater Washington, N.E. Sustainable Energy Assn., Ctr. for Analysis and Dissemination of Demonstrated Energy Techs. Avocations: socially responsible investing, residential energy efficiency and renewable energy, swimming, gardening. Office: Ctr for Study of Svcs 733 15th St NW Ste 820 Washington DC 20005

LIPPERT, ROBERT LAWRENCE, social services administrator; b. Detroit, Mar. 28, 1935; s. Lawrence and Isabel (Forman) L.; 1 child, David Alan. AB, San Francisco State, 1957; AM, U. Chgo., 1960. Lic. clin. social worker ACSW. Exec. dir. Boys and Girls Aid Soc., Spring Valley, Calif.; adminstr. Village of Childhelp, Beaumont, Calif.; bd. dirs. Mt. San Jacinto Coll. Found. Mem. Am. Orthopsychiat. Assn., Am. Assn. Children's Residential Ctrs., NASW. Home: 43839 Mandarin Hemet CA 92544 Office: Village of Childhelp PO Box 247 14700 Manzanita Park Rd Beaumont CA 92223

LIPPES, GERALD SANFORD, lawyer, business executive; b. Buffalo, Mar. 23, 1940; s. Thomas and Ruth (Landsman) L.; m. Sandra Franger; children: Tracy E., David S., Adam F. Student, U. Mich., 1958-61; JD, U. Buffalo, 1964. Bar: N.Y. 1964. Sr. ptnr. Lippes, Silverstein, Mathias & Wexler, Buffalo, 1964—; sec., dir., gen. counsel Mark IV, Industries, Inc., Amherst, N.Y., 1969—; chmn. Del. Photographic Products, Buffalo, 1970-88, Ingram Software, Buffalo, 1982-86, Abels Bagels, Inc., Buffalo, 1972-75; bd. dirs. Mark IV Industries, Inc., Amherst, N.Y., Gilbraltar Steel Corp., Buffalo, Upgrade Corp. Am., Buffalo, Nat. Health Care Affiliates, Inc., Buffalo, Niagara Envelope. Bd. dirs. Buffalo Fine Arts Acad. Ctr. for Entrepreneurial Leadership SUNY, Children's Hosp. Buffalo; chmn. bd. dirs. Roswell Park Meml. Inst., Buffalo, Downtown Med. Ctr., Inc., Buffalo; chmn. U. Buffalo Law Sch., Found. Jewish Philanthropies, Inc., U. Buffalo Found. Recipient Disting. Alumni award U. Buffalo Law Sch.; named Entrepreneur of Yr., 1993. Mem. N.Y. State Bar Assn., Erie County Bar Assn., Am. Soc. Corp. Secs. Office: Lippes Silverstein Mathias & Wexler 28 Church St Buffalo NY 14202-3908

LIPPES, RICHARD JAMES, lawyer; b. Buffalo, Mar. 18, 1944; s. Thomas and Ruth (Landsman) L.; m. Sharon Richmond, June 4, 1972; children: Amity, Joshua, Kevin. BA, U. Mich., 1966; JD cum laude, SUNY-Buffalo, 1969. Bar: N.Y. 1970, U.S. Dist. Ct. Md. 1970, U.S. Ct. Appeals (4th cir.) 1970, U.S. Ct. Appeals (2d cir.) 1971, U.S. Dist. Ct. (we. dist.) N.Y. 1971, U.S. Dist. Ct. (no. dist.) N.Y. 1973, U.S. Dist. Ct. (so. dist.) N.Y. 1985. Clk. Arnold & Porter, 1967, Hodgson, Russ, Andrews, Woods & Goodyear, 1968-69; clk. to presiding justice U.S. Ct. Appeals, Balt., 1970; exec. dir. Ctr. for Justice Through Law, Buffalo, 1971; pvt. practice law, Buffalo, 1971-77; ptnr. Moriarity, Allen, Lippes & Hoffman, Buffalo, 1977-79, Allen, Lippes & Shonn, Buffalo, 1979—; lectr. SUNY, Buffalo, 1978, 79; lead counsel and spl. environ. counsel for hazardous waste, mass toxic tort cases. Contbr. articles to profl. jours. Chmn. Atlantic chpt. Sierra Club, 1980-83; chmn. Buffalo chpt. Am. Jewish Com., 1986-88; chmn. lawyers com. Niagara Frontier chpt. N.Y. Civil Liberties Union, 1971, chpt. chairperson, 1972-74; chmn. City of Buffalo Environ. Mgmt. Commn., 1987—; bd. dirs. Empire State Ballet, N.Y. State Preservation League; also gen. counsel; chmn. City of Buffalo Task Force, 1986-87, N.Y. State Preservation League; various others. Recipient Am. Jurisprudence award, 1968; Urban and Environ. Law fellow, 1969. Mem. ABA, N.Y. State Bar Assn., Erie County Bar Assn. (former chmn. pub. interest law com., former chmn. prepaid legal svcs. com.). Democrat.

LIPPINCOTT, JAMES ANDREW, biochemistry and biological sciences educator; b. Cumberland County, Ill., Sept. 13, 1930; s. Marion Andrew and Esther Oral (Meeker) L.; m. Barbara Sue Barnes, June 2, 1956; children—Jeanne Marie, Thomas Russell, John James. A.B., Earlham Coll., 1954; A.M., Washington U., St. Louis, 1956, Ph.D., 1958. Lectr. botany Washington U., 1958-59; Jane Coffin Childs Meml. fellow Centre Nat. de la Recherche Scientifique, France, 1959-60; asst. prof. biol. scis. Northwestern U., Evanston, Ill., 1960-66; assoc. prof. Northwestern U., 1966-73, prof., 1973-81, prof. biochemistry, molecular biology and cell biology, 1981-94; prof. emeritus Northwestern U., Evanston, Ill., 1994—; assoc. dean biol. scis. Northwestern U., 1980-83. Contbr. articles to profl. jours. Grantee NIH, NSF, Am. Cancer Soc., USDA. Mem. Am. Soc. Biol. Chemists, Am. Soc. Plant Physiologists, Bot. Soc. Am., Am. Soc. Microbiology. Office: Dept Biochem Molecular Biol & Cell Biol Northwestern University Evanston IL 60208

LIPPINCOTT, JOSEPH P., photojournalist, educator; b. Somerset, Pa., Mar. 12, 1940; s. Joseph Britton and Louise Frances (Picking) L.; widowed; children: Douglas B., David S. BA in Journalism, U. Iowa, 1968. Staff photographer The Miami (Fla.) Herald, 1964-67; pub. rels. dir. Lock Haven (Pa.) State Coll., 1967-68; mag. editor Caterpillar Tractor Co., Peoria, Ill., 1968-69; photo editor, photographer The Detroit Free Press, 1969-75; photo advisor The State News Mich. State U., East Lansing, 1975-84; instr. Lansing C.C., 1977-84; photo editor The Detroit News, 1984-87, The Patriot Ledger, Quincy, Mass., 1988-95; lectr. Boston U., 1990—. Author: An Introduction to Camera Maintenance, 1980. Mem. Nat. Press Photographers Assn. (chmn. nat. portfolio critique 1994—, Pictures of the Yr. awards), Boston Press Photographers Assn. Avocation: unique photographic equipment. Home: 148 Old Colony Ave # 291 Quincy MA 02170-3897

LIPPINCOTT, LAURENE ALICE, electron device technician, artist; b. Phila., Feb. 9, 1950; d. Arthur Noel and Mabel Alice (Williams) Gardiner; m. Robert A. Roll, Nov. 28, 1970 (div. June 1982); m. Alan Jaye Lippincott, June 22, 1985 (dec. Nov. 1985); children: Kevin B., Christine M. Student, Raritain Valley C.C., North Branch, N.J., 1975; cert., Rutgers Labor Edn. Ctr., 1983, Amray Sem. Sch., Bedford, Mass., 1980, Cornell Leadership Acad., 1984. Sculptor Waylande Gregory, Bound Brook, N.J., 1964-70; lab. technician I and II Towne Labs., Somerville, N.J., 1968-70; sr. electron device mechanic, failure mode analysis microscopist ATT Bell Labs., Murray Hill, N.J., 1970—; artist Anatoly Ivanov, Bridgewater, N.J., 1982—; v.p. Alexandra, Inc., Flemmington, N.J., 1986—. Illustrator: My First Birthday, 1990; prin. works include Mountain Lion (2d prize 1969), Fight for Life (1st prize 1973); contbr., developer, co-author: Spin on Glass. Mem. Microscopy Soc. Am., Microbeam Analysis Soc., Internat. Fedn. Socs. for Electron Microscopy, Women of ATT Bell Labs., Comm. Workers Am. (exec. bd. 1986-87, legis. chair 1987-90), Hunterdor Art Ctr., ATT/CWA Allliance Com., Plainfield Musical Club (assoc., hospitality chair 1986-90). Democrat. Episcopalian. Avocations: painting, sculpting, music, roller skating, dancing.

LIPPINCOTT, PHILIP EDWARD, retired paper products company executive; b. Camden, N.J., Nov. 28, 1935; s. J. Edward and Marjorie Nix (Spooner) L.; m. Naomi Catherine Prindle, Aug. 22, 1959; children: Grant, Kevin, Kerry. BA, Dartmouth Coll., 1957; MBA with distinction, Mich. State U., 1964. With Scott Paper Co., Phila., 1959-94, staff v.p. corp. planning, 1971, div. v.p., consumer products mktg., 1971-72, corp. v.p., mktg., 1972-75, sr. v.p., mktg., 1975-77, v.p., group exec. packaged products div., 1977, dir., 1978-94, pres., COO, 1980-94, chief exec. officer, 1982-94, chmn., 1983-94; ret., 1994; bd. dirs. Campbell Soup Co., Exxon Corp., The Bus. Coun.; trustee Penn Mut. Life Ins. Co. Bd. overseers Wharton Sch., U. Pa., Dartmouth Inst.; chmn. bd. trustees Fox Chase Cancer Ctr., Phila. Capt. U.S. Army, 1957-59. Mem. Riverton Country Club, Pine Valley Country Club, Stone Harbor Country Club, Kappa Kappa Kappa, Pi Sigma Epsilon, Beta Gamma Sigma. Mem. Society of Friends.

LIPPINCOTT, SARAH LEE, astronomer, graphologist; b. Phila., Oct. 26, 1920; d. George E. and Sarah (Evans) L.; m. Dave Garroway. Student, Swarthmore Coll., 1938-39, M.A., 1950; B.A., U. Pa., 1942; D.Sc. (hon.), Villanova U., 1973. Research asst. Sproul Obs., Swarthmore (Pa.) Coll., 1941-50, research asso., 1951-72, dir., 1972-81, prof., 1977-81, prof. and dir. emeritus, 1981—, research astronomer, 1981—; vis. assoc. in astronomy Calif. Inst. Tech., 1977. Author: (with Joseph M. Joseph) Point to the Stars, 1963, 3d edit., 1977, (with Laurence Lafore) Philadelphia, the Unexpected City, 1965; contbr. articles to profl. jours. Mem. Savoy Opera Co., Phila., 1947—; bd. mgrs. Societe de Bienfaisance de Philadelphie, 1966-69. Recipient achievement award Kappa Kappa Gamma, 1966; Disting. Daus. of Pa. award, 1976; Fulbright fellow Paris, 1953-54; Jessie Kovalenko scholar, 1953-54. Mem. Am. Soc. Profl. Graphologists (treas. 1988-93), Rittenhouse Astron. Soc. (sec. 1946-48), Am. Astron. Soc. (lectr. 1961-84), Internat. Astron. Union (v.p. commn. 26, 1970-73, pres. 1971-730, Disting. Daus. Pa. (sec. 1988—), Sigma Xi (pres. chpt. 1959-60). Home: 306 Bell Rd Cinnaminson NJ 08770

LIPPINCOTT, WALTER HEULINGS, JR., publishing executive; b. Phila., Jan. 16, 1939; s. Walter Heulings and Helen B. (Howe) L.; m. Caroline Seebohm, June 8, 1974 (div. June 1993); children: Sophie, Hugh. A.B., Princeton U., 1960. With Morgan Guaranty Trust Co., N.Y.C., 1960-63; coll. traveler Harper & Row Pubs., 1963-65, editor, 1965-70, editor-in-chief, coll. dept., 1970-74; editorial dir. Cambridge Univ. Press, N.Y.C., 1974-81; assoc. dir. Cornell Univ. Press, 1982, dir., 1983-86; dir. Princeton U. Press, N.J., 1986—. Club: Knickerbocker (N.Y.C.). Home: 1 River Knoll Dr Titusville NJ 08560-1308 Office: Princeton U Press 41 William St Princeton NJ 08540-5237

LIPPITT, ELIZABETH CHARLOTTE, writer; b. San Francisco; d. Sidney Grant and Stella L. Student Mills Coll., U. Calif.-Berkeley. Writer, performer own satirical monologues, nat. and polit. affairs for 85 newspapers including Muncie Star, St. Louis Globe-Dem., Washington Times, Utah Ind., Jackson News, State Dept. Watch. Singer debut album Songs From the Heart; contbr. articles to 85 newspapers including N.Y. Post, L.A. Examiner, Orlando Sentinel, Phoenix Rep., The Blue Book; author: 40 Years of American History in Published Letters 1952-1992. Mem. Commn. for Free China, Conservative Caucus, Jefferson Ednl. Assn., Presdl. Adv. Commn. Recipient Congress of Freedom award, 1959, 71-73. Mem. Amvets, Nat. Trust for Hist. Preservation, Am. Security Coun., Internat. Platform Assn., Am. Conservative Union, Nat. Antivivisection Soc., High Frontier, For Our Children, Childhelp U.S.A., Free Afghanistan Com., Humane Soc. U.S., Young Ams. for Freedom, Coun. for Inter.-Am. Security, Internat. Med. Corps, Assn. Vets for Animal Rights, Met. Club, Olympic Club. Home: 2414 Pacific Ave San Francisco CA 94115-1238 *Personal philosophy: I believe in freedom of the individual.*

LIPPMAN, MARC ESTES, pharmacology educator; b. Bklyn., Jan. 15, 1945. BA, Cornell U., 1964; MD, Yale U., 1968. Intern Osler med. svc. Johns Hopkins Hosp., Balt., 1968-69, asst. resident, 1969-70; clin. assoc. leukemia svc. Nat. Cancer Inst., NIH, Washington, 1970-71, clin. assoc. lab. biochemistry, 1971-73, sr. investigator med. br., 1974-88, head med. breast cancer sect., 1976-88; clin. prof. medicine & pharmacology, uniformed svc. U. Health Sci., 1978—; dir. Vincent T. Lombardi Cancer Ctr. Georgetown U., Washington, 1988—, prof. medicine & pharmacology, 1988—; mem. merit rev. bd. oncology Vet. Adminstrn. Med. Rsch. Svc., 1977-81, endocrine treatment com. Nat. Surg. Adjuvant Breast Project, 1977-86; cons. dept. pharmacology George Washington Sch. Medicine, 1978-89; co-chmn. Gordon Rsch. Conf. on Hormone Action, 1984, chmn., 1985; treas. Internat. Congress Hormones & Cancer, 1984—; mem. med. adv. bd. Nat. Alliance Breast Cancer Orgn., 1986—; mem. stage III monitoring com. Nat. Surg. Adjuvant Project Breast & Bowel Cancers, 1987-89; bd. trustees Am. Cancer Soc., Washington, 1989-92; mem. sci. adv. bd. Coordinated Coun. Cancer Rsch., 1989—; hon. dir. Y-ME, Nat. Orgn. Breast Cancer Info. & Support, 1990—; Woodward vis. prof., mem. Sloan-Kettering, 1990; Sidney Sachs Meml. lectr. Case Western Reserve, 1985, D.R. Edwards lectr. Tenovus Inst., Wales, 1985, Gosse lectr. Dalhousie U., Halifax, N.S., 1987, Transatlantic lectr. Brit. Endocrine Socs., 1989, Barofsky lectr. Howard U., 1990, Rose Kushner Meml. lectr. Long Beach Meml. Med. Ctr., 1990, Constance Wood Meml. lectr. Hammersmith Hosp., Eng., 1991. Endocrinology fellow Yale Med. Sch., 1973-74; recipient Mallinckrodt award Clin. Radioassay Soc., 1978, D.R. Edwards medal Tenovus Inst., 1985, Transatlantic medal Brit. Endocrine Socs., 1989, Tiffany award of Distinction, Komen Found., 1989. Richard and Hinda Rosenthal Found. award Am. Assn. Cancer Rsch. 1994. Fellow ACP, Am. Fedn. Clin. Rsch., Am. Soc. Cell Biology, Am. Assn. Cancer Rsch. (program com. 1986), Am. Soc. Clin. Oncology (program com. 1987-89, chmn. local organizing com. 1989-90), Endocrine Soc. (pub. affairs com. 1980-81, Edward B. Astwood Lecture award 1991), Metastasis Rsch. Soc.; mem. Assn. Am. Physicians, Am. Soc. Clin. Investigators (program com. 1988), Am. Soc. Biol. Chemists. Achievements include research in growth regulation of cancer, breast cancer, cancer endocrinology, growth factor receptors. Office: Lombardi Caneer Center Research Bldg 3970 Reservoir Rd NW, Rm E501 Washington DC 20007

LIPPMAN, SHARON ROCHELLE, cultural organization educator, artist, writer; b. N.Y.C., Apr. 9, 1950; d. Emanuel and Sara (Goldberg) L. Student, Mills Coll., 1968; BFA, New Sch. Social Rsch., 1970, CCNY, 1972; MA in Cinema Studies, NYU, 1976, postgrad., 1987. Cert. secondary tchr., N.Y. Instr., dir. Sara Sch. of Creative Art, Sayville, N.Y., 1976-85; founder, exec. dir., tchr. Art Without Walls, Inc., Sayville and N.Y.C., 1985—; exec. dir., curator Profl. Artist Network for Artists Internationally; organizer Profl. Artist Network for Nat./Internat. Artists, 1994. Author: Patterns, 1968, College Poetry Press Anthology, 1970; contbr. articles to profl. jours. Vol. Schneider Children's Hosp., New Hyde Park, N.Y., 1992, New Light-AIDS Patients, Smithtown, N.Y., 1993, Helen Keller Svcs. for the Blind, Hempstead, N.Y., 1993-94. Recipient Suffolk County New Inspiration award, 1990, Am. Artist Art Svc. award Am. Artists mag., 1993, Suffolk County Legis. proclamation, 1993, Newsday Leadership Vol. award Newsday newspaper, 1994, Nat. Women's Month award Town of Islip, 1996, Disting. Women's award Town of Islip, 1996. Mem. Orgn. Through Rehab. and Tng., Coll. Art Assn., Met. Mus. Art, Mus. Modern Art Univ. Film Assn. Avocations: fine art, books, cinema, political science, inventions. Office: Art Without Walls Inc PO Box 341 Sayville NY 11782-0341 also: PO Box 6344FDR Sta New York NY 10150-1902

LIPPMAN, WILLIAM JENNINGS, investment company executive; b. N.Y.C., Feb. 13, 1925; s. Henry J. and Fanny (Schapira) L.; m. Doris Kaplan, July 11, 1948; children—Howard Mark, Deborah Ellen. B.B.A. cum laude, Coll. City N.Y., 1947; M.B.A., N.Y.U., 1957. Marketing mgr. Pavelle Color, Inc., N.Y.C., 1947-50; sales mgr. Terminal Home Sales Corp., N.Y.C., 1950-55; div. mgr. King Merritt & Co., Inc., Englewood, N.J., 1955-60; pres., dir. Pilgrim Distbrs. Inc., Ft. Lee, N.J., 1960-86; pres. L.F. Rothschild Managed Trust L.F. Rothschild Fund Mgmt. Inc., N.Y.C., 1986-88, also dir.; pres. Franklin Managed Trust, New York, 1988—; mem. faculty Fairleigh Dickinson U. Sch. Bus. Adminstrn., 1957-69; bd. govs. Investment Co. Inst. Contbg. author: Investment Dealer Digest. Mem. Nat. Assn. Securities Dealers (investment cos. com.). Home: 18 Daniel Dr Englewood NJ 07631-3736 Office: Franklin Managed Trust 1 Parker Plz Fort Lee NJ 07024-2937

LIPPOLD, NEAL WILLIAM, criminal justice educator; b. Aurora, Ill., Dec. 30, 1946; s. Daniel Carl and Ada Louise (Knudson) L.; children: Neal William II, Cara Jo, Kenneth Franklin; m. Carol Ann Duckwiler, Dec. 31, 1987. A of Gen. Edn., Waubonsee C.C., 1972; BA, Aurora U., 1974; MS, Chgo. State U., 1978. Truck driver Rwy. Express Agy., St. Charles, Ill., 1965-66; credit mgr. Sherwin Williams Paint Co., Aurora, 1969-70; counselor, parole agt. State of Ill., Chgo., 1971-75; prof. criminal justice Waubonsee C.C., Sugar Grove, Ill., 1975—; police officer/police chief Village of Sugar Grove, 1976-86; campus police chief Waubonsee C.C., Sugar Grove, 1976-82; police sgt. Fox Valley Park Dist., Aurora, 1987-92. Sgt. USAF, 1966-69. Recipient Award of Honor, Kane County Bar Assn., 1990. Mem. Ill. Assn. Police Planners (treas., past sec.), Midwest Criminal Justice Assn., Midwest Gang Investigations Assn. Avocations: camping, fishing, golf, computing. Home: 127 Mattek Ave De Kalb IL 60115-4647

LIPPOLD, RICHARD, sculptor; b. Milw., May 3, 1915; s. Adolph and Elsa (Schmidt) L.; m. Louise Greuel, Aug. 24, 1940; children—Lisa, Tiana, Ero. Student, U. Chgo., 1934-37; B.F.A., Art Inst. Chgo., 1937; D.F.A. (hon.), Ripon Coll., 1968. Tchr. Layton Sch. Art, Milw., 1940-41, U. Mich., 1941-44, Goddard Coll., 1945-47; head art sect. Trenton (N.J.) Jr. Coll., 1948-52; prof. Hunter Coll., N.Y.C., 1952-67. Works exhibited Inst. Arts, Detroit, 1946-47, St. Louis City Mus., 1946, Toronto (Ont.) Mus., 1947, Whitney Mus., N.Y.C., 1947, 49, 51-53, 76, Calif. Palace Legion of Honor, San Francisco, 1948, Fundacao de Arte Moderne, Sao Paulo, Brazil, 1948, Mus. Modern Art, N.Y.C., 1951-53, 63, Tate Gallery, London, 1953, Musée d'Art Moderne, Paris, 1955, Nat. Collection Fine Arts, Washington, 1976, Nat. Air and Space Mus., Washington, 1976, Biennale, Venice, 1988; one-man show Willard Gallery, N.Y.C., 1947-48, 50, 53, 62, 68, 73, Arts Club, Chgo., Layton Art Gallery, Milw., 1953, Haggerty Mus., Milw., 1990; represented in collections Addison Gallery Am. Art, Andover, Mass., Fogg Mus., Harvard U., Wadsworth Atheneum, Hartford, Mus. Modern Art, Whitney Mus., N.Y.C., Newark Mus., Met. Mus. Art, N.Y.C., Detroit Art Inst., Des Moines Art Inst., Brooks Gallery, Memphis, Mobile (Ala.) Art Mus., Musée de Vin, Pavillac, France, Munson-Williams-Proctor Inst., Utica, N.Y., Va. Mus. Fine Arts, Milw. Art Center, Yale U. Art Gallery, others, also pvt. collections, U.S. and Europe; commns. include Harvard U., 1950, Inland Steel Bldg, Chgo., 1958, Four Seasons Restaurant, Seagram Bldg., N.Y.C., 1959, Stage Set, Spoleto, Italy, 1959; Portsmouth (R.I.) Priory Ch, 1960, Pan Am Bldg., N.Y.C., 1961, Avery Fisher Hall, Lincoln Center, N.Y.C., 1961, Jesse Jones Hall, Houston, 1965, St. Mary's Cathedral, San Francisco, 1967, Christian Sci. Center, Boston, 1974, Hyatt Regency Atlanta, 1975, Fairlane Plaza, Dearborn, Mich., 1975; 115 foot stainless steel sculpture on mall in front, Air and Space Mus., Washington, 1976; King's Retiring Room, Riyadh, Saudi Arabia, 1977, Columbia (S.C.) Mall, 1977, Kish Island, Iran, 1978, Hyatt Regency, Milw., 1980, Shiga Sacred Garden, Kyoto, Japan, 1981; 250 foot sculpture Park Ave Atrium Bldg., N.Y.C., 1981, One Fin. Ctr., Boston, 1984, Deutsche Bank, Frankfurt, W. Ger., 1985, First Interstate Bank, Seattle, 1985, Sohio Hdqrs., Cleve., 1986, 200 foot high outdoor sculpture, Seoul, South Korea, 1986, Atrium Sculpture for Crystal City, Va., 1986, Marina Square, Singapore, 1986, Orange County Ctr. for Performing Arts, Costa Mesa, Calif., 1987, Atrium Sculpture and Tapestry, Alexandria, Va., 1988, Atrium Sculpture, San Diego, 1990, 95, Haggerty Mus. Retrospective, Marquette U., Milw., 1991, Montrone Residence, La Jolla, 1992, Conv. Ctr., Charlotte, N.C., 1995. Recipient 3d prize Internat. Sculpture Competition, Inst. Contemporary Arts, London, 1953, Creative Arts award Brandeis U., 1958, Silver medal Archtl. League N.Y., 1960, Honor award Mcpl. Art Soc. N.Y., 1963, Fine Arts medal AIA, 1970. Mem. Nat. Inst. Arts and Letters (v.p. 1966). Address: PO Box 248 Locust Valley NY 11560-0248

LIPPS, JERE HENRY, paleontology educator; b. L.A., Aug. 28, 1939; s. Henry John and Margaret (Rosaltha) L.; m. Karen Elizabeth Loeblich, June 25, 1964 (div. 1971); m. Susannah McClintock, Sept. 28, 1973; children: Jeremy Christian, Jamison William. BA, UCLA, 1962, PhD, 1966. Asst. prof. U. Calif., Davis, 1967-70, assoc. prof., 1970-75, prof., 1975-88; prof. U. Calif., Berkeley, 1988—, prof. paleontology, 1988-89, prof. integrative biology, 1989—; dir. Mus. Paleontology, Berkeley, 1989—; dir. Inst. Ecology U. Calif., Davis, 1972-73, chmn. dept. geology, 1971-72, 79-84, chmn. dept. integrative biology, Berkeley, 1991-94. Contbr. articles to sci. publs. Fellow, dir. Cushman Found. Recipient U.S. Antarctic medal NSF, 1975; Lipps Island, Antarctica named in his honor, 1979. Fellow AAAS, Calif. Acad. Scis., Geol. Soc. Am., Cushman Found.; mem. Paleontol. Soc. (pres. 1996—). Avocation: scuba diving. Office: Mus Paleontology U Calif 1101 Valley Life Scis Bldg Berkeley CA 94720

LIPPWE, ESIKIEL, broadcast specialist; b. Namoluk Island, Chuuk State, Dec. 12, 1936; m. Marigita C. Billy Lippwe, Aug. 3, 1958; children: Jacinta, Lucia, Amy, Bendery, Brenda, Rosalinda, Joverly, Jesney, Donny, Wagner. Jr. observer U.S. Weather Bur.; announcer, program dir. Sta. KVZA; announcer, program prodr., program dir., news dir., broadcast mgr. Sta. WSZC; with Trust Territory Govt. Hdqrs., Saipan, Mariana Islands, 1973-80; with Federated States Micronesia Nat. Govt., Ponape, 1980—, broadcast officer, broadcast adminstr., broadcast specialist, broadcast rep. to broadcast unions around the world, broadcast tng. coord.; chmn. Satellite Conf., Honolulu; mem. pres. inauguration com., mem. Congress Election Bd. Federated States of Micronesia; del. Namoluk Island Constitution; converted space communitor ATS-1 Satellite Ctr. Mem. Saipan Mariana Sch. Bd., Health Svcs. HIV Task Force, Forum Planning Com.; chmn. comm. and media Federated States of Micronesia FSM Games; mem. sub parish coun. evang. com. Pohnpei Cath. Ch.; bd. dirs. Pohnpe Cath. Sch. Mem. Pacific Islands Broadcasting Assn. (founder), Pacific Is. News Assn. (founder), Chuukese Govt. Employees Assn. (pres.), Nat. Geographic Soc., Pacific Islands Assn. Libr. and Archives (planning com.), Asia Pacific Broadcasting Union (radio juries). Roman Catholic. Avocations: fishing, swimming, collecting music, reading. Home: Box 144, Pohnpei 96941, FM Office: Fed States of Micronesia Pub Info PO Box PS34 Palikir Ponape FM 96941

LIPS, H. PETER, systems engineer director; b. Nov. 6, 1939. BEE, MEE. Dep. dir. Siemens Ag. Mem. IEEE (mem. DC and flexible AC transmission subcom., working group on performance and testing of HVDC transmission sys., working group on econs. and operating strategies, Uno Lamm award com., substas. com., chmn. DC converter stas. subcom., working group on clearance and creepages in HVDC stas., past chmn. working group on power losses in HVDC converter stas., working group on static var compensators), PES (exec. bd. mem.). Office: Siemens Ag/Asi D Pes T 2, Frauenauracherstr 80, 91056 Erlangen Germany*

LIPSCHUTZ, ILSE HEMPEL, language educator; b. Bönnigheim, Wurttemberg, Germany, Aug. 19, 1923; came to U.S., 1946; d. Joseph Martin Paul and Fanny (Würzburger) Hempel; m. Lewis D. Lipschutz, Feb. 6, 1952; children: Elizabeth, Marion, Marc Hempel, Margaret Hempel. Diplôme Institut des Professeurs de Français à l'Etranger, Sorbonne U., Paris, 1942, Licence ès Lettres, 1943, Diplôme d'Etudes Supérieures Lettr, 1944; Diploma de Estudios Hispánicos, U. Complutense, Madrid, 1945; MA, Harvard U., 1949, PhD, 1958. Teaching fellow Radcliffe Coll. Harvard U., 1947-50; instr. Vassar Coll., Poughkeepsie, N.Y., 1951-58, asst. prof., 1958-63, assoc. prof., 1963-72, prof., 1972-92, Andrew W. Mellon prof. Humanities, 1981-92; prof. emerita Vassar Coll., 1992—, chair dept., 1975-82; cons., collaborator Spanish Ministry of Culture, Madrid, 1979; lectr. Frick Collection, N.Y.C., 1976, Prado Mus., Madrid, 1983, Met. Mus., N.Y.C., 1989, Universidad Internacional Menéndez Pelayo, Santander, Spain, 1990, Fundación Ramón Areces, Madrid, 1991; vis. prof. U. Complutense, Madrid, 1990; invited mem. Ctr. Rsch. Origines de l'Espagne Contemporaine, Sorbonne, U. Paris, 1992. Author: Spanish Painting and the French Romantics, 1972, rev. Spanish edit., 1988, (with others) La Imagen romántica de España, 1981, Goya, nuevas visiones, 1987, Viajeros románticos a Andalucía, 1987; contbr. articles to profl. jours. Spanish Govt. fellow U. Madrid, 1945; N.Y. State fellow AAUW, 1950-51; Ann. Radcliffe fellow Radcliffe Coll.-Harvard U., 1950-51; faculty fellow Vassar Coll., 1960-61, 67-68; rsch. scholar U.S.-Spain Commn. on Edn., 1979-80; sr. rsch. fellow Fulbright-Hays Commn., 1983-84 (nat. fellowship com. 1972-75, 84-87); chevalier Palmes Académiques, 1984. Mem. AAUP, AAUW (nat. fellowship com. 1961-67), Soc. Théophile gautier (bd. dirs. 1986—), Soc. Etudes Romantiques, Am. Soc. for Hispanic Art Hist. Studies, Soc. for Spanish and Portuguese Hist. Studies. Home: 11 Park Ave Poughkeepsie NY 12603-3101 Office: Vassar Coll Mail Drop 394 Poughkeepsie NY 12601

LIPSCHUTZ, MICHAEL ELAZAR, chemistry educator, consultant, researcher; b. Phila., May 24, 1937; s. Maurice and Anna (Kaplan) L.; m. Linda Jane Lowenthal, June 21, 1959; children—Joshua Henry, Mark David, Jonathan Mayer. B.S., Pa. State U., 1958; S.M., U. Chgo., 1960, Ph.D., 1962. Gastdocent U. Bern, Switzerland, 1964-65; asst. prof. chemistry Purdue U., West Lafayette, Ind., 1965-68, assoc. prof., 1968-73, prof., 1973—, chmn. inorganic chemistry, 1978-82, assoc. head dept. of chemistry, 1993—; dir. chemistry ops. Purdue Rare Isotope Measurement Lab. (PRIME), 1990—; vis. assoc. prof. Tel Aviv U., 1971-72; vis. prof. Max-Planck Inst. fuer Chemie, Mainz, Fed. Republic Germany, 1987; mem. panel space sci. experts Com. on Space Rsch., Space Agy. Forum of the Internat. Space Yr., Internat. Coun. Sci. Unions, 1990-92; cons. in field. Assoc. editor 11th Lunar and Planetary Sci. Conf., 3 vols., 1980; fin. editor: Meteoritics and Planetary Sci., 1992—; contbr. numerous articles to profl. jours. Served to 1st lt. USAR, 1958-64. Recipient Cert. of Recognition, NASA, 1979, Cert. of Spl. Recognition, 1979, Group Achievement award, 1983, Cert. Appreciation, Nat. Commn. on Space, 1986; postdoctoral fellow NSF, 1964-65, NATO, 1964-65; Fulbright fellow, 1971-72. Fellow Meteoritical Soc. (treas. 1978-84, mem. joint com. on pubs. of Geochem. and Meteoritical Socs. 1985-93, fin. officer 1985-93, chmn. 1988-90); mem. AAAS, Am. Chem. Soc., Am. Geophys. Union, Planetary Soc., Internat. Astron. Union (U.S. rep. 1988—), Sigma Xi. Minor planet named in honor of Lipschutz by Internat. Astronomical Union, 1987. Office: Purdue U Dept Chemistry West Lafayette IN 47907

LIPSCOMB, ANNA ROSE FEENY, small business owner, arts organizer, fundraiser b. Greensboro, N.C., Oct. 29, 1945; d. Nathan and Matilda (Carotenuto) L. Student langs., Alliance Francaise, Paris, 1967-68; BA in English and French summa cum laude, Queens Coll., 1977; diploma advanced Spanish, Forester Instituto Internacional, San Jose, Costa Rica, 1990; postgrad. Inst. Allende San Miguel de Allende, Mex., 1991. Reservations agt. Am. Airlines, St. Louis, 1968-69, ticket agt., 1969-71; coll. rep. CBS, Holt Rinehart Winston, Providence, 1977-79, sr. acquisitions editor Dryden Press, Chgo., 1979-81; owner, mgr. Historic Taos (N.Mex.) Inn, 1981-89, Southwest Moccasin and Drum, Taos; pres., co-owner Southwest Products, Ltd., 1991—; fundraiser Taos Arts Celebrations, 1989—; bd. dirs. N.Mex. Hotel and Motel Assn., 1986—; sem. leader Taos Women Together, 1989; founder All One Tribe Found., 1994, All One Tribe Fall Drumming Workshop Series, 1992—. Editor: Intermediate Accounting, 1980; Business Law, 1981. Contbr. articles to profl. jours.; patentee in field. Bd. dirs., 1st v.p. Taos Arts Assn., 1982-85; founder, bd. dirs. Taos Spring Arts Celebration, 1983—; founder, dir. Meet-the-Artist Series, 1983—; bd. dirs. and co-founder Spring Arts N.Mex., 1986; founder Yuletide in Taos, 1988, A Taste of Taos, 1988; bd. dirs. Music from Angel Fire, 1988—; founding mem. Assn. Hist. Hotels, Boulder, 1983—; organizer Internat. Symposium on Arts, 1985; bd. dirs. Arts in Taos, 1983, Taoschool, Inc., 1985—; mem. adv. bd. Chamisa Mesa Ednl. Ctr., Taos, 1990—; founder All One Tribe Found., 1994; bd. dirs. Roadrunner Recyclers, 1995—. Recipient Outstanding English Student of Yr. award Queens Coll., 1977; named Single Outstanding Contbr. to the Arts in Taos, 1986. Mem. Millicent Rogers Mus. Assn., Taos Lodgers Assn. (mktg. task force 1989), Taos County C. of C. (1st v.p. 1988-89, bd. dirs. 1987-89, advt. com. 1986-89, chmn. nominating com. 1989), Internat. Platform Assn., Taos Women Bus. Owners, Phi Beta Kappa. Home: Talpa Rte Taos NM 87571 Office: PO Drawer N Taos NM 87571

LIPSCOMB, JEFFREY JON, fund specialist, insurance agent; b. San Diego, May 8, 1946; s. Willis L. and Marjorie (Jones) L.; m. Jo Ann Elaine Nielsen, Oct. 1, 1983; 1 child, Amanda Nielsen. Student, Occidental Coll., 1964-68, Harvard U., 1971, New Eng. Conservatory Music, 1972. Chief cash flow analyst St. Johnsbury Co., Cambridge, Mass., 1970-81; pvt. investor San Diego, 1981-88; registered rep. New Eng. Securities, Sacramento, 1988—. Columnist (fin. commentary) The Bus. Jour. Sacramento, 1990-91. Mem. East Sacramento (Calif.) Improvement Assn., 1988—; pianist celebrity benefit concerts Stanford Children's Home, Sacramento, 1989. Mem. Inst. Cert. Fund Specialists, Internat. Assn. Fin. Planning (practitioner divsn. 1993—), Nat. Assn. Life Underwriters, Sacramento Assn. Life Underwriters, New Eng. Leaders Assn., Sutter Lawn Tennis Club (pres. 1992-93), The Sutter Club, Investment Trust Boston Cornerstone Club. Republican. Presbyterian. Avocations: chamber music, genealogy, tennis, chess. Home: 2295 Gateway Oaks Dr Sacramento CA 95833 Office: The New Eng 1300 Ethan Way Sacramento CA 95825-2211

LIPSCOMB, OSCAR HUGH, archbishop; b. Mobile, AL, Sept. 21, 1931; s. Oscar Hugh and Margaret (Saunders) L. S.T.L., Gregorian U., Rome, 1957;

Ph.D., Cath. U. Am., 1963. Ordained priest Roman Cath. Ch., 1956; consecrated bishop Roman Cath. Ch., 1980. Asst. pastor Mobile, 1959-65; tchr. McGill Inst., Mobile, 1959-60, 61-62; vice chancellor Diocese of Mobile-Birmingham, 1963-66, chancellor, 1966-80; pastor St. Patrick Parish, Mobile, 1966-71; lectr. history Spring Hill Coll., Mobile, 1971-72; asst. pastor St. Matthew Parish, Mobile, 1971-79, Cathedral Immaculate Conception, Mobile, 1979-80; adminstr. sede vacante Diocese of Mobile, 1980, now archbishop; pres. Cath. Housing Mobile, Mobile Senate Priests, 1978-80; chmn. com. on doctrine Nat. Conf. Cath. Bishops, 1988-91. Author articles, papers in field. Pres. bd. dirs. Mobile Mus., 1966-76; trustee Ala. Dept. Archives and History, Cath. U. Am., Washington, 1983—, Spring Hill Coll., Mobile; chmn. NCCB Com. on Ecumenical and Interreligious Affairs; chmn. bd. govs. N.Am. Coll., Rome, 1982-85. Mem. Am. Cath. Hist. Assn., So. Hist. Assn., Ala. Hist. Assn. (pres. 1971-72, exec. com. 1981-88), Hist. Mobile Preservation Soc., Lions. Address: PO Box 1966 400 Government St Mobile AL 36602-2332

LIPSCOMB, PAUL ROGERS, orthopedic surgeon, educator; b. Clio, S.C., Mar. 23, 1914; s. Paul Holmes and Mary Emma (Rogers) L.; m. Phyllis M. Oesterreich, July 20, 1940; children—Susan L. Nachbaur, Paul Rogers. B.S., U. S.C., 1935; M.D., Med. U. S.C., 1938; M.S. in Orthopaedic Surgery, Mayo Found., U. Minn., 1942. Diplomate Am. Bd. Orthopaedic Surgery (sec. 1968-71, pres. 1971-73). Intern Cooper Hosp., Camden, N.J., 1938-39; resident in orthopaedic surgery Mayo Clinic, Rochester, Minn., 1939-43, asst. to staff orthopaedic surgery, 1941-43, staff assoc., 1943-69, v.p. staff, 1963; cons. Methodist, St. Mary's hosps., 1943-69; mem. faculty Mayo Grad. Sch. U. Minn., 1944-69, prof. orthopaedic surgery, 1961-69; mem. univ. senate from U. Minn. (Mayo Grad. Sch.), 1963-67; past mem. grad. and admissions com. and joint com. Grad. Sch. U. Minn. and Mayo Grad. Sch.; prof., chmn. dept. orthopedic surgery (Sch. of Medicine, U. Calif.), Davis, 1969-81, prof. emeritus, 1981—; pres. staff Sacramento Med. Center, 1980-81; mem. staff Woodland Clinic, 1981-86; ret., 1992; v.p. Woodland Clinic Research and Edn. Found., 1982-84, pres., 1984-85; hon. vis. prof. orthopaedics U. Auckland, New Zealand, 1978; cons. Disability Evaluation Group, Sacramento, 1988-92. Contbr. numerous articles to profl. jours. Mem. Am. Acad. Orthopedic Surgery (chmn. com. sci. investigation 1955-56, chmn. instrl. course com., editor instrl. course lectures 1961-63, chmn. com. on arthritis 1970), Orthopaedic Rsch. Soc. (chmn. membership com., mem. exec. com. 1956), AMA (chmn. orthopaedic sect. 1965), ACS, Am. Orthopaedic Assn. (pres. 1974-75), Western Orthopaedic Soc., Internat. Soc. Orthopaedic Surgery and Traumatology, Ctrl., Internat. orthopaedic clubs, New Zealand Orthopaedic Assn. (corr.), Sacramento County, Yolo County med. socs., Sterling Bunnell Found. (trustee 1984-86), Calif. Med. Assn., Sigma Xi, Alpha Omega Alpha. Presbyterian. Home: 749 Sycamore Ln Davis CA 95616-3432

LIPSCOMB, WILLIAM NUNN, JR., retired physical chemistry educator; b. Cleveland, Ohio, Dec. 9, 1919; s. William Nunn and Edna Patterson (Porter) L.; m. Mary Adele Sargent, May 20, 1944; children: Dorothy Jean, James Sargent; m. Jean Craig Evans, 1983. BS, U. Ky., 1941, DSc (hon.), 1963; PhD, Calif. Inst. Tech., 1946; DSc (hon.), U. Munich, 1976, L.I. U., 1977, Rutgers U., 1979, Gustavus Adolphus Coll., 1980, Marietta Coll., 1981, Miami U., 1983, U. Denver, 1985, Ohio State U., 1991; Transylvania U., 1992, Transylvania U., 1992. Phys. chemist Office of Sci. R&D, 1942-46; faculty U. Minn., Mpls., 1946-59, asst. prof., 1946-50, assoc. prof., 1950-54, acting chief phys. chemistry div., 1952-54, prof. and chief phys. chemistry div., 1954-59; prof. chemistry Harvard U., Cambridge, Mass., 1959-71, Abbott and James Lawrence prof., 1971-90, prof. emeritus, 1990—; mem. U.S. Nat. Commn. for Crystallography, 1954-59, 60-63, 65-67; chmn. program com. 4th Internat. Congress of crystallography, Montreal, 1957; mem. sci. adv. bd. Robert A. Welch Found.; mem. rsch. adv. bd. Mich. Molecular Biology Inst.; mem. adv. com. Inst. Amorphus Studies; mem. sci. adv. com. Nova Pharms., Daltex Med. Svc., Gensia Pharms., Binary Therapeutics. Author: The Boron Hydrides, 1963, (with G.R. Eaton) NMR Studies of Boron Hydrides and Related Compounds, 1969; assoc. editor: (with G.R. Eaton) Jour. Chemical Physics, 1955-57; contbr. articles to profl. jours.; clarinetist, mem.: Amateur Chamber Music Players. Guggenheim fellow Oxford U., Eng., 1954-55; Guggenheim fellow Cambridge U., Eng., 1972-73; NSF sr. postdoctoral fellow, 1965-66; Overseas fellow Churchill Coll., Cambridge, Eng., 1966, 73; Robert Welch Found. lectr., 1966, 71; Howard U. distinguished lecture series, 1966; George Fisher Baker lectr. Cornell U., 1969; centenary lectr. Chem. Soc., London, 1972; lectr. Weizmann Inst., Rehovoth, Israel, 1974; Evans award lectr. Ohio State U., 1974; Gilbert Newton Lewis Meml. lectr. U. Calif., Berkeley, 1974; also lectureships Mich. State U., 1975, U. Iowa, 1975, Ill. Inst. Tech., 1976, numerous others; also speaker confs.; Recipient Harrison Howe award in Chemistry, 1958; Distinguished Alumni Centennial award U. Ky., 1965; Distinguished Service in advancement inorganic chemistry Am. Chem. Soc., 1968; George Ledlie prize Harvard, 1971; Nobel prize in chemistry, 1976; Disting. Alumni award Calif. Inst. Tech., 1977; sr. U.S. scientist award Alexander von Humboldt-Stiftung, 1979; award lecture Internat. Acad. Quantum Molecular Sci., 1980. Fellow Am. Acad. Arts and Scis., Am. Phys. Soc.; mem. NAS, Am. Chem. Soc. (Peter Debye award phys. chemistry 1973, chmn. Minn. sect. 1949-50), Am. Crystallographic Assn. (pres. 1955), The Netherlands Acad. Arts and Scis. (fgn.), Math. Assn. Bioinorganic Scientists (hon.), Academie Europeenne des Sciences, des Arts et des Lettres, Royal Soc. Chemistry (hon.), Phi Beta Kappa, Sigma Xi, Alpha Chi Sigma, Phi Lambda Upsilon, Sigma Pi Sigma, Phi Mu Epsilon. Office: Harvard U Dept Chemistry 12 Oxford St Cambridge MA 02138-2902*

LIPSCOMB-BROWN, EDRA EVADEAN, retired childhood educator; b. Marion, Ill., Aug. 3, 1919; d. Edgar and Anna Josephine (Wiesbrodt) Turnage; m. July 5, 1939 (div. Sept. 1950); 1 son, H. Alan; m. Mark S. Brown, 1981. B.S., So. Ill. U., 1955; M.A., U. Mich., 1955; Ed.D., Ind. U., 1962; postgrad., U. Minn. Tchr. Benton (Ill.) Elem. Schs., 1939-54, DeKalb (Ill.) Consol. Schs., 1955-56; mem. faculty No. Ill. U., DeKalb, 1956-81; prof. elem. edn. No. Ill. U., 1967-81, chmn. elem. and childhood edn., 1978-81, ret., 1981; ednl. cons. to various schs., No. Ill.; mem. vis. accreditation com. Nat. Council Accreditation Tchr. Edn., Kent State U., 1974, U. Wis.-Stout, 1975; co-author, director numerous projects sponsored by U.S. Office Spl. Edn., 1979-81. Author: Lipscomb Teacher Attitude Scale; Contbr. articles to profl. jours. Research grantee No. Ill. U., 1965, 73; Research grantee State of Ill., 1972-73. Mem. Internat. Reading Assn., Internat. Assn. Supervision and Curriculum Devel., NEA, Ill. Edn. Assn., Assn. Higher Edn., Am. Ednl. Research Assn., Pi Lambda Theta. Democrat. *Throughout my life, I have striven toward professional achievement and personal happiness. I tried never to let disappointments become bitterness, life's traumas to become defeat or sadness to become self-pity.*

LIPSET, SEYMOUR MARTIN, sociologist, political scientist, educator; b. N.Y.C., Mar. 18, 1922; s. Max and Lena (Lippman) L.; m. Elsie Braun, Dec. 26, 1944 (dec. Feb. 1987); children: David, Daniel, Carola; m. Sydnee Guyer, July 29, 1990. BS, CCNY, 1943; PhD, Columbia U., 1949; MA (hon.), Harvard U., 1966; LLD (hon.), Villanova U., 1973, Hebrew U., 1981, U. Buenos Aires, 1987, Free U., Brussels, 1990, U. Judaism, 1991, Hebrew Union Coll., 1993, Boston Hebrew Coll., 1993, U. Guelph, 1996. Lectr. U. Toronto, 1946-48; asst. prof. U. Calif., Berkeley, 1948-50; asst., then assoc. prof. grad. faculty Columbia U., 1950-56, asst. dir. Bur. Applied Social Research, 1954-56; prof. sociology U. Calif., Berkeley, 1956-66, dir. Inst. Internat. Studies, 1962-66; vis. prof. social rels. and govt. Harvard U., 1965-66, prof. govt. and sociology, exec. com. Ctr. Internat. Affairs, 1966-75, George Markham prof. Ctr. Internat. Affairs, 1974-75; sr. fellow Hoover Inst. Stanford U., 1975—, prof. polit. sci. and sociology, 1975-92, Caroline S.G. Munro prof., 1981-92; Hazel prof. pub. policy George Mason U., Fairfax, Va., 1990—; Henry Ford vis. research prof. Yale U., 1960-61; Paley lectr. Hebrew U., 1973; Fulbright program 40th Anniversary Disting. lectr., 1987; vis. scholar Russell Sage Found., New York, 1988-89. Author: Agrarian Socialism, 1950, (with others) Union Democracy, 1956, (with R. Bendix) Social Mobility in Industrial Society, 1959, expanded edit., 1991, Political Man, 1960, expanded edit., 1981, The First New Nation, 1963, expanded edit., 1979, Revolution and Counter Revolution, 1968, expanded edit., 1988, (with Earl Raab) The Politics of Unreason, 1970, expanded edit., 1978, Rebellion in the University, 1972, (with Everett Ladd) Academics and the 1972 Election, 1973, Professors, Unions and American Higher Education, 1973, The Divided Academy, 1975, (with David Riesman) Education and Politics at Harvard, 1975, (with I.L. Horowitz) Dialogues on American Politics, 1978, (with William Schneider) The Confidence Gap, 1983, expanded edit., 1987, Consensus and Conflict, 1987, Continental Divide: The Institutions and Values of the United States and Canada, 1990, The Educational Background of American Jews, 1994; (with Earl Raab) Jews and the New American Scene, 1995, American Exceptionalism: A Double-Edged Sword, 1996; co-editor: Class, Status and Power, 1953, Labor and Trade Unionism, 1960, Sociology: The Progress of a Decade, 1961, Culture and Social Character, 1961, The Berkeley Student Revolt, 1965, Class, Status and Power in Comparative Perspective, 1966, Social Structure, Mobility and Economic Development, 1966, Elites in Latin America, 1967, Party Systems and Voter Alignments, 1967, Students in Revolt, 1969, Issues in Politics and Government, 1970, Failure of a Dream? Essays in the History of American Socialism, 1974, rev. edit., 1984; co-editor: Democracy in Developing Countries, 3 vols., Africa, Asia and Latin America, 1988, 89, Politics in Developing Countries, 1990, 95, The Encyclopedia of Democracy, 4 vols., 1995; co-editor Public Opinion mag., 1977-89, Internat. Jour. Pub. Opinion Rsch., 1989—; editor: Students and Politics, 1967, Politics and Social Science, 1969, Emerging Coalitions in American Politics, 1978, The Third Century, 1979, Party Coalitions in the Eighties, 1981, Unions in Transition, 1986, American Pluralism and the Jewish Community, 1990; adv. editor: various jours. including Sci., Comparative Politics. Mem. Bd. Fgn. Scholarships, 1968-71; bd. dirs. Aurora Found., 1985—, U.S. Inst. Peace, 1996—; nat. chmn. B'nai B'rith Hillel Found., 1975-79, chmn. nat. exec. com., 1979-84; assoc. pres. Am. Profs. for Peace in the Middle East, 1976-77, nat. pres., 1977-81; co-chmn. exec. com. Internat. Ctr. Peace in Middle East, 1982-92; co-chmn. Com. for Effective UNESCO, 1976-81; chmn. Com. for UN Integrity, 1981-83; chmn. nat. faculty cabinet United Jewish Appeal, 1981-84; pres. Progressive Found., 1991-95. Recipient Gunyar Myrdal prize, 1970, Tod Harris medal, 1971, 125th Anniversary alumni medal CCNY, 1963, M.B. Rawson award, 1986, No. Telecom. Gold Medal for Can. Studies, 1987, Marshall Sklare award Assn. Social Sci. Study of Jewry, 1993; fellow Social Sci. Rsch. Coun., 1945-46, Ctr. Advanced Study Behavioral Sci. fellow, 1971-72, Woodrow Wilson Ctr. for Internat. Scholars fellow, 1995-96. Fellow NAS, AAAS (v.p. 1974-78, chmn. sect. on econ. and social sci. 1975-76, 95-96), Nat. Acad. Edn., Am. Sociol. Assn. (coun. 1959-62, MacIver award 1962, pres. 1992-93), Japan Soc.; mem. Sociol. Rsch. Assn. (exec. com. 1981-84, pres. 1985), Am. Polit. Sci. Assn. (coun. 1975-77, pres. 1981-82, Leon Epstein prize 1989), Internat. Polit. Sci. Assn. (coun. 1981-88, v.p. 1982-88), Internat. Soc. Polit. Psychology (pres. 1979-80), Internat. Sociol. Assn. (chmn. com. polit. sociology 1959-71), World Assn. Pub. Opinion Rsch. (v.p. and pres.-elect 1982-84, pres. 1984-86), Am. Philos. Soc., Finnish Acad. Sci. (hon.), Paul Lazarsfeld Gesellschaft (social rsch. 1994—), Soc. for Comparative Rsch. Office: George Mason U Inst of Policy Studies Pohick Module Fairfax VA 22030 also: Stanford U 213 Herbert Hoover Meml Bu Stanford CA 94305

LIPSEY, HOWARD IRWIN, lawyer; b. Providence, Jan. 24, 1936; s. Harry David and Anna (Gershman) L.; children: Lewis Robert, Bruce Stephen. AB, Providence Coll., 1957; JD, Georgetown U., 1960. Bar: R.I. 1960, U.S. Dist. Ct. R.I. 1961, U.S. Supreme Ct. 1972. Assoc. Edward I. Friedman, 1963-67, Kirshenbaum & Kirshenbaum, 1967-82; ptnr. Abedon, Michaelson, Stanzler, Biener, Skolnik & Lipsey, 1982-83; ptnr. Lipsey & Skolnik, Esquires, Ltd., Providence, 1983—; assoc. justice R.I. Family Ct., 1993—; lectr. trial tactics Nat. Coll. Adv., 1986, U. Bridgeport Law Sch., Yale U., U. Denver Law Sch., Suffolk U. Law Sch., 1987—; adj. prof. U. Houston Law Sch., 1994—. Served to capt. JAGC, USAR, 1960-71. Fellow Am. Coll. Trial Lawyers, Am. Acad. Matrimonial Lawyers; mem. ABA (family law advocacy inst., chair trial advocacy inst., 1994—), R.I. Bar Assn., Assn. Trial Lawyers Am. Clubs: B'nai B'rith (Anti-Defamation League). Contbg. author: Valuation and Distribution of Marital Property, 1984. Office: RI Family Ct 1 Dorrance Plz Providence RI 02903-7108

LIPSEY, JOHN C. (JACK LIPSEY), insurance company executive; b. Chgo., Oct. 1, 1930; s. Albert Ellis and Mae (Smikler) L.; m. Elise Sandra Gross, Apr. 15, 1956; children—William, Laura, Abby. Ph.B., U. Chgo., 1948; postgrad., NYU, 1949-50. C.L.U.; chartered fin. cons. Spl. agt., mgr., v.p. Prudential Co., Chgo. and N.Y.C., 1956-80; sr. v.p. Home Life Ins. Co., N.Y.C., 1980-82, exec. v.p., 1982-84; pres. HL Fin. Services of N.Y., N.Y.C., 1984-88; v.p. Personal Lines Ins. Co., 1988—; pres. PLI Ins. Agy. of Fla., Inc., 1996—. Bd. govs. Am. Jewish Com., Boca Raton, Fla., 1991—, v.p. 1992-95, pres. 1995—. With Army N.G., 1950-52. Mem. Am. Soc. C.L.U.s, Internat. Assn. Fin. Planners, Nat. Assn. Life Underwriters, Round Table of N.Y., Mountain Ridge Country Club, Delaire Country Club. Republican. Jewish. Avocations: golf; travel. Office: Personal Lines Ins 7777 Glades Rd Ste 112 Boca Raton FL 33434-4150

LIPSEY, JOSEPH, JR., water bottling executive, retail and wholesale corporation executive; b. Selma, Ala., Sept. 12, 1934; s. Joseph and Anna (Bendersky) L.; m. Betty Fay Wellan, June 5, 1960; children: Debora, Joseph III, Elizabeth, Tami. BA, La. State U., 1955, LLB, 1957. Bar: La. 1957, U.S. Dist. Ct. La. 1957, Korea 1959, Ryukyu Island 1958. Ptnr., Howell & Lipsey, Baton Rouge, 1960-65; ptnr. IsraAm Venture Group, Tel Aviv; v.p. Lipsey's Wholesale, Baton Rouge, 1977—; pres. So. Media Rsch. Co., Monroe, La., 1984—; chmn. Composite Analysis Group, Inc., Alexandria, 1989—; CEO Lipsey Mountain Spring Water, Atlanta, 1990—, Nantahalla Spring Water Bottling Co., Highlands, N.C., 1994—; speaker OPM 10 Harvard U., 1985; lectr. La. State U. Law Sch., Baton Rouge, 1961-63; chmn. Fashion Mchts. Conf., N.Y.C., 1977-81; chmn., sec.-treas. EAS Pub. Co., Inc., 1994—. Mem. exec. com. Com. for a Better La., Baton Rouge, 1971-86; pres. La. State U. Found., 1980-81. Inducted into La. State U. Law Sch. Hall of Fame, 1987. Capt. USAF, 1957-60. Mem. La. State C. of C. (pres. 1973-75), Alexandria C. of C. (pres. 1971-72), Rotary. Democrat. Jewish.

LIPSEY, RICHARD GEORGE, economist, educator; b. Victoria, B.C., Can., Aug. 28, 1928; s. Richard Andrew and Faith Thirell (Ledingham) L.; m. Diana Louise Smart, Mar. 17, 1960; children: Mark Alexander (stepson), Mathew Richard, Joanna Louise, Claudia Amanda. B.A. with honours, U. B.C., 1950; M.A., U. Toronto, 1953; Ph.D., London Sch. Econs., 1958; LL.D. (hon.), McMaster U., 1984, Victoria U., 1985, Carleton U., 1986, Qeens U., 1990; D.Sc. (hon), Toronto U., 1992; D.Litt., Guelph U., 1993; LL.D (hon.), U. Western Ont., 1994. Research asst. B.C. Dept. Trade and Industry, 1950-53; from asst. lectr. to prof. econs. London Sch. Econs., 1955-63; prof. econs., chmn. dept., dean Sch. Social Studies, U. Essex, Eng., 1965-69; vis. prof. U. B.C., 1969-70, U. Colo., 1973-74; Irving Fisher vis. prof. Yale U., 1979-80; Sir Edward Peacock prof. econs. Queens U., Kingston, Ont., 1970-87; prof. Simon Fraser U., Vancouver, B.C., 1989—; sr. rsch. advisor C.D. Howe Inst., 1983-89; dir. rsch. into growth in U.K. Nat. Econ. Devel. Coun. U.K., 1961-63; mem. coun. and planning com. Nat. Inst. Econ. and Social Rsch. U.K., 1962-69; mem. bd. Social Sci. Rsch. Coun. U.K., 1966-69. Author: An Introduction to Positive Economics, 8th edit, 1995, The Theory of Customs Unions: A General Equilibrium Analysis, 1971; co-author: An Introduction to a Mathematical Treatment of Economics, 3d edit, 1977, Economics, 11th edit., 1995, Mathematical Economics, 1976, An Introduction to the U.K. Economy, 1983, 4th edit., 1993, Common Ground for the Canadian Common Market, 1984, Canada's Trade Options in a Turbulent World, 1985, Global Imbalances, 1987, First Principles of Economics, 1988, 2d edit., 1992, Evaluating the Free Trade Deal, 1988, The NAFTA, What's In, What's Out, What Next; editor: Rev. Econ. Studies, 1962-64. Decorated officer Order of Can.; Can. Inst. for Advanced Rsch. fellow, 1989—. Fellow Econometric Soc., Royal Soc. Can.; mem. Royal Econ. Soc. (council 1967-71), Econ. Study Soc. (chmn. 1965-69), Am. Econ. Assn., Can. Econ. Assn. (pres. 1980-81), Atlantic Econ. Soc. (chmn. 1986-87). Office: Simon Fraser U Harbour Centre, 515 W Hastings St, Vancouver, BC Canada V6B 5K3

LIPSEY, ROBERT EDWARD, economist, educator; b. N.Y.C., Aug. 14, 1926; s. Meyer Aaron and Anna (Weinstein) L.; m. Sally Irene Rothstein, Nov. 24, 1948; children: Marion (Mrs. William Greenlee), Carol (Mrs. William Hersh), Eleanor (Mrs. William Ho). B.A., Columbia, 1944, M.A., 1946, Ph.D., 1961. Research asst. Nat. Bur. Econ. Research, N.Y.C., 1945-53; research assoc. Nat. Bur. Econ. Research, 1953-60, sr. research staff, 1960—, v.p. research, 1970-75, dir. internat. studies, 1975-78, dir. N.Y. Office, 1978—; lectr. econs. Columbia U., 1961-64; prof. econs. Queens Coll. and Grad. Ctr., CUNY, 1967-95, prof. emeritus, 1995—; cons. Dept. Commerce, Fed. Res. Bd., UN, World Bank; mem. Pres. Adv. Bd. on Internat. Investment, 1977-78; bd. dirs. Rsch. Found. CUNY, 1994-95; exec. com. European Union Studies Ctr., CUNY, 1994—. Author: Price and Quantity Trends in the Foreign Trade of the U.S. 1963, (with Raymond W. Goldsmith) Studies in the National Balance Sheet of the U.S. 1963, (with Doris Preston) Source Book of Statistics Relating to Construction, 1966, (with Irving B. Kravis) Price Competitiveness in World Trade, 1971, (with Phillip Cagan) Financial Effects of Inflation, 1978, (with Irving B. Kravis) Saving and Economic Growth: Is the U.S. Really Falling Behind, 1987; editor: (with Helen Stone Tice) The Measurement of Saving, Investment and Wealth, 1989, (with Magnus Blomström and Lennart Ohlsson) Economic Relations Between the U.S. and Sweden, 1989; assoc. editor Rev. of Econs. and Stats., 1989-92; mem. editorial bd. Rev. of Income and Wealth, 1992—; contbr. articles to profl. jours. Fellow Am. Statis. Assn., Internat. Trade and Fin. Assn. (pres.-elect); mem. Acad. Internat. Bus., Nat. Assn. Bus. Economists, Am. Econ. Assn., Internat. Assn. for Rsch. in Income and Wealth, N.Y. Acad. Sci., Conf. on Rsch. in Income and Wealth, Econometric Soc., Western Econ. Assn. Home: 70 E 10th St New York NY 10003-5102 Office: 50 E 42 St New York NY 10017-5405

LIPSHIE, JOSEPH, retired apparel manufacturing company executive; b. Bklyn., Sept. 16, 1911; s. Arthur and Rose Hannah (Knopfer) L.; m. Mildred Lee Wright, Mar. 5, 1942; children—Arthur Bruce, Mary Jane, Samuel David. AB, Syracuse (N.Y.) U., 1932. With Salant Corp., N.Y.C., 1935-76; pres., chief exec. officer Salant Corp., 1965-74, chmn. bd., 1974-75, chmn. exec. com., 1976-80; dir. Internat. Health Found., Inc., Jackson, Tenn. Bd. dirs. West Tenn. council Boy Scouts Am. Served with USCGR, 1942-45. Mem. Am. Apparel Edn. Found. (pres. emeritus), Tau Epsilon Phi. Jewish. Club: Shriners. Home: 647 Russell Rd Jackson TN 38301-3444

LIPSHUTZ, ROBERT JEROME, lawyer, former government official; b. Atlanta, Dec. 27, 1921; s. Allen A. and Edith (Gavronski) L.; m. Barbara Sorelle Levin, Feb. 16, 1950 (dec.); children: Randall M., Judith Ann, Wendy Jean, Debbie Sue; m. Betty Beck Rosenberg, Feb. 10, 1973; stepchildren: Robert, Nancy Fay. J.D., U. Ga., 1943. Bar: Ga. 1943, D.C. 1980. Practice in Atlanta, 1947-77, 79—; ptnr. firm Lipshutz, Greenblatt & King, 1979—; counsel to Pres. U.S., Washington, 1977-79. Past vice chmn. Ga. Bd. Human Resources; treas., legal counsel Jimmy Carter Presdl. campaign com., 1976; trustee The Carter Ctr., Americans United for Separation of Ch. and State. Capt. AUS, 1944-46. Mem. Am., Ga., Atlanta, D.C. bar assns., Atlanta Lawyers Club, Atlanta, B'nai B'rith (past pres.). Jewish (past pres. The Temple). Office: Lipshutz Greenblatt & King Harris Tower Peachtree Ctr Ste 2300 Atlanta GA 30303

LIPSIG, ETHAN, lawyer; b. N.Y.C., Dec. 11, 1948; s. Daniel Allen and Haddassah (Adler) L. BA, Pomona Coll., 1969; postgrad., Oxford U., 1969-70; JD, UCLA, 1974. Bar: U.S. Dist. Ct. (cen. dist.) Calif. 1974, U.S. Ct. Appeals (9th cir.) 1974, U.S Tax Ct. 1978. Author: Individual Retirement Arrangements, 1980, Downsizing, 1996. Mem. ABA (tax and labor rels. sect.), Western Pension and Benefits Conf., Calif. C. of C., Order of Coif, Ctrl. City Assn., Soc. Fellows of Huntington Libr., Calif. Club, L.A. Men's Garden Club. Avocations: travel, horticulture, wine, music, art. Home: 280 California Ter Pasadena CA 91105-1515 Office: Paul Hastings Janofsky & Walker 555 S Flower St Fl 23 Los Angeles CA 90071-2300

LIPSINSKY, BETTE ELAINE, fine artist, secretary; b. St. Louis, June 24, 1943; d. Owen Paul Davis and Wilma Alma (Filsinger) Ingalls; m. Erwin Richard Lipsinsky, Aug. 1, 1964; children: Rebecca Ann, Jennifer Sue. Student, Washington U., 1963-64, Jefferson Coll., 1985-86, 89-92. Bookkeeper Southwest Bank, St. Louis, 1961-64; various svc. positions St. Louis, 1977-82; bookkeeper Pioneer Bank & Trust, Maplewood, Mo., 1983-87; underwriter Safeco Ins., St. Louis, 1987; sec. Laudry Dryer and Equipment Co., St. Louis, 1987-88, Mo. Goodwill Industries, St. Louis, 1988—; owner, mgr. Image Creations, Arnold, Mo., 1990—. Artist: (mural) Faces of the Services, 1976, Maxville, Mo. 1913; illustrator: (books) Messin' Around in the Kitchen, 1991, The Rainbow of Love, 1992; artist religious Christian paintings and portraits in pencil or oil. Dir. day camp Girl Scouts U.S., Arnold, 1974-76; mem. Concerned Women for Am., 1993. Republican. Avocations: reading, swimming, horseback riding, gardening. Home and Office: Image Creations 466 Oye Dr Arnold MO 63010-1749

LIPSITT, LEWIS PAEFF, psychology educator; b. New Bedford, Mass., June 28, 1929; s. Joseph and Anna Naomi (Paeff) L.; m. Edna Brill Duchin, June 8, 1952; children: Mark, Ann. BA, U. Chgo., 1950; MS, U. Mass., 1952; PhD, U. Iowa, 1957. Instr. dept. psychology Brown U., Providence, 1957; asst. prof. Brown U., 1958-61, assoc. prof., 1961-66, prof., 1966—, dir. Child Study Ctr., 1967-92, Wriston Lectr., 1993—; mem. Gov.'s Adv. Commn. on Mental Retardation, 1963-66; cons. NIH; mem. edn. task force Model Cities Program, Providence, 1969-71; fellow Stanford Ctr. for Advanced Study in Behavioral Scis., 1979-80; vis. scientist NIMH, 1986-87. Co-author: Child Development, 1979; founder, editor: Infant Behavior and Devel., 1978-82; founding co-editor: Advances in Child Development and Behavior, 1963-70, 78-82; co-editor: Research Readings in Child Psychology, 1963, Experimental Child Psychology, 1971, Advances in Infancy Research, Self-regulatory Behavior and Risk Taking, 1991; contbr. articles to profl. jours. Bd. dirs. Providence Child Guidance Clinic, 1960-63; trustee Butler Hosp., Providence, 1965-84; mem. bd. sci. counselor Nat. Ins. Child Health and Human Devel., 1984-88; nat. co-dir. Lee Salk Family Ctr., Kidspeace, Allentown, Pa., 1993—. Recipient Mentor award for lifetime achievement AAAS, 1995, Profl. Achievement citation U. Chgo., 1995; USPHS Spl. Rsch. fellow, 1966, Guggenheim fellow, 1972-73, USPHS fellow, 1973. Fellow AAAS (Lifetime Mentor award 1994), APA (exec. com. divsn. devel. psychology 1967-70, pres.-elect divsn. devel. psychology 1979-80, pres. divsn. devel. psychology 1980-81, bd. sci. affirs 1985-88, exec. dir. for sci. 1990-91, sci. officer 1991-92, Nicholas Hobbs award 1990); mem. AAUP, Soc. Rsch. in Child Devel., Internat. Soc. Study of Behavioral Devel. (membership sec. 1981-83, exec. com. 1984-89), Am. Psychol. Soc. (founding mem., charter fellow, bd. dirs. 1989-90), Can. Inst. for Advanced Rsch. (chair adv. com. human devel. group 1995—).

LIPSKY, STEPHEN EDWARD, engineering executive, electronic warfare engineer; b. N.Y.C., Jan. 18, 1932; s. Arthur Arnold and Sophie (Malsbrook) L.; m. Laura Roher, May 11, 1958 (div. 1978); children—Janice, Sharon, David; m. Hyla Schaffer, Apr. 7, 1979. B.E.E., NYU, 1953, M.E.E., 1962; PhD in Elec. Engring., Drexel U., 1993. Project engr. Fisher Radio Corp; div. mgr., staff scientist Loral Electronics, Yonkers, N.Y., 1958-63; corp. v.p. Polarad-Radiometrics, Lake Success, N.Y., 1963-70; dir. advanced systems Gen. Inst. Corp., Hicksville, N.Y., 1970-79; chief tech. officer, sr. v.p. Am. Electronic Labs., Lansdale, Pa., 1979-93; founder, chief tech. officer Bynetics Corp., Jenkintown, Pa., 1993—; adj. univ. prof. elec. engring. Drexel U., Phila. Author: Microwave Passive Direction Finding, 1987; patentee; contbr. articles to profl. jours. Served to lt. U.S. Army, 1953-55. Decorated Bronze AFCEA medal. Fellow IEEE (life), IEE (London/assoc.); mem. Assn. Old Crows (charter mem., bd. dirs. 1972-74, sr. Gold cert. merit 1990), Am. Radio Relay League, Masons, Navy League, Army Assn. Republican. Avocations: radio amateur, color photography, stamp collecting, antique radios.

LIPSON, LESLIE MICHAEL, political science educator; b. London, Nov. 14, 1912; came to U.S., 1947, naturalized, 1953; s. Alexander and Caroline Rachel (Goodman) L.; m. Helen M. Fruchtman, Oct. 2, 1980; 1 son by previous marriage, David Roger. B.A., Oxford U., 1935, M.A., 1945; Ph.D., U. Chgo., 1938. Prof. polit. sci. and dir. Sch. Public Adminstrn., Victoria U., Wellington, N.Z., 1939-46; prof. polit. sci. Swarthmore (Pa.) Coll., 1947-49, U. Calif., Berkeley, 1950-83; chmn. undergrad. program dept. polit. sci. U. Calif., 1977-80, prof. emeritus, 1980—; mem. faculty Fromm Inst. for Lifelong Learning, San Francisco, 1983—, acad. advisor, 1989—; civilian guest lectr. Nat. War Coll., Washington, 1948-75, Air War Coll., Montgomery, Ala., 1954-86; prof. polit. sci. UN program tech. assistance in L.Am., Fundacao Getulio Vargas, Rio de Janeiro, 1953; vis. prof. Columbia U., 1961, Stanford U., 1963, U. Copenhagen, 1970-71, also others; vis. lectr. Oxford U., Inst. Commonwealth Studies, London, U. Inst. Internat. Higher Studies, Geneva, U. Pavia, U. Zagreb, also others; panelist, reporter Brit. Press on PBS program World Press, Sta. KQED-TV, San Francisco, 1963-75; seminar leader Danforth Assocs. Conf., Estes Park, Colo., 1970; panelist weekly radio program World Affairs Coun., 1986-87; cons. in field. Author: The American Governor, 1939, reprinted, 1968, The Politics of Equality, 1948, The Great Issues of Politics, 1954, 9th edit., 1993, The Democratic Civilization, 1964, The Ethical Crises of Civilization, 1993, (with Elizabeth

M. Drews) Values and Humanity, 1971, I Do Not Itch to Etch, Views in Verse, 1987; contbr. articles to profl. jours. and Ency. Brit. Trustee World Affairs Council No. Calif., 1979-87. Served with Home Guard, 1941-44, N.Z. Commonwealth Fund fellow Harkness Found., 1935-38; Rockefeller fellow, 1955-56, 59-60, grantee, 1967. Mem. NOW, UN Assn. (bd. dirs. San Francisco chpt. 1988-92). Democrat. Jewish. Home: 25 Stoddard Way Berkeley CA 94708-1719 Office: U Calif Dept Polit Sci Berkeley CA 94720

LIPSON, MELVIN ALAN, technology and business management consultant; b. Providence, R.I., June 1, 1936; s. Nathan and Esta (Blumenthal) L.; m. Jacqueline Ann Barclay, July 2, 1961; children: Donna, Robert, Michelle, Judith. BS, U. R.I., 1957; PhD, Syracuse U., 1963. Chemist ICI Organics, Providence, 1963, Philip A. Hunt Chem. Co., Lincoln, R.I., 1964-67; rsch. mgr. Philip A. Hunt Chem. Co., Lincoln, 1967-69; tech. dir. Dynachem div. Morton Thiokol Inc., Tustin, Calif., 1969-72; v.p. Morton Thiokol Inc., Tustin, 1979-82, sr. v.p., 1972-82, 1982-85, exec. v.p., 1985-86, pres., 1986-89; v.p. tech. devel. Morton Internat. Inc., Chgo., 1989-92; pres. Lipson Assocs., Newport Beach, Calif., 1992—; chmn. of the bd., CEO Aurelon, Inc., Huntington Beach, Calif., 1993—, Pivotech., Inc., Carpenteria, Calif., 1996—. Home and Office: 1715 Plaza Del Sur Newport Beach CA 92661-1417

LIPSON, MYER JACK, lawyer; b. Munich, Germany, July 4, 1946; came to U.S., 1949; s. Sundel and Rachel (Bendalin) L.; m. Beth Rubin, June 22, 1969; children: Shane, Shelby. BBA, U. Tex., 1968, JD, 1972. Bar: Tex. 1972, U.S. Dist. Ct. (we. dist.) Tex. 1975. Asst. dist. atty. 34th and 205th Jud. Dist., El Paso, Tex., 1972-74; ptnr. Lipson, Dallas & Weiser P.C., El Paso, Tex., 1974—. Pres., bd. dirs. B'nai Zion Synagogue, El Paso, 1985-86, El Paso Holocaust Mus., 1989-92, El Paso Tennis Club, 1988, B'nai Brith, El Paso, 1978. Recipient Cert. of Merit, El Paso C.C., Cert. of Merit, El Paso Adult Probation Dept.; named to Soc. of Fellows, Anti Defamation League, 1987, Tree of Life award Jewish Nat. Fund, 1995. Mem. ABA, Tex. Trial Lawyers Assn., El Paso Young Lawyers Assn. (dir., v.p. 1973-80), El Paso Bar Assn. (dir.). Avocation: tennis. Office: Lipson Dallas and Weiser PC 1444 Montana Ave El Paso TX 79902-5659

LIPSTEIN, ROBERT A., lawyer; b. Wilmington, Del., Dec. 6, 1954; s. Eugene Joseph and Leona (Feld) L.; m. Cheryl A. Artibee-Wedlake, July 30, 1978; children: Rebecca Lynn, Matthew Wedlake. BA in Econs., Stanford U., 1975, JD, 1978. Bar: D.C. 1978, U.S. Dist. Ct. D.C., 1979, U.S. Ct. Appeals (D.C. cir.) 1980, U.S. Ct. Internat. Trade, 1984, U.S. Ct. Appeals (fed. cir.), U.S. Supreme Ct. 1990. Assoc. Morgan, Lewis & Bockius, Washington, 1978-84, Coudert Bros., Washington, 1984-86; ptnr. Coudert Bros., 1987-94; mng. ptnr. Lipstein, Jaffe & Lawson, L.L.P., 1994—. Mem. ABA (antitrust sect.), D.C. Bar Assn., Phi Beta Kappa. Avocations: golf, wood working, Tae Kwon Do (black belt). Home: 511 Stonington Rd Silver Spring MD 20902-1545 Office: Lipstein Jaffe & Lawson LLP 1615 M St NW Ste 710 Washington DC 20036-3209

LIPSTONE, HOWARD HAROLD, television production executive; b. Chgo., Apr. 28, 1928; s. Lewis R. and Ruth B. (Fischer) L.; m. Jane A. Nudelman, Apr. 7, 1957; children—Lewis, Gregory. BA in Cinema, U. So. Calif., 1950. Asst. to gen. mgr. Sta. KTLA, Los Angeles, 1950-54; program dir. Sta. KABC-TV, Los Angeles, 1955-61, film and program dir., 1961-63; exec. asst. to pres., exec. producer Selmur Prodns., Inc. subs. ABC-TV, Los Angeles, 1963-69; exec. v.p. Ivan Tors Films and Studios, Inc., 1969-70; pres. Alan Landsburg Prodns., Inc., Los Angeles, 1970-85; pres., chief oper. officer The Landsburg Co., Los Angeles, 1985—. Mem. NATAS, Soc. Motion Picture and TV Engrs., Motion Picture Acad. Arts and Scis., Radio Club Am. Office: The Landsburg Co 11811 W Olympic Blvd Los Angeles CA 90064-1113

LIPTON, ALLEN DAVID, retail executive; b. Bklyn., Aug. 10, 1940; s. Moses Meyer and Pearl (Schiff) L.; m. Nanci Mayer, Feb. 24, 1963 (div. 1991); 1 child, Dawn Natalie; m. Vicky Jordan, Sept. 9, 1995. AAS, N.Y.C. Community Coll., 1961. Salesman Bakers Shoe Store, N.Y.C., 1961, Fabrex, N.Y.C., 1962-63, Sporteens, N.Y.C., 1963; asst. buyer Hammacher & Schlemmer, N.Y.C., 1961-62, Gimbels Dept. Store, N.Y.C., 1963-65; area mgr. Gimbels Dept. Store, Paramus, N.J., 1965-69; corp. buyer Stone & Thomas Dept. Store, Charleston, W.Va., 1969—; seminar spokesperson Draperies & Window Coverings Mag., N. Palm Beach, Fla., 1984; chmn. steering com. Fredrick Atkins Wholesale Buying Office. Author: Drapery and Curtain Department Store Training Manual, 1972, Buying Curtains and Draperies, 1987, Buying Carpet, Broadloom and Orential Rugs, 1991. Firefighter, Parsippany-Troy Hills (N.J.) Vol. Fire Assn., 1966-69. With N.Y. Nat. Guard, 1962-68. Recipient Leadership award Kirsch Co., 1983. Mem. Kanawha Valley Aquarium Soc. (pres. 1972, v.p. 1973, treas. 1975), Lions Club (pres. Charleston 1996-97), Phi Kappa Rho (sec. 1960). Democrat. Jewish. Avocations: fishing, collecting and breeding tropical fish, collecting stamps and fish, coins. Home: 1619 Quarrier St Apt A Charleston WV 25311-2136 Office: Stone & Thomas Dept Store Lee at Dickinson Charleston WV 25326

LIPTON, ALVIN E(LLIOT), lawyer; b. Hackensack, N.J., Jan. 5, 1945; s. Irving and Goldie (Blickstein) L. BA, U. Rochester, 1966; JD, Boston U., 1969; LLM in Taxation, NYU, 1970. Bar: N.Y. 1972, U.S. Tax Ct. 1972, Conn. 1973, U.S. Ct. Claims 1977, U.S. Supreme Ct. 1977, Calif. 1983. Internat. tax analyst Price, Waterhouse & Co., N.Y.C., 1969-70; tax analyst Arthur Young & Co., N.Y.C., 1970; tax assoc. Weiss, Bronston, Rosenthal, Heller & Schwartzman, N.Y.C., 1971; tax atty, Conn. Gen. Life Ins. Co., Hartford, 1971-76; tax counsel Owens-Corning Fiberglas Corp., Toledo, 1976-80, Crown Zellerbach Corp., San Francisco, 1981-87; pvt. practice, San Francisco, 1988—. Bd. dirs. San Francisco Choral, Instrumental & Theatrical for Youth, 1985-92; bd. dirs. San Francisco Chanticleer, vice chmn. 1987-89; citizens amb. to People's Republic of China, 1987. Mem. ABA (tax sect. 1972—), Tax Execs. Inst., Calif. Bar Assn., San Francisco Bar Assn. (tax sect. 1982—). Avocations: reading, hiking, snorkling, choral and solo singing. Home: 1800 Franklin St San Francisco CA 94109-3481 Office: 1 Sansome St Ste 2000 San Francisco CA 94104-4448

LIPTON, BARBARA, museum director, curator; b. Newark, N.J.; m. Milton Lipton; children: Joshua, Sara, Beth. BA, U. Iowa; MA, U. Mich.; MLS, Rutgers U. Library dir. Newark Mus., 1970-75, spl. projects cons., 1975-82; asst. dir. Castle Gallery Coll. of New Rochelle, N.Y., 1982-83; guest curator Dept. Indian and No. Officers, Ottawa, Ont., Can., 1983-85; dir. Jacques Marchais Mus. Tibetan Art, S.I., N.Y., 1985—; tchr., lectr. various schs. and mus. including Mus. Natural History, Smithsonian Inst., Washington, 1976—; former guest curator many mus. Author: (catalogs) Survival Art Life of the Alaskian Eskimo, 1976, Arctic Vision, 1984, Treasures of Tibetan Art: Collections of the Jacques Marchais Museum of Tibetan Art, 1996; (bibliography) Westerners in Tibet, 1972; exec. producer, writer documentary film: Village of No River, 1981. Grantee NEH, 1976, 79, 80, 87, 91. Mem. Am. Assn. Museums. Avocation: photography. Office: Jacques Marchais Mus Tibetan Art PO Box 060198 Staten Island NY 10306

LIPTON, BRONNA JANE, marketing communications executive; b. Newark, May 10, 1951; d. Julius and Arlene (Davis) L.; m. Sheldon Robert Lipton, Sept. 23, 1984. BA in Spanish, Northwestern U., 1973. Tchr. Spanish Livingston (N.J.) High Sch., 1973-78; profl. dancer Broadway theater, film, TV, N.Y.C., 1978-82; v.p., mgr. Hispanic mktg. svcs. Burson-Marsteller Pub. Rels., N.Y.C., 1982-89; exec. v.p. Lipton Communications Group, Inc., N.Y.C., 1989—; mem. minority initiatives task force Am. Diabetes Assn., Alexandria, Va., 1987-90, mem. pub. rels. com., 1990-91, mem. visibility and image task force, 1991-92, bd. dirs. N.Y. Downstate affiliate, chmn. visibility and image com., 1992-93. Mem. rev. panel Hispanic Designers, Inc. Recipient Pinnacle award Am. Women in Radio and TV (N.Y. Chpt.), 1984, Value Added awards Burson-Marsteller, N.Y.C., 1982, 83, 84. Mem. Hispanic Pub. Rels. Assn. Avocations: ballet, jazz dance, tennis, fgn. travel, birding. Home: 1402 Chapel Hill Rd Mountainside NJ 07092-1405

LIPTON, CHARLES, public relations executive; b. N.Y.C., May 11, 1928; s. Jack B. and Bertha (Lesser) L.; m. Audrey Williams, Nov. 11, 1951; children—Susan, Jack. AB, Harvard U., 1948. Market researcher Cecil & Presbury, Inc., N.Y.C., 1948-49; spl. events dir. 20th Century Fox Film Corp., N.Y.C., 1949-52; account exec. Ruder & Finn, Inc., N.Y.C., 1953-58; v.p. Ruder & Finn, Inc., 1958-63, sr. v.p., 1963-69, vice-chmn., 1969-95; sr. counsel, 1995—, also bd. dirs.; guest lectr. Boston U., 1967-68. Mem. coun. Ctr. for Vocat. Arts, Norwalk, Conn., 1966-74; trustee Norwalk Jewish Ctr., 1966-70; treas., mem. exec. com. Norwalk Symphony Soc., 1972-85; chmn. parent's counsel Washington U., St. Louis, 1976-77, trustee, 1977—. Mem. Am. Soc. Colon and Rectal Surgeons (trustee), Internat. Pub. Rels. Assn., USIA (pub. rels., pvt. sector com. 1988-93), Nat. Emphysema Soc. (trustee), Nat. Investor Rels. Inst., Harvard Club, Harvard Varsity Club. Home: 4502 Hazleton Ln Lake Worth FL 33467-8633 Office: Ruder Finn Inc 301 E 57th St Fl 3 New York NY 10022-2900

LIPTON, CHARLES JULES, lawyer; b. N.Y.C., Oct. 26, 1931; m. Alice Garretson; children: Leah Jane, Emma Ely. AB, Syracuse (N.Y.) U., 1951; LLB, Yale U., 1954; LLM in Internat. Law, NYU, 1966. Bar: N.Y. 1954, U.S. Supreme Ct. 1958. Assoc. Hughes, Hubbard and Reed, N.Y.C., 1954-55; judge advocate, trial atty. U.S. Dept. of Air Force, Washington, 1955-57; assoc. Breed, Abbott and Morgan, N.Y.C., 1957-62; counsel Freeport Minerals Co., N.Y.C., 1962-69; interregional legal advisor UN, N.Y.C., 1969-74; sr. cons. UN Centre on Transnational Corps., N.Y.C., 1976-90, chief legal adviser, 1991-92; spl. counsel Am. Indian Coun. Energy Resource Tribes, Denver, 1978-84; bd. dirs. Havelock Asbestos Mines (Swaziland) Ltd., Sun Internat. of Lesotho Pty., Ltd., Dokolowayo Diamond Mines Ltd., Emaswati Coal Pty., Ltd.; cons. U.S. Commr. of Edn., 1965; legal advisor, cons. numerous govts.; comml. legal advisor to the Govt. of Lesotho, 1967—; legal advisor to Kings of Swaziland, 1969—; adj. prof. law NYU, 1975-88; vis. prof. law U. Swaziland, 1977-88, Nat. U. Lesotho, 1984-88; vis. lectr. in law U. Calif., Berkeley, 1974-82; vis. fellow U. NSW, Sydney, Australia, 1987; lectr. in field, participant in numerous workshops; Fulbright prof. law U. Tartu (Estonia), 1996. Contbr. articles to profl. jours. Capt. USAF, 1955-57. Mem. Am. Soc. Internat. Law, Am. Fgn. Law Assn., ABA (chmn. African law com. sect. on internat. and comparative law 1964-67), Assn. of Bar of City of N.Y., African Law Assn. in Am. (bd. dirs. 1969-72. Home: 1136 5th Ave New York NY 10128-0122

LIPTON, CLIFFORD CARWOOD, retired glass company executive; b. Huntington, W.Va., Jan. 30, 1920; s. Clifford Carwood and Zerelda (Adkins) L.; m. Alyce Jo Anne Eckley, Jan. 3, 1943 (dec. July 1975); children: Clifford Carwood III, Thomas Denton, Michael Forrester; m. Marie Hope Mahoney, May 26, 1976. B in Engring. Sci., Marshall U., 1948; postgrad. exec. mgmt. program, Pa. State U., 1959. Staff engr. Owens-Ill. Inc., Huntington, 1948-52; supr. engring. Owens-Ill. Inc., Streator, Ill., 1952-55; chief engr. divsn. Owens-Ill. Inc., Toledo, 1955-66; gen. mgr. Giralt Laporta SA, Madrid, 1966-71; dir. mfg. United Glass Ltd., London, 1971-74; mfg. and tech. dir. Owens-Ill. Internat., Geneva, 1974-82; dir. internat. devel. Owens-Ill. Inc., Toledo, 1982-83; ret., 1983; cons. Owens-Ill., Inc., China, Greece and U.S., 1983-85, Internat. Exec. Svc. Corps., 1986—. Mem. sch. bd. Am. Sch., Barcelona, Spain, 1966-67, Madrid, 1967-70; pres. Highland Trails Homeowners Assn., Southern Pines, N.C., 1987-93. 1st lt. Parachute Inf., U.S. Army, 1942-45. Mem. Benevolent and Protective Order Elks, 101st Airborne Divsn. Assn. Republican. Presbyterian. Avocations: travel, golf, reading, music, model engineering. Home: 104 Selkirk Trl Southern Pines NC 28387-7230

LIPTON, DANIEL BERNARD, conductor; b. Paris; s. Gerald David and Germaine (Chaison) L.; m. Olga Lucia Gaviria, Mar. 7, 1983 (div. Oct. 1985). BS in Music, Juilliard Sch., 1963, Mannes Coll., 1965; postgrad., Accademia Chigiana, Siena, Italy, 1965, 67, Ecole Normale Superieure, Paris, 1967. Artistic dir. Opera Hamilton, Ont., Can.; prof. McMaster U., Hamilton, 1988. Condr. Am. Ballet Theater, 1968, Denver Symphony Orch., 1969-70, Teatro Comunale, Firenze, Italy, 1970-71, Teatro Comunale, Bologna, Italy, 1972, Opernhaus Zürich, 1973-75, Teatro del Liceo, Barcelona, Spain, 1979-82, Grand Theatre, Dijon, France, 1980-81, 83, Theatre de l'Opera, Nice, 1982-83, 87, Châtelet, Paris, Teatro de la Zarzuela, Madrid, Teatro La Fenice, Venezia, 1982, Utah Opera, 1983-85, Orch. de l'Opera de Paris, 1986, Bayerische Staatsoper, München, Germany, 1986-87, National theater Mannheim, 1988, 90, Teatro Regio di Parma, Teatro San Carlo, Napoli, Opera in Seoul, Republic of Korea, 1988, Il Giorno di Nozze, Oper Dortmund, Festival in Jesi, Italy, Opera Buffalo, Oper Köln; artistic dir. Orquesta Sinfonica de Colombia, Opera de Colombia, 1975-83, Opera Hamilton, 1986 —, San Antonio Internat. Festival of Arts, 1986-89, dir. music Houston Grand Opera, 1984-85, Spoleto Festival, 1991, Deutsche Oper, Berlin, 1992; gen. music dir. Dessau, Germany, 1992; music dir., prin. conductor Anhaltische Philharmonie, Germany. Decorated Cruz de Boyaca (Colombia); recipient award Italian Govt.; Besançon conducting grantee, Fulbright grantee. Office: Opera Hamilton, 100 King St W, Hamilton, ON Canada L8P 1A2

LIPTON, ERIC, reporter. With Hartford Courant; now county govt. reporter The Washington Post, Fairfax, Va. Recipient Pulitzer Prize for explanatory journalism, 1992. Office: The Washington Post Fairfax County Bureau 4020 University Dr Ste 220 Fairfax VA 22030-6802

LIPTON, JOAN ELAINE, advertising executive; b. N.Y.C., July 12; 1 child, David Dean. B.A., Barnard Coll. With Young & Rubicam, Inc., N.Y.C., 1949-52, Robert W. Orr & Assocs., N.Y.C., 1952-57, Benton & Bowles, Inc., N.Y.C., 1957-64; asso. dir. Benton & Bowles, Ltd., London, Eng., 1964-68; with McCann-Erickson, Inc. (advt. agy.), N.Y.C., 1968-85; v.p. McCann-Erickson, Inc. (advt. agy.), 1970-79, sr. v.p., creative dir., 1979-85; pres. Martin & Lipton Advt. Inc., 1985—. Bd. trustees Film/Video Arts, Inc., 1983—, chmn., 1993—, pres., 1994—; mem. Bus. Coun. for the UN Decade for Women, 1977-78; bd. visitors PhD program in bus. CUNY, 1986—. Named Woman of Yr. Am. Advt. Fedn., 1974; recipient Honors award Ohio U. Sch. Journalism, 1976; Matrix award, 1979; YWCA award for women achievers, 1979; named Advt. Woman of Yr., 1984. Mem. Advt. Women N.Y. (1st v.p. 1975-76, v.p. Found. 1977-78), Women's Forum (bd. dirs. 1988-90), Women in Communications (pres. N.Y. chpt. 1974-76, named Nat. Headliner 1976). Office: 163 E 62nd St New York NY 10021-7613

LIPTON, LEAH, art historian, educator, museum curator; b. Kearny, N.J., Mar. 22, 1928; d. Abraham and Rose (Berman) Shneyer; m. Herbert Lipton, Sep. 19, 1951 (dec. 1979); children: David, Ivan, Rachel. BA, Douglass Coll. Rutgers U., New Brunswick, N.J., 1949; MA, Harvard U., Cambridge, Mass., 1950; postgrad., Harvard U., 1970-73, Wellesley Coll., 1970-73. Photo, library researcher Mus. Fine Arts, Boston, 1950-53, lectr., division edn., 1965-70; instr. Boston Coll., 1968-69; faculty, full prof. Framingham State Coll., Mass., 1969-94; ret., 1994; interim dir. Danforth Mus. Art, 1994-95; mem. bd. trustees Danforth Mus. Art, Framingham Mass., 1975—; curator Am. art Danforth Mus. Art, Framingham Mass., 1994—; chair exhibitions Com.; Collections Com. Danforth Mus., Framingham Mass., 1988, guest curator Nat. Portrait, Wash., 1985. Author: Book, 1985, Exhibition Catalogues, 1988-94; contbr. articles to profl. jours., 1981—. Co-Founder Danforth Mus. Art., Mass. 1973-75. Recipient Distinguished Service award Framingham State Coll., Mass. 1978, 87. Mem. Coll. Art Assn., Am. Studies Assn. Office: Danforth Mus of Art 123 Union Ave Framingham MA 01701-8223

LIPTON, LESTER, ophthalmologist, entrepreneur; b. N.Y.C., Mar. 14, 1936; s. George and Rita (Steinbaum) L.; m. Harriet Arfa, June 25, 1960; children: Sherri, Brandi, Shawn. BA, NYU, 1959; MD, Chgo. Med. Sch, 1964. Rsch. fellow Chgo. Med. Sch., 1959-60; intern Brookdale Hosp. Ctr., Bklyn., 1964-65; resident Harlem Eye and Ear Hosp., N.Y.C., 1965-68; assoc. attending Polyclinic French hosps., N.Y.C., 1968-75; asst. attending physician, ophthalmologist, surg. instr. St. Clare's Hosp., N.Y.C., 1975—; attending ophthalmologist Cabrini Med. Ctr., N.Y.C., 1982—, St. Vincent's Hosp., N.Y.C., 1995—; founder Lipton Eye Clinic, N.Y.C., 1981—; v.p. Van Arfa Realty, N.Y.C., 1984-88; pres. H&L Realty, Suffern, N.Y., 1981—; mem. bd. dirs. Salisbury (Conn.) Pub. Health Nursing Assn. Mem. U.S. Congl. Adv. Bd.; mem. bd. deacons Congregationalist Ch. With AUS, 1956-58. Named Internat. Amigo, OAS; recipient Presdl. Citation for outstanding community svc., 1991. Mem. N.Y. Med. Soc., Am. Assn. Individual Investors, Bronx High Sch. Sci. Alumni Assn., Sharon Country Club, United Shareholders Assn., Internat. Platform Assn., Wider Quaker Fellowship, Vanderbilt U. Cabinet Club. Republican. Home: Interlaken Estates Lakeville CT 06039 also: 1199 Park Ave New York NY 10128-1711 Office: Lipton Eye Clinic 51 E 90th St New York NY 10128-1205

LIPTON, LOIS JEAN, lawyer; b. Chgo., Jan. 14, 1946; d. Harold Lypski and Bernice (Reiter) Farber L.; m. Bertram Kraft, June 13, 1968 (div. 1977); 1 child, Rachel; m. R. Peter Carey, May 30, 1978; 1 child, Sara. B.A., U. Mich., 1966; J.D. summa cum laude, DePaul Coll. Law, Chgo., 1974; postgrad. Sheffield U., Eng., 1966. Bar: Ky. 1974, U.S. Dist. Ct. (we. dist.) Ky. 1974, U.S. Ct. Appeals (6th cir.) 1974, Ill. 1975, U.S. Dist. Ct. (no. dist.) Ill., 1975, U.S. Ct. Appeals (7th cir.) 1976. Staff counsel Roger Baldwin Found. of ACLU, Inc., Chgo., 1975-79, dir. reproductive rights project, 1979-83; atty. McDermott, Will & Emery, Chgo., 1984-86, G.D. Searle, Skokie, Ill., 1988-90; sr. atty. AT&T, Chgo., 1990—. Del White House Conf. on Families, Mpls., 1980. Recipient Durfee award, 1984. Mem. Am. Judicature Soc., ACLU (bd. dirs. Ill.), Chgo. Bar Assn., Chgo. Council Lawyers. Office: AT&T 227 W Monroe St Chicago IL 60606

LIPTON, MARTIN, lawyer; b. N.J., June 22, 1931; s. Samuel D. and Fannie L.; m. Susan Lytle, Feb. 17, 1982; children: James, Margaret, Katherine, Samantha. BS in Econs., U. Pa., 1952; LLB, NYU, 1955. Bar: N.Y. 1956. Ptnr. Wachtell Lipton Rosen & Katz, N.Y.C., 1965—; mem. coun. Am. Law Inst. Trustee NYU; pres. bd. trustees NYU Law Sch.; hon. chmn. Jerusalem Found.; chmn. bd. dirs. Prep for Prep; dir. Inst. Jud. Adminstrn. Office: Wachtell Lipton Rosen & Katz 51 W 52nd St New York NY 10019-6119

LIPTON, RICHARD M., lawyer; b. Youngstown, Ohio, Feb. 25, 1952; s. Sanford Y. Lipton and Sarah (Kentor) Goldman; m. Jane Brennan, May 24, 1981; children—Thomas, Anne, Martin, Patricia. B.A., Amherst Coll., 1974; J.D., U. Chgo., 1977. Bar: Ill. 1977, D.C. 1978, U.S. Dist. Ct. (no. dist.) Ill. 1979, U.S. Ct. Appeals (D.C. and 7th cirs.) 1979, U.S. Tax Ct. 1977, U.S. Ct. Claims 1979. Law clk. to judge Hall, U.S. Tax Ct., Washington, 1977-79; assoc. Isham, Lincoln & Beale, Chgo., 1979-83; ptnr. Ross & Hardies, Chgo., 1983-86; v.p. Pegasus Broadcasting, Chgo., 1986-88; ptnr. Sonnenschein Nath & Rosenthal, Chgo., 1988—. Contbr. articles to profl. jours. Recipient Order of Coif award U. Chgo. Law Sch., 1977. Fellow Am. Coll. Tax Counsel; mem. ABA (coun. dir. 1990-93, vice chair taxation sect. 1993—), Chgo. Bar Assn. (subcom. chair, chair fed. taxation com. 1991-92). Republican. Clubs: Union League, Mich. Shores, Conway Farms, Geneva Nat. Office: Sonnenschein Nath Rosenthal 233 S Wacker Dr Ste 8000 Chicago IL 60606-6404

LIPTON, ROBERT STEVEN, lawyer; b. N.Y.C., May 12, 1946; s. Max and Mildred (Goodman) L.; m. Stephanie F. Kass, Aug. 8, 1971. BA, NYU, 1967, JD, 1971. Bar: N.Y. 1972, U.S. Ct. Appeals (2d cir.) 1972, U.S. Dist. Ct. (so. dist.) N.Y. 1973, U.S. Supreme Ct. 1975. Assoc. Curtis, Mallet-Prevost, Colt & Mosle, N.Y.C., 1971-80, ptnr., 1980—. Editor NYU Law Rev., 1969-71. Mem. ABA, Fed. Bar Council, N.Y. State Bar Assn., Assn. of Bar of City of N.Y., Phi Beta Kappa. Club: India House (N.Y.C.). Office: Curtis Mallet-Prevost Colt & Mosle 101 Park Ave New York NY 10178

LIPTON, STUART ARTHUR, neuroscientist; b. Danbury, Conn., Jan. 11, 1950; s. Harold and Evelyn Ruth (Stein) L.; m. Elisabeth Kay Ament, Aug. 10, 1980; children: Jennifer Ann, Jeffrey Harris. BA, Cornell U., 1971; MD, U. Pa., 1977, PhD, 1977; postgrad., Cornell U., 1971, U. Oxford (Eng.), 1972, Harvard U., 1974-76. Diplomate Am. Bd. Psychiatry and Neurology. Intern Beth Israel Hosp. and Harvard Med. Sch., Boston, 1977-78; resident in neurology Beth Israel, Brigham and Women's, Children's Hosp., Boston, 1978-80; chief neurology resident Brigham and Women's, Children's Hosp., Boston, 1980-81; research fellow in neurobiology Harvard Med. Sch., Boston, 1980-83, instr. in neurology, 1981-83, asst. prof. neurology and neurosci., 1983-87, assoc. prof. neurology and neurosci., 1987—; dir. cellular and molecular neurosci. Children's Hosp., Harvard Med. Sch.; neurologist Mass. Gen. Hosp., Brigham and Women's Hosp., Beth Israel Hosp., Children's Hosp., Boston. Contbr. articles to profl. jours.; patentee in field; composer of popular songs including one that sold 1.5 million copies, 1968. Established investigator Am. Heart Assn., 1988-93. Hartford Found. fellow, 1981, 82, 83, 84, NIH fellow, 1984, 85, 86, 87, 88, 89; NIH grantee, 1984—; Rhodes scholar Oxford (Eng.) U., 1971-72; recipient Pattison award, 1989; Nobel lectr. Karolinska Inst., 1994. Mem. AAAS, Am. Acad. Neurology, Am. Neurol. Assn., Soc. for Neurosci., Assn. for Rsch. in Vision and Opthalmology, Biophys. Soc., Phi Beta Kappa, Alpha Omega Alpha. Avocations: musical composition, soccer. Office: Childrens Hosp & Harvard Med Sch 300 Longwood Ave Boston MA 02115-5737

LIPTON, SUSAN LYTLE, investment banker, lawyer; b. Ft. Warren, Wyo., Oct. 23, 1945; d. James and Bette Lytle; m. Martin Lipton, Feb. 17, 1982. AB, U. Miami, 1967, JD, 1970; LLM, Harvard U., 1971. Bar: Fla. 1970, N.Y. 1984. From assoc. to ptnr. Greenberg Traurig Askew, Miami, Fla., 1970-77; from assoc. to v.p. Goldman Sachs & Co., N.Y.C., 1977-81; from v.p. to mng. dir. L.F. Rothschild, Unterberg, Towbin, N.Y.C., 1981-86; trustee Jewish Mus., 1986—, Brearley Sch., 1991—, Wildlife Conservation Soc., 1991—; trustee, pres. Jewish Communal Fund, 1992—.

LIPTON, WILLIAM JAMES, accountant, lawyer; b. N.Y.C., July 11, 1947; s. Irvin Edward and Evelyn Deborah (Morris) L.; m. Carol Anne Miller, Jan. 3, 1982; children: Michael Jon, Bradley Scott, Marissa Kate. BS in Acctg., U. Pa., 1969; JD, St. John's U., N.Y.C., 1973; LLM, N.Y.U., 1977. Bar: N.Y. 1974; CPA, N.Y. Tax assoc. Ernst & Whinney, N.Y.C., 1973-80, ptnr., 1980-87; ptnr.-in-charge of tax Ernst & Whinney, Phila., 1987-89; dir. tax Ernst & Young, Stamford, Conn., 1989-91; mng. ptnr. Ernst & Whinney, Stamford, Conn., 1991-93; vice chmn. tax svcs. Ernst & Young, N.Y.C., 1993—. Assoc. editor St. John's Law Rev., 1972; contbr. articles to profl. jours. Mem. ABA, N.Y. State Bar Assn., Phila. Bar Assn., AICPA, N.Y. State Soc. CPAs (chmn. partnership com. 1985-87), Conn. State Soc. CPAs. Home: 255 Marvin Ridge Rd New Canaan CT 06840-6910 Office: Ernst & Young 787 7th Ave New York NY 10019-6018*

LIPTZIN, BENJAMIN, psychiatrist; b. N.Y.C., Sept. 17, 1945; s. David Murray and Mollie (Brody) L.; m. Sharon Leslie Rothstein, June 10, 1968; children: Shoshanna, Daniel, Deborah. BA, Yale U., 1966; MD, U. Rochester, N.Y., 1971. Diplomate Am. Bd. Psychiatry and Neurology. Resident in psychiatry U. Va. Hosp., Charlottesville, 1971-74; med. officer NIMH, Rockville, Md., 1974-78; dir. geriatric psychiatry McLean Hosp., Belmont, Mass., 1978-89, asst. gen. dir., 1989-90; chief dept. psychiatry Baystate Med. Ctr., Springfield, Mass., 1990—; prof., dep. chmn. dept. psychiatry Tufts U. Sch. Medicine, 1990—. Contbr. articles to profl. jours. With USPHS, 1972-78. Recipient Acad. award NIMH, 1983. Fellow Am. Psychiat. Assn. (trustee-at-large 1992-95), Gerontol. Soc. Am.; mem. AMA, Am. Coll. Psychiatrists. Democrat. Jewish. Office: Baystate Med Ctr Dept Psychiatry 140 High St Springfield MA 01199-1000

LIS, ANTHONY STANLEY, business administration educator; b. Easthampton, Mass., Aug. 11, 1918; s. Anthony Stanley and Anna Barbara (Kaczmarczyk) L.; m. Jane Ann Mikus, June 25, 1951 (dec.); children: Anthony, Judith A., Sandra J.; m. Sophie A. Pobieglo, June 24, 1983. B.S., Mass. State Coll., Salem, 1950; M.S., Okla. State U., 1951; Ph.D., U. Minn., 1961. Asst. prof. Okla. State U., Stillwater, 1951-55; assoc. prof. U. Tulsa, 1956-62; mem. faculty U. Okla., Norman, 1962-86, prof. bus. adminstrn., 1967-86, prof. emeritus, 1986—; vis. prof. Central Sch. Planning/Stats., Warsaw, Poland, 1984; del. II Congress Scholars of Polish Descent, Warsaw, 1979, III Congress, 1989 ; cons. to numerous bus. and govtl. agys. Served with U.S. Army, 1937-40, 1942-46. Decorated Bronze Star; recipient Superior Profl. and Univ. Service award U. Okla., 1981; Summer fellow Found. Econ. Edn., 1954. Mem. Am. Bus. Comm. Assn., Polish Am. Hist. Assn., Adminstrv. Mgmt. Soc., Southwestern Social Sci. Assn., Delta Pi Epsilon, Beta Gamma Sigma, Delta Sigma Pi. Roman Catholic. Lodge: Lions. Home: 1827 Peter Pan St Norman OK 73072-5837 Office: U Okla Coll Bus Adminstrn Norman OK 73019

LIS, EDWARD FRANCIS, pediatrician, consultant; b. Chgo., Apr. 1, 1918; s. Stephen and Stephanie L.; m. Sonne Nadine Kowalsen, Apr. 3, 1944; children—Jeffrey Warren, James Bryan. Student, DePaul U., 1936-37; B.S., M.D., U. Ill. Pvt. practice Park Forest, Ill., 1949-51; faculty U. Ill. Coll. Medicine, 1951-90, prof. pediatrics, also dir. div. services crippled children, 1959-90, prof. emeritus, 1990—; dir. center handicapped children Univ. Hosp., U. Ill., 1955-90; cons. in field. Contbr. to profl. jours. Chmn. research adv. com. Children's Bur., HEW, 1964-67; mem. Ill. Commn. Children. Served to capt. AUS, 1944-46. Fellow Am. Acad. Pediatrics, Am. Pub. Health Assn.; mem. Sigma Xi. Home: 3003 Balmoral Cres Flossmoor IL 60422-1404

LISA, ISABELLE O'NEILL, law firm administrator, mergers and acquisitions executive; b. Phila., Mar. 12, 1934; d. Thomas Daniel and Margaret Marie (Hayes) O'Neill; m. Donald Julius Lisa, June 15, 1957; children: Richard Allan, Steven Gregory. Student, Harper Community Coll., Rolling Meadows, Ill., 1976, Scottsdale Community Coll., 1980, Ariz. State U., 1981-82. Cost control clk. Curtis Pub. Co., Phila., 1952-56; sec. United Ins. Co., Annapolis, Md., 1956-57; firm adminstr., legal sec. Law Offices Donald J. Lisa, Bloomingdale, Ill., 1987; legal sec. Lisa & Kubida, P.C., Phoenix, 1987-88, firm adminstr., 1987-89; firm adminstr. Lisa & Assocs., Phoenix, 1989-90, Lisa & Lisa, Phoenix, 1990-91, Lisa & Assocs., Scottsdale, Ariz., 1991-95, Law Offices of Donald J. Lisa, Scottsdale, 1995—; Law Offices of Donald J. Lisa, 1995—; v.p. adminstrn. Lisa & Co., Scottsdale, 1987-91, 1991—. Den mother Cub Scouts Am., Millburn, N.J., 1965; founder, pres. Pro-Tem Rutgers U. Law Wives Assn., 1962-63; bd. advisors Am. Inst., Phoenix, 1991—. Mem. NAFE, Maricopa County Bar Assn. (legal adminstrs. sect. 1992-95), Internat. Platform Assn., Rotary. Republican. Roman Catholic. Avocations: painting, drawing, graphic design, photography. Home and Office: 8661 E Carol Way Scottsdale AZ 85260

LISANBY, JAMES WALKER, retired naval officer; b. Princeton, Ky., Jan. 31, 1928; s. Alvin and Rebecca L.; m. Gladys Elnora Kemp, Nov. 18, 1951; children: Elizabeth Ann, Sarah Hollingsworth. B.S. in Elec. Engring, U.S. Naval Acad., 1950; Engrs. Degree in Naval Architecture, MIT, 1953-56; student, Program for Mgmt. Devel., Harvard U., 1967. Commd. ensign U.S. Navy, 1950, advanced through grades to rear adm., 1977; ship supt. Charleston Naval Shipyard, 1956-59; main propulsion asst. U.S.S. Antietam (CVS 36), 1959-61; asst. for ship materials, staff, comdr.-in-chief Atlantic Fleet, 1961-63; asst. for new constrn. cruisers and destroyers Naval Ship Systems Command, Dept. Navy, Washington, 1963-65; head procurement and prodn. br., fast deployment logistic ship project office Naval Ship Systems Command, Dept. Navy, 1965-68, exec. asst. to comdr., 1969-70; dir. indsl. engring. office of asst. sec. of navy, installations and logistics, 1968-69; supr. shipbldg. Pascagoula, Miss., 1970-73; asst. for ship design, office chief naval ops., 1973-74, project mgr. LHA class amphibious assault ships, 1974-77; comdr. Naval Ship Engring. Center Navy Dept., Washington, 1977-79; dep. comdr. ship design and integration Naval Sea Systems Command, Dept. Navy, Washington, 1979-81; prin. dep. acquisition Naval Sea Systems Command, Dept. Navy, 1981-83, ret., 1983; founder, pres. Naval Services Internat. Inc., Washington, 1983—, pres., chief exec. officer; chmn. Naval Svc. Internat., Inc., Tech. Financing Inc. Recipient Engr. of Yr. award Soc. Mfg. Engrs., 1979; decorated Legion of Merit. Mem. Am. Soc. Naval Engrs. (nat. v.p. 1979-81), Soc. Naval Architects and Marine Engrs., Sigma Xi, Tau Beta Pi. Office: PO Box 15515 Arlington VA 22215-0515

LISBOA-FARROW, ELIZABETH OLIVER, public and government relations consultant; b. N.Y.C., Nov. 25, 1947; d. Eleuterio and Esperanza Oliver; student pvt. schs., N.Y.C.; m. Jeffrey Lloyd Farrow, Dec. 31, 1980; 1 child, Hamilton Oliver Farrow; 1 stepson, Maximillian Robbins Farrow. With Harold Rand & Co. and various other public relations firms, N.Y.C., 1966-75; dir. pub. rels. N.Y. Playboy Club and Playboy Clubs Internat., 1975-79; pres., CEO Lisboa Assocs., Inc., N.Y.C., 1979—; founder, pres. Lisboa Prodns., Inc., Washington, 1994—; counselor Am. Woman's Devel. Corp. Sec. Nat. Acad. Concert and Cabaret Arts; mem. nat. adv. council SBA, 1980-81, apptd., 1994—; exec. dir. Variety Club of Greater Washington, Inc., 1985-90, Children's Charity; bd. dirs. Variety Myoelectric Limb Bank Found., 1990-91; bd. trustees Hispanic Bus. Scholarship Fund, 1995—, Southeastern U., 1995—; adv. bd. Indsl. Bank, N.A., 1996; active Women and Heart Disease Task Force. Recipient Disting. award of Excellence SBA, 1992, Women Bus. Enterprise award U.S. Dept. Transp. NHTSA, 1994, Excellence in Entrepreneurship award Dialogue on Diversity, Inc., 1995; named Pub. Rels. Woman of Yr. Women in Pub. Rels. Mem. SAG, NATAS, U.S. Hispanic C. of C. (Blue Chip Enterprise award 1993), Small Bus. Advisory Coun., U.S. C. of C., Advt. Coun., Am. Heart Assn., Hispanic Bus. and Profl. Women's Assn., Ibero-Am. C. of C. (Small Bus. award 1993, bd. dirs. 1993—, v.p. 1995—), City Club Washington. Office: 1317 F St NW Washington DC 20004-1105

LISH, GORDON, author, educator, editor; b. Hewlett, N.Y., Feb. 11, 1934; s. Philip and Regina (Deutsch) L.; m. Loretta Frances Fokes, Nov. 7, 1956 (div. May 1967); children: Jennifer, Rebecca, Ethan; m. Barbara Works, May 30, 1969; 1 son, Atticus. LittD (hon.), SUNY, 1993. Editorial dir. Genesis West, 1961-65; editor in chief, dir. linguistic studies Behavioral Research Labs., Menlo Park, Calif., 1963-66; with Ednl. Devel. Corp., Palo Alto, 1966-69; fiction editor Esquire mag., N.Y.C., 1969-77; with Alfred A. Knopf, Inc., 1977-95; lectr. Yale U., 1970-74, guest fellow, 1974-80; tchr. fiction writing Columbia U., 1980—; prof. NYU Coll. Arts and Scis. Author fiction and non-fiction under several pen-names: English Grammar, 1964, The Gabbernot, 1965, Why Work, 1966, A Man's Work, 1967, New Sounds in American Fiction, 1969; author: (short stories) What I Know So Far, 1981, 84, Mourner at the Door, 1988, The Selected Stories of Gordon Lish, 1996; author (novels): Dear Mr. Capote, 1983, Peru, 1986, Extravaganza, 1989, My Romance, 1991, Zimzum, 1993, Epigraph, 1996; editor: The Secret of Life of Our Times, 1973, All Our Secrets Are the Same, 1976; editor-in-chief The Quarterly, 1987—; editor-in-chief Chrysalis Rev., 1959-61. Pres. Chrysalis West Found., 1962—. Office: 650 Madison Ave Ste 2600 New York NY 10022-1029

LISHER, JAMES RICHARD, lawyer; b. Aug. 28, 1947; s. Leonard B. and Mary Jane (Rafferty) L.; m. Martha Gettelfinger, June 16, 1973; children: Jennifer, James Richard II. A.B., Ind. U., 1969, J.D., 1975. Bar: Ind. 1975, U.S. Dist. Ct. (so. dist.) Ind. 1975. Assoc. Rafferty & Wood, Shelbyville, Ind., 1976, Rafferty & Lisher, Shelbyville, 1976-77; dep. prosecutor Shelby County Prosecutor's Office, Shelbyville, 1976-78; ptnr. Yeager, Lisher & Baldwin, Shelbyville, 1977-96; pvt. practice, Shelbyville, 1996—; pros. atty. Shelby County, Shelbyville, 1983-95. Speaker, faculty advisor Ind. Pros. Sch., 1986. Editor: (seminar manual) Traffic Case Defenses, 1982. Bd. dirs. Girls Club of Shelbyville, 1979-84, Bears of Blue River Festival, Shelbyville, 1982—. Recipient Citation of Merit, Young Lawyers Assn. Mem. Nat. Assn. of Criminals, State Bar Assn. (bd. dirs.), Ind. Pub. Defender Assn., Ind. State Bar Assn. (bd. dirs. young lawyer sect 1979-83), Shelby County Bar Assn. (sec./treas. 1986, v.p. 1987, pres. 1988), Ind. Pros. Attys. Assn. (bd. dirs. 1985-95, sec./treas. 1987, v.p. 1988, pres.-elect 1989, pres. 1990). Democrat. Lodges: Masons, Elks, Lions. Home: 106 Western Trce Shelbyville IN 46176-9765 Office: Courthouse Rm 303 Shelbyville IN 46176

LISHER, JOHN LEONARD, lawyer; b. Indpls., Sept. 19, 1950; s. Leonard Boyd and Mary Jane (Rafferty) L.; m. Mary Katherine Sturmon, Aug. 17, 1974. B.A. with honors in History, Ind. U., 1975, J.D., 1975. Bar: Ind. 1975. Dep. atty. gen. State of Ind., Indpls., 1975-78; asst. corp. counsel City of Indpls., 1978-81; assoc. Osborn & Hiner, Indpls., 1981-86; ptnr. Osborn, Hiner & Lisher, 1986—. Vol. Mayflower Classic, Indpls., 1981—; pres. Brendonwood Common Inc.; asst. vol. coord. Marion County Rep. Com., Indpls., 1979-80; vol. Don Bogard for Atty. Gen., Indpls., 1980, Steve Goldsmith for Prosecutor, Indpls., 1979, 83, Sheila Suess for Congress, Indpls., 1980. Recipient Outstanding Young Man of Am. award Jaycees, 1979, 85, Indpls. Jaycees, 1980. Mem. ABA, Ind. Bar Assn., Indpls. Bar Assn. (membership com.), Assn. Trial Lawyers Am., Ind. U. Alumni Assn., Hoosier Alumni Assn. (charter, founder, pres.), Ind. Trial Lawyers Assn., Ind. Def. Lawyers Assn., Ind. U. Coll. Arts and Scis. (bd. dirs. 1983-92, pres. 1986-87), Wabash Valley Alumni Assn. (charter), Founders Club, Presidents Club, Phi Beta Kappa, Eta Sigma Phi, Phi Eta Sigma, Delta Xi Alumni Assn. (charter, v.p., sec., Delta Xi chpt. Outstanding Alumnus award 1975, 76, 79, 83), Delta Xi Housing Corp. (pres.), Pi Kappa Alpha (midwest regional pres. 1977-86, parliamentarian nat. conv. 1982, del. convs. 1978-80, 82, 84, 86, trustee Meml. Found. 1986-91. Presbyterian. Avocations: reading; golf; jogging; Roman coin collecting. Home: 5725 Hunterglen Rd Indianapolis IN 46226-1019 Office: Osborn Hiner Lisher & Orzeska PC Ste 380 8330 Woodfield Crossing Blvd Indianapolis IN 46240-4382

LISI, MARY M., federal judge. BA, U. R.I., 1972; JD, Temple U., 1977. Tchr. history Prout Meml. High Sch., Wakefield, R.I., 1972-73; hall dir. U. R.I., 1973-74; law clerk to Prof. Jerome Sloan Temple U., Phila., 1975-76; law clerk U.S. Atty., Providence, R.I., 1976, Phila., 1976-77; asst. pub. defender R.I. Office Pub. Defender, 1977-81; asst. child advocate Office Child Advocate, 1981-82; also. pvt. practice atty. Providence, 1981-82; dir. office ct. appointed spl. advocate R.I. Family Ct., 1982-87; dep. disciplinary counsel office disciplinary counsel R.I. Supreme Ct., 1988-90, chief disciplinary counsel, 1990-94; mem. Select Com. to Investigate Failure of R.I. Share and Deposit Indemnity Corp., 1991-92. Recipient Providence 350 award, 1986, Meritorious Svc. to Children of Am. award, 1987. Office: Fed Bldg and US Courthouse 1 Exchange Ter Rm 113 Providence RI 02903-1720

LISIMACHIO, JEAN LOUIS, book publishing executive; b. Nice, France, 1946. Mng. dir. book group Grolier Inc.; 1982-91, chmn. bd. dirs., 1991—. Office: Grolier Inc Sherman Tpke Danbury CT 06816

LISIO, DONALD JOHN, historian, educator; b. Oak Park, Ill., May 27, 1934; s. Anthony and Dorothy (LoCelso) L.; m. Susanne Marie Swanson, Apr. 22, 1958; children: Denise Anne, Stephen Anthony. B.A., Knox Coll., 1956; M.A., Ohio U., 1958; Ph.D., U. Wis., 1965. Mem. faculty overseas div. U. Md., 1958-60; asst. prof. history Coe Coll., Cedar Rapids, Iowa, 1964-69, assoc. prof., 1969-74, prof., 1974—, chmn. dept., 1973-81, Henrietta Arnold prof. history, 1980—. Author: The President and Protest: Hoover, Conspiracy, and the Bonus Riot, 1974, Hoover, Blacks, and Lily-Whites: A Study of Southern Strategies, 1985; contbg. author: The War Generation, 1975; contbr. articles to hist. jours. Mem. exec. com. Cedar Rapids Com. Hist. Preservation, 1975-77. Served with U.S. Army, 1958-60. Recipient Outstanding Tchr. award Coe Coll., 1969, Charles J. Lynch Outstanding Teaching award Coe Coll., 1991, Favorite Prof. award, 1996; William F. Vilas rsch. fellow U. Wis., 1963-64; NEH fellow, 1969-70, rsch. fellow, 1984-85; Am. Coun. Learned Socs. grantee, 1971-72, fellow, 1977-78; U.S. Inst. of Peace rsch. grantee, 1990. Mem. Orgn. Am. Historians, Am. Hist. Assn., AAUP, ACLU. Roman Catholic. Home: 4203 Twin Ridge Ct SE Cedar Rapids IA 52403-3950 Office: Coe Coll Cedar Rapids IA 52402

LISK, PAMELA KONIECZKA, lawyer; b. Chgo., Oct. 8, 1959; m. Thomas Joseph Lisk; 1 child, Sarah. BA, Northwestern U., 1980; M of Pub. Policy, JD, Harvard U., 1984. Staff atty. SEC, Washington, 1984-86; assoc. Lord, Bissell & Brook, Chgo., 1986-89; sr. atty. Sundstrand Corp., Rockford, Ill., 1989—. Mem. Ill. Bar Assn., Phi Beta Kappa.

LISKA, GEORGE, political science educator, author; b. Pardubice, Czechoslovakia, June 30, 1922; came to U.S., 1949, naturalized, 1957; s. Bedrich and Karla (Slezakova) L.; m. Suzy Colombier, June 30, 1962; children: Ian Pierre, Anne Fernande. Dr.Jr., Charles U., Prague, Czechoslovakia, 1948; Ph.D. in Polit. Sci, Harvard U., 1955. Sec. to sec. gen. Czechoslovak Ministry Fgn. Affairs, 1946-48; exec. asst. Council Free Czechoslovakia, Washington, 1949-52; asst. prof. polit. sci. U. Chgo., 1958-61; prof. polit. sci. Johns Hopkins U. and Sch. Advanced Internat. Studies, Washington; also research assoc. Johns Hopkins' Washington Ctr. Fgn. Policy Research (succeeded by Fgn. Policy Inst.), 1964—. Author: International Equilibrium, 1957, The New Statecraft, 1960, Nations in Alliance, 1962, Europe Ascendant, 1964, Imperial America, 1967, War and Order, 1968, States in Evolution, 1973, Beyond Kinninger, 1975, Quest for Equilibrium, 1977, Career of Empire, 1978, Russia and World Order, 1980, Russia and the Road to Appeasement, 1982, Rethinking U.S.-Soviet Relations, 1987, Ways of Power, 1990, Fallen Dominions, 1990, The State and Foreign Policy, 1992, Return to the Heartland and Rebirth of the Old Order, 1994. Recipient Sumner prize Harvard U., 1955. Office: 1740 Massachusetts Ave NW Washington DC 20036-1984 also: Johns Hopkins U Dept Polit Sci Baltimore MD 21218 *The impetus behind my efforts as a writer on and academic teacher of international relations has been the effort to convert the impossibility of actual participation—due to the loss of an official role in my native Czechoslovakia—into a deepened insight into the processes ultimately responsible for my expatriation.*

LISKAMM, WILLIAM HUGO, architect, urban planner, educator; b. N.Y.C., Sept. 10, 1931; s. William J. and Johanne (Herz) L.; m. Karen Elizabeth Nunn, May 1979; children: Amanda Nunn, Mason Nunn; children by previous marriage—Erika, Thea, Fiona. B.Arch., Pratt Inst., 1954; Fulbright scholar, Technische Hochschule, Stuttgart, Germany, 1954-55; M.Arch., Harvard, 1956. Project architect maj. archtl. and urban planning programs Calif. and N.Y., 1958-63; exec. v.p. Okamoto & Liskamm, Inc. (planners and architects), San Francisco, 1963-71; ind. archtl. and urban planning cons., 1971-74; pres. William H. Liskamm, AIA, AIP, Inc., 1974—; dir. planning Woodward-Clyde Consultants, San Francisco, 1978-79; dir. campus planning office U. Calif., Berkeley, 1984-90; asst. prof. dept. architecture Coll. Environ. Design, U. Calif. at Berkeley, 1963-69, vice chmn., 1965-67, vis. sr. lectr. U. Coll., London, 1967-68; chmn. bd. Archtl. Found. No. Calif.; chmn. design rev. bd. San Francisco Bay Conservation and Devel. Commn., State of Calif., 1970-80; chmn. archtl. adv. com. Golden Gate Bridge Hwy. and Transp. Dist., 1980-81; prof., advisor major planning and design competitions Nat. Endowment for the Arts. Author: Appearance and Design Element, California Coastal Plan, 1974. Served to 1st lt. C.E. AUS, 1956-58. Recipient awards for profl. projects HUD; Am. Inst. Planners award for San Francisco Urban Design Plan, 1972; Wheelwright fellow Harvard, 1967-68; Nat. Endowment for Arts grantee. Mem. AIA (coll. of fellows).

LISLE, JANET TAYLOR, writer; b. Englewood, N.J., Feb. 13, 1947; d. Alden Mygatt and Janet Roberton (MacColl) Taylor; m. Richard Waterman Lisle, Oct. 17, 1976; 1 child, Elizabeth. BA, Smith Coll., 1969; cert. in journalism, Ga. State U., 1971. Author: (books) The Dancing Cats of Applesap, 1984, 93, Sirens and Spies, 1985, 90 (Booklist Best of the 80's 1990, Notable Children's Book ALA 1985, Best Book for Young Adults, Booklist Editor's Choice, Best Book of the Yr. Sch. Libr. Jour. 1986, Jr. Lit. Guild Selection), The Great Dimpole Oak, 1987 (Golden Kite Honor award, Booklist Editor's Choice), Afternoon of the Elves, 1989, 91, (Newbery Honor award Children's Lit., 1990, Best Book of the Yr. Sch. Libr. Jour., Notable Children's Book ALA, Booklist Editor's Choice 1990, 90, Jr. Libr. Guild Selection), The Lampfish of Twill, 1991, 92 (Best Book of the Yr. Sch. Libr. Jour., Best Children's Book of the Yr. N.Y. Times Book Rev.), Forest, 1993 (Best Book of the Yr. Sch. Libr. Jour., Am. Bookseller Pick of the Lists), The Gold Dust Letters, 1994 (Jr. Libr. Guild Selection), Looking For Juliette, 1994, A Message from the Match Girl, 1995, Angela's Aliens, 1996; (anthologized short stories) Those in Peril on the Sea, 1992, The Face in the Rafters, 1993. Mem. Author's Guild, Soc. Children's Book Writers. Avocations: choral activities, tennis, writing group. Office: care Orchard Books 95 Madison Ave New York NY 10016-7801

LISMAN, ERIC, publishing executive, lawyer. V.p. and gen. counsel Cahners Pub. Co. Office: 275 Washington St Newton MA 02158*

LISNEK, MARGARET DEBBELER, artist, educator; b. Covington, Ky., Sept. 26, 1940; d. Aloysius Frank and Mary Elizabeth (Haubold) Debbeler; m. Schiller William Lisnek, June 26, 1966 (dec. May 1995); 1 child, Kimberly Anne. AA with honors, Mt. San Antonio Coll., 1985; BA in Art with honors, Calif. State U., Fullerton, 1991. Cert. substitute tchr. Freelance artist, 1985—; tchr. art Rorimer Elem. Sch., La Puente, Calif., 1992-93, City of Walnut (Calif.) Recreation Svcs., 1992—, Christ Luth. Sch., West Covina, Calif., 1993—, Los Molinos Elem. Sch., Hacienda Heights, Calif., 1993—, Los Altos Elem. Sch., Hacienda Heights, 1993—; mem. Getty Inst. Insvc. Resource Team. One-woman shows include Calif. State U., Fullerton, 1990; exhibited in group shows. Sec., treas., social chair PTA, Los Altos Elem. Sch., Hacienda Heights, 1972-73; membership and social chair Friends of Libr., Hacienda Heights, 1974-75; active Nat. Mus. Women in the Arts, L.A. County Art Mus., Norton Simon Mus., Pasadena, Calif. Mem. Calif. Art Edn. Assn. Avocations: world travel, art history, collecting stamps, foreign languages, dancing.

LISOTA, GARY MARTIN, business executive, retired naval officer; b. Milw., Nov. 22, 1949; s. Martin Gerard and Shirley Rose (Francke) L.; m. Judith Ann Winnicki, May 25, 1970 (div. July 1986); 1 child, Mark Joseph; m. Karen Janelle Bennett, May 13, 1989. Student, Ill. Inst. Tech., 1967-68; BSEE, Purdue U., 1974. Commd. 2d lt. USN, 1969, advanced through grades to lt. comdr., ret., 1980; program mgr. SEACOR, Alexandria, Va., 1980-81; dir. corp. mktg. AMSEC, Arlington, Va., 1981-83, ops. ctr. mgr., 1983-87; v.p. Washington div. SAIC-AMSEC, Arlington, 1987-88; v.p. bus. devel. SAIC-AMSEC, Virginia Beach, Va., 1988-90, COO, 1990—, also bd. dirs. Mem. Am. Soc. Naval Engrs., Purdue Alumni Assn., Tau Beta Pi, Eta Kappa Nu. Roman Catholic. Office: SAIC-AMSEC 2829 Guardian Ln Virginia Beach VA 23452-7328*

LISS, HERBERT MYRON, newspaper publisher, communications company executive; b. Mpls., Mar. 23, 1931; s. Joseph Milton and Libby Diane (Kramer) L.; m. Barbara Lipson, Sept. 19, 1954; children: Lori-Ellen, Kenneth Allen, Michael David. BS in Econs., U. Pa., 1952. With mktg. mgmt. Procter & Gamble Co., Cin., 1954-63, Procter & Gamble Internat., various countries, 1963-74; gen. mgr. Procter & Gamble Comml. Co., San Juan, P.R., 1974-78; v.p., mgr. internat. ops. InterAm. Orange Crush Co. subs. Procter & Gamble Co., Cin., 1981-84; pres. River Cities (Ohio) Communications Inc, 1985—; pub. The Downtowner newspaper and others, Cin., 1985—. Bd. dirs. Charter Com., Cin., 1958-63, Promotion and Mktg. Assn. U.S., 1978-81, Jr. Achievement, Cin., 1980-87; bd. dirs. Downtown Coun., Cin., 1985-94, treas., 1991-92; bd. dirs. Downtown Cin. Inc., 1995—, mem. retail mktg. com., 1995—. Mem. Manila Yacht Club, Manila Polo, Club Escuela de Equitación De Somos Aquas, Madrid, Rotary (Cin. club), Cin. Racquet Club. Home: 8564 Wyoming Club Dr Cincinnati OH 45215-4243 Office: The Downtowner Newspaper 128 E 6th St Cincinnati OH 45202-3211

LISSENDEN, CAROLKAY, pediatrician; b. Newark, Aug. 22, 1937; d. George Cyrus Sr. and Irene Elizabeth (Hempel) L.; m. Bart Albert Barré, June 13, 1964; children: Lisa Kim Barré-Quick, Bart Christopher Barré. BA, U. Pa., 1959; MD, Med. Coll. Pa., 1964. Pediat. intern St. Luke's Hosp., N.Y.C., 1964-65; pediat. resident Columbia-Presbyn. Hosp., N.Y.C., 1965-67; pvt. practice Mountainside, N.J., 1967—. Fellow Am. Acad. Pediats.; mem. AMA, N.J. Med. Assn., Union County Med. Assn. Republican. Presbyterian. Avocations: gardening, roller skating, sewing. Home and Office: 135 Wild Hedge Ln Mountainside NJ 07092-2520

LISSIMORE, TROY, historic site director. BA in Polit. History, MA in Polit. History, MS in Environ. Sci. and Edn.; JD, John Marshall Law Sch. Historian Gettysburg Nat. Mil. Pk., 1966; pk. mgr. William Howard Taft Nat. Hist. Site; chief interpretation Jamaica Bay; mgr. Jamaica Wildlife Refugee Gateway Nat. Recreational Area; supt. Tuskegee Inst. Nat. Hist. Site; chief of interpretation, asst. supt. Martin Luther King Jr. Nat. Hist. Site; supt., staff pk. ranger S.E. regional office Martin Luther King Jr. Nat. Hist. and Preservation Dist., 1992—. Office: Martin Luther King Nat Hist 526 Auburn Ave NE Atlanta GA 30312

LIST, ERICSON JOHN, environmental engineering science educator, engineering consultant; b. Whakatane, New Zealand, Mar. 27, 1939; came to U.S., 1962; s. Ericson Bayliss and Freda Helen (Sunkel) L.; m. Olive Amoore, Feb. 3, 1962; children: Brooke Meredith, Antonia Michael. B.E. with honors, U. Auckland, N.Z., 1961, B.Sc., 1962, M.E., 1962; Ph.D., Calif. Inst. Tech., 1965. Registered profl. engr., Calif. Sr. lectr. U. Auckland, 1966-69; asst. prof. Calif. Inst. Tech., Pasadena, 1969-72, assoc. prof., 1972-78, prof. environ. engring. sci., 1978—, exec. officer, 1980-85; dir. Fluid Kinetics Corp., Ventura, Calif., 1972-82; bd. chmn. Flow Sci. Inc., Pasadena, 1983—; cons. So. Calif. Edison, Rosemead, Calif., 1973—, City and County of San Francisco, 1974—. Author: (with Hugo B. Fischer et al), Mixing in Inland and Coastal Waters, 1979, (with W. Rodi) Turbulent Jets and Plumes, 1982, (with Roscoe Moss Co.) Handbook of Ground Water Development, 1990. Mem. Blue Ribbon Commn. City of Pasadena, 1976-78. Recipient Spl. Creativity award NSF, 1982. Fellow ASCE (editor Jour. Hydraulic Engring. 1984-89). Republican. Club: Athenaeum (Pasadena) (chmn. wine com. 1981-83). Office: Calif Inst Tech 1201 E California Blvd Pasadena CA 91125-0001

LIST, ROLAND, physicist, educator, former UN official; b. Frauenfeld, Thurgau, Switzerland, Feb. 21, 1929; s. August Joseph and Anna (Kaufmann) L; m. Gertrud K. Egli, Apr. 14, 1956; children: Beat R., Claudia G. List Woolner. Diploma physics ETH, Swiss Fed. Inst. Tech., 1952, Dr. Sci. Nat., 1960. Head hail sect. Swiss Fed. Inst. for Snow and Avalance Rsch., Davos, Switzerland, 1952-63; prof. dept. physics U. Toronto, 1963-82, 84-94, prof. emeritus, 1994—; assoc. chmn. dept. physics U. Toronto, Can., 1968-73; dep. sec.-gen. World Meteorl. Orgn., Geneva, 1982-84; sec.-gen. Internat. Assn. Meteorology and Atmospheric Scis., 1995—; chmn. World Meteorol. Orgn.-EC Panels on Cloud Physics/Weather Modification, 1969-82, Italian Sci. Com. for Rain Enhancement, 1990—; vis. prof. Swiss Fed. Inst. for Tech., Zurich, Switzerland, 1974; bd. dirs. Univ. Corp.for Atmospheric Rsch., Boulder, Colo., 1974-77; mem. Sci. Coun. Space Shuttle Program, 1979-82. Author more than 220 papers in atmospheric and classical physics. Recipient Sesquicentennial medal St. Petersburg U., Russia, 1970, Patterson medal Can. Meterol. Soc., 1979, Recognition plaque Govt. of Thailand, 1986. Fellow Can. Acad. Sci./Royal Soc. Can., Royal Meteorol. Soc. (U.K.), Am. Meteorol. Soc.; mem. Can. Meteorol. Oceanic Soc., Am. Geophysics Soc., Am. Physics Soc., European Geophys. Soc., Swiss Phys. Soc., Swiss Acad. Natural Scis., Rotary. Home: 58 Olsen Dr, Toronto, ON Canada M3A 3J3 Office: U Toronto, Dept Physics, Toronto, ON Canada M5S 1A7

LISTACH, PATRICK ALAN, professional baseball player; b. Natchitoches, La., Sept. 12, 1967. Student, Ariz. State U. Baseball players Milwaukee Brewers, 1988—. Named Am. League Rookie of the Year, 1992. Office: Milw Brewers County Stadium PO Box 3099 Milwaukee WI 53201-3099

LISTER, EARLE EDWARD, animal science consultant; b. Harvey, N.B., Can., Apr. 14, 1934; s. Earle Edward and Elizabeth Hazel (Coburn) L.; m. Teresa Ann Moore, June 4, 1983. BSc in Agriculture, McGill U., Montreal, Can., 1955, MSc in Animal Nutrition, 1957; PhD in Animal Nutrition, Cornell U., 1960. Feed nutritionist Ogilvie Flour Mills, Montreal, 1960-65; rsch. scientist rsch. br. Animal Rsch. Ctr. Agriculture Can., Ottawa, 1965-74, dep. dir. rsch. br. Animal Rsch. Ctr., 1974-78, program specialist ctrl. region rsch. br., 1978-80; dir. gen. Atlantic region rsch. br. Agriculture Can., Halifax, N.S., 1980-85; dir. gen. plant health and plant products and pesticides, food prodn. and inspection br. Agriculture Can., Ottawa, 1985-87, dir. rsch. br. Animal Rsch. Ctr., 1987-91; dir. Ctr. Food and Animal Rsch., 1991-92; cons., 1992—; former mem. Ont. Agrl. Rsch. and Svc. Coms.; former chmn. Beef Rsch. Com.; invited presenter Atlantic Livestock Conf., 1968, Ea. CSAS meeting, 1969, Can. Com. Animal Nutrition, 1976, CSAS Symposium Laval U., 1974, Guelph Nutrition Conf., 1973, 74, Asst. Dep. Minister Dairy Rev. meeting, Toronto, 1985, U. Guelph ethics conf., 1991, Can. Consumers Assn., Saskatchewan, 1991. Contbr. 54 articles to profl. jours. co-chmn. United Way/Health Ptnrs. for Agriculture Can., Ottawa, 1991; former dir. N.S. Inst. Agrologists. McGill U. scholar, 1953-55; recipient Nat. Rsch. Coun. Post Grad. Spl. scholarship Cornell U., 1957-59. Mem. Am. Soc. Animal Sci., Am. Dairy Sci. Assn., Assn. Advancement Sci. in Can., Agrl. Inst. Can., Can. Soc. Animal Sci. (former dir.), Ont. Inst. Agrologists. Achievements include research in the determination of nutrient requirements of beef cows during winter pregnancy, determination of protein and energy levels and appropriate sources of nutrients fot young dairy calves for optimal growth; development of intensive feeding system for raising high quality beef from Holstein male calves. Home: 390 Hinton Ave, Ottawa, ON Canada K1Y 1B1 Office: Ctr for Food and Animal Rsch, NCC Driveway Bldg #55, Ottawa, ON Canada K1A 0C6

LISTER, HARRY JOSEPH, financial company executive, consultant; b. Teaneck, N.J., Jan. 27, 1936; s. Harry and Arline Audrey (Pinera) L.; m. Erika Anna Maria Englisch, Sept. 3, 1960; children: Harry Joseph Jr., Karen P. Lister Lawson, Leslie M. Lister Fidler, Andrea A. Lister Lytle, Michael P. BS in Fin. and Econs., Lehigh U., 1958. Security analyst Calvin Bullock, Ltd., N.Y.C., 1959-61, assoc. dir. estate planning, 1961-65, dir. estate planning, 1965-72, asst. v.p., 1969-72; v.p. N.Y. Venture Fund, Inc., N.Y.C., 1970-72; registered rep. Johnston, Lemon & Co., Inc., Washington, 1972—, dir., 1978-90, v.p., 1978-83, corp. sec., 1978-85, sr. v.p., 1984-90; v.p. Wash. Mgmt. Corp., 1972-81, corp. sec., 1978-81, exec. v.p., 1981-85, pres., 1985—, dir., 1978—; pres. JL Fin. Svcs., Inc., Washington, 1975-90; v.p. Washington Mut. Investors Fund, Inc., Washington, 1972-81, corp. sec., 1978-81, exec. v.p., 1981-85, pres., dir., 1985—; pres. The Growth Fund of Washington, Inc., 1985—, also bd. dirs.; registered prin., bd. dirs. Washington Funds Distbrs., Inc., 1985-93, pres., 1992-93; pres., trustee The Tax Exempt Fund of Md., 1986—, The Tax Exempt Fund of Va., 1986—; chmn., bd. dirs. Washington Investment Advisors, Inc., 1991—; cons. Capital Group, Inc.,

L.A., 1972—; regent Coll. for Fin. Planning, Denver, 1979-84, mem. exec. com., 1980-84, chmn. bd. regents, 1981-83; bd. dirs. Internat. Bd. Standards and Practices for Cert. Fin. Planners, 1985-86. Author: Your Guide to IRAs and 14 Other Retirement Plans, 1985. Bd. dirs. cen. Bergen chpt. ARC, Hackensack, N.J., 1968-72, chmn. exec. com., 1970-72; bd. dirs. Westwood, N.J. Planning Bd., 1969-72, vice-chmn., 1970-72; bd. dirs. Westwood N.J. Zoning Bd. Adjustment, 1970-72. Mem. Investment Co. Inst. (pension com., chmn. 1976-81, tax com., rsch. com.), Nat. Assn. Securities Dealers, Inc. (investment cos. com. 1984-87, bd. arbitrators 1987-93), Met. Club, Univ. Club. Home: Spinnaker Ct Reston VA 22091 Office: 1101 Vermont Ave NW Washington DC 20005-3521

LISTER, KEITH FENIMORE, publishing executive; b. Clio, Iowa, Aug. 29, 1917; s. W. Frank and Maude (Fenimore) L.; m. Margaret Boman, Sept. 1, 1941; children: Janet, Priscilla. Student, Drake U., 1936-41. Pres. Lister Investment Co., San Diego, 1955-61, Southcoast Capital Co., San Diego, 1961-65, City Bank San Diego, 1965-69; pub. San Diego Daily Transcript, 1972-94. Mem. San Diego Yacht Club, Univ. Club. Presbyterian. Avocation: sailing.

LISTER, THOMAS MOSIE, composer, lyricist, publishing company executive, minister; b. Empire, Ga., Sept. 8, 1921; s. Willis Waller and Orena Pearl (Holl) L.; m. Jewel Wylene Whitten, June 2, 1946; children—Brenda (Mrs. James Milton Vann), Barbara (Mrs. David Miller Williams). Attended, Rennsalaer Poly. Inst., 1944-45, Middle Ga. Coll., 1945-46, U. South Fla., 1968; studied privately at, Tampa U., 1958-63. Founder, pres. Mosie Lister Publs., Atlanta, 1952-56, Tampa, 1956—; affiliate for performance and synchronization rights SESAC, Inc., 1955—; affiliate Lillenas Pub. Co., Kansas City, Mo., 1969—; also cons. and dir.; ordained to ministry Baptist Ch., 1975; choral dir. Composer, lyricist numerous gospel songs, 1940—; singer, Tampa, Fla., and Atlanta, 1941, 46-47; Compiler song. collections, hymnbooks, and others; arranger religious music for choral groups and ensembles; songs include I'm Feeling Fine, Where No One Stands Alone, His Hand in Mine; contbg. arranger profl. singing groups. Served with USNR, 1942-45. Named Bapt. Layman of Year for Tampa, 1971; inducted into Gospel Hall of Fame, 1976; recipient Humanist award Sesac, Inc., 1976; Mosie Lister Day named in his honor Tampa, 1974. Mem. Gospel Music Assn. (dir. 1970-71), Fla. Bapt. Ministers of Music Assn. (hon. life). Democrat. Address: 17008 Winners Cir Odessa FL 33556-1828

LISTERUD, MARK BOYD, retired surgeon; b. Wolf Point, Mont., Nov. 19, 1924; s. Morris B. and Grace (Montgomery) L.; m. Sarah C. Mooney, May 26, 1954; children: John, Mathew, Ann, Mark, Sarah, Richard. BA magna cum laude, U. Minn., 1949, BS, 1950, MB, 1952, MD, 1953. Diplomate Am. Bd. Surgery. Intern King County Hosp., Seattle, 1952-53; resident in surgery U. Wash., Seattle, 1953-57; practice medicine specializing in surgery Wolf Point, 1958-93; mem. admission com. U. Wash. Med. Sch., Seattle, 1983-88; instr. Dept. Rural and Community Health, U. N.D. Med. Sch., 1991. Contbr. articles to med. jours. Mem. Mont. State Health Coordinating Council, 1983, chmn. 1986—; bd. dirs. Blue Shield, Mont., 1985-87. Served with USN, 1943-46. Fellow Am. Coll. Surgeons, Royal Soc. Medicine; mem. N.E. Mont. Med. Soc. (pres.), Mont. Med. Assn. (pres. 1968-69), AMA (alt. del., del. 1970-84). Clubs: Montana, Elks. Avocations: fishing, hunting. Home: Rodeo Rd Wolf Point MT 59201 Office: 100 Main St Wolf Point MT 59201-1530

LISTGARTEN, MAX ALBERT, periodontics educator; b. Paris, May 14, 1935; came to U.S., 1968; s. Samuel and Etla (Weber) L.; m. Eileen Anne Gregory, July 3, 1963; children: Karen, Sheralyn, Michael. DDS, U. Toronto, 1959; cert. in periodontics, Harvard U., 1963; MA (hon.), U. Pa., 1971; PhD (hon.), U. Athens, 1993. Research assoc. Harvard U., Boston, 1963-64; asst. prof. periodontics U. Toronto, Can., 1964-67, assoc. prof., 1967-68; assoc. prof. U. Pa., Phila., 1968-71, prof., 1971—; vis. prof. U. Gothenburg, Sweden, 1976-77, U. Berne, 1988-89; cons. Nat. Inst. Dental Research, Bethesda, Md., 1979-88, FDA, Rockville, Md., 1992—; cons. in field. Author textbooks and numerous articles on various aspects of periodontal anatomy, microbiology, histopathology, and diagnosis. Recipient Periodontology award William J. Gies Found., 1981; named Disting. Alumnus, Harvard U., 1986, U. Pa., 1994. Fellow AAAS, Am. Acad. Periodontology (Clin. Rsch. award 1987); mem. ADA, Am. Assn. for Dental Rsch. (pres. 1991-92), Internat. Assn. Dental Rsch. (award for basic rsch. in periodontology 1973). Jewish. Avocations: swimming, skiing, hiking, photography. Office: U Penn-School of Dental Medicine Dept of Periodontics 4001 Spruce St Philadelphia PA 19104-4118

LISTON, MARY FRANCES, retired nursing educator; b. N.Y.C., Dec. 17, 1920; d. Michael Joseph and Ellen Theresa (Shaughnessy) L. BS, Coll. Mt. St. Vincent, 1944; MS, Catholic U. Am., 1945; EdD, Columbia, 1962; HHD (hon.), Allentown Coll., 1987. Dir. psychiat. nursing and edn. Nat. League for Nursing, N.Y.C., 1958-66; prof. Sch. Nursing, Cath. U. Am., Washington, 1966-78; dean Sch. Nursing, Cath. U. Am., 1966-73; prof. Marywood Coll., 1984-87; spl. assignment Imperial Med. Center, Tehran, Iran, 1975-78; dep. dir. for program affairs Nat. League for Nursing, N.Y.C., 1978-84. Mem. Sigma Theta Tau. Home: 182 Garth Rd Scarsdale NY 10583-3863

LISTROM, LINDA L., lawyer; b. Topeka, Kans., Mar. 17, 1952. BA magna cum laude, U. Houston, 1974; JD, Harvard U., 1977. Bar: Ill. 1977. Ptnr. Jenner & Block, Chgo. Bd. dirs. Cook County Court Watching Project, Inc., 1983-92. Mem. ABA. Office: Jenner & Block 1 E Ibm Plz Chicago IL 60611*

LISZT, HOWARD PAUL, advertising executive; b. Mpls., Aug. 12, 1946; s. Melvin Sherman and Evalyn (Chapman) Schwartz; m. Roberta Jean Bregman, Feb. 14, 1970; children: Andrew Charles, Daniel Mark. BA, U. Minn., 1968, MBA, 1970. From market rsch. mgr. to sr. product mgr. Green Giant Co., Mpls., 1970-76; from. account exec. to exec. v.p., gen. mgr. Campbell-Mithun, Mpls., 1976-88, pres., chief oper. officer, 1988-94, CEO, 1995—; lectr. Augsburg Coll., Mpls., 1981-86. Bd. dirs. St. Paul Chamber Orch., 1984—, Minn. Children's Mus., St. Paul, 1979-86, Greater Mpls. C. of C., 1988-94, Blake Schs. 1990—, Boys and Girls Club 1996—. Mem. Am. Mktg. Assn., Am. Assn. Advt. Agys. (mem. client svc. com.), Oakridge Club. Jewish. Avocations: golfing, traveling, theater. Office: Campbell-Mithun-Esty Advt 222 S 9th St Minneapolis MN 55402-3389

LITAN, ROBERT ELI, lawyer, economist; b. Wichita, Kans., May 16, 1950; s. David and Shirley Hermine (Krischer) L.; BS in Econs. (Class of 1946 award, W. Gordon award 1972, Albert A. Berg award 1971, 72), Wharton Sch., U. Pa., 1972; MPhil in Econs., Yale U., 1976, JD (Felix S. Cohen award 1976), 1977, PhD in Econs., Yale U., 1987. Bar: D.C. 1980. m. Avivah D. Swirsky, Aug. 12, 1980. Res. asst. Brookings Instn., 1972-73; instr., then lectr. econs. Yale U., 1975-75; energy cons. Nat. Acad. Scis., 1975-77; regulation and energy specialist President's Council Econ. Advs., 1977-79; assoc. Arnold & Porter, Washington, 1979-82, assoc., then ptnr. and counsel, Powell, Goldstein, Frazer & Murphy, Washington, 1982-90; sr. fellow Brookings Instn., Washington, 1984-92; dir. Ctr. for Econ. Progress, Brookings Inst., 1987-93; dep. asst. atty. gen. U.S. Dept. Justice, 1993-95, assoc. dir. Office of Mgmt. and Budget, 1995-96; dir. econ. studies Brookings Inst., 1996—; cons. Inst. Liberty and Democracy, Lima, Peru, 1985-88; visiting lectr., Yale U. Law Sch., 1985-86; mem. Presdl. Congl. Commn. on Causes of the Savs. and Loan Crisis, 1991-92. Recipient Silver medal Royal Soc. Arts, 1972; Thouron fellow, Eng., 1972. Mem. ABA, Am. Econs. Assn. Democrat. Author or co-author: Energy Modeling for an Uncertain Future, 1978; Reforming Federal Regulation, 1983; Saving Free Trade: A Pragmatic Approach, 1986, What Should Banks Do?, 1987, Liability: Perspectives and Policy, 1988, American Living Standards: Threats and Challenges, 1988, Blueprint for Restructuring America's Financial Institutions, 1989, Banking Industry in Turmoil, 1990, The Revolution in U.S. Finance, 1991, The Liability Maze, 1991, The Revolution in U.S. Finance, 1991, Down in the Dumps: Adminstration of the Unfair Trade Laws, 1991, The Future of American Banking, 1992, Growth with Equity, 1993, Assessing Bank Reform, 1993, Verdict, 1993, Financial Regulation in a Global Economy, 1994, Footing the Bill for Superfund Cleanups, 1995; contbr. articles to profl. publs. Home: 3 Golden Crest Ct Rockville MD 20854-2982 Office: US Office Mgmt and Budget 246 Old Exec Office Bldg Washington DC 20503

LITCHFIELD, ROBERT LATTA, JR., lawyer; b. Tucson, Apr. 6, 1949; s. Robert Latta Sr. and Mary Wyatt (Palmer) L.; m. Suzanne Kay Zerby, Dec. 29, 1971; children: Melissa Marie, Robert Latta III, Paul Andrew, James Ryan. BS, West Point Acad., 1971; MA, Miami U., 1977; JD, McGeorge Sch. Law, 1980. Bar: Oreg. 1980, U.S. Dist. Ct. Oreg. 1980, Calif. 1981, U.S. Dist. Ct. (ea. dist.) Calif. 1985. Assoc. Hershner, Hunter, Miller, Moulton & Andrews, Eugene, Oreg., 1980-83; pvt. practice Eugene, 1983-85; assoc. Felderstein, Rosenberg & McManns, Sacramento, 1985-86, Felderstein, Rosenberg, McManns, Diepenbrock, Wulff, et al., Sacramento, 1986-87; pvt. practice Grass Valley, Calif., 1987—; adv. bd. Truckee River Bank, Grass Valley, 1992-94; radio talk show host KNCO Radio, Grass Valley, 1991-92. Author: The Man Who Had No Wings, 1977. Mem. adv. bd. Salvation Army, Grass Valley, 1991-94; team leader marriage encounter group Westminster Presbyn. Ch., Eugene, 1984—, deacon and elder, 1983-85; candidate Nev. County Superior Ct. Judge, 1996. Capt. USAF, 1971-77. Named Atty. of Yr., Consumer Bus. Rev., 1995. Mem. Nevada County Bar Assn., Tea Bag Tax Revolt (founder, chmn. 1990-94), Make a Difference, Inc. (bd. dirs. 1992-94), Angelian Soc. (founder, chmn. 1992—), Nevada County Gideons (pres. 1995). Republican. Avocations: scuba diving, writing, woodworking, Christian family enrichment. Office: 113 Presley Way Ste 9 Grass Valley CA 95945-5847

LITCHFORD, GEORGE B., aeronautical engineer; b. Long Beach, Calif., Aug. 12, 1918. BA, Reed Coll., 1941. Fellow IEEE (past chmn. awards com. K.I. sect., Pioneer award AES-S 1974, Lamme medal 1981, AIAA (Wright Bros. medal/lectureship 1978); mem. Aerospace and Electronic Sys. Soc. Office: Litchstreet Co 32 Cherrylawn Ln Northport NY 11768*

LITES, JAMES, professional hockey team executive; b. Pentwater, Mich.; m. Denise Lites; children: Brooke, Samuel. BA, U. Mich., 1975; JD, Wayne State U., 1978. Exec. v.p. Detroit Red Wings, 1982-93; v.p. Little Caesar's Internat., Inc.; president Dallas Stars, 1993—; team rep. bd. govs. NHL. Office: Dallas Stars 211 Cowboys Pky Irving TX 75063*

LITFIN, RICHARD ALBERT, retired news organization executive; b. The Dalles, Oreg., Sept. 9, 1918; s. Bernard R. and Alberta (Knappenberger) L.; m. Marie Foley, June 28, 1944; children: Maria Eschen, Mercedes Zingmark, Regina Dibble, Angela Provenzale, Thomas, Anthony. B.J., U. Mo., 1940. Bur. mgr. U.P.I., Olympia, Wash., 1946-47, Pacific Northwest bus. rep., 1946-52, San Francisco rep., 1953-54; bus. mgr. U.P.I. Pacific div., 1954-56, div. mgr., 1956-75, v.p. western region, 1976-79, sr. v.p., 1980-83; Former owner The Dalles, Oreg. Daily Chronicle. Bd. fellows U. Santa Clara. Midshipman Northwestern U., 1940, commd. ensign USNR, 1941, assigned Battleship Idaho, 1941, after flight tng., assigned Fighting 12, U.S.S. Saratoga, 1943, PTO; inactive status, 1946—. Decorated D.F.C., Air Medal with stars. Mem. SAR, Sigma Delta Chi, Alpha Delta Sigma, Sigma Alpha Epsilon. Republican. Roman Catholic. Home: 1790 Oak Ave Menlo Park CA 94025-5863

LITHERLAND, ALBERT EDWARD, physics educator; b. Wallasey, Eng., Mar. 12, 1928; emigrated to Can., 1953, naturalized, 1964; s. Albert and Ethel (Clement) L.; m. Anne Allen, May 12, 1956; children: Jane Elizabeth, Rosamund Mary. B.Sc., U. Liverpool, Eng., 1949, Ph.D., 1955. Rutherford scholar Atomic Energy of Can., Chalk River, Ont., 1953-55; sci. officer Atomic Energy of Can., 1955-66; prof. physics U. Toronto, 1966-79, Univ. prof., 1979-93, prof. emeritus, 1993—. Contbr. articles to profl. jours. Recipient Rutherford medal Inst. Physics, London, 1974, Silver medal for accelerator-based dating techniques Jour. Applied Radiation and Isotopes, 1980; Guggenheim fellow, 1986-87; recipient Henry Marshall Tory medal Royal Society of Canada1993. Fellow Royal Soc. Can. (Henry Marshall Tory medal 1993), Royal Soc. London, AAAS, Am. Phys. Soc.; mem. Can. Assn. Physicists (Gold medal for achievement in physics 1971). Home: 3 Hawthorn Gardens, Toronto, ON Canada M4W 1P4 Office: 60 Saint George St, Toronto, ON Canada M5S 1A7

LITHGOW, JOHN ARTHUR, actor, director; b. Rochester, N.Y., Oct. 19, 1945; s. Arthur and Sarah L.; m. Jean Taynton, Sept. 10, 1966 (div.); 1 child, Ian; m. Mary Yeager, 1981; children: Phoebe, Nathan. Grad. magna cum laude, Harvard U., 1967; postgrad., London Acad. Music and Dramatic Art, 1967-69. Printmaker, founder Lithgow Graphics. Appeared in plays: A Midsummer Night's Dream, 1953, The Prodigal Daughter, 1973, Patience, Beggar's Opera, La Perichole, Iolanthe, 1965, Pygmalion, Of Mice and Men, Troilus and Cressida, 1969-70, Roar of the Greasepaint, Hadrian VII, The Magistrate, 1970, The Changing Room, What Price Glory, Trelawny of the Wells, 1972; Broadway plays: The Changing Room, 1973, My Fat Friend, 1974, Beyond Therapy, 1982, Requiem For A Heavyweight, 1985, The Front Page, 1986, M. Butterfly, 1988; stock and regional theatre, 15 Shakespearean roles at Gt. Lakes Shakespeare Festival, Ohio, summers 1963-64; dir. plays: As You Like It, 1968, Much Ado About Nothing, 1969, The Way of the World, 1970, The Magistrate, Barefoot in the Park, 1970, Abduction from the Seraglio, 1970, Beaux' Stratagem, 1972, A Pagan Place, 1973; appeared in films: Dealing, 1972, Obsession, 1976, All That Jazz, 1979, Rich Kids, 1979, Mom, the Wolfman and Me, 1980, Blow Out, 1981, Kaufman at Large, 1981, The World According to Garp, 1982 (Acad. award nomination), The Twilight Zone, 1983, Terms of Endearment, 1983 (Acad. award nomination), Footloose, 1984, 2010, 1984, The Glitter Dome, 1984, The Adventures of Buckaroo Banzai: Across The 8th Dimension, 1984, Santa Claus, The Movie, 1985, Manhattan Project, 1986, Harry and the Hendersons, 1987, Distant Thunder, 1988, Memphis Belle, 1990; Out Cold, 1989, Ricochet, 1991, At Play in the Fields of the Lord, 1991, Raising Cain,1992, Cliffhanger, 1993, The Pelican Brief, 1993, A Good Man in Africa, 1994, Princess Caraboo, 1994, Silent Fall, 1994; appeared in TV show The Country Girl, 1974; TV film appearances include Not in Front of the Children, 1982, The Day After, 1983, Resting Place, 1986, Baby Girl Scott, 1987, Amazing Stories (Emmy award 1987), Mesmerized, The Traveling Man, The Last Elephant, 1990, The Boys, 1991, The Wrong Man, 1993, Love, Cheat and Steal, 1993, World War II: When Lions Roared, 1994; writer, producer, actor radio show Under the Gun, Sta. WBAI-FM, N.Y.C., 1972-73. Office: Creative Artists Agy 9830 Wilshire Blvd Beverly Hills CA 90212-1804*

LITKE, ARTHUR LUDWIG, business executive; b. Torrington, Conn., Apr. 4, 1922; s. Gustav and Julia (Weiman) L.; m. Stephanie Eleanore Lojewski, June 9, 1951; children: Arthur Lawrence, Suzanne Elizabeth. B.S. in Econs, Trinity Coll., 1944; M.B.A., U. Pa., 1947; grad., Advanced Mgmt. Program, Harvard U., 1961. CPA, N.C., C.G.F.M. With GAO, 1946-64, asso. dir. civil accounting and auditing div., 1963-64; chief accountant, chief Office Accounting and Fin., FPC (FERC), 1964-73; mem. Fin. Acctg. Standards Bd., 1973-78; asso. adminstr. econ. and regulatory adminstrn. Dept. Energy, Washington, 1978; cons. to comptroller gen. of U.S. GAO, 1978-81, 92—; sr. v.p. Zinder Assocs., 1981-93; v.p. and sec. Zinder Cos., 1985-89, sec., treas., 1990-92, vice chmn., 1993—; mem. teaching staff econs. dept. Cath. U. Am., 1966-67; professorial lectr. acctg. George Washington U., 1967-73; adj. prof. acctg. Georgetown U., 1981-83; pres. Internat. Consortium on Govtl. Fin. Mgmt., 1981-84. Contbr. articles to profl. jours. Bd. dirs. Potomac Swimming and Recreation Assn., 1958-72, McLean Citizens Assn., 1990—; adv. bd. Conn. State Opera Assn., 1973-78. Recipient Meritorious Service award GAO, 1959; Meritorious Service award FPC, 1969; Disting. Service award, 1973; Disting. Leadership award Assn. Govt. Accts., 1969; Robert W. King Meml. gold medal, 1975. Mem. AICPA (com. on auditing procedure 1967-70, ethics com. 1971-73), D.C. Inst. CPAs, Assn. Govt. Accts. (nat. pres. 1972-73, bd. dirs. Washington chpt. 1969-72), Am. Arbitration Assn., Am. Accts. Assn., World Affairs Coun., Rotary, Pi Kappa Alpha. Lutheran (council). Home: 1422 Lady Bird Dr Mc Lean VA 22101-3227 Office: 1828 L St NW Washington DC 20036-5118

LITKE, DONALD PAUL, business executive, retired military officer; b. Denver, Nov. 7, 1934; s. Walter Monroe and Alice Vivian (Fowler) L.; m. Myrna Kay McDonald, July 1, 1956; children—Bradley, Susan, Lisa. B.S. in Econs., Colo. A&M U., 1956; MS in Internat. Affairs, George Washington U., 1966. Ops. and staff positions U.S. Air Force, 1956-79; vice comdr. Oklahoma City Air Logistics Ctr., 1979-81; dep. dir. logistics and security assistance U.S. European Command, Stuttgart, Germany, 1981-83; comdr. U.S. Logistics Group, Ankara, Turkey, 1983-85; dep. dir. Def. Logistics Agy., Alexandria, VA., 1985-86; pres. Bus. Devel. Internat., Alexandria and Niceville, Fla., 1986—. Contbr. articles to profl. jours. Mem. Air Force Assn. (Middle Mgr. of Yr. 1970, award of excellence 1977), Alpha Tau Omega. Methodist. Avocations: automobile restoration; racquet sports. Home and Office: 2422 Edgewater Dr Niceville FL 32578-2305

LITMAN, BERNARD, electrical engineer, consultant; b. N.Y.C., Oct. 26, 1920; s. Nathan and Gussie (Friedman) L.; m. Ellen Ann Kaufman, Feb. 27, 1949; children—Barbara, Richard. B.S. in Elec. Engring, Columbia U., 1941, Ph.D., 1949; M.S., U. Pitts., 1943. Design engr. energy equipment Westinghouse Electric Co., Pitts., 1941-47; with AMBAC Industries div. United Tech. Corp., Garden City, N.Y., 1949-83; tech. dir. guidance equipment Atlas inter-continental missile AMBAC Industries div. United Tech. Corp., 1962-63, chief engr. systems devel. and research, 1964-83; dir. advanced tech. Gull Electronics Systems Div., Parker Hannifin Corp., 1983-93; tech. cons., 1994—; Westinghouse lectr. U. Pitts., 1944; lectr. Adelphi U., Garden City. Co-author: Gyroscopics, 1961. William Petit Trobridge fellow, 1948. Asso. fellow Am. Inst. Aeros. and Astronautics (Achievement award L.I. sect. 1966); mem. IEEE (sr.), Am. Automatic Control Council, N.Y.-N.J. Trail Conf., Sigma Xi. Jewish. Patentee rotary amplifiers, axial motors, gravity pendulums, inductors, 2 axis accellerometers, ballistic missile safety devices, gyro attenuators, thrust retainers. Home: 228 Wagon Wheel Ln Columbus NJ 08022-1119

LITMAN, HARRY PETER, lawyer, educator; b. Pitts., May 4, 1958; s. S. David and Roslyn M. (Margolis) L. BA, Harvard U., 1981; JD, U. Calif., Berkeley, 1986. Bar: Calif. 1987, U.S. Ct. Appeals (D.C. cir.) 1987, Pa. 1988, D.C. 1989, U.S. Ct. Appeals (9th cir.) 1990, U.S. Dist. Ct. (so. dist.) Tex. 1992, U.S. Supreme Ct. 1992, U.S. Dist. Ct. (ea. and we. dists.) Pa. 1993, U.S. Ct. Appeals (7th cir.) 1994. Prodn. asst. feature films N.Y.C., 1980-82; newsman, clk. baseball desk AP, N.Y.C., 1982-83; sports reporter AP, 1983-86; law clk. to Hon. Abner J. Mikva U.S. Ct. Appeals (D.C. cir.), 1986-87; law clk. to Hon. Thurgood Marshall U.S. Supreme Ct., Washington, 1987-88, law clk. to Hon. Anthony M. Kennedy, 1989; asst. U.S. atty., dep. chief appellate sect. Dept. Justice, San Francisco, 1990-92; dep. assoc. atty. gen. Dept. Justice, Washington, 1992-93, dep. asst. atty. gen., 1993—; adj. prof. Boalt Hall Sch. Law U. Calif., Berkeley, 1990-92, Georgetown U. Law Ctr., 1996—. Editor-in-chief Calif. Law Rev., Vol. 73; author various articles. Presdl. scholar, 1976. Mem. Pa. Bar Assn., State Bar Calif., D.C. Bar, Order of Coif. Office: Dept of Justice 10th & Constitution Ave NW Washington DC 20530-0001

LITMAN, RAYMOND STEPHEN, financial services consultant; b. Kingston, Pa., Nov. 2, 1936; s. Stephen Vincent and Mary Helen (Wisnewski) L.; m. Ann Mae Kosik, Nov. 24, 1960; children: Raymond Stephen II, A. Christine. BS in Commerce, Wilkes Coll., 1961. Credit mgr. Sears Roebuck & Co., eastern div., 1961-66; banking officer Phila. Nat. Bank, 1966-69; dir. Decision Dynamics Corp., Marlton, N.J., 1969-71; asst. v.p. Bankers Trust Co., N.Y.C., 1971-75; sr. banking officer Girard Bank, Phila., 1975-77; pres. World Wide Cons. Svcs., Plymouth Meeting, Pa., 1977-78; asso. dir. bank card divsn. Am. Bankers Assn., 1978-80; mng. dir. Chemical Bank, N.Y.C., 1981-92, pres., chief oper. officer, ECC Mgmt. Svcs. Inc., King of Prussia, Pa., 1992-93; pres., CEO Litman Assocs., Inc. Fin. Svcs. Cons.; mem. adv. coun. Credit Rsch Ctr. Purdue U. Served with USN, 1954-57; ETO. Mem. Am. Bankers Assn. (mem. bank card div. exec. com.), Govt. Rels. Coun. and Banking Leadership, Internat. Assn. Credit Card Investigators (pres. Del. Valley chpt. 1976-77, dir. nat. chpt. 1976-77, life mem.), Montgomery County Police Chiefs Assn., Police Chiefs Assn. Southeast Pa., Plymouth Meeting Hist. Soc., VFW, Am. Legion, Frat. Order of Police. Republican. Roman Catholic. Home: 2057 Sierra Rd Plymouth Meeting PA 19462-1826

LITMAN, ROBERT BARRY, physician, author, television and radio commentator; b. Phila., Nov. 17, 1947; s. Benjamin Norman and Bette Etta (Saunders) L.; m. Niki Thomas, Apr. 21, 1985; children: Riva Belle, Nadya Beth, Caila Tess, Benjamin David. BS, Yale U., 1967, MD, 1970, MS in Chemistry, 1972, MPhil in Anatomy, 1972, postgrad. (Life Ins. Med. Rsch. Fund fellow) Yale U., Univ. Coll. Hosp., U. London, 1969-70; Am. Cancer Soc. postdoctoral rsch. fellow Yale U., 1970-73. Diplomate Am. Bd. Family Practice. Resident in gen. surgery Bryn Mawr (Pa.) Hosp., 1973-74; USPHS fellow Yale U. Sch. Medicine, 1974-75; pvt. practice medicine and surgery, Ogdensburg, N.Y., 1977-93, San Ramon, Calif., 1993—; mem. med. staff A. Barton Hepburn Hosp., 1977-93, John Muir Med. Ctr., 1993—, San Ramon (Calif.) Regional Med. Ctr., 1993—, also chmn. med. edn.; commentator Family Medicine Stas. WWNY-TV and WTNY-Radio, TCI Cablevision, Contra Costa T.V.; clin. preceptor dept. family medicine State Univ. Health Sci. Ctr., Syracuse, 1978—. Author: Wynnefield and Limer, 1983, The Treblinka Virus, 1991, Allergy Shots, 1993; contbr. articles to numerous sci. publs. Pres. Am. Heart Assn. No. N.Y. chpt., 1980-84. Fellow Am. Coll. Allergy, Asthma, and Immunology, Am. Acad. Family Physicians; mem. AMA (Physicians Recognition award 1970—), Calif. State Med. Assn., Alameda-Contra Costa County Med. Assn., Joint Coun. Allergy and Immunology, Nat. Assn. Physician Broadcasters (charter), Acad. Radio and TV Health Communicators, Book and Snake Soc., Gibbs Soc. of Yale U. (founder), Sigma Xi, Nu Sigma Nu, Alpha Chi Sigma. Home and Office: PO Box 1857 San Ramon CA 94583-6857

LITMAN, ROSLYN MARGOLIS, lawyer, educator; b. N.Y.C., Sept. 30, 1928; d. Harry and Dorothy (Perlow) Margolis; m. S. David Litman, Nov. 22, 1950; children: Jessica, Hannah, Harry. B.A., U. Pitts., 1949, J.D., 1952. Bar: Pa. 1952. Practiced in Pitts., 1952—; partner firm Litman, Litman, Harris & Brown, P.C., 1952—; adj. prof. U. Pitts. Law Sch., 1958—; permanent del. Conf. U.S. Circuit Ct. Appeals for 3d Circuit; past chair dist. adv. group U.S. Dist. Ct. (we. dist.) Pa., 1991-94, mem. steering com. for dist. adv. group, 1991—; chmn. Pitts. Pub. Parking Authority, 1970-74; mem. curriculum com. Pa. Bar Inst., 1986—, bd. dirs., 1972-82. Recipient Roscoe Pound Found. award for Excellence in Tchg. Child Advocacy, 1996. Mem. ABA (del., litigation sect., anti-trust health care com.), ACLU (nat. bd. dirs.), Pa. Bar Assn. (bd. govs. 1976-79), Allegheny County Bar Assn. (bd. govs. 1972-74, pres. 1975), Allegheny County Acad. Trial Lawyers (charter), United Jewish Fedn. (cmty. rels. com.). Home: 5023 Frew Ave Pittsburgh PA 15213 Office: 3600 One Oxford Centre Pittsburgh PA 15219

LITOW, JOEL DAVID, strategic planning administrator; b. N.Y.C., Feb. 10, 1947; s. Herbert and Jean (Zaller) L.; m. Lorraine Aziz; children: Jason, Jennifer. BChemE, CCNY, 1968; MBA, Rutgers U., 1973. Chem. engr. Airco, N.Y.C., 1966-69, fin. analyst, 1969-73; mgr. fin. analysis Bali Co., N.J., 1973-75; mgr. cost acctg. M&T Chems. Inc., Rahway, N.J., 1976-77, dir. control devel., 1978-79, controller, 1979-86, v.p. fin., controller, 1986-90; v.p. fin. EIF Atochem N.A., 1990-93, v.p. strategic planning, 1994—. Avocations: tennis, basketball, softball.

LITOW, MERRILL, advertising executive; b. Chgo., Sept. 2, 1927; s. Abraham B. and Rose (Postelnek) L.; m. Myrna Hoffman, Feb. 23, 1952; children: Beth, Neal. BA, U. Ill. Owner, founder Barlit Prods. Inc., Chgo., 1951-59, Bentley, Barnes & Lynn Inc., Chgo., 1957—. Work with Child Abuse Prevention Svcs., 1987—, Arthritis Found. Cpl.T5 U.S. Army, 1946-47. Jewish. Home: 707 County Line Rd Highland Park IL 60035-5110

LITROWNIK, ALAN JAY, psychologist, educator; b. Los Angeles, June 25, 1945; s. Irving and Mildred Mae (Rosin) L.; m. Hollis Merle, Aug. 20, 1967; children: Allison Brook, Jordan Michael. BA, UCLA, 1967; MA, U. Ill., Champaign-Urbana, 1969, PhD, 1971. Psychologist Ill. Dept. Mental Health, Decatur, 1970-71; asst. prof. psychology San Diego State U., 1971-75, assoc. prof., 1975-78, prof., 1978—, chmn. dept. psychology, 1981-87, assoc. dean for curriculum and acad. planning, North County Campus, 1987-88; co-dir. Ctr. for Behavioral and Community Health Studies, San Diego, 1989—; cons. San Diego County Dept. Edn. Program Evaluation, 1975-81; project dir. Self-Concept and Self-Regulatory Processes in Developmentally Disabled Children and Adolescents, 1975-78; co-dir. Child Abuse Interdisciplinary Tng. Program, 1987—; project dir. tobacco use prevention in youth orgns., 1989-92. Research, publs. in field. Contbr. chpts. to books. Mem. San Diego County Juvenile Justice Commn., 1989-92; mem. juvenile systems adv. group San Diego County Bd. Suprs., 1989-91. Grantee U.S. Office Edn., 1975-78, 80-81, Nat. Ctr. Child Abuse, 1987—, Calif. Dept. Health, 1989-92, U. Calif. Tobacco-Related Disease Rsch. Program, 1992-94. Office: Ctr Behavioral/Comm Health Studies 9245 Sky Park Ct San Diego CA 92123-4311

LITSCHGI, A. BYRNE, lawyer; b. Charleston, S.C., Dec. 31, 1920; s. Albert William and Mary Catherine (Byrne) L.; m. Mary Elaine Herring, Sept. 13, 1952. B.B.A., U. Fla., 1941; J.D., Harvard U., 1948. Bar: Fla. 1948, D.C. 1950. Atty. Office Gen. Counsel, Treasury Dept., Washington, 1949-52; legis. asst. to U.S. senator, 1952; mem. firm Hedrick & Lane, Washington, 1953-60, Coles, Himes & Litschgi, Tampa, Fla., 1960-62, Shackleford, Farrior, Stallings & Evans, 1962-87, Dykema Gossett, Tampa, Fla., 1988-92; chmn. SL Industries, Inc., 1976-92; mem. firm Holland & Knight, Tampa, 1992—; incorporator, dir. Communications Satellite Corp., 1962-64; mem. Fla. Jud. Council, 1965-68, U.S. Internal Revenue Commn. Adv. Group, 1967-68. Mem. Harvard Law Sch. Assn. (nat. council 1956-61), ABA (chmn. excise and miscellaneous tax com. tax sect. 1956-59), Fla. Bar, Bar Assn. D.C. Home: PO Box 1288 Tampa FL 33601-1288 Office: Holland & Knight PO Box 1288 Tampa FL 33601-1288

LITSCHGI, RICHARD JOHN, computer manufacturing company executive; b. St. Louis, July 1, 1937; s. William J. and Mary F. (Eynatten) L.; m. Christine Ewert, Aug. 21, 1968. BS, St. Louis U., 1959; MS, U. Okla., 1964. Cert. meteorology St. Louis U./USAF. Supr., Bellcomm, Inc., Washington, 1964-67; mgr. Computer Scis., Brussels, 1967-68, Intranet Computing Co., L.A., 1968-71, Xerox Corp., El Segundo, Calif., 1971-76; dir. Honeywell, Inc., L.A., 1976-80, v.p., Phoenix, 1980-85, v.p. Mpls., 1985-87, v.p. Honeywell Bull Inc., 1987-88, v.p. Bull HN Inc., Boston, 1988-89; v.p. Groupe Bull, Boston and Paris, 1990-93; v.p. Vanguard Automation Inc., Tucson, 1993-94; ret., 1994. Bd. dirs. Arizonians for Cultural Devel., 1981-85; trustee Phoenix Art Mus., 1982-85 . Served to capt. USAF, 1959-62. Democrat. Home: 24 Tupelo Rd Falmouth MA 02540-1945

LITSTER, JAMES DAVID, physics educator, dean; b. Toronto, Ont., Can., June 19, 1938; s. James Creighton and Gladys May (Byers) L.; m. Cheryl Ella Schmidt, June 26, 1965; children: Robin Joyce, Heather Claire. B Engring., McMaster U., Hamilton, Ont., 1961; PhD, MIT, 1965. Instr. physics MIT, Cambridge, Mass., 1965-66, asst. prof. physics, 1966-71, assoc. prof. physics, 1971-75, prof. physics, 1975—, head div. atomic, condensed matter and plasma physics, dept. physics, 1979-83, dir. Ctr. for Materials Sci. and Engring., 1983-88, dir. Francis Bitter Nat. Magnet Lab., 1988-92, interim assoc. provost, v.p. for rsch., 1991, v.p., dean for rsch., 1991—; mem. rsch. staff Thomas J. Watson Rsch. Ctr. IBM, 1969, cons. to liquid crystal group Thomas J. Watson Rsch. Ctr., 1969-70; vis. prof. U. Paris, 1971-72; lectr. in physics Harvard Med. Sch., 1974-75; mem. ad hoc oversight com. Solid State Chemistry, NSF, 1977-78; cons. N.Y. State Edn. Dept., 1978; vis. scientist Risø Nat. Lab., Denmark, 1978; mem. condensed matter scis. subcom. NSF, 1978-81, materials rsch. adv. com., 1978-81, chmn., 1980-81; mem. solid state scis. panel NRC, 1986-95, chmn., 1991-92. Regional editor Molecular Crystals and Liquid Crystals, 1986-93. Recipient Gold medal Assn. Profl. Engrs. Ont., 1961, Chancellor's Gold medal McMaster U., 1961, Irving Langmuir Chem. Physics prize Am. Chemical Soc., 1993; Kennecott Copper Co. fellow, 1964-65, John Simon Guggenheim Meml. fellow, 1971-72. Fellow AAAS, Am. Phys. Soc., Am. Acad. Arts and Scis. Office: MIT 77 Massachusetts Ave Rm 3-240 Cambridge MA 02139-4301

LITT, IRIS FIGARSKY, pediatrics educator; b. N.Y.C., Dec. 25, 1940; d. Jacob and Bertha (Berson) Figarsky; m. Victor C. Vaughan, June 14, 1987; children from previous marriage: William M., Robert B. AB, Cornell U., 1961; MD, SUNY, Bklyn., 1965. Diplomate Am. Bd. Pediatrics (bd. dirs. 1989-94), sub-specialty bd. cert. in adolescent medicine. Intern, then resident in pediat. N.Y. Hosp., N.Y.C., 1965-68; assoc. prof. pediat. Stanford U. Sch. Medicine, Palo Alto, Calif., 1982-87, prof., 1987—, dir. divsn. adolescent medicine, 1976—, dir. Inst. for Rsch. on Women and Gender, 1990—; bd. dirs. Youth Law Ctr., San Francisco. Editor Jour. Adolescent Health. Mem. Soc. for Adolescent Medicine (charter), Am. Acad. Pediatrics (award sect. on adolescent health), Western Soc. Pediatric Rsch., Soc. Pediatric Rsch., Am. Pediatric Soc., Inst. of Medicine/NAS. Office: 750 Welch Rd Ste 325 Palo Alto CA 94304

LITT, MITCHELL, chemical engineer, educator, bioengineer; b. Bklyn., Oct. 11, 1932; s. Saul and Mollie (Steinbaum) L.; m. Zelda Sheila Levine, Sept. 6, 1955; children: Ellen Beth, Steven Eric. A.B., Columbia U., 1953, B.S. in Engring, 1954, M.S., 1956; D.Engring. Sci., Columbia, 1961. Research engr. Esso Research and Engring. Co., 1958-61; faculty U. Pa., 1961—, asso. prof. chem. engring., 1965-72, prof., 1972—, prof. bioengring., 1977—, chmn. dept. bioengring., 1981-90; vis. prof. environ. medicine Duke, 1971-72; vis. prof. Weizmann Inst., Israel, 1979; v.p. research and devel. KDL Med. Techs. Inc., 1984—. Co-editor: Rheology of Biological Systems, 1973; asso. editor: Biorheology; contbr. articles to profl. engrs. Mem. IEEE (engring. in medicine and biology soc.), Am. Inst. Chem. Engrs., Am. Soc. Engring. Edn., Am. Chem. Soc., Biomed. Engring. Soc., Internat. Soc. Biorheology, N.Am. Soc. Biorheology, Am. Inst. Med. Biol. Engring., Phi Beta Kappa, Sigma Xi, Tau Beta Pi, Phi Lambda Upsilon, Theta Tau. Spl. research biorheology transp. processes, chemically reacting systems, med. aspects engring. Home: 2420 Spruce St Philadelphia PA 19103-6423 Office: Univ Pa Dept Bioengring Philadelphia PA 19104

LITT, MORTON HERBERT, macromolecular science educator, researcher; b. N.Y.C., Apr. 10, 1926; s. Samuel Bernard and Minnie (Hertz) L.; m. Lola Natalie Abrahamson, July 7, 1957; children: Jonathan S., Jennifer A. B.S., CCNY, 1947; M.S., Bklyn. Poly. Inst., 1953, Ph.D., 1956. Turner and Newall fellow U. Manchester, Eng., 1956-57; sr. research fellow N.Y. State Coll. Forestry, Syracuse, N.Y., 1958-59; sr. scientist Allied Chem. Corp., Morristown, N.J., 1960-64, assoc. dir. research, 1965-67; assoc. prof. Case Western Res. U., Cleve., 1967-76, prof. macromolecular sci., 1976—; cons. Allied Corp., Morristown, N.J., 1967-93, Vistakon, Jacksonville, Fla., 1980—, Polaroid Corp., Cambridge, Mass., 1987-90. Patentee in field. Fellow AAAS, Am. Inst. Physics; mem. Am. Chem. Soc., Chem. Soc. London, J. Polymer Sci. Polymer Chem. (adv. bd.). Home: 2575 Charney Rd Cleveland OH 44118-4402 Office: Case Western Res U Olin Bldg Cleveland OH 44106

LITTEER, HAROLD HUNTER, JR., lawyer; b. Rochester, N.Y., Nov. 13, 1943; s. Harold Hunter and Winifred Gladys (Gemming) L.; m. Kathleen May Dool, July 14, 1964; children: Harold H. III, Raymond J. BS, Empire State Coll., 1988; JD, Syracuse U., 1990. Bar: N.Y. 1991. Ptnr. Murray & Litteer, Batavia, N.Y., 1991—. Mem. Wheatland Zoning Bd., Scottsville, N.Y.; town justice Town of Wheatland, Scottsville, N.Y. Mem. ABA, N.Y. State Bar Assn., N.Y. State Defenders Assn., Lions (bd. dirs. Caledonia-Mumford club). Democrat. Baptist. Avocations: golf, fishing, sports, music. Home: 460 Armstrong Rd Mumford NY 14511 Office: Murray & Litteer 23 Jackson St Batavia NY 14020-3201

LITTELL, FRANKLIN HAMLIN, theologian, educator; b. Syracuse, N.Y., June 20, 1917; s. Clair F. and Lena Augusta (Hamlin) L.; m. Harriet Davidson Lewis, June 15, 1939 (dec. 1978); children: Jennith, Karen, Miriam, Stephen; m. 2d Marcia S. Sachs, 1980. BA, Cornell Coll., 1937, DD, 1953; BD, Union Theol. Sem., 1940; PhD, Yale U., 1946; Dr. Theology (hon.), U. Marburg, 1957; ThD (hon.), Thiel Coll., 1968; other hon. degrees, Widener Coll., 1969, Hebrew Union Coll., 1975, Reconstructionist Rabbinical Coll., 1976, Gratz Coll., 1977, St. Joseph's U., 1988, Stockton State Coll., 1991. Dir. Lane Hall, U. Mich., 1944-49; chief protestant adviser to U.S. High Commr., other service in Germany, 1949-51, 53-58; prof. Chgo. Theol. Sem., 1962-69; pres. Iowa Wesleyan Coll., 1966-69; prof. religion Temple U., 1969-86; adj. prof. Inst. Contemporary Jewry, Hebrew U., Israel, 1973-94; inaugural Ida E. King disting. vis. prof. Holocaust Studies Stockton (N.J.) State Coll., 1990, 91, Robert Foster Cherry disting. vis. prof. Baylor U., 1993-94, guest prof. numerous univs. Author numerous books including The Anabaptist View of the Church: an Introduction to Sectarian Protestantism (Brewer award Am. Soc. Ch. History), 1952, rev. edit., 1958, 64, From State Church to Pluralism, 1962, rev., 1970; (with Hubert Locke) The German Church Struggle and the Holocaust, 1974, 90; The Crucifixion of the Jews, 1975, 86, The Macmillan Atlas History of Christianity, 1976, German edit., 1976, 89 , (with Marcia Sachs Littell) A Pilgrim's Interfaith Guide to the Holy Land, 1981; A Half-Century of Religious Dialogue: Amsterdam 1939-1989; editor or assoc. editor numerous jours. including Jour. Ecumenical Studies, A Jour. of Ch. and State and Holocaust Genocide Studies; author weekly syndicated columns, also over 300 major articles or chpts. of books in field of modern religious history. cons. NCCJ, 1958-83; mem. exec. com. Notre Dame Colloqium, 1961-68; vice chmn. Ctr. for Reformation Research, 1964-77; nat. chmn. Inst. for Am. Democracy, 1966-69, sr. scholar, 1969-76; co-founder, officer Ann. Scholars' Conf. on Ch. Struggle and Holocaust, 1970—; pres. Christians Concerned for Israel, 1971-78, Nat. Christian Leadership Conf. for Israel, 1978-84, pres. emeritus 1985—; founder, chmn. ecumenical com. Deutscher Evangelischer Kirchentag, 1953-58; co-founder, cons. Assn. Coordination Univ. Religious Affairs, 1959—; mem. U.S. Holocaust Meml. Council, 1979-93; founder, pres. Nat. Inst. on Holocaust, Temple U., 1975-83, Anne Frank Inst., Phila., 1983-89; co-founder, pres. Phila. Ctr. on Holocaust, Genocide and Human Rights, 1989—; mem. exec. com. Remembering For The Future, Oxford and London, 1988, Berlin, 1994; named observer to Vatican II; mem. Internat. Bd. of Yad Vashem, Jerusalem, 1981—. Decorated Grosse Verdienstkreuz (Fed. Republic Germany); recipient Jabotinsky medal, Israel, Ladislaus Laszt Internat. Ecumenical award Ben Gurion U. of Negev, 1991, Buber Rosenzweig medal, Germany, 1996. Mem. PEN, European Assn. Evang. Acads. (co-founder), Locust Club, Yale Club, Pen and Pencil Club, Phi Beta Kappa, Phi Beta Kappa Assocs. Home: PO Box 10 Merion Station PA 19066

LITTELL, MARCIA SACHS, educator, educational administrator; b. Phila., July 12, 1937; d. Leon Harry Sobel and Selma Fisher Goldstein Lipson; m. Robert L. Sachs, Apr. 3, 1955 (div. June 1978); children: Jonathan R., Robert L. Jr., Jen Sachs-Dahnert; m. Franklin H. Littell, Mar. 23, 1980; children: Jennith Lawrence, Karen, Miriam, Stephen. BS in Edn., Temple U., 1971, MS in Edn., 1975, EdD, 1990. Cert. tchr. secondary and social studies, Pa. Tchr. Lower Merion Sch. Dist., Ardmore, Pa., 1972-74; regional exec. dir. Brit. European Ctr., Paris, 1974-78; dir. confs. Bryn Mawr (Pa.) Coll., 1976-80; internat. exec. dir. Anne Frank Inst., Phla., 1981-89; adj. prof. Temple U., Phla., 1990—; exec. dir. Ann. Scholars' Conf. on the Holocaust & the Chs., Merion, Pa., 1990—; vis. prof. Phila. C.C., 1974-76; dir. Phila. Ctr. on the Holocaust, Genocide and Human Rights, 1989—; exec. com. Remembering for the Future, Oxford, Eng. and Berlin, 1986—; mem. edn. com. U.S. Holocaust Meml. Mus., Washington, 1987—, chmn.'s adv. com., 1985. Editl. adv. bd. Holocause & Genocide Studies, Oxford U. Press, volume I, 1987— ; editor: Holocaust Education: A Resource for Teachers and Professional Leaders, 1985, Liturgies on the Holocaust: An Interfaith Anthology, 1986, rev. edit., 1996 (Merit of Distinction award), The Holocaust: Forty Years After, 1989, The Netherlands and Nazi Genocide, 1992, From Prejudice to Destruction: Western Civilization in the Shadow of Auschwitz, 1995, Remembrance and Recollection: Essays on the Centennial Year of Martin Neimoller and Reinhold Niebuhr, 1995, The Uses and Abuses of Knowledge: The Holocaust and the German Church Struggle, 1996. Exec. com. YM/YWHA Arts Coun., Phila., 1980—; adv. bd. Child Welfare, Montgomery County, 1975-80; bd. govs. Lower Merion Scholarship Fund, 1972-80. Named Woman of the Yr., Brith Sholom Women, Phila., 1993, Eternal Flame award Anne Frank Inst., 1988, Hall of Fame award Sch. Dist. of Phila., 1988. Fellow Nat. Assn. Holocaust Educators, Assn. of Holocaust Orgns. (founding sec. 1985-88), Nat. Coun. for the Social Studies. Democrat. Jewish. Avocations: walking, travel, reading. Home: PO Box 10 Merion Station PA 19066

LITTELL, PHYLLIS MAUREEN, counselor; b. Albuquerque, N.Mex., Oct. 15, 1941; d. Maurice William Robinson and Hazel Maureen (Billings) Wood; m. Danny Lane Littell, June 15, 1963; children: Tammy Littell Boser, Linda Littell Boser. AB, Hanover Coll., 1963; BS, Ind. U., 1977. Tchr. Sch. Town of Clarksville, Ind., 1963-65; high sch. counselor Mooresville (Ind.) High Sch., 1977-79, Plainfield (Ind.) High Sch., 1979-84; ind. individual & family counselor Greenwood, Ind., 1984—. Contbr. articles to various mags. Pres. Hendricks County Coun. Prevention of Child Abuse, Ind., 1990-91. Mem. ACA, Kappa Kappa Kappa (v.p. 1991-92). Mem. Ch. of Christ. Avocations: organizing and teaching Bible classes, writing, traveling. Office: 512 S Madison Ave Greenwood IN 46142-3060

LITTIG, LAWRENCE WILLIAM, psychologist, educator; b. Madison, Wis., June 30, 1927; s. Lawrence Victor and Elsie Louise (Rosanske) L.; m. Iris Mark, June 15, 1957; children—Eve Alexandra, Amy Victoria, Sharon Elizabeth. B.S., U. Wis., 1950, M.S., 1955; Ph.D., U. Mich., 1959. Instr. dpet. psychology U. Mich., Ann Arbor, 1958-59; Asst. prof. psychology U. Buffalo, 1959-62; asst. program dir. instl. programs NSF, Washington, 1962-63; social psychologist W.E. Upjohn Inst. Employment Research, Washington, 1963-65; prof. social psychology Howard U., Washington, 1965-92, prof. emeritus social psychology, 1992—; prof. psychology Md. Inst. Coll. of Art, Balt., 1993—; Fulbright prof. U. Nottingham, 1961-62; vis. scholar U. London, 1971-72; cons. Brookings Instn., 1968-70, Dept. Labor, 1968-70; vis. prof. U. Wis., 1970. Cons. editor: Jour. Cross Cultural Psychology, 1969-74; contbr. articles to profl. jours. Port warden City of Annapolis. U.S. Office Edn. grantee, 1965-70; NIMH research grantee, 1968-69; NSF research grantee, 1961-62; Nat. Inst. Child Health and Human Devel. grantee, 1971-73. Fellow AAAS, Am. Psychol. Assn., Am. Psychol. Soc., Soc. for Personality and Social Psychology; mem. Psychonomic Soc., Brit. Psychol. Soc., Sigma Xi. Clubs: Cosmos (Washington); Md. Capital Yacht, Eastport Yacht (Annapolis, Md.); Amateur Fencing (London). Home: 2 Wells Lndg Annapolis MD 21403-2316 Office: Howard U Dept Psychology Washington DC 20059

LITTLE, ALAN BRIAN, obstetrician, gynecologist, educator; b. Montreal, Que., Can., Mar. 11, 1925; emigrated to U.S., 1951, naturalized, 1959; s. Herbert Melville and Mary Lizette (Campbell) L.; m. Nancy Alison Campbell, Aug. 20, 1949 (div.); children: Michael C. (dec.), Susan MacF. and Deborah MacF. (twins), Catherine E., Jane A., Mary L.; m. Bitten Stripp, Mar. 31, 1983. BA, McGill U., 1948, MD, CM, 1950. Intern Montreal Gen. Hosp., 1950-51; resident Boston Lying-in and Free Hosp. for Women, 1951-55, asst. obstetrician, asso. obstetrician and gynecologist, 1955-65; teaching fellow, asst. prof. Harvard Med. Sch., 1952-65; prof. ob-gyn, then Arthur H. Bill prof. ob-gyn Case Western Res. U. Sch. Medicine, Cleve., 1965-82; chmn. dept. reproductive biology Case Western Res. U. Sch. Medicine, 1972-82; prof. gynecology McGill U., Montreal, 1983—, chmn. dept. ob-gyn., 1983-94; clin. prof. ob-gyn U. Medicine and Dentistry N.J., Newark, 1994—; dir. dept. ob-gyn. Univ. Hosps., Cleve., to 1982, Royal Victoria Hosp., Montreal, 1983-94; mem. nat. adv. com. Nat. Inst. Child Health and Human Devel. Author: (with B. Tenney) Clinical Obstetrics, 1962; editor: (with others) Gynecology and Obstetrics-Health Care for Women, 1975, 2d edit., 1982; (with D. Tulchinsky) Maternal Fetal Endocrinology, 2d edit., 1994; contbr. articles to profl. jours. Served with RCAF, 1943-45. Fellow ACS, Royal Coll. Surgeons, Am. Coll. Obstetricians and Gynecologists; mem. AMA, Endocrine Soc., Am. Gynecol. and Obstet. Soc., Am., Central assns. ob-gyn., Assn. Profs. Ob-Gyn., Soc. Gynecol. Investigation, Soc. Ob-Gyn. Can. Office: 687 Pine Ave W, Montreal, PQ Canada H3A 1A1

LITTLE, ARTHUR DEHON, investment banker; b. Providence, Feb. 13, 1944; s. Royal and Augusta Willoughby (Ellis) L.; m. E. Janice Leeming, Sept. 6, 1974; children: Cameron Royal, Kimberley Murray. B.A. in History, Stanford U., 1966. With Narragansett Capital Corp., Providence, 1967—, asst. to pres., 1968-69, v.p., 1969-73, exec. v.p., treas., 1975-76, pres., treas., chief operating officer, dir., 1976-77, pres., treas., chief exec. officer, dir., 1977-80, pres., chief exec. officer, dir., 1980, chmn. bd., chief exec. officer, 1980-86; mng. dir. Narragansett Capital, Inc., Providence, 1986—; prin. The Little Investment Co., Boston, 1992—; bd. dirs. A.T. Wall Co., Quantum Internat., JDR Holdings, Inc., R.I. Zool. Soc., Lyford Cay Found., Nat. Am. Liver Found., New Eng. chpt. Am. Liver Found., Jr. Achievement No. New Eng., Jr. Achievement Nat. Bd.; chmn. Digital Vision, Inc., L & K Acquisitions, Quantum Internat., JDR Holdings, Inc. Chmn. JDR Holdings, Inc. Mem. Lyford Cay Club, Somerset Club, Kittansett Club, Bald Peak Colony Club. Office: 33 Broad St Ste 10 Boston MA 02109-4216

LITTLE, BRIAN F., oil company executive; b. Moncton, N.B., Can., Oct. 28, 1943; s. George E. and Marion M. (McCartney) L.; m. Dianne E. Rogers, Oct. 9, 1969; children: Michael William, Sara Elizabeth. BA, Am. Internat. Coll., 1966; LLB, Osgoode Hall Law Sch., 1974; LLM, London Sch. Econs., Eng., 1975. Indsl. devel. asst. Can. Nat., Moncton and Montreal, Can., 1967-71; articling student McMillan Binch, Toronto, Ont., Can., 1975-76, assoc., 1977-82, ptnr., 1982-83; v.p., gen. counsel Dome Petroleum, Calgary, Alta., Can., 1983-88; v.p. law and external affairs Amoco Can. Petroleum Co. Ltd., Calgary, 1988-89, sr. v.p. law, 1989-92, sr. v.p. law, gen. counsel, 1992—. Trustee Can. Athletic Found. Mem. Can. Bar Assn., Law Soc. Upper Can., Osgoode Hall Law Sch. Alumni Assn. (bd. dirs.). Office: Amoco Can Petroleum Co Ltd, 240 Fourth Ave SW, Calgary, AB Canada T2P 4H4

LITTLE, CARL MAURICE, performing arts administrator; b. Campbellton, N.B., Can., Mar. 17, 1924; s. George Everett and Ada (Boucher) L.; m. Frances R. Corner, Aug. 27, 1949; children: Christine, Jennifer, Geoffrey, Stephen; m. Barbara Wolfond, Dec. 8, 1978. B.Sc., Dalhousie U., Halifax, N.S., Can., 1945, Licentiate of Music, 1945, Diploma Engring., 1944; Asso., Royal Coll. Music, London, 1952; Licentiate, Royal Acad. Music, London, 1952. Tchr. music public schs. Outremont, Que., Can., 1949-50; pvt. tchr. music Montreal, Que., 1946-59, Toronto, Ont., 1959-70; producer music CBC Radio, Montreal, 1952-59; producer music CBC Radio, Toronto, 1959-65, nat. network supr. serious music, 1965-75; mgr. Nat. Arts Centre Orch., Ottawa, 1975-78; co-founder, pres. Little Gallery of the Arts, Ottawa, 1979-80; pres. Arts Connection, Victoria, B.C., 1980—; exec. dir., festival adminstr. Courtenay Youth Music Centre (B.C.), 1983; organist Holy Trinity Anglican Ch., Saanichton, B.C., 1984-93. Pianist, 1945-52; juror for internat. music competitions including Scriabin Piano Competition, Oslo, Norway, Internat. String Quartet, Stockholm, Sweden, Let The Peoples Sing, Choir, London; jury chmn. Kathaumixw Internat. Choral Festival Powell River, B.C., Can. Mem. Royal Can. Coll. Organists (program chmn. 1985), Can. Conf. of Arts, Can. Music Council, Can. Amateur Musicians Assn. (dir.; co-founder), Ont. Choral Fedn., Nat. Arts Centre Orch. Assn. Instrumental in founding and adminstrn. of CBC competitions, CBC music projects and programs. Address: 2171-2600 Ferguson Rd, Saanichton, BC Canada V8M 2C1

LITTLE, CHARLES GORDON, geophysicist; b. Liuyang, Hunan, China, Nov. 4, 1924; s. Charles Deane and Caroline Joan (Crawford) L.; m. Mary Zughaib, Aug. 21, 1954; children: Deane, Joan, Katherine, Margaret, Patricia. BSc with honors in Physics, U. Manchester, Eng., 1948; PhD in Radio Astronomy, U. Manchester, 1952. Jr. engr. Cosmos Mfg. Co. Ltd., Enfield, Middlesex, Eng., 1944-46; jr. physicist Ferranti Ltd., Manchester, Lancashire, Eng., 1946-47; asst. lectr. U. Manchester, 1952-53; prof. dept. geophysics U. Alaska, 1954-58, dep. dir. Geophys. Inst., 1954-58; cons. Ionosphere Radio Propagation Lab. U.S. Dept. Commerce Nat. Bur. Standards, Boulder, Colo., 1958-60, chief Upper Atmosphere and Space Physics divsn., 1960-62, dir. Central Radio Propagation Lab., 1962-65; dir. Inst. Telecommunication Sci. and Aeronomy, Environ. Sci. Services Adminstrn., Boulder, Colo., 1965-67; dir. Wave Propagation Lab. NOAA (formerly Environ. Sci. Services Adminstr.), Boulder, Colo., 1967-86; sr. UCAR fellow Naval Environ. Prediction Research Facility, Monterey, Calif., 1987-89; George J. Haltiner rsch. prof. Naval Postgrad. Sch., Monterey, 1989-90. Author numerous sci. articles. Recipient U.S. Dept. Commerce Gold medal, 1964, mgmt. and sci. research awards NOAA, 1969, 77, Presdl. Meritorious Exec. award, 1980. Fellow IEEE, Am. Meteorol. Soc. (Cleveland Abbe award 1984); mem. NAE, AIAA (R.M. Losey Atmos. Sci. award 1992). Address: 4907 Country Club Way Boulder CO 80301

LITTLE, CHARLES LAWSON, judge; b. Montgomery, Ala., Aug. 21, 1946; s. Horton Henry and Martha Roberta (Hogg) L.; m. Gloria Lane, Jan. 23, 1971; children: Jennifer Marie, Charles Lawson Jr. BS, Troy (Ala.) State U., 1969; JD, U. Ala., 1972. Bar: Ala. 1974, U.S. Dist. Ct. Ala. 1975, U.S. Ct. Appeals (11th cir.) 1975. Asst. atty. gen. State of Ala. Atty. Gen., Montgomery, 1974-79; chief asst. dist. atty. Houston and Henry Counties, Dothan, Ala., 1979-82; U.S. magistrate judge U.S. Dist. Ct., Mid. Dist. Ala., Dothan, 1986-92; pvt. practice Dothan, 1981-94; cir. judge 20th Jud. Cir., 1995—. Mem. Dothan Rescue Mission Bd., 1994; chmn. jud. govtl. and legis. com. Houston County Substance Abuse Bd., 1994. Sgt. Ala. NG, 1969-75. Mem. Houston County Bar Assn. (exec. com. 1991-92), Kiwanis Club (chmn. law and regulation com. 1988-90). Baptist. Avocation: guitar. Home: 2802 Briarcliff Rd Dothan AL 36303-2121 Office: Houston County Courthouse Dothan AL 36301

LITTLE, CHRISTOPHER MARK, publishing company executive, lawyer; b. Tazewell, Va., Mar. 11, 1941; s. Haskin Vincent and Janet Koe (Kessinger) L.; m. Virginia Elizabeth Silver, Dec. 27, 1963 (div. Oct. 1988); children: Timothy Mark, Margaret Elizabeth; m. Elizabeth Foster Anderson, Oct. 15, 1988. BA, Yale U., 1963; LLB, U. Tex., 1966. Bar: D.C. 1966. Assoc. Covington & Burling, Washington, 1966-68, 70-75; adminstrv. asst. to Congressman Bob Eckhardt, U.S. Ho. of Reps., Washington, 1968-70; asst. gen. counsel EPA, Washington, 1975-76; v.p., counsel The Washington Post, 1976-80; pres., pub. The Herald, Everett, Wash., 1980-84; sr. v.p. adminstrn. Newsweek, Inc., N.Y.C., 1984-86, pres., 1986-89; pres. Cowles Mags., Inc., Harrisburg, Pa., 1989-92; v.p. pub. dir. Meredith Corp., Des Moines, Iowa, 1992-94, pres. mag. group, 1994—. Internat. bd. trustees Am. Field Svc., N.Y.C., 1989-95, chmn., 1992-95. Mem. Mag. Pubs. Am. (chmn. govt. affairs coun. 1990—), Wakonda Club, Des Moines Club. Episcopalian. Avocations: landscape architecture, 18th century American history, classical music. Office: Meredith Corp. 1716 Locust St Des Moines IA 50309-3038*

LITTLE, DANIEL EASTMAN, philosophy educator, university program director; b. Rock Island, Ill., Apr. 7, 1949; s. William Charles and Emma Lou (Eastman) L.; m. Ronnie Alice Friedland, Sept. 12, 1976 (div. May 1995); children: Joshua Friedland-Little, Rebecca Friedland-Little. BS in Math. with highest honors, AB in Philosophy with high honors, U. Ill., 1971; PhD in Philosophy, Harvard U., 1977. Asst. prof. U. Wis.-Parkside, Kenosha, 1976-79; vis. assoc. prof. Wellesley (Mass.) Coll., 1985-87; vis. scholar Ctr. Internat. Affairs Harvard U., 1989-91, assoc. Ctr. Internat. Affairs, 1991-95; asst. prof. Colgate U., Hamilton, N.Y., 1979-85, assoc. prof., 1985-92, prof., 1992-96, chmn. dept. philosophy and religion, 1992-93, assoc. dean faculty, 1993-96; assoc. Ctr. for Population and Devel. Studies, Harvard U., 1996—; v.p. academic affairs Bucknell U., Lewisberg, Pa., 1996—, prof. philosophy, 1996—; teaching fellow Harvard U., 1973-76; participant internat. confs. Ctr. Asian and Pacific Studies, U. Oreg., 1992, Social Sci. Rsch. Coun./MacArthur Found., U. Calif., San Diego, 1991, Budapest, Hungary, 1990, Morelos, Mex., 1989, Rockefeller Found., Bellagio, Italy, 1990, U. Manchester, Eng., 1986; mem. screening com. on internat. peace and security Social Sci. Rsch. Coun./MacArthur Found., 1991-94; manuscript reviewer Yale U. Press, Cambridge U. Press, Princeton U. Press, Oxford U. Press, Westview Press, Harvard U. Press, Can. Jour. Philosophy, Philosophy Social Scis., Synthese, Am. Polit. Sci. Rev.; grant proposal reviewer NSF, Social Sci. Rsch. Coun., Nat. Endowment for Humanities; tenure and promotion reviewer U. Tenn., Bowdoin Coll., Duke U. Author: The Scientific Marx, 1986, Understanding Peasant China: Case Studies in the Philosophy of Social Science, 1989, Varieties of Social Explanation: An Introduction to the Philosophy of Social Science, 1991 (Outstanding Book award Choice 1992), On the Reliability of Economic Models, 1995; contbr. articles to profl. jours., books. Social Sci. Rsch. Postdoctoral fellow MacArthur Found., 1989-91, Rsch. grantee NSF, 1987, Woodrow Wilson Grad. fellow, 1971-72. Mem. Am. Philos. Assn., Am. Soc. for Polit. & Legal Philosophy, Assn. Asian Studies, Internat. Assn. Philosophy of Law & Social Philosophy, Internat. Devel. Ethics Assn., Phi Beta Kappa. Office: VPAA Marts Hall Bucknell U Lewisburg PA 17837

LITTLE, DENNIS GAGE, diversified business executive; b. Cambridge, Mass., June 22, 1935; s. Thomas Wolcott and Margaret (deRongé) L.; m. Susan Gay Walker, May 11, 1957 (div.); children: Heather Gage, Jennifer Wolcott; m. Joanne Bowers, Oct. 1, 1983. AB, Harvard U., 1956, MBA with distinction, 1961. Asst. to fin. v.p. J.P. Stevens & Co., Inc., 1961-67; treas. GK Techs., Inc. (name formerly Gen. Cable Corp.), 1967-82, v.p., 1969-78, v.p. indsl. rels., 1975-78, sr. v.p., CFO, 1979-82; exec. v.p., CFO Avco Corp., Greenwich, Conn., 1982-85, Textron Inc., 1985-92; bd. dirs. Winthrop Focus Funds, Russell Reynolds Assocs., Taco, Inc., Cranston. With supply corps, USNR, 1956-59. Mem. R.I. Country Club (Barrington), Hawks Nest Club (Vero Beach, Fla.). Home: The Moorings 1915 Cutlass Cove Vero Beach FL 32963

LITTLE, DON BARRON, clergyman; b. Rosebud, Tex., Sept. 5, 1936; s. Leonard Barron and Idamartha (Busse) L.; 1 child, Beth Ann; m. Eleanor Ann Wisler, Aug.24, 1958; 1 child, Donna Ruth Bennett. BA, Southwestern U., 1958; ThM, So. Meth. U., 1961; D Ministry, McCormick Sem., Chgo., 1987. Ordained elder United Meth. Ch., 1961. Sr. minister Van (Tex.) United Meth. Ch., 1970-74, 1st United Meth. Ch., Texas City, Tex., 1974-78, Pollard United Meth. Ch., Tyler, Tex., 1978-84, Lakewood United Meth.

Ch., Houston, 1984-91, Pasadena (Tex.) 1st United Meth. Ch., 1991-94, 1st United Meth. Ch., Conroe, Tex., 1994—. Chaplain U.S. Army, 1967-70, Vietnam. Decorated Bronze Star, Air medal; recipient Copeland Evangelism award Tex. Ann. Conf., United Meth. Ch., 1986, 92. Office: 1st United Meth Ch 207 W Phillips St Conroe TX 77301

LITTLE, EMILY BROWNING, architect; b. Austin, Tex., June 4, 1951; d. Betty (Browning) L. BA in Cultural Anthropology, U. Tex., 1973, MArch, 1979. Registered architect, Tex. Archtl. apprentice Austin Design Assocs., 1980-81; project mgr. Nutt, Wolters & Assocs., Austin, 1981-84; prin. Emily Little/Architect, Austin, 1984—. Prin. works include numerous residences, hist. restorations and comml. bldgs. Mem. citizens adv. com. Travis County Juvenile Ct., Austin, 1984-86; mem. adv. bd. Deborah Hay Dance Co., Austin, 1984—; chmn. Austin Design Commn., 1987-89. Recipient Archtl. Merit award Austin Bd. Realtors, 1989. Mem. AIA (commr. Austin chpt. 1987-88, Outstanding Young Arch. of Tex. 1993), Tex. Soc. Archs. (honors com. 1992), Austin Women in Arch. (pres. 1985-86), Nat. Trust for Hist. Preservation, Tex. Fine Arts Assn. (pres. 1990-92), Heritage Soc. Austin (bd. dirs. 1989—, pres. 1995, Bldg. award 1988, 90, 92, 93). Democrat. Avocations: travel, swimming. Office: 1001 E 8th St Austin TX 78702-3248

LITTLE, F. A., JR., federal judge; b. 1936; m. Gail Little; children: Sophie, Sabrina. BA, Tulane U., 1958, LLB, 1961. Assoc. Chaffe, McCall, Phillips, Toler & Sarpy, New Orleans, 1961-65, Gold, Little, Simon, Weems & Bruser, Alexandria, La., 1965-69; pres. Gold, Little, Simon, Weems & Bruser, Alexandria, 1968-84; judge U.S. Dist. Ct. (we. dist.) La., Alexandria, 1984—. Office: US Dist Ct PO Box 1031 Alexandria LA 71309-1031*

LITTLE, GEORGE DANIEL, clergyman; b. St. Louis, Dec. 18, 1929; s. Henry and Agathe Cox (Daniel) L.; m. Joan Phillips McCafferty, Aug. 22, 1953; children: Deborah Philips, Cynthia McCafferty (dec.), Alice Annette, Daniel Ross, Benjamin Harry. AB, Princeton U., 1951; MDiv, McCormick Theol. Sem., Chgo., 1954; LLD (hon.), Huron Coll., 1977. Ordained to ministry Presbyn. Ch., 1954; pastor East London Group Ministry, Presbyn. Ch. Eng., 1954-56, Friendship Presbyn. Ch., Pitts., 1956-62; assoc. dir. dept. urban ch., planning assoc. Bd. Nat. Missions, United Presbyterian Ch. U.S.A., N.Y.C., 1962-72; assoc. for budgeting Gen. Assembly Mission Council, 1973-76, exec. dir. council, 1976-84; pastor First Presbyn. Ch., Ithaca, N.Y., 1984-93; interim pres. McCormick Theol. Sem., Chgo., 1993-94; pastor-in-residence Village Presbyn. Ch., Prairie Village, Kans., 1995-96; ret., 1996. Home: PO Box 4302 Ithaca NY 14852-4302

LITTLE, H. MAURICE, vocational educator; b. Brenham, Tex., July 31, 1947; s. Hoxie and Bert Estelle (Jameson) L. BS, Tex. So. U., 1972; MEd, Prairie View A & M U., 1974, Tex. So. U., 1985. Office adminstrn. coop. coord. M.B. Smiley High Sch., Houston, 1972—; devel. reading instr. Houston Cmty. Coll., 1985—; bus. edn. prof. Tex. So. U., Houston, 1987—. Mem. Bus. Profls. of Am. Baptist. Home: PO Box 632 Dickinson TX 77539-0632 Office: MB Smiley HS 10726 Mesa Dr Houston TX 77078-1402

LITTLE, JOHN BERTRAM, physician, radiobiology educator, researcher; b. Boston, Oct. 5, 1929; s. Bertram Kimball and Nina (Fletcher) L.; m. Francoise Cottereau, Aug. 4, 1960; children—John Bertram, Frederic Fletcher. A.B. in Physics, Harvard U., 1951; M.D., Boston U., 1955. Diplomate Am. Bd. Radiology. Intern in medicine Johns Hopkins Hosp., Balt., 1955-56; resident in radiology Mass. Gen. Hosp., Boston, 1958-61; fellow Harvard U., Cambridge, Mass., 1961-63; from instr. to assoc. prof. radiobiology Harvard Sch. Pub. Health, Boston, 1963-75; prof. Harvard Sch. Pub. Health, 1975—, chmn. dept. physiology, 1980-83, James Stevens Simmons prof. radiobiology, 1987—; dir. Kresge Ctr. Environ. Health, Boston, 1982—; cons. radiology Mass. Gen. Hosp., Boston, 1965—, Brigham and Women's Hosp., Boston, 1968—; chmn. bd. sci. counsellors Nat. Inst. Environ. Health Sci., 1982-84; bd. sci. counsellors Nat. Toxicology Program, 1988-92; mem. sci. coun. Radiation Effects Rsch. Found., Hiroshima, Japan, 1993—; bd. dirs. on radiation effects rsch. Nat. Acad. of Scis. Mem. editorial bd. numerous nat. and internat. jours.; contbr. chpts. to books and articles to profl. jours. Mem. coun. Nat. Coun. on Radiation Protection and Measurements, 1993—; trustee various hist. and cultural orgns. Capt. U.S. Army, 1956-58. Am. Cancer Soc. grantee, 1965-68; recipient numerous rsch. and grants NIH, 1968—; named one of Outstanding Investigator grantee Nat. Cancer Inst., 1988—. Mem. AAAS (coun. in med. scis. 1988-91), Radiation Rsch. Soc. N.Am. (pres.-elect 1985, pres. 1986-87), Am. Assn. Cancer Rsch., Am. Physiol. Soc., Health Physics Soc., Am. Soc. Photobiology. Avocations: music, architectural history. Office: Harvard U Dept Radiobiology 665 Huntington Ave Boston MA 02115-6021

LITTLE, JOHN DUTTON CONANT, management scientist, educator; b. Boston, Feb. 1, 1928; s. John Dutton and Margaret (Jones) L.; m. Elizabeth Davenport Alden, Sept. 12, 1953; children: John Norris, Sarah Alden, Thomas Dunham Conant, Ruel Davenport. SB in Physics, MIT, 1948, PhD, 1955; PhD (hon.), U. Liege, Belgium, 1992. Engr. Gen. Electric Co., Schenectady, 1949-50; asst. prof. ops. research Case-Western Res. U., 1957-60, assoc. prof., 1960-62; research asst. MIT, 1951-54, assoc. prof. mgmt., 1962-67, prof., 1967-78, George M. Bunker prof. mgmt., 1978-89, Inst. prof., 1989—, dir. Ops. Research Ctr., 1969-76, head mgmt. sci. group Sloan Sch. Mgmt., 1972-82, head behavioral and policy scis. area, 1982-88; pres. Mgmt. Decision Systems, Inc., 1967-80, chmn. bd. dirs., 1967-85; dir., advisor to bd. dirs. Info. Resources, Inc., 1985—; cons. ops. rsch. indsl. govtl. orgns., 1958—; vis. prof. mktg. European Inst. Bus. Adminstrn., Fontainebleau, France, fall 1988; researcher math. programming, queuing theory, mktg., traffic control, decision support systems. Assoc. editor: Mgmt. Sci, 1967-71; contbr. articles to profl. jours. Trustee Mktg. Sci. Inst., 1983-89. Served with AUS, 1955-56. Fellow AAAS; mem. NAE, Ops. Rsch. Soc. Am. (coun. 1970-73, pres. 1979-80), Inst. Mgmt. Scis. (v.p. 1976-79, pres. 1984-85), Inst. for Ops. Rsch. and the Mgmt. Scis. (pres. 1995), Am. Mktg. Assn., Sigma Xi. Home: 37 Conant Rd RR 3 Lincoln MA 01773 Office: MIT Sloan Sch Mgmt Cambridge MA 02142-1347

LITTLE, JOHN WILLIAM, plastic surgeon, educator; b. Indpls., Mar. 12, 1944; s. John William Jr. and Naida (Jones) L.; m. Patricia Padgett Lea, May 26, 1969 (div. 1974); m. Teri Ann Tyson, Feb. 28, 1981 (div. 1982). AB, Dartmouth Coll., 1966, B. in Med. Scis., 1967; MD, Harvard U., 1969. Diplomate Am. Bd. Med. Examiners, Am. Bd. Surgery, Am. Bd. Plastic Surgery. Intern affiliated hosps. Case Western Res. U., Cleve., 1969-70, resident in surgery, 1970-74, resident in plastic surgery, 1973-75; fellow in plastic surgery affiliated hosp. U. Miami, 1975-77; asst. prof. Georgetown U., Washington, 1977-82, assoc. prof., 1982-87, prof., 1987-92, clin. prof., 1992—, dir. div. plastic surgery, residency tng. program, plastic surgeon-in-chief univ. hosp., 1979-92; dir. Nat. Capital Tng. Program in Plastic Surgery affiliated hosps. Georgetown U. and Howard U., 1988-92; dir. Georgetown Plastic Surgery Fellowship in Breast and Aesthetic Surgery, 1990-92; chief plastic surgery Medlantic Ctr. for Ambulatory Surgery, Inc., 1993—; cons. Nat. Cancer Inst., NIH, Bethesda, Md., 1977-92, Washington VA Med. Ctr., 1981-92, Reach to Recovery program Nat. Capital chpt. Am. Cancer Soc., 1981—, RENU program in breast reconstrn., 1982; specialist site visitor plastic surgery residency rev. com. Accreditation Coun. for Grad. Med. Edn., 1982—; vis. lect. various insts. Contbr. numerous articles to profl. jours.; manuscript reviewer Plastic and Reconstructive Surgery, Annals of Plastic Surgery. Bd. dirs. Triann reconstructive surgery teams to Caribbean and S.Am., 1981—, Georgetown Tissue Bank, 1986-88, Operation Luz del Sol, 1992—, Reconstructive Surgeons Vol. Program, 1993—; trustee Washington Opera, 1993—, mem. artistic com., 1994—. Mem. AMA, ACS (coord. plastic surgery audiovisual program Ann. Clin. Congress 1988-90, 92-93, Met. Washington chpt. councillor 1985-94, chmn. sci. program com. 1990-91, v.p. 1991-92, pres. 1992-93), Nat. Capital Soc. Plastic Surgeons (sec. treas. 1982-83, pres. 1984-85), Am. Soc. Plastic and Reconstructive Surgeons (audiovisual program dir. ann. meeting 1984-86, strategic planning com. 1987-96, fin. com. 1989-94, conv. policy com. 1993-96, ops. com. 1993-96, chmn. 1994-95, spokesperson network steering com. 1994-96, bd. dirs. 1994-96, exec. com. 1995-96), Am. Assn. Plastic Surgeons (co-chmn. various coms.), Plastic Surgery Ednl. Found. (bd. dirs. 1985—, chmn. various coms., rep. to Coun. Plastic Surg. Orgns. 1989-95, parlimentarian 1992-93, v.p. 1993-94, presdl. adv. coun. 1993-96, commr. various commns., pres.-elect, 1995, pres. 1995-96), Med. Soc. D.C. (chmn. plastic surgery sect. 1985), D.R. Millard Surg. Soc. and Ednl. Found. (pres. 1985-87), Am. Cleft Palate Assn., Am. Soc. Maxillofacial Surgeons, Washington Acad. Surgeons (coun. 1988-90), Am. Soc. Aesthetic Plastic Surgery, NE Soc. Plastic Surgeons (chmn. various coms., v.p. 1991-92, pres. 1992-93, historian 1995—), Internat. Soc. Aesthetic Plastic Surgery (chmn. bylaws com. 1990-93, 95—, parliamentarian 1990-93, mem. membership com. 1993—, chmn. 1993-95, historian 1995—), Am. Alpine Workshop in Plastic Surgery (founder, pres. 1991-92, historian 1995—), Internat. Fedn. Plastic Reconstructive and Aesthetic Surgery, Internat. Plastic, Reconstructive and Aesthetic Found., Aesthetic Surgery Edn. and Rsch. Found., Nat. Endowment Plast Surgery (bd. govs. 1995—). Republican. Presbyterian. Home: 4200 Massachusetts Ave NW Washington DC 20016-4744 Office: 1145 19th St NW Ste 802 Washington DC 20036-3701

LITTLE, LARRY CHATMON, head football coach; b. Groveland, Ga., Nov. 2, 1945; s. George Chatmon and Ida Mae (Haynes) L.; m. Rose DeJesus, Apr. 15, 1978; children: Damita, Learon. BS, Bethune-Cookman Coll., 1967; DSc, Biscayne Coll., 1972. Pro-football player San Diego Chargers, 1967-69, Miami Dolphins, 1969-80; athletic dir. Miami (Fla.) Edison High Sch., 1981-83; head football coach Bethune-Cookman Coll., Daytona Bch., Fla., 1983-92, Ohio Glory World League, Columbus, 1992, N.C. Ctrl. U., Durham, 1993—. Named All Pro, 1971, 72, 73, 74, 75, 76, Off Lineman of Yr. by NFL, 1971, 72, 73, Fla. Hall of Fame by Fla. Sports Writers, 1978, NFL Hall of Fame, 1993. Democrat. Baptist. Home: 5310 Lacy Rd Durham NC 27713-1626 Office: NC Ctrl U PO Box 19705 Durham NC 27707-0099*

LITTLE, LESTER KNOX, historian, educator; b. Providence, Oct. 21, 1935; s. Arthur Foster and Edith Caroline (Hyde) L.; m. Lella Gandini, Apr. 7, 1972; stepchildren: Andrea Dell'Antonio, Ian Dell'Antonio. AB, Dartmouth Coll., 1957; MA, Princeton U., 1960, PhD, 1962. History instr. Princeton U., 1961-63; asst. prof. history U. Chgo., 1963-69, assoc. prof., 1969-71; assoc. prof. history Smith Coll., Northampton, Mass., 1971-76, prof., 1976-82, Dwight W. Morrow prof. history, 1982—, chmn. dept. history, 1986-89; dir. Smith Coll. in Italy, 1989-91; vis. prof. history U. Calif., Berkeley, 1988, Yale U., 1995, Ecole des Hautes Etudes en Scis. sociales, Paris, 1996. Author: Religious Poverty and the Profit Economy in Medieval Europe, 1978, Liberty, Charity, Fraternity: Lay Religious Confraternites at Bergamo in the Age of the Commune, 1988, Benedictine Maledictions: Liturgical Cursing in Romanesque France, 1993; co-editor, translator: Nature, Man and Society in the Twelfth Century, 1968. Fellow Inst. Advanced Study, 1969-70, Am. Coun. Learned Socs., 1970-71, Guggenheim Found., 1983, NEH, 1992, resident fellow Am. Acad. in Rome, 1995; grantee Am. Philos. Soc., 1974-75, NEH, 1982. Mem. Am. Hist. Assn., Medieval Acad. Am. Home: 33 Washington Ave Northampton MA 01060-2822 Office: Smith College Dept History Northampton MA 01063

LITTLE, LOREN EVERTON, musician, ophthalmologist; b. Sioux Falls, S.D., Oct. 28, 1941; s. Everton A. and Maxine V. (Alcorn) L.; m. Christy Gyles; 1 child, Nicole Moses; children from previous marriage: Laurie, Richard. BA, Macalester Coll., 1963; BS, U. S.D., 1965; MD, U. Wash., 1967. Prin. trumpeter Sioux Falls Mcpl. Band, 1956-65; trumpeter St. Paul Civic Orch., 1960-62; leader, owner Swinging Scots Band, St. Paul, 1960-63; trumpeter Edgewater Inn Show Room, Seattle, 1966-67, Jazztet-Arts Council, Sioux Falls, 1970-71, Lee Maxwell Shows, Washington, 1971-74; residency in ophthalmology Walter Reed Med. Ctr., Washington, 1974; coleader, trumpeter El Paso (Tex.) All Stars, 1975; freelance trumpeter, soloist various casinos and hotels, Las Vegas, Nev., 1977—. Trumpeter (album) Journey by R. Romero Band, 1983; soloist for numerous entertainers including Tony Bennett, Burt Bacharach, Jack Jones, Sammy Davis Jr., Henry Mancini, Jerry Lewis Telethon, for video Star Salute to Live Music, 1989; with Stan Mark Band Nat. Pub. Radio Broadcast, 1994, 95; soloist on video Stan Mark Live at the 4 Queens Hotel, Las Vegas; prodr. Carl Saunders Solo Album, 1996. Trustee Nev. Sch. of the Arts, Las Vegas, 1983—. Served to lt. col. U.S. Army, 1968-76, Vietnam. Decorated Silver Star, Purple Heart, Bronze Star, Air medal; fellow Internat. Eye Found., 1974; Dewitt Wallace scholar Readers Digest, 1963-65. Fellow ACS, Am. Acad. Ophthalmology; mem. Am. Fedn. Musicians, Nat. Bd. Med. Examiners. Presbyterian. Avocations: history, music, medicine, sports, skiing.

LITTLE, LOYD HARRY, JR., author; b. Hickory, N.C., Sept. 12, 1940; s. Loyd Harry and Rebecca Lillian (Bailey) L.; m. Kris Petesch, 1993. BA in Journalism, U. N.C., 1962, postgrad., 1967-68. Editor Lumbee weekly newspaper, Pembroke, N.C., 1966; med. reporter Winston-Salem (N.C.) Jour., 1967-69; bus. editor Raleigh (N.C.) News and Observer, 1969; editor Carolina Fin. Times, Raleigh, 1970-75; spl. projects editor Durham (N.C.) Morning Herald, 1976-79; tchr. creative writing courses U. N.C., 1979-82; asst. city editor Greenville (S.C.) News, 1990-93; mng. editor Carteret County News-Times, Morehead City, N.C., 1993—. Author: Parthian Shot, 1975 (Ernest Hemingway award), In the Village of the Man, 1978, Smokehouse Jam, 1988. Chmn. Orange Grove Precinct Republican Com., 1972-73. With Green Berets U.S. Army, 1962-65. Decorated Commendation medal; Vietnamese Bronze Star medal; Hickory Daily Record scholar U. N.C., 1962. Mem. PEN, Chez Hickory Club. Home: 189 Hibbs Rd Ext Newport NC 28570-9419

LITTLE, RHODA SMELTZER, nursing administrator; b. Harrisburg, Pa., Jan. 31, 1938; d. Charles Anderson and Rhoda May (Lepperd) Smeltzer; m. Lawrence Jess Little, May 26, 1962; children: Robin Kimberly, Jonathan Sanders. Diploma in nursing, Thomas Jefferson U. Hosp., Phila., 1960; BSN, Grace Coll., 1960; MSN in Nursing Adminstrn., U. Ill., 1979. RN, Pa., Ill., N.J. Divsnl. dir. nursing and staff devel. Silver Cross Hosp., Joliet, Ill., 1978-82; dir. nursing svcs. Forkosh Meml. Hosp., Chgo., 1982-83; dir. edn. and nursing quality assurance Loyola U. Med. Ctr.-Mulcahy Outpatient Ctr., Maywood, Ill., 1985-88; asst. adminstr. patient care, dir. nursing, maternal/child, emergency and edn. Polyclinic Med. Ctr., Harrisburg, Pa., 1989—; cons. St. Francis Hosp., Blue Island, Ill., 1983-84. Contbr. articles to profl. jours. Recipient Edn. award Pa. Hosp. Assn., 1992. Mem. Am. Orgn. Nurse Execs., Pa. Orgn. Nurse Execs., Pa. South Ctrl. Orgn. Nurse Execs. (program and mktg. coms., mem.-at-large exec. com.), Sigma Theta Tau. Presbyterian. Avocations: decorating, music. Home: 833 Tallyho Dr Hershey PA 17033-1828

LITTLE, RICHARD CARUTHERS (RICH LITTLE), comedian, impressionist, actor; b. Ottawa, Ont., Can., Nov. 26, 1938; s. Lawrence Peniston and Elizabeth Maud (Wilson) L. Ed., Lisgar Collegiate, Ottawa, 1953-57; student drama, Ottawa Little Theatre, 1950-60. First TV appearance in U.S. on Judy Garland Show, 1964; appearances films, TV, night clubs; host: TV series The Rich Little Show, 1975-76 (Winner Entertainer of Year award 1974), You Asked For It, 1981-83; appeared on TV series Love on a Rooftop, 1966-71, The John Davidson Show, 1969, ABC Comedy Hour, 1972, The Julie Andrews Hour, 1972-73; TV film appearance Dirty Tricks, 1981, Rich Little's Christmas Card, Rich Little's Washington Follies, Parade of Stars, The Christmas Raccoons, Rich Little and Friends in New Orleans; others; rec. albums include My Fellow Canadians, The First Family Rides Again; appeared in films Dirty Tricks, 1981, Happy Hour, 1987. Recipient Maple Leaf Disting. Arts and Letters award, 1983. Office: William Morris Agy 151 S El Camino Dr Beverly Hills CA 90212-2704

LITTLE, ROBERT ANDREWS, architect, designer, painter; b. Brookline, Mass., Sept. 9, 1915; s. Clarence Cook and Katherine Day (Andrews) L.; m. Ann Murphy Halle, Dec., 27, 1940; children: Sam Robertson, Revere (dec.). A.B. cum laude, Harvard U., 1937, M.Arch., 1939. Designer G.H. Perkins, Cambridge, Mass., 1939-41; architect U.S. Navy, Washington, 1941-43; ops. analyst Air Staff Intelligence, Washington, 1943-45; prin. Robert A. Little & Assos., Cleve., 1946-58, 67-69; partner Little & Dalton, Cleve., 1958-67; dir. design Dalton-Dalton-Little-Newport, Cleve., 1969-78; owner Robert A. Little, Design and Architecture, 1978—; tchr., lectr. Harvard, U. Pa., Carnegie Inst. Tech., U. Mich., Smith Coll., U. Notre Dame, Kent State U. Exhibited art and graphics in Cleve., Phila., Boston., since 1970; works include Air Force Mus., Dayton, Ohio, Supreme Ct. and Tower, Columbus, Ohio.; one-person shows in Ohio, Maine, Mass. Trustee Cleve. Mus. Sci., 1952-56, Cleve. Inst. Music, 1956-58; mem. Cleve. Fine Arts Com. Served with U.S. Army, 1940. Fellow AIA (pres. Cleve. chpt. 1966-68, nat. and state design awards), Harvard Sch. of Design Alumni Assn. (past pres., internat. dir. of devel.). Home: 5 Pepper Ridge Rd Cleveland OH 44124-4904 Office: Robert A Little FAIA Design 5 Pepper Ridge Rd Cleveland OH 44124-4904 *As a child, I drew pictures all the time—and they were my current ideal—a face I thought pretty, a massive locomotive, a pine tree against the sea, or a castle in the sky. As an adult Designer and Artist, too, I have spent my whole life dreaming of beauty, and trying to create it—and, of course, never fully succeeding. But the great satisfaction has not been the results, but rather the breathless moments of the search itself, and the boundless horizons of the dream.*

LITTLE, ROBERT COLBY, physiologist, educator; b. Norwalk, Ohio, June 2, 1920; s. Edwin Robert and Eleanor Thresher (Colby) L.; m. Claire Campbell Means, Jan. 20, 1945; children—William C., Edwin C. A.B., Denison U., 1942; M.D., Western Res. U., 1944, M.S., 1948. Intern Grace Hosp., Detroit, 1944-45; USPHS postdoctoral research fellow Western Res. U., 1948-49; resident internal medicine Crile VA Hosp., Cleve., 1949-50; asst. prof. physiology, then assoc. prof. physiology and medicine U. Tenn. Sch. Medicine, 1950-54; rsch. participant Oak Ridge Inst. Nuclear Studies, 1952; dir. clin. research Mead Johnson & Co., 1954-57; lectr. medicine U. Louisville, 1955-57; dir. cardio pulmonary labs. Scott and White Clinic, Scott Sherwood and Brindley Found., Temple, Tex., 1957-59; prof. physiology, asst. prof. medicine Seton Hall Coll. Medicine and Dentistry, 1957-64, acting chmn. dept. physiology, 1961-63; prof. physiology, chmn. dept., also asst. prof. medicine Ohio State U. Sch. Medicine, 1964-73; prof. physiology, prof. medicine Med. Coll. Ga. Sch. Medicine, Augusta, 1973-89, chmn. dept. physiology, 1973-86, prof., chmn. emeritus, 1989—; cons. in field. Author: Physiology of the Heart and Circulation, 1977, 2d edit., 1981, 3d edit., 1985, 4th edit., 1989; editor: Physiology of Atrial Pacemakers and Conductive Tissues, 1980; contbr. articles to profl. jours. Served to capt. M.C. AUS, 1945-47. Mem. Am. Physiol. Soc., So. Soc. Clin. Investigation, Am. Heart Assn., Soc. Exptl. Biology and Medicine, Am. Fedn. Clin. Research, Sigma Xi, Sigma Chi, Alpha Kappa Kappa, Alpha Omega Alpha. Home: 523 Brandon Village 4275 Owens Rd Evans GA 30809

LITTLE, ROBERT DAVID, library science educator; b. Milw., July 11, 1937; s. Kenneth Edwin and Grace Elizabeth (Terwilliger) L. BA, U. Wis., Milw., 1959; MA, U. Wis., 1964, PhD, 1972. Tchr., sch. librarian Sevastapol Pub. Schs., Sturgeon Bay, Wis., 1959-62; sch. librarian Highland Park (Ill.) High Sch., 1962-63; supr. sch. libraries Sevastapol/Gilbraltor Pub. Sch., Sturgeon Bay, 1963-65; state sch. library supr. Wis. Dept. Pub. Instrn., Madison, 1965-69, program adminstr., 1969-70; asst. prof. libr. sci. U. Wis., Milw., 1970-71, acting dir. Sch. Libr. Sci., 1971; assoc. prof. libr. sci. Ind. State U., Terre Haute, 1971-77, prof., 1977—, chmn. dept., 1971-93; cons. Ind. Nat. Network Study, Terre Haute, 1978-79; cons., researcher Nat. Ctr. Edn. Stats., Washington, 1978-79; mem. Ind. State Libr. Adv. Coun., Indpls., 1981-91. Co-author: Public Library Users and Uses, 1988; editor: Cataloging, Processing, Administering AV Materials, 1972; contbr. articles to profl. jours. Pres. West Cen. Ind. chpt. Ind. Civil Liberties Union, 1988-92. Edn. Act fellow U. Wis., Madison, 1967, 68. Mem. ALA, Am. Assn. Sch. Librs., Assn. Ind. Media Educators (pres. 1981-82, Peggy Leach Pfeiffer Svc. award 1987), AAUP. Methodist. Avocations: reading, travel. Home: 376 Keane Ln Terre Haute IN 47803-2010 Office: Ind State U Ctr for Libr Sci Reeve Hall 336 Terre Haute IN 47809

LITTLE, ROBERT EUGENE, mechanical engineering educator, materials behavior researcher, consultant; b. Enfield, Ill., May 24, 1933; s. John Henry and Mary (Stephens) L.; m. Barbara Louina Farrell, Feb. 4, 1961; children: Susan Elizabeth, James Robert, Richard Roy, John William. BSME, U. Mich., 1959; MSME, Ohio State U., 1960; PhDME, U. Mich., 1963. Asst. prof. mech. engrng. Okla. State U., Stillwater, 1963-65; assoc. prof. U. Mich., Dearborn, 1965-68, prof., 1968—. Author: Statistical Design of Fatigue Experiments, 1975, Probability and Statistics for Engineers, 1978. Mershon fellow Ohio State U., 1960. Mem. ASTM, Am. Statis. Assn., Rehab. Engrng. Soc. N.Am. Home: 3230 Pine Lake Rd West Bloomfield MI 48324-1951 Office: U Mich 4901 Evergreen Rd Dearborn MI 48128-1491

LITTLE, SYLVIA FORD, oil industry executive. Student, So. Meth. U., Scottsdale Community Coll., Ariz. Owner, operator gas and oil properties San Juan Basin, N.Mex., 1977—; pres. Little Oil & Gas, Inc., San Juan Basin, N.Mex. Founder Farmington (N.Mex.) Totah Festival of Authentic Indian Art; chmn. residential com. Town Forum 2000, 1980; mem. exec. com., state ctrl. com. N.Mex. Rep. Com., 1984-86; bd. dirs. N.Mex. Fedn. Rep. Women, 1984-90, Farmington LWV, Four Corners Better Bus. Bur., 1993—; mem. industry adv. com. to N.Mex. Dept. Energy, 1993; mem. N.Mex. Bd. Econ. Devel. Commrs., 1994—. mem. Ind. Petroleum Assn. N.Mex. (pres.-elect 1990, pres. 1991-93), N.Mex. Oil and Gas Assn. (exec. com. 1993-96), Assn. Commerce and Industry N.Mex. (bd. dirs. 1988-92), Farmington C. of C. (pres. 1996, redcoats amb. com.), Rotary. Avocations: needlepoint, photography. Office: 2346 E 20th St Farmington NM 87401-8906

LITTLE, THOMAS MAYER, public relations executive; b. Columbus, Ohio, Dec. 21, 1935; s. John William and Eulalia Josephine (Mayer) L.; m. Susan Mulford, Sept. 29, 1959; children: Carin Andrea, Debora Mayer, Sharon Mulford, Patricia Anne. BS in Journalism, Northwestern U., 1958; postgrad., Bradley U., 1958. Account supr. Philip Lesly Co., Chgo., 1962-77; v.p., account supr. Burson-Marsteller, N.Y.C., 1977; v.p. Foote Cone & Belding, Inc., N.Y.C., 1977-78; pres. FCB Pub. Rels., N.Y.C., 1978-81, Bus. Orgn., Inc. div. Carl Byoir & Assocs., N.Y.C., 1982, Tracy-Locke/BBDO Pub. Rels., Dallas, 1983-85; exec. v.p., gen. mgr. Manning, Selvage & Lee, N.Y.C., 1986; pres. T.J. Ross & Assocs., N.Y.C., 1986-87; pres., gen. mgr. Golin/Harris Communication, N.Y., 1987-91; pub. rels. cons., 1992—. Bd. dirs. Damon Runyon-Walter Winchell Cancer Fund, N.Y.C. Lt. (j.g.) USN, 1959-62. Mem. Am. Mktg. Assn., Pub. Rels. Soc. Am., Publicity Club N.Y.C., Mt. Kisco (N.Y.) Country Club, Sea Pines Country Club (Hilton Head Island), Lotos Club (N.Y.C.), Sigma Alpha Epsilon. Roman Catholic. Home and Office: 2 Newhall Rd Hilton Head Island SC 29928-3112

LITTLE, THOMAS WARREN, broadcast executive; b. Portland, Oreg., June 24, 1939; s. Hollis R. and Bernice (Lesseg) L.; m. Ruth Brady, Aug. 31, 1958; children—Vincent Thomas, Elizabeth Ann. BA and MA in Radio-TV, UCLA. Stage mgr. Sta. KPIX-TV, San Francisco, 1969-61; producer, dir. Sta. KVCR-TV, San Bernadino, Calif., 1963-65; telecommunications prof. San Bernadino Valley Coll., 1965-75; gen. mgr. Sta. KVCR-TV, Sta. KVCR-FM, San Bernadino, 1975-77, dir. radio, TV, 1979—; dir. TV Sta. KVZK-TV, Pago Pago, Am. Samoa, 1977-79. Served with U.S. Army, 1961-63. Mem. Assn. Calif. Pub. TV Stations, Calif. Pub. Radio, Pub. Broadcasting Service, Pacific Mountain Network. Democrat. Office: Sta KVCR-TV 701 S Mount Vernon Ave San Bernardino CA 92410-2705

LITTLE, W(ILLIA)M A(LFRED), foreign language educator, researcher; b. Boston, July 28, 1929; s. Wm. A. and Myrle A. (Holmes) L. BA, Tufts U., 1951; LTCL, Trinity Coll., London, 1952; MA, Harvard U., 1953, PhD, 1961. Asst. prof. Williams Coll., Williamstown, Mass., 1957-63; assoc. prof., chair Tufts U., Medford, Mass., 1963-66; chair U. Va., Charlottesville, 1966-72, prof., 1966-95, prof. German and music emeritus, 1995—; vis. prof. musicology U. Rochester, N.Y., 1996—. Author: G.A. Bürger, 1974; editor: Mendelssohn-Complete Organ Works, 5 vols., 1987-90; editor The German Quarterly, 1970-78; contbr. articles to profl. jours. Cpl. U.S. Army, 1953-55. Sesquicentennial fellow U. Va., 1972-73, 78-79, 88-89. Mem. MLA (chair comp. lit. 1970-72), Am. Assn. Tchrs. German (nat. exec. coun. 1968-78), Am. Guild Organists (registrar Mass. chpt. 1949-53, dean Charlottesville chpt. 1977-78, registrar, archivist Ctrl. Fla. chpt. 1995—, nat. com. profl. edn. 1993—), Am. Mus. Soc., Orgn. Hist. Soc. Home: 6853 S Atlantic Ave New Smyrna Beach FL 32169

LITTLE, WILLIAM ARTHUR, physicist, educator; b. South Africa, Nov. 17, 1930; came to U.S., 1958, naturalized, 1964; s. William Henry and Margaret (Macleod) L.; m. Annie W. Smith, July 15, 1955; children—Lucy Claire, Linda Susan, Jonathan William. Ph.D., Rhodes U., S. Africa, 1953, Glasgow (Scotland) U., 1957. Faculty Stanford, 1958—, prof. physics, 1965-94; prof. emeritus, 1994—; cons. to industry, 1960—; co-founder, chmn. MMR Techs. Inc., 1980—. Recipient Deans award for disting. teaching Stanford U., 1975-76, Walter J. Gores award for excellence in teaching, Stanford U., 1979, IR-100 award Indsl. Rsch. and Devel., 1981; NRC Can. postdoctoral fellow Vancouver, Can., 1956-58, Sloan Found. fellow, 1959-63, John Simon Guggenheim fellow, 1964-65, NSF sr. postdoctoral fellow, 1970-71. Fellow Am. Phys. Soc. Spl. research low temperature physics, superconductivity, neural network theory cryogenics; holder 10 patents in area of cryogenics and med. instrumentation. Home: 15 Crescent Dr Palo Alto CA 94301-3106 Office: Stanford Univ Dept Physics Stanford CA 94305

LITTLE, WILLIAM CAMPBELL, cardiologist, physiologist; b. Cleve., May 1, 1950; s. Robert Colby and Claire (Means) L.; m. Constance Lydia Loydall, June 9, 1975; children: John Campbell, Elizabeth Loydall. BA in Physics, Oberlin Coll., 1972; MD, Ohio State U., 1975. Diplomate Am. Bd. of Internal Medicine, Am. Bd. Cardiovascular Disease. Intern, then resident in internal medicine U. Va. Hosp., 1975-78; fellow in cardiology Sch. of Medicine U. Ala.; instr. U. Ala. Sch. Medicine, Birmingham, 1980-81; asst. prof. medicine U. Tex. Health Sci. Ctr., San Antonio, 1981-84, assoc. prof. medicine, 1984-86; assoc. prof. medicine Bowman Gray Sch. Medicine, Winston-Salem, N.C., 1986-89, prof. medicine, 1989—, chief cardiology, 1990—; cons. study sec. NIH, Bethesda, Md., 1987—. Co-author: (book) Physiology of the Heart and Circulation, 1989; contbr. over 100 articles on cardiac physiology and clin. cardiology to profl. publs. Recipient Established Investigator award Am. Heart Assn., 1986-91, Young Investigator award So. Sec. Am. Fedn. Clin. Rsch., 1991; grantee NIH, 1985—. Mem. Am. Coll. Cardiology, Am. Physiological Soc. (Lamport award 1987), Am. Soc. Clin. Investigation (Harrison award 1993), Assn. Univ. Cardiologists. Presbyterian. Office: Bowman Gray Sch Medicine Medical Ctr Blvd Winston Salem NC 27157

LITTLEFIELD, EDMUND WATTIS, mining company executive; b. Ogden, Utah, Apr. 16, 1914; s. Edmond Arthur and Marguerite (Wattis) L.; m. Jeannik Mequet, June 14, 1945; children: Edmund Wattis, Jacques Mequet, Denise Renee. BA with great distinction, Stanford U., 1936, MBA, 1938. With Standard Oil Co. of Calif., 1938-41, Golden State Co., Ltd., 1946-50; v.p., treas. Utah Internat. Inc. (formerly Utah Constrn. & Mining Co.), San Francisco, 1951-56; exec. com., dir. Utah Internat. Inc. (formerly Utah Constrn. & Mining Co.), 1951—, exec. v.p., 1956, gen. mgr., 1958—, pres., 1961—, chmn. bd., 1971—, chief exec. officer, 1971-78, chmn. exec. com., dir., 1978-86; bd. dirs. SRI Internat., FMC Gold. Served as lt. (j.g.) USNR, 1941-43; spl. asst. to dep. adminstr. Petroleum Adminstrn. for War 1943-45. Recipient Ernest C. Arbuckle award Stanford Bus. Sch. Assn., 1970, Golden Beaver award, 1970, Bldg. Industry Achievement award, 1972, Harvard Bus. Statesman award, 1974, Internat. Achievement award World Trade Club, 1986; named to Nat. Mining Hall of Fame. Mem. San Francisco C. of C. (pres. 1956), Bus. Council (hon. mem., past chmn.), Conf. Bd., Phi Beta Kappa, Chi Psi. Clubs: Burlingame (Calif.) Country; Pacific Union, San Francisco Golf (San Francisco); Augusta National Golf, Eldorado Country; Bohemian, Cypress Point (Pebble Beach, Calif.); Vintage. Office: 550 California St San Francisco CA 94104-1006

LITTLEFIELD, JOHN WALLEY, physiology educator, geneticist, cell biologist, pediatrician; b. Providence, Dec. 3, 1925; s. Ivory and Mary Russell (Walley) L.; m. Elizabeth Legge, Nov. 11, 1950; children: Peter P., John W., Elizabeth L. M.D., Harvard U., 1947; MHS, Johns Hopkins U, 1992. Diplomate: Am. Bd. Internal Medicine. Intern Mass. Gen. Hosp., Boston, 1947-48; resident in medicine Mass. Gen. Hosp., 1948-50, staff, 1956-74, chief genetics unit children's service, 1966-73; asso. in medicine Harvard U. Med. Sch., 1956-62, asst. prof. medicine, 1962-66, asst. prof. pediatrics, 1966-69, prof. pediatrics, 1970-73; prof., chmn. dept. pediatrics Johns Hopkins U. Sch. Medicine, Balt., 1974-85; pediatrician-in-chief Johns Hopkins U. Hosp., 1974-85; prof., chmn. dept. physiology Johns Hopkins U. Sch. Medicine, Balt., 1985-92. Author: Variation, Senescence and Neoplasia in Cultured Somatic Cells, 1976. Served with USNR, 1952-54. Guggenheim fellow, 1965-66; Josiah Macy Jr. Found. fellow Oxford U. Mem. NAS, Am. Acad. Arts and Scis., Am. Soc. Biol. Chemists, Am. Soc. Clin. Investigation, Tissue Culture Assn., Soc. Pediatric Rsch., Am. Soc. Human Genetics, Am. Pediatric Soc., Assn. Am. Physicians, Phi Beta Kappa, Alpha Omega Alpha, Delta Omega. Home: 304 Golf Course Rd Owings Mills MD 21117-4114 Office: Johns Hopkins U Sch Medicine Dept Physiology Baltimore MD 21205

LITTLEFIELD, MARTIN (MARTIN KLEINWALD), book publishing executive; b. N.Y.C., 1940; m. Sheila Kleinwald; children: Susanne Camilleri, Lisa Wolf. Pres., CEO Vantage Press, Inc., N.Y.C. Office: Vantage Press Inc 516 W 34th St New York NY 10001-1311

LITTLEFIELD, PAUL DAMON, management consultant; b. Cambridge, Mass., June 8, 1920; s. W. Joseph and Sally Pastorius (Damon) L.; m. Emmy Farnsworth Neiley, June 19, 1943 (dec. Apr. 9, 1982); children: Diane Neiley Littlefield Ritsher, Elizabeth Damon Littlefield Lehman, Paul Damon Jr.; m. Lucy Jean Boyd, Dec. 30, 1983. A.B., Harvard U., 1942, M.B.A. with distinction (Baker scholar), 1948. Assoc., Freeport Minerals Co., N.Y.C., 1948-50, 52-62, treas., 1956-62; v.p. finance, treas. Arthur D. Little, Inc., Cambridge, 1962-73; sr. v.p., chief fin. officer Arthur D. Little, Inc., 1973-85, cons., 1985—; pres. Brynmere Assoc., Inc., 1991-92; asst. to pres. Coty, Inc., 1950-52; hon. bd. mem. Cambridge Trust Co.; mem. investment com. Cape Ann and N.E. Health Sys., Inc. Trustee Old Sturbridge Village, ESOP Arthur D. Little, Cambridge. Mem. Fin. Execs. Inst., Harvard Bus. Sch. Assn. Boston (past pres.), Treas.' Club of Boston. Home: 15 Norwood Heights Annisquam Gloucester MA 01930 Office: Acorn Pk Cambridge MA 02140

LITTLEFIELD, ROBERT STEPHEN, communication educator, training consultant; b. Moorhead, Minn., June 21, 1952; s. Harry Jr. and LeVoyne Irene (Berg) L.; m. Kathy Mae Soleim, May 24, 1974; children: Lindsay Jane, Brady Robert. BS in Edn., Moorhead State U., 1974; MA, N.D. State U., 1979; PhD, U. Minn., 1983. Tchr. Barnesville (Minn.) Pub. Schs., 1974-78; teaching asst. N.D. State U., Fargo, 1978-79, lectr., 1979-81; teaching assoc. U. Minn., Mpls., 1981-82; instr. N.D. State U., Fargo, 1982-83, asst. prof., chmn., 1983-89, assoc. prof., chmn., 1989-90, interim dean, 1990-92, assoc. prof., chmn., 1992-94, prof., 1994—; dir. Inst. for Study of Cultural Diversity, 1992—; owner KIDSPEAK Co., Moorhead, 1987—. Author, co-author: (series) KIDSPEAK, 1989-92; lyricist (centennial hymn) Built on a Triangle with Faith in the Triune, 1989; contbr. articles to profl. jours. Mem. Fargo Lions Club, 1984—, pres., 1990-91. Recipient Burlington No. award N.D. State U., 1988-89; named Outstanding Speech Educator, Nat. Fedn. High Sch. Activities Assn., 1990-91. Mem. Am. Forensic Assn. (sec. 1990-92), N.D. Speech and Theatre Assn. (historian 1989—, pres. 1985-87, past pres. 1987-89, Hall of Fame 1989, Scholar of Yr. 1989), N.D. Multicultural Assn., Speech Comm. Assn., Pi Kappa Delta (nat. pres. 1991-93). Democrat. Lutheran. Office: ND State U 321G Minard Hall Fargo ND 58105

LITTLEFIELD, ROY EVERETT, III, association executive, legal educator; b. Nashua, N.H., Dec. 6, 1952; s. Roy Everett and Mary Ann (Prestipino) L.; m. Amy Root; children: Leah Marie, Roy Everett IV, Christy Louise. BA, Dickinson Coll., 1975; MA, Catholic U. Am., 1976, PhD, 1979. Aide U.S. Senator Thomas McIntyre, Democrat, N.H., 1975-78, Nordy Hoffman, U.S. Senate Sergeant-at-arms, N.H., 1979; dir. govt. rels. Nat. Tire Dealers and Retreaders Assn., Washington, N.H., 1979-84; exec. dir. Svc. Sta. and Automotive Repair Assn., Washington, N.H., 1984—; exec. v.p. Svc. Sta. Dealers of Am., 1994—; cons. Am. Retreaders Assn., 1984; mem. faculty Cath. U. Am., Washington, 1979—. Author: William Randolph Hearst: His Role in American Progressivism, 1980, The Economic Recovery Act, 1982, The Surface: Transportation Assistance Act, 1984; editor Nozzle mag.; contbr. numerous articles to legal jours. Mem. Nat. Dem. Club, 1978—. Mem. Am. Soc. Legal History, Md. Hwy. User's Fedn. (pres.), Nat. Hwy. User's Fedn. (bd. dirs.), Nat. Capitol Area Transp. Fedn. (v.p.), N.H. Hist. Soc., Kansas City C. of C., Capitol Hill Club, Phi Alpha Theta. Roman Catholic. Home: 1707 Pepper Tree Ct Bowie MD 20721-3021 Office: 9420 Annapolis Rd Ste 307 Lanham Seabrook MD 20706-3021

LITTLEFIELD, VIVIAN MOORE, nursing educator, administrator; b. Princeton, Ky., Jan. 24, 1938; children: Darrell, Virginia. B.S. magna cum laude, Tex. Christian U., 1960; M.S., U. Colo., 1964; Ph.D., U. Denver, 1979. Staff nurse USPHS Hosp., Ft. Worth, Tex., 1960-61; instr. nursing Tex. Christian U., Ft. Worth, 1961-62; nursing supr. Colo. Gen. Hosp., Denver, 1964-65, pvt. patient practitioner, 1974-78; asst. prof. nursing U. Colo., Denver, 1965-69, asst. prof., clin. instr., 1971-74, asst. prof., 1974-76, acting asst. dean, assoc. prof. continuing edn., regional perinatal project, 1976-78; assoc. prof., chair dept. women's health care nursing U. Rochester Sch. Nursing, N.Y., 1979-84; clin. chief ob-gyn., nursing U. Rochester Strong Meml. Hosp., N.Y., 1979-84; prof., dean U. Wis. Sch. Nursing, Madison, 1984—; cons. and lectr. in field. Author: Maternity Nursing Today, 1973, 76, Health Education for Women: A guide for Nurses and Other Health Professionals, 1986; mem. editorial bd. Jour. Profl. Nursing; contbr. articles to profl. jours. Bur. Health Professions Fed. trainee, 1963-64; Nat. Sci. Service award, 1976-79. Mem. MAIN, AACN (bd. dirs.), NLN (bd. dirs.), Am. Acad. Nursing, Am. Nurses Assn., Consortium Prime Care Wis. (chair), Health Care for Women Internat., Midwest Nursing Research Soc., Sigma Theta Tau (pres. Beta Eta chpt., co-chair coun nursing practice and edn. 1995). Avocations: golf, biking. Office: U Wis Sch Nursing 600 Highland Ave # H6 150 Madison WI 53792-0001

LITTLEFIELD, WARREN, television executive; m. Theresa Littlefield; 2 children. Student, Am. U., Washington; grad. in psychology, Hobart Coll., Geneva, N.Y. With Westfall Prodns., N.Y.C.; dir. comedy devel. Warner Bros. TV, 1979; mgr. comedy devel. NBC, 1979-81, v.p. current comedy programs, 1981-85; sr. v.p series, spls. and variety programming NBC Entertainment, 1985-87, exec. v.p. prime time programs, 1987-90, pres., 1990—. Office: NBC Entertainment 3000 W Alameda Ave Burbank CA 91523-0001

LITTLEJOHN, DAVID, journalism educator, writer; b. San Francisco, May 8, 1937; s. George Thomas and Josephine Mildred (Cullen) L.; m. Sheila Beatrice Hageman, June 10, 1963; children: Victoria Schoenke, Gregory David. BA, U. Calif., Berkeley, 1959; MA, Harvard U., 1961, PhD, 1963. Asst. prof. English U. Calif., Berkeley, 1963-69, assoc. prof. journalism, 1969-76, prof., 1976—, chmn. com. ednl. policy, 1981-82, chmn. senate policy com., vice chmn. acad. senate, 1984-86, assoc. dean Grad. Sch. Journalism, 1974-78, 85-86, 87-89. Author: (novel) The Man Who Killed Mick Jagger, 1977, (novel) Going to California, 1981, Architect: The Life and Work of Charles W. Moore, 1984, The Ultimate Art: Essays around and about Opera, 1992, also 7 other books, over 200 articles and 200 TV programs; arts critic Sta. KQED-TV, San Francisco, 1965-75, PBS nationwide, 1971-72; critic and corr. London Times, 1975-89, Architecture mag., 1984-89, Wall St. Jour., 1990—. Fulbright lectr., Montpellier, France, 1966-67; Am. Coun. Learned Socs. rsch. fellow, London, 1972-73; NEH grantee 1976-77. Mem. Arts Club (Berkeley). Democrat. Roman Catholic. Home: 719 Coventry Rd Kensington CA 94707-1403 Office: U Calif Grad Sch Journalism Berkeley CA 94720

LITTLEJOHN, MICHAEL A., electrical engineer, educator; b. King Mountain, N.C., Aug. 11, 1940. BSEE, N.C. State U., 1962, MSEE, 1964, PhD, 1966. Prof. elec. engring. N.C. State U. Fellow IEEE (seccion chmn./organizer regional symposium 1972, program organizer/session chmn. 1981, organizer IEEE/NSF Cooperation and Sharing Among US Microelectronics Ctrs. workshop 1981, pub. chmn. Tech. Digest of Internat. Electron Devices meeting 1983, mem. program com./session chmn. Internat. Conf. on Indium Phosphide and Related Materials for Advanced Electronics and Optical Devices 1989, mem. engring. R & D com. 1986-92, adv. bd. awards program for innovative educators 1992—, jour. reviewer). Office: North Carolina State Univ Electrical Eng Dept 232 Daniels Hall Raleigh NC 27607*

LITTLER, GENE ALEC, professional golfer; b. San Diego, Calif., July 21, 1930; s. Stanley Fred and Dorothy (Paul) L.; m. Shirley Mae Warren, Jan. 5, 1951; children: Curt Michael, Suzanne. Student, San Diego State Coll. Mem. U.S. Ryder Cup Team, 61, 63, 65, 67, 69, 71, 75. Served with USN, 1951-54. Winner 29 PGA tour events including Nat. Jr. Championship, 1948, Nat. Amateur Championship, 1953, U.S. Open, 1961, Canadian Open, 1965, Tournament of Champions, 1955, 56, 57, World Series of Golf, 1966, Taheiyo Masters, Japan, 1974, 75, Australian Masters, 15 sr. tour titles and Coca Cola Grand Slam, Japan, 1983, 87.

LITTLE RICHARD (RICHARD WAYNE PENNIMAN), recording artist, pianist, songwriter, minister; b. Macon, Ga., Dec. 5, 1932; s. Bud and Leva Mae Penniman; m. Ernestine Campbell, 1957 (div.). BA, Oakwood Coll. Sem., Huntsville, Ala., 1961. Ordained to ministry Seventh Day Adventist Ch., 1961. Began singing and dancing on streets of Macon, Ga., 1942; won talent shows in Atlanta, 1943 and 1951; toured with Dr. Hudson's Medicine Show and other shows, 1949-51; worked with own band doing dances and clubs, 1951-52, with Tempo Toppers in New Orleans, 1953-54; recording artist Peacock Records, Houston, 1953-54, Splty. Records, 1955-58, 64; toured in Big 10 Package shows, U.S., Australia and Gt. Brit., 1957-58; recording artist Veejay Records, 1964-65. Songs include Long Tall Sally, Tutti Frutti, Slippin' and Slidin', Rip it Up, Ready Teddy, Lucille, Send Me Some Lovin', Jenny, Jenny, Miss Ann, Keep A-Knockin', Good Golly Miss Molly, Baby Face, True Fine Mama, Kansas City, Bama Lama Bama Loo, Freedom Blues, Greenwood Mississippi; albums include Here's Little Richard, 1958, Little Richard 2, 1958, The Fabulous, 1959, Well Alright, 1959, Sings Gospel, 1964, Coming Home, 1964, Sings Freedom Songs, 1964, King of Gospel Songs, 1965, Wild & Frantic, 1965, The Explosive, 1967, The Explosive & Roy Orbison, 1970, The Rill Thing, 1971, King of Rock N Roll, 1971, Second Coming, 1971, All Time Hits, 1972, Rock Hard Rock Heavy, 1972, The Very Best Of, 1975, Georgia Peach, 1980, Get Down With It, 1982, Ooh! My Soul, 1983, Lucile, 1984, Shut Up, 1988, The Specialty Sessions, 1990, Greatest Songs, 1995, Mega-Mix, 1995; film appearances include The Girl Can't Help It, 1956, Don't Knock the Rock, 1957, She's Got It, 1957, Mr. Rock and Roll, 1957, Jimi Plays Berkeley, 1970, Let the Good Times Roll, 1973, Jimi Hendrix, 1973, Down and Out in Beverly Hills, 1985; TV appearances include Tonight Show, Merv Griffin Show, Mike Douglas Show, Smothers Brothers Show, American Bandstand, Glen Campbell Good Time Hour, Tom Jones Show, Midnight Special, Donny & Marie Show; stage appearances include Paramount Theatre, The Felt Forum, Wembley Stadium, Hollywood Paladium. Inducted Rock & Roll Hall of Fame. Office: PO Box 29 Hollywood CA 90028

LITTLETON, CAROL, film editor. Editor: (films) The Mafu Cage, 1978, French Postcards, 1979, Roadie, 1980, Body Heat, 1981, E.T. The Extra-Terrestrial, 1982 (Academy award nomination best film editing 1982), The Big Chill, 1983, Places in the Heart, 1984, Silverado, 1985, Brighton Beach Memoirs, 1986, Swimming to Cambodia, 1987, The Accidental Tourist, 1988, Vibes, 1988, White Palace, 1990, Grand Canyon, 1991, Benny & Joon, 1993, China Moon, 1994, Wyatt Earp, 1994. Office: care United Talent 9560 Wilshire Blvd Ste 500 Beverly Hills CA 90212

LITTLETON, HARVEY KLINE, artist; b. Corning, N.Y., June 14, 1922; s. Jesse Talbot and Bessie (Cook) L.; m. Bess Toyo Tamura, Sept. 6, 1947; children—Carol Louise Littleton Shay, Thomas Harvey, Kathryn Tamra (dec.), Maurine Bess, John Christopher. Student, U. Mich., 1939-42, B.Design, 1947; M.F.A., Cranbrook Acad. Art, 1951; D.F.A., Phila. Coll. Art. Instr. ceramics Toledo Mus. Art, 1949-51; prof. art U. Wis., Madison, 1951-77; chmn. dept. U. Wis., 1964-67, 69-71, prof. emeritus, 1977—. Author: Glass Blowing - A Search for Form, 1971; recent one- and two-man exhbns. include Lee Nordness Galleries, N.Y.C., 1969-70, Maison de Culture, Liege, Belgium, 1974, J & L Lobmeyr, Vienna, 1974, Brooks Meml. Art Gallery, Memphis, 1975, Contemporary Art Glass Gallery, N.Y.C., 1977, 78, 79, Habatat Gallery, Detroit, 1980, 81, Heller Gallery, N.Y.C., 1980, 81, 82, 83, 84, 85, Glasmuseum Ebeltoft, Sweden, 1989, Royal Copenhagen Gallery, 1989, Finnish Glasmuseum, Riihimaki, Finland, 1989, Kunsthaus am Mus., Cologne, Germany, 1990, Immenhausen, Germany, 1990, Glasmuseum, Frauenau, Germany, 1992, Yokohama (Japan) Mus. Art, 1995, retrospective exhbn. originated by High Mus. Art, Atlanta, 1984, traveling to the Renwick Gallery, Am. Craft Mus., Iowa State U., Milw. Art Mus. and Portland (Maine) Mus. Art; represented in permanent collections, Victoria and Albert Mus., London, museums in, Germany, Holland, Switzerland, Belgium, Austria and, Czechoslovakia, also, Met. Mus. Art, N.Y.C., Mus. Modern Art, N.Y.C., Am. Craft Mus., N.Y.C., L.A. County Mus. Art., L.A., Corning Mus. of Glass, Toledo Mus. Art, Detroit Art Inst., Milw. Art Center, Smithsonian Instn., Washington, High Mus. Art, Atlanta, Chrysler Mus., Norfolk, Va., U. Mich., U. Ill., Ohio State U., Phila. Mus. Art, The White House, Washington, numerous other pub. and pvt. collections. Bd. dirs. Penland Sch., N.C., pres. bd. dirs., 1986-88; pres., chmn. Littleton Co., Inc., Spruce Pine, N.C., 1981—. With Signal Corps U.S. Army, 1942-45, ETO. Recipient Fine Arts award Gov. of N.C., 1987; Toledo Mus. Art research grantee, 1962; Louis Comfort Tiffany Found. grantee, 1970-71; Corning Glass Works grantee, 1974; U. Wis. research grantee, 1954, 57, 62, 73, 75; Nat. Endowment for Arts grantee, 1978-79; Diploma of Honor, Glass Mus. Frauenau, Fed. Republic Germany. Fellow Am. Crafts Coun. (trustee 1957, 61-64, trustee emeritus, gold medal 1983), Corning Mus. Glass (Rakow award for excellence in art of glass); mem. Nat. Coun. for Edn. in Ceramic Arts (hon.), Glass Art Soc. (hon. life, lifetime achievement award 1993), Am. Ceramic Soc. (hon. life).

LITTLETON, ISAAC THOMAS, III, retired university library administrator, consultant; b. Hartsville, Tenn., Jan. 28, 1921; s. Isaac Thomas Jr. and Bessie (Lowe) L.; m. Dorothy Etta Young, Aug. 12, 1949; children—Sally Lowe Littleton Phillips, Thomas Young, Elizabeth Ann. B.A., U. N.C., Chapel Hill, 1943; M.A., U. Tenn., Knoxville, 1950; M.S.L.S., U. Ill., Champaign-Urbana, 1951, Ph.D., 1968. Circulation librarian, asst. librarian U. N.C., Chapel Hill, 1951-58; asst. dir. then dir. libraries N.C. State U., Raleigh, 1959-87; emeritus dir. libraries N.C. State U., 1987—; mem. N.C. Libr. Networking Steering Com., Raleigh, 1982-85; bd. dirs. Southeastern Libr. Network, Atlanta, 1973-74, 83-86, chmn., 1985-86; chmn. Assn. Southeastern Rsch. Librs., 1969-71; mem. com. Gov.'s Conf. on Libr. and Info. Svcs., 1990. Author: The Literature of Agricultural Economics, 1969, State Systems of Higher Education and Libraries, 1977, D.H. Hill Library: An Informal Historu, 1993; editor: N.C. Union List of Scientific Serials, 1967. Bd. dirs., treas. Theater in Park, Raleigh, 1982-85, Friends of Wake County Pub. Librs.; sec. N.C. State U. Friends of Libr., Raleigh, 1964-87, bd. dirs., 1990-94; pres. Friends of N.C. Libr. for Blind and Physically Handicapped, 1989-93, bd. dirs. 1993—; v.p. Wake County UN Assn., 1994-95. Lt. (j.g.) USN, 1943-46, PTO. Council on Library Resources fellow, Washington, 1975-76. Mem. Southeastern Library Assn. (exec. bd. 1974-78), N.C. Library Assn. (exec. bd. 1969-71, hon. life). Mem. Community United Ch. of Christ. Club: Torch (pres. Raleigh, N.C. 1974-75). Avocations: theater; reading; concerts. Home: 4813 Brookhaven Dr Raleigh NC 27612-5706

LITTLETON, JESSE TALBOT, III, radiology educator; b. Corning, N.Y., Apr. 27, 1917; s. Jesse Talbot and Bessie (Cook) L.; m. Martha Louise Morrow, Apr. 17, 1943 (dec. 1994); children: Christine, Joanne, James, Robert, Denise; m. Mary Lou Durizch, Mar. 25, 1995. Student, Emory (Va.) and Henry Coll., 1934-35. Johns Hopkins U., 1935-39; MD, Syracuse U., 1939-43. Diplomate Am. Bd. Radiology, Intern Buffalo Gen. Hosp., 1943; resident in medicine, surgery and radiology Robert Packer Hosp., Sayre, Pa., 1946-51, assoc. radiologist, 1951-53, chmn. dept. radiology, 1953-76; prof. radiology U. South Ala., Mobile, 1976-87, prof. emeritus, 1987—; cons. in field. Author textbooks (3); contbr. chpts. to books and 100 articles to profl. jours., sci. exhibits to profl. confs. Served to capt. U.S. Army MC, 1944-46; Pacific. Fellow Am. Coll. Radiology; mem. AMA, Radiol. Soc. N.Am., Am. Roentgen Ray Soc., Ala. Acad. Radiology, Med. Assn. Ala., French Soc. Neuroradiology, Sigma Xi, Alpha Omega Alpha. Republican. Methodist. Club: Country of Mobile (Ala.). Research on conventional tomography, phys. principles, equipment devel. and testing and clin. applications; transp. and radiology of acutely ill and traumatized patient; angiography, devel. first sheet film serialograph; devel. of equipment for sectional radiographic anatomy. Home: 5504 Churchill Downs St Theodore AL 36582-9622 Office: U South Ala Med Ctr 2451 Fillingim St Mobile AL 36617-2238

LITTLETON, TAYLOR DOWE, humanities educator; b. Birmingham, Ala., Mar. 14, 1930; s. M. Taylor and Florence (Longcrier) L.; m. Lucy Williams, Aug. 7, 1954; children: Dowe, George, Franklin, Mary Wood. B.S., Fla. State U., 1951, M.A., 1952, Ph.D., 1960. Teaching fellow Fla. State U., Tallahassee, 1954-57; from instr. to prof. dept. English Auburn U., Ala., 1957—, dean undergrad. studies, 1968-71, v.p. for acad. affairs, 1972-83, W. Kelly Mosley prof. sci. and humanities, 1983—. Author: Advancing American Art: Painting, Politics, and Cultural Confrontation at Mid-century, 1989, Athletics and Academe: An Anatomy of Abuses and a Prescription for Reform, 1991; author, editor: To Prove A Villain: The Case of King Richard III, 1964, The Idea of Tragedy, 1965; editor: multi-vol. series The Franklin Lectures in Sci. and Humanities: Approaching the Benign Environment, 1970; The Shape of Likelihood, 1974, A Time To Hear and Answer, 1977, The Rights of Memory, 1985; assoc. editor So. Humanities Rev., 1967-70. Served with U.S. Army, 1952-54. Mem. So. Atlantic MLA, Phi Kappa Phi, Omicron Delta Kappa. Democrat. Episcopalian. Home: 415 Norman Cir Auburn AL 36830-6307 Office: Auburn U Dept Sci & Humanities Haley 9030 Auburn AL 36830

LITTLEWOOD, DOUGLAS BURDEN, business brokerage executive; b. Buffalo, Sept. 24, 1922; s. Frank and G. Joan (Burden) L.; m. Jevene Hope Baker, July 2, 1949; children—Douglas Baker, Dean Houston, Laurie Littlewood Vogelsang. B.S. in Mech. Engring, Rensselaer Poly. Inst., 1945; M.B.A., Harvard, 1947. Sales engr. Otis Elevator Co., 1948-49; asst. to sec. Nat Gypsum Co., Buffalo, 1949-52; sec. Nat Gypsum Co., 1952-67; investment banker Hornblower & Weeks, 1967-68; pres. Littlewood Assocs., Inc., 1968-95, chmn. bd., 1995—. Past pres. Greater Niagara Frontier coun. Boy Scouts Am.; active Buffalo YMCA, United Fund; bd. dirs. Presbyn. Homes of Western N.Y.; bd. dirs., chmn. emeritus Salvation Army; v.p. N.E. region Boy Scouts Am. Served to lt. (j.g.) USNR, 1943-46. Recipient Silver Beaver, 1965; recipient Silver Antelope, 1978, Disting. Eagle, 1979. Mem. Country Club of Sebring, Buffalo Jr. C. of C. (past dir., chmn. bd.), Am. Soc. Corp. Secs., Buffalo Canoe Club (past commodore), Buffalo Country Club. Home: 1925 SE Lakeview Dr Sebring FL 33870-4938 Office: 22 Dawnbrook Ln Buffalo NY 14221-4930 *If you truly believe you are happy and successful then, and only then, you truly are.*

LITTLEWOOD, THOMAS BENJAMIN, journalism educator; b. Flint, Mich., Nov. 30, 1928; s. Thomas Nelson and Louise Engela (Grebenkemper) L.; m. Barbara E. Badger, June 9, 1951; children: Linda S. Johnson, Lisa L. Ratchford, Thomas S., Leah J. Hamrick. Student, DePauw U., 1948-51; BS, Northwestern U., 1952, MS, 1953. Reporter Chgo. Sun-Times, 1953-76, chief Springfield State Capital Bur., 1955-64, corr. Washington Bur., 1965-76; prof. journalism U. Ill., Urbana-Champaign, 1977—, head dept., 1977-87. Author: Bipartisan Coalition in Illinois, 1959, Horner of Illinois, 1969, The Politics of Population Control, 1977, Coals of Fire, 1988, Arch, 1990. John F. Kennedy Inst. Politics Harvard U. fellow, 1975. Mem. Soc. Profl. Journalists (SDX Nat. award 1988), Ill. State Hist. Soc., N.Am. Soc. Sports History, Sigma Delta Chi, Kappa Tau Alpha. Office: Univ Ill Journalism Dept 119 Gregory Urbana IL 61801

LITTMAN, EARL, advertising and public relations executive; b. Bklyn., Jan. 29, 1927; s. David and Cele Littman; m. Natalie Carol Jacobson, Dec. 21, 1948; children: Erica Humphrey, Bonnie Likover, Michael L. Littman. BS, NYU, 1948. With George N. Kahn, N.Y.C., 1948-50, Jones & Brown, Pitts., 1950-52; chmn., CEO Goodwin, Dannenbaum, Littman & Wingfield Inc., Houston, 1952-92; pres. The Advertizing Firm, Inc., 1992Two Nerds and A Suit, Inc., 1994, Chmn. Anti Defamation League, Tex. 1984; bd. dirs. Am. Heart Assn., Houston, Glassell Sch.; active End Hunger Network, Houston, 1984, active NCCJ. With USN, 1944-45. Recipient Silver medal Am. Advt. Fedn., 1989, Outstanding Vol. award Savvy, 1990, Anti-Defamation League Popkin award, 1990, End Hunger Network award, 1992; Am. Heart Assn. honoree, 1988; Heritage award Am. Women in Radio and TV, 1992. Mem. Affiliated Advt. Agys. Internat. (pres. 1979-80), Am. Advt. Agy. Assn. (gov. Houston chpt. 1990, Paul Dudley White award 1991), Houston Advt. Fedn. (Living Legend award 1993), Winedale Hist. Assn. (pres.), Tex. Entrepreneurial Soc. (bd. dirs.). Jewish.

LITTMAN, HOWARD, chemical engineer, educator; b. Bklyn., Apr. 22, 1927; s. Morris and Gertrude (Goldberg) L.; m. Arline F. Caruso, July 3, 1955; children—Susan Joy, Vicki Kim, Paul William. BChemE, Cornell U., 1951; PhD, Yale U., 1956. Asst., then assoc. prof. Syracuse U., 1955-65; on leave to Brookhaven Nat. Lab., summer 1957, Argonne Nat. Lab., 1957-59; faculty Rensselaer Poly. Inst., Troy, N.Y., 1965—; prof. chem. engring. Rensselaer Poly. Inst., 1967—, chmn. faculty council, 1975-76; vis. prof. Imperial Coll., London, Eng., 1971-72, Chonn'am Nat. U., Kwangju, Korea, 1988; Fulbright lectr. U. Belgrade, Yugoslavia, 1972; pres. Particle Systems Internat. Corp., 1990—. Patentee in field; contbr. articles to profl. jours. A founder Onondaga Hill Free Library, 1961, trustee, 1961-65, pres., 1965; a founder Onondaga Library System, 1962, trustee, 1962-65, v.p., 1965; trustee Capital Dist. Library Council, 1969-75, pres., 1970, 73. Served with USN, 1945-46. IREX grantee U. Belgrade, summer 1973; recipient Disting. Faculty award Rensselaer Poly. Inst., 1988. Mem. Am. Inst. Chem. Engrs., Am. Chem. Soc., Sigma Xi. Home: 7 Tulip Tree Ln Niskayuna NY 12309-1837 Office: Rensselaer Poly Inst Troy NY 12180-3590

LITTMAN, IRVING, forest products company executive; b. Denver, Apr. 21, 1940; s. Maurice Littman and Cecile P. Zohn.; m. Gertrude Pepper, Aug. 16, 1964; children: Margaret R., Michael J., Elizabeth B. BS in Engring. (Applied Math.), U. Colo., 1964; MBA, U. Chgo., 1966. Mgr. corp. systems Boise Cascade Corp., Idaho, 1966-68, corp. mgr. budgeting, 1968-71, asst. to pres., 1971-73; asst. controller realty group Boise Cascade Corp., Palo Alto, Calif., 1973-76; dir. investor relations Boise Cascade Corp., 1976-84, treas., 1984-86, v.p., treas., 1986—. Bd. dirs. Idaho Humanities Council, Boise, 1985-88, vice chair, 1987-88; trustee Boise High Sch. Band Scholarship Endowment, 1987—; referee US Soccer Fedn., 1982—; investment com. Idaho Community Found., 1989—, chmn. investment com., 1991—. With U.S. Army, 1958-59. Mem. Bogus Basin Ski Area Assn. (bd. dirs. 1988—, treas. 1989-94, vice-chmn. 1991-94, chmn. 1994-96), Treas. Club San Francisco, Fin. Execs. Inst., Crane Creek Country Club, Arid Club (Boise). Office: Boise Cascade Corp 1 Jefferson Sq Boise ID 83728-0001

LITTMAN, RICHARD ANTON, psychologist, educator; b. N.Y.C., May 8, 1919; s. Joseph and Sarah (Feinberg) L.; m. Isabelle Cohen, Mar. 17, 1941; children—David, Barbara, Daniel, Rebecca. AB, George Washington U., 1943; postgrad., Ind. U., 1943- 44; PhD, Ohio State U., 1948. Faculty U. Oreg., 1948—, prof. psychology, 1959—, chmn. dept., 1963-68, vice provost acad. planning and resources, 1971-73; Vis. scientist Nat. Inst. Mental Health, 1958-59. Contbr. articles to profl. jours. Sr. postdoctoral fellow NSF, U. Paris, 1966-67; sr. fellow Nat. Endowment for Humanities, U. London, 1973-74; Ford Found. fellow, 1952-53; recipient U. Oreg. Charles H. Johnson Meml. award, 1980. Mem. Am., Western, psychol. assns., Soc. Research and Child Devel., Psychonomics Soc., Animal Behavior Soc., Soc. Psychol. Study of Social Issues, Internat. Soc. Developmental Psychobiology, History of Sci. Soc., Am. Philos. Assn., AAUP, Sigma Xi. Home: 3625 Glen Oak Dr Eugene OR 97405-4736 Office: U Oreg Dept Psychology Eugene OR 97403

LITTON, DAPHNE NAPIER RUDHMAN, special education educator; b. Schenectady, July 28, 1952; d. James Napier and Mary (Stathas) Rudhman; m. John Shelby Litton, Oct. 5, 1984; children: Christian Napier, Erin Elizabeth. BS in Elem. Edn., Ind. U., South Bend, 1974, MS in Elem. Edn., 1978, cert. learning disabled, 1978; cert. emotionally disturbed, Ind. U.-Purdue U., Indpls., 1982. Tchr. remedial reading, dir. motor skills, tchr. summer sch. Olive Twp. Elem. Sch., New Carlisle, Ind., 1976; tchr. learning disabled, gifted, remedial reading Ox Bow Elem. Sch., Elkhart, Ind., 1976-85, dir. motor skills, 1976-85; tchr. learning disabled Stafford (Va.) Community Schs., 1985-87, Yorkshire Elem. Sch., Manassas, Va., 1993-95; tchr. emotionally disturbed Elvin Hill Elem. Sch., Columbiana, Ala., 1987-88; dir., adminstr. Riverchase Presbyn. Presch./Mother's Day Out, Birmingham, Ala., 1989-90; tchr. leadning disabled Piney Grove Elem. Sch., Kernersville, N.C., 1995—; mem. Ind. State Com. for Svc. Personnel Devel., Elkhart, 1979-85; asst. girl's volleyball coach Ox Bow Elem. Sch., Elkhart, 1985-87; asst. dir. Sports Medicine 10K Run Vols., South Bend, 1986. Active Am. Cancer Soc., South Bend, 1975. Mem. Coun. Exceptional Children. Republican. Presbyterian. Avocations: mus. instruments, choir, travel, swimming. Home: 1820 Glen Ridge Dr Kernersville NC 27284

LITTON, ROBERT CLIFTON, marine engineer, consultant; b. Banner Elk, N.C., Jan. 11, 1934; s. Hailey Clifton and Edna (Walsh) L.; m. Michele Louise Gennette, July 1, 1961. B in Mech. Engring., U. Va., 1957; MS in Mech. Engring., Rensselaer Polytech. Inst., 1963. Commd. ensign USN, 1957, advanced through grades to capt., ret., 1984; pvt. practice marine engring. cons. Great Falls, Va., 1985-94; sr. cons. engr. Mech. Tech., Inc., Latham, N.Y., 1988-95; program mgr. Innovative Tech., Inc., McLean, Va., 1988-89, Sachse Engring. Assocs., Inc., San Diego, 1989-90; bus. area mgr. naval engring. RGS Assocs., Arlington, Va., 1994—. Mem. Soc. Naval Archs. and Marine Engrs., Am. Soc. Naval Engrs., U.S. Naval Inst., Naval Sub. League. Republican. Avocations: personal computers, audio and video systems, golf. Home and Office: 10334 Eclipse Ln Great Falls VA 22066-1730

LITVACK, SANFORD MARTIN, lawyer; b. Bklyn., Apr. 29, 1936; s. Murray and Lee M. (Korman) L.; m. Judith E. Goldenson, Dec. 30, 1956; children—Mark, Jonathan, Sharon, Daniel. BA, U. Conn., 1956; LLB, Georgetown U., 1959. Bar: N.Y. 1964, D.C. 1979. Trial atty. antitrust div. Dept. Justice, Washington, 1959-61; asst. atty. gen. Dept. Justice, 1980-81; asso. firm Donovan, Leisure, Newton & Irvine, N.Y.C., 1961-69; ptnr. Donovan, Leisure, Newton & Irvine, 1969-80, 81-86, Dewey, Ballantine, Bushby, Palmer & Wood, N.Y.C., 1987-91; sr. exec. v.p., chief of corp. ops., gen. counsel The Walt Disney Co., Burbank, Calif., 1991—, also bd. dirs. Bd. dirs. Bet Tzedek. Fellow Am. Coll. Trial Lawyers; mem. ABA, Fed. Bar Coun., N.Y. State Bar Assn. (sec. antitrust sect. 1974-77, chmn. antitrust sect. 1985-86), Va. Bar Assn. Office: The Walt Disney Co 500 S Buena Vista St Burbank CA 91521-0001

LITWACK, GERALD, biochemistry researcher, educator, administrator; b. Boston, Jan. 11, 1929; s. David and Edith Jean (Berkman) Lytell; m. Patricia Lynn Gorog, Feb., 1956 (div. 1973); 1 child, Claudia; m. Ellen Judith Schatz, Aug. 31, 1973; children: Geoffrey Sandor, Katherine Victoria. BA, Hobart Coll., 1949; MS, U. Wis., 1950, PhD, 1953. Postdoctoral fellow Biochem. Labs. U. Paris, 1953-54; asst. prof. Rutgers U., New Brunswick, N.J., 1954-60; assoc. prof. U. Pa., Phila., 1960-64; Carnell prof., dep. dir. Fels Inst., Sch. of Medicine Temple U., Phila., 1964-91; prof., chair dept. pharmacology Thomas Jefferson U., Phila., 1991—, also dep. dir. Jefferson Cancer Inst., 1991—; assoc. dir. for basic sci. Jefferson Cancer Ctr., Phila., 1992—; dir. Ctr. Apoptosis Rsch., acting assoc. dean sci. affairs, 1995—; chmn. adv. com. am. Cancer Soc., N.Y.C., 1977-80; mem. adv. panel NSF, Washington, 1980-84; mem. ad hoc panels NIH, Bethesda, 1985, 89, reviewer, 1977, 84, 91, cons. Nat. Inst. Environ. Health Scis., 1982; mem. ad hoc panels Israel Cancer Rsch. fund Sci. Rev. Panel, 1992-93, U.S. Army Breast Cancer Study Sect., 1994; councilor Soc. for Exptl. Biology and Medicine, N.Y.C., 1984-88; cons. Franklin Inst., 1976, Georgetown U., 1980; reviewer Haverford Coll., 1976; evaluator Roswell Park Meml. Inst., 1978; mem. sci. adv. bd. Norris Cotton Cancer Ctr. Dartmouth Med. Sch., 1984—; Jefferson rep. U. Catania, Sicily, 1994—. Author/co-author: Experimental Biochemistry, 1960, Hormones, 1987; editor: Biochemical Actions of Hormones, Vol. XIV, 1970-87, Receptor Purification, 1990; founder, editor-in-chief Receptor, Humana Press, 1990—; editor-in-chief Vitamins and Hormones, 1992—; co-editor Actions of Hormones on Molecular Processes, 1964; mem. editl. bd. Chemtracts, Cancer Comm., Cancer Rsch., Endocrinology, Anticancer Rsch., Oncology Rsch., 1992, Oncology Reports, 1993—, Critical Revs. and Eukaryotic Gene Expression, 1994—, Apoptosis, 1995—. Recipient Pub. Svc. award Chapel of Four Chaplains, 1977, Faculty Rsch. award Temple U., 1987. Mem. Endocrine Soc. (program com. 1991-93, sci. and edn. com. 1992-93), Am. Assn. Cancer Rsch. (chair task force on endocrinology 1995), Am. Chem. Soc. Achievements include discovery and identification of the glucocorticoid receptor; co-discovery of ligandin (glutathione S-Transferase family) mechanism of glucocorticoid receptor activation, studies in apoptosis. Home: 380 E Montgomery Ave Wynnewood PA 19096 Office: Thomas Jefferson U 10th and Locust St Philadelphia PA 19107-3197

LITWACK, LEON FRANK, historian, educator; b. Santa Barbara, Calif., Dec. 2, 1929; s. Julius and Minnie (Nitkin) L.; m. Rhoda Lee Goldberg, July 5, 1952; children: John Michael, Ann Katherine. BA, U. Calif., Berkeley, 1951, MA, 1952, PhD, 1958. Asst. prof., then assoc. prof. history U. Wis., Madison, 1958-65; mem. faculty U. Calif., Berkeley, 1965—, prof. history, 1971—, Alexander F. and May T. Morrison prof. history, 1987—; dir. NDEA Inst. Am. History, summer 1965; vis. prof. U. S.C., 1975, Colo. Coll., Sept. 1974, 79, La. State U., 1985; Fulbright prof. Am. history U. Sydney, Australia, 1991, Moscow (USSR) State U., 1980; vis. lectr. Peking U., (China), 1982; Walter Lynwood Fleming lectr. La. State U., 1983; Wentworth scholar-in-residence U. Fla., Spring 1983; mem. Nat. Afro-Am. History and Culture Commn., 1981-83; mem. screening com. Fulbright Sr. Scholar Awards, 1983-86; bd. acad. advisors The American Experience Sta. WGBH-TV, 1986—; Ford Found. prof. So. studies U. Miss., 1989; mem. exec. com. of dels. Am. Coun. of Learned Socs., 1993—. Author: North of Slavery: The Negro in the Free States, 1790-1860, 1961, Been in the Storm So Long: The Aftermath of Slavery, 1979; (film) To Look for America, 1971; co-author: The United States, 1981, rev. edit., 1991; editor: American Labor Movement, 1962; co-editor: Reconstruction, 1969, Black Leaders in the Nineteenth Century, 1988. Mem. Bradley Commn. on History in Schs., 1987-90, Schomburg Commn. for the Preservation of Black Culture; trustee Nat. Coun. for History Edn., 1990—, mem. steering com. 1994 NAEP History Consensus Project. Served with AUS, 1953-55. Recipient Excellence in Teaching award U. Calif., Berkeley, 1967, Disting. Teaching award, 1971; Francis Parkman prize, 1980; Pulitzer prize history, 1980; Gold medal Commonwealth Club Calif., 1980; Am. Book award in history, 1980; fellow Social Sci. Research Council, 1961-62; fellow Henry E. Huntington Library, summer 1964; fellow Guggenheim Found., 1967-68; fellow U. Calif., Berkeley, 1976, 80; fellow Rockefeller Found. Humanities, 1983; grantee Nat. Endowment Humanities, 1971; grantee NIMH, 1972-73. Mem. Orgn. Am. Historians (chmn. nominations bd. 1975-76, exec. bd. 1983-85, pres. 1986-87), Am. Hist. Assn. (chmn. program com. 1980-81), So. Hist. Assn., Soc. Am. Historians, Am. Acad. Arts and Scis., Am. Antiquarian Soc., U. Calif. Alumni Assn., Am. Studies Assn., PEN Am. Ctr. Office: U Calif Dept History Berkeley CA 94720

LITWEILER, JOHN BERKEY, writer, editor; b. South Bend, Ind., Feb. 21, 1940; s. John Ernest and Pauline Lucile (Yoder) L. BA, North Cen. Coll., Naperville, Ill., 1962. Indexer-researcher Urban Rsch. Corp., Chgo., 1970-74; editor Maher Publs., Chgo., 1974-75, 79-81; instr. Am. Sch., Chgo., 1975-79; writer Ency. Brittanica, 1992—; free-lance writer, editor, jazz critic Chgo., 1981—; vis. instr. Sch. of Art Inst., Chgo., 1982. Author: The Freedom Principle, 1984, Ornette Coleman: A Harmolodic Life, 1993; contbr. numerous articles to Reader, Chgo. Tribune, N.Y. Times, Kulchur, Down Beat, other publs. Bd. dirs. Jazz Inst. of Chgo., 1977-88; com. mem. DeMichael Jazz Archives, 1977-88, Chgo. Jazz Festival, 1984-88, Jazz Criticism Inst. Music Critics Assn. fellow, 1974, NEH fellow, 1981. Home: 5633 S Kenwood Ave Chicago IL 60637-1738

LITWIN, BURTON HOWARD, lawyer; b. Chgo., July 26, 1944; s. Manuel and Rose (Boehm) L.; m. Nancy Iris Stein, Aug. 25, 1968; children: Robin Meredith, Keith Harris, Jill Stacy. BBA with honors, Roosevelt U., 1966; JD cum laude, Northwestern U., 1970. Bar: Ill. 1970, U.S. Dist. Ct. (no. dist.) Ill. 1970, U.S. Tax Ct. 1971, U.S. Ct. Fed. Claims 1983; CPA, Ill. Ptnr. Hopkins & Sutter, Chgo., 1970—. Author chpts. of books; contbr. articles to profl. jours. Recipient Gold Watch award Fin. Execs. Inst., Chgo., 1965. Mem. ABA (chmn. nonfiler task force for No. Ill. 1992-94), Fed. Bar Assn., Chgo. bar Assn. (chmn. adminstrv. practice subcom., fed. taxation subcom. 1982-83), Rosarian-Am. Rose Soc. (cons.), Legal Club Chgo. Avocations: roses, painting, photography. Office: Hopkins & Sutter 3 First National Plz Chicago IL 60602

LITWIN, MARTIN STANLEY, surgeon; b. Florence, Ala., Jan. 8, 1930; s. Ben and Rose L.; m. Cheryl Denise Mason; children: Anna Marie, Rebecca, Benjamin, Martin. BS, U. Ala., 1951, MD, 1955. Diplomate Am. Bd. Surgery. Intern Michael Reese Hosp., Chgo., 1955-56; asst. in surgery to chief surg. resident Peter Bent Brigham Hosp., Boston, 1956-65; pvt. practice specializing in surgery New Orleans; asst. prof. to assoc. prof. surgery Tulane Med. Sch., New Orleans, 1966-75; prof. surgery Tulane Med. Sch., 1975—, assoc. dean, med. dir. faculty practice, 1976—, Robert and Viola Lobrano prof. surgery, 1977—; chmn. continuing edn., 1979-90; clin. investigator VA Hosp., West Roxbury, Mass., 1964-66; vis. surgeon Charity Hosp. of La., 1966; active staff Tulane Med. Ctr. Hosp., 1977—; univ. staff Touro Infirmary, 1967—. Contbr. articles to profl. jours.; assoc. editor Emergency Medicine, 1969-84. 1st lt. to col. USAR-MC, 1956-80. Fellow ACS; mem. Assn. Am. Med. Colls. (chmn. steering com. 1994—, group on Faculty Practice), Am. Burn Assn., Am. Surg. Assn., Am. Assn. Surgery of Trauma, Am. Coll. Phys. Execs., So. Surg. Assn., So. Med. Assn., Southeastern Surg. Congress, La. Med. Soc., New Orleans Surg. Soc. (pres. 1989), Orleans Parish Med. Soc.(mem. hosp. com. 1983), European Soc. Exptl. Surgery, Assn. Acad. Surgery, Soc. Surgeons of Alimentary Tract, Soc. Univ. Surgeons, Brigham Surg. Alumni Assn., Tulane Surg. Soc., others. Address: 5591 Bellaire Dr New Orleans LA 70124-1001 Office: Tulane U Med Ctr 1415 Tulane Ave New Orleans LA 70112-2605

LITWINOWICZ, ANTHONY, information specialist, researcher; b. Jelenia Gora, Poland, July 29, 1952; came to U.S., 1978; s. Anthony and Anna (Zdrojewski) L.; m. Catherine Veronica Gajdos, June 30, 1979; children: Catherine, Anthony, John Paul, Peter. MA in History and Philosophy, Lodz U., Poland, 1976; MS in Info. Studies, Drexel U., 1984, postgrad., 1985-90. Cert. in info. mgmt. Sr. info. specialist Laventhol & Horwath CPAs, Phila., 1984-89; instr. info. sci. Delaware Valley Coll., Doylestown, Pa., 1989-91; dir. Info. Ctr. Samsung Electronics, Ridgefield Park, N.J., 1992—. Author: Nazi Occupation of Poland, 1978; contbr. articles to profl. jours. Mem. Am. Soc. for Info. Sci. Republican. Roman Catholic. Avocations: collecting antiques, reading, martial arts. Home: 108 W Pumping Station Rd Quakertown PA 18951-4214 Office: Samsung Electronics Am 105 Challenger Rd Ridgefield Park NJ 07660-2106

LITZ, ARTHUR WALTON, JR., English language educator; b. Nashville, Oct. 31, 1929; s. Arthur Walton and Lucile (Courtney) L.; m. Marian Ann Weiler, Feb. 2, 1958 (div. 1993); children: Katharine, Andrew, Victoria, Emily. AB, Princeton U., 1951; DPhil (Rhodes scholar), Oxford (Eng.) U., 1954. Instr. Princeton U., 1956-58; lectr. Columbia U., 1957-58; mem. faculty Princeton U., 1958—, prof. English lit., 1968—, chmn. English dept., 1974-81; vis. prof. Bryn Mawr Coll., Swarthmore Coll., BreadLoaf Sch. of English, Temple U., Columbia U., U. Pa.; mem. editl. bd. Princeton U. Press, 1967-71. Author: The Art of James Joyce, 1961, Modern American Fiction: Essays in Criticism, 1963, Jane Austen, 1965, James Joyce, 1966, James Joyce's Dubliners, 1969, The Poetic Development of Wallace Stevens, 1972, Eliot in His Time, 1973, Scribner Quarto of Modern Literature, 1977, Major American Short Stories, 1980, rev. edit., 1994, Ezra Pound and Dorothy Shakespear: Their Letters, 1985, Collected Poems of William Carlos Williams, 1986, Personae: The Shorter Poems of Erza Pound, 1990, James Joyce: Poems and Shorter Writings, 1990, Ezra Pound's Poetry & Prose, 1992. With AUS, 1954-56. Recipient E. Harris Harbison award for gifted teaching Danforth Found., 1972; named Am. Coun. Learned Socs. fellow, 1960-61, NEH sr. fellow, 1974-75, Guggenheim fellow, 1982-83, Eastman prof. U. Oxford, 1989-90. Mem. Am. Philos. Soc. Home: 62 Western Way Princeton NJ 08540-7206

LITZSINGER, PAUL RICHARD, publishing company executive; b. Clayton, Mo., Jan. 8, 1932; s. Melvin Paul and Catherine (Mooney) L.; m. Dona Lucy Follett, July 10, 1954; children: Mark, Robin, Heidi, Shawn, Todd. B.S., U. Mo., 1954. With Follett Corp., Chgo., 1957—; retail stores supr. Follett Corp., 1962-66, pres. retail stores div., 1966-76, pres., chief exec. officer corp., 1977—; bd. dirs. Continental Water Corp., Chgo. Area dir. United Crusade; bd. dirs. Hinsdale Community House. Served with USAF, 1954-57. Mem. Nat. Assn. Coll. Stores (dir. 1971-73), Nat. Assn. Colls. Stores Corp. (pres. 1974-75, trustee), Am. Assn. Pubs., Fla. Assn. Coll. Stores, Nat. Assn. Aux. Enterprise Dirs., Nat. Assn. Bus. Mgrs., Nat. Assn. Coll. and Univ. Bus. Officers, Nat. Assn. Jr. Colls., Mgt. Assn. Ill. (bd. dirs. 1992—). Presbyterian. Club: Knollwood Golf. Home: 1650 Green Bay Rd Lake Bluff IL 60044-2306 Office: Follett Corp 2233 West St River Grove IL 60171-1895

LIU, BEDE, electrical engineering educator; b. Shanghai, China, Sept. 25, 1934; came to U.S., 1954, naturalized, 1960; s. Henry and Shan (Yao) L.; m. Maria Agatha Sang, Jan. 31, 1959; 1 dau., Beatrice Agatha. B.S. in Elec. Engring., Nat. Taiwan U., 1954; M.E.E., Poly. Inst. Bklyn., 1956, D.E.E., 1960. Equipment engr. Western Electric Co., N.Y.C., 1954-56; intermediate engr. A.B. DuMont Lab., Clifton, N.J., summer 1956; mem. tech. staff Bell Telephone Labs., Murray Hill, N.J., 1959-62, summers 1957, 58, 66; mem. faculty Princeton U., 1962—, prof. elec. engring., 1969—, dept. chmn., 1995—; vis. prof. Nat. Taiwan U., 1970-71, U. Calif., Berkeley, 1971, Shanghai Jiao Tong U., 1979. Co-author: Digital Signal Processing, 1976; editor: Digital Filters and the Fast Fourier Transform, 1975; patentee in field. Recipient Tech. Achievement award IEEE Acoustics Speech and Signal Processing Soc., 1985, Edn. award IEEE Cir. and Systems Soc, 1988; named Hon. Prof. Inst. Acoustics, Inst. Electronics, Academia Sinica, 1988. Fellow IEEE (bd. dirs., 1984-85, Centennial medal 1984, Best Paper award IEEE Trans Video Technology, 1994, 96); mem. IEEE Circuits and Systems Soc. (v.p. 1979, pres. 1982, Edn. award 1988). Home: 248 Hartley Ave Princeton NJ 08540-5656 Office: Princeton Univ Dept Elec Engring Princeton NJ 08540

LIU, BEN-CHIEH, economist; b. Chungking, China, Nov. 17, 1938; came to U.S., 1965, naturalized, 1973; s. Pei-juang and Chung-su L.; m. Jill Jyh-huey, Oct. 2, 1965; children—Tina Won-ting, Roger Won-jung, Milton Won-ming. B.A., Nat. Taiwan U., 1961; M.A., Meml. U. Nfld., 1965, Washington U., St. Louis, 1968; Ph.D., Washington U., St. Louis, 1971. Economist Chinese Air Force and Central Customs, Taiwan, 1961-63; resource economist Canadian Land Inventory and Forest Services, Nfld., 1963-65; research project dir. St. Louis Regional Indsl. Devel. Corp., 1968-72; prin. econs. Midwest Research Inst., Kansas City, Mo., 1972-80; mgr. Energy and Environ. Systems Div., Argonne (Ill.) Nat. Lab., 1980-81; prof. econs., assoc. dir. rsch. Oklahoma City U., 1981-82; prof. mgmt., mktg. and info. systems Chgo. State U., 1982—; pres. Liu & Assocs., Inc., 1982—; vis. prof. econs. U. Mo., 1970-78, Nat. Taiwan U., 1991-92; cons. UN, NSF; mem. Gov. Thompson's Adv. Com. on Agrl. Export, 1985-87, Congressman Fawell's Adv. Com. on Sci. and Tech., 1985—; commr. Nat. Commn. on Librs. and Info. Svcs., 1991-94. Author: Interindustrial Structure Analysis: An Input-Output Study for St. Louis Region, 1968, The Quality of Life in the United States, 1970, Rating, Index and Statistics, 1973, Quality of Life Indicators in U.S. Metropolitan Areas, 1975, Physical and Economic Damage Functions for Air Pollutants by Receptors, 1976, Earthquake Risk and Damage Functions, An Integrated Model, 1981, Income, Energy and Quality of Life: An Information Systems Approach to Decisions, 1988; mem. editorial bd.: Internat. Jour. Math. Social Sci, Am. Jour. Econs. and Sociology, Hong Kong Jour. Bus. Mgmt.; contbr. articles to profl. jours. Recipient rsch. study award Am. Indsl. Devel. Coun., 1969—, Fulbright Scholar awards, 1992, 96, Faculty Meritorious awards Chgo. State U., 1983, 86, 89, 90, 96; U.S. Econ. Devel. Adminstrn. fellow, 1967-68; Korean Govt. scholar, 1963-65; Fulbright scholar Mgmt. Devel. Inst., Delhi U., 1992. Fellow Am. Statis. Assn. (com. mem.); mem. Am. Econ. Assn. (com. mem.), Econometric Soc., Royal Econ. Soc., Internat. Statis. Instn., Assn. for Social Econs. (com. mem.), Tax Inst. Am., Chinese Acad. and Profl. Assn. (pres. 1984-85), Chinese Econ. Assn. in N.Am. (pres. 1988-90). Home: 5360 Pennywood Dr Lisle IL 60532-2032 Office: Chgo State U Chicago IL 60628 *The joy of living may temporarily rest on present or past glory, but it is the immersion in planning for the future—the living ahead of one's time—which ensures permanently the flourishing of the joy of life. In a commonwealth society, happiness does not come from doing what we like to do, but from liking what we have to do for the less-well-to-do-ones.*

LIU, BENJAMIN YOUNG-HWAI, engineering educator; b. Shanghai, China, Aug. 15, 1934; s. Wilson Wan-su and Dorothy Pao-ning (Cheng) L.; m. Helen Hai-ling Cheng, June 14, 1958; 1 son, Lawrence A.S. Student, Nat. Taiwan U., 1951-54; B.S. in Mech. Engring., U. Nebr., 1956; Ph.D., U. Minn., 1960. Asso. engr. Honeywell Co., Mpls., 1956; research asst., instr. U. Minn., 1956-60, asst. prof., 1960-67, asso. prof., 1967-69, prof., 1969-93, regent's prof., 1993—, dir. Particle Tech. Lab., 1973-95; dir. Ctr. for Filtration Rsch., 1995—; vis. prof. U. Paris, 1968-69; patentee in field. Contbg. author: Aerosol Science, 1966; editor: Fine Particles, 1976, Application of Solar Energy for Heating and Cooling Buildings, 1977, Aerosols in the Mining and Industrial Work Environment, 1983, Aerosols: Science, Technology and Industrial Application of Airborne Particles, 1984; editor-in-chief: Aerosol Sci. and Tech., 1983-93; contbr. articles to Ency. Chem. Tech. Guggenheim fellow, 1968-69; recipient Sr. U.S. Scientist award Alexander von Humboldt Found., 1982-83. Mem. ASME, ASHRAE, Inst. Environ. Scis. (v.p. 1993-95), Air and Waste Mgmt. Assn., Am. Assn. for Aerosol Rsch. (pres. 1986-88), Chinese Am. Assn. Minn. (pres. 1971-72), Nat. Acad. Engring. Home: 1 N Deep Lake Rd North Oaks MN 55127-6504 Office: U Minn Particle Tech Lab 111 Church St SE Minneapolis MN 55455-0150

LIU, BRIAN CHEONG-SENG, urology and oncology educator, researcher; b. Hong Kong, Jan. 15, 1959; came to U.S., 1968; s. Keh Ming and Yin Man (Au) L. BS in Microbiology summa cum laude, UCLA, 1980, PhD in Molecular Biology, 1984. Postdoctoral fellow in tumor immunology and tumor biology Sch. Medicine UCLA, 1984-88; instr. dept. urology Mt. Sinai Sch. Medicine, N.Y.C., 1988-89, asst. prof. dept. urology, dir. urologic rsch., 1989—; sr. rsch. fellow Jonsson Comprehensive Cancer Ctr., 1985-88; vis. investigator dept. pathology Henry Ford Hosp., Detroit, 1987-88. Mem. editl. bd. Jour. Urology, 1996—; contbr. articles to profl. jours. Recipient Edwin Beer award N.Y. Acad. Med., 1991-93, New Investigator award Am. Found. Urologic Diseases, 1994—, Cancer of the Prostate Rsch. award Capcure Found., 1995, Merck Young Investigator award in Urology, 1996; Nat. Cancer Inst. grantee, 1991—. Mem. Am. Urologic Assn., Soc. Basic Urologic Rsch. (treas.), Sigma Xi. Office: Mt Sinai Sch Med Dept Urology 1 Gustave L Levy Pl New York NY 10029-6504

LIU, CHUNG LAUNG, computer engineer, educator; b. Canton, China, Oct. 25, 1934; U.S. citizen; married; 1 child. BSc, Cheng Kung U., 1956; SM, MIT, 1960, ScD in Elec. Engring., 1962. From asst. prof. to assoc. prof. elec. engring. MIT, 1962-72; prof. computer sci. U. Ill., Urbana, 1973—. Fellow IEEE (Taylor L. Booth Edn. award Computer Soc. 1992); mem. Assn. Computing Machinery (Karl V. Karlstron Outstanding Educator award 1990). Office: Univ of Illinois Dept Computer Science 1304 West Springfield Ave Urbana IL 61801*

LIU, CHUNG-CHIUN, chemical engineering educator; b. Canton, Kwangtun, China, Oct. 8, 1936; came to U.S., 1961, naturalized, 1972; s. Pay-Yen and Chi-Wei (Chen) L.; m. Mary Lou Rice, Nov. 25, 1967; children: Peter S.H. B.S., Nat. Cheng-Kung U., Taiwan, 1959; M.S., Calif. Inst. Tech., 1962; Ph.D., Case Western Res. U., 1968. Grad. asst. Case Western Res. U., Cleve., 1963-68, postdoctoral fellow, 1968, prof. chem. engring., 1978—; asst. prof. chem. engring. U. Pitts., 1968-72, assoc. prof., 1972-76, prof., 1976-78; prof. chem. engring. Case Western Res. U., Cleve., 1978—; assoc. dir. Case Center for Electrochem. Scis., Cleve., 1982-86; dir. electronics design ctr. Case Center for Electrochem. Scis., 1986-89, Wallace R. Persons prof. sensor tech. and control, 1989—. Contbr. articles in field to profl. jours.; patentee in field. Mem. Electrochem. Soc. (summer fellowship award 1963, 66), Am. Inst. Chem. Engrs. Home: 2917 E Overlook Rd Cleveland OH 44118-2433 Office: Case Western Res U Dept Chem Engr 10900 Euclid Ave Cleveland OH 44106-7200

LIU, ERNEST K. H., international banking executive, international financial consultant; b. Hong Kong, Oct. 4, 1950; came to U.S., 1979; s. Sun-Ip and Mei-Choi (Man) L.; m. Lily Chan, Dec. 5, 1979; children—Aimee On-On, Alvin Lok-Tin. B.Social Sci., Hong Kong U., 1974; M.B.A. in Fin., NYU, 1986. Lending officer Bank of Am. NT and SA, Hong Kong, 1974-76; market officer Hong Kong Trade Devel. Council, Hong Kong, 1976-79; mgr. Hong Kong Trade Devel. Council, N.Y.C., 1979-82; asst. v.p. mktg. Honkong and Shanghi Banking Corp, N.Y.C., 1982-83; sr. account exec. Citibank, N.A., N.Y.C., 1984-88; asst. v.p. Merrill Lynch Internat. Pvt. Client Svcs., N.Y.C., 1988-91; dir. Asia-Pacific Internat. Trade Promotion Ltd., N.Y.C., 1991—.

LIU, GANG-YU, chemist, educator; b. Zhengzhou, Henan, China, Apr. 19, 1964; came to U.S., 1986; parents Zhen Kun and Quan Xian (Guo) L.; m. Xiaoyuan Li, Dec. 1, 1987. BS, Peking (China) U., 1988; MS, Princeton U., 1990, PhD, 1992. Postdoctoral assoc. U. Calif., Berkeley, 1992-94; asst. prof. chemistry Wayne State U., Detroit, 1994—. Camille & Henry Dreyfus fellow, 1994—, Miller Rsch. fellow The Miller Inst. for Basic Rsch. in Sci., 1992-94, Harold W. Dodds Honorific fellow Princeton U., 1991-92, CGP fellow Ministry of Edn., China, 1986-87. Mem. AAAS, Am. Chem. Soc., Am. Phys. Soc., Am. Vacuum Soc. Office: Wayne St U Dept Chemistry Detroit MI 48202

LIU, HAN-SHOU, space scientist, researcher; b. Hunan, China, Mar. 9, 1930; came to U.S., 1960, naturalized, 1972; s. Yu-Tin and Chun-Chen (Yeng) L.; m. Sun-Ling Yang Liu, May 2, 1957; children—Michael Fu-Yen, Peter Fu-Tze. Ph.D., Cornell U., 1963. Research asst. Cornell U., 1962-63; research assoc. Nat. Acad. Sci., Washington, 1963-65; scientist NASA Goddard Space Flight Center, Greenbelt, Md., 1965—; Pres. Mei-Hwa Chinese Sch., 1980-81. Contbr. articles to profl. jours. Fellow AAAS; mem. Am. Astron. Soc., Am. Geophys. Union, Planetary Soc., AIAA. Office: NASA Goddard Space Flight Ctr Code # 921 Greenbelt MD 20771

LIU, HENRY, engineering educator, researcher, consultant; b. Peking, China, June 3, 1936; came to U.S., 1961; s. Yen-Huai and Remei (Bardina) L.; m. Susie Dou-Mei Chou, Dec. 16, 1964; children: Jerry B., Jason C.,

Jeffrey H. B.S., Nat. Taiwan U., Taipei, 1959; M.S., Colo. State U., 1963, Ph.D., 1966. Registered profl. engr., Mo. Asst. prof. U. Mo., Columbia, 1965-69, assoc. prof., 1969-76, prof. engring., 1976—, Natural Gas Pipeline Co. prof. engring., 1983-90; James C. Dowell prof. engring., 1990—; dir. Capsule Pipeline Rsch. Ctr., 1991—; vis. expert Nat. Taiwan U., Taipei, 1980; vis. prof. U. Melbourne, Australia, 1980; cons. wind energy Taiwan Power Co., Taipei, 1982—. Contbr. articles to profl. jours.; patentee in coal-log and capsule pipelines; inventor coal log pipeline. Recipient Disting. Lecture award Internat. Symposium on Freight Pipelines, 1982. Mem. ASCE (chmn. aerodynamics com. 1976-80, chmn. exec. com. aerospace divsn. 1988-89, chmn. pipeline rsch. com. 1991-94, Aerospace Sci. & Tech. award 1983, Bechtel Pipeline Engring. award 1992), Am. Soc. Engring. Edn. (mem. exec. com. mechanics divsn. 1982-85), Internat. Freight Pipeline Soc. (pres. 1989-94), U.S. Wind Engring. Rsch. Coun. (bd. dirs. 1985-89). Unitarian Universalist. Home: 3212 Woodbine Dr Columbia MO 65203-0976 Office: Univ Mo Dept Civil Engring Columbia MO 65211

LIU, KATHERINE CHANG, artist, art educator; b. Kiang-si, China; came to U.S., 1963; d. Ming-fan and Ying (Yuan) Chang; m. Yet-zen Liu; children: Alan S., Laura Y. MS, U. Calif., Berkeley, 1965. Instr. U. Va. Ext., Longwood Coll.; mem. tchg. staff master class Hill Country Arts Found., Tex., 1995, 96; invited mem. L.A. Artcore Reviewing and Curatorial Bd., 1993; invited juror, lectr. over 75 exhbns. and orgns.; juror, lectr. Ala. Watercolor Soc. Ann., 1996, Midwest Watercolor Soc. Nat. Exhibit, 1996, Watercolor West Nat. Open, 1996. One-woman shows include Harrison Mus., Utah State U., Riverside (Calif.) Art Mus., Ventura (Calif.) Coll., Fla. A&M U., Louis Newman Galleries, L.A., L.A. Artcore, Lung-Men Gallery, Taipei, Republic of China, State of the Arts International Biennial, Parkland Coll. Ill., 1989, 91, Watercolor U.S.A. Hon. Soc. Invitationa, 1989, 91, 93, 95, Hunter Mus. Art, Tenn., 1993, Bakersfield Art Mus., 1994, Sandra Walters Gallery, Hong Kong, 1994, Horwitch-Newman Gallery, Scottsdale, Ariz., 1995, Hong Kong U. Sci. and Tech. Libr. Art Gallery, 1996, J.J. Brookings Gallery, San Francisco, 1996; Invitational, U. B.C. Art Gallery, 1992, U. Sydney Art Mus., 1992, Ruhr-West Art Mus., Wise, 1992, Macau Art Mus., 1992, Rosenfeld Gallery, Phila., 1994, Mandarin Oriental Fine Arts, Hong Kong, 1994, Watercolor USA Honor Soc. Biennial, 1995; contbr. works to 21 books and 33 periodicals. Co-curator Taiwan-USA-Australia Watermedia Survey Exhbn., Nat. Taiwan Art Inst., 1994; sole juror San Diego Watermedia Internat., 1993, Triton Mus. Open Competition, 1994, Northern Nat. Art Competition, 1994, Watercolor West Nat., 1993, Tenn., Utah, Hawaii, N.C. Watercolor Socs., North Am. Open, Midwest Southwest and over 30 state-wide competitions in watermedia or all-media; co-juror Rocky Mountain Nat., San Diego Internat. and West Fedn. Exhibits. Recipient Rex Brandt award San Diego Watercolor Internat., 1985, Purchase Selection award Watercolor USA and Springfield (Mo.) Art Mus., 1981, Gold medal, 1986, Mary Lou Fitzgerald meml. award Allied Arts Am. Nat. Arts Club, N.Y.C., 1987, Achievement award of Artists Painting in Acrylic Am. Artists Mag., 1993; NEA grantee, 1979-80. Mem. Nat. Watercolor Soc. (life, chmn. jury 1985, pres. 1983, Top award 1984, cash awards 1979, 87), Watercolor U.S.A. Honor Soc., Nat. Soc. Painters in Casein and Acrylic (2nd award 1985), Rocky Mountain Nat. Watermedia Soc. (juror 1984, awards 1978, 80, 86).

LIU, KEH-FEI FRANK, physicist, educator; b. Beijing, Jan. 11, 1947; came to U.S., 1969; s. Hsien-Chang and Juihua (Wang) L.; m. Yao-Chin Ko, Apr. 6, 1974; children: Helen, Alexander. BS, Tunghai U., Taichung, Taiwan, 1968; MS, SUNY, Stony Brook, 1972, PhD, 1975. Vis. scientist C.E.N. Saclay France, Paris, 1974-76; from rsch. assoc. to adj. asst. prof. UCLA, 1976-80; assoc. prof. U. Ky., Lexington, 1980-86, prof. physics, 1986—; vis. prof. SUNY, Stony Brook, 1985-86, 1990; univ. rsch. prof. U. Ky., 1992. Editor: Chiral Solitons, 1987; assoc. editor World Scientific Pub. Co., Singapore, 1985—; contbr. articles to profl. jours. Recipient First Prize in Theoretical Physics Academia Sinica, China, 1987, Grand Challenge award DOE, 1988, 1989, Alexander Von Humboldt Sr. Scientist award Humboldt Found., Germany, 1990. Mem. Am. Phys. Soc., European Phys. Soc., Overseas Chinese Physicists Assn. (coord. 1991—). Office: U Ky Dept Physics & Astronomy Lexington KY 40506

LIU, KHANG-LEE, dentist, educator; b. China, Aug. 5, 1939; came to U.S., 1972, naturalized, 1982; s. T.P. and K.H. (Lu) L.; m. Nancy S.Y. Lee (div.); children: Christine, Helen. B.D.S., Nat. Def. Med. Ctr., Faculty of Dentistry, Taipei, 1964; MA, U. Chgo., 1974. Asst., Nat. Def. Med. Ctr., Taipei, Taiwan, 1964-67; instr. Med. Ctr., Republic of China, 1968-72; asst. prof. U. Chgo., 1972-76; assoc. prof. Nat. Def. Med. Ctr., 1976-77; from asst. prof. to assoc. prof. dentistry Northwestern U., Chgo., 1977—; dir. McCormick Boys and Girls Dental Clin. Pres. midwest chpt. Coun. on Chinese Cultural Renaissance, 1984—. Mem. ADA, Chgo. Dental Soc., Am. Soc. Dentistry for Children, Internat. Assn. Dental Rsch., Am. Acad. Pediatric Dentistry, Chinese Am. Dentist Assn. (charter mem., 1st pres. 1990). Office: 2158-B S Archer Ave Chicago IL 60616

LIU, MARGARET M., fabric company executive; b. China, July 24, 1946; d. I-Yung and K-Ming (Huan) L.; m. Shau-Chung Hu, Feb. 14, 1984; 1 child, Z.G. BA, Christian Coll., Taipei, Taiwan, 1974; MBA, Lincoln U., 1983; BBA, Nat. Acad. Mgmt., Taipei, 1980. Dir., pres. Am. Hubei Assoc., N.Y.C.; dir. Nat. Acad. Mgmt., Taipei; dir., pres. China Natural Fabric Corp., Bklyn.; hostess TV and radio program Computer and You, China TV Co., Cen. Radio Sta., 1970-73. Mem. Nat. Rep. Congl. Com. Recipient award Fend Chia U., Taipei, Taiwan Internat. Conf. on Computerized Bus. Simulations, 1976, Taiwan Merchants Assn. N.Y., Inc. Home: 1025 45th St Apt 1D Brooklyn NY 11219-1904

LIU, MING-TSAN, computer engineering educator; b. Peikang, Taiwan, Aug. 30, 1934. BSEE, Nat. Cheng Kung U., Tainan, Taiwan, 1957; MSEE, U. Pa., 1961, PhD, 1964. Prof. dept. computer and info. sci. Ohio State U. Recipient Engring. Rsch. award Ohio State U., 1982, Best Paper award Computer Network Symposium 1984, Disting. Achievement award Nat. Cheng Kung U., 1987, Disting. Scholar award Ohio State U., 1991, Ameritech prize for excellence in telecom. Ameritech Found., 1991. Fellow IEEE (chmn. tech. com. on distbtd. processing Computer Soc. 1982-84, editor IEEE Transactions on Computers 1982-86, chmn. Eckert-Mauchly award com. 1984-85, 91-92, bd. govs. Computer Soc. 1984-90, chmn. tutorials com. 1982, program chmn. 1985, gen. chmn. 1986, chmn. steering com. 1989, gen. co-chmn. Internat. Conf. on Distbtd. Computing Sys. 1992, chmn. steering com. Symposium on Reliable Distbtd. Sys. 1986-89, v.p. membership and info. Computer Soc. 1984, mem. fellow com. 1986-88, editor-in-chief IEEE Transactions on Computers 1986-90, program chmn. IEEE Internat. Conf. on Data Engring. 1990, mem. TAB awards and recognition com. 1990-91, program chmn. Internat. Symposium on Comm. 1991, Internat. Phoenix Conf. on Computers and Comm. 1992, mem. TAB new tech. directions com. 1992-93, gen. co-chmn. Internat. Conf. on Parallel and Distbtd. Sys. 1992, Meritorious Svc. award Computer Soc. 1985, 87, 90, Outstanding Mem. Columbus sect. 1986-87). Office: Ohio State U Computer & Information Sci 2036 Neil Ave Columbus OH 43210-1226*

LIU, RAY HO, forensic science program director, educator; b. Taiwan, Apr. 3, 1942; s. Ku and Tsan (Hwang) L.; m. Hsiu-Lan Lin, Dec. 4, 1965; children: Yu-Ting, Eugene, Hubert. LLB, Cen. Police Coll., Taipei, Taiwan, 1965; PhD, So. Ill. U., 1976. Qualified as lab. dir., N.Y. State Dept. Health. Asst. prof. forensic sci. U. Ill., Chgo., 1976-80; mass spectrometrist Cen. Regional Lab, U.S. EPA, Chgo., 1980-82; ctr. mass spectrometrist Ea. Regional Rsch. Ctr. USDA, Phila., 1982-83; assoc. prof. forensic sci. U. Ala., Birmingham, 1984-89, prof., 1989—, dir. grad. program in forensic sci., 1991—; tech. dir. Environ. Health Rsch. and Testing, Birmingham, Ala., 1987-91, Environ. Chem. Corp., Birmingham, 1992-93; cons. in field; vis. prof. Taiwanese Nat. Sci. Coun., 1981, 1994; insp. Nat. Lab. Certification Program, Research Triangle Park, N.C., 1988—. Author: Approaches to Drug Sample Differentiation, 1982, Elements and Practice in Forensic Drug Urinalysis, 1994, Handbook of Workplace Drug Testing, 1995; editor-in-chief Forensic Sci. Rev., 1989—; contbr. numerous articles to profl. jours. Fellow Am. Acad. Forensic Scis., mem. Am. Chem. Soc., Am. Assn. for Clin. Chemistry, Am. Soc. for Mass Spectrometry, Sigma XI. Office: U Ala Dept Criminal Justice Birmingham AL 35294

LIU, SHI-KAU, microbiologist, research scientist; b. Kaohsiung, Taiwan, Nov. 3, 1962; s. Pao-Hen Liu and Chen-Nuo Yen; m. Thyr-Min Lin; 1 child, Chung-Song. BS, Soochow U., Taiwan, 1984; PhD, Purdue U., U.S.A., 1991. Postdoctoral rsch. fellow Stanford U., Calif., 1991-93; assoc. prof. National Sun Yat-Sen Univ., Kaohsiung, Taiwan, 1993-94; rsch. assoc. U. N.C., Chapel Hill, N.C., 1994—; specialist referee Hong Kong Rsch. Grants Coun., Hong Kong, 1994—. Contbr. to profl. jours. Recipient Excellent Achievement award Republic of China Army, 1986, Outstanding Grad. Rsch. award Purdue U., 1990, Outstanding Researcher award Republic of China Nat. Sci. Coun., 1993. Mem. Am. Soc. Microbiology. Avocations: photography, fishing. Home: 281 Jen-Ai Road, Yung-Ho Taiwan

LIU, TA-TSAI, former military officer, maritime consultant; b. Nanchang, Kiangsi, Republic of China, Sept. 24, 1929; s. Chia Liu and Shun-Yin Wang; m. Chun-Pin Chen,. Oct. 12, 1967; children: Shu-Yao, Shu-Shun. BS, Naval Acad., Tso-ying, Taiwan, 1949; MA, Naval War Coll., Newport, R.I., 1966, Armed Forces Indsl. Coll., Washington, 1974. Commd. Taiwanese Navy, 1949, advanced through grades to vice-adm., 1984; dir. plan and program Ministry Nat. Def., Taipei, 1969-70; v.p. Def. Inst. Tech., Tao-Yuan, Taiwan, 1974-76; comdr. 192d Squadron Command, Tso-Ying, 1976-79, 2d Naval Dist., Peng-Hu, Taiwan, 1979-82; comdt. Naval Command and Staff Coll., Taipei, 1982-86; vice min. Ministry of Def., Taipei, 1987-88; dep. comdr.-in-chief Combined Svc. Forces, Taipei, 1988-90; advisor Ministry of Def., 1990-95; sr. advisor Sandalwood Culture Found., Puli, Taiwan, 1993—; observer SEAPOL Conf., Bangkok, 1992, SEAPOL Conf., Kuala Lumpur, Malaysia, 1993, Asia-Pacific Def. Conf., Singapore, 1994, ISPA Conf., Boston, 1994, SEAPOL Tri-Regional Conf., Bangkok, 1994; spkr. Ctr. for Strategic Studies, U. Pretoria, South Africa, 1988. Author: The Direction of Naval Warfare, 1983, The Seapower Essays of VADM Liu Ta-Tsai, 1996; editor: (monographs) Chinese Seapower Symposium, I, 1990, II, 1992; pub. monthly naval mag., 1986. Recipient Order of Loyalty and Diligence, Ministry Nat. Def., 1984, Spl. Cravat of Order of Resplendent Banner, Ministry Nat. Def., 1986, Medal of the Armed Forces, Ministry Nat. Def., 1990, Disting. Svc. Medal, Ministry Nat. Def., 1990. Fellow Soc. for Strategic Studies (sr. rsch. fellow); mem. U.S. Naval Inst. Avocations: swimming, golf, classical music, reading, sight-seeing. Home: Sec 1, 5F 27 Ln 197 Chih-Yu Rd, Shihlin Taipei 111, Taiwan

LIU, VI-CHENG, aerospace engineering educator; b. Wu-ching, China, Sept. 1, 1917; came to U.S., 1946, naturalized, 1973; s. Bi-Ching and Shu-Fung (Keng) L.; m. Hsi-Yen Wang, Mar. 1, 1947. B.S., Chiao Tung U., 1940; M.S., U. Mich., 1947, Ph.D., 1951. Instr. Tsing-Hua U., Kunming, 1940-46; research engr. Engring. Research Inst., U. Mich., Ann Arbor, 1951-59; prof. aerospace engring. U. Mich., 1959-89, prof. emeritus, 1989—; vis. prof. Inst. of Mechanics, Chinese Acad. Sci., Peking, 1980—; ministry edn., vis. chair prof. Nanjing Aero. Inst., People's Republic China, 1989-91, hon. prof., 1991—; cons. NASA, 1964-65. Ministry of Edn. China research fellow, 1946-49; NASA research grantee, 1964-80, USAF Geophysical Rsch. grantee, 1958-64. Research and 100 sci. publs. in rarefied gas dynamics, ionospheric physics, space physics, geophys. fluid dynamics. Home: 2104 Vinewood Blvd Ann Arbor MI 48104-2762

LIU, WING KAM, mechanical and civil engineering educator; b. Hong Kong, May 15, 1952; came to U.S., 1973, naturalized, 1990; s. Yin Lam and Siu Lin (Chan) L.; m. Betty Hsia, Dec. 12, 1986; children: Melissa Margaret, Michael Kevin. BSc with highest honors, U. Ill., Chgo., 1976; MSc, Calif. Inst. Tech., 1977, PhD, 1981. Registered profl. engr., Ill. Asst. prof. mech. and civil engring. Northwestern U., Evanston, Ill., 1980-83, assoc. prof., 1983-88, prof., 1988—; prin. cons. reactor analysis and safety div. Argonne (Ill.) Nat. Lab., 1981—. Co-editor: Innovative Methods for Nonlinear Problems, 1984, Impact-Effects of Fasts Transient Loadings, 1988, Computational Mechanics of Probabilistic and Reliability Analysis, 1989. Recipient Thomas J. Jaeger prize Internat. Assn. for Structural Mechanics in Reactor Tech., 1989, Ralph R. Teetor award Soc. Automotive Engrs., 1983; grantee NSF, Army Rsch. Office, NASA, AFSOR, ONR. Fellow ASCE, ASME (Melville medal 1979, Pi Tau Sigma gold medal 1985, Gustus L. Larson Meml. award 1995), U.S. Assn. Computational Mechanics (pres.-elect); mem. Am. Acad. Mechanics. Office: Northwestern U Dept Mech Engring 2145 Sheridan Rd Evanston IL 60208-0834

LIU, YOSEN, nuclear engineer; b. Wuchang, Hupei, China, Oct. 31, 1935; came to U.S., 1977; s. Henry C. and Chin-Feen (Chou) L.; m. Johanna S. Lui, Sept. 2, 1967; children: Sieglinde, Siegrid, Steve. BS, Naval Coll. Tech., 1958; dipl. engr., Tech. Hochschule, Germany, 1966, D of Engring., 1970. Rsch. scientist Kernforschungsanlage, Juelich, Germany, 1966-70; assoc. prof. Nat. Tsing Hua U., Hsinchu, Taiwan, 1970-75; nuclear engr. Kraftwerk Union, Erlangen, Germany, 1975-77; prin. engr. Combustion Engring. Inc., Windsor, Conn., 1977-80; mgr. bus. devel. Combustion Engring. Inc., Taipei, Taiwan, 1980-87; sr. cons. physicist ABB Combustion Engring. Inc., Windsor, 1987-90; staff engr. Battelle Pacific Northwest Lab., Richland, Wash., 1990—. Mem. Am. Nuclear Soc., Rotary Internat. Roman Catholic. Avocation: golf. Home: 218 Sitka Ct Richland WA 99352 Office: Battelle Pacific NW Lab Battelle Blvd Richland WA 99352

LIU, YUAN HSIUNG, drafting and design educator; b. Tainan, Taiwan, Feb. 24, 1938; came to U.S., 1970; s. Chun Chang and Kong (Wong) L.; m. Ho Pe Tung, July 27, 1973; children: Joan Anshen, Joseph Pinyang. BEd, Nat. Taiwan Normal U., Taipei, 1961; MEd, Nat. Chengchi U., Taipei, 1967, U. Alta., Edmonton, 1970; PhD, Iowa State U., 1975. Cert. tchr. Tchr. indsl. arts and math. Nan Ning Jr. High Sch., Tainan, Taiwan, 1961-62, 63-64; tech. math. instr. Chung-Cheng Inst. Tech., Taipei, 1967-68; drafter Sundstrand Hydro-Transmission Corp., Ames, Iowa, 1973-75; assoc. prof. Fairmont (W.Va.) State Coll., 1975-80; per course instr. Sinclair Community Coll., Dayton, Ohio, 1985; assoc. prof. Miami U., Hamilton, Ohio, 1980-85, Southwest Mo. State U., Springfield, 1985—; cons. Monarch Indsl. Precision Co., Springfield, 1986, Gen. Electric Co., Springfield, 1988, Fasco Industries, Inc., Ozark, Mo., 1989, 95, Springfield Remfg. Corp., 1990, 92, Ctrl. States Indsl., Intercont Products, Inc., L&W Industries, Inc., ZERCO Mfg. Co., 1994, 95. 2d lt. R.O.C. Army, 1962-63. Recipient Excellent Teaching in Drafting award Charvoz-Carsen Corp., Fairfield, N.J., 1978. Mem. Am. Design Drafting Assn. Avocations: walking, watching TV. Office: S W Mo State U Tech Dept 901 S National Ave Springfield MO 65804-0094

LIUKKONEN, KAREN ELAINE, financial company executive; b. Gardner, Mass., Oct. 30, 1958; d. Kaarlo and Helvi Helena (Manty) L. BS in Chemistry, Worcester Polytechnic Inst., 1980; MBA, Babson Coll., 1982. Credit analyst John Hancock Mut. Life, Boston, 1982-84, investment specialist, 1984-85, treas. officer, 1985-86; dir. money market ops. Boston, 1986-89; spl. asst. Dept. of Health and Human Svcs., Washington, 1989-90; pres. John Hancock Capital Corp., Boston, 1990—, gen. dir. portfolio mgmt. and investment svcs., 1991—; bd. dirs. John Hancock Corp. Republican. Avocation: traveling. Office: John Hancock Capital Corp PO Box 111 John Hancock Pl Boston MA 02117-0111

LIUZZI, ROBERT C., chemical company executive; b. Boston, 1944; married. AB, Coll. of Holy Cross, 1965; LLB, U. Va., 1968. V.p., gen. counsel U.S. Fin., Inc., 1969-74; with CF Industries, Long Grove, Ill., 1975—, exec. v.p., chief fin. officer, 1977-80, exec. v.p., operating officer, 1980-84, pres., chief exec. officer, 1985—; chmn. ad hoc com. Domestic Nitrogen Prodrs., Washington; chmn., bd. dirs. Can. Fertilizers Ltd., The Fertilizer Inst., Nat. Coun. Farmer Coops., Fla. Phosphate Coun., Tampa; co-chmn. Petrochem. Trade Group, Washington; mem. Nat. Forum Nonpoint Source Pollution sponsored by Nat. Geographic Soc. and Conservation Fund of Washington. Mem. coun. Internat. Exec. Svc. Corps, Stamford, Conn.; mem. bus. adv. coun. Law Sch. U. Va., Charlottesville. Mem. Ill. Bus. Roundtable, Northwestern U. Assocs., Coun. of 100, Tampa Fla. Office: CF Industries Inc One Salem Lake Dr Long Grove IL 60047-8402

LIUZZO, JOSEPH ANTHONY, food science educator; b. Tampa, Fla., Dec. 16, 1926; s. Joseph and Annie (Minardi) L.; m. Elaine Grammer, Nov. 30, 1951; children: Paul Arthur, Patricia Joyce, Jolaine Marie. BS, U. Fla., 1950, MS, 1955; postgrad., U. So. Calif., 1952-53; PhD, Mich. State U., 1958. Microbiologist Stokely-Van Camp Co., Tampa, 1950; head, div. microbiology Nutrilite Products, Inc., Buena Park, Calif., 1951-54; asst. prof. biochemistry La. State U., Baton Rouge, 1958-62; assoc. prof. food sci. La. State U., 1962-69, prof., 1969—, faculty chmn. athletics, 1979-83; Chmn. Am. Legion Baseball Program, 1976-82. Contbr. articles to profl. jours. With U.S. Army, 1945-46. Recipient Outstanding Alumnus award Food Sci. and Human Nutrition, Mich. State U., 1994. Fellow AAAS, Am. Inst. Chemists, Inst. of Food Technologists; mem. Am. Inst. Nutrition, Am. chem. Soc., Kiwanis (pres. 1988-89, div. lt. gov. 1990-91), Sigma Xi, Phi Tau Sigma, Gamma Sigma Delta, Phi Sigma, Omicron Delta Kappa. Democrat. Mem. Ch. of Christ. Office: La State U Dept Food Science Baton Rouge LA 70803

LIVA, EDWARD LOUIS, eye surgeon; b. Lyndhurst, N.J., Aug. 30, 1925; s. Paul Francis and Lucy Agnes (Andreozzi) L.; m. Dorothea Lucille Carter, Aug. 29, 1946; children: Edward Jr., Bradford, Douglas, Jeffrey, Elaine. SB, Harvard U., 1946, MD, 1950. Diplomate Am. Bd. Ophthalmology. Internship Med. Coll. Va., Richmond, 1950-51; fellowship in eye pathology Mass. Eye and Ear, Boston, 1951; residency Brooklyn Eye and Ear, N.Y., 1952-53; chief ophthalmic examiner Workman's Compensation Bd., N.Y.C., 1957-63; sr. ophthalmic surgeon Hackensack (N.J.) Med. Ctr., 1957—, Valley Hosp., Ridgewood, N.J., 1963—; sr. ophthalmic surgeon, resident instr. oculoplastics Manhatten Eye, Ear and Throat, N.Y.C., 1957—; pres. Bergen Surg. Ctr., Paramus, N.J., 1991—, Eye Inst. of N.J., Paramus, 1987—. Author: Advances in Ophthalmic Plastic, 1983. Mem. Rep. Club, Ridgewood, 1960—. Capt. USAF, 1955-57. Fellow AMA, Am. Acad. Ophthalmology, Internat. Coll. of Surgeons, Am. Soc. of Ophtalmic Plastic and Reconstructive Surgery (chartered). Republican. Roman Catholic. Achievements include development new lid flaps oculoplastics, prototype of lid canal laceration repair, major modification of ptosis surgical procedures widely used, disproved Trichromatic theory of color vision in 1952. Home: 225 Sollas Ct Ridgewood NJ 07450 Office: Liva Eye Ctr One West Ridgewood Ave Paramus NJ 07652

LIVAS, EDUARDO, JR., milling company executive; b. 1945. PhD in Econs., U. Tex. With Gruma Mex. S.A., Monterrey, Mex., 1966-80; pres. Azteca Milling Co., Edinburg, Tex., 1990—. Office: Azteca Milling Co 501 W Chapin St Edinburg TX 78539-2412*

LIVAUDAIS, MARCEL, JR., federal judge; b. New Orleans, Mar. 3, 1925; m. Carol Black; children: Julie, Marc, Durel. BA, Tulane U., 1945, JD, 1949. Bar: La. Assoc. Boswell & Loeb, New Orleans, 1949-50, 52-56; ptnr. Boswell Loeb & Livaudais, New Orleans, 1956-60, Loeb & Livaudais, 1960-67, 71-77, Loeb Dillon & Livaudais, 1967-71; U.S. magistrate, 1977-84; judge U.S. Dist. Ct. (ea. dist.) La., New Orleans, 1984—. Mem. Am. Judicature Soc. Office: US Dist Ct C-313 US Courthouse 500 Camp St New Orleans LA 70130-3313*

LIVELY, CAROL A., professional society administrator; b. Chgo., Sept. 2, 1935; d. William Mann and Lillian (Juske) Haycock; m. E. Raymond Platig; children: Richard B., Laura Jean. L.P.N., Los Angeles Sch. Nursing, 1953; student, Columbia U., 1954, Boston U., 1956-57. Program dir. United Fund, Pittsfield, Mass., 1966-71; exec. dir. Western Mass. Health Council, 1971-74; asst. exec. dir. Genesse Health Council, Rochester, N.Y., 1974-76; dir. devel. Shimer Coll., Mt. Carroll, Ill., 1976-77; assoc. dir. Am. Hosp. Assn., Chgo., 1977-80; dir. health div., v.p. Smith Bucklin Assn., Washington, 1980-95, ret., 1995; mem. Achievement Rewards Coll. Scientists, Washington, 1980—; cons. Dept. Health Rep. Haiti, Washington, 1976—. Contbg. author: Politics of Health Planning, 1962; contbr. articles to profl. jours. Bd. dirs. Jacobs Pillow Dance Theatre, Pittsfield, 1968; bd. dirs. Albany Regional Med. Program, N.Y., 1971-74; active Jr. League, Washington, 1965—; mem. Commn. Drug Abuse Council, Boston, 1971-74. Recipient Woman of Yr. award Bus. and Profl. Women, 1971. Mem. New Eng. Pub. Health Assn., Mass. Council on Aging, Am. Soc. Hosp. Planning, Am. Pub. Health Assn. Home: 2138 California St NW Washington DC 20008-1876

LIVELY, EDWIN LESTER, retired oil company executive; b. Bowie, Tex., June 16, 1930; s. L. D. and Lois E. Lively; m. G. Marie Bryan; 1 child, James E. B.B.A., Midwestern State U., Wichita Falls, Tex., 1951; postgrad. in Advanced Mgmt., Emory U., 1967. Adminstr. recruiting Conoco, Inc. (subs. E.I. du Pont de Nemours), Houston, 1967-68; Lake Charles coordinator Conoco, Inc., Lake Charles, La., 1968-75, Gulf Coast coordinator, 1975-79, regional coordinator, 1979-85, v.p. and regional coordinator, so.western areas external affairs, 1985-86; gen. mgr. external affairs dept. State Affairs div. E.I. du Pont de Nemours & Co., 1987-88, retired. Served to sgt., U.S. Army, 1952-54. Avocations: golf; fishing. *Always remember, people are the most important asset in any business venture. Success and good friends are God's reward for following that principle.*

LIVELY, EDWIN LOWE, sociology educator; b. Fairmont, W.Va., Aug. 14, 1920; s. E.L. and Lucy (Ross) L.; m. Virginia Isabelle Reed, Aug. 25, 1940; children: Lynellen, Gerianne (Mrs. Michael Green), Edwin L. II. A.B. in Edn, Fairmont State Coll., 1940; M.A. in Sociology, Ohio State U., 1946, Ph.D., 1959. Tchr. high sch. Farmington, W.Va., 1940-42; instr. Kent State U., 1947-53, asst. prof., 1953-58, assoc. prof., 1958-63; prof. sociology, chmn. dept. Akron U., 1963-68, dean grad. studies and research, 1968-75, prof., 1975-78; lectr. Labor and Edn. Service, Ohio State U., 1966-68; cons. Ohio Youth Commn., Akron Urban Renewal, Akron Community Action Council, Akron Community Relations Commn., Canton (Ohio) Bd. Edn. Contbg. editor: Dynamic Urban Sociology, 1954; guest editor: Sociol. Focus, 1970; co-author: (with V. Lively) Sexual Development of Young Children, 1990. Pres. Greater Akron Area Council Alcoholism, 1969-71; chmn. Akron Commn. Civil Disorders, 1968-69; pres. United Community Council, 1972-74; bd. dirs. Goals for Greater Akron Area, 1974-80. Served with USAAF, 1942-45. Decorated Air medal with five oak leaf clusters.; Swift fellow, 1963; grantee Esso Edn. Found., 1966; grantee div. adult and vocational research Dept. Health, Edn. and Welfare, 1967; grantee Ohio Bd. Regents, 1967; grantee Ohio Dept. Health, 1968. Fellow Am. Sociol. Assn.; mem. Ohio Valley Sociol. Soc. (bd. dirs. 1964-68), Nat. Council Family Relations, Summit County Mental Health Assn. (pres. 1965-67). Club: Mason. Home: 634 Brackenwood Cv West Palm Beach FL 33418-9001

LIVELY, PIERCE, federal judge; b. Louisville, Aug. 17, 1921; s. Henry Thad and Ruby Durrett (Keating) L.; m. Amelia Harrington, May 25, 1946; children: Susan, Katherine, Thad. AB, Centre Coll., Ky., 1943; LL.B., U. Va., 1948. Bar: Ky. 1948. Individual practice law Danville, Ky., 1949-57; mem. firm Lively and Rodes, Danville, 1957-72; judge U.S. Ct. Appeals (6th cir.), Cin., 1972—, chief judge, 1983-88; now sr. judge; Mem. Ky. Commn. on Economy and Efficiency in Govt., 1963-65, Ky. Jud. Advisory Com., 1972. Trustee Centre Coll. Served with USNR, 1943-46. Mem. ABA, Am. Judicature Soc., Order of Coif, Raven Soc., Phi Beta Kappa, Omicron Delta Kappa. Presbyterian. Office: US Ct Appeals PO Box 1226 Danville KY 40423-5226 also: US Courthouse Rm 418 Cincinnati OH 45202

LIVENGOOD, CHARLOTTE LOUISE, employee development specialist; b. L.A., June 18, 1944; d. James Zollie and Zela (Cogburn) L. BS in Secondary Edn., Tex. A & I U., 1968; MEd in Pers. Guidance and Counseling, North Tex. U., 1971. Cert. secondary teaching, Tex.; cert. counselor, Tex. Counselor Gus Grissom H.S., Huntsville, Ala., 1971-72; tchr. West Springfield H.S., Springfield, Va., 1972-73; edn. specialist U.S. Dept. Def., El Paso, Tex., 1975-78; instr. El Paso (Tex.) C.C., 1977-78; employee devel. specialist U.S. Office Pers. Mgmt., Dallas, 1978-79; pers. mgmt. specialist Dept. Vets. Affairs, Houston, 1979-87; labor rels. specialist Dept. Vets. Affairs, VA Med. Ctr., Houston, 1987-89; pers. staffing specialist Dept. Vets. Affairs, Houston, 1989-90; employee devel. specialist, acad. tng. officer HUD, Ft. Worth, 1990—; assoc. prof. Ariz. State U., 1995—; tng. officer Bur. of Engraving and Printing, U.S. Tng. Officer Ft. Worth, 1995—; EEO investigator Dept. Vet. Affairs, 1984-87; speaker in field. Editor: (monthly office newspaper) Pipeline, 1980-87. Chairperson, forensics coach Jr. High Sch. Speech Dept., 1968-69; tchr. S. Grand Prarie H.S., 1969-71; mem. Dallas/Ft. Worth Quality Control Coun., Tex. War on Drugs Com., 1990—; hon. mem. Dallas/Ft. Worth Fed. Exec. Bd., 1993-94. Recipient Future Secs. of Am. scholarship, 1962. Mem. ASTD, AAUW, Am. Pers. and Guidance Assn., Assn. for Quality Participation, Internat. Transactional Analysis Assn., Tex. State Tchrs. Assn., Tex. Classroom Tchrs. Assn., Fed. Bus. Assn., VA Employee Assn., Intergovernmental Tng. Assn., Intergovernmental Tng. Coun. (chairperson 1993-94). Mem. Church of Christ. Avocations: reading, travel, bridge, fishing, theater. Office: US Dept Treasury Bur Engraving & Printing Western Currency Facility 9000 Blue Mound Rd Fort Worth TX 76131

LIVENGOOD, JOANNE DESLER, healthcare administrator; b. Omaha, Sept. 29, 1936; d. Arthur Frederick and Rosamond Christina (Knudsen) D.; m. Richard Vaughn Livengood, Aug. 11, 1962; children: Linda Renee, John David. BA, W.Va. State Coll.Inst., 1975; Diploma, Swedish Am. Hosp. Sch. Nursing, Rockford, Ill., 1961; MBA, Ea. Ill. U., Charleston, 1984. RN, Ill. W.Va. State Inst.; DON Hoopeston (Ill.) Hosp. and Nursing Home, 1981-84; adminstr. Vermilion Manor Nursing Home, Danville, Ill., 1984-88; asst. adminstr. R.E. Thomason Hosp., El Paso, Tex., 1989-91; adminstr. Horizon Splty. Hosp., El Paso, Tex., 1992-93, Ill. Vets. Home at Anna, 1994—; cons. J.D. Williams Ins. Agy., El Paso, Tex., 1991-92, The Regional Clinic, Carterville, Ill., 1994. Mem. Danville (Ill.) Dist. 118 Sch. Bd., 1976-82. Fellow Am. Coll. Healthcare Execs.; mem. S.W. Healthcare Execs. (treas. 1989-93), Anna-Jonesboro Rotary Club. Home: 1810 Paula Ln Marion IL 62959-1425 Office: Ill Vets Home at Anna 792 N Main St Anna IL 62906

LIVERGOOD, ROBERT FRANK, prosecutor; b. Akron, Ohio, Dec. 20, 1957; s. Robert Burton and Rita Veronica (Haidnick) L.; m. Sandra Anne Ko, Aug. 5, 1983; children: Robert Santos, Jacob Christopher, Sarah Nicole. BA, St. Louis U., 1981, M in Health Adminstrn., 1983, JD, 1988. Bar: Mo. 1988, Ill. 1989, U.S. Dist. Ct. (ea. dist.) Mo. 1989, U.S. Dist. Ct. (so. dist.) Ill. 1989. Dir. market rsch. St. Joseph's Hosp. Kirkwood, Mo., 1983-85; assoc. Husch & Eppenberger, St. Louis, 1988-90; asst. prosecuting atty. Office of the Prosecutor, Clayton, Mo., 1990—. Editor St. Louis U. Law Jour., 1986-87, mng. editor, 1987-88. Vol. lawyer Voluntary Lawyers Program, St. Louis, 1988-90; spkr. St. Louis (Mo.) County and Mcpl. Police Acad., 1993-94. Mem. ABA, Ill. State Bar Assn., Bar Assn. Met. St. Louis. Avocations: martial arts, amateur radio. Office: Office of the Prosecutor 7900 Carondelet Ave Clayton MO 63105-1720

LIVERMAN, LYNDA M., community health nurse; b. Bogalusa, La., Mar. 26, 1941; d. Warren LeRoy and Verdine jane (McTaggart) Mizell; m. Merlin C. Liverman, Jan. 28, 1962; children: David, Debra, Donna. Student, La. State U., 1959-61, Our Lady Holy Cross Coll., 1972-74; ADN, Northwestern State U., 1979. Cert. care mgmt. Staff nurse Schumpert Med. Ctr., Shreveport, La., 1979; staff, charge nurse North Caddo Meml. Hosp., Vivian, La., 1979-81, Highland Hosp., Shreveport, 1982-85; staff relief, pvt. duty nurse MAS Nursing, Inc., Shreveport, 1982-85, dir. pers. and med. adminstrn., 1985-89; br. mgr. Kimberly Quality Care, Shreveport, 1989-92; established Premier Family Healthcare, Inc., Shreveport, La., 1992—, Glen Home Health, Inc. (subs. Premier Family Healthcare, Inc.), Shreveport, La., 1995—; v.p. Premier Healthcare Mgmt., Inc., Shreveport, La., 1995—. Mem. Riverside Bapt. Ch. Named Nurse of the Yr. Shreveport Dist. Nurses Assn., 1989. Mem. ANA, NAHC, Shreveport Dist. Nurses Assn., Am. Soc. Parenteral and Enteral Nutrition, Ark.-La.-Tex. Assn. Home Health and Hospice Agys., Homecare Assn. La. Avocations: reading, travel, photography, art, music, family activities.

LIVERMORE, JOSEPH MCMASTER, judge; b. Portland, Oreg., Feb. 5, 1937; s. Ernest R. and Frances (McMaster) L.; m. Elaine Dufort, Mar. 18, 1966; 1 son, Caleb. A.B., Dartmouth, 1958; LL.B., Stanford, 1961. Bar: Calif. 1962, Minn. 1968, Ariz. 1974. Assoc. Brobeck, Phleger & Harrison, San Francisco, 1961, 64-65; prof. law U. Minn., Mpls., 1965-73; asst. U.S. atty., Mpls., 1971-72; dean Coll. Law, U. Ariz., Tucson, 1973-77, prof., 1977-85; judge Ariz. Ct. Appeals, 1985—. Served with JAG Corps AUS, 1962-63. Mem. ABA, Ariz. Bar Assn., State Bar Calif., Order of Coif, Phi Beta Kappa. Home: 3208 E 3rd St Tucson AZ 85716-4232 Office: Ariz Ct Appeals 400 W Congress St Tucson AZ 85701-1352

LIVERSAGE, RICHARD ALBERT, cell biologist; b. Fitchburg, Mass., July 8, 1925; s. Rodney Marcellus and Hazel Mildred (Huntting) L.; m. June Patricia Krebs, June 19, 1954; children: John Walter, Robert Richard, James Keith, Ross Andrew. B.A., Marlboro Coll., 1951; A.M., Amherst Coll., 1953, Princeton U., 1957; Ph.D., Princeton U., 1958. Fellow Bowdoin Coll., Brunswick, Maine, 1953-54; instr. Amherst Coll., 1954-55, Princeton, 1958-60; mem. faculty U. Toronto, 1960—, prof. zoology, 1969—, grad. sec. dept., 1975-77, asso. chmn. grad. affairs dept., 1978-84, acting chmn., 1980-81; Investigator Huntsman Marine Lab., St. Andrews, N.B., Can., 1968-71. Contbr. over 78 articles on role of nerves and endocrine secretions at cellular-molecular levels in vertebrate appendage regeneration to sci. jours. Served as flight engr. USAAF, 1943-45. Recipient 5 decorations. Mem. Soc. Devel. Biology, Can. Soc. Zoologists, Royal Can. Inst., Wound Healing Soc., Sigma Xi (exec. com., v.p., pres. U. Toronto chpt.). Home: 48 Ferndell Circle, Unionville, ON Canada L3R 3Y8 Office: U Toronto, Ramsay Wright Zool Lab, Toronto, ON Canada M5S 3G5

LIVESAY, THOMAS ANDREW, museum administrator, lecturer; b. Dallas, Feb. 1, 1945; s. Melvin Ewing Clay and Madge Almeda (Hall) L.; m. Amanda Haralson, 1985; children: Heather Marie, Russell Lee. BFA, U. Tex., Austin, 1968, MFA, 1972; postgrad., Harvard U. Inst. Arts Adminstrn., 1978. Curator Elisabet Ney Mus., Austin, 1971-73; dir. Longview (Tex.) Mus. and Arts Center, 1973-75; curator of art Amarillo (Tex.) Art Center, 1975-77, dir. center, 1977-80; asst. dir. for adminstrn. Dallas Mus. Fine Arts, 1980-85; dir. Mus. of N.Mex., Santa Fe, 1985—; mem. touring panel Tex. Commn. Arts; mem. panel Nat. Endowment Arts, Inst. Mus. Services; adj. tchr. U. Okla., Coll. Liberal Studies, 1992—, U. N.Mex., 1992—. Author: Young Texas Artists Series, 1978, Made in Texas, 1979; editor: video tape American Images, 1979, Ruth Abrams, Paintings, 1940-85, NYU Press. Served with U.S. Army, 1969-71. Mem. Am. Assn. Mus. (coun. 1986-89, commn. on ethics 1992—, accreditation commn. 1994—), Tex. Assn. Mus. (v.p. 1981, pres. 1983), N.Mex. State Records and Archives Commn. (chmn. 1986—), Rotary. Methodist. Office: Mus of New Mexico PO Box 2087 Santa Fe NM 87504-2087

LIVESAY, VALORIE ANN, lead security analyst; b. Greeley, Colo., Sept. 9, 1959; d. John Albert and Mary Magdalene Yurchak. BA in Edn., U. No. Colo., 1981; M in Computer Info. Sys., U. Denver, 1991. Drafter Computer Graphics, Denver, 1981, Advanced Cable Sys., Inc., Denver, 1981-82, Am. TV Comm. Corp., Englewood, Colo., 1982-83; janitor Rockwell Internat., Golden, Colo., 1983-84, analytical lab tech., 1984-86, metall. operator, 1986-88; nuclear material coord. EG&G Rocky Flats Inc., Golden, 1988-92, lead security analyst, 1992-95. Active Channel 6, Denver, 1985, World Wildlife Fund, Westminster, Colo., 1987, Denver Dumb Friends League, 1987, The Nature Conservancy, Boulder, Colo., 1989. Mem. NAFE, Am. Soc. Insdl. Security. Avocations: scuba diving, mountain biking, skiing, reading, boating. Home: 6344 W 115th Ave Broomfield CO 80020-3034 Office: EG&G Rocky Flats Inc PO Box 464 Rocky Flats Plant Golden CO 80402-0464

LIVICK, MALCOLM HARRIS, school administrator; b. Staunton, Va., Apr. 5, 1929; s. Arthur Crawford and Sallie (Harris) L.; m. Linda Moorman Roller, July 21, 1956; children: Malcolm Harris, Charles Roller, Linda Lee, Todd Stephenson, Taylor Crawford (dec.). Student, Hampden Sydney Coll., 1947-48; B.S., U. Va., 1951; M.Ed., Madison Coll., 1965. Instr., coach Augusta Mil. Acad., 1955-56; instr. Norfolk (Va.) pub. schs., 1956-57; underwriter Mutual of N.Y., Norfolk, 1957-58; coach, asst. prin. Augusta Mil. Acad., Fort Defiance, Va., 1958-66; supt. Augusta Mil. Acad., 1966-83; dir. ednl. devel. Blue Ridge Community Coll., 1984-85, dir. continuing edn., 1986; dir. Blue Ridge Community Coll. Waynesboro Ctr., 1986—. Chmn. Upper Valley Regional Park Authority, 1969-78; Trustee King's Daus. Hosp., Staunton, Massanetta Springs. Served with USAF, 1951-55. Mem. Va. Mil. Schs. League (pres. 1966-68), Va. Assn. Prep. Schs. (exec. com. 1967-73, pres. 1971-72), Nat., Va. assns. secondary sch. prins. Presbyn. (deacon 1963-65, elder 1965—). Lodge: Kiwanis (pres. 1970-71, lt. gov. 1971, gov. 1979-80). Address: PO Box 22 Fort Defiance VA 24437-0022

LIVICK, STEPHEN, fine art photographer; b. Leeds, Yorkshire, Eng., Feb. 11, 1945; arrived in Can., 1947; Student, Sir George Williams U., Montreal, Can., 1963-66. Self employed artist, 1970—. One man shows include Centaur Gallery, Montreal, 1972, London Art Gallery, Ont., 1973, George Eastman House, Rochester, N.Y., 1975, David Mirvish Gallery, Toronto, 1976, 77, Photography Gallery, Bowmanville, Ont., 1976, 77, Balt. Mus. Art, 1978, Lunn Graphics, Washington D.C., 1978, Gallery Graphics, Ottawa, 1978, Jane Corkin Gallery, Toronto, 1979, 80, 81, U. Western Ont., London, 1981, 93, George Dalsheimer Gallery, Balt., 1982, MacDonald Stewart Art Ctr., Guelph, 1983, 94, New Brunswick Craft Sch., Fredericton, 1986, Winnipeg Photographers Group, 1987, Galerie Sequence, Quebec, 1988, U .Sherbrooke, 1990, Can. Mus. Contemporary Photography, Ottawa, 1992, MacKenzie Art Gallery, Regina, 1994, Meml. U. Art Gallery, St. John's, 1994, Beaverbrook Art Gallery, Fredicton, 1995, Art Gallery Windsor, 1995; travelling exhibitions include George Eastman House, 1978-81, London Regional Art Gallery, 1976-77, Nat. Film Bd., 1976-84, Art Gallery Ont., 1980, 81, Can. Mus. Contemporary Photography, 1986, 87; exhibited in group shows at Nat. Art Gallery, Ottawa, 1975, London Pub. Art Gallery, 1976, Nat. Film Bd., Ottawa, Can., 1977, Mendal Art Gallery, Saskatoon, Can., 1977, Neikrug Galleries, N.Y.C., 1978, Banff-London Exchange, Alberta, Can., 1978, Smithsonian Instn., Washington, 1981, Carpenter Ctr. Visual Arts, Cambridge, Mass., 1981, U. Calgary, 1982, Saidy Bronfman Mus., Montreal, 1984, Photographers Gallery, London, Eng., 1984, Presentation House, Vancouver, B.C., 1985, Photo Union Gallery, Hamilton, Ont., 1986, Film In The City, St. Paul, 1989, Corcoran Gallery Art, Washington, 1989, London (Can.) Regional Art Mus., 1990, Can. Mus. Contemporary Photography, Ottowa, 1992, others; represented in permanent collections Nat. Art Gallery Can., Can Mus. Contemporary Photography, Art Gallery Ont., Can. Art Bank, Nat. Archives Can., Mus. Modern Art, N.Y., George Eastman House, Rochester, N.Y., Carnegie Mus. Art, Pitts., Mus. Fine Arts, Houston, Fogg Art Mus., Cambridge, Mass., Balt. Mus. Art, George Washington U., Washington, Norton Gallery Art, West Palm Beach, Fla., Syracuse (N.Y.) U., Middlebury (Vt.) Coll., Hickory (N.C.) Mus. Art, U. Iowa Mus., U. No. Iowa, Art Gallery Hamilton, Can., High Mus. Art, Atlanta, Ga., London Regional Art Gallery, Corcoran Gallery Art, Washington, Queens U., Kingston, Can., Winnipeg (Can.) Art Gallery, Sarnia (Ont.) Art Gallery, U. Western Ont., London, Macdonald Stewart Art Ctr., Guelph, Ont., numerous pvt., corp. collections. B level grantee Can. Coun., Ottawa; sr. grantee Ont. Arts Coun., Toronto. Home and Office: 22A Maitland St Studio, London, ON Canada N6B 3L2

LIVINGOOD, CLARENCE S., dermatologist; b. Elverson, Pa., Aug. 7, 1911; s. Clarence A. and Eliza (Zerr) L.; m. Louise Sinclair Woelpper, Oct. 24, 1947; children: Wilson, Louise S., Clarence, Susan, Elizabeth. B.S., Ursinus Coll., 1932, D.Sc. (hon.), 1982; M.D., U. Pa., 1936. Diplomate Am. Bd. Dermatology (exec. dir. 1968-92, exec. cons. 1993—). Intern, then resident dermatology Hosp. U. Pa., 1936-41; asst. prof. dermatology U. Pa. Med. Sch., 1946-48, U. Pa. Med. Sch. (Grad. Sch.), 1946-49; chief dermatology Children's Hosp. Pa., 1946-48; prof., chmn. dept. dermatology Jefferson Med. Sch., Phila., 1948-49, U. Tex. Sch. Medicine, 1949-53; chmn. dermatology dept. Henry Ford Hosp., Detroit, 1953-76; chmn. emeritus Henry Ford Hosp., 1976—; team physician Detroit Tigers Baseball Club, 1967—; clin. prof. dermatology U. Mich. Sch. Medicine; mem. com. on cutaneous diseases AFEB, 1956-72; chief cons. dermatology VA, 1953-59; sec.-gen. XII Internat. Congress Dermatology, 1962; mem. Am. Bd. Med. Spltys., 1963-92, mem. exec. com., 1974-76, spl. award, 1993; mem. residency rev. com. for dermatology AMA, 1957-67; mem. adv. com. Nat. Disease and Therapeutic Index, 1974—; bd. dirs., treas. Coun. Med. Splty. Socs., 1976-80, mem. liaison com. on grad. med. edn., 1978-83; mem. Accreditation Coun. for Grad. Med. Edn., 1977-83. Author: (with D.M. Pillsbury, M.B. Sulzberger) Manual of Dermatology; contbr. articles to med. jours. Trustee Dermatology Found., 1965-71, ECFMG, 1975-79. Served to lt. col. M.C. AUS, 1942-46. decorated Bronze Star, Legion of Merit; recipient Profl. Achievement award Wayne County Med. Soc., 1993, Dermatology Fedn. Practitioner of Yr. award, 1993. Fellow Am. Acad. Dermatology (dir., past pres., Gold medal 1975, Masters in Dermatology 1985, Presdl. Citation 1987, C.S. Livingood Ann. Lectureship established 1993), ACP; mem. AMA (ho. of dels., chmn. sect. dermatology 1958, Disting. Svc. award 1990), Soc. Investigative Dermatology (past pres., Stephen Rothman award 1980), Am. Dermatol. Assn. (past pres., dir. 1964-68, named hon. mem. 1981), Am. Bd. Dermatology (diplomate, exec. dir. 1968-92, exec. cons. 1993—), Coll. Physicians Phila., Pacific Dermatol. Soc. (hon. mem.), Phila. Dermatol Soc., Detroit Dermatol. Soc. (past pres.), Mich. Med. Soc. (jud. council, ho. dels. 1974-80), Med. Cons. Soc. World War II, Assn. Mil. Dermatologists, Detroit Acad. Medicine, Assn. Maj. League Team Physicians, Assn. Dermatology Argentina (corr.), N.Y. Acad. Scis. (internat. congress dermatology), Danish Soc. (hon.), Indian Assn. Dermatologists (hon.), Brit. Dermatol. Soc. (hon.), Yugoslavian Dermatol. Soc. (hon.), Israel Dermatol. Soc. (hon.), N.Y. Dermatol. Soc. (hon. 1992), 18th World Congress Dermatology (hon. pres. 1992). Clubs: Grosse Pointe, Witenagemote. Home: 345 University Pl Grosse Pointe MI 48230-1635 Office: Henry Ford Hosp 2799 W Grand Blvd Detroit MI 48202-2608

LIVINGSTON, DAVID MORSE, biomedical scientist, physician, internist; b. Cambridge, Mass., Mar. 29, 1941; s. Arthur Joshua and Phyllis Freda (Kanters) L.; m. Jacqueline Gutman, June 23, 1963 (div. 1983); m. Emily Rabb, Jan. 25, 1986; children: Catherine Ellen, Julie. AB cum laude, Harvard U., 1961; MD magna cum laude, Tufts U., 1965. Diplomate Nat. Bd. Med. Examiners, Am. Bd. Internal Medicine. Intern, resident Peter Bent Brigham Hosp., Boston, 1965-67; rsch. assoc., sr. staff fellow, sr. investigator NCI-NIH, Bethesda, Md., 1967-69, 71-73; rsch. fellow in biol. chemistry Harvard Med. Sch., Boston, 1969-71, asst. prof. medicine, 1973-76, assoc. prof. medicine, 1976-82, prof. medicine, 1982-92; Emil Frei III prof. medicine Harvard Med. Sch., 1992—; v.p. Dana-Farber Cancer Inst., Boston, 1989-91; dir., physician-in-chief Harvard Med. Sch., Boston, 1991-95, Emil Frei III prof. medicine, 1992—, chmn. res. exec. com., 1995—. Mem. editorial bd. Virology jour., 1989—; editor BBA Revs. on Cancer, 1988—; contbr. articles to profl. jours. Mem. sci. adv. com. Damon Runyan-Walter Winchell Cancer Fund, N.Y.C., 1988-92, chmn. sci. adv. com., 1989-92; bd. dirs. Cancer Rsch. Fund, 1992—, mem. exec. com., 1994—; vice chmn. sci. adv. com. Pexcoller Found., Trento, Italy, 1994—; mem. sci. adv. bd. Inst. Cancer Rsch., Fox Chase, Pa., 1991—, Lineburger Comprehensive Cancer Ctr., U. N.C., Chapel Hill, 1993-95, MIT Cancer Ctr., 1994—, Fred Hutchinson Cancer Ctr., 1992—. Comdr. USPHS, 1967-73. Recipient Claire & Richard Morse award for Rsch., Dana-Farber Cancer Inst., 1991. Mem. NAS, Am. Soc. for Clin. Investigation, Assn. Am. Physicians, Am. Soc. Biol. Chemistry and Molecular Biology, Am. Soc. Microbiology, Am. Soc. Virology, Inst. Medicine of NAS, Met. Club Washington, St. Botolph Club, Univ. Club (N.Y.C., Boston), Alpha Omega Alpha. Achievements include discovery of important aspects of the neoplastic transforming process and of the mechanisms governing control of the mammalian cell cycle. Office: Dana-Farber Cancer Inst 44 Binney St Boston MA 02115-6013

LIVINGSTON, DONALD RAY, lawyer; b. Oak Ridge, Tenn., Jan. 11, 1952; s. Tally R. and Pansy L. (Heiskell) L.; m. Anne Davis, May 2, 1992; 1 child, John Tally. AB in Econs., U. Ga., 1974, JD, 1977. Bar: Ga. 1977, U.S. Dist. Ct. (no. dist.) Ga. 1977, U.S. Dist. Ct. (mid. dist.) Ga. 1978, U.S. Dist. Ct. (no. dist.) Calif. 1984, U.S. Dist. Ct. (no. dist.) N.Y. 1994, U.S. Ct. Appeals (5th cir.) 1978, U.S. Ct. Appeals (4th and 11th cirs.) 1981, U.S. Ct. Appeals (6th cir.) 1984, U.S. Supreme Ct. 1983. Assoc. Adair, Goldthwaite, Stanford & Daniel, Atlanta, 1977-79; ptnr. Adair, Goldthwaite & Daniel, Atlanta, 1979-87; exec. asst. to gen. counsel EEOC, Washington, 1987-90, acting gen. counsel, 1990-91, gen. counsel, 1991-93; ptnr. Akin, Gump, Strauss, Hauer & Feld, Washington, 1993—; lectr. seminars on employment law, 1987—. Contbr. articles to profl. jours. Mem. ABA, Ga. Bar Assn. (chair labor law sect. 1985-86), D.C. Bar Assn. Office: Akin Gump Strauss Hauer & Feld 1333 New Hampshire Ave NW Washington DC 20036-1511

LIVINGSTON, DOUGLAS MARK, lawyer; b. Lawton, Okla., Nov. 2, 1945; s. Oscar Calloway and Irene (Norton) L.; m. Vicki Sue Ratts, Dec. 21, 1969; children: Lisa Marie, Stephen Mark, Anna Lee, Micah James. BS, Okla. Christian Coll., 1967; MPH, U. Okla., 1969, JD, 1980; MEd, Wayne State U., 1981. Bar: Okla. 1980, U.S. Dist. Ct. (we. dist.) Okla. 1987, U.S. Army Ct. Mil. Rev. 1989, U.S. Ct. Appeals for Armed Forces 1995, U.S. Ct. Appeals (fed. cir.) 1995. Intern Cleveland County Dist. Atty., Norman, Okla., 1979-80; gen. counsel Delphi Devel., Ltd., Norman, 1980-81, Pepco Devel., Inc., Norman, 1981-85, Pepco, Inc., Norman, 1981-85; owner, ptnr. Payne, Livingstin & Harold, P.C., Oklahoma City, 1985-86, Livingston Law Office, Norman, 1986-92, 93-94; staff atty. U.S. Dept. of Army, Ft. Sill, Okla., 1992-93, labor atty., 1994—; ptnr. Concord Investments, Ltd., Norman, 1982-88; staff judge adv. 4003d U.S. Army Garrison, Ft. Chaffee, Ark., 1993-95, 122nd USAR Command, North Little Rock, Ark., 1995; comdr. 1st Legal Support Orgn., San Antonio, 1995—. Editor coll. newspaper Talon, 1966; note editor Am. Indian Law Rev., 1979-80. Bd. dirs. Big Bros./Big Sisters, Norman, 1983-85, Rock Creek Youth Camp, Norman, 1985-94; Rep. precinct chmn., Oklahoma City, 1971. Capt. U.S. Army, 1973-77; col. USAR. Named one of Outstanding Young Men of Am., 1973. Mem. Okla. Bar Assn., Fed. Bar Assn., Cleveland County Bar Assn., Res. Officers Assn., Assn. U.S. Army. Mem. Ch. of Christ. Avocations: family activities, reading, running. Home: 911 S Lahoma Ave Norman OK 73069-4509 Office: Office of Staff Judge Adv Building 462 Fort Sill OK 73503

LIVINGSTON, GROVER D., newspaper publishing executive. V.p. information management The Dallas Morning News, Tex. Office: The Dallas Morning News Communication Ctr Young & Houston Sts Dallas TX 75202

LIVINGSTON, JAMES DUANE, physicist, educator; b. Bklyn., June 23, 1930; s. James Duane and Florence (Boullee) L.; m. Nancy Lee Clark, June 27, 1953 (div. 1976); children: Joan, Susan, Barbara; m. Sharon Hood Penney, Mar. 30, 1985. B in Engring. Physics, Cornell U., 1952; PhD in Applied Physics, Harvard U., 1956. Physicist R & D GE, Schenectady, N.Y., 1956-89; sr. lectr. dept. material sci. and engring. MIT, Cambridge, 1989—. Author: Driving Force: The Natural Magic of Magnets, 1996; author, co-author over 100 publications in field. Coolidge Fellow Gen. Electric Corp. R & D, 1987; recipient Disting. Career award Hudson-Mohawk chpt. AIME, 1986. Fellow Am. Soc. Metals, Am. Phys. Co.; mem. Nat. Acad. Engring., IEEE, AAAS, Materials Rsch. Soc., The Minerals, Metals and Materials Soc. Democrat. Unitarian. Achievements include 7 patents; advanced research in superconducting, ferromagnetic, and mechanical properties of materials. Home: 90 Albee Dr Braintree MA 02184-8252 Office: MIT 13 4066 Cambridge MA 02139

LIVINGSTON, JAMES EVERTTE, marine corps officer; b. Towns, Ga., Jan. 12, 1940; s. Myret Barrett and Ruth Leona (Browning) L.; m. Sara Craft, June 10, 1966; children: Kimberly Anne, Melissa Paige. BSCE, Auburn U., 1962; MA in Mgmt., Webster U., 1984. Commd. 2d lt. USMC, 1962, advanced through grades to maj. gen., 1991; platoon comdr. Co. A, Schs. Demonstration Troops, Quantico, Va., Co. H, 2d Tng. Bn., Officer Candidates Sch., Quantico, 1963, various units, 1963-65; stationed at MCAS, Cherry Point, N.C., 1965, MCRD, Parris Island, S.C., 1966; comdg. officer USMC detachment USS Wasp, 1966-67; comdg. officer Co. E, 2d Bn., 4th Marines, Republic of Vietnam, 1967-68; dir. div. schs. 1st Marine Div., Camp Pendleton, N.C., 1972-73; ops. officer 3d Bn., 7th Marines, 1973-75, 4th Marines, Okinawa, Japan, 1975; comdg. officer Marine Barracks, U.K., 1977-80; comdg. officer 3d Recruit Tng. Bn., then asst. chief of staff for ops. and tng. USMC Recruit Depot, Parris Island; asst. chief of staff for manpower, then for ops. and tng. 2d Marine Div.; comdg. officer 6th Marine Regiment, 2d Marine Div., Camp Lejeune, N.C., 1986-87; sr. Marine/joint plans and programs officer (chief) Joint U.S. Assistance Group, The Philippines, 1987-88; dep. dir. for ops. Nat. Mil. Command Ctr., Joint Staff, Washington, 1988-90; acting comdg. gen. USMC Air-Ground Combat Ctr., Twentynine Palms, Calif., 1990-91; comdg. gen. 1st Marine Expeditionary Brigade, Kaneohe Bay, Hawaii, 1991, 4th Marine Div. (Reinforced), New Orleans, 1991-95, Marine Res. Forces, USMCR, New Orleans, 1992—. Decorated Medal of Honor, Disting. Svc. medal, Silver Star, Bronze Star with combat V, Purple Heart with two stars, Def. Superior Svc. medal, Def. Meritorious Svc. medal, Meritorious Svc. medal with gold star, Combat Action Ribbon; Cross of Gallantry (Republic of Vietnam); named Man of Yr. Sigma Pi, 1990. Mem. Marine Corps Assn., 3d Marine Div. Assn., 2d Bn. 4th Marine Regiment Assn., Medal of Honor Soc. Republican. Baptist. Office: Ste 2050 909 Poydras Ste 2050 New Orleans LA 70112

LIVINGSTON, JAY HAROLD, composer, lyricist; b. McDonald, Pa., Mar. 28, 1915; s. Maurice and Rose (Wachtel) L.; m. Lynne Gordon, Mar. 19, 1947; m. Shirley Mitchell, May 16, 1992; children from previous marriage: Travilyn, Tammy. B.A., U. Pa., 1937. With Paramount Pictures, 1945-55. Writer songs for over 100 motion pictures; songs, spl. material for Broadway shows Sons O' Fun, Hellzapoppin, also for Bob Hope, 1947-89, 90; scores for Broadway prodns. Oh Captain, 1958, Let It Ride, 1961; 2 songs in Sugar Babies, 1979; TV theme songs including Bonanza, Mister Ed, To Rome With Love; songs To Each His Own, Silver Bells, Tammy, Golden Earrings, Dear Heart, Never Let Me Go. Recipient 3 Acad. Award Oscars for songs Buttons and Bows, Mona Lisa, Que Sera Sera, Star on Hollywood Blvd. Walk of Fame, 1995; named to Songwriters Hall of Fame, 1973. Mem. Acad. TV Arts and Scis., ASCAP, Acad. Motion Picture Arts and Scis. (exec. bd.), Nat. Acad. Rec. Arts and Scis. (gov.), Songwriters Guild (exec. com.), AFTRA, Dramatist's Guild. Office: care ASCAP 1 Lincoln Plz New York NY 10023-7129

LIVINGSTON, JOHNSTON R., manufacturing executive; b. Foochow, China, Dec. 18, 1923; s. Henry Walter V and Alice (Moorehead) L.; m. Caroline Johnson, Aug. 17, 1946 (dec.); children: Henry, Ann, Jane, David; m. Patricia Karolchuck, Sept. 4, 1965. BS in Engring. with honors, Yale U., 1947; MBA with distinction, Harvard U., 1949. With Mpls.-Honeywell Regulator Co., 1949-55; with Whirlpool Corp., 1956-66, v.p., until 1966; v.p. Redman Industries, Dallas, 1966-67; dir. Constrn. Tech., Inc., Dallas, 1967—; pres., chmn. bd. dirs. Constrn. Tech., Inc., Denver, 1974-89; chmn. bd. dirs. Enmark Corp., Denver, 1979—; pres. Marcor Housing Sys., Inc., Denver, 1971-74. Past mem. industry adv. com. Nat. Housing Ctr.; bd. dirs., past pres. Nat. Home Improvement Coun.; pres., chmn. bd. dirs. Denver Symphony Assn., 1977-81; bd. dirs., past chmn. bd. dirs. Rocky Mountain Regional Inst. Internat. Edn.; trustee, v.p. Bonfils-Stanton Found., Denver, 1980—; hon. trustee Inst. Internat. Edn., N.Y. Baker scholar Harvard U., 1949. Mem. Rocky Mountain World Trade Assn. (bd. dirs., past chmn. bd. dirs.), Denver Country Club, Sigma Xi, Tau Beta Pi. Home: 1649 Keystone Ranch Rd Dillon CO 80435-8384 Office: 5070 Oakland St Denver CO 80239-2724

LIVINGSTON, LOUIS BAYER, lawyer; b. N.Y.C., Dec. 12, 1941; s. Norman and Helen (Bayer) L.; m. Mari Livingston, Apr. 6, 1968; children: Diana, Alex, Ann. BA, Yale U., 1963; LLB, Harvard U., 1966. Bar: N.Y. 1967, Oreg. 1971. Atty. NLRB, Memphis, 1967-68, Poletti, Freidin et al., N.Y.C., 1968-71; ptnr. Miller, Nash, Wiener, Hager & Carlsen, Portland, Oreg., 1971—. Office: Miller Nash Wiener Hager & Carlsen 111 SW 5th Ave Portland OR 97204-3604

LIVINGSTON, MYRA COHN, poet, writer, educator; b. Omaha, Aug. 17, 1926; d. Mayer L. and Gertrude (Marks) Cohn; m. Richard Roland Livingston, Apr. 14, 1952 (dec. 1990); children: Joshua, Jonas Cohn, Jennie Marks. BA, Sarah Lawrence Coll., 1948. Profl. horn player, 1941-48; book reviewer Los Angeles Daily News, 1948-49, Los Angeles Mirror, 1949-50; asst. editor Campus Mag., 1949-50; various public relations positions and pvt. sec. to Hollywood (Calif.) personalities, 1950-52; tchr. creative writing Dallas (Tex.) public library and schs., 1958-63; poet-in-residence Beverly Hills (Calif.) Unified Sch. Dist., 1966-84; sr. instr. UCLA Extension, 1973—; cons. to various sch. dists., 1966-84, cons. poetry to publishers children's lit., 1975—. Author: Whispers and Other Poems, 1958, Wide Awake and Other Poems, 1959, I'm Hiding, 1961, See What I Found, 1962, I Talk to Elephants, 1962, I'm Not Me, 1963, Happy Birthday, 1964, The Moon and a Star and Other Poems, 1965, I'm Waiting, 1966, Old Mrs. Twindlytart and Other Rhymes, 1967, A Crazy Flight and Other Poems, 1968, The Malibu and Other Poems, 1972, When You Are Alone/It Keeps You Capone: An Approach to Creative Writing with Children, 1973, Come Away, 1974, The Way Things Are and Other Poems, 1974, 4-Way Stop and Other Poems, 1976, A Lollygag of Limericks, 1978, O Sliver of Liver and Other Poems, 1979, No Way of Knowing: Dallas Poems, 1980, A Circle of Seasons, 1982, How Pleasant to Know Mr. Lear!, 1982, Sky Songs, 1984, A Song I Sang to You, 1984, Monkey Puzzle, 1984, The Child as Poet: Myth or Reality?, 1984, Celebrations, 1985, Worlds I Know and Other Poems, 1985, Sea Songs, 1986, Earth Songs, 1986, 1987, Higgledy-Piggledy, 1986, Space Songs, 1988, There Was a Place and Other Poems, 1988, Up in the Air, 1989, Birthday Poems, 1989, Remembering and Other Poems, 1989, My Head Is Red and Other Riddle Rhymes, 1990, Climb Into the Bell Tower: Essays on Poetry, 1990, Poem-making: Ways to Begin Writing Poetry, 1991, Light and Shadow, 1992, I Never Told and Other Poems, 1992, Let Freedom Ring: A Ballad of Martin Luther King, Jr., 1992, Abraham Lincoln, A Man for All the People, 1993, Platero Y Yo/Platero and I (trans. 1994, Flights of Fancy and other poems, 1994, Keep on Singing: A Ballad of Marian Anderson, 1994; The Writing of Poetry, film strips; co-editor: The Scott-Foresman Anthology, 1984; editor 36 anthologies of poetry; contbr. articles on children's lit. to ednl. publs., essays on lit. and reading in edn. to various books; mem. editorial adv. bd. The New Advocate, The Reading Teacher. Officer Beverly Hills PTA Council, 1966-75; pres. Friends of Beverly Hills Public Library, 1979-81; bd. dirs. Poetry Therapy Inst., 1975—, Reading is Fundamental of So. Calif., 1981—. Recipient honor award N.Y. Herald

Tribune Spring Book Festival, 1958, excellence in poetry award Nat. Coun. Tchrs. of English, 1980, Commonwealth Club award, 1984, Nat. Jewish Book award, 1987, Kerlan award U. Minn., 1994, Transl. award Internat. Bd. on Books for Young People, 1994. Mem. Authors Guild, Internat. Reading Assn., Soc. Children's Book Writers (honor award 1975), Tex. Inst. Letters (awards 1961, 80), So. Calif. Council on Lit. for Children and Young People (Comprehensive Contribution award 1968, Notable Book award 1972, Poetry Quartet award 89), PEN, Nat. Acad. Recording Arts & Scis. (Best Historical Album, 1995 The Heifetz Collection). Address: 9308 Readcrest Dr Beverly Hills CA 90210-2533

LIVINGSTON, ROBERT GERALD, university official, political scientist; b. N.Y.C., Nov. 17, 1927; s. Robert Teviot and Geraldine (Gray) L.; m. Jeanne Andrée Nettel, May 12, 1955; children: Catherine Schuyler Livingston Fernandez, Robert Eric. AB, Harvard U., 1953, AM, 1953, PhD, 1959. Fgn. svc. officer U.S. Dept. State, Washington, 1956-74; v.p. German Marshall Fund U.S., Washington, 1974-77, pres., 1977-81; writer Washington, 1981-83; acting dir. Am. Inst. for Contemporary German Studies, Johns Hopkins U., Washington, 1983-87, dir. Am. Inst. for Contemporary German Studies, 1987-94, sr. devel. officer Am. Inst. for Contemporary German Studies, 1994-95, chief devel. officer, 1995—; commentator BBC German Svc., London, 1986—, Deutschlandfunk, Cologne, 1991—. Co-author, editor: The Federal Republic in the 1980s, 1983, West German Political Parties, 1986; contbr. over 200 articles to polit. jours. and newspapers. Sgt. U.S. Army, 1946-49. Mem. German Studies Assn. U.S., Harvard Grad. Sch. Alumni Assn. Coun., Coun. on Fgn. Rels., N.Y. Soc. Cons. of Cincinnati, Cosmos Club, Chevy Chase Club, Barnstable Yacht Club (Mass.), Phi Beta Kappa. Democrat. Episcopalian. Avocations: hiking, swimming, tennis. Office: Am Inst Contemporary German Studies 1400 16th St NW Ste 420 Washington DC 20036-2217

LIVINGSTON, ROBERT LINLITHGOW, JR. (BOB LIVINGSTON, JR.), congressman; b. Colorado Springs, Colo., Apr. 30, 1943; s. Robert L. and Dorothy (Godwin) L.; m. Bonnie Robichaux, Sept. 13, 1965; children: Robert Linlithgow, III, Richard Godwin, David Barkley; SuShan Alida. BA in Econs., Tulane U., 1967, JD, 1968; postgrad., Loyola Inst. Politics, 1973. Bar: La. 1968. Ptnr. Livingston & Powers, New Orleans, 1976-77; asst. U.S. atty., dep. chief criminals divsn. U.S. Attys. Office, 1970-73; chief spl. prosecutor, chief armed robbery divsn. Orleans Parish Dist. Atty.'s Office, 1974-75; chief prosecutor organized crime unit La. Atty. Gen.'s Office, 1975-76; mem. 95th-104th Congresses from 1st La. Dist., 1977—; chair appropriations com., 1996—; Mem. nat. adv. bd. Young Ams. for Freedom. Mem. nat. adv. bd. Young Ams. for Freedom; bd. suprs. Smithsonian Inst.; bd. dirs. Internat. Rep. Inst. Ctr. for Democracy. Named Outstanding Asst. U.S. Atty., 1973. Mem. ABA, Fed. Bar Assn., La. Bar Assn., New Orleans Bar Assn., Navy League, Am. Legion. Roman Catholic. Home: 111 Veterans Memorial Blvd Metairie LA 70005-3028 Office: US Ho of Reps 2406 Rayburn HOB Washington DC 20515*

LIVINGSTON, STANLEY C., architect. BArch, U. So. Calif., 1961; student, U. Calif., San Diego. Lic. architect Calif., N.Mex., Nev., Ariz., Colo.; cert. Nat. Coun. Archtl. Registration. Prin. Salerno/Livingston Architects, San Diego; lectr. numerous instns. Archtl. projects include Residence Hall Tower & Multi Purpose Bldg. San Diego State U., Pacific Southwest Airlines Adminstrv. Offices & Hangar Facility, Fujitsu Microelectronics, Inc., Belden Village Low Income Sr. Housing Project, Atkinson Marine Corp. Hdqs. & Ship Repair Facility, Campbell Industries, Islandia Hotel Tower, Marlin Club, Sportfishing Facility and 500 Boat Marina, Branch Libr., Belmont Park Master Plan, Expert Witness Projects; other comml. projects include U.S. Fin. Office Bldg., Lake Murray Office Bldg., San Diego Fed. Branch Bank (5 locations), Nat. U. Office Bldg., Harbor Boat & Yacht Shipyard Renovation, Pacific Southwest Airlines Passenger Lounges & Gates (2 locations), and others. Symposia chmn. "Frank Lloyd Wright-Living in the Wright Century...An Evaluation" San Diego Archtl. Found./San Diego Mus. Art, 1990; mem. design competition adv. panel Balboa Park Organ Pavilion Parking Garage, 1990; mem. urban design com. San Diego Centre City, 1982-86; founder Orchids and Onions Program, 1976, com. chmn. 1984, jury chmn. 1985; chmn. design adv. com. San Diego Center City Devel. Corp., 1980. Fellow AIA (San Diego chpt., past pres. 1978-79, chmn. urban design com. 1978-86, chmn. task force Balboa Pk. master plan); mem. Am. Planning Assn. (mem. bd. dirs. San Diego 1981-82), Soc. Mktg. Profl. Svcs., Am. Arbitration Assn. (mem. panel arbitrators 1988—), Urban Land Inst. (assoc.), Urban Design & Planning Com., Bldg. Industry Assn. (mem. construction quality com.), Community Assn. Inst., San Diego Archtl. Found. (bd. dirs.), SCARAB. Office: Salerno/Livingston Architects 363 5th Ave 3rd Fl San Diego CA 92101-6909

LIVINGSTON, WILLIAM SAMUEL, university administrator, political scientist; b. Ironton, Ohio, July 1, 1920; s. Samuel G. and Bata (Elkins) L.; m. Lana Sanor, July 10, 1943; children: Stephen Sanor, David Duncan. B.A., Ohio State U., 1943, M.A., 1943; Ph.D., Yale U., 1950. Asst. prof. U. Tex., Austin, 1949-54; asso. prof. U. Tex., 1954-61, prof. govt., 1961—, chmn. dept. govt., 1965-69, Jo Anne Christian centennial prof. Brit. studies, 1982-95, asst. dean Grad. Sch., 1954-58, chmn. Grad. Assembly, 1965-68, chmn. faculty senate, 1973-79, chmn. comparative studies program, 1978-79; vice chancellor acad. programs U. Tex. System, 1969-71; v.p., dean grad. studies U Tex. Austin, 1979-95; acting pres. U. Tex. Austin, 1992-93; sr. v.p., 1995—; vis. prof. Yale U., 1955-56, Duke U., 1960-61; sec.-treas. Assn. Grad. Schs., 1982-85; bd. dirs. Council Grad. Schs. in U.S., 1983-86. Author: Federalism and Constitutional Change, 1956; contbg. author: World Pressures on American Foreign Policy, 1962, Teaching Political Science, 1965, Federalism: Infinite Variety in Theory and Practice, 1968, Britain at the Polls 1979, 1981; editor: The Presidency and Congress: A Shifting Balance of Power, 1979; co-editor: Australia, New Zealand and the Pacific Islands Since the First World War, 1979; editor, contbr. author: Federalism in the Commonwealth, 1963, A Prospect of Liberal Democracy, 179, The Legacy of the Constitution: An Assessment for the Third Century, 1987; book rev. editor: Jour. Politics, 1965-68, editor-in-chief, 1968-72; mem. editl. bd. Publius: Jour. of Federalism, 1971-95; mem. bd. editors: P.S, 1976-78, chmn., 1978-82. Served to 1st lt. FA AUS, 1943-45. Decorated Bronze Star, Purple Heart.; Recipient Teaching Excellence award, 1959; Ford Found. fellow, 1952-53; Guggenheim fellow, 1959-60; USIS lectr. in U.K. and India, 1977. Mem. Am. Polit. Sci. Assn. (exec. coun. and adminstrv. com. 1972-74, chmn. nominating com. 1973-74, 78-79), So. Polit. Sci. Assn. (exec. coun. 1964-67, pres. 1974-75), Southwestern Polit. Sci. Assn. (pres. 1973-74), Hansard Soc. (London), Philos. Soc. Tex., Austin Soc. for Pub. Adminstrn. (pres. 1973-74), Southwestern Social Sci. Assn. (pres. 1977-78), Phi Beta Kappa, Omicron Delta Kappa, Phi Gamma Delta, Pi Sigma Alpha (nat. coun. 1976-84, nat. pres. 1980-82). Home: 3203 Greenlee Dr Austin TX 78703-1621 Office: U Tex Office Sr VP Austin TX 78712

LIVINGSTONE, DANIEL ARCHIBALD, zoology educator; b. Detroit, Aug. 3, 1927; s. Harrison Lincoln and Elizabeth Agnes (Matheson) L.; m. Bertha Griffin Ross, June 17, 1952 (div.); children: Laura Ross, Mary Lisa, John Malcolm, Christina Ann, Elizabeth; m. Patricia Greene Palmer, June 3, 1989. BS, Dalhousie U., Halifax, N.S., Can., 1948, MSc, 1950; PhD, Yale U., 1953. Postdoctoral fellow Cambridge U., Eng., 1953-54, Dalhousie U., Halifax, 1954-55; asst. prof. zoology U. Md., College Park, 1955-56; asst. prof. zoology Duke U., Durham, N.C., 1956-59, assoc. prof., 1959-66, prof., 1966—, James B. Duke prof. zoology, 1980—; prof. geology Duke U., Durham, 1990—; limnogist U.S. Geol. Survey, Washington, summers 1956-58; mem. adv. panel Environ. Biology br. NSF, 1964-67, Tundra Biome Project, 1974-76, mem. human origins panel, 1978, mem. river-ocean interaction panel, 1978; mem. U.S. Nat. Com. for Internat. Hydrological Decade, 1964; mem. adv. council for systematic and environ. biology Fgn. Currency program, Smithsonian Instn., 1977-80; mem. external rev. com. U. Minn. Dept. Ecology and Behavioral Biology, 1979; collaborator Nat. Park Service U.S. Dept. Interior, 1974; cons. on geochemistry to A.D. Little Inc., 1972-73, on study on mineral cycling in Volta Lake, Ghana, Smithsonian Instn., 1973, to South-East Consortium for Internat. Devel., Kakamega, Kenya, 1985; convenor various workshop sessions. Mem. editorial bd. Limnology and Oceanography, 1969-72, Ecology, 1970-72, Ann. Rev. Ecology and Systematics, 1975-80, African Archaeol. Rev., 1985—; assoc. editor Paleobiology, 1974-79; mem. editorial adv. bd. Tropical Freshwater Biology, 1987—; contbr. articles to profl. jours. NRC fellow, 1953, 54-55; John Simon Guggenheim Meml. Found. fellow, 1960-61. Fellow AAAS; mem. Nova Scotian Inst. Sci., Internat. Union for Quaternary Rsch. (U.S. nat. com. 1970-78, sub.-commn. for African stratigraphy 1973-82), Am. Quaternary Assn. (coun. 1982, counselor 1971-73, 81—), Am. Soc. Ichthyologists and Herpetologists, Ecol. Soc. Am. (coun. 1961-66, ecology study com. 1964, chmn. weather working group 1965-66), Am. Soc. Limnology and Oceanography (G.E. Hutchinson medal 1989), N.C. Acad. Scis., Freshwater Biol. Assn., U.K. Hydrobiol. Soc. East Africa, Can. Quaternary Assn., Am. Assn. Stratigraphic Palynologists, Internat. Assn. for Fundamental and Applied Limnology, Assn. Pour l'Etude Taxonomique de la Flore d'Afrique Tropicale, Sigma Xi. Avocation: woodworking. Home: 2671 Davis St Raleigh NC 27608-2029 Office: Duke U Dept Zoology Durham NC 27706

LIVINGSTONE, FRANK BROWN, anthropologist, educator; b. Winchester, Mass., Dec. 8, 1928; s. Guy Philip and Margery Stuart (Brown) L.; m. Carol Southworth Ludington, Aug. 13, 1960; 1 dau., Amy Fenner. A.B., Harvard U., 1950; Ph.D., U. Mich., 1957. Research assoc. Liberian Inst. Tropical Medicine, 1955-56, 57-58; asst. prof. anthropology U. Mich., Ann Arbor, 1959-63; assoc. prof. U. Mich., 1963-68, prof., 1968—, chmn. dept. anthropology, 1983-86; cons. in field. Author: Abnormal Hemoglobins in Human Populations, 1967; Frequencies of Hemoglobin Variants, 1985; contbr. articles to profl. jours. Constable, Ann Arbor Twp., 1963-65. Served with U.S. Army, 1951-53. NSF fellow, 1957-59; Recipient Martin Luther King award So. Christian Leadership Conf., 1972. Mem. Am. Anthrop. Assn., Human Biology Council, Am. Assn. Phys. Anthropologists. Home: 471 Rock Creek Dr Ann Arbor MI 48104-1863 Office: Univ Mich Dept Anthropology Ann Arbor MI 48109

LIVINGSTONE, JOHN LESLIE, accountant, management consultant, business economist, educator; b. Johannesburg, Republic of South Africa, Aug. 29, 1932; m. Trudy Dorothy Zweig, Aug. 7, 1977; children: Roger Miles, Adrienne Jill, Graham Ross, Robert Edward. B in Commerce, U. Witwatersrand, South Africa, 1956; MBA, Stanford U., 1963, PhD, 1966. C.P.A., N.Y., Tex. Budget dir. Edgars Stores Ltd., South Africa, 1958-61; asso. prof. Ohio State U., Columbus, 1966-69; Arthur Young Disting. prof. Ohio State U., 1970-73; Fuller E. Callaway prof. Ga. Inst. Tech., Atlanta, 1973-78; mem. exec. bd. Ga. Inst. Tech., 1976-78; ptnr. Coopers & Lybrand, N.Y.C., 1978-81; prin., v.p. Mgmt. Analysis Center, Inc., Cambridge, Mass., 1975-90; prof., chmn. div. acctg. and law Babson Coll., 1985-90,, 1990—; cons. FPC, SEC, HEW, also maj. corps. Author 10 books including Accounting for Changing Prices: Replacement Cost and General Price Level Adjustments, 1976, Management Planning and Control, 1987, The Portable MBA: Finance and Accounting, 1992; assoc. editor: Decision Scis., 1973-78; mem. editl. bd. The Acctg. Rev., 1969-72, 76-78, Acctg., Orgns. and Socs., 1975-78, Jour. Acctg. and Pub. Policy, 1983-95; contbr. numerous articles to profl. jours. Mem. AICPA, Fla. Inst. CPAs, N.Y. Soc. CPAs, Am. Acctg. Assn., Acad. of Experts, Nat. Assn. for Forensic Econs., Nat. Assn. Bus. Economists, Tex. Soc. CPAs, Am.Arbitration Assn., Palm Beach Nat. Golf and Country Club, Breakers Club (Palm Beach), Govs. Club (Palm Beach). Office: 2300 Palm Beach Lakes Blvd West Palm Beach FL 33409-3303

LIVINGSTONE, SUSAN MORRISEY, nonprofit administrator; b. Carthage, Mo., Jan. 13, 1946; d. Richard John II and Catherine Newell (Carmean) Morrisey; m. Neil C. Livingstone III, Aug. 30, 1968. AB, Coll. William and Mary, 1968; MA, U. Mont., 1973; postgrad., Tufts U., 1973, Fletcher Sch. Law and Diplomacy, 1973—. Researcher Senator Mark O. Hatfield, Washington, 1969-70; chief legis. and press asst. Congressman Richard H. Ichord, Washington, 1973-75, adminstrv. asst., 1975-81; cons. Congressman Wendell Bailey, Washington, 1981; exec. asst. VA, Washington, 1981-85, assoc. dep. adminstr. logistics and mgmt., 1985-86, sr. procurement exec., 1985-89, assoc. dep. adminstr. logistics, 1986-89; asst. sec. Army Dept. of Def., Washington, 1989-93; v.p. health and safety svcs. ARC, Washington, 1993—; mem interagy. com. on women's bus. enterprise The White House, 1985-89; mem. Pres.'s Coun. on Mgmt. Improvement, 1985-86. NDEA fellow. Mem. Exec. Women in Govt., Procurement Round Table (bd. dirs. 1994—), Assn. U.S. Army (bd. dirs. 1994-96, coun. trustees 1996—), Women in Internat. Security (adv. bd. 1994—). Republican. Episcopalian. Office: ARC 8111 Gatehouse Rd Falls Church VA 22042

LIVINGSTONE, TRUDY DOROTHY ZWEIG, dancer, educator; b. N.Y.C., June 9, 1946; d. Joseph and Anna (Feinberg) Zweig; m. John Leslie Livingstone, Aug. 7, 1977; 1 child, Robert Edward. Student, Charles Lowe Studios, N.Y.C., 1950-52, Nina Tinova Studio, N.Y.C., 1953-56, Ballet Russe de Monte Carlo, N.Y.C., 1956-57, Bklyn. Coll., 1964-66; BA in Psychology cum laude, Boston U., 1968, MEd, 1969; postgrad., Serena Studios, Carnegie Hall Ballet Arts, N.Y.C., 1973-74. Tchr. Millis (Mass.) Pub. Schs., 1969-72, Hebrew Acad. Atlanta, 1974-76; profl. dancer various orgns. including Rivermont Country Club, Jewish Community Ctr., Callanwolde Performing Arts Ctr., Atlanta, 1974-84; founder, owner, instr. dance Sasha Studios, Atlanta, 1974-77; owner Trudy Zweig Livingstone Studios, Wellesley, Needham, Mass., 1987-88, Palm Beach, Fla., 1989—; judge dance competition Atlanta Council Run-Offs, 1976. Vol. League Sch., Bklyn., 1965, Kennedy Meml. Hosp., Brighton, Mass., 1969, Nat. Affiliation for Literacy Advances, Santa Monica, Calif., 1982. Mem. Am. Alliance for Health, Phys. Edn., Recreation and Dance, Poets of the Palm Beaches, L.A. Athletic Club, Wellesley Coll. Club, Governor's Club (West Palm Beach). Jewish. Avocation: writing poetry.

LIVNAT, JOSHUA, accounting educator, consultant; b. Jerusalem, June 8, 1949; came to U.S., 1973; s. Hayim Livnat; m. Shoshana Livnat; children: Orit, Ofer, Shira. BSc in Math. & Stats., Hebrew U., 1973; MPhil, NYU, 1978, PhD in Acctg. and Quantitative Analysis, 1978. CPA, Tenn. Lectr. acctg. NYU, N.Y.C., 1978; asst. prof. Hebrew U., Jerusalem, 1979-81, 83, 84, assoc. prof., 1985; assoc. prof. acctg. NYU, 1988-90, prof., chmn. dept. acctg., taxation and bus. law, 1990—; vis. lectr. U. Tex., Austin, 1979, 89, NYU, 1980, U. Wash., Seattle, 1981, U. Calif., Berkeley, 1982, Vanderbilt U., Nashville, 1983, J.L. Kellogg grad. sch. mgmt. Northwestern U., 1984-85, Chulalongkorn U., Thailand, 1987-88, U. Auckland, New Zealand, 1990-91; vis. assoc. prof. Vanderbilt U., 1986-87; acting dir. Ross Inst. Acctg. Rsch. NYU, 1994—; com. chair Acceptance of Books of Accounts; lectr., expert witness in field. Author: Financial Accounting, 1986, Managerial Accounting, 1992; co-author: Cash Flow and Security Analysis, 1992; mem. editorial bd. Acctg. Rev., 1984-87; contbr. questions to Uniform CPA Exams., Israel; contbr. articles to profl. jours. Mem. acctg. adv. bd. Nassau C.C., Garden City, N.Y., 1992—. Lt. Israeli Army, 1968-70. Recipient Best Article award Roeh Hahesbon, 1978, Best Presentation of Rsch. Paper award Berlin conf. Inst. Quantitative Investment Rsch., 1991; Price Waterhouse fellow NYU, 1975-77, Lady Davis Post Doctoral fellow Hebrew U., 1978. Mem. Am. Acctg. Assn. (doctoral consortium fellow ann. conv. 1977). Jewish. Avocations: swimming, traveling. Office: NYU Stern Sch Bus Dept Acctg 40 W 4th St New York NY 10012-1118*

LIVSEY, ROBERT CALLISTER, lawyer; b. Salt Lake City, Aug. 7, 1936; s. Robert Frances and Rosezella Ann (Callister) L.; m. Renate Karla Guertler, Sept. 10, 1962; children: Scott, Rachel, Daniel, Benjamin. BS, U. Utah, 1962, JD, 1965; LLM, NYU, 1967. Bar: Utah 1965, Calif. 1967. Prof. Haile Selassie U., Addis Ababa, Ethiopia, 1965-66; spl. asst. to chief counsel IRS, Washington, 1977-79; assoc., then ptnr. Brobeck, Phleger & Harrison, San Francisco, 1967—; adj. prof. U. San Francisco Law Sch., 1970-77; mem. adv. com. IRS Dist. Dirs., 1986-89; mem. western region liason com IRS (chmn. 1989). Research editor U. Utah Law Rev., 1964-65; editor Tax Law Rev., 1966-67; contbr. articles to profl. jours. Bd. dirs. Gilead Group, 1986-88, East Bay Habitat for Humanity, 1987-88, Morning Song, 1992-94. Mem. ABA (chmn. subcom. real estate syndications 1981-84), State Bar Calif. (chmn. taxation sect. 1984-85), San Francisco Bar Assn. (chmn. taxation sect. 1982), Am. Coll. Tax Counsel, Am. Law Inst., Tax Litigation Club (pres. 1986-87), Order of Coif, Beta Gamma Sigma. Democrat. Mem. Evangelical Covenant Ch. Club: Commonwealth (San Francisco). Home: 128 La Salle Ave Piedmont CA 94610-1233 Office: Brobeck Phleger & Harrison 1 Market Plz San Francisco CA 94105

LIZARDOS, EVANS JOHN, mechanical engineer; b. N.Y.C., Mar. 25, 1936; s. John George and Pearl (Arapoudis) L.; m. Helen Samaras, May 15, 1960; children: John E., Paul E., Lynn Lizardos Bloecker. B in Mech. Engring., Poly. U., Bklyn., 1960. Lic. profl. engr., N.Y. Draftsman Clinton Bogert Assocs., N.Y.C., 1953-56; designer Guy B. Panero, N.Y.C., 1956-60; assoc. Piccirillo & Brown, N.Y.C., 1960-65; pres., CEO Lizardos Engring. Assocs., Albertson, N.Y., 1965—. Contbr. chpts. to books and articles to profl. jours. treas. L.I. Heart Coun., 1992-94, chmn. bd., 1994-96; contbr. Guide Dog Assn. for Blind. Fellow ASHRAE (bd. govs. 1974-75, rec. sec. 1975-76, v.p. 1977-78, pres. 1978-79, chmn. handbook); mem. Cons. Engrs. Coun. N.Y. State (pres. 1986-87), Assn. Energy Engrs. (charter), Am. Solar Energy Soc., ASME, Am. Soc. Plumbing Engrs. (charter, chpt. sec. 1975-77), Constrn. Specification Inst. (profl.), Internat. Dist. Heating and Cooling Assn., Inst. Noise Control Engring., Instrument Soc. Am. (sr.), Internat. Solar Energy Soc., Nat. Fire Protection Assn., NSPE, Refrigeration Engrs. and Techs. Assn. (mem.-at-large). Greek Orthodox. Avocations: model railroading, running. Office: 200 Old Country Rd Mineola NY 11501-4235

LIZT, SARA ENID VANEFSKY, lawyer, educator; b. USSR, Mar. 10, 1913; came to U.S., 1921; d. Max and Yocheved (Koval) Vanefsky; widowed. LLB, CUNY, Bklyn., 1941, LLM, 1962. Bar: N.Y. 1946, U.S. Dist. Ct. (so. and ea. dists.) N.Y. 1946. Pvt. practice Bklyn., 1946—; prof. CUNY, Bklyn., 1966-80. Address: 2060 E 19th St Brooklyn NY 11229-3943

LLAMANZARES, MAGDA CAROLINA GO VERA, nurse, clinical child psychologist; b. Manila, Oct. 23, 1940; d. Misael Poblete and Rosalina (Go) Vera; m. Teodoro Paraiso Llmanzares, Apr. 20, 1967; children: Michael Denis, Teodoro Misael Danile, Rachel Marie Dorothy. B in Liberal Arts, U. The Philippines, 1960; BSN, St. Paul Coll. Manila, 1967; M in Child Psychiat. Nursing and Cmty. Health, Wayne State U., 1972; PhD in Clin. Psychology, Ateneo U., The Philippines, 1988. Cert. psychiat. nurse, behavioral medicine specialist, counselor. Reporter Manila Chronicle, 1960-61; grade sch. tchr. Ateneo de Manila, 1961-62; vol. nurse Md. Mental Retardation Sch., Balt., 1972; nursing bd. examiner Profl. Regulation Commn., Manila, 1978-81; dir. child day care The Lamp Ctr., San Juan, The Philippines, 1974-94; counselor In Touch Found., Manila, 1982-86; ind. nurse practitioner Makati (The Philippines) Med. Ctr., 1974—, clin. child psychiatrist, 1988—; child cons. Internat. Sch., Manila, 1982-86; dir. psychol. svcs. Sulo ng Zonta, San Juan, 1981-90; dir. Holy Angels Day Care, Quezon City, The Philippines, 1985-90. Author: Practice of Filial Therapy in Philippines, 1988; editor Perspective in Mental Health and Psychiat. Nursing Jour., 1974-86; author, chmn. (booklet): Practice on Philippine Psychiatric Nursing Mental Health, 1984. Founding pres. Quezon City Barangay Lioness Club, 1985-86; chmn. Z-Club of Zonta Club of Mandaluyong, San Juan, 1990-92; sec. Zonta Club of Mandaluyong, San Juan, 1980-90; chmn. Cathetical Instrn. U. of Philippines Cath. Action, 1957-60. Named Most Outstanding UPSCAN, Univ. Philippines Cath. Action, 1960; recipient Mich. State Fund grant Wayne State U., 1970-72, First prize Free Paper category Philippines Pediat. Soc., 1977, 3M Internat. Coun. Nurses Fellowship award, Geneva, 1981-85, Brit. Coun. grant, London, summer, 1982, Cmty. Svc. award Barangay Lions Club, 1986, Philippine Outstanding Women in Nation Svc. in Nursing award Assn. TOWNS, 1986, Svc. award Zonta Club Mandaluyong San Juan, 1991, Mother Madeline Nursing award St. Paul Coll., Manila, Diamond Yr. Alumni Assn., 1992, Most Disting. Alumna Psychology & Child Devel. award La Consolacion Coll., 1995. Mem. Philippine Nurses Assn. (founder, pres./dir 1982-88, #M Philippines Nat. Nursing award 1981, Founding Pres. award 1983), Postillon Specialist Internat., Inc. (founder, pres. 1988—), Psychiat. Nursing Specialists Found. of Philippines (founder, pres. 1980-83, dir. 1974—), Sigma Theta Tau Lambda. Roman Catholic. Avocation: travel. Office: Makati Med Ctr, 2 Amorsolo St, Manila The Philippines

LLANUSA, STEVEN MICHAEL, elementary education educator; b. Burbank, Calif., Feb. 26, 1960; s. Louis Henry and Margaret Mary (Ferruzza) L.; life ptnr. Glenn Miya; 1 child, Anthony Gomez. AA, L.A. Valley Coll., Van Nuys, Calif., 1982; BA, UCLA, 1985. Cert. tchr., Calif. Tchr. nursery sch. Child Devel. Ctr., L.A. Valley Coll. Campus, 1979-82; asst. tchr. UCLA Child Devel. Ctr., 1982-85; tchr. L.A. Unified Sch. Dist., Lincoln Heights, Calif., 1987-89, Colton Unified Sch. Dist., Bloomington, Calif., 1989—; curriculum specialist Gerald Smith Sch., Bloomington, 1993—. Chmn. diversity com. UCLA, 1992-94. Recipient cmty. svc. award ARC, 1981; scholar Tau Alpha Epsilon, 1982. Mem. ASCD, San Bernardino Humane Soc., UCLA Alumni Assn. (bd. dirs.-at-large 1992-94, co-chmn. Lambda alumni 1993-94), U. So. Calif. Lambda Alumni Assn. (edn. com. 1993-94), Sigma Phi Epsilon. Roman Catholic. Avocations: computer philanthropy theatre. Home: 2627 San Andres Way Claremont CA 91711-1556 Office: Gerald Smith Sci Magnet Sch 9551 Linden Ave Bloomington CA 92316-1430

LLAURADO, JOSEP G., nuclear medicine physician, scientist; b. Barcelona, Catalonia, Spain, Feb. 6, 1927; s. José and Rosa (Llaurado) García; m. Deirdre Mooney, Nov. 9, 1966; children—Raymund, Wilfred, Mireya; m. Catherine D. Entwistle, June 28, 1958 (dec.); children—Thadd, Oleg, Montserrat. B.S., B.A., Balmes Inst., Barcelona, 1944; M.D., Barcelona U., 1950; Ph.D. in Pharmacology, 1960; M.Sc. Biomed. Engring., Drexel U., 1963. Diplomate: Am. Bd. Nuclear Medicine. Resident Royal Postgrad. Sch. Medicine, Hammersmith Hosp., London, 1952-54; fellow M.D. Anderson Hosp. and Tumor Inst., Houston, 1957-58, U. Utah Med. Coll., Salt Lake City, 1958-59; asst. prof. U. Otago Dunedin, N.Z., 1954-57; sr. endocrinologist Pfizer Med. Research Lab., Groton, Conn., 1959-60; assoc. prof. U. Pa., 1963-67; prof. Med. Coll. Wis., Milw., 1970-82, Marquette U., 1967-82; clin. dir. nuclear medicine service VA Med. Ctr., Milw., 1977-82; chief nuclear medicine service VA Hosp., Loma Linda, Calif., 1983—; prof. dept. radiation scis. Loma Linda U. Sch. Medicine, 1983—; U.S. rep. symposium on dynamic studies with radioisotypes in clin. medicine and research IAEA, Rotterdam, 1970, Knoxville, 1974. Editor: Internat. Jour. Biomed. Computing; dep. editor Environ. Mgmt. and Health; contbr. numerous articles to profl. jours. Merit badge counselor Boy Scouts Am., 1972—; pres. Hales Corners (Wis.) Hist. Soc., 1981-83. Recipient Commendation cert. Boy Scouts Am., 1980. Fellow Am. Coll. Nutrition; mem. Soc. Nuclear Medicine (computer and acad. councils), IEEE (sr.), IEEE in Medicine and Biology Soc. (nat. adminstrv. Com. 1986-89), Biomed. Engring. Soc. (charter), Am. Physiol. Soc., Am. Soc. Pharmacology and Exptl. Therapeutics, Soc. Math. Biology (founding), Endocrine Soc., Royal Soc. Health, Societat Catalana de Biologia, Casal dels Catalans de Calif. (pres. 1989-91), Calif. Med. Assn. (sci. adv. panel nuclear medicine 1983—). Office: Nuclear Med Svc #115 11201 Benton St Loma Linda CA 92357-0001

LL COOL J (JAMES TODD SMITH), rap singer, actor; b. Queens, N.Y., 1968; s. Jimmy Nunya. Albums: Radio, 1984, Bigger and Deffer, 1987, Walking with A Panther, 1989, Mama Said Knock You Out (Grammy award Best Rap Vocal), 1991; actor: (films) Krush Groove, 1984, The Hard Way, 1991, Toys, 1992; (TV series) In the House, 1995—. Grammy nomination (Best Rap Solo, 1994) for "Stand By Your Man". Office: Bad Boy Entertainment Inc 8-10 W 19th St New York NY 10011

LLEWELLYN, CHARLES ELROY, JR., psychiatrist; b. Richmond, Va., Jan. 16, 1922; s. Charles Elroy and Pearl Ann (Shield) L.; m. Grace Eldridge, Sept. 25, 1948; children: Charles Elroy III, George E. (dec.), Richard S. BS, Hampden-Sydney Coll., 1943; MD, Med. Coll. Va., 1946; MS in Psychiatry, U. Colo., 1953. Diplomate Am. Bd. Psychiatry and Neurology; lic. marriage and family therapist, N.C. Intern psychiatry Tucker Hosp., Inc., Richmond, 1946-47, asst. to staff, 1948-50; intern gen. medicine Bellevue Hosp., N.Y.C., 1947-48; fellow psychiatry Colo. Psychopathic Hosp. and U. Colo. Med. Ctr., Denver, 1950-53; assoc. dept. psychiatry Duke U., Durham, N.C., 1955-56, asst. prof., 1956-63, assoc. prof., 1963-87; asst. dir. adult psychiat. outpatient clinic Duke U. Med. Ctr., Durham, 1955-56, head adult psychiat. outpatient div., 1956-76, acting head divsn. cmty. and social psychiatry, 1976-81, chief tng. divsn. cmty. and social psychiatry, 1976-85, head divsn. cmty. and social psychiatry, 1985-87; pvt. practice Durham, 1987—; psychiat. cons., supr., seminar dir. pastoral counseling tng. programs Duke U. Med. Ctr., 1965-87, dir. student mental health svc. Duke U., 1959-68; psychiat. cons. N.C. Divsn. Social Svcs., 1955-79, N.C. Medicaid Program, 1971-75, N.C. Med. Peer Rev. Found., Inc., 1975-79; sr. psychiat. cons. Family Cons. Svc., Durham, 1966-87; mem.-at-large N.C. Substance Abuse Profl. Ctr. Bd., 1984-89; part-time cons., med. dir. Durham Substance Abuse Treatment Ctr., 1968-88. Contbr. articles to profl. jours, chpts. to books. Mem. adv. bd. Durham County Drug Counseling and Evaluation Svc., 1972-79; bd. dirs. Family Counseling Svc. Durham, 1973-78, pres., 1975; bd. dirs. United Health Svcs., 1975-84; trustee Epworth United Meth. Ch., 1959-62, dir. cmty. ministries com., 1961-62; cubmaster Boy Scouts Am., 1960-66; mem. ch. campus rels. com. The Meth. Ctr., Duke U., 1964-66. Capt. U.S.

Army, 1953-55. Recipient Outstanding Profl. Human Svcs. Am. Acad. Human Svcs., 1974-75; grantee U.S. Inst. Mental Health, 1967-71. Fellow Am. Psychiat. Assn. (life); mem. AMA (life), Am. Group Psychotherapy Assn., Pan Am. Med. Soc. (life), Am. Assn. Marriage and Family Therapy, Carolinas Group Psychotherapy Soc. (treas. 1983-94), N.C. Med. Soc. (life), N.C. Assn. Marriage and Family Therapists, Mental Health Assn. N.C., Durham-Orange County Med. Soc. (life). Avocations: fishing, electronic gadgets, gardening. Office: 3308 Chapel Hill Blvd Ste 110 Durham NC 27707-2643

LLEWELLYN, FREDERICK EATON, real estate executive; b. Mexico, Mo., Mar. 28, 1917; s. Frederick William and Mabel (Eaton) L.; BS, Calif. Inst. Tech., 1938; MBA (Baker scholar), Harvard, 1942; LLD, Pepperdine U., 1976; m. Yvonne Maples, July 18, 1990; children: Richard, John, Ann Marie. Asst. gen. mgr., dir. Forest Lawn Life Ins. Co., Glendale, Calif., 1940-41, pres., 1959-61; asst. to gen. mgr. Forest Lawn Meml. Park, Glendale, 1941-42, exec. v.p., 1946-66, gen. mgr., 1966-89; pres. Forest Lawn Found., 1961—, Forest Lawn Co., 1967-88; chmn. bd. Am. Security & Fidelity Corp., Forest Lawn Co., 1988—, Upstairs Galleries Inc., 1974-91, Met. Computer Center, 1973-81, Calif. Citrus Corp., 1971-80, Forest Lawn Mortgage Corp., 1976-92; dir. IT Corp., Trust Svcs. Am., Inc.(chmn. 1983-91). Mem. Found. for the 21st Century, 1986-91, Orthopaedic Hosp., 1976-82, chmn., 1980; chmn. Glendale Meml. Hosp., 1980, trustee, 1982-85; pres. So. Calif. Visitors Coun., 1976-77; chmn. Coun. of Regents, Meml. Ct. of Honor, 1966-93. Mem. Mayor's Ad Hoc Energy Com., L.A., 1973-74, L.A. County Reorgn. Commn., 1978; bd. dirs. L.A. County Heart Assn., 1957; trustee U. Redlands, 1966-77, chmn. bd., 1969-72; mem. Univ. Bd., Pepperdine Coll. (life), chmn. bd. regents, mem. exec. bd., 1977-86; bd. dirs. Pasadena Found. Med. Rsch., 1967-72, So. Calif. Bldg. Funds, 1975-85, Met. YMCA L.A., 1975—; trustee San Gabriel Valley coun. Boy Scouts Am., 1968-74; trustee Calif. Mus. Sci. and Industry, 1977-89, pres., 1983-85, chmn., 1985-86; bd. govs. Dept. Mus. Natural History, L.A. County, 1968-72; mem. L.A. County Energy Commn., 1974-80; chmn. Mayor's Ad Hoc Water Crisis Commn., 1977. Served with USNR, 1942-45. Decorated knight Order of Merit (Italy). Mem. Nat. Assn. Cemeteries (pres. 1956-57), L.A. Area C. of C. (dir. 1969-78, bd. chmn. 1974, pres. 1973), Calif. C. of C. (dir. 1977-89), Newcomen Soc., Tau Beta Pi. Clubs: California, Lincoln, One Hundred, Twilight. Contbr. articles to profl. jours. Home: 1521 Virginia Rd San Marino CA 91108-1933 Office: 1712 S Glendale Ave Glendale CA 91205-3320

LLEWELLYN, JOHN SCHOFIELD, JR., food company executive; b. Amsterdam, N.Y., Jan. 10, 1935; s. John S. and Dorothea (Breedon) L.; m. Mary Martha Pallotta, June 9, 1962; children: Mary M., John S. III, Robert J., James P., Timothy J. AB, Holy Cross Coll., 1956; MBA, Harvard U., 1961. With mktg. Gen. Foods Corp., White Plains, N.Y., 1961-69, Sunshine Biscuit div. Am. Brands, N.Y.C., 1973-77; exec. v.p. Morton Frozen Foods div. ITT Continental Baking Co., Charlottesville, Va., 1977-79; gen. mgr. Continental Kitchens ITT Continental Baking Co., Rye, 1980-81; sr. v.p. Ocean Spray Cranberries Inc., Plymouth, Mass., 1982-86; exec. v.p., chief operating officer Ocean Spray Cranberries Inc., Plymouth, 1986-87, pres., chief exec. officer, 1988—; bd. dirs. Dean Foods Co. Trustee Derby Acad., Hingham, Mass., 1984—, St. Sebastian's Country Day Sch., Needham, Mass., 1991—; bd. dirs. Mass. Environ. Trust, 1991—. Capt. USMC, 1957-63. Mem. Nat. Food Processors Assn. (bd. dirs., exec. com., vice chmn.), Grocery Mfrs. Am. (bd. dirs., fin. com., govt. affairs coun.). Roman Catholic. Home: Steamboat Ln Hingham MA 02043 Office: Ocean Spray Cranberries Inc 1 Ocean Spray Dr Middleboro MA 02349-1000*

LLEWELLYN, LEONARD FRANK, real estate broker; b. Harlowton, Mont., Oct. 31, 1933; s. Ralph Emory and Frances Louise (Ewing) L.; m. Patricia Lockrom, Aug. 16, 1951 (div. 1955); m. Corrie J. Spruit, Aug. 21, 1974 (div. 1995). BSEE, Eastern Mont. Coll. Edn., 1955. Enlisted USMC, 1957, advanced through grades to capt., 1960, ret., 1967; owner Capitol Fla. Assn., Inc., Alexandra, Va., 1966-74; pres., owner Fla. Properties, Inc., Balt., 1968-74; chmn. Marco Beach Realty, Inc., Marco Island, Fla., 1975-82, 82—, Cons., Inc. of S.W. Fla., Marco Island, 1982—; served as presdl. pilot for presidents Kennedy and Johnson, 1963-66; bd. dirs. Founders Nat. Bank and Trust Co. Author: (manual) Aero-Gunnery Tactics, 1958. Bd. dirs. Collier County Conservancy, 1978-83; trustee Naples (Fla.) Cmty. Hosp., 1980-93, Cmty. Found. Collier County; commr. Collier County Sheriff's Commn., Marco Island C. of C., bd. dirs. Citizens & So. Nat. Bank, 1981-91, past trustee Naples Cmty. Hosp., Inc. Named Top Gun, USN, USMC, 1958, Citizen of Yr. Marco Island N.Y. Times and Marco Island Eagle, 1982. Mem. Marco Island Bd. Realtors (pres. 1982), Marco Island C. of C. (pres. 1981-82, pres. emeritus 1984), Naples Forum (pres. 1985-86), masonic Lodge, nat. Aviation Club, Nat. Assn. Sales Masters, Hideaway Beach Assn. (past pres.), Marco Island Beach Assn. (past. bd. dirs., past v.p.), Rotary Club Internat. Republican. Home: PO Box 825 Marco Island FL 33969-0825 Office: Cons Inc of SW Fla Marco Island FL 33937

LLEWELLYN, RALPH ALVIN, physics educator; b. Detroit, June 27, 1933; s. Ralph A. and Mary (Green) L.; m. Laura Diane Alsop, June 12, 1955; children: Mark Jeffrey, Rita Annette, Lisa Suzanne, Eric Matthew. B.S. in Chem. Engrng. with high honors, Rose-Hulman Inst. Tech., 1955; Ph.D. in Physics, Purdue U., 1962. Mem. faculty Rose-Hulman Inst. Tech., Terre Haute, Ind., 1961-70, assoc. prof. physics, 1964-68, prof., 1968-70, chmn. dept. physics, 1969-70; prof., chmn. dept. Ind. State U., Terre Haute, 1970-72, 74-80; dean Coll. of Arts and Scis. U. Cen. Fla., Orlando, 1980-84, prof., 1984—; exec. sec. Energy Bd., staff officer environmental Studies Bd. NAS/NRC, Washington, 1972-74; vis. prof. Rensselaer Poly. Inst., Troy, N.Y., 1964; cons. Commn. on Coll. Physics, 1987-89, NSF, 1965-66; mem. Ind. Lt. Gov.'s Sci. Adv. Coun., 1974-80; adv. bd. Ind. Gov.'s Energy Extension Svc., Fla. Solar Energy Ctr., policy coun. Fla. Inst. Govt., Fla. Radon Adv. Coun., 1988—; mem. environ. adv. com. Fla. Inst. Phosphate Rsch.; mem. grievance com. Fla. Bar, nat. adv. coun. Nat. Commn. on Higher Edn. Issues, 1982. Assoc. editor: Phys. Rev. Letters; contbr. articles to profl. jours.; producer instructional films and TV. Trustee Merom (Ind.) Inst. NSF Coop. fellow, 1959-60, Am. Coun. Edn. Acad. Adminstrn. Internship Program fellow. Fellow Ind. Acad. Sci. (chmn. physics divsn. 1969-70, Speaker of Yr. award 9175, pres.-elect 1980, Fla. State Univ. System TEaching Incentive award 1994), mem. AAAS, AAUP, Am. Phys. Soc., Am. Assn. Physics Tchrs. (pres. Ind.), N.Y. Acad. Scis., Fla. Acad. Scis. (endowment com.), Internat. Oceanographic Found., Ind. Acad. Sci., Sigma Xi, Tau Beta Pi. Home: 1463 Palomino Way Oviedo FL 32765-9304 Office: U Cen Fla Dept Physics Orlando FL 32816

LLINÁS, RODOLFO RIASCOS, medical educator, researcher; b. Bogota, Colombia, Dec. 16, 1934; came to U.S., 1959, naturalized, 1973; s. Jorge Enrique (Llinas) and Bertha (Riascos) L.; m. Gillian Kimber, Dec. 24, 1965; children: Rafael Hugo, Alexander Jorge. B.S., Gimnasio Moderno, Bogota, 1952; M.D., U. Javeriana, Bogota, 1959; Ph.D., Australian Nat. U., 1965; M.D. (hon.), U. Salamanca, Spain, 1985; PhD (hon.), U. Barcelona, Spain, 193, U. Nacional Bogota, Colombia, 194. Research fellow Mass. Gen. Hosp.-Harvard U., 1960-61; NIH research fellow in physiology U. Minn., Mpls., 1961-63, assoc. prof., 1965-66; assoc. mem. AMA Inst. Biomed. Research, Chgo., 1966-68, mem., 1970, head neurobiology unit, 1967-70; assoc. prof. neurology and psychiatry Northwestern U., 1967-71; guest prof. physiology Wayne State U., 1967-74; professorial lectr. pharmacology U. Ill.-Chgo., 1967-68, clin. prof., 1968-72; prof. physiology, head neurobiology div. U. Iowa, 1970-76; prof., chmn. physiology and biophysics NYU, N.Y.C., 1976—; Thomas and Suzanne Murphy prof. neurosci. NYU, 1985—; mem. neurol. sci. research tng. com. Nat. Inst. Neurol. Diseases and Stroke, NIH, 1971-73; mem. neurology A study sect. div. research grants NIH, 1974-78; assoc. neurosci. research program MIT, 1974-83; mem. U.S. Nat. Com. for IBRO, 1978-81; acting chmn. U.S. Nat. Com. For IBRO, 1982, chmn., 1983-89, exec. com., 1985—; mem. sci. adv. bd. Max-Planck Inst. for Psychiatry, Munich, 1979-83; professorial lectr. Coll. de France, Paris, 1979, Nat. Poly. Inst., Mexico City, 1981; IBRO internat. lectr., S.Am., 1982; McDowall lectr. King's Coll., London, 1984. Author: (with Hubbard and Quastel) Electrophysiological Analysis of Synaptic Transmission, 1969; editor: Neurobiology of Cerebellar Evolution and Development, 1969, (with W. Precht) Frog Neurobiology: A Handbook, 1976; chief editor: Neurosci., 1974—; mem. editorial bd.: Jour. Neurobiology, 1980—; mem.: Pfluegers Archives, 1981—, Jour. Theoretical Neurobiology, 1981—. Recipient John C. Krantz award U. Md., 1976, Einstein Gold medal UNESCO, 1991, Signoret award in cognition, Fondation Ipsen La Salpâtrière, Paris, 1994. Mem. NAS, Soc. For Neurosci. (council 1974-78), Am. Physiol. Soc. (Bowditch Lectr. 1973), Am. Soc. Cell Biology, Biophys. Soc., Harvey Soc., Internat. Brain Research Orgn., N.Y. Acad. Scis., Alpha Omega Alpha (hon.). Office: NYU Med Ctr 550 1st Ave New York NY 10016-6481

LLOYD, ALBERT LAWRENCE, JR., German language educator; b. Evanston, Ill., Aug. 10, 1930; married; 1 child. A.B., George Washington U., 1951, M.A., 1954, Ph.D., 1957. Asso. in German, George Washington U., 1954-57; mem. faculty U. Pa., 1957—, prof. German, 1970—, chmn. dept., 1972-80; nat. adv. bd. Jr. Yr. in Munich and Freiburg Program, 1962-82. Author: The Manuscripts and Fragments of Notker's Psalter, 1958, Der Münchener Psalter des 14. Jahrhunderts: Eine Auswahl zusammen mit den entsprechenden Teilen von Notkers Psalter, 1969, Anatomy of the Verb: The Gothic Verb as a Model for a Unified Theory of Aspect, Actional Types, and Verbal Velocity, 1979; co-author: Deutsch und Deutschland heute, 1967, 2d edit., 1981, Etymologisches Wörterbuch des Althochdeutschen, Vol. I, 1988; also articles. Grantee Am. Philos. Soc., 1966; Nat. Endowment for Humanities grantee, 1978—. Mem. Inst. Deutsche Sprache, Linguistic Soc. Am., Am. Assn. Tchrs. of German, Mediaeval Acad. Am., Soc. for Germanic Philology, Phi Beta Kappa. Office: U Pa 745 Williams Hall Philadelphia PA 19104-6305

LLOYD, ALEX, lawyer; b. Atlantic, Iowa, Aug. 13, 1942; s. Norman and Ruth (R.) L.; m. Jacqueline Roe, Aug. 24, 1963; children: Erin, Andrea, John, Peter. BA in Econs., Colby Coll., 1964; LLB, Law Sch., Yale U., 1967. Bar: Conn., U.S. Dist. Ct. (Conn.), U.S. Ct. Appeals (2d cir.), U.S. Tax Ct., U.S. Supreme Ct. Assoc. Shipman & Goodwin, 1967-72, ptnr., 1972—, chmn. mgmt. com., 1985—; bd. dirs. Hartford Hosp., Conn. Health System, Inc., Conn. Bar Found., The VNA Group, Visiting Nurse and Home Care, Inc. Recipient Charles J. Parker award Conn. Bar Assn., Dist. Svc. award Conn. Legal Svcs. Mem. ABA, Am. Soc. of Hosp. Attys., Conn. Bar Assn. Avocations: golf, boating, fishing, raquet sports, piano. Office: Shipman & Goodwin 1 American Row Hartford CT 06103-2833

LLOYD, CHRISTOPHER, actor; b. Stamford, Conn., Oct. 22, 1938; m. Carol Lloyd. Actor, Neighborhood Playhouse, N.Y.C.; actor: summer stock and off-Broadway, including title role in Kaspar, 1973 (Obie award, Drama Desk award); Broadway appearances include White and Maddox, Macbeth, N.Y. Shakespeare Festival; films include Butch and Sundance, 1969, Three Warriors, The Onion Field, 1979, The Black Marble, 1980, The Legend of the Lone Ranger, 1981, Mr. Mom, 1983, To Be or Not to Be, 1983, Star Trek III, 1984, Adventures of Buckaroo Banzai, 1984, Back to the Future, 1985, Clue, 1985, Who Framed Roger Rabbit, 1988, Walk Like a Man, 1987, Eight Men Out, 1988, Why Me, The Dream Team, 1989, Back to the Future, Part II, 1989, Back to the Future, Part III, 1990, The Addams Family, 1991, Suburban Commando, 1991, Dennis the Menace, 1993, Twenty Bucks, 1993, Addams Family Values, 1993, Angels in the Outfield, 1994, The Pagemaster, 1994, Camp Nowhere, 1994, The Radioland Murders, 1994, Things To Do in Denver When You're Dead, 1995; TV films include Lacy and the Mississippi Queen, 1978, The Word, 1978, Stunt Seven, 1979, Money on the Side, 1982, September Gun, 1983, Avonlea, 1991 (Emmy award, Best Actor in a Drama Series, 1992); appeared as regular in TV series Taxi, 1978-83, Back to the Future, 1991-92. Office: c/o Guild Mgmt Corp Penthouse A Los Angeles CA 90035-2716*

LLOYD, CHRISTOPHER, television writer and producer. Writer TV series The Golden Girls, 1987-88, Down Home, 1990-91, Wings, 1991-92; exec. prodr. TV series Frasier, 1992— (Emmy award for outstanding comedy series 1995). Office: care Broder Kurland Webb Offner Agy 9242 Beverly Blvd Ste 200 Beverly Hills CA 90210

LLOYD, DAVID LIVINGSTONE, JR., lawyer; b. Butler, Pa., Aug. 28, 1952; s. David Livingstone and Jean Marie (Basher) L.; m. Dana L. Kadison, June 26, 1983; children: John Gabriel, Margaret Kadison. BS, AB, U. Pa., 1974, JD, 1977. Bar: N.Y. 1977. Assoc. Dewey Ballantine, N.Y.C., 1977-85, ptnr., 1986-93; sr. counsel Financing and transactions GE Aircraft Engines, Cin., 1993—. Office: GE Aircraft Engines 1 Neumann Way # F17 Cincinnati OH 45215-1915*

LLOYD, DOUGLAS SEWARD, physician, public health administrator; b. Bklyn., Oct. 16, 1939; s. Heber Hughes and Virginia Seward (Chamberlin) L. A.B. in Chemistry, Duke U., 1961, M.D., 1971; postgrad., Old Dominion U., 1965-67; M.P.H. in Health Planning, U. N.C., 1971. Diplomate Am. Bd. Preventive Medicine. Intern in pediatrics Duke U., Durham, N.C., 1971-72; clin. scholar Duke U., 1972, resident in family practice, 1972-73; commr. health Conn. Dept. Health Services, 1973-87; assoc. med. dir. Nat. Med. Rsch. Corp., Hartford, Conn., 1987-89; pres. Doug Lloyd Assocs., Farmington, Conn., 1989-92; assoc. adminstr. Health Resources and Svcs. Adminstrn., Rockville, Md., 1992—; lectr. Yale U., Conn., 1973-87; chmn. bd. Pub. Health Found., 1984-87. Contbr. articles to profl. jours. Served to capt. USNR. Recipient Lange Publ. award, 1971, McCormick award for excellence in pub. health, 1987. Fellow Am. Coll. Preventive Medicine; mem. AMA, Am. Pub. Health Assn., Assn. State and Territorial Health Ofcls. (past pres.). Home: 11410 Stonewood Ln Rockville MD 20852-4543 Office: Health Resources & Svcs Adminstrn 5600 Fishers Ln Rockville MD 20857-0001

LLOYD, EMILY (EMILY LLOYD PACK), actress; b. North London, England, Sept. 29, 1970; d. Roger Lloyd Pack. Grad., Italia Conti Sch. for Performing Arts. Films: Wish You Were Here, 1987, Cookie, 1989, In Country, 1989, Chicago Joe and the Showgirl, 1990, A River Runs Through It, 1992. Office: William Morris Agencyer Ltd 151 El Camino Beverly Hills CA 90212*

LLOYD, EUGENE WALTER, construction company executive; b. Bklyn., Apr. 9, 1943; s. Walter Vincent and Mary Regina (Conway) L.; m. Julia Ann Bain Menzies, May 6, 1967; children: Deborah Ann, Doreen Marie. AA in Constrn., N.Y. Tech. Coll., 1960-63. Estimator Stephen H. Falk & Assocs., Great Neck, N.Y., 1962-65, Builder's Estimating Service, N.Y.C., 1965-67, Humphreys & Harding, Inc., N.Y.C., 1967-68; chief estimator, corp. sec. Conforti & Eisele, Inc., N.Y.C., 1968-76; exec. v.p. Torcon, Inc., Westfield, N.J., 1976-93; v.p., dir. The Henderson Corp., Raritan, N.J., 1994—. Served with U.S. Army, 1963-69. Republican. Roman Catholic. Avocation: working on old cars. Home: 242 W Central Ave Pearl River NY 10965-2119 Office: The Henderson Corp 575 State Hwy 28 Raritan NJ 08869

LLOYD, GREGORY LENARD, professional football player; b. Miami, Fla., May 26, 1965. Student, Ft. Valley State Coll. Linebacker Pitts. Steelers, 1987—. Named to Sporting New NFL All-Pro Team, 1994, selected to Pro Bowl, 1991-94. Office: Pitts Steelers 300 Stadium Cir Pittsburgh PA 15212*

LLOYD, HUGH ADAMS, lawyer; b. Pine Apple, Ala., Oct. 5, 1918; s. James Adams and Kate (Compton) L.; m. Lydia Douglas, Sept. 18, 1942; children: Kathryn Lloyd Allen, Sally Douglas (Mrs. Charles Proctor), Elizabeth Anne (Mrs. Thomas Goodman), Hugh Adams Jr. Student, Oglethorpe U., 1936-37; A.B., U. Ala., 1941, LL.B., 1942. Bar: Ala. 1942, U.S. Supreme Ct 1958. Adjudicator VA, Montgomery, Ala., 1946-47; partner firm Lloyd, Dinning, Boggs & Dinning, Demopolis, Ala., 1947-95, ret., 1995; chmn. bd. dirs., chief exec. officer Robertson Banking Co., Demopolis. Active Boy Scouts Am.; chmn. Demopolis Indsl. Devel. Com., 1970; mem. Regional Com. Juvenile Delinquency, 1970; chmn. Marengo County Devel. Bd., 1972-73; mem. Demopolis City Coun., 1974; chmn. Indsl. Devel. Bd. Marengo County, 1980; pres. Marengo County Port Authority, 1987, Demopolis City Schs. Found., 1995-96; trustee Judson Coll., Marion, Ala., 1981, vice-chmn. bd., 1989, chmn., 1991. With AUS, 1943-45. Decorated Bronze Star; recipient Silver Beaver award Boy Scouts Am., 1972. Mem. Am. Judicature Soc., ABA, Ala. Bar Assn., 17th Jud. Circuit Bar Assn. (pres.), Marengo County Hist. Soc. (v.p. 1980), Demopolis C. of C. (pres.), Ala. Law Inst. (coun.), Bus. Coun. Ala. (bd. dirs.), Ala. Safety Coun., Demopolis Country Club (pres. 1967-68), Kiwanis (dist. gov. 1967, chmn. internat. com. Key clubs 1969, internat. com. on boys and girls work 1972, dist. chmn. laws and regulations com. Ala. dist. 1979). Baptist (past chmn. ch. bd. deacons). Home: 1409 Colony Dr Demopolis AL 36732-3445 Office: PO Drawer Z 501 N Walnut Ave Demopolis AL 36732-2037 also: Robertson Banking Co 216 N Walnut Ave Demopolis AL 36732-2032

LLOYD, JACQUELINE, English language educator; b. N.Y.C., Aug. 21, 1950; d. R.G. and Hortense (Collins) L. BA, Fisk U., 1972; MEd, U. North Fla., 1989. Instr. English Edward Waters Coll., Jacksonville, Fla., 1983, 90—. Mem. Nat. Coun. Tchrs. English. Democrat. Presbyterian. Avocation: movies. Home: 5006 Andrew Robinson Dr Jacksonville FL 32209-1002

LLOYD, JAMES T., air carrier corporation executive, corporate lawyer; b. 1941. BA, kans. State U., 1963; LLB, So. Meth. U., 1966. Atty. Hydeman, Mason Burzio & Lloyd, 1967-85, Preston, Thorgrimson, Ellis & Holman, 1985-87; sr. v.p., gen. counsel USAIR Inc., 1987—; exec. v.p., gen. counsel USAIR Group Inc., 1990—. Office: USAIR Group Inc 2345 Crystal Dr Arlington VA 22202-4801*

LLOYD, JEAN, early childhood educator, television producer; b. Montgomery, Ala., Mar. 3, 1935; d. James Jack and Dorothy Gladys (Brown) L.; 1 child, Jamie Angelica. BA, Queens Coll., 1957; MA, NYU, 1960, PhD, 1976. Tchr. jr. h.s. N.Y.C. Bd. of Edn., 1961, dir. head start ctr., 1966, 67 summer, tchr. early childhood, 1961-69, tchr. kindergarten, 1984—; instr., asst. prof. U. Coll. Rutgers U., Newark, 1969-83; cons. Bd. Examiners, N.Y.C., 1982, Dept. of Pers., N.Y.C., 1985; rsch. cons. Seymour Laskow CPA, 1983; chmn. bd. dirs. Your Family Inc., N.Y.C., 1989—; prodr. New Ventures cable TV show (Manhattan), 1987—. Author: Sociology and Social Life, 1979; contbr. over 10 articles to profl. jours. Recipient Ed Press award Ednl. Press Assn., 1968; Project Synergy fellow Tchrs. Coll., Columbia, 1991-93. Mem. ASCD, United Fedn. of Tchrs., Delta Kappa Gamma. Democrat. Methodist. Avocations: writing poetry and feature articles, singing in church choir. Home: 180 W End Ave New York NY 10023-4902 Office: PS 207 41 W 117th St New York NY 10026-1901

LLOYD, JOHN KOONS, hospital administrator; b. Phila., Apr. 6, 1946. B. Princeton U., 1968; MHA, Temple U., 1973. Adminstrv. asst. Episcopal Hosp., Phila., 1973-74, v.p., 1974-80, exec. v.p., 1980-82; exec. v.p., exec. dir. Jersey Shore Med. Ctr., Neptune, 1982-83, pres., 1983—. Mem. Am. Coll. Healthcare Execs. Home: 2313 Orchard Crest Blvd Manasquan NJ 08736-4003 Office: Jersey Shore Med Ctr 1945 State Route 33 Neptune NJ 07753-4859*

LLOYD, KATE RAND, magazine editor; b. Mpls., Dec. 25, 1923; d. Rufus Randall and Helen Starkweather (Chase) Rand; m. John Davis Lloyd, Feb. 25, 1950; children—Kate Angeline Lloyd Traverse, Ann Elizabeth Lloyd Ingrasci, John Rand. B.A. cum laude, Bryn Mawr Coll., 1945. Mem. staff, feature writer Vogue Mag., N.Y.C., 1945-54, sr. feature editor, 1963-74, mng. editor, 1974-77; mng. editor Glamour Mag., N.Y.C., 1974-77; editor-in-chief Working Woman Mag. div. HAL Publs., N.Y.C., 1977-83, editor-at-large, 1983-92, also mem. speaker's bur.; adj. lectr. Columbia U. Sch. Journalism, N.Y.C., 1975-80, NYU Sch. Continuing Edn., 1982-83. Editor: Glamour Magazine Party Book, 1965, Vogue Beauty and Health Guide, 1975, 76; editorial supr.: Vogue's Book of Etiquette, rev. edit., 1969. Commr. Nat. Commn. on Working Women, Washington, 1979-90, N.Y. State Job-Tng. Ptnrship Council, 1986—, N.Y.C. Commn. on Status of Women, 1982—; bd. dirs. Planned Parenthood Fedn. Am., 1978-84, bd. advocates, 1984—; mem. adv. bd. Nat. Women's Polit. Caucus (Pres.'s Media award 1991), Cornell U.; bd. dirs. Alan Guttmacher Inst., N.Y.C., 1984-90, Coun. on Econ. Priorities, 1986—, Women's Equity Action League, 1986-90; chair adv. coun. Women in Community Svcs., 1991—; bd. dirs. Child-Care Action Campaign, 1984—, v.p., 1990; trustee OEF Internat.; mem. Conf. Bd. Work and Family Rsch. Coun. Recipient Prix de Paris, Vogue, 1945, Women of Achievement award YWCA, 1978, Econ. award Women's Equity Action League, 1983, Outstanding Woman in Mag. Pub. award March of Dimes, 1983, Dr. Louis M. Spadaro award Fordham U. Sch. Bus., Disting. Woman award Northwood Inst., 1991. Mem. AAUW, Am. Soc. Mag. Editors, Women in Communications (Woman of Yr. award 1989), Advt. Women N.Y. (bd. dirs. 1982-84, Advt. Woman of Yr. award 1987), Fin. Women's Assn., Women's Econ. Round Table, Nat. Coun. Women, Internat. Women's Forum Club (v.p. 1984-85, 87-89), Colony Club.

LLOYD, LEWIS KEITH, JR., surgery and urology educator; b. Shreveport, La., Sept. 18, 1941; s. Lewis Keith Sr. and Cidney (Linxwiler) L.; m. Karen Hansen, June 9, 1970; children—Kristine Elizabeth, Lewis Keith III, Kevin Hansen. Student, Centenary Coll., 1959-62; M.D., Tulane Med. Sch., 1966. Diplomate Am. Bd. Urology. Intern USPHS Hosp., Norfolk, Va., 1966-67; resident in urology Tulane U. Med. Sch., New Orleans, 1970-74; from asst. to assoc. prof. surgery U. Ala., Birmingham, 1974-77, prof., 1981—; dir. Urol. Rehab. Rsch. Ctr., Birmingham, 1978, dir. urol. divsn., 1995; chmn. exec. com. Univ. Hosp., 1988-90. Adminstrv. bd. Highlands Meth. Ch., Birmingham, 1983-90; trustee Ala. chpt. Multiple Sclerosis Soc., Birmingham, 1984-85, 92—; bd. dirs. Am. Spinal Injury Assn., 1986-92. Lt. comdr. USPHS, 1966-70, Vietnam. Mem. AMA (Billings Gold medal 1978), Am. Urol. Assn. (bd. dirs. Southeastern sect. 1991-94), Am. Spinal Injury Assn., Birmingham Urology Club (pres. 1981-82), Greystone Golf Club. Republican. Clubs: Birmingham Urology (pres. 1981-82); Mountain Brook Swim and Tennis, Summit Club. Office: U Ala Med Sch 606 MEB Birmingham AL 35294

LLOYD, MICHAEL JEFFREY, recording producer; b. N.Y.C., Nov. 3, 1948; s. John and Suzanne (Lloyd) Sutton; m. Patricia Ann Varble, Sept. 6, 1980; children: Michael, Christopher, Jeni, Deborah. Student, U. So. Calif. V.p. artists and repertoire MGM Records, Inc., 1969-73; ind. record producer, 1973—; pres. Heaven Prodns., 1975—, Michael Lloyd Prodns., 1979—, Taines-Lloyd Film Prodns., 1984-85; music dir. TV series Happy Days; music dir. Kidsongs, Living Proof, NBC-TV movie, Kidsongs Videos; prodr. Love Lines, NBC-TV movie Swimsuit; guest lectr. UCLA; judge Am. Song Festival. Composer: (music for feature films) Tough Enough, If You Could See What I Hear, Dirty Dancing, All Dogs Go to Heaven; composer music for 8 Movies of the Week, 9 TV spls., 28 TV Series and 32 feature motion pictures. Recipient 50 Gold Album awards, 24 Platinum Album awards, 26 Gold Single awards, 2 Platinum Single awards, 3 Grammy awards, 41 Chart Album awards, 100 Chart Single awards, 10 Broadcast Music Inc. awards, 1 Am. Music award, 1 Dove award, 2 Nat. Assn. of Record Minets. Mem. ASCAP (12 awards), Am. Fedn. Musicians, Screen Actors Guild, Nat. Assn. Rec. Arts and Scis., AFTRA.

LLOYD, MICHAEL STUART, newspaper editor; b. Dickinson, N.D., Aug. 11, 1945; s. James William and Mary Marie (Ripley) L.; m. Judith Ann Baxter, May 24, 1966; children—Matthew James, Kristen Ann. B.Jour., U. Mo., 1967. Reporter Grand Rapids (Mich.) Press, 1967-72, asst. city editor, 1972-74, city editor, 1975-77, editor-in-chief, 1978—. Bd. dirs. Mary Free Bed Hosp., Grand Valley State Coll. Found., Celebration on Grand Com. Mem. Am. Soc. Newspaper Editors. Office: The Grand Rapids Press Booth Newspaper 155 Michigan St NW Grand Rapids MI 49503-2302

LLOYD, PHILIP ARMOUR, lawyer; b. Youngstown, Ohio, Feb. 13, 1947; s. Robert Brill and Blanche (Butler) L.; m. Margaret McDowell, Aug. 9, 1969; children—Kimberly, Beatrice. B.A., Ohio Wesleyan U., 1969; J.D., U. Akron, 1972. Bar: Ohio 1972. Mem. firm Brouse & McDowell, Akron, 1972—, ptnr., 1977—. Trustee U. Akron Sch. Law Alumni Assn., Bd. Mental Retardation, Summit County, Ohio, Akron City Hosp. Found., Summit County Defenders Assn., Fairlawn West United Ch.; past trustee Old Trail Sch., Perkiomen Sch., Akron City Club, United Cerebral Palsy and Services for Handicapped; pres. United Cerebral Palsy and Services for Handicapped, 1982-83. Mem. Akron Bar Assn., Ohio Bar Assn., ABA. Republican. Mem. United Ch. of Christ. Avocations: skiing; flying. Office: Brouse & Mc Dowell 500 1st National Tower Akron OH 44308-1471*

LLOYD, TIMOTHY L., art educator; b Canton, Ohio, May 31, 1937; s. Donald J. and Wilma A. (Little) L.; m. Susan J. Lloyd, Dec. 19, 1959; children: Timothy Jr., Stephen. BFA, Kent State U., 1960, postgrad, 1960; MFA, Rochester Inst. Tech., 1964. Prof. art Carleton Coll., Northfield, Minn., 1964—; instr. Haystack Mountain Sch. Crafts, Deer Isle, Maine, 1964; vis. artist Duncan of Jordanstone Coll. Art, Dundee, Scotland, 1978-

79. One-man shows include Stubhahn Gallery, Salzburg, Austria, 1971, Duncan of Jordanstone Coll., Dundee, Scotland, 1979, Clark Gallery, Lincoln, Mass., 1987, Raymond Ave. Gallery, St. Paul, 1988, 91, others; exhibited in group shows at Canton (Ohio) Art Inst., 1959, Akron (Ohio) Art Inst., 1960, Wichita Art Assn., Kans., 1960, 85, Amerika Hause, Heidelberg, Germany, 1961, Mus. Contemporary Crafts, N.Y.C., 1962, Am. Fedn. Arts. Traveling Exhibit: Young Americans, 1962-63, Everhart Mus., Scranton, Pa., 1967, Brooks Art Gallery, Memphis, Tenn., 1967, Cedar Rapids (Iowa) Art Ctr., 1970, First Nat. Bank, Mpls., 1973, Minn. Mus. Art, St. Paul, 1974, Rochester Art Ctr. Gallery, 1977, U. Wis., River Falls Gallery, 1978, Zaner Gallery, Rochester, N.Y., 1982, Aaron Faber Gallery, 1985, Downey (Calif.) Nus. Art, 1985, Helen Drutt Gallery, Phila., 1985, Smithsonian Inst., Washington, 1986, Esther Saks Gallery, Navy Pier, Chgo., 1986, 87, Javier Puig Decorative Arts, Mpls., 1991, others; represented in permenent collectins including Smithsonian Inst. Nat. Air and Space Mus., Washington, Duncan of Jordanstone Coll. Art, Dundee, CRM Russell Mus., Great Falls, Mont., St. John's Abbey, Collegeville, Minn., Northwestern Nat. Life Inst., Mpls., Maud Hill Family Found., St. Paul, Minn., Carleton Coll., Northfield, Minn.; prin. works include Carleton Centennial Medal, 1966, communion vessels Nidaros Luth. Ch., Ashland Wis., 1966, communion vessels St. Andrew's Luth. Ch., Ames Iowa, 1966, communion vessels, processional cross, 1973, Minn. State Art Ctr. award sculpture, 1969, 73, Pres.'s Medal, St. John's Coll., 1972, gift from city of Northfield to Sidney Rand, Amb. to Norway, 1980, raised sterling vessel, Trustee award, Carleton Coll., 1980, Presdl. medal, 1987, William Carleton medal, 1992. Mem. Soc. N.Am. Goldsmiths, Am. Crafts Coun., Minn. Crafts Coun. (exec. bd. 1986-89, 93-95). Avocations: fly fishing, kayaking, canoeing. Office: Carleton College One N College St Northfield MN 55057-4002

LLOYD, WALT, cinematographer. Cinematographer: (films) Dangerously Close, 1986, Down Twisted, 1987, The Wash, 1988, Sex, Lies, and Videotape, 1989, To Sleep with Anger, 1990, Pump Up the Volume, 1990, Kafka, 1992, Short Cuts, 1992, There Goes the Neighborhood, 1992, Amos & Andrew, 1993, (TV movies) Out On the Edge, 1989, Extreme Close-up, 1990. Office: Innovative Artists Ste 2850 1999 Avenue Of The Stars Los Angeles CA 90067-6082

LLOYD, WILLIAM F., lawyer; b. Youngstown, Ohio, Dec. 27, 1947. AB magna cum laude, Brown U., 1969; JD cum laude, U. Chgo., 1975. Bar: Ill. 1975, U.S. Supreme Ct. 1980. Ptnr. Sidley & Austin, Chgo. Mem. ABA (mem. litigation and bus. sects.), Chgo. Bar Assn., Legal Club Chgo. Office: Sidley & Austin 1 First Nat Plz Chicago IL 60603

LLOYD-JONES, DONALD J., transportation executive; b. N.Y.C., May 25, 1931; s. Silas and Esther (McDonald) L.-J.; m. Beverly Louise Miller, June 12, 1954; children: Anne, Lisa, Susan, Donald. BA, Swarthmore Coll., 1952; MBA, Columbia U., 1954, PhD, 1961. Sr. analyst Am. Airlines, N.Y.C., 1957-63, asst. v.p., 1963-66, v.p., 1966-69, chief fin. officer, 1969-72, chief oper. officer, 1972-82; pres. Air Fla., Miami, 1982-84; cons. Western Airlines, L.A., 1984-85, pres., 1985-87; pres. Am. Express Bank-Aviation Svcs., N.Y.C., 1987-95, Am. Geog. Soc., 1996—; dir. SL Industries, Mt. Laurel, N.J., 1972-93. Bd. dirs. Aeronautics and Space Engring. Bd., Washington, 1985, Swarthmore (Pa.) Coll., 1972-84; councilor Am. Geog. Soc., 1992—. Republican. Episcopalian.

LLOYD WEBBER, SIR ANDREW, composer; b. London, Mar. 22, 1948; s. of late William Southcombe and Jean Hermione (Johnstone) Lloyd W.; m. Sarah Jane Tudor Hugill, July 24, 1971 (div. 1983); children: Imogen, Nicholas; m. Sarah Brightman, Mar. 1984 (div. 1990); m. Madeleine Astrid Gurdon, Feb. 1, 1991; children: Alastair Adam, William Richard. Ed., Westminster Sch., Magdalen Coll., Oxford U., Royal Coll. Music. Composer: (with lyrics by Timothy Rice) Joseph and The Amazing Technicolor Dreamcoat, 1968, rev., 73, 81 (Best Score Tony award nominee 1982), 91, Jesus Christ Superstar, 1970 (Drama Desk award 1971, Best Original Score Tony award nominee 1972), (with lyrics by Alan Ayckbourn) Jeeves, 1975, (with lyrics by Timothy Rice) Evita, 1978 (Best Score Tony award 1980, Drama Desk award 1980), (with lyrics by Don Black) Tell Me On A Sunday, 1980, Cats, 1981 (Best Musical and Best ScoreTony awards 1983, Drama Desk award 1983), (with lyrics by Richard Stilgoe) Starlight Express, 1984, (with lyrics by Don Black) Song and Dance, 1985 (Best Score Tony award nominee 1986), (with lyrics by Richard Stilgoe and Charles Hart) The Phantom of the Opera, 1986 (Ivor Novello award 1987, Drama Desk award 1988, Best Score Tony award nominee 1988), (with lyrics by Don Black and Charles Hart) Aspects of Love, 1989, (with lyrics by Don Black and book by Christopher Hampton) Sunset Boulevard, 1993 (Tony award for best score, best musical, 1995); prodr.: Cats, 1981, Daisy Pulls It Off, 1983, The Hired Man, 1984, Starlight Express, 1984, On Your Toes, 1984, Shirley Valentine, 1986, Lend Me A Tenor, 1986, The Resistible Rise of Arturo Vi, 1987, Aspects of Love, 1989, Joseph and the Amazing Technicolor Dreamcoat, 1991, Sunset Boulevard, 1993; co-producer: Jeeves Takes Charge, 1975, Cats, 1981, Song and Dance, 1982, The Phantom of the Opera, 1986, GIE Puccini, 1986, La Bete, 1991; composer film scores: Gumshoe, 1971, The Odessa File, 1974; composer: Variations (based on A Minor Caprice #24 by Paganini), 1977, symphonic version, 1986, Requiem Mass, 1985. Decorated knight Order Brit. Empire; recipient Grammy awards, 1980, 83, 85, Triple Play award ASCAP, 1988, award City and Music Ctr. of L.A., 1991, Praemium Imperiale award for music, 1995; named a Living Legend Grammy, 1989; named to Queen's Birthday List, 1992. Fellow Royal Coll. Music. Avocations: architecture, art. Office: 22 Tower St, London WC2H 9NS, England

LLUBIÉN, JOSEPH HERMAN, psychotherapist, counselor; b. San Juan, PR, July 14, 1943; s. Herman LLubién-Torres and Guilliermina Diaz Vaquez-LLubién; children: Sanjay Alexander Llubiéen, Jiang Carlos Llubién, Jose Lorenzo, Jill Ann Jo Garcia; 1 adopted child, Darius Johann LLubién. BA in Psychology and English, Fordham U., 1973; MA in Lit. and Creative Writing, CUNY, 1981; PhD, Sch. for Social Rsch., 1984; PhD in Clin. Psychology and Human Svcs., Walden U. Inst. for Advanced Studies, Mpls., 1995. Adj. prof., 1969-70; nat. adminstr., dir. counseling Employment Tng. Adminstrn. U.S. Labor Dept., Washington, 1970-82, nat. dir. counseling and tng. Community Employment Tng. Adminstrn./Employment Tng. Adminstrn., 1971-82; adj. prof. English and poetry Coll. Human Svcs., Washington, 1979-80; adjunct prof. English and Composition Malcolm King Coll., N.Y.C., 1984; substance abuse treatment counselor, psychotherapist Alcohol Drug Addiction Svcs. Adminstrn. D.C. Gen. Hosp., Washington, 1989-90; psychotherapist, crisis counselor, bilingual guidance counselor, clin. mental health specialist JMC Assocs., Inc., Washington, 1990-91; bilingual guidance counselor D.C. Pub. Schs. Bancroft Elem. Sch., Washington, 1991-93; clin. mental health specialist, bilingual Dept. Human Svcs., Commn. on Mental Health, Washington, 1993; psychol. treatment counselor II Nat. Capital Systems, Inc. Methadone Therapy Treatment Ctr., Washington, 1993-95; behav. therapist, activity coord. P.S.I. Assocs., Inc., 1995—; clin. counselor Vesta Found., Inc., 1995—; curriculum co-writer (with others) Substance Abuse Prevention Curriculum for pre-kindergarten and primary grades; helped develop a bilingual activity workbook for elem. schs. with U.S. Dept. Justice and Nat. Crime Prevention Coun., 1992; mem. youth coun. U.S. State Dept. Fgn. Desk. Author: (poetry) From the Belly of the Shark, 1978, For Neruda La Luz Que Llega, 1979, Black Yellow Red Indian Songs, 1993, Black Streams, 1993. Vol. counselor Apache reservation in southern Tex., 1986-87, Northern Cheyenne reservation, Lamedeer, Mont.; vol. trainer for guidance counselors Washington elem. schs. in substance abuse prevention. With USAF, 1961-67, Vietnam, USAR, 1982-90. Furman fellow Am. Acad. Child and Adolescent Psychiatry, 1991, Doctoral fellow Walden U. Inst. Advanced Studies. Mem. NAACP, ACA, Assn. of Sch. Counselors, La Raza Unida, U.S. Karate Assn., Am. Karate Assn., U.S. Tai Chi Assn., Japan-USA Akeido Fedn., Internat. Kung Fu Assn., U.S. Akido Assn., Tai Chi Assn., All Japan Am. Akeido Fedn., Tai Chi Chinese Fedn., Tae Quan Do Am. Karate Fedn., Kung Fu Am. Fedn., Am. Kung Fu Assn., All Japan Akeido USA Fedn. Home: Woods of Marlton 8907 Heathermore Blvd Apt 201 Upper Marlboro MD 20772

LO, KWOK-YUNG, astronomer; b. Nanking, Jiangsu, China, Oct. 19, 1947; came to U.S., 1965; s. Pao-Chi and Ju-Hwa (Hsu) Lu; m. Helen Bo Kwan Chen Lo, Jan. 1, 1973; children: Jan Hsin, Derek. BS in Physics, MIT, 1969, PhD in Physics, 1974. Rsch. fellow Calif. Inst. Tech., Pasadena, 1974-76, sr. rsch. fellow, 1978-80, asst. prof., 1980-86; prof. U. Ill., Urbana, 1986—, assoc. Ctr. for Advanced Study, 1991-92, chmn. astronomy dept., 1995-98; chmn. vis. com. to Haystack Obs., Westford, Mass., 1991-92; mem. adv. panel Academic Sinica Inst. Astronomy and Astrophysics, Taipei, Taiwan, 1993—; mem. AUI vis. com. for Nat. Radio Astrophysics Obs., 1993—. Recipient Alexander von Humboldt award, 1995; grantee NSF, 1977-95; Miller fellow U. Calif., Berkeley, 1976-78, James Clerk Maxwell telescope fellow U. Hawaii, 1991. Mem. Am. Astron. Soc., Internat. Astron. Union. Achievements include identification of accretion of ionized gas in center of Galaxy, size measurement of compact radio source at Galactic Center, first suggestion of circumnuclear H2O masers in active galaxies and of star formation in galaxies. Office: U Ill Astronomy Dept 1002 W Green St Urbana IL 61801-3547

LO, SHUI-YIN, physicist; b. Canton, Peoples Republic of China, Oct. 20, 1941; came to the U.S., 1959; s. Long tin and Ty-Fong (Chow) L.; m. Angela Kwok-Kie Lau, Dec. 18, 1969; children: Alpha Wei-min, Fiona Ai-ming, Hao-min. BS, U. Ill., 1962; PhD, U. Chgo., 1966. Rsch. assoc. Rutherford High Energy Lab., Chilton, United Kingdom, 1966-69, Glasgow (United Kingdom) U., 1969-72; sr. lectr. U. Melbourne, Australia, 1972-89; pres. Inst. for Boson Studies, Pasadena, Calif., 1986—; dir. Sinotronic Co., Hong Kong, 1980—; exec. v.p., dir. rsch. Am. Environ. Tech. Group, Monrovia, Calif., 1993—; vis. assoc. Calif. Inst. Tech.; prof. physics Zhong Shan U. Author: Scientific Studies of Chinese Character, 1986; author, editor: Geometrical Picture of Hadron Scattering, 1986; contbr. over 100 articles to profl. jours. Prin. Chinese Sch. of Chinese Fellowship Victoria, Australia, 1977-84. Fellow Australian Inst. Physics; mem. Am. Phys. Soc. Achievements include patents for Chinese computer and BASER.

LOACH, PAUL ALLEN, biochemist, biophysicist, educator; b. Findlay, Ohio, July 18, 1934; s. Leland Oris and Dorothy Elizabeth (Davis) L.; m. Patricia A. Johnson, Dec. 27, 1957; children: Mark, Eric, Jennifer; m. Pamela Sue Parkes, Apr. 19, 1986; children: Matthew, Sarah, Andrew. B.S., U. Akron, 1957; Ph.D. (NIH fellow), Yale, 1961. Research assoc. Nat. Acad. Scis.-NRC; postdoctoral fellow U. Calif. at Berkeley, 1961-63; asst. prof. chemistry Northwestern U., 1963-68, assoc. prof., 1968-73, prof., 1973-74, prof. biochemistry and molecular biology, and chemistry, 1974—; mem. BBCA study sect. NIH, 1978-82. Assoc. editor: Photochemistry and Photobiology, 1973-80, Biophysics of Structure and Mechanism, 1973-82; Contbr. articles, revs. to profl. jours. Recipient C.P. award U. Akron, 1957, Research Career Devel. award USPHS, 1971-76. Mem. Am. Soc. Biol. Chemists, AAAS, Biophys. Soc., Am. Soc. Photobiology (pres. 1985-86).

LOACH, ROBERT EDWARD, federal agency administrator; b. Worcester, Mass., Aug. 18, 1946; s. Charles Henry and Elizabeth Josephine (Feeney) L.; m. Mary Regina Burke, May 10, 1969; children: Christopher, Matthew, Bethany. BS, Worcester State Coll., 1968; MS, SUNY, 1969; MA, Webster U., 1976. Cert. tchr., Mass. Commd. 2d lt. USAF, 1969, advanced through grades to capt., 1979; missile systems analyst USAF, Tucson, Ariz., 1970-72; comdr. deputy missle combat crew USAF, Jacksonville, Ark., 1972-74, comdr. evaluation missile combat crew, 1974-78; air staff tng. officer USAF, Washington, 1978-79; program analyst U.S. Nuclear Regulatory Commn., Bethesda, Md., 1979-80, sr. program analyst, 1980-86, chief programs analysis br., 1986-88, mgr. human resources info. systems, 1988—; dir. divsn. resource mgmt. and adminstrn. U.S. Nuclear Regulatory Commn., King of Prussia, Pa., 1988; cons. Quest Rsch., Falls Church, Va., 1979-80. Coach soccer Springfield (Va.) Youth Club, 1983-93; coach basketball Cath. Youth Orgn., Springfield, 1988-90; active PTO, Springfield, 1985—. Col. USAFR. Recipient commendation medal USAF, meritorious svc. medal (3 oak leaf clusters). Mem. ASTD, Internat. Pers. Mgmt. Assn., Reserve Officers' Assn., Disabled Am. Vets., Federal Exec. Inst. Alumni Assn., Am. Legion, U.S. Youth Soccer Coaches Assn. Republican. Avocations: reading, coaching. Office: US Nuclear Regulatory Commn Washington DC 20555

LOADER, JAY GORDON, retired utility company executive; b. Plainfield, N.J., Aug. 3, 1923; s. Carl and Madalyn (Wright) L.; m. Joan Merrell, Aug. 19, 1965; children: Patricia Kay, Michael Jay, Sandra Lee, Gigi Ann. B.S., U. Ala., 1951. C.P.A., Ga. Auditor Arthur Andersen & Co., Atlanta, 1951-55; with Fla. Power Corp., St. Petersburg, Fla., 1955-82; asst. sec., asst. treas. Fla. Power Corp., 1960-67, sec.-treas., 1967-82, v.p., 1980-89; v.p., sec. Fla. Progress Corp., St. Petersburg, 1983-89; ret., 1989. Served with AUS, 1943-44. Mem. Soc. CPAs, Am. Soc. Corporate Secs., Fin. Analysts Soc. Central Fla., U. Ala. Alumni Assn., Phi Eta Sigma, Beta Gamma Sigma, Beta Alpha Psi. Clubs: Redington Beach Bath; St. Petersburg Yacht; Treasure Island Tennis and Yacht. Home: 13325 108th Ave Largo FL 34644-4649

LOANE, EDWARD S., civil engineering consultant; b. Balt., Mar. 14, 1908. BEng, Johns Hopkins U., 1928. Cons. GPU Svcs. Corp. Fellow ASCE (Rickey medal 1976), IEEE (past sec., sys. engring. com.), Power Engring. Soc. (past chmn., subcom. application probability methods). Office: Baltimore MD*

LOARIE, THOMAS MERRITT, healthcare executive; b. Deerfield, Ill., June 12, 1946; s. Willard John and Lucile Veronica (Finnegan) L.; m. Stephanie Lane Fitts, Aug. 11, 1968 (div. Nov. 1987); children: Thomas M., Kristin Leigh Soule. BSME, U. Notre Dame, 1968; Student, U. Minn., 1969-70, U. Chgo., 1970-71, Columbia U., 1978. Registered profl. engr., Calif. Prodn. engr. Honeywell, Inc., Evanston, Ill., 1968-70; various positions Am. Hosp. Supply Co., Evanston, Ill., 1970-83, pres. Heyer-Schulte divsn., 1979-83; pres. COO Novacor Med. Corp., Oakland, Calif., 1984-85, also bd. dirs.; pres. ABA Bio Mgmt., Danville, Calif., 1985-87; chmn., CEO Keravision, Inc., Fremont, Calif., 1987—; founder, chmn., med. device CEO Roundtable, 1993—; asst. prof. surgery Creighton U. Med. Sch., Omaha, 1986-94; speaker in field. Contbr. articles on med. tech. and pub. policy to Wall St. Jour., others. Bd. dirs. Marymount Sch. Bd., 1981-84; bd. dirs. United Way Santa Barbara, 1981-84, assoc. chairperson, 1982-83, treas., 1983. Named One of 50 Rising Stars: Exec. Leaders for the 80's Industry Week mag., 1983. Mem. Assn. for Rsch. in Vision and Ophthalmology, Contact Lens Assn. Ophthalmology, Med. Mktg. Assn., Health Industry Mfrs. Assn. (spl. rep. bd. dirs. 1993—), Am. Entrepreneurs for Econ. Growth. Roman Catholic. Avocations: competitive running, snow skiing, backpacking, oil painting, the arts. Office: KeraVision Inc 48630 Milmont Dr Fremont CA 94538-7353

LOBANOV-ROSTOVSKY, OLEG, arts association executive; b. San Francisco, July 12, 1934; s. Andrei and Grace S. (Pope) L-R.; m. Susan Waters, Sept. 8, 1979; 1 child, Alexandra; children by previous marriage: Christopher, Nicholas. BA, U. Mich., 1956. Community concert rep. Columbia Artists Mgmt. Inc., 1958-59; mgr. Columbus (Ohio) Symphony Orch., 1959-62, Hartford (Conn.) Symphony Orch., 1962-65, Balt. Symphony, 1965-69; program officer div. humanities and arts Ford Found., 1969-75; exec. dir. Denver Symphony Orch., 1975-76; mng. dir. Nat. Symphony Orch., Washington, 1977-80; cons. Fed. Coun. on Arts, 1980-81; exec. dir. Del. Ctr. for Performing Arts, 1981-82; exec. v.p., mng. dir. Detroit Symphony Orch., 1982-83, pres., 1983-89; ind. cons., 1989-90; mng. ptnr. Middle Am. div. Jerold Panas, Young & Ptnrs. Inc., Chgo., 1990-91; pres. Calif. Ctr. for the Arts, Escondio, Calif., 1991—.

LOBB, WILLIAM ATKINSON, financial services executive; b. Arlington, Pa., Apr. 21, 1951; s. Anthony William and Annamarie (Hilpert) L.; m. Maureen Veronique O'Hagan, July 7, 1977; children: William Atkinson III, Anthony Hagan. BS, Georgetown U., 1977. Account exec. Johnston Lemon, Washington, 1977-78; sr. account exec. Merrill Lynch, Alexandria, Va., 1979-83; asst. v.p. E.F. Hutton, Washington, 1983-85; mng. dir., ptnr.-in-charge Oppenheimer and Co., Inc., Atlanta, 1985—. Bd. trustees The Howard Sch.; bd. dirs. Atlanta Charity Clays. Mem. Ga. Rep. Found., Nat. Assn. Securities Dealers (bd. arbitrators), Nat. Securities Traders Assn., Ga. Securities Assn., Am. Arbitration Assn., Univ. Club, Army-Navy Club, Settindown Creek Club, Burge Plantation Hunt Club. Avocation: squash. Office: Oppenheimer & Co Inc 1200 Monach Plz 3414 Peachtree Rd NE Atlanta GA 30326-1113

LOBBIA, JOHN E., utility company executive; b. 1941; married. BSEE, U. Detroit, 1964. With Detroit Edison Co., 1964—, asst. primary svc. engr. sales dept., 1964-68, acting asst. dist. mgr., dir. svc. planning, 1969-72, project mgr. constrn., 1972-74, dir. generation constrn. dept., 1974-75, mgr. Ann Arbor div., 1975-76, asst. mgr. Detroit div., 1976-78, mgr. Oakland div., 1978-80, asst. vice chmn., 1980-81, asst. v.p., mgr. fuel support, 1981-82, v.p. fin. svcs., 1982-87, exec. v.p., 1987-88, pres., chief operating officer, 1988—, also chmn., chief exec. officer, 1990—, also bd. dirs.; bd. dirs. Nat. Bank of Detroit, NBD Bancorp, Inc. Office: Detroit Edison Co 2000 2nd Ave Detroit MI 48226-1203*

LOBDELL, FRANK, artist; b. Kansas City, Mo., 1921; m. Ann Morency, 1952; children: Frank Saxton, Judson Earle. Studied, St. Paul Sch. Art, 1938-39, Calif. Sch. Fine Arts, 1947-50, Academie de la Grande Chaumiere, Paris, France, 1950-51. Tchr. Calif. Sch. Fine Arts, 1957-65; prof. art, Stanford, 1965—. One man shows, Lucien Labaudt Gallery, 1949, Martha Jackson Gallery, 1958, 60, 63, 72, 74, de Young Meml. Mus., San Francisco, 1959, Ferus Gallery, 1962, Pasadena Art Mus., 1961, San Francisco Mus. Art, 1969, Benador Gallerie, Geneva, Switzerland, 1964, Gallerie Anderson-Mayer, Paris, 1965, Smith-Anderson Gallery, San Francisco, 1982, Oscarsson Hood Gallery, N.Y.C., 1983, 84, 85, John Berggruen Gallery, San Francisco, 1987, Campbell-Thiebaud Gallery, San Francisco, 1988, 90, 92, 95, Stanford Mus. Art, 1988, retrospective show, Pasadena Art Mus. and Stanford Mus., 1966, San Francisco Mus. Modern Art, 1983, Stanford Mus., 1993; exhibited group Shows, Salon du Mai, Paris, 1950, III Sao Paulo Biennial, 1955, Whitney Mus. Am. Art, 1962-63, 72, Guggenheim Mus., N.Y.C., 1964, Van Abbemuseum, Eindhoven, Holland, 1970, Corcoran Gallery Art, Washington, 1971, U. Ill., 1974; represented in permanent collections, San Francisco Mus. Art, Oakland Mus. Art, L.A. County Mus., Nat. Gallery Washington, others. Served with AUS, 1942-46. Recipient Nealie Sullivan award San Francisco Art Inst., 1960, award of merit AAAL, 1988. Home: 2754 Octavia St San Francisco CA 94123-4304

LOBDELL, ROBERT CHARLES, retired newspaper executive; b. Mankato, Minn., Jan. 1, 1926; s. Darwin Norman and Hilda Cecelia (Peterson) L.; m. Nancy Marion Lower, July 12, 1952; children: Teresa M., Robert John, William Scott, James Marston. A.B., Stanford U., 1948, LL.B., 1950. Bar: Calif. 1951, U.S. Supreme Ct 1964. Atty. legal dept. Bank of Am., Los Angeles, 1951-52; atty., corp. officer Youngstown Sheet and Tube Co., 1952-65; asst. gen. counsel, asst. sec. Times Mirror Co., 1965-70, v.p., asst. sec., 1970-86; v.p., gen. counsel Los Angeles Times, 1970-86; bd. dirs. Embarcadero Pub. Co.; former sec., trustee Pfaffinger Found., Los Angeles Times Fund. Trustee, former pres. Long Beach Mus. of Art Found. Mem. Calif. Bar Assn., Beta Theta Pi. Home: 925 Hillside Dr Long Beach CA 90815-4720

LOBECK, CHARLES CHAMPLIN, JR., pediatrics educator; b. New Rochelle, N.Y., May 20, 1926; s. Charles Champlin and Jeanne (Weiss) L.; m. Isabelle Anne Emerson, Feb. 6, 1954; children: Charles III, Anne, Sarah, Jane. AB, Hobart Coll., 1948; MD, U. Rochester, 1952. Diplomate Am. Bd. Pediatrics. Instr. U. Rochester, N.Y., 1955-58; asst. prof. U. Wis., Madison, 1958-62, assoc. prof., 1962-66, chmn. dept. pediatrics, 1964-74, prof., 1966-75; dir. clin. affairs Univ. Hosp., Madison, 1974-75; dean U. Mo. Sch. Medicine, Columbia, 1975-83; assoc. dean U. Wis. Med. Sch., Madison, 1984-91, prof. emeritus, 1991—; mem. study sect. NIH, Bethesda, Md., 1968-72. Author: (with others) Metabolic Basis of Inherited Disease, 2d edit., 1965, 3d edit., 1972. V.P. Cystic Fibrosis Found., Rockville, Md., 1982-83. Sgt. USAAF, 1944-46, ETO. Recipient Rsch. Career Devel. award, NIH, 1962. Fellow Am. Acad. Pediatrics; mem. Soc. for Pediatric Rsch., Am. Pediatric Soc., Am. Coll. Physician Execs., Rotary, Am. Assn. Accreditation Lab Animal Care (chmn. bd. 1984-89, Bennet J. Cohen award 1990). Democrat. Avocations: fly-fishing, biking. Home: 3420 Valley Creek Cir Middleton WI 53562-1990 Office: Programs Health Mgmt 1300 University Ave Madison WI 53706-1510

LOBECK, WILLIAM E., rental company executive; b. 1940. With Little Creek Leasing Corp., Norfolk, Va., 1963-69; pres. Am. Internat. Rent-A-Car, Inc., Dallas, 1969-81; pres., chmn. bd. Thrifty Rent-A-Car System, Inc., Tulsa, 1981-93, Pentastar Transp. Group, Inc., Tulsa, 1981-93; pres., CEO Nat. Car Rental, Mpls., 1993—. Office: 7700 France Ave S Minneapolis MN 55435

LO BELLO, JOSEPH DAVID, banking executive; b. Northampton, Mass., Feb. 5, 1940; s. Joseph Vincenzo and Marie (Mandella) Lo B.; m. Karen Suzanne Martin, June 21, 1969; children: Mark, Kara, Kimberly. BS, Babson Coll., 1961; MBA, U. Mass., 1963; postgrad., Harvard Bus. Sch., 1987. Loan officer Third Nat. Bank Hampden County, Springfield, Mass., 1963-65, v.p., 1965-75, sr. v.p., 1975-81; exec. v.p. Bank of New Eng. West, N.A., Springfield, 1981-90; regional pres. Bank of New Eng. N.A., Springfield, 1990-92; pres., chief exec. officer Peoples Savs. Bank, Holyoke, Mass., 1992—. Dir. Mass. Indsl. Fin. Agy., Boston, 1987; treas., trustee Basketball Hall of Fame, Springfield, 1985; trustee Springfield Coll., 1984, Baystate Med. Ctr., Springfield, 1983. Mem. Rotary Club, Robert Morris Assn. Avocations: golf, hiking, theatre, travel. Home: 152 Meadowbrook Rd Longmeadow MA 01106-1341

LO BELLO, NINO, author, journalist; b. Bklyn., Sept. 8, 1921; s. Joseph and Rosalie (Moscarelli) Lo B.; m. Irene Helen Rooney, Feb. 22, 1948; children: Susan, Thomas. BA, Queens Coll., 1947; MA, NYU, 1948. Reporter and columnist Ridgewood (N.Y.) Times, 1946-50; instr. sociology U. Kans., 1950-55; Rome corr. Bus. Week mag., 1959-62, N.Y. Jour. Commerce, 1962-64; European editor corr. Opera Is My Hobby Syndicated Radio Show, 1960—; bus. news writer N.Y. Herald Tribune, 1964-66; Vienna corr. 103 U.S. and Can. dailies, 1966—; vis. prof. sociology Denison U., Ohio, spring 1956; vis. prof. journalism U. Alaska, summer 1974; writer in Italy, Austria, Switzerland, France, Germany, Eng. Author: The Vatican Empire (N.Y. Times Best Seller List), 1968, The Vatican's Wealth, 1971, Vatican, U.S.A., 1972, European Detours, 1981, The Vatican Papers, 1982, Guide to Offbeat Europe, 1985, English Well Speeched Here, 1986, Guide to the Vatican, 1987, Der Vatikan, 1988, Vatikan im Zwielicht, 1990, The Danube: Here And There, 1992, Travel Trivia Handbook of Oddball European Sights, 1992; contbr. articles to mags. and jours. With USAAF, 1942-46. Recipient Goldener Rathausmann award for Outstanding Fgn. Reporting, Vienna, 1974, Silver decoration (Austria), 1988, Gold plaque Austrian Nat. Tourist Office, 1988; named Alumnus of Yr., Grover Cleveland High Sch., Queens, N.Y., 1977. Mem. Overseas Press Club Am., Am. Soc. Journalists and Authors, Fgn. Press Club Vienna (bd. dirs.). Home: 5706 N 10th Rd Apt 7 Arlington VA 22205-2362 Office: 8 Bankgasse, Vienna 1010, Austria *Work hard, play hard!.*

LOBENHERZ, WILLIAM ERNEST, association executive, legislative counsel, lawyer; b. Muskegon, Mich., June 22, 1949; s. Ernest Pomeroy and Emajean (Krautheim) L.; m. Andrea Risdon L.; children: Jessica Anne, Rebecca Jean, Christopher William, Andrew William. BBA, U. Mich., 1971; JD cum laude, Wayne State U., 1974. Bar: Mich. 1974. Legal counsel Mich. Legis. Services Bur., Lansing, Mich., 1974-77; legal legis. cons. Mich. Assn. of Sch. Bds., Lansing, 1977, asst. exec. dir. for legal legis. affairs, 1977-79; asst. v.p. state and congl. relations Wayne State U., Detroit, 1979-81, assoc. v.p. state relations, 1981-82, v.p. govtl. affairs, 1982-87; assoc. Dykema Gossett, Lansing, Mich., 1987-89; pres., chief exec. officer Mich. Soft Drink Assn., 1989—; guest lectr. in govtl. affairs, Wayne State U., U. Mich., U. Detroit. Contbr. chpt. Mich. Handbook for School Business Officials, 1979, 2d ed. 1980, articles to profl. jours. and mags. Mem. govtl. affairs com. New Detroit Inc., 1984-87, chmn. state subcom. of govtl. affairs com., 1986-87; chmn. ind. schs. campaign Greater Metro Detroit United Fund Torch Dr., 1979, chmn. Colls. and Univs. campaign, 1980; bd. dirs. Mich. Epilepsy Ctr., 1991—; bd. dirs. Coun. for Mich. Pub. Univs. Recipient Book award Lawyer's Coop. Pub. Co., 1973, Outstanding Svc. award Mich. Assn. for Marriage and Family Therapy, 1992, 95; Silver scholar key Wayne State U. Law Sch., 1974. Mem. Mich. Bar Assn., NAACP, Coun. for Advancement and Support of Edn. (Mindpower citation 1982), Mich. Delta Found. (bd. dirs. 1977—, sec. 1981-84, v.p. 1987-88), Greater Metro Detroit C. of C. (contact interviewer bus. attraction and expansion coun. 1984-86), City Club. Home: 5905 Patriots Way East Lansing MI 48823-2336 Office: Mich Soft Drink Assn 634 Michigan Nat Towers Lansing MI 48933 *Notable cases include: Mich. Soft Drink Assn. vs. State of Mich., 1991, the first case to overturn on constl. grounds a state statute which tried to seize the unclaimed deposit monies of soft drink bottles.*

LOBIG, JANIE HOWELL, special education educator; b. Peoria, Ill., June 10, 1945; d. Thomas Edwin and Elizabeth Jane (Higdon) Howell; m. James

Frederick Lobig, Aug. 16, 1970; 1 child, Jill Christina. BS in Elem. Edn., So. Ill. U., 1969; MA in Spl. Edn. Severely Handicapped, San Jose State U., 1989. Cert. elem. tchr., Calif., Mo., Ill., handicapped edn., Calif., Mo.; ordained to ministry Presbyn. Ch. as deacon, 1984. Tchr. trainable mentally retarded children Spl. Luth. Sch., St. Louis, 1967-68; tchr. trainable mentally retarded and severly handicapped children Spl. Sch. Dist. St. Louis, 1969-80, head tchr., 1980-83; tchr. severly handicapped children San Jose (calif.) Unifed Sch. Dist., 1983-86; tchr. autistic students Santa Clara County Office Edn., San Jose, 1986—; tchr. Suzanne Dancers, 1991-92. Vol. Am. Cancer Soc., San Jose, 1986-89, 92, St. Louis Reps., 1976-82, Am. Heart Assn., 1985—, Multiple Sclerosis Soc., 1990—; troop leader Camp Fire Girls, San Jose, 1984-85; moderator bd. deacons Evergreen Presbyn. Ch., 1986-89; mem. exec. bd. Norwood Creek Elem. Sch. PTA, 1983-86. Mem. Council for Exceptional Children, Assn. for Severly Handicapped, Nat. Edn. Assn., Calif. Tchrs. Assn. Independent. Avocations: golf, bowling, bridge, needlework. Home: 3131 Creekmore Way San Jose CA 95148-2805 Office: Weller Elem Sch 345 Boulder Dr Milpitas CA 95035

LOBIONDO, FRANK A., congressman; m. Jan Dwyer; children: Adina, Amy. BA in Bus. Adminstrn., St. Joseph's U., 1968. Ops. mgr. LoBiondo Bros. Motor Express, Inc., Rosenhayn, N.J., 1968-94; mem. Cumberland County Bd. Chosen Freeholders, 1985-88; chmn. Gen. Assembly Econ. and Cmty. Devel., Ar. and Tourism Com., 1992-94; mem. First Legis. Dist. N.J. Gen. Assembly, 1988-94; mem. U.S. House Reps., 1995—. Dir. YMCA, 1978-84, bd. dirs., 1986-94; pres. Cumberland County Guidance Ctr., 1982-84; founder Cumberland County Environ. Health Task Force, 1987; chmn. Cumberland County chpt. Am. Heart Assn., 1989-90; hon. chmn. ann. fund raising drive Cumberland County Hospice, 1992. Office: US House Reps 513 Cannon House Office Bldg Washington DC 20515-3002

LOBITZ, WALTER CHARLES, JR., physician, educator; b. Cin., Dec. 13, 1911; s. Walter Charles and Elsa (Spangenberg) L.; m. Caroline Elizabeth Rockwell, July 11, 1942; children: Walter Charles III, John Rockwell, Susan Hastings. Student, Brown U., 1930-31; B.Sc., U. Cin., 1939, M.B., 1940, M.D., 1941; M.Sc., U. Minn., 1945; M.A. (hon.), Dartmouth, 1958; LL.D., Hokkaido U., 1976. Diplomate Am. Bd. Dermatology (bd. dirs. 1955-64, pres. 1962). Intern Cin. Gen. Hosp., 1940, resident medicine, 1941; fellow Mayo Found., 1942-45; 1st asst. Mayo Clinic, 1945-47; chmn. sect. dermatology Hitchcock Clinic, Hanover, N.H., 1947-59; bd. dirs. Hitchcock Clinic, 1955; faculty Dartmouth Med. Sch., 1947-59, prof. dermatology, 1957-59; prof. dermatology, head div. U. Oreg. Med. Sch., 1959-69, chmn. dept., 1969-77; prof. Oreg. Health Scis. Univ., until 1980; emeritus prof. U. Oreg. Health Scis. Ctr., 1980—; area cons. VA, 1949-59; mem. commn. cutaneous diseases Armed Forces Epidemiologic Bd., 1965-75; cons., mem. gen. med. study sect. USPHS, 1961-65; mem. grant rev. com. United Health Found., 1964-65; cons. dermatology tng. grants com. NIAMD, 1966-70; cons. VA Hosp., U. Oreg. Med. Sch., 1959—; civilian cons. to surgeon gen. USAF, 1969-79; U.S. Air Force-Nat. cons. to Surgeon Gen., 1970-80; Dohi Meml. lectr. Japanese Dermatol. Assn., 1964; lectr. U. Copenhagen, Denmark, 1969, 74. Author numerous articles in field.; Co-editor: The Epidermis; editorial bd.: Jour. Investigative Dermatology, 1958-61, Excerpta of Medicine, 1961-78, Clinics in Dermatology, 1982; mem. editorial bd.: Archives Dermatology, 1960-77, chief editor, 1963-68. Trustee Dermatology Found., Med. Research Found. Oreg., 1972, exec. com., 1977-80, v.p., 1975-76, pres., 1977-78; music adv. com. Oreg. Symphony Orch., 1970-73; mem. Oreg. Ballet Council, 1974; bd. govs. Hitchcock Hosp., 1955; trustee Hitchcock Found., 1958-59, exec. com., 1958-59. Recipient Outstanding Achievement award U. Minn., 1964, Disting. Alumni award U. Cin. Coll. Medicine, 1995; dedication of Lobitz-Jillson Libr., Dartmouth-Hitchcock Med. Ctr., 1992; decorated Japanese Order of the Sacred Treasure, Gold Rays with neck ribbon, Emperor of Japan, 1993. Fellow ACP, Am. Acad. Dermatology (hon., bd. dirs. 1958-61, 66-69, pres. 1969, gold medal 1985, Master in Dermatology 1987), Phila. Coll. Physicians (hon.); mem. AMA, AAAS, Am. Dermatol. Assn. (bd. dirs. 1962-67, pres. 1972, hon. 1982), Soc. Investigative Dermatology (hon., v.p. 1952, bd. dirs. 1953-58, pres. 1957, Stephan Rothman medal for disting. achievement 1989), N.H., Multnomah County, Oreg., med. socs., N.Y. Acad. Scis., Pacific N.W. Dermatol. Assn. (pres. 1971), Pacific Dermatol. Assn., Israel Dermatol. Assn. (hon.), N.W. Soc. Clin. Rsch., Oreg. Dermatol. Soc. (pres. 1969), Portland Acad. Medicine, Am. Fedn. Clin. Rsch., Pacific Interurban Clin. Club (councilor 1971), Internat. Soc. Tropical Dermatology, Assn. Univ. Profs. Dermatology (founder, bd. dirs. 1961-66, pres. 1965-66), Soc. Venezolana de Dermatologia & Leprologia (hon.), French Soc. Dermatology, Brit. Assn. Dermatology, Assn. parala Investigacion Dermatologica (Venezuela), Soc. Dermatol. Danicae, Italian, Japan, Hokkaido, Sapporo derm. socs., Sigma Xi, Pi Kappa Epsilon, alpha Omega Alpha. Presbyn. Home: 2211 SW 1st Ave Portland OR 97201-5060

LOBL, HERBERT MAX, lawyer; b. Vienna, Austria, Jan. 10, 1932; s. Walter Leo and Minnie (Neumann) L.; m. Dorothy Fullerton Hubbard, Sept. 12, 1960; children: Peter Walter, Michelle Alexandra. AB magna cum laude, Harvard U., 1953, LLB cum laude, 1959, Avocat honoraire, 1993. Bar: N.Y. 1960, U.S. Tax Ct. 1963, French Conseil Juridique 1973; French avocat, mem. Paris bar, 1992, avocat hon., 1993. Assoc. Davis, Polk & Wardwell, N.Y.C., 1959-60; assoc. counsel to Gov. Nelson Rockefeller, Albany, N.Y., 1960-62; assoc. Davis, Polk & Wardwell, N.Y. and Paris, 1963-69, ptnr., Paris, 1969-92, sr. counsel, 1993—; lectr. law Columbia U., N.Y.C., 1993-95; supervisory bd. mem. CII-HB Internationale, Amsterdam, Holland, 1977-82. Gov. Am. Hosp. Paris, 1981-83, 88-93; trustee Am. Libr., Paris, 1969-81. Served to 1st lt. USAF, 1954-56, Berlin. Fulbright scholar U. Bonn, Germany, 1954. Mem. Am. C. of C. (bd. dirs. France 1988-90), Univ. Club, Harvard Club (N.Y., Boston). Address: PO Box 2488 Nantucket MA 02584-2488 Home: 3 Weetamo Rd Nantucket MA 02554 also: 22 Waters Edge Rye NY 10580-3254 also: Davis Polk & Wardwell 450 Lexington Ave New York NY 10017

LOBLEY, ALAN HAIGH, lawyer; b. Elkhart, Ind., Aug. 26, 1927; s. Frederick Askew and Eva May (Haigh) L.; m. Kathleen Covert Nolan, Mar. 2, 1957; children: James, Sarah. BSChemE, Purdue U., 1949; JD, Ind. U., 1952. Bar: Ind. 1952, U.S. Dist. Ct. (so. dist.) Ind. 1955, U.S. Ct. Appeals (7th cir.) 1963, U.S. Supreme Ct. 1971, U.S. Ct. Appeals (6th cir.) 1979. Assoc., then ptnr. Ice, Miller, Donadio & Ryan (formerly Ross, McCord, Ice & Miller), Indpls., 1955—. 1st lt. USAF, 1952-54. Mem. ABA, Ind. Bar Assn., Indpls. Bar Assn., Indpls. Rowing Ctr. Democrat. Avocations: photography, music, sculling. Home: 4535 N Park Ave Indianapolis IN 46205-1836 Office: Ice Miller Donadio & Ryan 1 American Sq Indianapolis IN 46282-0001

LOBOSCO, ANNA FRANCES, state development disabilities program planner; b. Binghamton, N.Y., Nov. 13, 1952; d. James H. and Marie A. (Wilcox) Mee; m. Charles M. Lobosco, Apr. 27, 1974; children: Charles Jr., Amanda, Nicholas, Dennis. BA in History, Marist Coll., Poughkeepsie, N.Y., 1974; MS in Edn./Spl. Edn., Coll. St. Rose, Albany, 1978; PhD in Curriculum and Instrn., SUNY, Albany, 1989. Cert. tchr. elem., secondary and spl. edn., N.Y. Diagnostic remedial tchr. Orange County Assn. for Help of Retarded Children, Middletown/Newburgh, N.Y., 1973-78; instr., supr. student tchrs. Mt. St. Mary Coll., Newburgh, 1980-82; rsch. asst., assoc. dir. evaluation consortium SUNY, Albany, 1985-89; devel. disability program planner/prevention specialist N.Y. State Developmental Disabilities Planning Coun., Albany, 1989—; cons. N.Y. State Edn. Dept. Edn., 1987-89, N.Y. State Unified Tchrs., 1988-89, N.Y. State Coun. on Children's Families, 1986-88, N.Y. State Assn. Counties, 1987-88; instr. Coll. St. Rose, Albany, 1989-90. Contbr. articles to profl. jours; exec. producer viedeos Mary's Choice: The Effects of Prenatal Exposure to Alcohol and Other Drugs, 1992, Its Up to You, 1995. Named Advocate of the Yr., N.Y. Libr. Assn., 1993. Mem. Coun. Exceptional Children, Am. Evaluation Assn., Am. Ednl. Rsch. Assn., Am. Assn. Mental Retardation, Kappa Delta Pi. Avocations: needlework, sports, reading. Office: NYS Devel Disabilities Planning Coun 155 Washington Ave 2d fl Albany NY 12210-2329

LOBRON, BARBARA L., speech educator, writer, editor, photographer; b. Phila., Mar. 19, 1944; d. Martin Aaron and Elizabeth (Gots) L.; student Pa. State U., 1962-63; B.A. cum laude, Temple U., Phila., 1966; student photography Harold Feinstein, N.Y.C., 1970, 79-80; student art therapy Erika Steinberger, N.Y.C., 1994—. Reporter, writer Camden (N.J.) Courier-Post, 1966-68; editorial asst. Med. Insight mag., N.Y.C., 1970-71; mng. editor Camera 35 mag., N.Y.C., 1971-75, also assoc. editor photog. anns. for U.S. Camera/Camera 35, 1972, 73; freelance editor as Word Woman, N.Y.C., 1975-77, 79—; acct. exec. Bozell & Jacobs, N.Y.C., 1977-79; copy editor Camera Arts mag., N.Y.C., 1981-83; editorial coord. Center mag., Nat. Ctr. Health Edn., 1985; editorial coord. Popular Photography mag., 1986-95; assoc. editor Sony Style, 1995; tchr. speech improvement N.Y.C. Bd. Edn., 1995—; contbg. editor Photograph; participant 3M Editor's Conf. (1st woman), 1972. Photographs: group exhbns. include Internat. Women's Art Festival, N.Y.C., 1975, Rockefeller Ctr., N.Y.C., 1976, Photograph Gallery, N.Y.C., 1981 ; acrylic painting exhbns. at Tchrs. Coll., N.Y.C., 1994, Warwick Hotel, N.Y.C., 1995; represented in collection Library of Calif. Inst. Arts, Valencia. Tchr. Sch. Vol. Program, N.Y.C., 1994—. Recipient 1st pl. honors Dist. 1, Internat. Assn. Bus. Communicators, 1977. Copy editor: The Complete Guide to Cibachrome Printing, 1980, The Popular Photography Question and Answer Book, 1979, The Photography Catalog, 1976, Strand: Sixty Years of Photography, 1976, You and Your Lens, 1975; contbr. articles to comml. publs., chpts. to books. Dist. leader SGI-USA. Buddhist. Avocations: ceramics, reading, photography, singing, walking. Home: 85 Hicks St Apt 7 Brooklyn NY 11201-6825

LOBSENZ, HERBERT MUNTER, data base company executive; b. N.Y.C., June 10, 1932; s. Jacob Munter and Marjorie (Roset) L.; m. Viola Pedreira, Sept. 29, 1961 (div. 1975); children: Jonathan, Andrew; m. 2d Sheila Katharine Martin, Dec. 18, 1975; children: James, Elizabeth, Emily, Daniel. B.A., NYU, 1953; acad. diploma, Courtauld Inst. Art, U. London, 1959; cert. Spanish studies, U. Madrid, Spain, 1956; postgrad., U. Perugia, Italy, 1958. Sales promotion mgr. Remington Rand, N.Y.C., 1964-66, product planning mgr., 1966-67; long range planning mgr. Xerox Pub., Stamford, Conn., 1967-69; v.p. Houghton Mifflin, Boston, 1976-81; pres. Market Data Retrieval, Shelton, Conn., 1969—; exec. v.p. Dun & Bradstreet Bus. Mktg. Services, 1987; CEO D&B Receivables Mgmt. Svcs., 1991. Author: Vangel Griffin, 1961 (Harper Prize 1961). Chmn. Bd. Edn., Westport, Conn., 1975-85, 89-93; mem. town com. Republican party, Westport, 1970-72. Served with U.S. Army, 1953-55. Mem. Assn. Media Producers (bd. dirs. 1972-78), Direct Mktg. Assn. Jewish. Office: Market Data Retrieval 16 Progress Dr Shelton CT 06484-6216

LOBSINGER, THOMAS, bishop; b. Ayton, Ont., Can., Nov. 17, 1927. Ordained priest Roman Cath. Ch., 1954, bishop, 1987. Bishop Whitehorse, Y.T., Can., 1987—. Home: 5119 5th Ave, Whitehorse, YK Canada Y1A 1L5*

LOCALIO, S. ARTHUR, retired surgeon, educator; b. N.Y.C., Oct. 4, 1911; s. Joseph and Carmella (Franco) L.; m. Ruth Virginia Adkins, July 14, 1945; children: William Hale, Susan Emily, Arthur Russell, David Charles. A.B., Cornell U., 1932; M.D., U. Rochester, 1936; D.Sc., Columbia, 1942. Diplomate Am. Bd. Surgery. Intern pathology N.Y. U. Hosp., 1936-37, intern medicine, 1937-38, asst. resident in surgery, 1938-40, sr. resident, 1940-42, asst. surgeon, 1945-47, asst. attending surgeon, 1947-49, asso. attending surgeon, 1949-52, attending surgeon, 1952—; clin. asst. vis. surgeon 4th surg. div. Bellevue Hosp., N.Y.C., 1945-46; asst. vis. surgeon 4th surg. div. Bellevue Hosp., 1946-48, asso. vis. surgeon, 1948-52, vis. surgeon, 1952—; practice medicine specializing in surgery N.Y.C., 1945—; instr. surgery Columbia Postgrad. Med. Sch., 1945-48; asst. prof. Columbia Postgrad. Med. Sch., 1948-49; asst. prof. surgery N.Y. U. Schs. Medicine, N.Y.C., 1949-50; asso. prof. N.Y. U. Schs. Medicine, 1950-53, prof., 1953—; Johnson and Johnson Disting. prof. surgery N.Y.U. Schs. Medicine, 1972-92, Johnson and Johnson Disting. prof. surgery emeritus, 1992—; cons. in surgery Riverview Hosp., Red Bank, N.J., 1952—, Monmouth Meml. Hosp., Long Branch, N.J., 1952—, St. Barnabas Hosp., N.Y.C., 1958—, VA Hosp., N.Y.C., Wyckoff Heights Hosp., Bklyn., N.Y. Infirmary, N.Y.C., Booth Meml. Hosp., Flushing, N.Y., Brookhaven Meml. Hosp., Patchogue, N.Y. Contbr. articles to med. jours. Trustee Deerfield (Mass.) Acad. Served from capt. to lt. col. M.C. AUS, 1942-45, PTO. Mem. Am. Gastroent. Assn., N.Y. Gastroent. Assn., ACS, AMA, Am. Assn. for Surgery of Trauma, Soc. for Surgery Alimentary Tract, N.Y. Acad. Medicine (trustee 1971-75), N.Y. Acad. Scis., N.Y. Cancer Soc., N.Y. Soc. Colon and Rectal Surgeons, Pan Am. Med. Soc. (N.Am. chmn. sect. gen. surgery 1972—), N.Y. County Med. Soc., N.Y. State Med. Soc., Sociedad Colombiana de Cirujanos, Société Internationale de Chirurgie, Collegium Internationale Chirurgie Digestivae, Royal Soc. Medicine, N.Y. Surg. Soc., B.C. Surg. Soc., Transplantation Soc., Am. Surg. Assn., Sigma Xi. Home: Mill Village Rd # 147 Deerfield MA 01342-9724 Office: NYU Sch Medicine 530 1st Ave New York NY 10016-6402

LOCASCIO, SALVADORE JOSEPH, horticulturist; b. Hammond, La., Oct. 29, 1933; s. John A. and Mary (Dantone) L.; m. Sybil Olivette Johnson, Nov. 21, 1954 (dec. May 1991); children: John David, Judy Lynn, Paul Anthony; m. Carol Smith Riggall, Dec. 29, 1993. BS, Southeastern La. Coll., 1955; MS, La. State U., 1956; PhD, Purdue U., 1959. Grad. asst. La. State U., 1955-56, Purdue U., 1956-59; asst. horticulturist U. Fla., Gainesville, 1959-65; assoc. prof. U. Fla., 1965-69, prof., 1969—. Contbr. articles to profl. publs. Recipient Ann. Rsch. award Fla. Fruit and Vegetable Assn., 1993. Fellow Am. Soc. for Hort. Sci.; mem. Fla. State Hort. Soc. (v.p. vegetable sci. 1975-76, pres. 1994, chmn. bd. dirs. 1995, presdl. gold medal 1978), Fla. Weed Sci. Soc. (outstanding weed sci. of yr. 1989, pres.-elect 1989-90, pres. 1990-91). Democrat. Roman Catholic. Achievements include research in efficient use of fertilizer, polyethylene mulch, and water for the production of vegetable crops. Office: U Fla Dept Hort Scis 406 NW 32nd St Gainesville FL 32607-2532

LOCATELLI, PAUL LEO, university president; b. Santa Cruz, Calif., Sept. 16, 1938; s. Vincent Dino and Marie Josephine (Piccone) L. B.S. in Acctg., Santa Clara U., 1961; MDiv, Jesuit Sch. Theology, 1974; DBA, U. So. Calif., 1971. CPA, Calif. Ordained priest Roman Cath. Ch., 1974. Acct., Lautze & Lautze, San Jose, Calif., 1960-61, 1973-74; prof. acctg. Santa Clara (Calif.) U., 1974-86, assoc. dean Bus. Sch. and acad. v.p., 1978-86, pres., 1988—. bd dirs. Silicon Valley, Tech. Mus.; bd. gov., Inst. of Eur & Asian Studies; mem. Nat. Cath. Bishops and Pres.' Com., Acctg. Edn. Change Commn.; mem. adv. couns. Parents Helping Parents and Community Found.; past rector Jesuit Community at Loyola Marymount U. Trustee Regis U.; past trustee U. San Francisco, Seattle U., St. Louis U. and Loyola Marymount U.; past mem. Sr. Commn. of Western Assn. Schs. and Colls. Mem. AICPA, Calif. Soc. CPAs (Disting. Prof. of the Yr award, 1994), Am. Acctg. Assn., NCCJ (bd. dirs.), Assn. Jesuit Colls. and Univs. (chair), Ind. Colls. Calif., Am. Leadership Forum (bd. dirs.). Democrat. Office: Santa Clara U Office of Pres Santa Clara CA 95053

LOCHBIHLER, FREDERICK VINCENT, lawyer; b. Chgo., Jan. 30, 1951; s. Frederick Louis and Marion Helen (Rutkauskas) L.; m. Darlene Gotfryde Wantuch, Nov. 8, 1952; 1 child, Frederick Karlman. AB in Govt. summa cum laude, U. Notre Dame, 1973; JD with honors, U. Chgo., 1976. Bar: Ill. 1976, U.S. Dist. Ct. (no. dist.) Ill. 1977, U.S. Ct. Appeals (7th cir.) 1980, U.S. Ct. Appeals (8th cir.) 1981, U.S. Supreme Ct. 1982, U.S. Dist. Ct. (ctrl. dist.) Ill. 1983, U.S. Dist. Ct. Ariz. 1991. Assoc. Chapman and Cutler, Chgo., 1976-84, ptnr., 1984—. Mem. Phi Beta Kappa, Order of Coif. Avocations: military history, literature, travel. Home: PO Box 72 Golf IL 60029-0072 Office: Chapman and Cutler 111 W Monroe St Chicago IL 60603-4003

LOCHER, RICHARD EARL, editorial cartoonist; b. Dubuque, Iowa, June 4, 1929; s. Joseph John and Lucille (Jungk) L.; m. Mary Therese Cosgrove, June 15, 1957; children: Stephen Robert, John Joseph, Jana Lynne. Student, Loras Coll., 1948, Chgo. Acad. Fine Arts, 1949-51; BFA, Art Center, Los Angeles, 1954, postgrad., 1955-56; DHL (hon.), Ill. Benedictine Coll., 1992. founder, pres. Novamark Corp., Chgo., 1968-72; cons. McDonalds Corp., Oakbrook, Ill.; tchr. art at local high schs. and colls. Asst. writer, artist: Buck Rogers Comic Strip, 1954-57, Dick Tracy Comic Strip, 1957-61, Martin Aerospace co., Denver, 1962-63; art dir. Hansen Co., Chgo., N.Y.C., 1963-68; editorial cartoonist Chgo. Tribune, 1972—; artist Dick Tracy Comic Strip, 1983—; author: Dick Locher Draws Fire, 1980, Send in the Clowns, 1982, Vote for Me, 1988, The Dick Tracy Casebook, 1990, Dick Tracy's Fiendish Foes, 1991, None of the Above, 1992, The Daze of Whine and Neurosis, 1995, (with Michael Kilian) Flying Can Be Fun, 1985; patentee Poker Face device to play poker without cards. Trustee Ill. Benedictine Coll., 1984—. Served with USAF, 1951-53. Recipient Dragonslayer award U.S. Indsl. Coun., 1976, 77, 78, 80, 81, 82, Disting. Health Journalism award, 1981, 82, 83, 84, 85, 92, Overseas Press Club award, 1983, 84, Pulitzer prize, 1983, Sigma Delta Chi award, 1985, World Population Inst. award, 1986, John Fischetti award, 1987, Peter Lisagor award, 1987, 89, 91; Named Ill. FBI Man of Yr., 1993. Mem. Assn. Am. Editorial Cartoonists.

LOCHMILLER, KURTIS L., real estate entrepreneur; b. Sacramento, Dec. 30, 1952; s. Rodney Glen and Mary Margaret (Frauen) L.; m. Mariye Susan Mizuki, Nov. 9, 1951; children: Margaux Sian, Chase Jordan. BA in Econs. and Fin., U. Denver, 1975. Dist. sales mgr. Hertz Truck Div., Denver, 1975-76; drilling foreman Shell Oil, Alaska, Mont., Colo., 1976-79; pres., owner Kurtex Mortgage & Devel. Co., Denver, 1979—, Kurtex Properties Inc., Denver, 1980-86; pres., chief exec. officer Kurtex Inc., Denver, 1981—, Bankers Pacific Mortgage, Denver, 1980—, Bankers Fin. Escrow Corp., Denver, 1984—, Northwest Title & Escrow, Denver, 1984—; pres., chief exec. officer Steamboat Title, Steamboat Springs, Colo., 1985—, First Escrow, Denver, 1986—, Fidelity-Commonwealth-Continental Escrow, Denver, 1984—; pres. Colonnade Ltd., Denver, 1981-88; pres., bd. dirs. Breckridge (Colo.) Brewery. V.p., founder Colfax on the Hill, Denver, 1984; mediator, arbitrator Arbitrator/Mediation Assn., Denver, 1986; mem. Police Athletic League, Denver, 1988. Recipient Pres. Spl. Achievement/Founder award Colfax on the Hill, Denver, 1984, Spl. Mayor's award, City & County of Denver, 1985. Mem. Nat. Assn.of Real Estate Appraisers, Internat. Brotherhood of Teamsters, Colo. Mortgage Bankers Assn., Mortgage Banking Assn., Denver C. of C., Phi Beta Kappa, Omicron Delta Epsilon. Clubs: U.S. Karate Assn. (Phoenix) (3d degree Black Belt), Ferrari (Portland). Lodge: Internat. Supreme Council Order of Demolay. Avocations: collecting cars, karate, fishing, art collecting. Home: 1 Carriage Ln Littleton CO 80121-2010 Office: Bankers Fin Escrow Corp 9655 E 25th Ave Ste 101 Aurora CO 80010-1056

LOCHNER, PHILIP RAYMOND, JR., lawyer, communications executive; b. New Rochelle, N.Y., Mar. 3, 1943; s. Philip Raymond and Maryl (Browning) L.; m. Sally Soth, June 23, 1973; children: Lauren Soth, John Philip. BA, Yale U., 1964, LLB, 1967; PhD, Stanford U., 1971. Bar: N.Y. 1972, D.C. 1991. Assoc. dean SUNY Law Sch., Amherst, 1971-73; assoc. Cravath, Swaine & Moore, N.Y.C., 1973-78; assoc. gen. counsel Time Inc., N.Y.C., 1978-80, corp. assoc. gen. counsel, 1980-84, sr. v.p., gen. counsel video, 1984-86, v.p., 1986-88, gen. cousel, sec., 1988-90; commr. SEC, Washington, 1990-91; sr. v.p. Time Warner Inc., N.Y.C., 1991—; bd. dirs. Bklyn. Bancorp., N.Y.C., 1994-96; lectr. Practicing Law Inst., N.Y.C., 1980—; mem. legal adv. com. N.Y. Stock Exch., 1991-94; mem. corp. governance and fin. markets sub-coun. U.S. Competitiveness Policy Coun., 1992. Treas., Yale Class of 1964, 1979-84; bd. dirs. Henry St. Settlement, N.Y.C., 1991—, Canterbury Sch., New Milford, Conn., 1994—, Citizens Budget Commn., N.Y., 1994—, Nat. Assn. Securities Dealers Regulation, Inc., Washington D.C., 1996—. Fellow Am. Bar Found.; mem. N.Y. State Bar Assn. (chmn. corp. counsel sect. 1989-90), Internat. Bar Assn. (N.Am. adv. group bus. law sect. 1992—). Clubs: Greenwich Country. Office: Time Warner Inc 75 Rockefeller Plz New York NY 10019-6908

LOCICERO, JOSEPH A., insurance company executive. Sec. Buck Cons. Office: 2 Penn Pla Fl 23 New York NY 10121

LOCIGNO, PAUL ROBERT, public affairs executive; b. Cleve., Sept. 1, 1948; s. Paul Robert and Anna Mae (Zingale) L.; m. Ki Cho Rim; children: Tammy, Robert. AA, Cuyahoga Community Coll., Parma, Ohio, 1974; BA, Case Western Res. U., 1976; postgrad., Cleve. State U., 1977-78. Part-time faculty Cuyahoga Community Coll., 1979-83; vice chmn. Presdl. Inaugural Labor Com., Washington, 1980-81; vice chmn. labor com. Presdl. Inaugural Com., Washington, 1984-85; legis. agt. Internat. Brotherhood of Teamsters, Washington, 1977-90, dir. govt. internat. affairs, 1983-89; dir. Asian/Pacific br. Internat. Brotherhood of Teamsters, Taipei, Taiwan, 1985-88; spl. rep. of chmn. Hill & Knowlton Pub. Affairs Worldwide, Washington, 1989-91; pres., founding ptnr. Rollins Internat. Ltd., Alexandria, Va.; bd. dirs. Nanjing Ya Dong Corp. Mem. Pres.'s Export Coun., 1988-89; mem. Asia adv. com. Bicentennial of U.S. Constitution, 1990; bd. govs. Am. League for Exports and Security Assistance, 1989; mem. Nat. Commn. for Employment Policy, Washington, 1981-86. With USMC, 1968-70, Vietnam. Republican. Roman Catholic. Avocations: archery, hunting, fishing. Home: 8203 Cherry Ridge Rd Fairfax VA 22039-3011 Office: Rollins Internat Ltd 510 King St Ste 302 Alexandria VA 22314-3132

LOCK, GERALD SEYMOUR HUNTER, retired mechanical engineering educator; b. London, June 30, 1935; arrived in Can., 1962, naturalized, 1973; s. George and Mary (Hunter) L.; m. Edna Burness, Sept. 19, 1959; children: Graeme, Gareth, Grenville. B.Sc. with honors, U. Durham, Eng., 1959, Ph.D., 1962. Asst. prof. mech. engring. U. Alta. (Can.), Edmonton, 1962-64; assoc. prof. U. Alta. (Can.), 1964-70, prof., 1970-93, dean interdisciplinary studies, 1976-81; cons. mech. engr., Edmonton, 1993—; chmn. Internat. Arctic Sci. Commn. Regional Bd., 1993—. Vice chmn. Alta. Manpower Adv. Coun., 1979-84, chmn., 1984-89; chmn. Salvation Army Red Shield Appeal, 1980-82; bd. govs. Alta. Coll., chmn., 1982-85; founding pres. Alta. Poetry Festival Soc., 1981. Recipient Queen Elizabeth II Silver Jubilee medal, 1977. Fellow Engring. Inst. Can, Can. Soc. Mech. Engring. (pres. 1977-78), ASME; mem. Sci. Coun. Can., Can. Polar Commn. Mem. Progressive Conservative Party. Anglican. Home: 11711 83d Ave, Edmonton, AB Canada T6G 0V2 Office: U Alta, Edmonton, AB Canada T6G 2G3

LOCK, RICHARD WILLIAM, packaging company executive; b. N.Y.C., Oct. 5, 1931; s. Albert and Catherine Dorothy (Magnus) L.; m. Elizabeth Louise Kenney, Nov. 2, 1957; children—Albert William, Dorothy Louise Lock Kuhl, John David. B.S., Rutgers U., 1953; M.B.A., N.Y. U., 1958. Acct. Gen. Electric Co., 1953-54, Union Carbide Co., N.Y.C., 1956-58; div. controller St. Regis Paper Co., Houston, 1959-62; div. controller Owens-Illinois, Inc., Toledo, 1962-64, supr. programmer office methods and data processing, 1964-65, asst. mgr. data processing procedures, 1965-67, mgr. systems analysis and devel., 1967-68, mgr. corp. systems analysis and devel., 1968-70, dir. corp. systems and data processing, 1970-72, gen. mgr. electro/optical display, 1972-75, treas., 1975-80, v.p., dir. corp. planning, 1980-84, v.p., asst. chief fin. officer, treas., 1984-88; mng. dir. Magnus Assocs., 1989—. Mem. adv. bd. Toledo Salvation Army, 1973—, chmn., 1974-77; pres. Toledo Area Govtl. Research Assn., 1978-79; bd. dirs. Riverside Hosp. Found., Toledo, 1982—. Served with USAF, 1954-56. Mem. Fin. Execs. Inst., Am. Soc. Corp. Secs., Phi Beta Kappa. Republican. Lutheran. Club: Toledo. Home: 5831 Monroe St Apt 406 Sylvania OH 43560-2256

LOCKARD, JOHN ALLEN, naval officer; b. Mobile, Ala., July 30, 1944; s. John David and Mary Ethlyn (Wyatt) L.; m. Peggy Lee Cantrell, Apr. 25, 1970; children: Denise, Karen, John, Kelley. BS, U.S. Naval Postgrad. Sch., 1971. Commd. ensign USN, 1966; advanced through grades to rear adm. advanced through grades to vice adm., 1995; commanding officer Attack Squadron 25 USN, Lemoore, Calif., 1980-81, commanding officer Strike Fighter Squadron 125, 1983-84; exec. officer USS Coral Sea USN, Norfolk, Va., 1985-86; program mgr. F/A-18 Naval AIr Systems Command USN, Washington, 1986-90, asst. comdr. for systems engring., 1990-91, program exec. officer to sec. navy staff, 1991-95, commdr. naval air systems command, 1995—; chmn. retirement com., bd. dirs. Navy Fed. Credit Union, Merrifield, Va., 1991—. Mem. Assn. Naval Aviation. Office: 1421 Jefferson Davis Hwy Arlington VA 22201-1010

LOCKE, CARL EDWIN, JR., academic administrator, engineering educator; b. Palo Pinto County, Tex., Jan. 11, 1936; s. Carl Edwin Sr. and Caroline Jane (Brown) L.; m. Sammie Rhae Batchelor, Aug. 25, 1956; children: Stephen Curtis, Carlene Rhae. BSChemE, U. Tex., 1958, MSChemE, 1960, PhDChemE, 1972. Rsch. engr. Continental Oil Co., Ponca City, Okla., 1959-65; prodn. engr. R.L. Stone Co., Austin, Tex., 1965-66; prodn. rsch. engr. Tracor Inc., Austin, 1966-71; vis. assoc. prof. U. Tex., Austin, 1971-73; from asst. prof. to prof., dir. chem. engring. U. Okla., Norman, 1973-86; dean engring. U. Kans., Lawrence, 1986—; Co-author: Anodic Protection, 1981; contbr. articles to profl. jours. Disting. Engring. grad. U. Tex., 1993. Fellow Am. Inst. Chem. Engrs.; mem. ASTM, Nat. Assn. Corrosion Engrs. (regional chair 1988-89, Eben Junkin award South Cen. region 1990), Am. Soc. Engring. Edn., Lawrence C. of C., Rotary. Democrat. Presbyterian. Office: U Kans 2291 Irving Rd Lawrence KS 66044-7541

LOCKE, EDWIN ALLEN, JR., investment banker; b. Boston, June 8, 1910; s. Edwin Allen and Elizabeth (Ferguson) L.; m. Dorothy Q. Clark, June 16, 1934 (div.); children: Elizabeth Eliane, Edwin Allen III, Benjamin Clark; m. Karin Marsh, 1952; 1 son, Jonathan Winston. Grad., Phillips Acad., Exeter, N.H., 1928; A.B. cum laude, Harvard U., 1932. Assoc. Chase Nat. Bank, N.Y.C., 1932-33, assoc. Paris br., 1933-35, assoc. London br., 1935-36, assoc., N.Y.C., 1936-40, v.p., 1947-51; Office Coordinator Purchases, adv. commn. to Council Nat. Def., 1940-41; asst. dep. dir. priorities div. Office Prodn. Mgmt., 1941; dep. chief staff officer Supply Priorities and Allocation Bd., 1941-42; asst. to chmn. WPB, 1942-44; exec. asst. to personal rep. of Pres., 1944-45, personal rep. of, 1945-47; also spl. asst. to pres., 1946-47; spl. rep. Sec. State; ambassador to Near East, 1951-53; exec. asst. to pres. Union Tank Car Co., Chgo., 1953-54, exec. v.p., 1954-55, pres., CEO, dir., 1955-63; pres., CEO Modern Homes Constrn. Co., Valdosta, Ga., 1963-67, Coastal Products Corp., Blountstown, Fla., 1964-67, Am. Paper Inst., N.Y.C., 1967-77, Econ. Club of N.Y., 1977-85; investment banker, 1985—; dir. Alusit Holdings, L.P., 1993—; chmn., dir. Fed. Home Loan Bank of Chgo., 1956-63; overseer Harvard U., 1958-64; trustee Century Power Corp. Ariz., 1989-91. Mem. Presdl. Survey Mission to Liberia and Tunisia, 1963; mem. adv. com. on internat. bus. problems Dept. State, 1962-67; trustee China Med. Bd., 1947-80, Radio Officers Union Benefit Plans, 1988-93. Mem. Racquet and Tennis Club (N.Y.C.), Metropolitan Club (Washington). Home and Office: PO Box 2568 Daytona Beach FL 32115-2568

LOCKE, EDWIN ALLEN, III, psychologist, educator; b. N.Y.C., May 15, 1938; s. Edwin Allen and Dorothy (Clark) L.; m. Anne Hassard, June 13, 1968. B.A., Harvard U., 1960; M.A., Cornell U., 1962, Ph.D., 1964. Assoc. research scientist Am. Inst. Research, 1964-66, research scientist, 1966-70; asst. prof. psychology U. Md., College Park, 1967-69; assoc. prof. U. Md., 1969-70, assoc. prof. bus., mgmt. and psychology, 1970-73, prof., 1973-96; chmn. faculty mgt. and orgn. Coll. Bus. and Mgmt. U. Md., College Park, 1984-96. Author: A Guide to Effective Study, 1975; co-author: Goal Setting: A Motivational Technique That Works, 1984, A Theory of Goal Setting and Task Performance, 1990, The Essence of Leadership, 1991; editor: Generalizing from Laboratory to Field Settings, 1986; cons. editorial bd. Organizational Behavior and Human Decision Processes, J. Applied Psychology; contbr. articles to profl. jours. Office Naval Research grantee, 1964, 79; NIMH grantee, 1967; Army Rsch. Inst. grantee, 1993. Fellow APA, Acad. Mgmt., Am. Psychol. Soc., Soc. Indsl. and Orgnl. Psychology (Disting Scientific Contbn. award 1993). Home: 30 Old Mill Bottom Rd N Annapolis MD 21401 Office: U Md Coll Bus and Mgmt College Park MD 20742 *The most important literary/philosophical influence in my life has been Ayn Rand. Her philosophy of Objectivism demonstrates that man's highest moral purpose is the achievement of his own happiness and that reason is his only means to achieve it. Her novels, which portray man as an heroic being, are an inspiration to every man to achieve the best within him.*

LOCKE, ELIZABETH HUGHES, foundation administrator; b. Norfolk, Va., June 30, 1939; d. George Morris and Sallie Epps (Moss) Hughes; m. John Rae Locke, Jr., Sept. 13, 1958 (div. 1981); children—John Rae III, Sallie Curtis. B.A. magna cum laude with honors in English, Duke U., 1964, Ph.D., 1972; M.A., U. N.C., 1966. Instr. English, U. N.C., Chapel Hill, 1970-72; vis. prof. English, Duke U., Durham, N.C., 1972-73, dir. univ. pubs., 1973-79; corp. contbns. officer Bethlehem Steel Corp., Pa., 1979-82; dir. edn. div. and communications Duke Endowment, Charlotte, N.C., 1982-96, exec. dir., 1996—; past pres. Communications Philanthropy, Washington; mem. comms. com. Coun. on Founds., Washington, 1994—; mem. Ind. Sect. bd. com. on pub. edn. Editor: Duke Encounters, 1977, Prospectus for Change: American Private Higher Education, 1985, (mag.) Issues, 1985-96. Pres., Jr. League, Durham, 1976, Hist. Preservation Soc., Durham, 1977, Pub. Rels. Soc. Am., Charlotte chpt., 1988, Charlotte Area Donors Forum; past pres. Sch. of Arts, Charlotte; bd. visitors Davidson Coll., Charlotte Country Day Sch., Duke U., Johnson C. Smith U. Recipient Leadership award Charlotte C. of C., 1984; Danforth fellow, 1972. Mem. Nat. Task Force, English Speaking Union, Phi Beta Kappa. Democrat. Episcopalian. Club: Charlotte City. Office: 100 N Tryon St Ste 3500 Charlotte NC 28202-4000

LOCKE, MICHAEL, zoology educator; b. Nottingham, Eng., Feb. 14, 1929; came to U.S., 1961; s. R.H. and K.N. (Waite) L.; m. J. V. Collins; children by previous marriage, Vanessa , John, Timothy, Marius. B.A., Cambridge U., 1952, M.A., 1955, Ph.D., 1956, Sc.D., 1976. State scholar, found. scholar St. John's Coll., 1949-56; lectr. zoology Univ. Coll. W.I., 1956-61; guest investigator Rockefeller Inst., N.Y.C., 1960; assoc. prof. biology Case Western Res. U., Cleve., 1961-67, prof. biology, 1967-71; prof., chmn. dept. zoology U. Western Ont., London, Can., 1971-85; prof. zoology U. Western Ont., 1985-94; prof. emeritus, 1994—; Raman prof. U. Madras, India, 1969; vis. dir. rsch. Internat. Ctr. Insect Physiology and Ecology, Nairobi, Kenya, 1977-81. Editor Monographs on Ultrastructure, 1970—; mem. editorial bd. Tissue and Cell, 1968—, Jour. Insect Physiology, 1978—, Insect Sci. and Its Applications, 1979-89; former editor: Growth Soc. Symposia; contbr. over 200 articles to profl. jours. Served with RAF. Disting. Internat. award in Insect Morphology & Embryology, Gold medal, 1988; Killam fellow, 1988-90. Fellow Royal Soc. Can., AAAS; mem. Am. Soc. Cell Biology. Avocations: lapidary; gemologist. Office: Dept Zoology, U Western Ont, London, ON Canada N6A 5B7

LOCKE, NORTON, hotel management and construction company executive; b. Mpls., May 22, 1927; s. Ben and Harriet (Markus) L.; m. Peggy Jane Smith, Nov. 6, 1959; children: Alexandria, Jonina, Elizabeth, Victoria. B.S., U. Wis., 1951; M.B.A., Mich. State U., 1957, cert. food and beverage exec., 1984, cert. hotel adminstr., 1986, cert. food service profl., 1988. Corp. dir. food and beverage Kahler Corp., Rochester, Minn., 1970; gen. mgr., chief exec. officer Carolando Corp., Orlando, Fla., 1971-74; also dir.; gen. mgr. Radisson Muehlebach Hotel, Kansas City, Radisson Cadillac Hotel, Detroit, 1974-79; v.p., gen. mgr. White Co. Hospitality Div., Merrillville, Ind., 1979-80; dist. dir. I.D.M. Mgmt. Co., Chgo., 1980-83; v.p., gen. mgr. Skirvin Plaza Hotel, Oklahoma City, 1983-87; v.p., dir. ops. SBI Mgmt. Co., Oklahoma City, 1987-91; v.p., gen. mgr. Anaheim (Calif.) Plz. Hotel, 1991-93; corp. dir. Midwest Hospitality Mgmt., Anaheim, Calif., 1993—; faculty Vallencia Coll., 1971-74; adj. prof. Oklahoma City Community Coll., 1983-89; adj. prof. Century Coll., San Diego. Author: Hard Times Cook Book, World Without Milk Cookbook, Land of Milk and Honey, Heritage, A Taste of Tradition. Bd. dirs. U. Minn. Tech. Coll., 1970-75, Am. Hotel and Motel Assn. Sch., 1975-79, Detroit Conv. and Visitors Bur. Served with inf. AUS, 1944-46. Mem. Internat. Food Service Execs. Assn. (dir. 1971-74), Am. Hotel and Motel Assn. (cert.), Am. Chefs Assn., Mich. and Ind. Hotel Assns., Nat. Restaurant Assn., Hotel Sales Mgrs. Assn., Am. Fisheries Inst. (dir. 1970-71), Okla. State Hotel Assn. (Innkeeper of Yr. 1985, Bd. Mem. of Yr. 1986). Republican. Clubs: Masons (Scottish Rite 32 degree), Shriners, Rotary, SKAL Internat, Toastmasters Internat.

LOCKE, VIRGINIA OTIS, textbook editor, behavioral sciences writer; b. Tiffin, Ohio, Sept. 4, 1930; d. Charles Otis and Frances Virginia (Sherer) L. BA, Barnard Coll., 1953; MA in Psychology, Duke U., 1972, postgrad. Program officer, asst. corp. sec. Agrl. Devel. Coun., N.Y.C., 1954-66; staff psychologist St. Luke's-Roosevelt Med. Ctr., N.Y.C., 1973-75; freelance writer and editor N.Y.C., 1976-85; writer-editor Cornell U. Med. Coll./N.Y. Hosp. Med. Ctr., N.Y.C., 1986-89; sr. editor humanities and social scis. coll. divsn. Prentice Hall divsn. Simon & Schuster, Upper Saddle River, N.J., 1989—. Co-author: (coll. textbook) Introduction to Theories of Personality, 1985, The Agricultural Development Council: A History, 1989. Founder Help Our Neighbors Eat Year-Round (H.O.N.E.Y.), Inc., N.Y.C., chmn., 1983-87, vol., 1987—, newsletter editor, 1992—; reader Recording for the Blind, N.Y.C., 1978-84; vol. Reach to Recovery program Am. Cancer Soc., Bergen County, N.J., 1990—. Recipient Our Town Thanks You award, N.Y.C., 1984, Mayor's Vol. Svc. award, N.Y.C., 1986, Cert. of Appreciation for Community Svc. Manhattan Borough, 1986, Jefferson award Am. Ins. Pub. Svc., Washington, 1986.

LOCKE, WILLIAM, endocrinologist; b. Morden, Man., Can., Mar. 16, 1916; s. Corbet and Ruby Louise (Brown) L.; m. Katherine Elizabeth Acer Russell, Sept. 29, 1945 (dec.). MD, U. Man., Winnipeg, 1938; MS in Medicine, U. Minn., 1947. Diplomate Am. Bd. Internal Medicine. Intern Winnipeg (Man., Can.) Gen. Hosp., 1937-38; fellow in medicine Mayo Found., Rochester, Minn., 1938-40, 46-48; rsch. fellow Harvard U., Boston, 1948-50; mem. staff Ochsner Clinic, New Orleans, 1950—, sr. cons., 1987—; clin. prof. medicine Tulane U., New Orleans, 1968-86, prof. emeritus, 1986—; sec. Alton Ochsner Med. Found., New Orleans, 1950—; pres. med. staff Ochsner Found. Hosp., New Orleans, 1954-55, trustee, 1978—. Author, editor: Hypothalmus and Pituitary in Health and Disease, 1972; contbr. numerous chpts. to books and articles to sci. jours. Lt. comdr. RCNVR, 1940-46. NIH grantee, 1958-62. Fellow ACP; mem. Am. Diabetes Assn., Endocrine Soc., Sigma Xi, others. Republican. Episcopalian. Home: 4815 Dryades St New Orleans LA 70115-5533 Office: Ochsner Clinic 1514 Jefferson Hwy New Orleans LA 70121-2429

LOCKER, J. GARY, university official, civil engineering educator; b. Kenora, Ont., Can., Nov. 19, 1937; s. Lorne John and Gladys Sarah (Kirk) L.; m. Elaine June Letawsky, May 25, 1963; children: Laura Lee, Tiffany Dawn. BSCE, U. Man., Winnipeg, Can., 1961; MS, U. Alta., Edmonton, Can., 1963, PhD, 1969. Registered profl engr., Ont. Lectr. dept. civil engring., Royal Mil. Coll., Kingston, Ont., 1963-66, asst. prof., 1968-71; assoc. prof. faculty engring. U. Regina,, Sask., Can., 1971-73; chmn. dept. civil engring. Lakehead U., Thunder Bay, Ont., 1973-76, dir. Sch. Engring., 1976-94; dean Faculty Engring. Lakehead U., Thunder Bay, 1994—; mem., past chmn. Coun. Ont. Deans Engring., Nat. Coun. Deans Engring. and Applied Sci. Fellow Engring. Inst. Can.; mem. Can. Geotech. Inst., Profl. Engrs. Ont. (order of honor), Internat. Soc. Soil Mechanics and Found. Engring., Thunder Bay Fly Fishing Club. Geotech. engring. rsch. in organic soils and clay shales. Avocations: fly fishing and tying, gardening, trailer travel, cross-country skiing. Office: Lakehead U Faculty Engring, Oliver Rd, Thunder Bay, ON Canada P7B 5E1

LOCKER, RAYMOND DUNCAN, editor; b. Dunkirk, N.Y., Apr. 15, 1960; s. Robert Smith and Margaret Ellen (Duncan) L.; m. Debbie Elizabeth Long, July 2, 1988; 1 child, Margaret Katherine. BA in Political Sci., U. Cin., 1982; MS in Journalism, Ohio U., 1984. Reporter Lake Wales Highlander, Lake Wales, Fla., 1982-83, The Montgomery Advertiser, Montgomery, Ala., 1985-87; political reporter The Tampa Tribune, Tampa, Fla., 1987-89, Washington corr., 1989-91, political columnist, 1991-93, night metro editor, 1993-94, political editor, 1994—. Panelist Tampa Bay Week, WEDU-TV, 1993—, Bayside, WTOG-TV, 1994—. Roman Catholic. Office: The Tampa Tribune PO Box 191 Tampa FL 33601-0191

LOCKETT, BARBARA ANN, librarian; b. Northampton, Mass., Feb. 21, 1936; d. William M. and Anna A. (Vachula) Prabulos; m. Richard W. Rice, June 2, 1957 (div. Feb. 1966); 1 child, Annamarie Louise; m. Benjamin B. Lockett, June 7, 1985. BS, U. Mass., 1957; MLS, U. Calif., Berkeley, 1967. Documents librarian Knolls Atomic Power Lab., Schenectady, N.Y., 1968-74; coordinator bibliog. devel. SUNY, Albany, 1974-81; prin. librarian reference services N.Y. State Library, Albany, 1981-85; dir. libraries Rensselaer Poly. Inst., Troy, N.Y., 1985-94, libr. emeritus, 1994—; cons. Office Mgmt. Svcs., Assn. Rsch. Librs., Washington, 1981-86. Contbr. articles on collection devel., mgmt. and info. systems to profl. jours. Mem. ALA (cons. collection mgmt. and devel. com., Resources and Tech. Svcs. div. 1983-87), Assn. Coll. and Rsch. Librs. (chmn. standards and accreditation com. 1988-90), N.Y. State Edn. and Rsch. Network (chmn. info. resources com. 1988-89), N.Y. State Libr./NYSERNet (joint planning team 1991-94, del. N.Y. State Gov.'s Conf. on Librs., 1990), Sigma Xi, Phi Kappa Phi, Beta Phi Mu. Mem. Unitarian Ch. Avocations; tennis, master gardener. Home: 1772 Calle Poniente Santa Barbara CA 93101-4916

LOCKETT, PIERRE, dancer; b. Mobile, Ala.. Scholarship student, The Joffrey Ballet Sch., 1980-82, Robert Joffrey Workshop, 1981. Dancer Dance Theater of Harlem, N.Y.C., 1982-88, Princeton Ballet, 1988-89, The Joffrey Ballet, N.Y.C., 1989—. Office: The Joffrey Ballet 130 W 56th St New York NY 10019-3818

LOCKETT, TYLER CHARLES, state supreme court justice; b. Corpus Christi, Tex., Dec. 7, 1932; s. Tyler Coleman and Evelyn (Lemond) L.; m. Sue W. Lockett, Nov. 3, 1961; children: Charles, Patrick. AB, Washburn U., 1955, JD, 1962. Bar: Kans. 1962. Pvt. practice law Wichita, 1962—; judge Ct. Common Pleas, 1971-77, Kans. Dist. Ct. 18th Dist., 1977-83; justice Supreme Court Kans., Topeka, 1983—. Methodist. Office: Kans Supreme Ct 389 Kans Jud Ctr 301 W 10th St Topeka KS 66612*

LOCKETT/GARZA, CAROL DENISE, graphic designer, photographer; b. Memphis, July 25, 1959; d. Calvin Coolidge Miller and Betty Lee (Lockett) Scott; m. David Ramirez Garza, Mar. 24, 1983 (div. Oct. 1992); children: David Ramirez Garza II, Taylore Lauren. AA in Visual Comms., Md. Coll. Art and Design, 1991; BA in Graphic Design, Coll. Notre Dame of Md., 1993. Illustrator Urban Profile Mag., Balt., 1991; intern Patuxent Pub. Co., Columbia, Md., 1992; designer, illustrator Morrese, Inc., N.Y.C., 1993; freelance graphic designer, illustrator CLGraphics, Columbia, 1993—. Artist: calendar for Montgomery County Equal Housing Commn., 1991; artist, designer inauguration quilt for pres. of Coll. of Notre Dame of Md., 1992. Active Jeffers Hill Elem. Sch. PTA, Columbia, 1990-92; vol. Girl Scouts Am., Columbia, 1991-92. Mem. Nat. Mus. for Women in the Arts, Nat. Geographic Soc., Am. Mus. Natural History, Nat. Trust for Hist. Preservation, Graphic Artists Guild, Advt. and Graphic Arts Soc. Howard County, Alumnae Assn. Coll. Notre Dame of Md. Avocations: ice-skating, tennis, roller-skating, reading, spending time with children. Home: 8953 Footedridge Columbia MD 21045-4235

LOCKEY, RICHARD FUNK, allergist, educator; b. Lancaster, Pa., Jan. 15, 1940; s. Stephen Daniel and Anna (Funk) L.; m. Carol Lee Madill, July 3, 1982; children—Brian Christopher, Keith Edward. B.S., Haverford Coll., 1961; M.D., Temple U., 1965; M.S., U. Mich., 1972. Diplomate Am. Bd. Internal Medicine, Am. Bd. Allergy and Immunology. Intern Temple U. Med. Sch., Phila., 1965-66; asst. resident internal medicine Univ. Hosp. U. Mich., Ann Arbor, 1966-67, resident, 1966-68, fellow in allergy and immunology, 1969-70; asst. prof. medicine U. South Fl. Coll. Medicine, Tampa, 1973-77, assoc. prof. medicine, 1977-83, asst. dir. div. allergy and immunology, 1979-82, dir. allergy and immunology, 1982—, prof. medicine, 1983—, prof. pediats., 1983—, prof. pub. health, 1987—; asst. chief sect. allergy and immunology VA Hosp., Tampa, 1973-82, chief sect. allergy and immunology, 1983—; mem. allergenic adv. com. FDA, 1985-89. Editor: Allergy and Clinical Immunology, 1980; co-editor: (with S.C. Bukantz) Fundamentals of Immunology and Allergy, 1987, (with S.C. Bukantz) Principles of Immunology and Allergy, 1987, JAMA Primer on Allergic and Immunologic Diseases, 1987, (with S. C. Bukantz) Allergen Immunotherapy, 1991, (with M. Levine) Monograph on Insect Allergy, 1995; contbr. articles to profl. jours. and chpts. to books; author monographs. Served to maj. USAF, 1971-73. Named Outstanding Med. Specialist, Town and Country Mag., 1989, Claude P. Brown Meml. lectr. Assn. Clin. Scientists, ADA, 1981, Disting. Visitor Ann. Meeting of Coll. of Medicine, Republic of Costa Rica, 1979, spl. mem. Internat. Sci. Bd. Pharmacia Allergy Rsch. Found., 1992—; recipient Alumni Achievement award Temple U. Sch. of Medicine Alumni Assn., 1990, Outstanding Leadership in Chpt. Devel. and Patient Support, Nat. Asthma and Allergy Found. of Am. award, 1992, Cert. of Appreciation, Fla. Med. Assn., 1992. Fellow ACP, AAAS, AMA, Am. Coll. Chest Physicians, Am. Acad. Allergy and Immunology (chmn. com. on insects 1978-81, chmn. undergrad. and grad. edn. com. 1982-88, com. on occupational lung disease 1982—, chmn. com. on standardization of allergenic extracts 1983-86, exec. com. mem. at large 1986-88, historian 1988-89, sec. 1989-90, treas. 1990-91, pres.-elect 1991-92, pres. 1992-93, Am. Bd. Allergy and Immunology (bd. dirs. 1993—), Soc. Allergy and Immunology of Cordoba, Argentina (hon.), John M. Sheldon U. of Mich. Allergy Soc. (councilor 1977-80, pres. 1980-82), Fla. Allergy and Immunology Soc. (sec.-treas. 1979-80, pres. 1981-82), Southeastern Allergy Assn., Hillsborough County Med. Assn., Joint Coun. Allergy and Immunology, Clin. Immunology Soc., Fla. Thoracic Soc., Univ. Club, Carrollwood Village Club. Clubs: Carrollwood Village (Tampa), University. Avocation: antique cut glass and tools. Home: 3909 Northampton Way Tampa FL 33624-4443 Office: U So Fla VA Hosp 13000 Bruce B Downs Blvd Tampa FL 33612-4745

LOCKHART, AILEENE SIMPSON, retired dance, kinesiology and physical education educator; b. Atlanta, Mar. 18, 1911; d. Thomas Ellis and Aileene Reeves (Simpson) L. B.S., Tex. Woman's U., 1932; M.S., U. Wis., 1937, Ph.D., 1942; D.Sc. (hon.), U. Nebr., 1967. Mem. faculty Mary Hardin Baylor Coll., Belton, Tex., 1937-42, U. Wis., 1941-42; asst. prof., then assoc. prof. phys. edn. and pharmacology U. Nebr., 1942-49; assoc. prof., then prof. U. So. Calif., 1949-73; dean Coll. Health, Phys. Edn., Recreation and Dance Tex. Woman's U., 1973-78, prof. dance and phys. edn., chmn. dept. dance, 1978-83, adj. prof., 1983-88; Clare Small lectr. U. Colo., 1975; Ethel Martus Lawther lectr. U. N.C., 1978; Amy Morris Homans lectr., Milw., 1976; Donna Mae Miller Humanities scholar/lectr. , U. Ariz., Tucson, 1989; vis. prof./lectr. Iowa State U., univs., Wash., Oreg., Wis., Mass.; N.H., Calif. State U., Long Beach, Springfield (Mass.) Coll., Smith Coll., Wellesley Coll., U. Maine-Presque Isle, Dunfermline Coll., Edinburgh, Scotland, U. Brazil, Brasilia; cons. editor William C. Brown Publishing Co., Dubuque, Iowa, 1954—. Author or co-author 12 books; contbr. numerous articles profl. jours.; cons. editor or editor over 200 books. Recipient Disting. Alumnae award Tex. Woman's U., 1971, Disting. Alumnae award U. Wis.-Madison, 1981, Cornaro award, 1980, Honor award Ministry Edn., Taiwan, 1981, Minnie Stevens Piper Found. award State of Tex., 1983, Nat. Dance Assn. Heritage award, 1985, Amy Morris Homans fellow, 1961-62; honra ao Merito Ministerio de Educato and Cultura Brazilia, Brazil, 1977; Nat. Dance Assn. scholar, 1986-87; Tex. Assn. Health, Phys. Edn., Recreation and Dance scholar, 1986. Fellow Am. Coll. Sports Medicine, Am. Alliance Health, Phys. Edn., Recreation and Dance (Honor award 1963, Luther Halsey Gulick award 1980), Am. Acad. Phys. Edn. (pres. 1980-81, Hetherington award 1992); mem. Nat. Assn. Girls and Women in Sports (honor award 1991), Nat. Dance Assn., So. Assn. Phys. Edn. Coll. Women, Nat. Assn. Phys. Edn. in Higher Edn., Phi Kappa Phi. Presbyterian. *That my students, many now well respected scholars, others eager neophytes in the journey of learning, exemplify some of the goals, ideals and visions, the high standards and high expectancies we have shared together is to me the most meaningful and fulfilling aspect in my life as an educator.*

LOCKHART, GEMMA, producer, writer; b. Rapid City, S.D., Dec. 5, 1956; d. Jim and Teena L.; children: Mica, Nakca, Aaron. BA in English, Creative Writing, Dartmouth Coll., 1979. TV news reporter Duhamel Broadcasting Enterprises, Rapid City, S.D., 1974-80; TV producer Rural Ethnic Inst., Rapid City, 1981-83; instr. Oglala Lakota Coll., Kyle, S.D., 1983-86; horse rider Black Hills, S.D.; TV producer S.D. Pub. TV, Vermillion, 1989-90; ind. producer, 1990—; CEO Wambli Win Prodns., 1994—, Anpao Studio, Rapid City, 1995—; auditor Lakota Elders, Dakota Land, 1975—; freelance columnist various publs. including USA Today. Presdl. scholar, 1975, 85. Mem. NAFE, Dartmouth Coll. Alumni Coun., Nature Conservancy (bd. dirs. 1995-96). Republican. Avocation: walking. Home: Box 8044 Rapid City SD 57709-8044 also: Dark Canyon Rapid City SD 57702

LOCKHART, GREGORY GORDON, lawyer; b. Dayton, Ohio, Sept. 2, 1946; s. Lloyd Douglas and Evelyn (Gordon) L.; m. Paula Louise Jewett, May 20, 1978; children: David H., Sarah L. BS, Wright State U., 1973; JD, Ohio State U., 1976. Bar: Ohio 1976, U.S. Dist. Ct. (so. dist.) Ohio 1977, U.S. Ct. Appeals (6th cir.) 1988, U.S. Supreme Ct. 1993. Legal advisor Xenia and Fairborn (Ohio) Police Dept., 1977-78; asst. pros. atty. Greene County Prosecutor, Xenia, 1978-87; assoc. DeWine & Schenck, Xenia, 1978-82; ptnr. Schenck, Schmidt & Lockhart, Xenia, 1982-85, Ried & Lockhart, Beavercreek, Ohio, 1985-87; asst. U.S. atty. So. Dist. of Ohio, Columbus, 1987-89, Dayton, 1989—; adj. prof. Coll. Law U. Dayton, 1990—, Wright State U., Dayton, 1979—. Co-author: Federal Grand Jury Practice, 1996, Republicans. Pres. Greene County Young reps., Xenia, 1977-79. With USAF, 1966-70; Vietnam. Mem. Fed. Bar Assn. (chpt. pres. 1994-95), Kiwanis (pres. 1983-84, lt. gov. 1986-87), Jaycees (pres. 1976-79), Am. Inns of Ct. (master of bench). Methodist. Avocations: golf, tennis, hiking, camping. Office: US Attorney 200 W 2d St Rm 602 Federal Bldg Dayton OH 45402

LOCKHART, JAMES BICKNELL, III, investment banker; b. White Plains, N.Y., May 13, 1946; s. James Bicknell Jr. and Mary Ann (Riegel) L.; m. Carolyn Strahan Zoephel, June 17, 1972; children: James Bicknell IV, Grace Strahan. BA, Yale U., 1968; MBA, Harvard U., 1974. Asst. treas. Gulf Oil (E.H.), London, 1979-80; fin. dir. Gulf Oil Belgium, Brussels, 1980-81; sr. mgr. Gulf Oil Corp., Pitts., 1981-82, asst. treas., 1982-83; v.p., treas. Alexander and Alexander Services, N.Y.C., 1983-89; exec. dir. Pension Benefit Guaranty Corp., Washington, 1989-93; mng. dir., head pvt. fin. group Smith Barney, Inc., N.Y.C., 1993—. Contbr. articles to profl. jours. Treas. Reps. Abroad, London, 1978-80. Served to lt. (j.g.) USNR, 1969-72. Fellow Assn. Corp. Treas. (Eng.); mem. Assn. Pvt. Pension and Welfare Plans (bd. dirs.). Office: Smith Barney Inc 388 Greenwich St New York NY 10013

LOCKHART, JAMES BLAKELY, public affairs executive; b. N.Y.C., May 27, 1936; s. Edgar L. and Margaret Evelyn (Blakely) L.; m. Ruth Douglas, Oct. 30, 1976; children: Marc Blakely, Diallo Henry. BS, Boston U., 1956, JD, 1959. Bar: S.C. 1959, Ill. 1963. Sr. ptnr. Rivers, Lockhart, Clayter & Lawrence, Chgo., 1965-71; sr. v.p. legal affairs, sec., dir. Budget Rent-a-Car Corp., Chgo., 1972-79; v.p. public affairs Transam. Corp., San Francisco, 1979—; chmn. bd. Chgo. Community Ventures, Inc., 1975-79; bd. dir. Budget Rent-a-Car Internat., Inc. Mem. men's coun. Art Inst. of Chgo., 1970-72; bd. dirs., v.p., mem. exec. com. bd. Episcopal charities Diocese of Chgo.; mem. Gov.'s Task Force on Civil Rights, Calif., 1980; past chmn. bd. dirs. Bay Area Urban League, Sta. KQED-TV, pub. broadcasting, also Sta. KQEC-TV, KQED-FM; past chmn. St. Mary's Coll. Exec. Symposium; chmn. bus. coun., mem. exec. com., trustee emeritus Fine Arts Mus. San Francisco; bd. dirs., vice chmn. bd. dirs. Pub. Broadcasting Svcs.; commr., pres. Bd. of Port Commrs., Port of Oakland, 1992-96. Capt. JAGC, AUS, 1960-63. Recipient Sta. WBEE Radio Cmty. Svc. award, 1973, Corp. Leadership award, 1988, San Francisco Planning and Urban Rsch. Assn., 1989, Cert. of Honor, San Francisco Bd. Suprs., 1989, Citizen of Yr. award Union Bank of KQED, 1996. Mem. Internat. Franchise Assn. (bd. dirs. 1973-77), Ill. Bar Assn., S.C. Bar Assn., Bay Area Coun. (liaison), Pub. Affairs Coun. (bd. dirs.), Calif. Bus. Roundtable (dep.), Downtown Assn. San Francisco (past pres., bd. dirs.), San Francisco C. of C. (bd. dirs., exec. com., chmn. pub. affairs com.), Bohemian Club, City Club (past pres.), Lakeview Club, Boulé, Sigma Pi Phi. Episcopalian. Home: 6037 Ridgemont Dr Oakland CA 94619-3721 Office: Transam Corp 600 Montgomery St San Francisco CA 94111-2702

LOCKHART, JOHN MALLERY, management consultant; b. Mellen, Wis., May 17, 1911; s. Carl Wright and Gladys (Gale) L.; m. Judith Anne Wood, Feb. 26, 1938 (dec. June 1991); children: Wood Alexander, Gale, Thomas; m. Frances Whittaker, Jan. 7, 1993. BS, Northwestern U., 1931; JD, IIT, 1938. CPA, Ill. Teaching fellow Northwestern U., 1931; asst. v.p. Welsh, Davis & Co. (investment bankers), Chgo., 1935-41; treas. Transcontinental & Western Air, Inc., Kansas City, Mo., 1941-47; exec. v.p., CEO TACA Airways, S.A., 1944-45; v.p., dir. The Kroger Co., 1947-71, exec. v.p., 1961-71; pres. Kroger Family Ctr. Stores, 1969-71, Lockhart Co. (mgmt. cons.), 1971—; v.p. corp. fin. Gradison & Co., 1973-86; chmn. bd. dirs., CEO Ohio Real Estate Investment Co., Ohio Real Estate Equity Corp., 1974-76; bd. dirs. Employers Mut. Cos., Des Moines, Witt Co.; chmn. bd. dirs. Autotronics Systems, Inc., 1976-78; bd. dirs. Vectra Internat., Inc. Chmn. Hamilton County Hosp. Commn., 1965-84; mem. adv. bd. Greater Cin. Airport, 1961-86. Mem. Comml. Club, Cin. Country Club, Conquistadores del Cielo Club. Home and Office: 2770 Walsh Rd Cincinnati OH 45208-3425

LOCKHART, KEITH ALAN, orchestra conductor, musician, teacher; b. Poughkeepsie, N.Y., Nov. 7, 1959; s. Newton Frederick and Marilyn Jean (Woodyard) L.; m. Ann Louise Heatherington, Aug. 22, 1981 (div. 1983). B.A. summa cum laude in German, Furman U., 1981, Mus.B. summa cum laude in Piano Performance, 1981; M.F.A. in Orch. Conducting, Carnegie-Mellon U., 1983. Mem. condrs. faculty Carnegie-Mellon U., 1983-89; music dir. Pitts. Civic Orch., 1987-90; asst. condr. Akron Symphony Orch., 1988-90, Cin. Symphony Orch., Cin. Pops Orch., 1990-92; assoc. condr., 1992-95; music dir. Cin. Chamber Orch., 1992—; condr. Naples (Fla.) Philharmonic Orch., 1993—, Boston Pops Orch., Boston Symphony Orch. Youth Concerts, 1995—. Guest condr. Chgo. Symphony Orch., Cleve. Orch., L.A. Philharmonic, L.A. Chamber Orch., Toronto Symphony, Mont. Symphony Orch., Indpls. Symphony, Vt. Symphony, Eugene Symphony, Long Island Philharmonic, Orch. Sinfonica de Tucuman (Argentina). Co-editor, arranger performance edition opera John Gay: The Beggars' Opera, 1985; recordings: Telarc, Christmas Songs with Mel Torme, 1992, works by Glabraith,

Alonso-Crespo, 1995. Mem. Conductors' Guild Am., Symphony Orch. League, Am. Fedn. Musicians. Avocations: reading; cooking; skiing; raquetball; outdoor sports. Office: The Boston Pops Orchestra care Boston Symphony Orchestra Symphony Hall Boston MA 02115

LOCKHART, MICHAEL D., electric company executive; b. Muncie, Ind., Mar. 25, 1949; s. Roy Eugene and Marjorie Ilene (Thornburg) L.; children—Jennifer, Jessica, Kathleen Coleman. MBA, U. Chgo., 1975. Systems analyst Needham Harper & Steers, Chgo., 1969-74; v.p. Boston Consulting Group, Boston, 1975-81, GE Credit Corp., 1981-83, GE Corp. Exec. Office, Fairfield, Conn., 1984-85, GE Turbine Bus. Ops., Schenectady, N.Y., 1985-87, GE Aircraft Engines, Cin., 1987-88, GE Transp. Systems, Erie, Pa., 1989-91; v.p., gen. mgr. GE Aircraft Engines, Cin., 1992-94; pres. Gen. Signal Corp., Stamford, Conn., 1994—; chmn., CEO. Mem. Beta Gamma Sigma. Office: Gen Signal Corp PO Box 10010 High Ridge Park Stamford CT 06904

LOCKHEAD, GREGORY ROGER, psychology educator; b. Boston, Aug. 8, 1931; s. John Roger and Ester Mae (Bixby) L.; m. Jeanne Marie Hutchinson, June 9, 1957; children: Diane, Elaine, John. B.S., Tufts U., 1958; Ph.D., Johns Hopkins, 1965. Psychologist research staff IBM Research, Yorktown Heights, N.Y., 1958-61; research assoc., instr. Johns Hopkins, 1961-65; asst. prof. psychology Duke, 1965-68, assoc. prof., 1968-71, prof., 1971-91; chmn. dept. exptl. psychology Duke U., Durham, N.C., 1991—; scholar Stanford U.; research asso. U. Calif., Berkeley, 1971-72; fellow Wolfson Coll., Oxford (Eng.) U., 1980-81; scholar Fla. Atlantic U., 1981; Cons. in human engring. Cons. editor: Perception and Psychophysics, 1972-92; contbr. articles to profl. jours., co-author, editor chpts. in books. Served with USN, 1951-55. NSF grantee, 1966-69, 79-84, USPHS grantee, 1963-69, 70-79, Air Force Office Sci. Rsch., 1983-91. Fellow Am. Psychol. Assn., Am. Psychol. Soc.; mem. Psychonomic Soc., Internat. Soc. Psychophysics, Sigma Xi, Phi Beta Kappa (hon.). Home: 2900 Montgomery St Durham NC 27705-5638 Office: Duke U Dept Exptl Psychology Durham NC 27708

LOCKLAIR, GARY HAMPTON, computer science educator; b. Sacramento, May 1, 1956; s. Oliver Hampton and Frances Eleanor (Snyder) L.; m. Karen Ann Kellar, Aug. 13, 1977; children: Joshua, Sabrina, David, Daniel, Valerie. BA in Chemistry, Calif. State U., Sacramento, 1979, BS in Computer Sci., 1980; MS, U. Idaho, 1986. Programmer, analyst Calif. Dept. Transp., Sacramento, 1977-79; mem. tech. staff Hewlett-Packard Co., Cupertino, Calif., 1980-81; software quality engr. Hewlett-Packard Co., Corvallis, Oreg., 1981-83; software program mgr. Hewlett-Packard Co., Boise, Idaho, 1983-86; asst. prof. Concordia U. Wis., Mequon, 1986—, chair computer sci. dept., 1986—, dir. computer ctr., 1986-93; computing cons., Milw., 1986—. Author: All of the Above, 1992; contbr. articles to profl. jours. Dist. computer cons. Philomath (Oreg.) Sch. Dist., 1981-83. Recipient HP Customer Svc. award Hewlett-Packard and Exxon Corp., 1985. Mem. IEEE, Assn. for computing Machinery. Lutheran. Avocation: photography. Office: Concordia U Wis 12800 N Lake Shore Dr Mequon WI 53097-2418

LOCKLEAR, HEATHER, actress; b. L.A., Sept. 25, 1961; d. Bill and Diane L.; m. Tommy Lee, 1986 (div. 1994); m. Richie Sambora, 1994. Appeared in (TV series) Dynasty, 1981-89, T.J. Hooker, 1982-87, Going Places, 1990, Melrose Place, 1992—, (films) Firestarter, 1986, Return of the Swamp Thing, 1990, Wayne's World 2, 1993, (TV movies) Twil, 1981, City Killer, 1984, Blood Sport, 1986, Rich Men, Single Women, 1990, Texas Justice, 1995, Shattered Mind, 1996. Office: William Morris Agy 151 S El Camino Dr Beverly Hills CA 90212-2704*

LOCKLIN, WILBERT EDWIN, management consultant; b. Washington, Apr. 2, 1920; s. Wilbert Edwin and Margaret Mae (Franklin) L.; m. Olga Maria Osterwald, June 28, 1947; children: Kenneth, Patricia, Randall. BS, Johns Hopkins U., 1942; LLD, George Williams Coll., 1966; DHum, Springfield Coll., 1994. Vice-pres. Nat. Bur. Pvt. Schs., N.Y.C., 1947-49; account exec. Reuel Estill & Co., N.Y.C., 1949-51; asst. dir. admissions Johns Hopkins, 1945-47, asst. to pres., 1955-65; v.p. Johns Hopkins Fund, 1960-65; pres. Springfield (Mass.) Coll., 1965-85, Locklin Mgmt. Services, 1985—; chmn. bd. dirs., mem. exec. com., salary com., charitable funds com.; chmn. trust com. Bay Bank Valley Trust Co., 1966-91; mem. exec. com. Assn. Ind. Colls. and Univs. in Mass., 1971-83; founding mem. Cooperating Colls. of Greater Springfield.; pres. Cooperating Colls. of Greater Springfield, 1982-83; mem. exec. com., bd. dirs. Business Friends of Arts. Bd. dirs. Springfield Symphony Orch., 1973-83; campaign dir. Elms Coll., 1992-94; sr. advisor Mass. Soc. for Prevention of Cruelty to Animals, 1995—. Served with USAAF, 1942-45. Decorated DFC, Air medal. Home: 225 Prynnwood Rd Longmeadow MA 01106-2754

LOCKMAN, STUART M., lawyer; b. Jersey City, July 18, 1949; s. Albert Korey and Edna Sally (Easton) L.; m. Deena Laurel Young, Dec. 27, 1970; children: Jeffrey, Susan, Karen. BA, U. Mich., 1971, JD, 1974. Bar: Mich. 1974, Fla. 1991; bd. cert. health law specialist, Fla. Ptnr. Honigman Miller Schwartz and Cohn, Detroit, 1974—. Office: Honigman Miller Schwartz & Cohn 2290 1st National Bldg Detroit MI 48226

LOCKMILLER, DAVID ALEXANDER, lawyer, educator; b. Athens, Tenn., Aug. 30, 1906; s. George Franklin and Lotta May (Ulrey) L.; m. Alma Elizabeth Russell, Sept. 23, 1930; children: Franklin Russell, Carlotta Elizabeth Lockmiller Minnis; m. Virginia L. Wilkinson, May 20, 1996. B.Ph., Emory U., 1927, A.M., 1928, LL.D., 1954; J.D., Cumberland U., 1929, LL.D., 1940; Ph.D., U. N.C., 1935; postgrad. summers, Oxford U., Eng., 1937, U. Chgo., 1940, U. Paris, 1952; Litt.D., U. Chattanooga, 1960; L.H.D., Am. U., 1961; EdD, Tenn. Wesleyan Coll., 1962. Bar: Ohio, Mo., Okla., Ark., N.C., Tenn., Supreme Ct. U.S. Practiced in Monett, Mo., 1929-33; research asst. Inst. Research in Social Sci., U. N.C., 1934-35; instr. history and polit. sci. N.C. State U., 1935-36, asst. prof., 1936-38, asso. prof., 1938-41, prof., head dept., 1940-42; pres. U. Chattanooga, 1942-59, Ohio Wesleyan U., 1959-61; exec. dir. Distance Edn. and Tng. Coun., Washington, 1961-72; edn. cons., 1972—; vis. prof. Am. history Emory U., summer 1938, N.C. Coll., Durham, summer 1941; vis. prof. geography Meredith Coll., 1941-42; 1st vice chmn. Am. Council on Edn., 1952-53. Author: Magoon in Cuba, A History of the Second Intervention, 1906-09, 1938, 69, Sir William Blackstone, 1938, 70, History of N.C. State College of Agriculture and Engineering, 1889-1939, 1939, The Consolidation of the University of North Carolina, 1942, General Enoch H. Crowder: Father of Selective Service, 1955, Scholars on Parade: Academic Degrees and Costumes, 1969, 92; contbr. to hist., ednl. jours., encys. Mem. exec. com. N.C. Hist. Highway Markers, 1935-42, Nat. Mental Health Council USPHS; def. adv. com. edn. Armed Forces; mem. Pres.'s Commn. to Argentina Sesquicentennial, 1960; Past mem. U. Senate Meth. Ch. State dept. rep. to colls. and univs. Far East, 1953; hon. trustee U. Chattanooga Found., Rockefeller Found. Recipient Chattanooga Man of Yr. award, 1953, Hon. alumnus award N.C. State U., 1940, NTL Home Study Coun. Man of Yr. award, 1969, Disting. Svc. award United Schs. Bus., 1972, Spl. Achievement award Nat. Assn. Trade and Tech. Schs., 1972, Alumnus medal St. Andrew's Sch., 1980, Honor Leadership award Cleve. Inst. Electronics, 1982, Lifetime Achievement award Samford U., 1994; named to NTL Home Study Coun. Hall of Fame; Travel grantee to Brit. Univs., 1956. Fellow Am. Scandinavian Found.; mem. Assn. Am. Colls. and Univ. (pres. 1960-61), So. Univ. Conf. (exec. sec. 1956-59), Assn. Urban Univs. (past pres.), Internat. Conf. Correspondence Edn., Chattanooga Bar Assn., Chattanooga Exec. Club (ex-pres.), SAR, Am. Hist. Assn., Tenn. Coll. Assn. (pres. 1948-49), So. Assn. Colls. and Secondary Schs. (v.p. 1953), Am. Polit. Sci. Assn., So. Hist. Assn., Bar Assn. Ohio, Am. Mil. Inst., Conf. Latin Am. Studies, State Lit. and Hist. Assn. N.C., Newcomen Soc., Sovereign Order St. John of Jerusalem-Knights of Malta, Phi Beta Kappa, Phi Kappa Phi, Omicron Delta Kappa, Blue Key, Phi Delta Phi, Pi Gamma Mu, Pi Delta Epsilon, Tau Kappa Alpha, Sigma Chi, Alpha Pi Omega, Delta Sigma Rho, Alpha Beta Kappa (founder). Republican. Methodist. Clubs: Masons, KT, Shriners; Rotary (Washington) (past Chattanooga pres., dist. gov.), Kiwanis (Chattanooga) (hon.), Torch International (Washington), Cosmos (Washington). Home: McKendree Towers 4343 Lebanon Rd # 1711 Hermitage TN 37076-1221

LOCKNER, VERA JOANNE, farmer, rancher, legislator; b. St. Lawrence, S.D., May 19, 1937; d. Leonard and Zona R. (Ford) Verdugt; m. Frank O. Lockner, Aug. 7, 1955; children: Dean M., Clifford A. Grad., St. Lawrence (S.D.) High Sch., 1955. Bank teller/bookkeeper First Nat. Bank, Miller, S.D., 1963-66, Bank of Wessington, S.D., 1968-74; farmer/rancher Wessington, 1955—. Sunday sch. tchr. Trinity Luth. Ch., Miller, 1968-72; treas. PTO, Wessington, 1969-70; treas., vice chmn., chmn., state com. woman Hand County Dems., Miller, 1978—. Named one of Outstanding Young Women of Am., Women's Study Club, Wessington, 1970. Mem. Order of Ea. Star (warder, marshall, chaplain 1970—). Avocations: oil painting, crafts, gardening, photography. Home and Office: RR 2 Box 102 Wessington SD 57381-8932

LOCKSHIN, MICHAEL DAN, rheumatologist; b. Columbus, Ohio, Dec. 9, 1937; s. Samuel Dan and Florence (Levin) L.; m. Jane Toby Roberts, Sept. 2, 1965; 1 child, Amanda. AB, Harvard U., 1959, MD, 1963. Diplomate Am. Bd. Internal Medicine. From asst. prof. to prof. Cornell U. Med. Coll., N.Y.C., 1970-89; attending physician Hosp. for Spl. Surgery and N.Y. Hosp., N.Y.C., 1970-89; dir. extramural program Nat. Inst. Arthritis & Musculoskeletal Skin Diseases/NIH, Bethesda, Md., 1989—, acting dir., 1994-95. Contbr. over 100 articles to jours., chpts. to books. Mem. Am. Rheumatism Assn. (2d v.p. 1984-85), La Sociedad Chilena de Reumatologica (hon.), Alpha Omega Alpha. Office: NIAMS/NIH 10 Rm 2C-146 Bethesda MD 20892

LOCKWOOD, DEAN H., physician, pharmaceutical executive; b. Milford, Conn., June 17, 1937; s. Horace Musson and Lucille Ruth (Fengler) L.; m. Carol Hay, June 21, 1958 (div. Mar. 1979); children: Andrew Brooks, Craig Stewart, Wendy Susan; m. Elizabeth East, July 19, 1980. AB, Wesleyan U., 1959; MD, John Hopkin's U., 1963. Intern in medicine Olser Medical Svc., The John Hopkins Hosp., Balt., 1963-64, asst. resident in medicine, 1964-65; staff assoc. sect. of intermediary metabolism Nat. Inst. Arthritis and Metabolic Diseases, NIH, Bethesda, Md., 1965-67; fellow dept pharmacology and experimental therapeutics and of medicine The John Hopkins U., Balt., 1967-69, asst. prof. medicine Sch. Medicine, 1969-74, asst. prof. pharm. and exptl. therapeutics, 1971-76, assoc. prof. medicine, 1974-76; staff physician The John Hopkins Hosp., Balt., 1969-76; dir. Diabetes Mgmt. Clin., The John Hopkins Hosp., Balt., 1971-76; prof. medicine Sch. Medicine U. Rochester, N.Y., 1976-92, head endocrine metabolism unit, dept. medicine, Sch. Medicine, 1976-91; v.p. clin. rsch. Warner Lambert Co., Ann Arbor, Mich., 1991-92, 93—, acting sr. v.p. clin. rsch., 1992-93; staff physician Balt. City Hosp., 1969-76, Strong Meml. Hosp., 1976-91; med. cons. Highland Hospital of Rochester, 1977-91, attending cons. Park Ridge Hosp., 1989-91; assoc. chmn. rsch. dept. medicine U. Rochester, 1991; adj. prof. medicine Sch. Medicine U. Rochester, 1992-93; lectr. in the field. Editorial bd. mem.: Internat. Jour. Obesity, 1975-84, Endocrinology, 1981-85, Am. Jour. Physiology, 1982-88; cons. editor: Jour. Clin. Investigation, 1992—. Recipient Bordon Undergrad. Rsch. award, 1963, NIH Rsch. Career Devel. award, 1969-74; Henry Strong Denison scholar, 1962-63; Am. Diabetes Assn. grantee, 1986-91, NIH grantee, 1969-92. Mem. Am. Diabetes Assn., Am. Fedn. for Rsch., The Endocrine Soc., Am. Soc. Biol. Chemists, Am. Soc. Clin. Investigation, Sigma Xi, Alpha Omega Alpha, Phi Beta Kappa. Home: 3431 Wagner Woods Ct Ann Arbor MI 48103-2167 Office: Warner Lambert 2800 Plymouth Rd Ann Arbor MI 48105

LOCKWOOD, FRANK JAMES, manufacturing company executive; b. San Bernardino, Calif., Oct. 30, 1931; s. John Ellis and Sarah Grace (Roberts) L.; children from previous marraige: Fay, Frank, Hedy, Jonnie, George, Katherine, Bill, Dena; m. 2d. Crystal Marie Miller, 1986. Student, Southeast City Coll., Chgo., 1955, Ill. Inst. Tech., 1963-64, Bogan Jr. Coll., Chgo., 1966. Foreman Hupp Aviation, Chgo., 1951-60; dept. head UARCO, Inc., Chgo., 1960-68; pres. XACT Machine & Engring., Chgo., 1968—; chmn. bd., pres., bd. dirs. Lockwood Engring., Inc., Chgo.; Ill. Nat. Corp., Chgo., and cons. engr., Chgo. Patentee printing equipment, beverage cans, gasoline pump dispenser "Super Pin", bus. forms equipment. Participant Forest Land Mgmt. Program; mem. Ill. Ambassadors; commr. Econ. Devel. Commn., Mt. Vernon, Ill., 1985; mem. bd. County of Jefferson, Ill., 1992—; mem. exec. com., legis. com. Ill. County Bds. Coun. Named Chgo. Ridge Father of the Yr., 1964. Mem. Ill. Divers' Assn. (pres. 1961-62). Lodge: Masons (32 degree), Shriners (past master 2). Home: RR 1 Texico IL 62889-9801 Office: 7011 W Archer Ave Chicago IL 60638-2201

LOCKWOOD, GARY LEE, lawyer; b. Woodstock, Ill., Dec. 3, 1946; s. Howard and Luella Mae (Behrens) L.; m. Cheryl Lynn Wittrock, Jan. 5, 1967; children: Jennifer, Lee, Cynthia. BA magna cum laude, Iowa Wesleyan Coll., 1969; student, Albert Ludwig U., Freiburg in Breisgau, Fed. Republic Germany, 1968-69; JD, Northwestern U., 1976. Bar: Ill. 1976, U.S. Dist. Ct. (no. dist.) Ill. 1976. Assoc. Lord, Bissell & Brook, Chgo., 1976-85, ptnr., 1985—. Bd. dirs. McHenry Sch. Dist. 15, Ill., 1974-85, pres., 1979-80. Served to sgt. U.S. Army, 1970-72. Mem. ABA (bus. and ins. com. 1985—). Methodist. Avocations: sports. Home: 175 N Harbor Dr Chicago IL 60601-7344 Office: Lord Bissel & Brook 115 S La Salle St Ste 3600 Chicago IL 60603-3801

LOCKWOOD, JOANNE SMITH, mathematician educator; b. Quebec City, Can., Nov. 9, 1946; d. Donald William MacKay and Sylvia Eleanor (Howard) Smith; m. Bryce M. Lockwood Jr., Aug. 10, 1968; children: Daren MacKay, Keith McLellan. BA in English, St. Lawrence U., 1968; MBA, Plymouth State Coll., 1980, BA in Math., 1985. Editor Houghton Mifflin Co., Boston, 1969-86; tchr. New Hampton (N.H.) Sch., 1974-76, 80-81; lectr. Plymouth (N.H.) State Coll., 1988—. Author: (textbooks) Beginning Algebra with Applications, 1989, 92, 96, Intermediate Algebra with Applications, 1989, 92, 96, Business Mathematics, 1988, 94, Introductory Algebra with Basic Mathematics, 1989, 96, Algebra with Trigonometry for College Students, 1991, A Review of Geometry, 1993, Prealgebra, 1994, Algebra for College Students: A Functions Approach, 1994. Mem. Am. Math. Assn. of Two Yr. Colls., Text and Acad. Authors Assn. Home: RR 1 Box 180 New Hampton NH 03256-9717

LOCKWOOD, JOHN LEBARON, plant pathologist; b. Ann Arbor, Mich., May 28, 1924; s. George LeBaron and Mary Bonita (Leininger) L.; m. Jean Elizabeth Springborg, Mar. 21, 1959; children: James L., Laura A. Student, Western Mich. Coll., 1941-43; BA, Mich. State Coll., 1948, MS, 1950; PhD, U. Wis., 1953. Asst. prof. Ohio Agrl. Expt. Sta., Wooster, 1953-55; asst. prof. Mich. State U., East Lansing, 1955-61, assoc. prof., 1961-67, prof., 1967-90, prof. emeritus, 1990—. Served with U.S. Army, 1943-46. NSF research fellow, 1970-71. Fellow Am. Phytopathol. Soc. (pres. 1984-85). Home: 1931 Yuma Trl Okemos MI 48864-2744 Office: Mich State Univ Dept Botany And Pathol East Lansing MI 48824

LOCKWOOD, RHODES GREENE, retired lawyer; b. Buchanan, Va., Nov. 26, 1919; s. Rhodes G. and Violet (Bennett) L.; m. Mary Hitchcock, Jan. 22, 1949 (dec. Feb. 1991); children: Mary Howland, Rhodes G., Faith B., Rebecca Ingersoll; m. Linda Uttaro, Feb. 18, 1994. B.A., Williams Coll., 1941; postgrad. U. Va., 1941-42, Va. Poly. Inst., 1946-47; LL.B., Harvard U., 1949. Bar: Mass. bar 1949. Assoc. firm Choate, Hall & Stewart, Boston, 1949-59; ptnr. Choate, Hall & Stewart, 1959-92—. Trustee Brigham and Women's Hosp.; sec., trustee Univ. Hosp.; vice chmn. Wellesley (Mass.) Sch. Com., 1966, chmn., 1967-69; mem. Wellesley Bd. Health. Served with USNR, 1942-52. Mem. Boston Bar Assn., Am. Law Inst., Am. Soc. Hosp. Attys., Mass. Hosp. Assn., Harvard U. Law Sch. Alumni Assn. Democrat. Home: 1 Edgewater Dr Wellesley MA 02181-1617 Office: Choate Hall & Stewart 53 State St Exchange Pl Boston MA 02109

LOCKWOOD, RHONDA J., mental health services professional; b. Jacksonville, N.C., Apr. 4, 1960; d. George Barton and Sally Lynn (Hassell) L. BA, Newberry Coll., 1982; MS in Edn., Youngstown State U., 1988. nat. cert. counselor. Corrections/tng. officer Geauga County Sheriff's Dept., Chardon, Ohio, 1982-87; forensic counselor Human Svcs. Ctrs., Inc., New Castle, Pa., 1987-89; dir. children & family svcs. Marion Citrus Mental Health Ctrs., Inc., Ocala, Fla., 1989-96; co-founder Sexual Abuse Intervention Network, Ocala, 1990-96, chair, 1990-92, Family Svcs. Planning Team, 1992-94; cons. Health & Human Svcs. Bd. Dist. 13, 1993-96. Pol. vol. state campaigns Dem. Party, Warren, Ohio, 1978-85; mem. Sexual Abuse Prevention Edn. Network, New Castle, 1987-88; cons. to gov.'s task force Sex Offenders and Their Victims; cons. Mad Dads Orgn., Ocala, 1993; mem. Juvenile Justice Coun., Ocala, 1993-94; children's svc. rep. Fla. Coun. for Cmty. Mental Health, 1995-96. Recipient Outstanding Teen Vol. award Am. Red Cross, 1977. Fellow N. Eastern Ohio Police Benevolent Assn.; mem. Nat. Mus. for Women in the Arts, Nat. Bd. Cert. Counselors, Chi Sigma Iota, Phi Kappa Phi. Democrat. Avocations: softball, volleyball, golf, fishing. Home: 201 E Main St Archer FL 32618-5517

LOCKWOOD, ROBERT PHILIP, publishing executive; b. Yonkers, N.Y., Dec. 21, 1949; s. Albert Francis and Evelyn (Toburn) L.; m. Christiana Lynn Nowels, July 21, 1973; children—Ryan Robert, Theresa Lynn. B.A. in History, Fairfield U. Assoc. editor Our Sunday Visitor, Huntington, Ind., 1971-77, dir. books, 1982-90, editor, 1977-85, dir., editor in chief, 1985-87, pub., 1987-90, pres., chief exec. officer, 1990—. Author: 70 Years of Our Sunday Visitor, 1982; columnist Catholic Jour.; contbr. articles to profl. jours., numerous periodicals. Chmn. St. Mary's Sch. Bd., Huntington, 1984-85; coach Huntington Cath. H.S. Tennis, 1983-85; bd. dirs. Cath. League for Religious and Civil Rights, 1994—; nat. adv. bd. Cath. Campaign for Am., 1993—. Mem. Cath. Press Assn. (editl. com. 1983—, Best Regular Column 1992, 94). Avocations: writing; tennis. Home: 4919 Long Canon Pl Fort Wayne IN 46804-6534

LOCKWOOD, ROBERT W., management consultant; b. Boise, Idaho, June 11, 1924; s. Walter Thomas and Elizabeth C. (Chamberlain) L.; m. Lois M. Minely, Feb. 19, 1945; children—Linda Kay Lockwood Johnson, Craig H. B.S., U. Calif., Berkeley, 1949, M.B.A., 1950; LL.D. (hon.), Northrop U., 1971. Civilian chief mgmt. Los Angeles procurement dist. U.S. Army, 1955-56; cons. Booz Allen and Hamilton, Los Angeles, 1956-58; v.p. United Calif. Bank, Los Angeles, 1958-75; v.p. acad. affairs Northrop U., 1975-76; asst. to pres. Bradston Hurricane, 1979-80; pres. Diversified Baby Products Internat., West Covina, Calif., 1980—; grad. prof. mgmt. Northrop U., Nat. U., San Diego. Served to 1st lt. USAR, 1942-45. Fellow Am. Inst. Indsl. Engrs. (pres. 1971-72). Club: Masons.

LOCKWOOD, THEODORE DAVIDGE, former academic administrator; b. Hanover, N.H., Dec. 5, 1924; s. Harold John and Elizabeth (Van Campen) L.; m. Elizabeth Anne White, Apr. 13, 1944 (dec. Feb. 1980); children: Tamara Jane Lockwood Quinn, Richard Davidge, Mavis Ferens, Serena Katherine; m. Lucille LaRose Abbot, Sept. 7, 1980. B.A., Trinity Coll., 1948, Litt.D. (hon.), 1981; M.A., Princeton, 1950, Ph.D., 1952; L.H.D., Concord Coll., 1968; LL.D., Union Coll., 1968, U. Hartford, 1969; L.H.D., Wesleyan U., Middletown, Conn., 1970. Instr. great issues Dartmouth, 1952-53; asst. prof. history Juniata Coll., Huntingdon, Pa., 1953-55, Mass. Inst. Tech., 1955-60; dean faculty Concord Coll., Athens, W.Va., 1960-64; provost, dean faculty Union Coll., Schenectady, 1964-68; pres. Trinity Coll., Hartford, Conn., 1968-81, Armand Hammer United World Coll. of Am. West, Montezuma, N.Mex., 1981-93; chmn. Greater Hartford Consortium for Higher Edn., 1972-81. Author: Mountaineers, 1945, Studies in European Socialism, 1960, Our Mutual Concern: The Role of the Independent College, 1968. Bd. dirs. Vols. Internat. Tech. Assistance, 1965-85, chmn., 1966-71; Bd. fellows Trinity Coll., 1962-64, trustee, 1964-81; corporator Hartford Hosp., 1978-81, Hartford Pub. Libr., 1969-81; bd. dirs. Inst. for Living, 1969-81, Edn. Commn. of States, 1969-71, Am. Coun. on Edn., 1977-81; trustee Northwood Sch., Lake Placid, N.Y., 1969-78; dir. adv. coun. Audubon Soc. Expdn. Inst., 1978-90; bd. dirs. Harry Frank Guggenheim Found., 1979—, Nepal adv. com. World Wildlife Fund, 1985-95; dir. Ars Publica, 1989-95. With U.S. Army, 1943-45. Belgian-Am. Fellow, 1959. Mem. Assn. Am. Colls. (dir. 1973-78, chmn. 1976-77, mem. project on undergrad. edn. 1981-85), Greater Hartford C. of C. (dir. 1977-81), Phi Beta Kappa, Pi Gamma Mu. Unitarian.

LOCKWOOD, WILLARD ATKINSON, publisher; b. Washington, Mar. 4, 1924; s. Hanford Nichols and Anna Lillian Atkinson L.; m. Marie Louise Field, June 7, 1947 (div. 1979); children: Andree, Rachel, Winthrop; m. Eleanor Bloch, 1979. B.A., Wesleyan U., 1945; postgrad., Art Students League N.Y.C., 1949-50. Mem. staff book design, prodn. various pubs. N.Y.C., 1947-51; asso. art editor U. Okla. Press, Norman, 1951-53; art editor U. Okla. Press, 1953-55; asst. mng. editor Charles E. Merrill Books, Middletown, Conn., 1955-57; dir. Wesleyan U. Press, Middletown, 1957-80; editor Cornell Maritime Press, 1980-90; Treas. Assn. Am. Univ. Presses, 1970-72, pres., 1976-77. Contbr. articles to profl. publs. Mem. Publishers Lunch Club (N.Y.C.), Phi Beta Kappa. Democrat. Club: Rotarian. Home: 101 Idlewild Ave Easton MD 21601-2814

LOCKYER, CHARLES WARREN, JR., corporate executive; b. Phila., Apr. 6, 1944; s. Charles Warren and Mary Alice (Underwood) L.; B.A., Fordham U., 1966; M.A., Princeton U., 1968, Ph.D., 1971, J.D. Georgetown U., 1995; m. Karen A. Damiani, Jan. 22, 1966; children: Charles Warren III, Larissa A., Daphne M. Vice pres. Fidelity Bank, Phila., 1970-79; v.p., chief fin. officer Pubco Corp., Glenn Dale, Md., 1980-82; exec. v.p. Perpetual Savs. Bank, F.S.B., Alexandria, VA, 1982-90; pres. Alleco Inc., Cheverly, Md., 1991-95; assoc. Fred, Frank, Harris, Schriver & Jacobson, Washington, 1996—; dir. Gulfstream Land & Devel. Corp., Plantation, Fla., 1980-86. Trustee Jeanes Hosp., Phila., 1973-87; dir. Foulkeways at Gwynedd (Pa.), 1975-80; mem. adv. com. classics Princeton U., 1978-83. Woodrow Wilson fellow, 1966. Mem. Phi Beta Kappa. Home: 4409 Glenridge St Kensington MD 20895-4255 Office: Fried Frank Harris Schriver & Jacobson 1001 Pennsylvania Ave NW Washington DC 20004-2505

LODEN, RONALD LYNN, physicist; b. Corpus Christi, Tex., Dec. 23, 1968; s. Kenneth L. and Ethel M. (Sweeten) L. Lab. instr. Tex. A&M U., Kingsville, 1990—. Mem. Soc. Physics Students. Baptist. Avocation: stargazing. Office: Tex A&M U Physics Dept CB175 Kingsville TX 78363

LODER, VICTORIA KOSIOREK, information broker; b. Batavia, N.Y., May 27, 1945; d. Leon Stanley and Jennie Joann (Amatrano) Kosiorek; m. Ronald Raymond Loder, Nov. 6, 1965. BS in Bus. Mgmt., Roberts-Wesleyan Coll., Rochester, N.Y., 1989; MLS, SUNY, Buffalo, 1992; postgrad. in Religious Study, Liberty U., 1993—. Tech. info. specialist Eastman Kodak Co., Rochester, 1985-92; reference libr. Xerox Corp., Webster, N.Y., 1993-95; mgr. XPS strategy and integration libr. Xerox Corp., Fairport, N.Y., 1995—; v.p., treas. Victron Design Svc. USA, Kent, N.Y., 1988—; pres., owner Alpha Omega Info Source, Kent, N.Y., 1993—. Republican. Avocations: clothing design/construction, horticulture/landscape design, floral design.

LODEWICK, PHILIP HUGHES, equipment leasing company executive; b. Bklyn., Dec. 31, 1944; s. Robert John and Louise Mary (Bockhold) L.; m. Christine Helen Lobeck, July 5, 1969; children: Alyssa Erin, Kendra Blythe. BS, U. Conn., 1966, MBA, 1967. With sales dept. IBM Corp., N.Y.C., 1969-71; officer Boothe Fin. Corp., San Francisco, 1971-80; pres. The Tradewell Corp., equipment leasing co., Ridgefield, Conn., 1980—; gen. ptnr. Sierra Assoc. IV, San Francisco, 1981-88; CFO Wicklo's Maple Hill Farm, Ridgefield, 1983—; bd. dirs. Ancora Coffee Roasters Inc., U. Conn. Found.; bd. overseers U. Conn. Bus. Sch. Trustee U. Conn. Found.; bd. dirs. St. Andrew's Luth. Ch., Ridgefield, 1979—; mem. Conn. Refugee Resettlement Commn., 1985-88; bd. dirs., treas. Family Y in Ridgefield, 1985-89; founder, dir. Discovery Ctr., 1986—; founder, pres. A Better Chance in Ridgefield, 1987—. With AUS, 1967-69, Korea. Mem. Computer Lessors and Dealers Assn., Golden Bridge Hounds, L.I. Golden Retreiver Club (pres. 1979-80). Republican. Lutheran. Avocations: golf, tennis, basketball, travel, reading. Home: 201 Spring Valley Rd Ridgefield CT 06877-1229 Office: Tradewell Corp Ridgefield CT 06877

LODGE, ARTHUR SCOTT, mechanical engineering educator; b. Waterloo, Lancashire, Eng., Nov. 20, 1922; s. Wilfred Claude and Jean Dea (Scott) L.; m. Helen Catherine Bannatyne, July 18, 1945; children: Keith Bannatyne, Alison Mary Shambrook, Timothy Patrick. B.A., U. Oxford, 1945, M.A., 1948, D.Phil., 1948. Jr. sci. officer Admiralty, Eng., 1942-45; theoretical physicist NRC, Montreal, Que., Can., 1945-46, Brit. Rayon Research Assn., Manchester, Eng., 1948-60; sr. lectr. Math Inst. Sci. and Tech., U. Manchester, 1961-68; prof. dept. engring. mechanics U. Wis., Madison, 1968-91, Hougen vis. prof., 1991, prof. emeritus, 1991—; v.p. Bannatek Co., Inc., Madison, 1981—. Author: Elastic Liquids, 1964 (citation classics award 1981), Body Tensor Fields..., 1974; contbr. articles to profl. jours.; patentee stressmeter. Recipient Byron Bird award U. Wis.-Madison, 1980; grantee U.S. govt. agys. Fellow Inst. Physics London; mem. NAE, Soc. Rheology (Bingham medal 1971), Brit. Soc. Rheology (Gold medal 1983). Republican. Episcopalian. Avocation: piano playing.

LODGE, EDWARD JAMES, federal judge; b. 1933. BS cum laude, Coll. Idaho, 1957; JD, U. Idaho, 1969. Mem. firm Smith & Miller, 1962-63; probate judge Canyon County, Idaho, 1963-65; judge Idaho State Dist. Ct., 1965-88; U.S. bankruptcy judge State of Idaho, 1988; dist. judge, now chief judge U.S. Dist. Ct. Idaho, 1989—. Recipient Kramer award for excellence in jud. adminstrn.; named three time All-Am., disting. alumnus Coll. Idaho, Boise State U.; named to Hall of Fame Boise State U., Coll. Idaho. Mem. ABA, Idaho Trial Lawyer Assn., Idaho State Bar Assn., U.S. Fed. Judges Assn., Boise State Athletic Assn., Elks Club. Office: US Dist Ct PO Box 040 550 W Fort St Boise ID 83724-0101

LODGE, GEORGE C(ABOT), business administration educator; b. Boston, July 7, 1927; s. Henry Cabot Jr. and Emily (Sears) L.; m. Nancy Kunhardt, Apr. 23, 1949; children: Nancy Lodge Burmeister, Emily Lodge Pingeon, Dorothy Lodge Peabody, Henry, George Jr., David. AB cum laude, Harvard U., 1950; hon. doctorate, INCAE, 1994. Polit. reporter, columnist Boston Herald, 1950-54; dir. info. U.S. Dept. Labor, Washington, 1954-58, asst. sec. labor for internat. affairs, 1958-61, U.S. del. to ILO, chmn. governing body, 1960-61; lectr. Grad. Sch. Bus. Adminstr., Harvard U., Boston, 1961-68, assoc. prof., 1968-72, prof. bus. adminstrn., 1972-91, Jaime and Josefina Chua Tiampo prof. bus. adminstrn., 1991—. Author: Spearheads of Democracy: Labor in the Developing Countries, 1962, Engines of Change: United States Interests and Revolution in Latin America, 1970, The New American Ideology, 1975, The American Disease, 1984, Perestroika for America, 1990, Comparative Business-Government Relations, 1990, Managing Globalization in the Age of Interdependence, 1995; co-author: Ideology and National Competitiveness, 1987; editor: U.S. Competitiveness in the World Economy, 1984. Rep. candidate U.S. Senate, Mass., 1962. With USN, 1945-46. Named one of 10 Outstanding Youn Men in U.S., U.S. Jr. C. of C., 1961, Arthur S. Fleming award, 1961, Lee Kuan Yew fellow Gov. of Singapore, 1991. Mem. Coun. Fgn. Rels., Carnegie Endowment for Internat. Peace (trustee), Robert F. Kennedy Meml. (trustee). Office: Harvard U Bus Sch Soldiers Fld Boston MA 02163

LODGE, JAMES ROBERT, dairy science educator; b. Downey, Iowa, July 1, 1925; s. Labon Fertel Lodge and Margaret Clara (Elliott) Funk; m. Jean Agnes Wessel, June 15, 1947; children—Julie Beth, James Robert. B.S., Iowa State U., 1952, M.S., 1954; Ph.D., Mich. State U., 1957. Research asst. Mich. State U., East Lansing, 1954-57; research asso. U. Ill., Urbana, 1957-60; asst. prof. reproductive physiology U. Ill., 1960-63, asso. prof., 1963-69, prof., 1969-91, prof. emeritus, 1991—. Co-author: Reproductive Physiology and Artificial Insemination of Cattle, 2d edit, 1978; contbr. articles to profl. jours. Asst. coach girls softball Babe Ruth Little League, Urbana, 1972-74. Served with AUS, 1944-46. Recipient Outstanding Instr. award Dairy Club U. Ill., 1969, Alpha Zeta Outstanding Instr. award U. Ill. Coll. Agr., 1981, Campus award for excellence in undergrad. teaching U. Ill., 1984, D.E. Becker award, 1987, Outstanding Advisor award Student Affiliated div. Am. Dairy Sci. Assn., 1988; Alpha Zeta Outstanding Instr. award U. Ill. Coll. Agr., 1991, Karl E. Gardner Outstanding Undergrad. Adviser award, 1991; NIH rsch. fellow, 1969. Fellow Am. Soc. Animal Sci.; mem. Am. Physiol. Soc., AAAS, Soc. Study Reproduction, Am. Dairy Sci. Assn. (student affiliate advisor 1986-88), Am. Soc. Animal Sci., Soc. Cryobiology, N.Y. Acad. Sci., Masons, Sigma Xi, Phi Kappa Phi (chmn. scholarship com. 1973, 77), Gamma Sigma Delta. Mem. commn. edn. Methodist Ch., 1975-78. Home: 1701 S Cottage Grove Ave Urbana IL 61801-5925 Office: U Ill Dept Animal Scis 312 Animal Sci Lab 1207 W Gregory Dr Urbana IL 61801-3838

LODISH, HARVEY FRANKLIN, biologist, educator; b. Cleve., Nov. 16, 1941; s. Nathan H. and Sylvia B. (Friedman) L.; AB, Kenyon Coll., 1962, DSc (hon.), 1982; PhD, Rockefeller U., 1966; m. Pamela Chentow, Dec. 29, 1963; children: Heidi, Martin, Stephanie. Postdoctoral fellow Med. Rsch. Coun. Lab. of Molecular Biology, Cambridge, Eng., 1966-68; asst. prof. biology M.I.T., Cambridge, Mass., 1968-71, assoc. prof., 1971-76, prof., 1976—; vis. scientist Imperial Cancer Rsch. Fund, Lincoln's Inn Fields, London, 1977-78; vis. prof. U. Calif., San Francisco Med. Ctr., 1977, Pa. State U. Med. Ctr., 1977; Staples vis. prof. U. Maine, 1989; Wellcome vis. prof. U. Oreg., 1990; Roering vis. lectr. U. Wash. Med. Sch., 1991; Sackler vis. scholar Tel Aviv U., 1994; Berson Meml. lectr. Internat. Endocrinology Congress, 1992, Presdl. lectr. Internat. Hematology Congress, 1992, McGinnis Meml. lectr., 1994, Sigma Xi lectr., 1994, Harry Eagle Meml. lectr., 1994; cons. scientist medicine Children's Hosp. Med. Ctr., Boston, 1977—; cons. in pediatric oncology Sidney Farber Cancer Inst., 1977—; cons. Ministry Edn. and Rsch., Denmark, 1991-92; mem. Whitehead Inst. Biomed. Rsch.; sci. adv. bd. Damon Biotech., Inc., Fisher Sci. Group, Genzyme, Inc., Arris Pharm. Co., Millennium Corp., Astra AB, Sweden, Interactive Scis., Inc.; pres. Bioinfo. Assocs., Inc.; cons. biotech.; mem. NSF adv. panel in devel. and cellular biology; mem. NIH study sect. of molecular biology and cell biology; adv. bd. Biozentrum, U. Basel, Switzerland, Fred Hutchinson Cancer Ctr., chair, Seattle, Cleve. Clin. Rsch. Found., chair, European Molecular Biology Lab., Heidelberg, Germany; cons. NIH, Am. Cancer Soc. Vice chairperson Gordon Rsch. Conf., 1975, chairperson, 1976, 85, 89. Trustee Kenyon Coll., 1989—. Recipient NIH Career Devel. award, 1971-75, grantee, 1968—, Stadie award and lecture Am. Diabetes Assn., 1989; NSF grantee, 1971—; Am. Cancer Soc. grantee, 1971-76, Guggenheim fellow, 1977-78, Rockefeller fellow, 1962-66. Fellow AAAS, Am. Acad. Microbiology; mem. NAS (mem. editl. bd. proceedings 1996—), Am. Soc. for Microbiology, Am. Soc. of Biol. Chemists (nominating com. 1979, 86), Am. Soc. for Cell Biology (coun. 1983-85), Am. Chem. Soc., European Molecular Biol. Orgn. (assoc. fgn.), Phi Beta Kappa, Sigma Xi. Contbr. numerous articles on biochemistry to profl. jours.; mem. editorial bds. Jour. Biol. Chemistry, 1974-80, 82-87, Jour. Cell Biology, 1974-77, Nucleic Acids Rsch., 1976-88, Jour. Supramolecular Structure, 1978-88, Virology, 1979-84; assoc. editor Molecular and Cellular Biology, 1980-81; editor: Molecular and Cellular Biology, 1982-87; mem. bd. of reviewing editors Science, 1991—. Home: 195 Fisher Ave Brookline MA 02146-5706 Office: Whitehead Inst Biomed Rsch 9 Cambridge Ctr Cambridge MA 02142-1401

LODISH, LEONARD MELVIN, marketing educator, entrepreneur; b. Cleve., Aug. 1, 1943; s. Nathan H. and Sylvia (Friedman) L.; m. Susan Joyce Fischer, July 11, 1965; children: Max, Jacob, Chaim. AB magna cum laude, Kenyon Coll., 1965; PhD, MIT, 1968. Asst. prof. mktg. U. Pa., Phila., 1968-71, assoc. prof., 1971-75, prof. mktg., 1975-87, chmn. mktg. dept., 1991-92, 1984-88, Samuel R. Harrell prof., 1988—; founding dir. Evergreen Health Group, Inc., 1984-91; bd. dirs. Info. Resources, Inc., Chgo., Franklin Electronic Pub. Inc., Mt. Holly, N.J., J&J Snack Foods, Inc., Pennsauken, N.J.; co-founder, prin. Mgmt. Decisions Sys., Inc., Waltham, Mass., 1967-85; co-founder, dir. Shadow Broadcast Svcs., Bala Cynwyd, Pa., 1991—. Author: The Advertising and Promotion Challenge: Vaguely Right or Precisely Wrong?, 1986; mem. editorial bd. Mgmt. Sci., Jour. Mktg. Sci., Mktg. Sci., Jour. Personal Selling and Sales Mgmt.; contbr. articles to profl. jours. Pres. Temple Beth Hillel/Beth El, Wynnewood, Pa., 1983-85, bd. dirs. 1975—. Mem. Inst. Mgmt. Scis. (Franz Edelman award 1987), Ops. Research Soc. Am., Am. Mktg. Assn., Phi Beta Kappa. Jewish. Home: 301 Kent Rd Wynnewood PA 19096-1814 Office: U Pa Wharton Sch Mktg Dept Philadelphia PA 19104

LODWICK, GWILYM SAVAGE, radiologist, educator; b. Mystic, Iowa, Aug. 30, 1917; s. Gwylim S. and Lucy A. (Fuller) L.; m. Maria Antonia De Brito Barata; children by previous marriage: Gwilym Savage III, Philip Galligan, Malcolm Kerr, Terry Ann. Student, Drake U., 1934-35; B.S., State U. Iowa, 1942, M.D., 1943. Resident pathology State U. Iowa, 1947-48, resident radiology, 1948-50; fellow, sr. fellow radiologic and orthopedic pathology Armed Forces Inst. Pathology, 1951; asst., then asso. prof. State U. Iowa Med. Sch., 1951-56; prof. radiology, chmn. dept. U. Mo. at Columbia Med. Sch., 1956-78, research prof. radiology, 1978-83, interim chmn. dept. radiology, 1980-81, chmn. dept. radiology, 1981-83, prof. bioengring., 1969-83, acting dean, 1959, assoc. dean, 1959-64; assoc. radiologist Mass. Gen. Hosp., 1983-88, radiologist, 1988-91; hon. radiologist Mass. Gen. Hosp., Boston, 1991—; vis. prof. dept. radiology Harvard Med. Sch., 1983-93; cons. in field; vis. prof. Keio U. Sch. Medicine, Tokyo, 1974; chmn. sci. program com. Internat. Conf. on Med. Info., Amsterdam, 1983; trustee Am. Registry Radiologic Technologists, 1961-69, pres., 1964-65, 68-69; mem. radiology tng. com. Nat. Inst. Gen. Med. Scis., NIH, 1966-70; com. radiology Nat. Acad. Scis.-NRC, 1970-75; chmn. com. computers Am. Coll. Radiology, 1965, Internat. Commn. Radiol. Edn. and Info., 1969-73; cons. to health care tech. div. Nat. Ctr. for Health Services, Research and Devel., 1971-76; dir. Mid-Am. Bone Tumor Diagnostic Ctr. and Registry, 1971-83; adv. com. mem. NIH Biomed. Image Processing Grant Jet Propulsion Lab., 1969-73; nat. chmn. MUMPS Users Group, 1973-75; mem. radiation study sect. div. research grants NIH, 1976-79, mem. study sect. on diagnostic radiology and nuclear medicine div. research grants, 1979-82, chmn. study sect. on diagnostic radiology div. research grants, 1980-82; mem. bd. sci. counselors Nat. Library of Medicine, 1985, chmn. 1987-89; dir. radiology Spaulding Rehab. Hosp., 1986-92. Adv. editorial bd. Radiology, 1965-86, cons. to editor, 1986-91; adv. editorial bd. Current/Clin. Practice, 1972-88; mem. editorial bd. Jour. Med. Systems, 1976—, Radiol. Sci. Update div. Biomedia, Inc., 1975-83, Critical Revs. in Linguistic Imaging, 1990; mem. cons. editorial bd. Skeletal Radiology, 1977-92, Contemporary Diagnostic Radiology, 1978-80; assoc. editor Jour. Med. Imaging, 1988—. Served to maj. AUS, 1943-46, ETO. Decorated Sakari Mustakallio medal Finland; named Most Disting. Alumnus in Radiology, State U. Ia. Centennial, 1970; recipient Sigma Xi Research award U. Mo., Columbia, 1972, Gold medal XIII Internat. Conf. Radiology, Madrid, 1973, Founder's Gold medal Internat. Skeletal Soc., 1990. Fellow AMA (radiology rev. bd. coun. med. edn., coun. rep. on residency rev. com. for radiology 1969-74), Am. Coll. Radiology (co-chmn. ACR-NEMA standardization com. 1983-90, NEMA Med. Tech. Leadership award 1995); mem. NAS Inst. Medicine, Am. Coll. Med. Informatics (founding), Nat. Acad. Practice in Medicine, Radiol. Soc. N.Am. (3d v.p. 1974-75, chmn. ad hoc com. representing assoc. scis. 1979-87, chmn. assoc. scis. com. 1981-87), Assn. Univ. Radiologists, Mo. Radiol. Soc. (1st pres. 1961-62), Salutis Unitas; hon. mem. Portuguese Soc. Radiology and Nuclear Medicine, Tex. Radiol. Soc., Ind. Roentgen Soc., Phila. Roentgen Ray Soc., Finnish Radio. Soc. (ho.), Rotary, Harvard of Boston Club, Cosmos, Alpha Omega Alpha. Home: 3900 Galt Ocean Dr Apt 307 Fort Lauderdale FL 33308-6622

LÖE, HARALD, dentist, educator, researcher; b. Steinkjer, Norway, July 19, 1926; s. Haakon and Anna (Bruem) L.; m. Inga Johansen, July 3, 1948; children: Haakon, Marianne. DDS, U. Oslo, 1952; D in Odontology, 1961; hon. degree, U. Gothenburg, 1973, Royal Dental Coll., Aarhus, 1980, U. Athens, 1980, Cath. U., Leuven, 1980, U. Lund, 1983, Georgetown U., 1983, U. Bergen, 1985, U. Md., 1986, U. N.J., 1987, Royal Dental Coll., Copenhagen, 1988, U. Toronto, 1989, U. Detroit, 1990, S.C. Med. U., 1990, U. Helsinki, Finland, 1992, Pacific U., 1993, U. Milan, Italy, 1994. Instr. Sch. Dentistry, Oslo U., 1952-55; rsch. assoc. Norwegian Inst. Dental Rsch., 1956-62; Fulbright rsch. fellow, rsch. assoc. dept. oral pathology U. Ill., Chgo., 1957-58; Univ. rsch. fellow Oslo U., 1959-62, asso. prof. dept. periodontology, 1960-61; prof. dentistry, chmn. dept. periodontology Royal Dental Coll., Aarhus, Denmark, 1962-72; asso. dean, dean-elect Royal Dental Coll., 1971-72; prof., dir. Dental Rsch. Inst. U. Mich., Ann Arbor, 1972-74; dean, prof. periodontology Sch. Dental Medicine U. Conn., Farmington, 1974-82; dir. Nat. Inst. Dental Rsch. Nat. Inst. Dental Rsch., Bethesda, Md., 1983-94; univ. prof. Sch. Dental Medicine U. Conn. Health Ctr., Farmington, 1994—; vis. prof. periodontics Hebrew U., Jerusalem, 1966-67; hon. prof. Med. Scis. U. Beijing, 1987; cons. WHO, NIH. Contbr. over 300 articles to sci. publs. With Norwegian Army, 1944-48. Recipient 75th Anniversary award Norwegian Dental Assn., 1958, Aalborg Dental Soc. prize, Denmark, 1965, William J. Gies Periodontology award, 1978, U.S. Surgeon Gen.'s medal and Exemplary award, 1988, Internat. award Swedish Dental Assn., 1989; decorated Knight of Danebrog by Queen of Denmark, 1972, Comdr. of Royal Norwegian Order of Merit by King of Norway, 1989. Mem. AAAS, ADA (gold medal 1994, Callahan medal 1995, Spenadel medal 1995), Am. Coll. Dentists, Nat. Acad. Inst. Medicine, Danish Dental Assn., Am. Acad. Periodontology, Am. Assn. Dental Rsch., Am. Soc. Preventive Dentistry (internat. award), Mass. Dental Soc. (internat. award), Internat. Assn. Dental Rsch. (award for basic rsch. in periodongology 1969, pres. 1980), Internat. Coll. Dentists, Scandinavian Assn. Dental Rsch. Office: U Conn Health Ctr Sch Dental Medicine Farmington CT 06030-1710

LOEB, BEN FOHL, JR., lawyer, educator; b. Nashville, May 15, 1932; s. Ben Fohl and Frances (Paysinger) L.; m. Anne Nelson, Sept. 23, 1961 (div. 1982); children: Charles Nelson, William Nelson. BA, Vanderbilt U., 1955, JD, 1960. Bar: Tenn. 1960, U.S. Supreme Ct. 1966, N.C. 1975. Assoc. Crownover, Branstetter & Folk, Nashville, 1960-64; asst. dir. Inst. Govt. U. N.C., Chapel Hill, 1964—, prof. pub. law and govt. Inst. Govt., 1972—; counsel to N.C. legis. coms. on motor vehicle law and transp., Raleigh, 1973-83; cons. on alcohol beverage control, 1985-89; cons. on wildlife, natural and scenic areas, 1989-93; mem. U. N.C. Faculty Coun., 1994—. Author: Traffic Law and Highway Safety, 1970, Alcohol Beverage Control Law, 1971, Motor Vehicle Law, 1975, Legal Aspects of Dental Practice, 1977, Eminent Domain Procedure, 1984; assoc. editor Vanderbilt Law Rev., 1959-60. Served to 1st lt. U.S. Army, 1955-57. Mem. ABA, Tenn. Bar Assn., Phi Beta Kappa, Phi Delta Phi, Pi Kappa Alpha (chpt. pres. 1954-55), Carolina Club (Chapel Hill). Democrat. Baptist. Home: 17 Bluff Trl Chapel Hill NC 27516-1603 Office: U NC Inst Govt Cb 3330 Knapp Bldg Chapel Hill NC 27599

LOEB, FRANCES LEHMAN, civic leader; b. N.Y.C., Sept. 25, 1906; d. Arthur and Adele (Lewisohn) Lehman; student Vassar Coll., 1924-26; L.H.D. (hon.), NYU, 1977; m. John L. Loeb, Nov. 18, 1926; children: Judith Loeb Chiara, John L., Ann Loeb Bronfman, Arthur Lehman, Deborah Loeb Brice. N.Y.C. commr. for UN and Consular Corps, 1966-78. Exec. com. Population Action Com., Washington; life mem. bd. Children of Bellevue, Inc., 1974-96; bd. dirs. Internat. Presch., Inc., N.Y. Landmarks Conservancy; chmn. bd. East Side Internat. Community Ctr., Inc.; mem. UN Devel. Corp., 1972-94; life trustee Collegiate Sch. for Boys, N.Y.C.; trustee Cornell U., 1979-88, trustee emeritus, 1988-96; trustee Vassar Coll., 1988-96; bd. overseers Cornell U. Med. Coll., 1983-88 (life mem. 1988-96), Inst. Internat. Edn. (life). Mem. UN Assn. (dir.). Clubs: Cosmopolitan, Vassar, Women's City (N.Y.C.). Died May 17, 1996.

LOEB, JANE RUPLEY, university administrator, educator; b. Chgo., Feb. 22, 1938; d. John Edwards and Virginia Pentland (Marthens) Watkins; m. Peter Albert Loeb, June 14, 1958; children: Eric Peter, Gwendolyn Lisl, Aaron John. BA, Rider Coll., 1961; PhD, U. So. Calif., 1969. Clin. psychology intern Univ. Hosp., Seattle, 1966-67; asst. prof. ednl. psychology U. Ill., Urbana, 1968-69, asst. coord. rsch. and testing, 1968-69, coord. rsch. and testing, 1969-72, asst. to vice chancellor acad. affairs, 1971-72, dir. admissions and records, 1972-81, assoc. prof. ednl. psychology, 1973-82, assoc. vice chancellor acad. affairs, 1981-94, prof. edn. psychology, 1982—. Author: College Board Project: the Future of College Admissions, 1989. Chmn. Coll. Bd. Coun. on Entrance Svcs., 1977-82; bd. govs. Alliance for Undergrad. Edn., 1988-93; active charter com. Coll. Bd. Acad. Assembly, 1992-93. HEW grantee, 1975-76. Mem. APA, Am. Ednl. Rsch. Assn., Nat. Coun. Measurement in Edn., Harvard Inst. Ednl. Mgmt. Avocation: the french horn. Home: 1405 N Coler Ave Urbana IL 61801-1625 Office: U Ill 1310 S 6th St Champaign IL 61820-6925

LOEB, JEROME THOMAS, retail executive; b. St. Louis, Sept. 13, 1940; s. Harry W. and Marjorie T. Loeb; m. Carol Bodenheimer, June 15, 1963; children: Daniel W, Kelly E. BS, Tufts U., 1962; MA, Washington U., St. Louis, 1964. Asst. dir. rsch., dir. EDP, div. v.p., dir. mgmt. info. scvs. Famous-Barr div. May Dept. Stores Co., St. Louis, 1964-74, v.p. mgmt. info. svcs./EDP parent co., 1974-77, sr. v.p., CFO Hecht's div., Washington, 1977-79; exec. v.p. devel. May Dept. Stores Co., St. Louis, 1979-81, exec. v.p., CFO, 1981-86, vice chmn., CFO, 1986-93, pres., 1993—; also bd. dirs. Bd. dirs. Jr. Achievement of Mississippi Valley, 1980—, chmn., 1993-95; bd. dirs. Jr. Achievement Nat. Bd., 1988—; bd. commrs. St. Louis Sci. Ctr., 1991—, chmn., 1995—; bd. dirs. Barnes-Jewish Hosp., 1984—, vice chmn. 1988, bd. dirs. BJC Health Sys., 1992—; mem. pres. cabinet Am. Jewish Com., 1994—. Mem. Westwood Country Club, Boone Valley Golf Club. Office: May Dept Stores Co 611 Olive St Saint Louis MO 63101-1721

LOEB, JOHN LANGELOTH, banker, broker; b. St. Louis, Nov. 11, 1902; s. Carl Morris and Adeline (Moses) L.; m. Frances Lehman, Nov. 18, 1926; children: Judith Loeb Chiara, John Langeloth, Ann Loeb Bronfman, Arthur Lehman, Deborah Loeb Brice. Student, Dartmouth Coll., 1920-21; SB cum laude, Harvard U., 1924, LLD (hon.), 1971. With Am. Metal Co. (Pitts. office), 1924-26, 26-28, Wertheim & Co., 1929-30; ptnr. Loeb, Rhoades & Co. Inc., N.Y.C., 1931-55, sr. ptnr., 1955-77, chmn., 1977-79; chmn. fin. com. Loeb, Rhoades, Hornblower & Co., 1978-79; vice chmn. Loeb Ptnrs. Corp., N.Y.C., 1980—, also bd. dirs.; gov. N.Y. Stock Exchange, 1951-54; adv. com. on internat. bus. problems State Dept., 1967-69, 70—. Hon. trustee Montefiore Hosp.; chmn., CEO Jacob and Valeria Langeloth Found.; bd. overseers Harvard U., 1962-68; hon. gov. N.Y. Hosp.; trustee, hon. chmn. Inst. Fine Arts, NYU. With Treasury Dept., Office War Moblzn., 1942-44, Washington. Mem. Coun. Fgn. Rels., N.Y. C. of C., SAR, Sky Club, Century Country Club (White Plains, N.Y.), Harvard Club, Lyford Cay Club. Office: Loeb Ptnrs Corp 375 Park Ave New York NY 10152

LOEB, JOHN LANGELOTH, JR., investment counselor; b. N.Y.C., May 2, 1930; s. John Langeloth and Frances (Lehman) L.; children: Nicholas, Alexandra. Grad., Hotchkiss Sch., 1948; A.B. cum laude, Harvard, 1952, M.B.A., 1954; LL.D. (hon.), Georgetown U. With Loeb, Rhoades & Co., N.Y.C., from 1956; gen. ptnr., mem. mgmt. com. Loeb, Rhoades & Co., 1964-73, mng. ptnr., pres., 1971-73, ltd. ptnr., 1973-84; chmn. bd. Holly Sugar Co., Colo., 1969-71; amb. to Denmark Copenhagen, 1981-83; chmn. John L. Loeb, Jr. Assocs., N.Y.C., 1984—; U.S. del. to 38th session Gen. Assembly of UN; spl. advisor environ. matters to Gov. Nelson A. Rockefeller, 1967-73; chmn. Gov. N.Y. Coun. Environ. Advisors, 1970-75; pres. Winston Churchill Found., 1981—; trustee Ednl. Testing Svc., Princeton, N.J., 1986-93. Trustee Montefiore Hosp. and Med. Ctr. Mus. City N.Y., 1962-94, John and Frances L. Loeb Found., 1957—, Am. U., Washington; mem. vis. com. Sch. Pub. Health, and Loeb Drama Ctr., 1988-94. Lt. USAF, 1954-56. Decorated Grand Cross of the Order of Dannebrog (Denmark); recipient Lee Max Friedman award Am. Jewish Hist. Soc., Disting. Patriot award SAR; Hon. Comdr. of the Most Excellent Order of the Brit. Empire. Mem. Downtown Assn. (N.Y.C.), City Midday Club, Harvard Club, Century Country Club, Sleepy Hollow Club (Westchester, N.Y.), Buck's Club, Brooks's Club, Hurlingham Club (London), Royal Swedish Yacht Club (Stockholm), Royal Danish Yacht Club (Copenhagen), Lyford Cay Club (Nassau, Bahamas). Home: Ridgeleigh 194 Anderson Hill Rd Purchase NY 10577-2101 Office: Loeb Family Office 375 Park Ave Ste 801 New York NY 10152-0899

LOEB, JOYCE LICHTGARN, interior designer, civic worker; b. Portland, Oreg., May 20, 1936; d. Elias Lichtgarn and Sylvia Amy (Margulies) Freedman; m. Stanley Robinson Loeb, Aug. 14, 1960; children: Carl Eli, Eric Adam. Student U. Calif.-Berkeley, 1954-56; BS, Lewis and Clark Coll., 1958; postgrad. art and architecture, Portland State U., 1976. Tchr. art David Douglas Sch. Dist., Portland, 1958-59, 61-64; tchr., chmn. art dept. Grant Union High Sch. Dist., Sacramento, 1959-60; designer, pres. Joyce Loeb Interior Design, Inc., Portland, 1976—; cons. designer to various developers of health care facilities. Chairperson fundraisers for civic orgns. and Jewish orgns.; mem. women's com. Reed Coll.; bd. dirs., mem. exec. com. Inst. Judaic Studies, 1989-92; bd. dirs. Young Audiences, Inc., Portland, 1970-76, chmn. long range planning, 78-80; bd. dirs. Met. Family Svc., Portland, 1968-71, Portland Opera Assn., 1978-84, Arts Celebration, Inc., Portland, 1984—, Friends of Chamber Music; chmn. Artquake Festival, 1985, Operaball, 1987, Children's Charity Ball Com., 1989, Women's Bd. Jewish Fedn. Portland, 1993-96, pres. 1996—; sec. exec. com., bd. dir. Oreg. Children's Theatre, 1992—; v.p. Beth Israel Sisterhood, 1981-83; bd. dirs., trustee Congregation Beth Israel, 1986-92, chmn. art interior design com.; trustee Robison Home, 1990-96; bd. dirs. Friends of Chamber Music, 1994—, Nat. Found. for Jewish Culture, 1996. Recipient Women of Distinction award in architecture and design Girl Scouts Columbia River Coun., 1994. Mem. Am. Soc. Interior Design (allied, bd. dirs. 1993-95), Multnomah Athletic Club. Democrat. Home: 4371 NW Tam-O-Shanter Way Portland OR 97229

LOEB, MARSHALL ROBERT, journalist; b. Chgo., May 30, 1929; s. Monroe Harrison and Henrietta (Benjamin) L.; m. Elizabeth Peggy Loewe, Aug. 14, 1954; children: Michael, Margaret. BJ, U. Mo., 1950; postgrad., U. Goettingen, Germany, 1950-51. Reporter Garfield News and Austinite, Chgo., 1944-45; reporter, columnist Garfieldian and Austin News, Chgo., 1946-47, 49-51; reporter Columbia Missourian, 1948-50; staff corr. UP, Frankfurt, Germany, 1952-54; reporter St. Louis Globe-Democrat, 1955-56; contbg. editor Time mag., 1956-61, assoc. editor, 1961-65, sr. editor, 1965-80, econs. editor and columnist, 1978-80; mng. editor Money Mag., 1980-86; editor Time Inc. Mag. Devel., 1984-86; mng. editor Fortune, 1986-94, editor-at-large, 1994-96, columnist, 1996—; daily commentator CBS Radio Network; assoc. fellow Yale U., Berkeley Coll., 1977—. Author (with William Safire): Plunging Into Politics, 1962, Marshall Loeb's Money Guide, 1983, ann. edits. 1985—, Money Minutes, 1986, Lifetime Financial Strategies, 1996. Trustee NYU Stern Sch. of Bus. Recipient INGAA award U. Mo., 1966; Gerald M. Loeb award UCLA Sch. Mgmt., 1974; John Hancock award, 1974; Champion Media award for econ. understanding citation, 1978, first prize, 1981; Dallas Press Club award, 1978; Freedoms Found. award, 1978; N.Y. citation Sigma Delta Chi, 1979; Nat. Assn. Home Builders award, 1984; Great Am. Patriot award Jefferson Barracks Chapel Assn., 1988, Journalism medal U. Mo., 1988, N.Y. award Navy League, 1989, TJFR Bus. Journalism Luminaries award 1990. Fellow World Econ. Forum (Geneva), Nat. Neurofibromatosis Found. (dir.), Econ. Club of N.Y. (dir.), NYU Stern Sch. of Bus. (trustee), Knight-Bagehot Fellowship (chair bd. adv.), Recording for the Blind and Dyslexic (dir.); mem. Coun. Fgn. Rels., Brit.-Am. C. of C. (v.p. 1979-81, dir. 1979-84), Am. Soc. Mag. Editors (v.p. 1986-88, pres. 1988-90), Overseas Press Club Am. (dir. 1963-65, treas. 1964-65). Jewish. Home: 31 Montrose Rd Scarsdale NY 10583-1129 Office: Fortune Mag Time & Life Bldg 1271 Avenue Of The Americas New York NY 10020

LOEB, NACKEY SCRIPPS, publisher; b. Los Angeles, Feb. 24, 1924; d. Robert Paine and Margaret (Culbertson) Scripps; m. William Loeb, July 15, 1952 (dec. 1981); children—Nackey Loeb Scagliotti, Edith Loeb Tomasko. Student, Scripps Coll. Pub. Union-Leader Corp., Manchester, N.H., 1981—, Neighborhood Pubs., Inc., Goffstown, N.H., 1993—. Republican. Baptist. Home: Paige Hill Rd Goffstown NH 03045 Office: Union Leader Corp 100 William Loeb Dr Manchester NH 03109-5309

LOEB, PETER KENNETH, money manager; b. N.Y.C., Apr. 8, 1936; s. Carl M. and Lucille H. (Schamberg) L.; m. Jeanette Winter, Nov. 1, 1980; 1 child, Alexander Winter; children by previous marriage: Peter Kenneth Jr., Karen Elizabeth, James Matthew. BA, Yale U., 1958; MBA, Columbia U., 1961. Security analyst Loeb, Rhoades & Co., N.Y.C., 1961-66, syndicate dept. ptnr., 1966-71, with trading/instl. sales sect., 1971-79; mng. dir. corp. fin. Shearson Corp., N.Y.C., 1979-83; mng. dir., portfolio mgr. PaineWebber Inc., N.Y.C., 1983-92; ptnr. Shufro, Rose & Ehrman, N.Y.C., 1992—; mem. com. on securities Am. Stock Exch., 1978-80; mem. del. to Beijing symposium N.Y. Stock Exch., 1986. Coach, games ofcl. Manhattan Spl. Olympics, 1980—; bd. dirs., co-chmn. devel. com. N.Y. Spl. Olympics, 1985-89; chmn. devel. com. Spl. Olympics Internat., 1986—, bd. dirs., 1989—; mem. com. on univ. investments Columbia U., 1977-85, trustee, 1979-85, vice-chmn. alumni adv. bd., 1986-92; fund chmn. Columbia U. Bus. Sch., 1964-66, mem. alumni counseling bd., 1970—, pres. Columbia Bus. Sch. Assocs., 1971-73, mem. bd. overseers, 1976—; dir. City Ctr. Theatre Found.; trustee Allen Stevenson Sch., 1969—, Langeloth Found., 1972—, N.Y. Infirmary-Beekman Downtown Hosp., 1978-85; mem. adv. bd. Atoms Track Club Bedford-Stuyvesant, 1970—; cert. track ofcl. USA Track and Field, 1985—; mem. marshals com. Westchester Golf Classic, 1970—; contbg. mem. Mus. Modern Art, Met. Mus. Art; mem. Statue of Liberty/Ellis Island Found., Friends of Kennedy Ctr., Friends of the Philharm., Friends of Carnegie Hall; mem. Wall St. com. N.Y. Urban Coalition, 1969-71; mem. exec. bd. new leadership div. Fedn. Jewish Philanthropies, 1963-64; vice-chmn. Pacesetter com. Greater N.Y. coun. Boy Scouts Am., 1966-67. Recipient Alumni medal for conspicuous service Columbia U., 1975, Alumni medal for disting. service Columbia U. Bus. Sch., 1976. Mem. SAR, Securities Traders Assn. N.Y., Investment Assn. N.Y. (exec. bd. 1969), Securities Industry Assn. (governing council 1977-79, minority capital com. 1980-85, trustee Econ. Edn. Found. 1986—, vice chmn. 1992—), Nat. Assn. Security Dealers (chmn. dist. 12 com. 1981, gov. 1982-85, chmn. corp. fin. com. 1983-86, vice-chmn. fin. 1984, mem. arbitration com. 1986-89, NASDAQ qualifications com. 1989—), N.Y.C. Baseball Fedn. (pres. 1968-91, chmn. 1992—, award for disting. service 1976), Univ. Club, Doubles Club, Bond Club, Century Country Club, Beta Gamma Sigma, Alpha Kappa Psi, Phi Gamma Delta. Office: Shufro Rose & Ehrman 745 5th Ave New York NY 10151

LOEB, RONALD MARVIN, lawyer; b. Denver, Sept. 24, 1932; s. Ellis and Lillian (Mosko) L.; m. Shirley Ross; children: Joshua Ross, Gabriel Ross,

Daniel Seth, Jennifer Miriam, Rachel Sarah.. AB with highest honors, UCLA, 1954; LLB cum laude, Harvard U., 1959. Bar: Calif. 1960. Assoc. Irell & Manella Law Firm, L.A., 1959-64, ptnr., 1964—; bd. dirs. Mattel, Inc., Internat. Transpersonal Ctr.; course presenter The Esalen Inst., 1995-96. Co-editor: Duties and Responsibilities of Outside Directors. Mem. adv. bd. Securities Regulation Inst., U. Calif., San Diego; trustee Crossroads Sch. Arts and Scis., Santa Monica, Calif., 1987—; past chmn. Pacific Crest Outward Bound Sch.; founding trustee, dir. World Bus. Acad. Mem. ABA, State Bar Assn. Calif., L.A. County Bar Assn., Beverly Hills Bar Assn., Nat. Assn. Securities Dealers (legal adv. bd.). Office: Irell & Manella 1800 Avenue Of The Stars Los Angeles CA 90067-4211

LOEB, VERNON FREDERICK, journalist; b. Akron, Ohio, Mar. 10, 1956; s. David Frederick and Betty Jane (Miller) L.; m. Patricia Ford, Jan. 7, 1984; children: Kathryn Magdalen, David Frederick, Julia Miller, Frances Ford. BA, U. N.C., 1978. Del. corr. Phila. Inquirer, Dover, Del., 1978-79; capital corr. Phila. Inquirer, Harrisburg, Pa., 1979-82; edn. writer Phila. Inquirer, Phila., 1982-84, city hall bureau chief, 1984-89, 92—; S.E. Asia corr. Phila. Inquirer, Manila, Philippines, 1989-92; city hall bur. chief Phila. Inquirer, 1992—. Methodist. Avocations: photography, tennis, running. Office: Phila Inquirer 400 N Broad St Philadelphia PA 19130-4015

LOEBIG, WILFRED F., health care executive; b. Wesley, Iowa, Feb. 3, 1936; s. Wifred Francis and Faye Maxine L.; m. Margaret Ann Schmitz, Oct. 6, 1960; children: William, Brian, Mary, Margaret, Maria, Blaise. BS, U. Iowa, 1958, MS, 1960. Admistrv. asst. Mercy Hosp., Council Bluff, Iowa, 1958-60; assoc. adminstr. Ft. Dodge (Iowa) Mercy Hosp., 1960-71; pres. St. Elizabeth Hosp., Appleton, Wis., 1971-77; exec. dir. Timken Mercy Med. Ctr., Canon, Ohio, 1977-83; pres., chief exec. officer Wheaton (Ill.) Franciscan Svcs., Inc., 1983—; pres. Area Hosp. Adminstrs. Coun.; mem. Ohio Adv. Coun. to Bd. Nursing Edn. and Nurse Registration. Served with Med. Service Corps, USAF, 1960-63. Mem. Am. Coll. Hosp. Admistrs., Am. Hosp. Assn., Ohio Hosp. Assn. (trustee), Greater Canton C. of C., Rotary. Roman Catholic. Office: Wheaton Franciscan Svcs Inc PO Box 667 Wheaton IL 60189-0667*

LOEBLICH, HELEN NINA TAPPAN, paleontologist, educator; b. Norman, Okla., Oct. 12, 1917; d. Frank Girard and Mary (Jenks) Tappan; m. Alfred Richard Loeblich, Jr., June 18, 1939; children: Alfred Richard III, Karen Elizabeth Loeblich, Judith Anne Loeblich Covey, Daryl Louise Loeblich Valenzuela. BS, U. Okla., 1937, MS, 1939; PhD, U. Chgo., 1942. Instr. geology Tulane U., New Orleans, 1942-43; geologist U.S. Geol. Survey, Washington, 1943-45, 47-59; mem. faculty UCLA, 1958—, prof. geology, 1966-84, prof. emeritus, 1985—, vice chmn. dept. geology, 1973-75; research assoc. Smithsonian Instn., 1954-57; assoc. editor Cushman Found. Foraminiferal Research, 1950-51, incorporator, hon. dir., 1950—. Author: (with A.R. Loeblich Jr.) Treatise on Invertebrate Paleontology, part C, Protista 2, Foraminiferida, 2 vols., 1964, Foraminiferal Genera and Their Classification, 2 vols., 1987, Foraminifera of the Sahul Shelf and Timor Sea, 1994; author: The Paleobiology of Plant Protists, 1980; mem. editl. bd. Palaeoecology, 1972-82, Paleobiology, 1975-81; contbr. articles to profl. jours., govt. publs. and encys. Recipient Joseph A. Cushman award Cushman Found., 1982; named Woman of Yr. in Sci. Palm Springs Desert Mus., 1987; Guggenheim fellow, 1953-54. Fellow Geol. Soc. Am. (sr., councilor 1979-81); mem. Paleontol. Soc. (pres. 1984-85, patron 1987, medal 1982), Soc. Sedimentary Geology (councilor 1975-77, hon. mem. 1978, Raymond C. Moore medal 1984), UCLA Med. Ctr. Aux. (Woman of Yr. medal), AAUP, Internat. Paleontological Assn., Paleontol. Rsch. Inst., Am. Microscopical Soc., Am. Inst. Biol. Scis., Phi Beta Kappa, Sigma Xi. Home: 1556 W Crone Ave Anaheim CA 92802-1303

LOEB-MUNSON, STELLA MARIE, school system administrator; b. Cleve., Feb. 14, 1943; d. Charles Harold and Beulah Hortense (Franklin) Loeb; children: Charles William, Maisha Kwetu. BS in Elem. Edn., Kent State U., 1969; MS in Ednl. Adminstrn., St. John Coll., 1974. Tchr. Cleve. Pub. Schs., 1969-72; freshman advisor spl. svcs., dir. peer counseling Case Western Res. U., Cleve., 1977-80, asst. dir. spl. svcs., 1977-80; classroom tchr. East Cleveland (Ohio) City Schs., 1981-84, curriculum specialist, 1984-85, bldg. prin., 1985—; mem. adv. bd. Young Audiences of Greater Cleve., Inc.; dist. chair East Cleve. Computer Com., 1988—; facilitator, presenter Ohio Dept. Edn., 1991, Ohio Acad. for Prins., 1987-91; presenter Cleve. State U., Lakeland C.C., 1991. Mem. program adv. com. Young Audiences Greater Cleve., 1991. Stella Loeb-Munson day proclaimed by East Cleve. City Coun. and Mayor, 1991; recipient Disting. Arts Educator award Ohio Arts Edn. Assn., 1994, Ohio N.E. Regional Disting. Arts Educator award, 1994; named Nat. Disting. Prin. U.S. Secondary Edn., 1991, Prin. Leadership Nat. Safety Ctr., Nat. Assn. Elem. Sch. Prins., Nat. Assn. Secondary Sch. Prins., 1992. Mem. N.E. Ohio Computer Consortium (bd. dirs. 1988—), ASCD, Nat. Assn. Elem. Sch. Adminstrs., Ohio Assn. Elem. Sch. Adminstrs. (Disting. Prin. Ohio 1991), Phi Delta Kappa (greater Cleve. interuniv. chpt., named Disting. Educator of Yr. 1992). Democrat. Avocations: computers, reading, crochet. Office: Caledonia Sch 914 Caledonia Ave Cleveland OH 44112-2319

LOEFFEL, BRUCE, software company executive, consultant; b. Bklyn., Aug. 13, 1943; s. Samuel and Loretta (Bleiweiss) L.; children: Alisa, Joshua. BBA, Pace U., 1966; MBA, St. John's U., 1971. Certified data processor. Mgr. fin. systems Gibbs & Hill Inc., N.Y.C., 1973-76; mgr. sales, tech. support Mgmt. Sci. Am. Inc., Fort Lee, N.J., 1976-81; dir. mktg. Info. Scis., Inc., Montvale, N.J., 1981-82; dir. bus. devel. Cullinet Software, Inc., Westwood, Mass., 1982-85; exec. v.p. strategic planning Online Data Base Software Inc., Pearl River, N.Y., 1985-88; pres. Corp. Application Software, Inc., Nyack, N.Y., 1988-94; sr. dir. IMRS, Inc., Stamford, Conn., 1994—, Hyperion Software, Inc., 1994—. With U.S. Army, 1966-71. Mem. Inst. Cert. Computer Profls. Democrat. Jewish. Avocations: sports, electronics. Home: 107 High Ave Apt 308 Nyack NY 10960-2500 Office: 777 Long Ridge Rd Stamford CT 06902-1247

LOEFFLER, FRANK JOSEPH, physicist, educator; b. Ballston Spa, N.Y., Sept. 5, 1928; s. Frank Joseph and Florence (Farrell) L.; m. Eleanor Jane Chisholm, Sept. 8, 1951; children: Peter, James, Margaret, Anne Marie. B.S. in Engring. Physics, Cornell U., 1951, Ph.D. in Physics, 1957. Research asso. Princeton U., 1957-58; mem. faculty Purdue U., Lafayette, Ind., 1958—; prof. physics Purdue U., 1962—; vis. prof. Hamburg U., Germany, 1963-64, Heidelberg U., Germany, CERN, Switzerland, 1971, Stanford U. Linear Accelerator Ctr., 1980-83; trustee, mem. exec. com., chmn. high energy com. Argonne Univs. Assn., 1972-76, 78-79, mem. com. on fusion programs, 1979-80; vis. prof. U. Hawaii, 1985-86. Contbr. to profl. publs. Recipient Antarctic Svc. medal NSF/USN, 1990, Ruth and Joel Spira award for outstanding tchg., 1992. Fellow Am. Phys. Soc., Sigma Xi, Tau Beta Pi. Exptl. research in astrophysics, high energy gamma ray astronomy, high energy particle interactions using counter-wire chamber techniques, prodn. resonant state from strong and electromagnetic interactions and on-line data acquisition-processing systems, cold fusion research. Established gamma ray astronomy lab. at South Pole, Antarctica, 1989, 91, 92. Home: 437 Maple St West Lafayette IN 47906-3016 Office: Purdue U Dept Physics Lafayette IN 47907

LOEFFLER, GARRY ANTONE, principal, municipal official; b. Lewiston, Idaho, Mar. 12, 1941; s. John Antone and Germaine Agnes (Meyer) L.; m. Bonnie Louise Ferguson, Dec. 28, 1968; children: Stacey Anne, Brian John, Bradley Scott. BS in Edn., U. Idaho, 1963; MS in Sch. Adminstrn., Calif. State U., Hayward, 1983. Tchr. Roosevelt Sch., San Leandro, Calif., 1965-70, vice prin., 1970-74; prin. Wash. Sch., San Leandro, Calif., 1975-80, Wilson Sch., San Leandro, Calif., 1980-85; prin. Garfield Sch., San Leandro, Calif., 1985—, facilitator conversion to yr.-round edn. Mem. city coun. City of San Leandro, 1994—. Lt. U.S. Army, 1963-65. Mem. ASCD, Am. Assn. Sch. Adminstrs., Assn. Calif. Sch. Adminstrs., San Leandro Adminstrs. Assn. (pres. 1991, Outstanding Sch. Adminstr. award 1992), World Future Soc., Phi Delta Kappa. Democrat. Roman Catholic. Avocations: model railroading, reading, writing, cartooning, traveling. Home: 235 Begier Ave San Leandro CA 94577-2813 Office: Garfield YRE Sch 13050 Aurora Dr San Leandro CA 94577-3159

LOEFFLER, JAMES JOSEPH, lawyer; b. Evanston, Ill., Mar. 7, 1931; s. Charles Adolph and Margaret Bowe L.; m. Margo M. Loeffler, May 26, 1962; children—Charlotte Bowe, James J. B.S., Loyola U.; J.D., Northwestern U. Bar: Ill. 1956, Tex. 1956. Assoc. Fulbright & Jaworski, Houston, 1956-69, ptnr., 1969-86, sr. ptnr., 1986; sr. ptnr. Chamberlain, Hrdlicka, White, Johnson & Williams, Houston, 1986-90; pvt. practice law Houston, 1990—. Mem. ABA, Ill. Bar Assn., Tex. Bar Assn., Houston Bar Assn., Houston Country Club. Office: 808 Travis 1616 Niels Esperson Bldg Houston TX 77002

LOEFFLER, RICHARD HARLAN, retail and technology company executive; b. Kansas City, Mo., Sept. 15, 1934; s. Sidney A. and Lily (Cowell) L.; m. Sheila Kay Gilligan, July 7, 1984; children: Kimberly Anne, Melissa Anne; stepchildren: Patrick K. Gilligan, Todd M. Gilligan. Student, U. Mo.; M.B.A., Pepperdine U., 1975. Ptnr. Foristall & Co., L.A., 1960-65; pres. Beverly Hills Film Corp., Calif., 1962-65; v.p. Buttes Gas and Oil Corp., Oakland, Calif., 1965-66; exec. v.p. TRE Corp., Beverly Hills, Calif., 1966-72; chmn., pres. Simplex Industries, Adrian, Mich., 1972-76; pres., chief oper. officer TRE Corp., L.A., 1976-86; chmn., CEO, MemTech Corp., Beverly Hills, 1987-91; chmn. Am. Builders Hardware Corp., Beverly Hills, Calif., 1991—; chmn., CEO RHL Mgmt. Group, Inc., Beverly Hills, Calif., 1992—; pres., COO, bd. dirs. Standard Brands Paint Co., Torrance, Calif., 1992-93; bd. dirs. Alpha Microsystems, Santa Ana, Calif., Future Flow Sys. Inc., Newbury Park, Calif., Lorus Corp., Beverly Hills, Calif.; chmn., CEO Hawaiian Grocery Stores Ltd., 1996—. Mem. bus. coun. Nat. Democratic Com., Washington, 1983—; trustee Internat. Assn. for Shipboard Edn.; bd. dirs. U. So. Calif. Cancer Rsch. Assocs. Office: 2915 Kaihikapu St Honolulu HI 96819

LOEFFLER, ROBERT HUGH, lawyer; b. Chgo., May 27, 1943; s. Julius and Faye (Fink) L.; m. Jane Canter, Sept. 6, 1970; children: James Benjamin, Charles Edward. AB magna cum laude, Harvard Coll., 1965; JD cum laude, Columbia U., 1968. Bar: N.Y. 1969, U.S. Ct. Appeals (2d cir.) 1969, D.C. 1970, U.S. Ct. Appeals (D.C. cir.) 1972, U.S. Supreme Ct. 1976, U.S. Ct. Appeals (9th cir.) 1981, U.S. Ct. Appeals (Fed. cir.) 1992. Law clk. to Hon. Harold R. Medina U.S. Ct. Appeals, 1968-69; assoc. Covington & Burling, Washington, 1969-76; assoc., ptnr. Isham, Lincoln & Beale, Washington, 1976-79; mng. ptnr. Morrison & Foerster, Washington, 1980-89, sr. ptnr., 1990—. Chmn. consumer com. Muskie presdl. campaign, 1972. Mem. ABA (vice chmn. energy law com. adminstrv. law sect. 1980-85), Am. Intellectual Property Law Assn., Fed. Energy Bar Assn. (chmn. oil pipeline regulation), Columbia Law Sch. Assn. Washington (pres. 1993, nat. v.p. 1994—), Univ. Club, Std. Club, Harvard Club (N.Y.C.). Home: 2607 36th Pl NW Washington DC 20007-1414 Office: Morrison & Foerster Ste 5500 2000 Pennsylvania Ave NW Washington DC 20006-1812

LOEFFLER, WILLIAM ROBERT, quality productivity specialist, engineering educator; b. Cleve., Aug. 31, 1949; s. Harry T. and Frances R. (Pearson) L.; children: Lindsay Brooke, Kelly Lynn, Robert Jason. BA, Wittenberg U., 1971; MA, SUNY-Stony Brook, 1972; Ed. Specialist, U. Toledo, 1979; PhD, U. Mich., 1984. Dir. alt. learning ctr. Lucas County Schs., Toledo, 1977-79; dir. chem. and metall. svcs. Toledo Testing Lab., 1979-82; pres. Chem. Resources, Lambertville, Mich., 1982-83; v.p. Benchmark Techs., Toledo, 1983-86; pres. Loeffler Group, Inc., 1986—; pres. Tech. Soc. Toledo, 1985-86; conf. chmn. Am. Soc. Quality Control. Deming Conf., Toledo, 1984; mem. Nat. Task Force ALARA Atomic Indsl. Forum, Washington; congl. sci. counselor PACCOS, Ohio; Ford Motor Co. prof., endowed chair Statis. Quality Studies Eastern Mich. U., 1986; examiner, trainer Malcolm Baldrige Nat. Quality Award, 1988-90. Editor Jour. Toledo Tech. Topics 1982-92; asst. editor Jour. English Quarterly, 1976-77. Contbr. articles to profl. jours. Vice chmn. Pvt. Industry Coun., Monroe County, Mich., 1983, 84; chmn. Bus.-Industry-Edn. Day Toledo & Detroit C. of C., 1984, 85; trustee Bedford Pub. Schs., Mich., 1982-85; chmn. Robotics Internat., 1985; bd. dirs., trustee Wittenberg U., 1991-95, Franciscan Health Systems, 1991-94, Riverside Health Group, 1993—, North Coast Health Systems, 1994—, Corp. for Effective Government, 1995—. Recipient Harvard Book award, 1967, internat. man of yr. award for total quality mgmt. Cambridge Centre, Eng., 1992; fellow SUNY-Stony Brook 1975-76, Cambridge U. 1976-77. Fellow Am. Psychol. Soc.; mem. Am. Chem. Soc. (chmn. Toledo chapt. 1984), Am. Soc. Non-Destructive Testing, Phi Delta Kappa, Phi Kappa Phi. Methodist. Club: U. Mich. (Toledo). Lodge: Rotary. Office: Loeffler Group Inc 4230 N Holland Sylvania Rd Toledo OH 43623-2506

LOEHLE, BETTY BARNES, artist, painter; b. Montgomery, Ala., Mar. 21, 1923; d. Harry McGuinn and Elizabeth (Fowler) B.; m. Richard E. Loehle, Aug. 16, 1947; children—Craig Edward, Alan David, Bruce Barnes, Lynn Elizabeth. Student Auburn U., Harris Sch. Art, Nashville, 1942-46, Evanston Art Ctr., 1964-68. Layout artist Atlanta Art Studios, 1970-75; free lance designer, painter, Atlanta, 1975-80; full time painter, Atlanta, 1980—; dir., publicity chmn., exhibition chmn. Ga. Watercolor Soc., 1981-85; pres. Artists Assocs. Gallery, Atlanta, 1977-79, sec., 1985—. Represented by Abstein Gallery of Art, Atlanta, Little House on Linden Gallery, Birmingham, Ala., Little Art Gallery, Raleigh, N.C. Entries judge Arts Festival of Atlanta, 1974; chmn. Unitarian Ch. Art Com., Atlanta, 1973-76. Recipient Purchase award Decatur Sesquicentennial, Ga., 1974, Hunter Mus. of Art, Chattanooga, 1977, Ga. Council for the Arts, Atlanta, 1977, 1980. Mem. DeKalb Council for the Arts, Ga. Watercolor Soc. (signature mem.; merit awards 1980, 82, 83, 87, 88), So. Watercolor Soc. (signature mem.; silver award 1979, merit award 1980), Ky. Watercolor Soc. (artist mem.), Atlanta Artist Club (exhbn. chmn. 1972-74). Home: 2608 River Oak Dr Decatur GA 30033-2805

LOEHLIN, JOHN CLINTON, psychologist, educator; b. Ferozepore, India, Jan. 13, 1926; s. Clinton Herbert and Eunice (Cleland) L.; m. Marjorie Leafdale, Jan. 2, 1962; children—Jennifer Ann, James Norris. AB, Harvard U., 1947; PhD, U. Calif., Berkeley, 1957. With rsch. dept. McCann-Erickson, Inc., Cleve., 1947-49; instr. to asst. prof. psychology U. Nebr., Lincoln, 1957-64; mem. faculty U. Tex., Austin, 1964—, prof. psychology and computer scis., 1969-92, prof. emeritus, 1992—. Author: Computer Models of Personality, 1968, Latent Variable Models, 1987, Genes and Environment in Personality Development, 1992; co-author: Race Differences in Intelligence, 1975, Heredity, Environment and Personality, 1976, Introduction to Theories of Personality, 1985. With USNR, 1945-47, 51-53. Fellow Ctr. Advanced Study Behavioral Scis., 1971-72. Fellow Am. Psychol. Soc.; mem. Behavior Genetics Assn., Soc. Multivariate Exptl. Psychology. Home: 304 Almarion Dr Austin TX 78746-5644 Office: U Tex Dept Psychology Austin TX 78712

LOEHR, ARTHUR WILLIAM, JR., healthcare executive, nurse; b. Cleve., July 26, 1948; s. Arthur William and Margaret Osborne (Robison) L.; m. Carol Lynn Hiatt; children: Brett Lawrence, Melissa Margaret, Joshua Hiatt. Diploma, Jackson Meml. Hosp., 1971; BS in Health Sci., Fla. Internat. U., 1975, M of Healthcare Adminstrn., 1977. RN, Fla. Psychiat. nurse Jackson Meml. Hosp., Miami, Fla., 1971, nurse cons., 1972, adminstr. pediats., 1973-74, hosp. planner, 1975-77; hosp. planner Duke U. Med. Ctr., Durham, N.C., 1977-80; v.p. planning N.C. Hosp. Assn., Raleigh, 1980-84, Catawba Meml. Hosp., Hickory, N.C., 1984—; preceptor U. N.C., Chapel Hill, N.C., 1988—. V.p., pres. Hospice of Catawba Valley, Hickory, 1985-90, Rape Crisis Ctr., Hickory, 1987-92; mem. Catawba County United Way Bd., 1991—, Family Care Ctr. of Catawba County, bd. dirs., 1992—. Scholar B'nai Brith, Miami, 1971. Fellow Am. Coll. Healthcare Execs.; mem. Rotary Internat. (bd. dirs. 1990-93). Presbyerian. Avocations: golf, fishing, snow skiing. Home: 4322 3rd Street Pl NW Hickory NC 28601-9033 Office: Catawba Memorial Hospital 810 Fairgrove Church Rd Hickory NC 28602-9617

LOEHR, MARLA, college president; b. Cleve., Oct. 7, 1937; d. Joseph Richard and Eleanore Edith (Rothschuh) L. BS, Notre Dame Coll., South Euclid, Ohio, 1960; MAT, Ind. U., 1969; PhD, Boston Coll., 1988; Degree (hon.), Notre Dame Coll. Ohio, 1995. Joined Sisters of Notre Dame, Roman Cath. Ch., 1956; cert. high sch. tchr., counselor, Ohio. Mem. faculty Notre Dame Acad., Cleve., 1960-64, John F. Kennedy High Sch., Warren, Ohio, 1964-66; adminstrn. asst., dir. residence halls Notre Dame Acad., Chardon, Ohio, 1966-72; dean students Notre Dame Coll., South Euclid, Ohio, 1972-85, acting acad. dean, 1988, pres., 1988-95; facilitator Coun. for Ind. Colls., Washington, 1980-84. Author: Mentor Handbook, 1985; co-author: Notre Dame College Model for Student Development, 1980. Hon. mem. Segund Montes Solidarity City Campaign; trustee NCCJ, Notre Dame Coll., Womankind, Ohio Found. of Ind. Colls.; mem. sch. bd. Marotta Montessori Schs. Cleve.; mem. Cleve. Commn. on Higher Edn., Leadership Cleve. Class of 1990; vol. Hospice of Western Res. Recipient Career Woman of Achievement award YWCA, 1992; named One of 100 Cleve.'s Most Powerful Women, New Cleve. Woman. Mem. Am. Assn. for Higher Edn., Assn. Ind. Colls. and Univs. Ohio (bd. dirs.), Assn. Governing Bds., Pax Christi, Alpha Sigma Nu, Kappa Gamma Pi. Avocations: photography, hiking, reading, sports. Office: Notre Dame Coll Ohio Office of the President 4545 College Rd South Euclid OH 44121-4228

LOEHWING, RUDI CHARLES, JR., publicist, radio broadcasting executive; b. Newark, July 26, 1957; s. Rudy Charles Sr. and Joan Marie (Bell) L.; m. Claire Popham, Sept. 4, 1987; children: Aspasia Joyce, Tesia Victoria, Rudi Douglas, Anna Marie, Samantha Diane, Ian Ryan. Student, Biscayne U., 1975, Seton Hall U., 1977, Hubbard Acad., 1980. Announcer radio sta. WHBI FM, N.Y.C., 1970-72; producer Am. Culture Entertainment, Belleville, N.J., 1973-74; exec. producer Am. Culture Entertainment, Hollywood, Calif., 1988-94; CEO Broadcaster's Network Internat., Hollywood, U.K., also U.K., 1989—, Broadcaster's Network Internat., Ltd., Hollywood, also U.K.; dir. pub. rels. The Dohring Co.; bd. dirs. First Break, Hollywood, also U.K., 1988—. Author: Growing Pains, 1970; exec. producer TV documentaries and comml. advertisements, 1983; patentee in field. Devel. dir. Tricentennial Found., Washington, 1989-90; bd. dirs. Just Say No to Drugs, L.A., 1989, Hands Across the Atlantic, Internat. Country Top 10, The Rock of Russia, Job Search, Hollywood, U.K. and Russia. Named Youngest Comml. Radio Producer and Announcer for State of N.Y., Broadcaster's Network Internat., 1972. Mem. Broadcasters Network Assn. (bd. dirs. 1977—), Profl. Bus. Comms. Assn. (founder 1989), BNI News Bur. (chmn. 1991—). Avocations: flying, music, writing, photography, martial arts. Office: Broadcasters' Network Internat Ltd 2624 Medlow Ave Ste B Los Angeles CA 90065-4617

LOEKS, JAMES, theater chain executive. Co-CHB Sony Theatres, N.Y. Office: Sony Theatres 711 Fifth Ave New York NY 10022

LOENGARD, JOHN BORG, photographer; editor; b. N.Y.C., Sept. 5, 1934; s. Richard Otto and Margery (Borg) L.; m. Eleanor Sturgis, Aug. 25, 1963 (div. 1987); children: Charles, Jennifer, Anna. B.A., Harvard Coll., 1956. Staff photographer Life mag., N.Y.C., 1961-72, picture editor, 1973-87; freelance photographer, 1987—; columnist Popular Photography mag., N.Y.C., 1987, Am. Photographer, N.Y.C., 1988—. Author: Pictures Under Discussion, 1987, Life Classic Photographs: A Personal Interpretation by John Loengard, 1988, Life Faces: Commentary by John Loengard, 1991, Celebrating the Negative, 1994, Georgia O'Keeffe at Ghost Ranch, 1995; essays in Life mag., The Shakers, 1967, Georgia O'Keeffe, 1968, Vanishing Cowboys, 1970, Photographers Over 80, 1982, Henry Moore, 1983, Interstate 80, 1989. Recipient Ansel Adams award Am. Soc. Mag. Photographers, 1987. Home: 20 W 86th St New York NY 10024-3604 Office: Time & Life Bldg Rm 2841 New York NY 10020

LOENGARD, RICHARD OTTO, JR., lawyer; b. N.Y.C, Jan. 28, 1932; s. Richard Otto and Margery (Borg) L.; m. Janet Sara Senderowitz, Apr. 11, 1964; children: Maranda C., Philippa S.M. AB, Harvard U., 1953, LLB, 1956. Bar: N.Y. 1956, U.S. Dist. Ct. (so. dist.) N.Y. 1958. Assoc. Fried, Frank, Harris, Shriver & Jacobson, predecessor firms, N.Y.C., 1956-64, ptnr., 1967—; dep. tax legis. counsel, spl. asst. internat. tax affairs U.S. Dept. Treasury, Washington, 1964-67; mem. Commerce Clearing House, Riverwoods, Ill. Editl. bd. Tax Transaction Libr., 1982-94; contbr. articles to profl. publs. Fellow Am. Coll. Tax Counsel; mem. ABA, N.Y. State Bar Assn. (exec. com. tax sect. 1984—, sec. 1994-95, vice chair 1995-97), Assn. Bar City N.Y. Office: Fried Frank Harris Shriver & Jacobson 1 New York Plz New York NY 10004

LOEPER, F. JOSEPH, state senator; b. Dec. 23, 1944; m. Joann M. Loeper; children: F. Joseph III, James H., Joanne M. BS in Edn., West Chester U., 1966; MEd, Temple U., 1970; D of Law (hon.), Widener U., 1992. Tchr. social studies, asst. basketball coach, advisor sch. paper Aldan Sch. Dist., 1966-67; tchr. social studies, football coach Drexel Hill Jr. High Sch. Upper Darby Sch. Dist., 1967-68; dir. leisure svcs. Upper Darby Sch. Dist. Upper Darby Twp., 1968-78; instr. Pub. Svc. Inst. Millersville, Kutztown and West Chester U., 1972; mem. Rep. State Com. 26th Senatorial Dist., 1972-74; co-adj. instr. Delaware County Community Coll., 1973-74; mem. Upper Darby Gov. Study Commn., 1973-74; treas. Upper Darby Sch. Dist., 1973-78; senator Pa. Senate, 1978—, senate majority caucus sec., 1980-83, senate majority whip, 1984-87, senate majority leader, 1988-92, 94—, minority whip, 1992-93; chmn. Rules and Exec. Nominations com.; mem. Appropriations Com., Banking and Ins. Com.; bd. govs. State Systems of Higher Edn. com.; mem. exec. com. Joint State Gov. Commn. Past chmn. Eastern Delaware County Br. ARC, past bd. dirs. southeastern Pa. chpt.; past bd. dirs. Delaware County Assn. for Retarded Citizens; past pres. Garrettford-Drexel Hill Fire Co., Upper Darby Twp. Fireman's Relief Assn. Recipient Delaware County Citizen of Yr. award, 1990, West Chester Univ. Disting. Alumni award, 1989, Presdl. award Delaware County Fed. Sr. Svcs., 1988, Legis. award Fraternal Order Police, 1985, Legion Honor award Chapel Four Chaplains, 1982, St. Charles Cath. Youth Assn. award, Delaware County Saving League award, YMCA Youth in Gov. award, Citizen of Yr. award Del. C. of C., 1992, Pres. medal West Chester U., 1994. Mem. Pa. Recreation and Park Soc. (Governmental svc. award, 1982), Nat. Edn. Assn. (life), Upper Darby Assn. Suprs. and Adminstrators, Nat. Rep. Legislators Assn. (Legislator of Yr. 1988), Senate Rep. Campaign Com. (treas.). Office: Rm 362 Main Capitol Bldg Harrisburg PA 17120 also: 403 Burmont Rd Drexel Hill PA 19026-3003

LOEPP, HERMAN ALBERT, claims manager; b. Wichita, Kans., Sept. 30, 1953; s. Edward and Mary (Dennis) L.; m. Kerri Louise Huss, May 26, 1979; 1 child, Jonathan Aaron. AA, Hutchinson (Kans.) C.C., 1973; BS, Emporia State U., 1975; JD, Washburn U., 1981. Bar: Kans. 1982, U.S. Dist. Ct. Kans. 1982. Atty. Anderson County Kans., Garnett, Kans., 1982-88; claims atty. Associated Aviation Underwriters, Overland Park, Kans., 1988-94; claims mgr. Associated Aviation Underwriters, Atlanta, 1994-95. Mem. Lawyers Pilots Bar Assn., Rotary Internat. (pres. 1987). Republican. Avocations: golf, softball. Home and Office: 12490 Quirira Rd #2224 Overland Park KS 66213

LOERKE, WILLIAM CARL, art history educator; b. Toledo, Aug. 13, 1920; s. William Carl and Anna Louisa (Stallbaum) L.; m. Helen Trautmann, 1944; children—Anna Hurd, Timothy, Eric, Alison, Lisa Huff, Ellen, Martha. B.A., Oberlin Coll., 1942; M.F.A., Princeton U., 1948, Ph.D., 1957. Acad. positions history of art Brown U., 1949-59; assoc. prof. Bryn Mawr Coll., 1959-64; prof. art history U. Pitts., 1964-71, chmn. fine arts dept., 1964-69; prof. Byzantine art Harvard U., Dumbarton Oaks Research Library, 1971-88, prof. emeritus, 1988—; dir. studies Ctr. Byzantine Studies, 1971-77; vis. prof. Cath. U. Am., 1978-88; vis. prof. U. Md., 1988-92; mem. adv. bd. Ctr. for Advanced Study in Visual Arts, Nat. Gallery Art, Washington, 1979-82, 89-92; bd. dirs. Internat. Ctr. Medieval Art, 1973-91; mem. mng. com. Am. Sch. Classical Studies, 1973-93. Co-author: The Place of Book Illumination in Byzantine Art, Princeton, 1975, Monasticism and the Arts, 1984, Codex Rossanensis, Commentarium, Rome, 1987, Architecture: Fundamental Issues, N.Y., 1990; contbr. Byzantine East, Latin West: Art Historical Studies in Honor of Kurt Weitzman, 1995; contbr. articles to profl. jours.; contbr. Dictionary of Byzantium, 1991. Served with USNR, 1943-46. Jr. fellow Princeton U., 1946-48, Dumbarton Oaks Harvard U., 1948-49, Danforth Tchr. fellow, 1956-57; Fulbright Rsch. scholar Am. Acad. Rome, 1952-53; recipient A.K. Porter prize Coll. Art Assn., 1961. Mem. Coll. Art Assn., Medieval Acad. Am., Soc. Fellows, Am. Acad. at Rome, Internat. Ctr. Med. Art. Home: 227 Gralan Rd Catonsville MD 21228-4835

LOESCH, HAROLD C., retired marine biologist, consultant; b. Osage, Tex., Oct. 3, 1926; s. Eldor E. and Martha (Niemeier) L.; m. Mabel Treichler, Oct. 19, 1945; children: Stephen C., Gretchen Drinkard, Jonathan, Frederick. BS in Fisheries, Tex. A&M Univ., 1951; postgrad., Univ. Tex., Port Aransas, 1951, 52; MS in Biol. Oceanography, Tex. A&M Univ., 1954, PhD in Biol. Oceanography, 1962. Prin. marine biologist, acting lab. dir. Dept. Conservation, Bayou la Batre, Ala., 1952-57; teaching asst. Tex. A&M Univ., College Station, 1957-58; assoc. rsch. scientist Tex. A&M Rsch.

Found., College Station, 1958-60; shrimp biologist Food & Agrl. Orgn. of UN, Guatamala, 1960-62; fisheries biologist Food & Agrl. Orgn. of UN, Ecuador, 1962-66; fisheries officer Food & Agrl. Orgn. of UN, La Ceiba, Honduras, 1967-68; prof. zoology La. State U., Baton Rouge, 1968-69; prof. marine scis. La. State U., 1970-75; expert marine biologist United Nat. Edn. Social and Cultural Orgn., Guaymas, Sonora, Mex., 1976-79; sr. resource assessment surveyor, project mgr. FAO, UN, Dhaka, Bangladesh, 1981-85; cons. Pensacola, Fla., 1985—; vis. prof. Orgn. Am. States, Guayaquil, Ecuador, 1972, Sch. for Field Study, Beverly, Mass., S. Caicos Isl, BWI, 1990; cons. Univ. Mex. U. N. Ed. Soc. & Cult Orgn., 1979-80. Contbr. articles to profl. jours. With USAF, 1945-46. Mem. AAAS (life), Am. Fisheries Soc., Internat. Acad. Fisheries Sci., Tex. Acad. Sci. (life), World Mariculture Soc., Am. Soc. Ichthyologists and Herpetologists (life), Sigma Xi. Democrat. Lutheran. Avocations: canoeing, wilderness camping, photography, traveling. Home: 2140 E Scott St Pensacola FL 32503-4957

LOESCH, KATHARINE TAYLOR (MRS. JOHN GEORGE LOESCH), communication and theatre educator; b. Berkeley, Calif., Apr. 13, 1922; d. Paul Schuster and Katharine (Whiteside) Taylor; student Swarthmore Coll., 1939-41, U. Wash., 1942; BA, Columbia U., 1944, MA, 1949; grad. Neighborhood Playhouse Sch. of Theatre, 1946; postgrad. Ind. U., 1953; PhD, Northwestern U., 1961; m. John George Loesch, Aug. 28, 1948; 1 child, William Ross. Instr. speech Wellesley (Mass.) Coll., 1949-52, Loyola U., Chgo., 1956; asst. prof. English and speech Roosevelt U., Chgo., 1957, 62-65; assoc. prof. communication and theatre U. Ill. at Chgo., 1968—; assoc. prof. emerita speech in communication and theater, U. Ill., Chgo., 1987—. Contbr. writings to profl. jours.; poetry performances. Active ERA, Ill., 1975-76. Am. Philos. Soc. grantee, 1970; U. Ill., Chgo., grantee, 1970. Mem. MLA, Speech Communication Assn. (Golden Anniversary prize award 1969, chmn. interpretation div. 1979-80), Celtic Studies Assn. N.Am., Pi Beta Phi. Episcopalian. Home: 2129 N Sedgwick St Chicago IL 60614-4619 Office: U Ill Dept Performing Arts M/C 255 1040 W Harrison St Chicago IL 60607-7130

LOESCH, MABEL LORRAINE, social worker; b. Annandale, Minn., July 1, 1925; d. Rudolph and Hedwig (Zeidler) Treichler; m. Harold Carl Loesch, Oct. 19, 1945; children: Stephen, Gretchen, Jonathan, Frederick. BS, La. State U., 1972, MSW, 1974. Cert. Acad. Cert. Social Worker, bd. cert. diplomate. Tchr. Am. schs. Tegucigalpa, Honduras, 1960-61, Guayaquil, Ecuador, 1962-66, La Ceiba, Honduras, 1966-67; supr. clin. svc. Blundon Home, Baton Rouge, 1974-81; social worker, cons. Dhaka, Bangladesh, 1981-85; social worker Manna Food Bank, Pensacola, Fla., 1986—; adj. instr. social work dept. Southern U., Baton Rouge, 1976-81. Editor: Making Do, 1989, Making Do II, 1994. Mem. adv. com. Luth. Ministries of Fla., 1993—. Mem. NASW, Mensa (local sec. 1986-90, chair scholarships com.), Phi Kappa Phi. Democrat. Lutheran. Avocation: genealogy. Home: 2140 E Scott St Pensacola FL 32503-4957

LOESCHER, GILBURT DAMIAN, international relations educator; b. San Francisco, Mar. 7, 1945; s. Burt Garfield and Helen (Aachen) L.; m. Ann Gordon Dull, Sept. 25, 1971; children: Margaret Madeline, Claire Helen. BA, St. Mary's Coll. of Calif., 1967; MA, Monterey Inst. Internat. Study, 1969; PhD, London Sch. Econs./Polit. Sci., 1975. Asst. prof. U. Notre Dame, Ind., 1975-84, assoc. prof., 1984-90, prof., 1990—, asst. dean., 1977-79; vis. fellow London Sch. Econs., 1978-79, Princeton (N.J.) U., 1982-83; rsch. cons. U.S. Select Commn. on Immigration and Refugee Policy, Washington, 1989; sr. rsch. fellow Queen Elizabeth House, Oxford (Eng.) U., 1986-89; rsch. assoc. Internat. Inst. for Strategic Studies, London, 1990-91. Author: Refugee Movements and International Security, 1992, Beyond Charity: International Cooperation and the Global Refugee Problem, 1993; co-author: Calculated Kindness: Refugees and America's Half-Open Door, 1985 (Gustavas Meyers award 1986). Mem. exec. bd. Ind. Consortium for Internat. Programs, 1976-80; bd. dirs. Amnesty Internat., N.Y., 1980-82; chair adv. com. on internat. experts UN Commn. for Refugees, Geneva, 1992—; advisor UN High Commnr. for Refugees, 1996. Grantee Ford Found., 1982-84, 92-93, 96, Twentieth Century Fund, 1987-89, MacArthur Found., 1990-91. Mem. Internat. Studies Assn., Am. Polit. Sci. Assn., Royal Inst. Internat. Affairs, Internat. Inst. for Strategic Studies, Academic Coun. of UN Sys. Democrat. Roman Catholic. Avocations: basketball, walking, theater. Office: U Notre Dame Notre Dame IN 46556

LOESCHER, RICHARD ALVIN, gastroenterologist; b. Brockton, Mass., Feb. 6, 1940; s. Vernon Alvin and Anna Marie (Good) L.; m. Linda Rockwell Clifford Loescher, June 5, 1965 (div. Jan. 1982); children: Steven Clifford Loescher, Laura May Loescher. BA, De Pauw U., 1961; MD cum laude, Harvard U., 1965. Diplomate Am. Bd. Internal Medicine, 1972, Am. Bd. Gastroenterology, 1973. Chief Med. Svc. U.S. Pub. Health Svc. Hosp., Lawton, Okla., 1967-69; chief Med. Staff, 1968-69, svc. unit dir., 1969; attending physician Seattle, 1970-71, U. Hosp., Seattle, 1970-71; active staff Sacred Heart Med. Ctr., Eugene, Oreg., 1973—, Eugene (Oreg.) Hosp., 1972-88; courtesy staff McKenzie-Williamette Hosp., Springfield, Oreg., 1982—. Recipient Rector scholarship DePauw U., 1957-61, Maimonides award Harvard Med. Sch., 1965. Mem. AMA, Lane County Med. Soc., Oreg. Med. Assn., Oreg. Soc. Internal Medicine, Am. Soc. Internal Medicine, Am. Soc. for Gastrointestinal Endoscopy, Am. Acad. Med. Acupuncture, Alpha Omega Alpha, Phi Beta Kappa. Democrat. Unitarian. Avocations: physical fitness, personal growth, magic, outdoor activities. Home: 2345 Patterson St # 34 Eugene OR 97405 Office: 1162 Willamette St Eugene OR 97401

LOESER, HANS FERDINAND, lawyer; b. Kassel, Germany, Sept. 28, 1920; s. Max and Cecilia H. (Erlanger) L.; m. Herta Lewent, Dec. 14, 1944; children—Helen, Harris M., H. Thomas. Student CCNY, 1940-42, U. Pa., 1942-43; LL.B. magna cum laude, Harvard U., 1950. Bar: Mass. 1950, U.S. Supreme Ct. 1968. Asso. firm Foley, Hoag & Eliot, Boston, 1950-55, ptnr., 1956—; hon. consul-gen. Republic of Senegal; mem. Mass. Bd. Bar Overseers; trustee Vineyard Open Land Found., Martha's Vineyard, Mass.; mem. exec. com. and nat. bd. Lawyers' Com. for Civil Rights Under Law, steering com. and past chmn. Lawyer's Com. for Civil Rights Under Law of Boston Bar Assn.; incorporator Univ. Hosp., Boston, Mt. Auburn Hosp., Cambridge, Mass. Served to capt. U.S. Army, 1942-46. Decorated Bronze Star, Purple Heart; hon. fellow U. Pa. Law Sch., 1978-79, commencement speaker, 1978. Fellow Am. Bar Found., Mass. Bar Found.; mem. ABA, Mass. Bar Assn., Boston Bar Assn. Clubs: Union, Harvard, Cambridge. Office: Foley Hoag & Eliot 1 Post Office Sq Boston MA 02109-2103

LOESER, JOHN DAVID, neurosurgeon, educator; b. Newark, Dec. 14, 1935; s. Lewis Henry and Rhoda Sophie (Levy) L.; m. Susan Winifred Becker, June 11, 1961 (div. 1974); children: Sally Ann, Thomas Eric, Derek William; m. Karen Winslow, Dec. 29, 1977; 1 child, David Winslow. BA, Harvard U., 1957; MD, NYU, 1961. Diplomate Am. Bd. Neurol. Surgery; cert. Nat. Bd. Med. Examiners.; lic. neurosurgeon, Wash. Intern dept. surgery U. Calif., San Francisco, 1961-62; resident neurol. surgery U. Wash., Seattle, 1962-67; asst. prof. neurosurgery U. Calif., Irvine, 1967-68; asst. prof. neurol. surgery U. Wash., Seattle, 1969-75, assoc. prof., 1975-80, prof., 1980—, dir. Multidisciplinary Pain Clinic, 1983—; chief div. of neurosurgery Children's Hosp. & Med. Ctr., 1987-93; Fulbright sr. scholar, Australia, 1989-90. Contbr. articles to profl. jours.; editor profl. books. Served as maj. U.S. Army, 1968-70. Fellow AAAS; mem. Internat. Assn. Study of Pain (sec. 1984-90, pres. 1993—), Am. Pain Soc. (treas. 1980-85, pres. 1986-87), Am. Assn. Neurol. Surgeons, Am. Soc. Functional and Stereotactic Neurosurgery, North Pacific Soc. Neurology and Psychiatry, Wash. Assn. Neurosurgery, Western Neurosurg. Soc., Am. Assn. Pain Medicine, King County Med. Soc., Conf. Neurol. Surgeons, Phi Beta Kappa, Alpha Omega Alpha. Avocations: skiing, woodcarving. Office: University of Washington Box 3547501 4245 Roosevelt Way NE Seattle WA 98195

LOESS, HENRY BERNARD, psychology educator; b. Chgo., June 24, 1924; s. Henry William and Alice Cecilia (Mansfield) L.; m. Frances Mary Van Horn, May 26, 1951; children—Kurt, Karin, Andrew, Alan. BS, Northwestern U., 1949, MS, 1950; PhD, U. Iowa, 1952. Prof. psychology, chmn. dept. Lake Forest (Ill.) Coll., 1952-58; Prof. psychology, chmn. dept. Wooster (Ohio) Coll., 1958-88, prof. emeritus, 1988—; vis. lectr. Ohio State U., 1958-63; vis. research scholar U. Calif. at Berkeley, 1963-64, Cambridge (Eng.) U., 1968-69, U. Mich., 1973-74, Yale U., 1980-81; vis. scientist Ohio Acad. Sci., 1962-92; regional coord. Am. Inst. Rsch. Project Talent, 1961-69; assoc. North Ctrl. Assn. Colls. and Secondary Schs., 1970-86; bd. dirs. Habitat for Humanity, Wayne County, 1989—, Hospice of Wayne County, 1990—, Wayne County Bd. Mental Retardation and Devel. Disabilies, 1978-86, 93—. Author articles in field; cons. editor: Memory and Cognition, 1971-85. Served with USAAF, 1943-46. Mem. Am., Midwestern, Eastern psychol. assns., Psychonomic Soc., AAAS, Am. Assn. U. Profs., Sigma Xi. Home: 5410 Lehr Rd Wooster OH 44691-9288

LOEVINGER, LEE, lawyer, science writer; b. St. Paul, Apr. 24, 1913; s. Gustavus and Millie (Strouse) L.; m. Ruth Howe, Mar. 4, 1950; children: Barbara L., Eric H., Peter H. BA summa cum laude, U. Minn., 1933, JD, 1936. Bar: Minn. 1936, Mo. 1937, D.C. 1966, U.S. Supreme Ct., 1941. Assoc. Watson, Ess, Groner, Barnett & Whittaker, Kansas City, Mo., 1936-37; atty., regional atty. NLRB, 1937-41; with antitrust div. Dept. Justice, 1941-46; ptnr. Larson, Loevinger, Lindquist & Fraser, Mpls., 1946-60; assoc. justice Minn. Supreme Ct., 1960-61; asst. U.S. atty. gen. charge antitrust div. Dept. Justice, 1961-63; commr. FCC, 1963-68; ptnr. Hogan & Hartson, Washington, 1968-85; of counsel Hogan & Hartson, 1986—; v.p., dir. Craig-Hallum Corp., Mpls., 1968-73; dir. Petrolite Corp., St. Louis, 1978-83; U.S. rep. com. on restrictive bus. practices Orgn. for Econ. Coop. and Devel., 1961-64; spl. asst. to U.S. atty. gen., 1963-64; spl. counsel com. small bus. U.S. Senate, 1951-52; lectr. U. Minn., 1953-60; vis. prof. jurisprudence U. Minn. (Law Sch.), 1961; professorial lectr. Am. U., 1968-70; chmn. Minn. Atomic Devel. Problems Com., 1957-59; mem. Adminstrv. Conf. U.S., 1972-74; del. White House Conf. on Inflation, 1974; U.S. del. UNESCO Conf. on Mass Media, 1975, Internat. Telecomms. Conf. on Radio Frequencies, 1964, 66. Author: The Law of Free Enterprise, 1949, An Introduction to Legal Logic, 1952, Defending Antitrust Lawsuits, 1977, Science As Evidence, 1995; author first article to use term: jurimetrics, 1949; contbr. articles to profl. and sci. jours.; editor, contbr.: Basic Data on Atomic Devel. Problems in Minnesota, 1958; adv. bd. Antitrust Bull., Jurimetrics Jour. Served to lt. comdr. USNR, 1942-45. Recipient Outstanding Achievement award U. Minn., 1968; Freedoms Found. award, 1977, 84. Fellow Am. Acad. Appellate Lawyers; mem. ABA (del. of sci. and tech. sect. to Ho. of Dels. 1974-80, del. to joint conf. with AAAS 1974-76, co-chair 1990-93, liaison 1984-90, 93—, chmn. sci. and tech. sect. 1982-83, coun. 1986-89, standing com. on nat. conf. groups 1984-90), AAAS, Minn. Bar Assn., Hennepin County Bar Assn., N.Y. Acad. Sci., D.C. Bar Assn., FCC Bar Assn., Broadcast Pioneers, U.S. C. of C. (antitrust coun. 1980-94), Am. Arbitration Assn. (comml. panel), Atlantic Legal Found. (adv. coun.), Cosmos Club (pres. 1990), City Club (Washington), Phi Beta Kappa, Sigma Xi, Delta Sigma Rho, Sigma Delta Chi, Phi Delta Gamma, Tau Kappa Alpha, Alpha Epsilon Rho. Home: 5600 Wisconsin Ave Apt 17D Chevy Chase MD 20815-4414 Office: Hogan & Hartson 555 13th St NW Washington DC 20004-1109 *With age I come increasingly to believe that life is, and should be,a learning experience. This involves a peculiar paradox: Ignorance increases faster than knowledge, as each new fact or principle opens new frontiers for intellectual exploration. Thus, with greater learning comes intellectual humility and skepticism. So, after reaching 75 I am less certain of anything than at 25 I was of everything.*

LOEW, FRANKLIN MARTIN, medical and biological scientist; b. Syracuse, N.Y., Sept. 8, 1939; s. David Franklin and Sarah (Adelaide) L.; children: Timothy, Andrew. B.S., Cornell U., 1961, D.V.M., 1965; Ph.D., U. Sask., 1971. Lic. veterinarian; diplomate Am. Coll. Lab. Animal Medicine. Research asst. R.J. Reynolds Co., Winston-Salem, N.C., 1965-66; research asst. Tulane U., New Orleans, 1966-67; prof. U. Sask., Saskatoon, Can., 1967-77; dir. comparative medicine Johns Hopkins U., Balt., 1977-82; dean Sch. Vet. Medicine, Tufts U., Boston, 1982-95, Henry and Lois Foster prof. comparative medicine, 1985-95; v.p. Tufts U. Devel. Corp. Inc., Boston, 1991-95; pres. Tufts Biotech. Corp., Boston, 1993-95; dean Coll. Vet. Medicine, Cornell U., Ithaca, N.Y., 1995—; cons. Can. Coun. Animal Care, Ottawa, Ont., 1969-84; mem. life scis. com. Nat. Acad. Sci., Washington, 1981-88, chmn. Inst. Lab. Animal Resources, 1981-87; mem. FDA Commn. on Sr. Biomed. Rsch. Svc. Credentials, 1995—; N.B. lectr. Am. Soc. Microbiology; mem. nat. adv.. bd. Ctr. on Bioethics Lit., Kennedy Inst. Georgetown U., 1986—; Schofield lectr. U. Guelph, Can.; Smith lectr. U. Sask.; Schalm lectr. U. Calif.; univ. lectr. Tex. A&M U.; bd. dirs. Mass. Biotech. Rsch. Inst., Commonwealth BioVentures, Inc.; mem. sci. adv. com. Harvard Primate Rsch. Ctr., 1988—, Mass. Health Resources Inst.; sci. and tech. adv. com. State of Mass., 1988-92; mem. USDA Sec.'s Adv. Com. Nat. Rsch. Initiative, 1992—; pres. Tufts Biotech. Corp., 1993-95; bd. trustees Marine Biol. Lab., 1990-94, New Eng. Aquarium, 1991-95, Guys Drug Rsch. Unit, U.K., 1993-94; mem. panel animal health Nat. Rsch. Coun., 1992—. Author: Vet in the Saddle, 1978; editor: Laboratory Animal Medicine, 1984; contbr. numerous articles to profl. jours. Chmn. bd. trustees Boston Zool. Soc., 1984-88; trustee Worcester Acad. 1984-90; mem. Nat. Ctr. Rsch. Resources adv. coun. NIH, 1988-92, Blue Ribbon adv. coun. USDA, 1987-91; bd. dirs. Ea. States Exhbn,m 1988-85; bd. dirs. Mass. SPCA, 1996—;mem. bus. bd. Pharmacia & Upjohn, 1996—. Decorated Queen Elizabeth II Jubilee medal Gov.-Gen. Can., 1977; Med. Rsch. Coun. Can. fellow, 1969-71; recipient Charles River prize Am. Vet. Med. Assn., 1988, named Vet. of Yr., 1989; recipient Disting. Svc. award Mass. Vet. Med. Assn., 1992. Mem. NAS/Inst. Medicine, AAAS, Am. Inst. Nutrition, Soc. Toxicology, Assn. Am. Vet. Med. Colls. (pres. 1985-86), Am. Coll. Lab. Medicine (bd. dirs. 1979-82), Nat. Acads. Practice, Fedn. Am. Socs. for Exptl. Biology, Am. Antiquarian Soc., Mass. Agrl. Club. Office: Cornell U Coll Vet Medicine Ithaca NY 14853-6401

LOEW, GILDA HARRIS, research biophysicist, biology research executive; b. N.Y.C.; 4 children. BA, NYU, 1951; MA, Columbia U., 1952; PhD in Chem. Physics, U. Calif., Berkeley, 1957. Rsch. physicist Lawrence Radiation Lab., U. Calif., Berkeley, 1957-62, Lockheed Missiles and Space Co., 1962-64; assoc. quantum biophysics Biophys. Lab., Stanford U., 1964-66; from asst. prof. to assoc. prof. physics Pomona coll., 1966-69; rsch. biophysicist, instr. biophysics Stanford U. Med. Sch., 1969-79; adj. prof. genetics Stanford U. Med. Ctr., 1974-79; program dir. molecular theory Life Sci. divsn. Stanford Rsch. Inst., 1979—; adj. prof. Rockefeller U., 1979—. Grantee NSF, 1966—, NASA, 1969—, NIH, 1974—. Fellow Am. Phys. Soc.; mem. Biophys. Soc., Internat. Soc. Magnetic Resonance. Achievements include research in molecular orbital and crystal field quantum chemical calculations; models for protein active sites; mechanisms and requirements for specific drug action; theoretical studies related to chemical evolution of life. Office: Molecular Rsch Inst 845 Page Mill Rd Palo Alto CA 94304-1011*

LOEW, RALPH WILLIAM, clergyman, columnist; b. Columbus, Ohio, Dec. 29, 1907; s. William Louis and Wilhelmina (Bauer) L.; m. Genevra Maxine Uhl, June 8, 1939; children—Carolyn Maxine, Janet Elaine. A.B., Capital U., 1928; M.Divinity, Hamma Div. Sch., Springfield, Ohio, 1931; D.D., Wittenberg U., 1947; L.H.D., Susquehanna U., 1972, Wagner Coll., 1974; LL.D., Hartwick Coll., 1979. Ordained to ministry Luth. Ch., 1931. Pastor Millerburg (Ohio) Luth. Parish, 1931-37; asso. pastor Luth. Ch. Reformation, Washington, 1937-44; pastor Holy Trinity Luth. Ch., Buffalo, 1944-75; Del. Luth. World Fedn., Lund, Sweden, 1947, Helsinki, Finland, 1968; Knubel-Miller lectr. United Luth. Ch., 1955; lectr. Retreat for Chaplains, Nat. Luth. Council, Berchtesgaden, Germany, 1956; Brit-Am. exchange preacher, 1966, 72; participant Long Range Planning Conf., India, 1968; pres. bd. fgn. missions United Luth Ch. Am., 1956-60, mem. exec. council, 1962-66, pres. bd. world missions, 1970-72, chmn. div. world missions and ecumenism, 1972-76; dir. dept. religion Chautauqua Instn., 1973-84; pres. ct. adjudication Luth. Ch. Am. Author: The Hinges of Destiny, 1955, The Church and the Amateur Adult, 1955, Confronted by Jesus, 1957, Lutheran Way of Life, 1966, Christmas in the Shadows, 1968, He is Coming Soon, 1972; Contbr.: weekly column From My Window, Buffalo Courier-Express, 1952-82; syndicated column Finding The Way, 1960-67. Pres. Buffalo and Erie County Coun. Chs., 1950-51, Comty. Action Orgn., Buffalo and Erie County; pres. bd. trustees Margaret L. Wendt Found.; trustee Chautauqua Instn., 1988-92; pres. WNY Grantmakers, 1988-90; bd. trustees Habitat for Humanity Internat.; founder Habitat for Humanity, Buffalo, 1974. Recipient Chancellor's medal U. Buffalo, Notable Sermon award Life mag., 1957, numerous other awards. Home: 342 Depew Ave Buffalo NY 14214-1677 *Died Mar. 5, 1996.*

LOEWEN, ERWIN G., precision engineer, educator, consultant; b. Frankfurt, Germany, Apr. 12, 1921; came to U.S., 1937; s. Franz L. and Gladys M. (Marx) L.; m. Joanna M. Wills, Sept. 5, 1952; children: Oliver F., Heidi R. BMechE, NYU, 1941; MS, MIT, 1949, MMechE, 1950, ScD, 1952. Tech. dir. Taft-Pierce Mfg. Co., Woonsocket, R.I., 1952-60; dir. gratings and metrology Bausch & Lomb, Rochester, N.Y., 1960-85; v.p. R&D Milton Roy Co., Rochester, 1985-87, emeritus, 1987—; prof. optics U. Rochester, 1988—. contbr. numerous articles on metal cutting, precision engring., and diffraction grating to profl. jours., chpt. to book. Staff sgt. U.S. Army, 1944-46, PTO. Recipient David Richardson medal, 1983, Robert M. Burley prize Optical Soc. Am., 1993. Fellow ASME (v.p. standardization), Optical Soc. Am. (David Richardson medal, 1984), Soc. Mfg. Engrs.; mem. Am. Soc. Precision Engrs. (hon.), Soc. Photoinstrumentation Engrs., Internat. Instn. Prodn. Engring. Rsch., Sigma Xi. Avocations: photography, skiing, swimming. Home: 34A Brookhill Ln Rochester NY 14625-2212 Office: Spectronics Instruments Inc 820 Linden Ave Rochester NY 14625-2710

LOEWENBERG, GERHARD, political science educator; b. Berlin, Germany, Oct. 2, 1928; came to U.S., 1936, naturalized, 1943; s. Walter and Anne Marie (Cassirer) L.; m. Ina Perlstein, Aug. 22, 1950; children: Deborah, Michael. A.B., Cornell U., 1949, A.M., 1950, Ph.D., 1955. Mem. faculty Mount Holyoke Coll., 1953-69, chmn. dept. polit. sci., 1963-69, acting academic dean, 1968-69; prof. polit. sci. U. Iowa, Iowa City, 1970—, chmn. dept., 1982-84, dean Coll. Liberal Arts, 1984-92, dir. Comparative Legis. Research Center, 1971-82, 92—; vice chair East-West Parliamentary Practice Project, 1990—; vis. assoc. prof. Columbia, UCLA, 1966, U. Mass. summer session at Bologna, Italy, 1967, Cornell U., 1968; mem. council Inter-Univ. Consortium for Polit. Research, 1971-74, chmn., 1973-74. Author: Parliament in the German Political System, 1967, Parlamentarismus im politischen System der Bundesrepublik Deutschland, 1969, Modern Parliaments: Change or Decline, 1971; co-author: Comparing Legislatures, 1979; co-editor: Handbook of Legislative Research, 1985; co-editor: Legis. Studies Quar.; contbr. articles to profl. jours. Trustee Mt. Holyoke Coll., 1971-84, chmn., 1979-84. Fulbright fellow, 1957-58; Rockefeller fellow, 1961-62; Social Sci. Research Council faculty research fellow, 1964-65; Guggenheim fellow, 1969-70. Mem. Am. Polit. Sci. Assn. (coun. 1971-73, v.p. 1990-91), Midwest Polit. Sci. Assn., Phi Beta Kappa, Phi Kappa Phi, Pi Sigma Alpha. Office: 323 Seashore Hall U Iowa Iowa City IA 52242

LOEWENSTEIN, BENJAMIN STEINBERG, lawyer; b. Atlantic City, Aug. 22, 1912; s. Sidney and Cecilia (Steinberg) L.; m. Eleanor Lax Schieren, June 14, 1966; children: Sally L. (Mrs. David S. Well, Jr.), P. Edward: stepchildren: Susan (Mrs. Stanton A. Moss, dec.), Julie (Mrs. Robert Dreidink). A.B., Haverford Coll., 1934; J.D., U. Pa., 1937. Bar: Pa. 1937. Practiced in Phila., 1937—; sr. partner Abrahams & Loewenstein, 1937-87, of counsel, 1988—; Sec., dir. Rojess Corp., Gen. Syndicate Corp., Jonns Inc., Engelside Realty Corp., Sherill Corp., Oak Blvd. Inc., Kahn's Inc., Atlas Rug Cleaners, Inc.; Counsel Diamond Coun. Am., Phila. County Dental Soc.; Del. White House Conf. on Aging; chmn. Task Force on Aging, Pa. Comprehensive Health Plan, Regional Comprehensive Health Planning Delaware Valley, Pa., 1968; mem. Pa. Human Relations Commn., 1974-87. Hon. chmn. bd. Jewish Occupational Coun., 1971—; pres. Jewish Employment and Vocat. Service, 1954-59, hon. pres. 1976—; pres. So. Home for Children, 1968-69, Health and Welfare Coun. Phila., 1969-71; pres. Jewish Community Rels. Coun. Phila., 1974-77, hon. pres., 1978—; mem. bd. govs. Am. Jewish Com., 1968—, hon. chmn. Phila. chpt.; trustee Community Svcs. Pa., 1968-78; bd. mgrs. Haverford Coll., 1970—; bd. dirs. Vocat. Rsch. Inst., 1960—, United Way of Phila., Fedn. Jewish Agys., Phila., Pa. Law and Justice Inst., 1971-76, Fellowship Commn. Phila., 1972-86, Phila. Anti-Poverty Action Commn., 1976-87, Nat. Inst. on the Holocaust, 1977-82; treas. Interfaith Council on the Holocaust, 1986—; bd. dirs. Quadrangle Retirement Community, 1977—, Martins Run Retirement Community, 1981—. Recipient Community Service award Allied Jewish Appeal Phila., 1956, certificate of appreciation Phila. County Med. Soc., 1961, certificate appreciation Fedn. Jewish Agys., 1972, Phila. Commn. Human Relations award, 1974; certificate Merit Am. Cancer Soc., 1974; Samuel Greenberg Meml. award Nat. Assn. Jewish Vocat. Services, 1980; Human Relations award Am. Jewish Com., 1981; Legion of Honor Chapel of Four Chaplains, 1980. Mem. Am., Pa., Phila. bar assns., Lawyers Club Phila., Socialegal Club Phila., Haverford Coll. Alumni Assn. (pres. 1956-57), Am. Arbitration Assn. (nat. panel arbitrators). Home: 2804 Kennedy House 1901 John F Kennedy Blvd Philadelphia PA 19103-1502 Home: 198 NW 67th St Apt 306 Boca Raton FL 33487-8306 Office: 1650 Market St Ste 3100 Philadelphia PA 19103-7392

LOEWENSTEIN, DAVID ANDREW, clinical psychologist, neuropsychologist, educator; b. Miami, Fla., Dec. 31, 1959; s. Jack Meyer and Arline (Perry) L.; m. Susan Laurie Berkell, Nov. 15, 1992. BA in Psychology, U. S. Fla., 1981; MS in Clin. Psychology, Fla. State U., 1983, PhD in Clin. Psychology, 1986. Psychol. intern U. Washington Sch. Medicine, Seattle, 1985-86; rsch. asst. prof. U. Miami Sch. Medicine, 1986-90, assoc. prof. psychiatry, 1992—; dir. neuropsychology labs. Wien Ctr. for Alzheimers Disease Mt. Sinai Med. Ctr., Miami Beach, Fla., 1986—; dir. psychol. svcs. dept. psychiatry U. Miami/Mt. Sinai Med. Ctr., Miami Beach, 1990—. Author book chpts.; contbr. numerous articles to profl. jours. Grantee NIMH, 1992-97. Achievements include development of direct asesment of functional status (DAFS) scale which is utilized to provide objective functional assessment of the demented patient (used in clin. and rsch. labs. in U.S. and abroad); co-development of culture fair cognitive tests for research and clinical assessment of the older adult. Office: Mt Sinai Med Ctr Dept Psych 4300 Alton Rd Miami FL 33140

LOEWENSTEIN, WALTER BERNARD, nuclear power technologist; b. Gensungen, Hesse, Germany, Dec. 23, 1926; came to U.S., 1938; s. Louis and Johanna ((Katz) L.; m. Lenore C. Pearlman, June 21, 1959; children: Mark Victor, Marcia Beth. BS, U. Puget Sound, 1949; postgrad., U. Wash., 1949-50; PhD, Ohio State U., 1954. Registered profl. engr., Calif. Rsch. asst., fellow Ohio State U., Columbus, 1951-54; rsch. asst. Los Alamos Nat. Lab., 1952-54; sr. physicist, divsn. dir. Argonne (Ill.) Nat. Lab., 1954-73; dept. dir., dep. divsn. dir. Electric Power Rsch. Inst., Palo Alto, Calif., 1973-89, profl. cons., 1989—, mem. large aerosol containment experiment project bd., 1983-87; mem. Marviksen project bd. Studsvik Rsch. Ctr., Stockholm, 1978-85; mem. LOFT project bd. Nuclear Energy Agy., Paris, 1982-89; mem. tech. adv. nuclear safety Ontario Hydro Corp., 1990—; mem. nuclear engring. dept. adv. com. Brookhaven Nat. Lab., 1992—. With USNR, 1945-46. Recipient Alumnus Cum Laude award U. Puget Sound, 1976. Fellow Am. Phys. Soc., Am. Nuclear Soc. (v.p., pres. 1988-90); mem. Am. Assn. Engring. Socs. (sec., treas. 1990), Nat. Acad. Engring. Jewish. Avocations: history, golf. Home and Office: 515 Jefferson Dr Palo Alto CA 94303

LOEWENTHAL, NESSA PARKER, communications educator; b. Chgo., Oct. 13, 1930; d. Abner and Frances (Ness) Parker; m. Martin Moshe Loewenthal, July 7, 1951 (dec. Aug. 1973); children: Dann Marcus, Ronn Carl, Deena Miriam; m. Gerson B. Selk, Apr. 17, 1982 (dec. June 1987). BA in Edn. and Psychology, Stanford U., 1952. Faculty Stanford Inst. for Intercultural Communication, Palo Alto, Calif., 1973-87; dir. Trans Cultural Svcs., San Francisco, 1981-86, Portland, Oreg., 1986—; dir. dependent svcs. and internat. edn. Bechtel Group, San Francisco, 1973-81, internat. edn. cons., 1981-84; mem. adv. com. dept. internat. studies Lesley Coll., Cambridge, Mass., 1986—; mem. Oreg. Ethics Commons, 1990—; mem. Bay Area Ethics Consortium, Berkeley, 1985-90; chmn. ethics com. Sietar Internat., Washington, 1987—, mem. governing bd., 1992-95; mem. faculty Summer Inst. for Internat. Comms., Portland, Oreg., 1987—; core faculty Sch. Svc. Leadership, Salem, Oreg., 1995—. Author: Professional Integration, 1987, Update: Federal Republic of Germany, 1990, Update: Great Britain, 1987; author, editor book series Your International Assignment, 1973-81; contbr. articles to profl. jours. Mem. equal opportunity and social justice task force Nat. Jewish Rels. Adv. Coun.; bd. dirs. Kids on the Block, Portland, Portland Jewish Acad., Portland-Ashland Sister City Assn.; mem. Lafayette (Calif.) Traffic Commn., 1974-80; bd. dirs. Ctr. for Ethics and Social Policy, 1988-91; mem. exec. bd. and planning com. Temple Isaiah, Lafayette, 1978-82; bd. dirs. Calif. Symphony, Orinda, 1988-90; mem. exec. com. overseas schs. adv. com. U.S. Dept. State, 1976-82; mem. cmty. rels. coun. Portland Jewish Fedn.; mem. Nat. Jewish Cmty. Rels. task force; Social Justice and Econ. Opportunity, 1995—. Named Sr. Interculturalist, Sietar Internat., 1986. Mem. Am. Soc. of Training and Development, Soc. for Intercultural Edn., Tng. and Rsch. (chmn. 1986-87, nomination com. 1985-86, co-chmn. ethics com. 1989—, governing bd. 1992-95), World Affairs Coun. (exec. bd. internat. profl. performance area 1993—), Am. Women for Internat. Understanding, Portland City Club.

Democrat. Avocations: photography, swimming. Office: TransCultural Svcs 712 NW Westover Ter Portland OR 97210-3136

LOEWY, ROBERT GUSTAV, engineering educator, aeronautical engineering executive; b. Phila., Feb. 12, 1926; s. Samuel N. and Esther (Silverstein) L.; m. Lila Myrna Spinner, Jan. 16, 1955; children: David G., Esther Elizabeth, Joanne Victoria, Raymond Matthew. B in Aero. Engring., Rensselaer Poly. Inst., 1947; MS, MIT, 1948; PhD, U. Pa., 1962. Sr. vibrations engr. Martin Co., Balt., 1948-49; assoc. research engr. Cornell Aero. Lab., Buffalo, 1949-52, prin. engr., 1953-55; staff stress engr. Piasecki Helicopter Co., Morton, Pa., 1952-53; chief dynamics engr., then chief tech. engr. Vertol divsn. Boeing Co., Essington, Pa., 1955-62; from assoc. prof. to prof. mech. and aerospace scis. U. Rochester, 1962-73, dean Coll. Engring. and Applied Sci., 1967-74; dir. Space Sci. Center, 1966-71; v.p., provost Rensselaer Poly. Inst., Troy, N.Y., 1974-78, Inst. prof., 1978-93; dir. Rotorcraft Tech. Ctr., 1982-93; chmn. sch. aerospace engring. Ga. Inst. Tech., 1993—; chief scientist USAF, 1965-66; cons. govt. and industry, 1959—; mem. aircraft panel Pres.'s Sci. Adv. Coun., 1968-72; mem. Air Force Sci. Adv. Bd., 1966-75, 78-85, vice chmn., 1971, chmn., 1972-75, chmn. aero. systems div. adv. group, 1978-84; mem. Post Office Rsch. and Engring. Adv. Coun., 1966-68; mem. rsch. and tech. adv. com. on aeros. NASA, 1970-71, mem. rsch. and tech. adv. coun., 1976-77, chmn. aero. adv. com., 1978-83; mem. aerospace engring. bd. NRC, 1972-78, 1988-93, mem. bd. on army sci. and tech., 1986-90; mem. naval studies bd. NAS, 1979-82; chmn. tech. adv. com. FAA, 1976-77; bd. dirs. Vertical Flight Found. Contbr. articles to profl. jours. Served with USNR, 1944-46. Recipient NASA disting. pub. service award, 1983; Gotshall-Powell scholar Rensselaer Poly. Inst.; USAF Exceptional Civilian Service awards, 1966, 75, 85. Fellow AAAS; hon. fellow AIAA (Lawrence Sperry award 1958), Am. Helicopter Soc. (tech. dir. 1963-64); mem. Am. Soc. Engring. Edn., Nat. Acad. Engring., Sigma Xi, Sigma Gamma Tau, Tau Beta Pi. Achievements include research on unsteady rotor aerodynamics first showing it to be fundamentally different from fixed wing. Home: 3420 Wood Valley Rd NW Atlanta GA 30327-1518 Office: Ga Inst Tech Sch Aerospace Studies Atlanta GA 30332-0150 *Looking back, I was fortunate to have known somehow, from an early age, that I would be an aeronautical engineer. That profession, through positions in industry, research and education, has provided challenge, satisfaction and valued associations.*

LOEWY, STEVEN A., lawyer; b. N.Y.C., Dec. 21, 1952; s. Samuel Alexander and Irene Dorothy (Aber) L.; children: Tamar, David. BA, Washington U., St. Louis, 1974; JD, Yeshiva U., 1979. Bar: Md. 1980, U.S. Supreme Ct. 1983. Assoc. Gordon, Feinblatt, Rothman, Hoffberger & Hollander, Balt., 1980-81, Constable, Alexander, Daneker & Skeen, Balt., 1981-85, Weinberg & Green, Balt., 1985-87; ptnr. Ober, Kaler, Grimes & Shriver, Balt., 1987-92; pvt. practice Rockville, 1993—; lectr. in law U. Balt., 1981-84; active edn. appeal bd. U.S. Dept. Edn., Washington, 1985-90. Research grantee U.S. Dept. Housing and Devel., 1979. Mem. ABA (chmn. title ins. com. 1992-95, com. on coms. 1995—, real property sect.), Md. Bar Assn. (real property sect.). Republican. Jewish. Home: 6251 Rollins Ave Rockville MD 21215-2506 Office: 6110 Executive Blvd Ste 612 Rockville MD 20852-3903

LOFERSKI, JOSEPH JOHN, electrical engineering educator; b. Hudson, Pa., Aug. 7, 1925; s. Andrew and Mary (Kochuba) L.; m. Sylvia Sweeda, Aug. 27, 1949; children: Marianne Fleury, Patricia Seal, Joseph, Barbara, Michael, Sharon. BS in Physics, U. Scranton, 1948; MS, U. Pa., 1949, PhD, 1953. Research physicist RCA Labs., 1953-60; faculty Brown U., 1961—, prof. engring., 1966—, dean of engring., 1968-74, assoc. dean Grad. Sch., 1980-83; dir. R.I. Ctr. for Thin Film and Interface Rsch., 1987—; pres. Solamat, Inc., E. Providence, 1977-83; sci. counsellor U.S. Embassy, Warsaw, 1985-87; mem. U.S./Poland Joint Commn. for Sci. and Tech. Coop., 1988-91; U.S./Poland Nat. Acad. Scis. Exch. fellow Inst. Nuclear Rsch., Swierk, 1974-75; mem. New Eng. Energy Congress, 1978-79; mem. organizing coms. 25 IEEE Photovoltaic Conf., 1956-96, Internat. Photovoltaic Confs., 1984—; gen. chmn. Fifth Internat. Conf. on Solid Films and Surfaces, 1990; cons. in field; lectr. on solar photovoltaic energy, sci. and tech.; vis. chaired prof. Nat. Tsing Hua U., Hsinchu, Taiwan, 1994-96. Mem. editl. bd. Energy Conversion, 1972—, Jour. Solar Energy Materials, 1978-92, Jour. Solar Energy Materials and Solar Cells, 1992, Progress in Photovoltaics, 1992—, Ency. of Applied Physics, 1990—; contbr. numerous articles to profl. jours. Served with AUS, 1944-46. Recipient Freeman award Providence Engring. Soc., 1974; named to Internat. Solar Hall of Fame, 1989. Fellow AAAS, IEEE (William Cherry award 1981); mem. Sigma Xi, Tau Beta Pi. Home: 33 Slater Ave Providence RI 02906-5423 Office: Brown Univ Div Engring Box D Providence RI 02912

LOFGREN, CHARLES AUGUSTIN, legal and constitutional historian, history educator; b. Missoula, Mont., Sept. 8, 1939; s. Cornelius Willard and Helen Mary (Augustin) L.; m. Jennifer Jenkins Wood, Aug. 6, 1986. AB with great distinction, Stanford U., 1961, AM, 1962, PhD, 1966. Instr. history San Jose State Coll., 1965-66; asst. prof. Claremont McKenna Coll., 1966-71, assoc. prof., 1971-76, prof., 1976—, Roy P. Crocker prof. Am. history and politics, 1976—. Served with USAR, 1957-63. Mem. Am. Soc. Legal History, Orgn. Am. Historians, Am. Hist. Assn. Republican. Roman Catholic. Author: Government from Reflection and Choice, 1986, The Plessy Case, 1988; contbr. articles to profl. jours. Office: Claremont McKenna Coll Dept History 850 Columbia Ave Claremont CA 91711-6420

LOFGREN, DONNA LEE, geneticist; b. Bay Shore, N.Y., Apr. 13, 1957; d. Carl Oscar and Esther Louise (Kustes) L. BS, Cornell U., 1979; MS, Va. Polytech. Inst. and State U., 1981, PhD, 1984. Postdoctoral rsch. assoc. Dept. Animal Scis. Purdue U., West Lafayette, Ind., 1985-90; profl. assoc. in animal breeding Dept. Animal Scis. Purdue U., 1990—. Mem. Am. Soc. Animal Sci., Am. Dairy Sci. Assn., Sigma Xi (rsch. award 1985). Office: Dept Animal Sci Purdue U 1151 Lilly Hall West Lafayette IN 47907-1151

LOFGREN, KARL ADOLPH, surgeon; b. Killeberg, Sweden, Apr. 1, 1915; s. Hokan Albin and Teckla Elizabeth (Carlsson) L.; m. Jean Frances Taylor, Sept. 12, 1942; children: Karl Edward, Anne Elizabeth. Student, Northwestern U., 1934-37; M.D., Harvard U., 1941; M.S. in Surgery, U. Minn., 1947. Diplomate Am. Bd. Surgery. Intern U. Minn. Hosps., Mpls., 1941-42; Mayo Found. fellow in surgery, 1942-44, 46-48; asst. surgeon Royal Acad. Hosp., Uppsala, Sweden, 1949; asst. to surg. staff Mayo Clinic, Rochester, Minn., 1949-50; cons. sect. peripheral vein surgery Mayo Clinic, 1950-81; instr. in surgery Mayo Grad. Sch. Medicine, 1951-60, asst. prof. surgery, 1960-74; comdg. officer USNR Med. Co. Mayo Clinic, 1963-67, head sect. peripheral vein surgery, dept. surgery, 1966-79, sr. cons., 1980-81; assoc. prof. surgery Mayo Med. Sch., 1974-79, prof., 1979-81, emeritus prof., 1982—; cons. surg. staff Rochester Meth. Hosp., St. Mary's Hosp. Contbr. chpts. to textbooks, articles to profl. jours. Mem. adv. bd. Salvation Army, Rochester, 1959-81, 82—, pres., 1962-63. Served to capt. M.C. USNR, 1944-46. Decorated Bronze Star. Fellow ACS; mem. Soc. Vascular Surgery, Midwestern Vascular Surgery Soc., Internat. Cardiovascular Soc., Minn. Surg. Soc., Swedish Surg. Soc. (hon.), Swiss Soc. Phlebology (co-worker), So. Minn. Med. Assn. (pres. 1972-73), Scandinavian Soc. Phlebology (hon.), Am. Venous Forum, Rotary Club, Sigma Xi. Baptist. Home: 1001 7th Ave NE Rochester MN 55906-7074 Office: Mayo Clinic Rochester MN 55905

LOFGREN, ZOE, congresswoman; b. San Mateo, Calif., Dec. 21, 1947; d. Milton R. and Mary Violet L.; m. John Marshall Collins, Oct. 22, 1978; children: Sheila Zoe Lofgren Collins, John Charles Lofgren Collins. BA in Polit. Sci., Stanford U., 1970; JD cum laude, U. Santa Clara, 1975. Bar: Calif., 1975. D.C. Adminstrv. asst. to Congressman Don Edwards, San Jose, Calif., 1970-79; ptnr. Webber and Lofgren, San Jose, 1979-81; mem. Santa Clara County Bd. Suprs., 1981-94; congresswoman 104th U.S. Congress, Calif. 16th Dist., 1995—; part-time prof. Law, U. Santa Clara, 1978-80; jud. com., judiciary subcom. on comml. and adminstrv. law, subcom. on crime, sci. com. subcoms. on basic rsch. & tech.; house com. on sci., subcommittee on tech., basic rsch. Exec. dir. Community Housing Developers, Inc., 1979-80; trustee San Jose Community Coll. Dist., 1979-81; bd. dirs. Community Legal Svcs., 1978-81, San Jose Housing Svc. Ctr., 1978-79; mem. steering com. sr. citizens housing referendum, 1978; del. Calif. State Bar Conv., 1979-82, Dem. Nat. Conv., 1976; active Assn. Immigration and Nationality Lawyers, 1976-82, Calif. State Dem. Cen. Com., 1975-78, Santa Clara County Dem. Cen. Com., 1974-78, Notre Dame High Sch. Blue Ribbon Com., 1981-84, Victim-Witness Adv. Bd., 1981-94. Recipient Bancroft-Whitney award for Excellence in Criminal Procedure, 1973. Mem. Santa Clara County Bar Assn. (trustee 1979—), Santa Clara County Women Lawyers Com. (exec. bd. 1979-80), Sanata Clara Law Sch. Alumni Assn. (v.p. 1977, pres. 1978), Nat. Women's Polit. Caucus, Assn. of Bay Area Govts. (exec. bd. 1981-86). Office: US House Reps 118 Cannon House Office Bldg Washington DC 20515-0516 also: 635 N First St Ste B San Jose CA 95112

LOFLAND, JOHN FRANKLIN, sociologist, educator; b. Milford, Del., Mar. 4, 1936; s. John Purnell and Juanita (Jobe) L.; m. Lyn Hebert, Jan. 2, 1965. B.A., Swarthmore Coll., 1958; M.A., Columbia U., 1960; Ph.D., U. Calif., Berkeley, 1964. Asst. prof. sociology U. Mich., 1964-68; assoc. prof. sociology Calif. State U., Sonoma, 1968-70; asso. prof. sociology U. Calif., Davis, 1970-74; prof. U. Calif., 1974-94; prof. emeritus U. Calif., Davis, 1994—. Author: Doomsday Cult, 1966, 77, Analyzing Social Settings, 1971, 3d edit., (with L. H. Lofland) 1995, Protest, 1985, Polite Protestors, 1993, Social Movement Organizations, 1996, 6 other books; founding editor Jour. Contemporary Ethnography, 1970-74; contbr. articles and revs. to profl. lit. Mem. Am. Sociol. Assn. (chair sect. on collective behavior and social movements 1980-81, chair sect. on sociology of peace and war 1989-90, Outstanding Scholarship award 1987), Pacific Sociol. Assn. (pres. 1980-81), Soc. Study Symbolic Interaction (pres. 1986-87, G.H. Mead award for outstanding career contbns. 1995). Home: 523 E St Davis CA 95616-3816 Office: U Calif Sociology Dept Davis CA 95616

LOFLAND, LYN HEBERT, sociology educator; b. Everett, Wash., Dec. 2, 1937; d. Lisle Francis and Estelle Mae (Hogan) Hebert; m. Stuart A. Jones, Dec. 28, 1958 (div. 1964); m. John Franklin Lofland, Jan. 2, 1965. BA, Antioch Coll., Yellow Springs, Ohio, 1960; MA, U. Mich., 1966; PhD, U. Calif., San Francisco, 1971. Asst. prof. sociology U. Calif., Davis, 1971-77, assoc. prof., 1977-85, prof., 1985—, vice chair dept., 1986-89, acad. dir. Women's Resource and Rsch. Ctr., 1976-78. Author: A World of Strangers, 1973, The Craft of Dying, 1978; co-author: Analyzing Social Settings, 1984, 95; editor: Toward a Sociology of Death and Dying, 1976; co-editor: The Community of the Streets, 1994. Mem. Am. Sociol. Assn. (chair comty. and urban sociology sect. 1986-88, Robert and Helen Lynd award comty. and urban sociology sect. 1995), Pacific Sociol. Assn. (pres. 1989-90), Soc. for Study Symbolic Interaction (pres. 1980-81), Davis Faculty Assn. (chair 1988-89). Democratic Socialist. Avocations: reading, puzzles, indoor gardening. Home: 523 E St Davis CA 95616-3816 Office: U Calif Dept Sociology Davis CA 95616

LOFRISCO, ANTHONY F., lawyer; b. Bklyn., 1933. BS, Fordham U., 1955, LLB, 1958. Bar: N.Y. 1958, U.S. Supreme Ct. 1960. Ptnr. Winston & Strawn, N.Y.C. Office: Winston & Strawn 200 Park Ave New York NY 10166-4193

LÖFSTEDT, BENGT TORKEL MAGNUS, classics educator; b. Lund, Sweden, Nov. 14, 1931; came to U.S., 1967; s. Ernst Martin Hugo and Sigrid (Johanson) L.; m. Maija-Leena Kekomäki, Oct. 15, 1961; children: Ragnar, Torsten, Ritva, Ingvar. M.A., U. Uppsala, Sweden, 1954, Fil. Lic. (Ph.D.), 1957, Fil. doktor, 1961. Asst. prof. Latin U. Uppsala, 1962-67; asso. prof. Mediaeval Latin U. Calif. at Los Angeles, 1967-68, prof., 1968—; contbr. Swedish newspapers Fria Ord, Vägen Framåt. Author: Studien Über die Sprache der langobardischen Gesetze, 1961, Der hibernolateinische Grammatiker Malsachanus, 1965, Zenonis Veronensis Tractatus, 1971, Ars Laureshamensis, 1977, Sedulius Scottus: In Donati artem minorem, in Priscianum, in Eutychem, 1977, Ars Ambrosiana, 1982, Beatus Liebanensis: Adversus Elipandum, 1984 (with G.J. Gebauer) Bonifatius Ars Grammatica, 1980, (with L. Holtz and A. Kibre) Smaragdus: Liber in Partibus Donati, 1986, Sedulius Scottus: Kommentar zum Evangelium nach Matthäus 11,2 bis Schluss, 1991, (with B. Bischoff) Anonymus ad Cuimnanum, 1992, Vier Juvenal-Kommentare aus dem 12. Jh., 1995; contbr. articles to profl. jours. Served to lt. Swedish Army, 1959-60. Alexander von Humboldt-Stiftung fellow Munich, 1961-62; Humanities Inst., U. Calif. grantee, 1968, 71; Am. Philos. Soc. grantee, 1971, 74; Am. Council Learned Socs. grantee, 1972, 75. Lutheran. Office: UCLA Dept Classics 405 Hilgard Ave Los Angeles CA 90024-1475

LOFSTROM, MARK D., lawyer, educator, communications executive; b. Mpls., May 11, 1953; s. Dennis E. and Dorothy Dee (Schreiber) L. BA in Art History, Carleton Coll., 1979; MBA, Columbia U., 1989; JD, U. Hawaii, 1992. Bar: Hawaii 1992, Minn. 1995. Pub. rels. asst. Honolulu Acad. Arts, 1979, pub. rels. rep., 1980-84, pub. rels. officer, 1984-87; law clk. Kiefer Oshima Chun Fong and Chung, 1990-91; assoc. Cades Schutte Fleming & Wright, 1991-95; sole proprietor Law Offices of Mark D. Lofstrom, 1995—; instr. internat. bus. law/bus. law for accts. U. Hawaii Coll. Bus., 1995—; instr. art law U. Hawaii summer session, 1995—; organizer artists and writers exhbn., 1981; coord. rep. program Carleton Coll. Alumni Assn., Hawaii, 1984-87; co-editor and mktg. assoc. Pacific Telecomms. Coun., 1988-92, intern East-West Ctr., 1992. Editor mag. on preservation; exec. editor U. Hawaii Law Rev., 1991-92; co-editor: (newsletter) Pacific Comm. Coun. Procs., 1990-92; bd. editors Hawaii Bar Jour., 1992—; contbr. articles on current exhbns., intellectual property, art, and internat. law. Sec., bd. dirs. Arts Coun. Hawaii, 1985-86, chmn. ways and means com., 1986-87, pres. bd. dirs.; bd. dirs. Hawaii Alliance for Arts Edn., 1994-95, chair-elect, 1995—. Recipient NCR Stakeholders award, 1988, legal rsch. and writing award Hawaii State Bar Assn. Young Lawyers Div., 1991. Mem. ABA, Hawaii State Bar Assn. (sec. internat. law sect. 1994, chair internat. law sect. 1995—), Minn. Bar Assn. Office: PO Box 2481 Honolulu HI 96804-2481 also: PO Box 27 Brainerd MN 56401

LOFT, KURT, newspaper editor, science writer, music critic; b. Baltimore, Fla., Mar. 5, 1956; s. Ernest E. and Mary (Guilday) L. Student, U. Ctrl. Fla., 1972-79, U. Fla., 1979-81. Music critic Tampa (Fla.) Tribune, 1981—, sci. writer, 1987—. Office: Tampa Tribune 202 S Parker St Tampa FL 33606-2308

LOFTFIELD, ROBERT BERNER, biochemistry educator; b. Detroit, Dec. 15, 1919; s. Sigurd and Katherine (Roller) L.; m. Ella Bradford, Aug. 24, 1946 (dec. Dec. 1990); children: Lore Loftfield DeBower, Eric, Linda, Norman, Bjòrn, Curtis, Katherine, Earl, Allison, Ella-Kari. BS, Harvard U., 1941, MA, 1942, PhD, 1946. Research assoc. MIT, Cambridge, 1946-48; research assoc. to sr. research assoc. Mass. Gen. Hosp., Boston, 1948-64; asst. to assoc. prof. biochemistry Harvard U. Sch. Medicine, Boston, 1948-64; prof. biochemistry Sch. Medicine U. N.Mex., Albuquerque, 1964-90, chmn. dept. biochemistry, 1964-71, 78-90, prof. emeritus, 1990—. Contbr. articles on protein biosynthesis and enzymology to profl. jours. Served as corp. U.S. Army, 1945-46. Fellow Damon Runyon Fund, 1952-53, Guggenheim Found., 1961-62; Fulbright fellow, 1977, 83; sr. fellow NIH, 1971-72. Mem. AAAS, Am. Soc. Biol. Chemists, Am. Chem. Soc., Am. Assn. Cancer Research, Biophys. Soc., Marine Biol. Lab. Lutheran. Avocations: sailing, hiking, camping, skiing. Home: 707 Fairway Rd NW Albuquerque NM 87107-5718 Office: Univ NMex Sch of Medicine Dept of Biochemistry Albuquerque NM 87131

LOFTIN, DON DERICO, secondary education educator; b. Kinston, N.C., Feb. 12, 1954; s. Hosea Nathaniel Loftin and Mary Elizabeth (Fields) Loftin-Mitchell. BA in English and Secondary Edn., St. Vincent's Coll., Latrobe, Pa., 1977; postgrad., CUNY, 1982-85. Tchr. Port Richmond H.S.-N.Y.C. Bd. Edn., Bklyn., 1978-88, dean students, 1980-83; tchr., reading curriculum planner Automotive H.S., Bklyn., coord. student affairs, 1995—; adj. prof. outreach program City U., S.I., 1983, Mercy Coll., Dobbs Ferry, N.Y., 1983-84; program dir., acad. cons. First Ctrl. Family Life Ctr., S.I., 1990—, founder, artistic dir. drama dept. Unity Repertoire Theatre Inc., 1993—, Youth Theatre on the Move, The Silvertone Theatre Experience, cons. edn., bd. dirs., 1994—. Proposal com. chmn. Louis Lopez Found., S.I., 1994—. Mem. ASCD, NAACP (edn. com.), Mus. Natural History. Democrat. Baptist. Avocation: helping children. Home: 17 Bowen St Staten Island NY 10304-3513

LOFTIN, MARION THEO, sociologist, educator; b. Coushatta, La., Sept. 10, 1915; s. John Griffin and Ida Estella (Huckaby) L. B.A., Northwestern La. State Coll., 1936; M.A., La. State U., 1941; Ph.D., Vanderbilt U., 1952. Tchr. pub. high schs. Red River Parish, La., 1935-40; asso. prof. Southeastern La. State Coll., 1946-47; faculty Miss. State U., 1949—, Thomas L. Bailey prof. sociology and anthropology, head dept., 1961-67; assoc. dean Miss. State U. (Grad. Sch.), 1965-77, dean, 1977-79, v.p. grad. studies and research, 1980-85, prof. sociology, v.p. grad. studies and research emeritus, 1986—. Served with AUS, 1941-45. Mem. Am. Sociol. Assn., Rural Sociol. Soc., So. Sociol. Soc., Phi Kappa Phi, Omicron Delta Kappa. Home: 1214 Hillcrest cir Starkville MS 39759

LOFTIN, SISTER MARY FRANCES, religious organization administrator; b. Atlanta, Mar. 25, 1928. B, Marquette U., 1955; M, George Washington U., 1970. Various positions, 1955-66; dir. nursing svcs. Seton Med. Ctr., Austin, 1966-68; adminstrv. resident Med. Ctr. East, Birmingham, Ala., 1969-70, asst. adminstr., 1970-71; asst. adminstr. St. Joseph Hosp. & Health Care Ctr., Chgo., 1971-74; adminstr. St. Thomas Hosp., Nashville, 1974-81; pres. Daus. of Charity Health Sys., Evansville, Ind., 1981-87; pres., CEO Daus. of Charity Nat. Health Sys., St. Louis, 1992-94; chancellor Diocese of Birmingham, Ala., 1995—. Home: St Vincent's Residence 2724 Hanover Cir S Birmingham AL 35205-1706 Office: Chancellor's Office Diocese of Birmingham PO Box 12047 Birmingham AL 35202-2047

LOFTIS, JACK D., newspaper editor, newspaper executive. Exec. v.p., editor Houston Chronicle. Office: Houston Chronicle Pub Co 801 Texas St Houston TX 77002-2906*

LOFTIS, JOHN (CLYDE), JR., English language educator; b. Atlanta, May 16, 1919; s. John Clyde and Marbeth (Brown) L.; m. Anne Nevins, June 29, 1946; children: Mary, Laura, Lucy. BA, Emory U., 1940; MA, Princeton U., 1942, PhD, 1948. Instr. English Princeton, 1946-48; instr., then asst. prof. English UCLA, 1948-52; faculty Stanford U., 1952-81, prof. English, 1958-81, Bailey prof. English, 1977-81, Bailey prof. emeritus, 1981—, chmn. dept., 1973-76. Author: Steele at Drury Lane, 1952, Comedy and Society from Congreve to Fielding, 1959, La Independencia de la Literatura Norteamericana, 1961, The Politics of Drama in Augustan England, 1963, The Spanish Plays of Neoclassical England, 1973, (with others) The Revels History of Drama in English, Vol. V, 1976, Sheridan and the Drama of Georgian England, 1977, Renaissance Drama in England and Spain: Topical Allusion and History Plays, 1987; editor: (Steele) The Theatre, 1962, Restoration Drama: Modern Essays in Criticism, 1966, (with V.A. Dearing) The Works of John Dryden, Vol. IX, 1966, (Sheridan) The School for Scandal, 1966, (Nathaniel Lee) Lucius Junius Brutus, 1967, (Addison) Essays in Criticism and Literary Theory, 1975, The Memoirs of Anne, Lady Halkett and Ann, Lady Fanshawe, 1979, (with D.S. Rodes and V.A. Dearing) The Works of John Dryden, Vol. XI, 1978, (with P.H. Hardacre) Colonel Bampfield's Apology, 1993; co-editor Augustan Reprint Society, 1949-1952, English Literature, 1660-1800: A Current Bibliography, 1951-56; gen. editor: Regents Restoration Drama Series, 35 vols, 1962-81; mem. editorial bd.: Studies in English Literature, 1966-76, Huntington Library Quar., 1968-76, Wesleyan Edit. Works Henry Fielding, 1970-83 , Augustan Reprint Soc., 1985-90. Served with USNR, 1942-46, PTO. Fellow Fund Advancement Edn., 1955-56; Fulbright lectr. Am. studies Peru, 1959-60; Guggenheim fellow, 1966-67; fellow Folger Shakespeare Library, 1967; NEH fellow, 1978-79. Mem. MLA, Phi Beta Kappa, Kappa Alpha. Home: 7 Arastradero Rd Portola Valley CA 94028-8012 Office: Stanford Univ Dept English Stanford CA 94305

LOFTNESS, MARVIN O., electrical engineer; b. Altacortes, Wash., Feb. 20, 1920. BA in Chemistry, Pacific Luth. U., 1957. Owner, engr. Loftness Engrng. Fellow IEEE (co-organizer/instr. tutorial on power-line EMI), Power Engrng. Soc. (corona and field effects subcom.). Office: Loftness Engineering 115 W 20th Olympia WA 98501*

LOFTNESS, VIVIAN ELLEN, architecture educator. BS, MIT, 1974, MArch, 1975; postgrad., Harvard U. Instr. MIT, 1976; asst. prof. SUNY, Buffalo, 1977-78; prof., head dept. arch. Carnegie Mellon U., Pitts., 1981—; bldg. rsch. bd., com. mem. Nat. Acad. Scis., 1986-89, bd. applied climatology, 1983-85, adv. bd. for built environment, 1982-84; vis. critic dept. arch. U. Pa., 1985; coun. mem. Nat. Inst. Bldg. Scis., 1983-85; rsch. project mgr. Housing Urban Devel. Office Policy Devel. and Rsch.; spkr. and cons. in field. Author: (with others) The Office of the Future: The Japanese Approach to Tomorrows Workplace, 1992; co-author: (with others) Evaluating and Predicting Design Performance, 1992, Occupational Medicine: Building-Associated Illness, 1989, Building Evaluation, 1989, The Handbook of Climatology, 1987, Intelligent Buildings: Applications of IT and Building Automation to High Technology Construction Projects, 1988, The Ergonomic Payoff: Designing the Electronic Office, 1986, The Building Systems Integration Handbook, 1985; contbr. articles to profl. jours. Grantee NSF, 1988—, U.S. Army Constrn. Engring. Labs., 1993-94, State Pa. Energy Office, Nat. Endowment for the Arts, 1986-87; Rotary fellow, 1975-76, Grunsfeld Found. fellow, 1973; recipient N.Y. State Passive Solar Residential Design award, 1979. Mem. AIA, ASTM, ASHRAE, Pa. Soc. Arch., Internat. Facility Mgmt. Assn., Internat. Solar Energy Soc., Am. Solar Energy Soc., Ctr. Internat. Batiment. Office: Carnegie Mellon Univ Coll Fine Arts Pittsburgh PA 15213-3890

LOFTON, KENNETH, professional baseball player; b. East Chicago, Ind., May 31, 1967. Student, U. Ariz. Baseball player Houston Astros, 1988-91, Cleveland Indians, 1991—. Ranked 1st in Am. League for stolen bases, 1992; recipient Am. League Gold Glove award, 1993, 94; named to All-Star Team, 1994. Office: Cleveland Indians 2401 Ontario St Cleveland OH 44115

LOFTON, KEVIN EUGENE, medical facility administrator; b. Beaumont, Tex., Sept. 29, 1954. BS, Boston U., 1976; M Health Care Adminstrn., Ga. State U., 1979. Adminstrv. resident Meml. Med. Ctr., Corpus Christi, Tex., 1978-79; adminstr. emergency svcs. Univ. Hosp., Jacksonville, Fla., 1979-80, adminstr. material mgmt., 1980-81, asst. exec. dir. ambulatory care, 1981-82, asst. v.p. ambulatory svcs., 1982-83, v.p. profl. svcs., 1983-86; exec. v.p. Univ. Med. Ctr., Jacksonville, 1986-90; exec. dir. Howard Univ. Hosp., Washington, 1990-93; assoc. v.p., exec. dir. U. Ala. Hosp., Birmingham, 1993—. Contbr. articles to profl. publs. Fellow Am. Coll. Health Care Execs. (R.S. Hudgenw award 1993); mem. Am. Hosp. Assn., Nat. Assn. Health Svcs. Execs. (pres.-elect). Home: U Ala Hosp Room 246/OHB 2112 Lake Heather Way Hoover LA 35242 Office: U Ala Hosp 619 19th St Rm 246/OHB Birmingham AL 35233*

LOFTON, THOMAS MILTON, lawyer; b. Indpls., May 12, 1929; s. Milton Alexander and Jane (Routzong) L.; m. Betty Louise Blades, June 20, 1954; children: Stephanie Louise, Melissa Jane. BS, Ind. U., 1951, JD, 1954. Bar: Ind. 1954, U.S. Ct. Appeals (7th cir.) 1959, U.S. Supreme Ct. 1958. Law clk. to justice U.S. Supreme Ct., Washington, 1954-55; ptnr. Baker & Daniels, Indpls., 1958—; dir. Ind. U. Found., Bloomington, 1978—, Clowes Fund, 1980—, Bank One Indpls., 1993—; chmn. bd. Lilly Endowment, Indpls., 1991—; mem. bd. visitors Ind. U. Law, Bloomington, 1976—. Editor-in-chief Ind. Law Jour., 1953. 1st lt. U.S. Army, 1955-58. Recipient Peck award Wabash Coll., 1982. Mem. Order of Coif, Masons, Beta Gamma Sigma. Republican. Presbyterian. Home: 9060 Pickwick Dr Indianapolis IN 46260-1714 Office: Lilly Endowment 2800 N Meridian St Indianapolis IN 46208-9999

LOFTUS, THOMAS ADOLPH, ambassador; b. Stoughton, Wis., Apr. 24, 1945; s. Adolph Olean and Margaret Elaine (Nielson) L.; m. Barbara Carolyn Schasse, Aug. 23, 1969; children: Alec Kristian, Karl Edward. B.S., U. Wis.-Whitewater, 1970; M.A., U. Wis.-Madison, 1971. Analyst Wis. Assembly Dem. Caucus, Madison, 1974-75; adminstrv. asst. to speaker Wis. Assembly, Madison, 1975-76; mem. Wis. Assembly, 1977-91, majority leader, 1981-82, speaker, 1983-91; dir. WisKids Count Wis. Coun. Children and Families, 1991-93; amb. to Norway, Oslo, 1993—; adj. prof. polit. sci. U. Wis.-Whitewater; lectr. Edgewood Coll.; vis. prof. Rutgers U., Eagleton Inst. Author: The Art of Legislative Politics, 1994. Del. Dem. Nat. Conf., 1976, 82, 88, 92; mem. Dem. Nat. Com., 1989-91; Dem. nominee for Gov. of Wis., 1990. Served with U.S. Army, 1965-67. Fellow John F. Kennedy Sch. Govt. Harvard U. Democrat. Lutheran. Home and Office: Am Embassy Oslo PSC 69 Box 1000 APO AE 09707

LOFTUS, THOMAS DANIEL, lawyer; b. Seattle, Nov. 8, 1930; s. Glendon Francis and Martha Helen (Wall) L. BA, U. Wash., 1952, JD, 1957. Bar:

Wash. 1958, U.S. Ct. Appeals (9th cir.) 1958, U.S. Dist. Ct. Wash. 1958, U.S. Ct. Mil. Appeals 1964, U.S. Supreme Ct. 1964. Trial atty. Northwestern Mut. Ins. Co., Seattle, 1958-62; sr. trial atty. Unigard Security Ins. Co., Seattle, 1962-68, asst. gen. counsel, 1969-83, govt. rels. counsel, 1983-89; of counsel Groshong, LeHet & Thornton, 1990—; mem. Wash. Commn. on Jud. Conduct (formerly Jud. Qualifications Commn.), 1982-88, vice-chmn., 1987-88; judge pro tem Seattle Mcpl. Ct., 1973-81; mem. nat. panel of mediators Arbitration Forums, Inc., 1990—. Sec., treas. Seattle Opera Assn., 1980-91; pres., bd. dirs. Vis. Nurse Svcs., 1979-88; pres., v.p. Salvation Army Adult Rehab. Ctr., 1979-86; nat. committeeman Wash. Young Rep. Fedn., 1961-63, vice chmn., 1963-65; pres. Young Reps. King County, 1962-63; bd. dirs. Seattle Seafair, Inc., 1975; bd. dirs., gen. counsel Wash. Ins. Coun., 1984-86, sec., 1986-88, v.p., 1988-90, Am. Mediation Panel of Mediators; bd. dirs. Arson Alarm Found., 1987-90; bd. visitors law sch. U. Wash., 1993—. 1st lt. U.S. Army, 1952-54, col. Res., 1954-85. Fellow Am. Bar Found.; mem. Am. Arbitration Assn. (nat. panel arbitrators 1965—), Am. Arbitration Forums, Inc. (nat. panel arbitrators 1992), Am. Mediation Panel, Wash. Bar Assn. (gov. 1981-84), Seattle King County Bar Assn. (sec., trustee 1977-82), ABA (ho. of dels. 1984-90), Internat. Assn. Ins. Counsel, U.S. People to People (del. Moscow internat. law-econ. conf. 1990), Def. Rsch. Inst., Wash. Def. Trial Lawyers Assn., Wash. State Trial Lawyers Assn., Am. Judicature Soc., Res. Officers Assn., Judge Advocate General's Assn., U. Wash. Alumni Assn., Coll. Club Seattle, Wash. Athletic Club, Masons, Shriners, Ranier Club, Pi Sigma Alpha, Delta Sigma Rho, Phi Delta Phi, Theta Delta Chi. Republican. Presbyterian. Home: 3515 Magnolia Blvd W Seattle WA 98199-1841 Office: 2133 3rd Ave Seattle WA 98121-2321

LOGA, SANDA, physicist, educator; b. Bucharest, Romania, June 13, 1932; came to U.S., 1968; d. Stelian and Georgeta (Popescu) L.; m. Karl Heinz Werther, Mar. 1968 (div. 1970). MS in Physics, U. Bucharest, 1955; PhD in Biophysics, U. Pitts., 1978. Asst. prof. faculty medicine and pharmacy Bucharest, 1963-67; rsch. asst. Presbyn./St. Luke's Hosp., Chgo., 1968-69; assoc. rsch. scientist Miles Labs., Elkhart, Ind., 1969-70; rsch. asst. U. Pitts., 1971-78; rsch. assoc. Carnegie-Mellon U., Pitts., 1978-80; health physicist VA Med. Ctr., Westside, Chgo., 1980; med. physicist, VA Med. Ctr. N. Chgo, 1980—; assoc. prof. Chgo. Med. Sch., N. Chgo., 1985—. Mem. Am. Assn. Physicists in Medicine, Health Physics Soc. Office: Chgo Med Sch U Health Scis 3333 Green Bay Rd North Chicago IL 60064-3037

LOGAN, DAVID BRUCE, health care administrator; b. Grand Rapids, Mich., Jan. 30, 1942; s. Wesley Goldsmith and Ernestine (Sovereen) L.; m. Joann Fern Jordan, Nov. 5, 1961; children: Jennifer, Julie, Jeanine, David II, Douglas, Dean. MusB, U. Mich., 1964; B Zoology with honors, Mich. State U., 1970; MBA, U. Ill., 1978. Tchr. sci. Flint (Mich.) Pub. Schs., 1970-71; health care adminstr. USAF, Mpls., 1971-75; asst. chief, med. adminstrn. svc. trainee VA, Mpls., 1975-76; asst. chief med. adminstrn. svc. VA, Danville, Ill., 1976-78; asst. med. dist. coord. VA Med. Dist. 15, Indpls., 1978-80; med. dist. coord. VA Med. Dist. 8, Durham, N.C., 1980-87; nat. disaster med. system mgr. VA, Salisbury, N.C., 1987—. Dir. choir Kirk of Kildaire Presbyn. Ch., 1981-85; asst. scoutmaster, scoutmaster Boy Scouts Am., 1978-94. Capt. USAF, 1964-68, lt. col. Res. ret. Fellow Am. Coll. Healthcare Execs., Soc. Air Force Res. Med. Officers, Air Force Assn., Res. Officers Assn. (bd. dirs. Minn. 1973-74, jr. v.p. for air 1974-75). Office: Dept VA Med Ctr 1601 Brenner Ave Salisbury NC 28144-2515

LOGAN, FRANCIS DUMMER, lawyer; b. Evanston, Ill., May 23, 1931; s. Simon Rae and Frances (Dummer) L.; m. Claude Riviere, Apr. 13, 1957; children: Carolyn Gisele, Francis Dummer. B.A., U. Chgo., 1950; B.A. Juris, Oxford U., 1954; LL.B., Harvard U., 1955. Bar: N.Y. 1956, Calif. 1989. Assoc. Milbank, Tweed, Hadley & McCloy, N.Y.C., 1955-64; ptnr. Milbank, Tweed, Hadley & McCloy, 1965-96; chmn., 1992-96. Mem. ABA, N.Y. State Bar Assn., Assn. of Bar of City of N.Y., Calif. Bar Assn., Council on Fgn. Relations, Am. Law Inst. Home: 1726 Linda Vista Ave Pasadena CA 91103

LOGAN, HENRY VINCENT, transportation executive; b. Phila., Nov. 7, 1942; s. Edward Roger and Alberta (Gross) L.; m. Mary Genzano, Sept. 28, 1963; children: Michele Leah, Maureen Laura, Monica Lynn. BS in Commerce, DePaul U., 1975; M in Mgmt., Northwestern U., 1984. Successively supr. corp. acctg., asst. mgr. gen. acctg., mgr. gen. acctg., dir. corp. acctg. and taxes TTX Co., Chgo., 1962-70, controller, 1970-78, dir. fin. planning, 1978-83, mng. dir., fin. adminstr., 1983-85, v.p., chief fin. officer, 1985-88, sr. v.p. fleet mgmt., 1988—; bd. dirs. Calpro, Co., Mira Loma, Calif., RailGon Co., Chgo.; bd. dirs., fin. com. Railway Supply Assn. Treas. TTX Co. Polit. Action Com., Chgo., 1980; vol Sch. Dist. 87 Task Force, Glen Ellyn, Ill., 1986. Mem. Nat. Freight Transp. Assn., Intermodal Assn. N.Am. (chmn. legis. com. 1992-94), Union League Club (reception com. 1987-92, fin. com. 1993-95), Medinah (Ill.) Country Club. Republican. Roman Catholic. Avocations: golf, music, reading, bicycling. Home: 812 Abbey Dr Glen Ellyn IL 60137-6130

LOGAN, J. MURRAY, investment manager; b. Balt., Mar. 15, 1935; s. Lloyd and Helen Mildred (Gilbert) L.; m. Mary Page Cole, June 19, 1987 (dec. Sept. 1993); 1 child by previous marriage, Maria Charlotte. BA, Johns Hopkins U., 1959. Securities analyst Merrill Lynch Pierce Fenner & Smith, N.Y.C., 1959-62; ptnr. Wood Struthers & Winthrop, N.Y.C., 1962-70; v.p. EFC Mgmt. Corp., L.A., 1970-73, Faulkner, Dawkins & Sullivan, Inc., N.Y.C., 1973-75; chmn. investment policy com. Rockefeller & Co., Inc., N.Y.C., 1975—; bd. dirs. Mercury Selected Trust, Luxembourg, U.K. Fund, N.Y.C., Europe Fund, N.Y.C., World Trust Fund, Luxembourg, Berkshire Opera Co., Camphill Found. Trustee Johns Hopkins U., Balt., 1984-91. With USCG, 1954-56. Mem. Racquet and Tennis Club, The Leash. Office: Rockefeller & Co Inc 30 Rockefeller Plz # 5425 New York NY 10112

LOGAN, JAMES KENNETH, federal judge; b. Quenemo, Kans., Aug. 21, 1929; s. John Lysle and Esther Maurine (Price) L.; m. Beverly Jo Jennings, June 8, 1952; children: Daniel Jennings, Amy Logan Sliva, Sarah Logan Sherard, Samuel Price. A.B., U. Kans., 1952; LL.B. magna cum laude, Harvard, 1955. Bar: Kans. 1955, Calif. 1956. Law clk. U.S. Cir. Judge Huxman, 1955-56; with firm Gibson, Dunn & Crutcher, L.A., 1956-57; asst. prof. law U. Kans., 1957-61, prof., dean Law Sch., 1961-68; ptnr. Payne and Jones, Olathe, Kans., 1968-77; judge U.S. Ct. Appeals (10th cir.), 1977—; Ezra Ripley Thayer tchg. fellow Harvard Law Sch., 1961-62; vis. prof. U. Tex., 1964, Stanford U., 1969, U. Mich., 1976; sr. lectr. Duke U., 1987, 91, 93; commr. U.S. Dist. Ct., 1964-67. Author: (with W.B. Leach) Future Interests and Estate Planning, 1961, Kansas Estate Administration, 5th edit., 1986, (with A.R. Martin) Kansas Corporate Law and Practice, 2d edit., 1979, The Federal Courts of the Tenth Circuit: A History, 1992; also articles. Candidate for U.S. Senate, 1968. Served with AUS, 1947-48. Rhodes scholar, 1952; recipient Disting. Service citation U. Kans., 1986. Mem. Am., Kans. bar assns., Phi Beta Kappa, Order of Coif, Beta Gamma Sigma, Omicron Delta Kappa, Pi Sigma Alpha, Alpha Kappa Psi, Phi Delta Phi. Democrat. Presbyterian.

LOGAN, JOHN ARTHUR, JR., retired foundation executive; b. Chgo., Dec. 8, 1923; s. John Arthur and Dorothea (Halstead) L.; m. Ann Orr deForest, Aug. 30, 1960. Grad., Taft Sch., Watertown, Conn., 1942; B.A., Yale, 1949, M.A., 1951, Ph.D., 1954; LL.D., Western Md. Coll.; L.H.D., Hollins Coll. Faculty Yale, 1949-61, asst. prof. history, 1958-61; pres. Hollins Coll., 1961-75, Ind. Coll. Funds Am., N.Y.C., 1975-86; vis. lectr. Salzburg Seminar in Am. Studies, 1961. Author: No Transfer: An American Security Principle, 1961. Served to capt. AUS, 1942-46. Fellow Saybrook Coll., Yale, 1950—. Mem. Phi Beta Kappa. Clubs: Elizabethan (New Haven); Century Assn. (N.Y.C.), Yale (N.Y.C.). Home: 88 Notch Hill Rd Apt 353 North Branford CT 06471

LOGAN, JOHN FRANCIS, electronics company executive, management consultant; b. Norristown, Pa., Apr. 10, 1938; s. Francis Michael and Elizabeth V. L. BS in Bus. Adminstrn., Drexel U., 1961. CPA, N.Y. Auditor Hurdman and Cranston CPA's (merger KPMG Peat Warwick), N.Y.C., 1961-69; v.p. fin., chief fin. officer, treas. Aero Flow Dynamics, Inc., N.Y.C., 1969-84; v.p. fin. and adminstrn., chief fin. officer, treas. Codenoll Tech. Corp., Yonkers, N.Y., 1985-90; v.p. fin., chief fin. officer, treas. VTX Electronics Corp., Farmingdale, N.Y., 1991-92; mgmt. cons. Comtex Info. Systems, Inc./KLMB Group Inc., N.Y.C., 1992—. With U.S. Army, 1962-64. Mem. AICPAs, N.Y. State Soc. CPA's, Pa. Soc.

LOGAN, JOSEPH GRANVILLE, JR., physicist; b. Washington, June 8, 1920; s. Joseph Granville and Lula (Briggs) L.; m. Esther Taylor, June 30, 1944; children—Joseph Michael, Eileen Cecile. B.S., D.C. Tchrs. Coll., 1941; Ph.D. in Physics, U. Buffalo, 1955. Physicist Nat. Bur. Standards, 1944-47, Cornell Aero. Lab., 1947-58; head propulsion research dept. Space Tech. Labs., 1958-61; dir. aerodynamics and propulsion research lab. Aerospace Corp., 1961-67; spl. asst. to dir. research and devel. McDonnell Douglas Astronautics Co., Santa Monica, Calif., 1967-69; mgr. vulnerability and hardening, devel. engring. McDonnell Douglas Astronautics Co., 1969-74; pres. Applied Energy Scis., Inc., Los Angeles, 1974—; v.p. rsch. and devel. Advent Resources, Inc., Torrance, Calif., 1994—; mem. faculty dept. physics Calif. Poly. U., Pomona, 1977-78; bus. devel. specialist Urban U. Center, U. So. Calif., Los Angeles, 1978-79, assoc. dir., 1979-80, dir., 1980-88. Mem. Am. Phys. Soc., AIAA, Soc. Info. Display, N.Y. Acad. Scis. Home: 3652 Olympiad Dr Los Angeles CA 90043-1144 Office: Applied Engery Scis Consulting Svcs PO Box 36583 Los Angeles CA 90043

LOGAN, JOSEPH PRESCOTT, lawyer; b. Topeka, Jan. 21, 1921; s. Joseph Glenn and Corinne (Ripley) L.; m. Yvonne Marie Westrate, July 17, 1943; children: John Daniel, Kathleen Elisabeth, Laurie Prescott. AB, Dartmouth Coll., 1942; LLB, Harvard U., 1948. Bar: Mo. 1948, U.S. Dist. Ct. Mo. 1948. Ptnr. Thompson Coburn, St. Louis, 1958—. Pres., chmn. bd. Ranken Jordan Home for Covalescent Crippled Children, St. Louis, 1968-93. Lt. USNR, 1942-46. Mem. ACLU (bd. mem. 1988, civil liberties award 1982), Noonday Club. Democrat. Congregationalist. Avocations: hiking, mountain climbing, sailing. Home: 36 S Gore Ave Saint Louis MO 63119-2910 Office: Thompson Coburn Ste 3300 1 Mercantile Ctr Saint Louis MO 63101-1643

LOGAN, JOYCE POLLEY, education educator; b. Providence, Ky., Sept. 18, 1935; d. Vernon and Hattie Alice Polley; m. Jewell Wyatt Logan (dec.), June 4, 1956; 1 child, James Edward. BS, Murray State U., 1956, MA, 1960; EdD, Vanderbilt U., 1988. Cert. bus. tchr., vocat. adminstrn. Student sec. Murray (Ky.) State U., 1954-56; bus. tchr. Hopkins County Schs., Madisonville, Ky., 1956-68; regional coord. Vocational Region 2 Ky. Dept. Edn., Madisonville, 1968-83; prin. Health Occupations Sch., Madisonville, 1983-88; voc., tech. adminstr. Ky. Dept. Edn., Frankfort, 1988-90; asst. prof. dept. adminstrn. and supervision Coll. Edn. U. Ky., Lexington, 1990-95; exec. sec. Ky. Com. for Secondary and Middle Schs. Southern Assn. Colls. and Schs., 1995—; evaluator Nat. Home Study Coun., Washington, 1981—; field coord. military evaluations, Am. Coun. on Edn., Washington, 1984—. Author: (with A.C. Krizan) Basics of Writing, 1993. Mem. alumni bd. Murray (Ky.) State U. Coll. Bus., 1988—; fundraiser Ky. Spl. Olympics, Madisonville, 1983, YMCA, Madisonville, 1984; mem. edn. com. Greater Leadership Program Madisonville, Ky. C. of C., 1987-88. Named FFA Hon. State Farmer, Ky. FFA., 1979, Woman of the Year, Lion's Club, Madisonville, Ky., 1987, Outstanding Teacher Educator, 1992. Mem. Nat. Bus. Edn. Assn., Am. Vocat. Assn., Ky. Vocat. Assn., Southern Assn. of Colls. and Schs. (trustee 1973, 1976-78, chmn. Commn on Occupational Ednl. Insts. 1973), Ky. Assn. for Sch. Adminstrs., Assn. for Supervision and Curriculum Devel., Phi Delta Kappa, Omicron Delta Kappa (hon.). Avocations: jogging, tennis, reading, piano playing. Home: 1352 Gray Hawk Rd Lexington KY 40502-2739 Office: U Ky 11 Dickey Hall Coll of Edn Lexington KY 40506

LOGAN, KENNETH RICHARD, lawyer; b. N.Y.C., Dec. 26, 1944; s. John S. and Hazel (Mathias) L.; m. Grace Winter-Durennel, Aug. 12, 1967; children: Finlay, Emily. BA, Princeton U., 1967; JD, U. Pa., 1972. Bar: N.Y., U.S. Dist. Ct. (so. dist.) N.Y., U.S. Ct. Appeals (2nd cir.). Assoc. Simpson Thacher & Bartlett, N.Y.C., 1972-79; ptnr. Simpson, Thacher & Bartlett, N.Y.C., 1979—. Served with U.S. Army, 1969-70. Office: Simpson Thacher & Bartlett 425 Lexington Ave New York NY 10017-3903

LOGAN, LOX ALBERT, JR., museum director; b. Rutherfordton, N.C., Feb. 7, 1954; s. Lox Albert Sr. and Grace (Hawkins) L.; m. Bernadette Wall, May 6, 1978; children: Mark Thomas, Garrett Michael, Sean Timothy. BS, U.S. Mil. Acad., 1976; MA in History Mus. Studies, SUNY, Cooperstown, 1982; postgrad. Am. History, Marquette U., 1988-89. Exec. dir. Wyo. Hist. and Geol. Soc., Wilkes-Barre, Pa., 1983-86; dir. Manitowoc (Wis.) Maritime Mus., 1986-95; exec. dir. USS Constitution Mus., Boston, 1995—; field reviewer Inst. Mus. Svcs., Washington, 1986—; mem. exec. com. Pa. Fedn. Hist. Socs., Harrisburg, 1983-85. Author: (with others) Maritime America, 1988; contbr. to profl. jour. Bd. dirs. Manitowoc-Two Rivers YMCA, 1989-93, scholarship selection com., 1991-95; Pa. rep. admissions to U.S. Mil. Acad., 1984-85; coord. N.E. Pa. Records Coop., Wilkes-Barre, 1983-86; active Com. Econ. Growth, Wilkes-Barre, 1983-85, Govs. Commn. on USS Wis., 1988; rec. sec. adv. com. underwater archaeology State Hist. Soc. Wis., 1988; cabinet Manitowoc United Way Campaign, 1990-92; chmn. Mishabago dist. Boy Scouts Am., 1990-92; bd. dirs., pres. Riverwalk Festival, 1989-95. Nat. Mus. Act. fellow Smithsonian Instn., 1982; recipient award Hugenot Soc. N.Y., 1982. Mem. Am. Assn. Mus. (cons. mus. assessment program 1988—), Am. Assn. State and Local History, Wis. Fedn. Mus. (adv. com. 1988-89, treas. 1989-92, exec. com. 1989-93), Assn. Gt. Lakes Maritime History (bd. dirs. 1986-95), sec. 1986-89, pres. 1989-93), Coun. Am. Maritime Mus. (bd. dirs. 1989, v.p. 1991-93, pres. 1993-95), Presbyn. Hist. Assn. (adv. com. 1989-95, moderator 1991-95). Presbyterian. Avocations: gardening, running, canoeing. Office: USS Constitution Mus PO Box 1812 Boston MA 02129

LOGAN, LYNDA DIANNE, elementary education educator; b. Detroit, June 22, 1952; d. Horatio Bernard and Ruby (Newsom) Graham; m. Keith L. Logan, Aug. 16, 1980; 1 child, Lauren Nicole. BS, Ea. Mich. U., 1974, MA, 1980. Cert. tng. program quality rev., Calif.; cert. tchr., Calif., Miss., Mich.; lic. guidance counselor basic related edn., Miss.; cert. counselor pupil pers. svc. credential, Mich., Calif. Substitute tchr. Detroit Pub. Schs., 1974-76; mid. sch. tchr. Inkster (Mich.) Pub. Schs., 1976-80; CETA vocat. counselor Golden Triangle Vocat.-Tech. Ctr., Mayhew, Miss., 1980-82, basic related educator, 1980-82; elem. tchr. Inglewood (Calif.) Unified Sch. Dist., 1982-93, resource tchr., 1993—; mem. forecast adv. bd. COED Mag., N.Y.C., 1979-80; advisor/founder Newspaper Club Fellrath Mid. Sch., Inkster, 1979-80; mem. interviewing com. Golden Triangle Vocat.-Tech. Ctr., Mayhew, 1980-82, evaluation and follow-up com., 1980-82; pronouncer spelling bee Inglewood Unified Sch. Dist., 1991, 94; organizer student body team meetings Worthington Sch., Inglewood, 1993—, coord. reading program, 1993—, mem. interviewing com., 1987—, co-chairperson yearbook com., 1993-94, prin. adv. bd., 1987-92, ct.-liaison and child welfare attendance rep. L.A. County Edn., 1995—, supt. adv. coun., 1995—, reading is fundamental coord., 1993—, mem. team earthquake preparedness com., 1994—. youth co-chairperson March of Dimes, Detroit, 1976-80; com. mem. Nat. Coun. Negro Women, L.A. chpt., 1982-84; com. mem. Cmty. Action Program, Eternal Promise Bapt. Ch., L.A., 1991, pres. choir, 1991, v.p. hospitality com., 1987-88; co-chmn. women's com., 1990; mem. parent adv. com. Knox Presbyn. Ch. Nursery Sch., L.A., 1988-89. Mem. ASCD, AAUW, NAFE, Black Women's Forum, Ladies Aux. Knights of St. Peter Claver, Ea. Mich. U. Alumni Assn., Phi Gamma Nu. Avocations: bike riding, community organizational activities, travel, movies, theater. Office: Worthington Sch 11101 Yukon Ave Inglewood CA 90303-2728

LOGAN, MATHEW KUYKENDALL, journalist; b. Norman, Okla., Aug. 19, 1933; s. Leonard Marion and Floy-Elise (Duke) L.; m. Linda Dianne Elderkin, Dec. 31, 1964. B.A. in Journalism, U. Okla., 1955. Reporter UPI, 1957-58; city editor Daily Oklahoman, 1958-69; asst. mng. editor Houston Post, 1969-76, mng. editor, 1976-83; mng. editor Sta. KHOU-TV, Houston, 1984-87; asst. dean for community affairs Med. Sch. U. Tex., Houston, 1987-92; v.p. pub. affairs and mktg. Hermann Hosp., Houston, 1992—. Served with AUS, 1957. Mem. UPI Editors Tex. (pres. 1977), Tex. AP Mng. Editors Assn. (pres. 1983), Sigma Chi. Methodist. Home: 24 Sunlit Forest Dr The Woodlands TX 77381-2986

LOGAN, PATRICIA JEAN, interior designer; b. Aurora, Ill., Feb. 24, 1926; d. Harley J. and Svea (Andrews) Benjamin; m. Marcel Guillaume, June 21, 1974. BA, MA, UCLA, 1951. Interior designer, 1951—. Author: Maliblue, 1980, (videos) Contemporary American Art, 1993. Bd. dirs. League for Crippled Children. Recipient awards City of Santa Monica, Calif., 1960, City of L.A., 1974, L.A. Times, Chgo. Tribune. Mem. Am. Soc. Interior Designers (historian), Am. Mus. Contemporary Art (pres. 1989—).

LOGAN, RODMAN EMMASON, jurist; b. West Saint John, N.B., Can., Sept. 7, 1922; s. Gilbert Earle and Emma Zela (Irwin) L.; m. Evelyn Pearl DeWitt, June 19, 1948; children: John Bruce DeWitt, Ian David Alexander, Mary Jane Irwin, Bruce Rodman Hans. BA, U. N.B., 1949, BCL, 1951, DCL (hon.), 1988; DCL, St. Thomas U., Fredericton, N.B., 1974. Bar: N.B. 1951, created Queen's Counsel 1972. Partner firm Logan, Bell and Church, Saint John, N.B., 1951-70; elected to Legis. Assembly, 1963, 67, 70, 74, 78; minister of labor and provincial sec. Province of N.B., 1970-77; atty.-gen. and minister of justice, 1977-82; justice Ct. of Queen's Bench, 1982—. Served with Can. Armed Forces, 1942-45, U.K., N.W. Europe and Ctrl. Mediterranean Forces; hon. col. Royal N.B. Regt. Mem. Royal Commonwealth Soc. Anglican. Clubs: Royal Can. Legion, Carleton and York Regtl. Home: RR 2, 273 Nerepis Rd, Westfield, NB Canada E0G 3J0 Office: Provincial Bldg, 110 Charlotte St, Saint John, NB Canada E2L 2J3

LOGAN, VICKI, advertising executive; b. Oakland, Calif., Aug. 3, 1954; d. Robert Lee and Freida Elizabeth (Luckett) L. BS in Bus. Adminstrn. magna cum laude, Pepperdine U., 1976; M in Internat. Mgmt. with honors, Am. Grad. Sch. Internat. Mgmt., 1979. Asst. to dep. dir. HUD, Washington, 1978; account exec. Doyle Dane Bernbach Advt., Inc., N.Y.C., 1979-81; sr. v.p., creative dir. Jordan, McGrath, Case, Taylor & McGrath Advt., N.Y.C., 1981—. Office: Jordan McGrath Case & taylor Inc 445 Park Ave New York NY 10022-2606

LOGANATHAN, BOMMANNA GOUNDER, environmental chemist, biologist, researcher, educator; b. Mettupalayam, Coimbatore, India, Sept. 30, 1954; arrived in U.S., 1990; s. Nanjappa Bommanna Gounder and Periakkal (Subbayan) B.; m. Kalaiselvi Kurunthachalam; children: Sudan, Dheepa. BS in Zoology, U. Madras, India, 1977; MS in Marine Biology, Annamalai U., Porto Novo, India, 1979, PhD in Marine Biology, 1986; PhD in Ecotoxicology/Environ. Chemistry, Ehime U., Matsuyama, Japan, 1990. Rsch. sci. SUNY, Buffalo, 1990-93; asst. prof. Skidaway Inst. Oceanography (U. Ga. sys.), Savannah, Ga., 1993—. Author chpts. to books; mem. rev. panel Environ. Pollution, Marine Pollution Bull., Environ. Toxicology & Chemistry; contbr. articles to profl. jours. Recipient Outstanding Rsch. award, 1991; sr. rsch. fellow Indian Coun. Agrl. Rsch., 1980-83, Govt. India rsch. fellow Dept. Ocean Devel., 1985-86; Monbusho (Japanese Govt.) rsch. fellow, 1986-90; U.S. EPA rsch. grantee, 1993-95. Mem. AAAS, Soc. Environ. Toxicology and Chemistry, Japanese Soc. Environ. Chemistry, Skidaway Marine Sci. Found. Office: U Systems Ga Skidaway Inst Oceanography 10 Ocean Sci Cir Savannah GA 31411

LOGANBILL, G. BRUCE, logopedic pathologist; b. Newton, Kans., Sept. 6, 1938; s. Oscar and Warrene (Rose) L. B.A., Bethel Coll., Kans., 1956; M.A., U. Kans., 1958; Ph.D., Mich. State U., 1961; postdoctoral fellow, Inst. Logopedics, 1965-66. Mem. faculty Kalamazoo Coll., 1961-63; mem. faculty Fresno (Calif.) State U., 1966-68; mem. faculty Calif. State U., Long Beach, 1968—, prof., 1975—; lectr. on speech communication and pathologies, Argentina, Denmark, France, Japan, Can., India, Scotland, Czechoslovakia, USSR, Germany, People's Republic of China; U.S. rep. 2d Internat. Congress de Melodie-Therapie du Language en accord Nat. Coll. Psychiatry, Paris, 1990. Author: The Bases of Voice, Articulation and Pronunciation, 1974, 5th edit., 1992; contbr. more than 30 articles to profl. jours. Mem. Speech Comm. Assn., Western Speech Comm. Assn., Am. Speech and Hearing Assn., Calif. Speech and Hearing Assn., Internat. Assn. Logopedics and Phoniatrics, Internat. Phonetics Assn., Assn. Calif. State U. Profs. (univ. chpt. pres. 1985, Calif. del. NEA/Calif. Tchrs. Assn. 1990), others. Republican. Episcopalian. Office: Calif State U Long Beach 1250 N Bellflower Blvd Long Beach CA 90840-0006

LOGE, FRANK JEAN, II, hospital administrator; b. Redlands, Calif., May 28, 1945; s. J. Phillip Loge and Helen M. (Booker) Loge Power; m. Sharon Lee Entrekin, Feb. 11, 1967; children—Frank III, Christopher, Gregory. BA, Claremont Men's Coll., Long Beach, Calif., 1967; MBA, Calif. State U.-Long Beach, 1969; postgrad., UCLA Sch. Pub. Health, 1972-73. Mgr. mgmt. analysis UCLA, 1972-73, asst. dir. fin., 1973-74; dir. fin. U. Calif. Davis Med. Ctr., Sacramento, 1975-79, dep. dir. hosp. and clinics, 1979-84, dir. hosp. and clinics, 1984—. Office: U Calif Davis Med Ctr 2315 Stockton Blvd Sacramento CA 95817-2201

LOGEMANN, JERILYN ANN, speech pathologist, educator; b. Berwyn, Ill., May 21, 1942; d. Warren F. and Natalie M. (Killmer) L.; BS, Northwestern U., 1963; MA, 1964, PhD, 1968. Grad. asst. dept. communicative disorders Northwestern U., 1963-68; instr. speech and audiology DePaul U., 1964-65; instr. dept. communicative disorders Mundelein Coll., 1967-71; research assoc. depts. neurology and otolaryngology and maxillofacial surgery Northwestern U. Med. Sch., Chgo., 1970-74, asst. prof., 1974-78, dir. clin. and research activities of speech and lang., 1975—, assoc. prof. depts. neurology, otolaryngology and comm. scis. and disorders, 1978-83, prof., 1983, chmn. dept. communication scis. and disorders, 1982—, Ralph and Jean Sundin Prof. of Comm. Scis. and Disorders, 1995—; mem. assoc. staff Northwestern Meml. Hosp., 1976—, N. Chgo. VA Hosp., 1983—, Evanston (Ill.) Hosp., 1988—, Children's Meml. Hosp., Chgo., 1988—; cons. in field; assoc. dir. cancer control. Ill. Comprehensive Cancer Council, Chgo., 1980-82. Mem. rehab. com. Ill. div. Am. Cancer Soc., 1975-79, chmn., 1979—; mem. upper aerodigestive tract organ site com. Nat. Cancer Inst., 1986-89. Postdoctoral fellow Nat. Inst. Neurologic Disease, Communicative Disorders and Stroke, Northwestern U., 1968-70; fellow Inst. Medicine Chgo., 1981—; grantee Nat. Cancer Inst., 1975—, Am. Cancer Soc. , 1981-82; Honors award Conn. Speech Lang. Hearing Assn., 1995, Appreciation award Coun. Grad. Programs in Comms. Scis. and Disorders, 1995, Cellular One award Vanderbilt U. Fellow Am. Speech, Lang. and Hearing Assn. (pres.-elect 1993, pres. 1994, past pres. 1995), Inst. Medicine; mem. Internat. Assn. Logopedics and Phoniatrics, AAUP, Acoustic Soc. Am. (program com. Chgo. regional chpt.), Linguistic Soc. Am., Speech Comm. Assn., Am. Cleft Palate Assn., Ill. Speech and Hearing Assn. (DiCarlo award 1988), Chgo. Heart Assn., Chgo. Speech Therapy and Auditory Soc. Author: The Fisher-Logemann Test of Articulation Competence, 1971, Evaluation and Treatment of Swallowing Disorders, 1983; Manual for the Videofluorographic Evaluation of Swallowing, 1985, 93; assoc. editor Jour. Speech and Hearing Disorders, Jour. Head Trauma Rehab., Dysphagia jour., 1978-82. Office: Northwestern U Med Sch 303 E Chicago Ave Chicago IL 60611-3008 also: Dept Comm Sci & Disorder 2299 Sheridan Rd Evanston IL 60208-0837

LOGGIA, ROBERT, actor; b. S.I., N.Y., Jan. 3, 1930; s. Benjamin and Elena (Blandino) L.; m. Audrey O'Brien; children: Tracey, John, Kristina, Cynthia. Student, Wagner Coll., S.I., 1947-49; B. Journalism, U. Mo., Columbia, 1951. Appeared in Broadway prodns. Toys in the Attic, 1961, Three Sisters, 1964, Boom Boom Room, 1973-74; TV series T.H.E. Cat, 1968-69, The Nine Lives of Elfego Baca, 1958-59, Mancuso F.B.I., 1989-90 (Emmy Best Actor award nominee), Sunday Dinner, 1991; films include Somebody Up There Likes Me, 1956, The Garment Jungle, 1957, Cop Hater, The Lost Missile, 1958, Cattle King, 1963, Greatest Story Ever Told, 1965, Che!, 1969, First Love, 1977, Speed Trap, Revenge of the Pink Panther, 1978, The Ninth Configuration (Twinkle Twinkle Little Kane), S.O.B., 1981, An Officer and a Gentleman, 1982, Trail of the Pink Panther, 1982, Scarface, 1983, Psycho II, 1983, Curse of the Pink Panther, 1983, Prizzi's Honor, 1985, Jagged Edge, 1985 (Acad. Best Supporting Actor award nominee 1986), Armed and Dangerous, 1986, Over the Top, 1986, Hot Pursuit, 1986, That's Life, 1986, The Believers, Big, 1988, Oliver & Company (voice), 1988, Triumph of the Spirit, 1989, Gaby, 1989, Marrying Man, 1990, Opportunity Knocks, 1990, Necessary Roughness, 1991, Gladiator, 1992, Innocent Blood, 1992, Bad Girls, 1994, I Love Trouble, 1994, Independence Day, 1996, Lost Highway, 1996, Mistrial, 1996, Wide Awake, 1996, Smille's Sense of Snow, 1996; TV miniseries Echoes in the Darkness, Favorite Son, 1989, Wild Palms, 1993; TV appearances include Chicago Conspiracy Trial, 1988 (Ace Best Actor award nominee), Afterburn, 1992, Merry Christmas Baby, 1992, Nurses on the Line, 1993, Mercy Mission, 1993, White Mile, 1994, Lifepod, 1993, Between Love & Honor, 1995, Jake Lassiter, 1995. With U.S. Army, 1951-53. Office: Creative Artists Agy 9830 Wilshire Blvd Beverly Hills CA 90212-1804 *Pursue excellence.*

LOGGIE, JENNIFER MARY HILDRETH, medical educator, physician; b. Lusaka, Zambia, Feb. 4, 1936; came to U.S., 1964, naturalized, 1972; d. John and Jenny (Beattie) L. M.B., B.Ch., U. Witwatersrand, Johannesburg,

South Africa, 1959. Intern Harare Hosp., Salisbury, Rhodesia, 1960-61; gen. practice medicine Lusaka, 1961-62; sr. pediatric house officer Derby Children's Hosp., also St. John's Hosp., Chelmsford, Eng., 1962-64; resident in pediatrics Children's Hosp., Louisville, 1964, Cin., 1964-65; fellow clin. pharmacology Cin. Coll. Medicine, 1965-67; mem. faculty U. Cin. Med. Sch., 1967—, prof. pediatrics, 1975, asso. prof. pharmacology, 1972-77. Contbr. articles to med. publs.; editor Pediatric and Adolescent Hypertension, 1991. Grantee Am. Heart Assn., 1970-72, 89-90. Mem. Am. Pediatric Soc. (elected), Midwest Soc. Pediatric Research. Episcopalian. Home: 1133 Herschel Ave Cincinnati OH 45208-3112 Office: Children's Hosp Med Ctr Children's Hosp Rsch Found 3300 Burnet Ave Cincinnati OH 45229

LOGGINS, KENNY (KENNETH CLARKE LOGGINS), singer, songwriter; b. Everett, Wash., Jan. 17, 1947; s. Robert George and Lina Clelia (Massie) L.; m. Julia Cooper. Student, Pasadena City Coll. Mem. groups, Second Helping, Loggins & Messina, Electric Prunes, rec. artist, Columbia Records and Sony Wonder Records; songwriter, Milk Money and Gnossos Music Pub. Co.; solo albums include: Celebrate Me Home, 1977, Nightwatch, 1978, Keep the Fire, 1979, Alive, 1980, Footloose, 1984, Vox Humana, 1985, Back to Avalon, 1988, Leap of Faith, 1991, Outside From the Redwoods, 1993, Return to Pooh Corner, 1994; albums with Messina include: Sittin' In, 1971, Loggins & Messina, 1972, Full Sail, 1973, On Stage, 1974, Motherlode, 1975, So Fine, 1975, Native Sons, 1976, Best of Friends, 1977, Finale, 1978, Best of Loggins and Messina, 1980; other albums: stage: Kenny Loggins on Broadway, 1988; composed and performed theme for This Island Earth (The Disney Channel), 1993 (Cable Ace award, Best Original Song, Emmy award). Adv. bd. Earthtrust. Recipient Rock 'n Roll Sports Classic Gold medal, Grammy award for What A Fool Believes, 1980, Grammy award for This is It, 1981, Harry Chapin award We Are the World. Mem. ASCAP, Nat. Assn. Rec. Arts and Scis. Office: care William Morris Agy 151 S El Camino Dr Beverly Hills CA 90212-2704

LOGHRY, RICHARD M., architecture and engineering services executive. CEO Mason & Harger Engring. Office: Mason & Hanger-Silas Mason Co 2355 Harrodsburg Rd Lexington KY 40504-3324*

LOGIE, JOHN HOULT, mayor, lawyer; b. Ann Arbor, Mich., Aug. 11, 1939; s. James Wallace and Elizabeth (Hoult) L.; m. Susan G. Duerr, Aug. 15, 1964; children: John Hoult Jr., Susannah, Margaret Elizabeth. Student Williams Coll., 1957-59; BA, U. Mich., 1961, JD, 1968; MS, George Washington U., 1966. Bar: Mich. 1969, U.S. Dist. Ct. (we. and ea. dists. 1969) Mich., U.S. Ct. Appeals (6th cir. 1987). Assoc. Warner, Norcross & Judd, Grand Rapids, Mich., 1969-74, ptnr., 1974—; mayor City of Grand Rapids, 1992—; chmn. civil justice adv. group U.S. Dist. Ct. (we. dist.) Mich., 1995—. program coord. condemnation law sect. Inst. Continuing Legal Edn.; guest lectr. Grand Rapids C.C., Grand Valley State U., Western Mich. U., Mich. State U.; legal counsel to 15 West Mich. hosps.; instr. U.S. Naval Acad., 1964-66. Pres. Grand Rapids PTA Council, 1971-73, Heritage Hill Assn., 1976, sec., trustee 1971-84; chmn. Grand Rapids Urban Homesteading Commn., 1975-80, Grand Rapids Hist. Commn., 1985-90, Grand Rapids/Kent County Sesquicentennial Com., 1986-88; MEM. Headlee Blue Ribbon Commn., 1993-94; v.p. bd. dirs. Goodwill Industries, Grand Rapids, 1973-79, Am. Cancer Soc., Grand Rapids, 1970-81; pres., trustee Hist. Soc. Mich., 1984-90. Lt. USN, 1961-66. Mem. ABA (forum com. on health law 1980—), Mich. Bar Assn. (chmn. condemnation com. real property sect. 1985-88), Grand Rapids Bar Assn. (dir. young lawyers sect. 1970), Am. Acad. Hosp. Attys., Mich. Soc. Hosp. Attys. (pres. 1976-77), Nat. Health Lawyers Assn., Univ. Club (dir. 1979-82, pres. 1980-82), Peninsular Club, Williams Club (NYC). Avocations: sailing, hunting, fishing. Home: 601 Cherry St SE Grand Rapids MI 49503-4726 Office: Warner Norcross and Judd 900 Old Kent Bldg Grand Rapids MI 49503 also: Office of Mayor 300 Monroe Ave NW Grand Rapids MI 49503-2206

LOGUE, DENNIS EMHARDT, financial economics educator, consultant; b. Bklyn., Mar. 28, 1944; s. Joseph Paul and Helen Rose (Emhardt) L.; m. Marcella Julia Watson, June 11, 1966; children: Dennis E. Jr., Patrick G. A.B., Fordham U., 1964; M.B.A., Rutgers U., 1966; Ph.D., Cornell U., 1971. Asst. prof. Ind. U., Bloomington, 1971-73; sr. economist U.S. Treasury, Washington, 1973-74; prof. bus. Tuck Sch., Dartmouth Coll., Hanover, N.H., 1974—, now Steven Roth prof. mgr., former assoc. dean; founding bd. dirs. Ledyard Nat. Bank; bd. dirs. Blurb Comm. Author: Legislative Influence on Corporate Pension Plans, 1979, The Investment Performance of Corporate Pension Plans, 1988, Managing Corporate Pension Plans, 1991; editor: Handbook of Modern Finance, 1993; co-editor Fin. Mgmt., 1978-81. Served to 1st lt. U.S. Army, 1966-68. Mem. Am. Econ. Assn., Am. Fin. Assn. (bd. dirs. 1981-84), Fin. Mgmt. Assn. (bd. dirs., pres. 1995—), Knights of Malta, Order Holy Sepulchre, N.Y. Athletic Club, Rotary, Beta Gamma Sigma. Republican. Roman Catholic. Home: 1 River Ridge Rd Hanover NH 03755-1910 Office: Dartmouth Coll Amos Tuch Sch Bus Admi Hanover NH 03755

LOGUE, EDWARD JOSEPH, development company executive; b. Phila., Feb. 7, 1921; s. Edward J. and Resina (Fay) L.; m. Margaret DeVane, June 7, 1947; children: Katherine, William DeVane. B.A., Yale U., 1942, LL.B., 1947. Bar: Pa. 1948, Conn. 1950. Practiced in Phila., 1948; legal sec. Gov. Chester Bowles, Hartford, Conn., 1949-51; spl. asst. to ambassador Chester Bowles, New Delhi, 1952-53; devel. adminstr. City of New Haven, 1954-60, City of Boston, 1961-67; vis. Maxwell prof. govt. Boston U., 1967-68; pres., chief exec. officer N.Y. State Urban Devel. Corp., 1968-75; pres. Roosevelt Island Devel. Corp., 1969-75, Logue Devel. Co., Inc., 1976—, South Bronx Devel. Orgn., Inc., 1978-85; chief exec. officer Logue Boston, 1987-1994; Thomas Jefferson prof. Sch. Architecture, U. Va., spring 1985; sr. lectr. Sch. Architecture and Planning, MIT, 1985-89; prin. devel. cons. to Ft. Lincoln New Town, Washington, 1968; vis. lectr. Yale Sch. Law, 1957-77; chmn. Task Force on Housing and Neighborhood Improvement, N.Y.C., 1966; mem. Critical Choices Commn., 1973-76; founder Vineyard Open Land Found., 1970; mem. vis. com. Harvard U. Sch. Design, 1969-75; mem. resource team Mayor's Inst. on City Design. Chmn. Dukes County Charter Commn., 1991-92; advisor to Mayor Jackson and Corp. for Olympic Devel., Atlanta, 1993. With USAAF, 1943-45. Decorated Air medal with clusters. Mem. AIA (hon. mem.), Am. Acad. Arts and Scis., Tavern Club (Boston), Century Club (N.Y.C.), Union Boat Club (Boston), Saturday (Boston), Yale Club (N.Y.C.), Phi Beta Kappa (hon.). Democrat. Home: Scotchman's Bridge Ln West Tisbury MA 02575

LOGUE, FRANK, arbitrator, mediator, urban consultant, former mayor New Haven; b. Phila., Aug. 18, 1924; s. Edward J. and Resina (Fay) L.; m. Mary Ann Willson, June 10, 1950; children: Nancy, Jennifer, Jonathan. BA, Yale U., 1948, JD, 1951. Bar: Conn. 1951. Practiced in Bridgeport and Trumbull, Conn., 1951-64; dir. Community Action Inst., OEO Regional Tng. Center, New Haven, 1965-69, Nat. Urban Fellows, New Haven, 1969-75; alderman City of New Haven, 1972-75; mayor, 1976-79; prosecutor Town of Trumbull, 1955-57; town atty., 1957-61; regional cons. U.S. Civil Rights Commn., 1961-63; lectr. New Haven Police Acad., 1965-70; vis. asst. prof. So. Conn. State Coll., 1968-69; assoc. fellow Morse Coll., Yale U., 1968—; mem. adv. bd. Yale U. Sch. Mgmt., 1976-80, mem. faculty, 1980-81; vice chmn. Inst. Pub. Mgmt., 1975-82; chmn. task force on arts Nat. League Cities, 1977-79; mem. adv. bd. U.S. Conf. Mayors, 1977-79; panelist pub. programs div. Nat. Endowment for Humanities, 1974-78; mem. Pres.'s Adv. Commn. on the Holocaust; chmn. bd. dirs. Internat. Inst. Public Mgmt., 1979-82; mem. Conn. Adv. Com. Intergovtl. Relations, 1984-86; pub. interest arbitrator Conn. Dept. Edn., 1985—; pub. mem. alt. panel Conn. Bd. Mediation and Arbitration, 1986-89. Author: Who Administers—Access to Leadership Positions in the Administration of Government, 1972. Served with inf. AUS, 1944-45, ETO. Mem. Am. Arbitration Assn. (labor panel 1987—), Conn. Bar Assn. (exec. com. labor and employment law sect. 1989—). Home and Office: 173 Livingston St New Haven CT 06511-2209

LOGUE, JOHN J(OSEPH), psychologist; b. Phila., Nov. 16, 1929; s. Edwin J. and Ellen V. (Mallon) L.; m. Evelyn Bortnick, Apr. 24, 1954; 1 child, Eileen Logue Handel. BS, Temple U., 1954, MEd, 1958, EdD, 1966. Lic. psychologist Pa., Md., N.J., Del. Ptnr., sr. cons. RHR Internat., Phila., 1966-88; mgmt. psychologist pvt. practice Phila, 1988—. With U.S. Army, 1954-56. Mem. APA (indsl., orgn., cons., counseling, edn. divsns.), Quaker City Yacht Club. Home: 1942 Greymont St Philadelphia PA 19116-3926 Office: 205 Keith Valley Rd Horsham PA 19044-1408

LOGUE, JOSEPH CARL, electronics engineer, consultant; b. Phila., Dec. 20, 1920; s. Percival J. and Mathilda (Moser) L.; m. Jeanne Martha Neubecker, Mar. 28, 1943; children: Raymond, Marilyn, Paul. BEE, Cornell U., 1944, MEE, 1949. Instr. Cornell U., Ithaca, N.Y., 1944-49, asst. prof., 1949-51; engr. IBM, Poughkeepsie, N.Y., 1951-86; dir. IBM Research Div., Yorktown Heights, N.Y., 1986; cons. Lorex Industries Inc., Poughkeepsie, 1986—. 30 patents in field; contbr. papers to profl. publs. IBM fellow. Fellow IEEE, AAAS; mem. Nat. Acad. Engring., Research Soc. Am. Avocations: flying, scuba diving, photography. Home: 52 Boardman Rd Poughkeepsie NY 12603-4228

LOGUE-KINDER, JOAN, alcoholic beverages company executive; b. Richmond, Va., Oct. 26, 1943; d. John T. and Helen (Harvey) Logue; m. Lowell A. Henry Jr., Oct. 6, 1963 (div. Sept. 1981); children: Lowell A. Henry III, Catherine D. Henry, Christopher Logue Henry; m. Randolph S. Kinder, Dec. 13, 1986 (div. Nov. 1995). Student, Wheaton Coll., 1959-62; BA in Sociology, Adelphi U., 1964; cert. in edn., Mercy Coll., Dobbs Ferry, N.Y., 1971; postgrad., NYU, 1973; cert. in edn., St. John's U., 1974. Asst. to dist. mgr. U.S. Census Bur., N.Y.C., 1970; tchr. and adminstr. social studies Yonkers (N.Y.) Bd. Edn., 1971-75; dir. pub. rels. Nat. Black Network, N.Y.C., 1976-83; corp. v.p. NBN Broadcasting (formerly Nat. Black Network), N.Y.C., 1984-90; sr. v.p. The Mingo Group/Plus, N.Y.C., 1990-91; v.p. Edelman Pub. Rels. Worldwide, N.Y.C., 1991-93; dep. asst. sec. pub. affairs U.S. Dept. Treasury, Washington, 1993-94, asst. sec. pub. affairs, 1994-95; dir. corp. comm. programs The Seagram Co., N.Y.C., 1995—; cons. in field. Mem. alumnae recruitment coun. Wheaton Coll.; mem. Nigerian-Am. Friendship Soc., 1978-81; bd. dirs. Westchester Civil Liberties Union, 1974-77, Greater N.Y. coun. Girl Scouts U.S.A., 1985-93, Operation PUSH, 1985-93; del. White House Conf. on Small Bus.; active polit. campaigns, including Morris Udall for U.S. Pres., Howard Samuels for Gov.; sr. black media advisor Dukakis/Bentsen presdl. campaign, 1988; conv. del. N.Y. State Women's Polit. Caucus, 1975, pres. black caucus, 1976-77. Recipient Excellence in Media award Inst. New Cinema Artists, 1984. Mem. World Inst. Black Comm. (bd. dirs. 1983-91). Home: 1800 7th Ave Apt 9B New York NY 10026 Office: Seagram Corp Comm 375 Park Ave New York NY 10152

LOH, EUGENE C., physicist, educator; b. Soochow, China, Oct. 1, 1933; 3 children. BS, Va. Polytech. U., 1955; PhD, MIT, 1961. Rsch. assoc. in physics MIT, Cambridge, Mass., 1961-64; asst. prof. MIT, Cambridge, 1964-65; sr. rsch. assoc. in nuc. studies Cornell U., Ithaca, N.Y., 1965-75; assoc. prof physics U. Utah, Salt Lake City, 1975-77, prof., chmn. dept. physics, 1977-90, Disting. prof. physics, 1995, dir. High Energy Astrophysics Inst., 1993—; vis. sci. Stanford Linear Accelerator Ctr., 1980-81. Fellow Am. Physics Soc.; mem. Sigma Xi. Office: U Utah 201 James Fletcher Bldg Salt Lake City UT 84112-1195

LOH, HORACE H., pharmacology educator; b. Canton, Republic China, May 28, 1936. BS, Nat. Taiwan U., Taipei, Republic China, 1958; PhD, U. Iowa, 1965. Lectr. dept. pharmacology U. Calif. Sch. Medicine, San Francisco, 1967; assoc. prof. biochem. Wayne State U., Detroit, 1968-70; lectr., rsch. assoc. depts. psychiatry, pharmacology Langley Porter Neuropsychiatric Inst. U. Calif. Sch. Medicine, San Francisco, 1970-72, assoc. prof. depts. psychiatry, pharmacology Langley Porter Neuropsychiatric Inst., 1972-75, prof. depts. psychiatry, pharmacology Langley Porter Neuropsychiatric Inst., 1975-88; prof., head dept. pharmacology U. Minn. Med. Sch., Mpls., 1989—, Frederick and Alice Stark prof., head dept. pharmacology, 1990—; chmn. annual meeting theme com. on receptors Fedn. Am. Socs. for Exptl. Biology, 1984; mem. exec. com. Internat. Narcotic Rsch. Conf., 1984-87, chair sci. program annual meeting, 1986; mem. adv. com. Nat. Tsing Hua U. Inst. Life Scis., Taiwan, Republic China, 1985-89; mem. exec. com. Com. on Problems of Drug Dependence, Inc., 1985-88; mem. sci. adv. coun. Nat. Found. for Addicitive Diseases, 1987—; cons. U.S. Army R & D Dept. Defense, 1980-84. Mem. editorial adv. bd. Life Scis., 1978—, Substance and Alcohol Abuse, 1980—, Neurochemistry Internat., 1980-88, Neuropharmacology, 1982—, Neurosci. Series, 1982-83, Annual Rev. Pharmacology and Toxicology, 1984-89, Jour. Pharmacology and Exptl. Therapeutics, 1987—; assoc. editor Annual Rev. Pharmacology and Toxicology, 1990-95, CRC Critical Rev. in Pharmacological Scis., 1987-88; author 56 book chpts; editor 1 book; contbr. 300 articles to profl. jours. Recipient Career Devel. award USPHS, 1973-78, 78-83, Rsch. Scientist award, 1983-88, 1989-94, Humboldt award for sr. U.S. scientists (Fed. Republic Germany), 1977. Mem. Am. Coll. Neuropsychopharmacology (honorific awards com. 1988—), Am. Soc. Pharmacology and Exptl. Therapeutics (program com. 1976-86, trustee bd. publs. 1987-93, com. on confs. 1990-93), Soc. Chinese Bioscientists in Am. (pres. 1985-86), Western Pharmacology Soc. (councilor 1980-83, pres. 1984-85). Office: U Minn Med Sch Dept Pharmacology 3 249 Millard Hall Minneapolis MN 55455

LOH, ROBERT N. K., academic administrator, engineering educator; b. Lumut, Malaysia; arrived in Can., 1962, came to U.S., 1968; m. Annie Loh; children: John, Peter, Jennifer. BSc in Engring., Nat. Taiwan U., Taipei, 1961; MSc in Engring., U. Waterloo, Ont., Can., 1964, PhD, 1968. Asst. prof. U. Iowa, Iowa City, 1968-72, assoc. prof., 1973-78; prof. Oakland U., Rochester, Mich., 1978—, John F. Dodge prof., 1984—, assoc. dean, 1985—, dir. Ctr. for Robotics and Advanced Automation, 1984—. Mem. editorial bd. Info. Systems, 1975—, Jour. of Intelligent and Robotic Systems, 1987—, Asia-Pacific Engring. Jour., 1990—; contbr. over 190 jour. publs. and tech. reports. Recipient numerous research grants and contracts from Dept. Def., NSF and pvt. industry. Mem. IEEE, Soc. Machine Intelligence (bd. dirs. 1985—), Assn. Unmanned Vehicle Systems, 1987—, Sigma Xi, Tau Beta Pi. Office: Oakland U Ctr for Robotics and Advanced Automation Dodge Hall Engring Rochester MI 48309-4401

LOH, WALLACE D., university dean. Dean Sch. Law U. Wash.

LOHF, KENNETH A., librarian, writer; b. Milw., Jan. 14, 1925; s. Herman A. and Louise (Krause) L. AB, Northwestern U., 1949; AM, Columbia U., 1950, MS in Library Sci., 1952. Asst. librarian spl. collections Columbia U., N.Y.C., 1957-67; librarian rare books and manuscripts Columbia U., 1967-92. Author: Thirty Poems, 1966, Conrad at Mid-Century: Editions and Studies, 1957, The Achievement of Marianne Moore: A Bibliography, 1958, Yvor Winters: A Bibliography, 1959, Frank Norris: A Bibliography, 1959, Sherwood Anderson: A Bibliography, 1960, An Index to The Little Review, 1914-1929, 1961, The Collection of Books, Manuscripts and Autograph Letters in the Library of Jean and Donald Stralem, 1962, Indices to Little Magazines, 1953-64, The Literary Manuscripts of Hart Crane, 1967, The Jack Harris Samuels Library, 1974, The Centenary of John Masefield's Birth, 1978; (poems) Seasons, 1981, Arrivals, 1987, Fictions, 1990, Passages, 1991, Places, 1992, Endings/Beginnings, 1994; editor: Hart Crane, Seven Lyrics, 1966, Collections and Treasures of the Rare Book and Manuscript Library of Columbia University, 1985, Poets in a War, 1995, Hours, 1996; editor Columbia Library Columns, 1981-92; contbr. prefaces, afterwards, essays and articles to profl. publs. Sec.-treas. Friends of Columbia U. Librs., 1973-92; mem. coun. Am. Mus. Britain. 1st lt. USAAF, 1943-46. Mem. Knickerbocker Club, Century Club, Grolier Club (coun., sec. 1987-90, pres. 1990-94), Coun. Fellows Pierpont Morgan Libr. Episcopalian. Home: 560 Riverside Dr Apt 21B New York NY 10027-3236

LOHMAN, GORDON R., manufacturing executive; b. 1934. BS, MIT, 1955. Rsch. metallurgist, project engr. Amsted Industries, Inc., Chgo., 1958-61; project engr. Amstead Rsch. Labs. Amsted Rsch. Labs., Chgo., 1961-67; dir. rsch. Amstead Industries, Inc., Chgo., 1967-68, pres. rsch., 1968-76, pres. MacWhyte divsn., 1976-78, v.p., 1978-87, exec. v.p., then pres., 1987-88, pres., COO, 1988-90, pres., CEO, 1990—; trustee Ill. Inst. Tech.; bd. dirs. Am. Brands, Inc., CIPSCO. Lt. USAF, 1955-58. Office: Amsted Industries Inc 205 N Michigan Ave Chicago IL 60601-5925*

LOHMAN, JOHN FREDERICK, editor; b. Bismarck, N.D., Oct. 29, 1935; s. William Ernest and Viola (Paulson) L.; m. Dorothy Louise Stolp, July 13, 1962; children—Sheryl, Susan, Timothy, Jeffrey. B.S. in Engring., N.D. State U., 1960. Copy boy The Forum, Fargo, N.D., 1952-56, reporter, 1957-68, night editor, 1969-71, city editor, 1972-76, mng. editor, 1977-86, assoc. editor, 1987—; outdoor editor, 1988—. Mem. AP Mng. Editors Assn., Eagles. Avocations: hunting; fishing. Home: 2029 33rd Ave S Fargo ND 58104-6563

LOHMANN, GEORGE YOUNG, JR., neurosurgeon, hospital executive; b. Scranton, Pa., Aug. 9, 1947; s. George Young Lohmann and Elizabeth (Nichols) Frantzen; m. Joette Calabrese, May 15, 1973 (div. 1981); m. Rosemary Ei-Ling Ma, Sept. 24, 1988; 1 child, Norelle Christa Victoria. AB in Chemistry with honors, Hobart Coll., 1968; MD, SUNY, Buffalo, 1972. Diplomate Am. Bd. Neurol. Surgeons, Am. Acad. Pain Specialists. Resident gen. surgery Wesley Meml. Hosp., Chgo., 1972-73; from jr. resident to chief resident Georgetown U. Hosp., Washington, 1975-79; asst. med. dir. West Side Orgn., Chgo., 1973-74; emergency physician St. James Hosp., Chicago Heights, Ill., 1973-74; pvt. practice Baton Rouge, 1979-81, 81-84; dir. dept. neurosurgery Brookdale Hosp. Med. Ctr., Bklyn., 1984-93; pres. Bklyn. Neurosurg. Svcs., Inc., 1985—; mem. Med. Dir. Com., Risk Mgmt. Com., Exec. Quality Assurance Com., 1987-93; mem. Med. Bd. Com., 1985-93, Exec. Bd. Com., 1984-93, Pain Mgmt. Com., 1988-91. Named to Compton-Connolly Guide to Best Physicians in the New York Met. Area; patentee in field; contbr. articles to profl. jours. Mem. adv. bd. Ctr. Latin Affairs, Baton Rouge, 1982-84; mem. Senatorial Inner Cir., 1988; bd. trustees Christian Victory Ctr., Hempstead, N.Y., 1986-88; fellow Am. Coll. Pain Mgmt. Fellow ACS; mem. AMA, Am. Assn. Neurologic Surgeons (sect. on trauma), N.Y. State Neurosurg. Soc., N.Y. Soc. Neurosurgery, Congress Neurologic Surgeons (spine sect., sect. on trauma), So. Med. Soc. Presdl. Roundtable, Shanhai Tiffin Club, Donyin Sister City Assn., Senatorial Inner Circle, Midland C. of C. Avocations: skiing, painting, poetry, music, cooking.

LOHMANN, JACK R., engineering educator; b. Stillwater, Okla., Feb. 7, 1951. AS in engring., Ea. Okla. State Coll., 1971; BS in mech. engring., Okla. State U., 1974; MS in indsl. engring., Stanford U., 1975, PhD, 1979. Lic. profl. engr., Mich. Asst. prof. indsl. and ops. engring. U. Mich., Ann Arbor, 1979-85, assoc. prof., 1985-91, assoc. dean grad. and undergrad. studies, 1987-89; sr. program dir. NSF, Washington, 1989-91; prof. indsl. and systems engring. Ga. Inst. Tech., Atlanta, 1991—, assoc. dean acad. affairs, 1991—; vis. assoc. prof., U. So. Calif., L.A., 1985; professeur associé, École Centrale des Arts et Manufactures, Paris, 1986; EHR adv. com. NSF, Washington, 1994-96; nat. adv. bd. mem. Synthesis Engring. Edn. Coalition, Ithaca, N.Y., 1991—; witness Subcom. on Sci., U.S. House Reps., Washington, 1992, Com. on HUD, VA Ind. Agys., Washington, 1993. Editor: The Engineering Economist, Atlanta, 1991—; dept. editor IIE Tranactions, Atlanta, 1982-87; contbr. articles to profl. jours. Recipient Presdl. Young Investigator award, White House, Washington, 1984, Dirs. Award for Excellence, NSF, Washington, 1991. Mem. Am. Soc. Engring Edn. (chair engring. economy divsn. 1984-85, centennial cert. 1993), Inst. Indsl. Engrs. (program chair engring. economy divsn. 1984-85), Accreditation Bd. Engring. and Tech. Achievements include research in econ. decision analysis, replacement econs., risk and engring. and sci. edn. Office: Ga Inst Tech Coll Engring Atlanta GA 30332

LOHMILLER, JOHN M. (CHIP LOHMILLER), professional football player; b. Woodbury, Minn., July 16, 1966. Student, U. Minn. Placekicker Washington Redskins, 1988—. Named kicker The Sporting News NFL All-Pro team, 1991. Played in Pro Bowl, 1991. Office: Washington Redskins Dulles Internat. Airport PO Box 17247 Washington DC 20041

LOHMULLER, MARTIN NICHOLAS, bishop; b. Phila., Aug. 21, 1919; s. Martin Nicholas and Mary Frances (Doser) L. B.A., St. Charles Borromeo Sem., Phila., 1942; D.Canon Law, Catholic U. Am., 1947. Ordained priest Roman Catholic Ch., 1944; officialis Diocese Harrisburg, Pa., 1948-63; vicar for religious Diocese of Harrisburg, 1958-70; pastor Our Lady of Good Counsel parish, Marysville, Pa., 1954-64, St. Catherine Laboure Parish, Harrisburg, 1964-68; consecrated Bishop of Ramsbury, 1970; vicar gen. Archdiocese Phila., 1970-94; aux. bishop of Phila., 1970-94; pastor Old St. Mary's Parish, Phila., 1976-89, Holy Trinity Parish, Phila., 1976-89.

LOHN, ROGER LOWELL, management consultant; b. Wessington Springs, S.D., Feb. 6, 1934; s. Kenneth Fairbairn and Irma Gladys Lohn; m. Eleanor Terlinden, Nov. 7, 1958; children: Cinty Lou, Mark David, Matthew Eric. Student, Phoenix Jr. Coll., 1958-60, Ariz. State U., 1960-63. Quality assurance technician Sperry Phoenix, 1958-60; engr. Motorola Mil., 1961-65; reliability product mgr. Siemens, Scottsdale, Ariz., 1965-67; dir. quality assurance Motorola Mobile Comm. Products, Fort Worth, 1967-83; dir. quality and productivity Codex-Phoenix Ops., 1983-86; mgr. reliability and quality assurance Motorola, Inc., Schaumburg, Ill., 1986—, mem. semiconductor group, 1987-91, cons., 1991—. Editor: The Quality System, 1981, revised, 1990.contbr. articles to profl. jours. 1st lt. USAF, 1952-57. Mem. Am. Soc. Quality Control (various com. positions). Home: 145 N Centennial Way Mesa AZ 85201-6750

LOHNES, JOAN, alcohol and substance abuse services administrator and professional; b. N.Y.C., Jan. 31, 1942; d. Dominick and Anna (McSweeney) Pacenta; m. William Edward Lohnes, Aug. 29, 1964; children: Christopher, William. Grad. in nursing, Bellevue Hosp., 1963; BS in Cmty. Health Nursing, St. Joseph's Coll., 1985. RN, N.Y.; cert. chem. dependency nurse. Staff pediat. nurse Bellevue Hosp., N.Y.C., 1963-64; charge nurse methadone program Flushing Queens Med. Ctr., N.Y.C., 1973-78; substance abuse specialist Bd. Edn., N.Y.C., 1979-84; relief supr. St. Mary's Hosp. for Children, N.Y.C., 1985-87; facility nurse Outreach House, N.Y.C., 1987-89, nursing supr., 1991-94; dir. med. svcs. Outreach House I and II, 1992—; dir. health svcs. Outreach Project, 1994—; relief charge nurse in pediat., alcohol detoxification, pediatric intensive care City Hosp. at Elmhurst, N.Y.C., 1964-85; instr. ARC, 1990—, Am. Heart Assn., N.Y.C., 1990-93. Mem. choir Grace Episcopal Ch., N.Y.C., 1980—; chmn. health com. Pub. Sch. 79, N.Y.C., 1981-84; rep. to Queens Coun. on Alcoholism, 1984-86. Mem. N.Y. State Nurses Assn., Bellevue Alumnae, Nat. Consortium Chem. Dependency Nurses, Drug and Alcohol Nursing Assn., Nat. Assn. for Alcoholism Counselors (assoc.). Avocations: tennis, bicycling, stamp collecting, gardening, music. Office: Outreach Project 89-15 Woodhaven Blvd Woodhaven NY 11421

LOHNES, WALTER F. W., German language and literature educator; b. Frankfurt, Germany, Feb. 8, 1925; came to U.S., 1948, naturalized, 1954; s. Hans and Dina (Koch) L.; m. Claire Shane, 1950; children: Kristen, Peter, Claudia. Student, U. Frankfurt, 1945-48, Ohio Wesleyan U., 1948-49, U. Mo., 1949-50; PhD, Harvard U., 1961. Asst., Inst. German Folklore, U. Frankfurt, 1947-48; instr. German U. Mo., 1949-50; head dept. German, Phillips Acad., Andover, Mass., 1951-61; asst. prof. Stanford (Calif.) U., 1961-65, assoc. prof., 1965-68, prof., 1969-95, prof. emeritus, 1995—, dir. NDEA Inst. Advanced Study, 1961-68, chmn. dept. German studies, 1973-79, dir. Inst. Basic German, prin. investigator NEH grant, 1978-80; vis. prof. Woehler-Gymnasium, Frankfurt, 1956-57, Middlebury Coll., 1959, U. N.Mex., 1980, 81, 86, U. Vienna, 1990, Coll. de France, Paris, 1992; mem., chmn. various coms. of examiners Ednl. Testing Svc. and Coll. Bd.; chmn. German Grad. Record Exam. Author: (with V. Nollendorfs) German Studies in the United States, 1976, (with F. W. Strothmann) German: A Structural Approach, 1968, 4th rev. edit., 1988; (with E.A. Hopkins) Contrastive Grammar of English and German, 1982, (with Martha Woodmansee) Erkennen und Deuten, 1983, (with J.A. Pfeffer) Grunddeutsch, Texte zur gesprochenen deutschen Gegenwartssprache, 3 vols., 1984, (with D. Benseler and V. Nollendorfs) Teaching German in America: Prolegomena to a History, 1988; contbr. numerous articles to profl. jours.; editor; Unterrichtspraxis, 1971-74. Bd. dirs. Calif. Youth Symphony, 1977-78, Oakland (Calif.) Symphony Youth Orch., 1978-80. Decorated Fed. Order of Merit (Germany); Medal of Honor in Gold (Austria); German Govt. grantee, 1975, 76, 78. Mem. MLA, Am. Assn. Tchrs. German (v.p. 1961-62, 70-71, Outstanding Educator award; hon. 1995), Am. Assn. Applied Linguistics, Am. Coun. on Teaching Fgn. Langs., German Studies Assn., Internat. Vereinigung Germanische Sprach und Literaturwissenschaft. Home: 733 Covington Rd Los Altos CA 94024-4903 Office: Stanford U Dept German Studies Stanford CA 94305-2030

LOHR, GEORGE E., state supreme court justice; b. 1931. BS, S.D. State U.; JD, U. Mich. Bar: Colo. 1958, Calif. 1969. Former judge Colo. 9th Dist. Ct., Aspen; assoc. justice Colo. Supreme Ct., Denver, 1979—. Office: Supreme Ct Colo State Judicial Bldg 2 E 14th Ave Denver CO 80203-2115

LOHR, HAROLD RUSSELL, bishop; b. Gary, S.D., Aug. 31, 1922; s. Lester ALbert and Nora Helena (Fossum) L.; m. Theola Marie Kottke, June 21, 1947 (div. Dec. 1973); children: Philip Kyle, David Scott, Michael John;

m. Edith Mary Morgan, Dec. 31, 1973. BS summa cum laude, S.D. State U., 1947; PhD, U. Calif.-Berkeley, 1950; MDiv summa cum laude, Augustana Theol. Sem., Rock Island, Ill., 1958. Ordained to ministry Augustana Luth. Ch., 1958; installed as bishop, 1980. Research chemist Argonne Nat. lab., Lemont, Ill., 1950-54; pastor Luth. Ch. of Ascension, Northfield, Ill., 1958-70; assoc. exec. Bd. Coll. Edn., N.Y.C., 1970-73; dir. research Div. Profl. Leadership, Phila., 1973-77, assoc. exec., 1977-80; synodical bishop Luth. Ch. in Am., Fargo, N.D., 1980-87; synodical bishop Evang. Luth. Ch. in Am., Moorhead, Minn., 1988-91, ret., 1991; mem. exec. council Luth. Ch. in Am., N.Y.C., 1982-87; mem. commn. of peace and war, 1983-85. Contbg. author: Growth in Ministry, 1980; also articles to sci. jours. Bd. dirs. Gustavus Adolphus Coll., 1980-87, Luther Northwestern Sem., St. Paul, 1980-87, Concordia Coll., Moorhead, Minn., 1988-91; mem. ch. coun. Evang. Luth. Ch. in Am., Chgo., 1990-91, disciplinary hearing officer, 1992—, interim dir. synodical rels., 1993-94; mem. bd. govs. Chgo. Ctr. Religion and Sci., 1987—; mem. Summit on Environ., Joint Appeal in Religion and Sci., Washington, 1992; mem. adv. bd. Ctr. for Faith and Sci. Exch., Concord, Mass., 1995—. Recipient Suomi award Suomi Coll., 1983. Mem. Phi Kappa Phi. Democrat. Home: 154 Woodridge Rd Marlborough MA 01752-3327

LOHR, WALTER GEORGE, JR., lawyer; b. Balt., Mar. 3, 1944; s. Walter George and Janet Louise (Cartee) L.; children: Lila Meredith, Walter George III, Frederick Boyce. AB, Princeton U., 1966; LLB, Yale U., 1969. Bar: Md. 1969. Law clk.to Hon. Harrison L. Winter U.S. Cir. Ct., Richmond, Va., 1969-70; assoc. Piper & Marbury, Balt., 1970-74, ptnr., 1977-88; ptnr. Hogan & Hartson, Washington, 1992—; asst. atty. gen. State of Md., Balt., 1974-76; prin. Walter G. Lohr Jr., Balt., 1988-92; bd. dirs. Danaher Corp., Washington, Cmty. of Sci., Inc., Balt., Diginet Comm., Inc., Rockville, Md., Sky Alland Rsch., Inc., Laurel, Md.; mem. adv. bd. prudential Venture Ptnrs., N.Y.C., 1985-93. Trustee Balt. Mus. Art, Gilman Sch. Office: Hogan & Hartson 111 S Calvert St Ste 16 Baltimore MD 21202-6174

LOHRER, RICHARD BAKER, investment consultant; b. Boston, Nov. 30, 1932; s. Leo and Elizabeth Louise (Kaiser) L.; m. Ruth Willa Gutekunst, Feb. 15, 1958; children: Richard Baker, William L., Elizabeth G., Andrew M. AB, Harvard U., 1954; MBA, NYU, 1961. Asst. sec. comml. lending Irving Trust Co. (now Bank of N.Y.), N.Y.C., 1957-64; asst. to v.p. fin. and treas. Nat. Dairy Products Corp. (now Kraft Foods Divsn. of Philip Morris, Inc.), N.Y.C., 1964-71; asst. treas. Martin Marietta Corp. (now Lockheed Martin Corp.), N.Y.C., 1971-74; with Northrop Corp. (now Northrop Grumman Corp.), Los Angeles, 1974-90; treas. Northrop Corp. (now Northrop Grumman Corp.), 1977-87, v.p. trust investments, 1987-90; prin., pres. R.B. Lohrer Assocs., Inc., Palos Verdes Estates, Calif., 1990—. Bd. dirs., pres. Cmty. Helpline, Inc., 1992—; bd. dirs., vice chmn. Presbyn. Ch. (U.S.A.) Investment and Loan Program, Inc., 1995—. Mem. L.A. Treas. Club (pres. 1981), L.A. Pension Group, Boston Latin Sch. West Coast Alumni Assn. (bd. dirs., pres. 1982-84), Fin. Exec. Inst., Harvard Club of So. Calif., Palos Verdes Country Club, Masons. Republican. Presbyterian.

LOHSE, AUSTIN WEBB, banker; b. N.Y.C., Jan. 22, 1926; s. Henry Vincent and Gertrude (Schroeder) L.; m. Virginia Meyer Butler, May 14, 1949; children: Constance Butler, John Daniel. B.A., Dartmouth Coll., 1947. Credit analyst Irving Trust Co., N.Y.C., 1947-52; with Am. Express Internat. Banking Corp., N.Y.C., 1952-73; asst. v.p. Am. Express Internat. Banking Corp., 1958-61, v.p., 1961-68, sr. v.p., 1968-73; v.p. Charterhouse Group Internat. Inc., N.Y.C., 1973-78, R.T. Madden & Co. Inc., N.Y.C., 1978-81; pres. A.W. Lohse & Co. Inc., N.Y.C., 1981—; former dir. Am. Express Bank G.M.B.H., Frankfurt, Germany, Am. Express Bank S.P.A., Rome, Am. Express Securities S.A., Paris, LB/Amex Ltd., London, Eng. Mem. Casque and Gauntlet Soc., Beta Theta Pi. Republican. Episcopalian. Clubs: Short Hills (N.J.); Knickerbocker (N.Y.C.). Home: 7 Taylor Rd Short Hills NJ 07078-2225 Office: 630 5th Ave New York NY 10111-0001

LOIELLO, JOHN PETER, public affairs executive, consultant; b. Oceanside, N.Y., Aug. 16, 1943; s. Rosario Paul and Mary Agnes (Butler) L.; m. Elaine Margaret Robinson, June 14, 1944. BA in History, Fordham U., 1965; MA in History, SUNY, Buffalo, 1973; PhD in African History, U. London, 1980. Tchr. history The Gow Sch., South Wales, N.Y., 1967-71; instr. U. Md. (U.K.), London, 1976-78; exec. dir. Dem. Party Com. Abroad, Washington and London, 1978-80; sr. cons. Assn. Am. Chambers of Commerce in Latin Am., Washington, 1980; spl. asst. to chmn. NEH, Washington, 1978-82; assoc. dir. Democracy Prog., Washington, 1982-83; founding exec. dir. Nat. Dem. Inst. for Internat. Affairs, Washington, 1983-85; pres. Gowran Internat., Washington, 1985-93; assoc. dir. ednl. and cultural affairs U.S. Info. Agy., Washington, 1994—; pres. Alcide de Gaspari Found. (USA), Washington, 1987-89. Contbr. articles to profl. jours. Commr. Commn. on Platform Accountability, Dem. Nat. Com., Washington, 1981-85, chmn. fgn. policy subcom., 1980, platform com., 1980; sec. Tax Equity for Ams. Abroad, London, 1977-79; sec. Dems. Abroad, London, 1976-79. African Studies scholar, U. London, 1974-78, grantee, 1975. Mem. Nat. Italian Am. Found., Royal African Soc. Democrat. Roman Catholic. Avocations: travel, racquetball, swimming.

LOIN, E. LINNEA, social work administrator; b. Middletown, Conn., Nov. 20, 1942; d. Alfred William Skinner and Ada Patricia Moore; m. Peter Michael Loin, Sept. 16, 1972. BA, U. Conn., 1965. Social worker State of Conn., Middletown and Hartford, 1964-69; case supr. State of Conn., Hartford, 1969-74; program supr. State of Conn., Hartford, Manchester and, Rockville, Hartford, 1984-90, Willimantic, 1990—; state liaison Nat. Ctr. for Child Abuse and Neglect, Washington, 1985-90. Editor: Connecticut's Children, 1985, Common Ground, 1987-89. Town rep. Charter Cable Adv. Bd. Avocations: swimming, walking, reading, travel, water sports. Home: 29 Cowles Rd West Willington CT 06279-1705 Office: DCYS Region 6 1320 Main St Willimantic CT 06226-1910

LOIS, GEORGE, advertising agency executive; b. N.Y.C., June 26, 1931; s. Harry and Vasilike (Thanasoulis) L.; m. Rosemary Lewandowski, Aug. 27, 1951; children: Harry (dec.), Luke. Student, Pratt Inst., 1949-51, D.F.A. (hon.), 1982. Designer Reba Sochis, 1951; designer CBS-TV, 1954-56; art dir. Sudler & Hennessey, 1956-57, Doyle, Dane, Bernbach, 1958-59; partner, creative dir. Papert, Koenig, Lois, Inc., N.Y.C., 1960-67; chmn. bd., chief exec. officer Lois Holland Callaway Inc., N.Y.C., 1967-78; chmn. bd., creative dir. Lois/EJL, N.Y.C., 1978—. Author: George, Be Careful, 1972, The Art of Advertising, George Lois on Mass Communication, 1977, What's the Big Idea?, 1991, Covering The 60's/George Lois, The Esquire Era, 1996. Served with AUS, 1952-54, Korea. Elected to Art Dirs. Hall of Fame, 1978, Creative Hall of Fame, 1980. Mem. N.Y. Art Dirs. Club (pres. 1971-73). Office: Lois/EJL 40 W 57th St New York NY 10019-4001*

LOKEN, JAMES BURTON, federal judge; b. Madison, Wis., May 21, 1940; s. Burton Dwight and Anita (Nelson) L.; m. Caroline Brevard Hester, July 30, 1966; children: Kathryn Brevard, Kristina Ayres. BS, U. Wis., 1962; LLB magna cum laude, Harvard U., 1965. Law clk. to chief judge Lumbard U.S. Ct. Appeals (2d Cir.), N.Y.C., 1965-66; law clk. to assoc. justice Byron White U.S. Supreme Ct., Washington, 1966-67; assoc. atty. Faegre & Benson, Mpls., 1967-70, ptnr., 1973-90; gen. counsel Pres.'s Com. on Consumer Interests, Office of Pres. of U.S., Washington, 1970; staff asst. Office of Pres. of U.S., Washington, 1970-72; judge U.S. Ct. Appeals (8th cir.), St. Paul, 1991—. Editor Harvard Law Rev., 1964-65. Mem. Minn. State Bar Assn., Phi Beta Kappa, Phi Kappa Phi. Avocations: golf, running. Home: PO Box 75848 Saint Paul MN 55175-0848 Office: Cir Cts Appeals 8th Cir 510 Federal Bldg 316N Robert St Saint Paul MN 55101-1423*

LOKENSGARD, JON A., school system administrator. Supt. Sierra Vista (Ariz.) Unified Sch. Dist. State finalist Nat. Supt. Yr. award, 1993. Office: Sierra Vista Unified Dist 3555 E Fry Blvd Sierra Vista AZ 85635-2972

LOKER, ELIZABETH ST. JOHN, newspaper executive; b. Leonardtown, Md., Jan. 1, 1948; d. William Meverell and June Whiting (Farner) L.; m. Donald Scott Rice, Sept. 11, 1980. B.A., George Washington U., 1969. Analyst Met. Washington Council Govt., 1973-74; analyst, programmer Washington Post, 1974-75, mgr. systems research, 1976, dir. data processing, 1976-78, asst. to pub., 1979, v.p. advanced systems, 1979—, v.p. sys. and engring., 1992—. Contbr. chpt. to book. Trustee Greater Washington Research Ctr., also mem. exec. com.; mem. bus. coun. Washington Opera; bd. dirs. Washington Chamber Symphony. Mem. Newspaper Systems Group (past pres.), Assn. for Computing Machinery, Soc. Info. Mgmt., Ops. Research Soc. Am., Inst. Mgmt. Sci. Avocations: antiques; gardening; historic preservation. Office: Washington Post Co 1150 15th St NW Washington DC 20071-0001

LOKEY, FRANK MARION, JR., broadcast executive, consultant; b. Ft. Worth, Oct. 15, 1924; s. Frank Marion Sr. and Corinne (Whaley) L. Student, Smith-Hughes Evening Coll., 1955-59. Asst. gen. mgr., mgr. sales, news anchor Sta. WLW-A TV (now named WXIA-TV), Atlanta, 1955-66; co-owner, gen. mgr. Sta. WAIA, Atlanta, 1960-62; S.E. news corr., talk show host CBS News N.Y., N.Y.C., 1960-66; asst. to owner, gen. mgr. Sta. WBIE-AM-FM, Atlanta, 1962-64; asst. to pres., gen. mgr. Stas. KXAB-TV, KXJB-TV, KXMB-TV, Aberdeen, Fargo, Bismarck, S.D., N.D., 1966-67; exec. v.p., gen. mgr. St. WEMT-TV, Bangor, Maine, 1967-70; pres., gen. mgr. Stas. KMOM-TV, KWAB-TV, Odessa-Midland, Big Spring, Tex., 1970-75; exec. v.p., gen. mgr. Sta. KMUV-TV (now named KRBK-TV), Sacramento, Calif., 1975-77; CEO Lokey Enterprises, Inc., Sacramento, L.A., El Centro, Calif., 1977—, also chmn. bd. dirs.; cons., Troubleshooter 16 TV stas. nationwide, 1977—; cons., actor 5 movie prodn. cos., Hollywood, Calif., 1980—; cons., outside dir. Anderson Cons., Manhattan, L.I., N.Y., 1981—; network talk show host/news corr. for 7 news orgns. worldwide, 1984—; bd. dirs. Broadcast Audience Behavior Rsch., Manhattan, 1986—, mem. inner circle, 1986—; owner franchise The Party Place. Creator, originator approach to real estate mktg. Hon. mem. Imperial County Bd. Suprs., El Centro, 1986—, El Centro City Coun., 1987—. Mem. Am. Legion. Baptist. Avocations: producer big bands parties, movie acting, ancient history, tracing family tree. Home: 830 Olive Ave El Centro CA 92243-2821 Office: Lokey Enterprises Inc 626 W Main St El Centro CA 92243-2920

LOKMER, STEPHANIE ANN, public relations counselor; b. Wheeling, W.Va., Nov. 14, 1957; d. Joseph Steven and Mary Ann (Mozney) L. BA in Comm., Bethany Coll., 1980; cert., U. Tübingen, Germany, 1980, Sprach Inst. Tübingen, Germany 1980. V.p., Wheeling Coffee and Spice, W.Va., 1981—; pharm. mktg. rep. Bristol Labs., Wheeling, 1982-84, pharm. hosp. mktg. rep., 1984-85; pharm. mktg. rep. Boehringer Ingelheim, Nashville, 1985-87; owner, pres. Lokmer & Assocs. Inc. Pub. Relations, 1986—. Mem. Pub. Rels. Soc. Am. (accredited), Pub. Rels. Soc. Am. Internat., Counselors Acad., Zeta Tau Alpha. Republican. Roman Catholic. Avocations: flying, sailing, tennis, reading.

LOLLAR, KATHERINE LOUISE, social worker, therapist; b. Cin., Nov. 1, 1944; d. Robert Miller and Dorothy Marie L.; div.; 2 children. BA, U. Kans., 1966; MSW, Loyola U., 1971. Lic. clin. social worker, Oreg.; cert. social worker, Wash.; bd. cert. diplomate clin. social work. Head activity therapy dept. Fox Children's Ctr., Dwight, Ill., 1966-68; child care worker Madden Mental Health Ctr., Hines, Ill., 1968-69, social worker, 1971-74; pvt. practice therapy Wheaton and Oakbrook, Ill., 1977-82; intern Monticello Care Unit alcohol and drug treatment program, 1983; cons. Residential Facility for Developmentally Disabled Adults, Battle Ground, Wash., 1983-85; therapist Cath. Community Svcs., Vancouver, Wash., 1983-88; outsta. mgr. Wash. Div. Devel. Disabilities, Vancouver, 1987—; pvt. practice therapy Vancouver, 1988—. Troop cons. Columbia River coun. Girl Scouts Am., 1984-86, internat. trip leader, 1993, alt. leader, 1995-96, life mem.; com. mem. Friends of Sangam Internat. Com., 1994—; mem. Internat. Field Selection Team, 1994-96; mem. Unity of Vancouver. Mem. NASW (sec. Vancouver chpt. 1982-84, co-chair 1985-87, unit rep. Wash. state unit 1990-92), Singles on Sat. Sq. Dance Club, Recycles Sq. Dance Club (pres. 1995—). Avocations: travel, reading, camping, dancing, hiking, rafting. Office: 650 Officers Row Vancouver WA 98661-3836

LOLLEY, WILLIAM RANDALL, minister; b. Troy, Ala., June 2, 1931; s. Roscoe Lee and Mary Sara (Nunnelee) L.; m. Clara Lou Jacobs, Aug. 28, 1952; children: Charlotte, Pam. AB, Samford U., 1952, DD (hon.), 1980; BD, Southeastern Sem., 1957, ThM, 1958; ThD, Southwestern Sem., 1962; DD (hon.), Wake Forest U., 1971, U. Richmond, 1984; LLD (hon.), Campbell U., 1986; LittD (hon.), Mercer U., 1988. Ordained to ministry So. Bapt. Conv., 1951; pastor First Bapt. Ch., Winston-Salem, N.C., 1962-74; pres. Southeastern Bapt. Theol. Sem., Wake Forest, N.C., 1974-88; pastor First Bapt. Ch., Raleigh, N.C., 1988-90, Greensboro, N.C., 1990—. Author: Crises in Morality, 1963, Bold Preaching of Christ, 1979, Servant Songs, 1994. Democrat. Club: Rotary. Home: 3200 W Market St Greensboro NC 27403-1456 Office: First Bapt Ch Greensboro NC 27403

LOLLI, ANDREW RALPH, industrial engineer, former army officer; b. Seatonville, Ill., Oct. 15, 1907; s. Joseph Fredrick and Adolfa (Fiocchi) L. Student Armed Forces Staff Coll., 1950, Nat. War Coll., 1957, N.Y. Inst. Fin., 1971; BS, Dickinson Coll., 1952; postgrad. Fordham U., 1952. Enlisted in U.S. Army, 1940, advanced through grades to maj. gen., 1960; chief plans and priorities Allied Forces So. Europe, 1952-56; comdr. Air Def. units, N.Y. and San Francisco, 1957-60; comdr. XX U.S.A. Corps, 1961-62, XV, 1962-63, comdr. Western NORD Region, Hamilton AFB, Calif., 1963-66; ret., 1966; exec. asst. Hughes Aircraft Co., Fullerton, Calif., 1967; dir. gen. services State of Calif., Sacramento, 1967-70; v.p. Sigmatics, Newport Beach, Calif., 1970-73, Intercoast Investments Co., Sacramento, 1975-76; pres. Andrew R. Lolli Assocs. Inc., San Francisco, 1973—, Lolman Inc., San Francisco, 1976—; commr. Small Bus. Adv. Commn., San Francisco, 1989-93; pres. bd. trustees Commonwealth Equity Trust, 1974-80; vice chmn. Calif. Pub. Works bd., 1967-69; mem. adv. panel Nat. Acad. Scis. and Engring. in Research, Washington, 1968-70; mem. fed., state and local govt. adv. panel Fed. Gen. Services, Washington, 1968-69. Bd. dirs. Columbia Boys Park Club, San Francisco, Lab. for Survival, San Francisco; mem. Presido of San Francisco Restoration Adv. Bd., 1994. Decorated D.S.M., Legion of Merit with oak leaf cluster, Bronze Star with oak leaf cluster; named Man of Year, Italian Sons of Am., 1964. Mem. Nat. Assn. Uniformed Services, Assn. U.S. Army, Ret. Officers Assn. Roman Catholic. Developed short notice inspection system for army air def. missiles, 1960. Home: 1050 N Point St San Francisco CA 94109-8302 Office: 286 Jefferson St San Francisco CA 94133-1126

LOMAN, MARY LAVERNE, retired mathematics educator; b. Stratford, Okla., June 10, 1928; d. Thomas D. and Mary Ellen (Goodwin) Glass; m. Coy E. Loman, Dec. 23, 1944; 1 child, Sandra Leigh Loman Easton. BS, U. Okla., 1956, MA, 1957, PhD, 1961. Grad. asst., then instr. U. Okla., Norman, 1956-61; asst. prof. math. U. Ctrl. Okla., Edmond, 1961-62; assoc. prof. U. Cen. Okla., Edmond, 1962-66, prof., 1966-93; prof. emeritus U. Ctrl. Okla., Edmond, 1993—; ret., 1993. NSF fellow, 1965-67. Mem. Math. Assn. Am., Nat. Coun. Tchrs. Math., Okla. Coun. Tchrs. Math. (v.p. 1972-76), Higher Edn Alumni Coun. Okla., VFW Aux., Delta Kappa Gamma. Home: 2201 Tall Oaks Trl Edmond OK 73003-2325 *Strive to do each task to the best of your ability. Then don't look back, saying "If only I had ...", but look forward to the next with the comfort of knowing you gave your very best effort.*

LOMAS, BERNARD TAGG, college president emeritus; b. Mackinaw City, Mich., Aug. 14, 1924; s. Percy L. and Eva (Tagg) L.; m. Barbara Jean West, June 21, 1947; children: Paul Neil, David Mark. AB, Albion Coll., 1946, DD, 1965; BD, Oberlin Grad. Sch. Theology, 1948; MDiv., Vanderbilt U., 1967; LLD, Adrian U., 1983. Ordained minister Meth. Ch., 1948. Minister William St. Meth. Ch., Delaware, Ohio, 1950-54; counsellor to students Ohio Wesleyan U., 1950-54; sr. minister Trinity Meth. Ch., Portsmouth, Ohio, 1954-60; sr. minister heading staff of five ministers Epworth-Euclid Ch., Univ. Circle, Cleve., 1960-70; pres. Albion (Mich.) Coll., 1970-83, chancellor, 1983-88, pres. emeritus, 1988—; cons. Am. Enterprise Inst., Washington, 1980-81; pers. and human rels. cons. to U.S. and fgn. bus. Author 5 books; contbr. numerous articles to edn. and religious jours. Organizer, head Citizens Com. for Law Enforcement, Portsmouth, 1957-58; founding mem. pres. Christian Residences Found.; bd. dirs. Goodwill Industries Cleve., 1964-70; trustee St. Lukes Hosp., Cleve., 1965-70; bd. govs. Greater Mich. Found., 1978-83; bd. dirs. Christian Children's Fund, 1978-81; counselor Heritage Found., Washington, 1984—, Bd. Inst. Am. Univs., Aix En Provence-France, 1988—. Mem. Masons, Shriners, Rotary.

LOMAS, LYLE WAYNE, agricultural research administrator, educator; b. Monett, Mo., June 8, 1953; s. John Junior and Helen Irene Lomas; m. Connie Gail Frey, Sept. 4, 1976; children: Amy Lynn, Eric Wayne. BS, U. Mo., 1975, MS, 1976; PhD, Mich. State U., 1979. Asst. prof., animal scientist S.E. Agrl. Rsch. Ctr., Kans. State U., Parsons, 1979-85, assoc. prof., 1985-92, prof., 1992—, head, 1985—. Contbr. articles to refereed sci. jours. Mem. Am. Soc. Animal Sci., Am. Registry Profl. Animal Scientists, Am. Forage and Grassland Coun., Rsch. Ctr. Adminstrs. Soc. (bd. dirs. 1993—), Rotary (bd. dirs. Parsons 1992—, v.p. 1994-95, pres. 1995-96), Phi Kappa Phi, Gamma Sigma Delta. Presbyterian. Achievements include research in ruminant nutrition, forage utilization by grazing stocker cattle. Home: 24052 Douglas Rd Dennis KS 67341-8916 Office: Kans State U SE Agrl Rsch Ctr PO Box 316 Parsons KS 67357-0316

LOMASON, HARRY AUSTIN, II, automotive company executive; b. Detroit, Oct. 6, 1934; s. William Keithledge and Neva L.; children by previous marriage: Kimri Elizabeth Lomason Massey, Krista Anne Lomason Massell, William Keithledge, Peter Kevin; m. Mary Alice Pushkarsky, June 26, 1971; children: Harry Austin, Heather Alice. Student, Ga. Inst. Tech., 1953-56; BBA, Ga. State U., 1959. Asst. sec. Douglas & Lomason Co., Farmington Hills, Mich., 1966-72, v.p., sec., 1972-76, pres., 1976—, COO, 1976-82, pres., chief exec. officer, 1982—, also chmn. bd. dirs.; v.p. Douglas y Lomason de Mex. S.A. de C.V., 1987—, also bd. dirs.; chmn. bd. dirs. Bloomington-Normal (Ill.) Seating Co., Mich. Mfrs. Assn.; bd. dirs., mem. exec. com. Amerisure Cos., Detroit; mem. bd. examiners Malcolm Baldridge Nat. Quality Award Com., 1988. Mem. bd. trustees GMI Engring. and Mgmt. Inst., Citizens Rsch. Coun. Mich.; bd. dirs. Mich. Opera Theatre, Mich. Thanksgiving Parade Found., Detroit Symphony Orch. Hall, 1979—. Mem. Engring. Soc. Detroit, Soc. Automotive Engrs., Detroit Club, Detroit Athletic Club, Detroit Golf Club, Marianna (Ark.) Country Club, Pine Lake Country Club (Orchard Lake, Mich.). Episcopalian. Home: 2900 Pine Lake Rd Orchard Lake MI 48324-1945 Office: Douglas & Lomason Co 24600 Hallwood Ct Farmington WI 48335

LOMAX, JOHN H., financial service company executive; b. Macon, Ga., Mar. 28, 1924; s. John H. and Regis (Garrity) L.; m. Anne E. Davis, Dec. 30, 1947; children: J. Harvey, Jan (Mrs. Ben Teal). BBA, U. Ga., 1948; student, U. N.C., 1962. Exec. v.p. Am. Credit Corp., Charlotte, N.C., 1958-76; exec. v.p. Assocs. Corp. of N.Am., Dallas, 1976-87; dir. Gulf Coast Consol. Office Resolution Trust Corp., Houston, 1989-91, dir. north ctrl. region, 1991-92; v.p. S.W. region Resolution Trust Corp., Dallas, 1992-94; pres., chmn., CEO Policy Funding Corp., Dallas, 1994—; pres., CEO Utility Gen. Corp., Dallas, 1995—; chmn., CEO Ulitity Gen. Corp., Dallas, 1996—. Bd. dirs. Dallas Summer Musicals. Capt. USAF, 1942-46. Home: 4215 Glenaire Dr Dallas TX 75229-4140 Office: Utility General Corp 17754 Preston Rd Dallas TX 75252

LOMAX, PEGGY QUARLES, gifted and talented education educator; b. Bradenton, Fla., Dec. 21, 1941; d. Archie Eugene and Katherine Louise (Stowe) Q.; m. David W. Ridge, Dec. 27, 1958 (div. July 1972); m. Robert T. Lomax, Nov. 23, 1978; children: Anita Ann, Michael Wade. MA in Mid. Sch. Edn., Appapachian State U., 1977; MA im Mid. Sch. Edn., Lenoir Rhyne Coll., 1987. Cert. tchr., sch. adminstr. gifted edn., N.C. Media asst. J.B. Little Elem. Sch., Arlington, Tex., 1969-72; pub. info. officer Appalachian State U., Boone, N.C., 1974-77; tchr. academically gifted Gamewell Mid. Sch., Lenoir, N.C., 1977-89, William Lenoir (N.C.) Mid. Sch., 1989-93; tchr., coord. gifted and talented Mayflower (Ark.) Pub. Schs., 1993-95; secondary gifted and talented tchr. Vilonia (Ark.) Pub. Schs., 1995—. Pres. Lenoir Bus. and Profl. Orgn., 1984-85; spl. registration commr. Caldwell County, 1985-87; bd. dirs. Caldwell County Libr., 1985-87; mem. N.C. Commn. on Youth and Children, 1987-89; mem. youth com. Mt. Grove Bapt. Ch. Recipient Caldwell County Human Rels. award, 1987=88; grantee Caldwell County C. of C., 1992, Z. Smith Reynolds Found., 1993. Mem. NEA, ASCD, N.C. Assn. Educators (v.p. 1985-86, 90-91, pres. 1986-87, 92-93), N.C. League Mid. Schs. (bd. dirs. 1981-84, v.p.), N.C. Assn. Gifted Educators, Caldwell County Assn. Educators (pres. 1984-85), Arkansans for Gifted and Talented Edn., Caldwell County Parents for Academically Gifted Edn., Nat. Mid. Sch. Assn., Arkansans Assn. Gifted Adminstrs., Kappa Delta Pi. Office: Vilonia Pub Schs PO Box 160 Vilonia AR 72106

LOMBARD, ARTHUR J., judge; b. N.Y.C., Nov. 30, 1941; s. Maurice and Martha (Simons) L.; m. Frederica Koller, Aug. 18, 1968; children: David, Lisa. BS in Acctg. magna cum laude, Columbia U., 1961; JD, Harvard U., 1964. Bar: N.Y. 1964, U.S. Ct. Appeals (2d cir.) 1965, U.S. Supreme Ct. 1970, U.S. Ct. Appeals (6th cir.) 1972, Mich. 1976. Law clk. to J. Edward Lumbard chief judge U.S. Ct. Appeals (2d cir.), N.Y.C., 1964-65; teaching fellow law sch. Harvard U., Cambridge, Mass., 1965-66; instr. Orientation Program in Am. Law, Assn. Am. Law Schs., Princeton, N.J., 1966; prof. law Wayne State U., Detroit, 1966-87, assoc. dean law, 1978-85; prof. Detroit Coll. Law, 1987-94, dean, chief adminstrv. officer, 1987-93; judge Wayne County (Mich.) Cir. Ct., 1994—; chmn. revision of Mich. class action rule com. Mich. Supreme Ct., 1980-83; reporter rules com. U.S. Dist. Ct. (ea. dist.) Mich., 1978-94. Contbr. articles to profl. jours. Mem. Mich. Civil Rights Commn., 1991-94, co-chmn., 1992-93, chmn. 1993-94. Office: 1913 City County Bldg Detroit MI 48226

LOMBARD, DAVID NORMAN, lawyer; b. Seattle, Dec. 6, 1949; s. John Cutler and Dororthy Marie (Brandt) L.; m. Susan Elliott, Oct. 22, 1983; children: Matthew, Jeffrey, Megan. BA, U. Wash., 1973; JD, U. Puget Sound, Tacoma, 1976. Bar: Wash. 1976, U.S. Dist. Ct. (we. dist.) Wash. 1976, U.S. Dist. Ct. (ea. dist.) Wash. 1983, U.S. Ct. Appeals (9th cir.) 1976. Law clk. Wash. State Supreme Ct., Olympia, 1976-77; assoc. Schwabe, Williamson, Ferguson & Burdell, Seattle, 1977-82, ptnr., 1983-93; Jameson Babbitt Stites & Lombard Seattle, 1993—. Mem. Rainier Club, Wash. Athletic Club. Presbyterian. Office: Jameson Babbitt Stites & Lombard 999 Third Ave Ste 1900 Seattle WA 98104

LOMBARD, JOHN JAMES, JR., lawyer; b. Phila., Dec. 27, 1934; s. John James and Mary R. (O'Donnell) L.; m. Barbara Mallon, May 9, 1964; children: John James, William M., James G., Laura K., Barbara E. BA cum laude, LaSalle Coll., Phila., 1956; JD, U. Pa., 1959. Bar: Pa. 1960. Assoc., Obermayer, Rebmann, Maxwell & Hippel, Phila., 1960-65, ptnr., 1966-84, fin. ptnr., 1980-84; ptnr. Morgan, Lewis & Bockius, LLP, Phila., 1985—, mgr. personal law sect., 1986-90, vice chair personal law sect., 1990-92, chair, 1992—; sec., dir. Airline Hydraulics Corp., Phila., 1969—; mem. adv. com. on decedents estates laws Joint State Govt. Commn., 1992—, mem. subcom. on powers of atty., 1993—; co-chair So. Jersey Ethics Alliance. Bd. dirs. Redevel. Authority Montgomery County, Pa., 1980-87, Gwynedd-Mercy Coll., Gwynedd Valley, Pa., 1980-89, LaSalle College High Sch., Wyndmoor, Pa., 1991—. Recipient Treat award Nat. Coll. Probate Judges, 1992. Mem. ABA (chmn. com. simplification security transfers 1972-76, chmn. membership com. 1972-82, mem. council real property, probate and trust law sect. 1979-85, sec. 1985-87, div. dir. probate div. 1987-89, chair elect 1989-90, chair 1990-91, co-chair Nat. Conf. Lawyers & Corp. Fiduciaries), Pa. Bar Assn. (ho. of dels. 1979-81), Phila. Bar Assn. (chmn. probate sect. 1972), Am. Coll. Trust and Estate Counsel (editor Probate Notes 1983, bd. regents 1986-91, mem. exec. com. 1988-91, elder law com. 1993—), Internat. Acad. Estate and Trust Law (exec. com. 1984-88, 90—), Am. Bar Found., Internat. Fish and Game Assn. Clubs: Union League (Phila.); Ocean City (N.J.) Marlin and Tuna, Ocean City Yacht. Co-author: Durable Power of Attorney—A Systems Approach, 1984, 3d edit. 1994; contbr. articles to profl. jours. Office: Morgan Lewis & Bockius LLP 2000 One Logan Sq Philadelphia PA 19103

LOMBARD, RICHARD SPENCER, lawyer; b. Panama Canal Zone, Jan. 28, 1928; s. Eugene C. and Alice R. (Quinn) L.; m. Arlene Olson, Dec. 27, 1952; children: Anne, James. AB, Harvard U., 1949, JD, 1952. Bar: N.Y. 1953, Tex. 1971. Assoc. Haight, Gardner, Poor & Havens, N.Y.C., 1952-55; mem. law dept. Creole Petroleum Corp., Caracas, Venezuela, 1955-65, mgr., 1963-65; gen. counsel Esso Chem. Co., N.Y.C., 1966-69; assoc. gen. counsel Humble Oil & Refining Co., Houston, 1969-71; asst. gen. counsel Exxon Corp., N.Y.C., 1971-72, assoc. gen. counsel, 1972-73, gen. counsel, 1973-93, v.p., 1980-93; counsel Baker & Botts, Dallas, 1993-96; trustee Parker Sch. Fgn. and Comparative Law, Columbia U., 1977—, Southwestern Legal Found., 1978, Practicing Law Inst., 1980. Author: American-Venezuelan Private International Law, 1965. Served with AC AUS, 1946-47. Fellow Am. Bar Found.; mem. ABA, Am. Law Inst., Am. Arbitration Assn. (bd. dirs., chmn. bd. 1983-86), N.Y. State Bar Assn., Assn. Bar City of N.Y.,

State Bar of Tex., Dallas Bar Assn., Univ. Club (N.Y.C.). Office: 2626 Cole Ave Ste 400 Dallas TX 75204-1073

LOMBARDI, CELESTE, zoological park administrator; b. Columbus, Ohio, Feb. 16, 1955; d. Adam Dominic and Frances Elizabeth (Varda) L.; m. Terence Lawrence Smith, Mar. 26, 1990; 1 child Matthew Peachey. BS in Zoology, Ohio State U., 1978. Zoo keeper Children's Zoo Columbus Zoo, 1978-83, supr. Children's Zoo, 1983-90, asst. curator mammals, 1990-93, gen. curator, 1993—. TV appearances include David Letterman Show, Good Morning America, PM Magazine, and various local news shows. Mem. Am. Assn. Zool. Parks and Aquariums, Am. Assn. Zoo Keepers. Roman Catholic. Home: 4190 Rutherford Rd Powell OH 43065-9733 Office: Columbus Zoo PO Box 400 9990 Riverside Dr Powell OH 43065-9606

LOMBARDI, CORNELIUS ENNIS, JR., lawyer; b. Portland, Oreg., Feb. 12, 1926; s. Cornelius Ennis and Adele (Volk) L.; m. Ann Vivian Foster, Nov. 24, 1954; children—Cornelius Ennis, Gregg Foster, Matthew Volk. B.A., Yale, 1949; J.D., U. Mich., 1952. Bar: Mo. bar. Since practiced in Kansas City, Mo.; mem. firm Blackwell, Sanders, Matheny, Weary & Lombardi, 1957-92, of counsel. Former pres. Kansas City Mus. Assn., Estate Planning Coun. of Kansas City; trustee Pembroke Country Day Sch.; chmn. soc. of fellows Nelson Gallery Found. Served with USMCR, 1944-46. Mem. Order of Coif, Phi Alpha Delta, Kansas City Country Club. Home: 5049 Wornall Rd Kansas City MO 64112-2423 Office: 2 Pershing Sq 2300 Main St Ste 1100 Kansas City MO 64108-2415

LOMBARDI, DENNIS M., lawyer; b. L.A., May 15, 1951; s. Peter Joseph and Jean (Nelson) L.; m. Suan Choo Lim, Jan. 9, 1992; children: Alexis Jeanne, Erin Kalani. BA, U. Hawaii, 1974; JD summa cum laude, U. Santa Clara, 1977. Bar: Calif. 1977, U.S. Dist. Ct. Hawaii, 1981. Assoc. Frandzel & Share, Beverly Hills, Calif., 1977-79; pvt. practice Capistrano Beach, Calif., 1979-81; ptnr. Case, Myrdal, Bigelow & Lombardi, Honolulu, 1982—. Office: Case Myrdal Bigelow & Lombardi 737 Bishop St 26th Flr Honolulu HI 96813

LOMBARDI, EUGENE PATSY, orchestra conductor, violinist, educator, recording artist; b. North Braddock, Pa., July 7, 1923; s. Nunzio C. and Mary (Roberto) L.; m. Jacqueline Sue Davis, Mar. 1955; children: Robert, Genanne. BA, Westminster Coll., 1948; MA, Columbia U., 1948; Edn. Specialist, George Peabody Coll., 1972; MusD, Westminster Coll., 1981. Band dir. Lincoln High Sch., Midland, Pa., 1948-49; orch. dir. Male High Sch., Louisville, 1949-50, Phoenix Union High Sch., 1950-57; orch. dir., prof. Ariz. State U., Tempe, 1957-89. Condr. Phoenix Symphonette, 1954-61, 70-73, Phoenix Symphony Youth Orch., 1956-66, Phoenix Pops Orch., 1971-83, Fine Arts String Orch., 1995—; asst. concertmaster Phoenix Symphony Orch., 1950-62, concermaster, 1962-69, asst. condr., 1968-69; mem. Newart String Quartet, 1965-89; concertmaster Flagstaff Festival Symphony, 1967-81, Flagstaff Festival Chamber Orch., 1967-81, Phoenix Chamber Orch., 1970-83; condr., music dir. Sun City (Ariz.) Symphony Orch., 1983-87. Condr. fine arts strings, Phoenix, 1995—. With USAAF, 1943-46. Decorated Bronze Star; named Outstanding Grad. Westminster Coll., 1948; recipient Alumni Achievement award, 1976, gold medal Nat. Soc. Arts and Letters, 1973, Disting. Tchr. award Ariz. State U. Alumni, 1974, Phoenix Appreciation award, 1983. Mem. Music Educators Nat. Conf., Am. String Tchrs. Assn. (pres. Ariz. unit 1965-67), Am. Fedn. Musicians, Ariz. Music Educators Assn. (pres. higher edn. sect. 1973-75, Excellence in Teaching Music award 1989), Ind. Order Foresters, Phi Delta Kappa, Phi Mu Alpha. Republican. Presbyterian. Home: 920 E Manhatton Dr Tempe AZ 85282-5520

LOMBARDI, FREDERICK MCKEAN, lawyer; b. Akron, Ohio, Apr. 1, 1937; s. Leonard Anthony and Dorothy (McKean) L.; m. Margaret J. Gessler, Mar. 31, 1962; children: Marcus M., David G., John A., Joseph F. BA, U. Akron, 1960; LLB, Case Western Res., 1962. Bar: Ohio 1962, U.S. Dist. Ct. (no. dist.) Ohio 1964, U.S. Ct. Appeals (6th cir.) 1966. Prin., shareholder Buckingham, Doolittle & Burroughs, Akron, 1962—, chmn. comml. law and litigation dept., 1989—. Bd. editors Western Res. Law Rev., 1961-62. Trustee, mem. exec. com., v.p. Ohio Ballet, 1985-93; trustee Walsh Jesuit H.S., 1987-90, Akron Golf Charities; chmn. formation com., 1st pres. St. Hilary Parish Coun., trustee, 1976-78; past chmn. World Series of Golf. Mem. Ohio Bar Assn. (coun. of dels. 1995-97), Akron Bar Assn. (trustee 1991-94), Case Western Res. U. Law Alumni Assn. (bd. govs. 1995-98), Soc. Benchers (bd. govs. 1995-98), Fairlawn Swim and Tennis Club (past pres.), Portage Country Club (fin. com.), Akron City Club, Rotary (fin. com. Akron), Pi Sigma Alpha. Democrat. Roman Catholic. Office: Buckingham Doolittle & Burroughs 50 S Main St Akron OH 44308-1828

LOMBARDI, JOHN BARBA-LINARDO, broadcasting executive; b. Toronto, Ont., Can., Dec. 4, 1915; s. Léonardo and Teresa L.; m. Antonia Lena Crisologo, July 4, 1949; children: Leonard, Theresa Maria, Donina Antonia. Grad. high sch., Toronto; student, Toronto Cen. Tech. Sch. Trumpet player Benny Palmer's Band, London, Ont., 1930-42; with Lombardi Grocery; later pres. Lombardi Italian Foods Ltd.; producer Italian radio programs Stas. CHUM, CKFH, from 1946; founder, pres., mng. dir. CHIN Radio/TV Internat. (multilingual broadcasting), 1966—; pres. Bravo Records & Music Co. Ltd., Carpejon Investments Ltd., Italian Shows Ltd.; chmn., pres. Radio 1540 Ltd. Originator ann. Johnny Lombardi Talent and Song Festival. Originator CHIN Internat. Picnic, free ann. festival ethnocultural music, song, dance; mem. Toronto Gen. Hosp Found.; founding dir., gov. Villa Colombo; founding officer Italian Immigrant Aid Soc.; trustee Nat. Arts Centre Corp., 1982-85; patron Ont. Mus. Arts Ctre, 1989—; founder, host Italian Spring Festival, 1988; bd. dirs. Can. Coun. Christian and Jews, 1990; supporting mem. numerous civic organs., hosps. univs. and schs. including Easter Seal Soc., Boys/Girls Clubs Can., Kidney Found. Can., Cath. Charities, Hebrew Culture Orgn. Can., Can. Citizenship Found., Can. Opera Co., United Way; supporter elimination of apartheid in South Africa, eliminatin of anti-semitism, 1992; founding mem. Met. Toronto Police Community Projects Found., 1990. Sgt. Can. Army, 1942-46, ETO. Recipient Ethnic Entrepreneur of Yr. award, 1994, Fed. Citation of Citizenship, 1994, Silver medal for Elimination of Racial Discrimination, 1995; named Officer Brother-Order of St. John, 1994. Mem. Broadcast Execs. Soc., Can. Assn. Ethnic (Radio) Broadcasters (pres. 1981), Toronto Musicians Assn. Can., Can. Italian Bus. and Profl. Assn., Toronto, Soc. for Recognition of Can. Talent Inc., Ont. Multicultural Assn. (patron), Can. Coun., Nat. Coun. Boy Scouts Can. (hon.), Can./Holland 1945 Liberation Soc., Order of Can., Order of Ontario, Variety Club (award 1985). Office: CHIN, 622 College St, Toronto, ON Canada M6G 1B6

LOMBARDI, JOHN V., university administrator, historian; b. Los Angeles, Aug. 19, 1942; s. John and Janice P. Lombardi; m. Cathryn Lee; children: John Lee, Mary Ann. B.A., Pomona Coll., 1963; M.A., Columbia U., 1964, Ph.D., 1968. Prof. contratado Escuela de Historia, Universidad Central de Venezuela, Caracas, 1967; lectr. history Ind. U. S.E., Jeffersonville, 1967-68; asst. prof. Ind. U. S.E., 1968-69; vis. asst. prof. Ind. U., Bloomington, 1968-69; asst. prof. history Ind. U., 1969-71, assoc. prof., 1971-77, prof., 1977-87, dir. Latin Am. studies program, 1971-74, dean Internat. Programs, 1978-85, dean Coll. Arts and Scis., 1985-87; prof. history Johns Hopkins U., 1987-89, provost, vp. for acad. affairs, 1987-89; pres. U. Fla., Gainesville, 1989—. Author: (with others) Venezuelan History: A Comprehensive Working Bibliography, 1977, People and Places in Colonial Venezuela, 1976, Venezuela: Search for Order, Dream of Progress, 1982; Mem. editorial bd.: (with others) UCLA Statis. Abstracts Latin Am, 1977—; contbr. (with others) articles to profl. jours. Fulbright-Hayes research fellow, 1965-66. Mem. Am. Hist. Assn., Latin Am. Studies Assn., Pan Am. Inst. Geography and History, Academia Nacional de la Historia (corr. mem .). Office: U Fla Office of Pres Gainesville FL 32611

LOMBARDI, KENT BAILEY, insurance company administrator; b. Keene, N.H., Nov. 24, 1955; s. Louis Richard Lombardi and Jean (Thurston) Tacy; m. June M. Havas, Aug. 12, 1978; children: Marina, Anthony. BS in Mktg. & Mgmt., Siena Coll., 1977. CPCU. Claims adjuster Crawford & Co., Poughkeepsie, N.Y., 1977-78; adjuster-in-charge Crawford & Co., Middletown, N.Y., 1978-82, 83-85; adjuster Ft. Orange Claims, Clifton Park, N.Y., 1982-83; claims examiner Frontier Ins. Co., Monticello, N.Y., 1985-87, asst. claims mgr. property & casualty, 1987-92; asst. claims mgr. med./dental malpractice Frontier Ins. Co., Monticello & Rock Hill, N.Y., 1992-94; v.p., claims mgr. med./dental malpractice Frontier Ins. Co., Rock Hill, N.Y., 1993-96, v.p. med./dental malpractice, 1996—. Mem. Mid Hudson Claims Assn. Avocations: skiing, golf, music. Office: Frontier Ins Co Lake Louise Marie Rd Rock Hill NY 12775

LOMBARDO, GAETANO (GUY LOMBARDO), venture capitalist; b. Salemi, Italy, Feb. 4, 1940; came to U.S., 1947; s. Salvatore and Anna Maria L.; Sc.B. with honors, Brown U., 1962; Ph.D. in Physics, Cornell U., 1971; m. Nancy B. Emerson, Sept. 2, 1967 (div. 1993); children: Nicholas Emerson, Maryanne Chilton. Sr. staff Arthur D. Little Inc., Cambridge, Mass., 1967-77; v.p. logistics Morton Salt Co., Chgo., 1977-78; dir. logistics and distbn. Gould Inc., Chgo., 1978-80; corp. dir. Bendix Corp., Southfield, Mich., 1980-82; group v.p. Bendix Indsl. Group, 1982-84; founder, pres., chief exec. officer Comau Productivity Systems, 1984-86; pres. Nelmar Corp., 1983-90; chmn., chief exec. officer Courtesy Mfg. Co., Elk Grove, Ill., 1988—; pres. Poplar Industries, Inc., 1989—; chmn. I.A. Bedford, Ltd., Des Moines; vis. prof. ops. mgmt. Boston U., 1973. Contbr. articles on physics and bus. mgmt. to profl. jours. Office: Courtesy Mfg Co 1300 Pratt Blvd Elk Grove Village IL 60007

LOMBARDO, JANICE ELLEN, microbiologist; b. Chgo., Sept. 22, 1951; d. John Robert and Betty Jane (Westfall) Richardson; m. Peter Anthony Lombardo, Aug. 17, 1979; 1 child, Gina Ellen. BA in Biology, Northeastern Ill. U., 1972, MS in Biology, 1984, postgrad., 1994—. Tech. supr. St. Joseph's Hosp., Chgo., 1973-78; lab. leader, microbiologist Cabrini Hosp., Chgo., 1979-80, lab. mgr., 1980-84; med. technologist Stroink Pathology Lab., Bloomington, Ill., 1984-85; microbiology supr. Damon Clin. Labs., Berwyn, Ill., 1985-87; microbiology technologist Damon Clin. Labs., Berwyn, 1987-90; microbiology supr. Columbus-Cabrini Med. Ctr., Chgo., 1990-92, lab. adminstrv. dir., 1992-93; microbiology supr. Nat. Health Labs., Elmhurst, Ill., 1993-94; microbiologist Metpath/Corning Labs., Wooddale, Ill., 1994—; sci. tutor Taft High Sch., Chgo., 1995—. Author: (under pen name Ellen West) Andrea, 1992. Mem. social ministry com., Lutheran Meml. Ch., Chgo. Grantee Campaign for Human Devel., Des Moines, 1978. Mem. Am. Soc. Microbiology, Am. Soc. Clin. Pathologists, South Ctrl. Assn. Clin. Microbiology, N.Y. Acad. Sci., Clin. Lab. Mgmt. Assn., Nat. Cert. Agy., Crohn's and Colitis Found. of Am., Assoc. of Sci. Tchrs. Achievements include environmental study on Chicago River, botanical study on bacterial pathogens, and microbiological analysis in botulism litigation, 1985. Home: 5605 N Nagle Ave Chicago IL 60646-6132

LOMBARDO, JOSEPH SAMUEL, acoustical engineer; b. Chgo., Aug. 16, 1946; s. Joseph and Frances Lombardo; m. Maureen Frick, May 25, 1974; children: Christopher, Jennifer. BS in Elec. Engring., U. Ill., 1969; MS in Elec. Engring., Johns Hopkins U., 1974. Registered profl. engr., Ill. Instrumentation specialist Johns Hopkins U./Applied Physics Lab., Laurel, Md., 1970-78, sect. supr. acoustics group, 1978-84, program mgr. Navy undersea rsch., 1984—; com. mem. Adv. Group to Asst. Sec. of Navy, Washington, 1990. Contbr. articles to profl. jours. Bd. govs. Cape St. Claire (Md.) Improvement Assn., 1985. Mem. IEEE, Nat. Security Indsl. Assn. (com. 1992-95), Cape St. Claire Yacht Club (commodore 1984-86), Eta Kappa Nu, Tau Beta Pi, Sigma Tau. Achievements include patents for vibration sensor, large aperture element location sys., towing configuration hardware for geophys. exploration sys.; avocation: sailing. Office: Johns Hopkins U Applied Physics Lab Johns Hopkins Rd Laurel MD 20723

LOMBARDO, MICHAEL JOHN, lawyer, educator; b. Willimantic, Conn., Mar. 25, 1927; s. Frank Paul and Mary Margaret (Longo) L.; children: Nancy C., Claire M. BS, U. Conn., 1951, MS, 1961, JD, 1973. Bar: Conn. 1974, U.S. Dist. Ct. Conn. 1975, U.S. Supreme Ct. 1979, U.S. Ct. Appeals (2d cir.) 1980. Div. controller Jones & Laughlin Steel Corp., Willimantic, 1956-67; adminstrv. officer health ctr. U. Conn., Hartford, 1968-69; dir. adminstrv. svcs. South Central Community Coll., New Haven, 1969-70; asst. dir. adminstrn. Norwich (Conn.) Hosp., 1970-77; asst. atty. gen. State of Conn., Hartford, 1977-92; pvt. practice, Willimantic, 1992—; adj. asst. prof. U. Hartford, 1961-70; adj. prof. bus. Old Dominion U., 1973-81; adj. lectr. in law and bus. Ea. Conn. State U., 1973—, disting. adj. faculty, 1990. Vol. Windham Ctr. (Conn.) Fire Dept. Sgt. U.S. Army, 1945-46, 1st lt. USAFR, 1951-53, col. USAFR, 1953-87, col. USAF ret., 1987. Mem. AAUP, Retired Officers Assn., Conn. Bar Assn., Windham County Bar Assn., Mensa Internat., Am. Legion, VFW, Lions (bd. dirs. Willimantic chpt. 1960-64). Home: 35 Oakwood Dr Windham CT 06280-1520 Office: 37 Church St Willimantic CT 06226-2601

LOMBARDO, PHILIP JOSEPH, broadcasting company executive; b. Chgo., June 13, 1935; s. Joseph Pete and Josephine (Franco) L.; m. Marilyn Ann Tellefsen, June 22, 1963; children: Dean, Jeffrey. Student, U. Ill., 1953-55; BA in Speech, Journalism and Radio/TV, U. Mo., 1958, postgrad. speech, 1958; grad. advanced mgmt. program, Harvard U., 1976. Account exec. Sta. WWCA, Ind., 1959-60; producer-dir. Sta. WBBM-TV, Chgo., 1960-65; program mgr., acting gen. mgr. Sta. WLWT, Cin., 1965-67; v.p., gen. mgr. Sta. WGHP-TV, N.C., 1968-73; pres., chief exec. officer Corinthian Broadcasting Corp., N.Y.C., 1973-82; chmn., pres., chief exec. officer Champlain Communications Corp., N.Y.C., 1982-84; mng. gen. ptnr. Citadel Communications Co. Ltd., N.Y.C., 1982—; chmn., pres., chief exec. officer Citadel Communications, Co. Ltd., C.C.C. Communications Corp., Lombardo Communications II, Inc., P.J.L. Investments, Inc., N.Y.C., 1984—; mng. gen. ptnr., nat. sales rep. U.S. and Can. TV stas. Can. Communications Co., Toronto, 1985—; mng. gen. ptnr. Coronet Communications Co., N.Y.C., 1985—, Capital Comm. Co., Inc., 1994—, Citadel Comm., LLC, 1995—; bd. dirs. The Gabelli Group, The Lynch Corp., N.Y.C. Mem. adv. bd. Salvation Army; com. budget, bd. dirs. United Fund; mem. com. High Point (N.C.) United Schs.; 1st vice chmn. Central Carolina chpt. Nat. Multiple Sclerosis Soc., 1968-73; bd. dirs. High Point Arts Council, 1968-73. Served with AUS, 1959, 62. Recipient Disting. Svc. award Freedom Found., Am. Legion, High Point (N.C.) Youth Coun. Mem. Dirs. Guild Am., Internat. Radio and TV Soc. (bd. govs.). Clubs: Winged Foot Golf, Marco Polo, Board Room, Bronxville Field, Chgo. Press. Lodges: Rotary, Kiwanis. Home: 24 Masterton Rd Bronxville NY 10708-4804 Office: Citadel Comm Co 17 Kraft Ave Bronxville NY 10708-4103

LOMBARDO, TONY, film editor. Editor: (films) A Wedding, 1978, A Perfect Couple, 1979, Cheech & Chong's Nice Dreams, 1981, Blame It on the Night, 1984, Reckless, 1984, P.K. and the Kid, 1987, (with Thomas Stanford) Born to Race, 1988, Man Outside, 1988, Uncle Buck, 1989, (with Frank Morriss) The Hard Way, 1991, (with Barry B. Leirer) The Distinguished Gentleman, 1992, My Cousin Vinny, 1992, Greedy, 1994, (TV movie) By Dawn's early Light, 1989. Office: The Gersh Agency 232 N Canon Dr Beverly Hills CA 90210-5302

LOMICKA, WILLIAM HENRY, investor; b. Irwin, Pa., Mar. 9, 1937; s. William and Carabel L.; m. Carol L. Williams, Feb. 14, 1979; 1 son, Edward W. B.A., Coll. Wooster, Ohio, 1959; M.B.A., U. Pa., 1962. Sr. securities analyst Guardian Life Ins. Co., N.Y.C., 1962-65; treasury svcs. mgr. L.B. Foster Co., Pitts., 1966-68, Welch Foods Co., Westfield, N.Y., 1969-70; asst. treas. Ashland Oil, Inc., Ky., 1970-75; sr. v.p. fin. Humana Inc., Louisville, 1975-85; pres., fin. cons. Old South Life Ins. Co., Louisville, 1985-87; sec. econ. devel. Commonwealth of Ky., 1987-88; acting pres. Citizens Security Life Ins. Co., Louisville, 1988-89; pres. Mayfair Capital, Inc., Louisville, 1988—; bd. dirs. Vencor, Inc., Regal Cinemas, Inc., Advocat, Inc. Bd. dirs., vice chmn. Louisville Downtown Devel. Corp.; trustee Bellarmine Coll. Served with USAR, 1962-63. Home: 402 Mockingbird Valley Rd Louisville KY 40207-1322 Office: Capital Holding Ctr 400 W Market St Ste 2510 Louisville KY 40202-3376

LOMMATSCH, I. LAVON, retired business administration consultant; b. Denver, June 6, 1940; d. William Theodore and Iro (Watenpaugh) Fisher; m. Lynn Lommatsch, June 1, 1985; children: James Waldorf, Lance Waldorf, Stacy Waldorf, Eric, Keith. Student, U. Colo., 1960-61, Front Range C.C., Denver, 1984, Don Kagy Real Estate Sch., Denver, 1985. Lic. realtor, Colo. With juvenile divsn. Adams County Dist. Atty., Brighton, Colo., 1983-86; with Adams County Parks and Cmty. Resources, Brighton, 1986-95; ret. Charter mem. bd. dirs. Women In Crisis, Adams County, 1983; prodr., dir. walk-a-thons Adams County Trails and Greenway Found.; active fundraising Amaranth Diabetes Found., Alternatives to Domestic Violence, Cmty. Health Svcs., Hearing/Seeing Dogs, Santa's Workshop, Shriner's Burn Ctrs. Recipient Excellence award Nat. Assn. County Info. Officers, 1986, State Recognition award Heart Assn. Mem. Order Ea. Star (worthy matron 1977-78), Order Amaranth, Inc. (grand royal matron 1991-92), White Shrine Jerusalem. Lutheran. Avocations: music, outdoors, wildlife.

LOMO, LEIF, electrical manufacturing company executive; b. Aalesund, Norway, July 1, 1929; came to U.S., 1951, naturalized, 1962; s. Leif and Ingeborg Rebekka (Helseth) L.; m. Mary Goodbar, Sept. 5, 1959; children—Caroline H., Erik H., Leif G. B.S., in Aero. Engring., U. Colo., 1954, M.S. in Aero. Engring., 1959. Flight test engr. Cessna, Wichita, Kans., 1954-57; sales engr. Boeing Corp., Renton, Wash., 1959-65; pres. Murray Iron Works, Burlington, Iowa, 1965-73, Trane-Europe, Epinal, France, 1973-78, A. B. Chance, subs. Emerson Electric Co., Centralia, Mo., 1978-88; group v.p. Emerson Electric Co., St. Louis, 1983-88; chmn., pres., CEO A. B. Chance Industries Inc., Centralia, 1988-94; ret., 1994; pres. Marley Pump Co., Mission, Kans., 1994—. Served to chief petty officer Royal Norwegian Navy, 1949-50. Office: 19700 N Hwy 124 Centralia MO 65240-1395

LOMON, EARLE LEONARD, physicist, educator, consultant; b. Montreal, Nov. 15, 1930; came to U.S., 1951, naturalized, 1965; s. Harry and Etta (Rappaport) L.; m. Ruth Margaret Jones, Aug. 4, 1951; children: Martha Glynis, Christopher Dylan, Deirdre Naomi. B.Sc., McGill U., Montreal, 1951; Ph.D., MIT, 1954. NRC Can. overseas research fellow Inst. Theoretical Physics, Copenhagen, 1954-55; fellow Weizmann Inst., Rehovoth, Israel, 1955-56; research assoc. lab. nuclear studies Cornell U., Ithaca, N.Y., 1956-57; assoc. prof. theoretical physics McGill U., Montreal, 1957-60; assoc. prof. physics MIT, Cambridge, 1960-70, prof., 1970—; vis. staff mem. Los Alamos Nat. Lab., 1968—; project dir. Unified Scis. and Math. for Elem. Schs., Cambridge, 1970-77; adj. prof. U. Louvain-la-Neuve, Belgium, 1980; vis. prof. U. Paris, 1979-80, 86-87, UCLA, 1983, U. Wash., 1985; vis. rschr. Kernforschungsanlage Jülich, 1986-92, U. Geneva, 1993, CERN, Geneva, 1994, IPN, Orsay, 1994; Lady Davis vis. prof. Hebrew U., Jerusalem, 1993-94. Contbr. articles to profl. jours. Guggenheim Meml. Found. fellow CERN, Geneva, 1965-66; Dupont fellow, 1952-53; Ossabaw Island Project fellow (Ga.), 1978; Sci. Research Council fellow U. London, 1980. Fellow Am. Phys. Soc.; mem. Can. Assn. Physicists. Office: MIT 6-304 77 Massachusetts Ave Cambridge MA 02139-4301

LOMONOSOFF, JAMES MARC, marketing executive; b. Van Nuys, Calif., Apr. 29, 1951; s. Boris Marc and Eileen Fairfax (Thomson) L.; m. Elisabeth Maas, June 12, 1982; children; Marc Frederik, James Forrest. BA in Econs., Colgate U., 1973; MBA in Gen. Mgmt., U. Va., 1975. With Saatchi and Saatchi Advt., N.Y.C., 1975-93, v.p., account supr., 1975-85, sr. v.p., mgmt. supr., 1986-87, exec. v.p., mgmt. dir., 1987—, pres. Collateral Plus div., 1987-90; pres., chief exec. officer Saatchi & Saatchi Specialized Communications, 1991-92; account dir. VDB/Compton B.V., Amsterdam, The Netherlands, 1980-83; acct. dir. Saatchi and Saatchi Compton S.A., Madrid, 1983-84; regional acct. dir. Saatchi and Saatchi Compton Worldwide, London, 1984-86; mng. dir., CEO BSB/Saatchi and Saatchi, Prague, 1992-93; v.p. internat. mktg. Walt Disney Attractions Inc., Lake Buena Vista, Fla., 1994—. Mem. Beta Theta Pi. Republican. Home: 10905 Bayshore Dr Windermere FL 34786 Office: Walt Disney Attractions Inc PO Box 10000 Lake Buena Vista FL 32830-1000

LONBORG, JAMES REYNOLD, dentist, former professional baseball player; b. Santa Maria, Calif., Apr. 16, 1942; s. Reynold H. and Ada (Ryan) L.; m. Rosemary Irene Feeney, Nov. 21, 1970; children: Phoebe Lea, Claire Elizabeth, Nicholas James, Nora Kathleen, John Bartholomew, Jordon Michael. B.A., Stanford U., 1964; D.M.D., Tufts U. Dental Sch., 1983. Baseball player Boston Red Sox, 1965-71, Milw. Brewers, 1972; pitcher Phila. Phillies, 1973-79; gen. dentist; asst. to adminstr. New Eng. Rehab. Clinic, Woburn, Mass., 1972-74. Recipient Cy Young award, 1967. Recorded 1000th maj. league strikeout, Aug. 19, 1973; career record 157 wins, 137 losses. Home: 498 First Parish Rd Scituate MA 02066-3201 Office: 105 Webster St Hanover MA 02339-1227

LONCOSKY, WALTER BEUGGER, real estate manager; b. Gowanda, N.Y., Nov. 12, 1935; s. Walter Herman and Ida B. (Beugger) L.; m. Anita Lucile Thorp, June 27, 1964; 1 child, Helga B. BA in Journalism and Pub. Adminstrn., Columbia Pacific U., 1984, MA in Journalism and Pub. Adminstrn., 1985; diploma Gen. Bible, Liberty U., 1985. Lic. real estate broker, Pa.; cert. conservationist, Pa., erosion and sediment control inspector, Pa.; ordained to ministry Bapt. Ch., 1984. Sports editor Danville (Pa.) News, 1956-58; performance specialist U.S. Agr. Stabilization & Cons. Dept., Danville, 1961-68; info. specialist Pa. Dept. Agr., Harrisburg, 1968-70; editor, owner Montour News Svc., Danville, 1971-80; pres., owner Skyco, Inc., Bloomsburg, Pa., 1981—; chmn., dir. Conservation Dist., Montour County, Pa., 1967-80; mem. adv. bd. County Planning Commn., Danville, 1969-80; chmn. Environ. Adv. Coun., Derry Twp., Pa., 1971-78; panel mem. Pa. Rural Studies Program, Danville, 1975. Author: Preservation of Agricultural Land, 1969, Columbia-Pacific Press, 1984. Bd. mem. Area Agy. on Aging, Danville, 1972-80; chmn. Home Rule Task Force, Danville, 1973; constable Derry Twp., Pa., 1976-82; bd. mem. County Dem. Com., Montour County, 1976-80. With U.S. Army, 1958-60. Named Hon. Chpt. Farmer Future Farmers Am., Turbotville, Pa., 1971; W.K. Kellogg Found. fellow, 1973; recipient award of merit World of Poetry, 1987. Mem. Pa. Assn. Environ. Profls., Rainbow Morgan Horse Assn., Masons, Elks. Democrat. Avocations: gardening, hiking, political science, soccer. Office: Skyco Inc 1000 Market St Bloomsburg PA 17815-2601

LOND, HARLEY WELDON, editor, publisher; b. Chgo., Feb. 5, 1946; s. Henry Sidney and Dorothy (Shaps) L.; m. Marilyn Moss, Aug. 20, 1981. BA in Journalism, Calif. State U., L.A., 1972. Adminstrv. dir. Century City Ednl. Arts Project, L.A., 1972-76, hon. dir., 1982—; founder, editor Intermedia mag., L.A., 1974-80; prodn. mgr. FilmRow Publs., L.A., 1981; assoc. editor Box Office mag., Hollywood, Calif., 1981-84, editor, assoc. pub., 1984-94; dir. publs. Entertainment Data, Inc., 1994-95; pres. CyberPod Prodns., 1995—; syndicated columnist Continental Features, Washington, Tel-Aire Publs., Dallas, 1986—; hon dir. Monterey (Calif.) Film Festival, 1987; mem. media adv. bd. Cinetex Internat. Film Festival, 1988; cons. Take 3 Info. Svc. Editor: Entertainment Media Electronic Info. Svc.; contbr. articles to profl. publs. Calif. Arts Council grantee, 1975, Nat. Endowment for Arts grantee, 1976-77. Mem. MLA, Soc. Profl. Journalists, Assn. for Edn. in Journalism and Mass Communication, Speech Communication Assn., Soc. for Cinema Studies. Office: PO Box 17377 Beverly Hills CA 90209

LONDEREE, RAMONA GAYLE, art educator; b. Hammond, Ind., Apr. 22, 1949; d. Virgil Raymond and Emma Ettalene (Ford) Howard; m. William Patrick Londeree, July 6, 1969; children: James William, Kimberly Sarette. BA in Edn., U. Fla., 1971; MA in Edn., U. South Fla., 1981. Cert. art educator. Tchr. art Jewett Jr. High Sch., Winter Haven, Fla., 1973-84, Winter Haven High Sch., 1984-95, Lake Region High Sch., Eagle Lake, Fla., 1995—. Contbr. photos: Design Standards for Art Facilities. Grantee Fla. Arts for a Complete Edn., 1993-94. Mem. NEA, Nat. Art Edn. Assn., Fla. Art Edn. Assn., Polk Edn. Assn., Polk Art Edn. Assn., Am. Hemerocallis Soc. Avocations: reading, gardening. Home: 584 Somerset Dr Auburndale FL 33823-9570 Office: Lake Region HS 1995 Thunder Rd Eagle Lake FL 33839

LONDON, ANDREW BARRY, film editor; b. Bronx, N.Y., Jan. 1, 1949; s. Max Edward and Nellie (Steiner) L. BA in Cinema magna cum laude, U. So. Calif., 1970. Represented by Mont. Artists, Santa Monica, Calif. Prin. works include: (features) The Meteor Man, 1993, F/X 2, 1991, Ramblo III, 1988, Planes, Trains and Automobiles, 1987, Link, 1986, Cloak & Dagger, 1984, Psycho II, 1983, The True Story of Eskimo Nell, 1975, (TV shows) The Crying Child, 1996, Evil Has a Face, 1996, Don't Talk to Strangers, 1994, Day of Reckoning, 1993, Mortal Sins, 1992, Running Delilah, 1992, True Tales, 1992, Sweet Poison, 1991, Tales from the Crypt, 1989-90, (pilot) Beauty and the Beast, 1987, The Christmas Star, 1986; sound editor: Wolfen (MPSE Golden Reel award 1982), Hammett, Roadgames, Psycho II, I'm Dancing As Fast As I Can, Perfect, Protocol, Coal Miner's Daughter, The Long Riders, others. Mem. Acad. Motion Picture Arts and Scis., Motion Picture Sound Editors (Golden Reel award 1982), Phi Beta Kappa. Office: 2622 Armstrong Ave Los Angeles CA 90039-2613

LONDON, CHARLOTTE ISABELLA, secondary education educator, reading specialist; b. Guyana, S.Am., June 11, 1946; came to U.S., 1966, naturalized, 1980; d. Samuel Alphonso and Diana Dallett (Daniels) Edwards; m. David Timothy London, May 26, 1968 (div. May 1983); children: David Tshombe, Douglas Tshaka. BS, Fort Hays State U., 1971; MS, Pa. State U., 1974, PhD, 1977. Elem. sch. tch., Guyana, 1962-66, secondary sch. tchr., 1971-72; instr. lang. arts Pa. State U., University Park, 1973-74; reading specialist/ednl. cons. N.Y.C. Community Coll., 1975; dir. skills acquisition and devel. center Stockton (N.J.) State Coll., 1975-77; reading specialist Pleasantville (N.J.) Public Schs., 1977—; ind. specialist United Nations Devel. Programme , Guyana, 1988—; v.p. Atlantic County PTA, 1980-82; del. N.J. Gov.'s Conf. Future Edn. N.J., 1981; founder, pres. Guyana Assn. Reading and Lang. Devel., 1987. Sec. Atlantic County Minority Polit. Women's Caucus. Mem. Internat. Reading Assn., Nat. Council Tchrs. English, Assn. Supervision and Curriculum Devel., NEA, N.J. Ednl. Assn., AAUW, Pi Lambda Theta, Phi Delta Kappa (sec.). Mem. African Methodist Episcopal Ch. Home: 6319 Crocus St Mays Landing NJ 08330-1107 Office: Pleasantville Pub Schs W Decatur Ave Pleasantville NJ 08232

LONDON, HERBERT IRA, humanities educator; b. N.Y.C., Mar. 6, 1939; s. Jack and Esta (Epstein) L.; m. Joy Weinman, Oct. 13, 1942 (div. 1974); children: Staci, Nancy; m. Vicki Pops, Nov. 18, 1950; 1 child, Jaclyn. BA, Columbia U., 1960, MA, 1961; PhD, N.Y. U., 1966; DL, U. Aix.-Marseille, Aix-en-Provence, France, 1982, Grove City Coll., 1993. Teaching fellow N.Y. U., N.Y.C., 1963-64, instr., 1964-65, asst. prof., 1967-68, univ. ombudsman, 1968-69, assoc. prof., 1969-73, prof., 1973—, dean Gallatin div., 1972-92, John M. Olin U. Prof. Humanities, 1992—; instr. New Sch. for Social Research, N.Y.C., 1964-65; research scholar Australian Nat. U., Canberra, Australia, 1966-67; bd. overseers Ctr. for Naval Analysis, Washington, 1983—; trustee Hudson Inst., Indpls., 1979—, research fellow 1974—; sr. fellow Nat. Strategy Info. Ctr. Created TV programs: Myths That Rule America, The American Character; contbr. numerous articles to profl. jours. Bd. dirs., chmn. Nat. Assn. Scholars, N.Y.C., 1986; bd. advisors Coalition for Strategic Def. Initiative, Washington, 1986; candidate for mayor of N.Y.C., 1989; conservative candidate for gov., N.Y., 1990, 94; candidate for comptroller of N.Y. State, 1994. Recipient Def. Sci. award Def. Sci. Jour., 1985, Fulbright award U.S. Govt., 1966-67, Anderson award NYU, 1965, Martin Luther King award Congress of Racial Equality; named Danforth Assoc. Danforth Found., 1971. Mem. Freedom House, Am. Hist. Assn., Edn. Excellence Network, Heritage Found (assoc. scholar 1983—), Ethics and Pub. Policy Ctr. (assoc. scholar 1985—), Nat. Strategy Info. Ctr., N.Y.C., 1984. Republican. Jewish. Avocations: writing, tennis. Home: 2 Washington Square Vlg New York NY 10012-1732 Office: NYU 113 University Pl New York NY 10003-4527

LONDON, J. PHILLIP, information technology company executive; b. Oklahoma City, Apr. 30, 1937; s. Harry Riles and Laura Evalyn (Phillips) L.; children: J. Phillip Jr., Laura McLain. BSc, U.S. Naval Acad., 1959; MSc, U.S. Naval Postgrad. Sch., 1967; D in Bus. Adminstrn., George Washington U., 1971. Commd. ensign USN, 1959, advanced through grades to capt., resigned, 1971; program mgr. Challenger Research Inc., 1971-72; mgr. CACI Internat. Inc., Arlington, Va., 1972-76, v.p., 1976-77, sr. v.p., 1977-79, exec. v.p., 1979-82, pres. operating div., 1982-84, pres., chief exec. officer, 1984-90, chmn. bd., 1990—. Recipient Alumni of Yr. award George Washington U. Sch. Govt. & Bus. Adminstrn., Washington, 1987, High Tech Entrepreneur award KPMG Peat Marwick, 1995. Mem. George Town Club (Washington), Cosmos Club (Washington). Episcopalian. Office: CACI Internat Inc 1100 N Glebe Rd Arlington VA 22201-4798

LONDON, MARTIN, lawyer; b. Glen Cove, N.Y., Apr. 4, 1934; s. Abraham and Rebecca (Lasker) L.; m. Mellanie Bell, May, 1958 (div. 1973); children: Jesse, Lizbeth; m. Doris Wilke, July 28, 1983. AB, Cornell U., 1955; LLB, NYU, 1957. Bar: N.Y. 1958, U.S. Dist. Ct. (so. dist.) N.Y. 1962, U.S. Tax Ct. 1968, U.S. Dist. Ct. (ea. dist.) N.Y. 1969, U.S. Ct. Appeals (2d cir.) 1969, U.S. Dist. Ct. D.C. 1970, U.S. Supreme Ct. 1971, U.S. Ct. Appeals (6th and 7th cirs.) 1982, U.S. Ct. Appeals (4th cir.) 1990. Assoc. Gallop, Climenko & Gould, N.Y.C., 1958-61; assoc. Paul, Weiss, Rifkind, Wharton & Garrison, N.Y.C., 1962-68, ptnr., 1969—; spl. counsel judiciary relations com. First Judicial Dept., 1973-74, counsel gov.'s judicial nomination com., 1975-82, chmn. deptl. disciplinary com., 1980-85; spl. trial counsel Ct. on the Judiciary, 1977. Served as sgt. U.S. Army, 1957-58, 61-62. Mem. Am. Coll. Trial Lawyers, Assn. of Bar of City of N.Y., Fed. Bar Council, Am. Arbitration Assn. (nat. panel arbitrators). Avocations: deep sea fishing, skiing. Office: Paul Weiss Rifkind Wharton & Garrison 1285 Avenue Of The Americas New York NY 10019-6028*

LONDON, RAY WILLIAM, clinical and forensic psychologist, consultant, researcher; b. Burley, Idaho, May 29, 1943; s. Loo Richard and Maycelle Jerry (Moore) L. AS, Weber State Coll., 1965, BS, 1967; MSW, U. So. Calif., 1973, PhD, 1976, Exec. MBA, 1989, cert. in Dispute Resolution, Pepperdine U., 1993. Diplomate: Am. Bd. Psychol. Hypnosis (dir. 1984—, pres. 1989—), Am. Acad. Behavioral Medicine, Am. Bd. Med. Psychotherapy, Internat. Acad. Medicine and Psychology., Am. Bd. Profl. Neuropsychology, Am. Bd. Adminstrv. Psychology, Am. Bd. Examiners Clin. Soc. Work, Am. Bd. Clin. Hypnosis in Social Work (pres. 1989-91), Am. Bd. Profl. Psychology, Am. Bd. Family Psychology (dir. 1993—), Am. Bd. Child and Adolescent Psychology (dir. 1992—), NASW Clin. Soc. Work, Am. Bd. Forensic Examiners (cert.); cert. Am. Assn. Sex Therapists, Soc. Med. Analysts; registered internat. cons., cert. mgmt. cons., congl. asst. U.S. Ho. of Reps., 1964-65; rsch. assoc. Bus. Advs., Inc., Ogden, Utah, 1965-67; dir. counseling and consultation svcs. Meaning Found., Riverside, Calif., 1966-69; mental health and mental retardation liaison San Bernardino County (Calif.) Social Svcs., 1968-72; clin. trainee VA Outpatient Clinic, L.A., 1971-72, Children's Hosp., 1972-73, clin. fellow, 1973-74; clin. trainee Reiss Davis Child Study Ctr., L.A., 1973-74, L.A. County-U. So. Calif. Med. Ctr., 1973; psychotherapist Benjamin Rush Neuropsychiat. Ctr., Orange, Calif., 1973-75; clin. psychology postdoctoral intern Orange County (Calif.) Mental Health, 1976-77; postdoctoral fellow U. Calif.-Irvine-Calif. Coll. Medicine, 1978; clin. psychologist Orange Police Dept., 1974-80; pvt. practice consultation and assessment, Santa Ana, Calif., 1974—; chief oper. officer London Assocs. Internat., 1974-80; cons. to public schs., agys., hosps., bus., nationally and internationally, 1973—; presenter nat. and internat. lectures, seminars and workshops; pres. bd. govs. Human Factor Programs, Ltd., 1976—; pres. Internat. Bd. Medicine and Psychology, 1980-84; chief exec. officer Human Studies Ctr., 1987—; pres., chief exec. officer London Assocs. Internat.; Organizational Behavior-Crisis-Devel. Cons., 1980—; research affil. Ctr. for Crisis Mgmt. U. So. Calif. Grad. Sch. Bus. Adminstrn., 1988-90; pres., chief exec. officer Am. Bd. Clin. Hypnosis, Inc.; mem. faculty UCLA, U. So. Calif., Calif. State U., U. Calif., Irvine, Calif. Coll. Medicine, Internat. Cong. of Psychosomatic Medicine, Internat. Coll.; research assoc. Nat. Commn. for Protection of Human Subjects of Biomed. and Behavioral Research, 1976; fellow Inst. for Social Scientists on Neurobiology and Mental Illness, 1978. Editor: Internat. Bull. Medicine and Psychology, 1980—, A.B.C.D. Report, 1988— behavioral medicine Australian Jour., 1980, adv. editor Internat. Jour. Clin. and Exptl. Hypnosis, 1981-92, mng. editor, 1991—, assoc. editor, 1992—; cons. editor Internat. Jour. Psychosomatics, 1984—; Experimentelle und Klinische Hypnose, 1987—, cons. Am. Jour. Forensic Psychology, 1986, Jour. Mgmt. Consulting, 1992—; pub.: London Behavioral Medicine Assessment, 1982, A Behavior-Cris-Development newsletter, ABCD Newsnote; producer: TV series Being Human, 1980; contbg. author World Book Ency. and books; contbr. articles to profl. jours. Recipient Congl. recognition U.S. Ho. of Reps., 1978, Morton Prince award, 1993; named scholar laureate Erickson Advanced Inst., 1980. Fellow Internat. Acad. Medicine and Psychology (dir. 1981—), Soc. Clin. Social Work (dir. 1979-80), Royal Soc. Health, Am. Coll. Forensic Psychology, Soc. Clin and Experimental Hypnosis (bd. dirs. 1985—, treas. 1987-89), Profl. Acad. Custody Evaluators, Acad. Family Psychology; mem. Acad. Psychosomatic Medicine, Am. Psychol. Assn., Am. Group Psychotherapy Assn., Am. Orthopsychiat. Assn., N.Y. Acad. Sci., Soc. Behavioral Medicine, Internat. Psychosomatic Inst., Australian Coll. Pvt. Consulting Psychologists, Australian Psychol. Soc., Internat. Coun. Psychologists, Acad. Mgmt., AsInst. Mgmt. Cons., Internat. Forum Corp. Dirs., Nat. Assn. Corp. Dirs., Profl. and Tech. Cons. Assn., Soc. Indsl. and Orgnl. Psychology, So. Calif. Mediation Assn. (mem. law soc.), Acad. Family Mediators, Am. Coll. Forensic Examiners, Am. Soc. Trial Cons., Am. Psychology Law Soc., Nat. Assn. Expert Witnesses, Soc. Profls. in Dispute Resolution, Am. Registry of Arbitrators, Am. Soc. Clin. Hypnosis (approved cons.), Toastmasters, Phi Delta Kappa, Delta Sigma Rho, Tau Kappa Alpha, Pi RhoPhi, Lambda Iota Tau. Office: London Assocs Internat 18062 Irvine Blvd Ste 200 Tustin CA 92680-3328

LONDON, WILLIAM LORD, pediatrician; b. Durham, N.C., Nov. 1, 1930. MD, U. N.C., 1955. Intern Children's Med. Ctr., Boston, 1955-56, resident, 1956-57, 59-60, fellow in pediatric hematology, 1960-61; mem. staff Durham (N.C.) Gen. Hosp.; clin. assoc. prof. Duke U., Durham. Fellow Am. Acad. Pediatrics; mem. AMA. Office: 2609 N Duke St # 801 Durham NC 27704-3019*

LONDONER, DAVID JAY, investment banker, analyst; b. Bklyn., Mar. 23, 1937; s. David Marcus and Amy Blanche Londoner; m. Clara Fleischmann, Feb. 5, 1967; children: David-Marc, John Alexander. AB, Columbia U., 1958, MS, 1959. Chartered fin. analyst, N.Y. Analyst H. Hentz & Co., N.Y.C., 1960-67; v.p. E.F. Hutton & Co., N.Y.C., 1967-70; sr. v.p. Edward A. Viner & Co., N.Y.C., 1970-71; exec. v.p. Black Securities, N.Y.C., 1971-72; with Wertheim Schroder & Co. Inc., N.Y.C., 1972—, assoc. mng. dir., 1986-89, mng. dir., 1989—. Author: The Changing Economics of Entertainment, 1978, Moving Toward Consolidation in the Entertainment Industry, 1989. trustee Am. Mus. Moving Image, N.Y.C., 1985—. With USAR, 1969-75. Fellow Am. Inst. Chartered Fin. Analysts; mem. Fin. Analysts Fedn., N.Y. Soc. Security Analysts, Media and Entertainment Analysts of N.Y., Econ. Club of N.Y., Wyantenuck Country Club (Great Barrington, Mass.). Office: Schroder Wertheim & Co Inc 787 7th Ave New York NY 10019-6018

LONDRÉ, FELICIA MAE HARDISON, theater educator; b. Ft. Lewis, Wash., Apr. 1, 1941; d. Felix M. and Priscilla Mae (Graham) Hardison; m. Venne-Richard Londré, Dec. 16, 1967; children: Tristan Graham, Georgianna Rose. BA with high honors, U. Mont., 1962; MA, U. Wash., 1964; PhD, U. Wis., 1969. Asst. prof. U. Wis. at Rock County, Janesville, 1969-75; asst. prof., head theatre program U. Tex. at Dallas, Richardson, 1975-78; assoc. prof. U. Mo., Kansas City, 1978-82, prof. theatre, 1982-87, curators' prof., 1987—; women's chair in humanistic studies Marquette U., 1995; dramaturg Mo. Repertory Theatre, Kansas City, 1978—, Nebr. Shakespeare Festival, 1990—; guest dramaturg Gt. Lakes Theater Festival, 1988; mem. archives task force Folly Theatre, 1982-83; artistic advisor New Directions Theatre Co., 1983-90; hon. lectr. Mid.-Am. State Univs. Assn., 1986-87; mem. U.S.-U.S.S.R. Joint Commn. on Theatre Historiography, 1989, fgn. vis. prof. Hosei U., Tokyo, 1993; mem.adv. bd. Contemporary World Writers, 1991—; lectr. univs. Budapest, Pecs, Debrecen, Hungary, 1992—. Author: Tennessee Williams, 1979, Tom Stoppard, 1981, Federico Garcia Lorca, 1984, (play) Miss Millay Was Right, 1982 (John Gassner Meml. Playwriting award 1982), The History of the World Theatre: From the English Restoration to the Present, 1991 (Choice Outstanding Acad. Book award 1991), Chow Chow Pizza, 1995 (Kansas City Gorilla Theatre First Prize); (opera libretto) Duse and D'Annunzio, 1987; co-editor: Shakespeare Companies and Festivals: An International Guide, 1995; book rev. editor: Theatre Jour., 1984-86; assoc. editor: Shakespeare Around the Globe: A Guide to Notable Postwar Revivals; mem. editl. bd. Theatre History Studies, 1981-87, 89—, Studies in Am. Drama, 1945 to the present, 1984—, 19th Century Theatre Jour., 1984-95, Bookmark Press, Tennessee Williams Rev., 1985-87, (jours.) Dramatic Theory and Criticism, 1986—, On-Stage Studies, The Elizabethan Rev., 1992—, Theatre Symposium, 1994—; contbr. articles and book and theatre revs. to profl. publs. Hon. co-founder, bd. dirs. Heart of Am. Shakespeare Festival, 1991—; bd. dirs. Edgar Snow Meml. Fund, 1993—. Fulbright grantee U. Caen, Normandy, France, 1962-63, faculty rsch. grantee U. Mo., 1985, 86, 90, 91, tchr. seminar grantee Mo. Humanities Coun., 1993, 96; grad. fellow U. Wis., 1966-67, Trustees fellow U. Kansas City, 1987-88. Mem. MLA, Am. Soc. Theatre Rsch. (mem. exec. com. 1984-90, program chair 1995), Shakespeare Theatre Assn. Am. (sec. 1991-93), Internat. Fedn. for Theatre Rsch. (del. gen. assembly 1985), Am. Theatre Assn. (commn. on theatre rsch. 1981-87, chmn. 1984-86), Theatre Libr. Assn., Dramatists Guild, Literary Mgrs. and Dramaturgs Am., Am. Drama Soc., Shakespeare Oxford So., Mid.-Am. Theatre Conf. (chair grad. rsch. paper competition 1985), Am. Theatre and Drama Soc. (v.p. 1995—). Roman Catholic. Avocations: travel, theatre, continental cuisine. Home: 528 E 56th St Kansas City MO 64110-2769 Office: Mo Repertory Theatre 4949 Cherry St Kansas City MO 64110-2229

LONEGAN, THOMAS LEE, restaurant corporation executive; b. Kansas City, Mo., July 4, 1932; s. Thomas F. and Edna L. (Payton) L.; m. Donna F. Ednie, Apr. 11, 1958; children: Timothy L., John M. BSME, Gen. Motors Inst., 1955; MS in Mgmt., USN Post Grad Sch., 1963; grad., Indsl. Coll. Armed Forces, Washington, 1970; postgrad., Calif. State U., Long Beach, 1979-83; grad., Coll. for Fin. Planning, Denver, 1984. Registered profl. engr.; CFP. Commd. ensign USN, 1956, advanced through grades to comdr., 1978; dir. pub. works Naval Weapons Sta., Seal Beach, Calif., 1974-78; ret., 1978; dir. cen. staff McAthco Enterprises, Inc., Camarillo, Calif., 1985, exec. v.p., CFO, 1986-90, pres., CEO,, 1991-93, exec. v.p., CFO, 1994-95; ret.; gen. ptnr. Lozzy Anne's Café, Agoura Hills, Calif., 1995—. Author: Analysis and Attenuation of Air Borne Noise in Industrial Plants, 1955, Formalized Training of Maintenance Personnel, 1963. Vol. various couns. Boy Scouts Am., 1968-74. Decorated Bronze Star with combat device, Meritorious Svc. medal, Jt. Svcs. Commendation medal, Navy Achievement medal; recipient Order of Chamoro Govt.of Guam; named Sr. Engr./Arch. Yr. Naval Facilities Engr. Command, 1972. Fellow Soc. Am. Mil. Engrs., Inst. CFP's, Ret. Officers Assn., GM Inst: Robots Honor Soc.; mem. Beta Gamma Sigma. Avocations: reading, theater, music, foreign travel. Home: 8578 Amazon River Cir Fountain Valley CA 92708-5510

LONERGAN, WALLACE GUNN, economics educator, management consultant; b. Potlatch, Idaho, Mar. 18, 1928; s. Willis Gerald and Lois (Gunn) L.; m. Joan Laurie Penoyer, June 1, 1952; children: Steven Mark, Kevin James. BA, Coll. Idaho, 1950; MBA, U. Chgo., 1955, PhD, 1960. Asst. dir., asst. prof. bus. Indsl. Relations Ctr. U. Chgo., 1960-70, assoc. dir., assoc. prof., 1970-74, dir., prof., 1974-84; vis. prof. Rikkyo U., Tokyo, 1985; vis. fellow Merton Coll. Oxford (Eng.) U., 1986; chair, prof. bus., econs. divsn. Albertson Coll. Idaho, Caldwell, 1987—; v.p. Human Resources Research Cons., Chgo., 1980-87. Author: Leadership and Morale, 1960, Group Leadership, 1974, Performance Appriasal, 1978, Leadership and Management, 1979. Chmn. Episcopal Commn. on Higher Edn., Chgo., 1970-80, mgmt. com. United Way Chgo., 1982-85. 1st lt. U.S. Army, 1950-53, Korea. Named Disting. Alumni Coll. Idaho, 1962; vis. scholar Internat. Anglican Exchange, N.Y.C., 1976, Tokyo, 1986. Mem. Internat. House Japan, Internat. Indsl. Relations Research Assn., Acad. Mgmt., Rotary. Avocations: power walking, hiking. Home: 814 E Linden St Caldwell ID 83605-5335 Office: Albertson Coll Idaho Bus Econs Divsn 2112 Cleveland Blvd Caldwell ID 83605-4432

LONEY, GLENN MEREDITH, drama educator; b. Sacramento, Dec. 24, 1928; s. David Merton and Marion Gladys (Busher) L. BA, U. Calif., Berkeley, 1950; MA, U. Wis., 1951; PhD, Stanford U., 1953. Teaching asst. U. Calif., Berkeley, 1949-50, Stanford U., Calif., 1952-53; instr. San Francisco State U., 1955-56, U. Nev., Las Vegas, 1956; prof. U. Md., Europe, N. Africa, Middle East, 1956-59; instr. Hofstra U., Hempstead, N.Y., 1959-61, Adelphi U., Garden City, N.Y., 1959-61; prof. speech and theater Bklyn. Coll. and City U. Grad. Ctr., 1961-71, prof. theater, 1971—. Author: Briefing and Conference Techniques, 1959, Peter Brook Midsummer Night's Dream, 1974, The Shakespeare Complex, 1974, Young Vic Scapino, 1980, The House of Mirth-The Play of the Novel, 1981, Twentieth Century Theatre, 1983, California Gold Rush Drama, Musical Theatre in America, 1984, Unsung Genius, 1984, Creating Careers in Music Theatre, 1988, Staging Shakespeare, 1990, Peter Brook: Oxford to Orghast, 1996; editor: The Modernist. Served with AUS, 1953-55. Fellow Am. Scandinavian Found.; mem. AAUP, Am. Theatre Critics Assn., Outer Critics Circle (sec.), Am. Music Critics Assn., Am. Soc. Theatre Research, Internat. Fedn. Theatre Research, Theatre Library Assn., Theatre Hist. Soc., Phi Beta Kappa, Alpha Mu Gamma, Phi Eta Sigma, Phi Delta Phi. Democrat. Office: CUNY Grad Ctr Theater 33 W 42nd St New York NY 10036-8003

LONG, ALAN K., chemistry research administrator; b. Burlington, Vt., June 19, 1950; married; 2 children. BS, Yale U., 1971; MA, Harvard U., 1976, PhD, 1979. From rsch. assoc. to lab. dir. depts. chem. and earth sci. Harvard U., Cambridge, Mass., 1979—. Mem. Am. Chem. Soc. Office: Harvard U Chemical Labs 12 Oxford St Cambridge MA 02138-2902

LONG, ALFRED B., former oil company executive, consultant; b. Galveston, Tex., Aug. 4, 1909; s. Jessie A. and Ada (Beckwith) L.; student S. Park Jr. Coll., 1928-29, Lamar State Coll. Tech., 1947-56, U. Tex., 1941; m. Sylvia V. Thomas, Oct. 29, 1932; 1 child, Kathleen Sylvia (Mrs. E.A. Pearson, II). With Sun Oil Co., Beaumont, Tex., 1931-69, driller geophys. dept., surveyor engring. dept., engr. operating dept., engr. prodn. lab., 1931-59, regional supr., 1960-69, cons., 1969—. Sr.'s bd. dirs. Bapt. Hosp., Beaumont, Tex.; chaplain sr.'s vols. bd. dirs., S.E. Tex. Rehab. Hosp., Beaumont, Seniors-Lawmen Coun.; chaplain; Jefferson County Program Planning Com., 1964; mem. tech. adv. group Oil Well Drilling Inst., Lamar U., Beaumont. Grad. Citizens Police Acad. Mem. Soc. Petroleum Engrs., Am. Petroleum Inst., Am. Assn. Petroleum Geologists, IEEE, Houston Geol. Soc., Gulf Coast Engring. and Sci. Soc. (treas. 1962-65), U.S. Power Squadron, Soc. Wireless Pioneers. Recipient Nat. Jefferson award for Outstanding Pub. Svc. Am. Inst. for Pub. Svc., 1992, Community Svc. award Quarter Century Wireless Assn., 1994, Sensational Seniors of the U.S. honor CBS TV, 1994, Hometown Heroes CHGTV, 1995, Olympic torch bearer. Inventor various oil well devices. Office: PO Box 7266 Beaumont TX 77726-7266

LONG, ALVIN WILLIAM, title insurance company executive; b. Steubenville, Ohio, Oct. 9, 1923; s. Roger H. and Emma (Reilley) L.; m. Ethelle Sherman, Jan. 1, 1944; children—Roger H., Sherry Long McBain. J.D., John Marshall Law Sch., 1949, LL.D., 1977; M.B.A., U. Chgo., 1955. Bar: Ill. 1950. V.p. Chgo. Title & Trust Co., 1960-63, sr. v.p., 1966-69, pres., chief adminstrv. officer, 1969-71, pres., chief exec. officer, 1971—, chmn., 1981, hon. chmn. ret., 1982—, also dir.; sr. v.p. Chgo. Title Ins. Co., 1963-66, pres., 1967—, chmn. bd., 1981-82, hon. chmn. ret., 1982—, also dir. Bd. dirs. Bradner Central Co.; pres. Chgo. Central Area Com., 1980-82; trustee John Marshall Law Sch.; bd. dirs. Ill. Childrens Home and Aid Soc., pres., 1975-77; mem. citizens bd. and alumni council U. Chgo. Served to 1st lt. USAAF, 1943-45. Recipient Distinguished Alumni citation John Marshall Law Sch., 1968. Mem. Ill., Bar Assn., Am. Land Title Assn. (pres. 1970-71), Law Club Chgo., Comml. Club Chgo., Chgo. Club, Flossmoor (Ill.) Country Club, Quail Ridge Country Club (Fla.).

LONG, ANTHONY ARTHUR, classics educator; b. Manchester, Eng., Aug. 17, 1937; came to U.S. 1983; s. Tom Arthur and Phyllis Joan (LeGrice) L.; m. Janice Calloway, Dec. 30, 1960 (div. 1969); 1 child, Stephen Arthur; m. Mary Kay Flavell, May 25, 1970 (div. 1990); 1 child, Rebecca Jane. B.A., U. Coll. London, 1960; Ph.D., U. London, 1964. Lectr. classics U. Otago, Dunedin, N.Z., 1961-64; lectr. classics U. Nottingham, Eng., 1964-66; lectr. Greek and Latin U. Coll. London, 1966-71; reader in Greek and Latin U. London, 1971-73; Gladstone prof. Greek U. Liverpool, Eng., 1973-83; prof. classics U. Calif., Berkeley, 1982—; pub. orator U. Liverpool, Eng., 1981-83; Irving Stone prof. lit. U. Calif., Berkeley, 1991—, chmn. dept. classics, 1986-90; mem. Inst. Advanced Study, Princeton, N.J., 1970, 79; vis. prof. U. Munich, 1973, Ecole Normale Supérieure, Paris, 1993; Cardinal Mercier prof. philosophy U. Louvain, Belgium, 1991; mem. Mellon Fellowships Selection Com., 1984-90; mem. selection com. Stanford U. Humanities Coun., 1985-86. Author: Language and Thought in Sophocles, 1968 (Cromer Greek prize 1968), Problems in Stoicism, 1971, Hellenistic Philosophy, 1974, 2d edit., 1986, (with Fortenbaugh and Huby) Theophrastus of Eresus, 1985, (with Sedley) The Hellenistic Philosophers, 1987, (with Dillon) The Question of Eclecticism, 1988, (with Bastianini) Hierocles, 1992, (with others) Images and Ideologies, 1993, Stoic Studios, 1996; editor: Classical Quar., 1975-81, Classical Antiquity, 1987-90; gen. editor: (with Barnes) Clarendon Later Ancient Philosophers, 1987—. Served to lt. Royal Arty., Eng., 1955-57. Named hon. citizen City of Rhodes, Greece; sr. fellow humanities coun. Princeton U., 1978, Bye fellow Robinson Coll., Cambridge, 1982, Guggenheim fellow, 1986-87, sr. fellow Ctr. for Hellenic Studies, 1988-93, fellow NEH, 1990-91, Wissenschaftskolleg fellow, Berlin, 1991-92, William Evans fellow U. Otago, New Zealand, 1995. Fellow Am. Acad. Arts and Scis., Brit. Acad. (corr.); mem. Classical Assn., Aristotelian Soc., Am. Philol. Assn., Phi Beta Kappa (hon.). Avocations: music, walking, travel. Home: 1088 Tevlin St Albany CA 94706-2467 Office: U Calif Dept Classics Berkeley CA 94720

LONG, BARBARA ELLIS, psychologist; b. St. Louis, Mar. 8, 1923; d. Oliver Everett and Melva Augusta (Westcott) Ellis; m. Richard Rodne Long, June 18, 1946 (dec. 1975); children: Susan Long Hood, Roger Ellis. Student, Washington U., St. Louis, 1941-42; BS with honors, U. Ill., Urbana, 1945, MA, 1846; PhD, Union Inst., Cin., 1973. Lic. clin. psychologist, Calif. Clin. psychologist Community Child Guidance Ctr., Yale Child Study Ctr., Portland and New Haven, 1948-49, 51-52, Thurston County Child Guidance Ctr., Olympia, Wash., 1952-56, St. Louis County Child Guidance Clinic, Clayton, Mo., 1958, Richland County Mental Health Clinic, Columbia, S.C., 1959-61; pvt. practice Columbia and St. Louis, 1959-65, 71-73; project dir., methodologist St. Louis County Health Dept., Clayton, Mo., 1965-67; instr., rsch. psychologist Webster Coll., Webster Groves, Mo., 1967-68; clin. and rsch. psychologist St. Louis State Hosp., 1968-71; children's svc. coordinator Dept. Pub. Health and Welfare, San Mateo County, San Mateo, Calif., 1973-75; pvt. practice San Carlos, Calif., 1976—; cons. mental health agys. and schs., U.S.A., Gt. Britain, Denmark, UNESCO, Indonesia, 1970—; mem. adj. faculty U. Calif. Santa Cruz Extension, 1974, U. San Francisco, 1978-79, Palo Alto Sch. of Profl. Psychology, 1982; expert witness San Mateo County (Calif.) Family Ct. Svcs. Author: The Journey to Myself, 1978; editor People Watching, 1969-72, Jour. Clin. and Child Psychology, 1976-77; contbr. articles to profl. jours. Fellow Am. Psychol. Assn., Am. Orthopsychiat. Assn.; mem. San Mateo County Psychol. Assn., Calif. State Psychol. Assn., Soc. Personality Assessment, Bay Area Multiple Personality Soc., Assn. Family and Conciliation Cts., Profl. Acad. Custody Evaluators, Psi Chi, Alpha Kappa Delta. Episcopalian. Avocations: gardening, traveling, watercolors, jewelry making. Office: 1622 San Carlos Ave Ste D San Carlos CA 94070-2022

LONG, BERT LOUIS, JR., artist; b. Houston, Sept. 27, 1940; s. Bertran Louis and Tennessee (Morris) L.; m. Connie Dianne Kelly, Aug. 15, 1964; children: Deborah Denise Foster, John Alan, Bertran Louis III. Class A tchg. credential adult edn., UCLA, 1972. Tchr. adult edn. L.A. (Calif.) Unified Sch. Dist., 1972-75; owner, exec. chef Berts Gourmet Restaurant, Klamath Falls, Oreg., 1975-76; sous chef Hilton Hotels, Las Vegas, Nev., 1976; exec. sous chef Ritz Carlton Hotels, Chgo., 1976-77, Hyatt Regency Hotel, Houston, 1977-78; exec. chef Holiday Inn, Houston, 1978-79; chmn. Artists in Action, 1979-83; visual arts panelist allocations com. Cultural Arts Coun., visual arts sub-panelist selection com., 1988; adv. panel appointee Task Force Midtown Arts Ctr.; exec. com. mem. Houston Arts Alliance; panelist visual arts Tex. Commn. on the Arts, 1990; presenter in field. One-man shows include Butler Gallery, Houston, 1988, Art Mus. S.E. Tex., Beaumont, 1987-88, Dallas (Tex.) Mus. Art, 1988, Tex. A&M Meml. Student Ctr., College Station, 1989, Barry Whistler Gallery, Dallas, 1989, Allan Stone Gallery, N.Y.C., 1990, Lew Allen Gallery, Santa Fe, 1991, Contemporary Arts Mus., Houston, 1991, Lyons Matrix Gallery, Austin, 1992, The Fabric Workshop Mus., Phila., 1993, complejo Cultural San Francisco, Spain, 1996, San Francisco/Ctr. de Expericiones San Jorge de Caceres, others; exhibited in group shows at Dallas (Tex.) Mus. Art, 1990, Calif. Afro-Am. Mus., L.A., 1990, Duke U. Mus. Art, Durham, N.C., 1990, Studio Mus. in Harlem, N.Y.C., 1990, Palm Springs (Fla.) Desert Mus., 1990, Alternative Mus., N.Y.C., 1991, Contemporary Arts Mus., Houston, 1991, Barry Whistler Gallery, Dallas, 1991, Sala 1, Rome, 1991, Am. Acad. in Rome, Italy, 1991, Lewallen Gallery, Santa Fe, 1991, Dishman Art Gallery, Beaumont, 1991, The Painted Bride Gallery, Phila., 1993, Lyons Matrix Gallery, Dallas, 1993, Mus. Fine Arts, Houston, 1993, The Galveston (Tex.) Arts Ctr., 1993, Amazing Space, Cleveland, Tex., 1994, First Interstate Bank, 1994, Irving Arts Ctr., Tex., 1996, others; represented in permanent collections including Huntington Art Gallery, U. Tex., Mus. Fine Arts, Houston, Dallas (Tex.) Mus. Art, Bell Telephone, Met. Mus. Art, Dinos of Calif., Spikes Pers., Erenwert Produce, Pfeffer Interests, Fleming Prodns., Craig Washington Law Firm, Highland Distributing, Mus. Contemporary Art, Chgo. Libr., Ajuntamiento Berzocana, Fabric Workshop Mus., Mus. S.E. Tex., Inst. Mario Roso de Luna, Spain; pub. Houston ArtScene, 1979-88; performances include Fire/Falla Installations Canermero, Cáceres, Spain, 1994-96; contbr. articles to profl. jours. With USMC, 1959-64. Recipient proclamation State of Tex., Tex. Senate, 1990; named Outstanding Texan,

State of Tex. Ho. of Reps., 1991. Fellow Soc. Fellows Am. Acad. in Room; mem. Tex. Fine Art Assn. (internat. bd. dirs. 1992—). Avocations: traveling, reading, gardening, photography, writing. Home: PO Box 1254 Houston TX 77033 Home and Office: c/o Pilar S/N, 10129 Berzocana, Caceres Spain

LONG, BEVERLY GLENN, lawyer; b. Omaha, Mar. 1, 1923; d. Max Edgar and Allise Katherine Dorothea (Nielsen) Glenn; m. Jacob Emery Long, May 6, 1950. AB in Econs., U. Chgo., 1944; JD, Columbia U., 1947. Bar: N.Y. 1948, R.I. 1951, U.S. Dist. Ct. (so. dist.) N.Y. 1949, U.S. Tax Ct. 1949, U.S. Dist. Ct. R.I. 1951, U.S. Ct. Appeals (2d cir.) 1949, U.S. Ct. Appeals (1st cir.) 1958, U.S. Ct. Claims 1960, U.S. Supreme Ct. 1960. Assoc. Edwards & Angell, Providence, 1950-59, ptnr., 1959-86, of counsel, 1986—. Adv. com. child welfare svcs. R.I. Dept. Social Welfare, 1959-66; pers. com. Big Bros. R.I., 1964-67; mem. Gov.'s Com. on Status of Women, 1965; chmn. R.I. Children's Code Commn., 1967-74; fundraiser Columbia U. Sch. Law, 1947-88, R.I. area for U. Chgo., 1951—; bd. dirs. Child Welfare League of Am., Inc., 1975-80, Children's Friend and Svc., Inc., 1966-75, 77-79, Providence chpt. ARC, 1967-72; bd. dirs. St. Mary's Home for Children, 1966-80, v.p., 1978-80; bd. dirs. R.I. Conf. Social Work, 1961-66, Coun. Cmty. Svcs., Inc., 1957-64; task force evaluation of criminal justice program LEAA, 1974-78; active United Way Southeastern New Eng., Inc., 1951-81, ad hoc adv. com., exec. budget com., 1971-78, bd. dirs., 1973-74, ABA sr. lawyers divsn. coun., 1986-91, sec., 1991-95. Recipient citation for pub. service U. Chgo., 1959. Fellow Am. Bar Found., R.I. Bar Found.; mem. ABA (Outstanding State Membership Chmn. award 1984), R.I. Bar Assn. (ho. dels., exec. com., pres., Merit award 1990), New Eng. Bar Assn. (bd. dirs. 1982-85), Fed. Bar Assn., Am. Law Inst., Am. Judicature Soc. (bd. dirs. 1988-90), U.S. Supreme Ct. Hist. Soc., U. Club R.I. Republican. Home: 200 Elmgrove Ave Providence RI 02906-4233

LONG, CARL FERDINAND, engineering educator; b. N.Y.C., Aug. 6, 1928; s. Carl and Marie Victoria (Wellnitz) L.; m. Joanna Margarida Tavares, July 23, 1955; children: Carl Ferdinand, Barbara Anne. S.B., MIT, 1950, S.M., 1952; D.Eng., Yale U., 1964; A.M. (hon.), Dartmouth Coll., 1971. Registered profl. engr., N.H. Instr. Thayer Sch. Engring., Dartmouth Coll., Hanover, N.H., 1954-57; asst. prof. Thayer Sch. Engring., Dartmouth Coll., 1957-64, assoc. prof., 1964-70, prof., 1970-94, assoc. dean, 1970, dean, 1972-84, dean emeritus, 1984—; prof. emeritus, 1994—; dir. Cook Design Ctr. Thayer Sch. Engring., Dartmouth Coll., 1984-94; engr. Western Electric Co., Alaska, 1956-57; v.p. ops., dir. Controlled Enivronment, 1975-81; pres., dir. Q-S Oxygern Processes, Inc., 1979-84; N.H. Water Supply and Pollution Control Com., U.S. Army Small Arms Systems Agy.; mem. New Eng. Constrn. Edn. Adv. Coun., 1971-74; mem. adv. com. U.S. Patenta and Trademark Office, 1975-79; mem. ad hoc vis. com. Engrs. Coun. for Profl. Devel., 1973-81; pres., dir. Roan of Thayer, Inc., 1986-93; bd. dirs. Micro Tool Co., Inc., Micro Weighing Systems, Inc., 1986-91, Roan Ventures, Inc., 1987-91; pres., dir. Hanover Water Works Co., 1989—. Mem. Hanover Town Planning Bd., 1963-75, chmn., 1966-74; trustee Mt. Washington Obs., 1975-92; bd. dirs. Eastman Community Assn., 1977-80; mem. corp. Mary Hitchcock Meml. Hosp., 1974—. NSF Sci. Faculty fellow, 1961-62; recipient Robert Fletcher award Thayer Sch. of Engring., 1985, Fellow Members awd., Am. Soc. for Engineering Education, 1992. Fellow AAAS, ASCE, Am. Soc. Engring. Edn. (chmn. New Eng. sect. 1977-78, chmn. council of sects. Zone 1, dir. 1981-83); mem. Sigma Xi, Chi Epsilon, Tau Beta Pi. Republican. Baptist. Home: 25 Reservoir Rd Hanover NH 03755-1311

LONG, CHARLES FRANKLIN, corporate communications executive; b. Norman, Okla., Jan. 19, 1938; s. James Franklin and Mary Katherine (Nemecek) L.; m. Joan Hampton, Sept. 16, 1961; children: Charles Franklin, David Hampton, Stephen Andrew. B.A., U. Okla., 1961. Sports writer San Angelo (Tex.) Standard-Times, 1961-62; news reporter Norman Transcript, 1962-63; asso. editor Sooner mag., U. Okla., 1963-66; news editor Quill mag., Chgo., 1967-71; editor Quill mag., 1971-80; sr. editor Cahners Pub. Co., Des Plaines, Ill., 1981-83; mgr. internal communications Beatrice Cos., Inc., Chgo., 1983-86, dir. communications, 1986-88; dir. corp. communications Tellabs Ops., Inc., Lisle, Ill., 1989—. Author: With Optimism for the Morrow, 1965. Bd. dirs. Wheaton (Ill.) Youth Outreach, 1988-94, Western DuPage Spl. Recreation Assn. Found., 1994— (Vol. of Yr. 1994). Named to Okla. Journalism Hall of Fame, 1979. Mem. Pub. Relations Soc. Am., Internat. Assn. Bus. Communicators (Spectra Excellence award Chgo.), Am. Mktg. Assn., Soc. Profl. Journalists-Sigma Delta Chi, Beta Theta Pi. United Methodist. Home: 1106 N Washington St Wheaton IL 60187-3860 Office: Tellabs Ops Inc 1000 Remington Blvd Bolingbrook IL 60440 *My parents, through gentle persuasion and by their own example, taught their sons to be curious and conscientious. I suppose it was those principles which eventually led me into a career in journalism and to come to realize that the supreme test of any good journalism is the measure of its public service—to serve the truth; to subscribe to ethical standards; to enlighten the public as to the nature and meaning of journalistic pursuits, especially in how those efforts support the American people's stake in their First Amendment to the Constitution.*

LONG, CHARLES HOUSTON, history of religion educator; b. Little Rock, Aug. 23, 1926; s. Samuel Preston and Diamond Geneva (Thompson) L.; m. Alice Freeman, June 21, 1953; children—John, Carolyn, Christopher, David. Diploma, Dunbar Jr. Coll., 1946; B.D., U. Chgo., 1953, Ph.D., 1962; L.H.D., Dickinson Coll., 1971. Mem. faculty U. Chgo., 1956-74, prof. history of religions, 1971-74; mem. faculty U. Chgo. Div. Sch., 1956-74, prof., 1971-74, dean students, 1956-60; William Rand Kenan, Jr. prof. history of religions U. N.C., Chapel Hill, 1974-88; also bd. govs. U. N.C. (U. N.C. Press); prof. history of religions Duke U., 1974-88; Jeannette K. Watson prof. history of religions Syracuse U., 1988-91, dir. humanities doctoral program, 1988-91; prof. dept. religious studies, dir. Rsch. Ctr. in Black Studies U. Calif., Santa Barbara, 1991—; dir. seminar Nat. Endowment Humanities, summers 1977, 78, yr. 1979-80; bd. commrs. Assn. Am. Colls. ; bd. govs. U. N.C. Press, 1975-87. Author: Alpha: The Myths of Creation, 1963; founding editor (with others): History of Religions jour, 1961-74; editor (with Joseph Kitagawa and Mircea Eliade) History of Religions: Essays in Understanding, 1959, Myths and Symbols: Essays in Honor of Mircea Eliade, 1969, Significations, 1986; gen. editor series Studies in Religion, 1978—; editorial bd. cons. Ency. Britannica; founding editor, editorial advisor jour. History of Religions, 1990—; mem. editl. bd. jour. Ecumene, 1994—; contbr. articles to hist.-religious jours., Ency. Britannica., Ency. Religion. Mem. N.C. Humanities Council; bd. dirs. Fund for Theol. Edn. Served with USAAF, 1944-46. Recipient Alumnus of Yr. award Div. Sch., U. Chgo., 1987, profl. achievement citation U. Chgo. Alumni Assn., 1991; Guggenheim fellow, 1971-72. Mem. Am. Acad. Religion (pres. 1973-74), Internat. Assn. Historians Religion, Am. Soc. Study Religion (founding mem.), Soc. Study Black Religion (founding mem.). Office: U Calif Rsch Black Studies 4603 S Hall Santa Barbara CA 93106

LONG, CHARLES THOMAS, lawyer; b. Denver, Dec. 19, 1942; s. Charles Joseph and Jessie Elizabeth (Squire) L.; m. Susan Rae Kircheis, Aug. 9, 1967; children: Brian Christopher, Lara Elizabeth, Kevin Charles. BA, Dartmouth Coll., 1965; JD cum laude, Harvard U., 1970. Bar: Calif. 1971, U.S. Dist. Ct. (cen. dist.) Calif. 1971, U.S. Ct. Appeals (9th cir.) 1975, D.C. 1980, U.S. Dist. Ct. D.C. 1981. Assoc. Gibson, Dunn & Crutcher, Los Angeles, 1970-77, ptnr., 1977-79; ptnr. Gibson, Dunn & Crutcher, Washington, 1979-83; dep. gen. counsel Fed. Home Loan Bank Bd., Washington, 1984-85; ptnr. Jones, Day, Reavis & Pogue, Washington, 1985—; Bar: Calif. 1971, U.S. Dist. Ct. (ctrl. dist.) Calif. 1971, U.S. Ct. Appeals (9th cir.) 1975, D.C. 1980, U.S. Dist. Ct. 1981, U.S. Ct. Fed. Claims 1995. Contbr. articles to profl. jours. Pres. Leigh Mill Meadows Assn., Great Falls, Va., 1980. Served to lt. USNR, 1965-67. Mem. ABA, Calif. Bar Assn., D.C. Bar Assn., Coun. for Excellence in Govt., Women in Housing and Fin., Herrington Harbour Sailing Assn. (sec.-treas. 1996), Westwood Country Club (Vienna, Va.). Republican. Methodist. Avocations: sailing, photography. Office: Jones Day Reavis & Pogue Met Sq 1450 G St NW Ste 600 Washington DC 20005-2001

LONG, CLARENCE DICKINSON, III, lawyer; b. Princeton, N.J., Feb. 7, 1943; s. Clarence Dickinson and Susanna Eckings (Larter) L.; m. Clothilde Camille Jacxsens, June 24, 1972; children: Clarence IV, Andrew, Amanda, Victoria, Stephen. BA, Johns Hopkins U., 1965; JD, U. Md., 1971; postgrad. Judge Advocate Gen.'s Sch., 1979-80. Bar: Ct. Appeals Md. 1972, U.S. Dist. Ct. D.C. 1972, U.S. Ct. Mil. Appeals 1975, U.S. Supreme Ct. 1976, N.C. 1978, U.S. Ct. Claims 1982, U.S. Ct. Appeals (fed. cir.) 1990. Asst. state's atty., Balt., 1973-74; trial atty., trial team chief Office Chief Trial Atty. Contract Appeals div., U.S. Army, Washington, 1980-84; chief atty. Def. Supply Svc., Washington, 1984-87; trial team chief contact appeals divsn. U.S. Army, 1987-92. Lt. col. U.S. Army. Decorated Silver Star, Soldier's medal, Bronze Star, Purple Heart (2), Meritorious Svc. medal (2), Army Commendation medal (2), Cross of Gallantry with gold star, Combat Infantry badge, Legion of Merit. Mem. ABA, D.C. Bar Assn., N.C. Bar Assn. Home: 119 N Fairfax St Falls Church VA 22046-3528 Office: Sec of Air Force Office of Gen Counsel Pentagon Washington DC 20330-1740

LONG, CLARENCE WILLIAM, accountant; b. Hartford City, Ind., Apr. 17, 1917; s. Adam and Alice (Weschke) L.; m. Mildred Bernhardt, Aug. 8, 1940; children: William Randall, David John, Bruce Allen. B.S., Ind. U., 1939. With Ernst & Young, Indpls., 1939—, ptnr., 1953—; mem. econ. exec. com. Gov. Ind., 1968-73. Mem. nat. budget and consultation com. United Way of Am., 1968-70; bd. dirs. United Fund Greater Indpls., 1966—, treas., 1968—; bd. dirs. Jr. Achievement, Ind., 1966-67; mem. exec. com. Nat. Jr. Achievement, 1966-67; mem. fin. com. Indpls. Hosp. Devel. Assn., 1966-67; trustee Ind. U., 1975-84; trustee Art Assn. Indpls., pres., 1977-78; mem. adv. com. to dir. NIH, 1986-92. Mem. Am. Inst. C.P.A.'s (council 1959-62), Ind. Assn. C.P.A.'s, Nat. Assn. Accountants, Ind. C. of C. (dir.), Delta Chi, Beta Alpha Psi, Alpha Kappa Psi. Republican. Lutheran. Clubs: Woodstock (Indpls.) (dir. 1958-60), Columbia (Indpls.) (dir. 1971-77, pres. 1976), Royal Poinciana Golf Club (Naples, Fla.). Home: 607 Somerset Dr W Indianapolis IN 46260-2924 Office: 1 Indiana Sq Indianapolis IN 46204-2004

LONG, DAVID L., magazine publisher. Publisher Sports Illustrated, N.Y.C. Office: c/o Sports Illustrated Time Inc. 1271 Ave of the Americas New York NY 10020*

LONG, DONLIN MARTIN, surgeon, educator; b. Rolla, Mo., Apr. 14, 1934; s. Donlin M. and Davene E. (Johnson) L.; m. Harriett Page, June 13, 1959; children: Kimberley Page, Elisabeth Merchant, David Bradford. Student, Jefferson City Jr. Coll., 1951-52; M.D., U. Mo., 1959; Ph.D., U. Minn., 1964. Diplomate: Am. Bd. Surgery. Intern U. Minn. Hosps., Mpls., 1959-60; resident U. Minn. Hosps., 1960-64; resident in neurosurgery Peter Bent Brigham and Children's Hosp. Med. Center, Boston, 1965; practice medicine specializing in neurosurgery Balt., 1973—; asst. prof. dept. neurosurgery U. Minn. Hosps., 1967-70, neurosurgeon, 1967-73, asso. prof., 1970-73; neurosurgeon-in-chief dept. neurosurgery Johns Hopkins Hosp., 1973—; prof. and chmn. dept. neurosurgery Johns Hopkins U., 1973—; mem. prin. staff Applied Physics Lab., 1976—; cons. neurosurgery Mpls. VA Hosp., 1967-73, John F. Kennedy Inst., 1977, Balt. City Hosp., 1973—. Contbr. numerous articles on neuropathology and surgery to profl. jours.; contbr. to book chpts. in field. Served with USPHS, 1965-67. Mem. Soc. Neurosci., Am. Assn. Neuropathologists, Soc. Neurol. Surgeons, AAAS, AMA, Balt. Neurol. Soc., Internat. Assn. Study of Pain, Internat. Soc. Pediatric Neurosurgery, William T. Peyton Soc., Congress Neurol. Surgeons, Johns Hopkins Med. and Surg. Assn., Electron Microscopy Soc. Am., Md. Neurosurg. Soc., Am. Acad. Neurosurgery, Am. Assn. Neurol. Surgery, Neurol. Soc. Am., Cajal Club, Sigma Xi, Omicron Delta Kappa, Alpha Omega Alpha, Phi Eta Sigma, Pi Mu Epsilon, Mystical 7. Home: 9 Blythewood Rd Baltimore MD 21210-2401 Office: Johns Hopkins Hosp Dept Neurosurgery Meyer 7-109 600 N Wolfe St Baltimore MD 21205-2110

LONG, DOUGLAS CLARK, philosophy educator; b. Ann Arbor, Mich., May 25, 1932; s. Dwight Clark and Marjorie Isabel (Grant) L.; m. Annie Nicole Groven, Aug. 21, 1961; children—Matthew Groven, Jonathan Wilson. B.A., U. Mich., 1954; M.A., Harvard U., 1955, Ph.D., 1963; postgrad., Oxford U., Eng., 1958-59. Instr. UCLA, 1960-62, asst. prof., 1962-67; vis. asst. prof. U. Wash., Seattle, 1965; assoc. prof. U. N.C., Chapel Hill, 1967-79; prof. U. N.C., 1979—, asst. chmn. dept., 1979-82, 91-92; vis. assoc. prof. Brown U., Providence, 1969. Contbr. articles to profl. jours. Woodrow Wilson fellow, 1954; grantee NSF, 1967, NEH, 1976-77. Mem. Am. Philos. Assn., Phi Beta Kappa. Home: 419 Granville Rd Chapel Hill NC 27514-2723 Office: U N C CB # 3125 Dept Philosophy Chapel Hill NC 27599-3125

LONG, EDWARD ARLO, business consultant, retired manufacturing company executive; b. Detroit, May 5, 1927; s. Arlo Russell and Florence Viola (Magown) L.; m. Lorraine Ruth Nordin, May 21, 1947; children: Karin Louise Long Schelke, Marian Elizabeth Long Benton. B.S., Wayne State U., 1956, MBA, 1964. Mfg. mgr. Ex-Cell-O Corp., Detroit, 1950-68; v.p. mktg. Colonial Broach & Machine, Warren, Mich., 1968-70; group v.p. Blue Bird Body Co., Fort Valley, Ga., 1970-75; pres. tool equipment div. Chgo. Pneumatic Tool, Franklin, Pa., 1975-77; group v.p. Joy Mfg. Co., Pine Bluff, Ark., 1977-87; v.p., gen. mgr. Wheeling Machine Products Co./Cooper Industries, Pine Bluff, 1987-94; ret., 1994; dir. Security Nat. Bank, Wheeling, W.Va. Bd. dirs. Franklin Hosp., 1976-76, Oglebay Inst., Wheeling, 1981-83, Ohio Valley Hosp. Trust, Wheeling, 1982-83, Ark. Ind. Colls., 1984, Jefferson County Indsl. Found., 1985, Pine Bluff Fifty for the Future, 1985, Pine Bluff Symphony Orch., 1987, Leadership Pine Bluff, 1990; apptd. zoning commr., Pine Bluff, 1995. Served with USCG, 1945-46. Scholar Nat. Office Mgmt. Assn., 1952, Beta Gamma, Detroit, 1953. Mem. AIME, Am. Petroleum Inst., Duquesne (Pitts.) Club, Rotary, Alpha Kappa Psi, Psi Chi, Sigma Iota Epsilon. Democrat. Roman Catholic. Home and Office: 7409 S Laurel St Pine Bluff AR 71603-8121

LONG, EDWIN TUTT, surgeon, data base company executive; b. St. Louis, July 23, 1925; s. Forrest Edwin and Hazel (Tutt) L.; m. Mary M. Hull, Apr. 16, 1955; children: Jennifer Ann, Laura Ann, Peter Edwin. AB, Columbia U., 1944, M.D., 1947. Diplomate Am. Bd. Surgery, Am. Bd. Thoracic Surgery. Rotating intern Meth. Hosp., Bklyn., 1947-78; surg. intern U. Chgo. Clinics, 1948-49, resident in gen. surgery, 1952-55, resident in thoracic surgery, 1955-57; asst. prof. surgery U. Chgo., 1957-59; thoracic and cardiovascular surgeon, chief surgery dept. Watson Clinic, Lakeland, Fla., 1960-69; asso. prof. surgery U. Pa., Phila., 1970-73; thoracic and cardiovascular surgeon Allegheny Cardiovascular Surg. Assocs., Pitts, 1973-88; exec. v.p. Mailings Clearing Ho. and Roxbury Press, Inc., 1988-90, pres., 1990—, chmn., bd. dir., 1991—; dir. Watson Clinic Rsch. Found., 1965-69. bd. dirs. Roxbury Press, Inc., Cardiac Telecom, Inc., Pitts. Pressure Vectorography Rsch. grantee Alfred P. Sloan Found., 1963; patentee gas sterilizer, 1969. Capt. USAF, 1950-52. Mem. ACS, Am. Coll. Cardiology, Internat. Soc. for Cardiovascular Surg., Allegheny Vascular Soc. (pres. 1987), Ea. Vascular Soc. (founding mem.), Soc. Thoracic Surgery (founding mem.), Direct Mktg. Assn., Midwest Bioethics Ctr., Kansas City Club, Rotary, Sigma Xi, Beta Theta Pi. Home and Office: 1415 Torrey Pines Dr Columbia MO 65203-4830 Office: Roxbury Press Inc 601 E Marshall St Sweet Springs MO 65351-0295 *The important things in life are: Your health, your education, your spouse and family, your service. With these in order your life is a success.*

LONG, ELIZABETH VALK, magazine publisher; b. Winston-Salem, N.C., Apr. 29, 1950; d. Henry Lewis and Elizabeth (Fuller) V. BA, Hollins Coll., 1972; MBA, Harvard Bus. Sch., 1979. Clin. adminstr. Mass. Gen. Hosp., Boston, 1973-77; asst. to circulation dir. Time Mag.-Time Inc., N.Y.C., 1979-80, 81-82; circulation dir. Fortune Mag.-Time Inc., N.Y.C., 1982-84, Sports Illustrated-Time Inc., N.Y.C., 1984-85, Time Mag.-Time Inc., N.Y.C., 1985-86; publisher Life Mag.-Time Inc., N.Y.C., 1987-93; pres. Time Mag., 1993—. Trustee Hollins Coll., 1987—; mem. bus. com. Mus. Modern Art, N.Y.C.; mem. bd. visitors Wake Forest U., Winston-Salem, N.C.; bd. dirs. Hanover Direct, Inc., Weehawken, N.J.; mem. Com. of 200. Recipient Matrix award N.Y. Women in Comms., 1992, Silver Medal award Am. Advt. Fedn., 1993. Mem. Phi Beta Kappa. Avocations: golf, gardening. Office: Time Inc Time & Life Bldg 1271 Avenue Of The Americas New York NY 10020*

LONG, EUGENE THOMAS, III, philosophy educator, administrator; b. Richmond, Va., Mar. 16, 1935; s. Eugene Thomas and Emily Joyce (Barker) L.; m. Carolyn Macleod, June 25, 1960; children: Scott, Kathryn. BA, Randolph-Macon Coll., Ashland, Va., 1957; BD, Duke U., 1960; PhD, U. Glasgow (Scotland), 1964. Asst. prof. philosophy Randolph-Macon Coll., 1964-67, assoc. prof., 1967-70; assoc. prof., U. S.C., Columbia, 1970-73, prof., 1973—, chmn. dept., 1972-87. Mem. S.C. Com. for Humanities, 1980-85; mem. adv. bd. The Franklin J. Matchette Found., 1992—. Recipient Research award NEH, 1968, Duke U./U. N.C. Coop. Program in Humanities, 1968-69. Mem. Soc. Philosophy in Religion (pres. 1980-81), Metaphys. Soc. Am. (sec. treas. 1977-81, exec. coun. 1991-94, v.p./pres.- elect 1996—), So. Soc. Philosophy and Psychology (exec. council 1976-79), Am. Philos. Assn. (sec. treas. eastern div. 1985-94). Author: Jaspers and Bultmann, 1968; Existence, Being and God, 1985; contbr., editor: God, Secularization & History, 1974, Experience, Reason and God, 1980; contbr., editor Prospects for Natural Theology, 1992; editor in chief Internat. Jourl for Philosophy of religion, 1990—; assoc. editor Internat. Jour. Philosophy of Religion, 1975-90, So. Jour. Philosophy, 1978-93; contbr., co-editor: God and Temporality, 1984, Being and Truth, 1986; mem. adv. editorial bd. The Works of William James, 1974-88, The Correspondence of William James, 1988—; contbg. editor: God, Reason and Religions, 1995; contbr. articles to profl. jours. Office: U SC Dept Philosophy Columbia SC 29208

LONG, FRANCIS MARK, retired electrical engineer, educator; b. Iowa City, Nov. 10, 1929; s. Frank B. and Hilda B. (Rohret) L.; m. Mary Ann Coyne, June 8, 1964 (dec. Apr. 1994); children: Ann Brett, Mary Bronwyn, Thomas Martin Carver, Caitlin Frances. B.S., U. Iowa, 1953, M.S., 1956; Ph.D., Iowa State U., 1961; NIH fellow, Stanford U. and Lawrence Livermore Lab, 1972-73. With Collins Radio Co., Cedar Rapids, Iowa, summers 1952, 55, Douglas Aircraft Co., Santa Monica, Calif., summer 1953, USNAMTC, Point Mugu, Calif., summer 1956, Good All Electric Co., Ogallala, Nebr., summer 1957, Lawrence Radiation Lab., Livermore, Calif., summer 1967, Globe Union Co., Milw., summer 1975, Naval Rsch Lab., Washington, 1988, 89, 91; instr. U. Wyo., Laramie, 1956-58; prof. elec. engring. U. Wyo., 1960-95; prof. emeritus U. Wyo., Laramie, 1995—; head elec. engring. dept. U. Wyo., 1977-87; instr. Iowa State U., 1958-60; dir. Wyo. Biotelemetry, Inc., Rocky Mountain Bioengring. Symposium; pres. Alliance for Engring. in Medicine and Biology, 1983, 84, mem. exec. com., 1979-89; conf. chmn., procs. editor 1st, 2d, 3d and 5th Internat. Conf. on Wildlife Biotelemetry. Author: (with E.M. Lonsdale) Introductory Electrical Concepts, 1967, rev. edit., 1977; co-author: (with R.G. Jacquot) Introduction to Engineering Systems, 1988. Trustee St. Paul's Newman Center Parish, 1969-72; mem. City of Laramie Planning Commn., 1970-72. Served with C.E. U.S. Army, 1953-55. Decorated citation Republic of Korea Army C.E.; recipient G.D. Humphrey Outstanding Faculty award U. Wyo., 1973, Western Electric Fund award for engring. teaching, 1978. Mem. IEEE (life), Am. Soc. Engring. Edn. (v.p., dir., 1st Outstanding Biomed. Engring. Educator award biomed. engring. divsn. 1981, chmn. Elec. Engring. divsn. 1986-87), Internat. Soc. for Hybrid Microelectronics, Sigma Xi. Republican. Home: 1888 S Jackson St Apt 701 Denver CO 80210

LONG, GREGORY ALAN, lawyer; b. San Francisco, Aug. 28, 1948; s. William F. and Ellen L. (Webber) L.; m. Jane H. Barrett, Sept. 30, 1983; children: Matthew, Brian, Michael, Gregory. BA, magna cum laude, Claremont Men's Coll., Calif., 1970; JD cum laude, Harvard U., 1973. Bar: Calif. 1973, U.S. Dist. Ct. (cen. dist.) Calif. 1973, U.S. Ct. Appeals (9th cir.) 1976, U.S. Supreme Ct. 1977, U.S. Ct. Appeals (fed. cir.) 1984. Assoc. Overton, Lyman & Prince, L.A., 1973-78, ptnr., 1978-87; ptnr. Sheppard, Mullin, Richter & Hampton, 1987—; arbitrator L.A. Superior Ct. Fellow Am. Bar Found.; mem. ABA (young lawyers div. exec. coun. 1974-88, chmn. 1984-85, ho. of dels. 1983-89, exec. coun. litigation sect. 1981-83), Calif. Bar Assn. (del. 1976-82, 87-88), L.A. County Bar Assn. (exec. com. 1979-82, trustee 1979-82, barristers sect. exec. coun. 1976-82, pres. 1981-82, exec. council trial lawyers sect. 1984-88, chair amicus briefs com. 1989-92). Office: Sheppard Mullin Richter & Hampton 333 S Hope St Bldg 48 Los Angeles CA 90071-1406

LONG, GREGORY R., botanic garden administrator. Ceo. and pres. The N.Y. Bot. Garden, Bronx, N.Y. Office: NY Botanical Garden 200th St & Southern Blvd Bronx NY 10458

LONG, HARVEY SHENK, computer educational consultant; b. Cornwall, Pa., May 14, 1933; s. Harvey I. L.; m. Constance Mareen Root, June 14, 1956; children: Bradford, Dean, Jody. BS in Edn., Millersville State Tchrs. Coll, 1955; MS in Math., Carnegie Inst. Tech., 1957; PhD in Math. Edn., NYU, 1969. Assoc. adv. engr. IBM, Poughkeepsie, N.Y., 1957-70; sr. adminstr. IBM, San Jose, 1971, White Plains, N.Y., 1971-72; edn. systems cons. DiscoVision Assocs., Washington, 1979-82, IBM, Washington, 1972-79; edn. applications cons. IBM, Boca Raton, Fla., 1982-85; edn. cons. IBM, Washington, 1985—; cons. Am. Fedn. Tchrs., Washington, 1992—. Contbr. to books and articles to profl. jours. Pres. Somers (N.Y.) PTA, 1973, Music Assn., Rockville, Md., 1976-80. Assn. Devel. Computer Based Inst. fellow, 1986. Fellow Am. Tomorrow; mem. ALA, ASCD, Am. Soc. Tng. and Devel., Nat. Coun. Tchrs. Math., Nat. Sci. Tchrs. Avocations: gardening, walking, model building, bridge. Home: 11025 Rosemont Dr Rockville MD 20852-3650

LONG, HELEN HALTER, author, educator; b. St. Louis; d. Charles C. and Ida (May) Halter; m. Forrest E. Long, June 22, 1944. A.B., Washington U., St. Louis, 1927, A.M., 1928; Ph.D., N.Y. U., 1937. Grad. fellow Washington U., 1927-28; tchr. social studies Venice, Ill., 1928-30; asst. prof. social sci. N.Y. State Coll. for Tchrs., Albany, 1930-38; tchr. pub. schs. Mamaroneck, N.Y., 1938-42; prin. elem. and jr. high schs., 1942-54, asst. supt. schs., 1954-61; dir. Inst. Instructional Improvement, N.Y.C., 1962-88; pres. Books of World, Sweet Springs, Mo., 1962-73; bd. dirs. Roxbury Press, Sweet Springs, Mo., 1963—; teaching fellow, instr. Sch. Edn. NYU, 1936-43; assoc. editor Clearing House, 1935-55. Author: Society in Action, 1936, National Safety Council Lesson Units, 1944-52, (with Forrest E. Long) Social Studies Skills, 8th edit, 1976 (with Forrest E. Long); assoc. editor Clearing House, 1935-55. Mem. Phi Beta Kappa, Pi Gamma Mu, Kappa Delta Pi, Alpha Xi Delta (Diamond Jubilee Outstanding Women award 1968). Home: The Gatesworth One McKnight Pl Saint Louis MO 63124

LONG, HOWARD CHARLES, physics educator emeritus; b. Seizholtzville, Pa., Dec. 12, 1918; s. Howard William and Isabella Geneva (Reese) L.; m. Frances Monroe Hoke, Apr. 16, 1945; children—Howard Charles, David William, Carol Joyce. B.A., Northwestern U., 1941, postgrad., 1941-42; Ph.D., Ohio State U., 1948. Asst. prof. physics Washington and Jefferson Coll., 1948-51; head Electromagnetism Influence Fields sec., U.S. Naval Ordnance Lab., 1951-52; assoc. prof., dept. chmn. physics Am. U., 1952-53; prof. physics, chmn. dept. Gettysburg Coll., 1953-59; prof. physics Dickinson Coll., 1959-81, chmn. dept., 1963-75, Joseph Priestley Chair of Natural Philosophy, 1973, prof. emeritus, 1981—; cons. physicist Naval Ordnance Lab., White Oak, Md., 1952-73, McCoy Electronics Co., Mt. Holly Springs, Pa., 1958-59. Contbr. articles to ednl. jours. Active Boy Scouts Am. Served with USNR, 1944-45. Mem. Am. Assn. Physics Tchrs. (sec.-treas. Central Pa. sect. 1958-59, v.p. 1959-60, pres. 1960-61), A.A.U.P. (sec.-treas. Dickinson chpt. 1963-64, v.p. 1964-65, pres. 1965-66), A.A.A.S., Am. Phys. Soc., Cumberland Conservancy. Methodist (chmn. adminstrn. bd. 1961-62, chmn. ofcl. bd. 1957-59, mem. conf. bd. edn. 1971-73). Home: 240 Belvedere St Carlisle PA 17013-3501 Office: Dickinson Coll Carlisle PA 17013

LONG, JAN MICHAEL, state legislator; b. Pomeroy, Ohio, May 31, 1952; s. Lewis Franklin and Dorothy (Clatworthy) L.; m. Susan Louise Custer, May 12, 1978; children: John D., Justin M., Jason M. BA, Ohio State U., 1974; JD, Capitol U., 1979. Adminstrv. asst. Congressman Doug Applegate, Washington, 1974-77; asst. prosecuting atty. Pickaway County, Circleville, Ohio, 1979-80; mem. Ohio State Senate, Columbus, 1987—; asst. minority whip Ohio Senate, Columbus, 1995—. Named one of Outstanding Young Men Am. U.S. Jaycees, 1987. Mem. Pickaway County Bar Assn. (treas. 1985-86, sec. 1986-87). Democrat. Home: 522 Glenmont Dr Circleville OH 43113-1523 Office: Ohio Senate Rm 134 Statehouse Columbus OH 43215

LONG, JEANINE HUNDLEY, state legislator; b. Provo, Utah, Sept. 21, 1928; d. Ralph Conrad and Hazel Laurine (Snow) Hundley; m. McKay W. Christensen, Oct. 28, 1949 (div. 1967); children: Cathy Schuyler, Julie Schulleri, Kelly M. Christensen, C. Brett Christensen, Harold A. Christensen; m. Kenneth D. Long, Sept. 6, 1968. AA, Shoreline C.C., Seattle, 1975; BA in Psychology, U. Wash., 1977. Mem. Wash. Ho. of Reps., 1983-87, 93-94, mem. bd. joint com. pension policy, Inst. Pub. Policy; mem. Wash. Senate, 1995—. Mayor protem, mem. city coun. City of Brier, Wash., 1977-80. Republican. Office: PO Box 40482 Olympia WA 98504-0482

LONG, JILL LYNETTE, congresswoman; b. Warsaw, Ind., July 15, 1952. BS, Valparaiso U.; MBA, Ind. U., PhD. Prof. various colls. and univs.; mem. 101st-103rd Congresses from 4th Ind. dist., 1989-95; mem. agrl. com., mem. vets. affairs com.; under sec. for rural econ. & community development USDA, 1995—; cons. in small bus. mgmt. Councilwoman City of Valparaiso, Ind.; chair Congrl. Rural Congress. Democrat. Methodist. Office: Rural Econ. & Comm. Development USDA 14th & Independence Ave SW Washington DC 20250

LONG, JOHN BROADDUS, JR., economist, educator; b. Bklyn., Feb. 28, 1944; s. John Broaddus and Katherine Lumpkin (Wicker) L.; m. Carol Elaine Stephens, Aug. 6, 1966; children—Jennifer Tipton, Owen Rosser, John McCauley. B.A., Rice U., 1966; Ph.D., Carnegie-Mellon U., 1971. Asst. prof. U. Rochester, N.Y., 1969-74, assoc. prof., 1974-84, prof., 1984—. Editor Jour. Fin. Econs., 1982—; contbr. articles to profl. jours. Office: U Rochester William E Simon Grad Sch Bus Adminstrn Wilson Blvd Rochester NY 14627

LONG, JOHN D., retired insurance educator; b. Earlington, Ky., July 21, 1920; s. John Boyd and Effie (Yates) L.; m. Hazel Elinor Schnyder; children: Douglas P., Martha S. Caughey, Elinor J. Badanes. BS, U. Ky., 1942; MBA, Harvard U., 1947; D. Bus. Adminstrn., Indiana U., 1954. CLU, CPCU. Instr. De Pauw U., Greencastle, Ind., 1947; instr. Indiana U., Bloomington, 1947—, asst. prof., 1954-56, assoc. prof., 1956-59, prof., 1959-90, acting dean sch. bus., 1983-84, Arthur M. Weimer prof. bus., 1985-90, Arthur M. Weimer prof. bus. emeritus, 1990—; bd. dirs. Meridian Ins. Cos., Indpls., 1975—; property-liability ins. cons. and expert witness. Author: Ethics, Morality, and Insurance, 1971; co-editor: Property and Liability Insurance Handbook, 1965; editor: Issues in Insurance, 1978; author numerous ins. related monographs; contbr. articles to profl. jours. Served to capt. U.S. Army, 1943-46, 51-52. Mem. Soc. CPCUs, Am. Risk and Ins. Assn. (pres. 1966-67, Elizur Wright award 1975), Am. Inst. Propery and Liability Underwriters (trustee 1978-89). Republican. Office: Ind U Sch of Bus 447 Bloomington IN 47405

LONG, JOHN MADISON, elementary music educator; b. Brookhaven, Miss., Nov. 26, 1964; s. Troy Maxwell and Anna Lee (Madison) L.; m. Sheryl Ann Rogers, Dec. 16, 1995. MusB, East Tex. Bapt. U., 1988. Tchr. Roosevelt Elem. Sch., West Palm Beach, Fla., 1988—; mem. curriculum com. Sch. Dist. Palm Beach County, West Palm Beach, 1988-89; instrnl. innovation team Roosevelt Elem. Sch., West Palm Beach, 1992—, vice-chmn. sch. adv. coun., 1994—, chmn. tech. team, 1993—; grant writer. Author: (tech. plan) RESTECH, 1993; designer, implementor: Tech Tools for Our School, 1993. Republican. Baptist. Avocations: travel, music, science fiction, Disney memorabilia. Home: 1475 Forest Hill Blvd Apt 5 West Palm Beach FL 33406-6030 Office: Roosevelt Elem Sch 1220 15th St West Palm Beach FL 33401-2404

LONG, JOHN MALOY, university dean; b. Guntersville, Ala., Dec. 28, 1925; s. Sam James and Lilian (Letson) L.; m. Mary Lynn Adams, July 7, 1950; children: John Maloy, Deborra Lynn. B.S., Jacksonville State U., 1949, LL.D., 1971; M.A., U. Ala., 1956. Dir. bands Oneonta (Ala.) High Sch., 1949-50; dir. bands. Ft. Payne (Ala.) High Sch., 1950-55; dir. bands Robert Lee High Sch., Montgomery, Ala., 1955-65; dir. bands. Troy (Ala.) State U., 1965—, chmn. music dept., 1969, dean Sch. Fine Arts, 1971, dean Coll. Arts and Scis., 1972—. Contbr. articles to mags. Pres. Troy City Sch. Bd., 1977; mem. Ala. Hist. Commn., 1976—. Served with AUS, 1944-46. Recipient citation fo excellence Nat. Band Assn., 1972, Disting. Citizens Service award City of Montogomery, 1964, Cert. Appreciation State of Ala., 1964, Algernon Sydney Sullivan award, 1989, Sudler Order of Merit, 1994; named one of top 10 band dirs. in U.S. Sch. Musician Mag., 1969, to Bandmasters Hall of Fame, 1977; named Ala. Outstanding Educator, Ala. Music Educators Assn., 1984; new music bldg.l named in honor Troy State U., 1975, named Disting. prof., 1989. Mem. Am. Bandmaster Assn. (pres. 1987-88), Am. Sch. Band Dirs. Assn. (state pres. 1968-72), Coll. Band Dirs. Nat. Assn. (state pres.), Nat. Band Assn. (named to Hall of Fame, chmn. bd. Hall of Fame), Omicron Delta Kappa Phi, Mu Alpha, Pi Beta Mu, Phi Delta Kappa, Kappa Kappa Psi (Nat. Disting. Svc. to Music award 1979), Delta Chi. Democrat. Methodist. Lodges: Masons; Shriners; Rotary (past pres.). Office: Troy State U John M Long Hall Troy AL 36082

LONG, JOHN PAUL, pharmacologist, educator; b. Albia, Iowa, Oct. 4, 1926; s. John Edward and Bessie May L.; m. Marilyn Joy Stookesberry, June 11, 1950; children: Jeff, John, Jane. B.S., U. Iowa, 1950, M.S., 1952, Ph.D., 1954. Research scientist Sterling Winthrop Co., Albany, N.Y., 1954-56; asst. prof. U. Iowa, Iowa City, 1956-58, asso. prof., 1958-63, prof. pharmacology, 1963—, head dept., 1970-83. Author 315 research publs. in field. Served with U.S. Army, 1945-46. Recipient Abel award Am. Pharm. Assn., 1958; Ebert award Pharmacology Soc., 1962. Mem. Am. Soc. Pharm. Exptl. Therapy, Soc. Exptl. Biol. Medicine. Republican. Home: 1817 Kathlin Dr Iowa City IA 52246-4617 Office: U Iowa Coll Medicine Dept Pharmacology Iowa City IA 52242

LONG, KEVIN JAY, medicolegal consultant; b. Chgo., May 19, 1961. Student, Chgo. Med. Sch., 1983-86; BS in Math./Stats., Loyola U., Chgo., 1985; postgrad., John Marshall Law Sch., 1988-90. Researcher Cons. in Neurology, Ltd., Skokie, Ill., 1981-84, Assn. for Women's Health Care, Ltd., Chgo., 1982-83; researcher dept. neurology U. Ill., Chgo., 1985-86; law clk. Steven K. Jambois, Chgo., 1989; med. paralegal Hilfman & Fogel, P.C., Chgo., 1989-92; internal medicolegal cons. Robert A. Clifford & Assocs., Chgo., 1992; medicolegal cons. Chgo., 1992—. Contbr. articles to Current Problems in Obstetrics and Gynecology, Archives of Neurology, Archives of Internal Medicine, Pediatrics, Clin. Electroencephalography, Am. Jour. Medicine, Hosp. Pharmacy, Pediatric Emergency Care, Quality Management in Health Care, Houston Medicine, Nursing Quality Connection. Mem. Nat. Hon. Soc. Secondary Schs., Assn. Trial Lawyers Am., Am. Med. Student Assn., N.Y. Acad. Scis., Blue Key Nat. Hon. Frat., Beta Beta Beta Biol. Honor Soc., Alpha Epsilon Delta Premed. Honor Soc. Jewish. Home and Office: Ste 3-South 1325 W North Shore Ave Chicago IL 60626-4763

LONG, LELAND TIMOTHY, geophysics educator, seismologist; b. Auburn, N.Y., Sept. 6, 1940; s. Walter K. and Carmalita Rose Long; m. Sarah Alice Blackard, Mar. 1970; children: Sarah Alice, Katherine Rose, Amy Virginia. BS in Geology, U. Rochester, 1962; MS in Geophysics, N.Mex. Inst. Mining and Tech., 1964; PhD in Geophysics, Oreg. State U., 1968. Registered profl. geologist, Ga. From asst. to assoc. prof. sch. geophysical scis. Ga. Inst. Tech., Atlanta, 1968-81, prof., 1981, divsn. chmn. earth scis. divsn., 1982-84; collaborator in seismology USGS; cons. in seismology, seismic road vibrations and gravity data analysis. Contbr. articles to profl. jours. Office: Ga Inst Tech Earth and Atmospheric Scis Atlanta GA 30332

LONG, LEVITHA OWENS, special education educator; b. Washington, Aug. 5, 1951; d. Otha and Lola Mary (Robinson) Owens; m. Johnnie Edward Long, Aug. 22, 1987; 1 child, Owen Edward Robinson. BS, Va. State U., 1980; MA, U. D.C., 1983. Tchr., adminstrv. asst. Friendship House Inc., Washington, 1980-82; spl. edn. educator Prince George's County (Md.) Pub. Sch., 1982-84, Davis Elem. Sch., Washington, 1984-86; spl. edn. educator Weatherless Elem. Sch., Washington, 1986-92, co-chmn. gifted and talented com., 1989-92; spl. edn. educator Ketcham Elem. Sch., Washington, 1992-95, Roper Middle Sch. of Science and Math Technology; coord. spelling bee Ketcham Elem. Sch., Washington, 1992-94, chairperson music/drama club. Dir. summer program Girl Scouts Am., Washington, 1985-93; mem. voter registration com. Prince George's County, 1991-94, voter registration ward 7 Rylan-Epworth Civiv Assn., Washington, 1977-85; mem. polit. action com., Kaypark Civic Assn., Sutland, Md., 1985—. Mem. ASCD, Coun. for Exceptional Children, Black Child Devel. Inst., Va. State U. Alumni Assn. (chair 1991-93), Va. State U. Alumni Assn. (chair scholarship fundraising), Alpha Kappa Alpha (co-chair 1985-87, cotillion co-chair). Democrat. Methodist. Avocations: piano, gardening. Home: 2531 Fairhill Dr Suitland MD 20746-2306 Office: Roper Middle Sch/DC Pub Sch 415 12th St NW Washington DC 20001

LONG, MADELEINE J., mathematics and science educator; b. N.Y.C.; d. Harry L. and Irma (Silverman) L. B.A., Queens Coll., 1960; M.Ed., Harvard U., 1963; Ed.D., Columbia U., 1967. Tchr. Westbury (N.Y.) Sch. System, 1960-61; teaching fellow Harvard U., 1962-63; prof. edn. L.I. U., asst. to dean, 1967-69, chmn. dept., 1969-76, dir. div. edn., dir. grad. programs at Westchester br. campus, 1977-83, dir. Inst. Advancement Math. and Sci., 1983-91; program officer (on leave from L.I. U.) NSF, Washington, 1993—; vis. scientist, spl. asst. comprehensive design planning NSF, 1992-93, sr. program officer Urban Systemic Initiative, 1993-96, reader, 1973, 77, 79, 85, 88, 90, career access panelist and chair, 1988; dir. summer tng. programs N.Y.C. Bd. Edn., 1978, 79, 81; reader Fund for Impervement Postsecondary Edn., 1984, 85, 87, N.J. Bd. Higher Edn., Minority Instns. Sci. Improvement Program; cons. to various univs. and sch. sys.; lectr. in field; apptd. coun. on excellence and equity in math. and sci. edn. N.Y. State, 1986-91. Mem. editorial bd. Jour. Coll. Sci. Teaching, 1986-89; contbr. articles to profl. jours. Mem. edn. subcom. Mayor's Commn. on Sci. and Tech., 1989-91. Columbia U. fellow, 1963-64, grantee NSF, 1972, 78, 79, 80, 81, 84-87, 87-91, 91-94, Career Edn., 1975, Fund for Improvement Postsecondary Edn., 1983-87, Title II Edn. for Econ. Security Act N.Y. State. Fellow Philosophy of Edn. Soc.; mem. AAAS (chair sect. Q, Sci. Edn., chmn. edn. section) Assn. Supervision and Curriculum Devel., N.Y. Acad. Sci., Nat. Sci. Tchrs. Assn., Nat. Coun. Tchrs. Math., Am. Ednl. Rsch. Assn., Kappa Delta Pi. Office: NSF 4201 Wilson Blvd Arlington VA 22201

LONG, MARGARET KAREN, art educator; b. Bridgeport, Conn., Mar. 18, 1950; d. Felix Joseph and Clayda Erna (Town) Petko; m. James Ray Long, July 1, 1977 (div. May 1991); children: Mason Douglas, Megan Elizabeth. AA in Photography & Comml. Art, L.A. Harbor Coll., 1973; BFA in Art and Human Svcs., Calif. State U., Fullerton, 1976; MA in Philosophy & Art History, Calif. State U., Dominguez Hills, 1982; MA in Counselor Edn., Calif. State U., San Bernadino, 1993. Cert. secondary tchr. Calif. Photographer, artist pvt. practice, San Pedro, Calif., 1968-73; photographer Blalack Studios, Fullerton, Calif., 1973-76; artist 110 Wilshire Studios, Fullerton, Calif., 1974-77; med. recs. tech. Long Beach (Calif.) Meml. Hosp., 1977-80; instr. photography S.E. L.A. ROP Adult Edn., Cerritos, Calif., 1980; instr. art, social studies ABC Unified Sch. Dist., Cerritos, Calif., 1980-82; educator art, journalism, yearbook Coachella Unified Sch. Dist., Thermal, Calif., 1983—; mentor tchr. Calif. Dept. Edn., 1989-95; counselor to disturbed teens, Insight, Thermal, 1986-94; pres. Faculty Forum, Coachella Valley H.S., 1993-94; dept. chair Visual and Performing Arts Dept., Thermal, 1983-94, coord., site rep., 1988-91; mem. accreditation and steering coms., Calif. Accreditation for Schs., Thermal, 1976-77, 93-94. Exhibited in group shows Malden Gallery Invitational Show, 1975, Laguna All Calif. Show, 1976. Foster parent State Dept. Social Svcs., Rancho Mirage, Calif., 1991-92; mem. Friends of Coachella Libr., 1986-94. Mem. Calif. Art Edn. Assn., Hi-Desert Artists Coop. (exhibitor 1984-85). Avocations: painting, drawing, photography, land investments.

LONG, MAURICE WAYNE, physicist, electrical engineer, radar consultant; b. Madisonville, Ky., Apr. 20, 1925; s. Maurice K. and Martha Ann (Nourse) L.; m. Patricia Lee Holmes, Feb. 25, 1950 (dec. Aug. 1961); children: Anne Catherine Long Key, Jane Elizabeth Long Rice; m. Beverly Ann Benson, Jan. 1, 1963; stepchildren: Theodore Douglas Downing, Beverly Patricia Downing. BEE, Ga. Inst. Tech., 1946, MS in Physics, 1957, PhD, 1959; MSEE, U. Ky., 1948. Registered profl. engr., Ga. Rsch. asst. Ga. Inst. Tech., Atlanta, 1946-47, rsch. engr., then spl. rsch. engr., asst. rsch. prof., prin. rsch. physicist, 1950-68, prof. elec. engring., 1968-73, head radar devel. br., 1955-60, chief div. electronics, 1959-68, dir. Engring. Expt. Sta. (now Ga. Tech. Rsch. Inst.), 1968-75; dir. rsch., sec., asst. treas. Ga. Tech. Rsch. Inst., 1968-75; liaison scientist U.S. Office Naval Rsch. London Br., 1966-67; bd. dirs. Ga. Tech. Rsch. Inst., 1968-82; mem. com. on remote sensing programs for earth resources surveys NAS, 1977, space applications adv. com., subcom. on remote sensing NASA, 1983-86; mem. Acad. Electromagnetics, MIT, 1990; mem. various coms. on radar U.S. Army, Navy, Air Force, NASA, 1967—. Author: Radar Reflectivity of Land and Sea, 1975, 2d edit., 1983; editor, contbg. author: Airborne Early Warning System Concepts, 1992; contbr. numerous articles to profl. jours., chpts. to books; patentee in field. Mem. Ga. Gov.'s Sci. Adv. Coun., 1972-74, chmn. ad hoc com. on tech. growth in Ga., 1974. Fellow IEEE (life); mem. Acad. Electromagnetics, Internat. Union Radio Sci. (commn. F.), Assn. Old Crows, Sigma Xi. Avocations: sailing, traveling. Home: 1036 Somerset Dr NW Atlanta GA 30327-3736

LONG, MAXINE MASTER, lawyer; b. Pensacola, Fla., Oct. 20, 1943; d. Maxwell L. and Claudine E. (Smith) M.; m. Anthony Byrd Long, Aug. 27, 1966; children: Deborah E., David M. AB, Bryn Mawr Coll., 1965; MS, Georgetown U., 1971; JD, U. Miami, 1979. Bar: Fla. 1979, U.S. Ct. Appeals (5th cir.) 1980, U.S. Dist. Ct. (so. dist.) Fla. 1980, U.S. Ct. Appeals (11th cir.) 1981, U.S. Dist. Ct. (mid. and no. dists.) Fla. 1987. Law clk. to U.S. dist. judge U.S. Dist. Ct. (so. dist.) Fla., Miami, 1979-80; assoc. Shutts & Bowen, Miami, 1980-90, of counsel, 1990-92, ptnr., 1992—. Mem. Fla. Bar Assn. (bus. litigation cert. com., past chair bus. litigation com., exec. coun. bus. law sect.), Dade County Bar Assn. (mem. fed. cts. com., recipient pro bono award/Vol. Lawyers for the Arts 1989). Office: Shutts & Bowen 201 S Biscayne Blvd Miami FL 33131-4332

LONG, MELVIN DURWARD, university president; b. Daytona Beach, Fla., Nov. 12, 1931; s. Melvin Durward and Ramona Bernice (Robinson) L.; m. Estrella Niña Celorio; children: Melvin Durward III, Carl Patrick, Elena Colleen. BS, Troy (Ala.) State U., 1953; MA, Auburn U., 1956; PhD, U. Fla., 1959. Vice chancellor U. Wis., 1968-70, chancellor cen. system, 1971-73; exec. dir. select com. on Calif. master plan, assoc. dir. Calif. Coordinating Coun. for Higher Edn., 1970-71; v.p. U. Calif., Berkeley, 1973-75; v.p. for acad. affairs U. Hawaii System, Honolulu, 1975-79, v.p., 1981-84; chancellor U. Hawaii Manoa, Honolulu, 1979-81; interim v.p. for fin. U. Wyo., Laramie, 1981-83; scholar in residence Nat. Assn. State Univ. and Land Grant Colls., 1984; pres. Sangamon State U., Springfield, Ill., 1984-91, pres. emeritus, Regency prof. econ. history, 1991—; vice chancellor for strategic planning and devel. Ill. Bd. Regents, 1991-92; v.p. fin. and adminstrn., treas., bd. trustees Fashion Inst. Tech., N.Y.C., 1993—; sr. fellow Edn. Commn. on the State, vis. rsch. prof. U. Fla., 1991-92. Author, editor: Student Protest, 1970, The Future of State Public Universities, 1985; contbr. articles on U.S. history and higher edn. to profl. jours. Mem. Am. Assn. State Univs. and Colls. (com. on policies and purposes 1984-88, bd. dirs. 1988-90). Home: 108 E Hazel Dell Springfield IL 62707-9516 Office: Fashion Inst Technology 7th Ave and 27th St New York NY 10010

LONG, MEREDITH J., art dealer; b. Joplin, Mo., Sept. 14, 1928; s. Emery Meredith and Martha M. (Attebury) L.; m. Cornelia Cullen, June 23, 1967; children: Meredith, Jenny, Gretchen, Martha Katherine. B.A., U. Tex., 1950, postgrad. Law Sch., 1950-51, 53-54. Exec. Curtis Mathes Corp., Houston, 1953-57; owner Meredith Long & Co., Houston, 1957—, Meredith Long Contemporary, N.Y.C., 1977-80; prin. Davis & Long, N.Y.C., 1974-80, Watson-de Nagy and Co., Houston, 1974-80; dir. Bank S.W., 1975-84, S.W. Bancshares, 1984; bd. dirs. MCorp, Quintana Petroleum Corp., 1984-94, dir. 1983—. Editor: Americans at Home and Abroad Catalogue, 1971, Tradition and Innovation-American Paintings 1860-1870 Catalogue, 1974, Americans at Work and Play, 1845-1944 Catalogue, 1980. Chmn. mcpl. arts, City of Houston, 1976-78; bd. dirs., exec. com., trustee Mus. Fine Arts, 1977-79; bd. dirs., mem. exec. com. Houston, Alley Theatre, Houston, 1975—, chmn., 1989-93; trustee Houston Ballet Found., 1974-76, exec. com., 1976-77, adv. com., 1979-80; mem. exec. com. Contemporary Arts Mus., 1975-77; mem. pres.'s adv. bd. John F. Kennedy Center of Performing Arts, until 1980; v.p. devel. Houston Symphony Soc., dir., 1986, adv. bd., 1987—, past bd. dirs., pres.'s counc. Houston Grand Opera; mem. adv. council U. Tex. Coll. Fine Arts, Austin, 1979—; chmn. emeritus, 1993; trustee Houston chpt. Multiple Sclerosis Soc., 1981, Archives of Am. Art, 1989-95, Cultural Arts Coun. City of Houston, 1991—; chmn. Tex. Heart Inst., 1991—. Mem. Am. Assn. Museums, Am. Fedn. Arts, Visual Artists and Galleries Assn. (dir. 1977-78), Art Dealers Assn. Houston (past pres.), Ducks Unlimited Inc. (nat. trustee 1969-80, sponsor of yr. 1979), River Oaks Country Club, Bayou Club, Coronado (bd. dirs.), Ramada-Tejas, The Houstonian, Doubles Club (N.Y.C.), Knickerbocker Club (N.Y.C.). Home: 3722 Knollwood St Houston TX 77019-1110 Office: 2323 San Felipe Houston TX 77019

LONG, MICHAEL THOMAS, lawyer, manufacturing company executive; b. Hartford, Conn., Feb. 22, 1942; s. Michael Joseph and Mary Fagan (Maguire) L.; m. Ann Marie O'Connell, Sept. 9, 1967; children: Michael, Maura, Deirdre. BBA, U. Notre Dame, 1964; JD, U. Conn., 1967, postgrad., 1968. Bar: Conn. 1967. Law clk. U.S. Bankruptcy Ct., U.S. Dist. Ct., Hartford, 1966-68; supr. indsl. rels. Ensign-Bickford Industries, Inc., Simsbury, Conn., 1968-72, contract adminstr., 1972-74, div. controller, 1974-79, mgr. govt. and legal affairs, 1978-81, gen. counsel, sec., 1981-83, v.p., gen. counsel, sec., 1983—; bd. dirs. Ensign-Bickford Co.; pres., chief exec. officer, Ensign-Bickford Haz-Pros Inc., 1989—; U. Notre Dame Alumni Clubs of Greater Hartford scholarship chmn., 1990—. Chmn. Dem. Town Com., Simsbury, 1971-81, Dem. State Ctrl. Com. of Conn., 1992—, Bradley Internat. Airport Com., Windsor Locks, Conn., 1983—; mem. pub. bldg. com. Town of Simsbury, 1981-85, mem. cultural, parks and recreation com., 1986-87, mem. fin. bd., 1987—; mem. Simsbury Jr. Achievement, 1970-74; pres. parish council St. Mary's Ch., Simsbury, 1982-85; chmn. Bradley Internat. Airport Commn., 1983-91. Named Home Town Hero Town of Simsbury, 1987; recipient Man of Yr. award U. Notre Dame Alumni Clubs of Greater Hartford, 1995. Mem. ABA, Conn. Bar Assn., Hartford County Bar Assn., Inst. Makers of Explosives (bd. govs. 1987—, chmn. legal affairs com. 1986-93, 95—), Am. Corp. Counsel Assn. (bd. dirs. Hartford chpt. 1988—), Greater Harford C. of C. (bd. dirs. 1991-94), Internat. Soc. Explosive Engrs., Simsbury Farms Men's Club (founder 1972), Hop Meadow Country Club. Democrat. Roman Catholic. Home: 9 Metacom Dr Simsbury CT 06070-1851 Office: Ensign-Bickford Industries Inc 10 Mill Pond Ln PO Box 7 Simsbury CT 06070-0007

LONG, PHILIP LEE, information systems executive; b. Cleve., Jan. 24, 1943; s. Philip Joseph and Anne Catherine (Woodward) L.; BEE, Ohio State U., 1968, MSc, 1970; m. LeAnn Boyack Edvalson, Apr. 22, 1982; children: Sarah J., Caitlin T.; children by previous marriage: Philip Imants, Michael Oskar; Assoc. dir. Ohio Coll. Libr. Ctr., 1969-73; asso. for computer systems devel. SUNY, Albany, 1974-75; pres. Philip Long Assos., Inc., Salt Lake City, 1975-81; v.p. Novell Data Systems, 1981-82; v.p. Telerate Systems, Inc., 1983-93; pres. Philip Long Assocs., Ltd., South Orange, N.J., 1993—; instr. computer sci. Ohio State Univ., libr. sci. SUNY, Catholic U. Am.; cons. to UNESCO, Bibliotheque National de France, Lib. Congress, Nat. Comm. Library and Info. Sci. Grantee, Nat. Rsch. Coun., Nat. Acad. Sci., 1971. Mem. Am. Soc. Info. Sci., IEEE, ALA, Assn. Computing Machinery, Am. Nat. Stds. Inst. Contbr. articles to profl. jours. Office: 397 Thornden St South Orange NJ 07079-1423

LONG, PHILLIP CLIFFORD, museum director; b. Tucson, Oct. 11, 1942; s. Hugh-Blair Grigsby and Phyllis Margaret (Clay) L.; m. Martha Whitney Rowe, Aug. 26, 1972; children—Elisha Whitney, Charlotte Clay, Elliot Sherlock. B.A., Tulane U., 1965. Sec. Fifth Third Bancorp, Cin., 1974-94; sr. v.p., sec. Fifth Third Bank, Cin., 1988-94; dir. Taft Mus., Cin., 1994—. Trustee Contemporary Arts Ctr., 1974-84, Art Acad. Cin., 1980-94, Cin. Symphony Orch., 1981-87, Cin. Nature Ctr., 1982-88, Taft Mus., 1987-94, Cin. Country Day Sch., 1991—; trustee, treas. Cin. Music Hall, 1981-92, Convalescent Hosp. for Children, 1989—, Cin. Assn. for Arts, 1992—. Mem. The Camargo Club, Queen City Club. Home: 4795 Burley Hills Dr Cincinnati OH 45243-4007 Office: Taft Mus 316 Pike St Cincinnati OH 45202-4214

LONG, RALPH STEWART, clinical psychologist; b. Pitts., Feb. 23, 1926; s. Ralph S. and Virginia (Hawk) L.; m. Vera Lazorchak, June 16, 1951; children: Karen Virginia, Brian Reed, Lauri Michelle. BS, Lock Haven U., 1950; MEd, Pa. State U., 1951; PhD, Washington U., St. Louis, 1965. Lic. psychologist, Tex. Commd. 2d lt. USAF, 1951, advanced through grades to lt. col., 1968; psychologist various hosps. USAF, U.S. and Europe, 1951-71; ret., 1971; dir. psychol. svcs. Community Ctr. Mental Health, Mental Retardation, Wichita Falls, Tex., 1971-72; psychol. cons. Family Counseling Ctr., Wichita Falls, 1972-74; dir. psychol. svcs. Nueces County Mental Health-Mental Retardation Community Ctr, 1974-77; dir. Corpus Christi Counseling Ctr./Physicians-Surgeons Hosp., Tex., 1977-79, Psychol. Cons., Corpus Christi, 1979-82; exec. dir. Personal Dynamics Inst., Corpus Christi, 1982—, dir., 1988—; instr. dept. psychology McKendree Coll., Lebanon, Ill., 1962-63; instr. So. Ill. U., 1962-64; adj. prof. human rels. Webster U., Webster Groves, Mo., 1976-79, 88-93; adj. prof. psychology Del Mar Coll., Corpus Christi, 1977-83, adj. prof. bus. adminstrn., 1991-93; cons. Tex. Dept. Corrections, 1988-90; bd. dirs. Ctr. Creative Living, 1986—; cons., trainer Crisis Svcs., 1980—; profl. adv. bd. North Tex. Regional Coun. Alcoholism, 1971-74, Mental Health Assn. Coastal Bend, 1974-83, Wichita Mental Health Assn., 1965-67, 70-74; adj. prof. Embry-Riddle U., Corpus Christi, 1991-93; consulting psychologist Nueces County Juvenile Justice Ctr., Corpus Christi, 1992—, Warm Springs Rehab. Ctr., Corpus Christi, 1992—, MCC Managed Behavioral Care, Inc., Eden Prairie, Minn., 1992—, Champus Provider, 1972—; bd. dirs. Consumer Credit Counseling Svc. South Tex., 1983-92, emeritus, 1993—. Contbr. to profl. jours.; presenter in field. With USN, 1944-51. Named Am. Man Sci., 1962. Fellow Soc. Air Force Clin. Psychologists; mem. APA, DAV, VFW, Am. Inst. Hypnosis, U.S. Holocaust Meml. Mus. (charter), Libr. of Congress Assocs. (charter), Tex. Assn. Mental Health (exec. com. 1980-83), Air Force Assn., Nat. Register Health Svc. Providers in Psychology, Smithsonian, Sierra Club, Am. Assn. Ret. Persons, Masons, Shriners, Sigma Xi. Avocations: painting, writing, travel, camping, fishing. Office: Personal Dynamics Inst 1819 S Brownlee Blvd Corpus Christi TX 78404-2901

LONG, RICHARD PAUL, civil engineering educator, geotechnical engineering consultant; b. Allentown, Pa., Nov. 29, 1934; s. Peter Anthony and Matilda (Stier) L.; m. Mary Elizabeth Doyle, Aug. 29, 1964; children: Marybeth, Christopher. BCE, U. Cin., 1957; MCE, Rensselaer Poly. Inst., 1963, PhD, 1966. Registered profl. engr., Conn. NSF postdoctoral fellow Rensselaer Poly. Inst., Troy, N.Y., 1966-67; from asst. to assoc. prof. civil engring. U. Conn., Storrs, 1967-77, prof., head dept., 1977-90; com. mem. Transp. Research Bd., Washington, 1971—. Contbr. articles to profl. jours.; co-inventor, patentee prefabricated subsurface drain, stress laminated timber bridges. Pres. Mansfield Middle Sch. Assn., Storrs, 1977-79; commr. Mansfield Housing Authority, Storrs, 1987—, chmn., 1988-93. 1st lt. U.S. Army, 1958-61. Recipient T.A. Bedford prize Rensselaer Poly. Inst., 1966, AT&T Found. award for Teaching Excellence, 1988, Recognition award Conn. Soc. Profl. Engrs., 1989. Fellow ASCE; mem. Conn. Soc. Civil Engrs. (sec. 1986-88, pres.-elect 1988-89, pres. 1989-90), Am. Soc. Engring. Edn. Roman Catholic. Avocations: jogging, travel. Home: 31 Westgate Ln Storrs Mansfield CT 06268-1506 Office: Univ Conn U-37 Dept Of Civil Enging Storrs CT 06269-2037

LONG, ROBERT EMMET, author; b. Oswego, N.Y., June 7, 1934; s. Robert Emmet and Verda (Lindsley) L. BA, Columbia Coll., 1956; MA, Syracuse U., 1964; PhD, Columbia U., 1968. Instr. SUNY, Cortland, 1962-64; asst. prof. Queens Coll., CUNY, N.Y.C., 1968-71; writer, 1971—. Author: The Great Succession: Henry James and the Legacy of Hawthorne, 1979, The Achieving of the Great Gatsby, 1979, Henry James: The Early Years, 1983, John O'Hara, 1983, Nathanael West, 1985, Barbara Pym, 1986, James Thurber, 1968, James Fenimore Cooper, 1990, The Films of Merchant Ivory, 1991, Ingmar Bergman: Film and Stage, 1994; editor numerous books; contbr. articles to profl. jours. and popular mags. Democrat. Episcopalian. Avocations: films, theater, ballet, jazz, travel. Address: 254 S 3rd St Fulton NY 13069-2356

LONG, ROBERT EUGENE, banker; b. Yankton, S.D., Dec. 5, 1931; s. George Joseph and Malinda Ann (Hanson) L.; m. Patricia Louise Glass, June 19, 1959; children: Malinda Ann, Robert Eugene, Jennifer Lynn, Michael Joseph. B.S. in Acctg., U. S.D., 1956; M.B.A., U. Mich., 1965; grad., Madison Grad. Sch. Banking, 1973, Nat. Comml. Lending Grad. Sch., U. Okla., 1977. Cert. comml. lender. Financial analyst Chrysler Corp., 1958-59; supr. finance Ford Motor Co., 1966-67; with First Wis. Bankshares Corp., Milw., 1967—, v.p. fin. First Wis. Bankshares Corp., 1973—; exec. v.p. 1st Wis. Fond du Lac, 1978—; dir. 1st Wis. Nat. Bank of, Southgate, Waukesha and Fond du Lac; exec. v.p., dir. West Allis State Bank, 1979-81, pres., dir., 1981—, chief exec. officer, 1983—; sr. v.p. adminstrn. Park Banks, 1987—; speaker/chmn. banking seminars Am. Mgmt. Assn., 1970—. Pres. local br. Aid Assn. Luth., 1970—, corp. bd. dirs., 1982—; vice chmn. bd., 1989—; pres. Mt. Carmel Luth. Ch., Milw., 1972; team capt. Re-elect Nixon campaign, 1972; bd. dirs. Luth. Social Svcs. of Wis. and Upper Mich., 1978—, chmn. bd., 1983—; bd. dirs. Luther Manor, 1981, Luther Manor Found., 1984, pres. bd. dirs. United Luth. Program for Aging, 1986—; bd. dirs. Wis. Inst. Family Medicine, 1985, pres., 1992—; vice chmn. adv. coun. West Allis Meml. Hosp., 1993—. With USAF, 1951-52. Recipient Good

Citizenship award Am. Legion, 1948. Mem. Wis. Assn. Family Practice (bd. dirs. 1992—), Wauwatosa C. of C. (bd. dirs. 1992—), Alpha Tau Omega. Lutheran. Clubs: Western Racquet (Elm Grove, Wis.) (dir. 1976—); Bluemound Golf and Country; Elmbrook Swim (pres. 1977-78). Lodges: Masons, Shriners, Jesters. Home: N21w24052 Dorchester Dr Unit D Pewaukee WI 53072-4692 Office: Park Banks 330 E Kilbourn Ave Milwaukee WI 53202-6636

LONG, ROBERT LIVINGSTON, retired photographic equipment executive; b. Abbeville, S.C., Jan. 3, 1937; s. Clarance Blakely and Amy (Wolff) L.; m. Phyllis Jo Crews, May 30, 1959; children: J. Blake, Brynn Diane, Brant Wolff. BSCE, U. S.C., 1959; grad. in Indsl. Mgmt. Program, U. Tenn., 1967. Chem. engr. Tenn. div. Eastman Kodak Co., Kingsport, 1959-66, gen. mgmt. staff tech. Tenn. div., 1966-74, mgr. licensing chemicals div., 1974-80, dir. mfg. staff Tenn. div., 1980-83, v.p., dir. planning div., chemicals div., 1983-86; v.p., dir. corp. planning Eastman Kodak Co., Rochester, N.Y., 1986-92, sr. v.p., 1989; cons., Melbourne Beach, Fla., 1992—; bd. dirs. Sun Microsystems Inc., Mt. View, Calif., Boradband Comms. Products, Melbourne, Fla., 1995—. Participant Tenn. Exec. Devel. Program, Knoxville, 1974; multiple adv. bd. City of Kingsport, 1978-86; bd. dirs. Boy's Club Greater Kingsport, 1965-81, chmn., 1973-75; bd. dirs. Holston Valley Hosp. and Med. Ctr., Kingsport, 1983-86, Rochester Gen. Hosp., 1988-92. Sgt. U.S. Army N.G., 1955-63. Recipient Medallion, Boys Club Am., 1976, Bronze Keyston award Boys Club Am., 1985. Mem. Am. Inst. Chem. Engrs., Soc. for Info. Mgmt., Acad. Natural Scis. (bd. dirs. environ. assocs. 1982-85), Sigma Alpha Epsilon. Episcopalian. Lodge: Rotary (chmn. coms. Kingsport 1975-86).

LONG, ROBERT LYMAN JOHN, naval officer; b. Kansas City, Mo., May 29, 1920; s. Trigg A. and Margaret (Franklin) L.; m. Sara Helms, Aug. 28, 1944; children: Charles Allen, William Trigg, Robert Helms. BS, U.S. Naval Acad., 1943; grad., Naval War Coll., 1954. Commd. ensign USN, 1943, advanced through grades to adm., 1977; assigned PTO; comdr. two nuclear polaris submarines, 1966-68; comdr. service force for 7th fleet, 1968-69; dep. comdr. Naval Ship Systems Command, 1969-72; comdr. submarine force U.S. Atlantic Fleet, 1972-74; dep. chief naval ops. for submarine warfare Washington, 1974-77; vice chief naval ops., 1977-79; comdr.-in-chief U.S. Forces Pacific, 1979-83. Decorated D.S.M. (two), Legion of Merit (three), Bronze Star. Club: Cosmos. Home: 247 Heamans Way Annapolis MD 21401-6303

LONG, ROBERT M., newspaper publishing executive; m. June Long; children: Shannon, Bob. BBA, Dyke Coll. CPA, Ohio. From acct. to treas. and contr. Plain Dealer Pub. Co., Cleve., 1965-92, exec. v.p., 1992—; v.p. Plain Dealer Charities, Inc., Delcom, Inc. Trustee Dyke Coll., Cleve. Ballet, St. Vincent Quadrangle, Inc.; bd. dirs. Jr. Achievement; active Leadership Cleve., 1993. Mem. Internat. Newspaper Fin. Execs. (bd. dirs.), Ohio Soc. CPAs, Cleve. Treas. Club. Office: The Plain Dealer Pub Co 1801 Superior Ave E Cleveland OH 44114-2107

LONG, ROBERT MERRILL, retail drug company executive; b. Oakland, Calif., May 19, 1938; s. Joseph Milton and Vera Mai (Skaggs) L.; m. Eliane Quilloux, Dec. 13, 1969. Student, Brown U., 1956-58; BA, Claremont Men's Coll., 1960. With Longs Drug Stores Inc., Walnut Creek, Calif., 1960—, dist. mgr., 1970-72, exec. v.p., 1972-75, pres., 1975-77, pres., chief exec. officer, 1977-91; chmn., chief exec. officer Longs Drug Stores, Walnut Creek, Calif., 1991—. Mem. Nat. Assn. Chain Drug Stores (dir.). Office: Longs Drug Stores Corp PO Box 5222 141 N Civic Dr Walnut Creek CA 94596-3858

LONG, ROBERT RADCLIFFE, fluid mechanics educator; b. Glen Ridge, N.J., Oct. 24, 1919; s. Clarence D. and Gertrude (Cooper) L.; m. Cristina Nersing, 1962; children: John Radcliffe, Robert W. AB in Econs, Princeton, 1941; MS in Meteorology, U. Chgo., 1949, PhD, 1950. Meteorologist U.S. Weather Bur., Paris, France, 1946-47; asst. prof. Johns Hopkins U., Balt., 1951-56, assoc. prof., 1956-59, prof. fluid mechanics, 1959-88, prof. emeritus, 1988—, dir. hydrodynamics lab., 1951-88; assoc. dept. aero. and mech. engring. Ariz. State U. Author: Mechanics of Solids and Fluids, Engineering Science Mechanics; also articles in field. Home: PO Box 10381 Sarasota FL 34278-0381

LONG, RONALD ALEX, real estate and financial consultant, educator; b. Scranton, Pa., Dec. 9, 1948; s. Anthony James and Dorothy Agnas (Posgay) L.; m. Geraldine Sinneway, July 17, 1976; 1 child, Elizabeth Dorothy. BA, Bethany Coll., Lindsburg, Kans., 1971; MAT, Trenton (N.J.) State Coll., 1973; BS, Spring Garden Coll., 1980; MBA, St. Joseph's U., Phila., 1985; JD, Widener U., 1996; cert. new home sales profl., Grad. Realtor Inst., 1990. Cert. real estate instr. Substitute tchr. Hackettstown and Roxbury (N.J.) Sch. Bds., 1971-72; prof., chmn. bus. adminstrn. dept. Spring Garden Coll., Phila., 1973-92; sales assoc. Red Carpet Real Estate, Doylestown, Pa., 1980—; cons. real estate Doylestown, 1980—; cons. mgmt. Budd Wheel Corp., Phila., 1978-82; pres., prin. Aladdin Fin. Svcs., Inc.; prin. Loan Finders, Inc.; dir. Met. Real Estate Sch., Doylestown, 1991-95; cons. The Princeton Group Telecom. Specialist. Co-author: Explorations in Macroeconomics, 1988, Explorations in Microeconomics, 1989; contbr. articles to area newspapers. Site dir. ARC Blood Mobile, 1975-91; bd. dirs Buckingham (Pa.) PTA, 1984-88. Recipient Legion Honor award Chapel of the 4 Chaplains, Phila., 1984. Mem. Nat. Assn. Realtors, Pa. Assn. Realtors, Bucks County Assn. Realtors, U.S. Power Squadrons, Profl. Assn. Diving Instrs. (cert.), Moe Levine Trial Advocacy Honor Soc. (cert. achievement land transactions, ocean and coastal law), Bus. Club (treas. 1969-71, pres. 1970-71), Alpha Chi, Pi Sigma Chi, Eta Beta Phi, Delta Theta Phi. Republican. Avocations: scuba diving, karate, surface and underwater photography, running. Home: 2698 Cranberry Rd Doylestown PA 18901-1770

LONG, SARAH ANN, librarian; b. Atlanta, May 20, 1943; d. Jones Lloyd and Lelia Maria (Mitchell) Sanders; m. James Allen Long, 1961 (div. 1985); children: Andrew C., James Allen IV; m. Donald J. Sager, May 23, 1987. BA, Oglethorpe U., 1966; M in Librarianship, Emory U., 1967. Asst. libr. Coll. of St. Matthias, Bristol, Eng., 1970-74; cons. State Libr. of Ohio, Columbus, 1975-77; coord. Pub. Libr. of Columbus and Franklin County, Columbus, 1977-79, dir. Fairfield County Dist. Libr., Lancaster, Ohio, 1979-82, Dauphin County Libr. System, Harrisburg, Pa., 1982-85, Multnomah County Libr., Portland, Oreg., 1985-89; system dir. North Suburban Libr. System, Wheeling, Ill., 1989—; chmn. Portland State U. Libr. Adv. Coun., 1987-89. Contbr. articles to profl. jours. Bd. dirs. Dauphin County Hist. Soc., Harrisburg, 1983-85, ARC, Harrisburg, 1984-85; pres. Lancaster-Fairfield County YWCA, Lancaster, 1981-82; vice-chmn. govt. and edn. div. Lancaster-Fairfield County United Way, Lancaster, 1981-82; sec. Fairfield County Arts Coun., 1981-82; adv. bd. Portland State U., 1987-89; mentor Ohio Libr. Leadership Inst., 1993, 95. Recipient Dir.'s award Ohio Program in Humanities, Columbus, 1982; Sarah Long Day established in her honor Fairfield County, Lancaster, Bd. Commrs., 1982. Mem. ALA (elected coun. 1993—), Pub. Libr. Assn. (pres. 1989-90, chair legis. com. 1991-95, chair 1998 nat. conf. com. 1995—), Ill. Libr. Assn. (pub. policy com. 1991—). Office: N Suburban Libr Systems 200 W Dundee Rd Wheeling IL 60090-4750

LONG, SARAH ELIZABETH BRACKNEY, physician; b. Sidney, Ohio, Dec. 5, 1926; d. Robert LeRoy and Caroline Josephine (Shue) Brackney; m. John Frederick Long, June 15, 1948; children: George Lynas, Helen Lucille Corcoran, Harold Roy, Clara Alice Lawrence, Nancy Carol Sieber. BA, Ohio State U., 1948, MD, 1952. Intern Grant Hosp., Columbus, Ohio, 1952-53; resident internal medicine Mt. Carmel Med. Ctr., Columbus, 1966-69, chief resident internal medicine, 1968-69; med. cons. Ohio Bur. Disability Determination, Columbus, 1970—; physician student health Ohio State U., Columbus, 1970-73; sch. physician Bexley (Ohio) City Schs., 1973-83; physician advisor to peer rev. Mt. Carmel East Hosp., Columbus, 1979-86, med. dir. employee health, 1981-96; physician cons. Fed. Black Lung program U.S. Dept. Labor, Columbus, 1979—. Mem. AMA, Gerontol. Soc. Am., Ohio Hist. Soc., Ohio State Med. Assn., Franklin County Acad. Medicine, Alpha Epsilon Delta, Phi Beta Kappa. Home: 2765 Bexley Park Rd Columbus OH 43209-2231

LONG, SARAH S., pediatrician; b. Portland, Oreg., Oct. 31, 1944. MD, Jefferson Med. Coll., 1970. Intern St. Christopher Hosp. for Children, Phila., 1970-71, resident, 1971-73; fellow pediatric and infant depts. Temple U. Sch. Medicine, Phila., 1973-75; staff St. Christopher Hosp. for Children, Phila., 1975—; prof. Temple U. Sch. Medicine, 1975—; Diplomate Am. Bd. Pediatrics. Office: St Christopher Child Hosp Erie Ave at Front St Philadelphia PA 19134*

LONG, SHARON RUGEL, molecular biologist, plant biology educator; b. San Marcos, Tex., Mar. 2, 1951; d. Harold Eugene and Florence Jean (Rugel) Long; m. Harold James McGee, July 7, 1979; 2 children. BS, Calif. Inst. Tech., 1973; PhD, Yale U., 1979. Rsch. fellow Harvard U., Cambridge, Mass., 1979-81; asst. prof. molecular biology Stanford U., Palo Alto, Calif., 1982-87, assoc. prof., 1987-92, prof., 1992—; investigator Howard Hughes Med. Inst., 1994—; bd. dirs. Ann. Revs. Inc. Assoc. editor (jour.) Plant Physiology, 1992—; editor Jour. Bacteriology; mem. editl. bd. Devel. Biology; editl. com. Ann. Review Cell Biology. Recipient postdoctoral award NSF, 1979, NIH, 1980, Shell Rsch. Found. award 1985, Presdl. Young Investigator award NSF, 1984-89, Faculty awards for women, 1991; rsch. grantee NIH, Dept. Energy, NSF; MacArthur fellow, 1992-97. Fellow AAAS, Am. Acad. Arts and Scis., Am. Acad. Microbiology; mem. NAS, Genetics Soc. Am., Am. Soc. Plant Physiology (Charles Albert Shull award 1989), Am. Soc. Microbiology, Soc. Devel. Biology. Office: Stanford U Dept Biol Scis Stanford CA 94305-5020

LONG, SHELLEY, actress; b. Fort Wayne, Ind., Aug. 23, 1949; m. Bruce Tyson; 1 child, Juliana. Student, Northwestern U. Writer, assoc. prodr., co-host Chgo. TV program Sorting It Out, 1970s (3 local Emmys 1970); mem. Second City, Chgo.; guest TV appearances various shows including M.A.S.H., Love Boat, Family; regular TV series Cheers, 1982-87, Good Advice, 1993-94; motion pictures include A Small Circle of Friends, 1980, Caveman, 1981, Night Shift, 1982, Losin' It, 1983, Irreconcilable Differences, 1984, The Money Pit, 1986, Outrageous Fortune, 1987, Hello Again, 1987, Troop Beverly Hills, 1989, Don't Tell Her It's Me, 1990, Frozen Assets, 1992, The Brady Bunch Movie, 1995; TV films include The Cracker Factory, 1979, The Promise of Love, 1980, The Princess and the Cabbie, 1981, Memory of a Murder, 1992, A Message from Holly, 1992, The Women of Spring Break, 1995; TV mini-series, Voices Within: The Lives of Trudy Chase, 1990. Recipient Emmy award Outstanding Actress in a Comedy Series for Cheers, 1983. Office: Creative Artists Agy Ron Meyer 9830 Wilshire Blvd Beverly Hills CA 90212-1804*

LONG, THAD GLADDEN, lawyer; b. Dothan, Ala., Mar. 9, 1938; s. Lindon Alexander and Della Gladys (Pilcher) L.; m. Carolyn Wilson, Aug. 13, 1966; children: Louisa Frances, Wilson Alexander. AB, Columbia U., 1960; JD, U. Va., 1963. Bar: Ala. 1963, U.S. Dist. Ct. (no. dist., so. dist., mid. dist.) Ala., U.S. Ct. Appeals (11th cir., 5th cir.), U.S. Supreme Ct. Assoc. atty. Bradley, Arant, Rose & White, Birmingham, Ala., 1963-70; ptnr. Bradley, Arant, Rose & White, Birmingham, 1970—; adj. prof. U. Ala., Tuscaloosa, 1988—. Co-author: Unfair Competition Under Alabama Law, 1990, Protecting Intellectual Property, 1990; mem. editl. bd. The Trademark Reporter; contbr. articles to profl. jours. chmn. Columbia U. Secondary Schs. Com. Ala. Area, 1975—, Greater Birmingham Arts Alliance, 1977-79; trustee, treas. Birmingham Music Club; trustee Oscar Wells Trust for Mus. Art, Birmingham, 1983—, Canterbury Meth. Found., 1993—, sec., 1993—; chmn. Entrepreneurship Inst. Birmingham, 1989; vice chmn., trustee Sons Revolution Found., Ala., 1994—; pres. Birmingham-Jefferson Hist. Soc., 1995—; trustee Birmingham Music Club Endowment, 1995—; mem. Birmingham Com. Fgn. Rels. Mem. U.S. Patent Bar, Internat. Trademark Assn., Ala. Law Inst., Birmingham Legal Aid Soc., Ala. Bar Assn. (chmn., founder bus. torts and antitrust sect.), U. Va. Law Alumni (chmn. Birmingham chpt. 1984-89), S.R. (pres. 1994-95), Gen. Soc. S.R. (gen. solicitor 1994—), Am. Arbitration Assn., Order of the Coif, Omicron Delta Kappa. Republican. Methodist. Avocations: travel, writing, table tennis. Home: 2880 Balmoral Rd Birmingham AL 35223-1236 Office: Bradley Arant Rose & White 1400 Park Pl Tower Birmingham AL 35203

LONG, THOMAS LESLIE, lawyer; b. Mansfield, Ohio, May 30, 1951; s. Ralph Waldo and Rose Ann (Cloud) L.; m. Peggy L. Bryant, Apr. 24, 1982. AB in Govt., U. Notre Dame, 1973; JD, Ohio State U., 1976. Bar: Ohio 1976, U.S. Dist. Ct. (so. dist.) Ohio 1976, U.S. Dist. Ct. (no. dist.) Ohio 1977, U.S. Ct. Appeals (6th cir.) 1978. Assoc. Alexander, Ebinger, Fisher, McAlister & Lawrence, Columbus, Ohio, 1976-82, ptnr., 1982-85; ptnr. Baker & Hostetler, Columbus, 1985—. Mem. ABA, Ohio Bar Assn., Columbus Bar Assn., Fed. Bar Assn., Assn. Trial Lawyer Am. Democrat. Roman Catholic. Club: Capitol (Columbus). Home: 2565 Leeds Rd Columbus OH 43221-3613 Office: Baker & Hostetler 65 E State St Columbus OH 43215-4213

LONG, THOMAS MICHAEL, investment banker; b. Tulsa, June 30, 1943; s. Thomas Marvin Long and Marcia Acosta; m. Catherine Howell, Dec. 30, 1964; children: Jane Alexander, Hampton Howell. B.A. in Govt. cum laude, Harvard U., 1965; M.B.A. with distinction, Harvard U., Boston, 1971. Dir., Ohio Plan Ohio U., Athens, 1966-68; with Boston Cons. Group, 1968-69; ptnr. Brown Bros. Harriman & Co., pvt. bankers, N.Y.C., 1971—; co-mgr. 1818 Fund, L.P., 1818 Fund II, L.P., 1989—; bd. dirs. Nuevo Energy Co., Houston, Winrock Enterprises, Little Rock, Columbia/HCA Healthcare, Inc., Nashville, The Ekco Group, Nashua, N.H., Gulf Can. Resources, Ltd., Calgary, Govt. Property Investors, Inc., Washington. Contbr. articles on mergers and acquisitions and banking industry consolidation to Am. Banker, Bankers Mag., Investment Dealers Digest. Trustee Greenwich Country Day Sch., 1987-92, The Healthcare Chaplaincy, Inc., N.Y.C., 1992—. Corning Glass traveling fellow Harvard U., 1965-66. Mem. Knickerbocker Club (N.Y.C.), India House Club (N.Y.C.), Country Club Little Rock. Democrat. Roman Catholic. Home: 3 Old Mill Rd Greenwich CT 06830-3342 Office: Brown Bros Harriman & Co 59 Wall St New York NY 10005-2818

LONG, TIMOTHY SCOTT, chemist, consultant; b. Racine, Wis., Dec. 20, 1937; s. Leslie Alexander and Esther (Sand) L.; m. Karen M. Koniarski, July 13, 1985; children by previous marriage: Corinne, Christine. BS in Chemistry, Winona State U., 1975. Staff chemist IBM, Rochester, Minn., 1962-77; adv. chemist IBM, Harrison, N.Y., 1977-80, IBM Instruments, Inc., Danbury, Conn., 1980-81; mgr. Midwest Instrument Ctr. IBM Instruments, Inc., Chgo., 1981-85; mgr. corp. environ. engring. IBM, Stamford, Conn., 1985-89; industry cons. IBM, White Plains, N.Y., 1989-92; environ. cons. Geraghty & Miller, Inc., Rochelle Park, N.J., 1992-94, Indpls., 1994—; mem. World Environ. Ctr., N.Y.C., 1985-89; adv. bd. Coop. Ctr. Rsch. in Hazardous and Toxic Substances, Newark, 1985-89. Autohr: Testing for Prediction of Material Performance, 1972, Methods for Emissions Spectrochemical Analysis, 1977, 2d edit., 1982; contbr. articles to Applied Spectroscopy, Plating, Polymer Engring. and Sci. Mem. ASTM (com. emission spectroscopy), Soc. Applied Spectroscopy (chmn. Minn. sect. 1976-77), Assn. Am. Indian Affairs, Soc. Plastics Engrs. (bd. reviewers 1975-76). Achievements include demonstration of world's first application using ion chromatography in the analysis of indsl. waste water. Home: 559 E Lord St Indianapolis IN 46202

LONG, TOM, manufacturing company executive; b. Charleston, W.Va., Apr. 19, 1932; s. Mary (Saunders) Nielsen; m. Delores Faye Holt, Aug. 6, 1954; children: Gary, Tom Jr., Debra, Rex. BSEE, U. Dayton, 1965, MBA, 1967; grad. advanced mgmt. program, Harvard U., 1985. Field engr. Tektronix Inc., Chgo., 1960-61, Dayton, Ohio, 1961-67; mktg. mgr. Beaverton, Oreg., 1967-71, engring. mgr.-gen. instruments, 1971-74, div. gen. mgr., 1973-74, v.p., gen. mgr. communications group, 1981-83, v.p., gen. mgr. design automation group, 1984-87, v.p., gen. mgr. tech. group, 1988-91; ret. Tektronix Inc., Chgo., 1991; pres. Grass Valley (Calif.) Group, 1974-81; exec. v.p. Analogic, Peabody, Mass., 1983-84; trustee Tektronix Found., Beaverton, 1985-91; pres. Tektronix Devel. Co., Beaverton, 1984-91; chmn., chief exec. officer TriQuint Semicondr. Inc., Beaverton, 1985-91; dir. of programs Planar Advance Inc., Beaverton, 1994—; bd. dirs. Novellus Systems, San Jose, Calif. Served to staff sgt. USAF, 1950-54. Mem. Soc. Motion Picture and TV Engrs. Republican. Avocations: racquetball, volleyball. Office: Planar Advance Inc 13950 SW Karl Braun Dr PO Box 4001 Beaverton OR 97076-4001

LONG, WALTER EDWARD, international trade company executive, consultant; b. Little Rock, Nov. 11, 1935; s. James Edward and Daisy Mae (Cooper) L. BA summa cum laude, Philander Smith Coll., 1957; MA in Psychology, U. Pa., 1960. Mgr. indsl. and psychol. testing Richton Co. Inc., Newark, 1960-63; pres. Best Resume Co., Inc., N.Y.C., 1963-65; pres., chief exec. officer PHAT Advt. Cons., Inc., N.Y.C., 1965-74; chmn. Nubian Internationale, Ltd. PHAT Advt. Cons., Inc., 1973-78; sr. v.p. internat. trade Daniels & Cartwright, Inc., 1978-80; pres., chief exec. officer Epic Internat. Trade, Ltd., 1980—, Am. Gas & Energy Corp., 1988—; v.p. internat. trade Swiss Bullion Internat. Corp., 1988-91; CEO GlobalArk Internat. Trade Ltd., Little Rock, 1991—; pres. Walter Long Assocs., 1991—; v.p. internat. trade World Trade Ctr., Memphis, 1993-94; spl. trade and fin. devel. cons., Namabia, S. Africa, 1993—; sr. cons./coord. World Econ. Developers Unlimited, N.Y.C., 1995—; dir. Pepsi-Cola, Mali, West Africa, 1995—; bd. dirs. Harlem br. N.Y. Urban Coalition, N.Y.C., 1972-74; condr. internat. trade seminars Queens (N.Y.) Coll., 1968. With U.S. Army, 1958-60. N.Y. Film Inst. grantee, 1973. Mem. Am. Psychol. Assn., Masons. Democrat. African Methodist Episcopalian. Avocations: golf, chess, writing, video-sound buff, travel. Office: GlobalArk Internat Trade 7500 Azalea Dr Little Rock AR 72209-4417

LONG, WILLIAM ALLAN, retired forest products company executive; b. Columbus, Ohio, Aug. 25, 1928; s. Allan C. and Dorothy (Crates) L.; m. Ann Cors, Aug. 27, 1954; children: Leslie, David, Steven, Jeffrey. B.A., Ohio Wesleyan U., 1951. Vice pres. Diamond Internat., N.Y.C., 1951-70; exec. v.p. Overhead Door Corp., Dallas, 1970-75; v.p. St. Regis Paper Co., N.Y.C., 1975-79; group v.p. Inland Container Corp., Indpls., 1979-93; ret., 1993. Sgt. U.S. Army, 1946-47. Republican. Presbyterian. Home: 5010 Plantation Dr Indianapolis IN 46250-1639

LONG, WILLIAM D., retail company executive; b. Watertown, Wis., Nov. 30, 1937; s. William D. and Olive (Piper) L.; m. Doreen Loveall, Sept. 23, 1967; children—Angela, Scott, Irene, Jeffrey, William, Jennifer. Student U. Wis.-Madison. Store mgr. Safeway, Salt Lake City, 1961-68; pres., chief exec. officer Waremart Inc., Boise, Idaho, 1968—. Served to cpl. U.S. Army, 1957-60. Office: Waremart Inc PO Box 5756 Boise ID 83705-0756*

LONG, WILLIAM EVERETT, retired utility executive; b. Oklahoma City, Sept. 3, 1919; s. William Everett and Hazel Kathleen (Stafford) L.; m. Frances Jeanne Baum, Aug. 7, 1942; children: Susan Jeanne, Nancy Lee. Student, U. Colo., 1937-39, Northwestern U., 1940. With Houston Natural Gas Corp., 1949-84, sr. v.p., gen. mgr. distbn. div., 1971-78, sr. v.p., chief adminstrv. officer, 1981-84. Served with USAAF, 1941-46; Served with USAF, 1951-53; mem. Res. (ret.). Mem. Christian Ch. (Disciples of Christ). Clubs: Lakeside Country, Masons. Home: 9585 Longmont Dr Houston TX 77063-1026 *I am blessed with parents who, when I was a youth, instilled in me a good sense of social, moral and civic values. They prepared me to seek opportunity, accept responsibility and respect my fellow man.*

LONG, WILLIAM JOSEPH, software engineer; b. Kokomo, Ind., Feb. 1, 1956; s. George Alexander and Rebecca Bethina (Burgan) L. BA, Harvard U., 1979; cert. in project mgmt., U. Calif., Berkeley, 1994. Cons. Bechtel Corp., San Francisco, 1982-85; assoc. prof. Dalian (Liaoning, China) Inst. Tech., 1985-86; software engr. Bechtel Corp., San Francisco, 1986-92; EDI project mgr. Pacific Gas & Electric Co., San Francisco, 1992-94; software engr. Am. Pres. Lines, Oakland, Calif., 1994-95; mem. adv. bd. Synetics, Inc., San Francisco, 1987—; owner William J. Long and Assocs., Oakland, Calif., 1990—. Vol. English tutor, Oakland, Calif., 1983—. Rsch. grantee Smithsonian Astrophys. Obs., Cambridge, Mass., 1976. Mem. IEEE, Assn. Computing Machinery, Am. Assn. Artificial Intelligence, Math. Assn. Am. Avocations: languages, photography, playing hammer dulcimer, running, jogging. Home and Office: William J Long and Assocs 2225 7th Ave #33 Oakland CA 94606-1969

LONG, WILLIS FRANKLIN, electrical engineering educator, researcher; b. Lima, Ohio, Jan. 30, 1934; s. Jesse Raymond and Cerelda Elizabeth (Stepleton) L.; m. Ginger Carol Miller; children: Andrew Mark, Kristin Kay, David Franklin. BS in Engring. Physics, U. Toledo, 1957, MSEE, 1962; PhD, U. Wis., 1970. Registered profl. engr., Wis. Project engr. Doehler Jarvis div. Nat. Lead Co., Toledo, Ohio, 1957, 59-60; instr. U. Toledo, 1962-66; mem. tech. staff Hughes Rsch. Labs., Malibu, Calif., 1969-73; asst., then assoc. prof. depts. extension engring. and elec. engring. U. Wis., Madison, 1973-80, prof., chair dept. extension engring., 1980-83, prof. depts. engring., profl devel. and elec. and computer engring., 1985—; dir. ASEA Power System Ctr., New Berlin, Wis., 1983-85; prin. Long Assocs., Madison, 1973—; cons. Dept. Energy, Washington, 1978—, ABB Power Systems, Raleigh, N.C., 1985—. Editor EMTP Rev., 1987-91; contbr. articles to profl. jours.; patentee power switching. Mem. adv. com. energy conservation Wis. Dept. Labor, Industry and Human Rels., Maidson, 1976-77; chmn. Wis. chpt. Sierra Club, 1977; pres. bd. dirs. Madison Urban Ministries, 1993-95. 2d lt. Signal Corps., U.S. Army, 1958. Recipient Disting. Engring. Alumnus award U. Toledo, 1983, award of excellence U. Wis.-Extension, 1987; Sci. Faculty fellow NSF, 1966. Fellow IEEE (Meritorious Achievement in Continuing Edn. award 1991); mem. Internat. Conf. on Large High Voltage Electric Systems (expert advisor 1979—). Mem. United Ch. of Christ. Avocation: canoeing. Home: 1444 E Skyline Dr Madison WI 53705-1133 Office: U Wis 432 N Lake St Madison WI 53706-1415

LONGAKER, NANCY, elementary school principal. Prin. Tualatin (Oreg.) Elem. Sch. Recipient Elem. Sch. Recognition award U.S. Dept. Edn., 1989-90. Office: Tualatin Elem Sch 19945 SW Boones Ferry Rd Tualatin OR 97062-9005

LONGAKER, RICHARD PANCOAST, political science educator emeritus; b. Phila., July 1, 1924; s. Edwin P. and Emily (Downs) L.; m. Mollie M. Katz, Jan. 25, 1964; children—Richard Pancoast II, Stephen Edwin, Sarah Ellen, Rachel Elise. B.A. in Polit. Sci, Swarthmore Coll., 1949; M.A. in Am. History, U. Wis., 1950; Ph.D. in Govt, Cornell U., 1953. Teaching asst. Cornell U., 1950-53, vis. asso. prof., 1960-61; asst. prof. Kenyon Coll., 1953-54, asso. prof., 1955-60; asst. prof. U. Calif., Riverside, 1954-55; faculty U. Calif., Los Angeles, 1961-76, chmn. dept. polit. sci., 1963-67, prof., 1965-76, dean acad. affairs grad. div., 1970-71; prof. Johns Hopkins U., Balt., 1976-87, provost and v.p. for acad. affairs, 1976-87; prof. emeritus, cons. western states office Johns Hopkins U., Santa Monica, Calif., 1987—. Author: The Presidency and Individual Liberties, 1961; co-author: The Supreme Court and the Commander in Chief, 1976, also articles, revs. Served with AUS, 1943-45. Mem. Am. Polit. Sci. Assn. Office: 16550 Chalet Ter Pacific Palisades CA 90272-2344

LONGAN, GEORGE BAKER, III, real estate executive; b. Kansas City, Mo., Apr. 20, 1934; s. Benjamin Hyde and Georgette Longan O'Brien; divorced; 1 child, Nancy Ann Longan LaPoff. BSBA, U. Ariz., 1956; post-grad., U. Kans., 1956-57. Cert. real estate broker. Sr. v.p., gen. mgr. Paul Hamilton Co., Kansas City, 1963-84; pres. Eugene D. Brown Co., Kansas City, 1984-93; v.p. J.C. Nichols Real Estate, 1993-94; bd. dirs. Genesis Relocation Network, N.J. Served to staff sgt. USAF, 1958-62. Mem. Nat. Real Estate Assn. (bd. dirs. 1991-94), Mo. Real Estate Assn. (bd. dirs. 1987-90), Real Estate Bd. Kansas City (bd. dirs. 1987-90), Met. Kansas City Real Estate Bd. (pres. 1992), Beta Sigma Psi, Sigma Chi. Episcopal. Avocations: antique collecting, tennis. Home: 2701 E Camino Pablo Tucson AZ 85718-6625 Office: Long Realty Co 5683 N Swan Tucson AZ 85718

LONGANECKER, DAVID A., federal official. BA in Sociology, Wash. State U., 1968; MA in Student Personnel Work, George Washington U., 1971; EdD in Adminstrn. and Policy Analysis in Higher Edn., Stanford U., 1978. With student affairs and residence life dept. George Washington U., Washington; with Congl. Budget Office, Washington, 1977-81; with Minn. Higher Edn. Coordinating Bd., 1981-84, exec. dir., 1984-88; exec. dir., exec. dir. dept. higher edn., officer Gov. Roy Romer's cabinet Colo. Commn. Higher Edn., 1988-93; asst. sec. postsecondary edn. U.S. Dept. Edn., Washington, 1993—; past. pres. State Higher Edn. Exec. Officers orgn.; commr. We. Interstate Commn. Higher Edn.; mem. postsecondary edn. and tng. for workplace com. Nat. Acad. Scis., commn. on edn. credit and credentials Am. Coun. Edn.; mem. various bds. and comns. including Exec. Com. Minority Edn. Coalition Colo., Gov.'s Commn. Families and Children, Math.,

Sci. and Tech. Commn. Office: Dept Edn Post Secondary Edn Office 7th and D Sts SW Washington DC 20202-5100*

LONGBRAKE, WILLIAM ARTHUR, bank executive; b. Hershey, Pa., Mar. 15, 1943; s. William Van Fleet and Margaret Jane (Barr) L.; m. Martha Ann Curtis, Aug. 23, 1970; children: Derek Curtis, Mark William, David Robert, Dorothy Eleanor Lois. BA, Coll. of Wooster, 1965; MA, U. Wis., 1968, MBA, 1969; D. Bus. Adminstrn., U. Md., 1976. Jr. asst. planner Northeastern Ill. Planning Commn., Chgo., 1966; instr. Coll. Bus. and Mgmt., U. Md., 1969-71, lectr., 1976, 79-81; fin. economist FDIC, Washington, 1971-75, sr. planning specialist Office Corp. Planning, 1975-76, spl. asst. to chmn., acting contr., 1977-78; assoc. dir. div. banking rsch. Office Compt. of Currency, Treasury Dept., Washington, 1976, dep. dir. econ. rsch. and analysis div., 1976-77; dep. compt. for rsch. and econ. programs, 1978-81, acting sr. dep. compt. for policy, 1981-82, sr. dep. compt. for resource mgmt., 1982; exec. v.p., chief fin. officer Wash. Mut. Savs. Bank, Seattle, 1982-85; exec. v.p. finance and ops., 1985-86, sr. exec. v.p., 1986-88, sr. exec. v.p., chief fin. officer, 1988—, dir. Abarim Bus. Computers Inc., 1993—; WM Trust Co., 1989-93, WM Life Co., 1994—; trustee Washington Mutual Savings Bank Found., 1982—; small bus. cons. Mem. College Park (Md.) Citizen's Adv. Com. on Code Enforcement, 1973-74, cons., 1975; lectr. Albers Sch. Bus. Seattle U., 1985, student mentor, 1994—; bd. dirs. Puget Sound Coun. Fin. Insts., Seattle, dir. 1986-90, v.p., 1988, pres., 1989-90; mem. Seattle Mcpl. League, 1986—; treas., 1988-90, pres. 1990-93, mem. exec. com., chmn. fin. and pers. com. 1988—, devel. com., 1992—, bus. planning com., 1992-93, strategic planning com., 1993—, Capitol Hill Housing Improvement Program, Seattle, 1988—; mem. The King County Housing Partnership, Seattle, 1988—, exec. com., 1989—, chmn. outreach and tech. assistance com., 1990-92; bd. visitors Sch. Nursing U. Washington, 1991—; mem. adv. com. Ctr. for the Study of Banking and Fin. Markets U. Wash., Seattle, 1983-92, chmn., 1986-90; mem. of local initiative support corp. Seattle/Tacoma Adv. Bd., 1989-91; bd. dirs. Diabetes Rsch. Coun., Seattle, 1984-89, v.p., 1987-88; bd. dirs. N.W. Symphony Orch., Seattle, 1987-89, treas. 1988-89, adv. bd. 1989—; trustee Kenney Presbyn. Home, West Seattle, 1987—, treas., 1988—, exec. com., chmn. fin. com.; trustee Intiman Theatre Co., Seattle, 1988-92; chmn. tax com. Wash. Savs. League, 1987—, legis. regulatory com. 1991—; mem. Seattle Comprehensive Plan Implementation Task Force, 1993-94; chmn. adv. bd. Wash. State Affordable Housing, 1993—; dir. Nat. Assn. Housing Partnerships, 1993—; mem. King County Growth Mgmt., planning coun. affordable housing task force, 1992-93; co-chair Gov.'s Task Force on Affordable Housing, Washington, 1992-93, chmn. bd. dirs. Threshold Housing, 1992—; mem. Impact Fees commn., 1991-92, Coun. Washington's Future, arrangement's chair, 1988-91; devel. bd. Musicomedy Northwestm 1983-84, trustee 1984; mem. U.S. Soccer Fedn., referee Seattle Youth Soccer Assn., 1982—; dir., sec. Presbyn. Pub. Corp., 1993—. Recipient Kenneth E. Trefftz prize Western Fin. Assn., 1971, cert. of recognition William A. Jump Meml. Found., 1978. Mem. Am. Econs. Assn., Am. Fin. Assn., Fin. Mgmt. Assn. (dir. 1978-80), Fin. Execs. Inst. (Puget Sound chpt., bd. dirs. 1988—, chmn. acad. rels. com. 1988-89, chmn. tech. com. 1989-90, treas. 1990-91, v.p. 1991-93, pres. 1993-94, chmn. nominating com. 1994—), Coll. of Wooster Alumni Assn. (pres. Washington Alumni Assn. 1976, pres. Seattle Alumni Assn. 1983—, trustee 1988—, mem. fin., audit, religious dimension, student rels. com. alumni bd. 1988—), Columbia Tower Club. Presbyn. (trustee 1973-75, chmn. 1975, elder, 1979-82, clk. 1980-82, deacon 1985-88, treas. 1993—). Assoc. editor Fin. Mgmt., 1974-78; mem. editorial adv. bd. Issues in Bank Regulation, 1977-84, Jour. Econs. and Bus., 1980-83; contbr. articles to profl. jours. Mem. Nat. Coun. Savings Instns., (mortgage fin. com. 1989). Avocations: jogging, painting, si39 18th Ave E Seattle WA 98112-3929 Office: Wash Mut Savs Bank PO Box 834 1201 3rd Ave Seattle WA 98101 Office: FDIC Bd of Dirs 550 17th St NW Washington DC 20429*

LONGENECKER, HERBERT EUGENE, biochemist, former university president; b. Lititz, Pa., May 6, 1912; s. Abraham S. and Mary Ellen (Herr) L.; m. Marjorie Jane Segar, June 18, 1936; children: Herbert Eugene, Marjorie Segar Longenecker White, Geoffrey Herr, Stanton Lee. B.S., Pa. State U., 1933, M.S., 1934, Ph.D., 1936; D.Sc., Duquesne U., 1951; LL.D., Loyola U., 1962; Litt.D., U. Miami, 1972; D.Sc., U. Ill., 1976, Loyola U. of South, 1976. Instr. biochemistry Pa. State U., 1935-36; NRC fellow univs. Liverpool (Eng.), Cologne (Germany), Queen's, Kingston, Can., 1936-38; sr. research fellow and lectr. in chemistry U. Pitts., 1938-41, asst. research prof. chemistry, 1941-42; prof. chemistry and dir. Buhl Found. Research Project, 1942-44; dean research in natural scis. U. Pitts., 1944-55; dean U. Pitts. (Grad. Sch.), 1946-55; v.p. U. Ill. Med. Center, 1955-60; pres. Tulane U., 1960-75, pres. emeritus, 1975—; mng. dir. World Trade Ctr., New Orleans, 1976-79; dir. Equitable Life Ins. Soc. U.S., 1968-84, cons. dir., 1984-92; dir. CPC Internat., 1966-85; mem. food and nutrition bd. NRC, 1943-53, chmn. com. on food protection, 1948-53; mem. com. on chem. warfare R & D Bd., 1949-53; mem. rsch. coun. Chem. Corps. Adv. Bd., 1949-65; pres. Nat. Commn. on Accrediting, 1964-66; mem. coun. Nat. Inst. Gen. Med. Scis., 1963-66; mem. site selection panel for high energy accelerators NAS, 1964-66; mem. nat. selection com. Fulbright Student awards, 1953-55; chmn. West Europe sect. Fulbright Student Awards, 1954-55; mem. coun. Nat. Inst. Environ. Health Scis., 1970-71; mem. panel on sci. and tech. Ho. of Reps. Com. on Sci. and Astronautics, 1970-76; mem. adv. panel on ROTC affairs Office Sec. Def., 1961-75, chmn., 1968-75; mem. Commn. on Pvt. Philanthropy and Pub. Needs, 1973-77. Pres. Pitts. Housing Assn., 1948-51; bd. govs. Inst. Medicine Chgo., 1957-60; trustee Council of So. Univs., 1960-75, pres., 1964-65; pres. Univs. Research Assn., 1971-72; trustee Inst. Def. Analyses, 1959-88, vice chmn., 1984-88; chmn. acad. adv. bd. U.S. Naval Acad., 1966-72; trustee Nat. Med. Fellowships, Inc., 1965-72; bd. dirs. Council Fin. Aid to Edn., 1964-71; trustee Inst. Service to Edn., Inc., 1965-71; trustee Am. Univs. Field Staff, 1960-74, pres., 1962-63; sec.-treas. Assn. Am. Univs., 1969-72, pres., 1972-73; trustee S.W. Research Inst., 1960-69; bd. dirs. World Trade Ctr., New Orleans, 1961—, Nat. Merit Scholarship Corp., 1969-75; trustee Sloan Found., 1970-84, Inst. for Future, 1975-76, La. Expo, Inc., 1976-82, United Student Aid Funds, 1971-85, Pacific Tropical Bot. Garden, 1974-77, Council of the Ams., 1976-79; trustee Nutrition Found., 1961-85, chmn., 1965-72; mem. bd. Indian Springs Sch., 1987-88. Recipient Army and Navy Cert. for service during World War II, USN Disting. Pub. Service award; Disting. Alumni award Pa. State U., 1960; Papal award Bene Merenti, 1977. Fellow Am. Public Health Assn., Am. Inst. Nutrition, Am. Inst. Chemists; mem. Am. Chem. Soc. (chmn. Pitts. sect. 1946-47), Am. Soc. Biol. Chemists, Am. Council Edn. (chmn. commn. on fed. relations 1963-65, coordinating com. 1972-74), Am. Oil Chemists Soc. (v.p. 1946-47), Nat. League Nursing, Sigma Xi (exec. com. 1965-70, pres. 1980-81), Phi Delta Kappa, Sigma Pi. Club: Boston (New Orleans). Home: 2717 Highland Ave S Apt 1002 Birmingham AL 35205-1730

LONGENECKER, MARK HERSHEY, JR., lawyer; b. Akron, Ohio, Feb. 16, 1951; s. Mark Hershey and Katrina (Hetzner) L.; m. Ruth Rounding, June 17, 1978; children: Emily Irene, Mark Hershey III. BA, Denison U., 1973; JD, Harvard U., 1976. Bar: Ill. 1976, Ohio 1979. Atty. Lord, Bissell & Brook, Chgo., 1976-79; ptnr. Frost & Jacobs, Cin., 1979—. Bd. govs. Ohio Fair Plan Underwriting Assn., Columbus, 1989-92; dir. Seven Hills Neighborhood Houses, Cin., 1990—. Mem. Cin. Country Club, Queen City Club, Gyro Club, Harvard Club (Cin. pres. 1993-94). Office: Frost & Jacobs 2500 PNC Ct 201 E 5th St Cincinnati OH 45202-4117

LONGEST, BEAUFORT BROWN, health services administration educator, research director; b. Rose Hill, N.C., Oct. 22, 1942; s. Beaufort Brown and Mary (Faircloth) L.; m. Carolyn Hepler, Jan 23, 1965; children: Brant, Courtland. BS, Davidson Coll., 1965; MHA, Ga. State U., 1969, PhD in Bus. Adminstrn., 1972. Instr. health adminstrn. Coll. Bus. Adminstrn., Ga. State U., 1969-72, asst. prof. health adminstrn., 1972-75; clin. asst. prof. preventive medicine and community health Sch. Medicine, Emory U., 1974-75; asst. prof. hosp. and health svcs. mgmt. J.L. Kellogg Grad. Sch. Mgmt., Northwestern U., 1975-78, faculty assoc. Ctr. Health Svcs. and Policy Rsch., 1978-79, assoc. prof. hosp. and health svcs. mgmt., 1979; prof. health svcs. adminstrn. Grad. Sch. Pub. Health and Joseph M. Katz Grad. Sch. Bus., U. Pitts., 1980—, prof. bus. adminstrn., 1987—, dir. Health Policy Inst., 1980—, dir. Health Adminstrn. Program, 1984-91, faculty assoc. Ctr. Med. Ethics, 1987—; lectr. in field, 1976—; condr. seminars including Am. Assn. Clin. Chemists, Am. Soc. Woman Accts., Am. Soc. Med. Tech., Ga. Hosp. Assn., Hosp. Assn. Pa., Gov.'s Policy Group, Pa., Ohio Hosp. Assn., Ontario Hosp. Assn., VA., many others; mem. coms. U. Pitts.; dir. Midland-Colt Retiree Med. Plan, Media Info. Svc. Adv. Bd., Biomed. Tech. Devel. Corp. Adv. Bd.; cons. Am. Soc. Med. Tech., 1972-74, Fetter Family Health Ctr., Charleston, S.C., 1974-75, Hosp. Fin. Mgmt. Assn., 1974-75, Am. Acad. Pediatrics, 1977, DuPage County Health Systems Agy., 1978, Health Care Fin. Adminstrn., 1989, U.S. Agy. Internat. Devel., Kingston, Jamaica, Gov.'s Policy Group, Pa., 1989, Sec. Health, Pa., 1990-91, Mfrs. Assn. Northwest Pa., 1992, Pan Am. Health Orgn., 1992. Author: Principles of Hospital Business Office Management, 1975, Management Practices for the Health Professional, 1976, 4th edit., 1990, (with others) Hospital Cost Containment Programs, A Policy Analysis, 1978, (with J.S. Rakich and T.R. O'Donovan) Managing Health Care Organizations, 1977, (with J.S. Rakich and K. Darr) Cases in Health Services Management, 1983, 3d edit., 1992, Managing Health Services Organizations, 2d edit., 1985; contbr. numerous articles, book chpts. papers to anthologies, profl. jours.; author rsch. monograph; book reviewer in field; editorial cons. Harper and Row, Inc., Health Professions Press, Little, Brown Pub. Co., Nat. Health Pub., Reston Pub. Co., Inc., W.B. Saunders Co. Dir. The Grove Sch., 1978-80; Hosp. Utilization Project, 1985-87; mem. adv. bd. work-study program minority students Chgo. Hosp. Coun., 1978-79, rsch. adv. com. Hosp. Utilization Project, 1982-83, steering com. Pitts. Program Affordable Health Care, 1984-88, com. health policy and planning Hosp. Coun. Western Pa., 1986—, health care and human svcs. Task Force, Leadership Pitts., 1985, 87, community problem solving com. United Way Allegheny County, 1986-89, chmn. community problem solving com. on frail elderly and disabled, 1989-92, mem. resource panel health and human svcs. Allegheny County 2001 Project, 1992, steering com. HSR&D devel. grant VA Med. Ctr., 1992-93; external examiner U. West Indies, Kingston, Jamaica, 1985-89. W.K. Kellogg Found. fellow, 1977-78. Fellow Am. Coll. Healthcare Execs. (ad hoc com. univ. program faculty 1982, regent's advisor 1985-89, com. book of yr. 1985-88, chmn. com. book of yr. 1988, com. awards and testimonials 1988, membership com. subcom. recruitement 1991-92, chmn. membership com. subcom. recruitement 1991-92); mem. Acad. Mgmt. (1st place rsch proposal award 1976), Am. Hosp. Assn., Am. Pub. Health Assn., Assn. Health Svcs. Rsch., Assn. Pub. Policy Analysis and Mgmt., Assn. Univ. Programs Health Adminstrn. (nom. com. bd. dirs. 1987, 88, adv. panel clin. edn. health adminstrn. 1986), Beta Gamma Sigma. Avocation: gardening. Office: U Pitts Health Pol Inst Grad Sch Pub Health 130 Desoto St Pittsburgh PA 15213-2535

LONGFELLOW, LAYNE ALLEN, author, lecturer; b. Jackson, Ohio, Oct. 23, 1937; s. Hershel Herman and Opal Edna (Pursley) L. BA in Psychology magna cum laude with honors, Ohio U., 1959; MA, U. Mich., 1961, PhD, 1967. Asst. prof. psychology Reed Coll., Portland, Oreg., 1967-68; postdoctoral fellow Dr. Carl Rogers, La Jolla, Calif., 1968-70; asst. prof. psychology Prescott (Ariz.) Coll., 1970-71, chmn. dept., 1971-72, acad. v.p., 1972-74; dir. exec. seminars Menninger Found., Topeka, 1975-78; dir. wilderness exec. seminars Banff Ctr., Alta., Can., 1978-86; pres. Lecture Theatre, Inc., Prescott, Ariz., 1981—; dir. Inst. for Human Skills, 1985—; internat. lectr., cons. in field; adj. faculty Union Grad. Sch. and Humanistic Psychology Inst., 1974-84. Composer: Ten Songs, 1969, Uncommon Festival of Christmas, 1974; creator Body Talk, 1970, The Feel Wheel, 1972, The Mountain Waits, 1983 (Gold medal N.Y. Festival of TV); video producer, author: Generations of Excellence, 1992, Beyond Success, 1993, Sustainable Growth, 1994, Healty, Wealthy and Wise, 1994; author: (with W.M. Hubbard) Visual Feast, 1995. Active Found. for Ethics and Meaning. Woodrow Wilson fellow, NSF fellow, NIMH fellow. Mem. APA, Nat. Speakers Assn., Nature Conservancy, Phi Beta Kappa. Office: Lecture Theatre Inc PO Box 4317 Prescott AZ 86302-4317 *Through much of life, activity substitutes for meaning. It is the gentler pace of maturity that allows the deepest questions of life to be addressed directly, without the filters of frenzy and ambition.*

LONGFIELD, WILLIAM HERMAN, health care company executive; b. Chgo., Aug. 8, 1938; s. William A. and Elizabeth (Beringer) L.; m. Nancy Shofstall, June 10, 1960; children: William, Scott. BS, Drake U., 1960; grad. bus. mgmt. program, Northwestern U., 1972. Pres. Convertors div. Am. Hosp. Supply, Evanston, Ill., 1961-82; exec. v.p., dir. Lifemark, Inc., Houston, 1982-83; pres., chief exec. officer Cambridge Group, Inc., Dallas, 1983-89; chmn., CEO C.R. Bard, Inc., Murray Hill, N.J., 1989—, also bd. dirs.; bd. dirs. United Dental Care, Dallas, Atlantic Health Sys., Manor Care Inc., Balt., Centenary Coll., Health Industry Mfrs. Assn., The West Co., Pa., Horizon Mental Health Mgmt., Dallas; exec. resident U. Colo., 1980-82; chmn. bd. Internat. Non-Wovens Assn., N.Y.C., 1975-82. Chmn., dir. Deerfield (Ill.) Youth Orgn., 1975-80. Recipient Pres.' award Nat. Nurse Cons. Assn., 1980. Mem. Baltrusol Golf Club, Echo Lake Country Club, Metedecork Country Club. Republican. Presbyterian. Avocations: golf, tennis. Office: C R Bard Inc 730 Central Ave New Providence NJ 07974-1139

LONGHOFER, RONALD STEPHEN, lawyer; b. Junction City, Kans., Aug. 30, 1946; s. Oscar William and Anna Mathilda (Krause) L.; m. Elizabeth Norma McKenna; children: Adam, Nathan, Stefanie. BMus, U. Mich., 1968; JD, 1975. Bar: Mich. 1975, U.S. Dist. Ct. (ea. dist.) Mich., U.S. Ct. Appeals (6th cir.), U.S. Supreme Ct. Law clk. to judge U.S. Dist. Ct. (ea. dist.) Mich., Detroit, 1975-76; ptnr. Honigman, Miller, Schwartz & Cohn, Detroit, 1976—, chmn. litigation dept., 1993-96. Editor Mich. Law Rev., 1974-75. Served with U.S. Army, 1968-72. Mem. ABA, Detroit Bar Assn., Fed. Bar Assn., Detroit Club, Detroit Econ. Club, U. Mich. Pres. Club, Order of Coif, Phi Beta Kappa, Phi Kappa Phi, Pi Kappa Lambda. Home: 46401 W Main St Northville MI 48167-3035 Office: Honigman Miller Schwartz & Cohn 2290 1st National Bldg Detroit MI 48226

LONGIN, THOMAS CHARLES, academic administrator; b. Lewistown, Mont., Nov. 17, 1939; s. Charles Otto and Anne Dorothy (Vavrovsky) L.; m. Nancy Tillinghast; children: Kevin C., Teresa L., Karl T., Anne M. BA in History, Carroll Coll., 1962; MA in History, Creighton U., 1965; PhD in Am. History, U. Nebr., 1970. Instr. Carroll Coll., Helena, Mont., 1965-67; asst. prof. Va. Tech., Blacksburg, 1970-73; asst. prof., then assoc. prof. Ithaca (N.Y.) Coll., 1973-82, dean humanities and scis., 1976-82, provost, 1985—; v.p. acad. affairs Seattle U., 1982-85. Office: Ithaca Coll Office of the Provost 350 Job Hall Ithaca NY 14850-7012

LONGLEY, BERNIQUE, artist, painter, sculptor; b. Moline, Ill., Sept. 27, 1923; d. Eli James and Effie Marie (Coen) Wilderson; 1 child, Bernique Maria Glidden. Grad., Art Inst. Chgo., 1945. One-woman shows at Mus. N.Mex., 1947, 50, 52, Appleman Gallery, Denver, 1950, Van Dieman-Lilienfield Galleries, N.Y.C., 1953, Knopp-Hunter Gallery, Santa Fe, 1954, 57, 58, Gallery Five, Santa Fe, 1964, 65, Coll. Santa Fe, 1967, Sanger-Harris, Dallas, 1968, Lars Laine Gallery, Palm Springs, Calif., 1969, Canyon Rd. Gallery, Santa Fe, 1972, Summer Gallery, Santa Fe, 1973, 74, 75, 76, Cushing Galleries, Dallas, 1977, Gov.'s Gallery, N.Mex. State Capitol, 1978, Santa Fe East, Austin, Tex., 1979, Santa Fe East Gallery, 1985, 86, 88, Leslie Levy Gallery, 1985-86; Artists of Am. exhbn., Denver, 1993-94; group shows include Denver Art Mus., 1948, N.Mex. Highlands U., 1957, Lars Laine Gallery, 1961, 63, Santa Fe Festival of Arts, 1977, 78, 79, 80, Leslie Levy Gallery, Scottsdale, Ariz., 1985-86, Santa Fe East, 1985-86, 88, Invitational Mask Exhbn., Bank of Santa Fe, 1987, Hickory (N.C.) Mus., 1989, Contemporary S.W. Gallery, Santa Fe, 1989-90, Contemporary S.W. Gaallery, Santa Fe, 1989-90, 95—, El Prado Gallery, 1989-94, Contemporary Southwest Gallery, 1995—, many others; retrospective exhbn. Santa Fe East Gallery, 1982; represented in permanent collections Mus. N.Mex., Fine Arts Ctr., Colorado Springs, Colo., Coll. Santa Fe; collection of Oprah Winfrey, 1987, other pvt. collections; subject of book Bernique Longley- A Retrospective, 1982. Bryan Lathrop Fgn. Travelling fellow, 1945. Mem. Art Inst. Chgo. Alumni Assn., Artists Equity Assn. Home and Studio: 427 Camino Del Monte Sol Santa Fe NM 87501-2825

LONGLEY, GLENN, biology educator, research director; b. Del Rio, Tex., June 2, 1942; s. Glenn L. and Cleo M. (Tipton) L.; m. Francis Van Winkle, Aug. 5, 1961; children: Kelly Francis, Kristy Lee, Katherine Camille, Glenn C. BS in Biology, S.W. Tex. State U., 1964; MS in Zoology and Entomology, U. Utah, 1966, PhD in Environ. Biology, 1969. Lectr. U. Utah, 1968-69; from lectr. to prof. S.W. Tex. State U., San Marcos, 1969-79, prof. aquatic biology, dir. Edward Aquifer Rsch. Ctr., 1979—. Contbr. 138 papers to profl. jours. or meetings. Recipient more than 50 grants or contracts for water related studies; named Emminent Tex. Hydrologist, Am. Inst. Hydrology and Am. Water Resource Assn., Tex. sects., 1993. Fellow Tex. Acad. Sci. (past. pres.); mem. Am. Water Resource Assn., Tex. Orgn. for Endangered Species (past pres.), Tex. Water Conservation Assn., Tex. Water Pollution Control Assn. (past pres.), Assn. Groundwater Scientists and Engrs., Water Environment Fedn., Sigma Xi (life), Phi Sigma (former chpt. pres.). Achievements include research on redescription and assignment to the new Lirceolus of the Texas troglobitic water slater, Asellus smithii, the larva of a new subterranean water beetle, Haideoporus texanus, watchlist of endangered, threatened and peripheral vertebrates of Texas, the generic status and distribution of Monodella texana Maguire, the only known North American Thermosbaeneacean, the Edwards Aquifer, Hadoecrus taylori, a new genus and species of phreatic Hydrobiidae from South-Central Texas, Phreatoceras, a new name for Hadoceras Hershler and Longley, Phreatodrobia coronae, a new species of cavesnail from southwestern Texas, reproductive patterns of the subterranean shrimp Palaemonetes antrorum Benedict from Cental Texa, population size, distribution, and life history of Eurycea nana in the San Marcos River. Home: 814 Palomino Ln San Marcos TX 78666-1130 Office: SW Tex State U Edwards Aquifer Rsch Ctr San Marcos TX 78666

LONGLEY, JAMES B., JR., congressman; children: Matt, Sarah. AB in History, Holy Cross, 1974; JD, U. Me., 1980. Lawyer, small bus. operator, 1979; mem. 104th Congress from 1st Me. dist., 1995—; mem. House Nat. Security Com., Small Bus. and Nat. Resources Com., subcommitte on mil. procurement, maritime subcommittee, fisheries committee; part-time asst. to Gov.; del. White House Conf. Small Bus. Dir. pub. affairs Camp Lejeune. With USMC, 1976-79, Lt. col. USMCR. Office: US House Reps 1530 Longworth House Office Bldg Washington DC 20515-1901

LONGLEY, JAMES WILDON, mathematician, researcher; b. San Saba, Tex., Oct. 29, 1913; s. Leon and Emily Areminti (Patton) L.; m. Letitia J. Robinson, 1961 (dec. 1988); 1 child, Roger Wayne. BA, Tex. A&M U., 1936, MS, 1937; MA, Harvard U., 1946, PhD, 1947. Economist, numerical analyst Bur. Labor Stats. U.S. Dept. Labor, Washington, 1955-83, researcher in applied math. and stats., 1983—. Author: Least Squares Computations Using Orthogonalization Methods, 1984, 2d edit., 1989; contbr. articles on least squares and the Gram-Schmidt process for the computer to profl. jours. Mem. Am. Statis. Assn., Math. Soc. Am., Soc. Indsl. and Applied Math. Republican. Methodist. Home: 8200 Cedar St Silver Spring MD 20910-5558

LONGLEY, MARJORIE WATTERS, newspaper executive; b. Lockport, N.Y., Nov. 2, 1925; d. J. Randolph and Florence Lucille (Craine) Watters; m. Ralph R. Longley, Oct. 1, 1949 (dec.). B.A. in English with highest honors cum laude, St. Lawrence U., 1947. Sports editor, feature writer Lockport Union Sun and Jour., 1945; with N.Y. Times, N.Y.C., 1948-88, asst. to v.p. consumer mktg., 1975-78, circulation sales mgr., 1978-79, sales dir., 1979-81, dir. pub. affairs, 1981-88; pres. Gramercy Internat., Inc. (mktg. and pub. rels.), N.Y.C., 1988—; dir. pub. affairs and pub. info., N.Y.C. Off-Track Betting Corp., 1990-94; mem. Nat. Newspapers' Readership Coun., 1979-82; mem. adv. coun. API, 1980-85. Author: America's Taste, 1960. Trustee St. Lawrence U., 1969-75, 77—; chmn. bd. dirs. Am. Forum for Global Edn., 1977—; pres. N.Y. State Adult Edn. Coun., 1974-77; mem. N.Y. State Adv. Coun. for Vocat. Edn., 1976-81, postsecondary edn., 1978-81, Mayor's Coun. Environment of N.Y.C., 1983-96; bd. dirs. Nat. Charities Info. Bur.; chmn. 42d St. Edn., Theatre, Culture, 1984-88, chmn. emeritus, 1988—. Mem. Nat. Inst. Social Scis., Am. Mgmt. Assn. (nat. mktg. coun. 1972-89, bd. dirs. 1986-88), Nat. Arts Club, Overseas Press Club, Phi Beta Kappa. Democrat. Baptist. Office: Gramercy Internat Inc 34 Gramercy Park E New York NY 10003-1731

LONGMAN, ANNE STRICKLAND, special education educator, consultant; b. Metuchen, N.J., Sept. 17, 1924; d. Charles Hodges and Grace Anna (Moss) Eldridge; m. Henry Richard Strickland, June 22, 1946 (dec. 1960); m. Donald Rufus Longman, Jan. 20, 1979 (dec. 1987); children: James C., Robert H. BA in Bus. Adminstrn., Mich. State U., 1945; teaching credentials, U. Calif., Berkeley, 1959; postgrad., Stanford U., 1959-60; MA in Learning Hand, Santa Clara U., 1974. Lic. educator. Exptl. test engr. Pratt & Whitney Aircraft, East Hartford, Conn., 1945-47; indsl. engr. Marchant Calculators, Emeryville, Calif., 1957-58; with pub. rels. Homesmith, Palo Alto, Calif., 1959-62; cons. Right to Read Program, Calif., 1978-79; monitor, reviewer State of Calif., Sacramento, 1976-79; tchr. diagnosis edn. Cabrillo Coll., Aptos, Calif., 1970-79; lectr. edn. U. Calif., Santa Cruz, 1970-79; cons. Santa Cruz Bd. Edn., 1970-79; reading rschr. Gorilla Found., Woodside, Calif., 1982—; bd. mem. Western Inst. Alcoholic Studies, L.A., 1972-73; chmn. Evaluation Com., Tri-County, Calif., 1974; speaker Internat. Congress Learning Disabilities, Seattle, 1974; ednl. cons. rsch. on allergies, 1993—. Author: Word Patterns in English, 1974-92, Cramming 3D Kids, 1975—, 50 books for migrant students, 1970-79; contbr. articles on stress and alcoholism and TV crime prevention for police, 1960-79. Founder Literacy Ctr., Santa Cruz, 1968-092; leader Girl Scouts U.S.A., San Francisco, 1947-50; vol. Thursday's Child, Santa Cruz, 1976-79, Golden Gate Kindergarten, San Francisco, 1947-57. Recipient Fellowships Pratt & Whitney Aircraft, 1944, Stanford U., 1959. Mem. Internat. Reading Assn. (pres. Santa Cruz 1975), Santa Clara Valley Watercolor Soc., Los Altos Art Club (v.p. 1992), Eichler Swim and Tennis Club. Republican. Episcopalian. Avocations: watercolor painting, travel, drama. Home and Office: 153 Del Mesa Carmel Carmel CA 93923-7950

LONGMAN, GARY LEE, accountant; b. Kewanee, Ill., Apr. 25, 1948; s. Howard L. and Dorothy (Wenk) L.; m. Ruth Ann Biesboer; children: Gregory, Rebecca. AA, Joliet (Ill.) Jr. Coll., 1968; BS in Acctg., No. Ill. U., 1970. CPA, Ill. Staff acct. KPMG Peat Marwick, Chgo., 1970-72, sr. acct., 1972-74, mgr., 1974-80, ptnr., 1980-91, ptnr.-in-charge Chgo. office mfg. practice, 1991—, ptnr.-in-charge Chgo. audit dept., 1991-93, midwest ptnr.-in-charge info., comm. & entertainment, 1993—. Bus. adv. coun. Dept. Commerce, DePaul U., 1991—; bd. dirs. Jr. Achievement, Chgo. Mem. AICPAs, Ill. Soc. CPAs, LaGrange Country Club. Office: KPMG Peat Marwick 303 E Wacker Dr Chicago IL 60601-5212

LONGMIRE, WILLIAM POLK, JR., physician, surgeon; b. Sapulpa, Okla., Sept. 14, 1913; s. William Polk and Grace May (Weeks) L.; m. Jane Jarvis Cornelius, Oct. 28, 1939; children—William Polk III (dec.), Gill, Sarah Jane. A.B., U. Okla., 1934; M.D., Johns Hopkins, 1938; M.D. hon. degrees, U. Athens, Greece, 1972, Northwestern U., 1976, U. Lund, Sweden, 1976; M.D. (h.c.), U. Heidelberg, Germany, 1974. Diplomate Am. Bd. Surgery (chmn. 1961-62). Intern surgery Johns Hopkins Hosp., Balt., 1938-39, resident surgery, 1944, surgeon in charge plastic out-patient clinic, 1946-48, surgeon, 1947-48; Harvey Cushing fellow exptl. surgery Johns Hopkins, 1939-40, Halsted fellow surg. pathology, 1940, successively instr., asst. prof. assoc. prof. surgery, 1943-48; prof. surgery UCLA, 1948-81, prof. emeritus, 1981—, chmn. dept., 1948-76; cons. surgery Wadsworth VA Hosp., Los Angeles County Harbor Hosp., 1945-76, VA disting. physician, 1982-87; guest prof. spl. surgery Free U. Berlin, Fed. Republic Germany, 1952-54; vis. prof. surgery Mayo Grad. Sch. Medicine, 1968, Royal Coll. Physicians and Surgeons of Can., 1968; chmn. surgery study sect. NIH, USPHS, 1961-64; mem. Conf. Com. on Grad. Edn. in Surgery, 1959-66, chmn., 1964-66; mem. spl. med. adv. group to med. dir. VA, 1963-68, vice chmn., 1967-68; chmn. surgery tng. com. NIH, 1969-70; mem. pres.' cancer panel Nat. Cancer Inst., 1982-91; Wade vis. prof. Royal Coll. Surgeons Edinburgh, 1972; nat. civilian cons. surgery Air Surgeon USAF; surg. cons. Surgeon Gen. U.S. Army, 1961-88; commr. Joint Commn. on Accreditation of Hosps., 1975-80. Editor: Advances in Surgery, 1975-76; editorial bd.: Annals of Surgery, 1965—. Served as maj. USAF, 1952-54; spl. cons. Air Surgeon Gen.'s Office. Recipient hon. certificate for advancement cardiovascular surgery Free U. of Berlin, 1954, certificate for high profl. achievement USAF, 1954, Gold medal UCLA, 1980, prize Societe Internationale De Chirurgie, 1987; inducted into Okla. Hall of Fame, 1980. Fellow ACS (chmn. forum com. fundamental surg. problems 1961-62, regent 1962-71, chmn. bd. regents 1969-71, pres. 1971-73, Sheen award N.J. chpt. 1987); hon. fellow Assn. Surgeons Great Britain and Ireland, Royal Coll. Surgeons Ireland, Royal Coll. Surgeons Edinburgh, Royal Coll. Surgeons Eng., Italian Surg. Soc., Association Française de Chirurgie, Japan Surg. Soc.; mem. AMA (mem. council on med. edn. 1964-69), Soc. Scholars of Johns Hopkins U., Soc. Clin. Surgeons, Am. Surg. Assn. (pres. 1967-68), Pacific Coast Surg. Assn., Western Surg. Assn., So. Surg. Assn., Soc. U. Surgeons, Internat. Soc. Surgery, Internat. Fedn. Surg. Colls. (pres. 1984-87), Internat. Surgical Group, (pres. 1993), Am. Assn. Thoracic Surgery, Pan-Pacific Surg. Assn., Los Angeles Surg. Soc. (pres. 1956), Bay Dist. Surg. Soc., Soc. Surgery Alimentary Tract (pres. 1975-76), Calif. Med. Assn. (sec. surg. sect. 1950-51, chmn. sci. bd. 1966-67, Golden Apple award 1990), James IV Assn. Surgeons (pres. 1981), Soc. Surg. Chairmen (pres. 1970-72), Sociédad Argentina di Cirugia Digestiva (hon.), Italian Surg. Soc. (hon.), Phi Beta Kappa, Alpha Omega Alpha; corr. mem. Deutsche Gesellschaft fur Chirugie. Home: 10102 Empyrean Way Bldg 8 Unit 203 Los Angeles CA 90067 Office: U Calif Med Ctr Los Angeles CA 90024

LONGNECKER, DAVID E., anesthesiologist, educator; b. Kendallville, Ind., 1939. MD, Ind. U., 1964, MA in Anesthesiology, 1968. Diplomate Am. Bd. Anesthesiology. Intern Blodgett Meml. Hosp., Grand Rapids, Mich., 1964-65; resident in anesthesiology U. Ind., 1965-69; asst. prof. dept. anesthesiology U. Mo., 1970-73; assoc. prof. dept. anesthesiology U. Va., Charlottesville, 1974-78, prof., 1978-88; Robert D. Dripps prof., chmn. dept. anesthesia U. Pa., Phila., 1988—. With USPHS, 1968-70. Mem. Am. Soc. Anesthesiology, Inst. Medicine. Office: U Pa Medical Ctr Dept Anesthesia 3400 Spruce St Philadelphia PA 19104

LONGO, GEORGE P., superintendent. Supt. Sheboygan (Wis.) Area Sch. Dist. Named state finalist Nat. Supt. of Yr. award, 1993. Office: Sheboygan Area Sch Dist 830 Virginia Ave Sheboygan WI 53081-4427

LONGO, LAWRENCE DANIEL, physiologist, obstetrician-gynecologist; b. Los Angeles, Oct. 11, 1926; s. Frank Albert and Florine Azelia (Hall) L.; m. Betty Jeanne Mundall, Sept. 9, 1948; children: April Celeste, Lawrence Anthony, Elizabeth Lynn, Camilla Giselle. BA, Pacific Union Coll., 1949; MD, Coll. Med. Evangelists, Loma Linda, Calif., 1954. Diplomate: Am. Bd. Ob-Gyn. Intern Los Angeles County Gen. Hosp., 1954-55, resident, 1955-58; asst. prof. ob-gyn UCLA, 1962-64; asst. prof. physiology and ob-gyn U. Pa., 1964-68; prof. physiology and ob-gyn Loma Linda U., 1968—; head ctr. for perinatal biology Loma Linda U. Sch. Medicine, 1974—; mem. perinatal biology com. Nat. Inst. Child Health, NIH, 1973-77; chmn. reprodn. scientist devel. program NIH; NATO prof. Consiglio Nat. delle Richerche, Italian Govt. Editor: Respiratory Gas Exchange and Blood Flow in the Placenta, 1972, Fetal and Newborn Cardiovascular Physiology, 1978, Charles White and A Treatise on the Management of Pregnant and Lying-in Women, 1987; co-editor: Landmarks in Perinatology, 1975-76, Classics in Obstetrics Gynecology, 1993; editor classic pages in ob-gyn. Am. Jour. Ob-Gyn.; contbr. articles to profl. jours. Served with AUS, 1945-47. Founder Frank A. and Florine A. Longo lectureship in faith, knowledge, and human values Pacific Union Coll., 1993. Fellow Royal Coll. Ob-Gyns., Am. Coll. Ob-Gyns.; mem. Am. Assn. History Medicine (coun.), Am. Osler Soc. (bd. govs., sec.-treas.), Am. Physiol. Soc., Assn. Profs. Ob-Gyn., Perinatal Rsch. Soc., Soc. Gynecologic Investigation (past pres.), Neurosci. Soc., Royal Soc. Medicine. Adventist. Office: Loma Linda U Sch Medicine Ctr Perinatal Biology Loma Linda CA 92350

LONGOBARDI, JOSEPH J., federal judge; b. 1930; m. Maud L.; 2 children: Joseph J. Longobardi III, Cynthia Jean Hermann. BA, Washington Coll., 1952; LLB, Temple U., 1957. Deputy atty. Gen. State Del., Wilmington, 1959-61, tax appeal bd., 1973-74; ptnr. Longobardi & Schwartz, Wilmington, 1964-72, Murdoch, Longobardi, Schwartz & Walsh, Wilmington, 1972-74; judge Superior Ct. State of Del., Wilmington, 1974-82; vice chancellor Ct. Chancery, State Del., Wilmington, 1982-84; federal judge U.S. Dist. Ct. Del., Wilmington, 1984—, chief judge, 1989—; assoc. editor Temple Law Rev. Recipient Paul C. Reardon award Nat. Ctr. for State Cts., 1981, S.S. Shull Meml. awrd for excellence in legal rsch. and writing. Office: US Dist Ct 844 N King St # 40 Wilmington DE 19801-3519

LONGOBARDO, ANNA KAZANJIAN, engineering executive; b. N.Y.C.; d. Aram Michael and Zarouhy (Yazejian) Kazanjian; m. Guy S. Longobardo, July 12, 1952; children: Guy A., Alicia Longobardo Langston. Student, Barnard Coll., 1947; BSME, Columbia U., 1949, MSME, 1952. Sr. systems engr. Am. Bosch Arma Corp., Garden City, N.Y., 1950-65; rsch. sect. head gyroscope Sperry Rand Corp., Gt. Neck, N.Y., 1965-68, rsch. sect. head systems mgmt., 1968-73; mgr. engring. personnel, utilization dir. hdqrs. Sperry Corp., Gt. Neck, 1973-77, mgr. systems mgmt. program planning, 1977-8l, mgr. planning systems mgmt. group, 198l-82; dir. tech. svc. Systems Devel., Unisys Corp., Gt. Neck, 1982-89, dir. field engring., 1989-93, dir. strategic initiatives, 1993-95;, 1993-95, ret., 1995; bd. dirs. and chmn. exec. compensation com. Woodward-Clyde Group, Denver. Contbr. articles to profl. publs. Trustee Columbia U., N.Y.C., 1990—, chmn. engring. coun.,, 1987-91; mem. Bronxville (N.Y.) Planning Bd.; chmn. Bronxville Design Rev. Com. Recipient hon. citation Wilson Coll. Centennial, 1970, Alumni medal for conspicuous svc. Columbia U., 1980; named One of 100 N.Y. Women of Influence, New York Woman mag., 1986. Fellow Soc. Women Engrs. (founder, pioneer); mem. AIAA (sr.), Columbia U. Engring. Alunni Assn. (pres. 1977-81), Columbia U. Alumni Fedn. (pres. 1981-85), Bronxville Field Club.

LONGONE, DANIEL THOMAS, chemistry educator; b. Worcester, Mass., Sept. 16, 1932; s. Daniel Edward and Anne (Novick) L.; m. Janice B. Bluestein, June 13, 1954. B.S., Worcester Poly. Inst., 1954; Ph.D., Cornell U., 1958. Research fellow chemistry U. Ill., Urbana, 1958-59; mem. faculty dept. chemistry U. Mich., Ann Arbor, 1959—, assoc. prof., 1966-71, prof., 1971—; cons. Gen. Motors Research Co., 1965-77. Am. Chem. Soc.-Petroleum Research Fund internat. fellow, 1967-68; Fulbright scholar, 1970-71. Mem. Am. Chem. Soc., Sigma Xi, Tau Beta Pi, Phi Lambda Upsilon. Home: 1207 W Madison St Ann Arbor MI 48103-4729 Office: U Mich 3537 Chemistry Ann Arbor MI 48109

LONGSTAFF, RONALD E., federal judge; b. 1941. BA, Kans. State Coll., 1962; JD, U. Iowa, 1965. Law clk. to Hon. Roy L. Stephenson U.S. Dist. Ct. (so. dist.) Iowa, 1965-67, clk. of ct., 1968-76, U.S. magistrate judge, 1976-91; fed. judge U.S. Dist. Ct. (so. dist.) Iowa, Des Moines, 1991—; assoc. McWilliams, Gross and Kirtley, Des Moines, 1967-68; adj. prof. law Drake U., 1973-76. Mem. Iowa State Bar Assn. (chmn. spl. commn. to revise Iowa exemption law 1968-70, mem. adv. com. 8th cir. ct. appeals 1988—). Office: US Dist Ct 422 US Courthouse Des Moines IA 50309*

LONGSTREET, HARRY STEPHEN, television producer, director, scriptwriter; b. Bklyn., Feb. 24, 1940; s. Stephen and Ethel Muriel (Godoff) L.; m. Diana Gail Bodlander, Nov. 25, 1962 (div. Jan. 1977); children: Stacy Robyn, Gregory Stephen; m. Renee Myrna Schonfeld, Jan. 9, 1977. Student, U. So. Calif., 1962-64. Producer Voyagers, 1983, Trauma Center, 1983, Misfits of Science, 1986; supervising producer Hot Pursuit, 1984, Shadow Chasers, 1985; exec. producer TV show Fame, 1986-87, Rags to Riches, 1987—. Scriptwriter: (TV shows) Quincy, Father Murphy, Jack & Mike, Magnum PI, Designing Women, (TV films) The Gathering Part II, 1979, The Promise of Love, 1980, The Sky's No Limit, 1984, Gunsmoke: One Man's Justice, 1993, Alien Nation: Body and Soul, 1995, Alien Nation: The Udara Legacy, 1996, (feature films) Wounded, 1996; exec. prodr., scriptwriter: Night Walk, 1989; dir.: Identity Crisis, 1984, The Big Contract, 1987, The Jenifer Graham Story, 1989, Alien Nation, 1989-90, The Perfect Daughter, 1996; exec. prodr. With A Vengeance, 1992; writer, dir.: Sex, Love and Cold Hard Cash, 1993, A Vow to Kill, 1995. Served with USAR, 1960-67. Mem. Writers Guild Am. (Outstanding Script nominee 1984, 90, Genesis award 1989, Humanitas nominee 1990), Dirs. Guild Am., Acad. TV Arts and Scis.

LONGSTREET, STEPHEN (CHAUNCEY LONGSTREET), author, painter; b. N.Y.C., Apr. 18, 1907; m. Ethel Joan Godoff, Apr. 22, 1932; children: Joan, Harry. Student, Rutgers Coll., Harvard U.; grad., N.Y. Sch. Fine and Applied Art, 1929; student in Rome, Paris. Ind. artist, writer, 1930—; staff lectr. Los Angeles Art Assn., 1954, UCLA, 1955, 58-59, Los Angeles County Mus., 1958-59; staff mem. arts and humanities dept. UCLA, 1965—; prof. art, dir. dept. Viewpoints Inst. of Gen. Semantics, Los Angeles, 1965; prof. modern writing U. So. Calif., Los Angeles, 1975-80. Began as painter; contbr. to French, Am. and English mags.; also cartoonist; radio writer for NBC, CBS, and other networks, writer shows for Rudy Vallee, Deems Taylor, John Barrymore, Bob Hope, Ellery Queen; writer popular series detective stories for Lippincott and Morrow under pen name Paul Haggrad, 1936; film critic Saturday Rev., 1941; mem. editorial staff Time mag., 1942, Screenwriters mag., 1947-48; critic L.A. Daily News, Book Pages, 1948; assoc. producer Civil War series The Blue and Gray, NBC, 1959—; author: All or Nothing, 1983, Delilah's Fortune, 1984, Our Father's House, 1985; painting exhibited: L.A., 1946, 48, N.Y., 1946, London, 1947; one-man shows include Padlia Galleries, L.A., 1970, Memphis Mus., 1979, Erie Mus., 1981, Coll. of Libr. of Congress, 1980, Jazz Age Revisited, 1983, Smithsonian Nat. Portrait Gallery, 1983, Sr. Eye Gallery, Long Beach, Calif., 1990, Columbus (Ohio) Mus. Art, 1992, tour of Japan, 1994; retrospective show Longstreet the Mature Years, L.A., 1983, Jazz-The Chgo. Scene, Regenstein Libr. U. Chgo., 1989, Columbus (Ohio) Mus. Fine Arts; author: The Pedlocks, 1951, The Beach House, 1952, The World Revisited, 1953, A Century of Studebaker on Wheels, 1953, The Lion at Morning, 1954, The Boy in the Model-T, 1956, Real Jazz, 1956, The Promoters, 1957, The Bill Pearson Story, 1957, (in French), Complete Dictionary of Jazz, 1957, Man of Montmatre, 1958, The Burning Man, 1958, The Politician, 1959, The Crime, 1959, Geisha, 1960, Gettysburg, 1960, A Treasury of the World's Great Prints, 1961, Eagles Where I Walk, 1961, The Flesh Peddler, 1962, A Few Painted Feathers, 1963, War In Golden Weather, 1965, Pedlock & Sons, 1965, The Wilder Shore: San Francisco '49 to '06, 1968, A Salute to American Cooking, (with Ethel Longstreet), 1968, War Cries on Horseback, An Indian History, 1970, The Canvas Falcons, 1970, Chicago: 1860-1920; a history, 1973, The General, 1974, (with Ethel Longstreet) World Cookbook, 1973, Win or Lose, 1977, The Queen Bees, 1979, Storm Watch, 1979, Pembroke Colors, 1981, From Storyville to Harlem - 50 years of the Jazz Scene, 1987, Magic Trumpets--The Young Peoples Story of Jazz, 1989, (poems) Jazz Solos, 1990, My Three Nobel Prizes; Life with Faulkner, Hemingway and Sinclair Lewis, 1994; editor, illustrator: The Memoirs of W.W. Windstaff Lower Than Angels, 1993; writer screen plays including Uncle Harry, 1943, Rider on a Dead Horse, The Imposter, First Travelling Saleslady, Stallion Road, 1946, The Jolson Story, 1947, Helen Morgan Story, 1956, plays including High Button Shoes, 1947, Gauguin, 1948, All Star Cast, Los Angeles, A History, 1977, (TV series) Playhouse 90, TV writer for Readers Digest Theatre, 1955; contbr. dialogue for films Greatest Show on Earth, Duel In the Sun. Pres. Los Angeles Art Assn., 1973-90. Recipient Stafford medal London, 1946, Bowman prize, 1948, Photo-Play mag. Gold medal for The Jolson Story, 1948, Billboard-Donaldson Gold medal for High Button Shoes, 1948. Mem. Motion Picture Acad. Arts and Letters, Writers Guild Am. (bd. dirs. 1948), Phi Sigma (charter mem.). Clubs: Sketch, Daguerreotype Society, Winadu Players. *I seem to have stumbled into the most dangerous world history since the fall of Rome. This time little of civilization may survive. The vulgarization of the culture by TV and lack of an American greatness in the White House can bring Orwell's world into being. But mankind will most likely remain in some form in his polluted planet, recalling what was the past. Man will always remain an undomesticated animal; rather kill than think.*

LONGSTREET, VICTOR MENDELL, government official; b. Louisville, Jan. 1, 1907; s. Joseph Emens and Allan Bemus (McKinley) L.; m. Mary Margaret Landry, 1930 (dec.); 1 child, Katherine Allan; m. Dorothy Bennett, 1986. BS magna cum laude, Harvard U., 1930. Economist AT&T, 1930-31; sr. economist Fed. Res. Bd., 1931-43; assoc. chief div. econ. devel. Dept. State, 1945-48; program rev. officer ECA U.S. Spl. Mission to Netherlands, The Hague, 1948-49; dep. U.S. sr. rep. Fin. Com., NATO, 1950-51; dep. dir. Office Trade and Fin., Econ. Coop. Adminstrn., Paris, 1951-52; v.p., mgr. Louisville br. Fed. Res. Bank, St. Louis, 1953-57; dir. mgmt. rsch. Schering Corp., 1957-62; asst. sec. Dept. Navy, 1962-65; assoc. dir. Internat. Mgmt. Group of Boston, 1966-69; chmn. The Boston Group, Inc., 1970-79; bd. dirs. N.Am. Fund Mgmt. Corp. Author: Financial Control in Multi-National Companies, 1971. Served from capt. to lt. col. AC, U.S. Army, 1943-45. Mem. Harvard Club (N.Y.C.), Phi Beta Kappa. Address: 1201 Lyndon Lane C11 Louisville KY 40222 Address: 4000 Cathedral Ave NW Washington DC 20016-5249

LONGSTRETH, BEVIS, lawyer; b. N.Y.C., Jan. 29, 1934; s. Alfred Bevis and Mary Agnes (Shiras) L.; m. Clara St. John, Aug. 10, 1963; children: Katherine Shiras, Thomas Day, Benjamin Hoyt. B.S. cum laude, Princeton U., 1956; LL.M., Harvard U., 1961. Bar: N.Y. 1962. Assoc. Debevoise & Plimpton, N.Y.C., 1962-70, ptnr., 1970-81; commr. SEC, Washington, 1981-84; ptnr. Debevoise & Plimpton, 1984—; lectr. Columbia U. Law Sch., N.Y.C., 1975-81, adj. prof., 1994—; cons. Ford Found., 1971-72; cons. to Comptroller Gen. of U.S.; mem. pension fin. com. World Bank, 1987—; bd. govs. Am. Stock Exch., 1992—; bd. dirs. INVESCO, plc, Capstead Mortgage Co. Author books, numerous articles on investment, securities and law. Bd. dirs. Symphony Space Inc.; trustee Nathan Cummings Found., 1991—, trustee, 1993—; New Sch. for Social Rsch., 1987—; chmn. fin. com. Rockefeller Family Fund, 1972-81, 84—, mem., 1986—. Lt. USMC, 1956-58. Mem. Am. Law Inst., Assn. of Bar of City of N.Y. Democrat. Home: 322 Central Park W New York NY 10025-7629 Office: Debevoise & Plimpton 875 3rd Ave New York NY 10022-6225*

LONGSWORTH, CHARLES R., foundation administrator; b. Fort Wayne, Ind., Aug. 21, 1929; s. Maurice A. and Marjorie K. L.; m. Polly Ormsby, June 30, 1956; children: Amy Porter, Elizabeth King, Laura Cramer, Anne Graybill. B.A., Amherst Coll., 1951; M.B.A., Harvard U., 1953. Mktg. trainee Campbell Soup Co., Camden, N.J., 1955-58; account exec. Ogilvy & Mather, Inc., N.Y.C., 1958-60; asst. to pres. Amherst (Mass.) Coll., 1960-65; chmn. edn. trust Hampshire Coll., Amherst, 1966, v.p., sec., 1966-71, pres., 1971-77, pres. emeritus, 1992; pres., chief operating officer Colonial Williamsburg Found., Va., 1977-79, pres., CEO, 1979-92; chmn. Colonial Williamsburg Found., 1991-94, chmn. emeritus, 1994—; dir. Houghton Mifflin Co., Flight Safety Internat., Crestar Fin. Corp., Roadway Svcs. Inc., Saul Ctrs. Inc., Pub. Radio Internat., Va. Ea. Shore Corp. Author: (with others) The Making of a College, 1966, Five Colleges: Five Histories, 1993; contbr. articles to profl. jours. Chmn. bd. trustees Amherst Coll.; trustee Colonial Williamsburg Found., 1977-94, Emeritus Nat. Trust Hist. Preservation; bd. dirs. Ctr. for Pub. Resources, bd. advisors, trustee reservations. Lt. USMC, 1953-55. Mem. Am. Philos. Soc., Am. Antiquarian Soc., Phi Beta Kappa, Univ. Club (N.Y.C.), Century Assn. Club (N.Y.C.), Commonwealth Club (Richmond, Va.). Office: Colonial Williamsburg PO Box C Williamsburg VA 23187-3707

LONGSWORTH, EILEEN CATHERINE, library director; b. N.Y.C., Feb. 7, 1950; d. Francis L. and Maurine E. (Romkey) Brannigan; m. Laurence S. Woodworth, June 16, 1970 (div. 1982); 1 child, David; m. Bruce Todd Longsworth, May 28, 1983. Student, Dunbarton Coll., 1966-68; BA, U. Md., 1970; MS in Libr. Sci., Cath. U., Washington, 1973. Dept. head Anne Arundel County Pub. Libr., Annapolis, Md., 1974-75, br. librarian, 1975-79; adult services specialist Enoch Pratt Free Libr., Balt., 1979-84; asst. dir. Salt Lake City Pub. Libr., 1984-87; dir. Salt Lake County Libr. System, 1987—. Mem. ALA, Utah Libr. Assn. Democrat. Home: 860 Terrace Hills Dr Salt Lake City UT 84103-4021 Office: Salt Lake County Libr System 2197 E 7000 S Salt Lake City UT 84121-3139

LONGSWORTH, ROBERT MORROW, college professor; b. Canton, Ohio, Feb. 15, 1937; s. Robert H. and Margaret Elizabeth (Morrow) L.; m. Carol Herndon, Aug. 16, 1958; children—Eric D., Margaret W., Ann E. A.B., Duke U., 1958; M.A., Harvard U., 1960, Ph.D., 1965. Asst. prof. Oberlin Coll., 1964-70, assoc. prof., 1970-75, prof. English, 1975—, dean Coll. Arts and Scis., 1974-84. Author: The Cornish Ordinalia, 1967, The Design of Drama, 1972. Contbr. articles to profl. jours. Danforth Found. fellow. Fellow Am. Council Learned Socs., Nat. Humanities Ctr.; mem. MLA, Medieval Acad. Am., Cornwall Archaeol. Soc., Phi Beta Kappa.

LONGUEMARE, R. NOEL, JR., federal official; b. El Paso, Tex., Mar. 26, 1932; s. Robert Noel Sr. and Lorenza (Escajeda) L.; m. Julianna Josephine Isdebski, June 6, 1959; 1 child, Maria Christine. BSEE, U. Tex., El Paso, 1952; MSE, Johns Hopkins U., 1958. Corp. v.p., gen. mgr. electronic sys. group Westinghouse Electric, Balt., 1952-93; prin. dep. under sec. of def. acquisition and tech. Dept. Def., Washington, 1993—; cons. Def. Sci. Bd., Washington, 1988-91, mem., 1991-93; mem. Air Force Sci. Adv. Bd., Washington, 1990-93. Recipient Greer award Nat. Security Indsl. Assn., 1993, Excellence in Mfg. award, 1995. Fellow IEEE; mem. AAAS, AIAA (sr.). Democrat. Roman Catholic. Achievements include 8 patents. Avocation: piano. Office: Dept of Defense 3015 Defense Pentagon Washington DC 20301-3015

LONGWELL, JOHN PLOEGER, chemical engineering educator; b. Denver, Apr. 27, 1918; s. John Stalker and Martha Dorothea (Ploeger) L.; m. Marion Reed Valleau, Dec. 11, 1945; children: Martha Reed, Elizabeth Ann, John Dorney. B.S. in Mech. Engring, U. Calif., Berkeley, 1940; Sc.D. in Chem. Engring, M.I.T., 1943. With Exxon Research & Engring. Co., Linden, N.J., 1943-77; dir. Exxon Research & Engring. Co. Central Basic Research Lab., 1960-69; sr. sci. adv. Exxon Research & Engring. Co. (Central Basic Research Lab.), 1969-77; prof. chem. engring. M.I.T., Cambridge, 1977—. Contbr. articles to profl. jours. Recipient Sir Alfred Egerton medal for contbns. to combustion Nat. Acad. Engring., 1976. Mem. Am. Chem. Soc., Combustion Inst. (past pres.), Am. Inst. Chem. Engrs. (award 1979), Sigma Xi, Tau Beta Pi. Republican. Patentee in field. Home: 22 Follen St Cambridge MA 02138-3503 Office: MIT Rm 66-456 Cambridge MA 02139

LONGWORTH, RICHARD COLE, journalist; b. Des Moines, Mar. 13, 1935; s. Wallace Harlan and Helen (Cole) L.; m. Barbara Bem, July 19, 1958; children: Peter, Susan. BJ, Northwestern U., 1957; postgrad., Harvard U., 1968-69. Reporter UPI, Chgo., 1958-60; parliamentary corr. UPI, London, 1960-65; corr. UPI, Moscow, 1965-68, Vienna, 1969-72; diplomatic corr. UPI, Brussels, 1972-76; econ. and internat. affairs reporter Chgo. Tribune, 1976-86, bus. editor, econ. columnist, 1987-88, chief European corr., 1988-91, sr. writer, 1991—; internat. affairs commentator Sta. WBEZ-FM, Chgo., 1984—. Served with U.S. Army, 1957-58. Nieman fellow, 1968-69; recipient award for econ. reporting U. Mo., 1978, 80, John Hancock award for econ. reporting, 1978, 79, 82, Gerald Loeb award for econ. reporting, 1979, Media award for econ. understanding Dartmouth Coll., 1979, award Inter-Am. Press Assn., 1979, Peter Lisagor award Sigma Delta Chi, 1979, Sidney Hillman award, 1985, Lowell Thomas award for travel writing, 1985, Beck award for fgn. corr., 1986, Domestic Reporting award, 1987, Overseas Press Club award, 1994. Mem. Chgo. Com. of Council Fgn. Rels., Assn. Am. Corrs. in London. Office: Chicago Tribune 435 N Michigan Ave Chicago IL 60611-4001

LONNEBOTN, TRYGVE, battery company executive; b. Bergen, Norway, Oct. 4, 1937; came to U.S., 1965; s. Trygve and Nora Gertrude (Hoyland) L.; m. Aud Amalie Engesaeter, Sept. 28, 1963 (div.); children: Anne V., Paal T. MChemE, Tech. U. Norway, 1963. With Rayovac Corp., Madison, Wis., 1965—, project engr., then. project mgr., 1965-74, materials mgr., 1974-75, plant mgr., 1975-77, dir. ops., 1977-79, v.p. tech., 1979-82, v.p. ops., 1982-86, sr. v.p. ops., 1986-95, exec. v.p. ops., 1995—. Served to sgt. Norwegian Army, 1957-58. Mem. Norges Ingenior Furening (Norwegian Engring. Soc.), Torskeklubben Club (Madison). Lutheran. Avocations: hiking, soccer, music. Office: Rayovac Corp 601 Rayovac Dr Box 4960 Madison WI 53711

LONNEKE, MICHAEL DEAN, radio and television marketing executive; b. Wichita, Kans., Jan. 15, 1943; s. John Henry and Lillian Eleanor (Millspaugh) L.; m. Charlene Bertha Wilson, Apr. 10, 1975; children: Rebecca, Marietta, Alison. Student, Wichita State U., 1962-63, Friends U., 1961-66. Ops. mgr. Sta. KCMO, Kansas City, Mo., 1968-80; program dir. Sta. WCAU/CBS, Phila., 1980-81; v.p., gen. mgr. Sta. WGSO, New Orleans, 1981-83, Sta. KRNT/KRNQ-FM, Des Moines, 1983-85, Sta. KHOW, Denver, 1985-86, Sta. WMAQ/WKQX-FM (NBC Inc.), Chgo., 1986-89; pres. broadcast divsn. TransAm. Mktg. Svcs., Inc., Washington, 1989-94; v.p., gen. mgr. Metromedia Internat., Moscow, Russia, 1994—. Bd. dirs. Youth Symphony of DuPage (Ill.); pres. Loudoun Symphony Orch. Mem. Radio-TV News Dirs. Assn. (bd. dirs. 1970-72), Nat. Assn. Broadcasters, Am. Radio Relay League, Quarter Century Wireless Assn., U.S. Yacht Club, Masons. Republican. Episcopalian.

LONNGREN, KARL ERIK, electrical and computer engineering educator; b. Milw., Aug. 8, 1938; s. Bruno Leonard and Edith Irene (Osterlund) L.; m. Vicki Anne Mason, Feb. 16, 1963; children: Sondra Lyn, Jon Erik. B.S. in Elec. Engring., U. Wis., 1960, M.S., 1962, Ph.D., 1964. Postdoctoral appointment Royal Inst. Tech., Stockholm, 1964-65; asst. prof. elec. engring. U. Iowa, Iowa City, 1965-67; assoc. prof. U. Iowa, 1967-72, prof., 1972—; vis. scientist Danish Atomic Energy, Riso, 1982, Inst. Space and Astron. Sci., Tokyo, 1981, Los Alamos Sci. Labs. (N.M.), 1979, 80, Math. Research Ctr., Madison, 1976, Inst. Plasma Physics, Nagoya, Japan, 1972, others. Author: Introduction to Physical Electronics, 1988; co-author: Introduction to Wave Phenomena, 1985; co-editor: Solitons in Action, 1978. Recipient Disting. Svc. citation U. Wisc. Madison, 1992. Fellow Am. Phys. Soc., IEEE. Presbyterian. Home: 21 Prospect Pl Iowa City IA 52246-1932 Office: U Iowa Dept Elec & Computer Engring Iowa City IA 52242

LONNQUIST, GEORGE ERIC, lawyer; b. Lincoln, Nebr., Mar. 29, 1946; s. John Hall and Elizabeth Claire (Hanson) L.; m. Sandra Lynn Wise, May 7, 1971; children: Alethea, Courtenay, Barrett. BS, U. Tenn., 1968; JD, U. Nebr., 1971; LLM, NYU, 1974. Bar: Calif. 1983, Oreg. 1972, Nebr. 1971. Law clerk Oreg. Supreme Ct., Salem, 1971-72; dep. legis. counsel Oreg. Legislature, Salem, 1972-73; ptnr. Meysing & Lonnquist, Portland, 1974-78; v.p., assoc. gen. counsel Amfac, Inc., Portland and San Francisco, 1978-84; sr. v.p., gen. counsel Homestead Fin. Corp., Millbrae, Calif., 1984-91, Homestead Savings, Millbrae, 1984-93; pvt. practice law San Francisco, 1993—. Democrat. Roman Catholic. Avocation: woodcarving. Home: 846 E Greenwich Pl Palo Alto CA 94303-3416 Office: 101 Lincoln Center Dr Foster City CA 94404

LOO, BEVERLY JANE, publishing company executive; b. L.A.; d. Richard Y. and Bessie E. Sue Loo. B.A., U. Calif., Berkeley. Dir. subs. rights Prentice-Hall, Inc., N.Y.C., 1957-59; fiction editor McCall's mag., 1959-62; exec. editor and dir. subs. rights, gen. books div. McGraw-Hill Book Co., N.Y.C., 1962-82; pres. Beverly Jane Loo Assocs., Inc., N.Y.C., 1982-85; sr. editor, dir. subs. rights World Almanac Pharos Books, N.Y.C., 1985-88; dir. mktg. and subs. rights Paragon House, N.Y.C., 1988-91; dir. mktg. and sales Thomasson-Grant, Charlottesville, Va., 1991-93; dir. pub. and comm. programs U. Va. Div. Continuing Edn., Charlottesville, 1993—. Clubs: Arts (London); Overseas Press (N.Y.C.); Va. Writers. Home: Lewis & Clark Sq # 701 250 W Main St Charlottesville VA 22902-5079 Office: Zehmer Hall 104 Midmont Ln Charlottesville VA 22903-2449

LOO, THOMAS S., lawyer; b. 1943. BS, U. So. Calif., JD. Bar: Calif. 1969. Ptnr. Bryan Cave LLP, Santa Monica, Calif. Office: Bryan Cave LLP 120 Broadway St Ste 500 Santa Monica CA 90401-2386

LOOGES, PETER JOHN, systems engineer, architect; b. East Orange, N.J., Mar. 4, 1963; s. Edwin John and Ida Claire (Jacobus) L.; m. Heather Marta Evans, Apr. 6, 1989; 1 child, Adrian. BS in Computer Sci., Rensselaer Poly. Inst., 1985; MS in Computer Sci., Old Dominion U., 1991, PhD in Computer Sci., 1992. Commd. ensign USN, 1985, advanced through grades to lt., resigned, 1992; researcher, adj. prof. Old Dominion U., Norfolk, Va., 1992-93; adj. computer sci. prof. Old Dominion U., Norfolk, 1993—; chief engr., asst. v.p. Sci. Applications Internat. Corp., Hampton, Va., 1993—. Contbr. articles to profl. jours. Mem. IEEE, Assn. for Computing Machinery, Software Engring. Inst. Avocations: scuba, sky diving, raquetball. Office: Sci Applications Internat Corp 22 Enterprise Pky Ste 200 Hampton VA 23666-5844

LOOI, LAI-MENG, pathology educator; b. Bentong, Pahang, Malaysia, July 28, 1950; d. Choong-Foon Looi and Lin-Kiew Chai; m. Kwong-Choong Chang, June 13, 1981. MB BS, U. Singapore, 1975; M in Pathology, U. Malaya, Malaysia, 1979; MD, U. Malaya, 1987. Lectr. U. Malaya, Kuala Lumpur, Malaysia, 1979-85; assoc. prof. U. Malaya, Kuala Lumpur, 1985-86, prof., 1986—; dir. pathology U. Hosp., Kuala Lumpur, 1984—, sr. cons. pathologist, 1986—; external examiner U. Singapore, 1988-94; vis. prof. Harvard Med. Sch., Mass., 1991-92; external assesor U. Aberdeen, U.K., 1993. Editor Malaysian Jour. Pathology, 1986—; mem. editl. adv. bd. Histopathology, 1994—, Human Pathology, 1995—, Jour. Pathology, 1996—; contbr. articles to profl. jours. Coord. Brit. Coun. Edn. Projects Malaysia-U.K., 1984—; senate mem. U. Malaya, Malaysia, 1984—; elected mem. Med. Ctr. Rsch. Com., U. Malaya, 1992—; cons. Ofcl. Secrets Act Project, Malaysia, 1994. Found. fellow Acad. Scis. Malaysia, 1995. Fellow Royal Coll. Pathologists U.K. (examiner 1988—), Royal Coll. Pathologists Australasia (Malaysian rep. 1988—), Royal Soc. Medicine; mem. Malaysian Soc. Pathologists (pres. 1990-91, 93—), Acad. Medicine Malaysia (mem. coun. 1993-95), Internat. Acad. Cytology, Internat. Acad. Pathology, Malaysian Med. Coun. (councillor 1986—), N.Y. Acad. Scis., Royal Microscopical Soc. U.K., Assn. Clin. Pathologists, Arthur Purdy Stout Soc. Surg. Pathologists. Avocations: swimming, music, poetry. Office: Dept Pathology, Univ Malaya, Kuala Lumpur 59100, Malaysia

LOOK, DONA JEAN, artist; b. Port Washington, Wis., Mar. 30, 1948; m. Kenneth W. Loeber. BA, U. Wis., Oshkosh, 1970. Art tchr. Dept. Edn., NSW, Australia, 1976-78; ptnr. Look and Heaney Studio, Byron Bay, NSW, 1978-80; studio artist Algoma, Wis., 1980—. One person shows include Perimeter Gallery, Chgo., 1991; exhibited in group shows Perimeter Gallery, Chgo., 1983, 93, 94, Phila. Mus. Art, 1984, Civic Fine Arts Mus., Sioux Falls, S.D., 1985, Dacotah Prairie Mus., Aberdeen, S.D., 1985, Bergstrom-Mahler Mus., Neenah, Wis., 1985, Lawton Gallery, U. Wis.-Green Bay, 1985, J. B. Speed Art Mus., Louisville, 1986, Laguna (Calif.) Art Mus., Am. Craft Mus., N.Y.C., 1985, 86, 87, 89, Ark. Arts Ctr. Decorative Arts Mus., Little Rock, 1987, Cultural Ctr., Chgo., 1988, Erie (Pa.) Art Mus., 1988, Maine Crafts Assn., Colby Coll. Mus. Art, 1989, Ft. Wayne (Ind.) Mus. Art, 1989, The Forum, St. Louis, 1990, Palo Alto (Calif.) Cultural Ctr., 1990, Neville Pub. Mus., Green Bay, Wis., 1992, Waterloo (Iowa) Mus. Art, 1993, Sybaris Gallery, Royal Oak, Mich., 1993, 95, Sun Valley Ctr. for Arts and Humanities, Ketchum, Idaho, 1995, Nat. Mus. Am. Art, Smithsonian Instn., Washington, 1995; represented in permanent collections The White House Collection, Phila. Mus. Art, MCI Telecomms. Corp., Inc., Washington, Am. Craft Mus., N.Y.C., Ark. Arts Ctr., Little Rock, C. A. Wustum Mus. Fine Arts, Racine, Erie Art Mus.; works included in publs. The White House Collection of American Crafts, 1995, Craft Today: Poetry of the Physical, 1986, International Crafts, 1991, FIBERARTS Design Book Four, 1991, The Tactile Vessel, 1989, Creative Ideas for Living, 1988, The Basketmaker's Art: Contemporary Baskets and Their Makers, 1986. Recipient 1st prize award Phila. Craft Show, 1984, 2d prize award, 1985, Design award Am. Craft Mus., 1985, Craftsmen's award Phila. Craft Show, 1986; Nat. Endowment for Arts/Arts Midwest fellow, 1987, Nat. Endowment for Arts Fellowship grantee, 1988. Office: Perimeter Gallery 750 N Orleans Chicago IL 60610-3540

LOOK, JANET K., psychologist; b. Bklyn., Mar. 11, 1944; d. Harry and Isabelle (Chernoff) Kaplan; divorced; children: Howard, Erika (dec.). AB, NYU, 1964; EdM, Rutgers U., 1967, EdD, 1976. Lic. psychologist; cert. sch. psychologist. Asst. examiner Ednl. Testing Svc., Princeton, N.J., 1964-66; instr. Rutgers U., New Brunswick, N.J., 1968-69; psychologist Seattle Pub. Schs., 1991—; pvt. practice Kirkland, Wash., 1993—; adj. instr. U. Conn., Waterbury, 1973-91; appearances on various TV and radio shows including the Today Show; interviews include Litchfield County Times, 1987, Waterbury Rep.-Am., 1983-87, Manchester Jour. Inquirer, 1986, Danbury News-Times, 1985; presenter APA, San Francisco, 1991, Nation's Concern and Its Response, U. Wis., Milw., 1991, Nat. Assn. Sch. Psychologists, Dallas, 1991, Divorce Issues Inst., So. Conn. State U., New Haven, 1989. Author: (with others) The Troubled Adolescent, 1991; contbr. articles to newspapers, including N.Y. Times. Mem. APA, Wash. State Psychol. Assn., Nat. Assn. Sch. Psychologists, Wash. State Assn. Sch. Psychologists (area rep., bd. dirs. 1991-93). Avocations: writing, reading, dance, film, running. Office: 1104 Market St Kirkland WA 98033-5441

LOOKSTEIN, HASKEL, rabbi; b. N.Y.C., Mar. 21, 1932; s. Joseph H. and Gertrude S. (Schlang) L.; m. Audrey Katz, June 21, 1959; children: Mindy Cinnamon, Debbie Senders, Shira Baruch, Joshua. BA, Columbia U., 1953; MA, Yeshiva U., 1963, PhD, 1979. Ordained rabbi, 1958. Rabbi Congregation Kehilath Jeshurun, N.Y.C., 1958—; prin. Ramaz Sch., N.Y.C., 1966—; pres. N.Y. Bd. Rabbis, N.Y.C., 1986-88; chmn. rabbinic cabinet United Jewish Appeal, N.Y.C., 1985-87. Author: Were We Our Brothers' Keepers? The Public Response of American Jews to the Holocaust, 1938-44, 1985. Chmn. N.Y. Coalition for Soviet Jewry, N.Y.C., 1989—; v.p. United Jewish Appeal-Fedn., N.Y.C., 1988—. Mem. Rabbinical Coun. Am. (v.p. 1990—). Office: Synagogue Council of America 252 Soundview Ave White Plains NY 10606-3800

LOOMAN, JAMES R., lawyer; b. Vallejo, Calif., June 5, 1952; s. Alfred R. and Jane M. (Halter) L.; m. Donna G. Craven, Dec. 18, 1976; children: Alison Marie, Mark Andrew, Zachary Michael. BA, Valparaiso U., 1974; JD, U. Chgo., 1978. Bar: Ill. 1978, U.S. Dist. Ct. (no dist.) Ill. 1978, U.S. Claims Ct. 1979. Assoc. Isham, Lincoln & Beale, Chgo., 1978-83; assoc. Sidley & Austin, Chgo., 1983-86, ptnr., 1986—. Mem. ABA, Chgo. Bar Assn., Chgo. Athletic Assn., Skokie Country Club. Lutheran. Office: Sidley & Austin 1 First Nat Plz Chicago IL 60603

LOOMIS, CAROL J., journalist; b. Marshfield, Mo., June 25, 1929; d. Harold and Mildred (Case) Junge; m. John R. Loomis, Mar. 19, 1960; children: Barbara, Mark. Student, Drury Coll., 1947-49; B in Journalism, U. Mo., 1951. Editor Maytag News, Maytag Co., Newton, Iowa, 1951-54; rsch. assoc. Fortune mag., N.Y.C., 1954-58, assoc. editor, 1958-68, mem. bd. editors, 1968—. Office: Fortune Mag 1271 Avenue Of The Americas New York NY 10020

LOOMIS, HENRY, former broadcasting company executive, former government official; b. Tuxedo Park, N.Y., Apr. 19, 1919; s. Alfred Lee and Ellen Holman (Farnsworth) L.; m. Mary Paul Macleod, May 18, 1946 (div. Jan. 1974); children—Henry, Mary, Lucy, Gordon; m. Jacqueline C. Williams, Jan. 19, 1974; stepchildren—Charles Judson Williams, John Chalmers Williams, David Finley Williams, Robert Wood Williams. A.B., Harvard, 1941; ed., U. Calif., 1946. With radiation lab. U. Calif., 1945-47; asst. to pres. MIT, 1947-50; asst. to chmn. research and devel. bd. Dept. Def., 1950-51; cons. Psychol. Strategy Bd., Washington, 1951-52; staff Pres.'s Com. Internat. Info., 1953; chief Office Research and Intelligence, USIA, 1954-57; staff to Spl. Asst. to Pres. for Sci. and Tech., 1957-58; dir. broadcasting service Voice of Am. USIA, 1958-65; dep. commr. edn. HEW, 1965-66; ptnr. St. Vincents Island Co., N.Y.C., 1966-69; dep. dir. USIA, 1969-72; pres. Corp. for Pub. Broadcasting, Washington, 1972-78; trustee, vice chmn. bd. dirs. Mitre Corp., 1967-69, 78-91. Vice chmn. bd. dirs. Nat. Mus. Natural History, Smithsonian Instn., 1991-92, trustee, 1992-95; trustee Mus. Sci. and History, Jacksonville, 1991—; bd. dirs. Jacksonville Zool. Soc., 1991—. Recipient Rockefeller Pub. Service award for fgn. affairs, 1963. Home: 4661 Ortega Island Dr Jacksonville FL 32210-7500

LOOMIS, HOWARD KREY, banker; b. Omaha, Apr. 9, 1927; s. Arthur L. and Genevieve (Krey) L.; AB, Cornell U., 1949, MBA, 1950; m. Florence Porter, Apr. 24, 1954; children: Arthur L. II, Frederick S., Howard Krey, John Porter. Mgmt. trainee Hallmark Cards, Inc., Kansas City, Mo., 1953-56; sec., controller, dir. Mine Svc. Co., Inc., Ft. Smith, Ark., 1956-59; controller, dir. Electra Mfg. Co., Independence, Kans., 1959-63; v.p., dir. The Peoples Bank, Pratt, Kans., 1963-65, pres., 1966—; pres., dir. Gt. Plains Leasing, Inc., Pratt, 1966-80, Central States Inc., Pratt, 1970-76, Krey Co. Ltd., Pratt, 1978—; fin. chmn. Econ. Lifelines, Topeka; bd. dirs. All Ins., Inc., Pratt, Kans. Devel. Credit Corp., Topeka, Kans. Wildscape Found.; past dir. Fed. Reserve Bank of Kansas City, Mo.; past pres. Pratt County United Fund. Past chmn. Cannonball Trail chpt. ARC; bd. dirs., past comdg. gen. Kans. Cavalry; past pres. Investment Com., Kanza coun. Boy Scouts Am. With AUS, 1950-52. Mem. Kans. C. of C. and Industry (past transp. chmn., dir., v.p.), Pratt Area C. of C. (past pres., dir.), Kans. Bankers Assn. (past dir.), Fin. Execs. Inst. (Wichita chpt.), Sigma Delta Chi, Chi Psi. Republican. Presbyterian. Club: Park Hills Country (past pres.). Lodges: Elks, Rotary. Home: 502 Welton St Pratt KS 67124-0928 Office: The Peoples Bank 222 S Main St Pratt KS 67124-1102

LOOMIS, JOHN NORMAN, psychiatrist; b. Dallas, Aug. 9, 1933; s. Glenn LaVerne and Maria Jeanette (Doyle) L.; B.A., Rice U., 1954; M.D., Cornell U., 1958. Intern Meth. Hosp., Bklyn., 1958-59; resident Westchester div. N.Y. Hosp., White Plains, N.Y., 1959-62; practice medicine specializing in psychiatry, N.Y.C., 1962-78; asst. attending psychiatrist N.Y. Hosp., 1972-80; asst. prof. psychiatry Cornell U. Med. Coll., 1972-80; dir. Loomis Internat. Inc., oil field service co., Houston, 1964—, v.p., 1970-75, chmn. bd., 1975—. Bd. dirs. Madison Square Boys' and Girls' Club, N.Y.C., 1965-93, The Hudson Rev., N.Y.C., 1983—. Mem. Am. Psychiat. Assn., N.Y. Acad. Scis., Phi Beta Kappa. Clubs: Knickerbocker (N.Y.C.). Office: PO Box 6408 Pasadena TX 77506-0408

LOOMIS, PHILIP CLARK, investment executive; b. Plainville, Conn., Sept. 24, 1926; s. Winfield Hathaway and Lucy Erma (Clark) L.; m. Jean Ann Slater, 1950 (div. 1970); children: Philip Clark Jr., Leslie Jean, Martha Lynn; m. Greta Elaine Gustafson, 1970. BA in Econs., Yale U., 1949; MBA in Fin. with distinction, Wharton Sch. U. Pa., 1950. Chartered fin. analyst. Trust investment specialist No. Trust Co., Chgo., 1950-54; investment analyst, portfolio mgr. Hartford (Conn.) Ins. Group, 1954-61; ptnr./dir. of rsch. Eastman, Dillon Union, N.Y.C., 1961-66; ptnr.-in-charge, rsch. svcs. div. Francis I. duPont & Co., N.Y.C., 1967-70; v.p. rsch. Dean Witter & Co., N.Y.C., 1971-73; v.p., dir. rsch. Reynolds Securities, Inc., N.Y.C., 1974-78; dir. Office of Securities Markets Policy, Dept. Treasury, Washington, 1978-81; freelance cons. N.Y.C., 1981-86; v.p. Crispi Wagner & Co., N.Y.C., 1987-89; ind. cons. and money mgr., 1989—. Mem. N.Y. Soc. Security Analysts, Assn. for Investment Mgmt. and Rsch. Avocations: music, opera, ballet, do-it-yourself. Home and office: 130 E End Ave New York NY 10028-7553

LOOMIS, ROBERT DUANE, publishing company executive, author; b. Conneaut, Ohio, Aug. 24, 1926; s. Kline C. and Louise C. (Chapman) L.; m. Gloria Colliani, Apr. 12, 1956 (div.); 1 dau., Diana Rachel; m. Hilary Paterson Mills, Sept. 18, 1983; 1 child, Robert Miles. B.A., Duke U., 1950. Assoc. editor Rinehart & Co., N.Y.C., 1956-58; v.p., exec. editor Random House, Inc., N.Y.C., 1958—. Author: Story of the U.S. Air Force, 1959, Great American Fighter Pilots, 1961, All About Aviation, 1964. Served with USAF, 1945. Recipient Roger Klein award for creative editing, 1977. Home: 68 W 11th St New York NY 10011-8673 Office: Random House Inc 201 E 50th St New York NY 10022-7703

LOOMIS, WESLEY HORACE, III, former publishing company executive; b. Kansas City, Mo., July 29, 1913; s. Wesley Horace, Jr. and Mary (Gary) L.; m. Mary Bradford Paine, Apr. 17, 1937; children: Mary Elizabeth (Mrs. R.M. Norton), Jonathan Lee (dec.), Frederick Pierson. Grad., Hackley Sch., Tarrytown, N.Y., 1931; B.S. in Engring. and Bus. Adminstrn, MIT, 1935. Indsl. engr. Automatic Elec. Co., Chgo., 1935-42; pres. Loomis Advt. Co., 1946-55, Gen. Telephone Directory Co., Des Plaines, Ill., 1956-78; v.p. Dominion Directory Co., Vancouver, B.C., 1956-64; pres. Dominion Directory Co., 1964-78, Courtnay Pty., Ltd., Adelaide, Courtnay Pty., Ltd. S.A. Australia, Directories (Australia) Pty., Ltd., Melbourne, Australia, Gen. Telephone Directory Co. C por A, Santo Domingo, 1971-78, Directorio Telefonico Centroamericano, S.A., 1972-78; dir. Directorio Telefonico de El Salvador (SA). Pres. Episc. Charities 1969-70, dir., 1962-83, now life trustee; trustee emeritus U.S. Naval Acad. Found., Annapolis, Md.; bd. dirs. Traveler Aid Soc. Met. Chgo./Immigrants' Service League, 1957-80, pres., 1960-61; chmn. Travelers Aid Internat., Social Service Am., 1973-77; bd. dirs. Travelers Aid Assn. Am., 1977-82, pres., 1978-80; pres. Ind. Telephone Hist. Found., 1967-81, trustee, 1981—; trustee emeritus Colby-Sawyer Coll., New London, N.H., sec., 1976-81; mem. corp. devel. com. M.I.T., 1979-81; trustee Ill. Bus. Hall of Fame, 1981-83; bd. dirs., trustee, chmn. planning com. Mote Marine Lab., Sarasota, Fla., 1983—. Served to lt. col., Ordnance AUS, 1942-46. Decorated hon. mil. mem. Order Brit. Empire; laureate Am. Nat. Bus. Hall of Fame, 1980; elected to Ind. Telephone Hall of Fame, 1981, Calif. chpt., 1990. Mem. Ind. Telephone Pioneers Assn. (pres. 1964-66), Racquet Club (Chgo.), Field and Bird Key Yacht (Sarasota), Longboat Key Club, Masons (32 deg.), Phi Gamma Delta. Republican. Episcopalian (warden). Home: 700 John Ringling Blvd Apt 305 Sarasota FL 34236-1505

LOOMIS, WORTH (ALFRED WORTHINGTON LOOMIS), college president, manufacturer; b. N.Y.C., May 18, 1923; s. Alfred F. and Priscilla (Lockwood) L.; m. Louise Harding Earle, June 17, 1950; children: Lucy Williams, Ruth Lockwood, Susan Fellows, Alfred Fullerton II, Charles Harvey, Charlotte Earle. BS in Indsl. Engring., Yale U., 1947; MBA in Internat. Fin., NYU, 1955. Securities analyst Reynolds & Co., N.Y.C., 1948-50; indsl. engr., part owner Internat. R&D Corp., Istanbul, Turkey, 1950-51; prodn. mgr. automotive parts div. Clevite Corp., Cleve., 1951-58; with Medusa Portland Cement Co., Cleve., 1958-70, v.p. fin., sec., bd. dirs.; v.p. fin. Dexter Corp., Windsor Locks, Conn., 1970-75, pres., 1975-88, also bd. dirs.; pres. Hartford (Conn.) Grad. ctr., 1989—, also trustee; trustee Mechanics Savs. Bank, Hartford; bd. dirs. Capewell Components Co., Hartford, Chemstone Corp., Strasburg, Va., Cigna Funds, Springfield, Mass., Colt's Mfg. Co., Inc., Hartford, Conn. Natural Gas, Hartford, Covenant Mut. Ins. Co., Hartford, So. New Eng. Telephone Co., New Haven, Spencer Turbine Co., Windsor, Conn.; chmn. bd. dirs. Life Techs., Gaithersburg, Md.; pres. bd. trustees Colt Bequest Inc., Hartford, 1989—. Trustee Alpha Ctr., Washington, Am. Inst. for Mng. Diversity, Morehouse Coll., Atlanta, Hartford Sem., Kazanjian Econs. Found., Oneonta, N.Y., Trinity Coll., Hartford, Yale Berkeley Divinity Sch., New Haven; mem. Goodrich Social Settlement, Cleve., 1960-70, chair, 1964-66; mem. exec. com. Cuyahoga County Reps., 1963-70; mem. Cleveland Heights (Ohio) Bd. Edn., 1964-67, pres., 1967; mem. exec. com. Nat. Com. for Indsl. Mission, Detroit, chair, 1966-72; vice chair Cleve. subcom. U.S. Commn. on Civil Rights, 1966; mem. bd. overseers NYU Stern Sch. of Bus.; bd. dirs. Hartford Hosp., 1979-89, sec. bd., 1982-83; bd. dirs. Bus. Coalition on Health, Hartford, chmn. bd., 1983-89; trustee Hartford Coll. for Women, chmn. bd. trustees, 1986-89; trustee Hartford Courant Found., chmn. bd. trustees, 1982-84. Sgt. USAF, 1943-46, PTO. Mem. NAM (bd. dirs. 1978-81), Conn. Bus. and Industry Assn. (bd. dirs. 1982-86), Soc. of Cin., Century Assn., Cruising Club of Am., Economic Club, Hartford Golf Club, Royal Ocean Racing Club, Tavern Club. Episcopalian. Home: 70 Terry Rd Hartford CT 06105-1109 Office: Hartford Grad Ctr 275 Windsor St Hartford CT 06120-2910

LOOMSTEIN, ARTHUR, real estate company executive; b. St. Louis, July 27, 1939; s. Meyer and Ann (Mariam) L.; m. Kay Diane Oppenheim, Aug. 22, 1975; children: David Jay, Debi, Debra Ann. BSBA, Washington U., St. Louis, 1961, JD, 1964. Pres. Centerco Properties Inc., St. Louis, 1961—. Recipient Disting. Citizen Citation, St. Louis Regional Commerce and Growth Assn., 1973. Mem. Bldg. Owners and Mgrs. Assn. Met. St. Louis (bd. dirs. 1969-75, treas. 1971-72, pres. 1973-74), Soc. Real Property Adminstrs. (founding mem.). Clubs: Meadowbrook Country. Avocations: swimming, golfing, thoroughbred racing. Home: 5 Somerset Downs Saint Louis MO 63124-1031 Office: Centerco Properties Inc 7730 Carondelet Ave Saint Louis MO 63105-3314

LOONEY, CLAUDIA ARLENE, academic administrator; b. Fullerton, Calif., June 13, 1946; d. Donald F. and Mildred B. (Gage) Schneider; m. James K. Looney, Oct. 8, 1967; 1 child, Christopher K. BA, Calif. State U., 1969. Dir. youth YWCA No. Orange County, Fullerton, Calif., 1967-70; dir. dist. Camp Fire Girls, San Francisco, 1971-73; asst. exec. dir. Camp Fire Girls, Los Angeles, 1973-77; asst. dir. community resources Childrens Hosp., Los Angeles, 1977-80; dir. community devel. Orthopaedic Hosp., Los Angeles, 1980-82; sr. v.p. Saddleback Meml. Found./Saddleback Meml. Med. Ctr., Laguna Hills, Calif., 1982-92; v.p. planning and advancement Calif. Inst. Arts, Santa Clarita, Calif., 1992—; instr. U. Calif., Irvine, Univ. Irvine; mem. steering com. U. Irvine. Mem. steering com. United Way, Los Angeles, 1984-86. Fellow Assn. Healthcare Philanthropy (nat. chair-elect, chmn. program Nat. Edn. Conf. 1986, regional dir. 1985-89, fin. com. 1988—, pres., com. chn. 1987—, Give To Life com. chmn. 1987-91, Orange County Fund Raiser of Yr. 1992); mem. Nat. Soc. Fund Raising Execs. Found. (cert., vice chmn. 1985-90, chair 1993—), So. Calif. Assn. Hosp. Devel. (past pres., bd. dirs.), Profl. Ptnrs. (chmn. 1986, instr. 1988—), Philanthropic Ednl. Orgn. (past pres.). Avocations: swimming, sailing, photography. Office: Calif Inst of the Arts 24700 Mcbean Pky Valencia CA 91355-2340

LOONEY, NORMAN EARL, pomologist, plant physiologist; b. Adrian, Oreg., May 31, 1938; came to Can., 1966; s. Gaynor Parks and Lois Delilah (Francis) L.; m. Arlene Mae Willis, Oct. 4, 1957 (div. 1982); children: Pamela June, Patricia Lorene, Steven Paul; m. Norah Christine Keating, July 16, 1983. BSc in Agr. Edn., Washington State U., 1960, PhD in Horticulture, 1966. Rsch. scientist Agr. Can., Summerland, B.C., 1966-71, scientist, sect. head, 1972-81, sr. scientist, 1982-87, sr. scientist, sect. head, 1987-90, prin. scientist, sect. head, 1991-95; prin. scientist, 1995—; vis. scientist food rsch. divsn. CSIRO, Sydney, Australia, 1971-72, East Malling Rsch. Sta., Maidstone, Kent, 1981-82, Dept. Horticulture U. Lincoln, Christchurch, New Zealand, 1990-91; sec. Expert Com. on Horticulture, Ottawa, Ont., Can., 1986-90; chmn. Agrl. Can. Tree Fruit Rsch. Network, 1993—; chmn. working group on growth regulators in fruit prodn. Internat. Soc. Hort. Sci., Wageningen, The Netherlands, 1987-94, chmn. fruit sect., 1994—. Contbr. numerous articles and chpts. to sci. publs. Fellow Am. Soc. Hort. Sci. Achievements include patent for Promotion of Flowering in Fruit Trees (U.S. and foreign). Office: Agr Can Rsch Sta, Summerland, BC Canada V0H 1Z0

LOONEY, RALPH EDWIN, newspaper editor, author, photographer; b. Lexington, Ky., June 22, 1924; s. Arville Zone and Connie Elizabeth (Boyd) L.; m. Clarabel Richards, Dec. 7, 1944. BA, U. Ky., 1948. Various positions including proof reader, photographer, chief photographer, sports writer, reporter Lexington Leader, 1943-52; reporter Albuquerque Tribune, 1953-54; reporter, copy editor, chief copy editor St. Louis Globe-Democrat, 1955-56; city editor Albuquerque Tribune, 1956-68, asst. mng. editor, 1968-73, editor, 1973-80; editor Rocky Mountain News, Denver, 1980-89; columnist Scripps Howard News Svc., 1989-93, Tribune, Albuquerque, 1989-93. Author: Haunted Highways, the Ghost Towns of New Mexico, 1969, O'Keeffe and Me, 1995; contbr. articles to mags. including Nat. Observer, others; photographs to mags. Founder, N.Mex. Motion Picture Commn., 1967-76; v.p., bd. dirs. Albuquerque C. of C., 1971-75; bd. dirs. Albuquerque Indsl. Devel. Svc., 1971-80, Newspaper Features Coun., 1984-89; bd. advisors Lovelace Med. Ctr., Albuquerque, 1976-80, UPI, 1983-86; exec. coun. St. Joseph Hosp., 1986-89. Recipient N.Mex. medal of Merit, 1968, Robert F. Kennedy Journalism award, 1970, George Washington Honor medal Freedoms Found., 1969, 19 E.H. Shaffer awards N.Mex. Press Assn., 1965-80; named Colo. Newspaper Person of the Yr., 1988, Newspaper Features Coun. Jester award, 1989. Mem. N.Mex. Press Assn. (state pres. 1976), Colo. Press Assn. (bd. dirs. 1982-85), Sigma Delta Chi (N. Mex. pres. 1960). Methodist. Home: 6101 Casa De Vida Dr NE Albuquerque NM 87111-1140

LOONEY, RICHARD CARL, bishop; b. Hillsville, Va., Feb. 14, 1934; s. Carl and Ruth (Bourne) L.; m. Carolyn Adele McKeithen, Sept. 3, 1957; children: Teresa, David, Jonathan. BA, Emory and Henry Coll., 1954; postgrad., Edinburg (Scotland U.), 1956; BD, Emory U., 1957; postgrad., Union Theol. Sem., Richmond, Va. Ordained to ministry United Meth. Ch. as deacon, 1955, as elder, 1959. Pastor Rising Faawn (Ga.) Cir., 1957-61, Pleasant View-Wyndale Charge, Abington, Va., 1961-65, Pleasant View, Abington, Va., 1965-67, White Oak United Meth. Ch., Chattanooga, 1968-71, Broad St. United Meth. Ch., Cleveland, Tenn., 1972-75; dist. supt. Chattanooga Dist., 1976-78; pastor Munsey Meml. United Meth. Ch., Johnson City, Tenn., 1979-86, Church St. United Meth. Ch., Knoxville, Tenn., 1987-88; elected bishop Southeastern Jurisdiction, United Meth. Ch., Macon, Ga., 1988—. Office: The United Meth Ctr PO Box 13616 Macon GA 31208-3616

LOONEY, WILLIAM FRANCIS, JR., lawyer; b. Boston, Sept. 20, 1931; s. William Francis Sr. and Ursula Mary (Ryan) L.; m. Constance Mary O'Callaghan, Dec. 28, 1957; children: Willam F. III, Thomas M., Karen D., Martha A. AB, Harvard U., JD. Bar: Mass. 1958, D.C. 1972, U.S. Supreme Ct. 1972, U.S. Dist. Ct. (ea. dist.) Mich. 1986. Law clk. to presiding justice Mass. Supreme Jud. Ct., 1958-59; assoc. Goodwin, Procter & Hoar, Boston, 1959-62; chief civil div. U.S. Attys. Office, 1964-65; ptnr. Looney & Grossman, Boston, 1965-94, sr. counsel, 1995—; asst. U.S. atty. Dist. Mass., 1962-65; spl. hearing officer U.S. Dept. Justice, 1965-68; mem. Mass. Bd. Bar Overseers, 1985-91, vice chmn., 1990-91; corp. mem. Greater Boston Legal Svcs., Inc., 1994—. Mem. Zoning Bd. of Appeals, Dedham, Mass., 1971-74; bd. dirs. Boston Latin Sch. Found., 1981-85, pres. 1981-84, chmn. bd. dirs., 1984-86; trustee Social Law Libr., 1994—. Fellow Am. Coll. Trial Lawyers; mem. Mass. Bar Assn. (co-chmn. standing com. lawyers responsibility for pub. svc. 1987-88), Boston Bar Assn. (pres. 1984-85, coun. mem. 1985-90, chmn. sr. lawyers sect. 1992-94, Maguire award for professionalism 1995), Nat. Assn. Bar Pres.'s, Boston Latin Sch. Assn. (pres. 1980-82, life trustee 1982—, man of yr. 1985), USCG Found. (bd. dirs. 1987—), Norfolk Golf Club, Harvard Club, New Seabury Golf Club. Democrat. Roman Catholic. Home: 43 Coronation Dr Dedham MA 02026-6230 Office: 101 Arch St 9th Fl Boston MA 02110-1112

LOOPER, GEORGE KIRK, religious society executive; b. Gould, Okla., Feb. 18, 1943; s. Ishmel Guy and Edna Mae (Burge) L.; m. Vivian Kay Swanson, Dec. 13, 1963; children: Michael Edward, Steven Allen, Jodell Lin. BS in Sci., Northeastern Okla. Tchrs. Coll, 1966; MS in Physics, U. Wyo., 1973; MS in Elem. Edn., Western Carolina U., 1968. Exec. dir. Seventh Day Bapt. Missionary Soc., Westerly, R.I. Republican. Seventh Day Baptist. Home: 7 State St Westerly RI 02891

LOORY, STUART HUGH, journalist; b. Wilson, Pa., May 22, 1932; s. Harry and Eva (Holland) L.; m. Marjorie Helene Dretel, June 19, 1955 (div. July 1995); children: Joshua Alan, Adam Edward, Miriam Beth; m. Nina Nikolaevna Kudriavtseva, Aug. 17, 1995. B.A., Cornell U., 1954; M.S. with honors, Columbia U., 1958; postgrad., U. Vienna, Austria, 1958. Reporter Newark News, 1955-58; Reporter N.Y. Herald Tribune, 1959-61, sci. writer, 1961-63, Washington corr., 1963-64; fgn. corr. N.Y. Herald Tribune, Moscow, 1964-66; sci. editor Metromedia Radio Stas., 1962-64, Moscow corr., 1964-66; sci. writer N.Y. Times, 1966; White House corr. Los Angeles Times, 1967-71; fellow Woodrow Wilson Internat. Center for Scholars, Washington, 1971-72; exec. editor WNBC-TV News, 1973; Kiplinger prof. pub. affairs reporting Ohio State U., Columbus, 1973-75; assoc. editor Chgo. Sun-Times, 1975-76, mng. editor, 1976-80; v.p., mng. editor Washington bur. Cable News Network, 1980-82, Moscow bur. chief, 1983-86, sr. correspondent, 1986, exec. producer, 1987-90; exec. dir. internat. rels. Turner Broadcasting System, Inc., Atlanta, 1988—; editor-in-chief CNN World Report, 1990-91; v.p. CNN, 1990-95; exec. v.p. Turner Internat. Broadcasting, Russia, 1993—; v.p., supervising prodr. Turner Original Prodns., 1995; lectr. in field. Author: (with David Kraslow) The Secret Search for Peace in Vietnam, 1968, Defeated: Inside America's Military Machine, 1973, (with Ann Imse) Seven Days That Shook the World: The Collapse of Soviet Communism, 1991; contbr. articles mags. and encys. Recipient citation Overseas Press Club, 1966; Raymond Clapper award Congl. Press Gallery, 1968; George Polk award L.I.U., 1968; Du Mont award U. Calif. at, Los Angeles, 1968; Distinguished Alumni award Columbia, 1969; 50th Anniversary medal Columbia Sch. Journalism, 1963; Edwin Hood award for diplomatic corr. Nat. Press Club, 1987; Pulitzer traveling scholar, 1958. Jewish. Office: CNN Moscow Box 26 Post International Inc 666 5th Ave Ste 572 New York NY 10103

LOOSBROCK, CAROL MARIE, information management professional; b. Dubuque, Iowa, Aug. 21, 1936; d. Julius Carl and Elizabeth Cecilia (Kurz) L. BA, Clarke Coll., 1958; postgrad., Art Inst. Chgo., 1959-63; MS, Am. U., 1979. With Dept. Def., Washington, 1968—, analyst, 1979—. Mem. AAAS, Assn. Computing Machinery (Washington D.C. symposium steering coms. 1980-81, exec. coun. 1981-84); N.Y. Acad. Scis. (life), Am. Mgmt. Assn., Am. Security Coun. Found. (U.S. congl. adv. bd. 1984—, coalition for peace through strength leadership award, coalition for Desert Storm, coalition for internat. security), Am. Mus. Natural History. Republican. Home: 4514 Connecticut Ave NW Washington DC 20008 Office: The Pentagon Washington DC 20310

LOPACH, JAMES JOSEPH, political science educator; b. Great Falls, Mont., June 23, 1942; s. John Ernest and Alma Marie (Schapman) L.; divorced, Dec. 10, 1991; children: Christine, Paul. AB in Philosophy, Carroll Coll., 1964; MA in Am. Studies, U. Notre Dame, 1967, MAT in English Edn., 1968, PhD in Govt., 1973. Mgr. Pacific Telephone, Palo Alto, Calif., 1968-69; adminstr. City of South Bend, Ind., 1971-73; prof. U. Mont., Missoula, 1973—, chmn. dept. polit. sci., 1977-87, assoc. dean Coll. Arts and Scis., 1987-88, acting dir. Mansfield Ctr., 1984-85, spl. asst. to the univ. pres., 1988-92, assoc. provost, 1992-95; spl. asst. to provost Mansfield Ctr., 1995—; cons. local govts., state agys., 1973—. Author, editor: We the People of Montana, 1983, Tribal Government Today, 1990, Planning Small Town America, 1990; contbr. articles to profl. jours. Roman Catholic. Office: U Mont Dept Polit Sci Missoula MT 59812

LOPATA, HELENA ZNANIECKA, sociologist, researcher, educator; b. Poznan, Poland, Oct. 1, 1925; d. Florian Witold and Eileen (Markley) Znaniecki; m. Richard Stefan Lopata, Feb. 8, 1946 (wid. July 1994); children: Theodora Karen Lopata-Menasco. B.A., U. Ill., 1946, M.A., 1947; Ph.D., U. Chgo., 1954; DSc (hon.), Guelph U., Can., 1995. Lectr. U. Va. Extension, Langley AFB, 1951-52, DePaul U., 1956-60; lectr. Roosevelt U., 1960-64, asst. prof. sociology, 1964-67, assoc. prof., 1967-69; prof. sociology Loyola U., Chgo., 1969; chmn. dept. sociology Loyola U., 1970-72, dir. Center for Comparative Study of Social Roles, 1972—; mem. NIMH Rev. Bd., 1977-79; mem. Mayor's Council Manpower and Econ. Devel., 1974-79; mem. adv. com., chair tech. com. White House Conf. on Aging, 1979-81; adv. council Nat. Inst. Aging, 1978-83. Author: Occupation: Housewife, 1971, Widowhood in an American City, 1973, Polish Americans: Status Competition in an Ethnic Community, 1976, (with Debra Barnewolt and

Cheryl Miller) City Women: Work, Jobs, Occupations, Careers, Vol. I, America, 1984, Vol. II, Chicago, 1985, City Women in America, 1986, (with Henry Brehm) Widows and Dependent Wives: From Social Problem to Federal Policy, 1986, Polish Americans, 1994, Circles and Settings: Role Changes of American Women, 1994, Current Widowhood: Myths and Realities, 1996; adv. editor: Sociologist Quar., 1969-72, Jour. Marriage and Family, 1978-82, Symbolic Interaction, 1989—; editor: Marriages and Families, 1973, (with Nona Glazer and Judith Wittner) Research on the Interweave of Social Roles: vol. I, Women and Men, 1980, (with David Maines) vol. 2, Friendship, 1981, (with Joseph Pleck) vol. 3, Families and Jobs, 1983, vol. 4, Current Research on Occupations and Professions, 1987, vol. 5, 1987, Widows: The Middle East, Asia and the Pacific, 1987, Widows: North America, 1987, (with Anne Figeat) Current Research on Occupations and Professions: Vol. 9: Getting Down to Business, 1996, (with David Maines) Friendship in Context, 1990; adv. bd. Symbolic Interaction, 1977-89; contbr. articles to profl. jours. Bd. overseers Wellesley Ctr. of Rsch. and Women, 1979-84. Recipient Research award Radcliffe Coll., 1982; grantee Chgo. Tribune, 1956, Midwest Coun. Social Research on Aging, 1964-65, Adminstrn. on Aging, 1967-69, 68-71, Social Security Adminstrn., 1971-75, also 1975-79, Indo-Am. Fellowship Program: Coun. for Internat. Eschange Scholars, 1987-88, Rsch. Stimulation grantee Loyola U. Chgo., 1988, 92, Am. Coun. Learned Soc. travel grant, 1995, Internat. Rsch. Exchange Bd. short term travel grant, 1995; named Faculty Mem. of Yr., Loyola U., 1975. Fellow Midwest Coun. for Social Rsch. on Aging (pres. 1969-70, 91-92, postdoctoral tng. dir. 1971-77), Ill. Sociol. Assn. (pres. 1969-70), Gerontol. Soc. Am. (chmn. social and behavioral sci. sect. 1980-81), Internat. Gerontol. Assn.: mem. Soc. for Study Social Problems (chmn. spl. problems com. 1971, v.p. 1975, coun. 1978-80, pres. 1983, Disting. Scholar award family div. 1989), Am. Sociol. Assn. (coun. 1978-81, chmn. sect. family 1976, chmn. sect. sex roles 1975, Sorokin awwards com. 1970-73, publs. com. 1972-73, nominations com. 1977, chmn. sect. on aging 1982-83 (Disting. Career award, 1992 Section on Aging), Cooley-Blumer awards com., 1984, Jessie Bernard awards com. 1984-86, disting. scholarly publ. awards selection com. 1988-89, awards policy com. 1990-92, co-chair com. on internat. sociology, 1992-95), Soc. for the Study of Symbolic Interaction (mem 1977—, Mead award for Life Time Achievement, 1993), Internat. Sociol. Soc. (com. on family rsch. com. on work 1972—, rsch. com. on aging 1990—, bd. dirs. 1991-94), Midwest Sociol. Assn. (state dir. 1972-74, pres. 1975-76, chair 1994—, publs. com. 1993-95), Nat. Coun. Family Rels. (Burgess award 1990, chair internat. sect. 1991-93), Polish Inst. of Arts and Scis. in Am. (dir. 1976-82, with Zbigniew Brzezinski, Bronislaw Malinowski award in social scis. 1995), Polish Welfare Assn. (bd. dirs. 1988-91),ernat. Inst. Sociology, 1994—, Sociologists for Women in Society (mem. task force alternative work patterns, pres. 1993-94, adv. editor Gender and Society 1993-94), Soc. Study Symbolic Interaction (G.H. Mead award 1993), Hon. Doctor of Sci., Guelph U. Can. Home: 5815 N Sheridan Rd Apt 917 Chicago IL 60660-3829 Office: Loyola Univ Dept Sociology 6525 N Sheridan Rd Chicago IL 60626-5311

LOPATIN, ALAN G., lawyer; b. New Haven, Conn., May 25, 1956; s. Paul and Ruth (Rosen) L.; m. Debra Jo Engler, May 17, 1981; children: Jonah Adam, Asa Louis. BA, Yale U., 1978; JD, Am. U., 1981. Bar: D.C. 1981, U.S. Supreme Ct. 1985. Law clk. Fed. Merit Systems Commn., Washington, 1980-81; counsel com. on post office and civil service U.S. Ho. of Reps., Washington, 1981-82, counsel com. on budget, 1982-86, dep. chief counsel, 1986-87, counsel Temporary Joint Com. on Deficit Reduction, 1986, dep. gen. counsel Com. on P.O. and Civil Service, 1987-90; gen. counsel Com. on Edn. & Labor, Washington, 1991-94; pres. Ledge Counsel, Inc., Washington, 1994—; exec. dir. Nat. and Cmty. Svc. Coalition, 1995—; mem. presdl. task force Health Care Reform, Washington, 1993. Mem. ABA, D.C. Bar Assn., Nat. Dem. Club, Yale Club. Democratic. Jewish. Home: 4958 Butterworth Pl NW Washington DC 20016-4354 Office: Ledge Counsel Inc PO Box 40097 Washington DC 20016

LOPATIN, DENNIS EDWARD, immunologist, educator; b. Chgo., Oct. 26, 1948; s. Leonard Harold and Cynthia (Shifrin) L.; m. Marie S. Ludmer, June 6, 1971 (div. 1983); 1 child, Jeremy; m. Constance Maxine McLeod, July 24, 1983. BS, U. Ill., 1970, MS, 1972, PhD, 1974. Postdoctoral fellow Northwestern U. Med. Sch., Chgo., 1974-75; rsch. scientist U. Mich., Ann Arbor, 1976-90, prof., 1982—. Contbr. articles to sci. jours. Mem. Am. Assn. Immunologists, Am. Soc. Microbiology, Internat. Assn. Dental Rsch., Sigma Xi. Office: U Mich Sch Dentistry Ann Arbor MI 48109-1078

LOPATKA, SUSANA BEAIRD, maternal, child health nurse consultant; b. White Plains, N.Y., May 1, 1937; d. Paul J. and Dorothy V.L. (Jewell) Grueninger; m. John Rudolph Lopatka, Sept. 6, 1975. AB in Polit. Sci., Duke U., 1959; BSN, Columbia U., N.Y.C., 1962; MA in Parent/Child Nursing, NYU, N.Y.C., 1975. RN, Ill. Staff nurse Columbia-Presbyn. Med. Ctr., N.Y.C., 1962; pub. health nurse Dept. of Health, City of N.Y., 1962-66; pub. health nurse high-risk maternal and infant care project N.Y. Med. Coll., N.Y.C., 1966-67; nursing coord. Brownsville East N.Y. Ctr. Maternal and Infant Care Project City of N.Y., 1967-69; asst. supr. ambulatory care Mt. Sinai Med. Ctr., N.Y.C., 1969-70, sr. supr. ambulatory care, 1970-72, asst. DON ambulatory care, 1972-75; clin. specialist in maternity Chgo. Lying-In Hosp., U. Chgo. Med. Ctr., 1976-80, DON, 1980-86; maternal/child health nurse cons. Ill. Dept. Pub. Health, Chgo., 1986—; mem. perinatal nursing adv. coun. Greater Ill. chpt. March of Dimes, Chgo., 1979—. Founding pres., bd. dirs. Am. Scandinavian Assn. Ill., Chgo., 1983-95; active Chgo. Coun. Fgn. Rels., 1976—, Chgo. Hist. Soc., 1994—. Recipient Nurses Recognition award Greater Ill. chpt. March of Dimes, 1993. Mem. ANA, APHA, Ill. Nurses Assn., Chgo. Nurses Assn. (dist. 1), Ill. Pub. Health Assn. (chairperson maternal/child health sect. 1992-94, asst. chairperson 1990-92), Ill. Assn. Maternal/Child Health (pres. 1992-94, bd. dirs. 1989—), Sigma Theta Tau, Pi Sigma Alpha. Avocations: hiking, bicycling, classical music. Office: Ill Dept Pub Health 33 E Congress Pky Chicago IL 60605-1223

LOPER, CARL RICHARD, JR., metallurgical engineer, educator; b. Wauwatosa, Wis., July 3, 1932; s. Carl Richard S. and Valberg (Sundby) L.; m. Jane Louise Loehning, June 30, 1956; children: Cynthia Louise Loper Koch, Anne Elizabeth. BS in Metall. Engring., U. Wis., 1955, MS in Metall. Engring., 1958, PhD in Metall. Engring., 1961; postgrad., U. Mich., 1960. Metall. engr. Pelton Steel Casting Co., Milw., 1955-56; instr., rsch. assoc. U. Wis., Madison, 1956-61, asst. prof., 1961-64, assoc. prof., 1964-68, prof. metall. engring., 1968-88, prof. materials sci. and engring., 1988—; assoc. chmn. dept. metall. and mineral engring. U. Wis., 1979-82; rsch. metallurgist Allis Chalmers, Milw., 1961; cons., lectr. in field. Author: Principles of Metal Casting, 1965; contbr. over 400 articles to profl. jours. Chmn. 25th Anniversary of Ductile Iron Symposium, Montreal, 1973; pres. Ygdrasil Lit. Soc., 1989-90. Foundry Ednl. Found. fellow, 1953-55; Wheelabrator Corp. fellow, 1960; Ford Found. fellow, 1960; recipient Adams Meml. award Am. Welding Soc., 1963, Howard F. Taylor award, 1967, Service citation, 1969, 72, others; recipient Silver medal award of Sci. Merit Portuguese Foundry Assn., 1978, medal Chinese Foundrymen's Assn., 1989. Fellow Am. Soc. Metals (chmn. 1969-70), AIM; mem. Am. Foundrymen's Soc. (bd. dirs. 1967-70, 76-79, best paper award 1966, 67, 85, John A. Penton gold medal 1972, Hoyt Meml. lectr. 1992, aluminum divsn. award of sci. merit 1995, Foundry Ednl. Found. dirs. award 1994), Am. Welding Soc., Foundry Ednl. Found., Torske Klubben (bd. dirs., co-founder 1978—), Blackhawk Country Club, Sigma Xi, Gamma Alpha, Alpha Sigma Mu, Tau Beta Pi. Lutheran. Achievements include significant contributions to understanding the solidification and metallurgy of ferrous and non-ferrous alloys; recognized authority on solidification and cast iron metallurgy, and on education in metallurgy and materials science. Office: U Wis Cast Metals Lab 1509 University Ave Madison WI 53706-1538

LOPER, D. ROGER, retired oil company executive; b. Mpls., Dec. 14, 1920; s. Donald Rust and Agnes (Yerxa) L.; m. Sylvia Lee Brainard, Aug. 16, 1946 (dec. Apr. 1973); children: Ann Kathleen, Michael Brainard, Joyce Elizabeth, Nancy Jean Loper Woods; m. Genevieve Jean Kusles, May 4, 1974. BSMetE, Carnegie Tech. Inst., 1947. Registered chem. engr., Calif. Div. supr. Standard Oil of Calif., San Francisco, 1958-64, asst. chief engr., 1964-74; gen. mgr. Chevron Petroleum, London, 1974-80; pres. Chevron Shale Oil Co., Denver, 1980-82; v.p. Chevron Overseas Petroleum, San Francisco, 1982-85; cons. Loper Assocs., Carmel, Calif., 1985—. Inventor hydrocracking reactor, remote inspection device. Pres. Our Saviour Luth. Ch., Lafayette, Calif., 1971-72. Maj. U.S. Army, 1942-46. Republican. Home and Office: 2804 Pradera Rd Carmel CA 93923-9717

LOPER, DAVID ERIC, mathematics educator; b. Oswego, N.Y., Feb. 14, 1940; married, 1966; 4 children. BS, Carnegie Inst. Tech., 1961; MS, Case Inst. Tech., 1964, PhD in Mech. Engring., 1965. Sr. scientist Douglas Aircraft Corp., 1965-68; from asst. prof. to assoc. prof. Fla. State U., Tallahassee, 1968-77, prof. math., 1977—; dir. Geophysical Fluid Dynamics Inst., 1994—; sr. vis. fellow U. Newcastle-upon-Tyne, Eng., 1974-75. Nat. Ctr. Atmospheric Rsch. fellow, 1967-68, sr. vis. fellow U. Newcastle-upon-Tyne, Eng., 1974-75, Cambridge U., Eng., 1990; H.C. Webster fellow U. Queensland, Australia, 1983. Mem. Am. Phys. Soc., Am. Geophys. Union, Soc. Indsl. and Applied Math, Sigma Xi. Achievements include research on boundary layers in rotating, stably stratified, electrically conducting fluids; evolution of the earth's core including stratification, heat transfer, solidification and particle precipitation. Address: Florida State U Dept Math Tallahassee FL 32306 Office: Fla State U Geophys Fluid Dynamics Inst 18 Keen Bldg Tallahassee FL 32306

LOPER, GEORGE WILSON, JR., physical education educator; b. Phila., Sept. 1, 1927; s. George Wilson Sr. and Emma Margaretta (Davis) L.; m. Eleanor Ruth Shell, mar. 10, 1951 (div. Aug. 1967); children: George Wilson III, Carol Ann Loper Cloud; m. Jeanne Ann Lodeski, Aug. 12, 1967; children: Lynn Jeanne Loper Sakers, Anne Marie Loper Todd, John Vincent. BS, W. Chester State U., 1954; MEd, Temple U., 1957. Cert. tchr. Fla. Tchr., coach Media (Pa.) Pub. Schs., 1954-63, Duval County Sch. System, Jacksonville, Fla., 1963-67; tchr., dept. chmn., coach Bradford County Sch. System, Starke, Fla., 1967—. Dir. March Dimes Walkathon, Starke, 1970; coord. Spl. Olympics, Starke, 1970-89; chmn. Adminstrv. Bd. First Meth. Ch., Starke, 1970; co-chmn. Toys for Tots USMC, Starke, 1976, 78. With USMC Res., 1945-87. Named Coach of Yr. Fla. Times Union, 1966, 67, Coach of Yr. Cross Country Gainesville Sun, 1985, 86. Mem. AAHPERD (life), NEA, Nat. Health Assn. (life), Nat. High Sch. Coaches Assn., Fla. Athletic Coaches Assn. (state vice chmn. 1972—, Meritorious Svc. awrd 1988, Nat. Boys Track Coach of Yr. 1991, Life Membership award 1992), The Athletic Congress (lead instr. 1987—, internat. level track official 1983—, Track Hall of Fame 1987), Fla. Officials Assn. (high sch. games com. 1964—, state vice chmn. track 1972—), Bradford Edn. Assn. (v.p. 1977-79). Democrat. Methodist. Avocations: reading, music, art, swimming and track officiating. Home: RR 2 Box 1674 Starke FL 32091-9539 Office: Bradford High Sch 581 N Temple Ave Starke FL 32091-2609

LOPER, JAMES LEADERS, broadcasting executive; b. Phoenix, Sept. 4, 1931; s. John D. and Ellen Helen (Leaders) L.; m. Mary Louise Brion, Sept. 1, 1955; children: Elizabeth Margaret Sehran (Mrs. Michael K. Sehran), James Leaders Jr. BA, Ariz. State U., 1953; MA, U. Denver, 1957; PhD, U. So. Calif., 1967; DHL (hon.), Columbia Coll., 1973; LLD (hon.), Pepperdine U., 1978. Asst. dir. bur. broadcasting Ariz. State U., Tempe, 1953-59; news editor, announcer Sta. KTAR, Phoenix, 1955-56; dir. ednl. TV, Calif. State U., Los Angeles, 1960-64; v.p. Community TV So. Calif., Los Angeles, 1962-63; asst. to pres. Sta. KCET-Pub. TV, Los Angeles, 1963-65, sec., 1965-66, dir. ednl. services, 1964-65, asst. gen. mgr., 1965-66, v.p., gen. mgr., 1966-69, exec. v.p., gen. mgr., 1969-71, pres., gen. mgr., 1971-76, pres., CEO, 1976-82; exec. dir. Acad. TV Arts and Scis., 1983—; bd. dirs., chmn. audit com. Western Fed. Savs. and Loan Assn., L.A., 1979-93; bd. dirs. Global View, Washington; chmn. bd. dirs. Tennessee Ernie Ford Enterprises, 1994-95; chmn. bd. Pub. Broadcasting Service, Washington, 1969-72; dir. Calif. Arts Coun., 1991—; adj. prof. Sch. Cinema and TV U. So. Calif., 1984—; sr. lectr. U. So. Calif., Los Angeles, 1969-70; pres. Western Ednl. Network, 1968-70; mem. Gov.'s Ednl. TV and Radio Adv. Com., Calif., 1968-74; U.S. rep. CENTO Conf. Radio and TV, Turkey, 1978, trustee Internat. Council Nat. Acad. TV Arts and Scis., 1988—. Contbr. articles to profl. jours; contbr. to ETV: The Farther Vision, 1967, Broadcasting and Bargaining: Labor Relations in Radio and Television, 1970. Mem. adv. bd. Jr. League of Los Angeles, 1970-76, Jr. League of Pasadena, 1972-75, Los Angeles Jr. Arts Ctr., 1968-72; exec. v.p. Assocs. of Otis Art Inst., 1971-77, pres., 1975-77; chmn., dir. The Performing Tree, Los Angeles; bd. dirs. Sears-Roebuck Found., 1976-79; chmn. bd. visitors Annenburg Sch. Communications, U. So. Calif., 1975-80; trustee Poly. Sch., Pasadena; mem. Calif. State Arts Commn., 1991. Recipient Disting. Alumnus award Ariz. State U., 1972; Alumni award of Merit, U. So. Calif., 1975; Gov's. award Hollywood chpt. Nat. Acad. TV Arts and Scis., 1975; Alumni Achievement award Phi Sigma Kappa, 1975; named Centennial Alumnus Nat. Assn. of State Univs. and Land Grant Colls., 1988. Named to Hall of Fame Walter Cronkite Sch. Comms., Ariz. State U., 1994 Mem. Acad. TV Arts and Scis. (past gov., v.p. Hollywood chpt., trustee nat. acad.), TV Acad. Found., Hollywood Radio and TV Soc. (treas., dir.), Western Ednl. Soc. Telecommunications (past pres.), Assn. Calif. Pub. TV Stas. (past pres.), Young Pres.'s Orgn., Phi Sigma Kappa, Pi Delta Epsilon, Alpha Delta Sigma, Sigma Delta Chi. Presbyterian (chmn. Mass Media Task Force So. Calif. synod 1969-75). Clubs: Valley Hunt (Pasadena), Bel-Air Bay, California, Los Angeles, 100 of Los Angeles, Calif. (Los Angeles), Twilight Pasadena, Lincoln Club, L.A. Office: Acad TV Arts and Scis PO Box 7344 North Hollywood CA 91603-7344

LOPER, MERLE WILLIAM, lawyer, educator; b. Webster City, Iowa, July 9, 1940; s. Clifford Matthew and Alfrieda Sophia (Hiller) L.; m. Jean Allyn Kelley, Oct. 7, 1967; 1 dau., Kelley. B.A., Northwestern U., 1962; J.D., U. Chgo., 1965. Bar: Ind. 1966, Maine 1974, U.S. Supreme Ct. 1979. Law clk. U.S. Dist. Ct., Ft. Wayne, Ind., 1965-66; atty. div. civil rights Dept. Justice, 1966-69; teaching fellow Harvard U. Law Sch., 1969-71; assoc. prof. law U. Maine, 1971-75, prof., 1975—; vis. prof. Shanghai Maritime U., 1988; chief cons. Maine Probate Law Revision Commn., 1976-81; cons. probate rules com. Maine Supreme Ct., 1980-94; exec. sec., counsel Maine Com. Jud. Responsibility and Disability, 1983—; pvt. practice civil rights litigation law Portland, Maine, 1975-83; cons. on comm. in pub. affairs and law, civil rights litigation; cons. com. on ct. structure Maine Jud. Coun., 1984-85; convocation scholar on constn. U. So. Maine, 1987-88. Bd. dirs. Maine Civil Liberties Union., 1981-82; mem. legal panel Maine Civil Liberties Union, 1982-83. Mem. ABA. Office: 246 Deering Ave Portland ME 04102-2800 *Be open to the world.*

LOPER, ROBERT BRUCE, theater director, educator; b. Olathe, Colo., June 30, 1925; s. Roy Major and Charlotte (Matthews) L.; m. Shirley McClurg, Aug. 28, 1948; children—William, Matthew. B.A., U. Colo., 1948, M.A., 1951; Ph.D. in Elizabethan Lit. (Fulbright scholar Stratford-on-Avon 1951-53), Birmingham (Eng.) U., 1957. Actor, also documentary film writer N.Y.C., 1948-49; radio writer and newscaster Tacoma, 1949-50; faculty Stanford, 1953-68; prof., 1962-68, head dept. drama, 1963-68; founder Stanford Repertory Theatre, 1965; prof. drama U. Wash., 1968—; mem. San Francisco Actor's Workshop, 1960-64; dir., actor Oreg. Shakespeare Festival, Ashland, 1955—; vis. dir. Brecht's Caucasian Chalk Circle at Vancouver (Can.) Internat. Festival, 1959, Seattle Repertory Theatre, 1967; actor, dir. Contemporary Theatre, Empty Space Theatre, 1968—; dir. Joe Egg, The Price; guest dir. Talbot Theatre Centre, London, Ont., 1970. Actor, dir. Oedipus Rex, Death of a Salesman, Member of the Wedding, 1987, Seattle Repertory Theatre, 1967, Awake and Sing, Joe Egg, And Miss Reardon Drinks a Little, The Prize, 1987, A Contemporary Theatre, 1968—; dir. Billy Bishop, Old Times, Otherwise Engaged, Duet for One, 1985, Empty Space Theatre, 1975, Wozzeck; actor Fool for Love, 1984, Intiman Theatre, Waterworks, Kennedy Ctr., 1988; featured actor Bergen Internat. Festival, Norway, 1969; premiere Centralia (Pritchard), Stand Still (Arlin); producer (stage works) Am. premiere Dallapiccola's opera Night Flight, 1962, Alchemist, 1960. Mem. Phi Beta Kappa, Tau Kappa Delta. Home: 2641 E Helen St Seattle WA 98112-3619 *The theatre has been my obsession and my religion. Directing a play is a kind of communion, the sharing of a fictional struggle which illuminates the more chaotic struggles and obsessions of our day-to-day lives. In making us more civilized, less lonely, the theatre can be teaching at its best.*

LOPES, LOLA LYNN, psychologist, educator; b. Jackson Heights, N.Y., Mar. 14, 1941; d. Ivan Correa and Elizabeth (Edgemon) L.; m. Gregg Clifford Oden, Apr. 18, 1980. BA, U. Redlands, 1962; MA, Calif. State U., Long Beach, 1971; PhD, U. Calif. San Diego, La Jolla, 1974. Asst. prof. psychology U. Wis., Madison, 1974-81, assoc. prof., 1981-87, prof., 1987-90, chmn. dept., 1988-90; Pomerantz prof. bus. U. Iowa, Iowa City, 1990—, assoc. dean undergrad. programs Coll. Bus., 1995—. Contbr. articles to profl. jours. Sloan Found. fellow, U. Chgo., 1981. Mem. Soc. for Judgement and Decision Making (pres. 1989-90), Psychonomic Soc., Cognitive Sci. Soc., Soc. for Math. Psychology, Am. Psychol. Soc., Sigma Xi. Home: 2021 Laurence Ct NE Iowa City IA 52240-9150 Office: U Iowa Dept Mgmt And Orgns Iowa City IA 52242

LOPEZ, A. RUBEN, lawyer; b. San Juan, P.R., Oct. 1, 1955; s. Angel and Elizabeth (Hernandez) L.; m. Magaly Retamar, Oct. 17, 1993. BA in Psychology, SUNY, Buffalo, 1979; JD, U. Toledo, 1982. Bar: Ohio 1992. Instnl. care asst. Dept. Anti-Addiction Svcs., San Juan, 1984; instnl. social worker Dept. Social Svcs., San Juan, 1984-86; supr. location Child Support Enforcement Program, San Juan, 1986-88; chief of benefits Bur. Social Security for Chauffeurs, San Juan, 1988-90; pvt. practice Cleve., 1992-93; atty. Legal Aid Soc. of Columbus, Ohio, 1993—. Bd. trustees Ct. Apptd. Spl. Advocates of Franklin County, 1994—. Mem. Columbus Bar Assn. (family law sect.). SDA. Avocations: camping, jogging. Home: 263 Georgesville Rd # 42 Columbus OH 43228-4019

LOPEZ, ANDY, university athletic coach. Head coach Pepperdine U. Waves, 1989-94, U. Florida, 1994—. NCAA Divsn. 1A Champions, 1992. Office: U Florida P O Box 14485 Gainesville FL 32604*

LOPEZ, BARRY HOLSTUN, writer; b. Port Chester, N.Y., Jan. 6, 1945; s. Adrian Bernard and Mary Frances (Holstun) L.; m. Sandra Jean Landers, June 10, 1967. BA, U. Notre Dame, 1966, MA in Teaching, 1968; postgrad., U. Oreg., 1968-69; LHD (hon.), Whittier Coll., 1988, U. Portland, 1994. Free-lance writer, 1970—; assoc. The Freedom Forum Media Studies Ctr., N.Y.C., 1985—; mem. U.S. Cultural Delegation to China, 1988. Author: Desert Notes, 1976, Giving Birth to Thunder, 1978, Of Wolves and Men, 1978 (John Burroughs Soc. medal 1979, Christophers of N.Y. medal 1979, Pacific Northwest Booksellers award in nonfiction 1979), River Notes, 1979, Winter Count, 1981 (Disting. Recognition award Friends Am. Writers in Chgo. 1982), Arctic Dreams, 1986 (Nat. Book award in nonfiction Nat. Book Found. 1986, Christopher medal 1987, Pacific Northwest Booksellers award 1987, Frances Fuller Victor award in nonfiction Oreg. Inst. Literary Arts 1987), Crossing Open Ground, 1988, Crow and Weasel, 1990 (Parents Choice Found. award), The Rediscovery of North America, 1991, Field Notes, 1994 (Pacific Northwest Booksellers award in fiction 1995); also numerous articles, essays and short stories; contbg. editor Harper's mag., 1981-82, 84—, N.Am. Rev., 1977—; works translated into Japanese, Swedish, German, Dutch, Italian, French, Norwegian, Chinese, Finnish, Spanish. Recipient award in Lit., Am. Acad. Arts and Letters, 1986, Gov.'s award for Arts, 1990, Lannan Found. award, 1990, Antarctic Svc. medal USN/NSF, 1989; John Simon Guggenheim Found. fellow, 1987. Mem. PEN Am. Ctr., Authors Guild, Poets and Writers.

LOPEZ, CAROLE SINKS, paralegal; b. Chgo., Mar. 16, 1962; d. Donald Joseph and Shirley Carole (Stewart) Sinks; children: Shannon, Phillip. Grad., Am. Inst. Paralegal Studies. Paralegal McCarthy, Rowden & Faber, Decatur, Ill.; steering com. Coalition Consumer's Rights, Chgo.; mem. A.B.A.T.E. Motorcycle Safety, Decatur. Coord. ctrl. Ill. Families Advocating Injury Reduction, Decatur, 1993—. Mem. ATLA. Mem. Christian Ch. Avocations: gardening, family. Office: McCarthy Rowden & Faber 243 S Water St Decatur IL 62523

LOPEZ, DAVID TIBURCIO, lawyer, educator, arbitrator, mediator; b. Laredo, Tex., July 17, 1939; s. Tiburcio and Dora (Davila) L.; m. Romelia G. Guerra, Nov. 20, 1965; 1 child, Vianei López Robinson. Student, Laredo Jr. Coll., 1956-58; BJ, U. Tex., 1962; JD summa cum laude, South Tex. Coll. Law, 1971. Bar: Tex. 1971, U.S. Dist. Ct. (so. dist.) Tex. 1972, U.S. Ct. Appeals (5th cir.) 1973, U.S. Dist. Ct. (we. dist.) Tex. 1975, U.S. Ct. Claims 1975, U.S. Ct. Appeals (fed. cir.) 1975, U.S. Supreme Ct. 1976, U.S. Dist. Ct. (ea. dist.) Tex. 1978, U.S. Ct. Appeals (11th cir.) 1981, U.S. Ct. Appeals (9th cir.) 1984; cert. internat. com. arbitrator Internat. Ctr. for Arbitration; mediator tng. Atty.-Mediator Inst. Reporter Laredo Times, 1958-59; cons. Mexican Nat. Coll. Mag., Mexico City, 1961-62; reporter Corpus Christi (Tex.) Caller-Times, 1962-64; state capitol corr. Long News Svc., Austin, Tex., 1964-65; publs. dir. Interam. Regional Orgn. of Workers, Mexico City, 1965-67; nat. field rep. AFL-CIO, Washington, 1967-71, publs. dir. Tex. chpt., Austin, 1971-72; pvt. practice, Houston, 1971—; adj. prof. U. Houston, 1972-74, Thurgood Marshall Sch. Law, Houston, 1975-76; mem. adv. com. nat. Hispanic ednl. rsch. project One Million and Counting Tomas Rivera Ctr., 1989—; mem. adv. bd. Inst. Transnat. Arbitration; charter mem. Resolution Forum Inc.; mem. adv. bd. East Tex. Ctr. Profl. Responsibility. Bd. dirs. Pacifica Found., N.Y.C., 1970-72, Houston Community Coll., 1972-75; mem. bd. edn. Houston Ind. Sch. Dist., 1972-75. With U.S. Army. Mem. ABA (chair sub-com. atty. fees in appeals), FBA, ATLA, Tex. Bar Assn. (dir. State Bar Coll., task force on rules of civil procedures), Houston Bar Assn., Internat. Bar Assn., Interam. Bar Assn., Bar of U.S. Fed. Cir., Mex.-Am. Bar Assn., Inter-Pacific Bar Assn., Tex.-Mex. Bar Assn. (chair labor com.), Hispanic Bar Assn., World Assn. Lawyers (chair com. on law and the handicapped), Am. Judicature Soc., Indsl. Rels. Rsch. Assn., Kappa Tau Alpha, Phi Theta Kappa, Sigma Delta Chi, Phi Alpha Delta. Democrat. Roman Catholic. Home: 28 Farnham Ct Houston TX 77024 Office: 3900 Montrose Blvd Houston TX 77006-4908

LOPEZ, ESTRELLITA COLUMNA, trading company executive; b. Manila, Nov. 20, 1953; came to U.S., 1990; d. Tiburcio Leaban and Dionicia Flores (Madriaga) Columna; divorced; 1 child, Ricci Anne C. A Secretarial Sci., Feati U., Manila, 1972. Office helper Kraft Foods, Inc. (Philippines), Paranaque, 1970-72; office clk. Nestle Philippines, Makati, 1972-76; acctg. clk.-typist Ultra Internat. Trading, Makati, 1976-78; clk.-typist Constrn.-Devel. Corp. of Philippine Internat. Trading Co., Makati, 1979-82, sec., 1982-86; exec. sec. to pres. Duty Free Philippines, Paranaque, 1986-90; exec. asst. Colina Group, Beverly Hills, Calif., 1990-91; mng. dir., buyer internat. sales Asian Am. Trading Co., Ltd., L.A., 1991—. Avocations: bowling, dancing, racquetball, singing, outdoor activities. Home and Office: Asian Am Trading Co Ltd 4359 Clayton Ave Los Angeles CA 90027-5533

LOPEZ, FRANCISCA UY, secondary educator; b. Leyte, The Philippines, Mar. 9, 1925; d. Juan and Perpetua (Loyola) Uy; m. Elias Espiritu Lopez, Apr. 10, 1955; 1 child, Maria Elisa Lopez Stevens. BSE, Philippine Normal Coll., Manila, Philippines, 1952; MEd, Pa. State U., 1961; MA, Nat. Tchr. Coll., Manila, 1955. Cert. life standard tchr., Calif., tchr. (life cert.), Tex. Instructional resource tchr. El Tejon Union Sch. Dist., Mettler, Calif.; reading specialist Saudi Arabia Internat. Sch., Dhahran; facilitator staff devel. unit, instr. indsl. tng. ctr. Arabian Am. Oil Co., Dhahran; tchr. Dallas Ind. Sch. Dist. Leader Girl Scouts U.S. Fulbright Smith-Mundt grantee, 1960-61. Mem. NEA, Classroom Tchrs. Dallas (sch. rep.), Tex. State Tchrs. Assn. Home: 1816 Tawakoni Ln Plano TX 75075-6732

LOPEZ, FRANCISCO, IV, health care administrator; b. San Jose, Costa Rica, Costa Rica, Aug. 31, 1956; s. Francisco III and Myriam (Bolanos) L.; m. Marie Jeanne de Lassus; children: Matthew Chase, Kathryn Louise, Elizabeth Myriam Jane, James Austin. BS, La. State U., 1976; MHA, Tulane U., 1980. Adminstrv. asst. Mercy Hosp. of New Orleans, 1980-81, asst. v.p., 1981-82, v.p., 1982-85, exec. v.p., 1985-86, chief operating officer, 1986—; exec. v.p. Mercy Health Sys., 1995—; pres. St. Mary's/Mercy Hosp., 1995—; bd. cons. St. John's Place, New Orleans, 1986—. Bd. dirs. Enid Beautiful; trustee Enid Telecomms. Authority; v.p. Calhoun/Palmer Neighborhood Assn., New Orleans, 1984-85; bd. dirs. Holy Name of Jesus Sch., New Orleans, 1985, United Cerebral Palsy, New Orleans, 1986, Mount St. Mary H.S., Okla. Cath. Health Care Assn., bd. dirs. YMCA, Rotary Club. Recipient Associated U. Programs in Health Adminstrn. scholarship, 1979, Nat. Hispanic scholarship, 1980. Fellow Am. Coll. Health Care Execs. (Foster G. McGaw scholarship 1979); mem. Am. Hosp. Assn., Fedn. Am. Hosps., New Health Care Mgrs., So. Yacht Club (New Orleans), Greens Country Club (Oklahoma City), Oakwood Country Club. Clubs: So. Yacht (new Orleans); Greens Country (Oklahoma City). Avocations: tennis, travel, swimming. Home: 2029 Oak Leaf Cir Enid OK 73703 Office: St Mary's Mercy Hosp PO Box 232 Enid OK 73702

LOPEZ, GUILLERMO, obstetrician-gynecologist, educator; b. Bogota, Colombia, Oct. 3, 1919; came to U.S., 1944; s. Pedro P. and Sofia (Escobar) L.; m. Jeannie Pareja, July 16, 1955; children: Monica, Diana, Roberto, John

G. MD, U. Nacional, Bogota, 1943; MS in Ob-Gyn, St. Louis U., 1947; asst. etranger, U. Paris, 1954. BE Am. Bd. Ob-Gyn. Intern Hosp. San Juan de Dios, U. Nacional, Bogota, 1942-43; resident in ob-gyn St. Louis U. Group Hosps., 1944-47; head gynecol. svc. San Juan de Dios Hosp., U. Nacional, Bogota, 1949-53, prof. of ob-gyn, 1951, assoc. dean clin. scis., 1965-66; head dept. gynecol. Inst. Nacional Cancer, Bogota, 1950-68; rsch. assoc. UCLA Harbor Gen. Hosp., 1967-68; head population div. Colombian Assn. Med. Schs., Bogota, 1969-73; head dept. gynecology, obstetrics and reproduction Centro Medico de los Andes, Fundacion Santa Fe, Bogota, 1981-88; rsch. prof. dept. community and family health Coll. Pub. Health, U. South Fla., Tampa, 1989—; seminar cons., tchr. mother and child care Peruvian Assn. Acad. Med. programs, Paracas, Peru, 1970; pres. Corp. Cen. Regional Population, Bogota, 1973-89; cons. Pan-Am. Health Orgn. (WHO), UN Fund for Population Activities (UNFPA), 1989—; bd. dirs. Bogota Health Div., 1981-82; presenter in field. Editor: Reproduction, 1979, editor Reproductive Health in Americas, 1992; contbr. articles to profl. jours., including Am. Jour. Ob-Gyn., Med. Cir., Panamerican Health Orgn., Editorial Fotolito Garcia e Hijos, others. Bd. dirs. Floridians for a Sustainable Population. Fellow ACS, Am. Coll. Ob-Gyn.; mem. N.Y. Acad. Scis., Am. Fertility Soc., Nat. Acad. Medicine Colombia, Fla. Ob-Gyn. Soc., Am. Pub. Health Assn. Home: 6118 Kipps Colony Dr W Saint Petersburg FL 33707-3970 Office: U South Fla Coll Pub Health 13201 Bruce B Downs Blvd Tampa FL 33612-3805

LOPEZ, JOE A., school system administrator. Supt. Cuba (N.Mex.) Ind. Schs., 1978—. Recipient Nat. Superintendent of the Yr. award, New Mexico, Am. Assn. of School Administrators, 1993. Office: Cuba Ind Schs PO Box 70 Cuba NM 87013-0070

LOPEZ, JOE JESUS, safety engineer; b. San Francisco, July 28, 1926; s. Miguel Galvan and Julia (Calderon) L.; m. Teresa Bernadino, Nov. 28, 1970; children: Jose Miguel, Silvia, Ann Maria, David. BBA, Tex. Tech. U., 1957, postgrad., 1959-60; postgrad., U. So. Calif., 1978-79. Cert. safety profl. Ground safety officer Reese AFB, Tex., 1953-69; safety mgr. NASA Goddard Space Flight Ctr., Greenbelt, Md., 1969-80; phys. scientist U.S. Dept. Energy, Washington, 1980-83, safety and health mgr., 1983-85; dir. environ., safety and health Zia, Los Alamos, N.Mex., 1985-86; mgr. environ., safety and health Johnson Controls World Svc. Inc., Los Alamos, 1986—. With U.S. Army, 1944-46, staff sgt. USAF, 1951-53. Mem. Am. Soc. Safety Engrs. (sec. N.Mex. sect. 1990-92), K.C., Rotary (treas. Los Alamos club 1988-91). Roman Catholic. Avocations: collecting coins, golf. Home: 1604 Camino Uva Los Alamos NM 87544-2727 Office: Johnson Controls World Svcs Pajarito & W Jemez Rd Los Alamos NM 87544

LOPEZ, JOSEPH JACK, oil company executive, consultant; b. N.Y.C., July 26, 1932; s. Florentino Estrada and Leah (Bodner) L.; m. June Elliott, June 20, 1953; children: Karen Marie Lopez Lynch, Debra Jo Lopez Newton, Laura Jean Lopez Berrell. Student, CCNY, 1955-59. Project estimator Chem. Constrn.-Engrs., N.Y.C., 1960-64, Dorr Oliver-Engrs., Stamford, Conn., 1964-66; chief estimator R.M. Parsons-Engrs., Frankfurt, Germany, 1966-74; mgr. project svcs. A.G. McKee-Engrs., Berkley Heights, N.J., 1974-76; mgr. tech. svcs. Rsch. Cottrell Corp., Sommerville, N.J., 1976-78; cons. Booz Allen & Hamilton, Abu Dhabi, United Arab Emirates, 1978-84; v.p. XL Tech. Corp., N.Y.C., 1984-87; cons. Qatar Gen. Pete Corp., Doha, 1987-90; pres. J. Lopez Cons., Babylon, N.Y., 1990—; estimator Combustion Engring. Co., N.Y.C., 1955-60. With USAF, 1950-54. Mem. Am. Assn. Cost Engrs., Project Mgmt. Inst. Republican. Roman Catholic. Home and Office: 15 Hinton Ave Babylon NY 11702-1407

LOPEZ, JUDITH CARROLL, lawyer; b. Boulder, Colo., Dec. 22, 1945; d. Robert Warren and Irene Caroll (Young) Adams; m. Richard Manuel Lopez, Mar. 19, 1967 (div. Nov. 1975); children: Heather Linn, Amber Elise. BA, Colo. Coll., 1967; JD, U. Wyo., 1979. Assoc. R. Michael Mullikin, Jackson Hole, Wyo., 1979-81; pvt. practice Jackson Hole, 1981-82; atty. KN Energy, Inc., Lakewood, Colo., 1982-88; assoc. Hawley & Vanderwerf, Denver, 1988-89; corp. counsel ANR Freight System, Inc., Golden, Colo., 1990-96; with Coastal States Mgmt. Corp., Houston, 1996—; bd. dirs. Edit, Inc. Bd. mgrs. Stonebridge Townhomes Homeowners Assn., Lakewood, 1993—. Avocations: skiing, hiking, bridge. Office: Ste 888 Nine Greenway Pl Houston TX 77045-0995

LOPEZ, LOURDES, ballerina; b. Havana, Cuba, 1958; came to U.S., 1959; Studied with, Alexander Nigodoff and Martha Mahr, Miami, Perry Brunson; attended, Sch. of Am. Ballet, N.Y.C. Mem. corps de ballet N.Y.C. Ballet, 1974-80, soloist, 1980-84, prin., 1984—. Created roles in Peter Martins' Sonate di Scarlatti and Rejouissance; other repertory includes: La Sonnambula, Divertimento No. 15, Serenade, Stars and Stripes, Apollo, Kammermusik No. 2, Firebird, The Four Seasons, The Goldberg Variations, Moves, Violin Concerto, Concerto Barocco, Theme and Variations, N.Y.C. Ballet's Balanchine Celebration, 1993, Cortège Hongrois, others; appeared in PBS series Dance in Am. Office: care NYC Ballet Inc NY State Theater Lincoln Ctr Plz New York NY 10023

LOPEZ, LUIS ANTONIO, electrical engineer; b. Ponce, P.R., Oct. 19, 1952; s. Luis A. and Carmen R. (Martinez) L.; m. Magdalena Garcia, July 2, 1977; children: Maria del Carmen, Luis Emilio. BSEE, U. P.R., 1974; MSEE, Stanford U., 1975; MBA, Nova U., 1981. Registered profl. engr., P.R. Prof. Technol. Inst. San Juan, P.R., 1975-76; radio product engr. Motorola, Ft. Lauderdale, Fla., 1976-79, engring. group leader product support, 1979-81, engring. group leader test sys., 1981-82; mgr. product engring. Hewlett Packard, Aguadilla, P.R., 1982-85, mgr. test engring., 1985-88, mgr. process engring., 1988-94, mgr. mfg. engring., 1994—; mem. tech. com., session chmn. Hewlett Packard Electronic Assembly Mfg. Conf., Palo Alto, Calif., 1993-95; mem. bus. adv. bd. Inter Am. U., Aguadilla, 1993-96. Recipient plaque P.R. 2000, 1992; fellow Stanford U., 1973. Mem. IEEE, P.R. Soc. Elec. Engrs., Colegio Ingenieros y Agrimensores P.R. (bd. dirs. Aguadilla chpt. 1993-96, chmn. orientation com. to high sch. students of engring. and surveyor's careers 1994-96). Roman Catholic. Avocations: coin collecting, personal computers, gardening and landscaping. Office: Hewlett Packard PO Box 4048 Aguadilla PR 00605-4048

LOPEZ, MANUEL, immunology and allergy educator; b. Bucaramanga, Colombia, Sept. 30, 1939; married; 4 children. BS, Colegio San Pedro Claver, Bucaramanga, 1956; MD, Univ. Javeriana, Bogota, Colombia, 1963. Diplomate Am. Bd. Allergy and Immunology, Am. Bd. Diagnostic Lab. Immunology. Intern Hosp. San Juan De Dios, Bucaramanga, 1962-63, resident, 1963-64, med. dir., 1969-71; clin. and rsch. fellow dept. medicine allergy unit Harvard U. and Harvard Med. Sch. at Mass. Gen. Hosp., Boston, 1964-68; dir. med. rsch. Univ. Indsl. De Santander, Bucaramanga, 1968-69; dir. immunology svc. lab. La. State Med. Ctr., New Orleans, 1971-74; asst. prof. medicine med. ctr. La. State U., New Orleans, 1971-74; from clin. asst. prof. to assoc. prof. med. sch. Tulane U., New Orleans, 1974-89, prof., 1989—, dir. immunology diagnostic lab. med. sch., 1974-83, dir. clin. immunology labs., 1983—, program dir. allergy and immunology tng. program, 1990—, acting chief sect. allergy and clin. immunology, 1990-91, chief, 1991—; mem. med.-sci. adv. com. Asthma and Allergy Found. Am., 1986-89; ad hoc mem. immunological sci. study sect. NIH, 1987, allergy and clin. immunology spl. reviewer immunology and transplantation rsch. com., 1988, mem. gen. clin. rsch. ctrs. com., 1993—; reviewer merit rev. grants VA, 1988, 89, 90; grant program reviewer Ctrs. of Excellence, Dept. Health and Human Svcs., 1991; mem. allergic products adv. com. FDA, 1993—; mem. spl. rev. com. Nat. Inst. Allergy and Infectious Diseases, 1993; presenter in field. Mem. editl. bd. Jour. Allergy and Clin. Immunology, 1986-94, reviewer, 1987-88; contbr. articles to profl. jours. and chpts. to books. Fellow John Simmon Guggenheim Meml. Found., 1964-66. Fellow Am. Acad. Allergy and Clin. Immunology (mem. internat. com. 1986-89, mem. immunotherapy of asthma com. 1987—, mem. Latin Ctrl. and South Am. com. 1987—, chmn. internat. grant aids 1988-89, mem. continuing med. edn. com. 1992-94), Am. Coll. Chest Physicians; mem. Am. Assn. Immunologists, Am. Fedn. Clin. Rsch., Am. Thoracic Soc., U.S.-Colombian Med. Assn. (pres. IX Congress 1989), La. Allergy Soc., N.Y. Acad. Scis., Southeastern Allergy Assn., Assn. Med. Lab. Immunologists, Internat. Assn. Aerobiology, Cordoba Allergy Soc. (hon.), Sigma Xi. Office: Tulane U Med Sch Clin Immunology Sect 1700 Perdido St Fl 3 New Orleans LA 70112-1210

LOPEZ, NANCY, professional golfer; b. Torrance, Calif., Jan. 6, 1957; d. Domingo and Marina (Griego) L.; m. Ray Knight, Oct. 25, 1982; children: Ashley Marie, Erinn Shea, Torri Heather. Student, U. Tulsa, 1976-78. Author: The Education of a Woman Golfer, 1979. First victory at Bent Tree Classic, Sarasota, Fla., 1978; named AP Athlete for 1978; admitted to Ladies Profl. Golf Assn. Hall of Fame, 1987, to PGA World Golf Hall of Fame, 1989. Mem. Ladies Profl. Golf Assn. (Player and Rookie of Yr. 1978). Republican. Baptist. Wiiner 33 LPGA Tour events, 2 maj. championships. Office: care Internat Mgmt Group 1 Erieview Plz Ste 1300 Cleveland OH 44114-1715*

LOPEZ, RAMON, recording industry executive. Now chmn. bd. dirs. WEA Internat. Inc., N.Y.C. Office: WEA Internat Inc 75 Rockefeller Plz 20Th Fl New York NY 10019-6908*

LOPEZ, SYLVIA ANN, principal; b. San Angelo, Tex., Oct. 25, 1953; d. Vivian C. and Olivia (Trinidad) Dominguez; children: Celina D. Hernandez, Deanna D. Hernandez. BS in Bilingual Edn., Southwest Tex. State U., 1976; MA in Guidance & Counseling, So. Meth. U., 1979; degree in mid-mgmt., East Tex. State U., 1987. Elem. tchr. Dallas Pub. Schs., 1976-83, counselor, 1983-89; counselor Sunset High Sch., Dallas, 1989-90; asst. prin. Edwin J. Kiest Elem., Dallas, 1990-92; dean of instrn. W.W. Samuell High Sch., Dallas, 1992-93; prin. John H. Reagan Elem., Dallas, 1993—. Named One of Top Ten Women-Positive Role Models, Girls Club-West Dallas, 1989. Mem. Assn. Hispanic Sch. Adminstrs., Tex. Elem. Prin. of Sch. Adminstrs., Dallas Assn. Sch. Adminstrs. Democrat. Roman Catholic. Avocations: reading, aerobic exercising, cycling. Home: 1812 Williams Way Ln Dallas TX 75228-4703 Office: John H. Reagan Elem Sch 201 N Adams Ave Dallas TX 75208-4624

LOPEZ-BOYD, LINDA SUE, geriatrics nurse; b. Kankakee, Ill.; d. Delven H. and Reina M. (Soucy) Brandt; m. James D. Boyd (dec.); 1 child, Albert B. Diploma, St. Luke's Sch. Nursing, 1967; BSN, Ind. U. Sch. Nursing, 1975, MS in Nursing, 1978, postgrad. Cert. gerontol. nurse ANA. Critical care nurse, 1967-75; lectr. Ind. U. Sch. Nursing, Indpls., 1975-79; dir. Winona Meml. Hosp., Indpls., 1981-86; med./surg. clin. nurse specialist St. Francis Hosp., Indpls., 1986-88; dir. nursing edn. Evergreen Healthcare, Ltd., Indpls., 1988-93; instr. CPR. Mem. Nat. Coun. on Aging. Mem. Ind. State Nurses Assn., Am. Diabetes Assn., Gerontol. Soc. Am., Marion County AIDS Coalition, Intravenous Nurses Soc.

LOPEZ-COBOS, JESUS, conductor; b. Toro, Spain, Feb. 25, 1940; m. Alicia Ferrer, May 15, 1987; 3 children. PhD in philosophy and music, U. Madrid, 1964; diploma composition, Madrid Conservatory, 1966; diploma conducting, Viennna (Austria) Acad., 1969. Gen. music dir. Deutsche Oper Berlin, 1981-90; prin. guest condr. London Philharm., 1981-86; prin. condr., artistic dir. Spanish Nat. Orch., 1984-89; music dir. Cin. Orch., 1986—; music dir. Orchestre de Chambre de Lausanne, Switzerland, 1990, condr.; also condr. concerts Edinburgh Festival, London Symphony, Royal Philharm., N.Y. Philharm., L.A. Philharm., Chgo. Symphony, Cleve. Orch., Phila. Orch., Berlin Philharm., Berlin Radio Orch., Amsterdam Concertgebouw, Vienna Philharm., Swiss Romande, Muncih Philarharm., Hamburg NDR, Oslo Philharm., Zurich Tonhalle, Israel Philharm., opera prodns. at Royal Opera House, Covent Garden, London, La Scala, Milan, Italy, Met. Opera, N.Y.C., Paris Opera, others; recs. include Lucia di Lammermoor New Philham. Orch., Otello, recital and operatic disc with José Carrera and London Symphony Orch., Liszt's Dante Symphony with Swiss Romande, Falla's Three-Cornered Hat, R-K Capricio Espangnole, Chiabrier's Espana with L.A. Philharm., others. Recipient 1st prize Besancon Internat. Condr.'s Competition, 1969, Prince of Astrurias award Spanish Govt., 1981, 1st Class Disting. Svc. medal Fed. Republic of Germany, 1989. Office: Cin Symphony Orch 1241 Elm St Cincinnati OH 45210-2267 also: Orchestre de Chambre de Lausanne, Chemin de devin 72, CH-1012 Lausanne Switzerland

LÓPEZ-MORILLAS, JUAN, Spanish and comparative literature educator; b. Jaén, Spain, Aug. 11, 1913; came to U.S., 1935; s. Emilio López-Morillas and Teresa Ortiz; m. Frances Mapes, Aug. 12, 1937; children: Martin, Consuelo, Julian. BLitt, U. Madrid, 1929; PhD, U. Iowa, 1940; LHD (hon.), Brown U., 1979. Asst. prof. romance langs. U. Iowa, Iowa City, 1940-43; asst. prof. Spanish Brown U., Providence, 1943-47, assoc. prof. Spanish, 1947-51, prof. Spanish and comparative lit., 1951-65, Alumni/Alumnae Univ. prof., 1965-73, William R. Kenan prof. humanities, 1973-78, prof. emeritus, 1978—, chmn. dept. Spanish and Italian, 1960-67, chmn. dept. comparative lit., 1967-71; prof. Spanish and comparative lit. U. Tex., Austin, 1978-79, Ashbel Smith prof., 1979-89, prof. emeritus, 1989—; vis. scholar U. Ctr. in Va., 1976-77. Author: El Krausismo español, 1956, Intelectuales y espirituales, 1961, Hacia el 98, 1972, Racionalismo pragmatico, 1988; editor, translator books; contbr. articles to profl. jours. Decorated Order of Isabella the Catholic by King Juan Carlos of Spain, 1985; grantee Am. Coun. Learned Socs., Am. Philos. Soc.; Phi Beta Kappa vis. scholar, 1966-67; Guggenheim fellow, 1950-51, 57-58. Mem. Internat. Assn. Hispanists (pres. 1980-83), Hispanic Soc. Am., MLA (mem. exec. com. 1981-85), Academia Norteamericana de la Lengua Española, Royal Spanish Acad. (corr.). Democrat. Avocations: travel, photography. Home: 2200 Hartford Rd Austin TX 78703-3127 Office: U Tex Dept Spanish Portuguese Austin TX 78712

LOPEZ-NAKAZONO, BENITO, chemical and industrial engineer; b. Nuevo Laredo, Tam., Mex., Oct. 26, 1946; came to U.S., 1968; s. Benito and Ayko (Nakazono) Lopez-Ramos; m. Anastacia Espinoza, June 22, 1981; children: Benito Keizo, Tanzy Keiko, Mayeli, Aiko Michelle. BSc in Chem. and Indsl. Engring., ITESM, Monterrey, Mexico, 1968; MS in Chem. Engring., U. Houston, 1971. Prof. chem. engring. ITESM, Monterrey, 1971-72; vessel analytical design engr./process engr. M.W. Kellogg, Houston, 1973-79, 81; product mgr. Ind. Del Alcali, Monterrey, 1980-81; sr. process engr. Haldor Topsoe, Inc., Houston, 1982—. Pres. adminstrv. coun. United Meth. Ch., Houston, 1990-92, 96. ITESM fellow, 1963, U. Houston fellow, 1968. Mem. Tex. Soc. Profl. Engrs., Am. Inst. Chem. Engrs., Sigma Xi. Achievements include development and design of hydgogen, ammonia, methanol, formaldehyde and SNOx/WSA plants, start-up supervision of ammonia plants in Mexico, U.S., Canada., Russia, Somalia, India and Bangladesh. Home: 1805 Lanier Dr League City TX 77573-4720 Office: Haldor Topsoe Inc 17629 El Camino Real Ste 302 Houston TX 77058-3051

LOPICCOLO, JOSEPH, psychologist, educator, author; b. L.A., Sept. 13, 1943; s. Joseph E. and Adeline C. (Russo) Lo P.; m. Leslie Joan Matlen, June 20, 1964 (div. 1978); 1 child, Joseph Townsend; m. Cathryn Gail Pridal, Dec. 20, 1980; 1 child, Michael James. BA with highest honors, UCLA, 1965; MS, Yale U., 1968, PhD, 1969. Lic. psychologist, Mo. Asst. prof. U. Oreg., Eugene, 1969-73; assoc. prof. U. Houston, 1973-74; prof. SUNY, Stony Brook, 1974-84, Tex. A&M U., College Station, 1984-87; prof. psychology U. Mo., Columbia, 1987—, chmn. dept., 1987-90. Author: Becoming Orgasmic, 1976, 2d edit., 1988, also book chpts.; editor: Handbook of Sex Therapy, 1978; contbr. numerous articles to profl. jours. Woodrow Wilson Found. fellow; NIH rsch. grantee, 1973-84. Fellow Am. Psychol. Assn.; mem. Internat. Acad. Sex Rsch., Soc. for Sci. Study of Sex (pres. 1983-84, Alfred Kinsey Meml. Rsch. award), Phi Beta Kappa, Sigma Xi. Office: U Mo Dept Psychology 210 McAlester Hall Columbia MO 65211

LOPINA, LAWRENCE THOMAS, manufacturing executive; b. Chgo., Nov. 9, 1930; s. Thomas F. and Augustine A. (Schwantes) L.; PhB, U. Notre Dame, 1952; MBA, DePaul U., 1953; MBA, U. Chgo., 1963; m. Marion T. Toomey, Nov. 5, 1955; children: Joseph D., Lawrence M., Mary E., Celeste N., James P. Jr. CPA, Wis.; cert. mgmt. acct. Acct. Haskins & Sells, CPA's, Chgo., 1952-53; acctg. positions with Motorola, Inc., Chgo., 1953-63; div. contr. then v.p. fin. fluid power group Applied Power, Inc., Milw., 1963-74; sr. v.p. fin. Broan Mfg. Co., Inc., Hartford, Wis., 1974—, former dir. With AUS, 1953-55. Mem. AICPA, Inst. Mgmt. Accts., Fin. Execs. Inst. (past pres. Milw. chpt.), Wis. Inst. CPA's, Catholic League (Wisc. chpt. treas.), Beta Gamma Sigma. Club: KC. Office: 926 W State St Hartford WI 53027-1066

LOPPNOW, MILO ALVIN, clergyman, former church official; b. St. Charles, Minn., Jan. 13, 1914; s. William and Doretta (Penz) L.; m. Gertrude Stoltz, Feb. 6, 1942; children—Donald, Bruce, David. B.A., Moravian Coll., 1937; M.Div., Moravian Theol. Sem., 1940, D.D., 1970. Ordained to ministry Moravian Ch. in Am., 1940; pastor congregations nr. Wisconsin Rapids, Wis., 1940-41, Waconia, Minn., 1941-53; pastor congregations nr. Lakeview Ch., Madison, Wis., 1953-64; dist. pres. Western Dist. Moravian Ch., Madison, 1965-78; elected bishop, 1970. Chmn. Youth Commn., Madison, 1957-63; Trustee Moravian Coll., 1954-78, Moravian Theol. Sem., Bethlehem, Pa.; former chaplain, dir. devel. Marquardt Meml. Manor, Watertown, Wis.

LOPREATO, JOSEPH, sociology educator, author; b. Stefanaconi, Italy, July 13, 1928; came to U.S., 1952; s. Frank and Marianna (Pavone) L.; m. Carolyn H. Prestopino, July 18, 1954 (div. 1971); children: Gregory F., Marisa S. Schmidt; m. Sally A. Cook, Aug. 24, 1972 (div. 1978). BA in Sociology, U. Conn., 1956; MA in Sociology, Yale U., 1957, PhD in Sociology, 1960. Asst. prof. sociology U. Mass., Amherst, 1960-62; vis. lectr. U. Rome, 1962-64; assoc. prof. U. Conn., Storrs, 1964-66; prof. sociology U. Tex., Austin, 1968—; chmn. dept. sociology U. Tex., 1969-72; vis. prof. U. Catania, Italy, 1974, U. Calabria, Italy, 1980; mem. steering com. Council European Studies, Columbia U., 1977-80; chmn. sociology com. Council for Internat. Exchange of Scholars, 1977-79; mem. Internat. Com. Mezzogiorno, 1986—; Calabria Internat. Com., 1988—. Author: Italian Made Simple, 1959, Vilfredo Pareto, 1965, Peasants No More, 1967, Italian Americans, 1970, Class, Conflict and Mobility, 1972, Social Stratification, 1974, The Sociology of Vilfredo Pareto, 1975, La Stratificazione Sociale negli Stati Uniti, 1945-1975, 1977, Human Nature and Biocultural Evolution, 1984, Evoluzione e Natura Umana, 1990, Mai Più Contadini, 1990; contbr. articles to profl. jours. Mem. Nat. Italian-Am. Com. for U.S.A. Bicentennial; mem. exec. com. Congress Italian Politics, 1977-80. Served to cpl. U.S. Army, 1952-54. Fulbright faculty research fellow, 1962-64, 73-74; Social Sci. Research Council faculty research fellow, 1963-64; NSF faculty research fellow, 1965-68; U. Tex. Austin research fellow, spring 1985, spring 1993; Guido Dorso award for U.S.A., Italy, 1992. Mem. AAAS (behavioral sci. rsch. prize com. 1992-94), Internat. Sociol. Assn., Am. Sociol. Assn., European Sociobiolog. Soc., Evolution and Behavior Soc., So. Sociol. Soc. (assoc. editor Am. Sociol. Rev. 1970-72, Social Forces 1987-90, Jour. Polit. and Mil. Sociology 1980—), Internat. Soc. Human Ethology. Catholic-Episcopalian. Office: Univ of Tex Dept Sociology Austin TX 78712

LOPRETE, JAMES HUGH, lawyer; b. Detroit, Sept. 17, 1929; s. James Victor and Effie Hannah (Brown) LoP.; m. Marion Ann Garrison, Sept. 11, 1952; children: James Scott, Kimberly Anne, Kent Garrison, Robert Drew. AB, U. Mich., 1951, JD with Distinction, 1953. Bar: Mich. 1954. Practiced law Detroit, 1953—; atty. Chrysler Corp., Detroit, 1953; assoc. firm Monaghan, LoPrete, McDonald, Yakima & Grenke, P.C. and predecessor firms, Detroit, from 1954; mem. firm Monaghan, LoPrete, McDonald, Yakima & Grenke, P.C. and predecessor firms, 1966—, pres., 1979—; bd. dirs. Drake's Batter Mix Co., Orsco Inc.; instr. legal writing Wayne State U., Detroit, 1955-57. Trustee U. Mich. Club of Detroit Scholarship Fund, 1967, pres., 1982—, Samuel Westerman Found., 1971—, pres., 1984, John R. & M. Margrite Davis Found. Fellow Am. Coll. Trust and Estate Counsel, Internat. Acad. Estate and Trust Law; mem. ABA, Oakland County bar assns., State Bar Mich., Detroit Athletic Club (dir. 1983-88, sec. 1986-88), Orchard Lake Country Club, U. Mich. of Greater Detroit (pres. 1966). Home: 2829 Warner Dr Orchard Lake MI 48324-2449 Office: Monaghan LoPrete McDonald et al 1700 N Woodward Ave Ste A Bloomfield Hills MI 48304-2249

LORAN, ERLE, artist; b. Mpls., Oct. 3, 1905; m. Clyta Sisson, May 8, 1937 (dec. Mar. 1982); m. Ruth Schorer, July 22, 1993. Student, U. Minn., 1922-23; grad., Mpls. Sch. Art, 1926; M.F.A. (hon.), 1968. Travelled and painted in Europe, 1926-30; prof. art U. Calif., Berkeley; now prof. emeritus. U. Calif.; participant Cezanne, the Lateworks Symposium Mus. Modern Art, 1977. Represented in permanent collections of Denver Art Mus., San Francisco Mus. Art, U. Minn., Santa Barbara Mus. Art, San Diego Mus. Art, Krannert Art Mus. of U. Ill., 1965, Art. Mus. U. Calif. Berkeley, Oakland (Calif.) Mus., Smithsonian Instn., Washington, also numerous pvt. collections; U.S. Treasury Dept. purchases Great Shipyards and Last Year's Swamplands; works in large exhbns. in U.S. since 1933, numerous one-man shows, 1934—, including Oakland Mus., 1981, San Francisco Gallery, Paula Anglim, Bergruen Gallery, 1989, Univ. Art Mus., Berkeley, Calif., 1990, DeYoung Mus., San Francisco, 1994; invited nat. exhbns. Mus. Modern Art, 1935, Whitney Mus. Am. Art, 1943, 44, 46, 48, Carnegie Inst., 1942, Pa. Acad., 1945, Met. Mus. Art, 1950, 51, 53, also 9 other nat. mus.; author: Cezanne's Composition, 1943, 45, 46, 47, 63, 70, 77, 81, paperback edit., 1985; also author numerous critical essays on art; chpts. on Cezanne in Les Peintres Celebres (Lucien Mazenod), Paris, 1948. Recipient numerous prizes and awards.; Awarded Paris prize ($6,000) by John Armstrong Chaloner Found., N.Y.C., 1926. Club: Arts (Berkeley). Home: 10 Kenilworth Ct Kensington CA 94707-1320

LORANCE, ELMER DONALD, organic chemistry educator; b. Tupelo, Okla., Jan. 18, 1940; s. Elmer Dewey and Imogene (Triplett) L.; m. Phyllis Ilene Miller, Aug. 31, 1969; children: Edward Donald, Jonathan Andrew. BA, Okla. State U., 1962; MS, Kansas State U., 1967; PhD, U. Okla., 1977. NIH research trainee Okla. U., Norman, 1966-70; asst. prof. organic chemistry So. Calif. Coll., Costa Mesa, 1970-73, assoc. prof., 1973-80, prof., 1980—, chmn. div. natural scis. and math., 1985-89, chmn. chemistry dept., 1990-93, chmn. divsn. natural scis. and math., 1993—. Contbr. articles to profl. jours. Mem. AAAS, Am. Chem. Soc., Internat. Union Pure and Applied Chemistry (assoc.), Am. Inst. Chemists, Am. Sci. Affiliation, Phi Lambda Upsilon. Republican. Mem. Ch. Assembly of God. Avocations: reading, gardening, music. Office: So Calif Coll 55 Fair Dr Costa Mesa CA 92626-6520

LORBER, BARBARA HEYMAN, communications executive; b. N.Y.C.; d. David Benjamin and Gertrude (Meyer) Heyman; divorced. AB in Polit. Sci., Skidmore Coll., 1966; MA, Columbia U., 1973, postgrad., 1973-76. Asst. dir. young citizens divsn. Dem. Party, 1966-68; exec. asst. to dean Albert Einstein Coll. Medicine, Bronx, N.Y., 1968-72; exec. asst. to v.p. devel. Vanderbilt U., Nashville, 1976-77; spl. projects dir. Am. Acad. in Rome, N.Y.C., 1977-78; pub. affairs dir., assoc. devel. dir. Met. Opera, N.Y.C., 1978-84; sr. v.p. Hill and Knowlton, N.Y.C., 1985-88; pres. Lorber Group, Ltd., N.Y.C., 1989-95; v.p. comms. and planning N.Y.C. Partnership and C. of C., 1996—; guest lectr. Arts and Bus. Coun., N.Y.C., Internat. Soc. Performing Arts Adminstrs., N.Y.C., NYU Sch. Continuing Edn., Nat. Media Conf., Nat. Soc. Fund Raising Execs., N.Y.C.; exec. prodr., prodr., writer N.Y. Internat. Festival Arts, N.Y.C., 1988. Author chpts. to book; contbr. articles to profl. jours. Office: NYC Partnership and C of C One Battery Pk Plz New York NY 10004

LORBER, MORTIMER, physiology educator; b. N.Y.C., Aug. 30, 1926; s. Albert and Frieda (Levin) L.; m. Eileen Segal, May 20, 1956; children: Kenneth, Stephanie. BS, NYU, 1945; DMD cum laude, Harvard U., 1950, MD cum laude, 1952. Diplomate Nat. Bd. Med. Examiners. Rotating intern A.M. Billings Hosp., 1952-53; resident in hematology Mt. Sinai Hosp., N.Y.C., 1953-54, asst. resident in medicine, 1957; asst. resident medicine Georgetown U. Hosp., Washington, 1958; instr., asst. prof. dept. physiology and biophysics Georgetown U., Washington, 1959-68, assoc. prof., 1968; lectr. physiology U.S. Naval Dental Sch., Bethesda, Md., 1962-70, Walter Reed Army Inst. Dental Rsch., Washington, 1963-70; guest scientist Naval Med. Rsch. Inst., Bethesda, 1978-83. Contbr.: The Merck Manual, 14th, 15th and 16th edit., 1982, 87, 92; contbr. articles to profl. jours. Lt. USNR, 1954-56. Recipient Lederle Med. Faculty award Lederle Co., Pearl River, N.Y., 1960-63, USPHS Rsch. Career Devel. award Nat. Inst. Dental Rsch., Bethesda, 1963-70; grantee Am. Cancer Soc., USPHS. Mem. Am. Physiol. Soc., Am. Soc. Hematology, Assn. Rsch. in Vision and Ophthalmology, Internat. Assn. Dental Rsch. Jewish. Achievements include discovery that the ground substance is masked but not lost in calcification, removal of spleen is followed by a reticulocytosis that is permanent in dogs, dogs have many more young reticulocytes in their blood than man, stretching of skin increases mitoses in the rat showing physical factors can modulate DNA and cell division, adult Gaucher cells contain iron secondary to erythrophagocytosis, the spleen protects against insecticide-induced hematoxicity, biological armature provides internal stability to exocrine glands. Home: 5823

Osceola Rd Bethesda MD 20816-2032 Office: Georgetown U Sch Medicine 3900 Reservoir Rd NW Washington DC 20007-2187

LORCH, ERNEST HENRY, lawyer; b. Frankfurt, Germany, Oct. 11, 1932; came to U.S., 1940; s. Alexander and Kate (Freundt) L. AB, Middlebury Coll., 1954; JD, U. Va., 1957; JD (hon.), Fairfield U., 1987. Bar: N.Y. 1958. Assoc. Olwine, Connelly, Chase, O'Donnell & Weyher, N.Y.C., 1957-65, ptnr., 1965-84; pres., chief oper. officer Dyson-Kissner-Moran Corp., N.Y.C., 1984-90, pres., chief exec. officer, 1990-91; chmn., chief exec. officer, 1991-92, ret., 1992; of counsel Whitman, Breed, Abbott & Morgan, N.Y.C., 1992—; chmn. bd. dirs. Varlen Corp., Chgo.; bd. dirs. Tyler Corp. Dir. various inner city athletic assns., N.Y.C., 1959—; The DYSM Found., N.Y.C., 1985-92; trustee, officer, dir. The Riverside Ch., N.Y.C., 1961-82; treas., dir. Wheelchair Charters Inc., Religion in American Life, 1993—. Mem. ABA, N.Y. State Bar Assn. Office: Whitman Breed Abbott & Morgan 200 Park Ave New York NY 10166-0005

LORCH, GEORGE A., manufacturing company executive; b. Glenridge, N.J., 1941. BS, Va. Poly. Inst. & State U., 1963. With Armstrong World Industries, Inc., 1963—, v.p. mktg. E&B div., 1974-76, mktg. mgr., 1976-78, gen. sales mgr., 1978-83, then group v.p. carpet ops., from 1983, past exec. v.p., now chmn. bd., CEO, dir. Office: Armstrong World Industries Inc 313 W Liberty St Lancaster PA 17604*

LORCH, KENNETH F., lawyer; b. Indpls., July 24, 1951. BSBA, Washington U., 1973; JD, John Marshall Sch. Law, 1976. Bar: Ill. 1976, U.S. Dist. Ct. (no. dist.) Ill. 1977; CPA, Ill. Ptnr. Holleb & Coff, Chgo. Mem. Chgo. Bar Assn. (exec. com., Cook County Probate Ct. rules and forms com., mem. legis. com., mem. probate practice com. 1991, mem. trust law com., chmn. estate planning com., mem. young lawyers sect. 1983-85), Chgo. Estate Planning Coun., Com.-Agy./Ct. Sr. Citizen Issues, Jewish Fedn. Chgo. (vice chair profl. adv. com.). Office: Holleb & Coff 55 E Monroe St Ste 4100 Chicago IL 60603-5803

LORCH, MARISTELLA DE PANIZZA (MRS. INAMA VON BRUNNENWALD), Romance languages educator, writer, lecturer; b. Bolzano, Italy, Dec. 8, 1919; came to U.S., 1947, naturalized, 1951; d. Gino and Giuseppina (Cristoforetti) de Panizza; m. Claude Bové, Feb. 10, 1944 (div. 1955); 1 dau., Claudia; m. Edgar R. Lorch, Mar. 25, 1956; children: Lavinia Edgarda, Donatella Livia. Ed., Liceo Classico, Merano, 1929-37; Dott. in Lettere e Filosofia, U. Rome, 1942; DHL (hon.), Lehman Coll., CUNY, 1993. Prof. Latin and Greek Liceo Virgilio, Rome, 1941-44; assoc. prof. Italian and German Coll. St. Elizabeth, Convent Station, N.J., 1947-51; faculty Barnard Coll., 1951-90, prof., 1967—, chmn. dept., 1951—, chmn. medieval and renaissance program, 1972-86; founder, dir. Ctr. for Internat. Scholarly Exch., Barnard Coll., 1980-90; dir. Casa Italiana, Columbia U., 1969-76, chmn. exec. com. Italian studies, 1980-90, dir. Italian Acad. Advanced Studies in Am., 1991—. Author: Critical edit. L. Valla, De vero falsoque bono, Bari, 1970, (with W. Ludwig) critical edit. Michaelida, (with K. Hieatt), 1976, On Pleasure, 1981, A Defense of Life: L. Valla's Theory of Pleasure, 1985, (with E. Grassi) Folly and Insanity in Renaissance Literature, 1986, (with F. Colombo, M. Spaziani, Sinisca) All' America, 1990; editor: Il Teatro Italiano del Renascimento, 1981, Humanism in Rome, 1983, La Scuola, New York, 1987; mem. editorial bd. Italian jour. Romanic Review; also articles on Renaissance lit. and theater. Chmn. Am. Ariosto Centennial Celebration, 1974; chmn. bd. trustees La Scuola N.Y., 1986-91; trustee Lycée Française de N.Y., 1986—. Decorated Cavaliere della Repubblica Italiana, 1973, Commendatore della Repubblica Italiana, 1988; recipient AMITA award for Woman of Yr. in Italian Lit., 1973, Columbus '92 Countdown prize of excellence in humanities, 1990, Elen Cornaro award Sons of Italy Woman of Yr., 1990, Father Ford award, 1994. Mem. Medieval Acad. Am., Renaissance Soc. Am., Am. Assn. Tchrs. Italian, Am. Assn. Italian Studies (hon. pres. 1990-91), Internat. Assn. for Study of Italian Lit. (Am. rep., assoc. pres. 8th Congress 1973), Acad. Polit. Sci. (life), Pirandello Soc. (pres. 1972-78), Arcadia Acad. (Asteria Aretusa 1976). Home: 445 Riverside Dr New York NY 10027-6842

LORD, EVELYN MARLIN, former mayor; b. Melrose, Mass., Dec. 8, 1926; d. John Joseph and Mary Janette (Nourse) Marlin; m. Samuel Smith Lord Jr., Feb. 28, 1948; children: Steven Arthur, Jonathan Peter, Nathaniel Edward, Victoria Marlin, William Kenneth. BA, Boston U., 1948; MA, U. Del., 1956; JD, U. Louisville, 1969. Bar: Ky. 1969, U.S. Supreme Ct. 1973. Exec. dir. Block Blight Inc., Wilmington, Del., 1956-60; mem. Del. Senate, Dover, 1960-62; administrv. asst. county judge Jefferson County, Louisville, 1968-71; corr. No. Ireland News Jour. Co., Wilmington, 1972-74; legal adminstr. Orgain, Bell & Tucker, Beaumont, Tex., 1978-83; v.p. Tex. Commerce Bank, Beaumont, 1983-84; councilman City of Beaumont, 1980-82, mayor pro tem, 1982-84, mayor, 1990-94; tourism chmn. U.S. Conf. Mayors, 1994, mem. adv. bd., chmn. arts, culture and recreation, 1992-94; bd. dirs. Tex. Commerce Bank. Bd. dirs. Symphony Soc. S.E. Tex., 1990—, Beaumont Cmty. Found., 1990-96, S.E. Tex. Art Mus., 1990-96, Lincoln Inst. Land Policy, Beaumont Pub. Schs. Found., Cmtys. in Schs.; trustee, pres. United Way, Beaumont, 1995; exec. bd. Boy Scouts Am., Three Rivers, 1978-84, 89-96; pres. Girl Scouts Am., Louisville, 1966-70, Tex. Energy Mus.; active Sister City Comm. Recipient Silver Beaver award Boy Scouts Am., Beaumont, 1979, Disting. Alumni award Boston U., 1983, Disting. Leadership award Nat. Assn. Leadership Orgns., Indpls., 1991, Labor-Mgmt. Pub. Sector award, 1991, Disting. Grad. award Leadership Beaumont, 1993, Rotary Svc. Above Self award, 1994; named Citizen of Yr., Sales and Mktg. Assn., 1990, Beaumont "Man of Yr.", 1993. Mem. LWV (Del. state pres. 1960-62, bd. dirs. Tex. 1978-80), Bus. and Profl. Women Assns. (Woman of Yr. 1983), 100 Club (pres. 1995—), Girl Scouts Am. (life), Rotary (hon.), Sigma Kappa (life), Phi Kappa Phi, Delta Kappa Gamma (hon.), Sigma Iota Epsilon (hon.). Avocations: writing, reading, African violets, genealogy. Home: 1240 Nottingham Ln Beaumont TX 77706-4316 *Basically - I believe in "blooming where you're planted". Life with my husband has taken me all over the world but we've always managed to be "at home" wherever we've been able to give a bit of ourselves.*

LORD, GEORGE DEFOREST, English educator; b. N.Y.C., Dec. 2, 1919; s. George deForest and Hazen (Symington) L.; m. Ruth Ellen du Pont, Mar. 22, 1947 (div. 1978); children: Pauline, George deForest Jr., Edith (dec.), Henry; m. Louise Robins Hendrix, 1978 (div. 1992); m. Marcia Adkisson Babbidge, 1993. BA, Yale U., 1942, PhD, 1951. Instr. English Yale U., New Haven, 1947-66, prof., 1966—; master Trumbull Coll., 1963-66, dir. directed studies, 1968-70, assoc. chmn. English dept., 1983-86; dir. Fiduciary Trust, N.Y., 1969-91; cons. PBS TV program Transformations of Myth Through Time, 1982-90; lectr. in field. Author: Homeric Renaissance: the "Odyssey" of George Chapman, 1956, Poems on Affairs of State, 1963, Andrew Mavell, Complete Poetry, 1968, rev. edit., 1985, Andrew Marvell: A Collection of Critical Essays, 1968, Anthology of Poems on Affairs of State, 1975, Heroic Mockery: Variations on Epic Themes from Homer to Joyce, 1977, Trials of the Self: Heroic Ordeals in the Epic Tradition, 1983, Classical Presences in Seventeenth-Century English Poetry, 1987 (Outstanding acad. book 1987 Choice mag.); gen. editor Poems on Affairs of State: Augustan Satirical Verse: 1660-1714, 7 vols., 1963-75; contbr. articles, revs. to acad. jours. Trustee Winterthur Mus., 1952-80, Mary Holmes Coll., West Point, Miss., 1971-80, Fair Haven Housing, 1972-78; trustee, advisor Outward Bound USA, 1977—; vestryman Calvary Episcopal Ch., Stonington, Conn., 1986-89. Morse fellow 1954-55, NEH sr. fellow, 1982. Mem. MLA, English Inst., Renaissance Soc. Am., Am. Acad. in Rome, The Century Assn. Home: 3 Diving St Stonington CT 06378 Office: Yale U Dept English New Haven CT 06520

LORD, HAROLD WILBUR, electrical engineer, electronics consultant; b. Eureka, Calif., Aug. 20, 1905; s. Charles Wilbur and Rossina Camilla (Hansen) L.; B.S., Calif. Inst. Tech., 1926; m. Doris Shirley Huff, July 25, 1928; children—Joann Shirley (Mrs. Carl Cook Disbrow), Alan Wilbur, Nancy Louise (Mrs. Leslie Crandall), Harold Wayne. With Gen. Electric Co., Schenectady, 1926-66, electronics engr., 1960-66; pvt. cons. engr., Mill Valley, Calif., 1966—. Coffin Found. award Gen. Electric Co., 1933, GE Inventors award, 1966. Fellow IEEE (life, tech. v.p. 1962, Centennial medal 1984, IEEE Magnetics Soc. 1984 Achievement award). Contbr. articles to profl. jours. Patentee in field. Home and Office: 1565 Golf Course Dr Rohnert Park CA 94928-5638

LORD, JANE ANNE, insurance broker; b. Alton, Ill., Oct. 14, 1932; d. H. L. and Cora LaRue (Reeder) Neudecker; widowed; children: Brian B., Jane Elizabeth. BA, So. Ill. U., 1957; MA, Monticello Coll. for Women, 1962; PhD, UCLA, 1982. Ins. broker, 1957—. Bd. dirs. Am. Heart Assn., Found. for Retarded. Named to Lewis and Clark Hall of Fame. Mem. AAUW, Nat. Assn. Life Underwriters, Palm Springs C. of C., Nat. Assn. Ins. Women, Rotary Internat., Order of Eastern Star, Life Champion Circle, Tempo de los Ninos. Avocations: art, music, ballet. Office: 400 S Farrell Dr Ste B105 Palm Springs CA 92262

LORD, JERE JOHNS, retired physics educator; b. Portland, Oreg., Jan. 3, 1922; s. Percy Samuel and Hazel Marie (Worstel) L.; m. Miriam E. Hart, Dec. 30, 1947; children—David, Roger, Douglas. Physicist U. Calif. Radiation Lab., Berkeley, 1942-46; research asso. U. Chgo., 1950-52; asst. prof. physics U. Wash., Seattle, 1952-57; assoc. prof. U. Wash., 1957-62, prof., 1962-92, prof. emeritus, 1992—. Fellow AAAS, Am. Phys. Soc.; mem. Am. Assn. Physics Tchrs. Home: 6803 52nd Ave NE Seattle WA 98115-7746 Office: U Wash Dept Physics Box 351560 Seattle WA 98195-1560

LORD, JEROME EDMUND, education administrator, writer, businessman; b. Waterbury, Conn., Dec. 24, 1935; s. James Andrew and Mary Frances (Hayes) L.; m. Eleanor Louise Collins, Apr. 22, 1967; children: Hayes Alexander FitzWarin, Stavely Hampston deHodnet, Savile Collins de Montenay, Dorian Warfield d'Amours, Wallis Jennings dePantulf. BA, Georgetown U., 1957; MA, Boston Coll., 1962, Columbia U., 1963; PhD, Columbia U., 1969; diploma (hon.), U. Madrid, 1962. Tchr. The Taft Sch. Peekskill Mil. Acad., 1957-60; editor, lang. recs. supr. Allyn and Bacon Inc., Boston, 1961-62; adminstrv. assoc. internat. programs and services Tchrs. Coll. Columbia U., N.Y.C., 1963-65, assoc. in higher edn., 1965-66; asst. prof. edn., exec. asst. to dean acad. devel. CUNY, 1965-67, assoc. prof. edn., exec. asst. to vice chancellor exec. office, 1967-69; dir. rsch. Ford and Carnegie Study of Fed. Politics of Edn. Brookings Instn., Washington, 1969-70; program officer Nat. Ctr. for Ednl. Tech., U.S. Dept. Edn., Washington, 1971-73; sr. assoc. Nat. Inst. Edn., Washington, 1973-86, Office Ednl. Rsch. and Improvement, Dept. Edn., Washington, 1986—; pres. Jerome Lord Enterprises, Inc., Washington; advisor to vol. edn. policy group Office Dir. Def. Edn., U.S. Dept. Def., 1975-76; chmn. Fed. Interagy. Panel for Rsch. on Adulthood; mem. World Affairs Coun., Washington, other various nat. panels and coms.; cons. in field; lectr. in field. Playwright: Teresa, 1971, The Election, 1972, Audition!, 1973, Decent Exposure, 1979, Amazing Grace, 1987, Heads You Win, 1991, Making Believe, 1996; author: Perfectly Proper, 1993, Teacher Training Abroad: New Realities, Adult Literacy Programs: Guidelines for Effectiveness; contbr. articles to profl. jours. Trustee St. John's Child Devel. Ctr., Washington, 1978-83; mem. nat. bd. sponsors Protestant and Orthodox Ctr., N.Y. World's Fair, 1964; mem. adv. bd. N.Y.C. Urban Corps, 1965-69, others; mem. coun. of friends Folger Shakespeare Libr.; sponsor Nat. Symphony Orch.; mem., donor reception rooms Dept. State. Named Coakley scholar, 1953-57, M.T. Runyan scholar, 1967-68; fellow W.T. Kellogg Found., 1968-69, Rinehart Found., 1970-71, others. Mem. Pilgrim Soc., Soc. Friends St. George's and Desc. Knights of Garter, Friends of Blair House, Pilgrims of the U.S., World Affairs Coun., City Tavern Club, Met. Club, Kappa Delta Pi, Phi Delta Pi, Eta Sigma Phi. Episcopalian. Avocations: writing, historic preservation, music, art history, architecture. Office: 555 New Jersey Ave NW Washington DC 20208-0001

LORD, LINDA DOROTHY, chemical engineer; b. Phila., Nov. 15, 1944; d. Julius Born and Alma Irene Lord; m. Joseph K. Hillstrom, Aug. 25, 1974. BSChemE, Wayne State U., 1977; MBA, U. Houston, 1988. Chem. engr. E.I. DuPont de Nemours, Wilmington, Del., 1977-80, Arco Chem., Channelview, Tex., 1980-85; prin. engr. Lyondell Petrochem., Houston, 1985-91; cons. engr. Coastal Corp., Houston, 1991—. Mem. AICE. Office: Coastal Corp 9 E Greenway Plz Houston TX 77046

LORD, M. G., writer; b. La Jolla, Calif., Nov. 18, 1955; d. Charles Carroll and Mary (Pfister) L.; m. Glenn Horowitz, May 19, 1985. B.A., Yale U., 1977. Reporter N.Y. Bur. Wall St. Jour., N.Y.C., summer 1976; editorial artist Chgo. Tribune, 1977-78; editorial cartoonist, columnist Newsday, N.Y.C., 1978-94; cartoons syndicated L.A. Times Syndicate, 1984-89; column syndicated Copley News Svc., 1989-94. Author: Mean Sheets, 1982, Prig Tales, 1990, Forever Barbie: The Unauthorized Biography of a Real Doll, 1994. Resident humanities fellow U. Mich., 1986-87. Club: Yale (N.Y.C.). Office: c/o Eric Simonoff Janklow & Nesbit Assoc 598 Madison Ave New York NY 10022

LORD, MARION MANNS, retired academic director; b. Fort Huachuca, Ariz., Dec. 17, 1914; d. George Wiley and Annie May (Pellett) Manns; children: Caroline L. Gross (dec.), Polly Steadman, Jane Chapin Humphries. BS, Northwestern U.; MEd, Harvard U., 1962; MA, U. Wis., 1968, PhD, 1968. Columnist, exec. sec. Boston Am., 1936-38; dean women, dir. counseling Henniker, N.H., 1962-64; psychology tchr. Cen. Mich. U., Washington, 1975-79; higher edn. adminstr. U.S. Office Edn., Washington, 1968-75; dean faculty Borough of Manhattan Community Coll., CUNY, 1975-79, Cottey Coll., Nevada, Mo., 1979-80; English tchr. high sch., 1982-84, realtor, 1984-90; asst. dir. Franklin Pierce Coll., Concord, N.H., 1992; mem. faculty N.H. Coll., 1994-95; ednl. cons. N.H. Coll. and Univ. Coun., 1974-80, David W. Smith & Assocs., Washington, U.S. Office Edn., 1975-80. Editor, contbr.: A Survey of Women's Experiences and Perceptions Concerning Barriers to Their Continuing Education, Review of the Literature. State rep. Gen. Ct. N.H., 1957-62; active various polit. campaigns; active in past numerous civic orgns. E.B. Fred fellow, 1964-68; Breadloaf Coll. scholar, 1936, Northwestern U. scholar, 1933-36. Mem. Am. Psychol. Assn., Pi Lambda Theta. Republican. Avocations: gardening, hiking, writing, reading. Home: RR 4 Box 402 Laconia NH 03246-8907

LORD, MARVIN, apparel company executive; b. N.Y.C., Sept. 22, 1937; s. Harry and Irene (Taub) L.; m. Joan Simon, Aug. 5, 1961; children—Elisa Anne, Michael Harris. B.S., Long Island U., Bklyn., 1959. Mdse. mgr. Oxford Industries, Inc., N.Y.C., 1964-66, gen. mdse. mgr., 1966-70, v.p., gen. mgr., 1970-73; pres. Holbrook Co., Inc. Div Oxford Industries, Inc., N.Y.C., 1970-85; pres., chief exec. officer Crystal Brands, Inc.-Youthwear Group, N.Y.C., 1985—; pres. Cluett Shirtmakers, N.Y.C., 1988—, M.L. Enterprises, Roslyn Heights, N.Y., 1990—; pres., chief oper. officer Sanyo Fashion House, N.Y.C., 1991—; pres., CEO MAternity Resources Inc., N.Y.C., 1994—. Chmn. Fathers Day Coun., N.Y.C., 1984—. Recipient Disting. Alumni award L.I. U., 1987. Mem. Mens Fashion Assn., Young Menswear Assn. Jewish. Avocation: tennis. Home: 53 Parkway Dr Roslyn Heights NY 11577-2705 Office: Maternity Resources Inc 525 7th Ave New York NY 10018

LORD, ROY ALVIN, retired publisher; b. Middletown, Ohio, July 2, 1918; s. Arthur Edwin and Mary Marie (Bell) L.; m. Elizabeth Frances Powell, Nov. 1, 1941; children—Thomas A., Frances A., William F. B.A., Ohio Wesleyan U., 1941; postgrad., Harvard U. Bus. Sch., 1962. With advt. sales Time Inc., N.Y.C. and Chgo., 1946-55; upper midwest mgr. advt. sales Time Inc., Mpls., 1955-62; nat. advt. sales mgr. Time Inc., N.Y.C., 1963-68; pres. ML&A Inc., N.Y.C., 1968-73; v.p. In-Store Publs., N.Y.C., 1973-74; pres. The Weekend Co., Inc., 1974-76; pub. A.D. Publs., Inc., N.Y.C., from 1976. Bd. dirs. Minn. Orchestral Assn., 1957-62; Minn. state chmn. Crusade for Freedom, 1960-62. Served with AC U.S. Army, 1942-45. Presbyterian.

LORD, WALTER, author; b. Balt., Oct. 8, 1917; s. John Walter and Henrietta Mactier (Hoffman) L. B.A., Princeton U., 1939; LL.B., Yale U., 1946. Editor bus. information services, 1946-53, engaged in advt., 1953-56, civilian aide to sec. army for So. N.Y. area, 1964-66. Author: A Night to Remember, 1955, Day of Infamy, 1957, The Good Years, 1960, A Time to Stand, 1961, Peary at the Pole, 1963, The Past That Would Not Die, 1965, Incredible Victory, 1967, The Dawn's Early Light, 1972, Lonely Vigil, 1977, The Miracle of Dunkirk, 1982, The Night Lives On, 1986; editor: The Fremantle Diary, 1954. Bd. dirs. Union Settlement, N.Y.C., 1959—, chmn., 1962-64; bd. dirs. Mcpl. Art Soc., N.Y.C., 1958-67; trustee N.Y. Soc. Library, 1963—, Mus. City N.Y., 1964-72, N.Y. Hist. Soc., 1965—; trustee Soc. Am. Historians, 1972—, pres., 1981-84; trustee Gilman Sch., Balt., 1962-80, Council Authors Guild, Inc., 1966-72, Coun. Authors League, 1972-83, sec., 1975-80; trustee N.Y. State Maritime Mus., 1968-79, South St. Seaport Mus., 1980—, Ocean Liner Mus., 1982—; mem. adv. bd. Protect Historic Am. Mem. Soc. Am. Historians, Authors Guild, ASCAP. Clubs: 14 W. Hamilton St. (Balt.); Century Assn. (N.Y.C.); Metropolitan (Washington).

LORD, WILLIAM GROGAN, financial holding company executive; b. Hearne, Tex., Oct. 21, 1914; s. Otis G. and Erminee G. Lord; m. Dorothy Nell Manning, Dec. 28, 1938 (dec.); children: Roger Griffin, Sharon Lord Caskey; m. Betty Fowler Hendrick, May 24, 1986. L.H.D. (hon.), Southwestern U., Georgetown, Tex., 1967. Sr. chmn. bd. dirs. TCC Industries, Inc. (formerly TeleCom Corp.), Austin, 1958—; sr. chmn. First Tex. Bancorp, Inc., Georgetown, 1971—; bd. dirs. Frozen Food Express Industries, Inc., Dallas; sr. chmn. bd. 1st Tex. Bancorp, Inc., Georgetown; mem., chmn. State Securities Bd., 1971-83. Trustee, mem. exec. com., vice chmn. bd. Southwestern U., 1958. Served to 1st lt. F.A. AUS, World War II. Decorated Purple Heart, Air medal with 4 oak leaf clusters; named Most Worthy Citizen Georgetown C. of C., 1971. Mem. Nat. Assn. Small Bus. Investment Cos. (past pres.), Regional Assn. Small Bus. Investment Cos, Tex. Research League, Tex. Philosophical Soc. Republican. Methodist. Clubs: Ramada (Houston), River Oaks Country (Houston); Austin (Austin, Tex.), Headliners (Austin, Tex.); St. Anthony (San Antonio). Office: PO Box 649 Georgetown TX 78627-0649

LORDEMAN, FRANK L., health facility administrator. COO Cleve. Clinic Hosp. Office: Cleve Clinic Hosp 9500 Euclid Ave Cleveland OH 44195-0001

LORE, MARTIN MAXWELL, lawyer; b. Milw., June 13, 1914; s. Michael and Jean (Dinerstein) L.; m. Doris Silver, Mar. 19, 1944; children: Amy L. Kovner, Dr. Cathy Jo. BA, U. Wis., 1934, LLB, 1936; LLM, Harvard, 1937; BCS, Strayer Coll. Accountancy, 1939. Bar: Wis. 1936, N.Y. 1946, D.C. 1947, Fla. 1977, U.S. Supreme Ct. 1939; CPA, D.C. Assoc. Rubin, Zabel & Ruppa, Milw., 1936-37; with Office Undersec. Treasury, 1937-38; spl. atty. office chief counsel, bur. IRS, 1938-40; trial counsel IRS (New Eng. div. tech. staff), 1940-42, IRS (N.Y. div.), 1945-47; tax counsel S.J. Foosaner, Newark, 1947-48; pvt. law practice N.Y.C., 1948-72; mem. firm Zissu Lore Halper & Robson, N.Y.C., 1972-76; counsel Zissu Lore Halper & Robson, 1976-80; ptnr. Lore & Levy, N.Y.C., 1981—; pres. bd. Fed. Tax Forum, Inc.; lectr. Tax Workshop, 1953-55, law sch. St. John's U., 1954, Fairleigh Dickinson U., 1955-56; specialist fed. tax matters, lectr. taxation NYU, 1946-50, 65, Practising Law Inst., 1947-48, Tax Inst., 1948, Pa. State Coll., 1949-50, U. W.Va., U. San Francisco, 1951, SUNY, Stony Brook, 1978-79; tax cons. Med. Econs.; pres., dir. Estate Planning Coun. N.Y.C.; part-time employee Melnik & Karan, Milw., 1933-36. Author: The Administration of The Federal Income Tax Through the United States Board of Tax Appeals, 1937, How to Win a Tax Case, 1955, Thin Capitalization, 1958; co-editor: Jour. of Taxation; chmn. bd. editors: How To Work with the Internal Revenue Code of 1954; contbr. articles to legal and accounting jours. Lt. comdr. Office Gen. Counsel, USNR, 1942-44. Mem. ABA (com. income taxation estates and trusts), N.Y. State Bar Assn., Assn. Bar City of N.Y. (taxation com., com. on trusts, estates and surrogate's cts.), FBA (chmn. com. fed. taxation), AICPA (sec. fed. tax lawyers com.), D.C. Accts., County Lawyers Assn. (taxation com.), Seawane Club (bd. govs.), Lawyers Club (N.Y.C.), Harvard Club (N.Y.C.), Barristers (Washington). Home: 46 Broome Ave Atlantic Beach NY 11509-1214 Office: Lore & Levy 1 Madison Ave New York NY 10010-3603

LORELL, MONTE, newspaper editor. Managing editor Page One, USA Today, Arlington, Va. Office: USA Today 1000 Wilson Blvd Arlington VA 22209-3901

LORELLE, LINDA, journalist; b. Chgo., Aug. 11, 1955; d. Clay Henry and Anita Clarice (Steele) Jones; m. Louis Wesley Gregory, June 23, 1990; 1 child, Lindsey Lorelle Gregory. BA in Devel. Psychology and Italian, Stanford U., 1977; MJ, U. Mo., Columbia, 1987. Weekend anchor, reporter Sta. KOMU-TV, Columbia, Mo., 1986-87; gen. assignment reporter Sta. KMOV-TV, St. Louis, 1987-89; weekend anchor, reporter Sta. KPRC-TV, Houston, 1989-90, anchor 6 and 10 p.m., 1990—. Mem. adv. bd. Houston Zoo, 1994—. Recipient Sch. Bell award Tex. State Tchrs. Assn., 1990, 91, Media award Tex. Assn. for Yr.-Round Edn., 1992, Sampson award Houston Tennis Assn., 1992, Matrix award Women in Commn., 1993, Makeda award Nat. Coalitino of 100 Black Women, 1994, Commendation award Am. Women in Radio and TV, 1995, Media Cmty. Svc. award Cancer League, 1995, Media Excellence award Cancer Counseling, 1995. Mem. Soc. Profl. Journalists (mem. adv. bd. 1993—). Avocations: tennis, dance. Office: Sta KPRC-TV 8181 SW Freeway Houston TX 77252

LORELLI, MICHAEL KEVIN, consumer products and services executive; b. N.Y.C., Apr. 17, 1951; s. Domenic and Effie (Stankevich) L.; m. Judith Bryant; children: Karen, Elizabeth. BE, NYU, 1972, MBA in Mktg., 1973. Dir. mktg. Clairol Co., N.Y.C., 1973-81; v.p., gen. mgr. internat. div. Playtex, Stamford, Conn., 1981-84; v.p. mktg. Apple Computer, Cupertino, Calif., 1984-85; exec. v.p. Pepsi-Cola Co., Somers, N.Y., 1985-88; pres. Pepsi-Cola East, Somers, N.Y., 1989-92, Pizza Hut Internat., 1993-96; pres. Am. divsn. Tambrands, Inc., White Plains, N.Y., 1996—. Bd. dirs. Trident Internat., Inc., Keep Am. Beautiful, United Way, Rosenbluth Travel, Am. Health Found.; trustee Sarah Lawrence Coll., Madison Sq. Boys and Girls Club. Republican. Roman Catholic. Avocations: flying, golf, running. Office: Tambrands Inc 777 Westchester Ave White Plains NY 10604-3520

LOREN, DONALD PATRICK, naval officer; b. N.Y.C., Mar. 17, 1952; s. Nicholas A. and Helen T. (Carrado) L.; m. Maureen M. Lynch, Jan. 12, 1991. BS in Ops. Analysis, U.S. Naval Acad., 1974; MS in Edn., Old Dominion U., 1983; postgrad., Harvard U., 1993-94, MIT, 1994-95. Commd. ens. USN, 1974, advanced through grades to capt., 1994, combat sys. officer, comdr. Destroyer Squadron, 1978; ops. officer USS Peterson, 1979-80; ops. and readiness officer Destroyer Squadron Two Staff, 1981-82; asst. chief of staff for comms. Cruiser Destroyer Group Eight Staff, 1983-85; exec. officer USS John Hancock, 1985-86; flag sec. to comdr. in chief U.S. Naval Forces, Europe, 1986-88; NATO policy officer Strategic Plans and Policy Directory, Joint Staff, 1989-91; comdg. officer USS Elrod FFG-55, 1991-93; doctrine devel. officer Naval Doctrine Command, 1993; fed. exec. fellow Ctr. for Internat. Affairs Harvard U., Cambridge, Mass., 1993-94; profl. staff mem. Ind. Commn. on Roles and Missions of Armed Forces, 1993-94; comdr. Destroyer Squadron Twenty-eight, Virginia Beach, Va., 1994—; mem. joint U.S. counter-drug ops.; dep. congl. liaison for Chmn. Commn. on Roles and Missions of Armed Forces. Author: Shape Up! A Shipboard Program for Physical Fitness, 1981; contbr. articles to profl. publs. Mem. Phi Kappa Phi, Sigma Iota Epsilon. Avocations: jogging, weight training, classical music, ballet, opera. Home: 1613 Colliers Ln Virginia Beach VA 23455 Office: Comdr Destroyer Squadron 28 Norfolk VA 23456

LOREN, MARY ROONEY, controller; b. Monaghan, Ireland, Nov. 18, 1939; came to U.S., 1957; d. Peter Paul and Mary Alice (McKenna) Rooney; m. Thomas Leroy Loren, Aug. 22, 1959; children: Mary Teresa, Aileen Frances, Susan Marie. AAS in Acctg., Adirondack C.C., 1976; BS in Bus., Skidmore Coll., 1979; postgrad., SUNY, Plattsburgh, 1995—. Acctg. supr. Neles-Jamesbury, Glens Falls, N.Y., 1979-88; contr. Queensbury Hotel, Glens Falls, 1988-89; mgmt. acct. Ahlstrom Screen Pl., Glens Falls, 1989-92; mill contr. Hollingsworth & Vose, Greenwich, N.Y., 1993—; owner Heritage Heirlooms. Treas. Every Woman's Coun., Glens Falls, 1985—; lectr., eucharistic min. St. Michael's Roman Cath. Ch., Glens Falls, 1980—. Mem. Inst. Mgmt. Accts. (corp., acad. dir. 1993-94, pres. 1992-93, Achievement award 1992-93, Cmty. Svc. award 1993). Republican. Avocations: golf, hiking, genealogical research, travel.

LOREN, PAMELA, telecommunications executive; b. Paris, Jan. 11, 1944; d. Theodore and Martha (Ephron) L.; BS in Sociology, Columbia U., 1964; MS in Sociology, U. Madrid, 1968, MS in Langs., 1970; m. Morton P. Levy, June 2, 1963; children: Cristopher Aram, Stirling Brett, Cristina Sahula. Pres., Pamela Loren, Ltd., N.Y.C., 1969-74, Loren Communications Internat., Ltd., N.Y.C., 1972-74; chmn. bd. Loren Communications Internat., Caracas, Venezuela, London, Milan, Italy and N.Y.C., 1974—; exec. v.p. Cinnamon World Trade Corp., 1974—; pres., chief exec. officer LorenAire Aviation, N.Y. and Brazil, 1988—; dir. Panda Internat. Export Corp., Durable Housing Internat., Loren Group, Danbury, Conn., Crespi, Rosann & Ponti; speaker on interdependence of medicine and communications. Bd. dirs. Burden Ctr. for Aging. Recipient Humanitarian award Community

Service Soc., 1972, Burden Ctr. for Aging, 1977, Soc. Order Helpers, 1978, 82, 86, 88, 92, Otty award, 1986; named Young Woman of Achievement YWCA, 1983, Woman of Vision, Caracas, 1986, Woman of the Future, Madrid, 1988. Mem. Am. Arbitration Assn., Am. Mgmt. Assn., Soc. Latin-Am. Bus. Owners, N.Y. Assn. Women Bus. Owners, Women's Econ. Round Table, World Trade Coun., Am. Soc. Prevention Cruelty to Animals (bd. dirs., media adv. bd.). Club: Columbia University. Author: The Generation In-Between, 1977; Looking Ahead to Thirty-Five, 1978, Slowing Down in the Fast Lane, 1987, When Having It All Isn't Enough, 1988, New Patterns of Power: Women and Influence, 1989. Home: 7425 E 58th St New York NY 10022 Office: Loren Communications Internat 155 E 55th St New York NY 10022-4038

LOREN, SOPHIA, actress; b. Rome, Sept. 20, 1934; d. Riccardo Scicolone and Romilda Villani; m. Carlo Ponti, Apr. 12, 1967; children: Carlo Ponti, Edoardo. Student, Scuole Magistrali Superiori. Films include E Arrivato l'Accordatore, 1951, Africa sotto i Mari, La Favorita, La Tratta Delle Bianche, 1952, Aida, Tempi Nostri, Ci Troviamo in Gellera, La Domenica Della Buona Genti, Il Paese dei Campanelli, Un Giorno in Pretura, Due Notti con Cleopatra, Pelegrini d'Amore, Attila, Carosello Napoletano, 1953, Miseria e Nobilta, Gold of Naples, Woman of the River, Too Bad She's Bad (Best Actress award Buenos Aires Festival), 1954, Lucky To Be A Woman, Sign of Venus, The Millers Wife, Scandal in Sorrento, 1955, Pride and Passion, Boy on a Dolphin, Legend of The Lost, 1957, Desire Under the Elms, Houseboat, The Key (Best Actress award Japan), 1958, That Kind of Woman, Black Orchid, 1959 (Best Actress Venice Festival, David Di Donatello award Italy, Victoire Popularity award France), Heller in Pink Tights (Best Actress Rapallo Festival Italy), It Started in Naples, A Breath of Scandal, The Millionaires, 1960, Two Women, (11 Best Actress awards including Oscar, Hollywood, Di Donatello award, Cannes Film Festival, N.Y. Critics, Golden Globe, Brit. Film Acad., others from Ireland, Japan, Belgium, Spain, France, W. Ger., also other awards), El Cid, Madame, Bocaccio 70, 1961, The Condemned of Altona, Five Miles to Midnight, 1962, Yesterday, Today and Tomorrow, (Best Actress Di Donatello award, Golden Globe award), 1963, The Fall of the Roman Empire, Marriage Italian Style, 1964 (Best Actress Di Donatello award, Golden Globe award, Alexander Korda award Brit. Film Inst., others), Operation Crossbow, Lady L, Judith, 1965, Arabesque, A Countess From Hong Kong, 1966, Happily Ever After, Ghosts, Italian Style (Best Fgn. Actress Diploma USSR), 1967, More Than A Miracle, (Ramo d'Oro award Italy, other awards), 1968, Sunflower (Best Actress Di Donatello award), 1969, The Priest's Wife, 1970, Lady Liberty, White Sister, 1971, Man of La Mancha, 1972, The Voyage (Di Donatello award), 1973, Brief Encounter, The Verdict, 1974, The Cassandra Crossing, A Special Day, 1977, Firepower, 1978, Brass Target, 1979, Blood Feud, 1981; TV film appearances include Sophia Loren: Her Own Story, 1980, Angela, 1982, Aurora, 1985, Mother Courage, 1986, The Fortunate Pilgrim (Best Actress of Yr. for TV mini-series), 1987, La Ciociara, 1989, Ready to Wear (Prêt-à-Porter), 1994. Recipient numerous awards including Nastro d'Argento, Italy, 14 Bambi and Bravo Popularity awards, Fed. Republic Germany, 3 Prix Uilenspigoel Fiamingo award, Belgium, Popularity awards Am. Legion, Tex. Cinema Exhibitors, 4 Snosiki Popularity awards, Finland, 2 Best Actress awards Bengal Film Journalists Assn., India, Box-Office Favourite Medal, Italy, Helene Curtis award, U.S.A., Simpatia Popularity award, Italy, Rudolph Valentino Screen Svcs. award, Italy, Best Actress award Moscow Film Festival, Hon. Acad. award, 1990; named Most Popular Actress in Italy. Office: Via di Villa Ada 10, Rome I-00199, Italy*

LORENTZ, WILLIAM BEALL, pediatrician; b. Glenville, W.Va., July 8, 1937; s. William Beall and Mary Gay (Garrett) L.; m. Anne Lynne Hickman, June 20, 1960 (div. Aug. 30, 1977); children: Pamela Lynne, Lisa Anne, William Chad; m. Suzy Vernice Gibson, Sept. 5, 1977. BA, W.Va. U., 1959; MD, Jefferson Med. Coll., 1963. Diplomate Am. Bd. Pediatrics, Sub-board of Pediatric Nephrology. Internship Harrisburg (Pa.) Polyclinic Hosp., 1963-64, resident in pediatrics, 1964-65; resident in pediatrics U. Tex. Med. Br., Galveston, Tex., 1965-67; med. corp USN, Quantico (Va.) Naval Hosp., 1967-69; fellow in renal physiology U. N.C. Sch. of Medicine, Chapel Hill, 1969-71; asst. prof. pediatrics U. Tex. Med. Br., Galveston, 1971-74, Bowman Gray Sch. Medicine, Winston-Salem, N.C., 1974-75; assoc. prof. pediatrics Bowman Gray Sch. Medicine, Winston-Salem, 1975-81; prof. pediatrics Bowman Grey Sch. Medicine, Winston-Salem, 1981—; assoc. chief staff N.C. Bapt. Hosp., 1991—; med. dir. Medcost, Winston-Salem, 1989—; cons. physician Allegheny Regional Hosp., Low Moor, Va., 1988; pres. Piedmont Med. Found., Winston-Salem, 1983-88. Contbr. articles to profl. jours. Lt. comdr. USN, 1966-69. Mem. Soc. for Pediatric Rsch., Am. Pediatric Soc., Am. Acad. Pediatrics. Am. Soc. Nephrology, Am. Soc. for Pediatric Nephrology. Democrat. Presbyterian. Avocation: running. Office: Bowman Gray Sch Medicine 300 S Hawthorne Rd Winston Salem NC 27157-0002

LORENZ, ANNE PARTEE, special education educator, consultant; b. Nashville, Aug. 6, 1943; d. McCullough and Mary Elizabeth (Shemwell) Partee; m. Philip Jack Lorenz, Jr., Nov. 26, 1970; stepchildren: Brenna Ellen, Philip Jack III. Student, Rhodes Coll., 1961-63, 64; BS, George Peabody Coll., 1966; postgrad., Ga. State U., 1967-68; MS, George Peabody Coll., 1969. Clerk Tenn. State Libr. Archives, Nashville, 1963-64; tchr. learning disabilities Howard Sch., Atlanta, 1966-68; prin., tchr. learning disabilities Sewanee (Tenn.) Learning Ctr., 1969-78; tchr. learning disabilities Clark Meml. Sch., Winchester, Tenn., 1978-79; tutor, cons. learning disabilities Anne Partee Lorenz Tutoring Consultation Svc., Sewanee, 1979—; psychol. cons. U. of South, 1974-78; cons. St. Andrew's-Sewanee Sch., Tenn., 1980—. Active Coun. for Exceptional Children, 1968-79; treas. Franklin County Dem. Party; sec. Sewanee Precinct Dem. Party, 1974-76; del. dist. and state Dem. Conf.; judge John M. Templeton Laws of Life Essay Contest; vol. Cordelle-Lorenz Obs., U. of the South, 1970—; bd. dirs. Franklin County Adult Activities Ctr., 1979-82. Recipient letter of commendation Gov. Tenn., 1974. Mem. Tenn. LWV (pres., bd. dirs.), Franklin County LWV (pres.), Learning Disabilities Assn. Tenn. (1st Tchr. Yr. 1975), Children and Adults with Attention Deficit Disorders. Avocations: wild flowers, bird and wild animal watching, walking, reading, crocheting. Home and Office: 390 Onteora Ln Sewanee TN 37375-2639

LORENZ, HUGO ALBERT, insurance executive; b. Elmhurst, Ill., July 5, 1926; s. Hugo E. and Linda T. (Trampel) L. B.S., Northwestern U., 1949; LL.B., Harvard U., 1952. Bar: Ill. 1954. Mem. patent staff Bell Telephone Labs., Murray Hill, N.J., 1952-53; atty. First Nat. Bank Chgo., 1954-58; gen. counsel N.Am. Life Ins. Co. of Chgo., 1958-73; dir., v.p., gen. counsel, sec. Globe Life Ins. Co., Chgo., 1973-95; v.p. Union Fidelity Life Ins. Co., Chgo., 1993-96; sec. Gt. Equity Life Ins. Co., Chgo., 1977-80, Pat Ryan & Assos. Inc., Va. Surety Co., Chgo., 1977—. Bd. dirs. Sr. Ctrs. Met. Chgo., 1977-93, pres., 1983-85; trustee Hull House Assn., 1983-88. With USNR, 1944-46. Mem. ABA, Assn. Life Ins. Counsel, Connoisseurs Internat (bd. dirs. 1972—, pres. 1980-95), Internat. Wine and Food Soc. Chgo. (gov. and oenologist 1980—). Unitarian. Home: 950 A N Clark St Chicago IL 60610 Office: Aon Corp 123 N Wacker Dr Chicago IL 60606-1700

LORENZ, JOHN DOUGLAS, college official; b. Talmage, Nebr., July 2, 1942; s. Orville George and Twila Lucille (Larson) L.; m. Alice Louise Hentzen, Aug. 26, 1967; 1 child, Christian Douglas. BS, U. Nebr., 1965, MS, 1967, PhD, 1973. Systems analyst U. Nebr., Lincoln, 1967-73; asst. prof. GMI Engring. and Mgmt. Inst., Flint, Mich., 1973-74, assoc. prof., 1974-78, prof., 1978—, dept. head, 1984-87, asst. dean, 1986-88, provost, dean faculty, 1988-92, Richard L. Terrell prof. acad. leadership, 1990—, v.p. for acad. affairs, provost, 1992—; cons. GM, Detroit, 1973-82, various orgns. Contbr. articles to profl. jours. Judge Internat. Sci. and Engring. Fair, various locations, 1989—. Mem. NSPE, Soc. Mfg. Engrs. (sr.), So. Automotive Engrs., Engring. Accreditation Commn. of Accreditation Bd. for Engring. and Tech., Am. Soc. Engring. Edn., Antique Auto Racing Assn., Model Engine Collectors Assn., Antique Model Race Car Club. Home: 3122 Beechtree Ln Flushing MI 48433-1945 Office: GMI Engring and Mgmt Inst 1700 W 3rd Ave Flint MI 48504-4832

LORENZ, JOHN GEORGE, librarian, consultant; b. N.Y.C., Sept. 28, 1915; s. John W. and Theresa T. (Wurtz) L.; m. Josephine R. Trumbull, Oct. 1, 1944; children: Laurence T., Janice R. B.S. (Library fellow), CCNY, 1939; B.S. in L.S, Columbia U., 1940; M.S. in Pub. Adminstrn., Mich. State U., 1952. With Queens Borough (N.Y.) Library, then Schenectady Pub. Library, 1940-44; chief reference div. Grand Rapids Pub. Library, 1944-46; asst. librarian Mich. State Library, 1946-56; with U.S. Office Edn., 1957-65, dir. div. library services and ednl. facilities, 1964-65; dep. librarian of congress Library of Congress, Washington, 1965-76; exec. dir. Assn. Research Libraries, 1976-80; library cons., 1980—; interim dir. libraries Cath. U. Am., 1982-83; liaison mem. com. sci. and tech. info. exec. office, 1966-73; interim dir. CAPCON, 1985; spl. asst. to librarian Georgetown U. Library, 1985-87; interim dir. Washington Research Library Consortium, 1987-88; coord. libr. stats. program Nat. Commn. on Librs. and Inf. Sci., 1988—; exec. com. Nat. Book Com., 1968-74. Author numerous articles in field; contbr. to books. Presdl. appointee Nat. Hist. Publs. and Records Commn., 1979-83. Recipient Superior Svc. award HEW. Mem. ALA (coun. 1960-64, 69-73, chmn. panel UNESCO 1965-70, exec. bd. 1970-75, Lippincott award 1993), D.C. Libr. Assn., Internat. Fedn. Libr. Assn. (mem. program devel. group 1974-78), Am. Nat. Stds. Inst. (treas. libr. stds. com. 1980-88), Cosmos Club, Kenwood Golf and Country Club. Home: 5629 Newington Rd Bethesda MD 20816-3321 Office: US Nat Commn on Librs Info Sci 1110 Vermont Ave NW Washington DC 20005-3522

LORENZ, KATHERINE MARY, banker; b. Barrington, Ill., May 1, 1946; d. David George and Mary (Hogan) L. BA cum laude, Trinity Coll., 1968; MBA, Northwestern U., 1971; grad., Grad. Sch. for Bank Adminstrn., 1977. Ops. analyst Continental Bank, Chgo., 1968-69, supr. ops. analysis, 1969-71, asst. mgr. customer profitability analysis, 1971-73, acctg. officer, mgr. customer profitability analysis, 1973-77, 2d v.p., 1976, asst. gen. mgr. contr.'s dept., 1977-80, v.p., 1980, contr. ops. and mgmt. svcs. dept., 1981-84, v.p., sector contr. retail banking, corp. staff and ops. depts., 1984-88, v.p., sr. sector contr. pvt. banking, centralized ops. and corp. staff, 1988-90, v.p., sr. sector contr. bus. analysis group/mgmt. acctg., 1990-94, mgr. contrs. dept. adminstrn. and tng., 1990-94; v.p., chief of staff to chief adminstrv. officer Bank of Am. Ill., Chgo., 1994-96, v.p., mgr. adminstrv. svcs., 1996—. Mem. Execs. Club Chgo. Office: Bank of Am Ill 231 S La Salle St Rm 1320 Chicago IL 60697

LORENZ, LATISHA JAY, elementary education educator; b. Uniontown, Pa., June 16, 1967; d. Lou Jean Lorenz and Mary Lou (Sesler) Rupp; m. Donald Raye Shetley, May 25, 1991 (div. Oct. 1993). AA, U. S.C., Union, 1987; BS in Edn., Lander U., 1989. Cert. elem. edn. 6th grade tchr. Union (S.C.) Acad., 1990-93; 7th grade lang. arts tchr. Sims Jr. H.S., Union, 1993—. Mem. S.C. State Coun. of the Internat. Reading Assn., Union Jr. Charity League. Republican. Baptist. Avocations: cats, reading Stephen King, watching the Buffalo Bills, going to movies. Office: Sims Jr High 200 Sims Dr Union SC 29379

LORENZ, LEE SHARP, cartoonist; b. Hackensack, N.J., Oct. 17, 1932; s. Alfred Lloyd and Martha (Castagnetta) L.; m. Jill Allison Runcie, Sept., 1986; children: Christopher, Matthew, Martha, Ava. Student, Carnegie Inst. Tech., 1950-51; BFA, Pratt Inst., 1954. Staff cartoonist New Yorker mag., 1958—, art editor, 1973—; profl. cornetist, 1955—. Cartoonist: Here it Comes, 1968; author, illustrator: Scornful Simkin, 1980; collection Npw Look What You've Done, 1977; illustrator: Real Men Don't Eat Quiche, 1982, A Bridge Bestiary, 1986, Collection the Golden Age of Trash, 1987; author, illustrator: A Weekend in the Country, 1985; author: The Art of the New Yorker, 1995. Trustee Swann Coll. of Cartoon and Caricature, 1978—; dir. Mus. for African Art. Mem. Century Club. Home: PO Box 117 Easton CT 06612-0131 Office: 20 W 43rd St New York NY 10036-7400

LORENZ, LORETTA ROSE, English language educator; b. Chgo., Apr. 14, 1931; arrived in Japan, 1961; d. Karl Adolph and Juliana (Grunauer) L. BS in Humanities, Loyola U., Chgo., 1953; postgrad., U. Chgo., 1954-55, Am. Acad. Art, Chgo., 1956, Am. U., Washington, 1958-59. Part-time editl. asst. Poetry: A Mag. of Verse, Chgo., 1952-58; advt. copywriter Spiegel, Inc., Chgo., 1954-56; publicity and promotions writer Chgo. Ednl. TV Assn., Sta. WTTW, 1956-58; editl. asst. Cath. U. of Am. Press, Washington, 1959; copywriter, layout designer D.C. Health and Co., Boston, 1959-60; tchr., contbr. to books and tapes Seido Lang. Inst., Ashiya City, Japan, 1961-80; tchr. English Shimogamo Acad., Kyoto, Japan, 1964-86; lectr. Kyoto U. Fgn. Studies, 1964-86; prof. Nagasaki (Japan) Jr. Coll. Fgn. Langs., 1986—; lectr. various cmty. ctrs. Japan, 1986—. Contbg. author, cons.: (textbook series) Modern English: An Oral Approach, 1965-80, Modern English, Cycle Two, 1965-80; contbr. articles to profl. jours. Office: Nagasaki Jr Coll Fgn Langs, College Hill Togitsu-machi, Nagasaki 851-12, Japan

LORENZEN, COBY, emeritus engineering educator; b. Oakland, Calif., Nov. 30, 1905; s. Coby and Catherine (O'Keefe) L.; m. Ina Voss, Aug. 7, 1937; children: Robert, Jacklyn, Donald, Kenneth. BSME, U. Calif., Berkeley, 1929, MSME, 1934. Profl. engr., Calif. Rsch. engr. Nat. Adv. Com. for Aeronautics, 1929-31; rsch. asst. U. Calif., Berkeley, 1931-34; rsch. engr. Calif. Forest and Range Exptl. Sta., 1934-37; prof. engring. U. Calif., Davis, 1937-69. Recipient John Scott medal City of Phila., 1976, Cyrus McCormick Gold medal Am. Soc. Agrl. Engrs., Chgo., 1981. Achievements include design of first commercial mechanical harvester for canning tomatoes. Home: Country Club Dr Carmel Valley CA 93924

LORENZEN, LOUIS OTTO, art educator; b. Akron, Ohio, Apr. 20, 1935; s. Lorenz Jack and Anne (Strampher) L.; m. Veronica Ann Lorenzen, Dec. 10, 1978; children: Michelle Melody Raitt, Teresa Ann Hopkins, Lisette Marie Jackson, Anthony Frederick, Nicholas Joseph. BSEd in Art, Bowling Green (Ohio) State U., 1959; MEd in Adminstrv. Counseling, Bridgewater State Coll., 1964; MAT, Assumption Coll., 1970; MFA, Syracuse (N.Y.) U., 1982. Cert. art tchr., Mass.; cert. secondary English, counseling and guidance, secondary adminstrn., Mass. Art tchr. K-12 Bluffton (Ohio) City Schs., 1959; dir. pubs. Illustrator, graphic designer Greater Cleve. Regional Rsch. Coun., 1959; English tchr. DUEL Vocat. Inst. Calif. Dept. Corrections, Tracey, 1960-61; spl. needs tchr. Old Rochester Regional High Sch., Mattapoisett, Mass., 1961-62; English tchr. Roosevelt Jr. High Sch., New Bedford, Mass., 1962-63, New Bedford Vocat. High Sch., 1963-65; full prof. art Fitchburg (Mass.) State Coll., 1965—; chair program rev. com. Mass. Dept. Edn. Certification, Quincy, Mass., 1991, program rev. com., 1987-90; artist-in-residence Mt. Washington Hotel, 1981. One man shows include LaGardina Gallery, San Francisco, 1960, Fitchburg State Coll., 1968, 80, 82, Jaffrey Civic Ctr., 1972, The Elms Coll., 1985, Borgia Gallery; exhibited in group shows at Rockport Art Assn., 1980-82, 84, Fitchburg Art Mus., 1978, 79, 81-83, 90, Fitchburg State Coll. Faculty Shows, 1982-89, Brick House Gallery, Boothbay Harbor, Maine, 1984-90 (3 ann. shows), New Eng. Art Educators Conf. Show, 1983, also represented in permanent collections. Adv. bd. dirs. Boston Globe Art awards, 1980-85; judge ann. show Westfield (Mass.) State Coll. Dept. Art, 1985. Mem. NEA (life), Mass. Tchrs. Assn., State Coll. Edn. Assn. (local bd. dirs. 1989-90, promotion com. 1988-90, curricula com. 1991—), Mass. Art Edn. Assn. (recording sec. 1968-69, corr. sec. 1970-72, chmn. nominations com. 1972-74, v.p. 1981-83, pres. 1983-86), Mass. Art Edn. Assn., Nat. Art Edn. Assn. (chair authored coee of ethics 1985, ea. rep. to exec. com. for the com. of minority concerns 1986-90, Cert. of Appreciation), Internat. Soc. for Edn. Through Art (ea. alt. rep. nat. chpt. 1989-91), Amnesty Internat., Phi Delta Kappa. Office: Fitchburg State Coll 160 Pearl St Fitchburg MA 01420-2631

LORENZEN, ROBERT FREDERICK, ophthalmologist; b. Toledo, Ohio, Mar. 20, 1924; s. Martin Robert and Pearl Adeline (Bush) L.; m. Lucy Logsdon, Feb. 14, 1970; children: Roberta Jo, Richard Martin, Elizabeth Anne. BS, Duke, 1948, MD, 1948; MS, Tulane U., 1953. Intern, Presbyn. Hosp., Chgo., 1948-49; resident Duke Med. Center, 1949-51, Tulane U. Grad. Sch., 1951-53; practice medicine specializing in ophthalmology, Phoenix, 1953—; mem. staff St. Joseph's Hosp., St. Luke's Hosp., Good Samaritan Hosp., Surg. Eye Ctr. of Ariz. Pres. Ophthalmic Scis. Found., 1970-73; chmn. bd. trustees Rockefeller and Abbe Prentice Eye Inst. of St. Luke's Hosp., 1975—. Recipient Gold Headed Cane award, 1974; named to Honorable Order of Ky. Cols. Fellow ACS, Internat. Coll. Surgeons, Am. Acad. Ophthalmology and Otolaryngology, Pan Am. Assn. Ophthalmology, Soc. Eye Surgeons; mem. Am. Assn. Ophthalmology (sec. of ho. of dels. 1972-73, trustee 1973-76), Ariz. Ophthal. Soc. (pres. 1966-67), Ariz. Med. Assn. (bd. dirs. 1963-66, 69-70), Royal Soc. Medicine, Rotary (pres. Phoenix 1984-85). Republican. Editor in chief Ariz. Medicine, 1963-66, 69-70. Office: 367 E Virginia Ave Phoenix AZ 85004-1202

LORENZETTI, OLE JOHN, pharmaceutical research executive, ophthalmic research and development executive; b. Chgo., Oct. 25, 1936; s. Natale and Quintilia (Bertochinni) L.; m. Lorna Joyce Bailey, June 20, 1961; children: Elizabeth Anne, Maria Anne, Dario. BS, U. Ill., Chgo., 1958; MS, Ohio State U., 1963, PhD, 1965; MBA (hon.), MIT, 1989. Rsch. fellow Ohio State U., Columbus, 1964-65; scientist Miles Labs., Elkhardt, Ind., 1965-67; sr. scientist Dome Labs. div. Miles Labs., Elkhardt, 1967-69; sr. scientist R&D Alcon Labs., Ft. Worth, 1969-72, mgr. R&D div. pre clin. sci., 1972-75, assoc. dir. R&D div. dermatology, 1975-80, dir. ophthal. R&D, 1980-83, sr. dir. surg. R&D, 1983-92, sr. dir. therapeutic rsch./licensing, 1992-94; v.p. therapeutic rsch./licensing, 1994—; asst. prof. pharmacology Health Scis. Ctr. U. Tex., Dallas, 1970-90; clin. prof. dermatology Health Scis. Ctr., U. Tex., Dallas, 1974-80; adj. prof. Tex. Christian U., 1972-82; J.J. Able lectr. pharmacology Ohio No. U., 1965, 69; Kaufman-Lattimer lectr. Ohio State U., 1967, 70, 73, 78; vis. lectr. in therapeutic and drug rsch. U. Ill., 1973-80; toxicologist cons. South Bend, Ind. Municipality, 1967-69, Tarrant County, Tex., 1970-73; vis. lectr. U. Tex. Med. Schs., 1990—. Mem. editorial bd. Jour. Pharm. Sci., 1974-84, Cutis, 1977-89, Jour. Sci. Investigative Dermatology, 1978-82; contbr. articles to profl. jours., book chpts., govt. reports. Am. Heart Assn. fellow Ohio State U., 1964. Fellow Acad. Pharm. Scis. (pharmacology-toxicology sect.), Am. Acad. Clin. Toxicology, Soc. for Exptl. Biology and Medicine; mem. AAAS, Am. Pharm. Assn., N.Y. Acad. Sci., Am. Chem. Soc., Soc. Investigative Dermatology, Drug Metabolism Group, Am. Soc. Pharmacology and Exptl. Therapeutics, Western Pharmacology and Exptl. Therapeutics, Western Pharmacology Soc., Am. Coll. Toxicology, Inflammation Rsch. Assn., Am. Soc. Clin. Pharmacology, Am. Acad. Ophthalmology, Assn. for Rsch. and Vision and Ophthalmology, Drug Info. Assn., Rotary (pres. 1990), Sigma Xi. Avocations: ranching, horses, sailing, photography, marathon running. Office: Vice Pres Ther Rsch & Devel Alcon Labs Inc 6201 South Fwy Fort Worth TX 76134-2001

LORENZINI, PAUL G., manufacturing executive; b. 1939. BS in Edn., S.E. Mo. State, 1962. With Sunshine Biscuit, N.Y.C., 1963-67; dist. mgr. Mobil Chem., Rochester, N.Y., 1967-69; with Bunzl Distbn. USA, Inc., Saint Louis, 1969—, now chmn. bd. Office: Bunzl Distribution USA Inc 701 Emerson Rd Ste 410 Saint Louis MO 63141-6754*

LORENZO, ALBERT L., academic administrator. BS, U. Detroit, 1965, MBA, 1966; LLD (hon.), Walsh Coll. Accountancy and Bus. Adminstrn., 1987. Asst. dir. housing U. Detroit, 1964-65; staff acct. McManus, McGraw and Co., Detroit, 1964-66; asst. prof. acctg. Macomb Community Coll., Warren, Mich., 1966-68, bus. mgr., 1968-74, contr., 1974-75, v.p. bus., 1975-79, pres., 1979—; lectr., pub. speaker, presenter in field. Dir. rsch. SBA, 1966; mem. Mayor's Adv. Com. Small Bus., Detroit, 1967-70, base-community coun. Selfridge Air NG, 1978-86, steering com. March of Dimes, 1980-86, adv. coun. Met. Affairs Corp., 1982—, Mich. Competitive Enterprise Task Force, 1988-90, adv. bd. Nat. Inst. Leadership Devel., 1988—, Community Growth Alliance Macomb County, 1982—, selection panel Heart of Gold ann. awards Southeastern Mich. United Way, 1990; chair div. II United Found., 1981; apptd. commr. State Mich. High Edn. Faciltiies Authority, 1988-90; bd. dirs. N.E. Guidance Community Mental Health Ctr., 1976-79, Mich. Nat. Bank Macomb, 1981-87, Indsl. Tech. Inst., 1982—; trustee Nat. Commn. Coop. Edn., 1985—; trustee St. Joseph Hosp., 1984-87, sec. 1985-87, mem. adv. bd. 1981-83. Recipient Resolution of Tribute Mich. State Senate, 1979, Italian-Am. Citizen Recognition award, 1980, Volkswagen Am. Recognition award, 1982, Excellence in Speech Writing award Internat. Assn. Bus. Communicators, 1988, Nat. Leadership award U. Tex., 1989, Thomas J. Peters Nat. Leadership award, 1989; named Pres. of Yr. Am. Assn. Women in Community and Jr. Colls., 1985. Mem. Am. Assn. Community and Jr. Colls., World Future Soc., Met. Mus. Art, Mich. Community Coll. Assn., Econ. Club Detroit. Office: Macomb Community Coll 14500 E 12 Mile Rd Warren MI 48093-3870

LORENZO, MICHAEL, engineer, government official, real estate broker; b. Newton, N.J., 1920; m. Anastasia Hackett; 5 children. BS in Chemistry and Physics, Pa. State U., 1947; MEA, George Washington U., 1956, postgrad., 1975-78; postgrad., USDA Grad. Sch. Registered profl. engr., D.C., Md.; cert. Internat. Property Specialist (CIPS), FIPC. Field instrumentation engr. Fischer and Porter Co., Harboro, Pa., 1947-52; aerospace engr. Dept. Def., 1952-65; with Westinghouse Electric Corp., Friendship, Md., 1965-81; mgr. Air Resources Westinghouse Mgmt. Services, Inc., 1966-70, dir. environ. quality control, 1970-73; founder, pres. Tech. Protection Engring. Co., 1982—; dep. under-sec. def. Washington, 1981-82; founder, prin. broker First Lady Realty Corp., 1986—. Author: (with others) Chemical Equipment Costs, 1950; assoc. editor: Missile and Rockets, 1958-61; contbr. articles to profl. jours.; patentee stall surge sonic sensor. Rear Admiral AC USN, World War II, Korea. Decorated D.S.M., D.F.C. (2), Air medals (7). Mem. Profl. Tennis Registry. Office: First Lady Realty Corp 3126 Shadeland Dr Falls Church VA 22044-1726 *Healthy mind requires healthy body and vice versa. Per Winston Churchill "A Democracy is the worst form of Government that was ever invented except for all the others." It's my time in life to give back.*

LORENZO, NICHOLAS FRANCIS, JR., lawyer; b. Norfolk, Va., Nov. 22, 1942; s. Nicholas and Jean W. L.; m. Patricia C. Connare, Sept. 7, 1968; children: Nicholas Michael, Matthew Christopher. B.A., St. Francis Coll., 1964; J.D., Duquesne U., 1968. Bar: Pa. 1968, U.S. Dist. Ct. (we. dist.) Pa. 1969, U.S. Supreme Ct. 1976, U.S. Dist. Ct. (mid. dist.) Pa. 1977, U.S. Ct. Appeals (3d cir.) 1983. Assoc. R. Edward Ferrero, Punxsutawney, Pa., 1968-70; pvt. practice law, Punxsutawney, 1970-79; pres. Lorenzo and Lundy, P.C., Punxsutawney, 1979-81, Nicholas F. Lorenzo, Jr. P.C., Punxsutawney, 1981-90, Lorenzo & Kulakowski, P.C., 1990—; instr. Sch. Continuing Edn., Pa. State U., 1969-73. Bd. dirs. Punxsutawney Area Hosp., 1972-74; mem. parish council S.S.C.D. Roman Cath. Ch., 1978-84, pres., 1979-84; bd. dirs. dist. Council Boy Scouts Am., 1982-84. Mem. ABA, Jefferson County Bar Assn. (v.p. 1980-82, pres. 1982-84), Pa. Bar Assn., Pa. Bar Inst. (bd. dirs. 1988-94), Pa. Trial Lawyers Assn. (bd. govs), West Pa. Trial Lawyers Assn., Assn. Trial Lawyers Am., Nat. Bd. Trial Advocacy (civil cert.). Republican. Club: Punxsutawney Country. Lodges: K.C., Elks, Eagles Pat Rotary (pres. Punxsutawney 1973). Home: 180 Monticello Dr Punxsutawney PA 15767-2614 Office: 410 W Mahoning St Punxsutawney PA 15767-1908

LORENZO FRANCO, JOSÉ RAMúÓN, Mexican government official; b. Apizaco, Tlaxcala, Mexico, Jan. 2, 1935. Student, Naval Staff Sch., Mexico, Navy War Coll., U.S. Joined Mexican Army, 1952; adj. Mexican Navy, chief tech. dept. naval edn., chief of staff naval zone, dir. gen. Ctr. of Army Capacities, dir. Ctr. for Higher Naval Studies, comdr. of Naval Region, insp., comptr. gen.; Sec. of the Navy Govt. of Mexico, 1995—. Office: Embassy of Mexico 1911 Pennsylvania Ave NW Washington DC 20006*

LORGE, WILLIAM D., state legislator, farmer; b. Bear Creek, Wis., Aug. 31, 1960; s. Gerald D. and Christina C. (Ziegler) L.; m. Molly M. McGinty, Apr. 11, 1996. BA in Internat. Relations, U. Wis., 1983. Real estate broker W. Lorge Sales, Bear Creek, Wis., 1988—; mem. Wis. State Assembly, Madison, 1989—; chairperson Assembly state affairs com.; vice-chair Assembly state fed. rels. com., Assembly ins. securities and corp. policy com.; vice chair assembly ins., securities and corp. policy com., mem. excise and fees com., mem. tourism, hwys., consumer affairs com., criminal justice com., corrections com. Wis. State Assembly; vice chair assembly Fed. State Rels. Com.; mem. Wis. Trust for Hist. Preservation. Sponsor Christian Children's Fund, 1979—. Named outstanding young man in Am., 1990, legislator of yr. Wis. Conservation Congress, 1992. Mem. Nat. Conf. Ins. Legislators (exec. com. mem.), U.S. Jaycees, Lions, KC. Republican. Roman Catholic. Home: Rt 1 Bear Creek WI 54922

LORIAUX, MAURICE LUCIEN, artist, ecclesiologist; b. Chanute, Kans., Aug. 27, 1909; s. Amour Joseph and Eva (Goosens) L.; m. Susan Bowman, Oct. 17, 1935; children: Donald Lynn, Michael Maurice. B.A., U. Tulsa, 1931; M.A., Northwestern U., 1933; pvt. student, Berger Sandzen, Laura Requa, George Serraz. Dir. string dept. U. Tulsa, 1933-38; exec. dir. Santa Fe (N.Mex.) Studios of Church Art, 1947-66; pres. Art Horizons, 1961—; founder, pres. Southwest Art League Seminars; dir. Georgia O'Keeffe Country Workshops. Designer over 300 church interiors, Am. and abroad; condr. annual seminars art, Santa Fe; works include mural Healing, Tex. Med. Ctr., Houston, 1967; restoration of Old Mission, Santa Barbara, Calif., 1964, The Cabrini Shrine, Denver, 1956, Las Supper mural (1st distinctive award achievement Am. Assn. Arts), the Junipero Serra monument, Sacramento. Recipient First award of merit Church Property Adminstrn., 1966; Okla. Art and Humanities award of distinction in sculpture and arts, 1978; award of distinction Sierra Clubs Am. Fellow Stained Glass Assn. Am.; mem. Am. Internat. Stained Glass Inst. (founder, pres.), Artes Italia, Community Entertainment Assn. (pres. 1940-44). Home and Office: 812 Camino Acoma Santa Fe NM 87505-4932

LORIE, JAMES HIRSCH, business administration educator; b. Kansas City, Feb. 23, 1922; s. Alvin J. and Adele (Hirsch) L.; m. Sally Rosen, June 16, 1948 (div. 1953); 1 child Susan; m. Nancy A. Wexler, June 19, 1958 (dec. 1966); stepchildren: Katherine Wexler, Jeffrey Wexler; m. Vanna Metzenberg Lautman, Aug. 27, 1967; stepchildren: Erika Lautman, Victoria Lautman, Karl Lautman. A.B., Cornell U., 1942, A.M., 1945; Ph.D., U. Chgo., 1947. Research asst. Cornell U., Ithaca, N.Y., 1944-45; mem. staff seminar Am. civilization Salzburg, Austria, 1947; mem. faculty U. Chgo. Grad. Sch. Bus., 1947-92, prof. bus. adminstrn., asso. dean, 1956-61; dir. Center Research in Security Prices, 1960-75; cons. divsn. rsch. and statistics bd. govs. Fed. Res. Sys., 1950-52; cons. U.S. Treas. Dept., 1973-74; bd. dirs. Acorn Fund, N.Y.C., Thornburg Mortgage Asset Co., Inc., Ardco Inc., Chgo.; mem. Nat. Market Adv. Bd., 1975-77. Author: (with Harry V. Roberts) Basic Methods of Marketing Research, 1951, (with Richard A. Brealey) Modern Developments in Investment Management, 1972, (with Mary T. Hamilton) The Stock Market: Theories and Evidence, 1973; Contbr. articles to profl. jours. Served with USCGR, 1942-44. Mem. Am. Econ. Assn., Mont Pelerin Soc., Nat. Assn. Securities Dealers (dir. 1972-75), Phi Beta Kappa. Clubs: Arts (Chgo.); Quadrangle (U. Chgo.). Home: 2314 N Lincoln Park W Chicago IL 60614-3454

LORIMER, LINDA KOCH, college official; m. Ernest McFaul Lorimer; children: Katharine Elizabeth, Peter Brailler. AB, Hollins Coll., 1974; JD, Yale U., 1977; DHL, Green Mountain Coll., 1981, Washington Coll., 1992, Randolph-Macon Coll., 1992. Bar: N.Y. 1978, Conn. 1982. Assoc. Davis Polk and Wardwell, N.Y.C., 1977-78; asst. gen. counsel Yale U., New Haven, 1978-79, assoc. gen. counsel, 1979-84, assoc. provost, 1983-87, acting assoc. v.p. human resources, 1984-85; prof. law, pres. Randolph-Macon Woman's Coll., Lynchburg, Va., 1987-93; v.p., sec. Yale Univ., New Haven, 1993—; lectr. Yale Coll. Undergrad. Seminars, 1980, 83; bd. dirs. Spring, McGraw Hill; past pres., mem. exec. com. Women's Coll. Coalition; mem. corp. Yale U., 1990-93, chair Virginia Rhodes scholarship com., 1991-93. Chair editorial bd. Jour. Coll. and Univ. Law, 1983-87. Former trustee Hollins Coll., Berkeley Div. Sch.; mem. com. on responsible conduct rsch. Inst. Medicine, NAS, 1988; bd. dirs. Norfolk Acad.; cabinet mem. United Way of Greater New Haven. Mem. Nat. Assn. Coll. and Univ. Attys. (exec. bd. 1981-84), Nat. Assn. Schs. and Colls. of United Meth. Ch. (1st v.p.), Assn. Am. Colls.,(bd. dirs., chmn. bd.), Am. Assn. Theol. Schs. (bd. dirs.), Mory's Assn., Phi Beta Kappa. Episcopalian. Home: 87 Trumbull St New Haven CT 06511-3723 Office: Woodbridge Hall Yale Univ New Haven CT 06520-9999

LORINCZ, ALBERT BELA, physician, educator; b. Budapest, Hungary, Sept. 6, 1922; came to U.S., 1922, naturalized, 1944; s. Frank Coleman and Theresa (Csore) L.; m. Ann Marie Callaghan, Mar. 23, 1946; children: Margaret Alice, Albert Gregory, Paul Francis, Ann Elizabeth, Thomas Andrew, Catherine Bernadette, Peter Henry. B.S. in Biochemistry, U. Chgo., 1944, M.D., 1946. Diplomate: Am. Bd. Obstetrics and Gynecology. Intern Ill. Central Hosp., Chgo., 1946-47; resident obstetrics and gynecology Chgo. Lying-In Hosp., 1949-53; asst. prof. obstetrics and gynecology U. Chgo. Med. Sch., 1958-61, prof., 1966-71; clin. prof. Stanford U. Sch. Medicine, 1971—; prof. obstetrics and gynecology, chmn. dept. Creighton U. Sch. Medicine, 1961-66; dir. dept. obstetrics and gynecology Creighton Meml.-St. Joseph's Hosp., Omaha, 1961-66; chmn. dept. obstetrics and gynecology Archbishop Bergan Mercy Hosp., Omaha, 1964-66; chief obstetrics Booth Meml. Hosp., Omaha, 1961-66; cons. VA Hosp., Omaha, also; Douglas County Hosp., Omaha, 1962-66; attending physician Chgo. Lying-In Hosp., Billings Hosp., Chgo., 1966-71; med. dir., chief obstetrics and gynecology Valley West Gen. Hosp., Los Gatos, Calif., 1971-75; chief staff Valley West Gen. Hosp., 1976, 84; mem. staff O'Connor Hosp., San Jose Hosp.; mem. staff, sec. dept. ob-gyn Santa Clara Valley Med. Ctr., bd. dirs., 1982-88; mem. staff Alexian Bros. Hosp., Good Samaritan Hosp., others. Contbr. articles to profl. jours. Mem. med. adv. bd. Nat. Found.-March of Dimes; bd. dirs. Santa Clara Valley PSRO, 1978-84. Served to 1st lt., M.C. AUS, 1944-46; to lt. col. 1948-58; col. Res., 1966-82 (ret.). Fellow ACS, Am. Coll. Obstetricians and Gynecologists; mem. AASS, Am. Assn. Gynecologic Laparoscopists, Am. Chem. Soc., N.Y. Acad. Scis., Am. Fertility Soc., Am. Inst. Chemists, Assn. Profs. Gynecology and Obstetrics, Gynecol. Soc. for Study Breast Disease, Am. Soc. Reproductive Medicine, Am. Geriatric Soc., Royal Soc. Medicine (affiliate), Omaha-Midwest Clin. Soc., Chgo., San Francisco gynecol. socs., AMA, World Med. Assn., Am. Assn. for Lab. Animal Sci., Central Assn. Ostetricians and Gynecologists, Am. Assn. for Maternal and Infant Health, Assn. Mil. Surgeons U.S., Reticuloendothelial Soc., Shufelt Soc. Santa Clara County, Pan Pacific Surg. Assn., Peninsula Gynecologic Soc., AAUP, Internat. Fertility Assn., Pan Am. Med. Assn., Am. Soc. Abdominal Surgeons, Pro-Life Med. Assn. Calif. (pres.), Am. Assn. Pro-Life Obstetricians and Gynecologists, Assn. for Advancement Med. Instrumentation, Santa Clara Valley PSRO (pres., dir.), Calif. Assn. Obstetricians and Gynecologists, Sigma Xi. Democrat. Roman Catholic. Club: Central Travel. Home: 18816 Devon Ave Saratoga CA 95070-4606 Office: 15899 Los Gatos Almaden Rd Los Gatos CA 95032-3739

LORING, ARTHUR, lawyer, financial services company executive; b. N.Y.C., Oct. 13, 1947; s. Murray and Mildred (Rogers) L.; m. Vicki Hootstein, June 4, 1978. BS in Commerce, Washington and Lee U., 1969; JD cum laude, Boston U., 1972. Bar: Mass. 1972. Atty. Fidelity Mgmt. & Research Co., Boston, 1972; sr. legal counsel Fidelity Mgmt. & Research Co., 1980-82, v.p., gen. counsel, 1984-93; sr. v.p., gen. counsel, 1993—; v.p.-legal FMR Corp., Boston, 1982—; sec. Fidelity Group of Funds, Boston, 1982—; dir. Fidelity Capital Publs. Inc., 1991—; v.p. Fidelity Distbr. Corp., Boston, 1984—; sr. v.p., gen. counsel Fidelity Investments Instnl. Svcs., Inc., 1994—; bd. govs. Investment Co. Inst., 1988-90; chmn. ICI SEC Rules Com., 1990-95; adv. bd. Fund Directions, 1993—. Case editor Boston U. Law Rev., 1971-72. Mem. adv. bd. sch. of commerce Washington and Lee Univ., 1996—. Mem. ABA (securities regulation com.), Boston Bar Assn., Cavendish Club (dir. 1981-84), Boston Chess Club (pres. Brookline, Mass. 1981-83), Pinebrook Country Club, Polo Club of Boca Raton. Republican. Jewish. Avocations: golf, bridge, exercise. Home: 300 Boylston St #803 Boston MA 02116 Office: Fidelity Mgmt & Rsch Co 82 Devonshire St Boston MA 02109-3605

LORING, CALEB, JR., investment company executive; b. Boston, Feb. 5, 1921; s. Caleb and Suzanne (Bailey) L.; m. Rosemary Merrill, Feb. 12, 1943; children—Caleb, David, Rosemary, Keith. A.B., Harvard U., 1943, LL.B., 1948. Bar: Mass. 1948, U.S. Dist. Ct. Mass. 1948. Asso., then partner firm Gaston, Snow, Motley & Holt, Boston, 1948-70; dir., trustee Loring, Wolcott and Coolidge Office-Fiduciary Services, Boston, 1948-86; gen. counsel Fidelity Mgmt. and Rsch. Co., 1964-74; v.p., dir. Puritan Fund, Inc., and all other funds in Fidelity Group of Funds, Boston, 1973-86; treas. Fidelity Mgmt. & Research Co., Boston, 1977-86, ret., 1986; dir. Fidelity Mgmt. & Research Co., 1959-86; mng. dir. FMR Corp. (parent co. Fidelity Mgmt. & Rsch. Co.), Boston, 1986—; dir. Fidelity Investments, Boston, 1974—. Served with USNR, 1943-46. Mem. Am. Bar Assn., Mass. Bar Assn., Boston Bar Assn. Office: Fidelity Investments 82 Devonshire St Ste 8sa Boston MA 02109-3605

LORING, GLORIA JEAN, singer, actress; b. N.Y.C., Dec. 10, 1946; d. Gerald Louis and Dorothy Ann (Tobin) Goff; m. Alan Willis Thicke, Aug. 22, 1970 (div. 1986); children: Brennan Todd, Robin Alan; m. Christopher Beaumont, June 18, 1988 (div. 1993); m. René Lagler, Dec. 20, 1994. Grad. high sch. Owner Glitz Records, L.A., 1984—; pres. Only Silk Prodns., L.A., 1985-90; owner Silk Purse Prodns., 1992—. Began profl. singing, Miami Beach, 1965; appeared in numerous TV shows; featured singer: Bob Hope's Ann. Armed Forces Christmas Tour, 1970; featured several record albums; featured actress: Days of Our Lives, 1980-86; composer: TV themes Facts of Life, 1979, Diff'rent Strokes, 1978; author: Days of Our Lives Celebrity Cookbook, 1981, Vol. II, 1983, Living the Days of Our Lives, 1984, Kids, Food and Diabetes, 1986, Parenting a Diabetic Child, 1991, The Kids Food and Diabetes Family Cookbook, 1991. Celebrity chmn. Juvenile Diabetes Found. Recipient Humanitarian of Yr. award Juvenile Diabetes Found., 1982, 88, Parents of Yr. award, 1984, Woman of Yr. award Jeweler's Assn. Am., 1986. Mem. Nat. Acad. Songwriters (gold mem.). *I feel the most important element in any life is to continue reaching out, growing, and learning. Don't be afraid to ask. Don't be afraid to challenge. Don't be afraid.*

LORING, HONEY, small business owner; b. Phila.. BA in Psychology, U. Md., 1970; MEd, Wash. U., St. Louis, 1971. Lic. psychologist-master Vt.; directress cert. Assn. Montessori Internat. Counselor Gardenville Diagnostic Ctr., St. Louis, 1971-72; tchr. Early Learning Pre-Sch., St. Louis, 1972-74; music dir., cabin counselor Follow Through Day Camp, Brattleboro, Vt., 1972-74; tchr. Montessori Sch., Dublin, 1974-75; ednl. cons. children's books Left Bank Books, St. Louis, 1975-76; program dir. day camp Brattleboro Child Devel., 1975-79; behavioral therapist Behavioral Medicine Unit, Dartmouth Med. Sch., 1979-84; pvt. therapist Brattleboro, Vt., 1984-85; founder, pres. Gone to the Dogs, Putney, Vt.; dog groomer, 1979-92; founder, dir. Camp Come to the Dogs, 1990—; mfr. dog collars, 1984-96; founder Tails Up Inn, 1995—. Author: (with Jeremy Birch) You're On. . .Teaching Communication Skills, 1984, The Big Good Wolf; contbr. articles to profl. jours. Leader 4-H Dog Club; helper Riding for the Physically Handicapped, St. Louis, 1974. Home and Office: RR 1 Box 958 Putney VT 05346-9748

LORING, JOHN ROBBINS, artist; b. Chgo., Nov. 23, 1939; s. Edward D'Arcy and China Robbins (Logeman) L. B.A., Yale U., 1960; postgrad., Ecole Beaux Arts, Paris, 1960-63; Dr. Arts (hon.), Pratt Inst., 1996. Disting. vis. prof. U. Calif., Davis, 1977; bur. chief Archtl. Digest mag., N.Y.C., 1977-78; assoc. dir. Tiffany and Co., N.Y.C., 1979—, exec. v.p., design dir., 1981-84, sr. v.p. design and merchandising, 1984—; mem. acquisitions com. dept. prints and illustrated books Mus. Modern Art, N.Y.C., 1990—. Contbg. editor: Arts mag., 1973—; books include: The New Tiffany Tablesettings, 1981, Tiffany Taste, 1986, Tiffany's 150 Years, 1987, The Tiffany Wedding, 1988, Tiffany Parties, 1989, The Tiffany Gourmet, 1992, A Tiffany Christmas, 1996; one-man exhbns. include Balt. Mus. Art, 1972, Hundred Acres Gallery, N.Y., 1972, Pace Edits., 1973, 77, Long Beach Mus. Art, 1975, A.D.I. Gallery, San Francisco, 1976; group exhbns. include Phila. Mus. Art, 1971, N.Y. Cultural Ctr., 1972, Biennale graphic Art, Ljubljana, Yugoslavia, 1973, 77, Intergrafia 74, Krakow, Poland, 1974, Bklyn. Mus. Nat. Print Exhbn., 1974, Art Inst. Chgo., 1975, R.I. Sch. Design, 1976; represented in permanent collections Mus. Modern Art, N.Y.C., Whitney Mus. Am. Art, Chgo. Art Inst., Boston Mus. Fine Arts, R.I. Sch. Design, Balt. Mus. Art, Yale U. Art Gallery; commd. by U.S. Customhouse, N.Y.C., Prudential Ins. Co. Am. Eastern Home Office, Woodbridge, N.J., City of Scranton, Pa., Western Savs., Phila. Recipient Edith Wharton award Design & Art Soc., 1988. Office: Tiffany & Co 727 5th Ave New York NY 10022-2503 also: Doubleday 1540 Broadway New York NY 10036 *I look on whatever talents I may have as natural resources to be given freely wherever needed. A lot has been given out; a lot has come in.*

LORIO, PHILIP DONATIEN, III, lawyer; b. New Orleans, Jan. 6, 1948; s. Philip Donatien Jr. and Helen Irma (Mayeux) L.; m. Kathryn Georgia Venturatos, Nov. 16, 1974; children: Elisabeth Bon, Philip D. IV. BBA, Loyola U., New Orleans, 1969; JD, Loyola U., 1974. Bar: La. 1974, U.S. Dist. Ct. (ea. dist.) 1974, U.S. Ct. Appeals (5th cir.) 1975. Asst. city atty. City of New Orleans, 1974-78; ptnr. Deutsch, Kerrigan & Stiles, New Orleans, 1978—; hon. consul Republic of Austria for La. and Miss., 1991—; lectr. Continuing Legal Edn. Program, Loyola Law Sch. Bd. dirs. Coun. Internat. Visitors of Greater New Orleans, 1993—; bd. mem. Tulane European Legal Practices Program, 1991—. Mem. ABA, Fed. Bar Assn., La. Bar Assn., New Orleans Bar Assn., La. Assn. Def. Counsel, Thomas More Inn of Ct., France-Amerique, Soc. of Founders of New Orleans, Bienville Club, Fgn. Rels. Assn. New Orleans, World Trade Ctr. New Orleans, Phi Delta Phi. Office: Deutsch Kerrigan & Stiles 755 Magazine St New Orleans LA 70130-3629

LORSUNG, THOMAS NICHOLAS, editor-in-chief, director; b. Milw., June 9, 1938; s. Nicholas A. and Margaret (Senger) L.; m. Mary Jelen, Aug. 27, 1960; children: Kristin Lorsung Shulder, Anne K., Erin Lorsung Krauss. BJ, Marquette U., 1960. Reporter Journal-Times, Racine, Wis., 1961-63; reporter, photographer, news editor Cath. Rev., Balt., 1963-69; photo, copy editor The Sentinel, Milw., 1969-72; photo editor Nat. Cath. News Svc., Washington, 1972-75, news editor, 1975-76, mng. editor, 1976-89; dir., editor-in-chief Cath. News Svc. (formerly Nat. Cath. News Svc.), Washington, 1989-95; chmn. bd. dirs. Carroll Pub., Washington, 1993-95; cons. Pontifical Coun. for Social Comms., 1995—. Mem. Cath. Press Assn. (bd. dirs. 1991—, St. Francis de Sales award 1995), Internat. Cath. Union of the Press, Fed. Cath. News Agencies (v.p. 1992). Avocations: photography, running, biking, choral singing. Home: 5367 Iron Pen Pl Columbia MD 21044 Office: Catholic News Svc 3211 4th St NE Washington DC 20017-1106

LORTEL, LUCILLE, theatrical producer; b. N.Y.C., Dec. 16, 1905; d. Harry and Anna (Moes) Wadler; m. Louis Schweitzer, Mar. 23, 1931 (dec.). Student, Adelphi Coll., 1920, Am. Acad. Dramatic Arts, 1920-21, abroad; DFA (hon.), U. Bridgeport, 1985. Established White Barn Theatre, Westport, Conn., 1947—; owner, producer Lucille Lortel Theatre (originally Lucille Lortel's Theatre de Lys), N.Y.C., 1955—; artistic dir. ANTA Matinee Series, N.Y.C., 1956—; founder Am. Shakespeare Festival Theatre, Stratford, Conn., 1955. Appeared in various stage plays including: Caesar and Cleopatra, 1925; The Dove, 1925; One Man's Woman, 1926; radio appearances, 1935; producer various stage plays, including Three Penny Opera, 1955, I Knock at the Door, 1957, Cock a Doodle Dandy, 1958, The Balcony, 1960, The Blood Knot, 1964, A Streetcar Named Desire, 1973; co-producer plays including Angels Fall, 1983 (Tony nomination), As Is, 1984 (Tony nomination), Blood Knot, 1985 (Tony nomination), numerous others. V.p. exec. com. bd. dirs. Friends of Theatre Collection of Mus. City of N.Y.; mem. adv. bd. Nat. Theatre of Deaf, Chester, Conn.; trustee Goodspeed Opera House, East Haddam, Conn. Recipient 2 awards Greater N.Y. chpt. ANTA, 1958, Off-Broadway award, 1956, 58, 60, 84, Margo Jones award, 1962, award Nat. ANTA, 1962, Villager award, 1979, Cert. Merit City of N.Y., 1980, Arnold Weissberger award Theatre Hall Fame, 1982, Spl. citation N.Y. Drama Critics, 1983, Lee Strasberg Lifetime Achievement in Theatre award, 1985, Spl. Theatre World award, 1985, Exceptional Achievement award Women's Project Am. Pl. Theatre, 1986, George M. Cohan award Cath. Actors Guild Am., 1986, 1st citation Mus. Am. Theatre, New Haven, 1986, numerous others. Office: Lucille Lortel Theatre 121 Christopher St New York NY 10014-4204

LORTON, LEWIS, dentist, researcher, computer scientist; b. N.Y.C., Nov. 3, 1939; s. Frederick S. and Rosell (Engel) L.; divorced; children: Elizabeth, Mark, Michael S.; m. Jacqueline Carol Andor, Aug. 3, 1982; children: Michael E., Erin. BA, Brandeis U., 1960; DDS, U. Pa., 1964; MSD, Ind. U., 1978. Pvt. practice West Medway, Mass., 1964-66; commd. lt. U.S. Army, 1966, advanced through grades to col., 1983, researcher, tchr., 1976—; cons. Armed Forces Inst. Pathology, Washington, 1986—; chief info. mgr. Henry M. Jackson Found., 1989-91; v.p. Klemm Analysis Group, Inc., 1991-92; pres. Lorton Assoc., 1992-94; exec. dir. Health Care Open Systems & Trials, Inc., 1994—. Contbr. numerous articles to profl. jours. Recipient Carl Schlack award Assn. Mil. Surgeons U.S., 1988. Fellow Am. Forensic Soc.; mem. Internat. Assn. Dental Rsch., Am. Assn. Dental Rsch., Am. Soc. Forensic Odontology, Soc. for Clin. Trials. Avocations: statistics, computers, fly fishing, squash. Home: 10096 Hatbrim Ter Columbia MD 21046-1318 Office: 414 Hall of the States 444 N Capitol St NW Washington DC 20001-1512

LORY, MARC H., hospital administrator; b. Bklyn., June 23, 1948; s. Jerome and Mildred (Platzick) L.; m. Audrey Manheimer, Nov. 2, 1985; 1 child from previous marriage, Rebecca. BEd, U. Miami, 1971; MPA, NYU, 1976. Nuclear medicine technologist Albert Einstein Coll. Medicine, Bronx, N.Y., 1971-74; adminstrv. resident Montefiore Hosp. & Med. Ctr., Bronx, 1974-75, adminstr., dept. neurology, 1975-77, asst. dir., 1977-81; v.p. St. Luke's-Roosevelt Hosp. Ctr., N.Y.C., 1981-86; chief oper. officer Roosevelt Hosp., N.Y.C., 1981-86; v.p., chief exec. officer U. Medicine & Dentistry of N.J.-Univ. Hosp., Newark, 1986—; trustee Ctr. for Preventive Psychiatry, N.Y., Univ. Health Systems, N.J., Essex chpt. ARC, N.J. Contbr. articles to profl. jours. Mem. Am. Hosp. Assn., Transplant Found. N.J., N.J. Hosp. Assn. Jewish. Office: UMDNJ Hosp 150 Bergen St Newark NJ 07103-2406*

LOS, MARINUS, agrochemical researcher; b. Ridderkerk, The Netherlands, Sept. 18, 1933; came to U.S., 1960; s. Cornelis and Neeltje (Zoutewelle) L.; m. Lorraine Betty Lowe, May 11, 1957; children: Simon, Sija, Michael, Martin (dec.). BS, Edinburgh U., Scotland, 1955, PhD, 1957. Sr. rsch. chemist Am. Cyanamid Co., Princeton, N.J., 1960-71, group leader, 1971-84, sr. group leader, 1984-86, mgr. crop protection chems., 1986-88, assoc. dir. crop scis., 1988-92, rsch. dir. crop scis., 1992—. Recipient Disting. Inventor of 1990 award Intellectual Property Owners, Inc., Washington, 1990, Thomas Alva Edison Patent award R&D Coun. of N.J., 1991, Nat. Medal of Tech. NSF, 1993, Achievement award Indsl. Rsch. Inst. Inc., 1994. Mem. AAAS, Am. Chem. Soc. (Perkin medal, 1994, Creative Invention award, 1995), Plant Growth Regulator Soc. Achievements include 53 patents. Office: Am Cyanamid Co PO Box 400 Princeton NJ 08543-0400

LOSCALZO, JOSEPH, cardiologist, biochemist; b. Camden, N.J., Oct. 26, 1951; s. Joseph and Dolores Rita (Ventura) L.; m. Anita Beth Sendrow, Mar. 10, 1974; children: Julia, Alexander. AB summa cum laude, U. Pa., 1972, MD and PhD, 1978. Diplomate Am. Bd Internal Medicine; cert. in cardiovascular disease. Postdoctoral fellow U. Pa., Phila., 1978; resident in internal medicine Brigham and Women's Hosp., Boston, 1978-81, clin. fellow cardiology, 1981-83, chief med. resident, 1983-84, instr. medicine, 1983-85; clin. fellow medicine Harvard Med. Sch., Boston, 1978-81, asst. prof. medicine, 1985-88, assoc. prof., 1989-93; chief cardiol. sect. Brockton West Roxbury VA Med. Ctr., Boston, 1989-93; disting. prof. medicine, prof. biochemistry Boston U., 1994—, dir. Whitaker Cardiovasc. Inst., Sch. Medicine, 1994—, vice chmn. dept. medicine, chief cardiovasc. medicine, 1994—; mem. rsch. rev. com. Am. Heart Assn., 1988—; rsch. rev. coms. Nat. Heart, Lung and Blood Inst., Bethesda, Md., 1990—. Author: (with others) books on vascular biology and medicine, thrombosis and hemostasis; assoc. editor New England Journal of Medicine; contbr. mem. editorial bd.: Circulation, Circulation Research, Journal Thrombusis and Thrombolysis, Jouranl Vascular Medicine Biology, American Journal of Cardiology, articles to profl. jours. Recipient Med. Scientist Tng. award NIH, 1972-77, Rsch. Career Devel. award, 1989-94, Clin. Scientist award Am. Heart Assn., 1983-88. Fellow ACP, Am. Coll. Cardiology (mem. editl. bd. jour.); mem. Am. Fedn. Clin. Rsch., Am. Soc. Clin. Investigation, Assn. Univ. Cardiologists, Am. Soc. Biol. Chemistry, Phi Beta Kappa. Achievements include eight patents related to nitric oxide congeners. Office: Boston U Sch Medicine Whitaker Cardiovasc Inst 700 Albany St Boston MA 02118-2518

LOSCAVIO, ELIZABETH, dancer; b. Jacksonville, Fla.. Student, Contra Costa Ballet Sch., Pacific N.W. Ballet Sch., San Francisco Ballet Sch. Co. apprentice San Francisco Ballet, 1986, mem. corps de ballet, 1986-88, soloist, 1988-90, prin. dancer, 1990—. Performances include Romeo and Juliet, The Sleeping Beauty, Swan Lake, Nanna's Lied, Haffner Symphony, Con Brio, Handel-a Celebration, Menuetto, Contradanses, Ballet D'Isoline, Intimate Voices, La Fille mal gardée, Ballo della Regina, Tchaikovsky Pas de Deux, Theme and Variations, Who Cares?, Symphony in C, Tarantella, Rubies, Stars and Stripes, The Four Temperaments, A Midsummer Night's Dream, Rodeo, Maelstrom, La Pavane Rouge, Dark Elegies, Grand Pas de Deux, Flower Festival at Genzano, Rodin, Connotations, Le Corsaire Pas de Deux, Sunset, In the Night, Interplay, The End, The Comfort Zone, Dreams of Harmony, The Wanderer Fantasy, The Sons of Horus, Nutcracker, Divertissemet d'Auber, Vivaldi Concerto Grosso, New Sleep, La Sylphide. Recipient Isadora Duncan award, 1991. Office: San Francisco Ballet 455 Franklin St San Francisco CA 94102-4438

LO SCHIAVO, JOHN JOSEPH, university executive; b. San Francisco, Feb. 25, 1925; s. Joseph and Anne (Re) Lo S. A.B., Gonzaga U., 1948, Ph.L. and M.A., 1949; S.T.L., Alma Coll., 1962. Joined S.J., Roman Catholic Ch., 1942; tchr. St. Ignatius High Sch., San Francisco, 1949-50; instr. philosophy and theology U. San Francisco, 1950-52, 56-57, 61-62, v.p. for student affairs, dean of students, 1962-68, pres., 1977-91, chancellor, 1991—; pres. Bellarmine Coll. Prep. Sch., San Jose, 1968-75. Bd. dirs. St. Mary's Hosp. and Med. Ctr., Sch. of Sacred Heart. Mem. Olympic Club, Bohemian Club, Univ. Club. Office: U San Francisco 2130 Fulton St San Francisco CA 94117

LOSCHIAVO, LINDA BOSCO, library director; b. Rockville Ctr., N.Y., Aug. 31, 1950; d. Joseph and Jennie (DelRegno) Bosco; m. Joseph A. LoSchiavo, Sept. 7, 1974. BA, Fordham U., 1972, MA, 1990; MLS, Pratt Inst., 1974. Picture cataloguer Frick Art Reference Libr., N.Y.C., 1972-75; sr. cataloguer Fordham U. Libr., Bronx, N.Y., 1975-87, head of retrospective conversion, 1987-90, systems libr., 1990-91, dir. libr. at Lincoln Ctr., 1991—; libr. cons. Mus. Am. Folk Art Libr., N.Y.C., 1985-90; indexer Arco Books, N.Y.C., 1974. Editor: Macbeth, 1990, Julius Ceasar, 1990, Romeo and Juliet, 1990. Mng. producer Vineyard Opera, N.Y.C., 1981-88. Mem. ALA, N.Y. Tech. Svcs. Librs., Beta Phi Mu, Alpha Sigma Nu. Home: 317 Collins Ave Mount Vernon NY 10552-1601 Office: Fordham Univ Library 113 W 60th St New York NY 10023-7471

LOSEE, THOMAS PENNY, JR., publisher; b. Mineola, N.Y., Dec. 9, 1940; s. Thomas Penny and Jeanne Hubbell (Grandeman) L.; m. Muriel Frances Hahn, Apt. 25, 1964; children: Thomas Penny III, Kendall Louise; m. Clark Edward Graebner Jr., Aug. 28, 1993. A.B., Duke U., 1963. Advt. salesman Look mag., 1964-71; advt. dir. House Beautiful, 1971-72; pub. Harper's Bazaar, N.Y.C., 1972-76, House Beautiful, 1976—; v.p., asst. to gen. mgr. Hearst Mag. div., 1981—; v.p., pub. Sci. Digest mag., 1983—, Archtl. Digest mag., 1989-91; sr. v.p., pub. dir. Knapp Communications, 1991—; pub. Archtl. Digest mag. CondÉ Nast Publs., 1993—. Mem. editorial bd. Duke Mag. Trustee Taft Sch., Heckscher Mus. With USAR, 1963-69. Mem. Univ. Club, Creek Club, Cold Spring Harbor Beach Club, Coral Beach Club (Bermuda), Gulf Stream Bath and Tennis Club, Lawrence Beach Club, Beta Theta Pi. Republican. Episcopalian. Home: PO Box 471 Cold Spring Harbor NY 11724-0471 Office: 350 Madison Ave New York NY 10017-3704

LOSER, JOSEPH CARLTON, JR., dean, retired judge; b. Nashville, June 16, 1932; s. Joseph Carlton and Pearl Dean (Gupton) L.; m. Mildred Louise Nichols, May 25, 1972; 1 child, Joseph Carlton III. Student, U. Tenn., 1950-51, Vanderbilt U., 1952-55; LLB, Nashville YMCA Night Law Sch., 1959. Bar: Tenn. 1959. Pvt. practice, 1959-66; judge Gen. Sessions Ct., Davidson County, Tenn., 1966-69, Cir. Ct. 20th Jud. Dist. Tenn., 1969-86; dean Nashville Sch. Law, 1986—. Mem. ABA, Internat. Acad. Trial Judges, Tenn. Bar Assn., Nashville Bar Assn., Am. Legion, Masons, Shriners, Sigma Delta Kappa, Kappa Sigma, Rotary.

LOSEY, MICHAEL ROBERT, professional society administrator; b. Cin., Nov. 10, 1938; s. Clyde William And Hilda C. (Ploom) L.; m. Ann J. Liparoto, Aug. 27, 1960; children: Debra Lynn, Scott Douglas, Robert Michael. BBA, U. Mich., 1961, MBA, 1962. Labor relations assoc. Ford Motor Co., Ypsilanti, Mich., 1962-64; personnel mgr. Sperry New Holland, Lancaster, Pa., 1964-66, Grand Island, Nebr., 1966-69; dir. plant & field personnel Sperry New Holland, New Holland, Pa., 1969-72; dir. personnel relations Sperry New Holland, 1972-74, v.p. human resources, 1974-83; staff v.p. compensation & benefits Sperry Corp., N.Y.C., 1983-84, Sperry Corp. (now Unisys Corp.), 1984-86; v.p. human resources Unisys Corp., Blue Bell, Pa., 1986-90; pres., CEO Soc. for Human Resource Mgmt., Alexandria, Va., 1990—; speaker in field. Contbr. articles to profl. jours. Pres. United Way, Grand Island, Nebr., 1968; campaign chmn., mem. various coms. United Way, N.Y., Pa. and Nebr. Recipient Equal Employment Opportunity award City of Lancaster, Pa., 1983. Avocations: boating, golf, fishing. Office: Soc Human Resource Mgmt 606 N Washington St Alexandria VA 22314-1943

LOSH, SAMUEL JOHNSTON, engineering administrator; b. Hershey, Pa., Nov. 11, 1932; s. Charles Seibert and Esther Dora (Johnston) L.; m. Llewellyn Mathews Hall, Sept. 26, 1964 (div. Oct., 1994); children: Elizabeth Mathews, Stephen Johnston. BSME, MIT, 1954; postgrad., Syracuse U., Utica, 1956-57, UCLA, 1968-74, U. So. Calif., 1975-81. Cert. profl. mgr. Inst. Cert. Profl. Mgrs. Engr. RCA, Camden, N.J., 1954-55; instr. Syracuse U., Utica, 1956; mem. tech. staff TRW, L.A., 1957-59; systems engr.

Hoffman Electronics, L.A, 1959-62; spacecraft systems engr. Lockheed Calif. Co., Burbank, 1962-64; sr. systems specialist Xerox Spl. Info. Systems, Pasadena, Calif., 1964-87; sr. systems engr. Datametrics Corp., Chatsworth, Calif., 1987-89; pres. Milner Street, Inc., Pasadena, 1980—; sec. Regina Properties, Inc., Pasadena, 1981-92. Chmn. L.A. chpt. MIT Ednl. Coun., 1978—; facilitator Math. Standards Program, L.A. Unified Sch. Dist., 1994. Recipient George Morgan award MIT Ednl.Coun., 1987; named Silver Knight of Mgmt., Nat. Mgmt. Assn., 1980. Mem. IEEE, AIAA, MIT Alumni Assn. (bd. dirs. 1981-83). Republican. Unitarian. Avocations: skiing, travel, apt. mgmt. Home and Office: PO Box 50368 Pasadena CA 91115-0368

LOSHUERTOS, ROBERT HERMAN, clergyman; b. San Francisco, Apr. 28, 1937; s. Joseph Guillermo and Ruth Margarethe (Erdmann) L.; m. Carolyn Angela Reinartz, Aug. 6, 1960; children: William Frederick, John Martin. AA, San Francisco City Coll., 1957; BA, Wittenburg U., 1959; MDiv, Luth. Theol. So. Sem., Columbia, S.C., 1963. Ordained to ministry Evang. Luth. Ch. in Am., 1963. Asst. pastor Meml. Evang. Luth. Ch., 1963-64, Trinity Luth. Ch., Riverside, Calif., 1964-66; pastor Our Saviours Luth. Ch., Oxnard, Calif., 1966-71; assoc. pastor Luth. Ch. of Good Shepherd, Buena Park, Calif., 1971-73; pastor St. Mark's Luth. Ch., Huntsville, Ala., 1973-80; exec. min. Interfaith Mission Svc., Huntsville, 1980—; chmn. pers./mut. ministry com. Southeastern Synod Evang. Luth. Ch. in Am., Atlanta, 1988-93. Active Humanitarian Svcs. Com., Huntsville, 1985—, Leadership 2000, Huntsville, 1988-89; chmn. adminstrn. com., bd. dirs. Williams-Henson Luth. Home, Knoxville, Tenn., 1986-92; pres. Target Success task force Dept. Human Resources, City of Huntsville, 1988-91, chmn. Mayor's Homeless Adv. Com., 1989-91; mem. Synod Coun.-S.E. Synod ELCA, 1991—. Recipient Brotherhood award NCCJ, 1989, Martin Luther King Jr. Unity award Alpha Phi Alpha, 1990. Mem. Nat. Assn. Ecumenical Staff. Office: Interfaith Mission Svc 411B Holmes Ave NE Huntsville AL 35801-4142

LOSS, JOHN C., architect, retired educator; b. Muskegon, Mich., Mar. 6, 1931; s. Alton A. and Dorothy Ann (DeMars) Forward; m. LaMyrna Lois Draggoo, June 7, 1958. B.Arch., U. Mich., 1954, M.Arch., 1960. Registered architect, Md., Mich. Architect Eero Saarinen & Assocs., Bloomfield Hills, Mich., 1956-57; owner John Loss & Assocs, Detroit, 1960-75; prof., acting dean Sch. Architecture, U. Detroit, 1960-75; prof., head dept. architecture N.C. State U., Raleigh, 1975-79; assoc. dean. Sch. Architecture U. Md., College Park, 1981-83, prof. architecture, 1979-93, prof. emeritus architecture, 1993—; dir. Architecture and Engring. Performance Info. Ctr., 1982-93; pvt. practice, Annapolis, College Park, 1979-93, Whitehall, Mich., 1993—; mem. com. NRC-NAS, 1982-93; mem. bldg. diagnostics com. Adv. Bd. on Build Environ., 1983-93; mem. com. on earthquake engring. NRC, 1983-93; leader survey team for tornado damage in Pa. and Ohio, 1985. Author: Building Design for Natural Hazards in Eastern United States, 1981, Identification of Performance Failures in Large Structures and Buildings, 1987, Analysis of Performance Failures in Civil Structures and Large Buildings, 1990, Performance Failures in Buildings and Civil Works, 1991; works include med. clinic, N.C.; Aldersgate Multi Family Housing, Oscoda, Mich. Advisor Interfaith Housing Inc., Detroit, 1966-74; advisor Detroit Mayor's Office, 1967-69, Interim Housing Com. Mich. State Housing Devel. Authority, Lansing, 1969-71, Takoma Park Citizens for Schs. (Md.), 1981-82; advisor, cons. Hist. Preservation Commn., Prince George's County, Md.; mem. planning commn. Blue Lake Twp., Mich., 1994—. With U.S. Army, 1954-56. NSF grantee, 1978-81, 1982-84, 86-87, 88-90; named one of Men of Yr., Engring. News Record, 1984. Fellow AIA. Democrat. Roman Catholic. *To participate, as an architect, in the continuing saga of the creation of the built environment and, as a teacher, in the continuing rebirth of our intellectual and spiritual lives remains a very special honor. I feel a sincere debt of gratitude to my mother who read to me when I was a very small child and who launched me on a life of reading and service. Happiness is a spiritual thing - not a physical thing! Success (our happiness) begins with what we aspire to be - not what we have or want.*

LOSS, LOUIS, lawyer, retired educator; b. Lancaster, Pa., June 11, 1914; s. Zelig and Elizabeth (Wenger) L.; m. Bernice Segaloff, June 19, 1938; children: Margaret Ruth, Robert Stanley. B.S., U. Pa., 1934; LL.B., Yale U., 1937; A.M. (hon.), Harvard U., 1953. Bar: D.C. 1937, Mass. 1952, U.S. Supreme Ct. 1953. Atty. SEC, 1937-44, chief counsel div. trading and exchanges, 1944-48, assoc. gen. counsel, 1948-52; lectr. law Cath. U. Am., 1941-42; vis. lectr. law Yale U., 1947-52; professorial lectr. law George Washington U., 1949-52; prof. law Harvard U., 1952-62, William Nelson Cromwell prof. law, 1962-84, prof. emeritus, 1984—, dir. program instrn. for lawyers, 1976-84; prof. Faculté Internationale de Droit Comparé, Luxembourg, summer 1958, U. Witwatersrand, summer 1962, Salzburg (Austria) Seminar in Am. Studies, summers 1968, 77, Australian Nat. U., summer 1973; Ford prof. Inst. Advanced Legal Studies, U. London, 1969; Turner Meml. lectr. U. Tasmania, Australia, 1973; Kimber fellow U. Toronto, 1978; Taylor lectr. U. Lagos, Nigeria, 1981; vis. prof. U. Pa., 1989; scholar-in-residence, U. Ga., 1985, draftsman Uniform Securities Act, 1954-56; cons. Internat. Bank, 1963-65, various fgn. govts. Author: Securities Regulation, 1951, supplememt, 1955, 2d edit., 1961, supplement 1969 (6 vols.), 3d edit. (with Joel Seligman) 11 vols., 1988-93, Commentary on the Uniform Securities Act, 1976, Fundamentals of Securities Regulation, 1983, 2d edit., 1988, supplements, 1989-92, Japanese translation, 1989; co-author: Blue Sky Law, 1958; editor: Multinational Approaches-Corporate Insiders, 1976; sr. co-editor: Japanese Securities Regulation, 1983; reporter: Am. Law Inst.'s Fed. Securities Code, 1969-78. Vice chmn. bd., gen. counsel Harvard Coop. Soc., 1961-89, N.Y. Stock Exch. Legal Adv. Com., chmn., 1987-89. Fellow AAAS, Am. Bar Found. (ann. research award 1979); mem. ABA (coun. bus. law 1966-69, 1974-75), Am. Law Inst., Assn. Bar City N.Y. (assoc.), Soc. Pub. Tchrs. Law (assoc.)(Britain), Cosmos Club (Washington), Phi Beta Kappa (hon. Alpha chpt.-Harvard). Home: 39 Meadow Way Cambridge MA 02138-4635

LOSS, MARGARET RUTH, lawyer; b. Phila., June 17, 1946; d. Louis and Bernice Rose (Segaloff) L.; m. Harry Clark Johnson, 1986; 1 child, Elizabeth Loss Johnson. B.A., Radcliffe Coll., 1967; LL.B., Yale U., 1970. Bar: Conn. 1970, N.Y. 1973. Assoc. Sullivan & Cromwell, N.Y.C., 1971-77; with Equitable Life Assurance Soc. U.S., N.Y.C., 1977-88, asst. gen. counsel, 1979-85, v.p. and counsel, 1985-88; counsel LeBoeuf, Lamb, Greene & MacRae, N.Y.C., 1988—; dir. Yale Law Sch. Fund. Mem. ABA, Am. Law Inst., Conn. Bar Assn., Assn. of Bar of City N.Y. Office: LeBoeuf Lamb Greene & MacRae 125 W 55th St New York NY 10019-5369

LOSS, STUART HAROLD, financial executive; b. Lancaster, Pa., June 15, 1946; s. Nathan and Natalie M. (Koenigsberg) L.; m. Rachelle Smithline; children: Jessica Lauren, David Jonathan, Andrew Jordan. BS in Acctg., Syracuse U.; MBA in Fin., NYU. CPA, N.Y. With KPMG Peat Marwick, N.Y.C., 1971-77; exec. v.p., CFO TBWA Chiat/Day Inc.-East, N.Y.C., 1977—; sec. TBWA Chiat/Day Inc. Mem. AICPA, N.Y. State Soc. CPAs, N.Y. Credit and Fin. Mgmt. Assn., Treas. Club. Office: TBWA Advt Inc 292 Madison Ave New York NY 10017-6307

LOSSE, CATHERINE ANN, pediatric nurse, critical care nurse, educator, clinical nurse specialist; b. Mount Holly, N.J., Mar. 12, 1959; d. David C. and Bernice (Lewis) L. Diploma, Helene Fuld Sch. Nursing, 1980; BSN magna cum laude, Thomas Jefferson U., 1986; MSN, U. Pa., 1989; postgrad., Widener U., 1995—. RN; cert. pediat. and adult nurse. Staff nurse adult med.-surg. Meml. Hosp. Burlington County, Mount Holly, N.J., 1980-81; staff nurse pediatric home care Newborn Nurses, Moorestown, N.J., 1986-87; clin. nurse II surg. intensive care Deborah Heart & Lung Ctr., Browns Mills, N.J., 1986-87, clin. nurse III pediatric cardiology, 1981-86, 87—; clin. nurse specialist critical care The Children's Hosp., Phila., 1992-94; instr. nursing of families, maternal-child health, pediat., geriatrics Burlington County Coll., 1994-96; staff nurse pediatric home care Bayada Nurses, Burlington, N.J., 1995—; clin. instr. pediatrics Thomas Jefferson U., 1990; clin. instr. adult med. surg. Burlington County Coll., 1991. Mem. ANA, AACN (CCRN, pediat. spl. interest cons. 1995-96), NAPNAP, Soc. Pediat. Nurses, N.J. State Nurses Assn. (mem. cabinet on continuing edn. rev. team III 1992-96, mem. forum for nursing in advanced practice 1994—), Am. Heart Assn. (cert. instr. PALS and BLS, bd. dirs. Burlington County br. 1995—, vice chairperson cmty. site com. 1995—), Sigma Theta Tau. Home: 253 Spout Spring Ave Mount Holly NJ 08060-2041

LOSSE, JOHN WILLIAM, JR., mining company executive; b. St. Louis, Mar. 16, 1916; s. John William and Claire (Schmedtje) L.; m. Marjorie West Penney, Mar. 7, 1942; children: John William IV, Georgia Shane, Barbara Stevens, Mary Coulter, Penney Gregersen, Jane Momberger. BS, Washington U., St. Louis, 1937; MBA, Harvard U., 1939. Sec.-treas. J.W. Losse Tailoring Co., St. Louis, 1939-41, 45-55; treas., controller, asst. sec. Uranium Reduction Co., Salt Lake City, 1955-62; v.p. finance Atlas Minerals div. Atlas Corp., Salt Lake City, 1962-64; asst. v.p., asst. treas. Am. Zinc Co., St. Louis, 1965-66; v.p. finance, treas. Am. Zinc Co., 1966-70; v.p. finance Conrad, Inc., St. Louis, 1970-71; v.p. finance, sec., dir. Fed. Resources Corp., Salt Lake City, 1971-82, pres., chief exec. officer, dir., 1982-84, 85-86, chief fin. officer, dir., 1986-88, v.p., treas., 1988—, also bd. dirs., 1988-89; sec.-treas. Madawaska Mines Ltd., Bancroft, Ont., Can., 1976-82, pres., bd. dirs., 1983—; pres. Camp Bird Colo., Inc., Ouray, 1983-92; Pres. Utah Natural Resources Council, 1964; tax com. and fin. adv. com. Am. Mining Congress, 1965-84; bd. dirs. Episcopal Mgmt. Corp., Salt Lake City. Bd. dirs. St. Mark's Hosp., Salt Lake City, 1987-88, Arthritis Found., Salt Lake City, 1988-96; vice chmn., bd. dirs. St. Mark's Charities, Salt Lake City, 1987-92; mem. investment com. Corp. of the Bishop, Salt Lake City, 1989-96; mem. investment adv. com. Perpetual Trust of St. Peter and St. Paul, 1995—. Lt. comdr. USNR, 1941-45. Mem. Utah Mining Assn. (bd. dirs., legis. and tax coms. 1971-91), Country Club of Salt Lake City, Alta Club of Salt Lake City, Phi Delta Theta. Republican. Episcopalian. Office: Fed Resources Corp PO Box 806 Salt Lake City UT 84110-0806

LOSSING, FREDERICK PETTIT, retired chemist; b. Norwich, Ont., Can., Aug. 4, 1915; s. Frank Edgar and Evelyn (Pettit) L.; m. Frances Isabella Glazier; children—Wilda, Patricia, Catherine. B.A., U. Western Ont., London, 1938, M.A., 1940; Ph.D., McGill U., Montreal, Que., Can., 1942. Research chemist Shawinigan Chems. Ltd., Shawinigan Falls, Que., 1942-46; research officer Nat. Research Council Can., Ottawa, Ont., 1946-80; asso. dir. div. chemistry Nat. Research Council Can., 1969-77, prin. research officer, 1977-80; rsch. scientist dept. chemistry U. Ottawa, 1980-94. Fellow Royal Soc. Can., Chem. Inst. Can.; mem. Am. Soc. Mass. Spectrometry, Royal Astron. Soc. Can. Home: 95 Dorothea Dr, Ottawa, ON Canada K1V 7C6

LOSTEN, BASIL HARRY, bishop; b. Chesapeake City, Md., May 11, 1930; s. John and Julia (Petryshyn) L. BA, St. Basil's Coll., 1953; STL, Cath. U., Washington, 1957. Ordained priest Ukranian Cath. Ch., 1957. Personal sec. to archbishop, 1962-66; contr. Archdiocese, 1966-75; apptd. monsignor, 1968; apptd. titular bishop of Arcadiopolis and aux. bishop Ukrainian Cath. Archeparchy of Phila., 1971-77; vicar gen., 1971, apostolic adminstr., 1976-77; bishop of Stamford, Conn., 1977—. Pres. Ascension Manor. Club: Union League (Phila.). *

LOSTER, GARY LEE, personnel director; b. Birmingham, Ala., Aug. 8, 1946; s. Sylvester and Leola (Madison) L.; m. Allene Shells, Dec. 14, 1969; children: Jennifer, Jacqueline. Assoc. in Law Enforcement, Delta Coll., Bay City, Mich., 1977; BA, Saginaw Valley State U., 1988. Lic. pvt. investigator, Mich. Assembler GM, Saginaw, Mich., 1968-69, spl. investigator, 1978-83, security supr., 1984-85; supr. to assoc. adminstr. fire, security, vehicle adminstrn. Delphi Saginaw Steering Sys. GM Corp., Saginaw, Mich., 1985—; chief of police Buena Vista Twp. (Mich.) Police Dept., 1970-78; speaker law enforcement subjects to various ednl., govt., religious orgns. Council mem. Saginaw City Council, 1988; bd. dirs. Am. Heart Assn., Saginaw County Info. Ctr. on Alcoholism, Saginaw Bay County Substance Abuse Com. Sgt. USMC, 1964-68. Recipient numerous awards, certs. of appreciation from law enforcement agencies,schs., govt. agencies. Mem. Nat. Fire Protection Assn., Nat. Crime Prevention Assn., Am. Soc. for Indsl. Security, Law Enforcement Adv. Council Delta Coll., Citizen Band Assn. Saginaw County. Seventh Day Adventist. Avocations: weightlifting, swimming, scuba diving, youth work. Office: Delphi Saginaw Steering Sys GM Corp 3900 E Holland Rd Saginaw MI 48601-9494

LOSTY, BARBARA PAUL, college official; b. Norwich, N.Y., June 16, 1942; d. Henry Edward and Mary Frances (Crowell) Paul; m. Thomas August Losty, Nov. 27, 1965; children: Ellen Christine, Amanda Elizabeth. BA, Wellesley Coll., 1964; MA, U. Conn., 1969, PhD, 1971. Asst. prof. psychology Westminster Coll., Fulton, Mo., 1971-73; asst. prof. psychology Stephens Coll., Columbia, Mo., 1973-75, assoc. dir. sch. liberal and profl. studies, 1975-79, assoc. dean of faculty, 1979-85; dean U. Wis. Ctr.-Sheboygan County, Sheboygan, 1985-91; coord. human svcs. degrees Thomas Edison State Coll., Trenton, N.J., 1992-94; assoc. dean human svcs. degrees, 1994—. Home: Perrineville Hightstown NJ 08535-9621 Office: Thomas Edison State Coll 101 W State St Trenton NJ 08608-1176

LOTAS, JUDITH PATTON, advertising executive; b. Iowa City, Apr. 23, 1942; d. John Henry and Jane (Vandike) Patton; children: Amanda Bell, Alexandra Vandike. BA, Fla. State U., 1964. Copywriter Liller, Neal, Battle and Lindsey Advt., Atlanta, 1964-67, Grey Advt., N.Y.C., 1967-72; creative group head SSC&B Advt., N.Y.C., 1972-74, asso. creative dir., 1974-79, v.p., 1975-79, sr. v.p., 1979-82, exec. creative dir., 1982-86; founding ptnr. Lotas Minard Patton McIver, Inc., N.Y.C., 1986—. Active scholarship fund raising; bd. dirs. Samuel Eaxman Cancer Rsch., Found., N.Y.C., 1981-88; fundraiser Nat. Coalition for the Homeless, N.Y.C., 1986—. Recipient Clio award, Venice Film Festival award, Graphics award Am. Inst. Graphic Artists, 1970, Effie award, Grad. of Distinction award Fla. State U., 1993; named Woman of Achievement, YWCA, One of Advt. Agys. 100 Best Women Ad Age, 1989. Mem. Advt. Women N.Y. (1st v.p. 1984-87, bd. dirs. 1981-87, Advt. Woman of Yr. 1993), The Ad Coun. (mem. creative rev. bd. 1994—, bd. dirs. 1995—), Women's Venture Fund (bd. dirs. 1995—), Kappa Alpha Theta. Democrat. Home: 45 E 89th St New York NY 10128-1251

LOTHROP, KRISTIN CURTIS, sculptor; b. Tucson, Feb. 8, 1930; d. Thomas and Elizabeth (Longfellow) Curtis; m. Francis B. Lothrop, Jr., Dec. 27, 1951; children—Robin B., Thornton K. and Jonathan C. (twins). B.A., Bennington Coll., 1951. Exhbns. include: Nat. Sculpture Soc., 1967-71, NAD, 1968-71, Hudson Valley Art Assn., 1968, Allied Artists Am., 1969, Concord Art Assn., 1970; represented in permanent collection, Brookgreen Gardens, S.C. Recipient Mrs. Louis Bennett award Nat. Sculpture Soc., 1967; Thomas R. Procter award N.A.D., 1968; Dessie Greer award, 1969; Daniel Chester French medal, 1970; hon. mention Hudson Valley Art Assn., 1968; 1st prize Concord Art Assn., 1970, 83; 1st prize Manchester Arts Assn., 1975; 1st prize Hamilton-Wenham Art Show, 1980; Liskin purchase prize Nat. Sculpture Soc., 1986. Mem. Nat. Sculpture Soc., New Eng. Sculptors Assn. (1st prize 1987), The Copley Soc. of Boston (Copley master). Address: 71 Bridge St Manchester MA 01944-1412

LOTITO, MICHAEL JOSEPH, lawyer; b. Carbondale, Pa., July 22, 1948; s. Dominic Joseph and Margaret Mary (Miller) L.; m. Luanne R. McMaster, Nov. 9, 1985; 1 child, Kelly C. AB, Villanova U., 1970, JD, 1974. Bar: Pa. 1974, Calif. 1983; lic. sr. profl. human resources. Assoc. Barley, Snyder, Cooper & Barber, Lancaster, Pa., 1974-76, Jackson, Lewis, Schnitzler & Krupman, N.Y.C., 1976-81; mng. ptnr. Jackson, Lewis, Schnitzler & Krupman, San Francisco, 1982—; bd. dirs. No. Calif. Human Resource Coun., San Francisco. Co-author: Making the ADA Work for You, 1992, What Managers and Supervisors Need to Know About the ADA, 1992, The Americans With Disabilities Act: A Comprehensive Guide to Title I, 1992; contbr. articles to profl. jours. Mem. ABA, Calif. Bar Assn., Soc. for Human Resource Mgmt. (chmn. legis. affairs com. 1988-90, nat. employment law com. 1981-86, legal adv. bd. 1988—, bd. dirs. 1991—, chair edn. task force 1990-92, edn. com. 1993-94, vol. counsel to bd. dirs. 1993—), Calif. C. of C. (labor com. 1986-88). Republican. Roman Catholic. Home: 95 Deer Park Ave San Rafael CA 94901-2310 Office: Jackson Lewis Schnitzler & Krupman 525 Market St Ste 3400 San Francisco CA 94105-2742

LOTMAN, HERBERT, food processing executive; b. Phila., Oct. 9, 1933; s. Samuel Meyer and Gertrude L.; m. Karen Levin, Apr. 6, 1957; children: Shelly Hope, Jeffrey Mark. Pres., chmn. bd. Keystone Foods Corp., Bryn Mawr, Pa., 1951; pres. Keystone Foods Corp., 1960, chm. bd., 1960—. Bd. dirs. Nat. Juvenile Diabetes Found. Served with U.S. Army, 1952-54. Mem. Young Pres. Orgn. Office: Keystone Foods Corp 401 E City Ave # 800 Bala Cynwyd PA 19004-1122*

LOTOCKY, INNOCENT HILARIUS, bishop; b. Petlykivci Stari, Buchach, Ukraine, Nov. 3, 1915; came to U.S., 1946; s. Stefan and Maria (Tytyn) L. Student at various religious insts., Ukraine, Czechoslovakia; Ph.D. in Sacred Theology, U. Vienna, Austria, 1994. Ordained priest Ukrainian Catholic Ch., 1944, consecrated bishop, 1981; cert. tchr., Mich. Superior-novice master Order St. Basil, Dawson, Pa., 1946-51; provincial superior U.S. province Order St. Basil, N.Y., 1951-53; novice master Order St. Basil, Glen Cove, N.Y., 1958-60; pastor-superior St. George Ch., N.Y.C., 1953-58; pastor St. Nicholas Ch., Chgo., 1960-62; pastor-superior Immaculate Conception Ch., Hamtramck, Mich., 1962-81, also tchr., 1962-81; bishop Diocese St. Nicholas, Chgo., 1981-93, ret., 1993; provincial counselor U.S. province Order St. Basil, 1962-80, del. to gen. chpt. Rome, 1963. Active numerous civic orgns. Mem. Nat. Council Cath. Bishops. Home and Office: Diocese St Nicholas in Chgo 2245 W Rice St Chicago IL 60622-4858*

LOTSPEICH, ELLIN SUE, art specialist, educator; b. Spring Valley, Ill., July 2, 1952; d. Donald Robert and Mary Rita (Smith) Mason; m. Thomas Grant Weaver, Jan. 26, 1974 (dec. July 1989); children: Jennifer, Michelle, Patrick; m. Michael Charles Lotspeich, Apr. 9, 1994; 1 child, Michael Charles II. BS, Western Ill. U., 1974, M Ednl. Adminstrn., 1995. Unit art specialist Winola Unit Dist., Viola, Ill., 1974-84, Al Wood Unit Dist., Woodhull, Ill., 1984—; discipline based art cons. Getty Ctr. for Edn. in Arts, 1989—; exec. bd. Commn. on Edn. Diocese of Peoria, Ill., 1993—, exec. chmn. Religious Edn. Com., 1994—. Mem. Nat. Art Edn. Assn., Ill. Art Edn. Assn. (exec. bd. 1980—, state youth art chmn. 1990-93), Ill. Rembrandt State Assn. (editor newsletter 1987-90, bd. dirs.), Ill. Alliance for Arts, Henry Stark H.S. Art Tchrs. (pres. 1984-94). Home: 212 N 3d Ave New Windsor IL 61465 Office: Al Wood Unit Dist 201 E 5th Ave Woodhull IL 61490

LOTSTEIN, JAMES IRVING, lawyer; b. Steubenville, Ohio, Jan. 27, 1944; s. Jack and Dorothy (Nach) L.; m. Paulette L. Gutcheon, June 25, 1972; children: Melissa A., Amanda J. BSBA, Northwestern U., 1965; JD, U. Conn., 1968. Bar: Conn. 1969, U.S. Ct. Appeals (2d cir.) 1971, U.S. Supreme Ct. 1972. From assoc. to ptnr. Hoppin, Carey & Powell, Hartford, Conn., 1969-86; ptnr. Cummings & Lockwood, Hartford, 1986—, ptnr.-in-charge, 1988-95. Author: An Introduction to the Connecticut Business Corporation Act, 1994. Trustee Conn. Policy and Econ. Coun., Inc., 1990, mem. exec. com., 1995—; mem. Sec. of State's bus. adv. com. State of Conn. 1st lt. JAGC, USAR, 1968-74. Mem. ABA (chmn. dirs. and officers task force, mem. corp. laws com. 1992), Conn. Bar Assn. (chmn. mcpl. law and govtl. svc. com. 1981—, chmn. bus. law sect. 1990-92, co-chmn. Conn. bus. corp. act task force 1993—). Office: Cummings & Lockwood City Pl I Hartford CT 06103

LOTT, MELINDA JO, special education and secondary education educator; b. Detroit, July 16, 1954; d. Frank Norris and Nellie Virginia (Shumaker) L. AA, Mitchell Coll., 1974; BS, Pfeiffer Coll., 1978; M in Elem. Edn., Francis Marion U., 1993. Cert. learning disabilities, mental retardation, secondary, social studies, spl. edn. tchr. Spl. edn. educator Millers Creek (N.C.) Intermediate Sch., 1978-86, Kingstree (S.C.) Elem. Sch., 1986-89, Savannah Grove Elem. Sch., Effingham, S.C., 1989-94, Moore Intermediate Sch., Florence, S.C., 1994—; faculty adv. coun. rep. Florence Sch. Dist. 1, 1992—; student tchr. supr. Coker Coll., Hartsville, S.C., 1992-93; student placement adv. bd. Savannah Grove Elem. Sch., 1989-94, Moore Intermediate Sch., 1994—. Active First Bapt. Ch., Florence, 1989, Nat. Trust for Hist. Preservation, Washington, 1994, Wildlife Action, Inc., Florence, 1992. Mem. AAUW, S.C. Coun. for Exceptional Children, Children with Attention Deficit Disorders, Orton Dyslexia Soc. (Ednl. Conf. grant 1992, 93), Palmetti State Tchrs. Assn., Internat. Reading Assn., Phi Delta Kappa. Home: 1806 Meadow Green Pl Florence SC 29501-6466 Office: Moore Intermediate Sch 1101 Cheraw Dr Florence SC 29501-5619

LOTT, ROBERT VINCENT, newspaper editor; b. Quantico Marine Base, Va., Dec. 3, 1941; s. Vincent Lamar and Sara Mildred (Lawson) L.; m. Sara Jacquelen Lovelady, Jan. 26, 1963; children: Sam, Tim, Danny. BA in Journalism, U. Ala., 1990. Ward attendant Bryce State Hosp., Tuscaloosa, Ala., 1960-63; reporter Columbus (Ga.) Ledger, 1964-66, city editor, 1966-68; copy editor Atlanta Jour., 1968-69, copy desk chief, 1969-73, asst. mng. editor, 1973-79; editor Waco (Tex.) Tribune-Herald, 1979—. Bd. dirs. Tex. Media, Austin, 1992—, Tex. Freedom of Info. Found., Dallas 1993—; mem. student publs. bd. U. Tex., 1988-90, 96. Recipient James Madison award Tex. Freedom of Info. Found., 1994, Journalism Grad. of Yr. award U. Ala., 1994. Mem. Am. Soc. Newspaper Editors, Tex. Assn. Press Mng. Editors (Freedom of Info. chair 1995). Presbyterian. Avocations: sailboating, fly fishing. Office: Waco Tribune-Herald 900 Franklin Ave Waco TX 76701-1906

LOTT, RONNIE (RONALD MANDEL LOTT), professional football player; b. Albuquerque, May 8, 1959. BS in Pub. Adminstrn., U. So. Calif., 1981. With San Francisco 49ers, 1981-90, L.A. Raiders, 1991-93, N.Y. Jets, 1993-94, Kansas City Chiefs, 1994—. Named to Sporting News All-Am. team, 1980, Pro Bowl team, 1981-84, 86-91, Sporting News All-Pro team, 1981, 87, 90. Office: Kansas City Chiefs One Arrowhead Dr Kansas City MO 64129

LOTT, THADDEUS, principal. Prin. Wesley Elem. Sch. Office: Wesley Elem Sch 800 Dillard St Houston TX 77091-2301

LOTT, TRENT, senator; b. Grenada, Miss., Oct. 9, 1941; s. Chester P. and Iona (Watson) L.; m. Patricia E. Thompson, Dec. 27, 1964; children—Chester T., Jr., Tyler Elizabeth. B.P.A., U. Miss., 1963, J.D., 1967. Bar: Miss. 1967. Assoc. Bryan & Gordon, Pascagoula, Miss., 1967; adminstrv. asst. to Congressman William M. Colmer, 1968-72; mem. 93d-100th Congresses from 5th Miss. dist., 1973-89; Rep. whip 97th-100th Congresses from 5th Miss. dist., mem. Ho. Rules com.; U.S. senator from Miss., 1989—, Senate armed svcs. com., budget com., energy, natural resources com., 102d Congress, sec. Senate Rep. Conf., 103d Congress, majority whip 104th Congress; field rep. for U. Miss., 1963-65; acting alumni sec. Ole Miss Alumni Assn., 1966-67; named as observer from House to Geneva Arms Control talks; chmn. Commerce, Sci. & Transp. subcom. on surface transp. & merchant marine; mem. Senate Republican Policy Com. Recipient Golden Bulldog award, Guardian of Small Bus. award. Mem. ABA, Jackson County Bar Assn., Sigma Nu, Phi Alpha Delta. Republican. Baptist. Lodge: Mason. Office: 487 Russell Senate Office Bldg Washington DC 20510*

LOTTES, JOHN WILLIAM, arts administrator; b. Mpls., 1934; m. Nancy J. Sawyer; children: John E., Andrew C., Rachel L. Engler. AA, Concordia Coll., St. Paul, 1954; BFA, Mpls. Coll. Art and Design, 1963, MFA (hon.), 1973; DA (hon.), William Jewell Coll., Liberty, Mo., 1984; postgrad., Die Hochschule Fur Gestaltung, Ulm, Germany, U. Iowa. Graphic and indsl. designer, 1954-63; instr. Mpls. Coll. Art and Design, 1960-62, asst. prof., chmn. indsl. design, 1962-63; instr. indsl. design Kansas City (Mo.) Art Inst., 1964-65, asst. prof., acting dean, 1965-66, dean coll., registrar, 1966-68, pres., 1970-73; v.p. planning and devel. Corcoran Gallery, Washington, 1968-69; v.p. acad. affairs Calif. Coll. Arts and Crafts, 1969-70; cons. devel. officer Sch. Visual Arts, N.Y.C., 1986-87; pres., trustee Mpls. Soc. Fine Arts, 1983-87; pres. Oreg. Sch. Arts and Crafts, Portland, 1987-91, Art Inst. So. Calif., Laguna Beach, 1991—; mem. Kansas City Regional Coun. Higher Edn., 1965-83, Alliance/Union Ind. Colls. Art, 1965-93, Nat. Assn. Schs. Art and Design, 1963—, Commn. on Accreditation Site Visitor, 1978—, North Ctrl. Assn. Schs. and Colls., 1965-83, Assembly Nat. Arts Edn. Orgns., 1979-83, Portland Arts Alliance, 1987-91, U.S. Inst. TheatreTech., 1987-92, Western Assn. Schs. and Colls., 1991—; cons. Cornish Sch. Allied Arts, Seattle, 1978, Galveston County Cultural Arts Coun., Inc., Tex., 1979, Nat. Endowment Arts, 1978-79, Pa. Acad. Fine Arts, Phila., 1981, The Portfolio Ctr., Atlanta, 1982, Nat. Endowment Arts Locals Program, 1983-85, Notre Dame U., 1984, Moorhead (Minn.) State U., 1984, Otis Art Inst. Parsons Sch. Design, L.A., 1984, Laguna Beach Coll. Art, Calif., 1985, Memphis Coll. Art, 1986, Art Inst. So. Calif., 1986, Sch. Visual Arts, N.Y., 1987, Casper (Wyo.) Coll., 1989, Pacific-N.W.Coll. Art, Oreg., 1989, Cornish Sch. Allied Arts, Wash., 1990, 92, Vincennes (Ind.) U. Jr. Coll., 1990, Munson-Williams-Proctor Inst., N.Y., Design Inst. San Diego, 1995. Mem. Mcpl. Arts Commn., Kansas City, Mo., 1978-83, Kansas City Arts Coun., 1978-83; chmn. Mayor's Task Force to Save the Philharmonic Orch., 1982; local program panelist Nat. Endowment for Arts, 1980-83; mem. Gov.'s Task Force on

Arts H.S. for Minn., 1985-86; mem. Artquake Artists' Jury, City of Portland, 1990-91; juror Laguna Beach Festival of Arts, 1993 Exhbn.; HIV adv. com. City of Laguna Beach, 1993—; advisor Laguna Beach Arts Commn., 1994—; bd. dirs. Arts Orange County, 1994—; bd. dirs. City of Fountains Found., Kansas City, 1973-83; bd. regents St. Paul's Coll., Concordia, Mo., 1981-87, chmn., 1983-87; pres. bd. trustees Mpls. Soc. Fine Arts, 1983-86; bd. dirs. Zion Luth. Ch., Portland, 1983-87, chmn., 1986-87; bd. hon. trustees Osaka (Japan) U. Arts, 1973—; bd. dirs. St. Paul's Luth. Ch., Laguna Beach, 1992—, pres., 1993—; bd. dirs. Cameray Pointe Homeowners Assn., 1992—, pres., 1993—. Recipient Pub. Svc. award Baker U., Kans., 1982, Citation Kansas City Regional Coun. Higher Edn., 1983, Citation Mid-Am. Coll. Art Assn., 1983. Fellow Nat. Assn. Schs. Art and Design (life); mem. Am. Assn. Higher Edn., Am. Coun. Edn., Rotary Club (Laguna Beach, Calif.) (bd. dirs. 1994—), Laguna Beach C. of C. Office: Art Inst So Calif 2222 Laguna Canyon Rd Laguna Beach CA 92651

LOTTES, PATRICIA JOETTE HICKS, foundation administrator, retired nurse; b. Balt., Aug. 18, 1955; d. James Thomas and Linda Belle (Cadd) Hicks; m. Jeffrey Grant Gross, Aug. 18, 1979 (div. 1981); m. William Melamet Lottes, Sept. 10, 1983. Diploma in practical nursing, Union Meml. Hosp., 1978. Staff nurse Union Meml. Hosp., Balt., 1978-79, critical care nurse, 1979-81; vis. critical care nurse Balt., 1981-84; head nurse Pharmakinetics, Inc., Balt., 1984-85; dir. Arachnoiditis Info. and Support Network, Inc., Ballwin, Mo., 1991—, dir. nat. support groups, 1992—; nat. support group leader Arachnoid, 1993—. Sec., treas. O'Fallon (Mo.) Elks Ladies Aux., 1989-91, treas., 1991-92, incorporator, 1991, bd. dirs., 1991-94; co-chairperson 303d Field Hosp., U.S. Army Family Support Group, St. Louis, 1990-94. Mem. Nat. Disaster Med. Systems (assoc.), Elks Benevolent Trust, Elks Nat. Home Perpetual Trust. Republican. Baptist. Avocation: quilting. Home: 606 Barbara Dr O'Fallon MO 63366-1306

LOTTMAN, EVAN, film editor. Editor: (films) Puzzle of a Downfall Child, 1970, Panic in Needle Park, 1971, Scarecrow, 1973, The Effects of Gamma Rays on Man-in-the-Moon Marigolds, 1973, (with others) The Exorcist, 1973 (Academy award nomination best film editing 1973), (with Richard Fetterman) Sweet Revenge, 1976, The Seduction of Joe Tynan, 1979, (with Aram Avakian, Norman Gay, and Marc Laub) Honeysuckle Rose, 1980, Rollover, 1981, The Pilot, 1981, Sophie's Choice, 1982, The Muppets Take Manhattan, 1984, The Protector, 1985, Maximum Overdrive, 1986, On the Yard, 1987, Orphans, 1987, See You in the Morning, 1989, Presumed Innocent, 1990, Beyond Innocence, 1992, The Public Eye, 1992, Missing Pieces, 1992, Guilty as Sin, 1993, (TV movies) Gotham, 1988. Office: 15 W 72nd St New York NY 10023-3402

LOTWIN, STANFORD GERALD, lawyer; b. N.Y.C., June 23, 1930; s. Herman and Rita (Saltzman) L.; m. Judy Scott, Oct. 15, 1994; children: Lori Hope, David, Sean. BS, Bklyn. Coll., 1951, LLB, 1954, LLM, 1957. Bar: N.Y. 1954, U.S. Supreme Ct. 1961, Pa. 1986. Ptnr. Tenzer, Greenblatt, Fallon and Kaplan, N.Y.C., 1987—; of counsel Frankfurt, Garbus, Klein & Selz, N.Y.C., 1983-87. Served with U.S. Army, 1954-56. Fellow Am. Acad. Matrimonial Lawyers (bd. of mgrs. 1984—); mem. N.Y. State Bar Assn. (family law sect.), N.Y. County Trial Lawyers (lectr. 1980—). Office: 405 Lexington Ave New York NY 10174

LOTZ, DENTON, minister, church official; b. Flushing, N.Y., Jan. 18, 1939; s. John Milton and Adeline Helen (Kettell) L.; m. Janice Robinson, Mar. 15, 1970; children: John-Paul, Alena, Carsten. BA, U. N.C., 1961; STB, Harvard Div. Sch., 1966; ThD, U. Hamburg, Fed. Republic Germany, 1970; DD (hon.), Campbell U., 1982, Ea. Bapt. Sem., 1991, Alderson-Broadus, 1995. Prof. mission Bapt. Sem., Ruschlikon, Switzerland, 1972-80; dir. evangelism Bapt. World Alliance, McLean, Va., 1980-88, gen. sec., 1988—; fraternal rep. Am. Bapt. Internat. Ministries To Ea. Europe, Valley Forge, Pa., 1970-80. Author, editor: Baptists in the USSR, 1987; editor: Spring Has Returned to China, 1987. V.p. CARE, N.Y.C., 1981. 1st lt. USMC, 1961-63. Mem. Internat. Religious Liberty Assn. (pres. 1990-91). Office: Bapt World Alliance 6733 Curran St Mc Lean VA 22101-3804

LOTZE, BARBARA, physicist; b. Mezokovesd, Hungary, Jan. 4, 1924; d. Matyas and Borbala (Toth) Kalo; came to U.S., 1961, naturalized, 1967; Applied Mathematician Diploma with honors, Eotvos Lorand U. Scis., Budapest, Hungary, 1956; PhD, Innsbruck (Austria) U., 1961; m. Dieter P. Lotze, Oct. 6, 1958. Mathematician, Hungarian Cen. Statis. Bur., Budapest, 1955-56; tchr. math., Iselsberg, Austria, 1959-60; asst. prof. physics Allegheny Coll., 1963-69, assoc. prof., 1969-77, prof., 1977-90, prof. emeritus, 1990—, chmn. dept., 1981-84; lectr. in history of physics; speaker to civic groups. Mem. Am. Phys. Soc. (mem. com. internat. freedom of scientists 1993-95), Am. Inst. Physics (mem. adv. com. history of physics 1994—), Am. Assn. Physics Tchrs. (coun., sect. rep. Western Pa., chmn. nat. com. on women in physics 1983-84, com. internat. physics edn. 1991-93, Disting. Svc. award 1986, cert. of appreciation 1988), AAUW, N.Y. Acad. Scis., Am. Hungarian Educators Assn. (pres. 1980-82), Wilhelm Busch Gesellschaft (Hanover). Editor: Making Contributions: An Historical Overview of Women's Role in Physics, 1984; co-editor The First War Between Socialist States: The Hungarian Revolution of 1956 and Its Impact, 1984; contbr. articles to profl. jours. Home: 462 Hartz Ave Meadville PA 16335-1325 Office: Allegheny Coll Dept Physics Meadville PA 16335

LOTZENHISER, GEORGE WILLIAM, music educator, university administrator; b. Spokane, Wash., May 16, 1923; married; 1 child. BA cum laude, Ea. Wash. U., 1946, BEd in Social Sci., 1947; MusM, U. Mich., 1948; EdD, U. Oreg., 1956. Instr. brass U. Ariz., Tucson, 1948-49, asst. prof. music, 1949-56, assoc. prof., 1956-60; prof. Ea. Wash. U., Cheney, 1960-83, dir. High Sch. Creative arts summer series, 1960-83, dean Sch. Fine Arts, 1960-83, dean emeritus Sch. Fine Arts, 1983—; cons. and lectr. in field. Author: A Study of Faculty Loads in Member Schools of the National Association of Schools of Music, 1963, A Study of the Selection Process of Administrators of the Fine Arts in Colleges and Universities in the U.S., 1970; contbr. articles to profl. jours. Mem. Wash. State Music Adv. Com., 1967-83, exec. com. Alliance for Arts Edn., 1972-83; pres. Navy League, 1975-77; mem. Spokane Riverfront Festival of the Arts, 1976-78, Allied Arts of Wash. State, 1977-83. Served to rear adm. USNR, 1942-82. Decorated Legion of Merit; named Disting. Eagle Scout Boy Scouts Am. Mem. Nat. Assn. Schs. Music (accreditation com. chmn. 1960—), Nat. Music Educators Research Council, North Cen. Assn. Accreditation Coms., N.W. Assn. Accreditation Com., Western Assn. Schs. and Colls. Com., Eastern Wash. Music Educators. Congregationalist. Home: PO Box 1528 Coupeville WA 98239-1528

LOUARGAND, MARC ANDREW, real estate executive, financial consultant; b. San Francisco, July 3, 1945; s. Andrew Louargand and Edna Antoinette McNeil; m. Elizabeth A. Warner, June 18, 1966 (div. Oct. 1978); m. J. R. McDaniel, Feb. 14, 1986. BA, U. Calif., Santa Barbara, 1967; MBA, U. Calif., L.A., 1974, PhD, 1982. Asst. prof. Calif. State Polytech. U., Pomona, 1975-77; assoc. prof. Calif. State U., Northridge, 1977-83, U. Mass., Boston, 1983-88; sr. lectr. Ctr. for Real Estate Devel. MIT, Cambridge, 1986-93; 2d v.p., sr. officer Mass. Mut. Life Ins. Co., Springfield, Mass., 1993-94; mng. dir. Cornerstone Real Estate Advisors, 1993—; cons. in field. Author: CRE2000: Managing the Fifth Strategic Resource, Study Guide to Financial Management, 1986, (with others) Principles and Techniques of Appraisal Review, 1980, Handbook of Real Estate Portfolio Management; assoc. editor Jour. Real Estate Lit., Jour. Real Estate Portfolio Management; contbr. articles to profl. jours. Bd. dirs. Beverly Glen Assn., Bel Air, Calif., 1973-77, Citronia Homeowners Assn., Northridge, Calif., 1978-83; chmn. Carlisle (Mass.) Bd. Assessors, 1985-93. Mem. N. Am. Coun. of Real Estate Investment Fiduciaries, Am. Real Estate and Urban Economies Assn., Am.Real Estate Soc., Internat. Assn. Assessing Officers, Fin. Mgmt. Assn., Nat. Trust for Hist. Preservation, Vt. Land Trust. Republican. Avocations: tree farming, skiing, building restoration. Home: 32 Longmeadow St Longmeadow MA 01106-1015

LOUBE, SAMUEL DENNIS, physician; b. Rumania, Aug. 26, 1921; came to U.S., 1922, naturalized, 1927; s. Harry and Rebecca (Pollack) L.; m. Emily Wallace, Apr. 14, 1976; children—Julian M., Jonathan B., Susan C., Karen E., Patricia A., Pamela B., Brian R. A.B., George Washington U., 1941, M.D. cum laude, 1943. Diplomate: Am. Bd. Internal Medicine. Intern, then resident in medicine Gallinger Municipal Hosp., Washington, 1943-46; physician USPHS, 1946-48; postdoctoral fellow NIH, 1948-50; research fellow in endocrinology Michael Reese Hosp., Chgo., 1948-49; research fellow in metabolism and endocrinology May Inst. Jewish Hosp., Cin., 1949-50; mem. faculty George Washington U. Med. Sch., 1950-89, clin. prof. medicine, 1975-89, prof. emeritus, 1989; practice medicine specializing in endocrinology and metabolic diseases, Washington, 1950-88, mem. Washington Internal Medicine Group, 1965-88; former chmn. dept. medicine, chief sect. endocrinology Sibley Meml. Hosp. Contbr. articles to med. jours. Fellow ACP; mem. AMA, Am. Diabetes Assn., Endocrine Soc., Am. Soc. Internal Medicine, Diabetes Assn. D.C. (past pres.), Jacobi Med. Soc. (past pres.). Jewish.

LOUBET, JEFFREY W., lawyer; b. Mt. Vernon, N.Y., May 12, 1943; s. Nathaniel R. and Joan (Fleischer) L.; m. Susan Maria Thom, Aug. 29, 1972; 1 child, Thom Carlyle. BA, Colgate U., 1965; JD, St. John's U., 1968; LLM in Taxation, N.Y. U., 1970. Bar: N.Y. 1968, U.S. Tax Ct. 1969, U.S. Dist. Ct. (so. dist.) N.Y. 1969, N.Mex. 1976, U.S. Dist. Ct. N.Mex. 1977. Assoc. Poletti, Freidin, Prashker, Feldman & Gartner, N.Y.C., 1969-76; ptnr. Modrall, Sperling, Roehl, Harris & Sisk, Albuquerque, 1976-94; counsel Rodey, Dickason, Sloan, Akin & Robb, Albuquerque, 1994—; lectr. N.Mex. Estate Roundtable, Albuquerque, 1979—; vis. prof. Estate and Gift Tax U. N.Mex., Albuquerque, 1988-89. Contbr. articles to profl. jours. Mem. Lovelace Inst. Estate Planning Adv. Coun., 1993—; mem. adv. bd. on charitable giving Albuquerque Cmty. Found., 1995—. Masters World Record Holder, high hurdles and decathlon. Fellow Am. Coll. Trust and Estate Counsel; mem. N.Mex. Estate Planning Coun., Greater Albuquerque C. of C. (chair tax task force, 1992, chair state govt. com., 1993), YMCA (mem. bd. dirs.). Avocations: track & field, skiing, fly fishing. Home: PO Box 3754 Albuquerque NM 87190 Office: Rodey Dickason Sloan Akin & Robb PO Box 1888 Albuquerque NM 87103-1888

LOUCHHEIM, DONALD HARRY, journalist; b. N.Y.C., June 6, 1937; s. Joseph Harry and Aline (Bernstein) L.; m. Valerie Pingree Wright, Sept. 6, 1958; children: Jessica Wright, Joseph Pingree, Jeffrey Depew. B.A., Yale U., 1959; M.B.A., Harvard U., 1971. Reporter, New Haven Jour.-Courier, 1959-61; mem. staff Washington Post, 1961-71, Paris bur. chief, 1967-69; owner, pub. Southampton Press, L.I., N.Y., 1971—. Served with AUS, 1959. Office: Southampton Press 135 Windmill Ln Southampton NY 11968-4840

LOUCK, LISA ANN, lawyer; b. Davenport, Iowa, July 16, 1963; d. Richard Lane and Jo Ann (Frerkes) L. BSBA, Iowa State U., 1985; JD, South Tex. Coll. Law, 1991. Bar: Tex. 1992. Atty. Woodard, Hall & Primm, Houston, 1994—; mediator Tex. Registry Alt. Dispute Resolution Profls., 1992—. Recipient Am. Jurisprudence award Lawyers Coop. Pub., 1991. Mem. ABA, State Bar Tex., Houston Young Lawyers Assn., Phi Alpha Delta. Office: Woodard Hall & Primm PC 7100 Texas Commerce Tower Houston TX 77002

LOUCKS, DANIEL PETER, environmental systems engineer; b. Chambersburg, Pa., June 4, 1932; s. Emerson Hunsberger and Eleanor Wright (Johnson) L.; m. Marjorie Ann Grant, June 24, 1967; children: Jennifer Lee, Susan Louise. B.S., Pa. State U., 1954; M.S., Yale U., 1955; Ph.D., Cornell U., 1965. Asst. prof. environ. engring. Cornell U., Ithaca, N.Y., 1965-70; assoc. prof. Cornell U., 1970-74, prof., 1974—, chmn. dept., 1974-80; assoc. dean research and grad. studies Cornell U. (Coll. Engring.), 1980-81; rsch. fellow Harvard U., Cambridge, Mass., 1968; economist IBRD, Washington, 1972-73; vis. prof. MIT, Cambridge, 1977-78; rsch. scholar Internat. Inst. for Applied Sys. Analysis, 1981-82; vis. disting. prof. U. Colo., 1992, U. Adelaide, 1992, Tech. U. Aachen, Germany, 1993, U. Tech., Delft, The Netherlands, 1995; cons. NATO, UN, WHO, FAO, IRBD on water resources and regional devel. projects in Asia, Western and EAstern Europe, Africa and L.Am., 1970—, EPA on water quality planning USSR, 1975-77; vis. prof. Internat. Inst. Hydraulic and Environ. Engring., Delft, 1976-80, 86—; environ. adv. bd. U.S. Army Corps Engrs., 1994—; dir. NATO Advanced Rsch. Workshops, 1990, 95. Contbr. articles to jours. and books on math. models. for mng. water resources systems and environ. quality. Bd. dirs. Wilderness Corp., Plymouth, Vt., 1968-87, treas., 1987—; pres. Cmty. Improvement Assn., Ithaca, 1976-77. Capt., aviator USNR, 1956-81. Recipient U.S. Sr. Rsch. award Alexander von Humboldt Found., 1992, Joy Wyatt Challenge (EDUCOM) award, 1991, Disting. Lecture award Nat. Rsch. Coun. Taiwan, 1990; Fulbright-Hayes fellow Yugoslavia, 1975. Fellow ASCE (Walter Huber rsch. award 1970, Julian Hinds award 1986); mem. AAAS, NAE, Am. Geophys. Union, Inst. Mgmt. Scis., Internat. Water Resources Assn., Am. Water Resources Assn., Internat. Assn. Hydraulic Rsch., Internat. Assn. Hydrologic Scis., Sigma Xi. Home: 116 Crest Ln Ithaca NY 14850-2704 Office: Cornell U Hollister Hall Ithaca NY 14853

LOUCKS, RALPH BRUCE, JR., investment company executive; b. St. Louis, Dec. 10, 1924; s. Ralph Bruce and Dola (Blake) L.; m. Lois Holloway, June 4, 1949 (dec. Sept. 1983); children: Elizabeth, Mary Jane; m. Mary Sutliffe Stahl, June 2, 1984. BA, Lake Forest Coll., 1949; postgrad. U. Chgo., 1950-52. Registered prin. Nat. Assn. Securities Dealers. Investment fund mgr. No. Trust Co., Chgo., 1950-53, Brown Bros. Harriman & Co., Chgo., 1953-55; investment counsel, pres. Tilden, Loucks & Grannis, Chgo., 1955-80; sr. v.p. Bacon, Whipple & Co., 1981-88; sr. v.p. Roberts, Loucks & Co., 1988—. Served with 11th Armored Div., AUS, 1943-45. Decorated Bronze Star medal, Purple Heart. Mem. Investment Analysts Soc., Investment Counsel Assn. Am., Huguenot Soc. Ill. (pres. 1960-61), Nat. Assn. Security Dealers (registered prin.), Soc. Colonial Wars. Clubs: Economic, Racquet, Chgo. Yacht (Chgo.). Office: 250 S Wacker Dr Chicago IL 60606-5834

LOUCKS, VERNON R., JR., healthcare products and services company executive; b. Evanston, Ill., Oct. 24, 1934; s. Vernon Reece and Sue (Burton) L.; m. Linda Kay Olson, May 12, 1972; 6 children. B.A. in History, Yale U., 1957; M.B.A., Harvard U., 1963. Sr. mgmt. cons. George Fry & Assos., Chgo., 1963-65; with Baxter Travenol Labs., Inc (now Baxter Internat. Inc.), Deerfield, Ill., 1966—, exec. v.p., 1976, also bd. dirs., pres., chief oper. officer, 1980, chief exec. officer, chmn., 1987—; bd. dirs. Dun & Bradstreet Corp., Emerson Electric Co., Quaker Oats Co., Anheuser-Busch Cos.; bd. advisors Nestlé U.S.A. Trustee Rush-Presbyn.-St. Luke's Med. Ctr.; assoc. Northwestern U. 1st lt. USMC, 1957-60. Recipient Citizen Fellowship award Chgo. Inst. Medicine, 1982, Nat. Health Care award B'nai B'rith Youth Svcs., 1986, William McCormick Blair award Yale U., 1989, Semper Fidelis award USMC, 1989, Disting. Humanitarian award St. Barnabas Found., 1992, Alexis de Tocqueville award for community svc. United Way Lake County, 1993; named 1983's Outstanding Exec. Officer in the healthcare industry Fin. World; elected to Chgo.'s Bus. Hall of Fame, Jr. Achievement, 1987. Mem. Health Industry Mfrs. Assn. (chmn. 1983), Bus. Roundtable (conf. bd., mem. policy com.), Bus. Coun. Clubs: Chgo. Commonwealth, Commercial, Mid-America; Links (N.Y.C.). Office: Baxter Healthcare Corp One Baxter Pkwy Deerfield IL 60015

LOUD, WARREN SIMMS, mathematician; b. Boston, Sept. 13, 1921; s. Roger Perkins and Esther (Nickerson) L.; m. Mary Louise Strasburg, Dec. 27, 1947; children: Margaret Loud McCamant, Elizabeth Ann Loud Liebman, John Alden. S.B., Mass. Inst. Tech., 1942, Ph.D., 1946. Asst. prof. U. Minn., 1947-56, assoc. prof., 1956-59, prof. math., 1959-92, prof. emeritus, 1992—; vis. prof. Math. Rsch. Ctr., U. Wis., 1959-60, Technische Hochschule Darmstadt, Germany, 1964-65, Kyoto U., Japan, 1974-75, U. Florence, 1981-82, U. Trento, 1982, 83; vis. lectr. Math. Assn. Am., 1965—. Mem. Am. Math. Soc., Math. Assn. Am. (bd. govs. 1960-62, 77-80), Soc. Indsl. and Applied Math. (editor Rev. 1961-66, Jour. Applied Math. 1966-75, mem. editorial bd. 1975-79), AAAS. Congregationalist. Achievements include research, publs. in nonlinear ordinary differential equations. Home: 1235 Yale Pl # 504 Minneapolis MN 55403 Office: U Minn Sch of Math 206 Church St SE Minneapolis MN 55455-0488

LOUDEN, SUZANNE LOIS, educational consultant; b. Monroe, Mich., Apr. 3, 1937; d. James Clifford and Pauline Lois (Crumm) Brancheau; m. Roger William Lousen, Sept. 8, 1972; 1 child, Thomas James. BA in Edn./Music, U. Dayton, 1966; MA in Counseling and Guidance, John Carroll U., 1972; MA in Spl. Edn., U. Colo., 1976. Cert. sch. adminstr. Tchr. St. Joseph's (Mo.) Sch., Manteca (Calif.) Schs., St. Anthony's Sch., New Riegel, Ohio; youth dir. Dayton, Ohio; elem. sch. counselor Harrison Sch. Dist., Colorado Springs, Colo.; instr. U. Colo., Colorado Springs; cons. various schs., Colo.; instr. cooking classes, 1985—. Author (lesson plan books) The Sunshine Series, 1980. Mem. govt. team Leave No Child Behind, Denver, 1993. Mem. Am. Sch. Counselors Assn., Colo. Sch. Counselors Assn. (v.p., treas.), Nat. Assn. Mediation in Edn., Nat. Coun. Self-Esteem, Nat. Honor Soc. for Women. Roman Catholic. Avocations: cooking, reading, writing, walking. Home and Office: 14065 Gleneagle Dr Colorado Springs CO 80921-3219

LOUDEN, WILLARD CHARLES, artist, environmental consultant; b. Trinidad, Colo., Jan. 16, 1925; s. Roy D. and Zita P. (Bradley) L.; m. Virginia M. Hudson, Juen 1964 (div. 1969); 1 child, Tamara; m. Mary Ann Thiel, Jan. 1, 1973. AA, Trinidad (Colo.) State Coll., 1947; BA, U. Mo., 1949; postgrad., Colo. State U., 1973. Rancher Branson, Colo., 1946-86; tchr. Branson High Sch., 1952-57; wildlife cinematographer Branson, 1955-62; vol. Peace Corps, Iran, 1962-64; geology, anthropology, mus. tech. instr. Trinidad State Coll., 1973-76; bldg. renovator Trinidad, 1977—; environ. cons. Branson, 1977—; mus. dir., curator A.R. Mitchell Mus. & Gallery, Trinidad, 1980—; Bd. dirs. Louden-Henritze Archeol. Mus., 1990—. One man shows include Columbian Hotel, Trinidad, Colo., 1960, Colo. Bank and Trust, Delta, Colo., La Rennaisance, Pueblo, Colo., 1993; three person show A.R. Mitchell Mus. and Gallery, Trinidad, 1985; exhibited in group shows at Folsom Art Group, Raton, N.Mex., Trinidad, 1960-67, Trinidad Roundup Shows, 1975-87, Nat. Art Shows, LaJunta, Colo., 1979-90, Wildlife Art Exhbn., Denver, 1983, Artists of the West Show, Colorado Springs, 1988, Santa Fe Trail Days Show, Trinidad, 1989-90; included in permanent collections: Trinidad Nat. Bank, Otero Jr. Coll., LaJunta, Nuzum Nurseries, Boulder, Bob Doak Oil Explorations, Albuquerque. Pres. So. Colo. Heritage Conservancy, Pueblo, 1987—, S.E. Colo. Area Health Edn. Ctr., 1990—, Friends of Purgatory, 1993—; adv. com. Pinon Canyon Manuever Area Land Utilization Tech. Adv. Com., 1984—; chmn. bd. Mid-Town Investment Corp., Trinidad, 1975-87. With U.S. Army, 1943-46. Recipient Outstanding Svc. award, Colo. Nature Conservancy, 1986, Internat. Peace Prize, Beyond War, 1987, Stephen Hart award, Colo. State Hist. Soc., 1988, Outstanding Svc. award, A.R. Mitchell Mus. and Gallery, 1990. Mem. Colo. Archaeol. Soc. (chpt. pres.), Trinidad Art League (pres. 1975-77), Trinidad Hist. Soc. (hon. life mem.). Avocations: photography, backpacking, archaeology, Western history, organic gardening. Home: 83500 County Rd 10 Branson CO 81027-9501 Office: AR Mitchell Mus & Gallery PO Box 95 Trinidad CO 81082-0095

LOUDERMILK, PEGGY JOYCE, pediatrics nurse, public health nurse; b. Mar. 1, 1944; d. Marshall Brown and Esther Rebecca (Gaines) Fisher; m. George E. Loudermilk, Dec. 21, 1968; children: Darrell Wayne, Donna Lynn. ADN, Dabney South Lancaster C.C., 1985. Nursing asst. Alleghany Regional Hosp., Low Moor, Va., 1980-84, nursing extern, 1984-85, staff nurse med./surg., 1985-87, staff nurse ICU, 1987-92; nurse pediatrics Alleghany County/Covington (Va.) Health Dept., 1992—; CPR instr. ARC, Covington, 1984-92. Mem. sch. adv. bd. Alleghany County Sch. System, 1994; local interagy. coun. (State Mandated Orgn.), Clifton Forge, Va., 1993—. Nursing grantee Alleghany Regional Hosp., 1983-85. Fellow Nursing Coun. Alleghany Dist. Republican. Baptist. Avocations: reading, sewing, cross stitch, sports, hiking. Home: 2700 Sugar Maple Dr PO Box 52 Low Moor VA 24457

LOUDON, DONALD HOOVER, lawyer; b. Kansas City, Kans., Nov. 20, 1937; s. Donald Charles and Berenice (Hoover) L.; m. W. Sue Cantrell, Aug. 17, 1958; children: Donald H. Jr., Kurt William. BJ, U. Mo., 1959; LLB, U. Kans., 1962. Bar: Mo. 1962, U.S. Supreme Ct. 1977. Reporter Kansas City Times, 1959; assoc. Blackmar, Swanson & Midgley, Kansas City, Mo., 1962-65; asst. gen. counsel Commerce Bank of Kansas City (Mo.), 1965-68; dir., shareholder Morris, King, Stamper & Bold, Kansas City, Mo., 1968-87, Shughart, Thomson & Kilroy, P.C., Kansas City, Mo., 1987—; sec. Torotel, Inc., Grandview, Mo., 1984—. Elder, Presbyn. Ch. Mem. ABA, Met. Bar Assn. Kansas City, Lawyers Assn. Kansas City, Delta Tau Delta (pres., bd. dirs. Columbia, Mo. chpt.). Office: Shughart Thomson & Kilroy 12 Wyandotte Plz 120 W 12th St Kansas City MO 64105-1902

LOUDON, DOROTHY, actress; b. Boston, Sept. 17, 1933; d. James E. and Dorothy Helen (Shaw) L.; m. Norman Paris, Dec. 18, 1971 (dec.). Student, Syracuse U., 1950-51, Emerson Coll., summers 1950, 51, Alviene Sch. Dramatic Art, 1952, 53, The Am. Acad. Dramatic Art. Appeared in nat. repertory cos. of The Effect of Gamma Rays on Man in the Moon Marigolds, 1970, Plaza Suite, 1971, Luv, 1965, Anything Goes, 1967; appeared in Broadway prodns. Nowhere to Go But Up, 1962 (Theatre World award), Sweet Potato, 1968, Fig Leaves Are Falling, 1969 (Tony nominee), Three Men on a Horse, 1969 (Drama Desk award), The Women, 1973, Annie (Tony award, Drama Desk award, Outer Critics Circle award), 1976 (Dance Educators Am. award), Ballroom, 1979 (Tony nominee), Sweeney Todd, 1980, West Side Waltz, 1981 (Sarah Siddons award), Noises Off, 1983 (Tony nomination), Jerry's Girls, 1985 (Tony nomination), Driving Miss Daisy, 1988, Annie 2, 1990, Comedy Tonight, 1994; appeared in film Garbo Talks, 1984; numerous appearances on TV variety and talk shows; latest TV appearances In Performance at the White House, A Salute to Stephen Sondheim at Carnegie Hall, 1992; star TV show Dorothy, 1979; appeared in supper clubs The Blue Angel, Le Ruban Bleu, Persian Room; rec.: (CDs) Saloon, Broadway Baby. Mem. Actors Equity, Screen Actors Guild, AFTRA. *I have no "thoughts on my life" that do not include my late husband, Norman Paris. He loved the theatre, as do I, and was my reason for being and my constant inspiration to persevere. That perserverance brought me the coveted Tony award for Miss Hannigan in "Annie." My husband lived to share that glorious moment with me. The award is small consolation, indeed-but the letters of love and encouragement from people all over the country is wondrous. It is a tribute to my husband as well as to me. I will devote my life to the justification of the faith he had in me-and to the faith of all those everywhere who love the theatre.*

LOUGANIS, GREG E., former Olympic athlete, actor; b. San Diego, Jan. 29, 1960; s. Peter E. and Frances I. (Scott) L. Student, U. Miami, Fla., 1978-80; B.A. in Drama, U. Calif., Irvine, 1983. Mem. U.S. Nat. Diving Team, 1976—. Author: Breaking The Surface, 1995. Recipient Silver medal Olympic Games, 1976, 2 Olympic Gold medals, 1984, 2 Olympic Gold medals, 1988; James E. Sullivan award, Olympic Games, 1984; inducted into Olympic Hall of Fame, 1985; winner 48 U.S. nat. diving titles; World Diving Champion (platform and springboard) 1986, Jesse Owens award, 1987, Pan Am Gold medal, 1979, 83, 87; Gold medalist (platform and springboard) Seoul Olympics, 1988. Home: PO Box 4130 Malibu CA 90264-4130*

LOUGH, RICK LEO, sales and marketing professional; b. Belleville, Ont., Can., Sept. 15, 1948; came to U.S., 1990; s. Leslie Robert and Jessie Pearl (Logue) L. BA, U. Western Ont., London, Can., 1971; BS with honors, U. Guelph, Ont., 1972, DVM, 1976. Toxicologist Bio Rsch. Labs. Ltd., Montreal, Que., Can., 1976-78, head gen. toxicology, 1978-81, head gen. toxicology and animal health, 1981-83, assoc. dir. toxicology, 1983-84, dir. mktg., 1984-87, sr. dir. pacific rim bus. Devel., 1987-90; v.p. internat. sales and mktg. Internat. Rsch. and Devel. Corp., Mattawan, Mich., 1991-95; cons. environ. toxicology specialist Calif. State Pub. Health, L.A., 1984-87; cons. in regulatory toxicology Consultra Internat. Ltd., Tokyo, 1990-91. Hastings County Vet. scholarship Ont. Vet. Assn., 1972. Mem. Soc. of Toxicology of Can., European Soc. of Toxicology, Occupational Hygiene Assn. of Ont. (pub. rels. com. 1985-87), Am. Mgmt. Assn., Ont. Vet. Assn. Avocations: photography, philately, languages. Home: 631 Carrington Ct Kalamazoo MI 49009-2463 Office: Internat Rsch & Devel 500 N Main Mattawan MI 49071

LOUGHEED, PETER, lawyer, former Canadian official; b. Calgary, Alta., Can., July 26, 1928; s. Edgar Donald and Edna (Bauld) L.; m. Jeanne Estelle Rogers, June 21, 1952; children—Stephen, Andrea, Pamela, Joseph. B.A., U. Alta., 1950, LL.B., 1952; M.B.A., Harvard U., 1954. Bar: Alta 1955. With firm Fenerty, Fenerty, McGillivray & Robertson, Calgary, 1955-56; sec. Mannix Co., Ltd., 1956-58, gen. counsel, 1958-62, v.p., 1959-62, dir., 1960-62; individual practice law, from 1962; formerly mem. Alta. Legislature for Calgary West; formerly leader Progressive Conservative Party of Alta., 1965-85; premier of Alta., 1971-85; ptnr. Bennett Jones Verchere, Calgary,

1986—. Office: Bennett Jones Verchere, 4500 Bankers Hall E 855 2d St SW, Calgary, AB Canada T2P 4K7

LOUGHLIN, KEVIN RAYMOND, urological surgeon, researcher; b. N.Y.C., Aug. 10, 1949; s. Raymond Gerard and Josephine (McGrath) L. AB, Princeton U., 1971; MD, N.Y. Med. Coll., 1975. Diplomate Nat. Bd. Med. Examiners, Am. Bd. Urology. Surgery instr. Harvard Med. Sch. Brigham & Women's Hosp., Boston, 1983-86, asst. prof. surgery Harvard Med. Sch., 1986-90, dir. urologic rsch., 1987—, assoc. prof. surgery Harvard Med. Sch., 1991—; staff urologist Dana Farber Cancer Inst., Boston, 1991—; dir. urologic rsch. Brigham and Women's Hosp., Boston, 1987—. Contbr. over 90 articles to profl. jours. Fellow Am. Cancer Soc., 1982-83, Nat. Kidney Found., 1980-81. Fellow ACS; mem. AAAS, Am. Soc. Andrology, Am. Soc. Clin. Oncology, Am. Urologic Assn., Boston Surg. Soc., Soc. for Basic Urologic Rsch. Achievements include patent in laparoscopic surg. instruments, and other surg. instruments. Home: 30 Lime St Boston MA 02108-1103 Office: Brigham & Womens Hosp 75 Francis St Boston MA 02115-6110

LOUGHLIN, WILLIAM JOSEPH, priest, religious organization administrator; b. Wharton, N.J., Mar. 3, 1927; s. William Joseph and Theresa Catherine (May) L. AB, Seton Hall U., 1954, AM, 1957; MDiv, Pope John XXIII Sem., Weston, Mass., 1969; postgrad., Rutgers U., 1959. Ordained priest Roman Cath. Ch., 1969. Deacon St. Mary's Ch., Greenwich, Conn., summer 1968, parochial vicar, 1980-82, 90-92; parochial vicar St. Rose Ch., Newtown, Conn., 1969-70, Assumption Ch., Westport, Conn., 1970-73; defender of the bond Diocesan Marriage Tribunal, Bridgeport, Conn., 1973-82; parochial vicar St. Philip Ch., Norwalk, Conn., 1973-78, St. Augustine Cathedral, Bridgeport, Conn., 1978-80; pastor St. Joseph Ch., Shelton, Conn., 1982-90; dir. pilgrimages Diocese of Bridgeport, 1982—; parochial vicar St. Luke Ch., Westport, 1992-95, St. Thomas Aquinas Ch., Fairfield, Conn., 1995—; chaplain to His Holiness Pope John Paul II, Rome, 1988—. Mem. Am. Pers. and Guidance Assn. (evaluation com. Cath. counselors Phila. 1960, Denver 1961), Nat. Vocat. Guidance Assn., KC (Lafayette coun. Dover, N.J. 1947—, Walter J. Barrett Gen. Assembly 1950—). Avocations: collecting Hummel figurines, travel. Home: 16 Walnut St Wharton NJ 07885-2516

LOUGHNANE, LEE DAVID, trumpeter; b. Chgo., Oct. 21, 1946; s. Philip Louis and Juanita (Wall) L. Student, DePaul U., Chgo., 1964-66, Chgo. Conservatory Music, 1966-67. Mem. musical group The Big Thing, 1967, Chicago, 1967—; v.p. Chgo. Music, Inc. Rec. artist: Columbia Records. Named Entertainer of Yr., People's Choice Awards, 1974, Best Instrumental Band, Playboy mag., 1971-75; recipient 3 Grammy awards, 1977. Mem. AFTRA, Nat. Acad. Recording Arts and Scis., Screen Actors Guild, Psi Mu Alpha Sinfonia. Address: care Howard Rose Agy 8900 Wilshire Blvd # 320 Beverly Hills CA 90211-1906

LOUGHRAN, JAMES NEWMAN, philosophy educator, college president; b. Bklyn., Mar. 22, 1940; s. John Farley and Ethel Margaret (Newman) L. A.B., Fordham U., 1964, M.A., 1965, Ph.D. in Philosophy, 1975; Ph.D. (hon.), Loyola Coll., Balt., 1985. Joined S.J., 1958; ordained priest Roman Catholic Ch., 1970. Instr. philosophy St. Peter's Coll., Jersey City, 1965-67; asst. dean Fordham U., Bronx, N.Y., 1970-73; tchr. philosophy Fordham U., Bronx, 1974-79, 82-84, dean, 1979-82; pres. Loyola Marymount U., L.A., 1984-91; acting pres. Bklyn. Coll., 1992; Miller Prof. Philosophy John Carroll U., Cleve., 1992-93; interim pres. Mount St. Mary's Coll., Emmitsburg, Md., 1993-94; interim acad. v.p.. Fordham U., Bronx, N.Y., 1994-95; pres. St. Peter's Coll., 1995—. Contbr. numerous articles and revs. to popular and scholarly jours. Trustee St. Peter's Coll., Jersey City, 1972-78, 94—, Xavier U., Cin., 1981-84, Canisius Coll., Buffalo, 1994—. Mem. Am. Philos. Assn. Avocation: tennis.

LOUGHRIN, JAY RICHARDSON, mass communications educator, consultant; b. Mankato, Minn., Oct. 21, 1943; s. J. Richardson and Jane Aileen (Smith) L.; m. Helen Marie Struyk, Aug. 8, 1964 (div. Sept. 1985); children: Jennifer, Amy; m. Yolanda Christina Ramos, July 17, 1986; children: Tawny, Heather. BA in Drama, Calif. State U., Los Angeles, 1968; postgrad., San Diego State U., 1968-69, UCLA, 1970-71, U. Redlands, Calif., 1983-84, Fla. State U., 1990; MA, Whittier (Calif.) Coll., 1992. Prodn. asst. Andrews-Yagemann Prodns., Hollywood, Calif., 1961-63; with merchandising, sales Sta. KTTV-TV, Hollywood, 1963-64; assoc. producer Born Losers Am. Internat. Pictures, Hollywood, 1964; assoc. producer V.P.I. Prodns., Hollywood, 1964, Ralph Andrews Prodns., North Hollywood, Calif., 1965; producer Stein Erikson Ski Films, North Hollywood, 1965, F.K. Rocket Films, North Hollywood, 1966-68; dir. promotion and publicity Sta. KCST-TV, San Diego, 1968-69; prof. mass communication Rio Hondo Coll., Whittier, 1969—; sales mgr. Warren Miller Films, Hermosa Beach, Calif., 1984-85, cons., 1985-86; exec. producer Echo Prodns., Hollywood, 1985-87; cons. Radio Concepts, Los Angeles, 1978-80, Tom Cole Prodns., Los Angeles, 1985-87, Chuck Richards Whitewater, Lake Isabella, Calif., 1984-86; media relations cons. Police Officers Standards and Training, Sacramento, 1986—; venue mgr. Los Angeles Olympic Organizing Com., Long Beach, Calif., 1984. Contbr. articles to Review Publs., Orange Coast mag., Jet Am. mag., Ted Randall Report. Pres. Rue Le Charlene Homeowners Assn., Palos Verdes, Calif., 1984, Hilltop Homeowners Assn., Walnut, Calif., 1989-90; v.p. West Walnut Homeowners Assn., 1988-89. Recipient Pub. Service Programming award Advt. Council, N.Y.C., 1982; named Adviser of Yr., U. So. Calif.'s 50th Annual Journalism Awards, Los Angeles, 1985. Mem. Acad. TV Arts and Scis., Rio Hondo Coll. Faculty Assn. (pres. 1978), So. Calif. Broadcasters Assn. (Pub. Service award 1978). Republican. Avocations: sailing, skiing, whitewater rafting, motorcycling, bicycling. Office: Rio Hondo Coll 3600 Workman Mill Rd Whittier CA 90601-1616

LOUI, ALEXANDER CHAN PONG, electrical engineer; b. San Fernando, Trinidad and Tobago, Feb. 20, 1961; came to U.S., 1990; s. John Sue-Tang and Mary Loui; m. Jessie S.B. Chong, May 25, 1991. BSc in Elec. Engring., U. Toronto, 1983, MSc in Elec. Engring., 1986, PhD in Elec. Engring., 1990. Rsch. asst. Atomic Energy of Can. Ltd., Chalk River, Ont., 1982; teaching asst. dept. elec. engring. U. Toronto, Ont., 1983-89; rsch. assoc. signal processing lab. U. Toronto, 1985-90; mem. tech. staff applied rsch. Bellcore, Red Bank, N.J., 1990-94, rsch. scientist, 1995—; rsch. scientist Applied Rsch., Bellcore, Red Bank, N.J., 1995—. Contbr. articles to profl. jours. Founding mem., past pres. Jarvis Multicultural Soc., Toronto, 1988-90. Wallbery Undergrad scholar, 1981-82, NSERC postgrad. scholar, 1983-87. Mem. IEEE (mem. tech. com. Internat. Conf. on Image Processing 1994—), Soc. Motion Picture and TV Engrs. Baptist. Avocations: table tennis, skating, reading, hi-fi systems. Office: Bellcore 331 Newman Springs Rd Red Bank NJ 07701-5657

LOUI, PATRICIA M. L., marketing company executive; b. Honolulu, Sept. 17, 1949; d. Frederick H.M. and Alyce Masako (Karashimo) L.; m. Michael L. Schmicker, July 5, 1975; 1 child, Christopher. BS in Journalism, Northwestern U., 1971; MS in Asian Studies, U. Hawaii, 1974. Freelance journalist CBS News, N.Y.C., 1971-72; communications cons. UNESCO, Taiwan and Malaysia, 1973; regional communications cons. U.N. Devel. Program, Bangkok, Thailand, 1974-76; v.p. Honolulu Pub. Co., Ltd., Honolulu, 1977-79; v.p. mktg. Bank of Hawaii, Honolulu, 1979-84; pres., owner OmniTrak Group, Inc., Honolulu, 1984—; dir., ptnr. Acorn-Omni-Trak Mktg. Cons. Inc., Honolulu, 1989—; chmn., majority owner PacMar, Inc., Honolulu, 1987—; chmn., owner OmniTrak Internat., Calif., 1991, OmniTrak Mktg. Corp. Asia, Hong Kong, 1993, OmniTrak-Taiwan, 1994; bd. dirs. Pacific Marine and Supply Co. Ltd., Honolulu, INRAsia Pacific Ltd., Hong Kong, Acorn-OmniTrak, Bangkok. Pres. East West Ctr. Assn., Asia, 1984-89; bd. dirs. Oahu Pvt. Industry Coun., Honolulu, 1990-93, Pacific Asian Affairs Coun., Honolulu, 1990—; co-chmn. Gov.'s Internat. Congress, Honolulu, 1988-89. Recipient East-West Ctr. Two-Year fellowship U.S State Dept., 1973-74; Writing award Hawaii Med. Assn., 1970. Mem. Japan-Am. Soc., Com. on Fgn. Affairs, Hawaii C. of C. (dir., exec. com.). Office: Omnitrak Rsch & Mktg Group 220 S King St Ste 975 Honolulu HI 96813-4539

LOUIS, BARBRA SCHANTZ, dean; b. Dover, N.J., Nov. 26, 1940; d. Henry Albert and Priscilla Ruth (Schantz) L.; m. Roger Donald Coss, Sept. 1957 (div. 1973); children: Candee Lee Coss Spizzirri, Lynn Ellen Coss Brandimarte, Amber Mary Coss Gillespie. AA, County Coll. of Morris, Dover, N.J., 1971; BA, Montclair State Coll., 1973, MA, 1973; DEd, Rutgers U., 1985. Cert. secondary tchr. Counselor, adminstr. Bergen Community Coll., Paramus, N.J., 1974-77; exec. asst. to exec. dir. Bergen County Community Action Program, Hackensack, N.J., 1977-80; cons. Nat. Multiple Sclerosis Soc., Teaneck, N.J., 1984-85; dir. devel. Passaic County Community Coll., Paterson, N.J., 1985-90; dean for Continuing Edn. Santa Barbara (Calif.) City Coll., 1990—. Bd. dirs. Edwin Gould Svcs. for Children, N.Y.C., 1980-90, Planned Parenthood of Passaic County, Paterson, N.J., 1989-90, Santa Barbara, Ventura Counties, Calif.; bd. mem. Passaic County Cultural and Heritage Coun., Paterson, 1987-90, Found. for Santa Barbara City Coll., 1992—. Mem. The Hamilton Club (bd. govs. 1988-90). Democrat. Unitarian. Avocations: travel, antique collecting. Home: 126 San Clemente St Santa Barbara CA 93109-2130 Office: Santa Barbara City Coll Wake Ctr Continuing Edn Divsn 300 N Turnpike Rd Santa Barbara CA 93111-1931

LOUIS, LESTER See BROWN, LES

LOUIS, MURRAY, dancer, choreographer, dance teacher; b. N.Y.C., Nov. 4, 1926; s. Aaron and Rose (Mintzer) Fuchs. B.S., N.Y. U., 1951. Principal dancer Nikolais Dance Theatre, 1950-59; assoc. dir. dance div., Henry St. Playhouse, N.Y.C., 1953-70; artistic dir. Nikolais/Louis Found. Dance, N.Y.C., 1970—, Murray Louis Dance Co., 1953—; co-dir. Choreoarts, 1973—; choreographer numerous works, 1953—, including Porcelain Dialogues, 1974, Moments, 1975, Catalogue, 1975, Cleopatra, 1976, Ceremony, 1976, Deja Vu, 1976, Glances, 1976, Schubert, 1977, The Canarsie Venus, 1978, Figura, 1978, A Suite for Erik, 1979, Afternoon, 1979, The City, 1980, November Dances, 1980, Aperitif, 1982, A Stravinsky Montage, 1982, Repertoire, 1982, The After Boat, 1983, Frail Demons, 1984, Four Brubeck Pieces (with Dave Brubeck Quartet), 1984, Pug's Land, 1984, The Station, 1985, Revels, 1986, The Disenchantment of Pierrot, 1986, Black and White, 1987, Return to Go, 1987, Horizons, 1994, Alone, 1994; choreographer: By George (music by George Gershwin for Cleve. Ballet), 1987, Act I (with Dave Brubeck Quartet), 1987, Bach II, 1987, Asides, 1987; TV projects include Repertoire Workshop, CBS, N.Y.C., 1965, Proximities, Calligraph for Matyrs, ZDF-TV, Munich, 1974, Soundstage (with Dave Brubeck) PBS, Chgo., 1977, Studio Two, Polish Nat. TV, Warsaw, 1978, Murray Louis Dance Co., TeleFrance 1, Paris, 1982, video AT&T (with Dave Brubeck Quartet), 1988; 5 part film series Dance as an Art Form, 1974; choreographer for 23d, 27th Annual City Am. Fashion Critics awards; author: Inside Dance, Letters to Nik from India; Nik and Murray (film by Christian Blackwood), 1986, Murray Louis on Dance, 1992. Chmn. U.S. chpt. Conseil Internat. de la Danse (UNESCO). Served with USNR, 1945-46. Guggenheim fellow, 1969, 73; grantee Rockefeller Found., 1974; Nat. Endowment Arts, 1968, 70, 72, 74-78, Mellon Found., 1976; recipient Critics award Internat. Festival Weisbaden, Ger., 1972, Dance Mag. award, 1977, Grand Medaille de la Ville de Paris, 1979; decorated knight Order of Arts and Letters, France, 1984. Mem. Am. Guild Mus. Artists, Assn. Am. Dance Cos., Asso. Council Arts, Dance Notation Bur. Jewish. Office: Nikolais/Louis Found 375 W Broadway New York NY 10012-4324 *I think, to discover the intuitive force within oneself, and then know how to utilize and trust its judgment, is essential for the creative artist. My aesthetics were achieved by this intuitive judgment.*

LOUIS, PAUL ADOLPH, lawyer; b. Key West, Fla., Oct. 22, 1922; s. Louis and Rose Leah (Weinstein) L.; m. Nancy Ann Lapof, Dec. 28, 1971; children: Louis Benson, IV, Connor Cristina and Marshall Dore (twins). B.A., Va. Mil. Inst., Lexington, 1947; LL.B., U. Miami, Fla., 1950, J.D., 1967. Bar: Fla. 1950, U.S. Dist. Ct. (so. dist.) Fla. Asst. state atty., 1955-57; atty. Beverage Dept. Fla., 1957-60; spl. asst. atty. gen. State of Fla., 1970-71; partner firm Sinclair, Louis, Heath, Nussbaum & Zavertnik (P.A.), Miami, 1960—; mem. Fed. Jud. Nominating Commn., 1977-80; mem. peer rev. com. U.S. Dist. Ct. for So. Dist. Fla., 1983-85. Author: Defamation, How Far Can You Go, Trial and Tort Trends, 1969; contbr.: chpts. to Fla. Family Law, 1967, 72. Founder mem. Palm Springs Gen. Hosp. Scholarship Com., 1968; mem. Dade County Health Facilities Authority, 1979—; trustee Fla. Supreme Ct. Hist. Soc., 1994—. Served to maj. USAAF, 1943-45, ETO. Decorated Air medal with five oak leaf clusters, Bronze Star (7), Purple Heart. Mem. ABA, Fla. Bar (bd. cert. civil trial lawyer and marital and family law, bd. govs. 1970-74), Dade County Bar Assn. (dir. 1954-55, 66-69), Assn. Trial Lawyers Am., Am. Judicature Soc., Va. Mil. Inst. Alumni Assn. Democrat. Jewish. Club: Miami, Bath. Home: 4411 Palm Ln Miami FL 33137-3346 Office: 1125 A I duPont Bldg 169 E Flagler St Miami FL 33131

LOUIS, WILLIAM ROGER, historian, educator, editor; b. Detroit, May 8, 1936; s. Henry Edward and Bena May (Flood) L.; m. Dagmar Cecilia Friedrich; children: Antony Andrew, Catherine Ann. B.A., U. Okla., 1959; M.A., Harvard U., 1960; D.Phil., Oxford U., 1962, D.Litt., 1979. Asst., then assoc. prof. history Yale U., 1962-70; prof. history, curator hist. collections Humanities Research Center U. Tex., Austin, 1970-85; dir. British Studies, 1975—; Kerr chair English history and culture U. Tex., Austin, 1985—; supernumerary fellow St. Antony's Coll., U. Oxford, Eng., 1986-96, hon. fellow, 1996—; corr. fellow Brit. Acad., 1993—; Chichele lectr. All Souls Coll., U. Oxford, Eng., 1990; Disting. lectr. London Sch. Econs., 1992; Cust lectr. Nottingham (Eng.) U., 1995; Brit. Acad. Elie Kedorie Meml. lectr., 1996; dir. summer seminars NEH, 1985, 88, 90, 91, 96. Author: Ruanda-Urundi, 1963, Germany's Lost Colonies, 1967, (with Jean Stengers)The Congo Reform Movement, 1968, British Strategy in the Far East, 1919-1939, 1971, Imperialism at Bay, 1977 (History Book Club), British Empire in the Middle East, 1984 (George Louis Beer prize Am. Hist. Assn. and Tex. Inst. Letters award), In The Name of the God Go! Leo Amery and the British Empire in the Age of Churchill, 1992; editor British Documents on the End of Empire, 1988—; editor-in-chief Oxford History of the British Empire, 1993—; editor: (with P. Gifford) Britain and Germany in Africa, 1967, France and Britain in Africa, 1971, The Origins of the Second World War: A.J.P. Taylor and his Critics, 1972, National Security and International Trusteeship in the Pacific, 1972, Imperialism: The Robinson and Gallagher Controversy, 1976, (with William S. Livingston) Australia, New Zealand and the Pacific Islands since the First World War, 1979, (with P. Gifford) The Transfer of Power in Africa, 1982, (with R. Stookey) End of the Palestine Mandate, 1986, (with H. Bull) The Special Relationship: Anglo-American Relations Since 1945, 1986, (with P. Gifford) Decolonization and African Independence, 1988, (with James Bill) Musaddiq, Iranian Nationalism, and Oil, 1988, (with Roger Owen) Suez 1956: The Crisis and Its Consequences, 1989, (with Robert A. Fernea) The Iraqi Revolution of 1958, 1991, (with Robert Blake) Churchill, 1993, Adventures with Britannia, 1995. Marshall scholar; Woodrow Wilson fellow, NEH fellow, Am. Inst. Indian Studies fellow, Guggenheim fellow, vis. fellow All Souls Coll., U. Oxford, overseas fellow Churchill Coll., U. Cambridge, Eng., fellow Woodrow Wilson Internat. Ctr.; guest scholar Brookings Instn. Fellow Royal Hist. Soc.; mem. Am. Hist. Assn. (life), Coun. on Fgn. Rels. (N.Y.C.), Tex. Inst. Letters, Reform Club (London), Century (N.Y.C.), Met. Club (Washington). Democrat. Office: U Texas Dept History Austin TX 78712

LOUIS-COTTON D'ENGLESQUEVILLE, FRANCOIS PIERRE, automobile company executive; b. Neuilly Seine, France, Sept. 4, 1929; came to U.S., 1955; s. Georges Auguste and Paule Marie Cotton (d'Englesqueville) L.; m. Martine Combaluzier, Apr. 30, 1965 (div.); 1 child, Veronique; m. Mary Elizabeth Thames, June 14, 1986; children: George, Timothy, Jennifer, Mary Beth. BEE, Ecole Brequet, Paris, 1952. Engr. Demarais Freres, Paris, 1954-55, Cadillac Motor Cars div. GM, Detroit, 1955-58; nat. svc. mgr. Peugeot, S.A., N.Y.C., 1958-60; engr. Michelin Tire Group, Woodside, N.Y., 1960-61, Port Authority N.Y. and N.J., N.Y.C., 1962-68; dir. Renault USA, Inc., Washington, 1968-94; cons. Garden City, N.Y., 1994—. Mem. Conseiller du Commerce Exterieur de la France, Soc. Automotive Engrs., Assn. Internat. Automobile Mfrs. (bd. dirs. 1974-94), Cercle Militaire Paris, Army and Navy Club (Washington), Cherry Valley Club (Garden City). Avocations: photography, travel, cooking. Office: 101 3d St Garden City NY 11530

LOUIS-DREYFUS, JULIA, actress. TV appearances include Saturday Night Live, 1982-85, Day by Day, 1986-89, Seinfield, 1990— (Emmy nomination Supporting Actress-Comedy, 1993, 94); films include Soul Man, 1986, Troll, 1986, Hannah and Her Sisters, 1986, National Lampoon's Christmas Vacation, 1989, Jack the Bear, 1993, North, 1994. Emmy nominations 1992, 93, 94, 95. Office: TPEG Mgmt 9150 Wilshire Blvd Ste 205 Beverly Hills CA 90212-3429

LOUNSBERRY, ROBERT HORACE, former state government administrator; b. Carlisle, Iowa, June 22, 1918; s. Horace Charles and Alice Mae (Elmore) L.; m. Muriel Dirks, Aug. 2, 1942; children: William, Beth, Janet, Paul, Steven. BA, Luther Coll., 1940; postgrad., U. Iowa, 1940-42. Farmer McCallsburg, Iowa, 1946-69; dep. sec. agr. Iowa Dept. Agr., Des Moines, 1969-72, sec. agr., 1973-87. Chmn. Story County Bd. Edn., 1950-69; bd. dirs. Iowa Assn. Sch. Bds., 1961-68, Des Moines Area Community Coll., 1964-70; clk. Richland Twp., 1952-64; chmn. Story County Rep. Party, 1964-68, chmn. 5th Rep. Dist., 1968-70; dir Am. Legion Boys State, 1957-88; active Iowa Arboretum, Iowans Right to Work Com.; active Gov's. Conf. for Aging; elected to Older Iowa Legislature (spkr. of house 1989); nat. dir. Comm. for Agriculture (sr. citizens adv. com.); active Iowa Aging Coalition, Retired Sr. Vol. Program. With USAAF, 1942-45. Decorated D.F.C., Air medal with 4 oak leaf clusters. Mem. Nat. Assn. Depts. Agr., Am. Assn. Retired Persons, Midwest Assn. State Depts. Agr., Mid-Am. Internat. Agri-Trade Coun., Greater Des Moines C. of C., Davis County Sheeps Producers, Iowa Cattlemen's Assn., Story County Cattlemen's Assn., Res. Officers Assn., Am. Legion (mem. nat. exec. com. 1965-70, state comdr. 1953-54), Lions, Masons, Shriners. Home: RR Mc Callsburg IA 50154

LOUNSBURY, JOHN FREDERICK, geographer, educator; b. Perham, Minn., Oct. 26, 1918; s. Charles Edwin and Maude (Knight) L.; m. Dorothea Frances Eggers, Oct. 3, 1943; children—John Frederick, Craig Lawrence, James Gordon. B.S., U. Ill., 1942, M.S., 1946; Ph.D., Northwestern U., 1951. Asst. dir. rural land classification program Insular Govt., P.R., 1949-52; cons., research analyst Dayton Met. Studies, Inc., Ohio, 1957-60; chmn. dept. earth scis., prof. geography Antioch Coll., 1951-61; prof. geography, head dept. geography and geology Eastern Mich. U., 1961-69; chmn. dept. geography Ariz. State U., 1969-77; dir. Ctr. for Environ. Studies, 1977-80; prof. emeritus Ariz. State U., 1987—; project dir. Geography in Liberal Edn. Project, Assn. Am. Geographers, NSF, 1963-65, project dir. commn. on coll. geography, 1965-74; dir. environment based edn. project US. Office Edn., 1974-75; dir. spatial analysis of land use project NSF, 1975-85. Author articles, workbooks, textbooks. Mem. Yellow Springs Planning Commn., Ohio, dir. research, 1957-60; mem. Ypsilanti Planning Commn., 1961-66; research com. Washtenaw County Planning Commn., 1961-69; mem. cons. Ypsilanti Indsl. Devel. Corp., 1961-63. Served with AUS, 1942-46, ETO. Named Man of Yr., Yellow Springs C. of C., 1956-57. Fellow Ariz.-Nev. Acad. Sci.; mem. Assn. Am. Geographers (chmn. East Lakes div. 1959-61, mem. nat. exec. council 1961-64, chmn. liberal edn. com. 1961-65), Nat. Council Geog. Edn. (chmn. earth sci. com. 1961-68, regional coord. 1961-63, mem. exec. bd. 1968-71, 77-83, v.p. 1977-78, pres. 1979-80, Disting. Svc. award 1988, Disting. Mentor award 1990), Mich. Acad. Sci. Arts and Letters (chmn. pub. relations com. 1964-69, past chmn. geography sect.), Ohio Acad. Sci. (past exec. v.p.), Mich. Acad. Sci., Ariz. Acad. Sci., Am. Geog. Soc., AAAS, Sigma Xi, Delta Kappa Epsilon, Gamma Theta Upsilon. Home: 7850 E Vista Dr Scottsdale AZ 85250-7641 Office: Ariz State U Dept Geography Tempe AZ 85281

LOURENCO, RUY VALENTIM, physician, educator; b. Lisbon, Portugal, Mar. 25, 1929; came to U.S., 1959, naturalized, 1966; s. Raul Valentim and Maria Amalia (Gomes-Rosa) L.; children: Peter Edward, Margaret Philippa. M.D., U. Lisbon, 1951. Intern Lisbon City Hosps., 1951-53, resident internal medicine, 1953-55; instr. U. Lisbon, 1955-59; fellow dept. medicine Columbia U.-Presbyn. Med. Ctr., N.Y.C., 1959-63; asst. prof. medicine N.J. Coll. Medicine, 1963-66, assoc. prof., 1966-67; practice medicine specializing in pulmonary medicine, 1967—; assoc. prof. medicine and physiology U. Ill. Coll. Medicine, Chgo., 1967-69, prof., 1969-89, Foley prof. medicine, 1978-89, chmn. dept. medicine, 1977-89, exec. head dept. medicine, 1983-89; dir. respiratory rsch. lab. Hektoen Inst., Chgo., 1967-71; dir. pulmonary medicine Cook County Hosp., Chgo., 1969-70; attending physician U. Ill. Med. Ctr., Chgo., 1967-89; dir. pulmonary sect. and labs U. Ill. Med. Ctr., 1970-77, physician-in-chief, 1977-89, pres. med. staff, 1980-81; prof. medicine and physiology, dean N.J. Med. Sch. U. Medicine and Dentistry N.J., Newark, 1989—; cons. task force on rsch. in respiratory diseases NIH, 1972, mem. pathology study sect., 1972-76; mem. rev. bd. Spl. Ctrs. of Rsch. program, 1974; cons. career devel. program VA, 1972-90; mem. nat. com. Rev. Sci. Basis of Respiratory Therapy, 1973-74; pres. exec. com. U. Hosp., Neark, 1989—; mem. bd. govs. Hackensack U. Hosp., 1993—; mem. step II USMLE and fin. com. Nat. Bd. Med. Examiners, 1994—; mem. bd. trustees Bergen Pines County Hosp., 1994—. Editorial bd. Jour. Lab. and Clin. Medicine, 1973-77, 84-91, Am. Rev. Respiratory Diseases, 1985-91; contbr. numerous articles on pulmonary diseases, respiratory physiology and biochemistry to med. jours. Fellow AAAS, Am. Coll. Chest Physicians, ACP (pres. Ill. chpt. 1974-75, vice chmn. com. on environ. health 1981-82, gov. 1988-90, 93-95); mem. Assn. Am. Med. Colls. (coun. of deans 1989—, exec. com. project 3000 by 2000), Am. Fedn. Clin. Rsch., Am. Heart Assn., Am. Physiol. Soc., Am. Soc. Clin. Investigation, Am. Thoracic Soc. (chmn. sci. assembly 1974-75, bd. dirs. 1987-90, chmn. com. on internat. rels. 1989-91), Am. Soc. Internal Medicine, Chgo. Soc. Internal Medicine (pres. 1988-89), Am. Lung Assn. (com. smoking and health 181-84), Internat. Acad. Chest Physicians and Surgeons (chmn. nominating com. 1984-90), Chgo. Lung Assn. (bd. dirs. and mem. exec. com. 1974-82), Assn. Profs. Medicine, Soc. Exptl. Biology and Medicine, Sigma Xi, Alpha Omega Alpha, Phi Kappa Phi.

LOURIE, ALAN DAVID, federal judge; b. Boston, Mass., Jan. 13, 1935. AB, Harvard U., 1956; MS, U. Wis., 1958; PhD, U. Pa., 1965; JD, Temple U., 1970. Bar: Pa. 1970. Chemist Monsanto Co., St. Louis, 1957-59; lit. scientist, chemist, patent agt. Wyeth Labs., Radnor, Pa., 1959-64; counsel Smith Kline Beechum Corp., Phila., 1964-90, successively as patent agt., atty., dir. corp. patents, asst. gen. counsel, v.p. corp. patents; cir. judge U.S. Ct. Appeals (fed. cir.), Washington, 1990—; mem. Judicial Conf. Com. on Financial Disclosure, 1990—; mem. U.S. del. to Diplomatic Conf. on Revision of Paris Conv. for Protection of Indsl. Property, 1982, 84; vice chmn. industry functional adv. com. to U.S. Trade Rep. and Dept. Commerce, 1987-90; chmn. U.S. group of U.S.-Japan Bus. Coun. Task Force on Patents. Mem. ABA, Phila. Patent Law Assn. (pres. 1984-85), Am. Intellectual Property Law Assn. (bd. dirs. 1982-85), Assn. Corp. Patent Counsel (treas. 1987-89), Pharm. Mfrs. Assn. (chmn. patent com. 1981-86), Am. Chem. Soc., Cosmos Club, Harvard Club Washington. Office: US Ct Appeals Fed Cir 717 Madison Pl NW Washington DC 20439-0001

LOURIE, NORMAN VICTOR, government official, social worker; b. N.Y.C., Feb. 1, 1912; s. Inte and Elsie (Horowitz) L.; m. Betty Pokrassa, Dec. 31, 1945 (dec. 1975); children: Richard, Iven, Mary Ann, Susan, Sara; m. Dorothy Maxey, Sept. 1, 1991; stepchildren: Lynn Zimmerman, Karen Biondi, Matthew Maxey, Margaret Calnon. Student, Cornell U., 1932-35; BS, NYU, 1936; diploma, N.Y. Sch. Social Work; MSW, Columbia U., 1938; DHL, Adelphi U., 1976. Rsch. assoc. Russell Sage Foundation. Greater N.Y. Fund, N.Y.C. Health and Welfare Coun., 1937-39; asst. dir. Bronx House Settlement, N.Y.C., 1939- 41; dir. Madison Settlement House, 1941-43, Hawthorne Cedar Knoll Sch., 1946-51; DHL, PhD Adelphi Coll. Grad. Sch. Social Work, 1948-51; dir. Assn. Jewish Children, Phila., 1951-55; exec. dep. sec., and sec. Pa. Dept. Pub. Welfare, 1955-80; policy adv. Inst. Econ. Devel., Washington, 1979-82; cons. Pa. Dept. Public Welfare, 1980-81; vis. prof. U. Pa. Sch. Social Work; prof. Norman Lourie Archives, U. Pa. Van Pelt and Grad. Sch. Social Work Libraries, 1975, Philippine Women's U., 1982; sr. policy advisor Nat. Immigration, Refugee and Citizenship Forum, 1982-90; sr. policy advisor Schirm Assocs.-Head Injury, 1987-93; chmn. Nat. Task Force on Definition of Developmental Disabilities, 1977; mem. Vietnamese Children's Resettlement Adv. Com., 1976; chmn. Nat. Coalition for Refugee Resettlement, 1978-82; cons. NIMH, Office Econ. Opportunity, Nat. Commn. on Marijuana and Drug Abuse, Social Rehab. Service, Health and Human Services; speaker White House Conf. on Children and Youth, 1950, 60, 70, White House Conf. on Aging, 1960; welfare cons. Fels Inst., Wharton Sch., U. Pa., 1953-55; mem. bd. Joint Commn. Mental Health of Children, 1965-67, chmn. com. on studies, exec. com., 1965-67; adv. council Pres.'s Com. on Juvenile Delinquency and Youth; chmn. bd. trustees Community Mental Health and Family Services, Refugee Camps, Southeast Asia, 1982-84, emeritus, 1984-94; instr. part-time Grad. Sch. U. Pa., Pitts., Columbia U. Author books in field; chmn. editorial bd.: Jour. Jewish Communal Service, 1952-58, Child Welfare, 1962-64; editorial bd.: Social Casework, 1969-72, Jour. Social Work Edn, 1970-72, Jour. Adminstrn. and Social Work; contbr. to encys., jours. Bd. dirs. Am. Child Guidance Found.,

Indochinese Community Ctr., Washington, 1986-94, Inst. Child Mental Health, Nat. Accreditation Council for Blind; adv. com. Bryn. Mawr Sch. Social Work.; bd. dirs. Alan Gutmacher Inst., 1976-80, Soc. for Study Traumatic Stress Studies, 1985-87, Indochinese Cultural Ctr., Washington, 1985-89; mem. adv. bd. Indochinese Refugee Action Ctr., 1985-94; life sr. advisor Tri-County Planned Parenthood, Harrisburg, Pa., 1988-94; bd. dirs. Sr. Citizen's Ctr., Harrisburg, 1988-94. 1st lt., inf., Med. Service Corps, AUS, 1943-46; acting chief psychiat. social worker USAR, Pentagon, 1946-51. Recipient Man of Yr. award Am. Soc. Pub. Adminstrn., 1963, Heritage and Social Svcs. award Gov. of Pa., 1991. Fellow Am. Orthopsychiat. Assn. (chmn. legis. com. 1956-60, pres. 1966-67, Ortho Lourie Family award), Am. Psychiat. Assn. (hon.); mem. NASW (pres. 1961-63, chmn. commn. on social policy and action 1958-60, chmn. poverty com. 1964-66, Lifetime Svc. award Pa. chpt. 1990), Am. Pub. Welfare Assn. (dir., 1st v.p. 1965-66, chmn. fed. policy com., W.S. Terry Meml. merit award 1971), Nat. Council State Adminstrs. (exec. com. 1972-79, emeritus 1979-94, chmn. health com. 1974-75, chmn. supplementary security income liaison com. 1976-79), Child Welfare League Am. (dir. 1960-62, chmn. editorial bd.), Nat. Rehab. Assn., Internat. Child Welfare Union, Internat. Council Social Welfare (chmn. U.S. com. 1971-75, exec. com. 1975-79), Nat. Conf. Social Welfare (dir. 1971-75, v.p. 1972-73, pres. 1975-76), Alumni Assn. Columbia Sch. Social Work, Internat. Assn. Workers for Maladjusted Children (Am. br. chmn. 1972-79, permanent rep. to UN 1973-79), Nat. Inst. Pub. Mgmt. (bd. dirs. 1977-79), Soc. Traumatic Stress Studies (bd. dirs. 1968-86), Cosmos Club (Washington). Home: 5740 Union Deposit Rd Harrisburg PA 17111-4708 *Literature is full of solutions to the anger and violence which continue to characterize the current society. My current experience, in retirement, with refugee programs in Southeast Asia and other parts of the world, leads me to conclude that our glorious civilization of knowledge and science is still too much marred with hate and inequality. Our protestations of religion are suspect because of our behavior. Poverty and violence are our greatest sins, as is inequality. Only when we act out that each person is a holy place and we learn to love our children and our species more than we hate and fight, will we have the right to say we are civilized. We are good at rescue, but very poor at prevention. We should respect that every person is a holy place.*

LOUTREL, CLAUDE YVES, retired corporate official; b. Nanterre, France, Oct. 1, 1930; arrived in Belgium, 1957; s. Marcel and Odette (Diguet) L.; m. Anne Beatrice Dumont, July 6, 1957; children: Catherine, Bernard. Degree in engring., Ecole Centrale des Arts et Manufactures, Paris, 1954. Engr., various positions Solvay S.A., Brussels, 1957-72, Milan, 1972-74; mem. exec. com. Solvay S.A., Brussels, 1975-95, also bd. dirs.; ret., 1995; chmn. Solvay Polymers Corp., Houston, 1974—; vice chmn. Solvay Am., Houston, 1984—. Decorated chevalier de l'Ordre de la Couronne, officier de l'Ordre de Léopold (Belgium), commdr. Most Noble Order of Crown of Thailand. Office: Solvay SA, rue du Prince Albert 33, 1050 Brussels Belgium also: Solvay Am Inc 3333 Richmond Ave Houston TX 77098-3007

LOUTTIT, JAMES RUSSELL, retired publishing company executive; b. Monongahela, Pa., May 15, 1924; s. James S. and Orilla (Hutchinson) L.; m. Eleanor H. Ely, Mar. 19, 1986; children: J. Kipling, Dana M. B.A., U. Pitts., 1950. Reporter Canton (Ohio) Repository, 1950-51; feature writer, asst. city editor L.I. (N.Y.) Daily Press, 1951-56; advt. exec. McCann-Erickson, N.Y.C., 1956-57; speech writer Esso Standard Oil Co., N.Y.C., 1957-63; product mgr. Western Pub. Co., N.Y.C., 1963-69; exec. v.p. David McKay Co. Inc., N.Y.C., 1969-74; pres. David McKay Co. Inc., 1974-86, Fodor's Travel Guides, 1978-86; v.p. Morgan-Grampian, Inc., 1982-86; pres. Editorial Ink Ltd., Durham, N.C., 1986-90. Author: Adobe Walls, 1963, The New Skipper's Bowditch, 1984; co-author: (with Eleanor Louttit) Bantam's Scotland, 1991. Served with USNR, 1942-46, PTO.

LOUTTIT, WILLIAM A., supermarket chain executive; b. 1946; married. Grad., CUNY City Coll. With Grand Union Co., Wayne, N.J., fin. analyst N.Y. region, 1973-75, v.p. L.I. div., 1975-80, sr. v.p. Atlanta div., 1980-81, 1st. sr. v.p. Atlanta, from 1981, then exec. v.p. Atlanta ops., exec. v.p. merchandising, 1984—, also bd. dirs. Office: Grand Union Co 201 Willowbrook Blvd Wayne NJ 07470-7025*

LOUX, GORDON DALE, organization executive; b. Souderton, Pa., June 21, 1938; s. Curtis L. and Ruth (Derstine) L.; m. Elizabeth Ann Nordland, June 18, 1960; children: Mark, Alan, Jonathan. Diploma, Moody Bible Inst., Chgo., 1960; BA, Gordon Coll., Wenham, Mass., 1962; BD, No. Bapt. Sem., Oak Brook, Ill., 1965, MDiv, 1971; MS, Nat. Coll. Edn., Evanston,Ill., 1984; LHD (hon.), Sioux Falls Coll., 1985. Ordained to ministry, Bapt. Ch., 1965. Assoc. pastor Forest Park (Ill.) Bapt. Ch., 1962-65; alumni field dir. Moody Bible Inst., Chgo., 1965-66, dir. pub. rels., 1972-76; dir. devel. Phila. Coll. Bible, 1966-69; pres. Stewardship Svcs., Wheaton, Ill., 1969-72; exec. v.p. Prison Fellowship Ministries, Washington, 1976-84, pres., CEO, 1984-88; pres., CEO Prison Fellowship Internat., Washington, 1979-87, Internat. Students, Inc., Colorado Springs, Colo., 1988-93; pres. Stewardship Svcs. Group, Colorado Springs, 1994—; pres., CEO Trinity Cmty. Found., 1996—. Author: Uncommon Courage, 1987, You Can Be a Point of Light, 1991; contbg. author: Money for Ministries, 1989, Dictionary of Christianity in America, 1989. Bd. dirs. Evang. Coun. for Fin. Accountability, Washington, 1979-92, vice chmn., 1981-84, 86-87, chmn., 1987-89; vice chmn. Billy Graham Greater Washington Crusade, 1985-85; bd. dirs. Evang. Fellowship of Mission Agys., 1991—. Named Alumnus of Yr., Gordon Coll., 1986. Mem. Broadmoor Golf Club (Colo. Springs). Republican. Home: 740 Bear Paw Ln Colorado Springs CO 80906-3215 Office: PO Box 60037 Colorado Springs CO 80960-0037

LOUX, NORMAN LANDIS, psychiatrist; b. Souderton, Pa., June 27, 1919; s. Abram Clemmer and Martha Wasser (Landis) L.; m. Esther Elizabeth Brunk, June 4, 1941; children—Philip Michael, Elizabeth Ann, Peter David. Student, Eastern Mennonite Coll., 1940-42; B.A., Goshen Coll., 1943; M.D., Hahnemann Med. Coll., 1946; postgrad., Yale, 1950-51. Intern Hahnemann Hosp., Phila., 1947; gen. practice medicine Souderton, 1947-48; psychiat. resident Butler Hosp., Providence, 1949-50; chief service, clin. dir., asst. supt. Butler Hosp., 1951-55; founder Penn Found. Mental Health, Inc., Sellersville, Pa., 1955; med. dir. Penn Found. Mental Health, Inc., 1955-80; chief Psychiat. Svc. Grand View Hosp., Sellersville, 1955-80; pres. med. staff Grand View Hosp., 1963-64; exec. com., joint conf. com. Mem. Gov.'s Adv. Com. for Mental Health and Mental Retardation, 1955-80; mem. Pa. State Bd. Pub. Welfare, 1971-85. Bd. dirs. Dock Woods Retirement Community, 1989—, Adult Communities Total Svcs. Inc., 1990—. Co-recipient Earl D. Bond award, 1964; recipient Achievement award Souderton Lions Cub, 1963, Community Svc. award B'nai B'rith, 1976, citation for achievements Mennonite Med. Assn., 1978; dept. of psychiatry Grand View Hosp. rededicated in his name, 1992. Fellow Am. Psychiat. Assn., A.C.P., Pa. Psychiat. Soc., Am. Coll. Psychiatrists; mem. AMA, Pa., Bucks County med. socs., Group for Advancement Psychiatry, Southeastern Mental Health Assn., Acad. Religion and Mental Health. Mem. Mennonite Ch. Home: 138 Cowpath Rd Souderton PA 18964-2007 Office: Penn Found Mental Health Inc PO Box 32 Sellersville PA 18960-0032

LOVAS, SÁNDOR, chemist, researcher, educator; b. Kunmadaras, Hungary, Apr. 28, 1958; came to the U.S., 1990; s. Sándor and Mária (Diószegi) L.; m. Éva Ács, Apr. 19, 1980; 1 child, Veronika Éva. MS in Chemistry, József Attila U., Szeged, Hungary, 1982, PhD in Organic Chemistry, 1985. Rsch. asst. Biol. Rsch. Ctr., Szeged, 1982-85, rsch. fellow, 1985-90; postdoctoral fellow Creighton U., Omaha, 1990-93, asst. prof., 1994—. Contbr. articles to profl. jours. Grantee State of Nebr., 1994. Mem. Am. Chem. Soc., Am. Peptide Soc., Hungarian Chem. Soc., World Assn. Theoretical Chemists. Achievements include patent pending for specific anticancer activity of GNRH analogs; research in conformationally constrained peptides and molecular dynamics simulations of peptides. Office: Creighton Univ Dept Biomed Sci 2500 California Plaza Omaha NE 68178

LOVE, BEN HOWARD, retired organization executive; b. Trenton, Tenn., Sept. 26, 1930; s. Ben Drane and Virginia (Whitehead); m. Ann Claire Hugo, Mar. 4, 1933; children: Ben H. Jr., Phillip H., Leigh Ann, Mark E. BS, Lambuth Coll., 1955, HHD (hon.), 1986; Dr. Philanthropy (hon.), Pepperdine U., 1987; LHD (hon.), Montclair State U., 1991. With Boy Scouts Am., 1955—; dist. exec., Jackson, Tenn., 1955-60; scout exec. Delta area council, Clarksdale, Miss., 1960-64; dir. Nat. council, North Brunswick, N.J., 1964-68; scout exec. Longhorn council, Ft. Worth, 1968-71; scout exec. Sam Houston council, Houston, 1971-73; dir. Northeast region, Dayton, N.J., 1973-85; chief scout exec. Nat. council, Irving, Tex., 1985-93; bd. dirs. Am. Gen. Series Portfolio Co., Mid.-Am. Waste Sys. Inc. Served with U.S. Army, 1951-52. Recipient Gold medal SAR, Bronze Wolf award World Scout Orgn. Republican. Presbyterian. Club: La Cima (bd. dirs. Irving chpt. 1985—). Avocations: tennis, golf, swimming, reading, spectator sports. Office: 4407 Eaton Cir Colleyville TX 76034-4653

LOVE, DANIEL JOSEPH, consulting engineer; b. Fall River, Mass., Sept. 27, 1926; s. Henry Aloysius and Mary Ellen (Harrington) L.; m. Henrietta Maurisse Popper, June 10, 1950 (dec. Mar. 1986); children: Amy, Timothy, Terence, Kevin; m. Adeline Aponte Esquivel, Feb. 11, 1989; stepchildren: Eric, Brian, Jason. BSEE, Ill. Inst. Tech., 1951, MSEE, 1956; MBA, Calif. State U., Long Beach, 1973. registered profl. engr., Calif., Ariz., Ill., La.; cert. fire protection, Calif. Test engr. Internat. Harvester Co., Chgo., 1951-52; designer Pioneer Svc. & Engring. Co., Chgo., 1952-53; project engr., ops. mgr. Panellit Co., Skokie, Ill., 1953-60; mktg. mgr. Control Data Co., Mpls., 1961-62; mktg. mgr., asst. to pres. Emerson Electric Co., Pasadena, Calif., 1963-65; pres., gen. mgr. McKee Automation Co., North Hollywood, Calif., 1965-68; engring. specialist Bechtel Co., Vernon and Norwalk, Calif., 1968-80; chief elec. engr. Bechtel Co., Madrid, 1980-83; engring. specialist Bechtel Co., Norwalk, Calif., 1983-87; cons. engr. Hacienda Heights, Calif., 1987—. Contbr. articles to jours. in field. Pres. Wilson High Sch. Band Boosters, Hacienda Heights, 1971-73. With USN, 1944-46. Named Outstanding Engr., Inst. for Advancement Engring., 1986; recipient 3d place prize paper award Industry Application Soc., 1995. Fellow IEEE (disting. lectr., chmn. Met. L.A. sect. 1973-74, chmn. L.A. coun. 1977-78, chmn. protection com. 1990-91, Richard Harold Kaufmann award 1994, Ralph H. Lee prize paper award 1995); mem. NSPE, Instrument Soc. Am. (sr.), Soc. Fire Protection Engrs. Republican. Roman Catholic. Avocations: duplicate bridge, travel, walking, writing. Home: 16300 E Soriano Dr Hacienda Heights CA 91745

LOVE, DAVIS, III, professional golfer. Mem. Ryder Cup Team, 1993. Winner The Internat., 1990, MCI Heritage Classic Champion, 1991, 92, Tournament Players Championship, 1992, 93, Greater Greensboro Open, 1992. Address: care PGA Tour 112 TPC Blvd Ponte Vedra Beach FL 32082-3046*

LOVE, DENNIS M., consumer products company executive. CEO Printpack, Atlanta. Office: Printpack Inc 4335 Wendell Dr SW Atlanta GA 30336-1622

LOVE, DURAL LEE, professional football player; b. L.A., June 24, 1963. Student, UCLA. Guard Ariz. Cardinals, Phoenix. Named to NFL Pro Bowl Team, 1994. Office: Ariz Cardinals 8701 S Hardy Phoenix AZ 85284

LOVE, EDITH HOLMES, theater producer; b. Boston, Oct. 17, 1950; d. Theodore Rufus and Mary (Holmes) L. Student, Denison U., 1968-72; BFA, U. Colo., 1973. Freelance designer various orgns., Atlanta, 1974-75; costumer Atlanta Children's Theatre, 1975-77; prodn. acct. David Gerber Co., L.A., 1980-81; bus. mgr. Alliance Theatre/Atlanta Children's Theatre, 1977-79, adminstrv. dir., 1981-83, gen. mgr., 1983-85, mng. dir., 1985—; bd. dirs. Midtown Bus. Assocs., 1988-94; mem. adv. bd. Stage Hands, Inc., Atlanta, 1983-89; mem. exec. com. Prodn. Valves, Inc., Atlanta, 1985-89; mem. adv. com. arts mgmt. program Carnegie Mellon U.; panelist Nat. Endowment for Arts, 1994-96. Mem. Cultural Olympiad Task Force, 1996 Summer Olympic Games, 1992-96, Met. Atlanta Arts Fund Bd.; bd. dirs. Atlanta Convention and Visitor's Bur., 1993-95. Recipient Deca award for Outstanding Bus. Women in Atlanta, 1992. Mem. League Resident Theatres (treas. 1987—), Atlanta Theatre Coalition (exec. com. 1987-91, pres. 1989), Atlanta C. of C. (bd. dirs. bus. coun. for arts 1988—), Leadership Atlanta. Office: Alliance Theatre Co 1280 Peachtree St NE Atlanta GA 30309-3502

LOVE, FRANKLIN SADLER, retired trade association executive; b. Rock Hill, S.C., Nov. 9, 1915; s. Franklin Sadler and Edna (Hull) L.; m. Jessie Huggins, Apr. 10, 1943; children: Judith (Mrs. J. Lindsay Freeman), Beverly (Mrs. Ronald Sparrow), Franklin Sadler III, Glenn. A.B., Presbyn. Coll., Clinton, S.C., 1937. Sec. Cotton Mfrs. Assn. S.C., Clinton, 1937-42, Am. Cotton Mfrs. Assn., Charlotte, N.C., 1946-49; sec. treas. Am. Textile Mfrs. Inst., 1949-79, v.p., 1979-80, ret., 1980; speaker numerous civic and bus. groups; Adviser Internat. Cotton Adv. Com., 1958. Former mem. adv. bd. Charlotte Salvation Army; former bd. dirs. Charlotte Council on Alcoholism. Capt. Ordnance dept. AUS, 1942-46. Recipient Alumni citation for outstanding achievement Presbyn. Coll., 1955; certificate of merit Ala. Textile Mfrs. Assn., 1972. Mem. Def. Supply Assn. (pres. Carolinas chpt. 1952), Phi Psi, Rotary (pres. Charlotte chpt., del. internat. conf. 1961), Goodfellows Club (Charlotte), Charlotte Execs. Club (former sec.). Presbyterian. Home: 5100 Sharon Rd Charlotte NC 28210-4720

LOVE, GAYLE MAGALENE, special education educator, adult education educat; b. New Orleans, July 25, 1953; d. Lowell F. Sr. and Nathalie Mae (Adams) L.; children: Nathanael Dillard, Raphael. BMEd, Loyola U., New Orleans, 1975, MMEd, 1981. Cert. learning disabled, emotionally disturbed, gifted-talented, adult edn., mild-moderate, elem.-secondary vocal music, prin., spl. sch. prin., parish/city sch. supr. instrn., supervision of student tchg., supr. adult edn. & spl. edn., child search coord. Dean student svcs. Jefferson Parish Sch. Bd., Harvey, La., chmn. spl. edn. dept., 1990-93; adult educator instr., supr., spl. sch. prin., parish city dir. spl. education, 1995-96; chmn. Sch. Bldg. Level Com., 1994-96; presenter St. Joseph the Worker Cath. Ch., 1988, Very Spl. Arts Week Jefferson Parish Pub. Sch. Sys., 1989, 90, 91, 92, 93, 94, 95, 96; mem. spl. edn. alternative curriculum com., 1990—, Urban Ctr. Tchrs. Devel. com. U. New Orleans, 1990-91. Mem. NAFE, ASCD, Coun. Exceptional Children (workshop presenter 1990), Jefferson Assn. Pub. Sch. Adminstrs., East Bank Jefferson Parish Parent Adv. Coun., New Orleans C. of C. (com. Alliance for Quality, small bus. improvement team), La. Assn. Sch. Execs., Phi Beta, Kappa Delta Pi, Alpha Kappa Alpha. Home: 1740 Burnley Dr Marrero LA 70072-4522

LOVE, JOSEPH L., history educator, cultural studies center administrator; b. Austin, Tex., Feb. 28, 1938; s. Joseph L. Sr. and Virginia (Ellis) L.; m. Laurie Reynolds, Dec. 23, 1978; children: Catherine R., David A.; children from previous marriage: James A., Stephen N. AB in Econs. with honors, Harvard U., 1960; MA in History, Stanford U., 1963; PhD in History with distinction, Columbia U., 1967. From instr. to prof. U. Ill., Urbana-Champaign, 1966—, dir. ctr. Latin Am. and Caribbean studies, 1993—; rsch. assoc. St. Antony's Coll. Oxford U.; vis. prof. Pontifical Cath. U., Rio de Janeiro, 1987; presenter in field. Author: Rio Grande do Sul and Brazilian Regionalism, 1882-1930, 1971, Sao Paulo in the Brazilian Federation, 1889-1937, 1980, Crafting the Third World: Theorizing Underdevelopment in Rumania and Brazil, 1996; editor: (with Robert S. Byars) Quantitative Social Science Research on Latin America, 1973, (with Nils Jacobsen) Guiding the Invisible Hand: Economic Liberalism and the State in Latin American History, 1988; bd. editors Latin Am. Rsch. Rev., 1974-78, Hispanic Am. Hist. Rev., 1984-89, The Americas, 1995—; contbr. articles to profl. jours. Fulbright-Hays Rsch. grantee; fellow Social Sci. Rsch. Coun., IREX, Guggenheim; vis. fellow U. São Paulo, Inst. Ortega y Gasset, Madrid; sr. rsch. fellow NEH, others; sr. univ. scholar U. Ill., 1993-96. Mem. Am. Hist. Assn., Conf. Latin Am. History (chair Brazilian studies com. 1973, mem. gen. com. 1983, Conf. prize 1971), Latin Am. Studies Assn. Unitarian. Office: U Ill Ctr Latin Am and Caribbean Studies 910 S 5th St Rm 201 Champaign IL 61820-6216

LOVE, KIRK HARRY, stock broker; b. Detroit, Feb. 28, 1955; s. William and Irene (Opalinski) L.; m. Judith Slusser, May 19, 1979; 1 child, Kyle H. BS in Bus. Adminstrn., Ctrl. Mich. U., 1977; postgrad., Coll. Fin. Planning, 1991—. CFP; cert. investment mgmt. analyst; cert. investment mgmt. consulting assoc. Mfg. mgmt. tng. program GM, Saginaw, Mich., 1977-79; owner Retial Auto Rustproofing, Wayne, Mich., 1979-80; stock broker EF Hutton, Southfield, Mich., 1980-87, Prudential Securities, West Bloomfield, Mich., 1987—. Trustee Detroit (Mich.) Symphony Orch., 1987—; bd. dirs. Southeastern Mich. chpt. ARC, Detroit, 1990—. Mem. Investment Mgmt. Consulting, Internat. Assn. Fin. Planner. Avocations: golfing, flying. Office: Prudential Securities 7031 Orchard Lake Rd Ste 101 West Bloomfield MI 48322-3635

LOVE, MARGARET COLGATE, lawyer; b. Balt., June 9, 1942; d. H.A. and Margaret West (Dennis) L.; 1 child, Jenny West. BA, Sarah Lawrence Coll., 1963; MA, U. Pa., 1969; JD, Yale U., 1977. Bar: Washington, 1977. Lawyer Shea & Gardner, Washington, 1977-79; spl. counsel office of legal counsel U.S. Dept. Justice, Washington, 1979-88, dep. assoc. atty. gen., 1988-89, assoc. dep. atty. gen., 1989-90, pardon atty., 1990—. Mem. ABA (standing com. on ethics and profl. responsibility chair 1994—). Office: Dept Justice 500 1st St NW Fl 4 Washington DC 20530*

LOVE, MICHAEL KENNETH, lawyer; b. Richmond Height, Mo., Oct. 2, 1951; s. Clarence Kenneth and Helen (Schlapper) L.; m. Gloria Pia Miccioli, Sept. 8, 1979; children: Claire Pia, Patrick Kenneth. BS in Forestry, U. Mo., 1974; JD, George Washington U., 1977. Bar: Va. 1977, D.C. 1978, Md. 1981. Asst. dir. model procurement code project ABA, Washington, 1977-80; assoc. Wickwire, Gavin & Gibbs, P.C., Vienna, Va., 1980-84; ptnr. Wickwire, Gavin & Gibbs, P.C., Vienna, 1984-86, Smith, Pachter, McWhorter & D'Ambrosio, Vienna, 1986-94; corp. counsel Info. Sys. and Networks, Inc., Bethesda, 1994-95; sr. atty. Epstein, Becker & Green, Washington, 1995—. Contbr. articles to profl. publs. Mem. ABA (chmn. subcontracting and constrn. com. pub. contract law sect. 1984-92, constrn. com. 1990-91, chair constrn. divsn. 1993-94, mem. coun. 1994—), Nat. Contract Mgmt. Assn., Nat. Security Indsl. Assn., Va. Bar Assn. Office: Epstein Becker & Green 1227 25th St NW Washington DC 20037-1156

LOVE, MILDRED ALLISON, retired secondary school educator, historian, writer, volunteer; b. Moultrie, Ga., Mar. 12, 1915; d. Ulysees Simpson Sr. and Susie Marie (Dukes) Allison; m. George Alsobrook Love, Aug. 24, 1956 (dec. 1978). BSEd, U. Tampa (Fla.), 1941; MS in Home Econs., Fla. State U., 1953; MA in History, U. Miami, Coral Gables, Fla., 1969. Cert. tchr., Fla. Vocat. home econs. tchr. Hamilton County Pub. Schs., Jasper, Fla., 1941-43, Pinellas County Pub. Schs., Tarpon Springs, Fla., 1946-51; vocat. home econs. tchr. Dade County Pub. Schs., Miami, Fla., 1951-61, history tchr., 1961-73; supr. food svcs. Ft. Jackson (S.C.), 1944-46. Chmn. subcoun. for crime prevention Brickell Area, City of Miami, 1983-87; mem. Crisis Response Team, Miami Police Dept., 1983—; vol. VA Hosp., Miami, 1987—; historian, vol. vets affairs VFW Aux., Miami, 1988-89; precinct worker presdl. election, 1976, 80; sponsor history honor soc. Miami Edison Sr. H.S., 1961-73; mem. Mus. of Sci., St. Stephen's Episc. Ch., Coconut Grove, Fla.; mem. Dade Heritage Trust. Mem. AAUW, VFW (aux. post 471 Miami, Fla.), Inst. for Retired Profls., Hist. Assn. S. Fla., U. Miami Alumni Assn., Fla. Ret. Educators Assn., Nat. Wildlife Fedn., Am. Legion (aux. post 29 Miami, Fla.), Nat. Trust Hist. Preservation, Coll. of Arts and Scis. Assn. U. Miami, Fla. Vocat. Home Econs. Tchrs. (pres. 1947), Fla. Vocat. Home Econs. Assn. (pres. 1948-49), Dade Heritage Trust, Woman's Club of Miami Beach, Sierra Club, Phi Alpha Theta. Democrat. Episcopalian. Avocation: foreign languages. Home: 2411 S Miami Ave Miami FL 33129-1527

LOVE, MIRON ANDERSON, retired judge; b. Houston, Oct. 25, 1920; s. Robert William and Josephine (Moody) L.; m. Marjorie Skiles, Dec. 21, 1948; children: Ross, Mark. BA, So. Meth. U., 1948; LLB, So. Tex. Law Sch., 1951. Bar: Tex. 1951, U.S. Dist. Ct. Tex. 1952, U.S. Supreme Ct. 1967. Asst. dist. atty. Harris County (Tex.) Dist. Atty.'s Office, Houston, 1951-53; pvt. practice Houston, 1953-58; adminstrv. judge 177th Dist. Ct., Harris County, Houston, 1958-95. Pres. Nat. Conf. Met. Cts. 1st lt. USAF, 1944-46, PTO. Mem. Internat. Acad. Trial Judges (mem. bd. regents). Democrat. Unitarian. Office: 177th Dist Ct 301 San Jacinto St Rm 100 Houston TX 77002-2022

LOVE, RICHARD EMERSON, equipment manufacturing company executive; b. N.Y.C., Dec. 15, 1926; s. Emerson C. and Ruth A. (Mealley) L.; m. Margaret A. Lloyd, June 24, 1950; children—Mary-Ann, Nancy, Jane, Thomas. Grad., N.Y. State Maritime Coll., 1946; AAS, Hofstra Coll., 1955. Group v.p. Crane Co., N.Y.C., 1967-72, U.S. Filter Co., N.Y.C., 1972-75; group pres. Peabody Internat. Corp., Stamford, Conn., 1975-77; exec. v.p. Peabody Internat. Corp., Stamford, 1978-85; group v.p. Pullman Co. (merged with Peabody Internat. Corp.), Stamford, 1985-87; v.p. ops. Hosokowa Micron Internat. Inc., N.Y.C., 1987-93; dir., cons. Hosokawa Micron Internat., N.Y.C., 1993-95; ret., 1995; pres. Internat. Area Mgmt., Hilton Head, S.C., 1995—. Served with USN, 1948-49. Mem. ASME, Instruments Soc. Am. Office: Internat Area Mgmt 16 Old Fort Dr Hilton Head Island SC 29926

LOVE, RICHARD HARVEY, lawyer; b. Washington, Aug. 31, 1915; s. Leo Young and Grace Marie (Jett) L.; m. Betty Zane Schofield, Nov. 14, 1942 (dec. Sept. 1967); children: Richard, Robert, Edward, William, Elizabeth. AB, U. Md., 1936, LLB, 1938. Bar: Md., D.C. 1939. Law clk. U.S. Dist. Ct., Balt., Md., 1938-40; pvt. practice Washington, Md., 1940-41, 46—; counsel Bd. Zoning Appeals, Prince Georges County, Md., 1953-55. Editor Judge Adv. Jour., 1948-81. Served to maj. AUS, 1941-46; col. Judge Adv. Gen.'s Corps Res., 1946-75. Decorated Legion of Merit U.S. Army, 1972. Mem. ABA, Md. Bar Assn., Bar Assn. D.C., Prince Georges County Bar Assn., Judge Advocates Assn. (exec. sec. 1948-81, dir. emeritus 1981—), Res. Officers Assn., Mil. Order Fgn. Wars (past nat. comdr. gen.), Assn. U.S. Army, Army-Navy Club, Order of Coif, Phi Kappa Phi. Republican. Roman Catholic. Home: 6905 Carleton Ter College Park MD 20740-3620 Office: 6419 Baltimore Ave Riverdale MD 20737-1065

LOVE, ROBERT LYMAN, educational consulting company executive; b. Oswego, N.Y., July 28, 1925; s. Robert Barnum and Marion Alberta (Peavy) L.; m. Janet May Fuller, June 26, 1948; children: Robert H., Andrew L., Charles D., Cynthia S. Student U. Rochester, 1943-44; A.B., Syracuse U., 1945, postgrad. in medicine, 1946-48, M.Ed., 1949; postgrad., Cornell U., 1963-64. Sci. tchr. Middlesex Valley Central Sch., Rushville, N.Y., 1949-53; mem. faculty Agrl. and Tech. Coll., SUNY-Alfred, 1953-81; prof., dean Agrl. and Tech. Coll., SUNY (Sch. Allied Health Techs.), until 1981, dean emeritus, 1981—; pres. Edn. Cons. Services, Alfred Station, N.Y., 1981—; former mem. bd. dirs. Nat. Tech. Inst. Deaf; program evaluation steering com. AMA; allied health reviewer HEW; chmn. health sub-com. 39th Congl. Dist. Author: He and She, An Introduction to Human Sexuality and Birth Control, 1970; editor: Upward Mobility for Lab Personnel, 1970. Fin. sec., mem. adminstrv. bd. Alfred United Meth. Ch.; mem. Roving Vols. in Christ's Svc., 1982-91, bd. dirs. 1984-86, 89-91, chmn. bd. dirs., 1989-90; mem. Selected Vols. in Christ's Svc., 1987-88; litercy vol.; pres., bd. dirs. Genesee Valley Habitat for Humanity, Inc., 1993-95; treas. 1995—; Allegany County Office for Aging Handyman's Svc. Fellow Sci. Tchrs. Assn. N.Y. State, Am. Soc. Allied Health Professions; mem. Gideons Internat. (past pres. Hornell Camp), Literacy Vols. Am. (bd. dirs. Allegany County chpt. 1990-93), Masons, Order Eastern Star. Republican. Home: 5366 Jericho Hill Rd Alfred Station NY 14803-9736 Office: Edn Cons Svc 5366 Jericho Hill Rd Alfred Station NY 14803 *Having had the opportunity to work with young people has kept me young and knowing the Lord has saved me.*

LOVE, ROBERT WILLIAM, JR., retired physician, government administrator; b. Springfield, Mo., June 28, 1929; s. Robert William and Ruby Gladys (Teel) L.; m. Barbara Joyce Few, July 5, 1974; children—Robert William, III, Curry Maria, Rebecca Anne. A.B., Drury Coll., 1950, M.D., St. Louis U., 1954. Intern Kansas City (Mo.) Gen. Hosp., 1954-55, resident in surgery, 1955-59; staff surgeon VA Hosp., Asheville, N.C., 1961-62; chief gen. surgery VA Hosp., 1962-72, asst. chief surg. service, 1962-72; chief of staff VA Hosp., Mountain Home, Tenn., 1972-74; dir. field ops. VA Central Office, Washington, 1974-75, dir. ops. rev. and analysis, 1975-79; med. dir., evaluation and analysis office VA Central Office, 1979-85; dir. VA Outpatient Clinic, Pensacola, Fla., 1985-90; asst. clin. prof. surgery Duke U., 1967-72. Served to capt. M.C. USNR, 1959-61. Recipient dirs. commendation VA Hosp., Mountain Home, 1974, Adminstrs. commendation, VACO, 1985. Mem. A.C.S., Assn. VA Surgeons, Naval Res. Assn., Res. Officers Assn., Assn. Mil. Surgeons U.S., Escambia County Med. Soc., Alpha Omega Alpha. Research in magnification lymphangiographic radiography, Tb and gastric ulcer, med. treatment of spinal Tb. Home: 8774 Thunderbird Dr Pensacola FL 32514-5659

LOVE, SHARON IRENE, elementary education educator; b. Pontiac, Mich., July 27, 1950; d. James and Ethlyn (Cole) M.; married; 1 child, Sheralyn Reneé. BS, Western Mich. U., 1964; postgrad., Oakland U., Rochester, Mich. Cert. elem. educator, early childhood educator, Mich.

Tchr. kindergarten Pontiac Bd. Edn., 1964-69, 76-83, 87—, tchr. 1st grade, 1965-66, tchr. 4th grade, 1983-84, tchr. 2d grade, 1984-87; tchr. trainer triple I.E. classroom instruction Emerson Elem. Sch., Pontiac, 1988-89; trainer Math Their Way, Pontiac Sch. Sys., 1989, leadership, 1990; trainer Mich. Health Model Oakland Schs., Waterford, 1987; co-chair com. for developing and writing new Fine Arts curriculum for Pontiac Sch. Dist., 1993-94. Chair coord. coun. Walt Whitman Elem. Schs., Pontiac, 1987-91; mem. PTA, 1970-90; chair coord. coun. Webster Elem. Sch., 1993-94. Creative Art grantee Pontiac PTA, 1965; recipient cert. Appreciation Pontiac Blue Ribbon Com., 1991, cert. for outstanding educatorMich. Gov. Engler, 1991. Mem. NAACP, Mich. Edn. Assn., Pontiac Edn. Assn. (del. 1965-66). Avocations: art, writing poetry, sewing. Office: Pontiac Bd Edn 350 Wide Track Dr E Pontiac MI 48342-2243

LOVE, WARNER EDWARDS, biophysics educator; b. Phila., Dec. 1, 1922; s. J. Warner E. and Elizabeth (Ford) L.; m. Lois Jane Hosbach, Dec. 26, 1945; children: Rebecca Edwards Love Burton, Michael Warner. B.A. in Zoology, Swarthmore Coll., 1946; Ph.D. in Physiology, U. Pa., 1951. Fellow, then assoc. biophysics U. Pa., 1951-55; research fellow, then research assoc. physics Inst. Cancer Research, Fox Chase, Pa., 1955-57; faculty Johns Hopkins U., 1957—, prof. biophysics, 1965—, dept. chmn., 1971-74, 80-83. Served with Am. Field Service, 1943-45, with U.S. Army, 1945-46. Mentioned in dispatches AFS. Research on x-ray crystal structure analysis of biol macro-molecules, particularly hemoglobins. Office: Johns Hopkins U 3400 N Charles St Baltimore MD 21218-2684

LOVE, WILLIAM EDWARD, lawyer; b. Eugene, Oreg., Mar. 13, 1926; s. William Stewart and Ola A. (Kingsbury) L.; m. Sylvia Kathryn Jaureguy, Aug. 6, 1955; children: Kathryn Love Petersen, Jeffrey, Douglas, Gregory. B.S., U. Notre Dame, 1946; M.A. in Journalism, U. Oreg., 1950, J.D., 1952. Bar: Oreg., 1952. Newspaper reporter Eugene Register Guard, 1943-44, 47-52; asst. prof. law, asst. dean Sch. Law U. Wash., Seattle, 1952-56; ptnr. Cake, Jaureguy, Hardy, Buttler & McEwen, Portland, Oreg., 1956-69; pres., chmn., chief exec. officer Equitable Savs. & Loan, Portland, 1969-82; sr. ptnr. Schwabe, Williamson & Wyatt, Portland, 1983—; chmn. Oreg. Savs. League, 1976; dir. Portland Gen. Electric, 1976-83, Fed. Home Loan Bank of Seattle, 1976-79, 85—, adv. council, Washington, 1978-80; exec. dir. Health, Housing, Ednl. & Cultural Facilities Authority, 1990—. Author: (with Jaureguy) Oregon Probate Law and Practice, 2 vols., 1958. Contbr. articles to profl. jours. Commr., past chmn. Oreg. Racing Commn., 1963-79; pres. Nat. Assn. State Racing Commrs., 1977-78; commr. Port of Portland, 1979-86, pres., 1983; referee Pac-10 football, 1960-81, Rose Bowl, 1981; active United Way, Boy Scouts Am., Portland Rose Festival, polit. campaigns; mem. adv. coun. Jockeys' Guild, Inc., 1990—. Served to lt. (j.g.), USN, 1944-47. Mem. Oreg. Bar Assn., Multnomah County Bar Assn. Republican. Clubs: Arlington, Multnomah Athletic, Golf (Portland). Home: 10225 SW Melnore St Portland OR 97225-4356 Office: Schwabe Williamson & Wyatt 1211 SW 5th Ave Portland OR 97204-3713

LOVE, WILLIAM JENKINS, sales and marketing executive; b. Atlanta, June 12, 1962; s. James Erskine Jr. and Gay (McLawhorn) L.; m. Helen Elizabeth Brumley, Aug. 6, 1988. BS, Duke U., 1984, MBA, 1992. Comml. appraiser Coldwell Banker, Atlanta, 1985-88; mktg. specialist Printpack Inc., Atlanta, 1988-90, also bd. dirs.; sales rep. Printpack Inc., 1992—. Vol. Atlanta Symphony Assocs., 1987—, Project READ, 1995—; mem. Trinity Presbyn. Ch. Avocations: photography, travel, tennis, golf, softball. Office: Printpack Inc 4335 Wendell Dr SW Atlanta GA 30336-1622

LOVEALL, CLELLON LEWIS, transportation administrator, civil engineer; b. Carthage, Tenn., June 13, 1938; s. Clellon Reuben and Blanche Mavis (Thompson) L.; m. Jane Ellen Johnson, July 16, 1960; children: Lisa Renee, Sharon Kay, Angela Dawn. B in Engring., Vanderbilt U., 1959. Lic. profl. engr. Bridge design engr. Tenn. Dept. Transp., Nashville, 1959-63, sr. bridge design engr., 1963-66, chief bridge design engr., 1966-69, asst. state bridge engr., 1969-78, state bridge engr., 1978-86, asst. dir. planning and devel., 1986—; keynote speaker U.S.-European Conf. on Bridge Evaluation, Repair, and Rehab., Paris, 1987, Engring. Found. Conf. Mng. Am.'s Aging Bridge Sys., 1989, Pitts. Internat. Bridge Conf., 1989, Western Bridge Engrs. Seminar, 1991, U.S.-European Workshop on Bridge Rehab., Darmstadt, Germany, 1992. Mem. ASCE (chpt. dir. com. redundancy, Govt. Civil Engr. of Yr. 1984), ASTM (sec. C-27.20 precast concrete structure), Am. Concrete Inst., Prestressed Concrete Inst. (bridge com.), Post Tensioning Inst. (charter mem., tech. adv. bd.), Segmental Bridge Inst., Am. Iron and Steel Inst. (steel bridge rsch. task force), Am. Assn. State Hwy. and Transp. Ofcls. (subcom. on design, subcom. bridges and structures 1987-92), Tenn. Soc. Profl. Engrs. (state dir., state sec., Nashville pres. 1986-87, Engr. of Yr. 1990), Transp. Rsch. Bd. Roman Catholic. Avocations: golf, tennis. Office: Tenn Dept Transp Bur Planning & Devel James K Polk Bldg 505 Deaderick St Ste 700 Nashville TN 37243-0349*

LOVEDAY, WILLIAM JOHN, hospital administrator; b. Lynn, Mass., Nov. 4, 1943; Married. B, Colby Coll., 1967; MHA, U. Chgo., 1970. Adminstrv. asst. Meml. Med. Ctr., Long Beach, Calif., 1970-71, asst. adminstr., 1971-74, v.p., 1974-82, exec. v.p., 1982-88; pres., chief exec. officer Meth. Hosp. Ind., Inc., Indpls., 1988—. Home: 7828 Traders Cove Ln Indianapolis IN 46254-9614 Office: Meth Hosp Ind PO Box 1367 Indianapolis IN 46206-1367*

LOVEJOY, ALLEN FRASER, retired lawyer; b. Janesville, Wis., Oct. 9, 1919; s. Henry Stow and Mary Fraser (Beaton) L.; m. Betty Foote, Dec. 20, 1944; children: Jennifer Lovejoy Craddock, Charles F., Allen P. BA, Yale U., 1941, LLB, 1948. Bar: N.Y. 1949, U.S. Ct. Appeals (2d cir.) 1975. Assoc. Breed, Abbott & Morgan, N.Y.C., 1948-58, ptnr., 1958-87. Served with U.S. Army, 1941-46; ETO. Decorated Purple Heart with oak leaf cluster; recipient Frank M. Patterson award Yale U., 1941. Fellow Am. Numis. Soc. (life, councillor 1988—, 1st v.p. 1990—), Am. Numis. Assn. Republican. Episcopalian. Clubs: Pilgrims (N.Y.C.); Mid Ocean (Bermuda); Stanwich (Greenwich, Conn.); Riverside (Conn.) Yacht. Author: La Follette and the Establishment of the Direct Primary in Wisconsin, 1890-1904, 1941; co-author: Early United States Dimes, 1796-1837, 1984; contbr. articles to numismatic publs. Home: 100 Club Rd Riverside CT 06878-2032

LOVEJOY, ANN LOUISE, development director, insurance company executive; b. Baker, Oreg., Aug. 18, 1949; d. Victor and Norma (Peters) Lovejoy; m. Pierre Ventur, June 9, 1975; 1 child, Conrad Ventur. Bachelors, U. Wash., 1971, Masters, 1975. Bot. field asst. (grant) Yale U., San Luis, Guatemala, 1975-77; editorial asst., micro personal computer trainer Yale U., New Haven, Conn., 1977-86; tech. trainer Bunker Ramo/Allied Signal, Shelton, Conn., 1984-86; sr. training specialist Bank of Boston, Springfield, Mass., 1986-87, MassMutual Life Ins., Springfield, Mass., 1987-96, Cibna, Hartford, Conn., 1996—. Mem. bd. corporators Springfield Metro YMCA, 1994—. Mem. ASTD (bd. dirs. Pioneer Valley 1986-91), Assn. for Computing Machinery. Office: Cigna 900 Cottage Grove Rd Hartford CT 06152-1011

LOVEJOY, BARBARA CAMPBELL, sculptor, architectural designer; b. Detroit, Oct. 31, 1919; d. Robert Bruce and Mona (Goodwin) Campbell; m. William Edward Gibson, Oct. 27, 1941 (dec. Aug. 1969); children: Linda Dean Gibson Stoner, William Kent; m. John Marshall Lovejoy, Jan. 27, 1971 (dec. Nov. 1994). B of Design, Tulane U., 1941; studied sculpture with Lothar Kestenbaum; also studied with Yuri Hollosy, New Orleans. Archtl. designer Aurora Devel. Co., New Orleans, 1950-60; pvt. practice archtl. design New Orleans, 1960-70; chief designer D.H. Holmes Store Planning, New Orleans, 1970-78; dir. store planning and interior design Wray Williams Display Co., New Orleans, 1978-86. One-woman shows include D.H. Homes Canal St. Window Exhbn., New Orleans, 1981, Kaplan's Art Exhibit, Alexandria, La., 1983, 85, Ea. Art Assoc., Fairhope, Ala., 1985; exhibited in group shows at Salon de Refuses, New Orleans, 1967, Edgewater Mall, 1980, New Orleans Commodity Exchange, 1982, Palm Beach (Fla.) Art Galleries, 1984, (Patron's award in sculpture 1983), Peyton Meml. Arts Festival, Alexandria, 1983-85, 91, 93 (Patron's award 1983, Spl. Purchase award 1984), U. New Orleans Gallery, 1983-84, St. Tammany Art Assn., Covington, La., 1984, 90, New Orleans Women's Caucus for Art, 1985, New Orleans Acad. Art Summer Group Show, 1985, New Orleans Ctr. Contemporary Art, 1984-86, Grand Festival Art at Grand Hotel, Point Clear, La., 1985, 87, La. Women Artists, Baton Rouge, 1987, 5th Juried Exhbn. for La. Artists, 1987-88, Decatur Arts Alliance, 1990, Memphis Arts Festival, 1990 (Patron's award in sculpture), Mystic Conn. Art Gallery, 1991, Artist in Still Zinsel Gallery, New Orleans, 1988-91, Miriam Walmsley Gallery, 1992, Masur Mus. Art, Monroe, La., 1992, 95, La. Competition, Baton Rouge, 1993, 95, Art for Advocacy, La., 1993, 95, Carol Robinson Gallery, 1994-96, La. Arts & Sci. Ctr., Baton Rouge, 1996. Recipient 1st pl. Painting award Chevron Art Exhbn., 1965, 66, 1st pl. Sculpture award Nat. Art Appreciation Soc., 1984, other awards New Orleans Mus. Art, 1985, Art for Advocacy, 1993, Slidell Art League, 1995, Masur Mus. Art (Monroe, La.), 1995, Ben Weiner Found. (permanent display in Wilson Ctr., Tulane U.), 1995. Mem. Am. Soc. Interior Designers (prof.), Women's Caucus for Art, Southeastern Women's Caucus for Art. Presbyterian. Home and Studio: 100 Finland Pl New Orleans LA 70131-3904

LOVEJOY, RAY, film editor. Editor: (films) 2001: A Space Odyssey, 1968, The Ruling Class, 1972, A Day in the Death of Joe Egg, 1972, Fear Is the Key, 1973, Little Malcolm and His Struggle Against the Eunuchs, 1974, Ghost in the Noonday Sun, 1974, The Shining, 1980, Krull, 1983, The Dresser, 1983, Sheena, 1984, Eleni, 1985, Aliens, 1986, Suspect, 1987, The House on Carroll Street, 1988, Batman, 1989, Homeboy, 1989, Mr. Frost, 1990, Year of the Comet, 1992, A Far Off Place, 1993. Office: Sandra Marsh Mgt 9150 Wilshire Blvd Ste 220 Beverly Hills CA 90212-3429

LOVEJOY, WILLIAM JOSEPH, automotive company executive; b. Bklyn., Sept. 2, 1940; s. William G. and Catherine J. (Barry) L.; m. Geraldine V. Smith, Feb. 12, 1966; children: William Jerome, Catherine Elizabeth. BS, St. Francis Coll., 1975; MBA, Fairleigh Dickinson U., 1981. Teller First Nat. City Bank, Bklyn., 1959-62; mem. credit staff GMAC, Bklyn., 1962-71; mgr. GMAC, Parsippany, N.J., 1974-75; asst. control mgr. GMAC, Washington, 1975-78; regional mgr. GMAC, Denver, 1981-84; group v.p. mktg. GMAC, Detroit, 1988-89, exec. v.p. ops., 1990, pres., 1990-92; v.p., gen. mgr. GM Svc. Parts Operation, Flint, Mich., 1992—. With U.S. Army, 1961-62. Avocations: swimming, bicyling. Office: GM Svc Parts Operation 6060 W Bristol Rd Flint MI 48554-0001*

LOVELACE, ALAN MATHIESON, aerospace company executive; b. St. Petersburg, Fla., Sept. 4, 1929; married; 2 children. BA, U. Fla., 1951, MA, 1952, PhD in Chemistry, 1954. Staff mem. Air Force Materials Lab., Wright-Paterson AFB, 1954-72; dir. sci. and tech. Andrews AFB, Washington, 1972-73; prin. dep. asst. sec., dept. R & D USAF, 1973-74; assoc. adminstr. Aerospace Tech. Office, 1974-76; dep. NASA Aerospace Tech. Office, 1976-81; v.p. sci. and engring., space systems div. Gen. Dynamics Corp., San Diego, 1981-82, corp. v.p. quality assurance and productivity, 1982-85, corp. v.p., gen. mgr., 1985—; chmn. Nat. Acad. Engr., Washington, 1996—. Fellow AIAA (Goddard Astronautics award 1989, George M. Low Space Transp. award 1992); mem. NAE, Air Force Assn., Sigma Xi. Office: Nat Acad Engr 2101 Constitution Ave NW Washington DC 20418*

LOVELACE, BYRON KEITH, lawyer, management consultant; b. Vernon, Tex., Feb. 15, 1935; s. Joseph Edward and Hattie Pearl (Brians) L.; m. Sandra Alene Daniel, June 17, 1961; children: Kirk Daniel, Bethany Alene, Amy Kathleen. BS in Chem. Engring., U. Tex., 1958, MS, 1961, PhD, 1973; JD, South Tex. Coll. Law, 1978. Bar: Tex. 1978. R & D engr. Core Labs., Dallas, 1960-61; with Tex. Instruments, Inc., Dallas and Houston, 1961-78, mgr. process control for advanced tech., 1969-70, reliability mgr. metal oxide semicondr. (MOS) div., 1971-75, MOS reliability dir., 1975-78; pres. P-V-T Inc., Houston, 1978-80, Mgmt. Resources Internat., Houston, 1980—; pvt. practice Law Offices of Keith Lovelace, Houston, 1980—. Contbr. articles to profl. jours.; patentee in field. Mem. Houston Clean City Commn., 1991-94, Greater Southwest Houston C. of C. (bd. dirs. 1996—, vice chmn. 1996—). With U.S. Army, 1953. Tex. Instruments fellow, 1965-68; FMC Corp. fellow, 1958-60; Eastern States Petroleum and Chem. scholar, 1957-58; Ethyl Corp. scholar, 1956-57. Mem. ABA, AIChE, Am. Chem. Soc. (award 1958), Soc. Petroleum Engrs. (vice chmn. reservior group 1979-80), State Bar Tex., Trial Lawyers Am., S.W. Houston C. of C. (bd. dirs. 1988-91, pres. 1990-91), Greater S.W. Houston C. of C. (bd. dirs. 1996—, vice chmn. 1996—), Tau Beta Pi (chpt. v.p. 1958-59), Omega Chi Epsilon. Office: 7322 SW Freeway Ste 1480 Houston TX 77074

LOVELACE, ELDRIDGE HIRST, retired landscape architect, city planner; b. Kansas City, Kans., Mar. 16, 1913; s. Charles Wilson and Eva (Hirst) L.; m. Marjorie Van Evera, May 15, 1937; children: Jean (Mrs. William C. Stinchcombe), Richard. B.F.A. in Landscape Architecture, U. Ill., 1935. Registered profl. engr., Mo. With Harland Bartholomew & Assocs., Inc., St. Louis, 1935—81; mem. firm Harland Bartholomew & Assocs., Inc., 1943-79, chmn. bd., 1979—81; cons., 1981—; prepared comprehensive city plans numerous cities including Toledo, Baton Rouge, Oklahoma City, Vancouver, Waco, Lincoln, Washington; master plans for naval facilities Hawaiian Islands and P.I.; also plans parks, subdivs., housing projects.; Vice pres. Internat. Fedn. Landscape Architects, 1975-77, sec. gen., 1980—81. Author: Harland Bartholomew: His Contributions to American Urban Planning. Mem. bd. commrs. Tower Grove Park, 1971—, pres. 1986-94. Fellow Am. Soc. Landscape Architects (past sec.), ASCE; mem. Am. Inst. Cert. Planners. Clubs: Mo. Athletic (St. Louis). Home: 5 Brookside Ln Saint Louis MO 63124-1814

LOVELACE, JON B., investment management company executive; b. Detroit, Feb. 6, 1927; s. Jonathan Bell and Marie (Andersen) L.; m. Lillian Pierson, Dec. 29, 1950; children: Carey, James, Jeffrey, Robert. A.B. cum laude, Princeton U., 1950. Personnel asst. Pacific Finance Co., 1950-51; with Capital Research & Mgmt. Co., L.A., 1951—, treas., 1955-62, v.p., 1957-62, exec. v.p., 1962-64, pres., 1964-75, 82-83, chmn. bd., 1975-82, 83—, also dir.; chmn. bd. Investment Co. Am., 1982—, Capital Income Builder, 1987—, Am. Mut. Fund Inc., 1971—; bd. dirs. Capital Research Co., 1967—, Am. Pub. Radio; pres., dir. New Perspective Fund. Trustee Claremont McKenna Coll.; mem. bd. fellows Claremont U. Ctr.; mem. adv. bd. Stanford U. N.E. Asia/U.S. Forum on Internat. Policy; trustee Calif. Inst. Arts, chmn., 1983-88; trustee Santa Barbara Med. Found. Clinic, J. Paul Getty Mus., chmn. 1988—. Mem. Council on Fgn. Relations, Sierra Club. Clubs: Princeton (N.Y.C.), University (N.Y.C.); Calif. (Los Angeles). also: 780 El Bosque Rd Santa Barbara CA 93108-1310 Address: 333 S Hope 47th Fl Los Angeles CA 90071-9007*

LOVELACE, JULIANNE, library director; b. Jackson, Miss., July 30, 1941; d. Benjamin Travis and Julia Elizabeth (Knight) Robinson; m. William Frank Lovelance, July 6, 1963 (div. Mar. 17, 1972); 1 child, Julie Lynn. BA in History, So. Meth. U., 1963; MLS, U. North Tex., 1970. Clk. Dallas Pub. Libr., 1963-64, children's libr. asst., 1964-66, children's libr., 1966-69; libr. Richardson (Tex.) Pub. Libr., 1971-72, supr. pub. svcs., 1972-87, dir., 1987—. Mem. exec. bd. Youth Svcs. Coun., Richardson Adult Literacy Ctr.; mem. Altrusa Internat., Inc. Richardson, Leadership Richardson Alumni Assn., Friends of the Richardson Pub. Libr. Adminstrs., North Tex. Mem. ALA, Tex. Libr. Assn., Pub. Libr. Adminstrs. North Tex. Avocations: horse racing, blackjack. Office: Richardson Pub Libr 900 Civic Center Dr Richardson TX 75080-5210

LOVELACE, ROBERT FRANK, health science facility administrator, researcher; b. Elizabethton, Tenn., Oct. 7, 1950; s. Douglas Clayton and Doris Ivalee (Guy) L.; m. Diane Marie Wamsley, June 3, 1972; children: Jason Robert, Geoffrey Mark. BS, Phila. Coll. Bible, 1972; MA, Ea. Sem., Phila., 1974; PhD, Temple U., 1988. Lic. nursing home adminstr. Adminstr. research The Franklin Inst., Phila., 1974-79, adminstr. contracts, 1979-81; dir. research adminstrn. The Grad. Hosp., Phila., 1981-88; adminstr. Elm Terr. Gardens, Lansdale, Pa., 1988-95, pres., 1995—; adj. lectr. Temple U., Phila., 1983-86, Wilkes Coll., 1986-90, Rutgers U., 1989-93, St. Joseph's U., 1993—; exec. dir., sec.-treas. Gradtech, Phila., 1985-88. Contbr. articles to profl. jours. V.p., bd. dirs. Elm Terr. Gardens, Lansdale, 1986-88; dir. bd. Christian edn. 1st Bapt. Ch., Lansdale, 1985-88, 90-96, chmn. program com., 1987-90, chmn. worship svcs. com., 1992, chmn. search com., 1995. Mem. Am. Coll. Health Care Adminstrs., Nat. Coun. Univ. Rsch. Adminstrs., Soc. Rsch. Adminstrs. (mem. editorial bd. jour. 1986-90), Rsch. and Devel. Mgmt. Assn. Republican. Home: 553 Millers Way Lansdale PA 19446-4059 Office: Elm Terr Gardens 660 N Broad St Lansdale PA 19446-2361

LOVELADY, STEVEN M., newspaper editor; b. Morganfield, Ky., July 2, 1943; s. Talmage C. and Virginia Dell (Fortenberry) L.; m. Linda R. Higgins, June 18, 1965 (div. Apr. 1979); children—Stephanie, Sara; m. Ann Judith Kolson, Apr. 30, 1979. B.J., U. Mo., 1965. Midwest corr. Wall Street Jour., Chgo., 1965-66; west coast corr. Wall Street Jour., Los Angeles, 1966-69; page 1 rewriteman Wall Street Jour., N.Y.C., 1969-72; asst. mng. editor Phila. Inquirer, 1972-75, assoc. mng. editor, 1975-80, assoc. exec. editor, 1980-91, mng. editor, 1991—; directed Pulitzer prize-winning news coverage, 1977, 79, 85, 87, 88, 89; Pulitzer prize juror, 1989, 90; seminar leader Poynter Inst., St. Petersburg, Fla., 1981, 82, 85, 87. Active Center City Phila. Residents Assn. Mem. AP Mng. Editors. Avocation: breeding and racing thoroughbred horses. Office: Phila Inquirer 400 N Broad St Philadelphia PA 19130-4015

LOVELAND, DONALD WILLIAM, computer science educator; b. Rochester, N.Y., Dec. 26, 1934; s. Roger Platt and Dorothy (Dobbin) L.; m. Amy Straw, May 21, 1966; children: Robert Philip, Douglas Roger. AB, Oberlin Coll., 1956; SM, MIT, 1958; PhD, NYU, 1964. Mathematician, programmer IBM, Yorktown Heights, N.Y., 1958-59; asst. prof. math. NYU, 1964-67; asst. prof., then assoc. prof. math. and computer sci. Carnegie-Mellon U., Pitts., 1967-73; prof., chmn. dept. computer sci. Duke U., Durham, N.C., 1973-78, 91-92, prof. computer sci., 1973—; disting. faculty visitor IBM Rsch. Ctr., Yorktown Heights, 1979-80; program chmn., editor procs. 6th Conf. on Automated Deduction, 1982, trustee corp. controls, 1994—. Author: Automated Theorem Proving: A Logical Basis, 1978; co-editor: (with W.W. Bledsoe) Automated Theorem Proving: After 25 Years, 1984; mng. editor book series Artificial Intelligence, 1983-92; editorial bd. Artificial Intelligence, 1983-93, Jour. Automated Reasoning. Grantee NSF, 1970-73, 75-77, 88-92, 92-96, Air Force Office Sci. Rsch., 1981-86, Army Rsch. Office, 1984-91. Mem. Assn. for Computing Machinery, Assn. for Symbolic Logic, Am. Assn. for Artificial Intelligence (elected fellow 1993), AAAS. Home: 3417 Cambridge Dr Durham NC 27707-4507 Office: Duke Univ Box 90129 Durham NC 27708-0129

LOVELAND, EUGENE FRANKLIN, petroleum executive; b. Anderson, Ind., Sept. 11, 1920; s. Irving Eugene and Clare (McFarlane) L.; m. Joan King, Aug. 4, 1944; children: Jeffrey, David C. and Peter F. (twins), Mark, Laurie E. B.A., Wesleyan U., Middletown, Conn. With Shell Oil Co., 1946-80, v.p. central mktg. region, 1968-71; v.p. oil products Shell Oil Co., Houston, 1972-80; pres. Transworld Oil USA, Inc. (formerly T.W. Oil Inc.), Houston, 1981—; chmn., chief exec. officer T.W. Oil Inc., 1983-89, ret., 1989; bd. dirs. Transworld Oil Ltd.; Bermuda. Bd. dirs. Lyric Theatre, Houston, Am. Dance Cos.; chmn. Houston Ballet Found., Combined Arts Corp., Campaign, Houston, Greater Houston Skating Coun., vice chmn. Better Bus. Bur., Houston; hon. counsul gen. Republic of Malta in Tex.; dir. Cultural Arts Coun. Houston, 1989-93; chmn. Greater Houston Ice Skating Coun., 1989—; mem. exec. com. Houston Internat. Festival, 1992; chmn. devel. commn. Fay Sch., 1992. With USNR, 1943-45. Decorated D.F.C., Air medal (2); recipient Disting. Alumnus award Wesleyan U., 1993. Mem. Mil. and Hospitaller Order St. Lazarus Jerusalem, Petroleum Club of Houston. Office: Transworld Oil USA Inc 654 N Belt Dr E Ste 400 Houston TX 77060-5914

LOVELAND, JACQUELINE JANE, neuroscientist, biologist; b. Point Pleasant Borough, N.J., Feb. 16, 1952; d. George Clark and Virginia Mae (Skimmons) L.; m. Alan Dale Nunes, Aug. 22, 1974 (div. Aug. 1978); 1 child, Emmett Todd Nunes. BA, San Jose State U., 1981, MA, 1987. Rsch. assoc. NASA-Ames Rsch. Ctr., Mt. View, Calif., 1980-83; supr., sr. case mgr. Cmty. Companions, Inc., San Jose, Calif., 1983-85, cons., 1985; neurosci. biologist Syntex Rsch. Inst. of Pharmacology, San Jose, Calif., 1985-93; safety pharmacology biologist Syntex Rsch. Inst. of Pathology, Toxicology & Metalobism, Palo Alto, 1993—. Contbr. articles to profl. jours.; author abstracts. Mem. AAAS, Soc. Neurosci., Psi Chi, Phi Theta Kappa. Avocations: camping, dancing, swimming, skiing. Office: Syntex Rsch 3401 Hillview Ave Palo Alto CA 94304-1320

LOVELESS, EDWARD EUGENE, education educator, musician; b. Lafayette, Ind., July 29, 1919; s. Benjamin Moses and Belva Lucille (Bowles) L.; m. Jean Evelyn Skinner, May 18, 1941; children: Linda Louise Loveless Reeder, Kathleen Beal Loveless Bodine, Stephen Edward, Melissa Jane Loveless Campbell, Benjamin Warwick. B.S., Purdue U., 1940, M.S., 1941; Ed.D., Stanford U., 1960. Tchr., prin., supt. public schs. Ind., 1941-57; asst. Stanford U., 1957-60; prin. public schs. Palo Alto, Calif., 1961-65; asst. prof. sch. adminstrn. San Francisco State Coll. and assoc. prof. San Jose State Coll., 1960-65; assoc. prof. U. Nev., Reno, 1965-72; prof. U. Nev., 1972-85, prof. emeritus, 1986—; vis. prof. Purdue U., summers 1965, 68, 75; prof. exec. devel. program USAF, Crete, spring 1973. Author: (with Frank Krajewski) The Teacher and School Law: Cases and Materials in the Legal Foundations of Education, 1974, (with J. Clark Davis) The Administrator and Educational Facilities, 1982; contbr. over 70 articles to profl. jours.; editor: Who's Who in Northern Nevada Education, 1976; spkr. on sch. vandalism; clarinetist, saxaphonist, vocalist Jean and Ed (musical duo), 1984—; musical tours Ms World Discoverer, Singapore, The South Seas, New Guinea, Western Samoa, Tonga, Fiji, Tahiti, others, 1984-85; performance South Pacific Coll., Stanford U. Alumni Assn., 1985; royal command performance King Tauf-ahau Tupou IV, Tonga, 1985; commd. performance Trident submarine USS Nev., 1986; concert U.S. Embassy, Geneva, 1987; recs. include Songs of the 30's and 40's, The Gershwin Bros., The Best of Irving Berlin, Jerome Kern Favorites, Hoagy & Benny Revisited, An Evening with Cole Porter, We Like Rodgers & Hart, The Genius of Duke Ellington, Easy Listening, Songs of Jule Styne, A Tribute to Jimmy Van Heussen, Rodgers and Hammerstein Music, 1989, cassette tape series for Wickenburg (Ariz.) Hist. Mus., 1989, Golden Anniversary performance Purdue U., 1990, 74th Birthdays Cassette, 1993, Nat King Cole Songs, 1996. Performer, concert artist for retirement homes and hosps., Palo Alto, Calif., 1990—. Recipient Commendations for providing benefit concerts and performances Sierra Health Care Ctr., 1985, Salvation Army Family Emergency, 1986, VA Hosp., 1988, Daus. of Norway, 1988, Westwood Retirement Home, 1989, State of Nev. Employees Assn., 1989; recipient Certs. of Appreciation Riverside Hosp., 1986, Carson Convalescent Ctr., 1987, Reno Lions Club, 1987, Thank-U-Gram Physicians Hosp., 1988, Manor at Lakeside, 1988, award Washoe County Sr. Citizens Ctr., 1989, Sharon Heights Convalescent Hosp., Palo Alto, Calif., 1993. Mem. NEA, Nev. Edn. Assn., Internat. Soc. Gen. Semantics, Nat. Soc. Profs., Navy League, Kappa Sigma, Phi Delta Kappa (cert. for disting. service 1974, placque of appreciation Gamma Psi chpt. 1976). Democrat. Presbyterian (elder). Home: 2170 Princeton St Palo Alto CA 94306-1325 also: 2895 W Moana Ln Reno NV 89509 *Providing musical entertainment for retired and/or hospitalized people has a therapeutic effect that medicine cannot provide. Wynton Marsalis says that "music washes away the dust of everyday life from your feet".*

LOVELESS, GEORGE GROUP, lawyer; b. Baldwinsville, N.Y., Sept. 16, 1940; s. Frank Donald and Mayme (Lont) L.; m. Shirley Morrison, Nov. 27, 1965; children: Michael, Peter. BS, Cornell U., 1962, MBA, 1963; JD, U. Md., 1968. Bar: Pa. 1969, U.S. Dist. Ct. (ea. dist.) Pa., U.S. Ct. Appeals (3d cir.). Ptnr. Morgan, Lewis & Bockius, Phila., 1968—. With USAFR, 1963-68. Republican. Presbyterian. Home: 11 Rose Valley Rd Moylan PA 19063-4217 Office: Morgan Lewis & Bockius 2000 One Logan Sq Philadelphia PA 19103

LOVELESS, JAMES KING, art educator; b. Saginaw, Mich., Apr. 24, 1935; s. James Clifton and Edris Maureen (King) L.; m. Ruthann Speer, Oct. 5, 1974; children—Elizabeth, Ellen, Karen, Douglas, David. A.B., DePauw U., 1957; M.F.A., Ind. U., 1960. Asst. prof. art Hope Coll., Holland, Mich., 1960-64; asst. prof. U. Ky., Lexington, 1964-66; prof. Colgate U., Hamilton, N.Y., 1966—. One-man shows include: Everson Mus., Syracuse, N.Y., 1978, Fine Arts Gallery, SUNY, Oneonta, 1984; exhibited in group shows: Munson-Williams-Proctor Inst., Utica, N.Y., 1979, traveling exhbn. sponsored by Mus. Am. Art, Washington; 1981-83; represented in permanent collection: Munson-Williams-Proctor Inst., Utica, Picker Gallery, Colgate U., Hamilton, N.Y., Chase Manhattan Bank, N.Y.C., Gettysburg (Pa.) Coll. Fellow Yaddo, Millay Colony. Home: RR 1 Box 124 Hamilton NY 13346-9737 Office: Colgate Univ Art and Art History Dept Hamilton NY 13346

LOVELESS, KATHY LYNNE, computer specialist; b. Corsicana, Tex., Mar. 7, 1961; d. Vernon Ray and Barbara Alice (Brown) L. BA, Baylor U., 1983. Adminstrv. asst. InterFirst Bank, Dallas, 1983-85; adminstrv. asst. Chaparral Steel Co., Midlothian, Tex., 1985-89, audio/visual coord., 1989-93; freelance computer instr. Duncanville, Tex., 1993-94; tng. specialist U. Tex. Southwestern Med. Ctr., Dallas, 1994-95, supr. client svcs. ctr., 1995—. Pres., v.p. Midlothian Cmty. Theatre, 1990-93, mem., 1987-94; v.p. Lovers Ln. United Meth. Ch. Choir, Dallas, 1994, 95, Adminstrv. Bd., 1995-96; chmn. worship and mem. care com. Elmwood United Meth. Ch., 1990, 91; bd. dirs. Trinity River Mission, Dallas, 1994, 95, 96. Mem. NAFE, AAUW, USA Film Festival, Am. Film Inst. Avocations: sports, films, music, books, theatre. Home: 8918 Sweetwater Dallas TX 75228

LOVELESS, PATTY (PATTY RAMEY), country music singer; b. Pikeville, Ky., Jan. 4, 1957; m. Terry Lovelace (div.); m. Emory Gordy, Jr., Feb. 1989. Recording artist MCA, 1985-93, Sony Music, 1993—. Albums: Patty Loveless, 1987, If My Heart Had Windows, 1988, Honky Tonk Angel, 1988 (gold), On Down the Line, 1990, Up Against My Heart, 1991, Only What I Feel, 1993, Greatest Hits, 1993, When Fallen Angels Fly, 1994; # 1 hit singles Timber, I'm Falling in Love, Chains. Named Favorite New Country Artist by Am. Music Awards, 1989; recipient TNN Music City News Country Award, Female Artist, 1990; inductee Grand Ole Opry, 1988.

LOVELL, CHARLES C., federal judge; b. 1929; m. Ariliah Carter. BS, U. Mont., 1952, JD, 1959. Assoc. Church, Harris, Johnson & Williams, Great Falls, Mont., 1959-85; judge U.S. Dist. Ct. Mont., Helena, 1985—; chief counsel Mont. Atty Gen.'s Office, Helena, 1969-72. Served to capt. USAF, 1952-54. Mem. ABA, Am. Judicature Soc., Assn. Trial Lawyers Am. Office: US Dist Ct PO Drawer 10112 301 S Park Ave Helena MT 59626*

LOVELL, EDWARD GEORGE, mechanical engineering educator; b. Windsor, Ont., Can., May 25, 1939; s. George Andrew and Julia Anne (Kopacz) L.; children: Elise, Ethan. B.S., Wayne State U., 1960, M.S., 1961; Ph.D., U. Mich., 1967. Registered profl. engr., Wis. Project engr. Bur. Naval Weapons, Washington, 1959, Boeing Co., Seattle, 1962; test engr. Ford Motor Co., Troy, Mich., 1960; instr. U. Mich., Ann Arbor, 1963-67; design engr. United Tech., Hartford, Conn., 1970; prof. engring. U. Wis., Madison, 1968—, chmn. dept. engring. mechanics and astronautics, 1992-95; cons. structural engring. to govt. labs., indsl. orgns., maj. textbook pubs., 1968—. Contbr. numerous articles to profl. jours. Postdoctoral research fellow Nat. Acad. Sci., 1967; NATO Sci. fellow, 1973; NSF fellow, 1961. Mem. Wis. Fusion Tech. Inst., Wis. Ctr. for Applied Microelectronics, Sigma Xi, Tau Beta Pi, Phi Kappa Phi. Office: U Wis Dept Mech Engring Dept Mech Engring 1513 University Ave Madison WI 53706-1572

LOVELL, FRANCIS JOSEPH, investment company executive; b. Boston, Mar. 21, 1949; s. Frank J. and Patricia Anna (Donnellan) L. BBA, Nichols Coll., 1971. With Brown Bros. Harriman & Co., Boston, 1971—, deputy mgr., 1990—. alumni dir. St. Columbkille Sch., Brighton, Mass. Mem. New Eng. Hist. Gen. Soc., Union Club of Boston. Republican. Home: 25 Pomfret St West Roxbury MA 02132-1809 also (summer): 48 Hidden Village Rd West Falmouth MA 02574 Office: 40 Water St Boston MA 02109-3604

LOVELL, GLENN MICHAEL, film critic; b. Bishop Stortford, Eng., Sept. 21, 1948; came to U.S., 1952; s. Lester Eugene and Audrey Mary (Caton) L.; divorced; 1 child, Andrew Hurst Lovell. BA cum laude, Lycoming Coll., 1970; MA, Pa. State U., 1972. TV-film-book critic Hollywood Reporter, L.A., 1972; entertainment editor Richmond (Va.) Mercury, 1973, Miami Beach Sun-Reporter, 1974, Fort Lauderdale (Fla.) Sun-Sentinel, 1976-80; theater critic San Jose (Calif.) Mercury News, 1980-82, film critic, 1982—; Nat. Arts Journalism fellow U. So. Calif., 1995-96; film critic Sta. KARA-FM, San Jose, 1985-86, Sta. KOME-FM, San Jose, 1985-86; instr. film adult extension program San Jose State U., 1984-87; instr. De Anza Coll., Cupertino, Calif., 1989, 94; film commentary Sta. KGO, San Francisco, 1985—; judge Palo Alto (Calif.) Film Festival, 1983; panel moderator Screenwriter's Workshop, San Francisco, 1991, Cinequest panel, San Jose, 1994; profl.-in-residence journalism dept. U. Iowa, 1996. Revs. pub. in numerous newspapers, including Atlanta Constn., Boston Globe, Chgo. Tribune, Cin. Enquirer, Des Moines Register, Detroit Free Press, L.A. Daily News, Miami Herald, N.Y. Daily News, Phila. Inquirer, San Francisco Chronicle, Washington Post, others; also freelance work in L.A. Times, Miami Herald, Toronto Star, Aquarian Weekly, Calif. Theatre Ann., Cinefantistique Mag., Hollywood Reporter, L.A. Free Press.; co-writer (short film) Night Ride, Miami Film Festival, 1977. Union rep. Newspaper Guild, Bay Area, San Jose, 1991, 94. Nominee, Nat. Soc. Film Critics, 1995. Democrat. Avocations: running, scuba, skiing. Home: 975 Terra Bella Ave San Jose CA 95125-2656 Office: San Jose Mercury News 750 Ridder Park Dr San Jose CA 95131-2432

LOVELL, MALCOLM READ, JR., public policy institute executive, educator, former government official, former trade association executive; b. Greenwich, Conn., Jan. 1, 1921; s. Malcolm Read and Emily (Monihan) L.; m. Celia Coghlan, 1978; children by previous marriage: Lucie, Sara. Annette, Caroline. Grad., Lawrenceville Sch., 1939; student, Brown U., 1939-42; I.A., Harvard U., 1943; M.B.A., Harvard, 1946. With Ford Motor Co., Dearborn, Mich., 1946-58; mgr. employee services Am. Motors Corp., Detroit, 1958-61; chmn. State Labor Mediation Bd., Detroit, 1963; dir. Mich. Office Econ. Opportunity, 1964, Mich. Employment Security Commn., Detroit, 1965-69; exec. asso. Manpower, Urban Coalition, 1969; dep. asst. sec. of labor and manpower adminstr., 1969-70, asst. sec. of labor for manpower, 1970-73; pres. Rubber Mfrs. Assn., 1973-81; asst. dir. Office Policy Coordination and Econ. Affairs, Office Pres.-Elect, 1980; undersec. Dept. Labor, Washington, 1981-83; vis. scholar Brookings Instn., Washington, 1983-85; disting. vis. prof. govt. and dir. Labor Mgmt. Inst. George Washington U., 1985-92; pres. Nat. Planning Assn., 1992—; sr. fellow Hudson Inst., 1985-88; mem. Nat. Adv. Coun. on Vocat. Edn., 1975-79, Nat. Commn. for Manpower Policy, 1977-79; chmn. sec. labor Task Force on Econ. Adjustment and Worker Dislocation, 1985-86. Vice pres. Birmingham (Mich.) Sch. Bd., 1956-60; bd. dirs. Nat. Alliance Bus., 1984—; bd. dirs. Travelers Aid of Washington, 1983—, pres., 1985-86; Served to lt. USNR, 1943-46. Mem. City Tavern Club (Washington), Clean Plate (Washington), Cosmos Club (Washington), Alpha Delta Phi. Quaker. Office: Nat Planning Assn 1424 16th St NW Washington DC 20036-2211

LOVELL, THEODORE, electrical engineer, consultant; b. Paterson, N.J., May 10, 1928; s. George Whiting and Ethel Carol (Berner) L.; m. Wilma Syperda, May 8, 1948 (div. Oct. 1961); m. Joyce Smelik, July 15, 1962; children: Laurie, Dorothy Jane, Valerie, Cynthia, Karen, Barbara. BEE, Newark Coll. Engring., 1948; postgrad., Canadian Inst. Tech., 1950. Exec. dir. Lovell Electric Co., Franklin Lakes, N.J., 1955-82; ptnr., exec. dir. Lovell Design Services, Swedesboro, N.J., 1982—. Author engring. computer software, 1982. Bd. dirs., treas. Contact "Help" of Salem County, 1991-93; pres. Bloomingdale Bd. Edn., N.J., 1970-82; mem. Mcpl. Planning Bd., Bloomingdale, 1980-82, Swedesboro/Woolwich Bd. Edn., 1987-94, v.p., 1990-92, pres. 1993-94; mayoral candidate Borough of Bloomingdale, 1982. Recipient Outstanding Service award Lake Iosco Co., Bloomingdale, 1985, 20 Yr. Svc. award N.J. Sch. Bd. Assn., 1994. Mem. Am. Soc. Engring. Technicians, Radio Club Am., Dickinson Theater Organ Soc. Republican. Presbyterian. Avocations: Lincoln history, theater, organ music. Home: 502 Liberty Ct Swedesboro NJ 08085-9416 Office: Lovell Design Svcs PO Box 366 Swedesboro NJ 08085-0366 *It has become apparent to me, slowly perhaps that as I progress through life, the things that bring lasting joy and satisfaction are not personal achievements, but those things that help others.*

LOVELL, WALTER CARL, engineer, inventor; b. Springfield, Vt., May 7, 1934; s. John Vincent and Sophia Victoria (Klementowicz) L.; m. Patricia Ann Lawrence, May 6, 1951; children: Donna, Linda, Carol, Patricia, Diane, Walter Jr. B of Engring., Hillyer Coll., Hartford, Conn., 1959. Project engr. Hartford Machine Screw Co., Windsor, Conn., 1954-59; design engr. DeBell and Richardson Labs., Enfield, Conn., 1960-62; cons. engr. Longmeadow, Mass., 1962—; freelance inventor Wilbraham, Mass., 1965—. Numerous patents include Egg-Stir mixer, crown closure sealing gasket, circular unleakable bottle cap, sonic wave ram jet engine, solid state heating tapes, card key lock; composer over 50 country-and-Western songs. Achievements include patents for sonic wave ram jet engine, solid state heat and resistor tape, card key lock, security lock system, heat producing paints and ceramics.

LOVELY, THOMAS DIXON, banker; b. N.Y.C., Apr. 2, 1930; s. Thomas John and Margaret Mary (Browne) L.; AB, Adelphi U., 1954, MA, 1956, MBA, 1958; m. Erna Susan Fritz, June 16, 1956; children: Thomas John Hall, Richard Robert. Treas., Pepsi Cola Bottling Co., Garden City, N.Y., 1957-60; assoc. prof. mgmt. and communications CUNY, 1958-77; dist. adminstr. Lido Beach (N.Y.) Pub. Schs., 1971-80; chmn. bd., pres. Fidelity Fed. Savs. and Loan Assn., Floral Park, N.Y., 1980-82, chmn. bd., pres. Fidelity N.Y., 1982—; v.p., dir. N.Y. Enterprise Co. Trustee, SUNY, 1992, chmn. bd. SUNY Old Westbury Coll. Found., 1989—, vice chmn. bd. trustees Adelphi U., 1967-91, chmn. bd. govs. Univ. Sch. Banking and Money Mgmt., 1975—; trustee Nassau County (N.Y.) Med. Center, 1982—; exec. v.p., treas. Nassau County coun. Boy Scouts Am., 1986—, pres., 1989-92; regional chmn. campaign U.S. Treasury Savs. Bonds Sales, Long Island, 1987—; pres., trustee Meadowbrook Med. Edn. Found., Inc., 1987—. Mem. SAR, L.I. Insured Savs. Group (v.p.). Clubs: Pinehurst Country (N.C.), Cherry Valley Country (Garden City). Home: 52 Locust St Garden City NY 11530-6329 Office: Fidelity NY Fed Savs Bank 1000 Franklin Ave Garden City NY 11530-2910

LOVEN, ANDREW WITHERSPOON, environmental engineering company executive; b. Crossnore, N.C., Jan. 31, 1935; s. Andrew Witherspoon Loven and Annie Laura (Crowell) Stewart; m. Elizabeth Joann DeGroot, June 20, 1959 (dec.); children: Laura Elizabeth, James Edward. BS, Maryville Coll., 1957; PhD, U. N.C., 1962. Registered profl. engr., Va., Ga., Iowa, Md., N.C., S.C., D.C., Ohio, Fla., Mich. Rsch. assoc. U. N.C., Chapel Hill, 1962-63; sr. rsch. chemist Westvaco Corp., Charleston, S.C., 1963-66; mgr. carbon devel. Westvaco Corp., Charleston, 1966-71, mgr. Westvaco Wastewater Cons. Service, 1967-71; mgr. engring. concepts Engring.-Sci. Inc., McLean, Va., 1971-74; v.p., regional mgr. Engring.-Sci. Inc., Atlanta, 1974-80, group v.p., 1980-86; pres., chief exec. officer Engring. Sci. Inc., Pasadena, Calif., 1986-95, also chmn. bd. dirs.; exec. v.p. Parsons Engring. Sci. Inc., Pasadena, Calif., 1995; pres., CEO Millennium Sci. & Engring., Inc., McLean, Va., 1995—. Contbr. articles to profl. jours. NSF grantee, 1958-59; recipient Maryville Coll. Alumni Citation award, 1992. Mem. AIChE, NSPE, Am. Acad. Environ. Engrs. (diplomate, membership com. 1985—), Water Pollution Control Fedn., Am. Water Works Assn., Am. Pub. Works Assn., Constrn. Industry Pres. Forum, Willow Springs Club, Sigma Xi, Alpha Gamma Sigma. Avocations: golf, hiking. Home: # 103 7720 Tremyne Pl McLean VA 22102 Office: Millennium Sci & Engring Inc 1364 Beverly Rd Ste 301 Mc Lean VA 22101

LOVENTHAL, MILTON, writer, playwright, lyricist; b. Atlantic City; s. Harry and Clara (Feldman) L.; m. Jennifer McDowell, July 2, 1973. BA, U. Calif., Berkeley, 1950, MLS, 1958; MA in Sociology, San Jose State U., 1969. Researcher Hoover Instn., Stanford, Calif., 1952-53, spl. asst. to Slavic Curator, 1955-57; librarian San Diego Pub. Library, 1957-59; librarian, bibliographer San Jose (Calif.) State U., 1959-92; tchr. writing workshops, poetry readings, 1969-73; co-producer lit. and culture radio show Sta. KALX, Berkeley, 1971-72; editor, pub. Merlin Press, San Jose, 1973—. Author: Books on the USSR, 1951-57, 57, Black Politics, 1971 (featured at Smithsonian Inst. Special Event, 1992), A Bibliography of Material Relating to the Chicano, 1971, Autobiographies of Women, 1946-70, 72, Blacks in America, 1972, The Survivors, 1972, Contemporary Women Poets an Anthology, 1977, Ronnie Goose Rhymes for Grown-Ups, 1984; co-author: (Off-Off-Broadway plays) The Estrogen Party to End War, 1986, Mack the Knife, Your Friendly Dentist, 1986, Betsy & Phyllis, 1986, The Oatmeal Party Comes to Order, 1986, (plays) Betsy Meets the Wacky Iraqi, 1991, Bella and Phyllis, 1994; co-writer (mus. comedy) Russia's Secret Plot to Take Back Alaska, 1988. Recipient Bill Casey Award in Letters, 1980; grantee San Jose State U., 1962-63, 84. Mem. Assn. Calif. State Profs., Calif. Alumni Assn., Calif. Theatre Coun. Office: PO Box 5602 San Jose CA 95150-5602

LOVERDE, PAUL S., bishop; b. Framingham, Mass., Sept. 3, 1940. Grad., St. Thomas Sem., Bloomfield, Conn., 1960; B.A. summa cum laude, St. Bernard Sem., Rochester, N.Y.; Licentiate in Sacred Theology, Gregorian U., Rome, Italy, 1966; Licentiate in Canon Law, Cath. U., Washington, D.C., 1982. Ordained priest, Dec. 18, 1965. Asst. pastor St. Sebastian Church, Middletown, CT, 1966-69; Catholic chaplain Wesleyan U., Middletown, CT, 1966-68; chaplain, Religion instructor & chmn. of Religious Studies Dept. St. Bernard Girls' Sch., New London, CT, 1969-72; Religion instructor & chmn. Religious Studies Dept. St. Bernard HS, Montville, CT, 1972-73; assoc. defender of the Bond Diocesan Tribunal of Norwich, 1970-81; Catholic chaplain Conn. Coll., New London, CT, 1970-79; dir. of Campus Ministry Diocese of Norwich, 1973-79; campus min. Eastern Conn. State Coll., Willimantic, CT, 1973-76; mem. bd. of dirs. Conn. Catholic Conf., 1973-78; vicar for priests Wyndham Co., 1974-75; chmn. bd. of vicars for priests, Diocese of Norwich, 1975-79; vice-officialis Diocesan Tribunal, 1981-88; chmn. bd. of conciliation/arbitration for priests, 1982-85; exec. coord. bd. of conciliation & arbitration, 1983-89; mem. Presbyteral Council, 1983-90, chmn., 1985-89; priests' rep. Diocesan Pastoral Council, 1984-88, vice-chmn., 1984-87; Bishop's del. for clergy, 1985-88; mem. Coll. of Consulters, 1985-90; reg. rep. U.S. Catholic Bishop's Nat. Adv. Council, 1986-90; appointed titular bishop of Ottabia, 1988; aux. bishop Diocese of Hartford, 1988-94; bishop Diocese of Ogdensburg, 1994—; mem. Continuing Edn. for the Clergy Comm. for Diocese of Norwich, 1967-71; mem. Clergy Assn. of Middletown, 1966-69; bd. of dirs., Conn. Project Equality, 1968-73; vocation promoter Middletown area, 1968-69; Diocese of Norwich rep., Task Force on Race & Ministry with Minorities, 1970; mem. Senate of Priests of Norwich Diocese, 1971-75 (v.p. 1971-72, pres. 1972-75); v.p. Church Vocations Task Group, 1973-79; temp. admin., Holy Trinity Church, Pomfret, CT, 1981; temp. admin. St. Catherine of Siena Church, Preston, CT, 1982, 85-86. contributor of articles to The Priest, Pastoral Life, and Today's Parish. 1st Hon. Brother, Altruism House, New London, CT, 1970. Address: Bishops Residence 624 Washington St Ogdensburg NY 13669*

LOVERING, LORELI, nurse practitioner, secretary; b. Renton, Pa., Dec. 28, 1934; d. Harry and Mary (Romanco) Federoff; m. Francis J. Piekarski, May 4, 1957 (dec. Mar. 1973); children: Jill C., Beth S. Hammack, Karen, James; m. Larry J. Lovering. Diploma in nursing, West Pa. Hosp. Sch. Nursing, 1955; nurse practitioner, U. Pitts., 1969; cert. nurse practitioner, Russellton Med. Group, 1973. Cert. Nurse Practitioner, 1978; ordained to ministry Eckankar, 1990. Staff and rehab. nurse Angelus Rehab. Ctr., Pitts., 1955-56; psychiat. nurse Vets. Hosp., Pitts., 1956-58; nurse part-time Citizen Gen. Hosp./Columbia Hosp., New Kensington, Pa., 1958-63; from nurse to nurse practitioner Penn Plum Med. Bldg. (merged with Miners Clinic, Inc., New Kensington, 1963-78; nurse practitioner VA Nursing Home Care Unit, Phoenix, 1978—; coord. Profl. Hearing Healthcare Ctrs., Sun City, Ariz., 1987—; chmn. nursing com. VA, 1992-94; pres. Nat. Assurance Svcs., Inc., Phoenix, 1986—; owner, pres. Interiors by Loreli, 1987-93. Co-editor Ariz. Geriatrics Jour. Mem. Ariz. Geriatrics Soc. (bd. dirs. 1993-96) Women's Bus. Clubs (scholar 1952), Advanced Practice Nurses, Geriatric Jour. Club, Nat. Hospice Orgn., Coun. Hospice Profls., Ariz Coun. of Aging, Toastmasters. Republican. Avocations: reading, writing poetry, swimming, walking. Home: 2745 E Winchcomb Dr Phoenix AZ 85032-5037 Office: Carl T Hayden Vets Med Ctr 650 E Indian School Rd Phoenix AZ 85012

LOVETT, CLARA MARIA, university administrator, historian; b. Trieste, Italy, Aug. 4, 1939; came to U.S., 1962; m. Benjamin F. Brown. BA equivalent, U. Trieste, 1962; MA, U. Tex.-Austin, 1967, PhD, 1970. Prof. history Baruch Coll., CUNY, N.Y.C., 1971-82, asst. provost, 1980-82; chief European div. Library of Congress, Washington, 1982-84; dean Coll. Arts and Scis., George Washington U., Washington, 1984-88; provost, v.p. academic affairs, George Mason U., Fairfax, Va., 1988-93; on leave from George Mason U.; dir. Forum on Faculty Roles and Rewards Am. Assn. for Higher Edn., 1993-94; pres. No. Ariz. U., Flagstaff, 1994—; vis. lectr. Fgn. Service Inst., Washington, 1979-85; bd. dirs. Inst. for Research in History, N.Y.C., 1981-82; exec. council Conf. Group on Italian Politics, 1980-83, others; lectr., cons. Fgn. Service Inst. State Dept., 1979—; adv. bd. European program Wilson Ctr., 1986—; bd. dirs. Assn. Am. Colls., 1990—. Author: The Democratic Movement in Italy 1830-1876, 1982 (H.R. Marraro Prize, Soc. Italian Hist. Studies); Giuseppe Ferrari and the Italian Revolution, 1979 (Phi Alpha Theta book award); Carlo Cattaneo and the Politics of Risorgimento, 1972 (Soc. for Italian Hist. Studies Dissertation award), (bibliography) Contemporary Italy, 1985; co-editor: Women, War, and Revolution, 1980, (essays) State of Western European Studies, 1984; contbr. sects. to publs. U.S., Italy. Organizer Dem. clubs Bklyn., 1972-76; exec. com. Palisades Citizens Assn., Washington, 1985-87; vestry mem. St. David's Episc. Ch., Washington, 1986-89. Fellow Guggenheim Found., 1978-79, Woodrow Wilson Internat. Ctr. for Scholars, 1979 (adv. bd. West European program), Am. Council Learned Socs., 1976, Bunting Inst. of Radcliffe Coll., 1975-76, others. Named Educator of Yr., Va. Fedn. of Bus. and Profl. Women, 1992. Mem. Am. Hist. Assn. (officer 1984-87), Am. Assn. Higher Edn. (cons. 1979—), Council for European Studies, Soc. for Italian Hist. Studies, Conf. Group on Italian Politics, others. Avocations: choral singing, swimming. Office: No Ariz U Office of Pres PO Box 4092 Flagstaff AZ 86011

LOVETT, JOHN ROBERT, retired chemical company executive; b. Norristown, Pa., June 17, 1931; s. James and Margaret (Creighton) L.; m. Sandra Miller, May 26, 1956; children: Judy, Jackie, John Robert Jr. BS, Ursinus Coll., 1953; MS, U. Del., 1955, PhD, 1957. Rsch. chemist Exxon Rsch., Linden, N.J., 1957-64; lab. dir. Exxon Rsch./Exxon Chem., Linden, 1964-70; v.p. Paramins Exxon Chem., Houston, 1970-74; tech. mgr. Exxon Chem., Linden, 1974-76; v.p. rsch. Air Products and Chems., Inc., Allentown, Pa., 1976-81; pres. Europe Air Products and Chems., Inc., Hersham, Eng., 1981-88; group v.p. chems. Air Products and Chems., Inc., Allentown, 1988-92, exec. v.p. gases & equipment, 1992-93, exec. v.p. strategic planning and tech., 1993-96. Mem. AICE, Chem. Mfrs. Assn. (bd. dirs. 1990-95), Am. Chem. Soc., Soc. Chem. Industry.

LOVETT, LYLE, musician; b. Klein, Tex.; s. William and Bernell; m. Julia Roberts, Jun. 27, 1993. Degree in Journalism, Tex. A&M U., 1980, grad. studies in German. Albums: Lyle Lovett, 1986, Pontiac, 1988, Lyle Lovett and His Large Band (Grammy award), 1989, Joshua Judges Ruth, 1992, I Love Everybody, 1994; contbd. songs to Deadicated, all-star tribute to Grateful Dead; contbd. songs to films: The Switch, 1987, The Crying Game, 1992, The Firm, 1993; appeared in films: The Player, 1992, Short Cuts, 1993, Ready to Wear (Prêt-à-Porter), 1994, TV appearances: Austin City Limits. Office: c/o MCA Records 70 Universal City Plz Universal City CA 91608

LOVETT, ROBERT G., lawyer; b. York, Pa., Aug. 17, 1944. BA, U. Pitts., 1966; JD, Duquesne U., 1969. Bar: Pa. 1970. Office: Reed Smith Shaw & McClay 435 6th Ave Pittsburgh PA 15219-1886

LOVETT, WENDELL HARPER, architect; b. Seattle, Apr. 2, 1922; s. Wallace Herman and Pearl (Harper) L.; m. Eileen Whitson, Sept. 3, 1947; children: Corrie, Clare. Student, Pasadena Jr. Coll., 1943-44; B.Arch., U. Wash., 1947; M.Arch., Mass. Inst. Tech., 1948. Architect, designer Naramore, Bain, Brady & Johanson, Seattle, 1948; architect, assoc. Bassetti & Morse, Seattle, 1948-51; pvt. practice architect Seattle, 1951—; instr. architecture U. Wash., 1948-51, asst. prof., 1951-60, assoc. prof., 1960-65, prof., 1965-83, prof. emeritus, 1983—; lectr. Technische Hochschule, Stuttgart, 1959-60. Prin. works include nuclear reactor bldg. U. Wash., 1960, Villa Simonyi, Medina, Wash., 1989. Pres. Citizen's Planning Council, Seattle, 1968-71. Served with AUS, 1943-46. Recipient 2d prize Progressive Architecture U.S. Jr. C. of C., 1949; Internat. design award Decima Triennale di Milano, 1954; Arch. Record Homes awards, 1969, 72, 74; Interiors award, 1973; Sunset-AIA awards, 1959, 62, 69, 71; Fulbright grantee, 1959; AIA fellow, 1978. Mem. AIA (sec. Wash. chpt. 1953-54, bd. dirs. Found. Seattle chpt. 1991-92, Seattle chpt. medal 1993, pres. sr. coun. 1991-92), Plestcheeff Inst. (bd. dirs. 1992). Patentee in field. Home and Office: 420 34th Ave Seattle WA 98122-6408

LOVETT, WILLIAM ANTHONY, law and economics educator; b. Milw., Sept. 2, 1934. AB, Wabash Coll., 1956; JD, NYU, 1959; PhD in Econs., Mich. State U., 1969. Bar: N.Y. 1960. Atty. U.S. Dept. Justice, Washington, 1962; economist FTC, Washington, 1963-69; prof. Tulane U., New Orleans, 1969—, dir. internat. law, trade and fin. program, 1985—; Joseph Merrick Jones prof. law and econs., 1991—. Author: Inflation and Politics, 1982, Banking and Financial Institutions Law, 1984, 88, 92, World Trade Rivalry, 1987, U.S. Shipping Policies and the World Market, 1996. Root-Tilden scholar, 1956-59. Mem. ABA, Am. Econs. Assn., Am. Soc. Internat. Law, Phi Beta Kappa. Office: Tulane Law Sch New Orleans LA 70118

LOVETTE, BLAKE DUANE, food company executive; b. North Wilkesboro, N.C., Dec. 19, 1942; s. Charlie Odell and Ila Ruth (Bumgarner) L.; m. Julia Lee Wooten, June 30, 1963; children: Sena Maria Lovette Brown, Angela Blake, Amy Camille. BS in Poultry Sci., N.C. State U., 1965. With Holly Farms Poultry Ind., Inc., various locations, 1965-78; exec. v.p. Holly Farms Poultry Ind., Inc., Wilkesboro; pres. Valmac Industries, Tasty Birds Foods, Russellville, Ark., 1978-84; v.p. Tyson Foods, Onc., Russellville, 1984; pres. Shenandoah Products subs. Perdue Foods, Inc., Harrisonburg, Va., 1984; exec. v.p. Perdue Foods, Inc., Salisbury, Md., 1988; pres., COO Holly Farms Foods, Inc., Wilkesboro, 1988-90; pres. Lovettte Co., Inc., North Wilkesboro, N.C., 1990—; pres. NBC, 1984-85. Republican. Methodist. Avocation: skiing. Home: 102 Meadow Brook Ct North Wilkesboro NC 28659-4636 Office: Lovette Co Inc Hwy 115 S North Wilkesboro NC 28659*

LOVIN, KEITH HAROLD, university administrator, philosophy educator; b. Clayton, N.Mex., Apr. 1, 1943; s. Buddie and Wanda (Smith) L.; m. Marsha Kay Gunn, June 11, 1966; children—Camille Jenay, Lauren Kay. B.A., Baylor U., 1965; postgrad., Yale U., 1965-66; Ph.D., Rice U., 1971. Prof. philosophy Southwest Tex. State U., San Marcos, 1970-77, chmn. dept. philosophy, 1977-78; dean liberal arts Southwest Tex. State U., 1978-81; provost, v.p. acad. affairs Millersville U., Pa., 1981-86; provost, v.p. acad. and student affairs U. So. Colo., Pueblo, 1986-92; pres. Maryville U. St. Louis, 1992—. Contbr. articles on philosophy of law, philosophy of religion to profl. publs.; mem. adv. bd. Southwest Studies in Philosophy, 1981-90. Bd. dirs. St. Louis Symphony Orch., Boys Hope, Jr. Achievement Mississippi Valley, Inc., United Way, St. Luke's Hosp., Nat. Coun. Alcohol and Drug Abuse, St. Louis Intercollegiate Athletic Conf., Ind. Colls. and Univs. of Mo., Higher Edn. Coun., 1992—. Mem. Chesterfield C. of C. (leadership club), Univ. Club, Media Club. Avocation: fly fishing. Home: 13664 Conway Rd Saint Louis MO 63141-7234 Office: Maryville U 13550 Conway Rd Saint Louis MO 63141-7232

LOVIN, ROBIN WARREN, minister, university dean, educator; b. Peoria, Ill., Mar. 22, 1946; s. Harvey Gifford and Irene (Warren) L. BA, Northwestern U., 1968; BDiv, Harvard U., 1971, PhD, 1978. Pastor United Meth. Ch., Freeport, Ill., 1971-72, Fenton, Ill., 1972-74; assoc. prof. U. Chgo., 1978-91; dean Theol. Sch. Drew U., 1991—; bd. visitors Duke Divinity Sch., Durham, N.C., 1984-90. Author: Christian Faith & Public Choices, 1984; editor: Religion and American Public Life, 1986, (with others) Cosmogony and Ethical Order, 1985; editor: Jour. of Religion, 1985-91; mem. editorial bd. Jour. of Religious Ethics, 1982—, Jour. of Law & Religion, 1983—. Guggenheim Found. fellow, 1987-88. Mem. Am. Acad. Religion (sect. chair 1987-90), Soc. Christian Ethics (bd. dirs. 1986-90). Democrat. Home: 9321 Frenchmans Way Dallas TX 75220-5039 Office: Drew U Theological Sch Madison NJ 07940

LOVING, GEORGE GILMER, JR., retired air force officer; b. Roanoke, Va., Aug. 7, 1923; s. George Gilmer and Ora Page (Carr) L.; m. Mary Ambler Thomasson, Jan. 15, 1945; children—Cary Ambler, Betty Page Behler. Student, Lynchburg Coll., 1941; B.A., U. Ala., 1960; M.A. in Internat. Affairs, George Washington U., 1965; grad., Air War Coll., 1965. Commd. 2d lt. U.S. Army Air Force, 1943; advanced through grades to lt. gen. U.S. Air Force, 1975; fighter pilot, test pilot, operations officer, fighter squadron comdr., 1943-55; U.S. adviser (Nat. War Coll.), Republic of China, 1960-62; staff planner Hdqrs. U.S. Air Force, Washington, 1965-69; comdr. Air Command and Staff Coll., 1970-73; dir. plans Hdqrs. U.S. Air Force, Washington, 1973-75; Joint Chiefs Staff rep. for mut. and balanced force reductions Washington, 1975; comdr. 6th Allied Tactical Air Force Izmir, Turkey, 1975-77; comdr. U.S. forces Japan; comdr. 5th Air Force Yokota Air Base, Japan, 1977-79; ret., 1979; cons. RAND Corp., 1979-80; exec. dir. Marie Selby Bot. Gardens, Sarasota, Fla, 1981-88. Decorated D.S.M. with 2 oak leaf clusters, Silver Star medal, Legion of Merit, D.F.C. with oak leaf cluster, Meritorious Service medal, Air Force Commendation medal, Air medal with 25 oak leaf clusters.; N.Y.C. Council on Fgn. Relations fellow, 1969-70. Mem. Am. Fighter Aces Assn. Episcopalian. Club: Sarasaota Yacht. Home: 508 Whitfield Ave Sarasota FL 34243-1603

LOVING, SUSAN B., lawyer, former state official; m. Dan Loving; children: Lindsay, Andrew, Kendall. BA with distinction, U. Okla., 1972, JD, 1979. Asst. atty. gen. Office of Atty. Gen., 1983-87, first asst. atty. gen., 1987-91; atty. gen. State of Okla., Oklahoma City, 1991-94; atty. Lester & Bryant, P.C., Oklahoma City, 1995—; Master Ruth Bader Ginsburg Inn of Ct.; bd. dirs. Bd. for Freedom of Info., Okla., Inc., Boy Scouts Am., Legal Aid of West Okla., Okla. Com. for Prevention of Child Abuse, Inst. for Ch. Adv.; mem. med. steering com. Partnership for Drug Free Okla., 1993—; adv. bd. Law and You Found. Vice chmn. Pardon and Parole Bd., 1995—; bd. dirs. Bd. for Freedom of Info., Okla. Inc., Boy Scouts Am., Legal Aid of West Okla., Okla. Com. for Prevention of Child Abuse; mem. med. steering com. Partnership for Drug Free Okla., Inst. for Child Advocacy, 1996—; mem. adv. bd. Law and You Found. Recipient Nat. Red Ribbon Leadership award Nat. Fedn. Parents, Headliner award, By-liner award Okla. City and Tulsa Women in Comm., First Friend of Freedom award, Freedom of Info., Okla., Dir. award Okla. Dist. Attys. Assn. Mem. Okla. Bar Assn. (past chmn. adminstrv. law sect., mem. adminstrn. of justice com., profl. responsibility commn.), Phi Beta Kappa. Office: Lester Loving & Davies PLLC 601 N Kelly Ste 102 Edmond OK 73003

LOVINGER, WARREN CONRAD, emeritus university president; b. Big Sandy, Mont., July 29, 1915; s. Wilbur George and Ruth Katherine (Hokanson) L.; m. Dorothy Blackburn, Aug. 14, 1937; children—Patricia Mae, Jeanie, Warren Conrad. B.A., U. Mont., 1942, M.A., 1944; Ed.D., Columbia U., 1947. Tchr., prin. Pub. Schs. Mont., 1937-43; instr. history U. Mont., Missoula, 1943-44; pres. No. State Coll., Aberdeen, S.D., 1951-56; pres. Central Mo. State U., Warrensburg, 1956-79, pres. emeritus, 1979—; exec. sec. Am. Assn. Colls. for Tchr. Edn., 1947-51, nat. pres., 1963-64; nat. pres. Am. Assn. State Colls. and Univs., 1974-75; mem. del. to study effects of Marshall Plan on Western Europe, 1950; leader study of tchr. edn. in Fed. Republic of Germany, 1964; leader del. People's Republic of China, 1975; mem. comparative study tour of Republic of China, 1976. Author: General Education in Teachers Colleges, 1948; contbr. articles to profl. jours. Served as lt. USNR, 1944-46, ETO. Recipient Silver Beaver award Boys Scouts Am., 1970; Outstanding Civilian Service award Dept. Army, 1979. Mem. Mo. Tchrs. Assn., Am. Assn. Sch. Adminstrs., Mo. Assn. Sch. Adminstrs., Columbia U. Alumni Assn., Stover C. of C. , Am. Legion, Gideons Internat., Phi Kappa Phi, Phi Delta Kappa, Kappa Delta Pi,. Baptist. Lodges: Masons, Shriners, Rotary, Lions. Avocations: travelling; writing; fishing; farming.

LOVINS, AMORY BLOCH, physicist, energy consultant; b. Washington, Nov. 13, 1947; s. Gerald Hershel and Miriam (Bloch) L.; m. L. Hunter Sheldon, Sept. 6, 1979. Student, Harvard U., 1964-65, 66-67, Magdalen Coll., Oxford, Eng., 1967-69; MA, Oxford U., Oxford, 1971; DSc (hon.), Bates Coll., 1979, Williams Coll., 1981, Kalamazoo Coll., 1983, U. Maine, 1985; LLD (hon.), Ball State U., 1983; D of Environ. Sci. (hon.), Unity Coll., 1992. Jr. research fellow Merton Coll., Oxford, England, 1969-71; Brit. rep., policy advisor Friends of the Earth, San Francisco, 1971-84; regent's lectr. U. Calif., Berkeley and Riverside, 1978, 81; v.p., dir. research Rocky Mountain Inst., Old Snowmass, Colo., 1982—; govt. and indsl. energy cons., 1971—; vis. prof. Dartmouth Coll., 1982; disting. vis. prof. U. Colo., 1982; prin. tech. cons. E Source, 1989—; prin. The Lovins Group, 1994—. Author: (also layout artist and co-photographer) Eryri, The Mountains of Longing, 1971, The Stockholm Conference: Only One Earth, 1972, Openpit Mining, 1973, World Energy Strategies: Facts, Issues, and Options, 1975, Soft Energy Paths: Toward a Durable Peace, 1977; co-author: (with J. Price) Non-Nuclear Features: The Case: The Case for an Ethical Energy Strategy, 1975, (with L.H. Lovins) Energy/War: Breaking the Nuclear Link, 1980, Brittle Power: Energy Strategy for National Security, 1982, (with L.H. Lovins, F. Krause, and W. Bach) Least-Cost Energy: Solving the CO2 Problem, 1982, 89 (with P. O'heffernan, sr. author and L.H. Lovins) The First Nuclear World War, 1983, (with L.H. Lovins, sr. author and S. Zuckerman) Energy Unbound: A Fable for America's Future, 1986, (hardware reports) The State of the Art: Lighting, 1988, The State of the Art: Drivepower, 1989, The State of the Art: Appliances, 1990, The State of the Art: Water Heating, 1991, The State of the Art: Space Cooling and Air Handling, 1992, (with Ernst von Weizsaecker, sr. author and L.H. Lovins) Faktor Vier, 1995, (with M.M. Brylawski, D.R. Cramer, T.C. Moore) Hypercars: Materials and Policy Implications, 1995; co-photographer (book) At Home in the Wild: New England's White Mountains, 1978; author numerous poems; contbr. articles to profl. jours., reports to tech. jours.; patentee in field. Recipient Right Livelihood award Right Livelihood Found., 1983, Sprout award Internat. Studies Assn., 1977, Pub. Edn. award Nat. Energy Resources Orgn., 1978, Pub. Svc. award Nat. Assn. Environ. Edn., 1980; Mitchell prize Mitchell Energy Found., 1982, Delphi prize Onassis Found., 1989, Nissan prize Internat. Symposium Automotive Tech. and Automation, 1993, Award of Distinction, Rocky Mountain chpt. AIA, 1994; MacArthur fellow John D. and Catherine T. MacArthur Found., Chgo., 1993. Fellow AAAS, World Acad. Art and Sci., Lindisfarne Assn; mem. Fedn. Am. Scientists, Am. Phys. Soc. Avocations: mountaineering, photography, music. Home and Office: 1739 Snowmass Creek Rd Snowmass CO 81654-9115 *Personal philosophy: Devotion to efficient and sustainable use of resources as a path to global security, with emphasis on how advanced technologies, market economics, and Jeffersonian politics can provide new solutions to old problems, or better still, avoid them altogether.*

LOVINS, L. HUNTER, public policy institute executive; b. Middlebury, Vt., Feb. 26, 1950; d. Paul Millard and Farley (Hunter) Sheldon; m. Amory Bloch Lovins, Dept. 6, 1979; 1 child, Nanuq. BA in Sociology, Pitzer Coll., 1972, BA in Polit. Sci., 1972; JD, Loyola U., L.A., 1975; LHD, U. Maine, 1982. Bar: Calif. 1975. Asst. dir. Calif. Conservation Project, L.A., 1973-79; exec. dir., co-founder Rocky Mountain Inst., Snowmass, Colo., 1982—; vis. prof. U. Colo., Boulder, 1982; Henry R. Luce vis. prof. Dartmouth Coll., Hanover, N.H., 1982; pres. Nighthawk Horse Co., 1993, Lovins Group, 1994. Co-author: Brittle Power, 1982, Energy Unbound, 1986, Least-Cost Energy Solving the CO2 Problem, 2d edit., 1989. Bd. dirs. Renew Am., Basalt and Rural Fire Protection Dist., E Source, Roaring Park Polocrosse Assn.; vol. EMT and firefighter. Recipient Mitchell prize Woodlands Inst., 1982, Right Livelihood Found. award, 1983, Best of the New Generation award Esquire Mag., 1984. Mem. Calif. Bar Assn., Am. Quarter Horse Assn., Am. Pedocrosse Assn. Avocations: rodeo, fire rescue, polocrosse. Office: Rocky Mountain Inst 1739 Snowmass Creek Rd Snowmass CO 81654-9115

LOVITT, GEORGE HAROLD, advertising executive; b. Bridgeport, Conn., June 7, 1922; s. Leon H. and Sarah (Lubetkin) L.; m. Nancy Posner, Nov. 27, 1947 (dec. Apr. 1995); children: Alison Lovitt Reinfeld, Charles, Robert, Patricia Barrier. BA, NYU, 1944. Asst. to publicity dir. Prentice-Hall, Inc., N.Y.C., 1946-48; advt. and publicity dir. John Wiley & Sons, Inc., N.Y.C., 1948-52; successively account exec., v.p., pres., chmn. Franklin Spier, Inc., N.Y.C., 1952-82; pres. Keynote Mktg., Inc., N.Y.C., 1982-84; adj. prof. English dept. Hofstra U., 1986. Trustee Baldwin Pub. Library, 1971-76, 77-78. Served with inf. AUS, 1943-46. Decorated Purple Heart. Home: 40 Interlaken Est Lakeville CT 06039-2104

LOVITZ, JON, actor, comedian; b. Tarzana, Calif., July 21, 1957. Attended, U. Calif.-Irvine; studied acting, Film Actors Workshop. Began performing in comedy improvisation with the Groundlings, L.A.; TV work includes (series) Foley Square, 1985, Saturday Night Live, NBC, 1985-90, The Critic, 1994—, (voice); feature films include The Last Resort, 1986, Ratboy, 1986, Jumpin' Jack Flash, 1986, Three Amigos, 1986, Big, 1988, My Stepmother is an Alien, 1988, Brave Little Toaster, 1989 (voice), Mr. Destiny, 1990, An American Tail: Fievel Goes West, 1991 (voice), A League of Their Own, 1992, Mom and Dad Save the World, 1990, Coneheads, 1993, National Lampoon's Loaded Weapon I, 1993, City Slickers II: The Legend of Curley's Gold, 1994, North, 1994, Trapped in Paradise, 1994. Address: care Brillstein/Grey Entertainment 9150 Wilshire Blvd Ste 350 Beverly Hills CA 90212*

LOW, ANDREW M., lawyer; b. N.Y.C., Jan. 1, 1952; s. Martin Laurent and Alice Elizabeth (Bernstein) L.; m. Margaret Mary Stroock, Mar. 31, 1979; children: Roger, Ann. BA, Swarthmore Coll., 1973; JD, Cornell U., 1976. Bar: Colo. 1981, U.S. Dist. Ct. Colo. 1981, U.S. Ct. Appeals (10th cir.) 1986. Assoc. Rogers & Wells, N.Y.C., 1977-81; assoc. Davis, Graham & Stubbs, Denver, 1981-83, ptnr., 1984—. Editor: Colorado Appellate Handbook, 1984, 94. Pres. Colo. Freedom of Info. Coun., Denver, 1990-92, Colo. Bar Press Com., 1989, appellate practice subcom. Colo. Bar Assn. Litigation Coun., 1994—; bd. dirs. CLE in Colo., Inc., 1993—; bd. trustees 9 Health Fair, Denver, 1988—; mem. Colo. Sup. Ct. Joint Commn. on Appellate Rules, 1993—. Avocations: skiing, golfing, fly-fishing. Office: Davis Graham & Stubbs 370 17th St Ste 4700 Denver CO 80202-5647

LOW, ANTHONY, English language educator; b. San Francisco, May 31, 1935; s. Emerson and Clio (Caroli) L.; m. Pauline Iselin Mills, Dec. 28, 1961; children: Louise, Christopher, Georgianna, Elizabeth, Peter, Catherine, Nicholas, Alexandra, Michael, Frances, Jessica, Edward, Charlotte. A.B., Harvard U., 1957, M.A., 1959, Ph.D., 1965. Mem. faculty Seattle U., 1965-68; mem. faculty NYU, N.Y.C., 1968—; prof. English lit., 1978—, chmn. dept. English, 1989-95; vis. scholar Jesus Coll., Cambridge, Eng., 1974-75; pres. Conf. on Christianity and Lit., 1996-97. Author: Augustine Baker, 1970, The Blaze of Noon, 1974, Love's Architecture, 1978, The Georgic Revolution, 1985, The Reinvention of Love, 1993; editor: Urbane Milton, 1984. Pres. Conf. on Christianity and Lit., 1996-97. Pew Evangelical fellow, 1995. Mem. Milton Soc., Donne Soc., MLA, Renaissance Soc., Phi Beta Kappa. Home: 7 Christopher Rd Ridgefield CT 06877-2407 Office: NYU Dept English 19 University Pl New York NY 10003-4501

LOW, BARBARA WHARTON, biochemist, biophysicist; b. Lancaster, Eng., Mar. 23, 1920; came to U.S., 1946, naturalized, 1956; d. Matthew and Mary Jane (Wharton) L.; m. Metchie J.E. Budka, July 13, 1950 (dec. 1995). B.A. (Coll. scholar), Somerville Coll., Oxford (Eng.) U., 1942, M.A., 1946, DPhil, 1948. Research fellow Calif. Inst. Tech., 1946-47; research assoc. in phys. chemistry Harvard U. Med. Sch., 1948, assoc. in phys. chemistry, 1948-50; assoc. mem. Univ. Lab. Phys. Chemistry Related to Medicine and Public Health, 1950-54; asst. prof. phys. chemistry Harvard U., 1950-56; assoc. prof. biochemistry Columbia U. Coll. Physicians and Surgeons, 1956-66, prof., 1966-90, prof. emeritus, 1990—; cons. USPHS; mem. biophysics and biophys. chemistry study sect. div. rsch. grants NIH, 1961, spl. study sect., 1966-69, 1988, 90; rsch. coun. Pub. Health Rsch. Inst. City N.Y., 1973-78, bd. dirs., 1974-78; assoc. prof. U. Strasbourg, France, 1965; vis. prof. Japan Soc. Promotion Sci., Tohoku U., Sendai, Japan, 1975; invited lectr. Chinese Acad. Scis. 1981, Soviet Acad. Scis., 1988; mem. seminar on archaeology of Ea. Mediterranean, Ea. Europe and near East, Columbia U. Contbr. articles to chem., biochem., biophys., and crystallographic jours., also chpts. in books. Recipient Career Devel. award NIH, 1963-68; NIH sr. research fellow, 1959-63. Fellow Am. Acad. Arts and Scis.; mem. AAAS, Am. Crystallographic Assn., Am. Inst. Physics, Am. Soc. Biol. Chemists, Biophys. Soc., Royal Soc. Chemistry, Harvey Soc., Internat. Soc. Toxinology, Protein Soc., Soc. Neurosci. Achievements include determination of three dimensional structure of penicillin; structure determination of protein implicated in neurological block; discovery of pi helix; co-developer use of heavy atoms in protein crystal structure determination; introduction of low temperature studies for protein data collection and of polaroid photography of protein X-ray diffraction patterns; established probable binding site of snake venom neurotoxins to Acetylcholine receptor. Office: Columbia U Dept Biochem & Mo Bio 630 W 168th St New York NY 10032-3702

LOW, BOON CHYE, physicist; b. Singapore, Feb. 13, 1946; came to U.S., 1968; s. Kuei Huat and Ah Tow (Tee) Lau; m. Daphne Nai-Ling Yip, Mar. 31, 1971; 1 child, Yi-Kai. BSc, U. London, Eng., 1968; PhD, U. Chgo., 1972. Scientist High Altitude Observatory Nat. Ctr. for Atmospheric Rsch., Boulder, Colo., 1981-87, head coronal interplanetary physics sect., 1987-90, acting dir., 1989-90, sr. scientist, 1987—; mem. mission operation working group for solar physics NASA, 1992-94. Mem. editl. bd. Solar Physics, 1991—. Named Fellow Japan Soc. for Promotion of Sci., U. Tokyo, 1978, Sr. Rsch. Assoc., NASA Marshall Space Flight Ctr., 1980. Mem. Am. Physical Soc., Am. Astron. Soc., Am. Geophysical Union. Office: Nat Ctr for Atmosph Rsch PO Box 3000 Boulder CO 80307-3000

LOW, DONALD GOTTLOB, retired veterinary medicine educator; b. Cheyenne Wells, Colo., May 14, 1925; s. John Louis and Marie (Gabriel) L.; m. Jeanette Maxine Reedy, Dec. 4, 1948 (div. Feb. 1972); children: Ronald, Raymond, Richard, Christine, Cheryl; m. Jane M. Herschler, May 12, 1973. D.V.M., Kans. State U., 1947; Ph.D., U. Minn., 1956. Pvt. practice vet. medicine, 1947-49; dist. veterinarian U.S. Dept. Agr., 1949-50; instr. U. Minn., 1950-53, 55-56, asso. prof., 1956-60, prof., 1960-65, head dept. vet. hosps., 1965-70; prof., head dept. clin. scis. Colo. State U., 1971-74; prof. vet. medicine, dir. teaching hosp. U. Calif.-Davis, 1974-80, assoc. dean instrn., 1982-83, assoc. dean pub. programs, 1983-93; ret., 1993. Author: (with Osborne, Finco) Small Animal Urology, 1972; Contbr. articles to tech. jours. Active Boy Scouts Am., PTA; established Don Low/Calif. Vet. Med. Assn. Practitioner Fellowship, 1995. Served with AUS, 1943-44; as capt. 1953-55. Recipient Disting. Teaching award U. Minn., 1965, Disting. Svc. award, 1990, 91, Robert W. Kirk award for Disting. Svc., Am. Coll. Vet. Internal Medicine, Disting. Alumnus award Kans. State U. and the Vet. Med. Alumni Assn., 1994. Mem. Am. Coll. Vet. Internists (founder), Am., Colo., Vet. Med. Assns., Am. Animal Hosp. Assn. (Veterinarian of Yr. 1970), Nat. Acad. Practice-Vet. Medicine, Calif. Vet. Med. Assn. (pres. award 1988), Calif. Acad. Vet. Medicine (excellence in Continuing Edn. award 1989, disting. svc. award Wild West Vet. Conf. 1995), Phi Zeta. Methodist. Home: 26778 County Road 34 Winters CA 95694-9064

LOW, EMMET FRANCIS, JR., mathematics educator; b. Peoria, Ill., June 10, 1922; s. Charles Walter and Nettie Alys (Baker) Davis; m. Lana Carmen Wiles, Nov. 23, 1974. B.S. cum laude, Stetson U., 1948; M.S., U. Fla., 1950, Ph.D., 1953. Instr. physics U. Fla., 1950-54; aero. research scientist NACA, Langley Field, Va., 1954-55; asst. prof. math. U. Miami, Coral Gables, Fla., 1955-60; assoc. prof. U. Miami, 1960-67, prof., 1967-72, chmn. dept. math., 1961-66; acting dean U. Miami (Coll. Arts and Scis.), 1966-67, assoc. dean, 1967-68, assoc. dean faculties, 1968-72; prof. math. Clinch Valley Coll., U. Va., 1972-89, dean, 1972-86, chmn. dept. math. scis., 1986-89; emeritus prof. math., 1989—; vis. research scientist Courant Inst. Math. Scis., NYU, 1959-60. Contbr. articles to profl. jours. Mem. Wise County Indsl. Devel. Authority, 1992—, chmn., 1996—. Served with USAAF, 1942-46. Recipient award for excellence in tchg. Clinch Valley Coll., 1988; hon. Ky. Col. Mem. Am. Math. Soc., Math. Assn. Am., Soc. Indsl. and Applied Math., Nat. Council Tchrs. of Math., Southwest Va. Council Tchrs. of Math., AAUP, AAAS, Sigma Xi, Delta Theta Mu, Phi Delta Kappa, Phi Kappa Phi. Clubs: Univ. Yacht (Miami, Fla.); Kiwanis.

LOW, FRANCIS EUGENE, physics educator; b. N.Y.C., Oct. 27, 1921; s. Bela and Eugenia (Ingerman) L.; m. Natalie Sadigur, June 25, 1948; children—Julie, Peter, Margaret. B.S., Harvard U., 1942; M.A., Columbia U., 1947, Ph.D., 1949. Mem. Inst. Advanced Study, 1950-52; asst. prof. U. Ill., Urbana, 1952-55, asso. prof., 1955-56; prof. physics MIT, Cambridge, 1957-67, Karl Taylor Compton prof., 1968-85, Inst. prof., 1985-92, Inst. prof. emeritus, 1992—, dir. Center for Theoretical Physics, 1973-76, dir. Lab. for Nuclear Sci., 1979-80, provost, 1980-85; cons. in field; mem. high energy physics adv. panel Dept. Energy, 1972-76, chmn., 1987-90. Contbr. articles to profl. jours. Served with USAAF, 1942-43; Served with AUS, 1944-46. Mem. NAS (nat. coun. 1986-89), Am. Phys. Soc. (chmn. divsn. particles and fields 1974, councillor-at-large 1979-82), Fedn. Am. Scientists (nat. coun. 1973-77), Am. Acad. Arts and Scis., Internat. Union of Pure and Applied Physics (commn. on particles and fields 1976-82). Home: 28 Adams St Belmont MA 02178-3525 Office: MIT Rm 6-301 Cambridge MA 02139

LOW, FRANK NORMAN, anatomist, educator; b. Bklyn., Feb. 9, 1911; s. William Wans and Hilda (Nelson) L. BA, Cornell U., 1932, PhD, 1936; DSc (hon.), U. N.D., 1983. Postdoctoral Charlton fellow Sch. Medicine Tufts Coll., Boston, 1936-37; instr. to asst. prof. U. N.C., Chapel Hill, 1937-45; assoc. Sch. Medicine U. Md., Balt., 1945-46; assoc. prof. U. W.Va., Morgantown, 1946; asst. prof. Johns Hopkins Med. Sch., Balt., 1946-49; assoc. prof. to prof. anatomy Sch. Medicine La. State U., New Orleans, 1949-64, vis. prof., 1981—; rsch. prof. anatomy U. N.D., Grand Forks, 1964-81, emeritus, 1981—, Chester Fritz Disting. prof., 1975-77; mem. regional rev. bd. Am. Heart Assn., Grand Forks, 1971-74. Author: (with J.A. Freeman) Electron Microscopic Atlas of Normal and Leukemic Human Blood, 1958; assoc. editor Am. Jour. Anatomy, 1971-91; contbr. over 100 rsch. articles to profl. jours. Participant People's Republic China-U.S. exchange program, People to People; citizen amb. Soviet Union, 1991; del. Anniversary Caravan '91, People to People Internat., Russia, Uzbekistan. Mem. Am. Assn. Anatomists (exec. com. 1976-80, Henry Gray award 1989), Am. Soc. Cell Biology, La. Soc. Electron Microscopy (chmn. 1962), Am. Assn. History of Medicine, World Trade Ctr. (New Orleans), Sigma Xi (pres. U. N.D. chpt. 1977). Avocation: travel, history of medicine. Office: La State Med Ctr Dental Sch 1100 Florida Ave New Orleans LA 70119-2714

LOW, HARRY WILLIAM, judge; b. Oakdale, Calif., Mar. 12, 1931; s. Tong J. and Ying G. (Gong) L.; m. May Ling, Aug. 24, 1952; children: Larry, Kathy, Allan. AA, Modesto Jr. Coll., 1950; AB Polit. Sci. with honors, U. Calif., Berkeley, 1952, JD, 1955. Bar: Calif. 1955, U.S. Ct. Appeals (9th cir.) 1955. Commr. Workmen's Compensation Commn., 1966; teaching assoc. Boalt Hall, 1955-56; dep. atty. gen. Calif. Dept. Justice, 1956-66; judge Mcpl. Ct., San Francisco, 1966-74; presiding judge Mcpl. Ct., 1972-73; judge Superior Ct., San Francisco, 1974-82; presiding justice Calif. Ct. Appeals, 1st dist., 1982-92; pres. San Francisco Police Commn., 1992-96; mem. Jud. Arbitration and Mediation Svcs., 1992—, Commn. on Future of Cts., 1991-94, Commn. on Future of Legal Profession, 1993-95. Contbr. articles to profl. jours. Chmn. bd. Edn. Ctr. for Chinese, 1969—, Chinese-Am. Bilingual Sch.; bd. visitors U.S. Mil. Acad., 1980-83; bd. dirs. Friends of Recreation and Parks, Salesian Boys Club, World Affairs Coun., 1979-85, NCCJ, San Francisco chpt. St. Vincent's Boys Home, Coro Found., 1970-76, San Francisco Zool. Trust, 1987, Union Bank, 1993—; pres. San Francisco City Coll. Found., 1977-87, Inst. Chinese Western History U. San Francisco, 1987-89. Mem. ABA (chmn. appellate judges conf. 1990-91, commr. on minorities), San Francisco Bar Assn., Chinese Am. Citizens Alliance (pres. San Francisco chpt. 1976-77, nat. pres. 1989-93), Calif. Judges Assn. (pres. 1978-79), Calif. Jud. Coun., State Bar Calif. (rsch. editor publs. 1958-76, pub. affairs com. 1987-90, exec. bd. 1992-94), Calif. Conf. Judges (editor jour. cts. commentary 1973-76), Calif. Judges Assn. (exec. bd. 1976-79), Asian Bus. League (dir. 1986-93), Nat. Ctr. State Cts. (bd. dirs. 1986-91), San Francisco Bench Bar Media Commn. (chmn. bd. dirs. 1987-92), Phi Alpha Delta. *Try to enjoy whatever task you are doing and enjoy the good company of those with whom you associate. Be an active part of the community and try to improve it. Keep busy and try to understand and respect others.*

LOW, JAMES A., physician; b. Toronto, Ont., Can., Sept. 22, 1925; s. Donald M. and Doris V. (Van Duzer) L.; m. Margery Una, Oct. 5, 1952; children: Donald E., Margeret P., Norman I. M.D., U. Toronto, 1949. Intern Toronto Gen. Hosp., 1949-50; resident in ob-gyn U. Toronto, 1950-54, clin. instr. dept. ob-gyn, 1955-65; fellow ob/gyn Duke U., 1955; prof. and chmn. dept. ob-gyn Queens U., Kingston, Ont., Can., 1965-85; prof. Queens U., 1985—. Mem. editorial bd. Ob-Gyn., 1986-89, Am. Jour. Ob-Gyn., 1995—. Served with Can. Navy, 1943-45. Fellow Royal Coll. Physicians and Surgeons Can. (chmn. splty. com. 1976-82, chmn. manpower com. 1984-92); mem. Assn. Profs. Ob-Gyn Can. (sec.-treas. 1972-80, pres. 1983-84), Am. Gynecol. and Obstet. Soc., Soc. Gynecol. Investigation, Soc. Obstetricians and Gynecologists of Can., Can. Soc. Clin. Investigation, Am. Acad. Cerebral Palsy, Internat. Incontinence Soc. Home: 185 Fairway Hills, Kingston, ON Canada K7M 2B5 Office: Queens U, Dept Ob-Gyn, Kingston, ON Canada K7L 3N6

LOW, JOHN WAYLAND, lawyer; b. Denver, Aug. 7, 1923; s. Oscar Wayland and Rachel E. (Stander) L.; m. Merry C. Mullan, July 8, 1979; children: Lucinda A., Jan W. BA, Nebr. Wesleyan U., 1947; JD cum laude, U. Denver, 1951. Bar: Colo. 1951, U.S. Dist. Ct. (Colo. dist.) 1951, U.S. Ct. Appeals (10th cir.), U.S. Supreme Ct. 1960. Ptnr. Sherman & Howard LLC, Denver, 1951-93, counsel, 1993—. Trustee U. Denver, 1987—; chmn. bd. Denver Symphony Assn., 1989-90; vice chmn. Colo. Symphony Assn., 1990—; chmn. Colo. Alliance of Bus., Denver, 1983-87. 1st lt. U.S. Army, 1942-46, CBI. Recipient Learned Hand award Am. Jewish Com., 1989, Outstanding Alumni award U. Denver, 1994. Mem. ABA, Colo. Bar Assn., Denver Bar Assn., University Club of Denver, Garden of Gods Club (Colorado Springs). Republican. Mem. United Ch. of Christ. Office: Sherman & Howard 633 17th St Ste 3000 Denver CO 80202-3601

LOW, JOSEPH, artist; b. Coraopolis, Pa., Aug. 11, 1911; s. John Routh and Stella (Rent) L.; m. Ruth Hull, Oct. 21, 1940; children: Damaris, Jennifer. Student, U. Ill., 1930-32, Art Students League N.Y., 1935. founder, 1959; since propr. Eden Hill Press. Engaged in printmaking and graphic arts, 1943—; exhbns. include, Princeton, Dartmouth, Williams, U. Ill., Phila. Mus. Art, Brandeis U., Grinnell Coll., Carnegie Inst. Tech., Herron Art Inst., Indpls., U. Ky., others; rep. permanent collections, Princeton, Dartmouth, U. Ky., State Dept., Library of Congress, Chapin Library at Williams Coll., U. Ill., Wesleyan U., Middletown, Conn., Va. Mus. Fine Arts, San Francisco Pub. Library, Boston Atheneum, Boston Mus. Fine Arts, Harvard Coll. Library, Pratt Inst., U. Okla., Newberry Library, Chgo., Met. Mus. Art, Ohio State U., Bodleian Library, Oxford U., pvt. collections. Home: RFD 278 Chilmark MA 02535

LOW, MARY LOUISE (MOLLY LOW), documentary photographer; b. Quakertown, Pa., Jan. 3, 1926; d. James Harry and Dorothy Collyer (Krewson) Thomas; m. Antoine Francois Gagné, Nov. 3, 1945 (div.); children: James L., David W., Stephen J., Jeannie Wolff-Gagné; m. Paul Low, July 11, 1969 (dec. July 1991). Student, Oberlin Conservatory of Music, 1943-44, Oberlin Coll., 1944; cert., Katharine Gibbs Sec. Sch., 1945; degree in psychiat. rehab. work, Einstein Coll. Medicine, 1968-70. Sec. Dept. Store, N.Y.C., 1945; sec., treas. Gagné Assocs., Consulting Engrs., Binghamton, N.Y., 1951-66; psychiat. rsch. asst. Jacobi Hosp., Bronx, 1969-70; asst. to head of sch. Brearley Sch., N.Y.C., 1976-78; pvt. practice documentary photographer San Diego, 1984—. Contbr. articles to profl. jours. Pres., bd. trustees Unitarian-Universalist Ch. Recipient Dir.'s award for excellence Area Agy. on Aging, San Diego, 1993, Citizen Recognition award County of San Diego, Calif., 1993. Avocations: singing, directing church choir, traveling. Office: Molly Low Photography 5576 Caminito Herminia La Jolla CA 92037-7222

LOW, MORTON DAVID, physician, educator; b. Lethbridge, Alta., Can., Mar. 25, 1935; s. Solon Earl and Alice Fern (Litchfield) L.; m. Cecilia Margaret Comba, Aug. 22, 1959 (div. 1983); children—Cecilia Alice, Sarah Elizabeth, Peter Jon Eric; m. Barbara Joan McLeod, Aug. 25, 1984; 1 child, Kelsey Alexandra. M.D., C.M., Queen's U., 1960, M.Sc. in Medicine, 1962; Ph.D. with honors, Baylor U., 1966. From instr. to asst. prof. Baylor Coll. Medicine, Houston, 1965-68; assoc. prof. medicine U. B.C., Vancouver, Can., 1968-78, prof. medicine, 1978-89, clin. assoc. dean, 1974-76, assoc. dean rsch. and grad. studies, 1977-78, coord. health scis., 1985-89; creator Health Policy Rsch. Unit U. B.C., Vancouver, 1987; pres. U. Tex. Health Sci. Ctr., Houston, 1989—, prof. neural scis. Grad. Sch. Biomed. Scis., 1989—, dir. Health Policy Inst., 1990—; prof. neurology U. Tex. Med. Sch., Houston, 1989—; prof. health policy and mgmt. Sch. Pub. Health U. Tex., 1989—; cons. in neurology U. Hosp. Shaughnessy site, Vancouver, 1971-89, U. B.C. site, Vancouver, 1970-89; dir. dept. diagnostic neurophysiology Vancouver Gen. Hosp., 1968-87; cons. in EEG, 1987-89; exec. dir. Rsch. Inst., 1981-86; mem. med. sci. adv. com. USIA, 1991-93. Mem. editorial bd. numerous jours.; contbr. articles to profl. jours. Bd. dirs. Greater Houston Ptnrship., 1994—, mem. governing bd. Houston Mus. Natural Sci., 1991—; trustee Kinkaid Sch., Houston, 1991—. Med. Rsch. Coun. Can. grantee, 1968-80; recipient Tree of Life award Jewish Nat. Fund, 1995, Caring Spirit award Inst. Religion, 1995. Fellow Am. EEG Soc., Royal Coll. Physicians (Can.), Royal Soc. Medicine (London); mem. AMA, Tex. Med. Assn. (coun. on med. edn. 1990—), Can. Soc. Clin. Neurophysiology, Internat. Fedn. Socs. for EEG and Clin. Neurophysiology (rules com. 1977-81, sec. 1981-85), Assn. Acad. Health Ctrs. (task force on access to care and orgn. health svcs. 1988—, chmn. 1992, task force on instnl. values 1989—), Harris County Med. Soc., Am. Coun. Edn., Forum Club of Houston (governing bd. 1991—). Avocations: sailing instructing; photography; youth soccor coach; vol. ski-patrol; flying. Office: U Tex-Houston Health Sci PO Box 20036 Houston TX 77225-0036

LOW, PAUL M., mortgage banking executive, food service executive; b. Flint, Mich., Oct. 27, 1930; s. Samuel and Helen (Freed) L.; m. Nedda Luisa Alcazar, May 23, 1968; children: Lori Ellen Schwartz, Marcia Nedda Millard, Paul M. Jr. JD cum laude, U. Miami, 1956; BA magna cum laude, Kenyon Coll., 1994. V.p. The Lomas & Nettleton Co. (now Lomas Mortgage USA), Dallas, 1958-79, sr. v.p., 1979-84, exec. v.p., 1984-87, pres., 1987-90; chmn. Enterdine Inc., Dallas, 1984—; founder, former chmn. New Am. Fin. LP, Dallas, 1992-95; founder, mng. ptnr. Enterdine, Inc. dba. The Riviera, Dallas; bd. dirs. Capstead Mortgage Corp., Dallas. Bd. dirs. Mental Health Assn., Dallas County, 1986—; v.p., bd. dirs. Mental Health Assn. Tex.; exec. com. North Tex. chpt. March of Dimes, 1985-88; pres., bd. dirs. Cedars Med. Ctr., Miami, 1976-86; chmn. Parents Fund and Adv. Coun. Kenyon Coll. Staff sgt. USAF, 1950-53. Mem. Fla. Bar Assn., Tex. Bar Assn., Dallas Bar Assn., Mortgage Bankers Assn. Am., Brookhaven Country Club. Jewish. Avocations: reading, writing, research, travel. Office: PO Box 9068 Dallas TX 75209

LOW, PETER W., legal educator; b. Springfield, Mass., May 17, 1937; s. George W. and Doris J. Low; m. Carol Randolph, Sept. 10, 1960; children: Cathryn E., Diana R. AB, Princeton U., 1959; LLB, U. Va., 1963. Bar: Va. 1963, U.S. Supreme Ct. 1970. Law clk. to Chief Justice Earl Warren, U.S. Supreme Ct., Washington, 1963-64; mem. faculty U. Va. Law Sch., Charlottesville, 1964—, asst. dean, 1965-69, assoc. dean, 1969-76, 89-94, Hardy Cross Dillard prof. law, 1975—, v.p., provost, 1994—; vis. prof. Inst. Criminology, Cambridge, Eng., 1970; Salzburg Seminars in Am. Studies, 1972; U. Pa. Law Sch., 1974-75, Stanford Law Sch., 1977; cons. FBI Acad., Quantico, Va., 1972—. Mem. Am. Law Inst., Va. Bar Assn., Order of Coif. Author: (with Jeffries and Bonnie) Criminal Law-Cases and Materials, 2d edit., 1986; (with Jeffries) ALI, Model Penal Code and Commentaries, Part II, 3 vols., 1980, others. Office: U Va Sch Law Madison Hall Charlottesville VA 22901

LOW, PHILIP FUNK, soil chemistry educator, consultant, researcher; b. Carmangay, Alta., Can., Oct. 15, 1921; came to U.S., 1940; s. Philip and Pearl Helena (Funk) L.; m. Mayda Matilda Stewart, June 11, 1942; children—Roseanne, Jeannine, Philip, Lasca, Lorraine, Martin. B.S., Brigham Young U., 1943; M.S., Calif. Inst. Tech., 1944; Ph.D., Iowa State U., 1949. Soil chemistry faculty, agronomy dept. Purdue U., West Lafayette, Ind., 1949—, prof. soil chemistry, 1955-92, prof. emeritus, 1992—; cons. Exxon Prodn. Rsch. Co., Houston, 1960-80, Cold Regions Rsch. Lab., U.S. Army, Hanover, N.H., 1962-67, Battelle, Pacific N.W. Labs., 1980-81, U.S. Salinity Lab., Riverside, Calif., summer 1962; hon. prof. Zhejiang Agrl. U., Hangzhou, Peoples Republic of China, 1987—. Cons. editor Soil Sci., 1957—, Geoderma, 1981-88, Jour. Colloid and Interface Sci., 1993—; assoc. editor Clays and Clay Minerals, 1960-66; contbr. articles to profl. jours.; patentee in field. Pres., Indpls. Stake, Ch. of Jesus Christ of Latter Day Saints, 1959-73; regional rep. Ind. Regions, Ch. of Jesus Christ of Latter Day Saints, 1977-83; bd. dirs. Opera de Lafayette, 1984-85. Served to 1st lt. Air Corps, U.S. Army, 1943-45. Recipient Ann. Research award Purdue chpt. Sigma Xi, 1960, Disting. Visitor award to Australia, Fulbright Ednl. Exchange Program, 1968, Disting. Service award Brigham Young U., 1976, Herbert Newby McCoy Research award Purdue U., 1980; Thurburn Vis. fellow U. Sydney, 1983. Fellow Am. Soc. Agronomy (bd. dirs.), Soil Sci. Soc. Am. (pres.-elect 1971-72, pres. 1972-73, bd. dirs. 1971-74, Soil Sci. Achievement award 1963, Bouyoucus Disting. Career award 1984, Soil Sci. Disting. Svc. award 1993); mem. NAS, Clay Minerals Soc. (Disting. Mem. award 1992), Internat. Soc. Soil Sci., Internat. Assn. for Study Clay. Avocations: collecting art, classical music, hiking, collecting crystal, jade, ceramics. Home: 340 Hollowood Dr West Lafayette IN 47906-2146 Office: Purdue U Agronomy Dept West Lafayette IN 47907

LOW, RICHARD H., broadcasting executive, producer; b. Union City, N.J., Feb. 20, 1927; s. Irving and Regina (Krieger) L.; 1 dau., Jennifer Alix-e. Student, U. Mich., 1947-49; J.D., Columbia U., 1952. With CBS News, 1952-56; with CBS-TV Network, 1956-62, dir. contracts, facilities and program sales, 1959-62; with Young & Rubicam, 1962-84, v.p. TV-radio dept., 1970-72, v.p. programming, 1972-73, sr. v.p., 1973-81, responsible for network TV programming and purchasing, 1973-84, includes cable TV, 1980-84, exec. v.p., dir. broadcast programming and purchasing, 1981-84; pres. Manticore Prodns., Inc. 1985—; pres. Universal Holding Co.; advisor LWV presdl. TV debates, 1980; judge N.Y. World TV Festival, 1979-80, Internat. Emmy awards, 1981-83; panelist Nat. Assn. TV Programming Execs. Conf., 1981; keynote spkr. 25th Anniversary seminar Broadcasters Promotion Assn., 1981; presenter S.I. Newhouse Sch. Pub. Comm., 1981; discussant Ctr. for Comm., 1982; mem. Task Force on Pub. Broadcasting, 1983. Mem. media task force Nat. Coun. Arts, 1977, Aspen Inst., 1973; v.p., trustee Am. Mus. Immigration; trustee Town Hall Found.; bd. dirs. U.S. Organizing Com. 1983 Bicentennial of Air and Space. With U.S. Army, 1945-46. Mem. NATAS (gov. N.Y. 1979-83). Office: 1056 5th Ave New York NY 10028-0112 *In the beginner's mind, there are many possibilities.*

LOW, RON ALBERT, professional hockey coach; b. Birtle, Man., Can., June 21, 1950. Profl. hockey player Toronto Maple Leaves, Can., 1970-74, Washington Capitals, 1974-77, Detroit Red Wings, 1977-78, Quebec Nordiques, Can., 1979-80, Edmonton Oilers, Can., 1980-83, N.J. Devils, 1983-85; player Nova Scotia Oilers, Can., 1985-86, asst. coach, 1985-87; asst. coach Edmonton Oilers, 1989—. Recipient Tommy Ivan trophy, 1978-79; named to CHL All-Star 2d team, 1973-74, All Star 1st team, 1978-79. Office: Edmonton Oilers, Edmonton, AB Canada T5B 4M9

LOW, STEPHEN, foundation executive, educator, former diplomat; b. Cin., Dec. 2, 1927; s. Martin and Margaret (Friend) L.; m. Helen Sue Carpenter, Oct. 9, 1954; children: Diego, Rodman, Jesse. B.A., Yale U., 1950; M.A., Fletcher Sch. Law and Diplomacy, Tufts U., 1951, Ph.D., 1956. With Dept. State, various locations, 1956-74; sr. staff mem. NSC, 1974-76; U.S. ambassador to Zambia, 1976-79, U.S. ambassador to Nigeria, 1979-81; dir. Fgn. Service Inst. Dept. State, 1982-87; dir. Bologna (Italy) Ctr. Sch. Advanced Internat. Studies Johns Hopkins U., 1987-92; pres. Assn. Diplomatic Studies and Tng., 1992—. Served with AUS, 1946-47. Address: 2855 Tilden St NW Washington DC 20008-3820

LOWD, JUDSON DEAN, oil and gas processing equipment manufacturing executive; b. Chelsea, Mass., June 8, 1918; s. Dana Joseph and Olive Wanda (Dean) L.; m. Alice Carroll, Sept. 6, 1975; 1 dau., Dana. BS in Mech. Engring. with honors, Worcester Poly. Inst., Mass., 1940. Mgr. oil field equipment divsn. Parkersburg Rig & Reel Co., W.Va., 1948-56; exec. v.p. internat. mktg. ops. C-E Natco, Tulsa, 1957-73, pres., 1973-82; chmn. C-E Randall, 1980-84; bd. dirs. Ocean Corp., Houston; pres. Nat. Tank France, Paris; vice chmn. Williams TEch., Inc.1985-90. Trustee U. Tulsa, 1977-87, Goodland Children's Home, Hugo, Okla., 1976-82, Lebanese Am. U., Beirut, 1973-87, dir. and overseer acads.; bd. dirs. Jr. Achievement, Tulsa, 1978-81, Tulsa United Way, 1975-80; elder Presbyn. Ch., 1954—; mem. Tu lsa Execs. Svc. Corps, 1985-96, chmn. 1990. Office AUS, 1941-48, ETO. Decorated Bronze Star; named Marketer of Year, Am. Mktg. Assn., 1974. Mem. ASME (life), Inst. Petroleum (U.K.), Tulsa C. of C. (dir.), Sigma Xi, Tau Beta Pi. Republican. Clubs: So. Hills Country, Tulsa, Tulsa So. Tennis (Tulsa); Lost Hound Hunt (Edmond, Okla.). Office: 427 S Boston Ave Tulsa OK 74103

LOWDEN, JOHN L., retired corporate executive; b. Yakima, Wash., Oct. 29, 1921; s. Roy Ruben and Hildegarde Annie (Grommesch) L.; m. Janet Katherine Langan, Jan. 21, 1961; children: Susan Elizabeth, Jonathan Roy, Andrew Matthias. B.A., U. Nev., 1949. Account supr. Campbell-Ewald Advt., 1951-57, Erwin, Wasey Advt., 1957-59; advt. dir. Gen. Dynamics Corp., 1959-61; account supr. Foote, Cone & Belding, 1961-63; with ITT Corp., 1963-84, v.p. corp. rels. and advt., 1977-84. Author: Silent Wings at War, 1992. Served with USAAF, 1941-45. Decorated Air Medal with Oak Leaf Cluster and Order of William by the Queen of The Netherlands; seven unit battle stars. Roman Catholic.

LOWDEN, SUZANNE, state legislator; b. Camden, N.J., Feb. 8, 1952; m. Paul W. Lowden; children: Christopher, Jennifer, Paul, William. BA magna cum laude, Am. U.; MA cum laude, Fairleigh Dickinson U. Resort industry exec.; mem. Nev. State Senate, 1993—, majority whip, 1993—. Active Juvenile Diabetes Found., United Way of So. Nev. With USO, 1971, Vietnam. Recipient Woman of Achievement award Women's Coun. of Las Vegas C. of C. Republican. Home: 992 Pinehurst Dr Las Vegas NV 89109-1569 Office: Nev State Senate State Capitol Carson City NV 89710 also Office: 4949 N Ranelo Dr Las Vegas NV 89130*

LOWDER, RACHAEL DELLA, company executive, consultant; b. Winston Salem, N.C., July 10, 1942; d. Fred Noah and Evelyn Lucille (Mock) Motsinger; m. Larry L. Lowder, Feb. 8, 1964 (div. 1976); children: Jon Sheldon, Russell Stephen. BA, Wake Forest U., 1964; MS, N.C. State U., 1972. Tchr. various schs., 1964-72; editor, mgr. gen. svcs. Nat. Assn. Coll. Univ. Bus. Officers, Washington, 1973-77; pub. mgr., dir. pub. rels. Am. Automobile Assn., Falls Church, Va., 1977-80; dir. publicity and info. Resources for the Future, Inc., Washington, 1980-84; dir. comm., v.p. comm. and mktg., exec. v.p. World Pres.' Orgn., Washington, 1985—; editor, publicity cons. Project on the Fed. Social Rose, Washington, 1984-85, Am. Automobile Assn., Falls Church, 1989; editor Integon Corp., Winston-Salem, 1987-88; editor, rsch. asst. Bowman Gray Sch. of Medicine, Winston-Salem, 1989-90. Bd. advisors Advanced Mgmt. Inst., 1994—; mem. Assn. Chief Execs. Coun., 1994—; bd. visitors Md. U. Grad. Bus. Sch., 1994—. Mem. Am. Soc. Assn. Exec., Greater Washington Soc. Assn. Execs. Office: World Pres Orgn 601 Pennsylvania Ave NW Apt 520 Washington DC 20004-2610

LOWE, CLAYTON KENT, visual imagery, cinema, and video educator; b. Endicott, N.Y., July 10, 1936; s. Clayton Edwin and Loretta Arlene (Terry) L.; m. Janet E. Snider, 1957 (div. 1977); children: Steven Scott, Kim Ann Parker, David William, Rebecca Michelle Sobel; m. Robin S. McKell, 1980 (div. 1993). BA, Bethany Coll., 1958; MS, Butler U., 1967; PhD, Ohio State U., 1970; BD, Christian Theol. Sem., Indpls., 1962. Pastor Bellaire (Ohio) Christian Ch., 1957-58, Beallsville (Ohio) Christian Ch., 1958, Russellville (Ind.) Christian Ch., 1958-60, Montclair (Ind.) Christian Ch., 1960-61; youth dir. St. Paul United Ch. of Christ, Columbus, 1967-70; asst. prof. journalism U. Ga., 1970-72; asst. prof. comm. Ohio State U., Columbus, 1972-73, asst. prof. photography and cinema, 1973-74, assoc. prof., 1974—, chairperson photography and cinema, 1974-78, dir. grad. studies photography and cinema, 1989-92; assoc. prof. emeritus Ohio State U., 1992—; comml. TV prodr., dir., writer Stas. WISH-TV, 1960-66, WLWI-TV, 1966-67, WOSU-TV, 1967-70; moderator World Film Classics, Educable TV-25, 1991—, also bd. dirs.; E.R.I.C. evaluator-film theory, 1973-78; juror Columbus Internat. Film and TV Festival, 1993, 94. Book reviewer The Arts Edn. Rev. of Books; editor: The Movies on Media Catalog, 1995; host: Columbus Mus. of Art "Movies on Media" film series, 1995, 96. Eli Lilly Found. grantee, 1961-63, Ohio State U. Devel. of Media on Media Study Collection grantee, 1985; Recipient Casper award for A Thing Called Hope, WISH-TV, 1966, Regional Emmy for A Tribute to Dr. King, WOSU-TV, 1968; nominated for regional Emmys for Lucasville, WOSU-TV, 1970, High Street, WOSU-TV, 1975. Mem. AAAS, NATAS (bd. govs. Ohio chpt. 1973-74), Univ. Film and Video Assn., Ohio State U. Dept. Photography and Cinema Alumni Assn. (pres. 1994-95, bd. dirs. 1994—), Kiwanis. Home: 68 Walhalla Rd Columbus OH 43202-1441 *If these were my last words, I would write of the beauty that has filled me and that I in turn have filled. I would look past the darkness and pain-our too frequent companions-toward the light. Toward the radiant spots when family and friends were most open and life was at its wondrous best.*

LOWE, DONALD CAMERON, corporate executive; b. Oshawa, Ont., Can., Jan. 29, 1932; s. Samuel John and Carales Isobel (Cox) L.; m. Susan Margaret Plunkett, July 22, 1955; children: Michelle, Jeffrey, Steven. B.Applied Sci., U. Toronto, 1954; M.S. (Athlone fellow 1957), U. Birmingham, Eng., 1957; grad. internat. sr. mgrs. seminar, Harvard U., 1975. With Gen. Motors Can. Ltd., 1957-71; asst. gen. mgr., then gen. mgr. Gen. Motors Can. Ltd., St. Therese, Que., 1969-71; dir. mfg. Vauxhall Motors Ltd., Luton, Eng., 1971-75; pres., chief exec. officer Pratt & Whitney Aircraft Ltd., Can., 1975-80; also chmn. bd.; pres. comml. products div. Pratt & Whitney Aircraft Group, East Hartford, Conn., 1980-82; chmn., chief exec. officer Allied Can. Inc., 1982-83; pres., chief exec. officer Kidd Creek Mines Ltd., 1983-86, Canadair, Montreal, 1986-90; dep. chmn. Bombardier, Inc., Montreal, 1990-92; bd. dirs. Bayridge Resources, Trilon Fin., Can. Tire Corp., Alta Natural Gas, Devtek Corp., Fleet Aerospace; chmn. Sedgwick Ltd., Bombardier, Inc., Ingersoll-Rand Can., Haley Industries, Exal Aluminum Inc., Strong Equipment Co. Bd. govs. Université de Montréal; hon. dir. Can. Aviation Hall of Fame. Mem. Aerospace Industries Assn. Can., Conf. Bd. Can., Les Ambassadeurs Club (London), Muskoka Lakes Golf and Country Club (Port Carling), Donalda Club, Granite Club, Cambridge Club (Toronto). Office: Sedgwick Ltd, PO Box 439 Toronto Dominion Ctr, Toronto, ON Canada M5K 1M3

LOWE, E(DWIN) NOBLES, lawyer; b. Minturn, Ark., Oct. 4, 1912; s. James A. and Ether (Nobles) L.; m. Catherine McDonald, June 9, 1934 (div. 1959); children: Nancy, Edwin N.; m. Margaret Breece, Dec. 1, 1961; 1 son, James W. A.B., U. Ark., 1932, LL.B., 1934; postgrad., Harvard U. Bus. Sch. Advanced Mgmt. Program, 1950; JD, U. Ark., 1976. Bar: Ark. 1934, N.Y. 1936, U.S. Ct. Appeals (2d cir.) 1938, D.C. 1975, U.S. Ct. Internat. Trade 1979, U.S. Supreme Ct. 1942. Mem. staff Ark. Bond Refunding Bd., 1934; with legal dept. Electric Bond & Share Co., N.Y.C., 1934-35; assoc. mng. atty., ptnr. Reid & Priest, 1935-43; gen. counsel Westvaco Corp. (formerly W.Va. Pulp & Paper), N.Y.C., 1943-77; dir. pub. rels. Westvaco Corp., 1944-48, dir. govt. affairs, 1944-76, sec., 1947-66, v.p., 1966-77; spl. ptnr. Gadsby & Hannah, N.Y.C., 1978-79; mem. firm Lowe & Knapp, N.Y.C., 1979-84; pvt. practice N.Y.C., 1985-86, Carmel, N.Y., 1986—; mem. pub. affairs com. Community Svc. Soc. N.Y., 1956-72; sec., dir. Fund for Modern Cts., N.Y., 1974—; gen. counsel Photography in the Fine Arts, 1957-58; counsel, dir. Photographic Adminstrs., Inc., 1995—. Trustee Emma Willard Sch., Troy, N.Y.; chmn. Second Century Fund, 1956-64; pres. Bronxville (N.Y.) Adult Edn. Sch., 1953-57, hon. dir., 1957-84; dir. Merc. Libr., N.Y.C., 1943-83, pres., 1963-66; trustee Clinton Hall Assn., 1956—, pres., 1966-69, 85-90; mem. devel. bd. U. Ark., 1970-89; bd. dirs. Putnam Hosp. Ctr., 1984—, sec., 1986-94; dir. Putnam United Way, 1984-88, Putnam County Alliance, counsel dir., 1990—; dir. Putnam County Arts Coun., 1992—. Recipient Disting. Alumni cert. U. Ark., 1972, 50-Yr. award Fellows of Am. Bar Found., 1985, PLI Seligson CLE award, 1990, Disting. Svc. award U. Maine Pulp and Paper Found., 1990, Dist. Svc. award Am. Corp. Counsel, N.Y. chpt., 1995. Fellow Am. Bar Found. (50-yr. award 1985), Inst. Jud. Adminstrn.; mem. ABA (spl. and standing coms., chmn. com. corp. lawyers 1959-62, membership com. 1964-68, vice chmn. environ. law 1970-73, organizer, chmn. corp. law dept., bus. law sect. 1955-58, emeritus 1979—, chmn. membership 1965-68, mem. sect. coun. 1961-62, chmn. program 1972-74, chmn. continuing legal edn. 1974-80, mem. non-profit corps. 1988-94—, mem. com. arbitration 1970-94, chmn. book publ. subcom. 1991-95, coun. mem. 1992—, sr. lawyer divsn., Experience mag. 1990—, chmn. 1995—), Am. Law Inst. (life), Gen. Counsel Assn., Am. Soc. Corp. Secs. (pres. N.Y. regional group 1956-57, nat. dir. 1956-59), Assn. of Bar of City of N.Y. (exec. com. 1961-65, v.p. 1968-69, chmn. com. post-admission legal edn. 1965-68, organizer, chmn. corp. law dept. 1957-61, chmn. com. trade regulations 1953-57, mem. jud. com. 1977-79, chmn. membership com. 1981-85, internat. trade regulation com. 1985-90, sr. lawyers 1989-96), Am. Arbitration Assn. (exec. com. 1968—, chmn. 1972-77, chmn. bd. 1977-79, chmn. emeritus 1980—), N.Y. State Bar Assn. (antitrust, other coms.), Nat. Coun. Paper Industry for Air and Steam Improvement (bd. govs. 1956-74, chmn. bd. govs. 1966-69), Nat. Coun. Adminstrv. Justice (dir. 1980-83), Practicing Law Inst. (trustee 1966-86, pres. 1972-79, chmn. 1979-86, chmn. emeritus 1986—), Dutch Treat Club. (gov., sec. 1992—), Univ. Club (v.p. coun., chmn. club activities, charter revision com.), Sigma Nu. Methodist. Home and Office: The Knoll Gypsy Trail Rd Carmel NY 10512

LOWE, FELIX CALEB, publishing executive; b. Mountain City, Tenn., Nov. 12, 1933; s. Ned Tillie and Sarah (Lochery) L.; m. Susan Johnson, Nov. 24, 1961; children: Christopher, Joshua. B.S., East Tenn. State U., 1959, postgrad., 1960; postgrad., Ga. State U., Statesboro, 1961, Fed. Exec. Inst., Charlottesville, Va., 1983. Tchr. Arlington County Bd. Edn., Va., 1959-62; editor, mktg. mgr. Macmillan Co., N.Y.C., 1962-68; mktg. dir. Entelek Inc., Newburyport, Mass., 1968-69; sales mgr. Brookings Instn., Washington, 1969-76; dir. Smithsonian Instn. Press, Washington, 1976-94; with U.Va., 1994; pub. Rivilo Books, Bluffton, S.C., 1994—; lectr. George Washington U., 1978—, Howard U., East Tenn. State U.; mem. adv. bd. Nat. Hist. Pub. and Records Com., Washington, 1978—; mem. U.S. pub. del. to Soviet Union, 1987. Author: John Ross: Cherokee Indian Chief, 1989. Coach, Little River Soccer Club, Annandale Boys Club, Braddock Road Youth Club, 1974—. Named Alumni of Yr., East Tenn. State U., 1981. Mem. Assn. Am. Univ. Presses, Washington Book Pubs. (co-founder, exec. sec. 1981-82). Baptist. Club: Nat. Press (Washington). Home: 113 Gascoigne Bluff Rd Bluffton SC 29910 Office: Rivilo Books 113 Gascoigne Bluff Rd Bluffton SC 29910

LOWE, HARRY, museum director; b. Opelika, Ala., Apr. 9, 1922; s. Harry Foster and Lois (Fletcher) L. B.F.A., Auburn U., 1943, M.F.A., 1949; student, Cranbrook Acad., 1951, 53. Prof. art, dir. Art Gallery, Auburn U., 1957-59; dir. Tenn. Fine Arts Center, Nashville, 1959-64; curator exhibits Nat. Mus. Am. Art (formerly Nat. Collection Fine Arts), Smithsonian Instn., 1964-72, dep. commr. U.S. Exhbn. at Venice Biennale, 1966, asst. dir. for ops., 1972-74, asst. dir., 1974-81, acting dir., 1981-82, dep. dir., 1983-84, dep. dir. emeritus, 1985—; 1st pres. Tenn. Assn. Museums, 1960. Served with F.A. AUS, World War II, ETO. Home: 802 A St SE Washington DC 20003-1340 Office: Nat Mus Am Art Smithsonian Instn Washington DC 20560

LOWE, JAMES ALLEN, school superintendent; b. Pocatello, Idaho, Aug. 10, 1936; s. James Merwin and Ruby (Bennett) L.; m. Joanne Stanger, Dec. 28, 1955; children—Jill, Jann, James, Jeffrey A., Julie, Jared G. A.S., Weber Coll., 1956; B.S., U. Utah, 1958; M.S., N.Mex. Highlands Coll., 1963; Ed.D., Utah State U., 1973. Tchr. math., sci. Davis Sch. Dist., Farmington, Utah, 1961-68; grad. asst. Utah State U., Logan, 1968-69; asst. prof. Brigham Young U.-Hawaii campus, Laie Hawaii, 1969-71; tchr. math. Viewmont High Sch., Bountiful, Utah, 1971-74; prin. Star Valley High Sch., Afton, Wyo., 1974-77; supt. Lincoln County Sch. Dist. #2, Afton, 1977—; recipient Nat. Superintendent of the Yr. awd., Wyoming, Am. Assn. of School Administrators, 1992. Co-editor Brigham young U. Hawaii Edn. Dept., 1970-71. Contbr. articles to profl. jours. Bishop Ch. of Jesus Christ of Latter-day Saints, Afton, 1978-83. NSF fellow, 1962, 67. Mem. Wyo. Assn. Sch. Adminstrs., Phi Delta Kappa. Home: 225 E 9th Ave Afton WY 83110 Office: Lincoln County Sch Dist #2 PO Box 219 Afton WY 83110-0219

LOWE, JOHN, III, consulting civil engineer; b. N.Y.C., Mar. 14, 1916; s. John and Rose Marie (Jahoda) L.; m. Jeanne Wright, June 19, 1943; children: Jonathan Alan, Barbara Jean, Heather Ellen. B.S. in Engring., CCNY; M.S.C.E., MIT. Registered profl. engr., N.Y., La., PR., Calif. Instr. U. Md., College Park, 1937-40, MIT, Cambridge, Mass., 1941-44; physicist David Taylor Model Basin, Carderock, Md., 1945; chief soils engr. Tippetts-Abbett-McCarthy-Stratton, N.Y.C., 1945-55, assoc. ptnr., 1956-62, ptnr., 1962-83; pvt. practice geotech. and dam engring., 1984—; adj. assoc. prof. NYU, 1949-51; lectr. soil mechanics CCNY, 1953-60; 8th Terzaghi lectr., 1971, 4th Nabor Carrillo lectr., 1978, 2d U.S. Com. on Large Dams lectr., 1982, Marty Kapp lectr., 1986; keynote address Roller Compacted Concrete II, 1988; cons. Corps. Engrs., Washington, 1962-80. Contbr. chpts. to 4 books, 38 articles in field to profl. jours. Decorated comdr. Order of Alouites (Morocco); recipient Townsend Harris medal Alumni CCNY, 1982. Fellow ASCE; mem. NAE, U.S. Com. Large Dam (chmn. 1977-78), Nat. Com. Soil Mechanics and Found. Engring., Moles, Univ. Club, Bronxville Field Club.

LOWE, KATHLENE WINN, lawyer; b. San Diego, Dec. 1, 1949; d. Ralph and Grace (Rodes) Winn; m. Russell Howells Lowe, Oct. 7, 1977; 1 child, Taylor Rhodes. BA in English magna cum laude, U. Utah, 1971, MA in English, 1973, JD, 1976. Bar: Utah 1976, U.S. Dist. Ct. Utah 1976, U.S. Ct. Appeals (10th cir.) 1980, Calif. 1989, U.S. Dist. Ct. (ctrl. dist.) Calif. 1990. Assoc. Parsons, Behle & Latimer, Salt Lake City, 1976-80, ptnr., 1980-84; v.p. law Skaggs Alpha Beta Inc., Salt Lake City; now ptnr. Brobeck, Phleger & Harrison, Newport Beach, Calif. Contbg. editor Utah Law Rev., 1975-76. Mem. ABA, Utah Bar Assn., Salt Lake City Bar Assn., Phi Kappa Phi. Avocations: fly fishing, reading, skiing, golfing, traveling. Office: Brobeck Phleger & Harrison 4675 Macarthur Ct Ste 1000 Newport Beach CA 92660-1846*

LOWE, KENNETH STEPHEN, magazine editor; b. St. Paul, July 18, 1921; s. Malcolm and Erma Alta (Henderson) L.; m. Marie Elizabeth Contway, June 18, 1949; children—Stephen, Scott, Stuart. B.A., U. Mich., 1948. Telegraph editor Daily Mining Jour., Marquette, Mich., 1948-51, assoc. editor, 1951-55, editor, 1955-72; various pub. relations positions Mich., 1972-75; editor Mich. United Conservation Clubs, Lansing, 1975—. Mem. Mich. Conservation Commn., Lansing, 1961-63; pres. Upper Peninsula Child Guidance Clinic, Marquette, 1965-66, Peter White Library Bd., 1965-67. Mem. Outdoor Writers Assn. Am., Mich. Outdoor Writers Assn. (award 1951-52), Mich. United Conservation Clubs (Merit award 1958, Spl. Conservation award 1987). Democrat. Avocations: hunting; fishing; dogs; birding. Home: 1037 Blanchette Dr East Lansing MI 48823-1821

LOWE, MARVIN, artist; b. Bklyn., May 19, 1922; m. Juel Watkins, Apr. 1, 1949; 1 dau., Melissa. Student, Julliard Sch. Music, 1952-54; BA, Bklyn. Coll., 1956; MFA, U. Iowa, 1961. Prof. fine arts Ind. U., Bloomington, 1968-92, prof. emeritus, 1992—; vis. artist-lectr., 1970—. Exhibites in 62 one-person shows; over 200 group and invitational exhbns.; participated in U.S. info. exhbns. in Latin Am., Japan, USSR, and most European countries; represented in 84 permanent collections including Phila. Mus. Art, Bklyn. Mus., Smithsonian Instn., Brit. Mus., Japan Print Assn., N.Y.C. Pub. Libr., Calif. Palace Legion of Honor, San Francidso, Boston Pub. Libr., Columbia U., Libr. of Congress, Indpls. Mus. Art, Ringling Mus., Honolulu Acad. Art, Ft. Wayne Mus. Art, Purdue U. Mus. Fine Art, Springfield, Mass. Served with USNR, 1942-45. Fellow Nat. Endowment for Arts, 1975; fellow Ford Found., 1979, Ind. Arts Commn., 1987; recipient numerous Purchase awards, 1960—. Office: Ind U Sch Fine Arts Bloomington IN 47405 *As a visual artist, I have tried to refrain from making public statements about my work which ultimately must speak for itself.*

LOWE, MARY FRANCES, federal government official; b. Ft. Meade, Md., Apr. 15, 1952; d. Benno Powers and Peggy Catherine (Moore) L. B.A., Coll. William and Mary, 1972; M.A., Fletcher Sch. Law and Diplomacy, 1974, M.A. Law and Diplomacy in, 1975; diplome, Grad. Inst. Internat. Studies U. Geneva, Switzerland, 1975; M.P.H. in epidemiology, Johns Hopkins Sch. Hygiene and Pub. Health, 1986. External collaborator ILO, Geneva, 1974; legis. asst. to U.S. Senator Richard S. Schweiker Washington, 1975-76; profl. staff mem. health and sci. rsch. subcom. U.S. Senate Com. Labor and Human Resources, Washington, 1976-81; exec. sec. U.S. Dept. HHS, Washington, 1981-85; sr. asst. to commr. program policy FDA, 1985-89; sr. asst. pesticide programs EPA, 1989—; rep. U.S. delegations 34th and 35th World Health Assemblies, Geneva, 1981, 82; alt. trustee Woodrow Wilson Internat. Ctr. Scholars. Mem. Soc. for Epidemiologic Rsch., Am. Assn. World Health, Exec. Women in Govt., Soc. Risk Analysis, Washington World Affairs Coun., Delta Omega. Home: 7920 Spotswood Dr Alexandria VA 22308-1125 Office: EPA 401 M St SW Washington DC 20460-0001

LOWE, MARY JOHNSON, federal judge; b. N.Y.C., June 10, 1924; m. Ivan A. Michael, Nov. 4, 1961; children: Edward H. Lowe, Leslie H. Lowe, Bess J. Michael. BA, Hunter Coll., 1952; LLB, Bklyn. Law Sch., 1954; LLM, Columbia U., 1955; LLD, CUNY, 1990. Bar: N.Y. 1955. Pvt. practice law N.Y.C., 1955-71; judge N.Y.C. Criminal Ct., 1971-72; acting justice N.Y. State Supreme Ct., 1972-74; judge Bronx County Supreme Ct., 1974; justice N.Y. State Supreme Ct., 1977, 1st Jud. Dist., 1978; judge U.S. Dist. Ct. (so. dist.) N.Y., 1978-91, sr. judge, 1991—. Recipient award for outstanding service to criminal justice system Bronx County Criminal Cts. Bar Assn., 1974, award for work on narcotics cases Asst. Dist. Attys., 1974. Mem. Women in Criminal Justice, Harlem Lawyers Assn., Bronx Criminal Lawyers Assn., N.Y. County Lawyers Assn., Bronx County Bar Assn., N.Y. State Bar Assn. (award for outstanding jud. contbn. to criminal justice Sect. Criminal Justice 1978), NAACP, Nat. Urban League, Nat. Council Negro Women, NOW. Office: US Dist Ct US Courthouse 40 Foley Sq New York NY 10007*

LOWE, MELINDA MARIE, banker; b. Cleve., Feb. 23, 1966; d. James E. and Phyllis J. (King) Lowe. Student, U. N.C., Wilmington, 1988. Internat. letter of credit specialist NationsBank, Charlotte, N.C., 1989-94; cert. internat. letter of credit specialist First Union Nat. Bank, Charlotte, N.C., 1994-95; office mgr. Control Products Sales, Inc., Ft. Hill, S.C., 1995—. Republican. Avocations: reading, walking, needlepoint. Office: Control Products Sales Inc PO Box 242 Avon NC 27915

LOWE, PETER STEPHEN, non-profit company executive; b. Lahore, Pakistan, Oct. 23, 1958; s. Eric and Margaret Winnifred (Bradshaw) L.; m. Tamara Angela Forte, May 9, 1987. BA, Carleton U., Ottawa, Ont., Can., 1986. Pres. Lifemasters Tng. Co., Vancouver, B.C., Can., 1981-87, Global Achievers, New Orleans, 1987-90; pres., chief exec. officer Peter Lowe Internat., Inc., Tampa, Fla., 1990—. Mem. Nat. Speakers Assn., Nat. Christian Speakers Assn. (founder), Internat. Platform Assn. Office: 8405A Benjamin Rd Tampa FL 33634

LOWE, RALPH EDWARD, lawyer; b. Hinsdale, Ill., Nov. 24, 1931; s. Charles Russell and Eva Eleanor (Schroeder) L.; m. Patricia E. Eichhorst, Aug. 23, 1952; children: John Stuart, Michael Kevin, Timothy Edward. BA, Depauw U., 1953; LLB, U. Ill., 1956. Bar: Ill. 1956, U.S. Dist. Ct. (no. dist.) Ill. 1957, Ga. 1974, U.S. Dist. Ct. (no. dist.) Ga. 1980, S.C. 1990. Assoc. Ruddy & Brown, Aurora, Ill., 1956-58; ptnr. Lowe & Richards, Aurora, 1959-62, Vincent, Lowe & Richards, Aurora, 1963-71; pvt. practice Aurora, 1972-74, Aurora and Atlanta, 1974-85; prin. Lowe & Steinmetz, Ltd., Aurora and Atlanta, 1985-91; chmn. Inter-Am. Devel. Corp., Ill., 1965-67. Office: 407 W Galena Blvd Aurora IL 60506-3946

LOWE, RANDALL BRIAN, lawyer; b. Englewood, N.J., Nov. 20, 1948. BA, U. R.I., 1970; JD, Washington U., 1973. Bar: Ill. 1973, Conn. 1975, D.C. 1976, U.S. Ct. Appeals (2d and D.C. cirs.) 1976, N.J. 1977, U.S. Dist. Ct. N.J. 1977, U.S. Ct. Appeals (3d cir.) 1977, U.S. Ct. Appeals (9th cir.) 1979, N.Y. 1980, U.S. Dist. Ct. (ea. and so. dists.) N.Y. 1980. Atty. Callis & Filcoff, Granite City, Ill., 1973-75, AT&T, Washington and N.Y.C., 1975-78, ITT Corp, 1978-83, Surrey & Morse, Washington, 1983-86; ptnr. Jones, Day, Reavis & Pogue, Washington, 1986-94, Piper & Marbury, Washington, 1994—. Office: Piper & Marbury 1200 19th St NW Washington DC 20036*

LOWE, ROB, actor; b. Charlottesville, Va., Mar. 17, 1964; m. Sheryl Berkoff, July 22, 1991. Appeared in films including The Outsiders, 1983, Class, 1983, The Hotel New Hampshire, 1984, Oxford Blues, 1984, St. Elmo's Fire, 1985, Youngblood, About Last Night..., 1986, Square Dance, 1987, Illegally Yours, Masquerade, 1988, Bad Influence, 1991, The Dark Backward, 1991, Wayne's World, 1992, Frank and Jesse (also prodr.), 1994, Billy the Third, 1995; TV appearances include (series) A New Kind of Family, (movie) Thursday's Child, (spls.) A Matter of Time, Schoolboy Father, Stephen King's The Stand. Office: UTA 9560 Wilshire Blvd 5th fl Beverly Hills CA 90212*

LOWE, ROBERT CHARLES, lawyer; b. New Orleans, July 3, 1949; s. Carl Randall and Antonia (Morgan) L.; m. Theresa Louise Acree, Feb. 4, 1978. 1 child, Nicholas Stafford. BA, U. New Orleans, 1971; JD, La. State U., 1975. Bar: La. 1975, U.S. Dist. Ct. (ea. dist.) La. 1975, U.S. Ct. Appeals (5th cir.) 1980, U.S. Dist. Ct. (we. dist.) La. 1978, U.S. Supreme Ct. 1982. Assoc. Sessions, Fishman, Rosenson, Boisfontaine, and Nathan, New Orleans, 1975-80, ptnr., 1980-87; ptnr. Lowe, Stein, Hoffman, Allweiss and Hauver, 1987—. Author: Louisiana Divorce, 1984; mem. La. Law Rev., 1974-75; contbr. articles to profl. jours. Mem. ABA, La. State Bar Assn. (chmn. family law sect. 1984-85), La. Assn. Def. Counsel, New Orleans Bar Assn. (chmn. family law sect. 1991-92), La. State Law Inst., La. Trial Lawyers Assn., Order of Coif, Phi Kappa Phi. Republican. Home: 9625 Garden Oak Ln River Ridge LA 70123-2005 Office: 701 Poydras St Ste 3600 New Orleans LA 70139-6001

LOWE, ROBERT CHARLES, lawyer, banker; b. Seattle, Jan. 15, 1927; s. Martin M. and Helen (Yaster) L.; m. Hope Lucille Sperstad, Mar. 21, 1952; children: Karen, Karlton, Nelson, Inez. B.A., U. Wash., 1953; LL.B., U. Denver, 1959. Bar: Alaska 1961. Accountant Haskins & Sells (C.P.A.s), Los Angeles, 1953-54; agt. Internal Revenue Service, 1954-57; atty. State Alaska, 1960; mem. firm Hughes, Thorsness, Lowe, Gantz & Clark, Anchorage, 1960-75; pres. Safeco Title Agy., Inc., Anchorage, 1975-79; chmn. bd. Peoples Bank & Trust Co., Anchorage. Served with USNR, 1944-46. Mem. Am., Alaska, Anchorage bar assns., Anchorage Estate Planning Council (pres. 1970), Rotary. Home: 2765 S Saint Andrews Dr Sierra Vista AZ 85635-5221

LOWE, ROBERT EDWARD, insurance company executive; b. Winnipeg, Man., Can., Oct. 31, 1940; s. Mark Currie and Florence Irene L. Lowe; m. Isabella Love Hunter Liddell, Oct. 1, 1965; children: Susan Patricia, Donna Jane, Mark William. MBA, York U., Toronto, 1975. Chartered acct. Ptnr. Coopers & Lybrand, Toronto, 1971; pres. Coopers & Lybrand Ltd., Toronto, 1975-80, chmn. corp. reorgn. and bankruptcy, 1980—; bd. dirs. Olympia & York Devels. Ltd., Toronto, Olympia & York U.S.A., N.Y. Lt. Can. Army Res., 1958-61. Mem. Insolvency Inst. Can., Toronto Golf Club, Can. Club, Nat. Club. Mem. Conservative Party. Presbyterian. Avocations: golf, sailing. Office: Coopers & Lybrand, 145 King St W Ste 2300, Toronto, ON Canada M5H 1V8

LOWE, ROBERT STANLEY, lawyer; b. Herman, Nebr., Apr. 23, 1923; s. Stanley Robert and Ann Marguerite (Feese) L.; m. Anne Kirtland Selden, Dec. 19, 1959; children: Robert James, Margaret Anne. AB, U. Nebr., 1947, JD, 1949. Bar: Wyo. 1949. Ptnr. McAvoy & Lowe, Newcastle, 1949-51, Hickey & Lowe, Rawlins, 1951-55; county and pros. atty. Rawlins, 1955-59, pvt. practice, 1959-67; assoc. dir. Am. Judicature Soc., Chgo., 1967—; bd. dirs., exec. sec. Hilltop Nat. Bank, Casper, 1967-74; bd. dirs., sec. Hilltop Nat. Bank, Casper; legal adv. div. Nat. Ski Patrol Sys., 1975-88; city atty. City of Rawlins, 1963-65; atty., asst. sec. Casper Mountain Ski Patrol, 1988—. Mem. Wyo. Ho. of Reps., 1952-54; bd. dirs. Vols. in Probation, 1969-82; leader lawyer del. to China, People to People, 1986; mem. Wyo. Vets. Affairs Coun., 1994—, chmn., 1996—; mem. legis. com. United Vets, Coun. Wyo., 1993—; trustee, pres., Troopers Found., Inc., 1994—; pres. Casper WW II Commemorative Assn. Lt. (j.g.) U.S. Maritime Svc., U.S. Mcht. Marine, 1943-46. Recipient Dedicated Community Worker award Rawlins Jr. C. of C., 1967, Yellow merit award Nat. Ski Patrol System, 1982, 85, 87, 88. Fellow Am. Bar Found. (life); mem. VFW (post advisor 1991-96, nat. aide-de-camp 1993-94, judge advocate dist. 3 Dept. Wyo., 1994—, Mil. Order of Cootie grand judge advocate 1994—, Mil. Order of Cooter (grand judge advocate, ABA (sec. jud. adminstrn. divsn. lawyers conf., exec. com. 1975-76, chmn. 1977-78, chmn. judicial qualification and selection com. 1986-93, coun. jud. adminstrn. divsn. 1977-78, mem. com. to implement jud. adminstrn. standards 1978-83, Ho. of Dels. state bar del. 1978-80, 86-87, state del. 1987-93, Assembly del. 1980-83), Am. Judicature Soc. (dir. 1961-67, 85-89, bd. editors 1975-77, Herbert Harley award 1974), Wyo. State Bar (chmn. com. on cts. 1961-67, 77-87), Nebr. State Bar Assn., Ill. State Bar Assn., D.C. Bar, Inter-Am. Bar Assn., Selden Soc., Inst. Jud. Adminstrn., Rocky Mountain Oil and Gas Assn. (legal com. 1976—, chmn. 1979-82, 90-91), Rocky Mountain Mineral Law Found. (trustee 1980-94), Am. Law Inst., Order of Coif, Delta Theta Phi (dist. chancellor 1982-83, chief justice 1983-93, assoc. justice 1993—; Percy J. Power Meml. award 1983, Gold Medallion award 1990), Casper Rotary Club (pres. 1985-86), Casper Rotary Found. (dir., sec. 1990—). Mem. Ch. of Christ, Scientist. Home: 97 Primrose St Casper WY 82604-4018 Office: 895 River Cross Rd Casper WY 82601-1758

LOWE, ROY GOINS, lawyer; b. Lake Worth, Fla., Apr. 8, 1926; s. Roy Sereno and May (Goins) L.; A.B., U. Kans., 1948, LL.B., 1951. Admitted to Kans. bar, 1951; gen. practice, Olathe, 1951—; mem. firm Lowe, Farmer, Bacon & Roe and predecessor, 1951—. Served with USNR, 1944-46. Mem. Bar Assn. State Kans., Johnson County Bar Assn., Am. Legion, Phi Alpha Delta, Sigma Nu. Republican. Presbyn. Home: 701 W Park St Olathe KS 66061-3137 Office: Colonial Bldg Olathe KS 66061

LOWELL, HOWARD PARSONS, government records administrator; b. Rockland, Maine, May 10, 1945; s. Chauncey Vernon Lowell and Delia Coffin (Parsons) Morey; m. Marcia Barrell, Feb. 15, 1969 (div. 1980); m. Charlesa Ann Gatson, July 27, 1985, 1 stepson, Garrett Timmons. BA, U. Me., Orono, 1967; MS, Simmons Coll., 1974. Adminstrn. svcs. officer Maine state archives, Augusta, 1968-72; ednl. specialist Mass. bur. libr. ext., Boston, 1974-75; dir. Revere (Mass.) Pub. Libr., 1975-76; freelance cons. Salem, Oreg., 1976-81, Denver, 1976-81; adminstr. Okla. resources br. Okla. Dept. Librs., Oklahoma City, 1981-89; archivist and records administrator State of Del., 1990—; acting dir. N.E. Document Conservation Ctr., Andover, Mass., 1978. Mem. Acad. Cert. Archivists, Nat. Assn. Govt. Archives and Records Adminstrs. (bd. dirs. 1985-87, 1995-96, pres. 1992-94), Phi Beta Kappa, Phi Kappa Phi, Phi Alpha Theta, Beta Phi Mu. Democrat. Mem. Unitarian Ch. Office: Del Pub Archives Hall of Records PO box 1401 Dover DE 19903

LOWEN, GERARD GUNTHER, mechanical engineering educator; b. Munich, Germany, Oct. 25, 1921; came to U.S., 1939; s. Charles and Stefanie (Frank) L.; m. Doris Julie Wolff, July 2, 1952; children: Deborah Lowen-Klein, Nicole Vianna, Daniel. BSME, CCNY, 1954; M of Mech. Engring., Columbia U., 1958; D of Engring., Tech. U. Munich, 1963. Registered profl. engr., N.Y. Machinist, tool and diemaker Germany and the U.S., 1938-54; lectr. mech. engring. CCNY, 1954-59, asst. prof., 1959-64, assoc. prof., 1964-69, prof., 1969—, Herbert Kayser prof., 1987—, chmn. mech. engring. dept., 1987-90; assoc. dean grad. studies, engring., 1990—; cons. in field. Contbr. articles to profl. jours.; patentee in field. Named Outstanding Tchr., CCNY, 1984; NSF grantee, 1968-89. Fellow ASME (machine design award 1987); mem. AAAS, Am. Soc. Engring. Edn., Verein Deutscher Ingenieure (corr.), Soc. Mfg. Engrs., N.Y. Acad. Scis. Jewish. Avocations: reading, history, hiking. Home: 484 Eisenhower Ct Wyckoff NJ 07481-2206 Office: CCNY Grad Engring Office Convent Ave New York NY 10031-2604

LOWEN, WALTER, mechanical engineering educator; b. Cologne, Germany, May 17, 1921; came to U.S., 1936, naturalized, 1945; m. Sylvia Lowen, May 22, 1943; children: Robert Gary, John Gordon. B.S. in Mech. Engring, N.C. State Coll., 1943, M.S., 1947; student, Oak Ridge Sch. Reactor Tech., 1955; D.Sc., Swiss Fed. Inst. Tech., 1963. Instr. N.C. State Coll., 1943-47; faculty Union Coll., Schenectady, 1947-68; prof. mech. engring. Union Coll., 1956-68, chmn. div. engring., 1956-60, 66-67, acting chmn. mech. engring. dept., 1959-60, chmn. dept., 1966-67; prof., dir. Sch. Advanced Tech. SUNY, Binghamton, 1967-68, dean Sch. Advanced Tech., 1968-77, prof. systems sci., 1968-90, Thomas J. Watson sch. prof. emeritus, 1991—; cons. Oak Ridge Nat. Lab., Knolls Atomic Power Lab., Alco Products, Inst. Applied Tech. of Nat. Bur. Standards.; adj. faculty IBM Systems Research Inst., 1979-89; vice chmn. Niskayuna Sch. Centralization Bldg. Com., 1954; co-founder Vols. for Internat. Tech. Assistance, Inc., 1960—. Author: Dichotomies of the Mind, 1982. NSF fellow to Switzerland, 1961-62. Mem. ASME (sect. vice-chmn. local chpt. 1959-60), Am. Soc. Engring. Edn., Sigma Xi, Tau Beta Pi, Pi Tau Sigma, Phi Kappa Phi. Home: 152 Moore Ave Binghamton NY 13903-3124

LOWENBERG, MICHAEL, lawyer; b. Bklyn., Mar. 6, 1943; s. Leo and Edna (Hanft) L.; m. Julie Goldberg, June 13, 1965; children: Daniel, Frances, Anthony. BA, Bklyn. Coll., 1963; LLB, Harvard U., 1966. Bar: Tex. 1966, U.S. Dist. Ct. (no. dist.) Tex. 1966, U.S. Ct. Appeals (5th cir.) 1967. Assoc. Akin, Gump, Strauss, Hauer & Feld, L.L.P., Dallas, 1966-71; prof. corp. ptnr. Akin, Gump, Strauss, Hauer & Feld, P.C., Dallas, 1972—. Pres. Dallas Legal Services Found., 1972; chmn. Dallas chpt. Am. Jewish Com., 1973-74. Mem. ABA, Tex. Bar Assn., Bar Assn. of 5th Cir. (bd. dirs.), Dallas Bar Assn., Nat. Legal Aid and Defenders Assn., Def. Rsch. Inst. Democrat. Home: 5551 Montrose Dr Dallas TX 75209-5609 Office: Akin Gump Strauss Hauer & Feld 4100 First City Center 1700 Pacific Ave Dallas TX 75201-7322*

LOWENFELD, ANDREAS FRANK, law educator, arbitrator; b. Berlin, May 30, 1930; s. Henry and Yela (Herschkowitsch) L.; m. Elena Machado, Aug. 11, 1962; children: Julian, Marianna. AB magna cum laude, Harvard U., 1951, LLB magna cum laude, 1955. Bar: N.Y. 1955, U.S. Supreme Ct. 1961. Assoc. Hyde and de Vries, N.Y.C., 1957-61; spl. asst. to legal adv. U.S. Dept. State, 1961-63; asst. legal adviser for econ. affairs, 1963-65, dep. legal adviser, 1965-66; fellow John F. Kennedy Inst. Politics, Harvard U., Cambridge, Mass., 1966-67; prof. law Sch. Law, NYU, N.Y.C., 1967—, Charles L. Denison prof. law, 1981-94, Herbert and Rose Rubin prof. internat. law, 1994—; arbitrator internat. comml. panels ICC. Mem. ABA, Assn. of Bar of City of N.Y., Am. Soc. Internat. Law, Am. Arbitration Assn. (arbitrator), Coun. Fgn. Rels., Inst. de Droit Internat. Author: (with Abram Chayes and Thomas Ehrlich) International Legal Process, 1968-69; Aviation Law, Cases and Materials, 1972, 2d edit., 1981; International Economic Law, vol. I, 1975, 3d edit., 1996, vol. II, 1976, 2d edit., 1982, vol. III, 1977, 2d edit., 1983, vol. IV, 1977, 2d edit., 1984, vol. VI, 1979, 2d edit., 1983, Conflict of Laws, Federal, State and International Perspectives, 1986, International Litigation and Arbitration, 1993, International Litigation: The Quest for Reasonableness, 1996; editor, co-author: Expropriation in the Americas: A Comparative Law Study, 1971; assoc. reporter Am. Law Inst. Restatement on Foreign Relations Law; contbr. articles and book revs. on pub. internat. law, internat. econ. law, air law, conflict of laws, arbitration, history and politics to profl. jours. Home: 5776 Palisade Ave Bronx NY 10471-1212 Office: NYU Sch Law 40 Washington Sq S New York NY 10012-1005

LOWENFELS, FRED M., lawyer; b. Richmond, Va., Mar. 22, 1944; s. Fred C. and Joan (Weber) L.; m. Joan Roberta Brafman, June 10, 1974; children: Erica Anne, Helene Beth. AB, Harvard U., 1965, JD, 1968; postgrad., Univ. Libre de Bruxelles, 1968-69. Bar: N.Y. 1969. Assoc. Wolf, Haldenstein, Adler, Freeman & Herz, N.Y.C., 1970-74; sr. v.p., gen. counsel Transammonia Inc., N.Y.C., 1974—. Trustee Jewish Home and Hosp. for the Aged, N.Y.C., 1974—. Mem. Assn. Bar. City of N.Y., Am. Corp. Counsel Assn., Harvard Club N.Y.C. Office: Transammonia Inc 350 Park Ave New York NY 10022-6022

LOWENFELS, LEWIS DAVID, lawyer; b. N.Y.C., June 9, 1935; s. Seymour and Jane (Phillips) L.; m. Fern Gelford, Aug. 15, 1965; children: Joshua, Jacqueline. BA magna cum laude, Harvard U., 1957, LLB, 1961. Bar: N.Y. 1961. Ptnr. Tolins & Lowenfels, N.Y.C., 1967—; adj. prof. law Seton Hall U. Law Sch; lectr. law Practicing Law Inst., Southwestern Legal Found., U. Minn. Fed. Bar Assn., 1972; pub. gov. Am. Stock Exch., 1993-96. Co-author: Securities Fraud and Commodities Fraud, 6 vols., 1995; contbr. articles to profl. jours. With USAR, 1957-63. Mem. ABA (fed. regulation of securities com. 1978—, lectr.), N.Y. County Lawyers Assn. (securities and exchanges com. 1974—), Phi Beta Kappa, Harvard Club. Avocations: reading, writing, athletics. Office: Tolins & Lowenfels 12 E 49th St New York NY 10017-1028

LOWENKRON, LOU, brewing company executive. CEO G. Heileman Brewing, La Cross, Wis. Office: G Heileman Brewing 100 Harborview Plaza La Crosse WI 54601

LOWENSTEIN, ALAN VICTOR, lawyer; b. Newark, Aug. 30, 1913; s. Isaac and Florence (Cohen) L.; m. Amy Lieberman, Nov. 23, 1938; children: John, Roger, Jane Lowenstein Forsyth. A.B., U. Mich., 1933; M.A., U. Chgo., 1935; LL.B., Harvard U., 1936. Bar: N.J. 1936. Practiced in Newark and Roseland, 1936—; sr. partner Lowenstein, Sandler, Kohl, Fisher & Boylan, 1961—; assoc. atty. Temporary Nat. Econ. Com., 1938-39; asst. prof. Rutgers U. Law Sch., 1951-57; chmn. N.J. Corp. Law Revision Commn., 1959-72; spl. hearing officer Dept. Justice, 1961-65; chmn. bd. United Steel & Aluminum Corp., 1976-91. Pres. Jewish Community Council Essex County, 1950-53, United Way Essex and West Hudson, 1953-55; chmn. Newark Charter Commn., 1953, Newark Citizens Com. Mcpl. Govt., 1954-58, Newark Community Survey, 1959-60; v.p. Council Jewish Fedns., 1965-68, assoc. treas., 1981; pres. N.J. Symphony Orch., 1971-73, chmn. bd., 1973-76; mem. adv. council Rutgers U. Sch. Social Work, 1955-64; vice chmn. Liberty State Park Devel. Corp., 1984—; bd. overseers Rutgers U. Found., 1994—. Recipient Brotherhood award Nat. Conf. Christians and Jews, 1972, Trustees award for Disting. Community Service, N.J. Inst. Tech., 1984, Equal Justice award Legal Services N.J./N.J. State Bar Assn., 1988. Mem. ABA, N.J. Bar Assn., Essex County Bar Assn. (Pro-Bono Achievement award 1994), Am. Judicature Soc., Order of Coif, Phi Beta Kappa (v.p. N.J. 1951-52), Phi Kappa Phi, Tau Kappa Alpha. Home: 285 N Ridgewood Rd South Orange NJ 07079-1503 also: RR 3 Box 3892 Vergennes VT 05491-8601 Office: Lowenstein Sandler et al 65 Livingston Ave Roseland NJ 07068-1725

LOWENSTEIN, DANIEL HAYS, lawyer, educator; b. N.Y.C., May 10, 1943; s. Nathan and Elizabeth (Corn) L.; m. Sharon Yagi, Feb. 14, 1970; children—Aaron, Nathan. A.B., Yale U., 1964; LL.B., Harvard U., 1967. Bar: N.Y. 1968, Calif. 1969. Staff atty. Calif. Rural Legal Assistance, 1968-71; dep. sec. State of Calif., 1971-75; 1st chmn. Calif. Fair Polit. Practices Commn., 1975-79; prof. law UCLA, Los Angeles, 1979—; cons. on freedom of info. legislation, Que., Can., 1979. Contbr. articles on campaign fin., legis. districting, bribery and initiative elections to profl. publs.; author leading text on Am. election law. Bd. dirs. Common Cause, 1979-85, Ams. for Nonsmokder' Rights, 1980-93; counsel to House Dem. of Calif., 1981-82; draftsman Calif. Polit. Reform Act, 1974. Office: UCLA Law Sch 405 Hilgard Ave Los Angeles CA 90095-1476

LOWENSTEIN, DEREK IRVING, physicist; b. Hampton Court, Eng., Apr. 26, 1943; came to U.S., 1946; s. Siegfried and Ilse (Mildenberg) L.; m. Elaine Hartmann, July 6, 1968; children: Jessica R., Peter D. BS, CCNY, 1964; MS, U. Pa., 1965, PhD, 1969. Postdoctoral fellow U. Pa., Phila., 1969-70; research assoc. U. Pitts., 1970-73; asst. physicist Brookhaven Nat. Lab., Upton, N.Y., 1973-75; assoc. physicist Brookhaven Nat. Lab., 1975-77, physicist, 1977-83, sr. physicist, 1983—, head Exptl. Planning and Support div., 1977-84, dep. chmn. accelerator dept., 1981-84, chmn. Alternating Gradient Synchrotron dept., 1984—; assoc. mem. U.S.-Russia Joint Coordinating Commn. on Fundamental Properties of Matter, 1983—, U.S.-Japan Commn. on High Energy Physics, 1984—; mem. Dept. of Energy High Energy Physics Adv. Panel, 1993—. Contbr. articles on particle and accelerator physics to profl. jours. Fellow Am. Phys. Soc.; mem. AAAS, N.Y. Acad. Scis., Sigma Xi. Office: Brookhaven Nat Lab Ags Dept Upton NY 11973

LOWENSTEIN, JAMES GORDON, former diplomat, international consultant; b. Long Branch, N.J., Aug. 6, 1927; s. Melvyn Gordon and Katherine Price (Goldsmith) L.; m. Dora Laurinda Richardson, June 11, 1955 (div. 1977); children: Laurinda Vinson, Price Gordon; m. Anne Cornely de la Selle, July 4, 1981. Grad., Loomis Sch., 1945; B.A., Yale U., 1949; postgrad., Harvard Law Sch., 1955-56. With Office Spl. Rep. in Europe, Econ. Cooperation Adminstrn., Paris, 1950-51; mem. U.S. Spl. Mission to Yugoslavia, Sarajevo, 1951; fgn. svc. officer Bur. European Affairs Dept. State, 1957-58; fgn. service officer Am. Embassy, Colombo, Ceylon, 1959-61, Belgrade, Yugoslavia, 1961-64; cons. Fgn. Relations Com., U.S. Senate, Washington, 1965-74; prin. dep. asst. sec. state for European affairs Washington, 1974-77; ambassador to Luxembourg, 1977-81; with Bur. European Affairs, Dept. State, 1981-82; ptnr. IRC Group, Washington, 1982-87; sr. cons. APCO Assocs., Washington, 1988—; mem. internat. observer group Sri Lanka elections, 1993, 94, sr. elections adv. Osce Mission to Bosnia, 1996; vice chmn. U.S. Bus. Coun. for Southeastern Europe: chmn. bd. Baltic Investments, S.A., Luxembourg; bd. dirs. AIS Worldwide Fund Ltd.; past sec. bd. Emerging Eastern European Fund; co-founder, bd. dirs. French-Am. Found.; bd. dirs. Washington Found. for European Studies, Citizens Exch. Coun., Refugees Internat.; past mem. adv. coun. Sch. Advanced Internat. Studies and Bologna (Italy) Ctr. Johns Hopkins U. Past trustee Madeira Sch., Lacoste Sch. of the Arts in France; mem. staff naval war coll., 1954-55. Lt. (j.g.) USNR, 1952055. Decorated chevalier Légion d'Honneur (France); Grand Croix de la Couronne de Chene (Luxembourg). Mem. Coun. Fgn. Rels., Internat. Inst. Strategic Studies (London). Clubs: Metropolitan (Washington); Army-Navy Country (Arlington, Va.); Century Assn., Knickerbocker (N.Y.C.); Harbor (Seal Harbor, Maine); Travellers, Racing (Paris). Home: 3139 O St NW Washington DC 20007-3117 also: 32 Rue de Verneuil, 75007 Paris France Office: Ste 900 1615 L St NW Washington DC 20036-3308

LOWENSTEIN, LOUIS, legal educator; b. N.Y.C., June 13, 1925; s. Louis and Ralphina (Steinhardt) L.; m. Helen Libby Udell, Feb. 12, 1953; children: Roger Spector, Jane Ruth, Barbara Ann. B.S., Columbia, 1947, LL.B., 1953; M.F.S., U. Md., 1951. Bar: N.Y. 1953. Pvt. practice law N.Y.C., 1954-78; Assoc. Judge Stanley H. Fuld, N.Y. Ct. Appeals, 1953-54; assoc., then partner Hays, Sklar & Herzberg, 1954-68; partner Nickerson, Kramer, Lowenstein, Nessen, Kamin & Soll, 1968-78; Simon H. Rifkind prof. emeritus law and fin. Columbia U. Law Sch., 1980—, project dir. Instl. Investor Project, 1988-94; pres. Supermarkets Gen. Corp., Woodbridge, N.J., 1978-79; bd. dirs. Liz Claiborne, Inc. 1988-96. Author: What's Wrong with Wall Street, 1988, Sense and Nonsense in Corporate Finance, 1991; contbr., co-editor: Knights, Raiders and Targets, 1988; editor in chief Columbia Law Rev., 1951-53. Vice pres., mem. exec. com. Fedn. Jewish Philanthropies N.Y.; pres. Jewish Bd. Family and Children's Services N.Y., 1974-78; trustee Beth Israel Med. Center, N.Y.C., 1975-81. Served to lt. (j.g.) USNR, 1943-46. Mem. Am. Bar Assn., Assn. of Bar of City of N.Y., Am. Law Inst. Home: 1 Fountain Sq Larchmont NY 10538-4105 Office: Columbia U Law Sch 435 W 116th St New York NY 10027-7201

LOWENSTEIN, PETER DAVID, lawyer; b. N.Y.C., Dec. 31, 1935; s. Melvyn Gordon and Katherine Price (Goldsmith) L.; m. Constance Cohen; children from previous marriage: Anthony, Kate E., Christopher. BA, Trinity Coll., 1958; LLB, Georgetown U., 1961. Bar: Conn. 1962, N.Y. 1963. With SEC, Washington, 1961-63; assoc. Whitman & Ransom, N.Y.C., 1963-70, ptnr., 1970-83; sec., gen. counsel Value Line, Inc., N.Y.C., 1983-87; v.p., sec., gen. counsel Service Am. Corp., Stamford, Conn., 1988-90; ptnr. O'Connor, Morris & Jones, Greenwich, Conn., 1990-92, pvt. practice, 1992—; legal counsel Value Line Mutual Funds. Bd. dirs. Grand St. Settlement, N.Y.C., 1970-92, Greenwich Health Assn., Conn., 1978-85; bd. dirs. Greenwich chpt. ARC, 1989-94, vice chmn., 1991-93. Mem. Nantucket Yacht Club, Greenwich Field Club. Home: 496 Valley Rd Cos Cob CT 06807-1627 Office: Two Greenwich Plz Ste 100 Greenwich CT 06830-5436

LOWENSTEIN, RALPH LYNN, university dean emeritus; b. Danville, Va., Mar. 8, 1930; s. Henry and Rachel (Berman) L.; m. Bronia Grace Levenson, Feb. 6, 1955; children: Joan, Henry. BA, Columbia U., 1951, MS in Journalism, 1952; PhD in Journalism, U. Mo., 1967. Reporter Danville (Va.) Register, 1952, El Paso Times, 1954-57; asst. prof. journalism U. Tex. at El Paso, 1956-62, assoc. prof., 1962-65; publs. editor Freedom of Info. Ctr., Columbia, Mo., 1965-67; vis. prof., head journalistic studies Tel Aviv U., 1967-68; assoc. prof. Sch. Journalism, U. Mo., Columbia, 1968-70; prof. Sch. Journalism, U. Mo., 1970-76, chmn. news-editorial dept., 1975-76; press critic CBS Morning News, 1975-76; dean Coll. Journalism and Communications, U. Fla., Gainesville, 1976-94. Author: Bring My Sons from Far, 1966; (with John C. Merrill) Media, Messages and Men, 2nd edit., 1979, Macromedia, 1990; editor: (with Paul Fisher) Race and the News Media, 1967. Served with Israeli Army, 1948-49; AUS, 1952-54. Recipient Research in Journalism award Sigma Delta Chi, 1971, Disting. Svc. award Columbia Journalism Alumni, 1957, 30th Anniversary award State of Israel, 1978, Freedom Forum Journalism Adminstr. of Yr. award, 1994. Mem. Assn. Edn. in Journalism and Mass Comm. (pres. 1990-91), Kappa Tau Alpha. Home: 1705 NW 22nd Dr Gainesville FL 32605-3953

LOWENSTINE, MAURICE RICHARD, JR., retired steel executive; b. Valparaiso, Ind., Feb. 28, 1910; s. Maurice Richard and Etta (Hamburger) L.; m. Miriam Jean Richards, Nov. 9, 1940; children: Martha Jean, Linda Jane, Mark Richards. Student, U. Mich., 1928-29, U. Ariz., 1929-30. With Central Steel & Wire Co., Chgo., 1932-71, exec. v.p., treas., dir., 1942-71; Chmn. exec. com. Steel Service Center Inst., 1962-64. Chmn. bd. Greater Hinsdale Cmty. Chest, 1960; bd. dirs. Chgo. area coun. Boy Scouts Am., 1957-96, Hinsdale Cmty. House, 1961-64; vice commodore Chgo. Sea Explorer Scouts, 1973-96. Episcopalian. Clubs: Chgo. Yacht; Ruth Lake Country. Address: 407 E 3rd St Hinsdale IL 60521-4224

LOWENTHAL, ABRAHAM FREDERIC, international relations educator; b. Hyannis, Mass., Apr. 6, 1941; s. Eric Isaac and Suzanne (Moos) L.; m. Janet Wyzanski, June 24, 1962 (div. 1983); children: Linda Claudina, Michael Francis; m. Jane S. Jaquette, Jan. 20, 1991. A.B., Harvard U., 1961, M.P.A., 1964, Ph.D., 1971; postgrad., Harvard Law Sch., 1961-62. Tng. assoc. Ford Found., Dominican Republic, 1962-64; asst. rep. Ford Found., Lima, Peru, 1969-72; asst. dir., then dir. of studies Coun. Fgn. Rels., N.Y.C., 1974-76; dir. Latin Am. program Woodrow Wilson Internat. Ctr. for Scholars, Washington, 1977-83; exec. dir. Inter-Am. Dialogue, Washington, 1982-92; prof. Sch. Internat. Rels., U. So. Calif., Los Angeles, 1984—; dir., ctr. internat. studies U. So. Calif., 1992—; pres. Pacific Coun. Internat. Policy, L.A., 1995—; vis. fellow, rsch. assoc. Ctr. Internat. Studies, Princeton U., 1972-74; vis. lectr. polit. sci. Cath. U. Santiago, Dominican Republic, 1966; lectr. Princeton U., 1974; spl. cons. Commn. U.S.-L.Am. rels., N.Y.C., 1974-76; mem. internat. adv. bd. Ctr. U.S.-Mex. Rels., U. Calif.-San Diego, 1981-94; mem. internat. adv. bd. Helen Kellogg Inst., 1984-95; cons. Ford Found., 1974-90. Author: The Dominican Intervention, 1972, 2nd edit., 1995, Partners in Conflict: The United States and Latin

America in 1990s, 1991; editor, contbg. author: The Peruvian Experiment: Continuity and Change Under Military Rule, 1975, Armies and Politics in Latin America, 1976, Exporting Democracy: The United States and Latin America, 1991; co-editor, contbg. author: The Peruvian Experiment Reconsidered, 1983, The California-Mexico Connection, 1993; editor Latin Am. and Caribbean Record, vol. IV, 1985-86, vol. V, 1986-87, Latin America in a New World, 1994; mem. editorial bd. Jour. Inter-Am. Studies and World Affairs, Hemisphere, Internat. Security, 1977-85, Wilson Quar., 1977-83; contbr. articles to profl. jours. Mem. nat. adv. coun. Amnesty Internat., 1977-83, Ctr. for Nat. Policy, 1986—. Mem. Internat. Inst. Strategic Studies, Am. Polit. Sci. Assn. (coun. 1979-81), Latin Am. Studies (exec. coun. 1979-81), Coun. Fgn. Rels., Overseas Devel. Coun., Human Rights Watch, Calif. com. Democrat. Jewish. Home: 903 Stanford St Santa Monica CA 90403-2223 Office: Pacific Coun Internat Policy Los Angeles CA 90089-0035

LOWENTHAL, CONSTANCE, art historian; b. N.Y.C., Aug. 29, 1945; d. Jesse and Helen (Oberstein) L. BA cum laude, Brandeis U., 1967; AM, Inst. Fine Arts, NYU, 1969; PhD, Inst. Fine Arts, NYU, N.Y.C., 1976. Mem. faculty Sarah Lawrence Coll., Bronxville, N.Y., 1975-78; asst. mus. educator Met. Mus. Art, N.Y.C., 1978-85; exec. dir. Internat. Found. Art Research, N.Y.C., 1985-96; bd. dirs. Internat. Art and Antiques Loss Register Ltd., 19856, Ctr. for Edn. Studies, Inc. Regular contbr. Art Crime Update column Wall Street Jour., 1988—; contbr. articles to Mus. News and other profl. publs. Office: Internat. Found. for Art Rsch Ste 1234 500 Fifth Ave New York NY 10110

LOWENTHAL, HENRY, greeting card company executive; b. Frankfurt, Germany, Oct. 26, 1931; came to U.S., 1940, naturalized, 1945; s. Adolf and Kella (Suss) L.; m. Miriam Katzenstein, June 29, 1958; children—Sandra, Jeffry, Joan Chana, Benjamin, Avi. B.B.A. cum laude, City U. N.Y., 1952, M.B.A., 1953; J.D., N.Y. U., 1962. CPA. Lectr. acctg. Baruch Coll., N.Y.C., 1952-53; auditor Price Waterhouse & Co., N.Y.C., 1955-62; v.p., controller Am. Greetings Corp., Cleve., 1962-68, controller, 1966-68, sr. v.p., chief fin. officer, 1977-95, sr. v.p., 1995—; v.p. fin., treas. Tremco Inc., Cleve., 1968-77; mem. adv. bd. Case Western Res. U. Dept. Accountancy, 1986—. Chmn. bd. dirs. Rabbinical Coll. Telshe, 1974-77, v.p., 1977-90; v.p. Hebrew Acad. Cleve., 1977—; pres. Agudath Israel of Cleve., 1978-95, treas., 1995—; v.p. Agudath Israel Am., 1989—; bd. dirs. Jewish Cmty. Fedn., Cleve., 1979-88, 90-95, chmn. audit com., 1992-95; trustee Mt. Sinai Med. Ctr., Cleve., 1992—; chmn. citizens rev. com. Cleveland Heights-Univ. Heights Sch., 1972-73, mem. lay fin. com., 1974-79; mem. Cleveland Heights Citizens Adv. Com. for Cmty. Devel., 1976-79. With AUS, 1953-55. Mem. AICPA, Assn. of Publicly Traded Cos. (budget & fin. com. 1986—, bd. dirs. 1987—, treas. 1990—), Fin. Execs. Inst. (sec. N.E. Ohio chpt. 1979-80), Ohio Soc. CPA's, Greater Cleve. Growth Assn., Beta Gamma Sigma, Beta Alpha Psi. Home: 3394 Blanche Ave Cleveland OH 44118-2128 Office: Am Greetings Corp 1 American Rd Cleveland OH 44144-2301

LOWENTROUT, PETER MURRAY, religious studies educator; b. Salinas, Calif., Mar. 14, 1948; m. Christine Ione, Sept. 30, 1980; children: Mary, Brandon. AB, U. Calif., Riverside, 1973; PhD, U. So. Calif., L.A., 1983. Prof. religious studies Calif. State U., Long Beach, 1981—. Contbr. articles to profl. jours. Capt. Orange County Fire Dept., Orange, Calif., 1977-94. Mem. Am. Acad. Religion (regional pres. 1989-90), Ctr. for Theology and Lit. U. Durham (Eng.), Sci. Fi. Rsch. Assoc. (pres. 1991, 92). Office: Calif State U Dept Religious Studies 1250 N Bellflower Blvd Long Beach CA 90840-0006 *Though it is the hatred in life that seems most quickly to catch our attention, there is far more love in the world. Learning to see that love and helping others to do so is life's best work.*

LOWER, JOYCE Q., lawyer; b. Milford, Mass., July 15, 1943; d. Raymond Joseph and Marion (Little) Quenneville; m. Michael Rhodes Lower, Aug. 7, 1965; children: Anthony Miles, Courtney Anne. BA, Wellesley Coll., 1965; JD, U. Mich., 1967. Ptnr. Dickinson, Wright, Moon, VanDusen & Freeman, Detroit, 1968—. Co-author: Michigan Estate Planning, Drafting and Estate Administration, 1989. Pres. YMCA Met. Detroit, 1984-86; trustee Roeper City and Country Sch., Bloomfield Hills, Mich., 1981-86, Fin. and Estate Planning Coun., Detroit, Oakland County Estate Planning Coun.; bd. dirs. United Cmty. Svcs., Detroit, 1990-95, United Way Cmty. Svcs., 1995—, Alzheimers Assn., Detroit, 1990-92. Mem. ABA, Mich. Bar Assn., Oakland County Bar Assn., Village Club. Office: Dickinson Wright Moon VanDusen & Freeman PO Box 509 525 N Woodward Ave Bloomfield Hills MI 48304-2971

LOWER, LOUIS GORDON, II, insurance company executive; b. N.Y.C., July 3, 1945; s. Elmer Wilson and Gilberta Madeleine (Stengel) L.; m. Adrienne Adair Borger, Sept. 26, 1970; children—Brandon Wilson, Samatha June. BA, Yale U., 1967; MBA, Harvard U., 1970. Asst. v.p. Amprop, Inc., Miami, Fla., 1970-73; v.p. Gale Orgn., Miami, 1973-76; dir. real estate Allstate Ins. Co., Northbrook, Ill., 1976-80, v.p. investments, 1980-85, group v.p. investments, 1985-86, sr. v.p., treas., 1986-89; exec. v.p. Allstate Life Ins. Co., Northbrook, 1989, pres., 1990—; bd. dirs. Ill. Life Ins. Coun.; chmn. bd. dirs. Northbrook Life Ins. Co., Lincoln Benefit Life, Surety Life, Allstate Life Ins. Co. of N.Y. Bd. dirs. North Suburban YMCA, Northbrook, 1984—, Evanston (Ill.) Hosp. Corp., Chgo. Bot. Garden. Served with USAR, 1968-73. Clubs: Skokie Country (Glencoe, Ill.); Key Biscayne Yacht (Fla.). Avocations: tennis; waterskiing. Home: 76 Woodley Rd Winnetka IL 60093-3746 Office: Allstate Life Ins Co 3100 Sanders Rd Northbrook IL 60062-7155*

LOWER, ROBERT CASSEL, lawyer, educator; b. Oak Park, Ill., Jan. 8, 1947; s. Paul Elton and Doris Thatcher (Heaton) L.; m. Jean Louise Lower, Aug. 24, 1968 (dec. Aug. 1985); children: David Elton, Andrew Bennett, James Philip Thatcher; m. Cheryl Bray, July 26, 1986. A.B. magna cum laude with highest honors, Harvard U., 1969, J.D., 1972. Bar: Ga. 1972. Assoc. Alston & Bird, Atlanta, 1972-78, ptnr., 1978—; adj. prof. Emory U., 1978-85, 92. Contbr. articles to law jours. Co-founder, pres. Ga. Vol. Lawyers for the Arts, Inc., 1975-79; chmn. Fulton County (Ga.) Arts Council, 1979-87; trustee Woodruff Arts Ctr., 1988-95, Piedmont Coll., Ga. Found. Ind. Colls. Mem. Ga. Bar Assn., Atlanta Bar Assn., Midtown Bus. Assn. (bd. dirs. 1988-90), Author's Ct., Harvard Club (Ga.), Ansley Golf Club, Phi Beta Kappa. Presbyterian. Avocations: running, music, bonsai. Home: 935 Plymouth Rd NE Atlanta GA 30306-3009 Office: Alston & Bird One Atlantic Ctr 1201 W Peachtree St NW Atlanta GA 30309-3400

LOWERY, BARBARA J., psychiatric nurse, educator. RN, Reading Hosp. Sch., 1958; MSN, Villanova U., 1966; NSN, U. Pa., 1968; EdD, Temple U., 1973. Staff nurse, head nurse Danville State Hosp., Pa., 1958-62; unit and hosp. supr. Norristown (Pa.) State Hosp., 1960-63, instr. nursing edn., 1963-65; dir. nursing edn. Ea. Pa. Psychiat. Inst., 1968-69; instr. Sch. Nursing, U. Pa., Phila., 1970-72, assoc., 1972-73, from asst. prof. to assoc. prof., 1973-87, prof., 1987—, chmn. psychiat. mental health nursing, 1978-84, ombudsman, 1984-86, dir. Robert Wood Johnson clin. nurse scholars program, 1986-91; cons. in field. Author, co-author chpts. to books; assoc. editor Nursing Rsch., 1978-83. Fellow Am. Acad. Nursing; mem. NAS. Office: U Pa Sch Nursing 34th and Spruce Sts Philadelphia PA 19104

LOWERY, CHARLES DOUGLAS, history educator, academic administrator; b. Greenville, Ala., May 8, 1937; s. Reuben F. and Frances Louise (Jordan) L.; m. Sara Bradford, June 24, 1961; children: Thomas Bradford, Douglas Trenton, Charles Daniel. BA, Huntingdon Coll., 1959; MA, Fla. State U., 1961; PhD, U. Va., 1966. Asst. prof. history Ball State U., Muncie, Ind., 1964-66; from asst. prof. to prof. Miss. State U., Starkville, 1966—, head dept. history, 1985—, asst. dean Coll. Arts and Scis., 1971-74, assoc. dean, 1974-81, dir. Inst. for Humanities, 1981-85. Author: James Barbour: The Biography of A Jeffersonian Republican, 1984, (with others) America: The Middle Period, 1973; Encyclopedia of African-American Civil Rights: From Emancipation to the Present, 1992; contbr. articles to profl. jours. Mem. Citizen's Adv. Coun., Starkville, 1971; mem. Miss. Com. for Humanities, Jackson, 1986-88; vice chmn. Miss. Humanities Coun., Jackson, 1988-89. Grantee NEH, 1980, 81, 84, Miss. Humanities Coun., 1983, 84, 88. Mem. Orgn. Am. Historians, Soc. Historians of Early Am. Rep., So. Hist. Soc., Miss. Hist. Soc. (com. chmn. 1989-90). Democrat. Presbyterian. Avocations: camping, travel, fishing, historical preservation. Home: 609 Sherwood Rd Starkville MS 39759-4009 Office: Miss State U Dept History Drawer H Mississippi State MS 39762

LOWERY, JOSEPH E., clergyman; m. Evelyn Gibson; 3 daus. Student, Knoxville Coll., Ala. A&M Coll., Payne Coll., Wayne U., Payne Theol. Sem., Garrett Theol. Sem., Chgo. Ecumenical Inst.; AB, BD, LLD, Clark Coll., 1975; DD (hon.), Morehouse Coll.; DLitt (hon.), Dillard U.; LLD (hon.), Atlanta U. Ordained to ministry United Methodist Ch.; pastor Warren St. United Meth. Ch., Mobile, Ala., 1952-61; adminstrv. asst. to Bishop Golden, Nashville, 1961-64; pastor St. Paul United Meth. Ch., Birmingham, Ala., 1964-68, Central United Meth. Ch., Atlanta, 1968-86, Cascade United Meth. Ch., 1986-92; co-founder SCLC, v.p., until 1967, chmn. bd., 1967-77, pres., 1977—; mem. Commn. on Religion and Race, chmn. merger rev. com. United Meth. Ch., 1968-76; del. World Meth. Council, London, Gen. Confs. United Meth. Ch.; instr. Candler Sch. Theology and Nursing Sch., Emory U., 1970-71. Chmn. coordinating com. on civil rights in Nashville, 1963-64; pres. Ministerial Alliance, Birmingham, Birmingham OEO community Action Agy., Enterprises Now, Inc.; bd. dirs. Meth. Pub. Ho., 1960-72, Met. Atlanta Rapid Transit Authority, 1975—, Martin Luther King, Jr. Ctr. for Social Change; co-chair anniversary March on Washington, 1983, 88, 93; initiated Gun Buy Back Program, Atlanta, now nationally, 1993. Recipient Equal Opportunity award Atlanta Urban League, 1975, awards Nat. Conf. Black Mayors, Martin Luther King Jr. Peace prize, Martin Luther King, Jr. Ctr. for Non-Violent Social Change, 1990, Martin Luther King Jr. Human Rights award George Washington U., 1990, also awards Ebony mag., others; named one of 15 Greatest Black Preachers Ebony mag.; 1st recipient MLK award for freedom Boston U., 1992. Office: So Christian Leadership Conf 334 Auburn Ave NE Atlanta GA 30303-2604

LOWERY, LEE LEON, JR., civil engineer; b. Corpus Christi, Tex., Dec. 26, 1938; s. Lee Leon and Blanche (Dietrich) L.; children: Kelli Lane, Christianne Lindsey. B.S. in Civil Engring, Tex. A&M U., 1960, M.E., 1961, Ph.D., 1965. Prof. dept. civil engring. Tex. A&M U., 1960; rsch. engr. Tex. A&M Rsch. Found., 1962—; pres. Pile Dynamics Found. Engring., Inc., Bryan, Tex., 1962—; pres. Tex. Measurements, Inc., College Station, 1965—; pres. Interface Engring. Assos., Inc., College Station, 1969—; dir. Braver Corp. Bd. dirs. Deep Found. Inst. Recipient Faculty Disting. Achievement Teaching award Tex. A&M U., 1979, Zachary Teaching award, 1989, 91, award of merit Tex. A&M Hon. Soc., 1991; NDEA fellow, 1960-63. Mem. ASCE, NSPE, Tex. Soc. Profl. Engrs., Sigma Xi, Phi Kappa Phi, Tau Beta Pi. Baptist. Achievements include patents in field. Home: 2905 S College Ave Bryan TX 77801-2510 Office: Tex A&M U Dept Civil Engring College Station TX 77843

LOWERY, WILLIAM HERBERT, lawyer; b. Toledo, June 8, 1925; s. Kenneth Alden and Drusilla (Pfanner) L.; m. Carolyn Broadwell, June 27, 1947; children: Kenneth Latham, Marcia Mitchell. PhB, U. Chgo., 1947; JD, U. Mich., 1950. Bar: Pa. 1951, U.S. Supreme Ct. 1955. Assoc. Dechert Price & Rhoads, Phila., 1950-58, ptnr., 1958-89, mng. ptnr., 1970-72; mem. policy com., chmn. litigation dept., 1962-68, 81-84; of counsel Dechert Price & Rhoads, Phila., 1989—; counsel S.S. Huebner Found. Ins. Edn., Phila., 1970-89; faculty Am. Conf. of Legal Execs., Pa. Bar Inst.; permanent mem. com. of visitors U. Mich. Law Sch. Author: Insurance Litigation Problems, 1972, Insurance Litigation Disputes, 1977. Pres. Stafford Civic Assn., 1958; chmn. Tredyffrin Twp. Zoning Bd., Chester County, Pa., 1959-75; bd. dirs. Paoli (Pa.) Meml. Hosp., 1964-89, chmn., 1972-75; bd. dirs. Main Line Health, Radnor, Pa., 1984-89; permanent mem. Jud. Conf. 3d Cir. Ct. Served to 2d lt. USAF, 1943-46. Mem. ABA (chmn. life ins. com. 1984-85, chmn. Nat. Conf. Lawyers and Life Ins. Cos. 1984-88), Order of the Coif, Royal Poinciana Golf Club, Phi Gamma Delta, Phi Delta Phi. Home: 2777 Gulf Shore Blvd N Apt S-4 Naples FL 33940-4386 Office: Dechert Price & Rhoads 4000 Bell Atlantic Tower 1717 Arch St Philadelphia PA 19103-2713

LOWEY, NITA M., congresswoman; b. N.Y., July 5, 1937; m. Stephen Lowey, 1961; children: Dona, Jacqueline, Douglas. BS, Mt. Holyoke Coll., 1959. Community activist, prior to 1975; asst. sec. state State of N.Y., 1975-87; former mem. 101st-102nd Congresses from 20th N.Y. dist., 1989-92; mem. 103rd-104th Congresses from 18th N.Y. dist., 1993—; mem. appropriations com., 1993—. Democrat. Office: US Ho of Reps 2421 Rayburn HOB Washington DC 20515*

LOWI, THEODORE J(AY), political science educator; b. Gadsden, Ala., July 9, 1931; s. Alvin R. and Janice (Haas) L.; m. Angele M. Daniel, May 11, 1963; children: Anna Amelie, Jason Daniel. BA, Mich. State U., 1954; MA, Yale U., 1955, PhD, 1961; HLD (hon.), Oakland U., 1972; LittD (hon.), SUNY, Stony Brook, 1988; Docteur honoris causa, Fondation Nationale des, Sciences Politiques, Paris, 1992. Mem. faculty dept. govt. Cornell U., 1959-65, 72—, asst. prof., 1961-65, John L. Senior prof. Am. instns., 1972—; assoc. prof. U. Chgo., 1965-69, prof., 1969-72; Gannett disting. prof. Rochester Inst. Tech., 1986-87, 90-91; fellow Ctr. Advanced Study in Behavioral Scis., 1977-78; chair Am. civilization U. Paris, 1981-82. Author: At the Pleasur of the Mayor, 1964, (with Robert Kennedy) The Pursuit of Justice, 1964, The End of Liberalism, 2d edit., 1979, Japanese edit., 1981, French edit., 1987, The Politics of Disorder, 1971, Poliscide, 1976, (with others) Nationalizing Government: Public Policies in America, 1978, Incomplete Conquest: Governing America, 1981, The Personal President: Power Investe, Promise Unfulfilled, 1985, Spanish edit., 1994, (with B. Ginsberg) American Government: Freedom and Power, 1990, 4th edit., 1996, (with B. Ginsberg) Embattled Democracy, 1995, The End of the Republican Era, 1995; anthologies: Private Life and Public Order, 1968, Legislative Politics U.S.A., 3d edit., 1973. Recipient J. Kimbrough Owen award Am. Polit. Sci. Assn., 1962, French-Am. Found. award, 1981-82, Fulbright award, 1981-82, Harold Lasswell award Policy Studies Orgn., 1986, Richard Neustadt award for Best Book on Presidency, 1986; Social Sci. Rsch. Coun. fellow, 1963-64; Guggenheim Found. fellow, 1967-68; Nat. Endowment for Humanities fellow, 1977-78; Ford Found. fellow, 1977-78; Fulbright 40th Anniversary Disting. fellow, 1987. Mem. Am. Polit. Sci. Assn. (v.p. 1985-86, pres. 1991), Am. Acad. Arts and Sci., Policy Studies Orgn. (pres. 1977), Internat. Polit. Sci. Assn. (1st v.p. 1994—). Home: 101 Delaware Ave Ithaca NY 14850-4707 *If there is a how-to of success it is this: a passion for work, an ethic of workmanship, and an idea of what, in the end, is a good product.*

LOWITT, RICHARD, history educator; b. N.Y.C., Feb. 25, 1922; s. Eugene and Eleanor (Lebowitz) L.; m. Suzanne Catharine Carson, Sept., 1953; children: Peter Carson, Pamela Carson. B.S.S., CCNY, 1943; M.A., Columbia U., 1945, Ph.D., 1950. Instr. U. Md., College Park, 1948-52; asst. prof. U. R.I., Kingston, 1952-53; faculty mem. Conn. Coll., New London, 1953-66, prof. history, 1966; prof. history Fla. State U., Tallahassee, 1966-68, U. Ky., Lexington, 1968-77; prof., chmn. dept. history Iowa State U., Ames, 1977-87, prof., 1987-89; prof. U. Okla., Norman, 1990—; mem. Iowa Humanities Bd., 1987-89; mem. Okla. Humanities Bd., 1995—; vis. prof. U. Colo., summer 1953, Yale U., 1961-62, Brown U., 1965-66, U. Chattanooga, summer 1965, Emory U., Atlanta; Sutton vis. prof. U. Okla., 1989-90. Author: A Merchant Prince of the 19th Century, 1954, George W. Norris, 3 vols., 1963, 71, 78; editor: Nils Olsen and the Bureau of Agricultural Economics, 1980; co-editor: One Third of a Nation-Lorena Hickok Reports on the Great Depression, 1981, The New Deal and the West, 1984, Letters From An American Farmer: The Eastern European and Russian Correspondence by Roswell Garst, 1987, Henry A. Wallace's Irrigation Frontier: On the Trail of the Cornbelt Farmer, 1990, Bronson M. Cutting, Progressive Politican, 1992, Politics in the Postwar American West, 1995. Trustee Pub. Library, Lexington, 1973-77. NEH sr. fellow, 1974, John Simon Guggenheim Found. fellow, 1957; grantee Social Sci. Rsch. Coun., 1958, Am. Coun. Learned Socs., 1962, Am. Philos. Soc., 1964, Huntington Libr., 1986; recipient Gaspar Perez de Villagra award Hist. Soc. N.Mex., 1993. Mem. Am. Hist. Assn., So. Hist. Assn. (membership com. 1973, Ramsdell p rize com. 1975, program com. 1983, nominating com. 1990), Western History Assn. (bd. editors 1986-88, program com. 1995, merit award 1992), Orgn. Am. Historians (nominating com. 1970, Turner prize com. 1972-76, bd. editors 1985-87), Agrl. History Soc. (exec. com. 1973-75, pres. 1991-92). Democrat. Office: Univ Okla Dept History Norman OK 73019

LOWMAN, GEORGE FREDERICK, lawyer; b. N.Y.C., Oct. 29, 1916; s. William H. and Mary (Canty) L.; m. Mary Farrell, Oct. 4, 1947; children—John F., Peter H., Patricia A. A.B., Harvard U., 1938, J.D., 1942. Bar: Conn. 1946. Since practiced in Stamford; assoc. Cummings & Lockwood, 1946-52, ptnr., 1952—; chmn. bd. dirs., chmn. exec. com. Farrell Lines Tankers Inc.; bd. dirs. S.S. Owners Mus. Protection and Indemnity Assn., Inc.; bd. govs. Nat. Maritime Coun.; bd. mgrs. Am. Bur. Shipping. Chmn. Darien YMCA-YWCA fund campaign, 1956; chmn. fund campaign Darien ARC, 1953-54, bd. dirs., 1953-59; mem. exec. com. Alfred W. Dater council Boy Scouts Am., 1956; chmn. Darien Cancer Fund, 1959-60; pres., bd. dirs. Silvermine Guild Artists, 1967-77; bd. dirs., trustee King Sch., Stamford; trustee Low-Heywood Sch.; advisory com. U. Bridgeport Law Sch.; pres. B/G India House, N.Y.C., 1980—. Served to lt. col. AUS, 1942-46. Decorated Legion of Merit, Bronze Star. Fellow Am. Coll. Trial Lawyers, Internat. Acad. Trial Lawyers, Am. Bar Found.; mem. ABA, Conn. Bar Assn. (past pres.), Stamford Bar Assn. (past pres.), Harvard U. Alumni Assn. (v.p.), Marine Soc. N.Y.C. (hon.), St. Andrew's Soc., Conn. Srs. Golf Assn., Delta Upsilon. Home: 40 Allwood Rd Darien CT 06820-2416 Office: 10 Stamford Forum Stamford CT 06901-3253

LOWMAN, ROBERT PAUL, psychology educator, academic administrator; b. Lynwood, Calif., Jan. 23, 1947; s. Hubert Alden and Martha Guynn (Howard) L.; m. Kathleen Marie Drew, June 25, 1972; children: Sarah Guynn, Amy Katherine. AB, U. So. Calif., 1967; MA, Claremont U., 1969, PhD, 1973. Asst. prof. U. Wis., Milw., 1972-76; adminstrv. officer APA, Washington, 1976-81; asst. dean Kans. State U., Manhattan, 1981-86, assoc. dean grad. sch., 1986-90, assoc. vice provost, 1990-91; dir. rsch. svcs. and adj. assoc. prof. psychology U. N.C., Chapel Hill, 1991—, assoc. vice chancellor for rsch., 1994-96, assoc. vice provost for rsch., 1996—. Editor: APA's Guide to Rsch. Support, 1981; contbr. over 30 articles to profl. jours. Recipient numerous grants. Mem. APA (sec. bd. sci. affairs 1976-81, sec. com. on internat. rels. in psychology 1978-81), AAAS, Am. Psychol. Soc., Soc. for Psychologists in Mgmt. (newsletter editor 1994—, bd. dirs. 1996—), Nat. Coun. Univ. Rsch. Adminstrs., Soc. Rsch. Adminstrs., Phi Beta Kappa, Phi Kappa Phi, Phi Eta Sigma, Psi Chi. Democrat. Methodist. Home: 104 Chesley Ln Chapel Hill NC 27514-1459 Office: Univ NC Office Rsch Svcs CB# 4100 Chapel Hill NC 27599-4100

LOWN, BERNARD, cardiologist, educator; b. Utena, Lithuania, June 7, 1921; came to U.S., 1935; s. Nisson and Bella (Grossbard) L.; m. Louise Charlotte Lown, Dec. 29, 1946; children—Anne Lown Green, Frederick, Naomi Lown Lewiton. BS summa cum laude, U. Maine, 1942, DS (hon.), 1982; MD, Johns Hopkins U., 1945; DSc (hon.), Worcester State Coll., 1983, Charles U., Prague, 1987, Bowdoin Coll., 1988, SUNY, Syracuse, 1988, Columbia Coll., Chgo., 1989; LLD (hon.), Bates Coll., Lewiston, Maine, 1983, Queen's U., Kingston, Ont., Can., 1985; LHD (hon.), Colby Coll., 1986, Thomas Jefferson U., 1988; PhD (hon.), U. Buenos Aires, 1986; D honoris causa, Autonomous U. Barcelona, Spain, 1989; D Univ. (hon.), Hiroshima (Japan) Shudo U., 1989. Asst. in pathology Yale U.-New Haven Hosp., 1945-46; intern in medicine Jewish Hosp., N.Y.C., 1947-48; asst. resident in medicine Montefiore Hosp., N.Y.C., 1948-50; research fellow in cardiology Peter Bent Brigham Hosp., Boston, 1950-53, asst. in medicine, 1955-56, dir. Samuel A. Levine Cardiovascular Research Lab., 1956-58, jr. assoc. in medicine, 1956-62, research assoc. in medicine, 1958-59, assoc. in medicine, 1962-63, sr. assoc. in medicine, 1963-70, dir. Samuel A. Levine Coronary Care Unit, 1965-74, physician, 1973-81, sr. physician, 1982—; asst. in medicine Harvard U., Boston, 1955-58, asst. prof. medicine dept. nutrition Sch. Pub. Health, 1961-67, assoc. prof. cardiology, 1967-73, prof. cardiology, 1974—, dir. cardiovascular research lab. Sch. Pub. Health, 1961—; cons. in cardiology Newton-Wellesley Hosp., Mass., 1963-77, Beth Israel Hosp., Boston, 1963-94, Children's Hosp. Med. Ctr., Boston, 1964-82; spl. cons. WHO, Copenhagen, 1971; coordinator U.S.-USSR Coop. Study, 1973-81; mem. lipid metabolism adv. com. NIH, Bethesda, Md., 1975-79; vis. prof., lectr., guest speaker numerous univs., hosps., orgns. Author: (with Samuel A. Levine) Current Advances in Digitalis Therapy, 1954; (with Harold D. Levine) Atrial Arrhythmias, Digitalis and Potassium, 1958, (with A. Malliani) Neural Mechanisms and Cardiovascular Disease, 1986; mem. editorial bd. Circulation, Coeur et Medecine Interne, Jour. Electrocardiology; mem. editorial adv. bd. Jour. Soviet Research in Cardiovascular Diseases; contbr. numerous articles to profl. jours.; mem. internat. adv. bd. Internat. Med. Tribune, 1987—; inventor cardioverter; introduced Lidocaine as antiarrythmic drug. Recipient Modern Medicine award, 1972, Ray C. Fish award and Silver medal Tex. Heart Inst., Houston, 1978, A. Ross McIntyre award and Gold medal U. Nebr. Med. Ctr., Omaha, 1979, Richard and Hinda Rosenthal award Am. Heart Assn., 1980, George W. Thorn award Brigham and Women's Hosp., 1982, 1st Cardinal Medeiros Peace medallion, 1982, Nikolay Burdenko medal Acad. Med. Scis. USSR, 1983; co-recipient Peace Edn. award UN Edn., Sci. and Cultural Orgn., 1984, Beyond War award, 1984, Nobel Peace prize, 1985, Ghandi Peace award, 1985, New Priorities award, 1986, Andres Bello medal 1st class Ministry Edn. and Ministry Sci., Venezuela, 1986, Gold Shield, U. Havana, Cuba, 1986, Dr. Tomas Romay y Cahcon Medallion Acad. Sci., Havana, 1986, George F. Kennan award, 1986, Fritz Gietzelt Medaille Council of Medico-Sci. Socs. of German Democratic Republic, 1987; named hon. citizen City of New Orleans, 1978, Pasteur award Pasteur Inst., Leningrad, USSR, 1987, Alumni Humanitarian award U. Maine, Orono, 1988, Internat. Peace and Culture award Soka Gokkai, Tokyo, 1989, Golden Door award Internat. Inst. Boston, 1989; named Disting. Citizen and recipient Key to City Buenos Aires, 1986. Fellow Am. Coll. Cardiology; mem. Am. Soc. for Clin. Investigation, Am. Heart Assn., Assn. Am. Physicians, AAAS, Physicians for Social Responsibility (founder, 1st pres. 1960-70), U.S.-China Physicians Friendship Assn. (pres. 1974-78), Internat. Physicians for Prevention Nuclear War (pres. 1980-93); mem. Brit. Cardiac Soc. (corr.), Cardiac Soc. Australia and New Zealand, Swiss Soc. Cardiology, Belgian Royal Acad. Medicine, Acad. Medicine of Columbia (hon.), Harvard Club (Boston), Nat. Acad. Scis. (sr. mem. inst. medicine), Phi Beta Kappa, Alpha Omega Alpha. Club: Harvard (Boston). Avocations: photography; music; philosophy; bicycling. Office: Lown Cardiovascular Group PC 21 Longwood Ave Brookline MA 02146

LOWNSDALE, GARY RICHARD, mechanical engineer; b. Poplar Bluff, Mo., Nov. 2, 1946; s. Edward Lee and Margie Lee (Tesreau) L.; m. Paulette Ann Wermuth, Nov. 30, 1968; children: Charles Edgar, Larissa Renee. BSME, U. Cin., 1970. Registered profl. engr., Mich. Trainee engring. mgmt. Chrysler Corp., Highland Park, Mich., 1965-69; contact engr. Chrysler Corp., Hamtramck, Mich., 1970-71; prin. design engr. Ford Morot Co., Dearborn, Mich., 1971-82; exec. dir. advance programs Schlegel Corp., Madison heights, Mich., 1982-86; mgr. automotive design ctr. GE, Pittsfield, Mass., 1986-87; mgr. strategic projects GE, Southfield, Mich., 1990; v.p. design and engring. Autopolymer Design inc., Auburn Hills, Mich., 1987-88; chief engr. polymer body Saturn corp., Troy, Mich., 1988-90; industry dir. Hercules Incorp., Troy, Mich., 1990-92; dir. mktg. automotive systems group Johnson Controls, Inc., Plymouth, Mich., 1992; dir. comml. bus. APX Internat., Madison Heights, Mich., 1993-94; v.p., COO TRANS 2 Corp., Livonia, Mich., 1994-96; v.p. ops. Mastercraft Boat Co., Vonore, Tenn., 1996—. Presenter internat. and tech. papers; patentee in field. Sec. Coventry Gardens Homeowners Assn., Livonia, Mich., 1976-86; dist. leader Boy Scouts Am., Livonia, 1977—; pres. PTA, Livonia, 1982-84. Mem. ASME (sr.), Am. Soc. Body Engrs., Engring. Soc. Detroit (vice chmn. 1972-82), Soc. Plastics Engrs., Soc. Automotive Engrs. (co-chmn. com. 1991-92), Elfen Soc., Hadley Hills Homeowners Assn. (pres. 1990—), Sports Car Club Am. (solo chmn. 1972-76, Solo Nat. Champion award 1974). Avocations: classic car racing and restoration, horse ranching. Home: 4221 Meadow Pond Ln Metamora MI 48455-9751 Office: Mastercraft Boat Co 100 Cherokee Cove Dr Vonore TN 37885

LOWREY, ANNIE TSUNEE, retired cultural organization administrator; b. Osaka, Japan, Mar. 3, 1929; naturalized U.S. citizen, 1963; d. Shigeru Takahata and Kuniko Takahata Takahashi; m. Lawrence K. Lowrey, Mar. 17, 1953; children: Kristine K. Ricci, Jay. BS in Lit., Wakayama (Japan) Shin-Ai, 1949; BS in Art Edn., Kans. State U., 1967; MA in Indsl. Tech., Wichita State U., 1976. Cert. instr. Wichita-Tchr. Assessment and Assistance Program, 1987. Tchr. Minoshima Elem. Sch., Wakayama, Japan, 1945-46, Wakayama Jr. H.S., 1948-49, Truesdell Jr. H.S., Wichita, Kans., 1967-69; tchr., coord. dept. fine arts Wichita H.S. East, 1969-92, instr. Japanese, 1991-92; lectr. dept. art and indsl. tech. Wichita State U., 1974-88, instr. computer applications in industry, 1990-91; tchr. Woodman Elem. Sch., Wichita, summer 1987; instr. art appreciation Butler County C.C., McConnell and Wichita, 1988-92; dir. edn. and exhbn. Wichita Ctr. for Arts, 1992-95; ret., 1995; asst. to fine arts photographer Charles Phillips, Wichita, spring 1989; judge Sister City Art Contest, 1991, Wichita Botanica Photography Competition, painting competition Wichita Painter's Guild, design competition Kans. Aviation Mus., 1991-92; instr. art instrnl. strategy to elem. and secondary art tchrs. Ft. Collins and Loveland, Colo. sch. dists., 1989; presenter many profl. confs. and workshops, most Nat. Art Edn. Conf., Phoenix, 1992, Kans. Accessible Arts, 1994, Kans. State U., 1994. Chairperson writing team for Kans. Plan for Indsl. Edn.-TV, 1974-75; co-author tech. edn. curriculum Kans. State Bd. Regents, 1989. Judge Miss Asia contest 10th Ann. Asian Festival, Wichita, 1990; pres. pub. art adv. bd. City of Wichita, 1991—. Carnegie grantee for development of inter-disciplinary program on cultural literacy, 1984, Matsushita Electronic Co. grantee for curriculum devel., 1986; inductee Kans. Tchrs. Hall of Fame, 1994. Mem. NEA (presenter nat. conv. 1985), ASCD, Nat. Art Edn. Assn.Western Region Secondary Outstanding Educator of Yr. 1988), Kans. Alliance for Arts Edn. (bd. dirs. 1987-89), Phi Delta Kappa (pres. Wichita State U. chpt. 1983-84), Delta Phi Delta. Home: 2727 S Linden St Wichita KS 67210-2423

LOWRIE, JEAN ELIZABETH, librarian, educator; b. Northville, N.Y., Oct. 11, 1918; d. A. Sydney and Edith (Roos) L. A.B., Keuka Coll., 1940, LLD (hon.), 1973; B.L.S., Western Res. U., 1941, Ph.D., 1959; M.A., Western Mich. U., 1956. Childrens librarian Toledo Pub. Library, 1941-44; librarian Elementary Sch., Oak Ridge, Tenn., 1944-51; exhange tchr., librarian Nottingham, Eng., 1948-49; campus sch. librarian Western Mich. U., Kalamazoo, 1951-56; asso. prof. Western Mich. U. (Sch. Librarianship), 1958-61, prof., 1962-83, dir. sch., 1963-81; mem. faculty U. Ky., summer 1951, U. Calif. at Berkeley, summer 1958; Chmn. Internat. Steering Com. for Devel. Sch. Libraries; also del. World Conf. Orgns. Teaching Profession, meetings, Paris, 1964, Vancouver, 1967, Dublin, 1968, Abidjan, 1969, Sydney, 1970; pres. Internat. Assn. Sch. Librarianship, 1971-77, exec. sec., 1978—; mem. exec. bd. Internat. Fedn. Library Assns. and Instns., 1979-83. Author: Elementary School Libraries, rev. edit., 1970, School Libraries: International Developments, 1972, 2d edit., 1991, also articles.; adviser: film-strip Using the Library, 1962. Recipient Dutton-Macrae award ALA, 1957, Profl. Achievement award Keuka Coll. Alumni, 1963. Mem. ALA (pres. 1973-74), Mich. Library Assn., Assn. Libr. & Info. Sci. Educators, Am. Assn. Sch. Librarians (dir., past pres., 1st President's award 1978), Delta Kappa Gamma, Beta Phi Mu. Club: Altrusa (Kalamazoo). Home: 1006 Westmoreland Ave Kalamazoo MI 49006-5544

LOWRIE, WALTER OLIN, management consultant; b. North Braddock, Pa., Apr. 7, 1924; s. Robert Newell and Laura Rae (Essick) L.; m. Dorothy Ann Williams, Aug. 28, 1948; children: Susan, Allison, James. B.S. in Aero. Engring., MIT, 1948; Dr. Engring. (hon.), U. Central Fla., 1985. With Martin Marietta, 1948-86; v.p., program dir. Viking Program Martin Marietta, Denver, 1972-77; v.p., program dir. Missile X Martin Marietta, 1977-78, v.p. tech. ops. Denver div., 1978-80, v.p., gen. mgr. space and electronics, 1980-82; pres. Martin Marietta Orlando, Fla., 1982-86; pvt. practice mgmt. cons. Maitland, Fla., 1986—. Bd. dirs. U. Ctrl. Fla. Found., Orlando, 1983-91; gen. chmn. 42d Internat. Sci. and Engring. Fair, 1991; mayor City of Bow-Mar, Colo., 1964-68; mem. Colo. Gov.'s Adv. Commn. on Corrs., 1979-80; bd. dirs. Indsl. Devel. Commn. Mid-Fla. Inc., Orlando, 1983; chmn. Met. Transp. Authority of Greater Orlando, 1985-86; trustee Orlando Sci. Ctr., 1986—, chmn. bd. trustees, 1994—. 1st lt. USAAF, 1943-45, ETO. Decorated DFC; decorated Air medal with 6 oak leaf clusters; recipient Disting. Pub. Service award NASA, 1977. Fellow Am. Astronaut. Soc.; assoc. fellow AIAA (Space Systems Engr. of Yr. award 1977). Republican. Presbyterian.

LOWRIE, WILLIAM G., oil company executive; b. Painesville, Ohio, Nov. 17, 1943; s. Kenneth W. and Florence H. (Strickler) L.; m. Ernestine R. Rogers, Feb. 1, 1969; children: Kristen, Kimberly. BChemE, Ohio State U., 1966. Engr. Amoco Prodn. Co. subs. Standard Oil Co. (Ind.), New Orleans, 1966-74, area supt., Lake Charles, La., 1974-75, div. engr., Denver, 1975-78, div. prodn. mgr., Denver, 1978-79, v.p. prodn., Chgo., 1979-83; v.p. supply and marine transp. Standard Oil Co. (Ind.), Chgo., 1983-85; pres., Amoco Can., 1985-86; sr. v.p. prodn., Amoco Prodn. Co., 1986-87, exec. v.p. USA, 1987-88; exec. v.p. Amoco Oil Co., Chgo., 1989-90, pres., 1990-92; pres. Amoco Prodn. Co., 1992-94; exec. v.p. E&P sector Amoco Corp., 1994-95, pres. 1996—. Bd. dirs. Jr. Achievement, Northwestern Meml. Corp.; trustee, bd. dirs. Nat. 4-H Coun. Named Outstanding Engring. Alumnus, Ohio State U., 1979, Disting. Alumnis Ohio State U., 1985. Mem. Am. Petroleum Inst., Soc. Petroleum Engrs., Mid-Am. Club (Chgo.). Republican. Presbyterian. Office: Amoco Corp PO Box 87703 Chicago IL 60680-0703

LOWRY, A. ROBERT, federal government railroad arbitrator; b. Salem, Oreg., Jan. 16, 1919; s. Archie R. and Emaline (Hyland) L.; m. Nancy Jo Srb, May 3, 1975. Student, Albion (Idaho) Normal Coll., 1938. With U.P. R.R., 1937-53; local chmn., then asst. to pres. Order R.R. Telegraphers, 1949-64; v.p., then. pres. Transp.-Communications Employees Union, 1964-68; pres. TC div., internat. v.p. Brotherhood Ry. and Airline Clks., 1969-72; supt. ops. Amtrak, 1972-73, dir., top labor rels. officer, 1973-75, asst. v.p., top labor rels. officer, 1975-79; now neutral arbitrator for fed. govt. and R.R. industry San Antonio. Served to lt. col. AUS, 1941-46, USAR, 1946-65, ret. Lodge: Mason, Shriners. Home and Office: 13919 Bluff Wind San Antonio TX 78216-7923

LOWRY, ANN BENDIGO, school health nurse; b. Lebanon, Pa., Oct. 27, 1940; d. Glenn Emanuel and Leah Eleanor (Harpel) Bendigo; children: Kathryn Louise Lowry Bryant, Thomas Livingston. Diploma, Lankenau Hosp. Sch. Nursing, 1961; BS, Am. Internat. Coll., 1985. RN, Mass., Pa. Staff nurse Children's Hosp. of Phila., 1961-62, Prince George's Hosp., Prince George County, Md., 1962, North Adams (Mass.) Regional Hosp., 1963; pediatric staff nurse Hillcrest Hosp., Pittsfield, Mass., 1964-69; with Lenox (Mass.) Vis. Nurse, 1964-65; geriatric nurse Meadow Pl./Berkshire Pl., Lenox, 1969-72, Edgecombe Nursing Home, Lenox, 1971-72; sch. health nurse, elem. health edn. coord. Lenox Pub. Schs., 1973—; camp nurse Kehonka Camp, Lake Winnepasaukee, N.H., summers 1969, 70. Contbr. articles to profl. publs. Mem. adv. com. Rep. John Olver's Health Steering Com., Mass., 1992-93; mem. Nurses for Senator Edward Kennedy, Mass., 1994-95. Recipient Friend of Guidance award Berkshire County Guidance Assn., 1990; grantee Mass. Dept. Edn., 1984-85, 89-91. Mem. ANA (cert. cmty. health/sch. nurse), Mass. Nurses Assn., Nat. Assn. Sch. Nurses (pres. 1994-95), Mass. Sch. Nurses Orgn. (pres. 1986-88, Mass. Sch. Nurse of Yr. 1993-94), Mass. Tchrs. Assn. (bd. dirs. 1989-94, Sch. Nurse of Yr. 1993), Am. Sch. Health Assn. (sch. nurse study com. 1989—). Lutheran. Avocations: music, travel. Home: 108 Kemble St Lenox MA 01240-2814 Office: Nat Assn Sch Nurses PO Box 1300 Scarborough ME 04070-1300

LOWRY, BATES, art historian, museum director; b. Cin., June 21, 1923; s. Bates and Eleanor (Meyer) L.; m. Isabel Barrett, Dec. 7, 1946; children: Anne, Patricia. PhB, U. Chgo., 1944, MA, 1952, PhD, 1955. Asst. prof. U. Calif., Riverside, 1954-57, Inst. Fin. Arts NYU, 1957-59; prof., chmn. dept. art Pomona Coll., Claremont, 1959-63, Brown U., Providence, 1963-68; dir. Mus. Modern Art, N.Y.C., 1968-69; prof., chmn. dept. art U. Mass., Boston, 1971-80; dir. Nat. Bldg. Mus., Washington, 1980-87; cons. dept. photography Getty Mus., 1992; disting. vis. prof. U. Del. Newark, 1988-89; founder, pres. Com. to Rescue Italian Art, 1966-76; mem. arts coun. MIT, 1974-80. Author: Visual Experience, 1961, Renaissance Architecture, 1962, Muse or Ego, 1963, Building a National Image, 1985, Looking for Leonardo, 1993; editor: College Art Association Monograph Series, 1957-59, 65-68, Architecture of Washington, D.C., 1977-79, Art Bull., 1965-68; mem. editorial bd. Smithsonian Instn. Press, 1981-87. Mem. bd. cons. NEH, 1975-81. With U.S. Army, 1943-46. Decorated Grand Officer of Order of Star of Solidarity, Italy, 1967; recipient Gov.'s award for contbn. to art, R.I., 1967; fellow Guggenheim Found., 1972, Inst. for Advanced Study, 1971. Mem. Coll. Art Assn. (bd. dirs. 1962-65), Soc. Archtl. Historians (bd. dirs. 1959-61, 63-65), Dunlap Soc. (pres. 1974-92), Academia del Disegno (hon. mem. Italy). Home: 255 Massachusetts Ave Boston MA 02115-3505

LOWRY, BRUCE ROY, lawyer; b. Lima, Ohio, Mar. 4, 1952; s. Lewis Roy and Gloria May (Rekers) L.; m. Kathleen Ann Sherman, Sept. 1, 1973; children: Bruce Benjamin, Tyler Sherman. BA cum laude, Ohio State U., 1974, JD cum laude, 1977. Bar: Ohio 1977. Tax intern Coopers & Lybrand, CPAs, Columbus, Ohio, 1976-77; assoc. Smith & Schnacke, LPA, Dayton, Ohio, 1977-84; chmn. tax dept. Smith & Schnacke, LPA, 1984-89; tax ptnr. Thompson, Hine and Flory, Dayton, 1989—; discussion leader Ohio Soc. CPAs, Cleve., 1980-96; adj. prof. U. Dayton Coll. Law, 1981-82; mem. faculty Ohio Continuing Legal Edn. Inst., 1987-96, mem. tax curriculum com.; mem. faculty Banff (Alta., Can.), Ctr. for Mgmt.-Internat. Tax, 1991; mem. faculty, program chair Coun. Internat. Tax Edn., 1995, 96. Contbr. articles to profl. jours. Nat. swimming ofcl. YMCA, S.W. Ohio, 1990-93; chmn. Miami County Planning Commn., Troy, Ohio, 1991-96; bd. dirs. Miami Valley coun. Boy Scouts Am., Dayton, 1988-95. Recipient award of merit Ohio Legal Ctr. Inst., 1987, Golden Rule award, 1991, Up and Comer in Dayton award, 1991. Mem. Internat. Bar Assn., Internat. Fiscal Assn., Tipp City C. of C. (chmn. econ. devel. com. 1989-91), Rotary Club Tipp City (pres.). Avocations: tennis, golf. Office: Thompson Hine & Flory 2000 Courthouse Pla NE PO Box 8801 Dayton OH 45401-8801

LOWRY, CHARLES WESLEY, clergyman, lecturer; b. Checotah, Okla., Mar. 31, 1905; s. Charles Wesley and Sue (Price) L.; m. Edith Clark, June 14, 1930; children: Harriet Richards Lowry King, Charles Wesley, Atherton Clark, James Meredith Price; m. Kate Rowe Holland, Jan. 11, 1960. BA, Washington and Lee U., 1926, DD, 1959; MA, Harvard U., 1927; BD, Episcopal Theol. Sch., 1930; DPhil, Oxford (Eng.) U., 1933. Ordain deacon Episcopal Ch., 1930. Priest Episcopal Ch., 1931; traveling fellow Episc. Theol. Sch., 1930-32; Episc. chaplain U. Calif., 1933-34; prof. systematic theology Va. Theol. Sem., 1934-43; rector All Saints' Ch., Chevy Chase, Md., 1943-53; lectr. theology Seabury Western Theol. Sem., 1947, Phila. Div. Sch. (Bohlen lectr.), 1947, 49-50, Gen. Theol. Sem., 1951-52; chmn. Bd. Examining Chaplains, Diocese of Washington, 1945-53, sec., standing com., 1945-51; ofcl. del. from U.S. Internat. Conv. on Peace and Christian Civilization, Florence, Italy, 1952; chmn., exec. dir. Found. for Religious Action in Social and Civil Order, 1953-59, pres., 1960—, project research dir. on moral revolution, 1973-75; cons. FCDA, 1953-55; cons. Air War Coll., 1953, lectr., 1953-54; lectr. Naval War Coll., 1955, Nat. War Coll., 1957, 59-61, Command and Staff Coll., 1961-62, Indsl. Coll. Armed Forces, 1963, Inst. Lifetime Learning, 1964-66, Campbell Coll. Sch. Law, 1979, 80; also lectr. various seminars; lectr. philosophy and polit. sci. Sandhills Community Coll., 1967-69, 71, 89; spl. lectr. Oxford (Eng.) Poly. Coll., 1974; spl. lectr. Washington and Lee U., 1977, baccalaureate preacher, 1984; dir. Nat. Conf. on Spiritual Founds. Am. Democracy, Washington, 1954-55, 57, 59; minister The Village Chapel, Pinehurst, N.C., 1966-73; mem. faculty Wallace O'Neal Day Sch., Southern Pines, N.C., 1976—; columnist Pinehurst Outlook, 1977-78, Moore County News, 1978-79, The Pilot, 1979—; priest assoc. Emmanuel Epis. Ch., Southern Pines, 1981—. Author: The Trinity and Christian Devotion, 1946, Christianity and Materialism (Hale Sermon), 1948, Communism and Christ, rev. edit, 1962 (Brit. edit. 1954), Conflicting Faiths, 1953, The Ideology of Freedom vs. The Ideology of Communism, 1958, To Pray or Not to Pray, rev. edit, 1968, The Kingdom of Influence, 1969, William Temple: An Archbishop for All Seasons, 1982, The First Theologians, 1986, Constitution Commentary, 1989; (with others) Anglican Evangelicalism, 1943, Encyclopaedia of Religion, 1945, The Anglican Pulpit To-Day, 1953; editor: Blessings of Liberty, 1956-90; contbr. articles to profl. publs. Chmn. Nat. Jefferson Davis Hall of Fame Co., 1960, 64-65; candidate for U.S. Congress 10th Dist. Va., 1962; mem. N.C. Bicentennial Constn. Conv., 1985-89. Recipient George Washington medal Freedoms Found., 1955, 59, 61, 68, other award, 1953, 81. Mem. Am. Peace Soc. (past pres.), Am. Polit. Sci. Assn., Internat. Platform Assn., Am. Theol. Soc. (treas. 1955-70, 72, past v.p.), Cum Laude Soc. (pres. O'Neal chpt.), World Conf. Faith and Order, Phi Beta Kappa, Omicron Delta Kappa, Delta Sigma Rho, Sigma Upsilon. Clubs: Achilles (Oxford and Cambridge); Rotary (dist. gov. 1970-71), Chevy Chase, Pinehurst Country, Nat. Press. Address: 160 Longleaf Rd Southern Pines NC 28387-2832 *A religious view of life is not an easy optimism. The serious person knows the force of moral evil or sin. But when in the great religions we meet a Power that transforms, we see with new eyes. We are saved by hope and by faith and love.*

LOWRY, EDWARD FRANCIS, JR., lawyer; b. L.A., Aug. 13, 1930; s. Edward Francis and Mary Anita (Woodcock) L.; m. Patricia Ann Palmer, Feb. 16, 1963; children: Edward Palmer, Rachael Louise. Student, Ohio State U., 1948-50; A.B., Stanford, 1952, J.D., 1954. Bar: Ariz. 1955, D.C. 1970, U.S. Supreme Ct. 1969. Camp dir. Quarter Circle V Bar Ranch, 1954; tchr. Orme Sch., Mayer, Ariz., 1954-56; trust rep. Valley Nat. Bank Ariz., 1958-60; pvt. practice, Phoenix, 1960—; assoc. atty. Cunningham, Carson & Messinger, 1960-64; ptnr. Carson, Messinger, Elliott, Laughlin & Ragan, 1964-69, 70-80, Gray, Plant, Mooty, Mooty & Bennett, 1981-84, Eaton, Lazarus, Dodge & Lowry Ltd., 1985-86; exec. v.p., gen. counsel Bus. Realty Ariz., 1986-93; pvt. practice, Scottsdale, Ariz., 1986-88; ptnr. Lowry & Froeb, Scottsdale, 1988-89, Lowry, Froeb & Clements, P.C., Scottsdale, 1989-90, Lowry & Clements P.C., Scottsdale, 1990, Lowry, Clements & Powell, P.C., Scottsdale, 1991—; asst. legis. counsel Dept. Interior, Washington, 1969-70; mem. Ariz. Commn. Uniform Laws, 1972—, chmn., 1976-88; judge pro tem Ariz. State Ct. Appeals, 1986, 92-94. Chmn. Council of Stanford Law Socs., 1968; vice chmn. bd. trustees Orme Sch., 1972-74, treas., 1981-83; bd. trustees Heard Mus., 1965-91, life trustee, 1991—, pres., 1974-75; bd. visitors Stanford Sch. Law; magistrate Town of Paradise Valley, Ariz., 1976-83; juvenile ct. referee Maricopa County, 1978-83. Served to capt. USAF, 1956-58. Fellow Ariz. Bar Found. (founder); mem. ABA, Maricopa County Bar Assn., State Bar Ariz. (chmn. com. uniform laws 1979-85), Stanford Law Soc. Ariz. (past pres.), Scottsdale Bar Assn. (bd. dirs. 1991—, v.p. 1991, pres. 1992-95), Ariz. State U. Law Soc. (bd. dirs.), Nat. Conf. Commrs. Uniform State Laws, Delta Sigma Rho, Alpha Tau Omega, Phi Delta Phi. Home: 7600 N Moonlight Ln Paradise Valley AZ 85253-2938 Office: Lowry Clements & Powell PC Ste 1120 2901 N Central Ave Phoenix AZ 85012 also: Ste 1040 6900 E Camelback Rd Scottsdale AZ 85251

LOWRY, GLENN DAVID, art museum director; b. N.Y.C.; s. Warren and Laure (Lynn) L.; m. Susan Chambers, Aug. 24, 1974; children: Nicholas, Alexis, William. BA, Williams Coll., 1976; MA, Harvard U., 1978, PhD, 1982. Asst. curator Fogg Art Mus., Harvard U., Cambridge, Mass., 1978-80; rsch. asst. Archeol. Survey of Mediterranean Town of Amalfi, Italy, 1980; curator Oriental art Mus. Art, R.I. Sch. Design, Providence, 1981-82; dir. Joseph and Margaret Muscarelle Mus. Art, Williamsburg, Va., 1982-84; curator Nr. Ea. art Arthur M. Sackler and the Freer Gallery Art, Smithsonian Instn., Washington, 1984-90, curatorial coord., 1987-89; dir. Art Gallery Ont., Toronto, Can., 1990-95, Mus. Modern Art, N.Y.C., 1995—. Co-author: Fatehpur-Sikri: A Source Book, 1985, From Concept to Context: Approaches to Asian and Islamic Calligraphy, 1986, An Annotated Checklist of the Vever Collection, 1988, A Jeweler's Eye: Art of the Book from the Vever Collection, 1988, Timur and the Princely Vision: Persian Art and Culture in the Fifteenth Century, 1989, Europe and the Arts of Islam: The Politics of Taste, 1991. Trustee Metro Toronto Conv. and Visitors Assn. Recipient Inst. Turkish Studies Travel award Smithsonian Instn., 1980, Spl. Exhbns. award, 1987, Scholarly Studies award, 1990. Mem. Assn. Am. Art Mus. Dirs., Can. Assn. Mus. Dirs., Coll. Art Assn. Office: Mus Modern Art 11 W 53rd St New York NY 10019-5401

LOWRY, JAMES DAVID, author, consultant; b. Wichita, Kans., May 24, 1942; s. Frederick Brennan and Mary (Mullendore) L.; children: Anne Harrison, Blythe Brennan, Terrell Brennan, James Sargent. B.S., Okla. State U., 1965; LL.B., U. Okla., 1968. Bar: Pa. bar 1968. Mem. Liebert, Harvey, Bechtle & Short, Phila., 1968-69; counsel Systems Capital Corp., Phila., 1969-71; v.p., counsel Provident Nat. Bank, 1971-73; sr. v.p., sec., dir. ops. Provident Nat. Corp., Phila., 1973-76; exec. v.p., chief adminstrv. officer Provident Nat. Corp., 1976-78; also dir. subs.; v.p.-fin., gen. mgr. Petroleum Heat and Power Co., Phila., 1978-80; chmn., pres., chief exec. Bancshares of N.J., 1981-83, No. Nat. Corp.; chmn., pres. The Bank of N.J.; chmn. The Trustees' Pvt. Bank, 1981-84; pres., chief exec. officer Equibank, Equimark, 1984-85; mng. dir. Lowry Bittel, Perrot & Co., 1985-91; chmn. Hopper Soliday Corp., 1986-91, Blue Hill Conservatory, Blue Hill, Maine, 1991—; exec. producer Voices Across Am., 1995—. Served with U.S. Army, 1960-62. Mem. ABA, Pa. Bar Assn., Phila. Bar Assn., Racquet Club, Corinthian Yacht Club, Rittenhouse Club (Phila.), Mill Dam Club (Wayne, Pa.), Bar Harbor Yacht Club (Maine). Home: Beech Hill Rd Blue Hill ME 04614 Office: Blue Hill Conservatory PO Box 330 Blue Hill ME 04614-0330

LOWRY, JAMES HAMILTON, management consultant; b. Chgo., May 28, 1939; s. William E. and Camille C. L.; 1 child, Aisha. BA, Grinnell Coll., 1961; M in Polit. and Instl. Adminstrn., U. Pitts., 1965; PMD, Harvard U., 1973. Assoc. dir. Peace Corps, Lima, Peru, 1965-67; spl. asst. to pres., project mgr. Bedford-Stuyvesant Restoration Corp., Bklyn., 1967-68; sr. assoc. McKinsey & Co., Chgo., 1968-75; pres. James H. Lowry & Assos., Chgo., 1975—; ptnr. Opus Equity; mem. Small Bus. Adv. Com.; bd. dirs. Johnson Products Co., Burrell Advt. Mem. vis. com. Harvard U.; adv. bd. J.L. Kellogg Grad. Sch. Mgmt. Northwestern U., also adj. prof.; trustee Grinnell Coll.; bd. dirs. Chgo. United, Northwestern Hosp., Chgo. Pub. Libr., Chgo. Fgn. Affairs, African-Am. Inst. John Hay Whitney fellow, 1963-65; co-chmn. Chgo. United. Mem. Harvard Alumni Assn. (dir., vis. com.), Inst. Mgmt. Cons., Econ. Club, Monroe Club, Univ. Club, Comml. Club of Chgo. Home: 3100 N Sheridan Rd Chicago IL 60657-4954 Office: 676 N Michigan Ave Chicago IL 60611

LOWRY, LARRY LORN, management consulting company executive; b. Lima, Ohio, Apr. 12, 1947; s. Frank William and Viola Marie L.; m. Jean Carroll Greenbaum, June 23, 1973; 1 child, Alexandra Kristin. BSEE, MIT, 1969, MSEE, 1970; MBA, Harvard U., 1972. Mgr. Boston Consulting Group, Menlo Park, Calif., 1972-80; sr. v.p., mng. ptnr. Booz, Allen & Hamilton Inc, San Francisco, 1980—. Western Electric fellow, 1969, NASA fellow, 1970. Mem. Sigma Xi, Tau Beta Pi, Eta Kappa Nu. Presbyterian. Home: 137 Stockbridge Ave Atherton CA 94027-3942

LOWRY, LOIS (HAMMERSBERG), author; b. 1937. Author: A Summer to Die, 1977, Find A Stranger, Say Goodbye, 1978, Anastasia Krupnik, 1979, Autumn Street, 1980, Anastasia Again, 1981, Anastasia at Your Service, 1982, The One Hundredth Thing About Caroline, 1983, Taking Care of Terrific, 1983, Anastasia, Ask Your Analyst, 1984, Us and Uncle Fraud, 1984, Anastasia on Her Own, 1985, Switcharound, 1985, Anastasia Has the Answers, 1986, Anastasia's Chosen Career, 1987, Rabbie Starkey, 1987, All About Sam, 1988, Number the Stars, 1989 (John Newbery medal 1990), Your Move, J.P.!, 1990, Anastasia at This Address, 1991, Attaboy, Sam!, 1992, The Giver, 1993 (John Newbery medal 1994), Anastasia Absolutely, 1995, See You Around, Sam!, 1996. Address: 205 Brattle St Cambridge MA 02138-3319 Office: care Houghton Mifflin 222 Berkeley St Boston MA 02116-3748

LOWRY, MIKE, governor, former congressman; b. St. John, Wash., Mar. 8, 1939; s. Robert M. and Helen (White) L.; m. Mary Carlson, Apr. 6, 1968; 1 child, Diane. B.A., Wash. State U., Pullman, 1962. Chief fiscal analyst, staff dir. ways and means com. Wash. State Senate, 1969-73; govtl. affairs dir. Group Health Coop. Puget Sound, 1974-75; mem. council King County Govt., 1975-78, chmn., 1977; mem. 96th-100th congresses from 7th dist. Wash., 1979-1989; governor State of Wash., 1993—. Chmn. King County Housing and Community Devel. Block Grant Program, 1977; pres. Wash. Assn. Counties, 1978. Democrat. Address: Legislative Bldg PO Box 40002 Olympia WA 98504*

LOWRY, OLIVER HOWE, pharmacologist, biochemist; b. Chgo., July 18, 1910; married Adrienne Clark, 1935; children: Susan, Emily, Charles, Stephen, John. BS, Northwestern U., 1932; MD and PhD in Biochemistry, U. Chgo., 1937; DSc (hon.), Wash. U., 1981. Oliver H. Lowry lectr. prof. exptl. instr. biochemistry Harvard Med. Sch., 1937-42; mem. staff Pub. Health Rsch. Inst., N.Y., 1942-44, assoc. chief divsn. physiology and nutrition, 1944-47; prof. pharmacology Wash. U., 1947-79, head dept., 1947-76, dean, 1955-58, emeritus disting. prof. pharmacology Sch. Medicine, 1979—; Commonwealth Found. fellow Carlsberg Lab., Copenhagen U., 1939. Recipient Borden award Assn. Am. Med. Colls., 1955. Mem. NAS, Am. Soc. Pharmacology and Exptl. Therapeutics, Am. Soc. Biol. Chemistry, Am. Chem. Soc. (Midwest award 1962, Scott award 1963), Histochem. Soc., AAAS, Harvey Soc., Am. Acad. Arts and Scis., Royal Danish Acad. Sci. Office: Washington Unif Dept of Pharmacology Sci 660 S Euclid Ave Saint Louis MO 63110-1010*

LOWRY, RALPH JAMES, SR., history educator; b. Pitts., Dec. 30, 1928; s. Robert William and Elizabeth (Carter) L; 1 son. AB with hons., Lincoln U., 1955; MA, Temple U., 1957; PhD, U. N.Mex., 1972; postgrad., Carnegie-Mellon U., 1980. History tchr. William Penn High Sch. for Girls, Phila., 1957-58; asst. prof. dept. history So. Univ., Baton Rouge, La., 1959-64, Md. State U., Princess Anne, 1965-69; tchr. sixth grade John Marshall Elem. Sch., Albuquerque, 1969-70; assoc. prof. dept. history/geography Va. State U., Petersburg, 1970-78; tchr. English/social studies Schenley High Sch., Pitts., 1978-80; assoc. prof. history and geography Bishop Coll., Dallas, Tex., 1980-83; asst. prof. philosophy and history Alcorn State U., Lorman, Miss., 1983-90; assoc. prof. history and geography Lincoln Univ., Pa., 1991; ret. Lincoln Univ. of Pa., 1995; adj. prof. Black history, John Tyler C.C., Chester, Va., 1971-72, U. Va., Danville, 1972-74; substitute tchr. Dallas Ind. Sch. System, 1983; history scholar U.S. Mil. Acad., West Point, N.Y., summer 1985. Contbr. articles to profl. jours./publs. With USN, 1948-52, Korea. John Hay Whitney fellow, Jessie Smith Noyes scholar, others. Mem. Am. Hist. Soc., Miss. Polit. Sci. Assn., Western Pa. Psychiat. Clinic, Smithsonian Assocs., Western Pa. Rsch. and Hist. Soc., Phi Delta Kappa, Phi Alpha Theta, Alpha Phi Omega, Beta Sigma Tau, Pi Gamma Mu, Alpha Kappa Mu, Alpha Mu Gamma, Shriners. Democrat. Episcopalian. Home: 4717 Hazel Ave Philadelphia PA 19143-2022 Office: Dept History Lincoln Univ of Pa Lincoln University PA 19352

LOWRY, WILLIAM KETCHIN, JR., insurance company executive; b. Columbia, S.C., Oct. 4, 1951; s. William Ketchin and Beverly Hubbard (Frazee) L.; m. Elaine Diana Kent, June 22, 1984; children: Jennifer Lyn, Julia Ann, Samuel Ketchin. BSBA, U. S.C., 1972, M in Acctg., 1973. CPA, S.C. Supr. Ernst & Whinney, Columbia, 1973-81; sr. mgr. Price Waterhouse, Hartford, Conn., 1981-83, Phila., 1983-84; dir. corp. sys. devel. and analysis Am. Can Co., Greenwich, Conn., 1984-86; v.p., treas., CFO Phoenix Re Corp. and Reins. Co., N.Y.C., 1986-90, sr. v.p., treas., CFO, 1990; v.p., treas. Transnat. Ins. Co., N.Y.C., 1989-90; bd. dirs., v.p., treas. Nat. Bus. Brokers, Inc., Greenlawn, N.Y., 1989-90; sr. v.p., CFO SCOR U.S. Corp., SCOR Reins. Co. Gen. Security Assurance Corp., N.Y.C., 1990-93, Constn. Reins Corp., 1993-96; exec. v.p. CFO Constn. Reins. Corp., 1996—, 1996—; bd. dirs. Constn. Reins Corp., 1994—, Constn. Reins. Corp. Sirius Reins. Corp., 1993—; pres. CRC Corsair Inc, 1995—. Pres., bd. dirs. Groves Homes Assn., Columbia, 1980-81; diaconate West Side Presbyn. Ch., Ridgewood, N.J., 1989-91. Fellow Life Mgmt. Inst.; mem. AICPA, Am. Soc. CLUs, Fin. Execs. Inst., Soc. Ins. Rsch., Soc. Fin. Examiners, Inst. Mgmt. Accts., S.C. Assn. CPAs, City Midday Drug and Chem. Club, Forest Lake Club, Saddle River Valley Swim and Tennis Club, Beta Gamma Sigma, Omicron Delta Kappa, Beta Alpha Psi, Omicron Delta Epsilon, Sigma Phi Epsilon. Presbyterian. Avocations: horseback riding, golf. Home: 22 Autumn Ct U Saddle Riv NJ 07458-1853 Office: Constn Reins Corp 110 William St New York NY 10038-3901

LOWRY-JOHNSON, JUNIE, casting director. Films include Summer Heat, 1987, La Bamba, 1987, Born in East L.A., 1987, Powwow Highway, 1989, Blind Fury, 1990, Little Vegas, 1990, The Hand That Rocks the Cradle, 1992; TV series includes N.Y.P.D. Blue (Emmy award for outstanding individual achievement in casting 1995). Mem. Casting Soc. Am. Office: 20th Century Fox Bldg 26 Stage 2 10201 W Pico Blvd Los Angeles CA 90035

LOWTHER, FRANK EUGENE, research physicist; b. Orrville, Ohio, Feb. 3, 1929; s. John Finger and Mary Elizabeth (Mackey) L.; m. Elizabeth E. Koons, Apr. 21, 1951; children: Cynthia E., Victoria J., James A., Frank Eugene. Grad. Ohio State U., Columbus, 1952. Scientist missile systems div. Raytheon Corp., Boston, 1952-57, Gen. Electric Co., Syracuse, N.Y., and Daytona Beach, Fla., 1957-65; chief sci. Purification Sci., Inc., 1965-72; mgr. ozone rsch. and devel. W.R. Grace Co., Curtis Bay, Md., 1972-75; sr. engring. assoc. Linde div. Union Carbide Corp., Tonawanda, N.Y., 1975-80; chief sci., Atlantic Richfield-Energy Conversion and Materials Lab, 1980-83; prin. sci. Atlantic Richfield-Corp. Tech., 1983-85, sci. advisor, 1985-88, rsch. advisor, 1988-93, cons. tech. advisor, 1993—; advisor Energy Sci., Inc., Canandaigua, N.Y., 1993—, Custom Tech. Creations, Inc., Buffalo, N.Y., 1993—. Recipient Inventor of Yr. award Patent Law Assn. and Tech. Socs. Council, 1976. Assoc. fellow AIAA; mem. IEEE (sr.), AAAS, N.Y. Acad. Scis., Masons. Patentee in field of ozone tech., plasma generators, solid state power devices, internal combustion engines, electro-desorption, thermoelectrics, virus and bacteria disinfection systems, oil field technology, electric power distribution, nuclear fusion, chemical and physical reactors, exploding bridge wires, weapons. Home and Office: 817 Parkside Ave Buffalo NY 14216-2009

LOWTHER, GERALD HALBERT, lawyer; b. Slagle, La., Feb. 18, 1924; s. Fred B. and Beatrice (Halbert) L.; children by previous marriage: Teresa, Craig, Natalie, Lisa. A.B., Pepperdine Coll., 1951; J.D., U. Mo., 1951. Bar: Mo. 1951. Since practiced in Springfield; ptnr. firm Lowther, Johnson, Joyner, Lowther, Cully & Housley; Mem. Savs. and Loan Commn. Mo., 1965-68, Commerce and Indsl. Commn. Mo., 1967-73; lectr. U. Tex., 1955-57, Crested Butte, Colo., 1958-59. Contbr. articles law jours. Past pres. Ozarks Regional Heart Assn.; Del., mem. rules com. Democratic Nat. Conv., 1968; treas. Dem. Party Mo., 1968-72, mem. platform com., 1965, 67, mem. bi-partisan commn. to reapportion Mo. senate, 1966; Bd. dirs. Greene County Guidance Clinic, Ozark Christian Counseling Service, Greene County, Mo.; past pres. Cox Med. Center. Served with AUS, 1946-47; Col. staff of Gov. Hearnes 1964, 68, Mo. Mem. ABA, Mo. Bar Assn., Greene County Bar Assn., Def. Orientation Conf. Assn., Internat. Assn. Ins. Counsel, Def. Rsch. Inst., Springfield C. of C. Clubs: Kiwanian (pres. 1962), Quarterback (pres. 1958), Tip Off (pres. 1960). Home: 2320 Englewood 350 Hammons Pkwy Springfield MO 65806 Office: 300 S John Q Hammons Pky Springfield MO 65806-2545

LOWY, FREDERICK HANS, university president, psychiatrist; b. Grosspetersdorf, Austria, Jan. 1, 1933; arrived in Can., 1944; s. Eugen and Maria (Braun) L.; m. Anne Louise Cloudsley, June 25, 1965 (dec. 1973); children: David, Eric, Adam; m. Mary Kathleen O'Neil, June 1, 1975; 1 dau., Sarah. BA, McGill U., Montreal, Que., Can., 1955, MD, 1959. Intern, resident in internal medicine Royal Victoria Hosp., Montreal, Que., Can.; resident in psychiatry U. Cin. Hosp., Cin. VA Hosp.; psychoanalytic tng. Montreal Psychoanalytic Inst.; psychiatrist Allan Meml. Inst.-Royal Victoria Hosp., Montreal-McGill U. Faculty Medicine, 1965-70; psychiatrist-in-chief Ottawa Civic Hosp.; also prof. dept. psychiatry U. Ottawa Faculty Medicine, 1971-74; prof. psychiatry, chmn. dept. U. Toronto Faculty Medicine; also dir. Clarke Inst. Psychiatry U. Toronto, 1974-80, dean Sch. Medicine, 1980-87, dir. Ctr. for Bioethics, 1989-95; rector, vice chancellor Concordia U., Montreal, 1995—. Author numerous papers in field; co-editor: A Method of Psychiatry, 1980, Alzheimer's Disease Research, 1991. Fellow Royal Coll. Physicians and Surgeons, Am. Coll. Psychiatrists; mem. Internat. Psychoanalytic Assn., Can. Psychiat. Assn. (editor jour. 1972-76), Am. Psychiat. Assn., Am. Coll. Psychoanalysts, Am. Coll. Psychiatrists. Office: Concordia U Office Rector, 1455 de Maisonneuve Blvd W, Montreal, PQ Canada H3G 1M8

LOWY, GEORGE THEODORE, lawyer; b. N.Y.C., Oct. 6, 1931; s. Eugene and Elizabeth Lowy; m. Pier M. Foucault, Sept. 7, 1957. BA cum laude, LLB cum laude, NYU. Bar: N.Y. 1955, U.S. Dist. Ct. (so. dist.) N.Y. 1958, U.S. Supreme Ct. 1972, U.S. Ct Appeals (2d cir.) 1975. Assoc. Cravath, Swaine and Moore, N.Y.C., 1957-65, ptnr., 1965—; trustee NYU Law Ctr. Found.; bd. dirs. Equitable Life Assurance Soc. U.S., Eramet, Paris; adj. prof. NYU Law Sch., 1983—. Fellow ABA; mem. Am. Law Inst., Assn. of Bar of City of N.Y., Internat. Bar Assn., Union Internat. des Avocats, Cercle Interallie Paris. Home: 580 Park Ave New York NY 10021-7313 Office: Cravath Swaine & Moore World Wide Pla 825 8th Ave New York NY 10019-7416

LOWY, JAY STANTON, music industry executive; b. Chgo., Nov. 22, 1935; s. Joseph Alfred and Minnie Lowy; m. Diane Friedland, Oct. 10, 1959 (div.); children—Dana Kim, Jeffrey Mark; m. Brenda Belle Orloff, Mar. 22, 1982; 1 child, Jason Louis. Student, UCLA, 1954-58. Gen. mgr. Robbins Feist & Miller Music Pub. Cos., 1959-67, Famous Music Corp., 1967-69; v.p. Dot and Paramount Records, 1969-71; pres., chief operating officer Capitol-EMI Music Pub. Cos., 1971-73; v.p., gen. mgr. Jobete Music Co., Inc. (Motown Industries), Hollywood, Calif., 1976-86; cons., personal mgr., 1986—. Served with AUS, 1958. Named one of Top 200 Music Execs. Billboard Mag., 1976, Old Master Purdue U., 1979. Mem. Nat. Acad. Recording ARts and Scis. (nat. pres. and chmn. bd. trustees 1979-81), Calif. Copyright Conf. (pres. 1977-78), Tau Epsilon Phi. Democrat. Jewish. Home: 5516 Aura Ave Tarzana CA 91356-3006

LOXLEY, JOHN, economics educator; b. Sheffield, Eng., Nov. 12, 1942; arrived in Can., 1975; s. John and Elizabeth (Antcliff) L.; m. Zeeba Dawood, June 10, 1967 (div. 1985); children: Salim John, Camille Elizabeth; m. Aurelie Mogan, Sept. 15, 1989; children: Raina Ilène, Matthew Reuben. BA in Econs. with honors, U. Leeds, Eng., 1963, PhD in Econs., 1966. Lectr. econs. dept. Makerere U., Kampala, Uganda, 1966-67; rsch. mgr. Nat. Bank Commerce, Tanzania, 1967-69; sr. lectr. dept. econs. U. Dar es Salaam, Tanzania, 1969-72; first dir. Inst. Fin. Mgmt., Dar es Salaam, 1972-73, UN Devel. Program prof. econs. and planning, head dept., 1973-74; sec. (dep. minister) resource and econ. devel. sub-com. of cabinet Govt. of Man., Winnipeg, Can., 1975-77; prof. econs. U. Man., 1977—, head. dept., 1984—; chair Cmtys. Econ. Devel. Fund, Winnipeg, 1975-78; chair and pres. Channel Area Loggers, Man. Crown Corp., Winnipeg, 1976-78; vis. prof. U. Leeds, 1987-88; advisor, cons. Govt. Mozambique, 1978, 88, Govt. Tanzania, 1981, 82, 83, 84, Govt. Uganda, 1986, 87, Ctrl. Bank Madagascar, 1985, St. Kitts and Nevis, 1991, 92, ANC/COSATU, South Africa, 1991, 92, 93, Royal Commn. Aboriginal Peoples, 1993-95; ptnr., pres. HKL & Assocs. Ltd. Author: The International Monetary Fund and the Poorest Countries, 1984, Debt and Disorder, 1986; co-editor: Towards Socialist Plannings, 1972, Structural Adjustment in Africa, 1989; editorial bd. Studies in Polit. Economy, 1979-92, Can. Jours. Devel. Studies; Rev. African Polit. Economy, 1985—. Bd. dirs., mem. exec. bd. Soc. for Manitobans with Disabilities, Winnipeg, 1983-89, mem. hon. adv. coun., 1989-90; bd. dirs., mem. exec. bd. Can. Rehab. Coun. for Disabled, Winnipeg, 1987-89; pres. Can. Assn. for Study Internat. Devel.; chmn. CHOICES—A Coalition for Social Justice, 1990-92; mem. Can. Commonwealth Scholarship and Fellowship Com., 1991-94. N.-S. Inst. vis. fellow, Ottawa, Ont., Can., 1982-83. Mem. Can. Econs. Assn., Can. Assn. for Study Internat. Devel. (v.p.), Can. African Studies Assn. Avocations: soccer, squash. Office: U Man Dept Econs, 501 Fletcher Argue Bldg, Winnipeg, MB Canada R3T 2N2

LOY, FRANK ERNEST, conservation organization executive; b. Nuremberg, Germany, Dec. 25, 1928; came to U.S., 1939; s. Alfred Loewi and Elizabeth (Loeffler) L.; m. Dale Haven, 1963; children: Lisel, Eric Anthony. BA, UCLA, 1950; LLB, Harvard U., 1953. Bar: D.C. 1953, Calif. 1954. With O'Melveny & Myers, L.A., 1954-65; spl. asst. to adminstr. FAA, 1961-63; spl. cons. to adminstr. AID, 1963-64; dep. asst. sec. state for econ. affairs, 1965-70; sr. v.p. Pan Am. World Airways, Inc., N.Y.C., 1970-73; pres. Pennsylvania Co., Washington, 1974-79, Penn Ctrl. Corp., 1978-79; dir. Bur. Refugee Programs, Dept. State, Washington, 1980-81; pres. German Marshall Fund of U.S., 1981-95; chmn. League Conservation Voters, Washington, 1993—, pres., 1995-96; instr. corp. fin. Grad. Sch. Commerce, U. So. Calif., 1959-61; dir. Applied Bioscience Internat. Inc. Chmn. bd. trustees Goddard Coll., Vt., 1976-78, Environ. Def. Fund, 1983-90, Washington Ballet, 1991-94; U.S. mem. Bd. Regional Environ. Ctr. for Ctrl. and Ea. Europe, Budapest, Hungary. With U.S. Army, 1953-55. Home: 3230 Reservoir Rd NW Washington DC 20007-2955 Office: League Conservation Voters 1707 L St NW Washington DC 20036

LOY, RICHARD FRANKLIN, civil engineer; b. Dubuque, Iowa, July 6, 1950; s. Wayne Richard and Evelyn Mae (Dikeman) L.; m. Monica Lou Roberts, Sept. 2, 1972 (div.); children: Taneha Eve, Spencer Charles. BSCE, U. Wis., Platteville, 1973. Registered profl. engr., Wis., Ohio. Engr. aid Wis. Dept. of Transp., Superior, 1969; asst. assayer Am. Lead & Zinc Co., Shullsburg, Wis., 1970; asst. grade foreman Radandt Construction Co., Eau Claire, Wis., 1970; air quality technician U. Wis., Platteville, 1972-73; asst. city engr. City of Kaukauna, Wis., 1973-77; asst. city engr. City of Fairborn, Ohio, 1977-89, city engr., 1989-93; pub. works dir. City of Fairborn, 1993—. Bd. dirs. YMCA Fairborn, 1990-95; mem. coun. Trinity United Ch. of Christ, Fairborn, 1989-92; chmn. Chillicothe dist. Tecumseh coun. Boy Scouts Am., 1991-93. Recipient Blue Coat award, 1983; named to Exec. Hall of Fame, N.Y., 1990. Mem. ASCE, NSPE, Am. Pub. Works Assn., Am. Water Works Assn., Inst. Transp. Engrs.

LOYND, RICHARD BIRKETT, consumer products company executive; b. Norristown, Pa., Dec. 1, 1927; s. James B. and Elizabeth (Geigus) L.; m. Jacqueline Ann Seubert, Feb. 3, 1951; children: Constance, John, Cynthia, William, James, Michael. B.S. in Elec. Engring., Cornell U., 1950. Sales engr. Lincoln Electric Co., Cleve., 1950-55; with Emerson Electric Co., St. Louis, 1955-68; pres. Builder Products div. Emerson Electric Co., 1965-68, v.p. Electronics and Space div., 1961-65; v.p. ops. Gould, Inc., Chgo., 1968-71; exec. v.p. Eltra Corp., N.Y.C., 1971-74; pres. Eltra Corp., 1974-81; chmn. Converse, Inc., 1982-84; chmn., chief exec. officer Interco Inc., St. Louis, 1989—. Home: 19 Randall Dr Short Hills NJ 07078-1957 Office: Interco Inc 101 S Hanley Rd Saint Louis MO 63105-3406*

LOZANO, IGNACIO EUGENIO, JR., newspaper editor; b. San Antonio, Jan. 15, 1927; s. Ignacio E. and Alicia E. de Lozano; m. Marta Navarro, Feb. 24, 1951; children: Leticia Eugenia, José Ignacio, Monica Cecilia, Francisco Antonio. A.B. in Journalism, U. Notre Dame, 1947. Asst. pub. La Opinion, Los Angeles, 1947-53, pub., editor, 1953-76, 77-83, 84-86; pub. La Opinion, 1983-84, editor-in-chief, 1986—; ambassador El Salvador, 1976-77; Am. ambassador to El Salvador, 1976-77; bd. dirs. BankAmerica Corp., Bank of Am. NT & SA, Pacific Enterprises., The Walt Disney Co., Calif. Econ. Devel. Corp. Bd. dirs. Nat. Pub. Radio, Los Angeles World Affairs Council, Santa Anita Found., Youth Opportunity Found., Orange County Performing Arts Ctr.; mem. Council on Fgn. Relations, Council of Am. Ambassadors; trustee U. Notre Dame, Occidental Coll., South Coast Repertory Company; overseer The Rand Corp. Inst. for Civil Justice; bd. govs. Calif. Community Found. Mem. Calif. Newspaper Pubs. Assn. (bd. dirs.), Calif. Press Assn., Cath. Prss Council of So. Calif., Greater Los Angeles Press Club, Inter Am. Press Assn. (pres.), Sigma Delta Chi. Office: La Opinion 411 W 5th St Los Angeles CA 90013-1000

LOZANO, JOSE, nephrologist; b. San Vicente, El Salvador, Feb. 11, 1941; came to U.S., 1968; s. Jose E. and Transito Maria (Mendez) L.; m. Hilda Berganza, Jan. 27, 1965; children: Jose E., Claudia Maria. MD, U. El Salvador, 1965. Diplomate Am. Bd. Internal Medicine, Am. Bd. Nephrology. Rotating intern Nat. Med. Ctr., San Salvador, El Salvador, 1963-64; asst. resident in internal medicine Rosales Hosp., San Salvador, 1965-66, resident in internal medicine, 1966-67, chief resident in internal medicine, 1967-68; resident in internal medicine Baylor U. Affiliated Hosps., Houston, 1968-70, fellow in nephrology, 1970-71, 73-74; asst. prof. medicine U. El Salvador, 1971-72; internist and nephrologist Social Security Hosp., San Salvador, 1971-72; instr. in medicine Baylor Coll. Medicine, Houston, 1974-75, asst. prof. medicine in nephrology, 1975-76, clin. asst. prof. medicine, 1976-80; mem. staff internal medicine St. Elizabeth Hosp., Beaumont Med./Surg. Hosp., Bapt. Hosp., Beaumont, Tex., 1976; med. dir. Golden Triangle Dialysis Ctr., Beaumont, 1977—, BMA Jasper, Jasper, Tex., 1986, BMA Orange, Orange, Tex., 1987-90; med. dir. Golden Triangle Dialysis Ctr., Beaumont, 1977; med. dir. BMA Jasper, Tex., 1986, Orange, Tex., 1987-90; mem. Kidney Health Care Adv. Com., 1981-82; pesenter in field. Contbr. articles to profl. publs. Mem. AMA, ACP, Am. Soc. Nephrology, Internat. Soc. Nephrology, Tex. Med. Assn., Harris County Med. Soc., Jefferson County Med. Soc., Am. Coll. Physicians Execs., Physicians for A Nat. Health Plan. Avocations: study of socioeconomic factors in healthcare in U.S., Catholic theologies. Home: 4655 Ashdown St Beaumont TX 77706-7723 Office: Beaumont Nephrology Assocs 3282 College St Beaumont TX 77701-4610 *In terms of health care we need a system that provides easy, uncomplicated access to primary care services. We urgently need a health care system that provides universal and comprehensive access to health care without considerations given to the ability to pay, race, gender, religion or sexual orientation. We need a system that is independent of employment, in which people with existing conditions are not restricted from free and adequate access to health care. The creation of a universal health care system is in the best interests of all citizens of this country.*

LOZANO, JOSE I., publishing executive. Pub. La Opinion, L.A., 1993—. Office: La Opinion 411 W 5th St Los Angeles CA 90013-1000 also: 411 W 5th St Los Angeles CA 90013-1000

LOZANO, RUDOLPHO, federal judge; b. 1942. BS in Bus., Ind. U., 1963, LLB, 1966. Mem. firm Spangler, Jennings, Spangler & Dougherty. P.C., Merrillville, Ind., 1966-88; judge U.S. Dist. Ct. (no. dist.) Ind., Hammond, 1988—. With USAR, 1966-73. Mem. ABA, Ind. State Bar Assn., Def. Rsch. Inst. Office: US Dist Ct 205 Fed Bldg 507 State St Hammond IN 46320-1503*

LOZANSKY, EDWARD DMITRY, physicist, author, consultant; b. Kiev, Ukraine, Feb. 10, 1941; came to U.S., 1977; s. Dmitry R. and Dina M. (Chizhik) L.; m. Tatiana I. Yershov, Feb. 27, 1971; 1 child, Tania. MS, Moscow Phys. Engring. Inst., 1966; PhD, Inst. Atomic Energy, Moscow, 1969; LHD, Waynesburg Coll., 1995. Asst. prof. Moscow State U., 1969-71; assoc. prof. Mil. Tank Acad., Moscow, 1971-75; prof. U. Rochester, N.Y., 1977-80, Am. U., Washington, 1981-83, L.I. U., Bklyn., 1983-87; pres. Independent U., Washington, 1987-91; exec. dir. Andrei Sakharov Inst., Washington, 1981-86; pres. Russia House, Inc., 1991—, Am. U. in Moscow, 1992—, Am. Univs. in Russia, Ukraine and New Independent States, 1994—. Author: Theory of the Spark, 1976, For Tatiana, 1984, Andrei Sakharov, 1986, Mathematical Competitions, 1988, Democracy: USA-Russia, 1994. Mem. Russian Acad. of Soc. Scis. Avocations: skiing, chess, lecturing on Russia. Office: Russia House 1800 Connecticut Ave NW Washington DC 20009-5731

LOZIER, ALLAN G., manufacturing company executive; b. 1933. Student, U. Nebr. With Lozier Corp., Omaha, ltd. ptnr., 1953-57, gen. ptnr., 1957-64, pres., treas., 1964-82, chmn. bd. dirs., 1982—. Office: Lozier Corp 6336 Pershing Dr Omaha NE 68110-1100*

LOZNER, EUGENE LEONARD, internal medicine educator, consultant; b. Stamford, N.Y., Apr. 29, 1915; s. Samuel and Rebecca (Barnhard) L.; m. Jean MacPherson Culver, July 3, 1942; 1 child: Eugene Culver. BA, Columbia Coll., 1933; MD, Cornell U., 1937. Diplomate Am. Bd. Internal Medicine. Intern Albany (N.Y.) Hosp., 1937-38; resident Boston City Hosp., 1938-41; assoc. in pathology George Washington U., Washington, 1942-46; instr. medicine Harvard Med. Sch., Cambridge, Mass., 1946-47; assoc. prof. medicine Syracuse (N.Y.) U., 1947-50; assoc. prof. medicine SUNY, Syracuse, 1950-56, prof. medicine, 1956-75, emeritus prof., 1975—; prof. internal med. U. So. Fla., Tampa, 1976—; attending physician Univ. Hosp., Syracuse, 1948-75, Vet.'s Affairs Hosp., Tampa, 1980—; dir. clin. labs. Univ. Hosp., Syracuse, 1948-65; staff physician Vet.'s Affairs Hosp., Tampa, 1975-79. Contbr. over 80 articles to profl. jours. Chmn. Syracuse Regional Bd. Program, 1952; bd. dirs. Am. Cancer Soc., 1970; mem. nat. med. com. Planned Parenthood Fedn. Am., 1970-75; chmn. Syracuse and Onondaga County chpts. ARC, 1972-73. Comdr. USNR, 1941-47. Fellow Am. Coll. Physicians, Am. Soc. Hematology, Internat. Soc. Hematology; mem. Am. Soc. Clin. Investigation, Am. Fed. Clin. Rsch. (councillor 1941-47, pres. 1946-47), Phi Beta Kappa, Alpha Omega Alpha, Sigma Xi. Avocation: kite flying. Home and Office: 10364 Carrollwood Ln Apt 223 Tampa FL 33618-4728

LOZOFF, BETSY, pediatrician; b. Milw., Dec. 19, 1943; d. Milton and Marjorie (Morse) L.; 1 child, Claudia Brittenham. BA, Radcliffe Coll., 1965; MD, Case Western Res. U., 1971, MS, 1981. Diplomate Am. Bd. Pediat. From asst. prof. to prof. pediatrics Case Western Res. U., Cleve., 1974-93; prof. pediatrics U. Mich., Ann Arbor, 1993—, dir. Ctr. for Human Growth and Devel., 1993—. Recipient Rsch. Career Devel. award Nat. Inst. Child Health and Human Devel., 1984-88. Fellow Am. Acad. Pediatrics; mem. Soc. for Pediatric Rsch., Soc. Rsch. in Child Devel. (program com. 1988—), Soc. Behavioral Pediatrics (exec. com. 1985-88), Ambulatory Pediatric Soc. Office: Univ Mich Ctr Human Growth and Devel 300 N Ingalls St Ann Arbor MI 48109-2007

LOZOFF, BO, nonprofit organization administrator; b. Miami, Fla., Jan. 10, 1947; s. Eli Saul and Molly (Rubitzky) L.; m. Sita Linda Shrager, Sept. 25, 1966; 1 child, Joshua Elias Bo. Student, Tulane U., 1963-64, U. Fla., 1967. Rsch. assoc. Psychical Rsch. Found., Durham, N.C., 1972-74; mgr. Sunshine Farms Yoga Ashram, Durham, 1973-77; dir. Prison-Ashram Project, Durham, 1973—, Human Kindness Found., Durham, 1973—, Kindness House, Mebane, N.C., 1994—; cons. in field. Author: We're All Doing Time, 1984, Lineage and Other Stories, 1987, Inner Corrections, 1989, Just Another Spiritual Book, 1990. Recipient Quetlalcotyl award Xat Medicine Soc., 1986, Temple Award for Creative Altruism, Inst. of Noetic Scis., 1994. Office: Human Kindness Foundation RR 1 Box 201-n Durham NC 27705-9801*

LOZOYA-THALMANN, EMILIO, Mexican government official; b. Mexico City, May 15, 1947; s. Jesus Lozoya-Solis and Susana Thalmann-Richard; m. Gilda Austin-Solis de Lozoya, Mar. 27, 1971; children: Juan Jesus, Emilio Ricardo, Gilda Susana. Economist, Universidad Nacional Autónoma de Mexico (UNAM), 1969; MBA, Columbia U., 1972; MPA, Harvard U., 1974. Analyst, economic direction Secretariat of Programming and Budget, Mexico City, 1972-73; advisor to dep. gen. dir. Light and Power Co., Mexico City, 1974-75; dep. programming dir. Commn. Pub. Indsl. Policy, Mexico City, 1975-76; gen. treas. Mex. Inst. Social Security, Mexico City, 1977-80, dep. gen. adminstrv. dir., 1980-82; undersec. "B" Secretariat of Labour and Social Prevision, Mexico City, 1982-88; gen. dir. State Employees Social Security and Social Svcs. Inst., Mexico City, 1988-92; sec. Secretariat of Energy, Mines and State Industries, Mexico City, 1993—; councilor Banco Mexicano Somex; Serfin; Multibanco Comermex., Mexico, 1988-91; treas. Internat. Social Security Assn., Geneva, 1992-93; lectr. faculty economics, UNAM; ICAP-PRI, El Colegio de México. Contbr. articles to newspapers, jours. Pres. Oaxtepec Football Soccer Club, 1982; dir. internat. affair youth br. Partido Revolucionario Institucional, Mexico City, 1965, exec. sec., 1982, coord., 1987-88, mem. adv. coun. polit., econ., social studies inst.Partido Revolucionario Institucional. Recipient Colegio Alemán Alexander von Humbolt award, Mexico City, 1964. Mem. Nat. Coll. Economists (undersec. fgn. affairs 1977-79), Am. Economic Assn., Latinamerican Economic Assn. (pres. 1972), Club Aleman de Mexico. Home: Rinconda de Santa Teresa # 82, 14210 Mexico City Mexico Office: Insurgentes Sur 552 3, 06769 Mexico City Mexico

LOZYNIAK, ANDREW, manufacturing company executive; b. N.Y.C., July 28, 1931; s. Stephen and Helen (Pupchek) L.; m. Florence Slovitski, Nov. 24, 1955; children: Cynthia, Andrew, Richard, Wendy, Cathy. Grad., U. Conn., 1954. Pres. Fermont div. Dynamics Corp. Am., 1968-70; group v.p. Dynamics Corp. Am., Greenwich, Conn., 1970; exec. v.p. Dynamics Corp. Am., 1970, pres., 1970—, chmn. bd., 1978—, also dir.; bd. dirs. CTS Corp., Elkhart, Ind. Mem. Patterson, Indian Harbor Yacht Club. Office: Dynamics Corp Am 475 Steamboat Rd Greenwich CT 06830-7197

LU, DAN, systems analyst, mathematician; b. Beijing, Jan. 22, 1960; came to U.S., 1981; s. Yingzhong Lu and Huaiqing Chen; m. Hong Lou, Sept. 28, 1994; 1 child, Katherine H. BS in Physics, Beijing U., 1981; MS in Physics, U. Wash., 1983, PhD in Theoretical Physics, 1986. Tchg., rsch. asst. U. Wash., Seattle, 1981-86; postdoctoral rsch. assoc. Washington U., St. Louis, 1986-88; R&D mgr. Yu Feng Internat. Ltd., Hong Kong, 1988-90; sys. cons. Summit Computer Svcs., Charlotte, N.C., 1991-93; sr. sys. cons. Criterion Group, Charlotte, 1993-94; bus. sys. analyst, mathematician CMS, Inc., Winston-Salem, N.C., 1994—. Contbr. articles to profl. publs. China-U.S. Physics Examination and Application fellow, 1981. Mem. Am. Phys. Soc. Achievements include development of model for market promotion, forecasting system for coupon redemption, set of subroutines to calculate EXAFS electron energy losses. Home: 325 Craver Pointe Dr Clemmons NC 27012 Office: CMS Inc 2650 Pilgrim Ct Winston Salem NC 27106

LU, DAVID JOHN, history educator, writer; b. Keelung, Taiwan, Sept. 28, 1928; came to U.S., 1950, naturalized, 1960; s. Ming and Yeh (Lai) L.; m. Annabelle Compton, May 29, 1954; children: David John, Daniel Mark, Cynthia King, Stephen Paul. B.A. in Econs, Nat. Taiwan U., 1950; postgrad., Westminster Theol. Sem., Phila., 1950-52; M. Internat. Affairs, Columbia, 1954; certificate, East Asian Inst., 1954, Ph.D., 1960. Editor Prentice-Hall, Inc., 1956-60; instr. Rutgers U., 1959; asst. prof. history Bucknell U., Lewisburg, Pa., 1960-64; assoc. prof. Bucknell U., 1964-69, prof., 1969-94, prof. emeritus, 1994—, dir. Ctr. for Japanese Studies, 1965-94; cons. on global edn. Pa. Dept. Edn., 1961-62, 78, U.S. Dept. Edn., 1973-85; resident dir. associated Kyoto program Doshisha U., 1987-88. Author: From the Marco Polo Bridge to Pearl Harbor, 1961, (Japanese edit.) Taiheiyo Senso e no Dotei, 1967, Sources of Japanese History, 2 vols., 1974, Bicentennial History of the United States (in Japanese), 1976, The Life and Times of Matsuoka Yosuke, 1880-1946, 1981, Fumble-free Management, 1987, Japan: A Documentary History, 1996; translator: The China Quagmire, 1983, What Is Total Quality Control? The Japanese Way, 1985, Kanban, Just-in-Time at Toyota, 1986, Total Quality Control for Management: Strategies and Techniques from Toyota and Toyoda Gosei, 1987 TQC (Total Quality Control), The Wisdom of Japan, 1988; contbr. Sekai to Nippon, weekly, Tokyo. Fulbright-Hays scholar Japan, 1966-67. Presbyterian. Home: 635 Broadway St Milton PA 17847-2407

LU, GUIYANG, electrical engineer; b. Guiyang, China, May 10, 1946; came to U.S., 1982; s. Wen and Yunqiu Deng; m. Jing Du; 1 child, Jia. Degree in elec. engring., Tsing Hua U., Beijing, 1970; postgrad., South China U. Tech., Guangzhou, 1980-81; MA in Math., Calif. State U., Fresno, 1984; MSEE, Poly. U., N.Y.C., 1986. Instr. in elec. engring. South China U. Tech., Guangzhou, 1973-80; v.p. engring. Kawahara Corp., N.Y.C., 1986-88; H.S. math. tchr. N.Y.C. Bd. Edn., 1988-90; sr. R&D engr. Avid Inc., Norco, Calif., 1991—. Mem. IEEE. Home: 1718 Eastgate Ave Upland CA 91784-9210 Office: Avid Inc 3179 Hamner Ave Norco CA 91760-1983

LU, HUIZHU, computer scientist, educator; m. Yin Ming Wang; children: Serkuang, Qiang. BS in Physics, Fudan U., Shanghai; MS in Computer Science, U. Okla., PhD in Computer Science, 1988. Lectr. Shanghai U. Technology, Shanghai, China, 1961-80; visiting research associate, scientist U. Okla., Norman, 1981-85; asst. prof. Okla. State U., Stillwater, 1985-92, assoc. prof., 1992—; prin. investigator of projects Okla. Dept. Health, Okla. Dept. Environ. Quality. Co-author: Digital Measurement Techniques, 1980; contbr. numerous rsch. articles to profl. jours. Recipient numerous rsch. grants. Mem. Assn. for Computing Machinery, IEEE Computer Soc., Sigma Xi. Office: Oklahoma State U 213 Mathematical Sci Bldg Stillwater OK 74078

LU, PONZY, molecular biology educator; b. Shanghai, China, Oct. 7, 1942; came to U.S., 1949, naturalized, 1963; s. Abraham and Beth (Chou) L.; m. Heidi Fahl, Jan. 13, 1975; 1 child, Kristina. B.S., Calif. Inst. Tech., 1964; Ph.D., MIT, 1970. Arthritis Found. postdoctoral fellow Max Planck Inst., Goettingen, Fed. Republic Germany, 1970-73; asst. prof. dept. chemistry U. Pa., Phila., 1973-78; assoc. prof. U. Pa., 1978-82, prof., 1982—; mem. study sect. NIH, 1982-86, 92—; mem. Univ. Space Reseach Assn./NASA Biotechnology Discipline Working Group, microgravity sci. and applications div., 1986-91. Recipient Career Devel. award NIH, 1977-82. Mem. Am. Soc. Biochemistry, Molecular Biology, Biophys. Soc., Sigma Xi. Office: Univ Pa Dept Chemistry Philadelphia PA 19104

LU, SHIH-PENG, history educator; b. Kao-Yu, Chiang-Su, China, Sept. 16, 1928; s. Ch'un-Tai and Chu-Yin (Chia) L.; m. Wei-Chun Julia Lee; children: Ting Ting, Shin. BA, Nat. Taiwan U., Taipei, 1952. Cert. full prof., Ministry of Edn., Taiwan. Tchg. asst. Taiwan U., Taipei, 1953-55; rsch. asst. Acad. Sinica, Taipei, 1955-58; lectr. Tunghai U., Taichung, Taiwan, 1958-63, assoc. prof., 1963-67, prof., 1967—; vis. scholar Harvard U., Cambridge, Mass., 1961-63; rsch. fellow Yale U., New Haven, 1980-81; dir. evening divsn. Tunghai U., 1972-81, chmn. dept. history, 1981-87, dean Coll. Arts, 1988-94; dir. Chinese Culture Monthly, Taichung, 1988—. Author: Vietnam During the Period of Chinese Rule, 1964 (Nat. Sci. Coun. Publ. award 1965), The Modern History of China, 1979 (World Books Co. Authors award 1979), The Contemporary History of China, 1991 (Ministry of Edn. Outstanding Textbook award 1992); editor Chinese Culture Monthly, 1979— (Ministry of Edn. Best Jour. award 1991). 2nd lt. ROTC, Chinese Mil., 1952-53. Named Outstanding Youth, China Youth Corps, Taiwan, 1952, Outstanding Prof., Ministry of Edn., 1992. Mem. Assn. Modern History (chairperson bd. overseers 1994-96), Chinese Hist. Assn. (bd. dirs. 1983-94), Taiwan U. Alumni Assn. (chmn. 1987-89), Assn. for Ming Studies (exec. dir. 1995—). Avocations: reading, classical music, table tennis, jogging, Chinese opera. Home: 49 Tunghai Rd, 407 Taichung Taiwan Office: Tunghai Univ, Dept History, 407 Taichung Taiwan

LU, WUAN-TSUN, microbiologist, immunologist; b. Taichung, Taiwan, July 8, 1939; came to U.S., 1964; s. Yueh and Jinmien Lu; m. Rita Man Rom, July 25, 1970; children: Dorcia, Loretta. BS in Agrl. Econs., Nat. Taiwan U., 1960; MS in Microbiology, Brigham Young U., 1968; PhD, U. Okla., 1978. Microbiologist, chemist Murray Biol. Co., L.A., 1969-71; microbiologist Reference Lab., North Hollywood, Calif., 1971-73; rsch. assoc. U. Okla., Okla. City, 1973-78; lab. supr. Reference Med. Lab., San Jose,

Calif., 1980; mng. dir. Anakem Labs., Los Gatos, Calif., 1981-85; toxicologist SmithKline Labs., San Jose, 1981; founder, pres. United Biotech, Inc., Mountain View, Calif., 1983—, dir., chmn., mng. dir., 1987—; bd. dirs. Sino-U.S. Hunan Bioengrng. Co., Ltd. Mem. Am. Soc. Clin. Pathologists, Am. Soc. Clin. Chemists, Delta Group. Office: United Biotech Inc 110 Pioneer Way # C Mountain View CA 94041-1517

LUBAR, JEFFREY STUART, journalist; b. Rockville Centre, N.Y., Apr. 15, 1947; s. Sidney and Rose (Grupsmith) L.; m. Barbara Ruth Bigelman; children—Debra, Adam, Rachel. B.A., Am. U., 1969. Dir. Washington News Bur., Susquehanna Broadcasting Co., 1969-86; v.p. pub. affairs Nat. Assn. Realtors, 1987—; Mem. exec. com. of corrs. Radio-TV Assn. (U.S. Congress), 1974-75. Served with AUS, 1969-75. Mem. Burke Racquet Club, Nat. Press Club. Jewish. Home: 6307 Karmich St Fairfax VA 22039-1622 Office: 700 11th St NW Washington DC 20001-4507

LUBATTI, HENRY JOSEPH, physicist, educator; b. Oakland, Calif., Mar. 16, 1937; s. John and Pauline (Massimino) L.; m. Catherine Jeanne Berthe Ledoux, June 29, 1968; children: Karen E., Henry J., Stephen J.C. AA, U. Calif., Berkeley, 1957, AB, 1960; PhD, U. Calif., 1966; MS, U. Ill., 1963. Research assoc. Faculty Scis. U. Paris, Orsay, France, 1966-68; asst. prof. physics MIT, 1968-69; assoc. prof., sci. dir. visual techniques lab. U. Wash., 1969-74, prof., sci. dir. visual Techniques lab., 1974—; vis. lectr. Internat. Sch. Physics, Erice, Sicily, 1968, Herceg-Novi, Yugoslavia Internat. Sch., 1969, XII Cracow Sch. Theoretical Physics, Zapokane, Poland, 1972; vis. scientist CERN, Geneva, 1980-81; vis. staff Los Alamos Nat. Lab., 1983-86; guest scientist SSC Lab., 1991-93; mem. physics editorial adv. com. World Sci. Pub. Co. Ltd., 1982-93. Editor: Physics at Fermilab in the 1990's, 1990; contbr. numerous articles on high energy physics to profl. jours. Alfred P. Sloan research fellow, 1971-75. Fellow AAAS, Am. Phys. Soc.; mem. Sigma Xi, Tau Beta Pi. Office: U Wash Visual Techniques Lab Physics Box 351560 Seattle WA 98195-1560

LUBAWSKI, JAMES LAWRENCE, health care consultant; b. Chgo., June 4, 1946; s. Harry James and Stella Agnes (Pokorny) L.; m. Kathleen Felicity Donnellan, June 1, 1974; children: Kathleen N., James Lawrence, Kevin D., Edward H. BA, Northwestern U., 1968, MBA, 1969, MA, 1980. Asst. prof. U. Northern Iowa, Cedar Falls, 1969-72; instr. Loyola U., Chgo., 1974-76; dir., market planning Midwest Stock Exchange, Chgo., 1976-77; dir. mktg. Gambro Inc., Barrington, Ill., 1977-79; mktg. mgr. Travenol Labs., Deerfield, Ill., 1979-82; dir. mktg. Hollister Inc., Libertyville, Ill., 1982-84; pres., chief exec. officer Neomedica Inc., Chgo., 1984-86; v.p. bus. devel. Evangl. Health Svcs., Oak Brook, Ill., 1986-87; pres., chief exec. officer Cath. Health Alliance Met. Chgo., 1987-95; mng. dir. Ward Howell Internat., Chgo., 1995—. Author: Food and Man, 1974, Food and People, 1979; co-editor: Consumer Behavior in Theory and in Action, 1970. Am. Assn. Advt. Acys. Faculty fellow, 1973. Mem. Evanston Golf Club, Equestrian Order of Knights of Holy Sepulchre. Avocation: golf, fishing. Office: Ward Howell Internat Ste 2940 300 S Wacker Dr Chicago IL 60606

LUBBEN, DAVID J., lawyer; b. Cedar Rapids, Iowa, 1951. BA, Luther Coll., 1974; JD, U. Iowa, 1977. Bar: Minn. 1977. Ptnr. Dorsey & Whitney, Mpls. Office: Dorsey & Whitney LLP 220 S 6th St Minneapolis MN 55402-1498

LUBBERS, AREND DONSELAAR, academic administrator; b. Milw., July 23, 1931; s. Irwin Jacob and Margaret (Van Donselaar) L.; m. Eunice L. Mayo, June 19, 1953 (div.); children—Arend Donselaar, John Irwin Darrow, Mary Elizabeth; m. Nancy Vanderpol, Dec. 21, 1968; children—Robert Andrew, Caroline Jayne. AB, Hope Coll., 1953; AM, Rutgers U., 1956; LittD, Central Coll., 1977; DSc, U. Sarajevo, Yugoslavia, 1987; LHD, Hope Coll., 1988; DSc, Akademia Ekonomiczna, Krakow, Poland, 1989, U. Kingston Univ., Eng., 1995. Research asst. Rutgers U., 1954-55; research fellow Reformed Ch. in Am., 1955-56; instr. history and polit. sci. Wittenberg U., 1956-58; v.p. devel. Central Coll., Iowa, 1959-60; pres. Central Coll., 1960-69, Grand Valley State U., Allendale, Mich., 1969—; mem. Am. Assn. State Colls. and Univs. seminar in India, 1971, Fed. Commn. Orgn. Govt. for Conduct Fgn. Policy, 1972; USIA insp., Netherlands, 1976; mem. pres.'s commn. NCAA, 1984-87, 89—, pres. com., 1989-95; bd. dirs. Grand Bank, Grand Rapids, Mich. Student community amb. from Holland, Mich. to Yugoslavia, 1951; bd. dirs. Grand Rapids Symphony, 1976-82; bd. dirs. Butterworth Hosp., 1988. Recipient Golden Plate award San Diego Acad. Achievement, 1962, Golden-Emblem Order of Merit Polish Peoples Republic, 1988; named 1 of top 100 young men in U.S. Life mag., 1962. Mem. Mich. Coun. State Univs. Pres. (chmn. 1988), Grand Rapids World Affairs Council (pres. 1971-73), Phi Alpha Theta, Pi Kappa Delta, Pi Kappa Phi. Home: 801 Plymouth Ave SE Grand Rapids MI 49506-6555 Office: Grand Valley State U Coll Landing 1 Campus Dr Allendale MI 49401-9401

LUBECK, MARVIN JAY, ophthalmologist; b. Cleve., Mar. 20, 1929; s. Charles D. and Lillian (Jay) L. A.B., U. Mich., 1951, M.D., 1955, M.S., 1959. Diplomate Am. Bd. Opthamology; m. Arlene Sue Bitman, Dec. 28, 1955; children: David Mark, Daniel Jay, Robert Charles. Intern, U. Mich. Med. Ctr., 1955-56, resident ophthalmology, 1956-58, jr. clin. instr. ophthalmology, 1958-59; pvt. practice medicine, specializing in ophthalmology, Denver, 1961—; mem. staff Rose Hosp., Porter Hosp., Presbyn. Hosp., St. Luke's Hosp.; assoc. clin. prof. U. Colo. Med. Ctr.; cons. ophthalmologist State of Colo. With U.S. Army, 1959-61. Fellow ACS; mem. Am. Acad. Ophthalmology, Denver Med. Soc., Colo. Ophthalmol. Soc., Am. Soc. Cataract & Refractive Surgery. Home: 590 S Harrison Ln Denver CO 80209-3517 Office: 3600 E Alameda Ave Denver CO 80209-3803

LUBELL, HAROLD, economic consultant; b. N.Y.C., Mar. 29, 1925; s. Morris and Fannie (Bell) L.; m. Claudie Marchaut, 1962; children: Martin, Diane. BA, Bard Coll., 1944; MPA, Harvard U., 1947, MA in Econs., 1948, PhD in Econs., 1953. Economist Fed. Res. Bd., Washington, 1944-45, ECA/MSA, Paris, 1949-53; Economist AID, Ankara, Turkey, 1965-68, New Delhi, 1969-71, Washington, 1978-82, Cairo, 1982-85, Dakar, 1985-89; economist Falk Project for Econ. Research, Jerusalem, 1954-57, Rand Corp., Santa Monica, Calif., 1957-62; with Ford Found., Saigon, Vietnam, Kuala Lumpur, Malaysia, 1963-64; economist World Employment Program, ILO, Geneva, 1971-78; econ. cons. 1989—. Author: Middle East Oil Crises and Western Europe's Energy Supplies, 1963, Urban Development and Employment: the Prospects for Calcutta, 1974, The Informal Sector in the 1980s and the 1990s, 1990. Office: 25 Rue de Lille, Paris 75007, France

LUBER, AMANDA KIMMER, public relations executive, marketing professional; b. Aliquippa, Pa., June 21, 1961; d. William Cephus Jr. and Joan Elizabeth (Phillips) Kimmer; m. Jay Lance Luber, Dec. 10, 1988; 1 child, Matthew William. BA in Pub. Rels., Journalism, Econs., Fla. So. Coll., 1983. Cert. pub. rels. profl. Asst. dir. Ctrl. Fla. Health Fair, Orlando, 1983-84; prodn. editor Harcourt Brace Pub., Orlando, 1984-86; features writer The Independent, Winter Haven, Fla., 1986; pub. rels. dir. Palmview Hosp., Lakeland, Fla., 1986-87, Fantastic Sam's Regional Office, Tampa, Fla., 1987-90; mktg. supr. Manatee Community Blood Ctr., Bradenton, Fla., 1991-94; freelance writer, graphic artist Luber Comms. and Design, Riverview, Fla., 1993—; pub. affairs dir. ARC, Tampa Bay chpt., 1995—, state lead for pub. affairs, Fla., 1995—. Founder Reneé Turbeville Meml. Scholarship, Fla. So. Coll., Lakeland, 1984. Mem. Fla. Pub. Rels. Assn. (bd. dirs. 1993-94, newsletter editor 1993-94, Most Improved Chpt. Newsletter state award 1994, PR Profl. of Yr. 1994, Judges award 1993, Award of Distinction 1992). Democrat. Roman Catholic. Avocations: collecting Disney memorabilia, tennis, reading, music. Home: 10408 Deepbrook Dr Riverview FL 33569 Office: ARC Tampa Bay Chpt Pub Affairs PO Box 4236 Tampa FL 33677

LUBER, THOMAS J(ULIAN), lawyer; b. Louisville, Feb. 16, 1949; s. John J. and Martha E. (Cotton) L.; m. Dorothy Ann Carter, Dec. 19, 1975; children: Katharine Ann, Allison Julia. BS in Acctg., U. Louisville, 1972, JD with honors, 1976; LLM in Taxation, NYU, 1977. Bar: Ky. 1976. Agt. IRS, Louisville, 1972-73; assoc. Fahey & Gray, Louisville, 1977-79; from assoc. to ptnr. Wyatt, Tarrant & Combs and predecessor firms, Louisville, 1979—, chmn. tax sect., 1983—; lectr. U. Louisville, 1978-80; speaker in field; bd. advisors Jour. Multistate Taxation. Contbr. articles to profl. jours. Bd. dirs. Univ. Pediatrics Found., Louisville, Univ. Ob-gyn. Found., Louisville, Assumption High Sch., Louisville. With USAF, 1967-69. Mem. ABA, Ky. Bar Assn. (chmn. tax sect. 1983-84), Louisville Bar Assn., Ky. Inst. Fed. Taxation (mem. planning com. 1981—, chmn. 1984—), Jefferson Club, Big Spring Country Club. Democrat. Roman Catholic. Avocations: tennis, bicycling. Home: 2324 Saratoga Dr Louisville KY 40205-2021 Office: Wyatt Tarrant & Combs 2800 Citizens Plz Louisville KY 40202-2898

LUBERDA, GEORGE JOSEPH, lawyer, educator; b. N.Y.C., Apr. 27, 1930; s. Joseph George and Mary Loretta (Koslowski) L.; m. Beverly Louis Carey, Feb. 13, 1954; children: Margaret, Joseph, Eileen, Ann Marie, Julie. Bar: D.C. 1959, U.S. Ct. Appeals (D.C. cir.) 1959, Mich. 1970, Mo. 1973. Washington rep. Ford Motor Co., Washington, 1955-59; atty. FTC, Washington, 1960-64; trial atty. Antitrust Div. Dept. Justice, Washington, 1965-69; sr. atty. Bendix Corp., Mich., 1970-71; assoc. Butzel, Long, Gust, Klein & Van Zile, Detroit, 1972; antitrust counsel Monsanto Co., St. Louis, 1973-88; assoc. Herzog, Crebs and McGhee, 1988-93; ptnr. Luberda & Carp, St. Louis, 1993—; adj. prof. St. Louis U., 1985—. Mem. Mo. Bar Assn., Bar Assn. Met. St. Louis. Republican. Roman Catholic. Home: 716 Ridgeview Circle Ln Ballwin MO 63021-7810 Office: Luberda & Carp 225 S Meramec Ave Ste 325 Saint Louis MO 63105-3511

LUBETSKI, EDITH ESTHER, librarian; b. Bklyn., July 16, 1940; d. David and Leah (Aronson) Slomowitz; m. Meir Lubetski, Dec. 23, 1968; children: Shaul, Uriel, Leah. BA, Bklyn. Coll., 1962; MS in L.S., Columbia U., 1965; MA in Jewish Studies, Yeshiva U., 1968. Judaica librarian Stern Coll., N.Y.C., 1965-66, acquisitions librarian, 1966-69, head librarian, 1969—; Author: (with Meir Lubetski) Building a Judaica Library Collection, 1983; contbr. articles to profl. jours. Mem. ALA, Assn. Jewish Libraries (corr. sec. 1980-84, pres. N.Y. chpt. 1984-86, nat. v.p. 1984-86, nat. pres. 1986-88, Fanny Goldstein Merit award 1993), N.Y. Library Assn. Home: 1219 E 27th St Brooklyn NY 11210-4622 Office: Yeshiva U Hedi Steinberg Libr 245 Lexington Ave New York NY 10016-4605

LUBIC, RUTH WATSON, association executive, nurse midwife; b. Bucks County, Pa., Jan. 18, 1927; d. John Russell and Lillian (Kraft) Watson; m. William James Lubic, May 28, 1955; 1 son, Douglas Watson. Diploma, Sch. Nursing Hosp. U. Pa., 1955; BS, Columbia U., 1959, MA, 1961, EdD in Applied Anthropology, 1979; Cert. in Nurse Midwifery, SUNY, Bklyn., 1962; LLD (hon.), U. Pa., 1985; DSc (hon.), U. Medicine and Dentistry, N.J., 1986; LHD (hon.), Coll. New Rochelle, 1992; DSc (hon.), SUNY, Bklyn., 1993; LHD (hon.), Pace U., 1994. RN, Pa. Mem. faculty Sch. Nursing, N.Y. Med. Coll.; mem. faculty Maternity Ctr. Assn., SUNY Sch. Nurse-Midwifery, Downstate Med. Ctr.; staff nurse through head nurse Meml. Hosp. for Cancer and Allied Disease, N.Y.C., 1955-58; clin. assoc. Grad. Sch. Nursing N.Y. Med. Coll., N.Y.C., 1962-63; parent educator, cons. Maternity Ctr. Assn., N.Y.C., 1963-67, gen. dir., 1970-95; dir. clin. projects., 1995—; cons. in midwifery, nursing and maternal and child health Office of Pub. Health and Sci. HHS, 1995—; adj. prof. divsn. nursing, NYU, 1995—; bd. dirs., v.p. Am. Assn. for World Health U.S. Com. for WHO, 1975-94, pres. 1980-81; mem. bd. maternal child and family health NRC, 1974-80; mem. Commn. on Grads. Fgn. Nursing Schs., 1979-83, v.p. 1980-91, treas., 1982-83; bd. govs. Frontier Nursing Svc., 1982-92; bd. dirs. Pan Am. Health Edn. Found., pres. 1987-88; vis. prof. King Edward Meml. Hosp., Perth, Australia, 1991; Kate Hanna Harvey vis. prof. cmty. health nursing Frances Payne Bolton Sch. Nursing Case Western Res., 1991; Lansdowne lectr. U. Victoria, B.C., Can., 1992. Author: (with Gene Hawes) Childbearing: A Book of Choices, 1987; contbr. articles to profl. jours. Recipient Letitia White award, Florence Nightingale medal, 1955, Rockefeller Pub. Svc. award, 1981, Hattie Hemschemeyer award, 1983, Alumnae award Sch. Nursing U. Pa., 1986, Tchrs. Coll. Columbia U., 1992, Disting. Svc. award Francis Payne Bolton Sch. Nursing, 1993, MacArthur Fellowship award, 1993, Hon. Recognition N.Y. State Nurses Assn., 1993, Nurse-Midwifery Faculty award Columbia U., 1993, Spirit of Nursing award Vis. Nurses Svc. N.Y., 1994, Maes-MacInnes award Divsn. Nursing NYU, 1994, Hon. recognition ANA, 1994; named Maternal-Child Health Nurse of Yr., ANA, 1985. Fellow AAAS, Am. Acad. Nursing, N.Y. Acad. Medicine, Soc. for Applied Anthropology, Am. Coll. of Nurse Midwives; mem. APHA (mem. com. on internat. health, sec. maternal and child health coun. 1982, mem. governing coun. 1986-89, mem. nominating com. 1987, mem. action bd. 1988-90), Am. Coll. Nurse-Midwives (v.p. 1964-66, pres.-elect 1969-70), Soc. Applied Anthropology, Inst. Medicine of NAS, Nat. Assn. Childbearing Ctrs. (pres. 1983-91), Herman Biggs Soc. (sec., treas. 1989-90), Cosmopolitan Club, Sigma Theta Tau. Office: 48 E 92nd St New York NY 10128-1316 *As a professional nurse-midwife and public health scientist, the guiding principles of my professional life are to listen carefully to the families to be served and to combine their needs with proven scientific knowledge in constructing models for care. It is my belief that the primary purpose of maternal and child health programs is to assist families to achieve a sense of self-confidence about their ability to bring forth and rear offspring in conjunction with, but not dependent upon, professional guidance.*

LUBICK, DONALD CYRIL, lawyer; b. Buffalo, Apr. 29, 1926; s. Louis and Minna D. (Nabith) L.; m. Susan F. Cohen, June 5, 1960; children:Jonathan, Caroline, Lisa. BA summa cum laude, U. Buffalo, 1945; JD magna cum laude, Harvard U., 1949. Bar: N.Y. 1950, Fla. 1974, D.C. 1981; lic. fgn. law cons. Ont., 1989. Teaching fellow Harvard U. Law Sch., 1949-50; lectr. law U. Buffalo, 1950-61; assoc., then ptnr. Hodgson, Russ, Andrews, Woods & Goodyear, Buffalo and Washington, 1950-61, 64-77, 81-94; tax legis. counsel Treasury Dept., Washington, 1961-64; asst. sec. for tax policy Treasury Dept., 1977-81; dir. tax adv. program for countries of Ctrl. and Ea. Europe and former Soviet Union Treasury Dept., Paris, 1994—. Author: (with Hussey) Basic World Tax Code and Commentary, 1992, 95. Chmn. Tax Revision Com., City of Buffalo, 1958; mem. adv. com. to select Com. on Election Reform, N.Y. State Legislature, 1974, mem. adv. group to commr. internal revenue, 1976. Served with USAAF, 1945-46. Harvard Internat. Tax Program sr. fellow, 1991—. Mem. ABA, Am. Law Inst., Am. Bar Found., N.Y. State Bar Assn., Fla. Bar Assn., Erie County Bar Assn. Democrat. Jewish. Office: Paris Embassy OECD PSC 116 TAP APO AE 09777

LUBICK, SONNY, college football coach; b. Mar. 12, 1937; m. Carol Jo Lubick; children: Matthew, Michelle, Mark. BS, Western Mont. Coll., 1960; MS in Phys. Edn., Mont. State U., 1978. Head football coach Tutte (Mont.) H.S., 1963-69; asst. football coach Mont. State U., Bozeman, 1970-77, head coach, 1977-81; asst. coach Stanford U., Palo Alto, Calif., 1985-88; defensive coord. U. Miami, Fla., 1989-92; offensive coord. Colo. State U., Ft. Collins, 1982-84, head football coach, 1992—. Named Football Coach of Yr., State of Mont., 1968, Western Athletic Conf., 1994, Sports Illustrated, 1994, Nat. Coach of Yr., 1995. Office: Colo State U Football Dept Fort Collins CO 80000

LUBIN, BERNARD, psychologist, educator; b. Washington, Oct. 15, 1923; s. Israel Harry and Anne (Cohen) L.; m. Alice Weisbord, Aug. 5, 1957. B.A., George Washington U., 1952, M.A., 1953; Ph.D., Pa. State U., 1958. Diplomate: Am. Bd. Profl. Psychology, Am. Bd. Psychol. Hypnosis; lic. psychologist, Mo., Tex. Intern St. Elizabeths Hosp., 1952-53, Roanoke (Va.) VA Hosp., 1954-55, Wilkes-Barre (Pa.) VA Hosp., 1955; USPHS postdoctoral fellow, postdoctoral residency in psychotherapy U. Wis. Sch. Medicine, 1957-58; staff psychologist, instr. dept. psychiatry Ind. U. Sch. Medicine, Indpls., 1958-59; chief psychologist adult outpatient service Ind. U. Sch. Medicine, 1960-62, assoc. prof., 1964-67; dir. psychol. services Dept. Mental Health, Indpls., 1962-63; dir. div. research and tng. Dept. Mental Health, 1963-67; dir. div. psychology Greater Kansas City (Mo.) Mental Health Center, 1967-74; prof. dept. psychiatry U. Mo. Sch. Medicine, Kansas City, 1967-74, 76—; prof., dir. clin. tng. program dept. psychology U. Houston, 1974-76; prof., chmn. dept. psychology U. Mo. at Kansas City, 1976-83, Curators' prof., 1988; trustees' faculty fellow, 1994; cons. Am. Nurses Assn., Panhandle Eastern Pipeline Co., Eli Lilly Pharm. Co., U.S. Sprint, Inst. Psychiat. Research, Ind. U. Med. Center, Ind. U. Sch. Dentistry, Goodwill Industries, USPHS Bur. Health Services, mental retardation div., (univ.-affiliated facilities br.), U.S. VA, Baylor U. Med. Sch., U. Tex. Health Scis. Center, Houston, 1974-76; Mem. tng. staff Nat. Tng. Labs. Inst.; dean or faculty mem. numerous confs., 1960—; exec. sec. Ind. Assn. for Advancement Mental Health Research and Edn., 1962-67. Author: (with M. Zuckerman) Multiple Affect Adjective Check List: Manual, 1965, 2d edit., 1985, (with E.E. Levitt) The Clinical Psychologist: Background, Roles and Functions, 1967, Depression: Concepts, Controversies, and Some New Facts, 1975, 2d edit., 1983, Depression Adjective Check Lists: Manual, 1967, rev. edit., 1994, (with L.D. Goodstein and A.W. Lubin) Organizational Development Sourcebooks I and II, 1979; (with W.A. O'Connor) Ecological Approaches to Clinical and Community Psychology, 1984, (with D.C. Martin and R.A. Blanc) Study Guide and Readings for Abnormal Psychology, 1984, (with Alice W. Lubin) Comprehensive Index to the Group Psychotherapy Literature: 1906-1980, 1987, (with A.W. Lubin) Family Therapy: A Bibliography, 1937-86, 1988, (with R. Gist) Psychosocial Aspects of Disaster, 1989 (with R.V. Whitlock) Homelessness in America: A Bibliography with Selective Annotations, 1894-1994, also articles; editorial bd. Jour. Community Psychology; mem. editorial bd. Internat. Jour. Group Psychotherapy, Profl. Psychology: Research and Practice; cons. reader, bd. dirs. Jour. Cons. and Clin. Psychology. pres. Midwest Group for Human Resources, Inc., 1965-69, trustee, 1965. Recipient N.T. Veatch award for disting. rsch. and creative activity, 1983; faculty fellow U. Kansas City, 1994. Mem. AAAS, Mo. Psychol. Assn. (exec. bd.), Am. Group Psychotherapy Assn. (edit. com.); mem. APA (fellow div. group psychology and group psychotherapy, chmn. sponsor approval com., exec. bd. dir. cons. psychology, coun. rep., Disting. Sr. Contbr. to Counseling Psychology award 1995), Midwestern Psychol. Assn., Ind. Psychol. Assn. (pres. 1967), World Fedn. for Mental Health, Conf. Psychologist Dirs. and cons. in State, Fed. and Territorial Mental Health Programs (editor conf. procs. 1966-68, Perspective 1966-68, mem. exec. com. 1966-69), Inter-Am. Congress Psychology, Cert. Cons. Internat. (charter), NTL Inst. (bd. dirs. 1986-92), Sigma Xi, Phi Kappa Phi, Psi Chi (v.p. for midwest, mem. nat. coun. 1986-90, pres.-elect 1991-92, pres. 1992-93, past pres. 1993-94). Office: U Mo Kansas City Dept Psychology 5307 Holmes St Kansas City MO 64110-2437

LUBIN, DONALD G., lawyer; b. N.Y.C., Jan. 10, 1934; s. Harry and Edith (Tannenbaum) L.; m. Amy Schwartz, Feb. 2, 1956; children: Peter, Richard, Thomas, Alice Lubin Spahr. BS in Econs., U. Pa., 1954; LLB, Harvard U., 1957. Bar: Ill. 1957. Ptnr., chmn. exec. com. Sonnenschein Nath & Rosenthal, Chgo., 1957—; bd. dirs., mem. exec. com. McDonald's Corp.; bd. dirs. Molex, Inc., Daubert Industries Inc., Charles Levy Co., Tennis Corp. Am., Arcade Holdings, Inc.; former v.p., dir. San Diego Nat. League Baseball Club, Inc.; former dir., mem. exec. com. First Nat. Bank of Highland Park; former mem. Spl. Commn. on Adminstrn. of Justice in Cook County, Chgo. Former mem. Navy Pier Redevel. Corp., Highland Park Cultural Arts Commn.; life trustee, former chmn. bd. Highland Park Hosp., Ravinia Festival Assn.; trustee, mem. exec. com. Rush-Presbyn.-St. Luke's Med. Ctr.; life trustee Orchestral Assn. Chgo.; bd. dirs., v.p. and sec. Ronald McDonald Children's Charities, Inc., Chgo. Found. for Edn., Smithsonian Inst., Washington; pres., bd. dir. The Barr Fund; former bd. dirs., v.p., sec. Ragdale Found.; bd. govs. Art Inst. Chgo., Chgo. Lighthouse for the Blind; mem. citizens bd. U. Chgo.; mem. coun. Children's Meml. Hosp.; former bd. overseers Coll. Arts and Sci., U. Pa. Woodrow Wilson vis. fellow. Fellow Am. Bar Found., Ill. Bar Found., Chgo. Bar Found.; mem. ABA, Ill. Bar Assn., Chgo. Bar Assn., Law Club Chgo., Chgo. Hort. Soc. (past bd. dirs.), Econ. Club, Comml. Club (sec., civic com.), Chgo. Club, Std. Club, Lakeshore Club, Beta Gamma Sigma. Home: 2269 Egandale Rd Highland Park IL 60035-2501 Office: Sonnenschein Nath & Rosenthal 233 S Wacker Dr Ste 8000 Chicago IL 60606-6404

LUBIN, MARTIN, cell physiologist educator; b. N.Y.C., Mar. 30, 1923; m. Dorothy Alpern, Sept. 5, 1942; children—Peter, Adam, Thomas, John Caleb. B.A., Harvard U., 1942, M.D., 1945; Ph.D. in Biophysics, MIT, 1954. Research assoc. biology MIT, 1953-54; assoc. pharmacology then asst. prof. pharmacology Harvard U. Med. Sch., 1957-68; prof. microbiology Dartmouth Med. Sch., 1968—. Served with AUS, 1946-48. USPHS fellow, 1949-51; Childs Meml. Fund med. research fellow, 1951-53; Guggenheim fellow and Commonwealth Fund fellow Lab. Molecular Biology, Cambridge, Eng., 1965-67. Home: 21 Lyme Rd Hanover NH 03755-1406

LUBIN, MARY LUELLA, nursing consultant; b. Glastonbury, Conn., Apr. 24, 1932; d. Robert Harley and Luella (Sampson) Kellogg; m. Michael D. Lubin, Sept. 10, 1955; children: Elizabeth Lubin Hughes, James Kellogg. BS, Simmons Coll., 1954; MA, Calif. State U., 1970. RN, Calif.; cert. gerontol. nurse. Pub. health nurse New Haven VNA and Sacramento Health Depts., 1954-56; lectr. pub. health. nursing Boston Coll., Chestnut Hill, Mass., 1965-67; rehab. nurse specialist Internat. Rehab. Assn., Atlanta, 1975-76; dir. staff devel. Nat. Health Enterprises, San Leandro, Calif., 1980-81; dir. nursing services Hillhaven Corp., Alameda, Calif., 1981-85, adminstr., 1985-87, dist. dir., 1987-89; dir. hosp.-based svcs. Guardian Health Group, Corte Madera, Calif., 1989-95; pvt. cons. San Leandro, 1995—; co-owner Yram Applications Software, San Leandro, 1982-91. Vol. leader United Way, Sacramento, 1976-80; nurse vol. USAF and ARC, Sacramento, 1958-64, Japan, 1970-72; bd. dirs. Support Svcs. for Srs. of Alameda County, Hayward, Calif., 1986-91. Fellow Am. Coll. Health Care Adminstrs. (cert.). Avocations: oriental art, antiques. Home and Office: 1235 View Dr San Leandro CA 94577-5334

LUBIN, MICHAEL FREDERICK, physician, educator; b. Phila., Mar. 20, 1947; s. Leonard and Ethel Sybil (Stern) L. BA, Johns Hopkins U., 1969, MD, 1973. Resident Emory U. Affiliated Hosp., Atlanta, 1973-76; asst. prof. medicine Emory U. Sch. Medicine, Atlanta, 1976-82, assoc. prof. medicine, 1982—, dir. div. gen. medicine, 1989-95; dir. preoperative clinic Grady Hosp., Atlanta, 1995—; chmn. housestaff evaluation com. Dept. medicine Emory U. Sch. Medicine; chmn. pharmacy and therapeutics com. Grady Hosp. Editor: Medical Management of the Surgical Patient, 1982, 3d rev. edit., 1995, Med. Rounds, 1988-90; mem. editl. bd. I-M: Internal Medicine, 1992-95; contbr. to Med. Knowledge Self Assessment Program X, 1994. Mem. alumni coun. Johns Hopkins U., 1995—. Hartford scholar in Geriatrics UCLA, 1984-85. Fellow ACP; mem. Am. Geriatrics Soc., Soc. Gen. Internal Medicine. Office: Emory U Sch Medicine 69 Butler St SE Atlanta GA 30303-3033

LUBIN, STEVEN, concert pianist, musicologist; b. N.Y.C., Feb. 22, 1942; s. Jack and Sophie (Auslander) L.; m. Wendy Lubin, June 2, 1974; children: Benjamin, Nathaniel. AB in Philosophy, Harvard U., 1963; MS in Piano, Juilliard Sch. Music, 1965; PhD in Musicology, NYU, 1974. Mem. faculty Juilliard Sch. Music, N.Y.C., 1964-65, Aspen (Colo.) Music Sch., 1965; Mem. faculty Vassar Coll., Poughkeepsie, N.Y., 1970-71; coordinator grad. music theory program Cornell U., Ithaca, N.Y., 1971-75; adj. prof. Sch. Arts, SUNY, Purchase, 1975—; founding mem. The Mozartean Players, 1978—. Mem., NYU Electronic Composers Workshop, 1967-68; concert pianist tours in U.S. and Europe, 1976—; appeared as fortepiano soloist and condr. in Authentic-Instrument concert series, N.Y.C., 1981—; rec. artist Decca, Arabesque Records, Harmonia Mundi; filmed solo performances for Brit. documentary TV in London and Vienna, 1986; soloist in complete Beethoven piano concertos for London/Decca Records, 1987; performed complete cycle Beethoven concertos, London, 1987; solo recordings (new series) Decca including Beethoven Sonatas, 1991; contbr. articles to N.Y. Times, Keyboard Classics, others. Martha Baird Rockefeller grantee, 1968. Mem. Am. Mus. Soc., Soc. Music Theory.

LUBINSKY, MENACHEM YECHIEL, communications executive; b. Hanover, Germany, Apr. 13, 1949; arrived in country 1950; s. Chaim P. and Pesa (Lubinsky) L.; m. Hindy Deborah Fink, Jan. 14, 1973; children: Tziporah, Meiri, Tzviya. BBA, CUNY, 1975, MBA, 1982. Asst. to pres. Agudath Israel of Am., N.Y.C., 1971-72; dir. Boro Park Sr. Citizens Ctr., Bklyn., 1973-74, Project COPE, N.Y.C., 1975-80; dir. gov., pub. affairs Agudath Israel of Am., N.Y.C., 1981-84; pres. Lubinsky, Schild Assocs., N.Y.C., 1985-86, Lubicom, 1987-90, Integrated Mktg. & Comm. Inc., N.Y.C., 1990—; v.p. Agudath Israel of Am., Inc.; pres. Integrated Mktg. and Comm. Author: Op-Ed-Page, New York Times, 1984, Struggle and Splendor. Bd. dirs. Ohel Children's Home, Jewish Com. Rels. Coun., 1986; pres. Met. N.Y. Coordinating Coun. on Jewish Poverty; v.p. Agudath Israel of Am.; mem. domestic affairs com. United Jewish Appeal, 1992—; mem. Pvt. Industry Coun. City of N.Y. Mem. Pub. Relations Soc. Am., League of Advt. Avocation: tennis.

LUBKIN, GLORIA BECKER, physicist; b. Phila., May 16, 1933; d. Samuel Albert and Anne (Gorrin) B.; m. Yale Jay Lubkin, June 14, 1953 (div. Apr. 1968); children: David Craig, Sharon Rebecca. AB, Temple U., 1953; MA, Boston U., 1957; postgrad., Harvard U., 1974-75. Mathematician Fairchild Stratos Co., Hagerstown, Md., 1954, Letterkenny Ordnance Depot,

Chambersburg, Pa., 1955-56; physicist TRG Inc., N.Y.C., 1956-58; acting chmn. dept. physics Sarah Lawrence Coll., Bronxville, N.Y., 1961-62; v.p. Lubkin Assocs., electronic cons., Port Washington, N.Y., 1962-68; assoc. editor Physics Today Am. Inst. Physics, N.Y.C., 1963-69; sr. editor Physics Today Am. Inst. Physics, 1970-84, editor, 1985-94, editl. dir., 1994—; cons. in field; mem. Nieman adv. com. Harvard U., 1978-82; co-chmn. search/adv. com. Theoretical Physics Inst., U. Minn., 1987-89, co-chmn. oversight com. 1989—; mem. mng. com. Westinghouse Sci. Writing Prizes, 1988-91; mem. selection com. Knight Fellowships, 1990. Contbr. articles to profl. publs. Gloria Becker Lubkin Professorship of Theoretical Physics established in her honor U. Minn., 1990; Nieman fellow, 1974-75. Fellow AAAS (mem. nominating com. for sect. B phusics 1987-89, chair 1989), Am. Phys. Soc. (exec. com. history of physics divsn. 1983-86, 92-95, exec. com. forum on physics and soc. 1977-78); mem. N.Y. Acad. Scis. (chair The Scis. pub. com. 1992-93), Nat. assn. Sci. Writers, D.C. Science Writers Assn., Sigma Pi Sigma. Jewish. Office: Am Inst Physics One Physics Ellipse College Park MD 20740

LUBKIN, VIRGINIA LEILA, ophthalmologist; b. N.Y.C., Oct. 26, 1914; d. Joseph and Anna Fredericka (Stern) L.; m. Arnold Malkan, June 6, 1944 (div. 1949); m. Martin Bernstein, Aug. 28, 1949; children: Ellen Henrietta, James Ernst, Roger Joel, John Conrad. BS summa cum laude, NYU, 1933; MD, Columbia U., 1937. Diplomate Am. Bd. Ophthalmology. Intern Harlem Hosp., N.Y.C., 1938-40; asst. resident neurology Montefiore Hosp., N.Y.C., 1940, asst. resident pathology, 1940-41, fellow in ophthalmology, 1941-42; resident ophthalmology Kings County Hosp., Bklyn., 1942-43, Mt. Sinai Hosp., N.Y.C., 1943-44; attending ophthalmologist, assoc. clin. prof. emeritus Mt. Sinai Sch. Medicine, 1944—; also sr. attending surgeon N.Y. Eye and Ear Infirmary, Mt. Sinai Sch. Medicine; pvt. practice N.Y.C., 1945-90; surgeon, now sr. surgeon N.Y. Eye and Ear Infirmary, 1945—; rsch. prof. N.Y. Med. Coll., 1986—; co-creator, now chief of rsch. bioengineering lab. N.Y. Eye and Ear Infirmary (name now The Aborn), N.Y.C., 1978—; creator first grad. course in oculoplastics and bi-yearly symposia in devel. dyslexia Mt. Sinai Sch. Medicine; educator courses in psychosomatic ophthalmology Am. Acad. Ophthalmology, 1950-60, educator course in complications of blepharoplasty, 1980-90; bd. dirs. Jewish Guild for the Blind; tchr. surg. opthalmology in French Cameroon, Presbyn. Mission, 1951; lectr. in numerous countries including India, 1976, 92, Pakistan, 1976, 84, China, 1978, Sri Lanka, 1979, South Africa, 1982, Singapore, 1984, Thailand, 1984, Argentina, 1986, Peru, 1987. Author: (with others) Ophthalmic Plastic and Reconstructive Surgery, 1989; contbr. articles to profl. jours. Bd. dirs. Ctr. fo Environ. Therapeutics, 1995. Grantee Intraocular Lens Implant Mfrs., 1989. Fellow AMA, AAAS, Am. Soc. Ophthalmic Plastic and Reconstructive Surgery (founding), Am. Coll. Surgeons, N.Y. Acad. Medicine, N.Y. Acad. Scis., Am. Acad. Ophthalmology, Am. Soc. Cataract and Refractive Surgery, PanAm. Soc. Ophthalmology, N.Y. Soc. Clin. Ophthalmology, Soc. Light Treatment and Biol. Rhythms, Phi Beta Kappa, Alpha Omega Alpha. Home: 1 Blackstone Pl Bronx NY 10471-3607 Office: NY Eye and Ear Infirmary Apt 2C Residence Bldg 310 E 14th St New York NY 10003-4200

LUBLINSKI, MICHAEL, lawyer; b. Eskilstuna, Sweden, Sept. 11, 1951; came to U.S., 1956; s. Walter and Dora L. BA magna cum laude, CCNY, 1972; JD, Georgetown U., 1975. Bar: N.Y. 1976, Calif. 1980, Ct. Internat. Trade 1981, U.S. Dist. Ct. (cen. dist.) Calif. 1981, U.S. Dist. Ct. (so. dist.) N.Y. 1981, U.S. Ct. Appeals (D.C. cir.) 1982. Atty. U.S. Customs Service, Washington, 1975-79, U.S. Dept. Commerce, Washington, 1980; assoc. Mori & Ota, Los Angeles, 1980-84; assoc. Kelley Drye & Warren, Los Angeles, 1984-85, ptnr., 1986—. Panel moderator Calif. continuing edn. of bar Competitive Bus. Practices Inst., Los Angeles and San Francisco, 1984. Mem. ABA, Calif. Bar Assn., Los Angeles County Bar Assn. (arbitrator 1981-82, chmn. customs law sect. 1986). Avocations: travel, photography, movies. Home: 2609 Creston Dr Los Angeles CA 90068-2207 Office: Kelley Drye & Warren 515 S Flower St Los Angeles CA 90071-2201

LUBORSKY, FRED EVERETT, research physicist; b. Phila., May 14, 1923; s. Meyer and Cecelia (Miller) L.; m. Florence R. Glass, Aug. 25, 1946; children—Judith, Mark, Rhoda. B.S., U. Pa., 1947; Ph.D., Ill. Inst. Tech., 1952. Teaching-research asst. Ill. Inst. Tech., Chgo., 1947-51; research assoc. Gen. Elec. Co., Schnectady, 1951-52, West Lynn, Mass., 1952-58; research physicist Gen. Elec. Co., Schenectady, 1958-92; gen. chmn. 2d Joint Internat. Magnetism and Magnetic Materials Conf., 1979; chmn. adv. com. Conf. on Magnetism and Magnetic Materials, 1980. Editor: Amorphous Metallic Alloys, 1984; mem. editorial bd. Internat. Jour. Rapid Solidification, 1984—; mem. editorial adv. bd. Internat. Jour. Magnetism, 1972—; contbr. articles to profl. jours.; patentee in field. Served with USN, 1944-46. Recipient citation achievement in indsl. sci. AAAS, 1956; Brit. Sci. Research Council fellow, 1977; Coolidge fellow in research and devel. Gen. Elec. Corp., 1978. Fellow IEEE (editorial bd. Transactions on Magnetics jour. 1968—, editor-in-chief 1972-75, editorial bd. Spectrum jour. 1972-73, Centennial medal 1984, mem. Fellows com. 1993—), Am. Inst. Chemists, N.Y. Acad. Scis.; mem. Nat. Acad. Engring., Magnetics Soc. of IEEE (pres. 1975-77, named disting. lectr. 1979, achievement award 1981), Am. Chem. Soc., Materials Research Soc. Home: 1162 Lowell Rd Schenectady NY 12308-2512

LUBOVITCH, LAR, dancer, choreographer; b. Chgo.. Student, Art Inst. Chgo., U. Iowa, Juilliard Sch. Music, Am. Ballet Theatre Sch., Martha Graham, Anthony Tudor. Debut with Pearl Lang Dance Co., 1962; danced with modern cos. Glen Tetley, John Butler, Sophie Maslow and Donald McKayle; also with Manhattan Festival Ballet, Santa Fe Opera and Harkness Ballet; formed Lar Lubovitch Dance Co., 1968, choreographer, 1968—, guest choreographer, Bat-Dor Dance Co., Gulbenkian Ballet, Dutch Nat. Ballet, Ballet Rambert, Pa. Ballet, Am. Ballet Theatre, Royal Danish Ballet, Bejart Ballet XX Century, Alvin Ailey Am. Dance Theater, John Curry Ice Dancing Co., Les Grandes Ballets Canadiens, Stuttgart Ballet, N.Y.C. Ballet, Pacific N.W. Ballet, Paris Opera Ballet, White Oak Dance Project; ballets choreographed include Blue, 1968, Freddie's Bag, 1968, Journey Back, 1968, Greeting Sampler, 1969, Whirligogs, 1969, Unremembered Time-Forgotten Place, 1969, Variations and Theme, 1970, Ecstasy, 1970, Sam Nearlydeadman, 1970, The Teaching, 1970, Some of the Reactions,1970, The Time Before, 1971, Clear Lake, 1971, Air, 1972, Joy of Man's Desiring, 1972, Chariot Light Night, 1973, Scherzo for Massah Jack, 1973, Three Essays, 1974, Zig Zag, 1974, Avalanche, 1975, Rapid Transit, 1975, Session, 1975, Eight Easy Pieces, 1975, Girl on Fire, 1975, Marimba, 1976, Les Noces, 1976, Scriabin Dances, 1977, Exultate Jubilate, 1977, North Star, 1978, Valley, 1978, Tiltawhirl, 1979, Up Jump, 1979, Mistral, 1980, Cavalcade, 1980, American Gesture, 1981, Beau Danube, 1981, Big Shoulders, 1983, Tabernacle, 1983, Adagio and Rondo, 1984, A Brahms Symphony, 1985, Concerto Six Twenty-Two, 1986, Blood, 1986, Of My Soul, 1987, Musette, 1988, Rhapsody in Blue, 1988, Fandango, 1989, Just Before Jupiter, 1990, Hautbois, 1990, Sinfonia Concertante, 1991, Waiting for the Sunrise, 1991, American Gesture, 1992, So In Love, 1994, others; choreographer Sleeping Beauty (WGBH-TV), 1987, Into the Woods (Broadway), 1987, Salome, (Broadway), 1992, The Red Shoes (Broadway), 1993, The Planets (A&E-TV). Guggenheim fellow; CAPS grantee, NEA grantee; nominee Tony award, 1988, Astaire award, 1993-94. Address: care Lubovitch Dance Co 625 Broadway Ste 11-H New York NY 10012

LUBY, THOMAS STEWART, lawyer; b. Meriden, Conn., Jan. 12, 1952; s. Robert M. and Ruth (McGee) L.; m. Paula P. Falcigno, July 19, 1985; children: Elizabeth, Caroline, Katherine. BA, Yale U., 1974; JD, U. Conn., 1977. Bar: Conn., U.S. Dist. Ct. Conn., U.S. Ct. Appeals (2d cir.) Law clk. to Hon. T. F. Gilroy Daly U.S. Dist. Ct., Bridgeport, Conn., 1977-78; asst. U.S. atty. New Haven, Conn., 1978-81; ptnr. Luby, Olson, Mango & Gaffney, Meriden, 1981—; mem. grievance com. U.S. Dist. Ct. Conn., 1985-90, chmn., 1990-91; mem. U.S. Magistrate SelectionCom., 1996. Rep. Conn. Gen. Assembly, 1987-92, house majority leader, 1993-94; co-chair Conn. Task Force on Groundwater Strategy, 1987-89, chmn. commerce com., 1991-92. Recipient Spl. Achievement award U.S. Dept. Justice, 1980, Outstanding Pub. Service award United Way, 1986; named Legis. Leader of Yr., Greater Hartford C. of C., 1990, Person of Yr., Gov.'s Tourism Council, 1991. Mem. Conn. Bar Assn. Democrat. Roman Catholic. Home: 32 Westfield Rd Meriden CT 06450-2426

LUCANDER, HENRY, investment banker; b. Helsingfors, Finland, Dec. 21, 1940; came to U.S., 1965, naturalized, 1974; student Gronesche Handelsschule, Hamburg, W.Ger., 1961-62, Pontificia Universidade Católica, Rio de Janeiro, 1963-64; diploma Brazilian Coffee Inst., Rio de Janeiro, 1965; M.B.A., Columbia U., 1968; m. Karen-Jean Olson, Aug. 22, 1981. With Schenkers Internat. Forwarders, Inc., N.Y.C., 1965-66; coffee merchandizer Anderson Clayton & Co., Inc., N.Y.C., 1966-68; with Smith Barney & Co., Inc., N.Y.C., 1968-69, Kidder Peabody & Co., Inc., N.Y.C., 1969-70; with Lucander & Co., Inc., investment bankers, N.Y.C., 1970—, pres., 1972—. Served to lt. Finnish Army, 1960-61. Home: 333 Pearl St New York NY 10038-1609

LUCAS, ALEXANDER RALPH, child psychiatrist, educator; b. Vienna, Austria, July 30, 1931; came to U.S., 1940, naturalized, 1945; s. Eugene Hans and Margaret Ann (Weiss) L.; m. Margaret Alice Thompson, July 6, 1956; children: Thomas Alexander, Nancy Elizabeth Watson, Alexander Eugene, Peter Clayton. B.S., Mich. State U., 1953; M.D., U. Mich., 1957. Diplomate Am. Bd. Psychiatry and Neurology. Intern U. Mich. Hosp., 1957-58; resident in child psychiatry Hawthorn Ctr., Northville, Mich., 1958-59, 61-62, staff psychiatrist, 1963-65, sr. psychiatrist, 1965-67; resident in psychiatry Lafayette Clinic, Detroit, 1959-61, rsch. child psychiatrist, 1967-71, rsch. coord., 1969-71; asst. prof. psychiatry Wayne State U., 1967-69, assoc. prof., 1969-71; cons. child and adolescent psychiatry Mayo Clinic, 1971—; assoc. prof. Mayo Med Sch., 1973-76, prof., 1976—; head sect. child and adolescent psychiatry Mayo Clinic, Rochester, Minn., 1971-80. Author: (with C. R. Shaw) The Psychiatric Disorders of Childhood, 1970. Fellow Am. Acad. Child and Adolescent Psychiatry (editl. bd. jour. 1976-82), Am. Orthopsychiat. Assn. (life), Am. Psychiat. Assn. (life); mem. Minn. Soc. Child and Adolescent Psychiatry (pres. 1993-95), Soc. Biol. Psychiatry, Soc. Profs. Child and Adolescent Psychiatry, Sigma Xi. Research in biol. aspects of child psychiatry, psychopathology, psychopharmacology, eating disorders, psychiat. treatment of children, adolescents, and young adults. Office: Mayo Clinic 200 1st St SW Rochester MN 55905-0001

LUCAS, AUBREY KEITH, university president; b. State Line, Miss., July 12, 1934; s. Keith Caldwell and Audelle Margaret (Robertson) L.; m. Ella Frances Ginn, Dec. 18, 1955; children: Margaret Frances, Keith Godbold (dec.), Martha Carol, Alan Douglas, Mark Christopher. BS, U. So. Miss., 1955, MA, 1956; PhD, Fla. State U., 1966. Instr. Hinds Jr. Coll., Raymond, Miss., 1956-57; pres. Delta State U., Cleveland, Miss., 1971-75; asst. dir. reading clinic U. So. Miss., Hattiesburg, 1955-56, dir. admissions, 1957-61, registrar, 1963-69, dean Grad. Sch., 1969-71, pres., 1975—. Author: The Mississippi Legislature and Mississippi Public Higher Education, 1890-1960; contbg. author: A History of Mississippi, 1973. Bd. dirs. Pine Burr Area coun. Boy Scouts Am., Miss. Inst. Tech. Devel., Miss. Power Co., Miss. Assn. Coll., 1979-80, Miss. Arts Commn., 1977-87, Salvation Army, Pine Burr; mem. gen. bd. Global Ministries, United Meth. Ch., 1984-92, mem. gen. bd. higher edn. and ministry, 1992—; chmn. Miss. Arts Commn., 1983-85; campaign chmn. Forest United Way, 1979, So. U. Conf., 1995—; state chmn. Am. Cancer Soc., 1978; mem. Commn. on Nat. Devel. Postsecondary Edn., 97th Congress; pres. Miss. Econ. Coun., 1982-83; lay leader Miss. Meth. Conf., 1980-88, mem. adminstrv. bd., 1989-92; bd. visitors Air U., 1990-94, chmn., 1991-92; mem. exec. bd. Commn. on Colls. of So. Assn. Colls. and Schs., 1990-93. Mem. So. Assn. Colls. and Schs. (mem. exec. bd. commn. on colls. 1990-93, v.p. commn. on colls. 1993, mem. exec. coun.), Hattiesburg C. of C., Miss. Forestry Assn., Newcomen Soc. N.Am., Am. Assn. State Colls. and Univs. (bd. dirs. 1982-86, chmn. 1984-85), Am. Coun. Edn. (bd. dirs. 1984-86), Miss. Inst. Arts and Letters, Red Red Rose Club, Sigma Phi Epsilon, Omicron Delta Kappa, Phi Kappa Phi, Pi Gamma Mu, Pi Tau Chi, Kappa Delta Pi, Phi Delta Kappa, Kappa Pi. Home: 3701 Jamestown Rd Hattiesburg MS 39402-2336 Office: U So Miss PO Box 5001 Hattiesburg MS 39406-5001

LUCAS, BETH ANNE, television producer; b. Grand Rapids, Mich., Sept. 15, 1960; d. Gordon Patrick and Phyllis (Sablack) Galka; m. Mark Fordham, Mar. 19, 1982 (div. 1985); m. Gus Lucas, June 3, 1991. BA in Psychology, Antioch U., 1995. Segment producer Breakaway, Metromedia TV, Hollywood, Calif., 1983; asst. dir. Anything for Money, Paramount TV, Hollywood, 1984; post prodn. supr. Heathcliff DIC, Hollywood, 1984; post prodn. supr. Beauty and the Beast, Witt-Thomas Prodns., Hollywood, 1986-88; assoc. producer Anything But Love, 20th Century Fox, Hollywood, 1989; assoc. producer Easy Street Viacom Prodns., Hollywood, 1984-85; mgr. post prodn. Matlock, Perry Mason, Father Dowling, Jack and the Fatman, Hollywood, 1990-91; project coord. Teen Dating Violence Prevention Team, Haven Hills, Inc. Vol. Children Are Our Future, Haven Hills Battered Woman's Shelter; mem. AIDS Project, L.A. Mission, Children Def. Fund. Mem. APA, NOW, Amnesty Internat., Am. Profl. Soc. on the Abuse of Children, Calif. Profl. Soc. on the Abuse of Children, Nature Conservancy, Nat. Parks and Conservation Assn., Feminist Majority, Nat. Abortion Rights Action League, Greenpeace, Smithsonian Assocs., Mus. Contemporary Art, Los Angeles County Mus., Sta. KCET, UCLA Alumni Assn., Child Help USA, Childreach, Mus. of Tolerance. Avocations: world travel, skiing, writing, wine tasting, cooking.

LUCAS, C. PAYNE, development organization executive; b. Spring Hope, N.C., Sept. 14, 1933; s. James Russell and Minnie (Hendricks) L; m. Freddie Emily Myra Hill, Aug. 29, 1964; children: Therese Raymonde, C. Payne Jr., Hillary Hendricks. BA in History, U. Md.; LLD (hon.), U. Md., 1975; MA in Govt., Am. U. Asst. dir. Peace Corps, Togo, 1964; dir. Peace Corps, Niger, 1965-67; dir. Africa region Peace Corps, 1967-71; pres. Africare, Washington, 1971—; lectr. in field. Author: (with Kevin Lowther) Keeping Kennedy's Promise--The Peace Corps: Unmet Promise of the New Frontier, 1978; contbr. articles to profl. publs. Bd. dirs. Coun. Fgn. Rels., Overseas Devel. Coun. World Resources Inst., InterAction, Population Action Internat., Kagiso Trust USA, Nat. Planning Assn.; bd. dirs., chmn. Reach & Teach USA; bd. dirs., founding mem. Corp. Coun. on Africa. Recipient Disting. Fed. Svc. award Pres. Lyndon B. Johnson, Presdl. Hunger award for Outstanding Achievement, Pres. Ronald Reagan, 1984, Aggrey medal Phelps-Stokes Fund, 1986, Order of Disting. Svc. award Pres. Kenneth Kaunda of Zambia, 1986, Recognition awards Nat. Order of Rep. Niger, 1988, Zambia, Cote D'Iroire, Senegal, Benin, Disting. Bicentennial award Land Grant Coll., 1990, Hubert H. Humphrey Pub. Svc. award APSA, 1991. Mem. Cosmos Club, Omega Psi Phi. Office: Africare 440 R St NW Washington DC 20001-1918

LUCAS, CAROL LEE, biomedical engineer; b. Aberdeen, S.D., Feb. 13, 1940; d. Howard Cleveland and Sarah Ivy (Easterby) Nogle; B.A., Dakota Wesleyan U., 1961; M.S., U. Ariz., 1967; Ph.D., U. N.C., 1973; m. Richard Albert Lucas, Feb. 26, 1961; children—Wendy Lee, Sean Richard. Tchr. Spanish, Mitchell (S.D.) High Sch., 1960-61; tchr. math, English, sci. U.S. Army, Furth, Ger., 1961-62; systems analyst Cargill Inc., Mpls., 1962-65; research assoc. U. N.C., Chapel Hill, 1973-76, lectr., 1976-77, asst. prof. curriculum in biomed. engring. and math, 1977-84, assoc. prof. dept. surgery, 1984-89, prof. dept. surgery, 1989—, acting chmn. curriculum biomed. engring. and math., 1990-92, chmn. biomed. engring., 1992—; NIH trainee, 1968-73. Mem. IEEE, Am. Heart Assn., N.C. Heart Assn., Biomed. Engring. Soc., Cardiovascular System Dynamics Soc., Am. Inst. Biol. and Med. Engrs. Democrat. Methodist. Contbr. articles to profl. jours. Home: 2421 Sedgefield Dr Chapel Hill NC 27514-6810 Office: U NC Sch Medicine Dept Biomed Engring 152 Macnider Hall Chapel Hill NC 27599-7575

LUCAS, CHRISTOPHER, artist; b. Durham, N.C., Nov. 13, 1958; s. M.S.P. and Marie (Mendal) L. Student, Yale Summer Sch. Music and Art, 1979; BA, U. Kans., 1980. Tchr. extended day program kindergarten N.Y. St. Grade Sch., Lawrence, Kans., 1981-83; vis. artist lectr. Carnegie-Mellon, Pitts., 1985, 87; tchr. Nat. Mus. Contemporary Art, Kwachon-Si, Republic of Korea, 1990-91. One-man shows include Jack Tilton Gallery, N.Y.C., 1984, John Good Gallery, N.Y.C., 1986-87, 89, 92, Paolo Baldacci Gallery, N.Y.C., 1995; exhibited in group shows at Anderson Theatre Gallery, N.Y.C., 1983, Barbara Braathen Gallery, N.Y.C., 1984, Patrick Fox Gallery, N.Y.C., 1984, Anne Plumb Gallery, N.Y.C., 1985, Simard, Halm and Shee Gallery, L.A., 1986, Jan Turner Gallery, L.A., 1987, Carnegie Mus. Art, Pitts., 1988, Gilbert Brownstone Gallery, Paris, 1988, Gabrielle Bryers Gallery, N.Y.C., 1988, Greenberg Gallery, St. Louis, 1988, Michael Maloney Gallery, 1988, John Good Gallery, 1985, 87, 88, 89, 90, Luise Ross Gallery, N.Y.C., 1989, Karl Bornstein Gallery, Santa Monica, Calif., 1990, Nicole Klagsbrun Gallery, N.Y.C., 1990, Leopold-Hoesch Mus., Duren, Germany, 1990, Duke U. Mus. Art, Durham, N.C., 1991, Mario Diacono Gallery, Boston, 1992, Galleria Planta, Rome, 1992, Galleria Nazionale d'Arte, Moderna, San Marino, 1993; represented in permanent collections at High Mus. Art, Atlanta, Carnegie Mus. Art, Pitts., New Sch., N.Y.C. Recipient Nat. Endowment Arts fellowship, 1987, award Pollock-Krasner Found.; Fulbright profl. rsch. grantee USIS, South Korea, 1990-91. Home: PO Box 20308 New York NY 10011-0007

LUCAS, CYNTHIA, ballet mistress, dancer; b. San Rafael, Calif.. Studies with, Leona Norman. Formerly with Royal Winnipeg Ballet, Joffrey II Co.; mem. corps de ballet Nat. Ballet Can., Toronto, Ont., 1972-76, 2nd soloist, 1976-78, 1st solist, 1978-89, ballet mistress, 1989—. Created roles including Farmer's Daughter in Apples at the Shaw Festival, The Chic Couple in The Party for CBC-TV, Sweet Young Thing in La Ronde; performances include Isabelle-Marie in Mad Shadows, Catherine Sloper in Washington Square; leading role in Kudelka's The Rape of Lucerne, 1980, The Merry Widow, 1986; dancer in Toronto Internat. Festival premiere Onegin, 1984. Office: National Ballet of Canada, 157 King St East, Toronto, ON Canada M5C 1G9

LUCAS, DONALD LEO, private investor; b. Upland, Calif., Mar. 18, 1930; s. Leo J. and Mary G. (Schwamm) L.; BA, Stanford U., 1951, MBA, 1953; m. Lygia de Soto Harrison, July 15, 1961; children: Nancy Maria Lucas Thibodeau, Alexandra Maria Lucas Ertola, Donald Alexander Lucas. Assoc. corp. fin. dept. Smith, Barney & Co., N.Y.C., 1956-59; gen., ltd. ptnr. Draper, Gaither & Anderson, Palo Alto, Calif., 1959-66; pvt. investor, Menlo Park, Calif., 1966—; bd. dirs. Cadence Design Systems, San Jose, Calif., Delphi Info. Systems, Inc., Amati Comm., Corp., San Jose, Kahler Realty Corp., Rochester, Minn., Oracle Corp., Redwood Shores, Calif., Quantum Health Resources Inc., Racotek, Inc., Mpls., Macromedia, San Francisco, TriCord Systems, Inc., Plymouth, Minn., Trascend Svcs., Inc., Atlanta; Mem. bd. regents Bellarmine Coll. Prep., 1977—; regent emeritus U. Santa Clara, 1980—. 1st lt. AUS, 1953-55. Mem. Am. Coun. Capital Formation (dir.), Stanford U. Alumni Assn., Stanford Grad. Sch. Bus. Alumni Assn., Order of Malta, Stanford Buck Club, Vintage Club (Indian Wells, Calif.), Menlo Country Club (Woodside, Calif.), Menlo Circus Club (Atherton, Calif.), Jackson Hole Golf and Tennis Club, Teton Pines Club, Zeta Psi. Home: 224 Park Ln Atherton CA 94027-5411 Office: 3000 Sand Hill Rd # 3-210 Menlo Park CA 94025-7116

LUCAS, FRANK D., congressman; b. Cheyenne, Okla., Jan. 6, 1960; m. Lynda L. Bradshaw, 1988. BS, Okla. State U., 1982. Mem. Okla. Ho. of Reps., 1989-94, 103d Congress from 6th Okla. Dist., 1994—. Baptist. Office: US Ho of Reps 107 Cannon Bldg Washington DC 20515-0003 Home: Rte 2 Box 136A Cheyenne OK 73628

LUCAS, FRANK EDWARD, architect; b. Charleston, S.C., Oct. 31, 1934; m. Edith R. Dority; children: Susan R. Lucas Tezza, Kelly E., Julie C. Lucas Rodenberg. BArch, Clemson U., 1959. Registered architect, S.C., Fla., N.C., W.Va., Ala., Ga., Va., Ky. Founder, architect (now LS3P Architects Ltd.) Lucas and Stubbs Assocs., Charleston, S.C., 1964—; chmn. bd. dirs. LS3P Architects Ltd. Mem. Charleston County Bd. Rev., Bldg. and Elec. Codes, 1972-85; mem. St. Philip's Episcopal Ch., former vestryman, sr. warden, lay reader St. James Episcopal Ch.; trustee Cities in Schs., Charleston, 1990-94; past pres. nine county region Girl Scouts Am., 1988-90; affiliate S.C. Sch. Bds. Assn.; bd. dirs. Charleston World Trade Ctr., S.C. Golf Expo; hon. chmn. March of Dimes Walkathon, 1991; pres. adv. coun. Clemson U.; mem. Am. Cancer Soc., Trident Tech. Coll. Found., Coll. Charleston Found.; mem. S.C. State Commn. on Def. Base Devel.; bd. dirs. S.C. Athletic Hall of Fame. Recipient Elizabeth O'Neill Verner award S.C. Arts Commn., 1990; featured in exhibit at Gibbes Art Gallery titled 20 Yrs. of Design Excellence, 1988. Fellow AIA; mem. S.C. AIA (pres. 1970), S.C. Econ. Developers Assn., Soc. Am. Mil. Engrs., Charleston Trident C. of C., Preservation Soc. Charleston, S.C. Hist. Soc., Carolina Art Assn., S.C. Arts Found. (bd. dirs.), Executives Assn. Greater Charleston (pres. 1983), Greater Charleston Real Estate Bd., Clemson Archtl. Found. (bd. dirs. 1967-73, 77-81, 86—, pres. 1975, 81, 89), Hibernian Soc. (mng. com. 1984-96), Hibernian Soc. Found. (v.p. 1990-92, pres. 1992-94), Country Club of Charleston (bd. dirs. 1976-79, exec. com. 1991), S.C. State C. of C. (bd. dirs. 1989-90, com. to reorganize state govt. 1990, exec. com. 1992), S.C. Arts Commn. (bus. and arts awards adv. com.), Assn. of Citadel Men, IPTAY Clemson U., Clemson Alumni Assn., Clemson Low Country Assn., Palmetto State Tchrs. Assn. (affiliate), Carolina Yacht Club, Rotary (N. Charleston chpt., Paul Harris fellow), Country Club Charleston (bd. dirs. 1973-76), Health Scis. Found. (bd. dirs.), The Harbor Club (Charleston, founding dir.). Home: 607 North Shore Dr Charleston SC 29412 Office: 24 N Market St Ste 300 Charleston SC 29401-2640

LUCAS, FRED VANCE, pathology educator, university administrator; b. Grand Junction, Colo., Feb. 7, 1922; s. Lee H. and Katherine W. (Vance) L.; m. Rebecca Ross Dudley, Dec. 21, 1948; children: Fred Vance, Katherine Dudley Lucas Volk. A.B., U. Calif.-Berkeley, 1942; M.D., U. Rochester, 1950. Am. Bd. Patholgy. Intern, postgrad. fellow in pathology U. Rochester, 1950-51, asst. in pathology, 1951-53, Lilliy fellow, 1952-53, Gleason fellow, 1953-54, instr., 1953-54, asst. prof., 1954-55; chief resident in pathology Strong Meml. Hosp., 1953-54; practice medicine specializing in pathology; assoc. prof. Coll. Physicians and Surgeons, Columbia U., 1955-60; assoc. attending pathologist Presbyn. Hosp., N.Y.C., 1955-60; prof., chmn. pathology U. Mo.-Columbia Sch. Medicine, 1960-77; research assoc. Space Sci. Research Ctr., 1964-70; prof. pathology Vanderbilt U., 1977-89, dir. program planning, dir. med. services, 1977-79, acting assoc. v.p. med. affairs, 1979, assoc. v.p. med. affairs, 1979-81, acting exec. dir. hosp., assoc. v.p. med. affairs, 1981-82, assoc. vice-chancellor med. affairs, 1982-89; cons. in field. Contbr. numerous articles to med. jours. Del WHO, Geneva, 1971; bd. dirs. Univs. Assoc. Research and Edn. in Pathology; commr. for Mo. and Ark. Coll. Am. Pathologists, 1975-77. Served in U.S. Army, 1942-46. Recipient Lederle Faculty award, 1954-56; recipient Disting. Service award Columbia U., 1967, Edn. and Social Affairs medal U. Mo.-Columbia, 1975, Student exec. com. service award U. Mo.-Columbia, 1975. Fellow Coll. Am. Pathologists, Am. Soc. Clin. Pathologists; mem. Am. Pathology Assn., Internat. Acad. Pathology, Harvey Soc., Sigma Xi, Alpha Omega Alpha (lectr. 1977). Democrat. Roman Catholic. Home: 333 Lee Dr Apt G12 Baton Rouge LA 70808-4985

LUCAS, GEORGE RAMSDELL, JR., philosophy educator; b. San Angelo, Tex., Sept. 8, 1949; s. George Ramsdell and Clare Elizabeth (Baldwin) L.; m. Patricia Cook; children: Jessica, Kimberly, Theresa. BS summa cum laude, Coll. William and Mary, 1971; PhD, Northwestern U., 1978. Asst. prof., chmn. dept. philosophy Randolph-Macon Coll., Ashland, Va., 1978-82; assoc. prof., chmn. dept. philosophy Santa Clara (Calif.) U., 1982-86; assoc. prof. Emory U., Atlanta, 1986-87; prof. philosophy Clemson (S.C.) U., 1987-91; asst. dir. rsch. div. NEH, Washington, 1991-95; prof. bus. Georgetown U., Washington, 1996—. Author: The Genesis of Modern Process Thought, 1983, The Rehabilitation of Whitehead, 1989; editor: Lifeboat Ethics: Moral Dilemmas of World Hunger, 1976, Poverty, Justice and the Law, 1986; philosophy editor SUNY Press, Albany, 1989—; also articles. Am. Coun. Learned Socs. fellow, 1982; Fulbright rsch. fellow, 1989. Mem. Am. Philos. Assn., Metaphys. Soc. Am. (exec. coun. 1987-92), Hegel Soc. Am., Omicron Delta Kappa, Phi Beta Kappa. Office: Georgetown U Sch Bus Washington DC 20057

LUCAS, GEORGE W., JR., film director, producer, screenwriter; b. Modesto, Calif., May 14, 1944. Student, Modesto Jr. Coll.; BA, U. So. Calif., 1966. Chmn. Lucasfilm Ltd., San Rafael, Calif. Creator short film THX-1138 (Grand prize Nat. Student Film Festival, 1967); asst. to Francis Ford Coppola on The Rain People; dir. Filmmaker (documentary on making of The Rain People); dir., co-writer THX-1138, 1970, American Graffiti, 1973; dir., author screenplay Star Wars, 1977; exec. producer More American Graffiti, 1979, The Empire Strikes Back, 1980, Raiders of the Lost Ark, 1981, Indiana Jones and the Temple of Doom, 1984, Labyrinth, 1986, Howard the Duck, 1986, Willow, 1988, Tucker, 1988, Radioland Murders, 1994; exec. producer, co-author screenplay Return of the Jedi, 1983; co-exec. producer Mishima, 1985; co-author, co-exec. producer Indiana Jones and the Last Crusade, 1989; exec. producer (TV series) The Young Indiana Jones Chronicles, 1992-93. Office: Lucasfilm Ltd PO Box 2009 San Rafael CA 94912-2009

LUCAS, GEORGES, physicist, researcher; b. Marosvasarhely, Transylvania, Rumania, Dec. 11, 1914; arrived in France, 1933; s. Emeric and Hermine (Grun) Lukacs; m. Irene Weingrow, Jan. 10, 1948. Degree in Chem. Engring., U. Strasbourg, France, 1938; postgrad., Ecole Normale Superieure, Paris, 1938-40; PhD, U. Paris, Sorbonne, 1955. Rsch. assoc. astrophysics Centre Nat. de la Recherche Scientifique Observatory, Meudon, France, 1953-55; with rsch. dept. Tidewater Oil Co., Avon, Calif., 1956-65; with rsch. dept. Elf-Aquitaine, Paris, 1965-77, ret., 1977. Author: Transfer Theory for Trapped Electromagnetic Energy, 1983; contbr. articles to profl. jours., abstracts to profl. proceedings; patentee in field. Mem. Am. Phys. Soc., Am. Soc. Photobiology, European Photochemistry Assn., European Soc. Photobiology, N.Y. Acad. Scis. Avocation: drawing. Home: 83-85 rue Saint Charles, 75015 Paris France

LUCAS, HENRY CAMERON, JR., information systems educator, writer, consultant; b. Omaha, Sept. 4, 1944; s. Henry Cameron and Lois (Himes) L.; m. Ellen Kuhbach, June 8, 1968; children: Scott C., Jonathan G. B.S. in Indsl. Adminstrn. magna cum laude, Yale U., 1966; M.S., MIT, 1968, Ph.D., 1970. Cons. Arthur D. Little, Inc., Cambridge, Mass., 1966-70; asst. prof. computer and info. systems Stanford U., Calif., 1970-74; assoc. prof. computer applications and info. systems NYU, 1974-78, prof., chmn. dept. info. systems, 1978-84; on leave IBM European Systems Research Inst., Belgium, 1981; INSEAD Fontainebleau, France, 1985; prof. info. systems NYU, 1985—. Author: The T-Farm Organization, 1996 Computer-Based Information Systems in Organizations, 1973, The Infr=ormation Systems Environment, 1980 (with F. Land, T. Lincoln and K. Supper) Casebook for Management Information Systems, 3d edit., 1985, The Analysis, Design and Implementation of Information Systems, 4th edit., 1992, Information Technology for Management 5th edit., 1994, Coping with Computers: A Manager's Guide to Controlling Information Processing, 1982, Introduction to Computers and Information Systems, 1986, Managing Information Services, 1989; editor Indsl. Mgmt., 1967-68; mem. editorial bd. Sloan Mgmt. Rev., 1975-91; assoc. editor MIS Quar., 1977-83; editor in chief Systems, Objectives, Solutions, 1980—; contbr. articles to profl. jours. Recipient award for excellence in teaching NYU Sch. Bus., 1982. Mem. Assn. Computing Machinery, Inst. Mgmt. Scis., Phi Beta Kappa, Tau Beta Pi. Home: 18 Portland Rd Summit NJ 07901-3044 Office: NYU 44 W 4th St 9-67 New York NY 10012-1126

LUCAS, J. RICHARD, retired mining engineering educator; b. Scottdale, Pa., May 3, 1929; s. J.W. and Mary (Hirka) L.; m. Joan H. Hathaway, Aug. 30, 1952; children: Eric Scott, Jay Hathaway. Student, Pa. State U., 1947-48; B.S. in Math. and Physics, Waynesburg Coll., 1951; B.S. in Mining Engring, W.Va. U., 1952; M.S. in Mining Engring, U. Pitts., 1954; Ph.D., Columbia, 1965. Registered profl. engr., Va., Ohio, W.Va. Miner Crucible Steel Co., 1947-52; field engr. Joy Mfg. Co., 1952-54; mem. faculty Ohio State U., Columbus, 1954-61; head dept. mining engring. Va. Poly. Inst. and State U., Blacksburg, 1961-71, head div. minerals engring., 1971-76, head dept. mining and minerals engring., 1976-87, Massey prof. mining and minerals engring., 1987-92; dir. mining systems design and ground control Generic Mineral Tech. Ctr.; ret., 1992; chmn. exec. com. Ann. Inst. on Coal-Mining Health, Safety and Rsch., 1969-87. Mem. Am. Inst. Mining, Metall. and Petroleum Engrs., AAAS, Coal Mining Inst., W.Va. Coal Mining Inst., AAUP, Nat., Va. socs. profl. engrs., Am. Soc. Engring. Edn., Va. Acad. Sci., Soc. Mining Engrs. (bd. dirs., chmn. coal div.). Home: 408 Hemlock Dr Blacksburg VA 24060-5232

LUCAS, JAMES E(VANS), operatic director; b. San Antonio, Mar. 15, 1933; s. Mason Harley and Nora Norton (Evans) L. B.A., Hiram Coll., 1951; postgrad., Stanford U., 1951-52, Juilliard Sch. Music, 1952-53. mem. faculty Temple U., 1965-71, Mannes Coll. Music, 1964-70, Manhattan Sch. Music, 1970-78, Carnegie-Mellon U., 1977-79; prof. music, stage dir. Ind. U., 1987-94. Free-lance operatic stage dir.; worked for numerous opera cos. in U.S., Can., including, Met. Opera, San Francisco Opera, N.Y.C. Opera, Can. Opera Co.; dir. for various summer festivals. Mem. Am. Guild Musical Artists, Am. Fedn. Musicians, Can. Actors Equity. Home and Office: 201 W 85th St New York NY 10024-3917

LUCAS, JAMES WALTER, federal government official; b. Frankfort, Ind., Oct. 20, 1940; s. Walter Kenneth and Hester (Kesterson) L.; m. Sara Sue Stewart, Feb. 17, 1962; 1 dau., Catherine Anne. BS, Ball State U., 1963, MA, 1964; postgrad., Am. U., 1977, Harvard U., 1990; DA, George Mason U., 1995. Asst. dir. intelligence coordination Nat. Security Council, Washington, 1975-76; exec. asst. to dep. dir. CIA, Washington, 1976-77, dep. exec. sec., 1977-79; CIA program budget officer Intelligence Community Staff, 1979-81; dep. asst. sec. U.S. Dept. Air Force, 1981-82, prin. dep. asst. sec., 1982-83; dir. crisis mgmt. planning staff Nat. Security Council, 1983-85; Disting. prof., dean Def. Intelligence Coll., Washington, 1985-93; assoc. dir. liaison Def. Intelligence Agy., 1993-96; dep. dir. Open Source Info., CIA, 1996—; adj. prof. U. Md.-Far East div., 1970-71, Def. Intelligence Coll., 1974-83; guest lectr. Am. U., Washington, 1971-77; cons. Pres.'s Fgn. Intelligence Adv. Bd. Author: Intelligence and National Security in the Nixon Administration, 1972, Simulation and Strategic Intelligence Analysis, 1973, Information Needs of Presidents, 1989, Organizing the Presidency: The Role of the Director of Central Intelligence, 1995. Pres. Muncie Young Republican's Club, Ind., 1959-64; pres. Muncie Students for Goldwater, 1964; mem. Rep. Nat. Com., Reston Rep. Assn. With USAF, 1965-77, brig. gen. Res., 1977—. Decorated Legion of Merit, Bronze Star medal, Meritorious Svc. medal, Republic of Vietnam Gallantry Cross with palm. Mem. Am. Polit. Sci. Assn., Internat. Studies Assn., Air Force Assn., Nat. Mil. Intelligence Assn., Res. Officers Assn., Pi Sigma Alpha, Phi Gamma Mu, Sigma Chi. Lodge: Masons. Office: CIA Washington DC 20205

LUCAS, JOHN ALLEN, lawyer; b. Washington, Aug. 1, 1943; s. George Luther and Opal (McCollum) L.; m. Carol Kaine, June 7, 1969; children: John Christian, Helen Elizabeth, David Marshall, Kerri Christine. BS, U.S. Mil. Acad., 1969; JD, U. Tex., 1977. Bar: Va. 1978, Tenn. 1984, N.Y. 1986. Assoc. Hunton & Williams, Richmond, Va., 1977-83; ptnr. Hunton & Williams, Knoxville, Tenn., 1984—; prof. law U. Richmond, 1979-80; lectr. various legal seminars, 1979—. Contbr. articles to profl. jours. Bd. dirs. Knoxville Boys Club, 1984-88; bd. dirs. Tenn. Juvenile Diabetes Assn., 1989—. Capt. U.S. Army, 1969-74. Mem. ABA, Va. Bar Assn., Tenn. Bar Assn. Roman Catholic. Avocations: mountain climbing, sport parachuting, white-water kayaking, triathlons. Office: Hunton & Williams PO Box 951 Knoxville TN 37901-0951

LUCAS, JOHN KENNETH, lawyer; b. Chgo., July 9, 1946; s. John and Catherine (Sykes) L.; m. Mary Ellen McElligott, Oct. 14, 1972; 1 child, John Patrick. BS with distinction, Ill. Inst. Tech., 1968; JD, DePaul U., 1972. Bar: Ill. 1972. Shareholder Brinks, Hofer, Gilson & Lione, Chgo.; hearing officer Ill. Pollution Control Bd., 1981-86; adj. prof. De Paul U. Coll. of Law, 1986-93. Mem. ABA, Ill. Bar Assn., Chgo. Bar Assn., Fed. Cir. Bar Assn., Bar Assn. of 7th Fed. Cir., Am. Intellectual Property Law Assn., Patent Law Assn. Chgo., Lic. Execs. Soc., Internat. Assn. Protection Indsl. Property, Legal Club of Chgo., Phi Alpha Delta, Tau Beta Pi, Eta Kappa Nu. Office: Brinks Hofer et al 455 N Cityfront Plaza Dr Chicago IL 60611-5503

LUCAS, JUNE H., state legislator; children: Deven Armeni, Adrien. Student, Youngstown State U. Mem. Ohio Ho. of Reps., 1986—, mem. energy and environment, judiciary and criminal justice coms.; Mem. adv. com. ohio child support guidelines, women's policy and rsch. Com.; ranking minority mem. family svcs. com. Contbr. articles to Warren Tribune Chronicle. Active Animal Welfare League. Named Woman of Yr., Coalition Labor Union Women, YWCA, 1988. Mem. NOW (Trumbull County chpt.), LWV, Ohio Bus. and Profl. Women, Ohio Farm Bur., Mosquito Creek Devel. Assn., Farmer's Union, Sierra Club. Democrat. Home: 1435 Locust St Mineral Ridge OH 44440-9721 Office: Ohio House of Reps Office of House Mems Columbus OH 43215

LUCAS, LINDA LUCILLE, dean; b. Stockton, Calif., Apr. 22, 1940; d. Leslie Harold Lucas and Amy Elizabeth (Callow) Farnsworth. BA, San Jose State Coll., 1961, MA, 1969; EdD, U. San Francisco, 1982. Dist. libr. Livermore (Calif.) Elem. Schs., 1962-64; libr. Mission San Jose High Sch., Fremont, Calif., 1964-69; media reference libr. Chabot Coll., Hayward, Calif., 1969-75; asst. dean instrn. Chabot-Las Positas Coll., Livermore, 1975-91; assoc. dean instrn. Las Positas Coll., Livermore, 1991-94, dean acad. svcs., 1994—; participant Nat. Inst. for Leadership Devel., 1991. Bd. dirs. Tri-Valley Community TV, Livermore, 1991—, Valley Choral Soc., 1993—, Chabot-Las Positas Colls. Found., Pleasanton, Calif., 1991-94; mem. needs assessment com Performing Arts Coun., Pleasanton. Mem. ALA, Coun. Chief Librs., Assn. Calif. Community Coll. Adminstrs., Calif. Libr. Assn. Avocations: choral music, photography. Office: Las Positas Coll 3033 Collier Canyon Rd Livermore CA 94550-7650

LUCAS, ROBERT ELMER, soil scientist; b. Malolos, The Philippines, June 27, 1916; (parents Am. citizens); s. Charles Edmund and Harriet Grace (Deardorff) L.; m. Norma Emma Schultz, Apr. 27, 1941; children: Raymond and Richard (twins), Milton, Keith, Charles. BSA, Purdue U., 1939, MS, 1941; PhD, Mich. State U., 1947. Research asst. Va. Agrl. Research Sta., Norfolk, 1941-43; farmer Culver, Ind., 1943-44; grad. asst. Mich. State U., East Lansing, 1945, assoc. prof. soil sci., 1951-57, prof., 1957-77, prof. emeritus, 1977—; agronomist William Gehring, Inc., Rensselaer, Ind., 1946-50, 77-78; vis. prof. Everglades Research Sta. U. Fla., Belle Glade, 1979-80. Author chpts. in books, research reports. Leader Boy Scouts Am., Lansing, Mich., 1961-72, dist. chmn. Chief Okemos (Mich.) Coun. Boy Scouts Am., 1965-66; pres. Okemos Cmty. Sr. citizens, 1987-88, pres. Lansing Area Farmers Agrl. Club, 1992, sec.-treas., 1994-96. Named Outstanding Specialist Mich. Coop. Extension Specialist Assn., 1967. Fellow Soil Sci. Soc. Am., Am. Soc. Agronomy (contbr. articles to jour.); mem. Internat. Peat Soc. (del. 1963—), U.S. Peat Soc., Mich. Onion Growers Assn. (sec. 1953-72), Mich. Muck Farmers Assn. (sec. 1953-72, Assoc. Master-Farmers award 1966), Mich. Mint Growers Assn. (sec. 1953-60). Republican. Lutheran. Avocations: traveling, gardening, sports, genealogy. Home: 3827 Dobie Rd Okemos MI 48864-3703 Office: Mich State Univ Dept Of Crop & Soil Sci East Lansing MI 48824

LUCAS, ROY EDWARD, JR., minister; b. Shawnee, Okla., Dec. 19, 1955; s. Roy Edward Sr. and Shirley Ann (Padgett) L.; m. Roberta Lee Duncan, Feb. 28, 1975; children: Jonathon Edward, Jerebeth Glenae. BA, Okla. Bapt. U., 1978, BA in Edn., 1979; MDiv, Southwestern Bapt. Theol. Sem., Ft. Worth, 1984, MRE, 1985, PhD, 1993. Ordained to ministry So. Bapt. Conv., 1978; cert. elem. tchr., Okla. Assoc. pastor Temple Bapt. Ch., Shawnee, 1975, Calvary Bapt. Ch., Shawnee, 1975-79; pastor Brandon (Tex.) Bapt. Ch., 1982-85, Fox (Okla.) Bapt. Ch., 1985-90, Union Hill Bapt. Ch., Purcell, Okla., 1990—; instr. Sem. Ext.-Enon Assn., Ardmore, Okla., 1986-89; teaching fellow Southwestern Bapt. Sem., 1989; adj. prof. Ministry Tng. Inst. Okla. Bapt. U , 1996. Home: 612 N 6th Ave Purcell OK 73080-2202 Office: Union Hill Bapt Ch RR 2 Box 80 Purcell OK 73080-9630

LUCAS, SANDRA ROBERTS, city official, entertainment company executive; b. Riverhead, N.Y., Sept. 18, 1954; d. Newton David and Stella (Garawrecki) Roberts; divorced; 1 child, Gary Joseph. Student, Miami-Dade Jr. Coll., 1972. Gen. mgr., v.p. Parkway Entertainment Ctr, Miramar, Fla., 1981—; vice mayor, commr. City of Miramar, 1993—. Chmn. parks and recreation City of Miramar, 1989-93, mem. Planning and Zoning Commn., 1992-93. Democrat. Avocations: golf, bowling, snorkeling, ocean activities. Home: 3121 SW 65th Ave Miramar FL 33023-3849 Office: City of Miramar 6700 Miramar Pky Miramar FL 33023-4897

LUCAS, STANLEY JEROME, radiologist, physician; b. Cin., Mar. 23, 1929; s. Morris and Ruby (Schaen) L.; m. Judith Esther Schulzinger, May 14, 1953; children—Barbara Ellen, Daniel Nathan, Betsy Diane, Marvin Howard, Ronna Sue. B.S., U. Cin., 1948, M.D., 1951. Diplomate Am. Bd. Radiology. Intern Cin. Gen Hosp., 1951-52, resident, 1952-53, 55-57; practice medicine specializing in radiology Cin., 1957—; mem. staff William Booth Meml. Hosp., 1957-61, Speer Meml. Hosp., 1957-61, Jewish Hosp., Cin., 1961-94; past chmn. bd. Iona, Inc. Chmn. med. div. United Appeal, 1978, Jewish Welfare Fund, 1980; bd. dirs., treas. Midwest Found. Med. Care; founder Choicecare, Inc., 1978-86; mem. policy devel. com. Local Health Planning Agy., 1978-82. Capt. USAF, 1953-55. Honoree, Jewish Nat. Fund, 1994. Fellow Am. Coll. Radiology; mem. Radiol. Soc. N.Am., AMA (alt. del. 1982-87, del. 1987—), Ohio State Med. Assn. (del. 1975-85, 94—, 1st dist. councilor 1985-90, pres.-elect 1991, pres. 1992-93), Cin. Acad. Medicine (pres. 1976-77), Radiol. Soc. Cin. (pres. 1967), Am. Roentgen Ray Soc., Phi Beta Kappa, Phi Eta Sigma. Club: Losantiville Country. Jewish. Home: 6760 E Beechlands Dr Cincinnati OH 45237-3728 Office: 2905 Burnet Ave Cincinnati OH 45219-2403

LUCAS, THERESA EILEEN, elementary education educator; b. Bellingham, Wash., Jan. 6, 1948; d. John M. and Lillian Sigrid (Westford) Cairns; m. Paul T. Lucas, 1970 (div. June 1987); children: Jeffrey Thomas, Aimee Michelle. BA, U. No. Colo., 1970, MA, 1985. Cert. elem. edn. grades K-6, spl. edn. grades K-12, Colo. Tchr. spl. edn. Baker Elem. Sch. Adams County Sch. Dist. 50, Westminster, Colo., 1970-77, tchr. 1st grade Berkeley Gardens Elem. Sch., 1978-84, tchr. kindergarten Harris Park Elem. Sch., 1984-87, tchr. kindergarten Tennyson Knolls Elem. Sch., 1987—; mem. sch. coms. Baker Elem. Sch., Berkeley Gardens Elem. Sch., Harris Park Elem. Sch., Tennyson Knolls Elem. Sch., Adams County Sch. Dist. 50, Westminster, 1970—; co-author literacy grant Adams County Ednl. Found., 1994, Gov.'s Creativity grant Tennyson Knolls Elem. Sch., 1989-90. Vol. Rainbows for All God's Children, Spirit of Christ Ch., Arvada, Colo., 1988-90, vol. crisis hotline, 1990-91; campaign vol. pro-edn. candidates, Arvada, 1992. Mem. ASCD, NEA, Internat. Reading Assn., Colo. Edn. Assn., Colo. Coun. Internat. Reading Assn., West Adams County Coun. Internat. Reading Assn., Westminster Edn. Assn. (membership rep. Tennyson Knolls Elem. Sch. 1990-95). Democrat. Avocations: reading, biking, dancing, walking, crafts. Home: 8279 Iris St Arvada CO 80005-2136

LUCAS, WILLIAM MAX, JR., structural engineer, university dean; b. Lamar, Mo., July 23, 1934; s. William Max and Margaret (Jones) L.; children—Jennifer Lynn Lucas Wyatt, Sarah Frances Lucas Whittington, Amy Johanne. B.S., U. Kans., 1956, M.S., 1962; Ph.D., Okla. State U., 1970. Registered profl. engr., Kans., Mo. Structural engr. Finney & Turnipseed, Topeka, 1960-62; prof. structural engring. U. Kans., Lawrence, 1962-74, 78-80, dir. facilities planning, 1974-78, dean Sch. Architecture and Urban Design, 1980-94; prof. arch. and archtl. engring., 1962—; owner W.M. Lucas, Engr., Lawrence, 1964—. Author: Matrix Analysis for Structural Engineers, 1968, Structural Analysis for Engineers, 1978; contbr. articles to profl. jours. Mem. Lawrence Bd. Bldg. Code Appeals, 1967-73, Kans. Bldg. Commn., 1982-84; pres. bd. dirs. United Fund, Lawrence, 1976; chmn. Lawrence/Douglas County Planning Commn., 1977-79; mem. consultative coun. Nat. Inst. Bldg. Scis., 1993—. Mem. Am. Soc. for Engring. Edn., Assn. Collegiate Schs. Architecture, Nat. Soc. Archtl. Engrs., Sigma Xi, Tau Beta Pi, Tau Sigma Delta. Club: Lawrence Country. Home: 2629 Bardith Ct Lawrence KS 66046-4536 Office: U Kans Sch Architecture & Urban Design Lawrence KS 66045

LUCAS, WILLIAM RAY, aerospace consultant; b. Newbern, Tenn., Mar. 1, 1922; married 1948; 3 children. B.S., Memphis State U., 1943; M.S., Vanderbilt U., 1950, Ph.D. in Chem. Metallurgy, 1952; L.H.D. (hon.), Mobile Coll., 1977; D.Sc. (hon.), Southeastern Inst. Tech., 1980, U. Ala., Huntsville, 1981. Instr. chemistry Memphis State U., 1946-48; chemist guided missile devel. div. Redstone Arsenal, 1952-54, chief chem. sect., 1954-55; chief engr. material sect. Army Ballistic Missile Agy., 1955-56, chief engr. material br., 1956-60; with Marshall Space Flight Center, NASA, 1960—, material div., 1963-66, dir. propulsion and vehicle engring. lab., 1966-68, dir. program devel., 1968-71, dep. dir., 1971-74, dir., 1974-86; pvt. practice aerospace cons. Hunstville, Ala., 1986—. Served as Lt. USNR, 1943-46. Recipient Exceptional Sci. Achievement medal NASA, 1964, 2 Exceptional Service medals, 1969, Disting. Service medal, 1972, Disting. Service award, 1981, 86; Presdl. rank Disting. Exec., 1980; Roger W. Jones award for outstanding exec. leadership Am. U., 1981; Space award for outstanding contbns. in field of space VFW, 1983; Disting. Alumni award Memphis State U., 1984; Aubrey D. Green award Lions Club Ala., 1986; named one of Tenn. Outstanding Scientists and Engrs., Tenn. Tech. Found., 1986; named to Ala. Engring. Hall of Fame, 1990. Fellow Am. Soc. Metals, Am. Astronautical Soc. (Space Flight award 1982), AIAA (Oberth award 1965, Holger N. Toftoy award 1976, Elmer A. Sperry group award 1986); mem. Nat. Acad. Engring., Am. Chem. Soc., Sigma Xi, Tau Beta Pi. Research in materials engring. metallurgy, inorganic chemistry, environ. effects on materials, especially space environ. effects.

LUCASSEN, SIGURD, labor union administrator, retired. Gen. pres. United Brotherhood of Carpenters and Joiners of Am., Washington, D.C. Office: United Brotherhood Carpenters & Joiners Am Am Carpenters Blvd 101 Constitution Ave NW Washington DC 20001-2133

LUCCA, JOHN JAMES, retired dental educator; b. Bklyn., July 12, 1921; s. Thomas and Marie (Ciancia) L.; m. Mary A. Pascarell, June 22, 1946; children—Diane, Eileen, Denise, Nancy, John, William. A.B., NYU, 1941; D.D.S., Columbia, 1947. Diplomate: Am. Bd. Prosthodontics. Research fellow prosthetics Columbia Dental Sch., 1949-52, asst. prof., 1952-57, assoc. prof., 1957-64, head clin. prosthodontics; and postgrad. instr. 1st, 10th Dist. dental socs., 1954-87, prof. dentistry, 1964-87, dir. div. prosthondontics; prof. emeritus Columbia U., 1987—; cons. Westchester County Med. Ctr.; attending emeritus Presbyn. Hosp.; cons., lectr. U.S. Naval Dental Sch.; mem. examination com. N.E. Regional Bd. Dental Examiners; mem. med. staff Valley Hosp. Contbr. to dental jours., chpts. to various textbooks. Extraordinary minister of the Eucharist, 1974—; mem. parish council Mt. Carmel Ch., 1985—; hon. police surgeon N.Y.C. Police Dept., 1964—. Served with AUS, 1943-44. Recipient Ella M. Ewell medal Columbia, 1947. Fellow N.Y. Acad. Dentistry, Internat. Coll. Dentists Am. Coll. Dentists, Greater N.Y. Acad. Prosthodontics (pres. 1968), Internat. Coll. Prosthodontists, Am. Acad. Osseo Integration, Am. Coll. Prosthodontics (charter, pres. N.J. state sect. 1979-81); mem. Am. Equilibration Soc., First Dist. Dental Soc. (chmn. prosthodontia sect. 1971), Am. Prosthodontics Soc., William Jarvie Rsch. Soc., Chgo. Acad. Dental Rsch., Knight of Malta, Omicron Kappa Upsilon (pres. Epsilon Epsilon chpt. 1967). Home: 524 Eastgate Rd Ridgewood NJ 07450-2204

LUCCA, LANA KAY, manufacturing analyst; b. North Hornell, N.Y., Aug. 25, 1952; d. Irving Leroy Hazlett and Loraine Jacqueline (Cary) Singleton; m. Mark James Lucca, Jan. 28, 1972 (div. 1977); children: Leilani M., Leslie Kay. Student, Alfred State Coll., 1970-71, Airco Tech. Inst., 1979. Tchr.-model John Robert Powers, Buffalo, 1971-73; mgr., owner Lucca's Pizza, Alfred, N.Y., 1973-76; heavy equipment operator Carborundum Co., Niagara Falls, N.Y., 1977-78; stock room attendant, assembler, prodn. planner Conax Buffalo Corp., 1979—; asst. mgr. Lock, Stock and Barrel, Clarence, N.Y., 1983-86. Leader, assn. rep. Girl Scouts Am., Niagara Falls, Buffalo; chairperson Amherst (N.Y.) Community Intervention, 1988-90; rep. Youth-At-Risk Supts. Adv. Bd., Amherst, 1988-93; vol., conv. rep. PTA, Amherst, 1988-92. Recipient Green Angel award Girl Scouts U.S.A., 1988, Cert. of Appreciation Amherst Community Intervention, 1992. Mem. Am Prodn. and Inventory Control Soc. Episcopalian. Avocations: sewing, quilting, antiques, political activities.

LUCCHETTI, LYNN L., military officer; b. San Francisco, Calif., Aug. 21, 1939; d. Dante and Lillian (Bergeron) L. AB, San Jose State U., 1961; MS, San Francisco State U., 1967; grad. U.S. Army Basic Officer's Course, 1971, U.S. Army Advanced Officer Course, 1976, grad. U.S. Air Force Command and Staff Coll., 1982, U.S. Air Force War Coll., 1983, Sr. Pub. Affairs Officer Course, 1984. Media buyer Batten, Barton, Durstine & Osborn, Inc., San Francisco, 1961-67; producer-dir. Sta. KTVA-TV, Anchorage, 1967-68; media supr. Bennett, Luke and Teawell Advt., Phoenix, 1968-71; commd. 1st lt. U.S. Army, 1971; advanced through ranks to lt. col., 1985, col., 1989, brig. gen. nom. 1993; officer U.S. Army, 1971-74, D.C. N.G., , 1974-78, U.S. Air Force Res., 1978—, program advt. mgr. U.S. Navy Recruiting Command, 1974-76; exec. coordinator for the Joint Advt. Dirs. of Recruiting (JADOR), 1976-79; dir. U.S. Armed Forces Joint Recruiting Advt. Program (JRAP), Dept. Def., Washington, 1979-91; resources mgr. Exec. Leadership Devel. Program Dept. Def., Washington, 1991-94. Author: Broadcasting in Alaska, 1924-1966. Decorated U.S. Army Meritorious Svc. medal, Nat. Def. medal, U.S. Air Force Longevity Ribbon, U.S. Navy Meritorious Unit Commendation, Dept. Def. Joint Achievement medal, 1984. Sigma Delta Chi journalism scholar, 1960. Mem. Women in Def., Sr. Profl. Womens Assn. Home: 11401 Malaguena Ln NE Albuquerque NM 87111-6899

LUCCHINO, LAWRENCE, lawyer, sports executive; b. Pitts., Sept. 6, 1945; s. Dominic A. and Rose (Rizzo) L. A.B. cum laude, Princeton U., 1967; J.D., Yale U., 1972. Bar: Calif. and Pa. 1973, D.C. 1975. Counsel Impeachment Inquiry, House Judiciary Commn., Washington, DC, 1974; assoc. Williams & Connolly, Washington, 1975-79, ptnr., 1979—; sec., bd. dirs., gen. counsel Washington Redskins Football Club, 1978-85; bd. dirs., gen. counsel Balt. Orioles Baseball Club, from 1979, v.p., 1982-88, pres., CEO, 1988-93; CEO San Diego Padres Baseball Club, 1994—; bd. dirs. Army Times, Springfield, Va. Trustee Nat. Found. on Counseling, Princeton, N.J., 1984—; bd. dirs. Nat. Aquarium Natl., Balt. Symphony, Princeton Electronic Bd., Babe Ruth Mus. Mem. ABA. Democrat. Roman Catholic. Office: PO Box 2000 San Diego CA 92112-2000

LUCCI, SUSAN, actress; b. Scarsdale, N.Y., Dec. 23, 1946; d. Victor and Jeanette L.; m. Helmut Huber, 1969; children: Liza Victoria, Andreas Martin. BA, Marymount Coll., 1968. Portrays Erica in TV series All My Children, 1970—; appearances in other series include: Fantasy Island, The Love Boat, The Fall Guy; TV films: Invitation to Hell, 1985, Mafia Princess, 1985, (mini-series) Anastasia: The Mystery of Anna Anderson, 1986, Haunted by Her Past, 1988, Lady Mobster, 1988, The Bride in Black, 1990, The Women Who Sinned, 1991, Double Edge, 1992, Between Love and Hate, 1993, French Silk, 1994; host of spl. with Tony Danza 99 Ways to Attract the Right Man. Recipient 13 Emmy nominations for best actress in daytime drama series, numerous other awards. Office: All My Children 320 W 66th St New York NY 10023-6338 also: ICM care Sylvia Gold 8942 Wilshire Blvd Beverly Hills CA 90211-1934*

LUCE, CHARLES FRANKLIN, former utilities executive, lawyer; b. Platteville, Wis., Aug. 29, 1917; s. James Oliver and Wilma Fisher (Grindell) L.; m. Helen G. Oden, Oct. 24, 1942; children: James O., Christine Mary, Barbara Anne, Charles Franklin. B.A., LL.B., U. Wis., 1941; Sterling fellow, Yale U., 1941-42. Bar: Wis. 1941, Wash. 1946, Oreg. 1945, N.Y. 1981. Law clk. Justice Hugo L. Black, U.S. Supreme Ct., 1943-44; gen. practice law Walla Walla, Wash., 1946-61; adminstr. Bonneville Power Adminstrn., Dept. Interior, Portland, Oreg., 1961-66; under sec. interior Washington, 1966-67; chmn. bd. Consol. Edison Co. of N.Y., Inc., 1967-82, chief exec. officer, 1967-81, chmn. emeritus, 1982—; ptnr. Preston, Thorgrimson, Ellis & Holman, Portland, Oreg., 1982-86; spl. counsel Met. Life Ins. Co., 1987-94; dir. emeritus UAL and Met. Life Ins. Co.; trustee Hudson River Found., Henry M. Jackson Found.; trustee emeritus Columbia U., N.Y.C. Mem. N.Y., Wash., Wis. bar assns., Phi Beta Kappa, Order of Coif. Episcopalian. Office: Consol Edison 4 Irving Pl New York NY 10003-3502

LUCE, GREGORY M., lawyer. Bar: D.C., Va., Md. With Jones, Day, Reavis & Pogue, Washington. Mem. ABA, Nat. Health Lawyers Assn. (bd. dirs. 1996—), Am. Acad. Hosp. Attys., Va. State Bar (past chair, mem. bd. govs. health law sect.). Office: Jones Day Reavis & Pogue 1450 G St NW Washington DC 20005-2001

LUCE, HENRY, III, foundation executive; b. N.Y.C., Apr. 28, 1925; s. Henry Robinson and Lila Hotz (Tyng) L.; m. Patricia Potter, June 27, 1947 (div. 1954); children: Lila Frances, Henry Christopher; m. Claire McGill, Aug. 6, 1960 (dec. June 1971); stepchildren: Kenneth, William, James; m. Nancy Bryan Cassiday, Aug. 15, 1975 (dec. Mar. 1987); stepchildren: Richard, Bryan (dec.); m. Leila Eliott Burton Hadley, Jan. 5, 1990; stepchildren: Arthur T. Hadley III, Victoria Smitter Barlow, Matthew Smitter Eliott, Caroline Smitter Nicholson. L.H.D. (hon.), Yale U., 1945; L.H.D., St. Michael's, 1973, L.I. U., 1986, Pratt Inst., 1991; LLD (hon.), Coll. of Wooster, 1994. Commr.'s asst. Hoover Commn. on Orgn. Exec. Br. of Govt., 1948-49; reporter Cleve. Press, 1949-51; Washington corr. Time Inc., 1951-53, Time writer, 1953-55, head new bldg. dept., 1956-60, asst. to pub., 1960-61; circulation dir. Fortune and Archtl. Forum, 1961-64, House & Home, 1962-64; v.p. Time Inc., 1964-80, chief London bur., 1966-68; pub. Fortune, 1968-69; pub. Time, 1969-72, dir. corp. planning, 1972-80; dir. Time, Inc., 1967-89, Time Warner Inc., 1989-96; pres., chmn., CEO Henry Luce Found., Inc., 1958—; pres. The New Mus. Contemporary Art, 1977—; chmn. Am. Security Systems Inc. Trustee Princeton Theol. Sem., Coll. Wooster, Eisenhower Exch. Fellowships, Ctr. Theol. Inquiry, Temple of Understanding, China Inst. in Am., Christian Ministry in Nat. Pks., N.Y. Hist. Soc., Am. Russian Youth Orch.; mem. Am. Coun. UN Univ.; pres. Assn. Am. Corrs. in London, 1968; dir. Nat. Com. on U.S. China Rels.,

Fishers Island Devel. Co. Lt. (j.g.) USNR, 1943-46. 2nd Ann. recipient medal for disting. philanthropy Am. Assn. Museums, 1994, Ann. award Assn. N.Y. State Arts Coun., 1995. Mem. Univ. Club (coun. mem.), Pilgrims Club (exec. com.), Explorers Club, Fishers Island Club, Hay Harbor Club. Presbyterian (elder). Office: 720 5th Ave Ste 1500 New York NY 10019-4107 also: Fishers Island NY 06930 also: Mill Hill Rd Mill Neck NY 11765

LUCE, R(OBERT) DUNCAN, psychology educator; b. Scranton, Pa., May 16, 1925; s. Robert Rennselaer and Ruth Lillian (Downer) L.; m. Gay Gaer, June 6, 1950 (div.); m. Cynthia Newby, Oct. 5, 1968 (div.); m. Carolyn A. Scheer, Feb. 27, 1988; 1 child, Aurora Newby. BS, MIT, 1945, PhD, 1950; MA (hon.), Harvard U., 1976. Mem. staff research lab electronics MIT, 1950-53; asst. prof. Columbia U., 1953-57; lectr. social relations Harvard U., 1957-59; prof. psychology U. Pa., Phila., 1959-69; vis. prof. Inst. Advanced Study, Princeton, 1969-72; prof. Sch. Social Scis., U. Calif., Irvine, 1972-75; Alfred North Whitehead prof. psychology Harvard U., Cambridge, Mass., 1976-81, prof., 1981-83, Victor S. Thomas prof. psychology, 1983-88, Victor S. Thomas prof. emeritus, 1988; chmn. Harvard U., 1988-94; disting. prof. cognitive sci. U. Calif., Irvine, 1988-94, dir. Irvine Rsch. Unit in math. behavioral sci., 1988-92, disting. rsch. prof. cognitive sci. and rsch. prof. econs., 1994—; dir. Inst. for Math. Behavioral Sci., 1992—; chmn. assembly behavioral and social scis. NRC, 1976-79. Author: (with H. Raiffa) Games and Decisions, 1957, Individual Choice Behavior, 1959, (with others) Foundations of Measurement, I, 1971, II, 1989, III, 1990, Response Times, 1986, (with others) Stevens Handbook of Experimental Psychology, I and II, 1988, Sound & Hearing, 1993. Served with USNR, 1943-46. Ctr. Advanced Study in Behavioral Scis. fellow, 1954-55, 66-67, 87-88, NSF Sr. Postdoctoral fellow, 1966-67, Guggenheim fellow, 1980-81; recipient Disting. award for Rsch. U. Calif., Irvine, 1994. Fellow AAAS, APA (disting. sci. contbn. award 1970, bd. sci. affairs 1993-95), Am. Psychol. Soc. (bd. dirs. 1989-91); mem. Am. Acad. Arts and Scis., Am. Philos. Soc., Nat. Acad. Scis. (chmn. sect. psychology 1980-83, class behavioral and social scis. 1983-86), Am. Math. Soc., Math. assn. Am., Fedn. Behavioral Psychol. and Cognitive Scis. (pres. 1988-90), Psychometric Soc. (pres. 1976-77), Psychonomic Soc., Soc. Math. Psychology (pres. 1979), Sigma Xi, Phi Beta Kappa, Tau Beta Pi. Home: 20 Whitman Ct Irvine CA 92612-4057 Office: U Calif Social Sci Tower Irvine CA 92697-5100

LUCE, SUSAN MARIE, library director; b. Ypsilanti, Mich., Mar. 4, 1948; d. Walter Stanley and Irene Elizabeth (Gallaway) Rybka; m. Paul Trescott Jackson, July 10, 1971 (div. Apr. 1986); m. John Archer Luce, Jr., Nov. 19, 1988. BA in History, U. Mich., 1968, AMLS, 1969. Acquisitions libr. Oakland U., Rochester, Mich., 1969-71; head circulation dept. Lincoln Libr., Springfield, Ill., 1972-73; dir. Alpha Park Pub. Libr. Dist., Bartonville, Ill., 1973-87, Ontario (Calif.) City Libr., 1988—. Mem. ALA, Calif. Libr. Assn. Office: Ontario City Library 215 E C St Ontario CA 91764-4111

LUCENKO, LEONARD KONSTANTYN, sport, recreation management, and safety educator, coach, consultant; b. Ukraine, Aug. 2, 1937; came to U.S., 1949; s. Konstantyn and Pauline Lucenko; m. Larissa Rohowsky, June 7, 1963; children: Leonard Jr., Kristina. BA, Temple U., 1961; MA, NYU, 1962; PhD, U. Utah, 1972. Instr. Lehman Coll., N.Y.C., 1962-62; athletic dir. Eron Prep Sch., N.Y.C., 1962-65; coach, trainer Pratt Inst., Bklyn., 1965; prof. sport, recreation mgmt., and safety, coach, administrator Montclair (N.J.) State Coll., 1966—; mem. com. N.J. Vol. Coaches Com., Trenton, 1988-91; cons. soccer Pres.'s Coun. Phys. Fitness, Washington; bd. dirs. All Am. Soccer Camp, South Orange, N.J., 1966—, Montclair State Coaching Acad., 1980—. Author: (with others) U.S. Soccer Federation Official Book, 1982; contbr. articles to profl. jours. Named Coach of Yr. Met. Conf., N.Y., 1971, N.J. State Athletic Conf. Mem. Ea. N.Y. Soccer Assn. (bd. dirs. coaching sch. 1972—, Most Valuable Player 1983). Office: Montclair State Coll Normal Rd Montclair NJ 07043

LUCENTE, ROSEMARY DOLORES, educational administrator; b. Renton, Wash., Jan. 11, 1935; d. Joseph Anthony and Erminia Antoinette (Argano) Lucente; BA, Mt. St. Mary's Coll., 1956, MS, 1963. Tchr. pub. schs., Los Angeles, 1956-65, supr. tchr., 1958-65, asst. prin., 1965-69, prin. elem. sch., 1969-85, 86—, dir. instrn., 1985-86, 1986—; nat. cons., lectr. Dr. William Glasser's Educator Tng. Ctr., 1968—; nat. workshop leader Nat. Acad. for Sch. Execs.-Am. Assn. Sch. Adminstrs., 1980; L.A. Unified Sch. Dist. rep. for nat. pilot of Getty Inst. for Visual Arts, 1983-85, 92—, site coord., 1983-86, team leader, mem. supt.'s adv. cabinet, 1987—. Recipient Golden Apple award Stanford Ave. Sch. PTA, Faculty and Community Adv. Council, 1976, resolution for outstanding service South Gate City Council, 1976. Mem. Nat. Assn. Elem. Sch. Prins., L.A. Elem. Prins. Orgn. (v.p. 1979-80), Assn. Calif. Sch. Adminstrs. (charter mem.), Assn. Elem. Sch. Adminstrs. (vice-chmn. chpt. 1972-75, city-wide exec. bd., steering com. 1972-75, 79-80), Asso. Adminstrs. Los Angeles (charter), Pi Theta Mu, Kappa Delta Pi (v.p. 1982-84), Delta Kappa Gamma. Democrat. Roman Catholic. Home: 6501 Lindenhurst Ave Los Angeles CA 90048-4733 Office: Figueroa St Sch 510 W 111th St Los Angeles CA 90044-4231

LUCERO, CARLOS, federal judge; b. Antonito, Colo., Nov. 23, 1940; m. Dorothy Stuart; 1 child, Carla. BA, Adams State Coll.; JD, George Washington U., 1964. Law clk. to Judge William E. Doyle U.S. Dist. Ct., Colo., 1964-65; pvt. practice Alamosa, Colo.; sr. ptnr. Lucero, Lester & Sigmund, Alamosa, Colo.; judge U.S. Ct. Appeals (10th cir.), 1995—; mem. Pres. Carter's Presdl. Panel on Western State Water Policy. Bd. dirs. Colo. Hist. Soc., Santa Fe Opera Assn. of N.Mex. Recipient Outstanding Young Man of Colo. award Colo. Jaycees, Disting. Alumnus award George Washington U.; Paul Harris fellow Rotary Found. Fellow Am. Coll. Trial Lawyers, Am. Bar Found., Colo. Bar Found. (pres.), Internat. Acad. Trial Lawyers, Internat. Soc. Barristers; mem. ABA (mem. action com. to reduce ct. cost and delay, mem adv. bd. ABA jour., mem. com. on the availability of legal svcs.), Colo. Bar Assn. (pres. 1977-78, mem. ethics com.), San Luis Valley Bar Assn. (pres.), Nat. Hispanic Bar Assn., Colo. Hispanic Bar Assn. (profl. svc. award), Colo. Rural Legal Svcs. (bd. dirs.), Order of the Coif. Office: US Ct Appeals 1823 Stout St Denver CO 80257*

LUCERO, MICHAEL, sculptor; b. Tracy, Calif., Apr. 1, 1953. BA, Humboldt State U., 1975; MFA, U. Wash., 1978. instr. NYU, 1979-80, Parsons Sch. Design, 1981-82; guest lectr. RISD, Providence, 1979. One-man shows include Charles Cowles Gallery, Inc., N.Y., 1981, 83, 84, 86, Linda Farris Gallery, Seattle, 1982, 87, Hokin Kaufman Gallery, Chgo., 1983, 86, Fuller Goldeen Gallery, San Francisco, 1985, ACA Contemp, N.Y., 1988, Contemp ARts Ctr., Cin., 1990, Contemp Cutouts, Whitney Mus. Am. Art, N.Y., 1988, Ceramic Tradition: Figuration, Palo Alto Cultural Arts Ctr., Calif., 1989; two-man shows Reese Bullen Gallery, Humboldt State U., Arcata, Calif., 1989, Explorations-The Aesthetics of Excess, Am. Craft Mus., N.Y., 1990, Natural Image, Stanford Mus. and Nature Ctr., Conn., 1990, Seattle Art Mus., Nat. Mus. Contemp Art, Seoul, Corcoran Gallery Art, Washington, Mus. Fine Arts, Boston. Recipient award Nat. Endowment Arts, 1979, 81, 84; Creative Artists Pub. Svc. Program fellow, 1981, Nettie Marie Jones fellow Ctr. Music, Drama & Art, Lake Placid, N.Y., 1983. Office: c/o Fay Gold Gallery 247 Buckhead Ave NE Atlanta GA 30305

LUCEY, JEROLD FRANCIS, pediatrician; b. Holyoke, Mass., Mar. 26, 1926; s. Jeremiah F. and Pauline A. (Lally) L.; m. Ingela Barth, Oct. 7, 1972; 1 child, Patrick; children by previous marriage: Colleen, Cathy, David. AB, Dartmouth Coll., 1948; MD, NYU, 1952. Intern Bellevue Hosp., N.Y.C., 1952-53; resident in pediat. Columbia-Presbyn. Med. Ctr., 1953-55; rsch. fellow Harvard-Children's Hosp., 1955-56; rsch. fellow in biochemistry U. Vt., 1956-60, from asst. prof. to prof. pediat., 1961-74, prof., 1974—; rsch. fellow in biol. chemistry Harvard Coll., 1960-61; cons. NIH; vis. prof. Royal Soc. Medicine, Eng., 1980; Wallace prof. neonatology, 1995. Editor Pediatrics, 1974—; contbr. articles on neonatology, phototherapy and transcutaneous oxygen to profl. jours. With USNR, 1944-46. Recipient Humbolt Sr. Scientist awrd, 1978, United Cerebral Palsy Rsch. award, 1984, McDonald prize, 1991, Apgar award, 1993; Markel scholar, 1960-65, Humbolt scholar, 1978, Univ. scholar, 1991. Fellow Am. Acad. Pediat. (Grulee award 1988); mem. Royal Soc. Medicine, World congress on Perinatal Medicine (pres. 1993), Indian Pediat. Soc. (hon., Gold medal 1994). Home: 52 Overlake Park Burlington VT 05401-4012 Office: Mary Fletcher Hosp McClure Rm 718 111 Colchester Ave Burlington VT 05401-1473

LUCEY, JOHN DAVID, JR., lawyer; b. Phila., May 4, 1930; s. John David and Eleanor (Gallagher) L.; m. Carol Ann Henderson, Oct. 29, 1955; children—John David, Michael Dakin, Timothy Gallagher, Carol Anne. A.B., U. Pa., 1953, LL.B., 1956. Bar: Pa. 1957. Mem. firm LaBrum and Doak, Phila., 1957—; instr. estate counselling Temple U. Sch. Law, 1977-86; course planner, author, lectr. Pa. Bar Inst., 1967—. Mem. Phila. Bar Assn. (chmn. sect. probate and trust law 1976), Pa. Bar Assn., ABA, Am. Coll. Trust & Estate Counsel. Republican. Roman Catholic. Club: Union League of Phila. Home: 1237 Hagys Ford Rd Narberth PA 19072-1103 Office: LaBrum & Doak 1818 Market St Ste 2900 Philadelphia PA 19103-3629

LUCHAK, FRANK ALEXANDER, lawyer; b. Alberta, Can., Feb. 19, 1950; came to U.S., 1956; s. George and Elizabeth (Szilagyi) L. AB in Econs., Princeton U., 1972; JD, SUNY, Buffalo, 1978. Bar: Pa. 1978, N.J. 1979, U.S. Dist. Ct. N.J. 1979, U.S. Dist. Ct. (ea. dist.) Pa. 1980, U.S. Supreme Ct. 1986. Assoc. Harvey, Pennington et al, Phila., 1977-81; assoc. Duane, Morris & Heckscher, Phila., 1981-86, ptnr., 1986—; mng. ptnr. N.J. office, 1994—. Mem. ABA, Pa. Bar Assn., Phila. Bar Assn. (civil and jud. procedures rules com.), Pa. Assn. Def. Counsel, Phila. Assn. Def. Counsel, Def. Research Inst. Home: 27 S Hinchman Ave Haddonfield NJ 08033-3714 Office: Duane Morris & Heckscher 51 Haddonfield Rd Ste 340 Cherry Hill NJ 08002-4801

LUCHE, THOMAS CLIFFORD, foreign service officer; b. Bklyn., Jan. 24, 1934; s. Theodore Paul Albert and Jennie Kristine (Thompsen) L.; m. Winifred Jean Bogardus, May 26, 1959; children: Stephen Edward, Jenna Elizabeth, Sarah Hope. BS in Gen. Forestry, SUNY, Syracuse, 1955; student employment tng. program, Scandinavian Am. Found., Denmark and Finland, 1955-56. Various positions USAID, Saigon, Vietnam, 1957-63; rural devel. officer Joseph Z. Taylor Assocs., Chiang Mai, Thailand, 1967-70, USAID, Upper Volta, 1975-79; area coord. USAID, Arusha, Tanzania, 1979-81; grants officer USAID, Washington, 1981-83; gen. devel. officer USAID, Accra, Ghana, 1983-85; spl. projects officer USAID, Washington, 1985-87; rep. USAID, Praia, Cape Verde, 1987-92; rep. USAID, Burkina Faso, 1992-94, ret., 1994. Recipient Vietnam Civilian Service medal, 1968, HRH The Princess Mother's Memorial medal, Thailand, 1969. Mem. Am. Fgn. Svc. Assn., Sr. Fgn. Svc. of the USA, Soc. Am. Foresters. Democrat. Episcopalian. Avocations: fishing, hunting, water sports, opera, ballet.

LUCHT, JOHN CHARLES, management consultant, executive recruiter, writer; b. Reedsburg, Wis., June 1, 1933; s. Carl H. and Ruth A. (Shultis) L.; m. Catherine Ann Seyler, Dec. 11, 1965 (div. 1982). BS, U. Wis., 1955, LLB, 1960. News dir. Sta. WISC-AM/FM, Madison, Wis., 1952-55; merchandising dir. The Bartell Group (radio and TV stas.), Milw., 1955-56; instr. U. Wis. Law Sch., 1959-60; TV contracts exec., account exec. J. Walter Thompson Co., N.Y.C., 1960-64; product mgr., new products supr., dir. new product mktg. Bristol-Myers Co., N.Y.C., 1964-69; dir. mktg. W.A. Sheaffer Pen Co., Ft. Madison, Iowa, 1969-70; gen. mgr. Tetley Tea div. Squibb Beech-Nut Inc., N.Y.C., 1970-71; v.p. Heidrick & Struggles, N.Y.C., 1971-77; pres. The John Lucht Consultancy, Inc., N.Y.C., 1977—, The Viceroy Press Inc., 1987—; Lectr. in field. Author: Rites of Passage at $100,000 Plus, The Insiders's Guide to Executive Job-Changing, Executive Job-Changing Workbook. Mem. Soc. Am. Bus. Editors and Writers, Internat. Assn. Corp. and Profl. Recruiters, State Bar Wis., N.Y. Bd. Trade, Assn. Exec. Search Cons., Nat. Assn. Corp. Profl. Recruiters, N.Y. Acad. Scis., Overseas Press Club, Met. Club, Can. Club, Phi Beta Kappa, Phi Eta Sigma, Phi Kappa Phi, Phi Delta Phi, Sigma Alpha Epsilon. Office: Olympic Tower 641 5th Ave New York NY 10022-5908

LUCHTERHAND, RALPH EDWARD, financial advisor; b. Portland, Oreg., Feb. 9, 1952; s. Otto Charles II and Evelyn Alice (Isaac) L.; children: Anne Michelle, Eric Alexander, Nicholas Andrew. BS, Portland State U., 1974, MBA, 1986. Registered profl. engr., Oreg.; gen. securities broker NYSE/NASD, CFP. Mech. engr. Hyster Co., Portland, 1971-75, svc. engr., 1975-76; project engr. Lumber Systems Inc., Portland, 1976-79; prin. engr. Moore Internat., Portland, 1979-81, chief product engr., 1981-83; project engr. Irvington-Moore, Portland, 1983, chief engr., 1983-86; ind. cons. engr., 1986; engring. program mgr. Precision Castparts Corp., Portland, 1986-87; personal fin. adv., Am. Express Fin. Advs., Clackamas, Oreg., 1987-94, sr. fin. adv., 1994—; apptd. to Silver Team, 1991, Gold Team, 1994. Treas. Village Bapt. Ch., Beaverton, Oreg., 1988-91; bd. dirs. Carus Community Planning Orgn., Clackamas, Oreg., 1993—; active Rolling Hills Cmty. Ch., Tualatin, Oreg., 1995—. Republican. Home: 24440 S Eldorado Rd Mulino OR 97042-9629 Office: American Express Fin Advisors Inc 8800 SE Sunnyside Rd Ste 300 Clackamas OR 97015-9786

LUCIANO, GWENDOLYN KAYE, planning specialist, utility rates administrator; b. Cleve., Feb. 26, 1954; d. Charles Wayne and Lila (Cole) Rhodes. BA in Math. and Mktg., Lake Erie Coll., 1975, MBA, 1988. cert. project mgmt. profl. Scheduling engr. A.G. McKee & Co., Independence, Ohio, 1975-78; project scheduling supr. Perry Nuclear Plant Raymond Kaiser Engrs., Perry, Ohio, 1978-85; maintenance planning supr. Cleve. Electric Illuminating Co., 1985-89; mgmt. cons. Liberty Cons. Group, Balt., 1989-91; outage planning coord. Cleve. Electric Illuminating, 1991-94; mgr. fed. regulation Centerior Energy Corp., Independence, Ohio, 1994-96, mgr. fed. reg. and pricing, 1996—; instr. Nuclear Power Ops., Atlanta, 1993-94; bd. dirs. Learning About Bus., 1992-96. Mem. Am. Assn. Cost Engrs., Project Mgmt. Inst., Lake Erie Coll. Nat. Alumni Assn. (pres. 1996—). Republican. Episcopalian. Avocations: gourmet cooking, golf, tennis. Office: Centerior Energy Corp 6200 Oak Tree Blvd Independence OH 44131-2510

LUCIANO, PETER JOSEPH, professional society administrator; b. Washington, Dec. 10, 1946; s. Samuel Gabriel and Eleanor Claire Luciano. AB, Boston Coll., 1968; MA, Brown U., 1970. Sr. economist U.S. Dept. Commerce, 1970-76; dir. of policy devel. Transp. Inst., 1976-80, exec. dir., 1980-88; exec. dir. Nat. Bus. Travel Assn., 1988-90; v.p. APEX Property Mgmt., Inc., 1990-91; CEO Nat. Alliance of Sr. Citizens, 1991—; sec. and dir. NASC Clinkscales Found., 1992—; dir. Seniorcare Ins. Svcs., Washington, 1992—. Capt. USAR, 1964-78. Mem. Univ. Club, Nay League of the U.S. (life). Roman Catholic. Office: Nat Alliance of Sr Citizens 1700 18th St NW Fl 4 Washington DC 20009-2506

LUCIANO, ROBERT PETER, pharmaceutical company executive; b. N.Y.C., Oct. 9, 1933; s. Peter and Jennie (Mastro) L.; m. Barbara Ann Schiavone, June 21, 1953; children: Susan Ann, Richard Peter. BBA, CCNY, 1954; JD, U. Mich., 1958. Sr. tax assoc. Royall Koegel & Rogers (now Rogers & Wells), N.Y.C., 1958-66; atty. CIBA Corp., Summit, N.J., 1966-68, asst. sec., 1968-70; asst. gen. counsel, dir. pub. affairs CIBA Pharm. Co., Summit, 1970-71, v.p. mktg., 1973-75; v.p. planning and adminstrn. pharm. div. CIBA-GEIGY Corp., Summit, 1971-73, pres. pharm. div., 1975-77; pres. Lederle Labs. div. Am. Cyanamid Co., Pearl River, N.Y., 1977-78; sr. v.p. adminstrn. Schering-Plough Corp., Kenilworth, N.J., 1978-79, exec. v.p. pharm. ops., 1979-80, pres., chief operating officer, 1980-82, pres., chief exec. officer, 1982-84, chmn. bd., pres., chief exec. officer, 1984-86, chmn. bd., chief exec. officer, 1986—; bd. dirs. C.R. Bard Inc., Murray Hill, N.J., Bank of N.Y. Co. Inc., N.Y.C. Asst. editor: U. Mich. Law Rev., 1957-58. Served with U.S. Army, 1954-56. Mem. ABA, N.Y. Bar Assn., Nat. Assn. Mfrs. (bd. dirs. 1982—), N.J. State C. of C. (bd. dirs. 1986—). Republican. Clubs: Union League, Sky, Econ. (N.Y.C.). Office: Schering-Plough Corp PO Box 1000 1 Giralda Farms Madison NJ 07940-1027*

LUCID, ROBERT FRANCIS, English educator; b. Seattle, June 25, 1930; s. Philip Joseph and Nora May (Gorman) L.; m. Joanne K. Tharalson, Sept. 18, 1954; 1 son, John Michael. B.A., U. Wash., 1954; M.A., U. Chgo., 1955, Ph.D., 1958. Faculty U. Chgo., 1957-59, Wesleyan U., Middletown, Conn., 1959-64; mem. faculty U. Pa., Phila., 1964-97, prof. English, 1975-97, chmn. dept. English, 1980-85, 90-91, chmn. faculty senate, 1976-77, master Hill Coll. House, 1979-96. Editor: Journal of Richard Henry Dana, 1968, The Long Patrol, 1971, Norman Mailer, the Man and His Work, 1971. Served with USAF, 1951-53. Recipient Lindback award U. Pa., 1975, Abrams award, 1986; Yaddo fellow, 1970. Mem. MLA, AAUP, PEN (exec. bd. 1987-93), Am. Studies Assn. (exec. sec. 1964-69), Princeton Club (N.Y.C.), Penn Club (N.Y.C.). Office: U Pa Dept English Dept English Philadelphia PA 19104

LUCIDO, CHESTER CHARLES, JR., management consultant; b. Pitts., Dec. 5, 1939; s. Chester C. and Alma (Dolence) L.; m. Linda G. Firrell, June 16, 1962; children: Chester C. III, Bradley J., Kristen L. BS in Mgmt., Pa. State U., 1961. Sales rep. Prentice-Hall, Englewood Cliffs, N.J., 1962-63, supr. sales, 1963-66, dist. mgr., 1966-69, editor, 1969-71, mgr. regional sales, 1971-72, exec. editor, 1972; pub., v.p. Glencoe Press, Encino, Calif., 1972-77; v.p. Little, Brown & Co., Boston, 1977-86, sr. v.p., 1986-88; pres., chief exec. officer Van Nostrand Reinhold, N.Y.C., 1988-89, South-Western Pub. Co., Cin., 1990-93; COO Encore Mktg. Internat., Inc., Lanham, Md., 1994-95; mgmt. cons., 199—. With U.S. Army, 1961-62. Mem. Assn. Am. Pubs. (exec. coun. higher edn. 1977-87, chmn. 1987, profl. and scholarly exec. coun. 1988-89, sch. exec. coun. 1990-91). Republican. Episcopalian. Avocation: reading, running. Home: 5 Deepwater Ct Edgewater MD 21037-1216 Home and Office: Encore Mktg Internat 4501 Forbes Blvd Lanham Seabrook MD 20706

LUCIER, JAMES ALFRED, advertising executive; b. Grand Forks, N.D., Feb. 5, 1920; s. Alfred Joseph and Mildred Perry (Fahar) L.; B.A., U. Minn., 1946; postgrad. U. So. Methodist, 1965; m. Juliann K. Dunlap, July 26, 1991; children: Edward, Kelley, John, Jane, Teddi, James. Sales exec. Times, Ft. Smith, Ark., 1946-47; sales mgr. KRKN, Ft. Smith, 1947-48; dir. advt. Times, Fayetteville, Ark., 1948-51; sales exec. Express, San Antonio, 1952-53; mgr. Sunday mag. Times, Dallas, 1953-65; dir. advt. and advt. and pub. relations Home Furniture Co., Dallas, 1965-81; advt. mgr. Smith Furniture Co., Dallas, 1981-85; v.p./gen. mgr. Home Furnishings Internat. Assn., 1985—; owner Lucier Assocs. Advt., Dallas, 1965—. Assoc. pub. Home Furnishings Rev., 1986—. Unit chmn. United Way, 1965-81; precinct chmn. Democratic Party, 1974-85; mem. bd. Dem. Forum, 1974-75; pres. bd. dirs. Dallas council USO; mem. orgns. com. Greater Dallas Sesquicentennial Com., 1983-86. Served with inf., AUS, 1942-44, USAAF, 1944-45, USAF, 1951-52. Decorated Air medal with 2 oak leaf clusters. Mem. Retail Furniture Assn. Greater Dallas (pres. 1971-72, pres. 1983-84, dir. 1972-85), Sigma Delta Chi, Theta Chi. Episcopalian. Clubs: Exchange (pres. E.Dallas 1967, pres. Tex. dist. 1969-70, nat. dir. 1970-72, chmn. nat. edn. com. 1974-76, fin. com. 1976-80), U. Minn. Alumni (past pres.), Vagabond, Dallas Magic Circle (past pres.). Home: 4345 Meadowdale Ln Dallas TX 75229-5339 Office: Home Furnishings Internat Assn 110 World Trade Ctr Dallas TX 75258

LUCIER, P. JEFFREY, publishing executive; b. Manchester, N.H., June 20, 1941; s. Paul A. and Elaine (Wilson) Fraser L.; m. Judith Margaret Akers, Dec. 21, 1963 (div. 1975); children—Kathryn Elizabeth, Amy Wilson; m. Velma Lee Frye, Nov. 27, 1976 (div. 1981); m. Susan Elizabeth Hess, May 25, 1985; children: Madalyn Antonette, Caitlin Elaine. B.A., Union Coll., N.Y., 1963; M.A., U. Chgo., 1964. Instr. English Northwestern U., Evanston and Chgo., Ill., 1967-69; registered rep. Paine Webber, Akron, Ohio, 1969-71; asst. to pres. Banks-Baldwin Law Pub., Cleve., 1971-74, v.p. editorial, 1974-76, exec. v.p., 1977-78, pres., editor-in-chief, 1978—; mem. adv. bd. Cleve. Collaborative for Math. Edn. Trustee Horizon Montessori Sch.; pres. Cleve. chpt. Juvenile Diabetes Found. Internat. Mem. Graphic Communication Assn., Ohio Regional Assn. Law Libraries. Democrat. Roman Catholic. Club: Cleve. City. Office: Banks Baldwin Law Pub Co 6111 Oak Tree Blvd Cleveland OH 44131

LUCK, DAVID JONATHAN LEWIS, biologist, educator; b. Milw., Jan. 7, 1929; s. Max. and Sarah (Plonsker) L. S.B., U. Chgo., 1949; M.D., Harvard, 1953; Ph.D., Rockefeller U., 1962. House officer Mass. Gen. Hosp., Boston, 1953-54; resident physician Mass. Gen. Hosp., 1957-58; research asso. Rockefeller U., 1962—, mem. faculty, 1964—, prof. biology, 1968—; v.p. acad. affairs, 1994. Editor: Jour. Cell Biology, 1968-74. Served to capt. USAF, 1955-57. Decorated Commendation medal with oak leaf cluster. Mem. Am. Soc. Biol. Chemists, Am. Soc. Cell Biologists, Nat. Acad. Sci. Club: University (N.Y.C.). Home: 205 E 78th St New York NY 10021-1243

LUCK, EDWARD CARMICHAEL, professional society administrator; b. Urbana, Ill., Oct. 17, 1948; s. David Johnston and Adele Suzanne (Kanter) L.; m. Dana Dee Zaret, June 19, 1971; 1 dau., Jessica Robin. B.A. cum laude with high distinction in Internat. Relations, Dartmouth Coll., 1970; M.I.A., Columbia U., 1972, M.A., 1973, M.Ph., 1974. Project dir. conventional arms control UN Assn. of U.S.A., N.Y.C., 1974-77, dep. dir., dep. v.p. for policy studies, 1977-82, v.p. policy studies, 1982-83, exec. v.p., 1983-84, pres., 1984-94, pres. emeritus, sr. policy advisor, 1994—; cons. UN, 1995—; cons. book project 20th Century Fund, 1995—; cons. social sci. dept. Rand Corp., Santa Monica, Calif., 1973-76, U.N., 1995—. Co-editor, contbr. On The Endings of War, 1980; editor, contbr. Arms Control: The Multilateral Alternative, 1983; contbr. articles to profl. publs. Herbert H. Lehman fellow and Internat. fellow Columbia U., 1970-73; jr. fellow, cert. Russian Inst., Columbia U, 1973-74. Mem. Coun. Fgn. Rels., Century Assn. Democrat. Home: 136 Elm Rd Briarcliff Manor NY 10510-2225

LUCK, GEORG HANS BHAWANI, classics educator; b. Bern, Switzerland, Feb. 17, 1926; came to U.S., 1951; s. Hans and Hanna (Von Ow) L.; m. Harriet Richards Greenough, June 15, 1957; children: Annina, Hans, Stephanie. Student, U. Bern, 1945-49, 50-51, Ph.D., 1953; student, U. Paris, 1949-50; A.M. (Smith-Mundt fellow), Harvard, 1952. Instr. classics Yale U., 1952-53; instr. classics Brown U., 1953-55, vis. prof., 1969; instr. classics Harvard U., 1955-58; vis. prof. Summer Sch., 1968; lectr. classics U. Mainz, 1958-62; prof. classics U. Bonn, 1962-71; vis. prof. Johns Hopkins U., 1970-71, prof. classics, 1971-90; prof. emeritus, 1990—; chmn. dept. classics Johns Hopkins U., 1973-75; vis. prof. classics UCLA, 1974, U. Fribourg, 1989; lectr. Smithsonian Instutions, 1992. Author: Der Akademiker Antiochos, 1953, The Latin Love Elegy, 1959, 2d edit., 1969, Über einige Interjektionen, d. lat. Umgangssprache, 1964, Ovid, Tristia, text, transl. and commentary, 2 vols., 1967-77, Untersuchungen zur Textgeschichte Ovids, 1969, Eine Schwezerreise: Ausdem Tagebuch des Alfred Meill von Salisbury, 1981, Arcana Mundi: Magic and the Occult in the Greek and Roman World, 1985 (Spanish and Italian edits. 1994), Kulak, Der Bürgerkrieg, 1985, Der Dichter in der Kutsche, 1986; editor: Tibullus, Carmina, 1987, Magie und andere Geheimwissenschaften der Antike, 1990, Properz und Tibull, Elegien, 1996, Collected Essays on Ancient Religion, Magic and Philosophy, 1996; editor-in-chief Am. Jour. Philology, 1971-81, 86-89; editor Noctes Romanae, 1975—; contbr. articles to profl. jours. Guggenheim fellow, 1958-59; Swiss Nat. Research Council grantee, 1976-77. Mem. Johns Hopkins Club. Episcopalian. Avocations: gardening, hiking, classical guitar. Home: 1108 Bryn Mawr Rd Baltimore MD 21210-1213 Office: Johns Hopkins U Classics Dept Baltimore MD 21218 *I am not sure I know what success really means, but I do know today that the rewards for your work or your dedication or your experience and skill do not come from outside; they must be found within you, as a gift from God.*

LUCK, JAMES I., foundation executive; b. Akron, Ohio, Aug. 28, 1945; s. Milton William and Gertrude (Winer) L.; children: Andrew Brewer, Edward Aldrich, L. BA, Ohio State U., 1967; MA, U. Ga., 1970. Caseworker Franklin County Welfare Dept., Columbus, Ohio, 1967-69; dir. forensics Tex. Christian U., Ft. Worth, 1970-74; assoc. dir. Bicentennial Youth Debates, Washington, 1974-76; exec. dir. Nat. Congress on Volunteerism and Citizenship, Washington, 1976-77; fellow Acad. Contemporary Problems, Columbus, Ohio, 1977-79; exec. dir. Battelle Meml. Inst. Found., Columbus, 1980-82; pres. Columbus Found., 1981—; exec. dir. Columbus Youth Found. and Ingram-White Castle Found., Columbus, 1981—; bd. dirs. Cardinal Group of Founds.; co-chmn. Task Force on Citizen Edn., Washington, 1977; mediator Negotiated Investment Strategy, Columbus, 1979; chmn. Ohio Founds. Conf., 1985; cons. HEW, Peace Corps., U. Va.; bd. vis. McGregor Sch., Antioch U. Author: Ohio-The Next 25 Years, 1978, Bicentennial Issue Analysis, 1975; editor: Proceedings of the Nat. Conf. on Argumentation, 1973; contbr. articles to profl. jours. Trustee Godman Guild Settlement House, Columbus, 1979-81, Am. Diabetes Assn., Ohio, 1984-88; chmn. spl. com. on displacement Columbus City Coun., 1978-80; bd. dirs. Commn. on the Future of the Professions in Soc., 1979. Mem. Donors Forum Ohio. Clubs: Capital, University, Columbus Met., Kit-Kat. Lodge: Rotary. Avocations: travel, reading. Home: 1318 Hickory Ridge Ln Columbus OH 43235-1131 Office: The Columbus Found 1234 E Broad St Columbus OH 43205-1463

LUCKE, ROBERT VITO, merger and acquisition executive; b. Kingston, Pa., July 26, 1930; s. Vito Frank and Edith Ann (Adders) L.; m. Jane Ann

Rushin, Aug. 16, 1952; children: Thomas, Mark, Carl. BS in Chemistry, Pa. State U., 1952; MS in Mgmt., Rensselaer Polytech Inst., 1960. Polymer chemist Uniroyal Naugatuck (Conn.) Chem. Div., 1954-60; comml. devel. engr. Exxon Enjay Div., Elizabeth, N.J., 1960-66; gen. mgr. Celanese Advanced Composites, Summit, N.J., 1966-70; bus. mgr. polymer div. Hooker Chem., Burlington, N.J., 1970-74; gen. mgr. Oxy Metal Industries Environ. Equipment. Divs., Warren, Mich., 1974-79; v.p., gen. mgr. Hoover Universal Plastic Machinery Divs., Manchester, Mich., 1979-84; pres. Egan Machinery, Somerville, N.J., 1984-87; pres., chief exec. officer Krauss Maffei Corp., Cin., 1987-93; pres. Dubuc, Lucke, Koring Co., Inc., Cin., 1990—; instr., Chem. Market Rsch. Assn., 1974. Author: (with others) Plastics Handbook, 1972; inventor, patentee in field. 1st lt. Corp Engrs., 1952-54, Korea. Senatorial scholar, Pa. State U., 1948-52. Mem. Am. Chem. Soc., Soc. Plastics Engrs. (sect. engr. STDS com. 1969), Tech. Assn. Pulp Paper Industry, Comml. Devel. Assn., Assn. Corp. Growth. Avocations: golf, skiing, travel, gardening. Office: Dubuc Lucke & Co Ste 1005 120 W 5th St Cincinnati OH 45202-2710

LUCKER, JAY K., library education educator; b. N.Y.C., Feb. 23, 1930; s. Joseph Jerome and Ella (Schwartz) L.; m. Marjorie Stern, Aug. 17, 1952; children—Amy Ellen, Nancy Judith. A.B., Bklyn. Coll., City U. N.Y., 1951; M.S., Columbia, 1952; postgrad., N.Y. U., 1955-57. Head procurement br., acquisition div. New York Pub. Library, 1954-57, first asst., acting chief, sci. and tech. div., 1957-59; asst. univ. librarian for sci. and tech., asso. prof. Princeton U. Library, 1959-68, asso. univ. librarian, prof., 1968-75; dir. librs. MIT, Cambridge, 1975-95; vis. prof. Grad. Sch. Libr. and Info. Sci. Simmons Coll., Boston, 1995—; chmn. bd. dirs. Captain Libr. Svcs. Corp., 1972-75; vis. lectr. Drexel U. Grad. Sch. Libr. Svc., 1962-67; vice chmn. New Eng. Libr. Info. Network, 1978-79, chmn., 1980-82. Bd. dirs. Boston Libr. Consortium; mem. adv. coms. Brown U., Tufts U., Washington U., St. Louis, Libr. Congress, Engring. Info. Inc. Served with Signal Corps U.S. Army, 1952-54. Council on Library Resources fellow, 1970-71. Mem. ALA (council 1978-82), AAAS, Am. Soc. Info. Sci., N.J. Library Assn. (Distinguished Service award coll. and univ. sect. 1975), Assn. Research Libraries (chmn. interlibrary loan com. 1976-80, dir. 1977-80, pres. 1980-81), Spl. Libraries Assn., Phi Beta Kappa, Alpha Phi Omega, Beta Phi Mu. Office: Simmons Coll Grad Sch Libr & Info Sci Boston MA 02115

LUCKER, RAYMOND ALPHONSE, bishop; b. St. Paul, Feb. 24, 1927; s. Alphonse and Josephine (Schiltgen) L. B.A., St. Paul Sem., 1948, M.A., 1952; S.T.L., U. St. Thomas, Rome, 1965, S.T.D., 1966; Ph.D., U. Minn., 1969; LHD honoris causa, Coll. St. Catherine, 1993. Ordained priest Roman Cath. Ch., 1952, bishop, 1971. Asst. dir. Confrat. of Christian Doctrine, Archdiocese of St. Paul, 1952-58, dir., 1958-68; prof. catechetics St. Paul Sem., 1957-68; dir. dept. edn. U.S. Cath. Conf., Washington, 1969-71; consecrated bishop, 1971; aux. bishop of St. Paul and Mpls., 1971-76; bishop of New Ulm, Minn., 1976—. Author: Aims of Religious Education, 1966, Some Presuppositions on Released Time, 1969, My Experience: Reflections on Pastoring, 1988; editor: The People's Catechism, 1995; contbg. author: Catholic Social Thought, 1990, The Universal Catechism Reader, 1990, Living the Vision, 1992. Recipient Nat. Catechetical award, 1991. Home: 1400 6th St N New Ulm MN 56073-2057 Office: Catholic Pastoral Ctr 1400 6th St N New Ulm MN 56073-2057

LUCKETT, BYRON EDWARD, JR., air force chaplain; b. Mineral Wells, Tex., Feb. 2, 1951; s. Byron Edward and Helen Alma (Hart) L.; m. Kathryn Louise Lambertson, Dec. 30, 1979; children: Florence Louise, Byron Edward III, Barbara Elizabeth, Stephanie Hart. BS, U.S. Mil. Acad., 1973; MDiv, Princeton Theol. Sem., 1982; MA, Claremont Grad. Sch., 1987. Commd. 2d lt. U.S. Army, 1973, advanced through grades to maj.; stationed at Camp Edwards, Korea, 1974-75; bn. supply officer 563rd Engr. Bn., Kornwestheim, Germany, 1975-76; platoon leader, exec. officer 275th Engr. Co., Ludwigsburg, Germany, 1976-77; boy scout project officer Hdqrs., VII Corps, Stuttgart, Germany, 1977-78; student intern Moshannon Valley Larger Parish, Winburne, Penn., 1980-81; Protestant chaplain Philmont Scout Ranch, Cimarron, N.Mex., 1982; asst. pastor Immanuel Presbyn. Ch., Albuquerque, 1982-83, assoc. pastor, 1983-84; tchr. Claremont High Sch., 1985-86; Protestant chaplain 92nd Combat Support Group, Fairchild AFB, Wash., 1986-90; installation staff chaplain Pirinclik Air Station, Turkey, 1990-91; protestant chaplain Davis-Monthan AFB, Ariz., 1991-95; dir. readiness ministries Offutt AFB, Nebr., 1995, sr. protestant chaplain, 1996; mem. intern program coun. Claremont (Calif.) Grad. Sch. Contbr. articles to profl. jours. Bd. dirs. Parentcraft, Inc., Albuquerque, 1984, United Campus Ministries, Albuquerque, 1984, Proclaim Liberty, Inc., Spokane, 1987-90; bd. dirs. western region Nat. Assn. Presbyn. Scouters, Irving, Tex., 1986-89, chaplain, 1991-93; mem. N.Mex. Employer Co, in Support of the Guard and Reserve, Albuquerque, 1984, Old Baldy coun. Boy Scouts Am., 1986; chmn. Fairchild Parent Coop., Fairchild AFB, 1986-87; pres. Co. Grade Officers Coun., Fairchild AFB, 1987-88. Capt. U.S. Army Reserve; chaplain USAF Reserve 1983-86, maj. 1990—. Recipient Dist. Award of Merit for Disting. Svc. Boy Scouts Am., 1977. Mem. Soc. Cin. Md., Mil. Order Fgn. Wars U.S. Presbyterian. Home: 12909 S 29th Ave Bellevue NE 68123 Office: 55 WG/HC 301 Lincoln Hwy Offutt A F B NE 68113

LUCKETT, PAUL HERBERT, III, manufacturing executive; b. El Paso, Tex., Feb. 6, 1935; s. Paul Herbert Jr. and Maxine (Mooney) L.; m. Caroline Foisie, Oct. 6, 1956 (div. Mar. 1991); children: Elizabeth Winkler, Christopher Lloyd; m. Cheryl Elaine Kanoff, June 15, 1991. BSChemE, MIT, 1956. Various positions El Paso Products Co., El Paso Co., 1956-69; exec. v.p. Beaunit Corp., El Paso Co., Raleigh, N.C. and N.Y.C., 1969-77; pres. Penn Athletic Co., Gencorp., Monroesville, Pa., 1977-82; pres. wallcovering divsn. Gencorp., Hanckensack, N.J., 1982-89; COO Insilco, Midland, Tex., 1989-91; dir. bus. devel. Wagner & Brown, Midland, 1991—; pres., CEO Flamecoat Systems, Inc., 1991-94; assoc. Bariston, Inc., West Palm Beach, Fla., 1994—. 2d lt. U.S. Army, 1957. Mem. Union League Club (N.Y.C.), Racquet Club (Midland), Delta Kappa Epsilon. Roman Catholic. Avocations: bicycling, hiking, snorkeling, tennis. Office: Bariston (USA) Inc 400 N Congress Ave West Palm Beach FL 33401-9999

LUCKEY, ALWYN HALL, lawyer; b. Biloxi, Miss., Oct. 3, 1960; s. Toxie Hall and Joy Evelyn (Smith) L.; m. Jeanne Elaine Carter, Aug. 4, 1984; children: Laurel McKay, Taylor Leah. BA in Zoology, U. Miss., 1982, JD, 1985. Bar: Miss. 1985, U.S. Dist. Ct. (so. and no. dist.) Miss. 1985, U.S. Ct. Appeals (5th cir.) 1985. Assoc. Richard F. Scruggs, Pascagoula, Miss., 1985-88; shareholder Richard F. Scruggs, Pascagoula, 1988—, Asbestos Group P.A., 1988-93; prin. Alwyn H. Luckey, Atty. at Law, Ocean Springs, Miss., 1993—; v.p., bd. dirs. Marine Mgmt., Inc., Ocean Springs, Miss., 1987—. Author: Mississippi Landlord Tenant Law, 1985. Deacon First Presbyn. Ch., Ocean Springs, 1989; chmn. Dole for Pres. com., Jackson County, 1988. Mem. Am. Trial Lawyers Assn., Miss. Bar Assn., Miss. Trial Lawyers Assn., Jackson County Bar Assn., Jackson County Young Lawyers Assn. (v.p.), Ocean Springs Yacht Club, Bienville Club, Treasure Oak Country Club. Avocations: tennis, boating, traveling. Office: 705 Washington Ave Ocean Springs MS 39564

LUCKEY, DORIS WARING, civic volunteer; b. Union City, N.J., Sept. 17, 1929; d. Jay Deloss and Edna May (Ware) Waring; m. George William Luckey, Mar. 29, 1958; children: G. Robert, Jana Elizabeth, John Andrew. AB, U. Rochester, 1950; CLU, Am. Coll., Bryn Mawr, Pa., 1957. With pers. dept., supr. life dept. Travelers Ins. Co., Rochester, N.Y., 1952-58; agt. asst. life underwriting Mass. Mut. Ins. Co., Rochester, 1958. Chairperson, various past offices Bd. Coop. Ednl. Svcs. and State Edn. Dept., Vocat. Tech. Adv. Com., Rochester and Albany, 1975—, pres. Rochester, 1975-85, Monroe County Sch. Bds. Assn., Rochester, 1980-81; v.p. Penfield (N.Y.) Schs., 1978-81; various fin. ednl. and speaking engagements LWV, 1983—; pres. ch. coun., chair ch. and min. com., co-chair United Ch. Christ denomination, Genesee Valley; pres. William Warfield Scholarship Fund Bd.; former adv. to bd. St. John's Home for Aging, mem. bd.; vol. numerous other civic, cultural, ch. and artistic orgns. Mem. AAUW (past pres., past bd. dirs., dist. 1 state rep.). Republican.

LUCKEY, ROBERT REUEL RAPHAEL, retired academic administrator; b. Houghton, N.Y., Nov. 19, 1917; s. James Seymour and Edith Bedell (Curtis) L.; m. Ruth Ida Brooks, Aug. 25, 1945; children: James, John, Linda, Peter, Daniel (dec.), Thomas. BS, BA, Houghton Coll., 1937; MA, N.Y. U., 1939; PhD, Cornell U., 1942; LittD, Houghton Coll., 1980; LLD, Marion Coll., 1987. Secondary tchr. Wilson (N.Y.) Cen. Sch., 1937-39; math. & physics instr. Houghton Coll., 1942, assoc. prof., prof. math. and physics, alumni dir., 1954, dir. devel., v.p. in devel.; pres. Marion (Ind.) Coll., 1976-84, 1986-87. Pres. Seneca Council Boy Scouts Am., Olean, N.Y., 1964-65; assessor Township of Caneadea, N.Y., 1951-76. Recipient Silver Beaver award Boy Scouts Am., 1965; named Alumnus of Yr. Houghton Coll., 1976, Disting. Alumnus Houghton Coll., 1984, Sagamore of the Wabash by Gov. of Ind., 1980. Mem. Grant County C. of C. (bd. dirs. 1981-84). Republican. Wesleyan. Avocations: golfing, personal computers. Home: 7363 Campus Heights Houghton NY 14744-9718

LUCKING, PETER STEPHEN, marketing consultant, industrial engineer; b. Kalamazoo, Oct. 11, 1945; s. Henry William, Sr., and Mary (Lynn) L.; m. Marilyn Barbara Jensen, Dec. 18, 1971. BA, Western Mich. U., 1968; BS in Indsl. Engring., 1973. Indsl. engr. Motorola, Phoenix, 1974, Revlon, Inc., Phoenix, 1974-75; indsl. engr. Hooker Chem. and Plastics Co., Niagara Falls, N.Y., 1975-76, sr. corp. indsl. engr., 1976-77; indsl. engr. Carborundum Co., Niagara Falls, 1977-78; cons. H.B. Maynard and Co., Pitts., 1978-85; mgr. indsl. engring. Carrier, Tyler, Tex., 1985-88; cons. H.B. Maynard and Co., Pitts., 1988-92; pres., mktg. cons. MARPET Systems, Inc., 1992—; lectr. in field, 1989. Advisor, Jr. Achievement, Niagara Falls, 1977. Author chpts. to books. Served with U.S. Army, 1969-70, Vietnam. Mem. Inst. Indsl. Engrs. (sr. mem., region v.p. 1983-85), Inst. Indsl. Engrs. (pres. Niagara Frontier chpt. 1977-78, paper presented fall conf.). Democrat. Roman Catholic. Home: 12826 Weatherstone Dr Florissant MO 63033-4045 Office: MARPET Systems Inc 11220 W Flossant Ste 141 Saint Louis MO 63033

LUCKMAN, CHARLES, architect; b. Kansas City, Mo., May 16, 1909; m. Harriet McElroy, 1931; children: Charles, James M., Stephen A. Grad. magna cum laude, U. Ill., 1931; LLD, U. Miami, Fla., 1950; AFD (hon.), Calif. Coll. Arts and Crafts, 1958; DFA (hon.), Adelphi U., 1986; LLD (hon.), Pepperdine U., 1989. Lic. architect, 1931 Registered architect, 48 states and D.C. sr. registration Nat. Archtl. Registration Bds. Employed in architect's office for license qualifications, 2 years; joined Colgate- Palmolive-Peet Co. as retail salesman, 1931, Chgo. sales supr., 1933; mgr. Colgate-Palmolive-Peet Co. as retail salesman (Wis. dist.), 1934; divisional mgr. Colgate- Palmolive-Peet Co. as retail salesman (Cin. hdqrs.), 1935; with Pepsodent Co. (later Pepsodent Div. of Lever Bros. Co.), 1935-50, sales promotion mgr., sales mgr., 1935-36, v.p. in charge sales, 1936, in charge sales and advt., 1937, v.p., gen. mgr., 1938, exec. v.p., 1942-43, pres., 1943-46; exec. v.p. Lever Bros., Jan.-July 1946, pres., 1946-50; pres., partner Pereira & Luckman, Los Angeles, 1950-58; founder, ptnr. The Luckman Partnership, Inc., 1958—; chmn. bd., chief exec. officer Ogden Devel. Corp., 1968-74, Luckman Mgmt. Co., 1973—; dir. Hollywood Bowl. Maj. projects include Madison Sq. Garden, N.Y.C., Conv. and Exhbn. Center, Los Angeles, U.S. World's Fair Pavilion, N.Y.C., Los Angeles World Zoo, U. Calif. at Santa Barbara, Civic Plaza, Phoenix, Prudential Center, Boston, State Office Bldg, Madison, Wis., Phoenix Civic Plaza, Los Angeles Internat. Airport, First Nat. Bank of Ariz, Phoenix, Broadway Plaza, Los Angeles, United Calif. Bank, Los Angeles, U. Del. Student Living Center, La Jolla VA Hosp, Aloha Stadium, Honolulu, 9200 Sunset Tower, Los Angeles, Manned Space Craft Center, Houston, VA Hosp, West Los Angeles, Calif., Hoover Library and Linear Accelerator Center, Stanford U., 1st Natl Bank of Oreg, Portland, Forum, Inglewood, Calif., Ralph M. Parsons Co. hdqrs, Pasadena, Calif., Nat. Security and Resources Study Center, Los Alamos, Hyatt Regency Hotels, Dearborn, Mich., The Harriet & Charles Luckman Fine Arts Complex, L.A., The Harriet & Charles Luckman Child Guidance Clin., L.A., Phoenix, City Hall and Police Bldg., Inglewood, Xerox Corp. hdqrs., Stamford, Conn., Warner Bros. Office Bldg., Burbank, Calif., Orange County Conv./Civic Ctr., Orlando, Fla.; also numerous other pub. bldgs; author: (autobiography) Twice in a Lifetime, 1988. Pres., chmn. bd. Los Angeles Orchestral Soc., 1962; v.p., dir. So. Calif. Symphony Assn.; mem. bd. assocs., pres. council George Pepperdine Found., Los Angeles; trustee Calif. State Colls.; chmn. bd. trustees, 1963-65; bd. govs. Library Presdl. Papers; trustee Nat. Art Mus. Sport; mem. U. Ill. Found.; Calif. mem. Ednl. Commn. of States; mem. bd. Am. Nat. Red Cross, YMCA; bd. dirs., past pres. AID-United Givers.; Mem. Pres.'s Commn. on Equality of Treatment and Opportunity in Armed Services and Civil Rights, Gov.'s Commn. Met. Area Problems; dir. Advt. Council; trustee Adelphi U.; chmn. Citizens Food Com., 1947; mem. Commerce and Industry Assn. N.Y.C., Los Angeles World Affairs Council, Com. Econ. Devel., Council U.S. Assocs. of Internat. C. of C.; bd. dirs. Nat. Adv. Council Community Chest, Am. Heritage Found.; bd. assocs. Northwestern U., Calif. Inst. Tech.; chmn. Nat. Council Trustees of Freedoms Found. at Valley Forge, 1986. Decorated Star of Solidarity Republic of Italy; chevalier Nat. Order Legion of Honor France; Order of St. John; recipient Horatio Alger award Am. Schs. and Colls. Assn., George Washington Honor medal Freedom's Found., 1964, 67, 68, Make Am. Beautiful award Nat. Assn. Realty Bds.; named Outstanding Mgmt. Exec. N.Y. Mgmt. Club, Man of Year Constrn. Industries, 1974; Disting. Achievement award U. Ill., 1970; Henry Laurence Gantt medal Am. Mgmt. Assn. and ASMF, 1981. Mem. AIA (Fellowship award 1963), Ill. Soc. Architects, U.S. Jr. C. of C. (One of Outstanding Young Men 1945, dir.), Tau Beta Pi, Theta Tau, Gargoyle. Home and Office: The Luckman Management Co 9220 W Sunset Blvd West Hollywood CA 90069-3501

LUCKNER, HERMAN RICHARD, III, interior designer; b. Newark, Ohio, Mar. 14, 1933; s. Herman Richard and Helen (Friednour) L. BS, U. Cin., 1957. Cert. interior designer and appraiser. Interior designer Greiwe Inc., Cin., 1957-64; owner, internat. designer Designers Loft Interiors, Cin., 1964—; owner Designer Accents, Cin., 1991—. Mem. bd. adv. Ohio Valley Organ Procurement Ctr., Cin., 1987—, U. Cin. Fine Arts Collection and Hist. Southwest Ohio. Mem. Am. Soc. Interior Designers, Appraisers Assn. Am., Metropolitan Club. Republican. Avocations: needlepoint, collecting 18th century Chinese porcelain. Home and Office: 555 Compton Rd Cincinnati OH 45231-5005

LUCKOW, LYNN D. W., publishing executive; b. Hettinger, N.D., 1949. Grad., U. N.D., 1971, Ind. U., 1974. Pres., pub. Jossey-Bass Inc. Pub., San Francisco. Home: 666 Post St San Francisco CA 94109-8232 Office: Jossey-Bass Inc Pub 350 Sansome St Fl 5 San Francisco CA 94104-1304

LUCOW, MILTON, lawyer; b. Detroit, Oct. 4, 1924; s. Louis and Dora (Schupps) L.; m. Audrey B. Kline, Mar. 30, 1947; children: Celia (Mrs. James Stegman), Michael B. LLD, Wayne State U., 1948. Bar: Mich. bar 1948. Since practiced in Detroit; ptnr., pres. firm Garan, Lucow, Miller, Seward & Cooper (P.C.), Detroit, 1948-95; of counsel, 1995—; lectr. in field; mediator Wayne Circuit Ct. Mich., 1973—. Pres. Detroit Svc. Group, 1983-87; bd. dirs. Jewish Welfare Fedn. Detroit; pres. Temple Emanu-El, 1960-62; chmn. Madrasha Coll. Jewish Learning, 1977-80, United Found., atty.'s sec., 1985; pres. United Hebrew Schs. Detroit, 1974-77. Sgt. U.S. Army, 1943-45, ETO. Decorated Purple Heart, Metz medal, Bronze Star. Mem. ABA, Am. Arbitration Assn. (arbitrator), Detroit Bar Assn., Mich. Bar Assn. (mem. del. assembly 1979-80), Def. Rsch. Inst. Tam-O-Shanter Club (pres. 1971-72), Longboat Key Club. Avocations: golf, tennis, squash. Home: 7529 Danbury Dr West Bloomfield MI 48322-3564 Office: Garan Lucow Miller Seward & Cooper 1000 Woodbridge St Detroit MI 48207-3108 Home: Apt 94N 2301 Gulf of Mexico Dr Longboat Key FL 34228

LUCY, DENNIS DURWOOD, JR., neurologist; b. Little Rock, July 3, 1934; s. Dennis Durwood and Ann Louise (Besiegel) L.; m. Patricia Wilch, Nov. 26, 1958; children: Stephen H., Vincent A., Denise D., David D. B.S., U. Ark., 1959, M.D., 1959. Diplomate: Am. Bd. Psychiatry and Neurology. Intern U. Ark. Med. Scis., 1959-60, resident in internal medicine, 1960-62, resident in psychiatry, 1962-63; resident in neurology U. Iowa Hosp., 1963-64, 65-66; instr., acting head dept. neurology U. Ark., 1964-65, prof., 1974—, chmn. dept. neurology, 1966-94; mem. exec. com. U. Ark. Coll. Medicine, 1979-83, chmn. council Departmental Chairmen, 1980-81; chief of staff Univ. Hosp., 1973-76. Bd. dirs. Ark. chpt. Multiple Sclerosis Soc., 1965-78; mem. Ark. Council Devel. Disabilities, 1971-74; bd. dirs. Ark. chpt. Epilepsy Soc., 1972-76; bd. dirs. Holy Souls Cath. Sch., 1974-77, pres. bd., 1976-77. Recipient Golden Apple award U. Ark., 1968-69. Mem. AMA, Am. Acad. Neurology, Ark. Med. Soc., Pulaski County Med. Soc., Alpha Omega Alpha. Roman Catholic. Home: 17 Robinwood Little Rock AR 72227-2241 Office: 4301 W Markham St Little Rock AR 72205-7101

LUCY, ROBERT MEREDITH, lawyer; b. Poplar Bluff, Mo., Apr. 16, 1926; s. James Raymond and Lucile Hargrove (Meredith) L.; m. Mary White George, June 10, 1947; children—Meredith Lucy Knight, Celia Lucy Denton, John Rackley, Robert Meredith Jr. BS, U.S. Naval Acad., 1947; JD, George Washington U., 1954, MS in Internat. Affairs, 1968. Bar: Mo. 1954, D.C. 1954. Commd. 2d lt. USMC, 1947; advanced through grades to col., 1974; student Air War Coll. Maxwell AFB, Montgomery, Ala., 1967-68; staff judge adv. 1st Marine Div., Danang, Vietnam, 1969-70; asst. for legal affairs Office Asst. Sec. Navy for Manpower and Res. Affairs, Washington, 1970-71; legal advisor, legis. asst. to chmn. Joint Chiefs of Staff, Washington, 1971-74; ret., 1974; ptnr. Bryan Cave, St. Louis, 1974—; chmn. litigation dept. Bryan, Cave, St. Louis, 1992-94, vice chmn., 1994-95. Dir. St. Andrew's Episcopal Presbyn. Found., 1995—. Decorated Bronze Star, Legion of Merit (3). Mem. ABA (litigation sect.), TechLaw Group, Inc. (pres. 1994-95), Childrens Home Soc. of Mo. (trustee 1989—). Presbyterian. Home: 38 Picardy Ln Saint Louis MO 63124-1628 Office: Bryan Cave 1 Metropolitan Sq Saint Louis MO 63102-2750

LUCYK, WILLIAM, financial planner; b. Detroit, Apr. 5, 1932; s. William and Nellie (Swincicki) L.; m. Mariann V. Lucyk, May 2, 1958; children: Charron R., William, Steven, Matthew. AA, Shasta Coll., 1979. Cert. life and disability and variable Nat. Assn. Stock Dealers. Pvt. practice retirement, estate, tax reduction fin. planning Calif., 1980-94; account rep. United Resources, L.A., 1986, Bank of Am., Red Bluff, Calif., 1989. Home: 12420 Charron Ln Redding CA 96003-7533

LUDDEN, JOHN FRANKLIN, retired financial economist; b. Michigan City, Ind., May 6, 1930. BS in Econs., U. Wis., 1952, MS in Econs., 1955; postgrad., U. Mich., 1955-59. Wage and hour investigator U.S. Dept. Labor, 1960, mgmt. intern, 1960-61, labor economist, 1963; economist, instr. U.S. Bur. of Labor Statis., 1961-63; economist Office of Internat. Ops. IRS, 1963-68, fin. economist Audit div., 1968-86, fin. economist Office of the Asst. Commr. Internat., 1986-95; ret. Office of the Asst. Commr. Internat., 1995. With U.S. Army, 1952-54. Recipient spl. svc. award U.S. Dept. Treasury, 1967, 68, 87, spl. achievement award, 1984, Spl. Act award, 1990, Albert Gallatin award, 1995. Mem. Am. Econ. Assn.

LUDENIA, KRISTA, psychologist, health facility administrator; b. Alexandria, Minn., Dec. 20, 1942; d. Dell John and Ethel Agnes (Balder) L.; children: Peter Jonathan, John Thomas, Kristin Ashley. BA, BS, Quincy Coll., 1967; MS, Ind. U., 1969; PhD, U. Mo., 1972. With VA Med. Ctr., 1972—, asst. chief alcohol and drug unit, Danville, Ill., 1972-74, clin. psychologist, St. Cloud, Minn., 1974-76, coordinator mental hygiene clinic, 1976-78, chief psychology service, Wichita, Kans., 1978-80, chief psychology service, Bay Pines, Fla., 1980-82, health systems adminstr., St. Louis, 1982-84, assoc. med. ctr. dir., Danville, 1984-86, Boston, 1986-88, med. ctr. dir., Ft. Wayne, Ind., 1988-89, Saginaw, Mich., 1989-92, Cleve, 1992—. Recipient Dir.'s Commendation for EEO, 1978, Leadership award VA, 1978, 1979, VA Dir.'s Commendation, 1981, 1982, 84-88, 92. Mem. Am. Coll. Healthcare Exexs. Office: VA Med Ctr 10000 Brecksville Rd Brecksville OH 44141-3204

LUDERS, ADAM, ballet dancer; b. Copenhagen, Feb. 16, 1950; came to U.S., 1975; s. Sten Otto and Hanne Marie (Jansen) L. Student, Royal Danish Ballet Sch. Balletmaster, tchr. Royal Danish Ballet and Sch., 1995—. Mem., Royal Danish Ballet Co., 1968-72, prin. dancer, London Festival Ballet Co., 1972-75, N.Y.C. Ballet Co., 1975-94; TV appearance in Choreography by Balanchine; guest artist TV appearance in, Paris Opera Ballet Co., Royal Danish Ballet Co., tour of, Japan, 1979, appearance at, White House, 1978. Office: NYC Ballet Co NY State Theater Lincoln Ctr Plz New York NY 10023 *Although the road to becoming a successful dancer is hard and never ending, I have been fortunate in many respects: I have the Bournonville tradition in teaching and performing as a sound basis for my technique, and the choreography of George Balanchine.*

LUDGIN, CHESTER HALL, baritone, actor; b. N.Y.C., May 20, 1925; s. Michael and Dora Josephine L. Student, Lafayette Coll., 1943, Am. Theatre Wing Profl. Tng. Program, 1948-50. Premiere leading baritone roles in: The Crucible, 1961, The Golem, 1962, Angle of Repose, 1976, A Quiet Place, 1983; appeared in major opera houses throughout the world, including San Francisco Opera Co., N.Y.C. Opera Co., Netherlands Opera, La Scala Opera, Vienna State Opera; singing actor in: musical comedies including Kismet, summer 1972, Most Happy Fella, summer 1977, Shenandoah, summer, 1978, Student Prince, summer 1980, South Pacific, summer 1981, Fanny, summer 1986. Co-chmn. exec. com. Norman Treigle Meml. Fund, 1975—. Served with inf. U.S. Army, 1943-46. Mem. Am. Guild Musical Artists, Actors Equity, AGVA, AFTRA. Home: 205 W End Ave New York NY 10023-4804 Office: care Thea Dispeker Artists Rep 59 E 54th St New York NY 10022-4211 *In observing many of my colleagues in the performing arts as well as those in other walks of life, I long ago came to the conclusion that it is wiser and more personally fulfilling to avoid compromising one's principles in the hope of advancing one's career. If there is truly a talent present, the act of quietly going about one's business with maximum efficiency makes the ultimate statement. Awareness by others of that talent inevitably follows.*

LUDGUS, NANCY LUCKE, lawyer; b. Palo Alto, Calif., Oct. 28, 1953; d. Winston Slover and Betty Jean (Brilhart) Lucke; m. Lawrence John Ludgus, Apr. 8, 1983. BA in Polit. Sci. with highest honors, U. Calif., Berkeley, 1975; JD, U. Calif., Davis, 1978. Bar: Calif. 1978, U.S. Dist. Ct. (no. dist.) Calif. 1978. Staff atty. Crown Zellerbach Corp., San Francisco, 1978-80, Clorox Co., Oakland, Calif., 1980-82; staff atty. Nat. Semiconductor Corp., Santa Clara, Calif., 1982-85, corp. counsel, 1985-92, sr. corp. counsel, asst. sec., 1992—. Mem. ABA, Am. Corp. Counsel Assn., Calif. State Bar Assn., Phi Beta Kappa. Democrat. Avocations: travel, jogging, hiking. Office: Nat Semiconductor Corp 1090 Kifer Rd # 16 135 Sunnyvale CA 94086-5301

LUDINGTON, CHARLES TOWNSEND, JR., English and American studies educator; b. Bryn Mawr, Pa., Jan. 31, 1936; s. Charles Townsend and Constance (Cameron) L.; m. Jane Ross, Feb. 22, 1958; children: David, Charles, James, Sarah. BA, Yale U., 1957; MA, Duke U., 1964; PhD, Duke U, 1967. Tchr. English Ransom Sch., Miami, Fla., 1960-62; from asst. prof. to prof. English U. N.C., Chapel Hill, 1967-78, Cary C. Boshamer prof. English and Am. Studies, 1982—, chair Am. studies curriculum, 1986—; part-time instr. Duke U., 1963-66; resident scholar U.S. Internat. Communication Agy., 1980-81; vis. prof. U.S. Mil. Acad., West Point, N.Y., 1988-89. Author: John Dos Passos, 1980 (Mayflower award 1981), Marsden Hartley, 1992; editor: The Fourteenth Chronicle, 1973. 1st lt. USMCR, 1957-60. Recipient Outstanding Svc. medal U.S. Army, 1988-89; Fulbright fellow, 1971-72, Nat. Humanities Ctr. fellow, 1985-86. Mem. Am. Studies Assn., South Atlantic MLA, PEN. Democrat. Avocations: tennis, golf, reading. Office: U NC Curriculum in Am Studies Greenlaw Hall CB# 3520 Chapel Hill NC 27599-3520

LUDLAM, JAMES EDWARD, III, insurance company executive; b. L.A., Jan. 9, 1943; s. James Edward and Jane Bramen (Hyde) L.; m. Mary Patricia McVee, Apr. 12, 1969; children—Jay, Erin. B.A. in Econs., Claremont McKenna Coll., 1965. M.B.A. U. So. Calif. 1967. Vice pres. group pensions Prudential Ins. Co., Florham Park, N.J., 1968-82; sr. v.p. Home Life Ins. Co., N.Y.C., 1982-90; v.p. employer sponsored plans Security Life of Denver, Denver, 1991-93; pres., CEO First ING Life of N.Y., 1993-94; pres., COO Rocky Mountain Life Ins. Co., Denver, 1994—. Mem. corp. United Way, Morris County, N.J., 1980-91; campaign exec. United Way, Denver, 1991—, bd. dirs. Mile High United Way, 1995—. Democrat. Presbyterian. Avocations: reading; investing; golf; rafting.

LUDLOW, JAMES ALDEN, physicist; b. Salt Lake City, July 19, 1967; s. Walter Wilson Ludlow and Dawn Louise (Westhoff) Horne. BS in Physics, U. Utah, 1991. Rsch. physicist Ceramatec, Salt Lake City, 1990—; ski instr. Park City (Utah) Ski Area, 1986-95. Mem. Electrochem. Soc., Profl. Ski Instrs. of Am. (level III instr. 1986—), U.S. Ski Coaches Assn. (level II coach 1993—). Avocations: skiing, running, bicycling, ski racing, kayaking. Office: Ceramatec 900 W 2425 S Salt Lake City UT 84119

LUDLUM, DAVID BLODGETT, pharmacologist, educator; b. N.Y.C., Sept. 30, 1929; s. C. Daniel and Elsie B. (Blodgett) L.; B.A., Cornell U., 1951; Ph.D., U. Wis., 1954; M.D., N.Y.U., 1962; m. Carlene L. Dyke, Dec. 23, 1952; children: Valerie Jean Ludlum Wright, Kenneth David. Research scientist Dupont Co., Wilmington, Del., 1954-58; intern Bellevue Hosp., N.Y.C., 1962-63; asst. prof. pharmacology Yale U., 1963-68; assoc. prof. U. Md., 1968-70, prof., 1970-76; prof. pharmacology Albany (N.Y.) Med. Coll., 1976-86 , chmn. dept. pharmacology, 1976-80, prof. medicine, 1980-86, dir. oncology research, 1980-86; prof. pharmacology and medicine U. Mass. Med. Sch., 1986—; adj. prof. chemistry Rensselaer Poly. Inst., Troy, N.Y., 1977-80; vis. prof. oncology Johns Hopkins U., 1973-76; vis. prof. Courtauld Inst., London, 1970. WARF fellow, 1951-52; NSF fellow, 1952-54; Am. Heart Assn. fellow, 1960-62; recipient NIH Research Career Devel. award 1968; Markle scholar in acad. medicine, 1967-72; lic. physician, N.Y., Conn., Md. Mem. Am. Soc. Pharmacology and Exptl. Therapeutics, Am. Soc. Clin. Pharmacology and Therapeutics, Am. Assn. Cancer Research, Am. Soc. Biochem. and Molecular Biology, Am. Chem. Soc., Phi Beta Kappa, Sigma Xi, Phi Kappa Phi, Alpha Omega Alpha. Assoc. editor Cancer Rsch., 1980-87, 89—; contbr. articles to profl. jours.; patentee in field; grantee in field. Home: 24 Linda Ct Delmar NY 12054-3512 Office: U Mass Med Sch Worcester MA 01655-0126

LUDLUM, JAMES S., lawyer; b. Elk City, Okla., Jan. 15, 1952; s. James Norman and Dorothy Blanche (Standifer) L.; 1 child, Michael James. JD, Baylor U., 1974. Bar: Tex. 1974, U.S. Dist. Ct. (so., ea., we. and no. dists.) Tex. 1974, U.S. Ct. Appeals (5th cir.) 1974, U.S. Supreme Ct. 1974. Litigator Ludlum & Ludlum, Austin, 1974-84, litigation chief, 1984-87, chief exec., 1987—; gen. counsel Tex. Police Assn., Austin, 1991—; mem. nat. adv. bd. govtl. programs AON Spl. Group, Richmond, Va., 1988—; chmn., CEO, Am. News Svc. Corp., 1996—. Contbr. articles to profl. jours. Chmn. Amtrac Com.-Austin C. of C., 1970-78; vice chmn., mem. Police Retirement Bd., Austin, 1981-88. Named Def. Litigator of the Yr., So. Transport Group, 1990, 91, 93. Mem. ABA, Tex. Bar Assn., Tex. Assn. Def. Counsel, Def. Rsch. Inst., Travis County Bar Assn., The Defense Rsch. Inst. Mem. Ch. of Christ. Avocations: tennis, swimming, aviating, public speaking, writing professional articles. Office: Ludlum & Ludlum Enterprize Plz 13915 Burnet Rd Austin TX 78728

LUDLUM, ROBERT, author; b. N.Y.C., May 25, 1927; s. George Hartford and Margaret (Wadsworth) L.; m. Mary Ryducha, March 31, 1951; children: Michael R., Jonathan C., Glynis J. BA with distinction, Wesleyan U., 1951. Actor Broadway, TV, 1952-60; prodr. No. Jersey Playhouse, Ft. Lee, 1957-60, N.Y.C., 1960-69, Playhouse-on-the-Mall, Paramus, N.J., 1960-70; novelist, 1969—. Author: The Scarlatti Inheritance, 1971, The Osterman Weekend, 1972, The Matlock Paper, 1973, Trevayne, 1973, The Cry of the Halidon, 1974, The Rhinemann Exchange, 1974, The Road to Gandolfo, 1975, The Gemini Contenders, 1976, The Chancellor Manuscript, 1977, The Holcroft Covenant, 1978, The Matarese Circle, 1979, The Bourne Identity, 1980, The Parsifal Mosaic, 1982, The Aquitaine Progression, 1984, The Bourne Supremacy, 1986, The Icarus Agenda, 1988, The Bourne Ultimatum, 1990, The Road to Omaha, 1992, The Scorpio Illusion, 1993, The Apocalypse Watch, 1995. Served with USMC, World War II. Recipient Scroll of Achievement Am. Nat. Theatre and Acad., 1960. Mem. Authors Guild. Office: care Henry Morrison Inc PO Box 235 Bedford Hills NY 10507-0235

LUDOVICE, PETER JOHN, chemical engineer; b. Des Plaines, Ill., Apr. 1, 1962; s. William Peter and Mary Jane (Unger) L.; m. Jennifer Davis Clair, May 29, 1993. BSChemE, U. Ill., 1984; PhDChemE, MIT, 1989. Rsch. assoc. ETH-Zurich, Switzerland, 1988-89; vis. scientist IBM Almaden Rsch. Ctr., San Jose, Calif., 1989-91, NASA Ames Lab., Moffett Field, Calif., 1989-91; polymer product mgr. Polygen Inc., Waltham, Mass., 1991-92, Molecular Simulations Inc., Burlington, Mass., 1992-93; asst. prof. Ga. Inst. Tech., Atlanta, 1993—; tech. cons. Molecular Simulations, Inc., Burlington, Mass., 1992—; faculty mem. Polymer Edn. Rsch. Ctr., Atlanta, 1993—, Ga. Tech Bioengring. Program, Atlanta, 1994—. Mem. editorial bd. Chem. Design Automation News, N.Y.C., 1992—. Mem. AIChE, Am. Chem. Soc. (Sherwin Williams award 1988). Office: Ga Inst of Technology Sch of Chem Engring Atlanta GA 30332-0100

LUDTKE, JAMES BUREN, business and finance educator; b. Waterloo, Iowa, Mar. 4, 1924; s. Henry George and Eteska (Buren) L.; m. Jean Seaver Edwards, Sept. 8, 1948; children—Melissa, Leslie, Mark, Betty, Rebecca. Student, Iowa Tchrs. Coll., 1942-43, N.W. Mo. State Tchrs. Coll., 1943-44; B.A., State U. Iowa, 1947, M.A., 1948, Ph.D., 1951. Instr. econs. U. Iowa, 1947-51; mem. faculty U. Mass., Amherst, 1951-86, prof. fin., 1960-86, chmn. dept. gen. bus. and fin., 1958-70. Author: The American Financial System: Markets and Institutions, 2d edit, 1967. Served with USNR, 1943-46. Sloan fellow Mass. Inst. Tech., 1961-62; Ford Found. faculty fellow Harvard U., summers 1961, 66. Mem. Fin. Mgmt. Assn., AAUP (pres. Mass. state conf. 1977-80, treas. Assembly of State Confs. 1980-82). Home: 30 Wachusett Hyannis Port MA 02647-9999

LUDWIG, ALLAN IRA, photographer, author; b. N.Y.C., June 9, 1933; s. Daniel and Honey (Fox) L.; m. Janine Lowell, Aug., 1955 (div. 1991); children: Katherine Arabella, Pamela Vanessa, Adam Lowell; m. Gwendolyn Akin, 1992; children: Allan B. Ludwig Jr., Alison Ludwig. BFA, Yale U., 1956, MA, 1962, PhD, 1964. Instr., R.I. Sch. Design, 1956-58; asst. instr. Yale U., 1958-64; asst. prof. Dickinson Coll., 1964-65; assoc. prof., 1965-68; assoc. prof. Syracuse U., 1968-69; pres. Automated Communications, Inc., Verona, N.J., 1969-75; dir. Ludwig Portfolios, 1975-90; co-dir. Akin/Ludwig, 1990-96; mem. exec. bd. Alternative Mus. N.Y.C., 1978-88, chmn. bd. dirs., 1982-83; cons. presses U. Mass., U. Ga., Boston Mus. Fine Arts, Smithsonian Instn. Author: Graven Images: New England Stonecarving and its Symbols, 1966; author exhbn. catalogues; one-person shows include: Silvermine (Conn.) Guild of Art, 1955, Davison Art Ctr., Wesleyan U., Middletown, Conn., 1961, Portland Mus. of Art, Portland, 1962, Met. Mus. and Art Ctrs., Miami, Fla., 1976, Jorgenson Art Gallery, U. Conn., Storrs, 1976, Alternative Mus., N.Y.C., 1977, Watson Art Gallery, Norton, Mass., 1978, Alonzo Gallery, N.Y.C., 1978, 79, Cayman Gallery, N.Y.C., 1980, IL Diaframma, Milan, Italy, 1981, Simon Gallery, Montclair, N.J., 1983, art gallery Farleigh Dickinson U., Madison, N.J., 1984, Ctr. for Creative Photography, Tucson, 1986, The Twining Gallery, N.Y.C., 1986, Cepa Gallery, Buffalo, 1986, The Shadai Gallery, Tokyo Inst. of Tech, Tokyo, 1987, White Columns, N.Y.C., 1988, O'Kane Gallery, Houston, 1988, Farideh Cadot Gallery, N.Y.C., 1988, XYZ Gallery, Ghent, Belgium, 1989, Northlight Gallery, 1990, Ariz. State U., Tempe, 1990, Galerie Farideh Cadot, Paris, 1990, Pamela Auchincloss Gallery, N.Y.C., 1991, 92, 94, Gallery 954, Chgo., 1994, Gallery at 777, L.A., 1994, Houston Ctr. for Photography, 1995, Hudson River Mus. Westchester, Yonkers, N.Y., 1995—, The Chrysler Mus., Norfolk, Va., 1995, CEPA Gallery, Buffalo, 1995; exhibited in group shows at Bannister Art Gallery, Providence, 1979, Westmoreland County (Pa.) Mus. Art, 1979, Ind. Am. Photography exhbn., Warsaw, Cracow, Katowice, Gdynia, Poland, 1980, Alonzo Gallery, N.Y.C., 1980, Alternative Mus., N.Y.C., 1981, Floating Found. for Photography, N.Y.C., 1981, World Photographic Archive, Parma, Italy, 1984, Diverse Works, Houston, 1985, The State Mus., Trenton, N.J., 1985, San Francisco Mus. Modern Art, 1986, Mus. Photog. Arts, San Diego, 1987, Public Image Gallery, N.Y.C., 1985; Alternative Mus., N.Y.C., 1986, Internat. Ctr. for Photography, N.Y.C., 1987, Farideh Cadot Gallery, N.Y.C., 1987, 88, Farideh Cadot Gallery, Paris, 1988, de Cordova and Dana Mus., Lincoln, Mass., 1988, Musee d'Art Moderne de la Ville de Paris, 1988, Musee d'Art et Histoire, Fribourg, Switzerland, 1988, Nat. Mus. of Am. Art, Washington, 1988, Security Pacific Corp., Gallery At The Plaza, L.A., 1988, Houston Ctr. for Photography, 1988, Catherine Edelman Gallery, Chgo., 1989, Musee fur Minerologie und Geologie, Leiden, Holland, 1989, The Friends of Photography, Ansel Adams Ctr., San Francisco, 1989, Alternative Mus., N.Y.C., 1989, Mus. of Contemporary Art, Chgo., 1989, The Walker Art Ctr., Mpls., 1990, Musee Zool. U. Louis Pasteur, Strasbourg, France, 1990, Akin Gallery, Boston, 1990, Monserrat Gallery, Beverly, Mass., 1990, Hallwalls, Buffalo, 1990, Natur Mus. Seckenberg Forshungsinstitut, Frankfort, Germany, 1990, Art 21-90, Basel, Switzerland, 1990, The Walker Art Ctr., Mpls., 1990, Lights Works, St. Paul, 1990, The Boston Athenaeum, 1990, Arts Festival Braga, Portugal, 1991, Nat. Mus. Am. Art, Washington, 1991, Addison Gallery Am. Art, Andover, Mass., 1991, The New Mus., N.Y.C., 1991, Mus. Fine Arts, Houston, 1992, Ctr. for Photography-Mid-Town, N.Y.C., 1992, Univ. Gallery, Clark U., Worcester, Mass., 1992, Long Beach (Calif.) Mus. Art, 1992, Preservation House, B.C., Can., 1992, Henry Art Gallery, U. Wash., Seattle, 1992, Akin Gallery, Boston, 1992, Internat. Mus.Photography George Eastman House, Rochester, N.Y., 1993, Wadsworth Athanaeum, Hartford, Conn., 1993, The New Museum, N.Y.C., 1993, Akin Gallery, Boston, 1993, Ctr. for Photography at Woodstock, 1993, Montage, Rochester, N.Y., 1993, Gallery 954 Chgo., 1993, Parko Gallery, Tokyo, 1993, Addison Gallery Am. Art, Andover, Mass., 1994, New Mus., N.Y.C., 1994, Mus. Photographic Arts, San Diego, 1995, Mus. Contemporary Art, Chgo., 1995, The New Orleans Mus. Art, 1995, The Mercury Gallery, Boston, 1995, Thread Waxing Space, N.Y.C., 1995, Calif. Ctr. for the Arts Mus., Escondido, 1996; represented in permanent collections: Mus. Modern Art, N.Y.C., Library of Congress, Washington, Smithsonian Instn., Washington, Archives Am. Art, Washington, Snite Mus. Art, Notre Dame, Ind., Walker Art Ctr., Mpls., Mus. Photog. Art, San Diego, N.Y.C., Polaroid Found. Collection, Cambridge, Mass., Yale U. Art Gallery, New Haven, Conn., San Francisco Mus. Modern Art, Ctr. for Creative Photography Collection, Tucson, Shadai Gallery, Tokyo, Maison Europeenne de la Photographie, L.A. County Mus. of Art, Mus. Fine Arts, Houston, Metropolitan Mus. Art, N.Y.C., The State Mus., Trenton, N.J, The Chrysler Mus., Norfolk, Va., The New Orleans Mus. Art, Kiyosato (Japan) Mus. Photographic Arts. Regional chmn. Campaign for Yale Art Sch. Div., Met. N.Y.C. area, 1975-76. Bollingen Found. fellow, 1961-63; Am. Philos. Soc. fellow, 1964-66; Am. Coun. Learned Socs. fellow, 1967-68; NEH fellow, 1967; recipient USIS Merit award, 1966; Merit award Assn. State and Local History, 1967-68; Harriette Merrifield Forbes award Assn. Gravestone Studies, U. Conn., Storrs, 1981; Polaroid Found. grantee, 1987-88, Arts grantee N.J. State Coun., 1990, Agfa Corp. grantee, 1990, NEA grantee, 1990-91. Democrat.

LUDWIG, CHRISTA, mezzo-soprano; b. Berlin; d. Anton and Eugenie (Besalla) L.; m. Walter Berry, Sept. 29, 1957 (div. 1970); 1 son, Wolfgang; m. Paul-Emile Deiber, Mar. 3, 1972. Ed. German schs. Prof. H.S. Berlin, 1995; hon. mem. Vienna Philharm., 1995. Appeared at Staedtische Buehnenm, Frankfurt, W. Ger., 1946-52, Landestheatre, Darmstadt, W. Ger., 1952-54, Hannover, W. Ger., 1954-55, Vienna (Austria) State Opera, 1955—, Medaille, Ville de Paris, 1993, Shibuya-Price, Japan, 1993, others, U.S. appearances include Avery Fisher Hall, N.Y.C., 1978, Lyric Opera, Chgo., 1959-60, 70-71, 73-74, Philharmonic Hall, N.Y.C., 1968, 69, 72, 74, others; guest artist London, Buenos Aires, Munich, Berlin, Tokyo, Salzburg Festival, Athens Festival, Saratoga Festival, Hunter Coll., Met. Mus., Scala Milano, Expo 67, Montreal, and others; rec. artist. Decorated Commdr. des Arts et des Lettres, France, 1988, Goldenes Ehren Zeichen Stadt, Salzburg, 1988, Goldene Ehrennadel Stadt, Wien, Austria, 1988; chevalier Legion d'Honneur, France, 1989; recipient Mozart medal, Mahler medal, Hugo Wolf medal, Fidelio medal Opera Wien, 1991, Shibuya prize Japan, 1993, Medaille Paris, 1993, Medaille Ville de Dijon, 1993, Echo Deutscher Preis, 1994, Karajan preis, Berliner Bär, 1994, Grosses Ehrenzeichen Osterreich, 1994, Ehrenmitglied der Wiener Philharm., Silver Rose, Vienna Philharm., Golden Ring, Vienna Staatsoper, Musician of Yr. award Musical Am., 1994; named Kammersaengerin, Govt. of Austria, 1962. Mem. NARAS.

LUDWIG, EDMUND VINCENT, federal judge; b. Phila., May 20, 1928; s. Henry and Ruth (Viner) L.; children: Edmund Jr., John, Sarah, David. AB, Harvard U., 1949, LLB, 1952. Assoc. Duane, Morris & Heckscher, Phila., 1956-59; ptnr. Barnes, Biester & Ludwig, Doylestown, Pa., 1959-68; judge Common Pleas Ct., Bucks County, Pa., 1968-85, U.S. Dist. Ct. (ea. dist.), Phila., 1985—; mem. faculty Pa. Coll. of the Judiciary, 1974-85; presenter Villanova (Pa.) U. Law Sch., 1975-80, lectr., 1984—; vis. lectr. Temple Law Sch., 1977-80; clin. assoc. prof. Hahnemann U., Phila., 1977-85; mem. Pa. Juvenile Ct. Judge's Commn., 1978-85; chmn. Pa. Chief Justice's Ednl. Com., 1984-85; pres. Pa. Conf. State Trial Judges, 1981-82; mem. 3rd Cir. Ct. of Appeals Task Force on Equal Treatment in the Cts., 1994—. Contbr. articles to profl. jours. Chmn. Children and Youth Adv. Com., Bucks County, 1978-83; mem. Pa. Adv. Com. on Mental Health and Mental Retardation, 1980-85; founder, bd. dirs. Today, Inc., Newtown, Pa., 1971-85, Probation Vols., Bucks County, 1971-81; bd. dirs. New Directions for Women, Del. Valley, 1988—; mem. Pa. Joint Coun. Criminal Justice, Inc., 1979-80; mem. Joint Family Law Council Pa., 1979-85; vice chmn. Human Services Council Bucks County, 1979-81; mem. Com. to Study Unified Jud. System Pa., 1980-82, Pa. Legislative Task Force on Mental Health Laws, 1986-87; chmn. Juvenile Justice Alliance, Phila., 1992—; co-chmn. Doylestown (Pa.) Revitalization Bd., 1993—. Recipient Disting. Svc. award Bucks County Corrections Assn., 1978, Spl. Svc. award Big. Bros., 1989, Humanitarian award United Way Bucks County, 1980, Founder's award Vol. Svcs., 1982, Spl. award Bucks County Juvenile Ct., 1985, Humanitarian award Ctrl. Bucks County C. of C., 1994. Mem. ABA, Pa. Bar Assn. (chmn. com. legal svcs. to disabled 1990-92), Fed. Bar Assn. (hon.), Harvard Club (N.Y.C. and Phila., v.p. 1979-80), Harvard Law Sch. Assn. (mem. exec. com. 1993—). Office: 12614 US Courthouse Independence Mall W 601 Market St Philadelphia PA 19106-1510

LUDWIG, EUGENE ALLAN, U.S. comptroller of the currency, lawyer; b. Bklyn., Apr. 11, 1946; s. Jacob and Louise (Rabiner) L.; m. Carol Lynn Friedman, Mar. 11, 1978; children: Abigail Sarah, Elizabeth Madelaine Cathleen, David Maxwell. BA magna cum laude, Haverford Coll., 1968; BA, MA, Oxford U., Eng., 1970; LLB, Yale U., 1973. Bar: D.C. 1973. Assoc. Covington & Burling, Washington, 1973-81, ptnr., 1981-93; comptr. of the currency Dept. of the Treasury, Washington, 1993—; pres. Yale Legis. Svcs., 1972-73; guest lectr. Harvard U., Georgetown U., 1974-77, 79, Yale U., 1989. Editor Yale Law Jour., 1972-73; mem. editorial bd., Jour. Internat. Banking Law, 1989; contbr. articles to profl. jours. Office: Comptroller of the Currency Independence Sq 250 E St SW Washington DC 20219

LUDWIG, GEORGE HARRY, physicist; b. Johnson County, Iowa, Nov. 13, 1927; s. George McKinley and Alice (Heim) L.; m. Rosalie F. Vickers, July 21, 1950; children: Barbara Rose, Sharon Lee, George Vickers, Kathy Ann Ramsay. BA in Physics cum laude, U. Iowa, 1956, MS, 1959, PhD in Elec. Engring., 1960. Head fields and particles instrumentation sect. Goddard Space Flight Center, NASA, 1960-65, chief info. processing div., 1965-71, assoc. dir. for data ops., 1971-72; dir. systems integration Nat. Environ. Satellite Service, NOAA, 1972-75, dir. ops., 1975-80, tech. dir., 1980; sr. scientist Environ. Rsch. Labs. NOAA, Boulder, Colo., 1980-81; dir. Environ. Rsch. Labs. NOAA, 1981-83; asst. to chief scientist NASA, 1983-84 ret., ind. cons. data mgmt. and space sta. design, 1983-92; sr. rsch. assoc. Lab. for Atmospheric and Space Physics U. Colo., 1985-91; vis. sr. scientist NASA hdqrs., Calif. Inst. Tech., 1989-91; prin. designer radiation detection instrumentation for numerous sci. spacecraft including Explorer I, 1956-65; co-discoverer Van Allen radiation belts; expert on NASA sci. and applications research data processing; oversaw devel. and operation U.S. Nat. Environ. Satellite System, 1972-80; oversaw environ. research program Nat. Oceanic and Atmospheric Adminstrn., 1981-83. Served from pvt. to capt. USAF, 1946-52. Van Allen scholar, 1958; research fellow U.S. Steel Found., 1958-60; recipient Exceptional Service medal NASA, 1969, Program Adminstrn. and Mgmt. award NOAA, 1977, Exceptional Sci. Achievement medal NASA, 1984. Mem. IEEE (sr.), Am. Geophys. Union, Phi Beta Kappa, Sigma Xi, Phi Eta Sigma, Eta Kappa Nu. Home: 215 Aspen Trl Winchester VA 22602-1404

LUDWIG, KARL DAVID, psychiatrist; b. Johnstown, Pa., June 9, 1930; s. Karl Döring and Kathryn Bride (Palmer) L.; m. Darlene Ann Fisher, July 9, 1959; children: John D., Karl David Jr., Elizabeth Ann Craig, Mark D., Michael D. BA in Biology, St. Vincent Coll., 1952; postgrad., Pa. State U., 1952-53, St. Mary's Sem. & Univ., Balt., 1953-54; MD, U. Pitts., 1960. Intern U.S. Naval Hosp., Phila., 1960-61; resident psychiatry Ea. Pa. Psychiat. Inst., Phila., 1961-64; fellow psychiat. rsch. and teaching Jefferson Med. Coll., Phila., 1964-66; rsch. psychiatrist, dir alcoholism program Friends Hosp., Phila., 1966-73; staff psychiatrist Haverford State Hosp., Haverford, Pa., 1964-71; cons. in psychiatry VA Hosp., Coatesville, Pa., 1968-70; chief outpatient svcs. Northeast Community Mental Health Ctr., Phila., 1973; clin. dir. Northeast Community Mental Health Ctr., 1973-80; supt. Dixmont State Hosp., Sewickley, Pa., 1980-81; dir. inpatient psychiatry Sewickley Valley Hosp., Sewickley, 1981-95; asst. med. dir. Staunton Clin., 1990-95; pres. med. staff Friends Hosp., Phila., 1969-71, Northeast Community Mental Health Ctr., Phila., 1974-75. Pres. Phila. Navy chpt. Res. Officers Assn. of U.S., 1976-77, dept. Pa., 1978-79; bd. trustees Valley Care Assn., Sewickley, 1983-93; bd. dirs. Valley Care Nursing Home, Sewickley, 1983-93. Capt. med. corps USNR, ret. Fellow Am. Psychiat. Assn., Psychiat. Physicians Pa. (pres. 1990-91); mem. AMA, Pitts. Psychiat. soc. (pres. 1985-86), Pa. Med. Soc., Allegheny County Med. Soc., Am. Legion, Assn. Mil. Surgeons U.S., Navy League U.S., Mil. Order World Wars. Republican. Roman Catholic. Home and Office: 2168A Reis Run Rd Pittsburgh PA 15237-1425

LUDWIG, MYLES ERIC, writer, editor, publishing executive, art director; b. Bklyn., Apr. 12, 1942; s. Solomon and Muriel (Levine) L.; m. Hendrieka Van Riper (div.); 1 child, Lindsay Anne; m. Marsha Daniel (div.). BA, U. N.C., 1967, MA in Mass. Comms., 1969. Editl. dir. Art Direction Mag., N.Y.C., 1970-73; creative asst. to pub. Penthouse/Viva Internat., N.Y.C., 1973-75; editor, pub. Olympic mag., N.Y.C., 1978-80; editl. dir. SMC/Carnegie Corp., N.Y.C., 1978-82; founding editor, pub. North Shore/The Sandwich Islands Quar., Kauai Style, Visions, BayNotes, Kauai, Hawaii, 1985—; mng. dir. Inter-Pacific Media, Inc., Kauai, 1988—; cons. Ludwig/Christensen, N.Y.C., 1982-85, Leber/Katz Ptnrs., N.Y.C., 1983-84; instr. creative writing NYU, N.Y.C., Kauai Acad. Creative Arts, 1971-72; instr. concept design N.Y. Inst. Advt., N.Y.C.; exhbn. judge Art Dirs. Club Denver, Art Dirs. Club N.C., N.Y. Art Dirs. Club; mem. Garden Island Arts Coun., founding editor and pub. ARTS, Mirage Princeville Resort Mktg. Bd. Author: (novel) Golem, 1969, (non-fiction) Creativity, 1972, The Detectives, 1980, Kauai in the Eye of Iniki, 1992, The Handbook of Magazine Design; contbr. numerous articles to profl. and consumer publs. Active Hawaii Internat. Film Festival, 1000 Friends of Kauai; advisor to mayor County of Kauai, 1993; advisor to Rep. Carl Stepath, 1993-94. Recipient Pele award Am. Assn. Advt. Agys., 1993, Pa'l award (2) Hawaii Pub. Assn., 1993); MCA fellow in creative writing Thomas Wolfe Award for Fiction, N.Y. Art Dirs. Mem. Soc. Pub. Designers (pres. 1983-84), N.Y. Type Dirs. Club (Ozzie award), Kauai Hist. Soc. Jewish. Avocations: golf, photography, weightlifting. Home: 3667 Anini Beach Rd Hanalei HI 96714 Office: Inter-Pacific Media Inc PO Box 1545 Hanalei HI 96714-1545

LUDWIG, PATRIC E., health care group executive; b. Mpls., Jan. 18, 1939; s. Roy and Gertrude (Anderson) L.; m. Carol Elizabeth Grasley, Oct. 29, 1960; children: Jana Kaye, David James, Mark Thomas. BS in Engring., U. Mich., 1962, MBA, 1963. Assoc. dir. Community Systems Found., Md., 1963-67, Hosp. Assn. N.Y. State, 1967-74; formerly pres. Mich. Hosp. Assn., Lansing, from 1974; now pres., chief exec. officer Bronson Healthcare Group, Kalamazoo, Mich.; mem. Mich. Health Planning Adv. Coun., 1975-76, Mich. Statewide Health Coordinating Coun., 1976-83; cons. Nat. Ctr. Health Svcs. R&D, HEW, from 1972; chmn. Co-author: Management Engineering for Hospitals, 1970. Chmn. trustees Community Systems Found., 1969-70, 72; mem. placement commn. Mich. Commn. for Blind Employer, 1980—. Recipient Outstanding Svc. award Community Systems Found., 1972. Mem. Am. Hosp. Assn., Am. Soc. Assn. Execs. (cert. assn. exec.), Am. Pub. Health Assn., Hosp. Mgmt. Systems Soc. (Outstanding LIt. award 1971), State Hosp. Assn. Execs. Forum, Lay Adminstrs. Mut. Benefit Soc., Mich. Health Econs. Coalition, Orgn. Execs. Mich., Lansing C. of C., Hosp. Adminstrs. Study Soc., Rotary, Capitol Club. Office: Bronson Healthcare Group 1 Healthcare Plz Kalamazoo MI 49007-5333*

LUDWIG, RICHARD JOSEPH, ski resort executive; b. Lakewood, Ohio, July 28, 1937; s. Mathew Joseph and Catherine Elizabeth (Sepich) L.; m. Emily Kathleen Popovich, Dec. 2, 1961 (div. Feb. 1967); 1 dau., Susan Kay; m. Erleen Catherine Halambeck Ramus, July 22, 1977; children: Charleen, Tracey, Charles. Cassandra. Student, Ohio State U., 1955-59; BBA Fenn Coll., Cleve. State U, 1963. C.P.A., Ohio. Sr. acct. Ernst & Whinney, Cleve., 1964-66; supervising acct. Ernst & Young, 1966-70; asst. treas. Midland Ross Corp., Cleve., 1970-71; treas. Midland Ross Corp., 1971-76; v.p. fin., treas. U.S. Realty Investments, 1976-78, v.p.-fin., chief fin. officer, 1978-79; owner Boston Mills Ski Resort, Inc., Peninsula, Ohio, 1979—, Brandywine Ski Resort, Inc., Sagamore Hills, Ohio, 1990—. Mem. Firestone Country Club (Akron, Ohio), Saddlebrook Club (Wesley Chapel, Fla.), Black Diamond Ranch Club (Lecanto, Fla.), Walden Country Club (Aurora, Ohio). Home: 5106 Pinelake Rd Wesley Chapel FL 33543-4459 Office: PO Box 175 7100 Riverview Rd Peninsula OH 44264

LUDWIG, RICHARD MILTON, English literature educator, librarian; b. Reading, Pa., Nov. 24, 1920; s. Ralph O. and Millie (Smeltzer) L. A.B., U. Mich., 1942; A.M., Harvard U., 1943, Ph.D., 1950. Mem. faculty Princeton U., 1950-86, prof. English, 1968-86, dir. spl. program humanities, 1956-64; dir. Am. civilization program, 1969-71, assoc. univ. librarian for rare books and spl. collections, 1974-85; teaching fellow Harvard, 1946-50, mem. faculty summer sch., 1951, 52. Editor Princeton U. Library Chronicle, 1977-85; editor: Aspects of American Poetry, 1963, Letters of Ford Madox Ford, 1965, Dr. Panofsky & Mr. Tarkington, 1974; co-editor: Major American Writers, 1952, Nine Short Novels, 1952, Guide to American Literature and Its Backgrounds, Since 1890, 1972, Literary History of the United States, 1974, Advanced Composition, 1977, Annals of American Literature, 1986, 89. Served with AUS, 1944-46. Dexter traveling fellow Harvard, 1950; Jonathan Edwards preceptor Princeton, 1954-57; McCosh Faculty fellow, 1967-68. Mem. MLA, Am. Studies Assn. Home: 143 Hartley Ave Princeton NJ 08540-5613

LUDWIG, VERNELL PATRICK, gas pipeline company executive; b. Algona, Iowa, Nov. 5, 1944; s. Vernell Peter and Alice Marcella (Joynt) L.; m. Susan Lee, Nov. 30, 1968; children: Maryanne, David. BSME, Iowa State U, Ames, 1966; MBA, Harvard U., 1972. Sr. cons. Resource Planning Assocs., Cambridge, Mass., 1974-77; mgr. Tex. Ea. Gas Pipeline Co., Houston, 1977-80, asst. to pres., 1980-81, gen. mgr., 1981-82, v.p., 1982-83, sr. v.p., 1983-86; v.p. Transwestern Pipeline Co., Houston, 1982-83, sr. v.p., 1983-84; exec. v.p. Algonquin Energy, Inc., Boston, 1986-90, pres., 1991-93; v.p. corp. devel. PanEnergy Corp., Houston, 1993—. Mentor Greater Houston Partnership CEO Roundtable, 1994—; dir. Houston Soc. for Performing Arts, 1995—; chmn. Boston subcom. New Eng. com. for corp. support Joslin Diabetes Found., 1992-93. Lt. USN, 1967-70. Mem. ASME, Interstate Natural Gas Assn., Am. Gas Assn., New England Gas Assn. (bd. dirs. 1986-93), Pi Tau Sigma. Office: PanEnergy Corp 5400 Westheimer Ct Houston TX 77056-5310

LUDWIKOWSKI, RETT RYSZARD, law educator, researcher; b. Skawina, Cracow, Poland, Nov. 6, 1943; came to U.S., 1982; s. Ryszard and Maria Ludwikowski; m. Anna Ludwikowski; children: Mark, Agnes. MA, Jagiellonian U., Poland, 1966, PhD in Law, 1971, D in Legal/Polit. Ideas, 1976. Bar: D.C. 1987; cert. legal counselor, 1973. Chmn. modern polit. movement/ideas Jagiellonian U., Cracow, 1976-82, chmn. div. bus., 1976-81, chmn. div. law, 1980-81; sr. fellow Marguerite Eyer Wilbur Found., Santa Barbara, Calif., 1981-82; vis. prof. politics Elizabethtown (Pa.) Coll., 1983; vis. scholar Hoover Inst., Stanford (Calif.) U., 1983; vis. prof. politics Alfred U., N.Y.C., 1983; vis. prof. politics Cath. U. Am., Washington, 1984, prof. law, 1985—, dir. comparative and internat. law inst., 1992—; vis. scholar Max Planck Inst., Hamburg, Fed. Republic of Germany, 1990. Author: Conservatism of Kingdom of Poland, 1976 (Ministry of Sci. award 1977), Black Radicalism in USA, 1976 (Pres. of Univ. award), Main Currents of Polish Political Thought, 1982, The Crisis of Communism, 1986 (grants and awards of Wilbur Found., Hoover Inst., Stanford U.), Continuity and Change in Poland, 1991, (with W.F. Fox) The Beginning of the Constitutional Era, 1993, others; contbr. articles to profl. jours. 2d lt. Polish Army. Recipient Vis. Prof. award Earhart Found., 1982—, award of Wilbur Found.; Disting. scholar; Heritage Found. grantee, 1981-82; grantee Hoover Inst., Stanford U., Bradley Found., 1992, Earhart Found., 1992-94, Max Planck Inst. grantee, 1990. Mem. ABA, The Smithsonian Assocs., Polish Inst. Arts and Scis., Wilson Ctr. Assocs. (charter mem.). Avocations: tourism.

LUE, LOUIS PING-SION, insect toxicologist; b. Taipei, Taiwan, May 16, 1938; arrived in U.S., 1967; s. Yi-Lou and Ar-Chao (Chiang) L.; m. Martha C. Lue, Dec. 20, 1969; 1 child, Andrew L. BS, Taiwan U., 1963; MS, Auburn U., 1970, PhD, 1974. Postdoctoral rsch. assoc. U. Ark., Fayetteville, 1974-76, Purdue U., West Lafayette, Ind., 1976-78, La. State U., Baton Rouge, 1978-79; asst. prof. Va. State U., Petersburg, 1979-84; rsch. assoc. Med. Coll. of Va., Richmond, 1984-87; rsch. assoc. The Am. Tobacco Co., Hopewell, Va., 1987-90, sr. rsch. assoc., 1990—. Contbr. articles to profl. jours. Mem. Entomol. Soc. of Am., Am. Chem. Soc. (divsn. agrochems.), Genetics Soc. of Am., Va. Acad. Sci., Sigma Xi. Achievements include rsch. on cotton boll weevil karyology, toxicity of pesticides, pesticide persistence in environmental matrix, analytical identification of abused drugs and their pyrolitic products. Office: Am Tobacco Co PO Box 899 Hopewell VA 23860-0899

LUEBKE, NEIL ROBERT, philosophy educator; b. Pierce, Nebr., Sept. 15, 1936; s. Robert Carl and Cinderetta Amelia (Guthmann) L.; m. Phyllis Jean Madsen, June 15, 1957; children: Anne Elizabeth, Karen Marie. B.A., Midland Coll., 1958; M.A., Johns Hopkins U., 1962, Ph.D., 1968. Asst., assoc. then prof. philosophy Okla. State U., Stillwater, 1961-85, head philosophy dept., 1979-85, 89—; dir. Exxon Critical Thinking Project, 1971-74. Contbr. articles to profl. jours. Woodrow Wilson nat. fellow, 1958-59. Mem. Am. Philos. Assn., Soc. Bus. Ethics, Mountain-Plains Philos. Conf. (chmn. 1971-72, 80-81), Southwestern Philos. Soc. (pres. 1981-82), Phi Kappa Phi (nat. pres.-elect 1995—). Democrat. Lutheran. Home: 616 W Harned Ave Stillwater OK 74075-1303 Office: Okla State U Dept Philosophy 226 Hanner Bldg Stillwater OK 74078-5064

LUECKE, ELEANOR VIRGINIA ROHRBACHER, civic volunteer; b. St. Paul, Mar. 10, 1918; d. Adolph and Bertha (Lehman) Rohrbacher; m. Richard William Luecke, Nov. 1, 1941; children: Glenn Richard, Joan Eleanor Ratliff, Ruth Ann. Student, Macalester Coll., St. Paul, 1936-38, St. Paul Bus. U., 1938-40. Author lit. candidate and ballot issues, 1970—; producer TV local issues, 1981—; contbr. articles to profl. jours. Founder, officer, dir., pres. Liaison for Inter-Neighborhood Coop., Okemos, Mich., 1972—; chair countrywide special edn. millage proposals, 1958, 1969; trustee, v.p., pres. Ingham Intermediate Bd. Edn., 1959-83; sec., dir. Tri-County Cmty. Mental Health Bd., Lansing, 1964-72; founder, treas., pres. Concerned Citizens for Meridian Twp., Okemos, 1970-86; mental health rep. Partners of the Americas, Belize, Brit. Honduras, 1971; trustee Capital Area Comprehensive Health Planning, 1973-76; v.p., dir. Assn. Retarded Citizens Greater Lansing, 1973-83; chair, mem. Cmty. Svcs. for Developmentally Disabled Adv. Coun., 1973—; dir., founder, treas. Tacoma Hills Homeowners Assn., Okemos, 1985—; facilitator of mergers Lansing Child Guidance Clinic, Clinton and Easton counties Tri-County Cmty. Mental Health Bd., Lansing Adult Mental Health Clinic, founder. Recipient Greater Lansing Cmty. Svcs. Coun. "Oscar," United Way, 1955, state grant Mich. Devel. Disabilities Coun., Lansing, 1983, Disting. award Mich. Assn. Sch. Bds., Lansing, 1983, Pub. Svc. award C.A.R.E.ing, Okemos, 1988, Earth Angel award WKAR-TV 23, Mich. State U., East Lansing, 1990, Cert. for Cmty. Betterment People for Meridian, Okemos, 1990, 2nd pl. video competition East Lansing/Meridian Twp. Cable Comm. Commn., 1990, 1st pl. award video competition, 1992; Ingham Med. Hosp. Commons Area named in her honor, Lansing, 1971. Mem. Advocacy Orgn. for Patients and Providers (dir. 1994—). Avocations: reading, interior design, landscaping, gardening. Home: 1893 Birchwood Dr Okemos MI 48864-2766

LUECKE, RICHARD WILLIAM, biochemist; b. St. Paul, July 12, 1917; s. Frederick William and Susan (Trautz) L.; m. Eleanor Virginia Rohrbacher, Nov. 1, 1941; children—Glenn R., Joan E., Ruth A. B.A., Macalester Coll., 1939, M.S., 1941; Ph.D., U. Minn., 1943. Assoc. prof. A&M U., Tex., 1943-45; assoc. prof. biochemistry Mich. State U., East Lansing, 1945-49; prof. Mich. State U., 1949-87, prof. emeritus, 1987—; cons. Merck Sharpe & Dohme Labs., 1963-76; mem. nutrition bd. FAO. Contbr. articles to profl. jours.; mem. editorial bd.: Jour. Nutrition, 1974-78. Mem. Am. Assn. Animal Sci. (Research award 1956), Am. Chem. Soc., AAAS, Am. Inst. Nutrition, Brit. Nutrition Soc., Am. Soc. Biol. Chemists, N.Y. Acad. Sci., Soc. Exptl. Biology and Medicine. Home: 1893 Birchwood Dr Okemos MI 48864-2766 Office: Dept Biochemistry Mich State U East Lansing MI 48824

LUEDECKE, WILLIAM HENRY, engineer; b. Pittsburg, Tex., Apr. 5, 1918; s. Henry Herman and Lula May (Abernathy) L.; B.S., U. Tex., 1940; m. Mary Anne Copeland, June 3, 1939; children—William Henry, John Copeland. Mech. engr. Columbian Gasoline Corp., Monroe, La., 1940-41; supr. shipbldg., mech. engr. USN, Orange, Tex., 1941-42; gen. supr. factory mgrs. N. Am. Aviation Co., Dallas, 1944-46; mech. engr., charge Chrysler Airtemp. div. Chrysler Corp., Los Angeles, 1946-50; owner Luedecke Engring. Co., Austin, Tex., 1950—, also Luedecke Investment Co.; chmn. bd. dirs. Mut. Savs. Instn., Austin; dir. City Nat. Bank, Austin, 1st Tex. Fin. Corp., Dallas. Bd. dirs. Travis County Heart Fund, Austin YMCA. Named Man of Year, Tex. Barbed Wire Collectors Assn.; registered profl. engr., Tex. Mem. Am. Soc. Heating, Refrigerating and Air Conditioning Engrs. (dir., pres. Austin chpt.), Tex., Nat. socs. profl. engrs., C. of C., Econ. Devel. Council, Better Bus. Bur., Nat. Fedn. Ind. Bus. (nat. adv. council). Lutheran. Clubs: Rotary, Austin, Westwood Country (treas., dir.). Home: 15 Woodstone Sq Austin TX 78703-1159 Office: 1007 W 34th St Austin TX 78705-2008

LUEDERS, EDWARD GEORGE, author, poet, educator, editor; b. Chgo., Feb. 14, 1923; s. Carl G. and Vera (Simpson) L.; m. Julia Demaree, June 5, 1946 (div. Apr. 1991); children: Kurt D., Joel E., Julia Anne; m. Deborah Keniston, Aug. 11, 1992. A.B., Hanover Coll., 1947; M.A., Northwestern U., 1948; Ph.D., U. N.Mex., 1952. Instr. U. N.Mex., 1948-52, asst. prof. English and speech, 1952-57; asso. prof. English Long Beach State Coll., 1957-61; prof., chmn. dept. English Hanover Coll., 1961-66; prof. English U. Utah, Salt Lake City, 1966—; chmn. dept. U. Utah, 1969-71, dir. creative writing, 1980-83, univ. prof., 1987-88, prof. emeritus, 1988—; mem. faculty Bread Loaf Sch. English, 1990—; editorial chmn. Coll. and Adult Reading List of Books in Lit. and Fine Arts, 1962; dir. Seminar Am. Poetry, Am. Studies Rsch. Ctr., Hyderabad, India, 1971; writer-in-residence Sch. of Ozarks, 1971, Behrend campus Pa. State U., 1972, sch. arts, U. Wis., Madison, 1987, Deep Springs Coll., 1989. Author: Carl Van Vechten and the Twenties, 1955, Carl Van Vechten, 1965, Images and Impressions: Poems by Brewster Ghiselin, Edward Lueders and Clarice Short, 1969, The Gang from Percy's Hotel and Other Poems, 1971, The Clam Lake Papers, A Winter in the North Woods, 1977, The Wake of the General Bliss, 1989; editor: (with others) Reflections on a Gift of Watermelon Pickle and Other Modern Verse, 1966, 2d edit., 1995, Some Haystacks Don't Even Have Any Needle and Other Complete Modern Poems, 1969, (with Primus St. John), Zero Makes Me Hungry, 1976, Writing Natural History: Dialogues with Authors, 1989, co-translator (with Naoshi Koriyama) Like Underground Water, The Poetry of Mid-20th Century Japan, 1995, Western Humanities Rev., 1969-72; gen. editor Peregrine Smith Literary Naturalists Series, 1989-92, U. Utah Press Nature and Environmental Studies, 1993—. Bd. dirs. Ucross Found., 1989—. Served with USAAF, 1943-46, CBI. Recipient Poetry prize Utah Inst. Fine Arts Creative Writing Competition, 1969, Disting. Alumni award Hanover Coll., 1972, Nat. Endowment Arts Creative Writing fellow, 1983, Utah Humanities Coun. Gov.'s award in the Humanities, 1992. Home: 958 Windsor St Salt Lake City UT 84105-1308

LUEDERS, WAYNE RICHARD, lawyer; b. Milw., Sept. 23, 1947; s. Warren E. and Marjorie L. (Schramek) L.; m. Patricia L. Rasmus, Aug. 1, 1970 (div. Nov. 1990); children: Laurel, Daniel, Kristin. BBA with honors, U. Wis., 1969; JD, Yale U., 1973; Yale Law Sch. Bar: Wis. 1973. Acct. Arthur Andersen & Co., Milw., 1969-70; atty. Foley & Lardner, Milw., 1973-80, ptnr., 1980—; bd. dirs. numerous cos. Bd. dirs. Riveridge Nature Ctr., Milw., 1983-92, Milw. Pro Soccer, 1986—, Milw. Art Mus., 1992—, Child abuse Prevention Fund, Milw., 1989—, Michael Fields Agrl. Inst., 1991—; mem. adv. bd. Florentine Opera Co., 1992—; class agt. Yale Law Sch., 1978—. With U.S. Army, 1969-75. Mem. ABA, AICPA (Wisc.), Wis. Bar Assn., Milw. Bar Assn., Estate Counselors Forum, Univ. Club (Milw.), Phi Kappa Phi. Avocations: theater, racquetball, violin. Office: Foley & Lardner 777 E Wisconsin Ave Milwaukee WI 53202-5367

LUEDTKE, LUTHER S., academic administrator. Pres. Calif. Luth. U., Thousand Oaks. Office: Calif Luth U Office of President 60 Olsen Rd Thousand Oaks CA 91360-2700

LUEDTKE, ROLAND ALFRED, lawyer; b. Lincoln, Nebr., Jan. 4, 1924; s. Alfred C. and Caroline (Senne) L.; m. Helen Snyder, Dec. 1, 1951; children: Larry O., David A. B.S., U. Nebr., 1949, J.D., 1951. Bar: Nebr. 1951. Since practiced in Lincoln, 1951—; mem. Luedtke, Radcliffe & Evans (and predecessor), 1973-79; dep. sec. state State of Nebr., 1953-60; spl. legis. liaison Nebr. Dept. State, 1953-60; corps and elections counsel to sec. of state State of Nebr., 1960-65; senator Nebr. Unicameral Legislature, 1967-78, speaker, 1977-78; lt. gov. State of Nebr., 1979-83; mayor City of Lincoln, 1983-87; of counsel McHenry, Haszard & Flowers, Lincoln, 1987—; exec. sec. Gov. Nebr. Com. Refugee Relief, 1954-58; del., conferee nat. confs. Past pres. Lancaster County Cancer Soc.; crusade chmn. Nebr. div. Am. Cancer Soc., 1981-82; past dist. v.p., fin. chmn. Boy Scouts Am.; treas. Nebr. Young Republicans, 1953-54; jr. pres. Founders Day, Nebr. Rep. Com., 1958-59; chmn. Lancaster County Rep. Com., 1962-64; bd. dirs. Concordia Coll. Assn., Seward, Nebr., 1962-66, pres., 1965-66; bd. dirs. Lincoln Lutheran Sch. Assn., 1961-65, pres., 1964-65; bd. dirs. Immanuel Health Ctr. Omaha; Tabitha Found., Lincoln, 1986—, v.p., 1990-94; bd. dirs. Nebraskaland Found., Lincoln, 1980—, pres. 1990-93; bd. dirs. Coords. for Adult Literacy, Nebr., 1984—, v.p., 1990-92. Served with AUS, 1943-45, ETO. Decorated Bronze Star, Purple Heart; recipient Disting. Service award Concordia Tchrs. Coll., 1965, Disting. Alumni award Lincoln High Sch., 1983. Mem. Am. Bar Assn., Nat. Conf. State Legislators (chmn. criminal justice task force 1975-77, chmn. consumers affairs com. 1975-77, exec. com. 1977-78), Nat. Conf. Lt. Govs. (exec. com. 1981-83), U.S. Conf. Mayors (chmn. human devel. com.), Nat. Conf. Cities (bd. dirs., bd. advisor human devel. com. NLC), Nat. League Cities (bd. dirs.), Nebr. Bar Assn., Lincoln Bar Assn., Am. Legion, DAV, VFW, Lincoln C. of C., Lincoln Gateway Sertoma Club (pres. 1962-63, chmn. bd. 1963-64), Delta Theta Phi. Lutheran. Office: McHenry Haszard & Flowers Ste 870 NBC Ctr Lincoln NE 68508

LUELLEN, CHARLES J., retired oil company executive; b. Greenville, S.C., Oct. 18, 1929; s. John B. and Dorothy C. (Bell) L.; m. Jo S. Riddle, July 11, 1953; children: Margaret L. Briggs, Nancy L. Bissell. B.S., Ind. U., 1952. Sales rep. Ashland Oil, Inc., Ky., 1952-70, v.p. sales, 1970-72, group v.p. sales, 1972-80, pres., chief operating officer, 1986-92; also dir. emeritus Emeriti-Ashland, Inc., Ky.; pres. Ashland Petroleum Co., 1980-86; bd. dirs. Tosco Corp., Stamford, Conn. Bd. dirs. Kings Daus. Hosp., Ashland, 1981-87, Ashland Area YMCA, 1980-92, Nat. Chamber Found., Washington, 1987-92; trustee Centre Coll., Danville, Ky., 1988, Joint Coun. for Econ. Edn., N.Y.C. Mem. Beta Gamma Sigma. Home: 3409 Monte Vista Dr Austin TX 78731-5722 Office: Ashland Inc PO Box 391 Ashland KY 41105-0391 also: Ashland Inc 1000 Ashland Dr Russell KY 41169

LUENGO, CARLOS ALBERTO, physics educator; b. Buenos Aires, Aug. 12, 1943; arrived in Brazil, 1976; s. Aurelio and Hilda Esther (Blanco) L.; m. Maria Del Rosario Bianchi, Feb. 8, 1979; children: João Carlos, Ana Paula. BS in Physics, Inst. Balseiro, Bariloche, Argentina, 1967; D Physics, U. Cuyo, Bariloche, 1972. Rsch. asst. Centro Atomico Bariloche, 1968-70; vis. scientist U. Calif. at San Diego, La Jolla, 1971-72, rsch. physicist Inst. Pure and Applied Phys. Scis., 1973-76; prof. physics U. Campinas, Unicamp, Sao Paulo, Brazil, 1976—, prof. energy supply systems, 1988—; R&D project mgr. Finep, Rio de Janeiro, 1977-82, Petrobrás Rsch. Ctr., 1994—; cons. Bendix Corp., Campinas, Brazil, 1980, Copersucar Tech. Ctr., Piracicaba, Brazil, 1988—; chief tech. advisor UN Indsl. Devel. Orgn., Asuncion, Paraguay, 1983-87. Mem. editl. bd. Fuel mag., 1988-96. Scholar Liceo Almirante Brown, 1957, Atomic Energy Commn., Buenos Aires, 1962, sr. fellow Guggenheim Found., 1970. Mem. Am. Phys. Soc., Brazilian Phys. Soc.

LUENING, OTTO, composer, conductor, flutist, educator; b. Milw., June 15, 1900; s. Eugene and Emma (Jacobs) L.; m. Ethel Codd, Apr. 19, 1927 (div.); m. Catherine Brunson, Sept. 5, 1959. Student, State Acad. Music, Munich, 1915-17; diploma, Mcpl. Conservatory Music, Zurich, Switzerland, 1919; student, U. Zurich, 1919-20; D.Mus. (hon.), Wesleyan U., 1963, Wis. Conservatory of Music, 1979; D.Mus (hon.), U. Wis.-Milw., 1985; D.F.A. (hon.), U. Wis.-Madison, 1977; Litt.D. (hon.), Columbia U., 1981. Assoc. prof. U. Ariz., 1932-34; chmn. music dept. Bennington (Vt.) Coll., 1934-44; dir. music Bennington Sch. of Arts, 1940-41; assoc. prof., chmn. music dept. Barnard Coll., 1944-48; prof. music Columbia and Barnard Coll., 1948-68, prof. emeritus of music, 1968—; music chmn. Sch. Arts Columbia U., 1968-70; prof. Joline Found., 1947-64; mus. dir. Brander Matthews Theatre, Columbia U., 1944-59; mem. composition faculty Juilliard Sch., N.Y.C., 1971-73; co-dir. Columbia-Princeton Electronic Music Center, 1959-80; Bennington Coll. Disting. Hadley fellow, 1975; vis. composer U. S.C., 1978, U. Wis., Kenosha-Parkside, 1979, 80, 81, 82, N.Y. U., 1979, Bklyn. Coll., 1981; commd. N.Y. Philharmonic, BMI, NEA, McKim Fund at Library of Congress; Phi Beta Kappa vis. scholar and hon. mem., 1966; spl. cons. Silver Burdett Co.; mem. ednl. advisory com. Guggenheim Found., 1964-69; life mem. Nat. Inst. Arts and Letters, v.p., 1953; mem. music com. Yaddo, 1936, 37, 38, 40, 47; mem. exec. com. New Music Quar. Records; mem. advisory com. Fed. Music Project in Vt.; mem. Vt. Music Library Com.; co-founder Am. Music Ctr. N.Y.C., chmn., 1940-60; bd. dirs. Vt. Symphony Orch., 1939; founder, mem. Am. Composers Alliance, pres., 1945-51; co-founder Composer's Recs., Inc., pres., 1968-70, chmn. bd., 1970-75, co-pres., 1975-77; bd. mem. Am. Composers Orch., 1974—, Composers Forum; mem. exec. bd. League of Composers, 1943; bd. dirs. Internat. Soc. Contemporary Music, 1974-81; nat. chmn. Am. composition Nat. Fedn. Music Clubs, 1943; mem. com. Soc. for Publ. Am. Music, 1945, Com. on Contemporary Music in U.S.A., Music Educators Nat. Conf., 1943; U.S. del. Internat. Composers Conf., Stratford, Ont., 1960; U.S. music advisory com. UNESCO, 1953—; guest lectr. Bourges Internat. Music Festival. Flutist, condr. operetta and symphony orchs., Munich and Zurich, 1915-20; conducted first all-Am. opera performance, Chgo., 1922; coach, exec. dir. opera dept., Eastman Sch. Music, 1925-28, asst. condr., later condr., Rochester Am. Opera Co., guest condr., Am. Opera Co., N.Y.C., 1928; assoc. condr. N.Y. Philharm. Symphony Chamber Orch., 1936; guest condr. Vt. Symphony Orch., 1978, 85, Res Musica Balt., 1984, Internat. Festival of the Americas, Miami, 1984, vis. composer, trustee Am. Acad. in Rome, composer-in-residence, 1958, 61, 65; vis. composer Peabody Inst. Music, 1977, composer-in-residence, 1977-79; vis. composer, Bennington Coll. summer workshops, 1977-79, composer-in-residence Chamber Music Conf. and Composers' Forum, Bennington, 1988, Skaneateles Festival, 1991, Cin. Conservatory, Canonical Studies and Fanfare for Those We Have Lost for Wind Orch., 1993, Green Lake, Wis., 1993; retrospective concert and exhbn. of composers' collection, N.Y. Pub. Libr. of Performing Arts at Lincoln Ctr. for 90th Birthday ; other 90th Birthday performances include Sage City (Vt.) Symphony, New Paltz, N.Y., Conn. Early Music Festival, concert at Merkin Hall by Goodman Chamber Choir, N.Y.C.; commission performance Symphonic Fantasia #10, Woodstock Chamber Orch.; performances at Eastman Sch. Music, New Eng. Conservatory for 90th Birthday; also appeared as composer and flute soloist; appeared (with Ethel Luening) in concerts, U.S., Can. and Europe, 1928-41; author: The Odyssey of an American Composer: Autobiography, 1980; (with others) The Development and Practice of Electronic Music, 1975; contbr.: The Liberation of Sound, 1972, On the Wires of Our Nerves, 1989; also articles; composer over 300 works in varios musical forms, many compositions played by Am., fgn. symphony orchs., chamber music socs. and soloists, recs., Composer Recs. Inc.; also published: (in collaboration with Vladimir Ussachevsky) pioneer works for tape recorder including Rhapsodic Variations, Poem in Cycles & Bells, Concerted Piece for tape recorder and orch., taped electronic music solos and with orch.; recs. include Orchestra Works, 1917-92, 1994. Named hon. alumnus U. Wis., Parkside, 1981; named in his honor Otto Luening Day, N.Y.C., 1995; recipient David Bispham medal Am. opera, 1993, award Nat. Inst. of Arts and Letters, 1946, citation for outstanding achievements and contbns. to edn. and music Wis. Senate and Ho. of Reps., 1965, 76, Thorne Music Fund Found. award, 1972, citation Nat. Assn. Composers and Condrs., 1966, Am. Composers Alliance Laurel Leaf award, 1970, Laurel Wreath award, 1985, award NEA, 1974, 77, medallion and citation Wis. Acad. Scis., Arts and Letters, 1977, Creative Arts award and medal for music Brandeis U., 1981, Nat. Music Coun. Am. Eagle award, 1985, BMI citation, 1985, citation for svc. and dedication League Composers and Internat. Soc. for Contemporary Music, 1986, citation by Electro-Acoustic Soc. in U.S., Busoni award Busoni Found., 1991, proclamation and commendation Mayor of Milw. and Gov. of Wis., 1995; Guggenheim fellow, 1930-32, 74-75. Mem. N.Y. Acad. Scis. Clubs: Columbia U., Faculty, Century Assn. (N.Y.C.). Broadcasts and concerts in honor of 75th, 80th, 83d, 85th, 90th and 95th birthdays, N.Y.C., Milw., Munich, San Francisco, L.A., Houston, Washington, Boston, Denver, Louisville, Cologne (Germany), Bourges (France), Moscow, London, The Netherlands. Home: 460 Riverside Dr New York NY 10027-6820 *Be patient, healthy and practice.*

LUENING, ROBERT ADAMI, agricultural economics educator emeritus; b. Milw., Apr. 20, 1924; s. Edwin Garfield and Irma Barbara (Adami) L.; m. Dorothy Ellen Hodgskiss, Aug. 27, 1966. B.S., U. Wis., 1961, M.S., 1968. Dairy farmer Hartland, Wis., 1942-58; fieldman Waukesha County Dairy Herd Improvement Assn., Waukesha, Wis., 1958; adult agr. instr. Blair Sch. Dist., Wis., 1961-63; extension farm mgmt. agt. U. Wis.-Racine, 1963-69; extension farm record specialist Dept. Agrl. Econs. U. Wis.-Madison, 1969-88; free-lance work, 1988—. Author: (with others) The Farm Management Handbook, 1972, 7th edit., 1991, Teacher's Manual, 1991, Managing Your Financial Future Farm Record Book Series, 1980, 4th edit., 1987, USDA Yearbook of Agriculture, 1989, Beef, Sheep and Forage Production in Northern Wisconsin, 1992; writer mag. column: Agri-Vision, 1970-88. Founder, exec. pres. Lüning Family Orgns. U.S.A., Inc. Recipient John S. Donald Excellence in Teaching award U. Wis.-Madison, 1980; recipient Wis. State Farmer award Vocat. Agr. Inst. Wis., 1980, Second Mile award Wis. County Agts. Assn., 1980, Outstanding Svc. to Wis. Agr. award Farm and Industry Short Course, 1989. Mem. Am. Soc. Farm Mgrs. and Rural Appraisers (coll. v.p. 1976, chmn. editorial com. 1978-80, sec.-treas. 1968-80, pres. Wis. chpt. 1982, Silver Plow award 1988), Epsilon Sigma Phi (Disting. Service award 1988), Alpha Gamma Rho. Presbyterian. Lodge: Masons. Home: 5313 Fairway Dr Madison WI 53711-1038 Office: U Wis Dept Agrl and Applied Econs Rm 216 Rm 216 427 Lorch St Madison WI 53706-1513

LUEPKE, GRETCHEN, geologist; b. Tucson, Nov. 10, 1943; d. Gordon Maas and Janice (Campbell) Luepke; B.S., U. Ariz., 1965, M.S., 1967; U. Colo., summer, 1962. Geol. field asst. U.S. Geol. Survey, Flagstaff, Ariz., 1964; with U.S. Geol. Survey, Menlo Park, Calif., 1967—, geologist, Pacific Br. of Marine Geology, 1976—. Registered geologist, Ore. Mem. U.S. Congress Office Tech. Assessment Workshop, Mining and Processing Placers of EEZ, 1986. Mem. Soc. Econ. Paleontologists and Mineralogists (chmn. com. libraries in developing countries 1988-91), Geol. Soc. Am.(Interdisciplinary Perspectives on the Hist. Earth Scis., Penrose Conf. 1994), Ariz. Geol. Soc., Peninsula Geol. Soc., Bay Area Mineralogists (chmn. 1979-80), History of the Earth Scis. Soc., Internat. Assn. Sedimentologists, Internat. Marine Minerals Soc. (charter), Geospeakers Toastmasters Club (charter), Sigma Xi. Editor: Stability of Heavy CTM Minerals in Sediments, 1995; Econ. Analysis of Heavy Minerals in Sediments; editor book rev. Earth Scis. History, 1989—. Contbr. articles on heavy-mineral analysis to profl. jours. Office: 345 Middlefield Rd Menlo Park CA 94025-3561

LUEPKE, HENRY FRANCIS, JR., lawyer; b. St. Louis, May 12, 1935; s. Henry Francis and Genevieve (Barthold) L.; m. Judith Claire Schicker, Dec. 27, 1958; children: Caroline, Gretchen, Henry, Mary Claire. BA cum laude, U. Notre Dame, 1957; JD, St. Louis U., 1960. Bar: Mo. 1960, Ill. 1960, U.S. Dist. Ct. (ea. dist.) Mo. 1960, U.S. Dist. Ct. (so. dist.) Ill., 1960, U.S. Supreme Ct. 1973. Assoc. Lewis, Rice, Tucker, Allen & Chubb, St. Louis, 1960-68; mem. Lewis, Rice & Fingersh, L.C., St. Louis, 1968-86, mem. in charge of adminstrn., 1986-95; lectr. Sch. Commerce, St. Louis U., 1962-68; gen. counsel Environ. Improvement and Energy Resources Authority, Jefferson City, Mo., 1978—; chmn. lawyers div. Arts and Edn. Fund, St. Louis, 1988. Author: Guide to Probate Practice, 1962; mem. editorial bd. St. Louis U. Law Jour., 1959-60; contbr. articles to profl. jours. Chmn. Civil Svc. Bd., University City, Mo., 1974—; bd. dirs. Ozark Nat. Scenic River's Ways Commn., Van Buren, Mo., 1977-81; legal counsel, treas. Teasdale for Gov. Com., Jefferson City, Mo., 1977-81. Recipient Award of Yr. Notre Dame Club-St. Louis, 1984, Alumni Svc. award St. Louis U., 1987, Cross of Affiliation award Acad. of Visitation, 1988. Mem. ABA, Mo. Bar Assn., Ill. Bar Assn., Bar Assn. Met. St. Louis, Notre Dame U. Law Assn., Mo. Athletic Club (bd. dirs. 1991-94, pres. 1993-94), St. Louis Hinder Club. Democrat. Roman Catholic. Avocations: handball, fly fishing, bird hunting, canoeing. Office: Lewis Rice & Fingersh 500 N Broadway Ste 2000 Saint Louis MO 63102-2130

LUEPKER, RUSSELL VINCENT, epidemiology educator; b. Chgo., Oct. 1, 1942; s. Fred Joeseph and Anita Louise (Thornton) L.; m. Ellen Louise Thompson, Dec. 22, 1966; children: Ian, Carl. BA, Grinnell Coll., 1964; MD with distinction, U. Rochester, 1969; MS, Harvard U., 1976; MD (hon.), U. Lund, Sweden. Intern U. Calif., San Diego, 1969-70; resident Peter Bent Brigham Hosp., Boston, 1973-74; cardiology fellow Peter Bent Brigham Hosp./Med., Boston, 1974-76; asst. prof. divsn. epidemiology med. lab. physiol. hygiene U. Minn., Mpls., 1976-80, assoc. prof., 1980-87, prof. divsn. epidemiology and medicine, 1987—, dir. divsn. epidemiology, 1991—; cons. NIH, Bethesda, Md., 1980—, U. So. Calif., L.A., 1985—, Armed Forces Epidemiology Bd., 1993—; vis. prof. U. Goteborg, Sweden, 1986, Ninewells Med. Sch., Dundee, Scotland, 1995. Lt. comdr. USPHS, 1970-73. Harvard U. fellow, 1974-76, Bush Leadership fellow, 1990; recipient Prize for Med. Rsch. Am. Coll. Chest Physicians, 1970, Nat. Rsch. Svc. award Nat. Heart, Lung and Blood Inst., Bethesda, 1975-77, Disting. Alumni award Grinnell Coll., 1989. Fellow ACP, Am. Coll. Cardiology, Am. Heart Assn. Coun. on Epidemiology (chmn. 1992-94), Am. Heart Assn. Sci. Sessions (program com. chair 1995—), Am. Coll. Epidemiology; mem. Delta Omega Soc. (Nat. Merit award 1988). Office: Univ Minn Sch Pub Health Div Epidemiology 1300 S 2nd St Ste 300 Minneapolis MN 55454-1015

LUERS, WILLIAM HENRY, art museum administrator; b. Springfield, Ill., May 15, 1929; s. Carl U. and Ann L. (Lynd) L.; m. Wendy Woods Turnbull, Oct. 18, 1979; children by previous marriage: Mark B., David L., William F., Amy L. A.B., Hamilton Coll., 1951, LL.D. (hon.), 1984; M.A., Columbia U., 1957; postgrad., Northwestern U., 1951-52. Commd. fgn. service officer Dept. State, 1957; vice consul Naples, Italy, 1957-60; 2d sec. Am. Embassy, Moscow, 1963-65; polit. counselor Am. Embassy, Caracas, Venezuela, 1969-73; dep. exec. sec. Dept. State, 1973-75; dep. asst. sec. for inter Am. affairs, Washington, 1975-77; dep. asst. sec. European affairs (Soviet-Eastern Europe), 1977-78; ambassador to Venezuela, Caracas, 1978-82, Czechoslovakia, Prague, 1983-86; pres. Met. Mus. Art, N.Y.C., 1986—; bd. dirs. Wickes Lumber Co., Vernon Hills, Ill., IDEX Corp., Northbrook, Ill., Scudder New Europe Fund, N.Y., Scudder Global/Internat. Funds; dir.'s visitor Inst. Advanced Study, Princeton, N.J., 1982-83; vis. lectr. Woodrow Wilson Sch., Princeton U., 1983; trustee Rockefeller Bros. Found., N.Y.C. Active adv. coun. Trust for Mut. Understanding, N.Y.C.; trustee adv. coun. Appeal of Conscience Found., N.Y.C.; bd. dirs. Inst. for East West Studies, N.Y.C., Am. Acad. Diplomacy, Washington. Fellow Am. Acad. Arts and Scis.; mem. Coun. Fgn. Rels., Econ. Club N.Y. (bd. dirs.). Episcopalian. Office: Met Mus Art 1000 5th Ave New York NY 10028-0113

LUERSSEN, FRANK WONSON, retired steel company executive; b. Reading, Pa., Aug. 14, 1927; s. George V. and Mary Ann (Swoyer) L.; m. Joan M. Schlosser, June 17, 1950; children: Thomas, Mary Ellen, Catherine, Susan, Ann. BS in Physics, Pa., State U., 1950; MSMetE, Lehigh U., 1951; LLD (hon.), Calumet Coll.; DPS (hon.), Xavier U. Metallurgist research and devel. div. Inland Steel Co., East Chicago, Ind., 1952-54; mgr. various positions Inland Steel Co., 1954-64, mgr. research, 1964-68, v.p. research, 1968-77, v.p. steel mfg., 1977-78, pres., 1978-85, chmn., 1983-92; bd. dirs. Morton Internat., Inc. Contbr. articles on steelmaking tech. to various publs. Trustee Northwestern U., 1980—; trustee, sec., treas. Munster Sch. Bd., 1957-66. With USNR, 1945-47. Named disting. alumnus Pa. State U. Fellow Am. Soc. Metals; mem. AIME (Disting. life mem., B.F. Fairless award, Howe meml. lectr. 1988-91), Am. Iron and Steel Inst. (Gary medal, chmn. 1989-90), Nat. Acad. Eng. Home and Office: 8226 Parkview Ave Munster IN 46321-1419

LUETKEHOELTER, GOTTLIEB WERNER (LEE), retired bishop, clergyman; b. Wheatwyn, Sask., Can., Nov. 16, 1929; s. Henry William and Marie Louise (Schlepper) L.; m. Betty Edwards, July 25, 1959; children—David Lee, Jonathan Richard. B.A., U. Sask., 1952; B.D., Lutheran Coll. and Sem., Saskatoon, Sask., 1955; S.T.M., Vancouver Sch. Theology, 1975; DD, St. John's Coll., U. Manitoba, 1990. Ordained to ministry United Luth. Ch. in Am., 1955. Pastor Markinch-Wheatwyn-Cupar Parish, 1955-57; pastor St. Mark's Luth. Ch., Regina, Sask., 1957-61, Erloeser Luth. Ch., Phila., 1961-63, Faith Luth. Ch., Burnaby, B.C., Can., 1963-69, Trinity Luth. Ch., Edmonton, Alta., Can., 1969-76; bishop Central Can. Synod, Luth. Ch. in Am., Winnipeg, Man., Can., 1976-85; bishop Man./Northwestern Ont. Synod, Evang. Luth. Ch. in Can., Winnipeg, Man., 1985-94; ret., 1994; mem. exec. coun. Luth. Ch. in Am., N.Y.C., 1978-85, Anglican-Luth. Dialogue, Can., 1983-95; dir. Can. Luth. World Relief, 1989—. Bd. govs. Luth. Theol. Sem., Saskatoon, 1976-94, Schmieder resident, 1994-95. With Can. Navy, 1953-55. Avocations: golf; swimming.

LUFFSEY, WALTER STITH, transportation executive; b. Richmond, Va., Mar. 15, 1934; s. Roland Emmit and Bernice Irene (Hall) L.; m. Louise Arlington Hicks, Dec. 19, 1956; children: Dennis Glenn, Melinda Denise. Student, U. Richmond, 1952-55, Agrl. Dept. Grad. Sch., 1963-65.

With FAA, 1957—; supervisory air traffic control specialist FAA, Atlantic City, 1960-63; air traffic control specialist research FAA, 1963-65, sr. air traffic control analyst systems research and devel. service, 1965-71; chief program analysis and reports br. FAA, Washington, 1971-72; asst. chief program mgmt. staff FAA, 1972-73, spl. asst., assoc. adminstr. for engring. and devel., 1973-74, chief program mgmt. staff system research and devel. service, 1974-75, tech. asst., assoc. adminstr. policy devel. and rev., 1975-78, tech. asst., assoc. adminstr. policy and internat. aviation affairs, tech. asst. to the assoc. adminstr. for aviation standards, 1978-79, dep. assoc. adminstr. for aviation standards, 1979-80, assoc. adminstr. for aviation standards, 1980-85, assoc. adminstr. for air traffic, 1985-86, dir. advanced aviation system design team, 1986-89; sr. v.p. ops. and planning Tech. and Mgmt. Assistance, Washington, 1989-90, exec. v.p., 1990—; pres. WSL Enterprises, Arlington, 1989—. Author: Air Traffic Control: How to Become an FAA Air Traffic Controller, 1990; contbr. articles to profl. jours. Served with USAF, 1955-58. Recipient Meritorious Achievement award Air Traffic Control Assn., 1965; recipient Spl. Achievement award FAA, 1970, 78, 85, Disting. Service award Aviation Week and Space Tech.-Flight Safety Found., 1982; Sec.'s award for outstanding achievement, 1982; Meritorious Exec. award-Presdl. Rank, 1983; Adminstr.'s Superior Achievement award for excellence in equal employment opportunity, 1985, numerous others. Mem. AIAA (mem. aero. policy com.), Soc. Sr. Aerospace Execs., Nat. Aero. Assn., Exptl. Aircraft Assn., Aircraft Owners and Pilots Assn., Profl. Women Contrs. Assn., Air Traffic Control Assn. (hon. mem. award 1986, chair publs. com.), John Marshall Cadet Alumni Assn., Soc. Airway Pioneers, Va. Aero. Hist. Soc., Order of Quiet Birdmen, Aero Club, Nat. Aviation Club (past pres., gov. emeritus), Kiwanis (past pres. Crystal City club). Home: 1805 Crystal Dr #713-S Crystal Park Arlington VA 22202 Office: Tech & Mgmt Assistance 600 Maryland Ave SW Ste 420 Washington DC 20024-2520 also: WSL Enterprises PO Box 16223 Arlington VA 22215-1223

LUFKIN, LIZ, newspaper editor. Entertainment editor The San Francisco Chronicle, Calif. Office: The San Francisco Chronicle 901 Mission St San Francisco CA 94103-2905

LUFRANO, MICHAEL RICHARD, lawyer; b. Chgo., July 8, 1965; s. Ned Nathan and Joan Audrey (Gold) L. BA, U. Ill., 1987; JD, Harvard U., 1992. Bar: Ill. 1992, D.C. 1993, U.S. Dist. Ct. (no. dist.) Ill. 1995. Assoc. city atty. City of Atlanta, 1992-93; spl. asst. to pres., dep. dir. advance White House, Washington, 1993-95; media/intellectual property atty. Sonnenschein, Nath & Rosenthal, Chgo., 1995—; issues dir., speechwriter Dukakis for Pres., Boston, 1987-88. Rotary Internat. scholar, 1987. Office: Sonnenschein Nath Rosenthal 8000 Sears Tower Chicago IL 60606

LUFT, HAROLD S., health economist; b. Newark, N.J., Jan. 6, 1947; s. George and Kay (Grossman) L.; m. Lorraine Ellin Levinson, May 24, 1970; children: Shira Levinson, Jana Levinson. A.B., Harvard U., 1968, AM, 1970, Ph.D., 1973. Systems analyst, rsch. asst. Harvard Transport Rsch., Cambridge, Mass., 1965-68; systems analyst Harvard Econ. Rsch. Project, Cambridge, Mass., 1968-72; instr. econs. Tufts U., Medford, Mass., 1972-73; postdoctoral fellow Harvard Ctr. Community Health, Boston, 1972-73; asst. prof. health econs. Stanford U., Calif., 1973-78; prof. health econs., acting dir. Inst. Health Policy Studies, U. Calif., San Francisco, 1978—; cons. Applied Mgmt. Scis., Silver Spring, Md., 1979—, Robert Wood Johnson Found., Princeton, N.J., 1982—; study sect. Nat. Ctr. Health Svcs., Rockville, Md., 1981-83; mem. coun. Agy. for Health Care Policy and Rsch. Author: Poverty and Health, 1978, Health Maintenance Organizations, 1981, 2d edit., 1988, (with Deborah Garnick, David mark, Stephen McPhee) Hospital Volume, Physician Volume, and Patient Outcomes, 1990, HMOs and the Elderly, 1994; contbr. chpts. to books, articles to profl. jours. Advisor, fin. planning com. Mid-Peninsula Health Service, Palo Alto, Calif., 1984—. NSF fellow, Carnegie Found. fellow, Grad. Prize fellow Harvard U., 1968-72, fellow Ctr. for Advanced Study in Behavioral Scis., 1988-89. Mem. Am. Pub. Health Assn., Am. Econ. Assn., Inst. Medicine, Western Econ. Assn., Assn. for Health Svcs. Rsch. (bd. dirs.). Home: 1020 Ramona St Palo Alto CA 94301-2443 Office: U Calif Inst for Health Policy Studies 1388 Sutter St Fl 11 San Francisco CA 94109-5427

LUFT, RENE WILFRED, civil engineer; b. Santiago, Chile, Sept. 21, 1943; came to U.S., 1968; s. David and Malwina (Kelmy) L.; m. Monica Acevedo, Aug. 24, 1970; children: Deborah Elaine, Daniel Eduardo. CE, U. Chile, 1967; MS, MIT, 1969, DSc, 1971. Registered profl. engr., Alaska, Calif., Wash., Mass., N.H., R.I., Republic of Chile; registered structural engr., Vt. Asst. prof. civil engring. U. Chile, 1967-68; research asst. MIT, Cambridge, Mass., 1969-71, vis. lectr., 1983-84; staff engr. Simpson, Gumpertz & Heger Inc., Arlington, Mass., 1971-74, sr. staff engr., 1975-78, assoc., 1978-83, sr. assoc., 1984-90; prin. Simpson, Gumpertz & Heger Inc., San Francisco, 1990-91; head design div. Simpson, Gumpertz & Heger Inc., 1991—; sec. seismic adv. com. Mass. Bldg. Code Commn., 1978-80, chmn., 1981-82; mem. Boston seismic instrumentation com. U.S. Geol. Survey; mem. slabs on ground com. Post-Tensioning Inst., 1994—. Contbr. articles to profl. jours. Mem. design overview com., bldg. seismic safety coun. Earthquake Hazards Reduction Program, 1983-91, chmn. rsch. com. 1987-88. Mem. ASCE, Boston Soc. Civil Engrs. (chmn. seismic design adv. com. 1981-86, Clemens Herschel award for tech. paper 1980, pres.'s award for leadership in earthquake engring. 1984), Am. Concrete Inst., Earthquake Engring. Research Inst., Structural Engrs. Assn. Calif., NSPE (Young Engr. of Yr., 1979), Sigma Xi, Chi Epsilon. Home: 109 Ardith Dr Orinda CA 94563-4201 Office: 221 Main St Ste 1500 San Francisco CA 94105-1934

LUFTGLASS, MURRAY ARNOLD, manufacturing company executive; b. Bklyn., Jan. 2, 1931; s. Harry and Pauline (Yaged) L.; children by previous marriage: Paula Jean, Bryan Keith, Robert Andrew, Richard Eric; m. Christine L. Novick, May 29, 1988; 1 child, Andrew William. BS, Ill. Inst. Tech., 1952; MS, U. So. Calif., 1959; MBA, U. Conn., 1972.With Shell Chem. Co., Torrance, Calif., 1955-60, N.Y.C., 1960-61, Wallingford, Conn., 1961-64, Torrance, 1964-66, N.Y.C., 1966-69; asst. gen. mgr. Westchester Plastics div. Ametek, Inc., Mamaroneck, N.Y., 1969-75; dir. corp. devel. Ametek, Inc., N.Y.C., 1975-76, v.p., 1976-83, sr. v.p. corp. devel., 1984—. Served to lt. (j.g.) USN, 1952-55. Mem. NAM, Soc. Plastics Industry, Assn. Corp. Growth, Soc. Plastics Engrs., Tau Beta Pi, Beta Gamma Sigma, Phi Lambda Upsilon. Club: University (N.Y.C.). Contbr. articles to profl. jours., publs. Patentee in field. Office: Ametek Inc 410 Park Ave New York NY 10022-4407

LUGAR, RICHARD GREEN, senator; b. Indpls., Apr. 4, 1932; s. Marvin L. and Bertha (Green) L.; m. Charlene Smeltzer, Sept. 8, 1956; children: Mark, Robert, John, David. B.A., Denison U., 1954; B.A., M.A. (Rhodes scholar), Oxford (Eng.) U., 1956. Mayor Indpls., 1968-75; vis. prof. polit. sci. U. Indpls., 1976; mem. U.S. Senate, 1977—, chmn. com. fgn. relations, 1985-86, chmn. com. on agr.nut. and forestry, 1995—; chmn. Nat. Rep. Senatorial Com., 1983-84; Treas. Lugar Stock Farm, Inc.; mem. Indpls. Sch. Bd., 1964-67, v.p., 1965-66; vice chmn. Adv. Commn. on Intergovtl. Relations, 1969-75; pres. Nat. League of Cities, 1970-71; mem. Nat. Commn. Standards and Goals of Criminal Justice System, 1971-73; Del., mem. resolutions com. Republican Nat. Conv., 1968, del., mem. resolutions com., 1992, Keynote speaker, 1972, del., speaker, 1980; mem. internat. adv. council Inst. Internat. Studies. Author: Letters to the Next President, 1988. Trustee Denison U., U. Indpls.; bd. dirs. Nat. Endowment for Democracy, Am. Running and Fitness Assn.; bd. dirs. Youth for Understanding. Served to lt. (j.g.) USNR, 1957-60. Pembroke Coll., Oxford U. hon. fellow. Mem. Blue Key, Phi Beta Kappa, Omicron Delta Kappa, Pi Delta Epsilon, Pi Sigma Alpha, Beta Theta Pi. Methodist. Club: Rotary. Office: US Senate 306 Hart Senate Bldg Washington DC 20510

LUGAR, THOMAS R., manufacturing executive. With Allison Div. Gen. Motors Co., Indpls., 1955-57; pres. Thomas L. Green & Co., Indpls., 1957—. Office: Thomas L. Green & Co. Inc. 202 Miley Ave Indianapolis IN 46222-4341

LUGENBEEL, EDWARD ELMER, publisher; b. Balt., June 6, 1932; s. Nimrod Augustus and Victoria Elizabeth (Shilling) L.; m. Alice Marie Smith, June 12, 1953; children: Craig Edward, Susan Elizabeth, Douglas Paul, Leslie Jean. B.S., U. Md., 1954. With Prentice-Hall, Inc., N.J., 1957-76; exec. editor, asst. v.p. Prentice-Hall, Inc., 1972-76; pres. D. Van Nostrand Co., div. Litton Ednl. Pub., Inc. (pubs. coll. textbooks), N.Y.C., 1976-81; v.p. Lynne Palmer Exec. Recruitment, Inc., N.Y.C., 1981-83; v.p., editorial dir. W.B. Saunders Med. Pubs., Phila., 1983-85; exec. editor Columbia U. Press, N.Y.C., 1985—. Served as 1st lt. USAF, 1954-57. Mem. AAAS, Am. Inst. Biol. Scis., Am. Geophys. Union, Soc. Vertebrate Paleontology, Internat. Assn. Landscape Ecology, Soc. Conservation Biology, Delta Sigma Pi. Office: 136 S Broadway Irvington NY 10533-2500

LUGER, DONALD R., engineering company executive; b. Elizabeth, N.J., May 12, 1938; s. George A. and Elizabeth M. Luger; m. Pat Sanders, Feb. 17, 1968 (dec. 1982); m. Sharon L. Luger, May 14, 1983; children: Christopher Daniel, Morgan Kathleen. BCE, Auburn U., 1962, MSCE, Auburn U., 1964, exec. program Stanford U., 1979. Registered profl. engr., N.C., Ga., Mich., Va., N.Y. Structural engr. NASA, Huntsville, Ala., summer 1962; area engr. E.I. DuPont Co., Nashville, 1964; structural engr. Hayes Internat. Corp., Huntsville, 1964-65; resident engr. Fibers Industries, Inc., Shelby, N.C. and Greenville, S.C., 1965-66; project mgr. Lockwood Greene Engrs., Inc., Atlanta, 1967-71, sr. project mgr., 1971-74, v.p., corp. dir., 1974-78, sr. v.p., corp. dir., 1978-82, pres., 1982—, chief exec. officer, 1983—, chmn. 1989. Mem. ASCE, NSPE, Ga. Soc. Profl. Engrs., So. Ctr. for Internat. Studies, Auburn U. Alumni Assn., Auburn Alumni Engring. Coun., Stanford Alumni Assn., Constrn. Industry Pres. Forum, Commerce Club, Atlanta Athletic Club.

LUGO, ARIEL E., ecologist, botanist, federal agency administrator; b. Mayagüez, P.R., Apr. 28, 1943; m. Helen Nunci; 2 children. BS in Biology, U. P.R., 1963, MS in Biology, 1965; PhD in Ecology, U. N.C., 1969. Asst. prof. dept. Botany U. Fla., Gainesville, 1969-73, 75-76, assoc. prof., 1976-79, acting dir. ctr. for wetlands, 1977-78; asst. sec. planning and resource analysis P.R. Dept. Natural Resources, Puerta de Tierra, 1973-74, asst. sec. sci. and tech., 1974-75; staff mem. Coun. Environ. Quality Exec. Office Pres., Washington, 1978-79; head divsn. ctr. energy and environ. rsch. U. P.R., 1980-88; project. leader Internat. Inst. Tropical Forestry, USDA Forest Svc., Rio Piedras, P.R., 1980-92, dir., 1986-92, acting dir., supervisory rsch. ecologist, 1992—; dir., 1992—, Internat. Inst. Tropical Forestry, USDA Forest Svc., Washington, 1994—; cons. Save Our Bays Assn., 1970, Am. Oil Co., 1972, H.W. Lochner, Inc., 1972, U.S. Postal Svc., 1972, U.S. Forest Svc., 1972, U.S. Dept. Interior, 1972, 73, 76, 77, U.S. EPA, 1974, U.S. Justice Dept., 1974, 78, UNESCO, 1975-76, 78, 83, 85-86, P.R. Dept. Natural Resources, 1975, 76, S.W. Fla. Regional Planning Coun., 1976-77, Environ. Quality Bd., 1976, 77, Fla. Dept. Natural Resources, 1976, Rockefeller Found., 1976, Nat. Audubon Soc., 1977, County of Lee, Fla., 1977, Nat. Wildlife Fedn., 1978, World Bank, 1978, Orgn. Am. States, 1979, 80, Collier County Nature Conservancy, 1980; hon. prof., lectr. U. P.R., 1974-76, 80—, hon. assoc. prof., 1985-86; with dept. Environ. Engring. Scis., Ctr. Latin Am. Studies U. Fla., Gainesville, 1977, dept. Botany, 1980-92; co-chmn. Fed. Com. Ecol. Reserves, 1977-79; mem. Man and Biosphere directorate 7-B Caribbean Islands, 1978-79, chmn. directorate I Tropical Forest Ecosystems, 1980-89, chmn. directorate Tropical Ecosystems, 1990; mem. Endangered Species Scientific Authority, Interagy. Arctic Rsch. Coordinating Com., Interagy. Tropical Deforestation Task Force, 1978-79, Tropical Diversity Interagy. Com., 1985; chmn. rsch. com. Latin Am. Forestry Commn. UNESCO, 1980—; mem. commn. on ecology Internat. Union Conservation Nature and Natural Resources, 1980-86; nat. rsch. coun. com. ecol. problems associated with devel. humid tropics, 1980-82; exec. com. U.S. Man and Biosphere program, 1981-84, nat. com. 1990; sr. adv. com. to Pres. U. P.R., 1982-88, chmn., 1985-88; scientific advisor Inst. Energy Analysis, Oak Ridge, Tenn., 1982-84; active Decade of Tropics Internat. Union Biol. Scis., 1985-88; adv. com. Yale Tropical Resources Inst., 1985—; advisor coastal zone program tropical countries, R.I. U., 1985-88; review team dept. forestry, Sch. Forest Resources and Conservation U. Fla., 1989; nat. rsch. coun. com. sustainable agriculture and the environment in the humid tropics, 1990-93; mem. grad. faculty dept. Environ., Population and Organismic Biology, U. Colo., Boulder, 1990-91; apptd. Consejo Consultivo del Programa de Patrimonio Nacional, 1990-92; expert witness in field. Mem. editorial bd. Vegetatio, 1981-82, Jour. Litoral, 1982—, Acta Cientifica, 1987—, Jour. Sustainable Forestry, 1991—, Restoration Ecology, 1992—, assoc. editor; mem. editorial bd. Forest Ecology and Mgmt., 1994—; contbr. articles to profl. jours. Trustee Fla. Defenders of Environment, 1980-81; rsch. assoc. Islands Resources Found., U.S. Virgin Islands, 1980—; bd. overseers Harvard Coll., com. to visit dept. Organismic and Evolutionary Biology, 1989—; bd. govs. Soc. Conservation Biology, 1989-91; bd. dirs. P.R. Conservation Found., 1990—. Recipient Disting. Scientist award Interam. U., San Juan, P.R., 1992; grantee U. Fla., 1969, 70, 71-72, U.S. Forest Svc., 1970, U.S. Dept. Interior, 1971, 72-75, Br. Sport Fisheries and Wildlife, 1971-73, 73-76, , Am. Oil Co., 1972, Fla. Dept. Natural Resources, 1972-75, H.W. Lochner, Inc., 1972, State of Fla., 1972-74, Inst. Food and Agrl. Scis., 1973, NSF, 1974, 81-83, 88—, U.S. EPA, 1977-79, Conservation Found., 1977, U.S. Dept. Energy, 1978-82, , U.S. Man and the Biosphere Consortium, 1980-87, 90-91, U.S. AID, 1982-83, FAO, 1983, U.S. Oceanographic Adminstrn., 1984-85, Tech. Wetlands Coun., 1986, World Wildlife Fund, 1989; Fullbright-Hayes fellow U. La Plata, Argentina, 1978. Mem. AAAS (coun. Caribbean divsn. 1991-92), Ecology Soc. Am., Internat. Soc. Tropical Foresters (exec. com. 1990-93), Soc. Ecol. Restoration and Mgmt. (founding 1988, bd. dirs. 1992), Internat. Soc. Tropical Ecology (bd. bearers 1990-93), Internat. Assn. Ecology, Fla. Acad. Scis, Soc. Caribbean Ornithology, P.R. Acad. Arts and Scis., Sigma Xi, Beta Beta Beta (hon. Zeta Zeta chpt.). Achievements include research in assessment of role of tropical forests in the carbon cycle of the world; studies of tropical tree plantations in Puerto Rico; comparisons of plantations and natural forests; relations between forest management and soil and water quality in Caribbean forests; studies of tropical wetlands; study on rate of decomposition in the tropics. Home: 1528 Tamesis El Paraiso San Juan PR 00926 Office: USDA Forest Svc Internat Inst Tropical Forestry PO Box 25000 San Juan PR 00928-5000

LUGT, HANS JOSEF, physicist; b. Bonn, Germany, Sept. 12, 1930; came to U.S., 1960; s. Josef and Elisabeth (Pütz) L.; m. Anneliese W. Scheller, Nov. 22, 1957; children: Christian H., Brigitte M. Prae Diploma, Bonn U., Fed. Republic of Germany, 1952; diploma, Aachen U., Fed. Republic of Germany, 1954; PhD, Stuttgart U., Fed. Republic of Germany, 1960. Asst., physics lab. Ruhrgas Co., Essen, Fed. Republic of Germany, 1954-57, head, physics lab., 1957-60; rsch. physicist U.S. Naval Weapons Lab., Dahlgren, Va., 1960-66; sci. cons. David Taylor Rsch. Ctr., Bethesda, Md., 1967-74, div. head, 1974-78, sr. rsch. physicist, 1978—. Author: Vortex Flow in Nature and Technology, 1983, reprint, 1995, Introduction to Vortex Theory, 1996; also over 110 articles to profl. jours. and govt. reports. Recipient Humboldt award Fed. Republic of Germany, 1981, Disting. Civilian Svc. award USN, 1982. Fellow Am. Physical Soc., Washington Acad. Scis.; mem. Am. Hist. Soc., Am. Goethe Soc. (pres. 1985-87), German Soc. for Applied Math. and Mechanics, Sigma Xi. Achievements include discovery of vortex breakdown in pipes; explanation of autorotating plates, Navier-Stokes computer simulations. Office: Carderock Div Naval Surface Warfare Ctr Bethesda MD 20084-5000

LUHRING, JOHN WILLIAM, former bank executive; b. Los Angeles, Sept. 11, 1912; s. Otto August and Lillian Louise (Fritz) L.; m. Josephine Ferentzy, Nov. 12, 1958; children by previous marriage: Karen Maria, John Dietrich. J.D., Southwestern U., 1934, LL.D., 1974; grad., Pacific Coast Sch. Banking, 1950. Bar: Calif. 1936. With Union Bank, Los Angeles, 1931-74, trust counsel, gen. atty., 1931-43, asst. cashier, 1943-45, asst. v.p., 1945-53, regional v.p., 1953-63, v.p. charge So. Calif. dept. Bus. Devel. Div., 1960-63, regional v.p. Wilshire Center regional head office, 1963-67, regional v.p., gen. mgr. hdqrs. banking office, 1967-69, exec. dir. pub. affairs, 1969-74; past dir., mem. exec. com. Harbor Ins. Co.; dir. sec., former pres. Third Laguna Hills Mut.; exec. dir. Friends of Cultural Center, Inc., Palm Desert, Calif., 1974-79. Mem. adv. com. YWCA, 1955-60; mem. investment com. YMCA, 1951-74; past pres. bd. commrs. Dept. Water and Power; dir. Met. Water Dist. So. Calif., 1962-67; pres. Community TV So. Calif., 1967-72; mem. Nat. Adv. Com. Oceans and Atmosphere, 1972-76; pres., dir. Golden Rain Found. Laguna Hills; chmn. Airport Adv. Assos., 1964-74; pres. adv. council Liberty Park; pres. William H. Parker Meml. Scholarship Found, 1966-74; mem.-at-large Los Angeles council Boy Scouts Am., 1950-74; Bd. dirs. ARC, 1951-64, 66-68, exec. com., 1956-64; treas.; bd. dirs. Braille Inst., 1960-75, Vets. Service Center, 1950-60; bd. dirs., past pres. U.S.O., 1964-66; trustee Resthaven Sanitarium, 1956-58; trustee, chmn. exec. com. Southwestern U., pres., chmn. bd., 1974—80; bd. dirs. Saddleback Community Hosp. Found., 1980-83, also bd. dirs. hosp., 1981—83; chmn. bd. dirs. Aliso Viejo Housing Opportunities Corp., 1982—. Decorated knight Order St. Lazarus Jerusalem. Mem. ABA, Los Angeles Bar Assn., State Bar Calif., Beverly Hills Wine and Food Soc., Chevaliers du Tastevin (grand officer), Commanderie de Bordeaux, Wine and Food Soc. So. Calif. (past chmn. bd. govs.), L.A. C. of C. (past dir., chmn. aerospace com.), Founding Friends Harvey Mudd Coll., Ephebian Soc., Alpha Phi Gamma. Home: 55172H Paseo Del Lago Laguna Hills CA 92653-2601

LUHRS, H. RIC, toy manufacturing company executive; b. Chambersburg, Pa., Mar. 22, 1931; s. Henry E. and Pearl (Beistle) L.; m. Grace B. Walke, June 12, 1973; children by previous marriage: Stephen Frederick, Christine Michelle, Terriann, Patricia Denise. BA, Gettysburg Coll., 1953. With The Beistle Co., Shippensburg, Pa., 1948-53, 1959—; pres., gen. mgr. Beistle Co., 1962-90, chmn. bd., 1978—; bd. dirs. Mellon Bank, Commonwealth region; dir., vice chmn. CompuPix Tech. Inc., 1984-88, pres., 1986-88, gemologist, 1977—; owner Luhrs Gem Testing Lab., 1977—, Luhrs Jewelry, 1976—, Allied Leasing Co., Shippensburg, 1968; pres. South Lac Devel. Co., 1986-92; owner Gun Depot, Shippensburg, 1992; chmn. The Walking Quail, Sports Goods Store, Shippensburg, 1994—. Pres. Shippensburg Public Library, 1964-66, 1970-72, 76-78, bd. dirs., 1963-82; pres. Community Chest, 1965, bd. dir., 1963-72; pres. Shippensburg Area Devel. Corp., 1966-72; bd. dirs., trustee Carlisle (Pa.) Hosp., 1967-71, Chambersburg Hosp., 1969-75; mem. consumer adv. coun. Capital Blue Cross, 1976-78; bd. dirs. Fla. Atlantic U. Found., 1988-91, Shippensburg U. Found., 1991—. Capt. USAF, 1953-59. Mem. SAR (life), Shippensburg Hist. Soc. (life, bd. dirs. 1968), Shippensburg C. of C. (pres. 1965, bd. dirs. 1964-65), Toy Mfrs. Assn. (bd. dirs. 1969-71), Nat. Sml. Businessmen's Assn., NRA (life, benefactor), NRA Whittington Ctr. Founder's Club, NRA Golden Eagles, Shippensburg Fish and Game Assn. (life, pres. 1963), Carlisle Fish and Game Assn. (life), Am. Legion (life) VFW (life), Cumberland Valley Indsl. Mgmt. Club, York Printing House Craftsmen, Masons (32 deg.), Shriners, Tall Cedars of Lebanon. Lutheran. Office: 1 Beistle Plz Shippensburg PA 17257

LUICK, ROBERT BURNS, lawyer; b. Belmond, Iowa, Aug. 6, 1911; s. Albert Lee and Estella Margaret (Burns) L.; m. Evelyn Pelletier, Nov. 21, 1942 (dec.); children: Elisabeth, Susan, Sarah, Nancy. AB, U. Minn., 1933, LLB, 1936; MBA cum laude, Harvard U., 1939. Bar: Mass. 1941. Atty. New Eng. Mut. Life Ins. Co., Boston, 1939-43; ptnr. Sullivan & Worcester, Boston, 1943-93, of counsel, 1993; bd. dirs. Ionics, Inc., Watertown, Mass., Continental Cablevision, Inc., Boston, Setra Systems, Inc., Acton, Mass. and others; pres. and dir. Boston Investment Co. Mem. ABA, Boston Bar Assn., Knights of Malta, Union Club, Longwood Cricket Club. Avocations: tennis, painting, music. Home: 51 Rutledge Rd Belmont MA 02178-3322

LUIGS, CHARLES RUSSELL, gas and oil drilling industry executive; b. Evansville, Ind., Apr. 4, 1933; s. Charles Anthony and Agnes A. (Russell) L.; m. Mary M. McClaine, Sept. 7, 1957; children: Charles Edwin, James Russell, Carol Lynn, Susan Nadine, Michael Alan. B.S. in Petroleum Engring., U. Tex., 1957; student, St. Edwards U., 1951-52. With U.S. Industries, various locations, 1957-76; v.p. U.S. Industries, 1969-71, exec. v.p., 1971-74, pres., 1974-76; dir. U.S. Industries, 1971-76; pres., chief exec. officer, dir. Global Marine, Inc., 1977—, chmn. bd., 1982—. Mem. Internat. Assn. Drilling Contractors (dir.), Nat. Soc. Profl. Engrs., AIME. Clubs: Houstonian, Houston, Westlake (Houston). Home: PO Box 4577 Houston TX 77210-4577 Office: Global Marine Inc 777 N Eldridge Pky Houston TX 77079-4425

LUIKART, FORDYCE WHITNEY, management consultant; b. Cleve., Aug. 17, 1910; s. Louis Edward and Grace (Latham) L.; m. Margaret Clark, Sept. 7, 1935; children—Clark W., James L., John F. A.B. cum laude, Ohio Wesleyan U., 1933, teaching certificate, 1934. Teaching fellow, asst. Maxwell Grad. Sch. Citizenship and Pub. Affairs, Syracuse U., 1934-37; instr. social sci. State Tchrs. Coll., Brockport, N.Y., 1937-39; mgr. br. office U.S. CSC, Cleve., 1942-44; chief investigations div. U.S. CSC, Washington, 1944-45; chief orgn. and methods staff U.S. CSC, 1945-46, chief inspection div., 1947-50, dir. exec. devel. program, 1950-51, exec. vice chmn. fed. personnel council, 1951, chief examining and placement div., 1951-53; dep. dir. adminstrn. HEW, 1953-54, dir. adminstrn., 1954; vis. lectr. pub. personnel adminstrn. Maxwell Grad. Sch., 1946-62; sr. staff mem. Brookings Instn., 1962-76, cons., 1976—; pvt. cons. on govt. orgn. and mgmt., exec. devel. and tng., 1976—; cons. on govt. orgn. with Cresap, McCormick & Paget (mgmt. cons.), 1955-57; cons., staff dir. Pres.'s Com. on Career Exec. Service, Sept. 1957; dir. Fed. Aviation Orgn. Study, White House Staff, 1957-58; asst. adminstr. personnel and tng. FAA, 1958-62; lectr. Eisenhower Exchange Fellowship Inc. Program, 1979—. Author pub. personnel adminstrn. articles profl. jours. Pres. Group Health Assn., Inc.; trustee Community Group Health Found., Washington.; Spl. adv. asst. to mem. Commn. Orgn. of Exec. Br. (Hoover Commn.), 1948-49; spl. adv. personnel and civil service to Greek Govt., E.C.A. mission, 1949-50. Mem. Pub. Personnel Assn., Soc. Personnel Adminstrn. (pres. 1952-53), Phi Beta Kappa, Omicron Delta Kappa, Sigma Chi. Methodist. Home: 3257 Beech St NW Washington DC 20015-2207 Office: Brookings Instn Washington DC 20036

LUIKART, JOHN FORD, investment banker; b. Washington, Apr. 9, 1949; s. Fordyce Whitney and Margaret Lucille (Clark) L.; m. Lorry Adele Haycock, June 2, 1973; children: Erin Kristine, James Benjamin, John Thomas. BA, Ohio Weslyan U., 1971. Ptnr. Prescott Ball and Turben, Cleve., 1977, sr. v.p., mgr. fixed income, 1982-86, exec. v.p., also bd. dirs., 1986-88; pres. Sutro & Co. Inc., San Francisco, 1989—, CEO, 1995—; bd. dirs. John Hancock Freedom Securities, San Francisco; pres. Selected Money Mkt. Fund, Chgo., 1986, 1331 Advisors, Cleve., 1986; mgr. Ohio Bond Fund, Cleve., 1983—; chmn. NASD Dist. Bus. Conduct Com., 1994; bd. dirs. John Hancock Clearing Corp. Chmn. Ohio Mcpl. Adv. Council, Cleve., 1978-79. Mem. Cleve. Bond Club (pres. 1980). Methodist. Avocations: sports, reading. Office: Sutro & Co 201 California St San Francisco CA 94111

LUING, GARY ALAN, financial management educator; b. Collins, Iowa, Apr. 24, 1937; s. Dwight Orn and Marjorie Mae (Clemons) L.; m. Sherry Lea Gates, Dec. 19, 1954; 1 child, Heather Sherry-Anne. B.S. cum laude, Stetson U., 1960; M.A., U. Ill., 1961; Dr. Adminstrn. (hon.), Canadian Sch. Mgmt. Auditor Arthur Andersen & Co., Chgo., 1963; prof. Fla. Atlantic U., Boca Raton, 1965—, dean Sch. Bus., 1970-87; cons. U.S. Treasury; expert witness on valuing closely held corps., 1972—, lectr., U.S., various fgn. countries; dir. Fla. Liquid Assets, Templeton Trust Co.; mem. faculty Internat. Assn. Fin. Planners. Editor Fla. C.P.A., 1974; assoc. editor Intellect, 1975-79; tax editor Quick Print, 1988—; contbr. articles to profl. jours. Chmn. Palm Beach County Transp. Com., 1972-75. Served to 1st lt. U.S. Army, 1961-63. Recipient Disting. Service Fla. Accountants Assn., 1971. Hon. fellow Internat. Soc. Preventive Medicine, Canadian Sch. Mgmt.; mem. AICPA, Am. Acctg. Assn., Acctg. Rsch. Assn., Beta Gamma Sigma, Beta Alpha Psi, Phi Beta Phi (pres. 1974), Phi Kappa Phi. Baptist. Home: 9550 NW 42nd Ct Coral Springs FL 33065-1576 *In the professions, as in life, so much is owed to those who have gone before.*

LUISELLI FADDA, ANNA MARIA, philosophy educator; b. Cagliari, Italy, Nov. 27, 1931; d. Fadda Luigi and Fadda Scano Fernanda; m. Luiselli Bruno, 1964; children: Raffaele, Luca, Maria-Michela. Vol. asst. prof. U. Cagliari, Italy, 1957-61, extraordinary asst. prof., 1962-68, ordinary asst. prof., 1968-69; libero docente professorship U. Rome I, 1970-71, assoc. prof., 1971-79, full prof., 1980—. Editor: Filologia Germanica: Testi e Studi, Firenze, 1977—; author: Nuove Omelie Anglosassoni Benedettina, 1977, Tradizioni Manoscritte e Critica del Testo nel Medioevo Germanico, 1994. Mem. Ecclesiastical History Soc., Internat. Soc. Anglo-Saxonists, Royal Nat. Rose Soc. Avocation: gardening. Home: Via Olona 7, 00198 Rome Italy Office: U Rome Dept Comparative Lit, via Castro Pretorio 20, 00185 Rome Italy

LUISO, ANTHONY, international food company executive; b. Bari, Italy, Jan. 6, 1944; s. John and Antonia (Giustino) L.; divorced. BBA, Iona Coll., 1967; MBA, U. Chgo., 1982. Audit sr. Arthur Andersen & Co., Chgo., 1966-71; supr. auditing Beatrice Foods Co., Chgo., 1971-74, adminstr. asst. to exec. v.p., 1974-75, v.p. ops. internat. div., dairy div., 1975-77, exec. v.p. internat. div., 1977-82, prof. internat. div., 1982-83, chief operating officer internat. food group, 1984-86, pres. U.S. Food segment, from 1986; group v.p. Internat. Multifoods Corp., Mpls., until 1988, COO, 1988-89, chmn., CEO, pres., 1989—; bd. dirs. Black & Decker Co. Mem. adv. council U.

Chgo. Grad. Sch. of Bus. Served with USAR, 1968-74. Mem. AICPA. Republican. Roman Catholic. Clubs: Univ. (Chgo.), Internat. (Chgo.). Office: Internat Multifoods Corp 33 S Sixth St Minneapolis MN 55402

LUJAN, HERMAN D., academic administrator; m. Carla Lujan; 3 children. B in Polit. Sci., St. Mary's Coll. Calif.; M in Polit. Sci., U. Calif., Berkeley; PhD in Polit. Sci., U. Idaho. Faculty mem., adminstr. U. Kans., dir. inst. social and environ. studies, 1972-78; dir. divsn. state planning and rsch. Gov. of Kans., 1974-75; prof. polit. sci. dept. U. Wash., lectr. Japanese exec. mgmt. program, sch. bus., v.p. minority affairs, 1978-88, vice provost, 1988-91; pres. U. No. Colo., 1991—; bd. dirs. Bank One, Greeley, Colo. Author several books; contbr. articles to profl. jours. Bd. dirs. Boy Scouts Am., Latin Am. Ednl. Found. Mem. Rotary (Greeley). Office: U No Colo Office of Pres Greeley CO 80639

LUJAN, MANUEL, JR., former U.S. secretary of the interior, former congressman; b. San Idlefonso, N.Mex., May 12, 1928; s. Manuel and Lorenzita (Romero) L.; m. Jean Kay Couchman, Nov. 18, 1948; children: Terra Kay Everett, James Manuel, Barbara Frae, Robert Jeffrey. BA, Coll. Santa Fe, 1950; postgrad., St. Mary's (Calif.) Coll., 1946-47. Engaged in ins. bus. Santa Fe and Albuquerque, 1948; mem. 91st-100th Congresses 1st N.Mex. Dist., 1969-89; mem. interior and insular affairs com., energy and environ. subcom., sci. and tech. com. Dept. of Interior, 1969, sec., 1989-93. Office: Manuel Lujan Agys PO Box 3727 Albuquerque NM 87190-3727*

LUKAC, GEORGE JOSEPH, fundraising executive; b. Garfield, N.J., Mar. 6, 1937; s. Michael and Elizabeth (Gall) L.; m. Alice Louise Osborn, Nov. 8, 1958; children: Mark Robert (dec.), Amy Elizabeth. BA in Polit. Sci., Rutgers U., 1958. Trainee, systems reviewer Prudential Ins. Co., Newark, 1958-59; asst. editor comm. dept. Johnson & Johnson, New Brunswick, N.J., 1959-61; editor Rutgers Alumni Monthly Rutgers U., New Brunswick, 1961-66, asst. dir. alumni rels. and devel., 1966-77; exec. dir. Sangamon State U. Found., Springfield, Ill., 1977-81; dir. devel. and pub. rels. Mo. Hist. Soc., St. Louis, 1981-84; v.p. devel. Rio Grande (Ohio) U., 1984-86; exec. dir. St. Luke's Hosps. Meritcare Found., Fargo, N.D., 1986-90; pres., CEO Venice (Fla.) Hosp. Found., 1990-92; pres. Lehigh Valley Hosp. Trust Fund, Allentown, Pa., 1992—; vol. cons. Presbyn. chs., Fargo, Ballwin, Mo. and Venice, Fla., 1978-92, social welfare groups, Fargo, Ballwin, Venice and Allentown, 1978—; ofcl. cons. Ohio Arts Coun., Columbus, Ohio, 1986; instr., adviser, speaker univs., groups, confs., 1978—; jury mem. 1982 CASE Nat. Awards Contest. Editor: Aloud to Alma Mater, 1966, Copyright-The Librarian and the Law, 1972 (Citation N.J. Writers Conf. 1974); contbr.: Big Gifts, 1990; contbr. articles to mags. and profl. jours. Loaned exec. United Way, Fargo, 1987-88, capt., com. mem., 1988-90; bd. dirs. Red. River Dance Co., Fargo, 1989-90; v.p. bd. dirs. Ronald McDonald House, Fargo, 1987-90; mem. Indsl. Devel. Corp. of Lehigh Valley, 1992—; Rep. nat. com. Chmn.'s Campaign Adv. Panel, 1994—. Recipient Citation N.J. Writers Conf., 1974, Ashmead award Rutgers Fund, 1968,76, Spl. Recognition award CASE Nat. Alumni Mag. Competition, 1966, award Rutgers Fund, 1961. Mem. Nat. Soc. Fund Raising Execs. (cert., found. bd. dirs.), Inst. on Philanthropy U. Ind. (charter assoc.), Hawk Mt. Sanctuary Pa., Assn. Hosp. Philanthropy, Nat. Conf. Nonprofit Bds., Allentown Rotary Club. Republican. Presbyterian. Avocations: writing, volunteer consulting, nature, music. Home: 2085 Brook Cir Macungie PA 18062-9091 Office: Lehigh Valley Hosp Trust Fund 1243 S Cedar Crest Blvd Allentown PA 18103-6268

LUKACS, JOHN ADALBERT, historian, retired educator; b. Budapest, Hungary, Jan. 31, 1924; came to U.S., 1946, naturalized, 1953; s. Paul and Magdalena Maria L.; m. Helen Schofield, May 29, 1953 (dec. 1970); children: Paul, Annemarie; m. Stephanie Harvey, May 18, 1974. Ph.D., Palatine Joseph U., Budapest, 1946. Prof. history Chestnut Hill Coll., 1947-94, Chmn. dept. history, 1947-74, ret., 1994; vis. prof. history La Salle Coll., 1949-82, Columbia U., 1954-55, U. Toulouse, France, 1964-65, U. Pa., 1964, 67, 68, Johns Hopkins U., 1970-71, Fletcher Sch. Law, Diplomacy, 1971-72, Princeton U., 1988; vis. prof. U. Budapest, 1991, U. Pa., 1995—. Author books, including: The Great Powers and Eastern Europe, 1953, A History of the Cold War, 1961, Decline and Rise of Europe, 1965, The Passing of the Modern Age, 1970, Historical Consciousness, 1968, 2d edit., 1985, The Last European War, 1939-41, 1976; 1945, Year Zero, 1978, Philadelphia: Patricians and Philistines, 1900-1950, 1981, Outgrowing Democracy: A historical interpretation of the U.S. in the 20th Century, 1984, Budapest 1900, 1988, Confessions of an Original Sinner, 1990, The Duel (Hitler vs. Churchill 10 May-31 August 1940), 1991, the End of the 20th Century (and the End of the Modern Age), 1993, Destinations Past, 1994; contbr. numerous articles, essays, revs. to hist. and lit. jours. Mem. Schuylkill Twp. (Pa.) Planning Commn. Recipient Ingersoll prize, 1991, Order of Merit, Republic of Hungary, 1994. Fellow Soc. Am. Historians; mem. Am. Catholic Hist. Assn. (pres. 1977). Home: Valley Park Rd Phoenixville PA 19460

LUKAS, J. ANTHONY, journalist; b. N.Y.C., Apr. 25, 1933; s. Edwin Jay and Elizabeth (Schamberg) L.; m. Linda Healey, Sept. 18, 1982. BA magna cum laude, Harvard U., 1955; postgrad., Free U. Berlin, 1955-56; hon. degree, Northeastern U., 1986, Colby Coll., 1987. Reporter, city hall corr. Balt. Sun, 1958-62; mem. staff N.Y. Times, 1962-72, assigned to the Congo, 1962-65, assigned to India, 1965-67, assigned to N.Y.C., 1967-68; roving nat. corr. N.Y. Times, Chgo., 1969-70; staff writer Sunday mag., N.Y.C., 1970-72; Nieman fellow Harvard U., 1968-69, fellow Inst. Politics, 1976-77; vis. fellow NYU, 1991; fellow Yale U., 1973-78; adj. prof. journalism Sch. Pub. Comm., Boston U., 1977-78; adj. prof. Columbia U. Sch. of the Arts, 1995; vis. lectr. Yale U., 1973; adj. lectr. Kennedy Sch. Govt., Harvard U., 1979-80; cons. Hastings Ctr., 1979-80; mem. steering com. Reporter's Com. on Freedom of Press, 1970-84; mem. exec. com. PEN Am. Ctr., 1977-83; judge gen. non-fiction Am. Book Awards, 1983, 86, Pulitzer Prize, 1988; mem. study group urban sch. desegregation Am. Acad. Arts and Scis., 1977-78; mem. exec. bd. N.Y. Coun. Humanities, 1986-88; mem. faculty Wesleyan Writers Conf., 1986, New Orleans Writers Conf., 1991, N.Y. State Summer Writers Inst., 1987-88. Contbg. editor: New Times mag., 1973-75; sr. editor: More Journalism Rev., 1972-77, assoc. editor, 1977-78; mem. editorial bd. Book-of-the Month Club, 1989-94, The Am. Prospect; contbr. articles to Gentlemen's Quar., Rolling Stone, Atlantic, Harpers, Saturday Rev., The Nation, New Republic, Psychology Today, Esquire, Reader's Digest, New York, others, 1958—; host radio program: In Conversation, Sta. WOR, N.Y.C., 1973-74; author: The Barnyard Epithet and Other Obscenities: Notes On The Chicago Conspiracy Trial, 1970, Don't Shoot—We Are Your Children, 1971, Nightmare: The Underside of the Nixon Years, 1976, Common Ground: A Turbulent Decade in the Lives of Three American Families, 1985. Mem. exec. bd. N.Y. Coun. Humanities, 1986-88; mem. Com. for Pub. Justice, 1972-88. With AUS, 1956-58. Recipient George Polk Meml. award L.I. U., 1967, Pulitzer prize for local spl. reporting, 1968, Page One award N.Y. Newspaper Guild, 1968, Mike Berger award Columbia Sch. Journalism, 1968, Am. Book award, 1985, Pulitzer prize for gen. non-fiction, 1986, Nat. Book Critics Circle award, 1986, Robert F. Kennedy Book award, 1986, Polit. Book of Yr. award The Washington Monthly, 1986; named Literary Lion N.Y. Pub. Libr., 1986; Guggenheim fellow, 1979-80. Fellow Soc. Am. Historians; mem. Author's Guild (sec. 1989-91), Signet Soc., Phi Beta Kappa, Harvard Club, St. Botolph Club (Boston), The Century Assn.

LUKAS, JOSEPH FRANK, paralegal; b. Bronx, N.Y., Mar. 24, 1952; s. Francis Joseph and Theresa (Beaumont) L.; m. Jane Elizabeth Roberts, Dec. 23, 1989; 1 child, Matthew Joseph. AA, Fulton-Montgomery C.C., Johnstown, N.Y., 1972; BA, L.I. U., Southampton, N.Y., 1974, Miss. U. for Women and Men, Columbus, 1993. Cert. Miss. Assn. Legal Assts. Paralegal Webb, McLaurin & O'Neal, Tupelo, Miss., 1990-94; ind. paralegal Thorne & Assocs., Tupelo, 1994—. Mayoral candidate Guntown, Miss., 1992; justice ct. judge candidate No. Dist. Lee County, Miss. Republican. Avocations: photography, reading, swimming, landscaping. Home: PO Box 444 Tupelo MS 38802-0444 Office: Thorne & Assocs 210 W Main St Tupelo MS 38801

LUKASIK, STEPHEN JOSEPH, information technology executive; b. S.I., N.Y., Mar. 19, 1931; s. Stephen Joseph and Mildred Florence (Tynan) L.; m. Marilyn Bertha Trappiel, Jan. 31, 1953 (div. 1982); children: Carol J., Gregory C., Elizabeth A., Jeffrey P.; m. Virginia Dogan Armstrong, Feb. 11, 1983; stepchildren: Elizabeth L., Alan D. B.S., Rensselaer Poly. Inst., 1951; M.S., MIT, 1953, Ph.D., 1956. Dir. Advanced Research Project Agy., Washington, 1966-74; v.p. Xerox Corp., Rochester, N.Y., 1974-76; chief scientist and sr. v.p. Rand Corp., Santa Monica, Calif., 1977-79; chief scientist FCC, Washington, 1979-82; v.p. and mgr. Northrop Research and Tech. Ctr., Palos Verdes, Calif., 1982-85, corp. v.p. for tech., 1985-90; v.p. for tech. TRW Space and Def. Sector, Redondo Beach, Calif., 1990-92; CEO SAIC, San Diego, Calif., 1992—; dir. Face to Face Game Co.; cons. numerous gov. orgns. Assoc. editor: The Info. Soc. Trustee Stevens Inst. Tech., Hoboken, N.J., 1975-92; trustee Harvey Mudd Coll., Claremont, Calif., 1987—. Served to capt. USAR. Recipient Sec. Def. Disting. Civilian Service medal, 1973, 74. Mem. Am. Phys. Soc., AAAS. Club: Cosmos, D.C., George Town, D.C., Regency, Los Angeles. Home: 1714 Stone Canyon Rd Los Angeles CA 90077-1915

LUKE, DAVID LINCOLN, III, retired paper company executive; b. Tyrone, Pa., July 25, 1923; s. David Lincoln and Priscilla Warren (Silver) L.; m. Fanny R. Curtis, June 11, 1955. AB, Yale U., 1945; LLD (hon.), Juniata Coll., 1967, Lawrence U., 1976, Salem Coll., 1983, W. Va. U., 1984. V.p., dir. Westvaco Corp., N.Y.C., 1953-57, exec. v.p., dir., 1957-62, pres., bd. dirs., 1962-80, chief exec. officer, 1963-88, chmn. bd. dirs., 1980-96. Chmn. bd. trustees Cold Spring Harbor Lab.; bd. dirs. Josiah Macy Jr. Found.; past chmn., trustee emeritus Hotchkiss Sch. Served from aviation cadet to capt. USMCR., 1942-45. Mem. Links Club, The River Club, Piping Rock Club, Megantic Fish and Game Corp.

LUKE, DOUGLAS SIGLER, business executive; b. Middletown, N.Y., Oct. 1, 1941; s. Douglas Sigler Luke and Joanne (Benton) Cowles; m. Anne Sturgis Roosevelt, June 20, 1964 (div. Sept. 1976); m. Sarah Chappell Mullen, Mar. 23, 1991; children: Haven Roosevelt, David Russell, Lindsay Hall. Student, Mexico City Coll., 1961; BA Fgn. Affairs, U. Va., 1964; MBA, The Darden Sch., Charlottesville, Va., 1966. Mem. staff, chem. div. WestVaco Corp., Covington, Va., 1966-69; dir. corp. planning SCOA Industries, Columbus, Ohio, 1969-71; v.p. fin. Multicon Prop. div. Bethlehem Steel Corp., Columbus, 1971-72; gen. ptnr., chief exec. officer Personal Investments, Columbus, 1972-79; v.p. Rothschild, Inc. (formerly New Court Securities), N.Y.C., 1979-83, sr. v.p., 1984-87, mng. dir., 1987-90; pres, chief exec. officer WLD Enterprises, Inc., Ft. Lauderdale, Fla., 1991—; bd. dirs. DNA Plant Tech. Corp., Cinnaminson, N.J., Orbital Scis. Corp., Fairfax, Va. Founding donor Adopt-a-Class, N.Y.C., 1988;mem. space adv. bd. U. Colo., 1985-89; bd. dirs. condrs. com. Columbus Symphony Orch., 1972-75; trustee The Columbus Acad., Gahanna, Ohio, 1973-77, Girl Scouts U.S., Piedmont Region, Roanoke, Va., 1967-69; high tech. com. working group N.Y.C. Partnership Inc., 1988-90. Mem. Ausable Club (St. Huberts, N.Y.), Adirondack Mountain Reserve (St. Huberts, trustee 1985—, pres. 1988-91, chmn. 1991—), The Brook (N.Y.C.), Mashomack Fish and Game Preserve (Pine Plains, N.Y.), The Hillsboro Club (reciprocal, Hillsboro Bch., Fla.). Avocations: running, skiing, fly fishing.

LUKE, JAMES PHILLIP, manufacturing executive; b. Bklyn., Nov. 11, 1942; s. Edmon George and Gertrude Caroline (Sanial) L.; A.B., Princeton U., 1965; M.B.A., Columbia U., 1968; m. Elizabeth Joanne Hooke, Sept. 21, 1968; children—James Phillip, Karin Margaret, Shelby Elizabeth, Thomas Edmon. Exec. trainee WestPoint Pepperell, Inc., N.Y.C., 1968-69, salesman, Atlanta, 1969-70; venture devel. mgr. Internat. Paper Co., Inc., N.Y.C., 1970-71, dist. mgr. Formed Fabrics div., Atlanta, 1971-72, div. controller, Lewisburg, Pa., 1972-75; dir. planning Blessings Corp., Inc., N.Y.C., 1975-77, v.p. fin., Piscataway, N.J., 1977—, also sec.-treas., 1984-88, exec. v.p., sec.-treas. 1988—. Served to lt. USNR, 1965-67. Roman Catholic. Mem. Am. Soc. Corp. Secs. Clubs: Princeton of N.Y., Two Rivers Country. Home: 3012 Hearthstone Rd Williamsburg VA 23185-7523 Office: Blessings Corp 200 Enterprise Dr Newport News VA 23603-1300

LUKE, JOHN A., JR., paper, packaging and chemical company executive; b. Nov. 24, 1948; s. John Anderson Sr. and Joy (Carter) L.; m. Kathleen Allen, June 30, 1984; children: Lindsay Allen, Elizabeth Carter, John A. III. BA, Lawrence U., 1971; MBA, U. Pa., 1979. Unit sales mgr. Procter & Gamble, 1974-77; corp. assoc. Westvaco Corp., N.Y.C., 1979-81, sr. fin. analyst, 1981-82, asst. treas., 1982-83, treas., 1983-86, v.p., treas., 1986, 1986-87, sr. v.p. mktg., internat. and Brazilian subsidiary, 1987-90, exec. v.p., 1990-92, pres., CEO, 1992—; bd. dirs. Arkwright Ins. Boston, The Tinker Found., Americas Soc., Coun. of Ams.; bd. trustees Lawrence U.; mem. Coun. on Fgn. Rels. Bd. govs. NCASI; dir. United Negro Coll. Fund. Mem. Am. Forest and Paper Assn. (dir., exec. com.), UN Assn. of U.S.A. (gov.), Univ. Club. Office: Westvaco Corp 299 Park Ave New York NY 10171

LUKE, RANDALL DAN, retired tire and rubber company executive, lawyer; b. New Castle, Pa., June 4, 1935; s. Randall Beamer and Blanche Wilhelmina (Fisher) L.; m. Patricia Arlene Moody, Aug. 4, 1962 (div. Jan. 1977); children: Lisa Elin, Randall Sargent; m. Saralee Frances Krow, Mar. 1, 1979; 1 stepchild, Stephanie Sogg. BA in Econs. with honors, U. Pa., 1957, JD, 1960. Bar: Ohio 1960, Calif. 1962, Ill. 1989. Assoc., ptnr. Daus, Schwenger & Kottler, Cleve., 1965-70; ptnr. Kottler & Danzig, Cleve., 1970-75, Hahn, Loeser, Freedheim, Dean & Wellman, Cleve., 1975-81; assoc. gen. counsel The Firestone Tire & Rubber Co., Akron, Ohio, 1981-82, v.p., assoc. gen. counsel and sec., 1982-88; v.p., assoc. gen. counsel and sec. Bridgestone/Firestone, Inc., Akron, 1988-91; of counsel Hahn Loeser & Parks, Cleve., 1991—. Trustee, Akron Art Mus., 1982-87, Akron Symphony Orch., 1986-87, Cleve. Opera League, 1992—. Served to Capt. USNR, 1960-81; ret. 1981. Mem. ABA, Assn. Corp. Secs., Calif. Bar Assn., Ohio Bar Assn., Ill. Bar Assn. Republican. Clubs: Cleve. Skating (Shaker Heights, Ohio); Union (Cleve.); Univ. Club of Chgo. Avocations: tennis, jogging, skiing, swimming. Home: 13901 Shaker Blvd Cleveland OH 44120-1582 Office: Hahn Loeser & Parks 200 Public Sq Cleveland OH 44114-2301

LUKEHART, CHARLES MARTIN, chemistry educator; b. DuBois, Pa., Dec. 21, 1946; s. David Blair and Grace Dorothy (Lundgren) L.; m. Marilyn Orleana McKinney, Aug. 4, 1973; children: Mark, Brian, Laura. BS in Chemistry, Pa. State U., 1968; PhD in Inorganic Chemistry, MIT, 1972. Postdoctoral assoc. Tex. A&M U., College Sta., 1972-73; asst. prof. chemistry Vanderbilt U., Nashville, 1973-77, assoc. prof. chemistry, 1977-82, prof., 1982—. Author: Fundamental Transition Metal Organometallic Chemistry, 1985. Rsch. fellow Alfred P. Sloan Found., 1979-81. Mem. Am. Chem. Soc. (chmn. Nashville sect. 1979, 92), Materials Rsch. Soc. Office: Vanderbilt U Dept Chemistry Box 1822 Sta B Nashville TN 37235

LUKENBILL, GREGG, sports promoter, real estate developer; b. Sacramento, Aug. 15, 1954; s. Frank and Leona L.; children: Jake, Molly, Ben. BS in Bus. Adminstrn., Calif. State U., 1995. Owner, developer/builder Lukenbill Enterprises, Sacramento Valley Region; mng. gen. ptnr. Sacramento Kings Profl. Basketball/NBA, 1983-92, ARCO Arena, 1985-93; pres. Hyatt Regency, Sacramento, 1986-92; owner Sky King Inc.; pilot. Office: Lukenbill Enterprises 3600 Power Inn Rd Sacramento CA 95826-3826

LUKENS, ALAN WOOD, retired ambassador and foreign service officer; b. Phila., Feb. 12, 1924; s. Edward Clark and Frances (Day) L.; m. Susan Atkinson, Dec. 29, 1962; children: Lewis Alan, Susan Lukens Stone, Frances Lukens Bennett, Timothy Eric. AB, Princeton U., 1948; postgrad., U. Sorbonne, Paris, 1948, U. Madrid, 1948, Georgetown U., 1951; LLD (hon.), St. Lawrence U., 1987. Tchr. St. Albans Sch., Washington, 1950-51; joined U.S. Fgn. Svc., 1951; vice consul Ankara, Turkey, 1952, Istanbul, Turkey, 1953; pub. affairs officer Martinique, 1954-56; with news divsn. State Dept., 1956-57; U.S. del. 12th UN Gen. Assembly, 1957; mem. internat. staff NATO, Paris, 1958-60; consul Brazzaville, 1960; U.S. rep. to Independence of Congo, Brazzaville, Chad, Gabon, Central African Republic, 1961; charge d'affaires Am. Embassy, Bangui, Central African Republic, 1961, Paris, 1961-63, Rabat, Morocco, 1963-65; chief personnel Bur. African Affairs, State Dept., 1965-67; dep. chief mission, counselor embassy Dakar, 1967-70, Nairobi, 1970-72; chief jr. officer div. personnel State Dept., 1973-75; dir. Office Iberian Affairs, 1974-75; counselor, dep. chief mission Am. Embassy, Copenhagen, 1975-78; with Bur. African Affairs, Dept. State, Washington, 1978-79; consul gen. Cape Town, South Africa, 1979-82; dir. office analysis for Western Europe, Bur. Intelligence and Research, Dept. State, Washington, 1982-84; A.E.& P. People's Republic of Congo, 1984-87; cons. on internat. affairs and crisis mgmt. Dept. of State, 1987-93; lectr. on Africa. Pres. St. Barnabas Coll. Fund; co-chair, Peace Commn. Washington Nat. Cathedral. With AUS, 1943-46. Recipient Commendable Service award State Dept., 1961. Mem. Washington Inst. Fgn. Affairs (bd. sec. DACOR, Diplomatic and Consular Officers Ret.), Rotary, Princeton Club N.Y.C., Washington Club, Nairobi (pres. Paris chpt. 1961-63), Princeton U. Alumni Coun. (mem. exec. com.), Explorers Club Washington (bd. dirs.), Chevy Chase Club (gov.). Episcopalian. Home: 18 Grafton St Chevy Chase MD 20815-3428

LUKENS, PAUL BOURNE, financial executive; b. Meriden, Conn., Oct. 29, 1934; s. George Price and Elsie (Bourne) L.; m. Gail Perry Todd, July 7, 1956; children: Jennifer C. Lukens Holmes, Julie Lukens Belsky. B.S. in Accounting, U. Conn., 1956. C.P.A. Sr. accountant Webster Blanchard & Willard (merged with Price Waterhouse & Co. 1962), 1956-62; audit mgr. Price Waterhouse & Co., Hartford, Conn., 1962-69; with Aetna Life & Casualty Co., Hartford, Conn., 1969-77; v.p. treas. Aetna Variable Annuity Life Ins. Co. (subs), 1972-75, v.p. corp. planning dept. parent co., 1975-77; v.p., controller INA Corp., 1977-82, Cigna Corp., 1982-89; pres. CIGNA Holdings, Inc., 1989-90, chmn., 1990—; cons. corp. acctg. and fin. reporting, 1990—. Contbg. author: Property-Liability Insurance Accounting, 1974. Trustee Episcopal Hosp., Phila., 1981-85. Mem. Am. Inst. C.P.A.s (acctg. standards exec. com. 1983-85), Conn. Soc. C.P.A.s (bd. govs. 1973-75), Fin. Execs. Inst. (com. on corp. reporting 1979—, bd. dirs. Phila. chpt. 1982-85), Fin. Acctg. Standards Bd. (emerging issues task force). Home: 638 Glenwood Vlg West Chester PA 19380-5703 Office: Cigna Holdings Inc 1 Beaver Valley Rd Wilmington DE 19803-1115

LUKER, KRISTIN, sociology educator; b. San Francisco, Aug. 5, 1946; d. James Wester and Bess (Littlefield) L. BA, U. Calif., Berkeley, 1968; PhD, Yale U., 1975. Postdoctoral fellow U. Calif., Berkeley, 1974-75, asst. prof. sociology, San Diego, 1975-81, assoc. prof., 1981-85, prof., 1985-86, co-dir. women's studies program, 1984-85, prof. jurisprudence and social policy, sociology, Berkeley, 1986—; Doris Stevens prof. women's studies, prof. sociology Princeton (N.J.) U., 1993-95. Author: Taking Chances: Abortion and the Decision Not to Contracept, 1976 (hon. mention Jessie Bernard award), Abortion and the Politics of Motherhood, 1984 (Charles Horton Cooley award 1985), Dubious Conceptions: The Myths of Teenage Pregnancy, 1995. Bd. dirs. Ctr. for Women's Studies and Services, San Diego, Ctr. for Population Options, Washington. Recipient Disting. Teaching award U. Calif., San Diego, 1984; Guggenheim Found. grantee, 1985. Mem. Am. Sociol. Assn., Sociologists for Women in Soc. Office: U Calif Berkeley Jurisprudence & Social Policy 2240 Piedmont Ave Berkeley CA 94704

LUKEY, JOAN A., lawyer; b. Malden, Mass., Dec. 28, 1949; d. Philip Edward and Ada Joan (Roberti) L.; m. Philip Davis Stevenson. BA magna cum laude, Smith Coll., 1971; JD cum laude, Boston Coll., 1974. Bar: Mass. 1974, U.S. Dist. Ct. Mass. 1975, U.S. Ct. Appeals (1st cir.) 1976, U.S. Supreme Ct. 1985. Assoc. Hale & Dorr, Boston, 1974-79, jr. ptnr., 1979-83, sr. ptnr., 1983—. Mem. Joint Bar Com. on Judicial Appointments, Mass., 1985-87, steering com. Lawyers' Com. for Civil Rights Under the Law, Boston, 1987-90. Fellow Am. Coll. Trial Lawyers; mem. ABA, Mass. Bar Assn., Boston Bar Assn. (chair litigation sect. 1990-92, mem. coun. 1987-90), Women's Bar Assn. Mass., Boston Club. Office: Hale & Dorr 60 State St Boston MA 02109-1803

LUKS, ALLAN BARRY, executive director; b. N.Y.C., June 27, 1941; s. Joseph Moses and Evelyn (Gropper) L.; m. Karen Greenbaum, Feb. 22, 1969; children: Rachel, David. BA, U. N.C., 1963; JD, Georgetown Law Sch., 1966. Bar: N.Y. Vol. U.S. Peace Corps, Maracay, Venezuela, 1967-69; legal dir. Children's Aid Soc. East Harlem, N.Y.C., 1970-72; asst. dir. Life Ins. Industry Urban Investment Program, N.Y.C., 1972-75; sec.-treas. N.Y.C. Rand Inst., 1975-78; exec. dir. Alcoholism Coun. of Greater N.Y., N.Y.C., 1978-88, Inst. for the Advancement of Health, N.Y.C., 1988-90, Big Bros./Big Sisters of N.Y., N.Y.C., 1990—; author N.Y.C. law, warning posters on drinking during pregnancy, 1983; adj. prof. Fordham U. Grad. Sch. Social Svc., N.Y.C., 1979-88; chmn. legal sect. Internat. Coun. on Alcohol and Addictions, Lausanne, Switzerland, 1980-88; mem. NGO-Crime Prevention and Criminal Justice, UN, N.Y.C., 1982-90. Author: Will America Sober Up?, 1983, The Healing Power of Doing Good, 1991; co-author: You Are What You Drink, 1989; editor Having Been There, 1979. Pres. Cadman Towers Housing, Bklyn., 1971-75; sch. bd. mem. N.Y.C. Sch. Bd. #13, Bklyn., 1975-80; v.p. Brooklyn Heights Assn., N.Y.C., 1982-86; adv. coun. mem. Jr. League N.Y., N.Y.C., 1984-88. Recipient Vol. Leadership award Mayor of N.Y., N.Y.C., 1987, Pub. Svc. award Crains N.Y. Bus. Mag., N.Y.C., 1994. Office: Big Bros/Big Sisters NYC 223 East 30 St New York NY 10016

LUKSHA, ROSEMARY DOROTHY, art educator; b. Wilkes-Barre, Pa., Jan. 5, 1952; d. William Peter and Julia Catherine (Zavislak) L.; 1 child, Mary Rose. BS in Art Edn., Kutztown (Pa.) U., 1973, MEd, 1991; postgrad., Skidmore Coll., 1978, Marywood Coll., 1975, Wilkes U. Cert. instrnl. II art K-12. Art educator Wyoming Valley West Sch. Dist., Kingston, Pa., 1973-84; co. dancer Wilkes-Barre (Pa.) Ballet Theatre, 1973-80; dance instr. Coll. Misericordia, Dallas, Pa., 1980-81; art educator N.W. Area Sch. Dist., Shickshinny, Pa., 1988—; co. dancer Scranton (Pa.) Ballet Theatre, 1980-84; art cons. Wilkes U. Polish Rm. Com., Wilkes-Barre, 1976-92; mem. planning com. Wilkes-Barre Fine Arts Fiesta, 1980-82; illustrator Wilkes-Barre Ballet Theatre, N.E. Ballet, 1977-85, Wyo. Valley Oratorio, Wilkes-Barre, 1979. Choreographer: (dance work) Continue the Balance We Hold, Sisters, Young Choreographer's Performance inN.E. Regional Ballet Festival, 1979. Recipient Dance Scholarship N.E. Regional Ballet Festival, Melissa Hayden Ballet Sch., N.Y.C., 1979. Mem. N.W. Area Edn. Assn., Pa. Edn. Assn., Osterhout Libr. Soc., PTO State St. Sch. Republican. Roman Catholic. Avocations: reading, gardening, travel, bicycling, calligraphy. Office: NW Area Jr/Sr HS RR 2 Box 2271 Shickshinny PA 18655-9201

LULL, WILLIAM PAUL, engineering consultant; b. Indpls., Nov. 5, 1954; s. William Roger and Florence Elizabeth (Morris) L.; m. Mary Ann Garrison, Dec. 22, 1989. Student, Ind. State U., 1973-75; BS in Arts & Design, MIT, 1978. Systems designer James Assocs., Architects, Engrs., Indpls., 1978-79; architect TVA, Knoxville, Tenn., 1980; mgr. energy mgmt. div. Dubin-Bloome, Engrs., N.Y.C., 1981; asst. chief of design Syska & Hennessy, Engrs., N.Y.C., 1982-83; prin. Garrison/Lull Inc., Princeton Junction, N.J., 1984—; adj. assoc. prof. NYU, 1983—; lectr., presenter cons. environ. field. Author: Conservation Environment Guidelines for Libraries and Archives, 1990; co-author: Criteria for Storage of Paper-Based Archival Records, 1984; contbr. articles to profl. publs. Mem. ASHRAE (affiliate, conf. presenter 1983), Am. Assn. Mus. (registrars' com., presenter 1988, 93), Am. Inst. Conservation of Historic and Artistic Works (assoc.), Sigma Pi Sigma. Achievements include pioneering discipline of consulting on conservation environments for preservation of museum and archival collections. Home: 7 High St Allentown NJ 08501-1914 Office: Garrison/Lull Inc PO Box 337 Princeton Junction NJ 08550-0337

LUMB, WILLIAM VALJEAN, veterinarian; b. Sioux City, Iowa, Nov. 26, 1921; m. Lilly Carlson, 1949; 1 child, John W. DVM, Kans. State U., 1943; MS, Tex. A&M U., 1953; PhD in Vet. Medicine, U. Minn., 1957. Intern, resident Angell Meml. Animal Hosp., Boston, 1946-48; from instr. to assoc. prof. medicine and surgery Tex. A&M U., 1949-52; asst. prof. clin. surgery Colo. State U., 1954-58; assoc. prof. surgery and medicine Mich. State U., 1958-60; assoc. prof. medicine Coll. Vet. Medicine, Colo. State U., Ft. Collins, 1960-63, dir. surg. lab., 1963-79, prof. surgery, 1963-81, emeritus prof., 1981—. Mem. AVMA, AAAS, Am. Coll. Vet. Anesthesiologists, Am. Coll. Vet. Surgeons, Nat. Acad. Sci., N.Y. Acad. Sci., Am. Assn. Vet. Clinicians, Am. Coll. Vet. Surgery. Office: Vet Teaching Hosp Colo State U Fort Collins CO 80521*

LUMBARD, ELIOT HOWLAND, lawyer, educator; b. Fairhaven, Mass., May 6, 1925; s. Ralph E. and Constance Y. L.; m. Jean Ashmore, June 21, 1947 (div.); m. Kirsten Dehner, June 28, 1981 (div.); children: Susan, John, Ann, Joshua Abel, Marah Abel. BS in Marine Transp., U.S. Mcht. Marine Acad., 1945; BS in Econs., U. Pa., 1949; JD, Columbia U., 1952. Bar: N.Y. 1953, U.S. Supreme Ct. 1959, Pa. 1983. Assoc. Breed, Abbott and Morgan, N.Y.C., 1952-53; asst. U.S. atty. So. Dist. N.Y., 1953-56; assoc. Chadbourne, Parke, Whiteside & Wolff, N.Y.C., 1956-58; ptnr. Townsend & Lewis, N.Y.C., 1961-70; ptnr. Spear and Hill, N.Y.C., 1970-75; ptnr. Lumbard and

Phelan, P.C., N.Y.C., 1977-82, Saul, Ewing, Remick & Saul, N.Y.C., 1982-84; pvt. practice law, N.Y.C., 1984-86; ptnr. Haight, Gardner, Poor & Havens, N.Y.C., 1986-88; pvt. practice law, N.Y.C., 1988-92, ret.; chief counsel N.Y. State Commn. Investigation, 1958-61; spl. asst. counsel for law enforcement to Gov. N.Y., 1961-67; organizer N.Y. State Identification and Intelligence Sys., 1963-67; chair Oyster Bay Conf. on Organized Crime, 1962-67; criminal justice cons. to Gov. Fla. and other states, 1967; chief criminal justice cons. to N.J. Legis., 1968-69; chmn. com. on organized crime N.Y.C. Criminal Justice Coordinating Coun., 1971-74; organizer schs. of universal justice at SUNY Albany and Rutgers, Newark; mem. departmental disciplinary com. First Dept., N.Y. Supreme Ct., 1982-88; trustee bankruptcy Universal Money Order Co., Inc., 1977-82, Meritum Corp., 1983-89; spl. master in admiralty Hellenic Lines Ltd., 1984-86; chmn. Palisades Life Ins. Co. (former Equity Funding subs. 1974-75); bd. dir. RMC Industries Corp.; lectr. trial practice NYU Law Sch., 1963-65; mem. vis. com. Sch. Criminal Justice, SUNY-Albany, 1968-75; adj. prof. law and criminal justice John Jay Coll. Criminal Justice, CUNY, 1975-86; arbitrator Am. Arbitration Assn. and N.Y. Civil Ct.-Small Claims Part, N.Y. County; mem. Vol. Master Program U.S. Dist. Ct. (so. dist.) N.Y. Contbr. articles to profl. jours. Bd. dirs. Citizens Crime Commn. N.Y.C., Inc.; Big Bros. Movement, Citizens Union; trustee Trinity Sch. 1964-78, N.Y.C. Police Found., Inc., 1971-92, chmn., 1971-74, emeritus. Lt. j.g. USNR, 1943-52. Recipient First Disting. Svc. award Sch. Criminal Justice, SUNY-Albany, 1976. Mem. Assn. Bar City N.Y., N.Y. County Lawyers Assn., ABA, N.Y. State Bar Assn., Maritime Law Assn., Down Town Assn. Club. Republican. Home: 39B Apple Ln Hollis NH 03049-6311

LUMBARD, JOSEPH EDWARD, JR., federal judge; b. N.Y.C., Aug. 18, 1901; s. Joseph Edward and Martha Louise (Meier) L.; m. Polly Poindexter, Sept. 4, 1929; children: Abigail, Thomas. A.B. cum laude, Harvard U., 1922, LL.B., 1925, LL.D., 1970; LL.D., William Mitchell Coll., U. Bridgeport, Northwestern U., N.Y. Law Sch., Columbia U.; S.J.D. (hon.), Suffolk U. Asst. U.S. atty. So. Dist. N.Y., 1925-27; spl. asst. atty. gen. N.Y. State, in Queens Sewer investigation and prosecution of Maurice E. Connelly, 1928-29; mem. firm Fogarty, Lumbard & Quel, 1929-31; asst. to William J. Donovan in bankruptcy inquiry conducted by Assn. Bar City N.Y. and others, 1929; asst. U.S. atty. charge criminal div. So. Dist. N.Y., 1931-33; mem. firm Donovan, Leisure, Newton, Lumbard & Irvine (and predecessor firms), 1934-53; spl. asst. atty. gen. N.Y. State, in Drukman murder prosecutions, 1936; def. counsel U.S. vs. Standard Oil and 23 oil cos., 1937-38; spl. asst. atty. gen. N.Y. State charge Election Frauds Bur., 1943; justice Supreme Ct. N.Y. State, June-Dec. 1947; U.S. atty. So. Dist. N.Y., 1953-55; U.S. circuit judge 2d Circuit, 1955—; chief judge U.S. Court Appeals, 2d Circuit, 1959-71. Contbr. to law jours. Bd. overseers Harvard, 1959-65; trustee William Nelson Cromwell Found. Jud. fellow Am. Coll. Trial Lawyers; mem. ABA (chmn. spl. com. minimum standards for criminal justice 1964-68, Gold medal 1968), N.Y. State Bar Assn. (Gold medal 1969), Assn. Bar City N.Y., S.R. Republican. Unitarian. Clubs: Country (Fairfield); Harvard, Century (N.Y.C.). Home: 490 Hillside Rd Fairfield CT 06430-2145

LUMENG, LAWRENCE, physician, educator; b. Manila, Aug. 10, 1939; came to U.S., 1958; s. Ming and Lucia (Lim) Lu; m. Pauline Lumeng, Nov. 26, 1966; children: Carey, Emily. AB, Ind. U., 1960, MD, 1964, MS, 1969. Intern U. Chgo., 1964-65; resident Ind. U. Hosps., Indpls., 1965-67, fellow, 1967-69, asst. prof. Sch. of Medicine, 1971-73, assoc. prof. Sch. of Medicine, 1974-79, prof. Sch. of Medicine, 1979—, dir. div. gastroenterology and hepatology Sch. of Medieine, 1984—; chief gastroenterology sect. VA Med. Ctr., Indpls., 1979—; mem. merit rev. bd. VA. Cen. Office, Washington, 1981-84; mem. alcohol biomed. res. rev. com. NIAAA, Washington, 1982-86; mem. grant rev. panel USDA, Washington, 1985—. Contbr. articles to profl. jours. Maj. U.S. Army, 1969-71. Fellow ACP; mem. Am. Soc. Clin. Investigation, Am. Soc. Biol. Chemists, Rsch. Soc. on Alcoholism (treas. 1985-87, sec. 1987-89), Am. Gastroenterological Assn., Am. Assn. for the Study of Liver Diseases. Avocations: painting, music. Office: Ind U Med Ctr 975 W Walnut St Indianapolis IN 46202-5181

LUMET, SIDNEY, film director; b. Phila., June 25, 1924; s. Baruch and Eugenia (Wermus) L.; m. Rita Gam (div.); m. Gloria Vanderbilt, Aug. 27, 1956 (div. 1963); m. Gail Jones, Nov. 23, 1963 (div. 1978); m. Mary Gimbel, Oct. 1980; children: Amy, Jenny. Ed., Profl. Children's Sch.; student, Columbia. Tchr. acting High Sch. of Profl. Arts. Author: (with Alfred A. Knopf) Making Movies, 1995; appeared as child actor in several plays including Dead End, 1935, George Washington Slept Here, 1940-41, My Heart's in the Highlands, 1939; dir. summer stock, 1947-49; assoc. dir., CBS, 1950, dir., 1951-57; TV shows include Omnibus; films including Twelve Angry Men, 1957, Stage Struck, 1958, That Kind of Woman, 1959, The Fugitive Kind, 1960, A View from the Bridge, 1961, Long Days Journey into Night, 1962, Fail Safe, 1964, The Pawnbroker, 1965, The Hill, 1965, The Group, 1966, The Deadly Affair, 1967, The Sea Gull, 1968, Bye, Bye Braverman, 1968, The Appointment, 1969, (with Joseph L. Mankiewicz) King: A Filmed Record, 1969, Last of the Mobile Hot Shots, 1970, The Anderson Tapes, 1971, Child's Play, 1972, the Offence, 1973, Serpico, 1974, Lovin' Molly, 1974, Murder on the Orient Express, 1974, Dog Day Afternoon, 1975, Network, 1976, Equus, 1977, The Wiz, 1978, Just Tell Me What You Want, 1979, Prince of the City, 1981, Deathtrap, 1981, The Verdict, 1982, Daniel, 1983, Garbo Talks, 1984, Power, 1985, The Morning After, 1986, Running on Empty, 1988, Family Business, 1989, Q & A, 1990, A Stranger Among Us, 1992, Guilty As Sin, 1993; over 200 plays for, TV Playhouse 90, Kraft TV Theatre, Studio One; staged: play Caligula, 1960. Recipient D.W. Griffith Lifetime Achievement award, 1993. Mem. Dirs. Guild Am. (hon. life). Office: Amjen Entertainment Inc 259 W 54th St New York NY 10019-5501

LUMLEY, JOHN LEASK, physicist, educator; b. Detroit, Nov. 4, 1930; s. Charles S. and Jane Anderson Campbell (Leask) L.; m. Jane French, June 20, 1953; children: Katherine Leask, Jennifer French, John Christopher. B.A., Harvard, 1952; M.S. in Engring, Johns Hopkins, 1954, Ph.D., 1957; Haute Distinction Honoris Causa, Ecole Central de Lyon, France, 1987. Postdoctoral fellow Johns Hopkins, 1957-59; mem. faculty Pa. State U., 1959-77, prof. aerospace engring., 1963-74, Evan Pugh prof. aerospace engring., 1974-77; Willis H. Carrier prof. engring. Cornell U., 1977—; prof. d'echange U. d'Aix-Marseille, France, 1966-67; Fulbright sr. lectr. U. Liege; vis. prof. U. Louvain-La-Neuve, Belgium; Guggenheim fellow U. Provence and Ecole Centrale de Lyon, France, 1973-74. Author: (with H.A. Panofsky) Structure of Atmospheric Turbulence, 1964, Stochastic Tools for Turbulence, 1970, (with H. Tennekes) A First Course in Turbulence, 1971; also articles.; tech. editor: Statistical Fluid Mechanics, 1971, 75, Variability of the Oceans, 1977; assoc. editor: Physics of Fluids, 1971-73; assoc. editor Ann. Rev. of Fluid Mechanics, 1976-85, co-editor, 1986—; chmn. tech. editorial bd.: Izvestiya: Atmospheric and Oceanic Physics, 1971—; editorial bd.: Fluid Mechanics: Soviet Research, 1972-94; editor Theoretical and Computational Fluid Dynamics, 1989—; prin.: films Deformation of Continuous Media, 1963, Eulerian and Lagrangian Frames in Fluid Mechanics, 1968. Recipient medallion U. Liege, Belgium, 1971, Timoshenko medal ASME, 1993, Hugh LDryden lectureship Am. Inst. of Aeronautics and Astronautics, 1996. Fellow Am. Acad. Arts and Scis., Am. Acad. Mechanics, Am. Phys. Soc. (exec. com. divsn. fluid dynamics 1972-75, 81-84, chmn. exec. com. divsn. fluid dynamics 1982, 87-89, Fluid Dynamics prize 1990), AIAA (assoc., fluid and plasma dynamics award 1982, Hugh L. Dryden rsch. lectureship 1996); mem. NAE, AAAS, N.Y. Acad. Sci., Soc. Natural Philosophy, Am. Geophys. Union, Johns Hopkins Soc. Scholars (charter), Sigma Xi. Home: 743 Snyder Hill Rd Ithaca NY 14850-8708 Office: Cornell U 238 Upson Hall Ithaca NY 14853-7501

LUMLEY, SUSAN MCCABE, insurance company executive; b. Bristol, Conn., Mar. 26, 1944; d. James Cornelius and Jean Eleanor (Fucini) McCabe; m. William D. Lumley Jr., Jan. 29, 1984. Student, Ctrl. Conn. State U., 1962-64, Dartmouth Coll., 1983, U. Conn., 1983. Med. underwriter Aetna Life & Casualty, Hartford, Conn., 1964-66; v.p. mgr. Charles G. Marcus Agy., Wethersfield, Conn., 1966—; liaison Ind. Ins. Agts., Wethersfield, 1992. Dir. Better Bus. Bur., Hartford, 1985-89. Mem. Hartford Assn. Ins. Women (pres.-elect 1994—, Ins. Woman of Yr. 1994). Democrat. Roman Catholic. Home: 12 Chestnut Ln East Hartford CT 06118-3507

LUMPKIN, JOHN HENDERSON, retired banker; b. Fairbanks, Alaska, Jan. 28, 1916; s. Hope Henry and Mary Isobel (Henderson) L.; m. Caroline Sparrow Dalton, Apr. 8, 1942; children: John Henderson, Caroline Dalton (Mrs. Sozzi). BA, U. S.C., 1937, doctorate (hon.); LLB, Harvard U., 1940; doctorate (hon.), Columbia Coll., Coker Coll., Benedict Coll. Bar: N.Y. 1940. With firm White & Case, N.Y.C., 1940-41, Boyd, Bruton & Lumpkin, Columbia, S.C., 1946-64; sr. exec. v.p. S.C. Nat. Bank, Columbia, 1964-65, pres., 1965-70, chief exec. officer, 1965-81, chmn. bd., 1970-81; ret., 1981, hon. chmn. bd.; of counsel The McNair Firm, P.A., 1983-92. Chmn., trustee S.C. Found. Ind. Colls.; trustee Brookgreen Gardens (chmn. exec. com.). Lt. comdr. USNR, 1941-46. Decorated Commendation medal. Recipient Algernon Sydney Sullivan award U. S.C., 1963; inductee S.C. Bus. Hall of Fame, 1991. Mem. 4th Circuit Jud. Conv., S.C. C. of C. (pres. 1971-72), Columbia C. of C. (pres. 1953-54), ABA, S.C. Bar Assn., Richland County Bar Assn., S.C. Bankers Assn. (pres. 1974-75). Office: NCNB Tower PO Box 11390 Fl Columbia SC 29211-1390

LUMPKIN, JOHN ROBERT, public health physician, state official; b. Chgo., July 28, 1951; s. Frank and Beatrice (Shapiro) L.; m. Mary S. Blanks, Jan. 28, 1984; children: Alia, John R. Jr. BS, Northwestern U., Evanston, Ill., 1973; MD, Northwestern U., Chgo., 1974; MPH, U. Ill., Chgo., 1985. Diplomate Am. Bd. Emergency Medicine. Intern U. Chgo. Hosps., 1975, resident anesthesiology, 1976-78, vice chmn. emergency medicine, 1981-84; asst. prof. U. Chgo., 1978-84; asst. dir. emergency medicine South Chgo. Hosp., 1984-85; staff physician St. Mary of Nazareth Hosp., Chgo., 1985; assoc. dir. Ill. Dept. Pub. Health, Springfield and Chgo., 1985-90, dir., 1990—; cons. Egyptian Ministry Health, Cairo, 1986-90; mem. sec.'s adv. com. on injury control Ctrs. for Dis. Control, Atlanta, 1989-93. Fellow Am. Coll. Emergency Physicians (bd. dirs. 1987-93); mem. Soc. Tchrs. Emergency Medicine (pres. 1981-82), Ill. Coll. Emergency Physicians (pres. 1982-83, Bill B. Smiley award 1986), Assn. State and Territorial Health Ofcls. (pres. 1995-96). Avocations: racquetball, model trains, football, computers. Office: Ill Dept Pub Health 100 W Randolph St Ste 6-600 Chicago IL 60601-3219

LUMPKIN, LEE ROY, dermatologist, educator; b. Oklahoma City, Sept. 6, 1925; s. Lee R. and Martha L. (Lockard) L.; m. Mona F. Long, Jan. 28, 1953; children: Lee Roy III, Patricia J., Megan E., Julie A., William S. BA, U. Okla., 1949, MD, 1953. Intern Tripler Gen. Hosp., Honolulu, 1953-54; gen. practice medicine San Francisco, 1955-57; commd. capt. U.S. Air Force, 1957, advanced through grades to col., 1968; resident in dermatology Walter Reed Gen. Hosp., Washington, 1958-61; chief of dermatology Madrid, Spain, 1961-64; fellow in dermatopathology Armed Forces Inst. Pathology, Washington, 1964-65; chief USAF Regional Center, Carswell AFB, Tex., 1964-67; chief dermatology USAF Med Center, Lackland AFB, San Antonio, 1967-72; assoc. clin. prof. dermatology U. Tex. Sch. Medicine, San Antonio, 1969-72; ret. U. Tex. Sch. Medicine, 1972; clin. prof. dermatology Albany (N.Y.) Med. Center, 1972-92; ret. Editor: Bull. Assn. Mil. Dermatologists, 1968-71; mem. editorial bd. Mil. Medicine, 1968-76; contbr. articles to med. jours. Decorated Bronze Star medal, Air Force Commendation medal with oak leaf cluster, Meritorious Service medal; recipient James Clarke White award, 1971. Fellow Am. Acad. Dermatology, ACP, Am. Coll. Cryosurgery; mem. Assn. Profs. Dermatology, Dermatology Found., Internat. Soc. Pediatric Dermatology, N.Am. Clin. Dermatology Soc., Internat. Soc. Tropical Dermatology, Soc. Air Force Physicians (pres.-elect), New Eng. Dermatol. Soc., Central N.Y. Dermatol. Soc., N.Y. State Soc. Dermatology (bd. govs. 1980-83, pres. 1981-83). Episcopalian. Home: 223 Lancaster St Albany NY 12210-1131

LUMRY, RUFUS WORTH, II, chemist, educator; b. Bismarck, N.D., Nov. 3, 1920; s. Rufus Worth and Mabel (Will) L.; m. Gayle Kelly, Mar. 27, 1943 (div. Aug. 1973); children—Rufus Worth III, Ann Eliza, Stephen Ellis. A.B., Harvard U., 1942, M.S., 1948, Ph.D., 1948. Research chemist div. 8 Nat. Def. Research Council, 1942-45; NRC fellow Harvard U., 1946-48; Merck fellow nat. scis. U. Utah, 1948-51, asst. prof. chemistry and biochemistry, 1951-53; mem. faculty U. Minn., 1953—, prof. chemistry, 1956-91, prof. emeritus, 1991—; vis. prof. Inst. Protein Research, Osaka, Japan, 1961, U. Rome, Italy, 1964, U. Calif., San Diego, 1977, U. Va., 1978, U. Granada, Spain, 1985; cons. in field, 1948—. Author: (with W. Reynolds) Mechanisms of Electron Transfer, 1966, (with R. Gregory) The Fluctuating Enzyme, 1986; also articles. NSF sr. postdoctoral fellow Carlsberg (Denmark) Lab., 1959-60. Mem. Am. Chem. Soc., Am. Inst. Biol. Scis., Am. Biophysics Soc., Am. Soc. Biol. Chemists, Sigma Xi. Democrat. Home: 940 Franklin Ter Minneapolis MN 55406-1153

LUMSDEN, IAN GORDON, art gallery director; b. Montreal, Que., Can., June 8, 1945; s. Andrew Mark and Isobel Dallas (Wilson) L.; m. Katherine Elizabeth Carson, July 28, 1979; 1 child, Craig Ian. B.A., McGill U., 1968; postgrad., Mus. Mgmt. Inst., U. Calif., Berkeley, 1991. Curator art dept. N.B. Mus., Saint John, 1969; curator Beaverbrook Art Gallery, Fredericton, N.B., 1969-83, dir., 1983—; bd. dirs. ArtsAtlantic; mem. Cultural Property Export Rev. Bd., 1982-85; mem. program com. 49th Parallel Ctr. for Contemporary Can. Art., 1990-92. Author exhbn. catalogues; contbr. numerous articles to Can. art periodicals. Mem. Can. Museums Assn. (sec.-treas. 1973-75), Can. Art Mus. Dirs. Orgn. (1st v.p. 1977-83, pres. 1983-85), Atlantic Provinces Art Gallery Assn. (chmn. 1970-72), Am. Assn. Museums, Union Club (St. John, N.B.). Mem. Anglican Ch. of Can. Home: Fernholme, 725 George St, Fredericton, NB Canada E3B 1K6

LUMSDEN, LYNNE ANN, publishing company executive; b. Battle Creek, Mich., July 30, 1947; d. Arthur James and Ruth Julia (Pandy) L.; m. Jon B. Harden, May 3, 1986; 1 child, Heather Lynne. Student, U. Paris, 1967-69; BA, Sarah Lawrence Coll., 1969; postgrad., City Grad. Ctr., 1979-81, NYU, 1970-71; cert. of mgmt., Am. Mgmt. Assn., 1982. Copy editor Harcourt, Brace, Jovanovich, N.Y.C., 1970-71; editor Appleton-Century Crofts, N.Y.C., 1971-73, Coll. div. Prentice-Hall, Englewood Cliffs, N.J., 1974-78; sr. editor Coll. div. Prentice-Hall, 1978-81; asst. v.p., editor-in chief Spectrum Books, 1981-82; v.p. editorial dir., gen. pub. div., 1982-85; exec. v.p., publ., co-owner Dodd, Mead & Co., Inc., N.Y.C., 1985-89; owner, chmn. JBH Communications Inc., Hartford, Conn., 1989—; pub. Hartford News and Southside Media, 1989—. Bd. dirs. Greater Hartford Architecture Conservancy. Mem. Hartford Jr. League, Friends of Mark Twain (v.p.), Women Connect (bd. dirs.), Hartford Club, Lunch Club, N.Y.C. Sandbar Club, Town and Country Club, Hartford Golf Club. Episcopalian. Office: 191 Franklin Ave Hartford CT 06114-1373

LUNA, BARBARA CAROLE, expert witness, accountant, appraiser; b. N.Y.C., July 23, 1950; d. Edwin A. and Irma S. (Schub) Schlang; m. Dennis Rex Luna, Sept. 1, 1974; children: John S., Katherine E. BA, Wellesley Coll., 1971; MS in Applied Math. and Fin. Analysis, Harvard U., 1973, PhD in Applied Math. and Fin. Analysis, 1975. Investment banker Warburg Paribas Becker, L.A., 1975-77; cons./mgr. Price Waterhouse, L.A., 1977-83; sr. mgr. litigation Pannell Kerr Forster, L.A., 1983-86; nat. dir. litigation cons. Kenneth Leventhal & Co., L.A., 1986-88; ptnr. litigation svcs. Coopers & Lybrand, L.A., 1988-93; sr. ptnr. litigation svcs. White, Zuckerman, Warsavsky & Luna, Sherman Oaks, Calif., 1993—. Wellesley scholar, 1971. Mem. AICPA, Assn. Bus. Trial Lawyers (com. on experts), Am. Soc. Appraisers, Assn. Cert. Real Estate Apparaisers, Assn. Cert. Fraud Examiners, Assn. Insolvency Accts., Inst. Mgmt. Cons., Calif. Soc. CPAs (steering com. L.A. litigation svcs. com.). Avocations: golf, swimming. Home: 18026 Rodarte Way Encino CA 91316-4370 Office: White Zuckerman Warsavsky & Luna 14455 Ventura Blvd Ste 300 Sherman Oaks CA 91423

LUND, BERT OSCAR, JR., publisher; b. Stillwater, Minn., Nov. 8, 1920; s. Bert O. and Mary O. (Vordal) L.; m. Katherine Kingsley, July 31, 1943; children—Katherine Lund Cohen, Julie Lund Everett, Bert Oscar. B.B.A., U. Minn., 1942; postgrad., Harvard U., 1943. Advt. salesman Webb Co., St. Paul, 1946-54; advt. mgr. Webb Co., 1954-61; pub. Farmer Mag., 1961—, v.p. pub., 1963—, also dir.; v.p. pub. Pub. Cons., 1985—; dir. Audit Bur. Circulations, Gt. No. Ins. Co.; pres. Midwest unit Farm Papers, Inc., 1971; dir. Gt. No. Ins. Co., 1980—. Vice pres. Indianhead Council, Boy Scouts Am., 1974, Minn. Agrl. Soc., 1981; chmn. ops. com. St. Paul Civic Center Authority, 1972; bd. dirs. Minn. Council on Econ. Edn., 1969, Cath. Digest, 1980; chmn., trustee Dunwoody Inst., 1980, Hill Reference Library, 1984; trustee Minn. Med. Found. Served to lt. USNR, 1943-46. Mem. Agrl. Pubs. Assn. (past pres., dir.), State Farm Mag. Bur. (past pres., dir.), Advt. Club Minn (past pres.), U. Minn. Alumni Assn. (treas.), Sigma Alpha Epsilon. Republican. Episcopalian. Clubs: Minnesota, Royal Poinciana Country Club, Hole-in-Wall Golf, Somerset Country. Home: 2151 Upper St Dennis Rd Saint Paul MN 55116-2823

LUND, SISTER CANDIDA, college chancellor; b. Chgo.; d. Fred S. Lund and Katharine (Murray) Lund Heck. BA, Rosary Coll., River Forest, Ill.; MA, Catholic U. Am.; PhD, U. Chgo., 1963; DLitt (hon.), Lincoln Coll., 1968; LLD (hon.), John Marshall Law Sch., 1979; LHD honoris causa, Marymount Coll., 1979; LittD (hon.), St. Mary-of-the Woods Coll., 1994. Pres. Rosary Coll., 1964-81, chancellor, 1981—. Editor: Moments to Remember, 1980, The Days and the Nights: Prayers for Today's Woman, In Joy and in Sorrow, 1984, Coming of Age, 1992, Nunsuch, 1982, God and Me, 1988, Praymates, 1993; author, editor: If I Were Pope, 1987; contbr.: Why Catholic. Mem. women's bd. U. Chgo., 1984—; bd. dirs. The Chgo. Network, 1983-86, The Park Ridge Ctr., 1987-93, Gottlieb Hosp., 1991—. Recipient Profl. Achievement award U. Chgo. Alumni, 1974, U.S. Catholic award, 1984. Fellow Royal Soc. Arts; mem. Thomas More Assn. (bd. dirs. 1975—), The Arts Club (bd. dirs. 1987—). Home and Office: Rosary Coll 7900 Division St River Forest IL 60305-1066

LUND, DARYL BERT, agricultural studies educator; b. San Bernardino, Calif., Nov. 4, 1941; married June 15, 1963; children: Kristine, Eric. BS in Math., U. Wis., 1963, MS in food Sci., 1965, PhD in Food Sci., 1968. Rsch. asst. in food sci. U. Wis., Madison, 1963-67, instr., 1967-68, asst. prof., 1968-72, assoc. prof., 1972-77, prof. food sci., 1977-87, chmn. dept. food sci., 1984-87; chmn. dept. food sci., assoc. dir. agrl. experiment sta. Rutgers, the State U., New Brunswick, 1988-89; interim exec. dean agr. and natural resources Rutgers, the State U., New Brunswick, N.Y., 1989-91; exec. dean agr./natural resources Rutgers, the State U., New Brunswick, 1991-95, exec. dir. N.J. Agrl. Experiment Sta., dean Cook Coll., 1991-95; Ronald P. Lynch dean of agr. and life scis. Cornell U., Ithaca, N.Y., 1995—; vis. engr. Western Regional Rsch. Lab., Berkeley, Calif., 1970-71; advisor for evaluation of food tech. dept. Inst. Agr., Bogor, Indonesia, 1973; mem. four-man evaluation team to review grad. edn. programs Brazilian univs., 1976; vis. prof. food process engring. Agrl. U., Wageningen, The Netherlands, 1979; invited vis. prof. food process engring. Univ. Coll., Dublin, 1982; invited advisor Inter-Univ. Ctr. on Food Sci. and Nutrition, Bogor, 1991; advisor Agrl. U., Bogor, 1992; lectr. in field. Contbr. over 150 articles to profl. jours.; editor 5 books; co-author text book. Recipient Food Engring. award Dairy and Food Industries Supply Assn. and Am. Soc. Agrl. Engring., 1987. Fellow Inst. Food Technologists (Wis. sect. 1968-87, N.Y. sect. 1988—, Travel award as promising young scientist to Interatn. Congress on Food Sci. and tech., Madrid 1974); mem. AICE, Am. Inst. Nutrition, Am. Soc. Agrl. Engrs., Sigma Xi, Gamma Sigma Delta, Phi Tau Sigma. Avocations: golf, travel, wood working. Home: 56 Teeter Rd Ithaca NY 14850

LUND, DAVID NATHAN, artist; b. N.Y.C., Oct. 16, 1925; s. Isidore and Mollie (Hirschfield) Lifshitz; m. Sally Harriet Amster, June 17, 1961 (dec. Feb. 1988); children: Andrew Ethan, Giuliana Elizabeth; m. Judith Manelis. BA, Queens Coll., 1948; postgrad., NYU, 1948-50. Adj. asst. prof. painting, drawing, design Cooper Union Art Sch., 1955-57, 59-66, 67-74; instr. painting Cummington (Mass.) Sch. Arts, 1963; instr. in painting Haystack Sch., Deer Isle, Maine, 1963; instr. in drawing and painting Parsons Sch. Design, 1963-66, 67-69; lectr. in drawing Queens Coll., 1964-66; vis. prof. painting Washington U., St. Louis, 1966-67, 85; asst. prof. painting and drawing Columbia U., 1969-82; vis. prof. painting Boston U., 1975-76; vis. critic; lectr. in field; juror Nat. Selection Com., Fulbright Grants In Art; cons. in painting Creative Artists Public Service, 1979-81; vis. artist Winston-Salem Arts Council and Associated Artists of Winston-Salem, 1975. One-man shows include Grand Central Moderns Gallery, N.Y.C., 1954, Galleria Trastevere, Rome, 1959, Grace Borgenicht Gallery, N.Y.C., 1960, 63, 66, 67, 69, 76, 78, 80, 83, 86, Martin Schweig Gallery, St. Louis, 1966, Kirkland Coll., 1971, Arts Council Winston-Salem, N.C., 1975, Creiger-Seson Gallery, Boston, 1981, Meredith Contemporary Art Gallery, Balt., 1982, U. Alaska, Fairbanks, 1983, Washington U., St. Louis, 1985, Allport Gallery, San Francisco, 1984, A.J. Laderman Fine Arts, Hoboken, N.J., 1990; group shows include Whitney Mus., N.Y.C., 1958, 60, 61, 62, 77, Galleria Schneider, Rome, 1959, Palazzo Venezia, Rome, 1959, Galleria San Marco, Rome, 1959, Washington Gallery Art, 1963, Am. embassy, Athens, Greece, 1966-67, White House, Washington, 1966-67, 67-68, 68-69, Nat. Collection Fine Arts, Washington, 1972-73; represented in permanent collections Whitney Mus., Balt. Mus., Toronto (Ont., Can.) Gallery Art, Art Gallery Ont., Toronto, Corcoran Gallery Art, Washington, Ft. Worth Art Center, U. Mass., Montclair (N.J.) Mus., Haas Gallery at Bloomsburg State Coll., Kranert Art Gallery, Champagne, Ill., also other public and pvt. collections. Fulbright grantee Rome, 1957-59. Mem. Nat. Acad. Design, Artists Equity. Jewish. Subject of numerous profl. publs.

LUND, DORIS HIBBS, retired dietitian; b. Des Moines, Nov. 10, 1923; d. Loyal Burchard and Catharine Mae (McClymond) Hibbs; m. Richard Bodholdt Lund, Nov. 9, 1946; children: Laurel Anne, Richard Douglas, Kristi Jane Lund Lozier. Student, Duchesne Coll., Omaha, 1941-42; BS, Iowa State U., 1946; postgrad., Grand View Coll., Des Moines, 1965; MS, Iowa State U., 1968. Registered dietitian, lic. dietitian. Clk. Russell Stover Candies, Omaha, 1940-42; chemist Martin Bomber Plant, Omaha, 1942-43; dietitian Grand Lake (Colo.) Lodge, 1946; tailoring instr. Ottumwa Pub. Schs., 1952-53; cookery instr. Des Moines Pub. Schs., 1958-62; dietitian Calvin Manor, Des Moines, 1963; home economist Am. Wool Coun./Am. Lamb Coun., Denver, 1963-65, The Merchandising Group of N.Y., 1965-68, Thomas Wolff, Pub. Rels., 1968-70; home economist weekly TV program Iowa Power Co., 1968-70; cons. in child nutrition programs Iowa Dept. Edn., Des Moines, 1970-95; ret. Nutritioneering, Ltd., 1995; Mem. Iowa Home Economists in Bus. (pres. 1962-63), PEO, Pi Beta Phi (Iowa Gamma chpt. pres. 1945-46). Pres. Callanan Jr. H.S. PTA, 1964, Roosevelt H.S. PTA, 1966; pres., mem. Ctrl. Presbyn. Mariners, Des Moines; ruling elder, clk. of session Ctrl. Presbyn. Session, Des Moines, 1972-78; bd. dirs. Ctrl. Found., 1996; amb. Friendship Force Internat., 1982—. Duchesne Coll. 4 yr. scholar. Mem. Iowa Home Economists in Bus. (pres. 1962-63), PEO, Pi Beta Phi (pres. 1945-46). Republican. Avocations: international travel, writing, sailing, sewing, cooking. Home: 105 34th St Des Moines IA 50312-4526

LUND, GEORGE EDWARD, retired electrical engineer; b. Phila., Feb. 17, 1925; s. Harold White and Hannah (Lawford) L.; m. Shirley Bolton Stevens, Sept. 24, 1960; children: Marsha (Mrs. Donald Barnett), Roger, Sharon Stevens (Mrs. David Bailey), Gretchen (Mrs. Kevin J. Collette). BEE, Drexel U., 1952; MEE, U. Pa., 1959; postgrad. in computer sci., Villanova U., 1981-83. Project engr. Burroughs Corp., Paoli, Pa., 1952-86; project engr. UNISYS Corp., Paoli, 1986-90, ret., 1990. Assoc. editor, contbr.: Digital Applications of Magnetic Devices, 1960; patentee in field. With USN, 1943-46, ETO. Mem. IEEE (sr.), Eta Kappa Nu. Republican. Methodist. Avocations: photography, amateur radio. Home: 923 Pinecroft Rd Berwyn PA 19312-2123

LUND, LOIS A., food science and human nutrition educator; b. Thief River Falls, Minn., Aug. 9, 1927; d. Robert J. and E. Luella (Tosdal) L. BS, U. Minn., 1949, MS, 1954, PhD, 1966. Instr. foods U. Iowa, 1951-55, U. Minn., 1955-63; assoc. prof., dir. core studies program, asst. dir. Sch. Home Econs., 1966-68; research fellow U.S. Dept. Agrl., 1963-66; assoc. dean, dir. Sch. Home Econs. Ohio State U., 1969-72; dean Coll. Human Ecology Mich. State U., East Lansing, 1973-85, prof. food sci. and human nutrition, 1985—; bd. dirs. Consumers Power Co., Jackson, Mich., CMS Energy, Dearborn, Mich. Contbr. articles to profl. jours. Recipient Betty award for excellence in teaching U. Minn., 1958, 63, 68, Hon. Alumni award Mich. State U., 1977, Outstanding Achievement award U. Minn. Alumni Assn., 1977. Mem. Am. Coun. on Consumer Interest, Am. Assn. Cereal Chemists, Inst. Food Technologists, Am. Agrl. Econs. Assn., Soc. for Nutrition Edn., Pi Lambda Theta, Phi Kappa Phi, Phi Upsilon Omicron, Omicron Nu (nat. treas. 1971-74, 84-86), Sigma Delta Epsilon. Lutheran. Avocation: gardening. Home: 5927 Shadowlawn Dr East Lansing MI 48823-2379 Office: Mich State U Dept Food Sci and Human Nutrition East Lansing MI 48824

LUND, PETER ANTHONY, broadcast executive; b. Mpls., Jan. 12, 1941; s. Arthur Harold and Elizabeth (Rohan) L.; m. Theresa Mary Kessel, Sept. 3, 1960; children: Mark, Timothy. Ed., St. Thomas Coll., 1958-62. Announcer, sales rep. Sta. KCCR, Pierce, S.D., 1961-62; sales rep. Sta. KELO-

TV, Sioux Falls, S.D., 1962-64; sales rep., sales mgr. Sta. WTTC, Mpls., 1964-66; gen. sales mgr. Westinghouse Broadcasting Co., 1966-71; v.p., gen. mgr. Sta. KSDO, San Diego, Calif., 1972-75, Sta. WTOP, Washington, 1975-77; v.p. CBS owned AM Stas., N.Y.C., 1977-80; v.p., gen. mgr. WBBM-TV, Chgo., 1980-83, WCBS-TV, N.Y.C., 1983-84; exec. v.p. CBS Sports, N.Y.C., 1984-85, pres., 1985-87; pres. Multimedia Entertainment, N.Y.C., 1987-90; exec. v.p., pres. mktg. CBS, 1990-94; exec. v.p., pres. CBS TV Network, N.Y.C., 1994-95; pres. CBS Broadcast Group, N.Y.C., 1995—; pres., CEO CBS Inc., 1995—. Home: 100 Warwick Rd Bronxville NY 10708-5715 Office: CBS 51 W 52nd St New York NY 10019-6119

LUND, ROBERT W., newspaper editor. Editor L.A. Daily News, 1994—. Office: Los Angeles Daily News 21221 Oxnard St Woodland Hills CA 91367-5015

LUND, VICTOR L., retail food company executive; b. Salt Lake City, 1947; married. BA, U. Utah, 1969, MBA, 1972. Audit mgr. Ernst and Whinney, Salt Lake City, 1972-77; sr. v.p. Skaggs Cos. Inc., from 1977; v.p., contr. Am. Stores Co., 1980-83, sr. v.p., contr., from 1983, exec. v.p., co-chief exec. officer, vice-chmn., chief fin. and adminstrv. officer, now pres., CEO, dir., 1992—. Office: Am Stores Co PO Box 27447 Salt Lake City UT 84127-0447 also: Am Stores Co 709 E South Temple Salt Lake City UT 84102-1205

LUND, WENDELL LUTHER, lawyer; b. Prentice, Wis., Dec. 31, 1905; s. Rev. Carl A. and Bertha Elizabeth L.; m. Anne Catherine Greve, Nov. 8, 1934 (dec.); children: Judith (Mrs. Barton Biggs), Carole (Mrs. John A. Benning), Mary Wendell; m. Marian Alice Hope, 1981. A.B., Augustana Coll., Rock Island, Ill., 1927, D.H.L., 1968; A.M., Columbia U., 1930; J.D., Georgetown U., 1938; Ph.D., Princeton U., 1933. Checker C.&N.W. R.R. (iron ore docks), Escanaba, Mich., 1922-23; worked in tie yard and iron ore docks C.&N.W. R.R. (iron ore docks), summers 1924-27; tchr. Upsala Coll., E. Orange, N.J., 1927-29; asso. prof. English Augustana Coll., 1930-31, exec. sec., 1933-34; exec. sec. Upper Monongahela Valley Com., Washington, 1934; mem. Taylor Act Com., Dept. Interior, 1934; sec. Mich Adminstrv. Bd., Lansing, 1941; exec. dir. Mich. Unemployment Compensation Com., 1941-42; dir. labor prodn. div. WPB, also mem. War Manpower Commn., 1942-43; spl. asst. to chmn. WPB, 1943; practicing atty., mem. firm Lund & O'Brien & predecessor firms, Washington, 1943—; chmn., CEO Schonstedt Instrument Co., 1993; Del. World Council of Chs., Evanston, 1954, Uppsala, Sweden, 1968; mem. Bd. Pensions, Lutheran Ch. in Am., 1963-67, 70-79, pres., 1967-68, 74-79; Democratic nominee for Congress, 11th Mich. Dist., 1940; presdl. elector, 1944. Contbr. articles to profl. jours. Bd. dirs. Augustana Coll., 1974-88. Mem. ABA, Bar Assn. D.C., Congl. Country Club (Washington), Burning Tree (Washington), Met. Club (Washington), Univ. Club (Sarasota, Fla.). Home: 1255 N Gulfstream Ave Sarasota FL 34236-8920

LUNDBACK, STAFFAN BENGT GUNNAR, lawyer; b. Stockholm, Sweden, Mar. 23, 1947; came to U.S., 1965; s. B. Holger and Ingrid (Fjellstrom) L.; m. Lee Craig, June 14,1969; children: Hadley Elizabeth, Erik Burchfield. Student, U. Stockholm, 1966-67; BA, U. Rochester, 1970; JD, Boston U., 1974. Bar: N.Y. 1975, Fla. 1983. Assoc. Nixon, Hargrave, Devans & Doyle, Rochester, N.Y., 1974-83; ptnr. Nixon, Hargrave, Devans & Doyle, Rochester, 1983—; bd. dirs. Scandinavian Seminar, Amherst, Mass.; chmn. Scanamerican Properties, Inc., Atlanta, 1989—. Mem. Swedish-Am. C. of C. (sec., bd. dirs. 1994—), Genesee Valley Club, Phi Beta Kappa. Avocations: music, literature, sports, current events, photography. Office: Nixon Hargrave Devans & Doyle PO Box 1051 Clinton First Sq Rochester NY 14603

LUNDBERG, GEORGE DAVID, II, medical editor, pathologist; b. Pensacola, Fla., Mar. 21, 1933; s. George David and Esther Louise (Johnson) L.; m. Nancy Ware Sharp, Aug. 18, 1956 (div.); children: George David III, Charles William, Carol Jean; m. Patricia Blacklidge Lorimer, Mar. 6, 1983; children: Christopher Leif, Melinda Suzanne. AA, North Park Coll., Chgo., 1950; BS, U. Ala., Tuscaloosa, 1952; MS, Baylor U., Waco, Tex., 1963; MD, Med. Coll. Ala., Birmingham, 1957; ScD (hon.), SUNY, Syracuse, 1988, Thomas Jefferson U., 1993, U. Ala., Birmingham, 1994, Med. Coll. Ohio, 1995. Intern Tripler Hosp., Hawaii; resident Brooke Hosp., San Antonio; assoc. prof. pathology U. So. Calif., Los Angeles, 1967-72, prof., 1972-77; assoc. dir. labs. Los Angeles County-U. So. Calif. Med. Ctr., 1968-77; prof., chmn. dept. pathology U. Calif.-Davis, Sacramento, 1977-82; v.p. scientific info., editor Jour. AMA, Chgo., 1982—, editor in chief scientific publ., 1991-95; editor in chief AMA Sci. Info. and Multimedia, Chgo., 1995—; vis. prof. U. London, 1976, Lund U., Sweden, 1976; prof. clin. pathology Northwestern U., Chgo., 1982—; adj. prof. health policy Harvard U., Boston, 1993—; vis. prof. pathology, 1994-96. Author, editor: Managing the Patient Focused Laboratory, 1975, Using the Clinical Laboratory in Medical Decision Making, 1983, 51 Landmark Articles in Medicine, 1984, AIDS From the Beginning, 1986, Caring the the Uninsured and Underinsured, 1991, Violence, 1992; contbr. articles to profl. jours. Served to lt. col. M.C., U.S. Army, 1956-67. Fellow Am. Soc. Clin. Pathologists (past pres.), Am. Acad. Forensic Sci.; mem. N.Y. Acad. Scis., Inst. Medicine, Alpha Omega Alpha. Democrat. Episcopalian. Office: JAMA 515 N State St Chicago IL 60610-4320

LUNDBLAD, ROGER LAUREN, research director; b. San Francisco, Oct. 31, 1939; s. Lauren Alfred and Doris Ruth (Peterson) L.; m. Susan Hawly Taylor, Oct. 15, 1966 (div. 1985); children: Christina Susan, Cynthia Karin. BSc, Pacific Luth. U., 1961; PhD, U. Wash., 1965. Rsch. assoc. U. Wash., Seattle, 1965-66, Rockefeller U., N.Y.C., 1966-68; asst. prof. U. N.C., Chapel Hill, 1968-71, assoc. prof., 1971-77, prof. pathology and biochemistry, 1977-91; adj. prof., 1991—; dir. sci. tech. devel. Baxter-Biotech, Duarte, Calif., 1991—; vis. scientist Hyland div. Baxter Healthcare, Glendale, Calif., 1988-89. Author: Chemical Reagents for Protein Modification, 1984, 2d edit., 1990; editor: Chemistry and Biology of Thrombin, 1977, Chemistry and Biology of Heparin, 1980, Techniques in Protein Modification, 1994; editor-in-chief: Biotechnology and Applied Biochemistry, 1996—; contbr. articles to profl. jours. Recipient Career Achievement award U. N.C., 1986. Mem. Am. Soc. Biochem. Molecular Biology, Am. Soc. Microbiology, Am. Heart Assn., Sigma Xi. Office: Baxter Biotech Hyland Divsn 1720 Flower Ave Duarte CA 91010-2923

LUNDE, ASBJORN RUDOLPH, lawyer; b. S.I., N.Y., July 17, 1927; s. Karl and Elisa (Andenes) L.; AB, Columbia U., 1947, LLB, 1949. Bar: N.Y. 1949. Since practiced in N.Y.C.; with firm Kramer, Marx, Greenlee & Backus, and predecessors, 1950-68, mem., 1958-68; individual practice law, 1968—; mem. bd. dirs., v.p. Orchestra da Camera, Inc., 1964—; bd. dirs. Sara Roby Found., 1971—, The Drawing Soc., 1977—. Mem. ABA, N.Y. State Bar Assn., Assn. of Bar of City of N.Y., Met. Opera Club, East India Club (London); art collector, donator paintings and sculptures to Met. Mus. Art, N.Y.C., Nat. Gallery Art, Washington, Mus. Fine Arts, Boston, Clark Art Inst., Williamstown, Mass., others. Home and Office: 135 LaBranche Rd Hillsdale NY 12529-5713

LUNDE, DONALD THEODORE, physician; b. Milw., Mar. 2, 1937; m. Marilynn Krick; children: Montgomery, Christopher, Glenn, Evan, Bret. BA with distinction, Stanford U., 1958, MA in Psychology, 1964, MD, 1966. Diplomate Nat. Bd. Med. Examiners. Ward psychologist Palo Alto (Calif.) VA Hosp., 1965-66, chief resident in psychiatry, 1969-70, assoc. chief tng. and research sect., 1970-72, acting chief tng. and research sect., 1971-72; intern in internal medicine Palo Alto/Stanford Hosp., 1966-67; resident in psychiatry Stanford (Calif.) U. Sch. Medicine, 1967-69, instr. psychiatry, 1969-70, asst. prof. psychiatry, 1970-75, dir. med. sch. edn. in psychiatry, 1971-74, clin. assoc. prof. psychiatry, 1978-89, clin. prof. psychiatry, 1989—; lectr. Law Sch. Stanford U., 1971-81; staff physician Atascadero (Calif.) State Hosp., 1968. Author books and articles in field. Served with USN, 1958-61. Fellow Am. Psychiat. Assn., Am. Coll. Forensic Psychiatry; mem. No. Calif. Psychiat. Soc., Phi Beta Kappa, Alpha Omega Alpha. Office: Stanford U 900 Welch Rd Ste 400 Palo Alto CA 94304-1804

LUNDE, HAROLD IRVING, management educator; b. Austin, Minn., Apr. 18, 1929; s. Peter Oliver and Emma (Stoa) L.; m. Sarah Jeanette Lysne, June 25, 1955; children: Paul, James, John, Thomas. B.A., St. Olaf Coll., 1952; M.A., U. Minn., 1954, Ph.D., 1966. Assoc. prof. econs. Macalester Coll., St. Paul, 1957-64; fin. staff economist Gen. Motors Corp., N.Y.C., 1965-67; corp. sec. Dayton Hudson Corp., Mpls., 1967-70; mgr. planning and gen. research May Dept. Stores Co., St. Louis, 1970-72; v.p. planning and research May Dept. Stores Co., 1972-78; exec. v.p. adminstrn. Kobacker Stores, Inc., Columbus, Ohio, 1979; prof. mgmt. Bowling Green (Ohio) State U., 1980—. Mem. Acad. Internat. Bus., Acad. Mgmt., Am. Econ. Assn., Nat. Assn. Bus. Economists, Planning Forum, Case Research Assn., Decision Scis. Inst., Phi Beta Kappa, Phi Kappa Phi, Omicron Delta Kappa, Beta Gamma Sigma. Home: 880 Country Club Dr Bowling Green OH 43402-1602 Office: Bowling Green State U Dept Mgmt Bowling Green OH 43403

LUNDEBERG, PHILIP KARL BORAAS, curator; b. Mpls., June 14, 1923; s. Olav Knutson and Vivian Juliet (Boraas) L.; m. Eleanore Lillian Berntson, July 18, 1953; 1 son, Karl Fredrik. B.A. summa cum laude, Duke U., 1944, M.A., 1947; Ph.D. (Austin fellow 1949), Harvard U., 1954. Asst. to historian U.S. Naval Ops. in World War II, Navy Dept., 1950-53; asst. prof. history St. Olaf Coll., 1953-55, U.S. Naval Acad., 1955-59; assoc. curator naval history Nat. Mus. History and Tech., Smithsonian Instn., 1959-61, curator of naval history, 1961-84, curator emeritus, 1984—; v.p. Am. Mil. Inst., 1968-71, pres., 1971-73; chmn. Internat. Congress Maritime Museums, 1972-75; v.p. U.S. Commn. on Mil. History, 1975-79, pres., 1980-83; sec. Internat. Commn. Mus. Security, 1975-79; pres. Coun. Am. Maritime Museums, 1976-78. Author: The Continental Gunboat Philadelphia, 1966, 2d edit., 1995, Samuel Colt's Submarine Battery, 1974; co-author: Sea Power: A Naval History, 1960, 81; contbg. author: Guide to the Sources of U.S. Military History, 1975, 93, Seafaring and Society, 1987, To Die Gallantly, 1994, The Battle of the Atlantic (1939-1945), 1994; editor: Bibliographie de L'Histoire des Grandes Routes Maritimes: États-Uis D'Amèrique, 1970; exhibits: Armed Forces of U.S., 1961, By Sea and by Land, 1981. With USNR, 1943-83, 89, comdr. Res. ret., 1992. Decorated Bronze Star, Purple Heart; recipient Bronze medal Internat. Commn. Mil. History, 1975. Fellow Am. Mil. Inst. (Moncado prize 1964); mem. Coun. Am. Maritime Mus. (hon.), N.Am. Soc. for Oceanic History, Naval Hist. Found., Naval Order of U.S., Internat. Congress Maritime Mus. (life mem.), Soc. for Mil. History, Phi Beta Kappa. Home: 1107 Croton Dr Alexandria VA 22308-2009

LUNDEEN, BRADLEY CURTIS, lawyer; b. Karlstad, MN, Nov. 16, 1958; s. Curtis W. and LaVonne M. (Oistad) L.; m. Kristina Ogland, May 18, 1984 (div. Dec. 1991); 1 child, Jonathan B. BA, Moorhead State U, 1980; JD cum laude, William Mitchell Coll. Law, 1984. Bar: Minn. 1984, Wis. 1984. Assoc. Gwin, Gilbert, Gwin, Mudge & Porter, Hudson, Wis., 1984, Gilbert, Mudge & Porter, Hudson, 1985; ptnr. Gilbert, Mudge, Porter & Lundeen, Hudson, 1986-92; lawyer, shareholder Mudge, Porter & Lundeen S.C., Hudson, 1992-94, Mudge, Porter, Lundeen & Seguin S.C., Hudson, 1995—. Bd. dirs. Hudson Rotary, 1990-91, Bank St. Croix, Hudson, Wis., 1987-94. Mem. St. Croix Valley Bar Assn., St. Croix Valley Employers Assn., Masons, Shriners. Lutheran. Avocations: golf, skiing, travel, computers and cooking. Home: 714 Deer Path Rd N Hudson WI 54016 Office: Mudge Porter Lundeen & Seguin SC 110 Second St Hudson WI 54016

LUNDELIUS, ERNEST LUTHER, JR., vertebrate paleontologist, educator; b. Austin, Tex., Dec. 2, 1927; s. Ernest Luther and Hazel (Halton) L.; m. Judith Weiser, Sept. 28, 1953; children—Jennifer, Rolf Eric. B.S. in Geology, U. Tex., 1950; Ph.D. in Paleozoology, U. Chgo., 1954. Postdoctoral Fulbright scholar to Western Australia, 1954-55; postdoctoral research fellow Calif. Inst. Tech., 1956-57; mem. faculty U. Tex., Austin, 1957—; prof. vertebrate paleontology U. Tex., 1969; John Andrew Wilson prof. vertebrate paleontology, 1978—. Served with AUS, 1946-47. Fulbright sr. scholar to Australia, 1976. Home: 7310 Running Rope Austin TX 78731-2132 Office: U Tex Dept Geol Scis Austin TX 78712

LUNDEN, JOAN, television personality; b. Fair Oaks, CA, Sept. 19, 1950; d. Erle Murray and Gladyce Lorraine (Somervill) Blunden; children: Jamie Beryl, Lindsay Leigh, Sarah Emily. Student, Universidad de Las Americas, Mexico City, U. Calif., Calif. State U., Am. River Coll., Sacramento, Calif. Began broadcasting career as co-anchor and prodr. at Sta. KCRA-TV and Radio, Sacramento, 1973-75; with Sta. WABC-TV, N.Y.C., 1975—, co-anchor, 1976-80; co-host Good Morning America, ABC-TV, 1980—; host special report TV for Whittle Comm.; host Everyday with Joan Lunden, 1989; film appearances include: Macho Callahan, 1970, What About Bob?, 1991; co-author: (with Andy Friedburg) Good Morning, I'm Joan Lunden, 1986, (with Michael Krauss) Joan Lunden's Mother's Minutes, 1986, Your Newborn Baby; syndicated columnist: Parent's Notes. Recipient Outstanding Mother of Yr. award, Nat. Mother's Day Com., 1982; Albert Einstein Coll. of Yeshiva U. Spirit of Achievement award; Nat. Women's Polit. Caucus award; NJ Divsn. of Civil Rights award; Baylor U. Outstanding Woman of the Year award. Office: Good Morning Am 147 Columbus Ave New York NY 10023-5900

LUNDERGAN, BARBARA KEOUGH, lawyer; b. Chgo., Nov. 6, 1938; d. Edward E. and Eleanor A. (Erickson) Keough; m. James A. Lundergan, Dec. 29, 1962; children—Matthew K., Mary Alice. B.A., U. Ill., 1960; J.D., Loyola U., Chgo., 1964. Bar: Ill. 1964, U.S. Dist. Ct. (no. dist.) Ill. 1964, U.S. Tax Ct. 1974. With Seyfarth, Shaw, Fairweather & Geraldson, Chgo., 1964—, ptnr., 1971—. Fellow Am. Coll. Trust and Estate Counsel; mem. ABA (com. on fed. taxation), Ill. Bar Assn. (coun. sect. on fed. taxation 1983-91, chair 1989, coun. sect. on trusts and estates sect. coun. 1992—, sec. 1996—, editl. bd. Ill. Bar Jour. 1993-96), Chgo. Bar Assn. (chmn. trust law com. 1982-83, com. on fed. taxation). Office: Seyfarth Shaw Fairweather & Geraldson 55 E Monroe St Chicago IL 60603-5702

LUNDGREN, CARL WILLIAM, JR., physicist; b. Columbus, Sept. 17, 1933; s. Carl William and Anne Katherine (Kuntz) L.; BEE, U. Cin., 1957, MS, 1959, PhD, 1961; m. Virginia Anne Cullis, Dec. 7, 1963; children: David John, Janet Marie. Coop. undergrad. engr. Govt. Products div. Avco Corp., Cin. and Evendale, Ohio, 1953-56; asst. supr., research fellow Basic Sci. Research Lab., U. Cin., 1959-61; mem. tech. staff Bell Telephone Labs., Murray Hill, N.J., 1961-66, Holmdel, N.J., 1966-84; dist. mgr. advanced fiber optics planning Bell Communications Rsch. Inc., Red Bank, N.J., 1984-92; dir. transmission systems engring. Bellcore, Morristown and Red Bank. Capt., Signal Corps., U.S. Army, 1961-63. Mem. AAAS, IEEE, N.Y. Acad. Sci., Optical Soc. Am., Gideons Internat., Sierra Club, Delta Tau Delta, Tau Beta Pi, Eta Kappa Nu, Phi Eta Sigma, Omicron Delta Kappa. Republican. Episcopalian. Contbr. articles to profl. jours.; patentee in field. Home: 60 Woodhollow Rd Colts Neck NJ 07722-1323 Office: Bell Communications Research Inc Navesink Research & Engring Ctr 331 Newman Springs Rd Red Bank NJ 07701-5657

LUNDGREN, LEONARD, III, retired secondary education educator; b. San Francisco, June 22, 1933; s. Leonard II and Betty (Bosold) L.; m. Jane Gates, June 12, 1976. AA, City Coll. San Francisco, 1952; AB, San Francisco State U., 1954, MA, 1958, postgrad., 1958-71. Cert. tchr., Calif. Phys. edn. tchr., athletic coach Pelton Jr. High Sch., San Francisco, 1958-59; social studies tchr., dept. chair, phys. edn. tchr., athletic coach Luther Burbank Jr. High Sch., San Francisco, 1959-78; history, govt. econs., geography tchr. George Washington High Sch., San Francisco, 1978-93; water safety instr. ARC, San Francisco, 1946-61; mem. Calif. Quality Teaching Ctr. Conf. Bd., 1965-67. Author: Guide for Films and Filmstrips, 1966, Teacher's Handbook for Social Studies, 1966, Guide for Minority Studies, 1968. V.p. Lakeside Property Owners Assn., San Francisco, 1986-88, legis. advocate, 1988-95; v.p. West of Twin Peaks Coun., San Francisco, 1986-87; pub. affairs polit. econ. cons., Calif., 1993—. With USN, 1954-56. Fulbright scholar, Greece, 1963; recipient Svc. Pin, ARC, 1961. Mem. NEA (life, del. 1970, 72-76), Calif. Tchrs. Assn. (state coun. rep. 1963-74), Nat. Coun. Social Studies, Calif. Coun. Social Studies (v.p. San Francisco chpt. 1969-70), San Francisco Classroom Tchrs. Assn. (pres. 1972-73, Gavel award 1973), PTA (sch. v.p. 1980-81), Calif. Ret. Tchrs. Assn. (life, legislation chmn. San Francisco divsn. 1995-96), Am. Assn. Ret. Persons (cmty. coord. San Francisco 1996), San Francisco State U. Alumni Assn. (life, treas. 1959), Calif. Assn. Health, Phys. Edn., Recreation and Dance (life, treas. San Francisco chpt. 1959-60), Nat. Geog. Soc. (life), PhiDelta Kappa (life, pres. chpt. 1965-66). Avocations: travel, swimming, gardening, research, service. *A career in education for me is my life from learning to teaching over and over again. History, government, geography and economics are my major subjects. World travel gives me the chance to see the places I studied and taught.*

LUNDIN, BRUCE THEODORE, engineering and management consultant; b. Alameda, Calif., Dec. 28, 1919; s. Oscar Linus and Elizabeth Ellen (Erickson) L.; m. Barbara Ann Bliss, July 27, 1946 (wid. Feb. 1981); children: Dianne, Robert, Nancy; m. Jean Ann Oberlin, Mar. 22, 1982. BSME, U. Calif.-Berkeley, 1942; D of Engring. (hon.), U. Toledo, 1975. Chief engine research NASA Lewis Ctr., Cleve., 1952-58, asst. dir., 1958-61, assoc. dir., 1961-68, dir., 1969-77; dep. assoc. adminstrn. NASA, Washington, 1968-69; adv. U.S. Air Force Sci. Adv. Bd., Washington, 1961-77; mem. Aerospace Safety Adv. Bd., Washington, 1961-72; staff dir. Pres.'s Commn. on the Accident at Three Mile Island, 1981; mem. TM1-2 Safety Adv. Bd., 1981-89; chmn. Rockwell Internat. Safety Oversight Panel, 1988-89. Pres. Westshore Unitarian Ch., Rocky River, Ohio, 1967-68; trustee Southwest Gen. Hosp., Berea, Ohio, 1970-75. Recipient Outstanding Leadership medal NASA, 1965, Pub. Service award NASA, 1971, 75, Disting. Service medal NASA, 1971, 77, Engineer of the Year award Nat. Space Club, 1975. Fellow AIAA; mem. Nat. Acad. Engring. Avocations: woodworking; gardening; reading; travel. Home: 5859 Columbia Rd North Olmsted OH 44070-4611

LUNDIN, DAVID ERIK, lawyer; b. Middletown, Conn., May 8, 1949; s. Irving Erik and Majorie (Walker) L.; 1 child, Erik Stewart. BA, U. Redlands, 1971; JD, UCLA, 1974. Bar: Calif. 1974. Atty. advisor FTC, Washington, 1976-77; ptnr. Fredman, Silverberg & Lewis, San Diego, 1977-85, Sternberg, Eggers, Kidder & Fox, San Diego, 1985-87, Finley Kumble Wagner, San Diego, 1987-88, Lorenz, Alhadeff, Lundin and Oggel, San Diego, 1988-91; prin. David E. Lundin and Assocs., 1992—. Mem. bd. fellows U. Redlands, Calif., 1984-86; trustee San Diego Art Ctr., 1984-86, San Diego Bus. Innovations Ctr., 1992—, pres., 1994—. Mem. ABA (litigation and antitrust sects., pvt. antitrust litigation and antitrust exemptions com.), Western Behavioral Sci. Inst. (counsel 1981-86), Whispering Palms Country Club, Cotillion Club (sec. 1984-85). Mem. United Ch. Christ. Address: PO Box 3367 Rancho Santa Fe CA 92067-3367

LUNDIN, RICHARD ALLEN, career military officer, federal government administrator, educator; b. Holyoke, Mass., Feb. 19, 1937; s. Gustav Regner and Frances (Gaston) L.; m. Dolores Segovia, Nov. 19, 1962; children: Valerie Frances, Joanie Elizabeth. AA, Am. River Jr. Coll., 1970; BA, Golden Gate U., 1973, MBA, 1976; EdD, LaSalle U.; diploma, Command and Gen. Staff Coll. U.S. Army, 1985, Air War Coll., 1989. Cert. tchr., Calif.; instr. cert. U.S. Army. Commd. USAF, 1954, advanced through grades to lt. col., 1977; with res. USAR, Calif., 1962—; with Gen. Services Adminstrn. USN, USAF, Tex. and Calif.; col. Calif. NG, 1993; cons. Family Fin. Planning Group, Benicia, Calif., 1982—; instr. USAR, 1985—; adj. profl. Golden Gate U., San Francisco, 1978—; cons. contracts, mktg., edn.; adminstr. Chapman Coll., 1994. Asst. chmn. Waterfront Planning Commn., Benicia, Calif. 1982-84; mem. Utility User Tax Com., Benicia, 1984; Sister Cities Com., Benecia, 1982-86; active Calif. Rep. Assembly; Solano County Parole Commr., 1992-95; mem. WWII Commemorative Com. Calif., 1995; rep. ctrl. com.; Solano County U.S. Savings Bond rep., 1995-96. Recipient Sister Cities Com. Appreciation award Mayor of Tula, Hidalgo, Mex., 1985, Benicia City Appreciation award, Mayor of Benicia, 1984. Mem. Res. Officers Assn. U.S. Army (pres.), Nat. Contracts Mgmt. Assn. (mem. chmn.), Golden Gate U. Alumni Assn., Benicia C. of C., VFW, Am. Legion. Republican. Roman Catholic. Club: Yacht (Benicia). Lodge: K.C., Knights Templar.

LUNDING, CHRISTOPHER HANNA, lawyer; b. Evanston, Ill., June 15, 1946; s. Franklin J. and Virginia (Hanna) L.; children: Elizabeth, Nelson, Alexander, Andrew, Kirsten; m. Barbara J. Fontana, Aug. 19, 1989. BA, Harvard U., 1968; JD, Yale U., 1971. Bar: N.Y. 1972, Fla. 1972, U.S. Supreme Ct. 1975. Law clk. to judge 2d Cir. U.S. Ct. Appeals, N.Y.C., 1971-72; assoc. Cleary, Gottlieb, Steen & Hamilton, N.Y.C., 1973-79, ptnr., 1980—; chmn. Legal Svcs. N.Y.C., 1987-94. Chmn. Belle Haven Tax Dist., Greenwich, Conn., 1986-96. Fellow Am. Bar Found.; mem. N.Y. County Lawyers Assn. (bd. dirs. 1988-94). Episcopalian. Office: Cleary Gottlieb Steen & Hamilton Ste 4300 1 Liberty Plz New York NY 10006-1404

LUNDQUIST, DANA R., health insurance executive; b. Mpls., Sept. 12, 1941; s. R. Dana and Mary Jane (Norton) L.; children: Brenda A., Sheila R. BA, Valparaiso U., 1963; postgrad., U. Hawaii, 1963-64, U. Colo., 1963; MBA, U. Chgo., 1966. Adminstrv. asst. U. Chgo. Hosps. and Clinics, 1966-67, asst. supt., 1967-68, asst. dir., 1968-70; officer, bd. dirs. affiliates Hamot Health Systems, Inc., Erie, Pa., 1970-92, pres. parent co., 1981-92, cons. to bd., 1992—; cons. Blue Cross Western Pa., 1992-93, sr. v.p.,1993—; lectr. grad. program in hosp. adminstrn. U. Chgo., 1967-70; mem. Erie County Hosp. Coun., 1978-92, pres., 1982; bd. dirs. Hosp. Coun. Western Pa., 1978-92, vice chmn.; exec. com. Pa. Coun. Teaching Hosps., 1986-90; adv. coun. risk mgmt. Pa. Hosp. Ins. Co., 1982-90, bd. dirs. Vol. Hosps. Am. of Pa., 1985-92, chmn. bd.; bd. visitors The Behrend Coll., Pa. State U., 1990-92; bd. dirs. Pa. Med. Coll., 1991-92, Hardware Hawaii, 1989—. Mem. Erie Conf. on Community Devel., 1981-92, bd. dirs., 1988-92; bd. dirs. N.W. Pa. Buy Right Coun., 1986-92, United Way Erie County, 1983-92; mem. pres.'s coun. Villa Maria Coll., Erie, 1981-90, bd. incorporators Gannon U., Erie, 1981-92; mem. governing bd. St. Paul's Luth. Ch., Erie, 1973-78, v.p., 1974-78; mem. Erie Down Town Coalition Steering Com., 1990-92, chmn., 1991-92, numerous other activities. Mem. Am. Coll. Healthcare Execs. (former regents adv. coun. Pa.); mem. Am. Hosp. Assn. (governing coun. sect. met. hosps. 1987, alt. ho. of dels. 1988), Hosp. Assn. Pa. (polit. action com. 1981-92), Pa. C. of C., U. Chgo. Hosp. Alumni Assn. (exec. com. 1967-70, 87-92, sec.-treas. 1988, pres. 1990-91), Downtown Athletic Club, Rotary. Home: PO Box 22130 Pittsburgh PA 15222-0130 Office: Blue Cross Western PA 5th Ave Pl Ste 3012 Pittsburgh PA 15222-3099

LUNDQUIST, GENE ALAN, cotton company executive; b. Bakersfield, Calif., Feb. 25, 1943; s. Felix Waldemar and Elsia Geneva (Bartlett) L.; m. Linda Fern Smotherman, June 17, 1966; 1 child, Nels Eric. B.S., Colo. State U., 1964. Info. specialist Calcot Ltd., Bakersfield, 1969-71, field rep., 1971-74, asst. v.p., 1974-77, asst. v.p., corp. sec., 1977-80, v.p., corp. sec., 1980—; bd. dirs. Calif. Farm Water Coalition, Water Assn. Kern County; apptd. Calif. Gov.'s Agrl. Summit. Bd. dirs. Kern County Water Agy., Bakersfield, 1975-91, Bakersfield Salvation Army, 1985-88. Served with U.S. Army, 1965-67. Decorated Army Commendation medal; Calif. Agr. Leadership Found. fellow, 1973. Mem. Cotton Bd. (alt. dir. 1984—), Nat. Cotton Council Am. (del. 1984—), Calif. Cotton Growers Assn. (adv. com. 1976—), Calif. Planting Cotton Seed Distbrs. (adv. com. 1976—). Republican. Mem. Mennonite Brethren Ch. Avocations: golf; tennis; running; landscaping; reading. Office: Calcot Ltd 1601 E Brundage Ln PO Box 259 Bakersfield CA 93302

LUNDQUIST, JOHN MILTON, librarian, author, travel writer, photographer; b. Twin Falls, Idaho, Sept. 22, 1938; s. Milton Rocine and Mildred (Toolson) L.; m. Suzanne Evertsen, Sept. 6, 1966 (div. July 1985); children: Jennifer, Lila, Eric, Margaret, John, Jack. BA in History, Portland State U., 1970; MLS, Brigham Young U., 1972; MA in Near Eastern Studies, U. Mich., 1974, PhD in Near Eastern Studies, 1983. Instr. anthropology and religious instrn. Brigham Young U., Provo, Utah, 1979-83, asst. prof. anthropology and religious instrn., 1983-85; mem. faculty New Sch. for Social Rsch., N.Y.C., 1986-88; Susan and Douglas chief libr. Oriental divsn. N.Y. Pub. Libr., N.Y.C., 1985—; rschr. Archive for Rsch. in Archetypal Symbolism, N.Y.C., 1987—; lectr. Inst. for Asian Studies, Inc., N.Y.C., C.G. Jung Found., N.Y.; adj. assoc. prof. art history and archaeology Columbia U., N.Y.C., 1987-89; adj. assoc. prof. Near Eastern langs. and lit. NYU, 1987; spkr., lectr. in field; dir. excavation Am. Sch. Oriental Rsch., Tell Quarqur, Syria, 1981-85, field archaeologist, Syria, 1979-82; area supr. Am. Expedition to Tell Hadidi, Syria, summers 1974-76; extensive travel, rsch., field work China, Tibet, Japan, Hong Kong, Taiwan, India, Indonesia, others; guest scholar Japan Ctr. for Area Studies, Nat. Mus. Ethnology, Osaka, Mar. 1996. Author: The Temple: Meeting Place of Heaven and Earth, 1993, Japanese edit., 1994, Babylon in European Writing and Art Civilizations of the Ancient Near East, 1995; contbr. articles to The N.Y. Times and other publs.; translator langs. and lang. behavior abstracts. Bd. advisors The Asian Classics Inst., 1995—. Mem. Internat. Assn. Orientalist Librs., Am. Inst. Archaeology (bd. govs. N.Y.C. chpt.), Am. Schs. Oriental Rsch. (corp. instnl. rep. 1985—), Oriental Club N.Y.C. (pres. 1992-95), East Side Conservative Club, Phi Kappa Phi. Republican. Mormon. Avocations: marathon running, martial arts. Home: 881 7th Ave # 1001 New

York NY 10019-3210 Office: NY Pub Libr Oriental Divsn Fifth Ave and 42d St New York NY 10018

LUNDQUIST, MARVIN CARL ANDREW, agronomist researcher; b. Roxbury, Kans., Sept. 16, 1921; s. Carl Bernard and Myrtle Edla Amanda (Johnson) L.; m. Lillian Frances Violet Norland Cockriel, Mar. 4, 1995. BS, Kans. State U., 1950, MS, 1952. Cert. prof. agronomist. Asst. co. agrl. agt. Barton County Extension, Great Bend, Kans., 1953-56; supt. Sandyland expt. field Kans. State U. Agrl. Exptl. Sta., Manhattan, 1956-66, field agron., 1966-75, supt. S.W. expt. field, 1975-82, supt. cornbelt expt. field, 1982-85, ret., 1985; agron. cons. Soil Conservation Dist., McPherson, Kans., 1985-89, Agrl. Stabilization and Conservation Svc., McPherson, 1989-93; field inspector Kans. Crop Improvement Assn., Manhattan, 1985—; agron. cons. vol. Soil Conserv. Dist., McPherson, 1989—. Contbr. articles to profl. jours. Pres. McPherson Gem and Mineral Club, 1992—; chair City Tree Bd., 1995—. With USN, 1932-34. Grant Kans. Crop Imp. Assn. Mem. Am. Soc. Agronomy, Soil Conservation Soc. Am., Am. Soc. Range Mgmt., Lions Club, Lambda Chi Alpha (v.p. alumni housing bd.). Presbyterian. Achievements include pioneering work with subsurface tillage using v-blades; researching skew-treaders; developing other soil and water erosion control cropping strategies including a wheat-sorghum fallow rotation for grassy weed infested sandy soils. Home: 441 N Charles St Mc Pherson KS 67460

LUNDQUIST, WEYMAN IVAN, lawyer; b. Worcester, Mass., July 27, 1930; s. Hilding Ivan and Florence Cecilia (Westerholm) L.; m. Joan Durrell, Sept. 15, 1956 (div. July 1977); children—Weyman, Erica, Jettora, Kirk; m. Kathryn E. Taylor, Dec. 28, 1978; 1 child, Derek. BA magna cum laude, Dartmouth Coll., 1952; LLB, Harvard U., 1955. Bar: Mass. 1955, Alaska 1961, Calif. 1963, Vt. 1994. Assoc. Thayer, Smith & Gaskill, Worcester, 1957-60; atty. U.S. Attys. Office, Mass. and Alaska, 1960-62; assoc. Heller, Ehrman, White & McAuliffe, San Francisco, 1963-65, ptnr., 1967—; counsel, v.p. State Mut. Life Ins. Co., Worcester, 1965-67; vis. prof. environ. studies Dartmouth Coll., Hanover, N.H., 1980, 84; vis. scholar Dickey Ctr. for Internat. Understanding, 1994—; program chmn. 1990 Moscow Conf. on Law and Bilateral Econs. Rels.; mem. U.S. adv. com. Alaska/Can./Soviet No. Justice Conf., 1993-94, N.Y., San Francisco Cutting Edge Lawyer Liability Programs, 1989. Author: (fiction) The Promised Land, 1987; contbr. articles to profl. jours. Trustee Natural Resources Def. Coun., 1982-91. Recipient CPR Significant Achievement award, 1987. Fellow ABA (founder and chmn. litigation sect. 1978-79, chmn. Soviet Bar Assn. liaison com. 1986, co-chmn. spl. com. for study discovery abuse 1976-83, spl. com. on tort liability sys. 1981-84, superfund 301e study group advisor to U.S. Congress, 1983), Am. Coll. Trial Lawyers, Dartmouth Coll. Dickey Ctr. for Internat. Understanding (sr.); mem. Dartmouth Lawyer's Assn. (founding mem.), Am. Antiquarian Soc. (councillor), Fgn. Rels. Coun., Assn. Life Ins. Coun., U.S. Supreme Ct. Hist. Soc., No. Dist. Hist. Soc., Dartmouth Lawyers Assn., Swedish Am. C. of C. (pres., bd. dirs. western area U.S. 1982-89). Avocations: squash, skiing, writing. Home: 16 Occom Ridge Hanover NH 03755 Office: Heller Ehrman White & McAuliffe 333 Bush St San Francisco CA 94104 also: PO Box 200 Norwich VT 05055-0200

LUNDSGAARDE, HENRY PEDER, anthropology educator, researcher; b. Copenhagen, Dec. 22, 1938; came to U.S., 1957; s. Henry Thorvald and Ragnhild (Rasmussen) L.; m. Anette Rothenborg, June 24, 1967 (div. 1986); children—Peter, Thorsten, Allan, Erik. B.A., U. Calif., Santa Barbara, 1961; M.S., U. Wis., 1963, Ph.D., 1966. Research asst. dept. anthropology U. Oreg., 1964-65; asst. prof. anthropology U. Calif., Santa Barbara, 1965-70; fellow in law and anthropology Harvard U. Law Sch., Cambridge, Mass., 1969-70; assoc. prof. anthropology, chmn. dept. U. Houston, 1970-72; research assoc. dept. medicine Coll. Medicine U. Vt., 1976-78; prof. anthropology U. Kans., Lawrence, 1972—, chmn. dept. anthropology, 1972-76; assoc. dir. Salt Lake City Regional Med. Edn. Ctr., VA Med Ctr., Salt Lake City, 1987-89; cons. VA Regional Info. Sys. Ctr., Salt Lake City, 1989; adj. prof. med. informatics U. Utah Sch. Medicine, 1987-95; adj. rsch. asst. dept. anthropology U. Oreg., 1964-65; lectr. in field. Author: Cultural Adaptation in the Southern Gilbert Islands, 1966, Murder in Space City: A Cultural Analysis of Houston Homicide Patterns, 1977; (with others) Human Problems in Computerized Medicine, 1981; editor, author: Land Tenure in Oceania, 1974; contbr. articles to profl. jours. Fellow Woodrow Wilson Found., 1961, 64, Am. Council Learned Socs., 1963, 69, Harvard U. Law Sch., 1969, grantee NSF, NIH, Wenner-Gren Found. Home: 1502 W 25th Street Ct # D6 Lawrence KS 66046-4016 Office: U Kans Dept Anthropology Lawrence KS 66045

LUNDSTEDT, SVEN BERTIL, behavioral and social scientist, educator; b. N.Y.C., May 6, 1926; s. Sven David and Edith Maria L.; m. Jean Elizabeth Sanford, June 16, 1951; children: Margaret, Peter, Janet. AB, U. Chgo., 1952, PhD, 1955; SM, Harvard U., 1960. Lic. in psychology, N.Y., Ohio; cert. Council for Nat. Register of Health Services. Asst. dir. Found. for Research on Human Behavior, 1960-62; asst. prof. Case-Western Res. U., Cleve., 1962-64, assoc. prof., 1964-68; assoc. prof. adminstrv. sci. Ohio State U., Columbus, 1968-69, prof. pub. policy and mgmt., 1969—, Ameritech Research prof., 1987-89, prof. internat. bus. and pub. policy, 1988—; prof. mgmt. and human resources, 1990—; affiliate scientist Battelle PNL, 1994—; chmn. Battelle endowment program for tech. and human affairs, 1976-80, mem. Univ. Senate; dir. project on edn. of chief exec. officer Aspen Inst., 1978-80; advisor Task Force on Innovation, U.S. Ho. of Reps., 1983-84, Citizens Network for Fgn. Affairs, 1988—; mem. Am. Com. on U.S. Soviet Relations, 1985—, chair trade and negotiation project; cons. E.I. duPont de Nemours & Co., B.F. Goodrich Co., Bell Telephone Labs., Battelle Meml. Inst., Nat. Fulbright Award Com.; invited speaker Royal Swedish Acad. Scis., 1989. Author: Higher Education in Social Psychology, 1968; co-author: Managing Innovation, 1982, Managing Innovation and Change, 1989; author, editor: Telecommunications, Values and the Public Interest, 1990; contbr. articles to profl. jours. Pres., Cleve. Mental Health Assn., 1966-68; mem. Ohio Citizen's Task Force on Corrections, 1971-72. Served with U.S. Army, 1944-46. Harvard U. fellow, 1960; grantee Bell Telephone Labs., 1964-65, NSF, 1965-67, Kettering Found., 1978-80, Atlantic Richfield Found., 1980-82, German Marshall Fund of U.S. to conduct internat. ednl. joint ventures on econ. negotiations, Budapest, Hungary, 1990; recipient Ohio Ho. of Reps. award, 1986. Mem. Am. Psychol. Assn., Internat. Inst. for Applied Systems Analysis (innovation task force, nat. adv. com. project internat. negotiation with Am. Acad. Arts and Scis., founder, chmn. U.S. Midwest Assn. for IIASA 1986—, sr. social sci. advisor 1994—), Am. Acad. Arts and Scis. (chmn. PIN com. on east/west trade negotiation), Am. Soc. for Pub. Adminstrn. (pres. Central Ohio chpt. 1975-77, founder, chmn. com. on bus. govt. relations, 1977-79, editorial bd. Pub. Adminstrn. Rev., 1978-82), Internat. Soc. Panetics (sec. bd. govs., founding mem.). Unitarian. Home: 197 Riverview Park Dr Columbus OH 43214-2023 Office: Ohio State U Sch Pub Policy and Mgmt 1775 S College Rd Columbus OH 43210-1309

LUNDSTROM, GILBERT GENE, banker, lawyer; b. Gothenburg, Nebr., Sept. 27, 1941; s. Vernon G. and Imogene (Jackett) L.; m. Joyce Elaine Ronin, June 26, 1965; children: Trevor A., Gregory G. BS, U. Nebr., 1964, JD, 1969; MBA, Wayne State U., 1966. Bar: U.S. Dist. Ct. (1st dist.) Nebr. 1969, Nebr. 1969, U.S. Ct. Appeals (5th cir.) 1970, U.S. Ct. Appeals (10th cir.) 1971, U.S. Ct. Appeals (8th cir.) 1974, U.S. Ct. Appeals (3d cir.) 1986. Ptnr. Woods & Aitken, Lincoln, Nebr., 1969-93; pres., CEO First Fed. Lincoln Bank, 1994—; part-time faculty law sch. U. Nebr.-Lincoln, 1970-74; dir. First Fed. Lincoln Bank, TMS Corp. of Ams., First Fin. Corp.; bd. dirs. Sahara Enterprises, Inc., Sahara Coal Co., Chgo.; dir. Fed. Home Loan Bank Topeka. Bd. dirs. Folsom Children's Zoo, Lincoln, 1979-83, St. Elizabeth Hosp. Found. Fellow Nebr. State Bar Assn.; mem. ABA, ATLA, Lincoln Bar Assn., Nebr. Bar Assn., Newcomer Soc. U.S. Republican. Methodist. Club: Country Club of Lincoln. Lodge: Masons, Scottish Rite (33 degree). Home: 7441 N Hampton Rd Lincoln NE 68506-1633 Office: First Fed Lincoln 1235 N St Lincoln NE 68508-2008

LUNDSTROM, MARJIE, newspaper editor. Grad., U. Nebr. Columnist, editor, nat. corr. The Denver Post, 1981-89; with The Sacramento Bee, 1989-90, 91—; nat. corr. Gannett News Svc., Washington, 1990-91. Recipient Pulitzer Prize for nat. reporting, 1991. Office: The Sacramento Bee 2100 Q St PO Box 15779 Sacramento CA 95852

LUNDY, JOSEPH E., lawyer; b. Phila., Dec. 30, 1942; s. Martin L. and Adele E. (Zion) L.; m. Bonnie Verbit, Aug. 30, 1966; children: Seth Harris, Nancy Elizabeth. BS in Econs., U. Pa., 1965; JD, Temple U., 1968; LLM in Taxation, N.Y. U., 1969. Bar: Fla. 1968, Pa. 1969. Assoc. MacCoy, Evans & Lewis, Phila., 1969-73, ptnr., 1974-76; ptnr. Montgomery, McCracken, Walker & Rhodes, Phila., 1976-88, Ballard, Spahr, Andrews & Ingersoll, Phila., 1988—; adj. prof. law Temple U., 1974—. Editor-in-Chief Jour. Taxation of Exempt Orgns. Trustee Pa. Coll. Podiatric Medicine, Phila.; assoc. trustee U. Pa., Phila.; bd. overseers U. Pa. Univ. Mus., Phila. Fellow Am. Coll. Tax Counsel; mem. ABA (exempt orgn. com., com. govt. sub-coms.), Am. Acad. Hosp. Attys., Phila. Bar Assn. (vice chair tax sect. 1988-90, chair 1990-92). Office: Ballard Spahr Andrews & Ingersoll 1735 Market St Ste 51 Philadelphia PA 19103-7501

LUNDY, J(OSEPH) EDWARD, retired automobile company executive; b. Iowa, Jan. 6, 1915; s. Vern E. and Mary L. (Chambers) L. B.A., State U. Iowa, 1936. Fellow Princeton U., 1936-39, mem. econs. faculty, 1940-42, beginning as planning ofcl.; with Ford Motor Co., Dearborn, Mich., 1946-85, successively dir. fin. planning and analysis, gen. asst. contr., 1946-57, treas., 1957-61, v.p., contr., 1961-62, v.p. fin., 1962-67, exec. v.p., 1967-79, dir. and vice-chmn. fin. com., 1979-85; dir. research and analysis Office Statis. Control, Hdqrs. USAAF, 1945. Served from pvt. to maj. USAAF, 1943-45. Decorated Legion of Merit. Mem. Phi Beta Kappa, Delta Upsilon. Roman Catholic. Clubs: Detroit Princeton, Detroit. Home: 7 Brookwood Ln Dearborn MI 48120-1302

LUNDY, JOSEPH R., lawyer; b. Chgo., Jan. 21, 1940; s. Francis Lorain and Alice (Whitcomb) L. BA, Princeton U., 1962; JD, George Washington U., 1970. Bar: D.C. 1970, Ill. 1971, U.S. Supreme Ct. 1978. Legis. asst. to U.S. Congressman Abner J. Mikva, Washington, 1969-70; assoc. atty. Schiff Hardin & Waite, Chgo., 1971-73, 76-79; state rep. Ill. Gen. Assembly, Springfield, 1973-77; ptnr. Schiff Hardin & Waite, 1980—; adj. prof. Sch. of Law Northwestern U., 1994—. Commr. Ill. Commn. Uniform State Laws, 1976-79; dir. Legal Assistance Found. Chgo., 1980-83; mem. Gov.'s Commn. Administrv. Rules, Chgo., 1977-84. Mem. Chgo. Bar Assn. (chmn. antitrust com. 1983-84), Chgo. Coun. Lawyers (v.p. 1977-78, bd. govs. 1975-81), Am. Judicature Soc. Avocations: tennis, opera, piano, travel, reading. Office: Schiff Hardin & Waite 7200 Sears Tower Chicago IL 60606

LUNDY, MARY ANN WEESE, religious organization administrator. Dir. nat. bd. Nat. Student YWCA of USA, N.Y.C., 1982-87; dir. women's ministry unit Presbyn. Ch. (USA), Louisville, 1987-93, assoc. dir. gen. assembly, 1994; vis. scholar Hartford Sem., 1994—. Office: Presbyterian Church 100 Witherspoon St Louisville KY 40202-1396

LUNDY, ROLAND, publishing executive; b. 1950. Grad., Baylor U., 1972. With Word Inc., Irving, Tex., 1972—, now pres.

LUNDY, SHERMAN PERRY, secondary school educator; b. Kansas City, Mo., July 26, 1939; s. Loren F. and O. Metta (Brown) L.; m. Beverly J., Feb. 25, 1960; children: Paul, Carolyn. BA, U. Okla., 1963; MA, So. Meth. U., 1966; EdS, U. Iowa, 1975. Cert. tchr., Iowa. Tchr. Platte Canyon High Sch., Bailey, Colo., 1964-65, Lone Grove (Okla.) High Sch., 1966-68, Ardmore (Okla.) High Sch., 1968-69; tchr., sci. dept. chair Burlington (Iowa) High Sch., 1969—; geologist Basic Materials Corp., Waterloo, Iowa, 1983—, Raid Quarries, Burlington, 1975-80. Contbr. articles to profl. jours.; author curriculum guide: Environmental Activities, 1975. Mem., commr. Regional Solid Waste Commn., Des Moines County, 1990—; mem., pres. Conservation Bd., Des Moines County, 1978-88; bd. dirs. Iowa Conservation Bd. Assn., 1984-85; mem. Civil Rights Commn., City of Burlington, 1970-76. With USMC, 1960-64. Recipient Silver Beaver Boy Scouts Am., 1975, Service Recognition, Des Moines County Conservation Bd., 1988, Project ESTEEM agt., Harvard/Smithsonian, 1992. Mem. Geol. Soc. Am. (North Cen. edn. com. 1989—), Iowa Acad. Sci. (edn. com. 1990-91, chair earth sci. tchrs. sect. 1993-94, exec. bd. 1992-94), Nat. Assn. Geology Tchrs. (Outstanding Earth Sci. Tchr. 1992, v.p. ctrl. sect. 1994-95), Soc. Econ. and Sedimentary Geology, Geol. Soc. Iowa, Am. Chem. Soc., Unitarian Fellowship, Sons of Confederate Vets., SE Iowa Civil War Round Table (chair 1992-94). Unitarian. Avocations: civil war, stamp collecting, fossil collecting. Home: RR 1 Burlington IA 52601-9801

LUNDY, VICTOR ALFRED, architect, educator; b. N.Y.C., Feb. 1, 1923; s. Alfred Henry and Rachel Lundy; m. Shirley Corwin, 1947 (div. 1959); children: Christopher Mark, Jennifer Alison; m. Anstis Manton Burwell, Sept. 19, 1960; 1 child, Nicholas Burwell. BArch, Harvard U., 1947, MArch, 1948. Registered architect, Tex., N.Y., Calif. Pvt. practice architecture Sarasota, Fla., 1951-59, N.Y.C., 1960-75; prin. Victor A. Lundy & Assocs., Inc., Houston, 1976-84; design. prin., v.p. HKS Inc., Dallas, 1984—; vis. prof. Grad. Sch. Design, Harvard U., Sch. Architecture, Yale U., Columbia U., U. Calif., Berkeley, Calif. Poly. State U. San Luis Obispo, U. Houston, U. Rome, others; U.S. specialist-architect in U.S.I.A. exhibit, USSR, 1965. Responsible for design St. Paul's Luth. Ch., Sarasota, 1959, new sanctuary, 1970, 1st Unitarian Ch. of Fairfield County, Westport, Conn., 1961, 1st Unitarian Congl. Soc., Hartford, Conn., 1964, Ch. of Resurrection, East Harlem Protestant Parish, N.Y.C., 1966, exhbn. bldg. and exhibit for AEC in S.Am. (Buenos Aires, Rio de Janeiro, Bogota, Santiago), 1967 (Silver medal for exhbn. Archtl. League N.Y. 1965), recreation shelters for Nat. Mus. History and tech., Smithsonian Instn., Washington, 1967, U.S. States Tax Ct. bldg. and pla., Washington, 1976, U.S. Embassy, Colombo, Sri Lanka, for Office of Fgn. Bldgs., Dept. State, 1983 (U.S. Presdl. Design Awards Program 1988, Fed. Design Achievement award), Austin Centre-Omni Hotel, Austin, Tex., 1984, One Congress Pla., Austin, Tex., 1984, Walnut Glen Tower, Dallas, 1985, Mack Ctr. II, Tampa, Fla., 1990, Greyhound Corp. Ctr., Phoenix, 1991, GTE Telephone Ops. World Hdqrs., Irving, Tex., 1991, others; archtl. work represented in Berlin Internat. Archtl. Exposition, 1957, Sao Paulo Internat. Biennial Exposition, 1957, 5th Congress Union Internat. Des Architectes, Moscow, 1958, Expo '70 Exhbn., Osaka, Japan, 1970, travelling exhbn. of architecture in S.Am. Sgt. inf. U.S. Army, 1943-46, ETO. Decorated Purple Heart; recipient Gold medal award Buenos Aires Sesquicentennial Internat. Exhbn., 1960, Gold medal award Buenos Aires Sesquicentennial Internt.Exhbn., 1960; Silver medal Archtl. League N.Y., 1965; Charles Hayden Meml. Scholastic scholar, 1939-43, Edward H. Kendall scholar Harvard U., 1947-48, Rotch travelling scholar Boston Soc. Architects, 1948-50; travelling fellow Harvard U., 1948-50; Dept. State grantee, 1965. Fellow AIA. Avocations: painting, sculpture. Home: 701 Mulberry Ln Bellaire TX 77401-3805 Office: HKS Inc 1111 Pla of the Americas N Ste LB 307 Dallas TX 75201

LUNDY, WALKER, newspaper editor; b. St. Petersburg, Fla.; m. Saralyn Lundy; 2 children. BSJ, U. Fla. Reporter Atlanta Jour.-Constitution; reporter, city editor Detroit Free Press; mng. editor, exec. editor Tallahassee Democrat; mng. editor Ft. Worth Star-Telegram; editor Arkansas Gazette, Little Rock; gen. editor, sr. v.p. St. Paul Pioneer Press, 1990—, exec. editor, sr. v.p., 1990—. Office: Northwest Publs Inc 345 Cedar St Saint Paul MN 55101-1014

LUNEV, ALEKSANDR (SASHA), dancer; b. Leningrad, 1965. Grad., Choreographic Inst., 1983. Dancer Kirov, 1983; prin. dancer Boston Ballet; now premiere danseur, artistic advisor Tulsa Ballet Theatre, Tulsa, OK. Performed throughout the USSR, France, Italy, Germany, U.S., Can. and Japan; tour with Kirov to London and Paris; major dance roles include Giselle, Swan Lake, Sleeping Beauty, Chopiniana, La Sylphide, Les Sylphides, Fountain of Bakchisarai, Corsaire; debut in the U.S. with the Boston Ballet. Office: Tulsa Ballet Theatre 4512 S Peoria Ave Tulsa OK 74105-4563

LUNGER, IRVIN EUGENE, university president emeritus, clergyman; b. Williamsport, Pa., June 28, 1912; s. George Lee and Mabel Clara (Griggs) L.; m. Eleanor Jeanne Zink, Feb. 10, 1939 (dec. Aug. 1955); children: Susan Ann (Mrs. Lee C. Brown) (dec.), Kathryn Elizabeth (Mrs. Bob Willis) (dec.); m. Kay Walsh Ritchey, June 19, 1957; foster son, Owsley Ritchey. A.B. magna cum laude, Bethany Coll., 1934, Litt.D. (hon.), 1959; B.D., U. Chgo., 1935, A.M., 1936, Ph.D., 1938; postgrad., U. Munich, Germany, 1936-37; L.H.D. (hon.), U. Ala., 1965, Transylvania U., 1980; Litt.D. (hon.), Eastern Ky. U., 1974. Ordained to ministry Disciples of Christ Ch., 1932; minister Christian Ch., Morristown, 1930-34, University Ch. Disciples of Christ, Chgo., 1939-55; prof. religion, dean Morrison Chapel, Transylvania U., Lexington, Ky., 1955-56, acad. dean, 1956-57, pres., 1957-76, pres. emeritus, 1976—, interim pres., 1981-82; dir., pres., Bd. Higher Edn., Disciples of Christ, 1963-64; interim minister Christian Ch., Frankfort, Ky., 1980, Christian Ch., Danville, Ky., 1985. Contbr. to: Faith of the Free, 1940. Pres. bd. dirs. Henry Clay Found., Lexington, 1968-87 ; chmn. exec. com. Ky. Ind. Coll. Found., 1967-68, Ky. chmn. Rhodes Scholarship Selection Com., 1960-67; mem. Gov.'s Commn. Higher Edn., Ky., 1964-69; chmn. bd. dirs. Living Arts and Sci. Center, Inc., 1968-69; bd. dirs. Ednl. Adv. and Reference Corp., N.Y.C; bd. dirs. United Fund, 1959-65, pres., 1962-64; chmn. bd. dirs. Lexington Pub. Library, 1966-70; bd. dirs. Fund for Advancement of Edn. and Research, U. Ky. Med. Center, 1974-87 . Named Ky. col., 1959. Mem. Council Ind. Ky. Colls. and Univs. (pres. 1966, 68), Conf. Ch.-Related Colls. of South (pres. 1970), Omicron Delta Kappa, Tau Kappa Alpha, Beta Theta Pi. Democrat. Home: 461 Herrington Woods Harrodsburg KY 40330-9717

LUNGREN, DANIEL EDWARD, state attorney general; b. Long Beach, Calif., Sept. 22, 1946; s. John Charles and Lorain Kathleen (Youngberg) L.; m. Barbara Kolls, Aug. 2, 1969; children: Jeffrey Edward, Kelly Christine, Kathleen Marie. A.B. cum laude, Notre Dame U., 1968; postgrad., U. So. Calif. Law Sch., 1968-69; J.D., Georgetown U., 1971. Bar: Calif. 1972. Staff asst. Sen. George Murphy, Sen. William Brock, 1969-71; spl. asst. to co-chmn. Rep. Nat. Com., dir. spl. programs, 1971-72; assoc., selected as ptnr. Ball, Hunt, Hart, Brown & Baerwitz, Long Beach, 1973-78; mem. 96th-97th Congresses from 34th, 98th-100th Congresses from 42d Calif. Dist., 1979-1989, Rep. State Cen. Com. Calif., 1974-89; ptnr. Diepenbrock, Wulff, Plant & Hannegan, Sacramento, 1989-90; atty. gen. State of Calif., Sacramento, 1991—. Bd. dirs. Long Beach chpt. ARC, Boy's Club, 1976-88; committeeman Rep. Nat. Com., Calif., 1988—. Recipient Good Samaritan award Los Angeles Council Mormon Chs., 1976. Republican. Roman Catholic. Office: Office of the Atty Gen 1300 I St Sacramento CA 95814

LUNGSTRUM, JOHN W., federal judge; b. Topeka, Kans., Nov. 2, 1945; s. Jack Edward and Helen Alice (Watson) L.; m. Linda Eileen Ewing, June 21, 1969; children: Justin Matthew, Jordan Elizabeth, Alison Paige. BA magna cum laude, Yale Coll., 1967; JD, U. Kans., 1970. Bar: Kans. 1970, Calif. 1970, U.S. Dist. Ct. (ctrl. dist.) Calif., U.S. Ct. Appeals (10th crct.). Assoc. Latham & Watkins, L.A., 1970-71; ptnr. Stevens, Brand, Lungstrum, Golden & Winter, Lawrence, Kans., 1972-91; U.S. Dist. judge Dist. of Kans., Kansas City, Kans., 1991—; lectr. law U. Kans. Law Sch., 1973—; mem. faculty Kans. Bar Assn. Coll. Advocacy , Trial Tactics and Techniques Inst., 1983-86; chmn. Douglas County Rep. Ctrl. Com., 1975-81; mem. Rep. State Com.; del. State Rep. Convention, 1968, 76, 80. Chmn. bd. dirs. Lawrence C. of C., 1990-91; pres. Lawrence United Fund, 1979; pres. Independence Days Lawrence, Inc., 1984, 85, Seem-to-be-Players, Inc., Lawrence Rotary Club, 1978-79; bd. dirs. Lawrence Soc. Chamber Music, Swarthout Soc. (corp. fund-raising chmn.); mem. Lawrence Art Commn., Williams Scholarship Fund, Lawrence League Women Voters, Douglas County Hist. Soc.; bd. trustees, stewardship chmn. Plymouth Congl. Ch.; pres. Lawrence Round Ball Club; coach Lawrence Summertime Basketball; Vice chmn. U. Kans. Disciplinary Bd.; bd. govs. Kans Sch. Religion; bd. dirs. Kans. Day Club, 1980, 81. National Merit scholar, Yale Nat. scholar. Fellow Am. Bar Found.; mem. ABA (past mem. litigation and ins. sect.), Douglas County Bar Assn., Johnson County Bar Assn., Wyandotte County Bar Assn., Kans. Bar Assn. (vice chair legislative com., subcom. litigation, mem. continuing legal edn. com.), U Kans. Alumni Assn. (life), Phi Beta Kappa, Phi Gamma Delta, Phi Delta Phi. Avocations: basketball, hiking, skiing. Office: US Courthouse 500 State Ave Kansas City KS 66101*

LUNIN, JOSEPH, lawyer; b. Jersey City, Oct. 30, 1940; s. Benjamin Lunin and Ethel Ranz; m. Diana Sussman, Aug. 13, 1967; children: Jennifer, Benjamin. BA, Rutgers U., 1963, LLB, 1966; LLM, NYU, 1973. Bar: N.J. 1966. Legal sec. to judge appellate div. N.J. Superior Ct., 1966-67; assoc. Pitney, Hardin, Kipp & Szuch, Morristown, N.J., 1970-73, ptnr., 1974—; adj. faculty Rutgers U. Grad. Sch. Bus., Newark, 1972-77, adj. prof. Law Sch., 1988-93; cons. N.J. Corp. Law Revision Commn., 1970-73. Author: Forms for Practice Under the New Jersey Nonprofit Corporation Act, 1983, rev. edit., 1991, Forms for Practice Under the New Jersey Business Corporation Act, 1991; editor: Rutgers Law Rev., 1965-66, Organization and Sale of Small Business, 1968-70. Served to capt. U.S. Army, 1968-70, Vietnam, 1969. Mem. ABA, N.J. Bar Assn. (chmn. nonprofit law revision com. 1975—, chmn. corp. and bus. law sect. 1982-84), Morristown Club. Unitarian. Office: Pitney Hardin Kipp & Szuch PO Box 1945 Park Ave at Morris County Morristown NJ 07962-1945

LUNN, JANET LOUISE SWOBODA, writer; b. Dallas, Dec. 28, 1928; naturalized Can. citizen, 1950; m. Richard Lunn, 1950; children: Eric, Jeffrey, Alexander, Katherine, John. Student, Queen's U., Kingston, Ont., Can., 1947-50; LLD (hon.), Queen's U., 1992; hon. diploma, Loyalist Coll. Applied Arts, 1993. Author: (with Richard Lunn) The County, 1967, Double Spell, 1968, Larger Than Life, 1979, The Twelve Dancing Princesses, 1979 (IODE Children's Book award 1979, one of 10 best children's Can. Libr. Assn.), The Root Cellar, 1981 (Ruth Schwartz Children's Book of Yr. 1981, Children's Book of Yr., Can. Libr. Assn. 1982, Tchr.'s Choice for 1983, Internat. Bd. of Books for Young People honors list 1984, Am. Nat. Coun. Tchrs. English, Young Reader medal 1988, Reviewers' Choice Book-list), Shadow in Hawthorn Bay, 1986 (Honor list Internat. Bd. Books for Young People 1986, Young Adult Book of Yr. award Sask. Libr. Assn. 1986, Book of Yr. IDOE 1986, Can. Libr. Assn. Children's Lit. award, Can. Coun. Children's Book of Yr., Book of Yr. Internat. Children's Libr. Munich, Germany 1986), Amos's Sweater, 1988 (Ruth Schwartz award Can. Booksellers' Assn. 1989), Duck Cake for Sale, 1989, One Hundred Shining Candles: A Christmas Story, 1990, (with Christopher Moore) The Story of Canada, 1992 (Info. Book award Children's Lit. Round Tables fo Can. 1993, Mr. Christie Book award 1993, IODE 1993); editor: The Unseen, 1994. Recipient Vicki Metcalk award for body of work for children Can. Author's Assn., 1981. Mem. Can. Children's Book Ctr. (bd. dirs. 1989, v.p. 1990); IBBY Can. (bd. dirs. 1989), Writer's Union of Can. (2d vice chair 1979-80, 1st vice chair 1983-84, chair 1984-85), Can. Soc. Children's Authors, Illustrators and Performers, PEN Internat. Home and Office: RR #2, Hillier, ON Canada K0K 2J0

LUNN, JUDITH SASKA, newspaper editor, journalist; b. Budapest, Hungary, July 4, 1935; came to U.S., 1939; d. Laszlo and Mildred Amalia (Friedman) S.; m. Robert Charles Lunn, June 15, 1957; children: Susan Breedlove, Linda. BFA, RISD, 1956. Designer Jonathan Logan and Jack Horowitz, N.Y.C., 1955-57; copy writer Sanger's, Titche's, Dallas, 1958-66; reporter Fashion Week, Dallas and L.A., 1967-68; fashion and style editor Houston Post, 1972-82, fashion and H editor, 1983—; freelance Houston publs., 1982-83; lectr. Houston C.C., clubs, orgns., Houston, 1972—. Appeared Good Morning Houston TV talk show, 1982-92. Judge Textile and Costume Inst. Houston Mus. Fine Arts, 1991-94. Recipient Fashion Reporter's award, 1973, Lulu award Men's Fashion Assn. 1979, 80 (2), 82 (2), Dallas Market Ctr. 20th Ann. Editorial award/home furnishings, 1980, Penney-Mo. Journalism award U. Mo. Sch. Journalism, 1974, 76, Atrium award U. Ga. Coll. Journalism & Mass. Comm./Atlanta Apparel Mart, 1980, 85, 87, 88, 92, George A. Hough 3d award for Overall Superiority in Reporting on Apparel Industry, 1992. Mem. Fashion Group Internat. of Houston (chmn. bazaar 1978). Avocations: photography, travel writing, cooking, decorating. Home: 711 William St Ste 402 Houston TX 77002-1176

LUNN, REBECCA JO, nursing administrator; b. Warren, Pa., Nov. 18, 1949; d. Robert Arthur and Joyce Arlene (Winand) L.; divorced; 1 child, Joyce Anne Odom. Diploma in nursing, Ohio Valley Gen. Hosp., 1970. RN, Pa. Staff nurse Washington (Pa.) Hosp., 1970-74; head nurse Onslow Meml. Hosp., Jacksonville, N.C., 1976-77; charge nurse Portsmouth (Va.) Gen. Hosp., 1978-80; surg. asst. pvt. practice surgeon's office Milford, Conn., 1981-82; physicians' asst. pvt. practice pediatrics office Milford, 1982-87; charge nurse McMurray (Pa.) Manor Nursing Home, 1987-88; charge nurse Kade Nursing Home, Washington, 1988-90, dir. nursing, 1993-95; head trauma unit team leader Meadowlands Health Care Ctr., 1990-91; unit mgr. Washington County Health Ctr., 1991-93; physician asst. free pap test clinics, Washington, 1973-74. Author: (poems) Rainbows and Dreams, 1992, Echoes of a Legacy, 1993; contbr. poems to profl. publs. (Golden Poet award 1991, Internat. Poet Soc. of Poetry 1992, POetry Acad. award 1993). Advisor Washington County Youth Against Cancer program, 1973-74; past worthy advisor Rainbow Girls, Claysville, Pa., 1970; Miss Hope, Am. Cancer Soc., Washington, 1973-74, mem. pub. edn. com., speaker, 1973-74, mem. exec. bd., Charleroi, Pa., 1973-74. Lt. Nurse Corp USN, 1974-76. Avocations: writing, oil painting, piano, reading. Home: 1040 Michigan Ave Washington PA 15301-1842

LUNSFORD, JULIUS R(ODGERS), JR., lawyer; b. Weston, Ga., Jan. 22, 1915; s. Julius Rodgers and Mary (Robinson) L.; m. Mary Eugenia Vann, Aug. 24, 1941; children: J. Rodgers III, Clark V., Alan H. BA, Mercer U., 1935; JD, U. Ga., 1936. Bar: Ga. 1936, U.S. Ct. Custons and Patent Appeals 1953-82, U.S. Ct. Mil. Appeals 1955, U.S. Supreme Ct. 1955, U.S. Ct. Appeals (5th cir.) 1975, D.C. 1975, U.S. Ct. Appeals (11th cir.) 1981, U.S. Ct. Appeals for Fed. Cir. 1982. With legal dept. The Coca-Cola Co., 1936-75; asst. v.p., mgr. trademarks and unfair competition dept., 1972-75; ptnr. Beveridge, DeGrandi, Kline & Lunsford, Atlanta, 1975-79; sr. ptnr. Hurt, Richardson, Garner, Todd & Cadenhead, Atlanta, 1980-87; ptnr. Jones, Askew & Lunsford, Atlanta, 1987-92; cons., presenter expert testimony, 1992—; mem. law faculty Mercer U. Law Sch. 1990-95; lectr. in field. Contbr. numerous articles to profl. jours.; contbg. author: The Trademark Reporter, 1949—. Trustee, bd. dirs. Mercer U., Macon, Ga., 1988-93. Capt. USNR, 1942-75. Mem. ABA (chmn. state trademark rights and statues com. 1968-69), U.S. Trademark Assn. (pres. 1971-72, bd. dirs. 1969-66, 67-72, 74-77), Am. Intellectual Property Law Assn., Corp. Bar Assn., Atlanta Bar Assn., Lawyers Club Atlanta, Kiwanis, Phi Delta Phi, Kappa Alpha. Democrat. Baptist. Avocations: sports fan and spectator. Home: 4187 Conway Valley Rd NW Atlanta GA 30327-3607

LUNT, HARRY EDWARD, metallurgist, consultant; b. N.Y.C., Apr. 30, 1924; m. Carmela (Tamburri) Lunt, June 19, 1950; children: Teresa, Alan, Diana, Linda, Steven. AB, Syracuse U., 1948, postgrad., 1948-50; MS, Iowa State U., 1953. Registered profl. engr., Del., Calif. Rsch. asst. Ames (Iowa) Lab., U.S. AEC, 1950-53; devel. metallurgist U.S. Steel Corp. Applied Rsch. Labs., Monroeville and Homestead, Pa., 1953-63; sr. engr. Westinghouse Rsch. Labs., Churchill, Pa., 1963-66; corp. metallurgist Worthington Corp., Harrison, N.J., 1967-74; corp. cons. engr. Burns & Roe Enterprises, Inc., Oradell, N.J., 1974-94; cons. metallurgist Mendham, N.J., 1995—; mem. tech. adv. com. Materials Properties Coun., N.Y.C., 1980—. Author tech. papers and conf. proceedings in field. Fellow ASTM (chmn. com. on steel, stainless steel and related alloys 1986-92, bd. dirs. 1990-92, Merit award 1981), Standards Engring. Soc. (Robert J. Painter Meml. award 1989), Am. Soc. Metals (life; chmn. N.J. chpt. 1976-77); mem. Am. Welding Soc., Nat. Assn. Corrosion Engrs. (accredited corrosion specialist), Phi Beta Kappa. Home and Office: 13 Brockden Dr Mendham NJ 07945-3010

LUNT, HORACE GRAY, linguist, educator; b. Colorado Springs, Colo., Sept. 12, 1918; s. Horace Fletcher and Irene (Jewett) L.; m. Sally Herman, June 2, 1963; children: Elizabeth, Catherine. A.B., Harvard U., 1941; M.A., U. Calif., Berkeley, 1942; postgrad., Charles U., Prague, Czechoslovakia, 1946-47; Ph.D. (Rockefeller fellow), Columbia U., 1950. Lectr. in Serbo-Croatian Columbia U., 1948-49; asst. prof. Slavic langs. and lit. Harvard U., 1949-54, asso. prof., 1954-60, prof., 1960—, Samuel H. Cross prof. Slavic langs. and lits., 1965-89, Samuel H. Cross prof. Slavic langs. and lits., emeritus, 1989—, chmn. dept. Slavic langs. and lits., 1959-73, 75-76, 82-83; chmn. Slavic and East European Lang. and Area Ctr., 1983-89; mem. exec. com. Russian Rsch. Ctr., 1970-91, fellow, 1991—; mem. exec. com. Harvard Ukrainian Research Inst., 1974-91, fellow, 1991—. Author: Grammar of the Macedonian Literary Language, 1952, Old Church Slavonic Grammar, 1955, 6th, rev. edit., 1974, Fundamentals of Russian, 1958, 2d rev. edit., 1968, Progressive Palatalization of Common Slavic, 1981; editor: Harvard Slavic Studies, 1953-70. Served with U.S. Army, 1942-45. Guggenheim fellow, 1960-61. Mem. Macedonian Acad. Arts and Scis. (corr.). Home: 75 Bradford Rd Weston MA 02193-2142 Office: Harvard U Boylston 301 Cambridge MA 02138

LUNT, JACK, lawyer; b. Hartford, Conn., Oct. 19, 1944. BS magna cum laude, U. Utah, 1966, JD, 1969. Bar: Utah 1969. Assoc. Jones, Waldo, Holbrook & McDonough, Salt Lake City, 1969-73, ptnr., 1974-89; pres., exec. v.p. law and adminstrn. Am. Stores Properties, Inc., Salt Lake City, 1989-93; sr. v.p., asst. gen. counsel, corp. sec. Am. Stores Co., Salt Lake City, 1993—. Mem. ABA, Salt Lake County Bar Assn., Utah Bar Assn. Office: Am Stores Co 709 E South Temple Salt Lake City UT 84102-1205

LUNT, JENNIFER LEE, lawyer; b. Big Springs, Tex., July 18, 1965; d. John Daleton and Karen Adele (Olson) L. BS, Auburn U., 1986; JD, U. Ala., 1989, MLS, 1990. Bar: Ala. 1989, U.S. Ct. Appeals (11th cir.) 1990, U.S. Dist. Ct. (mid. dist.) Ala. 1991, U.S. Dist. Ct. (no. dist.) Ala. 1993. Rsch. asst. Supreme Ct. Ala., Tuscaloosa, 1988-90; cons. Gorham, Waldrep, Stewart, Kendrick & Bryant P.C., Birmingham, 1990; pvt. practice Montgomery, Ala., 1991—; legal asst. adv. bd. Auburn U., Montgomery, 1994—. Rsch. editor: Law and Psychology Rev., 1988-89. Mem. ABA (Young Lawyers Divsn. com. on criminal and juvenile justice 1995—), Ala. State Bar (task force on small firms and solo practitioners 1995—), Montgomery County Bar Assn. (com. on continuing legal edn. 1995—). Office: 207 Montgomery St Ste 224 Montgomery AL 36104-3528

LUOMA, GARY A., accounting educator; b. Pequaming, Mich., June 14, 1936; s. Otto Samuel and Ruth Eleanor (Braeger) L.; m. Evelyn Marie Gervais, July 7, 1956; children: Gary Jr., Valerie, Steven, Patricia. BA, Northern Mich. U., 1958; MA, Western Mich. U., 1959; D of Bus. Adminstrn., Washington U. St. Louis, 1966. CPA, CMA. Lectr., instr., asst. to dean Washington U., St. Louis, 1959-64; asst. prof., assoc. prof., prof., dir. BBA program Emory U., Atlanta, 1964-77; dir. sch. acctg., prof. Ga. State U., Atlanta, 1977-86, U. S.C., Columbia, 1986—; cons. in field. Author: Financial Aspects of Contract Negotiation and Administration, 1972, Fund Accounting for Colleges and Universities, 1973, Accounting and Record Keeping for Small Business, 1982, Cases on Business Ethics, 1988; contbr. articles to profl. jours. With USNR, 1954-58. Office: U SC Coll Bus Adminstrn Columbia SC 29208

LUONGO, C. PAUL, public relations executive; b. Winchester, Mass., Dec. 31, 1930; s. Carmine and Carmela (Gilberti) L. Grad., Cambridge Sch. Radio-TV, 1955; diploma, Bentley Coll., 1951; BSBA, Suffolk U., 1955; MBA, Babson Coll., 1956; AAS (hon.), Grahm Jr. Coll., 1970. Jr. exec. Raytheon Co., Lexington, Mass., 1956-59; account exec. Young & Rubicam, Inc., 1959-62; v.p. Copley Advt. Agy., Boston, 1962-64; pres. C. Paul Luongo Co., Boston, 1964—. Guest appearances include: (TV programs) Today Show, NBC-TV, 1984-89, Tomorrow Show, NBC-TV; TV-radio programs, Can.; author: America's Best!, 1980; contbr. syndicated newspaper-mag. features to Pub. Rels. Today; contbg. editor Travel Smart, N.Y., mo. newsletter. Pub. rels. dir. Anthony Spinazzola Meml. Scholarship Found., Boston U., 1986—; vol. U.S.S. Constn. Mus., Boston, Sta. WGBH-TV, Boston, TV Auctions, 1991—; mem. Boston Ctr. for Internat. Visitors, French Libr., Boston, Mus. Fine Arts, Black Ships Festival, Inc., Newport, R.I.; chmn. centennial ba.. Belcourt Castle, Newport, 1994. With AUS, 1952-54. Mem. Bostonian Soc., Boston Stockbrokers Club, Newcomen Soc. N.Am., Internat. Food, Wine and Travel Writers Assn., Am. Inst. Wine and Food, Japan-Am. Soc. R.I., Neighborhood Assn. of Back Bay, Inc., Back Bay Assn., Suffolk U. Gen. Alumni Assn. (bd. dirs. 1994—). Home: Copley Square Boston MA 02116 Office: 441 Stuart St Boston MA 02116-5019 *I believe in the work ethic, integrity and the maximum utilization of time for work and recreational activities. I loathe prejudice in any form, dishonesty and indolent people.*

LUPBERGER, EDWIN ADOLPH, utility executive; b. Atlanta, June 5, 1936; s. Adolph and Esma L.; m. Mary Jane McAlister Redmon, Jan. 6, 1989; children by previous marriage: David Todd, Edward Townsend. A.B. in Econs, Davidson (N.C.) Coll., 1958; M.B.A., Emory U., 1963. Asst. v.p. Southern Co. Services, Inc., Atlanta, 1963-69; v.p., treas. Gulf Power Co., Pensacola, Fla., 1969-77; sr. v.p. fin. Indpls. Power & Light Co., 1977-79; sr. v.p., chief fin. officer Middle South Utilities, Inc., New Orleans, 1979-85; chmn., CEO Entergy Corp., New Orleans, 1985—. Ensign USN, 1960. Mem. Edison Electric Inst., Univ. Club, Met. Club. Presbyterian. *

LUPERT, LESLIE ALLAN, lawyer; b. Syracuse, N.Y., May 24, 1946; s. Reuben and Miriam (Kaufman) L.; m. Roberta Gail Fellner, May 19, 1968; children: Jocelyn, Rachel, Susannah. BA, U. Buffalo, 1967; JD, Columbia U., 1971. Bar: N.Y. 1971. Ptnr. Orans Elsen & Lupert, N.Y.C., 1971—. Contbr. articles to profl. jours. Mem. ABA, N.Y. State Bar Assn. (trial lawyers sect.), Assn. of Bar of City of N.Y. (com. fed. legislation 1977-80, profl. and jud. ethics com. 1983-86, com. on fed. cts. 1986-89, 95—), Phi Beta Kappa. Office: Orans Elsen & Lupert 1 Rockefeller Plz New York NY 10020

LUPIENT, JAMES, automotive executive; b. 1934. With Iten Chevrolet, Mpls., 1964-69; pres. Lupient Oldsmobile Co., Inc., Mpls., 1969—; CEO Lupient Automotive Group, Mpls. Office: Lupient Automotive Group 750 Pennsylvania AVe Minneapolis MN 55246-2247*

LUPIN, ELLIS RALPH, physician, lawyer, coroner; b. New Orleans, Apr. 1, 1931; s. Albert I. and Yetta (Linneck) L.; m. Freda Merlin, Mar. 18, 1951; 1 child, Jay Stephen. BS in Pharmacy, Loyola U., New Orleans, 1952, PharmD, 1983; JD, Loyola U. South, New Orleans, 1988; MD, La. State U., 1956. Diplomate Am. Bd. Ob-Gyn. Bar: La. Practice medicine specializing in ob-gyn. Zoller, Lupin, Levinson, Cohen & Castillo, New Orleans, 1962—; atty. Middleberg, Riddle & Gianna; chief dep. coroner City of New Orleans, 1974-86; pvt. med.-legal practice; cons. Tenet Corp., E.R. Lupin, Ltd., 1984—; med. legal cons. Surgeon Gen., U.S. Army; mem. vis. com. Loyola Sch. Law. Bd. dirs. ARC, New Orleans, 1965-90, St. Charles Gen. Hosp., 1972-92, U. New Orleans Found., 1990-92, City of New Orleans of Vieux Carre Commn., 1995—; trustee New Orleans Symphony, 1982-90, Lupin Found., 1980—, Children's Hosp. of New Orleans, 1984—, Jewish Welfare Fedn. of New Orleans, 1972, 80, 84, Jewish Family and Children Svcs., 1972-76, New Orleans Mus. Art, 1993—; chmn. bd. dirs. La. State Mus., 1984-88, 92—; chmn. Upper Pontabla Commn., 1982-90; mem. adv. bd. Ladies Luekemia League, 1980—, Sophie Gumbel Guild, 1980—, others. With USAF, 1958-60, col. La. N.G. Fellow Am. Coll. Legal Medicine; mem. Jefferson Parish Med. So., Gyecology Laser So., Royal Soc. Medicine, New Orleans Ob-Gyn Soc., La. State Bar Assn. Jewish. Lodge: Masons. Avocation: collecting antiques. Home: 1021 Chartres St New Orleans LA 70116-3239 Office: Zoller Lupin Levinson Cohen & Castillo 515 Westbank Expy Gretna LA 70053-5644

LUPKE, DUANE EUGENE, insurance company executive; b. Ft. Wayne, Ind., July 17, 1930; s. Walter Herman and Lucy (Bell) L.; married, Sept. 14, 1957; children: Diane Carol, Mark Duane, David Burgess, Andrea Lucy. BS, Ind. U., 1952. CPCU. With Lupke Rice Clancy Assocs., Ft. Wayne, Ind., 1954—, pres., 1969—. Bd. dirs. Concordia Ednl. Found., Ft. Wayne; dir., treas. Luth. Health Found. Ind., 1995. Lt. U.S. Army, 1952-54. Lutheran. Home: 1407 Hawthorne Rd Fort Wayne IN 46802-4957 Office: Lupke Rice Clancy Assocs PO Box 11309 Fort Wayne IN 46857-1309

LUPKIN, STANLEY NEIL, lawyer; b. Bklyn., Mar. 27, 1941; s. David B. and Sylvia (Strassman) L.; m. Anne Rachel Fischler, June 3, 1962; children: Jonathan Daniel, Deborah Eve. BA, Columbia Coll., 1962; LLB, NYU, 1966. Bar: N.Y. 1966, U.S. Dist. Ct. (so. and ea. dists.) N.Y. 1970, U.S. Ct. Appeals (2d cir.) 1970, U.S. Supreme Ct. 1971. Asst. dist. atty., sr. trial atty., chief indictment bur. N.Y. County Dist. Atty.'s Office, N.Y.C., 1966-71; asst. commr. City of N.Y., 1966-71; 1st dep. commr., commr. Dept. Investigation, N.Y.C., 1978-82; ptnr. Litman, Asche, Lupkin, Gioiella & Bassin, N.Y.C., 1982-96; sr. v.p. and deputy gen. counsel Fairfax Group Ltd, New York, 1996—; mem. faculty Nat. Coll. Dist. Attys., Houston, 1974-75, FBI Nat. Acad., Quantico, Va., 1980-82; chmn. com. on criminal justice ops. Assn. of Bar of City of N.Y., 1982-85. Co-author book: Anatomy of A Municipal Franchise: N.Y.C. Bus Shelter Program, 1973-79, 4 vols., 1981. Trustee, counsel Solomon Schechter Sch. of Queens, Flushing, N.Y., 1974—; mem. secondary schs. com. admissions office Columbia Coll., N.Y.C., 1987—. With USAR, 1963-69. Mem. N.Y. State Bar Assn. (chmn. com. on def. 1985—, chmn. com. on prosecution 1977-85, exec. com. criminal justice sect. 1977—, Prosecutor of Yr. 1981), N.Y. State Assn. Criminal Def. Lawyers, Nat. Assn. Criminal Def. Lawyers, N.Y. Criminal Bar Assn., Soc. Columbia Grads. (v.p. 1989—). Avocations: classical music, Talmudic law. Office: Fairfax Group Ltd 505 Park Av New York NY 10022

LUPO, FRANK MICHAEL, architect; b. Buffalo, July 17, 1950; s. Michael and Raffaela (Giardina) L.; m. Mary Evelyn Stockton, May 4, 1985. BArch, U. Cin., 1974; MArch, Yale U., 1983. Registered architect, N.Y., Calif., N.J., Conn. With Studio Works, Los Angeles, 1978-79, Morphosis, Los Angeles, 1979-80, Gwathmey Siegel and Assocs., N.Y.C., 1983-85; ptnr., prin. N.Y. Architects, N.Y.C., 1985-93; prin. Frank Lupo Architect, N.Y.C., 1994-95; sr. designer Skidmore Owings and Merrill, N.Y.C., 1995—; participant Biennale di Venezia, 1985. Recipient Citation Progressive Architecture mag., 1980,82, N.Y.C. Design awards AIA, 1990, 91; William Wirt Wichester Traveling fellow, 1985. Office: Frank Lupo Architects Loft 12B 448 W 37th St New York NY 10018-4017

LUPONE, PATTI, actress; b. Northport, L.I., N.Y., Apr. 21, 1949; d. Orlando Joseph and Angela Louise (Patti) LuP.; m. Matt Johnston; 1 child, Joshua Luke. BFA, The Juilliard Sch., 1972. Off-Broadway prodns. include: The Woods, School for Scandal, The Lower Depths, Stage Directions; appeared in Broadway prodns.: Next Time I'll Sing to You, The Time of Your Life, The Three Sisters, The Robber Bridegroom (Tony award nominee), The Water Engine, The Beggar's Opera, Edward II, The Baker's Wife, 1976, The Woods, 1977, Working, 1978, Catchpenny Twist, 1978, As You Like It, 1982, The Cradle Will Rock, 1983, Stars of Broadway, 1983, Edmond, 1982, Oliver, 1984; star Broadway musicals Evita, 1979 (Best Actress in Musical Tony award 1980), Anything Goes, 1987, Pal Joey, 1995; London prodns. Les Miserables, 1985, Sunset Boulevard, 1993; films include: King of the Gypsies, 1978, 1941, 1979, Fighting Back, 1982, Witness, 1985, Wise Guys, 1986, Driving Miss Daisy, 1989; TV Appearances include: Kitty, The Time of Your Life, Lady Bird in LBJ, 1987, The Water Engine, 1992, Family Prayers, 1993; TV series, Life Goes On, 1989-93. Office: ICM 40 W 57th St New York NY 10019*

LUPU, RADU, pianist; b. Galati, Romania, Nov. 30, 1945; s. Meyer and Ana (Gabor) L. Attended Conservatoire, Moscow, USSR, 1961-69. London debut, 1969, Berlin, 1971, U.S. debut with Cleve. Orch. in N.Y.C., appearances with worldwide maj. orchs., including Berlin Philharmonic, Vienna Philharmonic, Israel Philharmonic, Orch. de Paris, Concertgebouw, N.Y. Philharmonic, Phila. Symphony Orch., Chgo. Symphony Orch., Cleve. Symphony Orch.; recs. include Beethoven cycle with Israel Philharmonic and Zubin Mehta, Schubert Sonatas, Beethoven Sonatas, Mozart Sonatas for Violin and Piano with Szymon Goldberg, Schubert Lieder with Barbara Hendricks, Mozart and Schubert duets and Mozart Concerto for 2 pianos, both with Murray Perahia, Brahms Piano Concerto #1 Mozart and Beethoven Quintets in E Flat. Recipient 1st prize Van Cliburn Internat. Piano Competition, 1966, Enescu Competition, 1967, Leeds Internat. Piano Competition, 1969, Grammy award for Schubert Sonatas D960 and D664, 1996.

LUPULESCU, AUREL PETER, medical educator, researcher, physician; b. Manastiur, Banat, Romania, Jan. 1, 1923; came to U.S., 1967, naturalized, 1973; s. Peter Vichentie and Maria Ann (Dragan) L. MD magna cum laude, Sch. Medicine, Bucharest, Romania, 1950; MS in Endocrinology, U. Bucharest, 1965; PhD in Biology, Faculty of Scis., U. Windsor, Ont., Can. Diplomate Am. Bd. Internal Medicine. Chief Lab. Investigations, Inst. Endocrinology, Bucharest, 1950-67; research assoc. SUNY Downstate Med. Ctr., 1968-69; asst. prof. medicine Wayne State U., 1969-72; assoc. prof., 1973—; vis. prof. Inst. Med. Pathology, Rome, 1967; cons. VA Hosp., Allen Park, Mich., 1971-73. Author: Steroid Hormones, 1958, Advances in Endocrinology and Metabolism, 1962, Experimental Pathophysiology of Thyroid Gland, 1963, Ultrastructure of Thyroid Gland, 1968, Hormones and Carcinogenesis, 1983, Hormones and Vitamins in Cancer Treatment, 1990; reviewer for various sci. jours.; contbr. chpts., numerous articles to profl. publs.; research on hormones and tumor biology; studies regarding role of hormones and vitamins in carcinogenesis. Fellow Fedn. Am. Socs. for Exptl. Biology; mem. Electron Microscopy Soc. Am., Soc. for Investigative Dermatology, N.Y. Acad. Sci., AMA (physician's recognition award 1983, 86), Am. Soc. Cell Biology, Soc. Exptl. Biology and Medicine, AAAS. Republican. Home: 21480 Mahon Dr Southfield MI 48075-7525 Office: Wayne State U Sch Medicine 540 E Canfield St Detroit MI 48201-1928

LURENSKY, MARCIA ADELE, lawyer; b. Newton, Mass., May 4, 1948. BA magna cum laude, Wheaton Coll., 1970; JD, Boston Coll. Law Sch., 1973. Bar: Mass. 1973, D.C. 1990, U.S. Dist. Ct. (we. dist.) Wis. 1978, U.S. Dist. Ct. Mass. 1974, U.S. Ct. Appeals (1st cir.) 1974, U.S. Ct. Appeals (3d cir.) 1982, U.S. Ct. Appeals (4th cir.) 1984, U.S. Ct. Appeals (5th cir.) 1995, U.S. Ct. Appeals (8th cir.) 1985, U.S. Ct. Appeals (9th cir.) 1976, U.S. Ct. Appeals (10th cir.) 1995, U.S. Ct. Appeals (11th cir.) 1982, U.S. Ct. Appeals (fed. cir.) 1989, U.S. Claims Ct. 1989, U.S. Supreme Ct. 1979. Atty. U.S. Dept. Labor, Washington, 1974-90, Fed. Energy Regulatory Commn., U.S. Dept. Energy, Washington, 1990—. Mem. Phi Beta Kappa. Office: Fed Energy Regulatory Commn 888 First St NE Washington DC 20426

LUREY, ALFRED SAUL, lawyer; b. Greenville, S.C., Oct. 17, 1942; s. Meyer and Pearl Sarah (Zaglin) L.; m. Betsy Ann Bennett, June 13, 1982; children: Mollie K., Allison A.; 1 stepchild, Amy E. Startari. AB, Duke U., 1964; LLB, Harvard U., 1967. Bar: Calif. 1967, U.S. Ct. Appeals (4th cir.) 1968, Ga. 1970, U.S. Dist. Ct. (no. dist.) Ga. 1971, U.S. Ct. Claims 1972, U.S. Ct. Appeals (5th cir.) 1976, U.S. Ct. Appeals (11th cir.) 1982. Law clk. to chief justice U.S. Ct. Appeals (4th cir.), Richmond, Va., 1967-69; assoc. Kilpatrick & Cody, Atlanta, 1969-75, ptnr., 1975—; adj. prof. law Emory U., 1989. With USAR, 1968-74. Am. Coll. of Bankruptcy fellow; Angier B. Duke Meml. scholar Duke U., 1960. Mem. Am. Bankruptcy Inst., Calif. Bar Assn., Ga. Bar Assn., Phi Beta Kappa, Phi Eta Sigma. Jewish. Avocations: physical fitness, tennis, reading. Home: 5115 Jett Forest Trl NW Atlanta GA 30327-4559 Office: Kilpatrick & Cody 1100 Peachtree St NE Ste 2800 Atlanta GA 30309-4528

LURIA, MARY MERCER, lawyer; b. Boston, Dec. 29, 1942; d. Albert and Mabel (Jacomb) Mercer; m. Nelson J. Luria, June 19, 1967. AB, Radcliffe Coll., 1964; LLB, Yale U., 1967. Bar: N.Y. 1968. Assoc. Simpson, Thacher & Bartlett, N.Y.C., 1967-68, Hale & Dorr, Boston, 1968-69; assoc. Satterlee & Stephens, N.Y.C., 1969-74, ptnr., 1974-86; ptnr. Patterson, Belknap, Webb & Tyler, N.Y.C., 1986—. Mem. ABA, N.Y. State Bar Assn., Assn. of Bar of City of N.Y., Metropolitan Club. Avocations: gardening, photography. Home: 45 E 85th St New York NY 10028-0957 Office: Patterson Belknap et al 1133 Avenue Of The Americas New York NY 10036-6710

LURIA, ZELLA HURWITZ, psychology educator; b. N.Y.C., Feb. 18, 1924; d. Hyman Hurwitz and Dora (Garbarsky) H.; m. Salvador Edward Luria, Apr. 18, 1945; 1 child, Daniel David. BA, Bklyn., 1944; MA, Ind. U., 1947, PhD, 1951. lic. clin. psychologist, Mass. Ford Found. post-doctoral fellow U. Ill., Urbana, 1951-53, Russell Sage found. fellow, 1953-56, clin. researcher, 1954-58; asst. prof. psychology Tufts U., Medford, Mass., 1958-62, assoc. prof., 1962-70, prof., 1970—; psychiatry lectr. Mass. Gen. Hosp., Boston, 1970-79; vis. scholar Stanford U., 1977, 83; vis. prof. UCLA, 1992, 94, U. Mich., 1993. Sr. author: Psychology of Human Sexuality, 1979, Human Sexuality, 1987. Postdoctoral fellow USPHS, Paris, 1963-64, Bunting fellow Radcliffe Coll., 1989-90; Mellon Found. Faculty grantee Wellesley Coll., 1979-80. Mem. Tufts U. Am. Assn. Univ. Profs. (pres. 1986-87). Office: Tufts Univ Dept Of Psychology Medford MA 02155

LURIE, ALISON, author; b. Chgo., Sept. 3, 1926; children: John, Jeremy, Joshua. AB, Radcliffe Coll., 1947. Lectr. English Cornell U., 1969-73; adj. assoc. prof. English Cornell U., Ithaca, N.Y., 1973-76, assoc. prof., 1976-79, prof., 1979—. Author: V.R. Lang: A Memoir, 1959, Love and Friendship, 1962, The Nowhere City, 1965, Imaginary Friends, 1967, Real People, 1969, The War Between the Tates, 1974, Only Children, 1979, The Language of Clothes, 1981, Foreign Affairs, 1984, The Truth About Lorin Jones, 1988, Don't Tell the Grownups, 1990, Women and Ghosts, 1994. Recipient award in lit. Am. Acad. Arts and Letters, 1978, Pulitzer prize in fiction, 1985; fellow Yaddo Found., 1963-64, 66, Guggenheim Found., 1965, Rockefeller Found., 1967. Office: Cornell U Dept English Ithaca NY 14853

LURIE, ALVIN DAVID, lawyer; b. N.Y.C., Apr. 16, 1923; s. Samuel and Rose L.; m. Marian Weinberg, Aug. 21, 1944; children: James, Jeanne, Margery, Jonathan. AB, Cornell U., 1943, LLB, 1944. Bar: N.Y. 1944, D.C. 1978. Ptnr. various N.Y.C. law firms, 1944-74, including Lurie & Rubin, 1961-68, Aranow, Brodsky, Bohlinger & Einhorn, 1968-74; asst. commr. for employee plans and exempt orgns. IRS, Washington, 1974-78; ptnr. Chadbourne, Parke, Whiteside & Wolff, N.Y.C., 1978-80; counsel Chadbourne, Parke, Whiteside & Wolff, 1980-84; ptnr. Meyers, Tersigni, Lurie, Feldman & Gray, N.Y.C., 1984-91; counsel Meyers, Tersigni, Lurie, Feldman & Gray, 1992-94; pvt. practice N.Y.C., 1994-95; ptnr. Lurie & Gelband, 1996—; mem. adv. bd. NYU Tax Inst., 1978-90, Tax Mgmt. adv. bd., 1978—. Author: Lurie's Commentaries on Pension Design, 1980, Lurie's Guide to VEBAs, 1983, Collected Commentaries on Pensions, 1984, ESOPs Made Easy, 1985. Contbr. articles to law revs., tax jours. Mem. ABA, Fed. Bar Assn., N.Y. State Bar Assn. (chmn. spl. com. pension simplification 1986—), Assn. Bar City N.Y., Am. Coll. Tax Counsel, N.Y. Bar Found. Office: 1890 Palmer Ave Larchmont NY 10538 *Hard work, in intensive spurts, is my formula. The work must be varied, permitting application of different skills in constantly changing, creative ways. But one thing more is needed: readiness to seize the moment; for only in that way will new opportunities come, with new achievements and recurrent gratification.*

LURIE, HAROLD, engineer, lawyer; b. Durban, South Africa, Mar. 28, 1919; came to U.S., 1946, naturalized, 1952; s. Samuel Isaac and Dora (Mitchell) L.; m. Patricia Elkin, Mar. 26, 1959 (div. 1978); children—Diana Isabel, David Andrew. BS, U. Natal, South Africa, 1940, MS, 1946; PhD, Calif. Inst. Tech., 1950; JD, Northeastern U., 1989. Bar: Mass. 1989, D.C. 1991, U.S. Supreme Ct. 1993. Lectr. aeros. Calif. Inst. Tech., 1948-50, asst. prof. applied mechanics, 1953-56, assoc. prof., 1956-64, prof. engring. sci., 1964-70, assoc. dean grad. studies, 1964-70; dir. research and devel. New Eng. Electric System, 1971-79; dean engring. Poly. Inst. N.Y., Bklyn., 1979-81; dean Coll. Engring. Northeastern U., Boston, 1981-86; acting dir. advanced systems dept. Electric Power Rsch. Inst., 1974-75; cons. Yankee Atomic Electric Co., 1970-71; head weapons effectiveness group RAND Corp., 1950-521 sr. devel. engr. Oak Ridge Nat. Lab., 1956-57; vis. scholar U. Wash. Law Sch., 1990-91; assoc. dir. Calif. Coun. on Sci. and Tech., 1992—. Office: Calif Coun on Sci and Tech 1201 Dove St Ste 680 Newport Beach CA 92660-2825

LURIE, HUGH JAMES, psychiatrist, educator; b. Chgo., May 22, 1935; s. Harold Hiram and Gertrude (Geitner) L.; m. Edythe Bruce Hammond, Oct. 7, 1961; children: Nicholas Hubbard, Jessica Stevens, Hugh Sterling. AB, Harvard U., 1955; MD, Yale U., 1961. Diplomate Am. Bd. Psychiatry and Neurology, Am. Bd. Child Psychiatry, Am. Gd. Geriatric Psychiatry. Resident in pediatrics Johns Hopkins U., Balt., 1961-63; resident in gen. psychiatry McLean Hosp.-Harvard U., Belmont, Mass., 1965-67; resident in child psychiatry Children's Hosp., Judge Baker Clinic, Harvard U., Boston, 1967-69; med. dir. Child Guidance Clinic, Tacoma, 1969-80; chief psychiatrist Good Samaritan Mental Health Ctr., Puyallup, Wash., 1980—; clin. asst. prof. psychiatry U. Wash. Sch. Medicine, Seattle, 1969-72, clin. assoc. prof., 1972-75, clin. prof., 1975—; coord. behavioral scis. Medex, physician asst. program, 1975—. Author: Clinical Psychiatry for the Primary Physician, 1985; writer, prod. about 85 ednl. videotapes for Am. Psychiat. Assn., U. Wash., Assn. Am. Med. Colls., Am. Acad. Family Practice, 1976—; exec. prodr. ednl. video Time Mirror, 1979 (bronze medal N.Y. Film and Video Festival 1979). Bd. dirs. Sta. KVOW, pub. radio, Seattle, 1988-94. Lt. M.C., USN, 1963-65. Recipient hon. mention Assn. for Acad. Psychiatry, 1990. Fellow Am. Psychiat. Assn. (mem., chmn. video subcom. 1978-95), Am. Acad. Child and Adolescent Psychiatry; mem. Group for Advancement Psychiatry (social issues com. 1992—), Wash. State Psychiat. Assn. (co-chmn. geriatrics com. 1992—), Wash. State Coun. Child and Adolescent Psychiatry. Avocations: playing chamber music (violin, viola), etching. Home: 1417 E Aloha St Seattle WA 98112-3931 Office: Good Samaritan Mental Health Ctr 325 E Pioneer Ave Puyallup WA 98372-3265

LURIE, JEFFREY, professional sports team executive; b. Sept. 8, 1951; married; 2 children. BA, Clark U.; MS in Psychology, Boston U.; PhD in Social Policy, Brandels U. Pres., CEO Chestnut Hills Prodn., L.A.; pvt. practice, internat. publishing, specialty retailing; owner Phila. Eagles, 1994—; mem. NFL expansion com. Former trustee Clark U.; dir. Autism Rsch. Found., Boston; active local charitable cmty., Phila. Mem. Phila. C. of C. (exec. com.). Office: Philadelphia Eagles Philadelphia PA

LURIE, PAUL MICHAEL, lawyer; b. Chgo., Apr. 9, 1941; s. Haskell and Fay (Weinstein) L.; m. Margaret Berman, Aug. 2, 1966; children: Alexander, Rachel, Daniel, Matthew. BA, U. Mich., 1962, JD, 1965. Bar: Ill. 1965, U.S. Dist. Ct. (no. dist.) Ill., U.S. Ct. Appeals (7th cir.), U.S. Supreme Ct. Assoc. Fischel & Kahn, Chgo., 1967-68; ptnr. Fohrman, Lurie, Sklar & Simon, Ltd., Chgo., 1968-86, Neal, Gerber, Eisenberg & Lurie, Chgo., 1987-89, Schiff, Hardin & Waite, Chgo., 1989—; adj. prof. U. Ill. Coll. Art, Architecture and Urban Scis.; cons. Australian Law Reform Commn.; founder, gen. counsel, bd. dirs. Chgo. Architecture Found., 1966-76; counsel, bd. dirs. Chgo. Archtl. Assistance Ctr., 1979-89. Mem. editorial bd. Fed. Publs., Inc., constrn. adv. bd.; contbr. articles to profl. jours. Fellow Am. Coll. Constrn. Lawyers; mem. ABA (forum com. on constrn. industry, tort and ins. practice sect., design and constrn. com.), ASCE (hon. affiliate mem.), AIA (hon. mem. Chgo. chpt.), Internat. Bar Assn., Ill. Bar Assn., Chgo. Bar Assn. (former chmn. and founder land devel. and constrn. com.), Chgo. Coun. Lawyers, Nat. Inst. Bldg. Sci. (consultive coun.), Am. Consulting Engrs. Counsel (gen. counsel's forum), Am. Arbitration Assn. (former chmn. constrn. adv. coun. Chgo. region, constrn. industry arbitrator), Internat. Constrn. Contracts Com., Chgo. Nat. Swedish Inst. for Bldg. Rsch., Com. on Post-constrn. Liability and Ins., Cliff Dwellers Club, Standard Club. Jewish. Office: Schiff Hardin & Waite 7200 Sears Tower Chicago IL 60606

LURIE, RANAN RAYMOND, political analyst, political cartoonist, artist, lecturer; b. Port Said, Egypt, May 26, 1932; came to U.S., 1968, naturalized, 1974; s. Joseph and Rose (Sam) L. (parents Israeli citizens); m. Tamar Fletcher, Feb. 25, 1958; children: Rod, Barry, Daphne, Danielle. Student, Herzelia High Sch., Tel Aviv, Israel, 1949; student, Jerusalem Art Coll., 1951. Corr. Maariv Daily, 1950-52; features editor Hador Daily, 1953-54; editor-in-chief Tevel mag., 1954-55; staff polit. cartoonist Yedioth Aharonot Daily, 1955-66, Honolulu Advertiser, 1979; lectr. polit. cartooning U. Hawaii; univ. lectr. in fine arts, polit. cartoon and polit. analysis Am. Program Bur., Boston.; polit. cartoonist Time Internat. mag., 1994—; Inventor 1st electronically syndicated bus.-news cartoon Lurie's Business World; 101 million readers of 1,-98 newspapers in 102 countries; 1996 Guiness Book of World Records. Author: Among the Suns, 1952, Lurie's Best Cartoons, 1961, Nixon Rated Cartoons, 1973, Pardon Me, Mr. President, 1974, Lurie's Worlds, 1980, So sieht es Lurie, 1981, Fed. Republic Germany, Lurie's Almanac (U.K.), 1982, (U.S.A.), 1983, Taro's International Politics, Japan, 1984, Lurie's Middle East, Israel, 1986; creator: The Expandable Painting, 1969; Cartoons used as guidelines in several encys., polit. sci. books.; 22 shows, Israel, Can., U.S., 1960-75, including, Expo 67, Can., Dominion Gallery, Montreal, Que., Can., Lim Gallery, Tel Aviv, 1965, Overseas Press Club, N.Y.C., 1962, 64, 75, U.S. Senate, Washington, Honolulu Acad. Fine Arts, 1979; represented by Circle Gallery, 1988—; exhibited numerous group shows including, Smithsonian Instn., 1972, Circle Gallery, Washington, 1989; creator Japan's nat. cartoon symbol Taro-San, Taiwan's nat. cartoon symbol Cousin Lee; polit. cartoonist, Life Mag., N.Y.C., 1968-73, polit. cartoonist, interviewer, Die Welt, Bonn, W. Ger., 1980-81; contbr.: N.Y. Times, 1970—; contbg. editor, polit. cartoonist, Newsweek Internat., 1974-76, editor, polit. cartoonist, Vision Mag. of South Am., 1974-76, syndicated, United Features Syndicate, 1971-73; syndicated nationally by Los Angeles Times, also internationally by, N.Y. Times to over 260 newspapers, 1973-75, internationally by Editors Press Syndicate (345 newspapers), King Features Syndicate, 1975-83; syndicated in U.S. by Universal Press Syndicate, 1982-86, Cartoonews Internat. Syndicat, 1986—; polit. cartoonist, The Times of London, 1981-83, ABC's Nightline, 1991—, World News Show, 1993; sr. polit. analyst, editorial cartoonist Asahi Shimbun, Japan's largest daily newspaper, 1983-84; sr. analyst and polit. cartoonist U.S. News & World Report, 1984-85; chief editorial dir. Editors Press Service, 1985; joined staff MacNeil/Lehrer News Hour (PBS) as daily polit. cartoonist, analyst. Served as maj. Combat Paratroop, Israeli Army Res., 1950-67. Recipient highest Israeli journalism award, 1954; U.S. Headliners award, 1972; named Outstanding Editorial Cartoonist of Nat. Cartoonist Soc., 1971-78; Salon award Montreal Cartoon, 1971; N.Y. Front Page award, 1972, 74, 77; cert. merit U.S. Publ. Designers, 1974; award Overseas Press Club, 1979; John Fischetti polit. cartoon award, 1982, 86; sr. adj. fellow Ctr. Strategic Internat. Studies, Washington; Ranan R. Lurie Internat. Polit. Cartoon ann. award created in his honor by Nat. Fedn. Hispanic Owned Newspapers, 1994, RananR. Lurie Internat. award for Polit. Cartooning created by U.N. Soc. of Writers, 1995. Mem. Soc. Profl. Journalists, Nat. Cartoonists Soc. Am., Assn. Editorial Cartoonists, Mensa, Overseas Press Club, Friars Club. Inventor 1st electronically animated TV news cartoon; creator 1st syndicated bus.-news cartoon Lurie's Business World; 102 million readers of 1,098 newspapers in 102 countries; 1995 Guiness Book of World Records. Office: Cartoonews Inc 9 Mountain Laurel Dr Greenwich CT 06831-2741 *The moment of truth will come when the cartoonist gauges the margin of time from the day he drew the cartoon. Then he can see how clearly or unclearly he has evaluated the situation through his work. Eventually, the simple facts and reality always win. Then it becomes apparent that wishful thinking is meaningless and the capacity to evaluate the project and even predict the events that are happening will eventually cement the professional status and integrity of the cartoonist.*

LURIE, ROD, film critic, writer, film director; b. Tel Aviv, May 15, 1962; came to U.S., 1966; s. Ranan R. and Tamar R. (Fletcher) L.; m. Gretchen Bean, June 24, 1989; children: Hunter Fletcher, Paige Clark. BS, U.S. Mil. Acad., West Point, N.Y., 1984. Film critic Greenwich (Conn.) News, 1986-89; entertainment reporter N.Y. Daily News, N.Y.C., 1988-89; contbg. editor L.A. Mag., 1990—, film critic, 1991—; American editor Emprie Mag., L.A., 1991—; TV commentator Paramount TV, L.A., 1994—. Author: Once Upon A Time in Hollywood, 1995; talk show host Sta. KMPC, L.A., 1994—; dir. Porkchop, 1996. Capt. U.S. Army, 1980-88. Mem. Broadcast Film Critic's Assn. (pres. 1995-96). Achievements include 1st Israeli born grad of West Point; profiled on Sixty Minutes. Office: 3815 W Olive Ave Ste 201 Burbank CA 91505

LURTON, H. WILLIAM, retired retail executive; b. Greenwich, Conn., Sept. 18, 1929; s. William Pearl and Elizabeth (McDow) L.; m. Susan Harvey, Oct. 26, 1980; children: Scott, Carrie, Nancy, Jennifer, Barbara, Diana, Deborah, Sarah. B.A., Principia Coll., 1951. Sales rep. Jostens Inc., Mpls., 1955-61; yearbook sales and plant mgr. Jostens Inc., Visalia, Calif., 1961-66; gen. sales mgr. yearbook div. Jostens Inc., v.p., gen. mgr. yearbook div., 1969-70, corp. exec. v.p., 1970-71, mem. exec. com., 1970-72, pres., 1971-75, chief operating officer, 1971-72, chief exec. officer, 1972-94, chmn. bd., 1975-94, also dir.; ret., 1994; dir. Deluxe Inc., Pentair, Inc. Bd. dirs. U.S. C. of C., Mpls. YMCA. Served with USMC, 1951-53. Mem. Quail Ridge Country Club (Boynton Beach, Fla.), La Quinta Resort Country Club (Calif.), Tammaron Country Club (Durango, Colo.), Mpls. Clubl. Clubs: Wayzata (Minn.) Country, Minneapolis. Home: 3135 Jamestown Rd Long Lake MN 55356-9648

LURTON, HORACE VANDEVENTER, brokerage house executive; b. Washington, Oct. 16, 1941; s. Horace Harmon III and Eleaner (Pentz) L.; m. Nancy Taylor Mackall, Aug. 30, 1964 (dec. 1992); children: Bowie VanDeventer, Sallie Taylor. Student, Gettysburg U., 1962; BS, Am. U., 1965. Registered prin. SEC. Stockbroker Thomson, McKinnon & Auchincloss, Washington, 1966-76, Dean Witter Reynolds, Chevy Chase, Md., 1977-79; stockbroker, branch mgr., dir. Johnston, Lemon & Co., Inc., Bethesda, Md., 1979-89; stockbroker, br. mgr., dir. Johnston, Lemon & Co., Inc., Washington, 1989-90; v.p., branch mgr. Janney, Montgomery, Scott, Washington, 1990—. Active various orgns. and charities, Washington, Md. Episcopalian. Avocation: biking. Home: 5004 Scarsdale Rd Bethesda MD 20816-2438 Office: Janney Montgomery Scott 1225 23rd St NW Washington DC 20037-1102

LURVEY, IRA HAROLD, lawyer; b. Chgo., Apr. 6, 1935; s. Louis and Faye (Grey) L.; m. Barbara Ann Sirvint, June 24, 1962; children: Nathana, Lawrence, Jennifer, Jonathan, David, Robert. BS, U. Ill., 1956; MS, Northwestern U., 1961; JD, U. Calif., Berkeley, 1965. Bar: Calif. 1965, Nev. 1966, U.S. Dist. Ct. (cen. dist.) Calif. 1966, U.S. Tax Ct. 1966, U.S. Ct. Appeals (9th cir.) 1966, U.S. Supreme Ct. 1975. Law clk. to hon. justices Nev. Supreme Ct., Carson City, 1965-66; from assoc. to ptnr. Pacht, Ross, Warne, Bernhard & Sears, Inc., 1966-84; predecessor firm Shea & Gould, Los Angeles; founding ptnr. Lurvey & Shapiro, Los Angeles, 1984—; lectr. legal edn. programs; mem. Chief Justice's Commns. on Ct. Reform, Weighted Caseloads; mediator family law L.A. Supreior Ct. Editor Community Property Jour., 1979-80, Primary Consultant CFL 2d, 1994; columnist Calif. Family Law Monthly; contbr. articles to profl. jours. Former chmn. L.A. Jr. Arts Ctr.; past pres. Cheviot Hills Homeowners Assn.; exec. v.p., counsel Hillel Acad. Sch., Beverly Hills, Calif., 1977—. With U.S. Army, 1957-58. Fellow Am. Acad. Matrimonial Lawyers (pres. So. Calif. chpt. 1991-92, mem. nat. bd. govs. 1992-94), Internat. Acad. Matrimonial Lawyers; mem. ABA (sec. 1993-94, vice-chair 1994-95, chair family law sect. 1996— governing coun. 1986—, fin. officer 1991-92, chmn. support com., chmn. CLE, chmn. policy and issues com., vice chmn. com. arbitration and mediation, bd. of editors Family Adv. mag.), Calif. Bar Assn. (editor jour. 1982-85, chmn. family law sect. 1986-87, exec. com. family law sect. 1982-88, specialization adv. bd. family law 1979-82), L.A. County Bar Assn. (chmn. family law sect. 1981-82, exec. com. family law 1989-92), Beverly Hills Bar Assn. (chmn. family law sect. 1976-77). Home: 2729 Motor Ave Los Angeles CA 90064-3441 Office: Lurvey & Shapiro Ste 1550 2121 Avenue Of The Stars Los Angeles CA 90067-5010

LÜST, KLAUS, astrophysicist, meteorology institute director; b. 1923. PhD, U. Gottingen. Dir. Max Planck Inst. Physics, 1963-72; pres. Max Planck Assn., 1972-84; dir. gen. European Space Agy., 1984-90; pres. Alexander von Humboldt Soc., Bonn, Germany, 1989—. Mem. AAAS, Bavarian Acad. Sci., Royal Astron. Soc., Austrian Acad. Sci., Royal Acad. Scis. Madrid, Internat. Acad. of Astronautics, Nat. Acad. Air and Space, European Acad., German Acad. Naturforscher Leopoldina, German Naturforshcer und Arzte, European Phys. Soc., German Phys. Soc. Office: Alexander von Humboldt Stiftung, Jean Paul Strasse 12, 53173 Bonn Germany Also: Alexander von Homboldt Soc, Bundesstrasse 55, W 2000 Hamburg 13, Germany*

LUSAS, EDMUND WILLIAM, food processing research executive; b. Woodbury, Conn., Nov. 25, 1931; s. Anton Frank and Damicele Nellie (Kasputis) L.; m. Jeannine Marie Muller, Feb. 2, 1957; children—Daniel, Ann, Paul. B.S., U. Conn., 1954; M.S., Iowa State U., 1955; Ph.D., U. Wis., 1958; M.B.A., U. Chgo., 1972. Project leader Quaker Oats Research Labs., Barrington, Ill., 1958-61, mgr. canned pet foods research, 1961-67, mgr. pet foods research, 1967-72, mgr. sci. services, 1972-77; assoc. dir. Food Protein Research and Devel. Ctr., Tex. A&M U., College Station, 1977-78, dir., 1978-93, head fats, oils and extrusion programs, 1993—. Author over 100 publs.; patentee in field. Assoc. editor Jour. Am. Oil Chem. Soc., 1980-88. Fund raiser YMCA, Crystal Lake, Ill., 1970-77, chmn. fin. com., 1977. Recipient F.N. Peters research award Quaker Oats Co., 1968. Mem. Am. Oil Chemists Soc., Inst. Food Technologists (Gen. Foods research fellow 1956, 57), Am. Chem. Soc., Am. Assn. Cereal Chemists, Am. Soc. Agrl. Engrs., R&D Assocs., Guayule Soc. Am., Sigma Xi, Phi Tau Sigma. Avocation: fishing. Home: 3604 Old Oaks Dr Bryan TX 77802-4743 Office: Texas A & M Univ Food Protein Rsch Devel Ctr College Station TX 77843

LUSBY, GRACE IRENE, infection control nurse practitioner; b. Huntington Park, Calif., Aug. 20, 1935; d. Fletcher Homer and Charlotte Ione (Hayden) L. BS in Nursing, U. Calif., San Francisco, 1964, MS, 1968; cert. program in epidemiology, U. Calif., San Diego, 1981. RN, pub. health nurse, psychiat. nurse. Staff nurse, head nurse cancer rsch. unit U. Calif., San Francisco, 1964-66; pvt. duty nurse open heart surgery Profl. Registry, San Francisco, 1966-68; infection control coord. San Francisco Gen. Hosp., 1969-92; infection control cons. Oakland, Calif., 1992—; infection control rep. Calif. Task Force on AIDS, Sacramento, 1983-87, U.S. AIDS Task Force, San Francisco, 1983-92; co-establisher 1st infection control program for AIDS, San Francisco Gen. Hosp., 1983; mem. infection control-adv. coms. Svc. Employees Internat. Union, Calif. Nurses Assn., Mayor's Homeless Com., CAL-OSHA, also others, San Francisco, 1985—; infection control cons. emergency, home care, skill nursing, psychiatry, San Francisco, 1985—. Contbr. chpts. to books. Recipient Founder's award U. Calif.-San Francisco AIDS/ARC Update, 1988. Mem. Assn. Practitioners Infection Control (past treas., rec. sec., chmn. AIDS resource group), Women's AIDS Network (charter), PEO (rec. sec., corr. sec.), Sigma Theta Tau. Avocations: hiking, genealogy, weaving. Home and Office: 5966 Chabolyn Ter Oakland CA 94618-1914

LUSCINSKI, STEVEN MICHAEL, corporate executive; b. Boston, Nov. 4, 1951; s. Anthony P. and Agnes V. (Nawoichek) L.; m. Cathryn Creveling, Jan. 9, 1982; children: Steven Jr., Keith, Laura. BSCE, Northeastern U., 1974; MSCE, MIT, 1976; MBA, Cornell U., 1980. Registered profl. engr. R.I. Engr. Stone & Webster, Boston, 1971-78; cons., researcher Brookhaven Nat. Labs., L.I., N.Y., 1978-80; mgr. corp. planning UGI, Valley Forge, Pa., 1980-84; chief fin. officer Accu-Sort Systems, Telford, Pa., 1984-85; exec. v.p., gen. mgr. Accu-Sort Systems, Telford, 1985—; bd. dirs. Accu-Sort Systems, Telford, ATS, Ellington, Conn., ScanQuest Corp., San Diego; mem. exec. com. Saga Ins. Home: Windsong Dr Doylestown PA 18901 Office: Accu Sort Systems 511 School House Rd Telford PA 18969-1148

LUSCOMBE, HERBERT ALFRED, physician, educator; b. Johnstown, Pa., Aug. 9, 1916; s. Herbert O. and Clara C. (Geiselhart) L.; m. Sally T. McHugh; children: Herbert J., Susan M., Jill A. B.S., St. Vincent Coll., 1936; M.D., Jefferson Med. Coll., 1940. Diplomate: Am. Bd. Dermatology. Intern Jefferson Hosp., Phila., 1940-42, resident, 1946-48; resident U. Pa., 1948-49; mem. faculty Jefferson Med. Coll. Thomas Jefferson U., Phila., 1949—, prof., chmn. dept. dermatology, 1959-86; chief attending dermatologist Thomas Jefferson U. Hosp., 1959—, prof. emeritus of dermatology, 1987—, sr. attending dermatologist, 1987—; cons. dermatology Wills Eye Hosp., Lankenau Hosp., Herbert A. Luscombe lectr. in dermatology, 1984—. Contbr. articles to profl. jours. Recipient Clark Finneraud award Dermatology Found., 1981. Fellow AMA, Soc. Investgative Dermatology, Am. Acad. Dermatologists, Sigma Xi; mem. Phila. Dermatologic Soc. (pres. 1963-64), Alpha Omega Alpha. Roman Catholic. Club: Aronimink Golf. Home: 600 Old Gulph Rd Narberth PA 19072-1622 Office: Jefferson Med Coll 111 S 11th St Philadelphia PA 19107-4824

LUSHER, JEANNE MARIE, pediatric hematologist, educator; b. Toledo, June 9, 1935; d. Arnold Christian and Violet Cecilia (French) L. BS summa cum laude, U. Cin., 1956, MD, 1960. Lic. physician, Mich.; cert. in pediat. and hematology/oncology, Am. Bd. Pediat. Resident in pediat. Tulane divsn. Charity Hosp. La., New Orleans, 1961-64; fellow in pediat. hematology-oncology Child Rsch. Ctr. Mich., Detroit, 1964-65, St. Louis Children's Hosp./Washington U., 1965-66; instr. pediat. Washington U., St. Louis, 1965-66; from instr. to assoc. prof. Sch. Medicine Wayne State U., Detroit, 1966-74, prof., 1974—; dir. divsn. hematology-oncology Children's Hosp. Mich., Detroit, 1976—; Marion I. Barnhart prof. hemostasis rsch. Sch. Medicine Wayne State U., Detroit, 1989—; med. dir. Nat. Hemophilia Found., N.Y.C., 1987-94, chmn. med. and sci. adv. coun., 1994—. Author, editor: Treatment of Bleeding Disorders with Blood Components, 1980, Sickle Cell, 1974, 76, 81, Hemophilia and von Willebrand Disease in the 1990's, 1991, Acquired Bleeding Disorder in Children, 1981, F VIII/von Willebrand Factor and Platelets in Health and Disease, 1987, Inhibitors to Factor VIII, 1994. Mem. Citizens Info. Com., Pontiac Township, Mich., 1980-82; apptd. mem. Hazardous Waste Incinerator Commn., Oakland County, Mich., 1981. Recipient Disting. Alumnus award U. Cin. Alumni Assn., 1990. Mem. Am. Bd. Pediat. (chmn. sub-bd. on hematology-oncology 1988-90), Am. Soc. Hematology (chmn. sci. com. pediat. 1991-92), Am. Pediat. Soc., Soc. Pediat. Rsch., Internat. Soc. Thrombosis-Hemostasis (chmn. factor VIII/IX subcom. 1985-90, sec., chmn.-elect sci. and standardization com. 1994—), Mich. Humane Soc. Avocations: nature, wildlife, hiking, gardening. Office: Children's Hosp Mich 3901 Beaubien St Detroit MI 48201-2119

LUSHT, KENNETH MICHAEL, business administration educator; b. N.Y.C., Dec. 22, 1942; m. Elizabeth Enloe Hall; children: Elizabeth, Alexander. BBA, Emory U., 1964; PhD, Ga. State U., 1973. Prof. bus. administrn. Pa. State U., University Park, 1973—, acad. program dir. continuing edn., 1983—, dir. inst. for real estate studies, 1986—, chmn. dept. ins. and real estate, 1989—; pres. Kenneth M. Lusht Cons., State College, 1983—. Author 2 textbooks; editorial bd. Jour. of the Am. Real Estate And Urban Econs. Assn., 1986-92, Jour. of Property Rsch., 1990—, Appraisal Jour., 1991—, Jour. of Real Estate Fin., 1993—; contbr. articles to profl. jours. Vis. fellow RMIT, 1989, 95, Vis. Rsch. fellow U. West Sydney, 1993, U. Hong Kong, 1994, 95; recipient Wagner award Am. Inst. of Real Estate Appraisers, 1986. Mem. Am. Real Estate and Urban Econs. Assn. (pres. 1987, bd. dirs. 1982-84, 88-90), Am. Real Estate Soc. Office: Coll Bus Pa State U 409 Bab University Park PA 16802

LUSIC, RONALD R., retail company executive; b. 1947; married. BA, U. Wis., 1975. Stock clk. Red Owl Foods Stores, 1965-67; from stock clk. to mgr. Sentry Food Stores, 1967-70; with Godfrey Co., Waukesha, Wis., 1970-82, 87—, labor rels. mgr., 1970-80, dist. mgr. labor rels., from 1980, now exec. v.p.; with Hub City Foods, 1982-87, v.p. sales, 1982-83, pres., 1983-87. Office: Godfrey Co 1200 W Sunset Dr Waukesha WI 53186-6513*

LUSK, HARLAN GILBERT, national park superintendent; b. Jersey City, June 22, 1943; s. Harlan H. and Mary M. (Kuhl) L.; m. Catherine L. Rutherford, Oct. 11, 1986. BA in History, Gettysburg Coll., 1965. Supervisory historian Cape Hatteras Nat. Seashore, Manteo, N.C., 1968; historian Nat. Pk. Svc., Washington, 1968-69; programs specialist So. Utah Group, Cedar City, 1968-70; pk. supt. Wolf Trap Farm Pk., Vienna, Va., 1970-72; supervisory pk. ranger Blue Ridge Pkwy., Roanoke, Va., 1972-74; pk. supt. Appomattox (Va.) Courthouse, Nat. Hist. Pk., 1974-76, Valley Forge (Pa.), Nat. Hist. Pk., 1976-81, Big Bend (Tex.) Nat. Pk., 1981-86, Glacier Nat. Pk., West Glacier, Mont., 1986-94; pk. supt. Albright Tng. Ctr. Grand Canyon Nat. Pk., Ariz., 1994—; chief, Divsn. Tng. and Employee Nat. Park Svc., Washington, 1995—; organizer 1st regional conf. Rio Grande Border, States on Pks. and Wildlife, Laredo, Tex., 1985. Bd. dirs. Tech. Com. on Pks. & Recreation Cen. Va. Planning Dist., 1972-74, Fed. Exec. Assn. Roanoke Valley, 1972-74, Flathead Basin Commn., 1986—, Flathead Conv. & Visitor Assn., 1986—, Sonoran Inst.; prin. founder, 1st pres., Appomattox County Hist. Soc., 1974-76; trustee Sci. Mus. Assn. Roanoke Valley, 1972-74, Nature Conservancy Mont., 1994—; ex-officio Friends of Valley Forge, 1977-81; founder, ex-officio, bd. dirs. Valley Forge Pk. Interpretive Assn., 1977-81; founder Big Bend Area Travel Assn., chmn., 1984-86. Recipient Meritorious Svc. award. Dept. Interior, 1986. Mem. Glacier Natural History Assn. (ex officio 1986-94), Glacier Nat. Pk. Assocs. (founder, ex-officio 1989-94), George Wright Soc., Lions, Rotary. Avocations: golf, antiques, computers, collecting artwork, hiking. Office: Grand Canyon Nat Pk Albright Tng Ctr Grand Canyon AZ 86023

LUSK, WILLIAM EDWARD, real estate, oil company executive; b. Medicine Lodge, Kans., May 16, 1916; s. William Edward and Teresa (Rhoades) L.; m. Anita Ballard, Feb. 1, 1942; children—William Edward, Janet Kathryn and James Raymond (twins). B.S. in Edn; A.B. in Econs, Ft. Hays State Coll., 1939; student, Washburn U., 1936; postgrad., Kans. U., 1940-41. Tchr. Protection (Kans.) High Sch., 1939-41; mgr. real estate dept. Wheeler, Kelly & Hagny Investment Co., Wichita, Kans., 1946-63; co-founder, exec. v.p., treas., dir. Clinton Oil Co., Wichita, 1963-73; pres. Lusk Real Estate Co., 1963—, Lusk Investment Co., 1973—; Pres. Wichita Real Estate Bd., 1961. Founder Lusk Found., 1968, William E. Lusk Scholarship, Ft. Hays State Coll., 1969; bd. dirs. Jr. Achievement Wichita. Served with USNR, 1942-46; comdr. Res. Named Kans. Realtor of Year Kans. Assn. Real Estate Bds., 1962; recipient Alumni Achievement award Ft. Hays Kan. State Coll., 1971. Mem. VFW, Sojourners, Res. Officers Assn., Naval Res. Officers Assn., Navy League, Phi Alpha Delta, Alpha Kappa Psi (hon.). Methodist (bd. dirs. 1965-70, fin. chmn. 1969—). Clubs: Wichita Country, Wichita (bd. dirs. 1969-72, pres. 1972), McConnell AFB Officers. Lodge: Masons (32 degree). Home: 6 W Parkway N Wichita KS 67206 Office: 1608 E Lewis St Wichita KS 67211-1823 *In business and personal relationships I have found strength in times of adversity and self-control in times of success by forming the habit of calling to mind this guideline: Things are never as good as they seem to be on the day they look good-nor are things as bad as they seem to be on the day they appear bad.*

LUSKIN, ROBERT DAVID, lawyer; b. Chgo., Jan. 21, 1950; s. Bert L. and S. Ruth (Katz) L.; m. Fairlea A. Sheehy, Aug. 23, 1975; children: Peter Duncan, Charles Cassimer. BA magna cum laude, Harvard U., 1972, JD magna cum laude, 1979; postgrad., Oxford (Eng.) U., 1972-75. Bar: D.C. 1979, U.S. Ct. Appeals (1st, 4th, 5th, 6th, 8th, 9th, 11th, D.C. cirs.) 1979, U.S. Supreme Ct., 1983. Law clk. to Hon. Louis F. Oberdorfer U.S. Dist. Ct. for D.C., Washington, 1979-80; spl. counsel organized crime racketeering sect. U.S. Dept. Justice, Washington, 1980-82; ptnr. Onek, Klein & Farr, Washington, 1982-89, Powell, Goldstein, Frazer & Murphy, Washington, 1989-93, Comey, Boyd & Luskin, Washington, 1993—; lectr. in law U. Va. Sch. Law, 1992—. Rhodes scholar, 1972-75. Mem. ABA (chmn. RICO Forfeitures and Civil Remedies com. 1986-94, vice chmn. task force on forfeitures), Harvard Law Sch. Assn. Washington (pres.). Home: 3244 38th St NW Washington DC 20016-3729 Office: Comey Boyd & Luskin Ste 200 2828 Pennsylvania Ave NW Washington DC 20007

LUSKY, LOUIS, legal educator; b. Columbus, Ohio, May 15, 1915; s. Leonard Morris and Amy (Kleeman) L.; m. Ruth Agnes Anderson, Aug. 31, 1946; children: Mary Hibbard Friedman, John Anderson; 1 child by previous marriage, Peter Joris. BA, U. Louisville, 1935; LLB, Columbia, 1937. Bar: N.Y. 1938, Ky. 1947. Law clk. to Supreme Ct. Justice Harlan F. Stone, 1937-38; assoc. Root, Clark, Buckner & Ballantine, N.Y.C., 1938-42, 44-45; civilian mem. ops. analysis sect. 8th Air Force, 1943-44; with legal div. U.S. Mil. Govt., Germany, 1945-46; ptnr. Wyatt & Grafton, Louisville, 1947-51; sole practice Louisville, 1952-63; prof. law Columbia Law Sch., 1963-85, Betts prof. law, 1979-85, prof. emeritus, 1985—. Author: (with others) Southern Justice, 1965, By What Right?, 1975, Our Nine Tribunes, 1993. Mem. ABA, ACLU (nat. com. 1963-67, nat. bd. 1967-70), Am. Law Inst. Home: 623 Eastbrook Rd Ridgewood NJ 07450-2114 Office: 435 W 116th St New York NY 10027-7201 also: 1250 E Ridgewood Ave Ridgewood NJ 07450-3930

LUSS, DAN, chemical engineering educator; b. Tel Aviv, Israel, May 5, 1938; came to U.S., 1963, naturalized, 1973; s. Manfred and Gertrude (Weinstein) L.; m. Amalia Rubin, Sept. 4, 1966; children: Noya, Limor. BS, Technion Inst. Tech., Haifa, Israel, 1960, MSc, 1963; PhD, U. Minn., 1966. Registered profl. engr., Tex. Asst. prof. chem. engring. U. Minn., Mpls., 1966-67; asst. prof. chem. engring. U. Houston, 1967-69, asso. prof., 1969-72, prof., 1972—, chmn. dept., 1975-95; assoc. dir. Tex. Ctr. for Superconductivity, 1988-92; cons. to several chem. cos. Editor: Revs. in Chem. Engring.; mem. editorial bd. Sci. and Engring, Catalysis Rev. Fellow Am. Inst. Chem. Engrs. (Allan P. Colburn award 1973, Profl. Progress award 1979, Wilhelm award 1986, chmn. awards com., former mem. editorial bd. jour.,former dir.), Am. Chem. Soc. (Honor scroll award of Indsl. Engring. Chemistry div. 1967); mem. NAE, Am. Soc. Engring. Edn. (Curtis McGraw award 1977 3M-Chem. Engring. lectureship award 1985). Home: 6242 Paisley St Houston TX 77096-3727 Office: U Houston Dept Chem Engring Houston TX 77204-4792

LUSSEN, JOHN FREDERICK, pharmaceutical laboratory executive; b. N.Y.C., Jan. 5, 1942; s. Frederick Maurice and Kathleen (Herlihy) L.; m. Kathleen Elizabeth Sheppard; children: Tara, Eric, Gregory. BS in Fin., Fordham U., 1963, JD, 1967; LLM in Tax, NYU, 1971. Bar: N.Y. 1967. Tax atty. Pfizer Inc., N.Y.C., 1971-74; mgr. taxes SCM Corp., N.Y.C., 1974-79; v.p. taxes Abbott Labs., Abbott Park, Ill., 1979—. Capt. U.S. Army, 1968-70. Mem. ABA, Tax Execs. Inst., Bus. Roundtable (tax subcom.), P.R. USA Found. Avocations: tennis, golf. Home: 1055 Westleigh Rd Lake Forest IL 60045 Office: Abbott Labs D367 AP6D 100 Abbott Park Rd Abbott Park IL 60064-3502

LUSSIER, GILLES, monsignor. Office: Evêché CP 470, 2 rue St Charles Borromee Nord, Joliette, PQ Canada J6E 6H6

LUSSIER, JEAN-PAUL, dentistry educator; b. Montreal, Sept. 17, 1917; s. Eugene and Parmelia (Gauthier) L.; m. Juliette Laurin, May 4, 1943; children: Louis, Renee Lussier Brecknock, Josee, Anne Lussier Morin, Pierre, Helene Lussier Black, Andre. BA, U. Montreal, 1938, DDS, 1942, MS, 1952; PhD, U. Calif., San Francisco, 1959; DSc (hon.), McGill U., 1972, Laval U., 1995. Mem. U. Montreal faculty medicine, dept. physiology, 1946-52, 54-57, mem. faculty dentistry, 1957-62, 79-83, prof. emeritus, 1983—, dean, 1962-79, chmn. health scis. coordinating com., 1979-83; rsch. fellow U. Calif.-San Francisco, 1952-54; cons. WHO, 1972—; bd. dirs. Sacred Heart Hosp., Montreal. Recipient award Am. Acad. Dental Medicine, 1958, award Alpha Omega, 1962. Fellow Am. Coll. Dentists, Internat. Coll. Dentists, Acad. Dentistry Internat. (hon.), Royal Coll. Dentists, Academie dentaire du

Quebec: mem. Fedn. Dentaire Internationale, Can. Dental Assn. (hon.). Home: 3507 Vendome St, Montreal, PQ Canada H4A 3M6

LUST, BARBARA C., psychology and linguistics educator; d. John Benedict and Virginia (Sleth) L. BA in English Lit., Manhattanville Coll., 1963; postgrad., Fairleigh Dickinson, 1965, The New Sch. for Social Rsch., 1965-66, U. Geneva, Switzerland, 1968-69; MA in English Lit., Fordham U., 1971; PhD Devel. Psychology, CUNY, 1975. Post doctoral fellow dept. linguistics and philosophy MIT, Cambridge, 1974-76; from asst. prof. to prof. dept. human development and family studies Cornell U., Ithaca, N.Y., 1976—, field rep. cognitive studies program, 1987—, co-dir., 1992—, prof. modern langs. & linguistics, 1990—; vis. prof. SUNY, Binghamton, 1977; vis. scientist MIT, 1984, 90; vis. scholar Kelaniya U., Sri Lanka, 1984, U.S. Edni. Found., 1984; cons. in field, lectr. various colls. and univs. Author: Studies in the Acquisition of Anaphora (vol I 1986, II 1987); co-editor, author: Syntactic Theory & First Language Acquisition, 1994 (vol. I and II); co-author: Studies in the Cognitive Basis of Language Development, 1975; contbr. articles to prof. jours., chpts. to books. Grantee NIMH, 1976, NSF, 1979-88, 92-93, 95; fellow Nat. Inst. Health, 1990, NSF, 1989-91; Smithsonian grant Am. Inst. Indian Studies, 1980-81; recipient Travel award Lingustistic Soc. Am. and NSF, 1982, Rsch. award NSF, 1988-89, James McKeen Cattell award, 1992-93, N.Y. State Coll. Human Ecology award, 1976-79, 83. Fellow AAAS (chair linguistics and the lang. scis. 1993-94); mem. APA, Linguistic Soc. Am. (del. to AAAS psychology sect. 1988—), Am. Psychological Soc., Internat. Assn. Study Child Language, Soc. Rsch. Child Devel., Internat. Soc. Woman in Cognitive Neuroscience, Internat. Soc. Korean Linguistics, New Eng. Child Lang. Assn., N.Y. Acad. Scis., Soc. Philosophy and Psychology, Linguistic Assn. Great Britian, Piaget Soc. Democrat. Office: Cornell U Human Devel & Family Studies Ng 28 Marth Van Rensse Ithaca NY 14853

LUST, HERBERT COHNFELDT, II, finance executive; b. Chgo., Oct. 31, 1926; s. Herbert Cohnfeldt and Jennie (Friedman) L.; m. Virginia Wertheimer; children: Herbert Cohnfeldt III, Conrad. MA, U. Chgo., 1948. Pres. Pvt. Water Supply, Inc. Greenwich Assocs., N.Y.C., 1961—, co-owner, dir. Gallery Bernard, 1969-87; dir. First Va. Real Estate Trust, Washington, 1981-83; chmn. bd. BRT, Great Neck, N.Y., 1983-85; chmn. United Mchts. & Mfg., Teaneck, N.J., 1991-93; lectr. comparative lit. U. Chgo., 1956-59; bd. dirs. Prime Hospitality, BRT. Author: 12 Principals of Art Investment, 1969, Alberto Giacometti, 1970, Enrico Baj, 1972, Violence and Defiance, 1983. Served in USN, 1944-46. Named Fulbright scholar, 1949-51. Jewish. Office: 1356 Madison Ave New York NY 10128-0826

LUSTENBERGER, LOUIS CHARLES, JR., lawyer; b. Chgo., Mar. 13, 1936; s. Louis Charles and Virginia (Chesrown) L.; m. Anita T. Anderson, June 17, 1961; children: Louis, Gwyn. BA, Williams Coll., 1959; LLB, Harvard U., 1962. Bar: N.Y. 1963, U.S. Dist. Ct. (so. and ea. dist.) N.Y. 1964, U.S. Dist. Ct. (we. dist.) N.Y. 1986, U.S. Ct. Appeals (2d cir.) 1964, U.S. Ct. Appeals (3d cir.) 1989, U.S. Ct. Appeals (5th cir.) 1980, U.S. Supreme Ct. 1978, U.S. Ct. Appeals (10th cir.) 1993, U.S. Dist Ct. (we. dist.) Mich., 1996. Assoc. Donovan, Leisure, Newton & Irvine, N.Y.C., 1962-71, ptnr., 1971—. Sr. warden St. Barnabas Ch., Irvington, N.Y., 1980-82; chmn. Irvington Zoning Bd., 1989—. Fellow Am. Coll. Trial Lawyers; mem. Assn. of Bar of City of N.Y., N.Y. State Bar Assn., N.Y. County Lawyers Assn., Phi Beta Kappa. Republican. Presbyterian. Home: 86 Fargo Ln Irvington NY 10533-1202 Office: Donovan Leisure Newton & Irvine 30 Rockefeller Plz New York NY 10112

LUSTER, GEORGE ORCHARD, professional society administrator; b. Pitts., Mar. 20, 1921; s. James W. and Gertrude (Orchard) L.; m. Edith A. Townsend, May 3, 1946 (dec. May 1989); children: Thomas, Carolea, Patricia; m. Mary Jane Herbolich, Oct. 1990. BS with honors, U. Pitts., 1949. CPA, Pa. Acct., Am. Inst. Rsch., Pitts., 1948-49; mgr. Price Waterhouse (CPAs), Pitts., 1949-59; treas., asst. sec. Mellon Inst., Pitts., 1959-67; treas. Carnegie-Mellon U., 1967-80; asst. sec., asst. treas., supervising com. Bellefield Boiler Plant, Pitts., 1962-71; treas., asst. sec. MPC Corp., Pitts., 1963-80; dir. adminstrn. Fin. Execs. Inst., 1980-86; instr. Robert Morris Sch., 1955-59, U. Pitts., 1959. Bd. dirs. Ctrl. Blood Bank, Pitts., 1973-80. With USAAF, 1943-46. Mem. AICPA, Fin. Execs. Inst., Air and Waste Mgmt. Assn. (treas. 1966-95), Pa. Inst. CPAs, River Bend Golf Club, Alpha Kappa Psi, Beta Gamma Sigma. Republican. Methodist. Home: 9238 SE Deerberry Pl Tequesta FL 33469-1804 *Individual success is relative to the challenges that one meets through life and how one perceives them as opportunities to learn, to be creative, and to be innovative in defining and planning actions to achieve one's goals.*

LUSTER, MARTIN ARNOLD, state legislator; b. N.Y.C., Apr. 4, 1942; s. Hyman I. and Esta G. (Green) L.; m. Barbara Kirschbaum, Apr. 11, 1964; children: Brian D., Ann D. BS, L.I. U., 1963; LLB, NYU, 1966. Bar: N.Y. 1966. Ptnr. Gaier & Luster, N.Y.C., 1967-76, Luster, Salk, Henry & Tischler and predecessor firm, Ithaca, N.Y., 1980-88; pvt. practice Trumansburg, N.Y., 1976-80; mem. N.Y. State Assembly, Albany, 1989—, chair task force on utility rate settlements, 1990, sec. majority conf., 1994, chair subcoms. on rural health and on librs.; chmn. Legis. Commn. on Govt. Adminstrn. Officer Tompkins County Econ. Opportunity Corp., Ithaca, 1972-83; bd. dirs. Alpha House, Trumansburg, 1979-83, Leadership Tompkins, Ithaca, 1992—; town supr. Town of Ulysses, N.Y., 1984-88. Named Newsmaker of Yr., Am. Community Cable TV, 1989; recipient Cert. of Recognition Atlantic chpt. Sierra Club, 1992, Cert. of Appreciation, Ithaca Neighborhood Housing Svcs, 1993. Democrat. Jewish. Avocations: sailing, hiking. Office: NY State Legislature Rm 639lob Albany NY 12248

LUSTGARTEN, IRA HOWARD, lawyer; b. N.Y.C., July 31, 1929; s. Louis and Florine Josephine (Van Mindeno) L.; m. Rhoda Manne, Oct. 24, 1954; children: Lise Anne, Nancy Ellen. AB, NYU, 1950; LLB, Columbia U., 1958. Bar: N.Y. 1958, Fla. 1978, U.S. Dist. Ct. (so. dist.) N.Y. 1959, U.S. Ct. Claims 1985, U.S. Ct. Appeals (fed. cir.) 1986. Assoc. Proskauer Rose Goetz Mendelsohn, N.Y.C., 1958-68, ptnr., 1968-79; ptnr. Willkie Farr & Gallagher, N.Y.C., 1979—; lectr. law Columbia U. Served to lt. USNR, 1951-55. Mem. ABA, Am. Law Inst., Am. Coll. Probate Counsel Found. (past pres.), Am. Coll. Probate Counsel, N.Y. Bar Assn. (past chmn. trusts and estates law sect.), Assn. of Bar of City of N.Y. (former chmn. trusts, estates, and surrogate cts.), Pub. Adminstrs. N.Y. (adm. bd. oversee), Fla. Bar Assn., Internat. Acad. Estate and Trust Law, N.Y. (legis. adv. com. to rev. law of trusts and estates). Office: Willkie Farr & Gallagher 1 Citicorp Ctr 153 E 53rd St New York NY 10022-4602

LUSZTIG, PETER ALFRED, university dean, educator; b. Budapest, Hungary, May 12, 1930; s. Alfred Peter and Susan (Szabo) L.; m. Penny Bicknell, Aug. 26, 1961; children: Michael, Cameron, Carrie. B in Com., U. B.C., Vancouver, Can., 1954; MBA, U. Western Ont., London, Can., 1955; PhD, Stanford U., 1964. Asst. to comptroller B.C. Electric, Vancouver, 1955-57; instr. fin. U. B.C., 1957-60, asst. prof. fin., 1962-64, assoc. prof., 1968-95, Killam sr. research fellow, 1968-69, prof., 1968—; dean Faculty Commerce, 1977-91; bd. trustees BC Health Benefit Trust; bd. dirs. Canfor Corp., Royal Ins. (Can.) Western Assurance, Roins Holding Co.; fed. commr. BC Treaty Commn.; vis. prof. IMEDE, Switzerland, 1973-74, London Grad. Sch. Bur. Studies, 1968-69, Pacific Coast Banking Sch., 1977—; sr. advisor B.C. Ministry of Econ. Devel., Small Bus. and Trade, 1991. Author: Report of the Royal Commission on Automobile Insurance, 2 vols., 1968, Financial Management in a Canadian Setting, 5th rev. edit., 1993, Report of the Commission on the B.C. Tree Fruit Industry, 1990. Ford Found. faculty dissertation fellow, Stanford U., 1964. Mem. Am. Fin. Assn., Fin. Mgmt. Assn. Lutheran. Office: Dept Commerce & Bus, Adminstrn BC, Vancouver, BC Canada V6T 1Z2

LUTALI, A. P., governor of American Samoa; b. Aunu'u, American Samoa, Dec. 24, 1919; married. Gov. Am. Samoa, 1985-89, 93—; spkr. of the House Senate, Am. Samoa, 1956-57, pres., 1965-67, v.p., 1988—; chair Constnl. Conv., 1966. Mem. Am. Samoa Bar Assn. (founder 1972). Office: Governor's Office Pago Pago AS 96799

LUTER, JOHN, news correspondent, educator; b. Knoxville, Tenn., Jan. 17, 1919; s. John Thomas and Bertha Mae (Carver) L.; m. Mary Hickey, 1948 (dec.); 1 child, Linda; m. Yvonne Spiegelberg, 1966 (div. 1971); m. Nan Hoyt Lawrence, 1974 (dec. 1996). BA, St. Mary's U., Tex., 1939, postgrad., 1939-42; fellow Time Inc., Sch. Advanced Internat. Studies, Washington, 1945. Reporter San Antonio Light, 1939-42, Washington Star, 1942-44; Wash. corr. Time mag., 1944-45; war corr. Time mag., Pacific, 1945; fgn. corr. Time and Life mags., Southeast Asia, 1945-46, Japan, 1946-47, Israel, 1948-49, Italy, 1949-54; asst. editor internat. edit. Life mag., 1954-56; reporter, writer CBS News, 1957-58; asso. editor Newsweek mag., 1958-61; radio news commentator Stas. WQXR and QXR-FM Network, 1960-61; coord. advanced internat. reporting program Columbia Grad. Sch. Journalism, 1961-72; dir. Maria Moors Cabot Prize Program, 1961-74; mem. profl. staff Bank St. Coll. Edn., N.Y.C., 1973-74; prof., dir. journalism U. Hawaii, Honolulu, from 1974, prof. and chmn. journalism dept., 1982-92, prof. journalism, 1992-94; prof emeritus, 1994—. Adv. editor: Columbia Journalism Rev., 1961-72. Chmn. internat. rels. com. N.Y.C. Protestant Coun., 1968-71; chmn. adv. screening com. communications Sr. Fulbright Program, 1970-73; trustee Overseas Press Club Found., 1962-72, chmn., 1964-65; bd. dirs. UN Assn. N.Y.C., 1973-74; chmn. Honolulu Community Media Coun., 1982-84. Mem. Assn. Edn. Journalism and Mass Comm., Assn. Schs. Journalism and Mass Comm., Honolulu Com. Fgn. Rels. and Pacific and Asian Affairs Coun., World Affairs Coun., San Antonio, 1974-94 Soc. Profl. Journalists (exec. coun. chpt. 1966-69, 89-90), Japan Am. Soc., Overseas Press Club (pres. N.Y.C. 1960-62), Outrigger Canoe Club. Home: 340 Alta Ave San Antonio TX 78209-4513

LUTER, JOSEPH WILLIAMSON, III, meat packing and processing company executive; b. Smithfield, Va., 1940; married. BBA, Wake Forest Coll., 1962. Pres. Smithfield Packing Co., Arlington, Va., 1964-69, Bryce Mountain Resort Inc., 1969-75; with Smithfield Foods Inc., Arlington, 1975—, pres., 1975-86, 89—, chief exec. officer, 1975—, chmn., 1977—, also bd. dirs. Office: Smithfield Foods Inc 501 N Church St Smithfield VA 23430*

LUTES, DONALD HENRY, architect; b. San Diego, Mar. 7, 1926; s. Charles McKinley and Helen (Bjoraker) L.; m. Donnie Wageman, Aug. 14, 1949; children: Laura Jo, Gail Eileen, Dana Charles. B.Arch., U. Oreg., 1950. Pvt. archtl. practice Springfield, Oreg., 1956-58; ptnr. John Amundson, Springfield, 1958-70; pres. Lutes & Amundson, Springfield, 1970-72; ptnr. Lutes/Sanetel, 1973-86; adj. assoc. prof. architecture U. Oreg., 1964-66, 89—; chmn. Springfield Planning Commn., 1956-64, Urban Design and Devel. Corp., 1968-70, Eugene Non-Profit Housing, Inc., 1970. Architect: Springfield Pub. Library, 1957, Mt. Hood Community Coll, 1965-79, Shoppers Paradise Expt. in Downtown Revitalization, 1957. Chmn. Springfield United Appeal, 1959. Served to 1st lt. AUS, 1943-46, 51-52. Decorate Bronze Star; named Jr. 1st Citizen, Springfield C. of C., 1957, 1st Citizen, 1968, Disting. Citizen, 1994. Fellow AIA (bd. dirs. 1987-90, v.p. 1991); mem. Rotary, Theta Chi. Home and Office: 778 Crest Ln Springfield OR 97477-3601

LUTES, JIM G. (JAMES LUTES), artist; b. Ft. Lewis, Wash., Dec. 5, 1955; s. James Gerald and Diane Gwendolyn (Schille) L.; m. Kimberly Ellen Piotrowski, Jan. 15, 1994. BA, Wash. State U., 1978; MFA, Art Inst. Chco., 1982. Assoc. prof. art Ill. State U., Normal, 1983-95; vis. artist The Sch. of The Art Inst. Chgo., 1983—; adj. assoc. prof. U. Ill., Chgo., 1995. One-man shows include Dart Gallery, Chgo., 1986, 87, 88, 91, 92, Michael Kohn Gallery, L.A., 1989, Temple Gallery, Phila., 1990, Vera Van Laer Gallery, Knokke-Heist, Belgium, 1993, Mus. Contemporary Art, Chgo., 1994, others; group shows include Hyde Park Art Ctr., Chgo., 1983, Dart Gallery, 1984, The Corcoran Gallery Art, Washington, 1984-86, Walker Art Ctr., Mpls., 1985, Artists Space, N.Y.C., 1986, The Whitney Mus., N.Y.C., 1987, The Contemporary Arts Ctr., Cin., 1989, Evanston (Ill.) Art Ctr., 1991, 95, Katonah (N.Y.) Mus. Art, 1992, Klein Gallery, Chgo., 1993, Edward Thorp Gallery, N.Y.C., 1993, others; represented in permanent collections at The Progressive Corp., Pepper Pike, Ohio, Ill. State Mus., Springfield, The Ruttenberg Family Found., Chgo., Larry and Evelyn Aronson, Chgo., James and Edie Cloonan, Chgo., Howard and Donna Stone, Chgo., Mus. of Contemproary Art, Chgo., Mus. van Hendendaagee Kinst, Ghent, Belgium, Paul and Camille Oliver-Hoffman, Chgo. NEA grantee, 1993; recipient Awards in Visual Arts award, 1987, Louis Comfort Tiffany Found. award, 1993.

LUTGEN, ROBERT R., newspaper editor; b. Fairmont, Minn., Oct. 27, 1949; s. William J. and Barbara Estella (Sanger) L.; m. Teresa L. Palm, July 17, 1971; children: Mark, Kyle, Laura. BA, Ctrl. Wash. State Coll., 1971. Reporter, asst. city editor Yakima (Wash.) Herald Republic, 1970-77; city editor Bryan (Tex.) Eagle, 1977-81; city editor Texarkana (Tex.) Gazette, 1981-83, mng. editor, 1983-87; asst. mng. editor Ark. Dem., 1987-91; mng. editor Ark. Dem.-Gazette, 1991—. Recipient Best News Story award, Editorial Writing award, Headline Writing award AP Mng. Editors Assn., 1985. Mem. Ark. AP (pres. 1989-90), Mng. Editors Assn. (bd. dirs. 1986-91). Avocations: travel, golf, reading. Home: 5 Nicole Ct North Little Rock AR 72118-3134 Office: Ark Dem-Gazette 121 E Capitol Ave Little Rock AR 72201-3819

LUTGENS, HARRY GERARDUS, food company executive; b. Geleen, The Netherlands; s. Hubertus and Antoinetta (Ramakers) L.; m. Denyse Richard; children: Louise, Carolyn. Cert. Adminstrv. Mgr., U. Toronto, Ont., Can., 1969, Cert. Gen. Acct., 1971. From acct. to mgr. fin. planning analysis Miracle Food Mart div. Steinberg Inc., Rexdale, Ont., 1963-74, regional mgr., 1974-78; various mgmt. positions to pres., gen. mgr. Valdi Foods Inc., Rexdale, 1978-93; ret., 1993. Mem. Cert. Gen. Accts. Assn., Cert. Adminstrv. Mgrs. Assn. Avocations: traveling, golf, home repair. Home: 20 Inverary Cres, Agincourt, ON Canada M1T 2W5

LUTH, WILLIAM CLAIR, research manager; b. Winterset, IA, June 28, 1934; s. William Henry Luth and Ora Anna (Klingaman) Sorenson; m. Betty L. Heubrock, Aug. 23, 1953; children: Linda Diane, Robert William, Sharon Jean. BA in Geology, U. of Iowa, 1958, MS in Geology, 1960; PhD in Geochemistry, Penn State U., 1963. Research assoc. in geochemistry Pa. State U., University Park, Pa., 1963-65; asst. prof. geochemistry MIT, Cambridge, Mass., 1965-68; assoc. prof. geology Stanford U., 1968-77, prof. of geology, 1977-79; supr. geophysics div. Sandia Nat. Labs, Albuquerque, N. Mex., 1979-82; mgr. geosciences dept. Sandia Nat. Labs, Albuquerque, 1982-90; mgr. geoscis. rsch. program U.S. Dept. Energy, Washington, 1990-95, acting dir. divsn. engring. & geosci., 1994-95, dir. divsn. engring and geosci., 1996—; geoscientist US ERDA/DOE Washington, 1976-78; faculty sabbatical Sandia Laboratories, Albuquerque, N. Mex., 1975, visiting staff mem. Los Alamos Nat. Lab, 1978. Contbr. articles to profl. jours. Served with U.S. Army, 1953-56. Grantee NSF, 1964-78. Avocations: photography, shooting. Home: 7516 Miller Fall Rd Rockville MD 20855-1122 Office: US Dept Energy ER-15 Washington DC 20545

LUTHER, DARLENE, state legislator; b. 1947; m. Bill Luther; 2 children. BA, U. St. Thomas. Mem. Minn. Ho. of Reps., 1993—. Home: 6809 Shingle Creek Dr Brooklyn Park MN 55445-2647 Office: Minn Ho of Reps State Capital Building Saint Paul MN 55155-1606

LUTHER, FLORENCE JOAN (MRS. CHARLES W. LUTHER), lawyer; b. N.Y.C. June 28, 1928; d. John Phillip and Catherine Elizabeth (Duffy) Thomas ; J.D. magna cum laude, U. Pacific, 1963; m. William J. Regan (dec.); children—Kevin P., Brian T.; m. 2d, Charles W. Luther, June 11, 1961. Admitted to Calif. bar; mem. firm Luther, Luther, O'Connor & Johnson, Sacramento, 1964—. Mem. faculty McGeorge Sch. Law, U. Pacific, Sacramento, 1966-88, prof., 1968-88, prof. emeritus, 1988—. Judge Bank Am. Achievement awards, 1969-71. Bd. dirs. Sacramento Suicide Prevention League, 1969-70. Mem. ABA, Calif., Sacramento County bar assns., AAUP, Womens Legal Groups, Am. Judicature Soc., Order of Coif, Iota Tau Tau. Mem. bd. advisors Community Property Jour., 1974—, state decision editor, 1974—. Home: 11101 Fair Oaks Blvd Fair Oaks CA 95628-5136 Office: PO Box 1030 Fair Oaks CA 95628-1030

LUTHER, GEORGE AUBREY, orthopedic surgeon; b. Keokuk, Iowa, Dec. 11, 1933; s. George August and Leda (Galbraith) L.; m. Dorothy Gould Luther, Aug. 18, 1956; children: Melinda, George Bradley. AB, Cen Meth. U., 1955; MD, Vanderbilt U., 1959. Diplomate Am. Bd. Orthopaedic Surgery. Intern Vanderbilt U. Hosp., Nashville, 1959-60, resident, 1961-64, instr., 1964; resident St. Louis City Hosp., 1960-61; pres. St. Louis Orthopedic Inst., 1965—; pres. med. staff St. Joseph Hosp., St. Louis, 1982-83; trustee St. Joseph Hosp., 1981-84. Contbr. article profl. jours. Served to maj. U.S. Army, 1967-69. Fellow Am. Acad. Orthopedic Surgery, ACS (admissions com. 1982—); mem. AMA, Mo. Orthopedic Soc. (v.p. 1985-86, pres. 1986-87), St. Louis Metro. Med. Soc. (counselor 1983-85), Vanderbilt Orthopedic Soc. (pres. 1981-82), Tenn. Soc. of St. Louis. Republican. Methodist. Club: Bellerive Country. Avocations: music, sports. Home: 177 Ladue Oaks Ct Saint Louis MO 63141-8128 *I have been most fortunate to be associated with the most important people in my life - great parents, a wonderful wife, and terrific friends. With the support and guidance of these individuals, one could not help but succeed in any and all endeavors.*

LUTHER, MARK ALAN, electrical deisgn engineer; b. Newport News, Dec. 9, 1963; s. Edward Morris and Brenda Lucille (Hill) L.; m. Anna Bessie Belt, Oct. 5, 1991; 1 child, Jessica Victoria. BSEE, Old Domionion U., Norfolk, Va., 1987. Elec. test engr. Newport News Shipbldg. and Drydock Co., 1990-92; design engr. Texcom, Inc., Portsmouth, Va., 1992—. Mem. Moose (legionnaire). Avocations: hunting, playing softball, volleyball. Home: 527 Beech Dr Newport News VA 23601 Office: Texcom Inc 801 Water St # 500 Portsmouth VA 23704

LUTHER, VICTORIA JEAN, prevention specialist, school nurse; b. Warren, Ohio, May 17, 1947; d. Albert William and Virginia Jean (Esau) Dyson; m. Hayward B. Luther, July 27, 1968; children: Michelle Luther, William Luther. RN diploma, Youngstown Hosp., 1968; student, Youngstown State U., 1988-91; BSHS, Thomas Edison State Coll., 1993. Cert. prevention cons., Ohio; cert. sch. nurse, Ohio. Sch. nurse Columbiana County JVS, Lisbon, Ohio, 1981-87, South Range Local Schs., North Lima, Ohio, 1987-91; prevention cons. Family Recovery Ctr., Lisbon, 1991—; sch. nurse Salem (Ohio) City Schs., 1992—; prevention cons. in field, 1981—. Recipient Ohio Exemplary Sch. award Ohio Dept. of Alcohol and Drug Addiction Svcs., 1992. Mem. Bus. and Profl. Womens Com. (chair), N.E. Ohio Nurse's Assn., Ohio Nurse's Assn. Home: 4150 W Middletown Rd Canfield OH 44406-9418 Office: Salem City Schs 1226 E State St Salem OH 44460-2222

LUTHER, WILLIAM P., congressman; b. Fergus Falls, Minn., June 27, 1945; s. Leonard and Eleanor L.; m. Darlene Luther, Dec. 16, 1967; children: Alexander, Alicia. BS in Elec. Engring. with high distinction, U. Minn., 1967; JD cum laude, U. Minn. Law Sch., 1970. Judicial clerkship 8th cir. U.S. Ct. Appeals, 1970-71; atty. Dorsey & Whitney Law Firm, Mpls., 1971-74, William P. Luther Law Office, Mpls., 1974-83; founder, sr. ptnr. Luther, Ballenthin & Carruthers Law Firm, Mpls., 1983-92; state sen. 47th dist. State of Minn., 1977-94, asst. maj. leader, 1983-94; rep. 6th dist. U.S. House of Reps., 1995—. Home: 6375 St. Croix Trail N # 147 Stillwater MN 55082 Office: US House Reps 1419 Longworth HOB Washington DC 20515 also: 1811 Weir Dr Ste 150 Woodbury MN 55125*

LUTHER-LEMMON, CAROL LEN, middle school educator; b. Waverly, N.Y., May 8, 1955; d. Carl Ross and Mary Edith (Auge) Luther; m. Mark Kevin Lemmon, June 21, 1986; children: Matthew C., Cathryn M. BS, Ithaca Coll., 1976; MS in Edn., Elmira Coll., 1982. Cert. elem. and secondary tchr., Pa., N.Y. Reading aide Waverly (N.Y.) Central Schs., 1978-80; tchr. reading N.Y. State Div. for Youth, Lansing, 1981-82; tchr. title I reading, mem. student assistance program and instructional support team Rowe Mid. Sch., Athens (Pa.) Area Sch. Dist., 1982—. Basketball coach Youth Activities Dept., Athens, 1982-85, asst. softball coach, 1990-91; mem. ad hoc com. Waverly Sch. Dist., 1990-91; mem. Goal G parents & edn. Mid. Sch. Implementation Team for WINGS-Waverly in a Global Soc. for Waverly Ctr. Sch. Dist. Strategic Plan; bd. dirs. SACC, 1995-96, Waverly Cmty. Ch., 1976-78; active Girls' Softball League Waverly, 1978-80, commr., 1980; choir mem. Meth. Ch., Wverly, 1976-90, adminstrv. bd., trustee, chmn. bd. trustees, 1995, 96; mem. Valley Chorus, Pa. and N.Y., 1983-86. With USAR, 1977-83. Mem. ASCD, AAUW (v.p. Waverly br. 1982-83, pres. Waverly br. 1992—), Am. Legion Aux. (girl's state rep. 1972, girl's state chmn. 1976-80 Waverly post, counselor 1977), Chemung Area Reading Coun., N.Y. State Reading Assn. Republican. Home: 490 Waverly St Waverly NY 14892-1102 Office: Athens Area Sch Dist Pennsylvania Ave Athens PA 18810-1440

LUTHEY, GRAYDON DEAN, JR., lawyer; b. Topeka, Sept. 18, 1955; s. Graydon Dean Sr. and S. Anne (Murphy) L.; m. Deborah Denise McCullough, May 26, 1979; children: Sarah Elizabeth, Katherine Alexandra. BA in Letters with highest honors, U. Okla., 1976, JD, 1979; Fellow in Theology, Oxford (Eng.) U., 1976. Bar: Okla. 1979, U.S. Ct. Appeals (10th cir.) 1979, U.S. Dist. Ct. (no., we. and ea. dists.) Okla. 1980, U.S. Supreme Ct. 1982. Assoc. Jones, Givens, Gotcher, Bogan & Hilborne, Tulsa, 1979-84, ptnr., 1984-92, also bd. dirs.; ptnr. Hall, Estill, Hardwick, Gable, Golden & Nelson, Tulsa, 1992—, also bd. dirs.; adj. assoc. prof. U. Tulsa, 1985-87, adj. prof., 1987—; vis. fellow in theology Keble Coll., Oxford (Eng.) U., 1976; presiding judge Okla. Temporary Ct. Appeals, 1992-93; mem. Okla. Supreme Ct. Rules Com., 1992—. bd. dirs. Tulsa Ballet, 1987—; chmn. Tulsa Pub. facilties Authority, 1990-93; trustee Episcopal Theol. Sem. of S.W., 1991—, exec. com., 1992—; vice chmn. Univ. Hosps. Authority, 1993-94, chmn. 1994—. Nat. Merit scholar U. Okla., 1973. Fellow Am. Bar Found.; mem. ABA, Okla. Bar Assn. (chmn. continuing legal edn. com. 1989-91), Tulsa County Bar Assn. (bd. dirs. 1983-89, Disting. Svc. award 1988), Am. Inns of Ct. (barrister), Summit Club, Golf Club Okla., Beta Theta Pi, Phi Beta Kappa, Omicron Delta Kappa. Office: Hall Estill Hardwick Gable Golden & Nelson 320 S Boston Ave Ste 400 Tulsa OK 74103-3704

LUTHRINGSHAUSER, DANIEL RENE, manufacturing company executive; b. Fontainebleau, France, July 23, 1935; came to U.S., 1937; s. Ernest Henri and Jeanne (Guerville) L.; m. Carol King; children: Mark Ernest, Heidi Elizabeth. BS, NYU, 1956, MBA, 1970. With exec. tng. program, internat. pub. relations Merck & Co. Inc., Rahway, N.J. and N.Y.C., 1962-65; dep. mktg. dir. Merck Sharp & Dohme Internat., Brussels, 1965-66; mktg. service dir. Paris, 1966-69; gen. mgr. Merck Sharp & Dohme/Chibret, Paris, 1970-74; v.p. mktg. Merrell (France), Paris, 1974-78; v.p. gen. mgr. Revlon Devel. Corp., Paris, 1978-82, Medtronic Europe, Paris, Africa, Middle East, 1982-86; v.p. internat. Medtronic Inc., Mpls., 1986—; bd. dirs. Medtronic Found., Mpls., 1986-91; chmn. Internat. Assn. of Prosthesis Mfrs., Paris, 1983-85. Bd. dirs. Am. Hosp. Paris, 1983-86, 94-95, Minn. Internat. Ctr., 1990—; mem. Am. Club Paris, 1970-80, Medtronic Found., Mpls., 1986-91. Served to capt. USAF, 1956-62. Recipient Gold medal Am. Mktg. Assn., 1956. Club: Ausable (Keene Valley, N.Y.). Avocations: gardening, golf, squash, skiing. Home: 480 Peavey Rd Wayzata MN 55391-1529 Office: Medtronic Inc 7000 Central Ave NE Minneapolis MN 55432-3568

LUTHY, JOHN FREDERICK, management consultant; b. Kansas City, Mo., Dec. 12, 1947; s. Walter Frederick Luthy and Loraine Florence Tramill; children: Rozlyn, Bryan, John Paul. BA, Baker U., 1969; MS, U. Mo., 1973; MPA, Boise State U., 1978; EdD, U. Idaho, 1991. Mgr. State Com. Disease Edn., Topeka, 1973; dir. Divsn. Health Edn., Johnson County, Kans., 1973-75; state dir. Bur. Health Edn., Boise, Idaho, 1975-80; dir. Gen. Svcs. Adminstrn., Boise, 1980-84; dir. bus. devel. Morrison Knudsen Techs. Inc., Boise, 1984-86; pres. The Futures Corp., Boise, 1986—; pres. Exec. Mgmt. Devel. Inst., Boise, 1991—; del. to China People to People, 1994. Author: (manual) Grantsmanship--A Time of Plenty, 1988; contbr. articles to profl. jours. Staff sgt. USAR, 1969-75. Recipient Nat. Early Career award APHA, 1978; named one of Outstanding Young Men of Am., U.S. Jaycees, 1977. Mem. ASTD, Am. Mgmt. Assn., U.S. Powerlifting Fedn. (exec. bd. dirs., regional chmn. 1981-86), Phi Delta Kappa. Avocations: mountain biking, power lifting, backpacking. Office: The Futures Corp 1109 Main St Ste 299A Boise ID 83702-5642

LUTHY, RICHARD GODFREY, environmental engineering educator; b. June 11, 1945; s. Robert Godfrey Luthy and Marian Ruth (Ireland) Haines; m. Mary Frances Sullivan, Nov. 22, 1967; children: Matthew Robert, Mara Catherine, Jessica Bethlin. BSChemE, U. Calif., Berkeley, 1967; MS in Ocean Engring., U. Hawaii, 1969; MSCE, U. Calif., Berkeley, 1974, PhDCE, 1976. Registered profl. engr., Pa.; diplomate Am. Acad. Environ. Engrs. Rsch. asst. dept. civil engring. U. Hawaii, Honolulu, 1968-69; rsch. asst. div. san. and hydraulic engring. U. Calif., Berkeley, 1973-75; asst. prof. civil engring. Carnegie Mellon U., Pitts., 1975-80, assoc. prof., 1980-83, prof., 1983—, assoc. dean Carnegie Inst. Tech., 1986-89, head dept. civil and environ. engring., 1989-96; cons. sci. adv. bd. U.S. EPA, 1983—, Bioremediation Action com., 1990-92; cons. U.S. Dept. Energy, 1978—, various pvt. industries; del. water sci. and tech. bd. NAE, Washington and Beijing, 1988; mem. tech. adv. bd. Remediation Techs., Inc., Concord, Mass., 1989-94, Fostin Capital, Pitts., 1991-94, Balt. Gas & Elec., 1992-95, Pa. Dept. Environ. Protection, 1994—; mem. sci. adv. com. Hazardous Substance Rsch. Ctr. Stanford U., 1994—; chair Gordon Rsch. Conf. Environ. Scis., 1994, Nat. Rsch. Coun. Commn. on Innovative Remediation Tech. Contbr. articles to tech. and sci. jours. Chmn. NSF/AEEP Conf. on Fundamental Rsch. Directions in Environ. Engring, Washington, 1988. Lt. C.E. Corps, USN, 1969-72. Recipient George Tallman Ladd award Carnegie Inst. Tech., 1977. Mem. ASCE (Pitts. sect. Prof. of Yr. award 1987), Assn. Environ. Engring. Profs. (pres. 1987-88, Nalco award 1978, 82, Engring. Sci. award 1988), Water Pollution Control Fedn. (rsch. com. 1982-86, awards com. 1981-84, 89-94, std. methods com. 1977—, groundwater com. 1989-90, editor jour. 1989-92, Eddy medal 1980), Internat. Assn. on Water Quality (Founders award U.S. Nat. Com. 1986, 93, orgnl. com. 16th Biennial Conf. Washington 1992), Am. Chem. Soc. (divsn. environ. chemistry, mem. editl. adv. bd. Environ. Sci. Tech. 1992-95). Presbyterian. Home: 620 S Linden Ave Pittsburgh PA 15208-2813 Office: Carnegie Mellon U Dept Civil & Environ Engring Pittsburgh PA 15213-3890

LUTLEY, JOHN H., precious metals company executive; b. Chefoo, China, Feb. 10, 1935; came to U.S., 1978; s. Albert French and Martha Davis (Bullitt) L.; m. Mary Heather Maingot, July 18, 1959; children: Elizabeth, Jennifer, Richard. B.A. in Metallurgy, Cambridge U., 1958. With Johnson Matthey Group, Malvern, Pa., Eng., Can., 1958-84; owner, pres. Klein & Saks, Inc., Washington, 1984—; pres. Gold Inst.; exec. dir. Silver Inst. Office: Klein & Saks Inc 1026 16th St NW Suite 101 Washington DC 20036

LUTRINGER, RICHARD EMIL, lawyer; b. N.Y.C., Feb. 4, 1943; s. Emil Vincent Lutringer and Alice Rich Danser; m. Dagmar Bonitz, May 1, 1970 (div. 1980); m. Clarinda Higgins, Oct. 11, 1980; children: Emily, Eric. AB, Coll. of William and Mary, 1964; JD in Internat. Affairs, Cornell U., 1967; MCL, U. Chgo., 1969. Bar: N.Y. 1972, U.S. Dist. Ct. (so. dist.) N.Y. 1972. Assoc. Whitman & Ransom, N.Y.C., 1971-80, ptnr., 1980-94; ptnr. Morgan, Lewis & Bockius, N.Y.C., 1994—. Vice pres. N.Y.-N.J. Trail Conf., N.Y.C., 1976-80. Mem. ABA, Internat. Bar Assn., Assn. of Bar of City of N.Y. (chmn. com. fgn. and comparative law 1990-93), Am. Fgn. Law Assn. (pres. 1989-93, treas. 1986-89), European-Am. C. of C. (vice chair trade com. 1992—). Avocations: sailing, hiking, skiing. Home: 2 Owenoke Park Westport CT 06880-6851 Office: Morgan Lewis & Bockius 101 Park Ave New York NY 10178

LUTTER, PAUL ALLEN, lawyer; b. Chgo., Feb. 28, 1946; s. Herbert W. and Lois (Muller) L. BA, Carleton Coll., 1968; JD, Yale U., 1971. Bar: Ill. 1971, U.S. Tax Ct. 1986. Assoc. Ross & Hardies, Chgo., 1971-77, ptnr., 1978—. Co-author: Illinois Estate Administration, 1993. Dir. ACLU of Ill., Howard Brown Health Ctr.; mem. chmn.'s coun. DIFFA Chgo. Mem. ABA, Chgo. Bar Assn. Home: 2214 N Magnolia Ave Chicago IL 60614-3104 Office: Ross & Hardies 150 N Michigan Ave Ste 2500 Chicago IL 60601-7525

LUTTIG, J. MICHAEL, federal judge; b. 1954. BA, Washington and Lee U., 1976; JD, U. Va., 1981. Asst. counsel The White House, 1981-82; law clk. to Judge Antonin Scalia U.S. Ct. of Appeals D.C. Cir., 1982-83; law clerk to chief justice Warren Burger Supreme Ct. of U.S., 1983-84, spl. asst. to chief justice Warren Burger, 1984-85; assoc. Davis Polk & Wardwell, 1985-89; prin. dep. asst. atty. gen., office of legal counsel U.S. Dept. of Justice, 1989-90, asst. atty. gen., office of legal counsel, counselor to atty. gen., 1990-91; judge U.S. Cir. Ct. (4th cir.), McLean, Va., 1991—. Mem. Nat. Adv. Com. of Lawyers for Bush, 1988, Lawyers for Bush Com., 1988. Mem. ABA, Va. Bar Assn., D.C. Bar Assn. Office: Circuit Ct 8280 Greensboro Dr Ste 780 Mc Lean VA 22102-3807

LUTTINGER, JOAQUIN MAZDAK, retired physics educator, researcher; b. N.Y.C., Dec. 2, 1923; s. Paul and Shirley Luttinger; m. Abigail Thomas, Oct. 13, 1942 (div.); 1 child, Catherine Thomas. SB, MIT, 1944, PhD, 1947. Asst. prof. physics U. Wis., 1950-52; mem. Inst. Advanced Study, 1952-53; assoc. prof. physics U. Mich., Ann Arbor, 1953-57; NRC sr. postdoctoral fellow École Normale Supérieure, Paris, 1957-58; prof. physics U. Pa., 1958-60; prof. physics Columbia U., 1960-93, chmn. dept., 1977-80; ret., 1993; exchange prof., Moscow, 1962. Contbr. over 80 articles to profl. jours. Swiss Am. Exchange fellow, 1947-48, Nat. Research fellow, 1948-49, Sr. Postdoctoral fellow Rockefeller U., 1968, Guggenheim fellow Rockefeller U., 1975-76. Mem. Nat. Acad. Scis., Am. Acad. Arts and Scis. Office: Columbia Univ Dept of Physics 826 Pupin Lab New York NY 10027

LUTTRULL, SHIRLEY JOANN, protective services official; b. Fordland, Mo., Feb. 26, 1937; d. Thomas Marion and Pauline (Sherrow) Pirtle; m. Leslie Allen Luttrull, June 3, 1956 (div. May 1978); children: Vicki Lynn, Ricki Allen; m. Orben Lowell Clark, Dec. 31, 1982 (div. Oct. 1987); m. Barry Mabe, June 1992 (div. Oct. 1994). Student, Southwest Mo. State U., 1979. Checker person Lea's Market, Fordland, Mo., 1955-56; plant supr. Mellers Photo Lab., Springfield, Mo., 1968-82; shopper Hopper and Hawkins, Dallas, 1982-83; crew leader Sentinal Security, Okla. City, Shrink Control Corp., Houston, 1984-86; sales mgr. Shrink Control Corp., 1986-88; owner Internal Theft Control, Springfield, 1988--. Mem. Mo. Retail Grocers Assn., Springfield C. of C. Republican. Avocations: water skiing, scuba diving, ballroom dancing. Home and Office: 1347 S Airwood Dr Springfield MO 65804-0520

LUTTS, RALPH HERBERT, museum administrator, scholar, educator; b. Quincy, Mass., Jan. 7, 1944; s. Herbert Warren Lutts and Jean May (MacKenzie) Easton. BA in Biology, Trinity U., San Antonio, 1967; EdD, U. Mass., 1978. Curator, educator Mus. Sci., Boston, 1967-73; naturalist Hampshire Coll., Amherst, Mass., 1973-80; natural sci. faculty Hampshire Coll., 1976-84; dir. Blue Hills Trailside Mus., Mass. Audubon Soc., Milton, 1980-90; dir. edn. Va. Mus. Natural History, Martinsville, 1990-92, dir. outreach div., 1992-94, rsch. assoc., 1994—; assoc.faculty Goddard Coll., Plainfield, Vt., 1995—; pres. Alliance for Environ. Edn., 1988-89; founding pres. New Eng. Environ. Edn. Alliance, 1980-84; assoc. Ctr. for Animals and Pub. Policy, Tufts U. Sch. Vet. Medicine, North Grafton, Mass., 1989-90; dept. dir. mid-atlantic region Global Network of Environ. Edn. Ctrs., 1993-95, bd. dirs., 1994—. Author: The Nature Fakers: Wildlife, Science and Sentiment, 1990; founding editor New Eng. Jour. Environ. Edn., 1985-88; contbr. articles to profl. jours. Pres. Hitchcock Ctr. for Environ., Amherst, Mass., 1977-79; treas. Mass. Environ. Edn. Soc., 1982-84; mem. Blue Hills citizens' adv. com. Met. Dist. Commn., 1988-89, mgmt. adv. com., 1989-90; mem. sec.'s adv. group on environ. edn. Mass. Exec. Office for Environ. Affairs, 1989-90. Recipient New Eng. Regional awrd for achievement New Eng. Environ. Edn. Alliance, 1989. Mem. AAAS, Am. Soc. Environ. History, Assn. for Study of Lit. and Environ., Forest History Soc. (Ralph W. Hidy award 1993), N.Am. Assn. Environ. Edn., Internat. Soc. Environ. Ethics, Am. Nature Study Soc. (bd. dirs., pres. 1995—), Authors Guild, Popular Culture Assn. (area chair 1993-95), Nat. Writers Union, Rotary Internat. (Paul Harris fellow). Avocations: natural history, woodworking, book collecting.

LUTTWAK, EDWARD NICOLAE, academic, writer policy and business consultant, writer; b. Arad, Transylvania, Nov. 4, 1942; came to U.S., 1972, naturalized, 1981; s. Josif Menashe and Clara (Baruch) L.; m. Dalya Iaari, Dec. 14, 1970; children: Yael Rachel, Joseph Emannuel. B.Sc. with honors, London Sch. Econs., 1964; Ph.D. (Univ. fellow), Johns Hopkins U., 1975. Vis. prof. polit. sci. Johns Hopkins U., 1973-78; sr. fellow Georgetown U. Center Strategic and Internat. Studies, 1978-87, research prof. internat. security affairs, 1978-82, Burke chair in strategy, 1987—, dir. geo-econs., 1991-94, sr. fellow, 1994—; sr. fellow in preventive diplomacy Office of Sec. of Def., Nat. Security Coun. and Dept. State; cons. Office of Sec. of Def., Nat. Security Coun., Dept. of Def. Army, Navy and U.S. Air Force, Fgn. (allied) Govs. and U.S., overseas bus. entities. Author: Coup d'Etat, 19 edits. including 12 for lang. translations, 1968-79, Dictionary of Modern War, 1971 (also Spanish edit.), The Political Uses of Sea Power, 1975 (also Japanese edit.), The Israeli Army, 1975, 85, (also Chinese edit.), The Grand Strategy of the Roman Empire, 1976 (also Hebrew, Italian and French edits.), Strategy and Politics: Collected Essays, 1980, The Grand Strategy of the Soviet Union, 1983 (also Italian and French edits.),The Pentagon and the Art of War: The Question of Military Reform, 1985 (also Italian, Japanese and Korean edits.), Strategy and History: Collected Essays, On the Meaning of Victory, 1986 (also Italian edit.), Strategy: The Logic of War and Peace, 1987 (also Chinese, French and Italian edits.), (with Stuart Koehl) Dictionary of Modern War, 1991 (also Italian edit.), The Endangered American Dream, 1993 (also French, Italian, German and Japanese edits.). Republican. Jewish. Office: CSIS 1800 K St NW Washington DC 20006-2202

LUTU, AFOA MOEGA, legislator, lawyer; b. Leulumoega-Fou, W.S., Feb. 24, 1947; s. Solofa Suesue and Vaituutuu (Leotaleuluaialii) L.; m. Etenauga Lam Yuen, Sept. 23, 1972; 10 children. BA in Polit. Sci., U. Hawaii, 1971; JD, Valparaiso U., 1974. Asst. law clk. High Ct. of Am. Samoa, Utulei, Pago Pago, 1972; rep. from 7th dist. Legislature of Am. Samoa, Utulei, 1993—, spl. counsel to senate, 1989-93; pvt. practice law Utulei, 1976-84; atty. gen. Govt. of Am. Samoa, Utulei, 1985-89; chmn. econ. devel. authority Govt. of Am. Samoa, 1986, legal counsel constnl. convention, 1986; chmn. judiciary com. Ho. of Reps., Am. Samoa, 1993—; chmn. Real Property Mgmt. Bd. and Indsl. Park Commn., Am. Samoa, 1985-89; chmn. adv. panel Western Pacific Regional Fishery Coun., Am. Samoa; chmn. 1st bond issue Am. Samoa Econ. Devel. Authority, 1987. Chief Afoafouvale, Fagatogo-Utulei Village Coun., 1990. Mem. ABA, Am. Samoa Bar Assn. (treas.), U.S. Supreme Ct. Bar Assn., Tautai-O-Samoa Fishing Assn. (pres.). Avocations: deep sea fishing, golf. Office: Fono PO Box 1029 Pago Pago AS 96799-1029

LUTVAK, MARK ALLEN, computer company executive; b. Chgo., Feb. 9, 1939; s. Joseph Issac and Jeanette Nettie (Pollock) L.; BS in Elec. Engring., U. Mich., 1962; MBA, Wayne State U., Detroit, 1969; m. Gayle Helene Rotofsky, May 24, 1964; children: Jeffrey, Eric. Sales rep. IBM Corp., 1962-64; successively sales rep., product mktg. mgr., corp. product mgr. Burroughs Corp., Detroit, 1964-76; mgr. product mktg. Memorex Corp., Santa Clara, Calif., 1976-80, product program gen. mgr., 1980-81; dir. product mktg. Personal Computer div. Atari, Inc., Sunnyvale, Calif., 1981-83; dir. mktg., v.p. Durango Systems, San Jose, Calif., 1983-85; dir. mktg. ITTQUME Corp., San Jose, 1985-87; v.p. mktg. Optimem, Mountain View, Calif., 1987-88; dir. mktg. Priam Corp., San Jose, 1988-91; dir. Memorex, Santa Clara, Calif. 1991-94; pres. Synergistic Mktg., 1994—; prof. Applied Mgmt. Center, Wayne State U., 1967-72, Walsh U., Troy, Mich., 1974-76, West Valley Coll., Saratoga, Calif., 1977-78. Trustee, pres. brotherhood Temple Emanuel, San Jose, Calif., 1979-80. Mem. IEEE, Soc. Applied Math., Alpha Epsilon Pi. Home: 1364 Box Canyon Rd San Jose CA 95120-5627

LUTZ, ALAN G., computer company executive; b. 1945. Pres. Switching Networks Group and Pub. Networks Group No. Teleco, pres. Kassandra Group; exec. v.p., pres. Computer Systems Group Unisys, Blue Bell, Pa., 1994—. Office: Unisys Corp Township Ln Nion Mtg Rads Blue Bell PA 19422*

LUTZ, CARL FREIHEIT, academic administrator; b. Lansing, Mich., Dec. 8, 1934; s. Paul and Edmunda (Freiheit) L.; m. Vivian Ericson; m. Aug. 18, 1959; children—Timothy Paul, Elizabeth. B.S. in Metallurgy, Mich. State U., 1956; M.S., Carnegie Inst. Tech., 1957, Ph.D., 1959; postgrad. student, Max Planck Inst. Physics, 1959-60. Asst. prof. USAF Acad., 1960-63; sr. engr. Rockwell-Standard Corp., Detroit, 1963-66, Kaiser Aluminum Co., Spokane, 1966-67; v.p., dean engring. S.D. Sch. Mines and Tech., Rapid City, 1967-74; dep. commr. higher edn. State of Ind., Indpls., 1974-79; chancellor Ivy Tech. State Coll., South Bend and others, 1979—. Served with USAF, 1960-63. Mem. Am. Soc. Engring. Edn., Am. Inst. Mining, Metall. and Petroleum Engrs., Am. Soc. Metals, Soc. Research Adminstrs., Sigma Xi, Delta Sigma Phi.

LUTZ, FRANCIS CHARLES, university dean, civil engineering educator; b. Pottsville, Pa., Apr. 5, 1944; s. Charles Henry and Pauline Anna (Weislo) L.; m. Evelyn Florence Zommer, Apr. 29, 1972; 1 child, Stephanie Diane. BSCE, N.J. Inst. Tech., 1966; MSCE, NYU, 1967, PhD, 1971. Assoc. M. Disko Assocs., West Orange, N.J., 1970-72; asst. prof. civil engring. Worcester Poly. Inst., Mass., 1972-76; prof. Worcester Poly. Inst., 1980—, assoc. dean, 1980-90, dean undergrad. studies, 1990-95; cons. Council on Environ. Quality, Washington, 1974-75; reviewer NSF. Co-editor: Studies in Science, Technology and Culture, Worcester Poly. Inst.; contbr. articles to profl. jours. Trustee Worcester Ctr. for Crafts, 1992—; mem. Boston Fed. Exec. Bd., 1972-74, Cen. Mass. Regional Planning Commn., Worcester, 1975-77. Am. Council on Edn. fellow, 1988-89; honors scholar NYU. Mem. ASCE, Am. Soc. Engring. Edn., Boynton Assn. (pres. 1982, 83), Sigma Xi, Chi Epsilon. Office: Worcester Poly Inst 100 Institute Rd Worcester MA 01609-2247

LUTZ, FRANK WENZEL, education administration educator; b. St. Louis, Sept. 24, 1928; s. Vincent J. and Helen M. (Scrivens) L.; m. Susan Virginia Bleikamp, July 12, 1958; children: Paul E., Andrew C., Lynn S. AA, Harris Tchrs. Coll., 1948; BS, Washington U., 1950, MS, 1954, EdD, 1962. Instr. Washington U., St. Louis, 1961-62; from asst. to assoc. prof. NYU, N.Y.C., 1964-68; dir. div. policy studies Pa. State U., State College, 1968-73; prof. edn. adminstrn. Pa. State U., 1974-80; dean Sch. Edn. Eastern Ill. U., 1980-82, asst. to v.p., 1982-83; prof., dir. Ctr. Policy Studies East Tex. State U., Commerce, Tex., 1983-92, prof. edn. adminstrn., 1991—; nat. lectr. Nova S.W. U., 1991—; mem., pres. Pattonville (Mo.) Sch. Bd., 1960-62; mem. adv. com. Opportunities Acad. Mgmt. Tng., Phila., 1975-90. Author seven books, numerous book chpts. in field; contbr. over 100 articles to profl. jours. Deacon 1st Presbyn. Ch., Commerce, Tex., 1989-91. Doctoral fellow Washington U., 1960-61; grantee U.S. Office Edn., OEO. Mem. Am. Edn. Rsch. Assn. (sec. Div. 1970-72, dir. rsch. pre-session 1969, program com. 1970), Commerce Rotary (pres. 1991-92, chair internat. svc. 1994-96), Phi Delta Kappa (life, pres. Washington U. chpt. 1960, 1st v.p. East Tex. State U. chpt. 1985, Lafferty Faculty Senate Disting. scholarship award 1996). Avocations: appaloosa horses, opera, classical music. Home: PO Box 51 Nederland CO 80466-0051 Office: East Tex State U Edn North Building Rm 214 Commerce TX 75428

LUTZ, GRETCHEN KAY, English language educator; b. Ft. Worth, Tex., Jan. 6, 1948. BA, Tex. Christian U., 1970; MA, U. Houston, 1974, Rice U., 1995; postgrad., Dartmouth Coll., 1994; MA, Rice U., 1995. High sch. and mid. sch. tchr. English Galveston and Deer Park (Tex.) Sch. Dists., 1970-77; instr. ESL and English Schreiner Coll., Kerrville, Tex., 1979-80; instr. English San Jacinto Coll. Ctr., Pasadena, Tex., 1981—. Contbr. articles to profl. jours. Mem. MLA, Nat. Symposium for Coherence in Liberal Arts, C.C. Humanities Assn., Am. Culture and Popular Culture Assn., U.S. European Command Mil. to Mil. Program Conf., Am. Studies Assn. Tex., South Ctrl. MLA, Conf. Coll. Tchrs. English (exec. coun.), S.W. Conf. Christianity and Lit., Western Soc. 18th Century Studies, Tex. Folklore Soc., S.W. Regional Conf. English in Two-Year Colls., Tex. Voices Sesquicentennial Series, Rice English Symposium, San Jacinto Coll. Faculty Symposium. Home: 3946 Sherwood Forest #135E Dallas TX 75220

LUTZ, JOHN SHAFROTH, lawyer; b. San Francisco, Sept. 10, 1943; s. Frederick Henry and Helena Morrison (Shafroth) L.; m. Elizabeth Boschen, Dec. 14, 1968; children: John Shafroth, Victoria. BA, Brown U., 1965; JD, U. Denver, 1971. Bar: Colo. 1971, U.S. Dist. Ct. Colo. 1971, U.S. Ct. Appeals (2d cir.) 1975, D.C. 1976, U.S. Supreme Ct. 1976, U.S. Dist. Ct. (so. dist.) N.Y. 1977, U.S. Tax Ct. 1977, U.S. Ct. Appeals (10th cir.) 1979, N.Y. 1984, U.S. Ct. Appeals (9th cir.) 1990, U.S. Dist. Ct. (no. dist.) Calif. 1993. Trial atty. Denver regional office U.S. SEC, 1971-74; spl. atty. organized crime, racketeering sect. U.S. Dept. Justice, So. Dist. N.Y., 1974-77; atty. Kelly, Stansfield and O'Donnell, Denver, 1977-78; gen. counsel Boettcher & Co., Denver, 1978-87, Kelly, Stansfield and O'Donnel, Denver, 1987; spl. counsel, 1987-88, ptnr., 1988-93; of counsel LeBoeuf, Lamb, Greene and Mac Rae, L.L.P., 1993-94, ptnr. 1995—; spkr. on broker, dealer, securities law and arbitration issues to various profl. orgns. Contbr. articles to profl. jours. Bd. dirs. Cherry Creek Improvement Assn., 1980-84, Spalding Rehab. Hosp., 1986-89; chmn., vice-chmn. securities sub sect. Bus. Law Sect. of Colo. Bar, 1990, chmn., 1990-91. Lt. (j.g.), USNR, 1965-67. Mem. ABA, Colo. Bar Assn., Denver Bar Assn., Am. Law Inst., Securities Industry Assn. (state regulations com. 1982-86), Nat. Assn. Securities Dealers, Inc. (nat. arbitration com. 1987-91), St. Nicholas Soc. N.Y.C., Denver Law Club, Denver Country Club, Denver Athletic Club (dir. 1990-93), Rocky Mountain Brown Club (founder, past pres.), Racquet and Tennis Club. Republican. Episcopalian. Office: LeBoeuf Lamb Greene & MacRae LLP 633 17th St Ste 2800 Denver CO 80202-3628

LUTZ, JULIE HAYNES, astronomy and mathematics educator; b. Mt. Vernon, Ohio, Dec. 17, 1944; d. Willard Damon and Julia Awilda (Way) Haynes; m. Thomas Edward Lutz, July 8, 1967 (dec. 1995); children: Melissa, Clea. BS, San Diego State U., 1965; MS, U. Ill., 1968, PhD, 1971. Asst. prof. astronomy Wash. State U., Pullman, 1972-78, asst. dean sci., 1978-79, assoc. prof., 1978-84, assoc. provost, 1981-82, prof., 1984—, chair math. and astronomy dept., 1992—; rsch. fellow Univ. Coll. London, England, 1976-77, 82-83; vis. resident astronomer Cerro Tololo Inter-Am. Obs., 1988-89; dir. div. astron. scis. NSF, 1990-92. Contbr. articles on astron. research to profl. jours. Fellow AAAS (mem. com. 1982-85, mem. nominating com. 1992—, chair sect. D 1993—), Royal Astron. Soc.; mem. Am. Astron., Soc. (chair publs. bd. 1986-88), Astron. Soc. Pacific (bd. dirs. 1988—, v.p. 1989, pres. 1990-92), Internat. Astron. Union. Avocations: cooking, backpacking, fishing. Home: 1200 NE Mcgee St Pullman WA 99163-3818 Office: Wash State U Program in Astronomy Pullman WA 99164-3113

LUTZ, KARL EVAN, lawyer; b. Dearborn, Mich., Dec. 18, 1949; s. Wallace G. and Marquerite E. (Smith) L.; m. Jeanne Daniel, June 30, 1973; children: Daniel Karl, Charles Littlefield, Kelsey Eldridge. BA, Yale U., 1972; JD, U. Mich., 1975. Bar: Ill. 1975, N.Y. 1990. Assoc. Kirkland & Ellis, Chgo., 1975-81, ptnr., 1981—. Office: Kirkland & Ellis 200 E Randolph St Chicago IL 60601-6436

LUTZ, LAWRENCE JOSEPH, family practice physician; b. Detroit, Dec. 16, 1949; s. Stephen A. and Eva B. (Groh) L.; m. Joan Regedanz, Dec. 27 (div. 1986); m. Ruthanne Rocki Ramsey, Apr. 29, 1989; 1 child, Alex Joseph. BS in Computer Sci., U. Mich., 1972; MD, Wayne State U., 1976; MSPH, U. Utah, 1982. Resident Saginaw Coop. Hosp., 1976-79; Robert Wood Johnson fellowship U. Utah, 1979-81; mem. faculty, divsn. dir. U. Utah, Salt Lake City, 1981-89; mem. faculty U. Colo., Denver, 1989-93; mem. faculty, chair family medicine Emory U., Atlanta, 1993—.

LUTZ, MATTHEW CHARLES, geologist, oil company executive; b. Bunkie, La., Mar. 28, 1934; s. John Matthew and Maxie Mae (Andrus) L.; m. Patricia Dawnn Feazel, Apr. 11, 1953; children: Matt, Jr., Cyndy, Tracey, Clay. BS, U. Southwestern La., 1956. Various geol. profl. positions Tidewater-Getty Oil Co., 1956-71; asst. dist. geologist Getty Oil Co., Houston, 1971-73, dist. geologist, Midland, Tex., 1973-78, central div. geologist, Tulsa, 1978-80, offshore dist. exploration mgr., Houston, 1980, so. div. exploration mgr., Houston, 1980-82, gen. mgr. offshore exploration and prodn., Houston, 1982-83, exploration mgr. so. div., Houston, 1983-84; sr. v.p. exploration Enserch Exploration Inc., Dallas, 1984-92, also dir.; vice chmn. & bus. devel. mgr. Hunter Resources, Inc., Irving, Tex., 1993-95, also bd. dirs.; vice chmn. exploration and bus. devel. mgr. Magnum Hunter Resources, Inc., Irving, Tex., 1995—; bd. dirs. Enserch Internat. Exploration Inc., Dallas, Enserch Processing Inc., Dallas, 1984-92. Mem. Am. Assn. Petroleum Geologists, Houston Geol. Soc., Dallas Geol. Soc., Mid-Continent Oil Gas Assn., Am. Petroleum Inst., Independent Petroleum Assn. Am. Republican. Baptist. Clubs: Dallas Petroleum, Las Colinas Sports. Avocations: travel, golf, hunting. Office: Magnum Hunter Resources Inc 600 Las Colinas Blvd E Ste 1200 Irving TX 75039-5616

LUTZ, RAYMOND PRICE, industrial engineer, educator; b. Oak Park, Ill., Feb. 27, 1935; s. Raymond Price and Sibyl Elizabeth (Haralson) L.; m. Nancy Marie Cole, Aug. 23, 1958. BSME, U. N.Mex., 1958, MBA, 1962; PhD, Iowa State U., 1964. Registered profl. engr., N.Mex., Okla. With Sandia Corp., Albuquerque, summers 1958-63; instr. mech. engring. U. N.Mex., 1958-62; asst. to assoc. prof. indsl. engring. N.Mex. State U., 1964-68; prof. head indsl. engring. U. Okla., 1968-73; prof., acting dean U. Tex. Sch. Mgmt., Dallas, 1973-76, dean, 1976-78, exec. dean grad. studies and research, 1979-92, prof. ops. mgmt., 1992—; cons. Bell Telephone Labs., Tex. Instruments, Kennecott Corp., Bath Iron Works, City of Dallas, Oklahoma City; cons. U.S. Army, USAF, U.S. Dept. Transp., Los Angeles and Seattle public schs.; mem. shipbldg. productivity panel NRC. Editor: The Engring. Economist, 1973-77, Indsl. Mgmt., 1983-87. Pres., bd. dirs. United Cerebral Palsy, Dallas, 1978, treas., 1984-88; bd. dirs., treas. Amigos Bibliographic Network, Dallas, 1984-90; chmn., bd. dirs. S.W. Police Inst., Dallas, 1980—; v.p., bd. dirs. Santa Fe Opera, 1988—; bdl dirs. Dallas Opera, 1989—, Santa Fe Opera Found., 1993—. Fellow AAAS, Am. Inst. Indsl. Engrs. (v.p. industry and mgmt. divsns., trustee, dir. engring. economy divsn., systems engring. group); mem. Am. Soc. Engring. Edn. (chmn. engring. economy divsn., Eugene L. Grant award 1972), Ops. Rsch. Soc. Am., Inst. Mgmt. Sci., Dallas Classic Guitar Soc. (bd. dirs. 1993—, v.p. 1994—), Ops. Mgmt. Assn. (bd. dirs. 1994—), Sigma Xi (bd. dirs. 1990—, chmn. capital campaign 1992—, exec. com. 1992-95). Avocation: jogging. Home: 10275 Hollow Way Dallas TX 75229 Office: U Tex at Dallas PO Box 830688 Richardson TX 75083-0688

LUTZ, ROBERT ANTHONY, automotive company executive; b. Zurich, Switzerland, Feb. 12, 1932; came to U.S., 1939; s. Robert H. and Marguerite (Schmid) L.; m. Betty D. Lutz, Dec. 12, 1956 (div. 1979); children: Jacqueline, Carolyn, Catherine, Alexandra; m. Heide Marie Schmid, Mar. 3, 1980 (div. Dec. 1993); m. Denise Ford, Apr. 17, 1994; 2 stepchildren. BS in Prodn. Mgmt., U. Calif., Berkeley, 1961, MBA in Mktg. with highest honors, 1962; LLD, Boston U., 1985. Research assoc., sr. analyst IMEDE, Lausanne, Switzerland, 1962-63; sr. analyst forward planning Gen. Motors Corp., N.Y.C., 1963-65; mgr. vehicle div. Paris, 1966-69; staff asst., mng. dir. Adam Opel, Russelsheim, Germany, 1965-66; asst. mgr. domestic sales Adam Opel, Russelsheim, Fed. Republic of Germany, 1969, dir. sales Vorstand, 1969-70; v.p. Vorstand BMW, Munich, 1972-74; gen. mgr. Ford of Germany, Cologne, Fed. Republic of Germany, 1974-76; v.p. truck ops Brentwood, Eng., 1976-77; pres. Ford of Europe, Brentwood, Eng., 1977-79, chmn., 1979-82; also bd. dirs. Brentwood, Eng.; exec. v.p. Ford Internat., Dearborn, Mich., 1982-84, Chrysler Motors Corp., Highland Park, Mich., from 1986; pres., COO Chrysler Corp., Highland Park, Mich., 1993—; bd. dirs. Silicon Graphics; adv. bd. Creditanstalt Bank, Vienna, Austria; bd. dirs. ASCOM, Switzerland; mem., former chmn. Hwy. Users Fedn. for Safety and Mobiligy. Trustee Mich. Cancer Found.; bd. dirs. United Way of Southeastern Mich.; bd. dirs. USMC Command and Staff Coll. Found.; adv. bd. Walter A. Haas Sch. Bus., U. Calif., Berkeley, 1979—. Capt. USMC, 1954-59. Named Alumnus of Yr., Sch. Bus., U. Calif., 1983; Kaiser Found. grantee 1962. Mem. Nat. Assn. Mfrs. (mem. exec. com.). Republican. Avocations: skiing, motorcycling, bicycling, helicopter flying. Office: Chrysler Corp 12000 Chrysler Dr Detroit MI 48288

LUTZ, THEODORE COMPTON, newspaper publishing executive. V.p. circulation, bus. mgr. The Washington Post, D.C. Office: Washington Post Co 1150 15th St NW Washington DC 20005-2780

LUTZ, WILLIAM LAN, lawyer; b. Chgo., May 18, 1944; s. Raymond Price and Sibyl (McCright) L.; m. Jeanne M. McAlister, Dec. 27, 1969; children: William Lan, David Price. B.S., U. Tex., 1965, J.D., 1969. Bar: Tex. 1969, N.Mex. 1970. Assoc. Martin, Lutz, Cresswell & Hubert and predecessor firms, Las Cruces, N.Mex., 1969-82; former U.S. atty. dist. N. Mex. U.S. Dept. Justice, Albuquerque, 1982-91; ptnr. Martin, Lutz & Brower, P.C., Las Cruces, N.Mex., 1991—. Mem. ABA, N.Mex. Bar Assn. (bd. of bar commrs. 1995—). Methodist. Office: Martin Lutz & Brower PO Drawer W 2100 N Main St Ste 3 Las Cruces NM 88001-1129

LUTZE, RUTH LOUISE, retired textbook editor, public relations executive; b. Boston, Apr. 19, 1917; d. Frederick Clemons and Louise (Rausch) L. BA with honors, Radcliffe Coll., 1938; postgrad., Boston U., 1938-39. Tchr. Winthrop (Mass.) Pub. Schs., 1938-39; with pub. rels. dept. Boston City Club, 1939-42; sr. projects editor D.C. Heath & Co., Lexington, Mass., 1942-82; book reviewer, lectr., cons. on pub. rels., lectr. textbook publ. Bd. dirs. Winthrop Improvement and Hist. Assn., 1980—; vol. tchr. Boston Pub. Schs., 1967-77; mem. Winthrop Rep. Town Com., 1970—; v.p. 1st Luth. Ch. Boston, 1986, deacon, 1980—. Recipient cert. appreciation for vol. in edn., Kiwanis Club of East Boston, 1972. Mem. Radcliffe Club Boston. Avocations: vol. work, theatre, birdwatching, reading, art exhibits. Home: 110 Circuit Rd Winthrop MA 02152-2819

LUVISI, LEE, concert pianist; b. Louisville, Dec. 12, 1937; m. Nina Hussey, June 20, 1959; 1 son, Brian. Student, Curtis Inst. Music, 1952-57. Mem. faculty Curtis Inst. Music, 1957-62; artist in residence U. Louisville Sch. Music. Artist-mem., Chamber Music soc. Lincoln Ctr. Office: U Louisville Sch Of Music Louisville KY 40292 also: Michal Schmidt Artists Int 59 E 54th St New York NY 10022-4211

LUX, MICHAEL SCOTT, federal government official; b. Lincoln, Nebr., May 13, 1960; s. John Elton and Ethel Carolyn (Carne) L.; m. Barbara Leigh Laur, Dec. 30, 1983. Exec. dir. Nebr. Project Energy Independence and Nebr. Energy Coalition, 1981-83; polit. dir. Iowa Citizen Action Network, 1983-84, exec. dir., 1984-87; nat. dep. polit. dir. Joe Biden for Pres. campaign, 1987; nat. cons. Paul Simon for Pres. Campaign, 1987-88; founding ptnr. Strategy Group, 1988-90; exec. v.p. Iowa Fedn. Labor, AFL-CIO, 1990-92; nat. constituency dir. Clinton-Gore Campaign, 1992; dir. Office of Constituency Outreach, Presdl. Transition, 1992-93; spl. asst. to Pres. for pub. liaison Washington, 1993-95; pres. Creative Devel. Group, Inc., 1995—; VISTA vol. Small Farms Action Group, 1980-81; summer organizer Nebraskans for Peace, 1981. Vol. Iowa Dem. Party, Des Moines and Cedar Rapids, 1983-92; co-founder, bd. mem. Green Vote, Boston, 1989-92; bd. mem. Health Policy Corp. Iowa, Des Moines, 1990-92, Iowa Workers' Compensation Adv. Bd., Des Moines, 1990-92; exec. v.p. Iowa Citizen Action Network, Des Moines, 1990-92. Mem. Internat. Assn. Machinists and Aerospace Workers. Democrat. Methodist. Avocations: basketball, reading.

LUXEMBURG, WILHELMUS ANTHONIUS JOSEPHUS, mathematics educator; b. Delft, Netherlands, Apr. 11, 1929; s. Everardus H. and Digna (Van Kranendonk) L.; m. Geetruida Zappeij, Aug. 2, 1955; children—Ronald P., Jacqueline T. B.A., U. Leiden, Netherlands, 1950, M.A., 1953; Ph.D., Delft Inst. Tech., 1955. Postdoctoral fellow NRC, Can., 1955-56; mem. faculty U. Toronto, 1956-58; faculty Calif. Inst. Tech., Pasadena, 1958—; prof. math. Calif. Inst. Tech., 1962—, exec. dir. for math., 1970-85; cons. Burroughs Corp., Pasadena, 1963-64. Mem. Am., Dutch math. socs., Math. Assn. Am., Canadian Math. Congress, Soc. for Indsl. and Applied Math., Royal Acad. Scis. Amsterdam (Humboldt award 1980). Research and publs. on theory of integration, spaces of measurable functions, ordinary differential equations, numerical analysis, topological linear spaces, Boolean algebras, axiomatic set theory, theory of Riesz spaces, non-standard analysis. Home: 817 S El Molino Ave Pasadena CA 91106-4411

LUXENBERG, MALCOLM NEUWAHL, ophthalmologist, educator; b. Philipsburg, Pa., July 29, 1935; s. Maurice and Henrietta (Neuwahl) L.; m. Sandra Diane Rosen, June 16, 1957; children: Steven Neuwahl, Cathy Ann. Student, Tulane U., 1953-56; M.D., U. Miami, Fla., 1960. Diplomate: Am. Bd. Ophthalmology. Intern Cin. Gen. Hosp., 1960-61; resident in neurology U. Vt. Affiliated Hosps., Burlington, 1961-63; resident in ophthalmology Bascom Palmer Eye Inst., U. Miami-Jackson Meml. Hosp., Miami, Fla., 1963-66; asst. prof. ophthalmology Coll. Medicine, U. Iowa, Iowa City, 1968-70; chief ophthalmology service VA Hosp., Iowa City, 1968-70; practice medicine specializing in ophthalmology West Palm Beach, Fla., 1970-72; clin. asst. prof. ophthalmology Bascom Palmer Eye Inst., Sch. Medicine, U. Miami, 1971-72; prof., chmn. dept. ophthalmology Med. Coll. Ga., Augusta, 1972—; cons. ophthalmology VA Hosp., Augusta, 1972—; Sr. surgeon USPHS, 1966-68; bd. dirs. Am. Bd. Ophthalmology. Recipient Outstanding Civilian Service Medal Dept. of Army, 1986. Mem. AMA, Am. Acad. Ophthalmology (hon. award 1986), Am. Ophthalmol. Soc., Assn. Univ. Profs. in Ophthalmology (pres. 1982-83), Ga. Soc. Ophthalmology, Med. Assn. Ga., Richmond County Med. Soc. Home: 512 Scotts Way Augusta GA 30909-3238 Office: Med Coll Ga Dept Ophthalmology Augusta GA 30912

LUXENBERG, STEVEN MARC, newspaper editor; b. Detroit, July 25, 1952; s. Julius Sam and Beth (Cohen) L.; m. Mary Jo Kirschman, June 28, 1981; children: Joshua K., Jill K. AB magna cum laude, Harvard U., 1974. Reporter Balt. Sun, 1974-79, 81-82, city editor, 1979-81, met. editor, 1982-84; dep. asst. mng. editor The Washington Post, 1985-91, asst. mng. editor investigative news/spl. projects, 1991—. Recipient Outstanding News Reporting award Nat. Headliners, 1975, award for state govt. reporting Md.-Del.-D.C. Press Assn., 1982, Feature Writing award, 1988. Office: Washington Post 1150 15th St NW Washington DC 20071

LUXMOORE, ROBERT JOHN, soil and plant scientist; b. Adelaide, South Australia, Australia, Nov. 7, 1940; came to U.S., 1966; s. John Alexander and Mary Elinor (Martin) L.; Annetta Paule Watson, Oct. 18, 1975. B Agrl. Sci., U. Adelaide, 1962, B. Agrl. Sci. with honours, 1963; PhD, U. Calif., Riverside, 1969. Cert. profl. soil scientist. Agronomist Dept. Agr., Adelaide, 1963-66; rsch. assoc. U. Ill., Champaign-Urbana, 1969-70; soil physicist U. Calif., Riverside, 1970-71; rsch. assoc. U. Wis., Madison, 1971-72; rsch. scientist Oak Ridge (Tenn.) Nat. Lab., 1973-86, sr. rsch. scientist, 1986—; cons. Ctr. for Law and Social Policy, Washington, 1979; com. mem. NRC, Washington, 1989-90. Editor: Coupling of Carbon, Water and Nutrient, 1986; contbr. articles to profl. jours. and chpts. to books. Com. mem. Rural Abandoned Mines Program, Morgan County, Tenn., 1979-81; bd. dirs. Tenn. Citizens for Wilderness Planning, Oak Ridge, 1988-91; bd. dirs. Save Our Cumberland Mountains, Lake City, Tenn., 1995—. Recipient Tech. Achievement award Martin Marietta Energy Systems, 1987; Australian Cattle & Beef Rsch. scholar, 1962. Fellow AAAS, Soil Sci. Soc. Am. (tech. editor 1988-90, editor-in-chief 1991-93, bd. dirs. 1994—); mem. Internat. Union Forestry Rsch. Orgns. (chmn. working party 1983-90, coord. dep. subject group 1991-95, exec bd. 1996—), Am. Geophys. Union. Home: 295 Solomon Hollow Rd Harriman TN 37748-9803 Office: Oak Ridge Nat Lab PO Box 2008 Oak Ridge TN 37831-2008

LUYENDYK, BRUCE PETER, geophysicist, educator, institution administrator; b. Freeport, N.Y., Feb. 23, 1943; s. Pieter Johannes and Frances Marie (Blakeney) L.; m. Linda Kay Taylor, Sept. 7, 1967 (div. 1979); 1 child, Loren Taylor Luyendyk; m. Jaye Ellen UpDeGraff, Oct. 12, 1984 (div. 1987). BS Geophysics, San Diego State Coll., 1965; PhD Marine Geophysics, Scripps Inst. Oceanography, 1969. Registered geophysicist, Calif. Geophysicist Arctic Sci. and Tech. Lab. USN Electronics Lab. Ctr., 1965; lectr. San Diego State Coll., 1967-68; postgrad rsch. geologist Scripps Inst. Oceanography, 1969; postdoctoral fellow dept. geology and geophysics Woods Hole Oceanographic Instn., 1969-70, asst. scientist dept. geology and geophysics, 1970-73; asst. prof. U. Calif., Santa Barbara, 1973-75, assoc. prof., 1975-81, prof. dept. geol. scis., 1981—, acting dir. Inst. Crustal Studies, 1987-88, dir. Inst. Crustal Studies, 1988—; com. marine geophysical formats NASCO, 1971; working group problems mid-Atlantic ridge NAS NRC, 1972; working group Inter-Union commn. Geodynamics; participant, chief sci. oceanographic cruises, geol. expeditions. Editorial bd. Geology, 1975-79, Marine Geophysical Rschs., 1976-92, Jour. Geophysical Rsch., 1982-84, Tectonophysics, 1988-92, Pageoph, 1988—; contbr. articles to profl. jours., chpts. to books, encys. Recipient Newcomb Cleveland prize AAAS, 1980, Antarctic Svc. medal U.S. NSF, Dept. Navy, 1990, numerous rsch. grants, 1971—. Fellow Geol. Soc. Am.; mem. Am. Geophysical Union, Soc. Exploration Geophysics. Home: 4645 Via Vistosa Santa Barbara CA 93110-2333 Office: Univ of Calif Santa Barbara Inst for Crustal Studies 1140 Girvetz Hall Santa Barbara CA 93106

LUZA, RADOMIR VACLAV, historian, educator; b. Prague, Czechoslovakia, Oct. 17, 1922; s. Vojtech V. and Milada (Vecera) L.; m. Libuse Ladislava Podhrazska, Feb. 5, 1949; children: Radomir V., Sabrina. JuDr, U. Brno, Czechoslovakia, 1948; MA, NYU, 1958, PhD, 1959. Assoc. prof. modern European history La. State U., New Orleans, 1966-67; prof. history Tulane U., New Orleans, 1967—; scholar-in-residence Rockefeller Found., Bellagio Study Ctr., 1988; prof. gen. history Masaryk U., Brno, 1993—. Author: The Transfer of the Sudeten Germans, 1964, History of the International Socialist Youth Movement, 1970, (with V. Mamatey) A History of the Czechoslovak Republic, 1918-1948, 1973, Austro-German Relations in the Anschluss Era, 1975, Österreich und die Grossdeutsche Idee in der NS-Zeit, 1977, Geschichte der Tschechoslowakischen Republik 1918-1948, 1980, A History of the Resistance in Austria, 1938-1945, 1984, Der Widerstand in Österreich, 1938-1945, 1985, La République Tchécoslovaque 1918-1948, 1987; mem. editl. bd. East European Quar., Contemporary Austrian Studies. With Czechoslovak Resistance, 1939-45. Recipient all Czechoslovak mil. decorations; prize Theodor Körner Found., Vienna, 1965, J. Hlavka Hon. medal Czechoslovak Acad. Arts and Scis., 1992; trantee Social Rsch. Coun., Am. Philos. Soc., Coun. Learned Socs., Fulbright Com., NEH. Mem. Am. Hist. Assn., Conf. on Slavic and East European History,Czechoslovak History Conf., So. Conf. Slavic Studies, Am. Assn. Advancement Slavic Studies, Am. Com. to Promote Studies of Habsburg Monarchy. Home: 18 Golf Club Dr Langhorne PA 19047-2163 Office: Tulane U Dept History New Orleans LA 70118

LUZKOW, JACK LAWRENCE, history educator, writer, consultant; b. Detroit, Dec. 18, 1941; s. Irving and Sally (Eagle) Farber; m. Susan Frankel, Mar. 27, 1964 (div. Dec. 1973); 1 child, Catherine Alexis; m. Virginia Ann Trieglaff, May 15, 1976; 1 child, Frank Jason. BA, Wayne State Univ., 1966; MA, St. Louis Univ., 1975, PhD, 1981. Bibliographic specialist Southern Ill. Univ., Carbondale, 1979-81; history prof. Union Coll., Barbourville, Ky., 1981-84, Marycrest Coll., Davenport, Iowa, 1984-90, Teikyo-Marycrest Univ., Davenport, Iowa, 1990—; pres. Cons. Global Learning, Davenport, 1992—; v.p. Lonetree Enterprises, Davenport, 1991—; v.p. Marycrest Acad. Senate, Davenport, 1990-91; past pres. Inst. Ednl. Seninars, Davenport, 1988; speaker Vis. Artists Series, Davenport, 1985. Contbr. articles to profl. jours. V.p. Latin Am. Human Rights Action Ctr., Iowa City, Iowa, 1988-90. Recipient Mellon-James Still fellowship, Univ. Ky., 1982, 84, rsch. grant Ky. Humanities Coun., Barbourville, 1984, dean's grant Marycrest Coll., 1986, 89, 90, Teikyo Marycrest Univ., 1991. Mem. Nat. Soc. Sci. Assn. (nat. governing & edn. bd. 1990—), European Studies Assn., Radical Historians of Am., Mo. Valley Hist. Assn. Office: Teikyo Marycrest U 1607 W 12th St Davenport IA 52804-4034 Home: 1804 Pershing Ave Davenport IA 52803-4327

LUZZATTO, EDGAR, lawyer; b. Milan, Italy, Nov. 25, 1914; s. Enrico and Maria (Norsa) L.; m. Mirella Del Monte, Apr. 4, 1948; children—Diana, Ariel, Kfir, Marco, Rossana. Dr. Chem. Engring., Polytechnic, Milan, 1935; Dr.Law, U. Milan, 1957. Patent agt. David Moscovitz, Atty., N.Y.C., 1946-48; sole practice, Milan, 1949-75, Ashkelon, Israel, 1976-81; sr. ptnr. Luzzatto & Luzzatto, Beer-Sheva, Israel, 1982—; lectr. Polytechnic, Milan, 1958-62; mem. Italian delegation to Lisbon Conf. for revision of Paris Conv., 1958. Author: Il Consulente Tecnico, 1954; Teoria e Tecnica Brevetti, 1960; The Industrial Property Factor in Industrial Research, 1978. Contbr. articles to profl. jours. Served with U.S. Army, 1941-46. Mem. Internat. Assn. for Protection Indsl. Property, Internat. Fedn. Indsl. Property Attys. Office: Omer Indsl Park 84965, PO Box 5352, Beersheba 84152, Israel

LUZZI, LAURA ANN, counselor, consultant; b. Belleville, N.J., Sept. 23, 1962; m. Kevin J. Skotnicki. BA in Psychology and Sociology, Purdue U., 1984; MS in Counseling, Villanova U., 1987. Lic. psychotherapist, Oreg.; cert. counselor. Youth counselor Joint Action in Cmty. Svcs., Phila., 1984-85; counselor Comprehensive Counseling Assn., N.J., 1987-88; sr. clinician S. Bergen Mental Health Ctr., Lyndhurst, N.J., 1987-89; asst. dir. Spectrum for Living, Inc., Hackensack, N.J., 1989-90; children's specialist supr. Psychiat. Emergency Screening Program Bergen County, Inc., Paramus, N.J., 1990; dir. family svcs. The Dougy Ctr. for Grieving Children, Portland, Oreg., 1991-93; workshop presenter for numerous cmty. orgns., Portland, 1993—; cons. cmty. profls., Portland, 1993—; vol., mem. Delta Soc., Rsch. and Pet Ptnrs. Coms., 1990—; freelance illustrator. Vol. edn. com. Wolf Haven, Inc., Wash., 1991-92. Mem. Am. Counseling Assn., Assn. for Play Therapy, Group Specialists and Multi-Cultural Counseling Assn. Avocations: pet-assisted therapy advocate, yoga, art. Home: 2050 NW Glisan St Portland OR 97209-1109

LYALL, KATHARINE C(ULBERT), academic administrator, economics educator; b. Lancaster, Pa., Apr. 26, 1941; d. John D. and Eleanor G. Lyall. BA in Econs., Cornell U., 1963, PhD in Econs., 1969; MBA, NYU, 1965. Economist Chase Manhattan Bank, N.Y.C., 1963-65; asst. prof. econs. Syracuse U., 1969-72; prof. econs. Johns Hopkins U., Balt., 1972-77; dir. grad. program in public policy Johns Hopkins U., 1979-81; dep. asst. sec. for econs. Office Econ. Affairs, HUD, Washington, 1977-79; v.p. acad. affairs U. Wis. System, 1981-85; prof. of econ. U. Wis., Madison, 1982—; acting pres. U. Wis. System, Madison, 1985-86, 91-92, exec v.p., 1986-91, pres., 1992—; bd. dirs. Kemper Ins. Cos.; mem. bd. Carnegie Found. for Advancement of Teaching. Author: Reforming Public Welfare, 1976, Microeconomic Issues of the 70s, 1978. Mem. Mcpl. Securities Rulemaking Bd., Washington, 1990-93. Mem. Am. Econ. Assn., Assn. Am. Univs., Phi Beta Kappa. Home: 6021 S Highlands Ave Madison WI 53705-1110 Office: U Wis System Office of Pres 1720 Van Hise Hall 1220 Linden Dr Madison WI 53706-1525

LYASHENKO, NIKOLAI NIKOLAEVICH, mathematician, educator; b. Leningrad, Russia, Jan. 19, 1946; came to U.S., 1990; s. Nikolai Makarovich and Rufina Stepanovna (Poshekhonova) L.; m. Tatiana Vasilievna Giga, June 21, 1969; 1 child, Anna Nikolaevna. BS, Leningrad U., 1966, MS, 1969, PhD in Physics and Math. Scis., 1974, D in Phys. Math. Scis., 1986. Assoc. prof. Leningrad Elec. Engring. Inst., 1975-85; prof. Leningrad Poly. Inst., 1986-88; dir. info. processing lab. Leningrad Inst. Informatics and Automation, 1988-90; vis. prof. George Mason U., Fairfax, Va., 1991—; pres. Knowledge Extraction Tools, Inc., L.A. Contbr. numerous articles to profl. jours.; patentee in field. Avocation: playing piano. Home: 4614 W 131st St Hawthorne CA 90250-5107 Office: 801 S Grand Ave 10th Fl Los Angeles CA 90017

LYBARGER, JEFFREY ALLEN, epidemiology research administrator; b. Granite, Ill., 1951. MD, So. Ill. U., 1976. Diplomate Am. Bd. Gen. Preventive Medicine, Am. Bd. Preventive Medicine in Pub. Health, Preventive Medicine and Occupl. Medicine. Intern in pediat. St. Louis U. Glennon Hosp., 1976-77; resident in occupl. medicine U. Cin., 1979-81; resident in pub. health, pub. medicine Ctrs. for Disease Control, Atlanta, 1982-84; dir. Agy. for Toxic Substances and Disease Registry Divsn. Health Studies, Atlanta. Mem. Soc. for Epidemiol. Rsch., Soc. for Occupl. and Environ. Health, Internat. Soc. for Environ. Epidemiology. Office: Agy Toxic Subs/Disease Reg Divsn Health Studies 1600 Clifton Rd NE Mail Stop E31 Atlanta GA 30333

LYBECKER, MARTIN EARL, lawyer; b. Lincoln, Nebr., Feb. 11, 1945; s. Earl Edward and Jeanette Frances (Kiefer) L.; m. Andrea Kristine Tollefson, Dec. 27, 1969; children: Carl Martin, Neil Anders. BBA, U. Wash., 1967, JD, 1970; LLM in Taxation, NYU, 1971; LLM, U. Pa., 1973. Bar: Wash. 1970, D.C. 1972, Pa. 1982. Atty. investment mgmt. div. SEC, Washington, 1972-75, assoc. dir. div., 1978-81; assoc. prof. SUNY, Buffalo, 1975-78; ptnr. Drinker Biddle & Reath, Washington, 1981-87, Ropes & Gray, Washington, 1987—; adj. prof. Georgetown U., Washington, 1974-75, 80-81; vis. assoc. prof. Duke U., Durham, N.C., 1977-78. Contbr. articles to law revs. Fellow U. Pa. Ctr. for Study of Fin. Instns., 1971-72. Mem. ABA (mem. subcom. on investment cos. and investment advisers, mem. subcom. on securities activities of banks, mem. com. on fed. regulation of securities bus. law sect., chairperson com. on devels. in investment svcs. bus. law sect., chairperson subcom. on bank holding co. activities and subcom. on fiduciary svcs. of com. of banking bus. law sect.), Univ. Club Washington. Home: 2806 Daniel Rd Bethesda MD 20815-3149 Office: Ropes & Gray Ste 800 East 1301 K St NW Washington DC 20005-2506

LYBRAND, THOMASINE LARKINS, tax specialist; b. Greenwood, S.C., Oct. 20, 1953; d. Robert Thomas and Elvena (McCoy) Larkins; m. Bobby Daniel Luker, Feb. 14, 1975 (dec. Mar. 1977); m. John William Lybrand III, Dec. 23, 1977; children: John William IV, Robert Thomas, Patrick Bryce. BS in Acctg., Lander U., 1994; postgrad., Clemson U. Computer oper. Parke-Davis, Greenwood, S.C., 1972-79; instr. data entry Piedmont Tech. Coll., Greenwood, S.C., 1979-82; computer oper. Cin. Milacron, Greenwood, 1982-85; data processing supr. Abbeville (S.C.) County Meml. Hosp., 1985-87, Hoke, Inc., Spartanburg, S.C., 1987-89; tax preparer, owner The Tax Ctr., Greenwood, 1990—; purchasing acct. GLEAMNS Human Resources Commn., Greenwood, 1994—. Sharon Jones Williams scholar Lander U., 1992-93, United Saving Bank scholar, 1993-94. Mem. Inst. Mgmt. Accts. Republican. Methodist. Home and Office: 208 Wellington Dr Greenwood SC 29649-9327 also: GLEAMNS Human Resources Commn 237 N Hosp St Greenwood SC 29646

LYDEN, TIMOTHY WORSLEY, microbiology and immunology educator, researcher; b. Princeton, N.J., Jan. 15, 1957; s. Edward F.X. and Marie Worsley (Barber) L.; m. Donella Lynn Searles, June 15, 1976; children: Heather, Jennifer. BS, U. Maine, Orono, 1986, PhD in Biol. Sci., 1992. Rsch. fellow dept. immunology U. Liverpool, U.K., 1989-90; rsch. asst. reproductive biology lab. Wright State U., Dayton, Ohio, 1990-92; asst. prof. dept. microbiology and immunology Wright State U., Dayton, 1992—; pres. Assn. Grad. Students, U. Maine, Orono, 1989-90. Contbr. articles to profl. jours. Judge Regional Sci. Fair, Dayton, Ohio and Bangor, Maine, 1987-95; com. mem. several coms. Wright State U., Dayton and U. Maine, Orono, 1986—; mentor minority H.S. and undergrad. rsch. programs Wright State U., 1994-95. Recipient Ob-Gyn. Rsch. award Nat. Student Rsch. Forum, Galveston, Tex., 1992, Young Investigator Travel awards Wright State U., 1993-94; James E. Totman scholar U. Maine, Orono, 1983, Trustee Tuition scholar U. Maine, Orono, 1989. Mem. AAAS, Am. Soc. for the Study of Reproductive Immunology, Soc. for the Study of Reproduction. Avocations: history, photography, computers. Office: Wright State Univ 1160 Xenia Ave Yellow Springs OH 45387-1101

LYDOLPH, PAUL EDWARD, geography educator; b. Bonaparte, Iowa, Jan. 4, 1924; s. Guy W. and Pauline (Ruschke) L.; m. Mary J. Klahn, Dec. 17, 1966; children by previous marriage—Edward, Donald, Paul, Thomas, Andrew. B.A., U. Iowa, 1948; M.S., U. Wis., 1951, Ph.D., 1955; student, Harvard U., 1944, MIT, 1945, UCLA, 1956, U. Calif. at Berkeley, 1956-57. Tchr. math. Pisgah (Iowa) Pub. Sch., 1946-47, Packwood (Iowa) Pub. Sch., 1947-49; asst. prof., then asso. prof. Los Angeles State Coll., 1952-59; mem. faculty U. Wis. at Milw., 1959—, prof. geography, 1962-92, emeritus, 1992—, chmn. dept., 1963-69, 71-72; Lectr. U. Hawaii, summer 1965, Oxford U., Stockholm Sch. Econs., 1970; C.I.C. Exchange prof. U. Mich., Ann Arbor, 1977, U. Iowa, Iowa City, 1978; Smithsonian Instn. tour dir. to, USSR, 1976, 77, 78, 79. Author: Geography of the USSR, 5th edit., 1990, Climates of the USSR, vol. 7, World Survey of Climatology, 1977, Weather and Climate, 1985, The Climate of the Earth, 1985, also articles; Festschrift written by colleagues in his honor: Soviet Geography Studies in Our Time, 1987. Served with USAAF, 1943-47. Ford Found. fellow, 1956-57. Home: N8328 Snake Rd Elkhart Lake WI 53020-2011 Office: U Wis Dept Geography Milwaukee WI 53201

LYDON, THOMAS J., federal judge; b. Portland, Maine, June 3, 1927. B.A., U. Maine, 1952; LL.B., Georgetown U., 1955, LL.M., 1957. Bars: Maine, D.C. Trial atty. civil div. Dept. Justice, Washington, 1955-67, chief Ct. Claims sect. civil div., 1967-72; sr. judge U.S. Ct. Clms., Washington, 1972—. Office: US Claims Ct 717 Madison Pl NW Washington DC 20005-1011*

LYE, WILLIAM FRANK, history educator; b. Kimberley, B.C., Can., Feb. 19, 1930; came to U.S., 1955, naturalized, 1981; s. Arthur Percy and Jessie Loretta (Prince) L.; m. Velda Campbell, Oct. 16, 1953; children: William Mark, Matthew Campbell, David Arthur, Victoria, Regina. Student Ricks Coll., 1953-55, Duke U., 1963; BS, Utah State U., 1959; MA, U. Calif.-Berkeley, 1959; PhD, UCLA, 1969. Instr. polit. sci. Ricks Coll., Rexburg, Idaho, 1959-63, 67-68, head dept. polit. sci., 1959-63; teaching asst. dept. history UCLA, 1964-65; asst. prof. Utah State U., Logan, 1968-69, acting head dept. history and geography, 1969-70, assoc. prof., head dept. history and geography, 1970-73, prof., head dept. history and geography, 1973-76, dean Coll. Humanities, Arts and Social Scis., 1976-83, v.p. for univ. relations, prof. dept. history and geography, 1983-91, prof. history, 1991-95, emeritus, 1996—; vis. lectr. dept. history Brigham Young U., Provo, Utah, 1970; temporary lectr. dept. history U. Cape Town, Republic of South Africa, 1974; social cons. for project design teams in land conservation, U.S. Agy. for Internat. Devel. Khartoum, Sudan, 1978, Maseru, Lesotho, 1979; mem. higher edn. taskforce on telecommunications, Utah, 1977-82; chmn. State of Utah Telecommunications Coop., 1987, Regents' Com. on Credit by Exam., Utah, 1976; mem. adv. com. Sta. KULC-TV, State Ednl. Telecommunications Operating Ctr., 1986-90; bd. dirs., exec. com. Children's Aid Soc. Utah, 1985-89, pres., 1990-91; mem. Utah Statehood Centennial Commn., 1989—, Utah Christopher Columbus Quincentenary Commn., 1990-91. Author: (with Colin Murray) Transformations on the Highveld: The Tswana and Southern Sotho, 1980, paperback edit., 1985; editor: Andrew Smith's Journal of His Expedition into the Interior of South Africa, 1834-36, 1975. Producer (TV series) Out of Africa, 1977, The God Seekers, 1978; contbr. articles and book revs. to profl. publs. Chmn. State Day celebration, Logan, Utah, 1973, univ. drive for new Logan Regional Hosp; bishop LDS Ch., 1993—. Recipient Leadership award Standard of Calif., 1957, Idea of Yr. award Utah State U., 1971, Faculty Service award Associated Students, Utah State U., 1977-78, Nicholas and Mary Kay Leone Leadership award, 1991; Woodrow Wilson Nat. fellow 1958, Foreign Area fellow Social Sci. Research Council, Republic of South Africa, England, 1966-67, 67-68; faculty devel. grantee Utah State U., 1972, Human Sci. Research Council of South Africa publ. grantee, 1975, Mauerberger Trust grantee, 1976. Mem. African Studies Assn., Royal African Soc., Western Assn. Africanists (program chmn. 1972-74, pres. 1974-76), Am. Soc. Landscape Architects (accreditation bd. 1967-93), Phi Kappa Phi, Phi Alpha Theta. Home: 696 E 400 N Logan UT 84321-4218 Office: Utah State U Dept History 650 N 1100 E Logan UT 84322-0710 *Personal philosophy: I support education for everyone as the means by which we make our fullest contribution to society, and it is by service to others that we earn our place on earth.*

LYERLA, BRADFORD PETER, lawyer; b. Savanna, Ill., Aug. 2, 1954; s. Ralph Herbert and Nancy Lee (Nelson) L.; m. Marilyn Wyse, Aug. 18, 1979; children: Claire, Joseph, Nina Rose. BA, U. Ill., 1976, JD, 1980. Bar: Ill. 1980, U.S. Dist. Ct. (no. dist.) Ill. 1980, U.S. Dist. Ct. (no. dist.) Ind. 1982, U.S. Dist. Ct. (no. dist.) Calif. 1991, U.S. Dist. Ct. (ctrl. dist.) Ill. 1991, U.S. Ct. Appeals (7th cir.) 1983, U.S. Ct. Appeals (fed. cir.) 1991, U.S. Supreme Ct. 1995. Ptnr. Jenner & Block, Chgo.; lectr. on litigation and intellectual property law. Author publications in field; editor U. Ill. Law Rev., 1978-80. Bd. dirs. North Suburban Bd., Wilmette, Ill., 1987-96, pres. 1993-94; bd. dirs. Traveler's and Immigrant's Aid, Chgo., 1991-95; bd. dirs., sec. Youth Svcs. Project, Inc., Chgo., 1987-91; mem. U. Ill. Pres.'s Coun.; founding mem. Cribbett Soc., U. Ill. Coll. Law; mem. Saints Faith Hope and Charity, Wilmette. Recipient John Powers Crowley Justice award People's Uptown Law Ctr., 1989. Fellow Am. Bar Found.; mem. ABA (editor litigation sect. intellectual property litigation newsletter 1990—, mem. intellectual property sect. com. on unfair competition litigation), Ill. Bar Assn. (sect. coun. mem. gen. practice sect. 1984-85, intellectual property sect. 1989—, co-editor intellectual property newsletter 1989—), Am. Intellectual Property Law Assn. (mem. antitrust and fed. lit. com.), Federalist Soc., Phi Beta Kappa, Phi Kappa Phi. Clubs: Lakeshore Athletic, Chgo., Mich. Shores, Wilmette. Office: Jenner & Block One IBM Pla Chicago IL 60611

LYERLY, HERBERT KIM, surgical oncology educator, researcher; b. San Diego, Aug. 26, 1958; s. Albert Elliot and Mitsu (Kinoshita) L. BS, U. Calif., Riverside, 1980; MD, UCLA, 1983. Diplomate Am. Bd. Surgery. Intern Duke U., Durham, N.C., 1983, resident, 1990-94, from asst. prof. to assoc. prof. surgery, 1990—, asst. prof. pathology, 1991—, clin. dir. molecular therapeutics, 1993—, asst. prof. immunology, 1995—. Editor: Surgical Intensive Care, 2d edit., 1989, co-editor: Surgical Intensive Care, 3d edit., 1991, Companion, 1992, Essentials of Surgery, 1994. Mem. Assn. Acad. Surgery, Soc. Surg. Oncology, Soc. Univ. Surgeons, Am. Coll. Surgeons. Office: Duke U Hosp Box 2606 Durham NC 27710

LYFORD, CABOT, sculptor; b. Sayre, Pa., May 22, 1925; s. Frederic Eugene and Eleanor (Cabot) L.; m. Joan Ardyth Richmond, June 22, 1953; children: Matthew, Julia, Thaddeus. BFA, Cornell U., 1950. Exec. trainee NBC, N.Y.C., 1952-54; producer and dir. J. Walter Thompson, N.Y.C., 1954-57, Sta. WGBH-TV, Boston, 1957-59; program mgr. Sta. WENH-TV, Durham, N.H., 1959-63; chmn. Dept. Art The Phillips Exeter (N.H.) Acad., 1963-86. Prin. sculptures include pub. monuments in Portland, Maine and Portsmouth, N.H., Berwick, Maine; represented in permanent collections at Portland Mus., Chattanooga Mus., Indpls. Mus., Wichita (Kans.) Mus., Ogunquit (Maine) Mus., Currier Gallery, Manchester, N.H., Addison Gallery, Andover, Mass. With inf. U.S. Army, 1943-46, PTO. Recipient Sculpture prize Nat. Design Acad., 1990. Home and Studio: PO Box 104 HC 62 New Harbor ME 04554-9005

LYGAS, MARJORIE MACGREGOR, critical care nurse; b. Cornwall, Ont., Canada, Oct. 14, 1942; came to U.S., 1966; d. James Clifton and Helen Isabel (McDonnell) MacGregor; m. Edward Allan Lygas, Nov. 13, 1965 (div. Oct. 1979); children: Marnie Elizabeth Krause, Andrew Walter

Lygas. Diploma in nursing, St. Joseph Sch. Nursing, Cornwall, Ont., 1963; BSN, Tex. Woman's U., 1992. RN, Tex.; cert. CEN; cert. ACLS instr., TNCC; cert. emergency nurse. Surg. fl. staff nurse King Edward VII Meml. Hosp., Hamilton, Bermuda, 1964-66; ICU staff nurse Upstate Med. Ctr., Syracuse, N.Y., 1966-68; critical care staff nurse Meml. City Med. Ctr., Houston, 1973-79, emergency staff nurse, 1979-81, emergency dept. coord., 1981-94; trauma coord. LBJ Hosp. of Harris County Hosp. Dist., Houston, 1994—; guest lectr. Houston C.C. ADN program, 1990—. Mem. Soc. Trauma Nurses, Trauma Coords. Forum, Am. Trauma Soc., Emergency Nurses Assn. Avocation: nursing education. Home: 10610 Holly Springs Houston TX 77042 Office: LBJ Hosp 5656 Kelley St Houston TX 77042

LYJAK CHORAZY, ANNA JULIA, pediatrician, medical administrator, educator; b. Braddock, Pa., Feb. 25, 1936; d. Walter and Cecilia (Swiatkowski) Lyjak; m. Chester John Chorazy, May 6, 1961; children: Paula Ann Chorazy, Mary Ellen Chorazy-Cuccaro, Mark Edward Chorazy. BS, Waynesburg Coll., 1958; MD, Women's Med. Coll. Pa., 1960. Diplomate Am. Bd. Pediats. Intern St. Francis Gen. Hosp., Pitts., 1960-61; resident in pediats., tchg. fellow Children's Hosp. of Pitts., 1961-63, pediatrician, devel. clinic, 1966-75; pediat. house physician Western Pa. Hosp., Pitts., 1963-66; med. dir. Rehab. Instn. Pitts., 1975—; clin. asst. prof. pediats. Children's Hosp. Pitts. and U. Pitts. Sch. Medicine, 1971-94, clin. assoc. prof. pediats., 1994—; pediat. cons. Children's Home Pitts., 1985—. Author chpts. to books. Co-chmn. EACH Joint Planning and Assessment, Pitts., 1980-85; mem. adv. com. 10th Nat. Conf. on Child Abuse, Pitts., 1993. Fellow Am. Acad. Pediats.; mem. AMA, Pa. Med. Soc., Pitts. Pediat. Soc., Allegheny County Med. Soc. Avocations: reading, comedy, theatre, music, opera. Home: 131 Washington Rd Pittsburgh PA 15221-4437 Office: Rehab Inst Pitts 6301 Northumberland St Pittsburgh PA 15217-1360

LYKES, JOSEPH T., III, shipping company executive; b. Galveston, Tex., Mar. 6, 1948. BA, Washington and Lee U., 1970. Sr. v.p. Lykes Bros. Steamship Co., Tampa. Office: 111 E Madison St Tampa FL 33602

LYKINS, MARSHALL HERBERT, insurance company executive; b. Cin., Mar. 5, 1944; s. Herbert Cooper and Hilda Freda (Krall) L.; m. Betty Foushee Sweaney, June 27, 1970; 1 child, Elizabeth Foushee. BS, U. Chgo., 1966; M in Actuarial Sci., U. Mich., 1968. Actuarial student New Eng. Mut. Life Ins. Co., Boston, 1970-72, asst. actuary, 1972-75, assoc. actuary, 1975-78, 2d v.p. and actuary, 1978-85, v.p. and actuary, 1986—. Active Beacon Hill Civic Assn., Boston, 1970—, Byron St. Assn., Boston, 1982—; treas. King's Chapel, 1995—. Served with USPHS, 1968-70. Fellow Soc. Actuaries; mem. Chartered Life Underwriters, Am. Council of Life Ins. (com. on N.Y. expense limitations 1982—), Life Office Mgmt. Assn. (com. on profitability studies 1985—), Actuaries Club of Boston (treas. 1979—), U. Chgo. Alumni of Boston, U. Mich. Alumni of Boston, Phi Kappa Phi, Beta Gamma Sigma. Unitarian. Club: U. Club (Boston). Avocations: skiing, jogging, bridge. Home: 14 Byron St Boston MA 02108-3401 Office: New Eng Mut Life Ins Co 501 Boylston St Boston MA 02116-3706

LYKOS, PETER GEORGE, educator, scientist; b. Chgo., Jan. 22, 1927; s. George Peter and Theodora (Psimoulis) L.; m. Marie Nina Shumicki, July 2, 1950; children—George, Kristina, Andrew. B.S., Northwestern U., 1950; Ph.D., Carnegie Inst. Tech., 1955. Prof. chemistry Ill. Inst. Tech., 1955—, dir. computation center and computer sci. dept., 1963-71, dir. Interactive Instrnl. TV, 1976-78; cons. solid state sci. Argonne Nat. Lab., 1958-66; assoc. dean for acad. planning Armour Coll. Engring. & Sci. Ill. Inst. Tech., 1993-95; cons. radiation therapy Michael Reese Hosp., Chgo., 1966-71; head computer impact on soc. NSF, 1971-73; pres. Four Pi, Inc., Oak Park, Ill., 1966-80; chmn. com. on computers in chemistry, chemistry divsn. NAS-NRC; dir. Assn. Media-based Continuing Engring. Edn.; sci. cons. NTU (video satellite), 1988—; dir. Project Chemnet, 1984—; Coll. Bd. Advanced Placement com. to create Advanced Placement Exam in Computer Sci., 1982. Author tech. articles. Bd. dirs. Oak Park Pub. Library, 1976-81; trustee Beacon Unitarian Ch. Served with USNR, 1944-46. Mem. Am. Chem. Soc. (chmn. edn. com. Chgo., co-dir. Operation Interface I, chmn. div. computers in chemistry, three term on com. profl. tng. 1980s, organizer materials chemistry secretariat 1988-91, adv. bd. Chemistry and Engring. News), Assn. Computing Machinery (chmn. Chgo., nat. lectr., chmn. spl. interest group on computers and soc., liaison to Am. Fedn. Info. Processing Socs. 1976-78, chmn. com. on computers and public policy), Sigma Xi (chmn. Chgo. chpt., program planning com.), Alpha Chi Sigma, Phi Sigma. Home: 316 N Ridgeland Ave Oak Park IL 60302-2325 Office: Ill Inst Tech Dept Chemistry Chicago IL 60616

LYLE, GLENDA SWANSON, state legislator; b. Knoxville, Tenn.; d. Richard and Olivia Swanson; Kipp Elise, Jennifer, Anthony. BA, U. Denver, 1964; MA, U. Colo., 1973. Former dir. cmty. and personal svcs., instr. early childhood edn., dir. preschool lab C.C. of Denver/Auraria; owner Planners, Etc.; mem. Colo. Ho. of Reps., 1992—, mem. various coms., 1993—. Del. White Ho. Conf. Small Bus., 1980-86; mem. Regional Transp. Dist. Bd., 1986-92, Regulatory Agy. Adv. Bd., Mayor's Planning Bd., Nat. Pub. Lands Adv. Coun., Gov.'s Small Bus. Coun., Colo. Mkt. and Distributive Edn. Adv. Coun., Va Neal Blue Ctr. Mem. Am. Planning Assn., Conf. Minority Transp. Ofcls. (nat. bd. dirs.), Black Women Polit. Action (founding mem.), Black C. of C. (bd. dirs.). Democrat. Office: Colo House of Reps State Capitol Denver CO 80203

LYLE, JAMES ARTHUR, real estate broker; b. Charlottesville, Va., Mar. 9, 1945; s. James Aaron and Sallie (Tuthill) Lyle; m. Martha Lee Gale, Jan. 28, 1978; children: Cory Jackson, Martha Jessica. BS in Indsl. Mgmt., Ga. Inst. Tech., 1968. Cert. comml. investment mem. Mktg. rep. IBM, Atlanta, 1970-71; investment cons. La Salle Ptnrs., El Paso, Tex., 1971-76; owner James Arthur Lyle and Assocs., El Paso, 1976—; v.p., bd. dirs. Hueco Mountain Estates, Inc., 1983-94; bd. dirs. Vista Hills Townhomes, 1977-78; bd. dirs. Southwestern Savs., 1984-86. Chmn., vice chmn. El Paso City Plan Commn., 1978-82; vice chmn. Internat. Airport Bd., 1982; adv. bd. El Paso Bikeway, 1986-88; mem. El Paso County Planning Commn., 1986-96; bd. dirs. NCCJ, 1978-82, Southwestern Gen. Hosp., 1979-83, El Paso Econ. Devel. Bd., 1980-82; bd. dirs. Am. Heart Assn., 1989-93. 1st lt. U.S. Army, 1968-70. Named Bus. Assoc. of Yr., Am. Bus. Women's Assn., 1984, S.W. Challenge Series Champion, 1991-95, Ironman World Triathlon Championship, 1992. Mem. Nat. Assn. Realtors, Realtors Nat. Mktg. Inst., Nat. Assn. Indsl. and Office Parks, Tex. Property Exchangors (Best Exch. 1979), Tex. Assn. Realtors, Tex. Real Estate Polit. Action Com. (life), El Paso Bd. Realtors (bd. dirs. 1975-88, cert. comml. investment mem. 1975—, El Paso/West Tex. cert. comml. investment mem., pres., sec., treas. 1975—, comml.-investment real estate coun. 1971—), El Paso Indsl. Devel. Bd., El Paso Investment Exch. Svc., SAR (dist. v.p.), Sons Confederate Vets., Sunturians (life), Half Fast Track Club (v.p. multisports), Triathlon Fedn. USA (bd. dirs. 1995-96), Team El Paso. Republican. Episcopalian. Avocation: triathlons. Home: 626 Blacker Ave El Paso TX 79902-2711 Office: James Arthur Lyle & Assocs 6028 Surety Dr Ste 204 El Paso TX 79905-2024

LYLE, JEAN STUART, social worker; b. Rock Hill, S.C., Jan. 13, 1912; d. David and Martha (Nash) L.; BA, U. S.C., 1949; MS in Social Work, Columbia U., 1951. Recreation dir. City of Rock Hill, 1938-44; commd. 1st lt. Med. Svc. Corps, U.S. Army, 1951, advanced through grades to lt. col., 1966; asst. chief social worker, Ft. Benning, Ga., 1951-55; chief social worker Fort Jay, N.Y., 1955-58, Fort McClellan, Ala., 1958-62, female inpatient svc. Walter Reed Gen. Hosp., Washington, 1962-66; dir. Army Cmty. Svc., U.S. Army, Hawaii, 1966-68, Walter Reed Army Med. Ctr., 1968-70; cons. group work to Med. Field Svc. Sch., Fort Sam Houston, Tex., 1969; ret., 1970; dir. vol. svcs. S.C. Dept. Health and Environ. Control, Columbia, 1970-74; pvt. practice social work, Rock Hill, 1974—; tchr. and supr. social work students Catholic U. Am., Washington, 1960-62. Decorated Legion of Merit; recipient Cmty. Svc. award U.S. Army, 1968. Mem. Nat. Assn. Social Workers, Acad. Cert. Social Workers. Democrat. Address: PO Box 2553 Rock Hill SC 29732-4553

LYLE, JOHN TILLMAN, landscape architecture educator; b. Houston, Aug. 10, 1934; s. Leo Tillman and Martha Ellen (Rawlins) L.; m. Harriett Laverna Fancher, Dec. 28, 1967; children: Alexander Tillman, Cybele Katsura. BArch, Tulane U., 1957; postgrad., Royal Acad. of Fine Arts, Copenhagen, 1965-67; M of Landscape Architecture, U. Calif., Berkeley, 1966. Registered architect, Calif. Architect Stanford (Calif.) U., 1959-62; urban designer John Carl Warnecke & Assocs., San Francisco, 1963-65; prof. Calif. State Poly. U., Pomona, 1968—; vis. prof. Liubliana (Yugoslavia) U., 1982, Instituto Universitario Di Architecture, Venice, Italy, 1988, U. Sao Paulo, Brazil, 1989, Kyushu Inst. Design, Fukuoka, Japan, 1990; dir. design bldg. and landscape Inst. for Regenerative Studies, 1984—. Author: Design for Human Ecosystems, 1985 (award Assn. Am. Pubs. 1985, Am. Soc. Landscape Architects 1986), Regenerative Design for Sustainable Development, 1994; contbr. articles to profl. jours. Mem. bd. govs. Desert Studies Consortium, Mojave Desert, 1984-88. Recipient Honor award Calif. Coun. Landscape Architects, 1988, Disting. Educator award Coun. Educators in Landscape Architecture, 1989; named Fulbright Disting. prof. U.S. Dept. State, 1982, Disting. Educator, Coun. Educators in Landscape Architecture, 1989; Fulbright scholar U.S. Dept. State, 1966-68. Fellow Am. Soc. Landscape Architects (Design for Sustainable Devel. award 1994, medal 1996). Democrat. Avocations: hiking, skiing. Home: 580 N Hermosa Ave Sierra Madre CA 91024-1117 Office: Calif State Poly U 3801 W Temple Ave Pomona CA 91768-2557

LYLE, JOHN WILLIAM, JR., former state senator, lawyer, social sciences educator, secondary school principal; b. Providence, May 19, 1950; s. John William and Lois (Smith) L.; m. Lori A. Lyle, Feb. 16, 1992. BA, Barrington Coll., 1973; MEd, Providence Coll., 1978; JD, Suffolk U., 1992 Tchr. Lincoln (R.I.) Sch. Dept., 1974-95, adminstr., 1995—; senator State of R.I., Dist. 34, 1981-86, 91-94, minority whip, 1993-94; tchr. William Davies Vo-cat. Sch.-Summer Sch., Lincoln, 1975, 77; dir. student affairs Brown U. Summer Acad., Providence, 1987; asst. prin. Lincoln H.S.; mem. adj. faculty R.I. Coll., Providence, 1990—, C.C. R.I., Lincoln, 1991—. Contbr. articles to profl. jour. Bd. dirs. Blackstone Valley Tourism Council; trustee Cumb-Line Boys and Girls Club, Cumberland, R.I., 1982; Rep. candidate for Sec. of State of R.I., 1986; tennis umpire USTA, N.Y.C., 1985—; 1st v.p. New Eng. Tennis Umpires Assn.; Robert A. Taft Inst. fellow, 1975, 79; recipient Outstanding Alumnus award Barrington Coll., 1982, Disting. Alumnus award, 1984; Appreciation award No. R.I. Sr. Services, 1983, John E. Fogarty award, 1995, Johns Hopkins U. Close Up fellow. Mem. R.I. Bar Assn., R.I. Assn. Social Studies Tchrs., Lincoln Fraternal Order Police, R.I. Assn. Secondary Sch. Prins., Lincoln Tchrs. Assn. (exec. bd. 1987-90).Avocations: travel, reading, running, tennis. Office: Lincoln HS 135 Old River Rd Lincoln RI 02865

LYLE, ROBERT EDWARD, chemist; b. Atlanta, Jan. 26, 1926; s. Robert Edward and Adaline (Cason) L.; m. Gloria Gilbert, Aug. 28, 1947. B.A., Emory U., 1945, M.S., 1946; Ph.D., U. Wis.-Madison, 1949. Asst. prof. Oberlin Coll., Ohio, 1949-51; asst. prof. U. N.H., Durham, 1951-53; assoc. prof. U. N.H., 1953-57, prof., 1957-76; prof., chmn. dept. chemistry U. North Tex., Denton, 1977-79; v.p. chemistry, chem. engr. S.W Rsch. Inst., San Antonio, 1979-91; v.p. GRL Cons., San Antonio, 1992—; vis. prof. U. Va., Charlottesville, 1973-74, U. Grenoble, France, 1976; adj. prof. Bowdoin Coll., Brunswick, Maine, 1975-79, U. Tex., San Antonio, 1985—. Mem. editorial bd. Index Chemicus, 1976—. USPHS fellow Oxford U., Eng., 1965; recipient honor scroll award Mass. chpt. Am. Inst. Chemistry, 1971; Harry and Carol Mosher awardee, 1986. Fellow AAAS; mem. Am. Chem. Soc. (councilor 1965-84, 86-92, medicinal chemistry divsn.), Royal Soc. Chemistry, Alpha Chi Sigma (editor Hexagon 1992—). Methodist. Office: GRL Cons 12814 Kings Forest St San Antonio TX 78230-1511

LYLES, JEAN ELIZABETH CAFFEY, journalist, church worker; b. Abilene, Tex., Mar. 2, 1942; d. Wiley Luther and Pauline Linn (Marlin) Caffey; m. James Vernon Lyles, Aug. 23, 1969 (div. Aug. 1987). Student, McMurry Coll., 1960-61; BA with honors, U. Tex., 1964. Copy editor Christian Century mag., Chgo., 1972-74, assoc. editor, 1974-84, editor at large, 1984—; assoc. editor Religious News Svc., N.Y.C., 1984-87; sr. news editor The Lutheran, Chgo., 1987-91; news dir. United Meth. News Svc., Evanston, Ill., 1991-94; freelance photojournalist, 1995—, freelance organist, 1995—. Author: A Practical Vision of Christian Unity, 1982; contbg. author: The First Amendment in a Free Society, 1979, Fearfully and Wonderfully Weird, 1990; contbg. editor Wittenburg Door, 1982-87; columnist Inside the Am. Religion Scene, 1985-87, The Underground Ecumenist, 1989-92; mem. editl. bd. Mid-Stream, Indpls., 1984—; mem. exec. com. Associated Ch. Press, 1989-91. Church organist. Mem. Religion Newswriters Assn., Am. Guild Organists, Hymn Soc. Am., United Meth. Assn. of Communicators. Democrat. Episcopalian. Home: 922 North Blvd Oak Park IL 60301-1243

LYLES, MARK BRADLEY, high technology company executive, dentist; b. Paducah, Ky., Dec. 3, 1957; s. Kendall Smith Lyles and Charlotte Dean (Ruley) Martell; m. Catherine Lynn Gregg, Mar. 17, 1984 (div. 1995); children: Austin Bradley, Dahlon Patrick. AS, BS, BA in Biology and Chemistry, Murray (Ky.) State U., 1978, MS, EdS, 1981; DMD, U. Louisville, 1986; postgrad., U. Tex., San Antonio, 1991—. Resident in oral and maxillofacial surgery U. Tex. Health Sci. Ctr., 1991—; founder, chief exec. officer, pres. Talis Techs., Inc., San Antonio, 1992—; founder, pres., chief sci. officer Materials Evolution and Devel. U.S.A., Inc. (M.E.D. USA), San Antonio, 1993—; presenter in filed. Contbr. articles to profl. jours.; inventor use of ultra-low density fused fibrous ceramics for indsl. applications, use of fused fibrous ceramics in dental materials, implantable sys. for cell growth control, filters for polynuclear aromatic hydrocarbon containing smoke. Lt. comdr. USNR, 1983—. Recipient Dentist-Scientist award Nat. Inst. Dental Rsch., 1991—; Dept. Chemistry and Bd. Regents scholar Murray State U., 1975-77; Grad. Coop. Edn. fellow Nat. Ctr. Toxicol. Rsch., EPA, FDA, 1979-80, Grad. fellow U. Louisville, 1981-82. Mem. Am. Coll. Oral and Maxillofacial Surgeons (Walter Lorenz Residents Rsch. award 1994), Acad. Osseointegration, Acad. Gen. Dentistry, Navy Inst., Assn. Mil. Surgeons U.S., Hon. Order Ky. Cols., Naval Res. Officers Assn., Phi Delta Kappa. Republican. Avocations: rifle and pistol marksmanship, weight training, sailing, travel, convertibles. Office: Materials Evolution & Devel USA Inc 8535 Wurzbach Rd Ste 104 San Antonio TX 78240-1040

LYMAN, ARTHUR JOSEPH, financial executive; b. Evergreen Park, Ill., May 18, 1953; s. Arthur Edward and Margaret (O'Conner) L.; m. Janet Lee Wenzel, Sept. 9, 1984; children: Christina Lee, Alissa Mary, Arthur Joseph Jr. BA, Knox Coll., 1975; M in Mgmt., Northwestern U., 1977. CPA, Ill.; CFP. Audit supr. Arthur Andersen & Co., Chgo., 1977-83; fin. planning analyst Montgomery Ward & Co., Chgo., 1983-84; dir. fin. and adminstrn. ctrl. region Coopers & Lybrand, Chgo., 1984-88, CFO Midwest region, 1989-93, nat. dir. fin. field ops., 1993—. Mem. AICPA, Fin. Execs. Inst. (bd. dirs. Chgo. chpt. 1992—), Ill. Inst. CPA's, Pi Sigma Alpha, Tau Kappa Epsilon (honor award 1988, chmn. bd. trustees 1988-93). Roman Catholic. Home: 3 Cornell Dr Lincolnshire IL 60069-3222 Office: Coopers & Lybrand 203 N La Salle St Chicago IL 60601-1210

LYMAN, CHARLES PEIRSON, comparative physiologist; b. Brookline, Mass., Sept. 23, 1912; s. Henry and Elizabeth (Cabot) L.; m. Jane Hunnewell Cheever, June 21, 1941; children—Charles Peirson, Jane Sargent, Theodore, David Russell, Elizabeth Anne. A.B., Harvard U., 1936, A.M., 1939, Ph.D., 1942. Asst. curator mammals Mus. Comparative Zoology, Harvard U., Cambridge, Mass., 1945-51; assoc. curator mammals Mus. Comparative Zoology, Harvard U., 1951-56, research assoc., 1956-58, curator in mammalogy, 1968-82; curator Warren Anat. Mus., Harvard Med. Sch., Boston, 1970-82; assoc. Harvard Med. Sch., 1949-60, asst. prof. anatomy, 1960-67, assoc. prof. anatomy, 1967-76, prof. biology, 1976-82; mem. NIH Study Sect., 1965-69; mem. nat. adv. bd. Biotron, 1965-75; mem. standing com. Trustees Public Reservations; trustee Mass. Soc. Promoting Agr. Contbr. articles, mostly on hibernation in mammals and reactions of mammals to environ. extremes, to profl. jours. Served to maj. USAF, 1942-45. NSF grantee, 1960-82; NIH grantee, 1955-76. Fellow AAAS; mem. Am. Zool. Soc., Am. Physiol. Soc., Am. Acad. Arts and Sci., Sigma Xi. Republican. Unitarian. Clubs: Harvard, Tavern, Dedham Country and Polo. Home: 105 Elm St Canton MA 02021-1255

LYMAN, DAVID, lawyer; b. Washington, Sept. 25, 1936; s. Albert Moses and Freda (Ring) L.; m. Yubol Pumsathit, Nov. 10, 1979. BS in Elec. Engring., Duke U., 1958; cert. U.S. Naval Officers Submarine Sch., 1960; JD, U. Calif.-San Francisco, 1965; postgrad. in fgn. and comparative law Columbia U., 1974. Bar: Calif. 1966; registered elec. engr., Thailand. Active minesweepers and submarine force U.S. Navy, 1958-62; assoc. Fitzsimmons & Petris, Oakland, Calif., 1965-66; Lempres & Seyranian, Oakland, 1966-67; Tilleke & Gibbins, R.O.P., Advocates and Solicitors, Bangkok, assoc. ptnr. 1967-84, sr. ptnr., 1984—; dir. Goodyear (Thailand) Ltd., Triumph Internat. (Thailand) Ltd.; founding mem. Prime Minister Thailand's Fgn. Investment Adv. Council, 1975, chmn. Fgn. C. of C. in Thailand Law Change Proj for the Prime Minister, 1992; mem. USAID Adv. Com. on U.S.-Thai Trade and Investment, 1988; founder, mem. steering com. tech. cooperation office U.S. Asia Environ. Partnership Program. 1994. Contbr. articles to profl. publs. Chmn. King Bhumiphol Rama IX Park U.S. Geodesic Dome Pavillion Com., 1987; founding mem. Thailand Bus. Coun. Sustainable Devel., 1993—; founder Davos Group World Economic Forum on Anti-Corruption Standards for Global Businesss, 1995—, co-founder, advisor Cmty. Svcs. Bangkok, 1985; advisor Thailand Soc. Prevention of Cruelty to Animals; co-founder Vietnam-Am. C. of C., 1992—. Served with U.S. Navy, 1958-68; lt. comdr. Res. Recipient U.S. Naval Inst. prize, 1958, Am. Jurisprudence prize, 1965, U.S. Dept. Commerce cert., 1987; Paul Harris fellow, 1987, Thai Prime Minister's Cert. of Achievement 1990, 92, Am. Cof C. Disting. Svc. Award, 1990. Mem. Am. C. of C. in Thailand (bd. govs. 1973—, v.p. 1974, 83-85, pres. 1975, 86), Asia-Pacific Coun. of Am. C. of C. (vice chmn. 1975-77, 85-89, 92-93, bd. dirs. 1975, 86), AmCham Environ. Coun. (founder, 1992), Environ. Bus. Exchange (creator 1993), Thai Bd. Trade (bd. dirs. 1975, 86), Fgn. Chambers of Commerce Working Group (sec. 1982-87, chmn. 1987-90), Thailand bd. of Investment Environ. Study Adv. Com., 1993, World Econ. Forum (program fellow Europe/East Asia Econ. Forum 1992-94), Lex Mundi (bd. dirs. 1989-91), ABA, Calif. Bar Assn., Intl. Bar Assn., LAWASIA, Thailand Trademark Assn., U.S. Naval Inst. (life), Naval Submarine League (life), Internat. Oceanographic Found. (life), Thailand Bus. Coalition AIDS Assn. (founder, 1994), 999 Wildlife Trust, Wildlife Fund Thailand, Chaine Des Rotisseurs (charge de mission), Jewish Assn. Thailand, Capital Club, Tau Epsilon Phi, Phi Alpha Delta, Beta Gamma Sigma (hon.). Republican. Jewish. Clubs: Royal Bangkok Sports, Heritage (founder Gov. 1985—), Fgn. Corrs. of Thailand (life). Lodge: Rotary (1969-89, sec. 1982-83, v.p. Bangkok 1984-85), Community Services of Bangkok (founder, acting pres. 1986, v.p. 1986-87, bd. dirs. 1985-88). Avocations: scuba diving, swimming, outdoor photography. Home: 39/221 Moo 3 Nichada Thani Soi 11, Tambol Bangtalad Amphur Pakkred, Nonthaburi 11120, Thailand Office: Tilleke and Gibbins ROP, 64/1 Soi Tonson, Ploenchit Rd, Bangkok 10330, Thailand

LYMAN, HENRY, retired publisher, marine fisheries consultant; b. Boston, Oct. 30, 1915; s. Henry and Elizabeth (Cabot) L.; m. Marjorie Borum, June 27, 1953 (dec. Mar. 1996). AB cum laude, Harvard Coll., 1937. Reporter Cape Cod Colonial, Hyannis, Mass., 1937-38; reporter Athol Daily News, Mass., 1938-40; editor Open Road Pub. Co., Boston, 1946-48; publisher Salt Water Sportsman, Boston, 1948-85, pub. emeritus, 1985—; advisor Internat. Conv. Conservation of Atlantic Tunas, Washington, 1976-86, New England Fishery Mgmt. Coun., Saugus, Mass., 1980—; bd. dirs. Atlantic Salmon Fedn., N.Y.C., Nat. Coalition for Marine Conservation, Savannah, Ga., Environ. League Mass., Boston; mem. U.S. sect. North Atlantic Salmon Conservation Orgn., Edinburgh, Scotland, 1983-92. Author: Bluefishing, 1953, rev. edit., 1987, Successful Bluefishing, 1974, (with others) The Complete Book of Striped Bass Fishing, 1954, The Complete Book of Weakfishing, 1959, Tackle Talk, 1971, Bottom Fishing, 1984; contbr. articles on marine fisheries matters. Trustee New England Aquarium, Boston, 1973-88, life trustee, 1988—; founding. trustee Coldwater Conservation Fund, Vienna, Va., 1993—; trustee Manomet Bird Obs., Mass., 1978-90, hon. trustee, 1990—; bd. dirs. Samual Cabot, Inc., Boston, 1974-91, Fund for Preservation of Wildlife and Natural Areas, Boston, 1979-89; incorporator Harvard Mag., Cambridge, Mass., 1979—. Comdr. USNR, 1940-46, 52-53. Mem. Nat. Wildlife Fedn. (bd. dirs. 1983-89), New England Outdoor Writers Assn. (life., bd. dirs. 1960-62), Outdoor Writers Assn. Am., Tavern Club (sec. 1980-83, pres. 1983-84), Harvard Club, Phi Beta Kappa. Avocations: angling; hunting. Home: 10 Longwood Dr Westwood MA 02090-1123 Office: Salt Water Sportsman 77 Franklin St Boston MA 02110-1510

LYMAN, JOHN, psychology and engineering educator; b. Santa Barbara, Calif., May 29, 1921; s. Oren Lee and Clara Augusta (Young) L. A.B. in Psychology and Math., UCLA, 1943, M.S., 1950, Ph.D. in Psychology, 1951. Research technician Lockheed Aircraft Corp., Burbank, Calif., 1940-43; mathematician Lockheed Aircraft Corp., 1943-44; with dept. psychology UCLA, 1947—, assoc. prof., 1957-63, prof., 1963—, from instr. to assoc. prof. Sch. Engring. and Applied Sci., 1950-63, prof. Sch. Engring. and Applied Sci., 1963—, chmn. engring. systems dept., 1978-84, head Biotech. Lab., 1958-80, head Human-Machine-Environment Engring. Lab., 1981-96; prof. materials sci. and engring., 1984-91; prof. emeritus Sch. Engring. and Applied Sci. UCLA, 1991—; research engr. Inst. Traffic and Transp., 1967-73; vis. prof. bioengring. Technol. Inst., Delft, Netherlands, 1965; spl. cons. Nat. Acad. Scis., Washington, 1973; cons. VA, Los Angeles, 1962-66, 67-76, NIH, 1963-66, 68-73, med. devices div. FDA, 1976-78, Perceptronics, Inc., Woodland Hills, Calif., 1978—, other agys. and cos.; bd. dirs. Perceptronics, Inc., Mega Graphics, Inc., also chmn. bd. Author chpts. in books, articles in profl. jours.; editor in field. Served to lt. (j.g.) U.S. Navy, 1944-46. Recipient Japanese Govt. Research award for Fgn. Specialists (Robotics), 1985, also numerous fellowships and grants. Fellow APA, Am. Psychol. Soc., Soc. Engring. Psychologists, AAAS, Human Factors and Ergonomics Soc. (Paul Fitts award 1971, pres. 1967-68, pres. disting. svc. award 1991); mem. Biomed. Engring. Soc. (pres. 1980-81), IEEE, Am. Soc. Engring. Edn., Am. Assn. Artificial Intelligence, Robotics Internat., Robotics Soc. Japan, Soc. Mfg. Engrs., Sigma Xi, Tau Beta Pi. Office: UCLA 6732 Boelter Hall Los Angeles CA 90024

LYMAN, PEGGY, dancer, choreographer, educator; b. Cin., June 28, 1950; d. James Louis and Anne Earlene (Weeks) Morner; m. David Stanley Lyman, Aug. 29, 1970 (div. 1979); m. Timothy Scott Lynch, June 21, 1982; 1 child, Kevin Kynch. Grad. high sch., Cin. Solo dancer Cin. Ballet Co., 1964-68, Contemporary Dance Theater, 1970-71; chorus dancer N.Y.C. Opera, 1969-70; Radio City Music Hall Ballet Co., 1970; chorus singer and dancer Sugar, Broadway musical, N.Y.C., 1971-73; prin. dancer Martha Graham Dance Co., N.Y.C., 1973-88, rehersal dir., 1989-90; artistic dir. Martha Graham Ensemble, N.Y.C., 1990-91; faculty Martha Graham Sch., 1975—; head dance div. No. Ky. U., 1977-78; artistic dir. Peggy Lyman Dance Co., N.Y.C., 1978-89; asst. prof. dance, guest choreographer Fla. State U., Tallahassee, 1982-89; guest choreographer So. Meth. U., Dallas, 1986; adjudicator Nat. Coll. Dance Festival Assn., 1983—; co-host To Make a Dance, QUBE cable TV, 1979; mem. guest faculty Am. Dance Festival, Durham, N.C., 1984; site adjudicator Nat. Endowment for Arts, 1982-84; tchr. Hartford Ballet Sch., 1992—, East Conn. Concert Ballet, 1992—; guest faculty Wesleyan U., Middletown, Conn., 1992; guest artist Conn. Coll., 1993; chair dance dept. Hartt sch. U. Hartford, Conn., 1994—; freelance master tch. internat. univs. Prin. dancer Dance in America, TV spls., 1976, 79, 84; guest with Rudolph Nureyev, Invitation to the Dance, CBS-TV, 1980; guest artist Theatre Choregraphique Rennes, Paris, 1981, Rennes, France, 1983, Adelaide U., 1991; site dir. Martha Graham's Diversion of Angels for student concert U. Mich., 1992, Martha Graham's Panorama, U. Ill., Champaign-Urbana, 1993, Martha Graham's Diversion of Angels for Dutch Nat. Ballet, 1995. Founding mem. Cin. Arts Coun., 1976-78. Mem. Am. Guild Mus. Artists. Office: Hartford Ballet 224 Farmington Ave Hartford CT 06105-3501

LYMAN, PRINCETON NATHAN, ambassador; b. San Francisco, Nov. 20, 1935; s. Arthur and Gertrude (Kramer) L.; m. Helen Carolyn Ermann, July 7, 1957; children: Cindy, Sheri, Lori. B.A., U. Calif., Berkeley, 1957; M.A., Harvard U., 1959, Ph.D., 1961. Program officer U.S. Aid Mission, Seoul, Korea, 1964-67; research assoc. Harvard U., Cambridge, Mass., 1967-68; dir. civic participation div. AID, Washington, 1968-71, equal employment counselor, 1969-71, dir. devel. resources for Africa, 1971-76; dir. U.S. Aid Mission, Addis Ababa, Ethiopia, 1976-78; dep. asst. sec. Africa Bur. U.S. Dept. State, Washington, 1981-86, U.S. amb. to Nigeria, 1986-89, dir. Bur. Refugee Programs, 1989-92, U.S. amb. to South Africa, 1992-95; asst. sec. Bureau of Int'l Org., 1995—; professorial lectr. Johns Hopkins U., Washington, 1980-86. Contbr. articles and book chpts. to profl. publs. Recipient AID Meritorious Honor award, 1966, Superior Honor award, 1970, 86, President's Meritorious Svc. award, 1989, 91; President's Disting. Svc. award, 1993. Mem. Am. Fgn. Service Assn. (v.p. 1969-70, bd. dirs.), Coun. Fgn. Rels.

LYMAN, RICHARD R., journalist; b. Gary, Ind., Dec. 30, 1954; s. Richard Walden and Willadean Mary (Volk) L.; m. Barbara Ann Whitaker, Sept.

12. Grad., Ind. U. Bus., labor writer The Times, Hammond, Ind., 1977; reporter UPI, Chgo., 1977-78; reporter, editor Kansas City Star, Mo., 1978-82; reporter Phila. Inquirer, 1982-83, movie critic, 1983—. Co-recipient Pulitzer Prize award, 1981. Mem. Sigma Delta Chi. Club: Pen and Pencil (Phila.).

LYMAN, RICHARD WALL, foundation and university executive, historian; b. Phila., Oct. 18, 1923; s. Charles M. and Aglae (Wall) L.; m. Elizabeth D. Schauffler, Aug. 20, 1947; children: Jennifer P., Holly Lyman Antolini, Christopher M., Timothy R. BA, Swarthmore Coll., 1947, LLD (hon.), 1974; MA, Harvard U., 1948, PhD, 1954, LLD (hon.), 1980; LLD (hon.), Washington U., St. Louis, 1971, Mills Coll., 1972, Yale U., 1975; LHD (hon.), U. Rochester, 1975, Coll. of Idaho, 1989. Teaching fellow, tutor Harvard U., 1949-51; instr. Swarthmore Coll., 1952-53; instr., then asst. prof. Washington U., St. Louis, 1953-58; mem. faculty Stanford U., 1958-80, 88-91, prof. history, 1962-80, 88-91, Sterling prof., 1980-91, assoc. dean Sch Humanities and Scis., 1964-66, v.p., provost, 1967-70, pres., 1970-80, pres. emeritus, 1980—, dir. Inst. Internat. Studies, 1988-91; pres. Rockefeller Found., 1980-88; spl. corr. The Economist, London, 1953-66; bd. dirs. Coun. on Founds., 1982-88, Independent Sector, 1980-88, chair, 1983-86, Nat. Com. on U.S.-China Rels., 1986-92; dir. IBM, 1978-92, Chase Manhattan Corp., 1981-91. Author: The First Labour Government, 1957; editor: (with Lewis W. Spitz) Major Crises in Western Civilization, 1965, (with Virginia A. Hodgkinson) The Future of the Nonprofit Sector, 1989; editorial bd. Jour. Modern History, 1958-61. Mem. Nat. Coun. on Humanities, 1976-82, vice chmn., 1980-82; chmn. Commn. on Humanities, 1978-80; trustee Rockefeller Found., 1976-88, Carnegie Found. Advancement of Tchg., 1976-82, World Affairs Coun. of No. Calif., 1992—; bd. dirs. Nat. Assn. Ind. Colls. and Univs., 1976-77, Assn. of Governing Bds. of Univs. and Colls., 1994—, Am. Alliance for Rights and Responsibilities, 1993—; chmn. Assn. Am. Univs., 1978-79. With USAAF, 1943-46. Decorated officier Legion of Honor; Fulbright fellow London Sch. Econs., 1951-52, hon. fellow, 1978—; Guggenheim fellow, 1959-60. Fellow Royal Hist. Soc.; mem. Am. Acad. Arts and Scis., Am. Hist. Assn., Council on Fgn. Relations, Conf. Brit. Studies, Phi Beta Kappa. Office: Stanford U Sch Edn Stanford CA 94305

LYMAN, WILLIAM WELLES, JR., retired architect; b. New London, Conn., Aug. 31, 1916; s. William Welles and Gladys Estelle (Latimer) L.; m. Margaret Helen Whittemore, July 12, 1941 (div. Sept. 1970); children: Cheryl, Steven, Philip, Susan, Donna, Patricia; m. Joan Evelyn Dalrymple, Sept. 26, 1970. BArch, U. Mich., 1939; MArch, Harvard U., 1940. Architect various orgns., Boston, 1941-42; pvt. practice Cambridge, Mass., 1947-53; chief designer Smith, Hinchman & Grylls, Detroit, 1953-56; architect Swanson Assocs., Bloomfield Hills, Mich., 1956-59, Smith & Smith Assocs., Royal Oak, Mich., 1959-62; architect Jickling Lyman & Powell Assocs., Inc., Birmingham, Mich., 1962-81, ret., 1981; mem. faculty Harvard U., Cambridge, Mass., 1947-53; lectr. on early Am. furniture, 1975—. Pres. Cambridge Coun. PTAs, 1950-52, Harlan Sch. PTA, 1960-61; treas. Mass. Coun. for Better Schs., 1950-52; chmn. Citizens Elem. Curriculum Study Birmingham Pub. Schs., 1962-63; bd. dirs. South Oakland Symphony Soc., 1960-63, Birmingham Teen. Ctr., 1965-67, Birmingham Community House, 1967-70, Profl. Skills Alliance, Detroit, 1973-75, Birmingham Hist. Bd., 1969-73, chmn., 1972-73; chmn. Birmingham Hist. Dist. Study Com., 1975-77, Community Devel. Svcs., Portsmouth, N.H., 1993—; pres. Birmingham Hist. Soc., 1980-81, bd. dirs. 1967-70; chmn. acquisitions com. John W. Hunter House, 1974-82; bd. govs. Warner House Assn., Portsmouth, N.H., 1983-91, chmn., 1986-88. U.S. Coast Guard, 1942-46. Fellow AIA; mem. Mich. Soc. Architects (pres. 1970). Unitarian. Home: 171 Gates St Portsmouth NH 03801-4607

LYN, GILLIAN H., artist, art educator; b. Midland Park, N.J., Jan. 31, 1965; d. Douglas William and Harriet Lynn (Trigere) L.; m. Kevin Balinger; children: Kimberly, Kenneth, Mandy. BFA, William Paterson Coll., 1986, MFA, 1988; postgrad., U. Boulder, 1992. Tchr. art Midland Park/Waldwick (N.J.) Cmty. Sch., 1985-92, Waldwick Middle Sch., 1988-90, Bayside (Wis.) Jr./Sr. High Sch., 1993—. Works exhibited in group shows at Bklyn. Mus., 1985, 86, 87, Brownstone Gallery, N.Y.C., 1986, Franklin lakes Libr., 1991, Ridgewood Libr., 1991, Oakland Pub. Libr., N.J., 1988, 90, 91, Ben Shan Gallery, N.J., 1990, 91, Bayside (Wis.) Gallery, 1992, 93, 95, Landry Gallery, 1993, 94, WinkWorks Gallery, Boulder, Colo. 1993, 95, 96, Flatirons Studios, 1996, West Moorhead Art Sch. and Gallery, 1995—. Grantee NEA, 1990, 93, 96. Mem. Typographers Assn. (award N.Y./N.J. br. 1989), Franklin Lakes Art Assn., Fair Lawn Art Assn., Salmagundi Club, N.Y.C., Boulder Arts and Artists' Guild.

LYNAM, JIM, professional basketball coach; b. Sept. 15, 1941; m. Kay Lynam; 3 children. Student, St. Joseph's U. Coll. basketball coach various univs.; asst. coach Portland Trailblazers (NBA), 1981-82; head coach San Diego Clippers (name now Los Angeles Clippers), 1983-85; asst. coach Phila. 76ers, 1985-88, head coach, 1988-94; head coach Washington Bullets, 1994—. Office: Washington Bullets US Air Arena Landover MD 20785*

LYNAM, TERENCE JOSEPH, lawyer; b. Dublin, Ireland, Mar. 25, 1953; came to U.S., 1958; s. Thomas Joseph and Bridget Anne (O'Carroll) L.; m. Melinda Anne Steagall, Aug. 23, 1980; children: Sean, Laura, Thomas. BA, U. Pa., 1975; JD, Georgetown U., 1978. Bar: D.C. 1978, Va. 1980, U.S. Supreme Ct. 1985. Law clk. D.C. Superior Ct., Washington, 1978-79; appellate atty. U.S. Dept. Justice, Washington, 1979-80, spl. asst. U.S. Atty., 1980, trial atty. fraud sect. criminal div., 1980-84; assoc. Heron, Burchette, Ruckert & Rothwell, Washington, 1984-86, ptnr., 1986-90; ptnr. Akin, Gump, Strauss, Hauer & Feld, Washington, 1990—. Vol. Gore for Pres., Washington, 1988. Roman Catholic. Avocations: sports, music. Office: Akin Gump Strauss Hauer & Feld Ste 400 1333 New Hampshire Ave NW Washington DC 20036-1511

LYNCH, BENJAMIN LEO, oral surgeon educator; b. Omaha, Dec. 29, 1923; s. William Patrick and Mary (Rauber) L.; m. Colleen D. Cook, Nov. 10, 1956; children: Kathleen Ann, Mary Elizabeth, Patrick, George, Martha, Estelle. BSD, Creighton U., 1945, DDS, 1947, MA, 1953; fellow, U. Tex., 1947-48; MSD, Northwestern U., 1954. Diplomate Am. Bd. Oral and Maxillofacial Surgery. Asst. instr. oral surgery Creighton U., 1948-50, instr., 1950-52, asst. prof., 1952-53; dean Creighton U. (Sch. Dentistry), 1954-61, assoc. prof. oral surgery, dir. dept., 1954-55, prof. oral surgery, 1957-86, prof. emeritus, 1986—, dir. oral surgery dept., 1954-67; also coordinator grad. and postgrad. programs; chief oral surgeon Douglas County Hosp., Omaha, 1951-63; pres. dental staff Children's Meml. Hosp., Omaha, 1952, 59; co-founder cleft palate team Children's Meml. Hosp., 1959; chmn. dept. dentistry Bergan-Mercy Hosp., Omaha, 1963-68; mem. exec. com., head dental staff Luth. Hosp., 1963-66; bd. dirs. Nebr. Dental Service Corp., 1972-78, pres., 1974-78; treas. Children's Meml. Hosp. Med.-dental staff, 1979-81; guest lectr. Walter Reed Grad. Sch. Medicine, 1957-58. Mem. Omaha-Douglas County Health Bd., 1966-68, v.p., 1967, pres., 1968; exec. com. Nebr. divsn. Am. Cancer Soc., 1963-67; bd. dirs. Nebr. Blue Cross, 1968-89, Creighton U. Alumni Coun., Omaha chpt., 1989-91; trustee United Cath. Social Svcs., 1989-95; adv. bd. to dean Creighton U. Dental Sch., 1984—, vice chmn., 1992-93, chmn., 1993-94; pres. Creighton U. Graybackers, 1991-94. Served at Walter Reed U.S. Army Med. Ctr., 1955-57. Recipient Alumni merit award Creighton U., 1978; named one of Ten Outstanding Young Omahans, 1952, 53, 58; inducted into Nebr. Dental Hall of Fame, 1981. Fellow Am. Coll. Dentists (pres. Nebr. chpt. 1973-74); mem. Am. Soc. Oral Surgeons, Midwest Soc. Oral Surgeons, Nebr. Soc. Oral Surgeons (founder 1957, pres. 1961), Nebr. Dental Soc. (trustee 1964-66), Omaha Dist. Dent Soc. (pres. 1963-64), Am. Coll. Oral-Maxillofacial Surgeons (founding mem.), Nebr. Soc. Dental Anesthesiology (founder, 1st pres.), Alpha Sigma Nu, Omicron Kappa Epsilon, Delta Sigma Delta. Home: 509 S Happy Hollow Blvd Omaha NE 68106-1224

LYNCH, BEVERLY PFEIFER, education and information studies educator; b. Moorhead, Minn., Dec. 27, 1935; d. Joseph B. and Nellie K. (Bailey) Pfeifer; m. John A. Lynch, Aug. 24, 1968. B.S., N.D. State U., 1957, L.H.D. (hon.); M.S., U. Ill., 1959; Ph.D., U. Wis., 1972. Librarian Marquette U., 1959-60, 62-63; exchange librarian Plymouth (Eng.) Pub. Library, 1960-61; asst. head serials div. Yale U. Library, 1963-65, head, 1965-68; vis. lectr. U. Wis., Madison, 1970-71, U. Chgo., 1975; exec. sec. Assn. Coll. and Research Libraries, 1972-76; univ. librarian U. Ill.-Chgo., 1977-89; dean Grad. Sch. Libr. and Info. Sci. UCLA, 1989-94, prof. Grad. Sch. Edn. and Info. Studies, 1989—. Author: (with Thomas J. Galvin) Priorities for Academic Libraries, 1982, Management Strategies for Libraries, 1985, Academic Library in Transition, 1989, Information Technology and the Remaking of the University Library, 1995. Named Acad. Libr. of Yr., 1982, one of top sixteen libr. leaders in Am., 1990. Mem. ALA (pres. 1985-86), Nat. Info. Standards Orgn. (bd. dirs. 1996—), Acad. Mgmt., Am. Sociol. Assn., Bibliog. Soc. Am., Caxton Club, The Chicago Network, Grolier Club, Arts Club Chgo., Phi Kappa Phi. Office: UCLA Grad Sch Edn and Info Mailbox 951521 3026 Moore Hall Los Angeles CA 90095-1521

LYNCH, CATHERINE GORES, social work administrator; b. Waynesboro, Pa., Nov. 23, 1943; d. Landis and Pamela (Whitmarsh) Gores; BA magna cum laude and honors, Bryn Mawr Coll., 1965; Fulbright scholar, Universidad Central de Venezuela, Caracas, 1965-66; postgrad. (Lehman fellow), Cornell U., 1966-67; m. Joseph C. Keefe, Nov. 29, 1981; children: Shannon Maria, Lisa Alison, Gregory T. Keefe, Michael D. Keefe. Mayor's intern, Human Resources Adminstrn., N.Y.C., 1967; rsch. asst. Orgn. for Social and Tech. Innovation, Cambridge, Mass., 1967-69; cons. Ford Found., Bogota, Colombia, 1970; staff Nat. Housing Census, Nat. Bur. Statistics, Bogota, 1971; evaluator Foster Parent Plan, Bogota, 1973; rsch. staff FEDESARROLLO, Bogota, 1973-74; dir. Dade County Advocates for Victims, Miami, Fla., 1974-86; asst. to dep. dir. Dept. Human Resources, Miami, 1986-87, computer liaison, 1987-88, asst. adminstr. placement svcs. program, 1988-89; exec. dir. Health Crisis Network, 1989—; guest lectr. local univs. Participant, co-chmn. various task forces rape, child abuse, incest, family violence, elderly victims of crime, nat., state, local levels, 1974-86; developer workshops in field; participant, chair, co-chair task forces on HIV/AIDS impact, long term care, children and AIDS, AIDS orgnl. issues, 1991—; mem. gov.'s task force on victims and witnesses, gov.'s task force on sex offenders and their victims, gov.'s Red Ribbon panel on AIDS, gov.'s interdepartmental work group; mem. ednl. review com. Am. Found. AIDS Rsch., 1991—; vice chair Metro-Dade HIV Svcs. Planning Council, 1991-93; active Fla. HIV Svcs. Adv. Coun., 1991-94; review panel Fed. Spl. Projects of Nat. Significance; cert. expert witness on battered women syndrome in civil and criminal cts. Recipient various public svc. awards including WINZ Citizen of Day, 1979, Outstanding Achievement award Fla. Network Victim Witness Svcs., 1982, Pioneer award Metro-Dade Women's Assn., 1989; cert. police instr. Mem. Nat. Orgn. of Victim Assistance Programs (bd. dirs. 1977-83; Outstanding Program award 1984). Fla. Network of Victim/Witness Programs (bd. dirs., treas., 1980-81), Nat. Assn. Social Workers, Am. Soc. Public Adminstrs., Dade County Fedn. Health and Welfare Workers, Fla. Assn. Health and Social Svcs. (Dade County chpt., treas., 1979-80), LWV (bd. dirs. Dade County chpt. 1989-92). Contbr. writings in field to publs. Office: Health Crisis Network 5050 Biscayne Blvd Miami FL 33137-3241

LYNCH, CHARLES ALLEN, investment executive, corporate director; b. Denver, Sept. 7, 1927; s. Laurence J. and Louanna (Robertson) L.; divorced; children: Charles A., Tara O'Hara, Casey Alexander; m. Justine Bailey, Dec. 27, 1992. BS, Yale U., 1950. With E.I. duPont de Nemours & Co., Inc., Wilmington, Del., 1950-69, dir. mktg., 1965-69; corp. v.p. SCOA Industries, Columbus, Ohio, 1969-72; corp. exec. v.p., also mem. rotating bd. W.R. Grace & Co., N.Y.C., 1972-78; chmn. bd., chief exec. officer Saga Corp., Menlo Park, Calif., 1978-86, also dir.; chmn., chief exec. officer DHL Airways, Inc., Redwood City, Calif., 1986-88; also dir.; pres., chief exec. officer Levolor Corp., 1988-89, also bd. dir., chmn. exec. com. of bd., 1989-90; chmn. Market Value Ptnrs. Co., Menlo Park, Calif., 1990-95; chmn., dir. Fresh Choice, Inc., Santa Clara, Calif., 1995—, chmn., 1995—; also bd. dirs.; bd. dirs. Pacific Mut. Life Inst. Co., Nordstrom, Inc., PST Vans, Inc., SRI Internat., Palo Alto Med. Found., Age Wave, Inc.; chmn. BJ Holdings, Inc., La Salsa Franchise, Inc. Bd. dirs. United Way, 1990-92, past chmn. Bay Area campaign, 1987; chmn., dir. Bay Area Coun.; past chmn. Calif. Bus. Roundtable; mem. adv. bd. U. Calif.-Berkeley Bus. Sch., Governance Bd. Mem. Yale Club (N.Y.C.), Internat. Lawn Tennis Club, Menlo Country Club (Calif.), Pacific Union Club (San Francisco), Coral Beach and Tennis Club (Bermuda), Vintage Club (Indian Wells, Calif.), Menlo Circus Club. Republican. Home: 96 Ridge View Dr Atherton CA 94027-6464 Office: 2901 Tasman Dr # 109 Santa Clara CA 95054

LYNCH, CHARLES ANDREW, chemical industry consultant; b. Bklyn., Jan. 6, 1935; s. Charles Andrew and Mary Martina (McEvoy) L.; m. Marilyn Anne Monaco, July 30, 1960; children: Nancy Callan, Cara Martina. BS, Manhattan Coll., 1956; PhD, U. Notre Dame, 1960. Rsch. chemist Esso Rsch. & Engring. Co., Linden, N.J., 1960-65; rsch. supr. FMC Corp., Organic Chem. Div., Balt., 1965-72; rsch. mgr. FMC Corp., Indsl. Chem. Div., Princeton, N.J., 1972-74; exec. v.p. Am. Oil & Supply Co., Newark, 1974-80; tech. dir., dir. sales & mktg., dir. rsch. & bus. devel., v.p. tech. Hatco Corp., Fords, N.J., 1981-95; with Calivera Cons., 1995—. Contbr. articles to profl. jours.; patentee in field (U.S. and foreign). Mem. Am. Chem. Soc., Am. Oil Chemists Soc., Soc. AutomotiveEngrs., Soc. Tribologists and Lubrication Engrs. (chmn. N.Y. sect. 1980-81), Ind. Lubricant Mfrs. Assn. (bd. dirs. 1985-88), Comml. Devel. Assn., Chem. Mgmt. and Resources Assn.

LYNCH, CHARLES J., secondary school principal. Prin. St. Isaac Joques Sch., Hinsdale, Ill. Recipient Elem. Sch. Recognition award U.S. Dept. Edn., 1989-90. Office: St Isaac Joques Sch 421 S Clay St Hinsdale IL 60521-4035

LYNCH, CHARLES THEODORE, SR., materials science engineering researcher, consultant, educator; b. Lima, Ohio, May 17, 1932; s. John Richard and Helen (Dunn) L.; m. Betty Ann Korkolis, Feb. 3, 1956; children: Karen Elaine Ostdiek, Charles Theodore Jr., Richard Anthony, Thomas Edward. BS, George Washington U., 1955; MS, U. Ill., 1957, PhD in Analytical Chemistry, 1960. Group leader ceramics div. Air Force Materials Lab., Wright-Patterson AFB, Ohio, 1962-66; lectr. in chemistry Wright State U., Dayton, Ohio, 1964-66; chief advanced metall. studies br. Air Force Materials Lab., Wright-Patterson AFB, Ohio, 1966-74, sr. scientist, 1974-81; head materials div. Office of Naval Rsch., Arlington, Va., 1981-85; pvt. practice cons. Washington, 1985-88; sr. engr. space ops. Vitro Corp., Washington, 1988-95; cons. Burke, Va., 1996—; USAF liaison mem. NMAB Panels on Solids Processing, Ion Implantation and Environ. Cracking, Washington, 1965-68, 78, 81; U.S. rep. AGARD structures and materials panel NATO, 1983-85. Co-author: Metal Matrix Composites, 1972; editor, author: Practical Handbook of Materials Science, 1989; editor: (series) Handbook of Materials Science, vol. I, 1974, vol. II, 1975, vol. III, 1975; vice chmn. editorial bd. Vitro Corp. Tech. Jour., 1989-92, chmn., 1993; contbr. articles to profl. jours. including Jour. Am. Ceramics Soc., Analytical Chemistry, Sci., Transactions AIME, Corr. Jour., Jour. Inorganic Chemistry, SAMPE, Jour. Less Common Metals. Mem., soloist George Washington U. Traveling Troubadours, Washington, 1950-55; choir dir. Trinity United Ch. of Christ, Fairborn, Ohio, 1966-81, Univ. Bapt. Ch., Champaign, Ill., 1957-60, Chapel II, Wright-Patterson AFB, Ohio, 1960-64; pres. Pub. Sch. PTO, 1967-69. 1st lt. USAF, 1960-62. Bailey scholar U. Ill., 1958-60; recipient Commendation medal USAF, 1962, Outstanding Achievement cert. NASA, 1992, award Soc. for Tech. Comm. Publ., 1993. Mem. Am. Chem. Soc. (treas. 1966-67, chmn. audit sect. 1967-68), ASM Internat. (sec. oxidation and corrosion com. 1980-81, chmn. 1981-82). Presbyterian. Achievements include patents for new corrosion inhibitors including encapsulated types, and for alkoxides and oxides; co-development of the refractory ceramic Zytrite, the first high density translucent zirconia made from thermal or hydrolytic decomposition of mixed alkoxides followed by hot pressing; pioneered general approach of organometallic compounds as precursors of high purity, fine particulate, materials. Home and Office: 5629 Kemp Ln Burke VA 22015-2041

LYNCH, DANIEL, newspaper editor, columnist, writer; b. Elmira, N.Y., Feb. 27, 1946; s. Joseph Patrick and Betty (Reed) L.; m. Donna L. Rimmer, Aug. 16, 1969; children: Kathleen Ellen, Kevin Rimmer. BS, Temple U., 1969. Polit. reporter Phila. Inquirer, 1970-74; Queens editor Newsday, L.I., N.Y., 1974-79; mng. editor Times Union, Albany, N.Y., 1979-95; columnist Hearts Newspapers, Albany, N.Y., 1995—. Author: (novels) Deadly Ernest, 1986, A Killing Frost, 1987, Deathly Pale, 1988, Brennan's Point, 1988, Bad Fortune, 1989, Yellow, 1992. Sgt. N.J. Air N.G., 1969-75. Named Author of Yr. Albany Pub. Libr., 1989; recipient first prize award for columns N.Y. AP, 1988, 95. Mem. N.Y. State Soc. Newspaper Editors (pres. 1990-91), N.Y. AP Assn. (pres. 1994-95). Roman Catholic. Avocations: sailing, fly fishing, painting. Office: Times Union News Pl PO Box 15000 Albany NY 12212-5000

LYNCH, DAVID K., film director, writer; b. Missoula, Mont., Jan. 20, 1946; s. Donald and Sunny L.; m. Peggy Reavey, 1967 (div.); daughter: Jennifer; m. Mary Fisk, 1977 (div.); son: Austin. Ed., Pa. Acad. Fine Arts, Philadelphia. Co-screenwriter, dir.: (films) Eraserhead, 1978, The Elephant Man, 1980 (Acad. award), Dune, 1984; screenwriter, dir.: (films) Blue Velvet, 1986, Wild at Heart, 1990 (Palme d'Or, Cannes Internat. Film Festival), Twin Peaks: Fire Walk With Me, 1992; creator: (TV series) Twin Peaks, 1990, American Chronicles, 1990, On the Air, 1992, Hotel Room, 1993, (performance piece) Industrial Symphony #1, 1989. Am. Film Inst. grantee. Mem. Dirs. Guild Am. Office: CAA 9830 Wilshire Blvd Beverly Hills CA 90212-1804

LYNCH, DAVID WILLIAM, physicist, educator; b. Rochester, N.Y., July 14, 1932; s. William J. and Eleanor (Fouratt) L.; m. Joan N. Hill, Aug. 29, 1954 (dec. Nov. 1989); children: Jean Louise, Richard William, David Allan; m. Glenys R. Bittick, Nov. 14, 1992. BS, Rensselaer Poly. Inst., 1954; MS, U. Ill., 1955, PhD, 1958. Asst. prof. physics Iowa State U., 1959-63, assoc. prof., 1963-66, prof., 1966—, chmn. dept., 1985-90, disting. prof. liberal arts and scis., 1985—; on leave at U. Hamburg, Germany; dir. microelectronics rsch. ctr. Iowa State Univ., 1995—; and U. Rome, Italy, 1968-69; sr. physicist Ames Lab. of Dept. of Energy; acting assoc. dir. Synchrotron Radiation Ctr., Stoughton, Wis., 1984; vis. prof. U. Hamburg, summer 1974; dir. Microelectronics Rsch. Ctr., Iowa State U., 1995—. Fulbright scholar U. Pavia, Italy, 1958-59. Fellow Am. Phys. Soc.; mem. AAAS, Optical Soc. Am. Achievements include research on solid state physics. Home: 3315 Ross Rd Ames IA 50014-3959

LYNCH, EDWARD STEPHEN, corporate executive; b. Holyoke, Mass., Oct. 5, 1911; s. Edward Joseph and Katherine Veronica (Moriarty) L.; m. Anna Azzariti, Aug. 3, 1946; children—Julia M., Edward G., Robert G., Stephen G. A.B., Amherst Coll., 1931; M.A., Harvard U., 1934, Ph.D., 1936. Instr. econs. Princeton, 1935-38; asst. prof. econs. Iowa State Coll., 1938-41; chief supply ops. Allied Commn., Rome and Unrra Italy, 1945-46; chief economist IBRD, Washington, 1946-48; chief economist, acting exec. v.p. Export-Import Bank Washington, 1948-59; v.p. overseas cos. Westinghouse Internat., 1960-66; v.p., treas. ITT Europe, Inc., Brussels, Belgium, 1966—; v.p. ITT Corp., 1973-76; cons., 1976—; cons., economist Sogen Swiss Internat. Corp., N.Y.C., 1977—; consultore Prefecture of Econ. Affairs of the Holy See, Vatican City, 1979-93. Served with AUS, 1943-45. Inducted into Holyoke High Sch. Hall of Fame, 1988; Amherst Meml. fellow, 1932, Henry Lee fellow, 1934-35; Christopher Weld scholar, 1933. Mem. Am. Econs. Assn., Council on Fgn. Relations, Phi Beta Kappa. Home: Via Salaria 408, 00199 Rome Italy

LYNCH, EUGENE F., federal judge; b. 1931. B.S., U. Santa Clara, 1953; LL.B., U. Calif., 1958. Assoc. O'Connor, Moran, Cohn & Lynch, San Francisco, 1959-64, ptnr., 1964-71; judge Mcpl. Ct., San Francisco, 1971-74; justice Superior Ct. City and County San Francisco, 1974-82; judge U.S. Dist. Ct. (no. dist.) Calif., San Francisco, 1982—. Office: US Dist Ct PO Box 36060 450 Golden Gate Ave San Francisco CA 94102*

LYNCH, FRANCIS CHARLES, lawyer; b. Pittsfield, Mass., Nov. 4, 1944; s. Frank Charles and Elizabeth Ellen (Dowd) L.; m. Sally Mapp Walker, June 24, 1972; children: William Mapp, Edward Walker, Katherine Francis. Student, London Sch. Econs., 1964-65; BS summa cum laude, Boston Coll., 1966; LLB, Yale U., 1969. Bar: S.D. 1969, Rosebud Sioux Tribal Ct. 1969, Oglala Sioux Tribal Ct. 1970, U.S. Dist. Ct. S.D. 1970, U.S. Dist. Ct. Mass. 1971, U.S. Ct. Appeals (1st cir.) 1973, U.S. Supreme Ct. 1980. Reginald Haber Smith fellow Rosebud Legal Svcs., Rosebud, S.D., 1969-70; assoc. Featherston, Homans & Klubock, Boston, 1971-73, Goodwin, Procter & Hoar, Boston, 1973-76; ptnr. Lynch & Walker, Boston, 1976; assoc. Newman & Meserve, Boston, 1977-78; assoc. Palmer & Dodge, Boston, 1978-79, ptnr., 1980—; asst. bar counsel Bd. Bar Overseers, Boston, 1976-77; commr. Mass. Com. Against Discrimination, Boston, 1973; lectr. profl. seminars. Contbr. articles to profl. jours. Trustee Bank Five for Savs., Arlington, Mass., 1980-87. Mem. Boston Bar Assn. (chair com. on fed. appointment of counsel/indigents plaintiffs in civil cases 1982-89). Democrat. Avocations: squash, tennis, golf. Home: 44 Woodland Rd Newton MA 02166-2322 Office: Palmer & Dodge 1 Beacon St Boston MA 02108-3106

LYNCH, GERALD WELDON, academic administrator, psychologist; b. N.Y.C., Mar. 24, 1937; s. Edward Dewey and Alice Margaret (Weldon) L.; m. Eleanor Gay Sherry, Dec. 5, 1970; children: Timothy, Elizabeth. B.S., Fordham Coll., 1958; Ph.D., N.Y. U., 1968. Tech. employment rep. Bell Telephone Labs., N.Y.C., 1958-63; psychologist VA Hosp., N.Y., Palo Alto, Calif., 1964-68; asst. prof. psychology John Jay Coll. Criminal Justice, N.Y.C., 1967-71; dir. student activities John Jay Coll. Criminal Justice, 1968-70, asso. prof., 1971-74, prof., 1974—, dean students, 1968-71, v.p., 1971-76, pres., 1976—; chmn. Use of Force in Jails, N.Y.C., 1987—. Contbr. articles to profl. jours. Chmn. N.Y.C. Police Found., 1979-92; chmn. N.Y. State Casino Gambling Study Panel, 1979, N.Y. State Fire Fighting Pers. Edn. and Stds. Com., 1980—, Westchester County Spl. Task Force on Dept. Pub. Safety Svcs.; mem. N.Y. State Fire Safety Task Force, 1981, N.Y. State Crime Control Planning Bd., 1979-86; chmn. bd. advisors Channel 13, 1984-87; chmn. N.Y.C. Fire Safety Found., 1984—; vice chmn. U.S. Marshals Found., 1987—; pres. Cath. Interracial Coun., 1990—; chmn. Mayoral Search Com. for Police and Fire Commn. Recipient Criminal Justice award N.Y. State Bar Assn., 1977; Disting. Alumni award in edn. Fordham Coll. Alumni Assn., 1978; Brotherhood award NCCJ, 1985; named Person of Yr., N.Y.C. chpt. Indsl. Security Soc., 1987, N.Y.C. Police Dept. Patrolwomen's Endowment Assn., 1987, Man of Yr., Police Self Support Group, 1989. Mem. Acad. Criminal Justice Scis., Am. Soc. Criminology, Am. Assn. State Colls. and Univs., AAAS, Am. Psychol. Assn. Democrat. Roman Catholic. Office: CUNY John Jay Coll Criminal Justice 899 10th Ave New York NY 10019-1029

LYNCH, GERARD E., law educator; b. N.Y.C., Sept. 4, 1951; s. Gerard Norman and Marjorie Ann (Werner) L.; m. Karen Marisak, June 10, 1972; 1 child, Christopher Marisak Lynch. BA, Columbia U., 1972, JD, 1975. Bar: N.Y. 1976, U.S. Supreme Ct., U.S. Ct. Appeals (2d, 4th and D.C. cirs.). Law clk. U.S. Ct. Appeals, N.Y.C., 1975-76, U.S. Supreme Ct., Washington, 1976-77; asst. U.S. atty. So. Dist. N.Y., N.Y.C., 1980-83; chief criminal div. U.S. Dist. Ct. (so. dist.) N.Y., N.Y.C., 1990-92; assoc. independent counsel Iran/Contra, 1988-90; asst. prof. Columbia U., N.Y.C., 1977-80, assoc. prof., 1980-87, prof. law, 1987—, vice dean, 1993—; of counsel Howard, Darby & Levin, N.Y.C., 1992—. Office: Columbia U Sch Law 435 W 116th St New York NY 10027-7201*

LYNCH, HARRY JAMES, biologist; b. Glenfield, Pa., Jan. 18, 1929; s. Harry James and Rachel (McComb) L.; m. Pokum Lee Lynch. BS, Geneva Coll., Beaver Falls, Pa., 1957; PhD, U. Pitts., 1971; postgrad. Bio-Space Tech. Tng. Program, NASA and U. Va., 1970. Clin. chemist West Penn Hosp., Pitts., 1955-56; grad. teaching asst. U. Pitts., 1966-71, sr. teaching fellow, 1971; postdoctoral fellow MIT, Cambridge, 1973-75, rsch. assoc. dept. nutrition, lab. neuroendocrine regulation, 1973-75, lectr., 1976-81, rsch. scientist dept. brain and cognitive sci., 1982-92; cons. Ctr. for Brain Scis. and Metabolism Charitable Trust, 1992—. Contbr. more than 60 articles on the pineal gland to profl. jours. and books; patentee on implantable programmed microinfusion apparatus, 1981. With USN, 1950-54. NIH postdoctoral fellow 1971-73. Mem. Soc. Light Treatment and Biol. Rhythms. Democrat. Avocation: study of animal behavior. Office: MIT E25-615 77 Massachusetts Ave Cambridge MA 02139-4301

LYNCH, JAMES ALEXANDER, architect; b. Ames, Iowa, July 24, 1923; s. Verne Marquis and Lorretta (Munson) L.; m. Edith Corrine Newlin, Oct. 1, 1951 (dec. 1954); m. Helen Peterson, Feb. 1, 1958; children: Michael J., Douglas R. BS, Iowa State U., 1949. Reg. profl. architect & engr., Iowa. Intern architect Brooks-Borg, Des Moines, 1949-52, James Allan, Omaha, 1952; architect Noel Wallace, Omaha, 1953-54, Amos Emery, Des Moines, 1955, Normile & Lynch, Des Moines, 1956-59, Russell & Lynch, Des Moines, 1959-65, James Lynch & Assocs., Des Moines, 1966-68, 79-95, Lynch Payne Champion Bernabe, Des Moines, 1969-79, Lynch & Quick

Assocs. PC, Des Moines, 1995—; pres. Iowa Bd. Architect Examiners, 1973-82; mem. City of Des Moines Archtl. Adv. Com., 1993—. Chmn. Archtl. Adv. Com. to Urban Renewal Bd., Des Moines, 1969-73; mem. Bldg. Code Bd. Appeals, Des Moines, 1958, Gov's. Economy Com., 1979. Mem. AIA (pres. Iowa chpt. 1966, bldg. design awards 1967, 68, 70), Des Moines Club (pres. 1976), Rotary. Republican. Avocations: flying, wine, cooking, photography, sketching. Office: Lynch & Quick Assocs PC 206 6th Ave Ste 700 Des Moines IA 50309

LYNCH, JAMES C., newspaper editor. Exec. editor The Daily News, N.Y.C. Office: The Daily News 220 E 42nd St Fl 817 New York NY 10017-5806

LYNCH, JAMES WALTER, mathematician, educator; b. Cornelia, Ga., Mar. 28, 1930; s. Ulysses Samuel and Ida Dell (Woodall) L.; m. Monika Antonie Fehrmann, May 2, 1959; children: Steve, David, Judith. AB, U. Ga., 1952, MA, 1956. Math. statistician Proving Ground, Aberdeen, Md., 1956-61; asst. prof. math. Ga. So. U., Statesboro, 1961-92, prof. emeritus math., 1992—. Contbr. articles to profl. jours.; author/contbr.: Crux Mathematicorum, 1982-92. NSF grantee, 1964. Mem. Ga. Coun. Tchrs. Math. (life), Ga. Coalition for Excellence in Teaching Math., Can. Math. Soc., Math. Assn. Am., Sigma Xi. Lutheran. Achievements include discovery that American Indians designed their projectile points to conform to the golden section ratio. Avocations: coin collecting, gardening, shooting. Home and Office: 411 College Blvd Statesboro GA 30458

LYNCH, JOHN A., lawyer, state senator; b. New Brunswick, N.J., Oct. 21, 1938; s. John A. Lynch; m. Deborah A. Lynch; children: Patricia, John P., Matthew J. L. Grad. Holy Cross Coll., 1960; LLB, Georgetown U., 1963. Bar: N.J. 1963; ptnr. Lynch, Martin, Philobosian, Chansky, Fitzgerald & Kane, North Brunswick, Brielle and Somerville; pres. N.J. Senate, 1990-92, minority leader, 1992—; mayor City of New Brunswick, 1979-91. Mem. Gov.'s Commn. on Sci. and Tech. Mem. Middlesex County Trial Lawyers Assn. (past pres.). Home: 11 Cotter Dr New Brunswick NJ 08901-1506 Office: 100 Bayard St New Brunswick NJ 08901-2165 also: NJ State Senate Trenton NJ 08625

LYNCH, JOHN BROWN, plastic surgeon, educator; b. Akron, Ohio, Feb. 5, 1929; s. John A. and Eloise L.; student Vanderbilt U., 1946-49; M.D., U. Tenn., 1952; children: John Brown, Margaret Frances Lynch Callihan; m. Mary Joyce Burrus, Dec. 1, 1994. Rotating intern John Gaston Hosp., Memphis, Tenn., 1953-54; resident in gen. surgery U. Tex. Med. Br., Galveston, 1956-59, resident in plastic surgery, 1959-62, instr., 1962, asst. prof. surgery, 1962-67, asso. prof., 1967-72, prof., 1972-73; prof., plastic surgery, chmn. dept. plastic surgery Vanderbilt U. Med. Center, 1973—. Served as capt. USAF, 1954-56. Diplomate Am. Bd. Plastic Surgery (chmn.). Fellow ACS; mem. Singleton Surg. Soc. (pres. 1982-83), AMA, Am. Soc. Plastic and Reconstructive Surgeons (pres. 1983-84), Am. Assn. Plastic Surgeons, Plastic Surgery Research Council, Am. Cleft Palate Assn., Am. Burn Assn., Soc. Head and Neck Surgeons, Internat. Burn Assn., Pan Am. Med. Assn., Am. Cancer Soc. (pres. Galveston County, Tex., Chpt. 1968), So. Med. Assn. (pres.-elect 1983-84), Tenn. med. Assn., Nashville Acad. Medicine, Tenn. Soc. Plastic Surgeons, Southeastern Soc. Plastic Surgeons, Southeastern Surg. Soc., H. William Scott, Jr. Soc., Nashville Surg. Soc., Am. Soc. Maxillofacial Surgeons, So. Surg. Assn., Am. Surg. Assn., Sigma Xi. Contbr. numerous articles to med. publs.; editor: (with S.R. Lewis) Symposium on the Treatment of Burns, 1973. Home: 5810 Hillsboro Pike Nashville TN 37215-4602 Office: Vanderbilt Hosp Rm 230mcs Nashville TN 37232

LYNCH, JOHN DANIEL, educator; b. Butte, Mont., Sept. 17, 1947; s. Leo and Queenie Veronica Lynch; m. Shannon Christine Crawford, May 7, 1983; 2 children: Kaitlin, Jennifer. B.S., West Mont. Coll.; M.S. No. Mont. Coll. Tchr. Butte High Sch., Mont., 1970-78, Butte Vo-Tech, 1978-89, Adult Basic Edn., 1989—; mem. Mont. State Legis., Helena, 1971-79, state senator, 1982—. Democrat. Roman Catholic. Lodge: KC.

LYNCH, JOHN EDWARD, JR., lawyer; b. Lansing, Mich., May 3, 1952; s. John Edward and Miriam Ann (Hyland) L.; m. Brenda Jayne Clark, Nov. 16, 1984; children: John E. III, Robert C., David B., Patrick D., Jacqueline E. AB, Hamilton Coll., 1974; JD, Case Western Res. U., 1977. Bar: Conn. 1978, Ohio 1980, U.S. Dist. Ct. (no. dist.) Ohio 1980, U.S. Ct. Appeals (6th cir.) 1980. Assoc. Thompson, Weir & Barclay, 1977-78; law clk. U.S. Dist. Judge, Cleve., 1978-80; assoc. Squire, Sanders and Dempsey, Cleve., 1980-86, ptnr., 1986—; master bencher Am. Inns of Ct. Found., 1987—; mem. civil justice reform act adv. group U.S. Dist. Ct. (no. dist.) Ohio. Del. Hamilton Coll. Alumni Coun., 1992—, regional chair alumni admissions, 1993—; trustee The Cath. Charities Corp., 1995—; mem. Cuyahoga County Rep. Exec. Com., Cleve., 1984—; mem. Seton Soc. St. Vincent Hosp. Fund. Mem. The Club (Cleve.). Roman Catholic. Avocations: golf, jogging. Home: 6075 Deepwood Dr Chagrin Falls OH 44022-2569 Office: Squire Sanders & Dempsey 4900 Society Ctr Cleveland OH 44114

LYNCH, JOHN JAMES, lawyer; b. Evergreen Park, Ill., Aug. 22, 1945; s. John J. and Agnes (Daly) L.; m. Kathleen Russell, Aug. 15, 1970; children: Kerry, Elizabeth, Erin. BA, St. Mary of the Lake Sem., 1967; MA in Philosophy, DePaul U., 1970, JD, 1973. Bar: Ill. 1973, U.S. Dist. Ct. (no. dist.) Ill. 1973, U.S. Ct. Appeals (7th cir.) 1976. Assoc. McKenna, Storer, Rowe, White & Haskell, Chgo., 1973-75; ptnr. Haskell & Perrin, Chgo., 1975—. Mem. ABA, Ill. State Bar Assn., Chgo. Bar Assn., Fedn. Ins. & Corp. Counsel. Office: Haskell & Perrin 200 W Adams St Chicago IL 60606

LYNCH, JOHN PETER, lawyer; b. Chgo., June 5, 1942; s. Charles Joseph and Anne Mae (Loughlin) L.; m. Judy Godvin, Sept. 21, 1968; children: Julie, Jennifer. AB, Marquette U., 1964; JD, Northwestern U., 1967. Bar: Ill. 1967, U.S. Ct. Appeals (7th cir.) 1979, U.S. Ct. Appeals (5th cir.) 1976, U.S. Supreme Ct. 1979. Ptnr. Kirkland & Ellis, Chgo., 1973-76, Hedlund, Hunter & Lynch, Chgo., 1976-82, Latham, Watkins, Hedlund, Hunter & Lynch, Chgo., 1982-85, Latham & Watkins, Chgo., 1985—. Mem. vis. com. Northwestern U. Law Sch. Served as lt. USN, 1968-71. Mem. ABA, Ill. Bar Assn., Assn. Trial Lawyers Am., Order of Coif, City Club, Exec. Club, Met. Club. Notes and Comments editor Northwestern U. Law Rev., 1967. Home: 439 Sheridan Rd Kenilworth IL 60043-1220 Office: Latham & Watkins Ste 5800 Sears Tower Chicago IL 60606

LYNCH, JOHN T., management consultant; b. 1948. With Towers Perrin, N.Y.C., 1969—, pres., 1990—; now chmn., CEO Towers Perrin, Stamford, Conn. Office: Towers Perrin 695 E Main St Stamford CT 06901*

LYNCH, JOHN THOMAS, science foundation administrator, physicist; b. Washington, Mar. 21, 1938; s. John Thomas and Mary Ellen (Kaye) L.; m. Leslie Gray, June 22, 1959 (div. June 1972); children: John Thomas III, Michael Gray; m. Carol Rollins, July 5, 1980. BS in Physics, Va. Poly. Inst., 1963; MS in Physics, U. Wis., 1965, PhD, 1972. Lab. technician Nat. Bur. Standards, Washington, 1957-60; rsch. scientist U. Wis., Madison, 1965-78; staff mem. Los Alamos (N.Mex.) Nat. Labs., 1978-81; program scientist NASA Hdqs., Washington, 1981-85; program dir. aeronomy and astrophysics Polar programs NSF, Washington, 1985—. Contbr. articles to sci. jours. Recipient Antarctic svc. medal USN, 1986. Mem. AAAS, Am. Geophys. Union, Astron. Soc. Pacific. Avocation: sailing. Office: NSF Polar Programs 4201 Wilson Blvd Arlington VA 22230-0001

LYNCH, KEVIN A., book publishing executive. Pub. Paulist Press, Mahwah, N.J. Office: Paulist Press 997 Macarthur Blvd Mahwah NJ 07430-2045

LYNCH, LAURA ELLEN, parochial school educator; b. Chgo., June 25, 1965; d. Edgar Lewis and Loretta Ann (Sheehar) Hield; m. Terrence Michael Lynch, June 22, 1991; children: Dennis Edgar, Ellen Rose. BA in Edn., St. Xavier U., 1987. Cert. tchr., Ill. Tchr. Queen of Martyrs Sch., Chgo., 1987-92.

LYNCH, MARK BRADLEY, electrical engineer, biomechanical researcher; b. Ft. Worth, Apr. 29, 1959; s. James Almon and Dolores (Heuring) L.; m. Amy Jo Fleming, Oct. 15, 1988; children: Abigail, Anthony, Emily. BSEE, U. Mo., Rolla, 1981, MS in Computer Sci., 1985; M of Engring. Mgmt., Washington U., St. Louis, 1989; PhD in Engring. Mgmt., U. Mo., Rolla, 1992. Registered profl. engr., Mo. Sr. design engr. Emerson Electric, St. Louis, 1981-85, Cencit Inc., St. Louis, 1985-89; project engr. Mark Andy Inc., St. Louis, 1989-90; univ. faculty La. Tech. U., Ruston, 1992-94; owner Beyond Inc., St. Louis, 1994—; rschr. Inst. for Micromanufacturing, Ruston, 1992-94; grad. rsch. asst. Intelligent Sys. Ctr., Rolla, 1991-92. Author: (book chpt.) Intelligent Systems in Design and Manufacturing, 1995. Grantee State of La., 1992; summer fellow U.S. Army, 1992. Mem. IEEE, Soc. Mfg. Engrs., Tau Beta Pi. Roman Catholic. Avocations: outdoor activities, sports. Home: 704 Summit Ave Saint Louis MO 63119 Office: Beyond Inc PO Box 1043 Maryland Heights MO 63043

LYNCH, MARTIN ANDREW, retail company executive; b. Chgo., Oct. 5, 1937; s. George Irwin and Cecilia Veronica (Corley) L.; m. Shirley Ann McKee, Oct. 20, 1962; children: Kathleen Marie, Kevin Michael, Karen Ann, Daniel Patrick, Michelle Eileen. BSc, DePaul U., 1962. CPA, Ill., Calif. Audit mgr. Price Waterhouse & Co., Chgo., 1962-69; asst. to pres. Scot Lad Foods, Chgo., 1969-70; v.p. fin. N.Am. Car Corp., Chgo., 1970-76; sr. v.p. fin. Tiger Internat. Inc., L.A., 1976-83; exec. v.p., chief fin. officer Duty Free Shoppers Group Ltd., San Francisco, 1983-89, Casino USA Inc., Santa Barbara, Calif., 1989—, Smart & Final Inc., Santa Barbara, 1989—. Mem. AICPA, Calif. CPA Soc., Fin. Execs. Inst., Nat. Assn. Whole Grogery, Inst. Food Distbn. Assn., Bel Air Country Club (L.A.). Roman Catholic. Avocations: jogging, swimming, skiing, golf. Office: Casino USA 524 Chapala St Santa Barbara CA 93101-3412

LYNCH, MAUREEN, communications executive; b. Jersey City, N.J., May 28, 1938; d. Thomas Edward and Mary Margaret (Doust) L. AA with honors, Marymount U., 1957; BA with honors, Rosemont Coll., 1959. Beauty and fashion editor Ladies Home Jour. Mag., 1974-82; pres. Maureen Lynch & Co., Inc., 1982—; dir. communications grad. sch. bus. adminstr. Fordham U., 1985—; bd. dirs. Blue Hill Troupe, Ltd., 410-57 Corp. Active Friends of Am. Ballet Theater. Recipient awards N.Y. Art Dirs. Club. Mem. Fashion Group Internat. (v.p. exec. com.), Cosmetic Exec. Women, Trends, West Side Tennis Club, Seabright Lawn Tennis and Cricket Club, NOW, Beta Gamma Sigma. Office: 113 W 60th St New York NY 10023-7471

LYNCH, MAXINE, newspaper publishing executive; b. Cleve.; children: Arana, Arrian. BS in Journalism, Kent State U., MPA, 1978. Publicist, dir. parks project Ohio Conservation Found.; copy desk intern Cleve. Press; reporter Akron Beacon Jour.; reporter Plain Dealer, Cleve., 1980-88, asst. city editor, 1988-89, asst. mng. editor personnel and adminstrn., 1989-90, mng. editor personnel, 1990—. Mem. Plymouth Ch., Shaker Heights. Mem. Am. Soc. Newspaper Editors, Soc. Profl. Journalists, AP Mng. Editors, Alpha Kappa Alpha, Press Club Cleve. Avocations: walking, creative dance. Office: The Plain Dealer 1801 Superior Ave E Cleveland OH 44114-2107

LYNCH, MILTON TERRENCE, retired advertising agency executive; b. Denver, Feb. 27, 1931; s. Thomas Lillis and Pauline Regina (Yaeger) L.; m. Katherine Marie Stamey, July 19, 1958; children—Carrie Elizabeth, Michael Thomas, Brian Wilson. B.F.A., Washington State U., Pullman, 1953. Promotion mgr. Gen. Mills, Inc., Palo Alto, Calif., 1956-62; v.p. Robert Ebey Co., Palo Alto, Calif., 1962-66; exec. v.p. Steedman, Cooper & Busse, San Francisco, 1966-74; owner, prin. Lynch & Assocs., San Francisco, 1974-78; exec. v.p. Lynch & Rockey Advt., San Francisco, 1978-84; pres., chief exec. officer Evans/Lynch Rockey, Inc., San Francisco, 1984-87; chmn., chief exec. officer Evans/San Francisco, 1987-90; dir. Evans Communications, Salt Lake City. Served to capt. Inf. U.S. Army, 1953-55. Mem. San Francisco Advt. Golf Assn. (pres. 1982-83). Republican. Roman Catholic. Avocations: golf; tennis; gardening. Home: 12779 Homes Dr Saratoga CA 95070-4016

LYNCH, NANCY ANN, computer scientist, educator; b. Bklyn., Jan. 19, 1948; d. Roland David and Marie Catherine (Adinolfi) Evraets; m. Dennis Christopher Lynch, June 14, 1969; children: Patrick, Kathleen (dec.), Mary. BS, Bklyn. Coll., 1968; PhD, MIT, 1972. Asst. prof. math. Tufts U., Medford, Mass., 1972-73, U. So. Calif., Los Angeles, 1973-76, Fla. Internat. U., Miami, 1976-77; assoc. prof. computer sci. Ga. Tech. U., Atlanta, 1977-82; assoc. prof. computer sci. MIT, Cambridge, 1982-86, prof. computer sci., 1986—; Ellen Swallow Richards chair MIT, 1982-87, Cecil H. Green chair, 1994-96; cons. Computer Corp. Am., Cambridge, 1984-86, Apollo Computer, Chelmsford, Mass., 1986-89, AT&T Bell Labs., Murray Hill, N.J., 1986-89, Digital Equipment Corp., 1990. Contbr. numerous articles to profl. jours. Mem. Assn. Computing Machinery. Roman Catholic. Office: MIT NE43-525 Dept Computer Sci Cambridge MA 02139

LYNCH, PATRICIA GATES, broadcasting organization executive consultant, former ambassador; b. Newark, Apr. 20, 1926; d. William Charles and Mary Frances (McNamee) Lawrence; m. Mahlon Eugene Gates, Dec. 19, 1942 (div. 1972); children: Pamela Townley Gates Sprague, Lawrence Alan; m. William Dennis Lynch. Student, Dartmouth Inst., 1975. Broadcaster Sta. WFAX-Radio, Falls Ch., Va., 1958-68; pub. TV host Sta. WETA, Washington, 1967-68; broadcaster NBC-Radio, Europe, Iran, USSR, 1960-61; internat. broadcaster, producer Voice of Am., Washington, 1962-69; staff asst. to First Lady The White House, Washington, 1969-70; host Voice of Am. Breakfast Show, Morning show, 1970-86; U.S. ambassador to Madagascar and the Comoros, 1986-89; dir. corp. affairs Radio Free Europe/Radio Liberty, Washington, 1989-94; worldwide lectr., 1968-86; adv. com. Ind. Fed. Savs. and Loan Assn., Washington, 1970-86. Author stories on Am. for English teaching dept. Radio Sweden, 1967-68, others on internat. broadcasting. Chair internat. svc. com. Washington chpt. ARC, 1979-86; bd. visitors Duke U. Primate Ctr., Durham, N.C. Grantee USIA, 1983; recipient Pub. Service award U.S. Army, 1960. Mem. Coun. Am. Ambs., (bd. dirs., v.p.), Assn. Diplomatic Studies and Tng. Dept. State (bd. dirs.), Am. Women in Radio and TV (pres. 1966-67), Am. News Women's Club, Washington Inst. Fgn. Affairs (bd. dirs.). Republican. Episcopalian. Avocations: travelling, reading, volunteer work, wildlife conservation.

LYNCH, PATRICK, lawyer; b. Pitts., Nov. 11, 1941; s. Thomas Patrick and Helen Mary (Grimes) L.; m. M. Linda Maturo, June 20, 1964; children: Megan, Kevin, Colin, Brendan, Erin, Brian, Liam, Eamonn, Kilian, Caitlin, Ryan, Declan, Cristin, Mairin, Sean. BA in Philosophy, Loyola U., Los Angeles, 1964, LLB, 1966. Bar: Calif. 1967, U.S. Dist. Ct. (cen., so., no. and ea. dists.) Calif., U.S. Ct. Appeals (9th cir.), U.S. Supreme Ct. Ptnr. O'Melveny & Myers, Los Angeles, 1966—; panelist PLI Annual Antitrust Law Inst., 1982-93. Bd. editors Matthew Bender Fed. Litigation Guide Reporter. Fellow Am. Coll. Trial Lawyers; mem. L.A. County Bar Assn. Office: O'Melveny & Myers 400 S Hope St Los Angeles CA 90071-2801

LYNCH, PATRICK, petroleum company executive; b. 1937. BBA, Iona Coll., 1959. Traveling auditor Texaco Inc., White Plains, N.Y., 1961-67, asst. mgr., 1967-74, asst. compt., 1974-79, dep. compt., 1979-80, assoc. compt., 1980-85, sr. asst. treas., gen. mgr. fin. dept., 1986-88, dep. treas., gen. mgr. fin. dept., 1986-88, compt., 1988—. Office: Texaco Inc 2000 Westchester Ave White Plains NY 10650-0001*

LYNCH, PAUL VINCENT, safety engineer, consultant; b. Bklyn., Apr. 11, 1932; s. John Andrew and Mary Catherine L.; m. Nancy Gates; children: David, Marianne. BA, St. Anselm's Coll., Manchester, N.H., 1954; postgrad. Fordham U., 1958-59, U. N.H., 1969-71. Registered profl. engr. in safety engring., Calif. Corp. ins. specialist Allied Chem. Corp., 1959-66; asst. to dir. risk mgmt. Am. Metal Climax, Inc., N.Y.C., 1966-68; lectr. risk mgmt., adminstr. safety U. N.H., Durham, 1969-71; assoc. prof. safety N.H. Vocat.-Tech. Coll., 1971-75; pres. Lynch Assocs., Inc., cons., Pittsfield, N.H., 1972-75; regional safety officer GSA, 1976-79; safety mgr. Calif., Bur. Land Mgmt., U.S. Dept. of Interior, Sacramento, 1979-86, bur. def. liaison officer and dep. dept. def. liaison officer Region IX Fed. Emergency Mgmt. Assn., 19979-86, emergency preparedness and disaster planning coord., 1979-86, chief safety mgmt. Bur. Land Mgmt. U.S. Dept. Interior, Washington, 1986-94, ret., 1994; guest lectr. in risk mgmt. Am. Mgmt. Assn., 1959-68; v.p. N.H. Safety Coun., 1972-74; mem. Vt. Roundtable for Fire and Bldg. Safety, 1972-75, Vt. Adv. Coun. on Fire Safety, 1972-75; advisor Vt. Occupl. Safety and Health Rev. Bd., 1972-75; instr. safety mgmt. Am. River Coll., Sacramento, 1975-76; pvt. cons., 1994—. Prodr., host Around Town, Hingham (Mass.) Cmty. TV, 1994—; weekly columnist for Hingham Times, 1995—. Active Boy Scouts Am., 1962—, dist. vice chmn. Nat. Capitol Area coun., 1987-92, membership chmn., mem. exec. bd. Golden Empire Coun., 1978-86, dist. chmn., 1984-85; pres. Deer Park PTA, 1961-62. With U.S. Army, 1955-57. Recipient Silver Beaver award Boy Scouts Am., 1977, Disting. Svc. award U.S. Dept. Interior, 1994, Disting. Svc. award Dept. Interior Safety and Health Coun., 1994. Mem. Am. Soc. Safety Engrs. (pres. Sacramento chpt. 1981-82; regional v.p., nat. long range planning com., chmn. legis. affairs com., adminstr. pub. sector divsn., named divsn. Safety Profl. of Yr. 1986, named pub. sector divsn. safety profl. of yr. 1986, Sacramento chpt. Safety Profl. Yr. 1986, chmn. sch. safety task force Nat. Safety Coun. 1988-91), Nat. Constructors Assn. (mem. ins. com.), Am. Indsl. Hygiene Assn., Vets of Safety (pres. Sacramento chpt. 1984-85), Rotary (sec. Pittsfield club 1970-73, vice-chmn. Hingham commn. on disability issues 1995—). Author, editor govt. publs.

LYNCH, PETER JOHN, dermatologist; b. Mpls., Oct. 22, 1936; s. Francis Watson and Viola Adeline (White) L.; m. Barbara Ann Lanzi, Jan. 18, 1964; children: Deborah, Timothy. Student, St. Thomas Coll., 1954-57; B.S., U. Minn., 1958, M.D., 1961. Intern U. Mich. Med. Center, 1961-62, resident in dermatology, 1962-65; clin. instr. U. Minn., 1965; chief dermatology and venereal disease Martin Army Hosp., Columbus, Ga., 1966-68; asst. prof. to asso. prof. dermatology U. Mich. Med. Center, 1968-73; asso. prof. to prof. dermatology U. Ariz., Tucson, 1973-86; chief sect. dermatology U. Ariz., 1973-86, asso. head dept. internal medicine, 1977-86; prof., head dermatology U. Minn. Med. Sch., Mpls., 1986-95; med. dir. ambulatory care U. Minn. Health System, 1993-95; prof., chmn. dept. dermatology U. Calif., Davis, 1995—. Author: (with S. Epstein) Burckhardt's Atlas and Manual of Dermatology and Venereology, 1977, Dermatology for the House Officer, 1982, 3d edit., 1994, (with W.M. Sams) Principels and Practice of Dermatology, 1992, 2 edit., 1996, (with I.E. Edwards) Genital Dermatology, 1994. Served with AUS, 1966-68. Served with AUS, 1966-68. Decorated Army Commendation Medal; recipient Disting. Service award for faculty U. Mich., 1970, Disting. Faculty award U. Ariz., 1981. Mem. Am. Acad. Dematology (bd. dirs. 1974-78, v.p. 1991-92), Assn. Profs. Dematology (bd. dirs. 1976-80, pres. 1994—), Internat. Soc. Study of Vulvar Disease (bd. dirs. 1976-79, pres. 1983), Soc. Investigative Dermatology, Am. Bd. Dermatology (bd. dirs. 1984-89), Gougerot Soc. (Bronze Medal award), Alpha Omega Alpha. Democrat. Roman Catholic. Home: 332 Sandpiper Dr Davis CA 95616 Office: U Calif Dept Dermatology 1605 Alhambra Blvd # 2300 Sacramento CA 95816

LYNCH, PETER S., retired portfolio manager; b. Boston, 1944; m. Carolyn Lynch; children: Mary, Annie, Beth. BA, Boston Coll., 1965; MBA, U. Pa., 1968. With Fidelity Investments, Boston, 1969-90; mgr. Fidelity Magellan Fund, 1977-90; trustee Fidelity Investments, 1990—; bd. dirs. Morrison Knudsen, W.R. Grace; guest lectr. Boston Coll. Author (with John Rothchild): One Up on Wall Street (1989), Beating the Street (1993), (best-selling books). Fin. advisor Lynch Fund, Boston Coll., Boston Pub. Libr., Third Century Found., Order of Malta, Cath. Schools Found., chmn. Named to Nat. Bus. Hall of Fame. Fellow Am. Acad. Arts & Scis. Office: 27 State St Boston MA 02109-2706*

LYNCH, PRISCILLA A., nursing educator, therapist; b. Joliet, Ill., Jan. 8, 1949; d. LaVerne L. and Ann M. (Zamkovitz) L. BS, U. Wyo., 1973; MS, St. Xavier Coll., Coll., 1981. RN, Ill. Staff nurse Rush-Presby.-St. Luke's Med. Ctr., Chgo., 1977-81, psychiat.-liaison cons., 1981-83, asst. prof. nursing, unit leader, 1985—; mgr. and therapist Oakside Clinic, Kankakee, Ill., 1987—; mem. adv. bd. Depressive and Manic Depression Assn., Chgo., 1986—; mem. consultation and mental health unit Riverside Med. Ctr., Kankakee, 1987—; speaker numerous nat. orgns. Contbr. numerous abstracts to profl. jours., chpts. to books. Bd. dirs. Cornerstone Svcs. Recipient total quality mgmt. award Rush-Presby.-St. Luke's Med. Ctr., 1991. Mem. ANA, Ill. Nurses Assn. (coms.), Coun. Clin. Nurse Specialists, Profl. Nursing Staff (sec. 1985-87, mem. coms.). Presbyterian. Home: 606 Darcy Ave Joliet IL 60436-1673

LYNCH, ROBERT EMMETT, mathematics educator; b. Chgo., Feb. 5, 1932; s. Joseph Burke and Mildred Cecilia (Bildhauser) L.; m. Martha Bolling Hacker, Oct. 8, 1955; children: Barbara Ann, William Robert, Pamela Elizabeth. B Engring. Physics, Cornell U., 1954; MS, Harvard, 1959, PhD, 1963. Sr. rsch. mathematician Gen. Motors Rsch. Lab., Warren, Mich, 1961-64; assoc. prof. computer sci. and math. U. Tex., Austin, 1964-67; assoc. prof. computer sci. and math. Purdue U., West Lafayette, Ind., 1967-85, prof., 1985—. Author: (with Garrett Birkhoff) Numerical Solution of Elliptic Problems, 1984; (with John R. Rice) Computers, Their Impact and Use/with Basic, 1975, Computers, Their Impact and Use/With Fortran, 1977, Computers, Their Impact and Use/with PL/1, 1978. Lt. USAF, 1955-57. Office: Purdue Univ Computer Sci Dept West Lafayette IN 47907

LYNCH, ROBERT MARTIN, lawyer, educator; b. St. Louis, Mar. 28, 1950; s. Raymond Burns and Nancy Winn (Roeder) L.; m. Cynthia Kay Allmeyer, June 7, 1974; children: Christopher, Kelly, Stephanie. AB, St. Louis U., 1972, JD, 1975. Bar: Mo. 1975, D.C. 1985, Tex. 1992. Law clk. to presiding justice Mo. Ct. Appeals, St. Louis, 1975-76; atty. Southwestern Bell Telephone Corp., St. Louis, 1976-79, atty. network, 1979-83, gen. atty., 1983-88, v.p., asst. gen. counsel, 1988-91; v.p., gen. counsel Tex. office Southwestern Bell Telephone Co., Dallas, 1991-93; v.p., gen. counsel external affairs Southwestern Bell Telephone Co., San Antonio, 1993—; instr. paralegal studies St. Louis Community Coll., 1977—. Mem. ABA, Tex. Bar, Dallas Bar Assn., Mo. Bar Assn. (adminstrv. law com. coun.), St. Louis Bar Assn. (chmn. adminstrv. law com. 1981-82), Am. Corp. Counsel Assn. (chmn. communications com. St. Louis chpt.). Republican. Avocations: racquetball, writing. Office: Southwestern Bell 175 E Houston St San Antonio TX 78205-2233

LYNCH, ROBERT N., clergy member. Gen. sec. Nat. Conf. Cath. Bishops, Washington. Office: US Cath Conf 3211 4th St NE Washington DC 20017-1106

LYNCH, ROSE PEABODY, retail executive; b. Dallas, June 6, 1949; d. Russell Vincent and Rose Peabody (Parsons) L.; m. Peter Stuart Milhaupt, Feb. 12, 1972 (div. 1977); m. James Alexander Torrey, Apr. 22, 1989. AAS, Bennett Coll., 1969; BA, Princeton U., 1971; MBA, Harvard U., 1982. Personal asst. Halston, Ltd., N.Y.C., 1975-76; assoc. dir. retail promotion Revlon, Inc., N.Y.C., 1976-80; dir. mktg. devel. Elizabeth Arden, N.Y.C., 1982-85; dir. mktg. Charles of the Ritz, N.Y.C., 1985-87; pres. Danskin, N.Y.C., 1987-89, Trowbridge Gallery, U.S., N.Y.C., 1989-93; cons., acting chief operating officer LeRoi Princeton Inc., 1991-92; v.p. merchandising-fragrance Victoria's Secret, Reynoldsburg, Ohio, 1993—. Republican. Episcopalian. Avocations: running, skiing, tennis, riding. Office: Three Limited Parkway Columbus OH 43218

LYNCH, SANDRA LEA, federal judge; b. Oak Park, Ill., July 31, 1946; d. Bernard Francis and Eugenia Tyus (Shepherd) L.; 1 child, Stephen Lynch Bowman. AB, Wellesley Coll., 1968; JD, Boston U., 1971. Bar: Mass. 1971, U.S. Dist. Ct. Mass. 1973, U.S. Dist. Ct. R.I., U.S. Ct. Appeals (1st cir.) 1974, U.S. Supreme Ct. 1974. Law clk. U.S. Dist. Ct., Providence, 1971-72; asst. atty. gen. Mass. Atty. Gen.'s Office, Boston, 1972-73; gen. counsel Mass. Dept. Edn., Boston, 1973-78; assoc. Foley, Hoag & Eliot, Boston, 1978-81, ptnr., 1981-95; apptd. U.S. cir. ct. judge U.S. Ct. of Appeals (1st cir.), Boston, 1995—; spl. counsel Jud. Conduct Commn., 1990-92. Contbr. articles to legal jours. Recipient Disting. Service award Planned Parenthood League of Mass., 1981. Mem. ABA (com. on partnership, ho. of dels. 1993-95), Boston Bar Assn. (pres. 1992-93, bd. bar overseers 1982-86, joint bar com. 1986). Office: US Ct Appeals 1st Cir 1617 US PO & CH Boston MA 02109

LYNCH, SONIA, data processing consultant; b. N.Y.C., Sept. 17, 1938; d. Espriela and Sadie Beatrice (Scales) Sarreals; m. Waldro Lynch, Sept. 18, 1981 (div. Oct. 1983). BA in Langs. summa cum laude, CCNY, 1960; cert. in French, Sorbonne, 1961. Systems engr. IBM, N.Y.C., 1963-69; cons. Babbage Systems, N.Y.C., 1969-70; project leader Touche Ross, N.Y.C., 1970-73; sr. programmer McGraw-Hill, Inc., Hightstown, N.J., 1973-78; staff data processing cons. Cin. Bell Info. Systems, 1978-89; sr. analyst AT&T, 1989-92; lead tech. analyst Automated Concepts Inc., Arlington, Va.,

1992—. Elder St. Andrew Luth. Ch., Silver Spring, 1992-96. Downer scholar CUNY, 1960, Dickman Inst. fellow Columbia U., 1960-61. Mem. Assn. for Computing Machinery, Phi Beta Kappa. Democrat. Avocations: needlework, sewing. Home: 13705 Beret Pl Silver Spring MD 20906-3030 Office: Automated Concepts Inc 4350 N Fairfax Dr Arlington VA 22203 Office: Automated Concepts Inc 4350 N Fairfax Dr Arlington VA 22203

LYNCH, THOMAS FRANCIS, archeologist, educator; b. Mpls., Feb. 25, 1938; s. Francis Watson and Viola Eugenia (Le Blanc) L.; m. Barbara Amy Deutsch, Feb. 4, 1961 (div. 1989); children: Elizabeth Ann, Jean Margaret, Julia Frances; m. Jane Ellen Flaherty, Oct. 7, 1989; children: Clare Viola, William Finn, Patrick Thomas. B.A., Cornell U., 1960; M.A., U. Chgo., 1962, Ph.D., 1967. Archeologist Idaho State U. Mus., Pocatello, 1963-64; instr. to prof. and chmn. anthropology dept. Cornell U., Ithaca, N.Y., 1964-93; dir. Cornell Intercollege Program in Archeology, 1971-74, 75-82; rsch. prof. Universidad Catolica del Norte, Antofagasta, Chile, 1976-77, rsch. assoc., 1983—, adj. prof., 1994—; adj. prof. Tex. A&M U.; dir. Brazos Valley Mus. Natural History, 1995—. Author: Guitarrero Cave: Early Man in the Andes, 1980; assoc. editor Am. Antiquity, 1986-90; mem. editorial bd. Latin Am. Antiquity, Andean Past, Chungara, Estudios Atacameños; contbr. articles to profl. jours. Recipient NSF, Nat. Geographic Soc., and other research grants for archeol. excavations in Peru, Chile and Ecuador, 1964—. Fellow AAAS; mem. Soc. for Am. Archeology, Tex. Archeol. Soc., Archeol. Inst. Am., Am. Quaternary Assn., Inst. Andean Rsch. (dir. 1976-79), N.Y. Archeology Coun., Am. Assn. Mus., Soc. for History Discoveries, Ctr. for Study First Ams. (sci. coun.), Inst. Andean Studies, Assn. Cornell U. Emeritus Profs., Centro de Estudios Andinos Cuzco (cons. mem.), Soc. Chilena de Arqueologia, Phi Beta Kappa.

LYNCH, THOMAS JOSEPH, museum manager; b. Omaha, Nebr., Feb. 15, 1960; s. James Humphery and Patricia Mae (Gaughan) L. BA in History, U. Nebr., 1984. Grad. tchng. asst. U. Nebr., 1984-86; mus. asst. Father Flanagan's Boys' Home, Boys Town, Nebr., 1986-88; mus. assoc. Father Flanagan's Boys' Home, Boys Town, 1988-93, mus. mgr., 1993—. Contbr. Boys Town: a Photographic History, 1992, Letters form the Front: Boys Town on the Battlefield from Pearl Harbor to the Persian Gulf, 1995. Vol. Omaha Metro Arts, 1988, Bot. Gardens, 1994; adv. bd. Metro Area History Day, Omaha, 1995. Named Most Valuable Player Father Flanagan's Boys' Home, 1992. Mem. Am. Assn. for State and Local History, Am. Mus. Assn., Nebr. Mus. Assn. Office: Boys Town Hall of History 14057 Flanagan Blvd Boys Town NE 68010-7509

LYNCH, THOMAS PETER, securities executive; b. N.Y.C., May 3, 1924; s. Michael Joseph and Margaret Mary (Fitzgerald) L.; m. Madeleine D'Eufemia, June 3, 1950; children: Francine, Richard. Student, Syracuse U., 1943-44; B.B.A., Baruch Coll., 1947. Acct. Deloitte, Haskins & Sells, N.Y.C., 1947-56; partner Bache & Co., N.Y.C., 1956-61; v.p. E.F. Hutton Co. Inc., N.Y.C., 1962-67; sr. v.p. E.F. Hutton Group Inc., 1967-72, exec. v.p., 1972-83, pres., dir., 1983-85; ret., 1985; pres., dir. Cash Res. Mgmt. Inc., 1976-85. Served with U.S. Army, 1943-46. Decorated Bronze Star. Mem. AICPA, Fin. Execs. Inst., India House, Canoe Brook Country Club, Baltusrol Golf Club, Johns Island Club, Morris County Golf Club.

LYNCH, THOMAS WIMP, lawyer; b. Monmouth, Ill., Mar. 5, 1930; s. William Brennan and Mildred Maurine (Wimp) L.; m. Elizabeth J. McDonald, July 30, 1952; children: Deborah, Michael, Maureen, Karen, Kathleen. BS in Geology, U. Ill., 1955, MS in Geology, 1958, JD, 1959. Bar: Ill. 1960, Okla. 1960, U.S. Supreme Ct. 1971, Tex. 1978. Staff atty. Amerada Hess Corp., Tulsa, 1959-72, asst. gen. counsel, 1972-75; mem. Hall, Estill, Hardwick, Gable, Collingsworth & Nelson, Tulsa, 1975; v.p., gen. counsel Tex. Pacific Oil Co., Inc., Dallas, 1975-80, Oryx Energy Co., Dallas, 1980-94; ret., 1994; adj. prof. law U. Tulsa, 1974; trustee Southwestern Legal Found., chmn., lectr. ann. Oil and Gas Short course, 1976—; chmn. Oil and Gas Edn. Ctr.; chmn. Oil, Gas and Mineral Law Coun. of State Bar of Tex. Served with USN, 1948-49, U.S. Army, 1951-53. Mem. ABA, Tex. Bar Assn. (chmn. oil, gas and mineral law sect.), Dallas County Bar Assn., Dallas Petroleum Club. Roman Catholic.

LYNCH, TIMOTHY JEREMIAH-MAHONEY, lawyer, educator, theologian, realtor, writer; b. June 10, 1952; s. Joseph David and Margaret Mary (Mahoney) L. MS, JD in Taxation, Golden Gate U., 1981; MA, PhD in Modern European History, U. San Francisco, 1983; Licentiate, Inter-Am. Acad., Rio de Janeiro, 1988; PhD in Classics and Divinity/Theology, Harvard U., 1988; JSD in Constl. Law, Hastings Law Ctr., 1990. Bar: D.C. 1989, Calif., U.S. Ct. Appeals (2d cir.) 1989, U.S. Ct. Appeals (4th cir.) 1990; mem. Bar/Outer Temple/Comml. Bar of U.K.; European Econ. Ct. of 1st Instance. Legal bus., tax, counsel Lynch Real Estate, San Francisco, 1981-85; researcher, writer Kolb, Roche & Sullivan, San Francisco, 1986-88; chmn. internat. law dept. Timothy J.M. Lynch & Assocs., San Francisco, 1987-88, chmn., mng. dir. law dept., 1988—; chmn., pres., CEO Lynch Real Estate Investment Corp., San Francisco, 1989—; ptnr. Lynch Investment Corp.; bd. lawyer/arbitrators Pacific Coast Stock Exch., NASD, 1994—; chmn. bd. Lynch Holdings Corp. Group; corp. counsel, sr. ptnr. L.A. Ctr. Internat. Comml. Arbitration, 1991—; vis. fellow classics, Inst. of Classical Studies, U. London; rsch. prof. Canon law and ecumenical ch. history grad. Theological Union U. Calif. Berkeley, 1992—; vis. scholar Patristic theology and classical philosophy of ecumenical doctrines, U. Laval, Quebec, Can., 1993—; vis. scholar Medieval ch. history U. Leeds, Eng., 1993-95; arbitrator Iran-U.S. Claims Tribunal, The Hague, 1993; mem. internat. corp. adv. bd. J.P. Morgan and Co., N.Y.C.; bd. dirs. Morgan-Stanley Corp., N.Y.C.; chmn. Latin Am., African and Middle East Corp. Groups J.P. Morgan Internat., Corp.; adv. bd. Morgan Stanley Corp., N.Y.C.; mem. Orgn. Econ. Cooperation and Devel., mem. adv. com. Internat. Labor Orgn.; participant Forum/A Group of Internat. Leaders, Calif., 1995, mem. adv. bd. U.S.-Saudi Arabia Bus. Coun., OECD on Industry and Fin., Paris, 1995, others; apptd. U.S. amb. Spl. Del. to Commn. Security/Coop. in Europe on Econ. and Pub. Reforms in Russian Republics; participant World Outlook Conf. on 21st Century, 1995; mem. Nat. Planning Assns., Washington, Brit.-North Am. Com. on Econ. and Pub. Policy Planning, Global Econ. Coun.; mem. adv. bd. Nat. Bus. Leadership Coun., Washington; mem. Arbitration Tribunal, Geneva; judge World Intellectual Property Orgns.; selected arbitrator, mem. tribunal; mem. arbitration bd., panel of arbitrators NAFTA Trade Policy; mem. adv. com. on private internat. law U.S. State Dept., Washington. Author: (10 vol. manuscript) History of Ecumenical Doctrines and Canon Law of Church; editorial bd. Internat. Tax Jour., 1993; author: Publishers National Endowment for Arts and Humanities Classical Translations: Latin, Greek, and Byzantine Literary Texts for Modern Theological-Philosophical Analysis of Social Issues; Essays on Issues of Religious Ethics and Social, Public Policy Issues, 1995, 96, others; editorial bd. Internat. Tax Jour., 1993; contbr. articles to profl. jours. Dir., vice chmn. Downtown Assn. San Francisco; councillor, dir. Atlantic Coun. U.S., 1984—; corp. counsel, chmn. spl. arbitrator's tribunal on U.S.-Brazil trade, fin. and banking rels. Inter-Am. Comml. Arbitration Commn., Washington; chmn. nat. adv. com. U.S.-Mid. East rels. U.S. Mid. East Policy Coun., U.S. State Dept., Washington, 1989—; mem. Pres. Bush's Adv. Commn. on Econ. and Public Policy Priorities, Washington, 1989; mem. conf. bd. Mid. East Policy Coun., U.S. State Dept., Washington, 1994—; elected mem. Coun. of Scholars U.S. Libr. Congress, Washington. Recipient Cmty. Svc. honors Mayor Dianne Feinstein, San Francisco, 1987, Leadership awards St. Ignatius Coll. Prep., 1984, Calif.'s Gold State award, 1990, AU-ABA Achievement award, 1990; named Civic Leader of Yr., Nat. Trust for Hist. Preservation, 1988, 89; named to Presdl. Order of Merit, 1991. Fellow World Jurist Assn., World Assn. Judges (Washington); mem. ATLA, Internat. Bar Assn. (various coms., internat. litigation, taxation, laborAm. Arbitration Assn. (panelist), Am. Fgn. Law Assn. (various coms.), Am. Soc. Ch. History, Am. Inst. Archaeology (Boston), Pontifical Inst. Medieval Studies (Toronto, Can.), Am. Hist. Assn., Am. Philol. Assn., Inst. European Law, Medieval Acad. Am., U.S. Supreme Ct. Hist. Soc., J Canon Law Soc. U.S., Nat. Planning Assn., Nat. Assn. Scholars (Eminent Scholar of Yr. 1993), Netherlands Arbitration Inst. (mem. Gen. Panels of Arbitrators, mem. Permanent Ct. Arbitration), Calif. Coun. Internat. Trade (GATT com., tax com., legis. com.), Practicing Law Inst., Am. Fgn. Law Assn. (mem. editl. bd. Working Groups on Rsch. Jour. for Legal systems of Africa, Mid. East, Latin Am., EEC and Soviet Union), U.S.-China Bus. Coun. (export com., GATT com., banking and fin. com., import com.), Bay Area Coun. (corp. mem.), Nat. Acad. Conciliators (Spl. award), Internat. Bar (mem. U.S. Group on Model on Insolvency Corp. Acts), Ctr. Internat. Comml. Arbitration, Comml. Club (various positions), Am. Soc. Internat. Law, Washington Fgn. Law Soc., Asia-Pacific Lawyers Assn., Soc. Profls. in Dispute Resolution, British Inst. Internat. and Comparative Law, Internat. Law Assn. (U.S. br.), Commercial Bar Assn. of United Kingdom (London), Inter-Pacific Bar Assn. (Tokyo; mem. arbitration intellectual property, consitutional taxation, labor, legal groups), Inst. European Law Faculty of Laws (United Kingdom), Urban Land Inst. Internat., Mid. East Inst. (Am.-Arab Affairs Coun.), Inter-Am. Bar Assn., 1987—, Calif. Trial Lawyers Assn., Ctr. Reformation Rsch. (co-chmn. Calif. State Com. on U.S-Mid. East Econ. and Polit. Rels.), Soc. Biblical Lit., Am. Acad. Arts and Letters, Am. Acad. Religion, World Lit. Acad., Coun. Scholars, Am. Com. on U.S.-Japan Rels., Japan Soc. No. Calif., Pan-Am. Assn. San Francisco, Soc. Indsl./Office Realtors, Assn. Entertainment Lawyers London, Royal Chartered Inst. Arbitrators (London), Soc. Indsl. and Office Realtors, Urban Land Inst., San Francisco Realtors Assn., Calif. Realtors Assn., Coun. Fgn. Rels., Chgo. Coun. Fgn. Rels., Conf. Bd., San Francisco Urban and Planning Assn., U.S. Trade Facilitation Coun., Asia Soc., Am. Petroleum Inst., Internat. Platform Assn., San Francisco C. of C. (bus. policy com., pub. policy com., co-chmn. congl. issues study group), Am. Inst. Diplomacy, Overseas Devel. Coun. (Mid. East, Russian Republics, Latin Am. studies group), Internat. Vis. Ctr. (adv. bd.), Fin. Execs. Inst., Nat. Assn. Corp. Dirs., Heritage Found. (bd. dirs.), Archaeological Inst. Am. (fellow coun. near east studies, Egyptology), Am. Literature Judicature Soc., Soc. of Biblical, Nat. Assn. Indsl. and Office Properties, World Literary Acad. (Cambridge, Eng.), Am. Acad. Arts & Letters, Am. Acad. Religion, Pres. Club, Nat. Assn. Bus. Economists, Villa Taverna Club, Palm Beach Yacht Club, Pebble Beach Tennis Club, Calif. Yacht Club, Commonwealth Club, City Club San Francisco, British Bankers Club, London, San Diego Track Club (registered athlete). Republican. Roman Catholic. Avocations: theater, social entertainment events, opera, ballet, fine arts. Home: 501 Forest Ave Palo Alto CA 94301-2631 Office: 540 Jones St Ste 201 San Francisco CA 94102-2022

LYNCH, VIRGINIA (LEE) M., art gallery director; b. Greenville, Tex., May 27, 1915; d. Oscar Roscoe and Catherine Claudine (Cooper) McGaughey; m. Eric Noble Dennard, June 16, 1938 (div. 1960); children: Katherine Fryer, Eric Jr. (dec.); m. William Stang Lynch, May 7, 1962 (dec. 1977); stepchildren: F. Bradley, James B., Mrs. Edward T. Barrett. BA, Baylor U., 1937, MA, 1960. Tchr. Tatum (Tex.) High Sch., 1937-38; part-time and substitute tchr. Waco (Tex.) Pub. Schs., Tyler (Tex.) Jr. Coll., 1950-60, Laselle Jr. Coll., Newton, Mass., 1959-60; dir. women Brandeis U., Waltham, Mass., 1960-62; owner Virginia Lynch Gallery, Tiverton, R.I., 1983—; guest curator Newport Art Mus., 1992-95. Trustee R.I. Sch. Design, Providence, 1980—; trustee Newport (R.I.) Art Mus., 1987-92, hon. life trustee, 1993—; mem. R.I. State com. Nat. Gallery Women in Arts, 1987—; mem. Town Planning Bd., Little Compton, R.I., 1980-86, Village Improvement Soc., Little Compton, 1963—, Save the Lighthouse Com., Little Compton; deacon United Congl. Ch., Little Compton, 1980-82; bd. dirs. Little Compton Hist. Soc., v.p., 1980-84. Recipient Citizen of Yr. award R.I. Sch. Design, 1983, State of the Arts award R.I. State Coun. on the Arts, 1992, Best Gallery award R.I. Monthly, 1992-94. Mem. Little Compton Garden Club (pres. 1975-77), Sakonnet Golf Club, Brown U. Faculty Club. Avocations: gardening, hiking, visiting museums, studios, and galleries. Home: 54 S Of Commons Rd Little Compton RI 02837-1522 Office: Virginia Lynch Gallery 3883 Main Rd Tiverton RI 02878-4843

LYNCH, WILLIAM DENNIS, JR., broadcast journalist; b. Salina, Kans., Sept. 11, 1945; s. William Dennis and Jean (Donelan) L.; children—Brendan Merrick, Patrick Hoctor. Student, U. Kans., 1963-66. Reporter, anchorman WTOP-AM-TV, Washington, 1968-70; newscaster WNEW-AM, N.Y.C., 1970-71; reporter WCBS Radio, N.Y.C., 1971-75, asst. news dir., 1975-76; corr. NBC News, N.Y.C. and Washington, 1977-81, CBS News, N.Y.C. and Washington, 1981—; anchor CBS World News Roundup, N.Y.C., 1985—; adj. prof. Sch. Journalism, Fordham U., N.Y.C., 1973-75. Served with U.S. Army, 1966-68. Recipient Rube Goldberg award N.Y. Sigma Delta Chi, 1973, N.Y. State AP Broadcasters' award, 1973, Champion-Tuck award 1985; inducted Radio Hall of Fame, 1995. Mem. AFTRA (N.Y. local bd. 1988-94), Mus. of Broadcasting (mem. creative coun. 1988—). Office: CBS News 524 W 57th St New York NY 10019-2902

LYNCH, WILLIAM FRANCIS, JR., secondary mathematics educator; b. Sharon Hill, Pa., July 9, 1956; s. William Francis Sr. and Patricia Claire Marie (Kilpatrick) L.; m. Marian Grace Geiger, Nov. 11, 1985. BS in Social Studies Edn., Temple U., 1978, postgrad., 1980-81; MA in Edn. in Math., Beaver Coll., 1984; postgrad., U. of the Arts, Phila., 1992-93. Social studies tchr. Ben Franklin H.S., Phila., 1978-79; math., English, reading, TV tchr. William Penn H.S., Phila., 1979; math., English, reading, social studies tchr. Stetson Jr. H.S., Phila., 1980-84; secondary sch. math. tchr. CAPA, Phila., 1984-85, Phila. H.S. for Girls, 1985, Kensington H.S., Phila., 1985, Edison H.S., Phila., 1985-86; math., sci., reading tchr. Jones Mid. Sch., Phila., 1986-90; math. tchr., head dept. LaBrum Mid. Sch., Phila., 1990—; acad. tutor, student advisor Phila. Sch. Dist., 1978—. Author curriculum in field. Mem. Phila. Fedn. Tchrs. Avocations: woodwork, music, sports, art, reading. Office: Gen J Harry LaBrum Mid Sch Brookview & Hawley Rds Philadelphia PA 19154

LYNCH, WILLIAM REDINGTON, lawyer; b. N.Y.C., Nov. 17, 1928; s. Francis Russell Vincent and Helen Adams (Barrett) L.; m. Mary Pomeroy Grant, Aug. 22, 1958; children: Melissa L. Woolford, Elizabeth Barrett, Cynthia Pomeroy, Kimberly Townsend, Sarah Phillips. Student, Phillips Exeter Acad., 1944-47; BA, Yale U., 1951; JD, Columbia U., 1958. Bar: N.Y. 1959, Conn. 1963. Assoc. Milbank Tweed Hadley & McCloy, N.Y.C., 1958-62; assoc. Cummings & Lockwood, Stamford, Conn., 1962-66, ptnr., 1966—, ptnr. in charge Greenwich office, 1978-88; bd. dirs. Greenwich Plaza Inc., 1970-74, Harrison & Ellis Inc., Cairo, Ga., 1985-87, Greenwich News Inc., 1986-90; chmn. ADM Mgmt. Corp., 1989-91. Chmn. Pub. Works Com., Greenwich, 1974-77, Greenwich United Way Campaign, 1975-76; vice chmn. Greenwich Bd. Edn., 1977-81, Rep. Town Meeting, 1967-77, dir., sec. Forum World Affairs, 1992-95. Lt. USNR, 1952-56. Mem. ABA, Conn. Bar Assn., Greenwich Bar Assn. (pres. 1979-80), Greenwich Field Club (pres. 1973-75), Round Hill Club (dir. 1992—, sec. 1993-96). Congregationalist. Home: 100 Bedford Rd Greenwich CT 06831-2535 Office: Cummings & Lockwood 2 Greenwich Plz Greenwich CT 06830-6353

LYNCH, WILLIAM THOMAS, JR., advertising agency executive; b. Evergreen Park, Ill., Dec. 3, 1942; s. William T. and Loretta J. L.; m. Virginia Louise Venteicher, Aug. 21, 1965; children: Kelly, Maureen, Kim, Meagan, Molly. BA, Loras Coll., 1964; MBA, U. Iowa, 1966. Media trainee Leo Burnett Co. Inc., chgo., 1966-68, asst. account exec., 1968-76, v.p., 1976-79, sr. v.p., 1979-82, exec. v.p., 1981-85; vice chmn. Leo Burnett USA, chgo., 1985-89; chmn., chief exec. officer Leo Burnett USA, Chgo., 1987-91; pres. Leo Burnett Co., Inc., Chgo., 1992-93; pres., chief exec. officer Leo Burnett Worldwide, Chgo., 1993; CEO, pres. Leo Burnett Worldwide, Leo Burnett Co. Inc., Chgo., 1993—. Mem. coun. U. Chgo. Grad. Sch. Bus.; bd. dirs. Chgo. United, Northwestern Meml. Hosp., Chgo. Mem. Econ. Club Chgo. Roman Catholic. Avocations: tennis, running, skiing, gardening, antiques. Office: Leo Burnett Co Inc 35 W Wacker Dr Chicago IL 60601*

LYNCH, WILLIAM WALKER, savings and loan association executive; b. Washington, Sept. 18, 1926; s. Talbott and Gertrude (Farrell) L.; m. Barbara Van Sant, Apr. 21, 1951; children: John S., William Walker, Franklin P., Mark F. BA, George Washington U., 1950. Vice pres., treas., dir. Met. Mortgage Co., Washington, 1950-55; dir., mem. exec. com. Prog. Fed. Savs. & Loan Assn., Washington, 1953-58; v.p., treas., dir. Anderson & Co., Inc., Washington, 1953-59; with 1st Fed. Savs. & Loan Assn. of Palm Beaches, West Palm Beach, Fla., 1959—, exec. v.p., 1966-89, pres., chief exec. officer, 1989-94, chmn. bd., 1994—; chmn. 1st Palm Beach Bancorp., 1994—; mem. tournament com. 53d PGA Championship, 1971; mem. tournament com. 19th World Cub, Internat. Golf Assn., 1971, 69th PGA Championship, 1987; dist. dir. Fla. League Fin. Instns., 1991; bd. dirs. Fla. Bankers Assn., 1994. Treas. Herbert Hoover Dike Dedication com., 1960; Asst. treas. Fla. Kennedy-Johnson campaign, 1960; bd. dirs. Am. Cancer Soc., 1967-69, 79—, hon. life dir. local United Way, 1962-64. With USNR, 1944-46. Recipient Free Enterprise Companion medal Palm Beach Atlantic Coll., 1989. Mem. West Palm Beach C. of C. (bd. dirs. 1970), Old Guard Soc. of Palm Beach Golfers, Kiwanis (bd. dirs. West Palm Beach club 1961, v.p. 1970-71, pres. 1971-72), City Club, No. Palm Beach Country Club, Bonnette Hunt Club, Pi Kappa Alpha. Republican. Roman Catholic. Office: First Federal Savings & Loan Assn 215 S Olive Ave West Palm Beach FL 33401-5617 Home: 1032 Country Club Dr North Palm Beach FL 33408-3716

LYNCH, WILLIAM WRIGHT, JR., investment executive, engineer; b. Dallas, Aug. 26, 1936; s. William Wright Sr. and Alma Martha (Hirsch) L.; m. June 11, 1960; children: Mary Margaret, Katherine. BSEE, U. Ariz., 1959; MBA, Stanford U., 1962. Pres. Ins. Bldg. Corp., Dallas, 1965-84; ptnr. Estacado Ptnrs., Dallas, 1985—, Encino Co., Dallas, 1970—, Cimarron Properties Co., Tucson, 1972-83; pres., bd. dirs. Argus Realty Corp., Dallas, 1972—; bd. dirs. Lynch Properties Inc., Dallas, Lynch Investment Co., Dallas, G.P. Bourrous Trucking Co., Inc., Dallas, Tex. Metal Works, Inc., Beaumont, Tex.; adv. dir. Sun Valley Fruit Co., Albuquerque, Patent Smith Tech., LTD, Enersyst Devel. Ctr., Inc., Dallas, 1995—. Bd. dirs. Dallas Symphony Orch., 1966-74, Dallas Civic Music, 1970-77, Ednl. Opportunities Inc., Dallas, 1973-90, Dallas Coun. World Affairs, 1990—; trustee W. W. Lynch Found., Dallas, 1968—. Capt. U.S. Army, 1959-60. Mem. Brook Hollow Club, Verandah Club, M.O. Club (Tuscon). Republican. Episcopalian. Office: Lynch Investment Co 1845 Woodall Rodgers Fwy Dallas TX 75201-2287

LYNCH-FIRCA, DIANA JOAN, secondary education educator; b. Kearny, N.J., Sept. 7, 1954; d. Joseph Daniel and Eleanor L. Lynch; m. John Nicholas Firca, Dec. 18, 1993. BA in Art History and Italian, U. Colo., 1976; MA in Art History, Rosary Coll. at Villa Schifanoia Grad. Sch. of Fine Arts (Italy), River Forest, Ill., 1979; BFA in Painting, Acad. Fine Arts, Milan, Venice, Bari, Italy, 1987; cert. in English as fgn. lang., Internat. House, London, 1990; postgrad., Monmouth Coll., 1990-91, Kean Coll. Cert. art, Italian, elem. edn. tchr. Tchr. English as foreign lang. Am. Inst., Florence, Italy, 1978-79, Brit. Sch., Venice, 1984-85, Am. Lang. Ctr., Matera, Italy, 1986-90; lectr. English U. Inst. Modern Lang., Milan, 1980-84, U. Studi di Bari, 1985-90; tchr. Italian Matawan Regional High Sch., Aberdeen, N.J., 1991—; tchr. art and ESL, Am. Sch., Montagnola, Switzerland, summers 1983-89; tchr. English as fgn. lang. Lord Byron Coll., London, summer 1990, Anglo Continental West Long Branch, N.J., 1990—; mem. adj. faculty ESL, fine art and art history Brookdale C.C., Lincroft, N.J., 1990—. Mem. N.J. Edn. Assn., Nat. Art Edn. Assn., Fgn. Lang. Educators N.J., Guild Creative Art, Art Educators N.J. Roman Catholic. Avocations: art, photography, languages, Irish dancing, music. Office: Matawan Regional High Sch Atlantic Ave Matawan NJ 07747

LYNCH-STAUNTON, JOHN, canadian senator; b. Montreal, Quebec, Canada, June 19, 1930. Student, Stanislas Coll., John de Brébeuf Coll., Georgetown U.; BSc, Queen's U. Councilman City of Montreal, 1960-74; Can. senator from Québec, 1990—; now leader of opposition Can. Senate; dep. leader govt. in senate, 1991; vice-chair exec. com. Montreal CityCoun., 1970-74; chmn. bd., CEO Soc. de Kuyper Can., Inc. Co-chair United Way Campaign, 1991. Mem. Canadian Club of Montreal (pres. 1976-77), Montreal Bd. Trade (pres. 1985-86). Office: Senate Bldg, Rm. 279, Ottawa, ON Canada K1A 0A4

LYNDEN, FREDERICK CHARLES, librarian; b. San Jose, Calif., Jan. 20, 1939; s. John Ross Jr. and Madeleine Lawton (Speik) L.; m. Deborah Reid Oehler, July 7, 1964; 1 child,Madeleine Scandrett. BA in Internat. Rels., Stanford U., 1960, MA in Am. History, 1961; MA in LS, U. Minn., 1963. Reference libr. Bancroft Libr., U. Calif., Berkeley, 1964-66, Meyer Libr., Stanford U., 1966-67; order libr., asst. chief acquisition dept. Stanford U. Libr., 1968-77; assoc. univ. libr. Brown U. Libr., Providence, 1977—. Assoc. editor Advances in Librarianship, 1991—, Pub. Rsch. Quar., 1985-94. Treas. Friends of Barrington (R.I.) Pub. Libr., 1984-86. Coun. on Libr. Resources fellow, 1977-78; Martinus Nijhoff Internat. travel grantee, The Hague, 1986; Blackwell N.Am. scholar, 1989. Mem. ALA (coun.), Assn. Coll. and Rsch. Librs. (pres. New Eng. chpt. 1990-91), Internat. Fedn. Libr. Assns. (standing com. on stats 1991—), Brown Faculty Club (sec. 1991—). Episcopalian. Avocations: tennis, gardening. Office: Brown U Libr Rockefeller Libr Box A Providence RI 02912

LYNDS, BEVERLY TURNER, retired astronomer; b. Shreveport, La., Aug. 19, 1929; d. Homer Emory and Nettie Lee (Robertson) Turner; m. Clarence Roger Lynds, June 19, 1954 (div. Oct. 1986); 1 dau., Susan Elizabeth; m. Leo Goldberg, Jan. 2, 1987 (dec. Nov. 1987). B.S., Centenary Coll., 1949; postgrad., Tulane U., 1949-50; Ph.D., U. Calif., Berkeley, 1955. Research assoc. U. Calif., 1955-58, Nat. Radio Astronomy Obs., Green Bank, W.Va., 1959-60; asst. prof. astronomy U. Ariz., 1961-65, assoc. prof., 1965-71; assoc. astronomer, asst. to dir. Kitt Peak Nat. Obs., Tucson, 1971-75; astronomer, asst. dir. Kitt Peak Nat. Obs., 1976-77, astronomer, 1977-86; cons. Assn. Univs. for Rsch. in Astronomy, 1986-87; assoc. Ctr. for Astrophysics and Space Astronomy U. Colo., Boulder, 1987—; edn. program coord. Unidata, UCAR, 1991—. Author: (with others) Elementary Astronomy, 1959; editor: (with others) Dark Nebulae, 1971. Mem. AAAS (chmn. sect. D), Internat. Astron. Union, Am. Astron. Soc. (councillor), Am. Meteorol. Soc., Am. Indian Sci. and Engring. Soc. *Knowing that there are many ways of making a contribution to the world we live in and choosing to use the opportunities available can result in a personal satisfaction which is the best form of success.*

LYNE, ADRIAN, director; b. Peterborough, Eng., Mar. 4, 1941. Dir. feature films: Foxes, 1980, Flashdance, 1983, 9 1/2 Weeks, 1986, Fatal Attraction, 1987 (Acad. award nomination), Jacob's Ladder, 1990, Indecent Proposal, 1993, Lolita, 1996. Mem. Dirs. Guild Am. Office: ICM 8942 Wilshire Blvd Beverly Hills CA 90211*

LYNE, AUSTIN FRANCIS, sporting goods business executive; b. Newton, Mass., Jan. 7, 1927; s. Daniel Joseph and Susan Markham O'Brien L.; m. Ann Blair, Nov. 27, 1954; children: Austin Francis, Jane Markham, Elizabeth Morgan, James Blair, Michael Davitt, Stephen Christopher. B.A., Harvard U., 1948; postgrad., U. Geneva, Switzerland, 1948-49. Store clk. 1st Nat. Stores Inc., Somerville, Mass., 1949-50, mgmt. trainee, 1950, warehouse supr., 1950, buyer, 1950-64, sales promotion mgr., 1964-67, advt. mgr., 1967, v.p. sales devel., 1968-73, sr. v.p. services, 1973-76, mgmt. cons., 1976-77; pres., treas. The Good Sport, Inc., Cohasset, Mass., 1977—. Coach Belmont Youth Hockey Assn., 1963-78; mem. Concord (Mass.) Rep. Town Com., 1964—, treas., 1967-74; dir. Internat. Friendship League, Elizabeth Peabody Settlement House, 1961-67, Concord-Carlisle Cmty. Chest, 1983-89; trustee Fenn Sch., 1972-78, Belmont Hill Sch., 1972-73, corporator, 1973—, Robert B. Brigham Hosp., 1971—. Served with USNR, 1945-46. Mem. Sorrento Village Improvement Assn. Clubs: Harvard in Concord (pres. 1965-67), Concord Country, Meganticook Rod and Gun, Harvard Varsity. Home: 68 Sudbury Rd Concord MA 01742-2420 Office: 166 Cushing Hwy Cohasset MA 02025

LYNE, SUSAN, magazine editor. Editor, publ. dir. Premiere mag., N.Y.C. Office: Premiere 2 Park Ave Fl 4 New York NY 10016-5603

LYNE, SUSAN MARKHAM, motion picture executive; b. Boston, Apr. 30, 1950; d. Eugene and Ruth (Lally) L.; m. George Crile III; children: Susan Markham, Jane Halle; stepchildren: Katherine Murphy, Elizabeth McCook. Assoc. editor City Mag., San Francisco, 1975-76; west coast editor New Times, San Francisco, 1976-77; mng. editor New Times, N.Y.C., 1978, The Village Voice, N.Y.C., 1978-82; v.p. creative devel. IPC Films, N.Y.C., 1982-85; ptnr. Lazar/Lyne Films, N.Y.C., 1985-86; founding editor Premiere mag., N.Y.C., 1987-96; exec. v.p. Walt Disney Motion Picture Group, 1996—. Bd. mem. babies heart fund Babies and childrens Hosp., 1990-94. Mem. Am. Soc. Mng. Editors (bd. dirs. 1993-96). Office: Premiere Mag 2 Park Ave New York NY 10016-5603

LYNES, JAMES WILLIAM, SR., communications company executive; b. Waverly, Iowa, July 26, 1928; s. James Kendall and Lenore Clara (Kuethe) L.; m. Opal Marie Kerdus, Aug. 24, 1954; 1 child, James William Jr. Student, U.S. Mil. Acad., 1946-47; BA in History, Wartburg Coll., 1950. Rural letter carrier U.S. Postal Svc., Plainfield, Iowa, 1951-86; corp. sec. Butler-Bremer Mut. Telephone Co., Plainfield, Iowa, 1962—, also bd. dirs.; pres. Iowa Rural Letter Carriers Assn., 1981-83, v.p., 1979-81, state bd. dirs. 1976-83. Vice chmn. Bremer County Bd. Health, Waverly, Iowa, 1969-84,

Waverly-Shell Rock Hospice, 1989-93, pres., 1992-93; fin. chmn. Bremer County Rep. Ctrl. Com., Waverly, 1987-92; mayor pro-tem City of Plainfield, Iowa, 1985-89, 91-94, mayor, 1994—, coun. mem., 1983-94; pres. Bremer County Hist. Soc., 1966—. With U.S. Army, 1951-53. Named Lion of Yr. Waverly Lions Club, 1988; Melvin Jones fellow, 1994. Mem. Plainfield Lions (sec. Plainfield chpt. 1971-72, pres. Waverly chpt. 1982-83, editor bulletin 1978—), Kopper Klowns (pres. 1980-81), Waterloo German-Am. (v.p., 1979-80), A.F. & A.M., Shriners. Lutheran. Home: 219 Main St # 218 Plainfield IA 50666-9753

LYNETT, GEORGE VINCENT, newspaper publisher; b. Scranton, Pa., Dec. 1, 1943; s. Edward James and Jean Marie (O'Hara) L.; m. Patricia Brady, June 4, 1966; children—Sheila Ellen, George Vincent, James Brady, Sharon Elizabeth. A.B. in English, Coll. of Holy Cross, 1965; M.B.A., U. Scranton, 1971; J.D., Georgetown U., 1978. Co-pub. Scranton Times and Sunday Times, 1967—; assoc. Haggerty, McDonnell, O'Brien & Wright, Scranton, 1978—; dir. 3d Nat. Bank and Trust Co., Scranton. Co-chmn. United Way of Lackawanna County, 1972; chmn. Lackawanna County Cancer Crusade, 1969; pres. Allied Services for Handicapped, 1973-75; trustee U. Scranton, 1970-76. Served with USNR, 1965-67. Mem. Lackawanna Bar Assn., Pa. Bar Assn., Pa. Newspaper Pubs. Assn., Am. Newspaper Pubs. Assn. Democrat. Roman Catholic. Club: Scranton Country. Office: The Scranton Times 147-149 Penn Ave Scranton PA 18503-2022

LYNETT, LAWRENCE WILSON, electronics company executive; b. N.Y.C., Sept. 11, 1921; s. James Degge and Lillian (Lonquist) L.; 1 dau., Michele. B.B.A., Manhattan Coll., 1943. With IBM Corp., 1946—, dir. adminstrv. rsch., 1966—; assoc. adminstrv. mgmt. Simmons Coll., 1966—; Mem. Nat. Adv. Com. for Bus. Edn. Curriculum Devel., 1973—. Chmn. editorial bd.: Impact, 1977—; mem. editorial bd. Adminstrv. Mgmt. Mag., 1983—. Chmn. bd. trustees AMS Rsch. Found. Lt. comdr. USNR, WWII, PTO. Decorated Navy Commendation ribbon; Presdl. Commendation for devel. adminstrv. mgmt. program for U.S. Govt. Mgrs., 1966. Mem. Adminstrv. Mgmt. Soc. (internat. pres. 1966-67, bd. dirs. 1980-83, Diamond Mgmt. key 1963, Internat. Mgmt. award 1967, Internat. Ambassador award 1985, Silver medal for mgmt. achievements 1988), Office Execs. Assn. N.Y. (pres. 1960-61, Leadership award 1961), Am. Mgmt. Assn. (v.p. gen. svcs. dir., bd. dirs. 1975-87). Home: 11 Purchase Hills Dr Purchase NY 10577-1615 Office: IBM Corp Old Orchard Rd Armonk NY 10504 *The most effective way to cope with change is to help create it.*

LYNETT, WILLIAM RUDDY, publishing, broadcasting company executive; b. Scranton, Pa., Jan. 18, 1947; s. Edward James and Jean O'Hara L.; children: Scott, Jennifer, Christopher P. B.S., U. Scranton, 1972. Pub. Scranton Times, 1966—; pres., chief exec. officer Shamrock Communications, Inc., 1971—; pres. Towanda Daily Rev., 1977-81, Owego Pennysaver Press, Inc., 1977-81; owner, Pres. Mgmt. Program, Harvard U., 1990. Bd. dirs. Community Med. ctr., Scanton; chmn. Mayor's Libr. Fund Drive, 1974; chmn. spl. gifts divsn. Heart Fund, 1975; bd. govs. Scranton Area Found.; trustee U. Scranton, 1990—; chmn. Steamtown Nat. Pk. Grand Opening com. Mem. Nat. Assn. Broadcasters, Pa. Assn. Broadcasters, Am. Newspaper Pubs. Assn., Pa. Newspaper Pubs. Assn., Greater Scranton C. of C. (chmn. membership drive 1980-81). Democrat. Roman Catholic. Clubs: Scranton Country, Elks, K.C. Office: 149 Penn Ave Scranton PA 18503-2022

LYNG, RICHARD EDMUND, former secretary of agriculture; b. San Francisco, June 29, 1918; s. Edmund John and Sarah Cecilia (McGrath) L.; m. Bethyl Ball, June 25, 1944; children: Jeanette (Mrs. Gary Robinson), Marilyn (Mrs. Daniel O'Connell). Ph.B. cum laude, U. Notre Dame, 1940; PhD (hon.), Carroll Coll., 1988. With Ed J. Lyng Co., Modesto, Calif., 1945-66, pres., 1949-66; dir. Calif. Dept. Agr., 1967-69; asst. sec. Dept. Agr., Washington, 1969-73, dep. sec., 1981-85; vice chmn. Commodity Credit Corp., 1981-85; pres. Lyng & Lesher, Inc., Washington, 1985-86; Sec. of Agr. Dept. Agr., Washington, 1986-89; pres. Am. Meat Inst., Washington, 1973-79; pvt. cons., 1980; dir. Commodity Credit Corp., 1969-73, Nat. Livestock and Meat Bd., 1973-76, Tri-Valley Growers, 1975-81; bd. govs. Refrigeration Rsch. Found., 1974-77, Chgo. Merc. Exch.; chmn. food industry trade adv. com. Commerce Dept.; chmn. U.S. Child Nutrition Adv. Com., 1971-73; mem. animal health com. NAS; sr. rsch. fellow Harvard U. Sch. Bus. Adminstrn., 1989-91; chmn. export adv. com. Nat. Dairy Bd., 1989—; bd. dirs. Ecosci., Corp, 1991—; trustee Internat. Life Sci. Inst., 1990—. Chmn. Stanislaus County (Calif.) Republican Central Com., 1961-62; dir. agr. div. Pres. Ford Com., 1976; co-dir. farm and food div. Reagan-Bush Campaign, 1980. Served with AUS, 1941-45. Mem. Washington Golf and Country Club, Del Rio Country Club (hon.). Roman Catholic. *

LYNGBYE, JØRGEN, hospital administrator, researcher; b. Andst, Denmark, July 23, 1929; arrived in Norway, 1988; s. Knud and Estrid Marie Schou (Nielsen) L.; m. Ulla von Holstein, July 15, 1967 (div. 1982); 1 child, Rie; m. Jintana Detwilaiphong, Jan. 3, 1994. MD, U. Copenhagen, 1956; PhD, U. Arhus, Denmark, 1969. Asst. U. Arhus, 1957-65; asst. prof. U. Copenhagen, 1966-72; sr. cons. Regional Hosp., Frederiksborg, Denmark, 1973-83, Førde, Norway, 1984; assoc. prof. molecular biology U.S., 1985-86; prof. U. Thailand, 1986-88; dir. Regional Hosp., Molde, Norway, 1988—. Author: Clinical Biochemistry, 1986, Twins--A Unique World Scenario, 1995; contbr. numerous articles to sci. and popular sci. jours. and newspapers. Sec. Danish Polit. Orgn., Copenhagen, 1977-81. Lt. Danish Army, 1951-66. Decorated WEO Order (Thailand); recipient prize Danish Sci. Soc., 1978, Prix Scientifique, France, 1980, prize Danish Soc. for Protection of Animals, 1987, Applied Physics award, 1993. Fellow N.Y. Acad. Scis.; mem. Danish Med. Assn. (rep. 1978-83). Avocations: world ecology, philosophy, mathematics, nuclear physics, music. Office: The Molde Hosp, Parkv 84, N-6400 Molde Norway

LYNHAM, C(HARLES) RICHARD, foundry company executive; b. Easton, Md., Feb. 24, 1942; s. John Cameron and Anna Louise (Lynch) L.; m. Elizabeth Joy Card, Sept. 19, 1964; children: Jennifer Beth, Thomas Richard. BME, Cornell U., 1965; MBA with distinction, Harvard U., 1969. Sales mgr. Nat. Carbide Die Co., McKeesport, Pa., 1969-71; v.p. sales Sinter-Met Corp., North Brunswick, N.J., 1971-72; sr. mgmt. analyst Am. Cyanamid Co., Wayne, N.J., 1972-74; gen. mgr. ceramics and additives div. Foseco Inc., Cleve., 1974-77, dir. mktg. steel mill products group, 1977-79; pres., chief exec. officer Exomet, Inc. subs. Foseco, Inc., Conneaut, Ohio, 1979-81, Fosbel Inc. subs. Foseco, Inc., Cleve., 1981-82; gen. mgr. splty. ceramics group Ferro Corp., Cleve., 1982-84, group v.p. splty. ceramics, 1984-92; owner, pres. Harbor Castings, Inc., North Canton, Ohio, 1992—; bd. dirs. Chick Master Incubator Inc., Corrpro Cos., Inc. Patentee foundry casting ladle, desulphurization of metals. Trustee Hospice of Medina County. Capt. C.E., U.S. Army, 1965-67. Decorated Bronze Star with one oak leaf cluster. Mem. Am. Foundrymen's Soc., Cornell U. Alumni Coun., Cornell U. Alumni Class 1963 (past v.p., past pres.), Cornell U. Alumni Fedn. (past pres., bd. dirs., past v.p.), Chippewa Yacht Club (commodore 1982), Cornell Club of N.E. Ohio (past pres., bd. dirs.). Republican. Congregationalist. Avocations: sailing, genealogy. Home: 970 Hickory Grove Ave Medina OH 44256-1616 Office: Harbor Castings Inc 4321 Strausser St NW North Canton OH 44720-7144

LYNN, ARTHUR DELLERT, JR., economist, educator; b. Portsmouth, Ohio, Nov. 12, 1921; s. Arthur Dellert and Helen B. (Willis) L.; m. Pauline Judith Wardlow, Dec. 29, 1943; children: Pamela Wardlow, Constance Karen, Deborah Joanne, Patricia Diane. Student, Va. Mil. Inst., 1938-39, U.S. Naval Acad., 1939; BA, Ohio State U., 1941, MA in Econs., 1943, JD, 1948, PhD in Econs., 1951; postgrad. in law, U. Mich., 1968-70. Bar: Ohio 1948, U.S. Supreme Ct. 1966. Upper Ohio Valley corr. Cin. Enquirer, 1937-38; ptnr. Lynn & Lynn, Portsmouth, 1949-50; chief clk. to dir. Ohio Dept. Hwys., 1957; mem. faculty Ohio State U., Columbus, 1941-86, prof. econs., 1961-86, asst. dean, 1959-62, assoc. dean Coll. Commerce and Adminstrn., 1962-65, assoc. dean faculties, assoc. provost, 1965-70, assoc. dean Coll. Adminstrv. Sci., 1984-86, assoc. dean emeritus Coll. Bus., 1986—, lectr. Coll. Law, 1961-67, adj. prof. law, 1967-86, prof. pub. adminstrn., 1969-86, prof. emeritus pub. policy and mgmt., 1986—, lectr. exec. devel. program, 1958-71, acting dir. divsn. pub. adminstrn., summers 1973, 74, acting dir. Sch. Pub. Adminstrn., summer 1975, 84-86; vis. prof. econs. Ohio Wesleyan U., 1958-59, U. Calif., Berkeley, summer 1972; vis. lectr. USAF Inst. Tech., Wright-Patterson AFB, Ohio, 1959-60; mem. Ohio Gov.'s Econ. Rsch. Coun., 1966-70; mem. assoc. faculty Lincoln Inst. Land Policy, Cambridge, Mass., 1989—. Author: Building the House: The Ohio State University School of Public Administration, 1969-89; editor: The Property Tax and Its Administration, 1970, Property Taxation, Land Use and Public Policy, 1976, Land Value Taxation, 1982; editorial adv. bd.: Tax Bramble Bush, 1959-70; assoc. editor: Nat. Tax Jour., 1971-88; bd. editors: Am. Jour. Econs. and Sociology, 1981—. Trustee Griffith Meml. Found. Ins. Edn.; chmn. external econs. adv. com. Marietta Coll., 1975-79; assoc. Nat. Regulatory Rsch. Inst., 1980—; mem. Alcohol, Drug Addiction and Mental Health Svcs. Bd., Franklin County, Ohio, 1990—; bd. dirs. Ohio Alliance for Mentally Ill, 1992-95, hon., 1995—; bd. dirs. Metro Behavioral Health Care Network, 1996—. 1st lt. F.A. AUS, 1942-46, PTO and Japan. Rsch. fellow Ohio Dept. Mental Health, 1991-92. Mem. ABA (chmn. com. state and local taxes sect. taxation 1961-63), Ohio Bar Assn., Columbus Bar Assn., Am. Econ. Assn., Royal Econ. Assn., Nat. Tax Assn. (chmn. com. model property tax assessment and equalization methods and procedures 1961-65, mem. exec. com. 1965-73, v.p., pres. 1969-70), Tax Inst. (adv. coun. 1960-63), Nat. Tax Assn.-Tax Inst. Am. (sec. 1975-84, treas. 1984-88, bd. dirs. 1975-88, counselor 1988—, hon. 1988—), Am. Arbitration Assn. (nat. panel), Ohio Coun. Econ. Edn. (bd. dirs. 1964-74), Com. on Taxation, Resources, and Econ. Devel. (co-chmn. 1979-87), Internat. Fiscal Assn., Internat. Assn. Assessing Officers (edn. adv. com.), Torch Club, Faculty Club, Rotary, Omicron Delta Epsilon, Beta Theta Pi, Phi Delta Phi, Beta Gamma Sigma, Pi Sigma Alpha, Pi Alpha Alpha. Republican. Episcopalian. Home: 2679 Wexford Rd Columbus OH 43221-3217 Office: 1775 S College Rd Columbus OH 43210-1309

LYNN, BARRY WILLIAM, religious organization executive; b. Harrisburg, Pa., July 20, 1948; s. Harold William and Edith Christine (Fairchild) L.; m. Dorcas Joanne Harley, June 6, 1970; children: Christina Dorcas, Nicholas Guy. BA summa cum laude, Dickinson Coll., 1970; ThM magna cum laude, Boston U., 1973; JD, Georgetown U., 1978. Bar: D.C.; ordained United Church of Christ. Tchr. religious studies dept. Cardinal Cushing Ctrl. H.S., South Boston, Mass., 1971-74; dir. To Heal A Nation program United Ch. of Christ, Washington, 1974-76, assoc. for emerging issues Ctr. for Social Action, 1976-77, legis. counsel Office for Ch. in Soc., 1978-80; pres. Draft Action, Inc., Washington, 1981-83; dir. Nat. Security Dissent Project William O. Douglas Inquiry into the State of Ind. Freedom, Washington, 1983; legis. counsel ACLU, Washington, 1984-91; exec. dir. Ams. United for Separation of Ch. and State, Washington, 1992—; cons. Ctr. for the Evaluative Clin. Scis., Hanover, N.H., 1992. Editor-in-chief Mil. Law Reporter, 1981-83; co-author: The Right to Religious Liberty: The Basic American Civil Liberties Union Guide to Religious Rights, 1994; co-host Battleline Radio Show, Washington, 1989-93, Pat Buchanan & Co. Radio Show, Washington, 1993-95; commentator on religion UPI Radio, Washington, 1993—; contbr. articles to profl. jours. Recipient Hugh Hefner First Amendment award Playboy Found., Chgo., 1986-87. Avocation: film. Home: 1406 Ingeborg Ct Mc Lean VA 22101 Office: Ams United for Separation of Ch and State 1816 Jefferson Pl NW Washington DC 20036

LYNN, CAROLYN IRVIN, pediatrics nurse, nursing administrator; b. Marshall, Tex., Feb. 8, 1945; d. Alva J. and Delphia Mae (Irvin); m. John F. Lynn, Mar. 21, 1965; children: John F. Jr., Vaughan Alva, Roseann Denise. Diploma, Tex. Ea. Sch. Nursing, Tyler, 1966. RN, Tex. Sch. nurse Beckville (Tex.) Ind. Sch. Dist.; nursing supr. Henderson (Tex.) Meml. Hosp. Mem. Tex. Nurses Assn. Home: RR 2 Box 236 Beckville TX 75631-9755

LYNN, C(HARLES) STEPHEN, franchising company executive; b. LaGrange, Ga., July 27, 1947; s. Charles Hubert and Norma Lee (Batey) L.; m. Milah Faith Pass, Sept. 4, 1976. B.S. in Indsl. Engring., Tenn. Tech. U., 1970; M.B.A., U. Louisville, 1973. Indsl. engr. Brown & Williamson Corp., Louisville, 1970-73; dir. distbn. div. Ky. Fried Chicken Corp., Louisville, 1973-77; pres., chief exec. officer MarQuest, Inc. subs. Century 21 Real Estate Corp., Irvine, Calif., 1978-80; v.p. Century 21 Real Estate Corp., Irvine, 1978-80; exec. v.p., dir., chief operating officer Burtson Corp., Marina Del Rey, Calif., 1980-83; chmn., pres., CEO Sonic Corp., Oklahoma City, 1983—; also bd. dirs. Sonic Industries, Inc., Oklahoma City; pres., ceo Shoney's Corp., Nashville, Tennessee; bd. dirs. Okla. Healthcare Corp., City Bank. Bd. dirs. Salvation Army, Oklahoma City, U. Okla. Sch. of Bus., Okla. Art Mus., Allied Arts, Oklahoma City U., Young Pres.'s Orgn., Bapt. Hosp. Found., Scope Ministry Internat., Tenn. Tech. Sch. Engring.; bd. trustees U. Louisville. Mem. Inst. Indsl. Engrs. (pres. 1973), Nat. Restaurant Assn., Internat. Franchise Assn. (bd. dirs. past chmn.), Okla. C. of C. (bd. dirs., past chmn.), Oklahoma City C. of C. (bd. dirs.), Nat. Cowboy Hall of Fame (bd. dirs.), Acad. State Goals, Fellowship Christian Athletes. Republican. Presbyterian. Avocations: tennis; basketball; reading; movies; travel. Home: 6907 Avondale Oklahoma City OK 73116 Office: Shoney's Corp 1727 Elm Hill Pike Nashville TN 37210*

LYNN, D. JOANNE, physician, ethicist, health services researcher; b. Oakland, Md., July 2, 1951; d. John B. and Mary Dorcas (Clark) Harley; m. Barry W. Lynn; children: Christina, Nicholas. BS summa cum laude, Dickinson Coll., 1970; MD cum laude, Boston U., 1974; MA in Philosophy and Social Policy, George Washington U., 1981; MS Clin. Evaluative Scis., Dartmouth Coll., 1995. Diplomate Am. Bd. Internal Medicine. Resident internal Medicine The George Washington U. Med. Ctr., 1974-77; emergency rm. physician, triage physician Washington VA Hosp., 1977-78; faculty assoc. for medicine and humanities divsn. experimental programs George Washington U., Washington, 1978-81, dir. divsn. aging studies, 1988-92, prof. health care scis. and medicine, 1991-92, assoc. chairperson dept. health care scis., 1990-92; dir of the Ctr. to Improve the Care of the Dying George Washington U., 1995—; prof. medicine, cmty. and family medicine, sr. assoc. Ctr. Evaluative Clin. Scis. Dartmouth-Hitchcock Med. Ctr., Hanover, N.H., 1992-95, assoc. dir. Ctr. for Aging, 1992-95; Robert Wood Johnson clin. scholar George Washington U., 1977-78, sr. fellow Ctr. Health Policy Rsch., 1991-92; asst. dir. med. studies The Pres. Commn. for Study of Ethical Problems in Medicine and Biomed. and Behavioral Rsch., 1981-83; med. dir. The Washington Home, 1983-89, Hospice of Washington, 1979-91, George Washington Cancer Home Care Program and Home Health Svcs. of The Washington Home, 1990-92, staff physician, 1979-92; fellow Hastings Ctr., 1984—; mem. working group on guidelines for care of terminally ill, 1985-87, rsch. project on ethical issues in care and treatment of chronically ill, 1985-87, working group on new physician-patient relationship, 1991-94, v.p., 1987, chair fellows nominating com., 1991; mem. coordinating coun. on life-sustaining med. treatment decision making by cts. Nat. Ctr. State Cts., 1989-93; fellow Kennedy Inst., 1991; mem. geriat. and gerontology adv. com. Dept. Vet. Affairs, 1991—; mem. bioethics com. Vets. Health Adminstrn., 1991-93; active Washington Area Seminar on Sci., Tech., and Ethics, 1982-92, Nat. Clin. Panel on High-Cost Hospice Care, Washington, 1991; presenter in field. Author chpts. to books; mem. editl. bd. The Ency. of Bioethics, 1994-95; mem. adv. editl. bd. Biolaw, 1983, The Hospice Jour., 1984—, Med. Ethics for the Physician, 1985-92, Med. Humanities Rev., 1986—, Cambridge Quar., 1991-95; contbr. articles, revs. to profl. jours. Peter Jeffries and Jeanne Arnold scholar, 1973; recipient Wellington Parlin Sci. Scholarship award, 1979, Dr. Bertha Curtis prize Boston U. Med. Sch., 1974, Nat. Bd. award Med. Coll. Pa., 1992. Fellow ACP (mem. subcom. on aging 1986-91), Am. Geriatrics Soc. (mem. com. public policy 1983—, mem. ethics com. 1988, chair subcom. on ethics and policy 1986, chair ethics com. 1991—, bd. dirs. 1991—); mem. AAAS, APHA, Am. Fedn. Clin. Rsch., Am. Health Care Assn. (mem. task force on AIDS 1987-89), Am. Hosp. Assn. (mem. spl. com. on biomedical ethics 1983-85, 89-94), Am. Med. Dirs. Assn., Am. Soc. Law and Medicine, Am. Coll. Health Care Adminstrs. (mem. nat. adv. com. wandering patients 1987-88), Nat. Inst. on Aging (mem. senile dementia of Alzheimer's type, mem. rsch. ethics task force 1981-82, Am. Geriatrics Soc. rep. 1984-86), Soc. Health and Human Values (mem. gov. coun. 1981-84), Inst. Medicine (mem. com. on future issues in med. tech. devel. 1992-94), N.H. Med. Soc., Soc. Health and Human Values (mem. gov. coun. 1981-84), Internat. Hospice Inst. (mem. physician's adv. com. 1984-86), Med. Soc. D.C. (mem. legis. affairs com. 1985-92, vice chairperson 1991-92), Soc. Gen. Internal Medicine (mem. editl. adv. bd. Jour. 1988-91). Office: Ctr Improve Care Dying George Washington Univ 1001 22d St NW 3820 Washington DC 20037

LYNN, EUGENE MATTHEW, insurance company executive; b. Kansas City, Mo., Nov. 6, 1918; s. Eugene M. and Marthield (Ellis) L.; m. Mary E. Spoors, Mar. 12, 1947 (dec.); 1 dau., Diane E.; m. Christine E. Koppl, Jan. 19, 1980. Student John B. Stetson U., 1937-39. Pilot Trans World Airlines, 1944-47; v.p. U.S. Epperson Underwriting Co., Boca Raton, Fla., 1949-55, pres., 1955—; pres. LIG Ins. Agy., Inc., Boca Raton, 1978—; v.p. Universal Underwriters Ins. Co., Kansas City, 1949-55, pres., 1955-82. Hon. chmn. bd., trustee Boca Raton Community Hosp.; trustee Lynn U. Boca Raton. Clubs: Boca Raton Hotel and Club, Royal Palm Yacht and Country (Boca Raton, Fla.), Delray Beach (Fla.), Ocean Reef (Key Largo, Fla.), Indian Creek Country, (Miami Beach), Fisher Island Surf (Miami Beach). Home: 565 Alexander Palm Rd Boca Raton FL 33432-7986 Office: Lumbermens Undwrt Aliance 2501 N Military Trl Boca Raton FL 33431-6356

LYNN, EVADNA SAYWELL, investment analyst; b. Oakland, Calif., June 1935; d. Lawrence G. Saywell; m. Richard Keppie Lynn, Dec. 28, 1962; children: Douglas, Lisa. BA, U. Calif., Berkeley, MA in Econs. With Dean Witter, San Francisco, 1958-61, 70-71, Dodge & Cox, San Francisco, 1961-69; v.p. Clark, Dodge & Co., San Francisco, 1971-73; chartered fin. analyst. V.p. Paine Webber, N.Y.C., 1974-77, Wainwright Securities, N.Y.C., 1977-78; 1st v.p. Merrill Lynch Capital Markets, N.Y.C., 1978-90; sr. v.p. Dean Witter Reynolds, N.Y.C., 1990—. Mem. N.Y. Soc. Security Analysts, San Francisco Security Analysts (treas. 1973-74). Mem. Fin. Women's Club of San Francisco (pres. 1967). Office: Dean Witter Reynolds 2 World Trade Ctr New York NY 10048-0203

LYNN, FREDRIC MICHAEL, sportscaster, former professional baseball player; b. Chgo., Feb. 3, 1952; s. Fredric Elwood and Marie Elizabeth (Marshall) L.; m. Natalie Brenda Cole, Oct. 7, 1986; children from previous marriage: Jason Andrew, Jennifer Andrea. Student, U. So. Calif., 1971-73. Center fielder Boston Red Sox, 1973-81, Calif. Angels, 1981-84, Balt. Orioles, 1985-88, Detroit Tigers, 1988-89, San Diego Padres, 1990; sportscaster ESPN, 1992—. Am. League batting champion, 1979; mem. Am. League All-Star Team, 1975-79, All-Star Team, 1975-83; named Most Valuable Player and Rookie of Yr., Am. League, 1975, Most Valuable Player in Play-Offs, Am. League, 1982, Most Valuable Player All Star Game, 1983, Center Fielder of 70's; recipient Rawlings Gold Glove award, 1975, 78, 79, 80, Seagrams Seven Crowns of Sports award, 1979. Mem. Major League Baseball Players Assn. Republican. Lutheran. Home: 7336 El Fuerte St Carlsbad CA 92009-6409

LYNN, JAMES DOUGAL, newspaper editor, journalist; b. Houlton, Maine, June 14, 1934; s. Charles Edward and Ethel Florence (Cripe) L.; m. Nancy Deborah Solomon, Jan. 30, 1965 (div. July 1979); children: Nina Vanessa, Nora Melissa. AB, Princeton U., 1955. Reporter L.I. Star-Jour., 1955-61; writer Newsweek, N.Y.C., 1961-63; copy editor, city hall reporter, state capital bur. chief N.Y. Herald Tribune, 1963-66; info. officer Temp. State Commn., N.Y.C., 1966-67; editorial dir. Sta. WABC-TV and Radio, N.Y.C., 1967-69; pub. affairs dir. Sta. WMCA-Radio, N.Y.C., 1969-72; editorial writer, dep. editorial page editor, opinion pages editor Newsday, L.I., 1972—. Jefferson fellow East-West Ctr., Honolulu, 1983. Office: Newsday Inc 235 Pinelawn Rd Melville NY 11747-4226

LYNN, JAMES THOMAS, investment banker, insurance company executive, government executive, lawyer; b. Cleve., Feb. 27, 1927. BA, Western Res. U., 1948; LLB, Harvard U., 1951. Bar: Ohio 1951, D.C. 1977. Gen. counsel U.S. Dept. Commerce, 1969-71, under sec., 1971-73; sec. HUD, 1973-75; dir. Office Mgmt. and Budget, 1975-77; asst. Pres. U.S., 1975-77; with Jones Day Reavis & Pogue, Cleve., 1951-69; with Jones Day Reavis & Pogue, Washington, 1977-84, ptnr., 1960-69, mng. ptnr., 1977-84; with Aetna Life & Casualty Co., Hartford, Conn., 1984, vice chmn., 1984, chmn., CEO, 1984-92, also bd. dirs.; sr. advisor Lazard Frères & Co., L.L.C., N.Y.C., 1992—; bd. dirs. Pfizer, Inc., TRW Inc. Case editor Harvard Law Rev., 1950-51. Served with USNR, 1945-46. Mem. Phi Beta Kappa. Office: Lazard Frères & Co LLC 5335 Wisconsin Ave NW Ste 440 Washington DC 20015-2030

LYNN, JANET (JANET LYNN NOWICKI SALOMON), professional figure skater; b. Chgo., Apr. 6, 1953; m. Richard Marc Salomon, 1975; 5 children. Figure skater, 1955—, profl. skater, 1973—; mem. Ice Follies, 1972—; Performed ice show to raise money for Shriners Hosps. Crippled Children and Burn Research Insts., 1973; mem. spkrs. bur. Fellowship Christian Athletes, 1970—; spokeswoman for the 1998 Olympics in Japan. Inducted to Skating Hall of Fame, 1994. U.S. Nat. Ladies Figure Skating champion, 1969-73; Olympic and World Bronze medallist, 1972; World Ladies Figure Skating Silver medalist, 1973. Home: 4215 Marsh Ave Rockford IL 61114-6143 *I have found that I want to do what is right for the Glory of God in Christ. As in anything, skating has been a challenge. I have tried to meet each challenge in my skating only with love for what I was doing instead of a selfish desire only to win.*

LYNN, LARRY (VERNE LAURISTON LYNN), engineering executive; b. Seattle, Sept. 5, 1930; s. Eldin Verne and Irma (Tuell) Lynn; m. Emily Jean Badger, Oct. 4, 1952 (div. 1988); m. Shirley Marie Pieczynski, Sept. 27, 1988. BS in Physics, Tufts U., 1951. Assoc. divsn. head, mem. steering com. Lincoln Lab. M.I.T., Lexington, Mass., 1953-79; dir. defensive systems Office of the Undersecretary of Defense, Washington, 1979-81; dep. dir. Adv. Rsch. Project Agy., Washington, 1981-85; v.p., COO Atlantic Aerospace Electronics, Greenbelt, Md., 1985-93; dep. under sec. defense Office Sec. Defense, Washington, 1993-95, dir. def. adv. rsch. project agy., 1995—. contbr. numerous articles to profl. jours. Lt. JG USNR, 1951-53. Mem. AIAA (sr. mem.), IEEE (sr. mem.). Home: 5911 Yates Ford Rd Manassas VA 22111 Office: DARPA 3701 N Fairfax Dr Arlington VA 22203-1714

LYNN, LAURENCE EDWIN, JR., university administrator, educator; b. Long Beach, Calif., June 10, 1937; s. Laurence Edwin and Marjorie Louise (Hart) L.; m. Patricia Ramsey Lynn; 1 dau., Katherine Bell; children from previous marriage—Stephen Louis, Daniel Laurence, Diana Jane, Julia Suzanne. A.B., U. Calif., 1959; Ph.D. (Ford Found. fellow), Yale, 1966. Dir., dep. asst. sec. def. (OASD/SA) Dept. Def., Washington, 1965-69; asst. for program analysis NSC, Washington, 1969-70; assoc. prof. bus. Grad. Sch. Bus., Stanford (Calif.) U., 1970-71, vis. prof. pub. policy, 1982-83; asst. sec. planning and evaluation HEW, Washington, 1971-73; asst. sec. program devel. and budget U.S. Dept. Interior, Washington, 1973-74; sr. fellow Brookings Instn., 1974-75; prof. pub. policy John Fitzgerald Kennedy Sch. Govt. Harvard U., Cambridge, Mass., 1975-83; dean Sch. Social Service Adminstrn. U. Chgo., 1983-88, prof., sch. of social svc. adminstrn. and Harris grad. sch. pub. policy studies, 1983—, dir. Ctr. for Urban Rsch. and Policy Studies, 1986—; dir. Mgmt. Inst., 1992—. Author: Designing Public Policy, 1980, The State and Human Services, 1980, Managing the Public's Business, 1981, Managing Public Policy, 1987, Public Management as Art, Science and Profession, 1996; co-author: The President as Policymaker, 1981; contbr. articles to profl. jours. Bd. dirs. Chgo. Met. Planning Coun., 1984-89, Leadership Greater Chgo., 1989-92; mem. coun. of scholars Libr. of Congress, 1989-93. 1st lt. AUS, 1963-65. Recipient Sec. Def. Meritorious Civilian Svc. medal, Presdl. Cert. of Disting. Achievment, Vernon prize. Fellow Nat. Acad. Public Adminstrn.; mem. U. Calif. Alumni Assn., Council on Fgn. Relations, Assn. Pub. Policy Analysis and Mgmt. (past pres.), Phi Beta Kappa. Home: 5000 S Cornell Ave Chicago IL 60615-3041 Office: Univ Chgo 969 E 60th St Chicago IL 60637-2640

LYNN, LORETTA WEBB (MRS. OLIVER LYNN, JR.), singer; b. Butcher Hollow, Ky., Apr. 14, 1935; d. Ted and Clara (Butcher) Webb; m. Oliver V. Lynn, Jr., Jan. 10, 1948; children—Betty Sue Lynn Markworth, Jack Benny (dec.), Clara Lynn Lyell, Ernest Ray, Peggy, Patsy. Student pub. schs. Sec.-treas. Loretta Lynn Enterprises; v.p. United Talent, Inc.; hon. chmn. bd. Loretta Lynn Western Stores. Country vocalist with MCA records, 1961—(numerous gold albums); most recent album Just a Woman, 1985, (with Conway Twitty) Making Believe, 1988, Greatest Hits Live, 1992, The Country Music Hall of Fame, 1991, Country's Favorite Daughter (reissue), 1993. Author: Coal Miner's Daughter, 1976. Hon. rep. United Giver's Fund, 1971. Named Country Music Assn. Female Vocalist of Year 1967, 72, 73, Entertainer of Year, 1972, named Top Duet of 1972, 73, 74, 75; recipient Grammy award 1971, Am. Music award 1978, named Entertainer of Decade, Acad. Country Music 1980; inducted into Country Music Hall of Fame, 1988; first country female vocalist to record certified Gold album. Office: care MCA Records Inc 70 Universal City Plz Universal City CA 91608

LYNN, NAOMI B., academic administrator; b. N.Y.C., Apr. 16, 1933; d. Carmelo Burgos and Maria (Lebron) Berly; m. Robert A. Lynn, Aug. 28, 1954; children: Mary Louise, Nancy, Judy Lynn Chance, Jo-An. BA, Maryville (Tenn.) Coll., 1954; MA, U. Ill., 1958; PhD, U. Kans., 1970. Instr. polit. sci. Cen. Mo. State Coll., Warrensburg, Mo., 1966-68; asst. prof. Kans. State U., Manhattan, 1970-75, assoc. prof., 1975-80, acting dept. head, prof., 1980-81, head polit. sci. dept., prof., 1982-84; dean Coll. Pub. and Urban Affairs, prof. Ga. State U., Atlanta, 1984-91; chancellor u. Ill., Springfield, 1991—; cons. fed., state and local govts., Manhattan, Topeka, Altanta, 1981-91; bd. dirs. Bank One Springfield. Author: The Fulbright Premise, 1973; editor: Public Administration, The State of Discipline, 1990, Women, Politics and the Constitution, 1990; contbr. articles and textbook chpts. to profl. pubs. Bd. dirs. United Way of Sangamon County, 1991—, Ill. Symphony Orch., 1992-95; bd. dirs. Urban League, 1993—. Recipient Disting. Alumni award Maryville Coll., 1986; fellow Nat. Acad. Pub. Adminstrn. Mem. Nat. Assn. Schs. Pub. Affairs and Adminstrn. (nat. pres.), Am. Soc. Pub. Adminstrn. (nat. pres. 1985-86), Am. Polit. Sci. Assn. (mem. exec. coun. 1981-83, trustee 1993—), Am. Assn. State Colls. and Univs. (bd. dirs.), Midwest Polit. Sci. Assn. (mem. exec. coun. 1976-79), Women's Caucus Polit. Sci. (pres. 1975-76), Greater Springfield C. of C. (bd. dirs. 1991—, accreditation task force 1992), Pi Sigma Alpha (nat. pres.). Presbyterian. Office: U Ill at Springfield Office of Chancellor Springfield IL 62794-9243

LYNN, OTIS CLYDE, former army officer; b. nr. Flynn's Lick, Tenn., Feb. 14, 1927; s. Dillard A. and Jennie Sue (Pruett) L.; m. Jacque Gilbert, Mar. 17, 1946; children: Clyde Gilbert, Gary Jackson. Student, Vanderbilt U., 1944-45; B.G.E., U. Omaha, 1963; M.S., George Washington U., 1968. Commd. 2d lt. U.S. Army, 1946, advanced through grades to maj. gen., 1972; chief of staff 2d Div., Korea, 1970; comdr. 1st Brigade 2d div., Korea, 1971; asst. div. comdr. 101st Div., Fort Campbell, Ky., 1974; chief of staff XVIII Airborne Corps, Fort Bragg, N.C., 1975, U.S. Forces, Japan, 1975-78; comdg. gen. 25th Inf. Div., Schofield Barracks, Hawaii, 1978-80; chief staff U.S. Army in Europe, Heidelberg, Fed. Republic Germany, 1980-82; ret., 1982, ret. real estate broker. Decorated Silver Star with two oak leaf clusters, Def. Superior Service medal, Legion of Merit (with two oak leaf clusters), Bronze Star, Air Medal, D.S.M., Purple Heart. Mem. Assn. of U.S. Army, Rotary. Mem. Ch. of Christ. Home: 140 Arborvitae Dr Pine Knoll Shores NC 28512-6200

LYNN, ROBERT PATRICK, JR., lawyer; b. N.Y.C., Nov. 17, 1943; s. Robert P. and Marie (Madeo) L.; m. Maria T. Zeccola, Nov. 18, 1967; children—Robert P. III, Stephanie M., Kerry Elizabeth. B.A., Villanova U., 1965; J.D., St. John's U., Bklyn., 1968. Bar: N.Y. 1969, U.S. Dist. Ct. (ea. dist.) N.Y. 1975, U.S. Ct. Appeals (1st cir.) 1978, U.S. Ct. Appeals (2d cir.) 1975, U.S. Supreme Ct. 1978. Clk., then assoc. Leboeuf, Lamb & Leiby, N.Y.C., 1966-69; dep. town atty. Town of North Hempstead, Manhasset, N.Y., 1969-71; assoc. Sprague Dwyer Aspland & Tobin, Mineola, N.Y., 1971-75, ptnr., 1975-76; ptnr. Lynn & Ledwith, Garden City, N.Y., 1976-92; spl. prosecutor Inc. Village of Bayville, 1975-76. Bd. dirs. Cath. Charities, 1971-89, chmn., 1982; vice chmn. Diocese of Rockville Centre Family Life Ctr., 1978-82. Mem. Nassau County Bar Assn., Suffolk County Bar Assn., N.Y. State Bar Assn. Roman Catholic. Clubs: Wheatley Hills Golf (East Williston, N.Y.); Lloyd Neck Bath (Lloyd Harbor, N.Y.), La Romana Country Club (Dominican Rep.). Home: Seaforth Ln Huntington NY 11743 Office: 200 Garden City Plz Garden City NY 11530-3301 also: GV269 Casade Campo La Romana Dominican Republic

LYNN, ROBERT WOOD, theologian, educator, dean; b. Wheatland, Wyo., Apr. 3, 1925; s. William McGregor and Janet (Reid) L.; m. Katharine Mitchell Wuerth, Mar. 8, 1952; children—Thomas Taylor, Janet MacGregor, Elizabeth Mitchell, Sarah McKee. A.B., Princeton U., 1948; B.D., Yale U., 1952; Th.D., Union Theol. Sem., N.Y.C., 1962. Ordained to ministry Presbyn. Ch., 1952; asst. minister Montview Presbyn. Ch., Denver, 1952-59; mem. faculty Union Theol. Sem., N.Y.C., 1959-75, dean Auburn program, 1960—, prof., 1965-75; v.p. Lilly Endowment, Inc., 1976-84, sr. v.p., 1985-89; vis. prof. Drew U., Andover Newton Theol. Sch., Fordham U., Tchrs. Coll., Columbia U.; scholar in residence Bangor Theol. Sem., 1989—. Author: Protestant Strategies in Education; co-author: The Big Little School; also articles. Trustee Louisville Sem., 1990-95, Yale U., 1991-95. Serve with AUS, 1943-44. Woodrow Wilson fellow, 1948-49; Presbyn. Grad. fellow, 1959-60. Home: PO Box 3290 Leeds ME 04263

LYNN, SHEILAH ANN, service executive, consultant; b. Anderson, Ind., Jan. 28, 1947; d. John Benton and Kathleen (Taylor) Bussabarger; m. John Hoftyzer, Dec. 21, 1968 (div. June 1982); children: Melanie Kay, John Theo; m. Guy C. Lynn, May 20, 1984. BS, Ind. U., 1969; postgrad., U. N.C., Greensboro, 1973, Webster U., 1994; diploma, Data Processing Inst., Tampa, Fla., 1983; MS, Ctrl. Mich. U., 1993. Bookkeeper John Hancock Life Ins. Co., Greensboro, 1970-72; freelance seminar leader and devel. Dhahran, Saudi Arabia, 1978-82; dir. programming Fla. Tech. Inst., Jacksonville, 1983-84, instr. in computer sci., 1984-85; real estate sales assoc. Fla. Recreational Ranches, Gainesville, 1985; instrnl. program coord., workforce tng. coord. Fla. C.C., Jacksonville, 1986—; handwriting analyst, cons. Sheilah A. Lynn & Assocs., Jacksonville, 1989—; cons. programmer, analyst Postmasters Co., Jacksonville, 1986—; pres. Options Cons., Jacksonville, 1986-89, Sheilah A. Lynn & Assocs., Jacksonville, 1989—; 6L cons. assocs. Dacum facilitator and curriculum developer. Mem. Jacksonville Community Council, Inc., 1986-87, Fla. Literacy Coalition, 1986-87. Mem. NAFE, ASTD, Fla. Assn. Ednl. Data Systems, Bus. and Profl. Women, Jacksonville C. of C. (bd. dirs. south coun. 1987, sec. 1989, treas. 1990, v.p. 1991, pres. 1992). Democrat. Avocations: duplicate bridge, reading, fishing, bowling.

LYNN, THEODORE STANLEY, lawyer; b. N.Y.C., Aug. 2, 1937; s. Irving and Sydell (Gorlie) L.; m. Linda Isabel Freeman, July 21, 1968; children: Jessica, Douglas. AB, Columbia U., 1958; LLB, Harvard U., 1961; LLM, NYU, 1962; SJD, George Washington U., 1972. Law clerk to Hon. Bruce M. Forrester, U.S. Tax Ct., Washington, 1962-64; teaching fellow in law George Washington U., Washington, 1963-64; ptnr. Webster & Sheffield, N.Y.C., 1964-90; ptnr. Stroock & Stroock & Lavan, N.Y.C., 1991—; cons. Adminstrv. Conf. U.S., Washington, 1974-75; founding counsel Pension Real Estate Assn., Washington, 1981-84 . Author: Real Estate Limited Partnerships, 3d edit., 1991, Real Estate Investment Trusts, 2d edit., 1994, supplement 1995; contbr. articles to profl. jours.; Spl. asst. Mayor John V. Lindsay, N.Y.C. 1966-69; sec. Manhattan Sch. of Dance, 1974-93; trustee Birch Wathen Lenox Sch., N.Y.C., 1975-93; bd. dirs. Manhattan Community Bd. #6, N.Y.C., 1977—, chair nominating com., 1992-94; bd. dirs. Citizens Union, 1991—, exec. com., 1995—, dir., Sutton Area Cmty., Inc., 1995—. Mem. ABA, Fed. Bar Council, Assn. of Bar of City of N.Y., Univ. Club, Inwood C. of C., Harvard Club. Office: Stroock & Stroock & Lavan 7 Hanover Sq New York NY 10004-2616

LYNN, THOMAS NEIL, JR., medical center administrator, physician; b. Ft. Worth, Feb. 14, 1930; s. Thomas Neil and Florence Van Zandt (Jennings) L.; m. Virginia Carolyn Harsh, July 26, 1952; children: Thomas Neil, Leslie Elizabeth, Kathryn Barry. B.S., U. Okla., 1951, M.D., 1955. Diplomate: Am. Bd. Internal Medicine, Am. Bd. Preventive Medicine. Intern Barnes Hosp., St. Louis, 1955-56; resident Barnes Hosp., 1956-57; clin. asso Nat. Heart Inst. NIH, Bethesda, Md., 1957-59; chief resident medicine U. Okla. Hosps., 1959-61; med. staff U. Hosps. and Clinics, 1970-72; staff Okla. Children's Meml. Hosp., Presbyn. Hosp., VA Hosp., Oklahoma City; instr. asst. prof. community health Okla. Med. Center, 1961-63, asso. prof., 1963-67, prof., chmn. dept., 1970-76; acting dean U. Okla. Coll. Medicine, 1974-76, dean, 1976-80; v.p. for med. staff affairs Bapt. Med. Ctr., Oklahoma City, 1980-95; mem. governing bd. Okla. Physician Manpower Tng. Commn., 1974-80, Ambulatory Health Care Consortium, Inc., 1977-78, Integris Mental Health Corp., 1996—, T.N. Lynn Inst. for Healthcare Rsch., 1996—; mem. Okla. Bd. Medicolegal Examiners. Contbr. articles to profl. jours. Bd. dirs. Okla. Arthritis Found., 1978-82, v.p., 1981-82; bd. dirs. North Care Mental Health Ctr., 1981-87, pres., 1986-87, Oklahoma City Community Coun., 1982-90; med. dir. Okla. Organ Sharing Network, 1989-90; mem. Bd. Health Oklahoma City-County Health Dept., 1983-85; bd. dirs. Okla. chpt. Am. Heart Assn., 1984-86; mem. Nat. Commn. on Cert. Physician Assts., 1987-90. Fellow Am. Coll. Preventive Medicine; mem. AMA, Okla. Med. Assn. (trustee 1981-87, chmn. bd. trustees 1986-87), Oklahoma County Med. Soc. (trustee), Am. Acad. Family Physicians, Okla. Acad. Family Physicians, Sigma Xi, Alpha Omega Alpha, Phi Sigma, Alpha Tau Omega. Presbyn. Home: 3136 Pine Ridge Rd Oklahoma City OK 73120-5918 *Individuals should live their life and conduct their affairs such that all succeeding generations will be benefitted and be glad that these people lived.*

LYNN, TONY LEE, import company executive; b. Burke City, N.C., Oct. 13, 1939; s. Craig and Marie (Lowman) L.; m. Cindy Robson; 1 child, Gretchen. Student, Lenoir Rhyne Coll., 1958-62, N.C. Sch. Banking, 1972, Sch. Banking of South, Baton Rouge, 1972-75, Am. Inst. Banking, 1976. Dist. mgr. Am. Credit Co., Atlanta, 1961-66; v.p. First Nat. Bank Catawba County, Hickory, N.C., 1966-76; exec. v.p. Dixie Boat Works, Newton, N.C., 1976-82; founder, pres. Friitala Am., Hickory, 1982—. Named one of Outstanding Young Men of Am., 1975. Mem. Am. Inst. Banking (past bd. dirs., pres. Hickory unit), Nat. Ski Patrol Alumni Assn. (lifetime mem., tng. officer, sr. profl.), Catawba County C. of C. (lifetime hon. mem.). Home: 5670 37th St NE Hickory NC 28601-9703 Office: Friitala Am 231 10th St NW Hickory NC 28601-4857

LYNN, WILLIAM J., III, federal agency administrator. BA, Dartmouth Coll., 1976; MA in Public Affairs, Princeton U., 1982; JD, Cornell Law Sch., 1980. Exec. dir. defense orgn. project Ctr. for Strategic and Internat. Studies, 1982-85; sr. fellow Strategic Devel. Ctr. Nat. Defense U., 1986-87; mem. staff Sen. Edward M. Kennedy, 1987-93; dir. Program Analysis and Evaluation Office of the Sec. of Def., 1993—. Author: (book) Toward A More Effective Defense, 1985; contbr. articles to profl. jours. Office: Office Sec Defense Rm 3E 836 The Pentagon Washington DC 20301

LYNNE, GILLIAN BARBARA, choreographer, dancer, actress, director; b. Bromley, Eng., Feb. 20, 1926; d. Leslie and Barbara (Hart) Pyrke; m. Peter Land, May 17, 1980. Ed., Baston Sch., Bromley; Arts Ednl. Sch. Leading soloist Sadler's Wells Ballet, 1944-51; star dancer London Palladium, 1951-53. Dancing debut with Royal Ballet; soloist roles included: The Black Queen (Checkmate), The Lilac Fairy (Sleeping Beauty), The Queen of the Wilis (Giselle) and The Black Ballerina (Ballet Imperial, Symphonic Variations); role in film, Master of Ballantrae, 1952; lead in Can-Can, Coliseum, 1954-55; Becky Sharp in Vanity Fair, Windsor Theatre, 1956; guest principal dancer: Samson and Delilah, Sadler's Wells Ballet, 1957, Aida, and Tannhauser, Covent Garden, 1957, Puck in A Midsummer Night's Dream, BBC TV, 1958; star dancer in Chelsea at Nine (featured dance segments), Granada TV, 1958; lead in New Cranks, Lyric and Hammersmith Theatres, 1959; roles in Wanda, Rose Marie, Cinderella, Out of My Mind, and lead in revue, 1960-61; leading lady, 5 Past Eight Show, Edinburgh, 1962, Queen of Cats, London, 1962-63; conceived, directed, choreographed, and starred in Collages, Edinburgh Festival, 1963, Royal Variety Performance Simple Man Extract, 1989; staged: England Our England, Revue, Princes Theatre, 1961; choreographer: The Owl and the Pussycat (1st ballet), Western Theatre Ballet, 1962, Queen of the Cats, London Palladium, 1962-63, Wonderful Life (1st film), 1963-64, Every Day's a Holiday, and Three Hats for Lisa (musical films), 1964, The Roar of the Greasepaint, and Pickwick, Broadway, 1965, The Flying Dutchman, Covent Garden, 1966, Half a Sixpence (film), 1966-67, How Now Dow Jones, Broadway, 1967, Midsummer Marriage, Covent Garden, 1968, The Trojans, Covent Garden, 1969, 1977, Breakaway (ballet), Scottish Theatre Ballet, 1969, Phil the Fluter, Palace Theatre, 1969, Ambassador Theatre, Her Majesty's Theatre, 1971, Man of La Mancha (film), 1972, The Card, Queen's, 1973, Hans Andersen, London Palladium, 1975, The Way of The World, Aldwych, 1978; My Fair Lady, nat. tour and Adelphi, 1979, Parsifal, Covent Garden, 1979, (also assoc. dir.) Cats, New London Theatre, 1981 (Olivier award 1981), Broadway 1982, nat. tour, 1983, dir. and choreographer prodn. in Vienna, 1983 (Silver Order of Merit, Austria, 1984), L.A., Sydney, 1985, East Berlin, 1987, also Can., Japan, Australia, Moscow, 1989, Paris, 1989 (Molière award Best Musical), Amsterdam, 1990, Café Soir (ballet), Houston Ballet Co., 1985, Cabaret, Strand, 1986, The Phantom of the Opera, Her Majesty's Theatre, 1986, Broadway, Japan, Vienna, 1989, Stockholm, Chgo., Hamburg, Australia, 1990, Canada, 1991, Amsterdam, 1993, Manchester, Eng., 1993, A Simple Man (ballet), Sadler's Wells, 1988, Aspects of Love, Prince of Wales Theatre, 1989, Broadway, 1990, The Brontës (ballet), Northern Ballet Theatre, 1995; choreographer, dir.: The Match Girls, Globe Theatre, 1966; Bluebeard, Sadlers Wells Opera, 1966, new prodn., Coliseum, 1969), Love on the Dole (musical), Nottingham Playhouse, 1970; Liberty Ranch, Greenwich, 1972, Once Upon a Time, Duke of York's, 1972, Jasperina, Amsterdam, 1978, Valentine's Day, Chichester, 1991, Globe, 1992, A Simple Man (BBC-TV) (Brit. Acad. award for conception, direction and choreography 1988); dir. Round Leicester Square, Prince Charles Theatre, 1963, Tonight at Eight, Hampstead, 1970, Fortune, 1971, Lillywhite Lies, Nottingham, 1971, A Midsummer Night's Dream, Stratford, 1977, Tomfoolery, Criterion, 1980, Jeeves Takes Charge, Fortune, 1980, off-Broadway, 1983, L.A., 1985, To Those Born Late, New End Theatre, 1981, La Ronde, RSC, Aldwych, 1982, (also appeared in) Alone Plus One, Newcastle, 1982, The Rehearsal, Yvonne Arnaud, Guildford and tour, 1983, Cabaret, Strand, 1986; staged: England Our England (revue), Princes, 1961, 200 Motels (pop-opera film), 1971, musical nos. in Quilp (film), 1974, A Comedy of Errors, Stratford, 1976 (Oliver award 1977), TV musical, 1977, As You Like It (musical), Stratford, 1977, Songbook, Globe Theatre, 1979, Once in a Lifetime, Aldwych Theatre, 1979 (Oliver award for best play 1978), new stage act for Tommy Steele, 1979, wedding sequence in Yentl (film), 1982, European Vacation II (film), Pirelli Calendar, 1988, Pickwick, Chichester and Sadler's Wells, 1993; conceived, directed dance for Life Gala, Her Majesty's Theatre, 1991; choreographer and staging: (films) Mr. Love, Under Milkwood, Quilp; choreographer for TV: Peter and the Wolf (narrated and mimed all 9 parts), 1958, At the Hawk's Well (ballet), 1975, There Was a Girl, 1975, The Fool on the Hill (1st Colour Spl. for ABC; Best Musical, Best Prodn. awards in Australia 1977), with Australian Ballet and Sydney Symphony Orch., staged Sydney Opera House, 1975, Muppet Show series, 1976-80 (Golden Rose Montreux award 1977); (also musical staging) Alice in Wonderland, 1985, shows and specials for Val Doonican, Perry Como, Petula Clark, Nana Mouskouri, John Curry, Harry Secombe, Ray Charles, and Mike Burstein, also produced and devised Noel Coward and Cleo Laine spls.; directed for TV: Mrs. F's Friends, 1981, Easy Money, 1982, Le Morte d'Arthur, 1983, A Simple Man, 1987 (BAFTA award), Gilliam Lynne and Friends Chichester Festival Theatre, 1994, The V.E. Day Gala Coliseum, 1995, (ballet in three acts) The Brontes, 1995; for internat. TV in various capacities as producer, deviser, stager, choreographer and dir.: 1989 Royal Variety Performance (Andrew Lloyd Webber segment), The Look of Love, BBC North West, (BBC) A Simple Man, The Morte D'Arthur, Easy Money, The Various Ends of Mrs. F.'s Friends, The Look of Love, Pickwick, It's Topol, Val Doonican, Nana Mouskouri, Soccer Dance, Tiptoes, There Was a Girl, A World of Music, The Great American Songbook; (ABC) The Fool on the Hill; (LTW) Marvellous Party, Tickertape Children's series, Cleo Laine Sings; (CBS/USA) Alice in Wonderland; (ATV) The Muppet Show, Marty Feldman Show; (VARA/Holland) The Mike Burstyn Show; (Thames) Comedy Tonight, The Royal Variety Show, 1991, 93, Sadlers Wells Theatre, 1993, Pickwick Chichester Festival Theatre, 1993; pub. contbr. to Cats, The Book of the Musical; articles in Dancing Times. Mem. Pickwick Club. Address: care Lean Two Prodns Ltd, 18 Rutland St Knightsbridge, London SW7 IEF, England

LYNNE, JEFF, rock musician, composer; b. Birmingham, Eng., Dec. 30, 1942. Musician with The Nightriders, Eng., The Move, also The Electric Light Orch.; albums include No Answer, 1971, ELO, II, 1973, On the Third Day, 1973, Eldorado, 1974, Face the Music, 1975, Ole ELO, 1976, A New World Record, 1976, The Light Shines On, 1977, 3 Light Years, 1978, ELO, 1978, Out of the Blue, 1978, Discovery, 1979, The Light Shines On, Vol. 2, 1979, Greatest Hits, 1979, Xanadu, 1980, Box of Their Best, 1980, Secret Messages, 1984, Balance of Power, 1986, Afterglow, 1990, ELO Part II, 1991, (with Traveling Willburys) Traveling Wilburys, 1988, Traveling Wilburys Vol. 3, 1990, (solo) Armchair Theatre, 1990; producer various artists including Dave Edmunds, George Harrison, Daryl Hall. Recipient Grammy award (with Traveling Wilburys), 1990.

LYNNE, SEYBOURN HARRIS, federal judge; b. Decatur, Ala., July 25, 1907; s. Seybourn Arthur and Annie Leigh (Harris) L.; m. Katherine Donaldson Brandau, June 16, 1937; 1 dau., Katherine Roberta (dec. Nov. 1988). B.S., Ala. Poly. Inst., 1927; LL.B., U. Ala., 1930, LL.D., 1973. Bar: Ala. 1930. Pvt. practice law Decatur, Ala., 1930-34; judge Morgan (Ala.) County Ct., 1934-41, 8th Jud. Cir. Ct. Ala., 1941-42; judge U.S. Dist. Ct. (no. dist.) Ala., 1946—, chief judge, 1953-73, sr. judge, 1973—. Served to lt. col., JAGC U.S. Army, 1942-46. Decorated Bronze Star; named to Ala. Acad. Honor, 1978. Mem. Ala. Bar Assn. (Award of Merit 1989), ABA, Blue Key, Scabbard and Blade, Pi Kappa Alpha, Phi Kappa Phi, Phi Delta Phi, Omicron Delta Kappa, Alpha Phi Epsilon. Democrat. Baptist. Clubs: Kiwanian (dist. gov. Ala. dist. 1938), Birmingham Country, Univ. of Ala. A. Office: US Dist Ct 419 US Courthouse 1729 5th Ave N Birmingham AL 35203-2000

LYNNES, R. MILTON, advertising executive; b. Chgo., Apr. 16, 1934; s. Roy Milton and Ethel (Wolfe) L.; m. Carol Rinehart, Aug. 30, 1958; children: Christopher, Katherine, Jeffrey, Jennifer. BS, Iowa State U., 1957. Advt. sales promotion supr. Interlake Steel, Chgo., 1961-62; copywriter Garfield-Linn, Chgo., 1963; account exec. Biddle Co., Appleton, Wis., 1964-66; exec. v.p. Marsteller HCM, Chgo., 1966-84; bd. dirs. Marsteller HCM, 1978-84; prin. Grant, Jacoby Inc., Chgo., 1985-89, pres., 1989-94, chmn. CEO, 1994—; bd. dirs. Worldwide Ptnrs., Denver. bd. dirs. MTW/WWP Media Venture, 1995, Better Bus. Bur., Chgo., 1984-87. Mem. Am. Assn. Advt. Agys. (vice chmn. ctrl. region, bd. dirs. 1981-82), Chgo. Advt. Club (bd. dirs. 1985-86), Exmoor Country Club, Bob O Link Golf Club, Pelican Bay Golf Club, Econs. Club, Tavern Club. Republican. Congregationalist. Office: Grant/Jacoby Inc 737 N Michigan Ave Chicago IL 60611-2615

LYNTON, ERNEST ALBERT, physicist, educator, former university official; b. Berlin, Germany, July 17, 1926; came to U.S., 1941, naturalized, 1945; s. Arthur J. and Lizzie (Kiefe) Lowenstein; m. Carla Ellen Kaufmann, Aug. 4, 1953; children—David Michael, Eric Daniel. B.S., Carnegie Inst. Tech., 1947, M.S., 1948; Ph.D., Yale, 1951. AEC postdoctoral fellow U. Leiden, Holland, 1951-52; faculty Rutgers U., 1952-74, prof. physics, 1962-74; dean Rutgers U. (Livingston Coll.), 1965-73; Commonwealth prof. U. Mass., Boston, 1974-95, sr. v.p. acad. affairs, 1974-80, sr. assoc. N.E. Resource Ctr. for Higher Edn.; vis. prof., Fulbright fellow U. Grenoble, France, 1959-60; cons. NSF, 1965-70, Ford Found., 1973, 80-82, Spelman Coll., 1980—, Cambridge Coll., 1982-83, OECD, 1981-93, Coun. of Europe, 1982-83, Carnegie Found., 1992—, Am. Assn. Higher Edn., 1992—; mem. Commn. on Higher Edn. Mid. States Assn., 1972-74; adv. bd. Princeton Sch. Architecture, 1971-80; chmn. Mass. Commn. Telecoms., 1981-83. Author: Superconductivity, 3d edit., 1968 (translated into French, Russian, German), Missing Connection Between Business and the Universities, 1984, (with Sandra Elman) New Priorities for the University, 1987, Making the Case for Professional Service, 1995; exec. editor Met. Univs., 1988—; contbr. articles to profl. jours. Pres. Princeton (N.J.) Jewish Ctr., 1964-66; bd. dirs. Princeton Assn. Human Rights, 1962-65, Mercer County chpt. ACLU, 1966-70; trustee Marlboro Music, 1982—. With AUS, 1944-46. Fellow Am. Phys. Soc. Home: 14 Allerton St Brookline MA 02146-7727

LYNTON, HAROLD STEPHEN, lawyer; b. N.Y.C., Nov. 2, 1909; widowed, Mar. 12, 1990; children: Stephen Jonathan, Richard David, Andrew Edward; m. Hattie Gruenstein Kalish, Jan. 27, 1991. AB magna cum laude, Yale U., 1929; JD cum laude, Harvard U., 1932. Bar: N.Y. 1933, U.S. Supreme Ct. 1947. Ptnr. Kaufman, Gallop, Gould, Climenko & Lynton, N.Y.C., 1934-51, Lynton & Klein and predecessors, N.Y.C., 1951-80; ptnr. Shea & Gould, N.Y.C., 1980-91, counsel, 1992-94; counsel Dornbush Mensch Mandelstam & Schaeffer, N.Y.C., 1994—; gen. counsel, trustee, mem. adv. bd. Barron Collier Cos., Naples, Fla., 1945—; also bd. dirs. Barron Collier Cos. and predecessors, Naples, Fla. Capt. AUS, 1943-45. Mem. ABA, N.Y. State Bar Assn., Assn. of Bar of City of N.Y., N.Y. County Lawyers Assn., Yale Club N.Y., Sunningdale Country Club, Phi Beta Kappa. Avocations: travel, theatre, tennis, swimming. Home: 870 UN Plz New York NY 10017-1807 Office: Dornbush Mensch et al 747 3rd Ave New York NY 10017-2803

LYON, ANDREW BENNET, economics educator; b. Elmhurst, Ill., June 6, 1958; s. Richard M. and Rhee Lyon; m. Jennifer A. Sour, May 31, 1987; 1 child, Sarah. AB, Stanford U., 1980; PhD, Princeton U., 1986. Economist Jt. Com. on Taxation, U.S. Congress, Washington D.C., 1985-87; asst. prof., dept. econ. U. Md., College Park; 1987-93, assoc. prof., dept. econ., 1993—; vis. fellow Brookings Inst., 1994-95; cons. and expert witness, 1987—; dir. Unisys Credit Corp., Detroit, 1991-92; sr. econ. Coun. Econ. Advisers, 1992-93. Contbr. numerous articles to profl. jours. Nat. Bur. Econc. fellow, 1987-94. Mem. Am. Econ. Assn., Nat. Tax Assn. (Outstanding Doctoral Dissertation award 1986, Fed. Tax Com. 1991), Phi Beta Kappa. Office: U Md Dept Econs College Park MD 20742

LYON, BRUCE ARNOLD, lawyer, educator; b. Sacramento, Sept. 24, 1951; s. Arnold E. and Arlene R. (Cox) L.; m. Patricia J. Gibson, Dec. 14, 1974; children: Barrett, Andrew. AB with honors, U. Pacific, 1974; JD, U. Calif.-Hastings Coll. Law, 1977. Bar: Calif. 1977, U.S. Dist. Ct. (ea. and no. dists.) Calif. 1977. Ptnr. Ingoglia, Marskey, Kearney & Lyon, Sacramento, 1977-84; sole practice, Auburn, Calif., 1984-91; ptnr. Robinson, Robinson & Lyon, Auburn, Calif., 1991—; counsel Placer Savs. Bank, Auburn, 1987—; instr. in law Sierra Coll., Rocklin, Calif., 1983—. Mng. editor Comment, A Jour. of Communications and Entertainment Law, 1974. Contbr. articles to trade publs. Mem. State Bar Calif., ABA (liaison student div. 1974), Calif. Trial Lawyers Assn., Placer County Bar Assn., Sacramento County Bar Assn., Thurston Soc., Mensa, Internat. Platform Assn., Order of Coif., Calif. League of Savings Inst. (atty's. com.), Native Sons of the Golden West. Office: Robinson Robinson & Lyon One California St Auburn CA 95603

LYON, CARL FRANCIS, JR., lawyer; b. Sumter, S.C., May 9, 1943; s. Carl Francis and Sophie (Goldstrum) L.; m. Maryann Mercier; children—Barbara Ruth, Sarah Frances, Carl Francis, III. A.B., Duke U., 1965, J.D. with honors, 1968. Bar: N.Y. 1969, D.C. 1977. Assoc., then ptnr. Mudge Rose Guthrie Alexander & Ferdon, N.Y.C., 1968-95, mem. exec. com., 1986-87, 94-95; ptnr. Orrick Herrington & Sutcliffe, N.Y.C., 1995—. Contbr. articles to profl. publs. Mem. ABA (vice-chmn. spl. com. on energy fin. 1988-91), N.Y. State Bar Assn., D.C. Bar Asns., Am. Pub. Power Assn., Duke U. Law Alumni Coun., Order of Coif, Phi Alpha Delta. Office: Orrick Herrington Sutcliffe 666 Fifth Ave New York NY 10103

LYON, DAVID WILLIAM, research executive; b. Lansing, Mich., Mar. 26, 1941; s. Herbert Reid and Mary Kathleen (Slack) L.; m. Catherine McHugh Dillon, July 8, 1967. BS, Mich. State U., 1963; M in City and Regional Planning, U. Calif., Berkeley, 1966, PhD, 1972. Regional economist Fed. Res. Bank Phila., 1969-71; research dir. human and econ. resources The N.Y.C.-Rand Inst., 1972-75, v.p., 1975; sr. economist The Rand Corp., Santa Monica, Calif., 1975-77, dep. v.p., 1977-79, v.p. domestic research div., 1979-93, v.p. external affairs, 1993-94; pres., CEO Pub. Policy Inst. Calif., 1994—; adj. prof. U. Pa., 1975; mem. adv. bd. Inst. for Civil Justice, 1987-93, Rand-Urban Inst. Program for Rsch. on Immigration Policy, 1988-91, Drug Policy Rsch. Ctr., 1989-93, So. Calif. Health Policy Rsch. Consortium, 1989-94, Rand Ctr. for U.S.-Japan Rels., 1989-93, Rand Ctr. for Asia-Pacific Policy, 1993-95; dir. Coll. Environ. Design Coun., U. Calif., Berkeley, 1979-90. Contbr. articles to profl. jours.; publs. com. Rand Jour. Econs., 1984-94. Bd. dirs. Sr. Health and Peer Counseling Ctr., Santa Monica, Calif., 1985-94, pres., 1989-91. Mellon fellow in city planning, 1966-68; Econ. Devel. Adminstrn. grad. fellow, 1966. Mem. Coun. on Fgn. Rels., Japan Am. Soc. So. Calif. (bd. dirs. 1990-94), Asia Soc. (So. Calif. adv. bd.), Riviera Tennis Club (Pacific Palisades, Calif.), Delta Phi Epsilon. Office: Pub Policy Inst Calif 500 Washington Ste 800 San Francisco CA 94111

LYON, JAMES BURROUGHS, lawyer; b. N.Y.C., May 11, 1930; s. Francis Murray and Edith May (Strong) L. BA, Amherst Coll., 1952; LLB, Yale U., 1955. Bar: Conn. 1955, U.S. Tax Ct. 1970. Asst. football coach Yale U., 1953-55; assoc. Murtha, Cullina, Richter and Pinney (and predecessor), Hartford, Conn., 1956-61, ptnr., 1961—; counsel, 1996—; mem. adv. com., lectr. and session leader NYU Inst. on Fed. Taxation, 1973-86; mem. IRS Northeast Key Dist.'s Exempt Orgns. Liaison Group, Bklyn., 1993—. Chmn. 13th Conf. Charitable Orgn. NYU on Fed. Taxation, 1982; mem. adv. bd. Charitable Giving, Trusts & Estates Mag., 1996—; trustee Kingswood-Oxford Sch., West Hartford, Conn., 1961-91, hon. trustee, 1991—, chmn. bd. trustees, 1975-78; trustee Old Sturbridge Village, Mass., 1974, chmn. bd. trustees, 1991-93; trustee Ella Vurr McManus Trust, Hartford, 1980—, Ellen Battell Stoeckel Trust, Norfolk, Conn., 1994—, Hartford YMCA, 1985—, St. Francis Found., 1991—, Watkinson Libr., 1990—; trustee Wadsorth Atheneum, Hartford, 1968—, pres., 1981-84, hon. trustee, 1993—; sec. bd. trustees Horace Bushnell Meml. Hall, Hartford,

1993—, trustee, 1994—; corporator Inst. Living, 1981—, Hartford Hosp., 1975—, St. Francis Hosp., Hartford, 1976, Hartford Pub. Libr., 1979—, Hartford Sem., 1991; bd. dirs. Conn. Policy and Econ. Com., Inc., 1991—; mem. Conn. adv. com. New Eng. Legal Found., 1991—; bd. vis. Hartford Art Sch., 1995—. Recipient Eminent Svc. medal Amherst Coll., 1967, Nathan Hale award Yale Club Hartford, 1982, Disting. Am. award No. Conn. chpt. Nat. Football Found. Hall of Fame, 1983, Community Svc. award United Way of the Capital Area, 1986. Fellow ABA (mem. exempt orgn. com., co-chairperson subcom. on mus. and other cultural orgns. sect. of taxation 1988—), Am. Coll. Tax Counsel; mem. Am. Law Inst., Hartford Golf Club, Yale Club, Union Club N.Y.C., Dauntless Club (Essex, Conn.), Wianno Club (Osterville, Mass.), Mory's Assn. (New Haven), Phi Beta Kappa. Office: 185 Asylum St Hartford CT 06103-3402

LYON, JAMES HUGH, educational rights specialist, consultant, political strategist; b. Clarksburg, W.Va., Apr. 17, 1936; s. James M. and Mildred E. Lyon; m. Marilyn Jean Lyon. BA in English, Salem Coll., 1960; MA, W.Va. U., 1967. Cert. English tchr., Ohio. Tchr. coll. preparatory English Harrison County (W.Va.) Schs., 1960-64, Urbana (Ohio) City Schs., 1964-70; edn. cons., lobbyist Ohio Edn. Assn., Columbus, 1970-93; edn. cons. Lyon Assocs., Canton, Ohio, 1993—. Mem. Nat. Assn. Lobbyists for Sch. Employees, Ohio Edn. Assn. (tchr. rights specialist in Ohio state legislature 1981-93, Outstanding Svc. award 1986), Elks. Home and Office: 6627 Avalon St NW Canton OH 44708

LYON, JAMES KARL, German language educator; b. Rotterdam, Holland, Feb. 17, 1934; came to U.S., 1937; s. T. Edgar and Hermana (Forsberg) L.; m. Dorothy Ann Burton, Dec. 22, 1959; children: James, John, Elizabeth, Sarah, Christina, Rebecca, Matthew, Melissa. BA, U. Utah, 1958, MA, 1959; PhD, Harvard U., 1963. Instr. German Harvard U., Cambridge, Mass., 1962-63, asst. prof., 1966-71; assoc. prof. U. Fla., Gainesville, 1971-74; prof. U. Calif. San Diego, La Jolla, 1974-94, provost Fifth Coll., 1987-94; prof. dept. Germanic and Slavic langs. Brigham Young U., Provo, Utah, 1994—; vis. prof. U. Augsburg, Germany, 1993. Author: Konkordanz zur Lyrik Gottfried Benns, 1971, Bertolt Brecht and Rudyard Kipling, 1975, Brecht's American Cicerone, 1978, Bertolt Brecht in America, 1980, Brecht in den USA, 1994. Capt. M.I., U.S. Army, 1963-66. NEH fellow, 1970, Guggenheim Found. fellow, 1974; Ford Found. grantee, 1988, 91. Mem. MLA, Am. Assn. Tchrs. German, Internat. Brecht. Soc., Phi Beta Kappa. Democrat. Mormon. Avocations: back-packing, fishing. Office: BYU Dept Germanic & Slavic Lang 4094 Jesse Knight Human Bld Provo UT 84602

LYON, JEFFREY, journalist, author; b. Chgo., Nov. 28, 1943; s. Herbert Theodore and Lyle (Hoffenberg) L.; m. Bonita S. Brodt, June, 20, 1981; children: Lindsay, Derek. BS in Journalism, Northwestern U., 1965. Reporter Miami (Fla.) Herald, 1964-66, Chgo. Today, 1966-74; reporter Chgo. Tribune, 1974-76, columnist, 1976-80, 94—, feature writer specializing in sci., 1980—; creative writing adj. prof.; coord. joint sci. and journalism programs Columbia Coll., Chgo., 1987—, dir., 1988—. Author: Playing God in the Nursery, 1985, Altered Fates: Gene Therapy and the Retooling of Human Life, 1995; also newspaper series Altered Fates, 1986 (Pulitzer Prize 1987). Mem. State of Ill. Perinatal Adv. Com., Springfield, 1986-90; mem. pediat. ethics com. U. Chgo. Hosps., 1985-90; bd. dirs. Shore Cmty. Svcs. to Retarded Citizens, Evanston, Ill., 1985-90; mem. bd. Little City, Palatine, Ill., 1979—. Recipient Nat. Headliner award Atlantic City Press Club, 1984, Citizen Fellow award Inst. Medicine of Chgo., 1987, Peter Lisagor award, 1990. Office: The Chgo Tribune 435 N Michigan Ave Chicago IL 60611

LYON, JOANNE B., psychologist; b. Little Rock, June 2, 1943; d. F. Ike and Marie (Graham) Beyer; m. Jas. Sherod Lyon, Dec. 1971 (div. Sept. 1975), m. John M. Lofton, May 22, 1983 (dec. Feb. 1990). BA, Webster U., 1966; MEd, U. Mo., St. Louis, 1976, PhD, 1986. Lic. psychologist, Kans. Reading specialist Rockwood Sch. Dist., St. Louis, 1976-79; psychology cons. handicapped component St. Louis Head Start, 1982-83; intern Topeka State Hosp., 1983-84; dir. partial hosp. programs Family Svc. & Guidance Ctr., Topeka, 1985-89; pvt. practitioner and joint owner Shadow Wood Clin. Assocs., Topeka, 1989—; clin. supr. Family Svc. & Guidance Ctr., Topeka, 1989-93. Mem. exec. bd. Interfaith of Topeka, I Have a Dream Coalition, Psychology Advisory Bd. Behavioral Sci. Regulatory Bd.; bd. dirs. Temple Beth Sholom Sisterhood. Sherman scholar U. Mo., St. Louis, 1982. Mem. APA, Kans. Psychol. Assn., Am. Orthopsychiatric Assn., Soc. for Personality Assessment. Jewish. Home: 3030 SW Arrowhead Rd Topeka KS 66614-4134 Office: Shadow Wood Clin Assocs 2933 SW Woodside Dr Topeka KS 66614-4181

LYON, PHILIP K(IRKLAND), lawyer; b. Warren, Ark., Jan. 19, 1944; s. Leroy and Maxine (Campbell) L.; children by previous marriage: Bradford F., Lucinda H., Bruce P., Suzette P., John P., Martin K., Meredith J.; m. Jayne Carol Jack, Aug. 12, 1982. JD with honors, U. Ark., 1967. Bar: Ark. 1967, U.S. Supreme Ct. 1970, Tenn. 1989. Sr. ptnr., dir. ops. House, Wallace, Nelson & Jewell, P.A., Little Rock, 1967-86; pres. Jack, Lyon & Jones, P.A, Little Rock & Nashville, 1986—; instr. bus. law, labor law, govt. bus. and collective bargaining U. Ark., Little Rock, 1969-72, lectr. practice skills and labor law, U. Ark. Law Sch., 1979-80; bd. dirs. Southwestern Legal Found., 1978—; editorial bd. dirs. Entertainment Law & Fin., 1993—. Co-author: Schlei and Grossman Employment Discrimination Law, 2d edit., 1982; editor-in-chief: Ark. Law Rev., 1966-67, bd. dirs., 1978-93, v.p., 1990-92; editor: Ark. Employment Law Letter, 1995. Mem. ABA (select com. liason office fed. contract compliance programs 1982—, select com. liason EEOC 1984—, select com. immigration law, forum com. entertainment and sports industries), Ark. State C. of C. (bd. dirs. 1984-88), Greater Little Rock C. of C. (chmn. community affairs com. 1982-84, minority bus. affairs 1985-89), Ark. Bar Assn. (chmn. labor law com. 1977-78, chmn. labor law sect. 1978-79, chmn. lawyers helping lawyers com. 1988-94), Tenn. Bar Assn. (labor sect., lawyers helping lawyers com. 1989—), Nashville Bar Assn. (entertainment law com., lawyers concerned for lawyers com., editor Ark. Employment Law Letter 1995—), Pulaski County Bar Assn., Country Music Assn., Acad. of Country Music, Nashville Entertainment Assn., Nashville Songwriters Assn. Internat., Copyright Soc. of South, Capitol Club. Recipient Golden Gavel award Ark. Bar Assn., 1978, Writing Excellence award Ark. Bar Found., 1980. Home: 350 Ardsley Pl Nashville TN 37215-3247 also: 17 Heritage Park Cir North Little Rock AR 72116-8528 Office: Jack Lyon & Jones PA 11 Music Cir S Nashville TN 37203-4335 also: Jack Lyon & Jones PA 425 W Capitol 3400 TCBY Tower Little Rock AR 72201 *One of the true secrets of success is to concentrate your efforts—for if you apply these efforts everywhere at once then you will accomplish very little anywhere.*

LYON, RICHARD, mayor, retired naval officer; b. Pasadena, Calif., July 14, 1923; s. Norman Morais and Ruth (Hollis) L.; m. Cynthia Gisslin, Aug. 8, 1975; children: Patricia, Michael, Sean; children by previous marriage: Mary, Edward, Sally, Kathryn, Patrick (dec.), Susan. B.E., Yale U., 1944; M.B.A., Stanford U., 1953. Commd. ensign USN, 1944; advanced through grades to rear adm. SEAL, 1974; served in Pacific and China, World War II; with Underwater Demolition Team Korea; recalled to active duty as dep. chief Naval Res. New Orleans, 1978-81; mayor City of Oceanside, Calif., 1992; mem. Chief Naval Ops. Res. Affairs Adv. Bd., 1978-81; exec. v.p. Nat. Assn. Employee Benefits, Newport Beach, Calif., 1981-90; mem. Bd. Control, U.S. Naval Inst., 1978-81; pres. Civil Svc. Commn., San Diego County, 1990, Oceanside Unified Sch. Bd., 1991. Pres. bd. trustees Children's Hosp. Orange County, 1965, 72. Decorated Legion of Merit. Mem. Nat. Assn. Securities Dealers (registered prin.), Newport Harbor Yacht Club, Rotary Club (Anaheim, Calif. pres. 1966). Republican. Episcopalian. Home: 4464 Inverness Dr Oceanside CA 92057-5052

LYON, RICHARD HAROLD, physicist educator,; b. Evansville, Ind., Aug. 24, 1929; s. Chester Clyde and Gertrude Lyon; m. Jean Wheaton; children: Katherine Ruth, Geoffrey Cleveland, Suzanne Marie. A.B., Evansville Coll., 1952; Ph.D. in Physics (Owens-Corning fellow), Mass. Inst. Tech., 1955; D.Eng., U. Evansville, 1976. Asst. prof. elec. engring. U. Minn., Mpls., 1956-59; Mem. research staff Mass. Inst. Tech., 1955-56, lectr. mech. engring., 1963-69, prof. mech. engring., 1970-95, prof. emeritus, 1995—, head mechanics and materials div., 1981-86; NSF postdoctoral fellow U. Manchester, Eng., 1959-60; sr. scientist Bolt Beranek & Newman, Cambridge, 1960-66, v.p., 1966-70; chmn. Cambridge Collaborative, Inc., 1972-90; v.p. Grozier Pub., Inc., 1972; pres. Grozier Tech. Systems, 1976-82, RH Lyon Corp., 1976—. Author: Transportation Noise, 1974, Theory and Applications of Statistical Energy Analysis, 1975, 2d edit. (with R. DeJong), 1994, Machinery Noise and Diagnostics, 1987. Bd. dirs. Boston Light Opera, Ltd., 1975; mem. alumni bd. U. Evansville, 1988—, bd. trustees, 1995—. Recipient Rayleigh medal Brit. Inst. Acoustics, 1995, Nat. Acad. Engring. award 1995. Fellow Acoustical Soc. Am. (assoc. editor jour. 1967-74, exec. coun. 1976-79, v.p. 1989-90, pres. 1993-94); mem. Sigma Xi, Sigma Pi Sigma, Nat. Acad. Engring., Brit. Inst. Acoustics (Rayleigh medal 1995). Research, publs. in fields of nonlinear random oscillations, energy transfer in complex structures, sound transmission in marine and aerospace vehicles, building acoustics, environmental noise, machinery diagnostics, home theater audio systems. Home: 60 Prentiss Ln Belmont MA 02178-2021 Office: RH Lyon Corp 691 Concord Ave Cambridge MA 02138-1002

LYON, RONALD EDWARD, management consultant, computer consultant; b. Kansas City, Kans., Apr. 13, 1936; s. William Edward and Lillian (Gee) L.; m. Josette Paula Larré, July 24, 1959; children: Michael Alan, Mark Alexander, Matthew Adam, Collette Allison. Owner Hansler Outboard & Austin Aqua Sports, Austin, Tex., 1959-63; gen. mgr. Wayne Green Ent.-73 Mag., Peterboro, N.H., 1963-65; with Computer Control Corp., Peterboro, N.H., 1965-71; sales person Radio Shack (Tandy) & Sterling Elec. Co., Maine, N.H., Vt. areas, 1971-82; sales engr. Pall Corp./Russell Assocs., Inc., Watertown, Mass., 1982-87; mgr. eastern region Fansteel/Wellman Dynamics, 1984-87; CEO, COO Laryon Assocs., Inc., Keene, N.H., 1987—. With USAF, 1955-59. Mem. U.S. Power Squadron, Soc. for Preservation and Encouragement of Barber Shop Quartet Singing in Am. Avocations: sailing, ham radio, computers, skiing, square dancing. Home: Mcintire Rd Munsonville NH 03457 Office: Laryon Assocs Inc 187D Main St Keene NH 03431-3739

LYON, STERLING RUFUS WEBSTER, justice; b. Windsor, Ont., Can., Jan. 30, 1927; s. David Rufus and Ella Mae (Cuthbert) L.; m. Barbara Jean Mayers, Sept. 26, 1953; children: Nancy, Andrea, Peter, Jennifer, Jonathan. B.A., U. Winnipeg, 1948; LL.B., U. Man., 1953. Bar: Man. 1953, created Queen's Counsel 1960. Crown atty., atty. gen. Man., 1953-57; mem. Man. Legis. Assembly, 1958-69, 76-86; atty. gen. Man., 1958-63, 66-69; minister of mcpl. affairs, 1960-61, of pub. utilities, 1961-63, of mines and natural resources, 1963-66, of tourism and recreation, 1966-68, commr. No. affairs, 1966-68; leader Man. Progressive Conservative Party, 1975-83; premier of Man., 1977-81; leader of the opposition, 1976-77, 81-83; mem. Her Majesty's Privy Council for Can., 1982; apptd. justice Man. Ct. of Appeal, Winnipeg, 1986—; chmn. 1st Can. Conf. on Pollution, Montreal, 1966, Can. Premier's Conf., 1980-81; pres. Can. Coun. Resource Ministers, 1965-66. Former trustee Ducks Unltd., Delta Waterfowl Found.; bd. regents U. Winnipeg, 1972-76; dir. Can. Royal Heritage Trust. With RCAF Res., 1950-53. Recipient U. Winnipeg Alumni Assn. Jubilee award, 1973. Office: Law Cts, Winnipeg, MB Canada R3C 0V8

LYON, WALDO KAMPMEIER, physicist; b. Los Angeles, May 19, 1914; s. Charles R. and Anna (Kampmeier) L.; m. Virginia Louise Backus, Aug. 28, 1937; children: Lorraine Mae, Russell Roy. A.B., UCLA, 1936, M.A., 1937, Ph.D., 1941. Research physicist, head submarine and Arctic research br. U.S. Naval Electronics Lab., 1941-66; sr. scientist wave measurement group Bikini Atom Bomb Test, 1946; submarine physicist USN-Byrd Antarctic Expdn., 1946; chief sci. Joint U.S.-Canadian Beaufort Sea Sci. Expdns., 1950-54, chief scientist Arctic submarine research, 1964—; dir. Arctic Submarine Lab., 1966-85; lectr., physicist U. Calif. at Los Angeles, 1948-49. Recipient Disting. Civilian Svc. award U.S. Navy, 1955, 58, Disting. Civilian Service award Dept. Def., 1956, President's Distinguished Fed. Civilian Svc. award, 1962, Edward Dickson UCLA Alumnus award, 1963, Gold medal award Am. Soc. Naval Engrs., 1959, Silver medal Societe de Geographie, Paris, 1983, Bronze medal Royal Inst. Navigation, 1985, Silver Bushnell award Am. Def. Preparedness Assn., 1993. Sr. scientist 1st submarine polar transit Arctic Ocean, U.S.S. Nautilus, 1958 1st winter North Pole transit U.S.S. Skate, 1959, 1st transpolar N.W. passage, U.S.S. Sea Dragon, 1960, sr. scientist 1st dual submarine North Pole expdn., 1962; chief scientist North Pole Submarine Expdns. by Queenfish, 1967, Whale, 1969, Hammerhead, 1970, Hawkbill, 1973, Bluefish, 1975, Gurnard, 1976, Flying Fish, 1977, Pintado, 1978, Archerfish, 1979, Silversides, 1981. Home: 1330 Alexandria Dr San Diego CA 92107-3937 Office: Arctic Submarine Lab Naval Ocean Systems Ctr 49250 Fleming Rd San Diego CA 92152-7202

LYON, WAYNE BARTON, manufacturing company executive; b. Dayton, Oct. 26, 1932; m. Maryann L., 1961; children: Karyn, Craig, Blair. B-SChemE, U. Cin., 1955; MBA in Mktg., U. Chgo., 1969. Registered profl. engr., Mich. Tech. rep. Union Carbide, Chgo., 1955-62; product devel. mgr., v.p. bus. devel. Ill. Tool Works, Chgo., 1962-72; group v.p., exec. v.p. Masco Corp., Taylor, Mich., 1972-85, pres., coo, 1985—, also bd. dirs.; bd. dirs. Masco Corp., Taylor, Mich., Payless Cashways, Inc.; lectr. AMA. Patentee in field. Bd. govs., trustees Cranbrook Kingswood Schs., Bloomfield Hills, Mich., 1984—, Orchard Lake Country Club, Mich., 1985-90. Capt. U.S. Army, 1955-63. Mem. Fairlane Club (Dearborn, Mich.), TPC of Mich. Club, Orchard Lake Country Club, Bloomfield Hills Country Club. Office: Masco Corp 21001 Van Born Rd Taylor MI 48180-1340

LYON, WILFORD CHARLES, JR., insurance executive; b. Blackfoot, Idaho, June 1, 1935; s. Wilford Charles and Nellie Anna (Estenson) L.; m. Eleanor Perkins, Aug. 23, 1957; children: Katherine Ann, Wilford Charles III. BS, Ga. Inst. Tech., 1958; MA in Actuarial Sci., Ga. State Coll., 1962. Asst. v.p. Ind. Life and Accident Ins. Co., Jacksonville, Fla., 1963-69, asst. v.p., dir. methods and planning dept., 1969-70, v.p., home office coordinator, 1970-79, pres., chief adminstrv. officer, 1979-84, chmn. bd., chief exec. officer, 1984-96; trustee, mem. exec. com. Edward Waters Coll., Jacksonville, 1983-96, chmn., bd. visitors, 1993-96. Trustee Gator Bowl Assn., Jacksonville, 1981—, pres., 1981; pres. Jacksonville C. of C., 1984; trustee community TV, Inc., Jacksonville, 1980-93, chmn., 1991-92; trustee Univ. Hosp., Jacksonville, Inc., 1985-86; bd. dirs. YMCA Fla.'s First Coast, 1985—, sec., 1986, vice chmn., 1987, chmn., 1988 (Svc. to Youth award 1991); chmn. 1991 Nat. Vol. Week, Vol. Jacksonville, Inc. Recipient Disting Svc. award Jacksonville Jaycees, 1972, Jack Donnell award Outstanding Businessman of the Year, 1983, Dick Hutchinson award Sertoma Club South Jacksonville, 1972, Svc. to Mankind award, 1972, Boss of Yr. award Profl. Secs. Internat., 1972-73, Victory Crusade award Fla. Cancer Soc., 1969, Ins. Industry Community Svc. award Jacksonville Assn. Life Underwriters, 1986, C.G. Snead Meml. award Jacksonville Assn. of Life Underwriters, 1991, Top Mgmt. award Sales and Mktg. Execs. of Jacksonville, 1990, Clanzel T. Brown award Jacksonville Urban League, 1991, Svc. to Youth award YMCA of Fla.'s First Coast, 1991, Humanitarian award NCCJ, 1994. Mem. Life Insurers Conf. (exec. com. 1981-91, chmn. membership com. 1981-86, sec. 1984-85, vice chmn. 1985-86, chmn. 1986-87), Am. Coun. Life Ins. (Fla. state v.p. 1981-96, bd. dirs. 1987-88, bd. dirs. Polit. Action Com. 1988-94), Southeastern Actuaries Club, Rotary Club Jacksonville (pres. Mandarin club 1977-78, Paul Harris fellow, dist. gov. 697 1985-86), Masons, York Rite, Scottish Rite Bodies, Shriners (potentate Morocco Temple 1973). Republican. Presbyterian. Home: 1129 Mapleton Rd Jacksonville FL 32207-5342

LYON, WILLIAM, builder; b. 1923. Student, U. So. Calif. With Lyon & son, Phoenix, 1945-50; with William Lyon Devel. Co., Newport Beach, Calif., 1954-72, pres.; with William Lyon Co., Newport Beach, 1972—, now chmn. bd. Office: William Lyon Co 4490 Von Karman Ave Newport Beach CA 92660-2008*

LYON, WILLIAM CARL, sports columnist; b. Carmi, Ill., Feb. 10, 1938; s. Clyde William and Harriet Kathryn (Murphy) L.; m. Ethel Gay Slade, Nov. 6, 1964; children—James Charles, John William. Student, Western Mil. Acad., Alton, Ill., 1956; B.S. in Liberal Arts, U. Ill., Champaign, 1961. Feature writer, sports writer, police reporter Champaign-Urbana News-Gazette, 1956-66; sports writer, gen. columnist Evansville (Ind.) Courier & Press, 1966-69; mng. editor East St. Louis (Ill.) Metro-East Jour., 1969-71, Champaign-Urbana News-Gazette, 1971-72; bus. editor Phila. Inquirer, 1972-73, sports writer, syndicated columnist, 1973—; Author: It's All in the Game, We Owed You One; contbr. numerous articles to mags. in U.S. and Can.; TV commentary twice weekly. Served with inf. U.S. Army, 1961. Named Sportswriter of the Yr., State of Pa., 1977, 79-85; recipient 69 state and nat. awards for writing, Best Newspaper Writing award Am. Soc. Newspaper Editors, 1980, Nat. Headliner award, 1988; inducted into Pa. Sports Hall of Fame, 1989. Mem. Baseball Writers Am., Profl. Hockey Writers Assn., Football Writers Assn. Am., Sigma Delta Chi. Methodist. Home: 89 Cherry Hill Ln Broomall PA 19008-1508 Office: Phila Inquirer 400 N Broad St Philadelphia PA 19130-4015

LYONS, CHAMP, JR., lawyer; b. Boston, Dec. 6, 1940; m. Emily Lee Oswalt, 1967; children—Emily Olive, Champ III. A.B., Harvard U., 1962; LL.B., U. Ala., 1965. Bar: Ala. 1965, U.S. Supreme Ct. 1973. Law clk. U.S. Dist. Ct., Mobile, Ala., 1965-67; assoc. Capell, Howard, Knabe & Cobbs, Montgomery, Ala., 1967-70; ptnr. Capell, Howard, Knabe & Cobbs, 1970-76, Helmsing, Lyons, Sims & Leach, Mobile, 1976—; mem. adv. commn. on civil procedure Ala. Supreme Ct., 1971—, chmn., 1985—. Author: Alabama Practice, 1973, 2d edit., 1986; contbr. articles to law jours. Mem. ABA, Ala. Bar Assn., Mobile Bar Assn. (pres. 1991), Am. Law Inst., Ala. Law Inst., Farrah Law Soc., Harvard U. Alumni Assn. (S.E. regional dir. 1988-91, v.p.-at-large 1992-94, 1st v.p. 1994-95, pres. 1995-96). Home: PO Box 1033 Point Clear AL 36564-1033 Office: Helmsing Lyons Sims & Leach 200 LaClede Bldg PO Box 2767 Mobile AL 36652-2767

LYONS, CHARLES, professional hockey team executive. Gov. Colo. Avalanche, Denver. Office: Colorado Avalanche 1635 Clay St Denver CO 80204*

LYONS, CHARLES R., drama educator and critic; b. Glendale, Calif., Apr. 27, 1933; s. James Grey and Daphne Mae (Burlingham) L.; m. Leila B. Phee, Dec. 22, 1956; children: John Christopher, James Charles. AB, Stanford U., 1955, AM, 1956, PhD, 1964. Asst. prof. Principia Coll., Elsah, Ill., 1964-68; assoc. prof. U. Calif., Berkeley, 1968-72, prof., assoc. dean, 1972-73; prof., chmn. Stanford (Calif.) U., 1973-85, Margery Bailey prof. english and dramatic lit., 1985—, chmn. grad. studies in drama, 1985-95, chmn. dept. drama, 1995—, chmn. Arts and Tech. Initiative, 1994—; vis. prof. Washington U., St. Louis, 1966. Author: Brecht: Despair and Polemic, 1968, Shakespeare and the Ambiguity of Love's Triumph, 1971, Ibsen: the Divided Consciousness, 1972, Samuel Beckett, 1983; editor: Critical Essays on Henrik Ibsen, 1987, Hedda Gabler: Gender, Role, and World, 1990; editorial bd. Comparative Drama, Kalamazoo, Mich., 1977—, Jour. Dramatic, Lit. and Theory, Lawrence, Kans, 1986—. Bd. dirs. San Francisco Archives for Performing Arts, 1985—. Served to lt. USNR, 1956-60. Recipient Younger Scholar award NEH, 1968; Guggenheim Found. fellow, 1977. Mem. Modern Language Assn., Samuel Beckett Soc. Democrat. Home: 728 Tolman Dr Palo Alto CA 94305-1045 Office: Stanford U Dept Drama Stanford CA 94305

LYONS, DAVID BARRY, philosophy and law educator; b. N.Y.C., Feb. 6, 1935; s. Joseph and Betty (Janower) L.; m. Sandra Yetta Nemiroff, Dec. 18, 1955; children—Matthew, Emily, Jeremy. Student, Cooper Union, 1952-54, 56-57; B.A., Bklyn. Coll., 1960; M.A. (Gen. Electric Found. fellow), Harvard U., 1963, Ph.D. (Woodrow Wilson dissertation fellow), 1963; postgrad., Oxford (Eng.) U., 1963-64. Asst. prof. philosophy Cornell U., Ithaca, N.Y., 1964-67; asso. prof. Cornell U., 1967-71, prof. philosophy, 1971-90, Susan Linn Sage prof. philosophy, 1990-95; chmn. dept. philosophy, 1978-84; prof. law, 1979-95, Boston U., 1995—. Author: Forms and Limits of Utilitarianism, 1965, In the Interest of the Governed, 1973, Ethics and the Rule of Law, 1984, Moral Aspects of Legal Theory, 1993, Rights, Welfare, and Mill's Moral Theory, 1994; editor: Philos Rev., 1968-70, 73-75. Recipient Clark award Cornell U., 1976; Woodrow Wilson hon. fellow, 1960-61, Knox travelling fellow, 1963-64; Guggenheim fellow, 1970-71, Soc. for Humanities fellow, 1972-73, Nat. Endowment for Humanities fellow, 1977-78, 84-85, 93-94. Mem. Am. Philos. Assn., Am. Soc. Polit. and Legal Philosophy, Soc. Philosophy and Pub. Affairs. Office: Boston U Law Sch 765 Commonwealth Ave Boston MA 02215

LYONS, EARLE VAUGHAN, JR., minister; b. Phila., Oct. 18, 1917; s. Earle Vaughan and Marie Meta (Anderson) L.; m. Eleanor Jean Morris, Sept. 6, 1946; children: Earle Vaughan III, William Morris, Jean Eleanor. BA, Maryville Coll., 1940; ThM, Princeton Theol. Sem., 1942; MA, U. Pa., 1952, Chapman U., 1977. Ordained to ministry Presbyn. Ch. (U.S.A.), 1943. Asst. pastor West Presbyn. Ch., Wilmington, Del., 1943-44; commd. lt. (j.g.) USN, 1944, chaplain WWII, Korea, Vietnam, ret., 1974; assoc. pastor Mission Hills Ch., San Diego, 1974-78, sr. pastor, 1978-85; interim pastor United Ch. Christ, La Jolla, Calif., 1991-92; officer in charge Chaplain Corps rsch. team, Washington, 1963-64, USN Chaplains Sch., Newport, R.I., 1967-71; chmn. planned giving So. Calif. conf. United Ch. of Christ, 1982-84, bd. dirs. San Diego county Ecumenical Conf., 1975—; team mem. Focus Five Daily TV program, 1976—; mem. ch. and ministry com. San Diego Assn. United Cch. of Christ, 1984—; mem. honor roll NCCJ, 1982-83; exec. dir. San Diego County Ecumenical Conf., 1987—; interim staff coord. Presbytery of San Diego, 1993-94, mem. nominating com. of ministry com., 1994. Contbr. articles to USN Chaplains Bull. Chmn. Vet's Conf. San Diego, 1975-76; bd. dirs. St. Paul's Manor, Green Manor, 1st Congl. Tower, San Diego, 1979-93; mem. Coalition for Equality, San Diego, 1992—; co-chair Coalition for Affordable Housing, San Diego. Decorated Legion of Merit with combat V, Commendation medal, Honor medal 1st class Govt. of Vietnam; recipient Honor medal Freedoms Found. at Valley Forge, 1974, Cath. Bishops Christian Unity award, 1985, Peacemaker award, 1990; named Samaritan of Yr. by San Diego Samarian Counseling Ctr., 1992. Mem. Calif. Coun. Chs. (bd. dirs.), UN Assn., Rotary. Home: 2727 Azalea Dr San Diego CA 92106-1132

LYONS, ELLIS, lawyer; b. Scranton, Pa., Mar. 24, 1915; s. Charles and Anna (Abrams) L.; m. Anita Chester, June 12, 1952; children: Charles, Cathy. Student, U. Scranton, 1933-34; A.B. (Coll. scholar), Oberlin Coll., 1936; J.D. (Univ. fellow), Northwestern U., 1939; LL.D. hon., Pa. Coll. Optometry, 1983. Bar: D.C. 1939, U.S. Supreme Ct 1946. Atty. Dept. Justice, 1940-43; spl. asst. to U.S. Atty. Gen., 1945-50; chief legal cons. U.S. Dept. Justice, 1950-53; acting asst. atty. gen. U.S., 1952-53; partner firm Perlman, Lyons and Emmerglick (and predecessors), Washington, 1953-65, Volpe, Boskey and Lyons, Washington, 1965-94; of counsel, 1995—; instr. bus. law Am. U., 1963-66; gen. counsel Am. Optometric Assn., 1968-94; gen. counsel, sec. Am. Automotive Leasing Assn., 1960-93, Equipment Leasing Assn. Am., 1961-94. Served to lt. USCG, 1943-45. Mem. D.C. Bar, Bar Assn. D.C., Fed. Bar Assn., Am. Bar Assn., Am. Law Inst., Phi Beta Kappa, Tau Epsilon Rho. Home: 4101 Blackthorn St Chevy Chase MD 20815-5053 Office: 918 16th St NW Ste 602 Washington DC 20006-2902

LYONS, GENE MARTIN, political scientist, educator; b. Revere, Mass., Feb. 29, 1924; s. Abraham M. and Mary (Karger) L.; m. Micheline Pohl, Sept. 5, 1951; children—Catherine Anne, Daniel Eugene, Mark Lucien. B.A., Tufts Coll., 1947; license en Scis. Politiques, Grad. Inst. Internat. Studies, Geneva, Switzerland, 1949; Ph.D., Columbia, 1958. Mgmt. officer Internat. Refugee Orgn., Geneva, 1948-52; budget and adminstrv. officer UN Korean Reconstrn. Agy., 1952-56; mem. faculty Dartmouth Coll., 1957-94, prof. govt., 1965-94, dir. Pub. Affairs Center, 1961-66, 73-75, asso. dean faculty social scis., 1974-78; rsch. fellow Dickey Ctr. Dartmouth Coll., Hanover, N.H., 1994—; vis. lectr. Sch. Mgmt. MIT, 1961-70; exec. sec. adv. com. govt. program behavioral scis. Nat. Acad. Scis., 1966-68; dir. dept. social scis. UNESCO, 1970-72; mem. U.S. Nat. Commn. for UNESCO, 1975-80, vice chmn., 1977-78; adv. U.S. del. UNESCO 19th Gen. Conf., 1976, 20th Gen. Conf., 1978; U.S. rep. to UNESCO European Conf., 1977; prof. associé U. Paris I, 1986; exec. dir. acad. council on the UN system, 1987-92. Author: Military Policy and Economic Aid: The Korean Case, 1961; co-author: (with J.W. Masland) Education and Military Leadership, 1959, (with L. Morton) Schools for Strategy, 1965, The Uneasy Partnrship, 1969; Editor: Social Research and Public Policies, 1975; editor, contbr. America: Purpose and Power, 1965, Social Science and the Federal Government, 1971; co-editor, contbr. Beyond Westphalia?, 1995, The United Nations System: The Policies of Member States, 1995. Served with AUS, 1943-46. Mem. Acad. Coun. on UN System, Internat. Studies Assn., Coun. on Fgn. Rels. Home: Main St Norwich VT 05055 Office: Dartmouth Coll Dickey Ctr Hanover NH 03755

LYONS, GEORGE SAGE, lawyer, oil industry executive, former state legislator; b. Mobile, Ala., Oct. 1, 1936; s. Mark, Jr. and Ruth (Kelly) L.; m. Elsie Crain, Feb. 5, 1960; children-George Sage, Amelia C. B.A. in Econs, Washington and Lee U., Lexington, Va., 1958; LL.B., U. Ala., 1960. Bar: Ala. 1960. Assoc. Lyons, Pipes & Cook, Mobile, 1963-66; ptnr. Lyons,

Pipes & Cook, 1966-82, sr. ptnr., 1982-87; pres. Lyons, Pipes & Cook, P.C., 1987-95, LPC Oil Co., Inc., 1988—, Amelia Land Co., Inc., 1978—; chmn., dir. Crain Oil Co., Inc., Guntersville, Ala., 1975—; commr. Ala. Dept. Rev., 1996—; dir. Jordan Industries, Inc., State Docks; mem. exec. com. Ala. Petroleum Coun.; mem. Tenn.-Tombignee Waterway Devel. Authority, 1966-70, 91-95; chmn. Ala. Commn. on Higher Edn., 1971-78. Trustee 11th cir. Hist. Soc. Served to capt., JAGC U.S. Army, 1960-62. Decorated Army Commendation medal. Fellow Am. Bar Found., Nat. Assn. Bond Lawyers, Coun. Ala. Law Inst., Farrah Law Soc. (trustee); mem. Am., Ala., Mobile County bar assns., Mid-Continent Oil and Gas Assn. (dir. Ala.-Miss. div.), Maritime Law Assn. U.S., Omicron Delta Kappa, Phi Delta Phi. Episcopalian. Home: 107 Carmel Dr E Mobile AL 36608-2479 Office: 2 N Royal St Mobile AL 36602-3802

LYONS, HARVEY ISAAC, mechanical engineering educator; b. N.Y.C., Sept. 26, 1931; s. Joseph and Betty (Janower) L.; m. Rebecca Anne Szeman, June 10, 1978; children: Neal Joshua, Leslie Eve. Cert. in indsl. design, Pratt Inst., 1952; BSME, The Cooper Union, 1962, ME in Mech. Engring., 1971; PhD in Mech. Engring., Ohio State U., 1978. Registered profl. engr., N.Y. From design engr. to sr. mech. engr. various orgns., N.Y.C., 1962-72; assoc. prof. mech. engring. Mont. State U., Bozeman, 1978-79, U. Wis.-Parkside, Kenosha, 1979-81, U. N.H., Durham, 1981-84, Seattle U., 1984-85; chmn. dept. mech. engring. Alfred (N.Y.) U., 1985-88; chair dept. mech. engring. Union Coll., Schenectady, 1988-92, Ind. Inst. Tech., Ft. Wayne, 1992-95; cons. engr. in pvt. practice Ft. Wayne, Ind., 1995—. Contbr. articles to profl. jours. Sgt. U.S. Army, 1952-54, Korea. Mem. ASME, NSPE, Am. Soc. Engring. Edn., Soc. Mfg. Engrs. Achievements include development of methods to investigate tribological phenomenon of Fretting-Wear in-situ, towards development of failure prediction criteria, development of mechanical engineering departments in industry and academe. Avocations: skiing, flying, karate, tennis, backpacking. Home and Office: 6303 Alvarez Dr Fort Wayne IN 46815

LYONS, J. ROLLAND, civil engineer; b. Cedar Rapids, Iowa, Apr. 27, 1909; s. Neen T. and Goldie N. (Hill) L.; BS, U. Iowa, 1933; m. Mary Jane Doht, June 10, 1924; children: Marlene R. Sparks, Sharon K. Hutson, Mary Lynn Lyons. Jr. hwy. engr. Works Projects Adminstrn. field engr. Dept. Transp., State Ill., Peoria, 1930-31, civil engr. I-IV Cen. Office, Springfield, 1934-53, civil engr. V, 1953-66, municipal sect. chief, civil engr. VI, 1966-72. Civil Def. radio officer Springfield and Sangamon County (Ill.) Civil Def. Agy., 1952—. Recipient Meritorious Service award Am. Assn. State Hwy. Ofcls., 1968, 25 Yr. Career Service award State Ill., 1966, Cert. Appreciation Ill. Mcpl. League, 1971. Registered profl. engr., Ill.; registered land surveyor, Ill. Mem. NSPE, Nat. Soc. Profl. Engrs., Ill. Soc. Profl. Engrs., Ill. Assn. State Hwy. Engrs., State Ill. Employees Assn., Am. Pub. Works Assn., Am. Assn. State Hwy. Ofcls., Amateur Trapshooters Assn., Sangamon Valley Radio Club, Lakewood Golf and Country Club, KC, Abe Lincoln Gun Club, South Fork Conservation Club (Ill.). Address: 3642 Lancaster Rd Springfield IL 62703-5022

LYONS, JAMES ALOYSIUS, JR., naval officer; b. Jersey City, Sept. 28, 1927; s. James Aloysius and Marion F. (Bach) L.; m. Renee Wilcox Chevalier, Apr. 10, 1954; children—Michele, Yvonne, James Aloysius, III. B.S., U.S. Naval Acad., 1952; student command and staff course, Naval War Coll., 1963-64, Nat. War Coll., 1970-71. Commd. ensign U.S. Navy, 1952, advanced through grades to vice adm., 1981; served at sea aboard 6th fleet flagship USS Salem, 1952-59, exec. officer U.S.S. Miller, 1959-61, antisubmarine warfare and weapons officer cruiser-destroyer Flotilla Four, 1961-63; dir. Navy plans, strategic plans div. Office of Chief of Naval Ops. Washington, 1964-66; comdr. USS Charles S. Sperry, 1966-68, exec. asst. and sr. aide to dep. chief naval ops. for plans and policy, 1971-74, comdr. guided missile cruiser USS Richmond K. Turner, 1974-75, chief of staff Carrier Group Four, 1975-76; sr. asst. on Joint Chiefs of Staff Matters, div. strategy, plans and policy, Office Chief Naval Ops. Washington, 1976-78; dep. dir. strategic plans and policy div., 1978; asst. dep. for polit. mil. affairs Directorate Orgn. Joint Chiefs of Staff U.S. Navy, Washington, 1978-79, dir. polit.-mil. affairs Directorate Orgn. Joint Chiefs of Staff, 1979-80; comdr. Task Force 72, also comdr. Naval Surface Group U.S. Navy, Western Pacific, 1980-81; comdr. U.S. 2d Fleet, Joint Task Force 120 and NATO Command Striking Fleet Atlantic U.S. Navy, 1981-83; dep. chief naval ops. Office of Chief Naval Ops. U.S. Navy, Washington, 1983—; U.S. rep. arms limitation talks with USSR, Helsinki, 1978, Mexico City, 1978; sr. U.S. rep. Incidents at Sea Talks with USSR, Moscow, 1984; sr. Navy mem. U.S. Del., UN Mil. Staff Com., 1983—. Decorated Legion of Merit, Meritorious Service medal with gold star, Navy Commendation medal with gold star, Navy Achievement medal. Mem. U.S. Naval Acad. Alumni Assn., U.S. Naval Acad. Athletic Assn. Roman Catholic. Home: QTRS O Washington Navy Yard Washington DC 20374 Office: Dep Chief Naval Ops Op-06 Navy Dept Washington DC 20350

LYONS, JAMES ELLIOTT, lawyer; b. Lexington, Mo., Mar. 10, 1951; s. james Elliott and Elouise (Blackman) L.; m. Mary Jane McCarthy, June 30, 1979; children: Sean Austin, Caitlan Maureen. BA with honors, U. Mo., 1973; JD, NYU, 1976. Bar: Mo. 1976, N.Y. 1977, Calif. 1984. Assoc. Stinson Mag Thompson McEvers & Fizzell, Kansas City, Mo., 1976-77; assoc. Skadden, Arps, Slate et al., N.Y.C., L.A., 1977-84; law clk. to Hon. Robert W. Sweet U.S. Dist. Ct. (so. dist.) N.Y., 1978; ptnr. Skadden, Arps, Slate et al., L.A. and San Francisco, 1984—. Mem. ABA, Los Angeles County Bar Assn., Bar Assn. San Francisco, Mo. Bar Assn. Democrat. Office: Skadden Arps Slate et al 4 Embarcadero Ctr Ste 3800 San Francisco CA 94111-9999

LYONS, JAMES ROBERT, federal official. BS in Forest and Wildlife Mgmt. with high honors, Rutgers U., 1977; M in Forestry, Yale U., 1979. Program analyst U.S. Fish and Wildlife Svc. Dept. Interior, 1979-82; dir. resource policy Soc. Am. Foresters, Bethesda, Md., 1982-86; staff dir. subcom. forests, family farms, energy Com. Agriculture, 1986, staff asst. com. agr., 1987-93; asst. sec. agr. natural resources and environ. USDA, Washington, 1993—, under sec. natural resources and environment; agrl. advisor Cong. Leon Panetta, 1989-91. Office: USDA Natural Resources & Environment 14th & Independence Ave SW Washington DC 20250-0002

LYONS, JEFFREY, film critic. Co-host Sneak Previews, Chgo. Office: Sneak Previews Sta WTTW-TV 5400 N Saint Louis Ave Chicago IL 60625-4623 also: Sta WCBS-AM 51 W 52nd St New York NY 10019-6119

LYONS, JERRY LEE, mechanical engineer; b. St. Louis, Apr. 2, 1939; s. Ferd H. and Edna T. Lyons. Diploma in Mech. Engring., Okla. Inst. Tech., 1964; MSME, S.W. U., 1983; PhD in Engring. Mgmt., Southwest U., 1984. Registered profl. engr., Calif. Project engr. Harris Mfg. Co., St. Louis, 1965-70, Essex Cryogenics Industries, St. Louis, 1970-73; mgr. engring. rsch. Chemetron Corp., St. Louis, 1973-77; cons. fluid controls Wis. U., 1977—; pres., chief exec. Yankee Ingenuity, Inc., St. Louis, 1974—; v.p., gen. mgr. engring. R & D Essex Fluid Controls divsn. Essex Industries, Inc., St. Louis, 1977-90; pres. Lyons Pub. Co., St. Louis, 1983—; pres., CEO Innovative Controls divsn. Yankee Ingenuity, Inc., Ft. Wayne, Ind., 1991—; chmn. exec. bd. continuing engring. edn. in St. Louis for U. Mo., Columbia, 1980-81; bd. dirs. Intertech., Inc., Houston; cons. fluid power dept. Bradley U., Peoria, 1977-84. Author: Home Study Series Course on Actuators and Accessories, 1977, The Valve Designers Handbook, 1983, The Lyons' Encyclopedia of Valves, 1975, 93, The Designers Handbook of Pressure Sensing Devices, 1980, Special Process Applications, 1980; co-author: Handbook of Product Liability, 1991; contbr. articles to profl. jours.; patentee in field. With USAF, 1957-62. Recipient Winston Churchill medal, 1988, Dwight D. Eisenhower Achievement award of honor, 1990; named Businessman of Week (KEZK radio), Eminent Churchill fellow Winston Churchill Wisdom Soc. Fellow ASME; mem. N.Y. Acad. Scis., Soc. Mfg. Engrs. (cert. product design, chmn. Mo. registration com. 1975-90, chmn. St. Louis chpt. 1979-80, internat. dir. 1982-84, 85-87, engr. of yr. 1984, internat. award of merit 1985), Nat. Soc. Profl. Engrs., Mo. Soc. Profl. Engrs., St. Louis Soc. Mfg. Engrs. (chmn. profl. devel., registration and cert. com. 1975-79), Instrument Soc. Am. (control valve stability com. 1978-84), Computer and Automated Sys. Assn. (1st chmn. St. Louis chpt. 1980-81), St. Louis Engrs. Club (award of merit 1977, wisdom award of honor 1987, Wisdom Hall of Fame 1987), Am. Security Coun. (committeeman 1976—), Nat. Fluid Power Assn. (com. on pressure ratings 1975-77), Am. Legion. Lutheran. Achievements include patentee in field. Home and Office: 2607 Northgate Blvd Fort Wayne IN 46835-2986

LYONS, JOHN DAVID, French, Italian and comparative literature educator; b. Springfield, Mass., Oct. 14, 1946; s. John Joseph and Loretta Francis (Feighery) L.; m. Patricia Stuart, July 31, 1971; 1 dau., Jennifer Catherine. A.B., Brown U., 1967; M.A., Yale U., 1968, Ph.D., 1972. Asst. prof. French, Italian and comparative lit. Dartmouth Coll., Hanover, N.H., 1972-78, assoc. prof., 1978-82, prof., 1982-87, chmn. comparative lit. program, 1981-84, chmn., prof. dept. French and Italian, 1987.; dir. Am. Univ. Ctr. for Film and Critical Studies, Paris, 1984-85; prof. French U. Va., Charlottesville, 1987-92, Commonwealth prof. French, 1993—, chmn. dept., 1989-92. Author: A Theatre of Disguise, 1978, The Listening Voice, 1982, Exemplum, 1989, The Tragedy of Origins, 1996; co-editor: Mimesis: Mirror to Method, 1982, Dialectic of Discovery, 1983, Critical Tales, 1993; editor: Art, Architecture, Text: The Late Renaissance, 1985; assoc. editor Continuum, 1987-93; editor Academe, 1994—; editl. adv. bd. Philosophy and Literature. Recipient Robert Fish award for teaching Dartmouth Coll., 1978; Woodrow Wilson fellow, 1967, ACLS study fellow, 1978, NEH fellow, 1985-89, 92-93, Ctr. for Advanced Studies U. Va. fellow, 1987-89. Office: U Va Dept French Lang and Lit Charlottesville VA 22903

LYONS, JOHN W(INSHIP), government official, chemist; b. Reading, Mass., Nov. 5, 1930. A.B. in Chemistry, Harvard U., 1952; A.M. in Phys. Chemistry, Washington U., St. Louis, 1963, Ph.D. in Phys. Chemistry, 1964. With Monsanto Co., 1955-73, group leader, sect. mgr. research dept., inorganic chems. div., 1962-69, mgr. comml. devel., head fire safety center, 1969-73; mem. ad hoc panel on fire research Nat. Bur. Standards, Washington, 1971-73; dir. Center for Fire Research, 1973-77, Inst. Applied Tech., 1977-78, Nat. Engring. Lab., 1978-89; acting dep. dir. Nat. Bur. Standards, 1983; dir. Nat. Inst. Standards and Tech., Gaithersburg, Md., 1990-93, Army Rsch. Lab., Adelphi, Md., 1993—; chmn. Products Rsch. Com. (trust which adminstrs. fire rsch. fund), 1974-79; vis. lectr. various univs.; co-chmn. U.S.-Japan Natural Resources Panel on Fire Rsch., 1975-78; mem. adv. com. on engring NSF, 1981-90; mem. bd. visitors U. Md. Coll. Engring., 1980-90; mem. adv. com. Naval Rsch. Lab., 1985; mem. com. on fed. labs. Office Sci. and Tech. Policy. Author: Viscosity and Flow Measurement, 1963, The Chemistry and Uses of Fire Retardants, 1970; Fire, 1985; contbr. numerous articles to profl. publs. Chmn. blue ribbon com. on rsch. and pub. svc. U. Md., 1993. Recipient gold medal Dept. Commerce, 1977, President's Mgmt. Improvement award White House, 1977, President's Disting. Exec. Rank award, 1981, E.U. Condon award, 1986; Disting. Svc. award U. Md. Coll. Engring., 1990, Centennial medal, 1994; 1st ann. Outstanding Achievement award Fire Retardant Chem. Assn., 1994. Fellow AAAS, Washington Acad. Sci.; mem. Am. Chem. Soc. (chmn. St. Louis sect. 1971-72), Nat. Fire Protection Assn. (bd. dirs. 1978-84), ASTM (bd. dirs. 1985-87), Nat. Acad. Engring., Sigma Xi. Office: Army Rsch Lab 2800 Powder Mill Rd Adelphi MD 20783-1197

LYONS, JOSEPH CHISHOLM, lawyer; b. Halifax, N.S., Can., Oct. 17, 1927; s. James Norbert and Frances (Chisholm) L.; m. Julianne Roach, Oct. 5, 1957; children: Juli, Catherine, Patricia, Chisholm, Elizabeth, John-Mark, Mathew. B.A., St. Francis-Xavier U., 1948; LL.B., Dalhousie Law Sch., 1951; M.B.A., Harvard U., 1953. Bar: created Queen's counsel 1966. Partner firm Smith, Lyons, Torrance, Stevenson & Mayer (barristers & solicitors), Toronto, Ont., Can.; vice chmn. Allen Group Inc., Cleve.; pres. Allen Group Can. Inc., Rothmans of Can. Ltd., Toronto Air King Ltd.; bd. dirs. Chas. T. Main Can. Ltd., Browning-Ferris Industries Can. Ltd., Can. Kawasaki Motors Ltd., Falk Can. Inc., Prestonia Products Inc. Mem. Can. Bar Assn. Mem. Progressive-Conservative Party. Roman Catholic. Clubs: National (Toronto), Toronto Golf (Toronto). Office: Scotia Pla Ste 6200, 40 King St W, Toronto, ON Canada M5H 3Z7

LYONS, LAURENCE, securities executive; b. Jersey City, Aug. 11, 1911; s. Louis and Teresa (Serge) L.; m. Gertrude Starr, Sept. 1, 1945; 1 son, Jonathan. BS, NYU, 1934, postgrad., 1935. Securities analyst Allen & Co., N.Y.C., 1935-52; with Allen Co., Inc., N.Y.C., 1952—, sr. v.p., 1989—. Mem. Soc. Security Analysts. Home: 1 Kensington Gate Apt 221 Great Neck NY 11021-1229 Office: Allen & Co Inc 711 Fifth Ave New York NY 10022-3109

LYONS, NATALIE BELLER, family counselor; b. Habana, Cuba, Apr. 3, 1926; d. Herman Lawrence and Jennie (Engler) B.; widowed, Apr. 18, 1986; children: Anne, Sara. BS in Surveying snd Land Appraising, Inst. Vedado, Habana, Cuba, 1943; BA, U. Mich., 1946; MEd, U. Miami, Fla., 1967. Family counselor, mem. staff furniture design and mfg. co. George B. Bent, Gardner, Mass., 1953-58; tchr. H.S., Winchendon, Mass., Hollywood, Fla., 1962; tchr. parochial sch. parochial sch., Ft. Lauderdale, Fla., 1963-64; family counselor Miami, 1967—; project dir. Cen. Am. fisheries program Peace Corps, 1972-74; counselor Svc. Corp. of Ret. Execs., Miami, 1993, bd. dirs., 1993—; bd. dirs., mem. Com. for Accuracy in Mid East Reporting, 1990—. Pres. Miami region Hadassah, 1989-91; bd. dirs. Greater Miami Jewish Fedn., 1985—; co-chair Greater Miami Jewish Fedn., 1985—; bd. dirs. Miami Civic Music Assn., 1985—, women's divsn. Greater Miami Jewish Fedns. Cmty. Rels. Coun.; mem. nat. bd. dirs. nat. women's divsn. Am. Soc. for Technion, 1991—, pres. 1984-86; co-chair Pro-Israel Rally, Tri County, 1991, Joint Action Com., Miami, 1989-91; tng. dir. Los Amigos de las Ams., 1975—; founder, dir. Cmty. Inst. Jewish Studies, Hollywood, Fla., 1962-64. Recipient Leadership award Hadassah, 1987, honoree Am. Soc. for Technion Scholarship Fund, 1991; named Woman of Yr., Hadassah, 1991. Democrat. Avocations: travel, reading, antiques, family, performing arts.

LYONS, PAUL MICHAEL, producer, film; b. Washington, Aug. 21, 1932; s. Thomas William and Nora (Bagley) L.; m. Bernadette Marie O'Rourke, Oct. 24, 1953; children—Stephen W., Loretta N., Sharon D. Student, Georgetown U., 1950-52. V.p. Charlie Papa Prodns., Rockville, Md., 1972-79; v.p., gen. mgr. Capital Film Labs., Washington, 1979-81; pres., chief exec. officer Am. Bus. Media Council, Inc., Washington, 1982-83; v.p., owner Images and Ideas, Vienna, Va., 1967—; exec. dir. Occupational Safety and Health Rev. Commn., Washington, 1984-90; dir. mktg. Nat. Empowerment TV, Washington, 1993—. Film editor Treasures of King Tut, 1977 (nominated Academy award); prodn. mgr. (film) Carry the Fire, Olympic Torch Relay, 1984. Mem. Vienna Town Council, 1968-76; chmn. Bicentennial Commn., Vienna, 1971-76; mem. Fairfax County Rep. Com., Va., 1978-84. Recipient Disting. Service award Jaycees of Vienna, 1965; named Citizen of the Yr. Vienna C. of C., 1976. Mem. Council on Internat. Nontheatrical Events (mem. adv. bd. 1979-92), Council on Nat. Policy (bd. govs. 1982—), Soc. Motion Picture & TV Engrs. (bd. mgrs.), White House News Photographers Assn. (pres. 1990-92), Washington Film Council (pres. 1982-83). Roman Catholic. Home: 603 Upham Pl NW Vienna VA 22180-4128

LYONS, PAUL VINCENT, lawyer; b. Boston, July 19, 1939; s. Joseph Vincent and Doris Irene (Griffin) L.; m. Elaine Marie Hurley, July 13, 1968; children: Judith Marie, Maureen Patricia, Paula Anne, Joseph Hurley. BS cum laude, Boston Coll., 1960; MBA, NYU, 1962; JD, Suffolk U., Boston, 1968. Bar: Mass. 1968, U.S. Cir. Ct. (1st cir.) 1969, U.S. Supreme Ct. 1991. Div. adminstrn. mgr. Pepsi-Cola Co., N.Y.C., 1962-64; mem. bus. faculty Burdett Coll., Boston, 1964-68; atty. NLRB, Boston, 1968-73; assoc. Foley, Hoag & Eliot, Boston, 1973-77, ptnr., 1978—; mem. faculty Boston U., 1972-74. Mem. Town Meeting, Milton, Mass., 1986—, mem. pers. bd., 1994—. Lt. U.S. Army, 1960-62. Mem. ABA, Mass. Bar Assn., Boston Bar Assn. Office: Foley Hoag & Eliot 1 Post Office Sq Boston MA 02109-2103

LYONS, RICHARD CHAPMAN, former urologist; b. Corry, Pa., Nov. 23, 1919; s. Arch C. and Araline (Drought) L.; m. Norma Lydia Wright, Dec. 25, 1945; children: Dorothy A., John C., Sanford D., Timothy R., Valerie A. Grad. U. Pa., 1941; MD, U. Pitts., 1944. Diplomate Am. Bd. Urology. Intern, St. Elizabeth Hosp., Washington, 1945; resident, Mayo Clinic, Rochester, Minn., 1945-46, 48-50; civilian physician U.S. Army, 1946-47; chmn. dept. urology, Hamot Med. Ctr., Erie, Pa., 1955-68, practitioner, surgeon, 1950-86, founder, head urology residency program, 1958-68; hon. mem. med. staffs St. Vincent Health Ctr., Erie, 1951-86; mem. Pa. State Bd. Med. Edn. and Licensure, 1971-85, chmn., 1976-78, 81-85; dir. NW Pa. Corp., Oil City, Mellon-North, Erie; mng. ptnr. Lyons Properties Ltd. Partnership. Trustee Gannon U. Named Disting. Pennsylvanian, Gannon U., 1981. Recipient Integrity award Soc. for Advancement Intergrity in Pub. Life. Fellow ACS (gov. 1975-81); mem. AMA, Pa. Med. Soc., Erie County Med. Soc., Pa. Urologic Assn. (pres. 1974), Mayo Clinic Alumni Assn., Mayo Urol. Alumni Assn. (pres. 1976), Erie Club, Kahkwa Club, Erie Yacht Club, Univ. Club (Pitts.), Elks. Republican. Roman Catholic. Home: 52 Royal Palm Dr Fort Lauderdale FL 33301-1409

LYONS, THOMAS PATRICK, economics educator; b. Groton, Conn., Sept. 8, 1953. BA in Asian Studies, Cornell U., 1979, MA in Econs., 1982, PhD in Econs., 1983. Asst. prof. econs. Dartmouth Coll., Hanover, N.H., 1983-87; vis. asst. prof. Cornell U., Ithaca, N.Y., 1986-88, asst. prof., 1988-91; assoc. prof., 1991—; dir. East Asia program Cornell U., Ithaca, N.Y., 1991-94; dir. undergrad. studies, econs., 1995—. Author: Economic Integration and Planning in Maoist China, 1987, China's War on Poverty, 1992, Economic Geography of Fujian: A Sourcebook, 1995; contbr. numerous articles to profl. jours. With USN, 1972-76. Rsch. grantee Ford Found., 1987. Mem. Am. Econ. Assn., Assn. for Asian Studies. Office: Cornell U Dept Econs Uris Hall Ithaca NY 14853-7601

LYONS, WILLIAM CLAYPOOL, engineering educator and consultant; b. Bronxville, N.Y., Nov. 26, 1937; s. Thomas Edward and Lucile (Marks) L.; m. Alahna Carter Weller, Feb. 25, 1961 (div. July 1980); children: Andrew W., Terrence W., Dale W. BS in Geol. Engring., U. Kans., Lawrence, 1961, MS in Engring. Mechanics, 1962, PhD, 1965. Registered profl. engr., N.Mex. Jr. engr. Phillips Petroleum Co., Bartlesville, Okla., 1961-62; instr. U. Kans., Lawrence, 1962-64; postdoctoral fellow Northwestern U., Evanston, Ill., 1964-65; staff mem. Sandia Nat. Lab., Albuquerque, 1965-69; asst. group leader Los Alamos (N.Mex.) Nat. Lab., 1969-76; tech. asst. to dir. U.S. ERDA/Fuel Cycle, Germantown, Md., 1976-77; pres. Rift Pneumatics Inc., Farmington, N.Mex., 1977-80; prof. N.Mex. Inst. Mining Tech., Socorro, 1977—; adj. prof. U. N.Mex., Albuquerque, 1966-68; rsch. fellow Polish Acad. Sci., Warsaw, 1963-64; Disting. vis. prof. U.S. Air Force Acad., Colorado Springs, 1993-94. Author: Air and Gas Drilling Manual, 1984; author, editor: Standard Petroleum & Natural Gas Engineers Handbook, 1995. Soccer referee NCAA, 1975-85. With USMCR, 1955-61. Recipient Energy Innovation award U.S. Dept. Energy, 1988. Mem. ASCE, NSPE, Soc. Petroleum Engrs., Am. Soc. Engring. Edn. Achievements include patents for drilling devices. Avocations: fishing, skiing, writing. Home: 1008 Rocky Rd Socorro NM 87801-4484 Office: NMex Inst Mining Tech Dept Petroleum Engring MSEC Bldg Rm 300 Socorro NM 87801

LYSAUGHT, PATRICK, lawyer; b. Kansas City, Kans., Sept. 12, 1949; s. Mathew Aloysius and Loretta Rose (Storen) L.; m. Patricia Caspar, June 27, 1970; children: Geoffrey James, Kevin Michael. BA, Creighton U., 1971, postgrad. Law Sch., 1971; JD with distinction, U. Mo., 1974. Bar: Mo. 1975, U.S. Dist. Ct. (we. dist.) Mo. 1975, U.S. Ct. Appeals (8th cir.) 1975. Law clk. to chief judge U.S. Dist. Ct. (we. dist.) Mo., Kansas City, 1975-76; assoc., then shareholder firm Jackson & Sherman, P.C., Kansas City, Mo., 1976-83; v.p., bd. dirs. Sherman, Wickens, Lysaught & Speck, P.C., Kansas City, Mo., 1983-91; ptnr., shareholder Shook, Hardy & Bacon, Kansas City, Mo., 1991—; bd. dirs. Western Mo. Def. Lawyers, 1985—; faculty mem. Trial Acad., 1990. Author: Techniques in the Use and Management of Demonstrative Evidence, 1984, Cross Examination of the Lay Witness, 1988, Federal Preemption As A Bar To State Tort Claims, 1988, Premises Liability Major Disasters-Structural Failures, Fires and Environmental. Mem. ABA (antitrust-civil practice com.), Kansas City Bar Assn. (fed. practice com., civil procedure com.), Mo. Orgn. Def. Lawyers (charter), Internat. Assn. Def. Counsel (pharm. med. device and biotech com., toxic and hazardous substance com., products liability com., excess and reins. com.), Am. Bd. Trial Advocates, Def. Research Inst. (products liability and profl. liability coms., lectr. drug and med. device), Leawood Country Manor Homes Assn. (bd. dirs., v.p., pres.), Phi Kappa Psi. Roman Catholic. Office: Shook Hardy & Bacon 1 Kansas City Pl 1200 Main St Kansas City MO 64105-2100

LYSAUGHT, THOMAS FRANCIS, publishing company executive; b. Chgo., July 5, 1936; s. Thomas Francis and Eleanor Annette (O'Brien) L.; children: Thomas, Mary Therese, Eileen, Ruth, Judy. B.S. in Elec. Engring., Ill. Inst. Tech., 1959, postgrad., 1959-61; J.D., Chgo.-Kent Coll. Law, 1966; M.B.A., U. Chgo., 1969. Bar: Ill. 1966, U.S. Ct. Custom and Patent Appeals 1972, U.S. Supreme Ct. 1973. Engr. Motorola Co., Chgo., 1959-61; patent counsel GTE Automatic Elec. Corp., Northlake, Ill., 1961-73; v.p. law GTE Directories Corp., Des Plaines, Ill., 1973-78, v.p. law and planning, 1978-81, v.p. info. service, law and planning, from 1981, dir., 1973-89; now pres., also bd. dirs. GTE Directories Corp., DFW Airport, Tex. Mem. ABA, Tex. Bar Assn., Dallas Bar Assn., Assn. for Corporate Growth, Planning Forum. Roman Catholic. Office: GTE Directories Corp PO Box 619810 W Airfield Dr Dallas TX 75261-9810*

LYST, JOHN HENRY, newspaper editor; b. Princeton, Ind., Mar. 28, 1933; s. John Henry and Marguerite (McQuinn) L.; m. Sharon Long, Dec. 29, 1956; children: Shannon M., Bettina A., Audrey K., Ellen K. AB, Ind. U., 1955. Reporter Indpls. Star, 1956-67, bus. columnist, from 1967, editor editl. page; corr. N.Y. Times, from 1964. Served with AUS, 1956-59. Mem. Indpls. Press Club (pres. 1968, bd. dirs. 1969), Sigma Delta Chi. Office: Ctrl Newspapers Inc PO Box 145 Indianapolis IN 46206-0145

LYSTAD, MARY HANEMANN (MRS. ROBERT LYSTAD), sociologist, author, consultant; b. New Orleans, Apr. 11, 1928; d. James and Mary (Douglass) Hanemann; m. Robert Lystad, June 20, 1953; children: Lisa Douglass, Anne Hanemann, Mary Lunde, Robert Douglass, James Hanemann. A.B. cum laude, Newcomb Coll., 1949; M.A., Columbia U., 1951; Ph.D., Tulane U., 1955. Postdoctoral fellow social psychology S.E. La. Hosp., Mandeville, 1955-57; field rsch. social psychology Ghana, 1957-58, South Africa and Swaziland, 1968, Peoples Republic of China, 1986; chief sociologist Collaborative Child Devel. Project, Charity Hosp. La., New Orleans, 1958-61; feature writer African div. Voice Am., Washington, 1964-73; program analyst NIMH, Washington, 1968-78; asso. dir. for planning and coordination div. spl. mental health programs NIMH, 1978-80; chief Nat. Ctr. for Prevention and Control of Rape, 1980-83, Ctr. Mental Health Studies of Emergencies, 1983-89; pvt. cons. specializing on mental health implications social and econ. problems Bethesda, Md., 1990—; cons. on youth Nat. Goals Research Staff, White House, Washington, 1969-70. Author: Millicent the Monster, 1968, Social Aspects of Alienation, 1969, Jennifer Takes Over P.S. 94, 1972, James the Jaguar, 1972, As They See It: Changing Values of College Youth, 1972, That New Boy, 1973, Halloween Parade, 1973, Violence at Home, 1974, A Child's World As Seen in His Stories and Drawings, 1974, From Dr. Mather to Dr. Seuss: 200 Years of American Books for Children, 1980, At Home in America, 1983; editor: Innovations in Mental Health Services to Disaster Victims, 1985, Violence in the Home: Interdisciplinary Perspectives, 1986, Mental Health Response to Mass Emergencies: Theory and Practice, 1988. Recipient Spl. Recognition award USPHS, 1983, Alumna Centennial award Newcomb Coll., 1986. Home and Office: 4900 Scarsdale Rd Bethesda MD 20816-2440

LYSTAD, ROBERT ARTHUR LUNDE, retired university dean, educator; b. Milw., Aug. 10, 1920; s. Arthur Frederick and Lulu Marion (Lunde) L.; m. Anita E. Firing, June 11, 1945 (dec. 1952); m. Mary Agnes Hanemann, June 20, 1953; children: Lisa Douglass, Anne Hanemann, Mary Lunde, Robert Douglass, James Hanemann. B.A., U. Wis., 1941; B.D., Drew Theol. Sem., 1944; Ph.D. in Anthropology, Northwestern U., 1951. Prof. anthropology Tulane U., 1951-61, head dept. sociology and anthropology Newcomb Coll., 1959-61; asso. prof. African studies Sch. Advanced Internat. Studies, Johns Hopkins U., 1961-64, prof., 1964-91, assoc. dean for acad. affairs, 1980-91; acting assoc. dean, 1992; cons. Voice of Am., various depts. U.S. govt., 1961-86, various ednl. and rsch. instns. in Japan, Korea, People's Republic of China, Taiwan, 1981. Author: The Ashanti: A Proud People, 1958; also articles in field.; editor: The African World: A Survey of Social Research, 1965. Mem. Ohio Conf. Methodist Ch., 1944-73. Recipient Founder's award Sch. Advanced Internat. Studies, 1991; fellow Social Sci. Research Council Gold Coast and Ivory Coast, 1949-50; grantee Carnegie Corp., Ghana, 1957-58. Home: 4900 Scarsdale Rd Bethesda MD 20816-2440

LYSYK, KENNETH MARTIN, judge; b. Weyburn, Sask., Can., July 1, 1934; s. Michael and Anna (Maradyn) L.; m. Patricia Kinnon, Oct. 2, 1959; children: Joanne, Karen (dec.), Stephanie. B.A., McGill U., 1954; LL.B., U. Sask., 1957; B.C.L., Oxford U., 1960. Bar: Sask., B.C., Yukon, apptd.

Queen's counsel 1973. Lectr. U. B.C., 1960-62, asst. prof., 1962-65, assoc. prof., 1965-68, prof., 1968-69; adviser Constl. Rev. sect. Privy Council Office, Govt. of Can., Ottawa, 1969-70; prof. Faculty of Law U. Toronto, 1970-72; dep. atty. gen. Govt. of Sask., Regina, 1972-76; dean Law Sch., U. B.C., Vancouver, 1976-82; judge Supreme Ct. of B.C., Vancouver, 1983—; dep. judge Supreme Ct. Yukon, 1991—, N.W. Territories, 1991—; judge ct. Martial Appeal Ct. Can., 1995—; assoc. dir. Nat. Jud. Inst., 1996—; chmn. Alaska Hwy. Pipeline Inquiry, 1977; sole commr. Yukon Electoral Boundaries Commn., 1991. Mem. Can. Bar Assn., Internat. Commn. Jurists (Can. sect.; v.p. for B.C. 1992—), Can. Inst. for Adminstrn. of Justice (pres. 1989-91). Office: Law Ct, 800 Smithe St, Vancouver, BC Canada V6Z 2E1

LYTHCOTT, MARCIA A., newspaper editor. Op-ed editor Chicago Tribune, Ill. Office: Chicago Tribune 435 N Michigan Ave Chicago IL 60611-4001

LYTLE, ELLEN JUANITA WILSON, special education educator; b. Port Arthur, Tex., Jan. 26, 1941; d. Walter Dean and Velma Juanita (Henry) Wilson; m. Donald L. Lytle, Jr., Apr. 12, 1963 (div. Jan. 1979); children: David Anthony, Shannon Wilson. BA in Elem. Edn., U. Southwestern La., 1963, MEd, 1972; spl. edn. cert., McNeese State U., 1992, postgrad., 1992-94; D of Psychology, Kennedy-Western U., 1994. Cert. tchr., spl. edn. assessor, computer lit., La. Tchr. Duson (La.) Elem. Sch. Lafayette Parish, 1963-65, N.P. Moss Elem. Sch. Lafayette Parish, Lafayette, 1965-70, St. Antoine Elem. Sch. Lafayette Parish, Lafayette, 1970-72; substitute tchr. French and band Merryville (La.) High Sch. Beauregard Parish, 1987; tchr. spl. edn. Pickering Elem. Sch. Vernon Parish, Leesville, La., 1989-92; alt. spl. edn. H.S. classes Pickering H.S. Vernon Parish, Leesville, 1992-94; ednl. diagnostician Vernon Parish Spl. Edn. Ctr., Leesville, 1994—; officer, pres. La. Divsn. Career Devel. and Transition, 1993—; spkr. spl. edn. super conf., 1992, 94. Author: (juvenile) Tales of the Circus, 1990, Histories of Louisiana Fairs, Festivals, and Historic Places, Book 1, 1993, Book 2, 1994, Louisiana: Festival of Color Coloring Book, 1994; illustrator: Chad and the Mighty Dragon, 1992; author and illustrator: Tales; creator classroom games. Officer Homemakers Club, Beauregard Parish, 1975-88; sec. La. Assn. Fairs and Festivals, 1985-89; sec.-treas. Beauregard Parish Fair Assn., DeRidder, 1980—. Mem. Coun. for Exceptional Children (sec. La. fedn. coun. 1995), Assn. Profl. La. Educators, La. Ednl. Diagnosticians Assn., Kappa Kappa Iota (pres. 1993-94). Methodist. Avocations: arts and crafts, sewing, travel, writing. Home: 3570 Neale Oil Field Rd Deridder LA 70634-9540 Office: Vernon Parish Spl Edn Ctr 201 Belview Rd Leesville LA 71446-2904

LYTLE, GUY FITCH, III, priest, educator, dean; b. Birmingham, Ala., Oct. 14, 1944; s. Guy Fitch and Nelle (Stewart) L.; m. Maria Rasco, Dec. 30, 1978; children: Elizabeth Eva Maria, Ashley Alexandra Gabriella. BA in History magna cum laude, Princeton U., 1966, MA in History, 1969, PhD in History, 1976; Marshall Scholar, U. Oxford, Eng., 1967-70. Ordained priest in Episcopalian Church, 1986. From instr. to asst. prof. history and medieval studies Cath. Univ. of Am., Washington, 1971-77; asst. prof. history U. Tex., Austin, 1977-84; assoc. prof. of church history The Church Divinity Sch. of the Pacific, Berkeley, Calif., 1984-89; prof. of church history and hist. theology The Church Divinity Sch. of the Pacific, Berkeley, 1989-91; doctoral prof. of history Grad. Theol. Union, Berkeley, Calif., 1984-91; dean, prof. Anglican studies Sch. of Theology, Univ. of the South, Sewanee, Tenn., 1991—, Juhan prof. divinity, 1992—; from asst. to rector All Souls Episcopal Ch., Berkeley, Calif., 1985; chaplain Merrithew Meml. Hosp., Martinez, Calif., 1986-87; assoc. rector Episcopal Ch. of St. John the Evangelist, San Francisco, 1987-90, rector, 1990; lectr. in history of sci. and medicine U. Ala., 1967; rsch. fellow, mem. sr. common rm., Corpus Christi Coll., 1971-73; vis. prof. Oxford U., Eng., 1980, 85, The Folger Shakespeare Libr., 1975-76, Australian Nat. Univ., 1983, Episcopal Sem. of the S.W., 1983-84; mem. Gen. Bd. Examining Chaplains, 1991—; pres. Conf. of Anglican Theologians, 1989-90, exec. com., 1990-95; mem. and theol. cons. Bishop's Commn. on Evangelism and Church Growth, Diocese of Calif., 1990-91; convenor Conf. of Anglican Ch. Historians, 1987-89; exec. bd. Coun. for Devel. of Min., 1994—; mem. Internat. Anglican-Meth. Ecumenical Commn., 1992—. Author: A Bishop's Household in Late Medieval England: an edition of the account roll of William of Wykeham, Bishop of Winchester for 1393, 1976, rev. edit., 1996, Reform and Authority in the Medieval and Reformation Church, 1981, paperback edit., 1987, Theological Education for the Future, 1988, Lambeth Conferences Past and Present, 1989, (with Stephen Orgel) Patronage in the Renaissance, 1981, paperback edit., 1982; mem. editl. bd. Anglican and Episcopal History, 1986—. Mem. Mayor's Task Force of Religious Leaders and Cmty. Problems, San Francisco, 1990. Avocations: tennis, rare books, music. Home: 484 Roarks Cove Rd Sewanee TN 37375 Office: Univ of the South Sch of Theology 335 Tennessee Ave Sewanee TN 37383

LYTLE, L(ARRY) BEN, insurance company executive, lawyer; b. Greenville, Tex., Sept. 30, 1946; children: Hugh, Larry. BS in Mgmt. Sci. and Indsl. Psychology, East Tex. State U., 1970; JD, Ind. U., 1980. Computer operator/programmer U.S. Govt., Ft. Smith, Ark., 1962-63; customer engr. Olivetti Corp., San Antonio, 1963-64; mgr. computer ops. and computer software LTV Electrosystems, Greenville, 1964-69; project mgr. electronic fin. system, dir. systems planning Assocs. Corp. N.Am., South Bend, Ind., 1969-74; asst. v.p. systems Am. Fletcher Nat. Bank, Indpls., 1974-76; with Assoc. Ins. Cos., Inc., Indpls., 1976—, pres., 1987—, COO, 1987-89, CEO, 1989—, now also chmn., bd. dirs.; CEO, chmn. bd. dirs. Anthem Cos., Inc., Acordia, Inc.; chmn. bd. dirs. AdminaStar, Inc., Health Networks Am., Inc., Novalis, Inc., Robinson-Conner Nev., Inc.; bd. dirs. The Shelby Ins. Group, Raffensperger, Hughes & Co., Inc., Acordia Benefits, Inc., Indpls. Power and Light Co., Indpls. Power and Light Co. Enterprises; mem. adv. bd. CID Venture Ptnrs., Ltd. Partnership; rschr., cons. state and fed. govt. orgns., including, Adv. Coun. on Social Security, Pepper Commn. of U.S. Congress, others. Chmn. health policy commn. State of Ind., Indpls., 1990-92; bd. dirs., mem. exec. com. Community Leaders Allied for Superior Schs.; bd. dirs. Indpls. Convention and Visitors Bur., Indpls. Symphony Orch.; mem. Corp. Community Coun.; active various civic orgns., including United Negro Coll. Fund, Indpls. Mus. Art. Mem. ABA, Ind. Bar Assn., Indpls. Bar Assn., Ind. State C. of C. (bd. dirs.), Indpls. C. of C. (bd. dirs.). Home: 426 E Vermont St Indianapolis IN 46202-3680 Office: Assoc Ins Cos Inc 120 Monument Cir Indianapolis IN 46204-4906*

LYTLE, VICTORIA ELIZABETH, writer, editor; b. Miami Beach, Fla., Aug. 25, 1951; d. Reginald Vivian and Antoinette (Whitfield) L.; m. Edward Hula, Apr. 5, 1975 (Div. Aug. 1979). BA in English, Fla. State U., 1971-74. Asst. pub. rels. dir. Marco Beach Hotel, Marco Island, Fla., 1975-76; assoc. editor Career Edn. Ctr., Tallahassee, 1976-78; writer, editor Am. Vocat. Assn., Alexandria, Va., 1978-80, 81-83; sr. writer, editor Azen, Kaplan & Assocs., Ft. Lauderdale, Fla., 1989; staff writer NEA Today, Washington, 1983-88, 89—; newsletter editor Nat. Urban Coalition, Washington, 1980-81. Contbr. articles to profl. jours. and popular publs. Mem. Women in Communications, Washington Ind. Writers, Toastmasters (v.p. Alexandria 1986-87). Avocations: traveling, reading, swimming. Home: 4650 36th St S # B-2 Arlington VA 22206-1741 Office: NEA 1201 16th St NW Washington DC 20036-3207

LYTTLE, DOUGLAS ALFRED, photographer, educator; b. Three Rivers, Mich., July 7, 1919; s. Stephen Henry and Ruth (Marshall) L.; m. Vivian M. Quell, October 12, 1991; children: Judith Ann Lyttle Nelson, Janet Ruth Lyttle Chobanian, Marsha Jane Lyttle Pidek. B.S. cum laude, U. Mich., 1941. Organic research chemist Merck and Co., Rahway, N.J., 1941-45, Upjohn Co., Kalamazoo, Mich., 1945-60; prin. Douglas Lyttle Photographer, Kalamazoo, 1961-69; mem. faculty Sch. Photog. Arts and Scis., Rochester (N.Y.) Inst. Tech., 1969-83, prof. emeritus, 1983—; freelance photographer. Exhibitor photographs; presenter audio-visual programs based on travels; contbr. photographs to mags. Mem. Profl. Photographers Am., Am. Soc. Photographers, Phi Beta Kappa. Office: 10 Downing Dr Pittsford NY 14534-3612 *The Christian faith, its morality, spirit and theology as active fellowship with God in Christ, is the basis for a life in which people are most important. Honesty with self and others, caring, commitment and a continuing reach for excellence and growth have been keystones for every endeavour. If there has been 'success' it has been a gift and a result.*

LYTTON, ROBERT LEONARD, civil engineer, educator; b. Port Arthur, Tex., Oct. 23, 1937; m. Robert Odell and Nora Mae (Verrett) L.; m. Eleanor Marilyn Anderson, Sept. 9, 1961; children: Lynn Elizabeth, Robert Douglas, John Kirby. BSCE, U. Tex., 1960, MSCE, 1961, PhD, 1967. Registered profl. engr., Tex., La.; registered land surveyor, La. Assoc. Dannenbaum and Assocs., Cons. Engrs., Houston, 1963-65; U.S. NSF fellow U. Tex., Austin, 1965-67, asst. prof., 1967-68; NSF postdoctoral fellow Australian Commonwealth Sci. & Indsl. Rsch. Orgn., Melbourne, Australia, 1969-70; assoc. prof. Tex. A&M U., College Station, 1971-76, prof., 1976-90, Wiley chair prof., 1990-95, dir. ctr. for infrastructure engring., 1991—, Benson chair prof., 1995—; divsn. head Tex. Transp. Inst., 1982-91, head infrastructure and transp. divsn. civil engring. dept., 1993-95; bd. dirs. MLA Labs., Inc., Austin, Trans-tec, Inc., Austin; v.p. bd. dirs. MLAW Cons., Inc., Austin, 1980—, ERES Cons., Inc., Champaign, Ill., 1981-95; prin. investigator strategic hwy. rsch. program A005 rsch. project, 1990-93. Patentee for sys. identification and analysis of subsurface radar signals. Mem. St. Vincent de Paul Soc., Houston, 1963-65, Redemptorist Lay Mission Soc., Melbourne, Australia, 1969-70. Capt. U.S. Army, 1961-63. Recipient SAR medal of honor St. Mary's U., 1957, Soc. Am. Mil. Engrs. Outstanding Sr. cadet U. Tex., 1959, Disting. Mil. grad. award, 1960, Hamilton Watch award Coll. Engring., 1960, Disting. Achievmeent award Tex. A&M U. Assn. Former Students. Fellow ASCE; mem. NSPE, Transp. Rsch. Bd. (chmn. com. A2L06 1987-93), Internat. Soc. for Soil Mechanics & Found. Engring. (U.S. rep. tech. com. TC-6 1987—, keynote address 7th internat. conf. on expansive soils 1992, keynote address 1st internat. conf. on unsaturated soils 1995), Assn. Asphalt Paving Technologists, Post-Tensioning Inst. (adv. bd.), Tex. Soc. Profl. Engrs., Internat. Soc. Asphalt Pavements, Sigma Xi, Phi Kappa Delta, Chi Epsilon, Tau Beta Pi, Phi Kappa Phi. Roman Catholic. Office: Tex A&M U 508G CE/TTI Bldg College Station TX 77843

LYU, SEUNG WON, metallurgical engineer, environmental scientist; b. Seoul, Korea, May 15, 1934; came to U.S., 1958; s. Yohan and Kyun Shin (Kim) L.; m. Yun O. Chung; children: John A., Lori K. BS in Chem. Engring., Ind. Inst. Tech., Ft. Wayne, 1961; BS in Metall. Engring., Ill. Inst. Tech., Chgo., 1975; MAS in Environ. Sci., Governors State U., University Park, Ill., 1981. Registered profl. engr. Ill., Calif.; cert. ind. wastewater treatment operator, Ill. Metallurgist Verson Allsteel Press Co., Chgo., 1962-65; metall. engr. Am. Std.-ARI, Franklin Park, Ill., 1965-67; sr. rsch. metallurgist Continental Group, Oak Brook, Ill., 1967-70; sr. prin. engr. Am. Nat. Can Co., Chgo., 1970-83; asst. prof. Ill. Inst. Tech., Glen Ellyn, Ill., 1983-88; pres., chief engr. Prospect Testing Labs., Des Plaines, Ill., 1985—; tech. cons. Korean Small and Medium Indsl. Promotion Corp., Seoul, 1983; metall. cons. Verson Allsteel Press Co., Chgo., 1985—. Bd. dirs. Korean-Am. Cmty. Svc., Chgo., 1989—, Niles (Ill.) Korean Sch., 1990—. Mem. ASTM. Republican. Presbyterian. Achievements include 6 patents in metallurgy, tooling and container application; method of making tin-layered stock material; die and method of assembly and application; split punch design and wall/bottom profile for containers. Home: 824 Shibley Ave Park Ridge IL 60068-2352 Office: Prospect Testing Labs Inc 1245 E Forest Ave Des Plaines IL 60018-1564

MA, ALAN WAI-CHUEN, lawyer; b. Hong Kong, Apr. 20, 1951; s. Pak Ping and Oi Quon (Hung) M.; m. Carrie Pak, Mar. 17, 1993. BBA, U. Hawaii, 1975; MBA, Chaminade U., 1981; JD, Golden Gate U., 1983. Bar: Hawaii 1984, U.S. Dist. Ct. Hawaii 1984, U.S. Ct. Appeals (9th cir.) 1986, U.S. Supreme Ct. 1989. Ptnr. Oldenberg & Ma, Honolulu, 1984-90; prin. Law Offices Alan W.C. Ma, Honolulu, 1990-95; counsel Goodsill Anderson Quinn & Stifel, Honolulu, 1995—; adj. prof. law U. Hawaii, Honolulu, 1988—. Co-editor: New Waves for Foreign Investors, 1990. Recipient Outstanding Vol. award Hawaii Cmty. Svc. Coun., 1990. Mem. ABA, Am. Immigration Lawyers Assn. (chpt. chair 1993-94), Internat. Bar Assn., Inter-Pacific Bar Assn., U.S. Japan Vols. Assn. (bd. dirs. 1989—), Overseas Chinese Am. Assn. (bd. dirs. 1993-94). Avocation: tennis. Office: Goodsill Anderson et al 1800 Alii Pl 1099 Alakea St Honolulu HI 96813

MA, FENGCHOW CLARENCE, agricultural engineering consultant; b. Kaifeng, Honan, China, Sept. 4, 1919; came to U.S., 1972; s. Chao-Hsiang and Wen-Chieh (Yang) Ma; m. Fanny Luisa Corvera-Achá, Jan. 20, 1963; 1 child, Fernando. BS in Agr., Nat. Chekiang U., Maytan, Kweichow, China, 1942; postgrad., Iowa State U., 1945-46. Cert. profl. agronomist, Republic of China, 1944; registered profl. agrl. engr., Calif. Chief dept. ops. Agrl. Machinery Operation and Mgmt. Office, Shanghai, China, 1946-49; sr. farm machinery specialist Sino-Am. Joint Commn. on Rural Reconstrn., Taipei, Taiwan, Republic of China, 1950-62; agrl. engring. adviser in Bolivia, Peru, Chile, Ecuador, Liberia, Honduras, Grenada, Bangladesh FAO, Rome, 1962-80; consulting agrl. engr. to USAID projects in Guyana & Peru IRI Rsch. Inst., Inc., Stamford, Conn., 1981-82, 83, 85; chief adviser Com. Internat. Tech. Coop., Taipei, 1984-85; pres. FCM Assocs., Inc., 1962—; short consulting missions to Paraguay, Saudi Arabia, Indonesia, Malawi, Swaziland, Barbados, Dominica, Ivory Coast, Vietnam, Philippines, Nicaragua and others. Author papers, studies; contbr. articles to profl. publs. Mem. Am. Soc. Agrl. Engrs. Avocations: reading, stamp and coin collecting. Home: 1004 Azalea Dr Sunnyvale CA 94086-6747 Office: PO Box 70096 Sunnyvale CA 94086-0096

MA, TAI-LOI, library curator, Chinese studies specialist; b. Canton, China, Oct. 14, 1945; came to U.S., 1970; s. James Chun-Woon and Mary (Wong) M. BA, U. Hong Kong, 1969; MA, U. Chgo., 1972, PhD, 1987. Cataloger East Asian Libr., U. Chgo., 1972-78, head cataloger, 1978-87, curator, 1987—; cons. Chinese collection Kinsey Inst. Rsch., Bloomington, Ind., 1983; fellowship paniel NEH, Washington, 1988—; mem. internat. adv. com. Chinese rare books project Rsch. Librs. Group, Mountain View, Calif., 1988—; mem. adv. bd. East Asian Libr. Jour., Princeton, N.J., 1990—; cons. Chinese collection Libr. Congress, 1995. Translator: Traditional Chinese Stories, 1978; contbr. articles to profl. publs. Fellow, scholar U. Chgo., 1970-73; Mellon Found. fellow Princeton U., summer 1980; conf. travel grantee Am. Coun. Learned Socs., Canton, 1983, Com. on Scholarly Comm. with China, Beijing, 1993. Mem. ALA, Assn. for Asian Studies (com. on East Asian librs. exec. group 1989-92, subcom. chmn. 1993-96, pres. coun. on East Asian librs. 1997—). Office: U Chgo East Asian Collection Regenstein Libr 1100 E 57th St Fl 5 Chicago IL 60637-1502

MA, TSO-PING, electrical engineering educator, researcher, consultant; b. Lan-Tsou, Gan-Su, China, Nov. 13, 1945; came to U.S., 1969; s. Liang-Kway and Zwey-Yueen (Liu) Ma; m. Pin-fang Lin, June 10, 1972; children: Mahau, Jasmine. BS, Nat. Taiwan U., 1968; MS, Yale U., 1972, PhD, 1974. Teaching asst. Yale U., New Haven, 1971-74, asst. prof. elec. engring., 1977-80, assoc. prof., 1980-85, prof., 1985—, chmn. dept. elec. engring., 1991-95, acting chmn. dept. elec. engring., 1988, vis. lectr., 1976-77, advisor Yale Chinese Student Svc., 1977—, Yale Mainland-Taiwan Soc.; staff engr. IBM, Hopewell Junction, N.Y., 1974-77; GE Whitney Symposium lectr., 1985; cons. in field. Contbr. articles to profl. jours. Patentee in field. Bd. dirs. New Haven Chinese Sch., 1982—. Grantee Rsch. Corp., 1978, Mobil Found., 1981-84, G.E. Found., 1984; recipient Conn. Yankee Ingenuity award, 1991, B.F. Goodrich Nat. Collegiate Inventor's Advisor award, 1993. Fellow IEEE (chmn. various coms. 1986—, officer semiconductor interface specialists conf. 1986-88); mem. Materials Rsch. Soc., Am. Phys. Soc., Orgn. of Chinese Ams. (pres. New Haven chpt. 1988-90, bd. dirs. 1990—), Electrochem. Soc., Conn. Acad. Sci. and Engring., Yale Figure Skating Club (v.p. 1991-93), Yale Sci. and Engring. Assn., Sigma Xi (v.p. Yale chpt. 1986, pres. 1987-88). Avocations: music, violin, skating. Home: 169 Northford Rd Branford CT 06405-2823 Office: Yale Univ Dept Elec Engring 15 Prospect St New Haven CT 06520-8284

MA, YO-YO, cellist; b. Paris, 1955; m. Jill; children: Nicholas, Emily. Studied with Janos Scholz; studied with Leonard Rose, Juilliard Sch. Music, N.Y.C., 1962; AB, Harvard U., 1976, MusD (hon.), 1991. Debut at age 9, Carnegie Hall, N.Y.C.; appeared with Pablo Casals, Isaac Stern, Leonard Bernstein, Emanuel Ax, Jaime Laredo, performs throughout world with maj. orchs.; rec. artist Sony Classical; recs. include Portrait of Yo-Yo Ma, China and Japan: Japanese Melodies, Anything Goes (with Stephanie Grapelli), Hush (with Bobby McFerrin), Yo-Yo Ma at Tanglewood, The New York Album. Recipient Avery Fisher prize, 1978, Ten-time Grammy award winning artist. Office: ICM Artists 40 W 57th St New York NY 10019 also: Harold Holt Ltd, 31 Sinclair Rd, London W14 0NS, England

MA, YUANXI, Chinese and English language and literature educator, translator; b. Shanghai, China, Feb. 18, 1933; came to U.S., 1985; d. Shu Yuan and Jingxing Ma; m. Zailiang Zhang, Feb. 16, 1958 (div. 1981); children: Xiaodan, Jia. BA, Beijing Fgn. Studies U., China, 1953, MA, 1956; MA, SUNY, Buffalo, 1988, PhD, 1992. Assoc. prof. Beijing Fgn. Studies U., 1953-82; assoc. prof., vice-chair English dept. Inst. Internat. Rels., Beijing, 1982-85; assoc. dir. Sch. Chinese Studies, China Inst., N.Y.C., 1989-95; dir. translation Baker & McKenzie Law Firm, Chgo., 1995—; adj. prof. NYU, 1990-95, The New Sch. for Social Rsch., 1991; interpreter, translator Conf. Internat. Coop. Alliance, Washington, 1985, interpreter, Am.-Chinese Friendship Group traveling in China, 1975. Author: College English, 1983, English, I-V, 1978, 79, TV English, I-III, 1980, English Textbooks, I, II, 1962; translator of lit. works; contbr. to profl. jours. and textbooks; numerous presentations in field. Mem. U.S.-China Friendship Assn., Chinese Lang. Tchr. Assn., Nat. Assn. Women's Studies, Assn. Asian Studies. Home: 333 E Ontario St # 2710 B Chicago IL 60611 Office: Baker & McKenzie Law Firm One Prudential Plz 130 E Randolph Dr Chicago IL 60601

MAAG, URS RICHARD, statistics educator; b. Winterthur, Switzerland, Jan. 20, 1938; m. Tannis Yvonne Arbuckle, July 31, 1965; children: Liane, Karin, Eric. Diploma in Math, Swiss Fed. Inst. Tech., Zurich, 1961; M.Sc., U. Toronto, Can., 1962, Ph.D., 1965. Asst. prof. U. Montreal, Que., Can., 1965-72; assoc. prof. U. Montreal, Can., 1972-78, prof., 1978—. Contbr. articles to profl. jours. Mem. Statis. Soc. Can. (sec. 1973-77, pres. 1980), Am. Statis. Assn. (pres. Montreal chpt. 1975-77), Internat. Statis. Inst., Can. Assn. Rd. Safety Profls., Inst. Math. Stats. Home: 3484 Marlowe Ave, Montreal, PQ Canada H4A 3L7 Office: U Montreal Dept Math and Stats, CP 6128 Succ Centre-ville, Montreal, PQ Canada H3C 3J7

MAAHS, KENNETH HENRY, SR., religion educator; b. Peoria, Ill., June 19, 1940; s. Silas Henry Maahs and Lydia Nettie (Heinold) Blessman; m. Vivian Louise Dawn Englert, Sept. 1, 1962; children: Kirsten Allison Dawn, Kenneth Henry Jr. BA in Philosophy/Theology magna cum laude, Simpson Coll., 1962; MDiv, Fuller Theol. Sem., Pasadena, Calif., 1965; ThM in N.T. Studies, Princeton Theol. Sem., 1966; PhD in Old Testament Studies, So. Bapt. Theol. Sem., Louisville, 1972. Ordained to ministry Missionary Ch./Am. Bapt. Conv., 1968. Instr. Nyack (N.Y.) Coll., 1966-67, Bethel Coll., Mishawaka, Ind., 1968; prof. Bibl. studies Ea. Coll., St. Davids, Pa., 1972—, Abram Clemens chair, 1986—, chmn. dept. religion-philosophy, 1985-88, chmn. humanities div., 1988-92, 95; faculty mem. The Jerusalem Ctr. for Biblical Studies, 1994—; interim pastor Columbus (N.J.) Bapt. Ch., 1975-76, Roxborough Bapt. Ch., Phila., 1980-81, Bapt. Temple, Blue Bell, Pa., 1981-83, Willowgrove (Pa.) Bapt. Ch., 1988, Belmont Bapt. Ch., Broomall, Pa., 1989, Lower Merion Bapt. Ch., Bryn Mawr, Pa., 1989-90, 2d Bapt. Ch. Germantown, Pa., 1990-92, Roxborough Bapt. Ch., Phila., 1992-93, No. Wales (Pa.) Bapt. Ch., 1994—; adj. prof. Ea. Bapt. Theol. Sem., 1980, 83, 85, 89, Lay Acad. of Phila. Bapt. Assn., 1984-86, 88, 90, 94, Fuller Theol. Sem./Young Life's Inst. Youth Ministries, 1986-87, 89.; keynote speaker Am. Bapt. Women's Regional Conf., 1983; feature lectr. Am. Bapt. Commn. on Continuing Edn., 1985. Recipient Legion of Honor award Chapel of Four Chaplains, 1983, Lindback award Ea. Coll., 1984; named Prof. of Yr. Ea. Coll., 1983-84. Mem. Bibl. Archaeology Soc., Soc. Bibl. Lit. Delta Epsilon Chi. Republican. Home: 346 E Valley Forge Rd King Of Prussa PA 19406-2035 Office: Eastern Coll Dept Bibl Studies Saint Davids PA 19087

MAARBJERG, MARY PENZOLD, office equipment company executive; b. Norfolk, Va., Oct. 2, 1943; d. Edmund Theodore and Lucy Adelaide (Singleton) Penzold; m. John Peder Maarbjerg, Oct. 20, 1966; 1 son, Martin Peder. A.B., Hollins Coll., 1965; M.B.A., Wharton Sch., Pa., 1969. Cons. bus. and fin., Stamford, Conn., 1977-78; corp. staff analyst Pitney Bowes, Inc., Stamford, Conn., 1978-80, mgr. pension and benefit fin. 1980-81, dir. investor relations, 1981-85; v.p. planning and devel. Pitney Bowes Credit Corp., Norwalk, Conn., 1985-86; treas., v.p. planning Pitney Bowes Credit Corp., 1986-94; v.p. mkt. devel. and mng. dir. Asia Pacific Bowes Fin. Svcs., 1994-95, v.p. ops. and mng. dir., 1995—. Mem. adv. com. City of Stamford Mcpl. Employees Retirement Fund, 1980-85; mem. fin. adv. com. YWCA, Stamford, 1982-86; bd. dirs. Stamford Symphony, 1985-95, Vis. Nurses Assn., 1984-86, Am. Recorder Soc., 1986—. Fellow Royal Statis. Soc.; mem. Fin. Execs. Inst., Phi Beta Kappa. Congregationalist. Office: Pitney Bowes Credit Corp 201 Merritt Seven Norwalk CT 06856

MAAS, DUANE HARRIS, distilling company executive; b. Tilleda, Wis., Aug. 26, 1927; s. John William and Adela (Giessel) M.; m. Sonja Johnson, Mar. 11, 1950; children: Jon Kermit, Duane Arthur, Thomas Ervin. B.S., U. Wis., 1951. With Shell Chem. Corp., 1951-59; plant mgr. Fleischmann Distilling Corp., Owensboro, Ky., 1959-63, Plainfield, Ill., 1963-65; asst. to v.p. Barton Distilling Co., Chgo., 1965-68; exec. asst. to pres. Barton Distilling Co., 1968, v.p. adminstrn., 1968; v.p., gen. mgr. Barton Brands, Inc., Chgo., 1968—72; pres. Leaf Confectionery div. W.R. Grace, Chgo., 1972-74; v.p., gen. mgr. Romano Bros., Chgo., 1974-79; v.p., sec.-treas. Marketing Directions Inc., Chgo., 1974-77; pres. Associated Wine Producers, Inc., 1979—; exec. v.p., chief exec. officer Mohawk Liqueur, Detroit, 1980-86; v.p. McKesson Wine & Spirits Group of N.Y., Detroit, 1982-86; pres. Mgmt. Cons. Services Co., Chgo., 1986—; past pres. Barton Distilling (Can.), Ltd.; past mng. dir. Barton Distilling (Scotland), Ltd.; past dir. Barton Distillers Europe, Barton Internat., Ltd. Sec.-treas. Plainfield Twp. Park Dist., 1967-70; chmn. Plainfield Planning and Zoning Commn., 1965-70. Served with USAAF, 1945-47. Mem. Wis. Alumni Assn. Lutheran. Home: 13264 W Highway 29 Bowler WI 54416 Office: 3135 Centennial Ct Highland Park IL 60035-1015

MAAS, JAMES BERYL, psychology educator, lecturer, filmmaker; b. Detroit, Aug. 9, 1938; s. Royal Sheldon and Mary Ann (Weiner) M.; m. Nancy Christine Neaher, July 28, 1979; children: Daniel, Justin. BA, Williams Coll., 1960; MA, Cornell U., 1963, PhD, 1966. Asst. prof. psychology Cornell U., Ithaca, N.Y., 1964-70, assoc. prof., 1970-79, prof., 1980—, chmn. dept., 1985-90, Stephen H. Weiss Presdl. fellow, 1993—; Fulbright prof. Uppsala (Sweden) U., 1969-70; observer BBC-TV, London, 1974; vis. prof. Stanford (Calif.) U., 1979; mgmt. cons. IBM, Armonk, N.Y., 1983—. Producer: (films) Until I Get Caught, 1980 (Am. FilmFest award 1980), Learning to See, 1983 (Am. FilmFest award 1983); producer, dir. Let's Build it Together, 1985 (Am. FilmFest award 1985), Where Have All the Teachers Gone, 1987; producer Bravo Gloria, 1988, Sleep Alert!, 1990, To Light a Fire, 1992, Asleep in the Fast Lane, 1995; producer 9 nat. PBS TV spls. Winner 42 film festivals for documentary films; recipient Clark Disting. Teaching award Cornell U., 1972, Rush Silver medal Psychiat. Assn., 1978, 79, 80. Mem. Am. Psychol. Assn. (pres. div. on teaching 1974-75, disting. teaching award 1973). Avocations: tennis, photography, sailing. Office: Cornell U 210 Uris Hall Ithaca NY 14853-7601

MAAS, JANE BROWN, advertising executive; b. Jersey City; d. Charles E. and Margaret (Beck) Brown; m. Michael Maas, Aug. 30, 1957; children: Katherine, Jennifer. BA, Bucknell U., 1953; postgrad., U. Dijon, France, 1954; MA, Cornell U., 1955; LittD, Ramapo Coll., 1986, St. John's U., 1988. Assoc. producer Name That Tune TV Program, N.Y.C., 1957-64; v.p. Ogilvy and Mather Inc., N.Y.C., 1964-76; sr. v.p. Wells, Rich, Greene, Inc., N.Y.C., 1976-82; pres. Muller Jordan Weiss Inc., N.Y.C., 1982-89; pres. Earle Palmer Brown Cos., N.Y.C., 1989-92, chmn., 1992-94, chmn. emeritus, 1994—. Co-author: How to Advertise, 1975, Better Brochures, 1981, Adventures of a Advertising Woman, 1986, The New How to Advertise, 1992, Christmas in Wales: a Homecoming, 1994. Trustee Bucknell U., Lewisburg, 1976-86, Fordham U., N.Y., 1983-91; bd. govs. com. Scholastic Achievement, 1985-92; active Girl Scouts U.S. Greater N.Y., 1970-76; mem. adv. bd. William E. Simon Grad. Sch. Bus. U. Rochester, 1989—, pub. dir. AIA, 1993-95. Recipient Matrix award Women in Communications, 1980, N.Y. Advt. Woman of Yr., 1986. Mem. AIA (hon.), Am. Archtl. Found. (regent 1993—), Am. Assn. Advt. Agys. (bd. govs.). Avocations: creative writing, jogging. Home: PO Box 1109 Westhampton Beach NY 11978-7109

MAAS, JOE (MELVIN JOSEPH MAAS), federal agency administrator; b. Washington; s. Melvin Joseph and Katherine (Endress) M.; m. Constance Mary Haile, June 13, 1965; children: Christine, Michael, Kevin. BS, U. Md., 1965; postgrad., Stanford U., 1972-73. Dir. career edn. U.S. Dept. Labor, Washington, 1969-73; dep. dir. pers. SBA, Washington, 1973-76, dir. pers., 1976-82, asst. adminstr., 1982-95; mem. Internat. Pers. Assn., 1981-83, chairperson, 1982. Bd. dirs., treas. Snowden Mill Assn., Silver Spring, Md., 1991; Wash. rep. Ind. Charities of Am., 1995—. Col. USMC, 1957-58.

Mem. Fed. Exec. Adminstrs. Assn., Sr. Exec. Assn., Pub. Employee Roundtable (bd. dirs. 1994—), Coun. Former Fed. Execs. (bd. dirs. 1995—), Volkswagen Club (pres. Washington club 1988-95). Roman Catholic. Home: 2213 Aventurine Way Silver Spring MD 20904-5253

MAAS, PETER, writer; b. N.Y.C., June 27, 1929; s. Carl and Madeleine (Fellheimer) M.; m. Audrey Gellen, Apr. 4, 1962 (dec. July 1975); 1 child, John Michael; m. Suzanne Jones, Feb. 1, 1986; 1 child, Terrence. B.A., Duke U., 1949; postgrad., The Sorbonne, Paris, 1950. Reporter N.Y. Herald Tribune, Paris, 1950-52; assoc. editor Collier's mag., 1954-56; sr. editor Look mag., 1959-61; contbg. writer Sat. Evening Post, 1961-66; cons. Curtis Pub. Co., 1966-67; contbg. editor New York mag., 1968-71. Free lance contbr. to nat. mags., newspapers, 1954—; author: The Rescuer, 1967, The Valachi Papers, 1969, Serpico, 1973, King of the Gypsies, 1975, Made in America, 1979, Marie: A True Story, 1983, Manhunt, 1986, Father and Son, 1989, In A Child's Name, 1990, China White, 1994, Killer Spy, 1995; works included in anthology. Served with USNR, 1952-54. Mem. PEN Am. Center, Author's Guild. Roman Catholic. Office: care Internat Creative Mgmt 40 W 57th St New York NY 10019-4001

MAAS, WERNER KARL, microbiology educator; b. Kaiserslautern, Germany, Apr. 27, 1921; came to U.S., 1936, naturalized, 1945; s. Albert and Esther (Meyer) M.; m. Renata Diringer, Oct. 15, 1960; children—Peter, Andrew, Helen. AB, Harvard U., 1943; PhD, Columbia U., 1948. Postdoctoral fellow Calif. Inst. Tech., Pasadena, 1946-48; commd. officer USPHS, Tb Research Lab., Cornell U. Sch., N.Y.C., 1948-54; asst. prof. pharmacology NYU, 1954-57, assoc. prof. microbiology, 1957-63, prof., 1963-94, prof. emeritus, 1994—, chmn. dept. basic med. scis., 1974-81. Career grantee USPHS, 1962-94. Mem. Am. Soc. Biol. Chemists, Genetics Soc. Am., Am. Soc. Microbiology. Home: 86 Villard Ave Hastings on Hudson NY 10706-1821 Office: 550 1st Ave New York NY 10016-6481

MAASS, ARTHUR, political science and environmental studies educator; b. Balt., July 24, 1917; s. Arthur Leopold and Selma (Rosenheim) M. A.B., Johns Hopkins, 1939; M.P.A., Harvard, 1941, Ph.D., 1949. Adminstrv. asst. Bur. Budget, 1939-40; intern Nat. Inst. Pub. Affairs, 1939-40; research technician Nat. Resources Planning Bd., 1941-42; budget analyst Dept. Navy, 1946; water resources analyst Natural Resources Task Force, Hoover Commn., 1948; faculty Harvard, 1949—, prof. govt., 1959-67, Frank G. Thomson prof. govt., 1967-84, prof. emeritus, 1984—, chmn. dept., 1963-67; cons. Office Dir. Budget, 1949, Office Sec. Interior, 1950-52, Pres.'s Materials Policy Commn., 1951-52, TVA, 1952, C.E., 1961—, Bur. Reclamation, 1971, Ministry Water Conservancy, People's Republic China, 1980—; vis. prof. polit. sci. U. Calif. at Berkeley, 1951, U. P.R., 1955, El Colegio de México, 1986, U. Internat. Menendez y Pelayo, Valencia, Spain, 1990. Author: Muddy Waters, The Army Engineers and the Nation's Rivers, 1951, Congress and the Common Good, 1983, Water Law and Institutions in the Western U.S.: Comparisons with Early Developments in California and Australia, Contemporary Developments in Australia and Recent Legislation Worldwide, 1990; co-author: Area and Power, 1959, Design of Water-Resource Systems: New Techniques for Relating Economic Objectives, Engineering Analysis and Governmental Planning, 1962, A Simulation of Irrigation Systems, 1971, rev., 1974, 78, 87, Chinese edit., 1980, . . . and the Desert Shall Rejoice: Conflict, Growth and Justice in Arid Environments, 1978, rev. edit., 1986, Un Modelo de Simulacion Para Sistemas de Regadio, 1985; contbr. articles to profl. jours. Served to lt. comdr. USNR, 1942-46. Guggenheim fellow, 1955; Fulbright research fellow Spain, 1960-61; Faculty research fellow Social Sci. Research Council, 1961. Club: Harvard (N.Y.C.). Home: 63 Atlantic Ave Boston MA 02110-3716 Office: Harvard U Littauer Ctr Cambridge MA 02138

MAATMAN, GERALD LEONARD, insurance company executive; b. Chgo., Mar. 11, 1930; s. Leonard Raymond and Cora Mae (Van Der Laag) M.; children: Gerald L. Jr., Mary Ellen; m. Bernice Catherine Brummer, June 3, 1971. BS, Ill. Inst. Tech., 1951. Asst. chief engineer Ill. Inspection & Rating Bur., Chgo., 1951-58; prof., dept. chmn. Ill. Inst. Tech., Chgo., 1959-65; v.p. engring. Kemper Group, Chgo., 1966-68, pres. Nat. Loss Control Svc. Corp., 1969-74; v.p. corp. planning Kemper Group, Long Grove, Ill., 1974-79, sr. v.p. info. svcs. group, 1979-85, exec. v.p. ins. ops., 1985-87; pres. Kemper Nat. Ins. Co., Long Grove, Ill., 1987-92, CEO, 1989-95, also bd. dirs., chmn. bd. dirs., 1991-95. Bd. dirs. Advs. for Auto and Hwy. Safety, 1992—, Nat. Down Syndrome Soc., Underwriters Labs. Lt. (j.g.) USCGR, 1952-54. Mem. Am. Inst. Assn. (bd. dirs. 1992-95), Ins. Inst. for Hwy. Safety (bd. dirs. 1991-95), Wynstone Golf Club, Tau Beta Pi. Republican. Roman Catholic.

MAATSCH, DEBORAH JOAN, trust administrator, compliance officer, paralegal tax specialist; b. Lincoln, Nebr., Mar. 26, 1950; d. Leon F. Forst and Jarolyn J. Hoffman Forst Conrad; m. Gordon F. Maatsch, Mar. 14, 1969; children: Jason, Diana. BS, U. Nebr., 1976. Acct., supr. U.S. Civil Svc., Heidelberg, Ger., 1971-73; paralegal Mattson Rickets Davies et al, Lincoln, Nebr., 1976-87; tax cons. Lincoln and Denver, 1981—; pres. DGJD Inc.-Bleachers, 1993—; paralegal Wade Ash Woods & Hill, P.C., Denver, 1986-94; sr. trust adminstr. Investment Trust Co., Denver, 1994—; compliance officer Nelson, Benson and Zellmer, Inc., 1995—; mem. Denver Trust Officers Assocs., bus. adv. bd. Ponderosa H.S., 1994—; officer The "O" Streeters, Lincoln, 1984-87; spkr., coord. Nebr. Continuing Legal Edn. Seminars, 1976-86. Contbr. articles to profl. jours. Officer The Aurorians Synchronized Swim Team Parents Orgn., Rocky Mt. Spash Parents' Corp.; youth edn. staff Ave Maria Cath. Ch., Parker, Colo., 1990-91; vol., chmn. activities PTSA Ponderosa H.S. Mem. Doane Coll. Alumni Assn. (dir. 1989-93), Rocky Mt. Legal Assts. (dir., sect. chair 1990-94), Am. Soc. Women Accts. (officer, dir.), Nebr. Assn. Legal Assts. (officer, dir. 1976-87), Colo. Bar Assn. (computer probate sect.), Phi Chi Theta (treas. 1988-89). Avocations: travel, snow skiing, outdoor activities, motorcycles, home decorating. Office: Investment Trust Co 455 Sherman St Ste 180 Denver CO 80203-4400

MAAZEL, LORIN, conductor, composer, violinist; b. Neuilly, France, Mar. 6, 1930; s. Lincoln and Marie (Varencove) M.; m. Dietlinde Turban, 1986; 3 children; 4 children from previous marriages. Studies with, Vladimir Bakaleinikoff; student, U. Pitts., Mus. D. (hon.), 1968; H.H.D., Beaver Coll., 1973. Debut as condr., 1938; condr. Am. symphony orchs., 1939—; violin recitalist; European debut, 1953; festivals include Bayreuth, Salzburg, Edinburgh; tours include S.Am., Australia, USSR, Japan, Korea, People's Republic China; artistic dir. Deutsche Opera Berlin, 1965-71; assoc. prin. condr. New Philharm. Orch., London, 1970-72; dir. Cleve. Orch., 1972-82, condr. emeritus, 1982-86; dir. Vienna State Opera, 1982-84; music dir. Pitts. Symphony Orch., 1988-96, Orchestre Nat. de France, 1988-90, Bavarian Radio Symphony Orch., Munich, 1993—. Decorated officer Legion d'Honneur 1981; Finnish Commdr. of the Lion; Portuguese Commdr.; Bundesverdienstkreuz, Germany.

MABBS, EDWARD CARL, management consultant; b. St. Louis, Sept. 8, 1921; s. Ralph I. and Anna (Renner) M.; m. Margaret E. von Paulsen, Oct. 16, 1943; children: Susan, Carl, Kenneth, Meg. BS in Mech. Engring., Cornell U., 1943. Registered profl. engr. With Linde div. Union Carbide Corp., Newark, Essington, Pa., Tonawanda, N.Y., 1946-55; plant mgr. Wright Hoist div., York, Pa., 1955-62; group v.p. Am. Chain & Cable Co., Bridgeport, Conn., 1962-68, exec. v.p., dir., 1968-71; pres., CEO, dir. Esterline Corp., N.Y.C., 1971-72; pres. Indsl. Components group Rockwell Internat. Corp., Pitts., 1972-75; pres., CEO, dir. Incom Internat. Inc., Pitts., 1975-81; mgmt. cons. Tavernier, Fla., 1981-84; chmn., CEO, dir. L.B. Foster Co., Pitts., 1984-86; past dir. Cross & Trecker Corp., Signode Industries, Arnold Corp., SPD Techs., Inc. Trustee emeritus Point Park Coll.; v.p. Pompeau coun. Boy Scouts Am.; past dir. Friends of Islamorada Area State Parks. Served to capt. U.S. Army, 1943-46, ETO. Mem. Internat. Materials Mgmt. Soc. (past dir.), Am. Prodn. and Inventory Control Soc. (past dir.), Bridgeport (Conn., York, Pa.) C. of C. (past dir.), Material Handling Inst. (past pres.). Home: PO Box 679 Tavernier FL 33070-0679

MABEE, CARLETON, historian, educator; b. Shanghai, China, Dec. 25, 1914; s. Fred Carleton and Miriam (Bentley) M.; m. Norma Dierking, Dec. 20, 1945; children: Timothy I., Susan (Mrs. Paul Newhouse). A.B., Bates Coll., 1936; M.A. (Perkins scholar), Columbia U., 1938, Ph.D., 1942. With Civilian Pub. Svc., 1941-45; Instr. history Swarthmore (Pa.) Coll., 1944; tutor Olivet (Mich.) Coll., 1947-49; asst. prof. liberal studies Clarkson Coll. Tech., Potsdam, N.Y., 1949-51; asso. prof. Clarkson Coll. Tech., 1951-55; prof., 1955-61; dir. social studies div. Delta Coll., University Center, Mich., 1961-64; prof., chmn. dept. humanities and social scis. Rose Poly. Inst., Terre Haute, Ind., 1964-65; prof. history State U. Coll. at New Paltz, N.Y., 1965-80; prof. emeritus State U. Coll. at New Paltz, 1980—; participant in projects for Am. Friends Service Com., 1941-47, 53, 63; Fulbright prof. Keio U., Tokyo, 1953-54. Author: The American Leonardo, A Life of Samuel F.B. Morse, 1943, The Seaway Story, 1961, Black Freedom: The Nonviolent Abolitionists from 1830 through the Civil War, 1970, Black Education in New York State: From Colonial to Modern Times, 1979; author: (with Susan Mabee Newhouse) Sojourner Truth: Slave, Prophet, Legend, 1993; Listen to the Whistle: An Ancedotal History of the Wallkill Valley Railroad in Ulster and Orange Counties, N.Y., 1995; also articles; editor: (with James A. Fletcher) A Quaker Speaks from the Black Experience: The Life and Selected Writings of Barrington Dunbar, 1979. Trustee Young-Morse Hist. Site, Poughkeepsie, N.Y.; bd. dirs. Wallkill Valley Land Trust, New Paltz, N.Y. Recipient Pulitzer prize in biography, 1944, Bergstein award for excellence in teaching Delta Coll., 1963, Anisfield-Wolf award race rels., 1971, Gustavus Myers award for outstanding book on human rights, 1994; rsch. grantee Rsch. Found. SUNY, 1965, 67, 68, 80, Am. Philos. Soc., 1970, Nat. Inst. Edn., 1973-76, NSF, 1982-83. Mem. N.Y. State Hist. Assn., Phi Beta Kappa, Delta Sigma Rho. Methodist. Home: 2121 Route 44-55 Gardiner NY 12525-5808

MABEY, RALPH R., lawyer; b. Salt Lake City, May 20, 1944; s. Rendell Noel and Rachel (Wilson) M.; m. Sylvia States, June 5, 1968; children: Rachel, Elizabeth, Emily, Sara. BA, U. Utah, 1968; JD, Columbia U., 1972. Bar: Utah 1972, U.S. Dist. Ct. Utah 1972, U.S. Ct. Appeals (10th cir.) 1976, N.Y. 1985, U.S. Supreme Ct. 1988, U.S. Ct. Appeals (4th cir.) 1988, U.S. Ct. Appeals (3d cir.) 1993. Law clk. Atty. Gen., Salt Lake City, 1970, U.S. Dist. Ct., Salt Lake City, 1972-73; ptnr. Irvine, Smith & Mabey, Salt Lake City, 1973-79; U.S. bankruptcy judge U.S. Ct., Salt Lake City, 1979-83; ptnr. LeBoeuf, Lamb, Greene & MacRae, Salt Lake City and N.Y.C., 1983—; adj. prof. Brigham Young U. Sch. Law, Provo, Utah, 1983—, U. Utah Coll. Law, Salt Lake City, 1983-85. Mng. editor Norton Bankruptcy Law Adviser, 1983-85; contbg. author: Collier Bankruptcy Manual, 1986—, Collier on Bankruptcy, 15th Edition. With USAR, 1968-74. Mem. ABA (bus. bankruptcy com., joint task force bankruptcy court structure and insolvency processes), Nat. Bankruptcy Conf., Am. Bankruptcy Inst., Am. Coll. Bankruptcy (bd. dirs.). Republican. Mormon. Avocation: running. Home: 253 S 1550 E Bountiful UT 84010-1350 Office: LeBoeuf Lamb Greene & MacRae 1000 Kearns Bldg 136 S Main St Salt Lake City UT 84101-1601 also: 125 W 55th St New York NY 10019-5369

MABLEY, JACK, newspaper columnist, communications consultant; b. Binghamton, N.Y., Oct. 26, 1915; s. Clarence Ware and Mabelle (Howe) M.; m. Frances Habeck, Aug. 29, 1940; children: Mike, Jill, Ann, Pat, Robert. B.S., U. Ill., 1938. With Chgo. Daily News, 1938-61, reporter, writer, columnist, 1957-61; columnist Chgo.'s Am., 1961-69, asst. mng. editor, 1966-69; asso. editor Chgo. Today, 1969-73; columnist Chgo. Today, Chgo. Tribune, 1973-74, Chgo. Tribune, 1974-82; pres. Mabley & Assocs., Corp. Communications, Glenview, Ill., 1982; columnist Daily Herald, Arlington Heights, Ill., 1987—; Lectr. journalism Northwestern U., 1949-50. Pres. Village of Glenview, Ill., 1957-61, Skokie Valley Community Hosp., Skokie, Ill., 1977-79. Served from ensign to lt. USNR, 1941-45. Recipient Media award Nat. Assn. for Retarded Citizens, 1977. Home and Office: 2275 Winnetka Rd Glenview IL 60025-1825

MABOUDIAN, MANSOUR, architect; b. Tehran, Iran, Mar. 21, 1960; came to U.S., 1978; s. Aliasghar and Sedigheh Maboudian. BArch, Cath. U. Am., 1982, MArch, 1984. Project architect Thomas Manion Architects, Cabin John, Md., 1985-87; sr. project architect Greenwell Goetz Architects, Washington, 1987—. Prin. works include Nasa Auditorium Project; featured in various arch. mags. Recipient Steelcase Design award Steelcase Mfg., 1990, AIA/DC Excellence award, 1993, Outstanding Achievement award IBD/Interior Design Mag., 1993, GSA Design award, 1994, ID 40th Annual Design Rev. award, 1994. Office: Greenwell Goetz Architects 1310 G St NW Washington DC 20005

MABRY, CATHY DARLENE, elementary school educator; b. Atlanta, Dec. 9, 1951; d. German William and Erma Isabel (Lyons) M. BA in Sociology and Psychology, U. Ga., 1975; Cert. in Edn., Oglethorpe U., Atlanta, 1983, MA in Elem. Edn., 1990. Cert. in early childhood edn., Ga. Charge account svcs. staff C&S Nat. Bank, Atlanta, 1974-75; with Rich's, Decatur, Ga., 1975-76, 79-84; mgr. trainee sales Sears Roebuck & Co., Decatur, 1974-75, 76-78; intermediate clk. Superior Ct. of DeKalb County, Decatur, 1978-81; paraprofl. kindergarten DeKalb County Sch. Sys., Decatur, 1979-81, tchr., 1984—; mem. sch.-based mgmt. com. Hooper Alexander Sch., Decatur, 1991-92, strategic planning com., 1990—; mem. social studies curriculum com. DeKalb County Sch. Sys., 1990-91, tchr. forum rep., 1992—. Author poetry in Am. Poetry Anthology, 1986. Sec. Lithonia Civic League, Inc., 1987—, Teen Scene, Inc., Lithonia, 1993-94; chair bd. dirs. DeKalb Econ. Opportunity Authority, Decatur, 1991-92, 93—; mem. Teach Well Wellness Program, Emory U. Sch. Pub. Health, 1994; active PTA. Mem. NAACP, Nat. Coun. of Negro Women, Inc., Nat. Geog. Soc., DeKalb Assn. Educators, Zeta Phi Beta. Democrat. Baptist. Avocations: reading, cooking, nature walks, writing poetry, listening to gospel/jazz. Home: 7109 Rhodes St Lithonia GA 30058-4235 Office: Hooper Alexander Sch 3414 Memorial Dr Decatur GA 30032-2708

MABRY, DONALD JOSEPH, university administrator, history educator; b. Atlanta, Apr. 21, 1941; s. Jerry Leon and Eunice Leigh (Harris) M.; m. Susan Strong Johnston, July 28, 1962 (div. Oct. 1986); children: Scott, Mark; m. Paula Ann Crockett, Dec. 18, 1992. BA, Kenyon Coll., Gambier, Ohio, 1963; MEd, Bowling Green State U., 1964; PhD, Syracuse U., 1970. Instr. St. Johns River Community Coll., Palatka, Fla., 1964-67; rsch. asst. fin. aid Syracuse (N.Y.) U., 1967-68, teaching fellow in history, 1968-69, Maxwell fellow, 1969-70, vis. lectr. dept. history, 1969, 70; asst. to chancellor U. Kans., Lawrence, 1978-79; from. asst. prof. to prof. dept. history Miss. State U., Mississippi State, 1970—, asst. to pres., 1979-81, assoc. dean for budget and rsch., 1991—; now dir., assoc. dean Biol. Physical Sciences Rsch. Inst., Mississippi State, Miss.; sr. fellow Ctr. for Internat. Security and Strategic Studies, Miss. State U., 1981—. Author: Mexico's Accion Nacional, 1973, The Mexican University and the State, 1982, (with others) Neighbors--Mexico and the United States, 1981; editor: The Latin American Narcotics Trade and U.S. National Security, 1989; contbr. articles to profl. jours. Mem. Am. Coun. on Edn. (exec. com. Coun. of Fellows 1980-83), South Ea. Coun. on Latin Am. Studies. Avocation: computer telecommunications. Home: 206 Hiwassee Dr Starkville MS 39759-2117 Office: Mississippi State U College of Arts & Sciences Box AS Mississippi State MS 39762

MABUS, BARBARA JEAN, special needs educator; b. Cleve., Nov. 6, 1950; d. Elmer Wilhelm and Florence Pauline Witzke; m. Stephen Michael Mabus, June 29, 1974; 1 child, Mark Samuel. BS in Edn., Bowling Green U., 1973, postgrad., 1991, 94; postgrad., Baldwin-Wallace Coll., 1991. Cert. 7-12 English and earth sci. educator, provision grad. tchr., Ohio. Tchr. lang. arts Bellefontaine (Ohio) City Schs., 1973-74; substitute tchr. Bryan (Ohio) City Schs., 1974-76, 90-93, spl. needs tutor, 1993—, vol. art appreciation tchr., 1988-91; substitute tchr. Williams County Schs., Bryan, 1974-76, 90-92; tchr. sci., health and phys. edn. St. Patrick Sch., Bryan, 1991. Leader 4-H, Bryan, 1987—; active Clowns of Grace, Bryan, 1991—; youth leader Grace Cmty. Ch., Bryan, 1992-93. Co-recipient Disting. Citizen of Yr. award N.W. Ohio Art Edn. Assn., 1990, tchr. recognition award Supporting Our Challenged Kids, 1995. Mem. NEA, Ohio Edn. Assn., Bryan Edn. Assn. (scholarship com. 1993-94), Coun. for Learning Disabilities. Avocations: colonial crafts, collecting memories, writing, hiking, clown ministry. Home: 115 W Trevitt St Bryan OH 43506-1229 Office: Bryan Mid Sch 1301 Center St Bryan OH 43506-9125

MACADAM, WALTER KAVANAGH, consulting engineering executive; b. N.Y.C., Nov. 16, 1913; s. John Moore and Mary (Kavanagh) MacA.; m. Rilla Reed, Jan. 30, 1941; children: Ann (Mrs. Dennis P. Delorier), Marie (Mrs. Paul Hoffman), Clair (Mrs. Bruno Aimi), Daniel, David, Barbara. B.S. and M.S. in Elec. Engring, Mass. Inst. Tech., 1937. With AT&T, 1937-68, with long lines dept., 1951-53, 54-56; supt. engring Distant Early Warning radar installation in Arctic for Western Electric Co., 1953-54; transmission engr. AT&T, 1956-59, bldg. and equipment engr., 1959, asst. chief engr., 1959-60, v.p. def., 1960-68; v.p. engring. N.Y. Telephone Co., 1968-73; cons. engr., 1973—. Bd. dirs. United Engring. Trustees, 1965-73, pres., 1971; mem. N.H. Legis. Acad. Sci. and Tech., 1980-82, N.H. Adv. Panel on Pub. Utility Legis., 1985-86. Recipient Vail medal AT&T, 1937. Fellow IEEE (dir. 1963-68, pres. 1967 Centennial medal); mem. ASME, Nat. Soc. Profl. Engrs., Sigma Xi, Tau Beta Pi, Eta Kappa Nu. Club: K.C. (4 deg.). Home: 9 Pinewood Vlg West Lebanon NH 03784-3120

MACAGBA, RUFINO L., JR., physician, international agency executive; b. San Fernando, Philippines, Feb. 3, 1933; came to U.S., 1974; s. Rufino N. Sr. and Crispina (Lorenzana) M.; m. Victoria D. Reyes, Apr. 10, 1957; children: Carol Lynn, Rufino III, Jonathan, Michelle. MD, U. Philippines, Manila, 1957; MPH, UCLA, 1975. Hosp. adminstr., chief surgeon Lorma Hosp., San Fernando, 1960-74; internat. health advisor World Vision Internat., Calif., 1975-88, exec. mgmt. trainer, 1982-84; pres. Lorma Hosp. and Coll., 1980—, Health Devel. Internat., Calif., 190—; internat. health coord. Food for the Hungry, Scottsdale, Ariz., 1990-95, head internat. tech. and managerial svcs., 1994-95; dir. MBA program Pacific Christian Coll., Fullerton, Calif., 1995—; freelance cons. to World Vision Relief and Devel., Inc., Monrovia, Calif., World Bank, Washington, U. of the Nations, Kona, Hawaii, Mercy Corps Internat., Portland, Oreg., Food for the Hungry Internat. Author books and booklets, including: Health Care Guidelines for Use in Developing Countries, 1977, Hospitals and Primary Health Care, 1984, What World Vision Staff Should Know About AIDS, 1987, (with Mike O. Minodin) Selected Publications for Community Health Care, 1987, also articles. Mem. Nat. Coun. for Internat. Health (bd. dirs. 1978-80), Internat. Hosp. Fedn. (travelling fellow 1982-84), Health Devel. Internat. (pres. 1991-95). Republican. Christian. Avocations: computers, travel, electronics. Home: 1352 Briarcroft Rd Claremont CA 91711-3001 Office: Pacific Christian Coll MBA Program 2500 E Nutwood Ave Fullerton CA 92631

MACAL, ZDENEK, conductor; b. Jan. 8, 1936. Ed., Janacek Music Acad. Music dir. Milw. Symphony Orch., 1986—; chief condr. Cologne Radio Orch., 1970-74; former chief condr. Prague Symphony, Hannover Radio Orch., Sydney Symphony Orch. Office: Milw Symphony Orch 330 E Kilbourn Ave Ste 900 Milwaukee WI 53202-3141

MACALUSO, FRANK AUGUSTUS, oil company executive; b. Cheyenne, Wyo., May 27, 1931; s. Frank R. and Thelma Elizabeth (Speight) M.; m. Margaret Ann Lynch, Oct. 14, 1950; children: Anne Marie Macaluso Foust, Elizabeth Mary Macaluso Nance, Margaret Mary Macaluso Walters, Teresa Marie Macaluso Fleming, Frank A. Jr. AB in Bus. Adminstrn., Regis Coll., 1950. Asst. cashier Merchants Bank, Gallup, N.Mex., 1950-52, Citizens Bank, Aztec, N.Mex., 1952-56; v.p. 1st Nat. Bank, Farmington, N.Mex., 1957-59; founder, chmn., CEO, Macaluso Oil Co., Farmington, 1959—; organizer, chmn. bd. dirs. Sunwest Bank, Farmington, 1974—; chmn. bd. dirs. Amigo Petroleum Co., Albuquerque, 1988—; chmn. Texaco Wholesale Coun., 1994. Mem. Gov's. Bus. Adv. Coun., 1991—, N.Mex. State Bd. Fin., Santa Fe, 1970-82, 91—, N.Mex. 1st, Albuquerque, 1986—; bd. dirs. U. N.Mex. Found., Albuquerque, 1988—. Named Boss of Yr. by Jaycees, 1971. Mem. N.Mex. Petroleum Marketers Assn. (pres. 1974-75), N.Mex. Amigos, San Juan Country Club (pres. 1980-82), Farmington C. of C., KC, Elks. Democrat. Roman Catholic. Avocation: golf. Office: 2501 E Main St # 90 Farmington NM 87401-7723

MACAN, WILLIAM ALEXANDER, IV, lawyer; b. Boston, Nov. 21, 1942; s. William Am. and Carol (Whitten) M.; m. Jane Mitchell Ahern, Sept. 3, 1965; children: Sandra Jane, William Andrew. BS, Haverford Coll., 1964; LLB, U. Pa., 1967. Bar: Pa. 1968, U.S. Tax Ct. 1970. Law clk. to judge U.S. Tax Ct., Washington, 1967-69; assoc. firm Morgan, Lewis & Bockius, Phila., 1969-76; ptnr. Morgan, Lewis & Bockius L.L.P., 1976—; lectr. legal instns., seminars. Author publs. on tax-oriented equipment leasing, other tax subjects. Mem. ABA, Pa. Bar Assn., Phila. Bar Assn. Republican. Presbyterian. Office: Morgan Lewis & Bockius LLP 101 Park Ave New York NY 10178 also: 2000 One Logan Sq Philadelphia PA 19103

MACARIO, ALBERTO JUAN LORENZO, physician; b. Naschel, Argentina, Dec. 1, 1935; came to U.S., 1974, naturalized, 1980; s. Alberto Carlos and Maria Elena (Giraudi) M.; MD, Nat. U. Buenos Aires, 1961; m. Everly Conway, Mar. 16, 1963; children: Alex, Everly. Intern, Ramos Mejia Hosp., Buenos Aires, 1958-60, resident 1960; resident Rivadavia Hosp., Buenos Aires, 1961-62, physician-hematologist, 1962-64; fellow NRC Argentina, Buenos Aires, 1964-69; head dept. radioactive isotopes Inst. Hematological Investigations, Nat. Acad. Medicine Argentina, Buenos Aires, 1967-69; Eleanor Roosevelt fellow Internat. Union Against Cancer, Dept. Tumorbiology, Karolinska Inst., Stockholm, 1969-71; mem. sci. staff Lab. Cell Biology, NRC Italy, Rome, 1971-73; head Lab. Immunology, Internat. Agy. Rsch. on Cancer, WHO, Lyons, France, 1973-74; research scientist Brown U., Providence, 1974-76, Div. Labs. and Rsch., N.Y. State Dept. Health, Albany, 1976-79; chief hematology Clin. Lab. Center, N.Y. State Dept. Health, Albany, 1979-81, dir. clin. and exptl. immunology sect. Lab. Medicine Inst., 1981-83; rsch. physician, 1981—, Wadsworth Ctr. for Labs. and Rsch. N.Y. State Dept. of Health; prof. Dept. Biomed. Scis. Sch. Pub. Health U. at Albany, 1985—, mem. senate at SUNY Albany, N.Y., 1989-94; adj. prof. pathology and lab. medicine Albany Med. Coll., 1991—; grant reviewer for nat. and internat. agys.; manuscript reviewer for sci. jours. Recipient Diploma de Honor prize Nat. U. Buenos Aires, 1961, Bernardino Rivadavia prize Nat. Acad. Medicine Argentina, 1967, Ciencia e Investigation prize Argentinian Soc. Advancement Sci., 1967; Ford Found.-NAS travel fellow, 1968, Eleanor Roosevelt fellow, 1969. Mem. Scandinavian Soc. Immunology, Italian Assn. Immunologists, French Soc. Immunology, Am. Assn. Immunologists, Am. Soc. Microbiology (sect. editor Manual of Clin. Lab. Immunology 5th edit. 1994—), Am. Soc. Investigative Pathology. Achievements include patents in field; discovered primary myeloperoxydase deficiency in leucocytes; developed method for immunologic identification of bacteria that produce methane gas; discovered antigenic diversity of these bacteria in natural and manufactured ecosystems; described structural topography of methanogenic bacteria and population dynamics in granular microbial consortia; found novel multicellular forms of archaebacteria; isolated for the first time the genes in the dnaK locus from an archaebacterium. Editor multivol. treatise Monoclonal Antibodies Against Bacteria and treatise Gene Probes for Bacteria; contbr. articles to profl. jours., chpts. to books. Office: Empire State Pla/Dept Health Wadsworth Ctr Labs Rsch PO Box 509 Albany NY 12201 *I am capable to walk alone, but with my wife by me I fly. We can both ascend toward the sky and together we reach the stars. Separately, alone, who knows, we might never have been able to rise above the mountains, perhaps not even the hills, we have conquered flapping our wings in unison.*

MACARTHUR, CAROL JEANNE, pediatric otolaryngology educator; b. Glendale, Calif., Aug. 23, 1957; d. Seth Gerald and Barbara Jeanne (Shaw) MacA.; m. Geoffrey Buncke, Dec. 14, 1990; children: Keith Davis, Michelle Jeanne. BS, Occidental Coll., 1979; MD, UCLA, 1984. Diplomate Am. Bd. Otolaryngology. Intern U. Calif., Davis, 1984-85, resident in otolaryngology, 1985-90; fellow in pediatric otolaryngology Boston Children's Hosp., 1990-91; instr. dept. otolaryngology U. Calif.-Davis, Sacramento, 1989-90; clin. fellow in otology and laryngology Harvard U. Med. Sch., Boston, 1990-91; asst. prof., dir. pediatric otolaryngology U. Calif., Irvine, 1991—, asst. prof. dept. pediatrics, 1993—, program dir. dept. otolaryngology-head and neck surgery, 1992-95. Recipient investigator devel. award Am. Acad. Facial Plastic and Reconstructive Surgery, 1993. Fellow ACS, Am. Acad. Pediatrics; mem. Am. Soc. Pediat. Otolaryngology, Soc. for Ear, Nose and Throat Advances in Children, Am. Cleft Palate Craniofacial Assn., Am. Acad. Otorhinolaryngology-Head and Neck Surgery, Alpha Omega Alpha. Office: U Calif Med Ctr 101 The City Dr S Bldg 25 Orange CA 92668-3201

MACARTHUR, JOHN RODERICK C. G. (RICK MACARTHUR), magazine publisher, journalist; b. N.Y.C., June 4, 1956; s. J. Roderick and Christiane (L'Etendart) MacA. BA, Columbia Coll., 1978. Reporter Wall Street Jour., Chgo., summer 1977, Washington Star, 1978, Bergen Record, Hackensack, N.J., 1978-79, Chgo. Sun Times, 1979-82; asst. fgn. editor UPI, N.Y.C., 1982; pres., pub. Harper's Mag., N.Y.C., 1983—. Author: Second Front: Censorship and Propaganda in the Gulf War, 1992. Bd. dirs. Com. to

Protect Journalists, Overseas Press Club, Death Penalty Info. Ctr. Fellow N.Y. Inst. Humanities; mem. Econ. Club of N.Y. Office: Harper's Mag 666 Broadway Fl 11 New York NY 10012-2317

MACAT, JULIO, cinematographer. Cinematographer: (films) Home Alone, 1990, Only the Lonely, 1991, Home Alone 2: Lost in New York, 1992, So I Married an Axe Murderer, 1993, Ace Ventura, Pet Detective, 1994. Office: care Spyros Skouras Sanford Skouras Gross & Assocs 1015 Gayley Ave Fl 3 Los Angeles CA 90024-3424

MACAULAY, COLIN ALEXANDER, mining engineer; b. Montreal, Que., Can., Dec. 26, 1931; s. Kenneth Douglas and Eunice S. (Guild) M.; m. Elizabeth Ann Rowsell, Aug. 27, 1955; children: Douglas C., James. R., Robert C. B.Engring. in Mining, McGill U., Montreal, 1954, M.Engring., 1955. Registered profl. engr., Ont. Gen. mgr., dir. Palabora Mining Co., Transvaal, Republic South Africa, 1972-82; dep. chmn., mng. dir., chief exec. Rössing Uranium Ltd., Namibia, 1982-88; pres., chief operating officer Rio Algom Ltd., Toronto, Ont., Can., 1988-91, pres., ceo, 1991—; chmn. bd. dirs. Highland Valley Copper, B.C. Mem. Ont. Mining Assn. (bd. dirs. 1990-91), Mining Assn. Can. (dir.), Can. Inst. Mining and Metallurgy, Assn. Profl. Engrs. Ont. Home: 70 Roxborough Dr, Toronto, ON Canada M4W 1X1 Office: Rio Algom Ltd, 120 Adelaide St W Ste 2600, Toronto, ON Canada M5H 1W5

MACAULAY, DAVID (ALEXANDER), author, illustrator; b. Burton-on-Trent, Eng., Dec. 2, 1946; s. James and Joan (Lowe) M.; m. Janice Elizabeth Michel, 1970 (div.); 1 child, Elizabeth Alexandra; m. Ruth Marris, 1978 (div.); m. Charlotte Valerie. BArch, R.I. Sch. Design, 1969. Instr. interior design R.I. Sch. Design, Providence, 1969-73, instr. two-dimensional design, 1974-76, adj. faculty dept. illustration, 1977-79; tchr. art Central Falls (R.I.) Pub. Schs., 1969-70, Newton, Mass., 1972-74; designer Morris Nathanson Design, 1969-72. Author, illustrator: Cathedral: The Story of Its Construction, 1973 (Caldecott Honor book 1973), City, 1974, Pyramid, 1975 (Christopher medal 1975), Underground, 1976, Castle, 1977 (Caldecott Honor book 1977), Great Moments in Architecture, 1978, Motel of the Mysteries, 1979, Unbuilding, 1980, Electricity, 1983, Mill, 1983, Baaa, 1985, Why the Chicken Crossed the Road, 1987, The Way Things Work, 1988, Black and White, 1990 (Caldecott medal 1991), Ship, 1993, Shortcut, 1995; illustrator: Help! Let Me Out!, 1982, The Amazing Brain, 1984; cons., presenter various TV projects. Recipient Wash. Children's Book Guild award, 1977, AIA medal, 1978, Bradford Washburn meda. Boston Mus. Sci., 1993, Charles Frankel prize NEH, 1995, Chevalier of Order of Arts and Letters, France, 1995.

MACAULAY, HUGH L., retail company executive; b. Toronto; s. Leopold and Hazel Charlton (Haight) M.; m. Dorothy Jean Taylor, Sept. 11, 1946; children—Barbara, Robert James, Andrew Taylor. B.A. in Journalism, U. Western Ont., 1948. With Pub. & Indsl. Relations Ltd., 1948-52; with Ford Motor Co., 1952-54, Lawrence Motors Ltd., 1954-55; owner York Mills Pontiac Ltd. and York Mills Leasing Ltd., 1955-70; vice chmn. Ont. Hydro, Toronto, 1979, chmn., 1979-83; chmn. Can. Tire Corp. Ltd., Toronto, 1984-94, CEO, 1985-87, also dir. Mem., chmn. bd. Ryerson Poly. Inst., 1964-71; bd. govs. York U.; mem. Commn. on Post-Secondary Edn., 1969-71; chmn. Commn. on Orgn. of Progressive Conservative Party, 1971-76. Served with Royal Can. Naval Vol. Res., 1943-45. Mem. Rosedale Golf Club, John's Island Club (Vero Beach, Fla.), Albany Club. Avocations: boating; golf. Office: Can Tire Corp Ltd/Sta K, 2180 Yonge St Box 770, Toronto, ON Canada M4P 2V8*

MACAULAY, LAWRENCE A., Canadian government official; b. St. Peters Bay, Sept. 9, 1946; s. Archibald and Bernadette MacAulay; m. Frances Elaine O'Connell, Aug. 16, 1972; children: Carolyn, Rita, Lynn. Mem. House of Commons, 1988—, apptd. assoc. critic for fisheries and oceans, 1989, apptd. critic for srs. and assoc. critic for fisheries, 1990; sec. of state for vets. Govt. of Can., 1993—; mem. standing com. on forestry and fisheries, caucus com. on health and social devel.; acclaimed chair Atlantic Caucus, 1992. Roman Catholic. Office: Veterans Affairs Can, 161 Grafton St PO Box 7700, Charlottetown, PE Canada C1A 8M9

MACAULAY, RONALD KERR STEVEN, linguistics educator, former college dean; b. West Kilbride, Ayrshire, Scotland, Nov. 3, 1927; came to U.S., 1965; s. Robert Wilson and Mary Robb (McDermid) M.; m. Janet Grey, July 25, 1956; children: Harvey, Anna. M.A., U. St. Andrews, 1955; Ph.D., UCLA, 1971. Lectr. Brit. Inst., Lisbon, Portugal, 1955-60, Brit Council, Buenos Aires, Argentina, 1960-64; asst. prof. linguistics Pitzer Coll., Claremont, Calif., 1965-67; assoc. prof. Pitzer Coll., 1967-73, prof., 1973—, dean faculty, 1980-86. Author: Language, Social Class and Education, 1977, Generally Speaking: How Children Learn Language, 1980, Locating Dialect in Disourse: The Language of Honest Men and Bonnie Lasses in Ayr, 1991, The Social Art: Language and Its Uses, 1994; editor: (with R.P. Stockwell) Linguistic Change and Generative Theory, 1972, (with D. Brenneis) The Matrix of Language: Contemporary Linguistic Anthropology, 1996. Home: 317 W 7th St Claremont CA 91711-4312 Office: Pitzer Coll 1050 N Mills Ave Claremont CA 91711-3908

MACAVOY, PAUL WEBSTER, economics educator, university dean; b. Haverhill, Mass., Apr. 21, 1934; s. Paul Everett and Louise Madeline (Webster) MacA.; m. Katherine Ann Manning, June 13, 1955; children: Libby, Matthew. A.B., Bates Coll., 1955, LL.D., 1976; M.A., Yale, 1956, Ph.D., 1960. Asst. to full prof. MIT, Cambridge, Mass., 1963-74, Henry R. Luce prof. pub. policy, 1974-75; mem. Pres.'s Coun. Econ. Advisers, 1975-76; prof. econs. and mgmt. Yale U., 1976-81, Beinecke prof. econs., 1981-83; dean W.E. Simon Grad. Sch. Bus. Admin. U. Rochester, 1983-91; Williams Bros. prof. Yale Sch. Mgmt. Yale U., 1991—, dean Yale Sch. Mgmt., 1992-94; bd. dirs. Chase Manhattan Bank Corp., Alumax Inc, Open Environment Corp., Lafarge Corp. Author: Price Formation in Natural Gas Fields, 1962, (with Stephen Breyer) Energy Regulation by the Federal Power Commission, 1974, (with R. Pindyck) The Economics of the Natural Gas Shortage, 1975, The Regulated Industries and the Economy, 1979, World Crude Oil Prices, 1981, Energy Policy, 1983, Explaining Metals Prices, 1988, Industry Regulation and the Performance of the American Economy, 1992, The Failure of Antitrust and Regulation to Establish Competition in Long Distance Telephone Service Markets, 1996; editor: Fort Administration Papers on Regulatory Reform, 8 vols., 1977-78, Privatization and State-Owned Enterprise: Assessment for the United Kingdom, Canada and the United States, 1988. Home: 420 Humphrey St New Haven CT 06511-3711 Office: Yale Sch Mgmt PO Box 208200 New Haven CT 06520-8200

MACAVOY, THOMAS COLEMAN, glass manufacturing executive, educator; b. Jamaica, N.Y., Apr. 24, 1928; s. Joseph V. and Edna M. Mac A.; m. Margaret M. Walsh, Dec. 27, 1952; children: Moira Mac Avoy Brown, Ellen Mac Avoy Jennings, Christopher, Neil. B.S. in Chemistry, Queens Coll., 1950; M.S. in Chemistry, St. John's U., 1952, D.Sc. (hon.), 1973; Ph.D. in Chemistry, U. Cin., 1952. Chemist, Charles Pfizer & Co., Bklyn., 1957-60; mgr. electronics research Corning Glass Works, N.Y., 1960-64; dir. phys. research Corning Glass Works, 1964-66, v.p. electronic products div., 1966-69, v.p. tech. products div., 1969-71, pres., 1971-83, vice-chmn., 1983-87; prof. mgmt. grad. sch. U. Va., 1988—; bd. dirs. Quaker Oats Co., Chubb Corp., Lubrizol Corp. Patentee in field; contbr. articles to tech. jours. Trustee Corning Mus. Glass; past pres. Boy Scouts Am. With USN, 1946; with USAF, 1952-53. Recipient Silver Antelope award Boy Scouts Am., 1976, Silver Beaver award, 1975, Silver Buffalo award, 1982, Bronze Wolf award, 1988. Roman Catholic. Office: U Va Darden Grad Sch Bus Adminstrn Charlottesville VA 22096

MACBAIN, WILLIAM HALLEY, minister, theology educator, seminary chancellor; b. Cambridge, Ont., Can., Aug. 12, 1916; s. George Alexander and Grace Ann (Wilkins) MacB.; m. Mary Ann Munday, Aug. 20, 1941; children: Grace Elizabeth MacBain Silvester, Constance Marilyn MacBain Parker. Licentiate in Theology, Toronto Baptist Sem., Ont., 1939; DD (hon.), Cen. Bapt. Sem., Toronto, 1962. Ordained to ministry Bapt. Ch., 1940. Pastor, founder Temple Bapt. Ch., Sarnia, Ont., 1937-64; pastor Forward Bapt. Ch., Toronto, 1964-73; dir., gen. sec. Fellowship Fgn. Missions, Toronto, 1973-81; chancellor Cen. Bapt. Sem., 1981-93, Heritage Bapt. Bible Coll. and Theol. Sem., Cambridge, Ont., Can., 1993—; pastor emeritus Forward Bapt. Ch., Toronto, 1994—; chmn. Can. Bd. Greater Europe Mission, 1963-73. Mem. Fellowship Evang. Bapt. Chs. in Can. (pres. 1953-54, 83-84). Conservative. Home: 35 Wynford Heights Crescent, Apt 2603, Don Mills, ON Canada M3C 1L1 Office: Heritage Bapt Bible Coll and Theol Sem, 175 Holiday Inn Dr, Cambridge, ON Canada N3C 3T2

MACBETH, ANGUS, lawyer; b. L.A., May 9, 1942. BA, Yale U., 1964, LLB, 1969. Bar: N.Y. 1970, D.C. 1981. Law clk. to Hon. Harold R. Tyler, Jr. U.S. Dist. Ct. (so. dist.) N.Y., 1969-70, asst. U.S. atty. criminal divsn., 1975-77; chief pollution control sect. Land and Natural Resources Divsn., U.S. Dept. Justice, 1977-79, dep. asst. atty. gen., 1979-81; ptnr. Sidley & Austin, Washington; adj. prof. law N.Y. Law Sch., 1985—; spl. counsel Wartime Relocation and Internment Civilians Commn., 1981-83. Mem. D.C. Bar (steering com. energy and natural resources divsn. 1982-84), N.Y. State Bar Assn. (exec. com. sect. environ. law 1981—), Phi Beta Kappa. Office: Sidley & Austin 1722 I St NW Washington DC 20006-3705

MACBRIDE, THOMAS JAMISON, federal judge; b. Sacramento, Mar. 25, 1914; s. Frank and Lotta Kirtley (Little) MacB.; m. Martha Harrold, Nov. 7, 1947; children—Peter, Thomas Jamison, David, Laurie. A.B., U. Calif. at Berkeley, 1936, J.D., 1940. Bar: Calif. 1940. Dep. atty. gen. Calif., 1941-42; pvt. practice Sacramento, 1946-61; U.S. dist. judge Eastern Dist. Calif., Sacramento, 1961-67; chief judge Eastern Dist. Calif., 1967-79, sr. judge, 1979—; mem. U.S. Temporary Emergency Ct. Appeals, 1982-87; mem. Criminal Justice Act Com., U.S. Jud. Conf., 1969-88; mem. U.S. Jud. Conf., 1975-78; chmn. Criminal Justice Act Com. of U.S. Jud. Conf., 1979-88; mem. U.S. Fgn. Intelligence Surveillance Ct., 1979-80. Pres. Town Hall, Sacramento, 1952, N.E. area YMCA, 1960; mem. Calif. Legislature from Sacramento County, 1955-60 mem. Nat. Commn. on Reform Fed. Criminal Laws, 1967-71; bd. dirs. Sacramento YMCA; trustee U. Calif., San Francisco Found., 1982—; bd. dirs. Sacramento Regional Found., 1988—; founding dir. League to Save Lake Tahoe, 1965. Lt. USNR., 1942-46. Mem. ABA, U. Calif. Alumni Assn. (v.p. 1955, 60), Mason (33 deg., Shriner, Jester), Rotarian (pres. 1966-67), Sutter Club, Univ. (pres. 1951-52), Comstock (pres. 1975-76), Senator Outing (sec.-treas.), Kappa Sigma, Phi Delta Phi. Democrat. Office: US Dist Ct US Courthouse 650 Capitol Mall Sacramento CA 95814-4708

MACBURNEY, EDWARD HARDING, bishop; b. Albany, N.Y., Oct. 30, 1927; s. Alfred Cadwell and F. Marion (McDowell) MacB.; m. Anne Farnsworth, Feb. 20, 1965; W. Norton Grubb, Page F. Grubb, James S. Grubb. AB, Darmouth Coll., 1949; STB, Berkeley Divinity Sch., 1952; HHD (hon.), St. Ambrose U., 1987; DD (hon.), Nashotah House, 1988. Ordained to ministry Episcopal Ch. as deacon, 1952, as priest, 1952, as bishop, 1988. Asst. St. Thomas' Ch., Hanover, N.H., 1953-63, rector, 1963-73; dean Trinity Cathedral, Davenport, Iowa, 1973-87; bishop Diocese of Quincy, Peoria, Ill., 1988—. Trustee Berkeley Divinity Sch., New Haven, 1964-70, St. Luke's Hosp., Davenport, 1973-87, Nat. Orgn. Episcopalians for Life, Fairfax, 1991—, Nashotah House, 1991—; v.p. Episcopal Synod Am., Ft. Worth, 1988—; mem. panel White House Fellowships, St. Louis, 1976-84; bd. dirs. Noel, 1991—. Democrat. Office: Diocese of Quincy 3601 N North St Peoria IL 61604-1548

MACCARTHY, TALBOT LELAND, civic volunteer; b. St. Louis, Jan. 28, 1936; d. Austin Porter Leland and Dorothy (Lund) Follansbee; m. John Peters MacCarthy, June 21, 1958; children: John Leland MacCarthy, Talbot MacCarthy Payne. BA, Vassar Coll., 1958. Sec., treas. Station List Pub. Co., St. Louis, 1975-85, pres., 1985-90. Trustee Robert E. Lee Meml. Assn., Arts and Edn. Coun. Greater St. Louis, pres., 1978-80, emerita; trustee St. Louis Art Mus.; past trsutee St. Louis Mercantile Libr. Assn., Family & Children's Svc. Greater St. Louis, Health and Welfare Coun., Greater St. Louis, Jr. Kindergarten St. Louis Page Park YMCA, Scholarship Fund. St. Louis, Friends St. Louis Art Mus. Bd., Ch. St. Michael and St. George Sch. Bd., Mid-Am. Arts Alliance; chmn. Mo. Arts Coun., 1980-85; past chmn. Vol. Action Ctr. Greater St. Louis; past vice chmn. bd. dirs. Mary Inst.; past pres. Jr. League St. Louis; mem. Nat. Coun. Arts, 1985-91. Recipient Woman of Achievement citation St. Louis Globe Democrat, 1979, Mo. Citizens for Arts/Arts Advocacy award, 1987, Mo. Arts Award, 1993. Mem. Vassar Club St. Louis (past pres.), Mary Inst. Alumnae Assn. (past pres.), Colonial Dames Am., Garden Club St. Louis. Republican. Episcopalian. Avocations: tennis, visual arts, performing arts.

MACCARTHY, TERENCE FRANCIS, lawyer; b. Chgo., Feb. 5, 1934; s. Frank E. and Catherine (McIntyre) MacC.; m. Marian Fulton, Nov. 25, 1961; children—Daniel Fulton, Sean Patrick, Terence Fulton, Megan Catherine. B.A. in Philosophy, St. Jospeh's Coll., 1955; J.D., DePaul U., 1960. Bar: Ill. 1960, U.S. Dist. Ct. (no. dist.) Ill. 1961, U.S. Ct. Appeals (7th cir.) 1961, U.S. Supreme Ct. 1966. Assoc. prof. law Chase Coll. Law, Cin., 1960-61; law clk. to chief judge U.S. Dist. Ct., 1961-66; spl. asst. atty. gen. Ill., 1965-67; exec. dir. Fed. Defender Program, U.S. Dist. Ct. (no. dist.) Ill., Chgo., 1966—; mem. nat. adv. com. on criminal rules; 7th cir. criminal jury instrn. com.; chmn. Nat. Defender Com.; chmn. bd. regents Nat. Coll. Criminal Def.; faculty Fed. Jud. Ctr., Nat. Coll. Criminal Def., Nat. Inst. Trial Advocacy, U. Va. Trial Advocacy Inst., Harvard Law Sch. Trial Advocacy Program, Western Trial Advocacy Inst., Northwestern U., U. Ill. Defender Trial Advocacy course, Loyola U. Trial Advocacy Program; lectr. in field. Contbr. articles on criminal law to profl. jours. Bd. dirs. U.S.O. Served as 1st lt. USMC, 1955-57. Recipient Nat. Legal Aid and Defender Assn./ABA Reginald Heber Smith award, 1986, Alumni Merit award St. Joseph Coll., 1970, Cert. of Distinction USO, 1977, Harrison Tweed Spl. Merit award Am. Law Inst./ABA, 1987, Bill of Rights award Ga. chpt. ACLU, 1986, William J. Brennan award U. Va., 1989, Alumni Svc. award DePaul U. Coll. Law, 1994, Ann. Significant Contbns. award Calif. Attys. for Criminal Justice; named to Outstanding Young Men of Am., 1970. Mem. ABA (past chmn. criminal justice sect., ho. of dels.), Ill. Bar Assn., Chgo. Bar Assn., 7th Cir. Bar Assn., Nat. Assn. Criminal Def. Lawyers (Disting. Svc. award 1993), Nat. Legal Aid and Defender Assn., Nat. coll. Criminal Def. (chair), Union League of Chgo. (pres.). Democrat. Roman Catholic. Office: US Dist Ct No Dist Ill 55 E Monroe Ste 2800 Chicago IL 60603

MACCARTY, COLLIN S., neurosurgeon; b. Rochester, Minn., Sept. 20, 1915; s. W.C. MacCarty; married; 3 children. AB, Dartmouth Coll., 1937; MD, Johns Hopkins U., Balt., 1940; MS in Neurosurgery, U. Minn., 1944. Diplomate Am. Bd. Neurol. Surgery. Surg. house officer Johns Hopkins Hosp., Balt., 1940-41; fellow in neurosurgery Mayo Found., Rochester, 1944; instr. neurol. surgery on grad. faculty U. Minn., Rochester, 1947-53, asst. prof., 1953-57, assoc. prof., 1957-61, prof., 1961-73; prof. Mayo Med. Sch./U. Minn., Rochester, 1973-80, assoc. dir. grad. edn., 1975-77, dir., 1977-80, prof. emeritus, 1980—; mem. neurosurg. staff Mayo Clinic, Rochester, 1946-75, sr. cons., 1975, chmn. med. staff, 1965-66; sec. for congress affairs World Fedn. Neurosurg. Socs., 1965-69, chmn. program com., mem. liaison com., mem. adminstrv. coun.; adv. com. to dean Dartmouth Med. Sch., 1968-72, bd. overseers, 1973—, chmn. bd., 1977-79; adv. bd. Bur. of Medicine and Surgery, Dept. of Navy, 1970; nat. cons. in neurosurgery Air Force, Wilford Hall Hosp., Lackland AFB, Tex., 1971; cons. in neursurgery to Surgeon Gen., USN, 1977-80; vis. prof. neurosurgery Western Res. U., Cleve., 1966, Johns Hopkins U., 1969, U. Okla., 1971, Ohio State U., 1977, U. Tex., 1979; Caldwell lectr. Am. Roentgen Ray Soc., 1974; Elsberg lectr. N.Y. Soc. Neurol. Surgery, 1981. Author: (monograph) The Surgical Treatment of Intracranial Meningiomas, 1961; co-author: Primary Intramedullary Tumors of the Spinal Cord and Filum Terminale, 1964; contbr. over 158 articles to various med. jours. With USN, 1944-46. Mem. AMA (residency rev. com., sect. on med. edn. 1967-72), ACS, Am. Assn. Neurol. Surgeons (v.p. 1965, pres. 1970, bd. dirs. 1965-73, del. to World Fedn. 1973-77), Neurosurg. Soc. of Am. (v.p. 1954, pres. 1959, rep. to AANS bd. dirs. 1965-69), Minn. Med. Assn., Zumbro Valley Med. Soc., Minn. Soc. Neurol. Scis., Soc. Neurol. Surgeons, So. Minn. Med. Assn., Minn. Neurosurg. Soc., Found. for Internat. Edn. in Neurol. Surgery, Inc., Societa Italiana de Neurochirurgia (corr. mem.), Egyptian Soc. Neurol. Surgeons (hon.), Japan Soc. Neurol. Surgeons (hon.), Internat. Travellers Club, Neurosurg. Travel Club, Sigma Xi (chpt. pres. 1979-80). Home: HC 60 Box 71A Cable WI 54821-9510

MACCAULEY, HUGH BOURNONVILLE, banker; b. Mt. Vernon, N.Y., Mar. 12, 1922; s. Morris Baker and Alma (Gardiner) MacC.; m. Rachael Gleaton, Aug. 30, 1943 (div. May 1980); m. Felice Cooper, Dec. 2, 1980. Student, Rutgers U., 1939-41, Tex. Christian U., 1948-50, U. Omaha, 1957-59. With 102nd Cavalry, Essex Troop N.J. Nat. Guard, 1940-42; commd. 2d lt. U.S. Army, 1943; advanced through grades to col. U.S. Army, USAF, Washington, 1943-73; v.p. Great Am. Securities, San Bernardino, Calif., 1979-94; founder., chmn. bd. Desert Cmty. Bank, Victorville, Calif., 1980-95, chmn. emeritus, 1995; account exec. Gorian Thornes, Inc., San Bernardino, Calif., 1995-96. bd. dirs. Air Force Village West, 1986-88; chmn. bd. and CEO Gen. and Mrs. Curtis E. Lemay Found., 1987—. Decorated Air medal, Legion of Merit. Mem. Daedalian Soc., Rotary, Internat. Platform Soc. Republican. Presbyterian. Avocation: golf. Home: 16505 Bordeaux Ln Huntington Beach CA 92649 *Personal philosophy: Whatever the game play by the rules.*

MACCHIAROLA, FRANK JOSEPH, academic administrator; b. N.Y.C., Apr. 7, 1941; s. Joseph John and Lucy (Bernardo) M.; m. Mary Teresa Collins, June 13, 1970; children: Joseph John, Michael Collins, Frank Joseph. B.A., St. Francis Coll., 1962, L.H.D. (hon.), 1981; LL.B., Columbia U., 1965, Ph.D., 1970; L.H.D. (hon.), Coll. S.I., 1983; LL.D. (hon.), Dominican Coll., 1983, Manhattan Coll., 1983. From fellow to prof. polit. sci. CUNY, 1964-83, v.p., 1977-78; asst. v.p. Columbia U., N.Y.C., 1973-74; dep. dir. N.Y. State Emergency Fin. Control Bd. for N.Y.C., 1976-77; chancellor of schs. N.Y.C. Public Sch. System, 1978-83; pres., chief exec. officer N.Y.C. Partnership, Inc., 1983-87; pres. Acad. of Polit. Sci., 1987-91; prof. bus. Columbia U., N.Y.C., 1987-91; dean Benjamin N. Cardozo Sch. of Law, Yeshiva U., N.Y.C., 1991—; of counsel Newman, Tannenbaum, Helpern, Syracuse and Hirschtritt, N.Y.C., 1991-96; pres. St. Francis Coll., N.Y., 1996—; bd. dirs. Jeffries Group Inc., Schuller; trustee Manville Personal Injury Settlement Trust. Mem., pres. Community Sch. Bd. 22, N.Y.C., 1973-78; mem., vice chmn. bd. trustees St. Joseph's Coll., 1977—. Decorated cavalieri Order of Merit Italy; recipient cert. of merit Dirigible Soc. Am., 1976. Democrat. Roman Catholic. Office: 900 3rd Ave New York NY 10022-4728 also: 180 Remsen St Brooklyn NY 11201

MACCINI, LOUIS JOHN, economic educator; b. Cambirdge, Mass., Aug. 3, 1942; s. Joseph and Jennie (Leccacorvi) M.; m. Carol Monterisi, June 25, 1965; children: Michael S., Sharon L. BS in Economics, Boston Coll., 1965; PhD in Economics, Northwestern U., 1970. From asst. prof. to assoc. prof. economics The Johns Hopkins U., Balt., 1969-86, prof., 1986—, chair, 1992—; ad hoc com. mem. graduate fin. aid, Johns Hopkins U., editorial bd., public interest investment adv. com., law sch. com., med. sch. com., and other coms.; mem. recruting chair dept. grad. student advisor dept., and other depts. Referee Am. Econ. Review, Jour. Econ. Dynamics and Control, Oxford Econ. Papers, and others; contbr. articles to profl. jours. Grantee NSF. Mem. Am. Econ. Assn., The Econometric Soc., Internat Soc. Inventory Rsch. Office: Johns Hopkins U 3400 N Charles St Baltimore MD 21218-2608

MACCLEAN, WALTER LEE, dentist; b. Sheridan, Wyo., July 10, 1935; s. Edward Satterlee and Eleanor Elizabeth (Weir) Mac.; m. Nancy Lee Strale, Sept. 4, 1965 (div. 1975); children: David Satterlee, Carrie Lynn. BS with honors, U. Wyo., 1957, postgrad., 1958; DMD, U. Oreg., Portland, 1962. Mil. dental adv. Korean Mil. Adv. Group, Wonju, 1962-63; chief dental svc. Dugway Chem. Testing Ctr., Utah, 1965-68; pvt. dental practice Cheyenne, Wyo., 1968-70; assoc. prof. Sheridan Coll., Wyo., 1970-76; staff dentist VA Hosp. Med. Ctr., Ft. Meade, S.D., 1976—; 1976-93, ret., 1993; cons., lectr. Health Edn. Program Svc., Ft. Meade, 1984-93. With U.S. Army 1962-68. Mem. ADA. Episcopalian. Home: PO Box 450 Hardin MT 59034-0450 also: Highbourne House, 13-15 Marylebone High St, London W1M 3PE, England

MACCLUGGAGE, REID, newspaper editor, publisher; b. Norwich, Conn., Oct. 18, 1938; s. Everett Reid and Edith Kathryn (Bowen) MacC.; m. Joellen Thompson, Mar. 29, 1965 (div. 1980); children: Stewart Reid, Scot Thompson; m. Linda Howell, May 30, 1981; 1 dau., Katherine Elizabeth. B.A., U. Hartford, 1962. Asst. state editor Hartford (Conn.) Courant, 1965-69, state editor, 1969-74, asst. mng. editor, 1974-82, mng. editor, 1982-84; editor, pub. New London (Conn.) Day, 1984—; bd. dirs. Day Pub. Co.; juror Pulitzer Prize. Trustee Day Trust, Dr. Martin Luther King Meml. Scholarship Trust Fund, Pine Point Sch.; commr. New London City Ctr. Dist.; bd. dirs. Family Svc. Assn.; founder Bodenwein Fellowship for Minorities; incorporator Lawrence and Meml. Hosp. Recipient Disting. Alumnus award U. Hartford, 1983. Mem. AP Mng. Editors Assn. (sec.). Office: The Day Pub Co 47 Eugene O'Neil Dr PO Box 1231 New London CT 06320

MACCOBY, ELEANOR EMMONS, psychology educator; b. Tacoma, May 15, 1917; d. Harry Eugene and Viva May (Johnson) Emmons; m. Nathan Maccoby, Sept. 16, 1938 (dec. Apr. 1992); children: Janice Maccoby Carmichael, Sarah Maccoby Bellina, Mark. BS, U Wash., 1939; MA, U. Mich., 1949, PhD, 1950. Study dir. div. program surveys USDA, Washington, 1942-46; study dir. Survey Rsch. Ctr. U. Mich., Ann Arbor, 1946-48; lectr., rsch. assoc. dept. social rels. Harvard U., Cambridge, Mass., 1950-58; from assoc. to full prof. Stanford (Calif.) U., 1958-87, chmn. dept. psychology, 1973-76, prof. emeritus, 1987—; elected Nat. Acad. of Sci., 1993. Author: (with R. Sears and H. Levin) Patterns of Child-Rearing, 1957, (with Carol Jacklin) Psychology of Sex Differences, 1974, Social Development, 1980, (with R.H. Mnookin) Dividing the Child: Social and Legal Dilemmas of Custody, 1992; editor: (with Newcomb and Hartley) Readings in Social Psychology, 1957, The Development of Sex Differences, 1966. Recipient Gores award for Excellence in Teaching Stanford U., 1981, Disting. Contbn. to Ednl. Research award Am. Edni. Research Assn., 1984, Disting. Sci. Contbn. to Child Devel. award Soc. for Research in Child Devel., 1987, Disting. Sci. Contbns. award Am. Psychol. Assn., 1988; named to Barbara Kimball Browning professorship Stanford U., 1979—. Fellow APA (pres. Divsn. 7, 1971-72, G. Stanley Hall award 1982), Soc. for Rsch. in Child Devel. (pres. 1981-83, mem. governing coun. 1963-66, Am. Psychol. Soc.; mem. NAS, Western Psychol. Assn. (pres. 1974-75), Inst. for Rsch. on Women and Gender, Social Sci. Rsch. Coun. (chmn. 1984-85), Inst. Medicine, Am. Acad. Arts and Scis., Consortium of Social Sci. Assns. Democrat. Avocations: tennis, vocal music. Home: 729 Mayfield Ave Palo Alto CA 94305-1016 Office: Stanford U Dept Psychology Stanford CA 94305-2130

MACCOMBIE, BRUCE FRANKLIN, composer, college administrator; b. Providence, Dec. 5, 1943; s. Franklin S. and Florence (Corbishley) MacC.; m. Frances Holliday, Sept. 4, 1965 (div. 1970); m. Turi Gundersen, Mar. 10, 1979; 1 child, Juliana. BA, U. Mass., 1967, M of Music, 1968, DFA (hon.), 1986; PhD, U. Iowa, 1971. Assoc. prof. Yale U., New Haven, 1975-80; v.p. G. Schirmer Mus. Publs., N.Y.C., 1980-85; dean, provost The Juilliard Sch., N.Y.C., 1986-92; dean Sch. for Arts Boston U., 1992—. Composer numerous musical works. Recipient Goddard Lieberson award Am. Acad. Inst. Arts and Letters, N.Y.C., 1979. Mem. Coll. Music Soc., Charles Ives Soc. (bd. dirs.). Office: Boston U Sch for Arts 855 Commonwealth Ave Boston MA 02215-1303

MACCONKEY, DOROTHY I., academic administrator; b. New Brunswick, N.J.; d. Donald Thurston and Dorothy Bennett (Hill) Ingling; m. Joseph W. MacConkey, June 19, 1949 (dec. Aug. 1975); children: Donald Franklin, Diane Margaret, Dorothy Frances; m. Karl Schmeidler, May 26, 1994. BA, Beaver Coll., 1947; MA, Wichita State U., 1953; PhD, U. Md., 1974; LLD (hon.), Beaver Coll., 1988. Lectr. Wichita (Kans.) State U., 1950-51; rsch.-campaign assoc. United Fund and Council, Wichita, 1951-62; rsch.- com. coordination Health and Welfare Council of Nat. Capital Area, Washington, 1963-65; exec. dir. multi-program agy. Prince Georges County Assn. for Retarded Children, Hyattsville, Md., 1965-66; asst. vice pres., acting dean, 1976-82; v.p., dean of coll. Hiram (Ohio) Coll., 1982-85; pres. Davis & Elkins (W.Va.) Coll., 1985—; bd. dirs. Davis Trust Co., Elkins, 1987—; adv. bd. George Mason U. Found., Fairfax, 1976—; trustee Beaver Coll., Glenside, Pa., 1971-87; cons., evaluator North Cen. Assn., Chgo., 1985—, commr., 1993—; mem. exec. com., pres. Assn. Presbyn. Colls. and Univs.; mem. bd. Svc. Opportunity Colls., Presbyn. Found., trustee, 1993—; chmn. North Area Cen. Com.; treas. Coun. of Ind. Colls. Pres. County Chasers of Am., 1985—. Recipient Citizen award for service to handicapped, Fairfax County, 1981, Goddin Women Alumni award, 1985, Woman of Yr. in Edn. award W.Va. Fedn. Women's Clubs, 1986. Mem. Coun. of Pres.', Nat. Assn. Intercollegiate Athletics, Coun. Ind. Colls. (bd. dirs.). Office: Davis and Elkins Coll Office of Pres 100 Campus Dr Elkins WV 26241-3971

MACCORMACK, CHARLES FREDERICK, academic administrator; b. Oct. 27, 1941; married; two children. AB, Middlebury Coll., 1963, EdD (hon.), 1982; MIA, Columbia U., 1965, PhD, 1974. Staff assoc. internat. div. First Nat. City Bank, Caracas, Venezuela, 1964; instr. latin-Am. politics U. N.H., Durham, 1967; asst. to dean Internat. Fellows Program Columbia U., N.Y.C., 1967-68; rsch. fellow fgn. policy studies Brookings Instn., Washington, 1969-70; dir. internat. career tng. program Experiment Internat. Living, Brattleboro, Vt., 1970-74; v.p. programs Save the Children Fedn./Community Devel. Found., Westport, Conn., 1974-77; pres. The Experiment Internat. Living/Sch. for Internat. Tng., Brattleboro, 1977—; bd. dirs. Arthur D. Little Mgmt. Edn. Inst., Ptnrs. Internat. Edn. and Tng., Am. Forum for Global Edn., Landmark Coll. Mng. editor Jour. Internat. Affairs. Mem. founding com. U., 1971-72, Vt. Commn. Edn. and the Econ. Future, 1982, coun. advisors Peace Corps Future Team, 1987, Coun. Fgn. Rels., N.Y.C., global awareness adv. bd. Wheaton Coll., Norton, Mass.; mem. exec. com., chair devel. assistance com., co-chair com. refugee svcs. Am. Coun. Voluntary Internat. Action. Universidad Cen. de Venezuela Fulbright fellow, Caracas, Venezuela, 1965-66, Universidad Nacional Autonoma de Mexico NSF fellow, Mexico City, 1968-69, Edward John Noble Leadership fellow, 1963-65; Gould scholar, Middlebury scholar, Travelli scholar, 1959-63. Home: 95 North St Easton CT 06612-1039 Office: The Experiment Internat Living Kipling Rd Brattleboro VT 05301

MACCORMACK, LAWRENCE LEE, chemicals marketing executive; b. N.Y.C., May 4, 1945; s. Donald George and Mary Louise (Flanagan) MacC.; m. Bonnie Lindsey Hall, June 10, 1967; children: Christopher Edward, Chad Eric. AB in History & Polit. Sci., Wagner Coll., 1967; MBA, U. Conn., 1974. Underwriting & programming trainee Great Am. Ins. Co., N.Y.C., 1967-68; systems analyst Am. Can. Co., Greenwich, Conn., 1970-73; sales mgr. Image Carrier Corp., N.Y.C., 1974; mng. dir. Dixie products Am. Can Co., 1975-81; dir. mktg. Lily-Tulip Cup Co., Augusta, Ga., 1982-85; v.p., gen. mgr. Ecolab Inc., St. Paul, 1985-96; exec. v.p., gen. mgr. Orchem Corp., Fairfield, Ohio, 1996—; mktg. cons. pvt. practice, New Fairfield, 1981. Mem. mgmt. decision lab. bd. NYU, Manhattanville, 1979-81; coach soccer and basketball Minnetonka (Minn.) Youth Assn., 1986-90; scoutmaster Boy Scouts Am., Excelsior, Minn., 1986-90. Sgt. U.S. Army, 1968-70. Avocations: sailboat racing, skiing, reading.

MACCRACKEN, PETER JAMES, marketing executive, communications executive; b. Trieste, Italy, Dec. 27, 1952; came to U.S., 1956; s. James and Kirsten (Koch) MacC.; m. Krishna Walker. BA summa cum laude, Albion Coll., 1975; MA, U. Calif., Santa Barbara, 1978. Asst. mgr. GranTree Furniture Rental, San Leandro, Calif., 1979-81; freelance writer San Diego, 1981-82; corp. editor Scripps Meml. Hosps., La Jolla, Calif., 1982-84; sr. v.p. Berkman & Daniels Mktg., San Diego, 1984-89; v.p. Stoorza Ziegaus & Metzger, Inc., San Diego, 1989-90; pres. MacCracken & McGaugh, San Diego, 1990—. Contbr. over 500 articles, photographs to numerous publs. Recipient 30 bus. comm. awards. Mem. Pub. Rels. Soc. Am. (bd. dirs. 1992—, pres. San Diego chpt. 1996), Internat. Assn. Bus. Communicators (pres. San Diego chpt. 1985), Am. Inst. Wine and Food (bd. dirs. 1990-95, sec. San Diego chpt. 1995), Phi Beta Kappa. Democrat. Avocations: photography, writing, wines, science fiction, fiction, music. Office: 701 B St Ste 2200 San Diego CA 92101-8111

MAC CRAWFORD, EDWIN, health facility administrator. Pres., CEO, chmn. bd. dirs. Charter Medical Corp., Macon, Ga. Office: Charter Medical Corporation 3414 Peachtree Rd Ste 1400 Atlanta GA 30326*

MAC CREADY, PAUL BEATTIE, aeronautical engineer; b. New Haven, Sept. 29, 1925. BS in Physics, Yale U., 1947; MS, Calif. Inst. Tech., 1948, PhD in Aeros. cum laude, 1952. Founder, pres. Meteorology Research Inc., 1951-70, Atmospheric Research Group, 1958-70; founder, 1971, chief exec. officer, chmn. AeroVironment Inc., Pasadena, Calif.; leader team that developed Gossamer Albatross for human-powered flight across English Channel, 1979, Solar Challenger, ultralight aircraft powered by solar cells, 1981, GM-Sunraycer, 1987, GM-Impact, 1990; cons. in field, 1951—; mem. numerous govt. tech. adv. coms. Author research papers in field. Recipient Collier trophy Nat. Aero. Assn., 1979, Edward Longsreth medal Franklin Inst., 1979, Gold Air medal Fedn. Aero. Internat., 1981; Inventor of Yr. award Assn. Advancement Innovation and Invention, 1981; named Engr. of Century ASME, 1980. Mem. AIAA (Reed Aero. award 1979), Nat. Acad. Engring., Am. Acad. Arts and Scis., Am. Meteorol. Soc. (chmn. com. atmospheric measurements 1968-69, councillor 1971-74). Office: Aerovironment Inc 222 E Huntington Dr Ste 200 Monrovia CA 91016-3500

MACCREERY, NEAL JOSEPH, education educator; b. Phila., Aug. 9, 1941; s. Joseph R. and Sophia (Pawluk) MacC.; m. Kathleen Marie MacCreery, Dec. 23, 1977; 1 child, Joshua Neal. BS in Edn., SUNY, Brockport, 1969; MEd, U. Rochester, 1972, CAS, 1982, EdD, 1992. Lic. elem. tchr., sch. prin., supt., N.Y. Elem. tchr. SUNY, Brockport, 1969-71; reading tchr. 7th-9th grade Rush-Henrietta (N.Y.) City Sch. Dist., 1971-73; dir. reading, spl. programs Marion (N.Y.) City Sch. Dist., 1973-76; elem. prin., dir. spl. edn. Herkimer (N.Y.) City Sch. Dist., 1976-84; dir. spl. edn. Utica (N.Y.) City Sch. Dist., 1984-87; asst. prof. Roberts Wesleyan Coll., Rochester, N.Y., 1987-88, SUNY, Oneonta, 1989—; right to read regional cons. N.Y. State Edn. Dept., Albany, 1973-78, test exam writer, 1978-82, 90; chairperson adv. bd. N.Y. State Devel. Disabilities Community Program, Herkimer, 1978-82. Contbr. articles to profl. jours. Coord. Spl. Olympics, Oneonta, 1990-92, vol. Holiday Project, Oneonta, 1990-91; v.p., mgr., exec. bd. mem. Oneonta Little League, 1990—; founder Kards for Kids, Oneonta, 1991-94. Profl. Devel. grantee N.Y. State United Tchrs., 1990. Mem. N.Y. State Assn. Tchr. Educators, N.Y. State Reading Assn., Assn. N.Y. State Educators of Emotionally Handicapped Students, Catskill Area Reading Coun., Phi Delta Kappa (chpt. pres., rsch. rep. 1985—, Outstanding Dissertation award). Avocations: desk-top publishing, computer technology, collecting sport cards, traveling, working with young children. Home: 57 Ford Ave Oneonta NY 13820-1512 Office: SUNY 420 Fitzelle Hall Oneonta NY 13820

MACCRINDLE, ROBERT ALEXANDER, lawyer; b. Glasgow, Scotland, Jan. 27, 1928; s. Fergus Robertson and Jean (Hill) MacC.; m. Pauline Dilys, Aug. 18, 1959; children: Guy Stephen, Claire. LLB, U. London, 1948; LLM, U. Cambridge, 1952. Called to Bar Eng. and Wales, 1952; created Queen's Counsel, 1963; bar: Hong Kong 1965; conseil juridique France, 1978-91. Barrister Temple, London, 1952-76; Bencher Gray's Inn, London, 1969—; ptnr. Shearman & Sterling, N.Y.C., 1976-94, of counsel, 1995—; Avocat au Barreau de Paris, 1991—. Flight lt. RAF, 1948-50. Fellow Am. Coll. Trial Lawyers. Club: University (N.Y.C.). Avocation: golf. Home: 88 Ave de Breteuil, Paris 75015, France also: Shearman & Sterling 599 Lexington Ave & 53d St New York NY 10022

MACCUBBIN, ROBERT PURKS, literature and culture educator; b. Balt., Oct. 30, 1939; s. Walter Aubrey and Mary Anna (Purks) M.; 1 child, Gwyneth Marie Gang; m. Martha J. Hamilton-Phillips, Sept., 1986; children: Charles Aubrey Phillips, Glencora Alison. BA in Biology, Johns Hopkins U., 1961; MA in English, U. Ill., 1962, PhD in English, 1968. From asst. prof. to prof. Coll. William and Mary, Williamsburg, Va., 1964-95; fellow Thomas Reid Inst. for Rsch. in Cultural Studies and the Humanities, Aberdeen (Scotland) U., 1995. Author: The Age of William III and Mary II: Power, Politics and Patronage, 1688-1702, 1989; editor: " 'Tis Nature's Fault": Unauthorized Sexuality During the Enlightenment, 1987, Science and Technology and Their Cultural Contexts, 1982, British Literature and Culture, 1986, English Culture at the End of the 17th Century, 1988, Manners of Reading, 1992, The Art and Architecture of Versailles, 1993, The South Pacific in the Eighteenth Century, 1994; editor: Eighteenth-Century Life, 1983— (Best Spl. Issue award Conf. Editors Learned Jours. 1984, 95); contbr. articles to profl. jours. NEH grantee, 1988-89. Mem. MLA, FHC Soc., Am. Soc. 18th-Century Studies (exec bd. east ctrl. chpt. 1983—, Clifford prize 1986, 87, Best Article award southeast chpt. 1987, 92), Soc. for Theatre Rsch., Pvt. Librs. Assn., Grolier Club. Avocations: gardening, acting, baseball. Office: Coll William & Mary English Dept Williamsburg VA 23185

MACCURDY, RAYMOND RALPH, JR., modern language educator; b. Oklahoma City, May 12, 1916; s. Raymond R. and Ada May (Eastl) MacC.; m. Blanche Hermine Wolf, June 2, 1939; children—George Grant II, William Douglas. B.A., La. State U., 1939; M.A., 1941; Ph.D., U. N.C., 1948. Assoc. prof. modern langs. U. Ga., 1948-49; Assoc. prof. modern langs. U. N.Mex., Albuquerque, 1949-53, prof., 1953—, chmn. dept. modern and classical langs., 1963-68; Nat. Def. Edn. Act. coordinator lang. Programs Am. Assn. Tchrs. Spanish and Portuguese, 1958-59. Author: The Spanish Dialect in St. Bernard Parish, Louisiana, 1950, Francisco de Rojas Zorrilla and the Tragedy, 1958, Francisco de Rojas Zorilla, 1969; Editor: La Vida en el Ataud, 1961, Lucrecia y Tarquino, 1963, Numancia Cercada y Numancia destruida, 1977, Tirso de Molina, El Burlador de Sevilla, 1965, Del rey abajo, ninguno, 1970, Spanish Drama of the Golden Age-Twelve Plays, 1971, The Tragic Fall: Don Alvaro de Luna and Other Favorites in Spanish Golden Age Drama, 1978, Caesar of Sante Fe, 1990. Served to maj. AUS, World War II, CBI. Julius Rosenwald fellow, 1941, 46; Fund for Advancement Edn. fellow, 1954-55; Fulbright research scholar Spain, 1960-61. Mem. Rocky Mountain Modern Lang. Assn. (pres. 1957), Hispanic Soc. Am. Home: 1804 Newton Pl NE Albuquerque NM 87106-2527

MACDERMOTT-COSTA, BARBARA, nursing educator, medical, surgical nurse; b. Easton, Pa., Dec. 7, 1932; d. Floyd F. and Sarah C. Laubach; m. Dexter B. MacDermott, July 10, 1954; children: Richard, Katherine, Martha; m. James V. Costa, May 13, 1994. BSN, Syracuse U., 1954, MS, 1971. RN, N.Y. Asst. prof. Syracuse U., 1964-76, assoc. prof., 1976-93, asst. dean nursing, 1984-92, prof. emeritus, 1993—. Author: Understanding Basic Pharmacology: Practical Approaches for Effective Appreciation, 1994, Instructor's Guide for Pharmocotherapeutics: A Nursing Process Approach, 1994. Mem. ANA, N.Y. League for Nursing, Sigma Theta Tau, Pi Lambda Theta.

MAC DIARMID, WILLIAM DONALD, physician; b. Arcola, Sask., Can., June 22, 1926; s. John Angus and Evaline (Reed) MacD.; m. Bette Nell Brown, May 16, 1953; children—John A., Margaret A., Donald G., Andrew L. B.A., U. Sask., 1947; M.D., U. Toronto, 1949. Intern Pasqua Hosp., Regina, Sask., 1949-50; family physician, mem. med. staff Pasqua Hosp. and Regina Gen. Hosp., 1950-53; mem. staff Shaunavon (Sask.) Union Hosp., 1953-58; resident in internal medicine, fellow in endocrinology and metabolism U. Utah Affiliated Hosps., Salt Lake City, 1958-62; research asst. in human genetics Univ. Coll. Hosp. Med. Sch., London, 1962-64; mem. faculty U. Utah Med. Sch., 1964-69; prof. medicine U. Man. Med. Sch., Winnipeg, 1969-75, 79-91, chmn. dept., 1979-85; physician-in-chief St. Boniface Gen. Hosp., 1969-75, St. John's Gen. Hosp. and Health Sci. Ctr., 1975-79, Health Sci. Ctr. of Winnipeg, 1979-85; health svcs. cons., 1986—; prof., chmn. dept. medicine Meml. U. Nfld. Med. Sch., 1975-79; pres. Swift Current and Dist. Med. Soc., 1956-57; mem. bd. Com. for Accreditation of Can. Med. Schs., 1985-91, chmn., 1988-91; cons. Health Care Systems, 1967—. Vol. Can. Cancer Soc., 1992—; bd. dirs. Man. Med. Svcs. found., 1986-91, Winnipeg Mcpl. Hosps., 1986-89; chmn. bd. Man. Cancer Treatment and Rsch. Found., 1987-88; v.p. Man. Med. Coll. Found., 1988-91. Fellow ACP, Royal Coll. Physicians and Surgeons Can., Can. Coll. Med. Geneticists; mem. Am. Soc. Human Genetics, Can. Med. Assn. (com. on ethics 1987-91, coun. on med. edn. 1988-91), Man. Med. Assn. (dir. 1981-83, 87—, chmn. bd. 1982-83, hon. sec. 1988-89, hon. treas. 1989-90, chmn. com. on ethics 1987-91). Home and Office: 4142 Cortez Pl, Victoria, BC Canada V8N 4R8

MACDONALD, ALAN HUGH, librarian, university administrator; b. Ottawa, Ont., Can., Mar. 3, 1943; s. Vincent C. and Hilda C. (Durney) MacD.; m. Elizabeth Whalen; children—Eric Paul Henry, Nigel Alan Christopher. B.A., Dalhousie U., Halifax N.S., 1963; B.L.S., U. Toronto, Ont., 1964. With Dalhousie U., 1964-78, law librarian, 1965-67, 69-71, asst. univ. librarian, 1970-72, health sci. librarian, 1972-78; lectr. Sch. Library Services, 1969-78; dir. info. svcs. U. Calgary, Alta., 1988—; dir. libraries U. Calgary, Alta., Can., 1979-92, univ. orator, 1989—; dir. U. Calgary Press, 1984-90; chmn. Alta. Library Network, 1981-89; librarian N.S. Barristers Soc., 1969-74; mem. adv. bd. Nat. Libr. Can., 1972-76, Health Scis. Resource Ctr., Can. Inst. Sci. and Tech. Info., 1977-79; mem. Coun. of Prairie Univ. Librs., 1979-92, chair, 1984-85, 89, 91; Bassam lectr. U. Toronto Faculty Info. Studies, 1994, Lorne MacRae lectr. Libr. Assn. Alta., 1996. Mem. editorial bd. America: History and Life (ABC-CLIO), 1985-93. Pres. TELED Cmty. Media Access Orgn., Halifax, N.S., 1972-74; mem. Minister's Com. on Univ. Affairs, Alta., 1979-83; bd. dirs. Alta. Found. for Can. Music Ctr., 1985-92, Can. Inst. for Hist. Microreprodn., 1990—, pres., 1996—. Council Library Resources fellow, 1975; exec. fellow Univ. Microfilms Internat., 1986; recipient Disting. Acad. Librarian award Can. Assn. of Coll. and Univ. Libraries, 1988. Mem. Can. Libr. Assn. (treas. 1977-79, pres. 1980-81), Atlantic Provinces Libr. Assn. (pres. 1977-78), Libr. Assn. Alta. (v.p. 1988-89, Pres.'s award 1992), Can. Health Libr. Assn. (treas. 1977-79), Australian Libr. and Info. Assn. (assoc. 1977), N.Z. Libr. Assn., Bibliog. Soc. Can., Foothills Libr. Assn., Can. Assn. Info. Sci. (pres. 1979-80), Can. Assn. Rsch. Librs. (bd. dirs. 1981-86, v.p. 1985-86), Calgary Free-Net Soc. (bd. dirs. 1994—). Office: U Calgary, 2500 University Dr NW A100, Calgary, AB Canada T2N 1N4

MACDONALD, ANDREW STEPHEN, management consulting firm executive; b. Fairbanks, Alaska, July 15, 1953; s. Bernard L. and Rosemary (Unger) MacD.; m. Josephine A. Joanne, Aug. 4, 1972; children: Peter, Stephen, Charles. BA in Acctg., Seattle U., 1974. CPA, cert. mgmt. cons. Acct. Boeing Aerospace, Seattle, 1976-79; owner, pres. Triak Corp., Seattle, 1977—; pres. Exec. Cons. Group, Inc., Seattle, 1979—. Mem. AICPA, Inst. Mgmt. Cons., Wash. Soc. CPAs, Columbia Tower Club. Home: 10030 Lake Shore Blvd NE Seattle WA 98125-8158 Office: Exec Cons Group Inc 1111 3rd Ave Ste 2700 Seattle WA 98101-3207

MACDONALD, BRIAN SCOTT, educational administrator; b. Sudbury, Ont., Can., June 6, 1939; s. David William and Katherine Lillian (McKinnon) MacD.; m. Margaret Louise Young, Aug. 11, 1962 (dec. Apr. 1985); children—Heather Anne, David Colin, Michael Alexander. B.A. with honors, Royal Mil. Coll., Kingston, Ont., 1961; M.B.A. cum laude, York U., Toronto, Ont., 1980; postgrad., U. Toronto, 1980—. Tchr., cons. Bd. Edn., Ont., Can., 1966-80; exec. dir. Can. Inst. Strategic Studies, Toronto, Ont., Can., 1982-89; pres. Strategic Insight Planning and Communications, 1989—. Editor: Parliament and Defence Policy, 1982, War in the 80's: Men Against High Tech, 1983, Canada's Strategies for Space, 1984, The Grand Strategy of the Soviet Union, 1984, Defence and the Canadian Economy, 1984, Canada's Strategies for the Pacific Rim, 1985, High Tech and the High Seas, 1985, Canada, the Caribbean, and Central Am., 1986, Terror, 1986, Tactics and Technology, 1987, A Grand Strategy for the United States?, 1988, Airwar 2000, 1989, Canadian Strategic Forecast 1989, 1989, Space Strategy: Three Dimensions, 1989; contbg. editor Def. Policy Rev., 1994—. Pres. Royal Can. Arty. Assn., Toronto, 1976; vice chmn. Conf. Def. Assns., Ottawa, Ont., 1975; gov. Can. Corps of Commissionaires, Toronto, 1984-86; hon. aide de camp to Gov. Gen. Can., Ottawa, 1984-86; comdr. Toronto Militia Dist., 1984-86; bd. dirs. Atlantic Coun. Can., 1986—, sr. v.p., 1991; bd dirs. Royal Can. Mil. Inst., 1986-87. Served to col. Can. Army, 1957-86. Marsh-McLennan scholar, 1977, Dept. Nat. Def. scholar, 1981-82. Mem. Toronto Bd. Trade, Can. Ops. Rsch. Soc.. Home: 169 Newton Dr, Willowdale, ON Canada M2M 2N6

MACDONALD, CAROLYN HELMS, gifted education educator; b. Leesburg, Va., Oct. 15, 1941; d. Edmund Davis and Mary Irene (Peters) Helms; m. John Mount MacDonald, July 27, 1963 (div. Dec. 1984); children: Christina Hope, Heather Laurel, Katherine Anne. BS, East Tenn. State U., 1964; MS, Nova U., 1979. Cert. elem. tchr., jr. coll. tchr., gifted tchr., Fla. Elem. tchr. Shoemaker Elem. Sch., Gate City, Va., 1964-65, Bakersfield Elem. Sch., Aberdeen, Md., 1965-66, Brookview Elem. Sch., Jacksonville, Fla., 1966-68, Holiday Hill Elem. Sch., Jacksonville, Fla., 1968-69, Arlington Annex 5th Grade Ctr., Jacksonville, 1972-73; elem. tchr., social studies, lang. arts specialist Loretto Elem. Sch., Jacksonville, 1973-81, tchr. gifted, 1981—; mem. steering com. for gifted edn. Duval County Sch. Bd., 1982-85; del to Murmansk, USSR, 1991, ESOL trainer, 1995—. Pres. Mandarin Cmty. Club, Jacksonville, 1980; mem. Panel on Sewage Treatment Problems, 1979, Neighborhood Cancer Drive Com., 1979-84, Com. to Assess Cmty. Recreation Needs, Jacksonville, 1981-82; sponsor ARC. Recipient placque Mandarin Community Club, Jacksonville, 1974-77; named Outstanding Safety Patrol Sponsor North Fla., 1993. Mem. Fla. Jr. Coll. Woman's Club (v.p. 1969-71, pres. 1971-72, Outstanding Young Woman Am. 1971), Southside Jr. Woman's Club (v.p. 1970-73), Phi Mu Alumnae (v.p. 1989-90), Delta Kappa Gamma. Democrat. Methodist. Avocations: reading, traveling, decorating, walking, the arts. Home: 9439 San Jose Blvd Apt 228 Jacksonville FL 32257 Office: Loretto Elem Sch # 30 3900 Loretto Rd Jacksonville FL 32223-2055

MACDONALD, DAVID RICHARD, industrial psychologist; b. Dowagiac, Mich., May 20, 1953; s. Jerrold Brewster and Shirley Ann (Shaffer) MacD.; m. Mary Elizabeth Olson, Dec. 20, 1975 (div. Sept. 5, 1995); 1 child, Sarah Ann. AS, Southwestern Mich. Coll., 1973; BBA, Western Mich. U., 1975, MA, 1976, EdS, 1979; PhD, Mich. State U., 1986. Announcer, boardman WDOW AM/FM, Dowagiac, Mich., 1969-72; mgmt. devel. specialist Interstate Motor Freight System, Grand Rapids, Mich., 1977-79; sr. mgmt. tng. instr. GTE Gen. Telephone Co. Mich., Muskegon, 1979-82; cons. human resources devel. Steelcase, Inc., Grand Rapids, 1982-86, mgr. performance devel., 1986—; asst. prof. grad. mgmt. Aquinas Coll., Grand Rapids, 1983—; cons., speaker in field; facilitator, program dir. Devel. Dimensions Internat., Pitts., 1981; facilitator Alamo Learning Systems, Southfield, Mich., 1983, 86, Wilson Learning Corp., Eden Prairie, Minn., 1983; job analysis program mgr. Barry M. Cohen & Assocs., Largo, Fla., 1985. Co-chair United Way Steelcase campaign, Grand Rapids, 1986. Mem. ASTD (sec. W. Mich. chpt. 1977-79), Soc. Indsl.-Orgnl. Psychology, Am. Psychol. Assn., Nat. Soc. for Performance and Instrn., Mensa, Phi Kappa Phi. Republican. Avocations: building harpsichords, stained glass, brewing, gardening, early music. Home: 2306 Prospect Ave SE Grand Rapids MI 49507-3159 Office: PO Box 1967 Grand Rapids MI 49501-1967

MACDONALD, DAVID ROBERT, lawyer; b. Chgo., Nov. 1, 1930; s. James Wear and Frances Esther (Wine) M.; m. Verna Joy Odell, Feb. 17, 1962; children: Martha, Emily, David, Rachel, Rebecca. B.S., Cornell U., 1952; J.D., U. Mich., 1955. Bar: Ill. 1955, Mich. 1955, D.C. 1983. Practiced in Chgo., 1957-74; mem. firm Kirkland, Ellis, Hodson, Chaffetz & Masters, Chgo., 1957-62, partner, 1962; partner Baker & McKenzie, Chgo., 1962-74, 77-81, 83—; asst. sec. of Treasury for enforcement, ops. and tariff affairs Dept. Treasury, Washington, 1974-76; undersec. of Navy, 1976-77; dep. U.S. Trade Rep., 1981-83; bd. dirs. Chgo. City Bank and Trust Co., Mestek, Inc. (N.Y. Stock Exch.); chmn. bd. Vylor Corp. Mem. vis. com. Harvard U. Grad. Sch. Design, 1981-86; chmn. Howard County United Way Campaign, Md., 1987, chmn. cmty. partnerships, 1991-94; bd. dirs. Nat. Inst. for Urban Wildlife, 1986-90, United Way Ctrl. Md., 1987-91, Howard County Gen. Hosp., 1988-94, Columbia Festival, Inc., 1988-91, NAHB Rsch. Found., 1989-92, Alliance to End Childhood Lead Poisoning, 1990-93; chmn. The Children of Separation and Divorce Ctr., Columbia, 1995—; mem. adv. bd. U. Md. Engring. Sch., 1990—; mem. adv. bd. continuing edn. Johns Hopkins U., 1988-91; mem. policy adv. bd. Harvard Joint Ctr. Housing Studies, 1984-94; chmn. chancellor's adv. coun. U. Md. Sys., 1988—; chmn. Univ. Md. Found., 1990-94, bd. dirs., 1990—; exec. fellow Kennedy Sch., Harvard U., 1990-92; chmn. Affordable Housing Initiative, Columbia, Md., 1990-92; bd. overseers U. Md., College Park, 1994—; mem. Victory '94 com. Md. State Rep. Party, chmn. election inquiry funding com., 1994-95. 2d lt. USAAF, 1944-46. Mem. ABA, Chgo. Bar Assn., D.C. Bar Assn., Chgo. Assn. Commerce and Industry (bd. dirs. 1977-81), Order of Coif, Econ. Club (Chgo.), Cosmos Club (Washington). Home: 6605 Radnor Rd Bethesda MD 20817-6324 Office: Baker & McKenzie 815 Connecticut Ave NW Washington DC 20006-4004

MACDONALD, DIGBY DONALD, scientist, science administrator; b. Thames, New Zealand, Dec. 7, 1943; came to U.S., 1977; s. Leslie Graham and Francis Helena (Verry) M.; m. Cynthia Lynch, 1969; m. Mirna Urquidi, July 6, 1985; children: Leigh Vanessa, Matthew Digby, Duncan Paul, Nahline. BS in Chemistry, U. Auckland, New Zealand, 1965; MS in Chemistry with honors, U. Auckland, 1966; PhD, U. Calgary, Alta., Can., 1969. Asst. research officer Atomic Energy of Can., Pinawa, Man., Can., 1969-72; lectr. Victoria U., Wellington, New Zealand, 1972-75; sr. research assoc., assoc prof. Alta. Sulfur Research U. Calgary, 1975-77; sr. metallurgist SRI Internat., Menlo Park, Calif., 1977-79; prof. metall. engring. Ohio State U., Columbus, Ohio, 1979-84; lab dir., dep. dir. phys. scis. divsn. SRI Internat., Menlo Park, 1984-91; prof. material sci. engring., dir. Ctr. Advanced Materials Pa. State U., 1991—; adj. prof. Ohio Stae U., 1984; W.B. Lewis Meml. lectr. Atomic Energy Can., 1993; mem. USAF Sci. Adv. Bd., 1994—; cons. in field. Author: Transient Techniques in Electrochemistry, 1977; contbr. numerous articles to profl. jours.; patentee in field. Nat. Research Council scholar, Ottawa, Can., 1967-69; recipient Research award Ohio State U., 1983. Fellow Nat. Assn. Corrosion Engrs. Internat. (pub. com. 1982-85, Whitney award), Electrochem. Soc. (divsn. editor 1982-84, C. Wagner Meml. award 1991). Avocations: sailing, flying. Home: 1010 Greenbriar Dr State College PA 16801-6935 Office: Pa State U Ctr Advanced Materials 517 Deike Bldg University Park PA 16802-2714

MACDONALD, DONALD ARTHUR, publishing executive; b. Union City, N.J., Nov. 30, 1919; s. Richard A. and Marie (McDonald) M.; m. Ruth Moran, Dec. 21, 1942; children: Ronald A., Martha J., Marie C., Donald A., Charles A. BS cum laude, NYU, 1948, MBA, 1950. Advt. sales rep. Wall St. Jour., Dow Jones & Co., Inc., N.Y.C., 1953-55, mgr. New Eng. and Can. ter., 1955-58, ea. advt. mgr., 1958-61, exec. advt. mgr., 1961-63, advt. dir. sales promotion and prodn. depts., 1963-67, v.p. advt. sales, 1970-74, sr. v.p., 1974—, also dir.; vice chmn. Dow Jones & Co. Inc., N.Y.C., 1979—; also dir. Dow Jones & Co. Inc.; dir. Far Ea. Econ. Rev., Hong Kong; chmn. coun. judges Advt. Hall of Fame, 1972-78. Author: An Arrow for Your Quiver, 1994. Capt. AUS, 1942-46, World War II. Named to Advt. Hall of Fame, 1985. Mem. Am. Advt. Fedn. (dir. 1962—, past chmn., Barton A. Cummings Gold Medal award, 1995), Advt. Fedn. Am. (past gov. 2d dist., past chmn. joint commn., past chmn.), Advt. Council (dir.), N.Y. Advt. Club (past dir., Silver medal award 1965), Beta Gamma Sigma. Clubs: Downtown Athletic (N.Y.C.), Yale (N.Y.C.); Rumson Country (N.J.). Home: 15 Buttonwood LnE Rumson NJ 07760-1045

MACDONALD, DONALD STOVEL, lawyer; b. Ottawa, Ont., Can., Mar. 1, 1932; s. Donald Angus and Marjorie (Stovel) M.; m. Ruth Hutchison, Mar. 4, 1961 (dec. Mar. 1987); children: Leigh, Nikki, Althea, Sonja; m. Adrian M. Lang, Sept. 10, 1988; step-children: Maria (dec.), Timothy, Gregory, Andrew, Elisabeth, Amanda, Adrian. Student, Ashbury Coll., Ottawa; BA, U. Toronto, 1951; LLB, Osgoode Hall Law Sch., 1955; LLM, Harvard, 1956; diploma internat. law, Cambridge U., 1957; LLD, St. Lawrence U., U N.B. Saint John, 1990; D.Eng., Colo. Sch. Mines. Bar: Called to Ont. bar 1955. Assoc. McCarthy & McCarthy, Toronto, 1957-62; M.P. for Toronto-Rosedale, 1962; reelected, 1963, 65, 68, 72, 74; parliamentary sec. to Minister of Justice, 1963-65, to Minister of Finance, 1965, to Sec. of State for External Affairs, 1966-68, to Minister of Industry, 1968; pres. Privy Council and Govt. House Leader, 1968; minister of nat. def., 1970-72, minister energy, mines and resources, 1972-75, minister of finance, 1975-77; ptnr. firm McCarthy & McCarthy, Toronto, 1977-88; high commr. for Canada to U.K., 1988-91; counsel McCarthy Tétrault, Toronto, 1991—; spl. lectr. U. Toronto Law Sch.; chmn. Royal Commn. on Econ. Union and Devel. Prospects for Can., 1982-85; chmn. adv. com. competition Ont. Electricity Sys., 1995—; chmn. Inst. for Rsch. on Pub. Policy, Montreal, 1991—, Siemens Electric Ltd., 1991—, Design Exch., Toronto, 1993—, Inst. Corp. Dirs., Toronto, 1995—; bd. dirs. Alta Energy Co. Ltd., Boise (Idaho) Cascade Corp., Celanese Can. Inc., Hambros Can. Inc., Banister Found. Inc., Slough Estates Can., Sun Life Assurance Co. Can., TransCan. Pipelines Ltd.; trustee The Clan Donald Lands Trust, Skye, Scotland, 1991—. Named Freeman of the City of London, 1990, hon. fellow Trinity Hall, Cambridge U., 1994, Companion of the Order of Can., 1994. Mem. Queen's Privy Coun. Can., Delta Kappa Epsilon. Liberal. Baptist. Office: McCarthy Tétrault PO Box 48, Toronto-Dominion Twr Ste 4700, Toronto, ON Canada M5K 1E6

MACDONALD, DONALD WILLIAM, architect; b. Calgary, Alta., Can., May 7, 1935; came to U.S., 1957; s. Wallace Harold and Dorothy Louise (DeFaye) MacD.; m. Kerstin Maria Lindberg, July 22, 1965 (div. 1979); children: Pia, Ian, Denise. BArch, U. Okla., 1962; MS, Columbia U., 1963. Registered architect, Calif., Nev., N.Mex., Colo. Archtl. draftsman Bell and McCulloch Architects, Edmonton, Alta., 1955-57; archtl. designer Anshen and Allen Architects, San Francisco, 1965-67; prin. Donald MacDonald Architects, San Francisco, 1967—; assoc. prof. U. Calif.-Berkeley, 1965-66; prof. advisor Cogswell Coll., San Francisco, 1979-81, U. Okla., Norman, 1982—; lectr. archtl. sch. Idaho State U., Pocatello, 1974, Posnan (Poland) Inst. Art and Architecture, 1974, Portsmouth Inst. Tech.,

Eng., 1974, U. Okla., Norman, 1982, Tex. Tech U., Lubbock, 1984, Auburn (Ala.) U., 1986, Tulane U., New Orleans, 1987, Moscow Inst. Architecture, 1987, U. Calif. Berkeley, 1987, Mich. State U., Lansing, 1988, Ga. Inst. Tech., 1993, San Francisco Inst. Architecture, 1992—, U. Okla. Coll. Architecture, 1992, Archtl. Inst. B.C. Vancouver, 1991, McGill U., 1991, U. Cin., 1991, Woodbury U., Burbank, 1993, Boston Archtl. Sch., 1993, San Jose State U., 1994; lectr. in field; jury mem. Nat. Competition of Plywood Structures, Seattle, 1972, La. AIA Archtl. Design Competition, 1988, Miss. AIA Archtl. Competition, 1988, McGill U., 1991, Northern Calif. Home and Garden, 1991, City Boston Pub. Facilities Dept., 1992, San Diego Housing Commn., 1992; mem. juror panel in field; mem. San Francisco Civil Service Archtl. Selection Com., 1974; examiner Calif. Archtl. Registration Bd., 1979; prof. Calif. Coll. Arts and Crafts, San Francisco, 1988; faculty design studio San Francisco Inst. Architecture, fall 1990; jury chmn. N.C. AIA Archtl. Design Competition, 1988, Alta. Assn. Archs. U. Calgary, 1994, panel mem. 1994; East-West advisor energy conservation in housing Greenpeace, U.S.A.; presenter 9th Ann. Monterey Design Conf., 1989. Author: (with others) Bruce Goff: Toward Absolute Architecture, 1988; guest editor: Architecture and Urbanism, 1978; contbr. articles to profl. and consumer jours., U.S., Eng., Germany, Can., Poland, Russia, China, Italy, Japan. Received recognition through the media ABC, CNN, NBC, Time, People, Internat. Herald Tribune, Der Spiegel, London Observer, etc. for the invention of the City Sleeper, an exptl. environment for the homeless, studio house, and earthquake bed, 1987-91; exhbns. of architectural designs include Royal Inst. British Architects, London, 1985, 92, Contract Design Ctr., San Francisco, 1989, Contemporary Coll. Arts and Crafts, San Francisco, 1989, Contemporary Realist Gallery, San Francisco, 1989, San Francisco chpt. AIA, 1989, Calif. Sch. Bd. Assn., San Jose, Calif., 1989, Philippe Bonnafont Archtl. Drawings, San Francisco, 1990, Columbia U., N.Y.C., 1991, Mill Valley (Calif.) City Hall, 1991, San Mateo (Calif.) County Fair, 1991, Randolph Street Gallery, Chgo., 1991, Portland (Oreg.) chpt. AIA, 1993, San Francisco Examiner Home Buyers and Sellers Fair, 1993, San Francisco Embarcadero Waterfront Competition Exhibit, 1993. Recipient Regolo d'Or award Domas Milan, Italy, 1966, Okla. U. Regent's Disting. Alumni award, 1988, Honor award Calif. Coun. AIA, 1987, Commendation award for Golden Gate Toll Plaza in San Francisco Calif. Counc. AIA, 1987, also for toll booth award of excellence in archtl. conservation Found. for San Francisco Archtl. Heritage, 1989, Community Assistance award for innovative housing Calif. Coun. AIA, 1989, selected projects award Rolex Awards for Excellence, 1990, Fed. Design Achievement award, Presdl. Design awards, Nat. Endowment for Arts, 1991, World Habitat awards, grand prize Bldg. and Social Housing Foundation World Habitat awards, 1990, Gold Nugget awards, Grand award, Merit award Pacific Coast Builders and Sun/Coast ArchitectBuilder mag., 1991, SF mag. and Showplace Sq. Group Designers on Parade award, 1991, Maxwell award of excelence Fannie Mae, 1992, Oakland Orchids award AIA and Oakland Design Advocates, 1992, WorldDesign 92 award City and County of San Francisco, 1992; winner Hon. Mention Am. Plywood Assn., 1986, first place Housing Cost Reduction Co., Mich. State Housing Authority, 1987, No. Calif. Home and Garden mag. DIFFA Design Competition, 1990. Fellow AIA (honor awards San Francisco chpt. 1983, jury mem. San Mateo (Calif.) design awards program 1990); mem. Constrn. Specification Inst., McIntosh Archtl. Soc. Scotland, Columbia Archtl. League N.Y., Archtl. Assn. London. Clubs: St. Andrews Soc. (San Francisco); Chelsea Art (London); Columbia N.Y. Home: 743 Northpoint St San Francisco CA 94109 Office: 91 S Van Ness Ave San Francisco CA 94103

MACDONALD, FLORA ISABEL, Canadian government official; b. North Sydney, N.S., Can., June 3, 1926; d. George Frederick and Mary Isabel (Royle) MacD. Attended Empire Bus. Coll.; grad., Nat. Def. Coll., 1972; DHL (hon.), Mt. St. Vincent U., 1979, various univs., U.S. and U.K. Exec. dir. Progressive Conservative Party Hdqs., Ottawa, Ont., Can., 1957-66; adminstrv. officer, tutor dept. polit. studies Queen's U., 1966-72; mem. Can. Parliament for Kingston and the Islands, Ont., 1972-88; Progressive Conservative spokesman for Indian affairs and no. devel. Can. Parliament, 1972; for housing and urban devel., 1974; chmn. Progressive Conservative Caucus Com. on Fed.-Provincial Relations, 1976; sec. of state for external affairs, 1979-80, minister employment and immigration, 1984-86, min. comms., 1986-89; chairperson Internat. Developmental Rsch. Ctr., 1992—; spl. adv. Commonwealth of Learning, 1990-91; nat. sec. Progressive Conservative Assn. of Can., 1966-69; exec. dir. Com. for Ind. Can., 1971; pres. Elizabeth Fry Soc. of Kingston, 1968-70; vis. fellow Ctr. for Can. Studies, U. Edinburgh, 1989; host T.V. series North South Vision T.V., 1990-94. Bd. dirs. Can. Crafts Coun., CARE CANADA, Carnegie Commn. Re-preventing Deadly Conflict, Ctr. for Refugee Studies York U., Friends of the Nat. Lib., Queen's U. Coun., Refugee Policy Group, Washington, Shashtri Indo-Can. Inst.; chairperson Capital Fundraising Campaign Mt. St. Vincent U., Halifax, 1990-94. Decorated Officer Order of Can., 1993, Order of Ont., 1959. Mem. Can. Inst. Fgn. Affairs (dir. 1969-73), Can. Polit. Sci. Assn. (dir. 1972-75), Can. Inst. Internat. Affairs, Can. Civil Liberties Assn. (bd. dirs.), Commonwealth Human Rights Initiative, Nat. Mus. of Scotland (hon. patron Can.); U.N. (Eminent Persons to study Trans-Nat. Corps. in South Africa). Mem. United Ch. of Canada. Office: Internat Devel Rsch Ctr, 250 Albert St PO Box 8500, Ottawa, ON Canada K1G 3H9

MACDONALD, GEORGE FREDERICK, anthropologist, Canadian museum director; b. Cambridge, Ont., Can., July 4, 1938; s. George and Jane (Gorton) MacD.; m. Joanne Elizabeth Rice, Sept. 9, 1961; children: Christine, Grant. BA, U. Toronto, 1961; PhD, Yale U., 1966. Joined archaeol. divsn. Nat. Mus. Can., 1964-66, with west coast archaeol., 1966-68, head west Can. sect., 1968-69, chief archaeol. divsn., 1969-72, chief archaeol. survey Can., 1972-78; rsch. fellow Mus. Fur Volkerkunde, Basel, Switzerland, 1977-78; sr. archaeologist Nat. Mus. Can., 1978-82; rsch. fellow Fla. State Mus., Gainesville, 1980-81; head new accomodation task force Nat. Mus. Can., 1982; exec. dir. Can. Mus. Civilization, 1982—; pres. Can. Mus. Civilization Corp., 1995—; vis. fellow Mus. Anthropology U. B.C., 1981; lectr. Trent U., U. Ottawa, Carleton U., Simon Fraser U.; bd. dirs. Nat. Hist. Sites & Monuments, Can., Can. Mus. Construction Corp. Author: Ninstints: Haida World Heritage Site, 1983, Haida Monumental Art, 1983, Museum for the Global Village, 1989; contbr. articles to profl. jours. Mem. Can. del. drafting com. UNESCO Conv. on World Heritage, Paris, 1972; Can. del. Commn. Experts, Mohenjo, Daro, Pakistan, 1973; mem. hon. com. Nat. Mus. Am. Indian Nat. campaign, Washington, 1991—. Recipient James award Victoria Coll. U. Toronto, 1961; Wenner Gren fellow Yale U., 1964-65; mem. Can. Coun. Govt. Can., Yale, 1962-63. Mem. Can. Archeol. Assn. (pres. 1968). Home: 29 Lynott St, Cantley, PQ Canada J0X 1L0 Office: Can Mus Civilization Sta B, 100 Laurier St PO Box 3100, Hull, PQ Canada J8X 4H2

MACDONALD, GORDON CHALMERS, management consultant; b. Boston, Sept. 27, 1928; s. Frank C. and Anna E. (MacLean) MacD.; m. Eileen T. Harkins, May 25, 1952; children: Brian P., Peter G., Keith A., Audrey A. AA, Boston U., 1950, BBA, 1952; grad. advanced mgmt. program, Harvard U., 1979. Grad. tng. program Westinghouse Electric Corp., Pitts., 1952-64, regional/zone mgr., 1953-60; nat. mdse. mgr. Westinghouse Electric Corp., Metuchen, N.J., 1960-64; asst. to v.p. sales mgr. Magnavox Co., N.Y.C., 1964-68; v.p. mktg. GTE Corp., Batavia, N.Y., 1968-69; dir. mktg. Mitsubishi Internat. Corp., Lincolnwood, Ill., 1969-75; v.p. Mitsubishi Internat. Corp., N.Y.C., 1975-88, sec., 1984-88; advisor Mitsubishi Internat. Corp., 1989-91; bd. dirs. Mitsubishi Internat. Corp., N.Y.C., 1976-88; prin., mgmt. cons. G.C. MacDonald & Assocs., Greenwich, Conn., 1988—. Chmn. Sea Explorers com. Boy Scouts Am., Greenwich, 1976-81. With U.S. Army, 1946-48. Club: U.S. Power Squadron (comdr. 1981-82, exec. com. 1987—) (Greenwich). Avocations: sailing, skiing, bridge. Home: 42 Birchwood Dr Greenwich CT 06831-3354

MACDONALD, GORDON JAMES FRASER, geophysicist; b. Mexico City, July 30, 1929; s. Gordon and Josephine (Bennett) MacD.; m. Marcelline Kuglen (dec.); children: Gordon James, Maureen, Michael; m. Betty Ann Kipniss; 1 son, Bruce; m. Margaret Stone Jennings. A.B. summa cum laude, Harvard U., 1950, A.M., 1952, Ph.D., 1954. Asst. prof. geology, geophysics Mass. Inst. Tech., 1954-55, assoc. prof. geology, geophysics, 1955-58; staff assoc. geophysics lab. Carnegie Inst. Washington, 1955-58; cons. U.S. Geol. Survey, 1955-60; prof. geophysics UCLA, 1958-68; dir. atmospheric rsch. lab., 1960-66, assoc. dir. UCLA (Inst. Geophysics and Planetary Physics), 1960-68; v.p. rsch. Inst. for Def. Analyses, 1966-67, exec. v.p., 1967-68, trustee, 1966-70; vice chancellor for rsch. and grad. affairs U. Calif. at Santa Barbara, 1968-70, prof. physics and geophysics, 1968-70; mem. coun. on Environ. Quality Washington, 1970-72; Henry R. Luce prof. environ. studies and policy, dir. environ. studies program Dartmouth Coll., 1972-79; trustee The MITRE Corp., McLean, Va., 1968-70, 72-77, exec. com., 1972-77; disting. vis. scholar The MITRE Corp., 1977-79, chief scientist, 1979-83, v.p., chief scientist, 1983-90; prof. internat. rels., rsch. dir. U. Calif., San Diego, 1990-96; dir. Internat. Inst. for Applied Sys. Analysis, Laxenburg, Austria, 1996—; cons. NASA, 1960-70, mem. lunar and planetary missions bd., 1967; mem. Def. Sci. Bd., Dept. Def., 1966-70; cons. Dept. State, 1967-70; mem. Pres.'s Sci. Adv. Com., 1965-69; adv. panel on nuclear effects Office Tech. Assessment, 1975-77. Author: The Rotation of the Earth, 1960; co-author: Sound and Light Phenomena: A Study of Historical and Modern Occurrences, 1978, The Long-Term Impacts of Increasing Atmospheric Carbon Dioxide Levels, 1982, Global Climate and Ecosystem Change, 1990; contbr. articles to sci., tech. jours. Fellow AAAS, Am. Mineral. Soc., Am. Meteorol. Soc., Geol. Soc. Am., Am. Geophys. Union, Am. Acad. Arts and Scis., Am. Philos. Soc.; mem. Am. Math. Soc., Nat. Acad. Scis. (chmn. environ. studies bd. 1970, 72-73, chmn. commn. on natural resources 1973-77), Royal Astron. Soc. (fgn. assoc.), Geochem. Soc. Am., Seismol. Soc. Am., Soc. Indsl. and Applied Math., Coun. Fgn. Rels., Cosmos Club, Sigma Xi. Office: Internat Inst Applied Sys Analysis, Schloss Laxenburg, A-2361 Laxenburg Austria

MACDONALD, HUGH IAN, university president emeritus, economist, educator; b. Toronto, Ont., Can., June 27, 1929; s. Hugh and Winnifred (Mitchell) M.; m. Dorothy Marion Vernon, June 4, 1960; 5 children. B.Com., U. Toronto, 1952; M.A. (Rhodes scholar), Oxford (Eng.) U., 1954, B.Phil., 1955; LLD (hon.), U. Toronto, 1974. Lectr. U. Toronto, 1955-62, asst. prof., 1962-65; dean of men U. Toronto (Univ. Coll.), 1956-65; chief economist Govt. Ont., Toronto, 1965-67; dep. treas. Govt. Ont., 1967, dep. treas., dep. minister econs., 1968, dep. treas., dep. minister econs. and intergovtl. affairs, 1972; pres. York U., North York, Ont., 1974-84; prof., dir. York Internat., 1984-94, prof., pres. emeritus, 1984—; past pres. World U. Univ. Svc. Can.; chmn. Hockey Can., The Commonwealth of Learning. Recipient Can. Centennial medal, 1967, Queen's Silver Jubilee medal, 1977, Officer, Order Can., 1977, Commemorative medal 125th Anniv. Can. Confederation, 1992. Office: York U, 4700 Keele St, North York, ON Canada M3J 1P3

MACDONALD, IAN DUNCAN, information executive; b. Sudbury, Ont., Can., Aug. 27, 1944; s. Charles Max and Ruth Gloria (Lyons) MacD.; m. Carmen Medora Payne, Aug. 16, 1969; children: Conrad Max, Scott Alexander, Tracy Anne. BA, McMaster U., Hamilton, Ont., 1967. Credit reporter Dun & Bradstreet Can. Ltd., Toronto, Ont., 1967-68, reporting supr., 1968-69, sales rep., 1969-71, gen. mgr. mktg. svcs. divsn., 1971-73, gen. sales mgr., 1973-76; gen. mgr. Screening Systems Internat. Ltd., Toronto, 1976-77; regional mgr. Creditel of Can. Ltd., Toronto, 1977-83, v.p. div. credit reporting, 1983-91, sr. v.p., 1991—; mem. Can. Credit and Fin. Exec. Inst., Toronto, 1967-91. Mem. Can. Credit Granters Assn., World Trade Centre Toronto, Toronto Bd. Trade, Columbus Ctr. Achievement: landscape painting, classical guitar playing. Home: 2 Vista Humber Dr, Weston, ON Canada M9P 3R7 Office: Creditel of Can Ltd, 110 Sheppard Ave East, North York, ON Canada M2N 6S1

MACDONALD, JAMES ROSS, physicist, educator; b. Savannah, Ga., Feb. 27, 1923; s. John Elwood and Antonina Jones (Hansell) M.; m. Margaret Milward Taylor, Aug. 3, 1946; children: Antonina Hansell, James Ross IV, William Taylor. B.A., Williams Coll., 1944; S.B., Mass. Inst. Tech., 1944, S.M., 1947; D.Phil. (Rhodes scholar), Oxford (Eng.) U., 1950, D.Sc., 1967. Mem. staff Digital Computer Lab., Mass. Inst. Tech., 1946-47; physicist Armour Research Found., Chgo., 1950-52; asso. physicist Argonne Nat. Lab., 1952-53; with Tex. Instruments Inc., Dallas, 1953-74; v.p. corporate research and engring. Tex. Instruments Inc., 1968-73, v.p. corporate research and devel., 1973-74; cons., 1974—; dir. Simmonds Precision Products Inc., 1979-83; William Rand Kenan Jr. prof. physics U. N.C., Chapel Hill, 1974-91, prof. emeritus, 1991—; mem. editorial bd. Jour. Applied Physics, 1984-86; adj. prof. biophysics U. Tex. Med. Sch., Dallas, 1954-74; mem. solid state scis. panel NRC, 1965-73; mem. adv. com. for sci. edn. NSF, 1971-73; mem. vis. com. physics Mass. Inst. Tech., 1971-74; mem. external adv. com. Engring. Expt. Sta., Ga. Inst. Tech., 1976-79. Editor, contbr.: Impedance Spectroscopy-Emphasizing Solid Materials and Systems, 1987; contbr. more than 200 articles to profl. jours. Mem. Dallas Radio Commn., 1967-71; mem. sci. adv. coun. Callier Hearing and Speech Ctr., Dallas, 1974-78; bd. dirs. League for Ednl. Advancement in Dallas, 1965-70; mem. adv. com. Weber Rsch. Inst., 1985-90. Fellow Am. Phys. Soc. (com. on edn. 1973-75, com. on applications of physics 1975-78, George E. Pake prize 1985), IEEE (awards 1962, 74, assoc. editor Transactions of Profl. Group on Audio 1961-66, Transactions on Audio and Electroacoustics 1966-73, recipient Edison Gold medal 1988), AAAS; mem. Nat. Acad. Engring. (exec. com. assembly of engring. 1975-78, coun. 1971-74), Nat. Acad. Scis. (chmn. numerical data adv. bd. 1970-74, mem. com. on motor vehicle emissions 1971-74, chmn. com. on motor vehicle emissions 1973-74, mem. com. on satellite power systems 1979-81, mem. com. on sci., engring., and pub. policy 1981-83, mem. commn. on phys. scis., math., and applications 1985-88, mem. report rev. com. 1990—), Am. Inst. Physcis (governing bd. 1975-78, chmn. com. on profl. concerns 1976-78), Electrochem. Soc., Audio Engring. Soc., Phi Beta Kappa, Sigma Xi, Tau Beta Pi. Achievements include 10 patents in field. Office: Univ NC Dept Physics and Astronomy Chapel Hill NC 27599-3255

MACDONALD, JOHN BARFOOT, research foundation executive; b. Toronto, Ont., Can., Feb. 23, 1918; s. Arthur Albert and Gladys Lillian (Barfoot) M.; m. Liba Bockova, July 10, 1967; children—Kaaren, Grant, Scott, Vivian, Linda. D.D.S. with honors, U. Toronto, 1942; M.S. in Bacteriology, U. Ill., 1948; Ph.D. in Bacteriology, Columbia U., 1953; A.M. (hon.), Harvard U., 1956; LL.D. (hon.), U. Man., 1962, Simon Fraser U., 1965, Wilfrid Laurier U., 1976, Brock U., 1976, U. Western Ont., 1977; D.Sc. (hon.), U. B.C., 1967, U. Windsor, 1977. Chmn. div. dental research U. Toronto, 1953-56, prof. bacteriology, 1956; dir. Forsyth Dental Infirmary, Boston, 1956-62; prof. microbiology Harvard U. Sch. Dental Medicine, 1956-62; pres. U. B.C., 1962-67; exec. dir. Council Ont. Univs., 1968-76; pres. Addiction Research Found., Toronto, 1976-81; chmn. Addiction Research Found., 1981-87; chmn. commn. pharm. services Can. Pharm. Assn., 1967; rev. officer unicameral expt. U. Toronto, 1977; bd. dirs. Donwood Found., 1966-79, chmn., 1972-75; bd. dirs. Banff Sch. Advanced Mgmt., 1962-67, chmn., 1966-67; vice chmn. Ont. Council Health, 1981-84; cons. in field. Served with Dental Corps Can. Army, 1944-46. Home: 30 Metropolitan Cres, Keswick, ON Canada L4P 1L5

MACDONALD, JOHN STEPHEN, oncologist, educator; b. Bklyn., June 2, 1943; s. John Stephen and Margaret (Martin) M.; m. Mary Suzanne Stock, July 11, 1964; children: Margaret Wilson, John Stephen, Kathleen Lenore, Frederick Stock. A.B., Dartmouth Coll., 1965, B.M.S., 1967; M.D., Harvard U., 1969. Diplomate Am. Bd. Internal Medicine (mem. med. oncology com. 1989-93, chmn. med. oncology self edn. process com. 1993—). Intern and resident in medicine Beth Israel Hosp., Boston, 1969-71; clin. assoc. immunology and med. oncology Nat. Cancer Inst., Bethesda, Md., 1971-74; assoc. dir. cancer therapy evaluation program, div. cancer treatment Nat. Cancer Inst., 1979-82, med. oncologist Washington Clin., 1982-84; instr., asst. prof., then assoc. prof. medicine Georgetown U., Washington, 1974-79; clin. assoc. prof. Georgetown U., 1979-84, George Washington U., 1980-84; prof. medicine, chief div. hematology-oncology U. Ky., Lexington, 1984-89, assoc. dir. Markey Cancer Center, 1984-89; prof. medicine, chief sect. med. oncology, dir. cancer ctr. Temple U., Phila., 1989—; chmn. gastrointestinal cancer com. S.W. Oncology Group, 1985—. Editor-in-chief: Cancer Treatment Reports, 1979-82; co-editor: Gastrointestinal Oncology, 1992; mem. editorial bd. Jour. Clin. Oncology, 1988-91; contbr. over 180 articles to med. jours. Bd. mgmt. YMCA, 1979-84; bd. dirs. CYO, 1979-84. Served with USPHS, 1971-74. Jr. faculty clin. fellow Am. Cancer Soc., 1974-76. Fellow ACP; mem. Am. Fedn. Clin. Research, Am. Soc. Clin. Oncology, Am. Assn. for Cancer Research, Am. Cancer Soc. (bd. dirs. Phila. chpt. 1994—). Roman Catholic. Home: 522 Ridgeview Ln Villanova PA 19085-1715 Office: Temple U PO Box 38346 3322 N Broad St Philadelphia PA 19140-5102

MACDONALD, JOHN THOMAS, educational administrator; b. Utica, N.Y., Nov. 21, 1932; s. Gerald Clement and Mildred (Hayes) MacD.; m. Marcia Sprague Gallup; children: Terrence, Anthony, Elizabeth, Michele, Elise, Denise. BS, Northeastern U., 1958, MEd, 1960; PhD, U. Conn., 1970. Cert. elem. and secondary sch. tchr., prin., supt., Mass., Conn. Supervising prin. Noank, Ft. Hill. and Poquonnock Elem. Schs., Groton, Conn., 1962-66, Robert E. Fitch Jr. High Sch., Groton, 1966-70; rsch. asst. Ednl. Resources and Devel. Ctr. U. Conn., Storrs, 1969-70; supt. schs. Wallingford (Conn.) Pub. Schs., 1970-73, Walpole (Mass.) Pub. Schs., 1973-78, Dartmouth (Mass.) Pub. Schs., 1978-86; commr. edn. State Dept. Edn., Concord, N.H., 1986-90; asst. sec. for elem. and secondary edn. U.S. Dept. Edn., Washington, 1990-93; dir. state leadership ctr. Coun. of Chief State Sch. Officers, Washington, 1993—; mem. Postsecondary Edn. Commn., Concord, 1986-90, Coun. for Tchr. Edn., Concord, 1986-90, Profl. Standards Bd., Concord, 1986-90; trustee Univ. System of N.H., Durham, 1986-90; mem. Surgeon Gen's Task Force, 1990-93; mem. White House Conf. on Indian Edn., 1990-93; mem. Interagy. Com. on Sch. Health, 1990-93, others. Contbr. articles to profl. jours. Co-chmn. Emergency Sch.-Aide Proposals, U.S. Office Edn., 1973-75; mem. Mass. Adv. Commn. for Ednl. TV, 1983-86; mem. N.H. Task Force on Child Abuse, 1987-90; mem. nat. adv. coun. Northeastern U., 1990—; mem. Galaxy Classroom Nat. Adv. Coun. Galaxy Inst. for Edn., 1992—; mem. sch. health policy initiative Ctr. for Population & Family Health Columbia U., 1992—; mem. Packard roundtable to children Ctr. for Health Policy George Washington U., 1992—; mem. adv. com. external program rev. CDC, 1992—. Recipient Sears B. Condit award, 1958, Alumni award Northwestern U., 1973, Recognition award Coun. of Chief State Sch. Officers, 1990. Fellow Phi Delta Kappa, Phi Alpha Theta; mem. N.H. Sch. Bldg. Authority, Mass. Assn. Sch. Supts. (pres. 1985-86). Office: Coun Chief State Sch 1 Massachusetts Ave NW Washington DC 20001-1401

MACDONALD, JOSEPH FABER, bishop; b. Little Pond, P.E.I., Can., Jan. 20, 1932. Ordained priest Roman Cath. Ch., 1963, bishop, 1980. Pres., bishop Atlantic Episcopal Assembly, Grand Falls, Nfld. *

MACDONALD, KAREN CRANE, occupational therapist, geriatric counselor; b. Denville, N.J., Feb. 24, 1955; d. Robert William and Jeanette Wilcox (Crane) M.; m. Geno Piacentini, Oct. 22, 1994. BS, Quinnipiac Coll., 1977; MS, U. Bridgeport, 1982; postgrad., NYU, 1983—. Cert. occupational therapist. Occupational therapist, coord. of spl. care unit Jewish Home for the Elderly, Conn., 1987-93, N.Y. Inst., N.Y.C., 1984-86; pvt. practice Fairfield County, Conn., 1977-88; occupl. therapist Rehab. Assocs., Fairfield, Conn., 1993—; instr. NYU, 1985-89, Quinnipiac Coll., 1986-92; lectr., cons. in field. Contbr. articles to profl. jours. Youth leader, deacon Union Meml. Ch., Stamford, Conn., 1980-88; deacon Southport Congl. Ch., 1992-94; chair consumer com. Alzheimer's Coalition of Conn., 1991-92. Teaching fellow NYU, 1983-86. Mem. World Fedn. Occupl. Therapy, Am. Occupl. Therapy Assn. (scholar 1985, coun. edn.), Conn. Occupl. Therapy Assn. (gerontology liaison 1980-83), Pi Lambda Theta. Avocations: photography, poetry writing, painting. Home: 1 Davenport St Norwalk CT 06851-4601 Office: Rehab Assocs 60 Katona Dr Fairfield CT 06430-3544

MACDONALD, KATHARINE MARCH, journalist, public relations executive; b. Los Angeles, Nov. 12, 1949; d. Ian G. and Eve (March) M. Grad. high sch., Beverly Hills, Calif.; student, Santa Monica Coll., 1971-73, Whittier Law Sch., Los Angeles, 1975-76. Scheduling asst. Jess Unruh for Gov., Los Angeles, 1969-70; dep. press. sec. Jess Unruh for Mayor, Los Angeles, 1973; polit. cons. various local campaigns, Los Angeles, 1973-78; researcher Washington Post-Los Angeles Bur., 1978-86; spl. corr. Washington Post-Los Angeles Bur., Washington, 1980-86; reporter State Capitol Bur. San Francisco Examiner, 1986-89; press dep. to L.A. City Councilman Zev Yaroslavsky, 1990-94; mng. dir. Hill and Knowlton, Inc., 1994—; guest lectr. journalism and polit. sci. various colleges and universities, 1984—. Office: One Capital Mall Ste 250 Sacramento CA 95814 also: 6500 Wilshire Blvd 21st fl Los Angeles CA 90048

MACDONALD, KEN CRAIG, geophysicist; b. San Francisco, Oct. 14, 1947; m. Rachel Haymon, 1984. BS in Engring. Physics, U. Calif. Berkeley, 1970; PhD in Marine Geophysics, MIT/Woods Hole, 1975. Cecil H. and Ida Green postdoctoral scholar Scripps Instn. of Oceanography, 1975-76, asst. rsch. geophysicist, lectr., 1976-80; assoc. prof. U. Calif., Santa Barbara, 1980-83; prof. U. Calif., 1983—; chief scientist on over 30 deep sea expeditions; prin. ALVIN diver on over 40 dives to the mid-ocean ridge. Assoc. editor Jour. of Geophys. Rsch., 1979-82, Earth and Planetary Sci. Letters, 1978-88; mem. editorial bd. Marine Sci. Revs., 1986—; editor Marine Geophys. Rschs., 1986-90; contbr. numerous articles to profl. jours. Mem. ALVIN Rev. Com., 1979-82; mem. Ocean Sci. Bd. of NAS, 1980-83, Lithosphere Panel Advanced Ocean Drilling Project, 1983-85, Ocean Scis. Panel, NSF, 1984-86, COSOD II planning com.; mem. various RIDGE coms., RIDGE steering com., 1987-90; mem. NSF Ocean Scis. Strategic Plan for Rsch. and Edn. Com., 1993-94. Regents scholar U. Calif., Berkeley, 1966-70, Mineral Tech. scholar, 1967-70, Cecil H. and Ida Green scholar Inst. Geophysics and Planetary Physics/U. Claif., San Diego, 1975-76; NSF Grad. fellow, 1970-73; recipient AAAS Newcomb-Cleveland prize, 1980, Robert L. and Bettie P. Cody prize and medal Scripps Instn. Oceanography, 1994; named U. Hawaii SOEST Disting. lectr., 1990. Fellow Am. Geophys. Union; mem. Geol. Soc. Am. Avocations: windsurfing, fly fishing. Office: U Calif Santa Barbara Dept Geol Sci Santa Barbara CA 93106

MACDONALD, KENNETH, journalist, former editor; b. Jefferson, Iowa, Sept. 3, 1905; s. William Arthur and Mabel (Swearingen) McD.; m. Helen Inman, June 17, 1929; 1 child, Stephen. A.B., U. Iowa, 1926. With Des Moines Register and Tribune, 1926-86, successively reporter, copyreader, telegraph editor, city editor, mng. editor, exec. editor, v.p., 1946-76, editor, 1953-76, editorial chmn., 1976-77, pub., 1960-70, dir., 1940-86; Bd. dirs. A.P., 1956-65, 1st v.p., 1963-65; adv. bd. Pulitzer prizes, 1958-70. Co-author: Drink Thy Wine With a Merry Heart, 1983. Trustee Simpson Coll., chmn. bd., 1957-59. Served as air combat intelligence officer USNR, World War II, PTO. Mem. Am. Soc. Newspaper Editors (dir. 1950-56, pres. 1955), Sigma Delta Chi. Mem. Episcopal Ch. Club: Des Moines. Home: 3412 Southern Hills Dr Des Moines IA 50321-1319

MACDONALD, LENNA RUTH, lawyer; b. Providence, July 16, 1962; d. Arthur Robert and Laina Ruth (Weake) Macd. BA, Brown U., 1984; postgrad., London Sch. Econs., 1984-85; JD, Emory U., 1988. Bar: Ohio 1988, R.I., 1989, Mass. 1992. With Erikson Internat. Biog. Database, Providence, 1983-86; assoc. Smith & Schnacke, Dayton, Ohio, 1988-89, Edwards & Angell, Providence, 1989-91, McDermott, Will & Emery, Boston, 1991-93; asst. gen. counsel, group mgr. Banc One N.H. Asset Mgmt. Corp., Manchester, 1993-96, Banc One Corp., Bank One, Ky., NA, Louisville, 1996—. Mem. Mass. Bar Assn., R.I. Bar Assn., Am. Friends London Sch. Econs., Phi Alpha Delta. Republican. Episcopalian. Avocations: sailing, pottery. Home: 1721 Devondale Dr Louisville KY 40222 Office: Banc One Bank One Ky NA Legal Dept 416 W Jefferson St Louisville KY 40202-3244

MAC DONALD, MALCOLM MURDOCH, editor, publisher; b. Uniontown, Pa., June 15, 1935; s. Morgan Bowman and Ruth (Newcomb) Greene Mac D.; m. Constance Emily Marsh, June 13, 1959; children—Randall Malcolm, Alison Margaret, Ellen Marsh. B.A., Trinity Coll., Conn., 1957. Coll. rep. Midwest D. Van Nostrand Co. Inc., Princeton, N.J., 1958-62, assoc. sci. editor, 1962, sci. editor, 1963-68; sci. editor Van Nostrand Reinhold Co., N.Y.C., 1968-70; editor Pa. State U. Press, State College, 1970-72; chief editor U. N.C. Press, Chapel Hill, 1972-76, asst. dir., 1975-76; asst. dir., editor U. Ga. Press, Athens, 1976-78; dir. U. Ala. Press, 1978-96; acting dir. U. Ala. Library, 1980-81; cons. in field. Author: (With Cecil E. Johnson) Society and the Environment, 1971, (with Robert E. Davis) Chemistry and Society, 1972. Mem. Assn. Am. Univ. Presses (bd. dirs. 1982-84), Omicron Delta Kappa. Office: U Ala Press Box 870380 Tuscaloosa AL 35487

MACDONALD, MARY ELIZABETH, nursing administrator, educator; b. Westboro, Mass., July 17, 1918; d. Hugh D. and Sarah (Campbell) MacD. Diploma, Mass. Gen. Hosp. Sch. Nursing, Boston, 1942; AB magna cum laude, Emmanuel Coll., Boston, 1939; MA, Columbia U., 1950, Suffolk U., Boston, 1987. Asst. prof., dir. basic nursing edn. program Boston Coll. Sch. Nursing, Chestnut Hill, Mass., 1950-53; assoc. dean, prof. nursing edn. U. Mass. Sch. Nursing, Amherst, 1953-67; dir. dept. analytical studies Mass. Gen. Hosp., Boston, 1967-68, dir. dept. nursing, 1968-83; cons. nursing adminstr. Surgeon Gen. U.S. Army; mem. HHS Coun. on Teaching Grants,

Policy Adv. Bd., Joint Commn. on Accreditation of Hosps.; cons. in nursing edn. to numerous schs. and profl. publs. Recipient Alumni Career Achievement award Emmanuel Coll., Boston, 1992. Fellow Am. Acad. Nursing; mem. AAUP, Internat. Coun. Nurses, Am. Nurses Assn., Nat. League Nursing, Mass. Nurses Assn., Mass. League Nursing, Sigma Theta Tau, Phi Lambda Theta, Kappa Delta Pi, Kappa Gamma Pi. Home: 8 Whittier Pl Apt 20 Boston MA 02114-1402

MACDONALD, MAURICE MARCUS, economics educator; b. Bozeman, Mont., Sept. 20, 1947; s. Bernard Marcus and Alice Mildred (Dira) MacD.; m. Jeanne Frances Reece, June 13, 1969; children: Nicole, Dantia, Anton, Micah, Jasper, Gabriel, Chester, Maurice Jr. AB in Econs., U. Calif., Santa Cruz, 1969; PhD in Econs., U. Mich., 1974. Project assoc. Inst. for Rsch. on Poverty U Wis., Madison, 1973-75, prof. consumer sci. Sch. Family Resources, 1975-95; chair human devel and family studies Iowa State U. Coll. Family and Consumer Scis., Ames, 1995—; mem. acad. adv. bd. Rockford (Ill.) Inst., 1989-95; cons. in field. Author: Food, Stamps and Income Maintanence, 1977. Adult edn. chair on Bishop's pastoral letter on economy Blessed Sacrament Parish, Madison, 1986. NIH grantee, 1978-79, 90-94. Mem. KC. Roman Catholic. Office: Coll Family and Consumer Scis 1086 LeBaron Hall Ames IA 50011

MACDONALD, MICHAEL R., retail executive. Exec. v.p., cfo asst. sec. P.A. Bergner & Co., Milw., Wis. Office: P A Bergner & Co 331 W Wisconsin Ave Milwaukee WI 53203-2201*

MACDONALD, PAUL CLOREN, biologist, physician. MD, U. Tex., 1955. Prof. ob-gyn. and biochemistry Cecil H. & Ida Cecil Green Ctr. Reproductive Biol. Scis., 1974—, dir. endocrinology, 1974—. Mem. Inst. Medicine, Nat. Acad. Scis. Office: Green Ctr Reproductive Biol 5323 Harry Hines Blvd Dallas TX 75235*

MACDONALD, PAUL EDWARD, electrical engineer; b. Syracuse, N.Y., Nov. 2, 1954; s. Cornelius J. and Virginia F. (Vassallo) MacD.; m. Linda Marie Fredrick, Aug. 20, 1983; children: Maeghen Leigh, Charles Fredrick. B Archtl. Engring., Pa. State U., 1977. Registered profl. engr., Va., Md., D.C., Conn., W.Va., Del., Ill. Engring. in tng. Syska & Hennessy, Washington, 1977-78, jr. engr., 1978-79, project engr., 1979-80; project engr. Meta Engrs. P.C., Washington, 1980-82, dir. elec. engring., 1982-88, chief elec. engring., 1988-91, v.p., chief elec. engring., 1991—. Leader Tiger Cubs, Boy Scouts Am., Alexandria, Va., 1994-95. Mem. NSPE, Nat. Soc. Archtl. Engrs., D.C. Soc. Profl. Engrs. (pres. 1991-92, bd. dirs. 1986, Outstanding Svc. award 1987, 88), Sierra Club. Roman Catholic. Avocations: woodworking, making stringed musical instruments, playing guitar, banjo and dulcimer, hiking. Home: 8801 Lukens Ln Alexandria VA 22309-4105 Office: Meta Engrs PC 1220 L St NW Washington DC 20005-4018

MACDONALD, R. FULTON, venture developer, business educator; b. Monmouth County, N.J., Dec. 24, 1940; s. James Fleming Smith Macdonald and Jane Macfarlane Barnes Abbott; m. Carol Jean Archer (div.); 1 child, Paige Brubaker Smith; m. Laura Boswell; children: George Dewey Boswell, James Fleming Smith Macdonald II. AB, U. Pa., 1963, MBA, 1969; postgrad. sr. mktg. mgmt., Stanford U., 1979. Systems mgr., mcht. John Wanamaker, Inc., Phila., 1969-74; prin. Booz, Allen & Hamilton, N.Y.C., 1974-79; pres. Irwill Industries, N.Y.C., 1979-82, Internat. Bus. Devel. Corp., N.Y.C., 1982—; chmn. IBEX Mktg. Corp., N.Y.C., 1988—; pres. Simfer Operational Internat., Inc., N.Y.C., 1984; vice chmn. Neusteter Co., Denver, 1984-85; dir. Fragrances Selective, Inc., 1985-87; mng. dir. Stuyvesant Group Internat., Dutch Am. Bus. Advisors, N.Y.C. and Amsterdam, 1987-88; chmn. Am. Bus. Media, Inc., 1989-90, One Ams., Inc., Washington, 1990—; mng. dir. Synoptics Devel. Corp., N.Y.C., 1992—; adj. prof. Grad. Bus. Sch., Columbia U., N.Y.C., 1984-85, Mgmt. Inst. NYU, 1992—, chmn. Globalization Adv. Bd., 1993—; strategic advisor Singapore, 1994—. Designer Manpower Mgmt. Concepts computer system, 1972—; contbr. articles to bus. publs. Capt. inf. U.S. Army, 1963-67, Vietnam. Decorated Bronze Star. Mem. Inst. Mgmt. Consultants (cert. mgmt. cons. 1989), Global Econ. Action Inst., Soc. Mayflower Descendants, Soc. Coll. Alumni U. Pa. (pres. 1973-74, bd. mgrs. 1975—), Ripon Soc. (Washington), Penn Club (N.Y.). Republican. Christian Scientist. Avocation: squash. Home: 40 Central Park S Penthouse A New York NY 10019 Office: Internat Bus Devel Corp 730 5th Ave Ste 900 New York NY 10019-4105

MACDONALD, RICHARD, production designer. Prodn. designer: (films) Eva, 1962, The Servant, 1964, King and Country, 1965, Modesty Blaise, 1966, Far from the Madding Crowd, 1967, Secret Ceremony, 1968, Boom!, 1968, A Severed Head, 1971, The Assassination of Trotsky, 1972, Jesus Christ Superstar, 1973, Galileo, 1975, The Romantic Englishwoman, 1975, The Day of the Locust, 1975, Marathon Man, 1976, Exorcist II: The Heretic, 1977, F.I.S.T., 1978, The Rose, 1979, ...And Justice for All, 1979, Altered States, 1980, Cannery Row, 1982, Something Wicked This Way Comes, 1983, Supergirl, 1984, Electric Dreams, 1984, Plenty, 1985, Spacecamp, 1986, Coming to America, 1988, The Russia House, 1990, The Addams Family, 1991, The Firm, 1993.

MACDONALD, ROBERT ALAN, language educator; b. Salamanca, N.Y., Mar. 25, 1927; s. Guy E. and Hildur V. (Helene) MacD. B.A., U. Buffalo, 1948; M.A., U. Wis., 1949, Ph.D., 1958. Asst. prof. U. Richmond, Va., 1955-61, assoc. prof., 1961-67, prof. Spanish, 1967-95, prof. emeritus, 1995; ofcl. project reviewer NEH, Washington, 1977-95, Social Sci. and Humanities Research Council, Ottawa, Ont., Can., 1981-95. Author: Espéculo, texto jurídico atribuído a Alfonso X, 1990, Alfonso X, Libro de las Tahurerías, 1995; editor Bull. of Fgn. Lang. Assn. Va., 1962-67, 72-86; contbr. articles to profl. jours. Served with U.S. Army, 1946-47, 51-53. A.L. Markham traveling fellow U. Wis., 1958-59; Am. Council Learned Socs. fellow, 1976; fellow and grantee U. Richmond, 1958-94; named Cultural Laureate of Va., 1977; recipient Disting. Service award Fgn. Lang. Assn. Va., 1981. Mem. Acad. Am. Rsch. Historians on Medieval Spain, Am. Assn. Tchrs. of Spanish and Portuguese (past pres. state chpt.), AAUP (past pres. local chpt.), Am. Council on Teaching Fgn. Langs., Medieval Acad. Am., MLA. Club: Torch (Richmond).

MACDONALD, ROBERT RIGG, JR., museum director; b. Pitts., May 11, 1942; s. Robert Rigg and Ruth (Johnson) M.; m. Catherine Ronan, Nov. 27, 1965; children: Matthew, Robert, Catherine. B.A., U. Notre Dame, 1964, M.A., 1965; M.A., U. Pa., 1970. Asst. curator Smithsonian Instn., Washington, 1965; curator Mercer Mus., Doylestown, Pa., 1966-70; dir. New Haven Colony Hist. Soc., 1970-74, La. State Mus., New Orleans, 1974-85, Mus. of City of N.Y., 1985—; adj. prof. mus. studies NYU, 1989—; mem. Commn. on Mus. for a New Century. Editor: New Haven Colony Furniture, 1973, Louisiana Images 1880-1920, 1975, Louisiana Black Heritage, 1977 Louisiana Portraitures, 1979, Louisiana Legal Heritage, 1981, The Sun King: Louis XIV and the New World, On Being Homeless in New York, 1987, Broadway! 125 Years of Musical Theater, Hives of Sickness: Public Health and Epidemics in New York City, 1995. Active Nat. Endowment for Humanities. Decorated chevalier de l'Ordre des Arts et des Lettres (France), cruz de Caballero de la Order de Isabel La Catolica (Spain); assoc. fellow Berkeley Coll., Yale U., 1978; Hagley fellow U. Del., 1970-71; Univ. scholar U. Notre Dame, 1964-65. Mem. Am. Assn. State and Local History (coun.), Am. Assn. Mus. (pres. 1985-88, chmn. ethics task force 1988-91), Century Assn. Roman Catholic. Home: 35 Edgewood Ln Bronxville NY 10708-1946 Office: Mus NYC 1220 5th Ave New York NY 10029-5221

MACDONALD, ROBERT TAYLOR, newspaper executive; b. Mt. Vernon, N.Y., Oct. 25, 1930; s. Joseph Taylor and Mary Gertrude (Broderick) MacD.; m. Christiana Barbara Besch, June 25, 1960 (div. 1977); children: Gregory, Michael, Jennifer; m. Gillian S. Tripier, 1978. B.S., Yale, 1952; M.B.A., Wharton Sch. of U. Pa., 1958. Pub. Mariner (monthly trade mag.), 1956; bus. mgmt. cons., 1958-61; v.p., adminstrn., dir. N.Y. Herald Tribune, Inc., 1961-63, exec. v.p., 1963-66; pub. N.Y. Herald Tribune-Washington Post Internat., 1966-67, Internat. Herald Tribune, 1967-77; chmn. Hudson Research Europe, Ltd., 1977-87; mng. dir. MacDonald & Co., 1980—; v.p. internat. ops. Washington Post Co., 1966-70, asst. to chmn., 1968-70. Bd. govs. Am. Hosp. of Paris. Served as lt. USNR, 1953-56. Mem. Fgn. Policy Assn., Am. C. of C. in Paris (dir.), Phi Gamma Delta. Clubs: Yale (N.Y.C.), Wharton MBA (N.Y.C.) (dir., past pres.); Apawamis (Rye, N.Y.); Travelers (Paris). Office: Ste 701 9393 Midnight Pass Rd Sarasota FL 34242-2959

MACDONALD, RODERICK, library director; b. Mpls., Mar. 13, 1931; s. Roderick and Frances Ruth (Lawrence) Mac D.; m. Joanne Gaffney, Jan. 4, 1958; children: Maria Halliday, Roderick III, David, Louise. B.A., Macalester Coll., 1953; M.A., U. Minn., 1959. City librarian Free Pub. Library, Kaukauna, Wis., 1959-61; reference librarian, asst. prof. Macalester Coll., 1961-66; dir. Anoka County Library, Mpls., 1966-69, Pub. Library, Des Moines, 1969-78, Dakota County Library System, Eagan, Minn., 1978-95; retired, 1996. Served with AUS, 1953-55. Mem. ALA, Iowa Library Assn. (legis. chmn. 1971), Minn. Library Assn. (pres. 1968). Democrat. Home: 4928 5th Ave S Minneapolis MN 55409-2645

MACDONALD, R(ONALD ANGUS) NEIL, physician, educator; b. Calgary, Alta., Can., Jan. 6, 1935; s. Angus Neil and Florence Mary (Macdonald) MacD.; m. Mary Jane Whiting, June 30, 1962; children: Cynthia, David, James, Gavin. BA, U. Toronto, 1955; MD, CM, McGill U., Montreal, 1959. Demonstrator, lectr. McGill U., 1965-67, assoc. dean, faculty of medicine, 1967-70; assoc. dir., dir. Oncology Day Ctr., Royal Victoria Hosp., Montreal, 1967-71; exec. dir. Provincial Cancer Hosps. Bd., Edmonton, Alta., Can., 1971-75; prof. medicine U. Alta., Edmonton, 1971-94; dir. Cross Cancer Inst., Edmonton, 1975-80, 1981-87; assoc. dir., prof. palliative care Royal Victoria Hosp., Montreal, 1980-81; prof. palliative medicine Alta. Cancer Found., Edmonton, 1987-94; dir. cancer ethics program Inst. Recherches Cliniques Montreal, 1994—; prof. oncology McGill U., 1994—; mem. cancer expert adv. panel WHO, Geneva, 1986—, Can. rep. Cancer Pain project, 1983—. Co-editor: Oxford Textbook of Palliative Medicine, 1993; contbr. articles on treatment of cancer pain and other topics to profl. jours. Recipient Queen's Jubilee medal, 1977, Alta. Achievement award, 1980, Blair award Nat. Cancer Inst., 1980, Edmonton Achievement award, 1994. Fellow Coll. Physicians and Surgeons Can., Royal Coll. Physicians Edinburgh (hon.); mem. Order of Can., Can. Cancer Soc. (nat. bd. dirs. 1981-87), Can. Oncology Soc. (pres. 1977-78), Am. Soc. Clin. Oncology (sec.-treas. 1980-82), Can. Soc. Palliative Care Physicians (pres. 1993-94). Roman Catholic. Avocations: squash, history. Office: Inst. Recherches Cliniques Montreal, 110 Pine Ave W, Montreal, PQ Canada H2W IR7

MACDONALD, THOMAS COOK, JR., lawyer; b. Atlanta, Oct. 11, 1929; s. Thomas Cook and Mary (Morgan) MacD.; m. Gay Anne Everiss, June 30, 1956; children: Margaret Anne, Thomas William. B.S. with high honors, U. Fla., 1951, LL.B. with high honors, 1953. Bar: Fla. 1953. Practice law Tampa, 1953—; mem. firm Shackleford, Farrior, Stallings & Evans, 1953—; spl. counsel Gov. of Fla., 1963, U. Fla., 1972—; del. 5th cir. Jud. Conf., 1970-81; mem. adv. com. U.S. Ct. Appeals (5th cir.), 1975-78, (11th cir.), 1988-93; mem. Fla. Jud. Qualifications Commn., 1983-88, vice chmn., 1987, chmn., 1988; mem. judicial nominating com. Fla. Supreme Ct., 1995—. Mem. Fla. Student Scholarship and Loan Commn., 1963-67, Fla. Jud. Qualifications Commn., Fla. Supreme Ct. Jud. Nominating Commn., 1995—, 1983-88, vice chmn., 1987, chmn., 1988; bd. dirs. Univ. Community Hosp., Tampa, 1968-78, Fla. West Coast Sports Assn., 1965-80, Hall of Fame Bowl Assn., 1989-93, Jim Walter Corp., 1979-87; mem. Hillsborough County Pub. Edn. Study Commn., 1965; lic. lay eucharistic min. Episcopal Ch., 1961—; chancellor Episcopal Diocese of S.W. Fla., 1990-93; bd. dirs. U. Fla. Found., 1978-86, Shands Teaching Hosp., U. Fla., 1981-95; counsel Tampa Sports Authority, 1983—. Recipient Disting. Alumnus award U. Fla., 1976, George C. Carr award Fed. Bar Assn., 1991, Fla. Bar Presdl. award of Merit, 1995, award Hillsborough County Bar Assn. Trial Lawyers, 1995. Fellow Am. Coll. Trial Lawyers (chmn. state com. 1990-91), Am. Bar Found., Fla. Bar Assn. (chmn. com. profl. ethics 1966-70, bd. govs. 1970-74, bar mem. Supreme Ct. com. on stds. conduct governing judges 1976, Fla. bd. cert. appellate lawyer); mem. ABA (com. on ethics and profl. responsibbility 1970-76), Am. Law Inst. (life), 11th Cir. Hist. Soc. (trustee 1982-95, pres. 1989-95), U. Fla. Nat. Alumni Assn. (pres. 1973), Phi Kappa Phi, Phi Delta Phi, Fla. Blue Key, Kappa Alpha. Episcopalian. Home: 1904 S Holly Ln Tampa FL 33629-7004 Office: PO Box 3324 Tampa FL 33601-3324

MACDONALD, WAYNE DOUGLAS, publisher; b. Port Elgin, Ont., Can., Sept. 20, 1940; s. John Murdock and Irene Juliana (Lunow) MacD.; m. Marjorie Anne Farwell, Apr. 28, 1968; children: Scott, Ryan. Journalist Kitchener (Ont.)-Waterloo Record, 1964-75, mgn. editor, 1975-79, dir. resource and devel., 1985-88, editor, 1988-90, pub., 1990—; assignment editor Toronto Star, 1979-82; comm. dir. Ministry of Consumer Affairs, Toronto, Canada, 1982-84, Ministry of Health, Toronto, Canada, 1984-85; bd. dirs. Can. Press, Toronto, 1992-93; mem. adv. coun. U. Western Ont. Sch. Journalism, London, Ont., 1993. Mem. Rotary of Kitchener-Waterloo (com. for ednl. excellence), Westmount Golf and Country Club, Univ. Club. Office: Kitchener-Waterloo Record, 225 Fairway Rd S, Kitchener, ON Canada N2G 4E5

MACDONALD, WILLIAM LLOYD, architectural historian; b. Putnam, Conn., July 12, 1921; s. William Lloyd and Susan Elisabeth (Elrod) MacD.; children: Noel, Nicholas. AB, Harvard U., 1949, AM, 1953, PhD, 1956. Instr. Boston Archtl. Ctr., Mass., 1950-54; from asst. prof. to assoc. prof. Yale U., 1956-65; A.P. Brown prof. Smith Coll., Northampton, Mass., 1965-80; archtl. historian, Washington, 1980—; exec. sec. Byzantine Inst., Boston, 1950-54. Author: Early Christian and Byzantine Architecture, 1962, Northampton Massachusetts Architecture and Buildings, 1976, Piranesi's Carceri: Sources of Invention, 1976, Architecture of the Roman Empire I, 1982, II, 1986 (Alice Davis Hitchcock prize, George Wittenborn Meml. award); The Pantheon, 1976, (with J.A. Pinto) Hadrian's Villa and its Legacy, 1995. Lt. USAAF, 1942-45. Recipient Kevin Lynch award Dept. of Urban Studies MIT; Emerton, Shaw fellow Harvard U., Cambridge, Mass., 1949, 50, Vets. Nat. scholar, 1948; J. Paul Getty Ctr. scholar, Santa Monica, 1985-86. Fellow Am. Acad. Arts and Scis., Am. Acad. Rome (Prize fellow 1954-56); mem. AIA (life), Soc. Archtl. Historians (bd. dirs.), Soc. for Promotion of Roman Studies (life), Soc. for Libyan Studies. Home: 3811 39th St NW Washington DC 20016-2835

MACDONOUGH, JOHN N., beverage company executive. Past pres., COO Miller Brewing Co., Milw., chmn. bd., CEO, 1994—. Office: Miller Brewing Co 3939 W Highland Blvd Milwaukee WI 53208-2816*

MACDOUGAL, GARY EDWARD, corporate director, foundation trustee; b. Chgo., July 3, 1936; s. Thomas William and Lorna Lee (McDougall) MacD.; children: Gary Edward, Michael Scott; m. Charlene Gehm, June 15, 1992. BS in Engring., UCLA, 1958; MBA with distinction, Harvard U., 1962. Cons. McKinsey & Co., L.A., 1963-68, ptnr., 1968-69; chmn. bd., chief exec. officer Mark Controls Corp. (formerly Clayton Mark & Co.), Evanston, Ill., 1969-87; gen. dir. N.Y.C. Ballet, 1993-94; chmn. Gov. Task Force on Human Svcs. Reform State of Ill., 1993—; sr. advisor and asst. campaign mgr. George Bush for Pres., Washington, 1988; apptd. chmn. Bulgarian-Am. Enterprise Fund, Chgo. and Sophia, Bulgaria, 1991-93, bd. dirs., 1991—; apptd. to U.S. Commn. on Effectiveness of UN, 1992-93; bd. dirs., chmn. fin. com. United Parcel Svc. Am., Inc., Atlanta; bd. dirs. Union Camp Corp., Wayne, N.J., CBI Industries, Oak Brook, Ill.; adv. dir. Saratoga Ptnrs., N.Y.; instr. UCLA, 1969. Contbr. articles to profl. jours., chpts. to books. Trustee Annie E. Casey Found., UCLA Found., 1973-79, W.T. Grant Found., 1992-94, Russell Sage Found., 1981-91, chair, 1987-90; apptd. by Pres. Bush as pub. del., alt. rep., U.S. Del. UN 44th Gen. Assembly, 1989-90; commr. Sec. Labor's Commn. on Workforce Quality and Productivity, Washington, 1988-89. Lt. USNR, 1958-61. Mem. Coun. Fgn. Rels., Harvard Club, Econ. Club, Harvard Bus. Sch. Club, Kappa Sigma. Episcopalian. Home: 505 N Lake Shore Dr Apt 2711 Chicago IL 60611-3406

MACDOUGALL, HARTLAND MOLSON, corporate director, retired bank executive; b. Montreal, Que., Can., Jan. 28, 1931; s. Hartland Campbell and Dorothy (Molson) MacD.; m. Eve Gordon, Oct. 29, 1954; children: Cynthia, Wendy, Keith, Willa, Tania. Ed., LeRosey, Switzerland, 1947-48, McGill U., 1949-53, Advanced Mgmt. Program, Harvard U., 1976. With Bank Montreal, various locations, 1953-84; vice chmn. Bank Montreal, 1981-84; chmn., dir. Royal Trustco Ltd., Toronto, 1984-93; dep. chmn. London Ins. Group, Inc.; dir. The Bermudiana Found. of Can. Founding chmn. Heritage Can., St. Michael's Hosp. Found., The Japan Soc., chmn., adv. com. Can.-Japan Bus. Com.; gov., past chmn. Coun. Can. Unity; dir. Friends of the Youth Awards Inc., U.S.; pres. Royal Agrl. Winter Fair; mem. Internat. Coun. Music Ctr. L.A., Adv. Coun. U. B.C.; gov. Olympic Trust; bd. dirs. Can. Soc. for Weismann Inst., Empire Club Found.; sen. Stratford Shakespearean Found.; former chmn. The Duke of Edinburgh Awards Internat. Coun. Decorated Order of Can., 1981, Comdr. Royal Victorian Order, 1989; recipient Order of the Rising Sun, Gold and Silver Star, Govt. of Japan, 1995. Avocations: skiing, tennis, farming.

MACDOUGALL, JOHN DOUGLAS, earth science educator; b. Toronto, Ont., Can., Mar. 9, 1944; s. Lorn Graham and Grace A. (Virtue) MacD.; m. Shiela Dawn Ward, June 8, 1968; children: Christopher David, Katherine Heather. BS, U. Toronto, 1967; MS, McMaster U., 1968; PhD, U. Calif.-San Diego, 1972. Asst. research geologist U. Calif., Berkeley, 1972-74; prof. earth scis. Scripps Inst. Oceanography U Calif.-San Diego, La Jolla, 1974—, chmn. geol. research div., 1985-89. Contbr. articles to profl. jours. Fellow Meteoritical Soc. ;mem. AAAS, Geochem. Soc., Am. Geophys. Union. Home: 534 Bonair St La Jolla CA 92037-6112 Office: Scripps Inst Oceanography # 0220 La Jolla CA 92093

MACDOUGALL, PETER, lawyer; b. Boston, Sept. 22, 1937; s. Duncan Peck and Hildegard (Moebius) MacD. AB, Harvard U., 1958, LLB, 1963. Assoc. Ropes & Gray, Boston, 1964-73, ptnr., 1973—. Sheldon fellow Harvard U., 1963-64. Club: Harvard (Boston). Avocations: concert and opera going, gardening, reading, travel. Office: Ropes & Gray 1 International Pl Boston MA 02110-2600

MACDOUGALL, PRISCILLA RUTH, lawyer; b. Evanston, Ill., Jan. 20, 1944; d. Curtis Daniel and Genevieve Maurine (Rockwood) MacDougall; m. Lester H. Brownlee, July 5, 1987. BA, Barnard Coll., 1965; grad. with honors, U. Paris, 1967; JD, U. Mich., 1970. Bar: Wis. 1970, Ill. 1970. Asst. atty. gen. State of Wis., 1970-74; lectr. law U. Wis., 1973-75; staff counsel Wis. Edn. Assn. Council, Madison, 1975—; instr. Columbia Coll., Chgo., 1988—; litigator, writer, speaker, educator women's and children's names and women's rights and labor issues. Mem. ABA, Wis. State Bar (founder sect. on individual rights and responsibilities, chairperson, 1973-75, 78-79), Legal Assn. Women Wis. (co-founder). Author: Married Women's Common Law Right to Their Own Surnames, 1972, (with Terri P. Tepper) Booklet for Women Who Wish to Determine Their Own Names After Marriage, 1974, supplement, 1975, The Right of Women to Name Their Children, 1985; contbr. articles to profl. jours. Home: 502 Engelhart Dr Madison WI 53713-4742 Office: 33 Nob Hill Dr Madison WI 53713-2198

MACDOUGALL, WILLIAM LOWELL, magazine editor; b. Des Moines, July 24, 1931; s. David Gregory and Elizabeth Jeanette (Dugan) MacD. A.B., Willamette U., Salem, Oreg., 1952; M.J. in Journalism (Pulitzer scholar 1953-54), Columbia U., 1953. Reporter Washington Star, 1958-62; corr. Los Angeles Times, 1962-63; asso. editor, then London corr. U.S. News & World Report, 1964-68; asst. mng. editor U.S. News & World Report, Washington, 1978-86; mng. editor Artsreview mag. NEA, 1987-8; pres. Atlantic Media Co., Arlington, Va., 1989. Author: American Revolutionary: A Biography of General Alexander McDougall, 1977. Served with USAF, 1954-57. Recipient George Washington medal Freedoms Found., 1978, citation U.S. Bicentennial Commn., 1976. Methodist. Office: Atlantic Media Co 5000 37th St N Arlington VA 22207-1823

MAC DOWELL, ANDIE (ROSE ANDERSON MACDOWELL), actress; b. Gaffney, S.C., Apr. 21, 1958. Films include: Greystoke, 1984, St. Elmo's Fire, 1985, sex, lies and videotape, 1989, Green Card, 1990, Hudson Hawk, 1991, The Object of Beauty, 1991, The Player, 1992, Ruby, 1992, Groundhog Day, 1993, Short Cuts, 1993, Four Weddings and a Funeral, 1994, Bad Girls, 1994, Unstrung Heroes, 1995; TV includes Women and Men 2: In Love There Are No Rules, 1991, Sahara's Secret. Office: ICM 321 Westminster Ave Los Angeles CA 90020-4652

MAC DOWELL, SAMUEL WALLACE, physics educator; b. Camaragibe, Brazil, Mar. 24, 1929; came to U.S., 1963; s. Samuel Wallace and Maria Anita (Amazonas) Mac D.; m. Myriam Ramos Da Silva, Feb. 2, 1953; children: Ana Myriam, Samuel Wallace, Maria Dolores. BSc in Engring., U. Pernambuco, Brazil, 1951; PhD in Math. Physics, Birmingham (Eng.) U., 1958. Rsch. assoc. Princeton (N.J.) U., 1959-60; assoc. prof. Centro Brasileiro De Fisicas Pesquisas, Rio de Janeiro, 1960-63; fellow Inst. for Advanced Study, Princeton, 1963-65; assoc. prof. Yale U., New Haven, 1965-67, prof., 1968—. Fellow Am. Phys. Soc.; mem. Brazilian Acad. Scis. Roman Catholic. Office: Yale U Sloane Physics Lab PO Box 6666 New Haven CT 06511-8167

MACE, JOHN WELDON, pediatrician; b. Buena Vista, Va., July 9, 1938; s. John Henry and Gladys Elizabeth (Edwards) M.; m. Janice Mace, Jan. 28, 1962; children: Karin E., John E., James E. B.A., Columbia Union Coll., 1960; M.D., Loma Linda U., 1964. Diplomate: Am. Bd. Pediatrics, Sub-bd. Pediatric Endocrinology. Intern U.S. Naval Hosp., San Diego, 1964-65, resident in pediatrics, 1966-68; fellow in endocrinology and metabolism U. Colo., 1970-72; asst. prof. pediatrics Loma Linda (Calif.) U. Med. Center, 1972-75, prof., chmn. dept., 1975—; med. dir. Loma Linda U. Children's Hosp., 1990-92, physician-in-chief, 1992—. Contbr. articles to profl. jours. Treas. Found. for Med. Care San Bernandino County, 1979-80, pres., 1980-82; mem. Congl. Adv. Bd., 1984-87; pres. So. Calif. affiliate Am. Diabetes Assn., 1985-86, dir., 1987-89; chmn. adv. bd. State Calif. Children's Svcs., 1986—; bd. dirs. So. Calif. Children's Cancer Svcs., 1993-94, Loma Linda Ronald McDonald House, 1991—, Aetna Health Plans of Calif., 1993-95; bd. dirs. Loma Linda U. Health Care, 1995—. Named Alumnist of Yr., Loma Linda U. Sch. Medicine, 1994. Mem. AAAS, N.Y. Acad. Sci., Calif. Med. Soc. (adv. panel genetic diseases State Calif., 1975—), Western Soc. Pediatric Rsch., Lawson Wilkens Pediatric Endocrine Soc., Assn. Med. Pediatric Dept. Chmn., Am. Acad. Pediatrics, Sigma Xi, Alpha Omega Alpha. Office: Loma Linda U Children's Hosp 11234 Anderson St Loma Linda CA 92354

MACEACHEN, ALLAN JOSEPH, senator; b. Inverness, N.S., Can., July 6, 1921; s. Angus and Annie (Gillis) M. B.A., St. Francis Xavier U., 1944, hon. degree, 1973; M.A., U. Toronto, 1946; postgrad. in indsl. relations, U. Chgo., MIT, 1951; hon. degree, Acadia U., 1973, Loyola Coll., Balt., 1973, St. Marys U., 1973, Dalhousie U., 1974, Sir Wilfrid Laurier U., 1976. Prof. econs. St. Francis Xavier U., 1946, head dept. social scis., 1948-51; M.P. from Inverness-Richmond dist. Ho. of Commons, 1953-57, 62-68, M.P. from Cape Breton-Highlands-Canso dist., 1968-84; minister labor, 1963-65, minister of nat. health and welfare, 1965-68, govt. house leader, 1967-68, minister of manpower and immigration, 1968-70; pres. Privy Council, 1970-74, 76-79, govt. house leader, 1967-68, 70-74, sec. state for external affairs, 1974-76, dep. prime minister, 1977-79, dep. leader of opposition, opposition house leader, 1979, dep. prime minister, minister of fin., 1980-82, dep. prime minister, sec. state for external affairs, 1982-84; govt. leader of Senate Ottawa, 1984—; leader of opposition of Senate, 1984-91; parliamentary observer 10th Gen. Assembly UN, 1955; alternate del. 22d session UN Econ. and Social Coun., Geneva, 1956; leader Can. delegation Commonwealth Parliamentary Conf., London, 1973; co-chmn. Conf. Internat. Econ. Cooperation, from 1975; chmn. Internat. Monetary Fund Group of Ten, 1980-81; chmn. interim com. IMF, 1980-81; chmn. GATT, 1982; chmn. adv. coun. Bank of Montreal, 1986-91. Trustee Royal Ottawa Health Care Group, 1987—. Office: The Senate of Canada, Ottawa, ON Canada K1A 0A4

MACEACHERN, JOHN DUNCAN, government executive; b. Glace Bay, N.S., Can., Nov. 8, 1946; s. Francis Archibald and Margaret Martina (MacSween) MacE.; m. Elaine MacEachern, July 4, 1970; children: Lori, Kevin, Rachel, Lynn. BSc, St. Francis Xavier U., Antigonish, N.S., 1969, EdB, 1971; EdM, Dalhousie U., Halifax, N.S., 1979. Tchr. Antigonish (N.S.) Regional H.S., 1970-72, St. Michael Sr. H.S., Glace Bay, N.S., 1972-84; vice prin. Donkin Morien Dist. H.S., Cape Breton, N.S., 1984-85, Morrison H.S., Glace Bay, 1985-88; tchr. Morrison Jr. H.S., Glace Bay, 1986-93; mem. legislature N.S. Govt., 1988—, min. of edn., 1993—. Home: 174 South St, Glace Bay, NS Canada B1A 1V8

MACEK, ANNA MICHAELLA, cosmetics executive; b. Lancashire, Eng., Aug. 10, 1950; came to U.S., 1974; d. Wasyl and Maria (Litynska) Flaszczak; m. Frank Macek, Aug. 18, 1977. MA, U. Manchester, Eng., 1973; grad., Ecole des Estheticiennes Inst. de Beaute, Geneva, 1974. Asst. to pres., chief exec. officer Reed-Ingram Corp., N.Y.C., 1974-77; coordinator corp. pub. relations Northrop Corp., Los Angeles, 1978-82; pres. Annastasia Cosmetics, Gardena, Calif., 1983—. Contbr. articles to profl. jours. Mem. Beauty and Barber Supply Inst. Avocations: tennis, gardening. *Personal philosophy: Express the limitless power of soul in anything you take up. Every position you hold in life will be the stepping stone to a higher one if you strive to climb upward.*

MACER, DAN JOHNSTONE, retired hospital administrator; b. Evansville, Ind., May 25, 1917; s. Clarence Guy and Ann (Johnstone) M.; m. Eugenia Loretta Andrews, June 1, 1943; children: Eugenia Ann, Dan James. B.S., Northwestern U., 1939, M.S. in Hosp. Adminstrn. with distinction, 1959. Chief hosp. ops. VA br. office, St. Paul, 1947-50; asst. mgr. VA hosps., Ft. Wayne, Ind., 1951, Kerrville, Tex., 1952, Augusta, Ga., 1952-56; mgr. VA Hosp., Sunmount, N.Y., 1956-58; dir. Va Research Hosp., Chgo., 1958-62; mem. hosp. adminstrn. faculty Northwestern U., 1959-61; dir. VA Hosps., Pitts., 1962-67; asst. vice chancellor health professions U. Pitts., 1968-71; prof. med. and hosp. adminstrn. U. Pitts. Grad. Sch. Pub. Health, 1962-71; prof. Coll. Health and Coll. Medicine, U. Okla., 1971-89, retired, 1989; dir. VA Hosps. and Clinics, Oklahoma City, 1971-76, VA Med. Dist. 20 (Okla.-Ark.), 1971-76; lectr. George Washington U., 1961-71; v.p. Hosp. Casualty Co., Oklahoma City, 1978-89; pres. Dan J. Macer & Assos., Inc.; cons. to health field; cons. nat. health profl. assns., indsl. corps., archtl. corps, health planners; cons. Health Services and Mental Health Adminstrn., HEW, 1968. Mem. editorial bd.: Nursing and Health Care, 1980-88; author articles in field. Coordinator civil def. and disaster planning all hosps., Chgo. nr. North Side, 1961; chmn. welfare and planning council Savannah River Community Chest, Augusta, 1954-56; chmn. group 17 fed. sect., govt. div. United Fund Allegheny County, 1964-65; mem. Fed. Interagy. Bd. Dirs., 1964-68; sec. U. Pitts. Health Center, 1969-71; chmn. health com. Health and Welfare Assn. Alleghany County, 1970-71; chmn. devel. com. Northwestern U. Alumni Program in Hosp. Adminstrn., 1962-63; chmn. adv. com. Regional Med. Program Western Pa., 1966-71; mem. steering com. Comprehensive Health Planning Western Pa.; dir. Am. States Regional Conf., 1971; vice chmn. procedures com., mem.-at-large exec. com. Okla. Regional Med. Program, 1971-78; mem. Gov's Adv. Com. Comprehensive Health Planning, 1971-80, Gov's Com. Employment of Handicapped, 1972, Pres.'s Com. Employment of Handicapped, 1962; chmn. VA chief med. dir.'s com. for evaluation and reorgn. VA health care delivery services, 1974-76; chmn. planning com. for constrn. New Children's Meml. Hosp., 1974-78; chmn. Gov.'s Ad Hoc Com on Fed.-State Planning, 1973-78; mem. Gov.'s Health Scis. Center planning and adv. com., 1973-78, State Health Planning Council, 1973-78; chmn. Okla. Health Goals and Planning Priorities Com., 1973-80; bd. dirs. Comprehensive Health Planning Agy., Western Pa.; bd. dirs. Health Services Corp., 1969-71, Okla. affiliate Am. Heart Assn., 1980-89; trustee Okla. Council Health Careers and Manpower, 1976-80; examiner Am. Coll. Hosp. Adminstrs. Lt. col. Med. Adminstrv. Corps, AUS, 1941-46. Decorated Bronze Star, Purple Heart; recipient citations VFW, 1959, citations Am. Legion, 1956, 58, citations DAV, 1964, citations Okla. Regional Med. Program, 1976, citations Okla. Gov.'s Office Health Planning, 1976, Laura G. Jackson award in recognition exceptional service in field of hosp. adminstrn., 1971, Disting. Service award Coll. Pub. Health U. Okla., 1987, Disting. Dedicated Service award Okla. Hosp. Assn., 1987; Leadership programs established in his honor Coll. Pub. Health, U. Okla. Fellow Am. Pub. Health Assn., Am. Coll. Health Care Execs. (life); mem. Am. Hosp. Assn. (life, mem. council med. edn. 1976-79), Hosp. Assn. Pa. (vice chmn. med. relations 1965-66, chmn. rehab. com. 1965-66, vice chmn. council on profl. practices, dir.), Hosp. Council Western Pa., Assn. Am. Med. Colls. (exec. com. council teaching hosps.), Oklahoma City C. of C. (vice chmn. research and edn. div. 1975-80), Northwestern U. Alumni Assn. (pres. Acacia chpt. 1961, hosp. adminstrn. chpt. 1962). Clubs: Kiwanian (Chgo.), University (Pitts.), Petroleum, Twin Hills Golf and Country (Oklahoma City), Faculty House (Oklahoma City). Home: 2925 Pelham Dr Oklahoma City OK 73120-4348

MACER, GEORGE ARMEN, JR., orthopedic hand surgeon; b. Pasadena, Calif., Oct. 17, 1948; s. George A. and Nevart Akullian M.; m. Celeste Angelle Lyons, Mar. 26, 1983; children: Christiana Marilu, Marina Lynn, Emily Sue. BA, U. So. Calif., 1971, MD, 1976. Diplomate Am. Bd. Med. Examiners, Am. Bd. Orthopaedic Surgery; cert. surgery of hand. Intern Meml. Hosp. Med. Ctr., Long Beach, Calif., 1976; resident Orthopaedic Hosp./U. So. Calif., 1977-81; pvt. practice hand surgery Long Beach, 1983—; asst. clin. prof. orthopaedics U. So. Calif., Long Beach, 1983-89, 1990—; cons. hand surgery svc. Rancho Los Amigos Hosp. Downey, 1990—; cons. Harbor UCLA Med. Ctr., Torrance, 1983—. Joseph Boyes Hand fellow, 1982; mem. AMA, Calif. Med. Assn., L.A. County Med. Assn., Western Orthopaedic Assn., Am. Soc. for Surgery of Hand, Am. Acad. Orthopaedic Surgery. Republican. Avocations: boating, skiing, scuba diving, carpentry. Office: 3550 Linden Ave Ste 2 Long Beach CA 90807 also: 8635 W 3d St Ste 965W Los Angeles CA 90048

MACERA, SALVATORE, industrial executive; b. Cambridge, Mass., May 3, 1931; s. Benedetto and Anna (DeVellis) M.; m. Josephine Guarnaccia (div.); children: Michael, Richard, Michelle; m. Daphne Lee. B.B.A., Northeastern U., 1960; grad., MIT Sloan Sr. Exec. Program, 1967. Financial analyst Ford Motor Co., 1955-58; v.p. finance and adminstrn. LFE Electronics div. Lab. for Electronics, Boston, 1958-63; v.p., chief financial officer Itek Corp., 1963-73, exec. v.p., 1973-82, also dir.; pres. Itek Electronics and Optical Industries, 1980-82; chmn., chief exec. officer Camelot Ind., 1981-82; chmn. Bristol Med. Elec., Boston; pres. R.V. Whitehall; chmn. The Fin. Adv. Ctre., Ltd.; bd. dirs. Harbor Nat. Bank, Boston., Fossella Assocs., Patriot Bancorp., Infinite Corp., Saxby Computer Corp., Baker & Lander, Internat. Ins. Corp., Whitman Group Inc., Conifer Group, David Banash and Co., Steinroe Variable Annuity Trust, Steinroe Variable Annuity Fund. Mem. budget com. Fin. Inst.; trustee Bentley Coll., Colonial Variable Annuity Fund; bd. dirs. Assoc. Industries Mass.; mem. bd. advisors N.Am. Corp. With AUS. Home: 507-509 Rowes Wharf Boston MA 02109

MACERO, TEO, composer, conductor; b. Glens Falls, N.Y., Oct. 30, 1925; s. Daniel and Angeline (De Fabio) M.; m. Jeanne Marie Crawley; 1 child, Suzanne E. BS, Juilliard Sch. Music, 1951, MS, 1953. Condr., composer, performer with N.Y. Philharm., Kansas City (Mo.) Symphony Orch., Buffalo Symphony, Santa Clara (Calif.) Symphony Orch.; composer with Pa. Ballet Co., Robert Joffrey Ballet Co., Anna Sokolow Ballet Co., Winnipeg (Can.) Ballet Co.; producer with various artists including Miles Davis, Dave Brubeck, Duke Ellington, Count Basie, Leonard Bernstein, Mahalia Jackson; lectr. Contemporary Am. music and jazz. Producer 18 Gold Records including Chorus Line (original cast album), Bitches Brew (Miles Davis), Sun Goddess (Ramsey Lewis), The Graduate (Simon & Garfunkel), Time Out (Dave Brubeck), Robert Palmer; composer, condr.: (TV films) Sgt. Matlovich vs. U.S. Army Air Corp, Top Secret, Teddy Kennedy Jr. Story, 1986, Special Friendships, 1987; (films) Cassius Clay, Skill, Brains & Guts, Jack Johnson; (documentary) The Body Human; (TV series) Lifeline, Omni; composer: Time Plus Seven, Acoustic Suspension, Christmas Tree; (ballet) Everything Goes, 1982; (opera) Once A Slave. Served with USN, 1943-47, PTO. Club: Metropolitan (N.Y.C.). Home: 320 E 46th St New York NY 10017-3042

MACER-STORY, EUGENIA ANN, writer, artist; b. Mpls., Jan. 20, 1945; d. Dan Johnstone and Eugenia Loretta (Andrews) Macer; divorced; 1 child, Ezra Arthur Story. BS in Speech, Northwestern U., 1965; MFA, Columbia U., 1968. Writing instr. Polyarts, Boston, 1970-72; theater instr. Joy of Movement, Boston, 1972-75; artistic dir. Magik Mirror, Salem, Mass., 1975-76, Magick Mirror Comm., 1977—. Author: Congratulations: The UFO Reality, 1978, Angels of Time, 1982, Project Midas, 1986, Dr. Fu Man Chu Meets the Lonesome Cowboy: Sorcery and the UFO Experience, 1991, 3d edit., 1994, Gypsy Fair, 1991, The Strawberry Man, 1991, Sea Condor/Dusty Sun, 1994, Awakening to the Light-After the Longest Night, 1995; (short stories) Battles with Dragons: Certain Tales of Political Yoga, 1993, 2d edit., 1994, Legacy of Daedulus, 1995; (plays) Fetching the Tree, Archeological Politics, Strange Inquiries, Divine Appliance, 1989, The Zig Zag Wall, 1990, The Only Qualified Huntress, 1990, Telephone Taps Written Up for Tabloids, 1991, Wars With Pigeons, 1992, Conquest of the Asteroids, 1993, Commander Galacticon, 1993, Meister Hemmelin, 1994, Six Way Time Play, 1994, Radish, 1996, others; philosophy writer; contbr. articles to profl. jours.; author poetry in Woodstock Times, Lamia Ink!, Manhattan Poetry Rev., Sensations, Kore, others; feature writer Borderlands Mag., 1995; editor Magick Mirror Newsletter. Shubert fellow, 1968. Mem. Dramatists Guild, U.S. Psychotronics Assn., Internat. Guild of Occult Scis. Democrat. Avocations: swimming, outdoor activities, hiking. Office: Magick Mirror Comm PO Box 741 New York NY 10116-0741

MACEWAN, BARBARA ANN, middle school educator; b. Adams, Mass., Apr. 22, 1938; d. Thomas Lawrence and Vera (Ziemba) Gaskalka; m. George Louie MacEwan, Feb. 16, 1963; children: Rebecca, Debra. BS in Edn. cum laude, North Adams State Coll., 1959; MEd with honors, Plymouth State Coll., 1994. Cert. K-8, secondary social studies tchr., sch. libr., Mass. Tchr. Town of Valatie, N.Y., 1959-61, 62-63, Dept. Def., Aachefensburg, Germany, 1961-62, Town of East Longmeadow, Mass., 1964; asst. children's libr. Springfield (Mass.) Libr., 1964; tchr. history Southwick (Mass.)-Tolland Regional Schs., 1971—, tchr. history, curriculum coord. mid. sch., 1995—; state coord. Nat. History Day, 1989-92. Author: The Old Cemetery: Southwick, 1977, Shays Rebellion, 1987, The Princess, 1995. Sec. Southwick Hist. Soc., 1976-79, treas., 1979-86, pres., 1986-94; trustee Moore House, Southwick, 1989—; chair Southwick Hist. Commn., 1994—; active Mass. Curriculum Framework Focus Group, 1994—. Recipient recognition New Eng. League Mid. Schs., 1991; Horace Mann grantee Southwick Sch. Com., 1982. Mem. ASCD, NEA, Mass. Tchrs. Assn., New Eng. Oral History Assn., Nat. Coun. for Social Studies, Mass. Coun. Social Studies (recognition 1992), Western Mass. Coun. for Social Studies (bd. dirs. 1987-95), Mass. Assn. Ednl. Media, Nat. Mus. Am. Indian, New Eng. Native Am. Inst., Pioneer Valley Reading Coun., Historic Mass., NAt. Trust Historic Preservation, Phi Delta Kappa. Roman Catholic. Avocations: gardening, walking, reading, travel. Office: Powder Mill Mid Sch 94 Powder Mill Rd Southwick MA 01077-9324

MACEWAN, NIGEL SAVAGE, merchant banker; b. Balt., Mar. 21, 1933; s. Nigel Savage and Ellen (Wharton) MacE.; children: Alison, Nigel, Pamela, Elizabeth. BA, Yale U., 1955; MBA, Harvard U., 1959. Assoc. Morgan Stanley & Co., N.Y.C., 1959-62, White, Weld & Co., N.Y.C., 1962-63; v.p. R.S. Dickson & Co., Charlotte, N.C., 1963-68; chmn. Fin. Cons. Internat. Ltd., Brussels, 1965-68; successively gen. ptnr., exec. v.p., pres., dir. White, Weld & Co., N.Y.C., 1968-78; sr. v.p., dir. Merrill Lynch, Pierce, Fenner & Smith, N.Y.C., 1978-87; chmn. Merrill Lynch Capital Ptnrs., N.Y.C., 1985-87; pres., CEO Kleinwort Benson, N.Am. Inc., N.Y.C., 1987-93, also bd. dirs.; chmn. Kleinwort Benson North Am., Inc., Kleinworth Benson Holdings, Inc., Alex Brown Kleinwort Benson Realty Advs.; bd. dirs. Kleinwort Benson Group plc, Kleinwort Benson Ltd., 1987-95, Kleinworth Benson Australian Income Fund, 1992—; adj. prof. bus. adminstrn. NYU, 1973-75. Pres. Tokeneke Tax Dist., Darien, 1978-80, later treas. Served with USN, 1955-57. Mem. Securities Industry Assn. (chmn. N.Y. group 1975-76), Links Club, N.Y. Yacht Club, Yale Club N.Y., Wee Burn Country Club, Tokeneke Club, Tarrantine Club (Dark Harbor, Maine). Republican. Episcopalian. Home: 153 Oenoke Ln New Canaan CT 06840 Office: Kleinwort Benson NAm Inc 200 Park Ave New York NY 10166-0005

MAC EWEN, GEORGE DEAN, physician, medical institute executive; b. Metcalfe, Ont., Can., Nov. 10, 1927; s. George W. and Catherine (Grant) MacE.; m. Marilyn Ruth Heidelberger, May 29, 1954; children: Kathryn, Jane, Nancy, David, John. MD, CM, Queen's U., Kingston, Ont., Can., 1953. Diplomate: Am. Bd. Orthopaedic Surgery (examiner 1971—). Intern D.C. Gen. Hosp., Washington, 1953-54; resident in gen. surgery Emergency Hosp., Washington, 1954-55; fellow in orthopaedic surgery Campbell Clinic, Memphis, 1955-58; asst. med. dir. Alfred I. duPont Inst., Wilmington, Del., 1958-68; surgeon-in-chief Alfred I. duPont Inst., 1961-79, med. dir., 1969-87; chmn. pediatric orthopaedic surgery Children's Hosp., New Orleans, 1987-93; sr. cons. Orthopedic Ctr. for Children St. Christopher's Hosp. for Children, Phila., 1995—; prof. orthopedic surgery Med. Coll. Pa. and Hahnemann U. Sch. Medicine, 1995—; chief orthopaedic svc. VA Hosp., Wilmington, 1960-66, cons. in orthopaedics, The Med. Ctr. Del., 1961—; cons. in orthopaedics Wilmington Med. Center, 1961—, St. Francis Hosp., Wilmington, 1961-86; cons. in orthopaedic surgery Surgeon Gen. U.S. Navy, 1964-72 , USAF Hosp., Dover, Del.; med. cons. John G. Leach Sch., Wilmington; cons. USAF Base, Dover, Del., 1961-86, Evan G. Shortlidge Sch., Wilmington, 1961-70, Pocono Med. Svcs., 1973-74, Walter Reed Army Hosp., Washington, 1978-86; med. adv. com. Del. Systems for Exceptional Children, 1973-86; cons. Surgeon Gen. U.S., 1982-86; emeritus in orthopaedic surgery St. Francis Hosp., Med. Ctr. Del., 1987—; assoc. prof. orthopaedic surgery Jefferson Med. Coll., Thomas Jefferson U., Phila., 1970-76, prof., 1976-86; clin. prof. U. Del., Newark, 1977-80; lectr. U.S. Naval Hosp., Phila., 1964-80; exec. com. Del. sch. health adv. com., 1966-86; med. adv. com. VA Hosp., 1965-79; mem. U. Del. Research Found., 1976-79; mem. subcom. Ctr. for Disease Control, 1990-93. Editor Orthopedic Resident, 1990—; mem. editorial bd. Del. Med. Jour., 1966-69; contbr. articles to books, jours. Bd. trustees Wilmington Coll., 1980—; bd. dirs. Arthritis Found., 1974-77; bd. dirs. Blood Bank of Del., 1969-78, exec. com., 1976-78, hon. mem., 1979—; editorial bd. of Evaluation and Health Professions, 1985—. Fellow Am. Acad. Cerebral Palsy; mem. Acad. of Medicine (Wilmington), Academia Mexicana de Cirugia (hon.), Am. Acad. Orthopaedic Surgeons (chmn., mem. various coms.), Am. Acad. Pediatrics (orthopaedic surg. fellow 1977—), ACS, AMA (ho. of dels. 1982-86), Am. Orthopaedic Assn. (traveling fellow 1967, pres. 1980-81, various coms.), Brit. Orthopaedic Assn. (corr.), Brazilian Orthopaedic Soc. (hon.), Campbell Club (pres. 1979), Can. Orthopaedic Assn. (trustee 1969-75), Coll. of Physicians (Phila.), Cosmos Club, Del. State Med. Soc., Eastern Orthopedic Assn., Fla. Orthopaedic Assn. (hon.), New Castle County Med. Soc. (del. 1970-72), Nat. Assn. Children's Hosps. and Related Instns. (bd. trustees 1980—), N.J. Orthopaedic Soc. (hon.), Del. Soc. Orthopedic Surgeons (charter), Orthopaedic Forum Club, Orthopaedic Rsch. Soc., Pan Am. Orthopedic Orgn., Pediatric Orthopaedic Soc. N.Am. (pres. 1972-73), Pa. Orthopaedic Soc. (hon.), Phila. Orthopaedic Soc. (pres. 1968-69), Scoliosis Rsch. Soc. (founding, exec. com. 1969-74, pres. 1971-73), Societe de Scoliose du Quebec (hon.), Societe Internationale de Chirurgie Orthopedique et de Traumatologie (exec com. 1979-86, SICOT Found. bd. dirs. 1990—), S. African Orthopaedic Assn. (hon.), Tex. Orthopaedic Assn. (hon.), Nat. Neurofibromatosis Found. (med. adv. bd. 1981—), German Orthopaedic Assn. (hon.), Costa Rican Orthopaedic Soc. (hon.), Mexican Orthopedic Soc. (hon.), Japanese Orthopaedic Assn. (hon.), Twentieth Century Orthopaedic Assn., Houston Orthopaedic Soc., La. Orthopaedic Assn., La. State Med. Soc., Mid-Am. Orthopaedic Assn. (hon.), Orleans Parish Med. Soc., So. Med. Assn., So. Orthopaedic Assn., Sociedad Mexicana de Ortopedia (hon.). Office: St Christophers Hosp for children Erie Ave at Front St Phia PA 19134

MACEY, JONATHAN R., law educator; b. 1955. BA, Harvard U., 1977; JD, Yale U., 1982. Bar: Ga. 1986. Law clk. to Hon. Henry J. Friendly U.S. Ct. Appeals (2nd cir.), N.Y.C., 1982-83; asst. prof. Emory U., 1983-86, assoc. prof., 1986-87; vis. assoc. prof. U. Va., 1986-87; prof. Cornell U., 1987-90; vis. prof. U. Chgo., fall 1989, prof., 1990—. Mem. ABA (com. on corp. laws), Nat. Assn. Security Dealers (bd. arbitrators). Office: U Chgo Law Sch 1111 E 60th St Chicago IL 60637-2702*

MACEY, MORRIS WILLIAM, lawyer; b. Camilla, Ga., Dec. 25, 1922; s. Isadore and Freda (Berman) M.; m. Dora Rosenfield, Dec. 28, 1950; children: Morris William, Jonathan Rosenfield, Rex Philip. A.B., U. Ga., 1946, LL.B., 1943; LL.M., Harvard, 1947. Bar: Ga. 1943, D.C. 1980. Practiced in Atlanta, 1947—; ptnr. Macey, Wilensky, Cohen, Wittner & Kessler; formerly adj. prof. Emory U. Law Sch., U. Ga. Law Sch.; Pres. Comml. Law League Am., 1966-67. Vice chmn., asso. editor: Comml. Law Jour. Chmn. bd. Associated Credit Union; former chmn. Southeastern Bankruptcy Law Inst.; former pres. Consumer Credit Counseling Svc.; former trustee Fisk U. Served with AUS, 1943-46. Mem. ABA (chmn. ad hoc com. on partnerships in bankruptcy, bus. law sect.), Internat. Bar Assn., Ga. Bar Assn., Atlanta Bar Assn., Nat. Bankruptcy Conf., Nat. Conf. Commrs. on Uniform State Laws, Nat. Assn. Comml. Fin. Attys., Am. Law Inst., Am. Coll. Bankruptcy, Am. Bankruptcy Inst., Nat. Conf. Lawyers and CPAs, Lawyers Club, Harvard Club, Std. Club, Commerce Club, Masons, Shriners, Phi Beta Kappa, Omicron Delta Kappa. Jewish (trustee Temple Sinai 1969-70). Home: 4175 Conway Valley Rd NW Atlanta GA 30327-3607 Office: 600 Marquis Two Tower 285 Peachtree Center Ave NE Atlanta GA 30303-1229

MACEY, SCOTT J., lawyer; b. San Francisco, Nov. 8, 1946; s. Arthur A. Macey and Miriam (Sherman) Breit; m. Virginia Kathleen Dodge Shrodo, Mar. 14, 1966 (div. 1978); children: Benjamin Scott, Pamela Michelle; m. Linda Sandborg, Feb. 10, 1990; children: Benjamin, Joshua, Sarah. Student, U. Calif., Santa Barbara, 1965-66; BA magna cum laude, U. San Francisco, 1969; postgrad., San Jose State U., 1969-72; JD summa cum laude, Santa Clara U., 1975. Bar: Calif. 1975, N.J. 1980, U.S. Ct. Appeals (2d cir.) 1979. Assoc. Parker, Milliken, Clark & O'Hara, L.A., 1975-77; gen. atty. AT&T, N.Y.C., 1977-86; exec. v.p., gen. counsel AT&T Actuarial Scis. Assocs., Inc., Somerset, N.J., 1986—; chmn. industry com. Employee Retirement Income Security Act of 1974 (ERISA), Washington; mem. Bur. of Nat. Affairs Pension Reporter Adv. Bd., Washington. Contbr. articles to legal jours., also other mags. and publs. Vol. various polit. campaigns; com. mem. United Fund, Somerset; youth activity counselor Cath. Youth Assn. Mem. ABA (chmn. fiduciary subcom. labor law sect.), N.J. Assn. Corp. Counsel (past chmn. labor law com.). Avocations: gardening, reading, sports, raising animals. Home: 11 Sugar Mill Rd Belle Mead NJ 08502 Office: AT&T Actuarial Scis Assocs Inc 270 Davidson Ave 7th Fl Somerset NJ 08873-4140

MACEY, WILLIAM BLACKMORE, oil company executive; b. Buffalo, Aug. 1, 1920; s. Richard Charles and Doris (Bourne) M.; m. Jean Olive Mullins, Oct. 6, 1945; 1 dau., Barbara Jean. B.S. in Petroleum Engring, N.Mex. Sch. Mines, 1942; D.Engring. (hon.), N.Mex. Inst. Mining and Tech., 1984. Dist. engr. N.Mex. Oil Conservation Commn., 1946-48; dist. supt. Am. Republics Corp., 1948-52; chief engr. N.Mex. Oil Conservation Commn., 1952-54, state geologist, dir., 1954-56; v.p. Internat. Oil & Gas Corp. (and predecessor co., developers mineral properties), Denver, 1956-60; then pres. Internat. Oil & Gas Corp. (and predecessor co., developers mineral properties), 1960-67; pres. Nielson Enterprises Inc., oil and gas prodn. and pipelines, livestock ranching, 1967-74; v.p., dir. Y-Tex Corp. (mfr. livestock identification tags), 1972-73; pres. GEN Oil Inc. (oil and gas prodn.), 1972-75, Col. Cody Inn (real estate and golf course devel.), 1970-73; pres., dir. Macey & Mershon Oil, Inc., 1974-93; dir. Juniper Oil and Gas Corp., Denver, 1981-83, Ruidoso (N.Mex.) State Bank Holding Co., 1987—; pres. The Macey Corp., Denver, 1985—. Served from 2d lt. to capt. USAAF, 1942-45. Mem. N.Mex. Oil and Gas Assn. (exec. com. 1949-52, 60-61). Episcopalian. Clubs: Garden of the Gods, Skyline Country (Tucson) (dir., treas. 1980-82, pres. 1982-83), Pres.'s N.Mex. Inst. Mines and Tech. (chmn. 1980-82), Pres.'s U. Ariz. Found, AltoLakes Golf and Country, Tucson Country, Ruidoso, N.Mex. Jockey Club (bd. dirs. 1985-88, 91-93, pres. 1993). Home: 7010 N Javelina Dr Tucson AZ 85718-1850 also: PO Box 360 Alto NM 88312-0360 Office: 1801 Broadway Ste 1600 PO Box 2210 Denver CO 80201

MACFARLAN, JOHN HOWARD, lawyer; b. Miami, Fla., Apr. 10, 1963. BA, Mars Hill Coll., 1985; JD, Stetson U., 1988. Bar: N.C. 1988. Assoc. McKeever, Edwards, Davis & Hays, Murphy, N.C., 1992—. Mem., musical dir. Licklog Players, 1993—. Capt. JAG, USAF, 1988-91. Mem. N.C. Trial Lawyers Assn. Mem. N.C. Trial Lawyers Assn., Phi Delta Phi. Avocations: music, acting, swimming. Office: McKeever Edwards Davis 4 & 5 Profl Bldg PO Box 596 Murphy NC 28906

MACFARLAND, CRAIG GEORGE, natural resource management professional; b. Great Falls, Mont., July 17, 1943; s. Paul Stanley and Jean Elizabeth (Graham) MacF.; m. Janice Lee Bennett, Dec. 23, 1963 (div. 1987); children: Bennett, Francisco; m. Marilyn Ann Swanson, Mar. 19, 1988; stepchildren: Alyssa, Krista, Sara. BA magna cum laude, Austin Coll., 1965; MA, U. Wis., Madison, 1969, PhD in Zoology, 1993; DSc (hon.), Austin Coll., 1978. Dir. Charles Darwin Rsch. Sta., Galapagos Islands, Ecuador, 1974-78; head Wildlands and watershed mgmt. program Cen. Am. Centro Agronomico Tropical de Investigacion Enseñanza, Turrialba, Costa Rica, 1978-85; pres. Charles Darwin Found. for Galapagos Islands, Ecuador, 1985—; cons. natural resources and sustainable use in Latin Am. Moscow, Idaho, 1985—; affiliate faculty dept. Resource, Recreation and Tourism, U. Idaho, Moscow, 1988—; affiliate faculty dept. natural resource recreation and tourism Colo. State U., Ft. Collins, 1992. Contbr. to numerous profl. publs. Recipient Internat. Conservation medal Zool. Soc. San Diego, 1978, Order of Golden Ark for internat. conservation, Prince Bernhard of Netherlands, 1984. Mem. Ecol. Soc. Am., Internat. Soc. Tropical Foresters, Assn. Tropical Biology, Soc. Conservation Biology, Nature Conservancy, World Wildlife Fund, Greenpeace. Avocations: cross-country skiing, hiking, camping, skiing. Office: Charles Darwin Found 836 Mabelle St Moscow ID 83843-3553

MACFARLANE, ALASTAIR IAIN ROBERT, business executive; b. Sydney, Australia, Mar. 7, 1940; came to U.S., 1978; s. Alexander Dunlop and Margaret Elizabeth (Swan) M.; m. Madge McCleary, Sept. 24, 1966; children: Douglas, Dennis, Robert, Jeffrey. B in Econs. with honours, U. Sydney, 1961; MBA, U. Hawaii, 1964; postgrad., Columbia U., 1964; AMP, Harvard U., 1977. Comml. cadet B.H.P. Ltd., Australia, 1958-62; product mgr. H.J. Heinz Co., Pitts., 1965-66; gen. mgr. new products div. H.J. Heinz Co., Melbourne, Australia, 1967-72; ptnr., dir., gen. mgr. Singleton, Palmer & Strauss McAllan Pty. Ltd., Sydney, 1972-73; dir., gen. mgr. successor co. Doyle Dane Bernbach Internat. Inc., Sydney, 1973-77; group sr. v.p. Doyle Dane Bernbach Internat. Inc., N.Y.C., 1978-84; pres., chief exec. officer PowerBase Systems, Inc., 1984-85, Productivity Software Internat. L.P., N.Y.C., 1985-86; div. pres., pub. Whittle Comm. L.P., Knoxville, Tenn., 1987-88; chmn., CEO Phyton Techs. Inc., Knoxville, 1988-94; pres., CEO Knox Internat. Corp., Knoxville, 1988-94; chmn., CEO Mich. Bulb Co., Grand Rapids, 1988-94; chmn., CEO Lansinoh Labs., Inc., Oak Ridge, Tenn., 1994—; lectr. Monash U., Melbourne, 1970-71; ind. mgmt. cons., Melbourne, 1970-72; dir. Univ. of Sydney USA Found., 1994—. Author papers in field. V.p. Waverley Dist. Cricket Club, 1975-77. East-West Ctr. fellow, 1962-64; Australian Commonwealth scholar, Australian Steel Industry scholar, 1961. Fellow Australian Inst. Mgmt. (assoc.); mem. Australian Soc. Accts. (assoc.), Harvard Club N.Y.C., Cherokee Country Club. Home: 5210 Rio Vista Ln Knoxville TN 37919-8987 Office: 1670 Oak Ridge Tpke Oak Ridge TN 37830-4933

MACFARLANE, ANDREW WALKER, media specialist, educator; b. Toronto, Ont., Can., Feb. 18, 1928; s. Joseph Arthur and Marguerite (Walker) MacF.; m. Betty Doris Wright Seldon; 1 stepchild, Elizabeth Seldon; children by previous marriage: Jeanie Andreas, Catriona Flora. Student, U. Sask., Can., 1945-46; B.A., U. Toronto, 1949; M.L.S., U. Western Ont., 1977. With Canadian Press, Toronto, 1949; reporter Halifax (N.S., Can.) Chronicle Herald, 1949-51, Scottish Daily Express, Glasgow, 1951-53; subeditor London Evening Standard, 1953-55; copy editor, night editor, feature editor, gen. reporter, daily columnist, asst. to pub. Telegram, Toronto, 1955-64; mng. editor, corporate dir. Telegram, 1964-69, dir. research and devel., 1969-71, exec. editor, 1971—; dir. Citizen's Inquiry br. Ministry Govt. Services, Province of Ont., 1971-72; chmn. dept., dean Grad. Sch. Journalism, U. Western Ont., 1973-80, prof., 1981-93; prof. emeritus U. Western Ont., 1993—; chair mass media studies, dir. Ctr. in Mass Media Studies Grad. Sch. Journalism, U. Western Ont., 1990-93; co-chmn. Ont.-Que. Journalist Exchange. Author: The Neverland of the Neglected Child, 1957, It Seemed Like a Good Idea at the Time, 1983, Local Flavor, 1990; editor: Byline, 1983, Byline Canada, 1984. Bd. dirs. Canadian Medic-Alert, 1959; past bd. dirs. Met. Toronto Children's Aid Soc.; chmn. advisory council Province of Ont. Medal Good Citizenship. Recipient Bowater award, 1960, Nat. Newspaper award, 1958, 59, Nat. Teaching award Poynter Inst. for Media Studies, 1987, Province Ont. Bicentennial medal; Southam fellow, 1961. Mem. Assn. for Edn. in Journalism and Mass Comm., Can. Comm. Assn., Commonwealth Assn. for Edn. in Journalism and Comm. (founding pres.), Toronto Press Club.

MACFARLANE, JOHN ALEXANDER, former federal housing agency administrator; b. Winnipeg, Man., Can., Sept. 6, 1916; s. John MacKay and Annie Catherine (Smith) MacF.; m. Gladys Valda Church, Dec. 20, 1941; children: John Lane, Elizabeth Ann, Janet Christine. BA with honours, U. Man., Winnipeg, 1939. With stats. br. Wartime Prices and Trade Bd., Ottawa, Ont., Can., 1940-46; supr. stats. dept. Cn. Mortgage and Housing Corp., Ottawa, 1946-65, asst. dir. econs. and stats. div., 1965-69, asst. dir. secretariat div., 1969-78; ret., 1978; treas. Caribbean and N.Am. area coun. World Alliance Ref. Chs., Ottawa, 1984—. Treas. Ottawa Valley Cricket Coun., 1946-70, 73-80, pres., 1970-73, 83-88; moderator Presbytery of Ottawa, Presbyn. Ch. Can., 1994-96. Recipient Long Svc. medal Boy Scouts Assn., 1945, Centennial medal Govt. of Can., 1967, spl. achievement award for amateur sport Govt. of Ont., 1991; mem. choir St. Andrew's Presbyn. Ch. Mem. Def. Cricket Club (sec.-treas. 1944-46, pres. 1951-76, 78-92). Avocation: stamp collecting. Address: 99 Acacia Ave, Ottawa, ON Canada

K1M 0P8 *I have touched many people as the years have passed; if I have helped one for the better I shall rest content.*

MACFARLANE, JOHN CHARLES, utility company executive; b. Hallock, Minn., Nov. 8, 1939; s. Ernest Edward and Mary Bell (Yates) MacF.; m. Eunice Darlene Axvig, Apr. 13, 1963; children: Charles, James, William. BSEE, U. N.D., 1961. Staff engr. Otter Tail Power Co., Fergus Falls, Mn., 1961-64; div. engr. Otter Tail Power Co., Jamestown, N.D., 1964-71; div. mgr. Otter Tail Power Co., Langdon, N.D., 1972-78; v.p. planning and control Otter Tail Power Co., Fergus Falls, 1978-80, exec. v.p., 1981-82, pres. and chief exec. officer, 1982—, also bd. dirs., now chmn.; bd. dirs. Northwest Bank, Fergus Falls, Pioneer Mut. Ins. Co. Pres. Langdon City Commn., 1974-78; chmn. Fergus Falls Port Authority, 1985-86; bd. dirs. Minn. Assn. Commerce and Industry, Minn. Safety Coun., Edison Electric Inst.; chmn. bd. dirs. U. N.D. Energy Rsch. Adv. Coun. Served with U.S. Army, 1962-64. Mem. Am. Mgmt. Assn., IEEE (chmn. Red River chpt.), U. N.D. Alumni Assn., Fergus Falls C. of C. Republican. Presbyterian. Lodges: Rotary, Masons. Office: Otter Tail Power Co 215 S Cascade St Fergus Falls MN 56537-2801

MACFARLANE, MALCOLM HARRIS, physics educator; b. Brechin, Scotland, May 22, 1933; came to U.S., 1956; s. Malcolm P. and Mary (Harris) M.; m. Eleanor Carman, May 30, 1957; children: Douglas, Kenneth, Sheila, Christine. M.A., U. Edinburgh, Scotland, 1955; Ph.D., U. Rochester, 1960. Research asso. Argonne (Ill.) Nat. Lab., 1959-60; asst. prof. physics U. Rochester, 1960-61; asso. physicist Argonne Nat. Lab., 1961-68, sr. physicist, 1968-80; prof. physics U. Chgo., 1968-80, Ind. U., Bloomington, 1980—; vis. fellow All Souls Coll., Oxford (Eng.) U., 1966-67; mem. nuclear scis. adv. com. Dept. Energy-NSF, 1983-87; cons. Ency. Brit. Contbr. articles of theoretical nuclear physics to profl. jours. Guggenheim fellow physics, 1966-67; Alexander von Humboldt Found. sr. scientist award, 1985. Fellow Am. Phys. Soc.; mem. Nuclear Physics sect. Am. Phys. Soc. (mem. exec. com. 1969-71). Home: 3510 E Homestead Dr Bloomington IN 47401-4217 Office: Dept Physics Indiana U Bloomington IN 47405

MACGARRAHAN, JOHN GOLDEN, project development and finance professional; b. Boston, Feb. 28, 1937; s. Owen Joseph and Ellen Catherine (Golden) McG.; m. Margaret Devon Gatheral, 1960; children: Sabina Gatheral, Ellen Golden, Sara Judge. AB, Harvard U., 1960, LLB, 1963. Assoc. Casey, Lane & Mittendorf, N.Y.C., 1963-67; asst. to mayor City of N.Y., 1967-70; assoc. Barrett Knapp, N.Y.C., 1970; sole practice N.Y.C., 1971-72; ptnr. McGarrahan & Heard, N.Y.C., 1973-91, Arent, Fox, McGarrahan & Heard, N.Y.C., 1992-93; prin. McGarrahan & Co., Inc., N.Y.C., 1993—. Cpl. U.S. Army, 1956-58. Avocations: sailing, photography. Office: McGarrahan Co Inc 50 Broadway New York NY 10004-1607

MACGILLIVRAY, LOIS ANN, organization executive; b. Phila., July 8, 1937; d. Alexander and Mary Ethel (Crosby) MacG. BA in History, Holy Names Coll., 1966; MA in Sociology, U. N.C., 1971, PhD in Sociology, 1973. Joined Sisters of Holy Names of Jesus and Mary, 1955. Research asst. U. N.C., Chapel Hill, 1969-70, 71-72, instr. sociology, 1970-71; sociologist Rsch. Triangle Inst., Durham, N.C., 1973-75, sr. sociologist, 1975-81; dir. Ctr. for Population and Urban-Rural Studies, Research Triangle Inst., Durham, 1976-81; pres. Holy Names Coll., Oakland, Calif., 1982-92; mem. steering com. Symposium for Bus. Leaders Holy Names Coll., 1982-92; prin. owner Svc. Orgns.: Planning and Evaluation, Chapel Hill, 1994—; vis. scholar dept. sociology U. N.C., Chapel Hill, 1992-94; mem. policy bd. U. Oakland Met. Forum, co-convenor panel on edn. and youth. Bd. dirs. Oakland Coun. Econ. Devel., 1984-86; bd. dirs. Bay Area Biosci. Ctr., 1990-92, mem. adv. com., 1992-94. Mem. Am. Sociol. Assn., Assn. Ind. Calif. Colls. and Univs. (exec. com. 1985-92, vice chmn. 1989-92), Regional Assn. East Bay Colls. and Univs. (past pres., bd. dirs. 1982-92). Avocation: birding. Home and Office: 101 N Hamilton Rd Chapel Hill NC 27514-5627

MACGINITIE, WALTER HAROLD, psychologist; b. Carmel, Calif., Aug. 14, 1928; s. George Eber and Nettie Lorene (Murray) MacG.; m. Ruth Olive Kilpatrick, Sept. 2, 1950; children: Mary Catherine, Laura Anne. B.A., UCLA, 1949; A.M., Stanford U., 1950; Ph.D., Columbia U., 1960. Tchr. Long Beach (Calif.) Unified Sch. Dist., 1950, 1955-56; mem. faculty Columbia U. Tchrs. Coll., 1959-80, prof. psychology and edn., 1970-80; Lansdowne scholar, prof. edn. U. Victoria, B.C., Can., 1980-84; research assoc. Lexington Sch. Deaf, N.Y.C., 1963-69; mem. sci. adv. bd. Ctr. for Study of Reading, 1977-80, chmn. 1979-80. Co-author: Gates-MacGinitie Reading Tests, 1965, 78, 89, Psychological Foundations of Education, 1968; Editor: Assessment Problems in Reading, 1972; co-editor: Verbal Behavior of the Deaf Child, 1969. Life mem. Calif. PTA. Served with USAF, 1950-54. Fellow APA, AAAS, Am. Psychol. Soc., Nat. Conf. Research English, N.Y. Acad. Scis.; mem. Internat. Reading Assn. (pres. 1976-77, Spl. Svc. award 1981), Reading Hall of Fame (pres. 1989-90). Home and Office: PO Box 1789 Friday Harbor WA 98250-1789

MACGOWAN, CHARLES FREDERIC, retired chemical company executive; b. Rock Island, Ill., Nov. 24, 1918; s. Charles John and Clara (Ohge) MacG.; m. Shirley Esther Sutherland, Feb. 22, 1941; children: Lynn Merle, Charles John II. Student, Wright Jr. Coll., Chgo., 1936-37, North Park Coll., Chgo., 1938-39, Harvard, 1955-56. Partner C.B. Isett Co., Chgo., 1946-49; indsl. engr. Graver Tank & Mfg. Co., East Chicago, Ind., 1949-50; asst. bus. mgr. Boilermakers Local 374 State Ind., 1950-54; internat. rep. Internat. Brotherhood Boilermakers, 1954-60; dir. Office Saline Water, U.S. Dept Interior, Washington, 1961-65; spl. asst. to sec. Office Saline Water, U.S. Dept Interior, 1965-66; coordinator intergovtl. relations Fed. Water Pollution Control Adminstrn., 1966-67; govt. relations mgr. Dow Chem. Co., Washington, from 1967; cons. nuclear desalting Internat. Atomic Energy Agy., Vienna, Austria; tech. cons. AFL-CIO.; Chmn. Ind. Boiler and Pressure Vessel Bd., 1960-61. Contbr. articles to profl. jours. Mem. Am. Water Works Assn., Aircraft Owners and Pilots Assn., Md. Acad. Sci. Democrat. Methodist. Club: Mason. Home: 10113 Nedra Dr Great Falls VA 22066-2836

MACGOWAN, MARY EUGENIA, lawyer; b. Turlock, Calif., Aug. 4, 1928; d. William Ray and Mary Bolling (Gilbert) Kern; m. Gordon Scott Millar, Jan. 2, 1970; 1 dau., Heather Mary. A.B., U. Calif., Berkeley, 1950; J.D., U. Calif., San Francisco, 1953. Bar: Calif. 1953; cert. family law specialist Calif. State Bar Bd. Legal Specialization. Research atty. Supreme Ct. Calif., 1954, Calif. Ct. Appeals, 1955; partner firm MacGowan & MacGowan, Calif., 1956-68; pvt. practice, San Francisco, 1968—. Bd. dirs. San Francisco Speech and Hearing Center, San Francisco Legal Aid Soc., J.A.C.K.I.E. Mem. Am., Calif., San Francisco bar assns., Queen's Bench. Clubs: San Francisco Lawyers, Forest Hill Garden. Office: 1 Sansome St Ste 1900 San Francisco CA 94104

MACGOWAN, SANDRA FIRELLI, publishing executive, publishing educator; b. Phila., Nov. 9, 1951; d. William Firelli and Barbara (Gimbel) Kapalcik. BS in Biology, BA in English, Pa. State U., 1973, MA in English Lit., 1978. Cert. supervisory analyst N.Y. Stock Exchange. Editor McGraw-Hill Pub. Co., N.Y.C., 1979-81; sr. acquisitions editor Harcourt Brace Jovanovich, Inc., N.Y.C., 1981-82; sr. editor The Coll. Bd., N.Y.C., 1982-88; v.p., head editorial CS First Boston Corp., N.Y.C., 1988-94; v.p. supervisory analyst internat. rsch. SBC Warburg, N.Y.C., 1994—; part time asst. prof. pub. NYU Sch. Continuing Edn., N.Y.C., 1985—. Author: 50 College Admission Directors Speak to Parents, 1988. Democrat. Avocations: art, reading, travel. Office: SBC Warburg 277 Park Ave New York NY 10172

MACGREGOR, DAVID BRUCE, lawyer; b. Miami Beach, Fla., Feb. 21, 1953; s. Bruce Herbert and Mary Don (Doty) MacG.; m. Carol Louise Edler, Aug. 21, 1976; children: Meredith Elder, Christine Elder, Scott Elder. BA magna cum laude, Bucknell U., 1975; JD magna cum laude, Georgetown U., 1978. Bar: Pa. 1978, U.S. Dist. Ct. (ea. dist.) Pa., U.S. Ct. Appeals (4th cir.). Law clk. to presiding justice U.S. Ct. Appeals (4th cir.), Richmond, Va., 1978-79; assoc. Morgan, Lewis & Bockius, Phila., 1979-85, ptnr., 1985—. Mem. ABA, Pa. Bar Assn., Phila. Bar Assn. Republican. Presbyterian. Avocation: golf. Home: 620 Pembroke Rd Bryn Mawr PA 19010-3614 Office: Morgan Lewis & Bockius 2000 One Logan Sq Philadelphia PA 19103*

MACGREGOR, DAVID LEE, lawyer; b. Cedar Rapids, Iowa, Sept. 17, 1932; s. John H. and Beulah A. (Morris) MacG.; m. Helen Jean Kolberg, Aug. 7, 1954; children—Scott J., William M., Brian K., Thomas D. B.B.A., U. Wis., 1954, LL.B., 1956. Assoc. Quarles & Brady and predecessor firms, Milw., 1959-64, ptnr., 1964—; pres. Milw. Estate Planning Council, 1972-73; mem. adv. bd. CCH Fin. and Estate Planning, N.Y.C., 1982-87. Fellow Am. Coll. Trust and Estate Counsel; mem. ABA, Milw. Bar Assn., State Bar Wis. (chmn. taxation sect. 1977-78), Nat. Assn. Estate Planning Councils (pres. 1979-80). Home: Apt 1608 929 N Astor St Unit 1608 Milwaukee WI 53202-3486 Office: Quarles & Brady 411 E Wisconsin Ave Milwaukee WI 53202-4409

MACGREGOR, DONALD LANE, JR., retired banker; b. Duluth, Minn., June 21, 1930; s. Donald Lane and Julia (Waldo) MacG.; m. Mary Jo Rouse, Sept. 27, 1959; children—Jeffrey Lane, Steven Scott, John Rouse. Student, Carleton Coll., 1948-51; B.A. in Econs., Macalester Coll., 1956. Asst. cashier 1st Nat. Bank of Mpls., 1956-61; v.p. United Calif. Bank, San Francisco, 1961-69; pres. Ormand Industries, Dallas, 1969-70; v.p. United Calif. Bank, Los Angeles, 1970-71; pres., COO Am. Security Bank (name now First Interstate Bank of Hawaii), Honolulu, 1972-83, pres., CEO, 1983-91. Hon. trustee Hawaii Army Mus. Soc., Honolulu, 1978-91; vice chmn., bd. regents Chaminade U., Honolulu; trustee Hawaii Conf. Found., 1985-91. Capt. USAF, 1951-55. Mem. Am. Bankers Assn. (leadership del. 1984-92), Hawaii Bankers Assn., Hawaii C. of C. (bd. dirs. 1985-91). Republican. Clubs: Outrigger Canoe, Pacific, Waialae Country (Honolulu).

MACGREGOR, GEORGE LESCHER, JR., freelance writer; b. Dallas, Sept. 15, 1936; s. George Lescher and Jean (Edge) MacG.; divorced; children: George Lescher III, Michael Fordtran. B.B.A., U. Tex., 1958. Asst. cashier First Nat. Bank in Dallas, 1960-64, asst. v.p., 1964-68; v.p. Nat. Bank of Commerce of Dallas, 1968-70, sr. v.p., 1970-73, exec. v.p., 1973-74; pres., chief exec. officer Mountain Banks Ltd., Colorado Springs, 1974-77; chief exec. officer Highfield Fin. (U.S.A.) Ltd., 1978-83; chmn. bd., chief exec. officer, dir. Dominion Nat. Bank, Denver, 1981-84; chmn. bd., chief exec. officer Royal Dominion Ltd., Denver; chmn. bd., chief exec. officer, dir. Market Bank of Denver, 1983-84; vice chmn., dir. Bank of Aurora, Denver, 1983-84; chmn., pres., chief exec. officer Alamosa Bancorp. of Colo., Denver, 1983-84; pres., chief exec. officer Am. Interstate Bancorp., 1984-88; pres. Banco, Inc., 1984-89; sr. mng. ptnr. Scotland Co., Denver, London, 1988-91; free-lance writer, 1992—. Served with M.C. AUS, 1958-60. Mem. Am. Inst. Banking (hon.), Young Pres.'s Orgn., Koon Kreek Club, Broadmoore Golf Club, Oxford Club, Phi Gamma Delta. Anglican Catholic. Home and Office: 1736 Blake St Denver CO 80202-1226

MACGREGOR, KENNETH ROBERT, former insurance company executive; b. Ottawa, Ont., Can., July 21, 1906; s. Robert and Margaret (Goundrey) MacG.; m. Charlotte Jessie Donnelly, June 29, 1935; children: Jayne Ennis, Kenneth Robert. B.Sc. in Mech. Engring (hon.), Queens U., 1929. Lectr. Queens U., 1929-30; joined Fed. Dept. Ins., Ottawa, 1930; served in actuarial and exam. brs., later in adminstrn. br., supt. ins. with rank of dep. minister Fed. Dept. Ins., 1953-64; pres. Mut. Life Assurance Co. of Can., 1964-73, chmn., 1973-82; chmn. exec. com. Mut. Life Assurance of Can., 1982-83; hon. chmn. Mut. Life Assurance Co. of Can., 1983-89; hon. dir. Econ. Mut. Ins. Co., Missisquoi Ins. Co., Speech Found. of Ont.; former dir., mem. exec. com. Can. Trust Co., Can. Trust Mortgage Co. Past trustee and hon. life mem. Queens U. Council; former chmn. fin. com. Nat. Cancer Inst. Can. Served as maj. Gov. Gen.'s Foot Guards, 1923-45; mem. Canadian Bisley Rifle Team, 1926-28; comdt. 1957. Fellow Soc. Actuaries (former gov., v.p.); mem. Dominion of Can. Rifle Assn. (life gov.), Canadian Life Ins. Assn. (pres. 1968-69), Can. Cancer Soc. (hon. life), Nat. Cancer Inst. of Can. (hon. life), Rideau Club, Westmount Golf and Country Club, York Club. Presbyterian. Home: 125 John Blvd, Waterloo, ON Canada N2L 1C4

MACGUIGAN, MARK RUDOLPH, judge; b. Charlottetown, P.E.I., Can., Feb. 17, 1931; s. Mark Rudolph and Agnes Violet (Trainor) MacG.; m. Patricia Alice Dougherty, Dec. 26, 1987; children from previous marriage: Ellen, Mark, Thomas, Beth, Buddy. BA summa cum laude, St. Dunstan's U., Charlottetown, 1951; MA, U. Toronto, 1953, PhD, 1957; LLB, York U., Toronto, 1958; LLM, Columbia U., 1959, JJD, 1961; LLD (hon.), U. Prince Edward Island, Charlottetown, 1971, St. Thomas U., Fredericton, N.B., Can., 1981, U. Windsor, Ont., 1983, Law Soc. of Upper Can., Toronto, 1983. Bar: Ont., Prince Edward Island, Newfoundland, Queen's Counsel-Ont. Asst. prof. law U. Toronto, 1960-63, assoc. prof. law, 1963-66; prof. law Osgoode Hall Law Sch., York U., Toronto, 1966-67; dean of law U. Windsor, Ont., 1967-68; mem. parliament for Windsor-Walkervidge House of Commons Can., Ottawa, 1968-84; joint chmn. spl. joint commn. on constn. of Can. Parliament of Can., Ottawa, 1970-72, 78; parliamentary sec. Min. of Manpower and Immigration, Ottawa, 1972-74, Min. of Labor, Ottawa, 1974-75; judge Fed. Ct. Appeals, Ottawa, 1984—; vis. assoc. prof. law NYU, N.Y.C., summer 1966; chmn. Justice Com., Ottawa, 1975-79, Sub-Com. on Penitentiaries, Ottawa, 1976-77; critic solicitor-gen., 1979; sec. State for External Affairs, Govt. of Can., Ottawa, 1980-82, min. of justice and atty. gen., 1982-84; founding dir. Can. Civil Liberties Assn., Toronto, 1965, chair, 1966-67; pres. Can. Sect.-Internat. Commn. of Jurists, 1988-90; founding dir. Parliamentarians for World Order, 1977. Author: (law casebooks) Jurisprudence: Readings and Cases, 2d edit., 1966, Cases and materials on Creditors' Rights, 2d edit., 1967. Recipient Tarnopolsky medal for human rights Internat. Commn. of Jurists-Can. Sect., 1995. Mem. Internat. Law Assn., Can. Inst. for the Adminstrn. of Justice, Can. Judges' Conf., Can. Bar Assn., Cercle Universitaire. Roman Catholic. Avocations: walking, bridge. Office: Fed Ct of Appeal, Ottawa, ON Canada K1A 0H9

MACGUINNESS, ROSEMARY ANNE, lawyer; b. Newry, County Down, No. Ireland, June 26, 1957; came to U.S., 1981.; d. Micahel Gerald and Maureen Rosemary (Leavy) MacG.; m. Philip Martin Bellber, Dec. 5, 1987; children: Sam Martin Bellber, Rhys Patrick Bellber, Mason Philip Bellber. B in Civil Law, U. Coll. Dublin, 1978, diploma in European Law, 1979; MS in Criminal Justice, Northeastern U., 1982. Bar: Ireland 1981, Calif. 1994. Legal asst. Bronson, Bronson & McKinnon, San Francisco, 1983; atty. McInerney & Dillon, Oakland, Calif., 1984-87; sr. counsel Pacific Stock Exch., San Francisco, 1987-90, sr. counsel, dir. arbitration, 1990—. Mem. Queen's Bench. Office: Pacific Stock Exch 301 Pine St San Francisco CA 94104-3301

MACHALE, JOSEPH P., financial executive; b. Aug. 17, 1951. BA with hons., Oxford U., 1973. With Price Waterhouse, London, 1973-78; mng. dir. J.P. Morgan Co., N.Y.C., 1979—. Office: J P Morgan & Co Inc 60 Wall St New York NY 10260

MACHAMER, SYLVIA GERALDINE, special education educator; b. Visalia, Calif., Oct. 3, 1939; d. Henry Ross and Lucille Marian (Alvarez) Mata; m. Milton Lynn Machamer, June 17, 1962; children: Jonathan (dec.), Leah, Anne Marie, Jill, Ryan, Daniel. AA, Coll. of Sequoia, Visalia, Calif., 1959; BA, San Jose State U., 1961, spl. edn. cert., 1977. Cert. elem. tchr., spl. edn. elem. and secondary, Calif. Tchr. 2nd and 3rd grade Noble Sch. Berryessa Dist., San Jose, Calif., 1961-62; 3rd grade tchr. L.A. Sch. Dist., 1962-63; 2nd and head start tchr. Toyon Sch. Berryessa Dist., San Jose, 1963-67; supplemental educator grade 1, 4, 6. Garden Gate Sch., Cupertino, Calif., 1969—; educator learninc handicapped students Garden Gate Sch., Cupertino, 1969—, educator severely handicapped students, 1969—; cons. and workshop presenter to sch. dists. state and nationwide, 1988—; video mentor tchr., Cupertino Union Sch. Dist., 1991-93; intervention specialist, 1994—. Developer Gift of Reading Program, Computerized I.E.P. Program. Chmn. Indian Edn. Parent Com. Fremont High Sch. Dist., 1991-93. Recipient Continuing Svc. award Garden Gate PTA, Cupertino, 1989, Eagle Feather award Title U Coalition, 1993. Mem. De Anza Coll. Cable TV, Computer Using Educators, Parents Helping Parents (Outstanding Educator 1991), Coastal Band of Chumash Nation. Avocations: video, computers, walking, reading, Native Am. affairs. Home: 21753 Castleton St Cupertino CA 95014-4704 Office: Garden Gate Sch 10500 Ann Arbor Ave Cupertino CA 95014-1661

MACHARE, PETER ALLEN, law librarian; b. Queens, N.Y., Mar. 7, 1954; s. Stanley H. and Marion G. (MacDougall) Symolon; m. Senn Patalinjug, June 21, 1991; 1 child, Erica Merifi. BA, Washington & Lee U., 1976; JD, Cath. U. Am., 1981; MLS, U. Md., 1988. Libr. Cath. U. Am., Washington, 1976-83, Nat. Gallery Art, Washington, 1983-89; law libr. U.S. Dept. Agr., Washington, 1989—. Office: US Dept Agr Law Libr Rm M-1406 S Bldg Washington DC 20250-1400

MACHASKEE, ALEX, newspaper publishing company executive; b. Warren, Ohio; m. Carol Machaskee. Degree, Cleve. State U. Sports reporter The Warren (Ohio) Tribune; dir. labor rels. and personnel The Plain Dealer, Cleve., asst. to pub., promotion dir., v.p., gen. mgr., 1985-90, pres., pub., 1990—. V.p. Mus. Arts Assn. (Cleve. Orch.); chmn. Greater Cleve. Roundtable; bd. dirs. Ohio Arts Coun., Cleve. Found., Univ. Hosps. Health Sys., Inc., Univ. Cir., Inc., Greater Cleve. Growth Assn., Cleve. Tomorrow, Nat. Conf., Gt. Lakes Sci. Mus., Cleve. Coun. on World Affairs, United Way Svcs., Cleve. Initiative for Edn., Rock and Roll Hall of Fame and Mus., Mus. Coun. of Cleve. Mus. Art and St. Vladimir's Orthodox Theol. Sem., Crestwood, N.Y.; mem. vis. com. Weatherhead Sch. Mgmt., Case Western Res. U.; mem. adv. com. Newspaper Mgmt. Ctr., Northwestern U. Mem. Newspaper Assn. Am. (mem. labor rels. subcom.). Office: Plain Dealer Pub Co 1801 Superior Ave E Cleveland OH 44114-2107

MACHATZKE, HEINZ WILHELM, dean, science administrator; b. Freiburg, West Germany, Oct. 26, 1932; came to U.S., 1968; s. Friedrich W. and Helene W. (Maluschke) M.; m. Gertraud Zimmermann, Apr. 22, 1962; children: Jorg, Jens. BS, U. Freiburg (West Germany), 1955, MS, 1958, DSci., 1960. Rsch. chemist Bayer AG, Germany, 1962-68; chief chemist Mobay Chem. Corp., Union, N.J., 1968-70, asst. to pres., 1971-72, v.p., 1972-74, gen. mgr. dyes and pigment divsn., 1974-86, group v.p. human resources and quality programs, 1986-89; industry advisor, adj. prof. Duquesne U., Pitts., 1989—, dean Sch. Natural and Environ. Scis., 1994—; rsch. fellow U. Mich., 1960-62. Contbr. articles to profl. jours.; patentee in field. Mem. Am. Chem. Soc. Home: Scaife Rd Sewickley PA 15143 Office: Duquesne U Dean's Office Pittsburgh PA 15282

MACHEN, ARTHUR WEBSTER, JR., lawyer; b. Balt., Dec. 16, 1920; s. Arthur W. and Helen Chase (Woods) M.; m. Rose Bradley Purves, Jan. 24, 1948; children: Arthur W. (dec.), John P., Henry Lewis. AB, Princeton U., 1942; LLB, Harvard U., 1948. Bar: Md. 1948, U.S. Dist. Ct. Md. 1949, U.S. Ct. Appeals (4th cir.) 1949, U.S. Supreme Ct. 1954. Assoc. Armstrong, Machen & Eney, Balt., 1948-51; assoc. Venable, Baetjer & Howard, Balt., 1951-57, ptnr., 1957-89, sr. counsel, 1989—; sec. Schenuit Investments, Inc., Balt., 1980—. Author: A Venerable Assembly: The History of Venable, Baetjer and Howard, 1900-90, 1991; contbr. articles to profl. jours. Trustee Samuel Ready Scholarships, Inc., 1977-89, trustee emeritus 1989—; bd. mgrs. Family and Children's Soc., 1956-69, pres., 1967-69; reporter Charter Bd. Balt. County, 1956; dep. Gen. Conv. Episcopal Ch., 1973, 76, 79, 82; chancellor Episcopal Diocese Md., Balt., 1972-85. Lt. USNR, 1942-46, PTO. Fellow Am. Bar Found., Md. Bar Found.; mem. ABA, Md. State Bar Assn., Balt. City Bar Assn., Am. Law Inst., Am. Judicature Soc., Hamilton Street Club, Phi Beta Kappa. Democrat. Home: 1055 W Joppa Rd Unit 612 Baltimore MD 21204-3748 Office: Venable Baetjer & Howard 1800 Merc Bank & Trust Bldg 2 Hopkins Plz Baltimore MD 21201-2930

MACHIZ, LEON, electronic equipment manufacturing executive; b. Bklyn., June 23, 1924; s. Isadore and Fanny (Klonsky) M.; m. Lorraine Block, Mar. 31, 1951; children: Marc, Linda, Gary. Grad., Cooper Union. Salesman Sun Radio Co., 1942-52; founder Time Electro Sales Co. (merged with Avnet, Inc. 1952-68), Electro Air of Ga. (merged with Avnet, Inc. 1968), 1957-68, Electro Air of Fla., 1960-68; sr. v.p., dir. Avnet Inc., N.Y.C., 1968-80, pres., dir., 1980—, vice chmn., chief exec. officer, from 1986, dir., chmn., chief exec. officer, 1988—. Trustee North Shore Univ. Hosp., Boys' Brotherhood Republic. Office: Avnet Inc 80 Cuttermill Rd Great Neck NY 11021-3108*

MACHKOVITZ, SUSAN JEAN, psychologist, mental health consultant, educator; b. Beaver Dam, Wis.; d. Harold John and Lovine Carol Marie (Knorr) Schmidt; m. David Allen Machkovitz, July 11, 1970 (dec. Dec. 1976). BS in Elem.-Spl. Edn. magna cum laude, U. Wis., Whitewater, 1980; MS in Behavior Disabilities, U. Wis., Madison, 1987, PhD in Rehab. Psychology, 1993. Lic. life spl. edn. tchr., lic. elem. edn. tchr., Wis.; lic. psychologist. Instr. behavior modification program Bethesda Luth. Home, Watertown, Wis., 1975-79, spl. educator, 1980-86, diagnostician, edn. specialist, mental health cons., 1986-87; tng. specialist, cons. Tng. Plus, Watertown, 1988; instr. Madison Area Tech. Coll., Watertown, 1988; tchg. and rsch. asst. U. Wis., Madison, 1988-91, supr. student tchrs., 1988-89; psychology intern Ethan Allen Sch. for Boys, State of Wis., Wales, 1991-92; instr. Edgewood Coll., Madison, 1993; psychotherapist River City Psychol. Svcs., Watertown, 1993-94; postdoctoral psychology trainee Luth. Social Svcs. Wis. and Upper Mich., 1994-95, family therapist, 1994—; lectr. U. Wis., Madison, summer, 1991; mental health cons. Head Start Dodge County, Wis., 1994. Contbg. author: Treatment of the Mentally Disabled Offender, 1993. Mem. APA, Wis. Psychol. Assn., Soc. Clin. and Cons. Psychologists, Chi Sigma Iota. Democrat. Roman Catholic. Home: 1409 E Main St Watertown WI 53094-4031 Office: Luth Social Svcs Wis & Upper Mich 1010 Declark St Beaver Dam WI 53916-1002

MACHLIN, EUGENE SOLOMON, metallurgy educator, consultant; b. N.Y.C., Dec. 29, 1920; s. Gershon and Rose (Kaplan) M.; m. Edda Servi, May 21, 1960; children: Rona Susan, Argia Debora; m. Gertrude Green, Oct. 15, 1943 (dec. May 1959); 1 child, Chester Elia. BME, CCNY, 1942; MS, Case Inst. Tech., 1948; ScD, MIT, 1950. Aero. rsch. scientist Nat. Adv. Commn. Aeronautics, Cleve., 1942-48; rsch. assoc., asst. prof. MIT, Cambridge, 1948-50, 50-51; asst. prof. Columbia U., N.Y.C., 1951-54, assoc. prof., 1954-58, prof. metallurgy, 1958-89, Howe prof., 1989-91, Howe prof. emeritus, 1991—; cons. Spl. Metals Corp., Utica, N.Y., 1951-76; cons., dir. UV Industries, N.Y.C., 1966-79; summer faculty fellow IBM T.J. Watson Res. Lab., 1984-90. Author: An Introduction to Aspects of Thermodynamics and Kinetics Relevant to Materials Science, 1990, Materials Science in Microelectronics—The Relationships Between Thin Film Processing and Structure, 1995; editor: Synthesis of Metastable Phases, 1980; inventor Udimet 700, 1960. Chmn. solid state scis. adv. com. Office Sci. Rsch. USAF, Washington, 1954-59. Recipient C.H. Mathewson Gold medal AIME, 1954; Guggenheim fellow, 1965. Fellow AIME; mem. Am. Soc. Metals (Achievement award 1961, Edn. award 1974). Democrat. Jewish. Office: Columbia U 500 W 120th St New York NY 10027-6623

MACHLIN, LAWRENCE J., nutritionist, biochemist, educator; b. N.Y.C., June 24, 1927; s. Morris Louis and Lilly (Manevitz) M.; m. Ruth Beerman, May 30, 1953; children: Marc, Steven, Paul. BS, Cornell U., 1948, M in Nutritional Sci., 1949; PhD, Georgetown U., 1953. Nutritional biochemist USDA, AEC, Beltsville, Md., 1949-56; group chief Monsanto Co., St. Louis, 1956-73; sr. group chief Hoffman-La Roche Inc., Nutley, N.J., 1973-85, dir., 1985-92; pres. Nutrition Rsch. and Info. Inc., Livingston, N.J., 1993—; lectr. in nutrition Washington U., St. Louis, 1969-72; adj. prof. nutrition NYU, 1977-82; adj. assoc. prof. nutrition in medicine Cornell U., 1979—; Samuel Brody lectr. U. Mo., Columbia, 1988; Gladys Emerson Vis. prof. UCLA, 1990. Editor: Vitamin E, 1980, Handbook of Vitamins, 1984, rev. edit. 1991; co-editor: Vitamin Intake & Health, 1991; contbr. over 120 articles to profl. jours. Mem. Am. Inst. Nutrition, Am. Soc. Clin. Nutrition, N.Y. Acad. Scis., N.Y. Lipid Club, Soc. for Exptl. Biology and Medicine. Achievements include 4 patents in field; first to demonstrate that growth hormone stimulates milk production in the dairy cow and lean meat production in the pig; demonstrated that vitamin E functioned as in vivo antioxidant and popularized the concept that antioxidant vitamins are important to human health. Home: 18 Locust Pl Livingston NJ 07039-1213 Office: Hoffmann-LaRoche Inc 45 Eisenhower Dr Paramus NJ 07652-1429

MACHLIN, MILTON ROBERT, magazine editor, writer; b. N.Y.C., June 26, 1924; s. Morris Lewis and Lillie (Manevetz) M.; 1 foster son, Jason Sheckley; m. Margaret Ryan, 1988. AB, Brown U., 1948; Degre Avance, U. Paris-Sorbonne, 1949. Reporter, columnist Clifton (N.J.) Morning Leader, 1950-52; editor Service Americain AFP (news wire service), 1952, Macfadden House, 1953-55, Hillman Periodicals, 1955-57; mng. editor Argosy mag., 1960—, editor, 1969—, dir. film div.; creative dir. Pelican Prodns., 1974; regional v.p. Council Writers Orgns., 1986. Author: Ninth Life, 1961, Private Hell of Hemingway, 1962, MacArthur—A Fighting Man, 1965, The Search for Michael Rockefeller, 1972, The Family Man, 1974, French Connection II, 1975, The Setup, 1975, Pipeline, 1976, Atlanta, 1979, The Complete UFO Book, 1979, Libby, 1980, Complete UFO Catalogue, 1980, The Gossip Wars, 1980, The Worldshakers, 1984, Strangers in the Land, 1985, Minsky's Burlesque, 1985, Joshua's Altar, 1990. With AUS, 1942-45. Recipient Mystery Writers spl. award, 1976, Porgie award, 1977. Mem. Mystery Writers Am. Club: Explorers. Home: 27 Washington Sq N New York NY 10011-9177

MACHOVER, CARL, computer graphics consultant; b. Bklyn., Mar. 26, 1927; s. John Herman and Rose (Alter) M.; m. Wilma Doris Simon, June 18, 1950; children: Tod, Julie, Linda. BEE, Rensselaer Poly. Inst., 1951; postgrad., NYU, 1953-56. Mgr. applied engring. Norden div. United A/C Corp., 1951-59; mgr. sales Skiatron Electronics & TV, N.Y.C., 1959-60; v.p. mktg., dir. Info. Displays, Inc. Info. Displays, Inc., Mount Kisco, N.Y., 1960-73; v.p., gen. mgr., Info. Displays, Inc., Mount Kisco, 1973-76; pres. Machover Assocs. Corp., White Plains, N.Y., 1976—; adj. prof. Rensselaer Poly. Inst. Author: Gyro Primer, 1957, Basics of Gyroscopes, 1958; mem. editorial bd. IEEE Computer Graphics and Applications, Computers and Graphics, Spectrum; editor C4 Handbook, 1989, 2d edit., 1995, The CAD/CAM Handbook, 1996; co-editor Computer Graphics Rev.; contbr. articles to profl. jours. Mem. adv. bd. Pratt Ctr. for Computer Graphics in Design. With USNR, 1945-46. Recipient Frank Oppenheimer award Am. Soc. for Engrng. Edn., 1971, Orthagonal award N.C. State U., 1988, Vanguard award Nat. Comp. Graphics Assn., 1993; named to Computer Graphics Hall of Fame Fine Arts Mus. of L.I., Hempstead, N.Y., 1988. Fellow Soc. for Info. Display (pres. 1968-70), mem. IEEE, Assn. for Computing Machinery, Am. Inst. Design and Drafting, Nat. Soc. Profl. Engrs., Nat. Computer Graphics Assn. (bd. dir., pres. 1989-90), Computer Graphics Pioneer, Art and Sci. Collaborators Inc. (pres. 1995—), Sigma Xi, Tau Beta Pi, Eta Kappa Nu. Home: 152 Longview Ave White Plains NY 10605-2314 Office: Machover Assocs Corp PO Box 308 152A Longview Ave White Plains NY 10605-2314

MACHTEI, ELI E., periodontist; b. Petaq-Tikva, Israel, June 6, 1952; s. Ahron and Nechama (Langer) M.; m. Orna Samov, Mar. 24, 1974; children: Avner, Ayelet, Itay. DMD, Hebrew U., 1979. Sr. clin. lectr. Hebrew U., Jerusalem, 1982-93; clin. assoc. prof. SUNY, Buffalo, 1989—. Maj. Israeli Def. Force, 1970-73. Mem. Am. Acad. Periodontology (editorial bd. jour. 1993—, Earl Robinson award for regenerative rsch. 1995), Internat. Assn. Dental Rsch., Internat. Team Oral Implantologists, Internat. Acad. Periodontology (editorial bd. jour. 1992—). Home: 14 Gordon St, Hod-Hasharon Israel 45203 Office: SUNY Dept Oral Biology 3435 Main St Buffalo NY 14214 also: Rambam U Hosp, Periodontal Unit, Haifa Israel

MACHULAK, EDWARD LEON, real estate, mining and financial corporation executive; b. Milw., July 14, 1926; s. Frank and Mary (Sokolowski) M.; BS in Accounting, U., Wis., 1949; student spl. courses various univs.; m. Sylvia Mary Jablonski, Sept. 2, 1950; children: Edward A., John E., Lauren A., Christine M., Paul E. Chmn. bd., pres., Commerce Group Corp., Milw., 1962—, San Luis Estates, Inc., 1973—, Homespan Realty Co., Inc., 1974—, Universal Developers, Inc., 1972—, Picadilly Advt. Agy., Inc., 1974—; chmn. bd., chief exec. officer, Gen. Lumber & Supply Co., Inc., 1949—; bd. dirs., v.p., San Sebastian Gold Mines, Inc., 1969-73, chmn. bd., pres., 1973—; bd. dirs, sec., LandPak, Inc., 1985—; bd. dirs. Edjo Ltd., 1974—, sec., 1976—; ptnr., Weem Assocs., 1974—; bd. dirs., designee Comseb Joint Venture Woodcreek Devel. Corp., 1987. Mem. nat. adv. coun. SBA, 1972-74, co-chmn. 1973, 74. Recipient Recognition award U.S. SBA, 1975, N.W. Festival Corp., 25 Yr. Recognition award San Sebastian Community, Santa Rosa de Lima, El Salvador, 1991, San Sebastian Community El Salvador award, 1992, El Salvador Ministry Edn. award, 1992. Edward L. Machulak Day proclaimed by students of Canton San Sebastian, El Salvador, May 9, 1992; recipient recognition award for valuable consideration of support and svc. to San Sebastian Community, 1992, Cmty. Recognition award Santa Rosa De Lima, 1994. Mem. Nat. Assn. Small Bus. Investment Co's (nat. chmn. legis. com. 1968-73, bd. govs. 1970-74, exec. com. 1971-74, sec. 1972-74, Disting. Service award to Am. Small Bus. 1970), Midwest Regional Assn. Small Bus. Investment Cos. (bd. dirs. 1968-74, v.p. 1970-71, pres. 1971-72, Outstanding Services award 1972), State of Wis. Council on Small Bus. Investment (chmn. 1973-74), Wis. Bd. Realtors (various coms. 1955-88), Milw. Bd. Realtors (various coms. 1955-88). Pres.' Council Marmion Mil. Acad., Aurora, Ill., 1966-79, lay life trustee, 1972, fin. advisor 1967-71, chmn. spl. fund raising com. 1966-67, planning com. 1972-79; chmn. adv. bd. Jesuit Retreat House, Oshkosh, Wis., 1966-68; chmn., bd. dirs. Spencarian Coll. of Bus., 1973-74; chmn. St. John Cathedral Symphony Concert Com., Milw., 1978; sustaining mem. Met. Mus. Art, 1974—. Served with AUS, 1945-46. Recognized bus. leader in Congl. Record, 1976; named Hon. Life Mem., Mid-Continental Railway, 1963. Clubs: Tripoli Golf (Milw.); Lodge: KC (4th degree 1971—, recognition award 1989). Home: 903 W Green Tree Rd Milwaukee WI 53217-3716 Office: 6001 N 91st St Milwaukee WI 53225-1721

MACIAS, EDWARD S., chemistry educator, university official and dean; b. Milw., Feb. 21, 1944; s. Arturo C. Macias and Minette (Schwenger) Wiederhold; m. Paula Wiederhold, June 17, 1967; children: Matthew Edward, Julia Katherine. AB, Colgate U., 1966; PhD, MIT, 1970. Asst. prof. Washington U., St. Louis, 1970-76, assoc. prof., 1976-84, prof. chemistry, 1984—, chmn. dept., 1984-88, provost, 1988-95, interim dean Faculty Arts and Scis., 1994-95, exec. vice chancellor and dean Faculty Arts and Scis., 1995—; cons. Meteorology Rsch., Inc., Altadina, Calif., 1978-81, Salt River Project, Phoenix, 1980-83, Santa Fe Rsch., Bloomington, Minn., 1985-88, AeroVironment, Inc., Monrovia, Calif., 1986-88. Author: Nuclear and Radiochemistry, 1981; editor: Atmospheric Aerosol, 1981; contbr. numerous articles to profl. jours. Bd. dirs. Mark Twain Summer Inst., St. Louis, 1984-87, 88-90, The Coll. Sch., St. Louis, 1984-88. Grantee NSF, EPA, Electric Power Rsch. Inst., So. Calif. Edison Co., Dept. Energy, AEC. Mem. Am. Chem. Soc., Am. Assn. Aerosol Rsch. (editorial bd.), Am. Phys. Soc., AAAS. Home: 6907 Waterman Ave Saint Louis MO 63130-4333 Office: Washington U Campus Box 1094 One Brookings Dr Saint Louis MO 63130

MACILVAINE, CHALMERS ACHESON, retired financial executive, former association executive; b. Bklyn., Oct. 25, 1921; s. James Andrew and Helen Marie (Acheson) MacI.; m. Elizabeth Jean Babcock, Mar. 26, 1943; children: Judith Anne, Joseph Chad, Martha Elizabeth. A.B., Stanford U., 1943. With Kaiser Steel Corp., 1946-73, asst. controller, 1953-62, treas., 1962-70, v.p., 1967-70, v.p. finance and planning, 1970-73; also v.p., dir. subsidiaries; v.p. project financing group Bank of Am., San Francisco, 1973-74; sr. v.p., dep. head Asia div. Bank of Am., 1974-77; sr. v.p.-fin. Peabody Coal Co., St. Louis, 1978-80; sr. v.p., dir. Stifel, Nicolaus & Co., Inc., St. Louis, 1980-83; exec. dir. Japan Am. Soc. of St. Louis, 1983-85; pres. Bamerical Internat. Fin. Corp., 1973-74. Served to lt. (j.g.) USNR, 1943-46. Mem. Phi Beta Kappa, Sigma Chi. Club: Tokyo Lawn Tennis, Burns Club of St. Louis. Home: Martin Point Rd PO Box 332 Friendship ME 04547-0332

MACILWINEN, WILLIAM LEE, JR., international business consultant; b. Abadan, Iran, Sept. 18, 1958; arrived in U.S., 1961; s. William Lee and Jean (Theabaut) MacI.; m. Teri Jo Teer, Aug. 15, 1981; children: Catherine, Brian. Student, U. Sevilla, Spain, 1979, U. Santiago, Santiago de Compostela, Spain, 1980-81; BA, U. N.C., 1980; M. of Internat. Bus., U. S.C., 1983. Adv. mktg. rep. IBM Corp., Hamden, Conn., Blythewood, S.C., 1983-90; dir. M. of Internat. Bus. Studies program U. S.C., Columbia, 1990-94; pres. The MacIlwinen Co., Inc., 1995—; mng. dir. World Trade Ctr. U. S.C., 1995—; ptnr. Solomon Industries, Inc.; founding bd. dirs. Columbia World Affairs Coun., 1992-93, pres., 1993, mem. exec. com., 1992—; bd. dirs. S.C. Internat. Trade and Econ. Devel. Coun. Advisor S.C. World Calss Partnership, Columbia, 1993; mem. S.C.-Israel Exch., Columbia, 1993; bd. dirs., treas. MIBS Alumni Partnership Orgn.; mem. planning com. S.C. State Mus. Found., 1996. Mem. Columbia C. of C. (mem. internat. com. 1990-93). Avocations: tennis, golf, biking, reading. Home: 6 Williamstown Ct Columbia SC 29212-8645 Office: PO Box 11536 Columbia SC 29211

MACINNIS, FRANK T., construction company executive, holding company executive; b. Camrose, Alta., Can., Nov. 10, 1946; came to U.S., 1978; s. H. Frank and Adele M. (Irving) MacI.; m. Beverley J. McAndrews, Nov. 3, 1977; children: Christopher, Katrina, Lauren, Robbie. BA, U. Alta., Edmonton, Can., 1968, LLB, 1971. Assoc. Liden, Ackroyd & Co., Edmonton, 1971-75; gen. counsel Banister-Price Internat., Tehran, Iran, 1975-77; dir. Banister-Price Overseas, London, 1977-78; exec. v.p. H.C. Price Co., Bartlesville, Okla., 1978-80; chmn., chief exec. officer H.C. Price Constrn. Co., Dallas, 1980-84; pres. Spie Group, Inc., Dallas, 1984—; exec. v.p. Comstock Group, Inc., Danbury, Conn., 1986—; chmn.pres., ceo Emcor Group Inc, Norwalk; mem. exec. com. Spie Batignolles, Paris, 1985—. Served to lt. Royal Can. Navy, 1964-68. Roman Catholic. Avocations: sports, coin collecting, music. Office: Emcor Group Inc 101 Merritt seven corp Park 7th Fl Norwalk CT 06851*

MACINTOSH, CHARLES WILLIAM, property development company executive; b. Halifax, N.S., Can., Nov. 4, 1928; s. Charles William and Jessie Lenore (Lawrence) MacI.; m. Geraldine Ethel Lawrence, May 15, 1964; children: C.W. Alexander, Constance E.S., Donald S.L. BA, Dalhousie U., Halifax, 1950, LLB, 1952. Barrister and solicitor, N.S. News and ct. reporter Halifax Mail Star, 1950-53; legal practitioner C.W. MacIntosh, Halifax, 1953-61; ptnr. law firm Pace, MacIntosh & Donahoe, Halifax, 1961-74; legal cons. to AG Provincial Govts. of N.S., N.B. and P.E.I., 1974-75; dir. legal svcs. Coun. Maritime Premiers, Halifax, 1975-80; dir. land titles and legal svcs. div. Land Registration and Info. Svc., Halifax, 1980-90; gen. counsel, corp. sec., bd. dirs. The Armour Group Ltd., Halifax, 1990—; mem. drafting com. Joint Land Titles Act, 1990. Author: Intro. to Real Property in the Maritime Provinces, 1980, N.S. Real Property Practice Manual, 1988; author legal articles and papers on Cadastral sci. Pub. rels. officer Progressive Conservative Assn. N.S., Halifax, 1956-57; v.p. Halifax South Progressive Conservative Assn., 1973-74; mem. Halifax Ct. House Commn., 1963-65; bd. dirs. N.S. Adv. Coun. on Heritage Property, 1980-86; gov. MacDonald Barr Meml. Found., Washington, 1988-90. Named Queen's Counsel, N.S., 1968. Mem. Can. Bar Assn. (mem. coun., com. chair), N.S. Barristers Soc. (mem. coun. 1963-66, 80-90, hon. pres. 1993-94), The Halifax Club, The Comml. Club of Halifax (pres. 1966), Clan Chattan Assn., Clan Chattan Soc. of N.S. (pres. 1980-83), Cape Breton Bar Soc. (hon. mem.). Progressive Conservative. Home: 854 Greenwood Ave, Halifax, NS Canada Office: The Armour Group Ltd, 1701 Hollis St Ste 1001, Halifax, NS Canada

MAC INTYRE, DONALD JOHN, college president; b. Detroit, Aug. 19, 1939; s. Donald MacLellan and Ellen (McGrath) MacI.; m. Antoinette Shen, June 2, 1979; children by previous marriage: Honey, Michele, James, John. A.B., U. Detroit, 1961; M.A., U. Iowa, 1963, Ph.D., 1966. Prof. U. Pacific, Stockton, Calif., 1966-73; acad. dean/pres. St. Francis Coll., Biddeford, Maine, 1973-75; acad. v.p. U. San Francisco, 1975-79; pres. Metro. State Coll., Denver, 1979-81, Canada Coll., Redwood City, Calif., 1981-83, Skyline Coll., San Bruno, Calif., 1983-85, John F. Kennedy U., Orinda, Calif., 1985-89, Patricia Montandon & Assocs., San Francisco, 1989-91, Tie Tone, Inc., Mill Valley, Calif., 1991-92, The Fielding Inst., Santa Barbara, Calif., 1993—; cons. Indsl. Rels. Workshops Seminars, Inc., 1978-81, State Bd. Agr. Colo., 1979; assoc. John A. Scalone & Assocs., Orinda, Calif., 1977-85; chmn. adv. com. office adult learning svcs. Coll. Entrance and Exam. Bd., 1980-81; evaluator Women's Equity in Edn. Act Program, 1981. Contbr. articles to profl. jours. Chmn. edn. div. Mile High United Way, Denver, 1980-81; bd. dirs. Nat. Hispanic Center for Advanced Studies and Policy Analysis, 1981-86, Nat. Hispanic U., 1982-86, Chinese Culture Found., 1983-89; chmn. Children As the Peacemakers Found. Recipient award for Commendable Service U. San Francisco, 1979, Henry Clay Hall award, 1976; Disting. Teaching award U. Pacific, 1971; U. Pacific grantee, 1969-71; Don Quixote award Nat. Hispanic U., 1983; hon. mem. World Trade Ctr. Club, Nanjing, Republic of China, 1985—. Mem. Assn. Public Coll. and Univ. Pres.'s (co-chmn. Colo. 1980-81), Internat. Cultural Soc. Korea,. Democrat. Roman Catholic. Club: World Trade Ctr. (hon.) (Nanjing, China). Office: 2112 Santa Barbara St Santa Barbara CA 93105-3544

MACINTYRE, PATRICIA COLOMBO, middle school educator; b. San Diego, Jan. 20, 1955; d. Vincent Christopher Colombo and Ellen Louise (Johnson) David; m. John Malcolm MacIntyre, July 25, 1981; children: Ann Marie, Katherine Christine. BA, San Diego State U., 1977; MA in Computer Edn., U.S. Internat. U., 1987. Cert. tchr., Calif. Math. and art tchr. Adams Jr. High Sch., Richmond, Calif., 1979-80; math. and computer tchr. Piedmont (Calif.) Middle Sch., 1980-81, La Jolla (Calif.) Country Day Sch., 1982-85; adminstrv. asst. to headmaster St. Michael's Sch., Newport, R.I., 1981-82; math. tchr. Kubasaki High Sch., Dept. Def. Dependents Sch., Okinawa, Japan, 1989-90; compuer tchr., tech. coord. Palm Middle Sch., Lemon Grove, Calif., 1985—; local telementor Calif. Tech. Project, 1994-95. Selected for KUSI TV's Class Act, 1995, One of 20 Top Tchrs. in San Diego County, 1995; recipient Honoring Our Own award San Diego Sch. Bds. Assn., 1995. Mem. San Diego Computer-Using Educators (grantee 1991), Phi Kappa Phi. Republican. Roman Catholic. Avocations: children, family activities. Office: Palm Middle Sch 8425 Palm St Lemon Grove CA 91945-3314

MACINTYRE, R. DOUGLAS, information technology executive; b. Bennettsville, S.C., Aug. 6, 1951; s. Wade Hampton and Lucy Allen (Tison) M.; m. Elizabeth Wallace, June 30, 1973; children—Robert, Carter, Stewart. BA, U.S. Mil. Acad., 1973; MSBA with honors, Boston U., 1976; postgrad., Harvard U., Boston, 1985, U. Pa., 1987; exec. program, Stanford U., 1989. Mktg. rep. McDonnell Douglas, Atlanta, 1978-79; mktg. rep. Mgmt. Sci. Am. Inc., Atlanta, 1980-81, dist. mgr., 1982, regional mgr., 1983, v.p., 1984, sr. v.p. mktg., 1985-87, div. pres., 1987-88, exec. vp. U.S. ops., 1988-89; pres., COO, dir. Software 2000, Inc., Hyannis, Mass., 1990-93; pres., CEO Dun & Bradstreet Software, Atlanta, 1994—. Bd. dis. Sci. and Tech. Mus., Atlanta, 1986-90, United Way Cape Code, 1991-94, U.S. Mil. Acad. Assn., 1988-89, Alliance Theatre, 1995—. Capt. U.S. Army, 1973-78. Mem. Am. Software Assn. (dir. 1993—, pres. 1995—), Info. Tech. Assn. of Am. (bd. dirs. 1995—). Methodist. Office: Dun & Bradstreet Software 66 Perimeter Center East Atlanta GA 30346

MACIOCE, FRANK MICHAEL, lawyer, financial services company executive; b. N.Y.C., Oct. 3, 1945; s. Frank Michael and Sylvia Maria (Morea) M.; children: Michael Peter, Lauren Decker, Theodore Kenneth; m. Helen Latourette Duffin, July 9, 1988. BS, Purdue U., 1967; JD, Vanderbilt U., 1972. Bar: N.Y. 1973, U.S. Dist. Ct. (so. dist.) N.Y. 1973, U.S. Ct. Appeals (2d cir.) 1975, U.S. Supreme Ct. 1976. Mem. law dept. Merrill Lynch, Pierce, Fenner & Smith Inc., N.Y.C., 1972-80, v.p., 1978-88, 1st v.p., 1988— ; mgr. corp. law dept. Merrill Lynch & Co., Inc., N.Y.C., 1980-93, asst. gen. counsel, 1982—; gen. counsel investment banking group, 1993-95, ops., sys. and telecomm. counsel, 1995—, sec. of audit, compensation and nominating coms. bd. dirs., 1978-83, sec. exec. com., 1981-83; mng. dir. Merrill Lynch Overseas Capital, N.V., Netherlands Antilles, 1980-85; sec., dir. Merrill Lynch Employees Fed. Credit Union, N.Y.C., 1978-82; dir. Merrill Lynch Pvt. Capital Inc., N.Y.C., 1981-87, Enhance Fin. Services Inc, N.Y.C., 1988-92; mem. fin. planning adv. bd. Purdue U., 1996—. Served with U.S. Army, 1969-70. Mem. ABA, Assn. of Bar of City of N.Y. (computer law com.). Home: 22 Essex Rd Summit NJ 07901-2802 Office: Merrill Lynch & Co Inc N Tower World Fin Ctr New York NY 10281-1334

MACIOCH, JAMES EDWARD, investment consultant, financial planner; b. Cleve., Mar. 30, 1947. Cert. fin. planner, Coll. for Fin. Planning, Denver, 1992; BS, U. Dayton, 1969. Lic. series 7, Nat. Assn. Securities Dealers. Registered floor broker Mid-Am. Commodity Exch., 1988-90; registered floor broker, mem. Chgo. Bd. Trade, 1990—; investment cons. Montano Securities Corp., Chgo., 1993-94, Dickinson & Co., Rosemont, Ill., 1995—. Mem. Internat. Soc. for Fin. Planning. Office: Dickinson & Co 5600 N River Rd Ste 180 Rosemont IL 60018-5184

MACIUSZKO, KATHLEEN LYNN, librarian, educator; b. Nogales, Ariz., Apr. 8, 1947; d. Thomas and Stephanie (Horowski) Mart; m. Jerzy Janusz Maciuszko, Dec. 11, 1976; 1 child, Christinia Alexsandra. BA, Ea. Mich. U., 1969; MLS, Kent State U., 1974; PhD, Case Western Res. U., 1987. Reference libr. Baldwin-Wallace Coll. Libr., Berea, Ohio, 1974-77, dir. Conservatory of Music Libr., 1977-85; dir. bus. info. svcs. Harcourt Brace Jovanovich, Inc., Cleve., 1985-89; staff asst. to exec. dir. Cuyahoga County Pub. Libr., Cleve., 1989-90; dir. Cleve. Area Met. Library System, Beachwood, Ohio, 1990; media specialist Cleve. Pub. Schs., 1991-93, Berea (Ohio) City Sch. Dist., 1993—. Author: OCLC: A Decade of Development, 1967-77, 1984; contbr. articles to profl. jours. Named Plenum Pub. scholar, 1986. Mem. Spl. Librs. Assn. (pres. Cleve. chpt. 1989-90, v.p. 1988-89, editor newsletter 1988-89), Baldwin-Wallace Coll. Faculty Women's Club (pres. 1975).. Avocation: piano. Office: Midpark HS 7000 Paula Dr Middleburg Heights OH 44130

MACIVER, JOHN KENNETH, lawyer; b. Milw., Mar. 22, 1931; s. Wallace and Elizabeth (MacRae) MacI.; m. Margaret J. Vail, Sept. 4, 1954; children: Douglas B., Carolyn V., Kenneth D., Laura E. BS, U. Wisc., 1953, LLB, 1955. Bar: Wisc. 1955. Sr. ptnr. Michael, Best & Friedrich, Milw., 1955—; mem. various bds. dirs. Chmn. Thompson for Gov. steering coms., 1986, 90, 94; state chmn. Wisc. Bush for Pres. coms., 1980, 88, 92; chmn. Wisc. Nixon for Pres. com., 1968, 72, Olson for Gov. com., 1970; vice chmn. Knowles for Gov. com., 1964, 66; bd. dirs. Milw. Symphony Orch., 1986-96, pres. 1981-82; trustee Milw. Symphony Endowment Trust, 1988—; chmn. exec. com., bd. govs. East-West Ctr., 1970-76 (Disting. svc. award Honolulu 1976); pres., chmn. bd. dirs. Nat. Coun. Alcoholism, 1974-77, bd. dirs. 1968-78 (Silver Key award N.Y. 1975); pres., campaign co-chmn. United Performing Arts Fund Greater Milw., 1974-76 (Stiemke award Arts 1988); bd. dirs., exec. com. Greater Milw. Edn. Trust, 1988—, Project New Hope, 1991—; sec., gen. counsel Wisc. Mfrs. and Commerce, 1980—; regent, sec., gen. counsel Milw. Sch. Engring., 1987—; bd. dirs., sec. Pettit Nat. Ice Tng. Ctr., 1992—; bd. dirs. Milw. Nat. Heart Project; bd. dirs., exec. com., founding mem., sec. Competitive Wisc. Inc., 1982—; bd. dirs., vice-chair Met. Milw. Assn. Commerce, 1987—; mem. Greater Milw. Com. 1985—; trustee Milw. County Pub. Mus., 1989-92. Recipient Wisc. Gov's. awards in Support of Arts, 1989. Mem. Wisc. Bar Assn. (chmn. commn. litigation costs and delay, past chmn. labor law sect.), Milw. Bar Assn. (chmn. jud. selection and qualifications com.), Milw. Club, Town Club. Republican. Avocations: Am. history, tennis, charities, politics. Home: 959 E Circle Dr Milwaukee WI 53217-5362 Office: Michael Best & Friedich 100 E Wisconsin Ave Milwaukee WI 53202-4107

MACIVER, LOREN, artist; b. N.Y.C., Feb. 2, 1909; d. Charles Augustus Paul and Julia (MacIver) Newman; m. Lloyd Frankenberg. Student, Art Students League, 1919. One-man shows East River Gallery, N.Y.C., 1938, Pierre Matisse Gallery, N.Y.C., 1940-44, 49, 56, 61, 66, 70, Mus. Modern Art Traveling Exhbn., 1941, Vassar Art Gallery, 1950, Wellesley Coll., 1951, Whitney Mus., 1953, Dallas Mus. Fine Arts, 1953, Venice Biennale, 1967, Musée des Beaux Arts, Lyons, France, 1968, Musée de l'Art Moderne de la Ville de Paris, 1968, Pierre Matisse Gallery, N.Y.C., 1981, Rutgers Art Gallery, 1982, U. Md. Art Gallery, 1982, Musée des Ponchettes, Nice, France, 1968, 50-yr. retrospective Newport Harbor Art Mus., Newport Beach, Calif., 1985, Pierre Matisse Gallery, 1987, Mus. Modern Art, 1991, Terry Dintenfass Gallery, 1993; works exhibited Mus. of Modern Art include Federal Art, 1937, Fantastic Art, Dada, Surrealism, 1938, Art In Our Time, 1939, Fourteen Americans, 1946; work in exhbns. Am. art, Jeu de Paume, Paris, 1938, St. Louis Mus., Whitney Mus., Bklyn. Mus., Corcoran Art Gallery, State Dept. exhbn. sent to Europe, 1946, Tolouse Mus. Fine Arts, 1967, Met. Mus. Art, N.Y.C., 1991; represented in permanent collections Mus. Modern Art, Met. Mus., Detroit Inst., Los Angeles, San Francisco, Newark museums, Addison Gallery, Whitney Mus., Wadsworth Atheneum, Smith Coll. Mus., Phillips Collection, Washington, Joseph Hirshhorn Collection, Washington, Williams Coll., Elliott Collection, others. Guggenheim fellow, 1976; recipient 1st prize Corcoran Art Gallery, 1957, 1st prize Art Inst. Chgo., 1961, purchase prize Kranner Art Mus. of U. Ill., 1963, Mark Rothko Found. award, 1972, Lee Krasner award, 1991; Ford Found. grantee, 1960. Mem. Nat. Inst. Arts and Letters. Office: Terry Dintenfass Gallery 50 W 57th St New York NY 10019-3914

MACK, CHARLES DANIEL, III, labor union executive; b. Oakland, Calif., Apr. 16, 1942; s. Charles Daniel and Bernadine Zoe (Ferguson) M.; m. Marlene Helen Fagundes, Oct. 15, 1960; children: Tammy, Kelly, Kerry, Shannon. B.A., San Francisco State Coll., 1964. Truck driver Garrett Freight Lines, Emeryville, Calif., 1962-66; bus. agt. Teamsters Local No. 70, Oakland, 1966-70, sec.-treas., 1972—; legis. rep. Calif. Teamsters Pub. Affairs Council, Sacramento, 1970-71; trustee Western Conf. Teamsters Pension Trust Fund, 1980—, mem. policy com., 1980-82, pres. Teamsters' Joint Council 7, San Francisco, 1982—; mem. Calif. Inst. for Fed. Policy Rsch., 1993—. Bd. dirs. Econ. Devel. Corp. of Oakland, 1980-90, Pvt. Industry Council, Oakland, 1983-84, Children's Hosp. of East Bay, 1981-83, Calif. Compensation Ins. Fund, San Francisco, 1980-86, Alameda County Easter Seals, 1983-85, United Way, 1978-82. Democrat. Roman Catholic. Office: Teamsters' Joint Counc 7 Executive Park Blvd San Francisco CA 94134-3301

MACK, CLIFFORD GLENN, investment banker, management consultant; b. Pitts., Feb. 23, 1927; s. Jay Oryd and Willa June (Shupe) M.; m. Judith McClain; children: Jeffrey, Cynthia, Marcia. B.B.A., U. Pitts., 1952; M.B.A., Temple U., 1955. Asst. treas. Air Products & Chems., Inc., Allentown, Pa., 1957-69; dir. internat. fin., asst. treas. Harris Corp., Cleve., 1969-75; treas. A.B. Dick Co., Chgo., 1975-83; pres. A.B. Dick Realty Corp., 1978-80, C.G. Mack Assocs. Ltd., Cons., 1983—; ptnr. AVM Fin. Group, Chgo., 1985-93. Contbg. author: Credit Management Handbook, 1955; also articles. Served with AUS, 1945-48. Home: 5100 Trent Woods Dr New Bern NC 28562-6726

MACK, CONNIE, III (CORNELIUS MACK), senator; b. Phila., Oct. 29, 1940; s. Cornelius Mack and Susan (Sheppard) McGillicuddy; children: Debra Lynn, Cornelius Harvey. Degree in bus., U. Fla., 1966. Mgmt. tng. Sun Bank, Cape Coral, Fla., 1966-68; v.p. bus. devel. First Nat. Bank, Ft. Myers, 1968-71; sr. v.p., dir. Sun Bank, Cape Coral, Fla., 1971-75; pres., dir. Fla. Nat. Bank, Cape Coral, 1975-82; mem. U.S. Ho. of Reps. from 13th Dist. Fla., Washington, 1983-89; U.S. Senator from Fla., 1989—, sec. Rep. conf. 104th Congress. Bd. dirs., chmn. Palmer Drug Abuse Program, Cape Coral; bd. dirs. Cape Coral Hosp. Mem. Met. Ft. Myers C. of C., Cape Coral C. of C. Republican. Roman Catholic. Office: US Senate 517 Senate Hart Bldg Washington DC 20510*

MACK, CONSUELO COTTER, news anchor and editor; d. J. Holland and Consuelo Cotter; m. Walter Mack; 1 child. BA in English Lit., History, Polit. Sci., Sarah Lawrence Coll. With various Wall St. investment firms; asst. press sec. Whitney North Seymour Campaign, 1982; founding news editor, co-anchor Bus. Times, ESPN, 1982-86; contbg. reporter The Today Show, NBC, 1986; achnor, exec. editor Today's Business, N.Y.C., 1986; anchor, editor The Wall St. Jour. Report, N.Y.C., 1987—, The Asian Wall St. Jour. Report, N.Y.C., 1993-95; guest panelist The Editors, The World in Rev. on PBS and Can. Broadcasting; speaker in field. Supr., vol. Helpline, N.Y. met. area; bd. dirs. Women's Econ. Round Table. Office: Wall St Jour Report 200 Liberty St Fl 10 New York NY 10281-1003

MACK, DANIEL RICHARD, furniture designer; b. Rochester, N.Y., Dec. 23, 1947; s. Richard Cornelius and Virginia Anne (Brayer) M.; m. Theresa Marie Husted, May 31, 1969; children: Kendra, Jessica, Eliza. BA, U. Toronto, Ont., Can., 1969; MA, New Sch. for Social Rsch., 1975. Journalist Sta. WRVR-FM, N.Y.C., 1971-73; spl. journalist NBC Radio, N.Y.C., 1973-75; journalist NBC TV, N.Y.C., 1981-83; asst. prof. Fordham U., Bronx, N.Y., 1975-81; pres. Daniel Mack Rustic Furnishings, Inc., Warwick, N.Y., 1983—; treework cons. Centerbrook Architects, Essex, Conn., 1990-91. Author: Making Rustic Furniture, 1992, The Rustic Furniture Companion, 1996; represented in permanent collections at Cooper Hewitt Mus., Mus. of Fine Arts, Houston, Mus. of Fine Arts, Boston, , Am. Craft Mus., The Hechinger Collection. Fellow N.Y. Found. for Arts, 1985-86, 90-91, Mid-Atlantic Arts Found., 1989-90. Home and Studio: 14 Welling Ave Warwick NY 10990-1514

MACK, DEBRA K., lawyer; b. New Orleans, Mar. 29; d. Willie Bell Mack and Dorothy (Maples) Watson. BA, Dillard U., 1976; JD, Loyola Law Sch., 1979. Bar: La. 1979. Recreational asst. New Orleans Recreation Dept., 1973-79; pub. defender Orleans Indigent Defender Program, New Orleans, 1979-81; staff atty. Larry P. Williams Law Firm, New Orleans, 1979-81; part-time instr. bus. law Ga. State U., Atlanta, 1982; spl. agt. atty. FBI, Newark, 1985-89; supervisory spl. agt., atty. FBI, Washington, 1989—; part-time instr. bus. law Dillard U., New Orleans, 1981; EEO counselor FBI, Newark, 1986—; legal advisor FBI, Newark, 1986—; gen. police instr. FBI, 1986—; target selection interviewer FBI, 1986—, mem. speaker's bur. Mem. Coalition of Black Women, Newark, 1989. Mem. Nat. Bar Assn., La. Bar Assn., Garden State Bar Assn., Assn. Black Women Lawyers, Nat. Orgn.

Black Law Enforcement. Democrat. Avocations: travel, reading, jogging, movies, plays. Office: FBI 600 Arch St 8th Fl Philadelphia PA 19106

MACK, DENNIS WAYNE, lawyer; b. Chgo., Sept. 11, 1943; s. Walter Andrew and Betty Jane (Klimek) M. B.A., Yale U., 1965; J.D., Harvard U., 1969. Bar: N.Y. 1970. Assoc. firm Curtis Mallet-Prevost Colt & Mosle, N.Y.C. and Paris, 1969-78; sec., gen. counsel Dominion Textile (USA) Inc., N.Y.C., 1978-91, v.p., 1986-91; pvt. practice N.Y.C., 1991—; alt. rep. Internat. Lesbian and Gay Assn. at ECOSOC of UN, 1994. Mem. dept. fin. Presbytery N.Y., 1978-83. Mem. ABA, N.Y. State Bar Assn., Bar Assn. City N.Y. Home: 180 Riverside Dr New York NY 10024-1021

MACK, EARLE IRVING, real estate company executive; b. N.Y.C., July 11, 1939; s. H. Bertram and Ruth (Kaufman) M.; m. Carol L. Dickey, July 26, 1990; children: Andrew Mack, Beatrice. BBA, Drexel U., 1960; postgrad., Fordham Law Sch., 1961-62; LHD (hon.), Yeshiva U., 1992. Owner, breeder thoroughbred horses Fla., Ky., N.J., N.Y., Md., Can., 1964—; sr. ptnr., CFO The Mack Co., Rochelle Park, N.J., since 1964; mem. adv. bd. N.Y. State Bus. Venture Partnership, 1988—; mem. transition team for Gov. George Pataki, 1994-95; chmn. N.Y. State Coun. Arts, 1996. Producer-dir. film The Children of Theater Street, 1977 (Acad. Award nomination). Bd. dirs. Benjamin N. Cardozo Sch. of Law, N.Y.C., 1980—, chmn. exec. com., 1990, vice chmn. bd. dirs., 1991, chmn. bd. dirs., 1992; bd. dirs. N.Y.C. Ballet, 1988—; chmn. N.Y. State Coun. on Arts, 1996, N.Y. State Racing Commn., 1983-90; mem. bldg. devel. com. N.Y.C. Holocaust Commn., 1985—, N.Y. State Thoroughbred Rading Capital Investment Fund, 1987—, The New 42d St., Inc., 1990-92; bd. dirs. Dance Theatre of Harlem, N.Y.C., 1987, elected co-chmn. bd., 1988-89; trustee N.Y. Racing Assn., Inc., 1990—; trustee, exec. com. Yeshiva U., 1992—. 1st lt. USAR, 1960-68. Recipient Can. Sovereign award Horse of Yr., 1993, Can. Sovereign award for best 3 yr. old horse, 1994; named One of Drexel 100, Drexel U., 1992. Mem. Nat. Realty Com. (bd. dirs., exec. com. 1986-88), Urban Land Inst., Union League Club, Univ. Club, Reading Room Club, Turf & Field Club. Avocations: skiing, swimming, jogging, nutrition. Office: The Mack Co 370 W Passaic St Rochelle Park NJ 07662-3009

MACK, EDWARD GIBSON, retired business executive; b. Toronto, Ont., Can., Dec. 4, 1917; s. Edward Gibson and Marion Margaret (Ward) M.; m. Ruth Harriet Davies, Aug. 3, 1940 (dec.); children: Edward Davies, Carol Mack Fuller, Susan Mack Vassel; m. Isolde Maderson, Sept. 30, 1978. Grad., Pickering Coll., 1938; student, Syracuse U., 1938-40, U. Pa., 1945-46. Investment analyst trust dept. Syracuse (N.Y.) Trust Co., 1939-43; acct. Hurdman & Cranstoun, Syracuse, 1943-44; from dist. sales mgr. to dir. mktg. and product research Easy Washing Machine Corp., Syracuse, 1948-55; dir. research Avco Corp., Connersville, Ind., 1955-58; exec. sec. planning and policy bd. Aeronca Mfg. Corp., Middletown, Ohio, 1958-60; pres. E.D.I., State College, Pa., 1960-62; pres., dir. Sherman Indsl. Electronics Inc., Eutectics Inc.; exec. Richards Musical Instruments, Inc., Elkhart, Ind., 1962-65; mgr. supply and distbn. plastic products Union Carbide Ltd., Lindsay, Ont., 1965-68; corp. sec. Dominion Dairies Ltd., Toronto, 1968-73; v.p., sec. Dominion Dairies Ltd., 1973-81; sec., dir. Sealtest (Can.) Ltd., 1968-81. Bd. mgmt. Pickering Coll. Served with U.S. Army, World War II. Mem. Inst. Chartered Secs. and Adminstrs. (assoc.), Am. Legion, Elks, Sigma Chi. Republican. Home: 217-5 Selby Ranch Rd American River Dr Sacramento CA 95864

MACK, FLOSSIE PHILLIPS, elementary educator; b. Mayodan, N.C., Aug. 22, 1944; d. Lewis H. and Hattie O. Phillips. BS, N.C. A&T State U., Greensboro, 1969; MEd, Rutgers U., 1973. Cert. early childhood tchr., bus. edn. tchr. Typist Capitol Collection Bur., 1964-65; receptionist U. N.C., Greensboro, 1969-70; legal sec. Smith & Patterson Law Firm, 1970-71; tchr. Greensboro City Schs., 1973—. State Tuition grantee; Work-Aid scholar; recipient LCH Civil award. Mem. NANBPWC, Tau Gamma Delta.

MACK, J. CURTIS, II, civic organization administrator; b. Los Angeles, Dec. 22, 1944; s. James Curtis and Ahli Christina (Youngren) M.; m. Tamara Jo Kriner, Jan. 23, 1988; children: James Curtis III, Robert Lee. BA cum laude, U. So. Calif., 1967, M in Pub. Adminstrn., 1969, MA, 1976. Asst. to regional dir. VA, Los Angeles, 1973-79; exec. dir. Citizens for the Republic, Santa Monica, Calif., 1979-85; asst. sec. oceans and atmosphere U.S. Dept. Commerce, Washington, 1985-88; pres. Los Angeles World Affairs Coun., 1988—; bd. dirs. Brentwood Bank of Calif. Col. USAFR, 1969—. Mem. Nat. Space Club (bd. dirs. 1987-88). Republican. Episcopalian. Avocation: philatelist. Office: Los Angeles World Affairs Coun 911 Wilshire Blvd Ste 1730 Los Angeles CA 90017-3409

MACK, JEROME D., banker; b. Albion, Mich., Nov. 6, 1920; s. Nate and Jennie (Solomon) M.; m. Joyce Jean Rosenberg, Mar. 30, 1947; children; children: Barbara Joan, Karen Diane, Marilynn Susan. BA, AA, UCLA, 1943; D.Law (hon.), U. Nev., Las Vegas, 1983. Vice chmn. Valley Capital Corp. (fomerly Valley Bank Nev.), Las Vegas, 1965-94; real estate developer Thomas & Mack Co., Las Vegas, 1992—; chmn., commr. Nev. State Tax Commn., 1970-89. Mem. Dem. Nat. Fin. Com., Washington; nat. coordinator Humphrey for Pres., Las Vegas, 1968; fin. chmn. Nev. State Dem. Party, 1968; state coordinator, treas., Cannon for Senate Com., 1958; trustee Boy Scouts Am., 1965-87, U. Nev. Las Vegas Land Found., 1965-87; trustee, bd. overseers UCLA. Recipient Israel's Peace award, 1981; named Outstanding Nev. Citizen U. Nev. Las Vegas Alumni, 1981. Democrat. Jewish. Club: Boys (founder, dir.). Avocations: boating, tennis. Office: Thomas & Mack Co Nev Fin Ctr 2300 W Sahara Ave Ste 530 Las Vegas NV 89102

MACK, JOHN EDWARD, III, utility company executive; b. Poughkeepsie, N.Y., Feb. 20, 1934; s. John Edward Jr. and Agnes D. (Albrecht) M.; m. Maureen Whitworth, Sept. 12, 1970; children: John, Todd, Ellen, David. BS, Siena Coll., 1956, LHD (hon.), 1966, MBA, 1966; LHD, Mt. St. Mary Coll., 1994. With Ctrl. Hudson Gas & Electric Corp., Poughkeepsie, 1958—, v.p. corp. svcs., 1974-76, v.p. customer svcs., 1976-79, exec. v.p., 1979-82, pres., 1982—, CEO, 1986—, also chmn. bd. dirs.; pres. Empire State Electric Energy Rsch. Corp.; bd. dirs. Mid Hudson Med. Ctr.; chmn. exec. com. N.Y. Power Pool. Mem. exec. com. Dutchess County (N.Y.) coun. Boy Scouts Am., pres. Hudson Valley coun.; bd. dirs. Astor Home for Children, Rhineback, N.Y., Marist Coll., N.Y. Bus. Devel. Corp. With U.S. Army, 1956-58. Recipient Alexis de Tocqueville Volunteerism award United Way, Poughkeepsie, 1988, Americanism award Anti Defamation League, 1988, Citizenship award Hudson-Del. Boy Scouts, 1987, Disting. Citizen award Dutchess County Boy Scouts Am. Mem. Am. Gas Assn., Edison Electric Inst. (bd. dirs.), Energy Assn. N.Y. State (chmn.). Roman Catholic. Office: Cen Hudson Gas & Electric 284 South Ave Poughkeepsie NY 12601-4838

MACK, JULIA COOPER, judge; b. Fayetteville, N.C., July 17, 1920; d. Dallas L. and Emily (McKay) Perry; m. Jerry S. Cooper, July 30, 1943; 1 dau., Cheryl; m. Clifford S. Mack, Nov. 21, 1957. B.S., Hampton Inst., 1940; LL.B., Howard U., 1951. Bar: D.C. 1952. Legal cons. OPS, Washington, 1952-53; atty.-advisor office gen. counsel Gen. Svcs. Adminstrn., Washington, 1953-54; trial appellate atty. criminal div. Dept. Justice, Washington, 1954-68; civil rights atty. Office Gen. Counsel, Equal Employment Opportunity Commn., Washington, 1968-75; assoc. judge Ct. Appeals, Washington, 1975-89; sr. judge, 1989—. Mem. Am., Fed., Washington, Nat. Bar Assns., Nat. Assn. Women Judges. Home: 1610 Varnum St NW Washington DC 20011-4206 Office: DC Ct Appeals 500 Indiana Ave NW Ste 6 Washington DC 20001-2131

MACK, KIRBIE LYN, municipal official; b. Chgo., Jan. 3, 1953; d. Robert Lee and Luvonia (Cheatham) Green; m. Jeffery Frazier Mack, Aug. 10, 1974; children: Maaina, Jeffery Jr., Anisha. BA in Psychology, Northeastern Ill. U., 1975; MA in Policy Analysis and Pub. Adminstrn., U. Wis., 1995. Pers. specialist City of Madison, Wis., 1975-76; program asst. planning budget analysis dept. natural resource State of Wis., Madison, 1976-79, dir. conservation corps, 1979-80, equal opportunity officer, mgr., 1980-85, chief negotiator employment rels., 1985-89; dir. affirmative action dept. City of Madison, 1989—. Co-host, prodr. (cable TV program) Focus On Equality, 1989—. Pres. Southside Raiders Football Booster Club, Madison, 1995. Recipient Gov.'s Orchid award State of Wis., 1987, Exemplary Leadership award Wis. Assn. Black State Employees, 1993, Leadership in Affirmative Action award Am. Soc. for Pub. Adminstrs., 1992, 93, Outstanding Cmty. Svc. award Prevention and Intervention Alcohol and Drug Abuse, 1992, Spirit of Am. Woman award Sta. WISC-TV, 1994, Pub. Svc. for Students award Links, Inc. and Madison Pub. Schs., 1994; named one of 100 Most Alluring Creative Influential and Entrepreneurial People Madison Mag., 1995. Mem. NAACP (life, 1st v.p. 1993—, 2d v.p., Outstanding Svc. award Madison br. 1990, 92, Unsung Heroine award 1993), Am. Contract Compliance Assn., Wis. Assn. Black State Employees (past pres. 1985, Pres.'s award 1989-90). Office: City of Madison Ste 130/MMB 215 Martin Luther King Jr Blvd Madison WI 53701

MACK, PATRICIA, secondary school principal. Prin. Walker Mid. Sch., Salem, Oreg. Recipient Elem. Sch. Recognition award U.S. Dept. Edn., 1989-90. Office: Walker Middle Sch 1075 8th St NW Salem OR 97304-3704

MACK, PATRICIA JOHNSON, newspaper editor; b. New Brunswick, N.J., Oct. 4, 1942; d. Henry Francis and Ann May (Monahan) Johnson; m. Parker Horton Moore, July 22, 1961 (div. 1971); m. Lonnie Burnell Mack, May 23, 1973; children: Tevis Ann, Kelaine Dorothy, Aidan Ruth. Student, Alderson-Broaddus Coll., 1960-61, U. W.Va., 1961, Harvard U., 1961-62, U. Ky., 1962-64. Reporter The Sentinel Greater Media Newspapers, East Brunswick, N.J., 1971-77; reporter, food editor, restaurant critic News Tribune, Woodbridge, N.J., 1977-92; food editor News Tribune/Record, Woodbridge and Hackensack, N.J., 1992—. Bd. dirs. Parents for Deaf Awareness, 1985-87; active Ctrl. Jersey Health Planning Commn., Woodbridge, 1987, Middlesex County Commn. for Handicapped, New Brunswick, 1987-89. Recipient 7 awards N.J. Press Assn., 1987-92, Cardiac Reporting award N.J. divsn. Am. Heart Assn., 1987, Nutrition Writing award Nestle, 1992, Disting. Svc. award N.J. Dietetic Assn., 1993. Mem. Assn. Food Journalists (Best Food Sect. awards 1987, 92, 93). Avocations: swimming, reading, cooking, film. Office: The Record 150 River St Hackensack NJ 07601-7110

MACK, RAYMOND FRANCIS, newspaper executive; b. Aitkin, Minn., Sept. 5, 1912; s. Raymond Frederick and Bertha (Tuller) M.; m. Betty Habes, Oct. 17, 1941; children—Patricia, Douglas. Student pub. schs., Va., Minn. Country circulation mgr. Duluth (Minn.) Herald News Tribune, 1930-40, St. Paul Dispatch Pioneer Press, 1940-42; circulation mgr. Washington Daily News, 1942-58, advt. dir., 1958-59, bus. mgr., 1959-72, pres., 1960-72; asst. gen. bus. mgr. Scripps-Howard Newspapers, 1972-79, exec. cons., 1979—; spl. adviser to pres. Washington Star-News, 1972-75. Past mem. exec. bd. Nat. Capitol council Boy Scouts Am.; past bd. dirs. Nat. Capital Com., YMCA Davis Meml. Goodwill Industries; bd. dirs. Washington area chpt. Nat. Multiple Sclerosis Soc. Mem. Inter-State Circulation Mgrs. Assn. (past pres.), Internat. Circulation Mgrs. Assn. (past dir.), Washington Bd. Trade (past dir.), Washington Conv. and Visitor's Bur. (past dir.). Clubs: Washington (Washington), Advertising (Washington), Nat. Press (Washington), Columbia Country (Washington), Kiwanis (Washington). Home: 3706 Leland St Chevy Chase MD 20815-4904 Office: Scripps Howard 1090 Vermont Ave NW Washington DC 20005-4905

MACK, RAYMOND WRIGHT, academic administrator; b. Ashtabula, Ohio, July 15, 1927; s. Wright R. and Hazel E. (Card) M.; m. Barbara Leonard, Mar. 1948 (div. 1953); 1 child, Donald Gene; m. Elizabeth Ann Hunter, Oct. 16, 1953; children: Meredith Lou, Julia Glen, Margaret Kingsley. AB with honors, Baldwin-Wallace Coll., 1949; MA, U. N.C., 1951, PhD, 1953; LHD (hon.), DePaul U., 1990. Asst. prof. sociology, anthropology U. Miss., Oxford, 1953; faculty Northwestern U., Evanston, Ill., 1953-95, assoc. prof. sociology, 1957-62, prof. sociology, 1962-95, prof. emeritus, 1995—, chmn. dept. sociology, 1959-67; dir. Ctr. for Urban Affairs, 1968-71, v.p., dean of faculties, 1971-74, provost, 1974-87; dir. program for Bell System execs., 1958-59. Author: (with Freeman and Yellin) Social Mobility, 1957, (with Kimball Young) Sociology and Social Life, 1959, Transforming America, 1967; editor: Principles of Sociology: A Reader in Theory and Research, 1960, Race, Class and Power, 1963, Our Children's Burden, 1967, The American Sociologist, 1968-70, The Changing South, 1970, Prejudice and Race Relations, 1970. Fellow Am. Sociol. Assn. (mem. council 1966-69); mem. Soc. Study Social Problems (pres. 1969-70), Midwest Sociol. Soc. (pres. 1967), Alpha Kappa Delta (pres. 1969-70). Office: Northwestern U Dept Sociology 1810 Chicago Ave Evanston IL 60208-0812

MACK, ROBERT EMMET, hospital administrator; b. Morris, Ill., 1924. M.D., St. Louis U., 1948. Diplomate: Am. Bd. Internal Medicine. Intern St. Marys Hosp. Group, 1948-49; asst. physician; asst. resident, then resident internal medicine St. Louis U., 1949-52; asst. chief radioisope clinic Walter Reed Army Med. Center, 1954-56; chief med. service, chief radioisotope service St. Louis VA Hosp., 1956-61; vis. physician St. Louis City Hosp., 1957-61; chmn. dept. medicine Womans Hosp., Detroit, 1961-66; dir. Hutzel Hosp., Detroit, 1966-71; pres. Hutzel Hosp., 1971-80; v.p. for academic affairs Detroit Med. Center Corp., 1980-96; asst. prof. medicine St. Louis U., 1957-61; assoc. prof. medicine, Wayne State U., Detroit, 1961-66, prof., 1966-96, emeritus prof. internal medicine, 1996—, dir. admissions, 1978-81, assoc. dean Med. Ctr. Rels., 1981-96. Fellow ACP, Am. Coll. Hosp. Adminstrs., Soc. Med. Adminstrs. (pres. 1987-89); mem. AMA, Am. Fedn. Clin. Rsch., Cen. Soc. Clin. Rsch., Am. Endocrine Soc., Am. Physiol. Soc. Home: 3020 S Westview Ct Bloomfield Hills MI 48304-2472 Office: Detroit Medical Ctr 4201 Saint Antoine St Detroit MI 48201-2153

MACK, ROBERT WHITING, lawyer; b. Cambridge, Mass., June 7, 1949; s. Robert Anthony and Caroline Marshall Mack. BA, Harvard U., 1971, JD, 1974. Bar: Mass. 1974. Assoc. Hale and Dorr, Boston, 1974-79, jr. ptnr., 1979-83, sr. ptnr., 1983-88, of counsel, 1988-89; computer cons., 1990—. Mem. Conservation Commn., Lincoln, Mass., 1981-91; bd. dirs. Harvard Gay and Lesbian Rev., 1994—; bd. dirs. Lincoln Homes Corp., 1991-95, pres., 1992-94; bd. dirs. Greater Boston coun. Am. Youth Hostels, 1990-92, pres., 1991-92. Mem. Chiltern Mountain Club (bd. dirs. 1992-95, co-chair 1993-95), Harvard Gay and Lesbian Caucus (bd. dirs. 1994—, co-chair 1994—). Home: 10 Magazine St 805 Cambridge MA 02139

MACK, ROBERT WILLIAM, secondary school educator; b. Elizabeth, N.J., Oct. 25, 1941; s. Edward A. and Genevieve Emma (Kollar) M.; m. D. Nadine Hixson, June 25, 1966; children: Timothy Robert, Gregory Dennis, Katherine Ann. AA, Union Jr. Coll., Cranford, N.J., 1961; BA, Rutgers U., Newark, 1963; MEd, Rutgers U., New Brunswick, N.J., 1970. Cert. tchr. secondary sch. history, English. Tchr. Readington (N.J.) Twp. Pub. Schs., 1963-70; tchr. social studies Bridgewater-Raritan (N.J.) Pub. Schs., 1970—, asst. wrestling coach, 1975-78; ESL GED instr. Sommerville Adult Sch., 1968-82. Mem. Hillsborough Twp. (N.J.) Bd. Edn., 1994—; com. mem. Hillsborough Dem. Party, 1975-82. NDEA Inst. grantee in econs. Colo. State U., 1969, in urban studies San Diego State U., 1970, East-West Inst. grantee, 1972, NEH Summer Seminar grantee, 1994. Mem. NEA, N.J. Edn. Assn., Somerset County Edn. Assn., Bridgewater Edn. Assn., Nat. Coun. Social Studies, N.J. Coun. Social Studies. Democrat. Roman Catholic. Avocations: reading, computers, photography. Home: 100 Flanders Dr Somerville NJ 08876-4616 Office: Bridgewater-Raritan Bd Edn 836 Newmans Ln Bridgewater NJ 08807

MACK, RONALD BRAND, dentist; b. San Francisco, Feb. 20, 1948; s. Edward Semmel and Susan Tabor (Brand) M.; m. Janet Berringer, July 12, 1986; children by previous marriage: Joshua Hamilton, Aaron Edward. Diplomate Am. Bd. Pediatric Dentistry. BS, U. Calif., Davis, 1969; DDS, U. Pacific, 1973; cert. pediatric dentistry Ind. U., 1975. Practice dentistry specializing in pediatric dentistry, San Francisco, 1975—; instr., mem. staff, Oakland (Calif.) Children's Hosp., 1976-82; instr. gen. practice residency Mt. Zion Hosp., San Francisco, 1978—; adj. assoc. prof. pediatric dentistry, U. Pacific Sch. Dentistry, 1983—. United Cerebral Palsy clinical fellow, 1973, 74; G.R. Baker fellow, 1975. Fellow Internat. Coll. Dentists, Am. Coll. Dentists, Am. Acad. Pediatric Dentistry, Acad. Dentistry for Handicapped, Am. Soc. Dentistry for Children, Acad. Dentistry Internat., Pierre Fouchard Acad.; mem. San Francisco Dental Soc., Bay Area Dental Guidance Council for the Disabled (co-founder, 1977), U. Pacific Sch. Dentistry Alumni Assn., Calif. Dental Assn., Coll. Diplomates of Am. Bd. Pediatric Dentistry, Calif (life, bd. dirs. 1994—). Soc. Pediatric Dentists (bd. dirs. 1979-81), No. Calif. Soc. Dentistry for Children (pres. 1981-82, 94-95), ADA, Am. Soc. Dentistry for Children (bd. trustees, 1988-94), Ind. U. Pediatric Dentistry Alumni Assn. (bd. dirs. 1981-95, pres. 1991-93), Bay Area Pediatric Dentistry Study Club (pres. 1983-84), Internat. Assn. Dentistry for Children, Internat. Assn. Dentistry for the Handicapped, Fédération Dentaire Internationale, Dolphin South End Runners, Roadrunners Club Am., Roa Tau Kappa Omega (pres. San Francisco alumni chpt. 1977-78). Contbr. numerous articles to profl. jours., chpts. to books. Home: 6 Locksley Ave Apt 9A San Francisco CA 94122-3852 Office: 632 Taraval St San Francisco CA 94116-2512

MACK, RONALD J., park superintendent; b. Ithaca, N.Y., Aug. 13, 1952; s. Voyce Joron and Margaret (Rogers) M.; m. Virlean Hill, Jan. 4, 1955; children: Terrence, Marquisha. BA, Syracuse U., 1973; postgrad., Fed. Law Enforcement Tng. Ctr., Glynco, Ga., 1981. Recreation specialist D.C. Pks. and Recreation, Washington, 1973-74; pk. ranger Nat. Pk. Svc., Washington, 1974-77, Bklyn., 1977-79, S.I., N.Y., 1979-80; supr. pk. ranger Nat. Pk. Svc., Sandy Hook, N.J., 1980-87; chief ranger activities Nat. Pk. Svc., Bklyn., 1987-88; supt. Nat. Pk. Svc., Hardy, Va., 1988-90, Independence, Mo., 1990-95; chief interpretation and edn. Nat. Pk. Svc., Washington, 1995—. Contbr. articles to profl. jours. Mem. City of Independence Heritage, 1990-95, Spl. Events Com., Independence, 1990-95. Mem. Dept. Interior fed. Credit Union, Cmty. of Concerned Citizens, Roundtable, Employee and Alumni Assn. Nat. Pk. Svc., Syracuse U. Alumni Assn. Avocations: swimming, historic preservation, recreation activities. Office: Nat Park Svc Nat Capital Area 1100 Ohio Dr SW Washington DC 20242

MACK, THEODORE, lawyer; b. Ft. Worth, Mar. 5, 1936; s. Henry and Norma (Harris) M.; m. Ellen Feinknopf, June 19, 1960; children: Katherine Norma, Elizabeth Ellen, Alexandra. AB cum laude, Harvard U., 1958, JD, 1961. Bar: Tex. 1961, U.S. Sup. Ct. 1971, U.S. Ct. Apls. (5th cir.) 1967, U.S. Ct. Apls. (11th cir.) 1981, U.S. Dist. Ct. (no. dist.) Tex. 1961, U.S. Dist. Ct. (we. dist.) Tex. 1968, U.S. Dist. Ct. (so. dist.) Tex. 1968. Assoc., Mack & Mack, Ft. Worth, 1961-62, ptnr., 1963-70; dir., pres., v.p., treas., ptnr. Renfro, Mack, Hudman, P.C., and predecessors, Ft. Worth, 1970-93; spl. counsel McLean & Sanders A Profl. Corp., Ft. Worth, 1993—. Trustee Ft. Worth Country Day Sch., 1976-82; bd. dirs. Beth-El Congregation, 1964-73, 75-78, pres., 1975-77; bd. dirs. Jewish Fedn. Ft. Worth, 1965-72; mem. Leadership Ft. Worth, 1973-74; bd. dirs. Sr. Citizens Ctrs., Inc., 1969-81, Family and Individual Svcs., 1981-84, Presbyn. Night Shelter Tarrant County, Inc., 1992—; pres. Harvard Law Sch. Assn. Tex., 1976-77. Fellow Tex. Bar Found. (life); mem. Tex. Bar Assn., ABA, Tarrant County Bar Assn., Bar Assn. 5th Cir. Ct., Colonial Country Club, Ft. Worth Club, City Club, Harvard Club (N.Y.C., Boston). Democrat. Jewish. Home: 2817 Harlanwood Dr Fort Worth TX 76109-1226 Office: 100 Main St Fort Worth TX 76102-3090

MACK, WAYNE A., lawyer; b. Chambersburg, Pa., Jan. 31, 1961; s. Wayne A. and Carol (Irwin) M.; m. L. Suzanne Forbis; children; Courtney L., Stephanie E., Ashley C., Audrey G. BS magna cum laude, Temple U., 1982; JD cum laude, U. Pa., 1986. Bar: Pa. 1986, U.S. Dist. Ct. (ea. dist.) Pa. 1986, U.S. Ct. Appeals (3d cir.) 1986, U.S. Supreme Ct. 1995. Assoc. Duane, Morris & Heckscher, Phila., 1986-94, ptnr., 1995—. Mem. ABA (forum com. on franchising, sect. bus. law. com. on bus. and corp. litigation), Pa. Bar Assn., Phila. Bar Assn., Nat. Health Lawyers Assn., U. Pa. Law Sch. Am. Inn of Ct., Order of Coif. Home: 346 Pelham Rd Philadelphia PA 19119-3110 Office: Duane Morris & Heckscher One Liberty Pl Philadelphia PA 19103

MACK, WHITTAKER, III, pharmaceutical chemist; b. Bklyn., Dec. 13, 1966; s. Whittaker Jr. and Ethel Mack; m. Jennifer Woodard, July 17, 1993. Bachelor's, Duke U., 1988. Intern analytical rsch. and devel. Am. Cyanamid, Pearl River, N.Y., 1988-89, control chemist, 1989-91, pharm. lab. supr. process formulations, 1991-94; tech. group leader Barr Labs., Pomona, N.Y., 1994-95; plant mgr. Solgar Vitamin and Herb Co., Leonia, N.J., 1995—. Chmn. Orange and Rockland Counties Duke U. Alumni com., Durham, N.C., 1989—; mem. Iron Duke Alumni Scholarship Found., Durham, 1990—; chmn. youth coun. NAACP, Spring Valley, N.Y., 1992-93; asst. coach to Pop Warner Football, Spring Valley, 1994—. Mem. AAAS, Am. Chem. Soc., Am. Assn. Pharm. Scientists. Achievements include research in active and excipient physico-chemical properties such as magnesium stearate, bisoproprol fumarate, methotrexate, calcium phosphate and microcrystalline cellulose; also research in the use and techniques of laser particle size analysis. Office: Solgar Vitamins & Herb Co 500 N Willow Tree Rd Leonia NJ 07605

MACKALL, LAIDLER BOWIE, lawyer; b. Washington, Aug. 8, 1916; s. Laidler and Evelyn (Bowie) M.; m. Nancy M. Taylor, Aug. 28, 1942; children: Nancy Taylor Mackall Lurton (dec.), Christie Beall Mackall Connard, Susan Somervell Mackall Smythe, Bruce Bowie Mackall Sloan; m. Prudence Robertson Colbert, July 26, 1978. A.B., Princeton U., 1938; postgrad., Georgetown U., 1938-40, J.D., 1946. Bar: D.C. bar 1947, ICC bar 1951, U.S. Supreme Ct. bar 1958. Law clk. to chief judge of predecessor to D.C. Ct. Appeals, 1946-47; assoc. Minor, Gatley & Drury, Washington, 1947-49, Steptoe & Johnson, Washington, 1949-51; ptnr. Steptoe & Johnson, 1952-86, of counsel, 1986—; mem. D.C. Ct. Appeals Com. on Admissions, 1974-78, D.C. Circuit Jud. Conf., 1983, 85, 86; bd. mgrs. Nat. Conf. Bar Examiners, 1974-77. Served with USAAF, 1940-46, 51. Decorated Silver Star, D.F.C. with oak leaf cluster, Air medal with 5 oak leaf clusters. Fellow Am. Coll. Trial Lawyers (emeritus); mem. ABA (past vice chmn. standing com. aviation ins. law), D.C. Bar, Bar Assn. D.C. (past chmn. com. on negligence, motor vehicle and compensation law), Barristers Club (v.p. 1964), Chevy Chase Country Club, Met. Club, Wilderness Country Club of Fla., Hawk's Nest Golf Club of Fla. Episcopalian. Home: 151 Passage Island Vero Beach FL 32963-4292 summer: 6400 Brookville Rd Chevy Chase MD 20815-3339 Office: 1330 Connecticut Ave NW Washington DC 20036-1704

MACKANESS, GEORGE BELLAMY, retired pharmaceutical company executive; b. Sydney, Australia, Aug. 20, 1922; came to U.S., 1965, naturalized, 1978; s. James Vincent and Eleanor Frances (Bellamy) M.; m. Gwynneth Patterson, May 5, 1945; 1 son, Miles Philip. M.B. B.S. with honors, U. Sydney, 1945; D.C.P., London U., 1949; M.A. with honors, U. Oxford, 1949, D.Phil., 1953. Demonstrator, tutor in pathology Sir William Dunn Sch. Pathology, Oxford, 1949-53; sr. fellow Australian Nat. U., 1954-58, asso. prof., 1958-60, professorial fellow, 1960-63; prof. microbiology U. Adelaide, 1963-65; dir. Trudeau Inst., 1965-76; pres. The Squibb Inst. for Med. Research, Princeton, N.J., 1976-88; clin. prof. dept. medicine Coll. of Medicine and Dentistry of N.J.; adj. prof. pathology N.Y. U. Author articles in field. Recipient Paul Ehrlich-Ludwig Darmstaedter prize, 1975. Fellow Royal Soc. London; mem. Am. Assn. Immunologists, AAAS, Am. Soc. Microbiologists, Internat. Soc. Immunopharmacology. Home: 2783 Little Creek Rd Johns Island SC 29455-6022

MACKAY, ALFRED F., dean, philosophy educator; b. Ocala, Fla., Oct. 1, 1938; s. Kenneth Hood and Julia Horsey (Farhum) MacK.; m. Ann Nadine Wilson, Feb. 4, 1962; children: Douglas Kevin, Robert Wilson. AB, Davidson Coll., 1960; PhD, U. N.C., 1967. Prof. philosophy Oberlin (Ohio) Coll., 1967—, dean Coll. Arts and Scis., 1984-95, acting pres., 1991; vis. asst. prof. philosophy dept. U. Ill., Urbana/Champaign, 1970-71; vis. prof. philosophy dept. Wayne State U., Detroit, 1983. Author: Arrow's Theories: The Paradox of Social Choice, 1980; editor: Society: Revolution and Reform, 1971, Issues in the Philosophy of Language, 1976. Campaign cons. Buddy MacKay for U.S. Senate, Fla., 1988. 1st lt. U.S. Army, Airborne, 1961-63. Fellow Woodrow Wilson Found., 1963-66, Am. Coun. of Learned Socs., 1973, Humanities fellow Rockefeller Found., 1981. Democrat. Avocations: choral singing, automobiles. Office: Oberlin Coll Office of Dean Coll Arts and Scis Oberlin OH 44074

MACKAY, HAROLD HUGH, lawyer; b. Regina, Sask., Can., Aug. 1, 1940; s. John Royden and Grace Madeliene (Irwin) MacK.; m. Jean Elizabeth Hutchison, Dec. 27, 1963; children: Carol, Donald. B.A., U. Sask., 1960; LL.B., Dalhousie U., Halifax, N.S., 1963. Bar: Sask. 1964, Queen's Counsel 1981. Assoc. MacPherson Leslie & Tyerman, Regina, 1963-69, ptnr., 1969-75, 76—, mng. ptnr., 1989—; bd. dirs. Ipsco Inc., Bank of Can., Weyerhauser Can. Ltd., Merfin Hygienic Products, INc. IMC Global Inc. Trustee Found. for Legal Rsch. Mem. Internat. Bar Assn., Can. Bar Assn., Law Soc. Sask. Mem. United Ch. Office: 1500-1874 Scarth St, Regina, SK Canada S4P 4E9

MACKAY, JACK WHITING, civil engineer; b. Asheville, N.C., Jan. 24, 1910; s. Daniel MacNeill and Emily Whiting (Walters) M.; m. Gweneth

Moxley, Sept. 24, 1938; children: Jack W., Marian MacKay Pfeiffer, Richard MacNeill. BS in aeronautical engr., U. Ala., 1935, BS in civil engr., 1936, Profl. Degree Civil Engring., 1956. Registered profl. engr., Ala. Instr. U. Ala., Tuscaloosa, 1933-36, Birmingham, Ala., 1936-45; engr. trainee Am. Cast Iron Pipe Co., Birmingham, Ala., 1936-40, asst. sales engr., 1947-50, asst. southern sales mgr., 1951-53, asst. gen. sales mgr., 1953-56, v.p., gen. sales mgr., 1956-75, bd. mgmt., 1956-75, bd. mgmt., sec., 1956-75; chmn. pub. rels. com. Cast Iron Pipe Rsch. Assn., Chgo., 1965-75; pres. Alloy Cast Inst., N.Y., 1960—; cons. engr. Caldwell MacKay Co., Birmingham, 1983-95. Author: American Pipe Manual, 1951; contbr. articles to profl. jours. Pres. Anti-Tuberculosis Soc., 1957-58. Named Birmingham Civil Engr. Yr., Ala. Soc. Am. Soc. Civil Engrs., 1969. Fellow ASCE (life, chmn. pub. com. pipe 1973); mem. Am. Water Works Assn. (Nat. Distribution award, 1956, dist. mktg. chair 1956, life), Ala. Soc. Profl. Engrs., Birmingham Kiwanis Club (chmn. coms.), Tau Beta Pi. Presbyterian. Achievements include invention of fastite pipe joint; co-inventor pipejoint conductive gasket and boltless river crossing pipe joint. Home: 3740 Country Club Dr Birmingham AL 35213-2862

MACKAY, JOHN, mechanical engineer; b. Stockport, Eng., Mar. 26, 1914; s. Frederick and Annie MacK.; m. Barbara Hinnell, Jan. 11, 1939; 1 child, Penelope; m. Veronica Hwang, Dec. 2, 1960; 1 child, Teresa. Student, Malvern Coll., 1927-31; BS, U. Manchester, 1936. Registered profl. engr., N.Y. Mng. dir. Industrial Gases (Malaya) Ltd., Singapore, 1947-50; dir. Saturn Oxygen Co. Ltd. & Group, London, 1950-52; supt. Am. Cyanamid, New Orleans, 1952-56; project mgr. M.W. Kellogg Co., N.Y.C., 1956-67, Union Carbide, N.Y.C., 1967-70; v.p. Procon Internat., Chgo., 1970-75; mgr. sales Davy Powergas, Houston, 1975-78; pres. Davy Corp. (Korea) Ltd., Seoul, 1978-80; v.p. Davy McKee Overseas Corp., Singapore, 1980-82; regional rep. Davy Corp. Ltd., Singapore, 1980-82; cons. Petronas, Kuala Lumpur, Malaysia, 1982-83; asst. dept. head cryogenics Superconducting Supercollider Lab./U. Rsch. Assocs., Waxahachie, Tex., 1989-93; cons. Lotepro Corp., Valhalla, N.Y., 1993-94. Lt. col. Brit. Army, 1939-46. Decorated Brit. Terr. decoration, Chevalier l'Ordre Leopold II avec Palme, Croix de Guerre avec Palme. Mem. ASME (life), Instn. Mech. Engrs., Sports Car Club Am. Republican. Home: Cypress Village Apt B 716 4600 Middleton Park Circle E Jacksonville FL 32224-6623

MACKAY, JOHN ROBERT, II, lawyer; b. Passaic, N.J., Aug. 17, 1934; s. John R. and Janice Faith (Miller) M.; m. Susan Kellett, July 4, 1959 (div. 1985); children: J. Scott, Lauren A., Amanda F.; m. Patricia Margitan, Feb. 14, 1987; 1 child, Paige Elizabeth. AB, Bowdoin Coll., 1956; LLB, Rutgers U., 1965. Bar: N.J. 1965, U.S. Dist. Ct. N.J., 1965. Tech. writer, editor ITT Communication System, Paramus, N.J., 1960-62; law sec. to Chief Justice Weintraub N.J. Supreme Ct., Newark, N.J., 1965-66; atty. Lowenstein Sandler, Roseland, N.J., 1966-70, ptnr., 1970—; chmn. N.J. Corp. Law Revision Com., 1977-88, sec., 1970-73; adj. faculty Seton Hall sch. Law, 1973-75, Rutgers Sch. Law, 1978-81, 95—. Author: New Jersey Business Corporations: Law and Practice, 1992; editor in chief Rutgers Law Review, 1964-65; contbr. articles to profl. jours. Trustee Newark Day Ctr., 1972-82, pres. 1975-77; exec. com., pres. Rutgers Law Alumni Assn., Newark, 1980-81; chmn. fin. com. ARC (Nutley chpt.), 1978-86; exec. com., sec. Williams Ctr. Performing Arts, Rutherford, N.J., 1986-92; trustee United Way Essex, West Hudson, 1979-86. Lt. USN 1956-60 PTO. Mem. ABA (commn. corp. laws 1979-87, com. negotiated acquisitions 1986—), N.J. Bar Assn., Essex County Bar Assn. Office: Lowenstein Sandler 65 Livingston Ave Roseland NJ 07068-1725

MACKAY, KENNETH DONALD, environmental services company executive; b. Detroit, July 18, 1942; s. John and Ina (Finlayson) M.; m. Bonnie Young, Aug. 15, 1964; children: Heather, Laurel. BS, U. Mich., 1964; PhD, U. Minn., 1968. Sr. rsch. chemist Gen. Mills., Mpls., 1968-73, group leader, 1973-77; tech. mgr. Henkel Corp., Mpls., 1977-80, assoc. dir. R & D, 1980-82, v.p., dir. rsch., 1982-86; pres. Henkel Rsch. Corp., Santa Rosa, Calif., 1986-91, Cognis, Inc., Santa Rosa, 1991—. Contbr. articles to profl. jours.; patentee in field. Mayor City of Circle Pines, Minn., 1971-77; mem. Santa Rosa Econ. Devel. Commn., 1987-88; mem. indsl. adv. bd. U. Calif., Berkeley, 1987—, L.A.; bd. dirs. Santa Rosa Symphony, 1987-88. Mem. Am. Chem. Soc., Indsl. Rsch. Inst. Avocations: fishing, tennis, golf. Office: Cognis Inc 2330 Circadian Way Santa Rosa CA 95407-5415

MACKAY, KENNETH HOOD (BUDDY MACKAY), state official, former congressman; b. Ocala, Fl, Mar. 22, 1933; m. Anne Selph; children: Ken, John, Ben, Andy. B.S., B.A., U. Fla., 1954, LL.B. with honors, 1961. Bar: Fla. 1961. Pvt. practice Raymond, Wilson & Karl, Daytona Beach, Fla., 1963; sole practice 98th-100th Congresses from 6th Dist. Fla., Ocala, Fla., 1963—; mem. Fla. Ho. of Reps. state of Fla., 1968-74; mem. Fla. State Senate, 1974-80, mem. U.S. Ho. Reps. from 6th dist. Fla., 1985-89; lt. gov. State of Fla. Elder Ft. King Presbyn. Ch. With USAF 1955-58. Recipient Nat. Legis. Leadership award, 1976; named Most Valuable Freshman Ho. Mem., 1968, Most Valuable Legislator St. Petersburg Times, 7 times; recipient Allen Morris award. Mem. ABA, Kiwanis. Democrat. Office: Office of Lt Gov The Capitol PL05 Tallahassee FL 32399-0001*

MACKAY, MALCOLM, executive search consultant; b. Bklyn., Nov. 6, 1940; s. John F. and Helen (Pflug) MacK.; m. Cynthia Johnson, Aug. 29, 1964; children: Robert Livingston, Hope Winthrop. A.B. Cum laude, Princeton U., 1963; J.D., Harvard U., 1966. Bar: N.Y. 1967. Assoc. Milbank, Tweed, Hadley and McCloy, N.Y.C., 1966-69; dep. supt. N.Y. State Ins. Dept., N.Y.C., 1969-71; 1st dep. supt. N.Y. State Ins. Dept., 1971-73; vice chancellor L.I. U., Greenvale, N.Y., 1973-75; sr. v.p. Blue Cross & Blue Shield of Greater New York, 1975-77, N.Y. Life Ins. Co., N.Y.C., 1977-89; mng. dir. Russell Reynolds Assocs., N.Y.C., 1989—; bd. dirs. Independence Savs. Bank, Bklyn., Empire Fidelity Investments Life Ins. Co. Trustee Hayden Found., Pratt Inst. Mem. Century Assn., Piping Rock Club. Home: 2 Montague Ter Brooklyn NY 11201-7102 Office: Russell Reynolds Assocs 200 Park Ave New York NY 10166-0005

MACKAY, NEIL DUNCAN, plastics company executive; b. Chelsea, Mass., Nov. 5, 1931; s. Allan Foster and Helen May (Smith) MacK.; m. Marcia Ann McCarthy, Aug. 22, 1953 (dec. 1979); children: Duncan, Jerry, Alan, Neil, Bonnie; m. Beverly J. Burke, May 31, 1991. BS, BA, Northeastern U., Boston, 1954. Gen. mgr. Plastic Molding Corp., Newtown, Conn., 1954-67; market specialist Chem. div. Uniroyal, N.Y.C., 1967-70; project mgr. Colt Ind. Korean Project, N.Y.C., 1970-76; pres. Automatic Injection Molding Corp., Berkeley Heights, N.J., 1976-87, Diamond Mgmt. Cons., Inc., Winchester, N.H., 1988—; bd. dirs. Frazier & Son, Inc., Clifton, N.J., 1987—, Lor-Tech Plastics, Inc., Berkeley Heights, N.J. Author: Korean Plastics, 1973. Mem. Rep. Nat. Com., Washington, 1986-92. Recipient Outstanding Performance award Ministry Nat. Def. Republic of Korea, 1974. Mem. Am. Profl. Capt.'s Assn., Soc. Plastics Engrs. (sec. 1963-70, treas. 1983-86), Scottish-Am. Cultural Soc., St. Andrews Soc. N.Y., Plastic Pioneers Assn., Stuyvesant Yacht Club, Am. Yacht Club. Republican. Presbyterian. Avocation: sailing. Home: 19 Lovely Ln Winchester NH 03470-2916 Office: Diamond Mgmt Cons Inc PO Box 40 Winchester NH 03470-0040

MACKAY, PATRICIA MCINTOSH, counselor; b. San Francisco, Sept. 12, 1922; d. William Carroll and Louise Edgerton (Keen) McIntosh; AB in Psychology, U. Calif., Berkeley, 1944, elem. teaching credential, 1951; MA in Psychology, John F. Kennedy U., Orinda, Calif., 1979; PhD in Nutrition, Donsbach U., Huntington Beach, Calif., 1981; m. Alden Thorndike Mackay, Dec. 15, 1945; children—Patricia Louise, James McIntosh, Donald Sage. Cert. marriage, family and child counselor. Elem. tchr. Mt. Diablo Unified Sch. Dist., Concord, Calif., 1950-60; exec. supr. No. Calif. Welcome Wagon Internat., 1960-67; wedding cons. Mackay Creative Svcs., Walnut Creek, Calif., 1969-70; co-owner Courtesy Calls, Greeters and Concord Welcoming Svcs., Walnut Creek, 1971-94; marriage, family and child counselor, nutrition cons., Walnut Creek, 1979—; coord. Alameda and Contra Costa County chpts. Parents United, 1985—, pres. region 2; bd. dirs. New Directions Counseling Ctr., Inc., 1975-81, founder, pres. aux., 1977-79. Bd. dirs. Ministry in the Marketplace, Inc.; founder, dir. Turning Point Counseling; active Walnut Creek Presbyn. Ch.; bd. dirs. counseling dir. Shepherd's Gate-shelter for homeless women and children, 1985-92, Contra Costa County Child Care Coun., 1993, 94, 95. Recipient Individual award New Directions Counseling Ctr., 1978, awards Neo-Life Co. Am. Prestige Club, yearly, 1977-86, Cmty. Svc. award Child Abuse Prevention Coun., 1990, 92, 94. Mem. Assn. Marriage and Family Therapists, Parents United Internat. (pres. region 2, bd. dirs. 1992), U. Calif. Berkeley Alumni (sec. 1979-94), C. of C., Prytanean Alumnae, Delta Gamma. Republican. Club: Soroptimist (dir. 1976, 86) (Walnut Creek). Home: 1101 Scots Ln Walnut Creek CA 94596-5432 Office: 1399 Ygnacio Valley Rd Ste 34 Walnut Creek CA 94598-2831

MACKAY, RAYMOND ARTHUR, chemist; b. N.Y.C., Oct. 30, 1939; s. Theodore Henry and Helen Marie (Cusack) M.; m. Mary Dilberian, Aug. 13, 1966; 1 child, Chelsea Christine; children by previous marriage: Brett, Edward. BS in Chemistry, Rensselaer Poly. Inst., 1961; PhD in Chemistry, SUNY-Stony Brook, 1966. Rsch. assoc. Brookhaven Nat. Lab., Upton, N.Y., 1966-67; prof. Drexel U., Phila., 1969-83; chief chem. div. Chem. Research and Devel. Ctr., Aberdeen Proving Ground, Md., 1983-91; prof. chemistry, dir. ctr. advanced materials processing Clarkson U., Potsdam, N.Y., 1991—. Contbr. articles to profl. jours. Served to capt. U.S. Army, 1967-69. Grantee U.S. Army, Dept. Energy, Army Rsch. Office, NSF, Acad. Applied Scis., 1972-83, 95—, NATO, 1982-86, NYSSTF, 1991—. Mem. Am. Chem. Soc., Am. Oil Chemists Soc. (assoc. editor), Sigma Xi. Office: Clarkson U PO Box 5665 Potsdam NY 13699-5665

MACKAY, ROBERT BATTIN, museum director; b. Bklyn., Jan. 24, 1945; s. John French and Helen (Pflug) MacK.; m. Anna V.; 1 child, Hale V. B.S., Boston U., 1968, Ph.D. in Am. Studies, 1980; M.Ed., Harvard U., 1972. With Archtl. Heritage, Inc., Boston, 1967-71; dir. So. Preservation of L.I. Antiquities, Setauket, N.Y., 1974—; chmn. N.Y. State Bd. Hist. Preservation; mem. curatorial com. Mystic Seaport Mus., Conn. Editor: Between Ocean and Empire: An Illustrated History of Long Island, 1985, AIA Architectural Guide of L.I. Trustee Theodore Roosevelt Assn., St. Giles Found. For Crippled Children. With U.S. Army, 1969-70, Vietnam. Mem. N.Y. State Coun. Pks. Club: N.Y. Yacht (chmn. fine arts com.). Home: PO Box 292 East Setauket NY 11733-0292 Office: Soc Preservation of LI Antiquities 93 N Country Rd Setauket NY 11733

MACKAY, WILLIAM ANDREW, judge; b. Halifax, N.S., Can., Mar. 20, 1929; s. Robert Alexander and Mary Kathleen (Junkin) MacK.; m. Alexa Eaton Wright, July 7, 1954; 1 dau., Margaret Kathleen. B.A., Dalhousie U., 1950, LL.B., 1953, LL.M., 1954; LL.M., Harvard U., 1970; LL.D. (hon.), Meml. U. Nfld., St. F.X. Univ., N.S. Bar: N.S.; Named queen's counsel. Fgn. service officer Dept. External Affairs, Ottawa, Ont., Can., 1954-57; asst. sec. Royal Com., Ottawa, 1955-57; sucessively asst. prof., assoc. prof., prof. law, dean Faculty of law Dalhousie U. (Halifax), N.S., Can., 1957-69, v.p., 1969-80, pres., vice-chancellor, 1980-86; ombudsman N.S., 1986-88; judge Fed. Ct. Can., trial div., Ottawa, Ont., Can., 1988—; chmn. Assn. Atlantic Univs., Halifax, 1981-83; v.p.. Assn. Univs. and Colls. Can., 1982-83, pres., 1983-85; pres. Conf. Gov. Bodies Legal Profession Can., 1968-69, Assn. Can. Law Tchrs., 1964-65. Chmn. N.S. Human Rights Com., Halifax, 1967-86; chmn. N.S. Commns. on Salary and Allowances of Elected Provincial Ofcls., 1974, 78, 81, 83, 84, 85; chmn. N.S. Task Force on AIDS, 1987-88. Mem. Can. Bar Assn. Home: 140 Rideau Terr, Apt 11, Ottawa, ON Canada K1M 0Z2 Office: Fed Ct Canada, Ottawa, ON Canada K1A 0H9

MACKE, KENNETH A., retail executive; b. Templeton, Iowa, Dec. 16, 1938; m. Kathleen O'Farrell; children: Michael, Jeffrey, Melissa. BS, Drake U., 1961. With Dayton Hudson Corp. and affiliates, 1961—, merchandising positions, 1961-73, sr. v.p., gen. merchandising mgr., 1973-76, pres., chief exec. officer, 1976-78, chmn., chief exec. officer, 1978-81, corp. sr. v.p., 1977-81, pres., 1981-82, pres., chief oper. officer, 1982-83, chief exec. officer, 1983-84, chmn., chief exec. officer, 1984—, also bd. dirs.; bd. dirs. 1st Bank Systems, Inc., Gen. Mills, Inc., Unisys Corp. Bd. dirs. United Way Mpls., J.L. Kellogg Grad. Sch. Mgmt., Northwestern U., Nat. Retail Fedn. Office: Dayton Hudson Corp 777 Nicollet Mall Minneapolis MN 55402-2004*

MACKENBACH, FREDERICK W., welding products manufacturing company executive; b. St. Marys, Ohio, Mar. 10, 1931; s. Frederick Jacob and Mabel (Tangeman) M.; m. Jo Ann Dietrich, Oct. 21, 1953; children: John Frederick, David Dietrich. BS in Econs., U. Pa., 1953. Various sales engr. positions The Lincoln Electric Co., Indpls., Ft. Wayne, L.A., 1956-64; asst. dist. mgr. The Lincoln Electric Co., L.A., 1973-76, dist. mgr., 1976-88; pres. Lincoln Electric Mexicana, 1988-91, Lincoln Electric Latin Am., 1991-92; pres., COO The Lincoln Electric Co., Cleve., 1992—; mem. Com. on Fgn. Rels. With U.S. Army 1953-55. Mem. NEMA, Econ. Roundtable in L.A., Am. Welding Soc., 50 Club of Cleve. Office: The Lincoln Electric Co 22801 Saint Clair Ave Cleveland OH 44117-2524

MACKENDRICK, PAUL LACHLAN, classics educator; b. Taunton, Mass., Feb. 11, 1914; s. Ralph Fulton and Sarah (Harvey) MacK.; m. Dorothy Grace Lau, Mar. 17, 1945; children: Andrew Lachlan, Sarah Ann. A.B. summa cum laude, Harvard U., 1934, A.M., 1937, Ph.D., 1938; postgrad., Balliol Coll., Oxford, 1934-36. Instr. Phillips Acad., 1938-41, Harvard U., 1946; asst. prof. U. Wis., 1946-48, assoc. prof., 1948-52, prof., 1952-75, Lily Ross Taylor prof., 1975-84, prof. emeritus, 1984—; prof. charge Sch. Classical Studies, Am. Acad. Rome, summers 1956-59; vis. prof. U. Colo., summer 1964; mem. Inst. for Advanced Study, Princeton, 1964-65; vis. prof. U. Ibadan, Nigeria, 1965-66, cons., 1990; prof. charge Intercoll. Ctr. for Classical Studies, Rome, 1973-74; Rockefeller scholar-in-residence Bellagio Center, Italy, 1977; vis. fellow Churchill Coll., Cambridge U., 1977-78; scholar-in-residence Fondation Hardt, Geneva, 1983; Phi Beta Kappa nat. lectr., 1970-71; Sec., dir. Am. Council Learned Socs., 1956-57, dir., 1960-63; vis. lectr. U. Canterbury; N.Z., 1985, Macquarie U., Australia, 1985, Universidade Fed. de Rio de Janeiro, 1987, Universidade de Coimbra, 1989; external examiner U. Tasmania, 1990. Author: (with Herbert M. Howe) Classics in Translation, 1952, (with V.M. Scramuzza) The Ancient World, 1958, The Roman Mind at Work, 1958, The Mute Stones Speak, 1960, 2d edit., 1983, The Greek Stones Speak, 1962, 2d edit., 1981, Western Civilization, 1968, The Athenian Aristocracy, 399-31 B.C, 1969, The Iberian Stones Speak, 1969, Romans on the Rhine, 1970, Roman France, 1972, Dacian Stones Speak, 1975, North African Stones Speak, 1980, The Philosophical Books of Cicero, 1989, Cicero's Speeches: Context, Law, Rhetoric, 1995. Trustee Am. Acad. in Rome, 1966-72; bd. dirs. Nat. Humanities Faculty, 1968-71, chmn., 1969-70. Served to lt. USNR, 1941-45. Fulbright fellow, 1950; Guggenheim fellow, 1957-58; Am. Philos. Soc. grantee, 1981. Mem. Classical Assn. Middle West and South (pres. 1969-70), Am. Philol. Assn. (sec.-treas. 1954-56), Archeol. Inst. Am. Madison Soc. (pres. 1963), Phi Beta Kappa (pres. Wis. 1965-66). Home: 208 Bordner Dr Madison WI 53705-2513

MACKENZIE, CHARLES SHERRARD, academic administrator; b. Quincy, Mass., Aug. 21, 1924; s. Charles Sherrard and Dorothy (Eaton) MacK.; m. Florence Evelyn Phelps Meyer, Aug. 28, 1964 (dec. 1981); 1 child, Robert Walter Meyer; m. Lavonne Rudolph Gaiser, Mar. 30, 1985. B.A., Gordon Coll., 1946; M.Div., Princeton Theol. Sem., 1949, Ph.D., 1955; student, Boston U., 1942-43, U. Paris, 1953. Ordained to ministry Congl. Christian Ch., 1949. Pastor Carversville (Pa.) Christian Ch., 1948-51; fellow faculty Princeton Theol. Sem., 1949-51, 53-54, Princeton U., 1954-64; pastor First Presbyn. Ch., Avenel, N.J., 1954-64, Broadway Presbyn. Ch., N.Y.C., 1964-67, First Presbyn. Ch., San Mateo, Calif., 1967-71; pres. Grove City (Pa.) Coll., 1971-91, chancellor, 1991-92; advisor to pres., prof. philosphy Reformed Seminary, Orlando, Fla., 1992—; sr. min. Eastminster Presbyn. Ch., Wichita, Kans., 1993; bd. dirs. Covenant Life Ins. Co.; cons. Oxford Project, 1992—, Provident Mutual Ins. Co.; lectr. Oxford U., 1965, U. Hamburg, 1968, Columbia U., 1964-67, Stanford U., 1967-71, U. Pitts., 1990-93. Author: The Anguish and Joy of Pascal, 1973, Freedom, Equality, Justice, 1980, The Trinity and Culture, 1985. Mem. Human Relations Commn., San Mateo, 1968-70; mem. Indsl. Devel. Council, Grove City, 1972-75. Served with USAF, 1951-53. Mem. Presbyn. Coll. Union, Am. Assn. Pres.'s Ind. Colls. and Univs. (dir., pres.), Nat. Assn. Ind. Colls. and Univs. (mem. secretariat 1985-91), Freedoms Found. (nat. jury), Duquesne Club (Pitts.), Univ. Club Boston, Citrus Club (Orlando), Evangelical initiative Notre Dame U., Rockford Inst. Main St. com. Republican. Address: PO Box 945120 Maitland FL 32794-5120

MACKENZIE, DONALD MURRAY, hospital administrator; b. Toronto, Ont., Can., June 5, 1947; s. Donald Alexander and June Cameron MacKenzie; m. Marilyn Adele McNaughton, Jan. 3, 1970; children: Jennifer, Katherine, Kenneth. BA in Econs., U. Toronto, 1968, MA in Polit. Sci., 1970, D Health Adminstr., 1974. Exec. asst. Mt. Sinai Hosp., Toronto, 1974-76, successively asst. exec. dir., assoc. exec. dir., v.p., 1974-89; pres. North York Gen. Hosp., Toronto, 1989—; asst. prof. U. Toronto, 1989—. Editor: History of Canadian Hospitals, 1972; contbr. articles to profl. jours. Bd. dirs. Ont. Cancer Treatment & Rsch. Found. Mem. Can. Coll. Health Svc. Execs. (cert., various coms.), Can. Cancer Soc. (hon. life, pres. Ont. div. 1989-91, award of merit 1988), Ont. Hosp. Assn. (bd. dirs.), Toronto Bd. Trade, Parkview Golf Club (bd. dirs.). Anglican. Avocations: golf, tennis, canoe tripping. Office: North York Gen Hosp, 4001 Leslie St, North York, ON Canada M2K 1E1

MACKENZIE, GEORGE ALLAN, diversified company executive; b. Kingston, Jamaica, Dec. 15, 1931; s. George Adam and Annette Louise (Maduro) MacK.; m. Valerie Ann Marchand, June 30, 1971; children from previous marriage: Richard Michael, Barbara Wynne. Student, Jamaica Coll., Kingston, 1944-48. Commd. flying officer Canadian Air Force, 1951, advanced through grades to lt. gen., 1978; comdr. Canadian Forces Air Command, Winnipeg, Man., 1978-80; resigned Canadian Forces Air Command, 1980; exec. v.p., COO Gendis Inc., 1980-89, pres., COO, 1989—, also bd. dirs.; bd. dirs. Sony of Can. Ltd., Willowdale, Ont., Can.; pres. Gendis Bus. Svcs.; chmn. exec.com. MMG MGmt. Group, Saan Stores Ltd.; bd. dirs. Tundra Oil and Gas Ltd., Chauvco Resources Ltd., Gendis Inc., bd. dirs.; pres. COO Met. Stores of Can. Ltd. Bd. dirs. St. Boniface Gen. Hosp. Rsch. Found.; coun. mem. Duke of Edinburgh's Award in Can.; mem. regional adv. bd. Carleton U.; mem. jud. coun. Province of Manitoba. Decorated comdr. Order of Mil. Merit, Order St. Johns, Can. Decoration, Knight of St. Lazarus of Jerusalem. Mem. United Services Inst. Can. (hon. v.p.), Canadian Corps Commissionaires (gov.), Police Chiefs Research Found. (co-chmn.), Pan Am. Games Soc. (hon.). Clubs: Rotary (Winnipeg); Lakewood Country (Delta); Manitoba; St. Charles Golf and Country. Home: Box 9, 383 Christie Rd, St Germain, MB Canada R0G 2A0 Office: Gendis Inc, 1370 Sony Pl, Winnipeg, MB Canada R3T 1N5

MACKENZIE, JOHN, retired oil industry executive; b. 1919. B.S., N.Y. U., 1948. Accountant S.Am. Devel. Co., N.Y.C., 1938-41; financial comptroller French Oil Ind. Agy.-Groupment D'Achat des Carburants, N.Y., 1946-53; v.p., treas. George Hall Corp., 1954-56; asst. treas. Am. Petrofina, Inc., 1956-61, sec., 1961-64, v.p., sec., 1964-68, sr. v.p., sec., 1968-84; ret., 1984. Decorated comdr. Order of Crown (Belgium). Address: 1304 Pagewynne Dr Plano TX 75093-2630

MACKENZIE, JOHN DOUGLAS, engineering educator; b. Hong Kong, Feb. 18, 1926; came to U.S., 1954, naturalized, 1963; s. John and Hannah (Wong) MacK.; m. Jennifer Russell, Oct. 2, 1954; children—Timothy John, Andrea Louise, Peter Neil. BS, U. London, 1952, PhD, 1954. Research asst., lectr. Princeton U., 1954-56; ICI fellow Cambridge (Eng.) U., 1956-57; research scientist Gen. Electric Research Ctr., N.Y.C., 1957-63; prof. materials sci. Rensselaer Poly. Inst., 1963-69; prof. engring. U. Calif., Los Angeles, 1969—; U.S. rep. Internat. Glass Commn., 1964-71. Author books in field (6); editor: Jour. Non-Crystalline Solids, 1968—; contbr. articles to profl. jours. Fellow Am. Ceramic Soc., Royal Inst. Chemistry; mem. Nat. Acad. Engring., Am. Phys. Soc., Electrochem. Soc., ASTM, Am. Chem. Soc., Soc. Glass Tech. Patentee in field. Office: 5732 Boelter Hall Univ of Calif Los Angeles CA 90024

MACKENZIE, JOHN PETTIBONE, journalist; b. Glen Ellyn, Ill., July 19, 1930; s. John W. P. and Elizabeth (Andersen) MacK.; m. Amanda Fisk, Oct. 24, 1959 (div. 1977); children—Bradley John, Alice Fisk, Douglas Bain. B.A. in Am. Studies cum laude, Amherst Coll., 1952; postgrad., Harvard U. Law Sch., 1964-65. Staff writer Washington Post, 1956-77, Supreme Ct. reporter, 1965-77; Walter E. Meyer vis. research prof. law N.Y. U., 1977-78; lectr. law SUNY Buffalo Law Sch., 1979; spl. contbr. to editorial page N.Y. Times, N.Y.C., 1977-79; editorial bd. N.Y. Times, 1980—. Author: The Appearance of Justice, 1974; contbr. articles to mags., law books, law revs. Served to lt. (j.g.) USN, 1952-55. Home: 250 W 89th St New York NY 10024-1700 Office: 229 W 43rd St New York NY 10036-3913

MACKENZIE, KENNETH DONALD, management consultant, educator; b. Salem, Oreg., Dec. 20, 1937; s. Kenneth Victor and Dorothy Vernon (Minaker) M.; m. Sally Jane McHenry, June 16, 1957; children: Dorothy Jane Rivette, Carolyn M. McFarland, Susan M. Treber, Nancy M. Kalb. AB in Math, U. Calif., Berkeley, 1960, PhD in Bus. Adminstrn, 1964. Cert. mgmt. cons. Asst. prof. indsl. adminstrn. Carnegie Mellon U., 1964-67; assoc. prof. industry Wharton Sch. U. Pa., 1967-71; prof. mgmt. scis. U. Waterloo, Ont., 1969-72; Edmund P. Learned disting. prof. Sch. Bus. U. Kans., Lawrence, 1971—; pres. Organizational Systems, Inc., Lawrence, 1976-84; founder, pres. Mackenzie and Co. Inc., Lawrence, 1983—. Author: An Introduction to Continuous Probability, 1969, A Theory of Group Structures, 2 vols., 1976, Basic Theory, 1976, A Theory of Group Structures, vol. II: Empirical Tests, 1976, Organizational Structures, 1978, Organizational Design: The Organizational Audit and Analysis Technology, 1986, The Organizational Hologram: The Effective Management of Organizational Change, 1991, Practitioner's Guide for Improving an Organization, 1995; editor: Organizations Behavior series; mem. editorial bd. of profl. jours. Served with USMCR, 1957-60, with Army N.G., 1960-64. Fellow AAAS; mem. Am. Mgmt. Assn., Acad. Mgmt., Am. Psychol. Assn., Ops. Research Soc., Inst. Mgmt. Scis. (chmn. coll. on orgns. 1983-93), Inst. Mgmt. Cons. Republican. Home: 502 Millstone Rd Lawrence KS 66049-2350 Office: Mackenzie & Co Inc 700 Massachusetts St Ste 301 Lawrence KS 66044-6604 also: U Kans Sch Bus Lawrence KS 66045 *While the pursuit of a better theory of organizations has led me from the classroom to the laboratory and then into the boardrooms of corporations, the thrust of all these many activities has been to develop the science of organizational behavior.*

MACKENZIE, LEWIS WHARTON, military officer; b. Truro, N.S., Can., Apr. 30, 1940; s. Eugene Murdock and Shirley Helena (Wharton) MacK.; m. Dora Rosalie McKinnon; 1 child, Kimm Katheryn. Student, NATO Def. Coll., Rome, 1977; BA in Polit. Sci., U. Manitoba, Winnipeg, Can., 1988; Phd (hon.), St. Francis Xavier U., 1993; LLB (hon.), St. Mary's U., 1993, Acadia U., 1993. Commd. 2d lt. Can. Armed Forces, 1972, advanced through grades to major gen., 1987; teamsite comdr. Internat. Commn. Control and Supervision, Vietnam, 1972; co. comdr. UN Emergency Peace Keeping Force, Cairo, 1973; exec. asst. to comdr. Can. Forces Europe, Lahr, Fed. Republic Germany, 1974-77; comdr. Nicosia dist. UN Peacekeeping Force, Cyprus, 1978; commdg. officer 1st bn. Princess Patricia's Can. Light Infantry, Calgary, 1977-79; faculty mem. Can. Forces Staff Coll., Toronto, 1979-82; dep. chief staff for tng. Can. Army, Montreal, 1983-85; dir. pers. careers officers Can. Armed Forces, Ottawa, 1985-87; dir. Combar Related Employment of Women, Ottawa, 1987-88; comdr. combat tng. ctr. Can. Armed Forces, Gagetown Can. Forces Base, N.B., 1988—; comdr. UN Peacekeeping Force, Ctrl. Am., 1990-91, chief staff Unprotection force, Yugoslavia, 1992, comdr. UN forces to open Sarajevo airport for humanitarian relief, 1992; internat. affairs commentator BATON Broadcasting; host TV documentary "A Soldier's Peace." Author: Peacekeeper, Road to Sarajevo, 1993. Bd. adv. Can. Fedn. for AIDS Rsch., Can. Spl. Olympics; bd. dirs. Pacific Body Armour. Decorated Meritorious Svc. Cross (3) (Can.); recipient Birks gold medal Xavier Jr. Coll., Sudney, N.S., Can., 1960, Vimy award, 1993; Internat. fellow U.S. Army War Coll., 1982-83; Nat. Sports Car champion, 1981; Nat. Formula Ford B Class champion, 1995; named to McLean's Honor Roll., 1993. Avocation: motor racing. Home and Office: RR 2, Bracebridge, ON Canada P1L 1WP

MACKENZIE, MALCOLM LEWIS, marketing executive, museum executive; b. El Paso, Tex., Jan. 19, 1926; s. William Forbes and Grace Meldon (Lewis) M.; m. Barbara Lee Webb, Apr. 4, 1952; children: David, Ellen; m. Marianne Eckerstrom, Nov. 22, 1980; stepchildren: Ann-Marie, Vicki, Adam, Lars. Graduate Maine Maritime Acad., 1946; student R.I. Sch. Design, 1948-51; B.A., Brown U., 1951. 3d mate Am. Export Lines, Jersey City, Pacific Tankers, San Francisco, 1946-48; 2d mate Sun Oil Co., Marcus Hook, Pa., 1948; plans dir., account exec. N. W. Ayer & Son, Phila., 1951-63; plans dir., head mktg. dept. Grey & Rogers Advt., Phila., 1963-64; v.p. Daily Svc., Phila., 1964-65; owner, pres. Malcolm L. Mackenzie & Assocs., Wilmington, Del., 1966—; dir., pres. Kalmar Nyckel Mus. Inst., 1990—; pres. Christina Marina, Inc., 1992—; dir., sec., treas. Fort Christina Marina, Inc., 1994—; incorporator, reg. agent Digital Design Group, Ltd.,

1994—; dir., v.p. Wilmington Shipbuilding Co., Inc., 1993—; adminstrv. mgr. Kalmar Nyckel Found., 1986-91; sec.-treas. North Star Charters Inc., Wilmington, 1984—, Kalmar Marine Supplies Ltd., 1992—, Lenape Corp., 1992—; pres. Delmarva Safe Sailing Assocs., Inc., Wilmington, 1977—, pres., bd. dirs., Beta Centaur Holding Co., 1992—; dir. devel., pres. Am. Prestige Arts, Inc., Wilmington, 1970-72; dir. Composite Structures, Inc., Wilmington, 1974-76; dir. Cutter Mohawk Corp., Wilmington, 1981-95; mgr., dir. Market Penetration, Wilmington, 1970—; cons. Del. Waterfront 2020; v.p. Landmark Properties, Inc., 1986—; incorporator, registered agt. Peace Please, Inc., Del. Fin. Accts., Inc., 1993—; pres. Active Young Reps., Brandywine Hundred, 1966, Windybush Civic Assn., Wilmington, Del., 1962-66; pres., dir. Coun. of Civic Orgns. of Brandywine Hundred, 1965; bd. dirs. Del. Safety Coun., 1965-73, 74-75, Wilmington Sister Cities, 1980—, Del. Maritime Ctr., 1989—; mem. New Castle County Rev. Bd., 1976-78; mem. CPAC Hwy. Dept. Adv. Bd., Dover, Del., 1979-82; vice chmn. No. New Castle County Land Use Study Group, 1990-95. With U.S. Mcht. Svc., 1944-48. Recipient Order of Merit, Boy Scouts Am., 1977, Order of the Arrow, 1974, Woodbadge, 1974; Commodore, Ships on the Shoreline, Inc., Del. Tall Ships Salute, 1982. Mem. Advt. Club Del., Colonial Period Ship Assn. (founding 1987), Del. Media Assn., Swedish Colonial Soc. (councilor), Wilmington Sailboat Show (mgr., owner 1981-89), Nat. Mariner Awards (mgr. 1982—), Cutter Mohawk (capt., 1982-85). Republican. Lutheran. Clubs: Kiwanis (Wilmington) (chmn. internat. com.); Brown U. of Phila. (pres. 1958-61), Brown U. of Del. (pres. 1974-84). Lodge: Masons. Office: 500 Concord Ave Wilmington DE 19802

MAC KENZIE, NORMAN HUGH, retired English educator, writer; b. Salisbury, Rhodesia, Mar. 8, 1915; s. Thomas Hugh and Ruth Blanche (Huskisson) MacK.; m. Rita Mavis Hofmann, Aug. 14, 1948; children: Catherine, Ronald. B.A., Rhodes U., South Africa, 1934, M.A., 1935, Diploma in Edn., 1936; Ph.D. (Union scholar), U. London, 1940; DLitt (hon.), St. Joseph's U., Phila., 1989. Lectr. in English Rhodes U., South Africa, 1937, U. Hong Kong, 1940-41, U. Melbourne, Australia, 1946-48; sr. lectr.-in-charge U. Natal, Durban, 1949-55; prof., head English dept. U. Coll., Rhodesia, 1955-65; dean Faculty Arts and Edn. U. Coll., 1957-60, 63-64; prof., head English dept. Laurentian U., Ont., Can., 1965-66; prof. English Queen's U., Kingston, Ont., 1966-80; emeritus prof. Queen's U., 1980—, dir. grad. studies in English, 1967-73, chmn. council grad. studies, 1971-73, chmn. editorial bd. Yeats Studies, 1972-74; Exec. Central Africa Drama League, 1959-65; mem. exec. com. Can. Assn. Irish Studies, 1968-73. Author: South African Travel Literature in the 17th Century, 1955, The Outlook for English in Central Africa, 1960, Hopkins, 1968, A Reader's Guide to G.M. Hopkins, 1981; editor: (with W.H. Gardner) The Poems of Gerard Manley Hopkins, 1967, rev. edit., 1970; Poems by Hopkins, 1974, U. Natal Gazette, 1954-55, The Early Poetic Manuscripts and Notebooks of Gerard Manley Hopkins in Facsimile, 1989, The Poetical Works of Gerard Manley Hopkins, 1990, rev. 1992, The Later Poetic Manuscripts of G.M. Hopkins in Facsimile, 1991; contbr.: chpts. to Testing the English Proficiency of Foreign Students, 1961, English Studies Today-Third Series, 1963, Sphere History of English Literature, Vol. VI, 1970, rev. edit., 1987, Readings of the Wreck of the Deutschland, 1976, Festschrift for E.R. Seary, 1975, British and American Literature 1880-1920, 1976, Myth and Reality in Irish Literature, 1977; articles to Internat. Rev. Edn., Bull. Inst. Hist. Research, Times Lit. Supplement, Modern Lang. Quar., Queen's Quar., others. Served with Hong Kong Vol. Def. Corps, 1940-45; prisoner of war, China and Japan 1941-45. Brit. Council scholar, 1954; Killam sr. fellow, 1979-81; Martin D'Arcy lectr. Oxford U., 1988-89. Fellow Royal Soc. Can.; mem. English Assn. Rhodesia (pres. 1957-65), So. Rhodesia Drama Assn. (vice chmn. 1957-65), Hopkins Soc. (pres. 1972-75), Yeats Soc. (life), MLA (life), Internat. Hopkins Assn. (bd. scholars 1979—). Home: 416 Windward Pl, Kingston, ON Canada K7M 4E4

MACKENZIE, PETER SEAN, computer-based training developer; b. L.A., Aug. 25, 1954; s. William Duncan and Patricia Ann (Kronschnabel) Mack; m. Carin Willette, Dec. 28, 1983; 1 child, Liam Reynolds. BA, Western Wash. U., 1976. Bus. editor Skagit Valley Herald, Mount Vernon, Wash., 1976-79; mng. editor Stanwood (Wash.)-Camano News, 1979-84; graphic artist Pacific Media Group, Seattle, 1985-90, editor, 1990-94; with Digital Systems Internat., Redmond, Wash., 1994—; instr. U. Wash. Exptl. Coll., Seattle, 1990-91, 96—. Author: Jumper, 1989; rec. artist LP KEZX Album Project, 1987, Victory Music Vol. # 2, 1988; speaker Viacom Cable Pub. Access TV, Seattle, 1990. V.p. Stanwood, Wash. C. of C., 1983. Recipient 1st place newswriting award Wash. Newspaper Pubs. Assn., 1981, 82, 2d place award for comprehensive coverage, 1982, 3d place awards in newswriting, features and spot news, 1983. Mem. Soc. Profl. Journalists (2d place award for investigative reporting 1982, 3d place award for editls. 1983), Greenpeace. Avocations: photography, music, political research, philosophy. Home: 316 NW 86th St Seattle WA 98117-3125 Office: Digital Systems Internat 6464 185th Ave NE Redmond WA 98052-6736

MACKENZIE, ROSS, newspaper editor; b. Evanston, Ill., Aug. 25, 1941; s. Henry Wallace Dundas and Marion Elizabeth (Gillies) M.; m. Virginia de Bruyn Kops; children: Alexander Ross, Ross Hale. Diploma, Phillips Exeter Acad., 1959; BA in History, Yale U., 1963; MA in Polit. Philosophy, U. Chgo., 1969. Editor editl. pages Richmond (Va.) News Leader, 1969-92, Richmond Times-Dispatch, 1992—; mem. adv. bd. Lincoln Rev., 1972—, Inst. for Polit. Journalism, 1993—. Author: Brief Points: An Almanac for Parents and Friends of the U.S. Naval Academy, 1993, revised, 1996; editor: Eyewitness: Writings From the Ordeal of Communism, 1993. Mem. adv. bd. Massey Cancer Ctr., 1992—. Recipient Eugene Pulliam fellow Sigma Delta Chi, 1978; runner-up Pulitzer Prize for Commentary, 1982. Mem. Am. Soc. Newspaper Editors (past mem. writing awards com.), Phila. Soc. (charter mem.), Nat. Press Club, Commonwealth Club (pres. 1985-87), Country Club of Va., Deep Run Hunt Club. Avocations: one-wall handball, tennis, amateur radio, nature. Office: Richmond Times-Dispatch 333 E Grace St Richmond VA 23293-1000

MACKERODT, FRED, public relations specialist; b. Bklyn., Sept. 17, 1938; s. Leroy and Margaret (Murphy) M.; m. Christy Woods, June 7, 1987. Student, NYU, 1958-59. Freelance writer, photographer N.Y.C. and Barcelona, Spain, 1968-73; editor Cars Mag., Popular Publs. Inc., N.Y.C., 1973-76; pres. Fred Mackerodt, Inc. (pub. relations and publicity), N.Y.C., 1976—. Contbr. articles to popular mags.; contbg. editor, sci. and tech.: Popular Mechanics, 1987—. Spl. Dep. Sheriff, Indian River County, Fla., 1994—. Mem. Aviation and Space Writers Am., Internat. Motor Press Assn. (dir.), Alcoholism Coun. of N.Y. (dir.), Publicity Club N.Y., Wings Club, N.Y. Zool. Soc. (aquarium field assoc. 1971—). Home: Ste 901 209 W 86th St New York NY 10024 Office: 110 Summit Ave Montvale NJ 07645

MACKERRAS, SIR (ALAN) CHARLES (MACLAURIN), conductor; b. Schenectady, N.Y. (parents Australian citizens), Nov. 17, 1925; s. Alan Patrick and Catherine M.; m. Helena Judith Wilkins, 1947; 2 children. Student with Vaclav Talich, Prague Acad. Music, 1947-48; DMus (hon.) Hull U., 1990, Nottingham U., 1991, U. Brno, Czech Republic, 1994, York (Eng.) U., 1994, Griffith U., Brisbane, 1994. Prin. oboist Sydney Symphony Orch., Australia, 1943-46; staff condr. English Nat. Opera (formerly Sadler's Wells Opera), London, 1949-53, musical dir., 1970-77; prin. condr. BBC Concert Orch., 1954-56; freelance condr. with most Brit. and many continental orchs., concert tours USSR, S. Africa, N. Am., Australia, 1957-66, U.S. coast-to-coast, 1983; first condr. Hamburg State Opera, 1966-69; chief guest condr. BBC Symphony Orch., 1976-79; chief condr. Sydney Symphony Orch., Australian Broadcasting Commn., 1982-85; prin. guest condr. Royal Liverpool Philharmonic Orch., 1986-88, Scottish Chamber Orch., 1992-95, condr. laureate, 1995, San Francisco Opera, 1993, Royal Philharmonic Orch., 1993Czech Philharmonic Orchestra, 1997; mus. dir. Welsh Nat. Opera, 1987-92, condr. emeritus, 1993—; appearances many internat. festivals and opera houses; frequent radio and TV broadcasts; many comml. recordings, notably Handel series for DGG and Janacek operas for Decca, Mozart series for Telarc. Published ballet arrangements Pineapple Poll (Sullivan), Lady and the Fool (Verdi), reconstrn. Sullivan's lost Cello Concerto. Contbr. appendices (book) A Musicians' Musician, articles to Opera Mag., Music and Musicians, other jours. Recipient Evening Standard award for opera 1977, Janacek medal, 1978, Gramophone Record of Yr. award, 1977, 80, Grammy award for best opera recording, 1981; prix Fondation Jacques Ibert, 1983, Record of Yr. award Stereo Rev., 1983, Gramophone Operatic Record of Yr. award, 1983-84, Gramophone Choral Recording of Yr., 1986, Gramophone Best Opera Recording award, 1994; decorated comdr. Order Brit. Empire, 1974; created Knight, 1979; Brit. Council scholar, 1947-48. Fellow Royal Coll. of Music (hon.), L.R.A.M. (hon.). Office: care Marks Mgmt Ltd. 14 New Burlington St, London W1X 1FF, England

MACKEY, DALLAS L., financial consultant, development officer; b. Upper Strasburg, Pa., June 7, 1920; s. Bard Dallas Mackey and Hattie (Kessinger) Mackey Rosenberry; widowed; 1 child, Pamela Dallas. Student, Coll. Charleston. V.p., dir. Seaboard Chem. Corp., Sanford, N.C., 1959-65, First Provident Corp., Florence, S.C., 1961-65; pres., dir. Lee Broadcasting Corp., Sanford, 1956-64; chmn., dir. The MuMac Corp., Charlotte, N.C., 1960—; regional dir. Ketchum, Inc., Charlotte, 1964-78; dir. emeritus office devel. Bowman Gray-Bapt. Hosp. Med. Ctr., Winston-Salem, N.C.; bd. dirs. First Citizens Bank and Trust, Winston-Salem; cons. U. Ill. Found., Champaign, 1980—; chmn. bd. dirs. First Counsel, Inc., Charlotte, 1993—. Bd. dirs., former chmn. Winston-Salem State U. Found., 1979—; bd. dirs. Triad United Meth. Home, Winston-Salem, 1984—, N.C. Cmty. Found.; life trustee Brevard Coll. With U.S. Army, 1940-45, ETO. Mem. Assn. Am. Med. Colls. (vice chmn. 1983-84), Assn. for Healthcare Philanthropy, Council Advancement and Support Edn., Newcomen Soc., Rotary Internat. Democrat. Methodist. Clubs: Twin City; Piedmont (Winston-Salem). Avocations: growing roses, public speaking. Home: 3606 Winding Creek Way Winston Salem NC 27106-4325 Office: Bowman Gray Bapt Hosp Med Ctr Medical Center Blvd Winston Salem NC 27157

MACKEY, LEONARD BRUCE, lawyer, former diversified manufacturing corporation executive; b. Washington, Aug. 31, 1925; s. Stuart J. and Margaret B. (Browne) M.; m. Britta Beckhaus, Mar. 2, 1974; children—Leonard B., Cathleen C., Wendy F. B.E.E., Rensselaer Poly. Inst., 1945; J.D., George Washington U., 1950. Bar: D.C. 1951, N.Y. 1954. Instr. elec. engring. Rensselaer Poly. Inst., Troy, N.Y., 1946-47; patent examiner U.S. Patent Office, Washington, 1947-50; atty. Gen. Electric Co., Schenectady and N.Y.C., 1953-60; dir. licensing, asst. sec. ITT, N.Y.C., 1960-73; v.p., gen. patent counsel, dir. licensing ITT, 1973-90; of counsel Davis Hoxie Faithfull & Hapgood, N.Y.C., 1990-93; cons. licensing and tech. transfer Sarasota, Fla., 1994—. Mem. Recreation Commn., Rye, N.Y., 1966-67; mem. Planning Commn., 1967-70, 72-75, city councilman, 1970-71. Served with USNR, 1943-45; to lt. 1951-53. Mem. ABA (coun. mem., intellectual property law sect. 1989-93), Am. Intellectual Property Law Assn. (bd. mgrs. 1968-70, pres. 1982-83), Licensing Execs. Soc. U.S.A. (pres. 1978), Licensing Execs. Soc. Internat. (pres. 1986), Eta Kappa Nu, Am. Yacht Club (sec. 1968-70), N.Y. Yacht Club, Masons, Apawamis. Republican. Presbyterian. Office: 219 S Orange Ave Sarasota FL 34236-6801

MACKEY, LOUIS HENRY, philosophy educator; b. Sidney, Ohio, Sept. 24, 1926; s. Louis Henry and Clara Emma (Maurer) M.; children: Stephen Louis, Thomas Adam, Jacob Louis, Eva Maria. B.A., Capital U., 1948; student, Duke, 1948-50; M.A., Yale, 1953, Ph.D., 1954. Instr. philosophy Yale U., 1953-55, asst. prof., Morse fellow, 1955-59; assoc. prof. philosophy Rice U., Houston, 1959-65, prof., 1965-67; prof. U. Tex., Austin, 1967—. Author: Kierkegaard: A Kind of Poet, 1971, Points of View: Readings of Kierkegaard, 1986; contbr. articles to profl. jours. Recipient Harry Ransom award for Tchng. Excellence, 1987, Pres.'s Assocs. award for Tchng. Excellence, 1991, Grad. Tchng. award 1994; NEH fellow, 1976-77. Episcopalian. Home: 4105 Victory Dr Apt A108 Austin TX 78704-7552 Office: Univ Texas 316 WAG Austin TX 78712

MACKEY, MAURICE CECIL, university president, economist, lawyer; b. Montgomery, Ala., Jan. 23, 1929; s. M. Cecil and Annie Laurie (Kimrey) M.; m. Clare Siewert, Aug. 29, 1953; children: Carol, John, Ann. B.A., U. Ala., 1949, M.A., 1953, LL.B., 1958; Ph.D., U. Ill., 1955; postgrad., Harvard U., 1958-59. Bar: Ala. 1958. Asst. prof. econs. U. Ill., 1955-56; assoc. prof. econs. U.S. Air Force Acad., 1956-57; asst. prof. law U. Ala., 1959-62; with FAA, 1963-65, U.S. Dept. Commerce, 1965-67; asst. sec. U.S. Dept. Transp., 1967-69; exec. v.p., prof. law Fla. State U., Tallahassee, 1969-71; pres. U. South Fla., Tampa, 1971-76; pres., prof. law Tex. Tech U., Lubbock, 1976-79; pres., prof. econs. Mich. State U., East Lansing, 1979-85, prof. econs., 1985—; asst. counsel Subcom. on Antitrust and Monopoly, U.S. Senate, 1962-63; bd. dirs. Community First Bank, Lansing, Mich.; mem. adv. com. U.S. Coast Guard Acad., 1969-71; chmn. Fla. Gov.'s Adv. Com. on Transp., 1975, Nat. Boating Safety Adv. Council, 1975—; mem. adv. council NSF, 1978-81; assoc. China Council, 1979—; Disting. vis. prof. United Arab Emirates U., 1990, 91, 92, 93; bd. dirs. Summit Holding Corp., Lansing. Bd. dirs. Gulf Ridge council Boy Scouts Am.; pres. Chief Okemos council, 1981-82; bd. dirs. Tampa United Fund, Lubbock United Way; chmn., bd. dirs. Debt for Devel. Coalition, 1989—. Served with USAF, 1956-57. Recipient Arthur S. Flemming award Washington Jaycees, 1967. Mem. Fla. Council 100, Tampa C. of C. (bd. govs.), Am. Assn. State Colls. and Univs. (pres., dir.), Artus, Phi Kappa Phi, Chi Alpha Phi. Office: Mich State U Marshall Hall East Lansing MI 48824

MACKEY, PATRICIA ELAINE, librarian; b. Balt., July 29, 1941; d. Timothy and Hazel Mozelle (Davis) M. BA in Anthropology, CUNY, 1978; MLS, Columbia U., 1981. Asst. libr. I, European Exch. Sys., Mainz-Kastel, Germany, 1966-68; interlibr. loan asst. Poly. U., Bklyn., 1968-72; interlibr. loan asst. Rockefeller U., N.Y.C., 1972-73, sr. libr. asst., 1974-80, libr., 1981-91, head libr., 1991—; mem. various libr. coms., N.Y.C., 1991—. Mentor pub. svc. scholars program for srs. Hunter Coll., CUNY, 1992—. Mem. ALA, N.Y. State Libr. Assn., Assn. Coll. and Rsch. Librs. Democrat. Roman Catholic. Avocations: reading, chess, gardening. Office: Rockefeller U Libr RU Box 263 1230 York Ave New York NY 10021-6307

MACKEY, SALLY SCHEAR, retired religious organization administrator; b. Seattle, Feb. 17, 1930; d. Rillmond Weible and Helen Annajane (Bovee) Schear; m. Hallie Willis Mackey, May 22, 1953; children: Melinda Kay, John Mark, Heather Lynn. BA, U. Wash., 1951; postgrad., San Francisco Theol. Sem., 1951-53. Teenage program dir., camp dir. YWCA, Seattle, 1953-55; sponsor, devel. Wash. Assn. Chs. Immigration and Refugee Program (affiliate Ch. World Svc.), Seattle, 1979-85, dir., 1985-90; bd. dirs., v.p. Ch. Coun. Greater Seattle, 1974-84; bd. dirs. Wash. Assn. Chs., 1976-79; mem. Gen. Assembly Mission Coun. Presbyn. Ch., N.Y.C., 1979-83, adv. com. on ecumenical rels., Presbyn. Ch. (U.S.A.), Louisville, 1989-92; Presbyn. Ch. (U.S.A.); del. to Caribbean Area Coun. World Alliance Reformed Chs., 1987-92. Home: 2127 SW 162nd St Seattle WA 98166-2654

MACKEY, SHELDON ELIAS, minister; b. Bethlehem, Pa., Nov. 20, 1913; s. Elias and Pearl Elizabeth (Cunningham) M.; m. Marie Louise Dillinger, Sept. 20, 1939; children—Peter David, John Harry, Mary Susan, Timothy Andrew, Philip James. AB, Moravian Coll., 1936; BD, Lancaster Theol. Sem., 1939; DD, Franklin and Marshall Coll., 1954; LLD, Ursinus Coll., 1958. Ordained to ministry Evang. and Reformed Ch., 1939; pastor Pa. congregations, 1939-54; adminstrv. asst. to pres. Evang. and Reformed Ch., 1954-57, sec., 1957-78; also editor Yearbook, dir. correlation and sec. gen. council Gen. Synod; ret.; co-sec. United Ch. of Christ, also sec. exec. coun., adminstrv. com., 1957-61, mem. fin. and budget com., exec. sec. stewardship coun., 1961-79. Contbr. articles to religious publs. Bd. dirs. Ursinus Coll.; trustee emeritus Lancaster Theol. Sem. Mem. Nat. Council Chs. in U.S.A. Club: Phi Alpha Clergy. Home: 30 Schuylkill Dr Wernersville PA 19565-2011 *Life has a dimension which lies beyond the visible or physical. I believe that this dimension which lies at the heart of my faith is also revealed in art, music and literature. We need to reach out into this dimension which makes life most real.*

MACKEY, WILLIAM ARTHUR GODFREY, computer software company executive; b. Glasgow, Scotland, Mar. 23, 1946; came to U.S., 1970; s. William Arthur and Joan Margaret (Sykes) M.; m. Bianca Ann Dell'Isola, June 9, 1973 (dec. Nov. 1993). BSc in Engring., U. London, 1968, MSc in Engring., 1970; MBA, Harvard U., 1972. Prodn. engr. Rolls-Royce PLC, Glasgow, 1969-70; securities analyst Tucker, Anthony & R.L. Day, Inc., Boston, 1972-74; sr. project engr. Fafnir Bearing divsn. Textron Inc., New Britain, Conn., 1974-76; mfg. contr. Loctite Corp., Newington, Conn., 1976-78, mgr. ops. and mktg. divisional, 1978-80, mgr. corp. productivity improvement, 1980-83; worldwide product mgr. Otis Elevator Co., Farmington, Conn., 1985-87; pres., CEO Signum Microsystems, Inc., Bloomfield, Conn., 1982—; bd. dirs. Signum Microsystems, Inc., Bloomfield; sr. cons. Coopers & Lybrand, L.L.P., Hartford, Conn., 1988-91. Vice chmn. Conn. Com. Newcomen Soc. in U.S., Exton, Pa., 1980—; mem. Wadsworth Ahteneum, Hartford, 1975—, coun., 1994—; mem. World Affairs Coun., Hartford, Conn., 1984—, bd. dirs., 1992—; chief staff City fo New Haven Blue Ribbon Commn., 1990. Rolls Royce scholar, 1964-69, 70-72. Mem. ASME, ACLU, Soc. Mfg. Engrs. (vice chmn. Hartford chpt. 1991-95, chmn. 1996—, Pres.'s award 1991-92), Conn. Bus. and Industry Assn., Greater Hartford C. of C., MIT Enterprise Forum Conn., Concord Coalition, Harvard Bus. Sch. Club No. Conn. (bd. dirs. 1991—), U.S. Amateur Ballroom Dancers Assn., Royal Scottish Automobile Club (Glasgow), Masons (Wyllys-St. John's lodge 4). Republican. Congregationalist. Avocations: economics and current affairs, 20th century music, special-interest automobiles and motorcycles. Home: 244 Steele Rd West Hartford CT 06117-2742 Office: Signum Microsystems Inc 11 Mountain Ave Bloomfield CT 06002-2343

MACKEY, WILLIAM STURGES, JR., investor, consultant; b. St. Louis, May 27, 1921; s. William Sturges and Dorothy Francis (Allison) M.; m. Margaret Powell, Dec. 10, 1943; children: Dorothy Mackey Lurie, John Powell, James Wescott; m. Barbara Drozdowski, May 26, 1988. B.A., Rice U., 1943; M.B.A., U. Tex., 1950. Assoc. prof. acctg. Rice U., 1946-62; v.p., treas. Mandrel Industries, 1962-66; v.p. fin. Tex. Internat. Airlines, 1966-69; chmn., chief exec. officer Lifemark Corp., 1969-84; cons. Whole Foods Market, Inc. Served to 1st lt. USAAF, 1943-46. AICPA, Houston Philos. Soc., The Houston Forum, Rice U. Assocs., Lakeside Country Club, Houston City Club. Unitarian. Home: 6333 Buffalo Speedway Houston TX 77005-3309 Office: PO Box 273202 Houston TX 77277-3202

MACKIE, FREDERICK DAVID, retired utility executive; b. Ashland, Wis., Aug. 3, 1910; s. David and Johanna (Zilisch) M.; m. Ruth Elizabeth Babcock, Aug. 27, 1937; children—Marilyn Ruth, Frederick D. B.S. in Elec. Engring, U. Wis., 1933. With Madison Gas & Electric Co., Wis., 1934—; exec. v.p. Madison Gas & Electric Co., 1964-66, pres., gen. mgr., 1966-78, chmn. bd., 1976-78, also dir. Recipient Disting. Service citation Coll. Engring., U. Wis., 1969. Mem. IEEE (life), Nat. Soc. Profl. Engrs., Wis. Soc. Profl. Engrs., Madison Tech. Club, Kiwanis, Madison Club. Lutheran. Home: 58 Golf Course Rd Madison WI 53704-1423

MAC'KIE, PAMELA S., lawyer; b. Jackson, Miss., Jan. 2, 1956; d. Charles Edward and Betty Jo (Moore) Spell; children: John Greene IV, Ann Katherine. BS, Delta State U., Cleveland, Miss., 1978; JD, U. Miss., Oxford, 1984. Bar: Miss. 1984, Fla. 1986. Assoc. Cummings & Lockwood, Naples, Fla., 1985-93; prin. Pamela S. Mac'Kie, P.A., Naples, 1993-95, pres., 1995—. Pres. Naples Better Govt., 1992-95; pres.-elect Women's Rep. Club, Naples, 1994; county commr. Collier County Bd., Naples, 1994—; dir. Youth Haven, 1992, YMCA, 1993, Collier County Women's Polit. Caucus, 1992—. Recipient Pro Bono award Fla. Bar, 1990, Leadership Collier C. of C., Naples, 1991. Recipient Pro Bono award Fla. Bar, 1990; grad. Leadership Collier, Naples, 1991, Leadership S.W. Fla., 1995. Republican. Episcopalian. Office: Ste 201 5551 Ridgewood Dr Naples FL 33963

MACKIE, ROBERT GORDON, costume and fashion designer; b. Monterey Park, Calif., Mar. 24, 1940; s. Charles Robert and Mildred Agnes (Smith) M.; m. Marianne Wolford, Mar. 14, 1960 (div.); 1 son, Robin Gordon. Student, Chouinard Art Inst., 1958-61. Sketch for Jean Louis, 1962-63; mem. staff Edith Head, 1962-63; pres. ptnr. Bob Mackie Originals, N.Y.C.; costume designer: (films) Brigadoon, 1954, Divorce, American Style, 1967, ...All the Marbles, 1981, Pennies from Heaven, 1981 (Academy award nomination best costume design 1981), Max Dugan Returns, 1983, (TV movies) Fresno, 1986, (TV series) The Carol Burnett Show, 1967-78, The Sonny and Cher Comedy Hour, 1971-74, Cher, 1975-76, The Diahann Carroll Show, 1976, The Sonny and Cher Show, 1976-77, Donny and Marie, 1976-79, Mama's Family, 1983-85, (TV spls.) Alice Through the Looking Glass, 1967, Carousel, 1967, Kismet, 1967, Fred Astaire Show, 1968, Diana Ross and the Supremes, 1969, Of Thee I Sing, 1972, Once Upon a Mattress, 1973, (theatrical prodns.) The Best Little Whorehouse Goes Public, 1994; co-costume designer: (films) Lady Sings the Blues, 1972 (Academy award nomination best costume design 1972), Funny Lady, 1975 (Academy award nomination best costume design 1975), The Villain, 1979, Butterfly, 1981, ... All the Marbles, 1983, Staying Alive, 1983, Brenda Starr, 1987, (theatrical prodns.) On the Town, 1971, Lorelei, 1972; author: Dressing for Glamour, 1969; appeared on Broadway and in TV prodn. Night of 100 Stars II, 1985. Recipient Emmy awards for outstanding costume design, 1966, 67, 69, 70, 76, 78, 84, 88, 95, Emmy award nominations for outstanding costume design, 1972, 74, 75, 76, 77, 79, 80, 83, 86, 87, Costume Designers Guild award, 1968, Fashion Achievement award Otis/Parsons Sch. Design, 1987; named most creative fashion designer in Am. US mag., 1982, 83; honored by Costume Inst. Fine Arts, Houston, 1987, AIDS Project L.A., 1989. Democrat.

MACKIEWICZ, EDWARD ROBERT, lawyer; b. Jersey City, July 2, 1951; s. Edward John and Irene Helen (Rakowicz) H. BA, Yale U., 1973; JD, Columbia U., 1976. Bar: N.J. 1976, U.S. Dist. Ct. N.J. 1976, N.Y. 1977, U.S. Dist. Ct. (so. and ea. dist.) N.Y. 1977, D.C. 1978, U.S. Dist. Ct. D.C. 1978, U.S. Ct. Appeals (D.C. cir.) 1978, U.S. Ct. Appeals (3d cir.) 1980, U.S. Supreme Ct. 1980, Md. 1984, U.S. Ct. Claims 1984, U.S. Ct. Appeals (4th cir.) 1986, U.S. Dist. Ct. Md. 1990. Assoc. Carter, Ledyard & Milburn, N.Y.C., 1976-77, Covington & Burling, Washington, 1977-82; counsel for civil rights litigation solicitor's office U.S. Dept. Labor, Washington, 1982-83; sr. assoc. Jones, Day, Reavis & Pogue, Washington, 1983-85; gen. counsel Pension Benefit Guaranty Corp., Washington, 1985-87; of counsel Pierson, Ball & Dowd, Washington, 1987-89; ptnr. Reed Smith Shaw & McClay, Washington, 1989; gen. counsel Masters, Mates & Pilots Benefit Plans, Linthicum Heights, Md., 1989-92; of counsel Steptoe & Johnson, Washington, 1992—; mem. adv. coun. Sec. of Labor's ERISA, 1991-93; profl. lectr. in law Nat. Law Ctr., George Washington U., 1993—. Mem. Am. Coun. Young Polit. Leaders (del. to Australia 1985), Univ. Club, Yale Club. Home: 3001 Veazey Ter NW Apt 1032 Washington DC 20008-5406 Office: 1330 Connecticut Ave NW Washington DC 20036-1704

MACKIN, COOPER RICHERSON, university chancellor; b. Selma, Ala., Apr. 26, 1933; s. Thomas R. and Muriel (Green) M.; m. Catherine Barragy, Feb. 15, 1958 (dec.); children: Michele, Patrick, Daniel; m. Mary Kathryn Ruetten, Dec. 14, 1985. B.A., Troy State Coll., 1956; M.A., Tulane U., 1958; Ph.D., Rice U., 1962. Instr. Tex. So. U., 1958-59; asst. prof. N. Tex. State U., Denton, 1962-63; asst. prof. U. New Orleans, 1963-66, assoc. prof., 1966-70, prof. English, 1970—, chmn. dept., 1966-69, dean Coll. Liberal Arts, 1969-80, vice chancellor for acad. affairs, 1980-83, acting chancellor, 1983-84, chancellor, 1984-87, chancellor emeritus, 1987—. Author: William Styron, 1969; Contbr. articles on 17th century English lit. to profl. jours. Bd. dirs. New Orleans chpt. NCCJ, 1969-79, Air U., 1986-88. Served with AUS, 1953-55. Mem. Milton Soc. Am., South Central MLA. Home: 18 Charlotte Dr New Orleans LA 70122-2532 Office: U New Orleans English Dept New Orleans LA 70148

MACKIN, J. STANLEY, banker; b. Birmingham, Ala., 1932. Grad., Auburn Univ., 1954. Chmn., pres., CEO and COO First Ala. Bancshares, Inc., Birmingham. Office: First Ala Bank PO Box 10247 Birmingham AL 35202-0247*

MAC KINNEY, ARCHIE ALLEN, JR., physician; b. St. Paul, Aug. 16, 1929; s. Archie Allen and Doris (Hoops) MacK.; m. Shirley Schaefer, Apr. 9, 1955; children—Julianne, Theodore, John. B.A., Wheaton (Ill.) Coll., 1951; M.D., U. Rochester, 1955. Intern, resident in medicine U. Wis. Hosp., 1955-59; clin. asso. NIH, 1959-61; clin. investigator VA, 1961-64; asst. prof. medicine U. Wis., Madison, 1964-68; assoc. prof. U. Wis., 1968-74, prof., 1974—, med. alumni prof., 1987; chief hematology VA Hosp., Madison, 1964—, chief nuclear medicine, 1964-73, 78-79. Author, editor Pathophysiology of Blood, 1984. Contbr. articles to med. jours. Trustee Intervarsity Christian Fellowship, 1985-88. Served with USPHS, 1959-61. Danforth asso., 1962. Mem. Am. Soc. Hematology, Am. Fedn. Clin. Research, Central Soc. Clin. Research. Republican. Baptist. Home: 190 N Prospect Ave Madison WI 53705-4071 Office: 2500 Overlook Ter Madison WI 53705-2254

MACKINNEY, ARTHUR CLINTON, JR., retired university official, psychologist; b. Kansas City, Mo., Oct. 16, 1928; s. Arthur Clinton and Doris (Long) MacK.; m. Lois Elizabeth Lineberry, Sept. 5, 1953; children: Arthur Clinton III, Gordon L., Nada L. B.A., William Jewell Coll., 1951; M.A., U. Minn., 1953, Ph.D., 1955. Instr. U. Minn., 1953-55, Macalester

Coll., 1955; cons. psychologist R.N. McMurry & Co., Chgo., 1953; research psychologist Gen. Motors Corp., 1955-57; asst. prof. to prof., head dept. psychology Iowa State U., 1957-70; dean grad. studies and Research Wright State U., Dayton, Ohio, 1971-76; vice chancellor for acad. affairs U. Mo.-St. Louis, 1976-86, interim chancellor, 1986; pres. and chief exec. officer U. Ctr. Tulsa, 1986-91, pres. emeritus, 1992-93; vis. disting. prof. U. Tulsa, 1992-94; vis. prof. U. Minn., 1960, U. Calif., 1962-63, 66; mem. Commn. on Instns. Higher Edn., North Cen. Assn., 1980-84; cons. to industry. Contbr. articles to profl. jours. Bd. dirs. Tulsa Edn. Fund. Served with AUS, 1946-47, 51. Fellow Am. Psychol. Assn. (Cattell research design award 1968, pres. div. indsl. and orgnl. psychology 1981-82); mem. Midwestern Psychol. Assn., Mo. Psychol. Assn. (sec. 1981, pres. 1983-84), Iowa Psychol. Assn. (pres. 1966), Sigma Xi, Psi Chi (nat. historian 1983—, nat. council 1983—, Midwestern regional v.p. 1984-85, pres. 1987-88), Kappa Alpha, Phi Kappa Phi. Unitarian. Research on long-term devel. complex human performance. Home: PO Box 105 Ellison Bay WI 54210

MACKINNON, CATHARINE A., lawyer, law educator, legal scholar, writer; d. George E. and Elizabeth V. (Davis) MacKinnon. BA in Govt. magna cum laude with distinction, Smith Coll., 1969; JD, Yale U., 1977, PhD in Polit. Sci., 1987. Vis. prof. U Chgo., Harvard U., Stanford U, Yale U., others, Osgoode Hall, York U., Canada; prof. of law U. Mich., 1990—. Author: Sexual Harassment of Working Women, 1979, Feminism Unmodified, 1987, Toward a Feminist Theory of the State, 1989, Only Words, 1993. Office: U Michigan Law School Ann Arbor MI 48109-1215

MACKINNON, DAVID CAMERON, research and development company executive; b. Ottawa, Ont., Can., Sept. 1, 1945; s. Frank and Daphne MacKinnon; m. Betsy MacKinnon, Dec. 29, 1973; children: Katy, Darcy. BA with honors, Dalhousie U., 1967; MBA, York U., 1969; postgrad., U. Western Ont., 1990. Dir. policy devel., small bus. secretariat Fed. Dept. Ind. Trade and Commerce, Can.; dir. planning and econs. Dept. Devl., N.S., Can.; dir. econ. devel. br. Ministry of Treasury and Econs., Ont.; sr. mgr. pub. affairs Bank of Montreal, Toronto; pres., CEO Ont. Devel. Corp., Toronto, 1986-93; pres. ORTECH Corp., Mississauga, Ont., 1993-96; with Ont. Hosp. Assn., 1996—; dir. Can. Comprehensive Auditing Found., Ottawa; mem. Rsch. Inst. of Queen Elizabeth Hosp. Mem. APRO, OCMR, Can. Rsch. Mgmt. Assn., Royal Can. Yacht Club. Avocation: sailing.

MACKINNON, JACQUELINE LOUISE, school nurse; b. Quincy, Mass., Aug. 1, 1943; d. Paul Richard and Doris Mae (Preston) Happel; m. George Harold MacKinnon; children: Scott Douglas, Heidi Jean MacKinnon Sargent, Daren Robert. BSN, Boston U., 1965. RN, Mass.; cert. sch. nurse. Vis. nurse Quincy Vis. Nurses, 1965-67; staff nurse South Shore Hosp., Weymouth, Mass., 1972-75; vis. nurse, supr. Town of Pembroke, Mass., 1974-76, Hanover (Mass.) Vis. Nurse Assn., 1984-88; sch. nurse Cedar Sch., Hanover, 1988—; continuing edn. cons. Wellness Assocs., Plymouth, Mass., 1984-88; mem. practice adv. com. Mass. Bd. of Registration in Nursing, 1994—. Mem. Mass. Nurses Assn. (continuing edn. com. 1988—), Mass. Sch. Nurses Assn. (continuing edn. com. 1985—), South Shore RNs (continuing edn. com. 1983—, pres. 1987-89, Profl. Growth award 1993), Mass. Coun. of Nurses Orgn. Avocations: basketmaking, painting, cross stitch, cooking, reading. Home: 334 Forest St Pembroke MA 02359-3711 Office: Cedar Sch 265 Cedar St Hanover MA 02339-1367

MACKINNON, JOHN ALEXANDER, lawyer; b. Glen Ridge, N.J., Feb. 5, 1949; s. John and Carol McNeir (Cox) M.; m. Anne Rider Patterson, Aug. 19, 1972; children: Lindsay Rider, John William. BA, Williams Coll., 1971; JD, U. Va., Charlottesville, 1974. Assoc. Brown & Wood, N.Y.C., 1974-82, ptnr., 1983—. Trustee, Tuxedo Park Libr., N.Y., 1982-89; mem. chmn., bd. zoning appeals, Tuxedo Park, 1987-89. Mem. The Tuxedo Club. Home: Mtn Farm Rd Tuxedo Park NY 10987 Office: Brown & Wood 1 World Trade Ctr New York NY 10048-0202

MACKINNON, MALCOLM D(AVID), retired insurance company executive, information systems executive; b. Guelph, Ont., Can., Mar. 9, 1931; came to U.S., 1955; s. A.L. and Jean (Butchart) Mack.; m. Betty Campbell, June 18, 1955; children: Sandra, Katherine, Donald. BA, U. Toronto, 1953. CLU; chartered fin. analyst. With Prudential Ins. Co., 1954-94, v.p., Newark, 1979-81, sr. v.p., 1981-82, sr. v.p., Roseland, N.J., 1982-94; retired 1994; commentator pub. radio, 1995—. Trustee Kean Coll., Union, N.J., 1990-93, Millburn Free Pub. Libr., 1996—; chmn. Milburn Short Hills Chpt. Am. Red Cross, 1992-94. Fellow Soc. Actuaries . Club: Canoe Brook Country (Summit, N.J.). Home: 23 Grosvenor Rd Short Hills NJ 07078

MACKINNON, RODRICK KEITH, corporate administration executive, lawyer; b. Berwick, N.S., Can., Mar. 25, 1943; s. Albert Forbes and Lilian Ruth (Grimm) MacK.; m. Mary Eleanor McAlpine, Aug. 23, 1968; children: Robert, Daniel. BA, Royal Mil. Coll., Kingston, Ont., Can., 1965; LLB, Dalhousie U., Halifax, N.S., 1971. Called to B.C. bar as barrister and solicitor, 1972. Barrister, solicitor various law firms, Vancouver, B.C., Can., 1972-79; legal counsel Genstar Corp., Vancouver, 1980-84, assoc. gen. counsel, sec., 1985-86; legal counsel Imasco Ltd., Montreal, Que., Can., 1987-88; sr. legal counsel Imasco Ltd., Montreal, Que., 1988-89, corp. sec., counsel, 1989-95; exec. asst. to pres. Seaspan Internat. Ltd., North Vancouver, B.C., Can., 1995-96; coach minor league baseball and soccer, Vancouver, 1977-85. Lt. Royal Can. Navy, 1965-68, mem. Res. ret. Mem. Can. Bar Assn., Inst. Corp. Secs. and Adminstrs., Law Soc. B.C., Can. Maritime Law Assn. (exec. com. Vancouver 1981-84), Naval Officers Assn. Can. (exec. com. Vancouver 1978-85), Royal Mil. Coll. Club (exec. com. coll. alumni Vancouver 1978-84), Vancouver Club, Beaconsfield Golf Club (Pointe Claire, Que.), Montreal Badminton and Squash Club.

MACKINNON, ROGER ALAN, psychiatrist, educator; b. Attleboro, Mass., Feb. 13, 1927; s. Irville Herbert and Helen (Junk) MacK.; m. Florence Lundgren, Apr. 8, 1949 (div. 1970); children: Carol Louise, Stuart Alan; m. Nadine Trassenster, May 28, 1971. Student, Princeton U., 1944-46; MD, Columbia U., 1950, Cert. Psychoanalytic Med., 1957. Diplomate Am. Bd. Psychiatry and Neurology. Intern E.W. Sparrow Hosp., Lansing, Mich., 1950-51; resident in psychiatry N.Y. State Psychiatric Inst., N.Y.C., 1951-52, 52-54; chief psychiatry Vanderbilt Clinic, Presbyn. Hosp., N.Y.C., 1959-77; prof. clin. psychiatry Coll. Physicians & Surgeons, Columbia U., N.Y.C., 1986—; tng., supervising analyst Columbia U. Psychoanalytic Ctr., 1970—, asst. dir. for selection, 1981-91, dir., 1991—; attending psychiatrist Presbyn. Hosp., N.Y.C., 1972—, N.Y. State Psychiatric Inst., N.Y.C., 1972—; asst. examiner Am. Bd. Psychiatry and Neurology, 1960-70; lectr. in field. Co-author textbook: The Psychiatric Interview, 1971, The Psychiatric Evaluation, 1986; contbr. articles to profl. jours., chpts. to books. Lt. USNR, 1952-54. Recipient George Goldman award, Columbia U. Psychoanalytic Ctr., 1989, George E. Daniels Merit award Assn. for Psychoanalytic Medicine, 1995. Fellow Am. Psychiat. Assn. (life), N.Y. Acad. Medicine; mem. Am. Psychoanalytic Assn., N.Y. Psychiat. Soc. (pres. 1987-88). Avocations: woodworking, boating, hiking. Home: 11 Edgewood St Tenafly NJ 07670-2909 Office: 11 E 87th St New York NY 10128-0527 also: Columbia U Ctr Psychoanalytic Tng Rsch 722 W 168th St New York NY 10032-2603

MACKINNON, SALLY ANNE, retired fast food company executive; b. Chgo., Apr. 20, 1938; d. Eugene and Anne Elizabeth (Jones) MacK. B.A., Smith Coll., 1960; postgrad., U. Ark., 1961-62. Brand mgr. Speidel div. of Textron, Providence, 1967-70; mktg. mgr. Candy Corp. Am., Bklyn., 1970-72; v.p. account service William Esty Advt., N.Y.C., 1972-76; mktg. mgr. R.J. Reynolds Tobacco, Winston-Salem, N.C., 1976-84, v.p. new brands, 1984-86; v.p. new products mktg. Ky. Fried Chicken, Louisville, 1986-88; ret., 1988. Democrat. Episcopalian. Avocation: travel. Home: 321 Lamplighter Cir Winston Salem NC 27104-3420

MACKINNON, STEPHEN R., Asian studies administrator, educator; b. Columbus, Nebr., Dec. 2, 1940; s. Cyrus Leland and Helen (Wigglesworth) MacK.; m. Janice Carolyn Rachie, July 15, 1967; children: Rebecca, Cyrus R. BA, Yale U., 1963, MA, 1964; PhD, U. Calif., Davis, 1971. Acting instr. Chinese U., Hong Kong, 1968-69; dir. Asian Studies, prof. History Ariz. State U., Tempe, 1971—; vis. assoc. Chinese Acad. Social Sci., Beijing, 1979-81, 85; mem. U.S. State Dept. Selection Bd., Washington, 1991, Nat. Com. on U.S.-China Rels., N.Y.C., 1991—; cons. PBS film documentary "Dragon and Eagle" on U.S.-China rels., San Francisco, 1986—. Author: (book) Power/Politics China, 1980; co-author: (books) Agnes Smedley, 1988, China Reporting, 1987; co-editor: (book) Chinese Women Revolution, 1976 (ALA notable book 1976); lectr. on China to local orgns. and TV, 1981—. Commr. Phoenix Sister Cities, 1986-91; treas. Com. on Fgn. Rels., Phoenix, 1988—. Rsch. fellow Am. Coun. Learned Socs., Hong Kong, 1978, Fulbright Found., India, 1977-78; rsch. sr. Com. on Scholarly Com. People's Republic China, Washington-Beijing, 1992. Mem. Assn. Asian Studies (bd. dirs. 1990-91), Am. Hist. Assn. (program com. 1990-91). Avocations: tennis, hiking, jazz. Office: History Dept Ctr for Asian Studies Ariz State Univ Tempe AZ 85287-2501

MACKINTOSH, CAMERON, musical theater producer; b. Enfield, Middlesex, Eng., Oct. 17, 1946; s. Ian Robert and Diana Gladys (Tonna) M. Student, Prior Pk. Coll., Somerset, Eng., Cen. Sch. for Speech and Drama. Asst. stage mgr. Oliver! tour, British cities, 1965; N.Y. debut as producer, deviser Tomfoolery, Top of the Gate, 1981; London debut producer Little Women, Jeanetta Cochrane, 1967; producer, deviser musicals Anything Goes, Saville, London, 1969, Trelawney, Sadler Wells, Prince of Wales, 1972, The Card, Queens, 1973, Winnie the Pooh, Phoenix, 1974, 75, Owl and the Pussycat Went To See, Westminster, 1975, Side By Side By Sondheim, Wyndhams and Garrick, 1976, Oliver!, Albery, 1977-80, Aldwych, 1983, Godspell, Phoenix, 1975, Her Majesty's P.O.W., Shaftsbury, 1977, Duke of York, 1978, Diary of a Madam, Phoenix, 1977, After Shave, Apollo, 1977, Out On a Limb, Vaudeville, 1977, Gingerbread Man, Old Vic, 1978, 79, Royalty, 1980, Westminster, 1981, My Fair Lady, Adelphi, 1979, Tomfoolery, Criterion, 1980, Jeeves Takes Charge, Fortune, 1981, Cats, New London, 1981, Song and Dance, Palace, 1982, Blondel, Old Vic, Aldwych, 1983, Little Shop of Horrors, Comedy, 1983, Abbacadabra, Lyric Hammersmith, 1983, The Boyfriend, Old Vic. and Albery, 1985, Les Misérables, 1985, The Phantom of the Opera, 1987, Follies, 1989, Miss Saigon, 1989, Five Guys Named Moe, 1990, Moby Dick: Putting It Together, 1992, Carousel, 1993 (Tony award, 1994), Oliver!, 1994, Martin Guerre, 1996; major tours in Britian include Little Women, 1967, Murder at the Vicarage, 1969, Rebecca, 1969, At Home with the Dales, 1970, Salad Days, 1972, Butley, 1973, Winnie the Pooh, 1973-74, Time and Time Again, 1974, Godspell, 1974-80, The Owl and The Pussycat Went To See, 1974, 75, 76, Relativeley Speaking, 1974-75, An Inspector Calls, 1974, Private Lives, 1974, Bell, Book and Candle, 1974, A Merry Whiff of Windsor, 1975, So Who Needs Marriage. 1975, John, Paul, George and Ringo, 1975-76, Rock Nativity, 1975-76, Touch of Spring, 1976, Virginia Woolf, 1976, Lauder, 1976, Oliver!, 1977, 83, Side By Side By Sondheim, 1978-79, My Fair Lady, 1978, 81-82, Rocky Horror Show, 1979-80, Gingerbread Man, 1979, Oklahoma, 1980; also tours various shows to Can., Republic S. Africa, Ireland, Scandinavia, Australia, U.S.A. Fellow St. Catherine's Coll. (hon., Oxford); mem. Soc. West End Theatres (exec. officer), Dramatists League, League Am. Theaters, Am. Dramatists Guild. Address: Number One, Bedford Sq, London England WC1B 3RA also: 226 W 47th St New York NY 10036-1413

MACKINTOSH, FREDERICK ROY, oncologist; b. Miami, Fla., Oct. 4, 1943; s. John Harris and Mary Carlotta (King) MacK.; m. Judith Jane Parnell, Oct. 2, 1961 (div. Aug. 1977); children: Lisa Lynn, Wendy Sue; m. Claudia Lizanne Flournoy, Jan. 7, 1984; 1 child, Gregory Warren. BS, MIT, 1964, PhD, 1968; MD, U. Miami, 1976. Intern then resident in gen. medicine Stanford (Calif.) U., 1976-78, fellow in oncology, 1978-81; asst. prof. med. U. Nev., Reno, 1981-85, assoc. prof., 1985-92, prof. medicine, 1992—. Contbr. articles to profl. jours. Fellow ACP; mem. Am. Soc. Clin. Oncology, Am. Cancer Soc. (pres. Nev. chpt. 1987-89, Washoe chpt. 1988-90), No. Nev. Cancer Coun. (bd. dirs. 1981-92), No. Calif. Cancer Program (bd. dirs. alt. 1983-87, bd. dirs. 1987-91). Avocation: bicycling. Office: Nev Med Group 781 Mill St Reno NV 89502-1320

MACKIW, VLADIMIR NICHOLAUS, metallurgical consultant; b. Stanislawiw, Western Ukraine, Sept. 4, 1923; came to Can., 1948, naturalized, 1953; s. Timothy and Irene (Iwanyckyj) M.; m. Bohdanna Irene Kebuz, Nov. 24, 1951. Dipl. Chemist, Univs. Breslau and Erlangen, Germany, 1946; postgrad., U. Louvain, Belgium, 1948; DSc (hon.), U. Alta., Edmonton, 1976. Chemist Lingman Lake Gold Mines, Winnipeg, Man., Can., 1948; with Man. Provincial Bur. Mines, 1949; research chemist Sherritt Gordon Mines Ltd., Toronto, Ont., Can., 1949, dir. research, 1952, dir. research and devel. div., 1955-68, dir., 1964, v.p., 1967, v.p. tech. and corp. devel., 1968-72, exec. v.p., 1972-88; cons. Toronto, 1988—; chmn. Nickel Devel. Inst., Toronto, 1984-86; mem. Nat. Research Council Can., 1971-77; former mem. Nat. Adv. Com. on Mining and Metall. Research; mem. adv. com. to minister energy, mines and resources, 1972-79, co-chmn., 1975-79; presented tech. papers and lectures Federal Republic of Germany, Belgium, Japan, Peoples Republic of China, Australia, Canada; participated in fed. gov. tech. missions to USSR, Belgium, Peoples Republic of China. Contbr. articles to profl. jours.; patentee in field. Recipient Jules Garnier prize Metall. Soc. France, 1966, Gold medal Instn. Mining and Metallurty, London, 1977, fellow award TMS, 1994. Fellow Can. Acad. Engring. (life), Can. Inst. Mining and Metallurgy (Inco Platinum medal 1966, Airey award 1972), Chem. Inst. Can. (R.S. Jane Meml. award 1967); mem. AIME (James Douglas Gold medal 1991), Can. Rsch. Mgmt. Assn. (R&D Mgmt. award 1990, Shevchenko Gold medal Ukranian Can. Congress), Am. Powder Metallurgy Inst., Am. Soc. Metallurgy Internat. (lectr. Can. chpts. 1990-91), Assn. Profl. Engrs. Alta., Soc. Chem. Industry (Can. sect.), Shevchenco Sci. Soc. (past pres.), Ont. Club. Ukrainian Catholic. Home: 9 Blair Athol Crescent, Toronto, ON Canada M9A 1X6 Office: Sherritt Internat Corp, 5 Hazelton Ave, Toronto, ON Canada M5R 2E1

MACKLEM, MICHAEL KIRKPATRICK, publisher; b. Toronto, Ont., Can., July 12, 1928; s. Hedley Clark and Mary Eileen (Kirkpatrick) M.; m. Anne Woodburne Hardy, Dec. 30, 1950; children—Timothy Street, Nicholas Hardy. B.A., U. Toronto, 1950; A.M. (Charles Scribner fellow), Princeton U., 1952, Ph.D. (Porter Ogden Jacobus fellow, Royal Soc. Can. fellow), 1954. Instr., English Yale U., New Haven, 1954-55; staff editor Ency. Canadiana, 1955-58; asst. to dir. Humanities Research Council of Can., 1958-60; gen. mgr. Oberon Press, Ottawa, Ont., 1966-85; pres. Michael, Hardy, Ltd., Ottawa, 1972—. Author: The Anatomy of the World: Relations Between Natural and Moral Law from Donne to Pope, 1958, God Have Mercy: The Life of John Fisher of Rochester, 1967, Cinderella, 1969, Voyages to New France 1615-1618, 1970, Voyages to New France 1599-1603, 1971, The Sleeping Beauty, 1973, Jacques the Woodcutter, 1977, Liberty and the Holy City, 1978. Can. Council fellow, 1964-65. Home: 555 Maple Ln, Ottawa, ON Canada K1M 0N7 Office: Oberon Press, 400-350 Sparks St, Ottawa, ON Canada K1R 7S8

MACKLER, TINA, artist; b. London; d. Leon and Ethel Mackler; divorced; 1 child, Leonore Bloom. Student, Arts Students League, N.Y.C., Indsl. Sch. Design, N.Y.C., New Sch., N.Y.C. Tchr. art Nat. Acad. Ballet, N.Y.C., 1966-69; tchr. adults West Side YMCA, N.Y.C.; asst. studio instr. Met. Mus. Art, N.Y.C., vol. program, 1990—. Illustrator: Informal Dictionary of Ballet, co-author, illustrator: To Dance, To Live; pub. Dance Horizons, 1977; one-person exhbns. Alfred Valente Gallery, N.Y.C., 1967, Mus. Performing Arts, Lincoln Ctr., N.Y.C., 1973, Adelphi U., L.I., N.Y., 1975, Phila. Art Alliance, 1976, Jackson (Miss.) Mus. Art, 1978, Northeastern U., Boston, 1980; exhibited in group shows Alfredo Gallery, N.Y.C., 1964, 1966, Dutchess Hall Gallery, Poughkeepsie, N.Y., 1969, Wright/Hepburn/Webster Gallery, N.Y.C., 1960, 70, N.Y. Pub. Library, 1973, O'Keefe Centre, Ont., Can., 1974, Ball State U., 1974, N.A.D. annual, 1974, Audubon Artists Annual, 1975, Nat. Pastel Show, 1975, Commedia Dell Art Adelphi U., 1974, Guild Gallery, N.Y.C., 1978, Dance Collections, Lincoln Ctr., N.Y.C., 1991, Jackson Gallery, 1994; works represented in permanent collections Nat. Collection Fine Prints, Smithsonian Instn., Washington, Israel Mus., Jerusalem, La Jolla (Calif.) Mus., U. Wis. Mus., Circus World Mus., Baraboo, Wis., Fairleigh Dickinson U., Circus Hall of Fame Mus., Sarasota, Fla., Adelphi U., Creative Dance Found. For Negro Arts, Tuskegee, Ala., Mus. Performing Arts Lincoln Center, N.Y.C., Jackson (Miss.) Mus. Art, Original Print Collectors Group Ltd., Northeastern U., also notable pvt. collections, Am. and abroad; completed series of studies on Spanish dance and impressions of Spain for Spanish Ministry Info. and Tourism, 1976, 88; represented in original stone lithographs of Rudolf Nureyev, Marcel Marceau, Margot Fonteyn and numerous dance soloists, N.Y. Times Mag., also nat. mags., 1975-78; History of International Art, Accademia Italia; works profiled Joe Franklin TV Show, 1979; represented in Works shown on TV NBC-TV preview, Mus. Performing Arts, Lincoln Center, 1973, Channel 13 TV Art Auction, 1978, 79, 80, 81, 82, 83; Meml. for Dame Margot Fonteyn oil painting; portrait of Margot Fonteyn & Rudolf Nureyev exhibited Lincoln Ctr. for Performing Arts, 1991; exhbn. ballet art with USA Internat. Ballet Competition, Jackson, Miss., 1994. Mem. Woman's Fedn. for World Peace, 1995—. Prints selected for promotional use Texaco, 1979. Home: 25 Central Park W New York NY 10023-7253 *I have long felt the influence which the arts exert on the minds and hearts of mankind. Believing, as I do, that the world today stands in need of spiritual truths, ideals and moral standards, it is my desire to reach out and set before the public some of the beauty and grandeur which reside in the human soul and expresses itself through that most primal art - the dance.*

MACKLIN, CROFFORD JOHNSON, JR., lawyer; b. Columbus, Ohio, Sept. 10, 1947; s. Crofford Johnson, Sr. and Dorothy Ann (Stevens) M.; m. Mary Carole Ward, July 5, 1969; children—Carrie E., David J. B.A., Ohio State U., 1969; B.A. summa cum laude, U. West Fla., 1974; J.D. cum laude, Ohio State U., 1976. Bar: Ohio 1977, U.S. Tax Ct. 1978. Acct., Touche Ross, Columbus, 1976-77; assoc. Smith & Schnacke, Dayton, 1977-81; ptnr. Porter, Wright, Morris & Arthur, Dayton, 1983-88; shareholder Smith & Schnacke, 1988-89; ptnr. Thompson, Hine & Flory, 1989—; sole practice, Dayton, 1981-82; adj. faculty Franklin U., 1977; adj. prof. U. Dayton Law Sch., 1981. Contbr. articles to profl. jours. Bd. dirs. Easter Seals, 1984-86. Served to capt. USMCR, 1969-74. Fellow Am. Coll. Trust and Estate Counsel; Emem. Dayton Bar Assn. (chmn. probate com. 1981-83), Dayton Trust & Estate Planning (pres. 1983-84), Ohio Bar Assn., ABA. Presbyterian. Home: 3 Forest Pl Glendale OH 45246-4407 Office: Thompson Hine & Flory 2000 Courthouse Pla NE PO Box 8801 Dayton OH 45401-8801

MACKLIN, F. DOUGLAS, bishop. Bishop Ch. of God in Christ, Memphis.

MACKLIN, PHILIP ALAN, physics educator; b. Richmond Hill, N.Y., Apr. 13, 1925; s. Egbert Chalmer and Margaret Griswold (Collins) M.; m. Cora Baldwin Galindo, Sept. 5, 1953; children: Susan, Steven, Peter. B.S. cum laude, Yale U., 1944; M.A., Columbia U., 1949, Ph.D., 1956. Physicist Carbide & Carbon Chems. Corp., Oak Ridge, 1946-47; research scientist AEC, Columbia U., 1949-51; instr. physics Middlebury Coll., Vt., 1951-54; acting chmn. dept. Middlebury Coll., 1953-54; mem. faculty Miami U., Oxford, Ohio, 1954—; prof. physics Miami U., 1961-93, chmn. dept., 1972-85, prof. emeritus, 1993—; research scientist Armco Steel Co., summers 1955-56; vis. prof. U. N.Mex., summers 1957-68, Boston U., fall 1985-86; physicist Los Alamos Sci. Labs., summers 1960-62; participant NSF summer insts., 1970-71; vis. scientist MIT, 1985-86. Author publs. in field. Vestryman Holy Trinity Episcopal Ch., Oxford , 1959-61, 67, 71-73, 75-77, mem. fin. com., chmn. blood assurance program, 1980—, lector, 1989—. With USN, 1944-46. Mem. AAAS, AAUP, LWV of Oxford (treas. 1986-88), Am. Phys. soc., Forum Physics and Soc., Am. Assn. Physics Tchrs., Kiwanis (bd. dirs. 1994—), Torch Club of Butler County (pres. 1982-83), 1809 Club (pres. 1964-65), Campus Ministry Ctr. (trustee 1994—), Union of Concerned Scientists, Phi Beta Kappa, Sigma Xi, Sigma Pi Sigma, Omicron Delta Kappa. Democrat. Achievements include patents in field. Home: 211 Oakhill Dr Oxford OH 45056-2710 Office: 117 Culler Hall Miami Univ Oxford OH 45056

MACKLIN, RUTH, bioethics educator; b. Newark, Mar. 27, 1938; d . Hyman and Frieda (Yaruss) Chimacoff; m. Martin Macklin, Sept. 1, 1957 (div. June 1969): children: Meryl, Shelley Macklin Taylor. BA with distinction, Cornell U., 1958; MA in Philosophy, Case Western Res. U., 1966, PhD in Philosophy, 1968. Instr. in philosophy Case Western Res. U., Cleve., 1967-68, asst. prof., 1968-71, assoc. prof., 1971-76; assoc. for behavioral studies The Hastings Ctr., Hastings-on-Hudson, N.Y., 1976-80; vis. assoc. prof. Albert Einstein Coll. Medicine, Bronx, N.Y., 1977-78, assoc. prof., 1978-84, prof. dept. epidemiology and social medicine, 1984—; cons. NIH, 1986—; advisor WHO, Geneva, 1989: apptd. mem. White House Adv. Com. on Human Radiation Experiments, Washington, 1994—. Author: Man, Mind and Morality, 1982, Mortal Choices, 1987, Enemies of Patients, 1993, Surrogates and Other Mothers, 1994; contbr. articles to ethics, law and med. jours. Fellow The Hastings Ctr., Inst. Medicine of NAS, Am. Philos. Assn. (life), Am. Pub. Health Assn., Am. Soc. Law, Medicine and Ethics; mem. Internat. Assn. Bioethics (bd. dirs.), Am. Assn. Bioethics (bd. dirs.), Phi Beta Kappa. Democrat. Office: A Einstein Coll Medicine Dept Epidemiology & Social Medicine 1300 Morris Park Ave Bronx NY 10461-1926

MACKNIGHT, WILLIAM JOHN, chemist, educator; b. N.Y.C., May 5, 1936; s. William John and Margaret Ann (Stuart) M.; m. Carol Marie Bernier, Aug. 19, 1967. B.S., Rochester U., N.Y., 1958; M.A., Princeton U., N.J., 1963, Ph.D., 1964. Research assoc. Princeton U., N.J., 1964-65; asst. prof. chemistry U. Mass., Amherst, 1965-69, assoc. prof. chemistry, 1969-74, prof. chemistry, 1974-76, dept. head polymer sci., 1976-85, prof. polymer sci. and engring., 1985-88, 95—, head dept. polymer sci. & engring., 1988-95; mem. sci. and tech. adv. bd. Alcoa, Pitts., 1984-86, Diversitech Gen., Akron, Ohio, 1985—; mem. panel for materials sci. Nat. Bur. Standards, Washington, 1983-89. Author: Polymeric Sulfur and Related Polymers, 1965; Introduction to Polymer Viscoelasticity, 2d edit., 1983. Served to lt. USN, 1958-61. Recipient Ford prize in high polymer physics Am. Phys. Soc., 1984; Guggenheim fellow, 1985. Fellow AAAS, Am. Phys. Soc. (exec. com. 1975-76); mem. Am. Chem. Soc., Am. Soc. Rheology. Club: Cosmos. Avocations: Music; sports. Home: 127 Sunset Ave Amherst MA 01002-2019 Office: U Mass Polymer Sci & Engring Dept Conte Bldg Amherst MA 01003

MACKOVIC, JOHN, college football coach, athletic director; b. Barberton, Ohio, Oct. 1, 1943; m. Arlene Francis; children: Aimee, John. BA in Spanish, Wake Forest U., 1965; MEd in Secondary Sch. Adminstrn., Miami U., Oxford, Ohio, 1966. Various coaching positions, 1965-72; offensive backfield coach U. Ariz., Tucson, 1973-74; offensive coord. U. Ariz., 1974-75, asst. head coach, 1976; asst. head coach, offensive coord. Purdue U., West Lafayette, Ind., 1976-78; head football coach Wake Forest U., Winston-Salem, N.C., 1978-81; asst. football coach Dallas Cowboys, 1981-83; head football coach Kansas City (Mo.) Chiefs, 1983-87; head football coach U. Ill., 1988-92, dir. of athletics, 1988-92; head coach football U. Tex., Austin, 1992—. Address: PO Box 7399 Austin TX 78713-7399*

MACKOWSKI, JOHN JOSEPH, retired insurance company executive; b. Westport, Mass., Feb. 1, 1926; s. John J. and Victoria K. (Skript) Mieczkowski; m. Ruth Williams, Feb. 3, 1951; children: Martha, John Matthew, Daniel, Joan. AB, Duke U., 1948; student, Harvard Advanced Mgmt. Program, 1970, 71. With Ins. Co. of N.Am., Boston, Phila., Chgo., 1948-51; with Atlantic Mut. Ins. Co., N.Y.C., 1951-88, chmn., CEO, to 1988; bd. dirs. F.W. Woolworth Co., RCB Trust Co., Stamford, Conn., Transatlantic Holdings, Inc. Bd. dirs. Seamen's Ch. Inst. N.Y. and N.J. Served to 1st lt. USMCR, 1943-46. Mem. Sawgrass Club (Ponte Vedra Beach, Fla.), Acoaxet Country Club (Westport Harbor, Mass.), Spindle Rock Yacht Club, Sigma Chi, Beta Lambda. Episcopalian. Home: 33 Widgeon Ln Little Compton RI 02837-1960 Other Home: 1506 Birkdale Ln Ponte Vedra Beach FL 32082-3500

MACKSOUD, MONA SALIM, clinical psychologist; b. Beirut, Oct. 31, 1955; d. Salim and Samia (Nassar) M.; m. Abdallah H. Nauphal, Aug. 27, 1993; 1 child, Maya. BA in Psychology with distinction, U. Calif., Davis, 1978; MS in Clin. Psychology, U. Surrey, Eng., 1980; PhD in Clin. Psychology, Columbia U., 1987. Chartered clin. psychologist, Eng.; lic. psychologist, N.Y. Clin. psychologist St. Francis Hosp., Haywards Heath, Eng., 1980-81; tng. psychotherapist Ctr. for Psychol. Svcs. Columbia U., N.Y.C., 1982-85, fellow psychology Ctr. for Infants and Parents, Tchrs. Coll., 1984-85; fellow psychology Am. U. Beirut Med. Ctr., 1985-86, rsch. assoc., 1988-89; vis. fellow Ctr. Ctr. for Lebanese Studies, Oxford, Eng., 1989; rsch. dir. Ctr. for Study of Human Rights Columbia U., N.Y.C., 1990—; hon. clin. psychologist St. George's Hosp., London, 1980-81; cons. UNICEF, 1990, 91, 92, 93; presenter in field. Contbr. articles to profl. jours. Mem. APA, Internat. Soc. for Traumatic Stress Studies, Brit. Psychol. Soc. (chartered clin. psychologist). Greek Orthodox. Avocations: sports, music, traveling. Office: Columbia U Project on Children & War 1108 Internat Affairs Bldg New York NY 10027

MACLACHLAN, DOUGLAS LEE, marketing educator; b. Hollywood, Calif., Aug. 27, 1940; s. Alexander D. and Patricia E. (Culver) MacL.; m.

Natalie Bowditch Knauth, July 23, 1966; children: Heather Bowditch, Trevor Douglas. A.B. in Physics, U. Calif., Berkeley, 1962, M.B.A., 1965, M.A. in Stats., 1970, Ph.D. in Bus. Adminstrn, 1971; student, Hastings Sch. Law, 1965-66. Instr. bus. adminstrn. U. Calif., Berkeley, 1969-70; v.p. Hartec Corp., Newport Beach, Calif., 1965-70; acting asst. prof. U. Wash., Seattle, 1970-71, asst. prof., 1971-74, asso. prof., 1974-78, prof., chmn. dept. mktg. and internat. bus., 1978-86, prof., acting chair dept. mktg. and internat. bus., 1993-94, Affiliate Program Disting. prof. mktg. and internat. bus., 1986-88, Nordstrom prof. retail mktg., 1988-89, Ford Motor Co. prof. mktg., 1989-90, assoc. dean, 1995—; vis. prof. bus. adminstrn. U. Calif., Berkeley, summer 1974; vis. prof. Institu Européen des Affaires, Fontainebleau, France, 1982-83, Cath. U. Leuven, Belgium, 1991-92; dir. Univ. Book Store, 1985—. Contbr. articles profl. jours.; editorial bd.: Jour. Mktg. Research, 1975-81. Mem. Am. Mktg. Assn. (dir. Puget Sound chpt. 1975-77, 90-91, pres. 1978-79), Inst. Mgmt. Scis., Am. Statis. Assn., Am. Inst. Decision Scis., Assn. Consumer Research, Alpha Kappa Psi, Kappa Delta Rho. Home: 16305 Inglewood Rd NE Bothell WA 98011-3908 Office: University Of Washington # 10 Seattle WA 98195-0005

MACLACHLAN, GORDON ALISTAIR, biology educator, researcher; b. Saskatoon, Sask., Can., June 30, 1930; s. Hector Ross and Nellie (Glass) M.; m. Sarah Dangerfield, June 26, 1959; children: Mary, Anna. B.A., U. Sask., 1952, M.A., 1954; Ph.D., U. Man., 1956. NRC postdoctoral fellow Imperial Coll., London, 1956-59; asst. prof. U. Alta., Edmonton, 1960-62; assoc. prof. biology McGill U., Montreal, 1962-69, prof., 1970—, chmn. dept., 1970-75, 95, dean. grad. studies vice prin. rsch., 1980-90. Assoc. editor Can. Jour. Botany, 1980-86; editor Jour. Plant Molecular Biology, 1988-90. Commonwealth prof. Australia, 1975. Mem. Can. Soc. Plant Physiologists (pres. 1973). Home: 561 Argyle Ave, Westmount, PQ Canada H3Y 3B8 Office: McGill U Biology Dept, 1205 Penfield Ave, Montreal, PQ Canada H3A 1B1

MACLACHLAN, KYLE, actor; b. 1960. Actor: film Dune, 1984, Blue Velvet, 1986, The Hidden, 1987, Don't Tell Her It's Me, 1990, The Doors, 1991, Twin Peaks: Fire Walk with Me, 1992, Where the Day Takes You, 1992, Rich in Love, 1993, The Trial, 1993, The Flintstones, 1994; TV series Twin Peaks, 1990-91; TV movies: Against the Wall, 1994, Roswell, 1994. Office: UTA 9560 Wilshire Blvd 5th Fl Beverly Hills CA 90212*

MACLACHLAN, PATRICIA, author; b. Cheyenne, Wyo., Mar. 3, 1938; d. Philo and Madonna (Moss) Pritzkau; m. Robert MacLachlan, Apr. 14, 1962; children: John, Jamie, Emily. BA, U. Conn., 1962. Tchr. English Bennett Jr. High Sch., Manchester, Conn., 1963-79; vis. lectr. Smith Coll., Northampton, Mass., 1986—. Author: The Sick Day, 1979, Arthur, for the Very First Time, 1980 (Golden Kite award Soc. Children's Book Writers 1980), Moon, Stars, Frogs, and Friends, 1980, Through Grandpa's Eyes, 1980, Cassie Binegar, 1982, Mama One, Mama Two, 1982, Tomorrow's Wizard, 1982, Seven Kisses in a Row, 1983, Unclaimed Treasures, 1984 (Boston Globe/Horn Book award 1984), Sarah, Plain and Tall, 1985 (Golden Kite award 1985, Scott O'Dell Historical Fiction award 1985, John Newbery medal 1986, Jefferson Cup award Va. Libr. Assn. 1986, Christopher award 1986, Garden State Children's Book award N.J. Libr. Assn. 1988), The Facts and Fictions of Minna Pratt, 1988 (Parent's Choice award Parent's Choice Found. 1988), Three Names, 1991, Journey, 1991, All the Places to Love, 1993, Baby, 1993, Skylark, 1994. Bd. dirs. Children's Aid Family Svc. Agency, 1970-80. recipient numerous awards for children's fiction. Office: Dept of Edn Smith Coll Northampton MA 01063*

MACLAGAN, JOHN LYALL, retired petroleum company executive; b. Lethbridge, Alta., Can., Oct. 26, 1929; s. Frederick Alexander Lyall and Dora Ellen (Dean) M.; m. Joan Lily Prince, July 15, 1965; 1 dau., Susan. B.Commerce, U. Alta., 1952. Chartered accountant, Alta. Staff auditor Price Waterhouse & Co., Calgary, 1952-56; accountant Union Oil Co. of Calif., Alta., 1956-61; mgr. accounting Union Oil Co. of Can., Ltd., Calgary, 1961-72; treas., comptroller Union Oil Co. of Can., Ltd., 1972-75, v.p. fin., treas., 1975-82; v.p. fin. Omega Hydrocarbons Ltd., Calgary, 1982-94; ret., 1994. Mem. Can. Inst. Chartered Accts. Club: Calgary Petroleum. Home: 308 Roxborough Rd SW, Calgary, AB Canada T2S 0R4

MACLAINE, ALLAN HUGH, English language educator; b. Montreal, Can., Oct. 24, 1924. B.A., McGill U., 1945; Ph.D. in English, Brown U., 1951. Instr. English McGill U., 1946-47, Brown U., 1947-50, U. Mass., 1951-54; from asst. prof. to prof. Tex. Christian U., 1954-62; prof. English U. R.I., 1962—, also dean div. univ. extension, 1967-71. Author: Student's Comprehensive Guide to the Canterbury Tales, 1964, Robert Fergusson, 1965, Allan Ramsay, 1985, also articles. Mem. Coll. English Assn. (pres. 1965, dir. 1961-66), Assn. for Scottish Literary Studies. Office: U Rhode Island Dept English Kingston RI 02881

MACLAINE, SHIRLEY, actress; b. Richmond, Va., Apr. 24, 1934; d. Ira O. and Kathlyn (MacLean) Beatty; m. Steve Parker, Sept. 17, 1954 (div.); 1 child, Stephanie Sachiko. Ed. high sch. Appearances include (Broadway plays) Me and Juliet, 1953, Pajama Game, 1954, (films) The Trouble With Harry, 1954, Artists and Models, 1954, Around the World in 80 Days, 1955-56, Hot Spell, 1957, The Matchmaker, 1957, The Sheepman, 1957, Some Came Running, 1958 (Fgn. Press award 1959), Ask Any Girl, 1959 (Silver Bear award as best actress Internat. Berlin Film Festival), Career, 1959, Can-Can, 1959, The Apartment, 1959 (Best Actress prize Venice Film Festival), Children's Hour, 1960, The Apartment, 1960, Two for the Seesaw, 1962, Irma La Douce, 1963, What A Way to Go, The Yellow Rolls Royce, 1964, John Goldfarb Please Come Home, 1965, Gambit and Woman Times Seven, 1967, The Bliss of Mrs. Blossom, Sweet Charity, 1969, Two Mules for Sister Sara, 1969, Desperate Characters, 1971, The Possession of Joel Delaney, 1972, The Other Half of the Sky: A China Memoir, 1975, The Turning Point, 1977, Being There, 1979, A Change of Seasons, 1980, Loving Couples, 1980, Terms of Endearment, 1983 (Acad. award 1984, Golden Globe-Best Actress), Cannonball Run II, 1984, Madame Sousatzka, 1988 (Best Actress Venice Film Festival, Golden Globe-Best Actress), Steel Magnolias, 1989, Waiting For the Light, 1990, Postcards From the Edge, 1990, Defending Your Life, 1991, Used People, 1992, Wrestling Ernest Hemingway, 1993, Guarding Tess, 1994, Evening Star, 1995, Mrs. Winterbourne, 1996; (TV shows) Shirley's World, 1971-72, Shirley MacLaine: If They Could See Me Now, 1974-75, Gypsy in My Soul, 1975-76, Where Do We Go From Here?, 1976-77, Shirley MacLaine at the Lido, 1979, Shirley MacLaine...Every Little Movement, 1980 (Emmy award 1980), (TV movie) Out On A Limb, 1987; prodr., co-dir. documentary: China The Other Half of the Sky; star U.S. tour stage musical Out There Tonight, 1990; author: Don't Fall Off the Mountain, 1970, The New Celebrity Cookbook, 1973, You Can Get There From Here, 1975, Out on a Limb, 1983, Dancing in the Light, 1985, It's All in the Playing, 1987, Going Within: A Guide for Inner Transformation, 1989, Dance While You Can, 1991; editor: McGovern: The Man and His Beliefs, 1972. Office: MacLaine Enterprises Inc 25200 Malibu Rd Ste 101 Santa Monica CA 90265*

MAC LAM, HELEN, periodical editor; b. N.Y.C., Aug. 17, 1933; d. Forrest Mearl and Bertha Margaret (Herzberger) Keen; m. David Carlyle MacLam, Feb. 7, 1953; children: Timothy David, David Andrew. AB Sociology, Heidelberg Coll., 1961; AMLS, U. Mich., 1967; MA African Am. Studies, Boston U., 1978. Dep. clerk Mcpl. Ct., Tiffin, Ohio, 1962-64; subprofessional asst. Heidelberg Coll. Libr., Tiffin, Ohio, 1964-66; collection devel. libr. social scis. Dartmouth Coll. Libr., Hanover, N.H., 1967-83; social scis. editor Choice Mag., Middletown, Conn., 1983—; cons. in field; spkr. in field. Editorial bd. Multicultural Review, 1992-95; contbr. articles to profl. jours. Bd. dirs. Headrest, 1976-80, Hanover Consumer Coop. Soc., 1969-72. Recipient Grant award Rsch. Program for Ethnic Studies Librarianship Fisk U., 1975. Mem. Nat. Assn. Ethnic Studies (pres. 1985-87, assoc. editor publs. 1980-83), African Studies Assn., Africana Libs. Coun. (exec. bd. 1989-91), Am. Soc. Indexers, Freelance Editorial Assn., Women in Scholarly Publishing, Assn. Coll. and Rsch. Librs. (New England chpt.). Home: 185 Upper Loveland Rd Norwich VT 05055-9724 Office: Choice Mag 100 Riverview Ctr Middletown CT 06457-3401

MACLANE, SAUNDERS, mathematician, educator; b. Taftville, Conn., Aug. 4, 1909; s. Donald Bradford and Winifred (Saunders) MacL.; m. Dorothy M. Jones, July 21, 1933 (dec. Feb. 1985); children: Margaret Ferguson, Cynthia M. Hay; m. Osa Skotting Segal, Aug. 16, 1986. PhB, Yale U., 1930; AM, U. Chgo., 1931; DPhil, Goettingen, Fed. Republic Germany, 1934; DSc (hon.), Purdue U., 1965, Yale U., 1969, Coe Coll., 1973, U. Pa., 1977, Union Coll., 1990; LLD (hon.), Glasgow U., Scotland, 1971. Sterling Research fellow Yale U., 1933-34; Benjamin Peirce instr. Harvard U., 1934-36; instr. Cornell U., 1936-37, U. Chgo., 1937-38; asst. prof. Harvard U., 1938-41, assoc. prof., 1941-46, prof., 1946-47; prof. math. U. Chgo., 1947-63, chmn. dept., 1952-58, Max Mason Disting. Service prof. of math., 1963-82, prof. emeritus, 1982—; exec. com. mem. Internat. Math. Union, 1954-58; research mathematician Applied Math. Group, Columbia, 1943-44, dir., 1944-45; Mem. Nat. Sci. Bd., 1974-80. Author: (with Garrett Birkhoff) Survey of Modern Algebra, 1942, Homology, 1963, Algebra, 1967, Categories for the Working Mathematician, 1971, Mathematics: Form and Function, 1985, (with I. Moerdijk) Sheaves in Geometry and Logic, A First Introduction to Topos Theory, 1992; editor: Bull. Am. Math. Soc., 1943-46, mng. editor, 1946-47; editor: Trans. Am. Math. Soc., 1949-54; chmn. editorial com., editor Carus Math. Monographs, 1940-45; contbr. articles to Annals Math., other jours. Recipient Nat. Medal of Sci. Nat. Sci. Found., 1989; John Simon Guggenheim fellow, 1947-48, 72-73. Mem. Am. Math. Soc. (coun. mem. 1939-41, v.p. 1946-47, pres. 1973-74, Leroy P. Steele prize 1986), Math. Assn. Am. (v.p. 1948-49, pres. 1950-52, Chauvenet prize for math. expn. 1941, Disting. Svc. award 1975, Proctor prize 1979), Nat. Acad. Sci. (coun. mem. 1958-61, 69-72, v.p. 1973-81, chmn. editorial bd. procs. 1960-68), Royal Danish Acad. Scis. (fgn. mem.), Am. Philos. Soc. (mem. council 1960-63, v.p. 1968-71), Akademie der Wissenschaften (Heidelberg), Royal Soc. Edinburgh, Assn. for Symbolic Logic (exec. com. 1945-47), Am. Acad. Arts and Sci. (coun. mem. 1981-85), Phi Beta Kappa, Sigma Xi. Congregationalist. Home: 5712 S Dorchester Ave Chicago IL 60637-1727

MAC LAREN, DAVID SERGEANT, manufacturing corporation executive, inventor; b. Cleve., Jan. 4, 1941; s. Albert Sergeant and Theadora Beidler (Potter) MacL.; children: Alison, Catherine, Carolyn. AB in Econs., Miami U., Oxford, Ohio, 1964. Chmn. bd., pres., Jet Inc., Cleve., 1967—; founder, chmn. bd., pres. Air Injector Corp., Cleve., 1966-78; founder, pres., chmn. bd. Fluid Equipment, Inc., Cleve., 1966-72; founder, chmn. bd., pres. T&M Co., Cleve., 1966-71, Alison Realty Co., Cleve., 1966—; chmn. bd., pres. Sergeant Realty, Inc., 1979-86; bd. dirs. Gilmore Industries, Cleve., 1975-77, MWL Systems, L.A., 1979-85; mem. tech. com. Nat. Sanitation Found., Ann Arbor, Mich., 1967-90. Patentee in field. Mem. Rep. State Cen. Com., 1968-72; bd. dirs. Cleve. State U. Found., 1986-90. Served with arty. AUS, 1964-66. Fellow Royal Soc. Health (London); mem. Nat. Environ. Health Assn., Am. Pub. Health Assn., Nat. Water Pollution Control Fedn., Cen. Taekwondo Assn. (2d Dan), Jiu-Jitsu/Karati Black Belt Fedn. (black belt instr.), Mercedes Benz Club N.Am. (pres. 1968), H.B. Leadership Soc. (sch. headmaster soc., devel. com. 1976-78), SAR, Soc. Mayflower Descendants, Delta Kappa Epsilon (nat. bd. dirs. 1974-86, dir. Kappa chpt. 1969—), Mentor Harbor Yachting Club, The Country Club, Cotillion Soc., Union League Club (N.Y.C.), Yale Club (N.Y.C.), Deke Club (N.Y.C.), N.Y. Acad. Scis. Home: West Hill Dr Gates Mills OH 44040 Office: Jet Inc 750 Alpha Dr Cleveland OH 44143-2125

MACLAREN, NOEL KEITH, pathologist, pediatrician, educator; naturalized U.S. citizen, 1986; MD, U. Otago. Resident Cook Hosp., Gisborne; resident Wellington (New Zealand) Hosp., from sr. resident to sr. registrar medicine and pediatrics, 1965-68; resident med. officer Queen Elizabeth Hosp. for Sick Children, London, 1969; cons. in pediatrics and internal medicine Gulf Oil Co., Kuwait, 1970-72; fellow in pediatric endocrinology and metabolism U. Md. Sch. Medicine and John's Hopkins Hosp., Balt., 1972-73; asst. prof. pediatric endocrinology and metabolism U. Md. Sch. Medicine, 1973-74, assoc. prof. pediatrics, dir. endocrinology and metabolism, 1975-78; dir. clin. chemistry Shands Tchg. Hosp., Gainesville, Fla., 1978-86; prof. pathology and pediatrics U. Fla. Coll. Medicine, Gainesville, 1978—, chmn. dept. pathology, 1988—; prof. comparative and experimental pathology U. Fla. Coll. Vet. Medicine, Gainesville, 1990—. Mem. editl. bd. Diabetes Care, 1986-89, Regional Immunology, 1987—, Autoimmunology, 1987—; reviewer numerous jours.; patentee in field; contbr. over 300 articles to jours. and books in field. Mem. med. adv. bd. Juvenile Diabetes Found., 1977-80, 95—; mem. sci. adv. bd. Nat. Coalition on Immune System Disorders, 1986—; mem. immunobiology study sect. NIH, 1988—; mem. Internat. Diabetes Found., 1989—; pres. Internat. Diabetes Immunotherapy Group, 1990-94. Recipient Mary Jane Kugel award for Diabetes Rsch., Juvenile Diabetes Assn., 1990, David Rumbaugh award, 1995, Connaught Novo Nordisk award Internat. Canadian Diabetes Assn., 1994, Rsch. Recognition award Am. Diabetes Assn., 1995. Mem. AMA, AAAS, Am. Acad. Pediatrics, Am. Diabetes Assn. (mem. sci. adv. bd. 1986-89), Am. Endocrine Soc., Am. Pediatric Soc., Am. Soc. Clin. Pathologists, Am. Soc. Histocompatibility and Immunogenetics, Am. Soc. Pathology, Internat. Assn. Pathologists, Acad. Clin. Lab. Physicians and Scientists, Assn. Pathology Chairs, Clin. Immunology Soc., Lawson Wilkins Pediatric Endocrine Soc., Soc. Pediatric Rsch., Alpha Omega Alpha Med. Soc.

MACLAREN, ROY, Canadian government official, publisher; b. Vancouver, B.C., Can., Oct. 26, 1934; s. Wilbur and Anne (Graham) MacL.; m. Alethea Mitchell, June 25, 1959; children: Ian, Vanessa, Malcolm. BA, U. B.C., 1955; MA, U. Cambridge, Eng., 1957; postgrad., Harvard U., 1974; MDiv, U. Toronto, 1991. Fgn. service officer Can. Diplomatic Service, Vietnam, Czechoslovakia, Switzerland, UN, 1957-69; dir. corporate pub. affairs Massey-Ferguson Ltd., Toronto, Ont., 1969-74; chmn., chief exec. officer Ogilvy & Mather, Can., Toronto, 1974-76; chmn. C.B. Media Ltd., 1976-93; mem. Toronto Planning Bd., 1974-76; mem. Parliament of Can., 1979-84, 88—, parliamentary sec. to minister energy, mines and resources, 1980-82, minister of state (fin.), 1983-84, minister of nat. revenue, 1984—, minister of internat. trade, 1993—; spl. lectr. U. Toronto, 1970-76; chmn. Can. Govt. Task Force on Rels. Between Govt. and Bus., 1976. Author: Canadians in Russia, 1918-19, 1976, Canadians on the Nile, 1882-1898, 1978, Canadians Behind Enemy Lines, 1939-1945, 1981, Honourable Mentions, 1986; contbr. articles to jours. Hon. col. 7th Toronto Regt., Royal Can. Arty. Fellow Royal Soc. Arts. Clubs: Royal Can. Yacht, Rideau. Office: House of Commons, Ottawa, ON Canada K1A 0A6

MACLAREN, WILLIAM GEORGE, JR., engineering executive; b. Chgo., May 6, 1928; s. William George Sr. and Dorothy Pauline (Costello) MacL.; m. Marie Lorraine Logan, Sept. 15, 1951 (div. Dec. 1977); children: Vanessa Ann MacLaren-Wray, Jon Mark, Scott William; m. Mary Patricia Loftus, Dec. 22, 1977 (div. Oct. 1995). BS in Indsl. Engring., U. Pitts., 1951; MS in Indsl. Engring., Syracuse U., 1958; PhD in Indsl. Mgmt., Columbia Pacific U., 1989. Commd. 2nd lt. USAF, 1951, advanced through grades to major gen., 1974; comdr. 5BW Minot AFB, N.D., 1972-74; chief of staff, 1975; comdr. Pacific Comm. Area, 1975-78; vice comdr. Air Force Comm. Command, 1978-79; dir. Command Control and Comm. Hdqs. USAF, 1979-81; dir. Comm. and Info. Sys. NATO, 1981-84; ret. USAF, 1984; v.p. Gia, Inc., Arlington, Va., 1984-90, 93—; dir. gen. NATO/NATO Air Command and Control Mgmt. Agy., Brussels, 1990-93. Contbr. articles to profl. jours. Regional bd. dirs. Boy Scout Am., Minot, N.D., 1972-74. Named Disting. Engring. Alumnus U. Pitts., 1986. Mem. AIAA, Inst. Indsl. Engrs., Air Force Assn., Armed Forces Comm. and Electronics Assn. (regional v.p. 1975-78, Gold medal 1983), Am. Def. Preparedness Assn., Order of Daedalians (chpt. pres. 1976-78, merit award 1979), Rotary. Republican. Avocations: golf, long distance bicycling, private flying. Home: 438 N Park Dr Arlington VA 22203-2344 Office: GIA Inc 1800 Diagonal Rd Ste 510 Alexandria VA 22314

MACLAUCHLIN, ROBERT KERWIN, communications artist, educator; b. Framingham, Mass., Oct. 8, 1931; s. Charles Lewis and Elinor Frances (Kerwin) MacL.; m. Elizabeth D'Ann Willson, June 13, 1964. BA in Sociology, U. Mass., Amherst, 1954; MEd, Bridgewater State Coll., 1958; MS in Radio and TV, Syracuse U., 1959; PhD in Speech, Radio, TV, Mich. State U., 1969. Personnel trainee Nat. Security Agy., Washington, 1954-55; elem. sch. tchr. Mattapoisett (Mass.) Pub. Schs., 1957-58; asst. prof., dir. programming Maine Ednl. TV Network, Orono, 1959-66; assoc. prof. speech communications, dir. TV-Radio instrn. Colo. State U., Ft. Collins, 1969-76, prof., dir. TV-Radio instrn., 1976—; cons. U. Maine, Orono, 1968, Ft. Collins Presbyn. Ch., 1976-78, Sta. KCOL-AM-FM, Ft. Collins, 1978, Pub. Health Assn., Ft. Collins, 1985; archives program guest Maine Pub. Broadcast, Orono, 1983. Served with inf. U.S. Army, 1955-57. Recipient Excellence in Teaching award Mich. State U., 1969, Friend of Broadcasting award Colo. Broadcasters Assn., 1985; named Disting. Vis. Prof. U. Vt., Burlington, 1983, A Teacher Who Makes A Difference Denver's Rocky Mountain News, KCNC-TV, 1987. Mem. NATA (panel Colo. chpt. 1989—), Broadcast Edn. Assn. (Industry State chmn. 1981-86, panel 1991—, chmn. faculty internship com. 1991—), Colo. Broadcasters Assn. (edn. com. 1972—, Hall of Fame com. 1980—, human resources com. 1991, Friends of Broadcast award 1985, panelist summer conv. 1994, panelist summer conv. 1995), Speech Comm. Assn., Kiwanis (Disting. past pres. 1979-80). Republican. Avocations: outdoor activities. Home: 1407 Country Club Rd Fort Collins CO 80524-1907 Office: Colo State U Dept Speech Communicat Fort Collins CO 80523 *Personal philosophy: Set high goals, enjoy people and laughter, and always seek to give back more to society than you take from it.*

MACLAUGHLIN, FRANCIS JOSEPH, lawyer; b. Davenport, Iowa, Oct. 5, 1933; s. Francis Joseph and Sylvia (Boone) MacL.; m. Joan Elizabeth Pfeiffer, Oct. 17, 1959; children: Lisa Ann, Christine Ann, Francis Joseph. B.A., Yale U., 1955; J.D., U. Mich., 1958. Bar: Ill. 1958, Calif. 1963. Assoc. Graham, Califf, Harper & Benson, Moline, Ill., 1958-59, Lillick, McHose & Charles, Los Angeles, 1963-70; ptnr. Lillick, McHose & Charles, L.A., 1970-90, White and Case, 1990—. Lt. USN, 1959-63. Mem. ABA, Calif. Bar Assn., Los Angeles County Bar Assn., Maritime Law Assn. U.S. Republican. Office: White & Case 633 W 5th St Ste 1900 Los Angeles CA 90071-2017

MACLAUGHLIN, HARRY HUNTER, federal judge; b. Breckenridge, Minn., Aug. 9, 1927; s. Harry Hunter and Grace (Swank) MacL.; m. Mary Jean Shaffer, June 25, 1958; children: David, Douglas. BBA with distinction, U. Minn., 1949, JD, 1956. Bar: Minn. 1956. Law clk. to justice Minn. Supreme Ct.; ptnr. MacLaughlin & Mondale, MacLaughlin & Harstad, Mpls., 1956-72; assoc. justice Minn. Supreme Ct., 1972-77; U.S. sr. dist. judge Dist. of Minn., Mpls., 1977—; part-time instr. William Mitchell Coll. Law, St. Paul, 1958-63; lectr. U. Minn. Law Sch., 1973-86; mem. 8th Cir. Jud. Council, 1981-83. Bd. editors: Minn. Law Rev, 1954-55. Mem. Mpls. Charter Commn., 1967-72, Minn. State Coll. Bd., 1971-72, Minn. Jud. Council, 1972; mem. nat. adv. council Small Bus. Adminstrn., 1967-69. Served with USNR, 1945-46. Recipient U. Minn. Outstanding Achievement award, 1995. Mem. ABA, Minn. Bar Assn., Hennepin County Bar Assn., Beta Gamma Sigma, Phi Delta Phi. Congregational. Office: US Dist Ct 684 US Courthouse 110 S 4th St Minneapolis MN 55401-2221

MACLAURY, BRUCE KING, research institution executive; b. Mount Kisco, N.Y., May 7, 1931; s. Bruce King and Edith Mae (Wills) MacL.; m. Virginia Doris Naef, Jan. 8, 1955; children—John, David. B.A., Princeton, 1953; M.A., Harvard, 1958, Ph.D., 1961. Successively mgr., v.p. fgn. dept. Fed. Res. Bank N.Y., N.Y.C., 1958-69; dep. under sec. for monetary affairs U.S. Treasury Dept., Washington, 1969-71; pres. Fed. Res. Bank of Mpls., 1971-77, Brookings Instn., Washington, 1977-95; pres. emeritus Brookings Instn., Wahsington, 1995—; bd. dirs. Am. Express Bank Ltd., St. Paul Cos., The Vanguard Group. Trustee Nat. Com. on Econ. Edn., 1978—, Com. for Econ. Devel., 1978—; mem. Coun. on Fgn. Rels., N.Y.C., 1962. Lt. AUS, 1954-56. Recipient Exceptional Service award U.S. Treasury Dept., 1971. Mem. Phi Beta Kappa, Cosmos. Home: 5109 Yuma Pl NW Washington DC 20016-4309 Office: Brookings Instn 1775 Massachusetts Ave NW Washington DC 20036-2188

MACLAY, DONALD MERLE, lawyer; b. Belleville, Pa., Feb. 16, 1934; s. Robert Barr and Grace Virginia (Royer) M.; m. Nancy Margaret Hixenbaugh, Sept. 13, 1958; children: Susan Jo (dec.), Timothy Dean. A.B. magna cum laude, Grove City Coll., 1956; LL.B., U. Pa., 1961. Bar: D.C. 1968, Pa. 1970. Commd. fgn. svc. officer U.S. Dept. State, 1961; assigned Am. embassy, Cotonou, Dahomey (Benin), 1962-64, Am. Consulate Gen., Frankfurt, Fed. Republic Germany, 1964-66, U.S. Dept. State, Washington, 1966-69; dir. courses of study Am. Law Inst.-ABA Com. on Continuing Profl. Edn., Phila., 1969-87, dep. exec. dir., 1987—. Served with U.S. Army, 1956-58. Mem. ABA, Pa. Bar Assn., Am. Law Inst. Democrat. Presbyterian. Home: 936 Church Rd Springfield PA 19064-3935 Office: 4025 Chestnut St Philadelphia PA 19104-3099

MACLAY, WILLIAM NEVIN, retired manufacturing and construction company executive; b. Belleville, Pa., Dec. 30, 1924; s. Robert Barr and Grace Virginia (Royer) M.; m. Betty Jane Boucher, June 4, 1949; children: Gary, Dennis, Rebekah, Bonnie, Beth. B.S. magna cum laude, Juniata Coll., 1947; Ph.D. in Phys. Chemistry, Yale U., 1950. Assoc. prof. chemistry Davis and Elkins Coll., Elkins, W.Va., 1950-51; research scientist B.F. Goodrich Co., Brecksville, Ohio, 1951-59; group mgr. Koppers Co., Inc., Monroeville, Pa., 1959-63, asst. sect. mgr., 1963-67; mgr. comml. devel. Koppers Co., Inc., Pitts., 1967-68; v.p. research Koppers Co., Inc., Monroeville, 1968-85; ret., 1985; dir. Indsl. Health Found., Pitts., 1974-77, Genex Corp., Rockville, Md., 1979-81, Kopvenco, Pitts., Ceramatec, Inc., Salt Lake City, 1981-85, Advanced Refractory Techs., Buffalo, 1984-85. Patentee in field. Deacon, ruling elder Presbyn. Ch., Pitts. Mem. Am. Chem. Soc. Republican. Presbyterian. Home: 539 Greenleaf Dr Monroeville PA 15146-1201

MACLEAN, BARRY L., plastic and metal products company executive; b. Evanston, Ill., Apr. 18, 1938; s. John A. Jr. and Dorothy Jean (Barker) MacL; m. Maude Callender, Aug. 29, 1959 (div. Aug. 1966); children: Elizabeth, Margaret; m. Mary Ann Shirley, Sept. 13, 1967; children: Duncan, Gillian, Adrian. BS, Dartmouth Coll., 1960, MS in Engring., 1961. Sec. MacLean-Fogg Co., Mundelein, Ill., 1961-72, pres., chief exec. officer, 1972—, also bd. dirs.; bd. dirs. Western Industries, Inc., Specialty Equipment, L.R. Nelson. Trustee Village of Mettawa, 1971—, Condell Meml. Hosp., Libertyville, Ill., 1973-82, Darmouth Coll.; bd. dirs., past pres. N.E. Ill. coun. Boy Scouts Am., 1973—; bd. overseers, former chmn. Thayer Sch. Engring., Dartmouth Coll., 1974—; chmn., former campaign mgr. Lake County Citizens for Jim Thompson Campaign, 1976; bd. dirs., officer Lake County Rep. Fedn., 1982—; com. chmn. Ill. Job Tng. Coun., 1989—; mem. Young Pres.'s Orgn., 1974-88, chmn. Chgo. chpt., 1987-88. Recipient Good Scout award Boy Scouts Am., 1986, Robert Fletcher award Thayer Sch., Dartmouth Coll., 1989. Mem. Indsl. Fasteners Inst. (bd. dirs. 1982—, chmn. 1988-89), Chief Execs. Orgn., Ill. Mfrs. Assn. (bd. dirs. 1977—, vice chmn. 1988-89, chmn. 1990—, chmn. mfrs. polit. action com. 1985-88, vice chmn. 1989—), Shoreacres Club (Lake Bluff, Ill.), Economic Club, Chicago Club, Onwentsia Club (Lake Forest, Ill.), Loblolly Pines Club (Hobe Sound, Fla.). Avocations: skiing, golf, construction, rare book and map collecting. Home: 15330 W Old School Rd Libertyville IL 60048-9661 Office: MacLean-Fogg Co 1000 Allanson Rd Mundelein IL 60060-3804*

MACLEAN, CHARLES (BERNARD MACLEAN), innovation team building organization consultant; b. Ann Arbor, Mich., Oct. 12, 1945. BS, Wis. State U., Oshkosh, 1967; MA, Mich. State U., 1969, PhD, 1973. Lic. profl. counselor, Tex. Dir. med. edn. Am. Coll. Emergency Physicians, Lansing, Mich. and Dallas, 1974-81; exec. dir. Soc. Tchrs. of Emergency Medicine, Lansing and Dallas, 1976-81; pres. Applied Foresight, Dallas, Tex., 1979—; ptnr. Inman, Maclean & Gaddy, Dallas, 1983-86; sr. v.p. Club Communities Retirement Ctrs., 1985-86; ptnr., exec. v.p. Metropolition Retirement Ctrs., 1986-88; pres. Tri-East Ventures, Inc., 1988-90. Author: (exec. briefing tapes) M.B.A.-Management by Acknowledgement, Acknowledgement-The Missing Piece in the Total Quality Puzzle, (video tng. package) Can't Happen...Here!, 1994, Workplace Violence, 1994, dir. (video documentary) Accelerated Career Transition for Ex-Military, 10 Virtual Commandments for Innovation; contbr. numerous articles to profl. jours. Chmn. community adv. bd. Youth at Risk, 1988-90; mem. Dallas Mayor's Adv. Com. on Crime, 1989-90. Mem. ASTD (v.p. profl. devel. 1982), Assn. for Quality Participation, Nat. Eagle Scout Assn., Oreg. Ethics Commons, An Electronics Assn. Innovation Now! Conf. Task Force, Delta Kappa, Psi Chi, Delta Tau Kappa, Delta Sigma Phi. Office: PO Box 14914 Portland OR 97293-0914

MACLEAN, DAVID BAILEY, chemistry educator, researcher; b. Summerside, P.E.I., Can., July 15, 1923; s. William and Lulu Adelaide (Stewart) McL.; m. Helen Shirley Canning, Dec. 28, 1945 (dec. 1950); 1 child, Susan; m. Regina Lane, Sept. 21, 1951; children—David, Richard, Robert, Gillian, stepchildren—Gary Hutton, Dariel Hutton. B.Sc., Acadia U., 1942; Ph.D., McGill U., 1946. Research chemist Dominion Rubber Co., Guelph, Ont., Can., 1946-49; assoc. prof. chemistry N.S. Tech. Coll., Halifax, Can., 1949-54; assoc. prof. chemistry McMaster U., Hamilton, Ont., 1954-60, prof., 1960-89, prof. emeritus, 1989—; mem. Council of Ont. Univs., Toronto, 1982-84. Fellow Royal Soc. Can., Chem. Inst. Can.; mem. Am. Chem. Soc.,

Am. Soc. Mass Spectroscopy. Home: 394 Queen St S, Hamilton, ON Canada L8P 3T9 Office: McMaster Univ, Dept Chemistry, Main St W, Hamilton, ON Canada L8S 4M1

MACLEAN, DOUG, hockey coach; b. Summerside, P.E.I., Can., Apr. 12, 1954. Student, P.E.I.; M in Ednl. Psychology, We. Ont. Asst. coach London Knights of OHL, 1984-85, St. Louis Blues, 1986-87, 87-88, Washington Capitals, 1988-89, 89-90; asst. coach Detroit Red Wings, 1990-91, asst. gen. mgr., 1992-93, 93-94; gen. mgr. Adirondack, Red Wing orgn., 1992-93, 93-94; dir. player devel., scout Fla. Panthers, 1994-95. Office: Florida Panthers 100 North East Third St 10th Fl Fort Lauderdale FL 33301*

MACLEAN, GUY ROBERTSON, retired university president; b. Sydney, N.S., Can., Dec. 21, 1929; s. Charles Whitmore and Mary Malinda (Nicholson) MacL.; m. Mary Judith Hunter, June 29, 1963; children—Colin Hunter, Mary Jocelyn. B.A., Dalhousie U., 1951, M.A., 1953; B.A. (Rhodes scholar), Oxford U., 1955, M.A., 1959; Ph.D., Duke, 1958. Asst. prof. Dalhousie U., Halifax, N.S., 1957-61, asso. prof., 1961-65, prof., 1965-80, dean of residence, 1961-63, acting chmn. dept. history, 1963-64, asst. dean faculty grad. studies, 1965-66, dean, 1966-69, dean faculty arts and scis., 1969-75, v.p. academic, 1974-80; pres. Mount Allison U., Sackville, N.S., 1980-86, pres. emeritus, 1986—; ombudsman of N.S., 1989-94; dean of men Kings Coll., 1957-61; lectr. U. Alta., 1963, N.S. Tech. Coll., 1965-66. Editor: introduction The Life and Times of A.T. Galt, 1966; Contbr. articles to profl. jours. Mem. Rhodes Scholarship Com., N.S.; mem. Maritime Provinces Higher Edn. Commn., Social Scis. and Humanities Research Council Can., 1978—; bd. dirs. Donner Canadian Found., Toronto; bd. govs. Coll. of Cape Breton; chmn. bd. dirs. Opera East. Served as 2d lt. Canadian Army, 1949-51. Recipient Centennial medal, 1967, Jubilee medal, 1978; Can. Council fellow, 1968-69. Mem. Canadian Hist. Assn. (exec. council 1967-68), Canadian Inst. Internat. Affairs (pres. Halifax 1965), Canadian Rhodes Scholar Assn., Nova Scotia Soccer Assn. (pres. 1976-78). Mem. United Ch. of Can. Club: Waegwoltic.

MACLEAN, JOHN ANGUS, former premier of Prince Edward Island; b. Lewes, P.E.I., Can., May 15, 1914; s. George Allen and Sarah MacL.; m. Gwendolyn Esther Burwash, Oct. 29, 1952; children—Sarah Jean, Allan Duart, Mary Esther, Robert Angus. Student, U. B.C., Can.), Vancouver; B.Sc., Mt. Allison U., 1939, LL.D. (hon.), 1958. Farmer Lewes; mem. Can. House of Commons, Ottawa, Ont., 1951-76, Privy Council Can., 1957—; minister of fisheries Govt. Can., 1957-63; mem. P.E.I. Legislature, 1976-82; premier P.E.I., 1979-81. Leader Progressive Conservative Party of P.E.I., 1976-81; del. NATO Parliamentary Conf., Paris, 1956, Commonwealth Parliametary Conf., Wellington, N.Z., 1965, 18th Parliametary Course, Westminster, Eng., 1969; del. Inter-Parliamentary Conf. on European Cooperation and Security, Helsinki, 1973, Belgrade, 1975; leader Can. del. Colombo Plan Conf., Tokyo, 1960, FAO Conf., Rome, 1961; mem. Can.-Japanese Ministerial Del., Tokyo, 1963; bd. regents Mt. Alison U.; bd. dirs. RCAF Meml. Fund. Served with RCAF, 1939-47; officer Most Venerable Order St. John of Jerusalem at Investiture Ceremony, Rideau Hall, Order of Can. Investiture, Rideau Hall, 1992; former mem. P.E.I. Energy Corp.; sr. adv. bd. Maritime Provinces Edn. Found.; P.E.I.'s Commr. to EXPO' 86; appointed officer of the Order of Can., 1992. Decorated D.F.C.; mentioned in Despatches. Mem. RAF Escaping Soc. (past pres. Can. br.), Commonwealth Parliamentary Assn. (past vice chmn. fed. br.), Mus. Nat. Scis., Nat. Mus. Can. Progressive Conservative. Presbyterian.

MACLEAN, JOHN RONALD, lawyer; b. Pueblo, Colo., Jan. 19, 1938; s. John Ronald and Mary Victoria (Curlin) MacL.; m. Carol Jean Turner, Aug. 18, 1962; children—Leslie Carol, John Ronald. Student, U. Okla., 1956; B.S., U.S. Mil. Acad., 1961; J.D., Vanderbilt U., 1967. Bar: Tex. 1967; cert. in personal injury trial law and criminal law Tex. Bd. Legal Splzn. Practicing atty. Turner & MacLean, Cleburne, Tex., 1967-68; county atty. Johnson County, Tex., 1968-76; dist. atty. 18th Jud. Dist. Tex., 1976-84; dist. judge 249th Jud. Dist. Tex., 1984-91; pvt. practice MacLean & Boulware, 1992—. Pres. Johnson County United Fund, 1976. Served with AUS, 1961-64. Fellow Tex. Bar Found.; mem. Tex. Bar Assn., Johnson County Bar Assn. (pres. 1969), Am. Bd. Trial Advocates (nat. dir.), Tex. Trial Lawyers Assn., Vanderbilt U. Law Sch. Bar Assn. (past pres.), Elks. Democrat. Methodist. Home: 1216 W Westhill Dr Cleburne TX 76031-6021 Office: 11 N Main St Cleburne TX 76031-5543

MAC LEAN, LLOYD DOUGLAS, surgeon; b. Calgary, Alta., Can., June 24, 1924; s. Fred Hugh and Azilda (Trudel) MacL.; m. Eleanor Colle, June 30, 1954; children—Hugh, Charles, Ian, James, Martha. B.Sc. (Viscount Bennett scholar), U. Alta., 1947, M.D. (Viscount Bennett scholar), 1949; Ph.D., U. Minn., 1957. Resident U. Minn. Hosp., Mpls., 1950-56; instr. dept. surgery U. Minn., Mpls., 1956-58, asst. prof. surgery, 1958-59, asso. prof., 1959-62; prof. McGill U., Montreal, Que., Can., 1962—, chmn. dept. surgery, 1968-73, 77-82, 87-88; surgeon-in-chief Ancker Hosp., St. Paul, 1957-62, Royal Victoria Hosp., Montreal, 1962-88; Edward Archibald prof. surgery McGill U., 1988-93, prof. surgery 1993—. Contbr. numerous articles on surgery, shock, host resistance and transplantation to profl. jours. Decorated officer Order Can. Fellow Royal Soc. Can.; mem. Am. Surg. Assn. (pres. 1992-93), A.C.S. (pres. 1993-94), Central Surg. Assn. (pres. 1985), Am. Physiol. Soc., Am. Assn. Thoracic and Cardiovascular Surgery, Soc. Surgery of Alimentary Tract. Home: # 1402-80 Berlioz, Montreal, PQ Canada H3E 1N9 Office: McGill Univ, 687 Pine Ave W, Montreal, PQ Canada H3A 1A1

MACLEAN, PAUL DONALD, government institute medical research official; b. Phelps, N.Y., May 1, 1913; s. Charles Chalmers and Elizabeth (Dreyfus) MacL.; m. Alison Stokes, July 16, 1942; children—Paul, David, Alexander, James, Alison. BA, Yale U., 1935; postgrad., U. Edinburgh, Scotland, 1935-36; MD cum laude, Yale U., 1940; DSci (hon.), SUNY, Binghamton, 1986. Intern in medicine Johns Hopkins U., 1940-41; asst. resident medicine New Haven Hosp., Yale Sch. Medicine, 1941-42, research asst. pathology, 1942, asst. prof. physiology, 1949-51, asst. prof. psychiatry, physiology and neurology, 1951-53, assoc. prof. physiology, 1956-57; clin. instr. medicine U. Wash. Med. Sch., Seattle, 1946-47; USPHS research fellow Harvard U. Med. Sch., also Mass. Gen. Hosp., 1947-49; dir. EEG lab. New Haven Hosp., 1951-52; assoc. prof. psychiatry, physiology and neurology, attending physician Grace-New Haven Hosp., 1953-56; sr. postdoctoral fellow NSF dept. physiology U. Zurich, 1956-57; chief sect. limbic integration and behavior Lab. Neurophysiology Intramural Research, NIMH, USPHS, Dept. Health and Human Services, Bethesda, Md., 1957-71; chief lab. brain evolution and behavior Intramural Research, Bethesda, Md., 1971-85; sr. research scientist Intramural Research Program, NIMH, 1985—. Author: The Triune Brain in Evolution, 1990; mem. editorial bd.: Jour. Nervous and Mental Disease. Emeritus trustee L.S.B. Leakey Found. Served to maj. M.C. AUS, 1942-46, PTO. Recipient award for disting. research Assn. for Research in Nervous and Mental Disease, 1964; Salmon medal and Lectureship award, 1966; Superior Service award HEW, 1967; Hincks Meml. lectr. Ont.; Spl. award Am. Psychopathol. Assn., 1971; G. Burroughs Mider NIH Lectureship award, 1972; Karl Spencer Lashley award Am. Philos. Soc., 1972; Adolph Meyer Lectureship award Am. Psychiat. Assn., 1982, Anokhin medal P.K. Anokhin Inst. Normal Physiology USSR Acad. Med. Scis., 1986. Mem. Am. Neurol. Assn., Am. Assn. History of Medicine, Am. Physiol. Soc., Am. Assn. Electroencephalographers, Eastern Assn. Electroencephalographers, Am. Assn. Neurol. Surgeons, Soc. Neurosci., Am. Assn. Anatomists, Sigma Xi, Alpha Omega Alpha. Home: 10450 Lottsford Rd Apt 1218 Mitchellville MD 20721-2746 Office: NIMH Neuroscience Ctr 2700 MLK Jr Ave SE Washington DC 20032

MACLEAN, VICTORIA GRAHAM, journalist, editor; b. Brockville, Ont., Can., June 2, 1948; d. Findlay Barnes and Helen Lois (Graham) MacL.; m. Robert E. Knight, Sept. 29, 1973 (div. Jan. 1985). Student, Trent U. Proofreader, adv. salesman, photo engraver, reporter, editor Brockville Recorder and Times, 1964-72; reporter, columnist, mng. editor St. Albert (Alta., Can.) Gazette, 1976-85; editor Edmonton (Alta.) Sun, 1988—. Columnist Can. Comty. Newspapers, 1980. Avocations: gardening, cooking, reading. Home: 8547 80th Ave, Edmonton, AB Canada T6C 0T2 Office: Edmonton Sun, Ste 250, 4990 92d Ave, Edmonton, AB Canada T6B 3A1

MACLEISH, ARCHIBALD BRUCE, museum director; b. White Plains, N.Y., May 6, 1947; s. Kenneth and Carolyn Elizabeth (de Chadenedes) MacL.; m. Patricia Ann McCue, Aug. 10, 1974; children: Kenneth Thomas, Padraic Andrew. BA, Johns Hopkins U., 1969; MA, SUNY, Oneonta, 1972. Asst. curator N.Y. State Hist. Assn., The Farmers' Mus., Cooperstown, 1972-73; assoc. curator N.Y. State Hist. Assn., Cooperstown, 1980-83, curator of collections, 1984-93, dir. collections, 1993—; curator of collections The Farmers' Mus., 1984-93, dir. collections, 1993—; curator The Ky. Mus., Bowling Green, 1973-80; mem. adj. tchg. faculty Cooperstown Grad. Program, 1980—. Author: Care of Antiques and Historical Collections, 1985; editor K.A.M. News, 1975-80. Sec. bd. dirs. Gallery 53, Cooperstown; mem. Ad Hoc Citizen's Com., Cooperstown, 1987—. Mem. Am. Assn. Mus., Am. Assn. for State and Local History, Mid-Atlantic Assn. Mus., Cooperstown Grad. Assn. Democrat. Methodist. Avocations: road running, gardening, guitar, fishing, cross-country skiing. Office: NY State Hist Assn PO Box 800 Lake Rd Cooperstown NY 13326

MACLENNAN, BERYCE WINIFRED, psychologist; b. Aberdeen, Scotland, Mar. 14, 1920; came to U.S., 1949, naturalized, 1965; d. William and Beatrice (MaCrae) Mellis; m. John Duncan MacLennan, Nov. 29, 1944. BSc with honors, London Sch. Econs., 1947; PhD, London U., 1960. Group psychotherapist, youth specialist cons. N.Y.C. and Washington, 1949-63; dir. Ctr. for Prevention Juvenile Delinquency and New Careers, Washington, 1963-66; sect. chief NIMH, Mental Health Study Ctr., Adelphi, Md., 1967-70, chief, 1971-74; regional adminstr. Mass. Dept. Mental Health, Springfield, 1974-75; sr. mental health adv. GAO, Washington, 1976-90; pvt. practice, specialist psychotherapy Bethesda, Md., 1990—; clin. prof. George Washington U., 1970—; group therapy cons. D.C. Mental Health Svcs., 1993—, Washington Assessement and Therapy Svcs., 1992—; lectr. Montgomery C.C., 1988-91; mem. tech. adv. com. Prince George's County Mental Health Assn., 1986-84; cons. Washington Bus. Group on Health, 1990-91, KOBA, 1991. Mem. NIMH Prevention Intervention Rsch. Task Force, 1990-91, Montgomery County Victims Assistance Programs, 1990-95; v.p. Compliance, Federally Employed Women, 1979-81; pres. Glenecho chpt. Older Women's League, 1993-94. Fellow APA, Am. Orthopsychiat. Assn.; disting. fellow Am. Group Psychotherapy Assn.; mem. Bethesda Garden Club, Washington Mushroom Club. Democrat.

MACLENNAN, DAVID HERMAN, research scientist, educator; b. Swan River, Man., Can., July 3, 1937; s. Douglas Henry and Sigridur (Sigurdson) MacL.; m. Linda Carol Vass, Aug. 18, 1965; children: Jessica Lynn (dec.), Jeremy Douglas, Jonathan David. B.S.A., U. Man., 1959; M.S., Purdue U., 1961, Ph.D., 1963. Postdoctoral fellow Inst. Enzyme Research, U. Wis., Madison, 1963-64; asst. prof. U. Wis., Madison, 1964-68; assoc. prof. U. Toronto, Ont., Can., 1969-74, prof., 1974-93; Ont.; John W. Billes prof. med. rsch. U. Toronto, Ont., Can., 1987—; Ont.; univ. prof. U. Toronto, Ont., Can., 1993—, acting chmn., 1978-80, chmn., 1980-90; prin. investigator Can. Genetic Diseases Network of Ctrs. of Excellence, 1991—; mem. med. adv. bd. Muscular Dystrophy Assn. Can., 1976-87; mem. scientists' rev. panel Med. Rsch. Coun., 1988-90; chmn. molecular biology and pathology grants com. Heart and Stroke Found. Can., 1995—; mem. rsch. rev. panel U. Ottawa Heart Inst., 1991—; cons. Merck, Sharp and Dohme, West Point, Pa., 1992—. Assoc. editor Can. Jour. Biochemistry, 1972-76; mem. editorial bd. Jour. Biol. Chemistry, 1975-80, 82-87; contbr. articles on muscle membrane biochemistry to profl. jours. Recipient Gairdner Found. Internat. award, 1991; Can. Med. Rsch. Coun. scholar, 1969-71, I.W. Killam Meml. scholar, 1977-78. Fellow Royal Soc. Can., Royal Soc. London; mem. Can. Biochem. Soc. (Ayerst award 1974), Am. Soc. Biol. Chemists, Biophys. Soc. (Internat. Lectr. award 1990). Home: 293 Lytton Blvd, Toronto, ON Canada M5N 1R7 Office: U Toronto-Banting & Best Med Rsch, 112 College St, Toronto, ON Canada M5G 1L6

MACLEOD, CYNTHIA ANN, national park service official, historian; b. Orange, N.J., Jan. 27, 1954; d. Robert Meredith and Martha Churchill (Shaw) MacL.; m. Douglas James Harnsberger, Oct. 23, 1993; 1 child, Anna Churchill Harnsberger. BA in Zoology, Comparative Lit., Duke U., 1975; M in Archtl. History, U. Va., 1979. Achitectural historian Va. Historic Landmarks Commn., Warrenston, Va., 1978-80; achitectural historian Nat. Park Svc., Omaha, Nebr., 1980-82, Phila., 1982-90; park supt. Nat. Park Svc., Richmond, Va., 1990—. Mem. Soc. Architectural Historians, Jr. League, Rotary Internat. Avocations: gardening, writing, antiques, photography. Office: Nat Park Svc 3215 E Broad St Richmond VA 23223

MACLEOD, DONALD, clergyman, educator; b. Broughton, N.S., Can., Dec. 31, 1914; s. Donald Archibald and Anne (MacKenzie) M.; m. Norma Eliner Harper, Jan. 5, 1948 (dec. Mar. 1972); children: John Fraser, David Ainslie, Anne, Leslie. A.B., Dalhousie U., Halifax, N.S., 1934, M.A., 1935, LL.D., 1978; B.D. (E.F. Grant scholar), Pine Hill Div. Hall, Halifax, 1938, D.D., 1970; Th.D., U. Toronto, 1947. Teaching fellow dept. English Dalhousie U., 1935-38; ordained to ministry Presbyn. Ch., 1938; minister First Ch., Louisburg, N.S., 1938-41; assoc. minister Bloor St. Ch., Toronto, 1941-45; sr. tutor Men's Residences Victoria Coll., Toronto, 1943-45; teaching fellow dept. homiletics Princeton Theol. Sem., 1946-47; asst. prof., 1947-53, assoc. prof., 1953-61, prof., 1961—, Francis L. Patton prof., 1982—; lectr. Princeton Summer Inst. Theology, 1948—; vis. lectr. Westminster Choir Coll., 1952, 55-58; lectr. Gettysburg Sem., 1952, Jr. Pastors Sch., Reading, Pa., 1954, Conf. on Evangelism, Whitby, Ont., 1957, Hampton (Va.) Inst., 1957, Union Sem., Richmond, Va., 1958, Crozier Sem., Chester, Pa., 1961, Ann. Pastors Conf. Am. Luth. Ch., Green Lake, Wis., 1966, Coll. Preachers, Nat. Cathedral Washington, 1967; lectr. continuing edn. Presbyn. Coll., Montreal, 1972-75; Mullins lectr. So. Baptist Theol. Sem., 1970; Kyes' lectr. Kirk in the Hills, Detroit, 1973; Oliver lectr. Nazarene Theol. Sem., 1985; Jameson Jones lectr. Duke U. Sch. Div., 1987; chmn. Synod Com. on Capital Ch., Trenton, N.J.; mem. coms. Christian edn., candidates and credentials, social edn. and action Presbytery New Brunswick; commr. Gen. Assembly United Presbyn. Ch., Oklahoma City, 1965; spl. preacher Princeton, Lehigh, Muhlenberg, Mt. Alison U., Duke U. and Rutgers U. Chapels, Chgo. Sunday Evening Club, Am. Preacher Series Eaton Meml. Ch., Toronto, Chatauqua Evangelist, Riverside Ch., N.Y.C., Fifth Ave. Presbyn Ch., N.Y.C., Nat. Presbyn. Ch., Washington, Preaching Mission McGuire AFB, Chaplains Seminars, USAF, 1967-68; adv. bd. Chapel of Princeton U. Author: Word and Sacrament, 1960, Presbyterian Worship, 1965, 2d edit., 1981, Higher Reaches, 1971, Proclamation, 1975; editor: Here Is My Method, 1952, Princeton Pulpit Prayers, 1987, Know the Way, Keep the Truth, Win the Life, 1987, The Problem of Preaching, 1987, Palms and Thorns, 1990; editor: Princeton Sem. Bull., 1956-82, Translator Dynamics of Worship, 1967; mem. editorial bd. Theology Today, 1948-61, Pulpit Preaching, 1970—, Pulpit Digest, 1980—; Am. corr.: The United Church Observer, 1947-56; N.J. corr.: The Christian Century, 1957-65; ecumenical editor Good News, Sunday Pubs. Inc., 1983—; author bimonthly book column. The Preachers Bookshelf, Monday Morning, 1985—; contbr. Vols. I, IV and VI of Great Sermons and articles profl. publs. Established biennial series: Donald Macleod Lectureship on Preaching, Congl. Ch., Short Hills, N.J., 1989. Fellow Am. Assn. Theol. Schs.; mem. Am. Assn. Theol. Profs. in Practical Fields (exec. com.), Ch. Service Soc. (past v.p.), Clan Macleod Soc. Am. (chaplain), Am. Acad. Homiletics (founder, pres.). Address: Minister in Residence Charlestown Retirement Com 719 Maiden Choice Ln # 238 Baltimore MD 21228-6117 *Too often we interpret the Boy Scouts' slogan "Be Prepared" as a caution against danger or disaster, but its thrust is largely positive. It implies being prepared for every opportunity. Never did I have any particular position in mind, but every door which has opened to me found me ready and equipped for it.*

MACLEOD, GORDON ALBERT, lawyer; b. Buffalo, Mar. 29, 1926; s. Alexander D. and Loraine (Shea) MacL.; m. Lorraine King, July 7, 1951; children: Bruce King, Heather Lea. AB, Hamilton Coll., 1948; LLB, Harvard U., 1951. Bar: N.Y. 1951. Ptnr. Hodgson, Russ Andrews, Woods & Goodyear, Buffalo, 1960-93, of counsel, 1994—; lectr. N.Y. State Bankers Assn., Am. Soc. CLUs. Contbr. articles to profl. jours., other publs.; inventor several internationally marketed games. Trustee Creative Edn. Found., Buffalo. Fellow Am. Coll.. Trust and Estate Counsel; mem. ABA, N.Y. State Bar Assn. (exec. com. trust and estates sect.), Phi Beta Kappa. Avocations: playing drums, backgammon, inventing toys and games, writing. Office: Hodgson Russ Andrews Woods 1800 One M & T Pla Buffalo NY 14203

MACLEOD, GORDON KENNETH, physician, educator; b. Boston, Jan. 30, 1929; s. Gordon Kenneth and Margaret J. MacL.; m. Janet B., Aug. 17, 1957; children—Gordon K. III, Alexander B. A.B., Blackburn Coll., 1954; M.D., U. Cin., 1960. Indsl. engr. Procter & Gamble Co., Cin., 1954-56; intern Boston City Hosp., 1960-61; resident, clin. fellow Mass. Gen. Hosp., Boston, 1961-64; research fellow Harvard U., 1962-64; sr. resident, sr. physician Boston VA hosp., 1964-66; asst. clin. prof. medicine Yale U., 1966-69, assoc. clin. prof. medicine and public health, 1969-71; dir. Health Maintenance Orgn. Service, HEW, 1971-73; prof. dept. health services adminstrn. Grad. Sch. Public Health, U. Pitts., 1974—, chmn. dept., 1974-83; assoc. clin. prof. medicine Grad. Sch. Public Health, U. Pitts. (Sch. Medicine), 1976-86, clin. prof. medicine, 1986—; sec. health, State of Pa., 1979; mem. staff W. Penn Hosp.; mem. nat. adv. coun. divsn. rsch. resources NIH, 1983-87; cons. Shadyside Hosp.; cons. in field. Editor: (with Mark Perlman) Health Care Capital: Competition and Control, 1978; contbr. articles to profl. jours. Served with U.S. Army, 1948-49. Ford Found. travel grantee, 1973. Fellow ACP; mem. Allegheny County Med. Soc., AMA (editorial bd. jour. 1989-94), Am. Pub. Health Assn., Med. Adminstrs. Conf., Group Health Assn. Am., Pa. Pub. Health Assn., Pa. State Med. Soc. (pres.), Pitts. Acad. Medicine. Office: 130 Desoto St Pittsburgh PA 15213-2535 *My first job as an industrial engineer with later training in internal medicine uniquely prepared me for an academic career in health management with intervals as a government executive at federal and state levels. My most challenging assignments were in initiating Health Maintenance Organizations nationally, in managing the health aspects of the nuclear accident at Three Mile Island, and in training young persons for careers in internal medicine and health management.*

MACLEOD, JOHN, college basketball coach; b. New Albany, Ind., Oct. 3, 1937; s. Dan J. and Ann Elizabeth (Welch) MacL.; m. Carol Ann McGroder, Jan. 18, 1974; children: Kathleen, Matthew. BA in History, Bellarmine Coll.; MA in History and Phys. Edn., Ind. State U., 1965. Coach high schs. Ky, Ind.; former coach U. Okla., Norman; head coach Phoenix Suns, NBA, 1973-87, Dallas Mavericks, NBA, 1987-89; former head coach New York Knicks, 1990; now head coach basketball program Notre Dame Univ., South Bend, Ind.; active hon. coach Ariz. Spl. Olympics. Active Soc. for Blind. Served with USAR, 1959-60. Named Coach of Yr. NBA, 1980. Mem. NBA Coaches Assn. (treas.). Office: care U Notre Dame Athletics Dept South Bend IN 46556*

MACLEOD, JOHN AMEND, lawyer; b. Manila, June 5, 1942; s. Anthony Macaulay and Dorothy Lillian (Amend) M.; m. Ann Klee; children: Kerry, Jack. BBA, U. Notre Dame, 1963, JD, 1969. Bar: D.C. 1969, U.S. Supreme Ct. 1980. Assoc. Jones, Day, Reavis & Pogue, D.C., 1969-73; ptnr., 1974-79; ptnr. Crowell & Moring, Washington, 1979—, mem. mgmt. com., 1979-82, 83-86, 91-94, chmn., 1984-85, 93-94. Editor-in-chief Notre Dame Law Review; contbr. articles to profl. jours; editor-in-chief Notre Dame Law Rev., 1968-69. Trustee, mem. exec. com. Eastern Mineral Law Found.; bd. dirs. St. Francis Ctr., 1982-91, C&M Internat. 1991-94. Served to lt. U.S. Army, 1963-65. Recipient Disting. Mining Lawyer award Nat. Mining Assn., 1995. Mem. ABA, D.C. Bar Assn., Notre Dame Law Assn. (dir., exec. bd.), Ptnrs. Leadership Forum, Metropolitan Club (Washington). Home: 4040 Swartz Rd Maurertown VA 22644-9759 Office: Crowell & Moring 1001 Pennsylvania Ave NW Washington DC 20004-2505

MACLEOD, JOHN DANIEL, JR., religious organization administrator; b. Robbins, N.C., Mar. 16, 1922; s. John Daniel Sr. and Sarah Cranor (McKay) MacL.; m. Helen Frances Boggs, Sept. 18, 1945 (dec. Aug. 1990); children: Sarah MacLeod Owens, Mary Marget MacLeod Silberstein, John Daniel III, William Boggs. AB, Davidson (N.C.) Coll., 1942; MDiv, Union Theol. Sem., Richmond, Va., 1945, ThM, 1949, ThD, 1952; DD (hon.), St. Andrews Presbyn. Coll., Laurinburg, N.C., 1992. Ordained to ministry Presbyn. Ch., 1945. Pastor Carolina Beach (N.C.) Presbyn. Ch., 1945-48, Brett-Reed Presbyn. Ch., Sweet Hall, Va., 1949-53, Keyser (W.Va.) Presbyn. Ch., 1953-63; exec. Appomattox Presbytery, Lynchburg, Va., 1963-67, Norfolk (Va.) Presbytery, 1967-76, Westminster Presbytery, St. Petersburg, Fla., 1976-81; exec. Synod of N.C., Raleigh, 1981-88, ret., 1988; interim exec. Coastal Carolina Presbytery, Fayetteville, 1991-93, Holston Presbytery, Kingsport, Tenn., 1993; interim parish assoc. White Meml. Presbyn. Ch., Raleigh, N.C., 1994; interim exec. Western N.C. Presbytery, Morganton, 1995, interim assoc. exec., 1996—; mem., chmn. various local and nat. Presbyn. Ch. Coms. Trustee Warren Wilson Coll., 1985-89, N.C. Presbyn. Hist. Soc., 1981—, Mary Baldwin Coll., 1960-68, Davis and Elkins Coll., 1955-61, Massanetta Springs Conf. Ctr., 1956-62; active Mineral County Redevel. Commn., Keyser, 1960-63; mem. N.C. Gov's. Adv. com. on Citizen Affairs, Raleigh, 1983-84; bd. advisors Wake Forest U. Div. Sch., 1991—. Nominee moderator Presbyn. Ch. USA Gen. Assembly, 1987, moderator Synod of Va., 1969, Synod of Mid-Atlantic, 1990. Fellow Soc. Antiquaries (Scotland); mem. St. Andrews Soc. (Southern Pines, N.C. chpt., bd. dirs. Tampa, Fla. chpt. 1976-81), N.C. Scottish Heritage Soc. (pres. 1992—), Clan MacLeod Soc. (chaplain, bd. dirs. 1994). Democrat. Avocations: genealogy, history, travel. Home: 114 Silver Creek Rd Morganton NC 28655-4205

MACLEOD, ROBERT ANGUS, microbiology educator, researcher; b. Athabasca, Alta., Can., July 13, 1921; s. Norman John and Eleonora Pauline Bertha (Westerhoff) MacL.; m. Patricia Rosemarie Robertson, Sept. 1, 1948; children—Douglas John, Alexander Robert, Kathleen Mary, David Gordon, Michael Norman, Susan Joan. B.A. with honors in Chemistry, U. B.C., Vancouver, Can., 1943, M.A. in Chemistry and Biology, 1945; Ph.D. in Biochemistry, U. Wis., Madison, 1949. Asst. prof. Queen's U., Kingston, Ont., Can., 1949-52; sr. biochemist Fisheries Research Bd. Can., Vancouver, B.C., 1952-60; assoc. prof. to prof., chmn. dept. microbiology Macdonald Coll., McGill U., Ste. Anne de Bellevue, Que., Can., 1960-86, prof. emeritus, 1986—; Cons. Def. Research Bd., Ottawa, Ont., 1965-75; assoc. editor Can. Jour. Microbiology, Ottawa, 1965-70. Author tech. papers. Recipient Harrison prize Royal Soc. Can., 1960; Can. Soc. Microbiologists award, 1973. Fellow Royal Soc. Can.; mem. Can. Soc. Microbiologists (pres. 1976-77, hon. mem. 1993), Am. Soc. Microbiology (hon. mem. 1992). Avocations: swimming, fishing. Home: 448 Greenwood Dr, Beaconsfield, PQ Canada H9W 4Z9 Office: MacDonald Coll, Dept Natural Resource Scis, 21111 Lakeshore Rd, Sainte Anne de Bellevue, PQ Canada H9X 3V9

MACLEOD, ROBERT FREDRIC, editor, publisher; b. Chgo., Oct. 15, 1917; s. Ernest F. and Martha W. (Ruzicka) MacL.; children—Merrill, Robert Fredric, E. Jay, Ian. B.A., Dartmouth Coll., 1939. Advt. mgr. Town & Country mag., N.Y.C., 1949; v.p., pub. Harper's Bazaar, N.Y.C., 1950-55, 55-60; v.p., advt. dir. Hearst Mags., N.Y.C., 1960-62; pub. Seventeen mag., N.Y.C., 1962-63; v.p., dir. mktg. Subscription TV Inc., Santa Monica, Calif., 1963-64; editor, pub. 'Teen Mag., Los Angeles, 1965—, now editorial dir., exec. pub.; sr. v.p. Petersen Pub. Co., L.A., 1976-95; ret., 1995, pub. cons., 1995—. Served to maj. USMC, 1941-46. Named to Football Hall of Fame, 1977. Club: Bel Air Country. Home: 110 Colony Dr Malibu CA 90265

MACLEOD, THOMAS D., feed company executive. V.p. Sara Lee Corp.; pres., chief exec. officer Kitchens of Sara Lee, 1990; pres., chief oper. officer Iams Co., Dayton, Ohio, 1990—. Office: Iams Co 7250 Poe Ave Dayton OH 45414-2572*

MACLEOD, WILLIAM BRIAN, hospital executive; b. Victoria, B.C., Can., June 12, 1951; s. Jacob Eugene and Winnifred Joan (Beecher) M.; m. Lucy Scarbo; children: Magenta Trishan, Collin Wilson, Andrew James. BS, U. Toronto, 1973, DHA, 1979. Comptr. Kootenay Lake Dist. Hosp., Nelson, B.C., Can., 1973-76, 79-80; asst. exec. dir. St. Joseph's Hosp., London, Ont., Can., 1980-85; pres. Peel Meml. Hosp., Brampton, Ont., Can., 1985-90; pres., CEO Women's Coll. Hosp., Toronto, Ont., Can., 1990—; asst. prof. health adminstrn. program U. Toronto. Mem. YMCA, Toronto. Recipient Robert Wood Johnson award, 1978. Mem. Can. Coll. Health Execs., Can. Coll. Health Svcs. Execs. Home: 740 Hurondale Dr, Mississaug, ON Canada M5S 1B2 Office: Womens Coll Hosp, 76 Grenville St, Toronto, ON Canada M5S 1B2

MACLIN, ALAN HALL, lawyer; b. DuQuoin, Ill., Dec. 22, 1949; s. John E. and Nora (Hall) M.; m. Joan Davidson (div. Dec. 1981); children: Molly, Tess, Anne; m. Jeanne Sittlow, Nov. 17, 1984. BA, magna cum laude, Vanderbilt U., 1971; J.D., U. Chgo., 1974. Bar: Minn. 1974, U.S. Dist. Ct.

Minn. 1974, U.S. Ct. Appeals (8th cir.) 1974, U.S. Ct. Appeals (5th cir.) 1975, U.S. Supreme Ct. 1978. Asst. atty. gen. Minn. Atty. Gen., St. Paul, 1974-80; chief anti-trust div. Briggs & Morgan, St. Paul, 1980—, mem. bd. dirs. 1993—. Mem. Minn. State Bar Assn. (treas. anti-trust sect. 1978-80), Ramsey County Bar Assn. (sec. jud. com. 1980-82), Phi Beta Kappa. Unitarian. Office: Briggs & Morgan 2200 First National Bank Bldg Saint Paul MN 55101

MACLIN, ERNEST, biomedical diagnostics company executive; b. N.Y.C., Jan. 25, 1931; s. Samuel and Dora (Sonsky) M.; m. Edith Samuel, Feb. 18, 1956; children—Alan David, Deborah Ellen, Julie Ann. B.M.E., CCNY, 1952, M.Engring., 1969. Registered profl. engr., N.Y., N.J. Engr. Reeves Instrument Corp., N.Y.C., 1952-54, Adrian Wilson Assocs., Nagoya, Japan, 1956-57; engr. Ford Instrument Co., L.I., N.Y., 1957-58; engr., unit head Kearfott div. Singer Corp., Little Falls, N.J., 1958-68; engr. Ford Instrument Co., L.I., N.Y., 1957-58, Technicon, Tarrytown, N.Y., 1968-69; v.p. research and devel. Electro-Nucleonics Inc., Fairfield, N.J., 1969-90; pres. The Product Devel. Group, 1990—; bd. dirs. Nat. Com. for Clin. Lab. Standards, Villanova, Pa., 1981-87. Contbr. articles to profl. jours.; patentee various instruments. Served to capt. USAF, 1954-57; mem. USAFR ret. Fellow ASME; mem. Am. Assn. Clin. Chemistry. Jewish. Home and Office: 659 Rutgers Pl Paramus NJ 07652-4207

MACMAHON, CHARLES HUTCHINS, JR., architect; b. Fort Seward, Alaska, June 6, 1918; s. Charles H. and Charlotte (Currie) MacM.; m. Ethel Hayward Pearce, Nov. 14, 1942; children—Charles H. III, Charlotte (Mrs. Douglas E. Neumann). Student, Bowdoin Coll., 1936-37, U. Pa., 1937-38; B.Arch., U. Mich., 1942. Dist. mgr. U.S. Gypsum Co., Chgo., 1947-52; gen. sales mgr. Spickelmeier Co., Indpls., 1952-55; with Smith, Tarapata, MacMahon, Inc., Birmingham, Mich., 1956-59; pres. Tarapata-MacMahon-Paulsen, Bloomfield Hills, Mich., 1959-73; cons. Tarapata-MacMahon-Paulsen, 1973—; pres. MacMahon-Cajacob Assos., DeLand, Fla., 1978-92; owner Charles MacMahon Architect, DeLand, Fla., 1992—; mem. Mich. Bd. Registration of Architects, Engrs. and Surveyors, 1964-68; mem. planning bd. City of DeLand, 1978-84. Works include Central Plaza, Canton, O., Gen. Motors Inst, Flint, Mich., Cloisters of DeLand, Fla., Washtenaw Community Coll, Ann Arbor, Mich. Chmn. bd. trustees Bloomfield Twp. Zoning Bd. Appeals, 1968-69; bd. dirs. Brookside Sch., Cranbrook, 1964-68; trustee Inst. for Advanced Pastoral Studies; mem. historic preservation bd. City of DeLand, 1993—. Lt. USNR, 1942-45. Fellow AIA; mem. Sch. Facilities Council (v.p., dir.), Mich. Soc. Architects (pres. 1962-64), Psi Upsilon. Episcopalian. Club: Lake Beresford Yacht. Address: 115 S Boundary Ave Deland FL 32720-5101

MACMAHON, PAUL, advertising executive; b. Orange, N.J., May 23, 1945; s. Paul J. and Joan (Schoenleber) MacM.; m. Mary Lee O'Neill, May 2, 1966 (div. May 1970); 1 child, Sandra; m. Barbara Jo Wernick, Mar. 8, 1972 (dec. Aug. 1988); children: Matthew, Timothy, Paul, Kathleen, Thomas, Julia; m. Ann Louise Dye, Aug. 7, 1993. A.A., Indian River Jr. Coll, 1966; B.S., Fla. State U., 1968; M.B.A., U. Mich., 1970. Acct. exec. Ted Bates & Co., N.Y.C., 1970-71; account dir. Ted Bates & Co., Ger. and Italy, 1972-74, v.p., 1975-79; sr. v.p. Ted Bates & Co., N.Y.C., 1979-80; sr. v.p. The Bloom Agy., Dallas, 1980-82, exec. v.p., 1982, gen. mgr., 1983-84, pres., 1984, chmn., 1985-88, chmn, ceo, 1988. Republican. Roman Catholic. Home: 126 Red Oak Ln Lewisville TX 75028-3501 Office: Publicis/Bloom 3500 Maple Ave Dallas TX 75219-3901*

MACMANUS, SUSAN ANN, political science educator, researcher; b. Tampa, Fla., Aug. 22, 1947; d. Harold Cameron and Elizabeth (Riegler) MacM. BA cum laude, Fla. State U., 1968, PhD, 1975; MA, U. Mich., 1969. Instr. Valencia Community Coll., Orlando, Fla., 1969-73; rsch. asst. Fla. State U., 1973-75; asst. prof. U. Houston, 1975-79, assoc. prof., 1979-85, dir. M of Pub. Adminstrn. program, 1983-85, rsch. assoc. Ctr Pub. Policy 1982-85; prof., dir. PhD program Cleve. State U., 1985-87; prof. pub. adminstrn. and polit. sci., U. South Fla., Tampa, 1987—, chairperson dept. govt. and internat. affairs, 1987-93; vis. prof. U. Okla., Norman, 1981—; field rsch. assoc. Brookings Instn., Washington, 1977-82, Columbia U., summer 1979, Princeton (N.J.) U., 1979—, Nat. Acad. Pub. Adminstrn., Washington, summer 1980, Cleve. State U., 1982-83, Westat, Inc., Washington, 1983—. Author: Revenue Patterns in U.S. Cities and Suburbs: A Comparative Analysis, 1978, Federal Aid to Houston, 1983, (with others) Governing A Changing America, 1984, (with Francis T. Borkowski) Visions for The Future: Creating New Institutional Relationships Among Academia, Business, Government, and Community, 1989, Reapportionment and Representation in Florida: A Historical Collection, 1991, Doing Business with Government: Federal, State, Local and Foreign Government Purchasing Practices for Every Business and Public Institution, 1992, Young v. Old: Generational Combat in the 21st Century, 1996; writer manuals in field; mem. editorial bds. various jours.; contbr. articles to jours. and chpts. to books. Bd. dirs. Houston Area Women's Ctr., 1977, past pres., v.p. fin., treas.; mem. LWV, Gov.'s Coun. Econ. Advisers, 1988-90, Harris County (Tex.) Women's Polit. Caucus, Houston; bd. dirs. USF Rsch. Found., Inc. Recipient U. Houston Coll. Social Scis. Teaching Excellence award, 1977, Herbert J. Simon Award for best article in 3d vol. Internat. Jour. Pub. Adminstrn., 1981, Theodore & Venette Askounes-Ashford Disting. Scholar award U. South Fla., 1991, Disting. Rsch. Scholar award, 1991; Ford Found. fellow, 1967-68; grantee Valencia Community Coll. Faculty, 1972, U. Houston, 1976-77, 79, 83; Fulbright Rsch. scholar, Korea, 1989. Mem. Am. Polit. Sci. Assn. (program com. 1983-84, chair sect. intergovtl. rels., award 1989, mem. exec. coun. 1994—, pres.-elect sect. urban politics 1994-95, pres. sect. urban politics 1995-96), So. Polit. Sci. Assn. (v.p. 1990-91, pres.-elect 1992-93, pres. 1993-94, V.O. key award com. 1983-84, best paper on women and politics 1988), Midwest Polit. Sci. Assn., Western Polit. Sci. Assn., Southwestern Polit. Sci. Assn. (local arrangements com. 1982-83, profession com. 1977-80), ASPA (nominating com. Houston chpt. 1983, bd. mem. Suncoast chpt., pres.-elect 1991, Lilly award 1992), Policy Studies Orgn. (mem. editorial bd. jour. 1981—, exec. coun. 1983-85), Women's Caucus Polit. Sci. (portfolio pre-decision rev. com. 1982-83, projects and programs com. 1981, fin.-budget com. 1980-81), Acad. Polit. Sci., Mcpl. Fin. Officers Assn., Phi Beta Kappa, Phi Kappa Phi, Pi Sigma Alpha (mem. exec. coun. 1994—), Pi Alpha Alpha. Republican. Methodist. Home: 2506 Collier Pky Land O'Lakes FL 34639-5228 Office: U South Fla Dept Govt & Internat Affairs Soc 107 Tampa FL 33620

MACMANUS, YVONNE CRISTINA, editor, videoscripter, writer, consultant; b. L.A., Mar. 18, 1931; d. Daniel S. and Josefina Lydia (Pina) MacM. Student, UCLA, NYU, U. So. Calif., U. London. Assoc. editor Bobbs-Merrill, N.Y.C., 1960-63; TV producer Leo Burnett Ltd., London, 1965-66; founding editor, editor-in-chief Leisure Books, L.A., 1970-72; tchr. pub. course UCLA Extension, 1972; sr. editor Major Books, 1974-77; copub., editor in chief Timely Books, Chattanooga, 1977; co-owner Write On...!, Chattanooga, 1977—; corp. videoscripting PR & video tng., 1983—; tchr. writing workshop Chattanooga State C.C., 1996. Author: Better Luck Elsewhere, 1966, With Fate Conspire, 1974, Bequeath Them No Tumbled House, 1977, Deadly Legacy, 1981, The Presence, 1982, You Can Write A Romance, 1983, (updated and expanded) 1996, (play) Hugo, 1990; contbr. articles to profl. publs. Home and Office: 4040 Mountain Creek Rd Ste 1304 Chattanooga TN 37415-6025

MACMASTER, DANIEL MILLER, retired museum official; b. Chgo., Feb. 11, 1913; s. Daniel Howard and Charlotte Louise (Miller) MacM.; m. Sylvia Jane Hill, Feb. 22, 1935; children—Daniel Miller, Jane Irene (Mrs. Robert W. Lightell). Student, Lakeside Press Tng. Sch., 1930-31, U. Chgo., 1931-34; L.H.D., Lincoln Coll., 1970; D.H.L., DePaul U., 1978. Mem. staff Mus. Sci. and Industry, Chgo., 1933—; acting dir. Mus. Sci. and Industry, 1950, dir., 1951-72, pres., 1968-78, pres. emeritus, 1978—, life trustee, 1968—; gen. mgr. Chgo. R.R. Fair, 1948-49. Author: (with others) Exploring the Mysteries of Physics and Chemistry, 1938; book reviewer; contbr. to newspapers, mags., encys. Mem. Homewood (Ill.) Bd. Edn., 1945-49, pres., 1948-49; mem. U. Ill. Citizen' Adv. Com., 1945—; sec. Higher Edn. Commn. Ill., 1955-59; dir. Hyde Park Bank and Trust Co., 1965-86; U.S. State Dept. Specialist to Ireland, Germany, Sweden, 1963; dir. Floating Seminar to Greece, 1960; guest mus. cons. Fed. Republic Germany, 1961, Iran, 1973, 74, 76, Hong Kong, 1978, 89, 90, 91, Singapore, Chili and Peru, 1978, Poland, Czechoslovakia and Hungary, 1979, Mexico, 1980, 81, Saudi Arabia, 1981, 82, 84, Columbia, Ecuador and Bolivia, 1983, Taiwan 1986-90, 92, 94, 96; mem. Nat. 4-H Svc. Com.; hon. dir. Chgo. Chamber Orch. Soc., pres., 1969-70; bd. dirs. Sears Roebuck Found., 1970-73, Internat. Coll. Surgeons Hall of Fame; mem. Lincoln Acad. Ill.; hon. trustee U. Chgo. Cancer Rsch. Found.; life trustee Adler Planetarium; dir. emeritus Monmouth Coll.; bd. govs. Chgo. Heart Assn., vice chmn., 1972-73. Decorated Golden Cross Royal Order Phoenix Greece; Officer's Cross Polonia Restituta Poland; Grand Badge of Honor Austria; Grand Badge of Honor of Burgenland Austria; Golden Badge of Honor Vienna; Officer's Cross 1st class Order of Merit Germany; Officer Order of Merit Luxembourg; Order Cultural Merit Poland; Royal Swedish Order North Star; recipient Patriotic Civilian Service award U.S. Army, St. Andrews Soc. Citizen of Yr. award, 1978. Fellow Assn. Sci. and Tech. Centers; mem. Kappa Sigma. Clubs: Tavern, Quadrangle, Commercial. Home: 2311 183rd St Apt 209B Homewood IL 60430-3146

MACMASTER, ROBERT ELLSWORTH, historian, educator; b. Winthrop, Mass., Oct. 10, 1919; s. Joseph Oscar and Ruby (Slocomb) MacM.; m. Ann Elizabeth Lynch, Apr. 28, 1942; children—Angus Michael, Martha Ann, David Joseph. A.B., Harvard, 1941, A.M., 1948, Ph.D., 1952. Mem. faculty MIT, 1952-90, prof. history and lit., 1967-90, prof. emeritus, 1990—, chmn. history sect., 1970-72. Author: Danilevsky: A Russian Totalitarian Philosopher, 1967. Served with AUS, 1941-46. Mem. Am. Assn. Advancement Slavic Studies. Home: 461 Main St Hingham MA 02043-4701 Office: MIT Dept History Cambridge MA 02139

MACMILLAN, DOUGLAS CLARK, naval architect; b. Dedham, Mass., July 15, 1912; s. James Duncan and Mary Grace (MacNeill) MacM.; m. Elizabeth Jane Smith, Sept. 9, 1939; children: Douglas Stuart, John Richard; m. Dorothy Hayford, Jan. 1, 1985. B.S., Mass. Inst. Tech., 1934. Registered profl. engr., N.Y., N.J. Engrs. Fed. Shipbldg. & Dry Dock Co., Kearny, N.J., 1934-41; from chief marine engr. to tech. mgr. George G. Sharp (N.A.), N.Y.C., 1941-51; pres. George G. Sharp, Inc., N.Y.C., 1951-69; chmn. bd. George G. Sharp, Inc., 1969-70; cons. naval architect, 1970-83; asst. to gen. mgr., cons. Quincy Shipbldg. div. Gen. Dynamics Corp., 1972-77; bd. dirs. Atomic Indsl. Forum, 1965-67; mem. coms. Nat. Acad. Scis.-NRC; mem. adv. coms. U.S, Navy, USCG. Author papers in field. Past trustee St. Johns Guild, N.Y.C. Recipient Elmer A. Sperry medal ASME-Soc. Naval Architects and Marine Engrs.-Soc. Automotive Engrs.-IEEE-Am. Inst. Aeros. and Astronautics, 1969. Fellow Soc. Naval Architects and Marine Engrs. (hon. v.p., David W. Taylor Gold medal 1969); mem. Nat. Acad. Engring., Am. Soc. Naval Engrs. Mem. United Ch. of Christ. Home: Box 834 Colony Dr East Orleans MA 02643

MACMILLAN, KENNETH, cinematographer. Cinematographer: (TV movies) Smiley's People, 1982, The Aerodrome, 1983, The Ghost Writer, 1984, Past Caring, 1985, Bleak House, 1985, Hotel du Lac, 1986, Pack of Lies, 1987, Day After the Fair, 1987, The Little Match Girl, 1987, (films) A Month in the Country, 1987, A Summer Story, 1988, The Tree of Hands, 1989, Henry V, 1989, King Ralph, 1991, Of Mice and Men, 1992, Rush, 1992, Lassie, 1994, Circle of Friends, 1995, Inventing the Abbotts, 1996. Office: Sandra Marsh Mgt 9150 Wilshire Blvd Ste 220 Beverly Hills CA 90212-3429

MACMILLAN, KIP VAN METRE, foundation executive; b. Evanston, Ill., Dec. 18, 1937; s. Charles Daniel and Janet Marvia (Van Metre) M.; m. Linda Jean Griesbach, Dec. 22, 1962; children: Christopher, Julia. Sgt., lt., div. comdr. Evanston Police Dept., 1961-88; supr. Polio Plus campaign Rotary Found., Evanston, 1988-90, ret., 1990. Bd. dirs. Youth Orgn. Umbrella, Evanston, 1974, McGaw YMCA, Evanston, 1976-89, Shore Cmty. Svcs. for Retarded Citizens, Evanston, 1986-90; pres. Teton Youth & Family Svcs.; chmn. Evanston March of Dimes, 1987; mem. adv. com. Cook County Dept. Children and Family Svcs., Chgo., 1987-90; mem. Ill. Coord. System Response Project-Mass Abuse of Children, Springfield, 1987-89; chmn. Wildcat dist. com. Boy Scouts Am.; dir., treas. Evanston Sister City Found., 1989-90; vol. Grand Teton Music Festival. Recipient Top Vol. of Yr. award North Shore mag., 1987, Jay Moore award Youth Orgn. Umbrella, 1988, William Harper award McGaw YMCA, 1975. Mem. Nat. Soc. Fundraising Execs., Internat. Assn. Chiefs of Police, Rotary (bd. dirs. Evanston club 1986-89, bd. dirs. Jackson Hole club, pres. Jackson Hole club 1994-95, Outstanding Rotarian Evanston club 1988), Am. Soc. Indsl. Security, Teton County Peace Officers Assn. (chair congressional awards com.). Republican. Episcopalian.

MACMILLAN, ROBERT SMITH, electronics engineer; b. L.A., Aug. 28, 1924; s. Andrew James and Moneta (Smith) M.; BS in Physics, Calif. Inst. Tech., 1948, MS in Elec. Engring., 1949, PhD in Elec. Engring. and Physics cum laude, 1954; m. Barbara Macmillan, Aug. 18, 1962; 1 son, Robert G. Rsch. engr. Jet Propulsion lab. Calif. Inst. Tech., Pasadena, 1951-55, asst. prof. elec. engring., 1955-58; assoc. prof. elec. engring. U. So. Calif., L.A., 1958-70; mem. sr. tech. staff Litton Systems, Inc., Van Nuys, Calif., 1969-79; dir. systems engring. Litton Data Command Systems, Agoura Hills, Calif., 1979-89; pres. The Macmillan Group, Tarzana, Calif., 1989—; treas., v.p. Video Color Corp., Inglewood, 1965-66. Cons. fgn. tech. div. USAF, Wright-Patterson AFB, Ohio, 1957-74, Space Tech. Labs., Inglewood, Calif., 1956-60, Space Gen. Corp., El Monte, Calif., 1960-63. With USAAF, 1943-46. Mem. IEEE, Am. Inst. Physics, Am. Phys. Soc., Sigma Xi, Tau Beta Pi, Eta Kappa Nu. Research in ionospheric, radio-wave, propagation; very low frequency radio-transmitting antennas; optical coherence and statist. optics. Home: 350 Starlight Crest Dr La Canada Flintridge CA 91011-2839 Office: The Macmillan Group 5700 Etiwanda Ave Unit 260 Tarzana CA 91356-2546

MACMILLAN, WHITNEY, food products and import/export company executive. Chmn., CEO Cargill, Wayzata, Minn.; mem. bd. dirs. Deluxe Corp., Minn. Office: Cargill PO Box 9300 Minneapolis MN 55440-9300*

MACMILLAN, WILLIAM HOOPER, university dean, educator; b. Boston, Oct. 21, 1923; s. Alexander Stewart and Leslie (Hooper) M.; m. Anne Stearns, May 29, 1948; children: Leslie Jean, Robert Bruce, William Ian. BA, McGill U., 1948; PhD, Yale U., 1954. Instr. pharmacology U. Vt. Coll. Medicine, 1954-55, asst. prof., 1955-59, asso. prof., 1959-64, chmn. dept. pharmacology, 1962-63, prof. pharmacology, 1964-76, dean Grad. Coll., 1963-69, 71-76; rsch. fellow USPHS, U. Oxford, Eng., 1958-59; cons. New Eng. Assn. Schs. and Colls., 1967-76; Ford Found. project specialist, sci. adv. to Haile Sellassie I U., Addis Ababa., Ethiopia, 1969-71; prof. biology, dean Grad. Sch. U. Ala., 1976-91, prof. biology, dean emeritus, 1991—; cons. So. Assn. Colls. and Schs., 1976-91; exec. com. African grad. Fellowship Program, African-Am. Inst., N.Y.C., 1971-92; chmn. com. biomed. scis. Coun. of Grad. Schs., Washington, 1973-77, bd. dirs., 1985-88; exec. com. N.E. Assn. Grad. Schs., 1975-76; v.p. Conf. So. Grad. Schs., 1981, pres., 1982; pres. New Eng. Assn. Grad. Schs., 1971; bd. dirs. Oak Ridge Associated Univs., 1987-93. Officer USNR, 1943-46. Mem. Am. Soc. Pharmacology and Exptl. Therapeutics, AAAS, N.Y. Acad. Sci., AAUP, Sigma Xi.

MACMILLEN, RICHARD EDWARD, biological sciences educator, researcher; b. Upland, Calif., Apr. 19, 1932; s. Hesper Nichols and Ruth Henrietta (Golder) MacM.; m. Ann Gray, June 12, 1953 (div. 1975); children: Jennifer Kathleen, Douglas Michael; m. Barbara Jean Morgan, Oct. 23, 1980; 1 child, Ian Richard. BA, Pomona Coll., 1954; MS, U. Mich., 1956; PhD, UCLA, 1961. From instr. to assoc. prof. Pomona Coll., Claremont, Calif., 1960-68, Wig Disting. prof., 1965; assoc. prof., then prof. U. Calif., Irvine, 1968—, chair dept. population and environ. biology, 1972-74, chair dept. ecology and evolutionary biology, 1984-90; prof. emeritus, 1993—; adj. prof. biology So. Oreg. State Coll., Ashland, 1996—; mem. advance panel NSF, Washington, 1976-80; coord. U. Calif. Multi-Campus Supercourse in Environ. Biology, White Mountain Rsch. Sta., spring 1996. Contbr. numerous articles to profl. jours. Chair sci. adv. bd. Endangered Habitats League, 1991-93. Recipient rsch. awards NSF, 1961-83; Fulbright-Hays advanced rsch. fellow Monash U., Australia, 1966-67. Fellow AAAS; mem. Am. Soc. Mammalogists (life), Ecol. Soc. Am. (cert. sr. ecologist), Am. Ornithologists Union, Cooper Ornithol. Soc. (life, bd. dirs. 1982-84). Democrat. Avocations: fly fishing, camping, hiking, nature photography. Home: 705 Foss Rd Talent OR 97540 Office: Dept Biology So Oreg State Coll Ashland OR 97520 *As world human populations continue to increase, our natural world continues to degrade. It is incumbent upon all of us to accept the responsibility of stewarding our land and its biota as precious and renewable resources.*

MACMILLIN, JAMES, religious organization administrator. Pres. John Milton Soc. for Blind Can., Toronto, Ont. Office: John Milton Soc For Blind, 40 St Clair Ave E Ste 202, Toronto, ON Canada M4T 1M9

MACMINN, ALEENE MERLE B(ARNES), newspaper editor, columnist, educator; b. Salt Lake City, Sept. 19, 1930; d. Harold Sansom and Allie (Rasmussen) Barnes; m. Fraser K. MacMinn, July 28, 1961; children: Margaret A., Gregor Geordie. AA, Glendale Coll., 1950; BA, U. So. Calif., L.A., 1952. Women's page reporter Glendale (Calif.) News-Press, 1948-52; women's page reporter L.A. Times, 1953-57, asst. family editor, 1957-60, asst. TV editor, 1960-65, exec. TV editor, 1965-69, asst. entertainment editor, 1969-72, TV Times editor, 1972-91, asst. Calendar editor, entertainment columnist, 1989-93; sr. lectr. U. So. Calif. Sch. Journalism, 1979-92. Mem. Women in Communications, Alpha Gamma Delta. Mem. LDS Ch.

MACMULLEN, DOUGLAS BURGOYNE, writer, editor, retired army officer, publisher; b. Berkeley, Calif., Dec. 26, 1919; s. T. Douglas and Florence (Burgoyne) MacM.; ed. San Francisco State U., 1937-41, Stanford U., U. Calif., Fgn. Svc. Inst., Strategic Intelligence Sch., Indsl. Coll. of the Armed Forces, Air War Coll., Army Mgmt. Sch.; m. Sherry Bernice Auerbach, Mar. 11, 1942; 1 child, Douglas Burgoyne Jr. Commd. 2d lt. F.A. Res. U.S. Army, 1941; advanced through grades to col. M.I., 1967; Army gen. staff Psychol. Ops. Fgn. Svc., PTO; ret., 1972; exec. editor Am. Rsch. Assoc., Sherman Oaks, Calif.; cons. in communication; accredited corr. Def. Dept. Bd. govs. Monte Vista Grove Homes, Pasadena, Calif., Shriners Hosps. for Crippled Children, L.A., Calif.; pres. Clan MacMillan Soc. N.Am., 1973-77, trustee, 1975—; mem. L.A. Olympics Citizens Adv. Commn., 1982-84; mem. L.A. Philanthropic Found.; bd. dirs. Masonic Press Club, L.A., 1975, 84-88; mem. steering com. Mayor L.A. Coun. Internat. Visitors and Sister Cities, 1969; chmn. Los Angeles-Glasgow Sister Cities Ad Hoc Com.; former mem. San Francisco Mayor's Mil. and Naval Affairs Com.; mem. wills and gifts com. Shriners Hosp. Crippled Children, Al Malaikah Temple, L.A., 1974-80; cons. com. on pub. info. Masons Grand Lodge of Calif., 1985-86. Decorated Legion of Merit, Army Commendation medal (U.S.), Knight Comdr. Order of Polonia Restituta (Free Poland), Red Cross of Constantine; Royal Order Scotland. Mem. Internat. Inst. Strategic Studies, Nat. Mil. Intelligence Assn., Assn. Former Intelligence Officers (pres. L.A. County chpt.), U.S. Naval Inst., Assn. U.S. Army, Company Mil. Historians, Am. Def. Preparedness Assn., St. Andrew's Soc. Los Angeles (past pres., trustee), Air Force Assn., Stanford U. Alumni Assn., Calif. Newspaper Pubs. Assn., Nat. Def. Exec. Res., Sigma Delta Chi. Republican. Presbyterian. Clubs: Press, Caledonian (London); Army & Navy Club (Washington), San Francisco Press. Lodges: Masons (32 deg.), K.T., Shriners (editor, pub. The Al Malaikahan, former imperial news editor Shrine of N.Am.), Quatuor Coronati C.C. Co-author: Psychological Profile of Cambodia, 1971; author-editor: A Sentimental Journey--The History of the First Hundred Years, 1988; numerous other publs. and articles; radio commentator and newspaper columnist on mil., polit. and internat. affairs. Address: PO Box 5201 Sherman Oaks CA 91413-5201

MACMULLEN, RAMSAY, retired history educator; b. N.Y.C., Mar. 3, 1928; s. Charles William and Margaret (Richmond) MacM.; m. Edith Merriman Nye, Aug. 7, 1954 (div. 1991); children: John A., Priscilla N., William R., Lucinda S.; m. Margaret McNeill, Aug. 1, 1992. A.B., Harvard, 1950, A.M., 1953, Ph.D., 1957. Instr., asst. prof. U. Oreg., 1956-61; asso. prof., prof. Brandeis U., 1961-67, chmn. dept. classics, 1965-66; prof. Yale U., 1967-93, Dunham prof. history and classics, 1979-93, chmn. dept. history, 1970-72, master Calhoun Coll., 1984-90. Author: Soldier and Civilian in the Later Roman Empire, 1963, Enemies of the Roman Order, 1966, Constantine, 1969, Roman Social Relations, 1974, Roman Government's Response to Crisis, 1976, Paganism in the Roman Empire, 1981, Christianizing the Roman Empire, 1984, Corruption and the Decline of Rome, 1988, Changes in the Roman Empire, 1990; (with E.N. Lane) Paganism and Christianity, 1992, Sisters of the Brush, 1996. Recipient Porter prize Coll. Art Assn., 1964; Fulbright fellow, 1960-61; Guggenheim fellow, 1964; Princeton Inst. for Advanced Study fellow, 1964-65; Nat. Endowment for Humanities sr. fellow, 1974-75. Mem. Soc. for Promotion Roman Studies, Assn. Ancient Historians (pres. 1978-81). Home: 25 Temple Ct New Haven CT 06511-6820 Office: Yale U Dept History New Haven CT 06520

MACMURREN, HAROLD HENRY, JR., psychologist, lawyer; b. Jersey City, Sept. 18, 1942; s. Harold Sr. and Evelyn (Almone) MacM.; m. Margaret Bartro, Nov. 21, 1970. BA, William Paterson Coll., Wayne, N.J., 1965; MA, Jersey City Coll., 1973; EdD, St. Johns U., N.Y.C., 1985; JD, Rutgers U., 1989. Cert. secondary tchr., N.J.; Bar: N.J. 1989. Instr. Wanaque (N.J.) Bd. Edn., 1965-66, cons. psychologist, 1983-84; instr. Elmwood Park (N.J.) Bd. Edn., 1967-70; coll. faculty mem., psychologist Assoc. Clinic, Jersey City, 1971-72; cons. psychologist Rockaway (N.J.) Bd. Edn., 1972-83; intern lawyer Environ. Law Clinic, Newark, N.J., 1988-89; cons. psychologist Pequannock (N.J.) Bd. Edn., 1984—; coord. of child study team Sandyston Walpack Sch. System; adj. prof. William Paterson Coll.; spkr. and writer in field. Mem. ABA, NEA, N.J. Edn. Assn., N.J. Psychologist Assn., N.J. Bar Assn., Sierra Club, Phi Delta Kappa. Avocations: reading, travel, skiing, hiking. Home: 4 Systema Pl Sussex NJ 07461-2833 Office: Pequanock Bd Edn Pequannock NJ 07440

MACMURREN, MARGARET PATRICIA, secondary education educator, consultant; b. Newark, Nov. 4, 1947; d. Kenneth F. and Doris E. (Lounsberry) Bartro; m. Harold MacMurren, Nov. 21, 1970. BA, Paterson State U., 1969; MA, William Paterson Coll., 1976; postgrad., Jersey City State Coll., 1976—. Tchr. Byram (N.J.) Twp. Schs., 1969-77; learning cons., child study team coord. Andover Regional Schs., Newton, N.J., 1977—. Mem. NEA, N.J. Edn. Assn., N.J. Assn. Learning Cons., Sussex Coutny Assn. Learning Cons. (pres. 1982-83, 93-94, sec.-treas. 1991-92, v.p. 1992-93), Andover Regional Edn. Assn. (pres. 1986-87). Avocations: skiing, dancing, weight training, travel, reading. Home: 4 Systema Pl Sussex NJ 07461-2833 Office: Andover Regional Schs 707 Limecrest Rd Newton NJ 07860-8801

MAC NAMARA, DONAL EOIN JOSEPH, criminologist; b. N.Y.C., Aug. 13, 1916; s. Daniel Patrick and Rita F.V. (Chambers) Mac N.; m. Margaret Elizabeth Scott, July 30, 1953 (dec. 1990); 1 child, Brian Scott. BS, Columbia U., 1939, M of Phil., 1948; M of Pub. Adminstrn., NYU, 1946; LLD (hon.), August Vollmer U., 1990. Instr. polit. sci. Rutgers U., New Brunswick, N.J., 1948-49; asst. dir. Delinquency Control Inst. L.A., 1949-50; dir. law enforcement program U. So. Calif., 1949-50; vis. prof. U. Louisville, 1950-71, Fla. State U., Tallahassee, 1958, St. Lawrence U., Canton, N.Y., 1954, 56; chmn. Law Enforcement Insts., NYU, 1950-57; coordinator police sci. programs Bklyn. Coll., 1954-57; with N.Y. Inst. Criminology, N.Y.C., 1950-63; assoc. dean N.Y. Inst. Criminology, 1955-56, dean, 1956-63; prof. criminology Center Corrections Tng., CUNY, 1966-67; in charge corrections programs John Jay Coll. Criminal Justice, 1965-85, emeritus disting. prof., 1985; dean doctoral programs August Vollmer U., Orange, Calif., 1987—; dir. summer session CUNY, Ireland, 1970; Disting. vis. prof. U. Melbourne, Australia, 1981; vis. prof. criminology Bar Ilan U., Ramat Gan, Israel, 1982-83; vis. prof. Calif. State U., Spring 1984, U. N.Mex., 1985, U. Tenn., 1986, Calif. State U., 1987-88, Bar Ilan U., Israel, Spring 1989; mng. ptnr. Flath-MacNamara Assocs., N.Y.C., 1958-64; dir. Crime Show Cons., N.Y.C., Traffic Mgmt. Survey Fund, Inc., N.Y.C.; Eastern regional dir. Character Underwriters, Inc., L.A.; vis. mem. faculty Hunter, Queens, Bklyn. colls., 1952-58; vis. lectr. criminology Brandeis U., Waltham, Mass., 1962; lectr. police adminstrn. SUNY, 1966-67; lectr. penology (CCNY), 1965-67; specialist police, correctional adminstrn. grad. program tng. pub. adminstrn., State of N.Y., Albany, 1951-56; criminol. cons. Am. Express Co., 1962-68; cons., Bergen County, N.J., 1967, N.J. Commn. Civil Disorders, 1967-68; vis. prof. criminology U. Utah, Salt Lake City, 1962; pres. League to Abolish Capital Punishment, 1958-70, chmn. bd., 1959-91; col. a.d.c. to commr. Ky. State Police, 1963; external assessor in police and pub. adminstrn. Republic of Ireland, 1975; vis. prof. Inst. Pub. Adminstrn., Dublin, 1974-75. Author: Problems of Sex Behavior, 1968, Perspectives on Correction, 1971, Corrections: Problems of Punishment and Rehabilitation, 1973, Police: Problems and Prospects, 1974, Criminal Justice, 1976, Sex, Crime and the Law, 1977, Incarceration: The Sociology of Imprisonment, 1978, Crime, Criminals and Corrections, 1981, Deviants: Victims or Victimizers, 1984, Deviance,

Denigration and Dominance, 1990, also articles.; Am. editor: Excerpta Criminologica, 1965-85; editor-in-chief: Criminology: An Interdisciplinary Jour., 1975-78; asso. editor: Jour. Corrective Psychiatry; editor: UN Crime Conference: Keynote Document Edit., 1981. Exec. v.p. Real Estate Bd., Bronx, N.Y., 1964-65. Served to maj. AUS, 1942-48. Recipient award of honor Internat. Assn. Women Police, 1960, Herbert A. Bloch award Am. Soc. Criminology, 1967, Bruce Smith award Am. Acad. of Criminal Justice Scis., 1990, Lifetime Achievement in Criminal Justice award Am. Soc. for Pub. Adminstrn., 1991. Fellow AAAS (chmn. sci. criminology sect., mem. council 1957-82), Am. Acad. Criminalistics (presiding); mem. Internat. Police Officers Assn. (life), Am. Soc. Criminology (pres. 1960-64), Assn. Psychiat. Treatment Offenders (program coordinator 1954-58), M.P. Assn., Internat. Criminol. Soc., Am. Assn. Criminologists (hon. life), Edn. Research Assn. (exec. dir. 1965-69), Nat. Police Officers Assn. Am. (research dir. 1963-67), Pi Sigma Alpha. Home: 76 Four Corners Rd Warwick NY 10990-3020 Office: 899 10th Ave New York NY 10019-1029

MACNAMARA, THOMAS EDWARD, physician, educator; b. Airdrie, Scotland, May 23, 1929; came to U.S., 1956, naturalized, 1962; s. Edward Francis and Bridget Monica (Fawcett) M.; m. Julia B. Caulfield, Sept. 22, 1956; children: Edward, Brian, Mary, Bridget, Anne. Student, Paisley Tech. Coll., Glasgow U., 1947, MBChB, 1952. Diplomate: Am. Bd. Anesthesiology. Intern Victoria Infirmary, Glasgow, 1953, Leith Hosp., Edinburgh, Bellsdyke Hosp., Larbert, 1954, St. Martins Hosp., Bath, 1954, Birmingham (Eng.) Accident Hosp., 1955; resident in anesthesiology Mass. Gen. Hosp., Boston, 1956; practice medicine specializing in anesthesia Washington, 1957-59, 62—, Boston, 1960-62; mem. staff Mass. Gen. Hosp., Boston; instr. anesthesia Georgetown U., 1957-60, prof., chmn. dept. anesthesia Med. Center, 1962-90; prof. emeritus, 1995—; dir. anethesia and surg. svcs. Walter Grant Magnuson Clin. Ctr., NIH, Bethesda, Md., 1990-92; mem. faculty senate Georgetown U., 1967-75, v.p. senate, 1967-70, pres. senate, 1973-75; chief anesthesiology NIH Clin. Center, Bethesda, Md., 1975-83, 92-93; asst. in anesthesia Mass. Gen. Hosp., Harvard U. Med. Sch., 1960-62; cons. VA Hosp., Washington, 1962-92. Editor: Surgical Digest, 1966-70, Clinical Therapeutics, 1976-82. Bd. dirs. Georgetown U. Fed. Credit Union. Fellow Am. Coll. Anesthesiologists (chmn. bd. govs. 1986-87); mem. Md.-D.C. Soc. Anesthesiology (pres. sect. II 1966-67). Home: PO Box 7137 Arlington VA 22207-0137 Office: NIH Walter Grant Magnuson Clin Ctr Bldg 10 Bethesda MD 20892

MACNAUGHTON, ANGUS ATHOLE, finance company executive; b. Montreal, July 15, 1931; s. Athole Austin and Emily Kidder (MacLean) MacN.; children: Gillian Heather, Angus Andrew. Student, Lakefield Coll. Sch., 1941-47, McGill U., 1949-54. Auditor Coopers & Lybrand, Montreal, 1949-55; acct. Genstar Ltd., Montreal, 1955; asst. treas. Genstar Ltd., 1956-61, treas., 1961-64, v.p., 1964-70, exec. v.p., 1970-73, pres., 1973-76, vice chmn., chief exec. officer, 1976-81, chmn. or pres., chief exec. officer, 1981-86; pres. Genstar Investment Corp., 1987—; bd. dirs. Can. Pacific Ltd., Sun Life Assurance Co. Can. ltd., Barrick Gold Corp., Varian Assocs., Inc.; past pres. Montreal chpt. Tax Execs. Inst. Bd. govs. Lakefield Coll. Sch.; past chmn. San Francisco Bay Area coun. Boy Scouts Am.; bd. dirs. San Francisco Opera. Mem. Pacific Union Club, World Trade Club, Villa Taverna (San Francisco), Mt. Royal Club (Montreal), Toronto Club. Office: Genstar Investment Corp 950 Tower Ln Ste 1170 Foster City CA 94404-2121 also: Barrick Gold Corp, 200 Bay St Ste 2700, Toronto, ON Canada M5J 2J3

MACNAUGHTON, DONALD SINCLAIR, health care company executive; b. Schenectady, N.Y., July 14, 1917; s. William and Marion (Colquhoun) MacN.; m. Winifred Thomas, Apr. 10, 1941; children: Donald, David. AB, Syracuse U., 1939, LLB, 1948. Bar: N.Y. 1948. Tchr. history Pulaski (N.Y.) Acad. and Central Sch., 1939-42; pvt. practice Pulaski, 1948-54; dep. supt. ins. N.Y. State, 1954-55; with Prudential Ins. Co. Am., 1955-78, pres., CEO, 1969-70, CEO, chmn. bd. dirs., 1970-78, also bd. dirs.; chmn. bd. dirs. Hosp. Corp. Am., Nashville, 1978-82; chmn. bd. Hosp. Corp. Am., 1982-85; chmn. exec. com. Healthtrust Inc., 1987—. Mem. capital campaign com. Harvard U., 1985—, mem. adv. bd. Bus. and Govt. Ctr., 1983—; trustee Vanderbilt U., Nashville, 1979-95. 1st lt. USAAF, 1942-46, PTO. Named Man of Yr. B'nai B'rith Youth Service, N.Y., 1985, The Ins. Field, 1969; recipient Gold Medal Founders award Internat. Ins. Seminars, N.Y., 1978, Exceptional Achievement citation Dept. Treasury, 1972. Mem. Hosp. Corp. Found. (chmn. 1985—), Bus. Coun. (hon.), Augusta Nat. Golf Club. Avocations: boating, skiing, golf, reading. Office: Health Trust Inc 4525 Harding Rd Nashville TN 37205-2101*

MACNAUGHTON, JOHN DAVID FRANCIS, aerospace company executive; b. Moose Jaw, Saskatchewan, Can., Apr. 10, 1932; s. Francis Maurice and Grace Elizabeth Ellen (Moore) MacN.; m. Joy Barbara Spencer; children: Paul, Neil, Jane. Diploma, deHavilland Aero. Tech. Sch., 1954; BSc, Hatfield Coll., U.K., 1954. Engring. supr. deHavilland's Guided Missile Div., 1954-57; chief engr. Garrett Mfg. Ltd., 1958-61; chief mech. engr. deHavilland's Spl. Projects and Applied Research, 1962-68; dir. mech. products dept. Spar Aerospace Ltd., Toronto, Ont., Can., 1968-69, v.p. mktg. and planning, 1969-74, v.p., gen. mgr. remote manipulator systems div., 1974-80, v.p., group exec. space & electronics group, 1981-82, sr. v.p. systems sector, from 1982, exec. v.p., 1988-89, pres., CEO, 1989—; also bd. dirs., 1989—; bd. dirs. Telesat Can., Ottawa; chmn. Nat. Quality Inst.; invited spkr. various profl. confs. Contbr. papers to profl. publs. and profl. confs. Dir.-at-large Jr. Achievement Can. Recipient Engring. medal Profl. Engrs. Ont., 1965, Pub. Service medal NASA, 1982, McGregor award Royal Can. Air Force Assn., 1983, Thomas W. Eadie medal Royal Soc. Can., 1984, 125th Can. Anniversary medal, 1993. Fellow Can. Aeronautics and Space Inst. (Casey Baldwin award 1963, McCurdy award 1983); mem. Assn. Profl. Engrs. of Province Ont., Info. Tech. Assn. Can. Rideau (Ottawa) Club, Mississauga Golf and Country Club, Bd. of Trade (Toronto), Founders Club (Toronto), Toronto Club. Home: 1054 Indian Rd, Mississauga, ON Canada L5H 1R7

MACNEAL, EDWARD ARTHUR, economic consultant; b. Winona Lake, Ind., Apr. 19, 1925; s. Kenneth Forsyth and Marguerite Josephine (Giroud) MacN.; m. Priscilla Creed Perry, Dec. 27, 1952; children: Catherine Wright, Madeleine Creed. Student Harvard, 1943; B.A., U. Chgo., 1948, M.A., 1951. Exec. sec. Internat. Soc. Gen. Semantics, Chgo., 1947-50; staff cons. James C. Buckley, Inc., N.Y.C., 1951-55; market researcher Socony Mobil Oil Co., N.Y.C., 1955-58; research dir. O.E. McIntyre, Inc., N.Y.C., 1958-61; econ. cons., N.Y., 1956-66, Wayne, Pa., 1966—; adv. local govt. agys. Served with AUS, 1943-46; ETO. Mem. ABA, Am. Statis. Assn., Am. Econ. Assn., Am. Mathematical Soc., Internat. Soc. Gen. Semantics (dir.), Inst. Gen. Semantics (dir.), Jean Piaget Soc., Am. Sociol. Assn., Am. Assn. Airport Execs., Travel Research Assn., Travel and Tourism Research Forum. Clubs: Nat. Aviation; Harvard (Phila.); Wings. Author: The Semantics of Air Passenger Transportation, 1981, MacNeal's Master Atlas of Decision Making, 1988, Mathsemantics: Making Numbers Talk Sense, 1994. Home: 348 Louella Ave Wayne PA 19087-4855 Office: PO Box 249 Wayne PA 19087-0249

MACNEE, ALAN BRECK, electrical engineer, educator; b. N.Y.C., Sept. 19, 1920; s. Forrest Frew and Ellen (Breck) M.; m. Lois Fuller Livermore, Feb. 16, 1946; children—Carol, Bruce Forrest, David Breck, Timothy Jay. S.B., S.M., M.I.T., 1943, Sc.D. (George Eastman fellow), 1948. Research asso. Chalmers Tech. U., Gothenburg, Sweden, 1949-50; vis. asso. prof. Chalmers Tech. U., 1961-62; mem. faculty U. Mich., Ann Arbor, 1950—; prof. elec. engring. U. Mich., 1959-89, prof. emeritus, 1989—; sr. research asso. Goddard Space Flight Center, NASA, 1971-72; mem. vis. tech. staff Sandia Labs., 1980-81. Co-author Modern Circuit Analysis, 1973; contbr. articles to profl. publs.; patentee in field. Recipient B.J. Thompson Meml. prize IRE, 1951, Western Electric Fund award Am. Soc. Engring. Edn., 1968-69. Fellow IEEE, AAAS; mem. Royal Soc. Sci. and Lit. (Gothenberg) (fgn. mem.), Sigma Xi, Eta Kappa Nu, Phi Kappa Phi. Congregationalist. Office: Univ Mich 1215 Eecs Bldg Ann Arbor MI 48109

MACNEE, (DANIEL) PATRICK, actor; b. London, Feb. 6, 1922; s. Daniel and Doratisea Mary (Henry) M.; m. Kate Woodwille, 1965 (div. 1969); children: Rupert, Jenny; m. Baba Majos de Nagyzsebyem Feb. 25, 1988. Student, Webber Douglas Academy Dramatic Art, 1940. Appearences include (theatre) in Eng., 1939-42, 46-52, in Can. and U.S., 1952-60, (films) The Life and Death Colonel Blimp, 1945, Dead of Night, 1946, Hamlet, 1948, The Fatal Night, 1948, All Over The Town, 1949, Hour of Glory, 1949, The Fighting Pimpernel, 1950, The Girl Is Mine, 1950, Dick Barton At Bay, 1950, A Christmas Carol, 1951, Flesh and Blood, 1951, Three Cases of Murder, 1955, Until They Sail, 1957, Les Girls, 1957, Pursuit of the Graf Spee, 1957, Mission of Danger, 1959, Incense for the Damned, 1970, King Solomon's Treasure, 1980, Dick Turpin, 1980, The Hot Touch, 1981, The Creature Wasn't Nice, 1981, The Howling, 1981, The Sea Wolves, 1981, Young Doctors in Love, 1982, Sweet Sixteen, 1983, This Is Spinal Tap, 1984, Shadey, 1985, A View to a Kill, 1985, For the Term of His Natural Life, 1985, Transformations, 1987, Waxwork, 1988, The Chill Factor, 1988, Lobster Man From Mars, 1989, A Stroke of Luck, (TV series) The Avengers, 1960-69, The New Avengers, 1978-80, Gavilan, 1982-83, Empire, 1984, Lime Street, 1985, Tales from the Darkside, 1985, (miniseries) Around the World in 80 Days, 1989, (TV movies) Mister Jerico, 1970, Sherlock Holmes in New York, 1976, Evening in Byzantium, 1978, Rehearsal for Murder, 1982, The Return of the Man From U.N.C.L.E., 1983, Club Med, 1986; author: (with Maggie Cameron) Blind in One Ear, 1988. 1st lt. Brit. Navy, 1942-46. Recipient Variety Artist award of Gt. Britain, 1963. Mem. Actors Equity, AFTRA, Screen Actors Guild, Assn. Can. TV and Radio Artists. Office: Irv Scechter Co 9300 Wilshire Blvd Ste 410 Beverly Hills CA 90212*

MACNEIL, IAN RODERICK, lawyer, educator; b. N.Y.C., June 20, 1929; s. Robert Lister and Kathleen Gertrude (Metcalf) Macneil; m. Nancy Carol Wilson, Mar. 29, 1952; children: Roderick, Jennifer, Duncan (dec.), Andrew. BA magna cum laude, U. Vt., 1950; LLB magna cum laude, Harvard U., 1955. Bar: N.H. 1956. Law clk. Hon. Peter Woodbury, 1955-56; asso. Sulloway Hollis Godfrey & Soden, Concord, N.H., 1956-59; mem. faculty Cornell U. Law Sch., Ithaca, N.Y., 1959-72, 74-80, Ingersoll prof. law, 1976-80; Wigmore prof. law Northwestern U. Sch. Law, Chgo., 1980—; vis. prof. U. East Africa, 1965-67, Duke U., 1971-72; prof. law, mem. Inst. Advanced Studies, U. Va., 1972-74; vis. fellow Centre for Socio-legal Studies and Wolfson Coll., Oxford U., 1979; hon. vis. fellow faculty law U. Edinburgh, 1979, 87; Rosenthal lectr. Northwestern U. Sch. Law, 1979; Braucher vis. prof. Harvard U., 1988-89. Author: Bankruptcy Law in East Africa, 1966, Contracts: Exchange Transactions and Relations, 2d edit., 1978, The New Social Contract, 1980, American Arbitration Law: Reformation Nationalization Internationalization, 1992; co-author: Federal Arbitration Law, 1994. Served with U.S. Army, 1951-53. Guggenheim fellow, 1978-79. Fellow Royal Soc. Antiquaries (Scotland); mem. ABA, Am. Law Inst., N.H. Bar Assn., Can. Assn. Law Tchrs., Soc. Pub. Tchrs. Law, Standing Coun. Scottish Chiefs. Office: Northwestern U Sch Law 357 E Chicago Ave Chicago IL 60611-3008 also: 5/8 Fountainhall Rd, Edinburgh EH9 2NL, Scotland

MAC NEIL, JOSEPH NEIL, archbishop; b. Sydney, N.S., Can., Apr. 15, 1924; s. John Martin and Kate (Mac Lean) Mac N. BA, St. Francis Xavier U., Antigonish, N.S., 1944; postgrad., Holy Heart Sem., Halifax, N.S., 1944-48, U. Perugia, 1956, U. Chgo., 1964; JCD, U. St. Thomas, Rome, 1958. Ordained priest Roman Cath. Ch., 1948. Pastor parishes in N.S., 1948-55; officialis Chancery Office, Antigonish, 1958-59; adminstrn. Diocese of Antigonish, 1959-60; rector Cathedral Antigonish, 1961; dir. extension dept. St. Francis Xavier U., Antigonish, 1961-69, v.p., 1962-69; bishop St. John, N.B., Can., 1969-73; chancellor U. St. Thomas, Fredericton, N.B., 1969-73; archbishop of Edmonton, Alta., 1973—; chmn. Alta Bishops' Conf., 1973—; chmn. bd. Newman Theol. Coll., Edmonton, 1973—, St. Joseph's Coll. U. Alta., Edmonton, 1973—. Vice chmn. N.S. Voluntary Econ. Planning Bd., 1965-69; bd. dirs. Program and Planning Agy., Govt. of N.S., 1969; exec. Atlantic Provinces Econ. Coun., 1968-73, Can. Coun. Rural Devel., 1965-75; bd. dirs. Futures Secretariat, 1981, Ctr. for Human Devel., Toronto, Ont., Can., 1985—; mem. bd. mgmt. Edmonton Gen. Hosp., 1983-92, Edmonton Caritas Health Group, 1992—; mem. Nat. Com. for Can. Participation in Habitat, 1976. Mem. Can. Assn. Adult Edn. (past pres. N.S.), Can. Assn. Dirs. Univ. Extension and Summer Schs. (past pres.), Inst. Rsch. on Pub. Policy (founding mem.), Can. Conf. Cath. Bishops (pres. 1979-81, mem. com. on ecumenism 1985-91, com. on missions 1991—, mem. permanent coun. 1993-95). Address: Archbishop of Edmonton, 8421 101st Ave, Edmonton, AB Canada T6A 0L1

MACNEIL, ROBERT BRECKENRIDGE WARE, broadcast journalist; b. Montreal, Que., Can., Jan. 19, 1931; came to U.S., 1963; s. Robert A.S. and Margaret Virginia (Oxner) MacN.; m. Rosemarie Anne Copland, 1956 (div. 1964); children: Catherine Anne, Ian B.; m. Jane J. Doherty, May 29, 1965 (div. 1983); children: Alison N., William H.; m. Donna P. Richards, Oct. 20, 1984. Student, Dalhousie U., 1949-51; BA, Carleton U., 1955; LHD (hon.), William Patterson Coll., 1977, Beaver Coll., Bates Coll., 1979, Lawrence U., 1980, Bucknell U., 1982, George Washington U., Kings Coll., Trinity Coll., U. Maine, 1983, Brown U., 1984, Colby Coll., Carleton Coll., U. S.C., 1985, Franklin and Marshall Coll., 1987, Nazareth Coll., Washington Coll., 1988, Kenyon Coll., 1990, U. Western Ont., 1992, U. Miami, Clark U., 1994, Clark U., 1994, U. L.I., 1995, Columbia U., 1995, Princeton U., 1995, The Cooper Union, 1996. Radio actor CBC, Halifax, N.S., Can., 1950-52; radio/TV announcer CBC, 1954-55; announcer Sta.-CJCH, Halifax, 1951-52; announcer, news writer Sta. CFRA, Ottawa, Ont., Can., 1952-54; sub-editor to filing editor Reuters News Agy., London, 1955-60; news corr. NBC, London, 1960-63, Washington, 1963-65, N.Y.C., 1965-67; corr. Panorama program BBC, London, 1967-71, 73-75; sr. corr. Nat. Public Affairs Center for TV, Washington, 1971-73; exec. editor, co-anchor MacNeil/Lehrer Report, Sta. -WNET-TV, N.Y.C., 1975—; exec. editor, co-anchor MacNeil/Lehrer News Hour, PBS, 1983-95, ret., 1995. Author: The People Machine, The Influence of Television on American Politics, 1968, The Right Place at the Right Time, 1982, Wordstruck, 1989, Burden of Desire, 1992, The Voyage, 1995; co-author: The Story of English, 1986; editor The Way We Were 1963, 1988. Recipient Lifetime Achievement award Overseas Press Club, 1995, Broadcaster of Yr. Internat. Radio and TV Soc., 1991, Paul White award Radio TV News Dirs. Assn., 1990, Medal of Honor U. Mo. Sch. Journalism, 1980. Fellow AAAS, The MacDowell Colony (chmn. 1993); mem. AFTRA, Assn. Radio and TV News Analysts, Writers Guild Am., Century Club (N.Y.C.). Office: c/o MacNeil-Lehrer Prodns 2700 S Quincy St Ste 240 Arlington VA 22206

MACNEILL, JAMES WILLIAM, international government consultant; b. Sask., Can., Apr. 22, 1928; s. Leslie William and Helga Ingeborg (Nohlgren) MacN.; m. Phyllis Beryl Ferguson, Nov. 30, 1953; children: Catherine Anne, Robin Lynne. BA, U. Sask., 1949, BE Mech., 1958, LLD (hon.), 1988; Diplome, U. Stockholm, 1951; DSc (hon.), McGill U., 1992; D of Environ. Studies (hon.), U. Waterloo, 1993; LHD (hon.), Lakehead U., 1994. Spl. adv. on constl. rev. Privy Council Office, Govt. Can., Ottawa, Ont., 1969-70; asst. sec. Can. Ministry of State for Urban Affairs, Ottawa, 1970-73; permanent sec. Can. Ministry of State for Urban Affairs, 1973-76; Can. AEP, Can. commr.-gen. UN Human Settlements Conf., Vancouver, B.C., 1975-78; dir. environ. directorate OECD, Paris, 1978-84; sec. gen. World Commn. Environment and Devel., Geneva, 1984-87; sr. fellow Inst. Research Pub. Policy, Ottawa, 1987-93; pres. J.W. MacNeill and Assocs., 1987—; chmn. Internat. Inst. for Sustainable Devel., 1994—; spl. advisor to adminstrn. UN Devel. Program, 1994—; apptd. officer Order of Can., 1995. Author: Environmental Management, 1971, Beyond Interdependence, 1991. Recipient Saskatchewan Achievement award, 1985, Silver medal City of Paris, 1984, Climate Inst. award, 1991, Swedish WASA award, 1991, Lifetime Achievement award Govt. of Can., 1993. Mem. Assn. Profl. Engrs. Ont., Assn. Profl. Engrs. Sask. Office: 13th Fl, 250 Albert St, Ottawa, ON Canada K2P 1L5

MAC NEISH, RICHARD STOCKTON, archaeologist, educator; b. N.Y.C., Apr. 29, 1918; s. Harris Franklin and Elizabeth (Stockton) MacN.; m. Phyllis Diana Walter, Sept. 26, 1963; children: Richard Roderick, Alexander Stockton. B.A., U. Chgo., 1940, M.A., 1944, Ph.D., 1949; LL.D. (hon.), Simon Frazer U., 1980; LL.D. Guggenheim fellow, Harvard U., 1956; LL.D. Aboriginal fellow, U. Mich., 1946. Supr., dir. U. Chgo. (W.P.A.), 1941-46; head dept. archaeology U. Calgary, 1964-68; anthropologist Nat. Mus. Can., 1949-62; dir. R.S. Peabody Found. for Archaeology, Andover, Mass., 1968-83; prof. dept. archeology Boston U., 1982-86; dir. Andover Found. for Archaeol. Research, 1986—. Contbr. numerous articles and revs. to profl. jours. Apptd. to U.S. Pres. Adv. Com. on Cultural Properties, 1992—. With AUS, 1942-43. Recipient Spinden medal for archaeology, 1964, Lucy Wharton Drexel medal for archaeol. research U. Pa. Mus., 1965, Addison Emery Verrill medal Peabody Mus., Yale U., 1966, hon. Disting. Prof. award Universidad Nacional de San Cristobal de Huamanga, Ayacucho, Peru, 1970, Cornplanter medal for Iroquois research Auburn, N.Y., 1977. Mem. Soc. Am. Archaeology (exec. council), Nat. Acad. Scis., Brit. Acad., Soc. Am. Archaeology (pres. 1971-72), Am. Anthrop. Assn. (Alfred Vincent Kidder award 1971), Sigma Psi, Alpha Tau Omega. Office: Andover Found Archaeol Research PO Box 83 Andover MA 01810-0002

MAC NELLY, JEFFREY KENNETH, cartoonist; b. N.Y.C., Sept. 17, 1947; s. Clarence Lamont and Ruth Ellen (Fox) Mac N.; m. Marguerite Dewey Daniels, July 19, 1969; children: Jeffrey Kenneth, Frank Daniels; m. Martha Scott Perry, July 13, 1985; 1 child, Matthew Perry; m. Susan Spekin, July 22, 1990. Grad., Phillips Acad., 1965; student, U. N.C., Chapel Hill, 1965-69. Cartoonist, staff artist Chapel Hill Weekly, 1969-70; cartoonist Richmond (Va.) News Leader, 1970-81, Chgo. Tribune, 1981—; creator syndicated comic strip Shoe. Recipient Pulitzer prize for editorial cartoons 1972, 78, 85. Office: Chicago Tribune 435 N Michigan Ave Chicago IL 60611

MACNICHOL, EDWARD FORD, JR., biophysicist, educator; b. Toledo, Oct. 24, 1918; s. Edward Ford and Adelaide (Foster) MacN.; m. Anne Proctor Ayer, Sept. 7, 1940; children—Edward Ford III, Anne (Mrs. David A. Brownell). A.B., Princeton, 1941; student, U. Pa., 1946-48; Ph.D., Johns Hopkins, 1952. Staff mem. radiation lab. Mass. Inst. Tech., 1941-46; from instr. to prof. biophysics Johns Hopkins, 1952-68; research biophysicist, asst. dir. Marine Biol. Lab., Woods Hole, Mass., 1972-76; dir. Lab. Sensory Physiology, 1973-84; prof. physiology Boston U. Med. Sch., 1973—; dir. Nat. Inst. Neurol. Diseases and Stroke, 1968-72; acting dir. Nat. Eye Inst., NIH, 1968-69; Mem. visual scis. study sect. NIH, 1963-66; mem. bd. sci. counsellors Nat. Inst. Neurol. Disease, and Blindness, 1965-68, chmn., 1968—; mem. U.S. Nat. Com. Photobiology, 1966-68, U.S. Nat. Com. Pure and Applied Biophysics, 1966. Co-editor: Sensory Processes, 1978-82. Bd. dirs. Deafness Research Found., 1973-83, sec., 1976-78. Recipient certificate of appreciation War Dept.-Navy Dept., 1947. Fellow IEEE (Engring. in Biology and Medicine prize award 1965, Centennial medal 1984, editor trans. biomed. engring. 1963-65); mem. AAAS, Am. Phys. Soc., Am. Physiol. Soc., Biophys. Soc., Soc. for Neurosci. Research in neurophysiology of vision; design instrumentation biol. research. Home: 120 Racing Beach Ave Falmouth MA 02540-1709 Office: Dept Physiology Boston Univ Sch Med 80 E Concord St Roxbury MA 02118-2307 *I have found a career, which has involved research, administration, engineering and teaching, to be both rewarding and challenging. I would regret not having had all these experiences; particularly the contact with different kinds of people having different ways of thinking. I would urge young people, above all, to understand thoroughly the basic principles involved in what they are doing, then work out the details, instead of just learning by rote the details of a narrow specialty.*

MACNIDER, JACK, retired cement company executive; b. Washington, Feb. 21, 1927; s. Hanford and Margaret Elizabeth (McAuley) MacN.; m. Margaret Hansen, Sept. 9, 1950; 1 son, Charles Hanford. Grad., Milton (Mass.) Acad., 1946; BA, Harvard U., 1950, MBA with distinction, 1952. With U.S. Steel Corp., 1952-54; with Northwestern States Portland Cement Co., Mason City, Iowa, 1954-90; v.p., asst. gen. mgr. Northwestern States Portland Cement Co., 1959-60, pres., gen. mgr., 1960-90, chmn. bd., 1979-90, ret., 1990; dir. Portland Cement Assn., 1962-9, chmn., 1974-76; sec.-treas., pres., dir. Mason City Hotel Corp.; pres., dir. Indian Farms, Inc., 1976—; trustee Equitable Life Ins. Co., Iowa, 1964-93. Chmn. North Iowa Med. Ctr., 1974-91; trustee Beloit Coll., Midwest Rsch. Inst., Kansas City, Mo., Iowa Natural Heritage Found., 1979-90, Herbert Hoover Presdl. Libr., 1985—; hon. trustee Upper Iowa U., Fayette; pres. Iowa Coll. Found., 1962. With USMCR, 1944-45. Mem. NAM (dir. 1978-85), Young Pres. Orgn., Portland Cement Assn. (chmn. bd. 1974-75, dir.), Iowa Mfrs. Assn. (chmn. 1971-72, dir.), Mason City C. of C. (pres. 1962), Am. Legion (past post comdr.), Masons, Euchre and Cycle Club (Mason City, Mason City Country Club, Mpls. Club, Univ. Club (Chgo.), Des Moines Club, Los Tree Club (Fla.). Republican. Congregationalist. Address: PO Box 623 Mason City IA 50402-0623

MACOMBER, JOHN D., construction executive; b. Boston, Oct. 8, 1955; s. George and Ann L. Macomber; m. Kristin Hodgkins, June 11, 1983; children: Ian D., Eric C. BA, Dartmouth Coll., 1978; MBA, Harvard U., 1983. Project mgr. George B.H. Macomber Co., Boston, 1987-90, v.p., 1983-87, pres., chief exec. officer, 1990—; lectr. MIT. Mem. exec. com. Appalachian Mountain Club, Boston, 1991—, Boys & Girls Clubs, Boston, 1989-93. Mem. U.S. Alpine Ski Team, 1974-76; NCAA All-America in skiing, 1974, 78. Mem. Harvard Bus. Sch. Assn., Young Pres. Orgn. Avocations: skiing, bicycling, tennis. Office: George BH Macomber Co 1 Design Ctr Pl Ste 600 Boston MA 02210

MACOMBER, JOHN D., industrialist; b. Rochester, N.Y., Jan. 13, 1928; s. William Butts and Elizabeth Currie (Ranlet) M.; m. Caroline Morgan, Oct. 21, 1955; children: Janet Morgan, Elizabeth Currie, William Butts II. B.A., Yale U., 1950; M.B.A., Harvard U., 1952. Mng. dir. McKinsey & Co., N.Y.C., France and Switzerland, 1954-73; chmn., CEO Celanese Corp., N.Y.C., 1973-87; chmn. J.D. Macomber & Co., N.Y.C., 1987-89; pres., chmn. Export-Import Bank of U.S., Washington, 1989-92; prin. JDM Investment Group, Washington, 1992—. 1st lt. USAF, 1952-54. Mem. Links (N.Y.C.), River Club (N.Y.C.), Union Club (N.Y.C.), Metropolitan (Washington). Office: JDM Investment Group 2806 N St NW Washington DC 20007-3339

MACOMBER, TRICIA, airport executive. Mgr. ops. Charlotte/Douglas Internat. Airport, Charlotte, N.C. Office: Charlotte/Douglas Internat Airpt PO Box 19066 Charlotte NC 28219-9066*

MACON, CAROL ANN GLOECKLER, micro-computer data base management company executive; b. Milw., Mar. 25, 1942; d. William Theodore and Gwendolyn Martha (Rice) Gloeckler; m. Jerry Lyn Macon, Aug. 28, 1981; children: Christian, Marie. BS in Edn. cum laude, U. Wis., Milw., 1969; postgrad., Midwestern State U., Wichita Falls, Tex., 1977, U. Tex., San Antonio, 1978, U. Colo., Colorado Springs. Tchr. Lubbock, Tex.; patient affairs coord. Cardiac Assocs., Colorado Springs; founder, CFO Macon Systems, Inc., Colorado Springs. Artist, Australia, Tex., Colo. Mem. Software Pubs. Assn., Colorado Springs Better Bus. Bur., Colorado Springs Fine Arts Ctr., Pikes Peak Rose Soc. (v.p.), Glen Eyrie Garden Soc., Bontantic Garden (mem. steering com.), Colo. Mountain Club, Phi Kappa Phi, Kappa Delta Pi, Sigma Tau Delta, Psi Chi.

MACON, JANE HAUN, lawyer; b. Corpus Christi, Tex., Sept. 26, 1946; d. E.H. and Johnnie Mae (De Mauri) Haun; m. R. Laurence Macon, Sept. 6, 1969. BA in Internat. Studies, U. Tex., 1967, JD, 1970. Bar: Tex. 1971, Ga. 1971, U.S. Dist. Ct. (we. dist.) Tex. 1973, U.S. Ct. Appeals (5th and 11th cirs.) 1973. Legal staff Office Econ. Opportunity, Atlanta, 1970-71; trial atty. City of San Antonio, 1972-77, city atty., 1977-83; ptnr. Fulbright & Jaworski, LLP, San Antonio, 1983—; pres. Internat. Women's Forum, Washington, 1987-89; mem. Com. of 200, 1988—; bd. dirs. Thousand Oaks Nat. Bank, San Antonio. Legal counsel Nat. Women's Polit. Caucus, 1981—; bd. dirs. Alamo council Boy Scouts Am., San Antonio, 1977—. Named to San Antonio Hall of Fame, 1984; named one of Rising Stars, 1984. Fellow Tex. Bar Found., Tex. Bar Assn. (chmn. women and the law 1984-85, client security fund com.), Southwest Research Found.; mem. San Antonio Bar Assn., San Antonio Young Lawyers Assn., Women Lawyers Tex. (pres. 1984-85), Tex. Banking Bd., Bexar County Women's Bar Assn. Democrat. Baptist. Home: 230 W Elsmere Pl San Antonio TX 78212-2349 Office: Fulbright & Jaworski LLP 300 Convent St Ste 2200 San Antonio TX 78205-3723

MACON, JERRY LYN, software company owner, software publisher; b. Okla., Jan. 10, 1941; s. James Westwood and Mary Isabelle (Hankins) M.; m. Carol Ann Gloeckler, Aug. 28, 1981; children: Heather, Scott, Karla. BS in Physics magna cum laude, Colo. Coll., 1963; MS in Physics, MIT, 1966; MBA in Fin., U. Colo., 1980. Physics instr. U.S. Naval Acad., Annapolis, Md., 1966-69; stockbroker Merrill Lynch, Colorado Springs, 1969-71; dir. systems analysis and programming Colorado Springs Pub. Schs., 1971-80; co-founder, pres. Alpine Software, Inc., Colorado Springs, 1980-82, Macon Systems Inc., Colorado Springs, 1981—. Author: (software) DB Master, 1980, Advanced DB Master, 1981, Advanced DB Master for Windows Version 6.0, 1995. Mem. Colorado Springs Fine Arts Ctr., 1982—, Colorado

Springs Symphony Coun., 1985—, Colorado Springs Better Bus. Bur., 1990—. Cmdr. USN, 1966-69, USNR, 1959-63, 69-82. Boettcher Found. scholar, 1959; Woodrow Wilson fellow, 1963; MIT rsch. assistantship, 1964. Mem. Nat. Fedn. Ind. Bus., Software Pubs. Assn., Pike Peak Rose Soc., Colo. Mountain Club, Phi Beta Kappa. Avocations: mountain climbing, hiking, travel, reading history, growing roses. Office: Macon Systems Inc 724 S Tejon St Colorado Springs CO 80903-4042

MACON, MYRA FAYE, retired library director; b. Slate Springs, Miss., Sept. 29, 1937; d. Thomas Howard and Reba Elizabeth (Edwards) M. BS in Edn., Delta State U., 1959; MLS, La. State U., 1965; postgrad., U. Akron, Ohio; EdD, Miss. State U., 1977. Librarian Greenwood (Miss.) Jr. High Sch., 1959-62, Greenwood High Sch., 1962-63, Grenada (Miss.) High Sch., 1963-64; library supr. Cuyahoga Falls (Ohio) City Schs., 1964-71; assoc. prof. U. Miss., Oxford, 1971-83; dir. libraries Delta State U., Cleve., 1983—. Editor: School Library Media Services for Handicapped; editor: ANRT Newsletter, Miss. Libraries; contbr. articles to profl. jours. Mem. ALA, Southeastern Library Assn., Miss. Library Assn., Exch. Club, Phi Delta Kappa, Beta Phi Mu, Delta Kappa Gamma, Omicron Delta Kappa. Home: Rt 3 Box 215A Calhoun City MS 38916 Office: WB Robers Library Delta State U Cleveland MS 38733

MACON, RICHARD LAURENCE, lawyer; b. Dallas, Dec. 31, 1944; s. Joseph Weldon and Dorothy Marie (Sikes) M.; m. Jane Arian Haun, Sept. 6, 1969. B of Arts in Am. Studies, Yale U., 1967; JD with honors, U. Tex., 1970. Bar: Ga. 1970, Tex. 1972, U.S. Dist. Ct. (we., ea., so. and no. dists.) Tex., U.S. Dist. Ct. (no. dist.) Ga., U.S. Ct. Appeals (5th and 11th cirs.), U.S. Supreme Ct. Assoc. Powell, Goldstein, Frazer & Murphy, Atlanta, 1970-72; ptnr. Cox & Smith, Inc., San Antonio, 1972-92, Akin, Gump, Strauss, Hauer & Feld, San Antonio, 1992—. Bd. dirs. Women Employment Network, Soc. Performing Arts, Monte Vista Hist. Soc., Target 90, Tex. Bank North, United Way Allocations Bd., San Antonio Free Clinic, San Antonio Edn. Employment, Inc., Com. for Alamodome, Com. for Supercollider, State Com. on Mental Retardation, Bexar County Women's Ctr., Bexar County Dem. Exec. Com.; chmn. 19th Senatorial Dist. Dem. Conv., Mayor's Commn. Energy; pres. Atlanta Tex. Execs.. Named as Man of Yr. San Antonio AFL-CIO, Rising Star Tex. Bus. Mag.; recipient Award of Appreciation YWCA, Award by Mexican Am. Legal Def. Fund, Award by Bexar County Edn. Found., Award by Bexar County Women's Polit. Caucus. Mem. Yale Club (pres. South Tex. chpt.), Order of Coif, Phi Delta Phi. Home: 230 W Elsmere Pl San Antonio TX 78212-2349 Office: Akin Gump Strauss Hauer & Feld 300 Convent St Ste 1500 San Antonio TX 78205-3716*

MACON, SETH CRAVEN, retired insurance company executive; b. Climax, N.C., Mar. 22, 1919; s. Oran T. and Kate (Craven) M.; m. Hazel Lee Monsees, June 27, 1942; children—Carol Susan, Randall Seth. A.B., Guilford Coll., 1940; grad., Am. Coll. Life Underwriters, 1949; postgrad., Inst. Ins. Marketing, So. Methodist U., 1947; exec. program, U. N.C., 1958. With Jefferson Standard Life Ins. Co., 1940-86, v.p., assoc. agy. mgr., 1964-67, v.p., agy. mgr., 1967-70, sr. v.p., dir., mem. finance com., 1970-74; v.p. Jefferson-Pilot Corp., 1974-86, also bd. dirs.; mem. adv. bd. Branch Bank & Trust Co. Author: Action in Recruiting, 1970, Recruiting—Today's Number One Priority in Agency Management, 1979. Trustee Guilford Coll., 1969—, chmn., 1980-88; trustee Life Underwriters Tng. Coun., 1974-76, So. Theol. Sem. Found., Louisville, 1983-93; bd. dirs. N.C. Bapt. Homes, 1983-92; mem. coordinating coun. Coop. Bapt. Fellowship, 1991-95. Recipient Disting. Alumnus award Guilford Coll., 1978. Mem. Life Ins. Marketing and Research Assn. (dir. 1974-78, chmn. 1976-77). Baptist (deacon 1960—, mem. fin. com. 1960-63). Lodge: Rotary. Home: 3803 Madison Ave Greensboro NC 27403-1035

MACOVSKI, ALBERT, electrical engineering educator; b. N.Y.C., May 2, 1929; s. Philip and Rose (Winogr) M.; m. Adelaide Paris, Aug. 5, 1950; children—Michael, Nancy. B.E.E., City Coll. N.Y., 1950; M.E.E., Poly. Inst. Bklyn., 1953; Ph.D., Stanford U., 1968. Mem. tech. staff RCA Labs., Princeton, N.J., 1950-57; asst. prof., then assoc. prof. Poly. Inst. Bklyn., 1957-60; staff scientist Stanford Research Inst., Menlo Park, Calif., 1960-71; fellow U. Calif. Med. Center San Francisco, 1971-72; prof. elec. engring. and radiology Stanford U., 1972—, endowed chair, Canon USA prof. engring., 1991—; dir. Magnetic Resonance Systems Research Lab.; cons. to industry. Author. Recipient Achievement award RCA Labs., 1952, 54; award for color TV circuits Inst. Radio Engrs., 1958; NIH spl. fellow, 1971. Fellow IEEE (Zworykin award 1973), Am. Inst. Med. Biol. Engring., Optical Soc. Am.; mem. NAE, Inst. of Medicine, Am. Assn. Physicists in Medicine, Soc. Magnetic Resonance in Medicine (former trustee), Sigma Xi, Eta Kappa Nu. Jewish. Achievements include patents in field. Home: 2505 Alpine Rd Menlo Park CA 94025-6314 Office: Stanford U Dept Elec Engring Stanford CA 94305

MACPHAIL, MORAY ST. JOHN, mathematics educator emeritus; b. Kingston, Ont., Can., May 27, 1912; s. James Alexander and Agnes Mary (Macmorine) M.; m. Frances Marian Patterson, Aug. 17, 1939; 1 child, James Alexander. B.A., Queen's U., 1933; M.A., McGill U., 1934; D.Phil., Oxford U., 1936; D.Sc. (hon.), Carleton U., 1978. Instr. Acadia U., Wolfville, N.S., Can., 1937-39, asst. prof., 1939-41, assoc. prof., 1942-44, prof., 1944-47; instr. Princeton U., N.J., 1941-42; vis. lectr. Queen's U., Kingston, Ont., Can., 1947-48; assoc. prof. Carleton U., Ottawa, Ont., Can., 1948-53, prof., 1953-67, 68-77, prof. emeritus, 1977—; vis. prof. U. Toronto, Ont., Can., 1967-68; assoc. dean Carleton U., Ottawa, Ont., Can., 1956-60, dir. grad. studies, 1960-63, dean grad. studies, 1963-69. Contbr. articles to profl. jours. Fellow Royal Soc. Can.; mem. Am. Math. Soc., Can. Math. Soc. Avocation: Music. Home: 165 Powell Ave, Ottawa, ON Canada K1S 2A2 Office: Carleton Univ, Dept Math and Stats, Ottawa, ON Canada K1S 5B6

MACPHEE, CRAIG ROBERT, economist, educator; b. Annapolis Royal, N.S., Can., July 10, 1944; came to U.S., 1950; s. Craig and Dorothy (Seney) MacP.; m. Kathleen Gray McCown, Feb. 6, 1966 (div. 1981); children: Paul, Heather, Rob; m. Andrea Joy Sime, June 26, 1983. BS, U. Idaho, 1966; MA, Mich. State U., 1968, PhD, 1970. Asst. prof., then assoc. prof. econs. U. Nebr., Lincoln, 1969-89, prof., 1989—, chmn. econs. dept., 1980-83, 89—; econ. affairs officer UN, Geneva, 1975-77; internat. economist U.S. Dept. Labor, Washington, 1983-84; cons. in field. Author: Economics of Medical Equipment and Supply, 1973, Restrictions on International Trade in Steel, 1974. Mem. Am. Econ. Assn., Midwest Econ. Assn., Nebr. Econ. and Bus. Assn., Delta Sigma Pi (faculty adviser 1982-95), Phi Eta Sigma, Omicron Delta Epsilon. Avocations: running, skiing, sailing, reading. Home: 631 Hazelwood Dr Lincoln NE 68510-4325 Office: U Nebr Coll Bus Dept Econ Lincoln NE 68588-0489

MACPHEE, DONALD ALBERT, academic administrator; b. Portland, Oreg., Jan. 3, 1928; s. Donald Lyman and Helen Adelaide (Randall) MacP.; m. Betty Jo Mincher, Sept. 9, 1950; children: Martha, William, Rebecca. BA, Seattle Pacific Coll., 1950; MA, U. Calif., Berkeley, 1952, PhD, 1959. Instr., asst., assoc. prof. history, acting dean ednl. svcs. and summer session San Francisco State Coll., 1956-64; assoc. prof. to prof. history Calif. State U., Dominguez Hills, 1964-85, mem. acad. planning staff, dean Sch. Social and Behavioral Scis., provost and v.p. acad. affairs, 1964-85; pres. SUNY Coll., Fredonia, 1985—. Contbr. scholarly articles on Am. politics, labor history, historiography, higher education to profl. jours. Bd. dirs. Fredonia (N.Y.) Coll. Found., Brooks Meml. Hosp., Dunkirk, N.Y., No. Chautauqua Community Found., Dunkirk, Chautauqua County Indsl. Devel. Agy., Mayville, N.Y. Mem. Am. Assn. State Colls. and Univs. (com. on policies and priorties), No. Chautauqua C. of C. Office: SUNY Coll at Fredonia Office of Pres Fredonia NY 14063

MACPHERSON, COLIN R(OBERTSON), pathologist, educator; b. Aberdeen, Scotland, Sept. 2, 1924; came to U.S., 1956; s. Donald J.R. and Nora (Tait) M.; m. Margaret E. Mitchell, Dec. 21, 1949; children: Shelagh, Catherine, Janet, Mary. MBChB, U. Cape Town, Union South Africa, 1946, M.Med., MD in Pathology, 1954. Diplomate Anatomic and Clinical Pathology, Blood Banking. Resident, instr. U. Cape Town, 1948-54; fellow Postgrad. Med. Sch., London, 1955-56; asst., assoc. then prof. pathology Ohio State U., Columbus, 1956-75, vice chmn. lab. med., 1961-75; dir. lab. medicine U. Cin., 1975-87, dep. dir. Hoxworth Blood Ctr., 1988-90, prof. dept. pathology and lab. medicine, 1991-95, prof. emeritus, 1995—. Contbr. articles to profl. jours. Chmn. bd. schs., rev. bd. Nat. Accrediting Agy. for Clin. Lab. Scis., 1968-74. Mem. Am. Assn. Blood Banks. Presbyterian. Avocations: music, color photography. Office: U Cin Med Ctr Goodman St Cincinnati OH 45267-0714

MACPHERSON, ELLE, model; b. Sydney, Australia, Mar. 29, 1964; m. Gilles Bensimon, May 24, 1986 (div.). Appeared on covers of Sports Illustrated swimsuit edit., 1986, 87, 88, 94, Elle, Cosmopolitan, Self; film appearences include Husbands and Wives, 1992, Sirens, 1994, If Lucy Fell, 1996. Office: Women Model Mgmt 107 Greene St Fl 2 New York NY 10012-3803

MACQUEEN, ROBERT MOFFAT, solar physicist; b. Memphis, Mar. 28, 1938; s. Marion Leigh and Grace (Gilfillan) MacQ.; m. Caroline Gibbs, June 25, 1960; children: Andrew, Marjorie. BS, Rhodes Coll., 1960; PhD, Johns Hopkins U., 1968. Asst. prof. physics Rhodes Coll., 1961-63; instr. physics and astronomy Goucher Coll., Towson, Md., 1964-66; sr. research scientist Nat. Ctr. for Atmospheric Research, Boulder, Colo., 1967-90, dir. High Altitude Obs., 1979-86, asst. dir., 1986-87, assoc. dir., 1987-89; prof. physics Rhodes Coll., Memphis, 1990—; prin. investigator NASA Apollo program, 1971-75, NASA Skylab program, 1970-76, NASA Solar Maximum Mission, 1976-79, NASA/ESA Internat. Solar Polar Mission, 1978-83; lectr. U. Colo., 1968-79, adj. prof., 1979-90; mem. com. on space astronomy Nat. Acad. Scis., 1973-76, mem. com. on space physics, 1977-79; mem. Space Sci. Bd., 1983-86. Recipient Exceptional Sci. Achievement medal NASA, 1974. Fellow Optical Soc. Am.; mem. Am. Astron. Soc. (chmn. solar physics div. 1976-78), Assn. Univ. Research Astronomy (dir.-at-large 1984-93, chmn. bd. 1989-92), Am. Assn. Physics Tchrs., Sigma Xi.

MAC RAE, ALFRED URQUHART, physicist, electrical engineer; b. N.Y.C., Apr. 14, 1932; s. Farquhar and Eliza J. (Urquhart) Mac R.; m. Peggy M. Hazard, May 13, 1967; children: Susan, Pamela. B.S. in Physics, Syracuse U., 1954, Ph.D. in Physics, 1960. Dir. integrated circuit devel. Bell Labs., Murray Hill, N.J., 1979-83; dir. satellite communications systems Bell Labs., Homdel, N.J., 1983-95; pres. Mac Tech., Berkeley Heights, N.J., 1995—; adv. com. to bd. trustees N.J. Inst. Tech., 1981-85. Bd. editor: Vacuum Sci. and Tech, 1965-67, Rev. Sci. Instruments, 1969-71; contbr. articles to jours.; patentee in field. Fellow IEEE (chmn. field awards 1991-93), Am. Phys. Soc.; mem. Bohmische Phys. Soc., IEEE Electron Devices Soc. (pres. 1986-87, chmn. field awards 1989-93, Ebers award 1994). Office: 72 Sherbrook Dr Berkeley Heights NJ 07922-2346

MACRAE, CAMERON FARQUHAR, III, lawyer; b. N.Y.C., Mar. 21, 1942; s. Cameron F. and Jane B. (Miller) MacR.; m. Ann Wooster Bedell, Nov. 30, 1974; children: Catherine Fairfax, Ann Cameron. A.B., Princeton U., 1963; LL.B., Yale U., 1966. Bar: N.Y. 1966, D.C. 1967, U.S. Dist. Ct. (so. dist.) N.Y. 1975. Atty.-advisor Office of Gen. Counsel to Sec. Air Force, Washington, 1966-69; assoc. Davis, Polk & Wardwell, N.Y.C., 1970-72; dep. supt. and counsel N.Y. State Banking Dept., N.Y.C., 1972-74; sr. ptnr., vice chmn. LeBoeuf, Lamb, Greene & MacRae, N.Y.C., 1975—. Trustee, sec. St. Andrew's Dune Ch., 1982—; hon. chmn. Clear Pool Inc., 1990—. Capt. USAF, 1966-69. Mem. Assn. of Bar of City of N.Y. (past mem. securities regulation com., banking law com.), D.C. Bar Assn. Republican. Episcopalian. Clubs: Links, Racquet and Tennis (N.Y.C.), Meadow (v.p., bd. govs.), Bathing Corp., Shinnecock Hills Golf (Southampton), Cottage (Princeton, N.J.). Note and comment editor Yale Law Jour., 1965-66. Office: LeBoeuf Lamb Greene & MacRae 125 W 55th St New York NY 10019-5369

MACRAE, DONALD ALEXANDER, astronomy educator; b. Halifax, Nova Scotia, Can., Feb. 19, 1916; s. Donald Alexander and Laura Geddes (Barnstead) M.; m. Margaret Elizabeth Malcolm, Aug. 25, 1939; children—David Malcolm, Charles Donald, Andrew Richard. B.A., U. Toronto, Ont., Can., 1937; A.M., Harvard U., Cambridge, Mass., 1940, Ph.D., 1943. Research asst. U. Pa., Phila., 1941-42; lectr. Cornell U., Ithaca, N.Y., 1942-44; scientist Carbide & Carbon Chem. Corp., Oak Ridge, Tenn., 1944-46; asst. prof. Case Inst. Tech., Cleve., 1946-53; assoc. prof. to prof. astronomy, dir. David Dunlap Observatory, U. Toronto, 1953-78, prof. and dir. emeritus, 1978—; trustee Univs. Space Research Assn., Lunar and Planetary Inst., Houston, 1969-76, Can.-France-Hawaii Telescope Corp., Kamuela, Hawaii, 1973-79, Cascatrust, 1991-94. Fellow Royal Soc. Can., Royal Astron. Soc. (London); mem. Can. Astron. Soc., Royal Astron. Soc. Can., Am. Astron. Soc. Home: 427 Glencairn Ave, Toronto, ON Canada M5N 1V4 Office: David Dunlap Observatory, Box 360, Richmond Hill, ON Canada L4C 4Y6

MACRAE, DUNCAN, JR., social scientist, educator; b. Glen Ridge, N.J., Sept. 30, 1921; s. Duncan and Rebecca Kyle (MacRae); m. Edith Judith Krugelis, June 24, 1950; 1 child, Amy Frances. A.B., Johns Hopkins U., 1942; A.M., Harvard U., 1943, Ph.D., 1950. Mem. staff Radiation Lab., Mass. Inst. Tech., 1943-46; instr., then lectr. sociology Princeton, 1949-51; rsch. assoc. Lab. Social Rels., Harvard U., 1951-53; asst. prof. sociology U. Calif., Berkeley, 1953-57; mem. faculty U. Chgo., 1957-72, prof. polit. sci. and sociology, 1964-72; William Rand Kenan, Jr. prof. polit. sci. and sociology U. N.C., Chapel Hill, 1972—; chmn. curriculum in public policy analysis U. N.C., 1980-85; Pres. Policy Studies Assn., 1974-75. Author: Dimensions of Congressional Voting, 1958, Parliament, Parties and Society in France, 1946-58, 1967, Issues and Parties in Legislative Voting, 1970, The Social Function of Social Science, 1976, (with James A. Wilde) Policy Analysis for Public Decisions, 1979, Policy Indicators, 1985; Editor: (with others) Electronic Instruments, 1948, Policies for America's Public Schools, 1988. Fulbright rsch. scholar France, 1956-57. Fellow AAAS, Am. Acad. Arts and Scis.; mem. Am. Polit. Sci. Assn., Am. Sociol. Assn., Am. Econ. Assn., Assn. Pub. Policy and Mgmt., Phi Beta Kappa. Home: 737 Gimghoul Rd Chapel Hill NC 27514-3815

MAC RAE, HERBERT FARQUHAR, retired college president; b. Middle River, N.S., Can., Mar. 30, 1926; s. Murdoch John and Jessie (Matheson) Mac R.; m. Mary Ruth Finlayson, Sept. 24, 1955; children—Roderick John, Elizabeth Anne, Christy Margaret, Mary Jean. Diploma NS, Agrl. Coll., 1952; BSc, McGill U., 1954, MSc, 1956, PhD, 1960, DSc (hon.), 1987. Chemist, food and drug directorate Dept. Nat. Health and Welfare, Ottawa, Ont., 1960-61; mem. faulty Macdonald Coll. McGill U., 1961-72, assoc. prof. animal sci. Macdonald Coll., 1967-70, prof., chmn. dept. Macdonald Coll., 1970-72; prin. N.S. Agrl. Coll., Truro, 1972-89, ret., 1989. Named to Can. Agrl. Hall of Fame, 1994. Fellow Agrl. Inst. Can.; mem. Can. Soc. Animal Sci., Mem. Order of Can., Rotary, Sigma Xi. Home: 7 Hickman Dr, Truro, NS Canada B2N 2Z2

MACRAKIS, KRISTIE IRENE, history of science educator; b. Boston, Mar. 11, 1958; d. Michael S. and Lily Macrakis. BA, Oberlin (Ohio) Coll., 1980; MA, Harvard U., 1983, PhD, 1989. Rsch. asst. Harvard U., Cambridge, Mass., 1980-82, lectr., 1989-90; postdoctoral fellow Humbolt Found., Bonn, Germany, 1990-91; asst. prof. Mich. State U., East Lansing, 1991—. Author: Surviving the Swastika, 1993; contbr. articles to profl. jours. AAUW fellow, WAshington, 1987-88; Social Sci. Rsch. Coun. fellow, N.Y.C., 1984-86; Inst. for Advanced Study fellow, 1993-94. Mem. Am. Hist. Assn., German Studies Assn., N.Y. Acad. Sci., History of Sci. Soc., Sigma Xi. Avocations: music, sports. Office: Mich State U Dept History Morrill Hall # 301 East Lansing MI 48824-1036

MACRI, THEODORE WILLIAM, book publisher; b. N.Y.C.; s. Francis Carl and Emma Julia (Fantini) M.; m. Joan Michele Damato; children: Alicia, Theodore William. AB, Villanova U.; MA, NYU. With Doubleday & Co. Inc., N.Y.C., dir. domestic rights, 1978-82, editorial group dir., 1982-83, asst. to pres., 1983; v.p., pub. R.R. Bowker Co., 1983-85; v.p., dir. subs. rights Contemporary Books, Inc., 1985-90; v.p. Carol Pub. Group, Inc., N.Y.C., 1990-94; pres. Ted Macri Assocs., 1994—; Bd. dirs. CUNY Ctr. for Pub., 1983—, Nat. Book Awards. Mem. N.Y. County Republican Com., 1980-81; mem. men's com. Mus. Natural History, N.Y.C., 1978. Served to lt. (j.g.) USNR. Named Disting. Alumnus Villanova U., 1983. Mem. Assn. Am. Pubs. (edn. com.), Am. Bookseller's Assn. Republican. Roman Catholic. Club: N.Y. Athletic (N.Y.C.). Office: 10 E End Ave Apt 4E New York NY 10021-1110

MACRO, LUCIA ANN, editor; b. Rhinebeck, N.Y., May 15, 1959; d. Virgil Jordan and Jeannette Anastasia (Jakelski) M.; m. Richard Marchione, 1992. BA, Fordham U., Bronx, 1981. Asst. editor, editor Silhouette Books, N.Y.C., 1985—, sr. editor, 1989—; speaker in field nat. convs. Romance Writers Am., 1985—; interviewed Bus. Week, 1987, CNN, 1991, Sta. WNBC, various newspapers including N.Y. Daily News, Washington Post. Author articles Romantic Times, 1988-89, 93, Romance Writers Report, 1988-89. Recipient Rita award Romance Writers Am., 1990, 92, 94, 95. Democrat. Office: Silhouette Books 300 E 42nd St New York NY 10017-5947

MACRURY, KING, management counselor; b. Manchester, N.H., Oct. 14, 1915; s. Colin H. and Lauretta C. (Shea) MacR.; 1 son, Colin C. A.B., Rollins Coll., 1938; postgrad., St. Anselms Coll., L.I. Coll. Medicine, Princeton. Asst. personnel dir. Lily-Tulip Cup Corp., 1939; asst. dir. market research Ward Baking Co., 1940-41; staff mem. Nat. Indsl. Conf. Bd., 1941-43; cons. indsl. relations and orgn. planning McKinsey & Co., 1946-48; internal cons. Oxford Paper Co., 1949-50; installer, dir. indsl. relations Champion Internat. Co., 1950-51; pvt. practice mgmt. counselor, 1951—; lectr. Indsl. Edn. Inst., 1962-68, Mgmt. Center, Cambridge, 1968-71, Dun & Bradstreet, 1979—; extension div. U. N.H., 1968—; extension program U. Maine, 1978—; also U. Bridgeport, extension program U. Conn.; coordinator mgmt. edn. extension div. U. Conn., 1964-68, Philippine Council Mgmt., 1969—, Econ. Devel. Found. Philippines, 1969—, Am. Metal Stamping Assn., 1969—; condr. mgmt. seminars for Asian Assn. Mgmt. Orgns. C.I.O.S., 1972; Mem. Indsl. Devel. Commn. Andover, 1957-58; manpower com. U.S. Dept. Labor Bus. Adv. Council, 1958-61. Author: Developing Your People Potential; Contbr. numerous articles in field to profl. jours. Served to lt. USNR, 1943-46. Mem. N.H. Dental Soc. (hon.), Smaller Bus. Assn. N.E., Res. Officers Assn. Office: PO Box 215 Rye NH 03870-0215 *As individuals or as corporations, we derive our vitality from the responsiveness of those to whom we are bound in interest or effort. So it becomes, necessarily, our primary goal to inspire and to nurture this elemental source of strength.*

MACSAI, JOHN, architect; b. Budapest, Hungary, May 20, 1926; came to U.S., 1947, naturalized, 1954; s. Ferenc and Margit (Rosenfeld) Lusztig; m. Geraldine Marcus, May 7, 1950; children: Pamela, Aaron, Marian, Gwen. Baccalaureate summa cum laude, Kolcsey Gimnasium, Budapest, 1944; student, Atelier Art Sch., Budapest, 1941-43, Poly. U., Budapest, 1945-47; BArch magna cum laude, Miami U., Oxford, Ohio, 1949. Archtl. designer Skidmore, Owings & Merrill, Chgo., Pace Assos., Chgo., Raymond Loewy Assos., Chgo., 1949-55; ptnr. Hausner & Macsai, Chgo., 1955-71, Campbell & Macsai, Chgo., 1971-74; prin. John Macsai & Assocs. Architects, Inc., Chgo., 1975-90, O'Donnell Wicklund Pigozzi & Peterson, Chgo., 1991—; prof. architecture U. Ill., Chgo., 1970—. Author: High Rise Apartment Buildings: A Design Primer, 1972, Housing, 1976, 2d edit., 1982, Russian edit., 1980, Mexican edit., 1984; co-author: Designing Environments for the Aged, 1977, Housing for a Maturing Population, 1983, (ency.) Highrise Apartment Buildings, 1988; prin. works include Nat. Opinion Rsch. Ctr., U. Chgo., 1967, High Energy Physics Bldg., 1968, Social Svcs. Ctr., 1970; apt. bldgs. Harbor House, 1965, Malibu East, 1972, Waterford apt. bldg., 1976, U. Chgo. faculty townhouses, 1986, Fairfield Ct. housing for the elderly, 1988, Evanston Pl. apt. bldg. and city garage, 1991, 2960 N. Lake Shore Dr. Housing for the Elderly, 1991. Fellow AIA (13 design award citations Chgo. chpt.). Jewish. Home: 1207 Judson Ave Evanston IL 60202-1316 Office: O Donnell Wicklund Pigozzi & Peterson 1 N Franklin St Chicago IL 60606-3421

MACTAGGART, BARRY, retired corporate executive; b. Kandos, Australia, Dec. 29, 1931; came to U.S., 1972; s. Malcolm Ian and Dorothy (Schroder) MacT.; m. Robin Margaret Wilson, Nov. 24, 1962; children: Susan, Ian, Cameron. Cert. acct., Inst. Chartered Accts., Australia, 1954. Audit mgr. Peat, Marwick, Mitchell, Sydney, Australia, 1950-58; auditor, controller eastern area Pfizer Internat., Hong Kong, 1959-64; controller Pfizer Asia, Tokyo, 1964-65, dir. adminstrn., 1966-67; mgr. country Pfizer Australia, 1967-68; pres. Pfizer Asia, Hong Kong, 1968-72; exec. v.p. Pfizer Internat., N.Y.C., 1972-80, pres., 1980-81, pres., chmn. bd. dirs., 1981-91. Mem. Indian Harbor Yacht Club, Hong Kong Club, The Pilgrims Club, John's Island Club, Riomar Bay Yacht Club, Univ. and Schs. Club. Home: 180 N Shore Pt Vero Beach FL 32963-3726

MACTAGGART, TERRENCE JOSEPH, academic administrator; b. Buffalo, Sept. 20, 1946; s. Joseph Carol and Genieve Mary (Quinn) MacT. BA in English and Philosophy, Canisius Coll., Buffalo, 1967; MA in Lit., St. Louis U., 1971, PhD in Lit., 1976; MBA, St. Cloud (Minn.) State U., 1986. Prof. Blackburn Coll., Carlinville, Ill., 1973-74; dir. Webster U., St. Louis, 1974-77; acting dean U. Alaska, Fairbanks, 1977-79; dean St. Cloud (Minn.) State U., 1979-83; v.p. Met. State U., St. Paul, 1983-86; vice chancellor Minn. State U. System, St. Paul, 1986-87; chancellor U. Wis., Superior, 1987-91, Minn. State U. System, 1991—. Editor: Cost Effective Assessment of Prior Learning, 1983; contbr. articles on higher edn. to profl. jours. Sgt. U.S. Army, 1969-71, Viet Nam. NDEA fellow, 1968-72. Mem. Phi Beta Kappa. Avocations: cross country skiing, sailing. Office: State U System of Minn System Office 555 Park St Ste 230 Saint Paul MN 55103-2142

MACURDY, JOHN EDWARD, basso; b. Detroit, Mar. 18, 1929; s. Blanchard Archibald and Dorathea Rosalie (Radtke) Mc Curdy; m. Justine May Votypka, Apr. 12, 1958; children—Allison Anne, John Blanchard. Student, Wayne State U., 1947; student of Avery Crew, Detroit, 1946. Mem. N.Y.C. Opera, 1959-62, Met. Opera, 1962—. Appeared in U.S., Europe, including San Francisco Opera, La Scala; performances include world premieres Mourning Becomes Electra, Met. Opera, 1967, opening night Anthony and Cleopatra, Met. Opera, 1966, Wuthering Heights, Santa Fe Opera, 1958, Six Characters in Search of an Author, N.Y.C. Opera, 1959, Griffalkin, Tanglewood Festival, 1957; Am. premieres Capriccio, Santa Fe Opera, 1958, Murder in the Cathedral, Empire State Music Festival, Bear Mountain Park, N.Y., 1959, Inspector General, N.Y.C. Opera, 1960; appeared with numerous orchs.; film Don Giovanni, 1979; participant 40th Anniversary Sud-Deutsche Rundfunk, 100th Anniversary Gala Met. Opera, 1983. Served with USAF, 1950-54. Recipient medal for artistic merit during Mich. Week City of Detroit, 1969; inducted into Acad. Vocal Hall of Fame, 1985. Mem. Bohemians. Presbyterian. Clubs: Bohemian (San Francisco); Greenwich Country (Conn.). Office: Met Opera Lincoln Ctr New York NY 10023

MAC VICAR, ROBERT WILLIAM, retired university administrator; b. Princeton, Minn., Sept. 28, 1918; s. George William and Elizabeth (Brennan) MacV.; m. Clarice Chambers, Dec. 23, 1948; children—Miriam J., John R. BA, U. Wyo., 1939, LLD, 1977; MS, Okla. State U., 1940; PhD, U. Wis., 1946; DSc (hon.), Dankook U., Korea, 1980; HLD, Nat. U., 1995. Assoc. prof., prof. biochemistry Okla. State U., 1946-64, dean grad. sch., 1953-64, v.p. acad. affairs, 1957-64; v.p. acad. affairs So. Ill. U., Carbondale, 1964-68; chancellor So. Ill. U., 1968-70; pres. Oreg. State U., Corvallis, 1970-84; pres. emeritus Oreg. State U., 1984—; acting pres. Coll. of Ganado, Ariz., 1985; founding mem., bd. dirs. Central Ednl. Midwest Research Lab., chmn. exec. com., 1969-70. Exec. dir. regents task force Ariz. Bd. of Regents, 1987-88; chmn. N.W. Acad. Computing Consortium, 1987-90. Served with U.S. Army, 1939-45. Rhodes scholar, 1939. Mem. Am. Soc. Biol. Chemists, Am. Chem. Soc., Am. Inst. Nutrition, Okla. Acad. Sci., Phi Beta Kappa, Sigma Xi, Phi Kappa Phi. Presbyterian. Home: 1440 NW 14th St Corvallis OR 97330-4660 Office: Oreg State U Office of the Pres Corvallis OR 97331

MACVITTIE, PAULA RAE, advertising executive; b. Rhinelander, Wis., Dec. 13, 1950; d. Paul R. and Geraldine Mae (Plant) Alfonsi; m. Ronald B. MacVittie, June 23, 1984. BS in Communication, U. Wis., 1973. Media sales rep. Sta. WAOW-Radio, Tomahawk, Wis., 1973-74; mgr. local sales Sta. WLFI-TV, Lafayette, Ind., 1975-78; pres. Concept Mktg., Inc., Lafayette, 1978-85; account supr. Caldwell VanRiper, Inc., Indpls., 1985-86, v.p., 1986-87, pres., chief exec. officer, 1987—. Mem. pres.'s circle Hudson Inst., Indpls., 1989, 94; Corp. Cmty. Coun., 1989—; exec. com. mem. Cmty. Leaders Allied for Superior Schs., 1989—; bd. dirs. Indpls. C. of C., Greater Indpls. Progress Com., United Way Ctrl. Ind. Mem. Am. Mktg. Assn., Ind. Fedn. Advt. Agys. (bd. dirs.), Japan-Am. Soc., Ad Club. Avocations: movies, aerobics, reading. Office: Caldwell VanRiper Inc PO Box 7046 Indianapolis IN 46207-7046

MAC VITTIE, ROBERT WILLIAM, retired college administrator; b. Middletown, N.Y., Dec. 29, 1920; s. Mortimer, Jr. and Mary (Thompson) MacV.; m. Margaret L. Cooper, July 15, 1944; children—Robert William II, Beth Ann, Geralyn Amy. B.Ed., State U. N.Y., Oneonta, 1944; M.A., N.Y. U., 1946; Ed.D., 1954. Elementary tchr. Pine Plains (N.Y.) Central Sch., 1944; social sci. tchr. Meml. Jr. High Sch., Middletown, N.Y., 1944-48; supervising prin. Montowese Sch., North Haven, Conn., 1948-52, Ridge Rd. Sch., North Haven, 1952-53; prof. sch. adminstrn., prin. lab. sch. N.Y. State Coll. Tchrs., Buffalo, 1954-56; dir. div. elementary and secondary edn. State U. N.Y. Coll., Buffalo, 1956-58; dean coll. State U. N.Y. Coll., 1958-63; pres. State U. Coll., Geneseo, 1963-79; emeritus State U. Coll., 1979—; interim pres. SUNY-Fredonia, N.Y., 1985, SUNY-Geneseo, 1988-89; Mem. regional adv. bd. Key Bank, N.A., Oneonta, N.Y., 1978-86; mem. SUNY Commn. Univ. Purposes and Priorities; exec. com. Rochester Area Colls., Inc., 1972-79, SUNY Council Pres.'s, 1970-72, 76-78; bd. dirs. Adams Art Gallery. Author: Handbook for Substitute Teachers, 3d edit, 1959, also numerous articles. Mem. citizens salary adv. com. Kenmore, N.Y., 1957; cons. sch. program evaluation team Tchrs. Coll., Temple U., 1956-57; mem. Livingston County Planning Bd., 1967-73, chmn., 1972-73; bd. dirs. Chautauqua Co. Automobile Club, Inc., Am. Automobile Assn., 1986-93, No. Chautauqua Community Foundation, 1985—, Chautauqua Adult Day Care Ctrs., 1991-92, D.R. Barker Libr., 1992—; mem. adv. bd. Auto Club Western N.Y., 1993—. Paul Harris fellow Rotary Internat. Mem. Am. Assn. Higher Edn., Am. Assn. Sch. Adminstrs., Am. Assn. Univ. Adminstrs. (pres. 1971-73, dir. 1977-79, gen. sec. 1979-81, Disting. Svc. award 1994), Am. Assn. State Colls. and Univs. (bd. dirs. 1977-79), Am. Acad. Polit. and Social Scis., Livingston C. of C. (dir. 1970-79), Phi Delta Kappa, Kappa Delta Pi, Rotary Internat., SUNY of N.Y. and Conferations of SUNY Alumni Assns. (spl. citation Disting. Alumni Svc. award 1994). Lodge: Rotary Internat. Robert W. MacVittie Coll. Union named in his honor SUNY-Geneseo, 1989. Home and Office: 187 Chestnut St Fredonia NY 14063-1601

MAC WATTERS, VIRGINIA ELIZABETH, singer, music educator, actress; b. Phila.; d. Frederick-Kennedy and Idoleein (Hallowell) Mac W.; m. Paul Abée, June 10, 1960. Grad., Phila. Normal Sch. for Tchrs., 1933; student, Curtis Inst. Music, Phila., 1936. With New Opera Co., N.Y.C., 1941-42; artist-in-residence Ind. U. Sch. Music, 1957-58; assoc. prof. U. Ind. Sch. Music, 1958-68, prof. voice, 1968-82, prof. emeritus, 1982—. Singer: leading roles Broadway mus. Rosalinda, 1942-44, Mr. Strauss Goes to Boston, 1945, leading opera roles New Opera Co., N.Y.C., 1941-42, San Francisco, 1944, N.Y.C. Ctr., 1946-51; leading soprano for reopening of Royal Opera House, Covent Garden, London, 1947-48, Guatemala, El Salvador, Cen. Am., 1948-49; debut at Met. Opera, N.Y.C., 1952; TV spls. on NBC include Menotti's Old Maid and the Thief, 1949, Would-be Gentleman (R. Strauss), 1955; leading singer with Met. Opera Co. on coast to coast tour of Die Fledermaus, 1951-52,, Met. Opera debut, N.Y.C., 1952, leading soprano Cen. City Opera Festival, Colo., 1952-56; performed with symphony orchs. in U.S., Can., S.Am.; concert recitalist U.S., Can., 1950-62; opened N.Y. Empire State Music Festival in Ariadne auf Naxos (Strauss), 1959; soloist Mozart Festival, Ann Arbor, Mich. Recipient Mile award Album Familiar Music, 1949, Ind. U. Disting. Tchg. award, 1979; named One of 10 Outstanding Women of the Yr.; Zeckwer Hahn Phila. Mus. Acad. scholar, 1941-42; MacWatters chair donated by New Auer Grand Concert Hall, U. Ind. Sch. Music. Mem. Nat. Fedn. of Music Clubs, Nat. Soc. Arts and Letters, Nat. Soc. Lit. and Arts, Soc. Am. Musicians, Nat. Assn. Tchrs. of Singing, Internat. Platform Assn., Sigma Alpha Iota. Club: Matinee Musical (hon. mem. Phila., Indpls. chpts.). Only original recorded version of Zerbinetta aria from Ariadne auf Naxos (Strauss). Home: 3800 Arlington Rd Bloomington IN 47404-1347 Office: Ind U Sch Music Bloomington IN 47401

MACWHORTER, ROBERT BRUCE, retired lawyer; b. Phila., July 12, 1930; s. George Merritt and Marion (Ritchie) MacW.; m. Althea Lucille Davis, June 23, 1956; children: Susan Elizabeth (Mrs. Steven Young), Nancy Jeanne (Mrs. Matthew Oja), Marjorie Anne (Mrs. Carl Friedrichs). A.B., Oberlin Coll., 1953; LL.B., U. Va., 1956. Bar: Va. 1956, N.Y. 1957. Assoc. Shearman & Sterling, N.Y.C., 1956-65, ptnr., 1965-91. Mem. ABA, N.Y. Bar Assn., Order of Coif. Home: 85 Jefferson Ave Maplewood NJ 07040-1228

MACWILLIAMS, KENNETH EDWARD, investment banker; b. Newburyport, Mass., Aug. 21, 1936; s. Harold Freeman and Helen (Melia) MacW.; m. Angelyn Wishnack, July 16, 1960 (div. 1975); children: Robert Hovey, James Stuart. BA, Harvard U., 1958, MBA, 1962. V.p. Morgan Guaranty Trust Co., N.Y.C., 1962-71; sr. assoc. Goldman Sachs & Co., N.Y.C., 1971-74; mng. dir., domestic merchant banking group Manfacturers Hanover Trust Co., N.Y.C., 1975-82; chmn., chief exec. officer Prudential Capital Corp. subs. Prudential Ins. Co. Am., Newark, 1982-90; pres. Prudential Equity Mgmt. Assn. subs. Prudential Ins. Co. Am., Newark, 1990-92, Woodrow Wilson House, Princeton, N.J., 1993—. Office: 10 State St Newburyport MA 01950

MACY, RICHARD J., state judge; b. Saranac Lake, N.Y., June 2, 1930; m. Emily Ann Macy; children: Anne, Patty, Mark. BS in Bus., U. Wyo., 1955, JD, 1958. Pvt. practice Sundance, Wyo., 1958-85; justice Wyo. Supreme Ct., Cheyenne, 1985—, former chief justice; Crook County atty., 1970-85; mem. Nat. Conf. Commrs. on Uniform State Laws, 1982—. Mem. Sigma Chi (Nat. Outstanding Sig award 1986). Office: Wyo Supreme Ct Supreme Ct Bldg Cheyenne WY 82002*

MADANSHETTY, SAMEER ISHWAR, mechanical engineer; b. Belgaum, Karnatak, India, Dec. 2, 1953; came to U.S., 1984; s. Ishwar Gurunath Mandanshetti; m. Isabel Morin Zambrano, Oct. 11, 1988. MS, Indian Inst. Tech., New Delhi, 1975; MA, Yale U., 1986, PhD, 1989. Engr. Telco Ltd., Poona, India, 1975-84; rsch. asst. Yale U., New Haven, 1984-89, tchg. fellow, 1987-88; lectr., rsch. assoc. engring. Harvard U., Cambridge, Mass., 1989-90; asst. prof. dept. mech. and aero. engring. Boston U., 1990—; with H.S. Outreach Program Boston U., North Andover H.S., 1991, 92; advisor Extracurricular Design Projects, Yale U., Harvard U., Boston U., 1988—; advisor Solar Car Club, Boston U., 1994. Contbr. articles to profl. jours. Recipient rsch. initiation award NSF, 1991; named Outstanding Engring. Prof. of Yr., Boston U., 1993. Mem. ASME, Acoustical Soc. Am., Am. Phys. Soc. Achievements include patents pending for apparatus for detection of particles in ultrapure liquids (acoustically), enhancing chemical reactions through acoustic cavitation, submicron particulate evictor. Home: 36 Amory St Cambridge MA 02139-1202 Office: Boston U Dept Engring 110 Cummington St Boston MA 02215-2407

MADANSKY, ALBERT, statistics educator; b. Chgo., May 16, 1934; s. Harry and Anna (Meidenberg) M.; m. Paula Barkan, June 10, 1990; children from previous marriage: Susan, Cynthia, Noreen, Michele. AB, U. Chgo., 1952, MS, 1955, PhD, 1958. Mathematician Rand Corp., Santa Monica, Calif., 1957-65; sr. v.p. Interpub. Group of Companies, N.Y.C., 1965-68; pres. Dataplan Inc, N.Y.C., 1968-70; prof. computer scis. CCNY, 1970-76; prof. bus. adminstrn. grad. sch. U. Chgo., 1976—, assoc. dean, 1985-90, dep. dean, 1990-93; bd. dirs. Analytic Services, Washington, 1975—. Author: Foundations of Econometrics, 1975, Prescriptions for Working Statisticians, 1988. Fellow: Ctr. for Advanced Study in Behavioral Scis., Am. Statis. Assn., Inst. Math. Stats., Econometric Soc. Home: 200 E Delaware Pl Apt 23F Chicago IL 60611-1736 Office: U of Chicago Grad Sch Business Chicago IL 60637

MADANSKY, LEON, particle physicist, educator; b. Bklyn., Jan. 11, 1923. B.S., U. Mich., 1942, M.S., 1944, Ph.D. in Physics, 1948. From asst. prof. to assoc. prof. Johns Hopkins U., Balt., 1948-58, chmn. dept., 1965-68, prof. physics, 1958-77, Decker prof., 1978—; research physicist Brookhaven Nat. Lab., 1952-53. Fellow NSF, 1961, 69, John S. Guggenheim Meml. Found., 1974-75. Fellow Am. Phys. Soc. Home: 6602 Edenvale Rd Baltimore MD 21209-2702 Office: Johns Hopkins U Dept Physics And Astro Baltimore MD 21218

MADARA, JAMES L., epitheliologist, pathologist, educator; b. Altoona, Pa., Sept. 16, 1950; s. Daniel Rodman and Margaret Jane (Hauser) M.; m. Victoria M. Madara, May 14, 1975; children: J. Maxwell, Alexis Lindsy. BA, Juniata Coll., 1971; MD, Hahnemann Med., 1975. Cert. anatomic and clin. pathology. Instr. pathology Harvard Med. Sch., Boston, 1980-81, asst. prof. pathology, 1981-85, assoc. prof. pathology, 1985-91; assoc. prof. of health scis. and tech. Harvard-M.I.T., Boston, 1986-91; prof. pathology Harvard U. Med. Sch., Boston, 1993—. Assoc. editor: Gastroenterology, 1986-91; editorial bd.: Jour. Clin. Investigation, 1987—; contbr. over 80 articles to profl. jours. Grantee NIH, 1980-91. Mem. Am. Soc. for Clin. Investigation (elected), Am. Soc. for Cell Biology, Am. Gastroenterological Assn. (rsch. coun. 1988-90, Ross Rsch. scholar award 1982), Am. Physiol. Soc., Am. Assn. Pathology (Parke/Davis award 1990). Achievements include description of functional sequellae of neutrophil-epithelial cell interactions; recognition that tight junctions between epithelial cells are regulated under physiological conditions. Office: Brigham and Womens Hosp 75 Francis St Boston MA 02115-6110

MADDALA, GANGADHARRAO SOUNDARYARAO, economics educator; b. Hyderabad, Andhra, India, May 21, 1933; came to U.S., 1960; s. Soundarya Rao and Veera Lakshmi (Gollakota) M.; m. Kameswari Modali, May 21, 1967; children: Tara, Vivek. BA, Andhra U., Waltair, India, 1955; MA, Bombay U., 1957; PhD, U. Chgo., 1963. Asst. prof. Stanford (Calif.) U., 1963-67; assoc. prof. U. Rochester (N.Y.), 1967-70, prof. econs., 1970-75; grad. rsch. prof. U. Fla., Gainesville, 1975-93; univ. eminent scholar dept. econs. Ohio State U., Columbus, 1992—; dir. Ctr. for Econometrics and Decision Scis., Gainesville, 1979-93. Author: Econometrics, 1977, Limdep Variables in Econometrics, 1983, Introduction to Econometrics, 1988, Microeconomics, 1989, Econometric Methods and Applications, 1994. Fellow Econometric Soc.; mem. Am. Econ. Assn., Am. Statis. Assn. Office: Ohio State U Arps Hall 1945 N High St Columbus OH 43210-1120

MADDALENA, LUCILLE ANN, management executive; b. Plainfield, N.J., Nov. 8, 1948; d. Mario Anthony and Josephine Dorothy (Longo) M.; m. James Samonte Hohn, Sept. 7, 1975; children: Vincent, Nicholas, Mitchell. AA, Rider Coll., 1968; BS, Monmouth Coll., 1971; EdD, Rutgers U., 1978. Newscaster, dir. pub. relations Sta. WBRW, Bridgewater, N.J., 1971-73; editor-in-chief Commerce mag., New Brunswick, N.J., 1973-74; dir. pub. relations Raritan Valley Regional C. of C., New Brunswick, N.J., 1973-74; aide pub. relations to mayor City of New Brunswick, 1974; dir. communications United Way Cen. Jersey, New Brunswick, 1974-77; mgmt. cons. United Way Am., Alexandria, Va., 1977-78; pres., owner Maddalena Assocs., Chester, N.J., 1978—; sr. cons. United Research Co., Morristown, N.J., 1980-81; sr. ptnr., dir. OCD Group, Parsippany, N.J., 1984-87; chmn. bd. dirs. OCD Group (subs. Xicom Inc.), Morristown, N.J., 1988; pres. Morris Bus. Group, Chester, 1989—; adj. faculty Somerset County Coll., Bridgewater, N.J., 1970, Fairleigh Dickinson U., 1980; guest lectr. Rutgers U., New Brunswick, N.J., 1975-80; designer publicly offered seminars for Bell Atlantic, 1992—; cons. change Howmet, Alloy, Dover, N.J., 1993; consortium trainer Johnson & Johnson, 1988—. Author: A Communications Manual for Non-Profit Organizations, 1980; editor New Directions for Instl. Advancement, 1980-81. Chmn. pers. com., police com. Chester Borough Coun., 1984-87; pres. Chester Consolidation Study Commn., 1990. Recipient Mayor's Commendation City of New Brunswick, 1973, Chester Borough, N.J., 1988. Mem. AAUW, LWV, Nat. Assn. Press Women, N.J. Elected Women Officials, Kappa Delta Pi. Republican. Roman Catholic. Club: N.J. Sled Dog Assn. Avocation: sled dog racing. Home: 75 Melrose Dr Chester NJ 07930-2321 Office: Morris Bus Group 415 State Route 24 Chester NJ 07930-2919

MADDEN, DAVID, author; b. Knoxville, Tenn., July 25, 1933; s. James Helvy and Emile (Merritt) M.; m. Roberta Margaret Young, Sept. 6, 1956; 1 son, Blake Dana. B.S., U. Tenn., 1957; M.A., San Francisco State Coll., 1958; postgrad., Yale Drama Sch., 1959-60. Faculty Appalachian State Tchrs. Coll., Boone, N.C., 1957-58, Centre Coll., Danville, Ky., 1960-62, U. Louisville, 1962-64, Kenyon Coll., Gambier, O., 1964-66, Ohio U., Athens, 1966-68; writer-in-residence La. State U., Baton Rouge, 1968-92, dir. creative writing program, 1992-94, dir. U.S. Civil War Ctr., 1992—; alumni prof. La. State U., 1994. Author: (novels) Cassandra Singing, 1969, Bijou, 1974, The Suicide's Wife, 1978, Pleasure Dome, 1979, On the Big Wind, 1980, (stories) The Shadow Knows (Nat. Coun. on Arts selection), 1970, The New Orleans of Possibilities (lit. criticism) Wright Morris, 1964, Poetic Image in Six Genres, 1969, James M. Cain, 1970, A Primer of the Novel, 1980, Writers' Revisions, 1981, Cain's Craft, 1985, Revising Fiction, 1988, Rediscoveries II, 1988; asst. editor: The Kenyon Rev., 1964-66; editor: Remembering James Agee, 1974; co-editor: (with P. Bach) Classics of Civil War Fiction, 1991, Sharpshooter, 1996. Served with AUS, 1953-55. Recipient Rockefeller grant in fiction, 1969; John Golden fellow in playwriting, 1959. Mem. Authors League, Associated Writing Programs (bd). Democrat. Office: US Civil War Ctr La State U Raphael Semmes Dr Baton Rouge LA 70803

MADDEN, DONALD PAUL, lawyer; b. Winthrop, Mass., Dec. 26, 1933; s. Francis Patrick and Mary Josephine (Doherty) M.; m. Sarah Anne Donovan, Aug. 12, 1966; children—Matthew James, Andrew Peter, Peter Thomas. A.B., Princeton U., 1955; J.D., Harvard U., 1961. Bar: N.Y. 1962, U.S. Dist. Ct. (so. dist.) N.Y. 1962. Assoc. White & Case, N.Y.C., 1961-69, ptnr., 1969—; resident ptnr. Paris office, 1971-76. dir., sec. Am. Hosp. of Paris Found. Served to lt. USMC, 1955-58. Mem. ABA, Assn. Bar City N.Y. Club: Links (N.Y.C.). Office: White & Case 1155 Ave Of The Americas New York NY 10036-2711

MADDEN, EDWARD HARRY, philosopher, educator; b. Gary, Ind., May 18, 1925; s. Harry Albert and Amelia Dorothy (Schepper) M.; m. Marian Sue Canaday, Sept. 15, 1946; children: Kerry Arthur, Dennis William. A.B., Oberlin Coll., 1946, A.M., 1947; Ph.D., U. Iowa, 1950. Prof. philosophy U. Conn., 1950-59, San Jose State Coll., 1959-64, SUNY, Buffalo, 1964-82, U. Ky., 1982—; vis. prof. Brown U., 1954-55, Amherst Coll., 1962, U. Toronto, 1967, Am. U. Beirut, Lebanon, 1969-70; sr. research fellow Linacre Coll., Oxford U., 1978, Inst. Advanced Study, Princeton, 1980-81. Author: Philosophical Problems of Psychology, 1962, Chauncey Wright and the Foundations of Pragmatism, 1963, Evil and the Concept of God, 1968, Civil Disobedience and Moral Law, 1968, The Structure of Scientific Thought, 1960, Causal Powers, 1975, Causing, Perceiving and Believing, 1975, Freedom and Grace, 1982, Reid and the Growth of His Tradition, 1996; co-author, editor: Theories of Scientific Method, 1960, Philosophical Perspectives on Punishment, 1968, The Idea of God, 1968; gen. editor: Harvard U. Press Source Books in History Sci.; mem. editl. bd.: The Works of William James, Thoreau Quar., History of Philosophy Quar.; mem. adv. bd.: A Critical Edition of the Correspondence of William James (Am. Coun. Learned Socs.). Served with USNR, 1943-45. Recipient Am. Philos. Soc. research grant, 1961, Fulbright-Hays award, 1969-70, Herbert W. Schneider award Soc. for Advancement Am. Philosophy, 1991. Fellow Asa Mahan Soc.; mem. C.S. Peirce Soc. (pres. 1962-63, sec.-treas., editorial bd. Transactions of Soc.), Am. Council Learned Socs. (selection com.), Am. Philos. Assn. (co-chmn. com. publs. 1960-77), Phi Kappa Phi. Home: 106 Pickett Dr Wilmore KY 40390-1223 Office: Univ Ky Dept Philosophy Lexington KY 40506

MADDEN, HEATHER ANN, aluminum company executive; b. Sharon, Pa., Dec. 20, 1967; d. Edward Arthur and Mary Ann (McWilliams) M. BS in Bus., Salisbury (Md.) State U., 1991; MS in Bus., Johns Hopkins U., 1994. With Delmarva Aluminum Co., Inc., Delmar, Del., 1984-95, exec.'s asst., 1987-95, also dir., 1990—; instr. office sys. tech. Del. Tech. & C.C., Georgetown, 1995—. Vol. The Holly Ctr., Salisbury, 1992-94. Recipient Holly Svc. award The Holly Found., Salisbury, 1994. Avocations: women's softball, personal computers, dogs, swimming, gardening. Home: 8300 Robin Hood Dr Salisbury MD 21804

MADDEN, JAMES COOPER, V, management consultant; b. Glen Cove, N.Y., June 18, 1961; s. James Cooper IV and Linda Marie (Lizza) M.; m. Jill Louise Howenstine, July 27, 1985; 1 child, Jennifer Louise. Student, Webb Inst. Naval Architecture, Glen Cove, 1979-80; BA cum laude, So. Meth. U., 1983, BBA magna cum laude, 1983. Cert. Soc. Naval Architects and Marine Engrs. Cons. Andersen Cons./Arthur Andersen, Houston, 1983-85, sr. cons., 1985-87; mgr. Andersen Cons./Arthur Andersen, L.A., 1987-90, sr. mgr., 1990-91; prin. Booz-Allen & Hamilton, L.A., 1991-93; v.p. mng. dir. SHL Systemhouse, L.A., 1993-95, pres. U.S. disvn., 1995—; mem. adv. bd. Claremont Grad. Sch., Mgmt. Info. Svcs. Program; mem. UCLA Anderson Sch., I.S. Assocs. Author industry papers. Scholar Webb Inst. Naval Architecture, 1979-80. Avocations: sailing, snow skiing, travel, reading. Home: 41 Bridgeport Rd Newport Coast CA 92657-1015 Office: SHL Systemhouse 12750 Center Court Dr S Cerritos CA 90701-4552

MADDEN, JAMES DESMOND, forensic engineer; b. Jersey City, Mar. 1, 1940; s. Louis A. and Ann (Desmond) M. BSChemE, U. S.C., 1963, ME, 1966. Lic. profl. engr., Ohio; cert. diplomate forensic engr. Process engr. Monsanto Co., Alvin, Tex., 1966-67; process and project engr. Union Carbide Corp., Houston, 1967-70; systems engr. M.W. Kellogg Co., Houston, 1970-73, prin. systems engr., 1974-77; sr. process engr. Litwin Co., Houston, 1973-74; sr. project engr. Davy Powergas, Houston, 1977-78, supervising project engr., 1978-79; mgr. equipment engring. DM Internat., Houston, 1979-80, project engring. mgr., 1980-83; owner, forensic engr. Madden Forensic Engring., Parma, Parma Heights and Brecksville, Ohio, 1983—. Pres. Houston Young Adult Rep. Club, 1970-73; chmn. Tex. Young Adult Rep. Clubs, 1973. NSF rsch. grantee, 1963; NASA fellow, 1963-65. Mem. ASTM, ASME, NSPE, Soc. Automotive Engrs., Nat. Fire Protection Assn., Am. Chem. Soc., Am. Inst. Chem. Engrs., Inst. Transp. Engrs., Transp. Rsch. Bd. (individual assoc.), Nat. Acad. Forensic Engrs., Sigma Xi, Sigma Pi Sigma, Tau Beta Pi, Omicron Delta Kappa. Office: 10175 Brecksville Rd Cleveland OH 44141-3205

MADDEN, JOHN, television sports commentator, former professional football coach; b. Austin, Minn., Apr. 10, 1936; s. Earl and Mary O'Flaherty M.; m. Virginia Madden; children: Mike, Joe. B.S., Calif. Poly. U., 1959, M.A., 1961. Player Phila. Eagles (NFL team), 1959; asst. coach Hancock Jr. Coll., Santa Maria, Calif., 1960-62; head coach Hancock Jr. Coll., 1962-64; defensive coordinator Calif. State U., San Diego, 1964-66; with Oakland Raiders, Am. Football League (now Am. Football Conf., Nat. Football League), 1967-79, linebacker coach, 1967-69, head coach, 1969-79; head coach NFL Pro Bowl team Am. Football Conf., 1971, 73, 74, 75; head coach 6 Western div. Am. Football Conf. championship teams, Super Bowl champions, 1976; sports commentator, football analyst CBS Sports, 1979-93; appears in TV and radio commls.; sports commentator, football analyst Fox Network, 1994—. Author: Hey, Wait a Minute, I Wrote a Book!, 1984; One Knee Equals Two Feet, 1986; developer (software) John Madden Football, 1988, John Madden Football II, 1993. Named Coach of Year Am. Football League, 1969, Sports Personality of the Yr., Am. Sportscasters Assn., 1985; recipient Emmy awards for sports broadcasting, 1982, 83, 85, 86, 87, 88. Office: care Fox Network PO Box 900 Beverly Hills CA 90213-0900

MADDEN, JOHN PATRICK, lawyer; b. N.Y.C., Sept. 9, 1945; s. Eugene Patrick and Eileen Mary (Gaughan) M.; m. Sally Williams, Apr. 21, 1984; children: Samuel, Christopher. BCE, Manhattan Coll., 1967; MSCE, NYU, 1969; JD, St. John's U., 1978. Bar: U.S. Patent Office 1978, N.Y. 1979, N.J. 1982, U.S. Dist. Ct. (so. and ea. dists.) N.Y. 1982, U.S. Dist. Ct. N.J. 1982, U.S. Supreme Ct. 1985; cert. internat. arbitrator, constrn. panelist, comml. mediator, D.O.D. instr. Law clk., assoc. Buckley, Treacy, Shaffel Mackey & Abbate, N.Y.C., 1977-80; cons. Contractors Consulting Svcs. Inc., Greatneck, N.Y., 1980-81; ptnr. Madden, Sciarra & Muirhead, N.Y., N.J., 1981-82, Canfield, Venusti, Madden & Rossi, Manhattan, N.Y., 1983—; lectr. in field. Contbr. articles to profl. jours. V.p. N.Y.C. Jaycees, 1975-95. ROTC USAF, 1963-65. Mem. ABA (pub. contract law sect., forum com. on constrn. industry), London Ct. Internat. Arbitration, Swiss Arbitration Assn., Am. Trial Lawyers Assn., N.Y. State Bar Assn., N.Y. State Trial Lawyers Assn., Assn. of Bar of City of N.Y., Nat. Arts Club. Office: Canfield Venusti et al 230 Park Ave Rm 2525 New York NY 10169-2599

MADDEN, JOSEPH DANIEL, trade association executive; b. N.Y.C., Dec. 25, 1921; s. Thomas A. and Margaret (McFadden) M.; m. Eileen M. MacDonnell, Sept. 8, 1951; children: Joseph Daniel, Jr., Maureen A. BS, Fordham U., 1951; MBA, N.Y. U., 1956. Credit investigator Dun & Bradstreet, N.Y.C., 1947-48; credit mgr. Devoe & Raynolds Co., N.Y.C., 1948-50; accounts supr. credit dept. Admiral Corp., N.Y.C., 1950-51; nat. credit mgr. Standard Toch Chems., Inc., S.I., N.Y., 1951-52; with chems. and plastics div. Union Carbide Corp., Danbury, Conn., 1952-62; mgr. Detroit sales office, 1958-60; sr. staff adminstr. Soc. Plastics Industry, Washington, 1962-69; exec. v.p. Drug, Chem. and Allied Trades Assn., Syosset, N.Y., 1969-88, cons. assn. mgmt., 1988—. With U.S. Army, 1942-43. Mem. Am. Soc. Assn. Execs. (cert.), N.Y. Soc. Assn. Execs. (past bd. dirs., Exec. of Yr. award 1988), Soc. Friendly Sons of St. Patrick, Kiwanis (past pres. Bayside, sec.), Am. Assn. Ret. Persons (pres. local chpt.), Toastmasters Internat. (past pres. local club). Home: 201-26 38th Ave Flushing NY 11361-1849

MADDEN, JOSEPH MICHAEL, microbiologist; b. Yokohama, Japan, July 19, 1949; s. John Joseph and Anne Louise (Johnson) M.; m. Rennie K. Robb, Aug. 4, 1973; children: Loren, Mary Kate, Julie. BA, U. Calif., 1971; MS, Ariz. State U., 1974, PhD, 1976. Chief microbiology Brook Army Med. Ctr., Ft. Sam Houston, Tex., 1976-78; rsch. microbiologist FDA Ctr. Food Safety and Applied Nutrition, Washington, 1978-88, dep. dir. microbiology divsn., 1988-91, dir., 1991-93, strategic mgr. microbiology, 1992—. Capt. U.S. Army, 1976-78, USPHS, 1978—. Fellow Am. Acad. Microbiology; mem. Am. Soc. Microbiology, Sigma Xi. Roman Catholic. Avocation: refereeing soccer. Office: FDA Ctr Food Safety and Applied Nutrition 200 C St SW Washington DC 20204-0001

MADDEN, MARTIN GERARD, state legislator, insurance agent; b. Washington, May 24, 1949; s. Anthony M. and Catherine W. (Tracey) M.; m. Julia Gatewood Spangler, July 29, 1988; children: Donald Gerard, Thomas Martin, Christina Lynn, Marguerite Allen Spangler. BA in Econs., Iona Coll., 1971. Owner Marty Madden Ins. Ctr., Lanham, Md., 1971—; state del. State of Md. Gen. Assembly, Annapolis, 1991-95; state senator, 1995—; mem. fin. com., chmn. subcom. on welfare reform. Bd. dirs. St. Vincent Pallotti H.S.; mem. Citizens Against Spousal Abuse, MADD. Mem. Nat. Assn. Life Underwriters, Prince Georges Life Underwriters, Sierra Club, Kiwanis, KC. Republican. Roman Catholic. Avocation: folk art collector. Office: James Senate Office Bldg 402-B Annapolis MD 21401-1991

MADDEN, MICHAEL DANIEL, finance company executive; b. Buffalo, Feb. 16, 1949; s. Daniel Francis and Miriam (Catron) M.; m. Mary Madden, May 1, 1976; children: Daniel, Kristina, Meagan, Michael. BA in Econs. magna cum laude, Le Moyne Coll., 1971; MBA with distinction, U. Pa., 1973. Assoc. Kidder, Peabody & Co., N.Y.C., 1973-77, v.p., 1977-80, mng. dir., 1980-85, dir. investment banking, 1985-88; head investment banking Lehman Bros., N.Y.C., 1989-93; exec. mng. dir. Global Capital Markets Kidder, Peabody Co., N.Y.C., 1993-94; vice chmn., chief origination officer Paine Webber Inc., N.Y.C., 1995—. Bd. dirs. Freeport Properties, Inc., Cath. TV Ctr., N.Y.C., 1981-85, LeMoyne Coll., Syracuse, N.Y., 1987—, Canisius Preparatory Sch., Buffalo, N.Y., 1992—. Mem. Am. Petroleum Inst., MBA Assn., Univ. Club, The Creek, Longboat Key Club. Republican. Roman Catholic. Avocations: boxing, hunting, tennis, coin collecting. Office: Paine Webber Inc 1285 Avenue Of The Americas New York NY 10019-6028

MADDEN, MURDAUGH STUART, lawyer; b. Morgantown, W.Va., Feb. 26, 1922; s. Joseph Warren and Margaret (Liddell) M.; m. Eileen Dillon, June 17, 1978; children by previous marriage: Liddell Louise, Murdaugh Stuart Jr., Michael Mann. Student, Oberlin Coll., 1939-40; BA, George Washington U., 1942; JD, Harvard U., 1948. Bar: D.C. 1948, Va. 1948, U.S. Supreme Ct. 1953. Asst. counsel Bur. Aero., Washington, 1948-50; sole practice Washington, 1950-61, 71—; sr. ptnr. Shaw, Pittman, Potts, Trowbridge & Madden, Washington, 1961-71; gen. counsel Humane Soc. U.S., Atlantic Devel. Co. and related corps. Author: (with Sherman L. Cohn) The Legal Status and Problems of the American Abroad, 1966. Trustee Inst. for Study Nat. Behavior, Princeton, N.J., Friends of India Com., Washington; pres. World Fedn. for Protection Animals, Zurich; v.p. World Soc. forProtection Animals, London. With USAAF, 1942-45, ETO. Mem. ABA (past chmn. internat. and comparative law com. internat. transp., chmn. subcom. on charitable orgns. internat. law sect. 1985—), D.C. Bar Assn., (past dir., past chmn. com. bar ethics), Va. Bar Assn., The Barristers, Am. Soc. Internat. Law, Harvard Law Sch. Assn., Oberlin Alumni Assn., Metropolitan Club, Harvard Club N.Y., Internat. Lawn Tennis Club U.S., Chevy Chase Club, Phi Sigma Kappa. Episcopalian. Home: 2530 Queen Annes Ln NW

Washington DC 20037-2148 Office: 2100 L St NW Washington DC 20037-1525

MADDEN, PALMER BROWN, lawyer; b. Milw., Sept. 19, 1945; m. Susan L. Paulus, Mar. 31, 1984. BA, Stanford U., 1968; JD, U. Calif., Berkeley, 1973. Bar: Calif. 1973, U.S. Dist. Ct. (no. dist.) Calif. 1973, U.S. Supreme Ct. 1982. Ptnr. McCutchen, Doyle Brown & Enersen, Walnut Creek, 1985—. Mem. bd. govs. Continuing Edn. of the Bar; judge pro tem Contra Costa Superior Ct., 1991-93. Mem. Contra Costa County Bar Assn. (dir. 1987—, pres. 1996). Democrat. Episcopalian. Office: McCutchen Doyle Brown & Enersen 1331 N California Blvd Walnut Creek CA 94596-4537

MADDEN, PAUL ROBERT, lawyer; b. St. Paul, Nov. 13, 1926; s. Ray Joseph and Margaret (Meyer) M.; m. Rosemary R. Sorel, Aug. 7, 1974; children: Margaret Jane, William, James Patrick, Derek R. Sorel, Lisa T. Sorel. Student, St. Thomas Coll., 1944; AB, U. Minn., 1948; JD, Georgetown U., 1951. Bar: Ariz. 1957, Minn. 1951, D.C. 1951. Assoc. Hamilton & Hamilton, Washington, 1951-55; legal asst. to commr. SEC, Washington, 1955-56; assoc. Lewis and Roca, Phoenix, Ariz., 1957-59, ptnr., 1959-90; ptnr. Beus, Gilbert & Morrill, Phoenix, 1991-94; ptnr. Chapman and Cutler, Phoenix, 1994—. Sec. Minn. Fedn. Coll. Rep. Clubs, 1947-48; chmn. 4th dist. Minn. Young Rep. Club, 1948; nat. co-chmn. Youth for Eisenhower, 1951-52; mem. Ariz. Rep. Com., 1960-62; bd. dirs. Found. Jr. Achievement Ctrl. Ariz., Cath. Community Found., Phoenix, Heritage Hills Homeowners Assn., St. Joseph the Worker; past bd. dirs. Camelback Charitable Trust, The Samaritan Found., Phoenix; past bd. dirs., past. pres. Ariz. Club, Phoenix, 1990-93; past bd. dirs., past chmn. Found. for Sr. Living; past bd. dirs., vice chmn., Cen. Ariz. chpt. ARC; past bd. dirs., vice chmn., Cen. Ariz. chpt. ARC; past bd. dirs., past pres. Jr. Achievement Cen. Ariz., Inc.; mem. nat. bd. vis. U. Ariz. Law Sch. With USNR, 1946-48. Mem. ABA, Ariz. Bar Assn., Maricopa County Bar Assn., Fed. Bar Assn., Fedn. Ins. Counsel, Nat. Health Lawyers Assn., Am. Soc. Hosp. Attys., Phi Delta Phi. Clubs: The Barristers (Washington), Arizona. Home: 5847 N 46th St Phoenix AZ 85018-1234 Office: Chapman & Cutler Two N Central Ave Ste 1100 Phoenix AZ 85004

MADDEN, RICHARD BLAINE, forest products executive; b. Short Hills, N.J., Apr. 27, 1929; s. James L. and Irma (Twining) M.; m. Joan Fairbairn, May 24, 1958; children: John Richard, Lynn Marie, Kathryn Ann, Andrew Twining. B.S., Princeton U., 1951; J.D., U. Mich., 1956; M.B.A., NYU, 1959; PhD (hon.), St. Scholastica Coll., 1994. Bar: Mich. 1956, N.Y. 1958. Gen. asst. treas.'s dept. Socony Mobil Oil Corp., N.Y.C., 1956-57; spl. asst. Socony Mobil Oil Corp., 1958-59, fin. rep., 1960; asst. to pres. Mobil Chem. Co.; also dir. Mobil Chems. Ltd. of Eng., 1960-63; exec. v.p., gen. mgr. Kordite Corp.; also v.p. Mobil Plastics, 1963-66; v.p. Mobil Chem. Co., N.Y.C., 1966-68; group v.p. Mobil Chem. Co., 1968-70; asst. treas. Mobil Oil Corp., 1970-71; chmn. Mobil Oil Estates Ltd., 1970-71; pres., chief exec. to chmn., chief exec. officer Potlatch Corp., San Francisco, 1971-94; ret., 1994; bd. dirs. Potlatch Corp., Pacific Gas and Electric Co., Consolidated Freightways, Inc., Pacific Gas Transmission Co., URS Corp.; former bd. dirs. Del Monte Corp., AMFAC Inc., Bank Calif. N.A. and BankCal Tri-State Corp.; from lectr. to adj. assoc. prof. fin. NYU, 1960-63. Bd. dirs. Smith-Kettlewell Eye Rsch. Inst., Nat. Park Found., mem. fin. com., devel. com.; trustee emeritus, former chmn. Am. Enterprise Inst.; bd. govs., mem. adminstrv. compensation, audit & labor rels. com. San Francisco Symphony; hon. trustee Com. for Econ. Devel. Lt. (j.g.) USNR, 1951-54. Mem. N.Y. Bar Assn., Mich. Bar Assn. Roman Catholic. Clubs: Bohemian (San Francisco); Lagunitas (Ross, Calif.); Metropolitan (Washington).

MADDEN, TERESA DARLEEN, insurance agency owner; b. Dallas, Aug. 4, 1960; d. Tommy Joe Frederick Dodd and Mary Helen (Sterner) Smith; m. Kim Ashley Madden, June 2, 1989. Student, Tex. Tech U., 1978-81. Cert. ins. counselor. With personal lines svc. Charles R. Ervin Ins., Midland, Tex., 1981, Bryant Scalf Ins., Richardson, Tex., 1981-82; with comml. ins. svc. Street & Assocs. Inc., Dallas, 1982-84; with comml. ins. sales/svc. Hotchkiss Ins., Dallas, 1984-85; mgr. sales Abbott-Rose Ins. Agy., Dallas, 1985-89; owner Glenn-Madden & Assocs. Ins., Dallas, 1990—. Methodist. Office: Glenn Madden & Assocs Inc Ste 1470 9330 Lyndon B Johnson Fwy Dallas TX 75243-3436

MADDEN, THERESA MARIE, elementary education educator; b. Phila., Feb. 12, 1950; d. James Anthony and Marie Margaret (Clark) M. BA in Social Sci., Neumann Coll., 1977; postgrad., Beaver Coll.; Immaculata Coll. Cert. tchr., Pa. Tchr. elem. grades St. Anthony Sch., Balt., 1971-73, St. Mary-St. Patrick Sch., Wilmington, Del., 1973-74, Queen of Heaven Sch., Cherry Hill, N.J., 1974-77, St. Bonaventure Sch., Phila., 1977-78, 79-83, St. Stanislaus Sch., Lansdale, Pa., 1978-79; substitute tchr. various schs. Phila., 1983-84; tchr. 8th grade math. St. Cecilia Sch., Phila., 1984-94; tchr. math., vice prin. Corpus Christi Sch., Lansdale, Pa., 1994—; mem. visiting team Mid. States Assn., Phila., 1992; presenter workshops. Mem. Nat. Coun. Tchrs. Math., Pa. Coun. Tchrs. Math., Assn. Tchrs. Math. of Phila. and Vicinity. Roman Catholic. Avocations: crochet, cross-stitch, baking, walking. Office: Corpus Christi Sch 920 Sumneytown Pike Lansdale PA 19446-5414

MADDEN, WALES HENDRIX, JR., lawyer; b. Amarillo, Tex., Sept. 1, 1927; s. Wales Hendrix and Kathryn (Nash) M.; m. Alma Faye Cowden, Nov. 8, 1952; children: Wales Hendrix III, Straughn. B.A., U. Tex., 1950, LL.B., 1952. Bar: Tex. 1952. Practiced in Amarillo; bd. dirs. First Nat. Bank of Amarillo, Mesa Inc.; mem. Tex. Constnl. Revision Commn., 1973. Bd. regents Amarillo Coll., 1958-59, U. Tex., 1959-65; mem. Tex. Coll. and Univ. System Coord. Bd., 1964-69, Amarillo Area Found., Cal Farley's Boys Ranch, Pres.'s Export Coun., 1981; trustee Trinity U., San Antonio; mem. Select Com. Higher Edn., 1985, 87; chmn. SWST Regional Panel, Pres.'s Commn. on White House Fellowships, 1989-90; chmn. bd. Internat. Food and Agrl. Devel., 1990-94. Served with USNR. Named Outstanding Man of Amarillo, 1972; Disting. Alumnus U. Tex., 1979, U. Tex. Law Sch., 1986. Mem. ABA, Amarillo Bar Assn. (pres. 1956), Tex. Philos. Soc., Amarillo C. of C. (pres. 1968), State Bar Tex., State Jr. Bar Tex. (pres. 1956), Friar Soc., Phi Alpha Delta, Phi Delta Theta, Phi Eta Sigma, Pi Sigma Alpha. Presbyterian (elder). Home: PO Box 15288 Amarillo TX 79105-5288 Office: P O Box 15288 Amarillo TX 79105

MADDEN, WILLIAM J., JR., lawyer; b. Washington, Jan. 9, 1939; s. William John and Anne Hayes M.; m. Imelda Moore, May 23, 1964 (div. 1982); children: Maureen, Edward. AB, Holy Cross Coll., 1961; JD, U. Mich., 1964. Trial atty. Fed. Power Commn., Washington, 1964-68; atty. Debevoise & Liberman, Washington, 1968-83; ptnr. Bishop, Cook, Purcell & Reynolds, Washington, 1983-90, Winston & Strawn, Washington, 1990—; bd. dirs. Fed. Energy Bar Assn., Washington. Bd. dirs. Fairfax County Water Authority, Falls Church, Va., 1977-87. Republican. Roman Catholic. Home: 1465 Hampton Ridge Dr Mc Lean VA 22101-6023 Office: Winston & Strawn 1400 L St NW Washington DC 20005-3509*

MADDEX, MYRON BROWN (MIKE MADDEX), broadcasting executive; b. Champaign County, Ohio, May 20, 1924; s. Walter Omer and Eva Mae (Brown) M.; m. Wilma Jean Anderson, Mar. 29, 1943; children: James Michael, John Eugene, Martha Jean. Student, Coyne Elec. Sch., Chgo., Moody Bible Inst., Chgo., eves., 1956-58. With R.W. Schetter Jewelry & Radio, Mechanicsburg, Ohio, 1946-51; owner Maddex Radio & TV, Mechanicsburg, 1952-53; chief engr. sta. WJEL-AM&FM, Springfield, Ohio, 1953-54; engr. staf. WMBI-AM&FM, Chgo., 1954-55; traffic supr., asst. to mgr., then asst. mgr. staf. WMBI-AM&FM, 1956-65; gen. mgr., then exec. v.p. sta. WEEC, Springfield, 1965-72; pres. sta. WEEC, 1972—; dir. World Evangelistic Enterprise Corp., 1965—; past bd. dirs. Springfield Youth for Christ. Served with AUS, 1943-45. Mem. Nat. Religious Broadcasters (dir. 1968-89, 1st Midwest chpt. pres. 1969-71, nat. sec. 1982-85), Nat. Assn Evangelicals, Ohio Assn. Evangelicals (bd. dirs. 1984-92, sec. 1985-87, 1st v.p. 1987-89, pres. 1989-91), Springfield C. of C. Home: Box 127 1300 Shrine Rd Lot 127 Springfield OH 45504-3966 Office: 2265 Troy Rd Springfield OH 45504-4229 *During high school, I felt radio was my field. That's about all that interested me. Pearl Harbor occurred 6 months prior to graduation, and the U.S. Army Signal Corps provided training and experience. Returning to civilian life in radio servicing came next. Then . . . I became a Christian. God directed me to Chicago and the pioneer Christian radio station, WMBI. From that day to this, radio, as a ministry, has been my calling.*

MADDIN, ROBERT, metallurgist educator; b. Hartford, Conn., Oct. 20, 1918; s. Isadore I. and Mae (Jacobs) Levine; married, July 8, 1945; children: Leslie, Jill. BS in Metall. Engring., Purdue U., 1942; DEng., Yale U., 1948. Registered profl. engr., Pa. Asst., assoc. prof. Johns Hopkins U., Balt., 1949-55; prof. U. Pa., phila., 1955-73, univ. prof., 1973-83; vis. prof. Harvard U., Cambridge, Mass., 1983-87, curator, 1987—; vis. prof. Oxford (Eng.) U., 1970, fellow Wolfson Coll., 1987; vis. prof. U. Birmingham, Eng., 1953-54; vis. scholar Hebrew U., Jerusalem, 1976; hon. prof. Beijing Sci. and Engring. U., 1986; hon. mem. Japan Metals. Contbr. more than 150 publs. to profl. jours. 1st Lt. USAF, 1942-45. Disting. Sr. Sci. fellow A. von Humboldt Found., Germany, 1989-90; recipient Pomerance award Archaeological Lust Am., 1994. Fellow Am. Soc. Metallurgists, TMS; mem. Mus. Fine Arts-Boston. Avocations: history early metallurgy.

MADDOCK, JEROME TORRENCE, information services specialist; b. Darby, Pa., Feb. 7, 1940; s. Richard Cotton and Isobel Louise (Mezger) M.; m. Karen Rhueama Weygand, Oct. 2, 1965. BS in Biology, Muhlenberg Coll., 1961; MS in Info. Sci., Drexel U., 1968. Editorial assoc. Biol. Abstracts, Phila., 1962-63; mgr. rsch. info. Merck & Co., West Point, Pa., 1963-72; sr. cons. Auerbach Assocs., Inc., Phila., 1972-79; mgr. libr. and info. svcs. Solar Energy Rsch. Inst., Golden, Colo., 1979-88; mgr. info. svcs. Transp. Rsch. Bd., Washington, 1988—; del. Gov.;s Conf. on Libr. and Info. Svc., Pa., 1978; mem. blue ribbon panel to select archivist of U.S., Washington, 1979; U.S. del. to ops. com. on transp. rsch. info. Orgn. for Econ. Cooperation and Devel., 1988—. Bd. dirs. Paoli (Pa.) Pub. Libr., 1976-77. With USAFR, 1962-68. Mem. AAAS, Am. Soc. Info. Sci. (chmn. 1974-75), Elks, Beta Phi Mu, Pi Delta Epsilon. Republican. Episcopalian. Achievements include projection of information science operations 10 years into the future. Home: 20517 Aspenwood Ln Gaithersburg MD 20879-1230 Office: Transp Rsch Bd 2101 Constitution Ave NW Washington DC 20879

MADDOCK, LAWRENCE HILL, language educator, writer; b. Ogden, Utah, July 14, 1923; s. Lawrence J. and Nellie (Hill) M. Student, U. Fla., 1941-42; BA, George Peabody Coll., 1946, PhD, 1965; MA, U. So. Calif., 1949. Tchr. pub. schs. Jacksonville, Fla., 1949-52; instr. U. Fla., Gainesville, 1952-53; asst. prof. California (Pa.) State Coll., 1955-56, assoc. prof., 1956-64; assoc. prof. N.E. La. State Coll., Monroe, 1964-67, U. West Fla., Pensacola, 1967-90. Author: The Door of Memory, 1974; contbr. chpts. to books and articles to profl. jours. Mem. MLA (bibliographer 1978-93), Thomas Wolfe Soc., Mormon History Assn. Republican. Mormon. Home: 1012 Gerhardt Dr Pensacola FL 32503-3222

MADDOCKS, ROBERT ALLEN, lawyer, manufacturing company executive; b. Missouri Valley, Ia., Dec. 25, 1933; s. Clarence A. and Helen Louise (Unger) M.; m. JoAnn Skaggs, June 2, 1956; children—Todd Duncan, Susan Colette, Amy Annette. B.S., Drake U., 1956; J.D., 1958. Bar: Iowa 1958, U.S. Supreme Ct. 1969, Ohio 1970, Mo. 1972, Colo. 1992. Pvt. practice law Clarion, Ia., 1958-67; atty. Massey Ferguson, Inc., Des Moines, 1967-68; div. gen. counsel Akron, Ohio, 1968-69; asst. sec., gen. counsel, dir. corp. relations Kellwood Co., St. Louis, 1970-73, sec., gen. counsel, 1973-90, v.p., 1978-90, also bd. dirs. subs. cos.; dep. chmn., dir. Smart Shirts Ltd., Hong Kong, 1980-90; sec. Midwest Credit Corp.; Wright County atty., Clarion, 1961-65. Trustee Maryville Coll., St. Louis, 1975-78, Drake U., 1987-94; bd. dirs. Kellwood Found., 1975-90. Mem. Am. Bar Assn., Inter-Am., Ia., Ohio, Mo., Colo. bar assns., Am. Trial Lawyers Assn., Nat. Corporate Secs. Assn., Comml. Law League, Licensing Execs. Soc., Am. Apparel Mfrs. Assn. (legal com. 1972-90). Home: 266 Lookout Point Dr Osprey FL 34229-9738

MADDOX, ALVA HUGH, state supreme court justice; b. Andalusia, Ala., Apr. 17, 1930; s. Christopher Columbus and Audie Louella Maddox; m. Virginia Roberts, June 14, 1958; children: Robert Hugh, Jane Maddox. AB in Journalism, U. Ala., Tuscaloosa, 1952, JD, 1957. Bar: Ala. 1957. Law clk. to Judge Aubrey Cates, Ala. Ct. Appeals, Montgomery, 1957-58; field examiner Chief Atty.'s Office, VA, Montgomery, 1958-59; law clk. to Judge Frank M. Johnson, U.S. Dist. Ct., Montgomery, 1959-61; pvt. practice, Montgomery, 1961-65; cir. judge, spl. cir. judge Montgomery Cir. Ct., 1963, asst. dist. atty., 1964; legal advisor to govs. State of Ala., Montgomery, 1965-69; assoc. justice Supreme Ct. Ala., Montgomery, 1969—; mem. adv. bd. JUSTEC Rsch. Author: Alabama Rules of Criminal Procedure, 1991, supplements, 1992—. Founder youth jud. program YMCA, Montgomery, 1987, also mem. metro. bd. dirs. 2d lt. USAF, 1952-54, col. USAF Res. ret. Recipient Man of Yr. award YMCA, 1988, Disting. Program Svc. award, 1989. Mem. ABA, Ala. Bar Assn., Inst. Jud. Adminstrn., Christian Legal Soc., Federalist Soc. (bd. dirs.), Montgomery County Inns of Ct. (charter, founding), Ala. Law Inst., Am. Jud. Soc., Kiwanis (past bd. dirs. Montgomery). Democrat. Baptist. Office: Supreme Ct Ala 300 Dexter Ave Montgomery AL 36104-3741

MADDOX, JESSE CORDELL, academic administrator; b. La Grange, Ga., Dec. 30, 1931; s. Jesse Garland and Esther Ann (Parmer) M.; m. Brona Faye Moorefield, Mar. 30, 1957; children: Cordell Jr., Michael, Brian, Gayle. BA, Furman U., 1954, LLD (hon.), 1976; M in Div., So. Bapt. Theol. Sem., 1957; DD (hon.), Bapt. Coll. at Charleston, S.C., 1972. Assoc. brotherhood dept. S.C. Bapt. Convention, Columbia, 1957-61; asst. to pres. Furman U., Greenville, S.C., 1961-71; pres. Anderson (S.C.) Coll., 1971-77, Carson Newman Coll., Jefferson City, Tenn., 1977—. Named Man. of Yr., Anderson Realtors, 1979; named to Athletic Hall of Fame Furman U., 1986. Mem. Nat. Jr. Coll. Council (pres. 1974-76), So. Assn. Colls. (commn. on colls. 1979-85), So. Assn., Ch. Related Colls. (pres. 1979), Assn. So. Bapt. Colls. and Schs. (pres. 1989-90). Lodge: Rotary (local pres. 1979). Avocations: tennis, jogging. Home: Laurel Hills RR 3 Jefferson Cy TN 37760-9803 Office: Carson-Newman Coll Office Pres Russell Ave Jefferson City TN 37760

MADDOX, ROBERT ALAN, atmospheric scientist; b. Granite City, Ill., July 12, 1944; s. Robert Alvin and Maxine Madeline (Elledge) M.; m. Rebecca Ann Speer, Dec. 27, 1967 (dec. Oct. 1995); children—Timothy Alan, Jason Robert. Student Purdue U., 1962-63; B.S., Tex. A&M U., 1967; M.S. in Atmospheric Sci., Colo. State U., 1973, Ph.D. in Atmospheric Sci., 1981. Meteorologist, Nat. Weather Service, Hazelwood, Mo., 1967; research meteorologist Geophys. Research & Devel. Corp., Ft. Collins, Colo., 1975-76; research meteorologist Atmospheric Physics and Chemistry Lab., NOAA-Environ. Research Labs., Boulder, Colo., 1976-79, meteorologist Office Weather Research and Modification, 1979-82, program mgr. weather analysis and storm prediction, 1982-83, dir. weather research program, 1983-84, program mgr. mesoscale studies, 1984-86; dir. Nat. Severe Storms Lab., Norman, Okla., 1986—; participant numerous sci. workshops; tchr. weather analysis, forecasting, mesoscale phenomena; presenter workshops on mesoscale analysis and heavy precipitation forecasting Nat. Weather Service Forecast Offices; cons. in field. Served to capt. USAF, 1967-75. Decorated Air Force Commendation medal with oak leaf cluster; recipient Superior Performance award NOAA, 1981, Outstanding Sci. Paper award, 1984. Fellow Am. Meteorol. Soc. (councilor 1989-92, chmn. severe storms com. 1991-92, Clarence Leroy Meisinger award 1983, co-editor, assoc. editor Monthly Weather Rev., assoc. editor Weather & Forecasting); mem. Nat. Weather Assn. (award for outstanding contbns. to operational meteorology 1981, co-editor Nat. Weather Digest, Mem. of Yr. award 1992, Silver medal, 1994), Sigma Xi, Phi Kappa Phi, Chi Epsilon Pi. Contbr. articles to profl. publs. Office: NOAA/ERL Nat Severe Storms 1313 Halley Cir Norman OK 73069-8480

MADDOX, ROBERT LYTTON, lawyer; b. Middlesboro, Ky., May 18, 1924; s. Robert Lytton and Sybil (Sipher) M.; m. Inez Bentley Pryor, Nov. 23, 1955; children: William Granville, Julie Thornton, Robert Lytton III. AB, Harvard U., 1947, LLB, 1950. Bar: Ky. 1950, U.S. Dist. Ct. (ea. dist.) Ky. 1972, U.S. Dist. Ct. (we. dist.) 1979, U.S. Ct. Appeals (6th cir.) 1974. Assoc. Wyatt, Grafton & Sloss, Louisville, 1950-58; ptnr. Wyatt, Grafton & Sloss, 1958-80, Wyatt, Tarrant & Combs, 1980—; bd. dirs. Whip-Mix Corp., Louisville, Nugent Sand Corp., Louisville, Ky. Tax-Free Income Fund, Lexington, Orr Safety Corp., Louisville. Trustee/treas. Louisville Collegiate Sch., 1976-83, Lees Coll., Jackson, Ky., 1974-86; trustee/pres. Estate Planning Coun., Louisville, 1984-88. With U.S. Army, 1943-45. Decorated Bronze Star medal. Mem. Louisville Country Club, Harmony Landing Country Club, Jefferson Club, Wynn-Stay Club, Rotary. Democrat. Presbyterian. Avocations: golf, bicycling, investing. Home: 1412 Northwind Rd Louisville KY 40207-1665 Office: Wyatt Tarrant & Combs 2800 Citizens Plz Louisville KY 40202

MADDOX, ROBERT NOTT, chemical engineer, educator; b. Winslow, Ark., Sept. 29, 1925; s. R.L. and Mabel (Nott) M.; m. Paula Robinson, Oct. 6, 1951 (dec. Apr. 1984); children—Deirdre O'Neil, Robert Dozier; m. Pauline Razook, Nov. 30, 1987. Student, Iowa State Coll., 1944-45; B.S., U. Ark., 1948; M.S., U. Okla., 1950; Ph.D., Okla. State U., 1955; Sc.D. (hon.), U. Ark., 1991. Registered profl. engr., Okla. Mem. faculty Sch. Chem. Engring., Okla. State U., 1950-51, 52-58, prof., head dept., 1958-77, Leonard F. Sheerar prof., 1976-86, dir. phys. properties lab., 1976-86; design engr. process div. Black, Sivalls & Bryson, Inc., Oklahoma City, 1951-52; adminstrv. v.p., tech. dir. Fluid Properties Research, Inc., 1972-85; chem. engring. cons. Author: Gas and Liquid Sweetening, 1971, rev. ed. 1978, 83, (with J. Erbar) Gas Conditioning and Processing Vol. 3 - Computer Techniques and Applications, 1981, rev. ed. (with L. Lilly), 1988, (with A. Hines) Mass Transfer - Fundamentals and Applications, 1985; also numerous tech. papers. Served with USNR, 1944-45. Recipient award for personal achievement Chem. Engring. mag., 1988; Phillips lectr. in chem. engring. edn., Oklahoma State U., 1989; inducted into Engring. Hall of Fame, U. Ark., 1989; Dr. Robert N. Maddox Professorship in Chem. Engring. established in his honor by Gas Processors Suppliers Assn. at Okla. State U., 1989, Founders award Am. Inst. of Chemical Engineers, 1994. Fellow AIChE (chpt. pres. 1956-57, André Wilkins Meml. award 1981, Founder's award 1994); mem. NSPE, Okla. Soc. Profl. Engrs. (chpt. pres. 1961-62, dir. 1966-68, Engr. of Yr. 1972), Am. Inst. Mining Engrs., Soc. Petroleum Engrs., Am. Chem. Soc. (treas. indsl. and engring. chemistry div. 1966-68, chmn. div. 1970, Stewart award 1971), Gas Processors Assn. (Hanlon award 1985, Svc. citation 1987), Gas Processors Suppliers Assn. (editorial adv. bd. Engring. Data Book 1972—), Sigma Xi, Omega Chi Epsilon (nat. pres. 1968-70), Tau Beta Pi, Alpha Chi Sigma, Om icron Deleta Kappa, Sigma Nu (high coun. 1966-70, regent 1972-74, Hall of Honor 1988). Episcopalian (lay reader, vestryman). Clubs: Elks, Masons. Home: 1710 Davinbrook Ln Stillwater OK 74074-2339

MADDREY, E. E., II, textile company executive. Pres., chief exec. officer Delta Woodside Industries Inc., Greenville, S.C. Office: Delta Woodside Industries Inc 233 N Main St Greenville SC 29601-2142*

MADDREY, WILLIS CROCKER, medical educator, internist, academic administrator, consultant, researcher; b. Roanoke Rapids, N.C., Mar. 29, 1939; s. Milner Crocker and Sara Jean (Willis) M.; m. Ann Marie Matt, Apr. 18, 1981; children: Jeffrey, Gregory, Thomas. BS, Wake Forest U., 1960; MD, Johns Hopkins U., 1964. Diplomate: Am. Bd. Internal Medicine. Intern Osler Med. Service Johns Hopkins Hosp., Balt., 1964-65, asst. resident, 1965-66, 68-69, chief resident, 1969-70; fellow in liver disease Yale U., 1970-71; asst. prof. medicine Johns Hopkins U., Balt., 1971-75, assoc. prof., 1975-79, prof., 1980-81, asst. dean Sch. Medicine, 1975-79; assoc. dir. dept. medicine Johns Hopkins U., Baltimore, 1979-82; prof., chmn. dept. medicine Jefferson Med. Coll., Phila., 1982-90; v.p. clin. affairs U. Tex. Southwestern Med. Ctr., Dallas, 1990-93, exec. v.p. clin. affairs, 1994—. Assoc. editor: Medicine, 1972-82, Hepatology, 1988-95, mem. editl. bd., 1981-84, 86-87, Gastroenterology, 1982-87, Am. Jour. Medicine, 1978-87; contbr. articles to profl. jours. Bd. dirs. Am. Liver Found., 1976-80; trustee Magee Rehab. Hosp., Phila., 1982-87. Served with USPHS, 1966-68. Mem. ACP (bd. regents 1984-94, pres. 92-93), Am. Soc. Clin. Investigation, Am. Gastroenterol. Assn., Am. Assn. Study Liver Disease (pres. 1982). Republican. Office: U Tex Southwestern Med Ctr 5323 Harry Hines Blvd Dallas TX 75235-7200

MADDUX, GREG(ORY ALAN), professional baseball player; b. San Angelo, Tex., Apr. 14, 1966. Grad. high sch., Las Vegas. Baseball player Chicago Cubs, 1984-92, Atlanta Braves, 1992—. Recipient Cy Young award Baseball Writers' Assn. Am., 1992, 93, 94, 95; named to All-Star team, 1988, 92, 94-5; recipient Gold Glove Award, 1990-94; Sporting News All-Star Team, 1992-94; named Nat. League Pitcher of Yr., Sporting News, 1993; Nat. League Innings Pitched Leader, 1991-92, earned run avg., 1995, fielding percentage, 1990-95. Mem. World Series championship team, 1995. Office: Atlanta Braves PO Box 4064 Atlanta GA 30302-4064*

MADDUX, PARKER AHRENS, lawyer; b. San Francisco, May 23, 1939; s. Jackson Walker and Jeanette Ahrens M.; m. Mathilde G.M. Landman, Mar. 20, 1966; 1 child, Jackson Wilhelmus Quentin. AB, U. Calif., 1961; JD, Harvard U., 1964. Bar: Calif. 1965, U.S. Dist. Ct. (no. so., ea., ctrl. dist.) Calif. 1965, U.S. Ct. Appeals (9th cir.) 1972, U.S. Ct. Claims, 1974, N.Y. 1981, U.S. Supreme Ct. 1982, Assoc., Pillsbury, Madison & Sutro, San Francisco, 1965-72, ptnr., 1973—; lectr. in field. Bd. dirs. Friends of Recreation and Parks, San Francisco; trustee Town Sch. for Boys, San Francisco; co-chair San Francisco Open Space Citizens Adv. Com. Fulbright fellow, 1964-65. Mem. ABA, Calif. Bar Assn., San Francisco Bar Assn., Harvard Club (N.Y.C., San Francisco), Pacific Union Club. Republican. Unitarian. Contbr. articles to profl. jours. Office: Pillsbury Madison & Sutro 225 Bush St San Francisco CA 94104-4207

MADDY, JANET MARIE, educator, dean of students; b. Crestline, Ohio, Feb. 20, 1939; d. Hubert Franklin and Mabel May (Hotelling) M. AA, Pasadena City Coll, 1959; BA, Calif. State U., L.A., 1965, MA, 1972. Instr. Calif. State Coll., L.A., fall 1965; tchr. phys. edn. Irving Jr. High, L.A. Unified Sch. Dist., spring 1966, Bret Harte Jr. High Sch., L.A. Unified Sch. Dist., 1966-67; tchr., phys. edn. tchr., dept. chair Walton Jr. High Sch.-Compton (Calif.) Unified Sch. Dist., 1967-72; tchr. phys. edn./coach Dominguez H.S., Compton, 1972-78; prin. Westchester Luth. Schs., L.A., 1978-84; tchr. phys. edn., dept. chair Nimitz Middle Sch., L.A. Unified Sch. Dist., Huntington Park, Calif., 1985-94, dean of students-C Track, 1995—; mem. shared decision making coun. Nimitz Middle Sch., Huntington Park, 1992—; mentor tchr. selection com. L.A. Unified Sch. Dist., 1993-94; women in sports delegation to China, Citizen Amb. Program, Spokane, Wash., 1994, U.S. China Joint Conf. on Women's Issues, China, 1995. Synod womens orgn. bd. ELCA Women, L.A., 1990-93, 94—, chair references and counsel com. triennial nat. conf., Washington, 1993; chair cmty. com. Police Activity League, Ingelwood, Calif., 1990-93; co-chair Neighborhood Watch, Inglewood, 1988—. Comdr. USNR, ret., 1960-83. Mem. CAHPER, AAHPER, CTA, UTLA. Democrat. Lutheran. Avocations: reading, sports, travel. Home: 412 W Spruce Ave Inglewood CA 90301 Office: Nimitz Middle Sch 6021 Carmelita Ave Huntington Park CA 90255-3320

MADDY, PENELOPE JO, philosopher; b. Tulsa, July 4, 1950; d. Richard and Suzanne (Lorimer) Parsons. BA in Math., U. Calif., Berkeley, 1972; PhD in Philosophy, Princeton U., 1979. Asst. prof. U. Notre Dame (Ind.), 1978-83; assoc. prof. U. Ill., Chgo., 1983-87; assoc. prof. U. Calif., Irvine, 1987-89, prof., 1989—, dept. chair, 1991-95; mem. editorial bd. Jour. Philos. Logic, 1985—. Author: Realism in Mathematics, 1990; editor: Notre Dame Jour. Formal Logic, 1979-84, editl. bd., 1984—; editl. bd. Jour. Symbolic Logic, 1995—, Philosophic Mathematics, 1993—. Fellow AAUW, 1982-83, U. Calif., 1988-89; NSF grantee, 1986, 88-89, 90-91, 94-95, Marshall scholar, 1982-83, Westinghouse Sci. scholar, 1968-72. Mem. Assn. Symbolic Logic (mem. exec. com. 1993-96), Am. Philos. Assn. (mem. exec. com. 1993-95), Philosophy of Sci. Assn. (mem. governing bd. 1993-95). Office: U Calif Dept Philosophy Irvine CA 92717

MADEIRA, EDWARD W(ALTER), JR., lawyer; b. Phila., Feb. 10, 1928; s. Edward W. and Alice T. (Thompson) M.; m. Grace Luquer, Oct. 13, 1956; children: Martha L., Melissa P., Amanda T. A.B., U. Pa., 1949, LL.B., 1952. Bar: Pa. 1953. Law clk. Justice John C. Bell, Jr., Phila., 1952-53; ptnr. Pepper, Hamilton & Scheetz, 1961—, co-chmn., 1992-94, chmn. emeritus, 1994—; adj. prof. law Villanova Law Sch., 1992—. Pres. bd. dirs. Defender Assn. Phila. (pub. defender); assoc. trustee U. Pa. 1989—. Fellow Am. Coll. Trial Lawyers; mem. ABA (ho. of dels. 1989-92, chmn. com. on fed. jud. improvements 1991—), Jud. Conf. 3d Cir., Phila. Bar Assn., Pa. Bar Assn., Internat. Assn. Ins. Counsel. Republican. Episcopalian. Home: 227 Atlee Rd Wayne PA 19087-3835 Office: Pepper Hamilton & Scheetz 3000 Two Logan Sq 18th Arch St Philadelphia PA 19103

MADEIRA, FRANCIS KING CAREY, conductor, educator; b. Jenkintown, Pa., Feb. 21, 1917; s. Percy Childs and Margaret (Carey) M.; m. Jean E. Browning, June 17, 1947. Grad., Avon Old Farms, 1934; student, Julliard Grad. Sch., 1937-43; D.F.A. (hon.), Providence Coll., 1966; D.H.L., R.I. Coll., 1969; Mus.D. (hon.), Brown U., 1976. Instr. music Brown U., 1943-46, asst. prof. music, 1946-56, assoc. prof. music, 1956-66; founder, condr. R.I. Philharm. Orch., 1945-78; concert pianist recitals and condr. concerts, U.S. and Europe; also guest condr. U.S. and fgn. orchs. World premiere Trilogy (JFK-MLK-RFK) (by Ron Nelson), R.I. Philharmonic Orch., 1969. Mem. music panel Maine State Arts Commn., 1987-90; bd. trustees Saco River Festival Assn., 1988-94. Recipient Gov.'s award for excellence in arts, 1972; John F. Kennedy award for service to community, 1978.

MADEIRA, ROBERT LEHMAN, professional society administrator; b. Elizabethtown, Pa., Aug. 30, 1915; s. Isaac Titus and Elsie Hernley (Lehman) M.; m. Mary Elizabeth Evans, Feb. 5, 1938; children: Terry Madeira Harsney, Chase Landre. Student, Juniata Coll., 1933-34; B.S. in Econs, Elizabethtown Coll., 1937; postgrad., Mpls. Honeywell Sch. Aero. Engring., U. Minn., 1945. Pianist, tchr. Elizabethtown, 1935-41; automobile salesman Packard Lancaster Co., Lancaster, Pa., 1937; owner, mgr. Conewago Foods, Elizabethtown, 1938-39; aircraft technician U.S. Air Force Middletown, Pa. and Columbia, S.C., 1941-42; project engr. Mpls. Honeywell, Chgo. and Mpls., 1942-45; mgr. Iceland, Inc., Elizabethtown, 1945-51; exec. sec. Nat. Frozen Food Locker Inst., Elizabethtown, 1951-55; exec. dir. Nat. Inst. Locker and Freezer Provisioners, Elizabethtown, 1955-73, Am. Assn. Meat Processors, Elizabethtown, 1973-80; exec. dir. emeritus Am. Assn. Meat Processors, 1980—; condr. internat. meat processing seminars, Europe, S.Am., Australia, New Zealand, The Orient, Africa, 1962-85. Chmn. Elizabethtown ARC, 1948-49, Elizabethtown Community Chest, 1952-53, Elizabethtown Park Dr., 1950; bd. dirs. Lancaster Com. of 100, 1953-57, Elizabethtown Music Found., 1951-57; bd. dirs. Norlanco Med. Center, Elizabethtown, 1972-75, chmn. fund dr., 1972-73. Recipient Man of Yr. award Nat. Inst. Locker and Freezer Provisioners, 1955; honor cert. Freedoms Found. at Valley Forge, 1976. Mem. Am. Soc. Assn. Execs. (Key award 1971, chartered assn. exec.), C. of C. U.S., Nat. Assn. Exhbn. Mgrs., Nat. Fedn. Ind. Bus., Gideons Internat., Nat. Right-to-Work Com. Republican. Presbyterian. Home: 660 Willow Valley Sq Apt M102 Lancaster PA 17602-4874 Office: Am Assn Meat Processors PO Box 269 Elizabethtown PA 17022-0269

MADER, BRYN JOHN, vertebrate paleontologist; b. N.Y.C., July 29, 1959; s. Walter Richard and Audrey Jeanne (Hargest) M. BS, SUNY, Stony Brook, 1982; MS, U. Mass., 1987, PhD, 1991. Curatorial asst. dept. vertebrate paleontology Am. Mus. Natural History, N.Y.C., 1982-83, asst. collection mgr., 1990-93, collections registrar dept. mammalogy, 1993—; trustee, founder, pres. L.I. Natural Hist. Mus., 1994—. Contbr. articles to profl. jours., chpts. to books. Mem. N.Y. Acad. Scis., Soc. Vertebrate Paleontology, Paleontol. Soc., Sigma Xi. Presbyterian. Achievements include publication of first and only significant review of brontotheres in almost 50 years (a major perissodactyl lineage known primarily from the Eocene and Oligocene epochs of North America and Central Asia). Office: Am Mus Natural History Cen Park West At 79th St W New York NY 10024

MADER, CHARLES LAVERN, chemist; b. Dewey, Okla., Aug. 8, 1930; s. George Edgar and Naomia Jane (Harer) M.; m. Emma Jean Sinclair, June 12, 1960; 1 child, Charles L. II. BS, Okla. State U., 1952, MS, 1954; PhD, Pacific Western U., 1980. Fellow Los Alamos (N.Mex.) Nat. Lab., 1955—; JIMAR sr. fellow U. Hawaii, Honolulu, 1985-94; pres. Mader Consulting Co., Honolulu, 1985—. Author: Numerical Modeling of Detonation, 1979, Numerical Modeling of Water Waves, 1988, LASL Data Volumes, 1980-82; contbr. numerous articles to profl. jours.; author 70 reports. Scoutmaster Boys Scouts Am., Los Alamos, 1971-85. Fellow Am. Inst. Chemists; mem. Am. Chem. Soc., Combustion Inst., Tsunami Soc. (editor 1985—), Marine Tech. Soc., Sigma Xi, Pi Mu Epsilon, Phi Lambda Upsilon. Methodist. Achievements include development and definition of field of numerical modeling of explosives and water waves. Home: 1049 Kamehame Dr Honolulu HI 96825-2860 Office: Mader Cons Co 1049 Kamehame Dr Honolulu HI 96825-2860

MADERA, JOSEPH J., bishop; b. San Francisco, Nov. 27, 1927. Ed., Domus Studiorum of the Missionaries of the Holy Spirit, Coyoacan, D.F., Mexico. Ordained priest Roman Cath. Ch., 1957. Coadjutor to bishop of Fresno, 1980; bishop of Fresno, 1980-91; aux. bishop Archdiocese for Mil. Svcs., Silver Springs, Md., 1991—.

MADEWELL, JOHN E., radiologist. MD, U. Okla., 1969. Intern Madigen Gen. Hosp., Tacoma, 1969-70; resident in diagnostic radiology Walter Reed Med. Ctr., Washington, 1970-73; fellow in radiol. pathology Armed Forces Inst. Pathology, Washington, 1973-74; radiologist Milton S. Hershey Med. Ctr.; prof., chmn. dept. Milton S. Hershey Med. Ctr./Pa. State U. Mem. ACR, ARRS, AUR, ISS, RSNA. Office: Pa State U Coll Medicine Hershey Med Ctr Dept Radiol PO Box 850 Hershey PA 17033-0850

MADEWELL, MARY ANN, nursing educator; b. Cin., Mar. 12, 1936; d. Joseph Anthony and Gertrude (Lietemeyer) Siegel; m. James Arthur Madewell, Sept. 12, 1959; children: Mary E., James J., Ann Marie, Larry J. BSN, U. Cin., 1958; MSN, Ind. U., 1982, D in Nursing Svc., 1994. RN, Ohio, Ind. Asst. head nurse The Christ Hosp., Cin., 1958; instr., tchr. trainer, evaluator Childbirth Edn. Assn., Cin., 1958-83; office, on-call nurse Drs. Graf's McCord, Cin., 1958-60; staff nurse Mt. Carmel Hosp., Columbus, Ohio, 1960-61; instr. U. Cin., 1977-78; tchr. asst. Ind. U., Indpls., 1981-82, 83-84; instr. adj. U. Cin., 1985-88; asst. vis. prof. Miami U., Hamilton, Ohio, 1992-94; asst. prof. U. Cin., 1994—; adv. bd. mem. Pregnancy Ctr. Cleremont, 1986—; cmty. educator abuse of children Women Helping Women, Cin., 1993—. Bd. dirs., 1st v.p. Great Rivers Girl Scout Coun., Cin., 1991—, presenter adolescent sexuality, 1987-91. Recipient Perinatal grant and nurse traineeship, 1978-79, 79-81, Rsch. award Sigma Theta Tau, 1985; prin. investigator March of Dimes, 1994, Ohio Dept. Health, 1994—. Mem. Midwest Nursing Rsch. Soc. (presenter 1984), Assn. Women's Health, Obstetrical Neonatal Nurses (presenter, hospitality 1972—), Nat. Perinatal Assn., Health Mothers, Health Babies, Childbirth Edn. Assn. (con. 1983—). Roman Catholic. Home: 5 Kris Cir Terrace Park OH 45174-1015

MADEY, THEODORE EUGENE, physics educator; b. Wilmington, Del., Oct. 24, 1937. BS, Loyola Coll., Balt., 1959; PhD in Physics, U. Notre Dame, 1963. Staff physicist Nat. Inst. Stds. & Tech., 1965-81, rsch. fellow, 1983-88, group leader surface structure & kinetics, 1981-88; dir. lab. surface modification, prof. dept. physics Rutgers U., Piscataway, N.J., 1988—; vis. scientist Inst. Phys. Chemistry Tech. U. Munich, 1973, Sandia Nat. Labs., Albuquerque, 1977, Fritz Haber Inst. of Max Planck, Gesellschaft, Berlin, 1982; Chevron vis. prof. chem. engring. Calif. Inst. Tech., 1981. Recipient Gold Medal award U.S. Dept. Commerce, 1981. Fellow Am. Phys. Soc., Am. Chem. Soc., Am. Vacuum Soc. (pres. 1981, M.W. Welch award 1985); mem. Internat. Union Vacuum Sci. Tech. & Applications (sec. gen. 1986-89, pres.-elect 1989-92, pres. 1992—), Am. Inst. Physics. Office: Rutgers U Lab Surface Modification PO Box 849 Serin Physics Lab Piscataway NJ 08855-0849*

MADGETT, NAOMI LONG, poet, editor, educator; b. Norfolk, Va., July 5, 1923; d. Clarence Marcellus and Maude Selena (Hilton) Long; m. Julian F. Witherspoon, Mar. 31, 1946 (div. Apr. 1949); 1 child, Jill Witherspoon Boyer; m. William H. Madgett, July 29, 1954 (div. Dec. 1960); m. Leonard P. Andrews, Mar. 31, 1972. BA, Va. State Coll., 1945; MEd, Wayne State U., 1956; PhD, Internat. Inst. for Advanced Studies, 1980; LHD (hon.), Siena Heights Coll., 1991, Loyola U., 1993; DFA (hon.), Mich. State U., 1994. Reporter, copyreader Mich. Chronicle, Detroit, 1945-46; svc. rep. Mich. Bell Telephone Co., Detroit, 1948-54; tchr. English pub. high schs. Detroit, 1955-65, 66-68; rsch. assoc. Oakland U., Rochester, Mich., 1965-66; mem. staff Detroit Women Writers Conf. Ann. Writers Conf., 1968—; lectr. English U. Mich., 1970-71; assoc. prof. English Eastern Mich. U., Ypsilanti, 1968-73, prof., 1973-84, prof. emeritus, 1984—; editor-pub. Lotus Press, 1974—; sr. editor Lotus Poetry Series, Mich. State U. Press, 1993—. Author: (poetry) Songs to a Phantom Nightingale (under name Naomi Cornelia Long), 1941, One and the Many, 1956, Star by Star, 1965, 70, Pink Ladies in the Afternoon, 1972, 90, Exits and Entrances, 1978, Phantom Nightingale: Juvenilia, 1981, Octavia and other Poems (Creative Achievement award Coll. Lang. Assn.), 1988, Remembrances of Spring: Collected Early Poems, 1993; (textbook) (with Ethel Tincher and Henry B. Maloney) Success in Language and Literature B, 1967, A Student's Guide to Creative Writing, 1980; editor: (anthology) A Milestone Sampler: 15th Anniversary Anthology, 1988, Adam of Ife: Black Women in Praise of Black Men, 1992; Tribute In Her Lifetime Afrikan Poets Theatre, 1989. Participant Creative Writers in Schs. program. Recipient Esther R. Beer Poetry award Nat. Writers Club, 1957, Disting. English Tchr. of Y.. award, 1967; Josephine Nevins Keal award, 1979; Mott fellow in English, 1965, Robert Hayden Rungate award, 1985, Creative Artist award Mich. Coun. for the Arts, 1987, award Nat. Coalition 100 Black Women, 1984, award Nat. Coun. Tchrs. English Black Caucus, 1984, award Chesapeake/Virginia Beach chpt. Links, Inc., 1981, Arts Found. Mich. award, 1990, Creative Achievement award Coll. Lang. Assn., 1988; Arts Achievement award Wayne State U., 1985, The Black Scholar Award of Excellence, 1992; Am. Book award, 1993, Mich. Artist award, 1993; Creative Contbrs. award Gwendolyn Brook Ctr. Black Lit. and Creative Writing Chgo. State U., 1993, George Kent award, 1995; Naomi Long Madgett Poetry award named for her, 1993—. Mem. NAACP, Coll. Lang. Assn., So. Poetry Law Ctr., Langston Hughes Soc., Nora Neale Hurston Soc., Am. Acad. Poets, Poetry Resource Ctr. Mich., Detroit Women Writers, Alpha Kappa Alpha. Congregationalist. Home: 18080 Santa Barbara Dr Detroit MI 48221-2531 Office: PO Box 21607 Detroit MI 48221-0607 *I have tried to set an example of excellence in the use of language, especially the language of poetry. If I can leave behind some enduring work—my own words and the words of others I have published—I will consider myself amply rewarded for my labors. The truly great people I have known have given a great deal of themselves in the service of others, have not been puffed up by their own importance, and have maintained integrity in their personal and professional lives. They have been my models.*

MADIGAN, JOHN WILLIAM, publishing executive; b. Chgo., June 7, 1937; s. Edward P. and Olive D. Madigan; m. Holly Williams, Nov. 24, 1962; children: Mark W., Griffith E., Melanie L. BBA, U. Mich., 1958, MBA, 1959. Fin. analyst Duff & Phelps, Chgo., 1960-62; audit mgr. Arthur Andersen & Co., Chgo., 1962-67; v.p. investment banking Paine, Webber, Jackson & Curtis, Chgo., 1967-69; v.p. corp. fin. Salomon Bros., Chgo., 1969-74; v.p., CFO, dir. Tribune Co., Chgo., 1975-81, exec. v.p., 1981-91, pub., 1990-94, pres., CEO, 1991-94, pres., COO, 1994-5, chmn., pres., CEO, 1996—, 1996—. Trustee Rush-Presbyn.-St. Luke's Med. Ctr., Mus. TV & Radio in N.Y., Northwestern U., Ill. Inst. Tech. Mem. Chicagoland C. of C. (bd. dirs.), Chgo. Coun. on Fgn. Rels. (bd. dirs.), Robert R. McCormick Tribune Found. (bd. dirs.), Newspaper Mgmt. Ctr. at Northwestern U. (exec. com.), Econ. Club Chgo., Comml. Club Chgo. Home: 1160 Laurel Ave Winnetka IL 60093-1820 Office: Tribune Co 435 N Michigan Ave Chicago IL 60611-4001

MADIGAN, JOSEPH EDWARD, financial executive, consultant, director; b. Bklyn., June 26, 1932; s. James Peter and Mary (Goldman) M.; m. Catherine Cashman, July 26, 1980; children: Kerri Ann, Kimberly Ann, Elizabeth Ann. BBA cum laude, Baruch Coll., CUNY, 1958; MBA, NYU, 1963. Adminstrv. asst. Assoc. Metals & Minerals Corp., 1961-63; fin. analyst, fgn. exch. trader, corp. portfolio trader AMAX, Inc., 1963-65; mgr. corp. portfolio, dir. cash mgmt., asst. treas. TWA, Inc., 1965-68; treas. Borden, Inc., 1968-76, v.p., treas., 1976-80; exec. v.p., chief fin. officer Wendy's Internat., Inc., Dublin, Ohio, 1980-87; bd. dirs. Cooker Restaurant Corp., Skyline Chili, Inc., Voca Corp., Columbus Parts Supply, Inc., Columbus Paper & Supply Co., Frank Gates Svc. Co., RWS Enterprises, Cardinal Realty Svcs., Inc., chmn. bd. dirs. With USN, 1951-55. Mem. Fin. Execs. Inst., Nat. Investor Rels. Inst., Investor Rels. Assn., Exec. Forum NYU, Baruch Coll.-CUNY Alumni Assn., NYU Alumni Assn., Treas. Club N.Y., Country Club at Muirfield Village, Capital Club (Columbus), Imperial Golf Club (Naples, Fla.), Beta Gamma Sigma. Republican. Roman Catholic. Home: 9457 Avemore Ct Dublin OH 43017-9674

MADIGAN, MARY JEAN, editor, writer; b. Nanticoke, Pa.; d. Melvin Smith and Irene (Bellegia) Wagner; m. Richard A. Madigan (div. 1975); children: Richard, Dana, Reese. BA, Cornell U.; MA, Am. U., Washington. Curator Hudson River Mus., Yonkers, N.Y., 1970-76, asst. dir., 1976-77; editor Art & Antiques mag., N.Y.C., 1978-82, editor, pub., 1983; dept. editor RN mag., Oradell, N.J., 1984; editor-in-chief, pub. Restaurant/Hotel Design Internat. mag., N.Y.C., 1984—; cons. N.Y. State Council on Arts, N.Y.C., 1976-78, NEH, 1977; book reviewer Mus. News, Washington, 1974-77. Author: Eastlake-Influenced American Furniture, 1974, Steuben Glass, 1981; editor: 19th Century Furniture, 1982, Americana: Folk and Decorative Art, 1982; contbr. articles to profl. jours. Harry M. Grier scholar Am. Assn. Art Mus. Dirs., 1975; recipient Jesse M. Neal award Am. Bus. Press, 1984. Mem. Am. Soc. Interior Designers (press affiliate 1987—, Presdl. citation 1987), Author's Guild, Author's League of Am., Inst. Bus. Designers, Am. Soc. Mag. Editors, Phi Beta Kappa. Democrat. Mem. Unitarian Ch. Home: 565 Broadway Apt 6F Hastings Hdsn NY 10706-1713 Office: Restaurant/Hotel Design Internat Mag 633 3rd Ave New York NY 10017-6706

MADIGAN, MICHAEL J., lawyer; b. Washington, Apr. 18, 1943; s. Helen B. (McGuire) M.; children: Mollie, Shana. BA, U. Conn., 1965; JD, Cath. U., 1968. Law clk. to Hon. Edward A. Tamm U.S. Ct. Appeals (D.C. crct.), 1968-69; asst. U.S. atty. Washington, 1969-73; asst. minority counsel Senate Watergate Com., Washington, 1973-74; counsel to Sen. Howard Baker, Jr. Washington, 1975-76; minority counsel Senate Intelligence Com., Washington, 1976-77; ptnr. Akin, Gump, Strauss, Hauer & Feld, Washington, 1977—, chmn. pro bono com., 1989—; spl. counsel Senate Fgn. Rels. Com. for confirmation hearings in nomination of Sec. of State Alexander Haig, 1981; mem. adv. com. law firm pro bono project ABA, 1991—; pres. Asst. U.S. Attys. Assn., Washington, 1987-88; chmn. Fed. Jud. Appointments Com., Washington, 1991-93; mem. D.C. Fed. Jud. Nominating Commn., Washington, 1993. Mem. Bar Assn. of D.C. (nominating com. 1992-93, budget com. 1992), D.C. Bar Bd. Govs., Women's Bar Assn. D.C. Republican. Roman Catholic. Home: 3909 Ivy Terrace Ct NW Washington DC 20007-2138 Office: Akin Gump Strauss Hauer & Feld 1333 New Hampshire Ave NW Washington DC 20036-1511*

MADIGAN, MICHAEL JOSEPH, state legislator; b. Chgo., Apr. 19, 1942; m. Shirley Roumagoux; children: Lisa, Tiffany, Nicole, Andrew. Ed., U. Notre Dame, Loyola U., Chgo. Mem. Ill. Ho. of Reps., 1971—, majority leader, 1977-80, minority leader, 1981-82, house speaker, 1983-94, Dem. leader, 1995—; lawyer. Sec. to Alderman David W. Healey; hearing officer Ill. Commerce Commn.; del. 6th Ill. Constnl. Conv.; trustee Holy Cross Hosp.; ex officio mem. adv. com. to pres. Richard J. Daley Coll.; adv. com. Fernley Harris Sch. for Handicapped; committeeman 13th Ward Democratic Orgn. Mem. Council Fgn. Relations, City Club Chgo. Office: House Reps State Capital Bldg Springfield IL 62706

MADIGAN, RICHARD ALLEN, museum director; b. Corning, N.Y., Oct. 29, 1937; s. Myles L. and Rebekah M. (Bacon) M.; AB, Drew U., 1959; m. Mary Jean Smith, June 11, 1960 (div. 1975); children: Richard Allen, Dana Smith, Reese Jennings; m. 2d, Alice Sturrock, Sept. 6, 1975 (div. May 1978); m. 3d, Cara Montgomery, Aug. 5, 1978 (div. July 1987); 1 son, James Myles. Pub. contact rep. Corning Glass Center, 1959, supr. visitor rels., 1959-60; dir. Andrew Dickson White Mus. Art, Cornell U., 1960-63; asst. dir., asst. sec. Corcoran Gallery Art, Washington, 1963-67; dir. N. Tex. Museums Resources Council, 1967-68, Bklyn. Children's Mus., 1968-69; exec. dir. Wave Hill Center Environ. Studies, 1969-74; instr. anthropology dept. Lehman Coll., 1968-74; dir. Norton Gallery and Sch. Art, West Palm Beach Fla., 1974-89; sec. Norton Gallery and Sch. of Art, Inc., 1974-80; pvt. art cons., 1989-91; columnist Palm Beach Daily News, 1990-91; contbr. Calif. mag.; exec. dir., CEO Atlantic Ctr. for Arts, New Smyrna Beach, Fla., 1990-91; dir. Decorative Arts Study Ctr., San Juan Capistrano, 1992-93, dep. dir., N.Y. Transit Mus. 1994—; past instr. art dept. George Washington U.; bd. dirs. Palm Beach Festival; lectr. Fgn. Svc. Inst., Dept. State. Mem. Am. Assn. Museums (chmn. coll. and univ. museums sect. 1962-63), Museums Council N.Y.C. (chmn. 1970-71), Fla. Art Mus. Dirs. Assn. (pres. 1978-79, 83-84), S.E. Museums Conf., Assn. Art Mus. Dirs., Palm Beach C. of C. (dir. 1979-91), West Palm Beach C. of C. (dir. 1981-82). Author: The Sculpture of Michael Schreck, 1983. Office: New York Transit Mus 130 Livingston St 9th Fl Box E Brooklyn NY 11201-5106

MADISON, BERNARD L., academic dean, mathematics educator; b. Rocky Hill, Ky., Aug. 1, 1941; s. George G. and Neva (Crump) M.; m. Lyda Sue Madison Wood, June 1, 1969; children: Eva Camille, Blair Bernard. B.S., Western Ky. U., 1958-62; M.S., U. Ky., 1964, Ph.D., 1966. Asst. prof. La. State U., Baton Rouge, 1966-71, assoc. prof., 1971-79, dir. basic and applied math., 1976-79, prof. dept. math., 1979-80; prof., chmn. dept. math. U. Ark., Fayetteville, 1979-89, dean Fulbright Coll. Arts and Scis., 1989—; cons. NRC, 1986-87, project dir., 1987-88. Contbr. articles to profl. jours. Recipient Ogden medal Western Ky. U., 1962. Mem. Am. Math. Soc., Math. Assn. Am., AAUP, Sigma Xi, Sigma Pi Sigma, Pi Mu Epsilon, Lambda Chi Alpha. Democrat. Presbyterian. Home: 573 Rockcliff Rd Fayetteville AR 72701-3809 Office: U Ark Fulbright Coll Old Main # 525 Fayetteville AR 72701

MADISON, JAMES RAYMOND, lawyer; b. White Plains, N.Y., Apr. 27, 1931; s. Raymond S. and Katherine (Sherwin) M.; m. Mary Massey, Sept. 19, 1953; children: Michael, Matthew, Molly. BS, Stanford U., 1953, LLB, 1959. Bar: Calif. 1960, U.S. Dist. Ct. (no. dist.) Calif. 1960, U.S. Ct. Appeals (9th cir.) 1960, U.S. Dist. Ct. (ctrl. dist.) Calif. 1970, U.S. Supreme Ct. 1973, U.S. Dist. Ct. (ea. dist.) Calif. 1981, U.S. Dist. Ct. (so. dist.) Calif. 1988. Assoc. Orrick, Herrington & Sutcliffe, San Francisco, 1959-67, ptnr., 1968-95. Trustee Antioch U., Yellow Springs, Ohio, 1980-87; bd. dirs. Planned Parenthood Alameda/San Francisco, 1984-89. Lt. (j.g.) USN, 1953-56. Mem. ABA, ASCE, State Bar Calif., Bar Assn. San Francisco, San Mateo County Bar Assn., Am. Arbitration Assn. (large complex case panel arbitrators and mediators, No. Calif. regional adv. coun.), Lawyers Club San Francisco. Democrat. Episcopalian. Avocation: soccer. Office: 417 Montgomery St 5th Fl San Francisco CA 94104 also: 750 Menlo Ave Ste 250 Menlo Park CA 94025

MADISON, OCTAVIA DIANNE, mental health services professional; b. Lynchburg, Va., Mar. 28, 1960; d. Raymond Barlow Sr. Madison and Doreatha Madison Anderson. BA, Hampton U., 1982; MEd, Lynchburg Coll., 1983; postgrad., George Mason U., Fairfax, Va., 1989-94, Va. Poly. Inst. and State U., 1994—. Lic. profl. counselor, addiction counselor. Resource counselor Lynchburg Community Action Group, 1983, placement specialist, 1984; program mgr. Lynchburg 70001 Program, 1985; therapist, case mgr. Cen. Va. Community Svcs., Lynchburg, 1985-88; substance abuse counselor II Fairfax County Govt., 1988—; therapist Women's Ctr. No. Va., Vienna, 1990—; psychotherapist Dr. Carolyn Jackson-Sahni-Assocs., 1993; mental health therapist Arlington County Dept. Human Svcs., 1994—; grad. asst. Va. Polytechnic Inst. and State U., 1994. Asst. sec. So. Christian Leadership Conf., Lynchburg, 1983-84; mem. single ministry, asst. chair youth adv. bd. Mt. Pleasant Bapt. Ch., Alexandria, Va., 1991—; bd. examiners Profl. Counselors, 1991—. Recipient 2-Star award United Way (coord.), 1989. Mem. Am. Assn. for Counseling and Devel., Women's Ctr. Career Network, Advs. for Infants and Mothers, Inc., Nat. Black Alcoholism Coun., Va. Counselor's Assn., Washington Met. Area Addictions Counselors, Nat. Bd. Cert. Counselors, Psi Chi, Beta Kappa Chi. Avocations: reading, swimming, sports, viewing mountains. Home: 3890 Lyndhurst Dr Apt 303 Fairfax VA 22031-3722

MADISON, ROBERT PRINCE, architect; b. Cleve., July 28, 1923; s. Robert J. and Nettie (Brown) M.; m. Leatrice L. Branch, Apr. 16, 1949; children: Jeanne Marie, Juliette Branch. Student, Howard U., 1940-43, HHD, 1987; B.Arch., Western Res. U., 1946-48; M.Arch., Harvard, 1952. Mem. various archtl. firms, 1948-52; instr. Howard U., Washington, 1952-54; chmn., CEO Robert P. Madison Internat., architects, engrs. and planners, Cleve., 1954—; trustee Am. Automobile Assn.; vis. prof. Howard U., 1961-62; lectr. Western Res. U., 1964-65; mem. U.S. architects del. Peoples Repub. China, 1974. Prin. works include U.S. Embassy Dakar, Senegal, West Africa, 1966, State of Ohio Computer Ctr., 1988, Cuyahoga County Jail, 1990, Continental Airlines Hub Concourse, Cleve. Internat. Airport, 1991. Mem. tech. adv. com. Cleve. Bd. Edn., 1960—; mem. adv. com. Cleve. Urban Renewal, 1963—; mem. fine arts adv. com. to mayor, Cleve.; mem. archtl. adv. coun. Cornell U.; trustee Case Western Res. U., Cleve. Opera, 1990, NCCJ, 1990, Commn. on Higher Edn., 1990; bd. dirs. Jr. Achievement Greater Cleve.; trustee Cuyahoga County Hosp. Found., 1983—, Univ. Circle Inc., Midtown Corridor Inc.; mem. Ohio Bd. Bldg. Standards, 1986, Cleveland Heights City Planning Commn., 1987. 1st lt., inf. AUS, 1943-46. Decorated Purple Heart; Fulbright fellow, 1952-53; recipient Disting. Svc. award Case Western Res. U., 1989, Disting. Archtl. Firm award Howard U., 1989, Entrepreneur of Yt. award Ernst Young, Inc., Merrill Lynch, 1991; named to Corp. Hall of Fame, Ohio Assembly of Cours., 1991. Fellow AIA (chpt. pres., nat. task force for creative econs. 1976, mem. jury of fellows 1983-85, mem. nat. judicial coun. 1993, Gold Medal Firm award Ohio 1994); mem. Architects Soc. Ohio, Epsilon Delta Rho, Alpha Phi Alpha, Sigma Pi Phi. Home: 2339 N Park Blvd Cleveland OH 44106-3139 Office: Robert P Madison Internat Inc 2930 Euclid Ave Cleveland OH 44115-2416

MADISON, ROBERTA ELEANOR, epidemiologist, educator, consultant; b. Bklyn., Feb. 10, 1932; d. A.I. and Grace (Weinstein) M.; children: Jerry Solomon, Sue Vann. AB in History, UCLA, 1966, MA, 1969, MSPH in Environ. Health, 1972, DrPH, 1974. Chief epidemiological analyst Los Angeles County, L.A., 1972-75; from asst. prof. to assoc. prof. Calif. State U., Northridge, 1975-83, prof. epidemiology and biostatistics, 1983-89; part-time epidemiologist City of Hope, Duarte, Calif., 1977-85; instr. biostatistics UCLA Sch. Pub. Health, 1978-84; v.p. Enrich; cons., biostatistician Northridge Hosp., 1983-91; cons. epidemiology and biostats. Thrasher & Assocs., Northridge, 1988-91, Cytosystems, Cupertino, Calif., 1988-90; cons. epidemiology Warner Day Care Ctr., Woodland Hills, Calif., 1988-90; cons. to phys. therapy masters program Coll. Osteo Medicine of Pacific, 1992-93. Mem. editorial rev. bd. Alzheimers Disease and Assoc. Disorders, 1985—; contbr. articles to profl. jours.; cons. editor: Informed Consent mag., 1994—. Bd. dirs. Basehart Theatre, Woodland Hills, 1986-94. Grantee Am. Lung Assn., Health and Human Svcs., 1995, others. Fellow Am. Coll. Epidemiology, Cancer Rsch. Ctr.; mem. Am. Statis. Assn. (sec. state edn. sect. 1982, workshop organizing com. State Calif. chpt. 1986—), Golden Key Honor Soc. (hon.), Sigma Xi (sec. chpt. 1982). Avocations: walking, camping, reading, concerts. Office: Calif State U 18111 Nordhoff St Northridge CA 91330-0001

MADISON, T. JEROME, business executive; b. N.Y.C., June 2, 1940; s. Theodore H. and Eleanor E. (Eveland) M.; m. Marsha A. Heeb, Sept. 26, 1964 (dec.); children: Jillian, Kimberly, Ryan. BS, U. Pa., 1962; MBA, Monmouth U., 1975. CPA, N.J. Mgr. KPMG Peat Marwick, Newark and Princeton, N.J., 1970-75; mgr. Abbott Labs., North Chicago, Ill., 1976; chief internal auditor Rorer Group, Inc., Fort Washington, Pa., 1977-78, corp. contr., 1979-82; v.p. fin. Cytogen Corp., Princeton, N.J., 1982-86; pres., chief exec. officer, dir. Outwater & Wells Ventures, Inc., 1981-85, Atlantic Capital Resources Group, Inc., 1985-87, Founders Court Investors Inc., Princeton, N.J., 1986-91, Montgomery Ptnrs. 1991—, Intrepid Capital Ptnr., 1995—; chmn., chief exec. officer Pilling Co., 1986-91; chmn., dir. Capital Controls Corp, 1987-91; chmn. MEECO Industries, Inc., 1988-91, Prince Gardner, Inc., 1989-91; dir., chmn. fin. com. Carrier Found.; bd. dirs. Cytogen Corp., Serex, Inc., Somerset Resources, Inc., U.S. Pharm. Explorations, Ltd. Naval flight officer USN, 1962-66. Mem. AICPA, Delaware Valley Venture Group, Fin. Execs. Inst. Office: Montgomery Ptnrs 1608 Walnut St Philadelphia PA 19103

MADIX, ROBERT JAMES, chemical engineer, educator; b. Beach Grove, Ind., June 22, 1938; s. James L. and Marjorie A. (Strohl) M.; children: Bradley Alan, David Eric, Micella Lynn, Evan Scott. BS, U. Ill., 1961; PhD, U. Calif., 1964. NSF postdoctoral fellow Max Planck Inst., Göttingen, Fed. Republic of Germany, 1964-65; asst. prof. chem. engr. Stanford (Calif.) U., 1965-72, assoc. prof., chem. engr., 1972-77; prof. chem. engring. Stanford U., 1977—, chmn., chem. engr., 1983-87, prof. chemistry, 1981—; cons. Monsanto Chem., St. Louis, 1975-84, Shell Oil Co., Houston, 1985-86; Peter Debye lectorship Cornell U., 1985; Eyring lectr. chemistry Ariz. State U., 1990; disting. prof. lectr. U. Tex., Austin, 1980; chmn. Gordon Rsch. Conf. on Reactions on Surfaces, 1995. Assoc. editor Catalysis Rev., 1986—, Catalysis Letters, 1992—, Rsch. on Chem. Intermediates, 1994—; contbr.

articles to profl. jours. Recipient Alpha Chi Sigma award Am. Inst. Chem. Engrs., 1990, Paul Emmett award Catalysis Soc. N.Am., 1984, Humboldt U.S. Sr. Scientist prize, 1978; For Found. fellow, 1969-72. Mem. Am. Chem. Soc. (Irving Langmuir Disting. Lectr. award 1981), Am. Phys. Soc., Am. Vacuum Soc., AIChE, Calif. Catalysis Soc. Office: Stanford Univ Dept Chemical Engrng Stanford CA 94305

MADNI, ASAD MOHAMED, engineering executive; b. Bombay, Sept. 8, 1947; came to U.S., 1966; s. Mohamed Taher and Sara Taher (Wadiwalla) M.; Gowhartaj Shahnawaz, Nov. 11, 1976; 1 child, Jamal Asad. Gen. cert. edn., U. Cambridge, Bombay, 1964; AAS in Electronics, RCA Insts., Inc., 1968; BS in Engring., UCLA, 1969, MS in Engring., 1972; postgrad. exec. inst., Stanford U., 1984; cert. in engring. mgmt., Calif. Inst. Tech., 1987; PhD in Engring., Calif. Coast U., 1987; sr. exec. program, MIT, 1990. Sr. instr. Pacific States U., L.A., 1969-71; electronics auditor Pertec Corp., Chatsworth, Calif., 1973-75; project engr., sr. engr., program mgr, dir. advanced program Microwave div. Systron Donner, Van Nuys, Calif., 1975-82, dir. engring., 1982-92; gen. mgr. Microwave and Instrument div. Systron Donner, Van Nuys, Calif., 1985-90; chmn., pres., chief exec. officer Systron Donner Corp., 1990-92; pres., CEO Sensors and Controls Group BEI Electronics, Inc., 1992-93, BEI Motion Sys. Co., 1993-94, BEI Sensors & Sys. Co., 1994—; vice-chmn. IEEE-MTTS, San Fernando Valley chpt., 1991-92, chmn., 1992-94; tech. advisor Test and Measurement World, Boston, 1982-90; adv. Calif. State U. Northridge. Mem. editorial rev. bd., West coast chmn. Microwave Systems News and Communications Tech., 1982-90; contbr. more than 50 articles to numerous tech. publs.; patentee in field. Mem. AAAS, IEEE (sr.), NRA (life), Soc. Automotive Engrs., N.Y. Acad. Scis., Assn. Old Crows (life, gold cert. of merit 1992), Calif. Rifle and Pistol Assn. (life), MIT Soc. Sr. Execs. (life), UCLA Alumni Assn. (life), MIT Alumni Assn. (life). Home: 3281 Woodbine St Los Angeles CA 90064-4836 Office: BEI Sensors & Systems Co 13100 Telfair Ave Sylmar CA 91342-3573 *Personal philosophy: There is no substitute for talent and vision complemented by perseverance, dedication and integrity.*

MADONIA, VALERIE, dancer; b. Buffalo. Dancer Nat. Ballet of Can., 1979-81, Am. Ballet Theater, 1981-86, The Joffrey Ballet, N.Y.C., 1987—; mem. Baryshnikov and Co. Tour 1985; guest artist with The Armitage Ballet, 1987, Lines Contemporary Ballet, 1994; dir. Telluride (Colo.) Dance Gallery, 1995—. Office: Telluride Dance Gallery PO Box 1303 Telluride CO 81435

MADONNA (MADONNA LOUISE VERONICA CICCONE), singer, actress; b. Bay City, Mich., Aug. 16, 1958; d. Sylvio and Madonna Ciccone; m. Sean Penn, Aug. 16, 1985 (div. 1989). Student, U. Mich., 1976-78. Dancer Alvin Ailey Dance Co., N.Y.C., 1979; CEO Maverick Records, L.A. Albums include Madonna, 1983, Like a Virgin, 1985, True Blue, 1986, (soundtrack)Who's That Girl, 1987, (with others) Vision Quest Soundtrack, 1983, You Can Dance, 1987, Like a Prayer, 1989, I'm Breathless: Music From and Inspired by the Film Dick Tracy, 1990, The Immaculate Collection, 1990, Erotica, 1992, Bedtime Stories, 1994, Something to Remember, 1995; film appearances include A Certain Sacrifice, 1980, Vision Quest, 1985, Desperately Seeking Susan, 1985, Shanghai Surprise, 1986, Who's That Girl, 1987, Bloodhounds of Broadway, 1989, Dick Tracy, 1990, Truth or Dare, 1991, Madonna, 1992, Body of Evidence, 1992, Dangerous Game, 1993, Blue in the Face, 1995, Four Rooms, 1996, Girl 6, 1996; Broadway theater debut in Speed-the-Plow, 1987; author: Sex, 1992. Roman Catholic. Office: Maverick Records 8000 Beverly Blvd Los Angeles CA 90048*

MADONNA, JON C., accounting firm executive. Chmn., CEO KPMG Peat Marwick, N.Y.C. Office: KPMG Peat Marwick 767 Fifth Ave 47th Fl New York NY 10153*

MADORE, JOYCE LOUISE, gerontology nurse; b. Madison, Kans., Dec. 15, 1936; d. Lionel Wiedmer and Mary Elizabeth (Piley) Murphy; m. Robert Madore, Aug. 15, 1969; children: Carl, Clay. BS, Emporia State U., 1980; diploma, Newman Hosp., 1981. RN, Kans., Mo.; cert. gerontol. nurse, non profit adminstr., nursing home adminstr. Med. charge nurse St. Mary's Hosp., Emporia, Kans., 1971-72; dir. nursing Madison (Kans.) Manor, 1974-81, 82-83; staff nurse Newman Meml. Hosp., Emporia, 1981-82; dir. Daybreak Adult Day Svcs., dir. HELP program Springfield (Mo.) Area Coun. of Chs., 1983—; mem. Gov.'s Com. to Establish Rules and Regulations on Adult Day Care Patients State of Mo.; cons. U. Mo. Coop. Extension Svc. Program Guides on Adult Day Care. Contbr. video Understanding Aging Program; developer Home Guide for the Homebound, 1996. Named one of Outstanding Nurses in Mo. St. Louis U., 1989. Mem. NANA, AFE, Adult Day Care Assn. (past sec., exec. past v.p. 1989-91), Mo. Nurses Assn., Mo. Adult Day Care assn. (pres. 1991-95, Exec. award 1995), Mo. League of Nursing. Home: 171 Hilltop Oaks Ln Sparta MO 65753-8911

MADORY, JAMES RICHARD, hospital administrator, former air force officer; b. Staten Island, N.Y., June 11, 1940; s. Eugene and Agnes (Gerner) M.; m. Karen James Clifford, Sept. 26, 1964; children: James E., Lynn Anne, Scott J., Elizabeth Anne, Joseph M. BS, Syracuse U., 1964; MHA, Med. Coll. Va., 1971. Enlisted USAF, 1958; x-ray technician Keesler Area Med. Ctr., Biloxi, Miss., 1959-62; commd. 2d lt. USAF, 1964, advanced through grades to maj., 1978; x-ray technician Keesler Area Med. Ctr., Biloxi, Miss., 1959-62; adminstr. Charleston (S.C.) Clinic, 1971-74, Beale Hosp., Calif., 1974-77; assoc. adminstr. Shaw Regional Hosp., S.C., 1977-79; ret. USAF, 1979; asst. adminstr. Raleigh Gen. Hosp., Beckley, W.Va., 1979-81; adminstr., dir., sec. bd. Chesterfield Gen. Hosp., Cheraw, S.C., 1981-87; pres., CEO Grand Strand Hosp., Myrtle Beach, S.C., 1987-95, trustee, 1987-95; cons. in health care adminstrn. Horry County Planning Commn., 1995—; cons. Healthcare Adminstrn., 1995—; mem. adv. bd. Cheraw Nursing Home, 1984-85. Contbr. articles to profl. publs. Chmn. bd. W.Va. Kidney Found., Charleston, 1980-81; chmn. youth bd. S.C. TB and Respiratory Disease Assn., Charleston, 1972-73; county chmn. Easter Seal Soc., Chesterfield County, S.C., 1984-85; campaign crusade chmn. Am. Cancer Soc., Chesterfield County, 1985-86; chmn. dist. advancement com. Boy Scouts Am., 1987-90; bd. dirs. Horry County United Way, 1989-91, Horry County Access Care, 1989-91; trustee Cheraw Acad., 1982-85, Grand Strand Gen. Hosp., 1987-94, Coastal Acad., 1988-90; commr. Horry County Planning Commn., 1995—. Decorated Bronze Star, Vietnamese Cross of Gallantry, Vietnamese Medal of Honor; named to S.C. Order of Palmetto Gov. David Beasley, 1995. Fellow Am. Coll. Hosp. Adminstrs., Am. Coll. Health Care Execs; mem. S.C. Hosp. Assn. (com on legislation 1984-86, trustee 1989-94), Am. Acad. Healthcare Adminstrs., Cheraw C. of C. (bd. dirs. 1982-83), Rotary (pres. 1984-85). Republican. Roman Catholic. Home and Office: 3710 Kinloch Dr Myrtle Beach SC 29577

MADOW, LEO, psychiatrist, educator; b. Cleve., Oct. 18, 1915; s. Solomon Martin and Anna (Meyers) M.; m. Jean Antoinette Weisman, Apr. 16, 1942; children: Michael, Robert. AB, Western Res. U., 1937, MD, 1942; MA, Ohio State U., 1938. Diplomate Am. Bd. Psychiatry and Neurology. Intern Phila. Gen. Hosp., 1942-43; resident Phila. Gen. Hosp., Jefferson Hosp., Inst. Pa. Hosp., 1943-46; practice medicine specializing in psychiatry Phila., 1948—; prof., chmn. dept. neurology Med. Coll. Pa., Phila., 1958-65; prof., chmn. dept. psychiatry and neurology Med. Coll. Pa., 1965-70, prof., chmn. dept. psychiatry, 1970-81, clin. prof. psychiatry Hershey Med. Ctr., 1982—; sr. cons. psychiatry Inst. Pa. Hosp., Phila., 1975—; tng. analyst, past pres. Phila. Psychoanalytic Inst.; past pres., mem. med. staff Inst. Pa. Hosp. Author: Anger, 1972, Love, 1983, Guilt, 1989; editor: Dreams, 1970, Sensory Deprivation, 1970, Psychomimetic Drugs, 1971, Integration of Child Psychiatry with Basic Resident Program, 1975. Served to capt. AUS, 1944-46. Named Outstanding Educator of Am. Med. Coll. Pa., 1972. Fellow ACP, Am. Psychiatric Assn. (life), Phila. Psychiatric Soc. (Lifetime Achievement award 1991) (past pres.), Am. Coll. Psychiatrists, Am. Coll. Psychoanalysts (pres. 1989-90, Laughlin award 1990); mem. Am. Psychoanalytic Assn., Am. Neurol. Assn., Phila. Psychoanalytic Soc. (past pres.), Alpha Omega Alpha, Phi Sec. Home: 135 Sibley Ave Narberth PA 19072-1318 Office: Inst of Pa Hosp 111 N 49th St Philadelphia PA 19139-2718

MADRID, OLGA HILDA GONZALEZ, retired elementary education educator, association executive; b. San Antonio, May 4, 1928; d. Victor A. and Elvira Ardilla Gonzalez; m. Sam Madrid, Jr., June 29, 1952; children: Ninette Marie, Samuel James. Student, U. Mex., San Antonio, St. Mary's U., San Antonio; BA, Our Lady of Lake U., 1956, MEd, 1963. Cert. bilingual tchr., adminstr., Tex. Sec. Lanier High Sch. San Antonio Ind. Sch. Dist., 1945-52, tchr. Collins Garden Elem. Sch., 1963-92; tutor Dayton, Ohio, 1952-54; bd. dirs., sch. rep. San Antonio Tchr.'s Coun., 1970-90; chair various coms. Collins Garden Elem., 1970-92. Elected dep. precinct, senatorial and state Dem. Convs., San Antonio, 1968—; apptd. commr. Keep San Antonio Beautiful, 1985; life mem., past pres. San Antonio YWCA; bd. dirs. Luth. Gen. Hosp., NCCJ, Cath. Family and Children's Svcs., St. Luke's Luth. Hosp.; nat. bd. dirs. YWCA, 1985—, also mem. exec. com.; mem. edn. commn. Holy Rosary Parish, 1994—; mem. bus. assocs. com. Our Lady of the Lake U., 1995—. Recipient Outstanding Our Lady Lake Alumni award Our Lady Lake U., 1975, Guadalupana medal San Antonio Cath. Archdiocese, 1975, Yellow Rose Tex. citation Gov. Briscoe, 1977; Olga H. Madrid Ctr. named in her honor, YWCA San Antonio and San Antonio City Coun., 1983; Lo Mejor De Lo Nuestro honoree San Antonio Light, 1991, honoree San Antonio Women's History Month Coalition, 1996. Mem. San Antonio Bus. and Profl. Women, Inc. (mem. exec. com.), Salute Quality Edn. (honoree 1993), Delta Kappa Gamma (Theta Beta chpt., mem. exec. com.). Avocations: reading, gardening. Home: 2726 Benrus Blvd San Antonio TX 78228-2319

MADRY-TAYLOR, JACQUELYN YVONNE, educational administrator; b. Jacksonville, Fla., Sept. 27, 1945; d. Arthur Chester and Janie (Cowart) Madry; 1 child, Jana LeMadry. BA, Fisk U., 1966; MA, Ohio State U., 1969; EdD, U. Fla., 1975. Cert. Inst. for Ednl. Mgmt., Harvard U., 1981. Tchr. Spanish Terry Parker Sr. High Sch., Jacksonville, 1967-72; instr. U. Fla., Gainesville, 1972-75; asst. to v.p. for acad. affairs. Morris Brown Coll., Atlanta, 1975-76; dean for instructional svcs. No. Va. Community Coll., Annandale, Va., 1976-83; dean undergrad. studies Bridgewater (Mass.) State Coll., 1983-92, exec. asst. to acting pres., 1988, acting v.p. acad. affairs, 1988-90; dir. Acad. Leadership Acad. Am. Assn. State Coll. and Univs., Washington, 1992-94; dir. ednl. programs and svcs. United Negro Coll. Fund Hdqs., 1994—; cons. W.K. Kellog Found., 1993—; bd. dirs. Bridgewater State Coll. Early Learning Ctr., 1984-88; evaluator U.S. Dept. State/Fgn. Svc., Washington, 1982—, U.S. Dept. Edn., 1989—; cons. in field. Vice chmn. No. Va. Manpower Planning Coun., Fairfax County, Va., 1981. Recipient Cert. Achievement Bridgewater State Coll. Black Alumni, 1988, Women Helping Women award Soroptimist Internat., 1983, Outstanding Young Women Am. award, 1976, 78; named Personalities of South, 1977; recipient Outstanding Tchr./Student Rels. Humanitarian award B'nai B'rith, 1972. Mem. Pub. Mem. Assn. U.S. Fgn. Svc., Soroptimist Internat., Boston Club (v.p. 1986-88), Jack and Jill of Am., Inc., Pi Lambda Theta, Phi Delta Kappa, Alpha Kappa Alpha, Links Inc. (Reston, Va. chpt.). Methodist. Avocations: playing piano, bike riding. Home: 12274 Angel Wing Ct Reston VA 22091 Office: United Negro College Fund PO Box 10444 8260 Willow Oaks Corp Dr Fairfax VA 22031-4511

MADSEN, BRIGHAM DWAINE, history educator; b. Magna, Utah, Oct. 21, 1914; s. Brigham and Lydia (Cushing) M.; m. Betty McAllister, Aug. 11, 1939; children—Karen Madsen Loos, David B., Linda Madsen Dunning, Steven M. B.A., U. Utah, 1938; M.A., U. Calif., Berkeley, 1940, Ph.D., 1948. Prin. Grade Sch. and Jr. High Sch., Pingree, Idaho, 1938-39; assoc. prof. history Brigham Young U., Provo, Utah, 1948-54; pres., mgr. Madsen Bros. Constrn. Co., Salt Lake City, 1954-61; prof. history Utah State U., Logan, 1961-64; asst. dir. tng. Peace Corps, Washington, 1964-65; first dir. tng. Vols. in Service to Am., Washington, 1965; dean div. continuing edn. U. Utah, Salt Lake City, 1965-66; dep. acad. v.p. U. Utah, 1966-67, adminstrv. v.p., 1967-71, dir. libraries, 1971-73, prof. history, 1973-84, chmn. dept. history, 1974-75. Author: Bannock of Idaho, 1958, The Lemhi: Sacajawea's People, 1980, Corinne: Gentile Capital of Utah, 1980, The Northern Shoshoni, 1980, (with Betty M. Madsen) North to Montana: Jehus, Bullwhackers and Muleskinners on the Montana Trail, 1980; Gold Rush Sojourners in Great Salt Lake City, 1849 and 1850, 1983, The Shoshoni Frontier and the Bear River Massacre, 1985, Chief Pocatello: The "White Plume", 1986, Glory Hunter: A Biography of Patrick Edward Connor, 1990; editor: The Now Generation, 1971, Letters of Long Ago, 1973, A Forty-niner in Utah: Letters and Journal of John Hudson, 1982, B.H. Roberts: Studies of the Book of Mormon, 1985, Exploring the Great Salt Lake: The Stansbury Expedition of 1849-50, 1989. Served to 1st lt., inf. AUS, 1943-46. Mem. Phi Beta Kappa, Phi Kappa Phi, Phi Alpha Theta. Mem. Ch. of Jesus Christ of Latter-day Saints. Home: 2181 Lincoln Ln Salt Lake City UT 84124-2759

MADSEN, DOROTHY LOUISE (MEG MADSEN), writer; b. Rochester, N.Y.; d. Charles Robert and Louise Anna Agnes Meyer; BA, Mundelein Coll., Chgo., 1978; m. Frederick George Madsen, Feb. 17, 1945 (dec.). Pub. rels. rep. Rochester Telephone Corp., 1941-42; feature writer Rochester Democrat & Chronicle, 1939-41; exec. dir. LaPorte (Ind.) chpt. ARC, 1964; dir. adminstrv. svcs. Bank Mktg. Assn., Chgo., 1971-74; exec. dir. The Eleanor Women's Found., Chgo., 1974-84; founder Meg Madsen Assocs., Chgo., 1984-88; women's career counselor; founder, Clearinghouse Internat. Newsletter; founder Eleanor Women's Forum, Clearinghouse Internat., Eleanor Intern Program Coll. Students and Returning Women. Served to lt. col. WAC, 1942-47, 67-70. Decorated Legion of Merit, Meritorious Svc. award. Mem. Res. Officers Assn., Mundelein Alumnae Assn., Phi Sigma Tau (charter mem. Ill. Kappa chpt.). Home and Office: 1030 N State St Chicago IL 60610-2844 also: 3902 Joliet Rd La Porte IN 46350

MADSEN, GEORGE FRANK, lawyer; b. Sioux City, Iowa, Mar. 24, 1933; s. Frank O. and Agnes (Cuhel) M.; m. Magnhild Norstog, June 28, 1959; 1 child, Michelle Marie. BA, St. Olaf Coll., 1954; LLB, Harvard U., 1959. Bar: Ohio 1960, Iowa 1961, U.S. Dist. Ct. (no. and so. dists.) Iowa, U.S. Ct. Appeals (8th cir.), U.S. Supreme Ct. 1991. Trainee Cargill, Inc., Mpls., 1954; assoc. Durfey, Martin, Browne & Hull, Springfield, Ohio, 1959-61; assoc., then ptnr. Shull, Marshall & Marks, Sioux City, 1961-85; ptnr. Marks & Madsen, Sioux City, 1985—. Author, editor: Iowa Title Opinions and Standards, 1978; contbg. author: The American Law of Real Property, 1991. Sec., bd.dirs. Sioux City Boys Club, 1969-76; mem. Sioux City Zoning Bd. Adjustment, 1963-65; past pres. Morningside Luth Ch., Sioux City; active Iowa Mo. River Preservation and Land Use Authority, 1992—. Lt. USAF, 1954-56. Fellow Iowa State Bar Found.; mem. ABA, Iowa Bar Assn., Woodbury County Bar Assn., St. Olaf Coll. Alumni Assn. (past pres. Siouxland chpt.), Nat. Wildlife Assn., Mont. Wildlife Assn., Rocky Mountain Elk Found., Pheasants Forever, Phi Beta Kappa (past pres. Siouxland chpt.), Rotary Internat. Avocations: skiing, hunting, swimming, reading. Office: 700 4th St Ste 303 PO Box 3226 Sioux City IA 51102-3226

MADSEN, H(ENRY) STEPHEN, retired lawyer; b. Momence, Ill., Feb. 5, 1924; s. Frederick and Christine (Landgren) M.; m. Carol Ruth Olmstead, Dec. 30, 1967; children: Stephen Stewart, Christie Morgan, Kelly Ann. M.B.A., U. Chgo., 1948; LL.B., Yale U., 1951. Bar: Wash. 1951, Ohio 1953, U.S. Supreme Ct. 1975. Research asst. Wash. Water Power Co., Spokane, 1951; assoc. Baker, Hostetler & Paterson, Cleve., 1952-59, ptnr., 1960-88, sr. ptnr., 1989-92; ret., 1992; chmn. bd. trustees Blue Cross Northeastern, Ohio, 1972-81; Danish consul for Ohio, 1973—. Trustee Breckenridge Retirement Cmty.; trustee Ohio Presbyn. Retirement Cmty. Served with AC U.S. Army, 1943-46. Decorated Knight Queen of Denmark, 1982. Fellow ABA; mem. Am. Coll. Trial Lawyers (life), Am. Law Inst., Am. Judicature Soc., Ohio Bar Assn., Cleve. Bar Assn., The Country Club of Cleve., The Club at Soc. Ctr. Office: Baker & Hostetler 3200 National City Ctr 1900 E 9th St Cleveland OH 44114-3401

MADSEN, LOREN WAKEFIELD, sculptor; b. Oakland, Calif., Mar. 29, 1943; s. Roy Sondergaard and Kathryn O. (Finerty) M.; m. Libbe Hurvitz, June 30, 1968; children: Anne Lea, Nora Karin. Student, Reed Coll., Portland, 1961-63; B.A., UCLA, 1966, M.A., 1970. One-man shows include Riko Mizuno Gallery, N.Y.C., 1976, 77, 82, 84, 86, 90, 92, 96, L.A. Louver Gallery, Venice, Calif., 1976, 78, Hansen Fuller Goldeen Gallery, San Francisco, 1980, Wright State U., Dayton, 1980, U. mass., 1981, Cheryl Haines Gallery, San Francisco, 1991; group shows include Los Angeles County Mus. Art, 1974, 76, 83, Hayward Gallery, London, 1975, Walker Art Ctr., Mpls., 1976, Biennale of Sculpture, Sydney, Australia, 1976, Ft. Worth Mus. Art, 1977, Joslyn Art Mus., Omaha, 1979, Hirshhorn Mus., Washington, 1979, Newport Harbor Art Mus., 1982, Freedman Gallery, Albright Coll., 1987, others. Nat. Endowment for Arts grantee, 1975-76, 80-81. Office: 426 Broome St New York NY 10013-3251

MADSEN, MICHAEL, actor; b. Chicago, IL, Sept. 25. films include: Wargames, 1983, The Natural, 1984, Racing with the Moon, 1984, The Killing Time, 1987, Shadows in the Storm, 1988, Iguana, 1988, Blood Red, 1989, Kill Me Again, 1990, The Doors, 1991, The End of Innocence, 1991, Thelma and Louise, 1991, Fatal Instinct, 1992, Inside Edge, 1992, Reservoir Dogs, 1992, Straight Talk, 1992, Almost Blue, 1992, Free Willy, 1993, A House in the Hills, 1993, Money for Nothing, 1993, Trouble Bound, 1993, Wyatt Earp, 1993, The Getaway, 1994, Dead Connection, 1994; TV movies include: Special Bulletin, 1983, War and Remembrance, 1988, Montana, 1990, Baby Snatcher, 1992, Beyond the Law, 1994; TV series include: Our Family Honor, 1985-86. Office: c/o Grant and Tane 9100 Wilshire Blvd Beverly Hills CA 90212*

MADSEN, PETER ERIC, architecture and real estate development firms executive; b. Boston, May 4, 1945; s. George Peter and May Isabelle (Alger) M.; m. Betsy Ridge, Oct. 12, 1969; children: Sarah Hall, Deane Alger, Joanna Morse, Samuel Alger (dec.). AB, Harvard U., 1967, MArch, 1972. Architect Perry, Dean & Stewart, Boston, 1967, Earl R. Flansburgh & Assoc., Boston, 1968; researcher Harvard U. Grad. Sch. Design, Cambridge, Mass., 1970; writer J. Scribner's, N.Y.C., 1972; architect John Andrews Architects, Toronto, Ont., Can., 1972; architect, prin. Graham Gund Architects, Inc., Cambridge, 1972—; pres. The Gunwyn Co., Cambridge, 1984—. Author: A Traveler's Guide to India, 1973, Essex, The Shipbuilding Town, 1976; editor: Dubbing, Hooping and Lofting, 1979. Pres. Castle Hill Found., Ipswich, Mass., 1984-87; v.p. trustees of Reservations, Beverly, Mass., 1987—; trustee Soc. Preservation of New Eng. Antiques, 1992—, vice-chmn., 1994—, vice-chmn. Boston Found. for Arch., 1995—, trustee, 1992—; overseer New Eng. Conservatory of Music, 1994—; mem. alumni coun. Grad. Sch. of Design Harvard U., 1980-86, 90-96. Fellow AIA; mem. Urban Land Inst., Boston Soc. Architects (bd. dirs. 1986-89, Honor award 1978, 85), Myopia Hunt Club, Hasty Pudding Club, Manchester Yacht Club, Somerset Club. Episcopalian. Avocations: sailing, music, golf. Office: Graham Gund Architects Inc 47 Thorndike St Cambridge MA 02141-1714

MADSEN, RICHARD WELLINGTON, lawyer; b. Portland, Oreg., Oct. 20, 1938; s. Richard W. Madsen and Adaline A. (Jeffries) Sarver; m. Priscilla A (Judy); children: Richard, Angela, Kristina. BA in Journalism, U. Nev., 1960; LLB, Georgetown U., 1963. Bar: Nev. 1963, D.C. 1967, Idaho 1971, Calif. 1974, D.C. Dep. atty. gen. Nev. Atty. Gen., Carson City, 1963-64; assoc. Jacobs & Speiler, Washington, 1966-69; asst. gen. counsel Boise Cascade Corp., Boise, Idaho, 1969-74; corp. counsel Rohr Industries Inc., Chula Vista, Calif., 1974-79, v.p., gen. counsel, sec., 1979—. Vice pres., sec., gen. counsel Nat. Kidney Found., 1983—; bd. dirs. Bowery Theater, San Diego, 1985—, pres., 1989-90. Capt. U.S. Army, 1963-64. Mem. Calif. Bar Assn., Nev. Bar Assn., Idaho Bar Assn., D.C. Bar Assn., Am. Soc. Corp. Secs. (pres. San Diego chpt. 1983), Am. Corp. Counsel Assn. (sec. San Diego chpt. 1987). Republican. Office: Rohr Inc 850 Lagoon Dr Chula Vista CA 91910

MADSEN, STEPHEN STEWART, lawyer; b. Spokane, Wash., Oct. 13, 1951; s. H. Stephen Madsen and Sarah Pope (Stewart) Ruth; m. Rebecca Wetherill Howard, July 28, 1984; children: Stephen Stewart Jr., Lawrence Wetherill, Christina Wetherill, Benton Howard. BA, Harvard U., 1973; JD, Columbia U., 1980. Bar: N.Y. 1981, U.S. Dist. Ct. (so. dist.) N.Y. 1981, U.S. Ct. Appeals (6th cir.) 1983, U.S. Ct. Appeals (8th cir.) 1985, U.S. Ct. Appeals (2d, 7th and D.C. cirs.) 1994. Law clk. to presiding judge U.S. Ct. Appeals (2d cir.), N.Y.C., 1980-81; assoc. Cravath, Swaine & Moore, N.Y.C., 1981-88, ptnr., 1988—. Bd. visitors Columbia U. Sch. Law, 1991—; bd. govs. Hill-Stead Mus., 1995—; mem. vestry St. Bartholomew's Ch., 1995—. Mem. ABA, N.Y. State Bar Assn., New York County Lawyers Assn. Office: Cravath Swaine & Moore Worldwide Pla 825 8th Ave New York NY 10019-7416

MADSON, JOHN ANDREW, architect; b. Mankato, Minn., Nov. 12, 1920; m. Joyce Helen Madson, Sept. 4, 1949; children: Brian A., David G., Paul J., Thomas R., John E., Tracy Ann. BA, U. Minn., 1949, BArch, 1950. Archtl. draftsman, designer Perry E. Crosier & Son, Mpls., 1950-53; architect-in-tng. Magney Tusler & Setter, Mpls., 1953-55; ptnr., prin. Patch Erickson Madson Watten, Inc., Mpls., 1955-89; chief exec. officer Madson & Assocs., Mpls., 1989—. Capt. USAF, 1944-45, ETO. Corp. mem. AIA. Republican. Lutheran. Avocations: playing and collecting jazz, classical music, golf, directing church choir. Home: 17419 N 130th Ave Sun City West AZ 85375-5061

MADURA, JAMES ANTHONY, surgical educator; b. Campbell, Ohio, June 10, 1938; s. Anthony Peter and Margaret Ethel (Sebest) M.; m. Loretta Jayne Sovak, Aug. 8, 1959; children: Debra Jean, James Anthony II, Vikki Sue. BA, Cogate U., 1959; MD, Western Res. U., 1963. Diplomate Am. Bd. Surgery. Intern in surgery Ohio State U., Columbus, 1963-64, resident in surgery, 1966-71; asst. prof. Surgery Ind. U., Indpls., 1971-76, assoc. prof. Surgery, 1976-80, prof. Surgery, 1980—; dir. gen. surgery Ind. U. Sch. Medicine, Indpls., 1985—. Contbr. articles to profl. jours. Capt. U.S. Army, 1964-66, Vietnam. Fellow Am. Coll. Surgeons; mem. Cen. Surg. Assn., Western Surg. Assn., Soc. Surgery Alimentary Tract, Midwest Surg. Assn., Internal Biliary Assn., Assn. Acad. Surgeons, The Columbia Club. Republican. Roman Catholic. Home: 9525 Copley Dr Indianapolis IN 46260-1422 Office: dept surgery Ind U 545 Barnhill Dr # 205 Indianapolis IN 46202-5112

MADVA, STEPHEN ALAN, lawyer; b. Pitts., July 27, 1948; s. Joseph Edward and Mary (Zulick) M.; m. Bernadette A. McKeon; children: Alexander, Elizabeth. BA cum laude, Yale U., 1970; JD, U. Pa., 1973. Bar: Pa. 1973, U.S. Dist. Ct. (ea. dist.) Pa. 1975, U.S. Ct. Appeals (3d cir.) 1976, U.S. Ct. Appeals (11th cir.) 1987, U.S. Supreme Ct. 1985, N.Y. 1990. Asst. defender Defender Assn. Phila., 1973-75, fed. defender, 1975-77, also bd. dirs., 1985—; assoc. Montgomery, McCracken, Walker & Rhoads, Phila., 1977-81, ptnr., 1981—, mem. mgmt. com., 1993—, chmn. litigation dept., 1996—; mem. Fed. Criminal Justice Act Panel; panelist Am. Arbitration Assn. Bd. dirs. Central Phila. Devel. Corp., 1995—. Mem. ABA, Am. Judicature Soc., Internat. Assn. Def. Counsel, Pa. Bar Assn., Phila. Bar Assn. (fed. cts. com.), Def. Rsch. Inst., Hist. Soc. Pa., Yale Alumni Assn. (schs. com.), Yale Rowing Assn. Democrat. Avocations: tennis, distance running. Home: 2055 Lombard St Philadelphia PA 19146-1314 Office: Montgomery McCracken Et Al 123 S Broad St Philadelphia PA 19109

MAECHLING, CHARLES, JR., lawyer, diplomat, educator, writer; b. N.Y.C., Apr. 18, 1920; s. Charles and Eugenie H. M.; m. Janet Leighton, Sept. 2, 1944; children: Philip Leighton and Eugenie Elisabeth (Mrs. David Buchan). Attended, Birch Wathen Sch., N.Y.C., 1924-37; BA, Yale U., 1941; LLB, U. Va., 1949. Bar: N.Y. 1949, D.C. 1957. Assoc. Sullivan & Cromwell, N.Y.C., 1949-51; atty. Office Sec. Air Force, 1951-52; counsel Electronics Industries Assn., Washington, 1953-56; ptnr. Shaw, Pittman, Potts & Maechling, 1956-61; dir. for internal def. Dept. State, Washington, 1961-63; spl. asst. to undersec. for polit. affairs and amb.-at-large Averell Harriman, 1963-66; dep. gen. counsel NSF, 1966-71, spl. asst. to dir., 1972-74; prof. law U. Va., 1974-76; spl. counsel Kirlin, Campbell & Keating, Washington, 1976-81; sr. fellow Carnegie Endowment for Internat. Peace, 1981-85; vis. fellow, mem. law faculty Cambridge U. (Wolfson Coll.), Eng., 1985-88; guest scholar internat. law Brookings Inst., Washington, 1989-93; internat. cons., 1993—; legal adviser internat. matters NAS, 1972-74, mem. ocean policy com.; mem. law-of-sea and other adv. coms. Dept. State; gen. counsel Fairways Corp., 1959-61; adj. prof. Sch. Internat. Svc., Am. U.; mem. adv. bd. Internat. Peace Acad.; lectr. Acad. Internat. Law, Hague, Netherlands, Knight Ctr. U. Md.; arbitrator complex internat. cases Am. Arbitration Assn., Internat. C. of C. Editor-in-chief Va. Law Rev., 1948-49; contbr. articles to N.Y. Times, Washington Post, L.A. Times, profl. and lit. jours.; columnist Newsday, Miami Herald. Bd. dirs. Coun. for Ocean Law, Washington Inst. Fgn. Affairs, U.S. Com. for IIASA; mem. secretariat Joint Chiefs Staff, 1943-44, del., 1943, Cairo Conf.; outside counsel to CIA, 1957-60. Lt. comdr. USNR, 1941-46. Recipient Ross Essay award Am. Bar Assn., 1969. Mem. ABA (past com. chair), Am. Soc. Internat. Law, City Tavern Club (Washington), Cosmos Club (Washington), Yale Club (Washington). Avocation: languages. Home: 3403 Lowell St NW Washington DC 20016-5024 also (summer): Bar Rd, Saint Andrews, NB Canada E0G 2X0

MAEDA, J. A., data processing executive; b. Mansfield, Ohio, Aug. 24, 1940; d. James Shunso and Doris Lucille Maeda; m. Robert Lee Hayes (div.

May 1970); 1 child, Brian Sentaro Hayes. BS in Math., Purdue U., 1962, postgrad., 1962-63; postgrad., Calif. State U., Northridge, 1968-75; cert. profl. designation in tech. of computer operating systems and tech. of info. processing, UCLA, 1971. Cons., rsch. asst. computer ctr. Purdue U., West Lafayette, Ind., 1962-63; computer operator, sr. tab operator, mem. faculty Calif. State U., Northridge, 1969, programmer cons., tech. asst. II, 1969-70, supr. acad. applicatons, EDP supr. II, 1970-72, project tech. support coord. programmer II, office of the chancellor, 1972-73, tech. support coord. statewide timesharing tech. support, programmer II, 1973-74, acad. coord., tech. support coord. instrn., computer cons. III, 1974-83; coord. user svcs. info. ctr., mem. tech. staff IV CADAM INC subs. Lockheed Corp., Burbank, Calif., 1983-86, coord. user svcs., tech. specialist computing dept., 1986-87; v.p., bd. dirs. Rainbow Computing, Inc., Northridge, 1976-85; dir. Aki Tech./Design Cons., Northridge, 1976—; mktg. mgr. thaumaturge Taro Quipu Cons., Northridge, 1987—; tech. cons. Digital Computer Cons., Chatsworth, Calif., 1988; computer tech., fin. and bus. mgmt., sys. integration, 1988-90; tech. customer software support Collection Data Sys., Westlake, Calif., 1991; tech. writer Sterling Software Info. Mgmt. Divsn., 1992—. Author, editor more than 275 user publs., tutorials, reference manuals, user guides; contbr. articles and photos to profl. jours. Mem. IEEE, SHARE, DECUS (editor spl. interest group 1977-83, ednl. steering com. RSIS/E 1979-82). Avocations: photography, photojournalism, vintage automobiles. Office: Sterling Software Info Mgmt Divsn 5900 Canoga Ave PO Box 4237 Woodland Hills CA 91365-4237

MAEDA, KENJI, medicine educator; b. Tsu-City, Japan, Apr. 1, 1939; s. Tamotsu and Sumi (Kubo) M.; m. Mayuko Matsunaga, Mar. 30, 1975; children: Kayaho, Mayuho. MD, Nagoya U., 1965, PhD, 1978. Asst. Nagoya U. Br. Hosp., 1973-79, assoc. prof., 1979-91, prof., 1991—, dir., 1992-96. Editor: Contributions to Nephrology, 1993, 94; contbr. articles to profl. jours. Recipient Jinkenkyukai award Japan Kidney Found., Tokyo, 1993. Mem. N.Y. Acad. Sci., AAAS, Am. Soc. Nephrology. Home: c-1514 1-2 Sunadabashi, Higashi-ku, Nagoya/Aichi 461, Japan Office: Nagoya U Br Hosp, Higashi-Ku, 20-1-1 Daiko-Minami, Nagoya 461, Japan

MAEDA, TOSHIHIDE MUNENOBU, spacecraft system engineer; b. Sagamihara, Kanagawa, Japan, Apr. 11, 1962; s. Mamoru and Yasuko Hiromi (Yamagishi) M. BS, U. Tokyo, 1986; postgrad., Internat. Space U., Cambridge, Mass., 1988. Engr. space systems div. Hitachi, Ltd., Tokyo, 1986-89, 92-95, 1995—; engr. Nat. Spece Devel. Agy. Japan, Tsukuba, 1990-92. Supr. Newton jour., 1991. Mem. AIAA, Nat. Space Soc., Planetary Soc., Remote Sensing Soc. Japan, Japan Soc. Aero. and Space Sci. Achievements include patents on thermal control technology for spacecraft components, structural test equipment. Home: 2349 Kamitsuruma, Sagamihara Kanagawa 228, Japan

MAEHL, WILLIAM HARVEY, historian, educator; b. Bklyn., May 28, 1915; s. William Henry and Antoinette Rose (Salamone) M.; m. Josephine Scholl McAllister, Dec. 29, 1941; children: Madeleine, Kathleen. BSc, Northwestern U., 1937, MA, 1939; PhD, U. Chgo., 1946. Asst. prof. history St. Louis U., 1941-42, Tex. A&M U., College Sta., 1943, De Paul U., Chgo., 1944-49; historian Dept. of Def., Karlsruhe, Stuttgart, Fed. Rep. Germany, 1950-52; chief briefing office U.S. hdqrs. U.S. Hdqs. European Command, Frankfurt, Germany, 1952-53; chief historian Arty. Sch., Okla., 1954; with War Plans Office, Hdqs. No. Air Materiel Area for Europe, Burtonwood, Eng., 1954-55; assoc. prof. European history Nebr. Wesleyan U., Lincoln, 1955-57, prof., 1958-62, 65-68; prof. German history Auburn (Ala.) U., 1968-81, prof. emeritus, 1981—; vis. prof. U. Nebr., 1962, U. Auckland, New Zealand, 1963-64, Midwestern U., Wichita Falls, Tex., 1965. Author: German Militarism and Socialism, 1968, History of Germany in Western Civilization, 1979, A World History Syllabus, 3 vols., 1980, August Bebel, Shadow Emperor of the German Workers, 1980, The German Socialist Party: Champion of the First Republic, 1918-33, 1986; author monographs for U.S. Army in Europe, chpts. in books, atomic, biol. and emergency war plans for No. Air Materiel Area for Europe; contbr. poetry to Question of Balance, Tears of Fire, Disting. Poets Am., Best Poems of 1995, Journey of Mind; contbr. articles to profl. jours. Grantee Nebr. Wesleyan U., 1959, Auburn U., 1969-73, 79-80, Am. Philosophical Soc., 1973-74, Deutscher Akademischer Austauschdienst, 1978. Mem. Am. Hist. Assn., Phi Kappa Phi, Phi Alpha Theta.

MAEHL, WILLIAM HENRY, historian, university administrator, educational consultant; b. Chicago Heights, Ill., June 13, 1930; s. William Henry and Marvel Lillian (Carlson) M.; m. Audrey Mae Ellsworth, Aug. 25, 1962; 1 child, Christine Amanda. B.A., U. Minn., 1950, M.A., 1951; postgrad (Fulbright fellow), King's Coll., U. Durham, Eng., 1955-56; Ph.D., U. Chgo., 1957; LHD (hon.), Fielding Inst., 1993. Asst. prof. Montclair (N.J.) State Coll., 1957-58; asst. prof. Washington Coll., Chestertown, Md., 1958-59, U. Okla., Norman, 1959-64; asso. prof. U. Okla., 1964-70, prof. English history, 1970-86; dean Coll. Liberal Studies, 1976-86, vice provost for continuing edn. and public service, 1979-86; pres. The Fielding Inst., Santa Barbara, Calif., 1987-93, pres. emeritus, 1993—; prin. investigator Project for a Nation of Lifelong Learners, Regents Coll., Albany, N.Y., 1994-96; vis. prof. U. Nebr., summer 1965; vis. fellow Wolfson Coll. Oxford (Eng.) U., spring 1975; fellow Salzburg Seminar in Am. Studies, 1976. Author: The Reform Bill of 1832, 1967; editor: R.G. Gammage, Chartist Reminiscences, 1981, Continuum: Jour. of the Nat. Continuing Edn. Assn., 1980-83, also articles. Bd. dirs. Alliance for Alternative Degree Programs, 1988-90; trustee Coun. for Adult and Exptl. Learning, 1990-94; mem. coun. Nat. Ctr. for Adult Learning, 1990—. Leverhulme Research fellow, 1961-62; grantee Am. Philos. Soc., 1961-62, 67-68, 71, 76. Fellow Royal Hist. Soc., Assn. of Grad. Liberal Studies Programs; mem. Am. Hist. Assn., Conf. on Brit. Studies, Soc. for Study Labour History.

MAEHR, MARTIN LOUIS, psychology educator; b. Guthrie, Okla., June 25, 1932; s. Martin J. and Regina (Meier) M.; m. Jane M. Pfeil, Aug. 9, 1959; children—Martin, Michael, Katherine. B.A., Concordia Coll., 1953, M.A., 1959; Ph.D., U. Nebr., 1960. Counselor U. Nebr., Lincoln, 1959-60; asst. prof. to assoc. prof. Concordia Sr. Coll., Fort Wayne, Ind., 1960-67; assoc. prof. ednl. psychology U. Ill., Urbana, 1967-70, prof., 1970—, chmn. dept. ednl. psychology, 1970-75, assoc. dean grad. and internat. programs prof., 1975-77, research prof., dir. Inst. Research on Human Devel., prof. ednl. psychology, 1977-88, assoc. dir. Office Gerontology and Aging Studies, 1980-82; prof. edn. and psychology U. Mich., Ann Arbor, 1988—, chair combined program edn. and psychology, 1988-92; vis. prof. U. Queensland, Australia, 1981; vis. prof., cons. to dean Faculty Edn. U. Tehran, Iran, 1973-74. Author: Sociocultural Origins of Achievement, 1974, (with others) Being a Parent in Today's World, 1980, (with L.A. Braskam) The Motivation Factor, 1986, (with Carol Midgley) Transforming School Cultures, 1996; editor: Advancement in Motivation and Achievement series; contbr. articles to profl. jours. Lutheran.

MAEROFF, GENE I., educational association administrator, journalist; b. Cleve., Jan. 8, 1939; s. Harry B. and Charlotte (Szabo) M.; children: Janine Amanda, Adam Jonathan, Rachel Judith. B.S., Ohio U., 1961; M.S., Boston U., 1962. Teaching fellow Boston U., 1961-62; news bur. dir. R.I. Coll., 1962-64; religion editor Akron (Ohio) Beacon Jour., 1964-65; with Cleve. Plain Dealer, 1965-71, assoc. editor, 1969-71; edn. writer N.Y. Times, N.Y.C., 1971-86; sr. fellow Carnegie Found. for the Advancement of Teaching, Princeton, N.J., 1986—; contbr. mags. Author: Don't Blame the Kids, 1981, School and College, 1983, The Empowerment of Teachers, 1988, The School-Smart Parent, 1989, Sources of Inspiration, 1992, Team Building for School Change, 1993; (with others) The New York Times Guide to Suburban Public Schools, 1976; contbr. The Human Encounter: Readings in Education, 1976, Human Dynamics in Psychology and Education, 1977, Social Problems, 1978, Education Reform in the '90's, 1992, Teachers As Leaders, 1994. Trustee Guild-Times Scholarship Fund, Ed Bang Journalism Scholarship Found.; mem. adv. bd. Inst. Ednl. Mgmt., Harvard U., Ednl. Resources Info. Ctr., U.S. Dept. Edn., Nat. Ctr. for Postsecondary Governance. Recipient writing awards Press Club Cleve., A.P. Soc. Ohio, Edn. Writers Assn., AAUP, Internat. Reading Assn. Mem. Blue Key, Omicron Delta Kappa, Kappa Tau Alpha, Phi Sigma Delta. Office: 23 Carriage Pl Edison NJ 08820-4023

MAESAKA, MARTHA H., special education educator; b. Honolulu, Apr. 28, 1940; d. Robert I. and Toshiko (Okasako) Tanaka; m. John K. Maesaka, July 21, 1962; children: Alan K., Robert K. BA, Washington U., 1962; MS, Bank Street Coll., 1992. Cert. special edn. educator, elem. edn. educator. Kindergarten tchr. Ritenour Sch. Dist., St. Louis, 1962-63, Ft. Sill (Okla.) Army Sch., 1963-64; substitute teaching N.Y.C. Pvt. Schs., 1968-69; tchr. Collegiate Sch., N.Y.C., 1983-87, dept. chair spl. edn., 1987—. Grantee Collegiste Sch., 1990, Oxford U., 1991. Mem. ASCD, Nat. Coun. Tchrs. English, N.Y. C. Orton Soc. Episcopalian. Avocations: reading, writing, tennis, classical music. Home: 1212 5th Ave New York NY 10029-5210 Office: Collegiate Sch 370 W End Ave New York NY 10024-6505

MAESTRINI, EMILIO, industrial projects contracts manager; b. São Paulo, Brazil, Jan. 15, 1939; came to U.S., 1963, naturalized, 1968; s. Mario and Trieste Yolanda (Sgueglia) M.; m. Virginia Wasson, Feb. 1969 (div. Oct. 1970); 1 child, Tracy; m. Noemia S.M. Pereira Da Silva, May 29, 1971; children: Andrew, Alessandra. AA, L.A. Harbor Coll., 1968; student, Long Beach State U., 1969-70, Escola Superior Adminstrn., Campinas, Brazil, 1976. Asst. gen. mgr. Inds. Texteis Barbero S.A., Sorocaba, Brazil, 1958-63; engring. adminstr. AiRearch Mfg. Co., Torrance, Calif., 1965-72; ptnr. bus. venture Textiles and Gas Stations, Sorocaba, 1972-75; contracts mgr. Kaiser Engrs. Internat. Inc., Oakland, Calif., 1975-89; sr. contracts mgr. Fluor Daniel Inc., Redwood City, Calif., 1989—. Avocations: languages. Office: Fluor Daniel Inc 3333 Michelson Dr Irvine CA 92715

MAESTRONE, FRANK EUSEBIO, diplomat; b. Springfield, Mass., Dec. 20, 1922; s. John Battista and Margaret Carlotta (Villanova) M.; m. Jo Colwell, Jan. 20, 1951; children: Mark, Anne. BA, Yale U., 1943; grad. Naval War Coll., 1963. Assignments in Vienna and Salzburg, Austria, 1948, 54, Hamburg, Fed. Republic Germany, 1949, Khorramshahr, Iran, 1960; with NATO, Paris, 1963, Brussels, 1968; dep. asst. sec. gen. NATO, Brussels, 1968-71; counselor of embassy for polit. affairs, Manila, 1971-73; Dept. State adviser to pres. Naval War Coll., 1973; min.-counselor, Cairo, 1974; amb. State of Kuwait, 1976-79; diplomat-in-residence U. Calif., San Diego, 1979; spl. rep. of pres., dir. U.S. Sinai Support Mission, 1980; exec. dir. World Affairs Coun. San Diego, 1984-86; adj. prof. internat. rels., amb.-in-residence U.S. Internat. U., San Diego, 1986-90; bd. dirs. World Affairs Coun., San Diego; mem. adv. bd. Hansen Inst. for World Peace, San Diego State U. Found. With AUS, 1943-46, U.S. Fgn. Svc., 1948-84. Decorated chevalier du Merite Agricole (France). Mem. Internat. Inst. Strategic Studies.

MAFFEO, VINCENT ANTHONY, lawyer, executive; b. N.J., Jan. 22, 1951; s. Michael Anthony and Marie M.; BA summa cum laude, Bklyn. Coll., 1971; JD, Harvard U., 1974; m. Debra, Dec. 16, 1972. Admitted to N.Y. State bar, 1975, Calif. bar, 1982, Va. 1988, D.C. 1988, Mich. 1994; assoc. firm Simpson Thacher & Bartlett, N.Y.C., 1974-77; legal counsel Communications Systems div. ITT, Hartford, Conn., 1977-79, v.p., gen. counsel Bus. Communications div., Des Plaines, Ill., 1979-80, asst. counsel Western region, 1980-83, group counsel ITT Europe, Inc., 1983-86, v.p. gen. coun. ITT Defense Inc., 1989-91, v.p., gen. coun. ITT Automotive, Inc., 1992-95; sr. v.p., gen. counsel ITT Industries, Inc., 1995—. Served to lt. Judge Adv. Gen. Corps, USNR, 1975. Mem. Am. Bar Assn., Calif. State Bar, N.Y. State Bar Assn., Phi Beta Kappa. Office: ITT Industries Inc 4 W Red Oak Ln White Plains NY 10604

MAFFIE, MICHAEL OTIS, utility executive; b. L.A., Jan. 26, 1948; s. Cornelius Michael and Elaine Minie (Wack) M.; m. Nickie Neville, Apr. 10, 1971; children—Wendy, Zachary. B.S. in Acctg, U. So. Calif., 1969, M.B.A. in Fin, 1970. Audit mgr. Arthur Andersen & Co., C.P.A.s, Los Angeles, 1970-78; with S.W. Gas Corp., Las Vegas, 1978—, v.p., treas., 1982-84, sr. v.p., treas., 1984-87, exec. v.p. fin., 1987-88, pres., chief. oper. officer, 1988—, also bd. dirs. *

MAFFITT, JAMES STRAWBRIDGE, lawyer; b. Raleigh, N.C., Oct. 29, 1942; s. James Strawbridge III and Lois (Handy) M.; children: Amy Maffitt Barkley, Margaret Maffitt Kramer; m. Frances Holton, Aug. 15, 1981. BA, Washington and Lee U., 1964, LLB, 1966. Bar: Va. 1966, Md. 1969. Assoc. Apostolou, Place & Thomas, Roanoke, Va., 1966-67; trust officer Mercantile-Safe Deposit & Trust Co., Balt., 1967-71; from assoc. to ptnr. Cable, McDaniel, Bowie & Bond, Balt., 1971-82; ptnr. Maffit & Rothschild, Balt., 1982-85, Anderson, Coe & King, Balt., 1986-90, Miles, Stockbridge & Easton, Balt., 1990—. Chmn. Acad. of the Arts, 1994—; mem. steering com. Upper Shore Regional Tech. Coun., 1992—; mem. exec. com. United Fund of Talbot County, 1994—. Fellow Md. Bar Found.; mem. ABA (ho. dels. 1986-88), Md. Bar Assn. (bd. govs. 1989-91), Va. Bar. Assn., Balt. City Bar Assn. (pres. 1985-86), Wednesday Law Club, Talbot Country Club, Harbortown Country Club. Republican. Episcopal. Club: Ctr. (Balt.). Avocations: boating, waterfowl hunting, golf. Home: 9498 Martingham Cir Saint Michaels MD 21663-2238 Office: Miles & Stockbridge 101 Bay St Easton MD 21601-2703 also: Miles & Stockbridge 10 Light St Baltimore MD 21202-1435

MAFFLY, ROY HERRICK, medical educator; b. Berkeley, Calif., Nov. 26, 1927; s. Alfred Emil and Frances Elizabeth (Henderson) M.; m. Marilyn Miles, Feb. 2, 1952; children: Robert, Nancy, Laurie. A.B., U. Calif.-Berkeley, 1949; M.D., U. Calif.-San Francisco, 1952. Intern U. Calif.-San Francisco, 1952-53, resident in medicine, 1953-54, research fellow in medicine, 1959-61; resident in medicine Herrick Meml. Hosp., Berkeley, 1954-55; research fellow in medicine Mass. Gen. Hosp., Boston, 1957-59; asst. prof. medicine Stanford U., Palo Alto, Calif., 1961-65, assoc. prof., 1965-70, prof., 1970-92, assoc. dean students Sch. Medicine, 1983-92, chmn. dept. physiology, 1986-88; ret., 1992; chief renal service VA Med. Ctr., Palo Alto, Calif., 1968-83; mem. adv. com. on renal dialysis ctrs. State of Calif., 1966-70; mem. gen. med. B study sect. NIH, 1967-71; dir. Health Edn. Network, 1980-83; mem. medicine test com. Nat. Bd. Med. Examiners, 1981-88, chmn. medicine test com., 1983-88, mem. com. for comprehensive part II exam., 1987-89; established investigator Am. Heart Assn., 1961-66, mem. rsch. study com., 1972-82, rsch. com., 1976-82. Served to lt. USNR, 1955-57, PTO. Recipient Kaiser award for teaching Stanford U. Sch. Medicine, 1970, 72, 77, 79, 86, 87; recipient Bloomfield award for teaching Stanford U. Sch. Medicine, 1977, Gores award for teaching Stanford U., 1982; Disting. Achievement award Am. Heart Assn. Sci. Council, 1984; Gift of Life award Nat. Kidney Found. No. Calif., 1985. Mem. Am. Heart Assn., Am. Physiol. Soc., Am. Soc. Clin. Investigation (editorial com. 1970-75), Nat. Kidney Found. (sci. adv. bd. 1970-77), Assn. Am. Med. Colls. Home: 1401 Webster St Palo Alto CA 94301-3649 Office: Stanford Univ M-105 Sch Medicine Stanford CA 94305

MAFFRE, MURIEL, ballet dancer; b. Enghien, Val D'Oise, France, Mar. 19, 1966; came to U.S., 1990; d. Bernard and Monique (Berteaux) M. Diploma, Paris Opera Ballet Sch., 1981; Baccalauréat (hon.), France, 1984. Dancer Hamburg Ballet, Fed. Republic Germany, 1983-84; soloist Sarragoza Ballet, Spain; premiere danseuse Monte Carlo Ballet, Monaco, 1985-90; prin. dancer San Francisco Ballet, 1990—; guest artist with Berlinor Staatsoper and Lines Contemporary Ballet. Recipient 1st prize Nat. Conservatory, Paris, 1983, Grand prize and Gold medal Paris Internat. Ballet Competition, 1984, Isadora Duncan award, 1990. Office: San Francisco Ballet 455 Franklin St San Francisco CA 94102-4438

MAFICO, TEMBA LEVI JACKSON, Old Testament and Semitic languages educator, clergy; b. Chipinge, Zimbabwe, Jan. 28, 1943; came to U.S., 1987; s. Mafico Ntondoyo Jackson Mhlanga and Lucy (Siqalaba Mpofu) Mafico Mhlanga; m. Thecla Chiza, Aug. 31, 1963; 1 child, David. AB, U. London, Salisbury, Rhodesia, 1970; ThM, Harvard U., 1973, MA, 1977, PhD, 1979. Ordained minister United Ch. of Christ, 1964. Ch. minister United Ch. of Christ, Harare, Zimbabwe, 1963-70; sch. chaplain Chikore High Sch., Chipinge, 1971; sr. lectr. U. Zimbabwe, Harare, 1979-86, univ. chaplain, 1979-86; prof. O.T. and Semitic langs. Interdenominational Theol. Ctr., Atlanta, 1988—; cons. globalizaion of theol. schs. Assn. Theol. Schs., 1988—; trustee U. Zimbabwe Evening Sch., 1987—. Contbr. articles to profl. jours. Sec.-treas. Student Christian Movement, Zimbabwe, 1965-70, Manicaland Devel. Asns., Zimbabwe, 1980-86; founder, dir. Univ. Evening Sch., Zimbabwe, 1980-86. Recipient Scholarship award Harvard U., 1971-78; grantee U. Zimbabwe, 1982, 86, Interdenominational Theol. Ctr., Atlanta, 1989, 90, Gammon Theol. Sch., Atlanta, 1990. Mem. Soc. Bibl. Lit., Internat. Assn. Mission Studies, Atlanta O.T. Colloquium (chmn.). Office: Interdenominational Theol Ctr 671 Beckwith St SW Atlanta GA 30314-4112

MAGA, JOSEPH ANDREW, food science educator; b. New Kensington, Pa., Dec. 25, 1940; s. John and Rose Maga; m. Andrea H. Vorperian, June 13, 1964; children: Elizabeth, John. BS, Pa. State U., 1962, MS, 1964; PhD, Kans. State U., 1970. Project leader Borden Foods Co., Syracuse, N.Y., 1964-66; group leader Cen. Soya Co., Chgo., 1966-68; asst. prof. Colo. State U., Ft. Collins, Colo., 1970-72, assoc. prof., 1972-74, prof. food sci., 1974—. Contbr. numerous articles to profl. jours. Mem. Inst. Food Technologists, Am. Chem. Soc., Am. Assn. Cereal Scientists. Office: Colo State U Dept Food Sci Nutritio Fort Collins CO 80523

MAGAD, SAMUEL, orchestra concertmaster, conductor; b. Chgo., May 14, 1932; s. Herman and Doris (Walder) M.; m. Miriam Seefor, Feb. 13, 1955; children: Debra, Carlen. Mus.B., De Paul U., 1955; student, Paul Stassevitch. Orch. violin soloist, beginning 1944; with Chgo. Symphony Orch., 1958—, asst. concertmaster, 1966-72, co-concertmaster, 1972—; concertmaster Grant Park Symphony Orch., 1970-71; dir., 1st violinist Chgo. Symphony Chamber Players; founder Chgo. Symphony Trio; music dir., condr. Kankakee Symphony Orch. (Ill.), from 1984; prof. violin Northwestern U., Evanston, Ill.; also 1st violinist Eckstein Quartet, Chgo. Symphony String Quartet; dir. music, condr. Northbrook Symphony Orch., 1980—; concertmaster Aspen Festival Orch., 1987—. Served with orch. AUS, 1955-58. Office: Northbrook Symphony Orch 801 Skokie Blvd Ste 213 Northbrook IL 60062-4027

MAGALNICK, ELLIOTT BEN, retail medical supply company executive; b. Cleve., Aug. 19, 1945; s. Joseph Hyman and Ann (Resnick) M.; m. Diane Kerner, May 26, 1968 (div. Feb. 1988); children: Joel A., David A.; m. Judy Banjavic, June 9, 1991; stepchildren: Daniel Banjavic, David Banjavic. BS in Bus. Mgmt., Temple U., 1968. Cert. orthopedic fitter Health Industries Dealer Assn. Retail mgr. Milner Surg. Supply Co., Phila., 1970-72, Colo. Surg. Supply Co., Denver, 1972-73; mgr. non wheelchair retail Wheelchairs, Inc., Englewood, Colo., 1973-77; asst. mgr. ops. Denver Surg. Supply Co., 1977-78; owner, founder The Get Well Shop, Inc., Aurora, Colo., 1978—. Mem. chorus Shir Ami Singers, Denver, 1978-95, Colo. Symphony Orch., Denver, 1986-95; vol. Allied Fedn. Denver, 1984-87; mem. Legion of Merit, Rep. Party, Denver, 1992; donor Belle Bonfils Blood Ctr., 1976—; active Cantor Temple Micah, Denver. Named Disting. Pres., Optimist Internat., 1987. Mem. Colo. Assn. Med. Equipment Suppliers (dealer mem.), Health Industries Dealer Assn. (cert. orthopedic fitter), Home Health Care Dealers Coop., Luncheon Optimist Club Windsor Gardens (pres. 1986), Masons (master mason Columbian lodge), Colo. Consistory, El Jebel Temple, Rocky Mtn. Cantors Assn. Jewish. Avocations: bicycling, cross-country skiing, singing, tennis, reading. Office: The Get Well Shop Inc 12028 E Mississippi Aurora CO 80012

MAGALSKI, ANTHONY, internist; b. Cleve., Apr. 3, 1963. MD, Washington U., St. Louis, 1989. Intern U. Tex. Southwestern Affiliated Hosp., Dallas, 1989-90, resident, 1990-92, fellow in cardiology, 1992—. Recipient Clinician-Scientist award Am. Heart Assn., 1995-96. Mem. ACP, Am. Coll. Cardiology, AMA. Office: U Tex Southwestern Med Ctr 3232 High Meadow Dr Dallas TX 76051-4284

MAGANZINI, BROTHER JOHN BERNARD, academic administrator; b. Somerville, Mass., Nov. 11, 1947; s. Bernard Louis and Eva (Alo) M. BS, St. Francis Coll., 1982; MS, Fordham U., 1987, postgrad., 1987—. Named to Order of Friars Ninor. Tchr. spl. religious edn. Kennedy Meml. Hosp. Day Program, Brighton, Mass., 1980-81; parish asst. Our Lady Queen of Peace, Hewitt, N.J., 1981; tchr. Holy Cross Sch., Bronx, N.Y., 1982, St. Anthony's Grade Sch., Washington, 1982-83; dir. religious edn. Holy Cross Parish & Sch., Bronx, 1983-84, tchr., 1984-88, dept. chmn., tchr., 1990-93, asst. prin., 1993—; tchr. East Boston (Mass.) Ctrl. Cath. Sch., 1988-90. With U.S. Army, 1967-69. Recipient John J. Duffy award Archdiocese of N.Y., 1987. Mem. Nat. Assn. Elem. Sch. Prins., Assn. Supervision and Curriculum Devel., Cath. Sch. Adminstrs. Assn. N.Y. State, Nat. Cath. Edn. Assn., 11th Armored Cavalry's Vets. Vietnam and Cambodia. Avocations: music, theater, youth work. Address: Saint Anthony Shrine 100 Arch St Boston MA 02107 Office: Holy Cross Sch 1846 Randall Ave Bronx NY 10473-2942

MAGARGEE, W(ILLIAM) SCOTT, III, lawyer; b. Abington, Pa., Sept. 3, 1940; m. Annette Bruno, July 6, 1963; children: Scott, Todd, Ashley. AB, Princeton U., 1962; LLB, Yale U., 1966. Bar: Pa. 1966, U.S. Dist. Ct. (ea. dist.) Pa. 1966, U.S. Tax Ct. 1973. Admission officer Princeton (N.J.) U., 1962-63; assoc. Dechert Price & Rhoads, Phila., 1966-75, ptnr., 1975—. Supr. Tredyffrin Twp., Chester County, Berwyn, Pa., 1973-87; bd. trustees Paoli Meml. Hosp., 1988—; mem. citizens adv. com. Southeastern Pa. Transp. Authority, 1988—; bd. dirs. United Way Southeastern Pa., 1994—, chair human resources com., 1993—. Mem. ABA (sect. taxation), Phila. Bar Assn. (pension com. 1981—, chair employee benefits com. sect. taxation 1993—), Princeton Club Phila., Princeton Univ. Alumni Coun. (chmn. 1985-87). Office: Dechert Price & Rhoads 4000 Bell Atlantic Tower 1717 Arch St Philadelphia PA 19103-2713*

MAGARIAN, ROBERT ARMEN, medicinal chemist, researcher, educator; b. East St. Louis, Ill., July 27, 1930; s. Leon and Pauline Mary (Struel) M.; m. Charmaine Virginia Kugler, June 24, 1950; children: Paula, Cindy, Leslie, Robert. Student, Washington U., St. Louis, 1951-52; B.A., U. Miss., 1956, B.S. in Pharmacy with highest honors, 1960, Ph.D., 1966. Registered pharmacist, Miss., Ill. Am. Found. for Pharm. Edn. fellow, 1961-66; NIH postdoctoral research fellow U. Kans., Lawrence, 1966-67; asst. prof. St. Louis Coll. Pharmacy, 1966-70; assoc. prof. U. Okla. Coll. Pharmacy, Norman, 1970-76; prof. Oklahoma City, 1978—; exec. dir. Kappa Psi, pharm. frat., 1980—. Assoc. editor Current Medicinal Chemistry. Served with U.S. Army, 1952-54, Korea. Recipient teaching awards Coll. Pharmacy, U. Okla., 1974, 786, 89, Excellence in Rsch. and Svc. award, 1985, Baldwin study-travel award, 1978, Assocs. Disting. Lectureship award, 1988; named Outstanding Prof. Okla. Soc. Hosp. Pharmacists, 1987, Alumni Teaching Excellence award, 1989, Outstanding Teaching award Gamma Omicron, 1990, 91, 92; Mead-Johnson grantee Am. Assn. Colls. Pharmacy, 1968, NSF grantee, 1968-70, Nat. Cancer Inst. grantee, 1987-93. Mem. Am. Assn. Colls. Pharmacy, Am. chem. soc., Sigma Xi, Phi Kappa Phi, Kappa Psi (exec. dir., assoc. editor Current Medicinal Chemistry, Tchr. Excellence award 1990, 92), Rho Chi (chpt. Rsch. award 1981). Episcopalian. Patentee in field. Office: U Okla Health Sci Ctr Coll of Pharmacy 1110 N Stonewall Ave Oklahoma City OK 73117-1223

MAGARITY, RUSSELL LYNN, banker; b. Corpus Christi, Tex., July 29, 1946; s. Roy Lee and Ira Oleuia (Patterson) M.; m. Susan Ann Byers, June 3, 1967; children: Jennifer Lynn, Jeffrey Alan, Allison Lee. BA in Internat. Rels., U. Okla., 1967; MBA in Fin., Thunderbird Sch. Internat. Mgmt., Ariz., 1973. Credit and mktg. officer Banco Lar Brasileiro, S.A., Rio de Janeiro, 1974-78; v.p., team leader Chase Manhattan Bank, N.A., N.Y.C., 1978; dir. adjutant, country corp. mgr. Banco Lar Brasileiro, S.A., Rio de Janeiro, 1979-80; country corp. mgr., country mgr. Chase Manhattan Bank, N.A., Mexico City, 1981-86; sr. v.p., credit supervising officer Asia Pacific Chase Manhattan Bank, N.A., Hong Kong, 1986-88; sr. v.p. Chase Manhattan Bank, N.A., N.Y.C., 1987—; chief exec. Chase Manhattan Asia Ltd., Hong Kong, 1989—; also bd. dirs. Chase Manhattan Asia Ltd., Hong Kong. Lt. USN, 1967-72, Vietnam. Mem. Young Reps., Am. C. of C. Avocations: sailing, flying, cycling, magic. Office: Chase Manhattan Asia Ltd, 39/F 1 Exchange Sq Central, Hong Kong Hong Kong

MAGAW, JOHN W., federal law enforcement official; b. Columbus, Ohio; m. Helen Mahley; 5 children. BA in Edn., Otterbein Coll., 1957. Patrolman State of Ohio, Columbus, 1958-66; joined U.S. Secret Svc., Columbus, 1967, spl. agt., 1967—; former head protection for U.S. President and First Lady U.S. Secret Svc., Washington, until 1992, 17th dir., 1992-93; dir. Bur. Alcohol, Tobacco & Firearms, Washington, 1993—. Bd. trustees Otterbein Coll., Westerville, Ohio. Recipient Presdl. Rank Meritorious award, 1991. Mem. Fed. Investigators Assn., Internat. Assn. Chiefs of Police (exec. com. adv. com. for internat. policy). Office: Dept Treasury Bur Alcohol Tobacco Firearm 650 Massachusetts Ave NW Washington DC 20001-3744

MAGAW, ROGER WAYNE, construction company executive; b. Beaver, Ohio, Feb. 8, 1933; s. Cecil Elsworth and Thelma Mae (Howerton) M.; m. Virginia May Burdette, July 2, 1955; children: Wayne Robert, Rex

Roger. BS, W.Va. State Coll., 1960. Exec. v.p., treas. Union Boiler Co., Nitro, W.Va., 1959—; bd. dirs. mgmt. chmn. Nat. Maintenance Agreements Policy Com., Washington, 1983—. Chmn. Putnam County Vocat. Adv. Com., W.Va., 1968-90. Served with U.S. Army, 1953-55. Mem. Am. Welding Soc., Nat. Assn. Constrn. Boilermaker Employers (pres., bd. dirs. 1983-87), Putnam County C. of C. (chmn., bd. dirs. 1985-87). Republican. Methodist. Lodges: Masons, Shriners. Avocations: motor home camping, farming. Home: RR 2 Box 112 Hurricane WV 25526-9683 Office: Union Boiler Co PO Box 425 Nitro WV 25143-0425

MAGAZINE, ALAN HARRISON, association executive, consultant; b. Cambridge, Mass., May 16, 1944; s. Arnold Lloyd and Ruth Magazine; m. June Ann O'Donohue, June 20, 1971 (div. Feb. 1984); children: Sarah Elizabeth, David Michael; m. Cynthia Louise Cordiner, Aug. 30, 1984. BA, Monmouth Coll., 1966; MPA, Kent State U., 1968; PhD, U.Md., 1976. Sr. cons. Real Estate Research Corp., Washington, 1969-72; exec. dir. Nat. Ctr. for Pub. Service Internships, Washington, 1972-75; nat. policy coordinator Internat. City Mgmt. Assn., Washington, 1973-76; dep. asst. dir. U.S. Commn. on Fed. Paperwork, Washington, 1976-78; dir. office of intergovernmental relations EPA, Washington, 1978-81; dir. Business-Higher Edn. Forum, Washington, 1981-86, pres. coun. on competitivenessadv. com. Congl. Tech. Policy Task Force, 1986-89; adv. bd. George Mason U. Ctr. Conflict Resolution, 1986-89; pres. Health Industry Mfgs. Assn., 1990—; adv. bd. George Mason U. Ctr. Conflict Resolution, 1986-89, Brookings Inst. Ctr. Econ. Progress and Employment, 1986-89; mem. U.S. China Joint Commn. on Commerce & Trade; bd. dirs. Congl. Econ. Leadership Inst., 1986-89—, Healthcare Tech. Inst. Bd. Advisors, 1992-95, Calif. Biomedical Found., 1994—. Author: Environmental Management in Local Government, 1977. Bd. dirs. Met. Washington Coun. of Govts., 1972-79; mem. Fairfax County Bd. Suprs., Va., 1972-79; chmn. No. Va. Transp. Commn., 1974-75; mem. No. Va. Planning Dist. Commn., Fairfax, 1976-79; mem. Dickinson Coll. Parents Coun., 1994—. Served with USAFR, 1968-71. Ford Found. fellow, 1970-71. Mem. Econ. Club of Washington D.C. Democrat. Jewish. Avocations: jogging, reading. Home: 1302 Chancel Pl Alexandria VA 22314-4707 Office: Health Industry Mfgs Assn 1200 G St NW Washington DC 20005-3814

MAGAZINER, ELLIOT ALBERT, musician, conductor, educator; b. Springfield, Mass., Dec. 25, 1921; m. Sari Fromkin; 2 children. Student, Nat. Orch. Assn., 1937-40, Princeton U., 1943, Juilliard School of Music, 1946-50. Music dir., prof. music Manhattanville Coll., Purchase, N.Y., 1970—; faculty Westchester Conservatory Music. Debut: Town Hall, N.Y.C., 1952; staff artist, concertmaster CBS-TV and Radio; Networks: condrs. Reiner, Ansermet, Beecham, Stokowski; condr. and sr. violin instr. Westchester Conservatory of Music; vis. condr. Dubuque Symphony; soloist N.Y. Philharm. Symphony, Symphony of the Air, Kol Visrael, symphonies in Chgo., Ft. Myers, Dubuque, York, St. Petersburg; recitals in N.Y.C., Washington, Detroit, Amsterdam, Paris, Jerusalem; star of CBS-TV, The Violin. Recs.: Charles Ives Sonata #2, Charles Ives Trio (with Frank Glazer and David Weber); Vivaldi Concerto in C and Concerto in B (with orchestre Symphonique de Paris); conductor Westchester All County Festival Orch. Mem. AAUP, N.Y. TV Musicians (pres.), CBS Musicians Fund (sec.). Avocations: collecting unique and ancient instruments. Home: 250 Garth Rd Apt 2b3 Scarsdale NY 10583-3922 Office: Westchester Conservatory Symphony Orch 20 Soundview Ave White Plains NY 10606-3302

MAGAZINER, FRED THOMAS, lawyer; b. Phila., July 4, 1947; s. Henry Jonas and Reba (Henken) M.; m. Phyllis Heller, June 28, 1970; children: Daniel, Andrew. BA, Columbia U., 1969, JD, 1976. Bar: Pa., U.S. Dist. Ct. (ea. dist.) Pa., U.S. Ct. Appeals (3rd cir.), U.S. Claims Ct. Law clk. to judge Max Rosenn U.S. Ct. Appeals (3rd cir.), Phila., 1976-77; assoc. Dechert, Price & Rhoads, Phila., 1977-84, ptnr., 1984—. Vice chair citizens adv. com. S.E. Pa. Transp. Authority, 1986—. Mem. ABA, Pa. Bar Assn., Phila. Bar Assn. Democrat. Jewish. Home: 1021 W Cliveden St Philadelphia PA 19119-3702 Office: Dechert Price & Rhoads 4000 Bell Atlantic Tower 1717 Arch St Philadelphia PA 19103-2713

MAGAZINER, HENRY JONAS, architect; b. Phila., Sept. 13, 1911; s. Louis and Selma (Jonas) M.; m. Reba Henken, June 19, 1938; children: Ellen Louise (Mrs. Alan I. Widiss), Fred Thomas. BArch, U. Pa., 1936. Cert. Nat. Coun. Arch. and Registration Bds.; registered arch. Pa., N.Y., N.J., Del., Md. Draftsman Phila. City Planning Project, 1936-37; draftsman Louis Magaziner (Architect), Phila., 1937-39, architect, 1946-48; chief Architects' Squad, Day & Zimmermann, Inc., Burlington, Iowa, 1940-41; architect Albert Kahn (Architect), Detroit, 1942; designer Wright Aero. Corp., Wood Ridge, N.J., 1943-45; ptnr. Louis & Henry Magaziner, Phila., 1948-56; architect, planner pvt. practice, 1956-72; regional hist. architect Mid-Atlantic region Nat. Pk. Svc., Phila., 1972-87; pvt. practice architecture, 1987—; archtl. adviser Phila. Hist. Commn., 1970-75, mem. archtl. com., 1979-85, chmn. archtl. com., 1972-75; mem. adv. bd. Preservation Coalition Greater Phila. Mem. Carpenters' Co. of City and County of Phila.; v.p. Phila. Health and Welfare Coun., 1957-61, Phila. chpt. Victorian Soc. Am., 1975; v.p. city planning Germantown Comty. Coun., 1957-62; bd. dirs. Downtown Children's (day care) Ctr., 1956-73, v.p., 1960-61; bd. dirs. Allens Ln. Art Ctr., 1945-67, Neighborhood Ctr. Phila., 1956-74, Hist. Soc. Pa., 1970-74, Chestnut Hill Hist. Soc., 1970-80, Phila. chpt. Assn. for Preservation Tech., 1991—, Clean Air Coun., 1980-92, Center City Residents Assn., 1995—, Rittenhouse Plz., Inc., 1995—; active Germantown Hist. Soc., bd. dirs., 1960-93; bd. dirs. Maxwell Mansion Mus., pres., 1964-67; trustee Stewardsom Meml. Fellowship in Arch., 1958-90. Recipient Presdl. award for Excellence in Design for the Govt., 1988; named to Germantown Hall of Fame, 1994. Fellow AIA (mem. com. on hist. resources); mem. ASTM (mem. com. on hist. preservation stds. 1981-90), Am. Inst. Conservation, Assn. for Preservation Tech., Ea. Nat. Pk. and Monument Assn., Fellows in Am. Studies (pres. 1983-84), Nat. Trust for Hist. Preservation (mem. preservation forum), Soc. Archtl. Historians (bd. dirs. 1977-80, mem. editl. bd. 58 vol. Buildings of the United States), Bldg. Conservation Internat., Am. Arbitration Assn. (arbitrator), Victorian Soc. Am., T-Square Atelier (pres. 1963-65), Pa. Soc. Architects, Pa. Acad. Fine Arts, Libr. Co. Phila., Sierra Club, Athenaeum of Phila., Preservation Action. Home: 1502 1901 Walnut St Philadelphia PA 19103-4664 *I do hope that we can pass on to future generations a prejudice-free America having a natural environment without pollution and a man-made environment with its best elements both preserved and appreciated. Achieving these objectives is an unending struggle but one certainly worth winning. God willing, I expect to continue to fight for these ends.*

MAGAZINER, IRA, federal official; b. N.Y.C.; s. Louis and Sylvia M.; m. Suzanne Magaziner, 1981; children: Seth, Jonathan, Sarah. Grad., Brown U. With Boston Consulting Group; co-founder Telesis, 1979-88; issues advisor Clinton campaign, 1992; sr. advisor policy devel. The White House, 1993—. chief architect Health Security Act, 1993. Rhodes scholar Oxford U. Office: Domestic Policy Coun 1600 Pennsylvania Ave NW Washington DC 20500*

MAGDOL, MICHAEL ORIN, bank executive; b. N.Y.C., May 18, 1937; s. David Aaron and Ruth (Wein) M.; m. Alice Jane Gates, Aug. 29, 1940 (div. Sept. 1974); 1 child, David; m. Patricia Elizabeth Marshall, Feb. 1, 1943; 1 child, Jennifer. BSE, U. Pa., 1959. Internat. officer Mfrs. Hanover Trust Co., N.Y.C., 1959-65; exec. v.p. J. Henry Schroder Bank, N.Y.C., 1965-87; vice chmn., chief fin. officer, dir. Fiduciary Trust Co. Internat., N.Y.C., 1987—. Bd. dirs. Boy Scouts Am., N.Y.C., 1975—, Children Oncology Soc. N.Y., Lingnan Found. Mem. Am. Bankers Assn. (internat. bd. dirs. 1980-83), N.Y. State Bankers Assn. (chmn. internat. com. 1982—), Univ. Econs. Club, Onteora Club (Tannersville, N.Y.). Office: Fiduciary Trust Co Internat 2 World Trade Ctr New York NY 10048-0203

MAGEE, A. ALAN, artist; b. Newtown, Pa., May 26, 1947; s. Richard Forrest and Rena (Cook) M.; m. Monika Gabriele Ruth Siekmann, Jan. 4, 1969. Student, Tyler Sch. of Art, 1965-66, Phila. Coll. Art, 1967-69. Contbr. articles to profl. jours.; one-person shows include Allport Assocs. Gallery, Larkspur, Calif., 1978, 81, Clark Gallery, Lincoln, Mass., 1979, Staempfli Gallery, N.Y.C., 1980, 82, FIAC Grand Palais, Paris, 1983, Norton Gallery and Sch. of Art, West Palm Beach, Fla., 1983, San Jose Mus. of Art, 1983, Newport Art Mus., 1984, Farnsworth Art Mus., Rockland, Maine, 1984, U. Maine, 1985, Fresno Art Ctr., 1985, Los Angeles, 1986, Schmidt-Bingham Gallery, N.Y.C., 1986, 88, 89, Allport Assocs. Gallery, San Francisco, 1986, Joan Whitney Payson Gallery at Westbrook Coll., Portland, Maine, 1990, Farnsworth Art Mus., 1991, James A. Michener Art Mus., Doylestown, Pa., 1991, Ringling Sch. Art & Design, Sarasota, Fla., 1992, Fine Arts Ctr. at Cheekwood, Nashville, 1992, Edith Caldwell Gallery, San Francisco, 1992, 93, 95, Edity Lambert Gallery, Santa Fe, 1995; group shows include Farnsworth Art Mus., Rockland, Maine, 1985, Akron (Ohio) Mus. of Art, 1985, Maine Coast Artists, Rockport, 1985, Ark. Art Ctr, Little Rock, 1985, Smithsonian Instn., Nat. Air and Space Mus., Washington, 1985, Wunderlich & Co., N.Y.C., 1986, Light Gallery, N.Y.C., 1986, Schmidt-Bingham Gallery, N.Y.C., 1986, 88, Mus. Fine Arts, Springfield, 1986, Butler Inst. Am. Art, Youngstown, Ohio, 1987, Am. Acad. and Inst. of Arts and Letters, N.Y.C., 1987, Nat. Invitationnal Drawing Exhbn., 1989, Staempfli Gallery, N.Y.C., 1990, Albrecht Art Mus., St. Joseph, 1990, Nat. Acad. of Design, N.Y.C., 1990; and others; pub. collections include Farnsworth Art Mus., Rockland, Arco Collection, Los Angeles, Achenbach Collection, Palace of the Legion of Honour, San Franciscco, Portland (Maine) Mus. of Art, Rutgers U. Art Mus., and others; author: Stones and Other Works, 1987, Alan Magee 1981-91; TV: Visions of Darkness and Light, 1988. Recipient Richard and Hinda Rosenthal Found. award N.Y.C., Am. Book award, Nevelson award, 1982; The Leo Meissner Prize, Nat. Acad. of Design, 1990. Home: Pleasant Point Rd RR 68 Box 132 Cushing ME 04563

MAGEE, DENNIS, cultural organization administrator; b. Pala, Calif., Oct. 9, 1937; s. Raymond Milton and Prudence Theresa (Golsh) M. BSBA, San Diego State U., San Diego, 1961. Wholesaler Kroshel Industries, San Diego, 1962-69; adminstr. Indian Health Council Inc., Pauma Valley, Calif., 1970—; adv. bd. Masters in Pub. Health Program for Native Americans, U. Calif., Berkeley; bd. trustees Robert F. Kennedy Meml. Found., Washington; bd. dirs. Comprehensive Health Planning Assn. of San Diego, Riverside and Imperial Counties, Nat. Indian Health Bd., Denver; mem. San Diego State U. Athletic Found, San Diego State U. Alumni Assn., San Diego Council of Community Clinics. Bd. dirs. United Way of San Diego County, Nat. Neighborhood Ctrs. Am., N.Y.C., Citizens Equal Opportunity Commn., San Diego, Mental Health Assn., Sacramento, San Diego County Regional Criminal Justice Planning bd.; mem. tribal health coun., Sacramento; mem. San Diego County Human Relations Commn. Recipient Nat. Disting. Cmty. Svc. award Nat. Soc. Workers Techni-Culture Coalition, Cin., 1973, Indian Health Ctr. dedicated to Dennis Magee, 1976, Letter of Commendation Pres. Jimmy Carter, 1980. Mem. Northern San Diego County Associated Cs. of C. (bd. dirs.). Democrat. Roman Catholic. Avocations: sports, bicycling, hunting, bullfighting. Home: Pala Mission Rd PO Box 86 Pala CA 92059-0086 Office: Indian Health Council Inc PO Box 406 Pauma Valley CA 92061-0406

MAGEE, DONALD EDWARD, retired national park service administrator; b. Trenton, N.J., Sept. 24, 1937; s. Donald A. and Anna C. (Bocskowics) M.; m. Linda Kimball, June 27, 1964; children: Kevin, Bonnie Magee Burch, Gale. BS in Forestry Mgmt., U. Mass., 1964. Pk. ranger Bryce Canyon (Utah) Nat. Pk., 1966-68; area mgr. Sunset Crater Nat. Monument, Flagstaff, Ariz., 1968-73; mgmt. analyst Nat. Capital Region, Washington, 1973-80; supt. Stones River Nat. Battlefield, Murfreesboro, Tenn., 1980-89, USS Ariz. Meml., Pearl Harbor, Hawaii, 1989-95; ret., 1995. With USN, 1956-58. Recipient Excellence of Svc. award Dept. of Interior, 1991. Home: 95-457 Kaukoe St Mililani HI 96789-1865

MAGEE, JOHN FRANCIS, research company executive; b. Bangor, Maine, Dec. 3, 1926; s. John Henry and Marie (Frawley) M.; m. Dorothy Elma Hundley, Nov. 19, 1949; children: Catherine Anne, John Hundley, Andrew Stephen. AB, Bowdoin Coll., 1947; MS, U. Maine, 1952; MBA, Harvard U., 1948. With Arthur D. Little, Inc., Cambridge, Mass., 1950—, v.p., 1961-72, pres., 1972-86, chief exec. officer, 1974-88, chmn., 1986—, also dir.; dir. John Hancock Mut. Life Ins. Co., Boston, Houghton-Mifflin Co., Boston. Author: Physical Distribution Systems, 1967, Industrial Logistics: Analysis and Management of Physical Supply and Distribution Systems, 1968, (with D. M. Boodman) Production Planning and Inventory Control, 1968; (with W. Capacino and W. Rosenfield) Modern Logistics Management, 1985. Trustee Boston U. Med. Ctr., New Eng. Aquarium, Woods Hole Oceanographic Instn., Bowdoin Coll. (emeritus), Emerson Hosp. (sec.), Thompson Island Outward Bound Edn. Ctr. (chmn.). Mem. Ops. Research Soc. Am. (pres. 1966-67), Inst. Mgmt. Scis. (pres. 1971-72), Phi Beta Kappa, Phi Kappa Psi. Clubs: Concord (Mass.) Country (gov. 1971-74); The Country (Brookline, Mass.); Somerset (Boston). Office: Arthur D Little Inc 25 Acorn Park Cambridge MA 02140-2301

MAGEE, PAUL TERRY, geneticist and molecular biologist, college dean; b. Los Angeles, Oct. 26, 1937; s. John Paul and Lois Lorene (Cowgill) M.; m. Beatrice Buten, Aug. 6, 1964; children: Alexander John, Amos Hart. B.S., Yale U., 1959; Ph.D., U. Calif., Berkeley, 1964. Am. Cancer Soc. postdoctoral fellow Lab. Enzymologie, Gif-sur-Yvette, France, 1964-66; mem. faculty Yale U., 1966-77, asst. prof. microbiology, 1966-72, assoc. prof. microbiology and human genetics, 1972-75, assoc. prof. human genetics, 1975-77; dean Trumbull Coll., 1969-72; prof. microbiology, chmn. dept. microbiology and pub. health Mich. State U., East Lansing, 1977-87, dir. Biotech. Research Ctr., 1985-87; dean Coll. Biol. Scis. U. Minn., 1987—, dean Coll. Med. Sci., 1987-95, prof. genetics and cell biology, 1995—; mem. genetics adv. panel NSF, 1978-83, mem. genetics adv. panel NSF, 1978-83, mem. adv. com. biology directorate, 1992—, chair, 1995—; chmn. BBS task force looking to 21st century, 1991; cons. Corning Glass Works, 1978-80, Pillsbury Rsch., 1990—; mem. pers. com. Am. Cancer Soc., 1983-87; mem. microbial genetics and physiology study sect. NIH, 1984-88; co-chmn. com. grad. record exam. biochemistry cell and molecular biology Ednl. Testing Svc., 1988—; mem. microbiology infectious disease rsch. adv. group NIH, 1994—, chair, 1996-98; chair Burrough Wellcome Fund Award Com. in Molecular Pathogenic Mycology, 1995—; traveling fellow Japanese Soc. for Promotion of Sci., 1995. Mem. editorial bd. Jour. Bacteriology, 1975-80, Molecular and Cell Biology, 1981-92. Named Mich. champion masters swimmming, 1978-84, 86, Minn. champion masters swimming, 1988, 89, 91-95, nat. YMCA swimming champion, 1990. Mem. AAAS, Am. Soc. Biochemistry and Molecular Biology (ednl. com. 1991-95), Am. Soc. Microbiologists, Genetics Soc. Am. Jewish. Office: U Minn Coll Biol Scis Saint Paul MN 55105-1095

MAGEE, ROBERT PAUL, accounting and information systems educator; b. Rochester, N.Y., Apr. 17, 1947; s. Charles Robert and Rosemond (Jones) M.; m. Margaret Ann Chandler, Dec. 28, 1968; children: Paul R., Michael D. AB, Cornell U., 1969, MS, 1972, PhD, 1974. Asst. prof. acctg. Grad. Sch. Bus. U. Chgo., 1973-76; assoc. prof. acctg. and info. systems Kellogg Grad. Sch. Mgmt. Northwestern U., Evanston, Ill., 1976-79, prof. acctg. and info. systems, 1979—, Eric L. Kohler prof., 1986-89, Keith I. DeLashmutt prof., 1989—. Author: Advanced Managerial Accounting, 1986; co-author: Efficient Capital Markets and Accounting, 1975; editor: The Acctg. Rev., 1993—; contbr. articles to Jour. of Acctg. Rsch., The Acctg. Rev., Jour. of Acctg. and Econs., others. Treas. Youth Orgns. Umbrella, Evanston, 1984-89, pres., 1989—. Recipient Notable Contbn. award AICPA, 1978. Mem. Am. Acctg. Assn., Phi Kappa Phi, Beta Gamma Sigma. Home: 2626 Lincolnwood Dr Evanston IL 60201-1227 Office: Northwestern Univ 2001 Sheriden Rd Rm 587 Evanston IL 60201-2962*

MAGEE, STEPHEN PAT, economics and finance educator; b. Wichita, Kans., Mar. 17, 1943; s. Lawrence Patrick and Edna Willard (Brock) M.; m. Naneska Nall, Aug. 20, 1965 (div. Dec. 1987); children: Christopher Sean Patrick, Theodore Parker; m. Frances Jean Toepperwein, July 28, 1988. BA in Econs., Tex. Tech. U., 1965, MA in Econs., 1966; PhD in Econs., MIT, 1969. Asst. prof. U. Calif., Berkeley, 1969-71; assoc. prof. U. Chgo., 1971-76; economist The White House, Washington, 1972-73; rsch. fellow Brookings Insts., Washington, 1973-74; prof. fin. and econs. U. Tex., Austin, 1976—, chmn. fin., 1980-84, McDermott prof., 1980-84, Fred H. Moore prof., 1984-92, Charles and Sarah Seay prof., 1992-94; Bayless/Enstar Corp. chairholder, 1994—; mem. econ. adv. bd. U.S. Sec. Commerce, Washington, 1978-79, NSF, 1979; expert witness Mesa Petroleum, Avis Rent-a-Car, El Paso Natural Gas, Kodak, Proctor & Gamble, AB Dick, Exxon; acad. lectr. in 11 fgn. countries for U.S. govt., 1977-88; vis. prof. bus. U. Chgo., 1990-91; expert effects of lawyers on U.S. economy. Author: International Trade (transl. to Japanese, Chinese, Korean), 1980, Black Hole Tariffs and Endogenous Policy Theory, 1989; mem. editorial bd. Rev. Econs. and Stats., 1972-79, Jour. Internat. Econs., 1977-79, Econs. and Politics, 1988-94, Rev. Internat. Econs., 1992-94; contbr. articles to scholarly publs., fin. publs. including Fortune Mag., Wall St. Jour. Capt., Tex. State Soccer Champions, 1984. Grantee NSF, 1972-77; recipient Joe Beasley Teaching award U. Tex. Grad. Sch. Bus., 1979, Outstanding Career Rsch. Contbn. award, 1990, named TopCore MBA prof., 1986. Avocations: soccer, drag racing, photography. Home: 1219 Castle Hill St Austin TX 78703-4125 Office: U Tex Dept Fin Austin TX 78712-1157

MAGEE, THOMAS HUGH, lawyer; b. Rochester, N.Y., Aug. 15, 1943; s. Edward Charles and Jane Kathleen (Cranmer) M.; m. Judith Joy Stone, Oct. 2, 1982; 1 child, Michael Julian. BSME, U. Rochester, N.Y., 1965; JD, Syracuse U., 1973. Bar: N.J. 1974, U.S. Dist. Ct. N.J. 1974, U.S. Ct. Appeals (D.C. cir.) 1975, N.Y. 1981, U.S. Supreme Ct. 1978, U.S. Patent and Trademark Office. Sr. patent counsel RCA Corp., Princeton, N.J., 1973-86, GE/RCA Licensing Operation, Princeton, 1986-88; sr. counsel E.I. duPont de Nemours & Co., Wilmington, Del., 1988—. Lt. USN, 1965-70, Capt. USNR (ret.), 1991. Navy commendation medal with combat V, Vietnam, 1969. Mem. Am. Intellectual Property Law Assn. (com. chair 1974—), Phila. Intellectual Property Law Assn. (com. chmn. 1974—), N.J. Patent Law Assn., Justinian hon. law soc., Phi Alpha Delta. Republican. Presbyterian. Avocations: tennis, handball, coin-collecting. Home: 721 Severn Rd Wilmington DE 19803 Office: E I duPont de Nemours & Co Barley Mill Plz BMP 36-2280 Wilmington DE 19880

MAGEE, WAYNE EDWARD, biochemistry educator, researcher; b. Big Rapids, Mich., Apr. 11, 1929; s. William Fredrick and Elsie E. (Gifford) M.; m. Nannette A. Pierce, June 11, 1951; children: Lawrence, William, John. BA magna cum laude in Chemistry, Kalamazoo Coll., 1951; MS in Biochemistry, U. Wis., 1953, PhD in Biochemistry, 1955. Sci., then sr. sci. Upjohn Co., Kalamazoo, 1955-71; prof. life sci. Ind. State U., 1971-74; prof. biology, head divsn. allied health and life sci. U. Tex., San Antonio, 1975-80, prof., 1980-81; prof. biochemistry, head dept. bacteriology and biochemistry U. Idaho, 1981-85; dir. divsn. Life Scis., prof., head dept. biosci. and biotech. Drexel U., Phila., 1985-92, prof. biosci., 1985-95, W.R. Nes prof. bioscience, 1995—; adj. prof. biology Western Mich. U., 1970-71. Wis. Alumni Found. Grad. fellow, 1951-52; Predoctoral fellow NSF, 1952-55. Fellow AAAS, Am. Chem. Soc., Am. Inst. Biol. Sci., Am. Soc. Biochemistry and Molecular Biology, Am. Soc. Microbiology. Contbr. articles and abstracts to profl. jours., chpts. in books. Research on phospholipid membranes, liposomes as drug carriers, immune modulation, monoclonal antibodies. Home: One Independence Pl 241 S 6th St Philadelphia PA 19106-3727 Office: Drexel U Dept Biosci Biotech Philadelphia PA 19104

MAGEN, MYRON SHIMIN, osteopathic physician, educator, university dean; b. Bklyn., Mar. 1, 1926; s. Barney and Gertrude Beatrice (Cohen) M.; m. Ruth Sherman, July 6, 1952; children—Jed, Ned, Randy. D.O., Coll. Osteo. Medicine and Surgery, 1951; Sc.D. (hon.), U. Osteo. Medicine and Health Scis., Des Moines, 1981. Rotating intern Coll. Hosp., Des Moines, 1951-52, resident in pediatrics, 1953-54; chmn. dept. pediatrics Coll. Osteo. Medicine and Surgery, Des Moines, 1958-62, Riverside Osteo. Hosp., Trenton, Mich., 1962-68, Detroit Osteo. Hosp., 1965-67; med. dir., dir. med. edn. Zieger-Botsford Hosps., Farmington, Mich., 1968-70; prof. pediatrics Mich. State Coll. Osteo. Medicine, East Lansing, 1970—, dean, 1970—; mem. spl. med. adv. group to chief med. dir. VA, 1973-77; mem. grad med. edn. nat. adv. com. HHS, Washington, 1978-80; James Watson disting. lectr. Ohio Ostio Assn., 1974, Grad. Med. Edn. Nat. Adv. Com.; Watson Meml. lectr. Am. Coll. Osteo. Pediatricians, 1987; chair Mich. Med. Schs. Coun. Deans, 1979-84, 90-91; mem. PEW Health Professions Com., 1991—. Contbr. articles to profl. jours. Served with USN, 1943-45. Recipient Disting. Service award Okla. Coll. Osteo. Medicine and Surgery, 1975; Founder's medal Tex. Coll. Osteo. Medicine, 1978;. Mem. Am. Assn. Colls. Osteo. Medicine (pres. 1977), Am. Osteo. Assn. (com. edn., chair com. on colls. 1987-90, La. Burns lectr. 1977, chair bur. profl. edn. 1990-92), Am. Coll. Osteo. Pediats. (pres. 1965-66), Mich. Assn. Osteo. Physicians and Surgeons. Home: 1251 Farwood Dr East Lansing MI 48823-1831 Office: Mich State Univ Coll Osteopathic Medicine 308 E Fee Hall East Lansing MI 48824-1316

MAGER, ARTUR, retired aerospace company executive, consultant; b. Nieglowice, Poland, Sept. 21, 1919; came to U.S., 1939, naturalized, 1944; s. Herman and Ella (Kornbluh) M.; m. Phyllis R. Weisman, Aug. 19, 1942; 1 child, Ilana Gail. BS, U. Mich., 1943; MS, Case Inst. Tech., 1951; PhD in Aeros., Calif. Inst. Tech., 1953. Aero. rsch. scientist NASA Lewis Labs., Cleve., 1946-51; rsch. scientist Marquardt Corp., Van Nuys, Calif., 1954-60; dir. Nat. Engring. Sci. Co., Pasadena, Calif., 1960-61; dir. spacecraft scis. Aerospace Corp., El Segundo, Calif., 1961-64, gen. mgr. applied mechanics div., 1964-68, v.p., gen. mgr. engring. sci. ops., 1968-78, v.p. engring. group, 1978-82, cons., 1982—; mem. BSD Re-entry Panel, 1961-63, NASA com. missile and space vehicle aerodynamics, 1963-65; mem. adv. com. AFML, 1971-72; mem. NASA Adv. Council, 1982-86 ; chmn. NASA Space Applications Adv. Com., 1982-86 ; mem. Aeros. and Space Engring. Bd., NRC, 1982-87; mem. Space Sta. Task Force, NRC, 1983-87, Shuttle Criticality and Hazard Analysis Rev. Bd., 1986-88, DSB NASP Task Force, 1987-88, AFSB Hypersonic Task Force, 1987-88. Contbr. articles to profl. jours. Mem. alumni fund coun. Calif. Inst. Tech., 1972-74; trustee West Coast U., 1980-92; bd. councilors U. So. Calif. Sch. Engring., 1976-86; mem. devel. disabilities bd. Area X, 1976-80, chmn., 1976-78; 1st v.p. Calif. Assn. Retarded, 1983-85 ; pres. Exceptional Children's Found., 1970-72. Recipient Disting. Alumni award U. Mich., 1969, Golden Rule award Calif. Assn. Retarded, 1977, 89. Fellow Inst. Advanced Engring., AIAA (chmn. Los Angeles sect. 1967-68, bd. dirs. 1975-77, pres. 1980-81), AAAS; mem. Technion Soc., Nat. Acad. Engring., Sigma Xi. Home and Office: 1353 Woodruff Ave Los Angeles CA 90024-5129

MAGER, EZRA PASCAL, automobile dealership vice chairman; b. N.Y.C., Nov. 1, 1941; s. Harold and Naomi (Levinson) M.; m. Sarah Johnson, Mar. 25, 1964 9div.); 1 child, Emma Rachel; m. Reeva Starkman, May 14, 1972; children: Camilla Elizabeth, Michael Johanon. B.A., Cornell U., 1963; M.B.A., Harvard, 1966. Successively v.p., sr. v.p., exec. v.p. and dir. Seiden & DeCuevas, Inc., N.Y.C., 1966-73; exec. v.p., dir. Furman Selz Mager Dietz & Birney, Inc., N.Y.C., 1973-90; vice chmn. United Auto Group, Inc., N.Y.C., 1990-96, Cross Country Auto Retailers, Inc., N.Y.C., 1996—. Pres. Baron de Hirsch Fund. Mem. N.Y. Soc. Security Analysts, Alpha Delta Phi. Democrat. Club: Harvard (N.Y.C.). Home: 141 E 72nd St New York NY 10021-4367 Office: Cross Country Auto Retailers Inc 540 Madison Ave Ste 3000 New York NY 10022

MAGGIN, BRUCE, communications executive; b. N.Y.C., Apr. 25, 1943; s. Sherwood and Bernice (Lush) M.; m. Jacqueline M. Montagne, Sept. 2, 1973; children: Benjamin M., Daniel M. BA, Lafayette Coll., 1965; JD, Cornell U., 1968, MBA, 1969. Bar: N.Y. 1969. Fin. analyst ABC, N.Y.C., 1970-71, dir. corp. planning, 1974-79, v.p. cost mgmt., 1982-83; sr. v.p. ABC Video Enterprises, Inc. div. Capital Cities/ABC, Inc., N.Y.C., 1983-88; exec. v.p. CC/ABC Video Enterprises, Inc., N.Y.C., 1988-93, CC/ABC Multimedia Group, 1993—; cons. Irving Trust Co., N.Y.C., 1972-73; v.p. planning, devel. Ziff Corp., N.Y.C., 1979-82; bd. dirs. ESPN, Inc., N.Y.C., O.T. Sports, Balt., Creative Wonders, San Francisco, Phillips Van Heusen, N.Y.C. Home: 8 Lawrence Farms Crsway Chappaqua NY 10514-1210 Office: CC/ABC Inc 77 W 66th St New York NY 10023-6201

MAGGIO, MICHAEL JOHN, artistic director; b. Chgo., July 3, 1951; s. Carlo and Genevieve (Sparacino) M.; m. Janice St. John, Sept. 7, 1974 (div. June 1977); m. Julie Carol Jackson, Mar. 29, 1980 (div. Dec. 1994); 1 child, Ben. BA, U. Ariz., 1973, MA, 1974. Artistic dir. Woodstock (Ill.) Music Theatre Festival, 1980-82, Northlight Theatre, Evanston, Ill., 1983-87; assoc. artistic dir. Goodman Theatre, Chgo., 1987—; artistic advisor Columbia Coll., Chgo., 1987—. Directed Another Midsummer Night, Brutality of Fact, Black Snow, Wings, Shakespeare's A Midsummer Night's Dream, Romeo and Juliet, Uncle Vanya, 1989-90, A Flea In Her Ear, A Christmas Carol, Sunday In The Park With George, Cyrano De Bergerac, The Front Page, The Dining Room; artistic dir. Northlight Theatre premieres of Dealing, City On The Make, Heart of A Dog, (Am. premiere) Ballerina, (world premiere) Sondheim Suite; dir. The Real Thing, West Memphis Mojo, Highest Standard of Living, Endgame, The Winter's Tale, Travesties, Tartuffe, Spokesong, Ladies In Waiting; dir. prodn. of Titus Andronicus for N.Y. Shakespeare Festival; prodns. include McCarter Theatre, Guthrie

Theater in Mpls., The Cleve. Playhouse, Ariz. Theatre Co., Actors Theatre of Louisville, Seattle Repertory Co. chmn. Michael Merritt Award and Endowment Fund, Colubmia Coll, Chgo. Recipient Joseph Jefferson "Jeff" Citation 1975-76. 78, 93-94, Father of Yr. award, Chgo. Father's Day Com., 1986, Excellence in Arts award De Paul U. Theatre Sch., 1993, Obie award, 1993,. Office: Goodman Theatre 200 S Columbus Dr Chicago IL 60603-6402

MAGGIORE, SUSAN, geophysical oceanographer; b. Newark, Mar. 14, 1957; d. John James and Marietta Nancy (Testa) M.; m. Stephen P. Garreffa, Oct. 21, 1989; children: Julianna Garreffa, Marietta Garreffa. BS in Geosci., Montclair State U., 1978; postgrad., U. So. Miss., 1981-84. Supr. rsch. and communications The Cousteau Soc., N.Y.C. and Norfolk, Va., 1979-81; geophysicist Naval Oceanographic Office, Bay St. Louis, Miss., 1981-85, NE Consortium Oceanographic Research, Narragansett, R.I., 1985-86; mem. tech. staff Lucent Technologies (formerly AT&T Bell Labs.), Whippany, N.J., 1986—; writer, creative cons. The Cousteau Soc., Los Angeles, 1981-89. Researcher book The Cousteau Almanac of the Environment, 1981; contbr. articles to profl. jours. Vol. Dover (N.J.) Gen. Hosp., 1987-88. Mem. Am. Geophys. Union, Marine Tech. Soc., Nat. Assn. Female Execs. Roman Catholic. Avocations: singing, playing musical instruments, reading, cooking. Office: Lucent Techs 67 Whippany Rd Whippany NJ 07981-1406

MAGGIPINTO, V. ANTHONY, lawyer; b. Tucson, Apr. 15, 1943; s. William Vito and Elizabeth Maria (Rice) M.; m. Maria Teresa Zequeira, Aug. 31, 1976; children: Marshall Albert Nicholas, Spencer William Jonathan. AB cum laude, Southampton Coll., 1970; JD, Fordham U., 1976. Bar: Fla. 1977, N.Y. 1978, U.S. Dist. Ct. (ea. and so. dists.) N.Y. 1979, U.S. Ct. Appeals (2d cir.) 1980. Asst. to pres. Interpub. Group of Cos., N.Y.C., 1965-66; asst. dean of admission Southampton (N.Y.) Coll., 1971-73; investigative aide N.Y. State Com. on Jud. Conduct, N.Y.C., 1974-76; asst. state atty. Dade County State Atty., Miami, Fla., 1977-78; asst. dist. atty. Suffolk Dist. Atty., Hauppage, N.Y., 1978-80; asst. county atty. Suffolk County Atty., Hauppauge, 1980-84; sole practice Riverhead and St. James, N.Y., 1982—; mem. spl. coms. on discovery, civil litigation U.S. Dist. Ct. (ea. dist.) N.Y., Bklyn., 1983-90, 95—, arbitrator, 1986—, ea. dist. N.Y. adv. group, 1990-95, chair jury task force, 1993—. Mem. appeals bd. SSS, 1982—, vice chmn., 1986—. Served with submarine svc. USN, 1961-65. Recipient Disting. Alumni award L.I. U., 1990. Mem. N.Y. State Bar Assn., Suffolk County Bar Assn., Fla. Bar, U.S. Naval Inst., Navy League (judge advocate L.I. coun. 1992—). Republican. Roman Catholic. Club: Nissequogue (N.Y.) Golf (counsel 1980—, bd. govs.). Avocations: hiking, horseback riding. Office: 1212 Roanoke Ave Riverhead NY 11901-2740

MAGGS, PETER BLOUNT, lawyer, educator; b. Durham, N.C., July 24, 1936; s. Douglas Blount and Dorothy (Mackay) M.; m. Barbara Ann Widenor, Feb. 27, 1960; children: Bruce MacDowell, Gregory Eaton, Stephanie Ann, Katherine Ellen. AB, Harvard U., 1957, JD, 1961; postgrad. (exchange student), Leningrad (USSR) State U., 1961-62. Bar: D.C. 1962. Research assoc. Law Sch. Harvard U., 1963-64; asst. prof. law U. Ill., 1964-67, assoc. prof., 1967-69, prof., 1969-88, William and Marie Corman prof., 1988—, acting dean, 1990; dir. rule of law program Washington, 1994; Fulbright lectr. Moscow State U., 1977; reporter Uniform Simplification of Land Transfers Act. Author: (with others) The Soviet Legal system, 1984, (with O.S. Ioffe) Soviet Law in Theory and Practice, 1983, (with others) Unfair Trade Practice and Consumer Protection, 1992; (with J. Sprowl) Computer Applications in the Law, 1987, (with others) Computer Law, 1992; designer talking computers for the blind. Fulbright rsch. scholar, Yugoslavia, 1967; East-West Ctr. fellow, 1972, Guggenheim fellow, 1979. Mem. ABA (chmn. com. on Soviet law sect. internat. law 1976-80), Bar Assn. of the Dist. of Columbia, Am. Assn. Advancement Slavic Studies, Assn. Am. Law Schs. (chmn. sect. comparative law 1977), Am. Law Inst. (consultative group, Restatement Law Unfair Competition), Am. Acad. Fgn. Law, Internat. Acad. Comparative Law. Office: U Ill Coll Law 504 E Pennsylvania Ave Champaign IL 61820-6909

MAGID, GAIL AVRUM, neurosurgeon, neurosurgery educator; b. Chgo., Oct. 15, 1934; s. Harry M. and Henrietta (Busch) M.; m. Janet Louise Reinhardt, June 15, 1962 (div.); children: Allison Magid London, Jonathan Alward; m. Roseanne Cipra Muirhead, Sept. 4, 1982. BSc, U. Ill., 1954; MD, Chgo. Med. Sch., 1958. Diplomate Am. Bd. Neurol. Surgery. Intern Cook County Hosp., Chgo., 1958-59; resident, then fellow neurol. surgery Mayo Clinic, Rochester, Minn., 1959-61, 63-65; clin. instr. neurosurgery U. Calif., San Francisco, 1965-70, asst. clin. prof., 1970-79, assoc. prof., 1979—; chmn. Dominican Neurol. Inst., Santa Cruz, Calif., 1975—; bd. dirs. Dominican Found.; cons. neurosurgery U.S. Army, San Francisco Gen. Hosp. Assoc. editor: Clinical Neurosurgery, 1974. Bd. dirs. Santa Cruz Symphony Assn., 1983-85, U. Calif. Friends of Arts, Santa Cruz, 1985-86. Served to lt. comdr. USN, 1961-63. Fellow ACS, Internat. Coll. Surgeons; mem. AMA, Calif. Med. Assn., Internat. Soc. Pediatric Neurosurgeons, Am. Assn. Neurol. Surgeons, Western Neurosurg. Soc., Cong. Neurol. Surgeons, San Francisco Neurol. Soc. (pres.-elect 1991, pres. 1992), St. Francis Yacht Club (San Francisco). Republican. Home: 241 4th Ave Santa Cruz CA 95062-3815 Office: 1661 Soquel Dr Santa Cruz CA 95065-1709

MAGIELNICKI, ROBERT L., lawyer; b. Perth Amboy, N.J., Mar. 28, 1947; s. Leon C. and Dorothy M. (Hudanish) M.; m. Kathleen J. Urban, June 14, 1969; children: Robert Jr., Kimberly, Peter, Matthew. AB with honors, Rutgers U., 1967; JD with distinction, Cornell U., 1970. Bar: N.Y. 1971, U.S. Supreme Ct. 1974, D.C. 1990. Commd. lt. USN, 1968; assoc. Donovan Leisure Newton & Irvine, N.Y.C., 1970-71, 74-80; asst. staff judge advocate U.S. Naval Base Subic Bay, Republic of Philippines, 1971-73; asst. prof. law U.S. Naval Acad., Annapolis, Md., 1973-74; assoc. litigation and antitrust counsel Gen. Elec. Corp. Hdqs., Fairfield, Conn., 1980-83, counsel, 1989-90; divsn. gen. counsel Gen. Elec. Factory Automation Products, Charlottesville, Va., 1983-88; ptnr. Kutak Rock, Washington, 1990—. Avocations: tennis, golf, swimming, reading. Office: Kutak Rock 1101 Connecticut Ave NW Washington DC 20036-4303

MAGIERA, FRANK EDWARD, journalist, critic; b. Webster, Mass., Nov. 28, 1945; s. Charles Frank and Marion Margaret (Kralik) M.; m. Janice Lee Rayner, Aug. 20, 1977. BS, Worcester Poly. Inst., 1967. Reporter Worcester (Mass.) Telegram & Gazette, 1970—, drama critic, 1978-89, art critic, 1989—. Lt. (j.g.) USN, 1968-70. Democrat. Avocations: farming, painting, woodworking. Home: Lawrence Rd Dudley MA 01571 Office: Worcester Telegram & Gazette 20 Franklin St Worcester MA 01608-1904

MAGILL, DODIE BURNS, early childhood education educator; b. Greenwood, S.C., July 10, 1952; d. Byron Bernard and Dora Curry B.; m. Charles Towner Magill, May 4, 1974; children: Charles Towner II, Emily Curry. BA, Furman U., 1974; MEd, U. S.C., 1978. Cert. tchr., early childhood, elementary, elementary principal, supv., S.C. Kindergarten tchr. Sch. Dist. Greenville County, 1974-83; early childhood edn. instr. Valdosta (Ga.) State Univ., 1983-84; dir. lower sch. Valwood Sch., Valdosta, 1984-86; kindergarten tchr. Sch. Dist. Greenville County, 1986—; tchr.-in-residence S.C. Ctr. for Tchr. Recruitment, Rock Hill, 1993, mem. policy bd.; workshop presenter and lectr. in various schs. and sch. dists. throughout U.S., 1974—; chmn. S.C. Pub. Kindergarten Celebration, 1994; giv. S.C. State Readiness Policy Group; mem. Southeastern Region Vision for Edn. Adv. Bd., S.C. Coun. Ednl. Collaboration. Demonstration tchr. S.C. ETV (TV show) Sch. Begins with Kindergarten. Mem. Gov. of S.C.'s State Readiness Policy Group, Southeastern Regional Vision for Edn. Adv. Bd., South Carolina Ctr. Tchr. Recruitment Policy Bd. Recipient Ralph Witherspoon award S.C. Assn. for Children Under Six; named Tchr. of Yr., Greenville County, 1992, 93, State of S.C., 1993, S.C. Tchr. of Yr. Coun. of Chief State Sch. Officers, 1993, 94. Mem. Assn. for Childhood Edn. Internat., S.C. Tchr. Forum (chmn. 1993-94), S.C. Early Childhood Assn., Alpha Delta Kappa. Presbyterian. Office: Mountain Park Elem Sch 1500 Pounds Rd SW Lilburn GA 30247

MAGILL, FRANK JOHN, federal judge; b. Verona, N.D., June 3, 1927; s. Thomas Charles and Viola Magill; m. Mary Louise Timlin, Nov. 22, 1955; children: Frank Jr., Marguerite Connolly, R. Daniel, Mary Elizabeth, Robert, John. BS in Fgn. Service, Georgetown U., 1951, LLB, 1955; MA, Columbia U., 1952. Ptnr. Nilles, Hansen, Magill & Davies, Ltd., Fargo, N.D., 1955-86; judge U.S. Ct. Appeals (8th cir.), Fargo, 1986—. Chmn. fin. disclosure com. U.S. Jud. Conf., 1993-96. Fellow Am. Coll. Trial Lawyers; mem. ABA (governing coun. pub. utilities sect. 1982-85, chmn. labor law com. 1981), N.D. Bar Assn. (chmn. legis com. 1975), Cass County Bar Assn. (pres. 1970). Republican. Avocations: tennis, sailing, skiing. Home: 1711 7th St S Fargo ND 58103-4945 Office: US Ct Appeals 8th Circuit 248 US PO & Fed Bldg 657 2nd Ave N Fargo ND 58102-4727

MAGILL, ROSALIND MAY, psychotherapist; b. Albany, N.Y., Apr. 27, 1944; d. Fenton Elliot Sr. and Rosalind Pearl (Gross) M.; m. Theodore T. Solomon, May 18, 1970 (div. 1980). Student, N.Y. Inst. Tech., 1963-64, Pace Coll., 1970-71; cert. in process piping design, Voorheese Tech. Inst., 1968; MEd in Counseling and Psychology, Cambridge Coll., 1994. Lic. master pipefitter, Mass.; EIT. Piping designer Badger Am., Inc., Cambridge, Mass., 1976-77; tchr. advanced math. Vision-in-Action, Natick, Mass., 1977-80; plumbing designer R. G. Vanderweil Assocs., Boston, 1980-81; vol. counselor alcohol/substance abuse social detox program Bergen County Hosp., Paramus, N.J., 1981-83; field engr. United Engrs. and Constructors, Phila., 1983-84; tchr. spl. edn. math. and sci. Amesbury (Mass.) High Sch., 1984-85; resident engr. Hoyle, Tanner Assocs., Londonderry, N.H., 1985-86; resident engr., constrn. mgr. dept. environ. mgmt. Commonwealth of Mass., Boston, 1986-89; clin. supr., counselor substance abuse Positive Lifestyles, Mattapan, Mass., 1990-93; dir. Respond Program, substance abuse therapist Ctr. for Family Devel., Lowell, Mass., 1993-94, dir. Respond Program, 1994—; counselor alcoholism and substance abuse Serenity House/Gift of Serenity, 1977-80; counselor substance abuse Baldpate Hosp., Georgetown, Mass., 1984.85. With USMC, 1962. N.Y. State Regent's scholar, 1962. Mem. ACA, Internat. Assn. Addictions and Offender Counselors, Women's Ordination Conf., Daus. Bilitis (pres. N.Y. chpt. 1968-70), Matachine Soc. (bd. dirs. 1968-70).

MAGILL, SAMUEL HAYS, retired academic administrator, higher education consultant; b. Decatur, Ga., July 19, 1928; s. Orrin Rankin and Ellen Howe (Bell) M.; m. Martha H. Carmichael, 1988; children: Samuel Hays Jr., Katherine Magill Walters, Suzanne Magill Weintraub. A.B., U. N.C., 1950; B.D., Yale U., 1953; Ph.D., Duke U., 1962; LHD (hon.), Stockton State Coll., 1990. Ordained to ministry Congl. Christian Ch., 1953; gen. sec. Davidson Coll. YMCA, 1953-55; dir. student activities U. N.C., Chapel Hill, 1955-58, asst. dean student affairs, 1958-59; chaplain Dickinson Coll., 1962-63, asst. prof. religion, 1962-66, asso. prof. religion, 1966-68, dean coll., 1963-68; pres. Council Protestant Colls. and Univs., Washington, 1968-70; exec. asso., chief office acad. affairs Assn. Am. Colls., 1971-76; pres. Simon's Rock Early Coll., Great Barrington, Mass., 1976-79; pres. Monmouth U., West Long Branch, N.J., 1980-93, pres. emeritus, 1993—; higher edn. cons., 1993—; adj. prof. Duke U., 1996. Trustee Jersey Shore Med. Ctr., 1985-93; bd. overseers N.J. Gov.'s Schs., 1986-93. Guerney Harris Kearns fellow in religion, 1960-61; Danforth Found. spl. grad. fellow, 1959-61. Fellow Soc. Values in Higher Edn. (dir. 1969-81); mem. Am. Assembly Collegiate Sch. Bus. (accreditation task force 1989-90), NCAA (pres.'s commn. 1990-93), Am. Coun. Edn. (commn. leadership devel. 1982-85, commn. on minority affairs 1986-89), Harvard Inst. Ednl. Mgmt., Assn. Ind. Colls. and Univs. N.J. (dir. 1980-93, exec. comm. 1983—, chair 1987-89), U.S. Assn. for Club of Rome, Order of Golden Fleece U. N.C., Delta Psi, Omicron Delta Kappa. Home: 1058 Fearrington Post Pittsboro NC 27312

MAGINN, STEPHEN ARTHUR, financial company executive; b. Orange, N.J., Mar. 5, 1952; s. Wallace Alton and La Verne (Chappell) M.; m. Linda Marie Stewart, Oct. 7, 1989; children: Brett Marshall, Todd Randall, Ryan Michael, Sean Christopher. BS in Commerce, U. Va., 1974. Cert. gen. securities prin. Nat. Assn. Securities Dealers. Securities broker Merrill Lynch, Newark, 1974-77, A.G. Becker, Inc., N.Y.C., 1977-79; regional v.p. Petro-Lewis Securities Corp., Denver, 1979-85; sr. v.p., co-founder Greystone Securities, Evergreen, Colo., 1985-86; regional v.p. NTS Securities, Louisville, 1986-87; sr. v.p., regional mgr. G.T. Global Fin. Svcs., San Francisco, 1987—. Mem. Internat. Assn. for Fin. Planning (nat. bd. dirs.). Avocations: golf, fine wine collecting, sailing. Home: 519 S Juanita Ave Redondo Beach CA 90277-3827 Office: 55 California St 27th Fl San Francisco CA 94111

MAGLACAS, A. MANGAY, nursing researcher. BSN, Vanderbilt U.; MPH, U. Minn.; DPH, Johns Hopkins U.; DS (hon.), U. Ill., 1987. Chief sci. for nursing divsn. health manpower devel. WHO, Cologny, Switzerland; adj. prof. Coll. Nursing, U. Ill., Chgo.; various vis. prof. positions in U.S., The Philippines, Thailand, Papua New Guinea, Japan, USSR, Australia; cons. in field. Rockefeller fellow, 1964-67; Fulbright-Smith-Mundt scholar, 1952-54. Mem. Internat. Coun. Nurses (bd. dirs.), NAS (fgn. assoc.). Office: 59 Chemin de Planta, CH-1223 Cologny Switzerland

MAGLICH, BOGDAN CASTLE, physicist; b. Yugoslavia, Aug. 5, 1938; came to U.S., 1956, naturalized, 1972; s. Cveta and Ivanka (Bingulac) M.; m. Victoria Vesna; children: Marko Castle, Ivanka Taylor, Roberta Cveta, Angelica Dara, Aleksandra Mara Nadine. Diploma physics, U. Belgrade, 1951; MS, U. Liverpool, Eng., 1955; PhD, MIT, 1959. Staff mem. Lawrence Berkeley Lab., 1959-62; dep. group leader Brit. group, 1962-63; leader Swiss group CERN European Orgn. Nuclear Rsch., 1964-67; vis. prof., joint faculty mem. Princeton U.-U. Pa. accelerator U. Pa., 1967-69; prof. physics, prin. investigator high energy physics Rutgers U., 1969-74; pres., chmn. Fusion Energy Corp., Princeton, N.J., 1972-81, Aneutronix, Inc., 1982-83, Sci. Transfer Assocs., Inc., 1981-84, United Scis., Inc., 1984-87, AE Labs Aneutronic Energy Lab., Inc., 1986-88; pres. Advanced Physics Corp., 1988-94; chmn. Advanced Projects Group, Inc., 1994—; chmn. The Tesla Found., 1985—; resident scientist UN-ILO Seminar Econ. Devel. East Africa, Kenya, 1967; lectr. Postdoctoral Sch. Physics, Yerevan, USSR, 1965, Internat. Sch. Majorana, Italy, 1969; mem. U.S. delegation Internat. Conf. High Energy Physics, Vienna, 1968, Kiev, 1970; spl. rep. of U.S. Pres. to Yugoslavia, 1976; sci. project dir. Univ. Research Ctr., King Abdulaziz U., Saudi Arabia, 1981-82; prin. investigator for aneutronic energy USAF Weapons Lab., 1985-87, USAF Space Tech. Ctr., 1988-89. Editor: Adventures in Exptl. Physics, 1972-80, Living Physics Video Jour. Chmn. Yugoslav-Am. Bicentennial Com., 1975-76; co-chmn. Serbian-Am. Com. for a Dem. Yugoslavia, 1989—; pres. World Serbian Union, Geneva, 1990-92. Recipient White House citation, 1961; Bourgeois d'honneur de Lens Switzerland, 1973; UNESCO fellow, 1957-58. Fellow Am. Phys. Soc.; mem. Serbian Acad. Scis. and Arts (Yugoslavia), Ripon Soc. (bd. govs.), Nassau Club, MIT Club, Sigma Xi. Mem. Serbian Orthodox Ch. Discoverer omega-meson, sonic spark chamber, missing-mass spectrometer, delta-meson, g-meson, S, T and U-mesons, precetron, self collider migma, aneutronic energy process; patentee in field.

MAGLIOCCO, JOHN, wholesale distribution executive; b. 1942. BS in Econs., U. Pa., 1963. With Peerless Importers Inc., 1963—, v.p., 1965-77, pres., 1978-85, chmn., 1986, CEO. Office: 16 Bridgewater St Brooklyn NY 11222

MAGNABOSCO, LOUIS MARIO, chemical engineer, researcher, consultant; b. Glarus, Switzerland, Nov. 29, 1938; s. Josef and Maria (Schlittler) M.; m. Vreni S. Zentner, Mar. 18, 1966 (div. Sept. 1985); 1 child, Henry Louis; m. D'Ella P. Phelon, Apr. 25, 1990; 1 child, Deon M. BSChemE, Swiss Fed. Inst. Tech., Zurich, 1961, MSChemE, 1963, ScD, 1967. Sr. scientist FMC Corp., Santa Clara, Calif., 1967-68; from engr. to project engr. Shell Devel. Co., Emeryville, Calif., 1968-72; sr. engr. Shell Devel. Co., Houston, 1972-74, staff engr., 1974-76; processing specialist ARCO, Harvey, Ill., 1976-79; mgr. process devel. ARCO, Harvey, 1979-85; cons. Magna Assocs., Olympia Fields, Ill., 1985-87; mgr. processes and catalysis Enimont, Zurich, 1987-90; pres. Chem. Engring. Ptnrs., Newport Beach, Calif., 1990-93; v.p. R&D Intercat, Sea Girt, N.J., 1993-94; cons. Magna Assocs., 1994—. Contbr. articles to internat. profl. jours.; conducted seminars and gave lectures on hydroprocessing internationally in petroleum field. Mem. AIChE, AAAS, Am. Chem. Soc. Catalysis Club. Achievements include: invention and development of Fluid Catalytic Cracking Sulfur Oxide Reduction Tech. (DESOX and NOSOX technologies); developer of math. models for: hydrotreating, hydrocracking, other petroleum processes, recycling tech. used motor oils, semi-synthetic lube oil process (H-H process). Avocations: reading, tennis, travels.

MAGNANO, SALVATORE PAUL, retired financial executive, treasurer; b. Portland, Conn., Jan. 10, 1934; s. Salvatore and Lucy (Dimodica) M.; m. Lois Jewel Johnson, July 16, 1955; children: Paul C., Mark J., Peter E. B.Metall. Engring., Rensselaer Poly. Inst., Troy, N.Y., 1955; MBA, Northwestern U., Chgo., 1959. Div. controller Sanders Assocs., Inc., Nashua, N.H., 1962-73; v.p., controller Teledyne Mec, Palo Alto, Calif., 1973-75; div. controller Sanders Assocs., Inc., Nashua, 1975-79; grp. controller Sanders Assocs., Inc., 1979-81, grp. v.p., controller, 1981-86, v.p. fin. and treas., 1986-96; ind. cons. Pres. Boys Club of Nashua, 1988-89, bd. dirs., 1981—; bd. dirs. Boys Club of Nashua Charitable Found., 1991—; trustee Daniel Webster Coll., Nashua, 1993—. Lt. USN, 1955-57. Mem. Am. Mgmt. Assn., Fin. Execs. Inst., Beta Gamma Sigma (award for excellence 1959).

MAGNANTI, THOMAS L., management and engineering educator; b. Omaha, Oct. 7, 1945; s. Leo A. and Florence L. Magnanti; m. Beverly A. McVinney, June 10, 1967; 1 child, R. Randall. BS in Chem. Engring., Syracuse U., 1967; MS in Stats., Stanford U., 1969, MS in Math., 1971, PhD in Ops. Rsch., 1972; Doktor honoris causa, Linköping U., 1995. Asst. prof. Alfred P. Sloan Sch. Mgmt. MIT, Cambridge, Mass., 1971-75; rsch. fellow, vis. prof. Ctr. for Ops. Rsch. and Econometrics Univ. Catholique de Louvain, 1976-77, 89; assoc. prof. Alfred P. Sloan Sch. Mgmt. MIT, 1975-79, prof., 1979-85, George Eastman prof. of mgmt. sci., 1985—, head mgmt. sci. area, 1982-88, co-dir. Ops. Rsch. Ctr., 1986—, founding co-dir. Leaders for Mfg. Program, 1988-94, prof. dept. elec. engring. and computer sci., 1995—; founding co-dir. System Design and Mgmt. Program, 1995—; vis. scientist Bell Labs., 1977, GTE Labs., 1989; vis. scholar Grad. Sch. Bus. Adminstrn., Harvard U., 1980-81; mem. corp. mfg. staff Digital Equipment Corp., 1990; mem. editl. bd. Jour. Computational Optimization and Applications; mem. adv. bd. North Holland Handbooks in Ops. Rsch. and Mgmt. Sci. Author: Applied Mathematical Programming, 1977, Network Flows, 1993; editor: Jour. Ops. Rsch., 1983-87; co-editor: Math. Programming, 1981-83; assoc. editor SIAM Jour. Algebraic and Discrete Methods, 1981-83, Mgmt. Sci., 1978-81, Ops. Rsch., 1978-81, SIAM Jour. Applied Math., 1976-81, Math. Programming, 1988—; adv. editor Transp. Sci., 1985—, Mktg. Sci., Math. of Artificial Intelligence, 1987-91; contbr. numerous articles to profl. jours. Mem. NSF Sci. and Tech. Exchange Delegation to Soviet Union, 1977, NSF Rsch. Initiation Grant panels, 1985, 90; advisor NSF program on decision, risk and mgmt. sci., 1988, 89; mem. mfg. studies bd. Nat. Rsch. Coun., 1993—. Recipient Gordon Billard award MIT, 1992; Mgmt. Program Exch. grantee IREX, Curriculum Devel. grantee Sloan Found., 1990-94. Mem. IEEE (com. on large scale systems 1979-83), TIMS (mem. and chmn. various coms.), Nat. Acad. Engring., Ops. Rsch. Soc. Am. (pres. 1988-89, mem. and chmn. various coms., coun. mem. computer sci. tech. sect. 1983-87, co-organizer 1st doctoral consortium 1983, plenary speaker conf. on telecom. 1983, Lanchester prize 1993, Kimball medal 1994), Tau Beta Pi, Pi Mu Epsilon, Phi Kappa Phi. Achievements include research in network analysis and optimization, network design and combinatorial optimization, and applications in manufacturing, telecommunications, and transportation; development of new engineering/management programs. Home: 33 School St Hopkinton MA 01748-2003 Office: MIT Ops Rsch Ctr 77 Massachusetts Ave Cambridge MA 02139-4301

MAGNER, FREDRIC MICHAEL, financial services executive; b. June 27, 1950; m. Rachel Harris, May 14, 1972. BA in Internat. Studies, U. S.C., 1971, MBA, 1972; M of Accountancy, U. So. Calif., 1976. Cert. in mgmt. acctg. Mktg. rep. IBM, L.A., 1976-79; v.p. First Interstate Services Co., El Segundo, Calif., 1979-82, First Interstate Bancorp, Los Angeles, 1982-83; sr. v.p. First Interstate System, L.A., 1983-86, First Interstate Bancorp, L.A., 1986-95; prin. Treasury Svcs. Corp., Santa Monica, Calif., 1995—. Capt. USAF, 1973-76. Mem. Carolina Club of So. Calif. (pres. 1990-95). Home: 2200 Pine Ave Manhattan Beach CA 90266-2833 Office: Treasury Svcs Corp 604 Arizona Ave Santa Monica CA 90401

MAGNER, JEROME ALLEN, entertainment company executive; b. Bklyn., Mar. 14, 1929; s. Herman and Evelyn I. (Wolfe) M.; BBA cum laude, CCNY, 1951; m. Frances Ogens, Mar. 22, 1953; children: Merrill, Steven. Asst. to treas., chief acct. Grayson-Robinson Stores, Inc., S. Klein Dept. Stores, Inc., N.Y.C., 1951-59; controller Food Fair Properties, N.Y.C., 1959-61; v.p., controller Am. Leisure Products Corp., N.Y.C. and Providence, 1961-69; sr. v.p. fin., treas., CFO Nat. Amusements, Inc., NE Theatre Corp., Dedham, 1969—. Mem. Met. Controllers Congress, Nat. Assn. Accts., Am. Mgmt. Assn., Nat. Assn. Theatre Owners (bd. dirs.), CCNY Alumni Assn. Office: Nat Amusements Inc 200 Elm St Dedham MA 02026-4536

MAGNESS, BOB JOHN, telecommunications executive; b. Clinton, Okla., 1924; married. Grad., South Western State Coll., 1949. Chmn. Tele-Communications, Inc., Denver; chmn. Community Tele-Communications, Inc.; bd. dirs. Republic Pictures Corp., WestMarc Communications, United Artists Communications, Inc. Office: Tele-Comm Inc PO Box 5630 Denver CO 80217-5630*

MAGNESS, RHONDA ANN, microbiologist; b. Stockton, Calif., Jan. 30, 1946; d. John Pershing and Dorothy Waneta (Kelley) Wetter; m. Barney LeRoy Bender, Aug. 26, 1965 (div. 1977); m. Gary D. Magness, Mar. 5, 1977; children: Jay D. (dec.), Troy D. BS, Calif. State U., 1977. Lic. clin. lab. technologist, Calif., med. technologist; cert. clin. lab. scientist. Med. asst. C. Fred Wilcox, MD, Stockton, 1965-66; clk. typist Dept. of U.S. Army, Ft. Eustis, Va., 1967, Def. Supply Agy., New Orleans, 1967-68; med. asst. James G. Cross, MD, Lodi, Calif., 1969, Arthur A. Kemalyan, MD, Lodi, 1969-71, 72-77; med. sec. Lodi Meml. Hosp., 1972; lab. aide Calif. State U., Sacramento, 1977; phlebotomist St. Joseph's Hosp., Stockton, 1978-79; supr. microbiology Dameron Hosp. Assn., Stockton, 1980—. Active Concerned Women Am., Washington, 1987—. Mem. AAUW, Calif. Assn. Clin. Lab. Technologists, San Joaquin County Med. Assts. Assn., Nat. Geog. Soc., Nat. Audubon Soc. Baptist. Lodge: Jobs Daus. (chaplain 1962-63). Avocations: boating, snow and water skiing, birding, sewing, reading. Home: 9627 Knight Ln Stockton CA 95209-1961 Office: Dameron Hosp Lab 525 W Acacia St Stockton CA 95203-2405

MAGNOLI, MICHAEL A., academic official. Pres. Mobile (Ala.) Coll. Office: Univ Mobile PO Box 13220 Mobile AL 36663-0220

MAGNUS, FREDERICK SAMUEL, investment banker; b. Montclair, N.J., Aug. 26, 1932; s. Robert Frederick and Cora (Argue) M. BA, Rutgers U., 1954. Rep., T.L. Watson Co., 1956-57, Goodbody & Co., 1957-58; pres., dir. Godfrey Hamilton & Magnus Co., 1958-61; pres., dir. Magnus & Co., Inc., Clifton, 1961—. With U.S. Army, 1954-56. Office: Magnus & Co Inc 575 Grove St Clifton NJ 07013-3177

MAGNUSON, HAROLD JOSEPH, physician; b. Halstead, Kans., Mar. 31, 1913; s. Joseph Simeon and Margaret Ethel (Matson) M.; m. Ruth Prusia, Feb. 16, 1935 (dec. 1941); children: Karen Margaret Magnuson Mauro), Ruth Ellen; m. Kathryne I. Bause, Dec. 20, 1941 (dec. 1993). AB, U. So. Calif., 1934, MD, 1938; MPH, Johns Hopkins U., 1942. Diplomate: Am. Bd. Preventive Medicine (mem. bd. 1964-75, vice chmn. occupational medicine 1968-75). Intern Los Angeles County Gen. Hosp., 1937-39; research fellow A.C.P., 1939-40; instr. medicine U. So. Calif., 1939-41; commd. asst. surgeon USPHS, 1941, med. dir., 1952; instr. medicine Johns Hopkins, 1943-46; research prof. exptl. medicine U. N.C., 1946-55; chief div. occupational health USPHS, 1956-62; ret., 1962; prof. internal medicine U. Mich. Sch. Medicine, prof. indsl. health, 1962-76, prof. emeritus, 1976—; chmn. dept. U. Mich. Sch. Pub. Health; also dir. U. Mich. Sch. Pub. Health (Inst. Indsl. Health), 1962-69; asso. dean U. Mich. Sch. Pub. Health (Sch. Pub. Health), 1969-76; Mem. U.S. delegation ILO Conf., 1958, 59; Chmn. U.S. indsl. toxicology delegation to, USSR, 1963. Fellow A.C.P., A.A.A.S., A.M.A. (chmn. sect. preventive medicine 1966, Hektoen bronze medal 1956), Am. Acad. Occupational Medicine, Am. Pub. Health Assn. (chmn. sect. occupational health 1966, Indsl. Med. Assn., Knudsen award 1970); mem. Soc. Clin. Investigation, Soc. Exptl. Biology and Medicine, Soc. Exptl. Pathology, Mich. Indsl. Med. Assn. (pres. 1965-66), Internat. Congress Indsl. Medicine (v.p. 1969), Rammazzini Soc., Phi Beta Kappa, Sigma Xi, Alpha Omega Alpha, Delta Omega. Home: 18755 W Bernardo Dr Apt 1125 San Diego CA 92127-3023

MAGNUSON, JOHN JOSEPH, zoology educator; b. Evanston, Ill., Mar. 8, 1934. BS, U. Minn., 1956, MS, 1958; PhD in Zoology, U. B.C., 1961. Chief tuna behavior program Biol. Lab. Bur. Comml. Fisheries U.S. Fish & Wildlife Svc., 1961-67; program dir. ecology NSF, 1975-76; asst. prof. to assoc. prof. Trout Lake Biol. Sta. U. Wis., Madison, 1968-74, chmn. oceanography & limnology grad. program, 1978-83, 86, prof. zoology, dir. Troup Lake Biol. Sta., 1974—, dir. Ctr. Limnology, 1982—; chmn. Aquatic Ecol. sect. Ecol. Soc. Am., 1975-76; chair Ocean Studies Bd. Com. Fisheries, Nat. Rsch. Coun., 1981-83, 93—; chmn. Com. Sea Turtle Conservancy, 1989-90, Com. Protection & Mgmt. Pacific N.W. Anadromous Salmonids, 1992-94; tri-chair Mgmt. Com. Coastal Ocean Program Coastal Fisheries Ecoysstems component, NOAA. NSF Midcareer fellow U. Wash., 1992. Fellow AAAS; mem. Am. Fisheries Soc. (pres. 1981, Disting. Svc. award 1980), Am. Soc. Limnology & Oceanography, Ecol. Soc. Am., Soc. Internat. Limnology. Office: Univ Wisconsin Madison Ctr Limnology 680 N Park St Madison WI 53706*

MAGNUSON, NANCY, librarian; b. Seattle, Aug. 15, 1944; d. James Leslie and Jeanette (Thomas) M.; 2 sons, Daniel Johnson, Erik Johnson. BA in History, 1977; MLS, U. Wash., 1978. With. King County Libr. System, Seattle, 1973-80; rsch. asst. Free Libr. Phila., 1980-81; asst. libr. Haverford (Pa.) Coll., 1981-87; libr. dir. Goucher Coll., Balt., Md., 1987—. Contbr. to profl. publs. Mem. ALA (com. on status of women in librarianship, various others), Online Computer Libr. Ctr. Users Coun., Md. Libr. Assn., Congress Acad. Libr. Dirs., NOW, Women's Internat. League for Peace and Freedom, Balt. Bibliophiles, Jane Austen Soc. N.Am. Democrat. Office: Goucher Coll Julia Rogers Libr 1021 Dulaney Valley Rd Baltimore MD 21204-2753

MAGNUSON, NORRIS ALDEN, librarian, history educator; b. Midale, Saskatchewan, Can., June 15, 1932; s. George August and Esther Lydia (Eliason) M.; m. Beverly Sue Carlson, Aug. 17, 1956; children: Douglas, Timothy, Kenneth, Daniel. BA, Bethel Coll., 1954; BD, Bethel Sem., 1958; MA, U. Minn., 1961, PhD, 1968. Instr., asst. libr. Bethel Theol. Sem., St. Paul, Minn., 1959-65, asst. prof., asst. libr., 1965-68, assoc. prof., assoc. libr., 1968-72, prof., head libr., 1972—; chair hist. com. Bapt. Gen. Conf., Arlington Heights, Ill., 1974—; mem. Conf. on Faith and History. Author: Salvation in the Slums, 1977, 2d edit., 1990, Missionsskolan: The History, 1982; editor: Proclaim the Good News, 1986; author: (with others) American Evangelism, 1990, 2d edit., 1996. Mem. Salem Bapt. Ch., chairperson, 1972-73. U. Minn. scholar, 1961-63; Inst. for Advanced Christian Studies fellow, 1968-69. Mem. Am. Theol. Libr. Assn., Minn. Theol. Libr. Assn. (pres. 1974-75, 79-80, 84-85, 88-89). Avocations: tennis, handball, racquetball, travelling. Office: Bethel Coll & Sem 3900 Bethel Dr Saint Paul MN 55112-6902

MAGNUSON, PAUL ARTHUR, federal judge; b. Carthage, S.D., Feb. 9, 1937; s. Arthur and Emma Elleda (Paulson) M.; m. Sharon Schultz, Dec. 21, 1959; children—Marlene, Margaret, Kevin, Kara. B.A., Gustavus Adolphus Coll, 1959; J.D., William Mitchell Coll., 1963. Bar: Minn. 1963, U.S. Dist. Ct. Minn. 1968. Claim adjuster Agrl. Ins. Co., 1960-62; clk. Bertie & Bettenberg Law Firm, 1962-63; ptnr. LeVander, Gillen, Miller & Magnuson, South St. Paul, Minn., 1963-81; judge U.S. Dist. Ct. Minn., St. Paul, 1981—, chief judge, 1995—; jurist-in-residence Hamline U. Law Sch., lectr., 1985; lectr. Augsberg Coll., 1986, Bethel Coll., 1986, Concordia Coll., St. Paul, 1987, U. Minn., Morris, 1987; instr. William Mitchell Coll. Law, 1984—. Mem. Met. Health Bd., St. Paul, 1970-72; legal counsel Ind. Republican Party Minn., St. Paul, 1979-81. Recipient Disting. Alumnus award Gustavus Adolphus Coll., 1982. Mem. ABA, 1st Dist. Bar Assn. (pres. 1974-75), Dakota County Bar Assn., Am. Judicature Soc. Presbyterian. Home: 3047 Klondike Ave N Lake Elmo MN 55042-9717 Office: US Dist Ct 730 Burger US Courthouse 316 Robert St N Saint Paul MN 55101-1423

MAGNUSON, ROBERT MARTIN, retired hospital administrator; b. Chgo., June 28, 1927; s. Martin David and Adena Marie (Hallberg) M.; m. Patricia Ann McNaughton, Dec. 30, 1960; children: Thomas Martin, Dana Caroline. B.S. cum laude, Lake Forest (Ill.) Coll., 1951; M.B.A., Harvard U., 1955. Factory budget mgr., asst. budget dir. Zenith Radio Corp., Chgo., 1955-57; asst. adminstr., controller Elmhurst Meml. Hosp., (Ill.), 1957-64; asso. adminstr. Elmhurst Meml. Hosp., 1964-66, pres., 1966-92; officer, dir. Chgo. Hosp. Council, 1972-79, chmn. bd. dirs., 1983; mem. hosp. adv. council Ill. Dept. Pub. Health, 1972-76; faculty preceptor U. Chgo. Program in Hosp. Adminstrn., 1971-92, Northwestern U. Program in Hosp. and Health Sci. Adminstrn., 1972-92; dir. DuPage County Community Nursing Service, 1964-67, Health Chgo. HMO, 1984-92, Elmhurst Fed. Savs. & Loan Assn., 1971-92; pres. Meml. Health Services, Inc., 1980-92. Pres. Elmhurst Meml. Hosp. Found., 1980-92. Served with USN, 1945-48, 51-52. Mem. Am. Coll. Health Care Execs., Ill. Hosp. Assn. (dist. pres. 1967-69, bd. dirs. 1985-90), Inter-Hosp. Planning Assn. of Western Suburbs (pres., dir.). Republican. Club: Medinah (Ill.) Country.

MAGNUSON, ROGER JAMES, lawyer; b. St. Paul, Jan. 25, 1945; s. Roy Gustaf and Ruth Lily (Edlund) M.; m. Elizabeth Cunningham Shaw, Sept. 11, 1982; children: James Roger, Peter Cunningham, Mary Kerstin, Sarah Ruth, Elizabeth Camilla, Anna Clara, John Edlund. BA, Stanford U., 1967; JD, Harvard U., 1971; BCL, Oxford U., 1972. Bar: Minn. 1973, U.S. Dist. Ct. Minn. 1973, U.S. Ct. Appeals (8th, 9th, 10th cirs.) 1974, U.S. Supreme Ct. 1978. Chief pub. defender Hennepin County Pub. Defender's Office, Mpls., 1973; ptnr. Dorsey & Whitney, Mpls., 1972—. Author: Shareholder Litigation, 1981, Are Gay Rights Right., The White-Collar Crime Explosion, 1992, Informed Answers To Gay Rights Questions, 1994; contbr. articles to profl. jours. Elder, Straitgate Ch., Mpls., 1980—. Mem. Christian Legal Soc., White Bear Yacht Club. Republican. Home: 625 Park Ave Saint Paul MN 55115-1663 Office: Dorsey & Whitney 220 S 6th St Minneapolis MN 55402-1498

MAGOR, LOUIS ROLAND, conductor; b. Auburn, Nebr., May 16, 1945; s. John William and Eleanor Lucille (Niemann) M. B.Mus. Edn., Northwestern U., 1967, Mus.M., 1974. Choral dir. Avoca Jr. High Sch., Wilmette, Ill., 1968-70; choral dir. Niles North High Sch., Skokie, Ill., 1970-73; dir. San Francisco Symphony Chorus, 1974-82, Schola Cantorum, 1982-85, San Francisco Boys Chorus, 1985-88; artistic dir. Seattle Bach Choir, 1990—; founder The Louis Magor Singers; mem. faculty San Francisco Conservatory of Music, 1976-78, San Francisco State U., 1979-80. Founder West Seattle Children's Chorus, 1990—; condr. Sing-It-Yourself Messiah, 1979-91, Calif. Symphony Chorus, 1990-92; exec. prodr. Sandy Bradley's Potluck, 1995—. Mem. Pi Kappa Lambda.

MAGOWAN, PETER ALDEN, professional baseball team executive, grocery chain executive; b. N.Y.C., Apr. 5, 1942; s. Robert Anderson and Doris (Merrill) M.; m. Jill Tarlau (div. July 1982; children—Kimberley, Margot, Hilary; m. Deborah Johnston, Aug. 14, 1982. BA, Stanford U.; MA, Oxford U., Eng.; postgrad., Johns Hopkins U. Store mgr. Safeway Stores Inc., Washington, 1968-70; dist. mgr. Safeway Stores Inc., Houston, 1970-71; retail ops. mgr. Safeway Stores Inc., Phoenix, 1971-72; div. mgr. Safeway Stores Inc., Tulsa, 1973-76; mgr. internat. div. Safeway Stores Inc., Toronto, Ont., Can., 1976-78; mgr. western region Safeway Stores Inc., San Francisco, 1978-79; chmn. bd., CEO Safeway Stores Inc., Oakland, Calif., 1980-93, chmn. bd., 1980—; pres., mng. gen. ptnr. San Francisco Giants, 1993—; bd. dirs. Chrysler Corp., Vons Cos. Inc., Caterpillar. Office: San Francisco Giants Candlestick Park San Francisco CA 94124

MAGRATH, C. PETER, educational association executive; b. N.Y.C., Apr. 23, 1933; s. Laurence Wilfrid and Giulia Maria (Dentice) M.; m. Deborah C. Howell, 1988; children: Valerie Ruth, Monette Fay. BA summa cum laude, U. N.H., 1955; PhD, Cornell U., 1962. Mem. faculty Brown U., Providence, 1961-68, prof. polit. sci., 1967-68, assoc. dean grad. sch., 1965-66; dean Coll. Arts and Scis. U. Nebr., Lincoln, 1968-69, dean faculties Coll. Arts and Scis., 1969-72, interim chancellor univ., 1971-72, prof. polit. sci., 1968-72, vice chancellor for acad. affairs, 1972; pres. SUNY, Binghamton, 1972-74, prof. polit. sci., 1972-74; pres. U. Minn., Mpls., 1974-84, U. Mo. System, 1985-91, Nat. Assn. State Univs. and Land Grant Colls., Washington, 1991—. Author: The Triumph of Character, 1963, Yazoo: Law and Politics in the New Republic, The Case of Fletcher v. Peck, 1966, Constitutionalism and Politics: Conflict and Consensus, 1968, Issues and Perspectives in American Government, 1971, (with others) The American Democracy, 2d edit., 1973, (with Robert L. Egbert) Strengthening Teacher Education, 1987; contbr. articles to profl. jours. Served with AUS, 1955-57. Mem. Assn. Am. Univs. (chmn. 1985-86), Phi Beta Kappa, Phi Kappa Phi, Pi Gamma Mu, Pi Sigma Alpha, Kappa Tau Alpha. Office: Nat Assn State U and Land Grant Colls 1 Dupont Cir NW Ste 710 Washington DC 20036-1110 *True personal success cannot be measured by public acclaim, recognition, or status. It grows out of an ability to recognize right from wrong, and to maintain principles of fairness and understanding in all human relationships - regardless of one's role in life. In my case I have tried to fulfill this ideal: I have been willing to exercise leadership by asserting my judgements and views openly and directly on the educational and human issues that came my way.*

MAGRILL, JOE RICHARD, JR., religious organization administrator, minister; b. Marshall, Tex., Aug. 7, 1946; s. Joe Richard and Mary Belle (Chadwick) M. BA summa cum laude, East Tex. State U., 1967; MDiv, Princeton Theol. Sem., 1970, MTh, 1972; MLS, Rutgers U., 1971. Ordained to ministry Cumberland Presbyn. Ch., 1970. Stated supply min. Newsome (Tex.) Cumberland Presbyn. Ch., 1966-67; Christian edn. asst. United Presbyn. Ch., Carlstadt, N.J., 1967-70; order libr. Princeton (N.J.) Theol. Sem., 1969-72; head libr., prof. Memphis Theol. Sem., 1972-79; pastor Brookhaven Cumberland Presbyn. Ch., Nashville, 1987-89; asst. to stated clk. Gen. Assembly Office, Cumberland Presbyn. Ch., Memphis, 1979-83, supr. ctrl. acctg. div., 1980-87, editor The Cumberland Presbyn., 1984-87, chief exec. bd. stewardship, 1989—, mem. Gen. Assembly Ctr., 1993—; mem. Trinity Presbytery of Cumberland Presbyn. Ch., 1970—; sec.-treas. Hist. Found. Cumberland Presbyn. Ch., Memphis, 1974—; bd. dirs. Hist. Found. Presbyn. Ch. U.S., Montreat, N.C., 1980-83. Editor: In the Valley of the Cauca, 1981, One Family Under God, 1982. Recipient achievement award Hist. Found. Cumberland Presbyn. Ch., 1980; scholar Phi Alpha Theta, 1967, Am. Theol. Libr. Assn., 1970. Democrat. Avocations: computers, historical research. Office: Cumberland Presbyn Ch Bd Stewardship 1978 Union Ave Memphis TN 38104-4134

MAGRILL, ROSE MARY, library director; b. Marshall, Tex., June 8, 1939; d. Joe Richard and Mary Belle (Chadwick) M. BS, E. Tex. State U., 1960, MA, 1961; MS, U. Ill., 1964, PhD, 1969. Asst. to dean women E. Tex. State U., Commerce, 1960-61, librarian II, 1961-63; teaching asst. U. Ill., Urbana, 1963-64; instr. to asst. prof. E. Tex. State U., Commerce, 1964-67; asst. prof. Ball State U., Muncie, 1969-70; asst. prof. to prof. U. Mich., Ann Arbor, 1970-81; prof. U. N. Tex., Denton, 1981—; dir. libr. E. Tex. Bapt. U., Marshall, 1987—; accreditation site visitor ALA, Chgo., 1975—; cons. in field. Co-author: Building Library Collections, 4th edit. 1974, Library Technical Services, 1977, Building Library Collections, 5th edit. 1979, Acquisition Management and Collection Development in Libraries, 2d edit. 1989. Trustee Memphis Theol. Sem., 1988—; treas. Mission Synod of Cumberland Presbyn. Ch., 1989—; bd. fin. Trinity Presbytery, 1989—; sec.-treas. Harrison County Hist. Commn., 1995—. Mem. ALA (RTSD Resources Sect. pub. award 1978), Tex. Libr. Assn. Home: 804 Caddo St Marshall TX 75670-2414 Office: E Tex Bapt Univ 1209 N Grove St Marshall TX 75670-1423

MAGRUDER, LAWSON WILLIAM, III, military officer; b. Bryan, Tex., Nov. 5, 1947; s. Lawson William Jr. and Maryanne (Windrow) M.; m. Gloria Ann Banton, July 26, 1969; children: Shannon, Loren, Matthew. BBA in Internat. Mktg., U. Tex., 1969; MA in Pers. Mgmt., Ctrl. Mich. U., 1979; student, U.S. Army Command Gen. Staff Coll., 1979, Army War Coll., 1986. Commd. 2d lt. U.S. Army, 1969, advanced through grades to maj. gen., 1995; rifle platoon leader 82d Airborne Divsn., Ft. Bragg, N.C., 1969-71, 23d Inf. Divsn., Vietnam; asst. brigade ops. officer, co. comdr. 82d Airborne Divsn., 1971-74; ranger co. comdr., bn. adj. 2d Ranger Bn., 1975-77; bn. ops. officer 9th Inf. Divsn., 1977-78; inf. assignment officer U.S. Total Army Pers. Command, 1979-82; brigade ops. officer 172d Light Inf. Brigade, Alaska; comdr. 5th bn. 327th Inf., Alaska, 1982-85; chief tactics, dep. dir. combined arms and tactics dept. U.S. Army Inf. Sch., Ft. Benning, Ga., 1986-88; comdr. 2d brigade 25th Inf. Divsn., Schofield Barracks, Hawaii, 1988-90; exec. asst. to dep. comdr.-in-chief, dep. dir. strategic policy and plans U.S. Pacific Command, 1990-92; asst. divsn. comdr. 10th Mountain Divsn.; comdr. Combined Task Force Kismayo, Somalia, 1992-93; comdg. gen. Joint Readiness Tng. Ctr. U.S. Army, Ft. Polk, La., 1993-95; comdg. gen. U.S. Army South, Ft. Clayton, Panama, 1995—. Pres. Ft. Benning Parish Coun., 1986-88; mem. Ft. Benning Sch. Bd., 1987-88. Decorated Bronze star medal with oak leaf cluster, Legion of Merit with two oak leaf clusters, Air medal, Army Commedation medal with one oak leaf cluster, Def. Superior Svc. medal, Meritorious Svc. medal with three oak leaf clusters. Roman Catholic. Avocations: golfing, running. Home: Quarters 1, Fort Amador Panama Office: Hqs US Army S Ft Clayton Panama APO AA 34004

MAGRY, MARTHA J., elementary education educator; b. Paragould, Ark., Jan. 6, 1936; d. Burrell F. and Georgia M. (Watkins) Spence; m. James Magry, June 28, 1958; 1 child, David J. BS, Wheaton (Ill.) Coll., 1957; MS, Ind. U. Northwest, Gary, 1985; postgrad., Ark. State U., Jonesboro, 1964. Cert. elem., gen. sci. tchr. 4th grade tchr. Gary City Schs., sci. tchr.; 2d grade tchr. Merrillville (Ind.) Community Schs. Mem. NEA, Ind. State Tchrs. Assn., Merrillville Classroom Tchrs. Assn. Home: 5312 Pierce St Merrillville IN 46410-1364

MAGUIRE, CHARLOTTE EDWARDS, retired physician; b. Richmond, Ind., Sept. 1, 1918; d. Joel Blaine and Lydia (Betscher) Edwards; m. Raymer Francis Maguire, Sept. 1, 1948 (dec.); children: Barbara, Thomas Clair II. Student, Stetson U., 1936-38, U. Wichita, 1938-39; BS, Memphis Tchrs. Coll., 1940; MD, U. Ark., 1944. Intern, resident Orange Meml. Hosp., Orlando, Fla., 1944-46; resident Bellevue Hosp. and Med. Ctr., NYU, N.Y.C., 1954, 55; instr. nurses Orange Meml. Hosp., 1947-57, staff mem., 1946-68; staff mem. Fla. Santarium and Hosp., Orlando, 1946-56, Holiday House and Hosp., Orlando, 1950-62; mem. courtesy and cons. staff West Orange Meml. Hosp., Winter Garden, Fla., 1952-67; active staff, chief dept. pediatrics Mercy Hosp., Orlando, 1965-68; med. dir. med. svcs. and basic care Fla. Dept. Health and Rehab. Svcs., 1975-84; med. exec. dir., med. svcs. divsn. worker's compensation Fla. Dept. Labor, Tallahassee, 1984-87; chief of staff physicians and dentists Ctrl. Fla. divsn. Children's Home Soc. Fla., 1947-56; dir. Orlando Child Health Clinic 1949-58; pvt. practice medicine Orlando, 1946-68; asst. regional dir. HEW, 1970-72; pediat. cons. Fla. Crippled Children's Commn., 1952-70, dir., 1968-70; med. dir. Office Med. Svcs. and Basic Care, sr. physician Office of Asst. Sec. Ops., Fla. Dept. Health and Rehab. Svcs.; clin. prof. dept. pediat. U. Fla. Coll. Medicine, Gainesville, 1980-87; mem. Fla. Drug Utilization Rev., 1983-87; real estate salesperson Investors Realty, 1982—; bd. dirs. Stavros Econ. Ctr. Fla. State U., Tallahassee; mem. pres.'s coun. Fla. State U., U. Fla., Gainesville. Mem. profl. adv. com. Fla. Center for Clin. Services at U. Fla., 1952-60; del. to Midcentury White House Conf. on Children and Youth, 1950; U.S. del from Nat. Soc. for Crippled Children to World Congress for Welfare of Cripples, Inc., London, 1957; pres of corp. Eccleston-Callahan Hosp. for Colored Crippled Children, 1956-58; sec. Fla. chpt. Nat. Doctor's Com. for Improved Med. Services, 1951-52; med. adv. com. Gateway Sch. for Mentally Retarded, 1959-62; bd. dirs. Forest Park Sch. for Spl. Edn. Crippled Children, 1949-54, mem. med. adv. com., 1955-68, chmn., 1957-68; mem. Fla. Adv. Council for Mentally Retarded, 1965-70; dir. central Fla. poison control Orange Meml. Hosp.; mem. orgn. com., chmn. com. for admissions and selection policies Camp Challenge; participant 12th session Fed. Exec. Inst., 1971; del. White House Conf. on Aging, 1980. Mem. AMA (life), Nat. Rehab. Assn., Am. Congress Phys. Medicine and Rehab., Fla. Soc. Crippled Children and Adults, Ctrl. Fla. Soc. Crippled Children and Adults (dir. 1949-58, pres. 1956-57), Am. Assn. Cleft Palate, Fla. Soc. Crippled Children (trustee 1951-57, v.p. 1956-57, profl. adv. com. 1957-68), Mental Health Assn. Orange County (charter mem.; pres. 1949-50, dir. 1947-52, chmn. exec. com. 1950-52, dir. 1963-65), Fla. Orange County Heart Assn., Am. Med. Women's Assn., Am. Acad. Med. Dirs., Fla. Med. Assn. (chmn. com. on mental retardation), Orange County Med. Assn., Orange Med. Soc. (life), Fla. Pediatric Soc. (pres. 1952-53), Fla. Cleft Palate Assn. (counselor-at-large, sec.), Nat. Inst. Geneal. Rsch., Nat. Geneal. Soc., Assn. Profl. Genealogists, Tallahassee Geneal. Soc., Fla. State U. Found. Inc. (bd. dirs. Stavoris Ctr. for Econ. Edn.). Club: Governors. Home: 4158 Covenant Ln Tallahassee FL 32308-5765

MAGUIRE, DEBORAH A., insurance and securities executive; b. Bronx, N.Y., Apr. 27, 1963; d. Richard and Marie (Odell) Nanfeldt; m. Gregory M. Maguire, Oct. 10, 1987. BA cum laude, Fairfield U., 1985. Lic. ins. and securities broker. Customer svc. rep. Shadow Lawn Savings and Loan Assn., Middletown, N.J., 1984-85; account rep. Hayt, Hayt and Landau, Esqs., Eatontown, N.J., 1985-87; from dist. svc. mgr. to asst. v.p., sr. account mgr. Liberty Securities Corp. (formerly Pamco Securities and Ins), Encino, Calif., 1988-94; now nat. dir. tng. Liberty Securities Corp. (formerly Pamco Securities and Ins), Boston, 1994—. Author: (screenplay) Consent of the Governed, 1983. Asst. to campaign mgr. Howard for Congress, Middletown, 1986, Pallone for Congress, Middletown, 1988; com. person Middletown Dem., 1990, 91; media cons. Jacki Walker for Assembly, Middletown, 1985. Mem. NAFE, Alpha Sigma Nu, Pi Sigma Alpha (v.p. 1984-85). Avocations: travel, furniture refinishing, reading, politics, writing. Office: Liberty Securities Corp 600 Atlantic Ave Boston MA 02210-2211

MAGUIRE, HENRY CLINTON, JR., dermatologist; b. N.Y.C., May 4, 1928; s. Henry Clinton Sr. and Elsie (Smith) M.; m. Elise Avallon; children: Jean Emily, Henry Clinton III, Albert Mahler. BA in Philosophy, Princeton U., 1947; MD, U. Chgo., 1954. Diplomate Am. Bd. Dermatology. Resident in dermatology U. Pa. Hosp., Phila., 1958-61, assoc., 1961-64, asst. prof. dermatology, 1964-66; guest investigator Rockefeller U., N.Y.C., 1966-67; assoc. prof. dermatology Hahnemann Med. Coll., Phila., 1967-77; vis. scientist Inst. Cancer Research, Phila., 1972-75; prof. dermatology, microbiology and immunology Hahnemann Med. Coll., Phila., 1975-87, chmn. dermatology, 1979-87, adj. prof. microbiology and immunology, 1987—; with pigmented lesion clinic Fox Chase Cancer Ctr., Phila., 1979-84; sr. research investigator dept. pathology U. Pa., Phila., 1986-90; adj. clin. rsch. prof. oncology Thomas Jefferson U. Med. Sch., Phila., 1984-90, rsch. prof. oncology and dermatology, 1990—; adj. prof. U. Pa. Sch. Vet. Medicine, Phila., 1978—; mem. study sect exptl. therapeutics 2 Nat. Cancer Inst., NIH, 1984-88; mem. biol. response modifier com. Ea. Coop. Oncology Group, 1983-86. Mem. editl. bd. Seminars in Oncology, 1983-93; contbr. articles to profl. jours. Served to capt. U.S. Army, 1956-58. Fellow Am. Acad. Dermatology, Phila. Coll. Physicians, Phila. Dermatol. Soc. (past pres.); mem. Am. Assn. Cancer Rsch., Am. Assn. Immunology, Soc. Investigative Dermatology, Am. Soc. Microbiology (past chmn. program com. ea. br.), Sigma Xi. Avocations: baroque music, tennis. Home: 409 N Latches Ln Merion Station PA 19066-1730 Office: Thomas Jefferson U Med Sch Divsn Med Oncology Curtis Bldg Ste 1024 Philadelphia PA 19107

MAGUIRE, JOHN DAVID, academic administrator, educator, writer; b. Montgomery, Ala., Aug. 7, 1932; s. John Henry and Clyde (Merrill) M.; m. Lillian Louise Parrish, Aug. 29, 1953; children: Catherine Merrill, Mary Elizabeth, Anne King. A.B. magna cum laude, Washington and Lee U., 1953, Litt.D. (hon.), 1979; Fulbright scholar, Edinburgh (Scotland) U., 1953-54; B.D. summa cum laude, Yale, 1956, Ph.D., 1960; postdoctoral research, Yale U. and U. Tübingen, Germany, 1964-65, U. Calif., Berkeley, 1968-69, Silliman U., Philippines, 1976-77; HLD (hon.), Transylvania U., 1990. Dir. Internat. Student Ctr., New Haven, 1956-58; mem. faculty Wesleyan U., Middletown, Conn., 1960-70; asso. provost Wesleyan U., 1967-68; vis. lectr. Pacific Sch. Religion and Grad. Theol. Union, Berkeley, 1968-69; pres. SUNY Coll. at Old Westbury, 1970-81, Claremont (Calif.) U. Ctr. and Grad. Sch., 1981—. Author: The Dance of the Pilgrim: A Christian Style of Life for Today, 1967; also numerous articles. Mem. Conn. adv. com. U.S. Commn. Civil Rights, 1961-70; participant White House Conf. on Civil Rights, 1966; advisor, permanent trustee and 1st chmn. bd. dirs. Martin Luther King Ctr. for Social Change, Atlanta, 1968—; bd. dirs. Nassau County Health and Welfare Coun., 1971-81, pres., 1974-76; trustee United Bd. Christian Higher Edn. in Asia, 1975-81, Inst. Internat. Edn., 1980-86, The Tomás Rivera Ctr., Claremont, Calif., 1984—, vice chmn., 1987-94, treas., 1995—, Assn. Ind. Calif. Colls. and Univs., 1985—, chmn. 1990-92, mem. exec. com., 1992—, The Calif. Achievement Coun., 1985-94, chmn. 1990-94, Transylvania U. Bingham Trust, 1987—, Lincoln Found. and Lincoln Inst. of Land Policy, Inc., 1987-94, The JL Found., 1988—, The Bus. Enterprise Trust, 1989—, Ednl. Found. for African Ams., 1991—; bd. dirs. Assn. Am. Colls. and Univs., 1981-86, chmn., 1984-85; bd. dirs. Legal Def. and Edn. Fund. NAACP, 1991—, west coast div., 1981—, Thacher Sch., Ojai, Calif., 1982-94, vice chmn., 1986-90, Salzburg Seminar, 1992—; charter mem. Pacific Coun. Internat. Policy, 1995—; mem. Am. Com. on U.S.-Soviet Rels., 1981-92, Blue Ribbon Calif. Commn. on Teaching Profession, 1984-86; mem. governing coun. Aspen Inst. Wye Faculty Seminar, 1984-94; mem. Coun. on Fgn. Rels., 1983—; adv. bd. RAND Ctr. Rsch. Immigration Policy, 1994—; mem. Pres.'s Adv. Coun. to Commn. on Calif. Master Plan for Higher Edn., 1986-87, L.A. Ednl. Alliance for Restructuring Now, 1992—, Calif. Bus. Higher Edn. Forum, 1992—. Recipient Julia A. Archibald High Scholarship award Yale Div. Sch., 1956; Day fellow Yale Grad. Sch., 1956-57; Kent fellow, 1957-60; Howard Found. postdoctoral fellow Brown U. Grad. Sch., 1964-65; Fenn lectr., 7 Asian countries, 1976-77; recipient Conn. Prince Hall Masons' award outstanding contbns. human rights in Conn., 1965; E. Harris Harbison Gt. Tchr. prize Danforth Found., 1968. Fellow Soc. Values Higher Edn. (pres. 1974-81, bd. dirs. 1972-88); mem. Phi Beta Kappa, Omicron Delta Kappa. Democrat. Office: Claremont U Ctr & Grad Sch Office of Pres 160 E 10th St Claremont CA 91711-5909

MAGUIRE, JOHN PATRICK, investment company executive; b. New Britain, Conn., Apr. 1, 1917; s. John Patrick and Edna Frances (Cashen) M.; m. Mary-Emily Jones, Sept. 8, 1945; children: Peter Dunbar (dec.), Joan Guilford. Student, Holy Cross Coll., 1933-34; degree in bus. adminstrn. with distinction, Babson Inst., 1936; A.B. cum laude, Princeton U., 1941; BS (hon.), Babson Inst., 1995, Babson Coll., 1995; J.D., Yale U., 1943; PhD (hon.), St. Bonaventure U., 1965. Bar: Conn. 1943, N.Y. 1944. Asso. Cravath, Swaine & Moore (and predecessor), N.Y.C., 1943-50, 52-54; v.p., dir. Forbes, Inc.; also mng. editor Investors Adv. Inst., 1951-52; asst. counsel Gen. Dynamics Corp., 1954-60, sec., 1962-87, v.p., 1981-87; sec., gen. counsel Tex. Butadiene and Chem. Corp., 1960-62; with J.P. Maguire Investment Advisors, 1987-95; exec. v.p. Fiduciary Asset Mgmt. Co., 1995—. Mem. bd. govs. N.Y. Young Rep. Club, 1951-52; chmn. fin. and investment coms. St. Louis Art Mus., 1984-94; trustee St. Bonaventure U., 1965-71, Webster U., 1983-85, John Burroughs Sch. (chmn. investment com.) 1976-85. Mem. ABA. Clubs: Piping Rock (Locust Valley, L.I.); University (St. Louis); St. Louis Country; Princeton (St. Louis); Tiger Inn (Princeton). Home: 8 Chatfield Place Rd Saint Louis MO 63141-7850

MAGUIRE, ROBERT ALAN, Slavic languages and literatures educator; b. Canton, Mass., June 21, 1930; s. Frederick William and Ruth Spalding (Plunkett) M. A.B., Dartmouth Coll., 1951; M.A., cert., Russian Inst., Columbia U., 1953, Ph.D., 1961. Instr. Russian Duke U., 1958-60; asst. prof. Russian Dartmouth Coll., 1960-62, dir. NDEA Russian Lang. Inst., 1962; faculty Sch. Internat. Affairs and Harriman Inst. Columbia U., N.Y.C., 1962—, asst. prof. Russian lang. and lit., 1962-66; assoc. prof. Columbia U., 1966-70, prof., 1970—; Bakhmeteff prof. Russian studies Columbia U., N.Y.C., 1992—; chmn. dept. Slavic langs. Columbia U., 1977-83, 85-88; vis. lectr. Ind. U., 1961, 66, 69; vis. prof. U. Ill., 1976, Yale U., New Haven, 1984, Princeton (N.J.) U., 1991-92, Harvard U., 1995-96; vis. fellow St. Antony's Coll., Oxford (Eng.) U., 1971-72; mem. adv. bd. Sr. Fulbright-Hays program NEH, 1971-74; mem. selection bd. Internat. Rsch. and Exchs. Bd., 1971-74, 77, Com. on Internat. Ednl. Exch., 1973, 78, 80; mem. planning and adv. bd. Am. Coun. Learned Socs.-USSR Acad. of Sci. Commn. on the Humanities and Social Scis., 1982; editor Soviet-Am. Lit. Project, Duke U./Leningrad U. Press; adv. com. on preservation of Russian periodicals N.Y. Pub. Libr.; mem. vis. com. dept. Slavic langs. Harvard U., 1988-95, chmn., 1990-95; selection com. Nat. Humanities Ctr. Author: Red Virgin Soil: Soviet Literature in the 2910's, 1968, 2d edit., 1987, Gogol from the Twentieth Century: Eleven Essays, 1974, 2d edit., 1976, others; translator: Gogol (V.V. Gippius), 1981, 2d edit., 1989; co-translator Russian Short Stories, II, 1965, The Survivor and Other Poems (Tadeusz Rozewicz), 1976, Petersburg (Andrei Bely), 1978, 80, 83, Building the Barricade (Anna Swirszczynska), 1979, Sounds, Feelings, Thoughts: Seventy Poems (Wislawa Szymborska), 1981, 89, Exploring Gogol, 1994, 2d edit., 1995; mem. edit. bd. Tchg. Lang. Through Lit., 1965-77, mng. editor, 1978-88; mem. editl. bd. Slavic Rev., 1966-69, 82-89, Polish Rev., 1980-88; mem. editl. adv. bd. Princeton Essays in Literature, 1972-77; contbr. articles to profl. jours. Sponsoring com. Leo Tolstoy Mus. and Rsch. Libr., 1979; bd. dirs. Chamber Music Conf. and Composers' Forum of the East, 1983-93. Served with U.S. Army, 1953-55. Mem. MLA (exec. com. divsn. on Slavic and East European langs. 1986-92, Aldo and Jeanne Scaglione prize 1995), Am. Assn. Advancement of Slavic Studies (dir. 1977-79), Am. Assn. Tchrs. Slavic and East European Langs., Nat. Assn. Scholars, Polish Inst. Arts and Scis., PEN, Kosciuszko Found., Irish-Am. Cultural Inst., Gogol Soc. Am. (pres. 1986). Mem. MLA (exec. com. divsn. on Slavic and E. European langs. 1986-92, Aldo and Jeanne Scaglione prize 1995), PEN, Am. Assn. Advancement of Slavic Studies (dir. 1977-79), Am. Assn. Tchrs. Slavic and E. European

Langs., Nat. Assn. Scholars, Polish Inst. Arts and Scis., Kosciuszko Found., Irish-Am. Cultural Inst., Gogol Soc. Am. (pres. 1986). Roman Catholic (parish coun. 1979-89). Home: PO Box 69 Davenport Center NY 13751-0069 Office: Dept Slavic Langs Columbia U New York NY 10027

MAGUIRE, ROBERT EDWARD, retired public utility executive; b. Somerville, Mass., Jan. 25, 1928; s. Hugh Edward and Alice Theresa (Garrity) M.; m. Leona Rosemarie Beaulieu, June 21, 1952; children—Lynne Marie, Steven Francis, Judith Anne, David Robert. B.S. in Chem. Engring., Northeastern U., 1950, B.B.A. in Engring. and Mgmt., 1953. Vice pres., mgr. Lawrence Gas Co., Mass., 1960-68; vice pres., mgr. Mystic Valley Gas Co., Malden, Mass., 1968-70; v.p., regional exec. Mass. Electric Co., North Andover, 1970-71; v.p. New Eng. Power Service Co., Westboro, Mass., 1971-72, New Eng. Electric System, Westboro, Mass., 1972-75; exec. v.p., trustee Eastern Utilities Assocs., Boston, 1975-91. Contbr. to Gas mag., 1959. Vice chmn. Greater Lawrence United Fund Budget Com., 1967; treas., dir. ARC, Lawrence, 1966; trustee Essex-Broadway Savs. Bank, Lawrence, 1966-78; pres., dir. Greater Lawrence C. of C., 1962-64. Recipient Paul Revere Leadership medal Boston C. of C., 1963. Roman Catholic. Club: Lanam (Andover, Mass.). Home: 22 Ivy Ln Andover MA 01810-5018

MAGUIRE, ROBERT FRANCIS, III, real estate investor; b. Portland, Oreg., Apr. 18, 1935; s. Robert Francis Jr. and Jean (Shepard) M. B.A., UCLA, 1960. Vice pres. Security Pacific Nat. Bank, L.A., 1960-64; chmn. Maguire Thomas Ptnrs., L.A., 1964—; Exec. bd. med. scis. UCLA. Chmn. bd. dirs. Los Angeles County Mus. Art; trustee UCLA Found., Bard Coll.; bd. dirs. St. John's Hosp., Music Ctr. Bd. Govs., Calif. Clubs: California (Los Angeles); Valley (Montecito, Calif.), L.A. Country.

MAGURNO, RICHARD PETER, lawyer; b. Suffern, N.Y., June 29, 1943; s. Eugene and Rose (Foresta) M. BS, Georgetown U., 1964; MS, U. Wis., 1965; JD, Fordham U., 1968. Bar: N.Y. 1970, Fla. 1982, U.S. Supreme Ct. 1974, U.S. Ct. Appeals (2d, 5th, 11th cirs.) 1976, U.S. Dist. Ct. (so. and ea. dists.) N.Y. 1979. Atty. Eastern Air Lines, N.Y.C., 1970-73, sr. atty., 1973-76, gen. atty., 1976-79; dir. legal Eastern Air Lines, Miami, Fla., 1980, v.p. legal, asst. sec., 1980-84; gen. counsel, sr. v.p. legal, sec. Eastern Air Lines, 1984-88; ptnr. Lord Day & Lord, Barrett Smith, 1989-94; gen. counsel, sr. v.p. legal Trans World Airlines, St. Louis, 1994—. Author: Romantic Suffern, 1773-1973, 1973. Served in Peace Corps, 1968-69. Mem. ABA, Bar Assn. City of N.Y., Fla. Bar Assn. Democrat. Roman Catholic.

MAH, FENG-HWA, economics educator; b. Kaifeng, Honan, China, Mar. 25, 1922; s. Chiao-Hsiang and Wen-Chieh (Yang) M.; m. Judy Jiann Ting, Sept. 14, 1975. B.L. in Econs., Nat. Peking U., 1947; M.A. in Econs., U. Mich., 1956, Ph.D., 1959. Research asst. U. Mich., Ann Arbor, 1955-58; research fellow U. Calif.-Berkeley, 1959-60; asst. prof. Calif. State U.-Los Angeles, 1960-61; asst. prof. U. Wash., Seattle, 1961-64, assoc. prof., 1964-76, co-chmn. China Program, 1975-83, prof. econs., 1976-87, prof. emeritus, 1987—. Author: Communist China's Foreign Trade: Price Structure and Behavior 1955-1959, 1963, The Foreign Trade of Mainland China, 1971, Literary Essays of Mah Feng-hwa (in Chinese), 1993; contbr. numerous articles on Chinese economy to profl. jours. Orla B. Taylor fellow U. Mich., 1958-59; Fulbright faculty research fellow, 1967-68; Social Sci. Research Council grantee, 1962-65, 71. Mem. Am. Econs. Assn., Assn. Comparative Econ. Studies, Assn. Asian Studies, Phi Kappa Phi. Address: PO Box 15311 Seattle WA 98115-0311

MAH, RICHARD SZE HAO, chemical engineering educator; b. Shanghai, China, Dec. 16, 1934; came to U.S., 1961, naturalized, 1972; s. Fabian Soh Pai and E. Shang (Chang) M.; m. Shopin Stella Lee, Aug. 31, 1962; 1 child, Christopher. B.Sc., U. Birmingham, 1957; D.I.C., Ph.D.; Leverhulme student, Imperial Coll. Sci. and Tech., U. London, 1961; DSc in Engring., U. London, 1992. Jr. chem. engr. A.P.V. Co., Ltd., Crawley, Sussex, Eng., 1957-58; research fellow U. Minn., 1961-63; research engr. Union Carbide Corp. Tech. Center, South Charleston, W.Va., 1963-67; group head/sr. project analyst Esso Maths. & Systems, Inc., Florham Park, N.J., 1967-72; assoc. prof. chem. engring. Northwestern U., Evanston, Ill., 1972-77; prof. Northwestern U., 1977—; trustee CACHE Corp., Cambridge, Mass., 1974—, sec., 1978-80, v.p., 1982-84, pres., 1984-86; cons. Argonne Nat. Lab., 1975-78, DuPont de Nemours & Co., 1981-89. Contbr. articles to profl. jours. Fellow Am. Inst. Chem. Engrs. (chmn. systems and process design com. 1978-80, chmn. cast div. programming bd. 1979-81, Computing in Chem. Engring. award 1981, E.W. Thiele award 1990); mem. Am. Chem. Soc., Am. Soc. Engring. Edn., Am. Soc. Quality Control (Youden prize 1986), Tau Beta Pi. Mem. United Ch. of Christ. Office: Northwestern U Dept Chem Engring Evanston IL 60208 *Live every day as if it is our last. Each day of life is a marvelous gift of God. Let us count all our blessings and put to use every minute of our day and every resource of our life. Every morning let us marvel at the miraculous world which He has created for us. Every night let us thank God for giving us another day of fulfillment and go to sleep with the expectation of another great day of miracles for tomorrow.*

MAHA, GEORGE EDWARD, research facility administrator, consultant; b. Elgin, Ill., Feb. 15, 1924; s. George William and Agnes (Lux) M.; m. Mary Andrea Rasmussen, June 6, 1953; children: George, Richard, Mary, Andrea, Sarah. BS, U. Notre Dame, 1950; MD, St. Louis U., 1953. Diplomate Am. Bd. Internal Medicine. Intern Mt. Carmel Mercy Hosp., Detroit, 1953-54; resident in internal medicine VA Hosp., St. Louis, 1954-55; fellow St. Louis U. Hosp., 1955-56; NIH fellow in cardiology Duke U., Durham, N.C., 1956-58; chief outpatient svc. VA Hosp., Pitts., 1962-64; staff physician FDA, Washington, 1964-66; exec. dir. clin. rsch. Merck, Sharp & Dohme Rsch. Labs., West Point, Pa., 1966-88; asst. to pres. Clin. Rsch. Internat., Research Triangle Park, N.C., 1988-89; med. dir. Burroughs Wellcome, Research Triangle Park, 1989-91; cons., 1991—; chmn. med. sect. Pharm. Mfr.'s Assn., Washington, 1982-83, mem. steering com., 1975-84. Contbr. 17 articles to profl. jours. Tech. sgt. USAF, 1943-46, PTO. Recipient Mosby award St. Louis U., 1953. Mem. AMA, AAAS, Am. Coll. Cardiology, N.Y. Acad. Sci., Am. Heart Assn., Am. Soc. Clin. Pharmacology and Therapeutics, Alpha Omega Alpha. Roman Catholic. Avocations: reading, fishing, tennis. Home: 313 Marina Bay 2550 Harbourside Dr Longboat Key FL 34228-4170

MAHADEVAN, KUMAR, marine laboratory director, researcher; b. Madras, Tamilnadu, India, Sept. 29, 1948; came to U.S., 1971; s. Sockalingam Ponnusamy and Pankajam (Nadar) M.; m. Linda Claire Goggin, Sept. 27, 1980; children: Andrew, Alexander, Chad, Vijayan. BS, Madras U., 1967; MS, Annamalai U., Chidambaram, India, 1971; PhD, Fla. State U., 1977. Instr. Chingleput (India) Med. Coll., 1967-68, Lakshman's Coll., Madras, 1968-69; rsch. asst. Fla. State U., Tallahassee, 1971-75; staff scientist Conservation Cons., Inc., Palmetto, Fla., 1975-78; sr. scientist Mote Marine Lab., Sarasota, Fla., 1978-79, dir. div., 1979-86, interim co-dir., 1984, exec. dir., 1986—; mem. Coun. on Ocean Affairs, Washington, 1989-91, steering com. Gulf of Mex. Program, Atlanta, 1988—; mem. South Atlantic and Gulf States Coastal Protection Commn., 1990—; vice chmn. NOAA Marine Rsch. Bd., Gulf of Mex., 1992—. Contbr. articles to profl. publs. Mem. sch. adv. bd., Sarasota, 1988-89; mem. tech. adv. bd. Myakka River, Sarasota, 1987-90; legis. liason Parents Assn. of Sarasota Schs., 1988-89; bd. dirs. Jason Found. for Edn., 1991—. Nat. Merit scholar Univ. Grants Commn., India, 1969-71. Mem. N. Am. Benthological Soc., Oceanographic Soc., World Aquaculture Soc., Deep Sea Biol. Soc. (hon.), Fla. Acad. Scis. (councillor 1975), So. Assn. Marine Labs (pres. 1990, exec. bd. 1986-91, treas. 1995—), Assn. Marine Labs Caribbean (pres. 1987-88, exec. bd. 1984—), Nat. Assn. Marine Labs. (pres. 1994-95), Sigma Xi. Republican. Avocations: racquetball, fishing, gardening. Office: Mote Marine Lab 1600 Ken Thompson Pky Sarasota FL 34236-1004

MAHAFFEY, JAMES PERRY, education educator, consultant; b. Greenville, S.C., Sept. 29, 1935; s. Earl Perry and Flora Virginia (Painter) M.; m. Nora Dean Padgett, Dec. 22, 1961; 1 child, Janet E. BA cum laude, Furman U., 1957; MA, Vanderbilt U., 1958; PhD, U. S.C., 1974. Cert. edn. specialist-reading. Tchr. Greenville (S.C.) County Schs., 1958-61, reading supr., 1961-65; S.C. state reading supr. S.C. Dept. Edn., Columbia, 1965-69; asst. supt. for instrn. Anderson (S.C.) Pub. Schs., 1969-77; assoc. prof. edn. Furman U., Greenville, 1977-79; assoc. supt. for instrn. Horry County Schs., Conway/Myrtle Beach, S.C., 1979-91; prof. edn. Wofford Coll., Spartanburg, S.C., 1991—; adj. prof. Converse Coll., Spartanburg, 1961-65; instr. U. S.C., Columbia, 1973-74; mem. S.C. Basic Skills Commn., Columbia, 1981-89; bd. trustees So. Assn. Colls./Schs., Atlanta, 1990-93. Author, editor: Teaching Reading in South Carolina Secondary Schools, 1969; contbg. author: Elementary School Criteria: Focusing on Desired Learner Outcomes, 1994; contbr. articles to profl. jours. Named Outstanding Sch. Adminstr., S.C. Assn. Sch. Adminstrs., Columbia, 1989, Outstanding Educator, So. Assn. Colls./Schs., Atlanta, 1990; Carnegie fellow Peabody Coll. of Vanderbilt U., Nashville, 1958. Mem. Internat. Reading Assn. (S.C. pres. 1977). Baptist. Avocation: gardening. Home: 101 Heritage Dr Spartanburg SC 29307-3146 Office: Wofford Coll Edn Dept 429 N Church St Spartanburg SC 29303-3612

MAHAFFEY, REDGE ALLAN, movie producer, director, writer, scientist; b. Bethesda, Md., Dec. 15, 1949; s. George Newton and Lila Katherine (Drum) M.; m. Ellen Cecilia Cranston, May 30, 1973 (div. Dec. 1980); m. Patricia Jane Guy, Apr. 29, 1984 (div. Sept. 1994); children: Travis Guy, Morgan Nicole; m. Veronica Bird, Sept. 24, 1994; children: Ryan Alexander, Ramsey Blake. BS, U. Md., 1971, MS, 1973, PhD, 1976. NRC postdoctoral fellow Nat. Acad. of Scis., Washington, 1976-77; research physicist Naval Research Lab., Washington, 1977-78; sr. research physicist Sachs/Freeman Assocs., Bladensburg, Md., 1978-79; dir. research Sachs/Freeman Assocs., Bowie, Md., 1979-81; sr. v.p., sec., treas. Sachs/Freeman Assocs., Landover, Md., 1981-91, also bd. dirs., 1985—; mng. ptnr. Ramsway Pictures, 1991—; instr. George Washington U., Washington, 1979-80, Prince George's Coll., 1987; pres. Capitol Contracts, Bowie, 1981-83. Author: A Higher Education, 1989, Me, Myself and I, 1992, Deadly Rivals, 1992; exec. prodr., writer Deadly Rivals, 1992, Quest for the Delta Knight, 1993; prodr., writer, dir. Life 1001, 1995, Mental Code, 1996; contbr. articles on lasers and particle beams to sci. jours., also short stories, essays and poems to mags.; patentee laser, x-rays and particle beams. Recipient Research Publ. award Naval Research Lab., 1978, 1st Place Novel Internat. Lit. Awards, 1988. Mem. IEEE, Am. Phys. Soc., MENSA, Intertel, Nat. Writer's Club, Internat. Platform Assn., Internat. Soc. Phil. Enquiry, Writer's Assn. Anne Arundel County, Bethesda Writer's Ctr., Inst. Noetic Scis. Republican. Club: Sea Dragons Martial Arts(Washington) (treas. 1984-85, instr. 1987-91). Avocations: martial arts, softball. Office: Ramsway Ltd 738 Intrepid Way Davidsonville MD 21035-1307

MAHAJAN, SUBHASH, electronic materials educator. BS with highest honors, Panjab U., India, 1959; BE in Metallyrgy with highest honors, Indian Inst. Sci., 1961; PhD in Materials Sci. and Engring., U. Calif., 1965. Rsch. asst. U. Calif., Berkeley, 1961-65; rsch. metallurgist U. Denver, 1965-68; Harwell fellow Atomic Energy Rsch. Establishment, Harwell, Eng., 1968-71; mem. tech. staff AT&T Bell Labs., Murray Hill, N.J., 1971-83, rsch. mgr., 1981-83; prof. electronic materials dept. material sci. and engring. Carnegie Mellon U., Pitts., 1983—; mem. site panel MRL, 1993; tech. dir. TMS bd.; vis. prof. U. Antwerp, Belgium, 1991, Ecole Ctrl. Lyon, Ecully, France, 1993; lectr., spkr., patentee, cons. in field. Editor: (with V.G. Keramidas) ECS Symposium volume, 1983; (with L.C. Kimberling) The Concise Encyclopedia of Semiconducting Materials and Related Technologies, 1992, Handbook on Semiconductors vol. 3, 1994; (with D. Bloor, R.J. Brook and M.C. Flemings) The Encyclopedia of Advanced Materials, 1994; contbr. over 160 articles to profl. jours. Mem. materials rsch. adv. com. divsn. materials rsch. NSF, 1989-92. DAAD fellow U. Göttingen, Germany, 1976. Fellow ASM Internat.; mem. Materials Rsch. Soc. (editor symposium volume 1983, organizer symposium Am. Assn. Crystal Growers), Electrochem. Soc. (mem. electronics divsn. 1976-83, divisional editor 1976-86), Minerals, Metals and Materials Soc. (mem. phys. metallurgy com. 1976-83, vice chmn. mech. metallurgy com. 1978-79, mem. 1975-80, mem. electronhic materials com. 1990-94, chmn. electronic, magnetic and photonic materials com. 1984-86), Sigma Xi. Office: Carnegie Mellon U Dept Materials Sci and Engring Wean Hall 3311 Pittsburgh PA 15213

MAHAL, TAJ (HENRY ST. CLAIR FREDERICKS), composer, musician; b. Mass., May 17, 1942; s. Henry St. Clair and Mildred (Shields) Fredericks; m. Inshirah Geter, Jan. 23, 1976; children: Aya, Taj, Gahmelah, Ahmen, Deva, Nani. BA, U. Mass., Amherst, 1964. Ind. musician, composer, rec. artist, 1964—. Early appearances at Club 47, Boston; rec. artist with Columbia, Warner Brothers, Gramavision labels; tours throughout U.S., Europe, Australia, including State Dept.-sponsored tour of Africa; composer: (album) Taj, Like Never Before, Dancin' the Blues-Private Music (Grammy nomination traditional blues 1993), (film soundtracks) Sounder, Sounder II, Brothers (Best Ethnic Music award, Bay Area Musics Awards 1979), (TV shows) Ewoks, The Man Who Broke a Thousand Chains, Brer Rabbit, The Hot Spot (Grammy nomination as Best Contemporary Blues Album 1990); actor: (films) King of Ragtime, Sounder, Sounder II., (theater) Mule Bone: assoc. artist, Mark Taper Forum, L.A., 1992—. Office: care Folklore Inc 1671 Appian Way Santa Monica CA 90401-3258

MAHAN, CLARENCE, retired govenment official, writer; b. Dayton, Ohio, Jan. 1, 1939; s. Clarence Mahan and Elsie (Crouch) Dilitz; m. Suky Mahan, May 27, 1962; children: Sean M., Christiane Elizabeth. BA, U. Md., 1963; MA, Am. U., 1968; MBA, Syracuse U., 1969. Dep. comtroller U.S. Army, Japan, 1974-76; dep. chief program and budget Defense Commn. Agy., Arlington, Va., 1976; aide Asst. Sec. Army, Washington, 1976-77; chief operating appropriations Dept. AF, Washington, 1979-80; dir. fin. and acctg. Dept. Energy, Washington, 1980-81, dep. comptroller, 1981-82; dir. fiscal and contracts mgmt. EPA, Washington, 1982-83, dep. comptroller, 1983-85, dir. Rsch. Mgmt. Mgmt. Office, 1985-95; instr., lectr. in field. Contbr. articles to profl. jours. and hort. mags. With U.S. Army, 1959-62, Korea. Mem. Am. Iris Soc. (bd. dirs., 2d v.p. 1991-95, 1st. v.p. 1995—), Hist. Iris Preservation Soc. (pres. 1991-93), Soc. Japanese Irises (pres. 1989-92), Reblooming Iris Soc. (bd. dirs. 1986-94). Democrat. Home and Office: 7311 Churchill Rd Mc Lean VA 22101-2001

MAHAN, (DANIEL) DULANY, JR., lawyer, real estate developer; b. Hannibal, Mo., Dec. 22, 1914; s. D. Dulany and Sarah (Marshall) M.; m. Eleanor F. Bethea, Sept. 14, 1948 (div. 1953). AB, U. Mo., Columbia; J.D., Harvard U., 1940. Assoc., Office of George M. Clark, N.Y.C., 1940-42; asst. atty. FTC, Washington, 1948-51; assoc. Adams & James, N.Y.C., 1951-68; assoc. Kurnick & Hackman, N.Y.C., 1968—; ptnr. Tall Pines Estates Devel., Jacksonville, Fla., 1971—. Served with U.S. Army, 1942-46. Mem. ABA, Internat. Bar Assn., World Assn. Lawyers, N.Y. Bar Assn., Fed. Bar Assn. Republican. Clubs: Harvard (N.Y.C.); Nat. Lawyers (Washington). Home: 98 Ralph Ave White Plains NY 10606-3609 Office: 450 Park Ave # 2305 New York NY 10022-2605

MAHAN, GERALD DENNIS, physics educator, researcher; b. Portland, Oreg., Nov. 24, 1937; s. Thomas Finley and Julia Kay (Swails) M.; m. Sally Ann Spaugh, Feb. 20, 1965; children—Christopher Parker, Susan Thayer, Roy Finley. A.B., Harvard U., 1959; Ph.D. in Physics, U. Calif.-Berkeley, 1964. Research physicist Gen. Electric Co., Schenectady, 1963-67; part-time Gen. Electric Co., 1967-84; assoc. prof. physics U. Oreg., Eugene, 1967-73; prof. physics Ind. U., Bloomington, 1973-82; disting. prof. Ind. U., 1982-84; disting. prof. physics U. Tenn., Knoxville; disting. scientist Oak Ridge Nat. Lab.; guest prof. Niels Bohr Inst., Copenhagen, 1977-78. Author: Many-Particle Physics, 1981; contbr. numerous articles on physics to profl. jours. Alfred Sloan fellow, 1968-70. Fellow NAS, Am. Phys. Soc. Office: U Tenn Dept Physics Knoxville TN 37996

MAHAN, JAMES CAMERON, lawyer; b. El Paso, Tex., Dec. 16, 1943; m. Eileen Agnes Casale, Jan. 13, 1968; 1 child, James Cameron Jr. BA, U. Charleston, 1965; JD, Vanderbilt U., 1973. Bar: Nev. 1974, U.S. Dist. Ct. Nev. 1974, U.S. Ct. Appeals (9th cir.) 1975, U.S. Tax Ct. 1980, U.S. Supreme Ct. 1980. Assoc. Lee & Beasey, Las Vegas, Nev., 1974-75; mem. firm John Peter Lee Ltd., Las Vegas, 1975-82; sr. ptnr. Mahan & Ellis, Chartered, Las Vegas, 1982—. With USN, 1966-69. Office: Mahan & Ellis Chartered 510 S 9th St Las Vegas NV 89101-7011

MAHANES, DAVID JAMES, JR., retired distillery executive; b. Lexington, Ky., June 19, 1923; s. David James and Ethel (Brock) M.; m. Dorothy Jean Richardson, Oct. 28, 1950; 1 child, David James III. BS, U. Ky., 1947; MBA, Harvard U., 1950. Regional mgr. Jack Daniel Distillery, Nashville, 1960-65, v.p., 1965-70, sr. v.p., 1970-71, exec. v.p., 1971-85, pres., 1985-88, chmn. bd. dirs.; chmn. bd. dirs. Early Times Distillery Co., Can. Mist Distilling Co., Thoroughbred Plastics Co. Lt. inf. AUS, 1943-45, ETO; lt. col. AG ret. Runnerup as outstanding sales exec. Gallagher Report, 1982. Mem. SAR (pres. Andrew Jackson chpt.), Soc. Colonial Wars in Tenn. (gov., dep. gov. gen.), English Speaking Union (pres.), Res. Officers Assn., So. Srs. Golf Assn., Belle Meade Country Club, Beaver Creek Club, Exch. Club, Tenn. Profl. Golfers Assn. (hon.), Kappa Alpha, Beta Gamma Sigma. Republican. Presbyterian. Home: 104 Adams Park Nashville TN 37205-4702

MAHANTHAPPA, KALYANA THIPPERUDRAIAH, physicist, educator; b. Hirehalli, Mysore, India, Oct. 29, 1934; s. Kalyana and Thippamma (Maddanappa) T.; m. Prameela Talkerappa, Oct. 30, 1961; children: Nagesh, Rudresh, Mahesh. BSc, Central Coll. Bangalore, India, 1954; MSc, Delhi U., 1956; PhD (Faculty Arts and Scis. fellow), Harvard, 1961. Research assoc. U. Cal. at Los Angeles, 1961-63; asst. prof. U. Pa., Phila., 1963-66; mem. Inst. Advanced Study, Princeton, N.J., 1964-65; assoc. prof. physics U. Colo., Boulder, 1966-69; prof. U. Colo., 1969—, faculty research fellow, 1970-71, 76-77, 83-84, 93-94; vis. prof./scientist U. Rome, 1970, Internat. Ctr. for Theoretical Physics, 1971, Cambridge U., 1976-77; cons. Aerojet-Gen., L.A., 1962-63; dir. Summer Inst. Theoretical Physics, Boulder, 1968-69, NATO Advanced Study Inst. in Elem. Particles, 1979, NATO Advanced Rsch. Workshop on Superstrings, 1987; gen. dir. Theoretical Advanced Study Inst. in Particle Physics, 1989—; sr. vis. rsch. fellow Imperial Coll., London, 1983-84. Contbr. articles to profl. jours. Fellow Am. Phys. Soc.; mem. AAAS, Sigma Xi. Research theoretical high energy and elementary particle physics. Home: 2865 Darley Ave Boulder CO 80303-6307

MAHAR, ELLEN PATRICIA, law librarian; b. Washington, Jan. 15, 1938; d. Richard A. and Lina C. (Chittick) M. BA, St. Joseph Coll., Emmitsburg, Md., 1959; MLS, U. Md., 1968. Asst. librarian Covington & Burling, Washington, 1971-73, libr. dir., 1978-92; librarian Shea & Gardner, Washington, 1974-78; mgr. info. ctr. Assn. Comml. Real Estate, Herndon, Va., 1992-94; head libr. Caplin & Drysdale Chtd., Washington, 1994—. Co-editor: Legislative History of the Securities Act of 1933 and the Securities Act of 1934, 11 vols., 1973. Mem. Am. Assn. Law Libraries, Spl. Libraries Assn., Law Librarians' Soc. Washington. Office: Caplin & Drysdale Chtd 1 Thomas Cir NW Washington DC 20005

MAHARIDGE, DALE DIMITRO, journalist, educator; b. Cleve., Oct. 24, 1956; s. Steve and Joan (Kopfstein) M. Student, Cleve. State U., 1974-75. Free-lance reporter various publs., Cleve., 1976; reporter The Gazette, Medina, Ohio, 1977-78; free-lance reporter Cleve. Plain Dealer, 1978-80; reporter The Sacramento Bee, 1980-91; lectr. Stanford U., Palo Alto, Calif., 1992—. Author: Journey to Nowhere: The Saga of the New Underclass, 1985, repub. with introduction by Bruce Springsteen, 1996, And Their Children After Them, 1989 (Pulitzer Prize for gen. nonfiction 1990), The Last Great American Hobo, 1993; contbr. articles to profl. jours. Nieman fellow Harvard U., 1988; grantee Pope Found., 1994, Freedom Forum, 1995. Democrat. Office: Stanford U Dept Comm Bldg 120 Stanford CA 94305

MAHER, BILL, talk show host, comedian, producer; b. N.Y.C., Jan. 20, 1956; s. Bill and Julie (Berman) M. BA, Cornell U., 1978. Creator, host Politically Incorrect, HBO, N.Y.C., 1993—. Performances include (theatre) Seymour Glick is Alive But Sick (Steve Allen); (stand-up) The Bob Monkhouse Show, Late Night with David Letterman, The Tonight Show Anniversary Show, The Tonight Show, HBO Spl., 1989, 92; (TV shows) Steve Allen's Music Room, Alice, Sara, Max Headroom, Hard Knocks, Newhart, Murder, She Wrote, The Midnight Hour, Say What?; (TV movies) Out of Time, Rags to Riches, Club Med; (films) D.C. Cab, Rat Boy, House II, Cannibal Women in the Avocado Jungle of Death, Pizza Man; author: (novel) True Story, 1994. Recipient Cableace award Nat. Acad. Cable Programming, 1990, Cableace award for best talk show series, 1995, Cableace award for best talk show host, 1995. Office: HBO Politically Incorrect 514 W 57th St New York NY 10019

MAHER, BRENDAN ARNOLD, psychology educator, editor; b. Widnes, Eng., Oct. 31, 1924; came to U.S., 1955; s. Thomas F. and Agnes (Power) M.; m. Winifred Barbara Brown, Aug. 27, 1952; children: Rebecca, Thomas, Nicholas, Liam, Niall. B.A. with honours, U. Manchester, Eng., 1950; M.A., Ohio State U., 1951, Ph.D., 1954; student, U. Ill. Med. Sch., 1952-53; A.M. (hon.), Harvard, 1972. Diplomate: Am. Bd. Examiners in Profl. Psychology. Psychologist Her Majesty's Prison, Wakefield, Eng., 1954-55; instr. Ohio State U., 1955-56; asst. prof. Northwestern U., 1956-58; asso. prof. La. State U., 1958-60; lectr. Harvard, 1960-64; chmn. Center Research Personality, 1962-64; prof. U. Wis., 1964-67, 71-72; vis. fellow U. Copenhagen, 1966-67, vis. fellow and research scientist, 1979; prof. psychology Brandeis U., 1967-72; dean Brandeis U. (Grad. Sch.), 1969-71, dean faculty, 1971-83; E. C. Henderson prof. psychology, 1983—; prof. Harvard U., 1972—, chmn. dept. psychology and social relations, 1973-78, chmn. dept. psychology, 1987-89, dean Grad. Sch. Arts and Scis., 1989-92; assoc. psychologist McLean Hosp., Belmont, Mass., 1968-77; psychologist McLean Hosp., 1977-84; cons. in medicine Peter Bent Brigham Hosp., Boston, 1977-85; cons. in psychology Mass. Gen. Hosp., 1977—. Author: Principles of Psychopathology, 1966, Introduction to Research in Psychopathology, 1970, A Passage to Sword Beach, 1966; co-editor: National Research Council: Research Doctorate Programs in the United States, 1995; editor Progress in Exptl. Personality Rsch., 1964-87, Jour. Cons. and Clin. Psychology, 1972-78; cons. editor Rev. Personality and Social Psychology, Clin. Psychology Rev. Served with Brit. Royal Navy, 1943-47. Fellow AAAS, Am. Psychol. Soc.; mem. Brit. Psychol. Assn. (chartered psychologist U.K.), Soc. Rsch. in Psychopathology (pres. 1985-87). Office: Harvard U William James Hall Cambridge MA 02138 also: Giffords Island, Mahone Bay, NS Canada

MAHER, DAVID L., drug store company executive; b. Iowa City, 1939. Grad., U. Iowa, 1964. Pres., COO Am. Stores Co., Salt Lake City. Office: American Drug Stores Inc 1818 Swift Dr Oak Brook IL 60521-1576

MAHER, DAVID ROBERT, quality assurance professional; b. Fall River, Mass., Oct. 2, 1964; s. Leo George and Virginia Dorothy (Maloney) M.; m. Deborah Ann Girard; children: Benjamin David, Matthew Bryan. BS in Elec. Engring., Northeastern U., Boston, 1987. Cert. quality engr. Quality engr. Sippican Inc., Marion, Mass., 1984-91; quality mgr. The First Years Inc., Avon, Mass., 1991-93, quality dir., 1993—. Mem. Am. Soc. Quality Control, Inst. Packaging Profls., Soc. Plastics Engrs. Avocations: commercial fishing, camping, skiing, hunting, computers. Office: The First Years Inc 1 Kiddie Dr Avon MA 02322

MAHER, DAVID WILLARD, lawyer; b. Aug. 14, 1934, Chgo.; s. Chauncey Carter and Martha (Peppers) M.; BA Harvard, 1955, LLB, 1959; m. Jill Waid Armagnac, Dec. 20, 1954; children: Philip Armagnac, Julia Armagnac. Bar: N.Y. 1960, Ill. 1961; pvt. practice Boston, N.Y.C., 1958-60; assoc. Kirkland & Ellis, and predecessor firm, 1960-65, ptnr. 1966-78; ptnr. Reuben & Proctor, 1978-86, Isham, Lincoln and Beale, 1986-88, Sonnenschein, Nath & Rosenthal, 1988—; gen. counsel BBB Chgo. and No. Ill.; lectr. DePaul U. Sch. Law, 1973-79, Law Sch. of Loyola U., Chgo., 1980-84. Mem. vis. com. to the Div. Sch., U. Chgo., 1986—. Served to 2d lt. USAF, 1955-56. Fellow Am. Bar Found. (lifetime); mem. ABA, Am. Law Inst., Ill. Bar Assn., Chgo. Bar Assn., Bull Valley Hunt Club, Chgo. Lit. Club, Union League Club, Tavern, Club. Roman Catholic. Home: 311 W Belden Ave Chicago IL 60614-3817 Office: Sonnenschein Nath & Rosenthal 233 S Wacker Dr Ste 8000 Chicago IL 60606-6404

MAHER, EDWARD JOSEPH, lawyer; b. Cleve., Sept. 18, 1939; s. Richard Leo and Lucile (Thompson) M.; m. Marilyn K. Maher, Oct. 8, 1966; children: Richard A., David C., Michael E, Colleen Therese. B.S., Georgetown U., 1961, LL.B., 1964; student U. Fribourg, Switzerland, 1959-61. Bar: Ohio 1964, U.S. dist. ct. (no. dist.) Ohio 1964. Assoc., Sweeney, Maher & Vlad, Cleve., 1964-71; sole practice, Cleve., 1971—. Pres. parish council St. Raphael's Ch., Bay Village, Ohio, 1983-84; former adv. bd. Catholic Family and Children's Services; adv. bd. Cath. Youth Orgn., 1973-79, pres., 1975-76; chmn. Elyria Cursillo Ctr., 1974-75; lay del. to Ohio Cath. Conf., Diocese of Cleve., 1973-75; chmn. adv. bd. Cath. Social Services of Cuyahoga County, 1978-79; trustee Cath. Charities Corp., 1977—, treas., 1979, sec., 1981, 1st v.p., 1983, gen. chmn. campaign, 1983, 84, pres., 1985-86; pres. Diocesan adv. bd. Cath. Youth Orgn., 1980-82; team capt. United Way Services Agy. Team Group, 1981, nominating com., 1983; mem. Tabor House, The Consultation Ctr. of the Diocese of Cleve., pres., 1992-94. Recipient Cardinal Robert Bellarmine S.J. award St. Ignatius High Sch., 1990, Cath. Man of the Year award, 1995. Mem. ABA, Ohio Bar Assn., Cuyahoga County Bar Assn., Cleve. Bar Assn., Cath. Lawyers Guild Cleve. (pres. 1970). Clubs: Irish Good Fellowship (pres.), First Friday of Cleve. (pres. 1990). Office: 1548 Standard Bldg Cleveland OH 44113

MAHER, FRANCESCA MARCINIAK, air transportation executive, lawyer; b. 1957. BA, Loyola U., 1978, JD, 1981. Ptnr. Mayer, Brown & Platt, Chgo., 1981-93; v.p., sec. UAL Corp., Elk Grove Village, Ill., 1993—. Bd. dirs. United Ctr. Mem. Ill. Humane Soc. (bd. dirs.). Office: UAL Corp PO Box 66100 Chicago IL 60666

MAHER, KIM LEVERTON, museum administrator; b. Washington, Feb. 25, 1946; d. Joseph Wilson and Helen Elizabeth (Bell) Leverton; m. William Fredrick Maher, June 12, 1965 (div. 1980); 1 child, Lauren Robinson. Student Duke U., 1963-65, George Washington U., 1966; B.A. in English, U. Fla., 1969. Social worker Fla. Health and Rehab. Service, Gainesville, 1969-71, Delray Beach, 1972-74, fraud unit supr., West Palm Beach, 1974-76, direct service supr., 1977-78; ctr. dir. Palm Beach County Employment and Tng. Adminstrn., West Palm Beach, 1979-81; exec. dir. Discovery Ctr., Inc., Ft. Lauderdale, Fla., 1981-92; exec. dir. Mus. Discovery & Sci., Ft. Lauderdale, 1992-94; CEO Va. Air and Space Ctr., Hampton, 1995—. Bd. dirs. Singing Pines Mus., Boca Raton, Fla., 1984—, Broward Art Guild, Ft. Lauderdale, 1985-91, Va. space grant consortium Va. Aerospace Bus. Roundtable, Hampton, 1995—; mem. Leadership Broward II, Ft. Lauderdale, 1983-84; mem. faculty Inst. New Sci. Ctrs., 1992. Recipient Cultural Arts award Broward Cultural Arts Found., 1985, Woman of Yr. award Women in Comm., 1990, Woman of Distinction award So. Fla. Mag., 1993. Mem. Am. Assn. Museums, Assn. Sci. and Tech. Ctrs., Southeastern Museums Conf., Fla. Sci. Tchrs. Assn. (bd. dirs.), Fla. Assn. Mus. (bd. dirs. 1989—, pres. 1993—), Leadership Broward Alumnae (curriculum com. 1984—), Fort Lauderdale Downtown Council (bd. dirs. 1992—),13), Women's Exec. Club, Phi Kappa Phi. Republican. Methodist. Avocations: scuba diving; piano; creative writing; collecting art and antiques; painting. Office: Va Air and Space Ctr 600 Settlers Landing Rd Hampton VA 23669-4033

MAHER, L. JAMES, III, molecular biologist; b. Mpls., Nov. 28, 1960; s. Louis James and Elizabeth Jane (Crawford) M.; m. Laura Lee Moseng, July 2, 1983; children: Elizabeth Lillian, Christina Ailene. BS in Molecular Biology, U. Wis., 1983, PhD in Molecular Biology, 1988. Fellow U. Wis., Madison, 1983-84, rsch. asst., 1984-88; postdoctoral fellow Calif. Inst. Tech., Pasadena, 1988-91; asst. prof. molecular biology Eppley Inst., U. Nebr. Med. Ctr., Omaha, 1991-95; assoc. prof. biochem. molecular biology Mayo Found., Rochester, Minn., 1995—. Editorial bd. Antisense Rsch. & Devel. Jour., 1991—; contbr. articles to profl. jours. Musician, Madison Symphony Orch., 1983-88, Calif. Inst. Tech. Symphony Orch., L.A., 1988-91. Gosney fellow, 1988; Am. Cancer Soc. postdoctoral fellow, 1988. Mem. AAAS, Phi Beta Kappa. Evangelical Christian Ch. Achievements include research in chemical and biochemical agents designed to artificially regulate the flow of genetic information in biological systems. Office: Mayo Found Dept Biochem and Molec Biol 200 1st St SW Rochester MN 55905

MAHER, LOUIS JAMES, JR., geologist, educator; b. Iowa City, Iowa, Dec. 18, 1933; s. Louis James and Edith Marie (Ham) M.; m. Elizabeth Jane Crawford, June 7, 1956; children: Louis James, Robert Crawford, Barbara Ruth. BA, U. Iowa, 1955, MS, 1959; PhD, U. Minn., 1961. Mem. faculty dept. geology and geophysics U. Wis.-Madison, 1962—, prof., 1970—, chmn. dept., 1980-84. Contbr. articles to profl. jours. Served with U.S. Army, 1956-58. Danforth fellow, 1955-61; NSF fellow, 1959-61; NATO fellow, 1961-62. Fellow AAAS, Geol. Soc. Am.; mem. Am. Quaternary Assn., Ecol. Soc. Am., Wis. Acad. Sci., Arts and Letters, Sigma Xi. Episcopalian. Office: U Wis Dept Geology and Geoph 1215 W Dayton St Madison WI 53706

MAHER, MICHAEL EDWARD, footwear executive; b. New Orleans, Sept. 20, 1948; s. Henry Oliver and Camille Dorothy (Ford) M.; m. Cynthia Gloria Creco, Dec. 26, 1970 (div. Nov. 1992); children: Wendi, Jaime; m. Susan Rene Koval, May 16, 1992. BBA, Loyola U., 1970, MBA, 1972. Sales rep. Ked's Corp., Cambridge, Mass., 1971-76, mktg. dir., 1976-81; sales rep. Famolare, Inc., N.Y.C., 1981-86, Mia Inc., Miami, Fla., 1986-89; regional v.p. Ked's Corp., 1989—; pres. Lakewood Bar & Grill, Limited Liability Co., 1994—. Vol. Spina Bifida Assn., Dallas. Mem. Two-Ten. Avocations: reading, football, racquetball. Office: Keds Corp 5 Cambridge Ctr Cambridge MA 02142-1493

MAHER, PATRICK JOSEPH, utility company executive; b. Dublin, Ireland, Apr. 20, 1936; came to U.S., 1946, naturalized, 1955; s. Pierce Albeus and Mary (Brady) M.; m. Catherine M. Sullivan, Oct. 13, 1962; children: Kathy, Kevin, Erin, Megan. BBA, Iona Coll., 1959; MBA, N.Y. U., 1965. With spl. devel. program Chase Manhattan Bank, N.Y.C., 1961-64, 2d v.p. fiduciary dept., 1964-68; asst. v.p. Nat. Comml. Bank, Albany, N.Y., 1968-70; chief sect. utility fin. N.Y. State Pub. Svc. Commn., Albany, 1970-74; v.p., chief fin. officer Washington Gas Light Co., 1974-80, exec. v.p. fin. and adminstrn., 1980-87, pres., 1987-92, 1992—, chmn. bd. dirs., CEO, 1993—. Served with USAR, 1960-61. Mem. Am. Gas Assn., Nat. Soc. Rate of Return Analysts, Natural Gas Men's Roundtable, Greater Washington Bd. Trade, Nat. Petroleum Coun., Inst. Gas Tech., U.S. C. of C., Rotary, N.Y. Athletic Club, Washington City Club. Roman Catholic. Home: 18781 Foggy Bottom Rd Bluemont VA 22012 Office: Washington Gas 1100 H St NW Washington DC 20080-0001

MAHER, PETER MICHAEL, university dean; b. North Battleford, Sask., Can., Mar. 4, 1940; s. Hugh James and Florence Andrea (Showell) M.; m. Illa Horning, Sept. 5, 1964; children: Andrea, Allison, Jennifer. BE, U. Sask., 1962; MBA, U. Western Ont., 1965; PhD, Northwestern U., 1970. Registered prof. engr., Sask., Alta. Devel. engr. DuPont of Can., 1962-64, new venture analyst, 1965-67; teaching asst. Sir George Williams U., 1966-70; rsch. engr. dept. indsl. engring. and mgmt. sci. Northwestern U., 1968-76; prof., rsch. coord. Faculty of Bus. Adminstrn. and Commerce, U. Alta., 1970-76; dean, prof. adminstrn. Coll. of Commerce, U. Sask., 1976-81; dean, prof. faculty of mgmt. U. Calgary, Alta., 1981—, mem. univ. senate, 1989-92; bd.d irs. Calgary Airport Authority, Computalog Ltd., Can. Inst. for Petroleum Industry Devel., Pratt & Whitney Can., Inc., Theatre Calgary; witness House of Commons Spl. Commn. Employment Opportunities, 1981; mem. exec. com. Nu-West Ltd., 1982-88; audit com. Contbr. articles to profl. jours. Chmn. edn. div., mem. cabinet United Way, Calgary, 1989-90; creditor Northland Bank, 1985; trustee CNIB White Cane Found., 1989—; bd. dirs. Calgary Econ. Devel. Authority, 1983-90, Banff Mountain Acad., 1990—, Banff Sch. Advanced Mgmt., 1990—, chmn. acad. coun., 1992—, Theatre Calgary, 1992—; mem. corp. St. Thomas More Coll., Saskatoon, 1983—. Mem. Nat. Rsch. Coun. Can., Can. C. of C. (bd. dirs. 1984-86), Calgary C. of C. (bd. dirs. 1982-86), Am. Assembly Collegiate Schs. Bus. (faculty supply com. 1986—, initial/continuing accreditation com. 1989-92), Can. Fedn. Deans Mgmt. and Adminstrn. Studies (vice chmn. 1981-82, chmn. 1982-84, sec.-treas. 1990—), Internat. Labour Orgn. (UN rep. 1985—), Can. Consortium Mgmt. Schs. (chmn. 1990—), Premier's Coun. on Sci. and Tech. (interman bd. dirs. 1984—). Home: 12 Varbrook Pl NW, Calgary, AB Canada T3A 0A2 Office: U Calgary Faculty Mgmt, 2500 University Dr NW, Calgary, AB Canada T2N 1N4

MAHER, SHEILA, secondary school principal. Prin. R. L. Turner High Sch., Carrollton, Tex. Recipient Blue Ribbon Sch. award U.S. Dept. Edn., 1990-91. Office: R.L. Turner HS 1600 Josey Ln Carrollton TX 75006

MAHER, SYLVIA ARLENE, nurse administrator; b. Kansas City, Mo., Nov. 12, 1946; d. Elmer Newton and Enid Louise (Olson) McKinley; m. A.C. Amborn Jr., 1969 (div. 1971); m. Mark Edward Maher, Oct. 14, 1977. Diploma in Nursing, Trinity Luth. Hosp., Kansas City, Mo., 1967; BSN, U. Kans. Med. Ctr., 1971, MA in Nursing, 1975. Nurse Trinity Luth. Hosp., Kansas City, Mo., 1967-71; head nurse emergency svcs. Baptist Meml. Hosp., Kansas City, Mo., 1971-77; clinical nurse specialist Bethany Med. Ctr., Kansas City, Mo., 1977-78, critical care div. dir., 1978-80, v.p. for nursing svcs., 1980-92, v.p. for patient care svcs., 1992—; adj. faculty William Jewell Coll., Liberty, Mo., 1975-77, U. Kans. Med. Ctr., Kansas City, 1979—, Avila Coll., Kansas City., 1981-82. Editorial bd. Jour. of AACN, 1978-84. Mem. Kansas City Nursing Adminstrs. (pres. and pres. elect 1987, 88, Nursing Adminstr. of Yr. 1988), Kans. Forum Women Execs., ANA, Sigma Theta Tau. Avocations: seamstress, rose gardener. Home: 262 Lakeshore Dr W Kansas City KS 66106-9521 Office: Bethany Med Ctr 51 N 12th St Kansas City KS 66102-5161

MAHER, WILLIAM JAMES, investment executive; b. Chgo., Feb. 23, 1937; s. Alexander E. and Merle G. M.; B.B.A., Marquette U., 1961. Merchandising exec. Montgomery Ward & Co., Inc., Chgo., 1962-68; mgmt. cons. Cresap, McCormack & Paget, N.Y.C., 1968-69; v.p., treas. Solar Prodns., Inc., L.A., 1969-72; v.p., sec., treas. Creative Mgmt. Assocs., L.A., 1972-74; v.p., dir. Josephson Internat., Inc., L. A., 1975-83; pres. Tipperary Prodns., Inc., Beverly Hills, Calif., 1983-88; pres. Winter Park Capital Assets, Inc., 1989—. Office: Winter Park Capital Assets Inc 1031 W Morse Blvd Winter Park FL 32789-3715

MAHESH, VIRENDRA BHUSHAN, endocrinologist; b. India, Apr. 25, 1932; came to U.S., 1958, naturalized, 1968; s. Narinjan Prasad and Sobhagyawati; m. Sushila Kumari Aggarwal, June 29, 1955; children: Anita Rani, Vinit Kumar. BSc with honors, Patna U., India, 1951; MSc in Chemistry, Delhi U., India, 1953, PhD, 1955; DPhil in Biol. Sci, Oxford U., 1958. James Hudson Brown Meml. fellow Yale U., 1958-59; asst. research prof. endocrinology Med. Coll. Ga., Augusta, 1959-63; assoc. research prof. endocrinology Med. Coll. Ga., 1963-66, prof., 1966-70, Regents prof. endocrinology, 1970-86, Robert B. Greenblatt prof., 1979—, chmn. endocrinology, 1972-86, chmn., Regents prof. physiology and endocrinology, 1986—, chmn. physiology and endocrinology, 1986—; dir. Ctr. for Population Studies, 1971—; mem. reproductive biology study sect. NIH, 1977-81, mem. human embryology and devel. study sect. NIH, 1982-86, 90-93, chmn., 1991-93. Contbr. articles to profl. jours., chpts. to books; editor: The Pituitary, a Current Review, Functional Correlates of Hormone Receptors in Reproduction, Recent Advances in Fertility Research, Hirsuitism and Virilism, Regulation of Ovarian and Testicular Function, Excitatory Amino Acids: Their Role in Neuroendocrine Function; mem. editl. bd. Steroids, 1963—, Jour. of Clin. Endocrinology and Metabolism, 1976-81, Jour. Steroid Biochemistry and Molecular Biology, 1991—, Assisted Reproductive Tech./ Andrology, 1993—; mem. adv. bd. Maturitas, 1977-81. Recipietn Rubin award Am. Soc. Study Sterility, 1962, Billings Silver medal, 1965; Best Tchr. award freshman class Sch. Medicine, Med. Coll. Ga., 1969, Outstanding Faculty award Sch. Medicine, 1992, Outstanding Faculty award Sch. Grad. Studies, 1981, 94, Disting. Teaching award, 1988, Excellence in Rsch. award Grad. Faculty Assembly, 1987-91, 93-95; Disting. Scientist award Assn. Scientist Indian Origin in Am., 1989, rsch. grantee NIH, 1960—. Mem. Chem. Soc. (Eng.), Soc. Biochem. and Molecular Biol., Soc. Neurosci., Endocrine Soc., Soc. for Gynecologic Investigation, Internat. Soc. Neuroendocrinology, Soc. for Study Reproduction (Carl G. Hartman award 1996), Am. Physiol. Soc., Internat. Soc. Reproductive Medicine (pres. 1980-82), Soc. Exptl. Biology and Medicine, Am. Fertility Soc., Am. Assn. Lab. Animal Sci., N.Y. Acad. Scis., AAUP, Sigma Xi. Office: Med Coll of Ga Dept Physiology & Endocrinology Augusta GA 30912-3000

MAHEU, SHIRLEY, Canadian legislator; b. Montreal, Que., Can., Oct. 7, 1931; d. George William Johnson and Bertha Hunt; m. René Albert Maheu, Sept. 5, 1953; children: Ronald, Richard, Daniel, Marc. Ed., O'Sullivan Bus. Coll. Cert. ins. broker. Ins. broker; mcpl. councillor City of Saint-Laurent, Que., 1982-88; mem. from Saint-Laurent Ho. of Commons, 1988-96; mem. Can. Senate, Ottawa, Ont., 1996—. Pres. Saint-Laurent br. Red Cross Soc. Mem. Saint-Laurent C. of C. Roman Catholic. Office: Canadian Senate, EB Rm 259, Wellington St, Ottawa, ON Canada K1A 0A6

MAHEY, JOHN ANDREW, museum director; b. DuBois, Pa., Mar. 30, 1932; s. Manasseh A. and Bernyce (Holdar) M. Student, Columbia U., 1950-52; B.A., Pa. State U., 1959, M.A., 1962. Asst. dir. Peale Mus., Balt., 1964-69; dir. E.B. Crocker Art Gallery, 1969-72, Cummer Gallery of Art, 1972-75, Meml. Art Gallery of U. Rochester, 1975-79; chief curator Philbrook Art Center, Tulsa, 1979-84; dir. San Antonio Mus. Art, 1984-89, Flint (Mich.) Inst. of Arts, 1989-96. Contbr. articles on artists to art his. jours.; author exhbn. catalogs. Served with USAF, 1952-57, 62-64. Fulbright scholar, 1962. Mem. Am. Assn. Museums, Assn. Art Mus. Dirs., Phi Beta Kappa, Phi Alpha Theta.

MAHL, GEORGE FRANKLIN, psychoanalyst, psychologist, educator; b. Akron, Ohio, Nov. 27, 1917; s. Floyd Alexander and Margaret (Strecker) M.; m. Martha Jane Fenn, Jan. 10, 1944; 1 dau., Barbara Jessica. A. B., Oberlin Coll., 1939, M.A., 1941; PhD, Yale U., 1948; certificate, Western New Eng. Inst. Psychoanalysis, 1962. Asst. psychology Oberlin Coll., 1939-41; rsch. asst. in psychology Yale U., New Haven, 1941-42, mem. faculty, 1947—, prof. psychiatry and psychology, 1964-88, prof. emeritus, 1988—; tchr. Western New Eng. Inst. Psychoanalysis, 1961-85, pres., 1972-74. Served to 1st lt. AUS, 1942-46. Fellow AAAS, APA; mem. Ea. Psychol. Assn., Western New Eng. Inst. Psychoanalysis, Western New Eng. Psychoanalytic Soc., Internat. Psychoanalytical Assn., Inst. Psychoanalytic Tng. and Rsch. (N.Y.). Home: 106 Bayard Ave North Haven CT 06473-4303

MAHLE, CHRISTOPH ERHARD, electrical engineer; b. Stuttgart, Germany, Mar. 7, 1938; came to U.S., 1968; s. Ernst Johannes and Else (Wurth) M.; m. Mary Heavenrich, Mar. 23, 1975; children: Lisa, Charles. Diploma engring., Swiss Fed. Inst. Polytech., Zurich, 1961, D of Sci. Tech., 1966. Rsch. asst. Swiss Fed. Inst. Tech., Zurich, Switzerland, 1961-67; with tech. staff Comsat Labs., Clarksburg, Md., 1968-71, sect. head, 1971-73, dept. mgr., 1973-81, dir., 1981-83, exec. dir., 1983-94, v.p., 1995-96; ret., 1996. Patentee in field; contbr. articles to profl. jours. Fellow IEEE. Avocations: music, mountain climbing.

MAHLER, HALFDAN THEODOR, physician, health organization executive; b. Vivild, Denmark, Apr. 21, 1923; s. Magnus and Benedicte (Suadicani) M.; m. Ebba Fischer-Simonsen, Aug. 31, 1957; children: Per Bo, Finn. MD, U. Copenhagen, 1948, postgrad. degree in pub. health; LLD (hon.), U. Nottingham, Eng., 1975; MD (hon.), Karolinska Inst., Stockholm, 1977; Docteur, de l'Universite des Scis. Sociales de Toulouse, France, 1977; DPH (hon.), Seoul Nat. U., 1979; ScD (hon.), U. Lagos, Nigeria, 1979, Emory U., 1989; MD (hon.), Warsaw Med. Acad., 1980; LHD, U. Nacional Federico Villareal, Lima, Peru, 1980; LHD (hon.), U. Gand, Belgium, 1983, CUNY, 1989; MD (hon.), Charles U., Prague, 1982, Mahidol U., Bangkok, Thailand, 1982, Aarhus U., Denmark, 1988, U. Copenhagen, 1988, Aga Khan U., Pakistan, 1989; LHD (hon.), U. Nacional Autonoma de Nicaragua, 1983; Dr. honoris causa, The Semmelweis U. of Medicine, Budapest, Hungary, 1987; LLD (hon.), McMaster U., Can., 1989; DSc (hon.), SUNY, 1990; MD (hon.), U. Newcastle Upon Tyne, 1990; LLD (hon.), U. Exeter, 1990; LLD (honoris causa), U. Toronto, 1990. Specialized tng. in TB, active field of internat. pub. health work; planning officer mass Tb campaign Ecuador, 1950-51; sr. officer nat. Tb program WHO, India, 1951-61; chief Tb unit, Hdqrs., WHO, Geneva, 1962-69, sec. to expert adv. panel on Tb, 1962-69, dir. project systems analysis, 1969-70, asst. dir.-gen. div. health services and div. family health, 1970-73, dir.-gen., 1973-88, dir. gen. emeritus, 1988; sec. gen. Internat. Planned Parenthood Fedn., 1989-95. Contbr. articles on epidemiology and control of Tb, polit., social, econ, and technol. priorities in health sector, application of systems analysis to health care problems to profl. jours. Decorated Grand Officier de l'Ordre Nat. du Benin, 1975, Grand Officier de l'Ordre Nat. du Voltaique, Upper Volta, 1978, comdr. de l'Ordre Nat. du Mali, 1982, Grand Officer de l'Ordre du Merite de la Rep. du Senegal, 1982, comdr. 1st class Order White Rose (Finland), Grand Officier de l'Ordre nat. malgache, Madagascar, 1987, Grand Cross Icelandic Order of the Falcon, 1988, Grand Cordon of Order Sacred Treasure, Japan, 1988, Bourgeoisie d'Honneur, Geneva, Switzererland, Grand Croix De L'Ordre De Merite, Luxenbourg, 1990; recipient Jana Evangelisty Purkyne medal (Presdl. award) Prague, 1974, Comenius U. gold medal Bratislava, 1974, Carlo Forlanini gold medal Federazione Italiana contro la Tubercolosi et le Malattie Polmonari Sociali Rome, 1975, Ernest Carlsens Found. Prize Copenhagen, 1980, Georg Barfred-Pedersen prize Copenhagen, 1982, Hagedorn medal and prize Denmark, 1986, Freedom From Want medal Roosevelt Inst., 1988, Storkors Af Dannebrogsordenen, Denmark, 1988; hon. prof. U. Nacional Mayor de San Marcos, Lima, Peru, U. Chile Faculty of Medicine, Beijing Med. Coll., Rep. of China, Shanghai Med. U.; Bartel World Affairs fellow Cornell U., 1988; U.N. Population award, 1995, Andrija Stampar award, 1995. Fellow Royal Coll. Physicians (London), Faculty Community Medicine of Royal Colls. Physicians U.K. (hon.), Indian Soc. for Malaria and other Communicable Diseases (hon.), Royal Soc. Medicine (London) (hon., U.K.-U.S. Hewitt award 1992), London Sch. Hygiene and Tropical Medicine (hon.); mem. Med. Assn. Argentina (hon.), Latin Am. Med. Assn. (hon.), Italian Soc. Tropical Medicine (hon.), Belgium Soc. Tropical Medicine (assoc.), Societe medicale de Geneve (hon.), Union internationale contre la Tuberculose (hon.), Societe francaise d'Hygiene, de Medecine sociale et de Genie sanitaire (hon.), Uganda Med. Assn. (hon. life), Coll. Physicians and Surgeons, Bangladesh Royal Coll. Gen. Practitioners (ad eundem), List of Honour of the Internat. Dental Fedn., Am. Pub. Health Assn. (hon.), Nat. Acad. Medicine Mex. (hon.), Nat. Acad. Buenos Aires (hon.), Swedish Soc. Medicine (hon.), Brit. Medal Assn. (hon. fgn. corr. 1990). Home and Office: 12 Chemin du Pont-Ceard, CH 1290 Versoix Switzerland

MAHLER, HARRY BEZ, architect, planner; b. Montclair, N.J., Aug. 8, 1928; s. Harry A. and Pauline Marie (Bez) M.; m. Elizabeth Willett, Oct. 2, 1954; children: Debra, Steven, Suzanne. B.Arch., Columbia U., 1954, William K. Fellows fellow, 1954-55. Successively draftsman, designer, chief designer, assoc., ptnr., sr. ptnr. for design, mem. mgmt. com. The Grad Partnership, Newark, 1949-90; chmn., chief exec. officer Grad. Assocs., P.A., Newark, 1990-94, chmn. emeritus, 1994—; prin. GLS Internat., 1994—; adj. prof. emeritus, curriculum coord. design and drawing Pratt Inst.; past mem. archtl. adv. bd. McGraw-Edison Corp.; chmn. adv. com., past chmn. fee com. N.J. Sch. Architecture; chmn. archtl. div. capital campaign, adv. com. Sch. Architecture N.J. Inst. Tech., mem. bd. overseers; design adv. com. State of N.J. Contbr. articles to profl. jours. Former commr., chmn. Montclair Redevel. Agy.; past chmn. barrier-free architecture com. Easter Seal Soc. N.J.; exec. v.p. Essex coun. Boy Scouts Am., chmn. camp study No. N.J. couns., mem. N.E. Regional Bd.; v.p. area 2 NE region Boy Scouts Am., mem. Nat. Properties Com. Boy Scouts of A., mem. nat. coun.; past chmn., mem. real estate and corp. devel. luncheon, past mem. exec. bd., bd. govs. N.J. com. NCCJ; past trustee Montclair YMCA; mem. baseball boosters and kickoff classic coms. N.J. Sports Authority; mem., chmn., pres. Montclair State U. Found. Bd., others; chmn. archtl. com., Eagle Rock Condominium Assn.; pres., trustee, First United Meth. Ch. of Montclair. Recipient awards AIA, Illuminating Engrs. Soc., N.J. Soc. Architects, Bell System, Am. Concrete Inst., N.J. Bus. Mag., Am. Cons. Engrs. Coun., Archtl. Record Mag., Am. Planning Assn.; Humanitarian Brotherhood award NCCJ, 1987; Sch. of Architecture award N.J. Inst. Tech., 1987; Silver Beaver award Boy Scouts of Am., 1987, Silver Antelope award, 1991, Northeast Region award, 1987; named Bus. Leader of the Yr., N.J. Mag., 1991. Fellow AIA (mem. nat. design com.); mem. N.J. Soc. Architects, Execs. Assn. N.J. (past chmn.), Regional Bus. Partnership (bd. dirs.), N.J. State C. of C. (bd. dirs.), N.J. Zool. Soc. (exec. v.p., past pres.), Beta Theta Pi. Methodist. Home: 214 Highland Ave Montclair NJ 07043-1010 Office: Grad Assocs PA 2 Gateway Ctr Newark NJ 07102-5003

MAHLER, RICHARD T., finance executive; b. Galt, Ont., Can., May 15, 1943; s. Lawrence Herman and Therese (Trepanier) M.; m. Susan Jane Campbell, May 25, 1968; children: Stephen, Katherine. BSc, U. Waterloo, 1966; MBA, McMaster U., Hamilton, 1975. Asst. contr. Ford Motor Can., Oakville, Ont., 1967-81; v.p. fin., chief fin. officer Amdahl Can. Ltd., Toronto, Ont., 1981-90; v.p., CFO Finning Ltd., Vancouver, B.C., 1990—. Chmn. Oakville Galleries, Ont., 1971-79; pres. U. Waterloo Adv. Coun., 1984-90; bd. dirs. Nat. Ballet Sch., Toronto, 1989—; chmn. coop. coun. Simon Fraser U., 1993-95; mem. bus. coun. B.C. Econ. Policy Adv. Group, 1994—. Mem. Fin. Execs. Inst., Coun. Fin. Execs. Conf. Bd. Can., Hollyburn Country Club, Seymour Golf Club, Canadian Club Vancouver. Office: Finning Ltd, 555 Great Northern Way, Vancouver, BC Canada V5T 1E2

MAHLER, ROBERT LOUIS, soil scientist, educator; b. Huntington Park, Calif., Jan. 7, 1954; s. Robert Alfred and Emily Chonita (Ortega) M.; 1 child, Claudia. BS, Wash. State U., 1976, MS, 1978; PhD, N.C. State U., 1980. Asst. prof., assoc. prof., now prof. soil sci. U. Idaho, Moscow, 1980—, soil fertility researcher, 1980—, extension soil scientist, 1989—, water quality coord., 1990—. Contbr. more than 200 articles to profl. jours. Environ. sciences tchr. Knights of Columbus. Mem. Am. Soc. Agronomy, Soil Sci. Soc. Am., Western Soc. Soil Sci., Rotary, KC, Gamma Sigma Delta (pres. 1989-90). Roman Catholic. Avocations: hiking, camping, collecting baseball cards. Office: U Idaho Soil Sci Divsn Moscow ID 83843

MAHLMAN, JERRY DAVID, research meteorologist; b. Crawford, Nebr., Feb. 21, 1940; s. Earl Lewis and Ruth Margaret (Callendar) M.; m. Janet Kay Hilgenberg, June 10, 1962; children—Gary Martin, Julie Kay. A.B., Chadron State Coll., Nebr., 1962; M.S., Colo. State U., 1964, Ph.D., 1967. Instr. Colo. State U., Fort Collins, 1964-67; from asst. prof. to assoc. prof. Naval Postgrad. Sch., Monterey, Calif., 1967-70; rsch. meteorologist NOAA Geophys. Fluid Dynamics Lab., Princeton, N.J., 1970-84, lab. dir., 1984—; lectr. with rank of prof. Princeton U., 1980—; chmn. panel on mid-atmosphere program NAS-NRC, 1982-84, mem. climate rsch. com., 1986-89, mem. panel on dynamic extended range forecasting, 1987-90; mem. U.S.-USSR Commn. on Global Ecology, 1989-92; mem. Bd. on Global Change, 1991-95, bd. on Sustainable Devel., 1995—; U.S. rep. world climate rsch. program Joint Sci. Commn., 1991—. Contbr. over 70 articles to profl. jours. Elder Monterey Presbyterian Ch., 1968-70, Lawrence Road Presbyn. Ch., Lawrenceville, N.J., 1972-75; bd. dirs. Lawrence Non-Profit Housing Inc., 1978-88. Recipient Disting. Authorship award Dept. Commerce, 1980, 81, Gold medal, 1986, Disting. Svc. award Chadron State Coll., 1984, Presdl. Rank award disting. exec. 1994, Honor Alumnus award Colo. State U. 1995. Fellow Am. Geophys. Union (Jule Charney lectr. 1993), Am. Meterol. Soc. (awards com. 1984, 95, chmn. upper atmosphere com. 1979, assoc. editor Jour. Atmospheric Sci. 1979-86, councilor 1991-94, Editor's award 1978, Carl-Gustaf Rossby Rsch. medal 1994). Democrat. Home: 9 Camelia Ct Lawrenceville NJ 08648-3201 Office: Princeton U Geophys Fluid Dynamics Lab PO Box 308/NOAA Princeton NJ 08542-0308

MAHLMANN, JOHN JAMES, music education association administrator; b. Washington, Jan. 21, 1942; s. Charles Victor and Mary Elizabeth (Deye) M.; m. Ning Ning Chang, Feb. 5, 1972; 1 son, Justin Geeng Ming. BFA, Boston U., 1962, MFA, 1963; postgrad., U. Notre Dame, summer 1962; EdD, Pa. State U., 1970. Grad. asst. Boston U., 1962-63, instr., supr. student tchrs., dir. masters degree candidates, 1964-66; grad. asst., research asst. Pa. State U., 1963-64, instr., 1966-67, dir. gallery, art edn. dept., 1966-67; asst. prof. Tex. Tech Coll., 1967-69; chmn. tenure and promotions com.; dir. publs., asst. exec. sec. Nat. Art Edn. Assn., Washington, 1969-71; exec. sec. Nat. Art Edn. Assn., 1971-82, also tour dir. to Japan and Orient; exec. dir. Music Educators Nat. Conf., 1983—; instr. drawing Lubbock Art Assn.; asst. debate coach, asst. coordinator forensics Boston U.; vis. instr., mem. staff George Washington U., No. Va. Community Coll., Tchrs. Coll. N.Y. Exhibited at, Boston U., Pa. State U., Harvard U., Tex. Tech. U., Salem (Mass.) State Coll., Botolph Gallery, Boston, Inst. Contemporary Art, Boston, Barncellar Gallery, Orleans, Mass., State Gallery, State College, Pa., Halls Gallery, Lubbock, Lubbock Art Assn., Loft Gallery, San Antonio, Llano Estacado Art Assn., Hobbs, N.Mex., Purdue U., Cushing Gallery, Dallas, Religious Art Exhbn., Cranbrook Acad. Art, Bloomfield Hills, Mich., Upstairs Gallery, Arlington, Tex., S.W. Tex. State Coll., San Marcos.; Editor: Art Edn., 1970-81, Art Tchr., 1971-80; contbr. articles to mags. Mem. Music Educators Nat. Conf., Nat. Art Edn. Assn., Am. Soc. Assn. Execs., Washington Soc. Assn. Execs., Phi Delta Kappa. Home: 10703 Cross School Rd Reston VA 22091-5105 Office: Music Ed Nat Conf 1806 Robert Fulton Dr Reston VA 22091-4348

MAHMOUD, ADEL A. F., physician, educator, investigator; b. Cairo, Aug. 24, 1941; s. Abdel Fattah and Fathia (Osman) M.; m. Sally L. Hodder. MD, U. Cairo, 1963; PhD, U. London, 1971. House officer U. Cairo Hosps., 1963-65; asst. lectr. U. Ain Shams Med. Faculty and Hosps., Cairo, 1965-68; clin. rsch. asst., WHO fellow Sch. Hygiene And Tropical Medicine U. London, 1969-72; rsch. assoc. to assoc. prof. medicine Dept. Medicine, Med. Sch. Case Western Res. U., Cleve., 1973-80; chief, div. geog. med. dept. medicine Univ. Hosps., Cleve., 1977-87, prof. medicine, 1980—; prof. molecular biology and microbiology, 1982—; John H. Hord prof., chmn., dept. medicine Case Western Reserve U., 1987—; physician-in-chief Univ. Hosps., 1987—; mem. com. on rsch. grants NAS, 1983-86; mem. nat. adv.

allergy and infectious diseases coun. NIH, 1988-92. Editor: (with K. Frank Austen) The Eosinophil in Health and Disease, 1979, (with K.S. Warren) Textbook on Tropical and Geographical Medicine, 1984, (with K.S. Warren) Geographic Medicine for the Practitioner, 1987, (with K.S. Warren) Tropical and Geographical Medicine, 2nd edit., 1990, Tropical and Geographical Medicine Companion Handbook, 2d edit., 1993; guest editor: Bailliere's Clinical Tropical Medicine and Communicable Diseases, 1987; contbr. articles to profl. jours., chpts. to books. Trustee Cleve. Mus. Natural History. Recipient Baily K. Ashford medal, 1983; WHO fellow, 1969-71; Squibb award 1984; Josiah Macy Found. scholar 1980. Mem. Inst. Medicine of NAS, Am. Soc. Clin. Investigation, Am. Soc. Hematology, Assn. Am. Physicians, Am. Assn. Immunology, Infectious Diseases Soc. Am., Am. Soc. Tropical Medicine and Hygiene, Internat. Soc. Infectious Diseases (pres. 1990-92), Cen. Soc. Clin. Rsch. (pres. 1992), Sigma Xi, Alpha Omega Alpha. Home: 25-21 83rd St Flushing NY 11370 Office: Univ Hosps Cleveland Dept Medicine 11100 Euclid Ave Cleveland OH 44106-1736*

MAHMOUD, ALY AHMED, electrical engineering educator; b. Cairo, Jan. 25, 1935; came to U.S., 1960, naturalized, 1970; s. Ahmed Aly and Amina Mohammed (Rashwan) M.; m. Lucinda Lou Keller, Dec. 20, 1962; children: Ramy, Samy. B.Sc. with distinction and honors (Nat. Honor student), Ain Shams U., Cairo, 1958; M.S., Purdue U., 1961, Ph.D., 1964. Diplomate: Registered profl. engr., Iowa, La. Instr. elec. engring. Ain Shams U., 1958-60; asst, prof. elec. engring. U. N.B., Fredericton, 1964; research engr. No. Electric Research and Devel. Lab., Ottawa, Ont., Can., summer 1964; asst. prof. elec. engring. U. Asyut, Egypt, 1964-66; sr. research elec. engr. Naval Civil Engring. Lab., Port Hueneme, Calif., 1968-69, summer 1970; asst. prof. elec. engring. U. Mo., Columbia, 1966-71; assoc. prof. U. Mo., 1971-73, prof., 1973-76; prof. elec. engring., dir. Iowa test and evaluation facility, program mgr. Power Affiliates Research Program; supr. Power System Computer Service, Iowa State U., Ames, 1976-85; dean Coll. Engring. U. New Orleans, 1985-88; dean Sch. Engring. and Tech. Ind. U.-Purdue U.-at Ft. Wayne, 1988—; with FPC, summer 1974; program mgr. NSF, 1975-76; cons. in field. Contbr. articles to profl. jours. Vice chmn. Water and Light Adv. Bd. City of Columbia, 1973-76. Am. Friends of Middle East fellow, 1960-68. Sr. mem. IEEE; Mem. Power Engring. Soc., Am. Phys. Soc., Egyptian Profl. Engring. Soc., Am. Soc. Engring. Edn., Sigma Xi, Tau Beta Pi, Eta Kappa Nu. Patentee in field. Home: 5640 Foxcross Ct Fort Wayne IN 46835-2802 Office: Ind U-Purdue U-Ft Wayne Dean Sch Engring and Tech 2101 E Coliseum Blvd Fort Wayne IN 46805-1445 *In this country there are outstanding opportunities for those who are willing to work hard to serve the society and their profession. I am thankful to be in the U.S. and to have found this type of opportunity.*

MAHNK, KAREN, law librarian, legal assistant; b. Bklyn., July 13, 1956; d. James V. and Mary M. (Jones) Mascari; 1 child, Adam Eugene. Student, Baruch Coll., 1974-75, Miami-Dade Community Coll., 1986-89, St. Thomas U., 1994. Asst. libr. Mershon, Sawyer et al, Miami, Fla., 1976-79; libr., legal asst. Steel Hecton & Davis, Miami, 1980-84; libr. Valdes-Fauli, et al, Miami, 1984-94, Pub. Defender's Office, 11th Jud. Cir., Miami, 1994—; asst. coord. Broward County Multi-Family Devel. Recycling Program, 1990-91. Chair ways and means com. Palm Cove Elem. PTO, 1993-94; active vol. Broward County Guardian Ad Litum Program, 1989-92. Mem. ABA (assoc. stat., family law sect., law libr. affiliate), Am. Assn. Law Librs., Southeastern Assn. Law Librs., South Fla. Assn. Law Librs. (bd. dirs. 1988-89, chair constn. and bylaws commn. 1988-91, sec. 1983-84, v.p.-elect 1986-88, nominating com. 1992, sec. 1993-95, chair union list com. 1995—), Spl. Librs. Assn., Internat. Platform Assn. Democrat. Baptist. Avocations: painting, sailing, chess. Office: 1320 NW 14th St Ste 313 Miami FL 33125-1609

MAHON, ARTHUR J., lawyer; b. N.Y.C., Jan. 13, 1934; s. Arthur Logan and Mary Agnes (Craine) M.; m. Myra E. Murphy, Aug. 10, 1957; children: Maura, Madonna, Arthur, Nancy. B.A., Manhattan Coll., 1955; JD, NYU, 1958. Bar: N.Y., Fla., D.C. Adj. prof. law NYU Sch. of Law, N.Y.C., 1964-78; ptnr. Mudge, Rose, Guthrie, Alexander & Ferdon, N.Y.C., 1970-94; counsel Donovan Leisure Newton & Irvine, N.Y.C., 1994—. Trustee Manhattan Coll., N.Y., 1988—, Adrian and Jesse Archbold Charitable Trust, N.Y.C., 1976—; mem. joint bd. N.Y. Hosp.-Cornell Med. Ctr., N.Y.C., 1990—; com. on trust and estate gift plans Rockefeller U., N.Y.C., 1984—; bd. dirs. United Way Internat., 1988-94, Alexandria, Va., chmn. planned giving and endowments com. Archdiocese, N.Y.C., 1985—; bd. overseers Cornell Med. Coll., N.Y.C., 1986-92, chmn., 1992-95; dir. Am. Skin Assn., N.Y.C., 1989—, Noel Found., San Francisco, 1990—; gov. N.Y. Hosp., N.Y.C., 1994—; counsel Ira W. De Camp Found., 1994—; dir. Catholic Found. for the Future, N.Y.C., 1995—; dir. Communal Fund of the Archdiocese of N.Y., N.Y.C., 1995—. Served to capt. USAF, 1958-60. Root-Tilden scholar NYU. Mem. N.Y. State Bar Assn., Bar Assn. City of N.Y., Fla. Bar Assn., D.C. Bar Assn. Home: 16 Cambridge Dr Madison CT 06443-3016 Office: Donovan Leisure 30 Rockefeller Plz New York NY 10112

MAHON, ELDON BROOKS, federal judge; b. Loraine, Tex., Apr. 9, 1918; s. John Bryan and Nola May (Muns) M.; m. Nova Lee Groom, June 1, 1941; children: Jana, Martha, Brad. B.A., McMurry Coll., 1939; LL.B., U. Tex., 1942. Bar: Tex. 1942. Law clk. Tex. Supreme Ct., 1945-46; county atty. Mitchell County, Tex., 1947; dist. atty. 32d Jud. Dist. Tex., 1948-60, dist. judge, 1960-63; v.p. Tex. Electric Service Co., Ft. Worth, 1963-64; mem. firm Mahon Pope & Gladden, Abilene, Tex., 1964-68; U.S. atty. U.S. Dist. Ct. (no. dist.) Tex., Ft. Worth, 1968-72, judge, 1972—, now sr. judge. Pres. W. Tex. council Girl Scouts U.S.A., 1966-68; Trustee McMurry Coll. Served with USAAF, 1942-45. Named an outstanding Tex. prosecutor Tex. Law Enforcement Found., 1957. Mem. ABA, Fed. Bar Assn., Ft.-Worth-Tarrant County Bar Assn., Am. Judicature Soc., State Bar Tex. Methodist (past del. confs.). Office: US Courthouse 501 W 10th St Rm 502 Fort Worth TX 76102*

MAHON, MALACHY THOMAS, lawyer, educator; b. N.Y.C., Jan. 4, 1934; s. James and Alice (Rooney) M.; m. Margaret Phyllis Kirwan, Jan. 25, 1958; children: Veronica Mahon Grover, Laura Mahon Chandonnet, Malachy. B.A., Manhattan Coll., 1954; J.D., Fordham U., 1960. Bar: N.Y. 1960. Law clk. to chief magistrate John M. Murtagh N.Y.C., 1959-60; law clk. to justice Tom C. Clark U.S. Supreme Ct., 1960-61; assoc. Hale Russell & Stentzel, N.Y.C., 1961-62, Mudge Rose Guthrie & Alexander, N.Y.C., 1979-80; of counsel Farrell, Fritz, Caemmerer, Cleary, Barnosky & Armentano, Mineola, NY, 1982-83, Havens & Lombard, Flushing, N.Y., 1994—; prof. Fordham U. Law Sch., 1962-68; prof. law Hofstra U. Law Sch., 1968—, founding dean, 1968-73, S.B. Wilzig disting. prof. banking, 1985—; vis. prof. U. Tex. Law Sch., 1973-74; exec. dir., spl. N.Y. State asst. atty. gen. Meyer Investigation Spl. Attica Prosecutor's Office, 1975; Chief counsel N.Y. Gov.'s Spl. Com. on Criminal Offenders, 1966; mem. Nassau County Bd. Ethics, 1983-96, chmn., 1989-96. Staff author: Mental Illness, Due Process and the Criminal Defendant, 1968; monthly comml. law columnist: N.Y. Law Jour, 1976-78. Served with U.S. Army, 1954-56. Mem. ABA, N.Y. State Bar Assn., Assn. Bar City N.Y., Am. Law Inst. Home: 14 Duke of Gloucester Manhasset NY 11030-3210 Office: Hofstra U Law Sch Hempstead NY 11550

MAHON, ROBERT, photographer; b. Wilmington, Del., Dec. 28, 1949; s. Clifton and Mary Veronica (Figash) M.; m. Carol Joyce, Apr. 24, 1983. BA in Am. Studies, U. Del., 1971. One-man show Twining Gallery, N.Y.C., 1985, Mercer Coll., Trenton, N.J., 1993; exhibited in group shows Whitney (Collection) Mus. Am. Art, 1982, Phila. Mus. Art, 1982, 95, Am. Ctr., Paris, 1982, Mus. Modern Art, N.Y.C., 1983, 84-85, 93, Kolnischer Kunstverein, 1983, Art Inst., Chgo., 1985, Twining Gallery, 1985-86, 88, 89, N.J. State Mus., 1990, Guggenheim Soho, 1994, also others; represented in permanent collections Phila. Mus. Art, Mus. Modern Art, Met. Mus. Art, N.Y. Pub. Libr., Humanities Rsch. Ctr., U. Tex., Austin, Princeton U. Libr., also pvt. collections. Guggenheim grantee, 1985. Home and Studio: PO Box Q Stockton NJ 08559-0390

MAHONE, BARBARA JEAN, automotive company executive; b. Notasulga, Ala., Apr. 19, 1946; d. Freddie Douglas M. and Sarah Lou (Simpson). BS, Ohio State U., 1968; MBA, U. Mich., 1972; PMD, Harvard U., 1981. Sys. analyst GM, Detroit, 1968-71, sr. staff asst., 1972-74, mgr. career planning, 1975-78; dir. pers. adminstrn. GM, Rochester, N.Y., 1979-81; mgr. indsl. rels. GM, Warren, Ohio, 1982-83; dir. human resources mgmt. Chevrolet-Pontiac-Can. group GM, 1984-86; dir. gen. pers. and pub. affairs Inland divsn. GM, Dayton, Ohio, 1986-88; gen. dir. pers. Indland Fisher Guide divsn. GM, Detroit, 1989-91, gen. dir. employee benefits, 1991-93; dir. human resources truck group GM, Pontiac, Mich., 1994—; chmn. Fed. Labor Rels. Authority, Washington, 1983-84, Spl. Panel on Appeals; dir. Metro Youth; mem. bd. govs. U. Mich. Alumni. Bd. dirs. ARC, Rochester, 1979-82, Urban League Rochester, 1979-82, Rochester Aea Multiple Sclerosis; mem. human resources com. YMCA, Rochester, 1980-82; mem. exec. bd. Nat. Coun. Negro Women; mem. allocations com. United Way Greater Rochester. Recipient Pub. Rels. award Nat. Assn. Bus. and Profl. Women, 1976, Mary McLeod Bethune award Nat. Coun. Negro Women, 1977, Senate resolution Mich. State Legislature, 1980; named Outstanding Woman, Mich. Chronicle, 1975, Woman of Yr., Nat. Assn. Bus. and Profl. Women, 1978, Disting. Bus. Person, U. Mich., 1978, one of 11 Mich. Women, Redbook mag., 1978. Mem. Nat. Black MBA Assn. (bd. dirs., nat. pres. Disting. Svc. award, bd. dirs., nat. pres. Outstanding MBA), Women Econ. Club (bd. dirs.), Indsl. Rels. Rsch. Assn., Internat. Assn. for Pers. Women, Engring. Soc. Detroit. Republican. Home: 175 Kirkwood Ct Bloomfield Hills MI 48304-2927 Office: 2000 Centerpoint Pkwy M/C 483-512-8G3 Pontiac MI 48341-3147

MAHONEY, DONALD SCOTT, financial industry marketing executive; b. Boston, May 18, 1953; s. Donald Richard and Gloria Joan (Lewis) M.; m. Cheryl Constance LeConche, Sept. 16, 1978; children: Brendon, Blake, Lawson, Gloria, Jacqueline. BS in Bus. Adminstrn., Fairleigh Dickinson U., 1977. Registered investment advisor. V.p. mktg. Fox & Carskadon Inc., San Mateo, Calif., 1984-87; 1st v.p. Met. Life Real Estate Investment Co., 1987-90; sr. v.p. The Colonial Group of Mut. Funds, Boston, 1990-95, cons. to adv. bd., 1993-94; sr. v.p. First Union Bank, Atlanta, 1996—. Bd. dirs. Northridge Civic Assn., Atlanta, 1994; mem. Ga. Republican Party, Atlanta, 1984-94. Mem. Internat. Assn. Fin. Planners, NRA. Roman Catholic. Avocations: jogging, Tai Kwan Do Karate (brown belt).

MAHONEY, GERALD FRANCIS, manufacturing company executive; b. Bklyn., July 31, 1943; s. Francis B. and Leona (Gray) M.; m. JoAnne A. Maselli, May 2, 1971; children: G. Scott, Ryan J. BA, Adelphi U., 1965; MBA, Northeastern U., 1966. CPA, N.Y. Mgr. Arthur Andersen & Co., N.Y.C., 1966-73; asst. contr. Bairnco Corp., N.Y.C., 1973-78, v.p. fin., 1980-81; gen. mgr. Bairnco Corp., Pensauken, N.J., 1979-80; v.p., div. pres. Bairnco Corp., Union, N.J., 1981-83; sr. v.p. fin. and adminstrn. Polychrome Corp., Yonkers, N.Y., 1984-87; pres. Transcrit Corp., Brewster, N.Y., 1987-90, Pavey Envelope & Tag Corp., Jersey City, 1991-94; chmn., CEO Mail-Well, Inc., Englewood, Colo., 1994—. Mem. AICPA, N.Y. State Soc. CPA's, Noyac Country Club (Sag Harbor, N.Y., bd. dirs. 1980-83), Glenmoor Country Club (Englewood, Colo.), Ridgewood Country Club (N.J.). Republican. Roman Catholic. Avocations: golf, tennis. Home: 21 Cherry Hills Farm Dr Englewood CO 80110-7170 Office: Mail-Well Inc 23 Inverness Way E Englewood CO 80112-5708

MAHONEY, GERALD T., medical facility administrator; b. Rochester, Minn., Nov. 10, 1933. AA, Rochester C.C., 1953; BS, Mankato State U., 1958. Constrn. supr. Murry Drake & Towey, 1958-59; credit counselor Mayo Clinic, Rochester, Minn., 1959-67, sys. and procedures specialist, 1967-69, adminstrv. asst., 1969-86; asst. to assoc. adminstr. St. Mary's Hosp. of Rochester, 1986-93, adminstr., 1993—. Mem. Am. Coll. Health Care Execs. (assoc.). Home: St Marys Hosp Rochester 1019 NW 1st St Rochester MN Office: St Mary's Hosp 1216 SW 2d St Rochester MN 55902*

MAHONEY, J. DANIEL, federal judge; b. Orange, N.J., Sept. 7, 1931; s. Daniel Vincent and Louisa (Dunbar) M.; m. Kathleen Mary O'Doherty, Oct. 22, 1955; children: J. Daniel, Kieran Vincent, Francis Kirk, Mary Louisa, Eileen Ann, Elizabeth Anne. B.A. magna cum laude, St. Bonaventure U., 1952; LL.B. (Kent scholar), Columbia U., 1955. Bar: N.Y. 1960. Asso. firm Simpson Thatcher & Bartlett, N.Y.C., 1958-62; partner firm Wormser, Keily, Alessandroni, Mahoney & McCann, N.Y.C., 1965-74, Windels, Marx, Davies & Ives, N.Y.C., 1974-86; state chmn. N.Y. Conservative Party, 1962-86; judge U.S. Ct. Appeals (2d cir.), Milford, Conn., 1986—; elected to Electoral Coll., 1980; dir. Nat. Rev., Inc., N.Y.C., 1972-86. Author: Actions Speak Louder, The Story of the New York Conservative Party, 1967. Mem. adv. coun. Pace U., 1985-87; dean's adv. coun. Hofstra U. Sch. Law, 1982-90; bd. fellows Poly. Inst. N.Y., 1981-91. Lt. (j.g.) USCGR, 1955-58. Roman Catholic. Office: 2 Corporate Dr Shelton CT 06484

MAHONEY, JERRY C. D., lawyer; b. Mpls., 1931. BSL, U. Minn., 1953, LLB, 1955. Bar: Minn. 1955. Ptnr. Dorsey & Whitney, Mpls. Office: Dorsey & Whitney 220 S 6th St Minneapolis MN 55402-4502*

MAHONEY, JOHN, actor; b. Manchester, Eng., June 20, 1940. MA in English, Western Ill. U.; student, Quincy Coll.; trained for the theater at St. Nicholas Theatre, Chgo. Stage performances include The Water Engine, 1977, The Hothouse, Taking Steps, Death of a Salesman, Orphans, 1985 (Theater World award), The House of Blue Leaves, 1986 (Tony award, Clarence Derwent award), The Subject Was Roses, 1991; films include Mission Hill, 1982, Voyeur, 1984, Code of Silence, 1985, The Manhattan Project, 1986, Streets of Gold, 1987, Tin Men, 1987, Suspect, 1987, Moonstruck, 1987, Frantic, 1988, Betrayed, 1988, Eight Men Out, 1988, Say Anything, 1989, Love Hurts, 1990, The Russia House, 1990, Barton Fink, 1991, Article 99, 1992, In the Line of Fire, 1993, Striking Distance, 1993, Reality Bites, 1994, The Hudsucker Proxy, 1994; TV series: Lady Blue, 1985-86, H.E.L.P., The Human Factor, 1991, Frasier, 1993—; TV movies Chicago Story, 1981, Listen to your Heart, 1983, Dance of the Phoenix, , 1984, The Killing Floor, 1984, First Steps, 1985, Trapped in Silence, 1986, Favorite Son, 1988, (TNT) Dinner at Eight, 1989, (HBO) The Image, 1990, The 10 Million Dollar Getaway, 1991, The Secret Passion of Robert Clayton, 1992; TV special The House of Blue Leaves, 1987. Served AUS. Office: care ICM c/o Paul Martino 8942 Wilshire Blvd Beverly Hills CA 90211*

MAHONEY, JOHN L., English literature educator; b. Somerville, Mass., Feb. 4, 1928. AB, Boston Coll., 1950, AM, 1952; PhD, Harvard U., 1957. Instr. of English Boston Coll., 1955-59, asst. prof. of English, 1959-62, assoc. prof., 1962-65, prof., 1965—, Rattigan prof. English, 1994—, chmn. dept., 1962-67, 69-70, dir. PhD program in English, 1970-75, 82-85, mem. ednl. policy com. Grad. Sch. Arts and Scis., 1985-87; vis. prof. of English Harvard U. summer sch., 1963, 65, 67, 71, 80, 83, 86; cons. for self-study Weston Coll. Schs. of Philosophy and Theology, Boston Coll., 1965; sem. leader programs for women, Boston Coll., Newton Coll., 1976, 78, 79; mem. numerous acad. coms. and couns.; cons., mem. English adv. com. Commonwealth of Mass., 1968-70; mem. acad. coun. Evening Coll. Arts and Scis. and Bus. Adminstrn., Boston Coll., 1969—, univ. core curriculum devel. com., 1991—; bd. trustees St. John's Sem., Brighton, Mass., com. on acad. affairs, 1980-86; sec. bd. trustees Katharine Gibbs Sch., Boston, 1982-90; mem. adv. bd. Jesuit Inst., Boston Coll., 1987—. Author: The Whole Internal Universe: Imitation and the New Defense of Literature in British Criticism, 1660-1830, 1985, The Persistence of Tragedy: Episodes in the History of Drama, 1985, The Logic of Passion: The Literary Criticism of William Hazlitt, rev. edit., 1981; editor, author intro. and notes: The Enlightenment and English Literature, 1980, The English Romantics: Major Poetry and Critical Theory, 1978, An Essay of Dramatic Poetry and Other Critical Writings by John Dryden, 1965, William Duff's Essay on Original Genius, 1964; contbr. Imagination and the Ways of Genius (in Approaches to Hazlitt), 1986, Teaching the Immortality Ode with Coleridge's Dejection: An Ode (in Approaches to Teaching Wordsworth's Poetry), 1986, and others; editor: (with J. Robert Barth, S.J.) Coleridge, Keats, and the Imagination: Romanticism and Adam's Dream, 1990, Teaching Shelley's Skylark and the Defence of Poetry, (in Approaches to Teaching Shelley's Poetry) 1990; mem. editl. bd. Boston Coll. Mag., 1981-90; author articles, papers delivered at profl. confs.; reviewer for Studies in Romanticism, The Wordsworth Circle, Nineteenth Century Contexts, So. Humanities Rev. Active Sacred Heart Parish, Lexington, Mass., del. to Lexington Coun. Chs., 1968, chmn. parish coun., 1969-72, mem. parish coun., 1995—, religious edn. commn., 1974-79, 90—, sem. leader Christian Youth Edn., 1969-73, lector, 1972—; mem. Archdiocese of Boston Commn. for Promotion of Parish Couns., 1969-74, Patron Book Selection Com., Cary Meml. Libr., Lexington. Boston Coll. Grad. Sch. fellow, 1950-52; Boston Coll. Faculty rsch. grantee, 1964, 68, 86, 92, Mellon Found. grantee for rsch. and faculty devel., 1981-82; grantee rsch. Am. Philos. Soc., 1987; recipient Boston Coll. Campus Coun. Tchr. of Yr. award, 1966, Boston Coll. alumni award for excellence in edn., 1978, Boston Coll. Faculty fellow, 1986, 94, Andrè Favat award Mass. Coun. Tchrs. English, 1988, Prof. of Yr. award Coun. for Advancement and Support of Edn. Mass., 1989. Mem. AAUP (pres. Boston Coll. chpt. 1962), MLA, N.E. MLA, Am. Soc. Eighteenth Century Studies, N.E. Soc. Eighteenth Century Studies, Wordsworth-Coleridge Assn. Am., Keats-Shelley Assn. Am., The Johnsonians, Alpha Sigma Nu, Phi Beta Kappa. Office: Boston Coll Dept English Chestnut Hill MA 02167

MAHONEY, KATHLEEN MARY, lawyer; b. Methuen, Mass., Oct. 24, 1954; d. Joseph Patrick and Beatrice Evelyn (Blackington) M.; m. Mark Dennis Schmitt, May 26, 1979; children: Alexis Anne Schmitt, Brynne Elizabeth Schmitt. BA, Keene (N.H.) State Coll., 1976; JD, Syracuse (N.Y.) U., 1979. Bar: Minn. 1979, U.S. Dist. Ct. Minn. 1980, U.S. Ct. Appeals (8th cir.) 1985, U.S. Supreme Ct. 1988. Instr. Sch. of Law Hamline U., St. Paul, 1979-80; law clk. to hon. justice Douglas K. Amdahl Minn. Supreme Ct., St. Paul, 1980-81; law clk. to hon. judge Neal P. McCurn U.S. Dist. Ct. (no. dist.) N.Y., Syracuse, 1981-83; spl. asst. atty. gen. Atty. Gen.'s Office State of Minn., St. Paul, 1983-89; assoc. Oppenheimer, Wolff & Donnelly, St. Paul, 1989-91, sr. assoc., 1991-93; ptnr., 1994—; cons. George Banzhaf Co., Milw., 1979-80; adj. prof. Hamline U. Sch. of Law, 1987-89. Mem. Dist. 621 Study Adv. Com., Shoreview, Minn., 1989-91, chair, 1991-93; mem. Turtle Lake Sch. Adv. Com., Shoreview, 1988—; mem. exec. com., bd. dirs. Voyageurs Regional Nat. Park Assn., 1993-95; mem. Class of '93; bd. dirs. St. Paul Vol. Ctr., 1994—; leader Girl Scouts Am., 1993—. Mem. ABA, Minn. Bar Assn., Ramsey County Bar Assn. Office: Oppenheimer Wolff & Donnelly First Bank Building Ste 1700 Saint Paul MN 55101

MAHONEY, MARGARET ELLERBE, foundation executive; b. Nashville, Oct. 24, 1924; d. Charles Hallam and Leslie Nelson (Savage) M.; BA magna cum laude, Vanderbilt U., 1946; LHD (hon.), Meharry Med. Coll., 1977, U. Fla., 1980, Med. Coll. Pa., 1982, Williams Coll., 1983, Smith Coll., 1985, Beaver Coll., 1985, Brandeis U., 1989, Marymount Coll., 1990, Rush U., 1993, SUNY, Bklyn., 1994, N.Y. Med. Coll., 1995. Fgn. affairs officer State Dept., Washington, 1946-53; exec. assoc., assoc. sec. Carnegie Corp., N.Y.C., 1953-72; v.p. Robert Wood Johnson Found., Princeton, N.J., 1972-80; pres. Commonwealth Fund, N.Y.C., 1980-94; pres. MEM Assocs., Inc., N.Y.C., 1995—. Contbr. articles to profl. jours. Trustee John D. and Catherine T. Mac Arthur Found., 1985—, Dole Found., 1984—, Smith Coll., 1988-93, Columbia U., 1991—, Goucher Coll., 1995—; vis. fellow Sch. Architecture and Urban Planning, Princeton U., 1973-80; bd. dirs. Council on Found., 1982-88; mem. N.Y.C. Commn. on the Yr. 2000, 1985-87, MIT Corp., 1984-89; bd. govs. Am. Stock Exchange, 1987-92; adv. bd. Office of the Chief Med. Examiner, N.Y.C., 1987—, Barnard Coll, Inst. Med. Research, 1986-92; vice chmn. N.Y.C. Mayor's Com. for Pub./Pvt. Partnerships, 1990-93; bd. dirs. Alliance for Aging Rsch., 1987—, Overseas Devel. Coun., 1988—, Nat. Found. Center for Disease Control and Prevention, Inc., 1994—; mem. vestry Parish of Trinity Ch., 1982-89, 91-95; active Atlantic Fellowships Selection Com., 1994—. Recipient Frank H. Lahey Meml. award, 1984, Women's Forum award, 1989, Walsh McDermott award, 1992, Disting. Grantmaker award Coun. Founds., 1993, Edward R. Loveland award Am. Coll. Physicians, 1994, Special Recognition award AAMC, 1994, Merit medal Lotos Club, 1994, Terrance Keenan Leadership award in Health Philanthrophy, Grantmakers in Health, 1995. Mem. AAAS, Inst. Medicine of NAS, Am. Acad. Arts and Scis., Am. Philos. Soc., Coun. Fgn. Rels., Fin. Women's Assn. N.Y., N.Y. Acad. Medicine (vice chmn. bd. govs.), N.Y. Acad. Scis., Alpha Omega Alpha. Office: MEM Assocs Inc 521 Fifth Ave Ste 2010 New York NY 10175

MAHONEY, MICHAEL ROBERT TAYLOR, art historian, educator; b. Worcester, Mass., Jan. 24, 1935; s. Michael J. and Mary (Taylor) M. Grad., Phillips Acad., 1953; B.A., Yale U., 1959; Ph.D., Courtauld Inst., U. London, 1965. Finley fellow Nat. Gallery Art, 1962-64; fellow Harvard Center Italian Studies, Villa I Tatti, 1963; museum curator Nat. Gallery Art, 1964-69; prof. fine arts, chmn. dept. Trinity Coll., Hartford, Conn., 1969-86; Genevieve Harlow Goodwin prof. fine arts Trinity Coll., 1974—; Incorporator Hartford Pub. Library, 1970—; elector Wadsworth Atheneum, Hartford, 1974-85. Author: The Drawings of Salvator Rosa, 1977, (with Jean Cadogan) Wadsworth Atheneum Paintings II: Italy and Spain; editor: National Gallery of Art Report and Studies in the History of Art, 1968-69. Trustee Cesare Barbieri Found., Trinity Coll., 1977—, Watkinson Libr., Trinity Coll., 1985—, Somerset House Art History Found., N.Y.C., 1985—; bd. govs. Hill-Stead Mus., Farmington, Conn., 1992-95. Office: Trinity Coll Dept Fine Arts Hartford CT 06106

MAHONEY, MICHAEL SEAN, history educator; b. N.Y.C., June 30, 1939; s. Thomas Michael and Dorothy (Hopkins) M.; m. Jean Carmel Angelilli, Aug. 20, 1960; children: Colin Sean, Bridget Elizabeth. AB, Harvard U., 1960; postgrad., U. Munich., 1960-62; PhD, Princeton U., 1967. Instr. history Princeton (N.J.) U., 1965-67, asst. prof., 1967-72, assoc. prof., 1972-80, prof., 1980—. Author: The Mathematical Career of Pierre de Fermat, 1973, 94, (in Japanese) Mathematics in History, 1982. Bd. edn. regional schs., Princeton, 1983-86; trustee Nat. Faculty of Humanities, Arts and Sci., 1986—, chair, 1994—. Deutscher Akademischer Anstauschdienst fellow, 1960, Dibner Inst. fellow, 1995-96, NSF fellow, 1964-69. Mem. History Sci. Soc. (council mem. 1980-82), Soc. for History of Tech. Home: 85 Harrison St Princeton NJ 08540-5355

MAHONEY, PATRICK MORGAN, retired judge; b. Winnipeg, Man., Can., Jan. 20, 1929; s. Paul Morgan and Joan Ethel Tracy (Patrick) M.; m. Mary Alma Sneath, June 28, 1958; children: Michael G., Patrick M., Sheila M., D'Arcy C. B.A., U. Alta., 1950, LL.B., 1951. Bar: Alta. 1952, apptd. Queen's counsel 1972, U.S. Ct. Mil. Appeals (hon.) 1983. Justice trial div. Fed. Ct. Can., Ottawa, Ont., 1973-83; judge Ct. Martial Appeal Ct. Can., Ottawa, 1973-82; chief justice Ct. Martial Appeal Ct. Can., 1982-94; ret.; judge Fed. Ct. Appeal, 1983-94; ret.; Mem. Parliament for Calgary South, 1968-72, sec. to minister of fin., 1970-71, minister of state, 1972. Mem. Can. Judges Conf. (dir. 1981), Calgary Golf and Country Club. Home: 3 Coltrin Pl, Ottawa, ON Canada K1M 0A5

MAHONEY, THOMAS HENRY DONALD, historian, educator, government official; b. Cambridge, Mass., Nov. 4, 1913; s. Thomas Henry, Jr. and Frances (Lucy) M.; m. Phyllis Norton, July 14, 1951; children: Thomas Henry IV, Linda, David, Peter, Philip. A.B., Boston Coll., 1936, A.M., 1937; Ph.D., George Washington U., 1944; M.P.A., Harvard U., 1967, D.P.A., 1989. Instr. Gonzaga Sch., Washington, 1937-39, Dunbarton Coll., Washington, 1938-39; instr., then asst. prof. history Boston Coll., 1939-44; asst. prof. history Holy Cross Coll., 1944-46; vis. lectr. history and govt. Smith Coll., 1944-45, Wellesley Coll., 1947-48; mem. faculty MIT, 1945-84, prof. history, 1961—, chmn. sect. history, 1963-65, 73-79; vis. prof. U. So. Calif., 1950; Lowell lectr. Boston, 1957; Carnegie fellow Harvard Law Sch., 1965-66; sec. elder affairs Commonwealth of Mass., 1979-83; head Mass. del. White House Conf. on Aging, 1981, mem. policy com., 1995; mem. ethnic com. U.S. Dept. Edn., 1979-83; mem. UNNGO Com. on Aging, N.Y.C., 1985—, chmn., 1987-91; corporator, trustee Cambridgeport Savs. Bank; adv. bd. Mildred & Claude Pepper Found., Washington, Tallahassee, 1989—; mem. adv. bd. Nat. Silver Haired Congress, 1995—; panelist, cons. numerous internat. confs. on gerentology; keynote spkr., cons., panelist Interparliamentarian Union meetings on aging, Bangkok, Guatemala City, Sofia, Budapest, London, 1986-89, New Delhi, Canberra, 1993, Paris, Copenhagen, 1994, Madrid, Bucharest, 1995, Istanbul, 1996; prin. spkr. MIT Alumni Club Dinners Istanbul, 1988, Paris, 1988, Singapore, 1993, Madrid, 1995, Berlin, 1995, London, 1996; rep. of Internat. Fedn. Aging, Montreal to UN, 1994—. Author: Edmund Burke and Ireland, 1960; co-author: Readings in International Order, 1951, China, Japan and the Powers, 3d edit., 1960, The U.S. in World History, 3d edit., 1963, Edmund Burke: The Enlightenment and the Modern World, 1977, 1776, 1977, Aging in Urbanization, 1990; editor: Burke's Reflections, 1955, Selected Writings and Speeches of Edmund Burke on America, 1964. Mem. Mass. Fulbright Com., 1953-74, chmn., 1966-74; observer Vatican City Consistories, 1956, 73, 85, World Assembly on Aging, Vienna, 1982; bd. dirs. Mass. Civic League, 1967—; state rep. Mass. Gen. Ct., 1971-78, chmn. energy and ethics coms., 1977-78; mem. community adv. coun. Jr. League Boston, 1982-86; UN rep. InterParliamentary Conf., Ottawa, 1985, Congress Latin Am. Socs. Gerontology and Geriatrics, Lima, 1984; N.Y. and Washington rep. Centre Internat. de Gérontologie, Paris,

1985-93; mem. Cambridge Sch. Com., 1948-54; chmn. trustees Cambridge Libr., 1948-54, Mass. State Libr., 1952-61; bd. dirs. Internat. Student Fedn.; mem. Cambridge City Coun., 1964-72; sr. advisor internat. issues and questions of aging Congressman Claude Pepper, 1985-88. Knight of Malta; Am. Coun. of Learned Socs. fellow, 1938, Guggenheim fellow, 1961-62, Carnegie fellow, 1954, Ford Internat. Rsch. fellow, 1975; recipient Humanitarian of Yr. award mass. Psychol. Soc., 1983. Fellow Royal Hist. Soc.; mem. Am. Hist. Assn., Am. Cath. Hist. Assn. (pres. 1957), Mass. Hist. Soc., Cath. Commn. Cultural and Intellectual Affairs, Conf. Brit. Studies, Nat. Conf. State Legislators (sci. and tech. com., intergovtl. rels. com. 1973-78, mem. del. People's Republic of China 1976 and Republic of China, Taiwan 1978, keynoter Singapore Internat. Conf. on Elders 1993), Japan-Am. Socs. (keynoter 1995). Home: 130 Mt Auburn St Apt 410 Cambridge MA 02138-5779

MAHONEY, WILLIAM FRANCIS, editor; b. Joliet, Ill., Jan. 24, 1935; s. Cletus George and Mildred Marie (Ochs) M.; m. Carroll Frances Johnson, June 28, 1958; children: Erin Michele Alderfer, Kevin William, Megan Ann, Sheila Marie, Nora Aileen. BS in Journalism, Marquette U., 1957. Reporter Ft. Wayne (Ind.) News Sentinel, 1958-59; pub. rels. mgr. Motorola, Inc., Franklin Park, Ill., 1959-66; sr. account exec. Young & Rubicam, Inc., Chgo., 1966-68; pub. info. dir. ABA, Chgo., 1969-71; investor rels. mgr. Chemetron Corp., Chgo., 1971-76; corp. comm. dir. Scott Paper Co., Phila., 1976-80; pub. rels. dir. Esmark Inc., Chgo., 1980-81; prin. Mahoney & Mitchell Incorp., Phila., 1981-89, Investor Rels. Ptnrs., Livingston, N.J., 1993—. Author: Investor Relations: The Professional's Guide to Financial and Marketing Communications, 1991, The Active Shareholder, 1993; editor Investor Rels. Update, Valuation Issues. Mem. Nat. Investor Rels. Inst., Pub. Rels. Soc. Am., Vesper Club. Republican. Roman Catholic. Home and Office: 716 S Brandywine St West Chester PA 19382-3511

MAHONY, ROGER M. CARDINAL, archbishop; b. Hollywood, Calif., Feb. 27, 1936; s. Victor James and Loretta Marie (Baron) M. A.A., Our Lady Queen of Angels Sem., 1956; B.A., St. John's Sem. Coll., 1958, B.S.T., 1962; M.S.W., Catholic U. Am., 1964. Ordained priest Roman Cath. Ch., 1962, ordained bishop, 1975, created cardinal priest, 1991. Asst. pastor St. John's Cathedral, Fresno, Calif., 1962, 68-73, rector, 1973-80; residence St. Genevieve's Parish, Fresno, Calif., 1964—, adminstr., 1964-67, pastor, 1967-68; titular bishop of Tamascani, aux. bishop of Fresno, 1975-80; chancellor Diocese of Fresno, 1970-77, vicar gen., 1975-80; bishop Diocese of Stockton (Calif.), 1980-85; archbishop Archdiocese of L.A., 1985-91, cardinal priest, 1991—; diocesan dir. Cath. Charities and Social Svc. Fresno, 1964-70, exec. dir. Cath. Welfare Bur., 1964-70; exec. dir. Cath. Welfare Bur. Infant of Prague Adoption Service, 1964-70; chaplain St. Vincent de Paul Soc., Fresno, 1964-70; named hon. chaplain to Pope Paul VI, 1967; mem. faculty extension div. Fresno State U., 1965-67; sec. U.S. Cath. bishops ad hoc com. on farm labor Nat. Conf. Bishops, 1970-75; chmn. com. on pub. welfare and income maintenance Nat. Conf. Cath. Charities, 1969-70; bd. dirs. West Coast Regional Office Bishops Com. for Spanish-Speaking, 1967-70; chmn. Calif. Assn. Cath. Charities Dirs., 1965-69; trustee St. Patrick's Sem., Archdiocese of San Francisco, 1974-75; mem. adminstrv. com. Nat. conf. Cath. Bishops, 1976-79, 82-85, 87-90, com. migration and refugees, 1976—, chmn. com. farm labor, 1981—, com. moral evaluation of deterrence, 1986-88; cons. com., chmn. for ProLife Activities, 1990—; mem. com. social devel. and world peace U.S. Cath. Conf., 1985, chmn. internat. policy sect., 1987-90; com. justice and peace, Pontifical Couns., 1984-89, 90—, pastoral care of migrants and itinerant people, 1986—, social communications, 1989—. Mem. Urban Coalition of Fresno, 1968-72, Fresno County Econ. Opportunities Commn., 1964-65, Fresno County Alcoholic Rehab. Com., 1966-67, Fresno City Charter Rev. Com., 1968-70, Mexican-Am. Council for Better Housing, 1968-72, Fresno Redevel. Agy., 1970-75, L.A. 2000 Com., 1985-88, Fed. Commn. Agrl. Workers, 1987—, Blue Ribbon Com. Affordable Housing City of L.A., 1988; mem. commn. to Draft an Ethics Code for L.A. City Govt., 1989-90; bd. dirs. Fresno Community Workshop, 1965-67; trustee St. Agnes Hosp., Fresno. Named Young Man of Yr. Fresno Jr. C. of C., 1967. Mem. Canon Law Soc. Am., Nat. Assn. Social Workers. Home: 114 E 2nd St Los Angeles CA 90012-3711 Office: Archdiocese of LA 1531 W 9th St Los Angeles CA 90015-1112

MAHOWALD, ANTHONY PETER, geneticist, cell biologist, educator; b. Albany, Minn., Nov. 24, 1932; s. Aloys and Cecilia (Maus) Mahowald; m. Mary Lou Briody, Apr. 11, 1971; children: Maureen, Lisa, Michael. BS, Spring Hill Coll., 1958; PhD, Johns Hopkins U., 1962. Asst. prof. Marquette U., Milw., 1966-70; asst. staff mem. Inst. Cancer Rsch., Phila., 1970-72; assoc. prof. Ind. U., Bloomington, 1972-76, prof., 1976-82; Henry Willson Payne prof. Case Western Res. U., Cleve., 1982-90, chmn. dept. anatomy, 1982-88, chmn. dept. genetics, 1988-90; Louis Block prof., chmn. dept molecular genetics and cell biology U. Chgo., 1990—; chmn. Com. Devel. Biology U. Chgo., 1991—. Woodrow Wilson Found. fellow, 1958, NSF fellow, 1958-62. Fellow AAAS, Am. Acad. Arts and Scis., Soc. Scholars Johns Hopkins U.; mem. Nat. Acad. Scis., Genetics Soc. Am. (sec. 1986-88), Soc. Devel. Biology (pres. 1989, editor-in-chief jour. 1980-85), Am. Soc. Cell Biology (coun. mem. 1995—). Office: U Chgo Dept Molecular Genetics/Cell Biology Chicago IL 60637

MAHR, GEORGE JOSEPH, financial service executive, real estate developer; b. Bklyn., Mar. 9, 1947; s. George Joseph and Mary Ann (Hanrahan) M.; m. Joan Valeroso, Mar. 21, 1970; children: Christopher, Courtney, Kelly. BS in Acctg., N.Y. Inst. Tech., 1970. Auditor Price Waterhouse & Co., Huntington Station, N.Y., 1973-77; mgr. internal audit United Techs. Corp., Hartford, Conn., 1977-83, contr., 1983-84, v.p. fin., chief fin. officer, 1985-86; v.p. fin., chief fin. officer Mostek Corp. div. United Techs. Corp., Carrollton, Tex., 1986, 1987; v.p. bus. devel. SGS-Thomson Microelectronics, Inc., Carrollton; mng. ptnr. Mahr Leonard Mgmt. Co., Dallas, 1988—; chmn. Semicondr. Insights, Inc., Kanata, Ont., Can., Mahr Devel. Corp., Dallas, Lenmar Devel. Corp., Dallas, Mahr Devel. Corp. Fla., Dallas, Sailfish Enterprises, Inc., Dallas; ptnr. DJ Enterprises, Dallas. Home: 2616 Rothland Ln Plano TX 75023-1421 Office: Mahr Leonard Mgmt Co Ste 626 5420 Lyndon B Johnson Fwy Dallas TX 75240-2643

MAHRE, PHIL, alpine ski racer, race car driver; b. Yakima, Wash., May 10, 1957; s. David Robert and Mary Ellen (Chotl) M.; m. Holly Mahre; 3 children. Student, pub. schs. Mem. U.S. Men's Pro Tour, 1989. Olympic Silver medalist in slalom Lake Placid, N.Y., 1980, Olympic Gold medalist, Sarajevo, Yugoslavia, 1984, winner World Cup, 1981, 82, 83, First Interstate Bank Cup slalom, 1989. Office: US Ski Team PO Box 100 Park City UT 84060-0100*

MAHRENHOLTZ, DAYLA DIANNE, elementary school principal; b. Glendale, Calif., Apr. 12, 1957; d. Preston Paul Buby and Evangeline Ruth (Sickler) B.; m. Laurence J. Mahrenholtz, Nov. 21, 1987 (div. Feb. 1993). AA, El Camino Jr. Coll., Torrance, Calif., 1975-77; BA, Calif. State U., Carson, 1979; MA, Calif. State U., L.A., 1990; EdD, U. LaVerne, Calif., 1996. Cert. edn. adminstr., Calif. Teller Ban of Am., Lawndale, Calif., 1977-79; tchr. Whittier (Calif.) City Sch. Dist., 1980-88, tchr., mentor, 1988-92; prin. Los Nietos Sch. Dist., Whittier, Calif., 1992—. Mem. AAUW, Calif. Assn. Bilingual Edn., Assn. Calif. Adminstrs., Computer Users in Edn., Whittier Area Sch. Adminstrs. (program chair 1993—). Democrat. Avocations: bird watching, running, bicycling, body building, reading. Office: Aeolian Sch 11600 Aeolian St Whittier CA 90606-3306

MAHSMAN, DAVID LAWRENCE, religious publications editor; b. Quincy, Ill., Aug. 16, 1950; s. Alvin Henry and Dorothy Marie (Schnack) M.; m. Lois Jean Mohn, July 27, 1975. BS in Journalism, So. Ill. U., 1972; MDiv, Concordia Theol. Seminary, Fort Wayne, Ind., 1983; STM, Concordia Sem., St. Louis, 1995. Staff writer Paddock Publs., Arlington Heights, Ill., 1972-73, Decatur (Ill.) Herald & Rev., 1973-76; press asst. Hon. Tom Railsback U.S. Ho. Reps., Washington, 1976-79; campaign press sec. Hon. Dan Coats U.S. Ho. Reps., Ft. Wayne, Ind., 1979-80, 82; pastor Trinity Luth. Ch., Glen Cove, N.Y., 1983-85; dir. news and info. Luth. Ch.-Mo. Synod, St. Louis, 1985—; exec. editor, contbr. Luth. Witness, St. Louis, 1985—; exec. editor Reporter, St. Louis, 1985—; mem. Inter-Luth. task force on pornography Luth. Coun. U.S.A., 1986; mem. Washington adv. coun. Mo. Synod, Office of Govt. Info., Washington, 1987—. Recipient Jacob Scher Investigative Reporting award Women in Comm., 1974, Commendation award Concordia Hist. Inst., 1988. Mem. Concordia Hist. Inst. (life). Republican. Avocations: travel, photography, flying. Office: Luth Ch-Mo Synod 1333 S Kirkwood Rd Saint Louis MO 63122-7295

MAI, CHAO CHEN, engineer; b. Kwangchow, Canton, China, Feb. 26, 1936; came to U.S. 1962, naturalized 1973; m. Shao Shen Yam; children: Glenn, Kenneth. M.S.E.E., Oreg. State U., 1964; Ph.D. in E.E., Utah State U., 1967. Project engr. Sylvania Electric Co., Woburn, Mass., 1967-70; mgr. research and devel. Mostek Corp., Carrollton, Tex., 1970-76, v.p. research and devel., 1976-84; founder, sr. v.p. Dallas Semiconductor Corp., 1984—. Patentee Silicon gate combined with depletion load process, 1974; method for making a semicondr. device, 1985. MOSFET Fabrication Process, 1984. Mem. IEEE, Electrochem. Soc. Current work: Advanced processing technology in integrated circuits. Subspecialties: Integrated circuits; Microchip technology (engineering).

MAI, ELIZABETH HARDY, lawyer; b. Ithaca, N.Y., Nov. 7, 1948; d. William Frederick and Barbara Lee (Morrell) M.; m. Edward John Gobrecht III, May 19, 1990. BA in Am. Studies, Cornell U., 1970; JD, Dickinson Sch. Law, 1975. Bar: Pa. 1975, U.S. Dist. Ct. (mid. dist.) Pa. 1976. Atty. Keystone Legal Svcs., Inc., State Coll., Pa., 1975-76; asst. atty. gen. Pa. Dept. Commerce, Harrisburg, Pa., 1976-77; chief counsel Pa. Dept. Commerce, Harrisburg, 1978; assoc. Wolf, Block, Schorr and Solis-Cohen, Phila., 1979-83, ptnr., 1986—; v.p., gen. counsel EQK Ptnrs., Bala Cynwyd, Pa., 1983-86; chair environ. dept. Wolf, Block, Schorr and Solis-Cohen; chair Pa. state govt. affairs Internat. Coun. Shopping Ctrs., 1988-93; founding dir., mem. Comml. Real Estate Women, Phila.; bd. dels. Nat. Network Comml. Real Estate Women; adj. prof. Villanova (Pa.) U. Sch. Law, 1986—. Active Cornell U. Real Estate Coun., 1990—. Mem. ABA, Am. Coll. Real Estate Lawyers, Pa. Bar Assn., Phila. Bar Assn. Office: Wolf Block Schorr and Solis-Cohen 15th & Chestnut Sts 12th fl Philadelphia PA 19102

MAI, HAROLD LEVERNE, retired judge; b. Casper, Wyo., Apr. 5, 1928. BA, U. Wyo., 1950, JD, 1952. Bar: Wyo. 1952, U.S. Supreme Ct. 1963. Sole practice, Cheyenne, Wyo., 1953-62, 67-71; judge Juvenile Ct., Cheyenne, 1962-67; U.S. bankruptcy judge, Cheyenne, 1971-93, ret., 1993. Mem. adv. bd. Salvation Army. Wyo. Mem. ABA, Wyo. Bar Assn., Laramie County Bar Assn., Nat. Conf. Bankruptcy Judges.

MAI, KLAUS L., oil research company executive; b. Changsha, China, Mar. 7, 1930; s. Ludwig H. and Ilse (Behrend) M.; m. Helen M. Martinchek, July 14, 1957; children: Martin, Michael, Mark, Matthew. BS in Chem. Engring., Gonzaga U., Spokane, Wash., 1951; MS, U. Wash., Seattle, 1952, PhD, 1954. Registered profl. engr., Wash. With Shell Chem. Co., Houston, 1957-74, 77-81; various overseas assignments Shell Chem. Co., 1974-75; v.p. Shell Chem. Co., Houston, 1979-82; v.p. transp. and supplies Shell Oil Co., 1976-82; pres. Shell Devel. Co., Houston, 1982-87; chmn., pres. World Petroleum Congresses, London and Houston, 1987—. Contbr. articles to profl. publs.; patentee. Chmn. bd. dirs. S.W. Rsch. Inst., San Antonio; mem. Gov.'s Sci. and Tech. Coun.; pres., bd. dirs. Keystone Ctr., René DuBos Ctr. Recipient Disting. Alumnus award Gonzaga U., 1982, U. Wash., 1988. Fellow Am. Inst. Chem. Engrs.; mem. Soc. Chem. Industry, Am. Petroleum Inst., Coun. Chem. Rsch. (chmn., bd. dirs.), Keystone Found, Am. Ind. Health Coun. (bd. dirs.), Chem. Indsl. Inst. Toxicology (bd. dirs.), Lakeside Country Club (Houston), Petroleum Club of Houston, Sigma Xi, Tau Beta Pi. Office: World Petroleum Congresses PO Box 79331 Houston TX 77279-9331

MAIBACH, BEN C., JR., service executive; b. Bay City, Mich., 1920. With Barton-Malow Co., Detroit, 1938—, v.p., dir.-in-charge field ops., 1949-53, exec. v.p., 1953-60, pres., 1960-76, chmn. bd., 1976; chmn. and dir. Barton-Malow Ent.; chmn. bd. Cloverdale Equipment Co. Trustee Barton-Malow Found, Maibach Found., 1967—, Greater Del Safety Coun.; chmn. Apostolic Christian Woodhaven, Detroit; bishop Apostolic Christian Ch., Mich., Ont., Fla.; nat. chmn. Apostolic Ch. European Relief Bd., 1991—; bd. dirs. S.E. Mich. chpt. ARC, United Found., Rural Gospel and Med. Missions of India. Home: 34050 Ramble Hills Dr Farmington MI 48331-4224 also: 5525 Azure Way Sarasota FL 34242-1857 Office: Barton-Malow Co 27777 Franklin Rd Ste 800 Southfield MI 48034-8258

MAIBACH, BEN C., III, construction company executive; b. 1946. BS, Mich. State U., 1969. With Barton-Malow Corp., Oak Park, Mich., 1964—, v.p. field ops., 1964-68, systems analyst, programmer, 1968-70, project adminstr., 1970-72, officer mgr., purchasing agt., 1972-73, v.p., 1973-76, exec. v.p., 1976-81, pres., 1981—. Office: Barton-Malow Co 27777 Franklin Rd Ste 800 Southfield MI 48034*

MAIBENCO, HELEN CRAIG, anatomist, educator; b. New Deer, Aberdeenshire, Scotland, June 9, 1917; came to U.S., 1917; d. Benjamin C. and Mary (Brown) Craig; children: Thomas Allen, Douglas Craig. BS, Wheaton (Ill.) Coll., 1948; MS, DePaul U., 1950; PhD, U. Ill., Chgo., 1956. Asst. prof., assoc. prof., then prof. U. Ill., Chgo., 1956-73; prof. Rush U., Chgo., 1973-86, prof. emeritus, 1993—; anatomist dept. anatomy, dept. rehab. medicine Rush-Presbyn.-St. Luke's Med. Ctr., Chgo., 1986—, rsch. cons., 1973—; prof. emeritus Rush-U. Chgo., 1986—; cons. on grant application NIH, Bethesda, Md. Contbr. articles to profl. jours. Mem. AAAS, Endocrine Soc., Am. Assn. Anatomists, Sigma Xi. Republican. Presbyterian. Home: 1324 S Main St Wheaton IL 60187-6480

MAICKEL, ROGER PHILIP, pharmacologist, educator; b. Floral Park, N.Y., Sept. 8, 1933; s. Philip Vincent and Margaret Mary (Rose) M.; m. Lois Louise Pivonka, Sept. 8, 1956; children: Nancy Ellen Maickel Ward, Carolyn Sue Maickel Anderson. B.S., Manhattan (N.Y.) Coll., 1954; postgrad., Poly. Inst. Bklyn., 1954-55; M.S., Georgetown U., 1957, Ph.D., 1960. Biochemist Nat. Heart Inst., Bethesda, Md., 1955-65; asso. prof. pharmacology Ind. U., 1965-69, prof., 1969—, head sect. pharmacology med. scis. program, 1971-77; prof. pharmacology and toxicology, head dept. Sch. Pharmacy and Pharmacal Scis. Purdue U., West Lafayette, Ind., 1977-83; dir. lab. animal program Purdue U., West Lafayette, 1988—; acting v.p. product acquisition and devel. BetaMED Pharms., Inc., Indpls., 1983-84. Adv. editor: Pergamon Press, 1970-88; adv. editorial bd.: Neuropharmacology, 1974-88. Bd. dirs. TEAMS, Inc., 1981-87, Am. Coun. on Sci. and Health, 1993—; trustee AAALAC, 1992-96. Recipient Alumni award in medicine Manhattan Coll., 1972. Fellow AAAS, Am. Coll. Neuropsychopharmacology, Am. Inst. Chemists (bd. dirs. 1989-92, pres.-elect 1992-94, pres. 1994-96, chmn. 1996—), Royal Soc. Chemistry, Collegium Internat. de Neuro-Psychopharmacologicum; mem. ASTM, Am. Chem. Soc., Am. Soc. Pharmacology and Exptl. Therapeutics, Am. Soc. Clin. Pharmacology and Therapeutics, Soc. Forensic Toxicologists, Internat. Assn. Chiefs Police, Internat. Soc. Psychoneuroendocrinology, N.Y. Acad. Scis., Soc. Neurosci., Soc. Toxicology, Sigma Xi, Rho Chi. Home: 3567 Canterbury Dr Lafayette IN 47905-3714 Office: R E Heine Pharmacy Bldg Purdue Univ Lafayette IN 47907-1334 *As a human being, I hope to be able to do my best in the roles of scientist, teacher, and citizen by fulfilling the academic criteria of teaching, research, and service to the utmost degree humanly possible.*

MAIDA, ADAM JOSEPH, cardinal; b. East Vandergrift, Pa., Mar. 18, 1930. Student, St. Vincent Coll., Latrobe, Pa., St. Mary's U., Balt., Lateran U., Rome, Duquesne U. Ordained priest Roman Cath. Ch., 1956, consecrated bishop, 1984. Bishop Green Bay, Wis., 1984-89; archbishop Detroit, 1990-95; cardinal, 1995—. Home: 75 E Boston Blvd Detroit MI 48202-1318 Office: Archdiocese of Detroit 1234 Washington Blvd Detroit MI 48226-1825

MAIDIQUE, MODESTO ALEX, academic administrator; b. Havana, Cuba, Mar. 20, 1940; s. Modesto Maidique and Hilda Rodriguez; m. Ana Hernandez, July 18, 1981; children: Ana Teresa, Mark Alex. BS, MIT, 1962, MS, 1964, PhD, 1970. Instr. MIT, Boston, 1976-79; v.p., gen. mgr. Analog Devices Semiconductor, Boston, 1970-76; asst. prof. Harvard U., Boston, 1976-81; assoc. prof. Stanford U., Palo Alto, Calif., 1981-84; sr. ptnr. Hambrecht and Quist Venture Ptnrs., Palo Alto, Calif., 1981-86; cofounder, dir. U. Miami (Fla.) Innovation and Entepreneurship Inst., 1984-86; pres. Fla. Internat. U., Miami, 1986—. Mem. Pres.'s Edn. Policy Adv. Com.; chmn. Beacon Coun., 1992-93. Recipient Citizenship award HEW, 1973, Teaching award Stanford U., 1983. Mem. IEEE, Assn. Cuban Engrs. Republican. Roman Catholic. Home: 6821 SW 104th St Miami FL 33156-3253 Office: Fla Internat U Office of President Miami FL 33199

MAIDMAN, RICHARD HARVEY MORTIMER, lawyer; b. N.Y.C., Nov. 17, 1933; s. William and Ada (Seegle) M.; m. Lynne Rochelle Lateiner, Apr. 3, 1960 (div. Sept. 1987); children: Patrick, Mitchel, Dagny. BA, Williams Coll., 1955; JD, Yale U., 1959; postgrad. N.Y. U. Grad. Sch. Bus., 1957, Grad. Sch. Law, 1960, 77. Bar: N.Y. 1961, Fla., 1961, U.S. Dist. Ct. 1962, 79, U.S. Ct. Appeals 1966, U.S. Supreme Ct., 1978. Assoc. Saxe, Bacon & O'Shea, N.Y.C., 1962-64; ptnr. Weiner, Maidman & Goldman, N.Y.C., 1964-67; pvt. practice, N.Y.C., and Fla., 1968—; pres. MBS Equities, Inc., 1970-88, Fashion Wear Realty Co., Inc., N.Y.C., 1975—; mng. gen. ptnr. Richard and David Maidman, N.Y.C., 1972—, Barcelona Hotel Ltd., Miami Beach, Fla., 1975-84, New Haven Projects Co., 1987—; dir. The Farr Companies, Washington, 1990-92; legis. counsel Theodore R. Kupferman, 17th Congl. Dist. N.Y., 1966-68; of counsel Shwal, Thompson & Bloch, N.Y.C. and Geneva, 1976-87; receiver Halloran House Hotel, N.Y.C., 1981. Contbr. articles to profl. jours. Mem. ABA, N.Y. State Bar Assn., Fla. Bar Assn., Assn. Bar City N.Y., Bankruptcy Lawyers Assn. N.Y.C., Real Estate Bd. of N.Y. Home: Steamboat Lndg Sands Point NY 11050 Office: 432 E 87th St New York NY 10128-6502

MAIDMENT, ANDREW DOUGLAS ARNOLD, medical physicist; b. Mississauga, Ont., Can., Oct. 17, 1964; came to U.S., 1993; s. Sidney Douglas and Jean (Grieveson) M.; m. Susan Ng, Aug. 21, 1993. B of Applied Sci., U. Toronto, Ont., 1987, PhD, 1993. Instr. Thomas Jefferson U., Phila., 1993-94, dir. radiol. imaging physics, 1993, asst. prof., 1994—; hon. adj. asst. prof. Drexel U., Phila., 1994—; cons. in field. Contbr. articles to jours. Med. Imaging, Radiology, Med. Physics, Physics in Medicine and Biology. Recipient Young Investigators award Internat. Union Phys. and Engring. in Medicine, 1994; grantee NIH-Nat. Cancer Inst.; scholar Radiol. Soc. N.A., Ont. Ministry of Edn., Univ. Toronto. Mem. IEEE, AAAS, Am. Coll. Radiology (mem. coms.), Am. Assn. Physicists in Medicine (mem. coms.), Pa. Radiol. Soc., Internat. Soc. Photo-optical Engring. Achievements include research in physics of medical imaging, image instrumentation. Office: Thomas Jefferson U 111 S 11th St Philadelphia PA 19107-4824

MAIDON, CAROLYN HOWSER, education director; b. Chgo., May 13, 1946; d. Lloyd Earl and Esther Lillian (Beck) Howser; m. Charles Randall Maidon, Nov. 21, 1970; children: Randall Scott, April Janel. BS in Edn., Okla. State U., 1968; MS in Edn., N.C. State U., 1984, postgrad., 1987—. Tchr. biology and English Cary (N.C.) High Sch., 1968-71; grad. instr. N.C. State U., Raleigh, 1984-85, asst. affirmative action officer, 1985-89, asst. dir. univ. undesignated program, 1989-95; dir. tchr. edn., 1995—. Home: 311 Hemlock St Cary NC 27513-4313 Office: NC State U Box 7801 Raleigh NC 27695-7801

MAIDON, GILLES, dancer; b. Paris. Studied with Raymond Franchetti, studied with Diane Carter. Soloist Ballet de Marseille, Paris, 1976-83; dancer Santiago (Chile) Ballet, 1983-90, Cin. Ballet, 1990-92; prin. artist Ballet West, Salt Lake City, 1992—; guest artist various ballet cos., galas and festivals. Dance performances include Notre Dame de Paris, Peer Gynt, Anna Karenina, Sergeant Early's Dream, Taming of the Shrew, The Great Gatsby, Swan Lake. Office: Ballet West 50 W 200 S Salt Lake City UT 84101-1642

MAIENSCHEIN, FRED C., physicist; b. Belleville, Ill., Oct. 28, 1925; s. Fred and Ethel (Forsythe) M.; m. Joyce Kylander, Aug. 14, 1948; children: Jane, Jon. B.S. in Chem. Engring, Rose Hulman Inst. Tech., 1945; M.S. in Physics, Ind. U., 1948, Ph.D. in Physics, 1949. Physicist Oak Ridge Nat. Lab., 1951-60, assoc. dir. engring. physics div., 1960-66; co-dir. Oak Ridge Electron Linear Accelerator, 1965-74, dir. engring. physics div., 1966-90, ret., 1990; current neurosci. scholar; mem. com. reactor physics Nuclear Energy Agy., 1962-89; mem. adv. com. radiation aspects of SST, FAA, 1969-74; mem. subcoms. Nat. Com. Radiation Protection, 1959-71. Contbr. articles profl. jours., chpts. in books. Fellow Am. Nuclear Soc.; mem. Am. Phys. Soc., AAAS, Soc. Neurosci., Tau Beta Pi. Home: 838 W Outer Dr Oak Ridge TN 37830-8402

MAIER, ALFRED, neuroscientist; b. Bamberg, Bavaria, Fed. Republic of Germany, Sept. 16, 1929; came to U.S., 1958; s. Johan and Barbara (Rauh) M. BS in Zooology, Calif State U., Long Beach, 1967; PhD in Anatomy, UCLA, 1972. Postdoctoral fellow Dept. Kinesiology, UCLA, 1972-74; instr. Dept. Cell Biology U. Ala., Birmingham, 1974-76, asst. prof. 1976-80, assoc. prof., 1980-89, prof., 1989—; sr. scientist cell adhesion and matrix rsch. ctr. U. Ala., Birmingham; rsch. sabbatical Faculty Biology U. Konstanz, Fed. Republic of Germany, 1984, Dept. Physiology U. Otago, Dunedin, New Zealand, 1990; vis. prof. Faculty of Biology, U. Konstanz, 1985, '86. Contbr. articles and sci. papers to profl. jours and seminars. Recipient Pres.'s award for Excellence in Tchg., U. Ala., 1994, Didactic Instr. of Yr. Sch. Dentistry, 1993, 94, Best Basic Sci. Instr. Sch. Dentistry, 1978, 79, 83, 84. Mem. Soc. for Neurosci., Am. Assn. Anatomists. Avocations: photography, gardening, travel, camping.

MAIER, CHARLES STEVEN, history educator; b. N.Y.C., N.Y., Feb. 23, 1939; s. Louis and Muriel (Krailsheimer) M.; m. Pauline Alice Rubbelke, June 17, 1961; children—Andrea Nicole, Nicholas Winterer, Jessica Elizabeth Heine. A.B., Harvard U., 1960; postgrad., St. Anthony's Coll., Oxford, Eng., 1960-61; Ph.D., Harvard U., 1967. Instr. history Harvard U., Cambridge, Mass., 1967-69, asst. prof., 1969-73, lectr., 1973-75; vis. prof. U. Bielefeld, Fed. Republic Germany, 1976; assoc. prof. history Duke U., Durham, N.C., 1976-79, prof., 1979-81; prof. history Harvard U., Cambridge, Mass., 1981-91, Krupp Found. prof. European studies, 1991—; dir. Ctr. for European Studies, 1994—; rsch. fellow Lehrman Inst., N.Y.C., 1975-76; mem. assoc. staff Brookings Instn., Washington, 1978-84; mem. coun. Fondation Jean Monnet pour l'Europe, Lausanne, Switzerland; mem. joint comm. on We. Europe Social Sci. Rsch. Coun. and Am. Coun. Learned Socs., 1978-84, chmn., 1979-81. Author: Recasting Bourgeois Europe, 1975 (Am. Hist. Assn. George Louis Beer award 1976, Herbert Baxter Adams award 1977), In Search of Stability, 1987, The Unmasterable Past, 1988; editor: The Origins of the Cold War and Contemporary Europe, 1978, rev. edit., 1990, (with Dan S. White) The Thirteenth of May and the Advent of de Gaulle's Republic, 1967, (with Leon Lindberg) The Politics of Inflation and Economic Stagnation, 1985, Changing Boundaries of the Political, 1987, The Marshall Plan and Germany, 1991. Fellow NEH, 1977-78, German Marshall Fund, 1980-81, Guggenheim Found., 1984-85; rsch. grantee MacArthur Found., 1988-89. Fellow Woodrow Wilson Ctr. for Scholars (Washington); mem. Council on Fgn. Relations, Am. Hist. Assn., Soc. Italian Hist. Studies, Soc. Historians of Am. Fgn. Rels., Am. Acad. Arts and Scis., Phi Beta Kappa. Home: 60 Larchwood Dr Cambridge MA 02138-4639 Office: Harvard U Ctr for European Studies Cambridge MA 02138

MAIER, CRAIG FRISCH, restaurant executive; b. Cin., Sept. 20, 1949; s. Jack Craig and Blanche June (Frisch) M. BA, Trinity Coll., Hartford, Conn., 1971; MBA, Columbia U., 1975. With Frisch's Restaurant, Cin., 1975—, exec. v.p., 1987-89, pres., chief exec. officer, 1989—. Bd. dirs. Cin. Mus. Natural History, 1990—, Cin. Playhouse in the Pk., 1992—, Dan Beard coun. Boy Scouts Am., 1992—, Cin. Bus. Com., 1994—, Greater Cin. Cov. and Visitors Bur., 1995—. Mem. Greater Cin. Restaurant Assn. (bd. dirs. 1991—). Republican. Avocations: jogging, gardening, golf. Office: Frisch's Restaurants Inc 2800 Gilbert Ave Cincinnati OH 45206-1206

MAIER, DONNA JANE-ELLEN, history educator; b. St. Louis, Feb. 20, 1948; d. A. Russell and Mary Virginia Maier; m. Stephen J. Rapp, Jan. 3, 1981; children: Alexander John, Stephanie Jane-Ellen. BA, Coll. of Wooster, 1969; MA, Northwestern U., 1972, PhD, 1975. Asst. prof. U. Tex. at Dallas, Richardson, 1975-78; asst. prof. history U. No. Iowa, Cedar Falls, 1978-81, assoc. prof., 1981-86, prof., 1986—; cons. Scott, Foresman Pub., Glenview, Ill., 1975-94; editl. cons. Children's Press, 1975-76, Macmillan Pubs., 1989-90, Haper-Collins Pubs., 1994. Co-author: History and Life, 1976, 4th edit., 1990; author: Priests and Power, 1983; co-editor African Economic History, 1992—; contbr. articles to profl. jours., essays to books. Mem. Iowa Dem. Cen. Com., 1982-90, chmn. budget com., 1986-90; chmn. 3d Congl. Dist. Cen. Com., 1986-88. Fulbright-Hays fellow, Ghana, 1972, Arab Republic Egypt, 1987; fellow Am. Philos. Soc., London, 1978. Mem. Am. Hist. Assn., African Studies Assn., AAUW (fellow Ghana 1973), Quota Club. Home: 219 Highland Blvd Waterloo IA 50703-4229 Office: U No Iowa Dept History Cedar Falls IA 50614

MAIER, GERALD JAMES, natural gas transmission and marketing company executive; b. Regina, Sask., Can., Sept. 22, 1928; s. John Joseph and Mary (Passler) M. Student, Notre Dame Coll. (Wilcox), U. Man., U. Alta., U. Western Ont. With petroleum and mining industries Can., U.S., Australia, U.K.; responsible for petroleum ops. Africa, United Arab Emirates, S.E. Asia; chmn. TransCan. PipeLines, Calgary, 1985-95, also bd. dirs.; bd. dirs. BCE Inc., Bank of N.S., TransAlta Corp., Du Pont Can. Inc., Alta. Nat. Gas Co., Ltd., Petro-Can.; immediate past chmn. Can. Nat. Com. for World Petroleum Congresses; chmn. Van Horne Inst. for Internat. Transp.; dep. chmn. Coun. Can. Unity. Named Hon. Col. King's Own Calgary Rgt., Resource Man of Yr. Alta. Chamber of Resources, 1990; recipient Can. Engr.'s Gold medal Can. Coun. Profl. Engrs., 1990, Disting. Alumni award U. Alta., 1992, Mgmt. award McGill U., 1993, Centennial award Alta Assn. Engrs., Geologists and Geophysicists. Fellow Can. Acad. Engring.; mem. Assn. Profl. Engrs., Geologists and Geophysicists Alta. (past pres.), Can. Inst. Mining and Metallurgy (Past Pres.'s Meml. medal 1971). Avocations: golf, downhill skiing, shooting, fishing. Office: TransCan PipeLines Ltd, 2900, 240-4th Ave SW, Calgary, AB Canada T2P 4L7

MAIER, HAROLD GEISTWEIT, law educator, lawyer; b. Cin., Mar. 25, 1937; s. Alfred F. and Alberta (Wilmes) M.; divorced; children: Marc L., Kurt S. BA in English Lit., U. Cin., 1959, JD, 1963; postgrad. Free U. Berlin, 1959-60; LLM, U. Mich., 1964; postgrad. U. Munich, 1964-65. Bar: Ohio 1963. Mem. faculty of law Vanderbilt U., Nashville, 1965—, prof., 1970—, dir. Transnat. Legal Studies Program, 1973—; David Daniels Allen prof. law, 1988—; faculty San Diego Internat. and Comparative Law Inst. King's Coll. U. London, 1986,87, Regent's Coll., 1989, 91, 96; vis. prof. law U. Pa., 1985, U. N.C., Chapel Hill, 1987; vis. Lyle T. Alverson prof. law George Washington U., Washington, 1987-88; vis. Woodruff prof. internat. law U. Ga., Atlanta, 1995; prof. law summer program LSU, Aix-en-Provence, France, 1995; cons. Office of Sec. Army, Panama Canal Treaty Negotiations, 1976; guest scholar Brookings Instn., Washington, 1976-77; dir. PDS Patrons, Inc. (Univ. Sch. of Nashville), 1975-87, pres., 1978-79; counselor on internat. law Office of Legal Adviser, U.S. Dept. State, 1983-84. Recipient Luftbrucke Dankstipendium, Free U. Berlin, 1959-60; Ford internat. studies fellow U. Mich., 1964-65; Vanderbilt U. faculty fellow, 1976-77. Mem. Am. Soc. Internat. Law (exec. coun. 1974-78, 84-87), Am. Soc. for Comparative Study of Law (bd. dirs. 1984—), Am. Law Inst., Order of Coif, Omicron Delta Kappa, Phi Alpha Delta, Tau Kappa Alpha, Pi Delta Epsilon. Bd. editors Am. Jour. Internat. Law, 1984-88; author: (with T. Buergenthal) Public International Law in A Nutshell, 1985, 2d edit., 1989, (with T. Buergenthal, K. Doehring, J. Kokott) Grundzüge des Völkerrechts, 1987, Manual de Derecho Internacional Publico, 1994; contbr. numerous articles in field to profl. jours. Office: Vanderbilt U Sch Law 21st Ave S Nashville TN 37240

MAIER, HENRY B., environmental engineer; b. Yonkers, N.Y., July 11, 1925; s. Henry and Adelaide (Boyce) M.; m. Elizabeth A. Maier, May 4, 1968. BA, Columbia U., 1947; postgrad., Adelphi U., Hofstra U. Prin. Maier Solar Developments, Hempstead, N.Y. Author: Techniques for Seascape Painting. Mem. AIAA, Am. Chem. Soc., N.Y. Acad. Scis. Achievements include patents for elapsed time indicator, multiple reflecting solar collecting system, electroresponsive coatings, fusion power pellets, and fusion power; design of initial stage of work for aerospace vehicle, comet flyby study; development of rapid method for perspective visualizations, for views of engineering and design concepts; definition of geometrics for placement of measuring points by approximation; research on inorganic sulfur and chlorine pollutants from combustion of fossil fuels and from incinerator processes, and their interactive roles in the progressive deterioration of the stratospheric ozone shield previously blocking frequencies in the infrared, far infrared and microwave frequencies, with particular regard to the prediction and pattern formation of major North Atlantic storm systems; study for a comet detecting telescope; design study for single span, steel beam highway bridge for enhanced safety from emerging conditions of high-speed trucks, severe weather conditions and limited maintenance. Home: 6 Sealey Ave Apt 3K Hempstead NY 11550-1232

MAIER, PAUL LUTHER, history educator, author, chaplain; b. St. Louis, May 31, 1930; s. Walter A. and Hulda (Eickhoff) M.; m. Joan M. Ludtke, 1967; children: Laura Ann, Julie Joan, Krista Lynn, Katherine Marie. MA, Harvard U., 1954; BD, Concordia Sem., St. Louis, 1955; postgrad., U. Heidelberg, Fed. Republic Germany; PhD summa cum laude, U. Basel, Switzerland, 1957; LittD (hon.), Concordia Sem., St. Louis, 1995. Campus chaplain, 1958—; prof. ancient history Western Mich. U., Kalamazoo, 1961—; lectr. in field. Author: A Man Spoke, A World Listened, 1963, Pontius Pilate, 1968, First Christmas, 1971, First Easter, 1973, First Christians, 1976, The Flames of Rome, 1981, In the Fullness of Time, 1991, A Skeleton in God's Closet, 1994; editor: The Best of Walter A. Maier, 1980; editor: Josephus—The Jewish War, 1982; editor, transl.: Josephus—The Essential Writings, 1988, Josephus—The Essential Works, 1995; contbr. over 200 articles and revs. to profl. jours. Recipient Gold Medallion Book award ECPA, 1989, Disting. Faculty Scholar Western Mich. U., 1981, Alumni award tchg. excellence, 1974; named Outstanding Educator in Am., 1974-75, Prof. of Yr. Coun. for Advancement and Support of Edn., 1984, citation Mich. Acad. of Sci., Arts and Letters, 1985. Home: 8383 W Main St Kalamazoo MI 49009-8211 Office: Western Mich U Dept of History Kalamazoo MI 49008

MAIER, PAUL VICTOR, pharmaceutical executive; b. Seattle, Nov. 6, 1947; s. Norman Alvin and Rosalie (Godek) M.; m. Shirley Diehl, Aug. 11, 1979. BS, Pa. State U., 1969; MBA, Harvard U., 1975. Fin. analyst Greyhound Corp, Phoenix, 1975-76; asst. mgr. Wells Service Wells Fargo Bank, San Francisco, 1976-78; v.p. Fin. Cummins Service and Sales, Los Angeles, 1978-84; v.p., treas. ICN Pharms, Inc., Costa Mesa, Calif., 1984-90; v.p. fin. DFS West, 1990-92; v.p., CFO Ligand Pharmaceuticals, Inc., San Diego, 1992—. Chmn. hosp. div. United Way Region V, L.A., 1983-84; bd. dirs. The Wellness Community, San Diego, 1993—. Served with USNR, 1969—. Mem. Fin. Execs. Inst., The Athletic Congress, Pa. State Club of S.D., Harvard Bus. Sch. Assn. So. Calif., Ctr. for Non-Profit Mgmt., Vis. Nurse Assn. L.A. (bd. dirs. 1979-92, chmn.), Protection Mut. Inst. (West Coast adv. bd. 1985-90), L.A. Athletic Club, Point Fermin Flyers. Republican. Roman Catholic. Office: Ligand Pharmaceuticals 9393 Towne Centre Dr Ste 100 San Diego CA 92121-3016

MAIER, PAULINE, history educator; b. St. Paul, Apr. 27, 1938; d. Irvin Louis and Charlotte (Winterer) Rubbelke; AB, Radcliffe Coll., 1960; postgrad. London Sch. Econs., 1960-61; PhD in History, Harvard U., 1968, LLD (hon.), Regis Coll., 1987, DHL (hon.), Williams Coll., 1993; m. Charles Steven Maier, June 17, 1961; children: Andrea Nicole, Nicholas Winterer, Jessica Elizabeth Heine. Asst. prof., then assoc. prof. history U. Mass., Boston, 1968-77; Robinson-Edwards prof. history U. Wis., Madison, 1977-78; prof. history MIT, Cambridge, 1978—, William R. Kenan Jr. prof. history, 1990—, dept. head, 1979-88; mem. coun. Inst. Early Am. History, 1982-84; trustee Regis Coll., 1988-93; trustee Commonwealth Sch., 1991-96; bd. mgrs. Old South Meeting House, 1987—. Recipient Douglass Adair award Claremont Grad. Sch.-Inst. Early Am. History, 1976, Kidger award New Eng. History Tchrs. Assn., 1981; fellow Nat. Endowment Humanities, 1974-75, 88-89; Charles Warren fellow, 1974-75; Guggenheim fellow, 1990. Mem. Orgn. Am. Historians (exec. bd. 1978-82), Am. Hist. Assn. (nominations com. 1983-85, chmn. 1985), Soc. Am. Historians, Am. Antiquarian Soc. (exec. council 1984-89), Colonial Soc. Mass. (exec. coun. 1990-93), Mass. Hist. Soc. Author: From Resistance to Revolution: Colonial Radicals and the Development of American Opposition to Britain, 1765-1766, 1972; The Old Revolutionaries: Political Lives in the Age of Samuel Adams, 1980; The American People: A History, 1986. Home: 60 Larchwood Dr Cambridge MA 02138-4639 Office: MIT E51-216 Dept History Cambridge MA 02139

MAIER, PETER KLAUS, law educator, investment adviser; b. Wurzburg, Germany, Nov. 20, 1929; came to U.S., 1939, naturalized, 1945; s. Bernard and Joan (Sonder) M.; m. Melanie L. Stoff, Dec. 15, 1963; children: Michele Margaret, Diana Lynn. BA cum laude, Claremont McKenna Coll., 1949; JD, U. Calif., Berkeley, 1952; LLM in Taxation, NYU, 1953. Bar: Calif. 1953, U.S. Supreme Ct. 1957; cert. specialist in taxation law, Calif. Atty. tax div. U.S. Dept Justice, Washington, 1956-59; mem. firm Bacigalupi, Elkus, Salinger & Rosenberg, San Francisco, 1959-69, Brookes & Maier, San Francisco, 1970-73, Winokur, Maier & Zang, San Francisco, 1974-81; of counsel Crosby, Heafy, Roach & May, Oakland, Calif., 1986—; prof. law Hastings Coll. Law, U. Calif., San Francisco, 1967-95; vis. prof. U. Calif. Boalt Sch. Law, Berkeley, 1988-89, Stanford U. Sch. Law, 1996—; pres. Maier & Siebel, Inc., Larkspur, Calif., 1981—; prin. Wood Island Investment Counsel, Inc., Larkspur, 1981—. Author books on taxation; contbr. articles to profl. jours. Chmn. Property Resources Inc., San Jose, Calif., 1968-77; pres. Calif. Property Devel. Corp., San Francisco, 1974-81. Capt. USAF, 1953-56. Mem. San Francisco Bar Assn. (chmn. sect. taxation 1970-71), Order of Coif. Home: PO Box 391 Belvedere CA 94920-0391 Office: Maier & Siebel Inc 80 E Sir Francis Drake Blvd Larkspur CA 94939

MAIER, ROBERT HAWTHORNE, biology educator; b. N.Y.C., Oct. 26, 1927; s. Ernest Henry and Clara Louise M.; m. Jane Hiob, Aug. 31, 1952; children: Pamela, David, Daniel. BS, U. Miami, 1951; MS, U. Ill., 1952, PhD, 1954. Asst. dean Grad. Coll., U. Ariz., 1966-67; asst. chancellor for instrn. and research U. Wis., Green Bay, 1967-69, vice chancellor and dep. chancellor, prof., 1969-75, prof. sci. and environ. change, public and environ. adminstrn., 1975-79; vice chancellor acad. affairs East Carolina U., Greenville, N.C., 1979-83; prof. exptl. surgery, biology, polit. sci. East Carolina U., 1983—, dir. Trace Element Ctr., Sch. Medicine, 1984—; pres., chmn. Nat. Investment Advisors, Inc., 1984—, M 4, Inc., 1988—; bd. dirs. Agronomic Sci. Found.; mem. coun. biotech. U. N.C.; reviewer NC Tech. Devel. Authority, 1989—, NRC, 1990—. Contbr. articles to profl. jours. Bd. dirs. Lakeland chpt. ARC, 1978-79, Children's Svcs. Ea. N.C., 1987-94; mem. Edn. Task Force, City of Green Bay, 1977-78, N.C. State Panel Advancement of Women in Adminstrn., 1981-84, Gov.'s Commn. on Future of N.C., 1981-84; treas. Ronald McDonald House, 1987-94; mem. Vision Task Force, Global Transpark Devel. Commn., Kinston, N.C., 1996—. With U.S. Army, 1954-56. Fellow AAAS, Am. Inst. Chemists, Am. Soc. Agronomy, Soil Sci. Soc. Am.; mem. Am. Chem. Soc., Am. Inst. Biol. Scis. Presbyterian. Office: East Carolina U Sch Med Bio Dept Greenville NC 27858-4354

MAIER, WALTER ARTHUR, church official; b. St. Louis, June 14, 1925; s. Walter Arthur and Hulda (Eickhoff) M.; m. Leah Martha Gach, Aug. 27, 1951; children: Walter Arthur III, David Peter Edmund. Student, Harvard U., 1942-43, Concordia Coll., 1943-44; BA, Concordia Sem., 1948; postgrad., Marquette U., 1961-62; STM, Concordia Seminary, 1967, ThD, 1970. Prof. exegetical theology Concordia Theol. Sem., Springfield and Ft. Wayne, 1965—; v.p. Luth. Ch.-Mo. Synod, St. Louis, 1973-95; parish pastor Elma, N.Y., Levittown, Pa. and Milw. Office: Concordia Theol Sem Fort Wayne IN 46825

MAIER, WILLIAM OTTO, martial arts school administrator, educator, consultant; b. Newark, July 15, 1949; s. Emil William Maier and Elizabeth Muriel Flader; children: William Wyatt, Kami Elizabeth. BA, Marietta (Ohio) Coll., 1971; MA, Coll. of Wooster (Ohio), 1973. Lic. master instr. Internat. Bujinkan Dojo, Noda City, Japan, 1991. Tchr. Howard County (Md.) Pub. Schs., 1975-78; dean Martial Arts Am., Columbia, Md., 1975—. Featured on CNN, NBC and CBS; contbr. articles to profl. jours. Named Sch. of Month Black Belt Mag., Sept. 1992; recipient State Md. Govs. citation, 1992, Nat. Sch. of Yr. award U.S. Martial Arts Assn., 1992, 93, Cmty. Svc. award, 1993. Mem. Marishi Kai Instrs. Guild (charter mem.), U.S. Marital Arts Assn. (cons., bd. dirs. 1986-95, named Man of Yr. 1991, recipient award for best student retention 1988-93, Top Sch. award 1994), Martial Arts Am. (bd. dirs. 1995, 96), Rotary. Office: Martial Arts Am 9042 Rt 108 Columbia MD 21045

MAIHAFER, HARRY JAMES, retired banker, former army officer; b. Watertown, N.Y., Aug. 8, 1924; s. George A. and Loretta Agnes (Daggett) M.; m. Jeanne Louise Mietzelfeld, June 9, 1949; children: Veronica Maihafer Barnes, Mary Maihafer Thompson, Margaret M., Douglas P. BS, U.S. Mil. Acad., 1949; MA, U. Mo., 1966. Commd. 2d lt. U.S. Army, 1949, col., 1968, ret., 1969; tng. dir. C&S Nat. Bank, Atlanta, 1970-73; sr. v.p., dir. pers. Union Planters Bank, Memphis, 1973-76; sr. v.p., dir. human resources Commerce Union Corp., Nashville, 1977-87, ret., 1987; pres. Middle Tenn. Human Resources Planners, Nashville, 1982-83. Author: From the Hudson to the Yalu--West Point '49 in the Korean War, 1993, Brave Decisions-Moral Courage from the American Revolution to Desert Storm, 1995; contbr. articles on mgmt. and mil. history to profl. jours. Pres. West Point Soc. Mid. Tenn., 1985-86; bd. dirs. St. Mary Villa, nashville, 1982-95, Cath. Charities Tenn., 1990-95. Mem. Assn. Grads. U.S. Mil. Acad., Ret. Officers Assn., Korean War Vets. Assn. Roman Catholic. Avocations: tennis, writing, gardening. Home: 6601 Fox Hollow Rd Nashville TN 37205-3956

MAIKOWSKI, THOMAS ROBERT, educational director, priest; b. Milwaukee, Wis., Oct. 20, 1947; s. Thomas Robert and Eugenia A. (Rogowski) M. BA, St. Francis Coll., Milw., 1970, MS in Edn., 1972; MA, Cardinal Stritch Coll., 1974; MDiv, Kenrick Sem., St. Louis, 1976; BA, Notre Dame Coll., St. Louis, 1976; MEd, Marquette U., 1977; PhD, St. Louis U., 1980; EdD, U. San Francisco, 1992. Ordained priest Roman Cath. Ch., 1976; cert. secondary sch. tchr. and adminstr., Ariz., N.Mex.; cert. elem. tchr., N.Mex. Tchr., adminstr. Cathedral High Sch., Gallup, N.Mex., 1976-78; supt. of schs. Diocese of Gallup, 1978-90; prin. tchr. The Cath. Acad., Farmington, N.Mex., 1980-90; dir. edn. Diocese of Gallup, 1990—. Contbr. articles to religious jours. Maj. USAFR. Mem. Nat. Cath. Ednl. Assn. (exec. com. 1978-81, 87-90), Religious Edn. Assn., Am. Assn. on Mental Retardation, Assn. for Supervision and Curriculum Devel., N.Mex. Assn. Non-pub. Schs. (bd. dirs. 1981-84), Phi Delta Kappa. Address: PO Box 1028 Gallup NM 87305-1028

MAILANDER, WILLIAM STEPHEN, lawyer; b. Dover, N.J., July 25, 1958; s. William Stephen and Doris Elizabeth (Post) M.; m. Judith Gay Burrows, May 20, 1989 (div. 1993). BA, NYU, 1984; JD, Temple U., 1988. Bar: Pa. 1988, N.J. 1991, D.C. 1996; U.S. Ct. Vets. Appeals 1991, U.S. Ct. Appeals (fed. cir.) 1993, U.S. Supreme Ct. 1994. Staff atty. Bd. Vets. Appeals, Washington, 1988-90, Coast Guard Chief Counsel, Washington, 1990-91, VA Gen. Counsel, Washington, 1991-93; asst. gen. counsel Paralyzed Vets. Am., Washington, 1993—; faculty continuing legal edn. seminars, various cities, 1993—. Contbr. articles to profl. jours. With USMC, 1976-79. Decorated Navy Achievement medal. Mem. Fed. Bar Assn. (chair membership vets. law sect. 1993-94). Avocations: reading, running. Office: Paralyzed Vets Am 801 18th St Washington DC 20006

MAILER, NORMAN, author; b. Long Branch, N.J., Jan. 31, 1923; s. Issac Barnett and Fanny (Schneider) M.; m. Beatrice Silverman, 1944 (div. 1952); 1 dau., Susan; m. Adele Morales, 1954 (div. 1962); children: Danielle, Elizabeth; m. Jeanne Campbell, 1962 (div. 1963); 1 dau., Kate; m. Beverly Bentley, 1963 (div. 1980); children: Michael, Steven; m. Carol Stevens, 1980 (div. 1980); 1 dau., Maggie; m. Norris Church, 1980; 1 son, John Buffalo. SB cum laude, Harvard U., 1943; postgrad., Sorbonne, Paris, France, 1947-48. columnist Village Voice, 1946, Commentary, 1962-63, Esquire, 1962-63; contbg. editor Dissent, 1953-69; co-founding editor Village Voice, 1955. Author: No Percentage, 1941, The Naked and the Dead, 1948, Barbary Shore, 1951, The Deer Park, 1955, The White Negro: Superficial Reflections on the Hipster, 1957, Advertisements for Myself, 1959, Deaths for the Ladies and Other Disasters, 1962, The Presidential Papers, 1963, An American Dream, 1965, Cannibals and Christians, 1966, Why Are We in Vietnam?, 1967 (Nat. Book award nomination 1967), The Short Fiction of Norman Mailer, 1967, The Bullfight, 1967, The Armies of the Night, 1968 (Pulitzer prize for non-fiction 1969, George Polk award 1969), Miami and the Siege of Chicago, 1968 (Nat. Book award for non-fiction 1968), The Idol and the Octopus, 1968, Of a Fire On The Moon, 1970, King of the Hill, 1971, The Prisoner of Sex, 1971, The Long Patrol, 1971, Existential Errands, 1972, St. George and the Godfather, 1972, Marilyn, 1973, The Faith of Graffiti, 1974, The Fight, 1975, Some Honorable Men, 1975, Genius and Lust, 1976, A Transit to Narcissus, 1978, The Executioner's Song, 1979 (Pulitzer Prize for fiction 1980, Nat. Book Critics Circle award nomination 1979, Am. Book award nomination 1980), Of a Small and Modest Malignancy, Wicked and Bristling with Dots, 1980, Of Women and Their Elegance, 1980, Pieces and Pontifications, 1982, Ancient Evenings, 1983, Tough Guys Don't Dance, 1984, The Last Night, 1984, Harlot's Ghost, 1991, How the Wimp Won the War, 1991, Oswald's Tale, 1995, Portrait of Picasso as a Young Man, 1995; (plays) The Deer Park: A Play, 1967, Strawhead, 1985; editor: Genius and Lust: A Journey Through the Major Writings of Henry Miller, 1976; screenwriter: (films) The Executioner's Song, 1982 (Emmy award nomination outstanding adapted screenplay 1983); screenwriter, prodr., dir., actor: (films) Wild 90, 1967, Maidstone: A Mystery, 1971; screenwriter, prodr.: (films) Beyond the Law, 1968; screenwriter, dir.: (films) Tough Guys Don't Dance, 1987; actor: (films) Ragtime, 1981. Served with AUS, 1944-46. Recipient Edward MacDowell medal MacDowell Colony, 1973, Nat. Arts Club Gold medal, 1976, Emerson-Thoreau Medal for lifetime of literary achievement, 1989; Nat. Inst. and Am. Acad. grantee, 1960; Pappas fellow U. Pa., 1983. Mem. PEN Am. Ctr. (pres. 1984-86), Nat. Inst. Arts and Letters. Office: care Random House Author's Mail 201 E 50th St New York NY 10022-7703

MAILES, MICHAEL, sound recording engineer. Recipient Grammy award for Best Classical Engineered Recording ("Bartok: Concerto for Orch.; Kossuth Symphonic Poem"), 1996. Office: London Records 825 8th Ave 26th Fl New York NY 10019*

MAILHOT, LOUISE, judge; b. Montreal, Que., Can., July 23, 1940; d.Gerard and Jeanne (Bousquet) M.; m. Michael Oliver Lloyd, 1974; 2 children. BA, U. Montreal, LLL. Atty. pvt. practice, 1966-80, Justice Superior Ct., 1980-87, Justice Ct. Appeals, 1987—. Office: Ct Appeals, 1 rue Notre Dame Est # 1786, Montreal, PQ Canada H2Y 1B6

MAILLARD, ALBERT ACHILLES JOSEPH, head and neck surgeon, educator; b. Santiago, Chile, Aug. 8, 1943; s. Albert Joseph and Amanda (Holtheuer) M.; 1 child, John David. BS, U. Houston, 1968; MD, U. Tex., Galveston, 1972. Cert. Tex. State Bd. Med. Examiners, Nat. Bd. Med. Examiners, Am. Bd. Otolaryngology. Resident gen. surgery U. Tex. Med. Sch., Houston (Tex.) Affiliated Hosps., 1972-73, U. Tex. Southwestern Med. Sch., Affiliated Hosp., 1973-74; resident gen. surgery U. Tex. Med. Sch. Houston Affiliated Hosp., 1974-75, resident otolaryngology head and neck surgery, 1975-77; resident U. Tex. Med. Sch. Houston, M.D. Anderson Hosp. & Tumor Inst., 1977-78; instr. otolaryngology U. Tex. Med. Sch., Houston, 1978-82, clin. asst. prof. otolaryngology, head and neck surgery, 1982-84, clin. assoc. prof. otolaryngology, head and neck surgery, 1984—, clin. prof. dept. family practice, 1993—, cons. dept. oncology, 1989—; mem. St. Joseph Hosp. Quality Assurance Rev. Com.-Gen. Surgery, 1989-93, Quality Assurance Rev. Com.-Otolaryngology-Head and Neck Surgery, 1989-93, Bylaws Rev. Com., 1990, Hermann Hosp. Credentials Com., 1990, Hermann Hosp. Tissue Com., 1993, Sci. and Tech. Com., 1993—; bd. dirs. Physicans, Inc., Tex.; pvt. practice, 1979-94; lectr. and presenter in field. Contbr. articles to profl. jours. Charter mem. The Statue of Liberty Found., N.Y., 1983-86, Ellis Island Found., N.Y., 1985-92, Market Sq. Restoration, Houston, 1991. Fellow ACS, Am. Acad. Otolaryngology-Head and Neck Surgery, Am. Soc. for Head & Neck Surgery; mem. AAAS, AMA, Tex. Med. Assn., Harris County Med. Soc., M.D. Anderson Surg. Alumni Assn., The Deafness Rsch. Found., Nature Conservancy, Phi Beta Pi. Roman Catholic. Avocations: anthropology, marine biology, flying, winter sports. Home: 2038 Suffolk Dr Houston TX 77027-3801 Office: AAJ Maillard MD 6410 Fannin St Ste 1508 Houston TX 77030-5306

MAILLET, ANTONINE, author, educator; b. Bouctouche, N.B., Can., May 10, 1929; d. Leonine Maillet and Virginie Cormier. BA, Coll. Notre-Dame D'Acadie, 1950; MA, Moncton U., N.B., 1959, D es L (hon.), 1972; LLD, Montreal U., Que., Can., 1962; PhD, Laval U., Que., 1970, DLitt (hon.), 1988; D es L (hon.), Acadia U., 1980, St. Mary's U., 1980, Laurentian U., 1981, McGill U., 1982; DLitt (hon.), Carleton U., 1978, Mount Allison U., 1979, St. Thomas U., 1986, Mt. St-Vincent U., 1987, U. Ste-Anne, 1987, Bowling Green U., 1988, Simon Fraser U., 1989. U. Maine, 1990, Concordia U., 1990; LLD (hon.), U. Alta., 1979, Dalhousie U., 1981, U. Toronto, 1982, Queen's U., 1982, St. Francis Xavier U., 1984, Lyon U., 1989, B.C. U., 1991, Royal Mil. Coll. Can., 1992; LittD (hon.), U. New Eng., 1994. Prof. Coll. Notre-Dame D'Acadie, Moncton, 1954-60, Moncton U., 1965-67, Coll. des Jesuites, Que., 1968-69, Laval U., Que., 1971-74, Montreal U., 1974-75, Nat. Drama Sch., Montreal, 1989-91; writer N.B. Hist. Resources Adminstrn., Central Registry, Fredericton, N.B.; assoc. prof. French studies Moncton U., chancelor, 1989; guest Michener Found., Queen's U., 1991. Author: (novels) Pointe-aux-coques, 1958 (Prix Champlain, 1960), On a mangé la dune, 1962, Don l'orignal, 1972 (Prix du Gouverneur General du Can. 1972), Par derrière chez mon père, 1972, Mariaagélas, 1973 (Prix des Volcans (France) 1975, Grand Prix Littéraire de la ville de Montréal, 1973, Prix France Can. 1975, Prix litteraire La Presse 1976), Emmanuel à Joseph à Dâvit, 1975, Les Cordes-de-Bois, 1977 (Prix des 4 jurys 1978), Pélagie-la-charrette, 1979 (Prix Goncourt 1979); Cent ans dans les bois, 1981, La Gribouille, 1982, Crache-à-Pic, 1984; Le Huitième Jour, 1986, L'Oursiade, 1990, Les Confessions de Jeanne de Valois, 1992; (plays): Poire-Acre, 1960 (Best Can. Play Vancouver Theatre Festival, 1960), Les Jeux d'Enfants sont faits, 1960 (Prix du Conseil des Arts 1960), Les Crasseux, 1968, Gapi et Sullivan, 1973, Evangéline Deusse, 1975, Gapi, 1976, La Veuve Enragée, 1977, Le Bourgeois Gentleman, 1978, La Contrebandière, 1981, Les drolatiques, horrifiques et épouvantables aventures de Panurge, ami de Pantagruel, 1983, Garrochés en Paradis, 1986, Margot la Folle, 1987, William S, 1991; (translations) Les Fantastiques (Tom Jones), 1988, Richard III (Shakespeare), 1989, (also adaptation) Valentine (Willy Russel), 1990, La Nuit des Rois (Shakespeare), 1993 (Prix de la traduction l'Association québécoise de critiques de théâtre saison 1992-93), (also adaptation) La Foire de la Saint-Barthélemy (Ben Jonson), 1994, La Fontaine ou la Comédie des Animaux, 1995: (other) L'Acadie pour quasiment rien, 1973; author short stories, and children's literature. Mem. Conseil Littéraire Fondation Prince Pierre de Monaco, Haut Conseil Francophonie, 1987, Queen's Privy Coun. Can.; chancellor Moncton U., 1989; Conseil des gouverneurs associés de l'Université de Montréal. Decorated officer, comdr. Order of Can., officier des Palmes académiques françaises, knight l'Ordre de la Pléiade (Fredericton), officier l'Ordre Nat. du Québec, officier des Arts et des Lettres (France), comdr. l'Ordre du mérite culturel (Monaco); recipient Prix de la meilleure piece canadienne presented at Festival de Theatre, 1958, Prix Litéraire de la Presse, 1976. Mem. Assn. des Ecrivains de Langue Francaise, l'Ordre des francophones d'Amérique, l'Académie des Grandes Montréalais, Soc. des Auteurs et Compositeurs Dramatiques de France (sec.), Soc. des Gens de Lettres de France, Soc. Royale du Canada, Academie Canadienne-Francaise, Pen Club of Que.

MAILLOUX, ROBERT JOSEPH, physicist; b. Lynn, Mass., June 20, 1938; s. Joseph H. and Nora S. M.; m. Marlene Schirf, Jan. 14, 1967; children: Patrice, Julie, Denise. BS, Northeastern U., 1961; SM, Harvard U., 1962, PhD, 1965. Physicist NASA Electronics Rsch. Ctr., Cambridge, Mass., 1965-70, Air Force Cambridge Rsch. Labs., Bedford, Mass., 1970-77, Rome Air Devel. Ctr., Bedford, 1977-80; chief antennas and components div., electromagnetic directorate Rome Air Devel. Ctr., 1980-91; sr. scientist Antennas Rome Lab., 1992—; lectr. Tufts U., Boston, 1985—. Author: Phased Array Antenna Handbook; contbr. chpts. to 8 textbooks, articles to sci. jours. Served with C.E. U.S. Army, 1966-68. Recipient Air Force Marcus O'Day paper award, 1971, Engineer of Yr. award RADC, 1988; RADC fellow, 1988. Fellow IEEE (spl. achievement award 1969, 76, nat. lectr., assoc. editor Transactions on Antennas and Propagation 1984-92, Harry Diamond award 1991); mem. Antenna and Propagation Soc. (chmn. Boston chpt. 1968, nat. meetings chmn. 1977-80, adcom mem. 1977-80, v.p. 1982, pres. 1983), Internat. Sci. Radio Union (Commn. B. tech. activities chmn. 1980—), Sigma Xi (pres. Hanscom chpt. 1980-81), Eta Kappa Nu, Tau Beta Pi. Achievements include 9 patents in field. Office: RL/ER 31 Grenier St Hanscom AFB MA 01731-3010

MAIN, A. DONALD, bishop. Bishop Upper Susquehanna region Evang. Luth. Ch. in Am., Lewisburg, Pa. Office: Evang Luth Ch in Am PO Box 36 192 Reitz Blvd Lewisburg PA 17837

MAIN, BETTY JO, management analyst; b. Hatch, N.Mex., May 22, 1939; d. Truman Oliver and Madeline Kate (Bennett) Hickerson; m. Andrew Allan Burich, June 21, 1958 (div. Sept. 1977); children: Cari Lynn, Andrew Allan Jr.; m. Ralph Monroe Main, Apr. 21, 1979; stepchildren: Michael, Randall, Kelly. AA in Liberal Arts, Marymount Coll., 1988; BS in Bus. & Mgmt., U. Redlands, 1993, MBA, 1996. Escrow officer Palos Verdes Escrow, San Pedro, Calif., 1975-80; sec. City of L.A., San Pedro, 1980-85, wharfinger, 1985-87, mgmt. aide, 1987-89, mgmt. analyst II, 1989—. Mem. City of L.A. Tutoring Program, City of L.A. Spkrs. Bur. Mem. AAUW, Marymount Coll. Alumni, U. Redlands Alumni, Alfred North Whitehead Leadership Soc., Emblem Club (L.A.). Episcopalian. Avocation: travel. Home: 2238 W

Paseo Del Mar San Pedro CA 90732-4521 Office: City of LA 425 S Palos Verdes St San Pedro CA 90731-3309

MAIN, JACKSON TURNER, history educator; b. Chgo., Aug. 6, 1917; s. John Smith and Dorothy Kinsey (Turner) M.; m. Gloria Jean Lund, June 16, 1956; children: Jackson Turner, Eifiona Llewelyn, Judson Kempton. B.A., U. Wis., 1939, M.A., 1940, Ph.D., 1949; LL.D. (hon.), Washington and Jefferson Coll., 1980. Asst. prof. Washington and Jefferson Coll., Washington, Pa., 1948-50; prof. San Jose State U. (Calif.), 1953-65, U. Md., College Park, 1965-66; prof. history State U. N.Y. at Stony Brook, 1966-83. Author: The Antifederalists 1781-1788, 1961, The Social Structure of Revolutionary America, 1965, The Upper House in Revolutionary America, 1967, Political Parties Before the Constitution, 1973, The Sovereign States, 1775-1783, 1973, Connecticut Society in the Era of the American Revolution, 1977, Society and Economy in Colonial Connecticut, 1985. Served to sgt. USAF, 1941-45. Am. Council Learned Socs. fellow, 1962-63; Nat. Endowment Humanities fellow Center Advanced Studies in Behavioral Scis., Stanford, Calif., 1980-81. Mem. Am. Hist. Soc., Orgn. Am. Historians, Wis. Hist. Soc., others. Office: Univ of Colo Dept History Boulder CO 80309

MAINARDI, CAROL MARGREITHER, artist, framer, bookbinder; b. Hackensack, N.J., Apr. 19, 1967; d. Alan René and Arlene Carol (Clark) Margreither; m. Christopher Louis Mainardi, Apr. 21, 1990; children: Robin Clark, Samantha Rose. BFA in Printmaking, William Paterson Coll., Wayne, N.J., 1990. Owner Prints and Books, Wayne, 1987-90, Pompton Plains, N.J., 1987—; conservation libr. intern N.Y. Bot. Garden, Bronx, 1992-93. Bd. dirs. Salute to Women in the Arts, 1991—, newsletter editor, 1991-94, pres., 1994—. Recipient Excellence in Mixed Media award Salute to Women in the Arts, Old Church Cultural Ctr., 1993. Presbyterian. Avocations: swimming, sewing, cooking, gardening, walking. Home and Office: 14 White Birch Ave Pompton Plains NJ 07444-1659

MAINOUS, BRUCE HALE, foreign language educator; b. Appalachia, Va., Aug. 2, 1914; s. William Lazarus and Sibyl (Hale) M.; m. Ruth Marie Daugherty, June 7, 1941; children: Mary Michele (Mrs. Robert F. Chinn), Martha Hale (Mrs. Gary Dougherty). A.B., Coll. William and Mary, 1935; M.A., U. Ill., 1939, Ph.D., 1948; certificates, Sorbonne, Paris, 1958, U. Besançon, France, 1975. Asst. d'anglais Lycée de Nîmes, France, 1935-36; prin. Derby Grade Sch., Va., 1936-37; mem. faculty U. Ill., Urbana, 1937—; prof. French U. Ill., 1964-84, prof. emeritus, 1984—, head dept., 1965-73; dir. Unit for Fgn. Lang. Study and Research, 1972-76, Lang. Learning Lab., 1976-84. Author: (with H.C. Woodbridge) A Sainte-Beuve Bibliography, 1954, Basic French, 2d edit, 1968, (with Donald J. Nolan) Basic French, Workbook and laboratory Manual, 1968; co-author: Spanish for Agricultural Purposes, 1984, (with Maria T. Rund) A Glossary of Spanish-American Agricultural Terms, 1987. Served to lt. USNR, 1942-46; comdr. Res. ret. Decorated officier Ordre des Palmes Académiques; Camargo Found. fellow, 1975. Mem. MLA, Am. Assn. Tchrs. French, Ill. Fgn. Lang. Tchrs. Assn. (pres. 1966-68), Am. Council Teaching Fgn. Langs., Inst. d'Etudes Occitanes, N.Am. Catalan Soc., Corda Fratres Assn. Cosmopolitan Clubs, Phi Kappa Phi, Sigma Delta Pi, Pi Delta Phi. Methodist. Clubs: Dial, Exchange. Home: 502 W Washington St Urbana IL 61801-4052

MAINWARING, THOMAS LLOYD, motor freight company executive; b. Cleve., Aug. 25, 1928; s. Hugh Trevor and Mary Beatrice (Ottman) M.; m. Gladys Fraser Mehr, June 10, 1983; children by previous marriage—Kevin, James, Eileen, Scott, Bruce. B.A., Albion Coll., 1950; M.B.A., Western Res. U., 1958. C.P.A., Ohio. Controller Cleve. Cartage Co., 1959-61, v.p., treas., 1961-64; controller Associated Truck Lines, Inc., Vandenberg Ctr., Grand Rapids, Mich., 1964-69; v.p. fin. Associated Transport, Inc., N.Y.C., 1969-70, exec. v.p. fin. and adminstrn., 1970-72; pres. Ryder Truck Lines Inc., Jacksonville, Fla., 1972-78, exec. v.p., chief operating officer, 1978-81, chief exec. officer, 1981-84; pres. Freight System div. Ryder System Inc., Miami, Fla., 1984-86; cons. trucking industry affairs Arlington, Va., 1986-88; pres., chief oper. officer H & M Internat. Transp., Inc., 1989-91, vice chmn., 1991-92; transp. cons., 1992-93; pres., gen. mgr. E.I. Kane Intermodal Transport, Inc., Balt., 1993-95, vice chmn., 1995—; bd. dirs. Trucking Mgmt., Inc. Mem. exec. com. United Way Jacksonville, 1981-84; trustee Albion Coll., 1977; bd. dirs. Goodwill Industries North Fla. Served with AUS, 1950-53. Mem. Am. Trucking Assn. (nat. acctg. and fin. council 1964, pres. 1971, chmn. ATA Found. 1986-88, exec. com. 1985-88), Fla. Trucking Assn. (bd. dirs. 1973, pres. 1979), Am. Mgmt. Assn. (lectr. seminars), Jacksonville Area C. of C. (bd. govs., com. of 100, v.p. internat. 1984), Cen. and So. Motor Freight Tariff Assn. (bd. dirs. 1981-84, pres. 1983, exec. com. transp. rsch. bd. 1987-89), Sigma Nu. Home: 248 Springs Ave Gettysburg PA 17325-1728

MAINWARING, WILLIAM LEWIS, publishing company executive, author; b. Portland, Oreg., Jan. 17, 1935; s. Bernard and Jennie (Lewis) M.; m. Mary E. Bell, Aug. 18, 1962; children: Anne Marie, Julia Kathleen, Douglas Bernard. B.S., U. Oreg., 1957; postgrad., Stanford U., 1957-58. With Salem (Oreg.) Capital Jour., 1958-76, editor, pub., 1962-76; pub. Oreg. Statesman, 1974-76; pres. Statesman-Jour. Co., Inc., Salem, 1974-76, Westridge Press, Ltd., 1977—; pres. MediAmerica, Inc., Portland, 1981-96, CEO, 1988-96; bd. dirs. MediAmerica, Inc. Author: Exploring the Oregon Coast, 1977, Exploring Oregon's Central and Southern Cascades, 1979, Exploring the Mount Hood Loop, 1992, Government, Oregon-Style, 1996. Pres. Salem Beautification Coun., 1968, Marion-Polk County United Good Neighbors, 1970, Salem Social Svcs. Commn., 1978-79, Salem Hosp. Found., 1978-81. 2d lt. AUS, 1958; capt. Res. Ret. Mem. Salem Area C. of C. (pres. 1972-73), Oreg. Symphony Soc. Salem (pres. 1973-75), Salem City Club (pres. 1977-78), Sigma Chi. Republican. Presbyterian (ruling elder). Home and Office: 1090 Southridge Pl S Salem OR 97302-5947

MAIO, F. ANTHONY, lawyer; b. Passaic, N.J., Mar. 30, 1937; s. Anthony J. and Santina (Sciarra) M.; m. Maureen Margaret McKeown, Dec. 30, 1960; children: Christopher, Duncan, Todd. BS in Mech. Engring., Stevens Inst. Tech., 1959; LLB cum laude, Boston Coll., 1968. Bar: Wis. 1968, D.C. 1971. Engr., project mgr. Hazeltine Corp., Greenlawn, N.Y. and Avon, Mass., 1959-64; project mgr. Raytheon Corp., Portsmouth, R.I., 1964-65; atty. Foley & Lardner, Milw., 1968-70; ptnr. Foley & Lardner, Washington, 1971-86, Milw., 1986—. Editor Boston Coll. Law Rev., 1967-68. Dir. Arthritis Found., Milw., 1986-88, ARC, Milw., 1986-94. Mem. Order of Coif, Milw. Yacht Club (dir. 1989-95). Avocations: boating, fishing. Home: 515 Third St N Naples FL 33940 Office: Foley & Lardner Firstar Ctr 777 E Wisconsin Ave Milwaukee WI 53202-5302

MAIOCCHI, CHRISTINE, lawyer; b. N.Y.C., Dec. 24, 1949; d. George and Andreina (Toneatto) M.; m. John Charles Kerecz, Aug. 16, 1980; children: Charles George, Joan Christine. BA in Polit. Sci., Fordham U., 1971, MA in Polit. Sci., 1971, JD, 1974; postgrad., NYU, 1977—. Bar: N.Y. 1975, U.S. Dist. Ct. (so. and ea. dists.), N.Y. 1975, U.S. Ct. Appeals (2nd cir) 1975. Law clk. to magistrate U.S. Dist. Ct. (so. dist.) N.Y., N.Y.C., 1973-74; atty. corp. legal dept. The Home Ins. Co., N.Y.C., 1974-76; asst. house counsel corp. legal dept. Allied Maintenance Corp., N.Y.C., 1976; atty. corp. legal dept. Getty Oil Co., N.Y.C., 1976-77; v.p., mgr. real estate Paine, Webber, Jackson & Curtis, Inc., N.Y.C., 1977-81; real estate mgr. GK Techs., Inc., Greenwich, Conn., 1981-85; real estate mgr., sr. atty. MCI Telecom. Corp., Rye Brook, N.Y., 1985-93; real estate and legal cons. Wallace Law Registry, 1994—. Bd. dirs. League Women Voters, Dobbs Ferry, N.Y., 1988; co-pres. The Home/Sch. Assn., Immaculate Conception Sch., Irvington, N.Y. Mem. ABA, Nat. Assn. Corp. Real Estate Execs. (pres. 1983-84, treas. 1985-86, bd. dirs. 1986), Indsl. Devel. Rsch. Coun. (program v.p. 1985, Profl. award 1987), N.Y. Bar Assn., Women's Bar Assn. Manhattan, The Corp. Bar (sec. real estate divsn. 1987-89, chmn. 1990-92), Home Sch. Assn. Immaculate Conception Sch. (co-pres.), Jr. League Club, Dobbs Ferry Women's Club (program dir. 1981-92, 94—, publicity dir. 1992-94). Avocations: sports, theatre, gardening. Home and Office: 84 Clinton Ave Dobbs Ferry NY 10522-3004

MAIR, BRUCE LOGAN, interior designer, company executive; b. Chgo., June 5, 1951; s. William Logan and Josephine (Lee) M. BFA, Drake U., 1973; postgrad., Ind. Wesleyan U., 1990—. Mgr., head designer Reifers of Indpls., 1973-79; pres. Interiors Internat., Indpls., 1979-87; sr. designer Kasler Group, Indpls., 1987-89; dir. devel. Tillery Interiors and Imports, Greenwood, Ind., 1990; v.p. Tillery Interiors and Imports, Indpls., 1990-92; owner Mair Interior Design Group, Indpls., 1992—; pres. Tokens Inc., Indpls., 1982-88, Meg-A-Wat Enterprises Inc., Indpls., 1985-87, Luxury Ice Creams Inc., Indpls., 1986-87. Cover designer Indpls. Home and Garden mag., 1978, feature designer 1980; feature designer Builder mag., 1979; co-designer feature Indpls. At Home mag., 1979. Campaigner Anderson for Pres., 1980. Mem. Am. Soc. Interior Designers (treas. Ind. chpt. 1982-83, Pres. awards 1981-82), U.S. Rowing Assn. (master 1987—), St. Joseph Hist. Neighborhood Assn., Columbia Club (rowing crew coxswain 1986—), Highland Model A Club, Tower Harbor Yacht Club (Douglas, Mich.), Alpha Epsilon Pi. Avocations: sculling, historic preservation, model A Ford restoration, fishing, farming. Home: 219 E 10th St Indianapolis IN 46202-3303 Office: Mair Interior Design Group 219 E 10th St Indianapolis IN 46202-3303

MAIRS, DAVID, symphony conductor; b. Morristown, N.J., Jan. 30, 1943; s. G. Donald and Frances P. (Johnson) M.; children from previous marriage: Stephen, Gregory: m. Elizabeth Ann Powell, May 24, 1975; children: Ellen, Sarah. BM, U. Mich., 1965, MM, 1966; MDiv, Pitts. Theol. Sem., 1983. Cert. tchr. K-12, Mich. 3d horn San Antonio Symphony, 1969-70; assoc. prin. horn Pitts. Symphony, 1970-80; condr. wind ensemble Duquesne U., Pitts., 1981-83; asst. pastor 1st Presbyn. Ch., Flint, Mich., 1983-86, 87-88; asst. condr., music adminstr. Flint Symphony, 1984-88; artistic advisor Adrian (Mich.) Symphony, 1987-88; resident condr. San Antonio Symphony, 1988—; pops condr. Charlotte (N.C.) Symphony, 1993-95; music dir. Mid-Tex. Symphony, 1996—; music dir. Flint Youth Symphony, 1986-88; chmn. vision 2000 com. N.E. Ind. Sch. Dist., San Antonio, 1990-92. Hon. life mem. Tex. PTA. With U.S. Army, 1966-69. Mem. Am. Symphony Orch. League, Condr.'s Guild. Avocation: tennis. Office: San Antonio Symphony 222 E Houston St Ste 200 San Antonio TX 78205-1836

MAISEL, HERBERT, computer science educator; b. N.Y.C., Sept. 22, 1930; s. Hyman and Dora (Goldstein) M.; m. Millicent Sherry Kushner, Apr. 13, 1957; children—Scott Alan, Raymond Bruce. B.S., CCNY, 1951; M.S., NYU, 1952; Ph.D., Catholic U. Am., 1964. Mathematician, statistician Dept. Army, Aberdeen, Md., Washington, 1954-63; dir. acad. computer ctr. Georgetown U., Washington, 1963-76, prof. computer sci., 1963—; systems advisor Social Security Adminstrn., Balt., 1976-84; cons. Nat. Bur. Standards, Gaithersburg, Md., 1968-72, Balt. Housing Authority, 1972-73, Social Security Adminstrn., Balt., 1966-73; mem. study group HHS, Washington, 1975-76. Author: An Introduction to Electronic Digital Computers, 1969; Simulation of Discrete Stochastic Systems, 1972; Computers for Social and Economic Development, 1974; Computers: Programming and Applications, 1975; also others. Contbr. articles to profl. jours. Mem. Community Housing Resources Bd., Montgomery County, Md., 1975. Recipient spl. service award Internat. Assn. Parents of Deaf, 1982. Fellow Assn. Computing Machinery (chmn. external activities bd. 1981-86, chmn. mems. and chpts. bd. 1978-80, chmn. nominating com. 1983-84, mem. council, chmn. Washington chpt. 1971-73, Outstanding Contribution award 1986); mem. Phi Beta Kappa (chmn. Georgetown chpt. 1974-76), Sigma Xi. Jewish. Office: Georgetown Univ Computer Sci Dept 37th & O Sts NW Washington DC 20057

MAISEL, MARGARET ROSE MEYER, lawyer; b. Manila, Philippines, Dec. 5, 1937; came to U.S., 1952; d. Paul Emil and Conchita (De La Riva) Meyer; m. Donald F. Maisel, Dec. 31, 1956; children: Vicky Colemere, Leslie Otero, Kristi Langford. BA, St. Mary's U., 1965, JD, 1971. Bar: Tex. 1971, U.S. Dist. Ct. (we. dist.) Tex. 1973. Atty., shareholder Tinsman-Houser, San Antonio, 1971-84, 85—; chmn. Tex in indsl. accident bd. State of Tex., 1984-85. Mem., adv. bd. Santa Rosa Health Care, San Antonio, 1993-94; bd. trustees St. mary's Univ., San Antonio, 1988-89; chmn. Santa Rosa Health Care Found., San Antonio, 1994—. Recipient Outstanding Law Alumnus St. Mary's U., 1989; named Outstanding Lawyers Bexar County Womens Bar. Fellow Tex. Bar Found., San Antonio Bar Found. (bd. dirs.); mem. San Antonio Trial Lawyers (bd. dirs.), Tex. Trial Lawyers (bd. dirs.). Roman Catholic. Avocations: antiques, reading, travel. Home: 1402 Fortune Hill San Antonio TX 78258-3201 Office: Tinsman Houser Inc 700 N Saint Marys St San Antonio TX 78205-3501

MAISEL, MICHAEL, shoe designer and manufacturer; b. Newark, Oct. 19, 1947; s. Irving and Betty (Markin) M.; m. Arlette Bernstein, Oct. 18, 1980; children: Ian Albert, Alicia Beth, Noah Shawn, Bette Gabrielle, Melissa Ann, Eunice Blanca. B.S. in Mktg., B.A. in Gen. Bus. Adminstrn., Ariz. State U., 1969. Asst. sales mgr. Mid-Atlantic Shoe Co. div. Beck Industries, N.Y.C., 1969-71; dir. imports Felsway Corp., Totowa, N.J., 1972-73; exec. v.p. Carber Enterprises, N.Y.C., 1973-80; v.p. S.R.O. div. Caressa, N.Y.C., 1980-84; pres. Sandler of Boston, N.Y.C., 1984-85, chmn. bd., 1986—; v.p. Lowell Shoe, Inc., Hudson, N.H., 1992-93; v.p. Selby, U.S. Shoe, Cin., 1993—; cons. in field. Mem. 210 Shoe Industry (life), Nat. Shoe Retailers Assn. (bd. dirs.), Nat. Shoe Mfrs. Assn. Republican. Jewish. Designer Carber's shoe, displayed in Met. Mus. Art; nominated for Coty design award, 1974-78; recipient Friendship award City of Cin. Human Rels. Commn., 1994. Office: 9 West Group 1 Eastwood Dr Cincinnati OH 45227-1197

MAISEL, SHERMAN JOSEPH, economist, educator; b. Buffalo, July 8, 1918; s. Louis and Sophia (Beck) M.; m. Lucy Cowdin, Sept. 26, 1942; children: Lawrence C., Margaret L. A.B., Harvard U., 1939, M.P.A., 1947, Ph.D., 1949. Mem. bd. govs. FRS, 1965-72; economist, fgn. service res. officer Dept. State, 1945-46; teaching fellow Harvard U., 1947-48; asst. prof., assoc. prof., prof. bus. adminstrn. U. Calif. at Berkeley, 1948-65, 72-86; sr. economist Nat. Bur. Econ. Research-West, 1973-78; chmn., bd. dirs. Farmers Savings & Loan, 1986-88; pres. Sherman J. Maisel & Asscs. Inc., 1986—; fellow Fund For Advancement Edn., 1952-53, Inst. Basic Math. with Application to Bus., 1959-60, Center for Advanced Study in Behavioral Scis., 1972; mem. adv. coms. to Bur. Census, FHA, State of Calif., Ford Found., Social Sci. Research Council; mem. bldg. research adv. bd. NRC. Author: Housebuilding in Transition, 1953, Fluctuations, Growth, and Forecasting, 1957, Managing the Dollar, 1973, Real Estate Investment and Finance, 1976, Risk and Capital Adequacy in Commercial Banks, 1981, Macroeconomics: Theories and Policies, 1982, Real Estate Finance, 1987, 2d edit., 1992. Bd. dirs. Berkeley Unified Sch. Dist., 1962-65. Served to capt. AUS, 1941-45. Mem. Am. Fin. Assn. (pres. 1973), Am. Econ. Assn., Am. Statis. Assn. Home: 2164 Hyde St San Francisco CA 94109-1701 Office: U Calif Haas Bus Sch Berkeley CA 94720

MAISLIN, ISIDORE, hospital administrator; b. N.Y.C., Aug. 4, 1919; s. Solomon and Rose (Baruch) M.; m. Frances Mussman, Jan. 18, 1948; children—Wendy Sue (Mrs. Neil Robbins), Steven William. B.S., Columbia, 1950, M.S., 1951. Asso. dir. Albert Einstein Med. Center, Phila., 1950-59; asso. dir. Mt. Sinai Hosp. Greater Miami, Mimai Beach, Fla., 1959-63; adminstr. Scranton (Pa.) Gen. Hosp., 1963-64; exec. dir. Jewish Home of Eastern Pa., Scranton, 1964-67; adminstr. South Mountain (Pa.) Restoration Center, 1967—. Served with AUS, 1943-46. Fellow Am. Coll. Hosp. Adminstrs., Am. Pub. Health Assn., Royal Soc. Health. Home and Office: 535 Colfax Ave Scranton PA 18510-2364

MAISSEL, LEON ISRAEL, physicist, engineer; b. Cape Town, South Africa, May 31, 1930; came to U.S., 1956; s. Charles and Emily (Cohen) M.; m. Raina Eve Corren, Jan. 26, 1956; children: Simon, Gerda, Joseph. B.Sc., U. Cape Town, 1949, M.Sc., 1951; Ph.D., U. London, 1955. Staff scientist Philco Corp., Phila., 1956-60; adv. physicist IBM Corp., Poughkeepsie, N.Y., 1960-63, sr. engr., 1963-81, sr. tech. staff mem., 1981-93; patent writer, 1994—. Author, editor: Handbook of Thin Film Technology, 1969, An Introduction to Thin Films, 1970; contbr. articles profl. jours.; patentee in field. Recipient Outstanding Invention award IBM Corp., 1968; recipient Outstanding Contbn. award IBM Corp., 1969. Fellow IEEE; mem. Am. Vacuum Soc. (Dir. 1966-68). Democrat. Jewish. Lodge: B'nai B'rith. Home: 16 Smoke Rise Ln Wappingers Falls NY 12590-1220 *Most people, properly trained, can solve well-defined problems. The ability to deal with poorly-defined problems is much rarer and is the key to success in science.*

MAITIN, SAM(UEL CALMAN) (SAM MAITIN), artist; b. Phila., Oct. 26, 1928; s. Isaac Boris and Ruth (Pollack) M.; m. Lilyan Miller, Aug. 29, 1964; children—Izak Joshua, Ana Raquel. Grad., Phila. Coll. Art, 1949; B.A., U. Pa., 1951. instr. art Phila. Coll. Art, 1949-59, Moore Coll. Art, 1950-52, Phila. Mus. Art, 1961-73, 80-81, Annenberg Sch. Comm. U. Pa., 1964-70; vis. lectr. Kent (Eng.) Inst. Art & Design, Canterbury, 1990, Camberwell Coll. Art, London, 1990. Creator 50 posters for YM/YWHA Arts Council.; one-man shows include: Yoseido Gallery, Tokyo, 1967, 69, 70, Curwen Gallery, London, 1969, Fleisher Gallery, Phila. Mus. Art, 1971, Associated Am. Artists Gallery, Phila., 1979, Joanne Lyon Gallery, Aspen, Colo., 1981, 82, 84, Dolan/Maxwell Gallery, Phila., 1985, 87, Noyes Mus., N.J., 1985, Woodmere Art Mus., Phila., 1994, Art Inst. Phila., 1994; group shows include Phila. Mus. Art Bicentennial Exhbns., 1976, Tate Gallery, 1977, Phila. Artists, Tel Aviv, 1978; represented in permanent collections Library of Congress, Mus. Modern Art, N.Y.C., Nat. Gallery Art, Oakland Mus., Calif., Phila. Mus. Art, Currier Gallery Art, Manchester, N.H., Tate Gallery, London, Pa. Acad Fine Arts, Smithsonian Instn., U. Pa., Picker Mus., Colgate U.; commissions include: (tapestry) Ark Covering, Adath Jeshurun Synagogue, Elkins Park, Pa., 1976, (mural painting) Phila. Dept. Recreation swimming pool, 1978, (mural) Academy House, Phila., 1984, (mural) Christian Assn., U. Pa., 1985, (tapestry) Abington Hosp., Pa., 1985, (dimensional mural) Annenberg Sch. Communications lobby, U. Pa., 1975, expanded, 1985, (3 story dimensional mural) law offices of Morgan, Lewis & Bockius, Miami, Fla., 1987, (ceiling and wall mural banners) Wharton Sch., U. Pa., 1988, (dimensional mural) Children's Hosp., Phila., 1992, (dimensional diptych) Kaiserman YM/YWHA, Haverford, Pa., 1992, (50 dimensional paintings) Brady Cancer Treatment Ctr., Voorhees, N.J., 1993, (mural) Settlement Music Sch., West Phila., (66 foot mural-banner) Tai Cang Tape Factory, Shanghai, China, 1996. Guggenheim fellow, 1968; recipient award of excellence Art Matters, 1988. Home and Studio: 704 Pine St Philadelphia PA 19106-4005

MAITRA, SUBIR RANJAN, medical educator; b. Calcutta, India, Oct. 2, 1943; came to U.S., 1983; s. Sudhir R. and Nilima (Sanyal) M.; m. Sakti Sanyal, July 6, 1975; 1 child, Soma. BS, Calcutta U., 1964, MS, 1966, PhD, 1971, DSc, 1990. Lectr. in Physiology Banaras U., Varanasi, India, 1973-78, 81-83; sr. Fulbright rsch. scholar Henry Ford Hosp., Detroit, 1979-80, rsch. assoc. in hypertension, 1983-85; rsch. assoc. in physiology Loyola U., Chgo., 1985-86, asst. prof. physiology, 1987-88; dir. trauma rsch. surgery SUNY, Stony Brook, 1988-90, asst. prof., dir. trauma rsch. emergency medicine, surgery, 1990-93, assoc. prof., dir. rsch. emergency medicine, 1993—. Recipient Gold medal Calcutta U., 1966; prin. investigator Indian Coun. Med. Rsch., 1981, Univ. Grants Commn., 1983. Mem. AAAS, Am. Physiol. Soc., Shock Soc. Avocations: travel, community activities, sports.

MAIWURM, JAMES JOHN, lawyer; b. Wooster, Ohio, Dec. 5, 1948; s. James Frederick and Virginia Anne (Jones) M.; m. Wendy S. Leeper, July 31, 1974; children: James G., Michelle K. BA, Coll. Wooster, 1971; JD, U. Mich., 1974. Bar: Ohio 1974, D.C. 1986, Md. 1987, N.Y., 1987. Ptnr. Squire, Sanders & Dempsey, Cleve. and Washington, 1974-90; ptnr., group head Crowell & Moring, Washington, 1990—. Contbr. articles to profl. jours. Mem. ABA, D.C. Bar Assn., Leadership Washington, Fed. City Coun., Econ. Club Washington, George Mason U. Century Club (bd. dirs. 1994—). Home: 9419 Brian Jac Ln Great Falls VA 22066-2002 Office: Crowell & Moring 1001 Pennsylvania Ave NW Washington DC 20004-2505

MAIZE, JOHN CHRISTOPHER, dermatology educator; b. Elizabeth, N.J., July 23, 1943; s. Donald Adam and Caroline Marie (Costanzo) M.; m. Janice Lee Bentley, May. 21, 1966; children: Sandra Kristine Tolly, John C. Jr., Jennifer Lee. MD, U. Mich., 1968. Diplomate Am. Bd. Dermatology. Intern U. Mich., Ann Arbor, 1968-69, residency in dermatology, 1969-72; asst. prof. dermatology SUNY, Buffalo, 1972-77, assoc. prof., 1977-80; assoc. prof. Med. U. of S.C., Charleston, 1980-83, prof., 1983-89, prof., chmn. dept. dermatology, 1989—; editor-in-chief Am. Jour. Dermatology, 1986-90; dir. Am. Bd. Dermatology. Author: Pigmented Lesions of the Skin, 1987. Fellow Am. Acad. Dermatology, Am. Soc. Dermapathology (pres. 1995); mem. Am. Dermatol. Assn., Internat. Soc. Dermatopathology (sec. 1987-89, pres. 1989-91), S.C. Med. Assn., S.C. Dermatol. Assn. Roman Catholic. Avocations: fishing, golfing, travelling. Office: Med U SC 171 Ashley Ave Charleston SC 29425-0001

MAJD, MASSOUD, radiology and nuclear medicine educator; b. Yazd, Iran, July 23, 1935; came to U.S., 1961; s. Jalil and Khadijeh Majd; m. Fereshteh H.S. Javadi, June 23, 1968; children: Kurosh, Katayoon. MD, Tehran U., 1960. Diplomate Am. Bd. Radiology, Am. Bd. Nuclear Medicine. Intern Deaconess Hosp., Buffalo, 1961-62; resident Georgetown U., Washington, 1962-66, instr. radiology, 1965-66, 68-70; asst. prof. Pahlavi U., Shiraz, Iran, 1966-68; asst. prof. George Washington U., 1970-72, assoc. prof., 1972-79, prof. radiology and pediatrics, 1979—; radiologist, dir. pediatric nuclear medicine Children's Nat. Med. Ctr., Washington, 1968—; adj. prof. radiology Georgetown U., 1981—; staff radiologist Georgetown U. Hosp., 1965-66; radiologist Pahlavi U. Hosps, Shiraz, 1966-68; assoc. staff radiology Children's Med. Ctr., 1968-72, sr. attending staff radiology, 1972—, founder dir. sect. nuclear medicine, 1969—; presenter in field. Contbr. chpts. to books and articles to profl. jours. Fellow Soc. Uroradiology, Am. Coll. Radiology, Am. Coll. Nuclear Physicians, Am. Acad. Pediatrics; mem. Am. Roetgen Ray Soc., Radiologic Soc. N.Am., European Soc. Pediatric Radiology (affiliate), Soc. Pediatric Radiology, Soc. Nuclear Medicine, Pediatric Imaging Coun., John Caffey Soc. Home: 8605 Stirrup Ct Potomac MD 20854-4843 Office: Childrens Nat Med Ctr 111 Michigan Ave NW Washington DC 20010-2970

MAJDA, ANDREW J., mathematician, educator; b. East Chicago, Ind., Jan. 30, 1949; m. Gerta Keller. BS, Purdue U., 1970; MS, Stanford U., 1971, PhD, 1973. Instr. Courant Inst. NYU, 1973-76; from asst. prof. to assoc. prof. U. Calif., L.A., 1976-78, prof., 1978; prof. U. Calif., Berkeley, 1979-84; vis. prof. Princeton (N.J.) U., 1984-85, prof., 1985-95; Morse prof. arts and sci. Courant Inst./NYU, N.Y.C., 1995—. Alfred P. Sloan Found. fellow, 1977-79; recipient medal of college de France, 1982, John von Neumann award Soc. for Indsl. and Applied Math., 1990. Mem. NAS (Applied Math. and Numerical Analysis award 1992). Office: Courant Institute 251 Mercer St New York NY 10012

MAJERLE, DANIEL LEWIS, professional basketball player, Olympic athlete; b. Traverse City, Mich., Sept. 9, 1965. Student, Ctrl. Mich. Forward Phoenix Suns, 1988—; now with Cleveland Cavaliers. Mem. Bronze Medal Winning Olympic Team, Seoul, Korea, 1988; mem. NBA All-Defensive second team, 1991, 93; mem. NBA All-Star team, 1992, 93; named to Dream Team II, 1994. Mem. All NBA second team, 1991; NBA All-Star, 1992; Shares NBA Finals single-game playoff record for most three point field goals made-8, 1993. Office: Cleveland Cavaliers 1 Center Ct Cleveland OH 44115-4001*

MAJERUS, PHILIP WARREN, physician; b. Chgo., July 10, 1936; s. Clarence Nicholas and Helen Louise (Mathis) M.; m. Janet Sue Brakensiek, Dec. 28, 1957; children: Suzanne, David, Juliet, Karen. BS, Notre Dame U., 1958; MD, Washington U., 1961. Resident in Medicine Mass. Gen. Hosp., Boston, 1961-63; research assoc. NIH, Bethesda, Md., 1963-66; asst. prof. biochemistry Washington U., St. Louis, 1966-75, asst. prof. medicine, 1966-69, assoc. prof. medicine, 1969-71, prof. medicine, 1971—, dir. div. hematology, 1973—, prof. biochemistry, 1976—. Mem. editorial bd. numerous jours. and profl. mags.; contbr. numerous articles to profl. jours. Recipient numerous awards including Am. Cancer Soc. Faculty Rsch. Assoc. award, 1966-75, Disting. Career award for Contbns. to Hemostasis Internat. Soc. for Thrombosis and Hemostasis, 1985, Alumni/Faculty award Washington U. Sch. Medicine, 1986, The Robert J. and Claire Pasarow Found. award, 1994. Fellow ACP; mem. NAS, Inst. Medicine of NAS, Am. Acad. Arts and Scis., Assn. Am. Physicians, Am. Soc. Hematology (pres. 1991), Am. Fedn. Clin. Rsch., Am. Soc. Biol. Chemists, Am. Soc. Clin. Investigation (pres. 1981-82), Sigma Xi, Alpha Omega Alpha. Home: 7220 Pershing Ave Saint Louis MO 63130 Office: Wash Univ Sch of Med Internal Med Saint Louis MO 63110

MAJERUS, RICK, collegiate basketball team coach; b. Sheboygan, Wis.. BS, Marquette U., 1970, MS, 1979. Asst. coach Marquette U., 1971-83, head coach, 1983-86; asst. coach Milw. Bucks, 1986-87; head coach Ball State U., 1987-89, U. Utah, Salt Lake City, 1989—; asst. coach U.S.A. Dream Team 2, summer 1994. Named Coach of Yr. Hoop Scoop, 1989, UPI Coach of Yr., 1991, Coach of Yr. Basketball Times, 1991, Utah Sports Person of Yr. 1992, Playboy Coach of Yr., 1992, Kodak Dist. Coach of Yr.,

1991, 93, 95, Western Athletic Conf. Coach of Yr., 1994, 95. Office: U Utah Jon M Huntsman Ctr Salt Lake City UT 84112*

MAJESTY, MELVIN SIDNEY, psychologist, consultant; b. New Orleans, June 6, 1928; s. Sidney Joseph and Marcella Cecilia (Kieffer) M.; m. Bettye Newanda Gordon, Dec. 18, 1955; 1 child, Diana Sue. BA, La. State U., 1949; MS, Western Res. U., 1951; PhD (USAF Inst. Tech. fellow), Case-Western Res. U., 1967. Commd. 2d lt. USAF, 1951, advanced through grades to lt. col., 1968; program mgr., ast. dir. tng. rsch. Air Force Human Resources Lab., 1967-69; dir. faculty and profl. ednl. rsch. USAF Acad., 1969-72; dir. plot tng. candidate selection program Officer Tng. Sch., Air Tng.Command, 1972-76; ret. USAF, 1976; personnel selection cons. to Calif. State Pers. Bd., Sacramento, 1976-92. Patentee listening center; founded pers. testing for ballistic missile and space systems; directed largest study of fighter pilot selection since World War II; pioneered use of phys. testing as replacement for the maximum age requirement in law enforcement jobs; developed phys. fitness tests and established psychol. screening standards for state highway patrol officer and police officers; contbr. numerous articles to profl. publs. Decorated Commendation medal (2), Meritorious Svc. medal (2). Mem. Am. Psychol. Assn., Internat. Pers. Mgmt. Assn., Calif. Psychol. Assn., Western Psychol. Assn., Soc. Indsl. and Orgnl. Psychology, Personnel Testing Coun., VFW, DAV, Am. Legion, Amvets. Office: 801 Capitol Mall Sacramento CA 95814-4806

MAJEV, HOWARD RUDOLPH, lawyer; b. N.Y.C., Dec. 10, 1952; s. Benny and Hela (Wolnowicz) M.; m. Janet Brandt; children: Brendan Joshua, Collin Campbell. BA, Johns Hopkins U., 1973; JD, U. Md., 1976. Bar: Md. 1978, D.C. 1995. Exec. asst. to city coun. pres. City of Balt., Balt., 1976-79; assoc. Weinberg and Green, Balt., 1979-84; ptnr. Weinberg & Green, Balt., 1985-94, Rudnick & Wolfe, Balt., Washington, 1994—. Author: (with K.S. Koenig) How to be a Legal Eagle: A Checklist for Remodelers, 1988; dir. Lex Mundi, 1992-94. Dir. Citizens Planning and Housing Assn., Balt., 1985-95, pres., 1990-92; bd. dirs. Md. Food Bank, Inc., 1988-92, Florence Crittenton Svcs. Balt., 1986-87, Sinai Hosp. Balt., 1990-92, Levindale Hebrew Geriat. Home and Hosp., 1991; devel. coun. The Kennedy Krieger Inst., 1988-92; participant Leadership-Greater Balt. Com., 1986. Mem. ABA, D.C. Bar Assn., Md. State Bar Assn., Balt. City Bar Assn. Avocations: running, rotisserie league baseball, reading, stamp collecting. Office: Rudnick & Wolfe 555 12th St NW Ste 600 Washington DC 20004

MAJOR, ANDRÉ, radio producer, writer, educator; b. Montréal, Que., Can., Apr. 22, 1942; s. Arthur and Anna (Sharp) M.; m. Ginette Lepage, June 30, 1970; children—Eric, Julie. Student, Coll. de Montréal, 1955-60. Lit. critic La Presse, Montreal, 1965-79, Le Devoir, Montreal, 1967-70; lecteur Editions du Jour, Montreal, 1964-67, Lemeac, Montreal, 1972-75; radio producer CBC, Radio Canada, Montreal, 1973—; prof. lit. and creative writing Ottawa U., 1977-78, U. Que., 1977, McGill U., 1990. Works include Le Chair de poule, 1965, L'Épouvantail, 1974, L'Epideie, 1975, Les Rescapés, 1978 (Gov. Gen. Can. award), Histoires de Deserteurs, 1991, La Vie Provisoire, 1995; poetry collections include Poèmes pour durer, 1969; dramas include Un Soirée en octobre, 1975; short stories include La Folle d'Elvis, 1981, L'Hiver au coeur, 1987 (Can.-Belgium award 1991, prix Athanase-David, 1992). Mem. Union des Ecrivains québécois (sec. 1976-79). Office: CBC Radio Can, 1400 E Blvd Rene-Levesque, Montreal, PQ Canada H2L 2M2

MAJOR, CLARENCE LEE, novelist, poet, educator; b. Atlanta, Dec. 31, 1936; s. Clarence and Inez (Huff) M.; m. Pamela Ritter, May 8, 1980. BS, SUNY, Albany; PhD, Union Inst. Prof. U. Colo., Boulder, 1977-89, U. Calif., Davis, 1989—. Author: All-Night Visitors, 1969, Dictionary of Afro-American Slang, 1970, No, 1973, Reflex and Bone Structure, 1975, rev. edit., 1996, Emergency Exit, 1979, My Amputations, 1986, Such Was the Season, 1987, Fun and Games, 1990, Calling the Wind, 1993, Juba to Jive: A Dictionary of African American Slang, 1994, Dirty Bird Blues, 1996; poetry: Swallow the Lake, 1970, Symptoms & Madness, 1971, Private Line, 1971, The Cotton Club, 1972, Inside Diameter: The France Poems, 1985, Painted Turtle, 1988, Surfaces and Masks, 1988, Some Observations of a Stranger at Zune in the Latter Part of the Century, 1989, Parking Lots, 1992, The Garden Thrives, 1996; contbr. articles to Washington Post Book World, L.A. Times Book Rev., N.Y. Times Book Rev. Recipient Nat. Council on Arts award, Washington, 1970; Western States Book award, Western States Found., Santa Fe, 1986; Fulbright grantee, 1981-83. Office: U Calif Dept of English Sproul Hall Davis CA 95616

MAJOR, COLEMAN JOSEPH, chemical engineer; b. Detroit, Sept. 7, 1915; s. Coleman I. and Anna (Galik) M.; m. Marjorie Lois Shenk, Nov. 21, 1941; children: Roy Coleman, Marilyn M. Phillips Bever. B.S., U. Ill., 1937; Ph.D., Cornell U., 1941. Chief prodn. engr., supt. services Sharples Chems., Inc., Wyandotte, Mich., 1941-50; asso. prof. chem. engring. U. Iowa, 1950-56; head high energy chems. Am. Potash & Chem. Corp., Whittier, Calif. and Henderson, Nev., 1956-59; prof. chem. engring. U. Iowa, 1959-64; prof., head dept. chem. engring. U. Akron, 1964-70; dean Coll. Engring., also dir. Inst. Technol. Assistance, 1970-80; dir. Inst. Biomed. Engring. Rsch., 1979-80; cons. computers. Contbr. articles to tech. jours. Named Chem. Engr. of Yr., 1979; C.J. Major Scholarship award established in his honor, 1990; recipient Disting. Svc. award U. Akron, 1993. Fellow Am. Inst. Chem. Engrs.; mem. Am. Chem. Soc., Sigma Xi, Tau Beta Pi. Patentee in field. Home: 7838 Jaymes St Dublin OH 43017-8812 *A few guidelines that I have used: 1. Work very hard but find time to relax. 2. Push yourself ahead, but don't hold anyone else back. 3. When gathering facts, be rigorous and unrelenting but when making decisions involving people, use the art of compromise.*

MAJOR, JAMES RUSSELL RICHARDS, historian, educator; b. Riverton, Va., Jan. 7, 1921; s. Julian Neville and Jean (Richards) M.; m. Blair Louise Rogers, June 9, 1945; children: Blair Louise, Randon Leigh, Clara Jean, James Russell Richards. AB, Va. Mil. Inst., 1942; MA, Princeton U., 1948, PhD, 1949. Mem. faculty Emory U., 1949-90, Charles Howard Candler prof. history, 1980-90, chmn. dept., 1966-70, 76-79, 87-89; vis. prof. Harvard, 1965-66; mem. Inst. Advanced Study Princeton, 1967-68, 79-80; Vice pres. H.W. Dick Co., 1975—. Author: The Estates General of 1560, 1951, Representative Instns. in Renaissance France, 1421-1559, 1960, The Deputies to the Estates General of Renaissance France, 1960, The Western World: Renaissance to the Present, 2d edit, 1971, The Age of the Renaissance and Reformation, 1970, Bellièvre, Sully and The Assembly of Notables of 1596, 1974, Representative Government in Early Modern France, 1980, The Monarchy, The Estates and The Aristocracy in Renaissance France, 1988, From Renaissance Monarchy to Absolute Monarchy: French Kings, Nobles, and Estates, 1994; also articles; bd. editors: Jour. Modern History, 1966-69, French History, 1986-90. Served to capt. AUS, 1942-46. Decorated Silver Star, Bronze Star, Purple Heart with 2 clusters; Fulbright fellow France, 1952-53; Guggenheim fellow, 1953-54, 67-68; Faculty Research fellow Soc. Sci. Research Council, 1955-58; fellow, 1961-62; sr. fellow Nat. Endowment for Humanities, 1973-74. Mem. AAUP (pres. S.E. regional conf. 1965-67, mem. nat. coun. 1966-69), Am. Hist. Assn. (com. on PhD programs in history 1969-71, program com. 1976, mem. rsch. divsn. 1978-81, Leo Gershoy prize com. 1990-92, Leo Gershoy award 1996), Internat. Commn. History Rep. and Parliamentary Instn. (pres. N.Am. sect. 1975-81), Renaissance Soc. Am. (mem. coun. 1971-73), Sixteenth Century Studies Conf. (Nancy Syman Roelker prize 1987), Soc. French Hist. Studies (William C. Koren prize 1966, co-winner 1987), So. Hist. Assn. (vice chmn. program com. 1967, chmn. European sect. 1970-71), So. History of France, European Acad. History, Phi Beta Kappa (senator United chpts. 1970-76). Home: 2223 Hill Park Ct Decatur GA 30033-2716

MAJOR, JEAN-LOUIS, author, French literature educator; b. Cornwall, Ont., Can., July 16, 1937; s. Joseph and Noella (Daoust) M.; m. Bibiane Landry, June 4, 1960; 1 dau., Marie-France. B.A. with honors, U. Ottawa, Ont., 1959, B.Phil., 1959, Licenciate of Philosophy, 1960, M.A., 1961, Ph.D., 1965; research fellow, Ecole Pratique des Hautes Etudes, Paris, 1968-69. Lectr. philosophy College Bruyere, Ottawa, 1960-61; lectr. dept. philosophy U. Ottawa, 1961-65, asst. prof. departement lettres Francaises, 1965-67, assoc. prof. lettres Francaises, 1967-71, prof. lettres Francaises, 1971—, assoc. dean rsch., Faculty of Arts, 1991—; lit. critic, dir. lit. sect. Le Droit (newspaper), 1963-65; vis. prof. U. Toronoto, Ont., 1970-71; editor Corpus d'editions critiques, 1981—, Bibliothèque du Nouveau Monde; chmn. acad. adv. com. Ont. Coun. on Univ. Affairs, 1991-93. Author books including Saint-Exupéry, l'écriture et la pensée, 1968, Léone de Jean Cocteau, 1975, Anne Hébert et le miracle de la parole, 1976, Radiquet, Cocteau "Les joues en feu, ", 1977, Le jeu en étoile, 1978, Paul-Marie Lapointe: la nuit incendiée, 1978, Entre l'ecriture et la parole, 1984, Journal d'Henriette Dessaulles, 1989, Ringuet, Trente arpents, 1991; also numerous articles. Fellow Can. Coun., 1968, 69, 71; grantee Humanities Rsch. Coun. Can., 1975, 85, 90, 95. Fellow Royal Soc. Can., Academie des Lettres et des Sciences humaines. Home: PO Box 357, St-Isidore, ON Canada K0C 2B0 Office: Faculty Arts, U Ottawa, Ottawa, ON Canada K1N 6N5

MAJOR, JOHN CHARLES, judge; b. Mattawa, Ont., Can., Feb. 20, 1931; s. William and Elsie (Thompson) M.; m. Hélène Provencher, 1959; children: Suzan, Peter, Paul, Steven. BComm, Loyola Coll., Montreal, 1953; LLB, U. Toronto, 1957. Bar: Alberta 1958, Queen's Counsel, 1972, Alberta Ct. of Appeal, 1991. With Bennett, Jones & Verchere, Calgary, 1957-91, sr. ptnr., 1967; sr. counsel City of Calgary Police Svc., 1975-85; counsel McDonald Commn., 1978-82; sr. counsel Province of Alta., 1987; mem. Supreme Ct. of Can., 1992—. Fellow Am. Coll. Trial Lawyers; mem. Can. Bar Assn., Can. Inst. of the Adminstrn. of Justice, Can. Judges Conf., The Glencoe Club (Calgary), Calgary Golf and Country Club, Ottawa Hunt and Golf Club. Avocation: golf. Office: Supreme Court of Can, Wellington St, Ottawa, ON Canada K1A 0J1

MAJOR, JOHN KEENE, radio broadcasting executive; b. Kansas City, Mo., Aug. 3, 1924; s. Ralph Hermon and Margaret Norman (Jackson) M.; m. Gracemary Somers Westing, Apr. 9, 1950 (div.); children: John Westing, Ann Somers, Richard Jackson; m. Lee Adair Jordan, June 25, 1970. Student, U. Kansas City, 1940-41; BS, Yale U., 1943; MS, 1947; DSc, U. Paris, 1951. Lab. asst. physics Yale U., 1943-44, instr., research asst. physics, 1952-55; sci. staff spl. studies group, div. war research Columbia U., 1944; instr. physics and chemistry Am. Community Sch., Paris, 1948-49; research fellow Centre National de la Recherche Scientifique, Laboratoire de Chimie Nucleaire, Coll. de France, Paris, 1951; Carnegie Found. fellow Laboratoire Curie, Institut du Radium, Paris, 1951; assoc. prof. physics Western Res. U., 1955-57, chmn. dept., 1955-60, 61-64, Perkins prof. physics, 1957-66; staff assoc. univ. sci. devel. sect. div. instl. programs NSF, 1964-68; prof. physics, dean Grad. Sch. Arts and Scis., U. Cin., 1968-71; prof. physics NYU, 1971-74, dean Grad. Sch. Arts and Scis., 1971-73; vis. scholar Alfred P. Sloan Sch. Mgmt., MIT, 1973-74; prof. physics Northeastern Ill. U., Chgo., 1974-77; v.p. acad. affairs Northeastern Ill. U., 1974-75; cons. NSF, 1968-69; sci. cons. Sonar Analysis Group, 1946-47; gen. mgr. Sta. WONO, Syracuse, N.Y., 1977; dir. research and mktg. Sta. WFMT, Chgo., 1978-81; chmn. bd., pres. KCMA, Inc., 1980—; gen. mgr. Sta. KCMA, 1981-88; mem. exec. com. radio project Ctr. for Pub. Resources, 1980-81; bd. dirs. T. Rowe Price Equity Funds. Contbr. articles to profl. jours. Bd. dirs. Concertime, 1985—, prs. 1993-95; bd. dirs. Tulsa Opera, 1984-95, Tulsa Philharm. Soc., 1988-95. Lt. (j.g.) USNR, 1944-46. Fellow at Lab. für Technische Physik, Technische Hochschule Munich, 1960-61; Fulbright fellow U. Paris, 1949-50. Mem. Classical Music Broadcasters Assn. (exec. v.p., 1979-80, bd. dir. 1979-82, 85-87, 89-93, pres. 1980-81, 90-91), Cosmos Club (Washington), Sigma Xi. Home: 126 E 26th Pl Tulsa OK 74114-2422

MAJOR, MARY JO, dance school artistic director; b. Joliet, Ill., Dec. 5, 1955; d. George Francis and Lucille Mae (Ballun) Schmidberger; m. Perry Rex Major, June 9, 1979. AA, Joliet Jr. Coll., 1976; BA, Lewis U., 1978; MS, Ill. State U., 1983; postgrad., No. Ill. U., Nat. Lewis U. and Gov.'s State U. Cert. tchr., Ill. Tchr., softball coach St. Rose Grade Sch., Wilmington, Ill., 1977-78; tchr., coach volleyball, basketball, softball Reed Custer High Sch., Braidwood, Ill., 1978-79; pvt. tutor, 1979; tchr. Coal City (Ill.) Middle Sc, 1980—, basketball coach, 1980-84; owner, dir., choreographer Major Sch. Dance, Inc., Coal City, 1984—; owner Technique Boutique, 1991; founder Major Motion Dancers, 1984—; aerobics instr. Wilmington Park Dist.,1977-82, Coal City Shape Shoppe, 1980-82; cheerleading sponsor Joliet Jr. Coll., 1976-77, aerobics instr., 1980-81; pvt. dance instr., Coal City, 1981; dancer, choreographer Coal City Bi-Centennial Celebration, 1981, Coal City Community Celebration, 1982; founder Major Motion Dancers, 1984-95; tchr., Russia, 1990; dancer, choreographer various performances for ch. and civic orgns.; televised half-time performance and tour Citrus Bowl. Commd. to choreograph and appear in video prodn.: Jacinta, Not an Ordinary Love, The Patty Waszak Show A Bit of Branson, 1995-96. Mem. Arts Coun. Co-op. Recipient Proclamation of Achievement award Dance Olympus, Chgo., 1986, 87, 88, 89, 90, 91, 92, 93, 94, 95, 96, Best Choreographer award 1990, Merit award Tremaine Dance Conv., 1991-92; named Best Actress, Joliet Kiwanis, 1989, Best Musician, 1990. Mem. NEA, Ill. Edn. Assn., Coal City Cmty. Unit Edn. Assn. Office: Major Sch Dance Inc 545 E 1st St Coal City IL 60416-1635

MAJOR, PATRICK WEBB, III, principal; b. Wai, Maharastra, India, Mar. 12, 1947; s. Patrick W. Jr. and Alice (Seeland) M.; m. Daphnelynn Jantz, June 26, 1971; children: Mindy Joy, Matthew Patrick Webb. BA, Biola U., 1972; MA, Point Loma Coll., 1979; postgrad., U. Calif., Irvine. Cert. secondary tchr., adminstr., Calif. Prin. Omega High Sch., Bakersfield, Calif., 1980-84; headmaster Bakersfield (Calif.) Christian Life Schs., 1984-86; prin. North Kern Christian Sch., Wasco, Calif., 1986-88; prin., adminstr. Yucaipa (Calif.) Christian Schs., 1988—. Mem. ASCD, Assn. Christian Schs. Internat. (former dist. rep., exec. bd. mem.), Ctrl. Redwood League (pres. 1985-86), CIF Ctrl Sect., Internat. Fellowship Christian Sch. Adminstrs., Nat. Assn. Elem. Sch. Prins.

MAJORS, JOHNNY (JOHN TERRILL MAJORS), university athletic coach; b. Lynchburg, Tenn., May 21, 1935; m. Mary Lynn Barnwell, June 27, 1959; children—John Ireland, Mary Elizabeth. B.S., U. Tenn., 1957. Head football coach Iowa State U., 1968-72, U. Pitts., 1973-76, U. Tenn., 1977-92, U. Pitts., 1993—. Chmn. E. Tenn. Easter Seals Com., 1977, March of Dimes, 1977. Named Nat. Coll. Coach of Yr., 1973, 76; won nat. championship NCAA Divsn. 1A, 1976; inducted into Nat. Football Hall of Fame, 1987, Tenn. Hall of Fame (charter). Mem. Am. Football Coaches Assn. (bd. dirs., past pres.), Pitts. Athletic Assn., Univ. Club, Pitts. Field Club, Honors Club in Ooltewah (Tenn.), Sigma Chi, Omicron Delta Kappa. Home: 4215 Bigelow Blvd Pittsburgh PA 15213-2649 Office: U Pitts PO Box 7436 Pittsburgh PA 15213-0436

MAJORS, LEE, actor; b. Wyandotte, Mich., Apr. 23, 1940; m. Farrah Fawcett, July 28, 1973 (div. 1982). Student, U. Ind.; grad., Eastern Ky. State Coll.; student acting with, Estelle Harmon, MGM Studio Acting Sch. Actor: (films) including Will Penny, 1967, The Liberation of L.B. Jones, 1970, Killer Fish, 1979, Agency, Steel, Scrooge, 1988, Keaton's Cop, 1988; (TV movies) including The Six Million Dollar Man, 1973, Just a Little Convenience, 1977, The Ballad of Andy Crocker, 1969, Weekend of Terror, 1970, The Gary Francis Powers Story: The U-2 Incident, 1977, High Noon Part II: The Return of Will Kane, 1980, Starflight: The Plane That Couldn't Land, 1983, The Cowboy and the Ballerina, 1984, Danger Down Under, 1988, Fire! Trapped on the 37th Floor, 1991, (TV series) The Big Valley, 1965-68, The Men from Shiloh, 1970-71, Owen Marshall, Counselor at Law, 1971-73, The Six Million Dollar Man, 1973-78, The Fall Guy, 1981-85, Tour of Duty, 1990, Raven, 1992-93; other TV appearances include: Gunsmoke, The Bionic Woman, Alias Smith and Jones, Bracken's World. Mem. AFTRA, Acad. Motion Picture Arts and Scis. Office: David Shapira & Assocs 15301 Ventura Blvd Ste 345 Sherman Oaks CA 91403*

MAJORS, NELDA FAYE, physical therapist; b. Houston, Aug. 3, 1938; d. Columbus Edward and Mary (Mills) M. Cert. in Phys. Therapy, Hermann Sch. Phys. Therapy, Houston, 1960; BS, U. Houston, 1963. Lic. phys. therapist, Tex. Staff therapist Tex. Med. Ctr. Hermann Hosp., Houston, 1960-61; phys. therapist Chelsea Orthopedic Clinic, Houston, 1961-63; dir. phys. therapy Meml. Hosp. Southwest, Houston, 1963-75; owner, pres. Nelda Majors, Inc., Houston, 1975—; mem. profl. adv. bd. Logos Home Health Agy., Houston, 1985-86; adv. dir. 1st Northwestern Bank, Houston. Active Meml. Dr. Meth. Ch., Houston, 1983—; ptnr. Houston Proud Ptnr., 1986—; founder, pres. Instnl. Safety Advs. Inc., 1994—; bd. dirs. Texans for the Improvement of Long Term Care Facilities, 1995—. Named All Am. Softball Pitcher, Amateur Softball Assn., 1964, All-Regional and All-State Pitcher, Tex. Amateur Softball Assn., 1954-70; named to Houston Amateur Softball Assn. Softball Hall of Fame, 1994. Mem. Am. Phys. Therapy Assn. (pvt. practice sect.), Tex. Phys. Therapy Assn., U. Houston Alumni Assn., E. Cullen Soc. (U. Houston), N.W. Crossing Optimist Club (Houston, charter mem., bd. dirs.), River Oaks Rotary (Houston), Phi Kappa Phi. Republican. Club: U. Houston Cougar. Avocations: softball, bicycling, traveling, golf, reading.

MAJORS, RICHARD GEORGE, psychology educator; b. Ithaca, N.Y.; s. Richard G. II and Fannie Sue Majors; legal guardian: Lillian A. McGill. AA, Auburn (N.Y.) Community Coll., 1974; BA in History, Plattsburgh State Coll., 1977; PhD in Ednl. Psychology, U. Ill., 1987. Various social svc. positions, 1976-79; probation officer, ct. investigator Plattsburgh, 1979; clin. intern McKinley Health Ctr., Urbana, Ill., 1981; rsch. asst. U. Minn., Mpls., 1981, U. Ill., Urbana, 1981-84; instr. Parkland Community Coll., Champaign, Ill., 1985; rsch. asst. U. Ill., Champaign, 1985-86; postdoctoral fellow U. Kans., Lawrence, 1987-89; postdoctoral fellow, clin. fellow Harvard Med. Sch., Boston, 1989-90; asst. prof. psychology U. Wis. System, 1990-93; sr. rsch. assoc. The Urban Inst., Washington, 1993-95; vis. fellow, scholar The David Walker Rsch. Inst., Mich. State U., 1995—; vis. fellow, scholar David Walker Rsch. Inst. Mich. State U.; presenter in field. Co-author: Coolpose: The Dilemmas of Black Manhood in America, 1992, The American Black Male: His Present Status and Future, 1994; founder Jour. of African Am. Men. Named one of Outstanding Young Men of Am., 1987. Fellow APA (predoctoral minority fellow 1984); mem. Nat. Coun. African Am. Men (chmn., co-founder), Soc. for Psychol. Study of Ethnic Minority Issues, Am. Orthopsychiat. Assn., Greenpeace, Kappa Delta Pi, Phi Delta Kappa. Avocations: reading, traveling, cycling. Office: David Walker Rsch Inst Mich State U B421 W Fee Hall East Lansing MI 48824

MAJORS, STEVEN WILLIAM, director art museum, artist, art consultant; b. Trenton, N.J., Apr. 16, 1955; s. Steven Andrew and Alvina Henrietta Margaret (Marion) M. AA in Visual Arts, Mercer County C.C., 1978; BFA in Painting and Printmaking, Va. Commonwealth U., 1980; MA in Painting and Studio Arts, C.W. Post Ctr. L.I. U., 1983. Installation design/lighting dir. Hillwood Art Gallery, C.W. Post Ctr. of L.I. U., Greenvale, N.Y., 1981-83; interpreter of exhibits Whaling Mus. Soc., Inc., Cold Spring Harbor, N.Y., 1983; curator Washington County Mus. of Fine Arts, Hagerstown, Md., 1984-88; dir. Torpedo Factory Art Ctr., Alexandria, Va., 1988-96; adj. faculty in visual arts, Mercer County C.C., 1983-84; adj. faculty in art and art edn., Frostburg (Md.) State U.,1986-87; adj. faculty in art history, Frederick (Md.) C.C., 1993—; bd. mem. Alexandria (Va.) Commn. for the Arts, 1988-89, Gov.'s Task Force on the Arts, Annapolis, Md., 1987. One-man shows include C.W. Post Ctr. L.I. U., Greenvale, N.Y., 1983, Shepherd Coll., Shepherdstown, W.Va., 1987, Wilson Coll, Chambersburg, Pa., 1988; group exhibitions include Wunsch Arts Ctr., Glen Cove, N.Y., 1983, Mercer County C.C., Trenton, N.J., 1984, Md. Art Place, Baltimore, 1985-86, Frederick (Md.) Festival of the Arts, 1987, Harford C.C., Bel Air, Md., 1989, Target Gallery Torpedo Factory Art Ctr., Alexandria, Va., 1992; speaker in field; contbr. layout, photography, and design, to numerous catalogs and brochures. Outstanding Young Men of Am., U.S. Jaycees, 1984. Mem. Coll. Art Assn., Am. Assn. Mus. Avocations: shotokan karate, softball, skiing, biking, hiking. Home: 1226 Martha Custis Dr Alexandria VA 22302

MAJZOUB, MONA KATHRYNE, lawyer; b. Memphis, June 19, 1949; d. A. Joseph and Mary Majzoub. BA, U. Mich., 1970, MA, 1972; JD, U. Detroit, 1976. Bar: Mich. 1977, U.S. Dist. Ct. (ea. dist.) Mich. 1977, U.S. Supreme Ct. 1988. Sr. prin. Kitch, Drutchas, Wagner & Kenney, P.C., Detroit, 1977—. Bd. dirs. Saratoga Community Hosp., Detroit, 1986—, Family Svcs. Detroit and Wayne County, 1988—. Mem. ABA, State Bar Mich. (tort law review com.), Detroit Bar Assn., Women Lawyers Assn. of Mich., Am. Arab Bar Assn. (treas. 1982-86, pres. 1986-94), Am. Hosp. Assn., Mich. Soc. of Hosp. Attys., Nat. Assn. of Women Lawyers, Assn. of Def. Trial Counsel, Inc., Assn. Trial Lawyers of Am., Mich. Def. Trial Counsel, Leadership Detroit XVI. Office: Kitch Drutchas Wagner et al 1 Woodward Ave Fl 10 Detroit MI 48226-3422

MAK, GILBERT KWOK KWONG, pediatric dentist, researcher; b. Hong Kong, 1963; came to U.S., 1987.; s. Lun and Sze Mak. B in Dental Surgery, U. London, 1986; Licentiate in Dental Surgery, Royal Coll. Surgeons, London, 1987; postgrad. cert. in pediat. dentistry, U. So. Calif., L.A., 1990. Asst. house surgeon Guy's Hops. Dental Sch. U. London, 1986, researcher dept. oral medicine and oral pathology, 1987; resident in pediatric dentistry U. So. Calif., 1987, clin. teaching faculty dept. pediatric dentistry, 1987—; resident in dentistry Children's Hosp. L.A., 1987-90, Long Beach Med. Ctr., 1990; asst. prof. U. So. Calif., L.A., 1990—; pvt. practice L.A., 1990—; attending physician Millier's Children Dental Residency Program Long Beach Meml. Med. Ctr., 1991—; with Dulwich Coll., London, 1980-82; univ. senator U. So. Calif., L.A., 1992-93. Contbr. articles to profl. jours. Recipient Fencing Bronze Proficiency award Amateur Fencing Assn., 1982, Med. Sickness Soc. Elective award Guy's Hosp. Dental Soc., 1986, Malleson Prize for Dental Rsch. Guy's Hosp., London, 1985, NIH Physician Scientist award, 1991—; USPHS grantee, 1987-88, 88-89; Dean's fellow U. So. Calif. Sch. Dentistry, 1989-90;. Mem. Internat. Assn. for Dental Rsch., Am. Acad. Pediatric Dentistry, ADA, Brit. Soc. for Dental Rsch., Brit. Dental Assn., Am. Soc. Dentistry for Children, Alumni Assn. Student Clinicians of ADA, Calif. Dental Assn., Harbor Dental Soc. Office: PO Box 661059 Arcadia CA 91066-1059

MAK, TAK WAH, biochemist, educator; b. Canton, Republic of China, Oct. 4, 1946; s. Kent and Linda (Chan) M.; m. Shirley Lau, June 7, 1969; children: Julie Shi-Lan, Jennifer Shi-yan. BSc, U. Wis., 1967, MSc, 1969; PhD, U. Alta., Edmonton, Can., 1972; ScD (hon.), Carlton U., Ottawa, 1989, Laurentian U., 1992. Research asst. U. Wis., Madison, 1967-69, U. Alta., Edmonton, 1969-72; postdoctoral fellow U. Toronto, Ont., Can., 1972-74, asst. prof., 1974-78, assoc. prof., 1978-84, prof., 1984—; sr. staff scientist Ontario Cancer Inst., Toronto; dir. and research v.p. Amgen Inst.; vis. prof. U. Wis., Madison, 1980; hon. prof. Beijing Union Med. U., 1986—. Editor: Molecular and Cellular Biology of Hemopolitic Stem Cell Differentiation, 1981, Molecular and Cellular Biology of Neiplasia, 1983, Cancer: Perspective for Control, 1986, The T Receptor, 1987, AIDS: Ten Years Later, 1991; contbr. over 250 sci. articles. Recipient E.W.R. Steacie prize, 1986, Ayerst award Can. Biochem. Soc., 1985, Emil Von Behring prize Marburg (Germany) U., 1986, Gairdner Internat. award Gairdner Found., 1989, McLaughlin medal Royal Soc. Can., 1990, King Faisal Internat. prize for medicine King Faisal Found., 1995; hon. mem. Beijing Union Med. U., 1986, rsch. award Can. Found. for AIDS Rsch., 1992; E.W.R. Steacie fellow Nat. Sci. and Engring. Rsch. Coun. Can., 1984. Fellow Royal Soc. London (King Faisal Internat. prize of medicine 1995); mem. Royal Soc. Can. (McLaughlin medal 1990), Chinese Acad. Med. Sci. (hon.). Avocations: classical music, tennis. Home: 130 Glen Rd, Toronto, ON Canada M4W 2W3 Office: Ont Cancer Inst, 610 University Ave Rm 8-712, Toronto, ON Canada M5G 2M9

MAK, TONY WAH-CHIU, microelectronics packaging engineering manager; b. Fatshan, China, July 19, 1950; came to U.S., 1971; s. Man-Sum and Yau-Harn (Liang) M.; m. Claire Y. Huang, May 28, 1977; children: Charles, Stephanie, Gary. BSCivilE with honors, Rutgers U., 1975; MS, Cornell U., 1977; PhD, U. Ill., 1981. Assoc. engr. Elliott Co., Jeannette, Pa., 1977-78; staff engr. IBM Corp., Hopewell Junction, N.Y., 1981-86, adv. engr., 1986-92; engring. mgr. Allegro Microsys., Inc., Worcester, Mass., 1992—; vis. assoc. prof. mech. engring. U. Bridgeport, Conn., 1985-86. Contbr. articles to profl. jours. Mem. IEEE (chmn. thermal mgmt. tech. com. 1994—), AIAA. Achievements include development of heat sink/cap design. Office: Allegro Microsys Inc PO Box 15036 Worcester MA 01615

MAKA, ANDREA, microbiologist, research scientist; b. Chgo., Jan. 20, 1957; d. Andrew and Helen (Adamek) M. BS in Biology, Loyola U., Chgo., 1979; MS in Biology, Ill. Inst. Tech., 1982, PhD in Microbiology, 1986. Microbiologist, researcher Inst. Gas Tech., Chgo., 1986-93; microbiologist Met. Water Reclamation Dist. Greater Chgo., Cicero, Ill., 1993—. Author: Encyclopedia of Microbiology, 1992; contbr. articles to profl. jours. Mem. Am. Soc. Microbiology, Soc. Indsl. Microbiology. Avocations: financial investing, world travel, reading. Home: 5252 S Newland Ave Chicago IL 60638-1125

MAKADOK, STANLEY, management consultant; b. N.Y.C., Mar. 30, 1941; s. Jack and Pauline (Speciner) M.; BME, CCNY, 1962; MS in Mgmt. Sci., Rutgers U., 1964; m. Neilia A. David, Nov. 12, 1989; 1 child from previous marriage, Richard. Bus. systems analyst Westinghouse Electric Corp., Balt., 1964-65; project engr., corp. cons. Am. Cyanamid Corp., Pearl River, N.Y., Wayne, N.J., 1965-68; v.p., bus. devel. and planning Pepsico Inc. and affiliates, Purchase, N.Y., Miami, Fla., 1968-75; mgr. fin. and planning cons. Coopers & Lybrand, N.Y.C., 1975-77; pres. Century Mgmt. Cons., Inc., Ridgewood, N.J., 1977—. Contbr. articles to profl. jours. Office: Century Mgmt Cons Inc 4 Wilsey Sq Ste 9 Ridgewood NJ 07450-3728

MAKAR, BOSHRA HALIM, mathematics educator; b. Sohag, Egypt, Sept. 23, 1928; came to U.S., 1966, naturalized, 1971; s. Halim and Hakima (Khair Mikhail) M.; m. Nadia E. Eissa, Jan. 1, 1960; children—Ralph, Roger, B.Sc., Cairo U., 1943-47, M.Sc., 1952, Ph.D., 1955. Mem. faculty Cairo U., 1948-65; vis. assoc. prof. Am. U., Beirut, Lebanon, 1966, Mich. Tech. U., Houghton, 1967; prof. math. St. Peter's Coll., Jersey City, 1967—. Mem. Math. Assn. Am., AAUP, U.S. Naval Inst. Republican. Roman Catholic. Clubs: Poetry Soc. London; United Poets Internat. (Philippines) (v.p.). Home: 410 Fairmount Ave Jersey City NJ 07306-5910 Office: St Peter's Coll Math Dept Kennedy Blvd Jersey City NJ 07306

MAKAR, NADIA EISSA, secondary education educator, educational administrator; b. Cairo, Oct. 7, 1938; came to U.S., 1966.; d. Michel and Yvonne (Bitar) Issa; m. Boshra Halim Makar, Jan. 1, 1960; children: Ralph, Roger. Cert., Moscow U., 1964; BA, St. Peter's Coll., 1969, MA, 1981; postgrad., Hope Coll. and Brown U., 1972, 1973. Cert. tchr., supr., prin., N.J. Tchr. Hudson Catholic High Sch., Jersey City, 1970-72, sci. dept. chairperson, 1972-79; Convocation Model Project coordinator Union City N.J. Bd. Edn., 1979-81, tchr., coord. industry and coll. rels., 1989—; mem. Bd. Edn., Jersey City; cons. Stevens Inst. Tech. Hughes Grant, Hoboken, N.J., 1989-94; cons./advisor Project RISE. Author: Health; Space; Environment, 1980; co-editor NSSA mag., 1974-76; contbr. articles to profl. jours. Co-founder N.J. Bus./Industry/Sci. Edn. Consortium, 1981; pres. Bus./Profl. Women, Jersey City, 1984-86, sec. N.J., 1985; treas. Mental Health Assn., Hudson County, 1977-80; bd. dirs. N.J. Math. Coalition; U.S. del. 1st U.S./Russian Meeting for Math. Educators. Recipient Outstanding Secondary Educator Am. award U.S. Sec. Edn., 1973, award Mfg. Chemists Assn., 1975, recognition award Gov. State of N.J., 1988, Presdl. award for excellence in math. and sci. teaching, 1989. Mem. Am. Chem. Soc. (chmn. Hudson-Bergen sect. 1980-82, sec. N.Y. sect. 1994—, reviewer for Chem. Edn. Jour., bd. dirs. Home PC Mag., Nicol award 1975, Outstanding Achievement award New Eng. region 1976), St. Peter's Coll. Alumni Assn. (v.p. 1982-88, treas.), Nat. Coun. Tchrs. Math (reviewer). Office: Union Hill High Sch 3800 Hudson Ave Union City NJ 07087-6020

MAKARA, CAROL PATTIE, education educator, consultant; b. Norwich, Conn., Feb. 27, 1943; d. Howard G. and Ruth R. Robinson; m. Benjamin Makara, Feb. 19, 1966; children: Cheryl A., John J. AS, Three Rivers Community-Tech. Coll., 1988; BS, Cen. Conn. State U., 1965; MA, U. Conn., 1967. Cert. tchr., Conn. Tchr. Ledyard (Conn.) Bd. of Edn., 1965-66, Preston (Conn.) Bd. of Edn., 1974—; continuing edn. unit mgr. Preston (Conn.) Pub. Schs., 1993—; computer analyst Clinton (Conn.) plant Stanley Bostitch, summers 1987-92; evening instr. Three Rivers Cmty. Tech. Coll., 1989—; evening mgr. AutoCad Tng. Ctr., 1990-95; coop. mentor tchr. Dept. Edn., Conn., 1988—; advisor Conn. Educators' Computer Assn., 1992—; tchr. assessor The Begining Educator Support and Tng. Program, Conn. State Dept. Edn., 1995—. Author: (with others) Pedagogical Guide: Strategies for Improving Instruction, 1992. Active Fellowship Program for Disting. Tchrs., 1987-94. Fellow Conn. Bus. and Industry Assn.; mem. NEA, Conn. Edn. Assn. Home: 89 Mathewson Mill Rd Ledyard CT 06339-1114 Office: Preston Plains Sch 1 Route 164 Preston CT 06365-8818

MAKE, ISABEL ROSE, multicultural studies educator, small business owner; b. Phila., Oct. 6, 1947; d. Aaron M. and Lillian (Simon) Rose; m. Barry Jay Make, June 13, 1970; children: Jonathan David, Jeremy Simon. BA, George Wash. U., 1969; EdM, Temple U., 1970; cert. advanced grad. studies, W.Va. U., 1975. Cert. tchr., Pa., Mich., W.Va., Mass. Dir. learning ctr. Kirkbride Elem. Sch., Phila., 1970-71, Huron High Sch., Ann Arbor, 1971-73; learning disabilities tutor Brookline (Mass.) Pub. Schs., 1976-82; ednl. cons. Newton, Mass., 1982-84; child care cons. Isabel Make Assocs., Newton, 1984-88; adj. prof. reading and multicultural studies Metro State Coll., Denver, 1989—; pres. Top Hat Gourmet, 1992—; bus. lectr. on The Art of Corp. Giving, 1993—; ednl. counselor Phila. Home for Emotionally Disturbed Girls, 1970; cons. Ann Arbor Pub. Schs., 1971; child care cons. Newton Community Schs., 1985; founding mem. Denver Parenting Ctr., 1989—; chairperson legis. and regulations subcom. Commonwealth of Mass., Boston, 1984-88. ednl. counselor Phila. Home for Emotionally Disturbed Girls, 1970; cons. Ann Arbor Pub. Schs., 1971; child care cons. Newton Cmty. Schs., 1985; founding mem. Denver Parenting Ctr., 1989—; chairperson legis. and regulations subcom. Commonwealth of Mass., Boston, 1984-88; adj. prof. Metro. State Coll., 1984-88, 94—, Cmty. Coll. Denver, 1992—. Founder Temple Shalom Nursery Sch., Newton, 1975; chmn. childcare task force The U. Hosp., Boston U. Med. Ctr., 1985-88; bd. dirs. Greenwood Village Arts and Humanites Coun., 1991—; mem. at large Colo. Consortium Community Arts Couns., 1992—, Greenwood Village Arts and Humanities Coun. (chair A Space of my Own, Parent-Child Art Day), 1991—; mem. steering com. Colo. Alliance for Arts in Edn., 1993. Democrat. Jewish. Avocations: gourmet cooking, swimming. Home and Office: 2600 E Belleview Ave Littleton CO 80121-1627

MAKELA, BENJAMIN R., editor, research director; b. Hancock, Mich., Mar. 23, 1922; s. Charles Robert and Engel (Kruka) M.; m. Betty Virginia Shade, June 26, 1954; 1 son, Gregory Strickler. B.A., George Washington U., 1943; M.A., Stanford, 1954. Statistician Dept. Commerce, 1946, Nat. Fertilizer Assn., 1947-48; research economist U.S. C. of C., 1948-53; asso. dir. Financial Execs. Inst., N.Y.C., 1953-63; editor Financial Exec., 1963-72; research dir. Financial Execs. Research Found., 1966-83; cons., 1983—. Editor: How to Use and Invest in Letter Stock, 1970, (with William Chatlos) Strategy of Corporate Tender Offers, 1971, (with D.R. Carmichael) Corporate Financial Reporting: The Benefits and Problems of Disclosure, 1976, (with Richard F. Vancil) The CFO's Handbook, 1985; mem. editorial adv. bd. also author chpt. Financial Exec.'s Handbook. Served with AUS, 1943-46, 51-53. Mem. Am. Acctg. Assn., Stanford Alumni Club, Squadron A Club, Halifax Club, Smyrna Yacht Club, Men's Garden Club of New Smyrna Beach, Phi Beta Kappa, Pi Gamma Mu, Omicron Delta Gamma, Sigma Nu. Republican. Baptist. Home: 686 Rochester Ct New Smyrna Beach FL 32168-2105

MAKEPEACE, DARRYL LEE, consulting company executive; b. Pitts., Oct. 24, 1941; s. Thomas Henry Makepeace and Nevada Ruth (Wagener) Desin. BS in Indsl. Engring., Pa. State U., 1969; MBA, Pepperdine U., 1982. Dept. mgr. Procter & Gamble, Cin., 1969-72; plant mgr. CBS Mus. Instruments, Fullerton, Calif., 1972-76; dir. mfg. Frigid Coil/Wolf Range, Whittier, Calif., 1977-79; mgr. materials mgmt. Nat. Supply, Los Nietos, Calif., 1979-85; assoc. prof. mgmt. Calif. State U., Fullerton, 1982-86; mgr. mfg. Nat. Supply, Los Nietos, Calif., 1985-86; program mgr. Armco Cumberland Group, Middletown, Ohio, 1986; ptnr., cons. Armco Cumberland Group, Mason, Ohio, 1986-87; prin., owner Cumberland Group, Cin., 1988—; owner Phoenix Cons., Inc., Cin., 1991—; owner, pres. D.L. Makepeace & Assocs., Mason, Ohio, 1991—; assoc. prof. mgmt. Wright State U., Dayton, Ohio, 1987-88, Miami U., Oxford, Ohio, 1988-89. Author: The System, American Iron and Steel Institute, Steel Body Panel Performance Characteristics, 1991; contbr. articles to profl. jours. Served with U.S. Army, 1960-61. Named to Honorable Order of Ky. Cols. Mem. Am. Prodn. and Inventory Control Soc., Inst. Indsl. Engrs., Alpha Pi Mu, Tau Beta Pi, Sigma Tau. Avocations: reading, chess.

MAKHIJA, MOHAN, nuclear medicine physician; b. Bombay, Oct. 1, 1941; came to U.S., 1969; m. Arlene Zambito, Nov. 11, 1978. MD, Bombay U., 1965. Diplomate Am. Bd. Nuclear Medicine, Am. Bd. Radiology; cert. spl. competence in nuclear radiology. Resident in radiology Morristown (N.J.) Meml. Hosp., 1972-75; resident in nuclear medicine Yale-New Haven Hosp., 1975-76; post-doctoral fellow Yale U. Sch. Medicine, New Haven, 1976-77; jr. attending physician Helene Fuld Med. Ctr., Trenton, N.J., 1977-78; acting dir. dept. nuclear medicine Monmouth Med. Ctr., Long Branch, N.J., 1978, dir. nuclear medicine sect., 1979—. asst. attending radiology, 1978-80, assoc. attending radiology, 1980-83, attending radiologist, 1983—; sr. instr. Hahneman U., Phila., 1978-80, clin. asst. prof., 1980-83, clin. assoc. prof., 1983-91, clin. prof., 1991-94, clin. prof. of Radiologic Scis., Med. Coll. of Pa. and Hahnemann U., 1994—; radiol. cons. to N.J. State Bd. Med. Examiners, 1994. Contbr. articles to profl. jours. Fellow ACP, Am. coll. Nuclear Physicians (spkr. ho. of dels. 1992-93), Am. Coll. Radiology; mem. Monmouth County Med. Soc. (pres. 1991-92), Radio Soc. N.J. (chmn. nuclear medicine 1988-94, treas. 1994-95, sec. 1995-96, v.p. 1996-97), Indo-Am. Soc. Nuclear Medicine (pres. 1992-93), Soc. Nuclear Medicine (bd. govs. greater N.Y. chpt. 1992—). Home: 5 High Ridge Rd Ocean NJ 07712-3460 Office: Monmouth Med Ctr 300 2nd Ave Long Branch NJ 07740-6300

MAKHOLM, MARK HENRY, lawyer, former insurance company executive; b. Maple Valley, Wis., Jan. 10, 1915; s. Henry and Emma Dorothy Agnet (Johnson) M.; m. Phylis Shoger, Nov. 11, 1950; children: Linda Marie, Mark Henry, Martha Marie. B.A. magna cum laude, Northland Coll., Ashland, Wis., 1937; JD, U. Wis., 1950. Bar: Wis. 1950, U.S. Supreme Ct 1950. Asst. prof. Northland Coll., 1937-38; high sch. tchr. Washburn, Wis., 1939-41; operational supr. E.I. duPont de Neumours & Co. Inc., also U.S. Rubber Co., Kankakee, Ill., 1941-45; high sch. tchr. West Bend, Wis., 1945-47; engaged in retail clothing bus. West Bend, 1947-48; practice in Ashland, 1950-52; mem. firm Anderson, Fisher, Shannon, O'Brien and Rice, Stevens Point, Wis., 1980-86; with Sentry Ins. a Mut. Co.-Sentry Life Ins. Co., Stevens Point, Wis., 1952-80; v.p., gen. counsel Sentry Ins. a Mut. Co.-Sentry Life Ins. Co., 1962-78, exec. v.p., 1978-80, also dir., until 1980; former dir. Middlesex Ins. Co., Gt. S.W. Fire Ins. Co., The Sentry Corp., Dairyland Ins. Co., Sentry Indemnity Co. Dir. Delta Dental Plan Wis., 1980—. Mem. Am., Wis. bar assns., Internat. Assn. Ins. Counsel, Order of Coif, Phi Delta Phi. Home: 3717 Combs Creek Ln Stevens Point WI 54481-7621

MAKHOUL, JOHN IBRAHIM, electrical engineer, researcher; b. Deirmimas, Lebanon, Sept. 19, 1942; came to U.S., 1964; s. Ibrahim Hanna and Badia (Masoud) M. BEE, Am. U. Beirut, 1964; MEE, Ohio State U., 1965; PhDEE, MIT, 1970. Successively scientist, sr. scientist, supervisory scientist, prin. scientist to chief scientist Bolt Beranek & Newman Inc., Cambridge, Mass., 1970—; rsch. affiliate MIT, Cambridge, 1970—; adj. prof. Northeastern U., Boston, 1982—. Contbr. over 100 articles on speech processing by computer and spectral estimation to profl. jours. Recipient Citation Classic award for paper on linear prediction Inst. Scientific Info., 1982. Fellow IEEE, Acoustical Soc. Am.; mem. Acoustics, Speech and Signal Processing Soc. of IEEE (Sr. award 1978, Tech. Achievement award 1982, Soc. award 1988), Computer Soc. of IEEE, Communications Soc. of IEEE, Info. Theory Soc. of IEEE. Avocation: music. Home: 18 Amberwood Dr Winchester MA 01890-2202 Office: BBN Sys & Tech 70 Fawcett St Cambridge MA 02138-1119

MAKI, DENNIS G., medical educator, researcher, clinician; b. River Falls, Wis., May 8, 1940; m. Gail Dawson, 1962; children: Kimberly, Sarah, Daniel. BS in Physics with honors, U. Wis., 1962, MS in Physics, 1964, MD, 1967. Diplomate Am. Bd. Internal Medicine, Am. Bd. Infectious Diseases, Am. Bd. Critical Care Medicine. Physicist, computer programmer Lawrence Radiation Lab., AEC, Livermore, Calif., 1962; intern, asst. resident Harvard Med. unit Boston City Hosp., 1967-69, chief resident, 1972-73; with Hosp. Infections sect. Ctrs. for Disease Control, USPHS, Atlanta, 1969-71; acting chief nat. nosocomial infections study Ctr. for Disease Control, USPHS, Atlanta, 1970-71; sr. resident dept. medicine Mass. Gen. Hosp., 1971-72, clin. and research fellow infectious disease unit, 1973-74; asst. prof. medicine U. Wis., Madison, 1974-78, assoc. prof., 1978-82, prof., 1982—; hosp. epidemiologist, U. Wis. Hosp. and Clinic, Madison, 1974—; Ovid O. Meyer chair in medicine U. Wis., Madison, 1975—, head sec. infectious diseases, 1979—; attending physician Ctr. for Trauma and Life Support U. Wis., 1976—; clinician, rschr., educator in field; mem. program com. Intersci. Conf. on Antimicrobial Agts. and Chemotherapy, 1987-94; mem. Am. Bd. Critical Care Medicine, 1989-95. Sr. assoc. editor Infection Control and Hosp. Epidemiology, 1979-93; mem. editl. bd. Jour. Lab. and Clin. Investigation, 1980-86, Jour. Critical Care, 1985—, Jour. Infectious Diseases, 1988-90, Critical Care Medicine, 1989-94; contbr. articles to med. jours. Recipient 1st award for disting. rsch. in Antibiotic Rev., 1980, Internat. CIPI award, 1994, numerous teaching awards and hon. lectrs. Fellow ACP, Am. Coll. Chest Physicians, Infectious Diseases Soc. Am. (coun. 1993-96), Soc. for Critical Care Medicine, Surg. Infection Soc.; mem. Soc. Hosp. Epidemiologists Am. (pres. 1990, program com. ann. meeting 1992-96), Ctrl. Soc. for Clin. Rsch., Am. Soc. Microbiology, Am. Fedn. Clin. Rsch., Alpha Omega Alpha (nat. bd. dirs. 1983-89). Office: U Wis Hosp and Clinics H4/574 Madison WI 53792

MAKI, JERROLD ALAN, health system executive; b. Duluth, Minn., Sept. 4, 1947; s. Willio John and Eleanor Edla (Savela) M.; m. Carolyn Helen Dack, Aug. 2, 1969; children: Eric Edward, Emily Miriam, David Dack. BA cum laude, U. Min., Duluth, 1969; MHA, U. Min., Mpls., 1973. Lic. nursing home adminstr., Ohio. Asst. to supr. Investors Diversified Svcs., Inc., Mpls., 1969-71; assoc. adminstr. North Ottawa Community Hosp., Grand Haven, Mich., 1973-77; v.p. St. Mary's Hosp., Grand Rapids, Mich., 1977-80, Bapt. Med. Ctr., Oklahoma City, 1980-85; exec. v.p., chief operating officer Svc. Frontiers, Inc., Lafayette, Ind., 1985-86; exec. v.p., chief operating officer Mercy Med. Ctr., Springfield, Ohio, 1986-90, pres., chief exec. officer, 1990-95, bd. dirs., 1987-95; sr. v.p. Mercy Health System-We. Ohio, Springfield, 1995-96; pres., CEO, Mercy Health Sys.-Western Ohio, Springfield, 1996—, also bd. dirs.; sr. v.p. Mercy Health System, Cin., 1996—; chairperson accreditation and quality com. Ohio Hosp. Assn., 1993—; mem. bd. dirs. Mercy Managed Care, Ltd., 1995—. Bd. dirs. Mental Health Svcs. Clark County, Springfield, 1987—, Friends of Mercy, Springfield, 1988-95, Springfield Physician-Hosp. Orgn., 1991—; v.p. Springfield Acad. for Cmty. Leadership, 1988-89; bd. deacons for ch., 1990-92, bd. trustees, 1993—, Mercy Found., 1996—. Fellow Am. Coll. Healthcare Execs.; mem. Springfield C. of C., Springfield CountryClub, Rotary. Presbyterian. Avocations: stamp and coin collecting, sailing, golf. Home: 2006 W Mile Rd Springfield OH 45503-2732 Office: Mercy Health Sys-Western Ohio 1 S Limestone St Ste # 600 Springfield OH 45501-0688

MAKI, KAZUMI, physicist, educator; b. Takamatsu, Japan, Jan. 27, 1936; s. Toshio and Hideko M.; m. Masako Tanaka, Sept. 21, 1969. B.S., Kyoto U., 1959, Ph.D., 1964. Research asso. Inst. for Math. Scis., Kyoto U., 1964; research asso. Fermi Inst., U. Chgo., 1964-65; asst. prof. physics U. Calif., San Diego, 1965-67; prof. Tohoku U., Sendai, Japan, 1967-74; vis. prof. Universite Paris-Sud, Orsay, France, 1969-70; prof. physics U. So. Calif., Los Angeles, 1974—; vis. prof. Inst. Laue-Langevin, U. Paris-Sud, France, 1979-80, Max Planck Inst. fur Festkorper Forschung, Stuttgart, Germany, 1986-87, U. Paris-7, 1990, Hokkaido U., Sapporo, Japan, 1993, Centre de Recherche sur Tres Basses Temperatures, Grenoble, France, 1993-94, Instituto de Ciencia de Materiales, Madrid, Spain, 1994. Assoc. editor Jour. Low Temperature Physics, 1969-91; contbr. articles to profl. jours. Guggenheim fellow, 1979-80, Japan Soc. Promotion of Sci. fellow, 1993; Fulbright scholar, 1964-65; recipient Nishina prize, 1972, Alexander von Humboldt award, 1986-87. Fellow Japan Soc. Promotion of Sci., Am. Phys. Soc.; mem. AAAS, Phys. Soc. Japan. Office: U So Calif Dept Physics Los Angeles CA 90089-0484

MAKIMOTO, KAZUO, otolaryngologist, educator; b. Nakatane-Cho, Tanegashima, Kagoshima, Japan, Dec. 24, 1933; s. Genshichi and Haru (Hidaka) M.; m. Chizuru Hayaishi, Nov. 15, 1959; children: Yoshimi, Yasushi, Yukiko. MD, Kyoto U., Japan, 1958, degree in med. sci., 1967. Chief of otolaryngology Kyoto Nat. Hosp., 1967-77; assoc. prof. otolaryngology Kyoto U., 1977-85, Osaka Med. Coll., Takatsuki, Osaka, Japan, 1985—; rsch. assoc. Presbyn. Med. Ctr., Phila., 1971-73. Contbr. articles to profl. jours. Mem. Nat. Geographic Soc. Budhist. Avocations: bird watching, cello playing. Home: 505 Manjyojiki-Cho, Okamedani Fushimi-ku Kyoto 612, Japan Office: Osaka Med Coll, 2-7 Daigaku-Cho, Takatsuki 569, Japan

MAKIN, EDWARD, food products executive; b. 1951. Grad., Concordia U., 1972. With Redpath Sugars, Toronto, Ont., Can., 1972-91; with Domino Sugar Corp., 1991-92, pres., CEO, 1992—. Office: Domino Sugar Corp 1114 Avenue Of The Americas New York NY 10036-7703*

MAKINEN, MARVIN WILLIAM, biophysicist, educator; b. Chassell, Mich., Aug. 19, 1939; s. William John and Milga Katarina (Myllyla) M.; m. Michele de Groot, July 30, 1966; children: Eric William, Stephen Matthew. AB, U. Pa., 1961; postgrad., Free U. Berlin, 1960-61; MD, U. Pa., 1968; DPhil, U. Oxford, Eng., 1976. Diplomate Am. Bd. Med. Examiners. Intern Columbia-Presbyn. Med. Ctr., N.Y.C., 1968-69; rsch. assoc. NIH, Bethesda, Md., 1969-71; vis. fellow U. Oxford, Eng., 1971-74; asst. prof. biophysics U. Chgo., 1974-80, assoc. prof., 1980-86, prof. biochemistry and molecular biology, 1986—, chmn. dept., 1988-93; established investigator Am. Heart Assn., 1975-80; lectr. in field. Contbr. numerous articles to profl. jours. Mem., advisor The Raoul Wallenberg Com. of U.S., 1991—. Sr. surgeon USPHS, 1969-71. John E. Fogarty Sr. Internat. fellow, 1984-85, European Molecular Biology Orgn. sr. fellow, 1984-85, NIH spl. fellow, 1971-74, Berquist fellow Am. Scandinavian Found., 1970. Fellow Am. Inst. Chemists; mem. Am. Chem. Soc., Biophys. Soc., Am. Soc. Biochemistry and Molecular Biology, The Protein Soc., AAAS. Office: U Chgo Dept Biochemistry/Mol Biol 920 E 58th St Chicago IL 60637-1432

MAKINO, SHOJIRO (MIKE MAKINO), chemicals executive; b. Roppongi, Tokyo, Japan, June 5, 1929; s. Taro and Tomiko M.; m. Sachi Hirose, Apr. 24, 1965; 1 child, Genta. BA, Keio U., Tokyo, 1951; MBA, U. Oreg., 1961. Salesman Getz Bros. Shokai, Tokyo, 1951-55; mgr. indsl. sales Getz Bros. and Co., Okinawa, Japan, 1955-59; mgmt. trainee Getz Bros. and Co., San Francisco, 1959-61; sales rep., mgr. Far East Omark Industries, Inc., Portland, Oreg., 1962-67; v.p., gen. mgr. Omark Japan, Inc., Tokyo, 1967-69; v.p. W.R. Grace K.K., Tokyo, 1969-70; pres. W.R. Grace K.K. changed to Grace Japan K.K. (1985), Tokyo, 1970—; corp. v.p. W.R. Grace and Co., N.Y.C., 1988—; v.p. W.R. Grace & Co., Asia Pacific, 1992—, also sr. advisor, bd. dirs., 1995; vice chmn. Polyfibron Techs., Inc., 1995. Past mem. Prime Min.'s Deregulation Com., 1994; mem. Govt. Adminstrn. Com. Mem. Am. C. of C. (bd. govs. Tokyo chpt. 1988—), Tokyo Golf Club, Hakone Country Club, Hodogaya Country Club, Tokyo East Rotary Club. Office: Polyfibron Techs Inc, 2-4-1 Nishi Shinjuku, Tokyo 163-08, Japan

MAKIOS, VASILIOS, electronics educator; b. Kavala, Greece, Dec. 31, 1938; s. Thrassivoulos and Sophia M. Dipl.Ing., Tech. U. Munich, 1962; Dr. Ing., Max Planck Inst. for Plasmaphysics and Tech. U. Munich, 1966. Profl. engr., Ger., Ont., Greece. Research assoc. Max Planck Inst., Munich, 1962-67; asst. prof. dept. electronics Carleton U., Ottawa, Ont., 1967-70, assoc. prof., 1970-73, prof., 1973-77; prof. and head electromagnetics lab. U. Patras, Greece, 1975—; cons. in field; dean engring. U. Patras, 1980-82; hon. adj. prof. Carleton U., 1977—. Contbr. over 120 articles to profl. jours. Patentee in field. Recipient Silver medal German Elec. Engring. Soc., 1984; numerous grants for research in Can., Greece and European community. Mem. IEEE, German Phys. Soc., German Inst. Elec. Engrs., Can. Assn. Physicists & Engrs., Greek Tech. Chamber. Greek Orthodox. Avocations: classical music; swimming; skiing. Home: 2 Lefkosias St, 26441 Patras 41, Greece Office: U Patras, Lab Electromagnetics, Patras Greece

MAKISE, YOSHIHIRO, lawyer; b. Osaka, Japan, Dec. 16, 1930; s. Yoshihiko and Keiko (Matsumoto) M. BL, U. Tokyo, 1955; D Pvt. Internat. Law, U. Paris, 1975. With Dai-Tokyo Fire & Marine Ins. Co., Tokyo, 1955-59; legal apprentice Legal Rsch. and Tng. Inst., Supreme Ct. Japan, Tokyo, 1960-62; staff lawyer Dai-ichi Tokyo Bar Assn., 1962-67; legal cons. in collaboration with French lawyers Paris, 1968-75; prin. Makise Law Office, Tokyo, 1975—. Author: The Legal Theory of Money, 1991, New Civil Law, 1992, Money and the Future of Japan, 1993. Scholar of Boursier technique Dept. Fgn. Affairs, Govt. of France, 1967-68. Mem. Japan Assn. Internat. Econ. Law, French-Japanese Soc. Legal Sci., Brit. Acad. Experts (London). Avocations: reading, classical music, photography, travel, museums. Home: 1-6-15-408 Kichijoji-Minami, Musashino Tokyo 180, Japan Office: Makise Law Office, 1-6-15-408 Kichijoji-Minami, Musashino Tokyo 180, Japan

MAKKAY, MAUREEN ANN, broadcast executive; b. Chgo.; d. John Paul and Bernice Ann (Williams) Monaghan; m. Albert Makkay, Oct. 20, 1962; children: Allison, Albert Jr., Colleen. BA, U. R.I., 1974. Cert. secondary sch. tchr., Mass. Adminstr. Ednl. Records Bur., Wellesley, Mass., 1979-81; local sales mgr. Sta. WKZE, Orleans, Mass., 1981-83; nat. sales mgr. Sta. WKFM, Syracuse, N.Y., 1983-85; pres. Sta. WPXC-FM, Hyannis, Mass., 1987—; v.p. Sta. WRZE, Nantucket, Mass., Sta. WCIB-FM, Falmouth, Mass. Pres. Cape and Islands unit Am. Cancer Soc., 1988-91, bd. dirs., 1989-95; mem. pers. bd. Town of Barnstable, Mass., 1989-94, chmn., 1990-91; bd. dirs. Cape Cod Alcoholism Intervention and Rehab., Inc., 1995—. Mem. Bus. and Profl. Women Cape Cod (bd. dirs. 1989—), Am. Women in Radio and TV, Nat. Assn. Broadcasters. Office: Sta WPXC-FM Radio 154 Barnstable Rd Hyannis MA 02601-2930

MAKOUS, WALTER LEON, visual scientist, educator; s. Lawrence and Ruth Lorraine (Luehring) M.; m. Marilyn Ann Carlson, Feb. 2, 1958 (div. 1974); children: Ann, James, Matthew; m. Joyce Brown Menconi, 1974 (div. 1981); m. Barbara Anne Duggins, Apr. 29, 1982. B.S., U. Wis., 1958; M.Sc., Brown U., 1961, Ph.D., 1964. Mem. staff IBM, Yorktown Heights, N.Y., 1963-66; asst. prof. psychology U. Wash., 1966-69, lectr. in physiology and biophysics, 1966-69, assoc. prof. psychology, 1969-74, prof. psychology, 1974-79; prof. psychology, ophthalmology and visual sci., U. Rochester, 1979-95; prof. brain and cognitive sci., ophthalmology & visual sci., 1995—; dir. Ctr. for Visual Sci. U. Rochester, 1979-90; northwest rep., charter mem. steering com. West Coast Regional Consortium Univs. in Neurosci., 1976-79; mem. coun. on energy saving through more efficient lighting, NAS-NRC, 1978-79, night vision coun., 1985-86; chmn. ctr. symposium U. Rochester, 1981-82; sensory processes panelist NSF, Washington, 1977-82, mem. adv. com. applied sci. and rsch. applications policy, 1978-81, rev. com. Presdl. Young Investigator award program, 1984; vis. scientist IBM Rsch., 1970-71. Cons. editor Sensory Processes, 1977-79, Jour. of the Optical Soc. Am., 1982-86; contbr. over 100 articles to profl. jours. Served with USNR, 1953-55. Grantee Nat. Eye Inst., 1969—; NSF grantee, 1959-62, 81-82. Fellow AAAS, Am. Psychol. Soc., Optical Soc. Am. (mem. coord. vision and physiol. optics com. 1983-89, coord. vision and med. optics com. 1983-89, publs. com. 1985-89, chmn. fellows and hon. mems. com. 1986, editor vision and color 1982-86, feature editor applied vision 1989-90); mem. Assn. Rsch. in Vision and Ophthalmology (chmn. sect. pshcyo-physics 1977), Soc. Neurosci., Psychonomic Soc., Human Factors and Ergonomics, Am. Nat. Standards Inst./Human Factor & Ergonomics Sic-100 (rev. com. 1992—). Office: U Rochester Ctr for Visual Sci Rochester NY 14627

MAKOWKA, LEONARD, medical educator, surgeon; b. Toronto, Ont., Can., Nov. 25, 1953. MD, U. Toronto, Can., 1977, MS in Pathology, 1979, PhD in Pathology, 1982. Intern in surgery The Mount Sinai Hosp., Toronto, Ont., Can., 1977-78; with gen. surgery course U. Toronto, Can., 1978; Can. fellow med. rsch. coun., dept. surgery and pathology Toronto Gen. Hosp., U. Toronto, Can., 1978-82; rsch. assoc., dept. surgery and pathology U. Toronto, Can., 1982; asst. resident gen. surgery Toronto Gen. Hosp., Can., 1982; sr. resident gen. surgery Women's Coll. Hosp., 1983; chief resident surgery Toronto Western Hosp., Can., 1983-84; fellow in hepatobiliary surgery Toronto Gen. Hosp., Can., 1984-85; rsch. assoc. dept. surgery and pathology U. Toronto, Can., 1984-85, asst. prof. dept. surgery and pathology, 1985; asst. prof. surgery, dept. surgery U. Pitts., Pa., 1986-87, assoc. prof. surgery, dept. surgery, 1987-89; dir. surgery and transplantation svcs., dept. surgery Cedars Sinai Med. Ctr., 1989-92; prof. surgery UCLA Med. Sch., 1989—; chmn. dept. surgery, dir. transplantation svcs. Cedars Sinai Med Ctr., 1992—; exec. dir. comprehensive liver disease & treatment ctr. St. Vincent Med. Ctr., L.A., 1995—; vis. asst. prof. U. Pitts., Pa., 1985; lectr. in the field. Contbr. to over 345 jours. Recipient Charles E. Frost Bronze medal, 1979, Royal Coll. Physicians and Surgeons of Can. Surgery medal, 1980, 85, First Place award Second Annual Assembly of Gen. Surgeons, 1979, Gallie Bateman Essay award, 1980, Davis and Geck Surgical Essay award, 1981-82, Can. Found. of Ileitis and Colitis Rsch. award, 1981, U. Toronto Rsch. Papers award, 1981; Charles E. Frost scholar, 1979, Schering scholar Am. Coll. Surgeons, 1981; Graham Campbell fellow Faculty of Medicine U. Toronto, 1982, Centennial fellow Med. Rsch. Coun. of Can., 1985-87; named Humanitarian of the Yr. World Children's Transplant Fund, 1992. Mem. Alpha Omega Alpha. Office: St Vincent Med Ctr Institute Plz 2200 W Third St Los Angeles CA 90057

MAKOWSKI, LEE, science administrator, biology and chemistry educator; b. Providence, Nov. 4, 1949; s. Chester Stanley and Frances Margaret (Brown) M.; m. Diane June Rodi, Mar. 25, 1983; children: James Aziz, Nicholas Prakash, Bryan Siva. BS in Physics, Brown U., 1971; MSEE, MIT,

1973, PhD in Elec. Engring., 1976. Postdoctoral fellow Brandeis U., Waltham, Mass., 1976-78, rsch. assoc., 1978-80; asst. prof. biochemistry Columbia U., N.Y.C., 1980-87; assoc. prof. physics Boston U., 1988-91, prof. physics, 1991-92; dir. Inst. Molecular Biophysics Fla. State U., Tallahassee, 1993—, prof. biology and chemistry, 1993—. Contbr. articles to profl. jours.; patentee in field. Rsch. grantee NIH, 1980-93, Tng. grantee, 1988-92; Rsch. grantee NSF, 1982-94. Mem. AAAS. Office: Fla State U Inst Molecular Biophysics Tallahassee FL 32306-3015

MAKOWSKI, M. PAUL, electronics research executive; b. Warsaw, Poland, Jan. 15, 1922; Arrived in U.S. July 1949.; s. Antoni and Stanislawa (Leszowska) M.; m. Eugenia Sawczyn, Dec. 1, 1945; children: Paul, Teresa. BA in Chem., Case Western Reserve U., 1957, MS in Physical Chem., 1961, PhD in Electrochem., 1964. Mgr. Smith Phoenix Co., Cleve., 1950-55; chemist Clevite Research Ctr., Clevite Corp., Cleve., 1955-64; mgr. chemistry Materials Research Lab., Gould Inc., Cleve., 1964-73; assoc. dir. Materials Research Gould Inc., Cleve.; dir. Materials Research Lab., Gould Inc., Cleve., 1976-80; v.p. tech. adminstrn. Gould Inc., Rolling Meadows, Ill., 1980-81, v.p. scientific affairs, 1981-87; pres. TECTRA Cons. Inc., Rolling Meadows, Ill., 1988-93; cons. Rolling Meadows, 1994—; mem. Frontiers in Chem. Com. Cleve. 1976-80; bd. dirs. Microelectronics and Computer Corp. Austin, Tex. 1986-87. Inventor several patents in electrodeposition and catalysis. Mem. Ill. Gov.'s Commn. on Sci. and Tech. Chgo., 1986-87, Tech. Commercialization Coun. Ill. Dept. Commerce and Community Affairs. Mem. Am. Chem. Soc., Electrochem. Soc. Chgo., Materials Rsch. Avocation: stamp collecting. Home: 305 Shady Dr Palatine IL 60067-7551

MAKRI, NANCY, chemistry educator; b. Athens, Greece, Sept. 5, 1962; came to the U.S., 1985; d. John and Vallie (Tsakona) M.; m. Martin Gruebele, July 9, 1992; 1 child, Alexander Makris Gruebele. BS, U. Athens, 1985; PhD, U. Calif., Berkeley, 1989. Teaching asst. U. Calif., Berkeley, 1985-87; rsch. asst. U. Calif., 1986-89; jr. fellow Harvard U., Cambridge, Mass., 1989-91; asst. prof. U. Ill., Urbana, 1991—. Recipient Beckman Young Investigator award Arnold & Mabel Beckman Found., 1993, Ann. medal Internat. Acad. Quantum Molecular Sci., 1995; named NSF Young Investigator, 1993; Packard fellow for sci. and engring. David and Lucille Packard Found., 1993, Sloan Rsch. fellow Alfred Sloan Found., 1994, Cottrell scholar Rsch. Corp., 1994. Home: 2208 Wyld Dr Urbana IL 61801-6753 Office: U Ill at Urbana Dept Chem 505 S Mathews Ave Urbana IL 61801-3617

MAKRIANES, JAMES KONSTANTIN, JR., management consultant; b. Springfield, Mass., Jan. 15, 1925; s. James K. and Clara (Allen) M.; m. Judith Alden Erdmann, Sept. 30, 1960; children—Mary, James, Susan, Jane, Mahady. B.A., Amherst Coll., 1949. V.p., gen. mgr. Nat. Paper Box Co. and Nat. Games, Inc., Springfield, 1949-59; merchandising and acct. exec. Young & Rubicam, Inc., N.Y.C., 1959-63; v.p., acct. supr. Young & Rubicam, Inc., 1963-67, sr. v.p., mgmt. supr., 1963-73, exec. v.p., dir., 1973-78; sr. v.p., dir. Haley Assocs., Inc., N.Y.C., 1978-80, pres., 1980—, chief exec. officer, 1985-89; ptnr., dir. Ward & Howell Internat., Inc., N.Y.C., 1989-95; dir. Webb Johnson Assocs., N.Y.C., 1995—. Trustee Boys' Club N.Y., 1976—. With USNR, 1943-46. Mem. Maidstone Club, Racquet and Tennis Club, Links. Home: 415 E 52nd St New York NY 10022-6424 Office: Webb Johnson Assocs 280 Park Ave New York NY 10017

MAKRIS, ANDREAS, composer; b. Salonica, Greece, Mar. 7, 1930; came to U.S., 1950, naturalized, 1962; s. Christos and Kallitza (Andreou) M.; m. Margaret Lubbe, June 12, 1959; children: Christos, Myron. Grad. with highest honors, Nat. Conservatory, Salonica, 1950; postgrad., Kansas City (Mo.) Conservatory, 1953, Mannes Coll. Music, 1956, Aspen Music Festival, 1956-57, Fontainbleau (France) Sch., 1958; pupil of Nadia Boulanger. adv. to Maestro Rostropovich for new music, 1979-90. Compositions premiered and performed in U.S., Can., S.Am., Europe, Japan, USSR; composer-in-residence Nat. Symphony Orch., 1979-90; prin. works include Scherzo for Violins, 1966, Concerto for Strings, 1966, Aegean Festival, 1967, Anamnesis, 1970, Viola Concerto, 1970, Concertino for Trombone, 1970, Efthymia, 1972, Five Miniatures, 1972, Mediterranean Holiday, 1974, Fantasy and Dance for Saxaphone, 1974, Chromatokinesis, 1978, In Memory, 1979, Variations and Song for Orchestra, 1979, Fanfare Alexander 1980, Fourth of July March, 1982, Violin Concerto, 1983, Nature-Life Symphonic Poem, 1983, Caprice "Tonatonal", 1986, Intrigues for Solo Clarinet and Wind Ensemble, 1987, Concertante for Violin, Cello, Clarinet, French Horn, Percussion and Orchestra, 1988, Sonata for Cello and Piano, 1989, Symphony to Youth for Full Orchestra, 1989, Trilogy for Orchestra, 1990, Polychornion Chorus and Orchestra, 1990, Procession Chorus and Brass Quintet, 1990, Intrigues for Solo Clarinet, Strings, Brass and Percussion, 1991, Concertino for Organ, Flute and Strings, 1992, A Symphony for Soprano and Strings, 1992, Woodwind Quintet, 1993, Decalog (ten songs for young students), 1995, Antithesis for Orch., 1995, J.F.K. Commemorative Fanfare for Strings and Snare Drum, 1995; also works for violin, string quartets, voice quintets, duets and arrangements of Paganini, Bach, Corelli and Fiorillo. Recipient citation Greek Govt., 1980; Student Program grantee Phillips U., Enid, Okla., 1950, grantee Nat. Endowment Arts, 1967, grantee Martha Baird Rockefeller Fund, 1970, grantee Damrosh Found., 1958. Mem. ASCAP (ann. awards 1980-92), Internat. Platform Assn. Greek Orthodox. Home: 11204 Oak Leaf Dr Silver Spring MD 20901-1313 Office: Nat Symphony Orch Kennedy Ctr Washington DC 20566 *Two important elements have contributed tremendously to my composing: As a child I was in the midst of war in Greece, and, while all wars are terrible, it taught me both self-discipline and an appreciation for simplicity. Just being alive and able to compose makes me very happy. As a student I was not able to have a piano, the most valuable instrument for a composer. I learned to write with only a pencil and paper for full orchestra, and this liberated me both musically and practically.*

MAKSI, GREGORY EARL, engineering educator; b. Wilkes-Barre, Pa., May 9, 1939; s. Stephen Cedric and Laura Victoria (Pytell) M.; children: Sabrina, Jared, Joshua. BSME, Ga. Inst. Tech., 1961, MS in Indsl. Mgmt., 1964; PhD in Edn. Adminstrn., U. Miss., 1983. Registered profl. engr., Tenn. Mech. engr. Ellicott Machine Corp., Balt., 1961-62; project engr. Celanese Corp., Rock Hill, S.C., 1964-67; assoc. prof. State Tech. Inst., Memphis, 1967-71, prof., 1971-73, program chmn. of indsl. engring., 1973-90, dept. chmn. mech. engring./indsl. engring., 1990—; cons. Tenn. Ednl. Alliance, Nashville, 1994—, U. Ark., Millington, Tenn., 1988, instr., 1988—; curriculm coord. Memphis City H.S., 1993—; quality-productivity adv., 1990—; CAD/CAM cons., 1995—. Hon. sheriff Shelby County Sheriff's Office, 1991; hon. state legis. Tenn. Ho. Reps., Nashville, 1992. Named Disting. Engr. Memphis Engrs. Coun., 1986. Mem. SME, Inst. of Indsl. Engrs., World Future Soc., Tenn. Profl. Engrs. Soc. Avocations: computers, tennis, racquetball, fishing. Office: State Tech Inst Memphis 5983 Macon Cv Memphis TN 38134-7642

MAKUPSON, AMYRE PORTER, television station executive; b. River Rouge, Mich., Sept. 30, 1947; d. Rudolph Hannibal and Amyre Ann (Porche) Porter; m. Walter H. Makupson, Nov. 1, 1975; children: Rudolph Porter, Amyre Nisi. BA, Fisk U., 1970; MA, Am. U., Washington, 1972. Asst. dir. news Sta. WGPR-TV, Detroit, 1975-76; dir. pub. rels. Mich. Health Maintenance Orgn., Detroit, 1974-76, Kirwood Gen. Hosp., Detroit, 1976-77; mgr. pub. affairs, news anchor Sta. WKBD-TV, Southfield, Mich., 1977—, Children's Miracle Network Telethon, 1989—. Mem. adv. com. Mich. Arthritis Found., Co-Ette Club, Inc., Met. Detroit Teen Conf. Coalition, Cystic Fibrosis Soc.; mem. adv. com., bd. dirs. Alzheimers Assn.; mem. exec. com. March of Dimes; pres. bd. dirs. Detroit Wheelchair Athletic Assn.; bd. dirs. Providence Hosp. Found., Sickle Cell Assn., Kids In Need of Direction, Drop-out Prevention Collaborative, Merrill Palmer Inst. Recipient Emmy award for best commentary NATAS, 1993, 12 Emmy nominations NATAS, Editorial Best Feature award AP, Media award UPI, Oakland County Bar Assn., TV Documentary award, Detroit Press Club, numerous svc. awards including Arthritis Found. Mich., Mich. Mchts. Assn., DAV, Jr. Achievement, City of Detroit, Salvation Army, Spirit award City of Detroit, Spirit award City of Pontiac, Golden Heritage award Little Rock Bapt. Ch., 1993; named Media Person of the Yr. So. Christian Leadership Conf., 1994, Humanitarian of the Yr. March of Dimes, 1995. Mem. Pub. Rels. Soc. Am., Am. Women in Radio and TV (Outstanding Achievement award 1981, Outstanding Woman in TV Top Mgmt. 1993, Mentor award 1993), Women in Communications, Nat. Acad. TV Arts and Scis., Detroit Press Club, Ad-Craft. Roman Catholic. Office: 26955 W 11 Mile Rd Southfield MI 48034-2292

MALA, THEODORE ANTHONY, physician, consultant; b. Santa Monica, Calif., Feb. 3, 1946; s. Ray and Galina (Liss) M.; children: Theodore S., Galina T. BA in Philosophy, DePaul U., 1972; MD, Autonomous U., Guadalajara, Mex., 1976; MPH, Harvard U., 1980. Spl. asst. for health affairs Alaska Fedn. Natives, Anchorage, 1977-78; chief health svcs. Alaska State Div. of Corrections, Anchorage, 1978-79; assoc. prof., founder, dir. Inst. for Circumpolar Health Studies, U. Alaska, Anchorage, 1982-90; founder Siberian med. rsch. program U. Alaska, Anchorage, 1982, founder Magadan (USSR) med. rsch. program, 1988; commr. Health and Social Svcs. State of Alaska, Juneau, 1990-93; pres. chief exec. officer Ted Mala, Inc., Anchorage, 1993—; pres., ptnr. Mexican-Siberian Trading Co., Monterrey, Mex., 1994—; mem. Alaska rsch. and publs. com. Indian Health Svc., USPHS, 1987-90; advisor Nordic Coun. Meeting, WHO, Greenland, 1985; mem. Internat. Organizing Com., Circumpolar Health Congress, Iceland, 1992-93; chmn. bd. govs. Alaska Psychiat. Inst., Anchorage, 1990-93; cabinet mem. Gov. Walter J. Hickel, Juneau, 1990-93; advisor humanitarian aid to Russian Far East U.S. Dept. State, 1992—; cons. USAID on U.S.-Russian Health Programs, 1994. Former columnist Tundra Times; contbr. articles to profl. jours. Trustee United Way Anchorage, 1978-79; chmn. bd. trustees Alaska Native Coll., 1993—. Recipient Gov.'s award, 1988, Outstanding Svc. award Alaska Commr. Health, 1979, Ministry of Health citation USSR Govt., 1989, Citation award Alaska State Legislature, 1989, 90, 94, Commendation award State of Alaska, 1990, Alaska State Legislature, 1994, Honor Kempton Svc. to Humanity award, 1989, citation Med. Comty. of Magadan region, USSR, 1989; Nat. Indian fellow U.S. Dept. Edn., 1979. Mem. Assn. Am. Indian Physicians, N.Y. Acad. Scis., Internat. Union for Circumpolar Health (permanent sec.-gen. 1987-90, organizing com. 8th Internat. Congress on Circumpolar Health 1987-90). Avocations: cross-country skiing, hiking, photography, travel. Office: 205 E Dimond Blvd Ste 544 Anchorage AK 99515-1909 *Personal philosophy: Progress in the North will come only when circumpolar countries put aside their geopolitical thinking and work together as one northern family.*

MALABRE, ALFRED LEOPOLD, JR., journalist, author; b. N.Y.C., Apr. 23, 1931; s. Alfred Leopold and Marie (Leonard) M.; m. Mary Patricia Wardropper, July 28, 1956; children: Richard C., E. Ann, John A. B.A., Yale U., 1952. Copy editor Hartford (Conn.) Courant, 1957-58; successively reporter, Bonn bur. chief, econs. editor, news editor and Outlook columnist Wall St. Jour., 1958-94, news editor, 1969-94; contbg. editor Harvard Bus. Review, 1995—. Author: Understanding the Economy: For People Who Can't Stand Economics, 1976, America's Dilemma: Jobs vs. Prices, 1978, Investing for Profit in the Eighties, 1982, Beyond Our Means, 1987, Understanding the New Economy, 1988, Within Our Means, 1991, Lost Prophets, 1993. Served with USNR, 1953-56, Korea. Poynter fellow, 1976; Hoover Instn. fellow, 1991; recipient Eccles prize Columbia U., 1988. Mem. Authors Guild, Pilgrim Soc. U.S., Union Club, Nat. Golf Links Am. Address: PO Box 208 Quogue NY 11959

MALACARNE, C. JOHN, insurance company executive, lawyer; b. St. Louis, Dec. 26, 1941; s. Claude John and Virginia E. (Miller) M.; m. Kathleen M. Morris, Aug. 27, 1966; children: Tracy, Kristen, Lisa. AA, Harris-Stowe State Coll., 1962; BS in Pub. Adminstrn., U. Mo., 1964, JD, 1967. Bar: Mo. 1967. Asst. counsel Kansas City (Mo.) Life, 1967-71, assoc. counsel, 1971-74, asst. gen. counsel, 1974-76, assoc. gen. counsel, 1976-80, gen. counsel, 1980-81, v.p., gen. counsel, sec., 1981—; bd. dirs. Kansas City Life Ins. Co., Sunset Life Ins. Co. Am., Calif. Life Ins. Guaranty Assn.; sec., bd. dirs. Old Am. Ins. Co. Sec., bd. dirs. Mid-Continent coun. Girl Scouts U.S.A., Kansas City, 1986-88; v.p., bd. dirs. Kansas City Eye Bank, 1986-91; pres., bd. dirs. Shepherd's Ctr., Kansas City, 1982-84; bd. dirs. Shepherd's Ctr. Internat., 1986-92, Community Mental Health Svcs. Found., sec. rsch., 1992-94, v.p., 1995—; mem. Bd. Edn. Consolidated Sch. Dist. #4, Jackson County, Mo., 1989-91. Mem. ABA, Kansas City Met. Bar Assn. (vice chmn. corp. counsel com. 1986-87, vice chmn. corp. law 1993-94, chmn. corp. law com. 1994-95), Lawyers Assn. Kansas City (bd. dirs. 1976), Internat. Assn. Def. Counsel (chmn. accident health and life sect. 1982-84, ins. exec. com. 1986, v.p., mem. exec. com. 1988-90), Jr. C. of C. (bd. dirs. 1972), Kiwanis (pres. Kansas City 1975-76). Home: 604 Tam O Shanter Dr Kansas City MO 64145-1240 Office: Kansas City Life Ins Co PO Box 419139 Kansas City MO 64141-6139

MALACH, MONTE, physician; b. Jersey City, Aug. 15, 1926; s. Charles and Yetta (Pascher) M.; m. Ann Elaine Glazer, June 15, 1952 (dec. June 1989); children: Barbara Sandra, Cathie Tara, Matthew David; m. Barbara Meryl Lipstein, Dec. 24, 1994; stepchildren: Heather Ilene, Jennifer Beth, Matthew Howard. BA, U. Mich., 1949, MD, 1949. Diplomate Am. Bd. Internal Medicine, Nat. Bd. Med. Examiners. Intern Beth Israel Hosp., Boston, 1949-50; resident Beth Israel Hosp., 1950-51, chief resident, 1951-52; chief resident Kings County Hosp., Bklyn., 1954-55; practice medicine specializing in internal medicine and cardiology Bklyn., 1955—; dir. CCU Bklyn. Hosp., 1955-91, dir. emeritus CCU, 1991—; med. dir. Medicare IPRO Downstate N.Y., 1990—; pres. profl. staff Bklyn. Hosp., 1966-69, chmn. med. bd., 1971-72; attending staff Caledonian Hosp., pres. profl. staff, 1984-85; pres. profl. staff Bklyn. Hosp.-Caledonian Hosp., 1987-89, chmn. med. bd., 1988-89; cons. Kings County Hosp.; tchg. fellow Tufts U. Med. Sch., 1951-52; instr. medicine Downstate Med. Ctr., Bklyn., 1955-59, clin. asst. prof. medicine, 1959-68, clin. assoc. prof., 1969-76, clin. prof., 1976—; clin. prof. medicine NYU Med. Ctr., 1994—; bd. dirs. Bay St. Landing One Owners Corp., 1985-87; v.p. Ocean View Condos, 1989-90, pres., 1990-95. Kings County committeeman Democratic Party, 1964, 65. Served with USNR, 1944-46, to 1st lt. M.C. U.S. Army, 1952-54. Recipient 1st Prize for Crisis Mgmt. Habitat Mag., 1987. Fellow Am. Coll. Chest Physicians, ACP, Am. Coll. Cardiology (task force Health Care Quality Improvement Initiative 1996—); mem. AMA (chmn. sect. coun. ofr internal medicine 1980), N.Y. Heart Assn., Am. Soc. Internal Medicine (trustee 1975-79, sec.-treas. 1979—, pres. elect 1981, pres. 1982-83, chmn. investment com. 1985-93), N.Y. State Soc. Internal Medicine (pres. 1973-74, dir. 1966-84, chmn. Bklyn. chpt., v.p. 1971, award of merit 1978), Bklyn. Soc. Internal Medicine (mem. council 1965, pres. 1969-72), Med. Soc. State of N.Y. (chmn. sect. internal medicine 1976, chmn. med. care ins. com. 1988-93), Federated Council for Internal Medicine (chmn. 1979-80), Med. Soc. County Kings (censor 1985-91). Office: 55 Rugby Rd Brooklyn NY 11226-2607 *There is a place for hard work, scrupulous ethics and pride of accomplishment. A great marriage and a fine close family are buffers against adversity.*

MALAFRONTE, DONALD, health executive; b. Bklyn., Dec. 16, 1931; s. Pasquale and Amalia (Castaldo) M.; m. Diane Freedenberg, Jan. 7, 1960 (dec. Nov. 14, 1970); children: Philip, Victor.; m. Hillary Demby, Oct. 30, 1982. B.S., NYU, 1954. Reporter L.I. Daily Press, 1956-58; reporter, editor Newark Star-Ledger, 1958-65, art columnist, 1963-70; adminstrv. asst. to mayor of Newark, 1965-70; dir. Newark Model Cities Program, 1967-70, Newark Community Devel. Adminstrn., 1968-70; chief urban field operations N.J. Regional Med. Program, 1970-73; pres. Urban Health Inst., Roseland, N.J., 1973—; cons. to hosps., local govts., 1970—. Author articles in field. Served with AUS, 1954-56. Recipient Joyce Kilmer fiction prize NYU, 1953. Home: 78 Crestview Rd Mountain Lakes NJ 07046-1223 Office: Urban Health Inst 101 Eisenhower Pky Roseland NJ 07068-1028

MALAGUE, MARIANNE TYNDALL, nursing educator; b. N.Y.C.; d. Henry Francis and Mary (Callan) Tyndall; m. Paul Joseph Malague, June 15, 1963; children: Paul, Marilu. BS, Coll. Mount St. Vincent, 1959; MA, NYU, 1962; postgrad., Tex. Women's U., U. Houston, 1981-85. Staff nurse VA Hosp., Fort Hamilton, N.Y., 1959-60; head nurse St. Vincent's Psychiat. Hosp., Harrison, N.Y., 1960-61; instr. ADN Bronx Community Coll., N.Y.C., 1962-65; instr. Baccalaureate Nursing Adelphi U., Garden City, N.Y., 1967-70; instr. ADN Howard C.C., Columbia, Md., 1973-76; instr. ADN North Harris County Coll., Houston, 1978-88, dist. curriculum coord., 1988-89, divsn. head health occupations, 1989-92; dean sci. and tech., 1992-95; dean of instrn. North Harris County Coll., Houston, 1995—; test item writer Nat. League Nursing, 1984-85. Mem. Am. Assn. Women in Community/Jr. Colls., Nat. Orgn. for ADN, Tex. Nurses Assn., Tex. Jr. Colls. Tchrs. Assn., Houston Orgn. Nursing Execs., Coll. Mt. St. Vincent Alumnae Assn., Sigma Theta Tau. Office: North Harris Coll 2700 W W Thorne Blvd Houston TX 77073-3410

MALAKHOV, VLADIMIR, dancer; b. Krivoy Rog, Ukraine, USSR, Jan. 7, 1968; arrived in Can., 1994; s. Anatoly and Elena Malakhov. Grad., Bolshoi Ballet Acad., Moscow, 1986. Prin. dancer Vienna State Opera, 1992—, Nat. Ballet Can., 1994—, Am. Ballet Theatre, N.Y.C., 1995—; guest artist Am. Ballet Theatre, 1994. Appeared in Giselle, Swan Lake, Nutcracker, Manon, Romeo and Juliette, others; performed in major opera houses worldwide. Recipient Gold medal Varna Ballet Competition, 1986, Gold medal Moscow Ballet Competition, 1986, Serge Lifar prize, 1991.

MALAKOFF, JAMES LEONARD, management information executive; b. Phila., June 20, 1933; s. John and Ida Vera (Partman) M.; m. Anne Bronstein Frisch, June 26, 1955; children: Randi Ellen, John Seymour. B in Aerospace Engring., Rensselaer Poly. Inst., 1954, MS, 1955. Structural methods specialist Grumman Aircraft, Bethpage, N.Y., 1955-62; mem. tech. staff Northrop Corp., Hawthorne, Calif., 1962-65; chief, math. analyst Beckman Instruments, Inc., Fullerton, Calif., 1965-68; dir. data processing Beckman Instruments, Inc., Fullerton, 1968-82, v.p. data processing, 1982-85, v.p., mgmt. info., 1985-93, cons. to mgmt., 1993—; bd. dirs. Little Co. Mary Health Svcs., Little Co. Mary Hosp., San Pedro (Calif.) Peninsula Hosp.; vis. prof. computer sci. Calif. State U., Fullerton, 1981-82, mem. indsl. adv. coun. Sch. Engring. and Computer Sci. Fellow AIAA (assoc.); mem. IEEE (computer group), U.S. Council Internat. Bus. (bus. and industry adv. com., West Coast com. Internat. Info. and Telecommunications Policy), Assn. Computing Machinery, Data Processing Mgmt. Assn.

MALAMED, SEYMOUR H., motion picture company executive; b. N.Y.C., June 17, 1921; s. Abraham and Bess (Kaisin) M.; m. Doris Raphael, May 19, 1946; children—Margery, Susan, Nancy. B.B.A., City Coll. N.Y., 1942. Engaged in entertainment field, 1954—; asst. to v.p., treas. Screen Gems Co., 1956-62; treas. parent co. Columbia Pictures Corp., 1962—, v.p., 1963-73, exec. v.p., 1973—. Served with AUS, World War II. Mem. Motion Picture Acad. Arts and Scis. Clubs: Friars (N.Y.C.); Metropolis Country (Westchester County); High Ridge Country (Palm Beach, Fla.), Metropolis Country Club. Home: 135 Central Park W Apt 9nc New York NY 10023-2465 Office: 301 W 57th St Ste 336 New York NY 10019-3101

MALAMUD, DANIEL, biochemistry educator; b. Detroit, June 5, 1939; s. Jack and Jennie (Ashe) M.; m. Judith Disner, Mar. 7, 1961; children: Randy, Lisa. BS, U. Mich., 1961; MA, Western Mich. U., 1962; PhD, U. Cin., 1965; MA, U. Pa., 1983. Post-doctoral fellow Temple U., Phila., 1966-68, asst. prof. pathology, 1968-69; asst. biologist Mass. Gen. Hosp., Boston, 1969-72, assoc. biologist, 1972-77; assoc. prof. biochemistry Sch. Dental Medicine, U. Pa., Phila., 1977-84, prof. biochemistry, 1984—, chmn. biochemistry, 1985—; asst. prof. pathology Harvard U., Boston, 1970-77; vis. assoc. prof., Fulbright lectr. U. Philippines, Manila, 1975; vis. scientist Wistar Inst., Phila., 1985; affiliated scientist Monell Chem. Senses Ctr., Phila., 1985—; exchange scientist Hebrew U., Jerusalem, 1982. Author: Autoradiography, 1969; contbr. over 80 articles to profl. jours. and chpts. to books. Recipient Career Devel. award NIH, 1972-77. Mem. Am. Soc. Biol. Chemists, N.Y. Acad. Scis., Am. Soc. Cell Biologists, Am. Soc. Microbiologists. Office: Univ of Pa Sch of Dental Medicine 4001 Spruce St Philadelphia PA 19104-6003

MALAMY, MICHAEL H(OWARD), molecular biology and microbiology educator; b. Bklyn., Apr. 20, 1938; s. Henry R. and Rhoda A. (Resnick) M.; m. Frances E. Siegel, June 15, 1958; children: Adam C., Jocelyn E. B.A., NYU, 1958, Ph.D., 1963. Postdoctoral fellow Pasteur Inst., Paris, 1963-65, Princeton U., N.J., 1965-66; asst. prof. microbiology Tufts U., Boston, 1966-71, assoc. prof. molecular biology, microbiology, 1971-76, prof., 1976—. Mem. editorial bd.: Jour. Bacteriology, Washington, 1971-80. Mem. Am. Soc. Biochemistry and Molecular Biology, Am. Soc. Microbiology. Home: 39 Wildwood St Winchester MA 01890-1748 Office: Tufts U/Molecular Biology 136 Harrison Ave Boston MA 02111-1800

MALARCHICK, TIMOTHY PAUL, lawyer; b. Hermiston, Oreg., Sept. 24, 1959; s. Mike and Yvonne (Grace) M.; m. Charlotte McMaster, May 31, 1986; children: Nathan, Adam, Kendall. BA, U. Idaho, 1984, JD, 1987. Bar: Wash. 1987, Idaho 1989, U.S. Dist. Ct. (we. dist.) Wash. 1990, U.S. Dist. Ct. (ea. dist.) Wash. 1987, U.S. Dist. Ct. Idaho 1989. Assoc. Evans, Craven & Lackie, Spokane, Wash., 1987-90, Burgess, Fitzer, Leighton & Phillips, Tacoma, Wash., 1990-94; pvt. practice Tacoma, 1994—. Mem. ABA, Tacoma Bar Assn., Pierce County Bar Assn., Wash. Def. Trial Lawyers Assn. Presbyterian. Avocations: family, sports, music. Home: 5912 55th St W Tacoma WA 98467-2961 Office: 917 Pacific Ave Ste 205 Tacoma WA 98402

MALARKEY, MARTIN FRANCIS, JR., cable television executive; b. Pottsville, Pa., May 1, 1918; s. Martin Francis and Gertrude (Cress) M.; m. Catherine Clare McCarthy, May 30, 1935; 1 child, Clare Ann (Mrs. John E. Hampford); m. Elizabeth Koehn Onesto, May 29, 1961. BS in Acctg., LaSalle U., Phila., 1939. V.p. Malarkey's, Inc., Pottsville, 1939-42; pres. Malarkey's Inc., 1946-50; pres., dir. Trans Video Corps., Washington, 1950-59; chmn. Malarkey, Taylor Assocs., Inc., Washington, 1959—; pres., dir. radio Sta. WRTA, Altoona, Pa., 1956-84; owner Eastern Shore Microwave Relay Co., Washington, 1961-75; pres. radio sta. WMBT, Shenandoah, Pa., 1970-86. Pres. Washington Internat. Horse Show Assn., 1976-77; trustee emeritus Am. U., Washington; trustee Washington Hosp. Ctr.; chmn. Washington Hosp. Ctr. Found. Served with USNR, World War II. Mem. Nat. Cable TV Assn. (founder, 1st pres.), Washington Club, City Tavern Assn., F St. Club, Unmiv. Club, Army and Navy Club. Pioneer in devel. cable television. Home: 1817 Kalorama Sq NW Washington DC 20008-4021

MALASHEVICH, BRUCE PETER, consulting economist; b. Ridgewood, N.J., Feb. 21, 1952; s. Peter Gabriel and Olga Julia (Pelenko) M.; m. Linda Christine Kauskay, May 11, 1985; children: Jason Kauskay, Jessica Alexandra Kauskay. B.A. cum laude, Woodrow Wilson Sch. Pub. and Internat. Affairs, Princeton U., 1974; M.A., Johns Hopkins U., 1976. Internat. economist U.S. Treasury Dept., Washington, 1975-76; asst. to dir. Econ. Cons. Services div. Wolf and Co., C.P.A.s, Washington, 1976-78; v.p. Econ. Cons. Services Inc., Washington, 1978-88, pres., chief exec. officer, 1988—, also dir. Contbr. articles to internat. studies jours. and nat. bus. newspapers. Crown-Zellerbach scholar Johns-Hopkins U., 1975. Clubs: Princeton of N.Y.; Princeton of Washington; Kenwood Golf and Country. Avocations: tennis; squash; travel; reading history. Office: Econ Cons Svcs Inc 1225 19th St NW Ste 210 Washington DC 20036-2411

MALASPINA, ALEX, soft drink company executive; b. Athens, Greece, Jan. 4, 1931; came to U.S., 1948; s. Spiros and Mary (Souyiouljoglou) M.; m. Doris Woodruff Gould, Sept. 25, 1954; children: Spiros, Ann, Paul, Mark. SB, MIT, 1952, Ph.D., 1955. Coord. new products Pfizer, Inc., N.Y.C., 1955-61; mgr. quality control Coca-Cola Export Corp., N.Y.C., 1961-69, v.p., 1969-78; v.p. Coca-Cola Co., Atlanta, 1978-86, sr. v.p., 1986—; pres. Internat. Life Scis. Inst., Washington, 1978—, Internat. Tech. Caramel Assn., Washington, 1977—; v.p. Toxicology Forum, Washington, 1979—, Brit. Indsl. Biol. Rsch. Assn., London, 1991—. Bd. overseers Tufts U. Sch. Medicine, 1995—. Mem. AAAS, N.Y. Acad. Scis., Am. Inst. Chemists, Inst. Food Technologists, Am. Chem. Soc. Greek Orthodox. Home: 425 Kenbrook Dr NW Atlanta GA 30327-4937 Office: Coca-Cola Co 1 Coca Cola Plz NW Atlanta GA 30313-2420

MALATESTA, ROSALIE ELINOR, accountant, owner bookkeeping company; b. San Francisco, Feb. 10, 1938; d. Albert Angelo and Alba (Botto) M.; m. Otto Henry Saltenberger, May 16, 1959 (div. Sept. 26, 1977). AA in Acctg., Am. River Coll., 1974; postgrad., Sacramento State U., 1974-76. Staff acct. D.E. Pomerantz & Co., CPA, San Francisco, 1956-63, 66-67; cost acct. Roberts Constrn. Co., San Mateo, Calif., 1963-67; staff acct. Goldsmith, Exline & Seidman, CPAs, San Mateo, Calif., 1968-72; tax examiner Franchise Tax Bd. State of Calif., Sacramento, 1976; staff acct. Phil A. Baender, Acctg. Corp., Danville, Calif., 1976-80; owner Profl. Bookkeeping Systems, Alamo, Calif., 1980—. Pres. Pacifica (Calif.) Police Wives Assn., 1969-71, Vallemar Women's Club, Pacifica, 1966-68; treas. San Ramon Valley Congl. Ch., Danville, 1978-80. Memn. Profl. Bookkeepers Assn. (sec. 1993-95), Inst. Mgmt. Accts. (manuscript chmn. 1984-86), Am. Inst. Profl. Bookkeepers, Diablo Network (treas. 1994—), Diablo Valley C. of C., Meadow Creek Homeowner's Assn. (treas. 1995—). Republican. Roman Catholic. Avocations: hiking, walking, golf, gardening, music appreciation. Office: Profl Bookkeeping Systems 3237 Danville Blvd Alamo CA 94507-1913

MALATO, STEPHEN H., lawyer; b. Chgo., Sept. 25, 1953. BA, Western Ill. U., 1975; JD with high honors, Chgo. Kent Coll. Law (now Ill. Inst. Tech.), 1978. Bar: Ill. 1978, U.S. Dist. Ct. (no. dist.) Ill. 1981, U.S. Dist. Ct. (no. dist. trial bar) Ill. 1981. Ptnr. Hinshaw & Culbertson, Chgo. Mem. Chgo. Bar Assn., Legal Club Chgo., Moot Ct. Address: Hinshaw & Culbertson 222 N La Salle St Ste 300 Chicago IL 60601-1005*

MALCOLM, ANDREW HOGARTH, journalist, writer; b. Cleve., June 22, 1943; s. Ralph Monteith and Beatrice Florence (Bowles) M.; m. Connie D'Amelio, Nov. 28, 1981; children: Christopher, Spencer, Emily, Keddy. BJ, Northwestern U., 1966, MJ, 1967. Clk. The N.Y. Times, N.Y.C., 1967-68, met. reporter, 1969-70; nat. corr. The N.Y. Times, Chgo., 1971-73, San Francisco, 1974-75; fgn. corr. The N.Y. Times, Vietnam, Thailand, Guam, 1975, Tokyo, 1975-78, Republic of Korea, 1975-78; bur. chief The N.Y. Times, Toronto, Ont., Can., 1978-82, Chgo., 1982-87; asst. nat. editor The N.Y. Times, N.Y.C., 1987-88, nat. affairs corr., columnist, 1988-93; exec. asst. policy and communications Govs. Office, Helena, Mont., 1993—. Author: Unknown America, 1975, The Canadians, 1985, Final Harvest, 1986, This Far and No More, 1987, Someday, 1991, U.S. 1: America's Original Main Street, 1991, The Land and People of Canada, 1991, Huddle: Fathers, Sons, and Football, 1992, Mississippi Currents: A Journey Through Time and A Valley, 1996. Recipient George Polk award L.I. U., 1975, Page One award N.Y. Newspaper Guild, 1975, 83. Office: Governor's Office State Capitol Helena MT 59620-0801

MALCOLM, ELLEN REIGHLEY, small business owner; b. Hackensack, N.J., Feb. 2, 1947; d. William Ford Reighley and Barbara (Hamilton) Malcolm. BA, Hollins Coll., 1969; MBA, George Washington U., 1984. Regional mgr. Common Cause, Washington, 1971-74, nat. issues coord., 1974-75, so. states coord., 1975-76; pub. info. coord. Nat. Women's Polit. Caucus, Washington, 1978-79, project dir., 1979; media coord. Cambodia Crisis Ctr., Washington, 1980; press sec. to spl. asst. to pres. for consumer affairs White House, Washington, 1980-81; pres. Windom Fund, Washington, 1980—, EMILY's List, Washington, 1985—. Bd. dirs. Ctr. for Policy Alternatives, Washington, 1989—; chair Women's Legal Def. Fund, Washington, 1984—. Mem. Washington Ednl. Telecomms. Assn. (bd. dirs. 1996—). Democrat. Office: EMILYs List 805 15th St NW Ste 400 Washington DC 20005

MALCOLM, GAROLD DEAN, architect; b. Belle Fouche, S.D., Apr. 25, 1940; s. Gifford Garold Malcolm and Ellen Eve Liming; m. Breta Lois Bailey, 1966 (div. 1982); children; Heather Marie, Allison Clare; m. Lucia Eagon Stenson, 1991. BArch, U. Oreg., 1966. Ptnr. McAdoo, Malcolm & Youel, Architects, 1981—. Prin. works include Creston-Nelson Elec. Substation, Seattle (Honor award Wash. Aggregates and Concrete Assn.), Arboretum Visitor's Ctr., Seattle (Honor award Builders Community Awards Program, People's Choice award Seattle chpt. AIA), Des Moines (Wash.) Libr., Queen Anne Swimming Pool, Seattle. Mem. AIA, Matsumura Kenpo Karate Assn. (black belt). Office: McAdoo Malcolm & Youel Architects 1718 E Olive Way Seattle WA 98102-5615

MALCOLM, RICHARD WARD, academic administrator, consultant; b. Columbus, Ohio, July 27, 1933; s. Ralph James and Beatrice (Ward) M.; m. Cheryl Wallace, Dec. 26, 1993; 1 child, Gwynn Malcolm Socolich. BS, U. Findlay (Ohio), 1956; MA, Ariz. State U., 1960; MEd, U. So. Calif., 1965, EdD, 1966. Acad. dean Martin Coll., Pulaski, Tenn., 1965-67; dean instrn. Arapahoe C.C., Littleton, Colo., 1967-71; chair edn. divsn. Chapman U., Orange, Calif., 1971-80; assoc. prof. U. So. Calif., 1976-77; dean instrn. Mesa (Ariz.) C.C., 1980-91; asst. to provost Chandler (Ariz.)/Gilbert C.C., 1991-92, chair divsn. social and behavioral scis., 1993-96; dir. R&D Williams campus Maricopa C.C., 1996—. Author: Mental Measurement Yearbook, 1972. Pres. Ariz. Rail Pasenger Assn., Phoenix, 1984-93. Mem. Am. Assn. Higher Edn., Ariz. Acad. Adminstrv. Assn. (treas. 1991—), Rotary. Methodist. Avocations: reading, travel, hiking, railroading, music. Office: Williams Edn Ctr 6001 S Power Rd Bldg 410 Mesa AZ 85206

MALCOM, JOSEPH ADAMS, military officer; b. Social Circle, Ga., Oct. 29, 1944; s. Archie Preston Malcom and Sarah Rebecca (Adams) Malcom-Anderson; m. Mary Carol Anderson, May 7, 1967; children: Mary Elizabeth, Susan Rebecca. BBA, North Ga. Coll., 1966; MS in Econs., Clemson U., 1968; grad., Command and Gen. Staff Coll., 1984. Commd. 2d lt. U.S. Army, 1966; advanced through grades to lt. col., 1985; chief, financial mgr. U.S. Army Inventory Control Ctr., Long Binh, Vietnam, 1971; instr., inventory mgt. U.S. Army Quartermaster Sch., Ft. Lee, Va., 1972-73; co. commdr. XVIII Airborne Corps, Ft. Bragg, N.C., 1974-77; asst. prof. U. Tenn., Martin, 1977-80; finance officer 3d Infantry Divsn., Wuerzburg, Germany, 1980-83; chief exercise divsn. U.S. Army Logistics Ctr., Ft. Lee, 1984-88; chief logistics assistance officer 82nd Airborne Divsn., Ft. Bragg, 1989-93; adj. prof. U. Richmond, Ft. Lee, 1970, Chapman Coll., Ft. Lee, 1972-74, U. Md., Wuerzburg, 1980-82. Author: Civil War Organization, 1979; editor: Civil War Press Corps newsletter, 1980-87. Decorated Bronze Star (2), Meritorious Svc. medal (4), Army Commendation medal (3). Mem. SAR, SCV, Assn. U.S. Army, Soc. Civil War Necrologists, Assn. Quartermaster Officers, Assn. for Gravestone Studies, 3d Inf. Divsn. Marne Assn. Republican. Baptist. Avocation: necrology, genealogy. Home: PO Box 722 Social Circle GA 30279-0722 Office: USA AMC LSE Bldg 200 Ft McPherson Atlanta GA 30330-6000

MALDE, HAROLD EDWIN, retired federal government geologist; b. Reedsport, Oreg., July 9, 1923; s. Emil and Bessie May (Alspaugh) M.; m. Caroline Elizabeth Rose, Dec. 21, 1954; children: Margaret Jean, Melissa Ruth. AB, Willamette U., 1947; postgrad. Harvard U., 1947-48, U. Colo., 1948-51. Geologist, U.S. Geol. Survey, Denver, 1951-87, emeritus, 1987—; mem. Colo. com. for Nat. Register Hist. Places, 1972-80; vol. photographer Nature Conservancy, 1987—; mem. paleoanthropology del. to Peoples Republic China, Nat. Acad. Scis., 1975, mem. various coms. for study surface mining; mem. oil shale environ. adv. panel U.S. Dept. Interior, 1976-80. Contbr. numerous sci. papers to profl. lit. Served to ensign USNR, 1942-44. Recipient Meritorious Service award U.S. Dept. Interior, 1979, Oak Leaf award Nature Conservancy, 1993. Fellow Geol. Soc. Am. (Kirk Bryan award 1970, assoc. editor 1982-88), AAAS, Ariz.-Nev. Acad. Sci.; mem. Am. Quaternary Assn., Explorers Club. Democrat. Unitarian. Home: 842 Grant Pl Boulder CO 80302-7415

MALDEN, KARL (MALDEN SEKULOVICH), actor; b. Chgo., Mar. 22, 1914; s. Peter and Minnie (Sebera) Sekulovich; m. Mona Graham, Dec. 18, 1938; children—Mila, Carla. Student, Goodman Theatre, Chgo., 1935-38. pres. Acad. of Motion Arts and Scis.; mem. Citizens Stamp Com., U.S. Govt., Washington. Actor, 1935—; stage plays include Golden Boy, 1938, Gentle People, 1939, Key Largo, 1940, Flight to the West, 1942, Uncle Harry, 1940, All My Sons, 1949, A Streetcar Named Desire, 1950, Desire Under the Elms, 1952, Desperate Hours, 1954; in motion pictures, 1940—, films include: Boomerang, Gunfighter, 1945, Halls of Montezuma, 1950, A Streetcar Named Desire (Acad. award for best supporting actor), 1951, Ruby Gentry, 1952, I Confess, 1953, On the Waterfront, 1954, Baby Doll, 1956, Desperate Hours, 1957, Fear Strikes Out, 1957, The Hanging Tree, 1959, Pollyanna, 1960, One Eyed Jacks, 1961, Parrish, The Adventures of Bullwhip Griffin, 1967, Patton, 1970, Beyond the Poseidon Affair, 1978, Meteor, 1979, Sting II, 1982, Twilight Time, 1982, Billy Galvin, 1987, Nuts, 1987; TV films include: Word of Honor, 1981, Miracle on Ice, 1981, Intent to Kill, 1983, Fatal Vision, 1984 (Emmy award), My Father My Son, 1988, The Hijacking of the Achille Lauro, 1989, Call Me Anna, 1990, Absolute Strangers, 1991, Back to the Streets of San Francisco, 1992; dir.: Time Limit, 1957, Billion Dollar Brain, 1967, Hot Millions, 1968, Hotel, Cat O'Nine Tails, 1971, Wild Rovers, 1971, Summertime Killer, 1973, Nuts, 1987; star TV series Streets of San Francisco, 1972-77, Skag, 1980. Recipient Donaldson award, 1950, Critic's award, 1950. Mem. Acad. Motion Picture Arts and Scis. (pres. 1989-92). Address: 1845 Mandeville Canyon Rd Los Angeles CA 90049-2222

MALDON, ALPHONSO, JR., federal official, retired military officer; b. Bonifey, Fla., Oct. 6, 1950; m. Carolyn Maldon; 1 child, Kiamesha Racha'el. BS, Fla. A&M U., 1972; M in Human Rels., U. Okla., 1975; grad., Armed Forces Staff Coll., 1985. Commd. U.S. Army, 1972, advanced through grades to lt. col.; chief orgnl. effectiveness mgmt. U.S. Army, Stuttgart, Germany, 1981-83; pers. officer, comdr. 259th Pers. Svc. Co. U.S. Army, Bamberg, Ger., 1983-84; exec. officer Armed Forces Staff U. U.S. Army, Norfolk, Va., 1985-89; congl. liaison officer U.S. Army Legis. Liaison, U.S. Ho. of Reps. U.S. Army, 1989-93, ret., 1993; spl. asst. to Pres., legis. affairs The White House, Washington, 1993-94, dep. asst. to Pres., milit. affairs, 1994—, dep. asst. to Pres., legis. affairs, 1994—; admissions, pub. affairs officer West Point. Contbr. features Army pubs. Decorated Def. Meritorious Svc. medal with 2 oak leaf clusters, Army Meritorious Svc. medal with 2 oak leaf clusters, Army Commendation medal with 2 oak leaf clusters, Legion of Merit; Congl. scholar. Office: Legis Affairs 1600 Pennsylvania Ave NW Washington DC 20500*

MALDONADO-BEAR, RITA MARINITA, economist, educator; b. Vega Alta, P.R., June 14, 1938; d. Victor and Marina (Davila) Maldonado; m. Larry Alan Bear, Mar. 29, 1975. BA, Auburn U., 1960; PhD, NYU, 1969. With Min. Wage Bd. & Econ. Devel. Adminstrn., Govt. of P.R., 1960-64; assoc. prof. fin. U. P.R., 1969-70; asst. prof. econs. Manhattan Coll., 1970-72; assoc. prof. econs. Bklyn. Coll., 1972-75; vis. assoc. prof. fin. Stanford (Calif.) Grad. Bus. Sch., 1973-74; assoc. prof. fin. and econs. Grad. div. Stern Sch. Bus. NYU, 1975-81, prof., 1981—, acting dir. markets, ethics and law, 1993-94; cons. Morgan Guaranty Trust Co., N.Y.C., 1972-77, Bank of Am., N.Y.C., 1982-84, Res. City Bankers, N.Y.C., 1978-87, Swedish Inst. Mgmt., Stockholm, 1982-91, Empresas Master of P.R., 1985-90; bd. dirs. Medallion Funding Corp., 1985-87; apptd. adv. bd. dirs. equity and diversity in ednl. environs. Mid. States Commn. on Higher Edn., 1991—; trustee Securities Industry Assn., N.Y. Dist. Econ. Edn. Found., 1994—; chairperson NSF, Nat. Vis. Com. Curriculum Devel. Project Networked Fin. Simulation, 1995—. Author: Role of the Financial Sector in the Economic Development of Puerto Rico, 1970; co-Author: Free Markets, Finance, Ethics, And Law, 1994; contbr. articles to profl. jours. Trustee Bd. Edn., Twp. of Mahwah, N.J., 1991-92. P.R. Econ. Devel. Adminstrn. fellow, 1960-65; Marcus Nadler fellow, NYU, 1966-67, Phillip Lods Dissertation fellow, 1967-68. Mem. Am. Econs. Assn., Am. Fin. Assn., Metro. Econ. Assn. N.Y., Assn. for Social Econs. (trustee exec. com. 1994—). Home: 95 Tam O Shanter Dr Mahwah NJ 07430-1526 Office: Mgmt Edn Ctr 44 W 4th St Ste 9-190 New York NY 10012-1126

MALE, ROY RAYMOND, English language educator; b. Bklyn., Mar. 15, 1919; s. Roy Raymond and Mary Edwards (Brooks) M.; m. Carolyn Kate Conlisk, Aug. 19, 1944; children: Marilyn, Frank. B.S., Hamilton Coll., 1939; M.A., Columbia U., 1940; Ph.D., U. Tex., 1950. Instr. English U. Tex., 1946-50; asst. prof. Tex. Tech. Coll., 1950-55; mem. faculty U. Okla., 1955-84, Boyd prof. English emeritus; vis. prof. Bowling Green U., 1962, U. Wash., 1968, U. Tex. at Arlington, 1971. Author: Hawthorne's Tragic Vision, 1957, Enter, Mysterious Stranger, 1979; editor: Types of Short Fiction, 2d edit, 1970, Money Talks, 1981; co-editor: Am. Literary Masters, 1974. Served with AUS, 1940-45. Ford Found. fellow, 1954-55; Recipient Regents award excellence teaching U. Okla., 1968. Mem. Modern Lang. Assn., South Central Modern Lang. Assn. (pres. 1968). Home: Hilton Head Plantation 40 Field Sparrow Rd Hilton Head Island SC 29926-1813

MALEC, WILLIAM FRANK, utilities company executive; b. Broadalbin, N.Y., June 22, 1940; s. Henry and Anna Frances M.; m. Sarah Powell, Sept. 11, 1965; children: Charles A., Mariah E. BS cum laude, Niagara U., 1962; MBA, Ind. U., 1967; AMP, Harvard U., 1987. Mgmt. trainee Marine Midland Bank, Buffalo, 1962-63; project budget analyst Cleve. Electric Illuminating Co., 1967-68; asst. treas. Mid-Continent Telephone Co., Hudson, Ohio, 1968-75; v.p., treas. Gulf States Utilities, Beaumont, Tex., 1975-78; treas. Cen. and S.W. Corp., C&W Leasing Inc., CSW Energy Inc., CSW Fin., Inc., Dallas; v.p., treas. Cen. and S.W. Services, Inc., Dallas, 1978-89; pres. C&W Credit, Inc., 1985-89; exec. v.p., CFO TVA, Knoxville, 1989-95. Served with U.S. Army, 1963-65. Mem. Nat. Mgmt. Assn., Leading Chief Fin. Officers. Republican. Roman Catholic. Office: TVA 110 N Nilam St No 123 Fredericksburg TX 78624

MALECHA, MARVIN JOHN, architect, academic administrator; b. Lonsdale, Minn., June 26, 1949; s. George and Barbara Malecha; m. Cynthia Marie Miller, Aug. 8, 1970; children: Peter, Michelle. Student, St. Thomas Coll.; BArch, U. Minn.; MArch, Harvard U. Registered architect, Calif. Designer Wallace and Mundt Architects, Edina, Minn., 1969-73, Hugh Stubbins and Assocs., Cambridge, Mass., 1973-76; instr. Cambridge Urban Awareness Program, 1973-76, Boston Archtl. Ctr., 1974-76; asst. chmn., asst. prof. dept. arch. Coll. Environ. Design Calif. State Poly. U., Pomona, 1976-77, chmn., assoc. prof., 1979-82, prof., dean Coll. Environ. Design, 1982-94; dean sch. design N.C. State U., 1994—; chmn. Univ. Fall Conf. com. Calif. State Poly. U., 1984; mem. steering com. Architects for Social Responsibility; mem. bd. advisors Tchrs. cert. program City Bldg. Edn. Program, planning com. So. Calif. Assn. Govts.; vis. critic UCLA, 1985, U. Minn., 1981-83, 87, U. So. Calif., 1980-87, Calif. Poly. State U., San Luis Obispo, 1979-87, Clemson U., 1988; lectr. to schs. and archtl. assns.; cons. in architecture and research, Claremont, Calif., 1976—; master juror Nat. Council Archtl. Registration Bds.; mem. edn. equity com. Calif. State U. System, 1985-86; pres. Calif. Coun. Archtl. Edn., 1986-88; mem. accreditation vis. team for collegiate programs in landscape architecture, 1988—; bd. dirs. Nat. Archtl. Accreditation Bd.; campus architect cons. U. Calif., Riverside, 1990-94. Author: Form of Performance, The Fabric of Architecture, The Pomona Method; co-sgner, author internat. protocol for internat. exch. in arch. edn.; contbr. articles to profl. jours. Mem. Art and Liturgy com. Our Lady Assumption Ch., Claremont, Calif., 1982-94; mem. bldg. and real estate com. Archdiocese of Raleigh; bd. dirs. United Arts Raleigh, City Gallery Raleigh, 1995—. Recipient Ellerbe Archtl. award, 1972, Hon. Mention Mass. Housing Dept., 1976; Rotch scholar, 1980. Fellow AIA (bd. dirs. L.A. chpt. 1982-83, chmn. state and nat. awards coms. 1983-85, chmn. Monterey design conf. com., Henry Adams award 1973, mem. steering com. archs. in edn. com. 1991, chair archs. in edn. com. 1994-95, presdl. citation L.A. chpt. 1987, mem. Calif. coun. 1994, Excellence in Arch. Edn. award), Soc. Am. Registered Archs., Assn. Collegiate Schs. Arch. (v.p. 1988-89, chair ann. meeting, pres. 1988-89, adminstrs. conf. Washington 1985), Calif. Coun. Archtl. Edn. (pres. 1988-89). Office: NC State U Sch Design Raleigh NC 27695

MALECHEK, JOHN CHARLES, ecology and range science educator; b. San Angelo, Tex., Aug. 6, 1942. BS, Tex. Tech. U., 1964; MS, Colo. State U., 1966; PhD in Range Sci., Tex. A&M U., 1970. From asst. prof. to assoc. prof. Utah State U., Logan, 1970-82, prof. range sci., 1982—. Mem. Am. Soc. Animal Sci., Soc. Range Mgmt. Office: Utah State Experimental Area UMC 2 Range Science Logan UT 84322*

MALECKI, EDWARD STANLEY, JR., political science educator; b. Chgo., Nov. 16, 1938; s. Edward Stanley and Lucille Clara (May) M.; m. Judith Evelyn Sobczak, Aug. 24, 1962; children: Stephen, Robert. B.A., U. Ill., 1961, LL.B., 1963, M.A., 1965, Ph.D. (Charles Merriam fellow), 1969. Bar: Ill. 1963. Asst. prof. polit. sci. Calif. State U., Los Angeles, 1967-71; assoc. prof. Calif. State U., 1971-76, prof., 1976—, chair dept. Polit. Sci., 1993—. Author: (with H.R. Mahood) Group Politics: A New Emphasis, 1972; contbr. articles to profl. jours. Chmn. Caucus for a New Polit. Sci., 1970-71; ednl. cons. Foothill Urban League, 1969-70; bd. dirs. Pasadena Area Democratic Council, 1974. Calif. State U. Los Angeles Found. grantee, 1971-72, 84-85; HEW-Urban League grantee, 1969-70; NEH fellow, 1987. Mem. Ill. Bar Assn., Am. Polit. Sci. Assn., Am. Sociol. Assn., United Profs. Calif. (chpt. sec. 1974), ACLU (chpt. pres. 1974, 85-86, bd. dirs. So. Calif. 1981), Phi Kappa Phi. Home: 2225 Midwick Dr Altadena CA 91001-2828 Office: 5151 State University Dr Los Angeles CA 90032-4221

MALEFAKIS, EDWARD E., history educator; b. Springfield, Mass., Jan. 2, 1932; s. Emmanuel A. and Despina (Sophoulakis) M.; m. Cali Doxiadis, 1988; children from previous marriage: Michael, Laura. A.B., Bates Coll., 1953; M.A., Johns Hopkins U., 1955; Ph.D., Columbia U., 1965. Instr. Northwestern U., 1962-63, assoc. prof., 1968-71; asst. prof. Wayne State U., Detroit, 1963-64; asst. prof. modern European history Columbia U., 1964-67, prof., 1975—; prof. U. Mich., Ann Arbor, 1971-74. Author: Agrarian Reform and Peasant Revolution in Spain, 1970, Southern Europe in the 19th and 20th Centuries, 1992; editor: Indalecio Prieto, 1975, La guerra civil en España, 1986. Recipient Herbert Baxter Adams award Am. Hist. Assn., 1971, Faculty Teaching award Northwestern U., 1971, medal of honor U. Internacional Menendez Pelayo, 1982, Orden de Merito Civico (Spain), 1988; Social Scis. Rsch. Coun. grantee, 1967, NEH grantee, 1977; Guggenheim fellow, 1974, Inst. Juan March fellow, 1991. Mem. Modern Greek Studies Assn. (exec. com. 1981-87), Soc. for Spanish and Portuguese Hist. Studies (exec. council 1969-72), Spanish Inst. N.Y.C. (bd. dirs. 1982—). Democrat. Greek Orthodox. Home: 380 Riverside Dr New York NY 10025-1858 Office: Columbia Univ 524 Fayerweather Hall New York NY 10027

MALEK, FREDERIC VINCENT, finance company executive; b. Oak Park, Ill., Dec. 22, 1936; s. Fred W. and Martha (Smickilas) M.; m. Marlene A. McArthur, Aug. 5, 1961; children: Fred W., Michelle A. BS, U.S. Mil. Acad., 1959; MBA, Harvard U., 1964; D of Humanities (hon.), St. Leo Coll., St. Petersburg, Fla., 1970. Assoc. McKinsey & Co., Inc., L.A., 1964-67; chmn. exec. com. Triangle Corp., Columbia, S.C., 1967-69; dep. under sec. HEW, Washington, 1969-70; spl. asst. to Pres. U.S., Washington, 1970-73; dep. dir. U.S. Office of Mgmt. and Budget, Washington, 1973-75; with Marriott Corp., Washington, 1975-88, sr. v.p., 1975-77, exec. v.p., 1978-88; pres. Marriott Hotels and Resorts, 1981-88; pres. Northwest Airlines, Mpls., 1989-90, vice chmn., 1990-91, also bd. dirs.; campaign mgr. Bush-Quayle '92, 1991-92; co-chmn. CB Comml. Real Estate Group, 1989—; chmn. Lodging Opportunities Fund, 1991—, Thayer Capital Ptnrs., 1992—, Thayer Hotel Investors, 1994—; chmn. 1996 Rep. Presdl. Trust, 1995—; bd. dirs. Automated Data Processing Corp., Am. Mgmt. Sys. Inc., Avis Inc., ICF Kaiser Inc., Nat. Edn. Corp., N.W. Airlines, FPL Group Inc., Paine Webber Funds, Manor Care Inc.; dir. with rank of amb., 1990 Econ. Smuuit, 1989—; adj. prof. U. S.C., 1986-89; lectr. Kennedy Sch. Govt., Harvard U., 1976. Mem. Pres.'s Commn. on White House Fellows, 1971-75, White House Domestic Coun., 1974-75, Pres.'s Commn. on Pers. Interchange, 1974-76; dep. dir. com. for Re-election of Pres., 1972; Pres.'s Commn. on Pvt. Sector Initiatives, 1982-85, dir. conv. Bush for Pres., 1988; mem. Nat. Coun. on Surface Transp. Rsch., 1993-95; nat. adv. bd. Nat. Ctr. Econ. Edn. of Children, 1980-82; mem. Pres.'s Coun. on Phys. Fitness and Sports, 1986-91. Mem. Harvard Club of So. Calif. (bd. dirs., 1st v.p. 1965-67), University Club (com. chmn. 1966-68). Episcopalian. Avocations: biking, skiing. Office: 901 15th St NW Washington DC 20005-2327

MALENKA, BERTRAM JULIAN, physicist, educator; b. N.Y.C., June 8, 1923; s. Morris and Mollie (Wichtel) M.; m. Ruth D. Stolper, Mar. 28, 1948; children—David Jonathan, Robert Charles. AB, Columbia, 1947; MA, Harvard, 1949, PhD, 1951. Research fellow Harvard, 1951-54; asst. prof. physics Washington U., St. Louis, 1954-56; asso. prof. Tufts U., Medford, Mass., 1956-60; faculty Northeastern U., Boston, 1960—; prof. physics Northeastern U., 1962-93, prof. emeritus, 1993—; Mem. sci. adv. group Harvard-Mass. Inst. Tech. Cambridge Electron Accelerator, 1956—. Mem. Am., Italian phys. socs., N.Y. Acad. Scis., Phi Beta Kappa, Sigma Xi. Research and publs. on theory of nuclear forces and structure of nucleus, explanation polarization phenomena in high-energy scattering, gamma radiation, electric polarization deuteron, accelerator design. Home: 16 Rutledge Rd Belmont MA 02178-3323 Office: Northeastern Univ Dept Of Physics Boston MA 02115

MALES, WILLIAM JAMES, film producer, make-up artist; b. Mesa, Ariz.; s. James W. and Oveta (Bradshaw) M. Student, Pepperdine U., 1982-86; studies with Vincent J. R. Kehoe, 1980-82, studies with Dick Smith, 1981-83. Make-up artist William J. Males and Assocs., Hollywood, Calif., 1976—; exec. v.p. Bonaire Films, 1984-88; producer AZRAK Films, Inc., Hollywood, Calif., 1986—; co-producer with Bruce Boxleitner Diplomatic Immunity Distbr. Fries Entertainment, Hollywood, Calif., 1991; mgr. market rsch. Universal Pictures, Universal City, Calif., 1993—; CFO Calif. Pension Adminstrs., 1993-95. Studio make-up artist for numerous projects including (films) Aftershock, Family Reunion, Winds of War, Necromancer, Conan the Barbarian, Return of the Living Dead, Scanners, Ragedy Anne, (TV shows) The Blue and the Gray, Crisis at Central High, Skyward, Printer to the Territory, Golden Girls, Hollywood Squares, 21 Jump Street, 9 to 5, (theatrical prodns.) Mama Bear Papa Bear, I'm Not Rappaport, Man of La Mancha, The Gospel Truth, Camelot, Chorus Line (nat. tour), Grease, Godspell, Crucible; line producer (films) Aftershock, (distbr. Paramount Pictures) Dead Time, Lock Down, Necromancer, Ms. Frankenstein, Family Reunion, Rocky I; assoc. producer (films) Castle of Revenge, Alien Warrior, Californio, (TV commls.) Coppertone, Pepsi, Beechcraft, Levi Strauss, Chanel; prodn. dir. Danza/Floricanto USA; prodr. Lord Chamberlain's Players. Mem. NATAS, Acad. TV Arts and Scis. (Emmy nomination 1982), Brit. Acad. Film and TV Arts, Am. Soc. Makeup Artists, Soc. Motion Picture and TV Engrs., Assn. Film Craftsmen (local 531), Nat. Assn. Broadcast Employees and Technicians, Prodrs. Guild Am. Republican. Office: Universal Pictures Ste 26 8721 Santa Monica Blvd West Hollywood CA 90069

MALESARDI, MICHAEL J., management consultant. Controller Wyatt Corp.

MALESKA, MARTIN EDMUND, publishing executive; b. Yonkers, N.Y., Apr. 3, 1944; s. Edmund Joseph and Marian (Kolton) M.; m. Elissa Mary Delfini, Apr. 27, 1968; children: Christine, Matthew, Danielle. BS in Chemistry, Fordham U., 1966; MBA in Fin., NYU, 1968. Dir. fin. Celanese do Brasil, São Paulo, Brazil, 1972-77; mng. dir. internat. ops. Pfizer Med. Systems, N.Y.C., 1977-80; dir. planning Macmillan Inc., N.Y.C., 1980-82, now bd. dirs., bd. dirs., v.p., group exec., 1984-88; pres. Nat. Register Pub. Co., N.Y.C., 1982-83; sr. v.p. corp. devel. Maxwell Communication Corp., N.Y.C., 1989-91; bd. dirs. Macmillan Inc., N.Y.C.; mng. dir. Verons, Suhler & Assocs., N.Y.C., 1991-95; pres. Internat. and Profl. Publishing Grps., Simon and Schuster Inc., 1995—. Capt. USAF, 1968-72. Republican. Roman Catholic. Avocation: racquet sports. Home: 3 Debra Ln Chappaqua NY 10514-3003 Office: Simon & Schuster 1230 Ave of the Americas New York NY 10020

MALETTA, DIANE STANLEY, gifted and talented educator, education educator; b. Fairmont, W.Va., July 1, 1960; d. Dan Jarrell and LaModa June (Forth) Stanley; m. Robert Thomas Maletta, May 22, 1993; children: Adam Robert, Derek Nathaniel, Jasmine Elizabeth. BS in Edn. with honors and distinction, Valparaiso U., 1982; MS in Edn. summa cum laude, Butler U., 1986; postgrad., Ind. U., 1989—; gifted/talented endorsement, Purdue U., 1992. State of Ind. life license: gen. elem., reading minor, gifted/talented endorsement. Tchr. grade 1, Spanish tchr. grades 7-8, coach St. John's Luth. Sch., Indpls., 1983-86; tchr. grade 1 River Grove (Ill.) Sch., 1986-87; tchr. grades 2 and 4, intramural dir. Washington Twp. Sch., Valparaiso, Ind., 1987-89; asst. prof. edn. Valparaiso (Ind.) U., 1989-92; tchr. gifted and talented Valparaiso (Ind.) Cmty. Schs., 1992—; mem., rec. sec. Ind. Dist. Luth. Tchrs., Indpls., 1983-85; mem. Luth. Edn. Assn., Indpls., 1983-86, Nat. Orgn. Tchr. Educators in Reading, 1989-92, Ind. Reading Profs., Indpls., 1989-92; adv. bd. mem. The Learning Pl., Valparaiso, 1990-92; asst. planner Nat. Assessment Symposium, 1990; adj. prof. edn. Ind. U. N.W., Gary, spring 1995; tutor, spkr. and conf. presenter in field. Choir mem. St. John's Luth. Ch., Indpls., 1983-86, Immanuel Luth. Ch., Valparaisoon 1987-89; road race runner Lakeshore Striders, Chgo., N.W. Ind., 1989-94; mem. Trinity Luth. Ch., Valparaiso, 1992—; runner, phone vol. Dem. Election Com., Porter,Ind., 1994. Mem. ASCD, Internat. Reading Assn. (past sec.), Porter County Reading Assn. (past sec., bd. mem., com. chairperson), Kappa Delta Pi, Pi Lambda Theta, Phi Delta Kappa, Mortar Bd. Avocations: running, biking, swimming, traveling, reading. Home: 1140 Dunes Meadows Dr Porter IN 46304-1286 Office: Valparaiso Cmty Schs 405 Campbell St Valparaiso IN 46383

MALETZ, HERBERT NAAMAN, federal judge; b. Boston, Oct. 30, 1913; s. Reuben and Frances (Sawyer) M.; m. Catherine B. Loebach, May 8, 1947; 1 son, David M. A.B., Harvard, 1935, LL.B., 1939. Bar: Mass. bar 1939, D.C. bar 1952. Mem. staff Truman com. U.S. Senate, 1941-42; atty. antitrust div. Dept. Justice, 1946-50; with OPS, 1950-53, chief counsel, 1952-53; chief counsel anti-trust subcom. U.S. Ho. of Reps., 1955-61; commr. U.S. Ct. Claims, 1961-67; judge U.S. Ct. Internat. Trade, N.Y.C., 1967-87; vis. judge U.S. Dist. Ct. Md., Balt., 1987—. Served with AUS, 1942-46; lt. col. Res. Office: US Dist Ct Md 101 W Lombard St Baltimore MD 21201-2626

MALEY, PATRICIA ANN, preservation planner; b. Wilmington, Del., Dec. 25, 1955; d. James Alfred and Frances Louise (Fenimore) M.; m. Scott A.

Stone, Dec. 7, 1991. AA, Cecil C.C., 1973; BA, U. Del., 1975, MA, 1981. Cert. planner: cert. secondary tchr., Del. Analyst econ. devel. City of Wilmington, 1977-78, evaluation specialist, 1978-80, planner II mayor's office, 1980-86, cons. preservation, 1986-87; dir. Belle Meade Mansion, Nashville, 1987-88; dir. planning, devel. Children's Bur. of Del., Wilmington, 1988; prin. preservation planner Environ. Mgmt. Ctr., Brandywine Conservancy, Chadds Ford, Pa., 1988-92; planning cons., 1992-95; design review and preservation commn. coord. Wilmington Dept. Planning, 1995—; cons. cultural resources M.A.A.R. Inc., Newark, Del., 1987, ITC Cons., Wilmington, 1985-86. Contbg. photographer America's City Halls, 1984; author numerous Nat. Register nominations, 1980-86; 88—. Pres., founder Haynes Park Civic Assn., Wilmington, 1977-80; photographer Biden U.S. Senate Campaign, New Castle County, Del., 1984; sec. parish coun. Our Lady Fatima Roman Cath. Ch., 1985-86, choir dir., 1983-87; mem. com. on design & renovation of worship spaces Diocese of Wilmington, also mem. com. on music; bd. dirs. Del. Children's Theatre; music dir. St. Elizabeth Ann Seton parish, Bear, Del., 1988—. U. Del. fellow, 1976-77. Mem. Nat. Trust Hist. Preservation, Am. Inst. Cert. Planners, Am. Planning Assn., Nat. Pastoral Musicians Assn., Del. Soc. Architects, Del. Archeol. Soc., Del. Hist. Soc., Pi Sigma Alpha. Democrat. Avocations: photography; choral, piano, organ music. Office: City of Wilmington Dept Planning 800 French St 7th Fl Wilmington DE 19801

MALEY, SAMUEL WAYNE, electrical engineering educator; b. Sidney, Neb., Mar. 1, 1928; s. Samuel Raymond and Inez (Moore) M.; m. Elizabeth Anne Green, June 11, 1963; children—Karen Margaret, Laura Elaine. B.S., U. Colo., 1952, M.S., 1957, Ph.D., 1959; student, U. N.M., 1957-58. Geophysicist Stanolind Oil Co., Lubbock, Tex., 1952; design engr. Beach Aircraft Corp., Wichita, Kan., 1952-53, Dynalectron Corp., Cheyenne, Wyo., 1953-56; research scientist U. Colo., Boulder, 1959-60, vis. lectr., 1960-61, asst. prof., 1961-62, assoc. prof. elec. engring., 1962-67, prof., 1967-91, prof. emeritus, 1991—; mem. Nat. Ctr. Computer Aided Design, Millimeter and Microwave Systems U. Colo., 1988—; cons. Nat. Center Atmospheric Research, 1964, Automation Industries Research Div., Boulder, Colo., 1960-71, Midwec Corp., Ogallala, Neb., 1969-70, IBM, Boulder, 1969—. Author: Combinational Logic Circuits, 1969; contbg. author to 5 survey books on sci. and engring. Served with AUS, 1946-47; Served with USAF, 1947-48. Mem. I.E.E.E., A.A.A.S., Soc. Indsl. and Applied Math. Research electromagnetic theory; communication theory; computer design. Home: 3760 57th St Boulder CO 80301-3016

MALEY, WAYNE ALLEN, engineering consultant; b. Stanley, Iowa, Mar. 9, 1927; s. Neil Gordon and Flossie Amelia (Wharram) M.; m. Marianne Nelson, Aug. 2, 1959; children: James G., Mary G., Mark A. BS in Agrl. Engring., Iowa State U., 1949; postgrad., Purdue U., Ga. Tech., IIT. Power use advisor Southwestern Electric, Greenville, Ill., 1949-53; field agt. Am. Zinc Inst., Lafayette, Ind., 1953-59; mktg. devel. specialist U.S. Steel, Des Moines, Iowa, 1959-65; mktg. rep. U.S. Steel, Pitts., 1965-71, bar products rep., 1972-76; assoc. Taylor Equipment, Pitts., 1977-81; mgr. pub. rels. Am. Soc. Agrl. Engrs., St. Joseph, Mich., 1981-84, dir. mem. svcs., 1984-92; cons. Tech. Tours, St. Joseph, 1992—. Author: Iowa Really Isn't Boring, 1992, (textbook) Farm Structures, 1957, (computer program/workbook) Rim Lift Material Handling, 1970 (Blue Ribbon award 1971); editor: Agriculture's Contract with Society, 1991. Pres. Ednl. Concerns for Hunger Orgn., Ft. Myers, Fla., 1979-81; dist. activity dir. Boy Scouts Am., Moon Twp., 1969-70. With USN, 1945-46. Named Hon. Star Farmer, FFA Ill., 1958. Fellow Am. Soc. Agrl. Engrs. (bd. dirs. 1979-81 hon. for forum leadership 1991); mem. Agrl. Editors Assn., Coun. Engring. Soc. Execs. (bd. dirs. 1984-85), Sigma Xi (pres./del. Whirlpool chpt. 1993-94). Presbyterian. Achievements include patent for fence building machine, for material handling system; design of cable fences; design and installation of steel beverage can recycling center. Home and Office: Tech Tours 2592 Stratford Dr Saint Joseph MI 49085-2714

MALFELD, DIANE D., lawyer; b. Marshalltown, Iowa, 1953. BA, U. Iowa, 1975, JD, 1978. Bar: Minn. 1978. Ptnr. Dorsey & Whitney, Mpls. Mem. Phi Beta Kappa. Office: Dorsey & Whitney 220 S 6th St Minneapolis MN 55402-4502

MALGIERI, NICK, chef, author, educator; b. Newark, Sept. 30, 1947; s. Nufre and Antoinette (LoConte) M. BA in French, Seton Hall U., 1970; AOS in Culinary Arts, Culinary Inst., Hyde Park, N.Y., 1973. Pastrycook Seehotel Meierhof, Zurich, 1973-74, Hotel de Paris, Monte Carlo, 1974, Sporting Club, Monte Carlo, 1974-76, Hotel la Reserve, Beaulieu, France, 1974; pastry chef Windows on the World, N.Y.C., 1976-79; asst. pastry chef Hotel Waldorf Astoria, N.Y.C., 1979; chmn. baking dept. N.Y. Restaurant Sch., N.Y.C., 1979-83; v.p., dir. baking program Peter Kump Cooking Sch., N.Y.C., 1984—; founder, owner Total Heaven Baking Co.; exec. chef Paine Webber; pastry chef Board Room; cons. Inhilco, Inc. Author: Nick Malgieri's Perfect Pastry, 1989, Great Italian Desserts, 1990, How to Bake, 1995 (James Beard Found. Cookbook award/Best Book on Baking/Deserts of 1995); contbr. articles, recipes to newspapers, profl. jours. Mem. Internat. Assn. Culinary Profls. (cert. culinary profl., chmn. certification 1989-91), Amicale Culinaire de Monaco, Societe Culinaire Philanthropique N.Y., Federazione Italiana dei Cuochi, James Beard Found. (coord. competitions 1991—), N.Y. Assn. Cooking Tchrs. (former bd. dirs.), Cooking Advancement, Rsch. and Edn. Found. (former trustee). Home: 277 W 10th St New York NY 10014-2583 Office: Peter Kump Cooking Sch 307 E 92nd St New York NY 10128-5401

MALHERBE, ABRAHAM JOHANNES, VI, religion educator, writer; b. Pretoria, South Africa, May 15, 1930; came to U.S., 1951; s. Abraham Johannes V and Cornelia Aletta (Meyer) M.; m. Phyllis Melton, May 28, 1953; children: Selina, Cornelia, Abraham Johannes VII. BA, Abilene Christian U., 1954; STB, Harvard U., 1957; student, U. Utrecht, The Netherlands, 1960-61; ThD, Harvard U., 1963; LLD (hon.), Pepperdine U., 1981; LHD (hon.), Centre Coll., 1990; STD (hon.), Providence Coll., 1994. Minister Ch. of Christ, Lexington, Mass., 1956-63; asst. and assoc. prof. Abilene (Tex.) Christian U., 1963-67; vis. scholar Harvard Divinity Sch., Cambridge, Mass., 1967-68; assoc. prof. Abilene Christian U., 1968-69, Dartmouth Coll., Hanover, N.H., 1969-70; assoc. prof. Yale Divinity Sch., New Haven, Conn., 1970-77, prof., 1977-81, Buckingham prof., 1981-94, assoc. dean acad. affairs, 1981-94; prof. eremitus, 1994—. Author: Social Aspects of Early Christianity, 1983, Moral Exhortation, 1986, Paul and the Thessalonians, 1987, Ancient Epistolary Theorists, 1988, Paul and the Popular Philosophers, 1989; contbr. articles to profl. jours.; inspiration for book: Greeks, Romans and Christians: Essays in Honor of Abraham J. Malherbe, 1990. Recipient tchg. award Abilene Christian U., 1965, 67, Outstanding Alumni citation, 1993; NEH fellow 1973. Mem. Soc. Biblical Lit., North Am. Patristic Soc., Studiorum Novi Testamenti Societas, South African New Testament Soc. (hon.), Religious Studies Rev. (editoral bd. 1980—), The Second Century, Novum Testamentum (editorial bd. 1991—). Mem. Ch. of Christ. Home: 71 Spring Garden St Hamden CT 06517-1913 Office: Yale Divinity Sch 409 Prospect St New Haven CT 06511-2167

MALHOTRA, ASHOK KUMAR, philosophy educator; b. Ferozepur, India, Apr. 1, 1940; came to U.S., 1963, naturalized, 1977; s. Nihal Chand and Vidya (Wanti) M.; m. Nina Judith Finestone, Oct. 24, 1966; children: Raj Kumar, Ravi Kumar. B.A., U. Rajasthan, 1961, M.A., 1963; Ph.D., U. Hawaii, 1969. Asst. prof. SUNY-Oneonta, 1967-70, assoc. prof., 1970-80, prof., 1980—, chmn. philosophy dept., 1975—; vis. prof. SUNY-Buffalo, summer 1970, Kurukshetra U. and Birla Inst., Pilani, India, spring 1980; grants reviewer NEH, 1978—. bd. dirs. SUNY Press editorial, 1989—, dir. SUNY study abroad, program to India, 1980—; cons. TV series Kung Fu: The Legend Continues. East-West Ctr. fellow, 1963-65, 66-67; N.Y. State Dept. Edn. grantee, 1967-68, 68-69, summer 1969; NEH grantee, summer 1979; recipient Excellence in Teaching award United Univ. Profession. Mem. Am. Philos. Assn., Soc. Asian and Comparative Philosophy, Assn. Asian Studies, N.Y. State Asian Studies Soc., Internat. Phenomenol. Soc. Author: Sartre's Existentialism in Nausea and Being and Nothingness, 1978, Pathways to Philosophy: A Multidisciplinary Approach, 1996; articles, revs. Home: 17 Center St Oneonta NY 13820-1445

MALHOTRA, NARESH KUMAR, management educator; b. Ambala, Punjab, India, Nov. 23, 1949; came to U.S., 1975; s. Har Narian and Satya (Kakkar) M.; m. Veena Bahl, Aug. 13, 1980; children: Ruth Veena, Paul Naresh. BTech with honors, I.I.T., Bombay, India, 1971; MBA, I.I.M., Ahmedabad, India, 1973; MS, SUNY, Buffalo, 1978, PhD, 1979. Mgmt. cons. ASCI, Hyderabad, India, 1971-73; asst. prof. Ga. Tech. Inst., Atlanta, 1979—, assoc. prof. mgmt., coord. mktg., 1982-87, 89—, prof., 1988, regents' prof. 1992—; organizer several nat., internat. mktg. mgmt. confs. Contbr. articles to profl. jours. Lay preacher of the Gospel. Ranked the Top Researcher in U.S.A. based on publs. in Jour. Mktg. Rsch., 1980-85, Top Researcher Jour. Health Care Mktg., 1980-94. Fellow Acad. Mktg. Sci. (disting., program chmn. 1984-85, 85-86, v.p. programs 1988-90, chmn. bd. 1990-92, pres.-elect 1992-94, pres. 94-96, chmn. found. 1996—), Decision Scis. Inst.(track chmn. 1984-86); mem. Am. Mktg. Assn. (track chmn. 1983-84), Am. Statis. Assn. Republican. Baptist. Avocations: reading, writing, church activities, outdoor activities. Home: 1956 Lenox Rd NE Atlanta GA 30306-3035 Office: Ga Tech Inst Sch Mgmt Atlanta GA 30332

MALHOTRA, SURIN M., aerospace manufacturing executive; b. New Delhi, Dec. 27, 1948; came to U.S., 1970; s. Shiv D. and Gur D. (Kaushalya) M.; m. Rita Kashyap, Mar. 11, 1977; children: Tina, Amie. BSME, Delhi U., 1970; MSME, Wichita State U., 1971, MS in Adminstrn., 1973; JD cum laude, U. Bridgeport, 1992. Grad. asst. Wichita State U., Wichita, Kans., 1971-73; proj. engr. Norco Inc., Ridgefield, Conn., 1973-75, data processing mgr., 1975-78, program mgr., 1978-81, dir. materials, 1981-84, dir. contracts, 1984-86, v.p. sales, 1986-88, v.p. mfg. and sales, 1988-89; v.p. ops. Ridgefield, Conn., 1989-95; exec. v.p., COO Norco Inc., Ridgefield, Conn., 1995—; advisor BHS Mock Trial Team; notary pub. Inventor, patentee reversing mechanism. Vice chmn. Bethel (Conn.) Ethics Commn. Bridgeport scholar, 1989. Mem. ABA, Conn. Bar Assn., Phi Delta Phi. Republican. Hindu. Home: 104 Rockwell Rd Bethel CT 06801-3006 Office: Norco Inc 139 Ethan Allen Hwy Ridgefield CT 06877-6207

MALHOTRA, VIVEK, medical educator. BS with honors, Stirling U., 1982; DPhil in Biochemistry, Oxford U., 1985. Asst. prof. biology U. Calif., San Diego, 1990-95, assoc. prof. biology, 1995—. Contbr. articles to profl. jours. postdoctoral fellow Stanford U., 1985-90, Am. Cancer Soc., Calif., 1988-90; Pirie-Reid scholar, Oxford U., 1982-85, Basil O'Connor Starter scholar, March of Dimes, 1992-95. Office: U Calif Dept Biology La Jolla CA 92093-0347

MALICKY, NEAL, college president; b. Sour Lake, Tex., Sept. 14, 1934; s. George and Ethel L. (Reed) M.; m. Margaret A. Wilson, Sept. 2, 1956; children: Michael Neal, Eric Scott, David Matthew. A.B., Baker U., 1956; B.D., So. Meth. U., 1959; Ph.D., Columbia U., 1968; postgrad., Harvard U., 1978. Ordained to ministry Meth. Ch., 1959; pastor Meth. Ch., Moran, Kans., 1959-62, Van Cortlandtville, N.Y., 1962-66; asst. prof., dir. semester on UN Drew U., 1966-69; prof. polit. sci., dean Coll., Baker U., Baldwin City, Kans., 1969-75; acting pres. Coll., Baker U., 1973-75; v.p. acad. affairs, also dean Baldwin-Wallace Coll., Berea, Ohio, 1975-81; pres. Baldwin-Wallace Coll., 1981—. Author: To Keep the Peace, 1965, Non-Governmental Organizations at the United Nations, 1968; contbr. articles to profl. jours. Mem. Leadership Cleve., Nat. Conf. Christian and Jews, Cleve. Commn. Higher Edn., Cleve. Coun. World Affairs, Greater Cleve. Roundtable (chmn. edn. com.), Cleve. Initiative Edn. (vice chmn.), Summit on Edn. (co-convenor), Assn. Independent Colls. Ohio (chmn.). Mem. UN Assn. Clubs: Union of Cleve., Fifty of Cleve. Office: Baldwin-Wallace Coll Office of Pres 275 Eastland Rd Berea OH 44017-2005

MALIK, HAFEEZ, political scientist, educator; b. Lahore, Pakistan, Mar. 17, 1930; m. Lynda P. Malik; children: Cyrus, Dean. BA, Government Coll., Lahore, Pakistan, 1949; grad. diploma in Journalism, U. Punjab, Lahore, 1952; MS in Journalism, Syracuse U., 1955, MA in Polit. Sci., 1957, PhD in Polit. Sci., 1961. Asst. prof. Polit. Sci. Villanova (Pa.) U., 1961-63, assoc. prof., 1963-67, prof., 1967—; pub. rels. officer City of Lahore, 1950-53; White House correspondent The Nawa-i-Waqt, 1958-61, The Shabaz, 1958-61; mem. grad. com. dept. Polit. Sci. Villanova U., 1961-67, chmn., 1967-78; vis. prof. Fgn. Svc. Inst., Washington, 1961-63, 66-68, 70-85, Syracuse U. 1964, 65, Drexel U., Phila., 1968-69; mem. grad. coun. com. rsch. and publs., 1969-70, grad. adv. com. liberal arts and social studies, 1964-67, faculty libr. com., 1964-67, undergrad. com. polit. sci., 1980—, rank and tenure com., 1991-92; pres. Am. Inst. Pakistan Studies, 1972-88, Pakistan Am. Found., 1972—; exec. dir. Am. Coun. Study of Islamic Socs., 1983—; cons. Soviet Acad. Scis., 1979, Dept. Defense, 1980, Pakistan-U.S. subcommn. edn. and culture, 1985, 88, USIA, 1986; presenter in field. News editor The Daily Magharabi Pakistan, 1948-50; tech. editor: Meteorological and Geoastrophysical Abstracts, Am. Meteorological Soc. 1960-63; author: Muslim Nationalism in India and Pakistan, 1963, rev. edit. 1980, Sir. Sayyid Ahmed Khan's History of the Bijnore Rebellion, 1972, rev. edit. 1980, Political Profile of Sir Sayyid Ahmed Khan: A Documentary Record, 1982, Domestic Determinants of Soviet Foreign Policy Towards South Asia and the Middle Ease, 1990, Dilemmas of National Security and Cooperation in India and Pakistan, 1993, Soviet-Pakistan Relations and Current Dynamics, 1993; editor: Iqbal: Poet-Philosopher of Pakistan, 1971, rev. edit., 1974, Sir Sayyid Ahmed Khan's History of the Bijnore Rebellion, 1972, rev. edit., 1982, Soviet-American Relations with Pakistan, Iran, and Afghanistan, 1986; mem. editorial adv. bd. Islam and the Modern Age, Islam Awr Aser-i Jadid, 1969-79; editor Jour. South Asian and Middle Eastern Studies, 1977—; contbr. articles to profl. jours., encyclopedias, chpts. to books. Grantee Office Health, Edn. Welfare, 1974, 1978, Assn. Pakistan and Indic-Islamic Studies/Pakistan Am. Found, 1982. Office: Villanova U Lancaster Pike Villanova PA 19085

MALIK, MOSADDEQUE RAHMAN, architect, consultant; b. Dhaka, Pakistan, May 6, 1957; came to U.S., 1971; s. Hafizur Rahman and Dilara Karim Malik; divorced; 1 child, Salsabil. BS in Architecture, Cath. U. Am., 1981; postgrad. Archtl. consortium, George Washington U., D.C., 1982; MArch, Cath. U. Am., 1983. Registered architect U.S.; cert. architect, Pakistan. Assoc. Glen Constrn. Co., Rockville, Md., 1978-82; sr. designer Davis & Carter P.C., McLean, Va., 1984-88; dir. of design Velsey Architects, Bethesda, Md., 1987-88, Barlows Design Group, Fairfax, Va., 1988-90; prin. Archtl. Designs, Inc., Silver Spring, Md., 1987—; prin., ptnr. Simmons, Malik Assocs., Silver Spring, 1991—, Simmons & Assocs., Ft. Washington, Md., 1992—; design cons. U.A. & Assocs., McLean, Va., 1990-91, Al Afandi Orgn., Jeddah, Saudi Arabia, 1992—, Simmons & Assocs., Hamilton, Bermuda, 1993. Editor Archtl. Record, 1988; author: (jour.) Islamic Architecture Vols. I & II, 1982; co-author: Mimar, 1991. Mem. Fraternal Order Police, Rockville, Md., 1979-81. Recipient. Hon. Mention, F.S.P. Competition, 1983, citation N. Va. AIA, 1985, hon. mention Mimar Competition, 1990. Mem. AIA (assoc. 1988-90, mem. 1990—), World Congress of Architects, Islamic Congress for World Peace (bd. dirs.), Royal Inst. British Architects.

MALIK, OM PARKASH, electrical engineering educator, researcher; b. Sargodha, Punjab, India, Apr. 20, 1932; arrived in Can., 1966; s. Arjan Dass and Kesar Bai (Ahuja) M.; m. Margareta Fagerstrom, Dec. 22, 1968; children: Ola Parkash, Mira, Maya. Nat. Diploma in Elec. Engring., Delhi (India) Poly., 1952; M in Engring., Roorkee (India) U., 1962; PhD, London U., 1965; D.I.C., Imperial Coll., London, 1966. Registered profl. engr., Ont., Alta. Asst. engr. Punjab State Elec. Bd., 1953-61, asst. to chief engr., 1957-59; rsch. engr. English Elec. Co., Eng., 1965-66; asst. prof. U. Windsor, Ont., Can., 1966-68; assoc. prof. U. Calgary, Alta., Can., 1968-74, prof., 1974—; assoc. dean student affairs, faculty engring. U. Calgary, Alta., Can., 1995—; assoc. acad. dean faculty engring. U. Calgary, Alta., Can., 1979-90, acting dean, 1981; cons. prof. Huazhong U. Sci. and Tech., Wuhan, People's Republic China, 1986—. Assoc. editor Can. Elec. and Computer Engring. Jour., 1988—; contbr. 400 articles to profl. jours. Indsl. tng. scholar Govt. India, 1952-53, sr. indsl. tng. scholar Confedn. Brit. Industries, 1959-60. Fellow IEEE (Centennial medal 1984, chmn. Western Can. coun. 1983-84, Merit award 1986, chmn. student activities Can. region 1979-82), Inst. Elec. Engrs.; mem. IEEE Power Engring. Soc. (machine theory subcom. 1979—, excitation sys. subcom. 1988—, sys. dynamic performance subcom. 1988—, energy devel. and power generation com. 1990—), Assn. Profl. Engrs., Geologists and Geophysicists Alta. (Vol. Svc. award 1990), Assn. Profl. Engrs. Ont., Am. Soc. Engring. Edn., Can. Elec. Assn. (assoc., controls com.1977-92, chmn. digital control com. 1977-85, chmn. edn. com. 1983-85, mem. expert sys. com. 1989-94), Confederacion Panamericana de Ingenieria Mecanica, Electica y Ramas Afines (v.p. 1987—, bd. dirs. region I, 1991-93). Hindu. Home: 1917-10A Street SW, Calgary, AB Canada T2T 3K2 Office: U Calgary Dept Elec & Computer Engring, 2500 University Dr NW, Calgary, AB Canada T2N 1N4

MALIK, RAYMOND HOWARD, economist, scientist, corporate executive, inventor, educator; b. Lebanon, Feb. 4, 1933; came to U.S., 1948, naturalized, 1963; s. John Z. and Clarice R. (Malik) M. BA, Valparaiso U., 1950; BSBA and Econs., Simpson Coll., 1951; MSBA, So. Ill. U., 1956, PhD in Electronics and Econs., 1959. Supr. Arabian Am. Oil Co., Beirut, 1952-54; mem. grad. faculty, advisor Ill. State U., 1954-59; prof., head world trade programs Central YMCA Community Coll., Chgo., 1966-74; pres. Malik Internat. Enterprises Ltd., Chgo., 1959—; advisor U.S. Congl. Adv. Bd. Author: The Guide to Youth, Health and Longevity, 1980, Do You Really Need Glasses, 1988; inventor selectric typing elements and mechanism, 1959, heater-humidifier-dehumidifier, 1963, ednl. math toy, 1965, circle of sound concept of sound propogation, 1967; designed, introduced Computer and Others, 1962; introduced modular concept in color TV (system-three and others), 1973, gamma ray breast cancer detector, 1976, auto-ignition instant hot water heater, 1981, water filter, purifier and softener, 1984, no doze warner, 1985, indoor-outdoor barbeque grill, 1985, infra-red heat massager, 1986; designed and introduced telephone shoulder rest with adjustable mechanism, 1962, electronic telephone (Trimline, others), 1964, modular telephone, 1975, video phone, 1991; pioneer developer interplanetary communications system, 1961. Deacon, mem. pastor-congl. com., youth and young adult ednl. com. St. George Orthodox Ch., Cicero, Ill.; fundraiser March of Dimes, St. Jude Hosp., Am. Cancer Soc., Am. Heart Fund, numerous others; mem. Am. Task Force for Lebanon, 1992—. Named to Wisdom Hall of Fame, 1987, Personality of Yr. 1995; Fulbright scholar, 1948-50, Meth. Ch. scholar, 1950-51; So. Ill. U. fellow, 1954-59. Mem. IEEE, AAAS, Am. Mgmt. Assn., Am. Econ. Assn., Am. Mktg. Assn., Import Clubs U.S., Internat. Bus. Coun., Internat. Platform Assn., Pres.'s Assn., Nat. Assn. Self-Employed, Imperial Austrian Legion of Honor, Internat. Students Assn., Soc. Mfg. Engrs., Am. Legion, Highlander Club, Phi Beta Kappa, Sigma Xi, Delta Rho, Beta Gamma Sigma, Alpha Phi Omega. Address: PO Box 3194 Chicago IL 60654-0194 *My duties and responsibilities are: to be of service to my community, working and aiding my countrymen and women in the development of leaders, for the betterment of America's future and the world.*

MALIN, HOWARD GERALD, podiatrist; b. Providence, Dec. 2, 1941; s. Leon Nathan and Rena Rose (Shapiro) M. AB, U. R.I., 1964; MA, Brigham Young U., 1969; BSc, Calif. Coll. Podiatric Medicine, 1969, DPM, 1972; MSC, Pepperdine U., 1978; postgrad. in classic, U. So. Calif., 1983—. Diplomate Am. Bd. Podiatric Pub. Health, Am. Bd. Podiatric Orthopedics. Extern in podiatry VA Med. Ctr., Wadsworth, Kans., 1971-72, Marine Corps Res. Dept., San Diego, 1972; resident in podiatric medicine and surgery N.Y. Coll. Podiatric-Medicine, N.Y.C., 1972-73; resident in podiatric surgery, instr. in podiatric surgery N.Y. Coll. Podiatric Medicine, N.Y.C., 1973-74; pvt. practitioner in podiatric medicine and surgery Bklyn., 1974-77; mem. staff Prospect Hosp., Bronx, N.Y., 1974-77; chief podiatry service, mem. staff, cons. sports medicine David Grant U.S. Air Force Med. Ctr., Travis AFB, Calif., 1977-80; chief podiatric sect., mem. staff VA Med. Ctr., Martinsburg, W.Va., 1980—; instr. ednl. devel. program VA Med. Ctr., Martinsburg, W.Va., 1980—; clin. prof. med. sci. Alderson-Broaddus Coll., U. Osteopathic Medicine and Health Scis.; adj. prof. Barry U. Sch. Podiatric Medicine; dir. extern program Pa. Coll. Podiatric Medicine. Editorial rev. bd. Jour. Contemporary Podiatric Physician, 1991—. Lt. col. USAF, 1977-80, with Res. Fellow Am. Coll. Foot Orthopedics, Am. Coll. Podiatric Physicians, Am. SOc. Podiatric Medicine (past pres., archivist), Am. Soc. Podiatric Radiologists (v.p., archivist), Royal Soc. Health; mem. Am. Acad. Podiatric Sports Medicine (assoc.), Assn. Mil. Surgeons U.S. (life), Am. Coll. Podiatric Surgery (assoc.), Am. Assn. Podiatric Med. Writers (archivist), Phi Kappa Theta, Phi Kappa Psi. Home: 210 Shenandoah Rd Apt 2D Martinsburg WV 25401-3723 Office: VA Med Ctr Dept Podiatry Martinsburg WV 25401

MALIN, IRVING, English literature educator, literary critic; b. N.Y.C., Mar. 18, 1934; s. Morris and Bertha (Silverman) M.; m. Ruth Lief, Dec. 18, 1955; 1 child, Mark. BA, Queens Coll., 1955; PhD, Stanford U., 1958. Acting instr. English Stanford U., 1955-58; instr. Ind. U., 1958-60; from instr. to prof. CCNY, 1960-72, prof., 1972—; cons. Jewish Publ. Soc., 1964, Am. Quar., 1964, NEH, 1972, 79, 80, 81, 82, B'nai B'rith, 1974-75, Yaddo, 1975-77, Jewish Book Coun., 1976, 79, PEN, 1978-82, Princeton U. Press, 1979, Fairleigh Dickinson Press, 1980, Wayne State U. Press, 1980, INternat. Coun. Exch. of Scholars, 1980-81, Duke U. Press, 1981, Jewish Daily Forward, 1981, U. Pitts. Press, 1981, Papers on Lang. and Lit., 1981, U. Ga. Press, 1983, UMI Rsch., 1989, Gordian Press, 1990, Ctr. for Study of Higher Edn., 1990, Mosiac, 1991, MacArthur Found., 1996. Author: William Faulkner: An Interpretation, 1957, New American Gothic, 1962, Jews and Americans, 1965, Saul Bellow's Fiction, 1969, Nathaneal West's Novels, 1972, Isaac Bashevis Singer, 1972; co-editor: Breakthrough: A Treasury of Contemporary American Jewish Literature, 1964, William Styron's The Confessions of Nat Turner: A Critical Handbook, 1970, The Achievement of William Styron, 1975; editor: Psychoanalysis and American Fiction, 1965, Saul Bellow and the Critics, 1967, Truman Capote's in Cold Blood: A Critical Handbook, 1968, Critical Views of Isaac Bashevis Singer, 1969, Contemporary American-Jewish Literature: Critical Essays, 1973, Conrad Alken's Prose, 1982; adv. editor: Studies in American Jewish Literature, Jour. Modern Literature, Review of Contemporary Fiction, Saul Bellow Jour., 20th Century Literature; reviewer: Rev. Contemporary Fiction, rev. Commonweal, Hollins Critic, So. Qaurterly; co-editor Paul Bowles, 1986, Spl. Issue of 20th Century Lit., James Dickey spl. Issue of S.C. Rev., 1994, So. Quarterly, 1995, James Dickey's Fiction Spl. Tex. Rev., 1996. Fellow Yaddo, 1963, Nat. Found. for Jewish Culture, 1963-64, Huntington Libr., 1978. Mem. MLA, AAUP, Am. Studies Assn., Am. Jewish Hist. Soc., Melville Soc., Authors League Am., Soc. Study of So. Lit., Poe Studies Assn., English Inst., Nathaniel Hawthorne Soc., N.Y. Acad. Scis., Poetry Soc. Am., Popular Culture Assn., Nat. Book Critics Circle, Sherwood Anderson Soc., Internat. Assn. Univ. Prof. English, Kafka Soc., English-Speaking Union, Multi-Ethnic Lit. U.S. Soc., Hastings Ctr., Am. Jewish Congress, Assoc. Writing Programs, Nat. Coun. Tchrs. of English, Vladimir Nabokov Soc., Phi Beta Kappa. Jewish. Home: 96-13 68th Ave Forest Hills NY 11375-5039 Office: CCNY Dept English New York NY 10031

MALIN, MICHAEL CHARLES, space scientist, former geology educator; b. Burbank, Calif., May 10, 1950; s. Jack and Beatryce (Solomon) M. AB, U. Calif., Berkeley, 1971; PhD, Calif. Inst. Tech., 1976. Sr. scientist Jet Propulsion Lab., Pasadena, Calif., 1975-78, mem. tech. staff, 1978-79; asst. prof. geology Ariz. State U., Tempe, 1979-82, assoc. prof., 1982-87, prof., 1987-91; pres. Malin Space Sci. Systems, San Diego, 1991—. Co-author: Earthlike Planets, 1981; contbr. articles to profl. jours. MacArthur fellow, 1987-92. Mem. Am. Geophys. Union, Am. Astron. Soc. (div. Planetary Scis.). Office: Malin Space Sci Systems PO Box 910148 San Diego CA 92191-0148

MALIN, ROBERT ABERNETHY, investment management executive; b. Mt. Vernon, N.Y., Dec. 13, 1931; s. Patrick Murphy and Caroline Cooper (Biddle) M.; m. Gail Lassiter, Nov. 5, 1960; children: Alison Campbell, Robert Lassiter. A.B., Dartmouth Coll., 1953, M.B.A., 1954. Asst. to comptroller Biddle Purchasing Co., N.Y.C., 1958-59; with Blyth & Co., Inc., N.Y.C., 1960-71; v.p. Blyth & Co., Inc., 1965-71, dir., 1968-71, sr. v.p., mem. exec. com., 1971-72; sr. v.p. corp. fin. Reynolds Securities Inc., N.Y.C., 1972-74; dir. Reynolds Securities Inc., 1973-74; mng. dir. First Boston Corp., N.Y.C., 1974-90; gen. ptnr. Tiedemann Investment Group, N.Y.C., 1991—. Mem. adv. council Fin. Acctg. Standards Bd., 1973-78. Served as lt. (j.g.) USNR, 1954-57. Mem. Investment Bankers Assn. Am. (v.p. exec. com. 1970-71), Securities Industry Assn. (acctg. com.), Links Club, Bond Club, Beacon Hill Club (Summit, N.J.), Morris County (N.J.) Club, Harbour Ridge Club (Stuart, Fla.). Republican. Home: 105 Whittredge Rd Summit NJ 07901-3709 Office: Tiedemann Investment Group 535 Madison Ave New York NY 10022-4212

MALINA, JUDITH, actress, director, producer, writer; b. Kiel, Germany, June 4, 1926; came to U.S., 1945; d. Max and Rosel (Zamora) M.; m. Julian Beck, Oct. 30, 1948 (dec.); m. Hanon Reznikov, May 6, 1988; children—Garrick Maxwell, Isha Manna. Graduate, Dramatic Workshop, New Sch. Social Research, 1945-47. adj. prof. Columbia U. Founder, producer, actress, dir. The Living Theatre, 1947—; dir., actress: The Thirteenth God, Childish Jokes, Ladies Voices, He Who Says Yes and He Who Says No, The Dialogue of the Mannequin and the Young Man, 1951, Man Is Man, 1962, Mysteries and Smaller Pieces, 1964, Antigone, 1965, Paradise Now, 1968, The Legacy of Cain (including Seven Meditations on Political Sadomasochism), 1970-77, Strike Support Oratorium, 1974, Six Public Acts, The Money Tower, 1975, Prometheus, 1978, Masse Mensch, 1980, The Living Theatre Retrospectacle, 1986, The Zero Method, 1991; dir.: Doctor Faustus Lights the Lights, 1951, Desire Trapped by the Tail, Faustina, Sweeney Agonistes, The Heroes, Ubu the King, 1952, The Age of Anxiety, The Spook Sonata, Orpheus, 1954, The Connection, 1959, In the Jungle of Cities, 1960, The Apple, 1961, The Mountain Giants 1962, The Brig, 1963, The Maids, Frankenstein, 1965, The Archeology of Sleep, 1983, Kassandra, 1987, Us, 1987, VKTMS, 1988, I and I, 1989, German Requiem, 1990, Not in My Name, 1994; actress: The Idiot King, 1954, Tonight We Improvise, Phedre, The Young Disciple, 1955, Many Loves, The Cave at Machpelah, 1959, Women of Trachis, 1960, The Yellow Methuselah, 1982, Poland/1931, 1988, Anarchia, 1993; appeared in films: Flaming Creatures, 1962, Amore, Amore, 1966, Wheel of Ashes, 1967, Le Compromise, 1968, Etre Libre, 1968, Paradise Now, 1969, Dog Day Afternoon, 1974, Signals Through the Flames, 1983, Radio Days, 1986, China Girl, 1987, Lost Paradise, 1988, Enemies, A Love Story, 1989, Awakenings, 1990, The Addams Family, 1991, Household Saints, 1993; author: Paradise Now, 1971, The Enormous Despair, 1972, The Legacy of Cain (3 pilot projects), 1973, Seven Meditations on Political Sadomasochism, 1977, Living Means Theater, 1978, Theatre Diaries: Brazil and Bologna, 1978, Poems of a Wandering Jewess, 1983, The Diaries of Judith Malina 1947-57, 1984; translator: Antigone (B. Brecht), 1990. Vice chmn. U.S. Com. for Justice to Latin Am. Polit. Prisoners, 1973-74; sponsor Am. Friends of Brazil, 1973; mem. exec. coun. War Resisters League. Recipient Lola D'Annunzio award, 1959, Page One award Newspaper Guild, 1960, Obie awards, 1960, 1964, 1969, 1975, 87, 89, Grand Prix de Theatre des Nations, 1961, Paris Critics Circle medallion, 1961, Prix de l'Universite Paris, 1961, New Eng. Theatre Conf. award, 1962, Olympio prize Italy, 1967, 9th Centennial medal U. Bologna, Italy, 1988; named Humanist of the Yr., 1984; Guggenheim fellow, 1985. Office: Writers & Artists Agency 19 W 44th St Ste 100 New York NY 10036*

MALINA, MICHAEL, lawyer; b. Bklyn., Mar. 20, 1936; s. William and Jean (Kutlowitz) M.; m. Anita May Oppenheim, June 22, 1958; children: Rachel Lynn, Stuart Charles, Joel Martin. AB, Harvard U., 1957, LLB, 1960. Bar: N.Y. 1961, U.S. Dist. Ct. (so. and ea. dists.) N.Y. 1962, U.S. Ct. Appeals (2d, 3d, 4th, 9th, and D.C. cirs.) 1965, U.S. Supreme Ct. 1965, U.S. Tax Ct. 1991. Assoc. Kaye, Scholer, Fierman, Hays & Handler, N.Y.C., 1960-69, ptnr., 1969—. Contbr. articles to profl. jours. Mem. ABA (antitrust sect.), N.Y. State Bar Assn. (exec. com. antitrust sect. 1995—, chmn. 1975-82, sec. 1996—, Robinson-Patman act com.), Assn. of Bar of City of N.Y. (profl. ethics com. 1985-88), Phi Beta Kappa. Democrat. Jewish. Home: 12 Innes Rd Scarsdale NY 10583-7110 Office: Kaye Scholer Fierman Hays & Handler 425 Park Ave New York NY 10022-3506

MALINA, ROBERT S., investment company executive; b. 1935. BA, Cornell U., 1960; JD, Harvard, 1963. Law clk. to Hon. Jay E Lombard U.S. Ct. Appeals, 1963-70; v.p. E.M. Wardburg, Pincus & Co., N.Y.C., 1970-80; pres. Robert S. Malina, Inc., N.Y.C., 1980—; chmn., CEO Supermarket Devel. Corp., Albuquerque; Independent Investment Banker. Office: Supermarket Development Corp 3 Lincoln Ctr New York NY 10023*

MALING, GEORGE CROSWELL, JR., physicist; b. Boston, Mass., Feb. 24, 1931; s. George Croswell and Marjory (Bell) M.; m. Norah J. Horsfield, Dec. 29, 1960; children: Ellen P., Barbara J., Jeffrey C. A.B., Bowdoin Coll., 1954; S.B., S.M., MIT, 1954, Elec. Engr., 1958, Ph.D., 1963. Rsch. asst., postdoctoral fellow MIT, 1957-65; adv. physicist IBM Corp., 1965-71; sr. physicist IBM Corp., Poughkeepsie, N.Y., 1971-92; pres. Empire State Software Systems, Ltd., 1992-93; dir. Noise Control Found., Inc., Poughkeepsie, 1975—; chmn. com. Sl-acoustics Am. Nat. Standards Com., 1976-79; dir. Inst. Noise Control Engring. Found., Inc., 1993—; mng. dir. Inst. of Noise Control Engring., 1994—. Editor: Noise/News, 1972-92; mng. editor: Noise/News, 1972-92; mng. editor: Noise/News Internat., 1993—; assoc. editor Jour. Acoustical Soc. Am., 1976-83; editor tech. proc.; contbr. numerous articles to profl. jours. Served with U.S. Army, 1955-57. Fellow IEEE, AAAS, Acoustical Soc. Am. (exec. coun. 1980-83, Silver medal in noise 1992), Audio Engring. Soc.; mem. Inst. Noise Control Engring. (bd. dirs. 1972-77, pres. 1975), Internat. Inst. Noise Control Engring. (bd. dirs. 1980-86, 90—). Office: Noise Control Foundation PO Box 2469 Arlington Br Poughkeepsie NY 12603-8880

MALINO, JEROME R., rabbi; b. N.Y.C., June 7, 1911; s. Wolf and Henrietta (Rosenbaum) M.; m. Rhoda Simon, June 9, 1936; children: Frances, Jonathan. B.A., CCNY, 1931; M.H.L., Jewish Inst. Religion, 1935; L.H.D. (hon.), Alfred (N.Y.) U., 1958; D.D. (hon.), Hebrew Union Coll., 1960. Rabbi Baldwin (N.Y.) Jewish Center, 1934-35, United Jewish Center, Danbury, Conn., 1935-81; rabbi emeritus United Jewish Center, 1981—; chaplain Fed. Correctional Inst., Danbury, 1940-83; lectr. Western Conn. State U., 1983-84; adj. lectr. Hebrew Union Coll.-Jewish Inst. Religion, 1983—; a founder Jewish Fedn. Danbury, pres., 1947-50. Mem. Danbury Bd. Edn., 1949-69, pres. alternate yrs., 1951-69; bd. dirs. Danbury Cmty. Action Com.; mem. Danbury Charter Revision Com., 1976, Mayor of Danbury Ad Hoc Com. Racism, 1976. Mem. Central Conf. Am. Rabbis (pres. 1979-81), Assn. Religious Communities (pres. 1982-84), Jewish Peace Fellowship, Inst. Religion in Age of Sci., Danbury Music Center, Danbury Concert Assn. Home: 77 Garfield Ave Danbury CT 06810-7906 Office: 141 Deer Hill Ave Danbury CT 06810-7726 *The best way to enhance the meaning of one's own life is to place human values everywhere before all other considerations.*

MALINO, JOHN GRAY, real estate executive; b. N.Y.C., Oct. 15, 1939; s. Joseph and Dorothy (Gray) M.; m. Geraldine Seibel, Mar. 24, 1963 (div.); m. Phyllis Susan Alter, Mar. 29, 1987; children: Joanne, Linda. BA, NYU, 1961. Lic. real estate broker, N.Y. Real estate broker Robert Joseph, N.Y.C., 1961-64; asst. v.p. Loews Corp., N.Y.C., 1964-83, v.p., 1983—. Chmn. Young Men's and Women's Real Estate Assn., N.Y., 1974, N.Y.C. Real Estate Bd., 1982. Lodge: B'nai B'rith (pres. real estate div.). Home: 553 Barnard Ave Woodmere NY 11598-2707 Office: Loews Corp 667 Madison Ave New York NY 10021-8029

MALIS, LEONARD IRVING, neurosurgeon; b. Phila., Nov. 23, 1919; s. Morris Melvin and Dorothy (Brodsky) M.; m. Ruth Gornstein, June 24, 1942; children: Larry Alan, Lynne Paula. MD, U. Va., 1943. Intern Phila. Gen. Hosp., 1943-44; resident in neurology Mt. Sinai Hosp., N.Y.C., 1947, resident in neurosurgery, 1948-50, neurosurgeon in chief, dir. dept. neurol. surgery, 1970-92; prof., chmn. dept. neurosurgery Mt. Sinai Sch. Medicine, CUNY, 1970-92, prof. emeritus dept. neurosurgery, 1993—; fellow in neurophysiology Med. Sch., Yale U., 1951; practice medicine specializing in neurosurgery N.Y.C., 1951—; cons. in field. Contbr. numerous articles to profl. jours.; developer various surg. and electronic instruments. Capt. M.C., U.S. Army, World War II. Mem. ACS, Am. Assn. Neurol. Surgery, Congress Neurol. Surgeons, Am. Physiol. Soc., Soc. Neurosci., Am. Acad. Neurol. Surgery, Soc. Neurol. Surgeons, Alpha Omega Alpha. Office: 1148 5th Ave New York NY 10128-0807

MALITZ, SIDNEY, psychiatrist, educator, researcher; b. N.Y.C., Apr. 20, 1923; s. Benjamin and Etta (Cohen) M. Student, NYU, 1940-42, Tulane U., 1942-43; BM, Chgo. Med. Coll., 1946, MD, 1947. Diplomate Am. Bd. Psychiatry and Neurology. Intern St. Mary's Hosp., Huntington, W.Va., 1946-47; sr. intern Bethesda, Hosp., Cin., 1947-48; resident N.Y. State Psychiat. Inst., N.Y.C., 1948-51; sr. research psychiatrist N.Y. State Psychiat. Inst., 1954-56, acting prin. research psychiatrist, 1956-58, acting chief psychiat. research, chief dept. exptl. psychiatry, 1958-64, chief psychiat. research dept. exptl. psychiatry, 1964-72, dep. dir., 1972-75, acting dir., 1975-76, 81-84, dep. dir., 1976-78, dir. dept. biol. psychiatry, 1984-91; in charge psychiat. drug clinic Vanderbilt Clinic, Presbyn. Hosp., N.Y.C., 1956-75, asst. attending psychiatrist, 1960-66, assoc. attending psychiatrist, 1966-71, attending psychiatrist, 1971-93, acting dir. psychiatry service, 1975-76, 81-84, 93—, consulting psychiatrist; asst. dept. psychiatry Coll. Physicians and Surgeons, Columbia U., N.Y.C., 1955-57, assoc., 1957-59, asst. clin. prof., 1959-65, assoc. prof., 1965-69, prof., 1969-93, vice chmn. dept. psychiatry, 1972-75, acting chmn., 1975-76, 81-84, vice chmn., 1976-78, prof. emeritus, 1993—; mem. panel impartial psychiat. experts N.Y. State Supreme Ct., 1960—; mem. adv. com. subcom.; cons. U.S. Pharmacopeia; mem. adv. com. subcom. health N.Y. State Constl. Conv.; cons. div. med. scis. NRC, Washington, 1967-70; cons. Rush Found., Los Angeles, 1968-75; mem. ad hoc rev. com. to select Nat. Drug Abuse Research Ctrs., Ctr. Studies Narcotic and Drug Abuse, NIMH, 1972-73. Contbr. numerous articles to profl. jours. Recipient Leonard Caemmer award N.Y. State Psychiatric Inst., 1984. Fellow Royal Soc. Medicine (life), Am. Psychiat. Assn. (life, chmn. com. biol. psychiatry 1961-62, program com. 1961-62, sec-treas. chpt. 1962-63, com. rsch. 1966-68, pres. chpt. 1969-70, chmn. Coun. Rsch. and Devel. 1971-73, History and Libr. com. 1989-91), Am. Coll. Neuropsychopharmacology (life); mem. AAAS (coun. 1969-72), N.Y. Acad. Medicine (life), Collegium Internationale Neuropsychopharmacologicum (life), Am. Coll. Psychiatrists (archivist-historian 1978—, liaison to Royal Coll. Psychiatrists 1985—, Bowis award 1989), Royal Coll. Psychiatrists, Am. Coll. Psychoanalysts, N.Y. Soc. Clin. Psychiatry, Assn. Research Nervous and Mental Disease, N.Y. State, N.Y. County med. socs., AMA (cons. coun.l drugs 1960-70), Group Advancement of Psychiatry (rsch. com. 1986-91), N.Y. Acad. Scis, N.Y. Psychiat. Soc. (v.p. 1989-91, pres. 1991-92), Am. Psychopath. Assn., Soc. Biol. Psychiatry, Benjamin Rush Soc. (pres.-elect 1989, pres. 1990-91), Vidonian Soc. (pres. 1989-93), Alpha Omega Alpha. Office: Columbia U Dept Psychiatry 161 Fort Washington Ave New York NY 10032-3713

MALKASIAN, GEORGE DURAND, JR., physician, educator; b. Springfield, Mass., Oct. 26, 1927; s. George Dur and Gladys Mildred (Trombley) M.; m. Mary Ellen Koch, Oct. 16, 1954; children: Linda Jeanne, Karen Diane, Martha Ellen. AB, Yale U., 1950; MD, Boston U., 1954; MS, U. Minn., 1963. Diplomate Am. Bd. Ob-Gyn. Intern Worcester (Mass.) City Hosp., 1954-55; resident in ob-gyn Mayo Grad. Sch. Hosp., Rochester, Minn., 1955-58, 60-61; mem. faculty Mayo Med. Sch., 1962—, prof. ob-gyn, 1976—, chmn. dept. ob-gyn, 1976-86. Author articles in field. Served to lt. comdr. M.C., USNR, 1958-60. Named Tchr. of Yr., Mayo Grad. Sch. Medicine, 1973, 77, Alumnus of Yr., Boston U. Sch. Med., 1990. Mem. ACS, Am. Coll. Obstetricians and Gynecologists, Am. Gynecol. and Obstet. Soc., Am. Radium Soc., Soc. Gynecologic Oncologists, Assn. Profs. Ob-gyn., N.Am. Ob-gyn. Soc., Ctrl. Assn. Obstetricians and Gynecologists, Minn. Soc. Obstetricians and Gynecologists, Am. Coll. Obstetricians and Gynecologists (pres. 1989-90), Zumbro Valley Med. Soc. (exec. dir. 1996—). Home: 1750 11th Ave NE Rochester MN 55906-4215 Office: Mayo Clinic 200 1st St SW Rochester MN 55905-0001

MALKAWI, ALI MAHMOUD, architecture educator, researcher; b. Irbid, Jordan, Feb. 12, 1967; came to U.S., 1989; s. Mahmoud Ahmed and Safia (Khatib) M.; m. Jenae Joy Huey, Dec. 21, 1991. BS in Archtl. Engring. with honors, Jordan U. Sci. and Tech., Irbid, 1989; MArch, U. Colo., Denver, 1990; PhD with honors, Ga. Inst. Tech., 1994. Project designer Malkawi Cons. Engrs., Amman, Jordan, 1989; instr. Ga. Inst. Tech., Atlanta, 1992-94, doctoral fellow, 1991-94, project coord., 1994; vis. asst. prof. architecture U. Mich., Ann Arbor, 1994—, postdoctoral/Oberdick fellow, 1994-95; pres. Intelligenet Energy Optimization Cons., Ann Arbor, 1995—. Mem. ASHRAE, Acoustical Soc. Am., Illumination Engring. Soc., Am. Solar Energy Soc. Achievements include copyrighted theory development and implementation of intelligent CAD software. Office: U Mich Coll Architecture 2000 Bonisteel Dr Ann Arbor MI 48109-2069

MALKIEL, BURTON GORDON, economics educator; b. Boston, Aug. 28, 1932; s. Sol and Celia (Gordon) M.; m. Judith Ann Atherton, July 16, 1954 (dec. 1987); 1 child, Jonathan; m. Nancy Weiss, July 31, 1988. BA, Harvard, 1953, MBA, 1955; PhD, Princeton, 1964. Assoc. Smith Barney & Co., N.Y.C., 1958-60; asst. prof. dept. econs. Princeton U., 1964-66, assoc. prof., 1966-68, prof., 1968-81, Rentschler prof. econs., 1969-81, chmn. dept. econs., 1974-75, 77-81; dean Sch. Orgn. and Mgmt., Yale U., 1981-87; Chem. Bank chmn.'s prof. econs. Princeton U., 1988—; mem. Pres.'s Council Econ. Advisors, 1975-77; bd. govs. Am. Stock Exchange; dir. Amdahl Corp., Jeffrey Co., So. New Eng. Telephone Co., Prudential Life Ins. Co. Am., Baker, Fentress & Co., Vanguard Group. Author: The Term Structure of Interest Rates, 1966, (with others) Strategies and Rational Decisions in the Securities Options Market, 1969, A Random Walk Down Wall Street, 1973, 6th edit., 1996, The Inflation-Beater's Investment Guide, 1980. Served to 1st lt. AUS, 1955-58. Mem. Am. Fin. Assn. (dir., pres. 1978). Home: 76 North Rd Princeton NJ 08540-2430 Office: Princeton U Dept Econs Princeton NJ 08544

MALKIEL, NANCY WEISS, college dean, history educator; b. Newark, Feb. 14, 1944; d. William and Ruth Sylvia (Puder) W.; m. Burton G. Malkiel, July 31, 1988. BA summa cum laude, Smith Coll., 1965; MA, Harvard U., 1966, PhD, 1970. Asst. prof. history Princeton (N.J.) U., 1969-75, assoc. prof., 1975-82, prof., 1982—, master Dean Mathey Coll., 1982-86, dean of coll., 1987—. Author (as Nancy J. Weiss): Charles Francis Murphy, 1858-1924: Respectability and Responsibility in Tammany Politics, 1968, (with others) Blacks in America: Bibliographical Essays, 1971, The National Urban League, 1910-1940, 1974, Farewell to the Party of Lincoln: Black Politics in the Age of FDR, 1983 (Berkshire Conf. of Women Historians prize 1984), Whitney M. Young Jr., and the Struggle for Civil Rights, 1989. Trustee Smith Coll., Northampton, Mass., 1984-94, Woodrow Wilson Nat. Fellowship Found., 1975—. Fellow Woodrow Wilson Found., 1965, Charles Warren Ctr. for Studies in Am. History, 1976-77, Radcliffe Inst., 1976-77, Ctr. for Advanced Study in Behavioral Scis., 1986-87. Mem. Am. Hist. Assn., Orgn. Am. Historians (chmn. status women hist. profession 1972-75), So. Hist. Assn., Phi Beta Kappa. Democrat. Jewish. Office: Princeton U Office Dean Of College Princeton NJ 08544

MALKIEL, YAKOV, linguistics educator; b. Kiev, Russia, July 22, 1914; came to U.S., 1940, naturalized, 1946; s. Léon and Claire (Saitzew) M.; m. María Rosa Lida, Mar. 2, 1948 (dec. Sept. 1962). Matura, Werner-Siemens Realgymnasium, Berlin-Schöneberg, 1933; PhD magna cum laude, Friedrich-Wilhelms Universität, Berlin, 1938; LHD (hon.), U. Chgo., 1969; LLD (hon.), U. Ill., 1976; Dr honoris causa, U. Paris, 1983, Free U., W. Berlin, 1983, Georgetown U., 1987, Oxford U., 1989, Salamanca U., 1992. Instr. U. Wyo., 1942; lectr. U. Calif.-Berkeley, 1942-45, instr., 1945-46, asst. prof., 1946-48, assoc. prof., 1948-52, prof. Romance philology, 1952-66, mem. grad. council, 1953-57, assoc. dean grad. div., 1963-66, prof. linguistics and Romance philology, 1966-85, 86, 88, research fellow in the humanities, 1968-69, research prof. humanities, 1981; research assoc. Mills Coll., summers 1942-43; vis. assoc. prof. U. So. Calif., summer 1949; vis. lectr. Ind. U., summer 1953; vis. prof. U. Colo., summer 1958, U. Tex. Linguistic Inst., summer 1960, Linguistic Inst., Ind. U., summer 1964, Linguistic Inst., UCLA, 1966; Collitz prof. Linguistics Inst., 1980; vis. lectr. cursos superiores Melsaga U., 1989-92; lectr. Jennifer summer inst., Soria, Spain; cons. various panels NEH, 1978—; participant symposium Inst. Italian Ency., Rome. Editor in chief Romance Philology Quar., 1947-82, cons. editor, 1982—; assoc. editor Hispanic Rev., Jour. Hispanic Rsch. (London), Romance Quar. (Ky.), Revista de Filologia Española, Voz y Letra (Málaga); author: Essays on Linguistic Themes, 1968, Etymological Dictionaries: A Typological Survey, 1976, Theory and Practice of Romance Etymology, 1989, Etymology; also monographs, articles U.S. and fgn. countries; contbr. to Dictionary of the Middle Ages, Ency. of Romance Linguistics, Ency. of Lexicography. Recipient Guggenheim Meml. Found. 3d award, 1967; Berkeley citation U. Calif., 1985; Faculty Rsch. lectr. U. Calif. Berkeley, 1988-89; Guggenheim fellow, 1948-49, 59; NSF sr. postdoctoral fellow, 1966; Princeton U. fellow, 1977. Mem. Am. Acad. Arts and Scis., Linguistic Soc. Am. (pres. 1965), MLA (founder Romance linguistics group 1946), Linguistic Soc. Paris, Am. Oriental Soc., Philol. Assn. Pacific Coast (v.p. 1963, pres. 1965), Société de Linguistique Romane (exec. com. 1977, 79, 89), Royal Spanish Acad. (corr. mem. 1987—), Società di linguistica italiana (hon.), Ctr. Romance Studies, U. London. Home: 1 Arlington Ln Kensington CA 94707-1108

MALKIN, BARRY, film editor, consultant; b. N.Y.C., Oct. 26, 1938; s. Richard and Helen (Kandix) M.; m. Stephanie Byer, Apr. 5, 1971; 1 child, Sacha Janine. BA, Adelphi U., 1960. Freelance film editor Sacha Prodns., Inc., N.Y.C., 1964—. Editor: (films) The Rain People, 1969, They Might Be Giants, 1971, Who is Harry Kellerman and Why Is He Saying All Those Terrible Things About Me?, 1971, Cops and Robbers, 1973, One Summer Love, 1976, Somebody Killed Her Husband, 1978, Last Embrace, 1979, (with Edward Beyer and David Ray) One Trick Pony, 1980, Windows, 1980, (with Mark Laub) Four Friends, 1981, (with Laub, Robert Q. Lovett and Randy Roberts) Hammett, 1982, Rumble Fish, 1983, (with Lovett) The Cotton Club, 1984 (Acad. award nominee for best film editing 1984), Peggy Sue Got Married, 1986, Gardens of Stone, 1987, Big, 1988, New York Stories ("Life Without Zoe"), 1989, The Freshman, 1990, (with Lisa Fruchtman and Walter Murch) The Godfather Part III, 1990 (Acad. award nominee for best film editing 1990), Honeymoon in Vegas, 1992, It Could Happen to You, 1994, Jack, 1996. Mem. Acad. Motion Picture Arts and Scis., Motion Picture Editors. Home and Office: 275 Central Park W New York NY 10024

MALKIN, CARY JAY, lawyer; b. Chgo., Oct. 6, 1949; s. Arthur D. and Perle (Slavin) M.; m. Lisa Klimley, Oct. 27, 1976; children: Dorothy R., Victoria S., Lydia R. BA, George Washington U., 1971; JD, Northwestern U., 1974. Bar: Ill. 1974, U.S. Dist. Ct. (no. dist.) Ill. 1974. Assoc., Mayer, Brown & Platt, Chgo., 1974-80, ptnr., 1981—. Chmn. spl. events com. Mental Health Assn., 1984-85; mem. steering com. Endowment Campaign of the Latin Sch. Chgo, 1988-92; chmn. annual fund The Latin Sch. of Chgo., 1990-91, trustee, 1991—, v.p., 1992—, chmn. capital campaign, 1995—; mem. exec. com. Friends of Prentice Women's Hosp., 1991-92; bd. dirs. SOS Children's Village Ill., 1992—; mem. M.S. Weiss fund bd. Children's Meml. Hosp., 1989-93; mem. Graziano Fund bd. Children's Meml. Hosp., 1993-96; mem. steering com. Founder's Coun. Field Mus., 1995—. Mem. Order of the Coif, Phi Beta Kappa. Clubs: Saddle and Cycle, Standard, Chicago. Home: 233 E Walton St Chicago IL 60611-1526 Office: Mayer Brown & Platt 190 S La Salle St Chicago IL 60603-3410

MALKIN, JUDD D., diversified corporation executive; b. 1937; married. BS, U. Ill., 1959. CPA, Ill. Pres. Amco Industries, until 1969, Mid-Southern Toyota Distbrs. Inc.; chmn. bd. JMB Realty Corp., Chgo., 1969—; also exec. v.p. Amfac Inc. subs. JMB Realty Corp. Office: JMB Realty Corp 900 N Michigan Ave Chicago IL 60611-1542*

MALKIN, MOSES MONTEFIORE, employee benefits administration company executive; b. Revere, Mass., Sept. 18, 1919; s. Irving and Annie (Helfant) M.; m. Hannah Lacob, Oct. 11, 1941. AB, U. N.C., 1941; BSME, Columbia U., 1948. Enrolled actuary and chartered life underwriter. Engr. GE, Schenectady, N.Y., 1948-50; engr. Gen. Bronze, Inc., Jersey City, 1950-51; v.p. Malkin Warehouse, Inc., New Haven, 1951-57; pvt. practice actuary New Haven, 1957-72; chmn., actuary Profl. Pensions, Inc., East Haven, Conn., 1972—; presenter pension issues at numerous confs., 1970-80. Pres., founder Milford, Conn., 1962, Milford Child Guidance Clinic, 1966; pres. Clifford Beers Child Guidance, New Haven, 1971, Jewish Family Svc., New Haven, 1973. With U.S. Army, 1941-46, ETO. Mem. Am. Acad. Actuaries, Am. Soc. Pension Actuaries (instr. 1984), Am. Soc. Chartered Life Underwriters, Grads. Club (New Haven), Phi Beta Kappa, Tau Beta Pi. Jewish. Home: Four Tumblebrook Rd Woodbridge CT 06525 Office: Profl Pensions Inc 444 Foxon Rd New Haven CT 06513-2019

MALKIN, PETER LAURENCE, lawyer; b. N.Y.C., Jan. 14, 1934; s. Samuel and Gertrude (Greenberger) M.; m. Isabel L. Wien, July 10, 1955; children: Scott David, Cynthia Allison, Anthony Edward. Grad. cum laude, Poly. Prep. Country Day Sch., 1951; AB summa cum laude, Harvard U., 1955, LLB magna cum laude, 1958. Bar: N.Y. 1958, Conn. 1976, Fla. 1977. Sr. ptnr., chmn. Wien, Malkin & Bettex, N.Y.C. and Palm Beach, Fla., 1960—; gen. ptnr. Empire State Bldg. Assocs., 1961—, 1185 Ave. of Ams. Assocs., N.Y.C., 1978—; bd. dirs. U.S. Trust Corp., N.Y.C. Partnership and C. of C., 1992—; chmn. W&M Properties, Inc., Grand Ctrl. Partnership Inc., 34th St. Partnership, Inc.; dir. Fashion Ctr. Bus. Improvement Dist.; dir. Realty Found. N.Y., 1981—, v.p., 1995—; mem. adv. com. Greenwich (Conn.) Japanese Sch., 1992—; gov. Real Estate Bd., N.Y., 1993—. Nat. vice chmn. Harvard Law Sch. Fund, 1967-71, chmn. nat. scholarship com., 1975-76, chmn. N.Y.C. com., 1981-83; founder, bd. dirs. Urban League Southwestern Fairfield County, 1969-73, treas., 1969-71; bd. dirs., mem. exec. com. Lincoln Ctr. for Performing Arts, 1979—; bd. dirs. Inst. Internat. Edn., 1983-89, hon. 1994—; mem. devel. com. N.Y. Pub. Libr., 1979—; trustee Nat. Trust for Hist. Preservation, 1988-91; founding chmn. Greenwich (Conn.) Green & Clean, Inc., 1986—; v.p., mem. exec. com. Greenwich chpt. NAACP, 1967-69; trustee Citizens Budget Commn., N.Y.C., 1971-91, Jewish Communal Fund, N.Y., 1976-81; hon. trustee Assoc. YM and YWHA Greater N.Y.; dean's coun., Harvard U., 1987—; chmn. capital campaign and mem. overseers com. to visit Kennedy Sch. Govt., 1976-82, 83-89, 90—, to visit Harvard Law Sch. 1977-83; mem. exec. com. Program for Ctr. for Jewish Studies, 1974-80; bd. overseers Harvard Coll., 1989-95, mem. overseers com. univ resources, 1972-75, exec. com., 1985—; dean's adv. com., Harvard Law Sch., 1988-90; chmn. steering com. N.Y. Major Gifts, Harvard Coll. Fund, 1989-93; elected dir. Harvard Alumni Assn., 1981-83; chmn. schs. and scholarship com. Harvard U., Greenwich, 1973-79; exec. com. Assn. Better N.Y., 1972—. Recipient Nat. Honor award Nat. Trust Hist. Preservation, 1987, President's award Grad. Sch. and Univ. Ctr. CCNY, 1989, Crain's All-Star award, 1994, Nacore Disting. Man of Yr. award, 1995; named Outstanding Young Man, N.Y.C. Jaycees, 1969, fellow Brandeis U., 1970—, Man of Yr., Hist. Soc. Greenwich, Conn., 1993. Mem. Harvard Law Sch. Assn. N.Y.C. (trustee 1968-70, v.p. 1973-74, mem. coun.), Assn. Bar City N.Y. (mem. com. admissions 1965-68, com. assn. bldgs. 1968-72, chmn. com. ins. assn. bldgs. 1967-68), Am. Arbitration Assn. (nat. panel arbitrators), Century Assn., The Links N.Y., The Hasty Pudding Inst. 1770, AD Hon., Harvard Varsity Club (Cambridge), Harvard Club N.Y.C. (bd. mgrs. 1979-81), Harvard Club (Fairfield County, Conn., v.p. 1974-75, bd. dirs. 1976-80), Bailwick Club (founding pres.), Blind Brook Club, Phi Beta Kappa. Office: 60 E 42nd St New York NY 10165 Also: Royal Poinciana Plz Palm Beach FL 33480-4020

MALKIN, ROGER D., agricultural products executive; b. 1931. With Federal Compress & Warehouse Co., Memphis, 1968-69, Southwide Inc., Scott, Miss., 1968-69; now chmn. bd. dirs., CEO Delta & Pine Land Co., Scott, Miss., 1972—. Office: Delta & Pine Land Co 1 Cotton Row Scott MS 38772*

MALKIN, STANLEY LEE, neurologist; b. Pitts., Nov. 11, 1942; s. Maurice and Bessie Beatrice (Serbin) M.; children: Justin Ross, Keith Richard. BA with honors, U. Pa., 1964; MD, U. Pitts., 1968; Intern, Montefiore Hosp., Pitts., 1968-69; resident in neurology Columbia-Presbyn. Med. Center, N.Y.C., 1969-72; chief neurology service Wright-Patterson AFB, Dayton, Ohio, 1972-74; practice medicine specializing in neurology, N.Y.C.; attending staff Mt. Sinai Hosp.; former dir. Neuro-Diagnostic Lab, Englewood; asst. clin. prof. neurology Mt. Sinai Sch. of Medicine; founder Bergen-Passaic Tomography Center, Fairlawn, N.J.; neurology cons. Regent Hosp.; med. dir. Pain Suppression Labs., Inc.; med. dir. Efficient Health Systems, Inc.-N.Y.C. Healthline; founder, med. dir., exec. v.p. Hosp. Diagnostic Equipment Corp., 1987—; pres. Cancer Treatment Holdings, Inc, 1993-95, dir. 1993-94, sr. med. dir. 1995—; founder Montvale Med. Imaging Assocs. (N.J.), N.Y. Med. Imaging, N.Y.C., Hosp. Diagnostic Equipment Corp. Co-mcpl. coord. Ft. Lee Citizens for McGovern, 1972; ptnr. Sall/Myers Med. Assocs., prin. 1995—; mem. Edgewater Rent Control Bd., 1978, Nat. Headache Found. Maj. M.C., USAF, 1972-74. Diplomate Am. Bd. Psychiatry and Neurology, Nat. Bd. Med. Examiners. Mem. Am. Acad. Neurology, Am. Assn. Electrodiagnostic Medicine, Am. Soc. Neuro-Imaging (charter), Am. Med. EEG Soc., Am. Assn. for Study of Headache, Nat. Headache Found., Internat. Headache Soc., N.Y. Acad. Scis., N.Y.U. Bellevue Psychiat. Soc. Office: 120 W 44th St Ste 701 New York NY 10036 also: 136 E 57th St Ste 600 New York NY 10022

MALKINSON, FREDERICK DAVID, dermatologist; b. Hartford, Conn., Feb. 26, 1924; s. John Walter and Rose (Volkenheim) M.; m. Una Zwick, June 15, 1979; children by previous marriage: Philip, Carol, John. Student, Loomis Inst., 1937-41; 3 yr. cert. cum laude, Harvard U., 1943, D.M.D., 1947, M.D., 1949. Intern Harvard-Beth Israel Hosp., Boston, 1949-50; resident in dermatology U. Chgo., 1950-54, from instr. to assoc. prof. dept. dermatology, 1954-68; prof. medicine and dermatology U. Ill., Chgo., 1968-71; chmn. dept. dermatology Rush Med. Coll. and Rush-Presbyn.-St. Luke's Med. Ctr., Chgo., 1971-92, Clark W. Finnerud, M.D. prof. dept. dermatology, 1981-95; trustee Sulzberger Inst. Dermatol. Comm. and Edn., 1976-96; pres. Sulzberger Inst. Dermatol. Communication and Edn., 1983-88, 93-96. Editor: Year Book of Dermatology, 1971-78; chief editor: AMA

Archives of Dermatology, 1979-83; bd. editors, 1976-84, Jour. AMA, 1979-83; editorial cons. World Book Medical Encyclopedia, 1991—; contbr. articles and abstracts to profl. jours., chpts. to books. Active Evanston (Ill.) Libr. Bd., 1988-94, pres., 1993-94. With M.C. USN, 1950-52. Grantee U.S. Army, 1955-61, USPHS, 1962-73. Mem. AAAS, Am. Acad. Dermatology (v.p. 1987-89, dir. 1964-67), Am. Dermatol. Assn., Soc. Investigative Dermatology (v.p. 1978-79, dir. 1963-68), Am. Fedn. Clin. Rsch., Cen. Soc. Clin. Rsch., Radiation Rsch. Soc., Assn. Profs. of Dermatology (dir. 1982-85), Dermatology Found. (trustee 1980-93, pres. 1983-85), Nat. Coun. on Radiation Protection and Measurements (mem. com. on cutaneous radiobiology 1986-92), Chgo. Dermatol. Soc. (pres. 1964-65, Gold Medal award 1992), Chgo. Lit. Club.

MALKKI, OLLI, paper company executive. Wtih Oy Warstila AB, Helsinki, Finland, 1974-85; pres. Ahlstrom Industrial Holdings, Glens Falls, N.Y., 1991—. Office: Ahlstrom Industrial Holdings 101 Ridge Ctr Glens Falls NY 12801*

MALKOVICH, JOHN, actor; b. Christopher, Ill., Dec. 9, 1953; m. Glenne Headley, 1982 (div.); children: Amandine and Loewy, with Nicoletta Peyran. Student, Eastern Ill. U., Ill. State U. Co-founder Steppenwolf Theatre, Chgo., 1976. Made N.Y.C. theatrical debut in True West, 1982 (Obie award, Clarence Derwent award); other theatrical appearances include: Death of a Salesman, 1984, Burn This, 1987, States of Shock; dir. Balm in Gilead, 1984-85, Arms and the Man, 1985, The Caretaker, 1986, Coyote Ugly, (Chgo., Kennedy Ctr. for Performing Arts, Washington) 1985, Libra, 1994, Steppenwolf, 1994; appeared in films Places in the Heart, 1984, The Killing Fields, 1984, Eleni, 1985, Making Mr. Right, 1987, Glass Menagerie, 1987, Empire of the Sun, 1987, Miles From Home, 1988, Dangerous Liaisons, 1988, The Sheltering Sky, 1990, Queen's Logic, 1991, The Object of Beauty, 1991, Shadows and Fog, 1992, Jennifer 8, 1992, Of Mice and Men, 1992, In The Line Of Fire, 1993 (Academy award nomination best supporting actor 1993), Alive, 1993, Touchstone, 1994, Para De La Nuages, 1994, Mary Reilly, 1994, Mulholland Falls, 1996; co-exec. prodr. The Accidental Tourist, 1988; appeared in TV films Word of Honor, 1981, American Dream, 1981, Death of a Salesman, 1985 (Emmy award 1986), Heart of Darkness, 1994. Office: ICM 8942 Wilshire Blvd Beverly Hills CA 90211*

MALKUS, DAVID STARR, mechanics educator, applied mathematician; b. Chgo., June 30, 1945; s. Willem V.R. Malkus and Joanne (Gerould) Simpson; m. Evelyn R. (div.); children: Christopher, Annelise, Byron, Renata. AB, Yale U., 1968; PhD, Boston U., 1976. Mathematician U.S. Nat. Bur. Standards, Gaithersburg, Md., 1975-77; asst. prof. math. Ill. Inst. Tech., Chgo., 1977-83, assoc. prof., 1983-84; assoc. prof. mechanics U. Wis., Madison, 1984-87, prof., 1987—, chmn. Rheology Rsch. Ctr., 1991-94; chair prof. Nanjing (People's Republic China) Aero. Inst., 1986. Co-author: Concepts and Applications of Finite Element Analysis, 1989; contbr. articles to Computer Methods Applied Mech. Engring., Jour. Computational Physics. Mem. Soc. Rheology. Achievements include research on finite element methods--reduced and selective integration techniques, a unification of concepts. Home: 5595 Mary Lake Rd Waunakee WI 53597-9124 Office: U Wis Dept NEEP 1500 Engineering Dr Madison WI 53706-1607

MALL, IDA, church administrator. Pres. Intl. Lutheran Women's Missionary League of the Lutheran Church MO Synod International Ctr., St. Louis. Office: Internat Luth Women's Missionary League 3558 S Jefferson Ave Saint Louis MO 63118-3910

MALL, WILLIAM JOHN, JR., aerospace executive, retired air force officer; b. Pitts., Jan. 13, 1933; s. William John and Margaret (Henry) M.; m. Vivian Lea Fenton; children—Michele, William, Catherine. B.B.A., U. Pitts., 1954; M.B.A., George Washington U., 1966; sr. mgrs. in govt. program, Harvard U., 1980. Commd. officer USAF, 1954, advanced through grades to maj. gen., 1981; insp. gen. Mil. Airlift Command., Scott AFB, Ill., 1978; comdr. 436 wing Mil. Airlift Command., Dover AFB, Del., 1979; DCS personnel Mil. Airlift Command, Scott AFB, Ill., 1979-81; comdr. Air Rescue Service, Scott AFB, Ill., 1981-83, 23d AF/MAC, Scott AFB, Ill., 1983-85; assigned to Hdqrs USAF, Bolling AFB, D.C., 1985-86; ret.; dir. integrated logistics support div. Douglas Aircraft Co., Long Beach, Calif., 1987-89, gen. mgr. human resources, 1989-91; exec. dir. LAX Two Corp., L.A., 1991—. Decorated Legion of Merit, Bronze Star, Air medal. Mem. Airlift Assn., Daedalians, Jolly Green Pilots Assn. Avocations: tennis, sailing. Office: LAX Two Corp 200 World Way Los Angeles CA 90045-5808

MALLARD, RUTH FRANCES, telecommunications company administrator; b. West Berlin, Germany, Apr. 21, 1963; came to U.S., 1971; d. Paul Bortner and Helen Joy (Higgins-Carter) Rohrbaugh; divorced. BSBA, U. Ctrl. Fla., 1985; postgrad., Rollins Coll., 1993—. Account exec. Metromedia, Orlando, Fla., 1985-87; account exec. MCI Telecomm., Orlando, 1987-91, mktg. mgr., 1991-94; area mgr. Alcoa, 1994—. Vol. WeCare, Orlando, 1992; asst. Dale Carnegie, Orlando, 1992. Mem. Orlando C. of C., So. Bell Large Users Group, Economie Devel. Commn., Toastmasters (Spl. award 1992). Lutheran. Avocations: tennis, walking, reading, travel. Home: 1435 Sunnyside Dr Winter Park FL 32789-1455 Office: MCI Telecomm 201 S Orange Ave Ste 600 Orlando FL 32801-3468

MALLARD, STEPHEN ANTHONY, retired utility company executive; b. Jersey City, Sept. 15, 1924; s. Stephen F. and Gertrude V. (Donahue) M.; m. Winifred Anne Carey, June 7, 1947; children: Stephen Kevin, Catherine Anne, Eileen Rosemary Mallard McClenehan. M.E., Stevens Inst. Tech, Hoboken, N.J., 1948, M.S.E.E., 1951. With elec. distbn., system planning and devel. Pub. Service Electric and Gas Co., Newark, 1951-77, v.p. system planning, 1977-80, sr. v.p. planning and research, 1980-88, sr. v.p. transmission systems, 1989; pvt. practice engring. Nutley, N.J., 1990—; advisor Brookhave Nat. Lab.; cons. Manhattan Coll. Bd. dirs. Essex chpt. ARC, East Orange, N.J., 1985—, bd. dirs. No. N.J. chpt., 1988—; bd. dirs. Essex County Grand Jury Assn., 1978-87. With USN, 1944-46, PTO. Fellow IEEE; mem. Nat. Soc. Profl. Engrs., , Conf. Internationale des Grands Reseaux Electriques a Haute Tension, Eta Kappa Nu, Tau Beta Pi. Roman Catholic. Home and Office: 68 High St Nutley NJ 07110-1134

MALLARDI, MICHAEL PATRICK, retired broadcasting company executive; b. N.Y.C., Mar. 17, 1934; s. Michael Cosmo and Gaetana M.; m. Sylvia J. Mandalios, Aug. 19, 1961; children: Karen, Stephanie. B.Phil magna cum laude, U. Notre Dame, 1956. With ABC, Inc., 1956-61, 71—; v.p. corp. planning ABC, Inc., N.Y.C., 1971-74; pres. ABC Records and Sales Corp., Seattle, 1974-75, Fairfield, N.J., 1974-75; v.p., chief fin. officer ABC, N.Y.C., 1975-83, exec. v.p., 1983-86, pres. broadcast group, 1986—, also dir.; sr. v.p. Capital Cities/ABC Inc., 1986-96; ret., 1996; location auditor Metro-Goldwyn-Mayer, Inc., L.A., 1961; bus. mgr. Radio-Press Internat., Inc., N.Y.C., 1961-65; treas. Straus Broadcasting Group, Inc., 1965-69, v.p., gen. mgr., 1969-71; mem. adv. bd. Chem. Bank; trustee Pierpont Fund, Pierpont Tax Exempt Fund; bd. dirs. MS-TV, Inc. Mem. Good Samaritan Planning Bd., Suffern, N.Y.; bd. dirs. Good Samaritan Hosp., Vets. Bedside Network, Am. Women Econ. Devel., Jr. Achievement. Mem. Internat. Radio and TV Soc. Roman Catholic. Office: Capital Cities/ABC Inc 77 W 66th St # 21 New York NY 10023-6201

MALLARDI, VINCENT, organization executive; b. N.Y.C., Sept. 5, 1942; s. Dominic and Wanda Ruth (Ballard) M.; m. Susan Snyder; m. Avril Y. Stone, Dec. 27, 1986; children: Douglas M., Karen R., Kevan Stone. BBA in Mgmt., St. John's U., N.Y.C., 1971; MBA in Fin., Lehigh U., 1979. Cert. mgmt. cons. Announcer Sta. WLIR-FM, N.Y.C., 1960-61; sound-recording prodr. Audio Rec. & Mfg. Co., N.Y.C., 1961-67; pub. G. Riccordi, music, N.Y.C. and Milan, Italy, 1965-67, Synectics Network Inc., news weekly, Bethlehem, Pa., 1967-72, SNI/Re:Print, Phila., 1973-84; cons. SNI/Caribbean, Miami, Fla., 1985-91; chmn. Printing Brokerage/Buyers Assn., Palm Beach, Fla., 1992—; bd. dirs., chmn. exec. com. IFH Capital Mgmt. Corp., Ft. Lauderdale, Fla., 1990—, Mapasa/Sistemas Unidas de Mex., Toluca, sec. Author over 12 books; contbg. editor Am. Printer mag., 1979—; editor-in-chief Who's Printing What Monthly, 1989—. Recipient Disting. Salesman award Sales and Mktg. Execs. Internat. Fellow Soderstrom Soc. of Nat. Assn. Printers and Lithographers; mem. Chaine des Rotisseurs (chevalier). Republican. Episcopalian. Office: Printing Brokerage/Buyers Assn 277 Royal Poinciana Way Palm Beach FL 33480

MALLARY, GERTRUDE ROBINSON, civic worker; b. Springfield, Mass., Aug. 19, 1902; d. George Edward and Jennie (Slater) Robinson; m. R. DeWitt Mallary, Sept. 15, 1923; children: R. DeWitt, Richard Walker; student, Bennett Coll., 1921-22, U. Conn., 1941-42; LLD (hon.), U. Vt., 1996. Co-owner, ptnr. Mallary Farm, Bradford, Vt., 1936-93; mem. Vt. Ho. of Reps., 1953-56, sec. agr. com., 1953, mem. appropriations com., 1955; mem. Vt. Senate, 1957-58, mem. appropriations com., clk. pub. health com., vice chmn. edn. com. Pres., Jr. League, Springfield, 1931-33; trustee Wesson Meml. Hosp., Springfield, 1937-42, chmn. nursing services, 1939-42; chmn. Springfield Council Social Agys., 1938-40; mem. Mass. Commn. Pub. Safety, 1941-42; pres. Vt. Holstein Club, 1951-53; mem. Vt. Bd. Recreation, 1959-65; trustee Fairlee (Vt.) Public Library, 1953-84, Asa Bloomer Found., 1963-71, Justin Smith Morrill Found., 1964-71, pres., 1968-71; chmn. Fairlee Bicentennial Com., 1974-77. Recipient Theresa R. Brungardt award, 1979, co-recipient with husband Master Breeders award Vt. Holstein Assn., 1979, Master Breeders award New Eng. Holstein Assn., 1969, Disting. Svc. award, 1989. Mem. Vt. Hist. Soc. (hon.), Bradford Hist. Soc. (pres. 1965-69), Fairlee Hist. Socs., Am. Antiquarian Soc. Editor New Eng. Holstein Bull., 1947-50. Address: Mallary Farm RR1 Box 620 Bradford VT 05033

MALLARY, ROBERT, sculptor; b. Toledo, Dec. 2, 1917; s. Benjamin E. and Laura (Grossman) M.; m. Margot Handrahan, Oct. 29, 1942; children: Michelle, Michael, Martine, Dion. Certificate, La Escuela de las Artes del Libro, Mexico D.F., 1939. mem. faculty U. N.M., 1955-59, Pratt Inst., 1959-67; prof. art U. Mass., Amherst, 1967—. Exhbt. One-man shows, San Francisco Mus. Art., 1944, one-man shows, Crocker Art Gallery, Sacramento, 1944; Calif. Exhibitors Gallery, Los Angeles, 1951, Santa Barbara Mus. Art, 1952, Gumps, San Francisco, 1953, Fine Arts Gallery San Diego, 1953, Urban Gallery, N.Y.C., 1954, Coll. Fine Arts, U. N.M., 1956, Jonson Gallery, Albuquerque, 1957-59, Santa Fe, 1958, Allan Stone Gallery, N.Y.C., 1961, 62, 66, Los Angeles Mus. Art, 1951, 53, 54, Colorado Springs Fine Art Center, 1953, Denver Art Mus., 1955, exhibited in group shows, Denver Art Mus., Sao Paulo, Brazil, 1955, 63, Mus. Modern Art, 1959, 61, 65, Gt. Jones Gallery, N.Y.C., 1959, Guggenheim Mus., 1960, Whitney Mus. Am. Art, 1960, 62, 64, 66, 68, Pace Gallery, Boston, 1960, Stable Gallery, N.Y.C., 1960, Martha Jackson Gallery, N.Y.C., 1961, Inst. Contemporary Art, Houston, 1961, 62, Am. Fedn. Art, Riverside Mus., N.Y.C., 1961, Paris, 1962, Exhbt., Seattle Worlds Fair, 1962, Carnegie Inst., 1962, Denver Mus. Fine Arts, 1962, Art Inst. Chgo., 1962, Allan Stone Gallery, 1961, 62, 66, N.Y. State Coll., Potsdam, 1969; represented in permanent collections, Mus. Modern Art, rep., Whitney Mus. Am. Art, Maremont Found., Smith Coll., Brandeis U., Womens Coll. of U. N.C., U. Tex., Kalamazoo Art Center, U. Cal. at Berkeley, Roswell (N.M.) Mus., Los Angeles Mus. Art, U. N.M., Santa Fe, Drew Coll., N.J.; commd. by, N.Y. Worlds Fair, 1963-64, collaborator (with Dale Owne), mural, Beverly Hilton Hotel, Beverly Hills, Cal., 1955; Dir.: Arstecnica: Interdisciplinary Center for Art and Tech. Guggenheim grantee, 1964-65; fellow Tamarind Workshop, 1962. Mem. Computer Arts Soc., Siggraph/ACM. Research in computer art and computer-supported studies in aesthetics; projects in art and tech.; aesthetics of surface mine reclamation; application of computer-aided design techniques to large-scale environ. sculpture and landscape design; devel. of library of art-oriented computer-graphic programs, subroutines and tutorial exercises for dedicated and time-sharing systems; creative work with computer-graphic paint and image-processing systems and research-and-development projects in computer and video stereographic projection; assemblage relief sculpture; and in stereoscopic projection, in assemblage relief sculpture, and in self-referential and self-documenting installations. Home: PO Box 605 Conway MA 01341-0605

MALLENBAUM, ALLAN ELIYAHU, marketing executive; b. Bklyn., Nov. 26, 1931; s. Arthur I. and Sophie Mallenbaum; m. Irene Bright, Nov. 16, 1953; children: Stephan J., David N., Sandra L., Cheryl D., Lisa G. B in Psychology, NYU, 1952; postgrad., Università Di Padova, Padua, Italy, 1956-60; MBA in Mktg./Internat. Commerce, Baruch Grad. Sch., 1968. Mktg. rsch. Lennon & Newell Advt., N.Y.C.; mktg. dir. Steifel Labs., Oak Hill, N.Y., Belvac Internat., L.I. City, N.Y.; pres. copeless Concepts, Ltd., N.Y.C.; adminstrv. v.p. Alliance Communication Group, N.Y.C., 1984-86; exec. v.p. Resource Network Internat., N.Y.C., 1986-88; mng. dir./founder Kensington High St. Assocs., Plainview, N.Y., 1988—; arbitrator Better Bus. Bur., N.Y.C. Founder United Zionists of the Americas, N.Y.C., Rosa Robota Found., Plainview, N.Y., Family Rsch. Found., Plainview, L.I. Genealogy Fed., Plainview; co-founder Jewish Survival Legion, N.Y.C.; pres. L.I. Genealogy Computer Soc.; v.p. L.I. Jewish Genealogy Soc. With U.S. Army, 1954-56. Mem. Jewish War Vets., Mensa. Avocations: computer science, new technologies, photography, genealogy.

MALLERY, ANNE LOUISE, elementary education educator, consultant; b. Myersdale, Pa., June 14, 1934; d. Samuel Addison and Ruth Elizabeth (Meehan) M.; m. Richard Gwen Jones, Mar. 9, 1953 (div. 1974); children: Valerie Anne, Joseph Samuel, Richard Alan (dec.). BS in Edn., Calif. U., Pa., 1970, MEd, 1972; EdD, Pa. State U., 1980. From proficiency coord. to prof. elem. edn. Millersville (Pa.) U., 1980—; asst. to pres. for planning MobileVision Tech., Inc., Coral Gables, Fla., 1990—; editor Innovative Learning Strategy, Nat. Publ., 1989—; cons. East Brunswick Pub. Schs., 1995; cons. Pequea Valley H.S., Lancaster, Pa., 1985, Cambridge Adult Edn. Co., 1987, Conawago Elem. Sch., York, Pa., 1991; co-dir. NEH grant, 1993-94. Co-author The Secret Cave Multimodal Reading Program; contbr. numerous articles to profl. jours. Judge Intelligencer Reg. Spelling Bee, Lancaster, 1990,91. Mem. Assn. Pa. State Coll. and U. Faculty, Internat. Reading Assn., Lancaster Lebanon Reading Assn., Assn. Tchr. Educators, Am. Assn. Colls. Tchr. Edn., Am. Reading Forum. Republican. Presbyterian. Avocations: swimming, walking, reading, films. Home: 24 Strawberry Ln Lancaster PA 17602-1639 Office: Millersville Univ Stayer Education Ctr Millersville PA 17551

MALLETT, CONRAD LEROY, JR., state supreme court justice; b. Detroit, Oct. 12, 1953; s. Conrad LeRoy and Claudia Gwendolyn (Jones) M.; m. Barbara Straughn, Dec. 22, 1984; children: Alex Conrad, Mio Thomas, Kristan Claudia. BA, UCLA, 1975; MPA, U. So. Calif., 1979, JD, 1979. Bar: Mich. 1979. Legal asst. to congressman Detroit, 1979-80; dep. pol. div. Dem. Nat. Com., Washington, 1980-81; assoc. Miller, Canfield, Paddock & Stone, Detroit, 1981-82; legal counsel, dir. to gov. State of Mich., Lansing, 1983-84; sr. exec. asst. to Mayor City of Detroit, 1985-86; ptnr. Jaffe, Raitt, Heuer & Weiss, Detroit, 1987-90; justice Mich. Supreme Ct., Lansing, 1990—. Mem. NAACP, Kappa Alpha Psi. Democrat. Roman Catholic. Avocations: writing, fiction. Office: Supreme Ct Office 500 Woodward Ave Fl 20 Detroit MI 48226-3435

MALLETT, DEBORAH GLENN, gifted talented education educator, coordinator; b. Beaumont, Tex., May 20, 1951; d. Gerald Gordon and Mildred (Long) Mallett; m. Eric Lee Newman, Aug. 10, 1985 (dec. Sept. 1987). BA in Elem. Edn., Baylor U., 1973; cert. in ins. mktg., U. Houston, 1983; MEd summa cum laude, U. Oreg., 1991. Cert. gifted edn. educator, Tex.; cert. tchr., Tex., N.Mex., Ala. Women's ministry coord. Campus Crusade for Christ, San Bernardino, Calif., 1973-79; tchr. Spring Br. Ind. Sch. Dist., Houston, 1979-81; paralegal Butler, Binion, Rice, Cook, Knapp, Houston, 1081-83, Fonts and Moore, 1983-84; owner fashion cons. bus. Design for Beauty, Houston, 1983-85, fashion cons., 1984-85; tchr. The Kinkaid Sch., Houston, 1985-89, Beaumont (Tex.) Ind. Sch. Dist., 1989-90; talented/gifted facilitator and coord. Alamogordo (N.Mex.) Pub. Sch. Sys., 1992-94; ednl. cons., Houston, 1990-92; mem. adv. bd. Marrs Hill Prodns., Houston, 1991-92, South Ctrl. Aviation Ministries, Houston, 1985-87; cons. Gifted Edn. Task Force, Albuquerque. Author numerous short stories. Mem. Young Reps., Houston, 1991, Fine Arts Mus., Houston, 1985-92. Named one of Notable Women of Tex., State of Tex., 1984-85. Mem. NEA, ASCD, Nat. Assn. for Gifted Child, U.S. Water Fitness Assn. (cert. instr.), Nat. Trust for Historic Preservation, State Bar Tex. Legal Assts. Divsn. (charter mem.), Baylor Alumni Assn. Republican. Baptist. Avocations: writing, painting, aerobics, skiing, fashion.

MALLETT, HELENE GETTLER, elementary education educator; b. Goshen, N.Y., Aug. 20, 1937; d. John and Anna Gettler; m. Richard David Mallett, July 29, 1967; 1 child, Anna Alma. BS in Fgn. Svc., Georgetown U., 1959; MA, SUNY, Stonybrook, 1989. Supr. Fulbright Program/Europe Inst. Internat. Edn., N.Y.C., 1961-65; editor Am. Assn. Fund Raising Coun., N.Y.C., 1965-67; coord. adult GED/ESL programs BOCES 3, Deer Park, N.Y., 1973-85; tchr. UFSD #3 and UFSD #4, Huntington, N.Y., 1967—; trustee Eastwood Sch., Oyster Bay, N.Y., 1977-83; alumni interviewer, Georgetown U., Washington, 1989—. Mem. ASCD, Nat. Coun. for the Social Studies, N.Y. State United Tchrs. (com. 100), Chemist Club. Avocations: travel, Angora rabbits, diplomatic history, robots, geography. Home: 79 Little Neck Rd Centerport NY 11721-1615

MALLETTE, MALCOLM FRANCIS, newspaper editor, educator; b. Syracuse, N.Y., Jan. 30, 1922; s. Ralph Joseph and Hermia Ruth (Barry) M.; m. Eleanor Christine Ingram, Sept. 21, 1946; children: Gary, Bruce, David. BS magna cum laude, Syracuse U., 1947. Profl. baseball pitcher Norfolk, Va., Newark, Kansas City, Memphis, Sacramento, Bklyn., Montreal, 1946-52; sports reporter Asheville (N.C.) Times, 1951-54; sports editor Asheville Citizen, 1954-56; sports dir. Winston-Salem (N.C.) Jour. & Sentinel, 1956-59; mng. editor Winston-Salem Jour., 1959-66; assoc. dir. Am. Press Inst., Reston, Va., 1966-69; mng. dir. Am. Press Inst., 1969-75, sec., dir., 1975-79, dir. devel., 1979-87; dir. projects World Press Freedom Com., 1987—; guest lectr. Grad. Sch. Journalism, Columbia, 1969-71, Am. Press. Inst., Columbia, 1961-66, U. N.C. Sch. Journalism, 1964; Def. Info. Sch. Ft. Benjamin Harrison, Ind., 1987. Author (with others), editor: Handbook for Journalists of Central and Eastern Europe, 1990, transl. to Polish, Czechoslovakian, Hungarian, Romanian, Bulgarian, Albanian, Russian; author (Seminar) The Story of the American Press Institute, 1992; contbr. articles to various mags. Served to capt. Signal Corps, AC AUS, 1943-46. Mem. AP Mng. Editors Assn. (dir. 1961-66, regent 1976—), AP News Coun. (pres. N.C. 1964), Assn. Profl. Baseball Players (life). Baptist. Club: Rotarian. Home: 2419 Silver Fox Ln Reston VA 22091-2628

MALLEY, JAMES HENRY MICHAEL, industrial engineer; b. Providence, Oct. 15, 1940; s. Leo Henry and Gladys Elizabeth (Canning) M.; children: James Michael, Julie Michele; m. Joyce Sue Marie Greenwell, Aug. 28, 1993. BS in Engring., U.S. Mil. Acad., 1962; MS in Indsl. Engring., U. R.I., 1977. Commd. U.S. Army, 1962-84, advanced through grades to lt. col., ret., 1984; milt. advisor U.S. Army, Rep. of Vietnam, 1964-65; co. comdr. Army Tng. Ctr., Ft. Benning, Ga., 1965-67; ops. and exec. officer First Air Cavalry Div., Vietnam, 1968-69; asst. prof. U. R.I., Kingston, 1969-73; asst. inspector gen. U.S. Army Criminal Investigation Command, Washington, 1973-76; ops. rsch. analyst and study dir. U.S. Army Concepts Analysis Agy., Bethesda, Md., 1977-80; dir. tng. U.S. 7th Army Combined Arms Tng. Ctr., Vilseck, Ger., 1980-81; chief of ops. rsch. and sys. analysis U.S. Army Europe, Heidelberg, Ger., 1981-84; mgr. engring. svcs. Orion Internat. Tech., Inc., Albuquerque, 1984-90; temp. recall, Ops. Desert Shield/Desert Storm U.S. Army, 1991; army after action report integrator ODCSOPS-HQDA, Washington, 1991; prin. analyst Gen. Rsch. Corp., Washington, 1992; ops. rsch. and analysis exec. Lockheed-Sanders, Merrimack, N.H., 1992—; mgmt. advisor to pres. PC Support, Inc., Albuquerque, 1986—; presenter numerous symposia, U.S. and Europe. Decorated Silver Stars (2), Legion of Merit, Bronze Stars (3), Air medals (4), Purple Heart, Vietnamese Cross of Gallantry with Gold Star (1) with Palm (2). Mem. Ops. Rsch. Soc. Am., Assn. of U.S. Army, U.S. Naval Inst., Am. Def. Preparedness Assn., Internat. Test & Evaluation Assn. Avocations: volksmarching, kayaking, skiing, rafting, mathematics. Home: PO Box 746 Merrimack NH 03054-0746

MALLEY, KENNETH CORNELIUS, corporation executive, retired military officer; b. Newark, Dec. 12, 1934; s. Raymond Cornelius and Catherine Mary (Pisarcik) M.; m. Catherine Margaret Potter, June 8, 1958; children: William B., Paul K. BS in Naval Sci., U.S. Naval Acad., 1957; MSEE, Naval Postgrad. Sch., 1963. Commd. ensign USN, 1957, advanced through grades to vice adm., 1991; gunnery officer USS Borden USN, Norfolk, Va., 1957-59, staff ops. officer Destroyer Divsn. 322, 1959-60; weapons officer USS Farragut USN, Mayport, Fla., 1963-64; proj. officer Bur. Naval Ordnance USN, Washington, 1964-67, head strategic sys. program, 1970-75, head missile br., 1971-80, tech. dir., 1980-85, dir., 1985-91, comdr. naval sea sys. command, 1991-94; pres. Malley Assocs., 1994-95; support dir. naval ordnance sta. USN, Indian Head, Md., 1975-76; head missile br. naval plan rep. office USN, Sunnyvale, Calif., head. engring div., 1969-70; mem. Draper Labs., Cambridge, Mass. Bd. dirs. Constellation Found., Balt.; vol. spkr. Chesapeake Bay Found., Annapolis, 1987, 89, 90, 91. Decorated DSM, Legion of Merit with oak leaf cluster, Meritorious Svc. medal, Navy Achievement medal. Mem. Am. Soc. Naval Engrs. (Gold medal 1986), U.S. Naval Inst., Naval Submarine League. Republican. Roman Catholic. Avocations: duck carving, boating. Home: 136 Riverside Rd Edgewater MD 21037-1405

MALLEY, ROBERT JOSEPH, manufacturing company executive; b. Nashwauk, Minn., July 17, 1923; s. Joseph Cyril and Eva May (Troumbly) M.; m. Betty Josephine Gregg, Aug. 10, 1957; children: Robert, Gregg Philip, Elizabeth Lee, Kelly Lynn, Kenneth John. B.S. in Mil. Engring, U.S. Mil. Acad., 1946; M.S. in Civil Engring, U. Minn., 1953. Commd. U.S. Army, 1946, advanced through grades to maj. gen., 1975; assignments in airborne and engring. units, 1946-56; instr. physics U.S. Mil. Acad., West Point, N.Y., 1956-59; with programs div. SHAPE Paris, 1960-63; bn. comdr. engring. bn. 1st cav. div. Ft. Benning, Ga. and, Vietnam, 1963-66; dist. engr. Los Angeles, 1969-71; with Americal div., 1971-72; project mgr. production base modernization Picatinny Arsenal, N.J., 1973-76; dir. combat support systems Dept. Army, Washington, 1976-78; ret., 1978; v.p. internat. ops. Chamberlain Mfg. Corp., Arlington, Va., 1978-91; v.p. mktg. Nuclear Metals Inc., Concord, Mass., 1991—. Decorated D.S.M., Legion of Merit with 3 oak leaf clusters, Bronze Star, Air Medal with 5 oak leaf clusters. Fellow Soc. Am. Mil. Engrs. (Wheeler award 1965); mem. Am. Def. Preparedness Assn. Roman Catholic. Clubs: Army-Navy Country, K.C. Home: 1122 Ormond Ct Mc Lean VA 22101-2960 Office: 1200 N Nash St Apt 218 Arlington VA 22209-3613

MALLEY, WILLIAM, production designer. Prodn. designer: (films) Prime Cut, 1972, The Exorcist, 1973 (Academy award nomination best art direction 1973), Huckleberry Finn, 1973, Alex & Gypsy, 1976, Citizen's Band, Handle with Care, 1977, The Fury, 1978, (with Dennis Washington) The Ninth Configuration, 1980, Defiance, 1980, Mommie Dearest, 1981, The Star Chamber, 1983, Deal of the Century, 1983, The House of God, 1984, Protocol, 1984, Uforia, 1985, Vision Quest, 1985, Walk Like a Man, 1987, Big Shots, 1987, (with Alan Locke) Dr. Giggles, 1992, (TV movies) The Great Ice Rip-Off, 1974, Pray for the Wildcats, 1974, The Red Badge of Courage, 1974, Griffin and Phoenix, 1976, World War III, 1982, Something About Amelia, 1984, Margaret Bourke-White, 1989, Common Ground, 1990, Dark Avenger, 1990, The Whereabouts of Jenny, 1991, (TV episodes) Alfred Hitchcock Presents, 1986. Office: Smith/Gosnell/Nicholson & Assoc PO Box 1166 1515 Palisades Dr Pacific Palisades CA 90272

MALLIK, MOHAMMAD ABDUL-BARI, soil microbiologist; b. Pabna, Bangladesh, Mar. 15, 1927; s. Monsur Ali and Ataharun-Nisa Mallik; m. Rowshan Jahan Hamida, Sept. 24, 1966; 1 child, Abds-Sami. BSc, Rajshahi (Bangladesh) Coll., 1949; MSc, Dhaka (Bangladesh) U., 1952; MS, Minn. U., 1961; PhD, Okla. U., 1964. Lectr. botany U. Karachi, Pakistan, 1956-59, asst. prof., 1964-68, 69-72; vis. scholar dept. botany Baghdad (Iraq) U., 1968-69; asst. prof. Dhaka (Bangladesh) U., 1973-74; rsch. assoc. dept. botany and microbiology u. Okla., Norman, 1974-75; assoc. rsch. prof. agrl. rsch. program Langston (Okla.) U., 1975-82, rsch. prof. agrl. rsch. program, 1982—. Author: Introduction to Fungi, 1973; contbr. articles to profl. and popular publs. Fulbright scholar Minn. U., St. Paul, 1961; rsch. grantee Pakistan Agrl. Rsch. Coun., Karachi, 1968-69, USDA, Langston, 1982—. Mem. Am. Soc. Agronomy, Internat. Allelopathy Soc., Okla. Acad. Sci., Bangladesh Bot. Soc. Democrat. Muslim. Avocation: gardening. Home: 2611 S Oxford Dr Stillwater OK 74074 Office: Langston Univ Agrl Rsch Program PO Box 730 Langston OK 73050

MALLINCKRODT, GEORGE W., bank executive; b. Eichholz, Germany, Aug. 19, 1930; s. Arnold Wilhelm and Valentine (von Joest) von M.; m. Charmaine Brenda Schroder, July 31, 1958; children: Claire, Philip, Edward, Sophie. Student, various bus. schs.; DCL (hon.), Bishops U., Lennoxville, Can., 1994. With AGFA A.G., Munich, 1948-51, Munchmeyer and Co., Hamburg, 1951-53, Kleinwort Sons and Co., London, 1953-54, J. Henry Schroder Banking Corp., N.Y.C., 1954-55, 57-60, Union Bank Switzerland, 1956; with J. Henry Schroder & Co. Ltd., London, 1960—, also bd. dirs.; chmn. Schroders PLC, London, 1984-95, pres., 1995—; chmn. bd. dirs. J.

Henry Schroder Bank A.G., Zurich, 1967; chmn., pres. Schroders Inc., N.Y.C., 1985; bd. dirs. Schroders Australia Ltd., Sydney, 1984—, Schroder Wertheim and Co. Inc., N.Y.C., 1986—, Schroders Ltd., Bermuda, 1991, British Invisibles, 1995—; bd. dirs. Euris S.A., Paris, Siemens plc., London, Schroder Internat. Mcht. Bankers Ltd., Singapore, Fgn. and Colonial German Investment Trust plc.; mem. Brit. N.Am. com., 1988—; trustee Kurt Hahn Trust, 1991—. V.p. German Brit. C. of C., London, 1992-95; chmn. Coun. World Econ. Forum, Davos, 1992—; mem. CBI City Adv. Group, London; mem. Brit. Mus. Devel. Trust, 1995—, Nat. Art Collection Devel. Coun., 1995—. Recipient Verdienstkreuz Am. Bande Des Verdienstordens Der Bundesrepublik Deutschland, 1986, Verdienstkeuz 1 Klasse Verdienstordens, 1990. Fellow Royal Soc. Arts; mem. Inst. Mgmt. (companion 1986—). Office: Schroders PLC, 120 Cheapside, London EC2V 6DS, England also: Schroders Inc 787 7th Ave New York NY 10019-6018

MALLISON, N DANIELE, elementary school educator; b. Portsmouth, Va., Aug. 16, 1962; d. Howard Danford and Norma Mae (Gibbs) M.; married. BFA in Art Edn., Va. Commonwealth U., 1984. Cert. tchr. K-12, Va.; cert. therapeutic recreation asst. Activity dir. Eldercare Gardens Nursing Home, Charlotteville, Va., 1985-86; itinerant art tchr. Henry County Pub. Schs., Collinsville, Va., 1986-87; contract substitute Louisa County (Va.) Pub. Schs., 1988; middle/h.s. art tchr. Grayson County Pub. Schs., Independence, Va., 1988-90; elem. art resource tchr. Orange County (Va.) Pub. Schs., 1990—; Upward Bound art tchr. Wytheville (Va.) C.C., summer 1990; tchr./cons. Henry County Pub. Schs. in conjunction with Va. Dept. Edn., Collinsville, 1987. Lifetime mem. Va. 4-H All Stars; chmn. young adults Gordonsville United Meth. Ch., 1994—. Folk Artist grantee Va. Commn. for the Arts, 1992-93, 93-94. Mem. NEA, Va. Edn. Assn., Nat. Art Edn. Assn., Va. Art Edn. Assn., Nat. Therapeutic Recreation Assn., Gordonsville Jaycees (sec. 1992, 94, state dir. 1993). Avocations: arts and crafts, reading, travel, horses, researching native American heritage. Office: Orange County Pub Schs PO Box 349 Orange VA 22960-0204

MALLO-GARRIDO, JOSEPHINE ANN, advertising agency owner; b. Agana, Guam, Mar. 20, 1955; d. Benjamin Corneja and Salvacion (Lacuesta) Mallo; m. John Marco Haniu Garrido, Feb. 16, 1980; children: Josiah Michael, Jordan Thaddeus. Student, U. Guam, Agana, 1972-74; BA in Journalism, Seattle U., 1976; MBA, Pepperdine U., 1982. Reporter Pacific Daily News, Agana, 1976, features editor, 1977-78, asst. city editor, 1978-79; copy editor features Honolulu Star-Bull., 1979-81; advt. copywriter Advt. Factors, Honolulu, 1981-83; communications specialist Liberty House, Honolulu, 1983-84; editor, advt. copywriter Safeway Stores Inc., Oakland, Calif., 1984-88; features writer Tracy (Calif.) Press, 1988-91; mktg. mgr. ComputerLand of Guam, Maite, 1992-93; mktg. officer Citibank, Agana, 1993-94; owner JMG Advt., 1994—; newspaper graphics cons. Pacific Daily News, 1984. Editor/writer Foods Unltd., 1984-88, Tracy Community Hosp. Health Beat and Update, 1988-91; editor Pacific Voice, 1977-78; contbr. articles to profl. jours. Vol. Engaged Encounter, Honolulu, 1989, Trans-Pacific Yacht Race, Honolulu, 1983, United Way, Oakland, 1986; organist St. Patrick's Ch., Honolulu, 1980-84, Immaculate Heart of Mary Ch., Toto, Guam, 1994—; advt. coord. Easter Seals, Oakland, 1987; mem. adv. bd. Cath. Social Svcs., Agana, Guam, 1993—. Recipient Cert. Achievement award Advt. Age Mag., 1985, Cert Appreciation award Am. Heart Food Festival, 1985, Best in the West award Am. Advt. Fedn., 1986, Retail Nutrition award Nat. Potato Promotion Bd., 1986, Spl. Achievement award Newspaper Spl. Sect. Mother's Day/Father's Day Coun., 1989, 90, Best Feature Story 2d place Calif. Newspaper Pubs. Assn., 1989, 1st place Classified Advt. Assn., 1989, 1st place appetizer Spam Food Festival, 1991. Mem. Guam C. of C. (media coord. 1993-95), Citiclub (exec. sec. 1994-95). Roman Catholic. Avocations: piano, travel.

MALLON, MEG, professional golfer. Winner Women's U.S. Open, 1991; 4th ranked woman LPGA Tour, 1992; 2d major LPGA championship, 1991; winner 6 LPGA titles. Office: care LPGA 2570 Volusia Ave Ste B Daytona Beach FL 32114-7103*

MALLON, PETER, archbishop; b. Prince Rupert, Can., Dec. 5, 1929; s. Joseph P. and Sheila M. (Keenan) D. Grad., Seminary Christ the King, Burnaby and Mission, B.C. ordained to ministry Roman Cath. Ch., 1956;. Asst. Holy Rosary Cath., Vancouver, B.C., 1956-64, rector, 1966-82; chancellor Archdiocese Vancouver, 1964-65, dir. religious edn., 1971-73; adminstr. Guardian Angels Parish, Vancouver, 1964-65; pastor St. Anthony's, West Vancouver, 1982-89; bishop Nelson, B.C., 1989-95; archbishop of Regina Sask., Can., 1995—. Address: 445 Broad St N, Regina, SK Canada S4R 2X8

MALLORY, ARTHUR LEE, university dean, retired state official; b. Springfield, Mo., Dec. 26, 1932; s. Dillard A. and Ferrell (Claxton) M.; m. Joann Peters, June 6, 1954; children: Dennis Arthur (dec.), Christopher Lee, Stephanie Ann, Jennifer Lyn. B.S., S.W. Mo. State Coll., 1954; M.Ed., U. Mo., 1957, Ed.D., 1959; H.H.D., S.W. Bapt. Coll., Mo., 1972. History supr. U. Mo. Lab. Sch., Columbia, 1956-57; asst. to supt. schs. Columbia, 1957-59; asst. supt. schs. Parkway Sch. Dist., St. Louis County, Mo., 1959-64; dean evening div. U. Mo., St. Louis, 1964; pres. S.W. Mo. State U., Springfield, 1964-70, dean Coll. Edn., 1991-94; commr. edn. Mo. Dept. Edn., Jefferson City, 1971-87; dir. Internat. House, U. Mo., Columbia, 1956-59. V.p. Ozarks coun. Boy Scouts Am., 1967, pres. Gt. Rivers coun., 1972-73, Greene County Assn. for Retarded Citizens, 1989—, pres., 1991-96, mem. north ctrl. region exec. bd., 1984—; bd. dirs. Meml. Cmty. Hosp., Mid-Continent Regional Ednl. Lab., Ozark Pub. Telecoms. Inc., 1989—; chmn. bd. Mo. Coun. on Econ. Edn.; bd. regents Mo. State Univs.; trustee Pub. Sch. Retirement, William Jewell Coll., 1972-74; chmn. com. bds. So. Bapt. Conv., 1972-73, mem. com. or bds., 1981—; mem .exec. bd. Mo. Bapt. Conv., 1972-75, 77-80, 2d v.p., 1995-96; trustee Southwestern Bapt. Theol. Sem., Fort Worth, 1995—; mem. adv. com. Young Audiences, Inc., 1986, ARC Bd., Greene County, 1986, Children's Svcs. Commn., chmn., 1986—, Edn. Commn. U.S.; bd. dirs. Ozark Pub. TV. With U.S. Army, 1954-56. Recipient Disting. Service award Mo. Jr. C. of C., 1966; Distinguished Service award U. Mo., 1976; Faculty/Alumni award U. Mo., 1976; Silver Beaver award Boy Scouts Am., 1983, Good Shepherd and Cross, 1986, Disting. Citizen award, 1986; hon. life mem. Mo. Congress Parents and Tchrs.; named Springfield's Outstanding Young Man of Yr., 1965; Champion of Excellence PUSH, 1978. Mem. Am. Assn. State Colls. and Univs., N. Central Assn. Colls. and Secondary Schs., Council Chief State Sch. Officers, Mo. Assn. Sch. Adminstrs., NEA, Mo. Tchrs. Assn. So. Baptist (deacon). Clubs: Masons (33 deg.), Rotary.

MALLORY, CHARLES KING, III, lawyer; b. Norfolk, Va., Nov. 16, 1936; s. Charles King Mallory Jr. and Dorothy Pratt (Williams) Swanke; m. Florence Beale Marshall; children: King, Raburn, Anne, Richard. BA, Yale U., 1958; JD, Tulane U., 1961. Bar: La. 1961, Calif. 1965, D.C. 1972. Ptnr. Monroe & Lemann, New Orleans, 1965-72; acting exec. dir. SEC, Washington, 1972; dep. asst. sec. U.S. Dept. Interior, Washington, 1973, acting asst. sec., 1974; v.p., gen. counsel Middle South Svcs., Inc., New Orleans, 1975-79; ptnr. Hunton & Williams, Washington, 1979—. Mem. Reagan-Bush Transition Team, Washington, 1980-81, Grace Commn. on Pvt. Sector Survey Cost in the Fed. Govt., Washington, 1983-84. Served to lt. USNR, 1961-65. Mem. ABA, La. Bar Assn., Calif. Bar Assn., D.C. Bar Assn., Fed. Energy Bar Assn., Nat. Assn. Bond Lawyers. Republican. Episcopalian. Office: Hunton & Williams 2000 Pennsylvania Ave NW Washington DC 20006*

MALLORY, FRANK BRYANT, chemistry educator; b. Omaha, Mar. 17, 1933; s. Deane Havercroft and Helen (Bryant) M.; m. Patricia Ann Livingston, June 30, 1951; children—Mary Susan, Paul Deane, Philip Howard (dec.), Michele; m. Clelia Sara Wood, Nov. 26, 1965. B.S., Yale U., 1954; Ph.D., Calif. Inst. Tech., 1958. Asst. prof. Bryn Mawr (Pa.) Coll., 1957-63, assoc. prof., 1963-69; prof. chemistry Bryn Mawr Coll. (Pa.), 1969—, W. Alton Jones prof. chemistry, 1985—, chmn. dept., 1982-92; acad. dep. to pres. Bryn Mawr (Pa.) Coll., 1978-81; vis. assoc. Calif. Inst. Tech., 1963-64; vis. prof. Yale U., 1968, 78-79, lectr., 1977-78; vis. prof. SUNY-Albany, summer 1967; vis. fellow Cornell U., 1970-71; vis. prof. U. Pa., 1988-89. Mem. adv. bd. Jour. Organic Chemistry, 1988-93; contbr. articles to profl. jours. Mem. sci. and arts com. Franklin Inst., Phila. Recipient Bond award Am. Oil Chemists Soc., 1970, Lindback award for disting. tchg., 1992; John Simon Guggenheim fellow, 1963-64, Alfred P. Sloan rsch. fellow, 1964-68, NSF sr. postdoctoral fellow, 1970-71. Mem. Am. Chem. Soc. (exec. com. of organic divsn. 1986-95, symposium officer 1989-95, award Phila. sect. 1989), Phila. Organic Chemists Club (past sec., chmn.). Home: 321 Caversham Rd Bryn Mawr PA 19010-2927 Office: Bryn Mawr Coll Dept Chemistry Bryn Mawr PA 19010

MALLORY, FRANK LINUS, lawyer; b. Calgary, Alta., Can., May 5, 1920; s. Frank Louis and Anna Amy (Allstrum) M.; m. Jean Ellen Lindsey, Jan. 29, 1944; children: Susan Mallory Remund, Ann, Bruce R. AB with distinction, Stanford U., 1941, LLB, 1947. Bar: Calif. 1948. Assoc. Gibson, Dunn & Crutcher, L.A., 1947-54; ptnr. L.A. and Orange County, Calif., 1955-88; cert. specialist taxation law Calif. Bd. Legal Specialization, 1973-89. Pres. Town Hall of Calif., L.A., 1970, Boys Republic, Chino, Calif., 1962-64; pres. Braille Inst. Am., L.A., 1988-92. Lt. (j.g.) USNR, 1942-46. Mem. ABA, Calif. Bar Assn., Los Angeles County Bar Assn., Orange County Bar Assn., Newport Harbor Yacht Club, Big Canyon Country Club, Transpacific Yacht Club (staff commodore). Republican. Home: 633 Bayside Dr Newport Beach CA 92660-7213

MALLORY, KENNETH W., religious organization administrator. Sec. Am. Indian Council of the Reformed Ch. in Am., N.Y.C. Office: Reformed Church in Am 475 Riverside Dr Ste 1811 New York NY 10115-0122

MALLORY, ROBERT MARK, controller, finance executive; b. Mattoon, Ill., Apr. 15, 1950; s. Robert Monroe and Betty Ann (Mudd) M.; m. Diana Marie Burde, Aug. 19, 1972; 1 child, Laura Elizabeth. BS in Accountancy, U. Ill., 1972; M Mgmt., Northwestern U., 1986. CPA, Ill. Staff acct. Price Waterhouse, Chgo., 1972-74, sr. acct., 1974-77, mgr., 1977-79; dir. internal audit Mark Controls Corp., Skokie, Ill., 1979-81; corp. contr. Mark Controls Corp., Skokie, 1981-86, v.p., contr., 1986-88; contr., dir. planning Tribune Co., Chgo., 1988-91, v.p., contr., 1991—. Mem. Am. Inst. CPA's (Elijah Watts Sells award 1972), Ill. CPA Soc., Fin. Execs. Inst., Beta Gamma Sigma. Methodist. Home: 3312 Lakewood Ct Glenview IL 60025-2505 Office: Tribune Co 435 N Michigan Ave Chicago IL 60611-4001

MALLORY, SARA BROCKWELL, education educator; b. Newberry, S.C., Feb. 20, 1940; d. Charles Wilbur and Amelia Georgianna (Wideman) Brockwell; m. Buddy Lee Mallory, Feb. 4, 1967. BA, Columbia (S.C.) Coll., 1962; MS in Edn., Old Dominion U., 1986. Cert. collegiate profl., Va. Tchr. English, Ryan Schs., Inc., Norfolk, Va., 1979-86; adj. instr. reading Old Dominion U., Norfolk, 1986-88, instr. ednl. curriculum and instrn., 1988—; tchr. Spanish, Norfolk Collegiate Sch., spring 1987; reading resource tchr., Virginia Beach, 1993. Sec.-treas. ch. sch. Miles Meml. United Meth. Ch., Norfolk, 1992-93, chmn. com. on higher edn. and campus ministry, 1993. Named Most Inspiring Faculty Mem., Coll. Edn., Old Dominion U., 1990, Most Outstanding Faculty Mem. Office Student Svcs., 1992. Mem. ASCD, Nat. Coun. Tchrs. English, Internat. Reading Assn., Va. Reading Assn., Va. Coll. Reading Educators, Dickens Fellowship. Avocations: reading, travel, playing piano, singing, sewing. Home: 8605 Meadow Brook Ln Norfolk VA 23503-5411 Office: Old Dominion U Edn Bldg Rm 244 Norfolk VA 23529

MALLORY, V(IRGIL) STANDISH, geologist, educator; b. Englewood, N.J., July 14, 1919; s. Virgil Sampson and Sarah Lauris (Baum) M.; m. Miriam Elizabeth Rowan, Feb. 3, 1946; children—Charles Standish, Stefan Douglas, Peter Sommers, Ingrid Lauris. A.B., Oberlin Coll., 1943; M.A., U. Calif. at Berkeley, 1948, Ph.D. (Standard Oil of Calif. fellow in paleontology), 1952. Preparator U. Calif. Museum Paleontology, Berkeley, 1946-48; curator foraminifera U. Calif. Museum Paleontology, 1948-50, cons., 1951; lectr. paleontology U. Calif. at Berkeley, 1951; asst. prof. geology U. Wash., 1952-59, asso. prof., 1959-62; prof., chmn. div. geology and paleontology, curator of paleontology Burke Meml. Wash. State Mus., 1962-84, prof. emeritus, mus. curator, 1984—; cons. in petroleum geology and mus. curation, in wines to restaurants; lectr. geology of wine; mem. Gov. of Wash. Commn. on Petroleum Regulations, 1956-57; mem. NSF Paris Basin Field Inst., Paris, Belgium and Luxembourg, 1964; co-dir. NSF Inst. Secondary Sch. Tchrs., Western Wash. State Coll., summers 1963, 65. Author: Lower Tertiary Biostratigraphy of California Coast Ranges, 1959, Lower Tertiary Foraminifera From Media Agua Creek Drainage Area, Kern County, California, 1970, Biostratigraphy—A Major Basis of Paleontologic Correlation, 1970; contbg. author: Lincoln Library Essential Knowledge, 1965, Ency. Brit., 15th edit, 1974; Editor paleontology: Quaternary Research Jour, 1970-77; Contbr. articles to profl. jours. Served with AUS, 1944-46, PTO. Am. Assn. Petroleum Geologists Revolving Fund grantee, 1957; U. Wash. Agnes Anderson Fund grantee, 1963. Fellow AAAS (coun. 1964—), Geologic Soc. Am.; mem. Am. Assn. Petroleum Geologists (sect. coun. 1964-84, com. on stratigrahic correlations 1979-85), Paleontologic Soc. (chmn. sect. 1956-58), Geol. Soc. Am., Soc. Econ. Paleontology and Mineralogy, Paleontol. Rsch. Soc., Paleontologische Gesellschaft, Geologische Gesellschaft, Internat. Paleontological Union, N.W. Sci. Soc., Am. Assn. Mus., Mineral Mus. (adv. coun. 1974-87), N.W. Fedn. Mineralogical Socs. (hon. award 1995, 96), N.W. Paleontol. Assn. (hon. mem.), Sigma Xi, Theta Tau. Home: 5209 Pullman Ave NE Seattle WA 98105-2139 Office: Burke Meml Wash State Mus DB10 U Wash Seattle WA 98195

MALLORY, WILLIAM BARTON, III, lawyer; b. New River, N.C., June 8, 1944; s. William B. and Marion (Lucas) M.; m. Margaret Mary Milnor; children: Barton, Bennett, Brian, Allison. BA, U. Va., 1966; JD, U. Tenn., 1969. Bar: Tenn. 1969. Assoc. Heiskell, Donelson, Adams, Williams & Wall, Memphis, 1969; gen. counsel Guardsmark Inc., N.Y.C., 1969-73; v.p., gen. counsel The Crump Cos. Inc., Memphis, 1973-86; vice chmn., gen. counsel Guardsmark Inc., Memphis, 1986-93; v.p., gen. counsel Terminix Internat., Memphis, 1994—. Mem. ABA. Club: Memphis Country.

MALLOY, EDWARD ALOYSIUS, priest, university administrator, educator; b. Washington, May 3, 1941; s. Edward Aloysius and Elizabeth (Clark) M. BA, U. Notre Dame, 1963, MA, 1967, ThM, 1969; PhD, Vanderbilt U., 1975. Joine Congregation Holy Cross, 1963, ordained priest Roman Cath. Ch., 1970. Instr. U. Notre Dame, Ind., 1974-75, asst. prof., 1975-81, assoc. prof., 1981-88, prof. theology, 1988—, assoc. provost, 1982-86, pres. elect, 1986, pres., 1987—; bd. regents U. Portland, Oreg., 1985—. Author: Homosexuality and the Christian Way of Life, 1981, The Ethics of Law Enforcement and Criminal Punishment, 1982, Culture and Commitment: The Challenge of Today's University, 1992; contbr. articles to profl. jours. Chmn. Am. Coun. on Edn.; bd. dirs. NCAA Found., 1989—; mem. Bishops and Pres.' com. Assn. Cath. Colls. and Univs., 1988—; bd. dirs. Internat. Fedn. Cath. Univs., 1988—; mem. Pres.'s Adv. Coun. on Drugs, 1989—; mem. adv. bd. AmeriCorps and Nat. Civilian Community Corps, 1994—; interim chmn. Ind. Commn. on Community Svc., 1994—; bd. dirs. Points of Light, Campus Compact. Mem. Cath. Theol. Soc., Am. Soc. Christian Ethics, Bus.-Higher Edn. Forum, Assn. Governing Bds. of Univs. and Colls. (vice chair 1996—), The Conf. Bd. Office: U Notre Dame Office Pres Notre Dame IN 46556

MALLOY, EILEEN ANNE, ambassador; b. Teaneck, N.J., July 9, 1954; d. John Joseph and Mary Kathryn (Langan) M.; m. Ilmar Paegle, Jan. 13, 1975 (div. Aug. 1982); 1 child, Mary Kathryn; m. James George McLachlan, July 6, 1985; 1 child, Christina Alana. BS, Georgetown U., 1975. Analyst, divsn. mgr. Dunn & Bradstreet, Staten Island, N.Y., 1975-78; consular officer, spl. asst. to amb. U.S. Embassy, London, 1978-79; counselor, sci. officer U.S. Embassy, Moscow, 1980-82, chief arms control unit, 1988-90; consul U.S. Consulate, Calgary, A.B., Can., 1982-85; chief consular sect. U.S. Consulate, Dublin, Ireland, 1987-88; sr. U.K. desk officer Dept. of State, Washington, 1990-92, asst. to under sec. political affairs, 1992-93, dir. sec. staff, 1993-94, U.S. ambassador to Kyrgyz Republic, 1994—. Mem. Am. Fgn. Svc. Assn., Georgetown Alumni Assn. Office: US Ambassador Bishkek Kyrgistan Dept of State Washington DC 20521-7040

MALLOY, JAMES MATTHEW, managed care executive, health care consultant; b. N.Y.C., Aug. 26, 1939; s. Peter Joseph and Catherine (Cunningham) M.; m. Joan Elizabeth Wagner, Sept. 9, 1967; children—Stephen, Christopher. B.S., Manhattan Coll., 1961; M.P.H., Yale U., 1967. Asst. to dir. Yale New Haven Hosp., New Haven, Conn., 1967; assoc. adminstr. Waterbury Hosp., Conn., 1969-75; exec. dir., CEO Jersey City Med. Ctr., N.J., 1975-77; dir., CEO U. Conn. Hosp., Farmington, 1977-82, U. Ill. Hosp. and Clinics, Chgo., 1982-87; exec. v.p. Our Lady of the Resurrection Med. Ctr., Chgo., 1988-89; pres., CEO, St. Dominic Jackson Meml. Hosp., Jackson, Miss., 1989-91; sr. v.p. health affairs Miss. and La. Blue Cross/Blue Shield, Jackson, Miss., 1991-92; health care cons., pres. Malloy Assocs., Jackson, 1992—; pres., CEO S.E. Managed Care Orgn., Jackson, 1993-95; cons. NIH, Bethesda, Md., 1976-84; dir. Univ. Health Consortium; chmn. Compass Health Plan, Chgo., 1983-87; dir. Hosp. Fund, Inc., New Haven, Comprends Inc., Chgo.; lectr. Yale U. Sch. Medicine; adj. prof. U. Ill. Coll. Medicine, Chgo.; assoc. prof. U. Ill. Sch. Pub. Health. Contbr. articles to profl. jours. Chmn. Miss. chpt. Nat. Multiple Sclerosis Assn. Dr. Stuart Hamilton fellow Capital Area Health Consortium, 1982. Fellow Inst. Medicine Chgo., Am. Coll. Healthcare Execs.; mem. Ill. Hosp. Assn. (bd. dirs. 1984-86), Met. Chgo. Healthcare Coun., Yale Alumni Fund, Yale Club (pres. Miss. chpt.), Miss. Bus. Coalition on Health Care (bd. dirs.). Avocations: golf, jogging. Home and Office: 177 St Andrews Dr Jackson MS 39211-2532

MALLOY, JOHN RICHARD, lawyer, chemical company executive; b. Boston, Nov. 26, 1932; s. Thomas Francis and Mary (Field) M.; m. Maraleta Ellerson, May 24, 1960; children: Maureen, John, Megan, Elizabeth. BA, St. John's Sem., Brighton, Mass., 1954; LLB, Boston Coll., 1957. Bar: Mass. 1957. V.p., dir. fin. Remington Arms Co., Inc., Bridgeport, Conn., 1975-78; chief counsel, energy and raw materials E. I. du Pont de Nemours and Co., Wilmington, Del., 1978-79, asst. gen. counsel legal, 1979-83, dir. pub. affairs, 1983-85, v.p. pub. affairs, 1983-85, sr. v.p. external affairs, 1985-92, v.p., spl. counsel to chmn. bd., 1992-93; ret. Chmn. Jobs for Del. Grads, Wilmington, 1985—, Del. Compensation Commn., 1988—; trustee Del. Multiple Sclerosis Soc., 1980—, Med. Ctr. of Del., Christiana, 1985—, Del. Pension Fund, 1993—; bd. dirs. Del. Cmty. Found., 1989—, Children's Beach House, 1993—; mem. Minner Commn. (Del.), 1993—; chmn. Del. Coun. on Transp., 1994—. Mem. ABA, Fed. Bar Assn. Democrat. Roman Catholic. Avocations: tennis, golf, skiing.

MALLOY, MICHAEL TERRENCE, journalist, newspaper editor; b. Chgo., Feb. 26, 1936; s. Medard Valentine and Lucille (Zehrol)M.; m. Ruth Gwendolyn Lor, June 5, 1965; children: Linda Jo, Terrence. Student, Reed Coll., 1953-54, Columbia U., 1966-67. Police reporter City News Bur. Chgo., 1956-58; reporter, then bur. chief and chief corr. S.E. Asia UPI, Japan, Laos, India, Vietnam and Thailand, 1960-66; reporter Nat. Observer, Washington, 1968-76, mng. editor, 1976-77; reporter Asian Wall St. Jour., Manila, 1977-80, mng. editor, Hong Kong, 1980-84; mng. editor Dow Jones Can., Toronto, Ont., 1984-94; chief corr. Dow Jones India Report, 1995. Author: Racing Today, 1967, The Art of Retirement, 1967. With U.S. Army, 1958-60.

MALLOY, WILLIAM MICHAEL, book editor, reviewer, writer; b. Cleve., Oct. 29, 1960; s. Leroy Joseph Francis and Betty Jayne (Kubicek) M.; m. Claire Zion, Feb. 14, 1989; children: Rose Zion, Quinn Zion. BA in Lit., Yale U., 1982. Copyright mgr. G. Schirmer, Inc., N.Y.C., 1982-84; creative dir. Cloverdale Press, N.Y.C., 1985; mng. editor The Mysterious Press, N.Y.C., 1985-88; editor-in-chief The Mysterious Press/Warner Books, N.Y.C., 1988—; cons. 20th Century Crime and Mystery Writers, London, 1989—. Author: The Mystery Book of Days, 1990; contbg. editor The Armchair Detective, 1989—; contbr. critical essays to reference work. Democrat. Avocations: saxophone, flute, reading, cooking. Office: The Mysterious Press/Warner 1271 Avenue Of The Americas New York NY 10020

MALLOZZI, COS M., public relations executive; b. Utica, N.Y., Aug. 16, 1951. BA, Syracuse U., 1973. Pub. rels. coun. and legis. intern Congressman D. Mitchell, Washington, 1973-74; assr. pub. rels. dir., sports info. dir. Siena Coll., 1974-75; pub. rels. dir. SUNY, 1975-76; acct. supv. group mgr. Gibbs & Soell, Inc., N.Y.C., 1978-80, gen. mgr., 1980-81, exec. v.p., gen. mgr., 1981-88, pres., 1988—, CEO, 1993—. Office: Gibbs & Soell Inc 600 3rd Ave New York NY 10016-1901*

MALLUCHE, HARTMUT HORST, nephrologist, medical educator; b. Breslau, Fed. Republic Germany, Jan. 1, 1943; came to U.S., 1975, naturalized, 1985; s. Harald E. and Renate (Muenzberg) M.; m. Gisela Gleich, Dec. 19, 1975; children: Nadine, Danielle, Tiffany. Abitur, Albertus Magnus Coll., Koenigstein, Germany, 1963; postgrad. Phillips U., Marburg/Lahn, Fed. Republic of Germany, 1963-65, U. Innsbruck, Austria, 1965-66, U. Vienna, Austria, 1966; MD, J. W. Goethe U., Frankfurt, Fed. Republic of Germany, 1969. Diplomate German Bd. Internal Medicine. Intern, County Hosp., Aichach, Fed. Republic of Germany, 1969-70; resident in internal medicine and fellow in nephrology Ctr. Internal Medicine, Univ. Hosp., Frankfurt am. Main, 1970-75, asst. prof. medicine U. So. Calif., Los Angeles, 1975-78, assoc. prof., 1978-81; prof., dir. Div. Nephrology, Bone and Mineral Metabolism U. Ky. Med. Ctr., Lexington, 1981—; cons. NIH, FDA; Va. merit Rev. bd. nephrology. Author (monograph) Atlas of Mineralized Bone Histology, 1986; contbr. articles to profl. jours. and books. Grantee NIH, 1982—, Shriner's Hosp. for Crippled Children, Lexington, 1982—. Fellow ACP; mem. Am. Soc. Nephrology, Am. Soc. Clin. Investigation, Am. Soc. Bone and Mineral Research, Am. Soc. Physiol. Endocrinology, European Dialysis and Transplantation Assn., Am. Fedn. Clin. Research, Internat. Soc. Nephrology, AAAS.

MALM, ROGER CHARLES, lawyer; b. Hot Springs, S.D., July 8, 1949; s. Harry Milton and Angeline Mae (Johnson) M.; m. Sandra M. Metz, July 15, 1972; children: Andrew, Elliott, Nicholas. BA, St. Olaf Coll., 1971; JD, U. N.D., 1974. Bar: N.D. 1974, Ariz. 1975, Minn. 1980, U.S. Dist. Ct. N.D. 1974, U.S. Dist. Ct. Ariz. 1976, U.S. Ct. Appeals (9th cir.) 1981, U.S. Supreme Ct. 1981, U.S. Ct. Appeals (8th cir) 1982, U.S. Dist. Ct. Minn. 1985, U.S. Claims Ct. 1985, U.S. Tax Ct. 1988. Ptnr. Brink, Sobolik, Severson, Vroom & Malm. P.A., Hallock, Minn., 1980—; county atty. Kittson County, Minn., 1995—. Hospice dir. Kittson County Hospice, Inc., 1984—; bd. dirs. Cmty. Theatre, Hallock, 1987—, Greater Grand Forks Cmty. Theater, 1991-95. Mem. ABA, Ariz. Bar Assn., N.D. Bar Assn., Minn. Bar Assn. (bd. govs. 1993—), Am. acad. Hosp. Attys. Lutheran. Avocations: skiing, sailing. Office: Brink Sobolik Severson Vroom & Malm 217 S Birch Box 790 Hallock MN 56728

MALME, CHARLES IRVING, acoustical engineer; b. Crookston, Minn., Aug. 13, 1931; s. Charles Martin and Idella Hilma (Efteland) M.; m. Jane Elton Hamlett, June 17, 1961; children: Robert, Karen. BS, BEE, U. Minn., 1954; MS, MIT, 1958, Elec. Engr., 1959. Ensign, lt.(j.g.) USNR, 1954-56; rsch. asst. Acoustics Lab. MIT, Cambridge, Mass., 1956-59; scientist Bolt Beranek and Newman Inc., Cambridge, Mass., 1960-65, mgr. instrumentation lab., 1965-67, sr. scientist, 1968-93; cons., owner C. Malme Engring. and Scientific Svcs., Hingham, Mass., 1993—; mem. sci. rev. bd. Minerals Mgmt. Svc., Anchorage, 1994-95. Contbr. chpts. to books, articles to profl. jours. Chmn. bldg. com. First Parish Ch., Hingham, Mass., 1994—. Mem. Acoustical Soc. Am. Democrat. Unitarian. Achievements include patent in Wide Range Electrostatic Loudspeaker, Method for Reducing the Bubble Pulse From Underwater Explosions; development of methods for determining the sensitivity of marine species to high level underwater sound. Home: 25 Rockwood Rd Hingham MA 02043-1937 Office: Engring & Scientific Svcs 25 Rockwood Rd Hingham MA 02043-1937

MALME, JANE HAMLETT, lawyer, education researcher; b. N.Y.C., Dec. 2, 1934; d. Robert T. and Minnie (Means) Hamlett; m. Charles I. Maime, June 17, 1961; children: Robert H., Karen I. AB, Brown U., 1956; cert., U. Kobenhavn, Copenhagen, Denmark, 1959; JD, Northeastern U., 1977. Bar: Mass., 1977. Counsel Mass. Tax Commn., Boston, 1978-79; chief bur. local assessment Mass. Dept. Revenue, Boston, 1978-90; owner Mcpl. Mgmt. and Taxation Cons. Svcs., Hingham, Mass., 1990—; fellow Lincoln Inst. Land Policy, Inc., Cambridge, Mass., 1993—; faculty Lincoln Inst. Land Policy, Inc., Cambridge, 1989—; cons. state, provincial coun. Internat. Assn. Assessing Officers Chgo., 1990—; advisor property tax OECD, Paris, 1993—; advisor property tax USAID, Russia, 1995-96, Korea Tax Inst., 1995-96. Co-author: (with Joan Youngman) Internat. Survey of Taxes on Land and Buildings, 1994; contbr. articles to tax jours., papers for Lincoln Inst. of Land Policy, Inc., 1991—. Mem. Dem. Town Com., Hingham, 1990-96; trustee Old Ship Ch., Hingham, 1992—; treas. Betty Taymor Scholarship Fund, Boston, 1992—; pres. Network for Women in Politics and Govt., McCormick Inst., Boston, 1992-94. Mem. Internat Assn. Assessing Officers (founder, state and prov. adminstrv. sec., Presidential citation 1983), Mass. Assn. Assessing Officers (hon. lifetime), Mass. Bar Assn., Womens Bar

Assn., Nat. Assn. Tax Adminstrs. (chair property tax sect. 1988). Unitarian Universalist. Avocations: community service, women in politics, travel. Office: Lincoln Inst Land Policy 113 Brattle St Cambridge MA 02138-3407

MALMGREN, HARALD BERNARD, economist; b. Boston, July 13, 1935; s. Berndt Birger and Magda Helena (Nilsson) M.; m. Patricia A. Malmgren, 1959 (div. 1975); children: Karen Philippa, Britt Patricia, Erika Nina; m. Linda V. Einberg, Oct. 3, 1987; children: Markus Harald, Liivia Linda, Viivianne Vaike. BA summa cum laude, Yale U., 1957; postgrad., Harvard U., 1959; PhD, Oxford U., 1961. Asst. prof. dept. engring. and econs. Cornell U., Ithaca, N.Y., 1961-62; head, econ. group Inst. for Def. Analyses, Washington, 1962-64; asst. U.S. trade rep. Exec. Office Pres. The White House, Washington, 1964-69; sr. fellow Overseas Devel. Coun., 1969-71; ambassador, dep. U.S. trade rep., 1972-75; sr. fellow Woodrow Wilson Internat. Ctr. for Scholars, Washington, 1975-76; prof. George Washington U., Washington, 1976-77; pres. Malmgren, Inc., Washington, 1977—; mng. dir. Malmgren, Golt, Kingston, Ltd., London, 1979—; mem. adv. coun. CSIS, Washington, 1987—; adv. Senate Fin. Com., Washington, 1970-71, 75-76, Interaction Coun., 1985—. Author: International Economic Peace Keeping, 1972; co-author: Assisting Developing Countries, 1972; editor: Pacific Basin Development, 1972; bd. editors: The International Economy, 1987—, The Washington Quarterly, 1987—, The World Economy, 1980-90; contbr. articles to profl. jours. Mem. Am. Econ. Assn. Met. Club, Reform Club. Home: Summerfield Farm 7620 Cannonball Gate Rd Warrenton VA 22186 Office: Malmgren Group Ste 901 1133 Connecticut Ave NW Washington DC 20036-4305

MALMSTAD, JOHN EARL, Slavic languages and literatures, educator; b. Bismarck, N.D., June 25, 1941; s. Manley Ellsworth and Joyce Evelyn (David) M. BA summa cum laude with distinction and departmental honors in Russian Lang. and Lit., Northwestern U., 1963; MA in Slavic Langs. and Lits., Princeton U., 1965, PhD in Slavic Langs. and Lits., 1969; AM (hon.), Harvard U., 1985. Instr. Columbia U., N.Y.C., 1968-69, asst. prof. Russian Lit., 1969-73, assoc. prof., 1973-79, prof. dept. slavic langs. and lits., 1979-85; Samuel Hazzard Cross prof. Slavic langs. and lits. Harvard U., Cambridge, Mass., 1985—, assoc. dean, 1993-94; vis. assoc. prof. Stanford U., 1971-72, U. Calif. Berkeley, 1977-78; vis. prof. Harvard U., fall 1982; cons., referee NEH translation awards; lectr. in field; attendee internat. symposia. Editor: (with others) The Poetry of Mikhail Kuzmin (3 vols.), 1977, The Poetry of Andrei Bely (3 vols.), 1982-85, Gibel Senatora, 1986, Vladislav Khodasevich Sobranie sochinenii, 1983, Andrei Bely, Spirit of Symbolism, 1987, Readings in Russian Modernism to Honor Vladimir Markov, 1993; Russian book rev. editor Slavic Rev., 1975-86; assoc. editor Russian Rev., 1986-88; mem. editl. bd. Minuvshee, Feniks, Opyty, Novoe Literaturnoe obozrenie, Experiment, Philologica; manuscript rev. profl. jours., univ. presses; contbr. articles to profl. jours. Woodrow Wilson fellow, 1963, NDFL fellow Columbia U., 1963-66, Princeton U., 1967-68, Fulbright-Hays fellow, 1966-67, spring 1981, spring 1987, Woodrow Wilson Dissertation fellow, 1966, ACLS rsch. fellow, 1972, Rsch. fellow Russian Inst. Columbia U., summer 1977, 79, 83, 84, IREX fellow, 1975, John Simon Guggenheim fellow, 1980-81; ACLS grant-in-aid, summer, 1980, IREX/ACLS grantee exch. Acad. Scis. USSR, fall 1981, spring 1987, 91, IREX travel grantee Moscow, 1992. Mem. Am. Assn. Advancement of Slavic Studies, Modern Lang. Assn., Assn. Tchrs. of Slavic and East European Langs., Institut d'Etudes Slaves (Paris), Phi Beta Kappa. Avocations: fine arts, ballet, reading. Home: 8A Cogswell Ave Cambridge MA 02140-2001 Office: Harvard U Dept Slavic Langs/Lit 301 Bolyston Hall Cambridge MA 02138

MALMUTH, NORMAN DAVID, program manager; b. Brooklyn, N.Y., Jan. 22, 1931; s. Jacob and Selma Malmuth; m. Constance Nelson, 1970; children: Kenneth, Jill. AE, U. Cin., 1953; MA in Aero. Engring., Polytech. Inst. of N.Y., 1956; PhD in Aeronautics, Calif. Inst. Tech., 1962. Rsch. engr. Grumman Aircraft Engring. Corp., 1953-56; preliminary design engr. N.A. Aviation Div., L.A., 1956-68; teaching asst. Calif. Inst. Tech., L.A., 1961; mem. maths. sci. group Rockwell Internat. Sci. Ctr., 1968-75, project mgr. fluid dynamics rsch., 1975-80, mgr. fluid dynamics group, 1980-82, program mgr. spl. projects, 1982—; cons. Aeroject Gen., 1986-89; lectr. UCLA, 1971-72; mem. adv. group for aerospace R&D Fluid Dynamics Panel, 1995. Referee AIAA Jour.; bd. editors Jour. Aircraft; contbr. articles to Jour. of Heat Transfer, Internat. Jour. Heat Mass Transfer, and others. Named Calif. Inst. Tech. fellow; recipient Outstanding Alumnus award Univ. Cin., 1990. Fellow AIAA (Aerodynamics award 1991); mem. Am. Acad. Mechanics, Am. Inst. Physics (fluid dynamics divsn.), Soc. Indsl. and Applied Math. Achievements include patent in Methods and Apparatus for Controlling Laser Welding; pioneering development of high aerodynamic efficiency of hypersonic delta wing body combinations, hypersonic boundary layer stability, transonic wind tunnel interference web dynamics, combined asymptotic and numerical methods in fluid dynamics and aerodynamics. Home: 182 Maple Rd Newbury Park CA 91320-4718 Office: Rockwell Sci Ctr PO Box 1085 1049 Camino Dos Rios Thousand Oaks CA 91358

MALONE, BRENDAN, coach, professional athlete; b. Apr. 21, 1942; m. Maureen Malone; 6 children. Degree, Iona Coll., 1962; MS in Physical Edn., New York U., 1968. Asst. coach New York Knicks, 1985-88, Detroit Pistons, 1988-95; head coach Toronto Raptors, 1995—. Office: Toronto Raptors, 20 Bay St Ste 1702, Toronto, ON Canada M5J 2N8

MALONE, CHARLES THOMAS, bible college president. Pres. Free Will Bapt. Bible Coll. Nat. Assn. Free Will Bapts., Antioch, Tenn. Office: Natl Assn of Free Will Baptists PO Box 5002 Antioch TN 37011-5002 also: Free Will Baptists Bible College 3606 W End Ave Nashville TN 37205-2403 also: Free Will Bapt Bible Coll 3606 West End Ave Nashville TN 37205

MALONE, DAN F., journalist; b. Dallas, Jan. 22, 1955; s. Charles Ted and Ela Grace (Darden) M.; m. Kathryn Jones, June 27, 1981. BJ, U. Tex., 1978. Editor-in-chief The Daily Texan, Austin, Tex., 1977-78; intern Harte-Hanks Austin Bur., 1978-79; staff writer Corpus Christi (Tex.) Caller-Times, 1979-81, Ft. Worth Star-Telegram, 1981-85; staff writer Dallas Morning News, 1985—, Ft. Worth bureau chief, 1992—; Fox fellow Nat. News Coun., N.Y.C., summer 1978. Recipient Pulitzer prize for investigative reporting, 1992, 1st Place Freedom of Info. Category award Tex. AP Mng. Editor's Assn., 1992, 1st Place Investigative Reporting Inst. Southern Studies, 1992. Office: Dallas Morning News 500 Main St Ste 220 Fort Worth TX 76102-3939

MALONE, DAVID ROY, state senator, university administrator; b. Beebe, Ark., Nov. 4, 1943; s. James Roy and Ila Mae (Griffin) M.; m. Judith Kaye Huff, June 20, 1965 (div. Feb. 1990); 1 child, Michael David. BSBA, U. Ark., 1965, JD, 1969, MBA, 1982. Bar: Ark. 1969, U.S. Dist. Ct. (we. dist.) Ark. 1969, U.S. Tax Ct. 1972, U.S. Ct. Appeals (8th cir.) 1972, U.S. Supreme Ct. 1972. Pvt. practice Fayetteville, Ark., 1969-72; atty. City of Fayetteville, 1969-72; asst. prof. bus. U. Ark., Fayetteville, 1972-76, asst. dean law, 1976-91; mem. Ark. Ho. of Reps., 1980-84, Ark. Senate, 1984—; exec. dir. U. Ark. Found., 1991—; bd. dirs. Bank of Elkins, S.W. Edn. Devel. Lab., Austin, Tex., 1988-94; legal adv. coun. So. Regional Edn. Bd., Atlanta, 1991—. Contbr. articles to profl. jours.; bd. dirs. Ark. Law Rev., 1978-92; contbg. author U. Ark. Press, 1989. Mayor City of Fayetteville, 1979-80; mem. Jud. Article Task Force, Little Rock, 1989-91; chair Motor Voter task force, 1994-95; bd. dirs. Music Festival Ark., 1989-91, Washington County Hist. Soc., 1993—, Walton Arts Ctr. Found., 1994—; chmn. bd. dirs. Washington County Law Libr., 1970-84. Recipient Svc. award Ark. Mcpl. League, 1980, Disting. Service award U. Ark., 1988. Mem. Ark. Bar Assn. (ho. of dels. 1977-81, award of merit 1980, exec. 1981-82, Outstanding Lawyer-Citizen award 1990), Washington County Bar Assn., Ark. Inst. Continuing Legal Edn. (bd. dirs. 1979-88), Fayetteville C. of C. (bd. dirs. 1984—), Ark. Genealogy Soc. (bd. dirs. 1990—). Democrat. Methodist. Avocations: genealogy, stamp collecting. Home: 1928 Austin Dr Fayetteville AR 72703-2713 Office: PO Box 1048 Fayetteville AR 72702-1048

MALONE, EDWARD H., financial executive; b. Forest Hills, N.Y., Nov. 11, 1924; s. Edward H. and Gertrude (Gibson) M.; m. Margaret A. Rakers, Sept. 8, 1951; children: Mary Malone Tilney, Edward, Patricia J. Malone Palmer, Jo-Ann Malone Huber. B.S., Columbia U., 1949; M.B.A., N.Y. U., 1950. Bank examiner Fed. Res. Bank of N.Y., N.Y.C., 1949-52; trust officer Lincoln Rochester (N.Y.) Trust Co., 1952-55; with Gen. Electric Co., 1955-86; mgr. private placement investments Gen. Electric Co., N.Y.C., 1959-61, mgr. trust portfolios, 1961-67, mgr. trust investment ops., 1967-70; v.p. Gen. Electric Co., Stamford, Conn., 1970-86; trustee Prudential Savs. Bank, 1966-77; bd. dirs. Allegheny Power Sys. Inc., Butler Capital Corp., GenRe Corp., Mattel Inc., Warburg Pincus Capital, Fidelity Mutual Funds; chmn. CT Ret. Sys. Investment Adv., 1985-87; mem. Pres.'s Commn. for Fin. Structure and Regulation, 1970-71; dir. Darien chpt. ARC, 1982-88. Trustee Rensselaer Poly. Inst.; bd. dirs. Naples Philharm. Ctr. for Arts. Served with USAAF, 1943-45.

MALONE, EDWIN SCOTT, III, radio and television producer, public relations consultant; b. Vernon, Tex., Mar. 25, 1938; s. Edwin Scott and Pauline (King) M.; m. Sandra Sue Ballard, Aug. 19, 1960; children: Melissa, Michael Scott, Paula Sue. BA, So. Meth. U., 1960; MA, Burton Coll.; PhD, Burton Coll. Seminary; HumD (hon.), Golden State U. Pres. Ed Malone Enterprises, Arlington, Tex., 1960—; account exec. David Wade & Assocs., Dallas, 1963-66; ptnr. COMAL Pub. Rels. Cons., Arlington, 1970-75; v.p. radio So. Baptist Radio-TV Commn., Ft. Worth, 1965—; cons. Tyndale House Pubs., Inc., Wheaton, Ill. Performer Gourmet TV series, Dallas and Ft. Worth, 1955-60; author: Douglas Genealogy, 1959, Malone Genealogy, 1960, Religious Landmarks of America, 1973; prodr. (series) Accent on Youth, Assignment Travel. Tex. del. White House Conf. on Children and Youth, 1960, 70; mem. exec. com. Longhorn coun. Boy Scouts Am.; active, past pres. Ft. Worth Religious Pub. Rels. Coun. Mem. SAR, NATAS, Am. Soc. Travel Writers, Ft. Worth C. of C., Religious Heritage Am., Nat. Press Club, Soc. War of 1812, Sertoma (past pres.), Acacia, Order of Pythagorus (hon.), Order of St. Dennis of Zante (grand cross, charge d'affair Tex.), Order of Crown of Thorns (grand master), Masons, Shriners (past presiding officer York Rite), DeMolay, Legion of Honor. Home: 1608 Hawthorne Dr Arlington TX 76012-2229

MALONE, JAMES L., lawyer, diplomat; b. Los Angeles, Calif.. BA magna cum laude, Pomona Coll., 1953; JD, Stanford U., 1959. Bar: Calif. 1961, U.S. Supreme Ct. 1970, D.C. 1977. Lectr. law, asst. dean Law Sch. UCLA, 1961-67; prof., dean-elect Coll. Law Willamette U., Salem, Oreg., 1967-68; vis. prof. Law Sch. U. Tex., 1969; atty. Fed. Maritime Commn., 1970-71; asst. gen. counsel, then gen. counsel Arms Control and Disarmament Agy., 1971-76, acting dir., 1981; atty. Doub and Muntzing, Washington, 1978-81; asst. sec. oceans and internat. environ. and sci. affairs Dept. State, Washington, 1981-85; Navy Chair Prof. of Internat. Law Naval Postgrad. Sch., Monterey, Calif., 1987-90; pvt. practice, 1990—; U.S. rep. with personal rank of amb. Conf. of Com. on Disarmament, 1976-77; spl. rep. of Pres. for Law of Sea, 1981-85; chmn. U.S. del. and amb. for Law of Sea Conf., 1981-82; adv. bd. Ctr. for Oceans Law and Policy U. Va. Sch. Law. Contbr. articles to profl. jours. Trustee World Affairs Coun. of Monterey Bay Area. 1st lt. U.S. Army, 1954-56. Mem. ABA, State Bar Calif., D.C. Adv. Coun. (chmn.), S.W. Ctr. for Environ. Rsch. and Policy, Coun. Am. Ambs., Rotary Internat., NMMI Alumni (bd. dirs.), Met. Club. (Washington), Capitol Hill Club (Washington), Order of Coif, Phi Beta Kappa. Office: 2600 Garden Rd Ste 222 Monterey CA 93940

MALONE, JAMES WILLIAM, retired bishop; b. Youngstown, Ohio, Mar. 8, 1920; s. James Patrick and Katherine V. (McGuire) M. AB, St. Mary Sem., Cleve., 1945; MA, Cath. U. Am., 1952, PhD, 1957. Ordained priest Roman Catholic Ch., 1945; asst. pastor Youngstown, 1945-50; supt. schs. Diocese of Youngstown, 1952-65; instr. ednl. adminstrn. St. John's Coll., Cleve., 1953; aux. bishop of Youngstown, 1960-68; bishop, 1968-96; ret. Diocese Youngstown, 1996; v.p. Nat. Conf. cath. Bishops, 1980-83; pres. Nat. Conf. Cath. Bishops, 1983-86, mem. Bishops' Com. Ecumencial and Interreligious Affairs; cons. Com. on Socia Devel. & World Peace; ad hoc com. on health care NCCB, ex corde ecclesiae com.; mem. Nat. Interfaith Com. for Worker Justice. consultor Com. on Social Devel. and World Peace; mem. ad. hoc com. on health care, ex corde ecclesiae com. Nat. Conf. Cath. Bishops; mem. Nat. Interfaith Commn. for Worker Justice. Trustee Cath. U. Am.

MALONE, JOHN C., telecommunications executive; b. 1941; m. Leslie. Attended Yale U., Johns Hopkins U. Formerly pres. Jerrold Electronics Corp.; pres., chief exec. officer Tele-Communications, Inc., Denver; chmn., dir. Liberty Media Corp., Denver. Office: Tele-Comm Inc 5619 DTC Pky Englewood CO 80111-3017*

MALONE, JOSEPH D., state treasurer; b. Newton, Mass., Nov. 18, 1954; m. Linda Ploen; children: Joe Jr., Sam, Carolyn Adele. Educated at Harvard Univ., 1978. Treas. state of Mass., 1991—. Office: State House Rm 227 Office Of Treasurer Boston MA 02133

MALONE, JOSEPH JAMES, mathematics educator, researcher; b. St. Louis, Sept. 9, 1932; s. Joseph James and Aurelia Theresa (Schomaker) M.; m. Dorothy Sue Cleary, Nov. 24, 1960; children: Michael, Barbara, Philip, Patrick. BS, St. Louis U., 1954, MS, 1958, PhD, 1962. Instr. math. Rockhurst Coll., Kansas City, Mo., 1960-62; asst. prof. U. Houston, 1962-67; assoc. prof. Tex. A&M U., College Station, 1967-70, prof., 1970-71; prof. Worcester (Mass.) Poly. Inst., 1971—, chmn. dept. math., 1971-78. Contbr. articles to profl. jours. Mem. Town of Westborough (Mass.) Pub. Schs. Bd., 1974-83, 84-87, Fin. Com., 1992—. With U.S. Army, 1954-56. Mem. AAUP, Am. Math. Soc., Math. Assn. Am. Democrat. Roman Catholic. Achievements include research in near-ring theory and group theory. Home: 45 Adams St Westborough MA 01581-3610 Office: Worcester Poly Inst 100 Institute Rd Worcester MA 01609-2280

MALONE, JOSEPH LAWRENCE, linguistics educator; b. N.Y.C., July 2, 1937; s. Joseph Timothy and Katherine Veronica (O'Connor) M.; m. Pamela Joan Altfeld, Jan. 31, 1964; children—Joseph Timothy II, Otis Taig. B.A., U. Calif.-Berkeley, 1963, Ph.D., 1967. Mem. faculty Barnard Coll., N.Y.C., 1967—, prof. linguistics, 1975—, chmn. dept., 1967—; vis. lectr. U. Pa., 1970; linguistics advisor Grolier Pub. Co. Author: The Science of Linguistics in the Art of Translation, 1988, Tiberian Hebrew Phonology, 1992; editor, contbr. Acad. Am. Ency.; mem. editorial bd. Hellas; contbr. articles to profl. jours. Served with U.S. Army, 1957-60. Grad. fellow U. Calif.-Berkeley, 1965-66, Am. Council Learned Socs., 1966-67. Mem. Linguistics Soc. Am., Am. Oriental Soc., AAUP, N.Am. Conf. Afro-Asiatic Linguistics, Phi Beta Kappa. Democrat. Home: 169 Prospect St Leonia NJ 07605-1929 Office: Barnard Coll New York NY 10027-6598

MALONE, JULIA LOUISE, news reporter, White House correspondent; b. Memphis, Sept. 16, 1947; d. William Battle and Alice Avery (Allen) M. BA, Vanderbilt U., 1969. Copy aide Christian Sci. Monitor, Boston, 1969-71, editorial asst., 1971-72, local reporter, 1972-73, editor Living Page, 1978-80, Congl. reporter, 1980-86; TV corr. Christian Sci. Monitor, Washington, 1987-88; bull. editor Harvard Div. Sch., Cambridge, Mass., 1971; reporter The Fauquier Democrat, Warrenton, Va., 1975-77; nat. reporter Cox Newspapers, Washington, 1986-87, 89—; elected mem. standing com. corrs. House and Senate press galleries, Washington, 1983-85. Recipient award for excellence in bus. and econ. reporting John Hancock Fin. Services, Boston, 1986. Mem. White House Corr. Assn., Gridiron Club. Home: 3101 New Mexico Ave Washington DC 20016 Office: Cox Newspapers 2000 Pennsylvania Ave NW Washington DC 20006-1812

MALONE, KARL (THE MAILMAN), professional basketball player; b. Summerfield, La., July 24, 1963. Student, La. Tech. U., 1981-85. Basketball player Utah Jazz, 1985—; mem. U.S. Olympic Basketball Team (received Gold medal), 1992. Mem. NBA All-Star team, 1988-94; recipient NBA All-Star Game MVP award, 1989, co-recipient, 1993; mem. All-NBA first team, 1989-94; mem. All-NBA second team, 1988; mem. NBA All-Defensive second team, 1988; mem. NBA All-Rookie Team, 1986; co-leader most seasons (8) with 2000 points, 1987-95. Office: Utah Jazz Delta Ctr 301 W So Temple Salt Lake City UT 84101*

MALONE, MICHAEL PETER, academic administrator, historian; b. Pomeroy, Wash., Apr. 18, 1940; s. John Albert and Dolores Frances (Cheyne) M.; m. Kathleen Malone, Apr. 17, 1983; children: John Thomas, Molly Christine. BA in History, Gonzaga U., 1962; PhD in Am. Studies, Wash. State U., Pullman, 1966. Asst. prof. history Tex. A&M U., College Station, 1966-67; asst. prof., prof. history Mont. State U., Bozeman, 1967—, dean grad. studies, 1979-89, v.p. acad. affairs, 1989-90; pres. Mont. State U., 1991—; bd. dirs. Buttrey Food and Drug, Commn. on Colls. of N.W. Assn. of Schs. and Colls. Author: The Battle for Butte, 1981 (Sick award 1981), Historians and The American West, 1983, (with others) Montana: A History of Two Centuries, 1976, 2d edit., 1991, The American West: A 20th Century History, 1989, James J. Hill, Empire Builder of the Northwest, 1995. Mem. Western History Assn. Home: 2310 Springcreek Dr Bozeman MT 59715-6035 Office: Mont State U Bozeman MT 59717

MALONE, NANCY, actor, director, producer; b. N.Y.C.; d. James and Bridget (Sheilds) M. Freelance actress, dir., producer, writer. Performer (TV series) The First Hundred Years, Naked City, The Long, Hot Summer (Best Performance by an Actress award); Broadway debut in Time Out For Ginger, other stage performances include Major Barbara, The Makropoulis Secret, A Touch of the Poet, The Trial of the Catonsville Nine; touring performances include The Chalk Garden, The Seven Yr. Itch, A Place For Dolly; actress (films) The Violators, I Cast No Shadow, An Affair of the Skin, Intimacy, The Trial of the Cantonsville Nine, The Man Who Loved Cat Dancing, Capricorn One; producer (TV series) including Bionic Woman, 1978, Husbands, Wives and Lovers, 1978, The Great Pretender, 1984, (special) Bob Hope: The First 90 Years, 1993 (Emmy award, Outstanding Variety, Musical or Comedy Special, 1993), Womanspeak, 1983; dir. (TV series) Dynasty, 1984-87, Hotel, 1984-87, Colbys, 1985, Cagney and Lacey, 1987, Rosie O'Niel (Emmy nomination), Sisters (Emmy nomination), Melrose Place, Beverly Hills, Picket Fences; producer, dir. (film) There Were Times Dear, 1986 (John Muir Trustees award, Cine Golden Eagle, Blue Ribbon); founder Nancy Malone Prodns., 1975, Lilac Prodns., 1979. Fellow Leaky Found.; mem. Am. Film Inst. (mem. founder), Women in Film (Chrystal award). Home: 9911 W Pico Blvd Los Angeles CA 90035-2703 Office: care Guild Mgmt 9911 W Pico Blvd Los Angeles CA 90035-2703

MALONE, PERRILLAH ATKINSON (PAT MALONE), retired state official; b. Montgomery, Ala., Mar. 17, 1922; d. Odolph Edgar and Myrtle (Fondren) Atkinson. BS, Oglethorpe U., 1956; MAT, Emory U., 1962. Asst. editor, then acting editor Emory U., 1958-64; asst. project officer Ga. Dept. Pub. Health, Atlanta, 1965-68; asst. project dir. Ga. Ednl. Improvement Coun., 1968-69, assoc. dir., 1970-71; dir. career svcs. State Scholarship Commn., Atlanta, 1971-74; rev. coord. Div. Phys. Health, Ga. Dept. Human Resources, Atlanta, 1974-79; project dir. So. Regional Edn. Bd., 1979-81; specialist Div. Family and Children Svcs., Atlanta, 1982-91, ret., 1991; mem. Gov.'s Commn. on Nursing Edn. and Nursing Practice, 1972-75, Aging Svcs. Task Force, Atlanta Regional Commn., 1985-95; book reviewer Atlanta Jour.-Constn., 1962-79. Recipient Recognition award Ga. Nursing Assn., 1976, Korsell award Ga. Ga. League for Nursing, 1974, Alumni Honor award Emory U., 1964. Mem. Am. Pub. Health Assn., Ga. Gerontology Soc. (editor GGS Newsletter 1988-92, Lewis Newmark award 1991). Methodist. Home: 1146 Oxford Rd NE Atlanta GA 30306-2608

MALONE, ROBERT JOSEPH, bank executive; b. Sept. 3, 1944. With Bank of Am., 1969-81; chmn., pres., CEO First Interstate Bank Boise, Idaho, 1981-84; pres., CEO First Interstate Bank Denver, 1984-90; chmn., pres., CEO Western Capital Investment Corp. (now First Bank System, Inc.), Denver, 1990-92; chmn., CEO Bank Western/Central Banks (now First Bank System, Inc.), Denver, 1992-93, Colo. Nat. Bank, Denver, 1993—. Office: Colorado Nat Bank 950 17th St Denver CO 80202-2827

MALONE, ROBERT ROY, artist, art educator; b. McColl, S.C., Aug. 8, 1933; s. Robert Roy and Anne (Matthews) M.; m. Cynthia Enid Taylor, Feb. 26, 1956; 1 child, Brendan Trevor. B.A., U. N.C., 1955; M.F.A., U. Chgo., 1958; postgrad., U. Iowa, 1959. Instr. art Union U., Jackson, Tenn., 1959-60, Lambuth Coll., 1959-61; asst. prof. art Wesleyan Coll., Macon, Ga., 1961-67; assoc. prof. Wesleyan Coll., 1967-68, W.Va. U., 1968-70, So. Ill. U., Edwardsville, 1970-75; prof. So. Ill. U., 1975—. One-man shows at Gallery Illien, Atlanta, 1969, De Cinque Gallery, Miami, 1968, 71, Ill. State Mus., Springfield, 1974, U. Del., Newark, 1978, Elliot Smith Gallery, St. Louis, 1985, Merida Galleries, Louisville, 1985, Yvonne Rapp Gallery, Louisville, 1990, 92, 93, St. John's Coll., Santa Fe, 1991, others; group shows include Bklyn. Mus., 1966, Assoc. Am. Artists Gallery, N.Y.C., 1968, Musée d'Art Modern, Paris, 1970, DeCordova Mus., 1973, 74, St. Louis Art Mus., 1985, Wake Forest U., 1985, New Orleans Mus. Art, 1990, Dakota Internat., Vermillion, 1994; represented in numerous permanent collections including Smithsonian Instn., Washington, USIA, Washington, Library of Congress, Calif. Palace of Legion of Honor, San Francisco, N.Y. Pub. Library, N.Y.C., Victoria and Albert Mus., London, Chgo. Art Inst., Indpls. Mus. Art, Humana Inc., Louisville, State of Ill. Ctr., Chgo., Speed Mus., Louisville, N. Ill. Univ., Capital Devel. Bd., Ill. Recipient numerous regional, nat. awards in competitive exhbns.; Ford fellow, 1977; So. Ill. U. at Edwardsville sr. research scholar, 1976, 84. Home: 600 Chapman St Edwardsville IL 62025-1260 Office: Dept Art and Design So Ill U Edwardsville IL 62025

MALONE, THOMAS FRANCIS, academic administrator, meteorologist; b. Sioux City, Iowa, May 3, 1917; s. John and Mary (Hourigan) M.; m. Rosalie Doran, Dec. 30, 1942; children—John H., Thomas Francis, Mary E., James K., Richard K., Dennis P. B.S., S.D. Sch. Mines, 1940, D.Eng., 1962; Sc.D., MIT, 1946; L.H.D., St. Joseph Coll., West Hartford, Conn., 1965; Sc.D. (hon.), Bates Coll., 1988. Instr. MIT, 1942-43, asst. prof., 1943-51, assoc. prof., 1951-56; dir. Travelers Research Ctr., Travelers Ins. Co., Hartford, Conn., 1955-56; dir. research Travelers Research Ctr., Travelers Ins. Co., 1956-69, sr. v.p., 1968-70; chmn. bd. Travelers Research Ctr., Inc., 1961-70; dean Grad. Sch., U. Conn., Storrs, 1970-73; chmn. bd. Center for Environment and Men, 1970-71; dir. emeritus Holcomb Research Inst., Butler U., Indpls., 1983—; scholar in residence St. Joseph Coll., 1983-91; Nat. Scis. fellow Resources for Future, 1983-84; chmn. bd. Univ. Corp. for Atmospheric Research.; mem. Conn. Weather Control Bd., 1959-73; mem. panel on sci. and tech., com. on sci. and astronautics U.S. Ho. of Reps., 1960-1970; nat. adv. com. community air pollution HEW, 1962-66; mem. sci. info. council NSF, 1962-66; rep. Am. Geophys. Union to U.S. Nat. Commn. for UNESCO, 1963-73 chmn. U.S. Nat. Commn., 1965-67; mem. nat. adv. com. on oceans and atmosphere, 1972-75, mem. Com. Research Commn., 1965-71; mem. com. application sci. and tech. New Eng. Council; chmn. Nat. Motor Vehicle Safety Adv. Council, 1967-70; mem. sci. adv. com. climate impact assessment and response program UN Environ. Program, 1992—. Editor: Compendium of Meteorology, 1951; contbg. editor: Environment, 1992—; bd. editors: Jour. of the Marine Tech. Soc., 1995—. Bd. dirs. Engrs. Joint Coun., 1968-70; bd. govs. Ins. Inst. Hwy. Safety, 1968-70; mem. oversight rev. bd. Nat. Acid Precipitation Assessment Program, 1990—. Recipient Robert M. Losey award Inst. Aero. Sci., 1960, Charter Oak Leadership medal Greater Hartford C. of C., 1962, Charles Franklin Brooks award, 1964, Cleveland Abbe award Am. Meteorol. Soc., 1968, Conn. Conservationist of Yr. award, 1966, Guy E. March Silver medal S.D. Sch. Mines, 1976, Internat. Meteorol. Orgn. prize, 1984, Internat. St. Francis Assissi prize for environment, 1991, AAAS Internat. prize, 1994; N.C. State U. disting. scholar, 1990—. Fellow AAAS (internat. sci. coop., 1994), N.Y. Acad. Scis., Am. Meteorol. Soc. (pres. 1960-62), Am. Geophys. Union (past pres., sec. internat. participation 1964, Waldo E. Smith award 1986); mem. Nat. Acad. Scis. (chmn. geophysics research bd. 1969-76, chmn. bd. on internat. orgns. and programs, dep. fgn. sec. 1969-73, fgn. sec. 1978-82), Am. Acad. Arts and Scis., Internat. Council Sci. Unions (v.p., sec.-gen. sci. com. problems environ. 1970-76, treas. 1978-82 Nat. Acad. Engring. (space applications bd. 1973-77), Am. Geog. Soc. (council 1971-77), Royal Irish Acad. (hon.), Conn. Acad. Sci. and Engring. (exec. scientist 1987-91), Sigma Xi (bd. dirs. 1983—, pres. 1988-89, dir. Sigma Xi Ctr. 1992—). Home: 5 Bishop Rd Apt 203 West Hartford CT 06119-1536 Office: NC State U Dept Marine and Atmospheric Scis Box 8208 Raleigh NC 27695

MALONE, WALLACE D., JR., bank executive; b. Dothan, Ala., 1936; married. BS, U. Ala., 1957; MBA, U. Pa., 1960. With First Nat. Bank, 1959-71; with SouthTrust Corp., Birmingham, Ala., 1972—, now chmn., chief exec. officer, dir. Office: Southtrust Corp 420 N 20th St PO Box 2554 Birmingham AL 35203*

MALONE, WILLIAM GRADY, lawyer; b. Minden, La., Feb. 19, 1915; s. William Gordon and Minnie Lucie (Hortman) M.; m. Marion Rowe Whitfield, Sept. 26, 1943; children: William Grady, Gordon Whitfield, Marion Elizabeth, Helen Ann, Margaret Catherine. BS, La. State U., 1941; JD, George Washington U., 1952. Bar: Va. 1952, U.S. Supreme Ct 1971. Statis. analyst Dept. Agr., Baton Rouge, 1941; investigator VA, Washington, 1946-

59; legal officer, dep., gen. counsel, asst. gen. counsel VA, 1959-79; pvt. practice law Arlington, Va., 1979—. Editor: Fed. Bar News, 1972-73. Pres. Aurora Hills Civic Assn., 1948-49; spl. asst. to treas. Com. of 100, 1979-81, chmn., 1982-83; pres. Children's Theater, 1968-69; trustee St. George's Episc. Ch., 1979—; chmn. Arlington County Fair Assn., 1979-83. Lt. col. AUS, 1941-46, ETO. Decorated Legion of Merit; recipient Disting. Svc. award, 1979, 3 Superior Performance awards, 1952-72, Outstanding Alumni award George Washington Law Sch., 1978. Mem. Fed. Bar Assn. (pres. D.C. chpt. 1970-71, nat. pres. 1978-79), Va. Bar Assn., Arlington County Bar Assn., Nat. Lawyers Club (dir.), Arlington Host Lions, Ft. Myer Officers Club. Home: 224 N Jackson St Arlington VA 22201-1253 Office: 2060 14th St N Ste 310 Arlington VA 22201-2519 *Success is not measured by dollars accumulated but by service to others.*

MALONE, WINFRED FRANCIS, health scientist; b. Revere, Mass., Feb. 10, 1935; s. Winfred and Margurite (Meehan) M.; m. Eleanor Malone, Aug. 1974. BS, U. Mass., 1957, MS, 1961; MS, Rutgers U., 1963; PhD, U. Mich., 1970. Health scientist Nat. Cancer Inst., Bethesda, Md., 1970-81, chief chemoprevention br., 1981-95, acting assoc. dir., 1991-93; chief ACRES Nat. Cancer Inst., 1995—. Contbr. articles on drug devel. scis. to profl. jours. Mem. AAAS, Am. Coll. Toxicology, N.Y. Acad. Scis., Drug Info. Assn. Home: 3209 Wake Dr Kensington MD 20895-3216 Office: Nat Cancer Inst EPN # 201 Bethesda MD 20892

MALONEY, CAROLYN BOSHER, congresswoman; b. Feb. 19, 1948; d. R.G. and Christine (Clegg) Bosher; m. C.H.W. Maloney, 1976; children: Christina, Virginia. Student, Greensboro Coll., New Sch. for Social Rsch., N.Y., U. Dijon, Paris. Former mem. N.Y. State Assembly Housing Com., N.Y.C Council dist. 8; mem. 103rd Congress from 14th N.Y. dist., Washington, D.C., 1993—. Past chmn. Common Cause; active Assn. for a Better N.Y., Manahattan Women's Polit. Caucus. Mem. NAACP, Nat. Orgn. Women, Hadassah. Home: 49 E 92nd St Apt 1A New York NY 10128-1326 Office: US Ho of Reps 1504 Longworth Washington DC 20515

MALONEY, DIANE RUTH, financial planner; b. Berwyn, Ill., Jan. 20, 1939; d. Dayton Willian and Ruth E. (Bollnow) Nordin; m. James Ralph Maloney, Nov. 25, 1964; children: Joel Nordin, Katherine Linnea. Student, North Ctrl. Coll., Naperville, Ill., 1957-59; BA with honors, U. Ill., 1961, MA, 1972. Cert. fin. planner; registered in Ill. Dist. advisor Girl Scouts Am., Gary, Ind., Joliet, Ill., 1961-67; tchr. social studies Joliet Twp. H.S., 1968-88; instr. anthropology Coll. of DuPage, Glen Ellyn, Ill., 1970s; pres., chmn. bd. Unica, Inc., Plainfield, Ill., 1979-86; fin. planner CMP Fin. Svcs., Inc., Chgo., 1988-89, Herbst Fin. Svcs., Plainfield, 1989-91; fin. planner, ptnr., officer Herbst, Maloney & Brown, Fin. Planning Svcs. Ltd., Plainfield, 1992—; ptnr., officer Prairie Mgmt. Group, Ltd., Plainfield, 1994—. Author Children's Activity Books Career Series, 1980. Chmn. bd., supt. Sunday sch., Ch. in Joliet, 1970—; pres. Downtown Bus. Assn., Plainfield, 1992. Recipient Master Tchr. award Ill. State Bd. Edn., 1984, Those That Excel award, 1988; Fulbright grantee to Egypt, 1977. Mem. Internat. Assn. Fin. Planners, Inst. Cert. Fin. Planners, Am. Interprofl. Inst. (pres. 1991), East-West Corp. Corridor Assn. Democrat. Christian Scientist. Office: Herbst Maloney & Brown Fin Planning Svcs Ltd 819 N Division St Plainfield IL 60544-1926

MALONEY, FRANCIS PATRICK, physiatrist, educator; b. Pitts., Mar. 4, 1936; s. Francis Barrington and Esther Elizabeth (Kuhn) M.; m. Kathryn Brassell Anderson, June 25, 1960 (dec. June 6, 1987); children: Timothy J., Kevin P., J. Christopher; m. Billie Barbara Galloway, Feb. 14, 1990. BA, St. Vincent Coll., 1958; MD, U. Pitts., 1962; MPH, Johns Hopkins U., 1966. Diplomate Am. Bd. Phys. Medicine and Rehab., Am. Bd. Preventive Medicine, Am. Bd. Med. Mgmt. Intern St. Francis Hosp., Pitts., 1962-63; resident gen. preventive medicine Johns Hopkins U. Sch. of Hygiene & Pub. Health, Balt., 1965-67; fellow medicine, med. genetics Johns Hopkins U. Sch. of Medicine, Balt., 1966-68; resident phys. medicine and rehab. U. Minn., Mpls., 1968-70; staff physician Sister Kenny Inst., Mpls., 1970-72; asst. clin. prof. U. Minn., Mpls., 1970-72; asst. prof. phys. medicine and rehab., assoc. prof. U. Colo., Denver, 1972-78, 78-84; prof. head div. of rehab. medicine U. Ark., Little Rock, 1984-91, prof., chmn. dept. phys. medicine and rehab., 1991—; med. dir. Bapt. Rehab. Inst., Little Rock, 1985—; chief rehab. medicine svc. VA Med. Ctr., Little Rock, 1984—. Editor: Interdisciplinary Rehabilitation of Multiple Sclerosis and Neuromuscular Disease, 1984; editor, author: Physical Medicine & Rehabilitation State of the Art Reviews, 1987, Primer on Management, 1987, Rehabilitation of Aging, 1989, Management for Rehabilitation Medicine II, 1993; alt. editor: Archives of Physical Medicine and Rehabilitation, 1989-93. Mem. exec. bd. Greater No. Colo. Chpt. of Muscular Dystrophy Assn. of Am., 1972-82; spl. edn. adv. com. Cherry Creek Sch. Dist., Denver, 1975, vice chmn., 1976, chmn., 1977; med. advisor Denver Commn. on Disabled and Coun. on Aging, Denver, 1980-82, Denver Commn. on Human Svcs., 1982-84; external examiner King Saud U. Med. Sch., Saudi Arabia, 1983; med. adv. bd. Ark. Multiple Sclerosis Soc., Little Rock, 1985-88; chmn. chmn's. coun. Assn. Acad. Physiatrists, Indpls., 1992-94. Fellow Am. Acad. Phys. and Rehab.; mem. AMA, Am. Congress of Rehab. Medicine, Am. Acad. Cerebral Palsy, Am. Pub. Health Assn., Am. Bd. Physical Medicine and Rehbilitation (dir. 1988—), Soc. for Exptl. Biology and Medicine, Assn. Acad. Physiatrists, Ark. Med. Soc., Pulaski County Med. Soc., Soc. for Neuroscis. Office: U Ark Med Scis 4301 W Markham Slot #602 Little Rock AR 72205

MALONEY, GERALD P., utility executive; b. Lawrence, Mass., Mar. 9, 1933; s. Thomas P. and Concetta M.; m. Dorothea Ames. BSEE, MIT, 1955, BSBA, 1955; MBA, Rutgers U., 1962. With Am. Electric Power Co., Inc., Columbus, Ohio, 1955—; controller Am. Electric Power Co., Inc., 1965-70, v.p. fin., 1970-75, sr. v.p. fin., 1975-90, exec. v.p., CFO, 1990—; dir., v.p. fin. Appalachian Power Co., Ind., Mich. Power Co., Ohio Power Co., Ky. Power Co., Wheeling Power Co., Kingsport Power Co., Columbus & So. Power Co.; bd. dirs. Energy Ins. Mut., Ltd., chmn., 1990-92; bd. dirs. Nuclear Electric Ins., Ltd. Mem. Edison Electric Inst. (fin. com.), Beta Gamma Sigma. Home: 275 S Parkview Ave Bexley OH 43209 Office: Am Electric Power Co 1 Riverside Plz Columbus OH 43215-2355

MALONEY, JAMES EDWARD, lawyer; b. Hackensack, N.J., Apr. 28, 1951; s. Edward James Maloney and Kathleen Elizabeth (Lamont) Leaf. BA, Yale U., 1972; JD, Harvard U., 1975. Bar: Tex. 1975, U.S. Dist. Ct. (no., so., ea. and we. dists.) Tex., U.S. Ct. Appeals (2d, 3d, 5th, 9th and D.C. cirs.), U.S. Supreme Ct. Assoc. Baker & Botts, Houston, 1975-82, ptnr., 1982—; chmn. bd. dirs. Fotofest, Inc.; bd. dirs. Houston Ctr. for Photography. Trustee Woodberry Forest (Va.) Sch., 1991—. Mem. ABA, Tex. Bar Assn., Tex. Bar Found., Houston Bar Assn., Houston Bar Found., Yale Club (Houston, Assn. Yale Alumni rep. 1984-86). Republican. Episcopalian. Home: 2129 Tangley St Houston TX 77005-1640 Office: Baker & Botts 3000 One Shell Plz 910 Louisiana St Houston TX 77002

MALONEY, JAMES HENRY, lawyer; b. Quincy, Mass., Sept. 17, 1948; s. James Henry Jr. and Katherine Smith (Murphy) M.; m. Mary Angela Draper, Aug. 16, 1980; children: Adele, Anna, Ellen. BA cum laude, Harvard U., 1972; JD, Boston U., 1980. Vol. VISTA, Gary, Ind., 1969-70; exec. dir. Community Action Com. Danbury, Conn., 1974-78; atty. Pinney, Payne, VanLenten, Burrell, Wolfe & Dillman, P.C., Danbury, 1980-86; ptnr. Dice, Maloney & Lenz, P.C., Danbury, 1986-93, Maloney, Leaphart & Assocs., PC, Danbury, 1995—; mem. Conn. Senate, Hartford, 1987-95; asst. majority leader and senate chair fin., revenue and bonding com., 1993-95. Chmn. Danbury Cmty. Endowment, 1984-94, dem. candidate for U.S. Congress, 1994, 96. Recipient Disting. Svc. award Jaycees North Fairfield County, 1984, Community Svc. award Midwestern Conn. Coun. on Alcoholism, 1990, Spl. Recognition award Jewish Home for the Elderly, Fairfield County, 1993; named Legislator of Yr., Caucus Conn. Dems., 1990, Conn. Assn. Ind. Ins. Agts., 1992. Roman Catholic. Avocation: sailing. Office: Maloney Leaphart & Assocs PC 301 Main St Ste 300 Danbury CT 06810

MALONEY, JOHN ALEXANDER, retired hospital administrator; b. Knoxville, Tenn., Mar. 1, 1927; s. Harry Lotspeich and Gertrude (Blaetz) M.; m. Doris Ann Akes, Oct. 21, 1964; children: John Patrick, Christopher Michael; stepchildren: Thomas Kent Gaskins, Shelley Arlene Gaskins, William Glenn Gaskins. Student, U. Tenn., 1947-50; certificate in hosp. adminstrn., Ga. State Coll., 1958. Adminstr. Lawrence County Gen. Hosp., Lawrenceburg, Tenn., 1958-60, Morristown-Hamblen (Tenn.) Hosp., 1960-64, Central State Psychiat. Hosp., Nashville, 1964-67, Eastern State Psychiat. Hosp., Knoxville, 1967-72; cons. Project Devel. Corp., Knoxville, 1971-72; adminstr. R.J. Taylor Meml. Hosp., Hawkinsville, Ga., 1972-73; health services cons., 1973-77; unit adminstr. dept. psychiatry and neurology Walter Reed Army Med. Center, Washington, 1977-79; assoc. adminstr. Walter Reed Army Med. Center, 1979-94, chief hosp. support div., 1991-94; ret., 1994; pres. Knoxville Hosp. Coun., 1971-72. Served with USNR, 1944-46; to 2d lt. AUS, 1952-53. Mem. Am. Coll. Hosp. Adminstrs., Tenn. Hosp. Assn., Knoxville Hosp. Council (pres. 1969-70), Am. Pub. Health Assn., Pi Epsilon Rho. Episcopalian. Lodges: Kiwanis, Rotary, Elks (lodge # 160). Address: 790 N Cedar Bluff Rd Apt 605 Knoxville TN 37923-2240

MALONEY, JOHN FREDERICK, retired marketing and opinion research specialist; b. Watertown, N.Y., Apr. 28, 1913; s. John Francis and Grace (Gott) M.; m. Lucia Howard McKellar, Apr. 27, 1940; children—John Frederick, Robert McKellar, Bonnie Patton, Lucia Howard. Grad., Mt. Hermon Sch., 1931; A.B., Princeton, 1935. With Gallup Poll, 1935-38; v.p. Peoples Research Corp., 1939-40; research analyst Young & Rubicam, 1940; Eastern mgr. Nat. Opinion Research Center, 1941; devel. analyst Curtis Pub. Co., 1946; research dir. internat. and U.S. Reader's Digest, 1946-66, corp. research dir., 1966-70; exec. v.p. Reader's Digest Found., 1970-71; cons. Advt. Research Found., N.Y.C., 1972-87; exec. dir. Council of Am. Survey Research Orgns., 1976-79; ret.; Pres. World Assn. Pub. Opinion Research, 1952-53, Market Research Council, 1958-59; chmn. research com. Mag. Pubs. Assn., 1961-65; vice chmn. tech. com. Advt. Research Found., 1956-70. Chmn. Westchester County Social Agys., 1953-57; v.p. Nat. Social Welfare Assembly, 1964-68; nat. chmn. Princeton Ann. Giving, 1968-69; vice-chmn. Princeton U. Fund, 1968-69; pres. United Way Westchester, 1968-71, Princeton Class 1935, 1970-75; chmn. Westchester County adv. com. N.Y. State Urban Devel. Corp., 1970-86; chmn. adv. com. Westchester Community Found., 1981-86. Lt. comdr. USNR, 1941-45; comdg. officer destroyer escort. Decorated Commendation medal. Mem. Am. Mktg. Assn. (pres. N.Y. chpt. 1960, v.p. internat. div. 1972-73). Conglist. (chmn. bd. deacons 1962-63). Clubs: Princeton (N.Y.C.), Coffee House (N.Y.C.). Home: 48 Hamilton Rd Chappaqua NY 10514-3222

MALONEY, JOHN WILLIAM, lawyer; b. Santa Barbara, Calif., Dec. 6, 1930; s. John Joseph and Mildred (Brunenmeyer); m. Jean Anderson, Nov. 18, 1966; children: Patrick Maloney, Cynthia Maloney. BA in Econs., U. Calif., Santa Barbara, 1953; JD, UCLA, 1958. Bar: Calif. 1959, U.S. Dist. Ct. (no., ctrl., ea., so. dists.) Calif. 1959. Assoc. Fogel McInery, Santa Monica, Calif., 1959-62; ptnr. Rhodes Barnard & Maloney, Santa Monica, 1963-82, Rhodes, Maloney et al., Santa Monica, 1983-88; prin. Maloney & Mullen, Santa Monica, 1989—; ptnr. Real Estate Investors, 1970—. Pres. Santa Monica Legal Aid Soc., 1960-63. Capt. U.S. Army, 1953-55. Mem. Lions. Republican. Roman Catholic. Avocations: fly fishing, duck hunting, tennis. Office: Maloney & Mullen 520 Broadway St Ste 300 Santa Monica CA 90401-2429

MALONEY, MICHAEL JAMES, research scientist; b. Madison, Wis., Aug. 29, 1942; s. James Edward and Wanda Marie (Berry) M; m. Diane Lois Best, Apr. 20, 1962; children—Lance, Robin Maloney Judd, Tracy, Scott. Staff scientist Bjorksten Research Labs., Inc., Madison, Wis., 1962-79, v.p., 1979-84, pres., 1984—. Inventor in field. Contbr. articles to profl. jours. Chmn., Fitchburg Parks Commn., Wis., 1972—; mem. Fitchburg Planning Commn., 1972—. Mem. ASTM, ASM, Soc. Plastics Engrs. Roman Catholic. Office: Bjorksten Rsch Labs Inc 2998 Syene Rd PO Box 259444 Madison WI 53725-9444

MALONEY, MICHAEL PATRICK, lawyer, corporate executive; b. Syracuse, N.Y., June 1, 1944; s. Randolph Bartholomew and Alice Mary (Loban) M.; m. Jane McBurney, May 21, 1977; children: Christopher, Kara. A.B., Georgetown U., 1966; M.B.A., Cornell U., 1968, J.D., 1971. Bar: N.Y. 1972. Assoc. Donovan Leisure Newton and Irvine, N.Y.C., 1971-78; asst. dir. div. market regulation SEC, Washington, 1978-79; v.p., gen. counsel, sec. Orion Capital Corp., N.Y.C., 1979—; bd. dirs. Am. Arbitration Assn.; mem. Corp. Governance Com. Mem. N.Y. Bar Assn., Am. Soc. Corp. Secs. (pres. N.Y. chpt.), Am. Corp. Counsel Assn. (bd. dirs. N.Y. chpt.), Scarsdale Golf Club (Hartsdale, N.Y.), Rockefeller Ctr. Club. Home: 7 Kings Grant Way Briarcliff Manor NY 10510-2521 Office: Orion Capital Corp 600 5th Ave New York NY 10020-2302

MALONEY, MILFORD CHARLES, retired internal medicine educator; b. Buffalo, Mar. 15, 1927; s. John Angelus Maloney and Winifred Hill; m. Dione Ethyl Sheppard. BS, Canisius Coll., 1947, postgrad., 1947-49; MD, U. Buffalo, 1953. Diplomate Am. Bd. Internal Medicine. Rsch. chemist Buffalo Electrochem. Co., 1947-49; intership Mercy Hosp./Georgetown U., 1953-54; med. residency Buffalo VA Hosp., 1954-56; cardiology fellow Buffalo Gen. Hosp., 1956-57; chmn. dept. medicine Mercy Hosp., 1969-94; program dir., internal medicine residency Mercy Hosp., Buffalo, 1972-89; with steering com. Assn. Program Dirs. in Internal Medicine, 1976, coun. mem., 1977-80; clin. prof. medicine SUNY, Buffalo, 1981-94; trustee Am. Soc. Internal Medicine, 1984-90; edn. leader med. seminar Am. Soc. Internal Medicine, Austria, Switzerland, France, 1987, Argentina, Brazil, Paraguay, 1988; bd. dirs. Internal Medicine Ctr. for Advancement and Rsch. Edn.; pres. Heart Assn. Western N.Y., Buffalo, 1969; sr. cancer rsch. physician Roswell Park Meml. Cancer Inst., 1959-62; mem. internal medicine liaison com. N.Y. State, 1980-90. Editor (newsletter) N.Y. State Soc. Internal Medicine, 1972-78. bd. dirs. Health Systems Agy. Western N.Y., Buffalo, 1981; exec. com., bd. dirs. Blue Cross Western N.Y., Buffalo, 1987; bd. regents Canisius Coll., Buffalo, 1987—; mem. pres. assocs. SUNY, Buffalo. Capt. M.C., U.S. Army, 1957-59. Recipient Merit award N.Y. State Soc. Internal Medicine, 1980, Man of Yr. award Heart Assn. Western N.Y., 1982, Ann. Honoree award Trocai Coll., 1986, Disting. Alumni award Canisius Coll., 1991, Berkson Excellence award in Tchg. and Art of Medicine, SUNY at Buffalo, 1992, Outstanding Med. Tchg. Attending award Mercy Hosp./SUNY Med. Residents, 1994; named to Sports Hall of Fame, Canisius Coll., 1978. Fellow ACP (Upstate Physician Recognition award 1989), Am. Coll. Cardiology; mem. AMA (SUNY rep. 1986-94, rep. to sect. med. schs. at ann. meetings 1984-94, chmn. sect. on internal medicine 1990-91), Am. Soc. Internal Medicine (bd. dirs. internal medicine purchasing group, trustee 1984-90, pres. 1990-91, chmn. long range planning com.), N.Y. State Soc. Internal Medicine (pres.), Alumni Assn. SUNY (pres. 1975), Med. Soc. County Erie (pres. 1969), Va. Soc. Internal Medicine (hon.). Home: 116 Cove Point Ln Williamsburg VA 23185-8613

MALONEY, ROBERT B., federal judge; b. 1933. BBA, So. Meth. U., 1956, Postgrad., 1960. Asst. dist. atty. County of Dallas, 1961-62; ptnr. Watts, Stallings & Maloney, 1962-65, Maloney, Miller & McDowell, 1966-75, Maloney & McDowell, 1976-78, Maloney & Hardcastle, 1979-80, Maloney & Maloney, 1981-84; assoc. judge Tex. Ct. Appeals (5th cir.), Tex., 1983-85; judge U.S. Dist. Ct. (no. dist.) Tex., Dallas, 1985—. State rep., Austin, Tex., 1973-82. Mem. Tex. Bar Assn. Office: US Dist Ct 15E26 US Courthouse 1100 Commerce St Dallas TX 75242-1027*

MALONEY, ROBERT E., JR., lawyer; b. San Francisco, Sept. 17, 1942; s. Robert E. and Mara A. (Murphy) M.; children: Michael, Sarah. BA magna cum laude, U. Portland, 1964; JD summa cum laude, Willamette U., Salem, Oreg., 1967. Bar: Oreg., Wash., U.S. Dist. Ct. Oreg., U.S. Dist. Ct. (we. dist.) Wash., U.S. Dist. Ct. (ea. dist.) Wash., U.S. Ct. Appeals (9th cir.). Ptnr. Lane Powell Spears Lubersky, Portland, 1967—; bd. dirs., sec. Norm Thompson Outfitters, Inc., Portland, 1981—; chmn. bd. visitors Willamette U. Law Sch., 1993-95; chair, mem. exec. com. Portland Trial Dept.; lawyers del. 9th Cir. Jud. Conf., 1995—. Judge Pro Tem Multnomah County Cir. Ct., 1994—. Mem. ABA (co-chair products liability com., trial practice com. 1990-94), Nat. Assn. R.R. Trial Counsel, Fedn. Ins. Corp. Counsel, Oreg. Assn. Def. Counsel (bd. dirs. 1987-94, sec. 1991-92, v.p. 1993-94, pres. 1994), Fed. Bar Assn. (exec. com. Oreg. divsn. 1988—, pres. 1994-95), Multnomah Athletic Club. Republican. Roman Catholic. Office: Lane Powell Spears Lubersky 520 SW Yamhill St Portland OR 97204-1335

MALONEY, THERESE ADELE, insurance company executive; b. Quincy, Mass., Sept. 15, 1929; d. James Henry and F. Adele (Powers) M. BA in Econs., Coll. St. Elizabeth, Convent Station, N.J., 1951; AMP, Harvard U. Bus. Sch., 1981. CPCU. With Liberty Mut. Ins. Co., Boston, 1951-94, asst. v.p., asst. mgr. nat. risks, 1974-77, v.p., asst. mgr. nat. risks, 1977-79, v.p., mgr. nat. risks, 1979-86, sr. v.p. underwriting mktg. and adminstrn. 1986-87, exec. v.p. underwriting, policy decision, 1987-94, also bd. dirs.; pres. and bd. dirs. subs. Liberty Mut. (Bermuda) Ltd., 1981-94, LEXCO Ltd.; bd. dirs., dep. chmn. Liberty Mut. (U.K.) Ltd., London; bd. dirs. Liberty Mut. Ins. Co., Liberty Mut. Fire Ins. Co., Liberty Mut. Life Assurance Co., Liberty Fin. Cos.; mem. faculty Inst. Inst., Northeastern U., Boston, 1969-74; mem. adv. bd., risk mgmt. studies Ins. Inst. Am., 1977-83; mem. adv. coun. Suffolk U. Sch. Mgmt., 1984-96; mem. adv. coun. to program in internat. bus. rels. Fletcher Sch. Law and Diplomacy, 1985-94. Mem. Soc. CPCUs (past pres. Boston chpt.), Univ. Club, Boston Club.

MALONEY, WILLIAM GERARD, retired investment company executive; b. Dansville, N.Y., Apr. 8, 1917; s. William J. and Fannie K. (Kirschner) M.; m. Katherine R. Kenney, Oct. 21, 1940; children: William J., Elizabeth Ann, Stephen G. B.S., U. Pa., 1939. Trainee Hemphill, Noyes & Co., N.Y.C., 1939; mem. research dept. Hemphill, Noyes & Co., 1940-42, 44-45, mgr. corporate fin. dept., 1949, partner, 1951-63, co-mng. partner, 1963-64; coordinating partner Hornblower & Weeks-Hemphill, Noyes, N.Y.C., 1965-71; mgr. br. office adminstrn. Hornblower & Weeks-Hemphill, Noyes, 1969-71, vice chmn. exec. com., dir., 1972-80; sr. mng. dir. Loeb Rhoades, Hornblower & Co., N.Y.C., 1978-80, Shearson, Am. Express Inc., 1979-84; mng. dir. Shearson Lehman Bros. Inc., 1985-87, adv. dir., 1988-89; bd. dirs. N.Am. Royalties Inc., St. Camillus Health Ctr.; mem. adv. bd. Advanced Tech. Ventures; dir., vice chmn. Hanover Petroleum Corp., 1969-76. Bd. dirs. Med. Biology Inst., 1980-83; trustee Coll. of New Rochelle, 1986-92. Served with U.S. Army, 1942-43. Mem. N.Y. Soc. Security Analysts. Republican. Roman Catholic. Clubs: Met, Nantucket Yacht, Knight Commander of Equestrian Order of Holy Sepulchre of Jerusalem, Knight of Malta, Knight Commander of St. Gregory. Home: 155 Oenoke Ln New Canaan CT 06840-4518 Office: Am Express Tower World Fin Ctr New York NY 10005

MALOOF, GILES WILSON, academic administrator, educator, author; b. San Bernardino, Calif., Jan. 4, 1932; s. Joseph Peters and Georgia (Wilson) M.; m. Mary Anne Ziniker, Sept. 5, 1958 (dec. Oct. 1976); children: Mary Jane, Margery Jo. BA, U. Calif. at Berkeley, 1953; MA, U. Oreg., 1958; PhD, Oreg. State U., 1962. Petroleum reservoir engr. Creole Petroleum Corp., Venezuela, 1953-54; mathematician electronics div. research dept. U.S. Naval Ordnance Rsch. Lab., Corona, Calif., 1958-59; asst. prof. math. Oreg. State U., Corvallis, 1962-68, rsch. assoc. dept. oceanography, 1963-68, vis. prof. math., 1977-78; prof. math. Boise (Idaho) State U., 1968—, head dept., 1968-75, dean grad. sch., 1970-75; project dir. Dept. Energy Citizens' Workshop Energy Environment Simulator for Eastern Oreg., No. Nev. and Idaho, 1976—. Served with Ordnance Corps, AUS, 1950, 54-56. Author, reviewer of coll. textbooks; contbr. to profl. jours. Recipient Carter award, 1963, Mosser prize, 1966, Oreg. State U. Mem. Math. Assn. Am., Am. Math. Soc., Soc. Indsl. and Applied Math., Northwest Coll. and Univ. Assn. for Sci. (dir. 1973—, pres. 1990-92), Northwest Sci. Assn. (trustee 1977-80), Assoc. Western Univs. (mem. edn. and rsch. com. 1993—), Sigma Xi, Pi Mu Epsilon, Phi Kappa Phi. Home: 1400 Longmont Ave Boise ID 83706-3730

MALOOF, JAMES A(LOYSIUS), mayor, real estate company executive; b. Peoria, Ill., Oct. 18, 1919; s. Nimer and Sarah (Hamady) M.; m. Gertrude Mae Burson, June 28, 1941; children—James Michael, Mark (dec.), Nicholas, Janice. Grad. high sch., Peoria. Pres., owner Jim Maloof Realtor, Peoria, 1969—; mayor City of Peoria, 1985—. Mem. adv. bd. Peoria Civic Ctr. Commn., Jr. League Peoria, Boy's Club Peoria, Lebanon Task Force, local Peoria County Emergency Planning Com., Bradley Community Action Advisory Council; mem. exec. mgmt. bd. St. Jude Children's Research Hosp., Memphis, chmn. bd. dirs. and co-founder midwest affiliate at Meth. Med. Ctr., chmn. first telethon, 1978, past nat. exec. v.p.; chmn. Christian edn. fund drive St. Philomena Parish, Bradley U. Athletic Fund Dr.; chmn. adv. com. Peoria Big Bros. and Big Sisters; mem. Gov.'s Build Ill. Com., Ill. Job Tng. Coordinating Council, Gov.'s Statewide Taskforce on the Homeless; mem. fundraising com. Lakeview Ctr.; bd. dirs. Econ. Devel. Council Peoria Area, Peoria Conv. and Visitors Bur., Peoria Symphony, Peoria YMCA, Meth. Med. Ctr. Found. Served with USAAF, 1943-45. Recipient Pope John award, Jefferson award, Midwest Fedn. Am-Syrian Lebanese Clubs award, Gov.'s Citation award, Cited Congl. Record, Silver Good Citizenship medal SAR, Internat. Communication and Leadership award Toastmasters Internat., County Old Settler's Assn. award, Appreciation award Zeller Clinic, Patriotism award U.S. Marine Corps, Boss of Yr. award Am. Bus. Womens Assn., Achievement award Phoenician Club, Enterprise award Observer newspaper; named Man of Yr. B'nai Brith, Tri-County Kiwanis. Mem. Peoria Area C. of C. (bd. dirs., exec. com.), Orpheus Club, Italian Am. Soc. (hon.), Peoria Fedn. Musicians (hon.), Epsilon Sigma Alpha (hon.). Republican. Roman Catholic. Club: Creve Coeur (bd. dirs.). Lodge: Kiwanis (past pres. Southwest Peoria chpt.). Established Jim Maloof Realtor scholarship, Bradley Univ. Office: City of Peoria City Hall Bldg 419 Fulton St Ste 207 Peoria IL 61602-1217

MALOON, CLEVE ALEXIS, music educator; b. St. Thomas, V.I., Sept. 22, 1965; came to U.S., 1989; s. Claude Devlin Sr. and Jaunita (Fahie) M.; m. Kimberly Louise Patton, Nov. 5, 1991. B in Music Edn., Augustana coll., 1987; MA in Music, U. Iowa, 1989. Cert. music tchr. K-12, Ill., Iowa. Tchr. instrumental music Rock Island (Ill.) Sch. Dist., 1989—, dist. music coord., tchr. alternative high sch., star pride, 1990—. Scholar Aid Assn. Luths.; Music Performance grantee U. V.I. Mem. NEA, Am. Fedn. Tchrs., Nat. Assn. Black Sch. Educators, Music Educators Nat. Conf. Internat. Trombone Assn., Internat. Assn. Jazz Educators, Nat. Band Assn., Rock Island-Milan Fedn. Tchrs. (v.p. 1993-94), Sinfonia Music Fraternity for Men in Music, Phi Mu Alpha, Kappa Alpha Psi (keeper records 1993). Office: Rock Island H S 1400 25th Ave Rock Island IL 61201

MALOON, JERRY L., lawyer, physician, medicolegal consultant; b. Union City, Ind., June 23, 1938; s. Charles Elias and Bertha Lucille (Creviston) M.; children: Jeffrey Lee, Jerry Lee II. BS, Ohio State U., 1960, MD, 1964; JD, Capital U. Law Sch., 1974. Intern Santa Monica (Calif.) Hosp., 1964-65; tng. psychiatry Cen. Ohio Psychiat. Hosp., 1969, Menninger Clinic, Topeka, 1970; clin. dir. Orient (Ohio) Devel. Ctr., 1967-69, med. dir., 1971-83; assoc. med. dir. Western Electric, Inc., Columbus, 1969-71; cons. State Med. Bd. Ohio, 1974-80; pvt. practice law, Columbus, 1978—; pres. Jerry L. Maloon Co., L.P.A., 1981—; medicolegal cons., 1972—; pres. Maloon, Maloon & Barclay Co., L.P.A., 1990-95; guest lectr. law and medicine Orient Devel. Ctr. and Columbus Devel. Ctr., 1969-71; dep. coroner Franklin County (Ohio), 1978-84. Served to capt. M.C., AUS, 1965-67. Fellow Am. Coll. Legal Medicine; mem. AMA, ABA, Ohio Bar Assn., Columbus Bar Assn., Am. Trial Lawyers Assn., Ohio Trial Lawyers Assn., Columbus Trial Lawyers Assn., Ohio State U. Alumni Assn., U.S. Trotting Assn., Am. Profl. Practice Assn. Clubs: Ohio State U. Pres.'s, Buckeye. Home: 2140 Cambridge Blvd Upper Arlngtn OH 43221-4104 Office: Jerry L Maloon Co LPA 475 E Town St Columbus OH 43215-4706

MALORZO, THOMAS VINCENT, lawyer; b. Rome, N.Y., Jan. 10, 1947; s. Helen Adeline (Grande) M.; m. CAtherine Marie Healy, Dec. 28, 1968; children: Amy, Craig, Mary, Thomas Jr. BA, Walsh U., Canton, Ohio, 1969; JD, Cleve. State U., 1979. Bar: Ohio 1979, Tex. 1981, U.S. Dist. Ct. (no. dist.) Ohio 1980, U.S. Dist. Ct. (no. dist.) Tex. 1981, U.S. Patent Office 1980, U.S. Ct. Appeals (7th cir.) 1994. Environ. regulations analyst Diamond Shamrock Corp., Dallas, 1979-81; ind. adv. counsel Southwestern Corp., Dallas, 1981-83; staff atty. NCH Corp., Irving, Tex., 1983-89; gen. counsel Wormald US, Inc., Dallas, 1989-90; patent atty. Otis Engrng. Corp., Carrollton, Tex., 1990-93; pvt. practice Addison, Tex., 1993-95; ptnr. Falk, Vestal & Fish, LLP, 1995-96; pvt. practice Addison, Tex., 1996—; asst. prof. law Dallas/Ft. Worth Sch. Law, Irving, Tex., 1990-92. Dist. com. Circle 10 Boy Scouts Am., Dallas, 1985—; first aid team ARC, Cleve., 1972-80. Mem. State Bar Tex. (chmn. trademark com. intellectual property sect. 1989). Office: 15800 Addison Rd Ste 112 Dallas TX 75248

MALOTT, ADELE RENEE, editor; b. St. Paul, July 19, 1935; d. Clarence R. and Julia Anne (Christensen) Lindgren; m. Gene E. Malott, Oct. 24, 1957. B.S., Northwestern U., 1957. Coordinator news KGB Radio, San Diego, 1958-60; asst. pub. relations dir. St. Paul C. of C., 1961-63; night editor Daily Local News, West Chester, Pa., 1963-65; editor, co-pub. Boutique and Villager, Burlingame, Calif., 1966-76; sr. editor mag. The Webb Co., St. Paul, 1978-84; editor GEM Pub. Group, Reno, 1985—; co-pub. The

Mature Traveler, 1987—; mem. faculty Reader's Digest Writers' Workshops. Co-author: Get Up and Go: A Guide for the Mature Traveler, 1989. Recipient numerous awards Nat. Fedn. Press Women, Calif. Newspaper Pubs. Assn., San Francisco Press Club, Calif. Taxpayers Assn., White House Citations. Mem. Internat. Assn. Bus. Communicators (Merit award 1984), Press Women Minn. (numerous awards), Press Women Nev. Avocations: historical research; golf; travel; photography; reading.

MALOTT, ROBERT HARVEY, manufacturing company executive; b. Boston, Oct. 6, 1926; s. Deane W. and Eleanor (Thrum) M.; m. Elizabeth Harwood Hubert, June 4, 1960; children: Elizabeth Malott Pohle, Barbara Holden, Robert Deane. A.B., U. Kans., 1948; M.B.A., Harvard U., 1950; postgrad., N.Y. U. Law Sch., 1953-55. Asst. to dean Harvard Grad. Sch. Bus. Adminstrn., 1950-52; with FMC Corp., 1952—; asst. to exec. v.p. chems. div. FMC Corp., N.Y.C., 1952-55; controller Niagara Chem. div. FMC Corp., Middleport, N.Y., 1955-59; controller organic chems. div. FMC Corp., N.Y.C., 1959-62; asst. div. mgr. FMC Corp., 1962-63, div. mgr., 1963-65, v.p., mgr. film ops. Am. Viscose div., 1966-67, exec. v.p., mem. president's office, 1967-70; mgr. machinery divs. FMC Corp., Chgo., 1970-72; pres. FMC Corp., from 1972, chief exec. officer, 1972-91, chmn., 1973-91, chmn., exec. com., 1991—; dir. FMC Corp., Amoco Corp., United Techs. Corp. Trustee U. Chgo.; bd. govs. Argonne Labs.; bd. overseers Hoover Instn.; mem. Nat. Bd. of Nat. Mus. of Nat. Hist. Smithsonian Inst.; bd. dirs. Nat. Park Found. Served with USNR, 1944-46. Mem. Explorers Club, Bus. Coun., U.S. C. of C., Econ. Club, Mid-Am. Club, Indian Hill Club, Bohemian Club, Phi Beta Kappa, Alpha Chi Sigma, Beta Theta Pi. Office: FMC Corp 200 E Randolph St Chicago IL 60601-6436

MALOUF, EDWARD WAYNE, lawyer; b. Dallas, Oct. 14, 1957; s. Edward Malouf and Marie Moossy; m. Marianne M. Walder, Feb. 11, 1984; children: Natalie, Anastasia, Monica. BA in English, St. Mary's U., San Antonio, 1980, JD, 1986; MA in Social Scis., U. Chgo., 1987. Bar: Tex. 1987, U.S. Ct. Appeals (5th cir.) 1990, U.S. Supreme Ct. 1990, U.S. Dist. Ct. (no. dist.) Tex. 1991. Tchr. Bishop Lynch High Sch., Dallas, 1983; briefing atty. to Justice Blair Reeves Ct. Appeals (4th cir.), San Antonio, 1986-87; atty. Brock & Kelfer, P.C., San Antonio, 1987-89, Milgrim, Thomajan & Lee, Dallas, 1989, Hutchison, Boyle, Brooks & Fisher, Dallas, 1989-91; pvt. practice Dallas, 1991—. Editor, writer Air Force News Svc., 1981. Chmn. bd. of advocates St. Mary's U. Sch. of Law, 1985. Mem. State Bar Tex. (jour. com. 1988-92), Nat. Order of Barristers (E. Davila Jr. award for Excellence in trial advocacy 1986). Office: 2651 N Harwood St Ste 360 Dallas TX 75201-1563

MALOUFF, FRANK JOSEPH, health care association executive; b. La Junta, Colo., Aug. 21, 1947; s. Phillip Francis and Lillian Aileen (Sayklay) M.; m. Virginia Lynn Frye, Aug. 24, 1968; children: Lynnea, Joseph, J. Daniel, David. BS in Journalism, U. Colo., Boulder, 1969; MS in Health Adminstrn., U. Colo., Denver, 1974; LLD (hon.), Ohio Coll. Podiatric Medicine, 1988. Program adminstr. U. Colo. Health Scis. Ctr., Denver, 1974-83; exec. dir. Ohio Podiatric Med. Assn., Columbus, 1983-89, Am. Podiatric Med. Assn., Bethesda, Md., 1989—; dir. Fund for Podiatric Med. Edn., Bethesda, 1986—, Foothealth Found. Am., Bethesda, 1991—. Contbg. author: Handbook of Healthcare Human Resources Management, 1981; co-author: Pursuing Mastery: Professional Development Tools and Techniques, 1991; columnist in field. Leader Boy Scouts Am., various locations. 1st lt. U.S. Army, 1969-72, Korea. Mem. Am. Soc. Healthcare Edn. and Tng. (officer 1977-81, Disting. Svc. award 1982, past dir.), Am. Soc. Assn. Execs., Am. Inst. Parliamentarians. Roman Catholic. Avocation: lay church ministry. Office: Am Podiatric Med Assn 9312 Old Georgetown Rd Bethesda MD 20814-1646

MALOUIN, JEAN-LOUIS, university dean, educator; b. Three-Rivers, Que., Can., Oct. 5, 1943; m. Hélène Pépin; children: Pascale, Philippe. B in Commerce, Université Laval, Que., 1965, MSc, 1966; PhD, UCLA, 1970. Prof. Bus. Sch., U. Laval, 1966-89, dir. OSD dept., 1971-75, 78-79, assoc. dean acad. affairs, 1979-84, dean, 1984-89; dean faculty of bus. U. Alta., Edmonton, Alta., Can., 1989-92; dean faculty of adminstrn. U. Ottawa, Ottawa, Ont., Can., 1992—; coord. Can. Consortium for the Suuport of the Sea. Editor: The Generation of Scientific Administrative Knowledge, 1986; co-author: L'Innovation Technologique dans les PME Manufacturières: études de cas enquête, 1992. Bd. dirs. Centre québécois de Productivité, du Vêtement, Montréal, 1983-86, Nat. Rsch. Ctr., London, 1986-87, Banff Sch. Advancement Mgmt., 1989-92. Mem. Can. Fedn. Deans (v.p. 1987), Edmonton C. of C. (bd. dirs. 1989-92). Home: 1410 Clay Ct, Gloucester, ON Canada K1C 4T2 Office: U Ottawa Fac Adminstrn, 136 Jean-Jacques Lussier St, Ottawa, ON Canada K1N 6N5

MALOVANCE, GREGORY J., lawyer; b. Munster, Ind., June 29, 1954. BA in Economics magna cum laude, Emory U., 1975; JD, U. Chgo., 1978. Bar: Ill. 1978, U.S. Dist. Ct. (no. dist.) Ill. 1978, U.S. Ct. Appeals (7th cir.) 1978. Ptnr. Winston & Strawn, Chgo. Mem. ABA (litigation sect., labor and employment rels. sect.), Ill. State Bar Assn., Phi Beta Kappa. Office: Winston & Strawn 35 W Wacker Dr Chicago IL 60601-1614*

MALOZEMOFF, PLATO, mining executive; b. Russia, 1909. BS, U. Calif., Berkeley, 1931; MS, Mont. Sch. Mines, 1932. Metall. engr. Pan-Am. Engring., Berkeley, 1933-39; mgr. of mines of pvt. co.'s Argentina and Costa Rica, 1939-42; mining analyst OPA, Washington, 1942-45; with Newmont Mining Corp., N.Y.C., 1945-87, chief exec. officer, 1954-85, chmn. emeritus, 1985—. Bd. dirs. Boys' and Girls' Clubs Am., Tolstoy Found., Inc.; dir., trustee Am. Mus. Natural History; mem. James Madison coun. Libr. of Congress. Office: 230 Park Ave Rm 1154 New York NY 10169-1199

MALPAS, ROBERT, company executive; b. Birkenhead, Eng., Aug. 9, 1927; s. Cheshyre and Louise M.; m. Effie Josephine Dickenson, June 30, 1956. BSc with honors, Durham (Eng.) U., 1948. With ICI, Ltd., Millbank, London, 1948-78, main bd. dir., 1975-78; pres. Halcon Internat., Inc., N.Y.C., 1978-82; mng. dir., mem. bd. Brit. Petroleum PLC, London, 1983-89; chmn. PowerGen. London, 1988-90, Cookson Group, PLC, 1991—; bd. dirs. BOC Group PLC, Eurotunnel PLC, Repsol SA (Spain). Decorated comdr. Order Brit. Empire; recipient Order of Civil Merit, Spain, 1967. Fellow Engring. Inst. Chem Engrs., Inst. Mech. Engrs., Inst. Energy, Royal Soc. Chemistry (hon.); mem. Royal Swedish Acad. Engring. Scis. (fgn.), Am. Acad. Engring. (fgn. assoc.), RAC Club (London), Mill Reef Club (Antigua).

MALPASS, LESLIE FREDERICK, retired university president; b. Hartford, Conn., May 16, 1922; s. Fred J. and Lilly (Elmslie) M.; m. Winona Helen Cassin, May 17, 1946; children: Susan Heather (Mrs. J. Poulton), Peter Gordon, Jennifer Joy (Mrs. T. Droege), Michael Andrew. BA, Syracuse U., 1947, MA, 1949, PhD, 1952. Diplomate Am. Bd. Profl. Psychology. Psychologist Onondaga County (N.Y.) Child Guidance Center Syracuse, 1948-52; lectr. Syracuse U., also U. Buffalo, 1949-52; asst. prof. then assoc. prof. So. Ill. U., 1952-60; vis. prof. U. Fla., 1959-60; prof. psychology, chmn. div. behavioral scis. U. So. Fla., 1960-65; dean Coll. Arts and Scis., Va. Poly Inst., Blacksburg, 1965-68; v.p. acad. affairs Va. Poly Inst., 1968-74; pres. Western Ill. U., Macomb, 1974-87, pres. emeritus, 1987—; cons. in field; lectr. Duke U., 1988-93. Author books and articles in field. Mem. Mayor's Adv. Coun., Durham, N.C., 1989-93; bd. dirs. N.C. Poverty Program, 1989-95; mem. N.C. Human Rels. Commn., 1994—; adv. bd. Durham Salvation Army, 1992—. Fellow APA; mem. AAAS, AAUP, Assn. for Higher Edn., Sigma Xi, Psi Chi, Theta Chi Beta, Omicron Delta Kappa, Beta Gamma Sigma, Phi Mu Alpha. Home: 3927 Swarthmore Dr Durham NC 27707-5313 Office: Western Ill U Adams St Macomb IL 61455

MALPHURS, ROGER EDWARD, biomedical marketing executive; b. Lake Worth, Fla., Dec. 15, 1933; s. Cecil Edward and Muriel Thelma (Ward) M.; m. Carolyn Sue Calapp, Feb. 2, 1963(div. 1993); children: Steven, Brian, Darren, Regina, Victoria. BS, U. Utah, 1961; D of Chiropractic, Palmer Coll. Chiropractic West, 1990. Cert. med. technologist; lic. chiropractor, Calif., Ariz. Supr. spl. chemistry Cen. Pathology Lab., Santa Rosa, Calif., 1968-73; mgr. lab. Community Hosp., Santa Rosa, 1973-76; supr. chem., staff asst. Meml. Hosp., Santa Rosa, 1976-85; pres., chief exec. officer R.E. Malphurs Co., Sunnyvale, Calif., 1972—; owner, developer REMCO Mktg. Assocs., Santa Rosa, 1970-71; pvt. commodity trader, 1974—; owner Better Bus. Forms and Typeset, Santa Rosa, 1977-81, commodity pool operator, 1979-80; dept. mgr. immunochemistry Spectra Labs., Fremont, Calif., 1990-95; clin. trials cons. hematology Abbott Diagnostics, Santa Clara, Calif., 1995—. Author: A New, Simple Way to Win at Blackjack, 1972. Served as squadron commdr. CAP USAF Aux., 1982-84. Mem. Am. Chiropractic Assn., Calif. Chiropractic Assn., Optimists Internat. (youth awards chmn. 1969-74), Am. Pub. Health Assn., Toastmasters (sec./treas. 1988-89), Rep. Senatorial Inner Circle. Republican. Avocations: flying, computers, pistol shooting, oil painting, writing.

MALSACK, JAMES THOMAS, retired manufacturing company executive; b. Milw., Apr. 4, 1921; s. Leonard Henry and Florence Alice (Webb) M.; m. Joyce Irene Niemi, Aug. 1, 1963; children: Thomas James, Claudia Irene, Robert Richard, Thomas John, Pamela Joyce. BSBA, Marquette U., 1946; D Pub. Svc. (hon.), No. Mich. U., 1990. Acct. Price Waterhouse & Co., Milw., 1946-51; with Lake Shore, Inc., Iron Mountain, Mich., 1951-88; exec. v.p. Lake Shore, Inc., 1959-72, pres., chief exec. officer, 1972-84, chmn., 1984-88; dir. First Nat. Bank, Iron Mountain. With USN, 1942-45. Mem. Masons, Shriners. Republican. Episcopalian. Home (winter): 8326 E LaSenda Scottsdale AZ 85255

MALSON, REX RICHARD, drug and health care corporation executive; b. Stanberry, Mo., Nov. 26, 1931; s. Albert J. Curtis and Nellie E. Coburn (Bussey) M.; m. Jimmie S., May 25, 1956 (dec. 1980); children: Richard Gary, Gregory Neil; m. Vicki L., Feb. 10, 1983 (div. Aug. 1984). B.B.A., Ga. State U., 1961; postgrad. grad. exec. program, U. Chgo., 1967; postgrad. exec. program hon., Stanford U., 1983; LHD (hon.), L.I. U., 1989. Gen. transp. mgr. John Sexton & Co., Chgo., 1964-68; dir. distbn. system Keebler Co., Chgo., 1968-73; with drug and health care group McKesson Corp., San Francisco, 1973-92, vice pres., 1984-86, exec. v.p. ops., 1986-89, pres. & chief operating officer, 1989-92, also vice chmn.,bd. dirs.; ret., 1992; bd. dirs. Sunbelt Beverage Co., Balt., Stationers Distbg. Co., Ft. Worth; chmn. bd. dirs. Armor All Products Corp. Served with U.S. Navy, 1951-55, Korea. Mem. Am. Soc. Traffic and Transp. Republican. Office: McKesson Corp 1 Post St San Francisco CA 94104-5203

MALSON, VERNA LEE, special education educator; b. Buffalo, Wyo., Mar. 29, 1937; d. Guy James and Vera Pearl (Curtis) Mayer; m. Jack Lee Malson, Apr. 20, 1955; children: Daniel Lee, Thomas James, Mark David, Scott Allen. BA in Elem. Edn. and Spl. Edn. magna cum laude, Met. State Coll., Denver, 1975; MA in Learning Disabilities, U. No. Colo., 1977. Cert. tchr., Colo. Tchr.-aide Wyo. State Tng. Sch., Lander, 1967-69; spl. edn. tchr. Bennett Sch. 29J, Colo., 1975-79, chmn. health, sci., social studies, 1977-79; spl. edn. tchr. Deer Trail Sch., Colo., 1979—, chmn. careers, gifted and talented, 1979-87, spl. edn./preschool tchr. 1992—; course cons. Regis Coll., Denver, 1990; mem. spl. edn. parent adv. com. East Central Bd. Coop. Ednl. Services, Limon, Colo. Colo. scholar Met. State Coll., 1974; Colo. Dept. Edn. grantee, 1979, 81; recipient Cert. of Achievement, Met. State Coll., 1993. Mem. Council Exceptional Children, Bennett Tchrs. Club (treas. 1977-79), Kappa Delta Pi. Republican. Presbyterian. Avocations: coin collecting; reading; sports. Home: PO Box 403 Deer Trail CO 80105-0403 Office: Deer Trail Pub Schs PO Box 26J Deer Trail CO 80105-0026

MALSTROM, ROBERT A., lawyer; b. Ancon, Panama, May 28, 1946. BS with highest honors, U. Ill., 1969; JD cum laude, U. Mich., 1973. Bar: Ill. 1974. Ptnr. Sidley & Austin, Chgo. With U.S. Army, 1969-71. Mem. Law Club Chgo., Chgo. Estate Planning Coun. Office: Sidley & Austin 1 First Nat Plz Chicago IL 60603*

MALTBY, RICHARD ELDRIDGE, JR., theater director, lyricist; b. Ripon, Wis., Oct. 6, 1937; s. Richard Eldridge and Virginia (Hosegood) D.; m. Janet Brenner, 1987; children: Nicholas Avery, David Stevenson, Jordan Brenner, Emily Celia, Charlotte Perry. B.A., Yale U., 1959. Lyricist: Starting Here, Starting Now, 1977, Big, 1996; dir.: Ain't Misbehavin', 1978 (N.Y. Drama Critics Circle award, Drama Desk award, Obie award Best Musical, Tony award Best Dir.); dir., lyricist: Baby, 1983 (3 Tony award nominations); dir., co-lyricist: Song and Dance, 1985 (Tony award nomination); co-lyricist: Miss Saigon, 1989 (London Evening Standard Best Musical, London Drama Critics award, 3 Tony awards); dir., lyricist: Closer Than Ever, 1989 (2 Outer Critics' Circle awards, Best Off-Broadway Musical, Best Score); ptnr. FWM Producing Group. Mem. ASCAP, Dramatists Guild, Soc. Stage Dirs. and Choreographers. Office: care Flora Roberts Inc 157 W 57th St New York NY 10019-2210

MALTER, JAMES SAMUEL, pathologist, educator; b. Tooele, Utah, May 18, 1956; s. Robert Henry Malter and Evvajean (Harris) Mintz; m. Elaine Gadzicki, May 26, 1988. AB, Dartmouth Coll., 1979; MD, Washington U., 1983. Diplomate Am. Bd. Clin. Pathology. Resident in pathology U. Pa., Phila., 1983-88, chief resident, 1987-88; asst. prof. pathology Tulane U., New Orleans, 1988-91; dir. exptl. pathology Tulane Med. Ctr., New Orleans, 1988-91, dir. Blood Ctr., 1989-91; asst. prof. pathology Sch. Medicine U. Wis., Madison, 1991—; med. dir. Blood Bank U. Wis. Hosp. & Clinic, Madison, 1991—. Mem. editorial bd. Hepatology jour., 1991—. Recipient Nat. Rsch. Svc. award NIH, 1986-88, Clin. Investigator award NCI-NIH, 1988-91, Ind. Investigator award NIH, 1991—. Mem. Am. Assn. Blood Banks, Am. Assn. Pathologists, Am. Coll. Pathologists (diplomate). Office: U Wis Hosp & Clinic 600 Highland Ave # B4 263 Madison WI 53792-0001

MALTESE, GEORGE JOHN, mathematics educator; b. Middletown, Conn., June 24, 1931; s. Giorgio and Sebastiana (Morello) M.; m. Marlene Erika Kunz, Apr. 14, 1956; children: Christopher, Michelle. BA, Wesleyan U., Middletown, Conn., 1953; postgrad., U. Frankfurt, Germany, 1953-54; PhD, Yale U., 1960. Instr. MIT, 1961-63; asst. prof. U. Md., College Park, 1963-66, assoc. prof., 1966-69; prof. U. Md., 1969-73, U. Münster, Fed. Republic Germany, 1973—; vis. prof. U. Frankfurt, 1966-67, 70-71, U. Palermo, Italy, 1967, 71, 76. U. Pisa, Italy, 1972, U. Kuwait, 1977, U. Bahrain, 1988, U. Oman, 1991. Contbr. articles to profl. jours. Served with AUS, 1954-56. Fulbright fellow, 1953-54; NATO postdoctoral fellow, 1960-61. Mem. Am. Math. Soc., Math. Assn. Am., Unione Matematica Italiana, Deutsche Mathematiker Verein. Home: Kampstrasse 9, 48147 Münster Germany Office: Math Inst, Einstein Strasse 62, 48149 Münster Germany

MALTESE, SERPHIN RALPH, state senator, lawyer; b. N.Y.C., Dec. 7, 1932; s. Paul and Frances (Scafidi) M.; m. Constance Mary Del Vecchio, Aug. 27, 1955; children—Andrea Constance, Leslie Serphine, Serphin Ralph (dec.). B.A., Manhattan Coll., 1958; LL.B., J.D. (War Service scholar 1958-62), Fordham U., 1962. Bar: N.Y. bar 1963. Trial atty. for ins. cos., 1963-66; asst. dist. atty., dep. chief homicide bur. Queens County, N.Y., 1966-69; asso. counsel N.Y. State Com. Campus Disorders, 1969-70; counsel N.Y. State Com. Deaf and Multiple Impaired, 1970; chmn. law com. Buckley for U.S. Senator, 1970; counsel N.Y. State Assembly, 1972-76; counsel N.Y. State Senate, Albany, 1976-88, state senator, 1988—, chmn. senate standing com. on elections, mem. com. on aging, alcoholism and drug abuse, mem. codes and investigations and govt. ops. com.; exec. dir. N.Y. State Conservative Party, 1971-86, exec. vice chmn., 1978-86, state chmn., 1986-88. Chmn. trustees Christ the King Regional H.S., 1976—; pres. We Care Civic Assn., 1968-76, chmn. exec. bd., 1978-88; past cmty. chmn. local Boy Scouts Am.; N.Y. State chmn. Conservatives for Ronald Reagan, 1980. With AUS, 1952-54, Korea. Recipient Charles Edison Meml. award N.Y. State Conservative Party, 1977, St. John's U. Pres.'s medal, 1994. Mem. N.Y. State Bar Assn., Queens Asst. Dist. Attys. Assn., Christopher Columbus Assn. (chmn. 1970—), Young Ams. for Freedom (nat. sr. adv. bd.), Am. Conservative Union (nat. bd. dirs.), Internat. Assn. Space Philatelists, Queens C. of C., Alexander Hamilton Conservative Club (chmn. exec. com. 1971-88), Harold Gray Collectors Soc. (pres.), Met. Post Card Collectors Club, Am. Legion, VFW, Alpha Phi Delta. Roman Catholic. Home: 60-16 74th St Flushing NY 11373-5218 Office: 71-04 Myrtle Ave Glendale NY 11385-7254 Office: 803 Legislative Office Bldg Albany NY 12247

MALTIN, LEONARD, television commentator, writer; b. N.Y.C., Dec. 18, 1950; s. Aaron Isaac and Jacqueline (Gould) M.; m. Alice Tlusty, Mar. 15, 1975; 1 child, Jessica Bennett. BA, NYU, 1972. Mem. faculty New Sch. for Social Rsch., N.Y.C., 1973-81; curator Am. Acad. Humor, N.Y.C., 1975-76; guest curator dept. film Mus. Modern Art, N.Y.C., 1976; film critic and corr. Entertainment Tonight, Hollywood, Calif., 1982—; columnist Microsoft Cinemania Online, 1996. Author: Movie Comedy Teams, 1970, rev. edit., 1985, Behind the Camera (reprinted as The Art of the Cinematographer), 1971, The Great Movie Shorts (reprinted as Selected Short Subjects), 1971, The Disney Films, 1973, rev. edit., 1995, The Great Movie Comedians, 1978, Of Mice and Magic: A History of American Animated Cartoons, 1980, rev. edit., 1987; co-author: Our Gang: The Life and Times of the Little Rascals, 1977, reprinted as The Little Rascals: The Life and Times of Our Gang, 1992; editor: Leonard Maltin's Movie & Video Guide, 1969, rev. annually, Leonard Maltin's Movie Encyclopedia, 1994; producer, writer, host (video) Cartoons for Big Kids, 1989; writer (TV spl.) Fantasia: The Making of a Disney Classic, 1990; writer, host (video) The Making of The Quiet Man, 1992, The Making of High Noon, 1992, Cartoon Madness: The Fantastic Max Fleischer Cartoons, 1993, Cliffhanger!, 1993. Mem. steering com. Hollywood Entertainment Mus., 1989—. Mem. Authors Guild, Soc. for Cinephiles (pres. 1990-91, Man of Yr. 1973), L.A. Film Critics Assn. (pres. 1995-96). Office: care Entertainment Tonight Paramount TV 5555 Melrose Ave Los Angeles CA 90038-3149

MALTZ, J. HERBERT, physician, hospital director; b. Passaic, N.J., Jan. 8, 1920; s. Michael and Esther (Rinzler) M.; m. Sybil Zun, Sept. 27, 1947; 1 child, Roger A. Student, U. Wis., 1938-41; B.A., U. Miami, 1942; M.D., Chgo. Med. Sch., 1947. Diplomate: Am. Bd. Psychiatry and Neurology. Intern Wilmington (Del.) Gen. Hosp., 1947-48; psychiat. resident Ill. Dept. Pub. Welfare, 1948-51; clin. instr. psychiatry Chgo. Med. Sch., 1951-55; practice medicine specializing in psychiatry Chgo., 1951—; asst. to supt. Chgo. State Hosp., 1956-58, supt., 1958-66; med. dir. Ridgeway Hosp., 1966-69, Chgo. Lake Shore Hosp., 1970-85; mem. staff St. Joseph's Hosp., Chgo., Barclay Hosp., Chgo., Ill. Masonic Hosp.; former mem. faculty Northwestern U. Med. Sch., Chgo. Med. Sch. Fellow Am. Psychiat. Assn. Jewish. Home: 3260 N Lake Shore Dr Chicago IL 60657-3955 Office: 4840 N Marine Dr Chicago IL 60640-4220

MALTZAN, MICHAEL THOMAS, architect; b. Roslyn Heights, N.Y., Oct. 10, 1959; s. William George and Jacqualine (Cain) M.; m. Amy Louise Murphy, Sept. 25, 1988. Student, Wentworth Inst. Tech., 1977-79; BFA, RISD, 1984, BArch, 1985; MArch, Harvard U., 1988. Lic. architect, Calif. Architect The Architects, Glastonbury, Conn., 1978-80, Williamd D. Warner Assocs., Exeter, R.I., 1980-83, Steven Lerner Assocs., Providence, 1983-84, Schwartz/Silver Assocs., Boston, 1984-86, Machado-Silvetti Assocs., Boston, 1986-88, Frank O. Gehry Assocs., L.A., 1988-95; pvt. practice architecture L.A., 1995—; instr. RISD, Providence, 1987, Harvard U., Cambridge, Mass., 1988; co-instr. UCLA, 1989; invited jury critic Harvard U., RISD, So. Calif. Inst. Architecture, L.A., Ariz. State U., tempe, Calif. Coll. Arts and Crafts, San Francisco, U. SO. Calif., L.A., UCLA, Iowa State U., Ames, Miami (Ohio) U. Prin. works include Sweat Equity Housing, Hartford, Conn., 1978-80, Unitarian-Universalist Ch., Vernon, Conn., 1979, Providence Riverfront Study, 1982, Harvard Law Sch. Alumni Bldg. Addition, Cambridge, 1984, 330 Congress St. Renovation, Boston, 1985, 280 Summer St. Renovation, Boston, 1986, City of Leonforte, Italy Master Plan, 1987 (Progressive Architecture award), North Park Apt. Complex Renovation, Chevy Chase, Md., 1988, Walt Disney Concert Hall, 1988— (Progressive Architecture award), Culver City (Calif.) Retail Complex Master Plan, 1990, Villa Olympica Retail and Entertainment Complex, Barcelona, Spain, 1992,, U. Toledo Art Sch., 1992 (AIA award), Inner-City Arts Sch., L.A., 1994, various pvt. resdl. bldgs.

MALTZMAN, IRVING MYRON, psychology educator; b. Bklyn., May 9, 1924; s. Israel and Lillian (Mass) M.; m. Diane Seiden, Aug. 21, 1949; children—Sara, Kenneth, Ilaine. B.A., N.Y. U., 1946; Ph.D., State U. Iowa, 1949. Mem. faculty UCLA, 1949—, assoc. prof., 1957-60, prof. psychology, 1961—, chmn. dept., 1970-77. Co-author: Handbook of Contemporary Soviet Psychology, 1969. Fellow APA, AAAS; mem. Phi Beta Kappa, Sigma Xi. Home: 11260-22B Overland Ave Culver City CA 90230-5559

MALVEAUX, FLOYD J., academic dean. Dean Howard U. Med. Sch., Washington. Office: Howard U Med Sch 520 W St NW Washington DC 20059

MALVERN, DONALD, retired aircraft manufacturing company executive; b. Sterling, Okla., Apr. 22, 1921; s. George Michael and Anna Francesca (Elsass) M.; m. Ruth Marie Vogler, June 4, 1949; 1 son, Michael John. BSME, U. Okla., 1946. Engr. Victory Architects and Engrs., Clinton, Okla., 1943, Douglas Aircraft Co., Santa Monica, Calif., 1943; with McDonnell Aircraft Co., St. Louis, 1946-88; exec. v.p. McDonnell Aircraft Co., 1973-82, pres., 1982-86; v.p. McDonnell Douglas Corp., 1973-88; aerospace cons. St. Louis, 1988—; pres. McDonnell Douglas Services, Inc., 1978-82. Trustee Falcon Found., 1983—; bd. visitors Def. Sys. Mgmt. Coll., 1983-86, U. Okla. Coll. Engring., 1988-91; pres. Wings of Hope, 1989-92, chmn., 1992—. 1st lt. USAAF, 1943-46; capt. Mo. Air NG, 1946-51. Inducted into Okla. Aviation and Space Mus.'s Hall of Fame, 1987. Fellow AIAA (Tech. Mgmt. award 1968, Reed Aeros. medal 1980); mem. Am. Def. Preparedness Assn. (pres. St. Louis chpt. 1979-80), Navy League U.S. (life), Nat. Aeros. Assn., Air Force Assn., Armed Forces Mgmt. Assn., Pi Tau Sigma, Tau Beta Pi, Tau Omega, Sigma Tau Beta. Clubs: Bellerive Country, St. Louis. Home: 213 Grand Banks Ct Chesterfield MO 63017-9507

MALVERN, LAWRENCE EARL, engineering educator, researcher; b. Sterling, Okla., Sept. 14, 1916; s. George Michael and Anna Francesca (Elsass) M.; m. Marjorie Malene McCarther, Aug. 8, 1939 (dec. Jan. 1985); 1 dau., Maureen; m. Myra Louise Engelhardt, Sept. 18, 1987. Sc.B., Southwestern Okla. State Coll., 1937; M.A., U. Okla., 1939; Ph.D., Brown U., 1949. High sch. tchr. Marlow, Clinton, El Reno, Okla., 1937-38, 39-40, 40-42; asst. prof. math and mechanics Carnegie-Mellon U., Pitts., 1949-53; assoc. prof. applied mechanics Mich. State U., East Lansing, 1953-58, prof., 1958-69; prof. engring. scis. U. Fla., Gainesville, 1969-93; prof. emeritus. Assoc. editor: Jour. Applied Mechanics, 1978-85; author: Introduction to the Mechanics of a Continuous Medium, 1969, Engineering Mechanics-Statics and Dynamics, 2 vols., 1976. Served to lt. (j.g.) USNR, 1944-46. Guggenheim fellow, 1959. Fellow ASME (Worcester Reed Warner medal 1989), Am. Acad. Mechanics; mem. Soc. Engring. Sci. (dir. 1967-70), Sigma Xi. Home: 3901 NW 21st Ln Gainesville FL 32605-3566 Office: U Fla 231 Aerospace Bldg Gainesville FL 32611

MALY, KURT JOHN, computer science educator; b. Modling, Austria, Aug. 20, 1944; came to U.S., 1969; s. Anton and Editha (Gneist) M.; m. Christiana Peterlik, Mar. 18, 1972; 1 child, Angela Claudia. Diplom Ingenieur summa cum laude, U. Tech., Austria, 1968; MS, Courant Inst. NYU, 1970, PhD, 1973. Asst. prof. U. Minn., Mpls., 1972-78, assoc. prof., 1978-85, acting head, 1980-82, head, 1982-85; eminent prof., chmn. computer sci. Old Dominion U., Norfolk, Va., 1985—, Kaufman prof., 1991—; hon. prof. Chengdu U. of Sci. and Tech., People's Republic of China, 1986—, Hefei U., People's Republic of China, 1991—, Guangxi Computer Inst., People's Republic of China, 1993—; bd. dirs. Inst. of Info. Tech., Ctr. for Innovative Tech., Blacksburg, Va., 1988-92; bd. dirs., exec. co-dir. Microelectronic and Info. Scis. Ctr., Mpls., 1980-85. Author: Fundamentals of the Computing Sciences, 1978; assoc. editor: Jour. for Microcomputer Application Tech., PRC; contbr. articles to profl. jours. Served with Austrian Air Force, 1963-64. Fellow Sorbonne U., Paris, 1966, Courant Inst., N.Y.C., 1968-72. Mem. Assn. Computing Machinery, IEEE, Sigma Xi. Roman Catholic. Office: Old Dominion U Norfolk VA 23508

MALZAHN, RAY ANDREW, chemistry educator, university dean; b. Fort Madison, Iowa, July 8, 1929; s. Arnold Frederick and Inez (Russel) M.; m. Elizabeth Mae Barrett, Aug. 23, 1953; children—Karen Louise, Janet Elizabeth. B.A., Gustavus Adolphus Coll., 1951; M.S., U. N.D., 1953; Ph.D., U. Md., 1962. Research assoc. U. Ariz., Tucson, 1961-63; asst. prof. chemistry West Tex. State U., Canyon, 1963-65, assoc. prof., 1965-67, prof. chemistry, 1967-80, dean Coll. Arts and Scis., 1967-71, v.p. acad. affairs, 1971-77; prof., dean Sch. Arts and Scis. Mo. So. State Coll., Joplin, 1980-95, interim v.p. for acad. affairs, 1993-94. Served with AUS, 1954-56. Mem. Am. Chem. Soc. Home: 1215 Goetz Blvd Joplin MO 64801-1433

MAMANA, JOSEPH, editor; b. Easton, Pa., Sept. 3, 1909; s. Domenico Louis and Maria Filippe (Sacchetti) M.; m. Julia Cericola, Sept. 20, 1935; children: Joseph Jr., James, John, Julianne, June. BS, U. Notre Dame, MA, 1932; postgrad., Muhlenberg Coll., 1932. Cert. tchr., guidance counselor, prin., supt. Tchr. Pocono Sch. for Girls, Pocono Manor, Pa., 1929-30; tchr. U. Notre Dame, Notre Dame, Ind., 1931-32, Easton Sch. Dist., Easton, Pa., 1933-46; guidance counselor Easton Sch. Dist., 1947-50, prin., 1951-72;

editor PASSP Schoolmaster Publs., Harrisburg, Pa., 1970-92, editor emeritus, 1992—; investment mgr. Boyd Investment Svcs., Easton, 1974—; pres. Easton Edn. Assn., 1957-59; dist. XI commr. Pa. Interscholastic Athletic Assn., Easton High Sch. Assn., 1955-72; pres. Investment Svcs. Cons., 1974—. Contbr. edn. articles to PASSP Jour., 1970— . Edn. chmn. N.C. Am. Cancer Soc., Bethlehem, Pa., 1947-57, N.C. Am. Heart Assn., Bethlehem, 1957-67; mem. bd. 112U.S. SSS, Easton, 1967-73; police commn. mem. to study police brutality, Easton. Recipient Medal of Honor (educator) Freedoms Found., Valley Forge, Pa., 1965, Notre Dame U. Alumni award, 1992; named Nat. Prin. of Yr., A.C. Croft Publs., Vision Inc., N.J., 1963; named to Dist. XI Wrestling Hall of Fame, Pa. Interscholastic Athletic Assn., 1981; established Joseph Mamana Award of Merit, Pa. Prins. Assn., 1990. Mem. NEA (life, del. 1957-59), Pa. Assn. Secondary Sch. Prins. (life, chmn. real estate com. 1980-90), Easton Area Schoolmen's Assn. (life, pres. 1948-72, Schoolman of Yr. 1955, 89), Prins. Assn., Notre Dame Univ. Club (Alumni Svc. award 1992), Investments Club (mgr. 1974-96). Avocations: stone masonry, swimming, track, wrestling, collecting rare books. Home: 200 Burke St Easton PA 18042

MAMAT, FRANK TRUSTICK, lawyer; b. Syracuse, N.Y., Sept. 4, 1949; s. Harvey Sanford and Annette (Trustick) M.; m. Kathy Lou Winters, June 23, 1975; children: Jonathan Adam, Steven Kenneth. BA, U. Rochester, 1971; JD, Syracuse U., 1974. Bar: D.C. 1976, U.S. Ct. Appeals (D.C. cir.) 1976, Fla. 1977, U.S. Supreme Ct. 1979, U.S. Dist. Ct. (ea. dist.) 1983, U.S. Ct. Appeals (6th cir.) 1983, Mich. 1984, U.S. Dist. Ct. (no. dist.) Ind. 1984. Atty. NLRB, Washington, 1975-79; assoc. Proskauer, Rose, Goetz & Mendelsohn, Washington, N.Y.C. and L.A., 1979-83; assoc. Fishman Group, Bloomfield Hills, Mich., 1983-85, ptnr., 1985-87; sr. ptnr. Honigman, Miller, Schwartz and Cohn, 1987-94; pres. Morgan Daniels Co., Inc., West Bloomfield, Mich., 1995—; ptnr. Clark Klein & Beaumont, P.L.C., Detroit, 1995-96, Clark Hill, P.L.C., Detroit, 1996—; bd. dirs. Mich. Food and Beverage Assn., Air Conditioning Contractors of Am., Air Conditioning Contractors of Mich., Associated Builders and Contractors, Am. Subcontractors Assn., Mich. Mfrs. Assn. Labor Counsel. Gen. counsel Rep. Com. of Oakland County, 1986-89, 93—, Constrn. Code commn. Mich., 1993—; bd. dirs. 300 Club, Mich., 1984-90; pres. 400 Club, 1990-93, chmn., 1993—; mem. Associated Gen. Contractors Labor Lawyers Coun.; mem. Rep. Nat. Com. Nat. Rep. Senatorial Com., Presdl. Task Force, Rep. Labor Coun., Washington; city dir. West Bloomfield, 1985-87; pres. West Bloomfield Rep. Club, 1985-87; fin. com. Rep. Com. of Oakland County, 1984-93; pres. Oakland County Lincoln Rep. Club, 1989-90; bd. dirs. camping svcs. and human resources com. YMCA, 1989-93, Anti-Defamation League, 1989—; vice chmn. Lawyers for Reagan-Bush, 1984; v.p. Fruehauf Farms, West Bloomfield, Mich., 1985-88; mem. staff Exec. Office of Pres. of U.S. Inquiries/Comments, Washington, 1981-83. Mem. ABA, Fed. Bar Assn., Mich. Bar Assn., Fla. Bar Assn. (labor com. 1977—), Mich. Bus. and Profl. Assn., Am. Subcontractors Assn. (Southeastern Mich., bd. dirs.), Founders Soc. (Detroit Inst. Art), D.C. Bar Assn., Detroit Bar Assn., Oakland County Bar Assn., B'nai B'rith (v.p. 1982-83, trustee Detroit coun. 1987-88, bd. dirs. Detroit Barristers unit 1983-91, pres. 1985-87), Detroit Club, Oakpointe Country Club, Detroit Soc. Clubs. Office: Clark Hill PLC 1600 First Fed Bldg Detroit MI 48226 also: Morgan Daniels Co Inc 5484 Crispin Way Rd West Bloomfield MI 48323

MAMATEY, VICTOR SAMUEL, history educator; b. North Braddock, Pa., Feb. 19, 1917; s. Albert Paul and Olga (Darmek) M.; m. Denise M. Perrone, Nov. 20, 1945; children: Albert R., Peter V. Student, Wittenberg Coll., 1938-39, U. Chgo., 1939-40; AM, Harvard U., 1941; PhD, U. Paris, 1949. Asst. prof. history Fla. State U., Tallahassee, 1949-55, assoc. prof., 1955-58, prof., 1958-67, chmn. dept. history, 1964-67; rsch. prof. hist. U. Ga., Athens, 1967-82, acting dean Coll. Arts and Scis., 1972-73; vis. prof. Columbia U., 1961, Tulane U., 1963. Author: The United States and East Central Europe, 1914-18, 1957, Soviet RussianImperialism, 1964, (with Geoffrey Brunn) The World in the Twentieth Century, 1967, The Rise of the Hapsburg Empire, 1526-1815, 1971, (with Radomir Luza) History of the Czechoslovak Republic, 1918-1948, 1973. With U.S. Army, 1942-46. Guggenheim fellow, 1959. Mem. Am. Hist. Assn. (George Louis Beer prize for best book on internat. history 1958), Am. Assn. For Advancement Slavic Studies. Home: 142 Spruce Valley Rd Athens GA 30605-3332

MAMER, STUART MIES, lawyer; b. East Hardin, Ill., Feb. 23, 1921; s. Louis H. and Anna (Mies) M.; m. Donna E. Jordan, Sept. 10, 1944; children: Richard A., John S., Bruce J. A.B., U. Ill., 1942, J.D., 1947. Bar: Ill. bar 1947. Assoc. Thomas & Mulliken, Champaign, 1947-55; partner firm Thomas, Mamer & Haughey, Champaign, 1955—; lectr. U. Ill. Coll. Law, Urbana, 1965-85; Mem. Atty. Registration and Disciplinary Commn. Ill., 1976-82. Chmn. fund drive Champaign County Community Chest, 1955; 1st pres. Champaign County United Fund, 1957; Pres., dir. U. Ill. McKinley Found., Champaign, 1957-69; trustee Children's Home and Aid Soc. of Ill., v.p., 1977—. Served as pilot USAAF, 1943-45. Mem. Am. Coll. Trust and Estate Counsel (bd. regents 1984-90), Phi Beta Kappa, Phi Gamma Delta. Republican. Presbyterian. Home: 6 Montclair Rd Urbana IL 61801-5824 Office: Thomas Mamer & Haughey 30 E Main St Fl 5 Champaign IL 61820-3629

MAMET, DAVID ALAN, playwright, director, essayist; b. Chgo., Nov. 30, 1947; s. Bernard Morris and Lenore June (Silver) M.; m. Lindsay Crouse, Dec. 1977 (div.), m. Rebecca Pidgeon, Sept. 22, 1991. B.A., Goddard Coll., Plainfield, Vt., 1969. Artist-in-residence Goddard Coll., 1971-73; artistic dir. St. Nicholas Theatre Co., Chgo., 1973-75; guest lectr. U. Chgo., 1975, 79, NYU, 1981; assoc. artistic dir. Goodman Theater, Chgo., 1978; assoc. prof. film Columbia U., 1988; chmn. bd. Atlantic Theater Co. Author: (plays) The Duck Variations, 1971, Sexual Perversity in Chicago, 1973 (Village Voice Obie award 1976), Reunion, 1973, Squirrels, 1974, American Buffalo, 1976 (Village Voice Obie award, N.Y. Drama Critics Circle award), A Life in the Theatre, 1976, The Water Engine, 1976, The Woods, 1977, Lone Canoe, 1978, Prairie du Chien, 1978, Lakeboat, 1980, Donny March, 1981, Edmond, 1982 (Village Voice Obie award 1983), The Disappearance of the Jews, 1983, The Shawl, 1985, Glengarry Glen Ross, 1984 (Pulitzer prize for drama, N.Y. Drama Critics Circle award), Speed-The-Plow, 1987, Bobby Gould in Hell, 1989, The Old Neighborhood, 1991, Oleanna, 1992, The Cryptogram, 1994 (Obie award 1995), (dir. only) Ricky Jay and His 52 Assistants, 1994, (one act) Death Defying Acts, 1995; screenplays: The Postman Always Rings Twice, 1979, The Verdict, 1980, The Untouchables, 1986, House of Games, 1986, (with Shel Silverstein) Things Change, 1987, We're No Angels, 1987, Homicide, 1991 (also dir.), Hoffa, 1991, Oleanna, 1994, Bookworm, 1996, The Spanish Pragner, 1996; (children's books) Warm and Cold with drawings by Donald Sultan, 1985; (essays) Writing In Restaurants, 1986, Some Freaks, 1989, on Directing Film, 1990, The Cabin, 1992; (novel) The Village, 1994, (books) Passover, The Duck and the Goat, 1996, Make-Believe-Town, 1996, (poetry) The Hero Pony, 1990; dir. (films) House of Games, 1986, Things Change, 1987, Homicide, 1991, Oleanna, 1994, (play) Dangerous Corner (J.B. Pirestly), 1995. Recipient Outer Critics Circle award for contbn. to Am. theater, 1978; Acad. award nominee for best screen play adaptation, 1983; Rockefeller grantee, 1977; CBS Creative Writing fellow Yale U. Drama Sch., 1976-77.

MAMLOK, URSULA, composer, educator; b. Berlin, Feb. 1, 1928; d. John and Dorothy Lewis; m. Dwight G. Mamlok, Nov. 27, 1947. Student, Mannes Coll. Music, 1942-45; MusB, Manhattan Sch. Music, 1955, MusM, 1958. Mem. faculty dept. music NYU, 1967-74, CUNY, 1971-74; prof. composition Manhattan Sch. Music, N.Y.C., 1974—. Composer: numerous works including Variations and Interludes for 4 percussionists, 1973, Sextet, 1977, Festive Sounds, 1978, When Summer Sang, 1980, piano trio Panta rhei, 1981, 5 recital pieces for young pianists, 1983, From My Garden for solo viola or solo violin, 1983, Concertino for wind quintet, Strings and percussion, 1984, Der Andreas Garten for voice, flute and harp, 1986, Alariana for recorder, clarinet, bassoon, violin and cello, 1986, 3 Bagatelles for harpsichord, 1987, 5 Bagatelles for clarinet, violin, cello, 1988, Rhapsody for clarinet, viola, piano Inward Journey for Piano, 1989, Sonata for violin and piano, 1989, Music for flute, violin, cello, 1990, Girasol, a sextet for flute, violin, viola, cello and piano, 1991, Constellations for orch., 1993, Polarities for flute, violin, cello, piano, 1995. Recipient Serge Koussevitzky Found. commn., 1988, Walter Hinrichsen award Acad. Inst. Arts and Letters, 1989, commn. San Francisco Symphony, 1990; Nat. Endowment Arts grantee, 1974, Am. Inst. Acad. Arts and Letters grantee, 1981, 89, Martha Baird Rockefeller grantee, 1982; John Simon Gugenheim fellow, 1995. Mem. Am. Composers Alliance (dir., Opus One Rec. award 1987), Am. Soc. Univ. Composers, Am. Women Composers, N.Y. Women Composers, Internat. League Women Composers, Music Theory Soc. N.Y., Am. Music Ctr., Internat. Soc Contemporary Music (bd. dirs.), Fromm Found. Commn., Am. Guild Organists Com. Address: 315 E 86th St New York NY 10028-4714 *In my music, I have never striven for novelty nor originality for its own sake. Rather, my primary concern as a composer has been the consolidation of older and newer techniques, as they best serve the work at hand.*

MAMMEL, RUSSELL NORMAN, retired food distribution company executive; b. Hutchinson, Kans., Apr. 28, 1926; s. Vyvian E. and Mabel Edwina (Hursh) M.; m. Betty Crawford, Oct. 29, 1949 (dec. Oct. 1994); children: Mark, Christopher, Elizabeth, Nancy. BS, U. Kans., 1949. With Mammel's Inc., Hutchinson, 1949-57, pres., 1957-59; retail gen. mgr. Kans. divsn. Nash Finch Co., Hutchinson, 1959-61; retail gen. mgr. Iowa divsn. Nash Finch Co., Cedar Rapids, 1961-66; dir. store devel. Nash Finch Co., Mpls., 1966-75, v.p., 1975-83, exec. v.p., 1983-85, pres., COO, 1985-91; also bd. dirs. Nash Finch Co., Mpls., Mpls., 1991; pvt. investments, 1991—. With AUS, 1944-46. Home: 6808 Cornelia Dr Minneapolis MN 55435-1608 Office: Nash Finch Co 7600 France Ave S Minneapolis MN 55435-5924

MAMMEN, SAM, publishing executive, entrepreneur; b. Kerala, India, June 22, 1949; came to U.S., 1972; s. K.O. and Mariamma M.; m. Lori J. Hummel, Dec. 20, 1973; children: Sarah Nalini, Suzanne Kamala, Christopher Ashok. BS in Biology and Chemistry, U. Kerala, 1969; MA in English Lit., Kanpur (India) U., 1971; MA in Edn., U. Tex., San Antonio, 1979. Cert. profl. supr., Tex. Edn. Agy. Tchr. St. James Sch., San Antonio, 1973-76, St. Gerard Sch., San Antonio, 1976-77, Comal Ind. Sch. Dist., Bulverde, Tex., 1978-83; owner Ednl. Cons. Svc., San Antonio, 1982-86; pres. ECS Learning Systems, Inc., San Antonio, 1986—; coach Tex. Future Problem Solving Program State Finals, 1981-83. Founding pres. Assn. Educators Gifted Students, San Antonio, 1980-81; pres. San Antonio Assn. for Gifted and Talented Children, San Antonio, 1987-88. Teaching grantee Tex. Assn. for the Improvement Reading, 1978, Tchr. Tng. grantee Tex. Dept. Human Resources, 1986; Grad. Student scholar Nat. Assn. for Gifted Children, 1983. Mem. Ednl. Press Assn. Am. (regional rep. 1993-94), Am. Creativity Assn., Ednl. Dealers and Suppliers Assn., Nat. Sch. Supply and Equipment Assn., India/Asia Entrepreneur's Assn., Tex. Assn. for the Gifted and Talented (charter mem., 2d v.p. 1981-82, exec. bd. dirs. 1979-82). Avocations: travel, reading, gardening, tennis, San Antonio Spurs fan. Office: ECS Learning Systems Inc PO Box 791437 San Antonio TX 78279-1437

MAMPRE, VIRGINIA ELIZABETH, communications executive; b. Chgo., Sept. 12, 1949; d. Albert Leon and Virginia S. (Joboul) M. BA with honors, U. Iowa, 1971; Masters degree, Ind. U., 1972; spl. cert., Harvard U., 1981. Cert. tchr. Harris Intern WTTW-TV Sta., Chgo., 1972, asst. dir., 1972-73; prod. and dir. WSIU/WUSI-TV Sta., Carbondale, Ill., 1973-74; instr. So. Ill. U., Carbondale, 1972-77; prog. and prod. mgr. WSIU/WUSI-TV, Carbondale, 1974-77; prog. dir. KUHT-TV Sta., Houston, 1977-83; pres. Victory Media, Inc., Houston, 1984-89, Mampre Media Internat., Houston, 1984—; pres. A.I.C.B.; cons. Corp. for Pub. Broadcasting, Washington, 1981-83; chmn. AWRT/YCOC Houston Metro Area, 1983-85, pres., 1983—, nat. v.p., 1985-90; adv. coun. PBS, Washington, 1981-83; bd. and programming chmn. So. Edn. Comms., Columbia, S.C., 1978-83; bd. dirs. TVPC; program bd. EEN. Contbg. author/editor to mags. including Focus, 1989, News & Views, 1987-88, In the Black, 1984-93; creator: (report card campaign) Multi-media, U.S., 1985—; exec. prodr. TV spls., pub. affairs and info., 1977-83 (awards 1978-91). Pres. bd. dirs. Houston Fin. Coun., 1983—; pres. Child Abuse Prevention Coun., Houston, 1984—; bd. dirs. Child Abuse Prevention Network, 1990—; officer bd. dirs. Crime Stoppers Houston, 1984—; chmn. exhbns. Mayor's 1st Hearing, Children and Youth, Houston, 1985-88; founder, bd. dirs. Friends of WSIU-TV, 1974-77; chmn. Evening Guild St. John the Divine, St. Kevork/ACYO Nat. sports fair, 1990; rep. for Houston 2d World Conf. on Mayors, Japan, 1989; exec. bd. nat. com. to prevent child abuse, 1990—; bd. dirs. Houston Read Com., 1995—; mem. nat. faculty Ctr. for Children's Issues, 1995—. Fellow W.K. Kellogg Found., Battle Creek, Mich., 1987-90; recipient award for Excellence Pres. Pvt. Sector, White House, Washington, 1987, Ohio State U., Columbus, 1983, Feddersen award for excellence in Pub. TV Ind. U., Bloomington, 1981, Heritage award Child Abuse Prevention Coun., 1990, Dona J. Stone Founders award Nat. Assn. for Prevention of Child Abuse, 1990; named among Outstanding Women Vols. for community, civic and profl. contbns., Fedn. Houston Profl. Women, 1989; finalist Woman on the Move, 1987, Rising Star, 1987. Mem. Am. Women in Radio and TV (nat. v.p. 1986-90, award 1987, pres. Houston chpt. 1990, bd. dirs. 1985—), Houston Fed. Profl. Women (pres., del. 1986-93, chmn. 1994), Nat. Assn. Ednl. Broadcasters (presenter nat. conv. 1975-76), Tex. Lyceum (v.p., bd. dirs. 1990—), Dephians, Nat. Assn. for Programming TV Execs., Fedn. Houston Profl. Women Ednl. Found. (bd. dirs. 1994—), Ctr. for Bus. Women's Deve. (bd. dirs. 1993-94). Republican. Episcopalian. Avocations: photography, swimming, sailing, languages, travel. Office: Mampre Media Internat 5123 Del Monte Dr Houston TX 77056-4316

MAMUT, MARY CATHERINE, retired entrepreneur; b. Calabria, Italy, Oct. 17, 1923; came to U.S., 1928; d. Carmelo Charles and Caterina (Tripodi) Cogliandro; m. Michael Matthew Mamut, May 15, 1954; children: Anthony Carl, Charles Terrance. Student, Stenotype Comml. Coll., 1946-50. Sec. to pres. Thomas Goodfellow, Inc., Detroit, 1942-50; asst. to v.p. R.G. Moeller Co., Detroit, 1951-52; sec. to pres. United Steel Supply Co., Detroit, 1952-54; sec. to libr. Farmington (Mich.) Schs., 1962-68; real estate agt., 1969; owner, mgr. Crystal Fair, Birmingham, Mich., 1969-88; ret. Crystal Fair, Mich.; tchr. Stenotype Comml. Coll., Detroit, 1952-54. Vol. Henry Ford Mus., Dearborn, Mich., 1989-90, Greenfield Village, 1989-90, West Bloomfield Libr., 1993—. Recipient World Lifetime Achievement award Am. Biog. Inst. U.S.A., 1993. Mem. Am. Bus. Women's Assn., Birmingham-Bloomfield C. of C., Profl. Secs. Internat, NAFE. Roman Catholic. Avocations: reading, music, art, theater. Home: 7423 Coach Ln West Bloomfield MI 48322-4022

MAN, CAMERON ROBERT JAMES, landscape architect, educator; b. Russell, Man., Can., Feb. 25, 1935; s. Robert John and Helen (Middleton) M.; m. Sharron Jewel Jackson, Apr. 21, 1962 (div. 1977); children—Caius Alexander, Calrossie Robert; m. 2d, Agnes Marie Bourdon, May 26, 1978; children: Alexandre Cameron, Cassandre Helen. B.Arch., U. Man., Ft. Garry, 1959; M. Landscape Architecture, U. Calif.-Berkeley, 1964. Registered landscape architect, B.C. Sr. ptnr. Man, Taylor, Muret & Lantzius, Winnipeg, Man., 1966-72; chmn. dept. landscape architecture Sch. Environ. Design, Calif. State Poly. U., Pomona, 1972-75; pres. Landplan Collaborative, Guelph, Ont., Can., 1977-85; prof., head Sch. Landscape Architecture, U. Guelph, 1975-86. Bd. dirs. Landscape Architecture Found., Miss. State U., 1976-83, pres., 1982. Mem. Am. Soc. Landscape Architects (v.p. 1981-83, pres. elect 1991, pres. 1992), Council Educators in Landscape Architecture (v.p. 1974-75, pres. 1975-76). Prog. Conservative. Presbyterian. Office: Miss State U Sch Landscape Architecture Rm 100 Montgomery Hall Mississippi State MS 39762 Home: 108 Tanglewood Dr Starkville MS 39759-2356

MAN, EUGENE HERBERT, chemist, educator, business executive; b. Scranton, Pa., Dec. 14, 1923; s. E. Lester and Celia (Cohen) M.; m. Priscilla R. Perry, Sept. 15, 1976; children—Elizabeth Sue Man Eichenberger, Barbara Ruth, Linda Jeanne Man Manley, Bruce Jonathan, Pamela Irene Perry, Aaron Benjamin Perry. A.B., Oberlin Coll., 1948; Ph.D. (Office Naval Research fellow, E.I. duPont fellow), Duke, 1952. Rsch. chemist E.I. duPont de Nemours & Co., Inc., Wilmington, Del., 1952-60; supr. tech. sect. E.I. duPont de Nemours & Co., Inc., Chattanooga, 1960-61; sr. supr. E.I. duPont de Nemours & Co., Inc., 1961-62; coordinator research U. Miami, Coral Gables, Fla., 1962-66; dean rsch. coordination U. Miami, 1966-77, dean research and sponsored programs, 1977-79, prof. chemistry, 1967-93, prof. marine and atmospheric chemistry, 1971-93, prof. emeritus, 1994—; pres., chief exec. officer Ctr. for Health Techs. Inc., Miami, 1990—; vis. investigator Scripps Instn. Oceanography, 1971-72; Lady Davis faculty fellow Technion, Israel, 1990; bd. dirs. Health Planning Coun., Dade County, Fla., 1970-71; dir. Gulf Univs. Rsch. Consortium, Galveston, Tex., chmn., 1969-71, cons., 1979-81. Contbr. articles profl. jours. Trustee, v.p. Cmty. Mental Health Svc., Dade County, 1967-71; trustee United Fund Dade County, 1967-69; mem., chmn. exec. com. Mental Health Consortium, Dade County, 1966-71; mem. Met. Dade County Cultural Affairs Coun., 1984-89, chmn. sci. com., 1986-90, 1st vice chmn., 1988-89; mem. exec. com. Nat. Coun. Univ. Rsch. Adminstrs., 1967-72; trustee, vice chmn. Hospice Found. of Am., 1992—; mem. coun. Oak Ridge Assoc. Univs., 1973-79; trustee Miami Mus. Sci., 1990-94, adv. bd., 1995—; trustee Greater Miami C. of C., co-chmn. incubator com. 1st lt. AUS, 1943-46. Recipient Harry N. Holmes award in chemistry Oberlin Coll., 1948; NIH grantee, 1983-91. Fellow Am. Inst. Chemists; mem. Am. Chem. Soc., AAAS, Phi Beta Kappa, Sigma Xi (pres. U. Miami chpt. 1981-82), Phi Lambda Upsilon. Patentee in field. Home: 1627 Brickell Ave Apt 1107 Miami FL 33129-1249

MAN, LAWRENCE KONG, architect; b. Kowloon, Hong Kong, July 4, 1953; s. Hon-Kwong Man and Sau-Ching Luk. Student, U. Redlands, 1971-72; BArch, U. Oreg., 1977; MArch, Harvard U., 1978. Registered architect, Mass. Designer, project architect Shepley Bulfinch Richardson & Abbott, Boston, 1978-86; project designer, project architect E. Verner Johnson & Assoc., Boston, 1987-91; owner Lawrence Man Architect, Cambridge, Mass., 1992-95, L.A., 1994-95. Prin. works include LCP Studio, Somerville, Mass., New Asia Restaurants, Danvers and Arlington, Mass., Tai Pan Restaurant, Cambridge, Mass. (Honor award AIA 1993, New Eng. award Excellence in Architecture 1993, Design Excellence award Nat. Orgn. Minority Architects 1993), Ti-Sales Office, Sudbury, Mass. (Design Excellence award Nat. Orgn. Minority Architects 1993), Dental Clinic, Reading, Mass. (AIA Interior Architecture award 1992, Interior Design Project award Am. Soc. Interior Designers 1991, Boston Exports citation AIA 1990, Boston Soc. of Architects/New Eng. Healthcare Assembly honor award, 1994), Mus. Ctr. Union Terminal, Cin. (Reconstrn. award 1991), Ramesses Pavilion Boston Mus. Sci. (Double Vision award/Double Silver Soc. Environ. Graphics 1990), Smithsonian South Quadrangle Mus., Washington (Boston Exports award/citation AIA 1990, Honor award AIA 1989), Pub. Mus. Grand Rapids (Mich.) River Front Devel., U. Vt. Student Ctr., Burlington, Campus Ctr. Study and Libr. addition Franklin & Marshall Coll., Andover (Mass.) Co. Corp. Hdqs., Emerson Hosp., Concord, Mass., pvt. residences, others. Mem. AIA, Am. Assn. Mus., Boston Soc. Architects, Nat. Orgn. Minority Architects. Avocations: dancing, traveling, music. Home: 2158 Valentine Pl San Marino CA 91108 *There are ups and downs in life. It is more rewarding to experience them all, nomatter how hard it may get sometimes. It allows you to become a more complete person. That is, in my view, a ture achievement.*

MAN, MARY ANN, medical technologist; b. Durham, N.C., Apr. 14, 1945; d. Robert Martin and Edna Lee (Henley) M. BS, Ctrl. Mich. U., 1968. Med. technologist Branch County Community Health Ctr., Coldwater, Mich., 1967-68, Good Samaritan Hosp., Cin., 1968-77, Lykes Meml. Hosp., Brooksville, Fla., 1977, South Fla. Bapt. Hosp., Plant City, 1977-78; med. technologist James A. Haley Vets. Hosp., Tampa, Fla., 1978—, social chmn. lab. svc., 1990. Mem. disability com. Vets. Hosp., 1990-92; mem. abilities guild Abilities of Fla., 1993, Ams. with Disabilities Act Ctr., 1993—. Named Outstanding Handicapped Fed. Employee of Yr., Vets. Adminstrn., 1981. Democrat. Episcopalian. Avocations: tennis, swimming, biking, collecting hummingbirds and shells. Office: James A Haley Vets Hosp 13000 Bruce B Downs Blvd Tampa FL 33612-4745

MANABE, SYUKURO, climatologist; b. Shingu-Mura, Uma-Gun, Ehime-ken, Japan, Sept. 21, 1931; came to U.S., 1958; s. Seiichi and Sueko (Akashi) M.; m. Nobuko Nakamura, Jan. 21, 1962; children: Nagisa M. Bianchini, Yukari C. BS, Tokyo U., 1953, MS, 1955, DS, 1958. Rsch. meteorologist U.S. Weather Bur., Washington, 1958-63; sr. rsch. meteorologist Geophys. Fluid Dynamics Lab. NOAA, Washington, 1963-68; sr. rsch. meterologist geophys. fluid dynamics lab. NOAA, Princeton, N.J., 1968-95, mem. sr. exec. svc. of U.S., 1979-95, sr. scientist, 1995—; lectr. with rank of prof. Princeton U., 1968—; mem. joint sci. com. World Climate Rsch. Program, 1981-87; mem. bd. on atmospheric sci. and climate NRC, 1988-91; mem. Commn. on Geoscis., Environ. and Resources, NRC, 1990-93; mem. panel on climate and global change NOAA, 1988—. Recipient Fujiwara award Japan Meterol. Soc., 1967, gold medal U.S. Dept. Commerce, 1970, Presdl. Rank Meritorious Exec. award Pres. of U.S., 1989, Acad. award of Blue Planet prize Asahi Glass Found., 1992, Asahi prize Asahi Shinbun newspaper, 1996. Fellow Am. Geophys. Union (Revelle medal 1993), Am. Meteorol. Soc. (Meisinger award 1967, 2d half century award 1977, Rossby medal 1992); mem. NAS, Acad. Europaea (fgn.), Royal Soc. Can. (fgn.). Achievements include the first modeling study of global warming. Home: 8 Princeton Ave Princeton NJ 08540-5236 Office: NOAA Geophys Fluid Dynamics Lab Princeton U PO Box 308 Princeton NJ 08542

MANALAC, GAUDENCIO SERRANO, retired business executive; b. Feb. 12, 1915; m. Consuelo Beltran Manalac (dec. Mar. 1994); children: Nelinda, Manuel, Ernesto, Eloisa, Evalinda, Ophelia, Mercy, Eleazar, Francisco. BSc, Far Eastern U. CPA. Chmn. emeritus Mansons Corp.; chmn. Mansons Internat. Inc., The Consuelo B. Mañalac Found., Inc., Tanglaw Found., PEPOA Luzon Grid of Cos.; mem. 3 man trade mission to USSR and Socialist countries; chief of mission 2nd European econ. community Philippine trade mission to Europe; mem. Inter-Agency Com., NEDA, co-chmn. Confederation of Philippine Exporters, REgion III; chmn. First Producers and Exporters Conv.; chmn. com. on energy PCCI, First Nat. Energy Congress; vice-chmn. UN Food Agriculture Orgn. Wood-Based Industry Com., Rome; mem. Philippine delegation to ESCAP (UN) former ECAFE; hon. dean Coll. of Forestry, Mt. Apo, others. Editor-in-chief Rotary Govs. Monthly Newsletter, 1988; editor: The Rotary Found. newsletter, The New Horizons newsletter; author: Peace Thru Rotary, Vision of Tomorrow; bus. mgr., mng. editor Philippine Rotary Mag.; pub., editor Indsl. Philippines; contbr. numerous articles to profl. jours. Chmn. fin. com. Paskuhan Latern Festival, chmn. fin. com. Tanglaw Found., trustee, exec. v.p. Mindanao-Sulu Devel. Found., Inc.; trustee Kiwanis Heart Found.; dir. Kilusang Pusong Pilipino; founder., mem. United Way of Tariac, Inc. Recipient 241 awards, citations and commendations from trade and civic orgns., govt. agencies, univs., others. Fellow Am. Biog. Inst.; mem. Assn. of Philippine Ice & Cold Storage, Inc. (past pres.), Philippine Electric Plant Owners Assn., Inc. (past pres.), Planetary Soc. of the USA, Philippine C. of C. and Industry, Philippine Philharmonic Soc., Kapwa Ko, Mahal Ko, Nat. Geographic Soc., Am. Mgmt. Assn., FEU Alumni Assn. (past pres.), Coll. Editors Guild Alumni Assn., Internat. Chamber of Trade and Industry Inc., Lions Club of Davao (pres.), Rotary (numerous coms., numerous awards), numerous others. Home: 255 La Salle, Greenhills East, Mandaluyong The Philippines Office: Mansons Corp, 255 La Salle Connecticut, Mandaluyong The Philippines

MANASSON, VLADIMIR ALEXANDROVICH, physicist; b. Chernovtsy, Ukraine, Mar. 4, 1952; came to U.S., 1991; s. Alexander and Chaya (Finkelsteyn) M.; m. Katrine Kokhanovskaya, Aug. 2, 1975; children: Alexander, Julia. BSEE, Moscow Inst. Electronic Mfg., 1973, MSEE, 1974; PhD in Physics, Chernovtsy U., 1984. Entr. Acad. of Scis. of the Ukraine Material Sci. Inst., 1975-78, sr. engr., 1978-80, jr. rsch. assoc., 1980-85, sr. rsch. assoc., 1985-90; rsch. scientist Phys. Optics Corp., Torrance, Calif., 1991-94, sr. scientist, 1994-95; sr. scientist Wave Band Corp., Torrance, Calif., 1996—. Patentee several photosensitive devices and antennae. Grantee: NSF, 1993-94, Dept. Def., 1994-96. Mem. IEEE (lasers and electro-optic soc.), Internat. Soc. Optical Engring, Optical Soc. Am., Assn. of Old Crows. Avocations: playing piano, reading, children. Office: WaveBand Corp Ste 1105 375 Van Ness Ave Torrance CA 90501

MANATOS, ANDREW EMANUEL, policy consultant, former government official; b. Washington, July 7, 1944; s. Mike N. and Dorothy V. (Varanakis) M.; m. Tina G. Weber, June 25, 1967; children: Mike A., Nick A., Tom A., George A. B.A., Am. U., 1968, M.A., 1969. Staff post office and civil service com. U.S. Senate, Washington, 1969-73; assoc. staff dir. post office com., legis. asst. Senator Thomas Eagleton, 1973-77; asst. sec. congl. affairs Dept. Commerce, Washington, 1977-81; owner Manatos & Manatos Inc., Washington, 1981—; creator White House Conf. on Productivity, U.S. Senate Productivity Award, (videotapes) U.S. Congress and You, Your Court System and You; bd. dirs. Washington Coord. Coun. Productivity, 1981-88, Com. for Citizen Awareness, 1985—. Contbr. articles to N.Y. Times, Washington Post, Indianapolis Star. Pres. Brookmont Civic Assn., Bethesda, Md., 1974-76, Tulip Hill Civic Assn, Bethesda, 1978-80, PTA, 1981; Dem. precinct chmn., 1974-81; chmn. Montgomery County Dollars for Dems., 1975; bd. dirs., mem. nat. fin. com., co-chmn. Washington fin. com. Dukakis for Pres., 1987-88, Inst. Confidence in Cong.; mng. trustee Dem. Nat. Com. Victory Fund, 1988. Recipient Cross of Holy Sepulcher, Medal of St. Andrew; named Archon, Greek Orthodox Ch. Office: Manatos & Manatos 601 13th St NW Ste 1150 S Washington DC 20005-3807

MANATT, CHARLES TAYLOR, lawyer; b. Chgo., June 9, 1936. BS, Iowa State U., 1958; JD, George Washington U., 1962. Bar: Calif. 1962, U.S. Supreme Ct. 1967, D.C. 1985. Ptnr. Manatt, Phelps & Phillips, Washington. Bd. editors George WAshington Law Rev., 1960-62. Mem. ABA, Calif. State Bar, L.A. County Bar Assn., San Fernando Valley Bar Assn. (pres. 1971-72), Century City Bar Assn., Phi Delta Phi, Delta Sigma Rho. also: Manatt Phelps & Phillips Trident Ctr E Tower 11355 W Olympic Blvd Los Angeles CA 90064-1614

MANATT, RICHARD, education educator; b. Odebolt, Iowa, Dec. 13, 1931; s. William Price and Lucille (Taylor) M.; m. Sally Jo Johnson, Aug. 20, 1952; children—Tamra Jo, Ann Lea, Joel Price; m. Jacquelyn M. Nesset, Feb. 25, 1970; 1 child, Megan Sue. B.Sc., Iowa State U., 1953, M.S., 1956; Ph.D., U. Iowa, 1964. Prin. Oskloosa (Iowa) Schs., 1959-62; research asso. U. Iowa, Iowa City, 1962-64; mem. faculty Iowa State U., Ames, 1964—; prof. Iowa State U., 1972—, chmn. dept. ednl. adminstrn., 1970-80, 93—, dir. Sch. Improvement Model Projects, 1980—; cons. performance evaluation for public and independent schs.; disting. vis. prof. Calif. State U., L.A. Author: Educator's Guide to the New Design, When Right is Wrong, The Fundamentalists and the Public Schools, The Clinical Manual for Teacher Performance Evaluation Compendias of Professional Growth Plans, (computer software program) Computer Assisted Teach Evaluation/Supervision; editor Coll. Scene, Internat. Jour. Ednl. Reform. Served with AUS, 1953-55. Named Disting. Prof., Nat. Acad. Sch. Execs., 1979, Regents' Prof. Edn., 1994. Mem. NEA, Nat. Assn. Secondary Sch. Prins., Am. Assn. Sch. Adminstrs., Assn. Supervision and Curriculum Devel. (named Outstanding Cons. 1981), Phi Kappa Phi, Phi Delta Kappa, Delta Chi. Democrat. Methodist. Home: 2926 Monroe Dr Ames IA 50010-4362

MANBECK, HARRY FREDERICK, JR., lawyer; b. Honesdale, Pa., June 26, 1926; s. Harry Frederick Sr. and Pauline (Holley) M.; m. Lois Marie Lange, May 30, 1953 (dec. July 1973); children: Holley Manbeck Dey, Peter Charles; m. Julia Pauline McCarthy, June 30, 1989; 1 child, Emily Elisabeth. BEE, Lehigh U., 1949; LLB, U. Louisville, 1955. Bar: Ky. 1955, Ind. 1962, Mass. 1965, U.S. Ct. Appeals (fed. cir.) 1982, Conn. 1988, D.C. 1992. From trainee to patent atty. GE, various locations, 1950-57; counsel patent div. GE, Ft. Wayne, Ind., 1957-64; counsel patent air eng. div. GE, Lynn, Mass., 1964-67; patent counsel major appliance group Louisville, 1967-69; former gen. patent counsel Fairfield, Conn., 1970-90; asst. sec. commerce, commr. patents and trademarks U.S. Patent and Trademark Office, Washington, 1990-92; ptnr. Morgan & Finnegan, Washington, 1992—. Mem. ABA (chmn. patent, trademark and copyright sect. 1989-90), Bar Assn. of Ct. Appeals Fed. Cir. (bd. dirs. 1984-87), Assn. Corp. Patent Counsel (pres. 1978-79), Am. Arbitration Assn. (Whitney North Seymour Sr. award 1984), Patterson Club, Belleair Club, Westwood Club. Avocations: golf, boating. Home: 1460 Mayhurst Blvd McLean VA 22102 Office: Morgan & Finnegan NW Ste 960 1299 Pennsylvania Ave Washington DC 20004

MANBECK, HARVEY B., agricultural engineer, wood engineer, educator; b. Reading, Pa., Jan. 11, 1942; m. Glenda Manbeck; children: Eric, Christina. BS, Pa. State U., 1963, MS in Agrl. Engring., 1965; PhD in Engring., Okla. State U., 1970. Rsch. assoc. agrl. engring. dept. Pa. State U., 1965, instr. agrl. engring. dept., 1966, prof. agrl. engring., 1980—; asst. prof. agrl engring. dept. U. Ga., 1970-75, assoc. prof. agrl. engring. dept., 1977-80; assoc. prof., extension agrl. engr. Ohio State U., 1975-77; adminstrv. intern rsch. office Pa. Agrl. Experiment Sta., 1991-92; vis. prof. agrl. engring. U. Manitoba, 1986-87, Shenyang Agrl. U., 1988; interim dir. Housing Rsch. Ctr., Pa. State U., 1995. Contbr. chpts. to books and articles to profl. jours. Coach Little League Baseball, 1981-84, leader YMCA Indian Princess Longhouse, 1983-85, Webelo's Cub Scouts 1984, com. mem. Troop 31 Boy Scouts of Am. 1985—. Recipient Outstanding and Premier Teaching award, Outstanding Rsch. award Coll. of Engring., Pa. State U., Atherton Excellence in Teaching award Pa. State U. Mem. ASCE, Am. Soc. Agrl. Engrs. (mem. structures group, vice chair 1978-79, chair, 1979-81, Pa. State sect. sec.-treas. 1983-84, chair 1985-86, tech. dir. S.E. divsn. 1993-95, Henry Giese S & E award 1990), Nat. Frame Builders Assn. (mem. editl. rev. com. for the post-frame profl., chair 1988—), Ga. Soc. Profl. Engrs (state dir. at large 1974-75, named Outstanding Young Engr. of the Year, 1972, recipient Outstanding Chpt. Pres. award, 1974, various other coms.), Ohio Soc. Profl. Engrs., Am. Soc. for Engring. Edn., Forest Products Rsch. Soc., Gamma Sigma Delta, Alpha Epsilon, Sigma Xi, numerous others. Achievements include development of standard designs and specs for hardwood glulam highway birdges, authorship of national engineering practice for post-frame structural diaphragm design, development of FEM for predicting thermal pressures in grain bins, development of FEM for predicting structural performance of wood-framed, metal-clad diaphagm and development of quality control schemes for poultry housing systems. Home: 912 Anna St Boalsburg PA 16827-1214 Office: Penn State U 210 Agr Engring Bldg University Park PA 16802

MANCALL, ELLIOTT LEE, neurologist, educator; b. Hartford, Conn., July 31, 1927; s. Nicholas and Bess Tuch M.; m. Jacqueline Sue Cooper, Dec. 27, 1953; children: Andrew Cooper, Peter Cooper. BS, Trinity Coll., Hartford, 1948; MD, U. Pa., 1952. Diplomate Am. Bd. Psychiatry and Neurology (dir. 1983-91, dir. emeritus, 1991—). Intern Hartford Hosp., 1952-54; clk. in neurology Nat. Hosp. Nervous Disease, London, 1954-55; asst. resident neurology Neurol. Inst. N.Y., 1955-56; resident neuropathology Mass. Gen. Hosp., 1956-57, also clin. and research fellow, 1957-58; teaching fellow neuropathology Harvard Med. Sch., 1956-57; asst. prof. neurology Jefferson Med. Coll., 1958-64, asso. prof., 1964-65; prof. medicine Hahnemann Med. Coll. and Hosp., 1965-76, prof. neurology, chmn. dept., 1976-93; prof. neurology Jefferson Med. Coll., Phila., 1995—, Med. Coll. Pa.-Hahnemann U., 1993-95; dir. Hahnemann U. ALS Clinic; chmn. bd. dirs. Phila. Profl. Standards Rev. Orgn., 1981-84; del. Am. Bd. Med. Specialties, 1984—. Author: (with others) The Human Cerebellum: A Topographical Atlas, 1961, (with B.J. Alpers) Clinical Neurology, 1971, Essentials of the Neurological Examination, 1971, 81; contbr. numerous articles to profl. jours. Served with USN, 1945-47. Recipient Christian R. and Mary F. Lindback award, 1969; Oliver Meml. prize ophthalmology U. Pa., 1952. Fellow Am. Acad. Neurology (alt. del. to AMA 1982-86, gen. editor CONTINUUM 1991—); mem. Am. Neurol. Assn., Am. Assn. Neuropathology, Assn. Rsch. in Nervous and Mental Diseases, Soc. Neurosci., AAUP, Pa. Med. Peer Rev. Orgn. (dir. 1979-84), Phila. Neurol. Soc., Alpers Soc. Clin. Neurology, Coll. Physicians Phila., Sydenham Coterie, Phila. County Med. Soc., Pa. State Med. Soc., AMA (sec.-treas. sect. coun. neurology 1983-86), Am. Med. Soc. on Alcoholism, Neurology Intersoc. Liaison Group, Intersoc. Com. Neurol. Resources, Assn. Univ. Prof. Neurology (pres. 1988-90), Soc. for Exptl. Neuropathology, Am. Bd. Med. Specialities (exec. bd., chair COSEP, 1992—), Am. Bd. Psychiatry and Neurology (v.p. 1990, del. to Am. Bd. Med. Specialities, emeritus dir. 1991—), Pa. Blue Shield (profl. adv. coun. 1991—). Home: PO Box 498 Lafayette Hill PA 19444 Office: 1025 Walnut St Philadelphia PA 19107

MANCEL, CLAUDE PAUL, household product company executive; b. Paris, Oct. 27, 1942; s. Pierre Mancel and Marcelle E. (Grimaud) Mirowicz; m. Annie Simon, Sept., 1967; children: Pacome, Elodie, Sebastien. Diploma in engring., E.N.S.C., Bordeaux, France, 1966, ENSIC, Nancy, France, 1967; MS in Chem. Engring., Worcester (Mass.) Poly. Inst., 1971, PhD in Chem. Engring., 1974; hon. doctorate, Worcester Poly Inst., 1990. Mem. R & D staff Procter & Gamble European Tech. Ctr., Brussels, 1973-80; dir. R & D Procter & Gamble European Tech. Ctr., 1981-85, Procter & Gamble U.S., Cin., 1986-87; mgr. R & D Procter & Gamble European Tech. Ctr., Brussels, 1987-88; v.p. R & D Procter & Gamble Europe and Middle East, 1989-92, v.p. R & D Europe and Middle East and worldwide (dish, hard surface cleaner and bleach products), 1993—; chmn. adv. com. dept. chem. engring. Worcester Poly. Inst., 1988—, bd. trustees, 1992—; bd. trustees ENSIC, 1996—; vice chmn., treas., bd. dirs. Assn. Internat. Savonnerie, 1990; bd. dirs., vice chmn., treas. European Ctr. Ecotoxicology and Toxicology of Chems. Fulbright Found. grantee, 1969. Mem. Sigma Xi. Home: 115 Ave Bellevue, 1410 Waterloo Belgium Office: Procter & Gamble, Temselaan 100, 1853 Strombeek Bever Belgium

MANCHER, RHODA ROSS, federal agency administrator, strategic planner; b. N.Y.C., Sept. 28, 1935; d. Joseph and Hannah (Karpf) Ross; m. Melvin Mancher, May 27, 1962 (dec.); children: Amy Meg, James Marc. B.S. in Physics, Columbia U., 1960; M.S. in Ops. Research, George Washington U., 1978. Cons. pvt. practice, Bethesda, Md., 1994—; staff FEA, Washington, 1974-77; dir. info. systems devel. div. The White House, Washington, 1977-79; dir. office systems devel. Social Security Adminstrn., Balt., 1979-80; dep. asst. atty. gen. Office Info. Tech., Dept. Justice, Washington, 1980-84; assoc. dir. info. resources mgmt. Dept. Navy, Washington, 1985-87; dir. Office Info. Tech. VA, Washington, 1987-94; mem. ad hoc com. on recommendations to merge chem. and biol. info. systems Nat. Cancer Inst., Washington; chmn. permanent com. on info. tech. Iternat. Criminal Police Orgn. (INTERPOL); mem. curriculum com. USDA, adv. bd. computer system security and privacy U.S. Govt.; internat. tech. com. AFCEA. Contbr. articles to profl. publs. Recipient Assoc. Commr.'s citation Social Security Adminstrn., 1980, managerial excellence award Interagy. Com. on ADP, 1983; Meritorious award Sr. Exec. Svc., 1982, 83, 85, 87, 88, 91-93, Presdl. Rank of Meritorious Exec., 1990. Mem. Am. Fedn. Info. Processing Socs. (nat. info. issues panel).

MANCHESKI, FREDERICK JOHN, automotive company executive; b. Stevens Point, Wis., July 21, 1926; s. John Stanley and Luella (Zwaska) M.; m. Judith Knox; children: Mary Lou, Laura, Marcia, Bruce, Amy Frederick-a. BS in Mech. Engring., U. Wis., 1948; LLD (hon.), U. New Haven, 1986; LHD (hon.), Quinnipiac Coll., 1992; DSc (hon.), Albertus Magnus Coll., New Haven, Conn., 1994, U. Wis., 1996. With Timken Roller Bearing Co., Canton, Ohio, 1948-57, McKinsey & Co. (mgmt. cons.), N.Y.C., 1957-63, Echlin Inc., Branford, Conn., 1963—; chmn. bd., chief exec. officer Echlin Inc., 1969—; bd. dirs. Portec. Inc., Automotive Hall of Fame. Contbg. author: Turnaround Management, 1974. Co-chmn. Conn. Hospice, Inc.; chmn. bd. Quinnipiac Coll., Hamden, Conn.; bd. dirs. Jr. Achievement; former trustee Conn. Pub. Expenditure Coun.; mem. New Haven Regional Leadership Coun. Recipient Gold award Wall Street Transcript, 1985; named Automotive Man of Yr. Automotive Warehouse Distbrs. Assn., 1973, Chief Exec. of Decade (Bronze award) Fin. World, 1989, Automotive Industry Leader of Yr. Automotive Hall of Fame, 1992, Aftermarket Exec. of Yr. Automotive Parts and Accessories Assn., 1993; named to Automotive Hall of Fame, 1985; Disting. Bartels fellow U. New Haven, 1995. Mem. Nat. Acad. Engring., World Bus. Council, Young Pres.'s Orgn., Nat. Soc. Profl. Engrs., NAM (former dir.), Conn. Bus. Industry Assn. (former dir.), Greater New Haven Co. of C. (former dir.), Sigma Alpha Epsilon. Clubs: Pine Orchard Country (New Haven), Quinnipiack (New Haven), New Haven Country (New Haven). Home: 10 Old Farm Rd North Haven CT 06473-4416 Office: Echlin Inc PO Box 451 100 Double Beach Rd Branford CT 06405-4909

MANCHESTER, JUDY HAIGHT, occupational health nurse; b. Sayre, Pa., Sept. 2, 1942; d. Seward Miles Haight and Leola Irene (Reeve) Abbott; m. Thomas Leon Powell, Jan. 25, 1964 (div. Jan. 1980); children: Rae Lynne Powell Chapman, Thomas Brett Powell; m. Dennis D. Manchester, May 23, 1980; 1 child, Matthew Sean. Diploma, Robert Packer Sch. Nursing, 1963; BS in Edn., Mansfield U., 1973; MS in Edn., Elmira coll., 1981; postgrad., Boston U., 1987—. Cert. occupational health nurse. Nurse surg.-emergency Towanda (Pa.) Meml. Hosp., 1963-66; sch. nurse Towanda Area Schs., 1966-76; occupational health nurse GTE Sylvania, Towanda, 1979-85; corp. mgr. health svcs. Osram Sylvania, Danvers, Mass., 1985—; mem. grant slection com. Dept. Indsl. Accidents, Boston, 1989-92; mem. edn. adv. com. Harvard U. Ednl. Resource Ctr., Boston, 1993—; mem. practice adv. com. Bd. Registration in Nursing, Boston, 1993—. Author (manual) Policies and Procedures, OSI, 1993, (newsletter) Health Svcs. News and Vies, 1985—. Bd. dirs. Sch. Com., Rockport, Mass., 1992—, Leraysville, Pa., 1977-80. Recipient Spl. Contbns. award Leraysville Sch. Com., 1979. Mem. ANA, Am. Assn. Occupational Health Nurses, Mass. Assn. Occupational Health Nurses (sec. 1988-92, v.p. 1990-92, pres. 1992—). Avocations: gardening, swimming, skiing, hiking, travel. Home: 42 Highview Rd Rockport MA 01966-2209 Office: Osram Sylvania Inc 100 Endicott St Danvers MA 01923-3623

MANCHESTER, KENNETH EDWARD, electronics executive, consultant; b. Winona, Minn., Mar. 22, 1925; s. Laurence Edwin and Daisy Idel (Finley) M.; m. Bonnie Lee Hardgrave, June 24, 1946; children: Cynthia Lee, David Scott. AB, San Jose State Coll., 1949; MS, Stanford U., 1950, PhD, 1955. Sr. chemist Shell Devel. Co., Emeryville, Calif., 1955-62; head chemistry sect. Sprague Electric Co., North Adams, Mass., 1962-63, head chemistry dept., 1963-69, dir. semiconductor rsch., devel. and engring., 1969-79; dir. quality assurance and reliability Sprague Electric Co., Worcester, Mass., 1979-85; v.p. corp. R & D Sprague Electric Co., North Adams, 1985-89, Sprague fellow, 1985; cons. semiconductor industry, 1989—; lectr. Rensselaer Poly. Inst., Troy, N.Y., 1967. Contbr. articles to profl. jours.; patentee in field. Chmn. com. Troop 70 Boy Scouts Am. Sgt. U.S. Army Ground Forces, 1943-46, ETO. Mem. Am. Chem. Soc., AIME, Optimist Club, Sigma Xi. Republican. Avocations: woodworking, golf.

MANCHESTER, ROBERT D., venture capitalist; b. Windsor, Ont., Can., Dec. 16, 1942; came to U.S., 1956; s. Lewis R. and Mary I. (Suave) M.; m. Shirley A. Manchester, Sept. 24, 1971; children: Sara A., Robert D., Geoffrey A. B.S., Boston U., 1974; M.B.A., Amos Tuck Sch., Dartmouth U., 1976. Shipping mgr. N. Am. Pharmacal, Dearborn, Mich., 1961-64, plant mgr., 1968-72; investment analyst Narragansett Capital Corp., Providence, 1976-78, v.p., 1978-80, pres., chief operating officer, 1980-86; mng. dir. Narragansett Capital, Inc., Providence, 1986-88; pres., chief exec. officer Manchester & Co., Inc., 1989-91; pres. Manchester Humphreys Inc., 1992—, also bd. dirs.; bd. dirs. Data Indsl. Corp. Served to capt. U.S. Army, 1964-68. Home: 2 Harbour Rd Barrington RI 02806-4411 Office: Manchester Humphreys Inc 101 Dyer St Providence RI 02903-3908

MANCHESTER, WILLIAM, writer; b. Attleboro, Mass., Apr. 1, 1922; s. William Raymond and Sallie Elizabeth (Thompson) M.; m. Julia Brown Marshall, Mar. 27, 1948; children: John Kennerly, Julie Thompson, Laurie. BA, U. Mass., 1946; AM, U. Mo., 1947; LHD (hon.), U. Mass., 1965, U. New Haven, 1979, Russell Sage Coll., 1990; LittD (hon.), Skidmore Coll., 1987, U. Richmond, 1988. Reporter Daily Oklahoman, 1945-46; reporter, fgn. corr., war corr. Balt. Sun, 1947-55; mng. editor Wesleyan U. Publs., 1955-64; fellow Ctr. for Advanced Studies Wesleyan U., Middletown, Conn., 1959-60; writer-in-residence Wesleyan U., Middletown, 1975—, adj. prof. history, 1979-92; fellow Pierson Coll. Yale U., 1991—; prof. of history emeritus Wesleyan U., 1992—. Author: Disturber of the Peace, 1951, The City of Anger, 1953, Shadow of the Monsoon, 1956, Beard the Lion, 1958, A Rockefeller Family Portrait, 1959, The Long Gainer, 1961, Portrait of a President, 1962, The Death of a President, 1967 (Book-of-the-Month Club selection), The Arms of Krupp, 1968 (Lit. Guild selection), The Glory and the Dream, 1974 (Lit. Guild selection), Controversy and Other Essays in Journalism, 1976, American Caesar: Douglas MacArthur, 1880-1964, 1978 (Book-of-Month Club selection), Goodbye, Darkness, 1980 (Book-of-the-Month Club selection), The Last Lion: Winston Spencer Churchill Visions of Glory 1874-1932, 1983 (Book-of-the-Month Club selection), One Brief Shining Moment: Remembering Kennedy, 1983 (Book-of-the-Month Club selection), The Last Lion: Winston Spencer Churchill Alone 1932-1940, 1988 (Book-of-the-Month Club selection), In Our Time, 1989, A World Lit Only by Fire: The Medieval Mind and the Renaissance, Portrait of an Age, 1992; contbr. to Ency. Brit., various publs. Pres. bd. trustees Friends of U. Mass. Libr., 1970-71, trustee, 1970-74; bd. dirs. Winston Churchill Travelling Fellowships, 1990—. Sgt. USMC, 1942-45, PTO. Decorated Purple Heart; recipient Dag Hammarskjöld prize Assn. Internationale Correspondents Diplomatiques, Rome, 1967, citation for best book on fgn. affairs Overseas Press Club, 1968, U. Mo. Honor award for disting. svc. in journalism, 1969, Conn. Book award, 1975, Pres.'s Cabinet award U. Detroit, 1981, Frederick S. Troy medal U. Mass., 1981, McConnaughy award Wesleyan U., 1981, N.Y. Pub. Libr. Lit. Lion award, 1983, Disting. Pub. Svc. award Conn. Bar Assn., 1985, Lincoln Lit. award Union League Club N.Y., 1983, Blenheim award Internat. Churchill Soc., 1986, Washington Irving award, 1988, Sarah Josepha Hale award, 1993; Guggenheim fellow, 1959-60. Mem. PEN, Soc. Am. Historians, Am. Hist. Assn., Authors Guild, Century Club. Democrat. Avocation: photography. Office: Wesleyan U History Dept Middletown CT 06459

MANCINI, ERNEST ANTHONY, geologist, educator, researcher; b. Reading, Pa., Feb. 27, 1947; s. Ernest and Marian K. (Filbert) M.; m. Marilyn E. Lee, Dec. 27, 1969; children—Lisa L., Lauren N. B.S., Albright Coll., 1969; M.S., So. Ill. U., 1972; Ph.D., Tex. A&M U., 1974. Petroleum exploration geologist Cities Service Oil Co., Denver, 1974-76; asst. prof. geology U. Ala., Tuscaloosa, 1976-79, assoc. prof., 1979-84, prof., 1984—; state geologist, oil and gas supr. State Ala., Tuscaloosa, 1982-96. Cushman Found. fellow; recipient Nat. Coun. citation Albright Coll., 1983, Pratt-Haas Disting. Lectr. award, 1987-88. Fellow Geol. Soc. Am.; mem. Am. Assn. Petroleum Geologists (A.I. Levorsen petroleum geology Meml. award Gulf Coast assn., geol. socs. sect. 1980), Assn. Am. State Geologists (past pres.), Soc. Econ. Paleontologists and Mineralogists Gulf Coast sect. (hon., past pres.), Paleontol. Soc. (past pres. southeast sect.), N.Am. Micropaleontology Soc., Internat. Micropaleontology Soc., Ala. Geol. Soc. (past pres.), Sigma Xi (chpt. pres.), Phi Kappa Phi (past chpt. pres.), Phi Sigma. Presbyterian. Contbr. articles to profl. jours. Home: 15271 Four Winds Loop Northport AL 35476-9120 Office: Geological Survey of Ala 420 Hackberry Ln PO Box O Tuscaloosa AL 35486

MANCINI, FRANK, insurance executive. Treas. Hay/Huggins Co., Inc. Office: 229 S 18th St Ste 6 Philadelphia PA 19103

MANCINI, ROCCO ANTHONY, civil engineer; b. Prezza, Abruzzi, Italy, Aug. 16, 1931; came to U.S., 1940; s. Salvatore and Bambina (Tulliani) M.; m. Eileen Clifford, Apr. 11, 1959; children: Charles V., Ann Marie, Linda E., Donna. BSCE, MIT, 1953; cert. in transp. engring., Yale U., 1958. Registered profl. engr., Mass. Supr. devel. planning Mass. Bay Transp. Authority, Quincy, 1966-68, project mgr. traffic engring., devel., 1976-79, mgr. transp. systems mgmt. projects, 1979-80, acting dir. program devel., 1980-82, rep. to Met. Planning Orgn., 1982-87, project mgr. constrn. office, 1987-89, asst. dir. constrn., 1989-92, asst. dir. design and constrn., 1992—; cons. spl. transp. projects, City of Honolulu, 1968-69, Sao Paulo, Brazil, 1968-69; prin. transp. engr. Wilbur Smith and Assocs., 1969-70; New Eng. regional mgr. Tippetts-Abbett-McCarthy-Stratton, 1970-76. Contbr. articles to profl. publs. Mem. Milton (Mass.) Town Meeting, active various town coms. With U.S. Army, 1954-55. Automotive Safety Found. fellow Yale U., 1957-58. Fellow Inst. Transp. Engrs. (pres. New Eng. sect. 1965-66); mem. ASCE (transp. com. 1953—). Achievements include development, design and supervision of transportation construction projects.

MANCINI, VALERIE, health facility administrator; b. Apr. 23, 1947; came to U.S., 1955; d. John Battista and Theresa (Franco) Mingolla; m. Anthony Michael, May 10, 1969; children: Lisa, Beth. Cert., St. Vincent Hosp. Sch. Nursing, 1968; BSN, Worcester State U., 1981; MBA, Anna Maria Coll., 1984; EdD, U. Mass., 1990. RN, Mass.; cert. childbirth educator. Supr. nursing St. Vincent Hosp., Worcester, Mass., 1978-87, acting dir. patient care svcs., 1987-88, dir. patient care svcs., 1988-89, asst. v.p., 1989, v.p. nursing, 1989—; assoc. prof. grad. sch. nursing U. Mass., 1989—; prof. Anna Maria Coll., Paxton, Mass., 1995—; part-time childbirth educator Childbirth Edn. Assn. of Cen. Mass., 1972-88, dir. ednl. svcs., 1984-88; instr. nursing Quinsigamond Community Coll., Worcester, 1981-87; adj. prof. Worcester State Coll. Mem. Am. Orgn. Nurse Execs., Am. Hosp. Assn., Mass. Orgn. Nurse Execs., Cen. Mass. Nurse Execs., Nat. League for Nursing, Northeast Orgn. for Nursing, Sigma Theta Tau. Office: St Vincent Hosp 25 Winthrop St Worcester MA 01604-4543

MANCINO, DOUGLAS MICHAEL, lawyer; b. Cleve., May 8, 1949; s. Paul and Adele (Brazaitis) M.; m. Carol Keith, June 16, 1973. BA, Kent State U., 1971; JD, Ohio State U., 1974. Bar: Ohio 1974, U.S. Tax Ct. 1977; Calif. 1981, D.C. 1981. Assoc. Baker & Hostetler, Cleve., 1974-1980; ptnr. Memel & Ellsworth, Los Angeles, 1980-87, McDermott, Will & Emery, Los Angeles, 1987—; bd. dirs. Health Systems Internat., Inc. Author: Taxation of Hospitals and Health Care Organizations, 1995, (with others) Hospital Survival Guide, 1984, Navigating the Federal Physician Self-Referral Law, 1995; co-author quar. tax column Am. Hosp. Assn. publ. Health Law Vigil, (with L. Burns) Joint Ventures Between Hosps. and Physicians, 1987; contbr. articles to profl. jours. Chmn. bd. dirs. The Children's Burn Found. Mem. ABA (tax, bus., real property, probate and trust sects., chair exempt orgns. com. 1995—), Calif. State Bar Assn. (tax, bus. law sects.), Ohio Bar Assn., Greater Cleve. Bar Assn., D.C. Bar Assn., Beverly Hills Bar Assn. (chmn. health law com. 1982-84), Nat. Health Lawyers Assn., Am. Acad. Healthcare Attys. (bd. dirs. 1986-95, pres. 1993-94), Calif. Soc. for Healthcare Attys., Bel Air Country Club, The Regency Club. Home: 2727 Patricia Ave Los Angeles CA 90064-4422

MANCKE, RICHARD BELL, economics writer and investor; b. Bethlehem, Pa., Jan. 11, 1943; s. Donald Bell and Elizabeth (Schlottman) M.; m. Barbara Hobbie, Sept. 4, 1970; 1 child, Max. BA, Colgate U., 1965; PhD, MIT, 1969. Instr. MIT, Cambridge, Mass., 1968-69; staff economist U.S. President's Oil Imports Task Force, Washington, 1969-70; asst. prof. Grad. Sch. Bus., U. Chgo., 1969-71; asst. prof. econs. and law U. Mich. Law Sch., Ann Arbor, 1971-74; assoc. prof. Fletcher Sch. Tufts U., Medford, Mass., 1974-81, prof., 1981-86; mng. ptnr. Wolfeboro (N.H.) Ventures, 1985-92; vis. prof. Fgn. Affairs Coll., Beijing, 1987, Colgate U., Hamilton, N.Y., 1990; prof. Fletcher Sch. Tufts U., 1990-96; acad. dean Fletcher Sch., Tufts U., 1991-94; interim dean Fletcher Sch. Tufts U., Medford, Mass., 1994-95; expert witness Cravath, Swaine & Moore, N.Y.C., 1974-82; dir. Intellitech Corp., Key Largo, Fla., 1985-90; rsch. dir. Twentieth Century Fund Energy Policy Task Force, N.Y.C., 1976-77. Author: The Failure of U.S. Energy Policy, 1974, Squeaking By, 1976, Mexican Oil and Natural Gas, 1979; co-author: IBM and the U.S. Data Processing Industry, 1983 (outstanding acad. book award Choice) 1984. Testified before various coms. U.S. Senate, 1972-76; mem. various town bds., Wolfeboro, N.H., 1981-94. Fellow NSF, 1967, Earhart Found., 1981, Goethe Inst., 1995. Mem. Am. Econs. Assn., Appalachian Mountain Club. Avocations: reading, cycling, hiking. Home: PO Box 432 Wolfeboro NH 03894-0432

MANCOFF, NEAL ALAN, lawyer; b. Chgo., May 7, 1939; s. Isadore and Sarah (Leviton) M.; m. Alys Belofsky, June 26, 1966; children: Wesley, Frederick, Daniel. BBA, U. Wis., 1961; JD, Northwestern U., 1965. Bar: Ill. 1965, U.S. Dist. Ct. (no. dist.) Ill. 1965. Assoc. Aaron Aaron Schimberg & Hess, Chgo., 1965-72, ptnr., 1972-80; ptnr. Schiff Hardin & Waite, Chgo., 1980—. Author: Qualified Deferred Compensation Plans, 1983, Nonqualified Deferred Compensation Agreements, 1987. 1st lt. U.S. Army, 1961-62. Mem. Chgo. Bar Assn. (chmn. employee benefits com. 1984). Office: Schiff Hardin & Waite 7500 Sears Towers Chicago IL 60606

MANCUSO, FRANK G., entertainment company executive; b. Buffalo, July 25, 1933; married. Ed., SUNY. Film buyer, ops. supr. Basil Enterprises, 1958-62; joined Paramount Pictures Corp., 1962, booker Buffalo br., 1962-64, sales rep. Buffalo br., 1964-67, br. mgr., 1967-70; v.p., gen. sales mgr. Paramount Pictures Can. Ltd., 1970-72, pres., 1972-76; U.S. Western div. mgr. Paramount Pictures Can. Ltd., Los Angeles, 1976-77; gen. sales mgr. Paramount Pictures Can. Ltd., N.Y.C., 1977; v.p. domestic distbn. Paramount Pictures Can. Ltd., 1977-79, exec. v.p. distbn. and mktg., 1979-83, pres. Paramount Motion Picture div., 1983-84; chmn., chief exec. officer Paramount Pictures Corp., N.Y.C., 1984-91; chmn, CEO Metro-Goldwyn-Mayer, 1993—. Bd. dirs. Will Rogers Meml. Fund, N.Y.-Cornell Med. Ctr., Burke Rehab. Ctr., UCLA Med. Ctr., Mus. of Broadcasting. Mem. Acad. Motion Picture Arts and Scis. (bd. dirs.), Motion Picture Assn. (bd. dirs.), Am. Film Inst. (bd. dirs.), Motion Picture Pioneers (bd. dirs.), Variety Clubs Internat. (bd. dirs.). also: Metro-Goldwyn-Mayer Inc 2500 Broadway Santa Monica CA 90404-3061 also: Metro-Goldwyn-Mayer Inc 1350 Avenue Of The Americas New York NY 10019-4702*

MANCUSO, JAMES VINCENT, automobile columnist; b. Batavia, N.Y., June 18, 1916; s. Benjamin J. and Laura (LaRussa) M.; student Gen. Motors Inst., Flint, Mich., 1949, Army War Coll., 1988; m. Clarissa R. Pope, Sept. 8, 1945; children: Richard J., Robert P., Linda M., Laura Lee. Auto salesman C. Mancuso & Son, Inc., 1934-39, gen. mgr., 1939-42; gen. mgr. Batavia Motors (N.Y.), 1945-49; sales rep. Cadillac Motor Car div. Gen. Motors Corp., 1950-53; pres., gen. mgr. Mancuso Chevrolet, Inc., Skokie, Ill., 1953-74, chmn. bd., 1974-84; pres. Mancuso Cadillac/Honda, Inc., Barrington, Ill., 1974-76, chmn. bd., 1976—; pres. Mancuso Co., 1984—; pres., Service Survey Systems, 1985—; adv. council Consol. Am. Life Ins. Co.; dir. Lake States Life Ins. Co.; mem. faculty Chevrolet Acad., Wayne State U.,

1964; dir. Auto Industries Hwy. Safety Com. Svc. columnist Ward's Auto Dealer mag., 1987-90, Auto Age Mag., 1989—, Dealer Bus. Mag. Chmn. Niles Twp. Jud. Reform Com.; gen. mgr. Niles Twp. Community Fund, 1955; chmn. Skokie's All Am. City Com., 1961. Served from pvt. to maj. USAAF, 1942-46. Mem. Am. Legion, Nat. Auto Dealers Assn. (dir. chmn. pub. relations com.), Chgo. Better Bus. Bur. (dir.), Asso. Employers Ill. (dir.), Skokie C. of C. (pres. 1956), Chgo. Auto Dealers Assn. (dir. 1959-68), Chgo. Auto Trade Assn. (v.p. 1959-60), Chgo. Met. Chevrolet Dealers Assn. (pres. 1957-59), Chgo. Chevrolet Dealers Advt. Assn. (pres. 1969-70). Roman Catholic. Clubs: Rotary (pres. 1960-61), Evanston Golf (pres. 1969-70); Boca (Boca Raton, Fla.). Office: The Mancuso Co 560 Green Bay Rd Winnetka IL 60093-2238

MAND, MARTIN G., financial executive; b. Norfolk, Va., Sept. 26, 1936; s. Meyer J. and Lena (Sutton) M.; m. Shelly Cohen, Aug. 29, 1965; children: Gregory S., Michael E., Brian C. BS in Commerce, U. Va., 1958; MBA, U. Del., 1964. Various fin. staff and mgmt. positions E.I. du Pont de Nemours & Co., Wilmington, Del., 1961-83, v.p. taxes and fin. services, 1983-84; v.p., comptroller, 1984-88, v.p., treas. 1989-90 ; sr. v.p., CFO No. Telecon Ltd., Mississauga, Ont., Can., 1990-93, exec. v.p., CFO, 1993-94; chmn. pres., CEO Mand Assocs., Ltd., 1995—; dir. First Fed. Savs. and Loan, Wilmington, 1977-83, Bimcor, Inc., Toronto, Can., 1990-94, Fuji Bank & Trust Co, N.Y.C., 1995—, Sun Healthcare Group, Inc., Albuquerque, 1996—; pres. Fin. Execs. Research Found., 1988-90. Lt. USN, 1958-61. Mem. Fin. Execs. Inst., Am. Mgmt. Assn (chmn. fin. coun.).

MANDEL, BABALOO, scriptwriter; b. N.Y.C.. Screenwriter: (with Lowell Ganz) Night Shift, 1982, (and with Bruce Jay Friedman) Splash, 1984 (Academy award nomination best original screenplay 1984), (and with Dan Aykroyd) Spies Like Us, 1985, Gung Ho, 1986, Vibes, 1988, Parenthood, 1989, City Slickers, 1991, A League of Their Own, 1992, (and with Billy Crystal) Mr. Saturday Night, 1992, Greedy, 1994, City Slickers II: The Legend of Curley's Gold, 1994, (and with Crystal) Forget Paris, 1995; writer: (TV series) Laverne and Shirley, 1976-83, Busting Loose, 1977, (TV pilots) Herndon and Me, 1983; writer, exec. prodr.: (TV pilots) Gung Ho, 1986, Channel 99, 1988, Knight and Daye, 1989, Parenthood, 1990, A League of their Own, 1993; creator, writer, creative cons.: (with Ganz) Take Five, 1987; appearances include (film) Splash, 1984, (TV) Naked Hollywood, 1991. Office: CAA 9830 Wilshire Blvd Beverly Hills CA 90212-1804

MANDEL, CAROLA PANERAI (MRS. LEON MANDEL), foundation trustee; b. Havana, Cuba; d. Camilo and Elvira (Bertini) Panerai; ed. pvt. schs., Havana and Europe; m. Leon Mandel, Apr. 9, 1938. Mem. women's bd. Northwestern Meml. Hosp., Chgo. Trustee Carola and Leon Mandel Fund Loyola U., Chgo. Life mem. Chgo. Hist. Soc., Guild of Chgo. Hist. Soc., Smithsonian Assos., Nat. Skeet Shooting Assn. Frequently named among Ten Best Dressed Women in U.S.; chevalier Confrerie des Chevaliers du Tastevin. Capt. All-Am. Women's Skeet Team, 1952, 53, 54, 55, 56; only woman to win a men's nat. championship, 20 gauge, 1954, also high average in world over men, 1956, in 12 gauge with 99.4 per cent; European women's live bird shooting championship, Venice, Italy, 1957, Porto, Portugal, 1961; European woman's target championship, Torino, Italy, 1958; woman's world champion live-bird shooting, Sevilla, Spain, 1959, Am. Contract Bridge League Life Master, 1987. Named to Nat. Skeet Shooting Assn. Hall of Fame, 1970; inducted in U.S. Pigeon shooting Fedn. Hall of Fame, 1992. Mem. Soc. Four Arts. Club: Everglades (Palm Beach, Fla.), The Beach. Home: 324 Barton Ave Palm Beach FL 33480-6116

MANDEL, H(AROLD) GEORGE, pharmacologist; b. Berlin, June 6, 1924; came to U.S., 1937, naturalized, 1944; s. Ernest A. and Else (Crail) M.; m. Marianne Klein, July 25, 1953; children: Marcia Mandel Halgren, Audrey Lynn Mandel Todd. BS, Yale U., 1944, PhD, 1949. Lab. instr. in chemistry Yale U., 1942-44, 47-49; research asso. dept. pharmacology George Washington U., 1949-50, asst. research prof., 1950-52, assoc. prof. pharmacology, 1952-58, prof., 1958—, chmn. dept. pharmacology, 1960—; Advanced Commonwealth Fund fellow Molteno Inst. Cambridge (Eng.) U., 1956; Commonwealth Fund fellow U. Auckland (N.Z.) and U. Med. Scis., Bangkok, Thailand, 1964; Am. Cancer Soc. Eleanor Roosevelt Internat. fellow Chester Beatty Research Inst. London, 1970-71; Am. Cancer Soc. scholar U. Calif., San Francisco, 1978-79; fellow Med. Research Council toxicology unit, Carshalton, Eng., 1986; Burroughs Wellcome Rsch. travel grant, Carshalton, 1988; hon. rsch. fellow dept. biochemistry and molecular biology U. Coll., London, 1993; mem. cancer chemotherapy com. Internat. Union Against Cancer, 1966-73, fellow, Lyon, France, 1989; mem. external rev. com. Howard U. Cancer Research Center, 1972-74 ; cons. Bur. Drugs, 1975-79, EPA, 1978-82; mem. toxicology adv. com. FDA, 1975-78; mem. med. research service merit rev. bd. in alcoholism and drug dependence VA, 1975-78; mem. cancer spl. program adv. com. Nat. Cancer Inst., 1974-78, chmn., 1976-78; mem. Nat. Large Bowel Cancer Project Working Cadre, 1980-84; mem. com. on toxicology NRC-Nat. Acad. Sci., 1978-82; mem. Kettering award selection com. Gen. Motors Cancer Research Found., 1979-81. Editorial bd.: Jour. Pharmacology and Exptl. Therapeutics, 1960-65, field editor, 1978-94; editorial bd.: Molecular Pharmacology, 1965-69, Rsch. Comm. in Chem. Pathology, Pharmacology, 1972—, Cancer Drug Delivery, Selective Cancer Therapeutics, 1983-92, Cancer Research, 1974-76, assoc. editor, 1977-81. Served with AUS, 1944-46. Recipient John J. Abel award in pharmacology Eli Lilly and Co., 1958, Disting. Achievement award Washington Acad. Scis., 1958, Golden Apple Teaching award AMA, 1969, 85. Mem. AAAS, Am. Chem. Soc., Am. Soc. Biochemistry and Molecular Biology, Am. Soc. Pharmacology and Exptl. Therapeutics (pres. 1973-74), Am. Assn. Cancer rsch., Assn. Med. Sch. Pharmacology (pres. 1976-78), Nat. Caucus of Basic Biomed. Sci. Chairs (chmn. 1991—), Cosmos Club (Washington), Sigma Xi, Alpha Omega Alpha. Democrat. Research, numerous publs. on cancer chemotherapy, mechanism of growth inhibition, antimetabolites, drug disposition, chemical carcinogenesis. Home: 4956 Sentinel Dr Bethesda MD 20816-3594 Office: George Washington U Dept Pharmacology 2300 I St NW Washington DC 20037-2337

MANDEL, HERBERT MAURICE, civil engineer; b. Port Chester, N.Y., May 11, 1924; s. Arthur William and Rose (Schmeiser) M.; m. Charlotte Feldman, Aug. 22, 1954; children: Rosanne Mandel Levine, Elliott D., Arthur M. BSCE, Va. Poly. Inst., 1948, M Engring., Yale U., 1949. Registered profl. engr., N.Y., Conn., Fla., Md., Mich., Minn., Ohio, Pa., Va., W.Va. Structural engr. Madigan Hyland Co., Long Island City, N.Y., 1949-50; with firm Parsons, Brinckerhoff, Quade & Douglas, Inc., 1950-86; v.p. GAI Cons. Inc., 1986—, prin. staff cons., 1993—, project mgr., Atlanta, 1962, N.Y.C., 1963-70, Honolulu, 1970-74, v.p., 1974, sr. v.p., Pitts., 1977-86; faculty Yale U., 1948-49; adj. faculty Bklyn. Poly. Inst., 1956-64, U. Pitts., 1986; gen. chmn. 6th Internat. Bridge Conf., Pitts., 1989. Author tech. papers; prin. works include (prin.-in-charge) Williamstown-Marietta Bridge, W.Va.-Ohio, Dunbar Bridge, W.Va., I-64 Bridge over Big Sandy River, W.Va.-Kentucky, Davis Creek Bridge, Charleston, W.Va., Tygart R. Bridge, W.Va., Easley Bridge, Bluefield, W.Va., Fayette Sta. Bridge, Fayetteville, W.Va., Mon Valley Expwy., W.Va., (project mgr.) Newport Bridge, Narragansett Bay, R.I., (designer/project engr.) Hackensack River Bridge, N.J., Housatonic River Bridge, Conn., Arthur Kill Vertical Lift R.R. Bridge, S.I., N.Y., 62nd St. Bridge, Pitts., Savannah River Cantilever Bridge, Ga., I-84 Bridges, Danbury, Conn., (structural rehab designer) Avondale Bridge, N.J., Lincoln Bridge, N.J., B&O R.R. Bridge, Vincennes, Ind., Hawk St. Viaduct, Albany, N.Y., Congress Ave. Bridge, Austin, Tex., Ohio St. Bridge, Buffalo, Panhandle Bridge, Pitts.; project mgr. Interstate Rt. H-3, Honolulu, 1970-74; project dir. design and constrn. Pitts. Light Rail Transit System, 1977-84; designer Elizabeth R. Tunnel, Norfolk, Va., 1950. Served to 1st lt. U.S. Army, 1943-46, 50-52; ETO. Fellow ASCE, Soc. Am. Mil. Engrs. (pres. Pitts. post 1987-88); mem. Am. Ry. Engring. Assn. (steel structures specifications com., 1974—), Nat. Soc. Profl. Engrs. , Profl. Engrs. in Pvt. Practice (bd. govs.), Pa. Profl. Engrs. in Pvt. Practice (state vice-chmn. 1992-94, chmn. 1994-96), Internat. Assn. Bridge and Structural Engring., Assn. for Bridge Constrn. and Design, Tau Beta Pi, Chi Epsilon, Omicron Delta Kappa, Phi Kappa Phi, Pi Delta Epsilon, Scabbard and Blade. Jewish. Club: Engineers (Pitts.). Home: 920 Parkview Dr Pittsburgh PA 15243-1116 Office: GAI Cons Inc 570 Beatty Rd Monroeville PA 15146-1334

MANDEL, IRWIN DANIEL, dentist; b. Bklyn., Apr. 9, 1922; s. Samuel A. and Shirley (Blankstein) M.; m. Charlotte Lifschutz, Apr. 1, 1944; children: Carol, Nora, Richard. BS, CCNY, 1942; DDS, Columbia U., 1945; DSc (hon.), U. Medicine and Dentistry of N.J., 1981; DOdont (hon.), U. Göteborg, 1984. Rsch. asst. Dental Sch. Columbia U., 1946-48, mem. faculty Dental Sch., 1946—, prof. dentistry, dir. div. preventive dentistry Dental Sch., 1969-84, dir. Ctr. Clin. Rsch. in Dentistry Dental Sch., 1984-91, assoc. dean rsch., 1991-92; prof. emeritus Dental Sch., 1992—; pvt. practice dentistry, 1946-68; vis. prof. various dental schs.; chmn. oral biology and medicine study sect. Nat. Inst. Dental Rsch., 1974-76. Co-author: The Plaque Diseases, 1972; contbr. over 240 articles to profl. publs., chpts. to books. Active local chpt. ACLU, Peace Action, Physicians for Social Responsibility. Lt. Dental Corps USNR, 1945-46, 52-54. Recipient Career Scientist award N.Y.C. Health Rsch. Council, 1969-72, Leadership award in periodontology Tufts U. Dental Sch., 1971, Internat. award U. Conn. Sch. Dental Medicine, 1979, ann. Seymour J. Kreshover NIDR lecture award, 1986. Fellow AAAS, Am. Coll. Dentists; mem. ADA (chmn. coun. dental rsch. 1978-80, Gold medal for excellence in rsch. 1985), Dental Soc. (Henry Spenadel award 1973, Jarvie-Burkhart Internat. award 1990), Am. Assn. Dental Rsch. (pres. 1980), Am. Assn. Pub. Health Dentists (Disting. Svc. award 1991), Fed. Dentair Internat. (W. D. Miller prize 1992), Internat. Assn. Dental Rsch. (Salivary Rsch. award 1994), N.Y. Acad. Scis., Sigma Xi, Omicron Kappa Upsilon. Home: 60 Pine Dr Cedar Grove NJ 07009-1036 Office: 630 W 168th St New York NY 10032-3702

MANDEL, JACK N., manufacturing company executive; b. Austria, July 16, 1911; s. Sam and Rose M.; m. Lilyan, Aug. 14, 1938. Student, Fenn Coll., 1930-33. Founder, now chmn. fin. com. Premier Indsl. Corp., Cleve. Mem. exec. com. NCCJ; trustee Wood Hosp., 1969—, Fla. Soc. for Blind; life trustee South Broward Jewish Fedn., Cleve. Jewish Welfare Fedn.; pres. Montefiore Home for Aged; pres. adv. bd. Barry U.; hon. trustee Hebrew U.; trustee Tel Aviv U. Mus. of the Diaspora; life trustee The Temple, Woodruff Found.; trustee Cleve. Play House. Mem. Emerald Hills Country Club, Beachmont Country Club, Commede Club. Office: Premier Indsl Corp 4500 Euclid Ave Cleveland OH 44103-3736

MANDEL, JOSEPH DAVID, university official, lawyer; b. N.Y.C., Mar. 26, 1940; s. Max and Charlotte Lee (Goodman) M.; m. Jean Carol Westerman, Aug. 18, 1963; children: Jonathan Scott, Eric David. AB, Dartmouth Coll., 1960, MBA, 1961; JD, Yale U., 1964. Bar: Calif. 1965. Law clk. U.S. Ct. Appeals, 9th crct., L.A., 1964-65; lectr. law U. So. Calif. Law Ctr., L.A., 1965-68; assoc. atty. Tuttle & Taylor, L.A., 1965-69, mem., 1970-82, 90-91, of counsel, 1984-90; vice chancellor UCLA, 1991—; lectr. UCLA Law Sch., 1993; v.p., gen. counsel, sec. Natomas Co., San Francisco, 1983; mem. Calif. Legal Corps, 1993—; bd. dirs. Legal Rsch. Network, Inc., 1993—. Pres. Legal Aid Found., L.A., 1978-79; trustee Southwestern U. Sch. Law, 1982, UCLA Pub. Interest Law Found., 1981-82, L.A. County Bar Found., 1974-79, 82, Coro Found., 1989-92, Armed Hammer Mus. Art and Cultural Ctr., 1995—, Westwood Playhouse, Inc., Geffen Playhouse, 1995—; trustee Coro Soc. Calif. Ctr., 1985-92, bd. dirs. pub. coun., 1989-94, cmty. v.p., 1992-94; mem. L.A. Bd. Zoning Appeals, 1984-90, vice chmn., 1985-86, 89-90, chmn., 1986-87; bd. dirs. Western Justice Ctr. Found., 1989—, v.p., 1992-95, 1st v.p., 1995—; bd. dirs. Harvard Water Polo Found., 1990—; bd. advisors Pub. Svc. Challenge Nat. Assn. for Pub. Interest Law, 1990—; bd. govs. Inner City Law Ctr., 1991—; mem. alumni coun. Dartmouth Coll., 1992-95. Recipient Maynard Toll award Legal Aid Found. of L.A., 1991, Shattuck-Price award L.A. County Bar Assn., 1993, West Coast Liberty award Lambda Legal Def. and Edn. Fund, 1994, Cmty. Achievement award Pub. Coun., 1996. Mem. State Bar Calif. (legal svcs. trust fund commn. 1985-87, chmn. 1985-86), Yale U. Law Sch. Assn. (exec. com. 1983-88, 90—, v.p. 1986-88, chmn. planning com. 1990-92, pres. 1992-94, chmn. exec. com. 1994—). Democrat. Jewish. Home: 15478 Longbow Dr Sherman Oaks CA 91403-4910 Office: UCLA Office of the Chancellor 2135 Murphy Hall Los Angeles CA 90095

MANDEL, LEONARD, physics and optics educator; m. Jeanne Elizabeth Kear, Aug. 20, 1953; children: Karen Rose, Barry Paul. B.Sc., U. London, Eng., 1947, U. London, Eng., 1948; Ph.D., U. London, Eng., 1951. Tech. officer Imperial Chem. Industries, 1951-54; lectr., sr. lectr. Imperial Coll., U. London, 1954-64; prof. physics U. Rochester, N.Y., 1964—, prof. optics, 1977-80, Lee Du Bridge prof. physics and optics, 1994—; joint sec. Rochester Confs. on Coherence and Quantum Optics, 1966, 72, 77, 83, 89,, 1995; vis. prof. U. Tex., Austin, 1984; vis. scientist Am. Inst. Physics; Internat. Commn. Optics traveling lectr., 1992. Editor books; co-author: (with E. Wolf) Optical Coherence and Quantum Optics; contbr. more than 280 articles to profl. jours.. Recipient Marconi medal Italian Nat. Rsch. Coun., 1987, Thomas Young medal Inst. Physics Gt. Britain, 1989, 1st recipient Max Born medal, 1982, Ives medal, 1993. Fellow AAAS, Am. Phys. Soc., Optical Soc. Am. (bd. dirs. 1985-87, assoc. editor jour. 1970-76, 82-84, Optics Letters 1977-79, bd. editors Phys Rev. 1987-89, Jour. Quantum Optics 1989-93, chmn. com. for society objectives and policy 1977, Wood prize com. 1988, Max Bohr medal com. 1994), N.Y. Acad. Scis. Office: U Rochester Dept Physics Astronomy Rochester NY 14627

MANDEL, MORTON, molecular biologist; b. Bklyn., July 6, 1924; s. Barnet and Rose (Kliner) M.; m. Florence H. Goodman, Apr. 1, 1952; children: Robert, Leslie. BCE, CUNY, 1944; MS, Columbia U., 1949, PhD in Physics, 1957. Scientist Bell Telephone Labs., Murray Hill, N.J., 1956-57; asst. prof. physics dept. Stanford (Calif.) U., 1957-61; scientist Gen. Telephone & Telegraph, Mountain View, Calif., 1961-63; rsch. assoc. dept. genetics Stanford U., 1963-64; rsch. fellow Karolinska Inst., Stockholm, Sweden, 1964-66; assoc. prof. sch. of medicine U. Hawaii, Honolulu, 1966-68, prof., 1968—; founder, dir. Hawaii Biotechnology Group, Inc., 1982-95; cons. Fairchild Semiconductor, Hewlett Packard, Lockheed, Rheem, Palo Alto, Calif., 1957-61. Contbr. articles to profl. jours. Lt. (j.g.) USN, 1944-46. Recipient Am. Cancer Soc. Scholar award Am. Cancer Soc., 1979-80, Eleanor Roosevelt Internat. Cancer fellowship, 1979; named NIH Spl. fellow Karolinska Inst., 1964-66. Fellow Am. Phys. Soc.; mem. Sigma Xi. Achievements include citation classics; optional conditions for mutagenesis by N-methyl-N-nitro-N-nitrosoguanidine in E. coli K12; calcium dependent bacteriophage DNA infection. Office: Dept of Biochemistry 1960 E West Rd Honolulu HI 96822-2319

MANDEL, MORTON LEON, industrial corporation executive; b. Cleve., Sept. 19, 1921; s. Simon and Rose (Nusbaum) M.; m. Barbara Abrams, Feb. 27, 1949; children: Amy, Thomas, Stacy. Student, Case Western Res. U., 1939-40, Pomona Coll., 1943; LDH (hon.), Gratz Coll., 1984; LHD (hon.), Hebrew Union Coll., 1986; LDH (hon.), Brandeis U., 1989; LHD (hon.), Yeshiva U., 1993, Hebrew U., 1993, Cleve. Coll. Jewish Studies, 1993. With Premier Indsl. Corp., Cleve., 1940—; sec.-treas. Premier Indus Corp., Cleve., 1946-58, pres., 1958-70, chmn., 1970-96; also bd. dirs. Premier Indsl. Corp., Cleve.; dep. chmn. Premier Farnell, PLC, 1996—. Pres. Jewish Community Ctrs. of Cleve., 1952-57, now life trustee, Jewish Community Fedn., 1974-77, now life trustee, 1970-74, now hon. pres.; pres. Jewish Comty. Ctrs. Assn.; pres. Coun. Initiatives in Jewish Edn., 1991—; pres. United Way Cleve., 1977-79, chmn., 1979-81, now life trustee; mem. Commn. on Health and Social Services, City of Cleve., 1970-71; trustee Case Western Res. U., 1977-92, now hon. trustee, Mt. Sinai Med. Ctr., Cleve., 1970-79, now trustee emeritus, Cleve. Zool. Soc., 1970-73, Greater Cleve. Roundtable, 1981-83; founding pres. World Confedn. Jewish Community Centers, 1977-81, now hon. pres.; founding chair Nat. Jewish Dem. Coun., 1990-93; bd. govs. Jewish Agy., 1979-88, Hebrew U., 1995—; trustee United Israel Appeal, 1977-88, United Jewish Appeal, 1978-82, Am. Jewish Joint Distbn. Com., 1975-88; founder Cleve. Project MOVE, 1981; founder Clean-Land Ohio, 1981, trustee, 1981—; vice chmn. Cleve. Tomorrow, 1982-88, trustee, 1982—; founder, chmn. Mid-Town Corridor, 1982-85, trustee, 1982—; trustee United Way of Am., 1985-91; trustee Ctr. Social Policy Studies, 1983—, Cleve. Mus. Art, 1990-93, Mus. Arts Assn., 1990-93; co-chmn. Operation Independence, 1985-88. Recipient Outstanding Young Man of Yr. award Cleve. Jr. C. of C., 1956, Businessman of Yr. award Urban League of Cleve., 1973, Frank L. Weil award JCC Assn., 1974, Citizen of Yr. award Cleve. Area Bd. Realtors, 1974, Charles Eisenman award Cleve. Jewish Community Fedn., 1977, Mgmt. Performance award Case Western Res. U., 1982, Business Statesman of Yr. award Harvard Bus. Sch. Club of Cleve., 1985, Dively award Corp. Leadership in Urban Devel., 1986, Ben-Gurion Centennial medal State of Israel Bonds, 1986, Presdl. award for Pvt. Sector Initiatives, 1988, Newton D. Baker Disting. Svc. award Case Western Res. U., 1992; named Man of Yr., B'nai Brith, 1980, Leader of Yr., Clean-Land Ohio, 1983, Cleve. Bus. Exec. of Yr., Sales & Mktg. Execs. of Cleve., 1990. Home: 1063 North Ocean Blvd Palm Beach FL 33480 Office: Premier Farnell Corp 4500 Euclid Ave Cleveland OH 44103-3736

MANDEL, OSCAR, literature educator, writer; b. Antwerp, Belgium, Aug. 24, 1926; came to U.S., 1940; m. Adrienne Schizzano. BA, NYU, 1947; MA, Columbia U., 1948; PhD, Ohio State U., 1951. Asst. prof. English U. Nebr., 1955-60; Fulbright lectr. U. Amsterdam, 1960-61; vis. assoc. prof. English Calif. Inst. Tech., 1961-62, assoc. prof. English, 1962-68, prof. Lit., 1968—. Author: A Definition of Tragedy, 1961, The Theater of Don Juan, 1963, Seven Comedies by Marivaux, 1968, Ariadne, 1982, Collected Lyrics and Epigrams, 1981, Three Classic Don Juan Plays, 1981, Philoctetes and the Fall of Troy, 1981, Annotations to Vanity Fair, 1981, The Book of Elaborations, 1985, The Kukkurrik Fables, 1987, Sigismund, Prince of Poland, 1989, August von Kotzebue: The Comedy, The Man, 1990, The Virgin and the Unicorn: Four Plays, 1993, The Art of Alessandro Magnasco: An Essay on the Recovery of Meaning, 1994, The Cheerfulness of Dutch Art: A Rescue Operation, 1996; contbr. articles to profl. jours. Office: Calif Inst Tech Humanities Divsn Pasadena CA 91125

MANDELBAUM, HOWARD ARNOLD, marketing/management consultant; b. Newark, May 17, 1941; s. Morris and Minna (Eisenberg) M.; m. Susan Ganz, June 9, 1963; children: Joel Barry, Sari Beth, Matthew Gary. BS in Indsl. Engring., Lafayette Coll., 1963; MS in Mgmt., MIT, 1965. Advt. rsch. mgr. Hoffmann-La Roche Inc., Nutley, N.J., 1965-68; mgr. mktg. rsch. USV Pharms., N.Y.C., 1968-69; product mgr. Warner-Chilcott, Morris Plains, N.J., 1969-71; v.p. Mabico Automotive Warehouse, Maplewood, N.J., 1972; exec. v.p. William Douglas McAdams Inc., N.Y.C., 1973-93; pres. Mng. Dynamics, Inc., Livingston, N.J., 1994—. Trustee Temple Beth Shalom, Livingston, N.J., 1984-91. Mem. Pharm. Advt. Coun. Office: Mng Dynamics Inc 50 Tremont Ter Livingston NJ 07039-3340

MANDELBAUM, KEN, advertising executive; b. Newark, Dec. 29, 1962; s. Barry Richard and Judith (Solomon) M.; m. Liza Townsend Heath, Oct. 10, 1987. BFA, Hampshire Coll., 1982. Copywriter David H. Block Advt., N.J., 1979-82; sr. copywriter Ally & Gargano, Inc., N.Y.C., 1982-86, Hal Riney & Ptnrs., Inc., San Francisco, 1986-88; pres., chief exec. officer Mandelbaum Mooney Ashley, Inc., San Francisco, 1988—; instr. Sch. of Visual Arts, N.Y.C., 1985-86. Bd. dirs. Food and Hunger Hotline, N.Y.C., 1986; advisor Assn. for Retarded Citizens, San Francisco, 1989—. Avocations: bicycle racing, running.

MANDELBROT, BENOIT B., mathematician, scientist, educator; b. Warsaw, Poland, Nov. 20, 1924; came to U.S., 1958; s. Charles and Belle (Lurie) M.; m. Aliette Kagan, Nov. 5, 1955; children: Laurent, Didier. Diploma, Ecole Polytechnique, Paris, 1947; MS in Aeronautics, Calif. Inst. Tech., 1948; PhD in Math., U. Paris, 1952; DSc (hon.), Syracuse U., 1986, Syracuse U., 1985, Laurentian U., 1986, Boston U., 1987, SUNY, 1988, U. Bremen, 1988, U. Guelph, Ont., Can., 1989, U. Dallas, 1992, Union Coll., 1993, U. Buenos Aires, 1993, U. Tel Aviv, 1995; DHL (hon.), Pace U., 1989. Jr. mem. and Rockefeller scholar Inst. for Advanced Study, Princeton, N.J., 1953-54; jr. prof. math. U. Geneva, Switzerland, 1955-57, U. Lille and Ecole Polytechnique, Paris, 1957-58; rsch. staff mem. IBM Watson Rsch. Ctr., Yorktown Heights, N.Y., 1958-74, IBM fellow, 1974-93, IBM fellow emeritus, 1993—; prof. math. scis. Yale U., New Haven, 1987—; prof. L'Acad. des Scis., Paris, 1995; vis. prof. econs. Harvard U., 1962-63, vis. prof. Applied math., 1963-64, vis. prof. math., 1979-80, prof. practice math., 1984-87; vis. prof. engring. Yale U., 1970; vis. prof. physiology Einstein Coll. Medicine, 1970; Hitchcock prof. U. Calif., Berkeley, 1992; visitor MIT, 1953, also Inst. lectr.; visitor U. Paris, 1966, Coll. de France, Paris, 1973, Institut des Hautes Etudes Scientifiques, Bures, 1980, Mittag-Leffler Inst., Sweden, 1984, Max Planck Inst. Math., Bonn, 1988; lectr. Yale U., 1970, Cambridge U., 1990, Oxford U., 1990, Imperial Coll., London, 1991, Accademia di Lincei, Rome; spkr. and organizer profl. confs. Author: Logique, Langage et Théorie de l'Information, 1957, Les Objets Fractals: Forme, Hasard et Dimension, 1975, 4th edit., 1995, Fractals: Form, Chance and Dimension, 1977, The Fractal Geometry of Nature, 1982, La Geometria della Natura, 1987; contbr. articles to profl. jours. Recipient Franklin medal Franklin Inst., 1986, Alexander von Humboldt Preis, 1987, Caltech disting. svc. award, 1988, Moet-Hennessy prize, 1988, Harvey prize, 1989, Nev. prize U. Nev. Sys., 1991, Wolf prize for physics, 1993, Honda prize, 1994; nat. lectr. Sigma Xi, 1980-82; Guggenheim fellow, 1968. Fellow AAAS, IEEE (Charles Proteus Steinmetz medal 1988), Am. Acad. Arts and Scis., European Acad. Arts, Scis. and Humanities, Am. Phys. Soc., Inst. Math. Stats., Econometric Soc., Am. Geophys. Union, Am. Statistic Assn.; mem. NAS U.S.A. (fgn. assoc., Barnard medal 1985), Internat. Statis. Inst. (elected), Am. Math. Soc., French Math. Soc. Achievements include orgination of theory of fractals, an interdisciplinary enterprise concerned with financial data and all other shapes and phenomena that are equally rough, irregular or broken-up at all scales. Office: IBM PO Box 218 Yorktown Heights NY 10598-0218 also: Yale Univ Math Dept New Haven CT 06520-8283 *Science would be ruined if (like sports) it were to put competition above everything else, and if it were to clarify the rules of competition by withdrawing entirely into narrowly defined specialties. The rare scholars who are wanderers-by-choice are essential to the intellectual welfare of the settled disciplines.*

MANDELKER, DANIEL ROBERT, law educator; b. Milw., July 18, 1926; s. Adolph Irwin and Marie (Manner) M.; divorced; children: Amy Jo, John David. BA, U. Wis., 1947, LLB, 1949; JD, Yale U., 1956. Bar: Wis. 1949. Asst. prof. law Drake U., 1949-51; atty. HHFA, Washington, 1952-53; asst. prof., then assoc. prof. law Ind. U., 1953-62; mem. faculty Washington U., St. Louis, 1962—; prof. law Washington U., 1963-74, Howard A. Stamper prof. law, 1974—; Walter E. Meyer rsch. prof. law Columbia U., 1971-72; Ford Found. law faculty fellow, London, 1959-60; cons. State of Hawaii Dept. Planning and Econ. Devel., 1972-78, State of Hawaii Office of State Planning, 1993-94; legal resources adv. group Transp. Rsch. Bd., 1991-94; mem. local govt. adv. bd. intergovtl. rels. U.S. Adv. Commn., 1985-88; mem. devel. regulations coun. Urban Land Inst., 1980-96; cons. housing subcom., banking and currency com. U.S. Ho. of Reps., 1970-71, cons. policy studies, ins. subcom., banking, fin., urban affairs coms., 1989-91; cons. state and local govts. on land use regulation; Nat. Disting. lectr. Fla. State Jour. Land Use and Environ. Law, 1992; 15th Denman lectr. U. Cambridge, Eng., 1992. Author: Green Belts and Urban Growth: English Town and Country Planning in Action, 1962, Controlling Planned Residential Developments, 1966, Managing Our Urban Environment-Cases, Text and Problems, 1966, 2d edit., 1971, Case Studies in Land Planning and Development, 1968, The Zoning Dilemma, 1971, (with W.R. Ewald) Street Graphics and the Law, 1971, 2d edit., 1988, (with R. Montgomery) Housing in America: Problems and Perspectives, 1973, 2d edit., 1979, Housing Subsidies in the United States and England, 1973, New Developments in Land and Environmental Controls, 1974, Environmental and Land Controls Legislation, 1976, supplement, 1982, (with D. Netsch) State and Local Government in a Federal System, 1977, supplement, 1981, (with D. Netsch and P. Salsich) 2d edit., 1983, supplement, 1987, (with Netsch, Salsich and Wegner) 3rd edit., 1990, supplement, 1992, (with R. Cunningham) Planning and Control of Land Development, 1979, 3d edit., 1990, (with R. Cunningham and J. Payne) 4th edit., 1995, Environment and Equity, 1981, (with others) Cases and Materials on Housing and Urban Development, 1981, 2d edit., 1989, Land Use Law, 1982, 3d edit., 1993, supplement, 1995, (with F. Anderson and D. Tarlock) Environmental Protection Law and Policy, 2d edit., 1990, NEPA Law and Litigation, 2d edit., 1992, supplement, 1996, (with J. Gerard and T. Sullivan) Federal Land Use Law, 1986, supplement, 1995; mem. editl. adv. bd. various land use jours. Mem. nat. adv. com. on outdoor advt. and motorist info. Dept. Transp., 1980-81; mem. adv. com. on housing Dem. Caucus, U.S. Ho. of Reps., 1981-82; pres. Nat. Coalition for Scenic Beauty, 1987-88; sr. fellow Urban Land Inst., 1989-95; mem. law sch. editl. bd. Michie Co., 1989—. Mem. NAS (com. social and behavioral urban rsch. 1967-68), Am. Planning Assn. (bd. dirs. 1981-84, Housing Policy Task Force 1990-93, property rights task force 1994-95), Order of Coif, Phi Beta Kappa, Phi Kappa Phi. Office: Washington U Sch Law Campus Box 1120 Saint Louis MO 63130

MANDELKERN, LEO, biophysics and chemistry educator; b. N.Y.C., Feb. 23, 1922; s. Israel and Gussie (Krostich) M.; m. Berdie Medvedoff, May, 1946; children: I. Paul, Marshal, David. BA, Cornell U., 1942, PhD, 1949. Postdoctoral rsch. assoc. Cornell U., Ithaca, N.Y., 1949-52; phys. chemist Nat. Bur. Standards, Washington, 1952-62; prof. chemistry and biophysics

Fla. State U., Tallahassee, 1962—, R.O. Lawton Disting. prof., 1984—; vis. prof. U. Miami (Fla.) Med. Sch., 1963, U. Calif. Med. Sch., San Francisco, 1964, Cornell U., 1967; mem. biophysics fellowship com. NIH, 1967-70; mem. study panel crystal growth and morphology NRC, 1960; cons. in field. Author: Crystallization of Polymers, 1964, An Introduction to Macromolecules, 1972, 1983; contbr. numerous articles to profl. jours. 1st lt. USAAF, 1942-46, PTO. Recipient Meritorious Svc. award U.S. Dept. Commerce, 1957, Arthur S. Fleming award Washington Jaycees, 1958, Mettler award N.Am. Thermal Analysis Soc., Phila., 1984, Disting. Svc. in Advancement of Polymer Sci. award Soc. Polymer Sci., Japan, 1993. Mem. AAAS, N.Y. Acad. Scis., Am. Inst. Chemists, Am. Chem. Soc. (Polymer Chemistry award 1975, Fla. award 1984, Rubber divsn. Whitby award 1988, Charles Goodyear medal 1993, Applied Polymer Sci. award 1989, Disting. Svc. in Advancement of Polymer Sci. 1993, Polymer Divsn. P.J. Flory award 1994, Polymer Materials Sci. & Engring. Divsn. Coop. Rsch. award 1995), Polymer Soc. Japan, Biophys. Soc., Am. Phys. Soc. (Outstanding Educator of Am. 1973, 75), Cosmos Club Washington, Alpha Epsilon Pi. Home: 1503 Old Ft Dr Tallahassee FL 32301-5637 Office: Fla State U Dept Chemistry Tallahassee FL 32306

MANDELL, ARLENE LINDA, writing and communications educator; b. Bklyn., Feb. 19, 1941; d. George and Esther Kostick; m. Lawrence W. Mandell, May 23, 1982; children by previous marriage: Bruce R. Rosenblum, Tracey B. Grimaldi. BA magna cum laude, William Paterson Coll., 1973; MA Columbia U., 1989. Newspaper reporter Suburban Trends, Riverdale, N.J., 1972-73; writer Good Housekeeping mag., N.Y.C., 1976-78; account exec. Carl Byoir & Assocs., N.Y.C., 1978-86; v.p. Porter/Novelli, N.Y.C., 1986-88; adj. prof. composition, lit., poetry, women's studies William Paterson Coll., Wayne, N.J., 1989—. Contbr. articles to profl. jours. and newspapers, poetry to N.Y. Times and poetry jours. Recipient 1st place women's interest writing N.J. Press Assn., 1973; named John W. Stahr Writer of Yr., Carl Byoir & Assocs., N.Y.C., 1981. Mem. N.J. Coll. English Assn.

MANDELL, FLOYD A., lawyer; b. Chgo., June 17, 1948; s. Marvin M. and Estelle (Witt) M.; m. Pamela Sue Cohen, Aug. 31, 1975; children: Chad, Craig. BA magna cum laude, No. Ill. U., 1970; JD, U. Ill., Champaign, 1973. Bar: Ill. 1973, Fla. 1973. Assoc. Dettishell, McAuliffe & Hifestiter, Chgo., 1973-76; sr. ptnr. Katten, Muchin & Zavis, Chgo., 1976—; dir. Chgo. Bar Assn., 1978-80; planning chmn. Ill. Continuing Legal Edn., Intellectual Property Litigation, Chgo., 1985—. Cpl. USAR, 1969-73. Office: Katten Muchin & Zavis 525 W Monroe St Ste 1600 Chicago IL 60661-3629*

MANDELL, GERALD LEE, physician, medicine educator; b. N.Y.C., Aug. 20, 1936; s. Herman and Sylvia (Keller) M.; m. Judith Rensin Mandell, Dec. 22, 1960; children: James, Pamela, Scott. BA, Cornell U., 1958; MD, Cornell U., N.Y.C., 1962. Diplomate Am. Bd. Internal Medicine. Intern, resident N.Y. Hosp. Cornell Med. Ctr., N.Y.C., 1965-67; instr. Med. Coll., Cornell U., N.Y.C., 1968-69; asst. prof. U. Va., Charlottesville, 1969-71, assoc. prof., 1972-75, prof., 1976—, Owen R. Cheatham prof. sci., 1981—, head infectious diseases, 1970—. Editor: Principles and Practice of Infectious Diseases, 1979, 4th edit., 1995. Lt. comdr. USPHS, 1963-65. Recipient MERIT award NIH, 1986. Master ACP; mem. Assn. Am. Physicians, Am. Soc. Clin. Investigation, Phi Beta Kappa, Alpha Omega Alpha. Jewish. Avocations: photography, tropical fish, sculling. Office: U Va Med Ctr PO Box 385 Charlottesville VA 22902-0385

MANDELSON, RICHARD S., lawyer; b. N.Y.C., Dec. 14, 1947. BA with honors, U. Denver, 1970, MBA, 1974; JD cum laude, Washington & Lee U., 1973. Bar: Colo. 1974, U.S. Dist. Ct. (Colo. dist.) 1974, U.S. Ct. Appeals (10th cir.) 1975. Ptnr. Baker & Hostetler, Denver; assoc. prof. bus. and adminstrv. law U. Denver, 1973—. Mem. ABA, Colo. Bar Assn., Denver Bar Assn., Phi Alpha Delta, Omicron Delta Epsilon. Office: Baker & Hostetler 303 E 17th Ave Ste 1100 Denver CO 80203-1264*

MANDELSTAM, CHARLES LAWRENCE, lawyer; b. Brookline, Mass., July 6, 1927; s. Felix and Sarah (Odence) M.; m. Gloria Messinger, June 2, 1957; children: Emily F., Peter D. BA, Harvard Coll., 1949; LLB, Yale U., 1952. Bar: Conn. 1952, N.Y. 1953, D.C. 1953. Mem. staff office of gen. counsel Internat. Ladies' Garment Workers Union, N.Y.C., 1952-56; assoc. Kaye, Scholer, Fierman, Hays & Handler, N.Y.C., 1956-60; ptnr. Dornbush Mensch Mandelstam & Schaeffer, LLP, N.Y.C., 1968—; bd. dirs. Société d' Exploitation Agricole Rhodanienne, Ampuis, France; counsel North Salem (N.Y.) Open Land Found., 1975—. Comment editor Yale Law Jour., 1951-52; contbr. articles to Yale Law Jour., 1951, 52;. Bd. dirs. Samuel Rubin Found., 1975—, N.Y.C. Sch. Vol. Program, 1991—. With U.S. Army, 1945-46. Mem. Assn. of the Bar City of N.Y., Phi Beta Kappa. Home: 27 W 86th St New York NY 10024-3615 Office: 747 3rd Ave New York NY 10017-2803

MANDELSTAM, STANLEY, physicist; b. Johannesburg, South Africa, Dec. 12, 1928; came to U.S., 1963; s. Boris and Beatrice (Liknaitzky) M. BSc, U. Witwatersrand, Johannesburg, 1952; BA, Cambridge U., Eng., 1954; PhD, Birmingham U., Eng., 1956. Boese postdoctoral fellow Columbia U., N.Y.C., 1957-58; asst. rsch. physicist U. Calif., Berkeley, 1958-60, prof. physics, 1963—; prof. of math. physics U. Birmingham, 1960-63; vis. prof. physics Harvard U., Cambridge, Mass., 1965-66, Univ. de Paris, Paris Sud, 1979-80, 84-85. Editorial bd. The Phys. Rev. jour., 1978-81, 85-88; contbr. articles to profl. jours. Recipient Dirac medal and prize Internat. Ctr. for Theoretical Physics, 1991. Fellow AAAS, Royal Soc. London, Am. Phys. Soc. (Dannie N. Heineman Math. Physics prize 1992). Jewish. Office: Univ of Calif Dept Of Physics Berkeley CA 94720

MANDELSTAMM, JEROME ROBERT, lawyer; b. St. Louis, Apr. 3, 1932; s. Henry and Estelle (London) M.; stepchildren: Amy E., John M. Gagliardi, Maria A. Amundson. A.B., U. Pa., 1954; LL.B., Harvard U., 1957. Bar: Mo. 1957. Since practiced in St. Louis; partner Greenfield, Davidson, Mandelstamm & Voorhees, 1969-81, Schmitz, Mandelstamm, Hawker & Fischer, 1981-82; sole practice, 1982—; bd. dirs. Legal Aid Soc. City and County St. Louis, 1967-75, pres., 1969-70; bd. dirs. Lawyers Reference Service Met. St. Louis, 1976-83, chmn., 1978-83; bd. dirs. Mo. Legal Aid Soc., 1977-82; mem. 22d Jud. Cir. Bar Com., 1983-85, gen. chmn., 1984-85. Mem. St. Louis County Bd. Election Commrs., 1973-77. Served with AUS, 1957. Mem. ABA, Mo. Bar Assn., Am. Arbitration Assn. (panel of arbitrators 1984—), Bar Assn. Met. St. Louis (v.p. 1974-75, treas. 1975-76). Home: 4525 Laclede Ave # 3 Saint Louis MO 63108-2117 Office: 1010 Market St Ste 1600 Saint Louis MO 63101-2000

MANDELSTEIN, PAUL STANLEY, book publishing executive; b. Bklyn., May 18, 1946; s. Max and Esther (Friedman) M.; m. Cornelia S. Pratt, Feb. 21, 1973 (div. June 1993); children: Zachary, Naomi, Nicolas. Student, Bklyn. Coll., 1965. Pres. Quantum Pub., Mill Valley, Calif., 1984—, The Book Pub. Co., Summertown, Tenn.; mktg. cons. Farm Foods, Summertown, Tenn., 1975—, Solar Electronics, Summertown, 1976—, Shambhala Pubs., 1994—; bus. cons. Audio Scholar, Mendocino, Calif., 1991. Author: The Nightingale and the Wind, 1993, The Lute Player, 1994. Avocations: tennis, mythology, mythopoetics, basketball, music. Home: 1204 El Cide Ct Mill Valley CA 94941-3401 Office: PO Box 1738 Mill Valley CA 94942-1738

MANDERS, KARL LEE, neurosurgeon; b. Rochester, N.Y., Jan. 21, 1927; s. David Bert and Frances Edna (Cohan) Mendelson; m. Ann Laprell, July 28, 1969; children: Karlanna, Maidena; children by previous marriage: Karl, Kerry, Kristine. Student, Cornell U., 1946; MD, U. Buffalo, 1950. Diplomate Am. Bd. Neurol. Surgery, Am. Bd. Clin. Biofeedback, Am. Bd. Hyperbaric Medicine, Am. Bd. Pain Medicine, Nat. Bd. Med. Examiners. Intern U. Va. Hosp., Charlottesville, 1950-51, resident in neurol. surgery, 1951-52; resident in neurol. surgery Henry Ford Hosp., Detroit, 1954-56; pvt. practice Indpls., 1956—; med. dir. Cmty. Hosp. Rehab. Ctr. for Pain, 1973—; chief hosp. med. and surg. neurology Cmty. Hosp., 1983, 93; coroner Marion County, Ind., 1977-85, 92-96. Served with USN, 1952-54, Korea. Recipient cert. achievement Dept. Army, 1969. Fellow ACS, Internat. Coll Surgeons, Am. Acad. Neurology; mem. Am. Assn. Neurol. Surgery, Congress Neurol. Surgery, Internat. Assn. Study of Pain, Am. Assn. Study of Headache, N.Y. Acad. Sci., Am. Coll. Angiology, Am. Soc. Contemporary Medicine and Surgery, Am. Holistic Med. Assn. (co-founder), Undersea Med. Soc., Am. Acad. Forensic Sci., Am. Assn. Biofeedback Clinicians, Soc. Cryosurgery, Pan Pacific Surg. Assn., Biofeedback Soc. Am., Acad. Psychosomatic Medicine, Pan Am. Med. Assn., Internat. Back Pain Soc., North Am. Spine Soc., Am. Soc. Stereotaxic and Functional Neurosurgery, Soc. for Computerized Tomography and Neuroimaging, Ind. Coroners Assn. (pres. 1979), Royal Soc. Medicine, Nat. Assn. Med. Examiners, Am. Pain Soc., Midwest Pain Soc. (pres. 1988), Am. Acad. Pain Medicine, Cen. Neurol. Soc., Interurban Neurosurg. Soc., Internat. Soc. Aquatic Medicine, James A. Gibson Anat. Soc., Am. Bd. Med. Psychotherapists (mem. profl. adv. council), James McClure Surg. Soc., Brendonwood Country Club, Highland Country Club. Home: 5845 High Fall Rd Indianapolis IN 46226-1017 Office: 7209 N Shadeland Ave Indianapolis IN 46250-2021

MANDERS, SUSAN KAY, artist; b. Burbank, Calif., Dec. 29, 1948; d. Gus H. and Erika (Stadelbauer) M.; m. Allan D. Yasnyi, Dec. 18, 1992; children: Brian Mallut. Attended, U. Guadalajara, 1969; BA, Calif. State U., 1971; postgrad., Otis Parsons, L.A., 1985, Royal Coll. of the Arts, London, 1987; grad., Silicon Digital Arts. Owner, dir., tchr. The Art Experience Sch. and Gallery, Studio City, Calif., 1978—; cons. in field. One-woman shows include La Logia, Studio City, Calif., 1991, Il Mito, Studio City, 1991, Bamboo, Sherman Oaks, Calif., 1991—, L.A. Art Installations, 1990, 92, Fed. Bldg., L.A., 1993, Art Experience, Studio City, 1993, Emerson's Gallery, Sherman Oaks, 1994, Raphael's, Beverly Hills, Calif., 1994; group shows include Beverly Hills Affair in the Gardens, 1984, 94, Otis Parsons, L.A., 1987, Hilderbrand Galleries, New Orleans, 1993, Studio City Art Festival, 1994, Parents Found., New Haven, Conn., 1994, Project Studio 8, San Francisco, 1994, Bistango Studio-Gallery, Irvine, Calif., 1994—, Montserrat Gallery, N.Y.C., 1995; creator, publ. prints Iron Jane Collections, 1994, Children's Hosp. Docent UCLA; active Tuesday's Child, Pillars of Hope Project San Fernando Valley County Fair, 1995. Mem. L.A. Art Assn., Beverley Hills Art Assn., Nat. Mus. Women in the Arts, L.A. County Mus. of Art, Dada, L.A., Mus. Contemporary Art Coun. Office: The Art Experience 11830 Ventura Blvd Studio City CA 91604-2617

MANDERSCHEID, LESTER VINCENT, agricultural economics educator; b. Andrew, Iowa, Oct. 9, 1930; s. Vincent John and Alma (Sprank) M.; m. Dorothy Helen Varnum, Aug. 29, 1953; children: David, Paul, Laura, Jane. BS, Iowa State U., 1951, MS, 1952; PhD, Stanford U., 1961. Grad. asst. Iowa State U., Ames, 1951-52, Stanford (Calif.) U., 1952-56; asst. prof. Mich. State U., East Lansing, 1956-65, assoc. prof., 1965-70, prof., 1970-73, prof., assoc. chmn., 1973-87, prof., chmn., 1987-92, prof., 1992—; reviewer Tex. A&M Agrl. Econ. Program, College Station, 1989; con. Consortium Internat. Earth Sci. Info. Network, Ann Arbor, 1990. Co-author: Improving Undergraduate Education, 1967; contbr. articles to jours. in field. Pres. parish coun. St. Thomas, East Lansing, 1984-87; coll. coord. United Way, East Lansing, 1983-84. Recipient Disting. Faculty award Mich. State U., 1977. Mem. Am. Agrl. Econ. Assn. (pres. 1988-89, bd. dirs. 1982-85, excellence in teaching award 1974), Am. Statis. Assn., Am. Evaluation Assn., Am. Econ. Assn., University Club, Sigma Xi (pres. 1986-87), Phi Kappa Phi (pres. 1979-80). Roman Catholic. Home: 2372 Burcham Dr East Lansing MI 48823-7242 Office: Mich State U Dept of Agrl Econs Circle Dr East Lansing MI 48824-1039

MANDERY, MATHEW M., principal. BS, Bklyn. Coll., 1965, MA, 1971; EdD, Fordham U., 1990. Asst. prin. supr. math. Midwood H.S., Bklyn.; prin. Newtown H.S., Bklyn. Tech. H.S., Jericho (N.Y.) High Sch., 1987—. Author: Achieving Competence in Mathematics, 1987, Achieving Proficiency in Mathematics, 1994. Recipient Blue Ribbon Sch. award U. S. Dept. Edn., 1990-91; named N.Y. State Prin. of Yr., 1992-93, Educator of Yr. Assn. Tchrs. N.Y.C., 1985; Danforth fellow; recipient Disting. Svc. award for Contbns. to Math. Edn., 1984, Cert. of Honor Westinghouse Sci. Talent Search, Disting. Alumnus award Bklyn. Tech. H.S. Alumni Assn., 1993. Mem. Nassau County Secondary Sch. Adminstrs. Assn. (pres.), Headmasters Assn., Phi Delta Kappa (past pres. St. John's U. chpt., Educator of Yr., 1995). Office: Jericho High Sch Cedar Swamp Rd Jericho NY 11753

MANDEVILLE, CRAIG H., aircraft company executive, retired military officer; b. Chickasha, Okla., Sept. 22, 1940. BA, Okla. State U., 1963. Commd. 2d lt. U.S. Army, 1963, advanced through grades to lt. col., 1979; battery comdr. Battery A 2d Battalion 320th Field Artillery, 101st AIrborne Divsn. U.S. Army, Vietnam, 1967-68, dep. regimental advisor 15th Inf. Regiment, 9th ARVN Divsn., 1971-72; staff officer, dep. chief of staff ops. and plans, requirements directorate Hdqrs. DA U.S. Army, Washington, 1978-82; battalion comdr. 1st Battalion (LANCE) 12th Field Artillery U.S. Army, Ft. Sill, Okla., 1982-83; ret. U.S. Army, 1983; mgr. C-17 program devel. Douglas Aircraft Co.-McDonnell Douglas Corp., Long Beach, Calif., 1983-89, bus. unit mgr. C-17 program devel., 1989-91, acting gen. mgr. C-17 program exts., 1991, now exec. asst. to C-17 sr. v.p., program mgr. Founder, dir. L.A. Rams Pro-Am Celebrity Tennis Tournament; assisted clubs with tennis clinics, tournaments; instr. tennis. Decorated Silver Star (2), Bronze Star (3), Legion of Merit, Purple Heart (3), Combat Infantryman's Badge, Parachute Badge, others. Mem. U.S. Tennis Assn. Avocations: running, aerobics, cert. profl. U.S. profl. tennis registry. Home: 16521 Grunion Apt 200 Huntington Beach CA 92649-3484 Office: McDonnell Douglas Aerospace 54-44 2401 E Wardlow Rd Long Beach CA 90807-5309

MANDEVILLE, GILBERT HARRISON, consulting engineering executive; b. Bklyn., July 6, 1910; s. Gilbert Spier and Minnie (Ross) M.; m. Mildred Schwagerman, June 20, 1936; 1 child, Terry Melinda. B.S., Seattle U., 1953. Registered profl. engr., Wash. Exec. dir., v.p. Leo O. Daly Co., Seattle, 1952-57; ptnr., cons. engr. Mandeville & Berge, Architects and Engrs., Seattle, 1957-83; dir., sec.-treas. Riverfront Assocs.; dir. U.S. Devel. Co. Chmn. Seattle City Planning Commn., 1960-62, Puget Sound Regional Planning Coun., 1960-62. Lt. comdr. USNR, 1947-52. Fellow ASCE (life); mem. IEEE (life), Am. Arbitration Assn. Presbyterian. Clubs: Seattle Engring. Home: 1132 2d Ave S PO Box 895 Edmonds WA 98020 Office: Mandeville & Berge Archs & Engrs 500 Union St Seattle WA 98101-2332

MANDEVILLE, ROBERT CLARK, JR., former naval officer, business executive; b. Princeton, W.Va., July 18, 1927; s. Robert Clark and Grace (Oney) M.; m. Elizabeth Anne Perry, Oct. 10, 1953; children: Cathy, Karen, Christy, Scott. B.S., U.S. Naval Acad., 1950; M.S., Princeton U., 1959. Commd. ensign U.S. Navy, 1950, advanced through grades to rear adm., 1976; assigned carrier-based fighter and attack squadrons; project mgr. A-6/EA-6 Weapons Systems, Washington, 1970-73; comdg. officer Naval Air Sta. Oceana, Virginia Beach, Va., 1973-74; dir. aviation plans and requirements Navy Dept., Washington, 1974-78; comdr. Light Attack Wing, Pacific, Lemoore, Calif., 1978-80; dep. chief Naval Material for Logistics, Washington, 1980-81; ret., 1981; v.p. Science Applications, Inc., 1981-83; sr. v.p. ManTech Internat., Fairfax, Va., 1983-94; ind. cons., 1994—. Decorated D.F.C. (6), Air medal (13), Bronze Star, Meritorious Service medal, Legion of Merit (2). Mem. Assn. Naval Aviation, Tailhook Assn., Soc. Old Crows, Sigma Xi. Home: 5016 Althea Dr Annandale VA 22003-4144

MANDIL, I. HARRY, nuclear engineer; b. Istanbul, Turkey, Dec. 11, 1919; s. Harry Robert and Bertha (Presente) M. (parents Am. citizens); m. Beverly Ericson, June 22, 1946; children: Jean Dale, Eric Robert. B.S., U. London, Eng., 1939; M.S., MIT, 1941; grad., Oak Ridge Sch. Reactor Tech., 1950; D.Sc. (hon.), Thiel Coll., Greenville, Pa., 1960. Devel., design process controls for textile mills and chem. plants Norcross Corp., 1941-42, asst. to pres. charge field engring., 1946-49; asst. to tech. dir. naval reactors br. reactor devel. div. AEC, 1950-54, dir. reactor engring. div., 1954-64; prin. officer, dir. MPR Assos., Inc. (engrs.), Washington, 1964-85; cons., dir. MPR Assos., Inc. (engrs.), Alexandria, Va., 1985—; developer nuclear power for propulsion naval vessels, also for Shippingport Atomic Power Ctrl. Sta.; mem., sec. Energy Adv. Bd., Washington, 1990—; mem. corp. vis. com. for nuclear engring. dept. MIT, 1984-93; mem. sr. tech. rev. group for plutonium, Amarillo, Tex., 1995—. Author numerous papers in field. Served with USNR, 1942-46. Recipient Naval Letter of Commendation, 1946, Meritorious Civilian Svc. award Navy Dept., 1952, ASME Prime Movers award, 1956, Disting. Civilian Svc. award, 1959. Home: 701 Heathery Ln Pelican Bay Naples FL 33963 Office: 320 King St Alexandria VA 22314-3238

MANDINO, OG, author; b. Boston, Dec. 12, 1923; s. Silvio and Margaret T. (Lee) M.; m. Bette L. Lang, Dec. 9, 1957; children: Dana, Matthew. Student, Bucknell Jr. Coll., 1941. Sales mgr. Combined Ins. Co., Chgo., 1960-65; sales rep. Met. Life Ins. Co., Boston, 1948-60; exec. editor Success Unlimited mag., Chgo., 1965-72; pres. Success Unltd., Inc., Chgo., 1972-76; pres. Matt-Dana Ltd., 1974—, also dir. Author: A Treasury of Success Unlimited, 1967, The Greatest Salesman in the World, 1968, (with Edward R. Dewey) Cycles, The Mysterious Forces That Trigger Events, 1970, U.S. in a Nutshell, 1971, The Greatest Secret in the World, 1972, The Greatest Miracle in the World, 1975, (with Buddy Kaye) The Gift of Acabar, 1978, The Christ Commission, 1980, The Greatest Success in the World, 1981, Og Mandino's University of Success, 1982, The Choice, 1984, Mission: Success!, 1986, The Greatest Salesman in the World, Part II, End of the Story, 1988, A Better Way to Live, 1990, The Return of the Ragpicker, 1992, The Twelfth Angel, 1993, The Spellbinder's Gift, 1994, Secrets For Success and Happiness, 1995. Served to 1st lt. USAAF, 1942-45. Decorated D.F.C., Air medal with 5 oak leaf clusters. Mem. Authors Guild, Authors League, Nat. Speakers Assn., Internat. Speakers Hall of Fame.

MANDL, ALEX J(OHANN), telecommunications company executive; b. Vienna, Austria, Dec. 14, 1943; came to U.S., 1958, naturalized, 1968; s. Otto William and Charlotte J. (Peshek) M.; m. Nancy J. Scott, June 10, 1967; 1 dau., Melanie. BA, Willamette U., 1967; MBA, U. Calif., Berkeley, 1969. With Boise Cascade Corp., 1969-80; dir. internat. fin., asst. treas., then fin. chmn. Boise Cascade Corp., Boise, Idaho, 1973-80; sr. v.p. fin. and corp. planning Seaboard System R.R. Co., Jacksonville, Fla., 1980-85; sr. v.p. corp. devel. and adminstrn. CSX Corp., Richmond, Va., 1985-86; chmn., CEO CSX Tech., 1986-88, Sea-Land Corp. subs. CSX Corp., Iselin, N.J., 1988-91; exec. v.p. comm. svc. group AT&T, N.Y.C., 1991—; bd. dirs. CSX Comm., CSX Transp., Inc., Richmond Renaissance, Cybernetics and Systems Inc. Trustee Jacksonville Art Mus. Mem. Fin. Execs. Inst., Soc. Internat. Treasurers, Young Pres. Orgn., Bus. Week Corp. Planning 100, Mgmt. Policy Council, Council Planning Execs. (conf. bd.), Fin. Execs. Inst. (com. on corp. fin.). Clubs: River, University, The Bull and Bear. Office: AT&T 32 Avenue Of The Americas New York NY 10013-2473*

MANDLE, EARL ROGER, academic administrator, former museum administrator; b. Hackensack, N.J., May 13, 1941; s. Earl and Phyllis (Key) M.; m. Gayle Wells Jenkins, July 11, 1964; children: Luke Harrison, Julia Barnes. BA cum laude, Williams Coll., 1963; MA, NYU, 1967, cert. in Museum Training, 1967, postgrad.; DFA (hon.), U. Toledo, 1983, Kenyon Coll., 1986. Intern in drawings Met. Mus. Art, N.Y.C.; intern in sculpture and architecture Victoria and Albert Mus., London, 1966-67; assoc. dir. Mpls. Inst. Arts, 1967-74; assoc. dir. Toledo Mus. Art, 1974-76, dir., 1977-88; dep. dir. Nat. Gallery of Art, Washington, 1988-93; pres. Rhode Island Sch. Design, Providence, R.I., 1993—; chmn. exec. com. Am. Fedn. of Arts, 1987-93; mem. adv. panel New Zealand-U.S. Arts Found.; trustee Internat. Exhbns. Found., Sterling & Francine Clark Art Inst.; adv. panel Mus. Mgmt. Inst.; mem. NEA, Nat. Coun. on Arts; mem. adv. council Nat. Mus. Act, Smithsonian Instn.; mem. adv. com. on mus. mgmt. J. Paul Getty Trust; adv. bd. Charles Hosmer Morse Found., Inc.; trustee Spanish Found. for Restoration of Toledo (Spain); chmn. U.S. Com. on Restoration of Toledo; cons. Nat. Mus. Western Art, Tokyo, Kerr Found., Oklahoma City; chair cultural adv. council Netherlands-Am. Amity Trust, Inc., mem., exec. Ohio Arts Council; mem. exec. com. Williams Coll. Mus. Art; mem. arts adv. com. Barnes Found., 1991—; com. for the preservation of the Treasury Bldg., hist. advisor, 1989—; vis. prof. Robert Sterling Clark Prof. of Art Williams Coll., Williamstown, Mass., 1993. Contbr. to profl. mags. and jours. Decorated by the His Majesty Juan Carlos Knight of the Order of Isabel the Cath., Spain, 1985; Andover teaching fellow, 1963-64; Ford Found. fellow, 1966; Nat. Endowment Arts fellow, 1974; recipient Am. Hellenic Educational Progressive award, 1983, Distinguished Citizen for Art award Ohio Art Edn. Assn., 1983, Resolution for Leadership award Ohio Senate, 1983, Governor's award State of Ohio, 1983, Marketer of the Year award Am. Marketing Assn., 1983. Mem. Am. Assn. Mus. (trustee, v.p.), Art Mus. Assn. (pres.), Assn. Art Mus. Dirs., Am. Arts Alliance (trustee, policy com.), Coll. Art Assn., Internat. Council Mus., Intermus. Conservation Assn. (exec. com.), Ohio Found. for Arts, Ohio Art Council, Am. Assn. 18th Century Studies (treas.), Young Pres. Orgn., R.I. Ind. Higher Edn. Assn., Providence C. of C., R.I. Commodores, Confrerie des Chevaliers du Tastevin, Phi Kappa Phi. (hon. mem.), Providence Art Club, Hope Club, Univ. Club, Brown Faculty Club, Tile Club, Century Club (N.Y.C.), The Answer Club, Williams Club (N.Y.C.). Office: Rhode Island Sch Design Office of the President 2 College St Providence RI 02903-2717

MANDLER, GEORGE, psychologist; b. Vienna, Austria, June 11, 1924; came to U.S., 1940, naturalized, 1943; s. Richard and Hede (Goldschmied) M.; m. Jean Matter, Jan. 19, 1957; children: Peter Clark, Michael Allen. B.A., NYU, 1949; M.S., Yale U., 1950, Ph.D., 1953; postgrad., U. Basel, Switzerland, 1947-48. Asst. prof. Harvard U., 1953-57, lectr., 1957-60; prof. U. Toronto, Ont., Can., 1960-65; prof. psychology U. Calif., San Diego, 1965-94, chmn. dept. psychology, 1965-70, prof. emeritus, 1994—; dir. Ctr. Human Info. Processing, U. Calif., San Diego, 1965-90; hon. rsch. fellow Univ. Coll. London., 1977-78, 82-90, vis. prof., 1990—. Author: Mind and Emotion, 1975, (German edit.), 1980, Mind and Body, 1984, (Japanese edit.), 1987, Cognitive Psychology, 1985, Japanese edit., 1991; contbr. articles and revs. to profl. jours.; editor: Psychol. Rev., 1970-76. Served with U.S. Army, 1943-46. Fellow Ctr. for Advanced Study in Behavioral Scis., 1959-60; vis. fellow Oxford U., Eng., 1971-72, 78; Guggenheim fellow, 1971-72. Fellow AAAS, Am. Acad. Arts and Scis.; mem. AAUP, Am. Assn. Advancement Psychology (1974-82); Psychonomic Soc. (governing bd., chmn. 1983), Am. Psychol. Soc., Am. Psychol. Assn. (pres. div. exptl. psychology 1978-79, pres. div. gen psychology 1982-83, mem. coun. reps. 1978-82, William James prize 1986), Internat. Union Psychol. Scis. (U.S. com. 1985-90), Soc. Exptl. Psychologists, Fedn. Behavioral Psychol. and Cognitive Scis. (pres. 1981). Home: 1406 La Jolla Knoll La Jolla CA 92037-5236 Office: U Calif San Diego Dept Psychology La Jolla CA 92093-0109 also: 3 Perrins Ln, London NW3 1QY, England

MANDLER, JEAN MATTER, psychologist, educator; b. Oak Park, Ill., Nov. 6, 1929; d. Joseph Allen and May Roberts (Finch) Matter; m. George Mandler, Jan. 19, 1957; children: Peter Clark, Michael Allen. Student, Carleton Coll., 1947-49; BA with highest honors, Swarthmore Coll., 1951; PhD, Harvard U., 1956. Rsch. assoc. lab. social rels. Harvard U., 1957-60; rsch. assoc. dept. psychology U. Toronto, Ont., Can., 1961-65; assoc. rsch. psychologist, lectr. U. Calif. at San Diego, La Jolla, 1965-73, assoc. prof., 1973-77, prof. psychology, 1977-88, prof. cognitive sci., 1988—; mem. adv. com. on memory and cognitive processes NSF, 1978-81; hon. rsch. fellow U. Coll., London, 1978-89, vis. prof., 1990—; hon. mem. Med. Rsch. Coun. Cognitive Devel. Unit, 1982—. Author: (G. Mandler) Thinking: From Association to Gestalt, 1964, Stories, Scripts and Scenes, 1984; assoc. editor Psychol. rev., 1970-76; mem. editl. bd. Child Devel., 1976-89, Discourse Processes, 1977-94, Jour. Exptl. Psychology, 1977-85, Text, 1979—, Jour. Verbal Learning and Verbal Behavior, 1980-88, Lang. and Cognitive Processes, 1985—, Cognitive Devel., 1990—; contbr. articles to profl. jours. Pres. San Diego Assn. Gifted Children, 1968-71; v.p. Calif. Parents for Gifted, 1970-71; mem. alumni council Swarthmore Coll., 1975-78. NIMH research grantee, 1968-81; NSF research grantee, 1981—. Fellow APA (mem. exec. com. divsn. 3 1983-85), Am. Acad. Arts and Scis.; mem. Psychonomic Soc. (mem. governing bd. 1982-87, chmn. 1985-86), Soc. Rsch. in Child Devel., Cognitive Sci. Soc., Soc. Exptl. Psychologists, Phi Beta Kappa. Office: Dept Cognitive Sci U Calif San Diego La Jolla CA 92093-0515

MANDLER, SUSAN RUTH, dance company administrator; b. Kew Gardens, N.Y., Feb. 11, 1949; d. Ernest and Clea (Reisner) M.; m. Robert Morgan Barnett, July 30, 1982. B.S., Boston U., 1971. Mgr. Pilobolus, Inc., Washington, Conn., mgr., 1977—. Address: PO Box 166 Washington Depot CT 06794-0388

MANDRA, YORK T., geology educator; b. N.Y.C., Nov. 24, 1922; s. Raymond and Irene (Farruggio) M.; m. Highoohi Kechijian, Jan. 26, 1946. BA, U. Calif., Berkeley, 1947, MA in Paleontology, 1949; PhD in Geology, Stanford U., 1958. From instr. to assoc. prof. geology San Francisco State U., 1950-63, prof., 1964—, head geology sect., chmn. dept., 1960-67; vis. prof. U. Aix-Marseille, France, 1959, Syracuse U., summer

1963, U. Maine, summer 1969, U. Calif., Santa Barbara, summers 1972—; research assoc. U. Glasgow, 1959, Calif. Acad. Scis., 1966-88; vis. scientist New Zealand Geol. Survey, fall 1970. Contbr. numerous articles to profl. jours. Pres. David S. Sohigian Found., 1975—. Served with USAAF, 1942-46. Recipient Neil A. Miner Disting. Coll. Teaching award, 1984; Danforth Found. teaching fellow, 1958, NSF fellow, 1959; NSF rsch. grantee, 1967-77. Fellow Geol. Soc. Am. (Sr.), Calif. Acad. Scis., AAAS; mem. Nat. Assn. Geology Tchrs. (pres. Far Western sect. 1953-54, 73-74, Robert Wallace Webb award 1977), Paleontol. Soc., Soc. Econ. Mineralogists and Paleontologists, Soc. for Environ. Geochemistry and Health. Avocations: walking, reading, music. Office: San Francisco State U Dept Geosci 1600 Holloway Ave San Francisco CA 94132-1722

MANDRELL, BARBARA ANN, singer, entertainer; b. Houston, Dec. 25, 1948; d. Irby Matthew and Mary Ellen (McGill) M.; m. Kenneth Lee Dudney, May 28, 1967; children: Kenneth Matthew, Jaime Nicole, Nathaniel. Grad. high sch. Country music singer and entertainer, 1959—, performed throughout U.S. and in various fgn. countries; mem., Grand Ole Opry, Nashville, 1972—; star TV series Barbara Mandrell and the Mandrell Sisters, 1980-82, Barbara Mandrell: Get to the Heart, 1987; albums include Midnight Oil, Treat Him Right, He Set My Life To Music, This Time I Almost Made It, This is Barbara Mandrell, Midnight Angel, Barbara Mandrell's Greatest Hits, Christmas at Our House, 1987, Morning Sun, 1990, Greatest Country Hits, 1990, Standing Room Only, 1993. Author (with George Vecsey): Get To the Heart: My Story, 1990. Named Miss Oceanside, Calif., 1965; Named Most Promising Female Singer, Acad. Country and Western Music, 1971; Female Vocalist of Yr., 1978; Female Vocalist of Yr., Music City News Cover Awards, 1979; Female Vocalist of Yr., Country Music Assn., 1979; Entertainer of Yr., 1980, 81; People's Choice awards (6), 1982-84. Mem. Musicians Union, Screen Actors Guild, AFTRA, Country Music Assn. (v.p.). Mem. Order Eastern Star. Home: PO Box 620 Hendersonville TN 37077-0620 Office: Creative Artists Agy 3310 W End Ave Fl 5 Nashville TN 37203-1083

MANDT, JOHN F., religious organization executive. Pres. Am Baptist Historical Soc., Rochester, N.Y. Office: Am Baptist Historical Soc 1106 Goodman St S Rochester NY 14620-2532

MANDULA, JEFFREY ELLIS, physicist; b. N.Y.C., July 23, 1941; s. Andrew and Gertrude Phyllis (Entenberg) M.; m. Barbara Blumenstein, June 2, 1963. BA, Columbia U., 1962; MA, Harvard U., 1964, PhD, 1966. Postdoctoral fellow Harvard U., Cambridge, Mass., 1966-67; research fellow Calif. Inst. Tech., Pasadena, 1967-69, asst. prof. theoretical physics, 1970-73; mem. Inst. for Advanced Study, Princeton, N.J., 1969-70; assoc. prof. applied math. MIT, Cambridge, 1973-79; prof. physics Washington U., St. Louis, 1979-87; sr. scientist theoretical physics Dept. Energy, Washington, 1987—; program dir. for theoretical physics NSF, Washington, 1980-81; sec. Signition Corp., Los Alamos, N.Mex., 1986—; vis. prof. U. Minn., Mpls., 1979, U. Southampton, Eng., 1979; invited prof. U. Louvain, Belgium, 1980; adj. prof. physics Washington U., St. Louis, 1987—. Contbr. over 80 articles to profl. jours. NSF fellow, 1966, Alfred P. Sloan Found. fellow 1973; recipient Cottrel Research award Research Corp., 1984. Mem. AAAS, Am. Phys. Soc., Fedn. Am. Scientists. Home: 500 23rd St NW Washington DC 20037-2828 Office: US Dept Energy Divsn High Energy Physics Washington DC 20585

MANEA, NORMAN, writer, educator; b. Suceava, Bukovina, Romania, July 19, 1936; came to U.S., 1988; s. Marcu and Janeta (Braunstein) M.; m. Josette-Cella Boiangiu, June 28, 1969. MS in Engring., Inst. Constrn., Bucharest, Romania, 1954. Engr. Romania, 1959-74, writer, 1969-86; fellow Deutscher Akademischer Austauschdienst, West Berlin, Germany, 1987; fellow Internat. Acad. Scholarship and the Arts Bard Coll., Annandale On Hudson, N.Y., 1989-92, writer in residence, 1992—. Author: October, eight o'clock, 1992, On Clowns: The Dictator & the Artist, 1992, Compulsory Happiness, 1993, The Black Envelope, 1995; contbr. articles, stories to profl. jours. Recipient MacArthur Found. award, 1992, Nat. Jewish Book award Jewish Book Coun., 1993, Literary Lion award Nat. Pub. Libr., 1993; Guggenheim grantee, 1992; Fulbright fellow, 1988. Mem. Am. Pen. Home: 201 W 70th St Apt 10-i New York NY 10023-4301 Office: Bard Coll Dept Lang And Literatu Annandale On Hudson NY 12504

MANEATIS, GEORGE A., retired utility company executive; b. 1926. BSEE, Stanford U., 1949, MSEE, 1950. With GE, 1950-53; with Pacific Gas & Elec. Co., San Francisco, 1953-91, v.p., 1979-81, sr. v.p., 1981-82, exec. v.p., 1982-86, pres., 1986-91, also bd. dirs. Office: Pacific Gas & Electric Co PO Box 770000 123 Mission St H17F San Francisco CA 94177

MANEKER, DEANNA MARIE, advertising executive; b. Albany, N.Y., Dec. 13, 1938; d. Marion K. and Florence R. (Krell) Colle; m. Morton Maneker, Sept. 15, 1957 (div. Feb., 1981); children: Meryl C., Amy J., Marion Kenneth. AB, Barnard Coll., 1960. Dir. circulation Westchester Mag., Mamaroneck, N.Y., 1971-73; pub. Change Mag., New Rochelle, N.Y., 1973-78; gen. mgr. Ctr. for Direct Mktg., Westport, Conn., 1978-81; sr. v.p. The Stenrich Group, Glen Allen, Va., 1981-88, exec. v.p., 1988-94; COO Martin Direct (formerly The Stenrich Group), Glen Allen, Va., 1994-96, exec. v.p. applied info. mgmt. divsn., 1995—. Home: 206 Tamarack Rd Richmond VA 23229-7039 Office: The Martin Agency 4413 Cox Rd Glen Allen VA 23060

MANEKER, MORTON M., lawyer; b. N.Y.C., Nov. 14, 1932; s. Arthur and Estelle (Hochberg) M.; m. Roberta S. Wexler, 1985; children: Meryl Colle, Amy Jill, Marion Kenneth. A.B., Harvard U., 1954, LL.B., 1957. Bar: N.Y. State 1957. Assoc. Shearman & Sterling, N.Y.C., 1957-62; trial atty. antitrust div. Dept. Justice, 1962-63; ptnr. Proskauer, Rose, Goetz & Mendelsohn, N.Y.C., 1963-94; arbitrator, 1995—. Trustee Beth Israel Hosp., N.Y.C., 1977—. Mem. ABA, Am. Law Inst., N.Y. State Bar Assn., Harvard Club N.Y.C. Jewish. Home: 30 E 65th St New York NY 10021-7048

MANELLI, DONALD DEAN, screenwriter, film producer; b. Burlington, Iowa, Oct. 20, 1936; s. Daniel Anthony and Mignon Marie (Dean) M.; m. Susan Linda Allen, June 16, 1964 (div. Aug. 1973); children: Daniel, Lisa. BA, U. Notre Dame, 1959. Communications specialist Jewel Cos., Melrose Park, Ill., 1959; script writer Coronet Films, Chgo., 1960-62; freelance writer Chgo., 1962-63; creative dir. Fred A. Niles Communications Ctrs., Chgo., 1963-67; sr. writer Wild Kingdom NBC-TV, Chgo., 1967-70; freelance film writer, producer Chgo., 1970-76; pres. Donald Manelli & Assocs., Inc., Chgo. and Paris, 1976—. Screenwriter, prodr. over 200 documentary films, 1970—, numerous episodes Wild Kingdom, 1967-82 (Emmy award 1969, 70). Recipient numerous awards various orgns. including N.Y. Internat. Film Festival, Houston Internat. Film Festival, Berlin, Paris, Venice Internat. Film Festivals, CINE, 1976—. Mem. Writers Guild Am. Roman Catholic. Avocations: photography, traveling, tennis. Office: 400 W Erie St Chicago IL 60610-4041 also: 1 Rue Goethe, 75116 Paris France *A simple truth is played out in most lives: what we believe ourselves to be, we are. We may be tested with adversity, our own failed efforts, and plain bad luck, but our personal vision gives us strength and persistence. Success brings the satisfaction of fulfilled dreams, and the responsibility to help others form and follow their own visions.*

MANERI, REMO R., management consultant; b. Cleve., Aug. 16, 1928; s. Quinto Peter and Lucia (Massenzi) M.; m. Camille Ann Caranna, Aug. 26, 1950; children: Peter, Alisa, Leonard, Celia. B.S. in Chem. Engring., Case Inst. Tech., 1950; grad., Advanced Mgmt. Program, Harvard U., 1969. Devel. engr. Dow Corning, 1950-53, market researcher, 1956, comml. devel. mgr., 1957-63, chief engr., 1964-66, unit mfg. mgr., 1967-69, dir. tech. service and devel., 1970-72, bus. mgr., v.p., 1973-74, mgr. bus., group v.p., 1975-76; pres. Dow Corning U.S.A., 1977-80; exec. v.p. Dow Corning Corp., 1981-82, also bd. dirs.; chmn. bd. Quantum Composites, 1982-85, pres., chmn. bd., 1985-87, chmn. bd., 1987-89, also bd. dirs.; mgmt. cons., 1989—; bd. dirs. Comerica Bank-Midland, Duro-Last Roofing, Inc., Quantum Composites, Inc.; cons. in field. Contbr. articles to profl. jours. Bd. dirs. Midland Hosp. Assn. Served with Signal Corps, U.S. Army, 1954-56. Named Man of Year Adhesives and Sealants Coun., 1988. Mem. Chem. Spltys. Mfg. Assn. (dir.), Am. Chem. Soc., AAAS, Sigma Xi, Tau Beta Pi, Alpha Chi Sigma. Roman Catholic. Club: Midland Country. Patentee in field. Home and Office: 5808 Siebert St Midland MI 48640-2753

MANES, STEPHEN GABRIEL, concert pianist, educator; b. Bennington, Vt., Apr. 11, 1940; s. Julius H. and Edna E. (Silberstein) M.; m. Frieda Green, July 7, 1963; children: Sonya Ruth, Daniel Ira. B.S., Juilliard Sch. Music, 1961, M.S., 1963; postgrad. (Fulbright fellow), Acad. Music, Vienna, 1963-64. Vis. instr. music Oberlin Coll. Conservatory, Ohio, 1966-67; asst. prof. Ball State U., Muncie, Ind., 1967-68; prof. music SUNY-Buffalo, 1968—, chair, 1989-93; co-music dir. Sebago-Long Lake Region Chamber Music Festival, North Bridgton, Maine, 1982-85. Concert piano soloist maj. orchs. U.S. and abroad; debuts in Washington, 1962, N.Y.C., 1963, Vienna, Austria, 1964, Berlin, 1975, Amsterdam, 1975, London, 1975, chamber music concerts, radio, TV appearances, four-hand piano recitals with Frieda Manes in U.S., Australia, Can. and P.R.; rec. artist Orion Master Records, 1974—, Spectrum Records, 1986—; mem. Baird Piano Trio, 1986-90. Recipient Kosciuszko Chopin prize, 1960, Town Hall award Concert Artists Guild, 1962; finalist Leventritt Internat. Competition, 1962; Harriet Cohen Internat. Beethoven prize, 1964. Mem. Music Tchrs. Nat. Assn., Coll. Music Soc., Am. Fedn. Musicians. Home: 89 High Park Blvd Amherst NY 14226-4210 Office: SUNY-Buffalo Dept of Music 414 Baird Hall Buffalo NY 14260

MANESS, MILDRED, reading specialist; b. Caldwell, N.J., Dec. 10, 1928; d. Joseph and Olympia (Gaito) Raimo; m. Frank W. Maness, Aug. 3, 1958. Masters, Kean Coll., 1975. Cert. elem. tchr., learning cons., reading specialist, N.J. Tchr. Piscataway Twp. (N.J.) Schs., 1951-59; tchr. Parsippany-Troy Hills Schls., Parsippany, N.J., 1959-94, reading specialist, 1978-93; founder outdoor reading program, 1967-94; bd. dirs. Parsippany Day Care Ctr.; mem. awards com. Rudolph Rsch., Flanders, N.J. Co-author curriculum programs, 1968-94. Coord. Parsippany-Troy Hills Twp. Tree-Arbor, environ. projects and sr. citizen twp. parade, 1959-94. Named Outstanding Educator, Parsippany Rotary, 1975, one of Outstanding Elem. Tchrs. Am., 1973; recipient A+ for Tchrs. award Sta. 9 TV, , 1989, 92, Gov.'s Recognition, 1990, Disney Am. Tchr. award 1992. Mem. NEA, N.J. Edn. Assn., Alpha Delta Kappa. Home: PO Box 455 Caldwell NJ 07006-0455 Office: Intervale Sch PO Box 52 60 Pitt Rd Parsippany NJ 07054

MANEY, MICHAEL MASON, lawyer; b. Taihoku, Japan, Aug. 13, 1936; s. Edward Strait and Helen M. M.; m. Suzanne Cochran, Oct. 22, 1960; 1 child, Michele. B.A., Yale U., 1956; M.A., Fletcher Sch. Law and Diplomacy, Tufts U., 1957; LL.B., U. Pa., 1964. Bar: N.Y. 1966, D.C. 1977. Case officer CIA, 1957-61; law clk. Justice John Harlan, Supreme Ct. U.S., Washington, 1964-65; asso. Sullivan & Cromwell, N.Y.C., 1965-70; partner Sullivan & Cromwell, 1971-77, 81—; mng. partner Sullivan & Cromwell, Washington, 1977-81; law fellow Salzburg Seminar in Am. Studies, 1967; bd. vis. Fletcher Sch. Law and Diplomacy. Trustee, chmn. bd. Am. Found. for the Blind, Inc. Lt. USAF, 1958-60. Mem. ABA, Am. Law Inst., Am. Coll. Trial Lawyers, N.Y. State Bar Assn., Union Club, Harvard Club of Boston, Down Town Assn., Madison Beach Club, Madison Country Club, Met. Opera Club. Home: 1220 Park Ave New York NY 10128-1733 also: 48 Neptune Ave Madison CT 06443-3210 Office: Sullivan & Cromwell 125 Broad St New York NY 10004-2498

MANFREDI, DAVID PETER, architect; b. Hartford, Conn., Aug. 9, 1951; s. Domenic George and Elizabeth Frances (Ferrando) M. BA, U. Notre Dame, 1973; MA, U. Chgo., 1976; BArch, U. Notre Dame, 1979. Registered architect. V.p. The Architects Collaborative, San Francisco & Cambridge, Mass., 1979-88, Elkus/Manfredi Architects, Boston, 1988—. Prin. works include SONY Gallery, 1992 (Chgo. Interiors Grand Prize 1993), West Roxbury Dist. Courthouse, 1992, Franklin Pierce Law Ctr., 1992. Mem. AIA, Boston Soc. Architects, Phi Beta Kappa. Office: Elkus/Manfredi Architects 530 Atlantic Ave Boston MA 02210-2218

MANFREDI, DEANNA ANN, marketing researcher; b. Wilmington, Del., Mar. 12, 1968; d. Richard Lewis and Anna Gloria (Vallorani) M. BA, Franklin & Marshall Coll., Lancaster, Pa., 1990; MA, Princeton U., 1992, PhD, 1994. Lab. technician U. Pa. State Med. Sch., Hershey, Pa., 1987; teaching asst. Franklin & Marshall Coll., Lancaster, Pa., 1989; asst. instr. Princeton (N.J.) U., 1990-93; assoc. project mgr. Nat. Analysts, Inc., Phila., 1994—. Contbr. chpt. to book and articles to profl. jours. Faculty grantee Franklin & Marshall Coll., 1988. Mem. Am. Psychol. Soc., Sigma Xi. Republican. Roman Catholic. Home: Apt 2607 1815 John F Kennedy Blvd Philadelphia PA 19103-1701 Office: Nat Analysts Inc 1700 Market St Philadelphia PA 19103-3913

MANFREDI, JOHN FREDERICK, food products executive; b. N.Y.C., Dec. 1, 1940; s. John Frederick and Angela (Morano) M.; m. Doreen Honore Molloy, July 19, 19180; children: Nicole, Kendre, Hadley. Student, Yale U., 1958-61; BA, Columbia U., 1967. Asst. trader Singer & Mackie, N.Y.C., 1964; editor New Haven Jour. Carrier, Fairchild Publs., 1965-68; dir. pub. rels. Gen. Foods, White Plains, N.Y., 1968-74, dir. corp. communications, 1975-80, dir. internat. pub. affairs, 1981-86, dir. pub. affairs worldwide, 1986-87; v.p. pub. affairs Nabisco, Inc., Parsippany, N.J., 1988, sr. v.p. external and govt. affairs, 1988—; chmn. Internat. Food Info. Coun., Washington, 1990—; chmn. Commn. on Mktg. and Advt., U.S. Coun. for Internat. Bus., N.Y.C., 1990—, Internat. C. of C., Paris, 1990—; mem. govt. affairs coun. GMA, 1995. Mem. Internat. Advt. Assn. (bd. dirs. 1990—), U.S. Olympic Com. N.J. (chmn.), Internat. Pub. Rels. Assn., Pub. Rels. Soc. Am., Arthur Page Soc., The Wisemen, Nat. Press Club. Office: Nabisco Foods Group 7 Campus Dr Parsippany NJ 07054-4407

MANGAN, FRANK THOMAS, advertising executive; b. Bklyn., Nov. 14, 1944; s. Francis T. and Margaret M. Mangan; m. Kerry Kilmartin, Nov. 16, 1945; children: Michael T., Jeffrey D. BS, Mt. St. Mary's Coll., Emmitsburg, Md., 1966; postgrad., Fordham U., 1970-72. With Joseph E. Seagram & Sons, N.Y.C., 1967-74; sr. v.p. The Marschalk Co., Inc., N.Y.C., 1974-85, Wells, Rich, Greene, Inc., N.Y.C., 1985-86; v.p. Lord, Geller Federico, Einstein, Inc., N.Y.C., 1986-88; sr. v.p. LINTAS, N.Y.C., 1988-91, Y & R Cos., N.Y.C., 1991—. Republican. Roman Catholic. Club: Tokeneke (Darien, Conn.).

MANGAN, JOHN LEO, retired electrical manufacturing company executive, international trade and trade policy specialist; b. Lakewood, Ohio, May 24, 1920; s. Mark A. and Celia M. (Motley) M.; m. Mildred J. Livingston, June 21, 1946; children: John, Scott. BSME, Carnegie Inst. Tech., 1942. Registered profl. engr., Mass., N.Y. Turbine design engr. Gen. Electric Co., Lynn, Mass., 1946-48; turbine application and sales engr. Gen. Electric Co., Fitchburg and Lynn,, Mass., Schenectady, St. Louis,, 1948-55; mgr. gas turbine indsl. sales Gen. Electric Co., Schenectady, 1955-60, mgr. gas turbine product planning, 1960-64, mgr. turbine strategy devel., 1966-86; mgr. turbine indsl. customer requirements Boeing Co., Seattle, 1964-66. Contbr. articles profl. jours., chpts. in books; inventor in field. Mem. com. Boy Scouts Am., 1955-59, 64-66; bd. dirs. United Way Schenectady County, Inc., 1991—, chmn., 1992-93. 1st lt. U.S. Army, 1942-46. Recipient Profl. and Social Activities award Gen. Electric Co., 1977. Fellow ASME (v.p. 1975-79, bd. govs. 1983-87, Gas Turbine citation, Centennial medal 1980, Dedicated Svc. award 1988); mem. Internat. Combustion Engine Coun. (permanent com. 1974-81, v.p. 1977-81), Mohawk Golf Club (Schenectady). Home: 1345 Ruffner Rd Niskayuna NY 12309-2505

MANGAN, MAVOURNEEN, medical nurse, educator, administrator, researcher; b. Bklyn., Aug. 25, 1946; d. Francis Patrick and Edna May Mangan. Dipl. nursing, Southampton Hosp. Sch. Nursing, 1967; BA in Psychology, L.I. U., 1970; BSN, SUNY, Stony Brook, 1977, MSN, 1979. RN, N.Y., N.J.; cert. advanced practice nurse, BLS. Surg. nurse Bklyn. State Hosp., 1967-68; nurse L.I. U., Southampton, N.Y., 1968-70; psychiat. nurse South Oaks Hosp., Amityville, N.Y., 1970-75; psychiat. nurse, adult nurse practitioner VA Med. Ctr., East Orange, N.J., 1975-86; coord. diabetes edn. and treatment ctr. VA Med. Ctr., East Orange, 1986—; regional diabetes coord.; clin. asst. prof. U. Medicine and Dentistry of N.J., Newark. Contbr. articles to profl. jours. Named N.J. Nurse Practitioner of Yr. Am. Acad. Nurse Practitioners, 1994; grantee N.J. Dept. Health, 1993-96, 92-96. Mem. ANA, Am. Diabetes Assn., Am. Assn. Diabetes Educators, Nurses Orgn. Vets. Affairs, Dept. Vets. Affairs Diabetes Educators Group, N.J. State Nurses Assn., N.J. Pub. Health Assn. (exec. bd.), Garden State Nurses Assn. Diabetes Educators. Roman Catholic. Home: 238 Perth Hill Ct Aberdeen NJ 07747 Office: VA Med Ctr 385 Tremont Ave East Orange NJ 07018-1095

MANGAN, MONA, association executive, lawyer; b. Pittston, Pa., Dec. 29, 1945; d. Joseph H. and Mona C. Mangan; m. Roy N. Watanabe, Oct. 24, 1987; 1 child, Julia. BA, Lock Haven U., 1966; AM, Duke U., 1969; JD, Columbia U., 1975. Bar: N.Y. 1976, U.S. Dist. Ct. (ea. and so. dists.) N.Y. 1979. Congl. staff Senator Wayne Morse of Oreg., 1967-68; staff atty. U.S. Dept. Labor, N.Y.C., 1975-79; trial atty. EEOC, N.Y.C., 1979; asst. exec. dir. Writers Guild Am. East, Inc., N.Y.C., 1979-84, assoc. exec. dir., 1984, exec. dir., 1984—. Recipient Gross award for contbn. to journalism Lock Haven U., 1984. Mem. Assn. Bar City N.Y., ABA, Coalition Motion Picture and TV Unions (v.p.), Pan Am. Fedn. Arts, Mass Media and Entertainment Unions (regional v.p. 1993—), Unions for Performing Arts (treas.), Internat. Affiliation Writers Guilds (treas.), Columbia U. Law Sch. Alumni Assn. Office: Writers Guild Am East Inc 555 W 57th St New York NY 10019-2925

MANGANARO, FRANCIS FERDINAND, naval officer; b. Providence, Feb. 27, 1925; s. Ralph and Ada Susanna (Hobden) M.; m. Carol Anne Slater, Sept. 8, 1948; children: Carol Sue, William Francis, John Thomas, Linda Anne, Mary Kathryn. Student, U. R.I., 1943-44; B.S. in Elec. Engring, U.S. Naval Acad., 1944-47; Naval Engr., MIT, 1956; cert., Advanced Mgmt. Program, Harvard U. Sch. Bus., 1971; cert. pub. utilities exec. program, U. Mich., 1984. Registered profl. engr., Conn. Commd. ensign U.S. Navy, 1947, advanced through grades to rear adm., 1975; served in destroyers Atlantic Fleet, 1947-49, served in submarines Pacific Fleet, 1949-53, repair officer, submarines Pearl Harbor Naval Shipyard, 1956-59, design project officer, submarines Bur Ships, 1959-63; inspection and planning officer Office Supr. of Shipbldg. Groton, Conn., 1963-68; prodn. officer Portsmouth Naval Shipyard, 1968-72, comdg. officer Puget Sound Naval Shipyard, 1972-76, chmn. navy claims settlement bd. Naval Material Command, 1976-78; vice comdr. Naval Sea Systems Command Washington, 1978-80; ret. (Naval Sea Systems Command), 1980; v.p., dir. GPU Nuclear Corp., 1980-90; cons. Burns & Roe Utility Mgmt. Cons., 1990-94; cons. Raytheon Engrs. & Constructors, Inc., 1994—. Decorated Legion of Merit, DSM. Mem. Soc. Naval Architects and Marine Engrs., Am. Soc. Naval Engrs., Sigma Xi, Tau Beta Pi, Beta Psi Alpha.

MANGANO, LOUIS, lawyer; b. Passaic, N.J., Sept. 19, 1939; s. Salvatore and Mary Mangano; m. Arlene M. Triolo, Sept. 20, 1964; children: Kenneth L., Eileen M., Louis M., Michael S. BS in Bus. Adminstrn., Seton Hall U., 1970; MA in Criminal Justice, John Jay Coll., 1973; JD, Seton Hall U., 1979. Bar: N.J. 1981, U.S. Dist. Ct. N.J. 1981, U.S. Supreme Ct. 1985. With Elmwood Park (N.J.) Police Dept., 1966-83; pvt. practice atty. Elmwood Park, 1981—; adj. prof. Fairleigh Dickinson U., Rutherford, N.J., 1973-75, Jersey City (N.J.) State Coll., 1973-75; asst. prof. William Paterson Coll., Wayne, N.J., 1983-84; adv. bd. mem. Berkeley Coll., West Paterson, N.J., 1983—. Trustee, pres. Elmwood Park (N.J.) Bd. Edn., 1980-83, 89-93. With U.S. Army, 1959-61. Mem. Bergen County Bar Assn. Office: PO Box 305 395 River Dr Elmwood Park NJ 07407

MANGER, WILLIAM MUIR, internist; b. Greenwich, Conn., Aug. 13, 1920; s. Julius and Lilian (Weissinger) M.; m. Lynn Seymour Sheppard, May 30, 1964; children: William Muir, Jr., Lilian Wade (Mrs. Porter Fleming), Stewart Sheppard, Charles Seymour. BS, Yale U., 1944; MD, Columbia U., 1946; PhD, Mayo Found., U. Minn., 1958. Intern, Presbyn. Hosp., N.Y.C., 1946-47, resident, 1949-50; fellow internal medicine Mayo Found., 1950-55; asst. physician Presbyn. Hosp., 1957—; dir. Manger Rsch. Found., 1961-77; clin. asst. vis. physician Columbia div. Bellevue Hosp., 1964-68; asst. attending physician NYU Bellevue Hosp. 1969-77; assoc. attending physician, 1977-83, attending physician, 1983—; instr. medicine Columbia U. Coll. Phys. and Surg., 1957-66, assoc. medicine, 1966-70, lectr., 1981—; asst. attending physician Presbyn. Hosp., 1966-68; asst. clin. prof. medicine N.Y.U. Med. Ctr., 1968-75, assoc. clin. prof. medicine, 1975-83, prof. clin. medicine, 1983—; mem. devel. com. Mayo Clinic, 1981-87; vice chmn. bd. Manger Hotels, Inc., 1957-73. Mem. bd. govs. St. Albans Sch., Washington, 1958-64, 67-73, 83-89, chmn., 1967-69; trustee Found. Rsch. in Medicine and Biology, 1971-77, Buckley Sch., 1975-85, Found. for Advancement Internat. Rsch. in Microbiology, 1977-82, Thyroid Found., 1980-85; mem. bd. visitors Boston U. Med. Sch., 1992—; trustee Found. for Depression and Manic Depression, 1978-89, pres., 1980-89; elder Presbyn. Ch., 1968-70, 92-93, trustee, 1962-67, 80-84, deacon, 1959-61. Lt. (j.g.) M.C., USNR, 1947-49. Recipient Mayo Found. Alumni award for Meritorious Rsch., 1955, Disting. Alumnus award, 1992. Diplomate Nat. Bd. Med. Examiners, Am. Bd. Internal Medicine. Fellow ACP, Acad. Psychosomatic Medicine, Am. Geriatric Soc., Coun. on Geriatric Cardiology, N.Y. Acad. Medicine (admission com. 1976-78, edn. com. 1979-92), Am. Coll. Cardiology, Am. Coll. Clin. Pharmacology, Royal Soc. Health, Am. Inst. Chemists; trustee Nat. Hypertension Assn. (chmn. 1977—), AMA, Am. Soc. Internal Medicine, N.Y. State Med. Soc., N.Y. County Med. Soc., Am. Heart Assn. (fellow council on circulation and council for high blood pressure rsch.), Nat. High Blood Pressure Edn. Program (mem. Coord. Com.), Inter-Am. Soc. Hypertension, Internat. Soc. Hypertension, Am. Soc. Hypertension, Am. Thoracic Soc., N.Y. Acad. Sci., AAAS, Am. Physiol. Soc., Am. Chem. Soc., Am. Soc. Pharmacology and Exptl. Therapeutics, Am. Soc. for Clin. Pharmacology and Therapeutics, Clin. Autonomic Rsch. Soc., Am. Autonomic Soc., Med. Strollers, N.Y.C., Endocrine Soc., Pan Am. Med. Assn., Harvey Soc., Soc. Exptl. Biology and Medicine, Rsch. Discussion Group (founding mem., sec.-treas. 1958-80), Am. Fedn. Clin. Rsch., Am. Soc. Nephrology, Royal Soc. Medicine (affiliate), Fellows Assn. Mayo Found. (v.p., pres. 1953), Mayo Alumni Assn. (v.p. 1981-82, exec. com. 1981-89, pres. elect 1982-85, pres. 1985-87), Catecholamine Club (founder, sec.-treas. 1967-80, pres. 1981-82), Doctors Mayo Soc., Albert Gallatin Assos., New Eng. Soc., S.R. (chmn. admissions com. 1959-67, bd. mgrs. 1959-67, 69-70), Soc. Colonial Wars, Sigma Xi, Nu Sigma Nu, Phi Delta Theta, Explorers, Meadow (L.I., N.Y.); Univ.; Yale; N.Y. Athletic (N.Y.C.); Southampton Bathing Corp.; Jupiter Island. Co-author: Chemical Quantitation of Epinephrine and Norepinephrine in Plasma, 1959, Pheochromocytoma, 1977; author: Catecholamines in Normal and Abnormal Cardiac Function; editor, contbr. Hormones and Hypertension, 1966; editor: Am. Lecture Series in Endocrinology, 1962-75; guest editor First Irvine H. Page Internat. Hypertension Rsch. Symposium; contbr. articles to profl. and lay jours. Achievements include research on the mechanism of salt-induced hypertension, and on pheochromocytoma. Home: 8 E 81st St New York NY 10028-0201

MANGES, JAMES HORACE, investment banker; b. N.Y.C., Oct. 8, 1927; s. Horace S. and Natalie (Bloch) M.; m. Joan Brownell, Oct., 1969 (div.); m. Mary Seymour, Mar. 28, 1974; children: Alison, James H. Jr. Grad., Phillips Exeter Acad., 1945; BA, Yale U., 1950; MBA, Harvard U., 1953. With Kuhn, Loeb & Co., N.Y.C., 1954-77, ptnr., 1967-77; mng. dir. Lehman Bros., Kuhn Loeb Inc., N.Y.C., 1977-84, Shearson Lehman Hutton, Inc., N.Y.C., 1984-90; adv. dir. Lehman Bros., N.Y.C., 1990—; dir. Baker Industries, Inc., 1967-77; dir., exec. com. Metromedia, Inc. 1970-86. Trustee The Episcopal Sch., 1978-92, St. Bernard's Sch., 1985—, Phillips Exeter Acad., 1985-89, mem. trustee coun., 1989-95. Mem. Bond Club, Yale Club (N.Y.C.), City Midday, Century Country Club (Purchase, N.Y.). Home: 875 Park Ave New York NY 10021-0341 Office: Lehman Bros 3 World Financial Ctr New York NY 10285-1700

MANGHAM, R. HAROLD, church administrator. V.p. for ch. ministries The Christian and Missionary Alliance. Office: Christian & Missionary Alliance PO Box 35000 Colorado Springs CO 80935-3500

MANGHIRMALANI, RAMESH, international trade corporation executive; b. Bombay, Dec. 31, 1953; came to U.S., 1968; s. Chatur Thakurdas and Maya Mansukhani; m. Mona Gour, 1988. BA in History, Oxford U., 1975; MBA, London Sch. Econs., 1977; cert. internat. law and trade, U. Paris, 1979; diploma Exec. Devel. Program, Harvard U., 1984. Chief planner UN, Geneva, 1977-81; cons. Fin. Corp. Am., L.A., 1981-85; mgr. mktg. Calif. Fed. Savs. and Loan, L.A., 1985-86; pres. Marco Polo Assocs., San Francisco, 1986—; dir. Wall St. Cons. Assn., 1986—; pres. Indian Tourism Devel. Corp., 1988—; spl. advisor Hoover Inst., Stanford U., Palo Alto, Calif. Author: Thirld World Debt Solution, 1987, Marketing of Financial Instruments, 1988, India's Role in International Economy, 1988. Dir. Indian Children's Assn., New Delhi; pres. Children's World. Mem. Am. Mgmt.

Assn., World Affairs Coun., Commonwealth Club. Office: Global Markets Ltd 230 Powhattan Ct Danville CA 94526-5500

MANGIERI, JOHN NICHOLAS, university administrator; b. New Castle, Pa., Nov. 1, 1946; s. John and Rose Marie (Audino) M.; m. Deborah Ann Hoerner, Aug. 23, 1969; children: Jeffrey Michael, Deanna Ashley. B.S. in Edn., Slippery Rock State Coll., 1968; M.Ed., Westminster Coll., 1969; Ph.D., U. Pitts., 1972. Grad. asst. U. Pitts., 1970-72; asst. prof. edn. Ohio U., Athens, 1972-74, dir. tchr. corps., 1974-78; prof. edn. U. S.C., Columbia, 1978-82; dean Sch. Edn. Tex. Christian U., Fort Worth, 1982-87, dean grad. studies and rsch., 1987-89; provost, vice chancellor acad. affairs U. New Orleans, 1989-92; pres AR St Univ, State Univ, AR, 1992—. Author: (with Scott Baldwin) Effective Reading Techniques, 1978, (with Bader and Walker) Elementary Reading: A Comprehensive Approach, 1982, (with Staley and Wilhide) Teaching Language Arts: Classroom Application, 1984; contbr. numerous articles to profl. jours. Pres. Appalachian Reading Council, Ohio, 1973-74; pres. Columbia Area Reading Council, 1981-82; bd. dirs. Midwestern Tchr. Corps Network, 1976-80. Mem. Internat. Reading Assn. Office: Ark State U 2806 Covey Dr Jonesboro AR 72401-6909

MANGIN, CHARLES-HENRI, electronics company executive; b. Riom, France, Apr. 16, 1942; s. Louis Eugene and Monique (Mathivon) M.; m. Marguerite Stern, Nov. 27, 1974; children: Charlotte, Louis-David, Maxence. MBA, Ecole Superieure de Commerce, Reims, France, 1965. Computer salesman IBM, Paris, 1967-68; asst. to pres. EDC, Rome, 1969-71; gen. mgr. CEGI, Paris, 1971-77; pres. CEERIS, Paris, 1977-81, CEERIS Internat., Inc., Old Lyme, Conn., 1982—; cons. The Mitre Corp., Washington, 1973-78, Coyne & Bellier, Paris, 1973-76, IITRI, Chgo., 1979-81, PRC, London, 1980-81. Author: Lebanon, 1965, The Atlantic Facade, 1973, Flights Over Europe, 1974, Surface Mount Technology, 1986, Managing the SMT Challenge, 1990; contbg. editor Electronic Packaging and Prodn., 1988-91; contbr. articles to profl. jours. Mem. Surface Mount Tech. Assn., Soc. Mfg. Engrs., Internat. Electronics Packaging Soc., Am. Soc. Test Engrs., Internat. Soc. Hybrid Microelectronics, N.Y. Yacht Club, Ocean Cruising Club, Ski Club (Les Arcs, France). Roman Catholic. Avocations: sailing, skiing, opera. Office: Ceeris Internat Inc PO Box 939 Old Lyme CT 06371-0939

MANGINO, ROBERT, insurance company executive; b. 1936. Grad., Rutgers U., 1954-58, post grad., 1958-60. With Mutual Benefit Co., N.Y.C., 1960-70; sr. v.p. N. Am. Reassurance Co. subs. Swissre Holding N. Am., N.Y.C., 1970—. Office: Swissre Holding N Amer Inc 100 E 46th St # 13 New York NY 10017-2601*

MANGION, RICHARD MICHAEL, health care executive; b. Haverhill, Mass., Apr. 26, 1941; s. Michael Anthony and Evelyn (Cote) M.; m. Gail Elizabeth Donne, Apr. 27, 1968; children: Catherine Jean, James Richard, Ian Kyle. BBA, Suffolk U., 1963; MBA, Syracuse U., 1965; MPH, U. Calif., Berkeley, 1972. Asst. adminstr. Nashua (N.H.) Meml. Hosp., 1972-75, assoc. adminstr., 1975-77; pres. and chief exec. officer Harrington Meml. Hosp., Southbridge, Mass., 1977—; lectr. U. N.H., Durham, 1972-74. Pres. Tri-Community Devel. Corp., Southbridge, 1983-88. Capt. USAF, 1966-70. Fellow Am. Coll. Health Care Execs. (regent Mass. area B 1995—); mem. Am. Hosp. Assn., Mass. Hosp. Assn., Ctrl. Mass. Hosp. Coun. (pres. 1982-84), Ctrl. Mass. Health Care Found., Tri-Cmty. C. of C. (pres. 1983-84). Democrat. Roman Catholic. Club: Hosp. Supts. Lodge: Rotary. Avocations: tennis, swimming, hiking. Home: 50 Old Village Rd Sturbridge MA 01566-1069 Office: Harrington Meml Hosp 100 South St Southbridge MA 01550-4051

MANGIONE, CHUCK (CHARLES FRANK MANGIONE), jazz musician, composer; b. Rochester, N.Y., Nov. 29, 1940; children: Nancy, Diana. MusB in Music Edn., Eastman Sch. Music, U. Rochester, 1963, MusD (hon.), 1985. Formed quintet with brother Gap, Jazz Bros., 1958-64; tchr. elem. sch. music Rochester, 1963-64; dir. Eastman Jazz Ensemble; mem. faculty Eastman Sch. Music, 1968-72. Freelance musician with bands of Maynard Ferguson and Kai Winding, 1965, trumpet player with, Art Blakey's Jazz Messengers, 1965-67; formed Chuck Mangione Quartet, 1968; guest condr. Rochester Philharm. Orch., 1970, appeared at Montreux Internat. Jazz Festival, 1972; starred on PBS-TV spl. Live from Wolftrap; performed on PBS-TV spl. Grammy Awards show, 1981; ann. tours to Europe, Japan, Australia and S. Am.; performed benefit concerts for Spl. Olympics; also 8-hour marathon to aid Italy's earthquake victims; compositions include Hill Where the Lord Hides (Grammy nomination 1971), Land of Make Believe, 1973 (Grammy nomination for Best Big Band Performance and Best Instrumental Arrangement Accompanying a Vocalist), Bellavia, 1976 (Grammy award), Give It All You Got; theme for 1980 Winter Olympics (Emmy award Music Composition/Direction), 1980 (Grammy nomination for Best Instrumental Composition); albums include Chuck Mangione Quartet, 1972, Chase the Clouds Away, 1975 (gold album, 2 Grammy nominations), Main Squeeze, 1976, Feels So Good, 1977 (gold, platinum and double-platinum album), Children of Sanchez, Save Tonight For Me, 1986 Eyes of the Veiled Temptress, 1988; movie soundtrack, 1978 (Grammy award Best Pop Instrumental Performance), Live at the Hollywood Bowl, 1979, Fun and Games, 1980 (Grammy nomination), Tarentella, 1981. Commd. by Sesquicentennial Com. of City of Rochester to compose and premier spl. work in honor of city's 150th birthday. Made acting debut in film Paradise Blues, 1984; guest star Magnum PI; 1st music video Diana D, completed 1984 (directed by Zbigniew Rybczynski). Named Most Promising Male Jazz Artist, Record World 1975, Jazz Artist of Yr., Instrumentalist of Yr., Most Promising Instrumentalist, Top Fusion Artist, Top Producer, Top Instrumentalist, Outstanding Jazz Artist, Internat. Jazz award winner 1978-79, Georgie award for Instrumental Act of Yr., AGVA 1980, winner Playboy mag. ann. music poll, several times, also 1980 winner for Best Brass, Best Composer and Best Group.; recipient Entertainment award Big Bros. 4th Ann. Sidewalks of N.Y. Awards Dinner, 1983, Regents medal of excellence N.Y. State Bd. Regents, 1984, Jazz Music Campus Entertainment award Nat. Assn. Campus Activities, 1987. His performance at Montreal Internat. Jazz Festival, July 1986, drew largest crowd in history of the event.

MANGIONE, JERRE GERLANDO, author, educator; b. Rochester, N.Y., Mar. 20, 1909; s. Gaspare and Giuseppina (Polizzi) M.; m. Patricia Anthony, Feb. 18, 1957. BA, Syracuse U., 1931; MA (hon.), U. Pa., 1971, LittD (hon.), 1980; LHD (hon.), SUNY, Brockport, 1987. Writer, Time mag., 1931; book editor Robert M. McBride & Co., N.Y.C., 1934-37; nat. coordinating editor Fed. Writers' Project, 1937-39; spl. asst. to U.S. commr. immigration and naturalization, 1942-48; advt. writer, pub. relations dir., 1948-61; mem. faculty U. Pa., 1961—, dir. writing program, 1965-77, prof. English, 1968-77, emeritus, 1977—, founding dir. Italian Studies Center, 1978-80, coord. cultural events, 1980-82; vis. lectr. Bryn Mawr Coll., 1966-67; vis. prof. Trinity Coll., Rome, summer 1973, Queens Coll., 1980; chmn. Leon lectr. com. U. Pa., 1964-85; acting dir. Yaddo, 1977-78; editor WFLM Phila. Guide, 1960-61; book reviewer, 1931—; adv. editor Italian Americana, 1974-84, 90—; mem. lit. panel NEA, 1980-81; spkr. main address Symposium on Italian and Italian-Am. Women in '90s, SUNY, Stony Brook, 1993. Author: Mount Allegro: A Memoir of Italian Life, 1943, 6th edit., 1989 (hist. marker commemorating area erected in Rochester, 1986, stage adaptation premiere, Rochester), 1992, Spanish edit., 1944, Italian edit., 1947, rev., 1983, (novel) Ship and the Flame, 1948, Swedish edit., 1949, Reunion in Sicily, 1950, 2d edit., 1984, Italian edit., 1992, Night Search, 1965, To Walk the Night, Brit. edit., 1966, Italian edit., 1987, Life Sentences for Everybody, 1966, (fables) A Passion for Sicilians: The World Around Danilo Dolci, 1968, 3d edit., 1985, America is Also Italian, 1969, The Dream and the Deal: Federal Writers Project (1935-43), 1972, 3d edit., 1983 (nominated for Nat. Book award 1972), Mussolini's March on Rome, 1975, An Ethnic At Large: A Memoir of America in the Thirties and Forties, 1978, 2d edit., 1983, (with Ben Morreale) La Storia: Five Centuries of the Italian American Experience, 1992; (pamphlet on Phila. lit. history) By Reason of Birth or Residence, 1988; contbr. to newspapers and mags. Chmn. lit. arts com. Phila. Art Alliance, 1958-61; mem. adv. bd. U. Pa. Press, 1983-84; founding mem. exec. bd. Am.-Italy Soc., 1959-94, Inst. Contemporary Art U. Pa., 1964-77, Am. Italian Hist. Assn., 1969—, Am. Inst. Italian Studies, 1975-82, Amici, 1981—; pres. Friends Danilo Dolci, Inc., 1969-71. Guggenhiem fellow,1945; Fulbright Rsch. fellow, 1965; MacDowell Colony fellow, Yaddo fellow; Va. Ctr. Arts fellow; Rockefeller grantee, 1968; Am. Philos. Soc. grantee, 1971; Earhart Found. grantee, 1975; NEH grantee, 1980-83; decorated Knight Comdr. Order Star Solidarity, Italy, 1971; recipient Key to City Rochester, 1963, 10th Ann. Lit. award Friends Rochester Pub. Libr., 1966, Justinian Soc. award, 1966, Phila. Athenaeum Lit. award, 1973, Presdl. award Am. Inst. for Italian Culture, 1979, Outstanding Achievement award Am.-Italian Hist. Assn., 1985, Key to City New Orleans, 1988, Pa. Gov.'s award for Excellence in Humanities, 1989, Leonardo da Vinci award Italian Heritage and Culture Month Com., 1989; named Person of Yr. Italian Ams. Delaware County, 197, 86, Premio Nazionale Empedocie, 1984, Legion of Honor medal Chapel Four Chaplains, 1984; Mangione papers housed at U. Rochester; recipient Internat. Arts award Columbus Countdown, 1990, 92; honored by Libr. of Congress for lit. career with an exhibit titled: Jerre Mangione, An Ethnic at Large, 1992, Fed. Writer's Project, Christopher Columbus Quincentenary award, 1992, Mariano DiVito Human Achievement award, 1993, Distinction in Lit. Achievement award Columbus Citizens Found., 1993. Fellow Soc. Am. Historians; mem. Author's Guild, Franklin Inn, Assn. Writers of Agrigento in Sicily (nominated hon. pres. 1994), Sons of Italy. Home: 3300 Darby Rd Apt 7315 Haverford PA 19041-1075 Office: U Pa Dept English Philadelphia PA 19104

MANGLER, ROBERT JAMES, lawyer; b. Chgo., Aug. 15, 1930; s. Robert H. and Agnes E. (Sugrue) M.; m. Geraldine M. Delich, May 2, 1959; children: Robert Jr., Paul, John, Barbara. BS, Loyola U., Chgo., 1952, MA, 1983; JD, Northwestern U., 1955. Bar: Ill. 1958, U.S. Dist. Ct. (no. dist.) Ill. 1959, U.S. Supreme Ct. 1976, U.S. Ct. Appeals (7th cir.) 1980. Author: (with others) Illinois Land Use Law, Illinois Municipal Law. Village atty., prosecutor Village of Wilmette, 1965-93; mcpl. prosecutor City of Evanston, 1963-65; chmn. Ill. Traffic Ct. Conf., 1977—; pres. Ill. Inst. Local Govt. Law; mem. home rule attys. com. Ill. Mcpl. League. Mem. ABA (chmn. adv. com. traffic ct. program), Nat. Inst. Mcpl. Law Officers (past pres.), Ill. Bar Assn. (former chmn. traffic laws and ct. com.), Chgo. Bar Assn. (chmn. traffic ct. seminar, chmn. traffic laws com.), Caxton Club, Phi Alpha Delta.

MANGLONA, BENJAMIN T., commonwealth official; b. Rota, Mariana Islands; s. Prudencio M. and Maria T. M.; m. Magdalena Manglona Manglona, 1959; children: Lillian Manglona Matsumoto, Rebecca Manglona Taisague, Theodore, Marie Manglona Apatng, Joann Manglona San Nicolas, Benjamin M., Jr., Harold M., Debra M. Diaz, Selina Manglona Mesa. Grad., Surveyor's Sch., Palau, 1957; student Internat. Correspondence Sch., Scranton, Pa., 1964-65, Honolulu Community Coll., 1966-67; AS Civil Engring. Tech., U. Guam, 1973; constrn. insp. tng, OICC, Guam, 1971-73. Registered profl. land surveyor. Jr. engring. aide Rota Dist. Adminstrn., 1957, sr. engring. aide, 1958, supr. engring., 1958-59, asst. surveyor and cartographic engr., 1959-68, asst. clk. ct., Rota, part-time 1962-66, sta. mgr. Continental/Air Micronesia, Rota, 1968-69; pub. works officer, Rota, 1970-75; pres. Rota Petroleum Co., B & M Constrn. Co., Rota Community Project Assn.; mem. Mariana Islands Dist. Legislature, 1962-65; mem. Ho. of Reps. Congress of Micronesia, 1965-70, resigned; chmn. Ho. resources and devel. com. 1969-70; appointed Mariana Islands Dist. Legislature, 1975; mem. No. Marianas Legislature, 1976-78; mem. No. Mariana Islands Commonwealth Legislature (Senate), 1978-90, Senate floor leader, chmn. exec. appointments and govt. investigation com., chmn. fiscal affairs com. 1978-80, v.p., chmn. senate fiscal affairs com., 1980-82, v.p., legis. sec., chmn. 1984-85, chmn. fiscal affairs com., 1986-88; elected Senate pres., 1988-90; lt. gov., 1990—; trust terr. rep. S. Pacific Commn. Conf., New Caledonia, 1968; mem. Congress of Micronesia Joint Commn. on Polit. Status, Washington, 1969-70; No. Marianas rep. to numerous USA, UN confs.; 1st v.p. No. Mariana Constl. Conv., 1976; numerous other govtl. appointments and coms.; mem. Trust Terr. Bd. of Land Surveying Examiners, 1972-75; mem. Rota Mcpl. Scholarship Bd., 1969-75; mem. 902 Cons., 1988-90, chmn., 1990—, chmn. 702 multi-yr. covenant funding negotiation, 1991. Mem. Am. Soc. Bldg. and Constrn. Inspectors. Roman Catholic. Home: Songsong Village Rota MP 96951*

MANGO, WILFRED GILBERT, JR., construction company executive; b. Weehawkin, N.J., July 11, 1940; s. Wilfred Gilbert and Mildred B.M.; children from previous marriage: Christian P., Peter H.; m. Charlene Holt, Feb. 14, 1985; children: Alison L., David H. BS, Lehigh U., 1963; M.B.A., NYU, 1969. Auditor Hurdman & Cranstown, N.Y.C., 1963-69; dir. fin. Thomas Crimmins Contracting Co., N.Y.C., 1969-77; v.p. fin., mgr. fin. controls ITT Teleplant, Inc., N.Y.C., 1977-78; v.p. fin. George A. Fuller Co. div. Northrop Corp., N.Y.C., 1978-81, now pres., chief exec. officer, dir., 1981—. Past chmn. bd. trustees Marymount Manhattan Coll.; adv. bd. N.Y. Real Estate Inst.; bus. adv. coun. Lehigh U.; bus. coun. Lighthouse for the Blind; mem. Urban Land Inst. Mem. Am. Soc. C.P.A.s, N.Y. State Soc. C.P.A.s. Clubs: Lehigh U. of N.Y., Univ. (N.Y.C.). Home: 17 Khakum Wood Rd Greenwich CT 06831 Office: Fuller Group Inc 451 Park Ave S New York NY 10016-7390

MANGO-HURDMAN, CHRISTINA ROSE, psychiatric art therapist; b. Garden City, N.Y., May 13, 1962; d. Camillo Andrew and Dorothy Mae (Harrison) Mango; Keith Hurdman, Sept. 11, 1993; 1 child, Clarissa Rose Hurdman. BFA summa cum laude, Coll. of New Rochelle, 1984; MA, NYU, 1987. Registered art therapist; cert. structural family therapy tng.; cert. psycho-edn. multi family therapy tng. Art therapist Bronx Mcpl. Hosp. Ctr., 1984-88; art therapist, clin. supr. Fordham-Tremont Cmty. Mental Health Ctr., Bronx, 1988—; art therapy fieldworker Bronx State Hosp., 1984, art therapy intern Bronx Children's Hosp., 1985, Saint Lukes Hosp., N.Y.C., 1986. Contbr. articles to profl. jours. Mem. N.Y. Art Therapy Assn., No. N.J. Art Therapists Assn., Am. Art Therapy Assn. Home: 11 Turnure St Bergenfield NJ 07621-2035

MANGOLD, GLENN EDWARD, securities industry executive; b. Newark, June 22, 1942; s. Wilbur Ernest and Beverly Ruth (Martinson) M.; m. Diane Eleanor Fredricks, Dec. 7, 1963; children: Kimberly, Scott, Russell, Jill. BA, Rutgers U., 1963; MBA, NYU, 1969. Corp. trust adminstr. Chase Manhattan Bank, NA, N.Y.C., 1963-66, corp. trust officer, 1966-68, 2d v.p., 1968-73, v.p., 1973-80; sr. v.p. European Am. Bank, N.Y.C., 1980-84, Depository Trust Co., N.Y.C., 1985-88, 1988-95, exec. v.p., 1996—. Home: 113 Sutton Dr Berkeley Heights NJ 07922-2510 Office: Depository Trust Co Inc 55 Water St New York NY 10041

MANGOLD, JOHN FREDERIC, manufacturing company executive, former naval officer; b. La Grange, Ill., Jan. 24, 1927; s. John Frederic and Helvig Victoria (Anderson) M.; m. Margaret Ellen Gore, Oct. 25, 1947; children: John, Andrew, Jennifer. BS, U.S. Naval Acad., 1947; MSEE, U.S. Naval Postgrad. Sch., Monterey, Calif., 1958. Registered profl. engr., Conn. Commd. ensign USN, 1947, advanced through grades to comdr., 1962, comdg. officer nuclear submarine U.S.S. Halibut, 1962-63, comdg. officer nuclear tng. unit, 1963-67, ret., 1967; v.p. mfg. Combustion Engring., Inc., Windsor, Conn., 1972-78, group pres., 1982-86, v.p. utility boilers, 1990-91; pres. Vetco, Inc., Ventura, Calif., 1978-82; cons., 1992; pres. Detrex Corp., Southfield, Mich., 1992-93, bd. dirs., 1993—; bd. dirs. Detrex Corp. Mem. IEEE, U.S. C. of C. (energy com. 1984-87). Republican. Office: 1000 Prospect Hill Rd Windsor CT 06095-1521

MANGOLD, SYLVIA PLIMACK, artist; b. N.Y.C., Sept. 18, 1938; d. Maurice and Ethel (Rein) Plimack; m. Robert Mangold. Student, Cooper Union, 1956-59; BFA, Yale U., 1961. Exhibited one-person shows Daniel Weinberg Gallery, San Francisco, 1974, Fischbach Gallery, N.Y.C., 1974, 75, Annemarie Verna Gallery, Zurich, 1978, 91, Droll-Kolbert Gallery, N.Y.C., 1978, 80, Young Hoffman Gallery, Chgo., 1980, Ohio State U., Columbus, 1980, Pa. Acad., 1981, Contemporary Arts Mus., Houston, 1981, Madison Art Ctr., (Wis.), 1982, Brooke Alexander, Inc., 1982, 83, 84, 85, 86, 89, 92, 95, Duke Art Mus., N.C., 1982, Rhona Hoffman Gallery, Chgo., 1985, Tex. Gallery, 1986, Fuller Goldeen Gallery, San Francisco, 1987, U. Mich, Ann Arbor, 1992, Minn. Inst. Arts, 1992, Grunwald Ctr. for Graphic Arts, UCLA, 1992, Neuberger Mus. Art, SUNY, Purchase, 1993, Davison Art Ctr., Wesleyan U., Middletown, Conn., 1993, Albright-Knox Art Gallery, Buffalo, 1994, Wadsworth Atheneum, Hartford, Conn., 1994, Blaffer Gallery U. Houston, 1994, Mus. Fine Arts, Boston; group shows at Young Hoffman Gallery, Chgo., 1979, Walker Art Ctr., Mpls., 1979, Droll-Kolbert Gallery, 1979, Denver Art Mus., 1979, U. So. Calif., 1979, Honolulu Acad. Art, 1979, Oakland Mus., (Calif.), 1979, Univ. Art Mus. of U. Tex.-Austin, 1979, Internat. Biennial Ljibljana, Yugoslavia, Phoenix Art Mus., 1979, Art Latitute Gallery, N.Y.C., 1980, Thorpe Intermedia Gallery, Sparkhill, N.Y., 1980, U. Colo. Art Galleries, Boulder, 1980, Nina Freudenheim Gallery, Buffalo, 1980, U.S. Pavillion of Venice Biennial, 1980-81, Inst. Contemporary Art of U. Pa., Phila, 1980-81, Yale U. Art Gallery, 1981, San Antonio Mus. Art, 1981, Indpls. Mus. Art, 1981, Tucson Mus. Art, 1981, Pa. Acad., 1981, Mus. Art of Carnegie Inst., Pitts., 1981, Brooke Alexander, Inc., N.Y.C., 1982, Ben Shahn Ctr. Visual Arts, 1982, Castle Gallery, Coll. of New Rochelle, N.Y., 1983, Thomas Segal Gallery, Boston, 1982-83, Siegel Contemporary Art, N.Y., 1983, Freedman Gallery, Albright Coll., Reading, Pa., 1983, Fuller Goldeen, San Francisco, 1983, Yale U. Art Gallery, New Haven, 1983-84, 86, Wilcox Gallery, Swarthmore, Pa., 1984, The Hudson River Mus., Yonkers, N.Y., 1984, Sardonia Art Gallery, Wilkes Coll., Wilkes-Barre, Pa., 1985, Kent State U. Gallery, Ohio, 1985, Brooke Alexander, N.Y., 1985, John C. Stoller Co., Minn., 1985, Knight Gallery, Spirit Sq. Arts Ctr., Charlotte, N.C., 1986, Mus. Art, R.I. Sch. Design, Providence, 1986, Yale U. Gallery, 1986, CUNY, 1986-87, Lorence Monk Gallery, N.Y.C., Vanquard Gallery, Phila., 1986-087, Aldrich Mus., Ridgefield, 1986-87. Flander's Contemporary Art, Mpls., 1987, Annemarie Verna Galerie, Zurich, 1988, U. N.C., 1988, R.I. Sch. Design, 1988, Grace Borgenicht Gallery, N.Y.C., 1988, Fay Gold Gallery, Atlanta, 1988, U. N.C., Greensboro, Three Rivers Arts Festival, Pitts., 1989, Cin. Art Mus., New Orleans Mus. Art, Denver Art Mus., Pa. Acad. Fine Arts, 1989, U. Mich., 1992, Mpls. Inst. Arts, 1992, Grunwald Ctr. Graphic Arts, UCLA, L.A., Neuberger Mus. Art, SUNY Purchase, 1993, Davisob Art Ctr., 1993; exhibited in permanent collections, Albright-Knox Art Gallery, Buffalo, Allen Meml. Art Mus., Oberlin, Ohio, Bklyn. Mus., Dallas Mus. Fine Arts, Detroit Inst. Art, Mus. Fine Arts, Houston, Indpls. Mus. Art, Madison (Wis.) Art Ctr., Milw. Art Mus., Yale U. Art Gallery, Mus. Modern Art, N.Y.C., Mus. Fine Arts, U. Utah, Tampa (Fla.) Mus., Walker Art Mus., Mpls., Whitney Mus. Am. Art, N.Y., Weatherspoon Art Gallery, Greensboro, N.C., Wadsworth Athenaeum, Hartford, U. Mich., Utah Mus. Fine Art. Work reviewed in newspapers and mags.

MANGONE, GERARD J., international and maritime law educator; b. N.Y.C., Oct. 10, 1918; s. Gerard Francis and Viola (Schumm) M.; m. Emma Haddad, Apr. 13, 1958; children—Cleopatra, Regina, Flaminia. A.B., CCNY, 1938; M.A., Harvard, 1947, Ph.D. (Charles Summer prize), 1949. Asst. prof. polit. sci. Wesleyan U., Middletown, Conn., 1948-51; assoc. prof. Swarthmore Coll., 1951-56; prof. polit. sci. and internat. relations Syracuse U., 1956-67; dir. grad. overseas tng. program, exec. officer Maxwell Center Study Overseas Operations, 1958-60; exec. asst. to dean Maxwell Grad. Sch., 1961-64, asso. dean dir. internat. relations program, 1961-67; dean Coll. Liberal Arts, v.p., provost Temple U., Phila., 1967-69; sr. fellow Woodrow Wilson Internat. Ctr., 1970-72; prof. internat. law U. Del., Newark, 1972-74, dir. Ctr. for Study of Marine Policy, 1973-89, H. Rodney Sharp prof. internat. law and orgn., 1975-89, univ. rsch. prof. internat. and maritime law, 1989—, coord. grad. studies, 1976-79; adj. prof. Maine Maritime Acad., 1992—; vis. prof. Trinity Coll., Mt. Holyoke Coll., Yale, Princeton, Johns Hopkins; Tagore law prof. U. Calcutta, 1979; disting. lectr. U. Ind., 1980; vis. scholar U. Western Australia, 1983, 87, Peking U., 1984, Capetown U., 1986, 89, U. Natal, 1989; mem. Presdl. Commn. Trust Territory Pacific, 1963; cons. AID, 1965-67, Nat. Commn. Marine Resources and Engring. and State Dept., 1967-73, UN, 1965, U.S. Corps Engrs., 1975; vice chmn. exec. com. Commn. Study Orgn. Peace; exec. dir. Pres.' Commn. on UN, 1970-71. Author: The Idea and Practice of World Government, 1951, A Short History of International Organization, 1954, The Elements of International Law, 2d edit, 1967, Marine Policy for America, 1977, 2d edit., 1989, Law for the World Ocean, 1981, Mangone's Concise Marine Almanac, 2d edit., 1991; co-author, editor: The Art of Overseasmanship, 1958, The Overseas Americans, 1960, European Political Systems, 1960, UN Administration of Economic and Social Programs, 1966, Energy Policies of the World, 3 vols, 1976-79, Internat. Straits of the World, 11 vols., 1978-89; editor: Future of Gas and Oil from Sea, American Strategic Minerals, 1984; editor in chief: Marine Policy Reports, 1981-91, Internat. Jour. Marine and Coastal Law, 1991— . Capt. AUS, 1942-46. Mem. Am. Soc. Internat. Law, Internat. Law Assn., Maritime Law Assn., Port of Wilmington Maritime Soc. (bd. dirs. 1980—, chmn. 1989), Francis Alison Soc. (sec. 1990—, award 1983), Del. Acad. Sci. (pres. 1993), Cosmos Club (Washington), Harvard Club (N.Y.C.). Home: 201 Unami Trl Newark DE 19711-7508 Office: Univ Del Grad Coll Marine Studi Newark DE 19716

MANGOUNI, NORMAN, publisher; b. Detroit, Oct. 19, 1932; s. Nazareth Lazarus and Isabelle (Garabedian) M.; m. Anahid Apelian, May 10, 1964; 1 child, Marie-Isabelle. A.B., U. Mich., 1954; M.S., Columbia U., 1955; postgrad., U. Mich. Law Sch., 1957-58. Reporter Ann Arbor (Mich.) News, 1957-59; editor Mich. Alumnus, U. Mich., Ann Arbor, 1959-62; sr. editor Coll. Entrance Exam. Bd., N.Y.C., 1962-64; dir. fin. aid U. Miami, Coral Gables, Fla., 1965-66; dir. State U. N.Y. Press, Albany, 1966-78; pres., gen. editor Scholars' Facsimiles & Reprints, Delmar, N.Y., 1972—; pres. Caravan Books, Delmar, 1972—, Acad. Resources Corp., Las Vegas, Nev., 1988—; corr. DuPont-Columbia Survey and Awards, 1976-78; rep. to com. on standards in field of library work, documentation and related pub. practices Am. Nat. Standards Inst., 1974-78; Exec. asst. to majority caucus Mich. State Senate, 1964. Co-translator: The Gaucho Martin Fierro, 1974; contbr. articles to profl. jours.; mem. editorial bd.: Ararat mag, 1962-66, 77-78. Served to lt. USAF, 1955-57. Mem. Modern Lang. Assn. Am., Middle East Studies Assn. N.Am., Mensa, Phi Sigma Kappa, Sigma Delta Chi, Phi Alpha Delta. Club: Rotary Internat. Home: 410 Lenawee Dr Ann Arbor MI 48104-1866 Office: 410 Lenawee Dr Ann Arbor MI 48104-1866

MANGRUM, DEBRA KIRKSEY, elementary school educator; b. Jonesboro, Ark., May 17, 1955; d. Hayward Leon and Marguerite (Bailey) Kirksey; m. Michael Edgar Mangrum, Jan. 11, 1974; children: Wayne, Marissa, Martina. BS in Mktg., Ark. State U., Jonesboro, 1979, BSE in Edn., 1990, MSE in Counselor Edn., 1992; postgrad. Cert. elem. edn. tchr. Ark. Adminstrv. sec. to pres. Planters Prodn. Credit Assn., Jonesboro, 1983-85; owner, mgr. Goodship Lollipop Children's Shop, Jonesboro, 1985-88; grad. and rsch. asst. Ark. State U., Jonesboro, 1990-92; mem. MSE in Counselor Edn. curriculum com. Ark. State U., 1990-91, mem. tchr. edn. program com., 1991-92; presenter papers ann. conf. Mid.-South Ednl. Rsch. Assn., ann. spring conf. Ark. Assn. Colls. of Tchr. Edn./Assn. Tchr. Educators, 1992. Mem. Valley View PTA, Jonesboro, 1979—, Valley View Athletic Booster Club, Jonesboro, 1979—; cert. judge Miss Ark. Pageant Sys., Hot Springs, 1989—; dir. Miss Mistletoe Pageant, Jonesboro, 1989-93. Mem. ASCD, Am. Sch. Counselor Assn., Ark. Edn. Assn., Phi Delta Kappa, Kappa Delta Pi. Avocation: reading. Home: PO Box 9077 Jonesboro AR 72403-9077

MANGUM, JOHN K., lawyer; b. Phoenix, Mar. 7, 1942; s. Otto K. and Catherine F. Mangum; m. Deidre Jansen, Jan. 10, 1969; children: John Jansen, Jeffery Jansen. Student, Phoenix Coll. 1960-62; BS, U. Ariz., 1965, JD, 1969. Bar: Ariz. 1969. Sr. trial atty. criminal div. Maricopa County Atty.'s Office, Phoenix, 1969-71; ptnr. Carmichael, McClue and Stephens, P.C., Phoenix, 1972-74; sr. ptnr. O'Connor, Cavanagh, 1992-94, Phoenix; pvt. practice, Phoenix, 1994—; ct. commr., judge pro tem Maricopa County super. ct., Phoenix, 1974-78, spl. commr., 1979-82; legal csl. to speaker of Ariz. Ho. of Reps., Phoenix, 1975-86; mem. John K. Mangum and Assocs., P.C., Phoenix, 1974-92; sr. mem. O'Connor & Cavanagh, 1992-94; pvt. practice, 1994—. Mem. Maricopa County Bd. Health, 1974-79, Ariz. State Commn. on Elected Ofcls. Salaries, 1987-93; chmn. curriculum com., mem. legal asst. adv. com. Phoenix Coll., 1973-75; legal counsel Maricopa County Rep. Com., 1986-90; mem. task force com. on career edn. Phoenix Mayor's Youth Commn., 1972-73; v.p. The Samaritans, 1984-87. Mem. State Bar Ariz. (exec. bd. young lawyers sect. 1974-76), Maricopa County Bar Assn. (pres. young lawyers sect. 1974-75, dir. 1973-75), Ariz. C. of C. (dir. 1974-79), Phoenix Country Club, Ariz. Club, Rotary. Republican. Office: 340 E Palm Ln Ste 100 Phoenix AZ 85004-4529

MANHART, MARCIA Y(OCKEY), art museum director; b. Wichita, Kans., Jan. 14, 1943; d. Everett W. and Ruth C. (Correll) Yockey; children: Caroline Manhart Sanderson, Emily Alexandrea Morrison. BA in Art, U. Tulsa, 1965, MA in Ceramics, 1971. Dir. edn. Philbrook Art Ctr., Tulsa, 1972-77, exec. v.p., asst. dir., 1977-83, acting dir., 1983-84; exec. dir. Philbrook Mus. Art (formerly Philbrook Art Ctr.), Tulsa, 1984—; instr. Philbrook Art Ctr. Mus. Sch., Tulsa, 1963-72; gallery dir. Alexandre Hogue Gallery, Tulsa U., 1967-69; NEH Challenge Grant panelist, 1991, presenter to AAM Conv., 1991; MAAA Craft Fellowship panelist, 1988, 93, NEA

Craft Fellowship panelist, 1990; curator nat. touring exhibit Nature's Forms/ Nature's Forces: The Art of Alexandre Hogue, 1984-85; co-curator internat. exhbn.: The Eloquent Object, 1987-90; curator Sanford and Diane Besser Collection exhbn., 1992. Vis. com. Smithsonian Instn./Renwick Gallery, Washington, 1986; cultural negotiator Gov. George Nigh's World Trade Mission (Okla.), China., 1985; com. mem. State Art Coll. of Okla., 1985—; mem. Assocs. of Hillcrest Med. Ctr., 1983-88, exec. com., 1985-88; com. mem. Neighborhood Housing Services, 1985-87; mem. Mapleridge Hist. Dist. Assn., 1982—; steering com. Harwelden Isnt. for Aesthetic Edn., 1983; com. mem. River Parks Authority, 1976; mem. Jr. League of Tulsa Inc., 1974-78; adv. panel mem. Nat. Craft Planning Project, NEA, Washington, 1978-81; craft adv. panel mem. Okla. Arts and Humanities Council, 1974-76; juror numerous art festivals, competitions, programs; reviewer Inst. Mus. Services, Washington, 1985, 88, 92; auditor Symposium on Language & Scholarship of Modern Crafts, NEA and NEH, Washington, 1981; nominator MacArthur Fellows Program, 1988. Recipient Harwelden award for Individual Contbrn. in the Arts, 1989, Gov.'s award State of Okla., 1992. Mem. Assn. Am. Mus., Assn. Art Mus. Dirs., Art Mus. Assn. Am., Mountain Plains Assn. Mus., Am. Craft Coun., Okla. Mus. Assn., Rotary. Office: Philbrook Mus Art PO Box 52510 Tulsa OK 74152-0510

MANHEIM, MARGARET DONOVAN, educational association administrator; b. Boston, Sept. 4, 1946; d. George Henry and Margaret Mary (Gilligan) Donovan; m. Marvin Lee Manheim, July 20, 1974; children: Susannah Leigh, Marisa Kara. BA, Boston U., 1969; MEd, Boston State Coll., 1971. Cert. tchr. English, history, social studies, Mass. Homebound tchr. Somerville (Mass.) Pub. Schs., 1971-73, English tchr., 1973-75; mem. Evanston Sch. Dist. 202 Cmty. Task Force, 1995—. Bd. dirs. Invest Evanston, 1994—; mem. parents' coun. Shady Hill Sch., Cambridge, Mass., 1981-83; mem. parents' assn. North Shore Country Day Sch., Winnetka, Ill., 1984-86, v.p., 19877-88; v.p. PTA, King Lab. Sch., Evanston, Ill., 1990-91; sec. PTA Coun., Evanston/Skokie County ot PTAs, 1991-92, pres., 1992-94; v.p. Dist. 202 Parent/Tchr./Student Assn., Evanston Twp. H.S., 1994—, mem. curriculum forum, 1994—, writer sch.-based health clinic com., 1994—; mem. curriculum adv. coun. Sch. Dist. 65, Evanston, 1992-94; co-founder, co-chair, sec. Mothers Against Gangs, Evanston, 1992—; founder HIV Edn. Task Force, PTA Coun., Evanston, 1992—; observer Dist. 65 Sch. Bd., LWV, 1992—; bd. dirs. Youth Orgns. Umbrella, Evanston, 1993—; mem. violence prevention curriculum task force Ill. Coun. for Prevention of Violence, Chgo., 1994—; bd. dirs. Evanston Symphony Orch., 1987-92. Recipient State PTA HIV Edn. award Ill. PTA, 1993. Mem. North End Mothers Club. Democrat. Roman Catholic. Avocations: reading, travel. Home: 2855 Sheridan Pl Evanston IL 60201-1725 Office: Mothers Against Gangs 2100 Ridge Ave # 4701 Evanston IL 60201-2796

MANIATIS, THOMAS PETER, molecular biology educator; b. Denver, May 8, 1943; s. Peter T. and Jane V. (Swearingen) M.; m. Jessie Marion Klyce, Aug. 27, 1968; children: Ethan David, Silas Dana. BA, U. Colo., 1965, MA, 1967; PhD in Molecular Biology, Vanderbilt U., 1971. European molecular biology rsch. fellow Med. Rsch. Coun. Molecular Biology, Cambridge, England, 1973-74; NIH fellow Harvard U., 1971-73, rsch. assoc. in biology, 1974-75; asst. prof. Harvard U., Cambridge, Mass., 1975-77, prof. molecular biology, 1981—; sr. staff investigator Cold Spring Harbor Lab., N.Y., 1975-77; assoc. prof. Calif. Inst. Tech., Pasadena, 1977-79, prof., 1979-81; co-founder, advisor Genetics Inst., Boston, 1981—; chmn. dept. biochemistry and molecular biology Harvard U., 1985-88, prof. biochemistry and molecular biology, 1981—. Author: Molecular Cloning, 1982; assoc. editor: Cell. jour., 1978—. Recipient award Rita Allen Found., 1978; recipient Eli Lilly research award Am. Soc. Microbiology, 1981; Richard Lounsbery award for biology and medicine U.S. and French Acads. Sci., 1985. Fellow Am. Acad. Scis.; mem. Nat. Acad. Scis. Office: Harvard U Dept Molecular/Cellular Biology 7 Divinity Ave Cambridge MA 02138-2092

MANIERI-HARVEY, MICHELE DAWN, elementary education educator, musician; b. Melbourne, Fla., Apr. 25, 1955; d. Ettore Don and June Laclaire (Spaur) Manieri; m. Joseph Howard Harvey, May 27, 1989. AA, U. Fla., 1976, B in Music Edn., 1978; M in Elem. Edn., Nova U., 1983; M in Guidance and Counseling, U. South Fla., 1993. Cert. tchr., Fla. Profl. vocalist Fla., 1973—; vocal tchr. in pvt. practice Gainesville, Fla., 1978-80; substitute tchr. Alachua Sch. Bd., Gainesville, 1978-80; music specialist Levy County Sch. Bd., Williston, Fla., 1979-82, kindergarten tchr., 1982-83; tchr. 2d grade Hernando County/Moton Elem., Brooksville, Fla., 1983-84, tchr. 1st grade, 1984-86, music specialist with integrated counseling concepts, 1986—; adj. prof. St. Leo Coll., 1984—; Fla. cert. observer and peer tchr., 1986—. Featured vocalist Hernando Symphony Orch., Spring Hill, Fla., 1992, 95, 96; dir., prodr. 14 sacred cantata-dramas. Music dir. 1st Bapt. Ch., Brooksville, 1989—. Named 1994 Hernando County Tchr. of Yr., 1994 Best Musical Actress Stage West, 1995 Best Musical Supporting Actress. Mem. FTP-NEA, Nat. Music Educators Assn., Fla. Music Educators Assn., Fla. Counseling Assn., Hernando Counseling Assn. (Counseling Advocate of Yr. 1994), Hernando County Bd. Fine Arts Coun., Hernando Edn. Found. (sec. 1983—), Hernando Classroom Tchrs. Assn. (exec. bd. 1985-86). Office: Moton Elem Sch 7175 Emerson Rd Brooksville FL 34601

MANIFOLD, REBECCA MARCH, elementary school art educator; b. Frederick, Md., Mar. 11, 1949; d. William Dean and June Lois (March) M. BA, W.Va. U., 1971; postgrad., Kutztown U., 1972-75, Shippensburg U., 1976-77. Cert. art and comprehensive English tchr., Pa. Elem. and secondary art tchr. Fannett-Metal Sch. Dist., Willow Hill, Pa., 1971-73; elem. art tchr. Greencastle (Pa.)-Antrim Sch. Dist., 1973—. Vol. in fashion archives Shippensburg (Pa.) U., 1985—. Mem. NEA, Nat. Art Edn. Assn., Greencastle Area Arts Coun. Republican. Presbyterian. Avocations: collecting and studying historic costume, antique dolls, travel, reading. Office: Greencastle-Antrim Sch Dist 500 Leitersburg Rd Greencastle PA 17225-9571

MANIGAULT, PETER, media executive; b. Charleston, S.C., Jan. 13, 1927; s. Edward and Mary (Hamilton) M.; m. Landine Sanford Legendre, Aug. 8, 1959 (div.); children: Gabrielle, Pierre; m. Patricia Lucas Bennett, Dec. 14, 1986. A.B., Princeton U., 1950. With Eve. Post Pub. Co. and subs., Charleston, 1959—; pres., pub. Eve. Post Pub. Co. and subs., 1960-85, chmn., 1985—. Trustee Nat. Trust Historic Preservation, 1963, vice chmn., 1965-74. Served with USNR, 1945-46, 52-53; capt. Res. Decorated Legion of Merit with combat V; Order Mil. Merit (Republic of Korea). Mem. Nat. Audubon Soc. (dir. 1968-74). Office: 134 Columbus St Charleston SC 29403-4809

MANILOFF, JACK, biophysicist, educator; b. Balt., Nov. 6, 1938; s. Boris and Edith (Cohen) M.; m. Sandra Sue Steele, Dec. 22, 1960; children: Beth Susan, Eric Steele. BA in Biology, Johns Hopkins U., 1960; MS in Biophysics, Yale U., 1964, PhD in Biophysics, 1965. Research assoc. in chemistry Brown U., Providence, 1964-66; asst. prof. microbiology Sch. Medicine and Dentistry, U. Rochester, N.Y., 1966-71; assoc. prof. Sch. Medicine and Dentistry, U. Rochester, 1971-79, prof., 1979—; dir. core nucleic acid lab. U. Rochester; lectr. Am. Soc. Microbiology Found., 1989-90; mem. Internat. Com. on Taxonomy of Viruses, 1975—, mem. exec. com., 1990—, chair bacterial virus subcom., 1993—; cons. subcom. on taxonomy of mycoplasmatales Internat. Com. Systematic Bacteriology, 1978—. Adv. bd. Archives of Virology, 1995—; contbr. articles to profl. jours. Recipient Research Career Devel. award USPHS, 1970-75; Fogarty Sr. Internat. fellow, 1987-88; Disting. vis. fellow Christ's Coll., Cambridge, Eng., 1987-88; Lady Margaret lectr. Christ's Coll., 1988. Mem. Am. Soc. Microbiology (chmn. mycoplasma divsn. 1993-94), Am. Soc. Virology, Sigma Xi. Office: Univ Rochester Med Ctr Dept Microbiology & Immunology Box 672 Rochester NY 14642-8672

MANILOW, BARRY, singer, composer, arranger; b. N.Y.C., June 17, 1946; s. Harold Pincus and Edna M. Student, N.Y. Coll. Music. Former positions include mailroom CBS; film editor WCBS-TV. Dir. music Callback series, Ed. Sullivan's Pilots; dir. music, condr., arranger, producer for Bette Midler, singer and composer; recorded hit songs: Can't Smile Without You, I Write the Songs, At the Copa (Grammy award, best male pop performance, 1979), Mandy, Looks Like We Made It; albums include Even Now, 1977, Manilow, 1985, 2 A.M. Paradise Cafe, 1985, Swing Street, 1987, Barry Manilow, 1989, Because It's Christmas, 1990, Showstoppers, 1991, The Complete Collection, Then Some, 1992, Manilow Box Set, 1992; star TV movie Copacabana, 1985; appeared TV specials The Barry Manilow Special (Emmy award, 1977), The Second Barry Manilow Special, also Big Fun on Swing Street, 1988, Barry Manilow: SRO on Broadway, 1989; TV appearances Murphy Brown, 1992; Broadway prodn.: Barry Manilow at the Gershwin, 1989; author Sweet Life: Adventures on the Way to Paradise; recipient Spl. Tony award, 1977, Ruby award After Dark mag. 1976, Photoplay Gold medal award 1976.

MANINGER, R(ALPH) CARROLL, engineering executive, consultant; b. Harper, Kans., Dec. 24, 1918; s. Earl Dotterer and Mabel Velma (Haskin) M.; m. Jean Graves Kidder, July 1, 1942; children: Margaret Elisabeth, Mary Carroll, Emily Catherine. BS, Calif. Inst. Tech., 1941. Br. mgr. Gen. Precision Inc., Sunnyvale, Calif., 1953-62; head electronic engring. rsch. Lawrence Livermore Nat. Lab., Livermore, Calif., 1962-72, sr. scientist, 1972-85; owner Holidyne, Danville, Calif., 1985—. Contbr. articles to profl. jours.; patentee in field. Pres. Contra Costa (Calif.) Concert Guild, 1972-76. Fellow IEEE (life); mem. Nuclear and Plasma Scis. Soc. of IEEE (pres. 1980-82). Home and Office: Holidyne 146 Roan Dr Danville CA 94526-1915

MANION, BARBARA ANNE, sales representative; b. Phila., Nov. 7, 1954; d. Joseph L. and Helen R. (McKeown) M. Diploma, Laukenau Hosp., 1975; BSN, Villanova U., 1982, cert. in mgmt., 1990. RN, Pa. Staff nurse Laukenau Hosp., Phila., Haverford Dialysis Ctr., Bryn Mawr, Pa.; nurse adminstr. Chestnut Hill Dialysis Ctr., Phila.; pres. Med.-RN, Ltd., Phila.; sales rep. Minntech Corp., Mpls. Mem. Am. Nephrology Nurses Assn. (past pres. local chpt.), Nat. Kidney Found., Coun. Nephrology Nurses and Technicians. Home: 8 Shetland Cir Horsham PA 19044-1146

MANION, DANIEL ANTHONY, federal judge; b. South Bend, Ind., Feb. 1, 1942; s. Clarence E. and Virginia (O'Brien) M.; m. Ann Murphy, June 29, 1984. BA, U. Notre Dame, 1964; JD, Ind. U., 1973. Bar: Ind., U.S. Dist. Ct. (no. dist.) Ind., U.S. Dist. Ct. (so. dist.) Ind. Dep. atty. gen. State of Ind., 1973-74; from assoc. to ptnr. Doran, Manion, Boynton, Kamm & Esmont, South Bend, 1974-86; judge U.S. Ct. Appeals (7th cir.), South Bend, 1986—. Mem. Ind. State Senate, Indpls., 1978-82. Home: 20725 Riverlan Rd South Bend IN 46637-1029 Office: US Ct Appeals 301 Federal Bldg 204 S Main St South Bend IN 46601-2122

MANION, THOMAS A., college president; b. Aug. 10, 1934; m. Maureen O'Mara; children: Gregory, Marcy, Andrew, Margaret, Vicki, Tina, Thomas. B.B.A., St. Bonaventure U., 1959; M.B.A., Boston Coll., 1962; Ph.D., Clark U., 1968; D.Pedagogy, Bryant Coll., 1973. Chmn. econs. dept., dean grad. sch., acad. provost v.p. Bryant Coll., Smithfield, R.I.; pres. Coll. Saint Rose, Albany, N.Y., 1973-83, St. Nobert Coll., De Pere, Wis., 1983—; bd. dirs. Associated Kellogg Bank, Green Bay, Wis. Bd. dirs. Higher Edn. Aids Bd., State of Wis. Mem. NCAA, Nat. Assn. Ind. Colls. and Univs. (mem. commn. on campus concerns), Am. Assn. Higher Edn., Am. Coun. Edn., Nat. Cath. Edn. Assn., Assn. Cath. Colls. and Univs., Coun. Ind. Colls. (bd. dirs.), Wis. Assn. Ind. Colls. and Univs. (pres.), Wis. Found. Ind. Colls., Delta Epsilon, Delta Mu Delta. Office: St Norbert Coll De Pere WI 54115

MANIRE, GEORGE PHILIP, bacteriologist, educator; b. Roanoke, Tex., Mar. 25, 1919; s. Ernest L. and Zera (Ballew) M.; m. Ruth Jacobs, Apr. 10, 1943; children—Sarah, Philip. B.S., N. Tex. State Coll., 1940, M.S., 1941; Ph.D., U. Calif. at Berkeley, 1949. Instr. Southwestern Med. Sch., U. Tex., Dallas, 1949-50; mem. faculty U. N.C. Med. Sch., Chapel Hill, 1950—; prof. bacteriology and immunology U. N.C. Med. Sch., 1959-89, asst. vice chancellor health affairs, 1965-66, chmn. dept., 1966-79, Kenan prof., 1971—, vice chancellor, dean grad. sch., 1979-87; vis. scientist Lister Inst., London, Eng., 1971-72; Fulbright Research scholar Statens Seruminstut, Copenhagen, Denmark, 1956; Alan Gregg Travel Fellow in med. edn. China Med. Bd., 1963-64; vis. prof. Inst. for Virus Research, Kyoto (Japan) U., 1963-64, Inst. for Virus Research, Kyoto (Japan) U. (Japan Soc. Promotion Sci.), 1979. Club: Cosmos (Washington), Carolina Club (Chapel Hill). Research, publs. on chem. biol. and structural characteristics of chlamydiae, microbial pathogenesis. Home: 708 Coker Ln Chapel Hill NC 27514-4945

MANIRE, JAMES MCDONNELL, lawyer; b. Memphis, Feb. 22, 1918; s. Clarence Herbert and Elizabeth (McDonnell) M.; m. Nathalie Davant Latham, Nov. 21, 1951 (div. 1979); children: James McDonnell, Michael Latham, Nathalie Manire Willard; m. Nancy Whitman Colbert, Dec. 30, 1995. LL.B., U. Va., 1948. Bar: Tenn. 1948, U.S. Supreme Ct. 1957. Pvt. practice Memphis, 1948—, city atty., 1968-71; of counsel Waring Cox, Memphis, 1986—. Editor in chief Va. Law Rev., 1947-48. Served to lt. comdr. USNR, 1941-46. Fellow Am. Coll. Trial Lawyers, Am. Bar Found. (life); mem. ABA, Tenn. Bar Assn. (pres. 1966-67), Memphis and Shelby County Bar Assn. (pres. 1963-64), Tenn. Bar Found. (charter), 6th Circuit Jud. Conf. (life), Raven Soc. Clubs: Memphis Country, Memphis Hunt and Polo. Home: 2927 Frances Pl Memphis TN 38111-2401 Office: Waring Cox PLC 1300 Morgan Keegan Twr 50 N Front St Memphis TN 38103-2126

MANIS, MELVIN, psychologist, educator; b. N.Y.C., Feb. 18, 1931; s. Alex and Hanna (Oyle) M.; m. Jean Denby, May 28, 1954; children: Peter Eugene, David Denby. AB in Psychology, Franklin and Marshall Coll., 1951; PhD, U. Ill., 1954. Instr. psychology U. Pitts., 1956-58; rsch. psychologist Ann Arbor VA Med. Ctr., Mich., 1958-89; prof. psychology U. Mich., Ann Arbor, 1966—, assoc. chair dept. psychology, 1990-91. Author: Cognitive Processes, 1966, An Introduction to Cognitive Psychology, 1971; editor Jour. Personality and Social Psychology, 1980-84. Served with USPHS, 1954-56. Mem. APA, Am. Psychol. Soc., Midwestern Psychol. Assn., Soc. Exptl. Social Psychology, AAUP, Phi Beta Kappa, Sigma Xi. Democrat. Jewish. Club: Racquet (Ann Arbor). Home: 20 Harvard Pl Ann Arbor MI 48104-1726 Office: U Mich Dept Psychology Ann Arbor MI 48109

MANKA, RONALD EUGENE, lawyer; b. Wichita, Kans., Dec. 12, 1944; s. James Ashford and Jane Bunn (Meeks) M.; m. Frances Ann Patterson, Aug. 7, 19665 (dec. Dec. 1985); children: Kimberly Ann, Lora Christine; m. Linda I. Bailey, Mar. 11, 1995. BBA cum laude, U. Kans., 1967; JD cum laude, U. Mich., 1970. Bar: Conn. 1970, Mo. 1974, Kans. 1985. Assoc. Day, Barry & Howard, Hartford, Conn., 1970-73; assoc. Lathrop & Gage L.C., Kansas City, Mo., 1973-78, mem., 1979-82, 85—; group counsel Butler Mfg. Co., Kansas City, 1982-83, div. gen. mgr., 1983-84. Trustee, clk., elder Village Presbyn. Ch., Prairie Village, Kans.; dir., treas. Lyric Opera of Kansas City, 1995—; pres. Genesis Sch., Kansas City, 1987-89; devel. chmn. Kansas City Friends of Alvin Ailey, 1987-89; chmn. Kansas City Mus., 1988-92, gen. counsel, 1994—; gen. counsel Spirit Festival, Kansas City, 1985-87, Kansas City C. of C., 1989—; pres. Ctr. for Mgmt. Assistance, Kansas City, 1991-93. Mem. ABA, Mo. Bar Assn. (alt. dispute resolution com. 1986—), Lawyers Assn. Kansas City, Silicon Prairie Tech. Assn. (bd. dirs. 1990-92), Homestead Country Club (pres. 1984-85). Republican. Avocations: bicycling, swimming. Office: Lathrop & Norquist PC Ste 2600 2345 Grand Ave Kansas City MO 64108-2684

MANKEL, FRANCIS XAVIER, former principal, priest; b. Knoxville, Tenn., Nov. 8, 1935; s. George Whitehead Sr. and Willia Frances (Duncan) M. BA, St. Ambrose U., 1957; STB, St. Mary's Coll., Balt., 1959, STL, 1961; MEd, Loyola Coll., Balt., 1965. Ordained priest, Roman Cath. Ch., 1961. Assoc. pastor Holy Ghost Ch., Knoxville, 1962-67; prin. Knoxville Cath. High Sch., 1967-79; pastor Sacred Heart Ch., Lawrenceburg, Tenn., 1979-84, St. John Neumann Ch., Knoxville, 1984-87, Sacred Heart Cathedral, Knoxville, 1987—; vicar gen., chancellor Cath. Diocese Knoxville, 1988—; supt. Cath. Schs., Diocese of Knoxville, 1989-92. Bd. dirs. Knoxville area chpt. ARC, 1986—. Mem. Am. Guild Organists, Knoxville Ministerial Assn. Home: 711 Northshore Dr SW Knoxville TN 37919-7549 Office: 805 Northshore Dr Knoxville TN 37919

MANKIEWICZ, FRANK F., journalist; b. N.Y.C., May 16, 1924; s. Herman J. and Sara (Aaronson) M.; m. Holly Jolley, 1952 (div.); children: Joshua, Benjamin; m. Patricia O'Brien, 1988. A.B., UCLA, 1947; M.S., Columbia U., 1948; LL.B., U. Calif.-Berkeley, 1955. Bar: Calif. 1955, D.C. 1985. Engaged in journalism Washington and Los Angeles, 1948-52; practice law Beverly Hills, 1955-61; dir. Peace Corps, Lima, Peru, 1962-64; Latin Am. regional dir. Peace Corps, Washington, 1964-66; press sec. Senator Robert F. Kennedy, 1966-68; syndicated columnist and TV news commentator, 1968-71; nat. polit. dir. Presdl. campaign of Senator George McGovern, 1971-72; columnist Washington Post, 1976-77; pres. Nat. Pub. Radio, 1977-83; vice-chmn. Hill and Knowlton (formerly Gray and Co.), 1983—. Author: Perfectly Clear: Nixon from Whittier to Watergate, 1973, U.S. v. Richard M. Nixon: The Final Crisis, 1974, With Fidel: A Portrait of Castro and Cuba, 1975, Remote Control: Television and the Manipulation of American Life, 1977; contbr. articles to newspapers and mags. Served with inf. AUS, 1943-46.

MANKILLER, WILMA PEARL, tribal leader; b. Stilwell, Okla., Nov. 18, 1945; d. Charley and Clara Irene (Sitton) M.; m. Hector N. Olaya, Nov. 13, 1963 (div. 1975); children: Felicia Marie Olaya, Gina Irene Olaya; m. Charlie Soap, Oct. 13, 1986. Student, Skyline Coll., San Bruno Coll., 1973, San Francisco State Coll., 1973-75; BA in Social Sci., Flaming Rainbow Coll., 1977; postgrad., U. Ark., 1979. Cmty. devel. dir. Cherokee Nation, Tahlequah, Okla., 1977-83, dep. chief, 1983-85, prin. chief, 1985-87; pres. Inter-Tribal Coun. Okla.; mem. exec. bd. Coun. Energy Resource Tribes; bd. dirs. Okla. Indsl. Devel. Commn. Author: Mankiller: A Chief and Her People, 1993. Bd. dirs. Okla. Acad. for State Goals, 1985—. Recipient Donna Nigh First Lady award Okla. Commn. for Status of Women, 1985, Am. Leadership award Harvard U., 1986; inducted Okla. Women's Hall of Fame, 1986. Mem. Nat. Tribal Chmn. Assn., Nat. Congress Am. Indians, Cherokee County Dem. Women's Club. Avocations: reading, writing. Home: PO Box 308 Park Hill OK 74451 Office: Cherokee Prin Chief PO Box 948 Tahlequah OK 74465-0948

MANKIN, CHARLES JOHN, geology educator; b. Dallas, Jan. 15, 1932; s. Green and Myla Carolyn (Bohmert) M.; m. Mildred Helen Hahn, Sept. 6, 1953 (dec. Oct. 26, 1995); children: Sally Carol, Helen Francis, Laura Kay. Student, U. N.Mex., 1949-50; B.S., U. Tex. at Austin, 1954, M.A., 1955, Ph.D., 1958. Asst. prof. geology Calif. Inst. Tech., 1958-59; asst. prof. geology U. Okla., 1959-63, assoc. prof., 1963-64, prof., 1964—; dir. Sch. Geology and Geophysics, 1963-77, Energy Resources Inst., 1978-87; mem. U.S. Nat. Commn. on Geology, 1977-80; dir. Okla. Geol. Survey, 1967—; former chmn. bd. mineral and energy resources, former mem. commn. on phys. sci., math. and resources Nat. Acad. Scis.; former commr. Commn. Fiscal Accountability of Nation's Energy Resources; former chmn. Royalty Mgmt. Adv. Com. Dept. Interior; bd. dirs. Environ. Inst. for Waste Mgmt. Studies, U. Ala. Contbr. articles profl. jours. Recipient Conservation Service award Dept. Interior, 1983. Fellow Geol. Soc. Am. (co-project leader Decade N.Am. Geology, former councillor, chmn. found.), Mineral. Soc. Am.; mem. Am. Assn. Petroleum Geologists (pub. svc. award 1988), Am. Inst. Profl. Geologists (v.p., past pres., Martin Van Couvering Meml. award 1988, mem. found.), Clay Minerals Soc., Geochem. Soc., AAAS, Assn. Am. State Geologists (past pres.), Am. Geol. Inst. (past pres., Ian Campbell medal 1987), Soc. Econ. Paleontologists and Mineralogists (past pres. Mid-Continent sect.), Oklahoma City Geol. Soc. (hon., life), Sigma Gamma Epsilon (nat. sec.-treas.). Home: 2220 Forister Ct Norman OK 73069-5120 Office: Okla Geol Survey Energy Ctr 100 E Boyd St Rm 131N Norman OK 73019-1000

MANKIN, HENRY JAY, physician, educator; b. Pitts., Oct. 9, 1928; s. Hyman Isaac and Mary (Simons) M.; m. Carole Jane Pinkney, Aug. 20, 1952; children: Allison Joan, David Philip, Keith Pinkney. B.S. magna cum laude, U. Pitts., 1952, M.D., 1953; M.A. (hon.), Harvard U., 1973. Diplomate Am. Bd. Orthopaedic Surgery (mem. bd. 1976-82, pres. bd. 1980-81). Intern U. Chgo. Clinics, 1953-54; resident orthopaedics Hosp. for Joint Diseases, N.Y.C., 1957-60; instr. orthopaedics U. Pitts. Sch. Medicine, 1960-62, asst. prof., 1962-64, assoc. prof., 1964-66; dir., prof. orthopaedics Hosp. for Joint Diseases and Mt. Sinai Sch. Medicine, 1966-72; chief orthopaedics Mass. Gen. Hosp., Boston, 1972—; Edith M. Ashley prof. orthopaedics Harvard Med. Sch., 1972—; mem. surgery B study sect. NIH, 1969-73; mem. adv. com. on surg. treatment FDA, 1973-75; corporator Boston Five Cent Savs. Bank, 1982-83; mem. exec. com. Am. Bd. Med. Spltys., 1982-85; adv. council on grad. med. edn., 1986—; mem. Nat. Arthritis Avd. Bd., 1986-89; mem. human resources and research rev. group A Nat. Inst. Arthritis, Metabolism and Digestive Diseases, 1981-85, chmn., 1983-85. Assoc. editor Arthritis and Rheumatism, 1967-77, Jour. Bone and Joint Surgery, 1967-82; mem. editorial bd. Jour. Orthopedic Research, 1982-85; trustee Jour. Bone and Joint Surgery, 1985-91, chmn. bd., 1988-91; contbr. numerous articles to profl., med. jours. Served to lt. comdr. USNR, 1955-57. Fellow ACS, Royal Coll. Surgeons (hon.); mem. Am. Acad. Orthopaedic Surgeons, Acad. Orthopaedic Soc. (pres. 1991-92), Am. Orthopaedic Assn. (pres. 1982-83), Orthopaedic Research Soc. (pres. 1969-70), Musculoskeletal Tumor Soc. (pres. 1991-92), Brit. Orthopaedic Research Soc., Argentine Orthopedic Assn. (hon.), N.Y. Acad. Medicine (chmn. orthopaedic sect. 1971-72), Am. Rheumatism Assn., Soc. Internat. Chirurgerie Orthopaedice et Traumatologia, Hip Soc., Interurban, Forum Orthopaedic clubs, Brit. Orthopaedic Assn. (hon.), Can. Orthopaedic Assn. (hon.), Australian Orthopaedic Assn. (hon.), N.Z. Orthopaedic Assn. (hon.), Japanese Orthopaedic Assn. (hon.), Israel Orthopaedic Assn. (hon.), Thai Orthopaedic Assn (hon.). Home: 185 Dean Rd Brookline MA 02146-4201 Office: Mass Gen Hosp 32 Fruit St Boston MA 02114-2620

MANKIN, ROBERT STEPHEN, financial executive; b. N.Y.C., Mar. 26, 1939; s. Samuel Harry Mankin and Dorothy (Rosenblum) Goldstein; m. Joyce Marie Cabel, June 13, 1971; children: Seth Howard, Laura Nicole, Gina Danielle. BA cum laude, Bklyn. Coll., 1961; MBA, Bernard Baruch Coll., 1970; Dr. Profl. Studies with distinction, Pace U., 1982. Mgr. ABC, N.Y.C., 1969-71, Babcock and Wilcox, N.Y.C., 1971-74; v.p. Chase Manhattan Bank, N.Y.C., 1974-84; sr. v.p. 1st Interstate Bank, N.Y.C., 1984-87; mng. dir., sr. v.p., co-head fixed income, mem. mgmt. com. Nomura Securities Internat., N.Y.C., 1987-94; mng. dir. Paine Webber, N.Y.C., 1994-95; pres., CEO Lakeside Fin. Svcs., Hoboken, N.J., 1995—; bd. dirs., sec. Nomura Mortgage Capital Corp., N.Y.C.; bd. dirs., pres., CEO Nomura Asset Capital Corp., N.Y.C., 1988-94; bd. dirs. PaineWebber Real Estate, 1994-95. Contbr. articles to profl. jours. Mem. Planning Forum, Assn. for Computing Machinery, Assn. Computer Programmers and Analysts (chmn. bd. 1971). Home: 21 Shield Dr Woodcliff Lake NJ 07675-8127 Office: Lakeside Fin Svcs L L C 209 Garden St Hoboken NJ 07030

MANKO, JOSEPH MARTIN, SR., lawyer; b. Phila., Oct. 7, 1939; s. Horace David and Vivian (Greenberg) M.; m. Lynn Kimmelman, June 17, 1962; children: Joseph Jr., Glenn, Wendy. BA magna cum laude, Yale U., 1961; JD cum laude, Harvard U., 1964. Bar: Pa. 1964. Regional counsel EPA, Phila., 1973-75; assoc. Wolf, Block, Schorr & Solis-Cohen, Phila., 1964-72, ptnr., 1972-73, 75-89, chmn. environ. law, 1978-89; founding ptnr. Manko, Gold & Katcher, Phila., 1989—; adj. prof. U. Pa. Law Sch., 1988—, Grant Irey lectr., 1989-90; dir. Pa. Environ. Council, Phila., 1978-85, treas., 1986-87, pres., 1987-89, chmn. 1989—; chair or co-chair numerous environ. bar assn. coms. Commr. Lower Merion Twp., Ardmore, Pa., 1979-91, 94—, v.p., 1992, pres. 1993; mem. Com. of 70, Phila., 1978-88; pres. Beth David Reform Congregation, Gladwyne, Pa., 1983-86, trustee, 1978-83, 86—; trustee Fedn. Jewish Agys., Phila., 1982-86; bd. dirs. Golden Slipper Camp, 1981-84, 88—, Jewish Cmty. Rels. Coun., 1983-88, Lower Merion Conservancy, 1976—, Phila. Geriatric Ctr., 1990—, Delaware River Basin Water Resources Assn., 1993—; mem. Dem. State Com., 1986-90. Mem. ABA, Pa. Bar Assn., Phila. Bar Assn., Phi Beta Kappa. Clubs: Germantown Cricket, Bala Golf (Phila.), Hamilton Bridge, Vesper. Avocations: tennis, golf, walking, classical music. Home: 96 E Levering Mill Rd Bala Cynwyd PA 19004-2611 Office: Manko Gold & Katcher 401 E City Ave Ste 500 Bala Cynwyd PA 19004-1122

MANKOFF, ALBERT WILLIAM, cultural organization administrator, consultant; b. Newark, Aug. 24, 1926; s. Albert and Dorothy M.; m. Audrey Emery, Mar. 18, 1972; 1 child, Robert Morgan. BLS, U. Okla., 1967. With Am. Airlines, Inc., 1947-69; mgr. mgmt. tng. and devel. Am. Airlines Inc., 1957-67; mgr. orgn. devel. Am. Airlines, Inc., Tulsa, 1968-69; dir. personnel Peat, Marwick, Mitchell & Co., Chgo., 1969-72; ptnr. Lexicon, Inc. Cons., Raleigh, N.C., 1972-77; Pacific area mgr. safety and tng. Trailways, Inc., L.A., 1978-80; tng. cons. State of Sacramento, Sacramento, 1980-91; pres. Inst. Am. Hist. Tech., Weaverville, N.C., 1987—. Author: Trolley Treasures, 4 vols., 1986-87, The Glory Days, 1989, Tracks of Triumph, 1993, Tarnished Triumph, The Edison Paradigm, 1994, Sacramento's Shining Rails, 1995, Trolleys in America: The Long Road Back, 1995; contbr. articles to profl. jours. Bd. dirs., v.p. OASIS; Midwest Centre for Human Potential, Chgo., 1970-72, Tulsa Urban League, 1962-69; v.p., bd. dirs. Meditation Groups Inc., Ojai, Calif., Psychosynthesis Internat., Ojai Internat. Assn. Managerial and Orgnl. Psychosynthesis, Thousand Oaks, Calif. Avocations: street car and light rail technology, historical trolley photographs, cat humor. Home and Office: 36 Cedar Hill Ln Weaverville NC 28787 *Personal philosophy: I believe that the love principle is the most powerful force in the universe, and fear is the most destructive; that we create our own heaven or hell as a consequence of our thought; that we die and are reborn countless times until we master life in the human framework.*

MANKOFF, DAVID A., nuclear medicine physician; b. July 10, 1959. BS in Physics summa cum laude, Yale U., 1981; MD, PhD in Bioengring., U. Pa., 1988. Diplomate Am. Bd. Internal Medicine. Rsch. scientist UGM Med. Systems, Phila., 1988-89, dir. engring., 1989-90; rsch. assoc. nuclear medicine sect. U. Pa., Phila., 1988-90; resident in internal medicine U. Wash., Seattle, 1990-92, resident in nuclear medicine, 1992—. Office: Divsn Nuclear Medicine U Wash Med Ctr RC 70 1959 NE Pacific Seattle WA 98195

MANKOFF, RONALD MORTON, lawyer; b. Gettysburg, S.D., Oct. 13, 1931; s. Harry B. and Sarah (Frank) M.; m. Joy Faith Shechtman, Nov. 3, 1959; children: Jeffrey Walker, Douglas Frank. BSL, U. Minn., JD, 1954; LLM in Taxation, NYU, 1959. Bar: Minn. 1954, Tex. 1959. With Leonard, Street & Deinard, Mpls., 1957-58; research analyst Inst. Jud. Adminstrn., N.Y.C., 1958-59; assoc. Lyne, Blanchette, Smith & Shelton, Dallas, 1959-60; ptnr. Durant and Mankoff, Dallas, 1960-85; pres. Brice & Mankoff P.C., Dallas, 1985-89, Mankoff, Hill, Held & Metzger, L.L.P., Dallas, 1989-95; chmn./gen. counsel RAC Fin. Group, Inc., 1994—; pvt. practice Dallas, 1995—; lectr. law So. Meth. U., 1974-77; speaker in field. Contbr. articles to profl. jours. Chmn. bd. Dallas chpt. Am. Cancer Soc., 1976-77, bd. dirs. Tex. divsn., 1981-94; chmn. Dallas Crusade, 1974-75, bd. dirs., mem. exec. com., 1963-88; mem. Dallas Mcpl. Libr., 1973-75; exec. com. Dallas Citizens Charter Assn., 1971-75; pres. Dallas Arts Found., Inc., 1973-75; mem. exec. com. Nat. Pooled Income Fund, Coun. Jewish Welfare Fedns. and Funds, 1975-77; adv. dir. Dallas Cmty. Chest Trust Fund, 1976-78; chmn. Found. Dallas Jewish Fedn., 1976-77; pres. Temple Emanu-el, Dallas, 1977-79; bd. dirs. Jewish Fedn. Greater Dallas, 1977-79, Dallas Civic Opera, 1981-83, World Union Progressive Judaism, 1981-90; mem. S.W. regional liaison com. IRS, 1980-83; exec. com. Union Am. Hebrew Congregations, 1979-89, trustee, 1979—, chmn. nat. coll. com., 1983-87, vice chmn. bd. dirs., 1984-88; sec. Dallas Assembly, 1979-84; exec. com. Jewish Cmty. Rels. Coun., 1982-83, Com. for Qualified Judiciary, 1982—; sec. Child Care Partnership, 1984-86, bd. dirs., 1986-88; bd. dirs. Dallas Women's Found., 1985-89, adv. coun., 1989—; bd. dirs. Am. Jewish Com., 1982-88, pres. Dallas chpt. 1986-90; bd. dirs. Tex. coun. Girl Scouts U.S., 1982-85, Goodwill Industries of Greater Dallas, 1979-83, Title One Home Improvement Lender's Assn., 1994—; mem. Mayor's Task Force on Child Care, 1984; bd. govs. Dallas Symphony Assn., 1988—; chmn. Temple Emanu El Found., 1988—. Lt. (j.g.) USN, 1954-57. Mem. ABA, State Bar Tex., Dalls Bar Assn., North Dallas C. of C. (adv. bd. 1986-88), Columbian Country Club (bd. dirs. 1967-73), Zeta Beta Tau, Delta Sigma Rho. Democrat. Jewish. Home: 22 Lakeside Park Dallas TX 75225-8110 Office: 16901 Dallas Pkwy Ste 16901 Dallas TX 75248-1932

MANLEY, AUDREY FORBES, medical administrator, physician; b. Jackson, Miss., Mar. 25, 1934; d. Jesse Lee and Ora Lee (Buckhalter) Forbes; m. Albert Edward Manley, Apr. 3, 1970. A.B. with honors (tuition scholar), Spelman Coll., Atlanta, 1955; M.D. (Jesse Smith Noyes Found. scholar), Meharry Med. Coll., 1959; MPH, Johns Hopkins U.-USPHS traineeship, 1987; LHD (hon.), Tougaloo (Miss.) Coll., 1990, Meharry Med. Coll., Nashville, 1991; LLD (hon.), Spelman Coll., 1991. Diplomate: Am. Bd. Pediatrics. Intern St. Mary Mercy Hosp., Gary, Ind., 1960; from jr. to chief resident in pediatrics Cook County Children's Hosp., Chgo., 1960-62; NIH fellow neonatology U. Ill. Rsch. and Ednl. Hosp., Chgo., 1963-65; staff pediatrician Chgo. Bd. Health, 1963-66; practice medicine specializing in pediatrics Chgo., 1963-66; assoc. Lawndale Neighborhood Health Ctr. North, 1966-67; asst. med. dir., 1967-69; asst. prof. Chgo. Med. Coll., 1966-67; instr. Pritzker Sch. Medicine, U. Chgo., 1967-69; asst. dir. ambulatory pediatrics, asst. dir. pediatrics Mt. Zion Hosp. and Med. Center, San Francisco, 1969-70; med. cons. Spelman Coll., 1970-71, med. dir. family planning program, chmn. health careers adv. com., 1972-76; med. dir. Grady Meml. Hosp. Family Planning Clinic, 1972-76; with Health Services Adminstrs., Dept. Health and Human Services, 1976—; commd. officer USPHS, 1976—; chief genetic diseases services br. Office Maternal and Child Health, Bur. Community Health Services, Rockville, Md., 1976-81; acting assoc. adminstr. clin. affairs Office of Adminstr. Health Resources and Services Adminstrn., 1981-83, chief med. officer, dep. assoc. adminstr. planning, evaluation and legis., 1983-85; sabbatical leave USPHS Johns Hopkins Sch. Hygiene and Pub. Health, 1986-87; dir. Nat. Health Service Corps.; asst. surgeon gen., 1988; dep. asst. Sec. for Health USPHS/HHS, 1989-93, acting asst. Sec. Health, 1993, dep. asst. Sec. Health/intergovtl. affairs, 1993-94; dep. surgeon gen., acting dep. asst. Sec. for minority health USPHS, 1994-95; acting surgeon gen., 1995—; mem. U.S. del. UNICEF, 1990-94. Author numerous articles, reports in field. Trustee Spelman Coll., 1966-70. Recipient Meritorious Svc. award USPHS, 1981, Mary McLeod Bethune award Nat Coun. Negro Women, 1979, Dr. John P. McGovern Ann. Lectureship award Am. Sch. Health Assn., Disting. Alumni award Meharry Med. Coll., 1989, Spelman Coll. 108 Founder's Day Convocation, 1989, Disting. Svc. medal USPHS, 1992, Hildrus A. Poindexter award OSG/PHS, 1993, numerous other svc. and achievement awards. Fellow Am. Acad. Pediatrics; mem. Nat. Inst. Medicine of Nat. Acad. Sci., Nat. Med. Assn., APHA, AAUW, AAAS, Spelman Coll. Alumnae Assn., Meharry Alumni Assn., Operation Crossroads Africa Alumni Assn., Delta Sigma Theta (hon.). Home: 2807 18th St NW Washington DC 20009-2205 Office: 200 Independence Ave SW Washington DC 20201-0004

MANLEY, BARBARA LEE DEAN, occupational health nurse, hospital administrator, safety and health consultant; b. Washington, Nov. 5, 1946; d. Robert L. Dean and Mary L. (Jenkins) Dean Smallwood. BS, St. Mary-of-the-Woods, Terre Haute, Ind., 1973; MA, Central Mich. U., 1981. Cert. occupl. health nurse specialist. Indsl. nurse Ford Motor Co., Indpls., 1973-80; employee health nurse Starplex, Inc., Washington, 1981-84, Doctor's Hosp., Lanham, Md., 1984-85; regional occupational health nurse coordinator Naval Hosp., Long Beach, Calif., 1985-88; project mgr. East Coast Health Care Network, Inc., San Francisco, 1980-84; occupl. health nurse cons. HHS, Washington, 1980-84; occupational health and safety cons., mgr. FPE Group, Torrence, Calif., 1988-91; safety and loss control mgr. Assn. Calif. Hosp. Dists., Sacramento, 1991-93, v.p. loss control svcs., 1993-96; exec. dir. Quantum Inst., Sacramento, 1996—; part-time lectr. Compton (Calif.) Coll., 1986. Vol. ARC, Ft. Lewis, Wash., 1974-76, Ft. Harrison, Ind., 1978-80; counselor Crisis Hot-Line, Laurel, Md., 1981-83, Laurel Boy's and Girls Club, 1981-84. Recipient Navy's Meritorious Civilian Svc. Medal, 1989, Women of Excellence award Long Beach Press-Telegram Newspaper Guild, 1990, LCM Profl. of Yr. Acad. Loss Control Mgmt., 1995. Fellow Acad. Ambulatory Nursing Adminstrs. (Honor plaque 1981); mem. SCVAOHN (chair govt. affairs 1994—), Assn. Exec. Females, Am. Nurses Assn., Nat. Safety Mgmt. Soc. (2d v.p. 1992-96, 1st v.p. 1996—), Am. Assn. Occupational Health Nurses, Assn. Occupl. Healthcare Profls. (sec. 1986-88, conf. chairperson 1988, Outstanding Nurse of Yr. 1987), Fed. Safety and Health Council, Cen. Mich. U. Alumni Assn. (sec. 1985-88), Chi Eta Phi (regional bd. dirs. 1978-81). Presbyterian. Avocations: reading; crocheting; traveling; music. Office: Assn Calif Hosp Dists 2260 Park Towne Cir # Cl Sacramento CA 95825-0402

MANLEY, FRANK, English language educator; b. Scranton, Pa., Nov. 13, 1930; s. Aloysius F. and Kathryn L. (Needham) M.; m. Carolyn Mary Holliday, Mar. 14, 1952; children: Evelyn, Mary. B.A., Emory U., 1952, M.A., 1953; Ph.D., Johns Hopkins U., 1959. Instr., then asst. prof. Yale U., New Haven, 1959-64; assoc. prof., then prof. dept. English Emory U., Atlanta, 1964—; chmn. dept. Emory U., 1968-70, Candler prof. English, 1982—, dir. creative writing program, 1990—. Editor: The Anniversaries (John Donne), 1963, A Dialogue of Comfort (St. Thomas More), vol. 12, 1977 and Epistola ad Pomeranum, vol. 7, 1990, Yale edit. More's complete works; author: Resultances, 1980 (Devins award for poetry 1980), Two Masters (co-winner Gt. Am. New Play Contest 9th Ann. Humana Festival New Am. Plays 1985), (with F. Watkins) Some Poems and Some Talk About Poetry, 1985, Within the Ribbons: 9 Stories, 1989, (play) The Trap, 1993. With U.S. Army, 1952-55. Guggenheim Found. fellow, 1966-67, 78-79; recipient NEH transl. program fellowship, 1981-83, Nat. Endowment Arts Creative Writing Fellowship in Fiction, 1995—, Disting. Teaching award, 1984, Univ. scholar/Tchr. of yr. award, 1989, Disting. Alumnus award The Marist Sch., 1993. Mem. MLA, AAUP. Roman Catholic. Home: 401 Adams St Decatur GA 30030-5207 also: RR5 Box 228 Ellijay GA 30540 Office: Emory U Dept English Atlanta GA 30322

MANLEY, JOAN A(DELE) DANIELS, retired publisher; b. San Luis Obispo, Calif., Sept. 23, 1932; d. Carl and Della (Weinmann) Daniels; m. Jeremy C. Lanning, Mar. 17, 1956 (div. Sept. 1963); m. Donald H. Manley, Sept. 12, 1964 (div. 1985); m. William G. Houlton, May 31, 1991. BA, U. Calif., Berkeley, 1954; DBA (hon.), U. New Haven, 1974; LLD (hon.), Babson Coll., 1978. Sec. Doubleday & Co., Inc., N.Y.C., 1954-60; sales exec. Time Inc., 1960-66, v.p., 1971-75, group v.p., 1975-84, also bd. dir.; circulation dir. Time-Life Books, 1966-68, dir. sales, 1968-70, pub., 1970-76; chmn. bd. Time-Life Books Inc., 1976-80; vice chmn. bd. Book-of-the-Month Club, Inc., N.Y.C., until 1984; supervising dir. Time-Life Internat. (Nederland) B.V., Amsterdam, until 1984; bd. dirs. Scholastic Inc., Viking Office Products Inc., AON Corp., Sara Lee Corp., BFP Holdings, Inc. Past trustee Mayo Found., Rochester, Minn., Nat. Repertory Orch., William Benton Found.; former mem. adv. coun. Stanford U. Bus. Sch., Haas Sch. Bus. U. Calif.; trustee Vail Valley Inst., Keystone Ctr. Named to Direct Mktg. Hall of Fame, 1993; U. Calif.-Berkeley fellow, 1989. Mem. Assn. Am. Pubs. (past chmn.).

MANLEY, JOHN, Canadian government official; b. Ottawa, Ontario, Canada, Jan. 5, 1950; s. John Joseph Manley and Mildred Charlotte (Scharf) M.; m. Judith Mary Rae, April 21, 1973; children: Rebecca Jane, David John, Sarah Kathleen. Attended, Carleton U., U. Ottawa. Law clerk for Rt. Hon. Bora Laskin Chief Justice Can., 1976-77; chair Ottawa-Carleton Bd. Trade, 1985-86; min. industry Canada, 1993—, min. western economic diversificatio & min. of industry, min. for the atlantic Canada oppurtunities agency & min. responsible for the off. of reg. dev, 1996. elected to H. of C. g.e., 1988. Office: Industry, 235 Queen St 11th Fl East, Ottawa, ON Canada K1A 0H5 also: 200 1885 Bank St, Ottawa, ON Canada K1V 0W3*

MANLEY, JOHN FREDERICK, political scientist, educator; b. Utica, N.Y., Feb. 20, 1939; s. John A. and Gertrude Manley; children from previous marriage: John, Laura; m. Kathy Lynn Sharp, 1991; 1 child, Cole Sharp Manley. B.S., Le Moyne Coll., 1961; Ph.D., Syracuse U., 1966. Asst. prof. polit. sci. U. Wis., 1966, assoc. prof., 1969-71; prof., chmn. dept. polit. sci. Stanford U., 1977-80; fellow Center for Advanced Study in Behavioral Scis., 1976-77; vis. prof. Stanford in Oxford, 1996. Author: The Politics of Finance, 1970, American Government and Public Policy, 1976; author, co-editor: The Case Against the Constitution, 1987. Congressional fellow, 1963-64; Brookings Instn. fellow, 1965-66; Guggenheim fellow, 1974-75; Fulbright fellow U. Bologna, 1992. Office: Stanford U Dept Polit Sci Stanford CA 94305

MANLEY, JOHN HUGO, computing technology executive, educator; b. Highland Park, Mich., July 9, 1932; s. Hugo Edward and Linda Amelia (Kuure) M.; m. Josephine Theresa Catanzaro, Sept. 3, 1958; children: Lisa Linn, Michele Ann, John David, Marc Darrin. B. Metall. Engring., Cornell U., 1955; MS Indsl. Engring., U. Pitts., 1965, PhD, 1971. Metall. engr. GE, Schenectady, N.Y., 1955-56; commd. 2d lt. USAF, 1956, advanced through grades to lt. col., 1973, ret., 1976; asst. to dir. Johns Hopkins Applied Physics Lab., Laurel, Md., 1976-80; exec. ITT Corp., Stratford, Conn., 1980-83; v.p. Nastec Corp., Southfield, Mich., 1983-85; dir. Software Engring. Inst. Software Engring. Inst. Carnegie Mellon U., Pitts., 1985-87; pres., chmn. Computing Tech. Transition, Inc., Wilmington, Del., 1983—; prof. manufacturing and info. tech. systems engring., dir. mfg. sys. engring. prog. U. Pitts., 1987—; mem. tech. adv. bd. Tartan Inc., Pitts.; dir. Concurrent Techs. Corp., Johnstown, Pa.; mem. com. on nat. weather svc. modernization NRC, 1991-94. Editor-in-chief Jour. Systems and Software, 1978-82; contbr. articles to profl. jours. Pres. Point Field Community Assn., Millersville, Md., 1979-80; v.p. Greater Severna Park Coun., Severna Park, Md., 1980. Lt. col. USAF, 1955-76, Vietnam. Decorated Legion of Merit, Bronze Star. Mem. IEEE Computer Soc. (TC exec. bd.), Soc. Mfg. Engrs., Assn. Computing Machinery, Am. Soc. Engring. Edn., Pitts. Athletic Assn. Republican. Episcopalian.

MANLEY, NORLEE K., nurse, chemical dependence program administrator; b. Middleport, Ohio; d. James Norwood Van Cooney and Esther Marie Searles; m. Virgil James Manley; children: Michael James, Sandra René. ADN, Cuyahoga Community Coll., 1975; BSN, Kent State U., 1986; MNS in Adminstrn., U. Akron, 1991. Cert. in nursing adminstrn.; cert. chem. dependence counselor. Head nurse Vets. Addiction Recovery Ctr. VA Med. Ctr., Cleve., coord. Drug Depencence Treatment prog., dep. dir. Vets. Addiction Recovery Ctr., dir. Vets. Addiction Recovery Ctr. Contbr. to profl. jours. Chairperson 24th Ann. Nurses Conf. Recipient award for outstanding supr. Fed. Exec. Bd., 1991. Mem. ANA, Ohio Nurses Assn., Greater Cleve. Nurses Assn., Nat. Consortium of Chem. Dependence Nurses, Nurses Orgn. of VA (bd. dirs., Excellence in Nursing award 1986, Regional Adminstrs. award for Excellence in Nursing 1990), Sigma Theta Tau. Home: 4820 Sentinel Dr Cleveland OH 44141-3149

MANLEY, RICHARD WALTER, insurance executive; b. Malone, N.Y., Dec. 26, 1934; s. Walter E. and Ruth (St. Mary) M.; m. Linda Kimberlin, Dec. 18, 1965; children: Stephanie, Christopher. BS in Bus., U. So. Miss., 1960. Cert. real estate broker. Account exec. Colonial Life and Accident, Hattiesburg, Miss., 1960-63; dist. mgr. Colonial Life and Accident, Oklahoma City, 1963-66; regional dir. Colonial Life and Accident, Denver, 1966-76, zone dir., 1976-82; pres. Commonwealth Gen. Group, Denver, 1982-92, Manley Properties Inc., Denver, 1982-90, Richard W. Manley Commonwealth Gen. Grps., Inc., Denver, 1982—; cons. Capitol Am. Life Ins. Co., Cleve., 1987-92; bd. dirs. (merco) Mercy Hosp., Denver, 1982-87. With USAF, 1956-59. Mem. Nat. Life Underwriters, Sertoma, Cherry Hills C. of C., Rotary, Elks, Alpha Tau Omega. Roman Catholic. Avocations: golfing, racquetball, running. Home: 6510 E Lake Pl Englewood CO 80111-4411

MANLEY, ROBERT EDWARD, lawyer, economist; b. Cin., Nov. 24, 1935; s. John M. and Helen Catherine (McCarthy) M.; m. Roberta L. Anzinger, Oct. 21, 1971 (div. 1980); 1 child, Robert Edward. ScB in Econs, Xavier U., 1956; AM in Econ. Theory, U. Cin., 1957; JD, Harvard U., 1960; postgrad., London Sch. Econs. and Polit. Sci., 1960, MIT, 1972. Bar: Ohio 1960, U.S. Supreme Ct. 1970. Pvt. practice law Cin., 1960—; pres. Manley, Burke, Lipton & Cook, 1977; Taft teaching fellow econs. U. Cin., 1956-57, vis. lectr. community planning law Coll. Design, Architecture and Art, 1967-73, adj. assoc. prof. urban planning Coll. Design, Architecture, Art and Planning, 1972-81, adj. prof., 1981—, adj. prof. law, 1980—. Author: Metropolitan School Desegregation, 1978, (with Robert N. Cook) Management of Land and Environment, 1981, others; chmn. editl. adv. bd. Urban Lawyer, 1986-95. Mem. Hamilton County Pub. Defender Commn., 1976-79; trustee HOPE, Cin., Albert J. Ryan Found.; counsel, co-founder Action Housing for Greater Cin.; mem. Spl. Commn. on Formation U. Cin. Health Maintenance Orgn., Mayor Cin. Spl. Com. on Housing; chmn. Cin. Environ. Adv. Coun., 1975-76; trustee The Americas Fund for Ind. Univs., 1987—; trustee Ohio Planning Conf., 1982-91, pres., 1987-89, trustee, 1987-90; sec. Cin. Mounted Patrol Com., 1993—; active Bd. Cin. Downtown Coun., 1991—. Mem. ABA (coun. sect. local govt. law 1976-80, 81-85, 88-92), Ohio Bar Assn., Cin. Bar Assn., Am. Judicature Soc., Law and Soc. Assn., Nat. Coun. Crime and Delinquency, Harvard U. Law Sch. Assn. Cin. (pres. 1970-71), Am. Econ. Assn., Am. Acad. Polit. and Social Sci., Queen City Club, Explorers Club (N.Y.C.) (trustee, sec. Clark chpt. 1992—), Athenaeum Club (Phila.), S.Am. Explorers Club (Lima, Peru). Republican. Roman Catholic. Office: Manley Burke Lipton & Cook 225 W Court St Cincinnati OH 45202-1098

MANLY, CAROL ANN, speech pathologist; b. Canton, Ohio, Nov. 21; d. William George and Florence L. (Parrish) M.; m. William Merget, Sept. 19, 1992; children: William, John. MA, U. Cin., 1970; PhD, NYU, 1988. Instr. U. Cin. Med. Ctr., 1970-72; asst. dir. Goldwater Hosp. NYU, 1972-83; pvt. practice N.Y.C., 1983—; cons. Mary Manning Walsh Home, N.Y.C., 1974-85, Beth Israel Med. Ctr.-North Divsn., N.Y.C., 1983—; adj. asst. prof. NYU, 1989-90, C.W. Post campus L.I. U., Brookville, 1990—. Author: (with others) Current Therapy in Physiatry, 1984, Communication Disorders of the Older Adult: A Practical Handbook for Health Care Professionals, 1993; contbr. articles to profl. jours. Mem. N.Y. Acad. Scis., Am. Speech-Lang.-Hearing Assn., N.Y. State Speech-Lang.-Hearing Assn., N.Y. Neuropsychology Group, NOW. Achievements include development of new diagnostic and treatment procedures for oral-pharyngeal dysphagia in neurologically impaired adults. Office: 360 E 65th St Ste 21D New York NY 10021-6726

MANLY, MARC EDWARD, lawyer; b. Knoxville, Tenn., Mar. 11, 1952; s. William Donald and Jane (Wilden) M.; m. Colby A. Chapman, July 20, 1974; children: Justin C., Allison C. BA summa cum laude, Amherst Coll., 1974; MA in Econs., JD magna cum laude, U. Mich., 1977. Bar: Ill. 1978, D.C. 1988, U.S. Dist. Ct. (no. dist.) Ill. 1978. Assoc. Sidley & Austin, Chgo., 1978-84, ptnr., 1985—; ptnr. AT&T, 1995—. Mem. ABA, Order of Coif, Phi Beta Kappa. Office: AT&T Corp Office 150 Allen Rd Ste 3000 Washington DC 07138*

MANLY, WILLIAM DONALD, metallurgist; b. Malta, Ohio, Jan. 13, 1923; s. Edward James and Thelma (Campbell) M.; m. Jane Wilden, Feb. 9, 1949; children—Hugh, Ann, Marc, David. Student, Antioch Coll., 1941-42; B.S., U. Notre Dame, 1947, M.S., 1949; postgrad., U. Tenn., 1950-55. Metallurgist Oak Ridge Nat. Lab., 1949-60, mgr. gas cooled reactor program, 1960-64; mgr. materials research Union Carbide Corp., N.Y.C., 1964-65; gen. mgr. Union Carbide Corp. (Stellite div.), N.Y.C., 1967-69; v.p. Union Carbide Corp. (Stellite div.), Kokomo, Ind., 1969-70; sr. v.p. Cabot Corp., Boston, 1970-83; exec. v.p. Cabot Corp., 1983-86; ret., 1986; also dir. chmn. adv. com. for reactor safety AEC, 1964-65. Served with USMC, 1943-46. Recipient Honor award U. Notre Dame, 1974, Nat. Medal of Tech., Nat. Sci. Found., 1993. Fellow Am. Soc. Metals (hon. mem., pres. 1972-73, medal for advanced rsch. 1987), AIME, Am. Nuclear Soc. (Merit award 1966); mem. Nat. Acad. Engring., Nat. Assn. Corrosion Engrs., Metall. Soc., Cosmos Club, Masons. Presbyterian. Home: 300 Chamberlain Cove Rd Kingston TN 37763-6030

MANN, ALFRED, musicology educator, choral conductor; b. Hamburg, Germany, Apr. 28, 1917; came to U.S. May 2, 1939, naturalized, 1943; s. Wilhelm and Edith (Weiss) M.; m. Carolyn Owens, Aug. 23, 1948; children: Adrian, John, Timothy. Cert., State Acad. Music, Berlin, Germany, 1937, Royal Conservatory, Milan, Italy, 1938; diploma, Curtis Inst. Music, Phila., 1942; M.A., Columbia U., 1950, Ph.D., 1955; MusD (hon.), Whitworth Coll., 1947, Baldwin-Wallace Coll., 1984, Muhlenberg Coll., Allentown, Pa., 1985. Instr. State Acad. Music, Berlin, 1937-38; instr. Scuola Musicale, Milan, Italy, 1938-39; research asst. Curtis Inst. Music, Phila., 1939-42; chmn. to prof. emeritus Rutgers U., New Brunswick, N.J., 1947—; prof. emeritus musicology Eastman Sch. Music/U. Rochester, N.Y., 1980—; condr. Cantata Singers, N.Y., 1952-59, Bach Choir, Bethlehem, Pa., 1970-80, recs. G.F. Handel, Chandos Anthems, 3 vols., 1964, 65, 66; dir. publs. Am. Choral Found., Phila., 1962—. Author: Study of Fugue, 1958, Theory and Practice, 1987, Bach and Handel: Choral Performance Practice, 1992; editor vols. for Complete Works of Handel, Mozart, Schubert, 1965—, J.J. Fux, Gradus ad Parnassum, 1938, 43, 85, Messiah critical edit. of Handel's conducting score, 1959, 65, 89, Am. Choral Rev., 1962—, Handel, The Orchestra Music, 1996. Bd. dirs. G.F. Handel Gesellschaft, Halle, Germany. Served with CIC, U.S. Army, 1943-45. Guggenheim fellow, 1958. Fellow Am. Coun. Learned Soc., Am. Philos. Soc., Nat. Found. Humanities; mem. Am. Musicological Soc., Internat. Musicological Soc., Am. Bach Soc. (sec. 1972—), Am. Handel Soc. (hon., bd. dirs. 1965—), Internat. Bach Soc. (hon.), Internat. Schuetz Soc. (bd. dirs. Am. chpt. 1983—), Bach Riemenschneider Inst. (hon.). Home: 1536 Scribner Rd Penfield NY 14526-9723 Office: Eastman Sch Music 26 Gibbs St Rochester NY 14604-2505

MANN, BERNARD (BERNIE MANN), professional basketball team executive. Former pres. N.J. Nets, East Rutherford, now bd. dirs. Office: NJ Nets Meadowlands Arena East Rutherford NJ 07073*

MANN, BRUCE ALAN, lawyer; b. Chgo., Nov. 28, 1934; s. David I. and Lillian (Segal) M.; m. Naomi Cooks, Aug. 31, 1980; children: Sally Mann Stull, Jonathan Hugh, Andrew Ross. BBA, U. Wis., 1955, SJD, 1957. Bar: Wis. 1957, N.Y. 1958, Calif. 1961. Assoc. Davis, Polk & Wardwell, N.Y.C., 1957-60; assoc. Pillsbury, Madison & Sutro, San Francisco, 1960-66, ptnr., 1967-83; adminstrv. mng. dir. L.F. Rothschild Unterberg Towbin, San Francisco, 1983-87; ptnr. Morrison & Foerster, San Francisco, 1987—; cons. SEC, 1978; vis. prof. law Georgetown U., 1978; lectr. in field; mem. adv. bd. U. Calif. Securities Regulation Inst., 1973—. Contbr. articles to profl. jours. Served with USAR, 1957. Mem. Am. Law Inst., Am. Bar Assn. (chmn. fed. regulation of securities com. 1981-83), State Bar Calif., Bar Assn. San Francisco (bd. dirs. 1974-75), Nat. Assn. Securities Dealers (gov. at large 1981-83). Club: The Family. Office: Morrison & Foerster 345 California St San Francisco CA 94104-2635

MANN, CEDRIC ROBERT, retired institute administrator, oceanographer; b. Auckland, N.Z., Feb. 14, 1926; came to Can., 1949; s. Duncan and Winifred Mary (Wood) M.; m. Muriel Frances May, Dec. 19, 1950; 1 child, Robin Carl. B.Sc., U. N.Z., Auckland, 1948, M.Sc., 1950; Ph.D., U. B.C., Vancouver, Can., 1953; D.Eng., N.S. Tech. Coll., Halifax, Can., 1972. Physicist Naval Research Establishment, Halifax, N.S., Can., 1953-61; oceanographer Atlantic Oceanographic Lab., Halifax, N.S., Can., 1961-75, dir., 1975-78; dir. gen. Bedford Inst. Oceanography, Halifax, N.S., Can., 1978-79, Inst. Ocean Scis., Sidney, B.C., Can., 1979-87; Assoc. prof. Dalhousie U., Halifax, 1961-75; chmn. sci. adv. bd. Intergovtl. Oceanographic Commn., Paris, 1978-81; mem. Can. Climate Planning Bd., Ottawa, 1983-86; chmn. Sea Use Council, Seattle, 1981-86. Contbr. articles to profl. jours. Fellow Royal Soc. Can.; mem. Can. Meteorol. and Oceanographic Soc. (life, recipient J.P. Tully medal in Oceanography, 1994). Anglican. Avocations: golf; gardening. Home: 9751 Ardmore Dr, Sidney, BC Canada V8L 5H5

MANN, DAVID SCOTT, lawyer; b. Cin., Ohio, Sept. 25, 1939; s. Henry M. and Helen Faye M.; m. Elizabeth Taliaferro, Oct. 5, 1963; children: Michael, Deborah, Marshall. AB cum laude, Harvard Coll., 1961, LLB magna cum laude, 1968. Bar: Ohio 1968. Assoc. Dinsmore & Shohl, Cin., 1968-74, ptnr., 1974-83; ptnr. Taliaferro and Mann, Cin., 1983-92; councilman City of Cin., 1974-92, mayor, 1980-82, 91; mem. 103d Congress 1st Ohio dist., Washington, 1993-94; mem. armed svcs. com., mem. jud. com. Washington; of counsel Thompson, Hine and Flory, Cin., 1995—; vis. prof. Coll. of Law, U. Cin., 1995—. Editor Harvard Law Rev., 1966-68, notes editor, 1967-68; contbr. articles to profl. jours. Mem., chmn. Cin. Bd. Health, 1972-74. With USN, 1961-65. Mem. Cin. Bar Assn. Democrat. Methodist. Home: 568 Evanswood Pl Cincinnati OH 45220-1527

MANN, DAVID WILLIAM, minister; b. Elkhart, Ind., Apr. 17, 1947; s. Herbert Richard and Kathryn (Bontrager) M.; m. Brenda Marie Frantz, June 7, 1969; children: Troy, Todd, Erika. BA, Bethel Coll., 1969; MS, Nat. Louis U., 1986. Ordained to ministry Missionary Ch., 1978. Campus life dir. Youth for Christ, Elkhart, 1969-77; denominational youth dir. Missionary Ch., Ft. Wayne, Ind., 1977-81, Christian edn. dir., 1981-88, U.S. dir. missions, 1990—; assoc. dir. World Ptnrs., Ft. Wayne, 1988-90; dir. Missionary Ch. Vol. Svc., Ft. Wayne, 1983—. Author: (with others) Youth Leaders Source Book, 1985; contbr. articles to profl. jour. Mgr. Little League, Ft. Wayne, 1981-89, bd. dirs. 1986. Mem. Nat. Assn. Evangelicals, Evangelical Fgn. Mission Assn., Denominational Execs. in Christian Edn. (chmn. 1988), Aldersgate Pub. Assn. (bd. dirs. 1985, 87), Nat. Christian Edn. Assn. (exec. com. 1987-89). Avocations: baseball, skiing, fishing, woodworking. Home: 10025 Crown Point Dr Fort Wayne IN 46804-4391 Office: Missionary Ch 3811 Vanguard Dr Fort Wayne IN 46809-3304

MANN, DELBERT, film, theater, television director and producer; b. Lawrence, Kans., Jan. 30, 1920; s. Delbert Martin and Ora (Patton) M.; m. Ann Caroline Gillespie, Jan. 13, 1942; children: David Martin, Frederick G., Barbara Susan, Steven P. B.A., Vanderbilt U., 1941; M.F.A., Yale U.; LL.D. (hon.), Northland Coll. Dir. Town Theatre, Columbia, S.C., 1947-49; stage mgr. Wellesley Summer Theater, 1947-48; floor mgr., asst. dir. NBC-TV, N.Y.C., 1949, dir., 1949-55; freelance film and TV dir., 1954—; former bd. govs. Acad. TV Arts and Scis.; former co-chmn. Tenn. Film, Tape and Music Commn.; former pres. Dirs. Guild, Ednl. and Benevolent Found., Cinema Circulus; former lectr. Claremont (Calif.) McKenna Coll. Dir.,

Philco-Goodyear TV Playhouse, 1949-55, also Omnibus, Ford Star Jubilee, Playwrights 56, Producers Showcase, DuPont Show of the Month, Playhouse 90; films Marty, 1954 (Palme d'Or, Cannes Internat. Film Festival, Acad. Award), The Bachelor Party, 1956, Desire Under the Elms, 1957, Separate Tables, 1958, Middle of the Night, 1959, The Dark at the Top of the Stairs, 1960, The Outsider, 1960, Lover Come Back, 1961, That Touch of Mink, 1962, A Gathering of Eagles, 1962, Dear Heart, 1963, Mister Buddwing, 1965, Fitzwilly, 1967, Kidnapped, 1972, Birch Interval, 1976, Night Crossing, 1982; TV spl. Heidi, 1968, David Copperfield, 1970, Jane Eyre, 1971, The Man Without a Country, 1973, A Girl Named Sooner, 1975, Breaking Up, 1977, Tell Me My Name, 1977, Home To Stay, 1978, All Quiet on the Western Front, 1979, To Find My Son, 1980, All the Way Home, 1981, Bronte, 1982, The Member of the Wedding, 1982, The Gift of Love, 1983, Love Leads the Way, 1984, A Death in California, 1985, The Last Days of Patton, 1986, The Ted Kennedy Jr. Story, 1986, April Morning, 1987, Ironclads, 1991, Against Her Will: An Incident in Baltimore, 1992, Incident in a Small Town, 1993, Lily in Winter, 1994, The Memoirs of Abraham Lincoln, 1996; plays include A Quiet Place, 1956, Speaking of Murder, 1957, Zelda, 1969, The Memoirs of Abraham Lincoln, 1996,; opera Wuthering Heights, N.Y.C. Ctr., 1959. Bd. trustees Vanderbilt U., 1962—. 1st lt. USAAF, WWII; B-24 pilot and squadron intelligence officer, 1944-45. Recipient Acad. Award for dir. Marty, 1955. Mem. Dirs. Guild Am. (past pres. 1967-71) (Dirs. Guild award, 1955), Kappa Alpha. Democrat. Presbyterian. Avocation: reading history. Home and Office: Caroline Prodns Inc 401 S Burnside Ave Apt 11D Los Angeles CA 90036-5305

MANN, DONEGAN, lawyer; b. Birmingham, Ala., Mar. 6, 1922; s. Ephriam DeValse and Edna Atkins (Donegan) M.; m. Frances Virginia Hindman, Apr. 6, 1957 (dec. May 1993); m. Frances M. Jenkins, Jan. 7, 1995. Student, Birmingham-So., 1940-41; AB, George Washington U., 1947, JD, 1950. Bar: U.S. Dist. Ct. D.C. 1950, U.S. Ct. Appeals (D.C. cir.) 1950, U.S. Ct. Claims 1957, U.S. Supreme Ct. 1961, U.S. Ct. Appeals (fed. cir.) 1982. Acting bur. counsel Civil Aeronautics Bd., Washington, 1953-55; gen. rates atty. GAO, Washington, 1955-57; spl. rate counsel Gen. Svcs. Administrn., Washington, 1957-60; assoc. Wolf & Case, Washington, 1960-66; sr. atty., office gen. counsel. U.S. Dept. Treasury, Washington, 1966-79; of counsel Shands & Stupar, Washington, 1979-82; pvt. practice Washington, 1984—. Pres. Friends of Great Falls Tavern, Inc., Potomac, Md., 1977-80, bd. dirs., 1981-82. With USN, 1943-46, PTO. Mem. ABA (treas. pub. contracts sect. 1965-66, chair awards com. 1975-76, Svc. award sr. lawyers' divsn. 1991, counsel sr. lawyers divsn., 1995—, chair guardianship and conservatorship com. 1989-95, sr. lawyers' divsn. task force to reform guardianship laws 1992-94, vice chair, will's probate and trust com., 1995—), Bar Assn. D.C., Fed. Energy Bar Assn., Fed. Bar Assn., D.C. Bar Assn., Montgomery County Hist. Soc. (exec. v.p. 1980-83, bd. dirs. 1984-86). Democrat. Episcopalian. Avocations: fishing, hunting, golf, tennis, gardening. Office: 1000 Connecticut Ave NW Ste 204 Washington DC 20036-5302

MANN, EMILY BETSY, writer, artistic director, theater and film director; b. Boston, Apr. 12, 1952; d. Arthur and Sylvia (Blut) M.; 1 child, Nicholas Isaac Bamman. BA, Harvard U., 1974; MFA, U. Minn., 1976. Resident dir. Guthrie Theater, Mpls., 1976-79; dir. BAM Theater Co., Bklyn., 1980-81; freelance writer, dir. N.Y.C., 1981-90; artistic dir. McCarter Theater Ctr. for the Performing Arts, Princeton, N.J., 1990—; cons. N.Y. Theatre Workshop, 1987. Author: (plays) Annulla, An Autobiography, Still Life (6 Obie awards 1981, Fringe First award 1985), Execution of Justice (Helen Hayes award, Bay Area Theatre Critics Circle award, HBO/USA award, Playwriting award Women's Com. Dramtists Guild for Dramatizing Issues of Conscience 1986), Greensboro: A Requiem; co-author: (with Ntozake Shange) (musical) Betsey Brown; (screenplays) Naked, Fanny Kelly, The Winnie Mandela Story, The Greensboro Massacre; dir. Hedda Gabbler, A Doll House, Annulla, Still Life (Obie award), Execution of Justice (Guthrie and Broadway), Betsey Brown, The Glass Menagerie, Three Sisters, Cat on a Hot Tin Roof, Twilight: L.A., 1992 (L.A. NAACP award for best dir.), The Perfectionist, The Matchmaker: adaptor, dir. Miss Julie, Having Our Say (Tony nomination-direction of a play 1995, Dramatist Guild's Hull Warriner award), Greensboro, A Requiem; translator: Nights and Days (Pierre Laville), 1985; pub. in New Plays U.S.A. 1, New Plays 3, American Plays and the Vietnam War, The Ten Best Plays of 1986, Out Front. Recipient BUSH fellowship, 1975-76, Rosamond Gilder award New Drama Forum Assn., 1983, NEA Assocs. grant, 1984, Guggenheim fellowship, 1985, McKnight fellowship, 1985, CAPS award, 1985, NEA Playwrights fellowship, 1986. Mem. Soc. Stage Dirs. and Choreographers, Theatre Comms. Group (v.p.), New Dramatists, PEN, Writers' Guild, Dramatists' Guild, Phi Beta Kappa.

MANN, GEORGE STANLEY, real estate and financial services corporation executive; b. Toronto, Ont., Can., Dec. 23, 1932; s. David Philip and Elizabeth (Green) M.; m. Saundra Sair, Jan. 2, 1955; children: Michael, Tracy. Attended, North Toronto Collegiate Sch.; LLD (hon.), U. Windsor. Ptnr. Mann & Martel Co. Ltd., 1959-68, chief exec. officer, 1968-70; chief exec. officer United Trust Co., 1970-76; pres. Unicorp Canada Corp., Toronto, 1972-76, chmn. bd., 1976-90; dir. Nat. Bank Canada, 1978-91; chmn. bd. Union Gas Ltd., 1986-93; pres. chmn. bd. Lincorp Holdings, Inc., N.Y.C. Bd. govs. Mt. Sinai Hosp., Toronto. Clubs: Oakdale Golf & Country (Toronto); High Ridge Country (Palm Beach, Fla.). Avocation: golf. Office: Ste 1004, 2 St Clair Ave W, Toronto, ON Canada M4V 1L5 Home: 18 Old Forest Hill Rd, Toronto, ON Canada M5P 2P7 also: 930 S Ocean Blvd Palm Beach FL 33480-4909

MANN, H. GEORGE, lawyer; b. Chgo., Apr. 10, 1937. AB, Harvard U., 1958; JD, Columbia U., 1961. Bar: Ill. 1961. Ptnr. McDermott, Will & Emery, Chgo. Office: McDermott Will & Emery 227 W Monroe St Chicago IL 60606-5016

MANN, HENRY DEAN, accountant; b. El Dorado, Ark., Feb. 8, 1943; s. Paul L. and Mary Louise (Capps) M.; m. Rebecca Balch, Aug. 14, 1965; children: Julie Elizabeth, Betsey Sawyer Mann. BSBA, U. Ark., 1965. CPA, Mo., Tex. Staff acct., mgr. Ernst & Whinney, Houston, 1967-76, ptnr., 1976-77; regional personnel ptnr. Ernst & Whinney (now Ernst & Young), St. Louis, 1977-78, mng. ptnr., 1978-88; pres. Mann Industries, Inc., St. Louis, 1988-89; pres., dir. 1st Capital Corp., St. Louis, 1989—; chmn. bd. dirs. Humble (Tex.) Nat. Bank, 1992—, Citizens Nat. Bank, Ft. Scott, Kans., 1994—; adv. bd. U. Mo. Sch. Accountancy, Columbia, 1979-82; bd. dirs. Cupples Co. Mfrs., St. Louis. Treas. Jr. Achievement, St. Louis, 1984—, bd. dirs., 1986—; treas., bd. dirs. United Way, St. Louis, 1986-92, Art and Edn. Coun., St. Louis, 1986-91; bd. dirs. St. Louis Symphony, 1988-89, Kammergild Chamber Orch., St. Louis, 1986, pres., 1983-85. Mem. AICPA, Mo. Soc. CPAs, Bellerive Country Club (treas. 1986-87, v.p. 1988-89), Beta Gamma Sigma, Beta Alpha Psi. Presbyterian.

MANN, HERBIE, flutist; b. N.Y.C., Apr. 16, 1930; s. Harry C. and Ruth (Brecher) Solomon; m. Ruth Shore, Sept. 8, 1956 (div. 1971); children: Paul J., Claudia; m. Jan Clonts, July 11, 1971 (div. 1990); 2 children: Laura, Geoffrey; m. Susan Janeal Arison, 1991. Student, Manhattan Sch. Music, 1952-54. Founder, pres. Herbie Mann Music Corp., N.Y.C., 1959—; founder Kokopelli Music, Santa Fe, 1992—; toured Africa for Dept. State, 1960, Brazil, 1961-62, Japan, 1964, Scandanavia, Cyprus and Turkey, 1971; pres. Herbie Mann Orch., Inc., 5 Face of Music Prodns., Inc., Rupadia Music, Inc. Recorded over 100 albums under own name, 1954—; Memphis Underground, 1969, Push, Push, 1971, Missippi Gambler, 1974, Bird in a Silver Cage, 1977, Caminho De Casa, 1990. Deep Pocket, 1992, The Evolution of Mann: The Herbie Mann Anthology, 1994. Served with AUS, 1948-52. Recipient Downbeat award for flute, 1958-70. Mem. ASCAP, Nat. Acad. Rec. Arts and Scis. Office: Kokopelli Music PO Box 8200 Santa Fe NM 87504-8200

MANN, J. KEITH, arbitrator, law educator, lawyer; b. May 28, 1924; s. William Young and Lillian Myrle (Bailey) M.; m. Virginia McKinnon, July 7, 1950; children: William Christopher, Marilyn Keith, John Kevin, Susan Bailey, Andrew Curry. BS, Ind. U., 1948, LLB, 1949; LLD, Monmouth Coll., 1989. Bar: Ind. 1949, D.C. 1951. Law clk. Justice Wiley Rutledge and Justice Sherman Minton, 1949-50; practice, Washington, 1950; with Wage Stblzn. Bd., 1951; asst. prof. U. Wis., 1952; asst. prof. Stanford U. Law Sch., 1952-54, assoc. prof., 1954-58, prof., 1958-88, prof. emeritus 1988—, assoc. dean, 1961-85, acting dean, 1976, 81-82, cons. to provost, 1986-87; vis. prof. U. Chgo., 1953; mem. Sec. of Labor's Adv. Com., 1955-57; mem. Pres.'s Commn. Airlines Controversy, 1961; mem. COLC Aerospace Spl. Panel, 1973-74; chmn., mem. Presdl. Emergency Bds. or Bds. of Inquiry, 1962-63, 67, 71-72; spl. master U.S. vs. Alaska, U.S. Supreme Ct., 1980—. Ensign USN, 1944-46. Sunderland fellow U. Mich., 1959-60; scholar in residence Duke U., 1972. Mem. ABA, AAUP, Nat. Acad. Arbitrators, Indsl. Rels. Rsch. Assn., Acad. Law Alumni Fellows Ind. U., Order of Coif, Tau Kappa Epsilon, Phi Delta Phi. Editor: book rev. and articles Ind. U. Law Jour. Democrat. Presbyterian. Home: 872 Lathrop Dr Stanford CA 94305-1053 Office: Stanford U Law Sch Stanford CA 94305-8610

MANN, JAMES ROBERT, congressman; b. Greenville, S.C., Apr. 27, 1920; s. Alfred Cleo and Nina (Griffin) M.; m. Virginia Thomason Brunson, Jan. 15, 1945; children—James Robert, David Brunson, William Walker, Virginia Brunson. B.A., The Citadel, 1941, LL.D. (hon.), 1978; JD, U. S.C., 1947. Bar: S.C. 1947, U.S. Ct. Appeals (4th cir.) 1948, U.S. Supreme Ct. 1970. Practice in Greenville, 1947—; del. S.C. Ho. of Reps. from, Greenville County, 1949-52; solicitor 13th Jud. Circuit, 1953-63; mem. 91st-95th Congresses 4th Dist., S.C. Sec. Greenville County Planning Commn., 1963-67; Trustee Greenville Hosp. System, 1965-68; bd. govs. Greenville Shriners Hosp., 1983-90. Served to lt. col. AUS, 1941-46; col. USAR ret. Mem. Am., S.C., Greenville County bar assns., Am. Judicature Soc., Greater Greenville C. of C. (pres. 1965), V.F.W. (dep. comdr. 1951-52), Am. Legion. Democrat. Baptist. Lodges: Mason; Shriners; Kiwanis; Elks; Woodmen of World. Office: 812 E North St Greenville SC 29601-3102

MANN, JEFF, special effects expert, executive. With Indsl. Light & Magic, San Rafael, Calif., 1981—, mgr. model and creature shops, 1986—. Creator model and creature projects various films including Star Trek IV: The Voyage Home, 1986, Empire of the Sun, 1987, Star Tours, 1987, Witches of Eastwick, 1987, Batteries Not Included, 1987, Innerspace, 1987, Star Trek: The Next Generation, 1987, Who Framed Roger Rabbit, 2988, Willow, 1988, Indiana Jones and the Last Crusade, 1989, Ghostbusters II, 1989, The Abyss, 1989, Back to the Future II, 1989, Always, 1989, Dreams, 1989, Joe Versus the Volcano, 1990, The Hunt for Red October, 1990, Ghost, 1990, Back to the Future III, 1990, Die Hard II, 1990. Office: Indsl Light & Magic PO Box 2459 San Rafael CA 94912-2459

MANN, JIM (JAMES WILLIAM MANOUSOS), editor, publisher; b. Cambridge, Mass., Dec. 9, 1919; s. Demetrios Peter and Germaine (Lambertz) Manousos; m. Mary Dimitrakis, July 21, 1962. MFA, Fordham U., 1954. Assoc. editor View mag., Yonkers, N.Y., 1951-58; various editorial jobs N.Y.C., 1959-71; pres., editor The Gallagher Report, N.Y.C., 1971-74; pres., treas. Jim Mann & Assocs., Gales Ferry, Conn., 1974—; editor, pub. Media Mgmt. Monographs, 1978-90; editor in chief Pub. Trends & Trendsetters, 1991-95; adj. prof. mktg. U. New Haven, Orange, Conn., 1976-82. Author: Solving Publishing's Toughest Problems, 1982, Magazine Editing, 1985, Ad Sales, 1987. Pres. Cmty. Action Network, 1990-95. *Success is realizing one's potential; happiness is exercising it.*

MANN, JONATHAN MAX, international agency administrator, public health director; b. Boston, July 30, 1947; s. James and Ida (Laskow) M.; m. Marie-Paule Bondat, Jan. 30, 1970; children: Naomi, Lydia, Aaron. BA, Harvard U., 1969, MPH, 1980; MD, Washington U., St. Louis, 1974. Epidemic intelligence service officer USPHS, Ctrs. Disease Control, Atlanta and Santa Fe, 1975-77; med. epidemiologist, dir. AIDS research program, Kinshasa, Zaire, 1984-86; dir. global program AIDS, WHO, Geneva, 1986-90; state epidemiologist, chief med. officer N.Mex. Health Dept., Santa Fe, 1977-84. Mem. editorial bd. Control of Communicable Diseases in Man, Western Jour. Medicine, 1984—. Contbr. articles to profl. jours. Recipient Spl. Commendation N.Mex. Med. Soc., 1980, Friend of N.Mex. Journalism award Sigma Delta Chi, 1979, Disting. Service award School Nursing Com., 1979. Fellow Am. Coll. Preventive Medicine (Recognition award 1982), Am. Coll. Epidemiology; mem. Santa Fe County Med. Soc. (treas. 1981-82, pres. 1983-84), U.S.-Mex. Border Health Assn., Am. Pub. Health Assn.*

MANN, KENNETH HENRY, marine ecologist; b. Dovercourt, Essex, Eng., Aug. 15, 1923; emigrated to arrived Canada, 1967, naturalized, 1973; s. Harry and Mabel (Ashby) M.; m. Isabella Gilmour Ness, Apr. 18, 1946; children: Ian Malcolm, Sheila Helen, Colin Gilmour. B.Sc., U. London, 1949; Ph.D., U. Reading, 1953; D.Sc., U. London, 1965. Lectr. zoology, then reader U. Reading, Eng., 1949-64; 64-67; sr. biologist marine ecology lab. Bedford Inst. Oceanography, Dartmouth, Can., 1967-72, dir. marine ecology lab., 1980-86, sr. rsch. scientist, 1986-93, emeritus rsch. scientist, 1993—; prof., chmn. biology Dalhousie U., Halifax, N.S., Can., 1972-80, adj. prof. biology, 1980—. Author: Leeches: Their Structure, Phyiology, Ecology and Embryology, 1961, Ecology of Coastal Waters: A Systems Approach, 1982; co-author: (with J. Lazier) Dynamics of Marine Ecosystems: Biological-Physical Interactions in the Sea, 1991; 2d edit., 1996; (with R.S. Barnes) Fundamentals of Aquatic Ecology, 1991; editor, contbr.: Network Analysis in Marine Ecology, 1989; editor Jour. Animal Ecology, 1966-67. Served with Royal Air Force, 1942-46. Fellow Royal Soc. Can.; mem. Brit. Ecol. Soc., Am. Assn. Limnology and Oceanography. Home: 23 Woodward Cres, Halifax, NS Canada B3M 1J6 Office: Bedford Inst Oceanography, Box 1006, Dartmouth, NS Canada B2Y 4A2

MANN, KENNETH WALKER, retired minister, psychologist; b. Nyack, N.Y., Aug. 22, 1914; s. Arthur Hungerford and Ethel Livingston (Walker) M. AB, Princeton U., 1937; STB, Gen. Theol. Sem., N.Y.C., 1942; MS, U. Mich., 1950, PhD, 1956. Ordained priest Episcopal Ch., 1942; diplomate Am. Assn. Pastoral Counselors; lic. clin. psychologist, Calif., Conn.; lic. marriage, family and child counselor, Calif. Vicar in Valley Cottage, Pearl River, N.Y., 1941-43; priest in charge Yonkers, N.Y., 1943-45; dir. youth work and Christian edn. Diocese L.A., 1945-47; curate in Beverly Hills, Calif., 1947-49; counselor Bur. Psychol. Svcs., U. Mich., 1951-52; chaplain, clin. psychologist dept. psychiatry St. Luke's Hosp., N.Y.C., also priest-psychotherapist Cathedral St. John Divine, N.Y.C., psychol. examiner ministerial candidates Diocese N.Y., 1952-58; assoc. chaplain Hosp. Good Samaritan, L.A., 1958-65; exec. pastoral svcs., exec. coun. Episc. Ch. N.Y.C., 1965-70; program officer Acad. Religion and Mental Health, N.Y.C., 1970-72; sr. adviser profl. affairs Inst. Religion and Health, 1972-74; sr. psychol. staff Silver Hill Found., New Canaan, Conn., 1974-84; pres. Rockland County (N.Y.) Mins. Assn., 1942-43; exec. sec. social svc. commn. Diocese N.Y., 1943-45; chmn. div. pastoral svcs. Diocese L.A., 1958-65; field dir. Western region Acad. Religion and Mental Health, 1958-61; assoc. nat. chaplain U.S. Power Squadrons, 1956-57. Author: On Pills and Needles, 1969, Deadline for Survival—A Survey of Moral Issues in Science and Medicine, 1970; contbr. articles to profl. jours. Pres. Adoption Inst. L.A., 1964; mem. edn. com. Calif. Heart Assn., 1962-64; trustee, treas. Acad. Religion and Mental Health, 1954-59, mem. profl. bd., 1960-70; trustee Vis. Nurse Assn. L.A., 1963-65, Children's Home Soc. Calif. in L.A., 1964-65, North Conway Inst., 1966-80. USPHS grantee, 1950-51. Fellow AAAS; mem. APA (chmn. com. rels. between psychology and religion 1956-58), Western Psychol. Assn., Calif. Psychol. Assn., L.A. County Psychol. Assn., N.Y. Acad. Scis., Planetary Soc., Assembly Episc. Hosps. and Chaplains, Upper Nyack Tennis Club, The Club (Diocese N.Y.), Princeton Club N.Y. Republican. Home: 32 Tallman Ave Nyack NY 10960-1606 *I have strongly held to the principle that the total "health" of mankind cannot be considered apart from the values and aspirations by which people live, and by which they may even be prepared to die. Amidst the confusions that exist today over loyalties, traditions, and ideals, many are asking: What is the right way to behave? How should I think? What kind of person am I supposed to be? To help such people in quandary to live responsibly, and still be true to their individuality, is a large task, but it is one that is central to a religious ministry. It has always been my chief concern.*

MANN, LINDA MARIE, elementary school educator; b. Pitts., July 11, 1949; d. Howard Robert and Matilda Elizabeth (Baumann) M. BA in Edn., Syracuse U., 1972; MS in Instructional Systems Tech., Ind.U., 1975; post-grad. studies Edn.-related, SUNY, Oswego, Plattsburgh, Albany, 1991-92. Cert. tchr. lifetime (N-6), libr. media specialist (K-12), English (7-12) permanent, N.Y. Secondary English tchr. Liverpool (N.Y.) Ctrl. Schs., 1972-74, media specialist, 1975-91, elem. tchr. vertical team grades 3-4-5, 1992, elem. tchr., 1992—; edn. cons., mem. educators' adv. bd. Ste Marie Mus., Liverpool, 1976-92; tour guide, guest speaker Hist. Assn. Greater Liverpool, 1989-92. Tchr., tchr. trainer, supt. Sunday sch., chairperson curriculum com., coord. ref. libr. Greater Love in Christ Ch., Syracuse, N.Y., 1985-92. Mem. ASCD, Internat. Reading Assn., Tchrs. Applying Whole Lang., Ctrl. N.Y. Coun. Social Studies, Delta Kappa Gamma. Avocations: journal writing, literature, singing, speedwlking, bicycling, hiking. Office: Liverpool Ctrl Sch 800 4th St Liverpool NY 13088-4455

MANN, LOUIS EUGENE, financial planner; b. Balt., Jan. 24, 1947; s. Manfred and Ruth Eleanor (Kates) M.; m. Marjorie Ruth Friedman, Mar. 23, 1971; children: Lisa Renee, Brian Michael. Student, Balt. Poly. Inst., 1964, Towson State Coll., 1964-67; postgrad., U. Pa., 1969-70; CFP, Coll. for Fin. Planning, 1993. CFP; securities licenses; lic. ins. broker, N.J., Pa. Clk. Food Fair Stores, Inc., Balt., 1964-68; v.p. Friendly Grocer, Inc., Cherry Hill, N.J., 1968-79; sales mgr. Frito-Lay Inc., Cinnaminson, N.J., 1979-82; salesman N.Y. Life Ins. Co., Cherry Hill, N.J., 1982-89; ptnr. Custom Fin. Svcs., Marlton, N.J., 1988-93; pres. Louis E. Mann Fin. Svcs., Inc., Phila., 1993—; v.p. Orion Fin. Svcs., Inc., Phila., 1994—; cons. employee benefits and fin. Congregation Beth Tikvah, Marlton; mem. adv. bd. planned charitable giving Rotary Dists. of N.J., Point Pleasant. Theorist, author: (math. formula) Law of Squares of Consecutive Numbers, 1963. Mgr., coach Greentree Athletic Assn., Mount Laurel, N.J., 1985-94; pres. Congregation Beth Tikvah Men's Club, Marlton, 1988-89, 90-91, 94-95, bd. dirs., exec. bd. mem., 1994-95. Recipient Coll. scholarship State of Md.-Senatorial, 1964. Mem. Inst. CFPs, Million Dollar Round Table (membership com. 1984), Rotary Club of Moorestown (com. chmn., bd. dirs. 1984-94, 1st v.p. 1996-97), Rotary Internat. (dist. planned giving chmn. Dist. 7500, 1994-95), Fedn. Jewish Men's Clubs (bd. trustees mid. Atlantic region). Democrat. Jewish. Avocations: sports, hist. readings, fin. readings, music, gardening. Home: 121 Colony Pl Mount Laurel NJ 08054-2404 Office: Orion Fin Svcs Inc 2112 Walnut St Philadelphia PA 19103-4808

MANN, LOWELL D., religious organization executive. Chmn. Bd. for World Missions.

MANN, LOWELL KIMSEY, retired manufacturing executive; b. LaGrange, Ga., June 28, 1917; s. Otis A. and Georgia B. (Mundy) M.; m. Helen Margaret Dukes, Feb. 11, 1944; children: Margaret Ellen, Lowell Kimsey. Grad., Advanced Mgmt. Program, Harvard, 1962. Foreman Callaway Mills, LaGrange, 1935-39, indsl. engr., 1939-42; indsl. engr. Blue Bell, Inc., Greenboro, N.C., 1946-52, chief engr., 1952-61, v.p. engring., 1961-62, v.p. mfg., 1962-68, exec. v.p., 1968-73, pres., 1973-82, chief exec. officer, 1974-83, chmn. bd., 1982-84, ret., 1984; dir. Shadowline Inc., Morganton, N.C., Wachovia Bank & Trust Co., Greensboro, Quality Mills, Mt. Airy, N.C.; mem. So. adv. bd. Arkwright-Boston Ins. Co., 1975-84. Bd. dirs. Learning Inst., N.C., 1969-76; trustee Southeastern Legal Found., 1977-84; deacon Bapt. Ch., 1984-88, chmn., 1986-87. Served to capt. AUS, 1942-46. Recipient Disting. Citizen award Greensboro C. of C., 1983; named Clothing Mfg. Industry CEO of Yr. Fin. World, 1978. Mem. Piedmont Assoc. Industries (bd. dirs, pres. 1966-68), Am. Apparel Mfrs. Assn. (bd. dirs. 1972-78), Nat. MS Soc., NAM (bd. dirs. 1977-84), Beta Gamma Sigma (hon.). Democrat. Club: Sedgefield Country (bd. dirs. 1970-73, 85-88, pres. 1986-88) (Greensboro). Home: Sedgefield 5503 Currituck Pl Greensboro NC 27407-7217 *I believe that honesty, integrity, and fairness are essential in our relationships with others. These shared values will encourage understanding, and, in turn, will create pride in us, opportunities for us, and accomplishments by us.*

MANN, MARION, physician, educator; b. Atlanta, Mar. 29, 1920; s. Levi James and Cora (Casey) M.; m. Ruth Maurine Reagin, Jan. 16, 1943; children: Marion Jr., Judith (Mrs. Kenneth Walk). B.S. in Edn, Tuskegee Inst., Ala., 1940; M.D., Howard U., 1954; Ph.D., Georgetown U., 1961, D.Sc. (hon.), 1979; D.Sc. (hon.), U. Mass., 1984; grad., U.S. Army Command and Gen. Staff Coll., 1965, U.S. Army War Coll., 1970. Diplomate: Nat. Bd. Med. Examiners, Am. Bd. Pathology. Intern USPHS Hosp., Staten Island, N.Y., 1954-55; resident Georgetown U. Hosp., 1956-60; practice medicine, specializing in pathology Washington, 1961—; instr. pathology Georgetown U., 1960-61; professorial lectr. Georgetown U. (Sch. Medicine), 1970-73; asst. prof. pathology Howard U. Coll. Medicine, 1961-67, assoc. prof., 1967-70, prof., 1970, dean, 1970-79; v.p. rsch. Howard U., 1988-91. Capt. AUS, 1942-50; brig. gen. Res. Mem. Inst. Medicine, Nat. Acad. Scis., Alpha Omega Alpha. Mem. United Ch. of Christ. Home: 1453 Whittier Pl NW Washington DC 20012-2845 Office: 520 W St NW Washington DC 20001-2337

MANN, MARVIN L., electronics executive; b. Birmingham, Ala., Apr. 22, 1933; s. Jesse Marvin and Nannie Leola (Thomason) M.; m. Frances Nell Marlin, Dec. 24, 1953; children: Tara Jane, Jeffery Loy. BS, Samford U., 1954; MBA, U. Ala., 1958. Chmn., pres., chief exec. officer Lexmark Internat., Inc., Greenwich, Conn. Office: Lexmark Internat Inc 55 Railroad Ave Greenwich CT 06830-6378*

MANN, MICHAEL K., producer, director, writer; b. Chgo. Ed., U. Wis. Dir.: (documentary) 17 Days Down the Line; scriptwriter, dir.: (TV movie) The Jericho Mile, 1979 (Best Dir. award Dir. Guild Am., Emmy award), sceenwriter, exec. prodr. dir.; Thief, 1981; (film) The Keep, 1983; screenwriter, dir., prodr.: Manhunter, 1986, Last of the Mohicans, 1992; screenwriter, dir., prodr. Heat, 1995, exec. prodr. (TV show) Miami Vice, Crime Story, (TV miniseries) Drug Wars: Camarena Story (Emmy award), Drug Wars: Cocaine Cartel; scriptwriter: (TV episodes) Police Story, Starsky and Hutch. Mem. Writers Guild., Dirs. Guild. Office: care CAA 9830 Wilshire Blvd Beverly Hills CA 90212-1804

MANN, MICHAEL MARTIN, electronics company executive; b. N.Y.C., Nov. 28, 1939; s. Herbert and Rosalind (Kaplan) M.; m. Mariel Joy Steinberg, Apr. 25, 1965. BSEE, Calif. Inst. Tech., 1960, MSEE, 1961; PhD in Elec. Engring. and Physics, U. So. Calif., 1969; MBA, UCLA, 1984. Cert. bus. appraiser, profl. cons., mgmt. cons., lic. real estate broker, Calif. Mgr. high power laser programs office Northrop Corp., Hawthorne, Calif., 1969-76; mgr. high energy laser systems lab. Hughes Aircraft Co., El Segundo, Calif., 1976-78; mgr. E-0 control systems labs. Hughes Aircraft Co., El Segundo, 1978-83, asst. to v.p., space & strategic, 1983-84; exec. v.p. Helionetics Inc., Irvine, Calif., 1984-85, pres., chief exec. officer, 1985-86, also bd. dirs.; ptnr. Mann Kavanaugh Chernove, 1986-87; sr. cons. Arthur D. Little, Inc., 1987-88; chmn. bd., pres., CEO, Blue Marble Devel. Group, Inc., 1988—; exec. assoc. Ctr. Internat. Cooperation and Trade, 1989—; sr. assoc. Corp. Fin. Assocs., 1990—; exec. assoc. Reece and Assocs., 1991—; dir. Reece & Assocs., 1991—; mng. dir. Blue Marble Ptnrs. Ltd, 1991—; chmn. bd. dirs., CEO Blue Marble Ptnrs., 1992—; chmn., CEO, En Compass Techs., Inc., Torrance, Calif., 1994—; mem. Army Sci. Bd., Dept. Army, Washington, 1986-91; chmn. Ballistic Missile Def. Panel, Directed Energy Weapon Panel, Rsch. and New Initiatives Panel; cons. Office of Sec. of Army, Washington, 1986—, Inst. of Def. Analysis, Washington, 1978—, Dept. Energy, 1988—, Nat. Riverside Rsch. Inst., 1990—; bd. dirs. Datum, Inc.,1988—, Fail-Safe Tech., Corp., 1989-90, Safeguard Health Enterprises, Inc., 1988—, Am. Video Communications, Inc., Meck Industries, Inc., 1987-88, Decade Optical Systems, Inc., 1990—, Forum Mil. Application Directed Energy, 1992—, Am. Bus. Consultants, Inc., 1993—; chmn. bd. Mgmt. Tech., Inc. 1991—, Encompass Tech., Inc., 1994—; bd. dirs., mem. adv. bd. Micro-Frame, Inc., 1988-91; chmn. bd. HLX Laser, Inc., 1984-86; bd. dirs. Cons's. Roundtable, 1992—, Am. Bus. Cons., Inc., 1993—; rsch. assoc., mem. extension teaching staff U. So. Calif., L.A., 1964-70; chmn. Ballistic Missile Def. Subgroup, 1989-90, Tactical Directed Energy Weapons Subgroup, 1988-90; chmn., chief exec. officer Mgmt. Tech., Inc., 1991—; dir. Am. Bus. Cons., Inc., 1993—. Contbg. editor, mem. adv. bd. Calif. High-Tech Funding Jour., 1989-90; contbr. over 50 tech. articles to profl. jours.; patentee in field. Adv. com. to Engring. Sch., Calif. State U., Long Beach, 1985—; chmn. polit. affairs Am. Electronics Assn., Orange County Coun., 1986-87, mem. exec. com., 1986-88; adv. com. several Calif. congressmen, 1985—; mem. dean's coun. UCLA Grad. Sch. Mgmt., 1984-85; bd. dirs. Archimedes Circle U. So. Calif., 1983-85, Ctr. for Innovation and Entrepreneurship, 1986-90, Caltech/MIT Venture Forum, 1987-91. Hicks fellow in Indsl. Rels. Calif. Inst. Tech., 1961, Hewlett Packard fellow. Mem. IEEE (sr.), So. Calif. Tech. Execs. Network, Orange County CEO's Network, Orange County CEO's Roundtable, Pres. Roundtable, Nat. Assn. Corp. Dirs., Aerospace-Def. CEO's Roundtable, Am. Def. Preparedness Assn., Security Affairs Support Assn., Acad. Profl. Cons. and Advisors, Internat. Platform Assn., Inst. Mgmt. Cons. (bd. dirs. So. Calif. chpt.), Pres.

Assn., Cons. Roundtable, King Harbor Yacht Club. Republican. Avocations: sailing, photography, writing. Home: 4248 Via Alondra Palos Verdes Peninsula CA 90274-1545 Office: Blue Marble Partners 406 Amapola Ave Ste 200 Torrance CA 90501-6229

MANN, NANCY LOUISE (NANCY LOUISE ROBBINS), entrepreneur; b. Chillicothe, Ohio, May 6, 1925; d. Everett Chaney and Pauline Elizabeth R.; m. Kenneth Douglas Mann, June 19, 1949 (div. June 1979); children: Bryan Wilkinson, Laura Elizabeth. BA in Math., UCLA, 1948, MA in Math., 1949, PhD in Biostatistics, 1965. Sr. scientist Rocketdyne Div. of Rockwell Internat., Canoga Park, Calif., 1962-75; mem. tech. staff Rockwell Sci. Ctr., Thousand Oaks, Calif., 1975-78; rsch. prof. UCLA Biomath., L.A., 1978-87; pres., CEO, owner Quality Enhancement Seminars, Inc., L.A., 1982—; pres., CEO Quality and Productivity, Inc., L.A., 1987—; curriculum adv. UCLA Ext. Dept. of Bus. and Mgmt., L.A., 1991—; mem. com. on Nat. Statistics, Nat. Acad. Scis., Washington, 1978-82; mem adv. bd. to supt. U.S. Naval Posgrad. Sch., Monterey, Calif., 1979-82. Co-author: Methods for Analysis of Reliability and Life Data, 1974; author: Keys to Excellence, 1985, The Story of the Deming Philosophy, 2d edit., 1987, 3d edit., 1989; contbr. articles to profl. jours. Recipient award IEEE Reliability Soc., 1982, ASQC Reliability Divsn., 1986. Fellow Am. Statis. Assn. (v.p. 1982-84); mem. Internat. Statis. Inst. Office: Quality and Productivity Inc 1081 Westwood Blvd # 217 Los Angeles CA 90024-2911

MANN, OSCAR, physician, internist, educator; b. Paris, Oct. 13, 1934; came to U.S., 1953; s. Aron and Helen (Biegun) M.; m. Amy S. Mann, July 19, 1964; children: Adriana, Karen. AA with distinction, George Washington U., 1958; MD cum laude, Georgetown U., 1962. Diplomate Am. Bd. Med. Examiners, Am. Bd. Internal Medicine, Am. Bd. Internal Medicine subspecialty Cardiovascular Disease; cert. advanced achievement in internal medicine; re-cert. in internal medicine. Intern Georgetown U. Med. Ctr., Washington, 1962-63, jr. asst. med. resident, 1963-64, clin. fellow in cardiology with Proctor Harvey program, 1965-66; sr. asst. resident in medicine Georgetown svc. D.C. Gen. Hosp., Washington, 1964-65; clin. prof. medicine Georgetown U. Sch. Medicine, 1985—; nat. chmn. med. alumi fund Georgetown U. Med. Sch., Washington, 1993-95; pvt. practice internal medicine and cardiology, Washington, 1966—; mem. Med.-Nursing Audit Com., CME adv. com., teaching. adv. com., Opthamology dept. rev. com., surgery dept. rev. com., faculty com., search com. for a new dean for acad. affairs Georgetown U. Med. Ctr.; appointed coun. to the dean Georgetown U. Sch. Medicine, 1977—; mem. Instnl. Self Study Task Force. Contbr. articles to profl. jours. Served with the U.S. Army, 1953-55. Recipient Mead Johnson Postgrad. Scholar ACP, 1964-65, Physicians Recognition award AMA, 1987-96, Advanced Achievement in Internal Medicine, 1987. Fellow ACP, Am. Coll. Cardiology, Am. Coll. Chest Physicians; mem. AMA, Am. Soc. Internal Medicine, Am. Heart Assn. (coun. clin. cardiology), Med. Soc. D.C., Cosmos Club, Geogetown U. Alumni Assn. (bd. govs. 1993—, chmn. med. alumni bd. 1995—), Alpha Omega Alpha, Phi Delta Epsilon. Home: 4925 Weaver Ter NW Washington DC 20016-2660 Office: Foxhall Internists PC 3301 New Mexico Ave NW Washington DC 20016-3622

MANN, ROBERT NATHANIEL, violinist; b. Portland, Oreg., July 19, 1920; s. Charles Emanuel and Anna (Schnitzer) M.; m. Lucy Rowan, July 27, 1951; children: Lisa, Nicholas. Grad., Inst. Musical Art; diploma, Juilliard Sch. Music; hon. doctorate, Earlham Coll., Mich. State U., Jacksonville U. Mem. faculty Juilliard Sch., 1946—; resident mem. quartet Library of Congress, 1963-88; artistic dir. Revenia Stearns Inst., 1988—; panelist Nat. Endowment for Arts; pres. Walter Naumburg Found. First violinist, Juilliard Quartet, 1946—; composer numerous works for violin, piano, orch., chamber music. Bd. dirs. N.Y. Philharmonic. Served with AUS, 1943-46. Recipient Chamber Music Svc. award, 1991, String Tchrs. award, 1991, Peabody medal of honor, 1991. Mem. Am. Composers Alliance, Juilliard Sch. Music Alumni Assn. Clubs: Century, Bohemian.

MANN, ROBERT WELLESLEY, biomedical engineer, educator; b. Bklyn., Oct. 6, 1924; s. Arthur Wellesley and Helen (Rieger) M.; m. Margaret Ida Florencourt, Sept. 4, 1950; children: Robert Wellesley, Catherine Louise. SB, MIT, 1950, SM, 1951, ScD, 1957. With Bell Telephone Labs., N.Y.C., 1942-43, 46-47; with U.S. Army Signal Corps, 1943-46; research engr. MIT, 1951-52, rsch. supr., 1952, mem. faculty, 1953—, prof. mech. engring., 1963-70, Germeshausen prof., 1970-72, prof. engring., 1972-74, Whitaker prof. biomed. engring., 1974-92, Whitaker prof. emeritus, sr. lectr., 1992—, head systems and design div., mech. engring. dept., 1957-68, 82-83, founder, dir. engring. projects lab., 1959-62; founder, chmn. steering com. Center Sensory Aids Evaluation and Devel., 1964-86, chmn. div. health scis., tech., planning and mgmt., 1972-74, founder, dir. Newman biomechanics and human rehab. lab., 1975-92; dir. bioengring. programs Whitaker Coll. MIT, 1986-89; dir. Harvard-MIT Rehab. Engring. Ctr., 1988-93; mem. exec. com. Divsn. Health Scis. and Tech. Harvard U. MIT, 1972-85; prof., 1979—, mem. Com. on Use of Humans and Exptl. Subjects MIT, 1984-93, co-chair Pub. Svc. Ctr., 1988-92; lectr. engring. Faculty of Medicine, Harvard U., 1973-79; rsch. assocs. in orthopedic surgery Children's Hosp. Med. Ctr., 1973—; cons. in engring. sci. Mass. Gen. Hosp., 1969—; cons. in field, 1953—; mem. Nat. Commn. Engring. Edn., 1962-69; com. prosthetics rsch. and devel. NRC, 1963-69; chmn. sensory aids subcom., 1965-68, com. skeletal sys., 1969; mem. com. interplay engring. with biology and medicine Nat. Acad. Engring., 1969-73; mem. bd. health scis. policy Inst. Medicine, 1973-74, 82-86; mem. com. on nat. needs for rehab. physically handicapped Nat. Acad. Scis., 1975-76; mem.-at-large confs. com. Engring. Found., 1975-81; chair sensory aids panel scis. merit rev. bd. Rehab., R & D, Dept. Vets. Affairs, 1983-85; mem. Commn. on Life Scis. NRC, 1984-88, Com. on Strategic Tech. for U.S. Army, 1989-93; NRC Com. on Space Biology and Medicine, 1992-95. Consulting editor: Ency. Sci. and Tech.; assoc. editor: IEEE Trans. in Biomed. Engring., 1969-78, ASME Jour. Biomech. Engring., 1976-82; mem. editl. bd. Jour. Visual Impairment and Blindness, 1976-80, SOMA, 1986-92; mem. editl. adv. bd. new liberal arts program Alfred P. Sloan Found., 1986-92; contbr. over 330 articles to profl. jours. Pres., trustee Amanda Caroline Payson Scholarship Fund, 1965-86; bd. dirs. Carroll Ctr. for Blind, 1967-74, pres., 1968-74; mem. corp. Perkins Sch. for Blind, 1970—, Mt. Auburn Hosp., 1972—; trustee Nat. Braille Press, 1982—, pres., 1990-94; mem. Cardinal's adv. com. on social justice Archdiocese of Boston, 1993—; bd. overseers St. Marguerite D'Youville Found., Youville Lifecare Inc., 1994—. With U.S. Army Signal Corps, 1943-46. Recipient Sloan award for Outstanding Performance, 1957, Talbert Abrams Photogrammetry award, 1962, Assn. Blind of Mass. award, 1969, IR-100 award for Braillemboss, 1972, Bronze Beaver award MIT, 1975, UCP Goldenson Rsch. for Handicapped award, 1976, H.R. Lissner award, 1977, New Eng. award, 1979, J.R. Killian Faculty Achievement award MIT, 1983, Martin Luther King Leadership award MIT, 1995. Fellow Am. Acad. Arts and Scis., Am. Inst. Med. and Biol. Engring., IEEE (mem. editl. bd. Spectrum 1984-86), AAAS, ASME (gold medal 1977); mem. NAS, Inst. Medicine NAS, NAE, Biomed. Engring. Soc. (bd. dirs. 1981-84), Orthopedic Rsch. Soc., Rehab. Soc. N.Am., MIT Alumni Asssn. (pres. 1983-84, Alumni Fund Bd. 1978-80, bd. dirs. 1980-86, 93-95, corp. joint adv. com. 1983-84, chair nat. selector com. 1985-88, awards com. 1992-94, chmn. 1994, bd. Tech. Rev. 1986-95, chmn. 1993-95), Sigma Xi (nat. lectr. 1979-81), Tau Beta Pi, Pi Tau Sigma, Sigma Xi. Roman Catholic. Achievements include patents on missile power units, founding of computer aided design in 1963, earliest braille translation software and hardware in 1962, cybernetic amputation prosthesis, 1966, in vivo measurements of cartssures, 1984. Home: 5 Pelham Rd Lexington MA 02173-5707 Office: MIT 77 Massachusetts Ave Rm 3-137 Cambridge MA 02139-4301

MANN, SALLY, photographer; b. Lexington, Va., 1951. Student, Putney Sch., 1966-69, Bennington Coll., 1969-71, Praestegaard Film Sch., Denmark, 1971-72, Aegean Sch. Fine Arts, Greece, 1971-72; BA summa cum laude, Hollins Coll., 1974, MA, 1975. guest lectr. Honolulu Acad. Arts, 1989, Women Photog. Conf., 1989, Md. Inst. Art, 1989, Bard Coll., 1989, San Francisco Cameraworks, 1990, Photog.-Retrospect/Prospect Conf., 1990, others; instr. Maine Photog. Workshops, 1985-89, Palm Beach Photog. Workshops, 1987-89, Ctr. Photog. Woodstock, 1988, 90, Internat. Ctr. Photog., N.Y., 1989, Image Found., Honolulu, 1989, Okla. Arts Found., 1989, Friends Photog. Workshops, 1990. One-woman shows include Cleve. Ctr. Contemporary Art, 1990, Edwynn Houk Gallery, Chgo., 1990, 92, Tartt Gallery, Washington, 1990, Md. Art Pl., Balt., 1991, Houk Friedman, N.Y., 1992-94, Mus. Contemporary Photog., Chgo., 1993-94, Mus. Modern Art, N.Y., 1991, Milw. Mus. Art, 1991, Whitney Mus. Am. Art, N.Y., 1991, Met. Mus. Art, N.Y., 1991, Frumpkin Adams Gallery, N.Y., 1994, Elizabeth Leach Gallery, Portland, Oreg., 1994, Bard Coll., Mass., 1994, Wellesley Coll., Mass., 1995; exhibited in group shows Corcoran Gallery Art, Washington, 1977, Va. Mus. Fine Arts, Richmond, 1988, New Orleans Mus. Art, 1990; represented in permanent collections Addison Gallery Am. Art, Andover, Mass., Balt. Mus. Art, Birmingham (Ala.) Mus. Art, Boston Mus. Fine Art, Corcoran Gallery Art, Hirshhorn Mus. and Sculpture Garden, Nat. Mus. Am. Art, Smithsonian Inst., Washington, Met. Mus. Art, N.Y., Mus. Modern Art, N.Y., Whitney Mus. Am. Art, N.Y., San Francisco Mus. Art, Va. Mus. Fine Arts, Richmond, others. Fellow Nat. Endowment Arts, 1982, 88, 92, Guggenheim Found., 1987, Southeastern Ctr. Contemporary Arts, 1989, Artists Visual Arts, 1989. Office: c/o Houk Friedman 851 Madison Ave New York NY 10021

MANN, SAM HENRY, JR., lawyer; b. St. Petersburg, Fla., Aug. 2, 1925; s. Sam Henry and Vivian (Moore) M.; m. Mary Joan Bishop, Sept. 7, 1948; children: Vivian Louise, Sam Henry III, Wallace Bishop. BA, Yale U., 1948; LLB, Fla. U., 1951. Bar: Fla. 1951, U.S. Dist. Ct. (so. dist.) Fla. 1951, U.S. Ct. Appeals 1955, U.S. Supreme Ct. 1971. Ptnr. Greene, Mann, Rowe, Stanton, Mastry & Burton, St. Petersburg, 1951-84, Harris, Barrett, Mann & Dew, St. Petersburg, 1984—. Trustee, v.p. Mus. Fine Arts, St. Petersburg, 1980-94, Eckerd Coll., St. Petersburg, 1976-79, Webb Sch., Bell Buckle, Tenn., 1966-75; bd. dirs. Regional Community Blood Ctr., St. Petersburg, 1966—, Fla. Blood Svcs., 1993-94; mem., chmn. H. Milton Rogers Heart Found.; bd. dirs., pres. Family and Children's Svc., Inc., 1956-61. With USNR, 1943-46. Fellow Am. Coll. Trial Lawyers, Am. Bar Found., Fla. Bar Found.; mem. ABA, Fla. Bar Assn., Am. Counsel Assn., Def. Rsch. Inst., Internat. Assn. Def. Counsel, Phi Alpha Delta. Republican. Presbyterian. Avocations: RV travel, boating, gardening, workshop. Home: 531 Brightwaters Blvd NE Saint Petersburg FL 33704-3713 Office: Harris Barrett Mann & Dew Ste 1500 Southtrust Bank Bldg Saint Petersburg FL 33731-1441

MANN, SEYMOUR ZALMON, political science and public administration educator emeritus, union official; b. Chgo., Mar. 29, 1921; s. Morris and Sarah (Julius) M.; m. Irene Eincig, Aug. 30, 1942; children: Martin R., Sheldon H., Jeanette P. Student, Wright Coll., 1938-40; BE, No. Ill. U. (formerly No., Ill. State Tchr.'s Coll.), 1942; MA, U. Chgo., 1948, PhD, 1951. Instr. polit. sci. Triple Cities Coll., Syracuse U., 1948-51; asst. prof. Harpur Coll., State U. N.Y., 1951-55, asso. prof. polit. sci., 1955-60, chmn. dept., 1953-58; dir. pub. adminstrn. and met. affairs program, prof. govt. So. Ill. U., Edwardsville, 1960-67; chmn., prof. urban affairs dept. urban affairs Hunter Coll./CUNY, 1967-77; dir. Urban Research Center, 1967-68, chmn. dept. urban affairs, 1968-73; dep. to execs. dist. council 37, Am. Fedn. State, County and Mcpl. Employees, AFL-CIO, 1977-79; prof. govt. and public adminstrn., asso. dir. Nat. Center Public Productivity, John Jay Coll. Criminal Justice, CUNY, 1980-86; mem. profl. staff Congress; vis. expert rsch. staff Office Pub. Affairs, High Commr.'s Office, Germany, 1954; cons. Southwestern Ill. Govtl. Study Commn., 1961-62; vis. prof. U. So. Calif. Sch. Pub. Adminstrn., 1967; co-chmn. Ill. U.-State Agy. Coun., 1965-67; chmn. nat. commn. on urban affairs Am. Jewish Congress, 1977-81, mem. nat. governing coun., 1991—; cons., coord. spl. projects dist. coun. 37 Am. Fedn. State, County and Mcpl. Employees, N.Y.C., 1972-77. Author: (with others) From the Wagner Act to the Taft-Hartley Act, 1950, (with Charlotte B. Smart) Land Use and Planning in the Cleveland Metropolitan Area, 1959, (with R.R. Boyce) Urbanism in Illinois: Its Nature Importance and Problems, 1965, Chicago's War on poverty, 1966; contbr. to: Cases in State and Local Government, 1961, Cases in American National Government and Politics, 1978, The Politics of Productivity: State and Local Focus, 1980, Labor Management Cooperation and Worker Participation: A Public Sector Focus, 1989, play Summing Up in Public Voices, 1993; mem. editl. bd. Public Productivity and Management Rev., Pub. Voices. Served with AUS, 1943-45, ETO. Fellow Social Sci. Research Council, 1949-50; Fulbright prof. W. Germany, 1953-54; Fulbright prof. Tel Aviv (Israel) U., 1974-75. Mem. Am. Polit. Sci. Assn., Am. Soc. for Pub. Adminstrn. (pres. St. Louis met. chpt. 1964-65), Am. Arbitration Assn. (nat. labor panel), Soc. of Children's Book Writers and Illustrators, Poetry Soc. Va. Home and Office: 203 S Yoakum Pky Apt 1111 Alexandria VA 22304-3731 *It will have to be left to others to judge what success I may have obtained. There have, however, been some guiding principles which seemed to have given direction to my life's course and undoubtedly impacted on whatever professional recognition has come my way. These include: a profound respect for democratic ideology—particularly the notion that each person should have the opportunity to achieve his/her fullest potential; a clear recognition that wisdom and knowledge are not the same; and that listening is harder than talking, though it is the most important element in human communication.*

MANN, SUSAN, university president; b. Ottawa, Ont., Can., Feb. 10, 1941; d. Walter (dec.) and Marjorie Mann; m. Nicholas Trofimenkoff; 1 child, Britt. BA in Modern History, U. Toronto, 1963; MA in History, U. Western Ont., 1965; PhD, U. Laval, Que., Can., 1970; LLD (hon.), Concordia U., Montreal, Que, Can., 1989, U. Ottawa, 1994. Lectr. English Toyo Eiwa Jogakuin, Tokyo, 1963-64; lectr. in history U. Montreal, 1966-70; asst. prof. history U. Calgary, Alta., Can., 1970-72; from asst. to assoc. prof. U. Ottawa, Ont., Can., 1972-83, prof. history, 1983—, chmn. dept. history, 1977-80, vice rector acad., 1984-90; pres. York U., Toronto, Ont., 1992—; mem. stamp adv. com. Can. Post Corp., Ottawa, 1988-92; chmn. adv. bd. Nat. Archives Can., 1989-91. Author: (as Susan Mann Trofimenkoff) Action Française: French Canadian Nationalism in the 1920s, 1975, Stanley Knowles: The Man From Winnipeg North Centre, 1982, Dream of Nation: A Social and Intellectual History of Quebec, 1983 (Sec. of State Canadian Studies prize 1984), Visions nationales: Une histoire du Québec, 1986; editor: The Twenties in Western Canada, 1972, Abbé Groulx: Variations on a Nationalist Theme, 1973, (with Alison Prentice) The Neglected Majority: Essays in Canadian Women's History, vol. I, 1977, vol II, 1985; acad. editor Social Scis. in Can., 1974-76; assoc. editor Social History, 1982-84; contbr. articles to profl. jours. Assessor of projects SSHRCC, 1972—; chmn., aid to scholarly publs. com. Social Sci. Fedn. Can., 1976-79; mem. appraisals com. Ont. Coun. Grad. Studies, 1983-84; pres. Can. Hist. Assn., 1984-85; chair status of women com. Coun. Ont. Univs., 1985-88; mem. Summer Inst. Women in Higher Edn. Adminstrn. Bryn Mawr (Pa.) Coll., 1986; co-founder Sr. Women Acad. Adminstrs. Can. Publ. grantee SSHRCC, 1975, Leave fellow, 1980-81, Doctoral fellow Can. Coun., 1968-70; U. Toronto scholar, 1959-61, U. Western Ont. scholar, 1964. Fellow Royal Soc. Can., Canadian Rsch. Inst. Advancement Women (hon., life, founder, bd. dirs. 1976-78). Office: York Univ Office of Pres, 4700 Keele St, North York, ON Canada M3J 1P3

MANN, TED, screenwriter. Screenwriter VT series Bionic Showdown: The Six-Million Dollar Man and the Bionic Woman, 1989, Miami Vice, 1989, Civil Wars, 1991-92; prodr. N.Y.P.D. Blue (Emmy award for outstanding drama series 1995). Office: Warder White & Kane Inc 8444 Wilshire Blvd 4th Fl Beverly Hills CA 90211

MANN, THEODORE, theatrical producer and artistic director; b. N.Y.C., May 13, 1924; s. Martin M. and Gwen (Artson) Goldman; m. Patricia A. Brooks, Oct. 5, 1953; children: Andrew, Jonathan. Asso. B.A., Salinas (Calif.) Jr. Coll., 1945; LL.B., Bklyn. Law Sch., 1949. Co-founder, co-prodr., co-artistic dir. Circle in the Square Theatre, N.Y.C., 1951—; co-founder Circle in the Sq. Theatre Sch., 1961. Co-prodr.: Long Day's Journey into Night, 1956 (Tony award best prodn. of yr. 1956-57, Pulitzer prize, N.Y. Drama Critics award); prodr.: Carnegie Hall Concert Series, 1955-69; co-founder: Washington Sq. Park Concert Series, 1955; dir.: A Moon for the Misbegotten, Ah Wilderness!, Mourning Becomes Electra, Trumpets of the Lord, Morning, Noon and Night, Arsenic and Old Lace, John and Abigail, The Iceman Cometh, Where's Charley?, The Glass Menagerie, Pal Joey, Romeo and Juliet, Awake and Sing, Seven Days of Mourning, The Last Analysis, F. Jasmine Addams, An American Millionaire, Past Tense, The Boys in Autumn, The Night of the Iguana, Anna Karenina, (mus. and opera) The Small Jewel Box; prodr.-dir.: Ford's Theatre, Washington, 1968—; host: radio show Conversations with Circle in the Square Sta., WNYC, 1978; author: Producers on Producing, 1975. Served with USAAF, 1943-45. Recipient Vernon Rice award, 1956, Page One award Newspaper Guild, 1960, Tony spl. award, 1976, Tony award nomination for best revival, 1995. Office: Circle in the Sq Theatre 1633 Broadway New York NY 10019-6708

MANN, THEODORE R., lawyer; b. Kosica, Czechoslovakia, Jan. 31, 1928; came to U.S., 1929, naturalized, 1930; s. Aaron and Bertha (Schreiber) M.; m. Rowena Joan Weiss, 1954; children: Julie Ellen, Rachel Beth, Marcus Eliyahu. Pvt. practice Phila., 1953—; ptnr. Mann, Ungar, Spector & Lebovitz; advocate in civil liberties, anti-trust and securities fraud cases. Chmn., pres. Nat. Jewish Community Rels. Adv. Coun., 1976-80; Conf. Pres. Major Am. Jewish Orgns., 1978-80; Nat. Conf. Soviet Jewry, 1981-83; Am. Jewish Congress, 1984-88; Mazon-A Jewish Response to Hunger, 1985-90; co-chair Project Nishma, 1988—; trustee New Israel Fund, Jewish Fund for Christian Rescuers. Fellow Temple U. Alumni. Office: 1709 Spruce St Philadelphia PA 19103-6103

MANN, THOMAS EDWARD, political scientist; b. Milw., Sept. 10, 1944; s. Edward Emil and Eleanor (Hoffman) M.; m. Sheilah Rosenhack, June 4, 1976; children: Edward Matthew, Stephanie Rachael. B.A., U. Fla., 1966; M.A., U. Mich., 1968, Ph.D., 1977. Staff assoc. Am. Polit. Sci. Assn., Washington, 1970-76, asst. dir., 1977-81, exec. dir., 1981-87; co-dir. congress project Am. Enterprise Inst., Washington, 1979-81; dir. govtl. studies Brookings Instn., 1987—, W. Averell Harrimann sr. fellow in Am. governance, 1991—; mem. bd. overseers Nat. Election Study, 1987-94, chmn., 1990-94. Author: Unsafe At Any Margin, 1978; co-author: Vital Statistics on Congress, 1980, 82, 84-85, 87-88, 89-90, 91-92, 93-94, 95-96; Renewing Congress, 1992, 93; co-editor: The New Congress, 1981, The American Elections of 1982, 1983, Media Polls in American Politics, 1992, Values and Public Policy, 1994, Elections at Home and Abroad, 1994, Congress, the Press, and the Public, 1994, Intensive Care: How Congress Shapes Health Policy, 1995; editor: A Question of Balance: The President, The Congress and Foreign Policy, 1990. Mem. Democratic Nat. Com.'s Commn. on Presdl. Nomination and Party Structure, 1975-78; mem. tech. com. Dem. Nat. Com. Commn. on Presdl. Nominations, 1981-82, The Fairness Commn., 1985. U. Mich. NDEA grad. fellow, 1966-69; Am. Polit. Sci. Assn. Congl. fellow, 1969-70. Fellow Am. Acad. Arts and Scis., Nat. Acad. Pub. Adminstrn.; mem. Coun. on Fgn. Rels., Phi Beta Kappa. Home: 6508 Goldleaf Dr Bethesda MD 20817-5837 Office: Brookings Instn 1775 Massachusetts Ave NW Washington DC 20036-2188

MANN, TIMOTHY, corporate executive; b. Hackensack, N.J., July 24, 1942; s. Conklin and Hermione (Hatch) M.; m. Rosemary Teresa Connell, Feb. 26, 1965 (div. July 1993); children: Timothy, Sean Douglas, Patrick Devlin; m. Margaret Ann Tyrie, Nov. 20, 1993. Student U. Colo., 1960-61, Monmouth Coll., 1961-65, BS, 1965; postgrad. U. North Fla., 1980. Product mgr. Am. Brands, Inc., N.Y.C., 1965-70; account supr. Cargill Wilson & Acree, Inc., Richmond, Va., 1970-74; sr. mktg. mgr. Liggett & Myers Tobacco Co., Durham, N.C., 1974-78; sr. v.p. mktg. and sales Swisher Internat., Inc., Jacksonville, Fla., 1978-86, pres., 1986—, mem. mgmt. com., 1978—; pres., CEO export divsn. Swisher Internat., Inc., 1990—. Bd. dirs. Jr. Achievement of Jacksonville, Jacksonville Pvt. Industry Coun.; active Jacksonville Community Coun., Inc., 1980-87, N.E. Fla. Coun. Boy Scouts Am. Recipient N.J. Mortgage Bankers award, 1965. Mem. Cigar Assn. Am. (dir., v.p.), Am. Wholesale Marketers Assn., Tobacco Mchts. Assn. (bd. dirs.), Am. Mgmt. Assn., River Club. Office: Swisher Internat Inc PO Box 2230 Jacksonville FL 32203-2230

MANN, TRUE SANDLIN, psychologist, consultant; b. Longview, Tex., Aug. 4, 1934; d. Bob Murphy and Stella True (Williams) Sandlin; m. Jack Matthewson Mann, Sept. 4, 1954 (div. Dec. 1989); children: Jack Matthewson Jr., Bob Sandlin, Daniel Williams, Nathaniel Currier. BS, Stephen F. Austin State U., Nacogdoches, Tex., 1973, MA, 1977; PhD, East Tex. State U., 1982. Lic. psychologist, Tex., Ark. Instr. Stephen F. Austin State U., 1975-76, vis. asst. prof. psychology, 1986-87; instr. East Tex. State U., Commerce, 1980-81; postdoctoral fellow Southwestern Med. Sch., Dallas, 1982-83; pvt. practice, Longview, Tex., 1983-92; psychologist dept. family practice U. Tex. Health Sci. Ctr., Tyler, 1990-92; dir. psychol. svcs. St. Michael's Hosp., Texarkana, Tex., 1992-93; cons. psychologist, Longview, 1993—; weekly newspaper columnist HARBUS, Cambridge Mass., 1959-60; cons. Made-Rite Co., Longview, 1989—. Mem. candidate com. Assoc. Reps. Tex., Austin, 1990—; bd. dirs. Mental Health Assn. Tex., 1977-82, 84-92, Longview Symphony, 1995, Longview Mus. of Art, 1995; mem. Leadership Tex., 1988—. Mem. APA, Tex. Psychol. Assn. Episcopalian. Avocations: photography, travel, history of civilizations. Home: 1309 Inverness St Longview TX 75601-3548 Office: 1203 Montclair St Longview TX 75601-3565

MANN, WESLEY F., newspaper editor. Editor Investor's Business Daily, L.A. Office: Investor's Business Daily 1941 Armacost Ave Los Angeles CA 90025-5210

MANNE, HENRY GIRARD, lawyer, educator; b. New Orleans, May 10, 1928; s. Geoffrey and Eva (Shainberg) M.; m. Bobbette Lee Taxer, Aug. 19, 1968; children: Emily Kay, Geoffrey Adam. B.A., Vanderbilt U., 1950; J.D., U. Chgo., 1952; LL.M., Yale U., 1953, J.S.D., 1966; LLD, U. Puget Sound, 1987, U. Francisco Marroquin, Guatemala, 1987. Bar: Ill. 1952, N.Y. 1969. Practice in Chgo., 1953-54; asso. prof. Law Sch., St. Louis U., 1956-57, 59-62; prof. Law Sch., George Washington U., 1962-68; Kenan prof. law and polit. sci. U. Rochester, 1968-74; Disting. prof. law, dir. Law and Econs. Center, U. Miami Law Sch., 1974-80; prof. law and Econs. Center, Emory U., Atlanta, 1980-86; dean, univ. prof., chmn. Law and Econs. Ctr. George Mason U. Sch. Law, 1986—; vis. prof. law U. Wis., Madison, 1957-59, Stanford (Calif.) Law Sch., 1971-72; dir. Econs. Insts. Fed. Judges, 1976-89. Author: Insider Trading and the Stock Market, 1966, (with H. Wallich) The Modern Corporation and Social Responsibility, 1973, (with E. Solomon) Wall Street in Transition, 1974, Med. Malpractice Guidebook: Law and Economics, 1985; editor: (with Roger LeRoy Miller) Gold, Money and the Law, 1975; editor: (with Roger LeRoy Miller) Auto Safety Regulation: The Cure or the Problem, 1976, Economic Policy and the Regulation of Corporate Securities, 1968, The Economics of Legal Relationships, 1975; editor: (with James Dorn) Econ. Liberties and the Judiciary, 1987. Served to 1st lt. USAF, 1954-56. Recipient Salvatori award Excellence in Acad. Leadership, 1994; named Cultural Laureate of Va., 1992. Fellow Am. Bar Found.; mem. Am. Law Inst., Am. Econs. Assn., Am. Law and Econs. Assn. (hon. life, Salvatori award for excellence in acad. leadership 1994), Mont Pelerin Soc., Order of Coif, Phi Beta Kappa.

MANNERING, JERRY VINCENT, agronomist, educator; b. Custer, Okla., June 14, 1929; s. James Bryan and Verta (Bates) M.; m. Marjorye McVicker, June 20, 1953; children: Debra Lynn Mannering Zerman, Stephen Scott, Lisa Gaye Mannering Schwingendorf. B.S., Okla. State U., 1951; M.S., Purdue U., 1956, Ph.D., 1967. Cert. profl. soil scientist, profl. soil erosion and sediment control specialist. Grad. asst. Purdue U., West Lafayette, Ind., 1954-56, extension agronomist, prof. agronomy, 1967-89; prof. emeritus, 1990—; research agronomist U. Idaho, Aberdeen, 1956-58; research soil scientist Agrl. Research Sta., USDA, West Lafayette, 1958-67; cons. FAO, Bulgaria, 1972, Govt. of Brazil, 1975. Contbr. numerous articles on agronomy to profl. jours. Served to 1st lt. U.S. Army, 1951-54. Decorated Purple Heart; recipient Hovde award Purdue U. and Ind. Farm Bur., 1982. Fellow Soil Conservation Soc. Am., Soil Sci. Soc. Am., Am. Soc. Agronomy; mem. Internat. Soil Sci. Soc., Internat. Soil Tillage Research Orgn., Lions Club. Office: Purdue Univ Dept Agronomy West Lafayette IN 47907

MANNERS, GEORGE EMANUEL, business educator, emeritus dean; b. N.Y.C., Nov. 26, 1910; s. John Emanuel and Demetra (Kremida) M.; m. Claire Gibson, Oct. 14, 1939; children—George Emanuel, Susan Demetra. B.S. in Commerce, Ga. State U., 1935; M.B.A. in Econs, U. Ga., 1946; Ph.D. in History, Emory U., 1959. Bookkeeper and acct. Ga., 1927-37; pub. acct., 1937; high sch. tchr. Atlanta, 1937-39, 41-42, 46-47; test technician merit system Ga. Labor Dept., 1939-41; mem. faculty Ga. State U. (and predecessor), 1947—; dean Sch. Bus. Adminstrn. Ga. State U., 1950-69, asst. v.p., 1969-70, assoc. v.p., 1970—, Regents' prof., 1971—, dean emeritus, 1977—; dean Sch. Mgmt., Rensselaer Poly. Inst., Troy, N.Y., 1979-80; dir. Univ. Ctr. in Ga., Inc., 1980-83; dean protem, Sch. Bus. and Econs. Mercer U. Atlanta, 1986-87; Mem. Met. Planning Commn., Atlanta, 1949-59, Atlanta Regional Export Expansion Council. Also author: History of Life Insurance Company in Georgia, 1891-1955, 1959, also articles. Served to maj. AUS, 1942-46. Mem. So. Econ. Assn., So. Hist. Assn., Atlanta C. of C., Hellenic Study Group, Delta Sigma Pi, Beta Gamma Sigma. Methodist (Sunday sch. tchr.). Club: Kiwanian. Home: 338 Nelson Ferry Rd Decatur

GA 30030-2320 Office: 33 Gilmer St SE Atlanta GA 30303-3044 *I have noted that a life devoted to a sound ideal, pursued steadily with character and tolerance, brings the keenest and most lasting happiness. Others feel the fire and assist on the way; impediments become adventures. Challenge and zest accompany one each day; horizons widen. This spirit can be applied by all, in every walk of life, in every field of endeavor, in every land, at all times in history.*

MANNERS, ROBERT ALAN, anthropologist; b. N.Y.C., Aug. 21, 1913; m. Margaret D. Hall, July 6, 1943 (div. July 1955); children: Karen Elizabeth, John Hall; m. Jean I. Hall, Sept. 12, 1955; children: Stephen David, Katherine Dora. B.S., Columbia U., 1935, M.A., 1939, Ph.D., 1950. Instr. U. Rochester, 1950-52; lectr., asst. prof., asso. prof., prof. Brandeis U., Waltham, Mass., 1952—; Ralph Levitz prof. anthropology Brandeis U., 1973-80, Ralph Levitz prof. emeritus, 1980—, chmn. dept. anthropology, 1963-68, 78-79; vis. prof. Columbia U., summer 1956, Harvard U., summer 1967, Ibero-Am. U., Mexico, 1969-70; mem. social sci. subcom. NIH, 1965-69; Bd. dirs. Research Inst. For Study Man. Co-author: People of Puerto Rico, 1956; editor: (with James Duffy) Africa Speaks, 1961, Process and Pattern in Culture, 1964, The Kipsigis of Kenya, 1967, (with David Kaplan) Theory in Anthropology: A Sourcebook, 1968 and Culture Theory, 1972, Southern Paiute and Chemehuevi: An Ethnohistorical Report, 1974, An Ethnological Report on the Hualapai Indians of Arizona, 1975, Havasupai Indians: An Ethnohistorical Report, 1975; editor-in-chief Am. Anthropologist, 1974-76; contbr. articles to jours. Served to capt. AUS, 1942-46. Fellow Am. Anthrop. Assn.; mem. N.E. Anthrop. Assn. (pres. 1978-79). Home: 134 Sumner St Newton MA 02159-1957

MANNES, ELENA SABIN, film and television producer, director; b. N.Y.C., Dec. 3, 1943; d. Leopold Damrosch and Evelyn (Sabin) M. BA, Smith Coll., 1965; MA, Johns Hopkins U., 1967. Researcher Pub. Broadcast Lab. Nat. Ednl. TV, N.Y.C., 1968-70; writer Sta. WPIX-TV, N.Y.C., 1970-73; assignment editor Sta. ABC-TV, N.Y.C., 1973-76; producer, writer Sta. WCBS-TV, N.Y.C., 1976-80; producer CBS News, N.Y.C., 1980-87, Pub. Affairs TV/Bill Moyers PBS Documentaries, N.Y.C., 1987-90; ind. documentary dir. and producer, 1987—. Recipient Emmy award NATAS, 1984, 85, 87, 90, 94, 96, Peabody award, 1985, Cine Golden Eagle award, 1988, 90, 93, 94, 95, Robert F. Kennedy journalism award, 1989, DGA awards, 1987, 90. Mem. Writers Guild Am., Dirs. Guild Am., Am. Film Inst. (dir. Workshop for Women). Avocations: tennis, still photography.

MANNICK, JOHN ANTHONY, surgeon; b. Deadwood, S.D., Mar. 24, 1928; s. Alfred and Catherine Elizabeth (Schuster) M.; m. Alice Virginia Gossard, June 9, 1952; children—Catherine Virginia, Elizabeth Eleanor, Joan Barbara. BA, Harvard U., 1949, MD, 1953. Diplomate: Am. Bd. Surgery (dir. 1971-77). Intern Mass. Gen. Hosp., 1953-54, resident in surgery, 1956-60; instr. in surgery to asst. prof. Med. Coll. Va., 1960-64; asso. prof. to prof. surgery Boston U., 1964-76, chmn. div. surgery, 1973-76; Moseley prof. surgery Harvard U., 1976-94, Moseley Disting. prof. surgery, 1994—; dir. ednl. programs Harvard Med. Internat., 1994—; chmn. dept. surgery Peter Bent Brigham Hosp. and Brigham and Women's Hosp., Boston, 1976-94; dir. ednl. programs Harvard Med. Internat., 1994—; mem. surgery, anesthesiology and trauma study sect. NIH, 1978-82, mem. medicine study sect., 1967-70; rsch. com. Med. Found., Inc., 1970-76. Author: (with others) Modern Surgery, 1970, Core Textbook of Surgery, 1972, Surgery of Ischemic Limbs, 1972, The Cause and Management of Aneurysms, 1990; mem. editorial bd. AMA Archives of Surgery, 1973-84, Clin. Immunology and Immunopathology, 1972-84, Surgery, 1982—, Brit. Jour. Surgery, 1982-92, European Jour. Vascular Surgery, 1988—; mem. editorial bd. Advances in Surgery, 1979—, editor, 1984-86; mem. editorial bd. Jour. Vascular Surgery, 1984—, assoc. editor, 1990—; also articles. Served to capt. M.C. USAF, 1954-56. Markle scholar in acad. medicine, 1961-66. Fellow ACS (gov.), Royal Coll. Surgeons (hon., Eng.), Royal Coll. Surgeons (hon., Edinburgh); mem. Am. Fedn. Clin. Rsch., Am. Assn. Immunologists, Am. Soc. Exptl. Pathology, Soc. Clin. Investigation, Soc. Clin. Surgery, Soc. Univ. Surgeons, Soc. Surg. Chmn. (sec. 1985-87, pres. 1987-88), Am. Surg. Assn. (pres. 1989-90), Internat. Cardiovascular Soc. (recorder N.Am. chpt., 1973-76, pres. 1991-92, v.p. 1993), Soc. Vascular Surgery (pres. 1981), N.E. Surg. Soc., New Eng. Soc. Vascular Surgery (pres. 1994-95), So. Surg. Assn., So. Soc. Vascular Surgery, Surg. Infection Soc., Halstead Soc., Phi Beta Kappa. Home: 81 Bogle St Weston MA 02193-1056 Office: 75 Francis St Boston MA 02115-6110

MANNIELLO, JOHN BAPTISTE LOUIS, research scientist; b. N.Y.C., Oct. 31, 1923; s. George and Susan Manniello; m. Rosa Ann Gulotta; children: George, John, Stephen. B of Mech. Engring., Poly. Inst. N.Y., 1953; cert. with honors, Indsl. Coll. Armed Forces, 1962; DSc (hon.), N.Y. Inst. Tech., 1989, DMS, 1991. Engring. exec. Fairchild Camera, N.Y.C., 1946-60; dir. labs. div. CBS, Stamford, Conn., 1960-73, v.p. govt. ops. labs. div., 1973-77; diplomat State Dept., Rome, 1977-78; chief Am. scientist NATO Labs., 1978-79; with Office of Chmn. Western Union, Mahwah, N.J., 1978-79; v.p. N.Y. Inst. Tech., N.Y.C., 1979-91; exec. v.p. Artificial Intelligence Techs., Inc., N.Y.C., 1991-94; mem. adv. bd. CUNY, 1968-70; advisor to pres. Staten Island (N.Y.) C.C., 1970-72; permanent chair Inst. Mech. Studies, Trieste, Italy, 1975—; vis. prof. Med. Coll., U. Rome, 1977—, Hahnemann Med. Ctr., 1967—, U. Naples; pres., chief exec. officer San Marino (Italy) Telecom., 1958-59; instr. physics and engring. Hofstra U.; mem. governing bd. Clinica Moscati, Rome; apptd. mem. Commn. on Application Am. Sci. and Tech. to improvement of Italian med. care delivery, sci. advisor Nat. Rsch. Coun., Pres. of Italy; chmn. various confs., symposiums and workshops; active Office Navy Intelligence Adv. Com., 1991—, Def. Intelligence Agy. Adv. Com., 1990-91; sci. advisor Vatican, 1994; with info. sci. divsn. Argonne Nat. Labs. Author: Marketing Research and Developmentt for the Government, vols. 1 and 2, 1972, The NATO Market, 1978, (autobiography) A Life, 1993; mem. adv. panel Electronics Mag., contbr. to books, papers and publs. Chmn. N.Y. Civic Assn., 1962-63; co-chmn. Cerebral Palsy Assn., N.Y., 1965-66; counselor Eagle Scouts; mem. VITA; founder Arnaldo Marie Angelini Scholarship Fund, John Manniello Scholarship Fund; sponsor Lennard Perroots Intelligence Rsch. fellowship, William Doyle Internat. Rels. award; bd. dirs. Office Teleport. With USAAF, 1942-46, ETO, prisoner of war. Decorated Purple Heart with three oak leaf clusters, Air medal with three oak leaf clusters, DFC, Ordine Merito, Republic of Italy, 1977, comdr. and knight Cavaliere di Gran Croce-Etoile de la Paix, Order of St. John; recipient Presdl. Service award, ECO Gold Medal award. Mem. Am. Astron. Soc. (sr.), Soc. Photo-Optical Instrumentation Engrs., Soc. Photographic Scientists and Engrs., Am. Soc. Photogrammetry, Soc. for Info. Display, Am. Mgmt. Soc., Mus. Holography (bd. dirs.), N.Y. Acad. Scis., Internat. Innovation Group, Exec. Service Corps, Pan Am. Med. Assn., Acad. Incammenatti, Acad. Gentium Pro Pace, Marconi Inst. (mem. telecommunications commn.), Tau Beta Pi, Pi Tau Sigma, Sigma Alpha. Republican. Roman Catholic. Clubs: Army and Navy (Washington), Caterpillar (N.J.), Pres.'s (N.Y.), Goldfish. Achievements include implementation of ultrasound for medical diagnosis, compass link system for transmission and reception of hi-resolution photography between Vietnam and the U.S., color TV on the moon, pioneer wireless TV, videoconferencing. Home: 9 Island Ave Unit 801 Miami FL 33139

MANNING, BLANCHE M., federal judge; b. 1934. BEd, Chgo. Tchrs. Coll., 1961; JD, John Marshall Law Sch., 1967; MA, Roosevelt Univ., 1972; LLM, Univ. of Va. Law Sch., 1992. Asst. states atty. State's Atty.'s Office (no. dist.), Ill., 1968-73; supervisory trial atty. U.S. EEOC, Chgo., 1973-77; gen. atty. United Airlines, Chgo., 1977-78; asst. U.S. atty. U.S. Dist. Ct. (no. dist.) Ill., 1978-79; assoc. judge Cir. Ct. of Cook County, 1979-86, circuit judge, 1986-87; appellate court judge Ct. of Review Ill. Appellate Ct., 1987-94; district judge U.S. Dist. Ct. (no. dist.) Ill., Chgo., 1994—; tchr. A. O. Sexton Elem. Sch. James Wadsworth Elem. Sch., Wendell Phillips H.S. Adult Program, Morgan Park H.S. Summer Sch. Program, South Shore H.S. Summer Sch. Program, Carver H.S. Adult Edn. Program; lectr. Malcolm X C.C., 1970-71; adj. prof. NCBL C.C. of Law, 1978-79, DePaul Univ. Law Sch., 1992-94; tchg. team mem. Trial Advocacy Workshop, Harvard Law Sch., U. Chgo. Law Sch., 1991-94; chmn. Com. on Recent Devels. in Evidence, Ill. Judicial Conf., 1991; faculty mem. New Judges Seminar, Ill. Judicial Conf.; past faculty mem. Profl. Devel. Seminar for New Assoc. Judges, Cook County Cir. Ct.; mem. bd. dirs., trained intervenor Lawyers' Assistance Program, Inc.; mem. adv. coun. Lawyer's Asst. Program, Roosevelt U. Trustee Sherwood Music Conservatory Bd. Mem. Cook County Bar Assn. (second v-p 1974), Nat. Bar Assn., Nat. Judicial Coun., Ill. Judicial Coun. (treas. 1982-85, chmn. 1988, chmn. judiciary com. 1992), Ill. Judges Assn., Women's Bar Assn. of Ill., Nat. Assn. of Women Lawyers, Ill. State Bar Assn. (bd. dirs. Lawyers Assistance Program Inc.), Am. Bar Assn. (fellow 1991), Chgo. Bar Assn. (bd. dirs. Lawyers Assistance Program Inc.), Nat. Assn. of Women Judges, Appellate Lawyers Assn. (hon.); John Marshall Law Sch. Alumni Assn. (bd. dirs.), Chgo. State Univ. Alumni Assn. (bd. dirs.). Office: US Dist Ct 2156 US Courthouse 219 S Dearborn St Chicago IL 60604-1706

MANNING, BRENT V., lawyer; b. Preston, Idaho, Jan. 18, 1950; s. Leon W. and Gwen (Briscoe) M.; m. J. Christine Coffin, Oct. 25, 1969; children: Justin, Britten, John. BA, Idaho State U., 1972; JD, Harvard U., 1975. Bar: Colo. 1975, Utah 1981, U.S. Ct. Appeals (10th cir.) 1978. Assoc. Holme Roberts & Owen, Denver, 1975-80, ptnr., 1980—; ptnr. Holme Roberts & Owen, Salt Lake City, 1981—; cooperating atty. ACLU, Denver, 1979-81, Salt Lake City, 1987-91; mem. panel mediators and arbitrators U.S. Dist. Ct. Utah, 1993—; mediation & settlement judge pro tempore 3rd Jud. Dist. State of Utah, 1996—. Trustee Bountiful (Utah) Davis Art Found., 1985-91, Utah Tibetan Resettlement Project. Mem. ABA, Utah Bar Assn. (chmn. continuing legal edn. com. 1988, mem. disciplinary com. 1991-93, cts. and judges com. 1993—), Am. Inns of Ct. (master of bench 1988—), Sierra Club, Am. Alpine Club (N.Y.C.). Democrat. Avocations: climbing, bicycling, running. Home: 2079 Maple Grove Way Bountiful UT 84010-1005 Office: Holme Roberts & Owen 111 E Broadway Ste 1100 Salt Lake City UT 84111-5233

MANNING, BURT, advertising executive; b. 1931. Chmn., chief exec. officer J. Walter Thompson Co., Worldwide, N.Y.C., 1987—. Bd. dirs. nat. Assn. for Depressive Illness, Nat. Players Co., Advt. Edn. Found.; trustee Neuroscis. Inst., New Sch. for Social Rsch. Mem. Lotus Club. Office: J Walter Thompson Co 466 Lexington Ave New York NY 10017-3140*

MANNING, CHARLES TERRILL, retired lawyer; b. Empress, Alta., Can., Mar. 27, 1925; s. N. Folsom and Mary E. (Terrill) M.; m. H. Joyce Johnson, 1946; children—A. Terrill, Timothy F., Heather J., Annabelle H. B.A., Bishop's U., 1946; B.C.L., McGill U., 1949. Bar: Que. Ptnr. Hackett-Mulvena-Hackett, Montreal, Que., Can., 1946-56; gen. counsel, v.p. Brit. Newfoundland Corp., Montreal, Que., Can., 1956-69; v.p., sec., chief legal officer Royal Trust, Montreal and Toronto, Can., 1970-85; counsel McMaster Meighen, Montreal, Que., Can., 1985-90; assoc. Meighen Demers, Toronto, Ont., Can., 1991-94; ret., 1994. Served with Royal Can. Navy, 1944-45. Named to Queen's Counsel, Minister of Justice, Que., Can., 1968. Mem. Can. Bar Assn., Que. Bar Assn. Anglican. Home: 1000 King St W 703, Kingston, ON Canada K7M 8H3

MANNING, DANIEL RICARDO, professional basketball player; b. Hattiesburg, Miss., May 17, 1966; s. Ed Manning. Student, U. Kans. Basketball player L.A. Clippers, 1988-94, Atlanta Hawks, 1994, Phoenix Suns, 1994—. Recipient Bronze medal U.S. Olympic Basketball Team, 1988; named Most Outstanding Player NCAA Divsn. I Tournament, 1988, Naismith award, 1988, Wooden award, 1988; named to Sporting News NCAA All-Am. first team, 1987, 88, NBA All-Star Team, 1993-94. First pick overall NCAA draft, 1988; mem. NCAA Divsn. I Championship team, 1988. Office: Phoenix Suns 201 E Jefferson St Phoenix AZ 85004-2412*

MANNING, DAVID LEE, health care executive; b. Birmingham, Ala., Jan. 30, 1950; s. William L. and Lula L. (Lively) M.; m. Donna H. Holley, Dec. 29, 1972; children: Emily Anne, Laura Elizabeth. BA, U. Ala., Tuscaloosa, 1973, MPA, 1974. Budget analyst State of Tenn., Nashville, 1974-79, asst. state treas., 1979-87, commr. fin. and adminstrn., 1987-95; v.p. Columbia/HCA Healthcare Corp., 1995—. So. Regional Tng. Program in Pub. Adminstrn. fellow, 1973. Democrat. Baptist. Office: Columbia/HCA Healthcare Corp One Park Plz PO Box 550 Nashville TN 37202-0550

MANNING, ERIC, computer science and engineering educator, university dean, researcher; b. Windsor, Ont., Can., Aug. 4, 1940; g. George Gorman and Eleanor Katherine (Koehler) M.; m. Betty Goldring, Sept. 16, 1961; children: David, Paula. BSc, U. Waterloo, Ont., 1961, MSc, 1962; PhD, U. Ill., 1965. Registered profl. engr., B.C. Various positions MIT and Bell Telephone Labs., 1965-68; prof. computer sci. U. Waterloo, 1968-86, founding dir. computer comms. networks group, 1973-82; founding dir. Inst. for Computer Rsch., 1982-86; prof., dean engring. U. Victoria, B.C., Can., 1986-92, prof. computer sci., elec. engring., 1993—; dir. Natural Sci. and Engring. Rsch. Coun. Can., mem. exec. com., chair strategic grants com., 1982-87; dir. Comms. Rsch. Centre, Govt. of Can., 1995—; trustee B.C. Advanced Sys. Found., 1986-93; dir. Sci. Coun. B.C., 1988-91; bd. dirs. Can. Microelectric Corp.; mem. adv. com. on artificial intelligence NRC, 1987-91; IBM chair computer sci. Keio U., Yokohama, 1992-93; hon. prof. South East U., Nanjing, People's Republic of China. Author: Fault Diagnosis of Digital Systems, 1970; also numerous articles. V.p. Greater Victoria Concert Band, 1995-96. Fellow IEEE, Engring. Inst. Can.; mem. Assn. Profl. Engrs. B.C., Soc. for Computer Simulation, Can. Inst. for Advanced Rsch. (adv. com. on artificial intelligence and robotics 1986), Can. Assn. for Computer Sci. (pres. 1994—), Can. Soc. for Fifth Generation Rsch. (trustee 1987-88), B.C. Microelectronics Soc. (bd. dirs. 1986-87). Avocations: squash, scuba diving, sailing, flying, music. Home: 2909 Phyllis St, Victoria, BC Canada V8N 1Y8 Office: U Victoria Faculty Engring, PO Box 3055, Victoria, BC Canada V8W 3P6

MANNING, FARLEY, investment company executive; b. Shelburne, Mass., Oct. 30, 1909; s. John Farley and Bessie (Learmont) M.; m. Ruth Fulton Koegel, 1932 (div. 1968); 1 child, Toni Ruth; m. Jean Yeager, Nov. 17, 1982. Student Northeastern U., 1927-29, Boston U., 1929-31. Reporter, editor various newspapers, New Eng., 1931-42; acct. exec. Dudley Anderson Yutzy, N.Y.C., 1946-54; pres., chmn. Manning Selvage & Lee, N.Y.C., 1954-79; chmn. G. & M. Creative Svcs., 1958-81; treas. Cascade Olympic Corp., Olympia, Wash., 1982—; dir. Cascade Olympic Corp., Capital Cascade Inc., Capitol Ctr. Inc. Contbr. articles on dog care and tng. to nat. mags. Maj. USAF, 1943-46. Mem. Pub. Rels. Soc. Am., Olympia Yacht Club, N.Y. Yacht Club, Beaverkill Fly Fishers Club, Overseas Press Club, Thunderbird Country Club, Comm. 25 Club, Rotary. Home and Office: 5510 Cooper Point Rd NW Olympia WA 98502-3646

MANNING, FREDERICK JAMES, insurance company executive; b. Chgo., Oct. 20, 1947; s. Herbert and June Betty (Cohen) M.; m. Gail Hilary Phillips, Feb. 9, 1980; children: Elizabeth Sarah, David Charles. BS, U. Pa., 1969; JD, Harvard U., 1972. Treas. The Marmon Group, Inc., Chgo., 1973-77; chmn. bd. dirs., chief exec. officer Celtic Life Ins. Co., Chgo., 1978—; also chmn. bd. dirs., pres., chief exec. officer Celtic Group, Inc., Chgo.; bd. dirs. Engineered ControlsInternat., Inc. Trustee, chmn. bd. trustees Michael Reese Health Trust; trustee, v.p., asst. sec. Pritzker Family Philanthropic Fund; mem., pres. coun. U. Pa.; mem. adv. com. Dispute Resolution Rsch. Ctr., Kellogg Grad. Sch. Mgmt., Northwestern U., Evanston, Ill.; trustee, mem. planning and mktg. com., mem. budget com. Children's Meml. Med. Ctr. Mem. Young President's Orgn., Std. Club, East Bank Club, Met. Club, Northmoor Country Club (Highland Park, Ill.). Home: 442 W Wellington Ave Chicago IL 60657-5804 Office: Celtic Life Ins Co 233 S Wacker Dr Ste 700 Chicago IL 60606-6393

MANNING, FREDERICK WILLIAM, retired retail executive; b. Youngstown, Ohio, Aug. 15, 1924; s. John Carroll and Mary Matilda Manning; m. Martha Ann Gross, May 9, 1953 (dec. Feb. 1992); children: William, Patricia, Joan, Donna, David. BS, Youngstown U., 1948; LLB, Case Western Res. U., 1951. With F.W. Woolworth Co., N.Y.C., 1951-88, dir. real estate N.Y. office, 1960-79, v.p., 1980-88, ret., 1988. 2nd lt. USAAF, 1943-45. Mem. Ohio State Bar. Roman Catholic. Home: 77 Huron Dr Chatham NJ 07928-1205

MANNING, JACK, photographer, columnist, author; b. N.Y.C., Nov. 21, 1920; s. Mathew and Sally (Markowitz) Mendelsohn; m. Marie Louise Koch, Oct. 9, 1970; 1 child, Sarah-Jeanne. Student, CCNY. Free-lance photographer for nat. mags., 1941-63; staff photographer N.Y. Times, N.Y.C., 1964—, photographic columnist, 1976—. Author: Venezuela, 1958, Young Puerto Rico, 1966; Young Spain, 1967, Young Ireland, 1968, Young Brazil, 1969, Portrait of Spain, 1970, The Fine 35mm Portrait, 1979, 82; photographs represented in permanent collections Mus. Modern Art, Met. Mus. Art, Nat. Gallery Arts, Toronto. Recipient numerous photog. awards. Mem. Nat. Press Photographers, N.Y. Press Photographers. Home: 75 Pearce Pky Pearl River NY 10965-1923 Office: NY Times 229 W 43rd St New York NY 10036-3913

MANNING, JAMES FORREST, computer executive; b. Washington, July 31, 1929; s. James Forrest and Marguerite (Wise) M.; m. Joan Morris, Nov. 5, 1955; children: Katherine W., James Forrest IV, Robert M. Student in Math., Dayton U., 1951-53; B.A. in Econs., Williams Coll., 1954. With IBM Corp., 1954—, sales rep. data processing div., Pittsfield, Mass., 1954-57, branch mgr., Erie, Pa., from 1957, custom systems mgr., systems devel. div., 1965-66, systems mgr., intermediate systems, 1966-68, dir. intermediate/medium systems, systems devel. div., 1968-69, v.p. mktg., data products div., 1969-71, group dir. operational programs, data processing group, 1971-72, v.p. plans and controls, gen. products div., 1972-78, v.p. plans and controls, systems products div., 1978-81, asst. group exec., from 1981, corp. v.p., asst. group exec. business info. systems group, 1985-87; pvt. practice cons., 1987-95; pres. Staff Leasing, Bradenton, Fla., 1995—. Served to tech. sgt. USAF, 1950-53. Avocations: reading; sports. Home: Hilltop Rd Wilson Pt Norwalk CT 06854

MANNING, JEROME ALAN, lawyer; b. Bklyn., Dec. 31, 1929; s. Emanuel J. and Dorothy (Levine) M.; m. Naomi Jacobs, Oct. 31, 1954; children: Joy, Stephen, Susan. BA, NYU, 1950, LLB, 1952; LLM, Yale U., 1953. Bar: N.Y. 1953, Fla. 1977. Assoc. Joseph Trachtman, N.Y.C., 1956-61; ptnr. Stroock & Stroock & Lavan, N.Y.C., 1961—; prof. NYU Sch. Law, 1956—. Editor: NYU Law Review; author: Estate Planning, 1980, rev. edit. 1995, Estate Planning for Laymen, 1992. Trustee Jewish Communal Fund, N.Y. Capt. USAF, 1953-56. Mem. ABA, N.Y. State Bar Assn., Am. Coll. Trust & Estate Counsel, Internat. Acad. Estate and Trust Law. Home: 45 E 72d St New York NY 10021-2761 Office: Stroock & Stroock & Lavan 7 Hanover Sq New York NY 10004-2616

MANNING, JOAN ELIZABETH, health association administrator; b. Davenport, Iowa, July 7, 1953; d. George John and Eugenie Joan (Thomas) Stolze; m. Michael Anthony Manning, July 30, 1977. BA, U. No. Iowa, 1975; MPH, U. Minn., 1990. Traveling collegiate sec. Alpha Delta Pi Nat. Sorority, Atlanta, 1975-76; recreational therapist Americana Healthcare Ctr., Mason City, Iowa, 1976-81; communication coord. Area Agy. on Aging, Mason City, 1981-83; exec. dir. United Way Cerro Gordo County, Mason City, 1983-85, Health Fair of the Midlands, Omaha, 1985-87; dir. health services ARC, Omaha, 1987-90, chief ops. officer, 1990—; vis. rsch. prof. Niels Bohr Inst., Denmark, 1995-96. Bd. dirs. YMCA of U.S.A., Chgo., 1981-83, Mason City YMCA, 1980-84, Mason City Parks and Recreation Bd., 1983-85, Camp Fire Coun., 1989—, Potters Therapy House, 1989—; mem. spl. adv. bd. Cerro Gordo County Human Svcs. Bd., 1983-85; mem. spl. activities com. Omaha Wellness Coun. of Midlands, 1986-89; chmn. wider opportunity task force Great Plains (Nebr.) Girl Scouts U.S., 1986-89; bd. dirs. Omaha South YMCA; mem. Jr. League of Omaha. Mem. U. Minn. Alumnae Assn., Suburban Rotary, Alpha Delta Pi. Republican. Roman Catholic. Office: ARC 3838 Dewey Ave Omaha NE 68105-1148

MANNING, JOHN WARREN, III, retired surgeon, medical educator; b. Phila., Nov. 24, 1919; s. John Warren Jr. and Edith Margaret (Reagan) M.; m. Muriel Elizabeth Johnson, Oct. 11, 1944; children: John, Melissa, Susan. BS in Chemistry with honors, Ursinus Coll., 1940; MD, U. Pa., 1943; postgrad., 1978. Diplomate Am. Bd. Surgery. Naval intern Pa. Naval Hosp., 1946; resident Saginaw (Mich.) Gen. Hosp., 1947-50; preceptor Dr. H.M. Bishop, 1950-52; pvt. practice Saginaw, 1950—; sr. staff mem. Saginaw Gen. Hosp., St. Luke's Hosp., Saginaw; past chief of surgery, chmn. tissue com. St. Mary's Hosp., Saginaw; cons. VA Hosp., Saginaw; assoc. clin. prof. surgery Mich. State U., assoc. prof. surgery, 1976-92, prof. emeritus, 1992—; mem. search com. Saginaw Coop. Hosp. Contbr. articles to profl. publs. Lt. USN, 1942-46, PTO. Fellow ACS; mem. AMA, Mich. State Med. Soc., Saginaw Surg. Soc., Soc. Abdominal Surgeons, Am. Coll. Angiology, Soc. Am. Gastrointestinal Endoscopic Surgeons. Home: PO Box 3236 Key Largo FL 33037 Office: 140 Camelot Apt i-11 Saginaw MI 48603

MANNING, KENNETH ALAN, lawyer; b. Buffalo, July 22, 1951; Jack Edwin and Dorothea Ann (Ruhland) M.; m. Diane Louise Garrold, Aug. 11, 1973; children: Michael John, Kathryn Ann. BS in Engring. Sci., SUNY, Buffalo, 1974, JD, 1977. Bar: N.Y. 1978, U.S. Dist. Ct. (we. dist.) N.Y. 1978, U.S. Dist. Ct. (no. dist.) N.Y. 1980, U.S. Ct. Appeals (2d cir.) 1983, U.S. Ct. Appeals (3d cir.) 1988. Confidential law asst. to assoc. justice Appellate Div. 4th Dept., Buffalo, 1977-79; assoc. Phillips, Lytle, Hitchcock, Blaine & Huber, Buffalo, 1979-84, ptnr., 1985—. Vol. Lawyers Project, Erie County, 1985—, Criminal Appeals Program, Erie County, 1988-89; mem. coun. Western N.Y. region NCCJ. Woodburn fellow SUNY, Buffalo, 1973-76. Mem. ABA (TIP sect.), N.Y. State Bar Assn. (ins. negligence sect.), Erie County Bar Assn., Gyro Club (pres. 1988), Park Club. Avocations: sports, hunting. Office: Phillips Lytle Hitchcock Blaine & Huber 3400 Marine Midland Ctr Buffalo NY 14203-2887

MANNING, KENNETH PAUL, food company executive; b. N.Y.C., Jan. 18, 1942; s. John Joseph and Edith Helen (Hoffmann) M.; m. Maureen Lambert, Sept. 12, 1964; children: Kenneth J., John J., Elise, Paul, Caroline, Jacqueline. BMechEngring., Rensselaer Poly. Inst., 1963; postgrad. in Statistics George Washington U., 1965-66; M.B.A. in Ops. Research, Am. U., 1968. With W.R. Grace & Co., N.Y.C., 1973-87, v.p. European consumer div., 1975-76, pres. ednl. products div., 1976-79, pres. real estate div., 1979-81, v.p. corp. tech. group, 1981-83, pres., chief exec. officer Ambrosia Chocolate Co. div., Milw., 1983-87; with Universal Foods Corp., Milw., 1987—, group v.p., 1987-89, exec. v.p., dir., 1989-92, pres., COO, dir., 1992—; bd. dirs. Firstar Trust Co., Milw.; trustees Cardinal Stritch Coll. Served as lt. USN, 1963-67; rear adm., USNR, (ret.). Decorated Legion of Merit, Nat. Def. medal, Armed Forces Res. medal. Mem. Greater Milw. Com., Navy League, US. Naval Inst., Naval Res. Assn. Republican. Roman Catholic. Clubs: Union League (N.Y.C.), Milw. Club. Home: 2914 E Newberry Blvd Milwaukee WI 53211-3429 Office: Universal Foods Corp 433 E Michigan St Milwaukee WI 53202-5104

MANNING, KEVIN JAMES, academic administrator; b. N.Y.C., Nov. 8, 1944; s. James and Helen (Gurry) M.; m. Sara Garrity; children: Elizabeth Ann, Meagan Garrity, Kevin James. BA in Theatre, Webster U., St. Louis, 1967; MS in Pers., Shippensburg (Pa.) U., 1976; PhD in Ednl. Adminstrn., Ohio State U., 1982; attended, Inst. Ednl. Mgmt., Harvard U., 1989. Adminstr., intr. Webster U., St. Louis, 1967-68; mgmt recruiter L.S. Brady, Inc., St. Louis, 1969; adminstr. Washington U., St. Louis, 1969-71; admissions counselor Elizabethtown (Pa.) Coll., 1972-76, dir. admissions, 1976-80, spl. asst. to pres., 1982-83; rsch. asst. Ohio State U., Columbus, 1980-82; chief staff Gov.'s Commn. Higher Edn., Harrisburg, Pa., 1983-84; v.p. devel. Immaculata (Pa.) Coll., 1984—. Bd. dirs. Chester County Export Ctr., Exton, Pa., 1990; mem. attractions com. Phila. Econ. Devel. Coalition, 1988—. Mem. Coun. Advancements and Support Edn., Solutions Now, Am. Assn. Higher Edn. (chmn. 1994-95), Sr. Devel. Officers Phila. (chmn.), Great Valley C. of C. (bd. dirs.). Avocations: reading, arts, film. Home: 17 Pine Rd Malvern PA 19355-1623 Office: Immaculata Coll Villa Maria Hall Immaculata PA 19345

MANNING, MICHAEL C., lawyer; b. Kansas City, Mo., July 17, 1949. BA, Emporia State U., 1971; postgrad., U. Kans.; JD cum laude, Washburn U., 1977. Bar: Mo. 1977, Kans. 1978, D.C. 1988, U.S. Dist. Ct. Ariz. 1990. Ptnr. Morrison & Hecker, Phoenix; spl. asst. to Gov. Kans., 1974-75. Editor-in-chief Washburn Law Jour., 1976-77. Mem. Phi Kappa Phi. Office: Morrison & Hecker 2800 N Central Ave Ste 1600 Phoenix AZ 85004-1047

MANNING, NOEL THOMAS, publishing company executive; b. Ayden, N.C., Oct. 10, 1939; s. James Samuel and Tinie (McGlohon) M.; m. Edith Joyce Reagan, Jan. 1, 1964 (div. Jan. 1973); 1 son, Noel Thomas. BS in Intermediate Edn., East Carolina U.; student, Free Will Bapt. Coll., 1960. Cert. tchr. reading diagnosis, Eng., lang. arts, social studies and art. Staff illustrator Free Will Bapt. Press, Ayden, 1959-61, 1963-68; editor Free Will Bapt. Press Found., 1968-80; tchr. creative wrtiting Pitt Community Coll., Greenville, N.C., 1972-80; instr. piano, 1974-80; tchr. composition and creative writing Greenville Recreational Dept., 1974—; mng. editor The Christian Jew Found., San Antonio, Tex., 1980—. Youth dir. Cragmont Assembly Religious Camp, Black Mountain, N.C., 1968-80; musician Reedy Br. Free-Will Bapt. Ch., organist, 1968-80; choir dir. Good Shepherd Presbyn. Ch., San Antonio, 1983—. East Carolina U. honor scholar, Columbus (Ohio) Sch. Art scholar, 1959; recipient nat. awards for poetry. Democrat. Baptist. Composer church music. Home: 2503 Jackson Keller Rd Apt 619 San Antonio TX 78230-5249 Office: Christian Jew Found 611 Broadway St San Antonio TX 78215-1823 *How be it so? I have the choice to live or die—and in my hands I hold the tools to make life good—or to make it bad...One abbreviates his life when he dissociates himself from others and their concerns. In order to relate meaningfully, one must share both the sorrows and the joys of his fellowman. Identifying thus has certainly made life for me more beneficial. Accordingly, each day I live, I try to make life more livable for at least one person—be it a needed pat on the back or an extended word of greeting. I am convinced that the manner in which one approaches all situations will determine the outcome. I further believe that a smile communicates all messages best and receives in like measure.*

MANNING, PETER KIRBY, sociology educator; b. Salem, Oreg., Sept. 27, 1940; s. Kenneth Gilbert and Esther Amelia (Gibbard) M.; m. Victoria Francis Shaughnessy, Sept. 1, 1961 (div. 1981); children—Kerry Patricia, Sean Peter, Merry Kathleen; m. Betsy Cullum-Swan, Aug. 4, 1991. B.A., Willamette U., 1961; M.A., Duke U., 1963, Ph.D., 1966; M.A. (hon.), Oxford U., Eng., 1983. Instr. sociology Duke U., 1964-65; asst. prof. sociology U. Mo., 1965-66, Mich. State U., East Lansing, 1966-70; assoc. prof. sociology and psychiatry Mich. State U., 1970-74, prof., 1974—; prof. criminal justice, 1993—; Beto chair lectr. Sam Houston State U., 1990; Ameritech lectr. E. Ky. U., 1993; cons. Nat. Inst. Law Enforcement and Criminal Justice (now Nat. Inst. Justice), U.S. Dept. Justice, Rsch. Triangle Inst., NSF, Nat. Health and Med. Rsch. Coun., Australia, 1980—, Social Sci. Rsch. Coun. Eng., AID (Jamaica), 1991, Sheehy com. Police Pay and Performance, Eng., 1993. Author: Sociology of Mental Health and Illness, 1975, Police Work, 1977, The Narcs' Game, 1980, Semiotics and Fieldwork, 1987, Symbolic Communication, 1988, Organizational Communication, 1992, other books; also book chpts., articles in profl. jours.; cons. editor series: Principal Themes in Sociology; co-editor Sage Series in Qualitative Methods, Communications and Social Order Aldine/deGruyter; adv. editor, mem. editorial bd. numerous jours. in social scis. Recipient Bruce Smith Sr. award Acad. Criminal Justice Scis., 1993, Charles H. Cooley award Mich. Sociol. Assn., 1994; NDEA fellow, 1962-64, NSF fellow, 1965, fellow Balliol Coll., Oxford U., 1982-83, vis. fellow Wolfson Coll., Oxford U., 1981, 82-83, fellow, 1984-86. Mem. Am. Soc. Criminology, Am. Sociol. Assn., Brit. Soc. Criminology, Internat. Sociol. Assn., Midwest Sociol. Soc., Soc. Study of Social Problems, Soc. for the Study of Symbolic Interaction (spl. recognition award 1990, v.p. 1992-93, program chair 1993), Internat. Soc. for Semiotics and Law. Office: Mich State U 516 Baker Hall East Lansing MI 48824-1118

MANNING, RICHARD DALE, writer; b. Flint, Mich., Feb. 7, 1951; s. Harold J. Manning and Juanita Mayo; m. Margaret B. Saretsky, June 5, 1971 (div.); 1 child, Joshua; m. Tracy M. Stone, Sept. 8, 1990. AB in Polit. Sci., U. Mich., 1973. News dir. Sta. WATZ, Alpena, Mich., 1975-79; reporter Alpena News, 1977-79; city editor Post-Register, Idaho Falls, Idaho, 1979-81; editor, columnist Wood River Jour., Hailey, Idaho, 1981-82; city editor, columnist Times-News, Twin Falls, Idaho, 1982-85; reporter, columnist Missoulian, Missoula, Mont., 1985-89; John S. Knight fellow in journalism Stanford (Calif.) U., 1994-95. Author: Last Stand: Timber, Journalism and the Case for Humility, 1991, A Good House, 1993, Grassland, 1995. Recipient Blethen award for investigative reporting Allied Newspapers, 1986-87.

MANNING, ROBERT HENDRICK, development director; b. Soerabaja, Java, Indonesia, Aug. 23, 1941; s. William and Gertrude (Unk) M. BS, No. Mich. U., 1974. Instr. sailing USCG Acad., New London, Conn., 1959-63; dir. audio visual svcs. No. Mich. U., Marquette, 1965-93; dir. devel. Bresnan Comm. Co., Marquette, 1993—; ind. media cons., Marquette, 1969—. Pub. TV host PBS Sta. WNMU-TV, 1977—. Hon. mem. Marquette-Alger County Med. Soc. (exec. dir. 1970—, capt. U. Rsch. Vessel 1977-79). Avocations: astronomy, navigation, med. history, sailing, amateur radio. Home: PO Box 309 Marquette MI 49855-0309 Office: Bresnan Comm Co PO Box 190 Marquette MI 49855-0190

MANNING, ROBERT JOSEPH, editor; b. Binghamton, N.Y., Dec. 25, 1919; s. Joseph James and Agnes Pauline (Brown) M.; m. Margaret Marinda Raymond, Dec. 28, 1944 (dec. 1984); children: Richard Raymond, Brian Gould, Robert Brown; m. Theresa M. Slomkowski, July 11, 1987. Nieman fellow, Harvard, 1945-46; LittD (hon.), Tufts U., 1966; LHD, St. Lawrence U., 1971. Reporter Binghamton (N.Y.) Press, 1936-41, AP, 1942; State Dept. and White House corr. UPI, 1944-46; chief UN corr. United Press, 1946-49; writer Time mag., 1949-55, sr. editor, 1955-58; chief London bur. Time, Life, Fortune, Sports Illus. mags., 1958-61; Sunday editor N.Y. Herald Tribune, 1961-62; asst. sec. state for pub. affairs Washington, 1962-64; exec. editor Atlantic Monthly, 1964-66, editor-in-chief, 1966-80; v.p. Atlantic Monthly Co., 1966-80; editor-in-chief Boston Pub. Co., 1981-87; pres., editor-in-chief Bobcat Books Inc., Boston, 1987—. Served with AUS, 1942-43. Fellow Kennedy Inst. Politics, Harvard U., 1980. Mem. AAAS, Century Assn. (N.Y.C.), Tavern Club, St. Botolph Club. Home and Office: 191 Commonwealth Ave Boston MA 02116-2210

MANNING, ROBERT THOMAS, physician, educator; b. Wichita, Kans., Oct. 16, 1927; s. Thomas Earl and Mary Francis (Schlegel) M.; m. Jane Bell, July 29, 1949; children: Mary Kay Travers, Phillip Trenton, Susan Ann Shiba. A.B., Wichita U., 1950; M.D., Kans. U., 1954; DHL, Med. Coll. Hampton Rds., 1991. Diplomate Am. Bd. Internal Medicine. Intern Kansas City (Mo.) Gen. Hosp., 1954-55; resident Kans. U., Kansas City, 1955-58; from assoc. prof. to prof. Kans. U. Med. Ctr. Sch. of Medicine, Kansas City, 1958-71; assoc. dean students Kans. U. Med. Ctr. Sch. of Medicine, 1969-71; dean Eastern Va. Med. Sch., Norfolk, Va., 1971-74; chmn., prof. internal medicine Eastern Va. Med. Sch., 1974-77; prof. internal medicine U. Kans. Sch. of Medicine, Wichita, 1977-93; prof. emeritus U. Kans. Sch. Medicine, Wichita, 1993—; assoc. dean, clin. affairs U. Kans. Sch. of Medicine, Wichita, 1985-89; chmn. internal medicine U. Kans. Sch. Medicine, Wichita, 1991-93; pres. Wesley Med. Rsch. Inst., 1986-88; nat. cons. surgeon gen. USAF, 1973-78. Author: Major's Physical Diagnosis, 9th edit., 1982; contbr. articles to profl. jours. Served with USAF, 1945-47. Recipient Advanced Achievement award Am. Bd. Internal Medicine, 1987. Fellow ACP (laureate Kans. chpt., bd. govs. Kans. 1984-88); mem. Am. Fedn. Clin. Rsch., Cen. Soc. Clin. Rsch., Am. Assn. Study Liver Disease, Sigma Xi, Alpha Omega Alpha. Presbyterian. Avocations: hunting, fishing. Home: 156 N Maize Rd # 31 Wichita KS 67212-4649 Office: U Kans Sch Medicine 1010 N Kansas St Wichita KS 67214-3124

MANNING, SYLVIA, English studies educator; b. Montreal, Que., Can., Dec. 2, 1943; came to U.S., 1967; d. Bruno and Lea Bank; m. Peter J. Manning, Aug. 20, 1967; children—Bruce David, Jason Maurice. B.A., McGill U., 1963; M.A., Yale U., 1964, Ph.D. in English, 1967. Asst. prof. English Calif. State U.-Hayward, 1967-71, assoc. prof., 1971-75, assoc. dean, 1972-75; assoc. prof. U. So. Calif., 1975-94, prof., assoc. dir. Ctr. for Humanities, 1975-77, assoc. dir. Ctr. for Humanities, 1975-77, chmn. freshman writing, 1977-80, chmn. dept. English, 1980-83, vice provost, exec. v.p., 1984-94; prof. English U. Ill., 1994—, v.p. for acad. affairs, prof. English, 1994—. Author: Dickens as Satirist, 1971; Hard Times: An Annotated Bibliography, 1984. Contbr. essays to mags. Woodrow Wilson fellow, 1963-64, 66-67. Mem. MLA, Dickens Soc. Office: U of Ill 377 Henry Adm Bldg 506 S Wright St Urbana IL 61801-3614

MANNING, THOMAS EDWIN, II, aeronautical engineer; b. Randolph, Vt., Feb. 2, 1969; s. Thomas Edwin Manning and Jane Kate (Sadd) Fletcher. BS, Pa. State U., 1991, MS, 1993. Commd. USAF, 1993, advanced through grades to capt., 1996; chief joint STARS aircraft engring. USAF, Hanscom AFB, Mass., 1996—. 1st lt. USAF, 1993—. Mem. AIAA, Pa. State U. Alumni Assn., U.S. Hang Gliding Assn. (pilot), Company Grade Officers Assn. Avocations: physical fitness, hang gliding, computers. Home: 45 Georgetown Dr Apt 12 Framingham MA 01702 Office: ESC/SSIP 75 Vandenberg Ddr Hanscom AFB MA 01731-2119

MANNING, WALTER SCOTT, accountant, former educator, consultant; b. nr. Yoakum, Tex., Oct. 4, 1912; BBA, Tex. Coll. Arts and Industries, 1932; MBA, U. Tex., 1940; m. Eleanor Mary Jones, Aug. 27, 1937; children: Sharon Frances, Walter Scott, Robert Kenneth. Asst. to bus. mgr. Tex. Coll. Arts and Industries, Kingsville, 1932; tchr. Sinton (Tex.) High Sch., 1933-37, Robstown (Tex.) High Sch., 1937-41; prof. Tex. A&M U., College Station, 1941-77; cons. C.P.A., Tex. Walter Manning Outstanding Jr. and Outstanding Sr. awards at Coll. Bus. Adminstrn., Tex. A&M U. named in his honor. Mem. AICPA, AAUP, Am. Acctg. Assn., Tex. Soc. CPAs, College Station C. of C. (past pres.), Tex. Assn. Univ. Instrs. Acctg. (pres. 1963-64), SAR (independence chpt. past pres.), Knights York Cross of Honor, Alpha Chi, Beta Gamma Sigma, Beta Alpha Psi. Democrat. Presbyterian (elder). Clubs: Masons, (32 degree), Shriners, K.T., Kiwanis (past pres., past lt. gov. div. IX Tex. Okla. dist., Kiwanis Internat. Legion of Honor). Home: 405 Walton Dr College Station TX 77840-2224

MANNING, WALTER SCOTT, JR., veterinarian; b. Bryan, Tex., Mar. 3, 1945; s. Walter Scott and Eleanor Mary (Jones) M.; m. Mary Ann Hurliman, Mar. 11, 1972; children: Adrienne Emily, Walter Scott III. BS, Tex. A&M U., 1967, 76; MS, East Tex. State Univ., 1972; DVM, Tex. A&M U., 1977, PhD, 1986. Mixed practitioner Benton (Ark) Veterinary Hosp., 1977-81; veterinary clin. assoc. Coll. Veterinary Medicine Tex. A&M U., College Station, Tex., 1981-84; regional animal care specialist USDA Animal and Plant Health Inspec. Svc., Regulatory Enforcement Animal Care, Ft. Worth, 1986-89; clin. veterinarian Alcon labs., Inc., Ft. Worth, 1989-90, mgr., 1990-94, asst. dir., 1995—. Com. chmn. troop 431 Santa Fe Dist., Longhorn Coun., Boy Scouts Am. Mem. AVMA, Tex. Vet. Med. Assn., Tarrant County Vet. Med. Assn., Dallas County Vet. Med. Assn., Am. Soc. Lab. Animal Practitioners, Am. Assn. Lab. Animal Sci., Tex. Br. Lab. Animal Sci., Assn. Primate Veterinarians, Nat. Eagle Scout Assn., SAR, Beta Beta Beta, Phi Eta Sigma. Lutheran. Avocations: genealogy, numismatics, photography. Home: 2055 Mary Ann Ln Burleson TX 76028-9470 Office: Alcon Labs Inc 6201 South Freeway (R3-12) Fort Worth TX 76134

MANNING, WILLIAM DUDLEY, JR., retired specialty chemical company executive; b. Tampa, Fla., Mar. 7, 1934; s. William Dudley and Rebecca (Reid) M.; m. Carol Randolph Gillis, June 30, 1962; children: Carol Randolph, Rebecca Barrett, Anne Gillis. BA in Chemistry, Fla. State U., 1957. Sales rep. Amoco Chem. Co., St. Louis and Cleve., 1959-63; sales engr. The Lubrizol Corp., Tulsa, 1963-64, southwestern regional sales mgr., 1964-66; mgr. chem. product sales The Lubrizol Corp., Wickliffe, Ohio, 1966-72, sales mgr., western U.S., 1972, gen. sales mgr., asst. div. head-sales, 1972-79, mktg. mgr., asst. div. head-sales, 1979-80, v.p. mktg., 1980-81, v.p., bus. devel. div., 1981-85, sr. v.p. sales and mktg., 1985-87; pres. Lubrizol Petroleum Chems. Co., Wickliffe, 1987-94; sr. v.p., asst. to pres. The Lubrizol Corp., 1994; cons., investor, 1994—; bd. dirs. Fletcher Paper Co., Alpena, Mich., Robbins and Myers, Dayton, Ohio. Chmn. bd. trustees Vocat. Guidance Svcs., Cleve., 1991—. With USAR, 1957-63. Mem. Soc. Automotive Engrs. (assoc.), Am. Petroleum Inst., Nat. Petroleum Refiners Assn., Soc. of Chem. Industry, Kirtland Country Club (v.p. 1986-88, pres. 1988-89), Tavern Club (trustee 1986—), Chagrin Valley Hunt Club. Republican. Roman Catholic. Office: 2550 50M Center Rd Ste 105 Willoughby OH 44094

MANNING, WILLIAM FREDERICK, wire service photographer; b. Gardner, Mass., Aug. 18, 1920; s. Seth Newton and Jennie May (Bennett) M.; m. Yvonne J.C. Winslow, Feb. 29, 1964; children: Pamela Ann, Jeffrey Newton. A.A., Boston U., 1950, B.S. in Communications, 1952. With AP, Boston, 1951-53; photographer UPI, Boston, 1953-88, ret. Contbr. photos to books, mags., newspapers throughout the world. Served with USN, 1940-46, PTO. Recipient Look 1st Prize All Sports award, 1958; Pictures of the Yr. award U. Mo., 1964, 74; Nat. Headliners Club award for outstanding syndicate photography, 1974. Mem. Boston Press Photographers Assn., Delta Kappa Alpha. Congregationalist. Club: Nat. Headliners. Home: 23 Sunset Dr Beverly MA 01915-2319 Office: One Herald Sq 300 Harrison Ave Boston MA 02118-2237

MANNING, WILLIAM HENRY, lawyer; b. Dallas, Feb. 5, 1951. BA, Creighton U., 1973; JD, Hamline U., 1978. Bar: Minn. 1978, U.S. Dist. Ct. Minn. 1978, U.S. Ct. Appeals (8th cir.) 1979; cert. civil trial specialist. Spl. asst. atty. gen. Minn. Atty. Gen.'s Office, St. Paul, 1980-83, dir. tort litigation div., 1984-86; ptnr. Robins, Kaplan, Miller & Ciresi, Mpls., 1986—. Office: Robins Kaplan Miller & Ciresi 800 Lasalle Ave Minneapolis MN 55402-2006

MANNING, WILLIAM JOSEPH, lawyer; b. N.Y.C., Aug. 11, 1926; s. Joseph Michael and Eileen Johanna (Walsh) M.; m. Maryanne Cullen, June 23, 1956; children—William Joseph, Michael P., Maura G., Marian T., John A., Mary E. B.B.A. magna cum laude, St. John's U., N.Y.C., 1949, LL.B. magna cum laude, 1952. Bar: N.Y. 1952. Assoc. firm Simpson Thacher & Bartlett, N.Y.C., 1952-62; ptnr. Simpson Thacher & Bartlett, 1962—, sr. ptnr., 1968-88, of counsel, 1989—; dir. Brascan Ltd., Toronto, Ont., Can., 1970-79; bd. dirs. N.Y. Lawyers for Public Interest, 1977-88. Notes editor: St. John's Law Rev, 1951-52. Trustee Inst. for Muscle Disease, N.Y.C., 1963-70; bd. dirs. Mercy Hosp., Rockville Centre, N.Y., 1975-87. Served with inf. U.S. Army, 1944-46. Fellow Am. Coll. Trial Lawyers, Am. Law Inst., Am. Bar Found.; mem. ABA (chmn. sect. litigation 1977-78, founding mem. coun. 1973), Assn. Bar City N.Y., N.Y. State Bar Assn., N.Y. County Lawyers Assn., Am. Judicature Soc., Downtown Assn., Garden City Golf Club, Westhampton Country Club (pres. 1989—), Cherry Valley Club. Roman Catholic. Home: 64 1st St Garden City NY 11530-4321 also: 156 Dune Rd Westhampton Beach NY 11978-3003 also: 15865 Westerly Ter Jupiter FL 33477-1337 Office: Simpson Thacher & Bartlett 425 Lexington Ave New York NY 10017-3903

MANNING, WILLIAM RAYMOND, retired state official; b. Vancouver, C., Can., May 17, 1920; came to U.S., 1922; s. William and Mary (Gysels) M.; m. Louise B. Graham, Mar. 11, 1982. B.A., San Jose (Calif.) State Coll., 1941; M.A., U. Pacific, 1949; Ed.D., Stanford U., 1956. Tchr. Galt, Calif., 1946-49; prin. Lodi, Calif., 1949-50; supt. schs. Orangevale, Calif., 1950-58, Petaluma, Calif., 1958-64, Lansing, Mich., 1964-67, Washington, 1967-70; chmn. ednl. bd. Xerox Edn. Publs., 1969-73; pres. BFE Ednl. Consultants, 1973—; city mgr. Bel Air, Md., 1973-79; dir. adminstrn. Va. Housing Devel. Authority, Richmond, 1980-92; ret., 1992; vis. prof. U. Hawaii, Sacramento State Coll., San Francisco State Coll., No. Mich. U., Mich. State U. Contbr. to books and profl. jours. Served with USAAF, 1942-46. Recipient community and profl. awards. Home: 11807 Goodwick Sq Richmond VA 23233-3424

MANNING, WINTON HOWARD, psychologist, educational administrator; b. St. Louis, Feb. 9, 1930; s. Winton Harry and Jane (Swanson) M.; m. Nancy Mercedes Groves, Aug. 1, 1959; children: Cecelia Groves Tazelaar, Winton H. III. AB with honors, William Jewell Coll., 1947; PhD in Psychology, Washington U., St. Louis, 1959. Instr. psychology William Jewell Coll., Liberty, Mo., 1954-55, asst. prof., acting head dept. psychology, 1955-56; rsch. psychologist Washington U., St. Louis, 1956-58, rsch. assoc., 1958-59; vis. lectr. Washington U., summer, 1961, 62; asst. prof. psychology Tex. Christian U., Fort Worth, 1959-61, assoc. prof., 1961-64, prof., 1964-65, assoc. dir. univ. honors program, 1962-65; assoc. dir. rsch. Coll. Entrance Examination Bd., N.Y.C., 1965-66, dir. program devel., 1966-68, exec. dir. rsch.and devel., 1968-69; dir. devel. rsch. div. Ednl. Testing Svc., Princeton, N.J., 1969-70, v.p., 1970-77, sr. v.p. devel. and rsch., 1977-83, sr. scholar, 1983-93; pres. Ednl. Devel. Svc., Princeton, 1993—; vis. fellow Princeton U., 1982-83; cons. Gallup Internat. Inst., 1990—, Applied Ednl. Rsch., 1993-95; cons. Grad. Mgmt. Admissions Coun., 1992-95, Carnegie Found. for the Advancement of Tchg. 1993-95. Author: The Pursuit of Fairness in Admissions to Higher Education, 1977; Student Manual for Essentials of Psychology, 1960. Contbr. articles on ednl. measurement and psychology of learning to profl. publs. Patentee in field U.S. and Europe. Trustee Assn. for Advancement of Handicapped People, 1975-78, Nat. Chicano Coun. on Higher Edn., 1977-85, N.J. Arts Festival, 1980-85; vice-chair Found. for Books to China, 1980—; chair bd. trustees Princeton Day Sch., 1981-93; trustee Princeton Area Found., 1991-94, Our House Found., 1991-92, The Priceton's Singers, 1992%, Christian Renewal Effort in Emerging Democracies, 1992-94, George H. Gallup Internat. Inst., 1992—; chair, trustee Trinity-All Saints' Cemetery, 1993—; chair Affordable Housing Bd. of Princeton Borough, 1987-89; commr. Princeton Pub. Housing Authority, 1995—; sr. warden All Saints Epsic. Ch., 1987-89; chair ins. com. Diocese N.J., 1993-95; mem. Diocese Coun., Diocese of N.J., 1996—; adv. coun. U. Okla. Ctr. for Rsch. on Minority Edn., 1987-92, Ind. Sch. Chmn. Assn., 1987-92; trustee Friends of Princeton Open Space, 1995—; cons. Carnegie Found. for Advancement of Tchr., 1987-95; cons. The Coll. Bd., 1988-91; spl. cons. Comm. on Admission to Grad. Mgmt. Edn., 1987-89. Recipient Alumni Achievement citation William Jewell Coll., 1970; named Gallup Scholar in Edn., 1995. Fellow Am. Psychol. Soc. (charter), Eastern Psychol. Assn., Psychometric Soc., Am. Ednl. Rsch. Assn., Nat. Coun. on Measurement in Edn. (mem. com. on legal issues in measurement 1977-79), N.Y. Acad. Scis., Nassau Club, Pendragon Club, Oratory of Good Shepherd, Phi Beta Kappa, Sigma Xi. Home: 12 Morven Pl Princeton NJ 08540-3024 Office: Ednl Devel Svc PO Box 441 Princeton NJ 08542-0441

MANNINO, EDWARD FRANCIS, lawyer; b. Abington, Pa., Dec. 5, 1941; s. Sante Francis and Martha Anne (Hines) M.; m. Mary Ann Vigilante, July 17, 1965 (div. 1990); m. Antoinette K. O'Connell, June 25, 1993; children: Robert John, Jennifer Elaine. B.A. with distinction, U. Pa., 1963, LL.B. magna cum laude, 1966. Bar: Pa. 1967. Law clk. 3d cir. U.S. Ct. Appeals, 1966-67; assoc. firm Dilworth, Paxson, Kalish & Kauffman, Phila., 1967-71; ptnr. Dilworth, Paxson, Kalish & Kauffman, 1972-86, co-chmn. litigation dept., 1980-86, sr. ptnr., 1982-86; sr. prin. Elliott, Mannino & Flaherty, P.C., Phila., 1986-90; chmn. Mannino Griffith P.C., Phila., 1990-95; sr. ptnr. Wolf, Block, Schorr & Solis-Cohen, Phila., 1995—; hearing examiner disciplinary bd. Supreme Ct. Pa., 1986-89; lectr. Temple U. Law Sch., 1968-69, 71-72; mem. Phila. Mayor's Sci. and Tech. Adv. Com., 1976-79; mem. adv. com. on appellate ct. rules Supreme Ct. Pa., 1989-95; project mgr. Pa. Environ. Master Plan, 1973; chmn. Pa. Land Use Policy Study Adv. Com., 1973-75; chmn. adv. com., hon. mem. faculty history dept. U. Pa., 1980-85. Author: Lender Liability and Banking Litigation, 1989, Business and Commercial Litigation: A Trial Lawyer's Handbook, 1995, The Civil RICO Primer, 1996; mem. editl. bd. Litigation mag., 1985-87, Lender Liability News, 1988—, Bank Bailout Litigation News, 1989-93, Bus. Torts Reporter, 1988—, Practical Litigator, 1989—, Civil RICO Report, 1991—; contbr. articles to profl. jours. Pres. parish coun. Our Mother of Consolation Ch., 1977-79; bd. overseers U. Pa. Sch. Arts and Scis., 1985-89, chmn. recruitment and retention of faculty com.; commonwealth trustee Temple U., 1987-90, mem. audit, bus. and fin. coms. Named one of Nation's Top Litigators Nat. Law Jour., 1990. Fellow ABA (chmn. various coms.), Am. Law Inst., Hist. Soc. U.S. Dist. Ct. Ea. Dist. Pa. (bd. dirs.), Pa. Bar Assn., Phila. Bar Assn. (gov. 1975), Pyramid Club, Sharswood Law Club, Order of Coif, Phi Beta Kappa, Phi Beta Kappa Assocs. Democrat. Office: Wolf Block Schorr et al 12th Fl Packard Bldg 15th & Chestnut Sts Philadelphia PA 19102

MANNIX, KEVIN LEESE, lawyer; b. Queens, N.Y., Nov. 26, 1949; s. John Warren Sr. and Editta Gorrell M.; m. Susanna Bernadette Chiocca, June 1, 1974; children: Nicholas Chiocca, Gabriel Leese, Emily Kemper. BA, U. Va., 1971, JD, 1974. Bar: Oreg. 1974, U.S. Ct. Appeals (9th cir.) 1976, U.S. Supreme Ct. 1978, Guam 1979. Law clk. to judge Oreg. Ct. Appeals, Salem, 1974-75; asst. atty. gen. Oreg. Dept. Justice, Salem, 1975-77, Govt. of Guam, Agana, 1977-79; judge adminstrv. law Oreg. Workers' Compensation Bd., Salem, 1980-83; assoc. Lindsay, Hart, Neil & Weigler, Portland, Oreg., 1983-86; pres. Kevin L. Mannix Profl. Corp., Salem, 1986—. Chmn. St. Joseph Sch. Bd., Salem, 1981-86; pres. Salem Cath. Schs. Corp., 1985; v.p. Salem Cath. Schs. Found., 1985-88, pres., 1988-90, 91-94, state rep., 1989—; pres. bd. dirs. Blanchet Sch. Mem. Marion Bar Assn., Rotary (bd. dirs. East Salem 1985-89, pres. 1987-88), KC. Democrat. Avocations: photography, scuba diving, travel. Home: 375 18th St NE Salem OR 97301-4307 Office: 2003 State St Salem OR 97301-4349

MANNO, VINCENT PAUL, engineering educator; b. N.Y.C., Dec. 4, 1954; s. Paul Thomas and Jennie (Toia) M.; m. Mariann Margaret Montine, Feb. 16, 1980; children: Elizabeth Ellen, Michael Vincent, Christopher Lawrence. BS, Columbia U., 1976; MS, MIT, 1978, ScD, 1983. Engr. Am. Electric Power Co., N.Y.C., 1978-81; engr. Stone & Webster Corp., Boston, 1981-82; postdoctoral assoc. MIT, Cambridge, 1983-84; assoc. prof. Tufts U., Medford, Mass., 1984—; chmn. mech. engring. dept., 1993—; cons. high tech. and power industry, 1983—. Contbr. articles to engring. sci. and energy jours.; reviewer for tech. jours. and pub. cos.; guest editor tech. jours. Recipient Student award Am. Nuclear Soc., Ralph R. Teetor award, 1986; U.S. Dept. Energy fellow, 1983, sr. faculty fellow USN, 1988. Mem. AAAS, Am. Soc. Engring. Edn., AAUP, ASME, IEEE (chair conf. and program com.), Am. Nuclear Soc. (tech. conf. session chmn.), Sigma Xi. Roman Catholic. Office: Tufts U Dept Mech Engring Medford MA 02155

MANNY, CARTER HUGH, JR., architect, foundation administrator; b. Michigan City, Ind., Nov. 16, 1918; s. Carter Hugh and Ada Gage (Barnes) M.; m. Mary Alice Kellett, Dec. 6, 1942 (dec. Jan. 1994); children: Elizabeth, Carter Hugh III; m. Maya Moran, Dec. 27, 1995. A.B. magna cum laude, Harvard U., 1941, Indsl. Adminstr., 1942; Taliesin fellow, Scottsdale, Ariz., 1946; B.S. in Architecture, Ill. Inst. Tech., 1948. With Murphy/Jahn (name formerly Naess & Murphy and C.F. Murphy Assocs.), Chgo., 1948-83; partner Murphy/Jahn (name formerly Naess & Murphy and C.F. Murphy Assocs.), 1957-61; dir. 1st Citizens Bank, Michigan City, Ind., 1970-86; sr. v.p. Murphy/Jahn (name formerly Naess & Murphy and C.F. Murphy Assocs.), 1978-83; mem. adv. com. on architecture Art Inst. of Chgo., 1982—, oversight com. Ill. Inst. Tech. Sch. of Architecture, Chgo., 1989-94; trustee Graham Found. Advanced Studies in Fine Arts 1956-74, exec. dir., 1972-93, hon. trustee, 1994—. Projects include O'Hare Internat. Airport, Chgo., FBI Hdqrs, Washington, First Nat. Bank Chgo, Chgo. Civic Center, Chgo. Bd. Trade. Fellow AIA (pres. Chgo. chpt. 1973, dir. Ill. council 1972-73), Soc. Archtl. Historians (dir. 1982-85), Chgo. Bldg. Congress (dir. 1978-83); mem. Phi Beta Kappa, Pottawattomie Country Club, Mich. City Yacht Club, Tavern Club, Arts Club, Cliff Dwellers Club (Chgo., hon.). Home: 200 Lake Ave Michigan City IN 46360 also: 1448 N Lake Shore Dr Chicago IL 60610-1625 Office: Graham Found 4 W Burton Pl Chicago IL 60610-1405

MANOFF, DINAH BETH, actress; b. N.Y.C., Jan. 25, 1958; d. Arnold and Lyova (Rosenthal) (Lee Grant) M. Student public schs., N.Y. and Calif. Appeared in: TV series Soap, 1977-78, Empty Nest, 1989-95; TV movie appearances include Raid on Entebbe, 1977, High Terror, 1977, The Possessed, 1977, For Ladies Only, 1981, A Matter of Sex, 1984, The Seduction of Gina, 1984, Celebrity, 1984, Flight #90, 1984, Classified Love, 1986, The Cover Girl and The Cop, 1989, Babies, 1990, (also co-exec. prodr.) Maid for Each Other, 1992; stage performances include I Ought To Be In Pictures, 1980 (Tony award, Theatre World award), Leader of the Pack, 1985, Alfred and Victoria: A Life, Los Angeles Theatre Ctr., 1986-87; films include Grease, 1977, Ordinary People, 1979, I Ought To Be in Pictures, 1981, Gifted Children, 1983, Child's Play, 1988, Staying Together, 1989, Bloodhounds of Broadway, 1989, Welcome Home Roxy Carmichael, 1990. Mem. Screen Actors Guild, Actors Equity, AFTRA. Jewish. Office: The Gersh Agy 232 N Canon Dr Beverly Hills CA 90210 *So far, so good.**

MANOFF, RICHARD KALMAN, advertising executive, nutrition policy consultant; b. Bklyn., June 24, 1916; s. Kalman and Sarah (Glatman) M.; m. Lucy B. Deutscher, Nov. 27, 1942; children: Robert K., Gregory P. B.S., CCNY, 1937, M.S., 1940. Asst. regional dir. War Manpower Commn., 1942-45; marketing dir. Welch Grape Juice Co., 1949-53; v.p. Kenyon & Eckhardt Advt., N.Y.C., 1953-56; pres., chmn. bd. Richard K. Manoff Inc. Advt., N.Y.C., from 1956; now pres. Manoff Internat. Inc.; spl. adv. mktg. and communications to exec. dir. UNICEF, 1980—; dir. Thomas J. Lipton, Inc., 1963-78; adj. prof. dept. health Scis. Sargent Coll. Allied Health Professions, Boston U., 1978—; lectr. pub. health Columbia U. Sch. Medicine, 1982-83; Mem. U.S. del. FAO World Conf., Rome, Italy, 1966; spl. advisor UNICEF and WHO, 1968-78; cons. spl. mission to Food and Agr. Ministry, Govt. India, AID, 1969; Ford Found. offices Pub. Edn. Pub. Broadcasting for children's TV; participant 1st World Conf. on Social Communication for Devel. Mass Communications, Mexico, 1970, 7th Asian Advt. Congress, Delhi, 1970, 3d Western Hemisphere Nutrition Congress, Fla., 1971, Internat. Conf. Nutrition, Nat. Devel. and Planning, Mass. Inst. Tech., 1971, Symposium Eating Patterns and Their Influence on Purchasing Behavior and Nutrition, Nev., 1971, Nutrition Workshop, AID, 1971, 9th Annual Summer Workshop Family Planning, 1971, 4th & 5th Seminar Workshop on Mgmt. and Planning of Population Family Planning Programs, 1971, New Products Symposium, 1971, Communication Seminar series Cornell U., 1971, Exploration The Frontiers of Nutritional Edn. Seminar, 1972, 9th Internat. Congress of Nutrition, Mexico, 1972, East-West Center Comml. Resources Conf. on Family Planning, Hawaii, 1972; Protein adv. group UN Systems Annual Mtg., 1973; mem. panel White House Conf. Food, Nutrition and Health, 1969; mem. Sec.'s Adv. Com. on Population Affairs, Dept. HEW, 1971-76; mem. adv. com. Population Reference Bur., Washington, 1977—, Population Inst., 1980—; mem. Nelson A. Rockefeller's Commn. on Critical Choices for Ams.; cons. HRSA Healthy Start Campaign to reduce infant mortality, 1991; bd. dirs. Population Comm. Internat.; Martin J. Forman Meml. lectr., Washington, 1993. Author: Social Marketing: New Imperative for Public Health, 1985. Bd. dirs. Planned Parenthood World Population, Pathfinder Fund, Boston, 1977-80, United Nutrition Edn. Found., Alexandria, Va., 1978—; mem. com. on internat. nutrition programs NAS-NRC, 1973; founder, mem. Com. for Shakespeare Festival, N.Y.C.; bd. visitors Grad. Sch. and Univ. Ctr., CUNY; mem. adv. bd., cons. to the pres. Henry J. Kaiser Family Found., 1987-91. Recipient 5th Ann. Global award for media excellence Population Inst., China, 1985, Townsend Harris medal Alumni Assn. CCNY, 1986. Mem. Am. Assn. Advt. Agys. (gov. 1967—, sec.-treas. 1975—), City Club, City Coll. Club., Friars Club, Harmonie Club (N.Y.C.), Century Assn. Home: 14 Donahue Rd Litchfield CT 06759 also: 322 E 57th St New York NY 10022-2949

MANOLIU-MANEA, MARIA, linguist; b. Galatz, Romania, Mar. 12, 1934; came to U.S., 1978, naturalized, 1987; d. Ion T. and Ana S. (Codescu) Manoliu; m. Ion S. Manea, Nov. 26, 1968. BA, French Coll., Galatz, 1951; MA, U. Bucharest, Romania, 1955, PhD, 1966. Asst. prof. Romance linguistics U. Bucharest, 1957-61, assoc. prof., 1961-68, prof., 1968-77; prof. linguistics U. Calif., Davis, 1978—; vis. prof. U. Chgo., 1972-74, H. Heine Universitat, Dusseldorf, 1994; cons. NEH, 1980—; mem. adv. bd. Revue Romane, Copenhagen, 1972—, Romance Philology, Berkeley, Calif., 1984—, Philologica Canariensia, Spain, 1992—. Author: Sistematica Substitutelor, 1968 (Ministry of Edn. award 1968), Gramatica Comparată a limbilor romanice, 1971, El Estructuralismo Lingüístico, 1979, Tipología e Historia, 1985, Gramatică, Pragmasemantică si Discurs, 1993, Discourse and Pragmatic Constraints on Grammatical Choices. A Grammar of Surprises, 1994; editor-in-chief Bull. de la S.R.L.R., Bucharest, 1975-78; contbr. articles to profl. jours. Recipient Evenimentul award for Outstanding Contbn. to Romanian Culture, 1991; grantee Internat. Com., Linguists, 1972, Fulbright Found., 1972-74, 91-92, IREX, 1993, U. Calif., 1970, 81-96. Mem. MLA, Am. Romanian Acad. (pres. 1982-95, hon. pres. 1995—), Academia Română (hon.), Soc. de Linguistique Romane, Soc. Roumaine de Linguistique Romane (v.p. 1974-78), Internat. Assn. Hist. Linguistics, Linguistics Soc. Am., Internat. Assn. Pragmatics, Romanian Studies Assn. Am. (pres. 1986-88). Avocations: tourism, classical music, cinema. Office: U Calif Dept French and Italian 509 Sproul Hall Davis CA 95616

MANOOGIAN, RICHARD ALEXANDER, manufacturing company executive; b. Long Branch, N.J., July 30, 1936; s. Alex and Marie (Tatian) M.; children: James, Richard, Bridget. B.A. in Econs, Yale U., 1958. Asst. to pres. Masco Corp., Taylor, Mich., 1958-62, exec. v.p., 1962-68, pres., 1968-85, chmn. bd., CEO, 1985—; chmn., dir. Mascotech, Inc., Trimas Corp.; dir. NBD Bancorp, Inc., Detroit Renaissance, Am. Bus. Conf. Trustee U. Liggett Sch., State Dept. Fine Arts Comsn., Founder's Soc., Detroit Inst. Arts, Center for Creative Studies; trustee coun. Nat. Gallery Art. Mem. Young Presidents Orgn., Yale Alumni Assn. Clubs: Grosse Pointe Yacht, Grosse Pointe Hunt, Country Club Detroit, Detroit Athletic. Office: Masco Corp 21001 Van Born Rd Taylor MI 48180-1340

MANOOGIAN, WILLIAM, lawyer; b. Fresno, Calif., Mar. 29, 1946; s. Morris Anthony and Doris Eunice (Parigian) M.; m. Margaret Ann Solt, Oct. 18, 1975; children: Nicole-Helene, Claire-Louise. BA, Stanford U., 1968; postgrad., U. Paris, 1968-70; JD, Am. U., Washington, 1973. Legis. atty. Rep. Nat. Com., Washington, 1973-75; minority counsel Civil Svc. com. Civic Svc. com. Ho. of Reps., Washington, 1975-83; spl. counsel Dept. of Edn., Washington, 1983-84; counsel to Amb. John Gavin Dept. of State, Mexico City, 1984-86; cons. to Dr. Armand Hammer Occidental Petroleum, L.A., 1986-87; gen. atty. Criminal divsn., Dept. of Justice, Washington, 1987-89, Immigration and Naturalization Svc., San Diego, 1989—; advisor to William Saroyan, Paris, 1969-70. Contbr. articles to profl. jours. Legal advisor to Rep. campaigns, Washington, 1974. Mem. D.C. Bar Assn., Chi Psi. Armenian Orthodox. Avocations: swimming, foreign languages. Home: 13771 Mercado Dr Del Mar CA 92014-3415 Office: Justice Dept 880 Front St Ste 1234 San Diego CA 92101-8803

MANOR, ANDREA JOAN, nursing administrator; b. Milw., Apr. 27, 1951; m. William Phillip Manor, Nov. 11, 1978; children: Arianne, Adam, Ashley, Alexis. BSN, Valparaiso (Ind.) U., 1973; MS in Nursing, Marquette U., 1986. Staff nurse St. Michael Hosp., Milw., 1976-77; devel. dir. Mt. Sinai Med. Ctr., Milw., 1977-88; dir. nursing svcs. Waukesha (Wis.) Meml. Hosp., 1989—. Capt., Nurse Corps, U.S. Army, 1973-76. Mem. ANA, Am. Orgn. Nurse Execs., Wis. Orgn. Nurse Execs. Home: 10504 N Magnolia Dr Mequon WI 53092-5533 Office: Waukesha Meml Hosp 725 American Ave Waukesha WI 53188-5031

MANOS, JOHN, editor-in-chief. Editor-in-chief Consumer's Digest, Chgo. Office: Consumer's Digest 5705 N Lincoln Ave Chicago IL 60659*

MANOS, JOHN M., federal judge; b. 1922. BS, Case Inst. Tech., 1944; JD, Cleve.-Marshall Coll. Law, 1950. Bar: Ohio. Judge Ohio Ct. Common Pleas, 1963-69, Ohio Ct. Appeals, 1969-76, U.S. Dist. Ct. (6th dist.) Ohio, Cleve., 1976—. Mem. ABA, Fed. Bar Assn., Ohio Bar Assn. Office: US Dist Ct US Courthouse 201 Superior Ave E Cleveland OH 44114-1201

MANOS, PETE LAZAROS, supermarket executive; b. Washington, Dec. 29, 1936; s. George and Ardemecia (Saranides) M.; m. Barbara Lorraine Isper, July 16, 1960; children—Helene Deborah, Cynthia Denise. B. Comml. Sci., Benjamin Franklin U., Washington, 1956, M. Comml. Sci., 1962. C.P.A., Md. Buyer Giant Food Inc., Washington, 1961-63, sr. buyer, 1963-70, mgr., 1970-74, dir., 1974-77, v.p., 1977-81, sr. v.p., 1981-92, pres., 1992—; pres. Giant Food Fed. Credit Union, Greenbelt, Md., 1980-86. Mem. Prince George's Environ. Trust, Prince George's County, Md., 1969-70; mem. U.S. Selective Svc. bd., Prince George's County, 1974-76; mem. Prince George's Solid Waste Disposal Task Force, 1972-73; chmn. Balt.-Washington Food Industry Friends of Children's Cancer Found., 1988—. With USN, 1956-59. Recipient Disting. Alumni award Ben Franklin U., 1993, George Washington U., 1994, Am. Hellenic Heritage award, 1994. Mem. United Fresh Fruit and Vegetable Assn. (bd. dirs. 1983-86), Product Mktg. Assn. Democrat. Greek Orthodox. Lodge: Masons. Home: 947 Coachway Annapolis MD 21401-6409 Office: Giant Food Inc 6300 Sheriff Rd Hyattsville MD 20785-4303

MANOSEVITZ, MARTIN, psychologist; b. Mpls., June 22, 1938; s. Julius and Ethel (Cohen) M.; m. Carolyn Heather Margulius, Sept. 17, 1959; children—Bradley, Jason. B.A., U. Minn., Mpls., 1960, Ph.D., 1964. Diplomate in clin. psychology Am. Bd. Profl. Psychology. Asst. prof. psychology Rutgers U., 1964-67; asst. prof. psychology U. Tex., Austin, 1967-69; assoc. prof. U. Tex., 1969-75, prof., 1975-87; pvt. practice clin. psychology Austin, 1975—; adj. prof. psychology U. Tex., 1987-93; dir. psychol. svcs. CPC Capital Hosp., Austin, 1987-93, Shoal Creek Hosp., Austin, 1994-95. Trustee Austin-Travis County Mental Health-Mental Retardation Center, 1978-80. Fellow APA, Am. Orthopsychiat. Assn.; mem. Soc. Rsch. and Child Devel., Tex. Psychol. ASsn., Capital Area Psychol. Assn., Austin Soc. for Psychoanalytic Psychology (pres. 1994-95). Home: 3703 Kennelwood Rd Austin TX 78703-2008 Office: Ste 245 8140 N Mo Pac Expy Bldg 1 Austin TX 78759-8858

MANOUSOS, JAMES WILLIAM See **MANN, JIM**

MANOV, LESLIE JOAN BOYLE (LESLIE JOAN BOYLE MANOV BRONN), radiologist, medical administrator; b. White Plains, N.Y., Aug. 23, 1948; d. Myles Joseph and Harriet Geib (Warburton) Boyle; m. Gregory A. Manov; children from previous marriage: Jay Alexander Bronn, Natasha Nisa Bronn; children from current marriage: John Joseph Manov, Ann Esther Manov. BS, Ohio State U., 1970, MD, 1976. Diplomate Am. Bd. Radiology. Intern internal medicine Ohio State U. Hosp., Columbus, 1976-77, resident internal medicine, 1977-78, resident diagnostic radiology, 1978-81; chief radiology service VA Outpatient Clinic, Columbus, 1981-86; chief diagnostic radiology service Allen Park (Mich.) VA Hosp. Med. Ctr., 1986-87, chief nuclear medicine and diagnostic radiology services, 1987-94; chief radiology svc. Miami (Fla.) VA Med. Ctr., 1994—; clin. asst. prof. radiology Ohio State U. Coll. Medicine, 1981-86, Wayne State U. Sch. Medicine, 1986-94, U. Miami Sch. Medicine, 1995—. mem. Am. Coll. Radiology, Radiol. Soc. N.Am., Assn. VA Chiefs of Radiology, Am. Assn. Women Radiologists, Am. Women's Med. Assn., Am. Inst. Ultrasound in Medicine, South Dade Women's Physicians, South Fla. Radiology Soc., Fla. Radiology Soc., Phi Beta Kappa, Alpha Lambda Delta. Office: Miami VA Med Ctr Radiology Svc Miami FL 33146

MANSBERGER, ARLIE ROLAND, JR., surgeon; b. Pitts., Oct. 13, 1922; s. Arlie Rol and Mayme (Smith) M.; m. Anna Ellen Piel, July 27, 1946; children—Ellen Lynn, John Arlie, Leigh Ann. B.A., Western Md. Coll., 1943, D.Sc. (hon.), 1974; M.D., U. Md., 1947, D.Sc. (hon.), 1978. Diplomate: Am. Bd. Surgery (dir., vice chmn.). Intern U. Md. Hosp., 1947-49, resident in surgery, 1947-54; chief wound shock br. biophysics div. Army Chem. Center, 1954-56; instr. surgery U. Md., 1956-59, asst. prof., 1959-61, asso. prof., 1961-69, prof. surgery, 1969-73; clin. dir. shock-trauma unit, 1962-73; prof. surgery, chmn. dept. Med. Coll. Ga., Augusta, 1973-91; prof. surgery emeritus, chmn., 1991—; cons. surgeon Dwight David Eisenhower Army Med. Center, VA Hosp. Editor: Essence of General Surgery, 1975; chmn. editorial bd.: Bull. U. Md, 1971-73; editor-in-chief: The Am. Surgeon, 1973-89; surg. editor: Resident and Staff Physician, 1979-91; contbr. articles to profl. jours., chpts. to books. Trustee Western Md. Coll., 1971—, Med. Research Found. Ga., 1973-91; bd. dirs. Nicholas J. Pisican Found., 1993—. Served to col. U.S. Army, 1943-46, 54-56. Recipient Man of Yr. award U. Md., 1970, 72, Golden Apple teaching award U. Md., 1968, 72, Disting. Faculty award Med. Coll. Ga., 1979, Gold Medal Alumni award U. Md., 1989, Disting. Svc. award (medal) Southeastern Surg. Congress, 1990. Fellow A.C.S. (gov.); mem. Am. Surg. Assn., Soc. Univ. Surgeons, So. Surg. Assn., Soc. Internationale de Chirurgie, Am. Assn. Surgery of Trauma, Southeastern Surg. Congress, Soc. Surgery of Alimentary Tract, AMA, Soc. Consultants to Armed Forces, Med. Assn. Ga. (editorial bd. 1987-92), Am. Bd. Family Practice (bd. dirs. 1987-92), 29th Div. Assn., Alpha Omega Alpha. Episcopalian. Home: One 7th St Unit 1502 Augusta GA 30901-1343 Office: Dept Surgery Med Coll Ga Augusta GA 30912

MANSBRIDGE, JOHN B., art director, production designer. Prodn. designer: (films) The Love Bug, 1969, Bedknobs and Broomsticks, 1971 (Academy award nomination best art direction 1971), Deliverance, 1972, (with Mark Mansbridge) Amy, 1981, (with Leon Harris) The Devil and Max Devlin, 1981, Baby: Secret of the Lost Legend, 1985, Stone Cold, 1991; art dir.: (films) The Island at the Top of the World, 1974 (Academy award nomination best art direction 1974), No Deposit, No Return, 1976, The Shaggy D.A., 1976, Treasure of Matecumbe, 1976, Freaky Friday, 1976, Herbie Goes to Monte Carlo, 1977, Pete's Dragon, 1977, Hot Lead and Cold Feet, 1978, Return from Witch Mountain, 1978, The North Avenue Irregulars, 1979, The Last Flight of Noah's Ark, 1980, Midnight Madness, 1980, Herbie Goes Bananas, 1980, Tex, 1982, Tron, 1982, Something Wicked This Way Comes, 1983, Trenchcoat, 1983, Splash, 1984, Country, 1984, The River Wild, 1994, (TV movies) The Man Who Fell to Earth, 1987, (TV series) Beauty and the Beast, 1988 (Emmy award outstanding art direction 1989). Office: care Art Directors Guild 11365 Ventura Blvd Ste 315 Studio City CA 91604-3148

MANSBRIDGE, MARK, art director, production designer. Art dir.: (films) Smokey and the Bandit, 1977, Amy, 1981, The Man with Two Brains, 1983, 8 Million Ways to Die, 1986, The Witches of Eastwick, 1987, The War of the Roses, 1989, Ghost, 1990, Chaplin, 1992 (Academy award nomination best art direction 1992), Fire in the Sky, 1993; prodn. designer: (films) Say Anything, 1989, (TV movies) Dream Breakers, 1989. Office: care Art Directors Guild 11365 Ventura Blvd Ste 315 Studio City CA 91604-3148

MANSELL, DARREL LEE, JR., English educator; b. Canton, Ohio, Apr. 9, 1934; s. Darrel Lee and Virginia (Shepherd) M.; m. Elizabeth Meihack, Jan. 1957 (div. July 1970); 1 child, Benjamin Lloyd; m. Adriana Saviane, July 16, 1983. BA, Oberlin Coll., 1956; student, Oxford U., 1961-62; PhD, Yale U., 1963; MA (hon.), Dartmouth Coll., 1975. Instr. Dartmouth Coll., Hanover, N.H., 1962-64, asst. prof., 1964-68, assoc. prof., 1968-74, prof., 1974—. Author: The Novels of Jane Austen, 1973; contbr. articles to scholarly jours. Mem. Victorian Lit. Assn., Internat. Assn. for Phenomenology and Lit., Soc. for Literature and Sci., Jane Austen Soc. N.Am. (founding patron), Phi Beta Kappa. Home: 2 Dana Rd Hanover NH 03755-2227 Office: Dartmouth Coll Dept English Hanover NH 03755

MANSELL, JOYCE MARILYN, special education educator; b. Minot, N.D., Dec. 17, 1934; d. Einar Axel and Gladys Ellen (Wall) Alm; m. Dudley J. Mansell, Oct. 31, 1954; children: Michael, Debra Mansell Richards. BS, U. Houston, 1968; MEd, Sam Houston State U., 1980. Cert. provisional elem. tchr. 1-8, provisional mentally retarded tchr., provisional lang. and/or learning disabilities tchr., profl. elem. tchr. gen. 1-8, profl. reading specialist. 1st grade tchr. Johnson Elem. Sch., 1968-72, 2nd grade tchr., 1972-76, 3rd grade tchr., 1976-77; spl. edn. tchr. mentally retarded/learning disabled Meml. Parkway Jr. H.S., 1982-86, Waller Mid. Sch., 1986-90; spl. edn. tchr. mentally retarded Royal Mid. Sch., Tex., 1990—, Royal H.S., 1995-96; ret., 1996; tchr. Am. sign lang. for retarded students Holy Three and One Luth. Ch. of Deaf. Lutheran. Avocations: reading, fishing, grandchildren and family, signing choir. Home: 2155 Paso Rello Dr Houston TX 77077-5622

MANSFIELD, CARL MAJOR, radiation oncology educator; b. Phila., Dec. 24, 1928; m. Sarah Lynn Flower; children: Joel, Kara. AB in Chemistry, Lincoln U., 1951; postgrad., Temple U., 1952; MD, Howard U., 1956; ScD (hon.), Lincoln U., 1991. Diplomate Am. Bd. Radiology, Am. Bd. Nuclear Medicine. Rotating intern Episcopal Hosp., Phila., 1956-57, resident in radiology, 1957-58, 60, 61-62; resident in radiation therapy and nuclear medicine Thomas Jefferson Med. Coll. Hosp., Phila., 1960-61, NIH fellow in radiation therapy and nuclear medicine, 1962-63, instr. radiology, chief div. nuclear medicine, 1964-65, Chernicoff fellow in pediatric radiation therapy, 1964-66, assoc. in radiology, chief div. nuclear medicine, 1966-67, asst. prof. radiology, chief div. nuclear medicine, 1967-69, assoc. prof. dept. radiation therapy and nuclear medicine, chief sect. of ultrasound, 1970-74, prof., chief div. nuclear medicine and sect. of ultrasound, 1974-76, prof., chmn. dept. radiation therapy and nuclear medicine, 1983-95; assoc. dir. divsn. cancer treatment Nat. Cancer Inst. NIH, Bethesda, Md., 1995—; NIH postdoctoral fellow in radiation therapy Middlesex Hosp. and Med. Sch., London, 1963-64; lectr. in radiology U. Pa. Sch. Medicine, Phila., 1967-73; vis. prof. radiation therapy and nuclear medicine Hahnemann Med. Coll. Hosp., 1971; sabbatical leave Myerestein Inst. Radiotherapy, Middlesex Hosp. and Med. Sch., London, 1972-73; mem. grad. faculty in radiation biophysics U. Kans. Med. Ctr., Kansas City, 1977-83, prof., chmn. dept. radiation therapy, 1976-83; chmn. dept. radiation therapy Menorah Med. Ctr., Kansas City, Mo., 1977-83. Author 2 books, also author or co-author over 129 articles in med. jours. Served with USAF, 1958-60. Fellow Am. Coll. Radiology, Coll. Physicians of Phila., Am. Coll. Nuclear Medicine; mem. AMA, Am. Coll. Radiology, Am. Cancer Soc. (dir.-at-large, nat. bd. dirs. 1981-85, med. and sci. com. 1981-88, profl. edn. com. 1981-88, pres. Phila. divsn. 1989), Am. Radium Soc. (pres. 1988), Radiation Rsch. Program Nat. Cancer Inst. (dir.), Sigma Xi. Office: NIH Bldg EPN Rm 800 Bethesda MD 20892

MANSFIELD, CHRISTOPHER CHARLES, insurance company legal executive; b. 1950; married. BA, Boston Coll., 1972, JD, 1975. With Liberty Mut. Ins. Co., Boston, 1975—, v.p., 1983, sr. v.p., gen. counsel, 1983—; underwriter Liberty Lloyds of Tex. Ins. Co., 1984—; v.p., dir. Liberty Ins. Corp., 1985—; v.p. Liberty Mut. Fire Ins. Co., 1985—, Stein Roe Svcs. Co., 1986—; v.p., gen. counsel LEXCO Ltd., 1986—, Liberty Mut. Capital Corp., 1986—; bd. dirs. Liberty Fin. Cos., Liberty Mut. Bermuda, Liberty Internat. Office: Liberty Mut Ins Co PO Box 140 175 Berkeley St Boston MA 02117

MANSFIELD, EDWARD PATRICK, JR., advertising executive; b. Warren, Pa., Oct. 29, 1947; s. Edward Patrick and Frieda (Dahler) M.; m. Norma L. Johnson, Apr. 17, 1971. AS in Acctg., Jamestown Bus. Coll., 1967; BS in Mktg. Advt., David N. Myers Coll., 1970. Promotion mgr., ad dir. The News-Herald, Lake County, Ohio, 1973-77; dir. advt. The Eagle, Butler, Pa., 1977-78; dir. mktg. Baltimore Mag., 1978-79; dir. advt. The Washingtonian, Washington, 1979—. Founder, chmn. Warm-A-Heart Fund, 1988—; bd. dirs. Columbia Lighthouse for the Blind, 1988—, chmn., 1988-93; bd. dirs. The Lighthouse; mem. adv. bd. Ann Arundel County Mental Health. Avocations: amateur radio operator gen. class, sailing. Home: 347 Cottswold Pl Riva MD 21140-1528 Office: Washingtonian Mag 1828 L St NW Ste 200 Washington DC 20036-5104

MANSFIELD, EDWIN, economist, educator; b. Kingston, N.Y., June 8, 1930; s. Raymond and Sarah M.; m. Lucile Howe, Feb. 21, 1955; children: Edward, Elizabeth. AB, Dartmouth Coll., 1951; MA, Duke U., 1953, PhD, 1955; cert. diploma, Royal Statis. Soc., 1955; MA (hon.), U. Pa., 1971. Asst. prof., assoc. prof. econs. Carnegie-Mellon U., 1955-60, 62-63; vis. assoc. prof. econs. Yale U., New Haven, 1961-62; vis. prof. econs. Harvard U., Cambridge, Mass., 1963-64, Calif. Inst. Tech., Pasadena, 1967-68; prof. econs. U. Pa., Phila., 1964—; dir. Ctr. Econs. and Tech. U. Pa., 1985—; guest prof. Chalmers U. Tech. Gothenburg, Sweden, 1983, Nat. Technol. U., 1989-95; cons. Exec. Office Pres. of U.S., U.S. Dept. Commerce, U.S. Gen. Acctg. Office, U.S. Dept. Labor, HHS, NSF, Nat. Inst. Edn., Fed. Power Commn., Inst. for Def. Analysis, SBA, FTC, U.S. Army, Ford Found., RAND Corp., Can. Royal Commn., New Zealand Rsch. Inst., Nat. Inst. Standards and Tech., Internat. Fin. Corp., World Bank, others; mem. Gov.'s Sci. Adv. Com., 1965-66; chmn. U.S.-USSR Working Party on Sci. and Tech., 1974-75; panelist Nat. Bur. Standards/NAS, 1974-76; bd. examiners Grad. Record Exam, 1975-76; econ. adv. com. U.S. Bur. Census, 1982-85; Nat. Tech. Medal Com., 1984-87; chmn. vis. com. Rensselaer Poly. Inst., 1986-91. Author: The Economics of Technological Change, 1968, Industrial Research and Technological Innovation, 1968, Defense, Science and Public Policy, 1968, Research and Innovation in the Modern Corporation, 1971, The Production and Application of New Industrial Technology, 1977, Monopoly Power and Economic Performance, 4th edit., 1978, Technology Transfer, Productivity and Economic Policy, 1982, Managerial Economics and Operations Research, 5th edit., 1987, Economics, 7th edit., 1992, Economics USA, 4th edit., 1995, Managerial Economics, 1990, 3d edit., 1996, Microeconomics, 8th edit., 1994, Statistics, 5th edit., 1994, (with Elizabeth Mansfield) The Economics of Technical Change, 1993, Applied Microeconomics, 1994, Leading Economic Controversies, 1995, Innovation, Technology, and the Economy, 1995, others; editor Jour. of the Am. Statistical Assn., 1964-67, Am. Economist, 1969-90, Jour. of Econ. Edn., 1982-90, Review of Industrial Organization, 1984—, IEEE Transactions on Engring. Mgmt., 1985—, Managerial and Decision Econs., 1988-92, Univ. Wis. series on tech. change, 1984-88, Pub. Rsch. Quar., 1993—, and others. Fulbright fellow, 1954-55, Ford Found. rsch. fellow, 1960-61, Ctr. for Advanced Study Behavioral Scis. fellow, 1971-72; NSF grantee, 1962—; recipient Cert. Appreciation U.S. Sec. Commerce, 1979, Publ. award Patent Law Assn., 1984, Honor award Nat. Tech. U., 1992, Citation Classic award Inst. for Sci. Info., 1992, Spl. Creativity award NSF, 1994, Hall of Fame award Prentice Hall, 1995, Enterprise award Kenan Charitable Trust, 1996. Fellow Econometric Soc., Am. Acad. Arts and Scis.; mem. AAAS (sci., engring. and pub. policy com. 1981-84), Am. Econ. Assn., Royal Statis. Soc. (cert.), Phi Beta Kappa. Home: 202 Plush Mill Rd Wallingford PA 19086-6021 Office: Dept Econs U Pa Philadelphia PA 19104

MANSFIELD, JOHN H., legal educator; b. 1928. AB, Harvard U., 1952, LLB, 1956. Bar: Calif., Mass. John H. W., Jr. prof. law Harvard U., Cambridge, Mass. Mem. Assn. for Asian Studies. Editor: (with Weinstein, Abrams and Berger) Cases and Materials on Evidence, 1988. Office: Sch Law Harvard U Cambridge MA 02138

MANSFIELD, KAREN LEE, lawyer; b. Chgo., Mar. 17, 1942; d. Ralph and Hilda (Blum) Mansfield; children: Nicole Rafaela, Lori Michele. BA in Polit. Sci., Roosevelt U., 1963; JD, DePaul U., 1971; student U. Chgo., 1959-60. Bar: Ill. 1972, U.S. Dist. Ct. (no. dist.) Ill. 1972. Legis. intern Ill. State Senate, Springfield, 1966-67; tchr. Chgo. Pub. Schs., 1967-70; atty. CNA Ins., Chgo., 1971-73; law clk. Ill. Apellate Ct., Chgo., 1973-75; sr. trial atty. U.S. Dept. Labor, Chgo., 1975—, mentor Adopt-a-Sch. Program, 1992-95. Contbr. articles to profl. jours. Vol. Big Sister, 1975-81; bd. dirs. Altgeld Nursery Sch., 1963-66, Ill. div. UN Assn., 1966-72, Hull House Jane Addams Ctr., 1977-82, Broadway Children's Ctr., 1986-90, Acorn Family Entertainment, 1993-95; mem. Oak Park Farmers' Market Commn., 1996—; rsch. asst. Citizens for Gov. Otto Kerner, Chgo., 1964; com. mem. Ill. Commn. on Status of Women, Chgo., 1964-70; del. Nat. Conf. on Status of Women, 1968; candidate for del. Ill. Constl. Conv., 1969. Mem. Chgo. Council Lawyers, Women's Bar Assn. Ill., Lawyer Pilots Bar Assn., Fed. Bar Assn. Unitarian. Clubs: Friends of Gamelan (performer), 99's Internat. Orgn. Women Pilots (legis. chmn. Chgo. area chpt. 1983-86, legis. chmn. North Cen. sect. 1986-88, legis. award 1983, 85). Home: 204 S Taylor Ave Oak Park IL 60302-3307 Office: US Dept Labor Office Solicitor 230 S Dearborn St Fl 8 Chicago IL 60604-1505

MANSFIELD, LOIS EDNA, mathematics educator, researcher; b. Portland, Maine, Jan. 2, 1941; d. R. Carleton and Mary (Bowdish) M. BS, U. Mich., 1962; MS, U. Utah, 1966, PhD, 1969. Vis. asst. prof. computer sci. Purdue U., 1969-70; asst. prof. computer sci. U. Kans., Lawrence, 1970-74, assoc. prof., 1974-78; assoc. prof. math. N.C. State U., Raleigh, 1978-79; assoc. prof. applied math. U. Va., Charlottesville, 1979-83, prof., 1983—; mem. adv. panel computer sci. NSF, 1975-78; cons., vis. scientist Inst. Computer Applications in Sci. and Engring., Hampton, Va., 1976-78. Contbr. articles to profl. jours. Grantee NSF and DOE. Mem. Am. Math. Soc., Soc. Indsl. and Applied Math. (mem. editorial bd. Jour. Sci. Statis. Computing, 1979-88), Assn. Computing Machinery (bd. dirs. SIGNUM 1980-83). Office: U Va Dept Applied Math Thornton Hall Charlottesville VA 22903

MANSFIELD, MARC LEWIS, chemist, research scientist; b. Vernal, Utah, Mar. 30, 1955; s. Henry A. and Mildred (Lind) M.; m. Susan G. Bratton, Mar. 19, 1977; children: Katharine, Heather, Eric. BA, U. Utah, 1977; PhD, Dartmouth Coll., 1980. Postdoctoral assoc. Colo. State U., Ft. Collins, 1980-83; asst. prof. U. Md., College Park, 1983-85; rsch. scientist Mich. Molecular Inst., Midland, 1985—. Recipient Presdl. Young Investigator award NSF, 1985, Initiatives in Rsch. award NAS, 1988. Mem. Am. Chem. Soc., Am. Phys. Soc. Mem. LDS Ch. Office: Mich Molecular Inst 1910 W St Andrews Rd Midland MI 48640-2657

MANSFIELD, MICHAEL JOSEPH, former ambassador, former senator; b. N.Y.C., Mar. 16, 1903; s. Patrick and Josephine (O'Brien) M.; m. Maureen Hayes, Sept. 13, 1932; 1 dau., Anne Mansfield Marris. Student, Mont. Sch. Mines, 1927-28; A.B., U. Mont., 1933, A.M., 1934; student, U. Calif., 1936, 37. Seaman U.S. Navy, 1918-19; with U.S. Army, 1919-20, U.S. Marines, 1920-22; miner and mining engr., 1922-1931; prof. history and polit. sci. U. Mont., 1933-42; mem. 78th-82d Congresses from 1st Dist. Mont., 1943-53; U.S. Senator from Mont., 1953-77, asst. majority leader, 1957-61, majority leader, 1961-77; mem. Com. on Fgn. Relations, Appropriations Com.; chmn. Dem. Conf., Policy Com., Steering Com.; ambassador to Japan Tokyo, 1977-89; Presdl. rep. in, China, 1944; U.S. del. IX Inter-Am. Conf., Colombia, 1948, 6th UN Assembly, Paris, 1951-52, Southeast Asia Conf., Manila, 1954, 13th UN Gen. Assembly, 1958; Presdl. assignment, West Berlin, Southeast Asia, Vietnam, 1962, Europe, Southeast Asia, 1965, 69, visited People's Republic of China on invitation of Premier Chou-En-lai, 1972, on invitation of Govt. of People's Republic of China, 1974, 76, 77, 78. Recipient Nelson Rockefeller Pub. Service award, 1988. Office: Ste 900 1101 Pennsylvania Ave NW Washington DC 20004-2514

MANSFIELD, STEPHEN W., judge; b. Brookline, Mass., Aug. 21, 1952; s. Clarence E. and Mary Ann (Zeyer) M.; divorced; children: Eric, Mark, Greg. BA cum laude, Tufts U., 1974; JD, Boston U., 1977. Bar: Tex., Mass. Assoc. gen. counsel Corbel & Co., Jacksonville, Fla., 1984-86; sr. counsel VALIC, Houston, 1986-94; pvt. practice Houston, 1994; judge Tex. Ct. of Criminal Appeals, Austin, 1995—. Republican. Avocations: numismatics, rugby, running. Office: Ct Criminal Appeals Box 12308 Austin TX 78711*

MANSHIP, DOUGLAS, broadcast and newspaper executive; b. Baton Rouge, Nov. 3, 1918; s. Charles P. and Leora (Douthit) M.; m. Jane French, Jan. 31, 1942 (div. 1981); children—Douglas Lewis, Richard French, David Charles, Dina. Student, La. State U., 1936-41, U. Heidelberg, 1937, U.

Colo., 1938-39. Reporter State Times and Morning Advocate, 1945-47, pub., 1970—; with Baton Rouge Broadcasting Co., 1947—, pres., 1948—; pres., chmn. bd. La IV Broadcasting Corp., 1953—; vice chmn. bd. Radio Free Europe/Radio Liberty, 1978—; chmn. Mobile Video Tapes, Inc., 1960; pres. Capital City Press, 1970; bd. dirs. City Nat. Bank, TV Stas. Inc. Campaign chmn. Community Chest, 1950, bd. dirs., 1950-52, pres., 1951. With USAAF, World War II. Mem. Baton Rouge C. of C. (pres. 1963), La. C. of C. (v.p.), Assn. for Profl. Broadcasting Edn., Council for A Better La., Assn. La. Chambers Commerce, So. Newspaper Pubs. Assn. (pres. 1977-78), Kappa Alpha, Sigma Delta Chi. Episcopalian. Office: Capital City Press 525 Lafayette St Baton Rouge LA 70802-5410

MANSI, JOSEPH ANNEILLO, public relations company executive; b. Oct. 8, 1935; s. Joseph C. and Vinnie (Chirico) M.; m. Mary P. Fusco, Aug. 1, 1959; children: Karen M. D'Attore, Jeanine V. Dimenna. B.S., NYU, 1957. Newsman Internat. News Service, UPI, 1953-58; mem. pub. relations staff Lawrence Orgn., N.Y.C., 1960-63; acct. supr. Philip Lesly Co., N.Y.C., 1963-67; dir. corp. communications Ward Foods, Inc., N.Y.C., 1967-72; dir. pub. relations Metromedia Inc., N.Y.C., 1973-75; pres. Corp. Relations Network, Inc., N.Y.C., 1975-80; mng. ptnr. KCSA Pub. Rels., N.Y.C., 1980—. Served with AUS, 1958-60. Mem. Pub. Rels. Soc. Am. (accredited). Home: 10 Beatrice Ln Glen Cove NY 11542-1202 Office: KCSA Pub Rels 820 2nd Ave New York NY 10017-4504

MANSKE, PAUL ROBERT, orthopedic hand surgeon, educator; b. Ft. Wayne, Ind., Apr. 29, 1938; s. Alfred R. and Elsa E. (Streufert) M.; m. Sandra H. Henricks, Nov. 29, 1975; children: Ethan Paul, Claire Bruch, Louisa Hendricks. BA, Valparaiso U., 1960, DSc (hon.), 1985; MD, Washington U., St. Louis, 1964. Diplomate Am. Bd. Surgery. Surg. intern U. Wash., Seattle, 1964-65, surg. resident, 1965-66; orthopedic surg. resident Washington U., St. Louis, 1969-72; hand surgery fellow U. Louisville, 1971; instr. orthopedic surgery Washington U. Med. Sch., St. Louis, 1972-76, asst. prof. orthopedic surgery, 1976-83, prof., 1983—, chmn. dept., 1983-95. Editor-in-chief Jour. Hand Surgery, 1996—; contbr. more than 215 articles and abstracts to profl. jours. Lt. comdr. USN, 1966-69, Vietnam. Lt. comdr. USN, 1966-69, Vietnam. Fellow AMA, Am. Acad. Orthopaedic Surgery, Am. Orthopaedic Assn.; mem. Am. Soc. Surgery of the Hand, Alpha Omega Alpha. Lutheran. Office: Washington Univ Dept Orthop Surgery 1 Barnes Hosp Plz Saint Louis MO 63110

MANSKI, WLADYSLAW JULIAN, microbiology educator, medical scientist; b. Lwow, Poland, May 15, 1915; came to U.S., 1958, naturalized, 1964; s. Julian and Helena (Lewicka) M.; m. Anna Z. Artymowicz, June 20, 1941; children: Chris, Louis. M.Phil., U. Warsaw, Poland, 1939, D.Sc., 1951. Instr. U. Warsaw, 1936-39; rsch. asst. Inst. Lwow, 1940-41, Inst. Lwow (Inst. Agr.), Pulawy, Poland, 1942-44; instr. U. Lublin, Poland, 1944-45; instr. dept. microbiology Med. Sch., Wroclaw, Poland, 1945-49; Rockefeller fellow Columbia U., N.Y.C., 1949-50; head immunochemistry lab. Inst. Immunology and Exptl. Therapy, Polish Acad. Sci., Wroclaw, 1951-55; head Macromolecular Biochemistry Lab. Inst. Immunology and Exptl. Therapy, Polish Acad. Sci., Warsaw, 1955-57; head dept. virology Biochemistry Lab., State Inst. Hygiene, Warsaw, 1955-57; research worker Coll. Physicians and Surgeons, Columbia U., 1958-62, rsch. assoc., 1962-64, asst. prof., 1964-67, assoc. prof. microbiology, 1967-74, prof. microbiology, 1974-85, prof. emeritus, 1986; dir. rsch. Harkness Eye Inst., Columbia U., N.Y.C., 1985-90. Contbr. articles to profl. jours. NIH grantee, 1960-86. Mem. AAAS, Am. Assn. Immunologists, AAUP, Research in Vision and Ophthalmology Assn., Am. Chem. Soc., Brit. Biochemical Soc., N.Y. Acad. Scis., Soc. Exptl. Biology and Medicine, Soc. Study of Evolution, Internat. Soc. Eye Research, Harvey Soc., Transplantation Soc. Home: 10 Downing St New York NY 10014-4734 Office: 630 W 168th St New York NY 10032-3702

MANSMANN, CAROL LOS, federal judge, law educator; b. Pittsburgh, Pa., Aug. 7, 1942; d. Walter Joseph and Regina Mary (Pilarski) Los; m. J. Jerome Mansmann, June 27, 1970; children: Casey, Megan, Patrick. B.A., J.D., Duquesne U., 1964, 67; LL.D., Seton Hill Coll., Greensburg, Pa., 1985; PhD, La Roche Coll., 1990. Asst. dist. atty. Allegheny County, Pitts., 1968-72; assoc. McVerry Baxter & Mansmann, Pitts., 1973-79; assoc. prof. law Duquesne U., Pitts., 1973-82; judge west dist. U.S. Dist. Ct. Pa., Pitts., 1982-85; judge U.S. Ct. Appeals (3rd cir.), Phila., 1985—; Mem. Pa. Criminal Procedural Rules Com., Pitts., 1972-77; spl. asst. atty. gen. Commonwealth of Pa., 1974-79; bd. dirs. Pa. Bar Inst., Harrisburg, 1984-90; adj. prof. law U. Pitts., 1987—. Mem. adv. bd. Villanova U. Law Sch., 1985-91; bd. dirs. Duquesne U., 1987—, Sewickley Acad., 1988-91. Recipient St. Thomas More award, Pitts., 1983, Phila., 1984. Mem. ABA, Nat. Assn. Women Judges, Pa. Bar Assn., Fed. Judges Assn., Am. Judicature Soc., Allegheny County Bar Assn., Phi Alpha Delta. Republican. Roman Catholic. Office: US Ct Appeals 1036 US Courthouse Pittsburgh PA 15219*

MANSMANN, J. JEROME, lawyer; b. Pitts., Aug. 14, 1942; s. C. Rex and Margaret G. (McArdle) M.; m. Carol M. Los, June 27, 1970; children: Kathleen, Megan, Patrick. BA, U. Dayton, 1963; JD, Duquesne U., 1967. Bar: Pa., U.S. Dist. Ct. (we. dist.) Pa., U.S. Ct. Appeals (3d cir.), U.S. Supreme Ct. Assoc. Law Offices of P.J. MCArdle, Pitts., 1969-70; ptnr. Mansmann & Mansmann, Pitts., 1970-72, Gondelman, Baxter, Mansmann McVerry & Cindrich, Pitts., 1972-81, Mansmann Cindrich & Titus, Pitts., 1981-91; shareholder Buchanan Ingersoll, P.C., Pitts., 1991—; spl. asst. Atty. Gen. Commonwealth of Pa., Pitts., 1974-80. Past legal svcs. com. Cath. Health Assn., St. Louis. With USAF, 1967-68. Mem. Pa. Bar Assn., Allegheny County Bar Assn. Home: Backbone Rd Sewickley PA 15143 Office: Buchanan Ingersoll PC One Oxford Ctr 301 Grant St 20th Fl Pittsburgh PA 15219-2703

MANSON, JOSEPH LLOYD, III, lawyer; b. Richmond, Va., May 5, 1949; s. Joseph Lloyd Jr. and Nan Smith (Copley) M.; m. Martha Forman Foltz, Sept. 8, 1973; children: Martha Stuart, Joseph Scott, Rachel Smith. BS, U. Va., 1970; JD, Emory U., 1974. Assoc. Verner, Liipfert, Bernhard & McPherson, Washington, 1974-80; ptnr. Verner, Liipfert, Bernhard, McPherson & Hand, Washington, 1981—; bd. dirs. Barrow Grocery Co. Founder Alexandria Youth Sports Found., 1993. 2d lt. U.S. Army, 1973. Mem. ABA (ry. and airline labor law com., co-chmn. mgmt. 1993-94), D.C. Bar Assn. Republican. Episcopalian. Avocations: music, tennis, theatre, movies. Office: Verner Liipfert Bernhard McPherson & Hand 901 15th St NW Ste 700 Washington DC 20005-2327

MANSON, KEITH ALAN MICHAEL, lawyer; b. Warwick, RI, Oct. 26, 1962; s. Ronald Frederick and Joan Patricia (Reardon) M.; m. Jennifer Annette Stearns; children: Kristin Elizabeth, Michelle Nicole. BA, R.I. Coll., 1985; cert. computer info. systems, Bryant Coll., 1988; cert. law, U. Notre Dame, London, 1990; JD, Thomas M. Cooley Law Sch., 1991. Bar: Ind. 1991, U.S. Dist. Ct. (no. dist.) Ind. 1991, U.S. Dist. Ct. (so. dist.) Ind. 1991, U.S. Dist. Ct. (so. dist.) Ga. 1992, U.S. Dist. Ct. Mil. Appeals 1991. Spl. asst. U.S. atty. U.S. Dist. Ct. Ga., Brunswick, 1992-93; pvt. practice Fernandina Beach, Fla., 1994—; cons. The Law Store Ltd. Paralegal Svcs., Fernandina Beach., 1994—. Contbr. articles to profl. jours. Commnr. Fla. coun. Boy Scouts Am., Jacksonville, 1993—; com. mem. sea scout ship 660 St. Peters Ch., Fernandina Beach, 1994—; chmn. Scouting for Food Dr., Nassau County, Fla., 1994. Lt. USN, 1985-86, 90-94. F.C. Tanner Trust, Fed. Products Inc. scholar, Providence, 1981-85, Esterline Corp. scholar, Providence, 1986. Mem. ABA, Judge Advocate Assn., Jacksonville Bar Assn., Navy League U.S., Rotary (project mgr. Webster-Dudley Mass. chpt. 1986-88), Phi Alpha Delta. Avocations: gardening, rugby, sports history, military history, collecting historical items. Home and Office: 1908 Reatta Ln Fernandina Beach FL 32034-8936

MANSON, LEWIS AUMAN, energy research executive; b. Cleve., July 12, 1918; s. Lewis Frederick and Ina Josephine (Auman) M.; m. Alva Anne London, Sept. 3, 1960 (div. 1982); children: Anita, Howard; m. Shirley Anne Traeger, Jan. 27, 1982; children: Lewis, Jean, Phillip, Edward. Student, Gen. Motors Tech. U., 1944, Purdue U., 1942-43, Rice U., 1950-54. Cons. numerous oil, gas, and mining cos., 1951-57; cons. The Space Agy., Washington, 1958-59, Douglas Aircraft, El Segundo, Calif., 1964; dir. Copper Range Mines, Wyo., 1965; dir. explorations, cons. Nico Internat., S.A. de C.V., Mex., 1968-71; builder Spring, Tex., 1971-74; dir., conductor explorations Minerals of the Sun, S.A. de C.V., Honduras, 1975; dir. Asheville Petroleum Corp., Ill., 1976; conductor explorations Neozoic Minerals & Petroleum, Ltd., Colo., N.Mex., Tex., 1976-77; conductor explorations, dir. Primal Energy Rsch. Found., Houston, 1982—; pres. Transzoic Orebody Locators, Ltd., Vancouver, B.C., Pleiades Petroleum Corp., Lexington, Tenn. and Houston; lectr. grade schs., high schs., Kiwanis, and Rotary, 1962—. Author: The Primal Energy Transverter, 1966, Birth of the Moon, 1978, Origins of Solar Flares and Keys to Predicting Them, 1978, Automatic Recording of Deep Space (interplanetary) Gravity, 1978, Arriving Ionospheric High Energy (Solar Generated), 1978, Out of the Grey Mist, 1992, Life's Continuum, 1992, The Real Origin of Stellar Energy, 1993, The Great Mystery, 1994; patentee in field; inventor Quakaster, Affinity Sys., The Cradle System equipment to prevent and/or cure decubitis ulcers by "ocean motion." Scoutmaster Boy Scouts Am., Houston, 1956-63; cubmaster Cub Scouts, Pasadena, Calif., 1962. With Ind. NG, 1942-43. Republican. Avocations: mineral and fossil collecting, mountaineering, boating, archeology, metal and wood working. Office: Primal Energy Rsch Found Apt 113 11250 Taylor Draper Ln Austin TX 78759-3976

MANSON, PAUL DAVID, retired military officer, electronics executive; b. Trail, B.C., Can., Aug. 20, 1934; s. Robert Edwin and Mary Leonora (McLeod) M.; m. Margaret Nickel, May 11, 1957; children: Robert, Catherine, Peter, Karen. Diploma, Royal Roads Mil. Coll., Victoria, B.C., Can., 1954, Royal Mil. Coll., Kingston, Ont., Can., 1956; BS, Queen's U., 1957; D Mil. Sci. honoris causa, Royal Roads, 1990. Joined RCAF, 1957; advanced through grades to gen. Can. Armed Forces, 1989; various squadron duties Can. Armed Forces, France and Federal Republic of Germany, 1957-62, 67-72; ops. research, Hqrs. Can. Armed Forces, Ottawa, 1963-66; exec. asst. to chief of def. staff Nat. Def. Hdqrs., Can. Armed Forces, Ottawa, 1972-73, chief of air doctrine and ops., 1982-83, asst. dep. minister personnel, 1985-86, chief of def. staff, 1986-89; student Nat. Def. Coll., Kingston, 1973-74; base comdr. Can. Forces Base, Chatham, 1974-76; program mgr. New Fighter Aircraft Program, Ottawa, 1977-80; comdr. 1 Can. Air Group, Fed. Republic of Germany, 1980-81, Air Command, Winnipeg, Man., Can., 1983-85; pres. Lockheed Martin Electronic Systems Can., Inc., Montreal. Recipient Order of Mil. Merit Govt. of Can., 1981, Comdr. Legion of Merit U.S., 1989, C.D. Howe award for achievements in aeronautics and space, 1992. Mem. Aerospace Industries Assn. Can. (past chmn.). Anglican. Avocations: astronomy, music, golfing, home computing. Office: Lockheed Martin Electronic, Systems Can Inc, 6111 Royalmount Ave, Montreal, PQ Canada H4P 1K6

MANSON, PAUL NELLIS, plastic surgeon; b. Kansas City, Mo., Dec. 28, 1943; s. Nellis Emanuel and Alice Winifred (Olson) M.; m. Kathryn Garland, Mar. 1949; children: Ted, Jenner. BA in Chemistry, Northwestern U., 1965, MD, 1968. Prof., chmn. plastic surgery Johns Hopkins Sch. Medicine, Balt., 1990—. Maj. U.S. Army, 1970-73. Republican. Presbyterian. Office: 8152 F McElderry Wins 601 N Caroline St Baltimore MD 21205-1809

MANSON-HING, LINCOLN ROY, dental educator; b. Georgetown, Guyana, May 20, 1927; m. Joyce Louise Chin, Aug. 21, 1949; children: Collin James, Jennifer Lynn, Jeffrey Paul. D.M.D. cum laude, Tufts U., 1948; M.S., U. Ala., 1961. Practice dentistry Kingston, Jamaica; also dir. Schs.' Dental Clinic, St. Mary Parish, Jamaica, 1948-56; asst. prof. dentistry U. Ala., 1956-59, asso. prof., 1959-68, prof. dentistry, 1968-88, chmn. dept. dental radiology, 1962-88, prof. emeritus dentistry, 1988—; Cons. Am. Dental Assn., Am. Standards Assn., VA Hosp., Birmingham, Ala., Tuskegee, Ala.; cons. USAF, Ala. State Crippled Children Cleft Palate Clinic, 1957-69; Fulbright-Hays lectr., Egypt., 1964-65. Author: (with A.H. Wuehrmann) Dental Radiology, 1965, Panoramic Dental Radiology, 1975, Fundamentals of Dental Radiology, 1979; also articles, textbook chpts.; sect. editor: Jour. Oral Surgery, Oral Medicine and Pathology, 1967-80. Mem. ADA, Am. Acad. Dental Radiology (pres. 1967, editor 1967-80), Internat. Assn. Dento-maxillofacial Radiology (v.p. 41977—), Internat. Assn. Dental Research, AAAS, Sigma Xi, Omicron Kappa Upsilon. Home: 205 Mecca Ave Birmingham AL 35209-3459 Office: 1919 7th Ave S Birmingham AL 35233-2005

MANSOUR, FATEN SPIRONOUS, interior designer, realtor; b. Amman, Jordan, May 8, 1958; came to U.S., 1981; d. Spironous Mansour and Margret Mousa Nijmeh; 1 child, Lara. AS in Bus. Adminstrn., Wasifia Coll., Amman, 1977; AS in Computer Sci., Sec. Bus. Adminstrn., West Valley Coll., 1988; BS in Interior Design, Art, San Jose State U., 1992, M in Physiology, 1994. Tchr. French Rawdat Al-Sa'adeh, Amman, 1976-78; office mgr. of Min. of Transp. Queen Alia Internat. Airport, Amman, 1977-88; coord. banquets and weddings Marquee Club and Café, San Jose, Calif., 1988-93; interior designer, realtor, multi-media computer designer Esquisite, San Jose, 1992—. Prodr. Arab Am. TV, L.A., 1990—. Active Arab Am. Anti-Discrimination Com. Avocations: multi-media painting, photography, poetry, painting, internet cruising. Home: PO Box 10355 San Jose CA 95157-1355 Office: Esquisite PO Box 10355 San Jose CA 95157-1355

MANSOUR, GEORGE P., Spanish language and literature educator; b. Huntington, W.Va., Sept. 4, 1939; s. Elia and Marie (Yazbek) M.; m. Mary Ann Rogers, Dec. 27, 1961; children: Alicia, Philip. AB, Marshall U., 1961; MA, Mich. State U., 1963, PhD, 1965. Assoc. prof. Mich. State U., East Lansing, 1968-77, prof., 1977—, chmn. dept. Romance and Classical langs., 1982—; cons. Mich. Dept. Edn., Lansing, 1984-85. Contbr. articles to profl. jours. Mem. Am. Assn. Tchrs. Spanish and Portuguese (v.p. 1969-71), Mich. Fgn. Lang. Assn. (pres. 1982-84). Democrat. Mem. Eastern Orthodox Ch. Avocations: Pysanky, golf. Home: 1303 Lucerne Dewitt MI 48820 Office: Mich State U Dept Romance & Classical Langs East Lansing MI 48824

MANSOUR, TAG ELDIN, pharmacologist, educator; b. Belkas, Egypt, Nov. 6, 1924; came to U.S., 1951, naturalized, 1956; s. Elsayed and Rokaya (Elzayat) M.; m. Joan Adela MacKinnon, Aug. 6, 1955; children—Suzanne, Jeanne, Dean. DVM, Cairo U., 1946; PhD, U. Birmingham, Eng., 1949, DSc, 1974. Lectr. U. Cairo, 1950-51; Fulbright instr. physiology Howard U., Washington, 1951-52; sr. instr. pharmacology Case Western Res. U., 1952-54; asst. prof., asso. prof. pharmacology La. State U. Med. Sch., New Orleans, 1954-61; assoc. prof., prof. pharmacology Stanford U. Sch. Medicine, 1961—, chmn. dept. pharmacology, 1977-91, Donald E. Baxter prof., 1977—; cons. USPHS, WHO, Nat. Acad. Scis.; Mem. adv. bd. Med. Sch., Kuwait U.; Heath Clarke lectr. London Sch. Hygiene and Tropical Medicine, 1981. Contrbr. sci. articles to profl. jours. Commonwealth Fund fellow, 1965; Macy Found. scholar NIMR, London, 1982. Fellow AAAS; mem. Am. Soc. Pharmacology and Exptl. Therapeutics, Am. Soc. Biol. Chemists, Am. Heart Assn., Sierra Club, Stanford Faculty Club. Office: 300 Pasteur Dr Stanford CA 94305-5332

MANSOURI, LOTFOLLAH, opera stage director; b. Tehran, June 15, 1929; arrived in Can., 1976; s. Hassan and Mehri (Jalili) M.; m. Marjorie Anne Thompson, Sept. 18, 1954; 1 child, Shireen Melinda. AB, UCLA, 1953. Asst. prof. UCLA, 1957-60; resident stage dir. Zurich Opera, 1960-65; chief stage dir. Geneva Opera, 1965-75; gen. dir. Can. Opera Co., Toronto, Ont., 1976-88, San Francisco Opera, 1988—; dramatic coach Music Acad. West, Santa Barbara, Calif., 1959; dir. dramatics Zurich Internat. Opera Studio, 1961-65, Centre Lyrique, Geneva, 1967-72; artistic adviser Tehran Opera, 1973-75; opera adviser Nat. Arts Centre, Ottawa, Ont., 1977; v.p. Opera America, 1979—; operatic cons. dir. Yes, Giorgio, MGM, 1981; dir. opera sequence for film Moonstruck (Norman Jewison), 1987. Guest dir. opera cos. including Met. Opera, San Francisco Opera, N.Y.C. Opera, Lyric Opera of Chgo., Houston Grand Opera, La Scala, Covent Garden, Verona Opera, Kirov Opera, Australian Opera, Vienna Staatsoper, Vienna Volksoper, Salzburg Festival, Amsterdam Opera, Holland Festival, Nice (France) Opera, Festival D'Orange, France: co-author: An Operatic Life, 1982. Mem. Am. Guild Mus. Artists, Can. Actors Equity Assn. Initiated above-stage projection of subtitles as a simultaneous translation of opera, 1983.

MANSPEIZER, SUSAN R., artist, educator; b. N.Y.C., Oct. 17, 1940. BA cum laude, CCNY, 1962, MA in Art Edn., 1966; postgrad., Corcoran Gallery, 1966-68, Art Students League, 1976-81. Art tchr. N.Y.C. Pub. Schs., Coll. of New Rochelle, N.Y., 1974, Kipp St. Art Ctr., Chappaqua, N.Y., 1983, Arts Ctr. of No. N.J., 1990—; tchr. collage workshop Acad. Orthopaedic Surgeons, 1983; tchr. Art Students League, summer 1993; represented by Viridian Gallery, N.Y.C., Nat. Assn. Women Artists, N.Y.C., Hudson River Contemporary Artists, Yonkers, N.Y., Westchester Coun. for the Arts, N.Y., Mamaroneck Artist Guild. One woman shows include Greenburgh Pub. Libr., 1974, 85, Westchester C.C., Valhalla, N.Y., 1975, Chappaqua Libr. Gallery, 1980, The Gallery, Tarrytown, N.Y., 1987, Viridian Gallery, N.Y.C., 1987, 90, 93, Mus. of the Hudson Highlands, Cornwall, N.Y., 1987, Lever Ho., N.Y.C., 1988, Concordia Coll., Bronxville, 1989, Concordia Coll., Bronxville, N.Y., 1989, Kirkland Art Ctr., Clinton, N.Y., 1991, S.W. State U., Marshall, Minn., 1991; group exhbns. include Silvermine Guild of Artists, New Canaan, Conn., 1992, Berkshire Artisans, Pittsfield, Mass., 1994, Onward Gallery, Tokyo, 1994, numerous others; juried exhibitions include Silvermine New Mems. Exhbn., 1990, Hastings-on-Hudson Sculpture Invitational, 1990, No. Westchester Ctr. for the Arts, 1990, Bergen Mus. Art & Sci., 1991, Silvermine-Charlotta Kotik, Juror, 1991, Tweed Gallery, N.Y., 1991, Nabisco Brands, Hanover, N.J., 1992, Hammond Mus., North Salem, N.Y., 1992, Photography and Small Sculptures, Silvermine, 1993, City Coll. Art Alumni, 1993, Arts Ctr. No. N.J., 1993, Katonah Library, N.Y., 1993, Middlesex County Coll., Edison, N.J., 1993, Westbeth Gallery, N.Y.C., 1993, Nexus Gallery, Phila., 1994. Recipient Honorable Mention award Nat. Arts Club, 1985, 1st Place Sculpture award Greenwich Art Soc., 1985, Best in Show award Gallery 54 Soho, 1988, 2d Prize Sculpture award Katonah Libr., 1993. Mem. Nat. Assn. Women Artists, Mamaroneck Artists Guild, Silvermine Artist Guild.

MANSUR, SHARIF SAMIR, counselor, education educator; b. Cleve., Feb. 26, 1963; s. Aasim and Fareeda Mansur. BA, Knox Coll., 1985; MA in Psychology, Valparaiso U., 1988, MEd, 1990. Cert. sch. counselor, cert. profl. counselor. Clin. therapist Christian Haven Homes, Wheatfield, Ind., 1988-92, Tri-City Cmty. Mental Health, East Chicago, Ind., 1988-92; instr. edn. and psychology Valparaiso (Ind.) U., 1989-91; lectr. psychology Chgo. (Ill.) State U., 1991-92; tchr., counselor Michigan City (Ind.) Area Schs., 1991-92; lectr. psychology Cardinal Stritch Coll., Milw., 1992-94; sch. counselor Menomonee Falls (Wis.) Sch. Dist., 1992-94; lectr. edn. Carroll Coll., Waukesha, Wis., 1994—; asst. dir. career svcs. Cardinal Stritch Coll., Milw., 1994-95; counseling cons. Knox (Ind.) Elem. Sch.-Social Svc., 1989-92; ednl. cons. Our Lady Lourdes Sch., Chgo., 1991-92; human rels. cons. in field. Mem. Wis. Assn. for Counseling and Devel. (exec. bd. mem. 1994), Wis. Assn. for Multicultural Counseling and Devel. (pres. 1994-96), Met. Milw. Alliance Black Sch. Educators (co-chair higher edn. commn.), Cardinal Stritch Coll. Tchr. Edn. Adv. Coun. Home: N 89 W 16045 Main St Menomonee Falls WI 53051 Office: Carroll College Waukesha WI 53186

MANTEGNA, JOE ANTHONY, actor, playwright; b. Chgo., Nov. 13, 1947; s. Joseph Anthony and Mary Ann (Novelli) M.; m. Arlene Vrhel, Oct. 3, 1975; children: Mia Marie, Gina Cristine. Student, Goodman Sch. of Drama, Chgo., 1967-69. Author: (play) Bleacher Bums, 1979 (Emmy award 1979); appeared in plays including Glengarry Glen Ross, 1984-86 (Tony award, Jeff award), Speed-the-Plow; appeared in films Compromising Positions, 1984, Offbeat, 1985, Money Pit, 1986, 3 Amigos, 1986, Critical Condition, 1986, House of Games, 1987, Suspect, 1987, Weeds, 1987, Things Change, 1988 (Best Actor award Venice Film Festival 1988), Wait Until Spring Bandini, 1990, Alice, 1990, The Godfather Part III, 1990, Queens Logic, 1991, Homicide, 1991, Bugsy, 1991, Body of Evidence, 1992, Family Prayers, 1993, Searching for Bobby Fischer, 1993, Airheads, 1994, Baby's Day Out, 1994, Stranger Things, 1995, Above Suspicion, 1995, Forget Paris, 1995; TV films include Elvis, 1979, Comrades of Summer, 1992, The Water Engine, 1992, State of Emergency, 1994. Recipient Drama Desk Award N.Y. Drama Desk, 1984. Mem. Actors Equity, Screen Actors Guild, Am. Fedn. TV and Radio Artists. Office: care Peter Strain 1501 Broadway Ste 2900 New York NY 10036-5601*

MANTEL, SAMUEL JOSEPH, JR., management educator, consultant; b. Indpls., Nov. 17, 1921; s. Samuel Joseph and Beatrice Smith (Talmas) M.; m. Dorothy Jean Friedland, June 28, 1950; children—Michael Lee, Samuel Joseph, III, Margaret Irene, Elizabeth Baer. A.B., Harvard U., 1948, M.P.A., 1950, Ph.D., 1952. Asst. prof. social sci. Ga. Inst. Tech., 1953-56; asst. prof., then assoc. prof. econs., dir. Econs.-in-Action program, Case Western Res. U., 1956-69; prof. mgmt. and quantitative analysis U. Cin., 1969-89, prof. emeritus quantitative analysis and info. systems, 1989—, Joseph S. Stern prof. mgmt., 1973-89, emeritus, 1989, exec. dir. Grad. Ctr. for Mgmt. of Advanced Tech. and Innovation, 1987-89, emeritus, 1989; mgmt. cons., condr. mgmt. seminars. Author: Cases in Managerial Decisions, 1964, Project Management: A Managerial Perspective, 1985, 2d edit. 1989, 3d edit. 1995, Operations Management for Pharmacists: Strategy and Tactics, 1992; co-author several books; mem. editl. bd. Technovation; contbr. articles to profl. jours. Vice pres. Jewish Fedn. Cin., 1978-80; past pres., life mem. Cin. Hillel Found., Cleve. Hillel Found.; historian Rockdale Temple, 1969-77; mem. mgmt. and adminstrn. com. Anti-Defamation League, B'nai B'rith, 1976; trustee Jewish Hosp., Cin., 1975-84, Sarah Marvin Found. for Performing Arts, 1990—; mem. mgmt. adv. com. Cin. Police Dept., 1991-92. Maj. USMCR, 1942-46, 51-53. Decorated D.F.C. with 3 oak leaf clusters, Air medal with 11 oak leaf clusters; Econs.-in-Action fellow, 1955; fellow Inst. Policy Research, 1980; named Prof. of Year, Delta Sigma Pi, 1974. Mem. Project Mgmt. Inst., Iota Epsilon, Beta Gamma Sigma. Home: 608 Flagstaff Dr Cincinnati OH 45215-2525

MANTELL, SUZANNE RUTH, editor; b. West Orange, N.J., Nov. 26, 1944; d. Milton A. and Florence B. M.; m. Peter Gray Friedman, 1985; 1 child, Erica Mantell Friedman. Student, U. Chgo., 1962; B.F.A., Pratt Inst., 1967. Formerly assoc. editor Harper's mag., N.Y.C., exec. editor, 1977-80; editor Harper's Bookletter, 1974-77, Learning Mag., 1980-81, Family Learning Mag., 1983-84; reader Book of the Month Club, 1985-87, 91—; editor Travel Bookstore Catalogue, Banana Republic, 1985-87; assoc. editor The N.Y. Observer, N.Y.C., 1987-91; acting Book News editor Pubs. Weekly, 1992-93, contbg. editor, 1993—; also lectr. mag. writing Stanford U. Calif. at Santa Cruz. Consulting editor Spelman Coll. Messenger, 1994—. Mem. PEN, Nat. Book Critics Circle. Home: 601 W 113th St Apt 2B New York NY 10025-9701

MANTHEI, RICHARD DALE, lawyer, health care company executive; b. Olivia, Minn., Dec. 23, 1935; s. Alvin R. and Sidonia (Klatt) M.; m. Karen J. Peterson, Sept. 6, 1959 (dec. Mar. 1985); children: Steven, Jana, Kari, John, Rebecca; m. Lynn E. Graham, Aug. 9, 1986. B.S. in Pharmacy (Rexall award 1960), S.D. State U., 1960; J.D., U. Minn., 1967. Bar: Ind. 1967, Ill. 1970, D.C. 1987, U.S. Supreme Ct. 1987. Sales rep. Eli Lilly & Co., Indpls., 1962-64, atty., 1967-70; atty., then asst. corp. sec., dir. regulatory affairs Am. Hosp. Supply Corp., Evanston, Ill., 1970-79, corp. sec., dep. gen. counsel, 1979-85; assoc. gen. counsel Baxter Travenol Labs., Deerfield, Ill., 1986-87; ptnr. Burditt, Bowles & Radzius, Washington, 1987-90, McKenna & Cuneo, Washington, 1990—. Author articles in field.; Editorial adv. staff: Med. Devices and Diagnostic Industry, 1979. Mem. bd. edn. Libertyville High Sch., 1984-87; mem. governing bd. Spl. Edn. Dist. of Lake County, Ill., 1985-87. Served with AUS, 1954-56. Mem. ABA, Health Industry Mfrs. Assn. (chmn. law sect. 1976), Health Industry Assn. (chmn. legal com. 1973), Am. Soc. Corp. Secs. (corp. practices com. 1983-88, group pres. 1985-86, Chgo. regional group 1986-87), Ill. Bar Assn., Ind. Bar Assn., D.C. Bar Assn., Univ. Club (Evanston, Ill., bd. dirs. 1984-86), Hidden Creek Country Club (Reston, Va.). Home: 3845 N Tazewell St Arlington VA 22207-4544 Office: McKenna & Cuneo 1575 I St NW Washington DC 20005-1105

MANTHEY, FRANK ANTHONY, physician, director; b. N.Y.C., Dec. 2, 1933; s. Frank A.J. and Josephine (Roth) M.; m. Douglas Susan Falvey, Sept. 14 1958 (div. 1979, dec. 1989); children: Michael P., Susan M., Peter J.; m. Doris Jean Pulley, Oct. 11, 1979. BS, Fordham U., 1954; MD, SUNY, Syracuse, 1958. Diplomate Am. Bd. Anesthesiology, Am. Bd. Med. Examiners. Intern Upstate Med. Ctr., Syracuse, 1958-59; resident in anesthesiology Yale-New Haven Med. Ctr., 1962-64; physician Yale-New Haven Hosp., 1964-75; pvt. practice medicine Illmo, Mo., 1975-79; dir. Manthey Med. Clinic, Elkton, Ky., 1979—; clin. instr. anesthesiology Yale U. Med. Sch., New Haven, 1964-69, asst. clin. prof. anesthesiology, 1969-75; cons. Conn. Dept. Aeros., Hartford, 1969-70; sr. med. examiner Fed. Aviation Adminstrn., Illmo, 1975-79. Contbr. articles to profl. jours. Chmn. gen. works Little Folks Fair, Guilford, Conn., 1967-71; mem. Rep. Town Com., Guilford, 1969-75; chmn. Guilford Sch. Bldg. Com., 1973-75. Capt. USAF (M.C.), 1956-62. Mem. Ky. Med. Assn., Aerospace Med. Assn. (assoc. fellow 1973-75), Flying Physicians Assn. (v.p. NE chpt. 1973-75, v.p. nat. 1974-75, 79-80, bd. dirs. 1970-73, 75-78, bd. dirs. nat. 1975-78), Aircraft Owners and Pilots Assn., Mercedes Benz Club Am., Alpha Kappa Kappa.

Avocations: philately, aviation, skiing, automobile mechanics and restoration, photography. Home: 105 Sunset Dr Elkton KY 42220-9257 Office: Manthey Family Practice Clinic 203 Allensville St PO Box 368 Elkton KY 42220

MANTHEY, THOMAS RICHARD, lawyer; b. St. Cloud, Minn., May 5, 1942; s. Richard Jesse and Dolores Theresa (Terhaar) M.; m. Janet S. Barth, Dec. 18, 1965; children: Molly, Andrew, Luke. BA cum laude, St. John's U., Collegeville, Minn., 1964; JD cum laude, Harvard U., 1967. Bar: Minn. 1967. Assoc. Dorsey & Whitney, Mpls., 1967-73, ptnr., 1974—, also mem. Indian and gaming law practice group, chmn. real estate workout practice group. Contbr. articles to profl. jours. Capt. U.S. Army, 1968-70. Mem. Minn. State Bar Assn. (real estate sect.), Hennepin County Bar Assn. (real estate sect.). Roman Catholic. Avocations: volleyball, golf, fishing. Home: 1834 Summit Ave Saint Paul MN 55105-1427 Office: Dorsey & Whitney 220 S 6th St Minneapolis MN 55402-4502

MANTLE, RAYMOND ALLAN, lawyer; b. Painesville, Ohio, Oct. 15, 1937; s. Junius Dow and Ada Louise (Stinchcomb) M.; m. Judith Ann LaGrange, Nov. 26, 1967; children: Amanda Lee, Rachel Ann, Leah Amy. BSBA summa cum laude, BA summa cum laude Kent State U., 1961; LLB cum laude, NYU, 1964. Bar: N.Y. 1964, N.J. 1976, U.S. Supreme Ct. Asst. counsel Gov. Nelson A. Rockefeller, N.Y., 1964-65; assoc. Paul Weiss Rifkind Wharton & Garrison, 1967-69; mem. firm Varet & Fink P.C. (formerly Milgrim Thomajan & Lee, P.C.), N.Y.C., 1969-95; ptnr. Peper & Marbury L.L.P., N.Y.C., 1995—; lectr. in computer law field. Contbg. author Doing Business in China. Served to capt. U.S. Army, 1965-67. Mem. N.Y. State Bar Assn., N.J. Bar Assn. Republican. Methodist. Office: Piper & Marbury LLP 53 Wall St New York NY 10005-2834

MANTON, EDWIN ALFRED GRENVILLE, insurance company executive; b. Earls Colne, Essex, Eng., Jan. 22, 1909; came to U.S., 1933; s. John Horace and Emily Clara (Denton) M.; m. Florence V. Brewer, Feb. 1, 1936; 1 child, Diana H. Manton Morton. Student, London (Eng.) U., 1925-27, N.Y. Ins. Soc., 1933-35; DHL (hon.), Coll. of Ins., 1994. With B.W. Noble Ltd., Paris, 1927-33; casualty underwriter Am. Internat. Underwriters Corp., N.Y.C., 1933-37, sec., 1937-38, v.p., 1938-42, pres., 1942-69, chmn., 1969-75; sr. advisor Am. Internat. Group, Inc.; hon. dir. C.V. Starr & Co., Inc. Trustee St. Luke's-Roosevelt Hosp., N.Y.C. Mem. Salmagundi Club, City Midday Drug and Chem. Club, Mendelssohn Glee Club, Williams Club, St. George's Soc. Episcopalian. Home: 40 5th Ave New York NY 10011-8843 Office: Am Internat Group Inc 70 Pine St New York NY 10270-0002

MANTON, THOMAS JOSEPH, congressman; b. N.Y.C., Nov. 3, 1932; m. Diane Schley; children: Cathy, Tom, John, Jeanne. BBA, St. John's U., 1958, LLB, 1962. Mem. N.Y.C. Police Dept., 1955-60; mktg. rep. IBM, 1960-64; practice law, 1964-84; mem. 99th-104th Congresses from 9th (now 7th) N.Y. Dist., Washington, 1984—; mem. commerce com., Dem. steering and policy com. Mem. N.Y.C. Council, 1970-84. Served with USMC, 1951-53. Democrat. Office: US Ho of Reps 2235 Rayburn HOB Washington DC 20515

MANTONYA, JOHN BUTCHER, lawyer; b. Columbus, Ohio, May 26, 1922; s. Elroy Letts and Blanche (Butcher) M.; m. Mary E. Reynolds, June 14, 1947 (dec. 1987); children: Elizabeth Claire, Mary Kay, Lee Ann; m. Carole L. Lugar, Sept. 28, 1989. A.B. cum laude, Washington and Jefferson Coll., 1943; postgrad., U. Mich. Law Sch., 1946-47; J.D., Ohio State U., 1949. Bar: Ohio 1949. Assoc. A.S. Mitchell (Atty.), Newark, Ohio, 1949-50, C.D. Lindrooth, Newark, 1950-57; partner firm Lindrooth & Mantonya, Newark, 1957-74; firm John B. Mantonya, 1974-81, John B. Mantonya, L.P.A., 1981—. Mem. North Fork Local Bd. Edn., 1962-69; adv. com. Salvation Army, Licking County, 1965—, Mayor of, Utica, Ohio, 1953-59. Served with AUS, 1943-45. Mem. Am. Bar Assn., Ohio Bar Assn., Licking County Bar Assn. (pres. 1967), Phi Delta Phi, Beta Theta Pi. Home: 11055 Reynolds Rd Utica OH 43080-9549 Office: 3 N 3rd St Newark OH 43055-5506

MANTOR-CLARYSSE, JUSTINE CLAIRE, fine arts educator; b. Neenah, Wis., Aug. 12, 1943; d. Jack Allen and Ann Elizabeth (Suchy) Mantor; m. John Allan Wantz, June 18, 1968 (div. 1983); m. Omer T. Clarysse, July 28, 1994. BFA, Sch. Art Inst. Chgo., 1967; MA, No. Ill. U., 1969, MFA, 1971. Assoc. prof. fine arts Loyola U., Chgo., 1971-93, dir. women's studies, 1982-83; represented by Artisimo Gallery, Scottsdale, Ariz.; instr. Coll. of DuPage, Glen Ellyn, Ill., 1971-72, North Shore Art League, Winnetka, Ill., 1972-73, DuPage Art League, Wheaton, Ill., 1972; gallery dir. Water Tower Gallery, Loyola U., Chgo., 1973-82; lectr. Ill. Conf. L.Am. Studies, U. Ill., 1990, Chantauqua Conf. Fgn. Lang. Tchrs., Pheasant Run, Ill., 1991, U. Wis., Madison, 1991, Mid-Am. Coll. Art Assn., Madison, Wis., 1991, 92, Mid-Am. South-East Coll. Art Assn., Birmingham, Ala, 1992, Nat. Coll. Art Assn., Seattle, 1993, N.Y., 94. Solo exhbns. include U. Ill. Med. Ctr., Chgo., 1979, Springfield (Ill.) Art Assn., 1979, John Nelson Bergstrom Art Ctr. and Mus., Neenah, Wis., 1980, Aurora (Ill.) Coll., 1980, Arc Gallery, Chgo., 1981, 83, Illini Union Gallery, Champaign, Ill., 1982, Fountain Hills Cmty. Ctr., Ariz., 1990, Downtown Gallery, Phoenix, 1994, others; permanent collections include Ill. State Mus., Rockford Mus., Kemper Ins. Co., Gillman Gallery, Chgo., Byer Mus., No. Ill. U. Student Ctr. and Fine Arts Dept., Loyola U. Gallery Coll., Chgo., others. Named Best of Show, Fountain Hills Art Fair, Ariz., 1993, 94, Best of Show and 1st Pl. Acrylic, Juried Competition, 1994, Fountain Hills Art Fair; grantee Ill. Arts Coun., 1978, Ill. Art Coun./Mellon Found., 1979, Nat. Humanities Assn., 1980, Ill. Humanities Coun., 1980-81. Mem. AAUP, Nat. Coll. Art Assn. (lectr. 1993), Mid-Am. Coll. Art Assn. (lectr. 1991, 92), Internat. Friends of Transformative Art (co-editor The Transformer newsletter) Fountain Hills Art League, Ariz. Artists' Guild, Chgo. Artists' Coalition, Sch. Art Inst. Chgo. Alumni Assn., Ariz. Women's Caucus for Art (pres. 1994). Democrat. Presbyterian. Avocations: painting, bookbinding, archaeology, Mexican culture. Office: Loyola U Chgo Crown Ctr Humanities 6525 N Sheridan Rd Chicago IL 60626-5311

MANTSCH, HENRY HORST, chemistry educator; b. Mediasch, Transylvania, Romania, July 30, 1935; emigrated to Can., 1968; s. Heinrich Johann and Olga Augusta (Gondosch) M.; m. Amy Emilia Kory, Nov. 2, 1959; children: Monica, Marietta. B.Sc., U. Cluj, Transylvania, 1958, Ph.D., 1964. Rsch. scientist Romanian Acad. Sci., Cluj, 1958-65, Tech. U. Munich, Germany, 1966-68; with NRC, Ottawa, Can., 1968-72; prof. biochemistry U. Cluj, 1973-74, Liebig U., Giessen, Germany, 1975-76; head molecular spectroscopy NRC, Ottawa, 1977—; mem. Can. Rsch. Coun., Ottawa, 1977-91, Winnipeg, Can., 1992—; adj. prof. Carleton U., Ottawa, 1978-90, U. Ottawa, 1990-92, U. Manitoba, Winnipeg, 1992—. Contbr. articles to profl. jours.; patentee in field. Recipient medal Ministry of Edn., Bucharest, 1972; recipient Humboldt Found. award and medal Bonn, 1980; Chem. Inst. Can. fellow, 1979; Royal Soc. Can. fellow, 1982; recipient Herzberg award, 1984. Mem. Am. Biophys. Soc., Soc. Applied Spectroscopy, Chem. Inst. Can. (chmn. biol. chem. div. 1980-81), Can. Spectroscopy Soc. (mem. nat. exec. com. 1981-90). Home: 2222 W Taylor Blvd, Winnipeg, MB Canada R3P 2J5 Office: NRC Can, 435 Ellice Ave, Winnipeg, MB Canada R3B 1Y6

MANTULIN, WILLIAM W., biophysicist, laboratory director; b. Munich, Bavaria, Germany, Apr. 5, 1946; came to U.S., 1950; BS, U. Rochester, 1968; PhD, Northeastern U., 1972. Postdoctoral fellow Tex. Tech U., Lubbock, 1972-74; postdoctoral fellow U. Ill., Urbana, 1975-77, adj. assoc. prof., 1986—, dir. Lab. Fluorescence Dynamics, 1986—; instr. Baylor Coll. Medicine, Houston, 1978-83, asst. prof., 1984-86; cons. Exxon Corp., Houston, 1980-84. Author: (book chpt.) Fluorescent Biomolecules, 1989; contbr. articles to Bioimaging, Biochemistry. Recipient Paul Naney award Am. Heart Assn., 1987. Mem. Am. Chem. Soc., Am. Assn. Biochemistry and Molecular Biologists, Biophys. Soc. Achievements include patent for near infrared optical imaging. Office: U Ill Lab Fluorescence Dynamics 1110 W Green St Urbana IL 61801-3003

MANTYLA, KAREN, sales executive; b. Bronx, N.Y., Dec. 31, 1944; d. Milton and Sylvia (Diamond) Fischer; m. John A Mantyla, May 30, 1970 (div. 1980); 1 child, Michael Alan. Student, Rockland Community Coll., Suffern, N.Y., 1962, NYU, 1967, Mercer U., 1981. Mktg. coordinator Credit Bur., Inc., Miami, Fla., 1973-79; dist. mgr. The Research Inst. Am., N.Y.C., 1979-80, regional dir., 1980-85, field sales mgr., 1985-86, nat. sales mgr., 1986-87; dir. mktg. TempsAmerica, N.Y.C., 1987-88; nat. accounts mgr. The Rsch. Inst. Am., N.Y.C., 1989; v.p. sales Bur. Bus. Practice/Paramount Comm., Inc., Waterford, Conn., 1989-93; pres. Quiet Power, Inc., Washington, 1993—. Author: Consultative Sales Power, 1995. Mem. ASTD, Sales and Mktg. Execs. (past bd. dirs. N.Y. chpt., v.p. Ft. Lauderdale chpt. 1979), U.S. Distance Learning Assn., Nat. Assn. Women Bus. Owners, U.S. C. of C., Women Entrepreneurs. Avocations: antiques, tennis, writing, swimming. Home: 5449 Grove Ridge Way Rockville MD 20852-4648 Office: Quiet Power Inc 655 15th St NW Ste 300 Washington DC 20005-5701

MANUEL, RALPH NIXON, private school executive; b. Frederick, Md., Apr. 21, 1936; s. Ralph Walter and Frances Rebecca (Nixon) M.; m. Sarah Jane Warner, July 22, 1960; children: Mark, David, Stephen, Bradley. A.B., Dartmouth Coll., 1958; M.Ed., Boston U., 1967; Ph.D., U. Ill., 1971. Assoc. dean Dartmouth Coll., Hanover, N.H., 1971-72, dean of freshmen, 1972-75, dean, 1975-82; pres. Culver (Ind.) Acad. and Culver Edn. Found., 1982—. Bd. dirs. Ind. Sch. Cen. States, 1986—, chair, 1993-95. NDEA fellow, 1968-69. Mem. Assn. Mil. Colls. and Schs. of U.S. (pres., bd. dirs.), Nat. Assn. Ind. Schs. (bd. dirs. 1995—). Office: Culver Acads 1300 Academy Rd Culver IN 46511-1234

MANULIS, MARTIN, film producer; b. N.Y.C., May 30, 1915; s. Abraham and Anne (Silverstein) M.; m. Katharine Bard, June 14, 1939; children: Laurie, Karen, John Bard. BA, Columbia, 1935. Mng. dir. Bahamas Playhouse, 1951-52; exec. head TV prodn. Twentieth Century Fox, 1958-60, ind. motion picture producer, 1960—; artistic dir. Ahmanson Theatre, Music Ctr., Los Angeles, 1987-89; dir. Am. Film Inst. West, 1974-76. Producer, dir. (with John C. Wilson) Broadway; dir. Private Lives, Laura, Made in Heaven, The Show Off, Westport Country Playhouse, 1946-50, (CBS-TV shows) Suspense, Studio One, Best of Broadway, Climax, Playhouse 90, 1952-58, Requiem for a Heavyweight (Emmy award Best Show 1956-57), Miracle Worker (Emmy Best Show 1957-58); producer films Dear Heart, Days of Wine and Roses, Luv and Duffy; producer TV miniseries Chiefs, James Michener's Space, Grass Roots. Served as lt. USNR, 1942-45. Recipient spl. Svc. award Crusade for Freedom, 1954, Look TV award for Best Dramatic Series, 1955, 56, 57, eleven TV Emmy awards for Playhouse 90 Nat. Acad. TV Arts and Scis., 1956, 57; named to Producers Guild of Am. Hall of Fame for Playhouse 90, 1992. Office: Martin Manulis Prodns Ltd PO Box 818 Beverly Hills CA 90213-0818

MANUTA, DAVID MARK, research chemist; b. Bklyn., June 10, 1957; s. Gerald and Vivian Bernice (Chartoff) M.; m. Ruth Pauline Krog, Mar. 27, 1988 (dec. Dec. 1993). BS in Chemistry, SUNY, Oneonta, 1979; PhD in Chemistry, SUNY, Binghamton, 1985. Lab. tech. Scientific Process & Rsch., Somerset, N.J., 1980-81; from tchg. asst. to postdoctoral fellow SUNY, Binghamton, 1981-86; asst. prof. Upper Iowa U., Fayette, 1986-88; asst. prof. II Shawnee State U., Portsmouth, Ohio, 1989-90; rsch. staff Martin Marietta Utility Svcs., Piketon, Ohio, 1990—; tchr. Christ the King Regional H.S., N.Y.C., 1986; instr. Stanley Kaplan Exam. Prep. Svcs., Garden City, N.Y., 1986; cons. City of Portsmouth, 1989. Served in U.S. Navy, 1978-79. IBM Corp. grad. fellow, 1984-85. Mem. AAAS, Am. Chem. Soc. Avocations: chess, reading, running, bicycling, traveling. Home: 431 Gordon Ave Waverly OH 45690-1208 Office: Martin Marietta Utility Svc 3930 US Rte 23 S PO Box 628 M/S 2142 Piketon OH 45661-0628

MANVEL, ALLEN DAILEY, fiscal economist; b. Spokane, Wash., June 29, 1912; s. Arthur Orlando and Agnes Louise (Johnson) M.; m. Helen Louise de Werthern, Oct. 9, 1937; children: Sarah Katherine, Bennet. AB in Econs., Occidental Coll., 1934; postgrad., U. Chgo., 1935-36, Harvard U., 1939-40; DSc (hon.), Ohio State U., 1976. Rsch. assoc. Ill. Dept. Fin., Springfield, 1936-41; rsch. dir. Ill. Agrl. Assn., Chgo., 1941-42; state budget supr. Ill. Dept. Fin., Springfield, 1942-43; adminstrv. analyst U.S. Bur. Budget, Washington, 1943-46; chief govts. div. U.S. Bur. Census, Washington, 1946-67; assoc. dir. Nat. Com. on Urban Problems, Washington, 1967-68; asst. dir. Adv. Com. on Intergovt. Rels., Washington, 1968-71; rsch. asst., sr. fellow The Brookings Instn., Washington, 1972-75; econ. cons. Tax Analysts, Inc., Arlington, Va., from 1976; now ret.; lectr. in pub. adminstrn. George Washington U., Washington, 1946-48; cons. Fiscal Div. UN, N.Y.C., 1953, N.Y.C. Commn. on Statis. Programs, 1954-55. Author: (book) Paying for Civilized Society, 1986; co-author: (books) Measuring Fiscal Capacity and Effort, 1971, Monitoring Revenue Sharing, 1975; contbr. numerous articles to profl. jours. Recipient Louis Brownlow award, Nat. Mcpl. League, 1966. Mem. Nat. Tax Assn. (past. bd. dirs.), Nat. Acad. Pub. Adminstrn., Cosmos Club, Washington. Democrat. Unitarian. Avocations: reading, travel. Home and Office: 10450 Lottsford Rd Unit 3009 Mitchellville MD 20721

MANVILLE, STEWART ROEBLING, archivist; b. White Plains, N.Y., Jan. 15, 1927; s. Leo and Margaret (Roebling) M.; m. Ella V. Grainger, Jan. 19, 1972 (dec.). Student U. Wyo., 1944-46; BS, Columbia U., 1962. Various office positions, N.Y.C., 1947-51, 56-58; asst. stage dir. several European opera houses, 1951-55; editor Jas. T. White & Co., N.Y.C., 1959-63; archivist, curator Percy Grainger Library, White Plains, N.Y., 1963—. Mem. SAR, Hist. House Assn. Am., Nat. Trust Hist. Preservation, Victorian Soc. in Am. (past dir. N.Y. chpt.), Société des Antiquaires de Picardie, Soc. Archtl. Historians, Westchester County Hist. Soc., Titanic Hist. Soc., White Plains Battle Monument Com., Appalachian Trail Conf., Westchester Trails Assn. (past dir.), St. Nicholas Soc. N.Y., Quaker. Author: The Manville/Manvel Families in America; contbr. articles and revs. on music to mags. and newspapers. Office: 7 Cromwell Pl White Plains NY 10601-5005

MANWORREN, DONALD B., church administrator; b. Galesburg, Ill., Jan. 25, 1937; m. Elaine K. Jensen, June 15, 1957; children: Julia, Susan, John. BA, Drake U., 1957, BD, 1961, DD (hon.), 1981; STM, Yale U., 1962; postgrad., Sch. Theology, Claremont, Calif., 1977, Assumption Coll., 1980. Pastor 1st Christian Ch., Keota, Iowa, 1962-64, Convenant Christian Ch., Urbandale, Iowa, 1965-71, Ctrl. Christian Ch., Waterloo, Iowa, 1971-77; exec. coord. Iowa Inter-Ch. Forum, Des Moines, 1977-85; dep. gen. min., pres. Christian Ch. (Disciples of Christ) U.S. and Can., 1986—; mem. gen. bd. Christian Ch. (Disciples of Christ) U.S. and Can., 1975-83, mem. adminstrv. com., 1975-81, mem. regional commn. witness and Soc., 1979-81, mem. Upper Midwest regional bd., parliamentarian, 1981-85; mem. Disciples Ecumenical Consultative Coun., Jamaica, 1979; bd. dirs. Coun. Christian Unity, 1979-85. Commr. Iowa Commn. Aging, 1976-80; bd. dirs. Ramsey Meml. Home, Des Moines, 1975-85; trustee Christian Theol. Sem., Indpls., 1976-87, 89—. Rsch. fellow Yale U., 1983. Mem. NCCC-USA (chmn. commn. regional and local ecumenism 1985-87), Nat. Coun. Chs. (mem. governing bd. 1979-87, mem. study panel ecumenical commitment and purposes 1979-87), Phi Beta Kappa. Home: 783 Woodview N Dr Carmel IN 46032 Office: Box 1986 Indianapolis IN 46206

MANZ, BETTY ANN, nurse administrator; b. Paterson, N.J., Nov. 30, 1935; d. James Albert and Elsie (Basse) Brown; diploma Newark Beth Israel Hosp. Sch. Nursing, 1955; BSN, Seton Hall U., 1964; m. Roger A. Johnson, Feb. 1988; children: Laura, Richard, Garry. Staff nurse oper. room Newark Beth Israel Hosp., 1955-56, recovery room head nurse, 1956-57, oper. room head nurse, 1957-58, supr. oper. room, 1958-60; substitute tchr. pub. schs. Harding Twp., 1966-70; charge nurse St. Barnabas Med. Ctr., Livingston, N.J., 1965-70, head nurse emergency room, 1970-72; oper. room supr. St. Clares Hosp., Denville, N.J., 1972-77; asst. dir. for oper. rooms and post anesthesia rooms Newark Beth Israel Med. Ctr., 1977-82; asst. dir. nursing oper. room care program Thomas Jefferson U. Hosp., Phila., 1982-84; asst. dir./assoc. nursing dir. oper. room, anesthesia ICU, ambulatory surgery Univ. Hosp., SUNY-Stony Brook, 1984-87 dir. oper. room/post anesthesia care ambulatory surgery Med. Ctr. Del., Wilmington and Christiana, Del., 1987-88; practice mgr. Del. Orthopaedic Ctr., Wilmington, 1989—; faculty mem. postgrad. course in microsurgy for Am. Coll. Obstetricians and Gynecologists, Newark, 1982; profl. cons. oper. room products, also health cons. Henry E. Wessel Assocs., Moraga, Calif.; profl. tech. cons., lectr. Surgicot, Inc., Smithtown, N.Y. Dep. dir. Harding Twp. CD, 1967-75. Recipient Service award Essex County Med. Soc., 1979. Mem. AAMI, MGMA, Nat. Assn. Orthopaedic Nurses, Assn. Oper. Room Nurses, Am. Soc. Post Anesthesia Nurses, Del. Med. Group Mgmt. Assn. (sec.), Bones Soc. Orthopedic Mgrs., Newark Beth Israel Hosp. Nursing Alumnae Assn., Seton Hall U. Alumnae Assn., Harding Twp. Civic Assn., Am. Field Svc., Colonial States Knitters Guild (pres.). Republican. Club: Mt. Kemble Lake Community. Editor operating room sect. SCORE mag. Home & Office: 2620 Lamper Ln Wilmington DE 19808-3808

MANZ, CHARLES C., management educator. Prof. mgmt. Ariz. State U., Tempe. Author: The Art of Self Leadership: Achieving Personal Effectiveness in Your Life and Work, 1983, Mastering Self-Leadership: Empowering Yourself for Personal Excellence, 1991; co-author: Superleadership, 1990, Business Without Bosses: How Self-Managing Teams are Building High-Performance Companies, 1993, Company of Heroes: Unleashing the Power of Self-Leadership, 1996. Office: Ariz State U Dept Mgmt Tempe AZ 85287

MANZ, JOHANNES JAKOB, Swiss diplomat; b. Zurich, Switzerland, Dec. 15, 1938; s. Jakob J. and Margaret (Ruegg) M.; m. Marie-Antoinette Kunz, May 26, 1966; children: Alexander Cyril, Isabel Carmela. Student, Oreg. State U., 1958-59; LLD, U. Zurich, 1969. Sec. Mission of Switzerland, N.Y.C., 1971-75; counselor Swiss Embassy, Vienna, Austria, 1975-81; min., dep. head mission Mission of Switzerland, Geneva, 1981-84; amb., chief protocol Swiss Confedn., Bern, 1984-88; amb., dir. adminstrn. and pers. Swiss Dept. for Fgn. Affairs, Bern, 1988-91; under sec. gen., spl. rep. to sec. gen. for Western Sahara, UN, N.Y.C., 1990-91; amb., head of mission, permanent observer to UN, Mission of Switzerland, N.Y.C., 1992—. Contbg. author: Manual of Swiss Foreign Policy, 1991. Pres. Platform for Young Citizens, Zollikon, Switzerland, 1967-68. Mem. Delta Upsilon (hon. Oreg. State U. chpt.). Avocations: cross-country skiing, golf, swimming, classical music. Office: Mission of Switzerland 757 3rd Ave Fl 21 New York NY 10017-2013

MANZI, JIM, computer software company executive; b. N.Y.C., Dec. 22, 1951; s. Walter Edward and Ann (Smirka) M.; m. Glenda Baugh, May 20, 1978. B.A., Colgate U., 1973; M.A.L.D., Fletcher Sch., Tufts U., 1979. Editorial asst. Nat. Rev. Mag., N.Y.C., 1973-74; news reporter Gannet Newspapers, Port Chester, N.Y., 1974-77; cons. McKinsey & Co., Los Angeles, Boston and N.Y.C., 1979-83; v.p. mktg. and sales Lotus Devel. Corp., Cambridge, Mass., 1983-84, pres., 1984-86, 89-1996, CEO, 1986-1996; pres., CEO Industry Net, 1996. Recipient In-Depth Reporting award AP, N.Y., 1976, 77, Investigative Reporting award N.Y. State Pubs. Assn., 1976, 77. Office: Industry Net 5 Cambridge Ctr 8th Fl Cambridge MA 02102*

MANZO, SALVATORE EDWARD, business developer; b. Bklyn., Oct. 23, 1917; s. Salvatore and Mary (Sireci) M.; B.S., U.S. Mil. Acad., 1939; m. Flournoy Davis, Mar. 11, 1960; children: Janeen, John, Joanne, Molly. Commd. 2d lt. USAF, 1939, advanced through grades to col., 1944, ret., 1962; v.p. C.H. Leavell & Co., El Paso, 1962-65; exec. dir. Met. Airlines Com., N.Y.C., 1965-67; dir. aviation City of Houston, 1967-69; pres. Trans-East Air Inc., Bangor, Maine, 1969-70; aviation mgmt. cons., Bangor, 1970-72, Sao Paulo, Brazil, 1972-74; exec. asst. to pres. Hidroservice, Sao Paulo, 1974-77; assoc. Charter Fin. Group, Inc., Houston, 1977-79; dir. exec. devel. Jesse H. Jones Grad. Sch. Adminstrn., Rice U., Houston, 1979-85, asst. dean for exec. devel., 1985-89; pres., bd. dirs. Manzo Devel. Co., 1969-90; 1st Tex. Venture Capital Corp., 1983-89; dir. Headlines U.S.A., Houston, 1987-91; ind. gen. partner Equus Capital Ptnrs., Ltd. 1989—; pres. El Paso Indsl. Devel. Corp., 1965; dir. Bus. Devel. and Financing Greater Houston Partnership's Econ. Devel. Div., 1989—. Vestryman Christ Ch. Cathedral, Houston, 1979-81. Decorated Silver Star, Legion of Merit, D.F.C. (2), Soldier's medal, Air medal (5), Commendation medal (2); Croix de Guerre with palm (France); recipient Entrepreneur of Yr. award Arthur Young and Venture Mag., 1988. Mem. Houston C. of C., El Paso C. of C. (pres. 1965). Republican. Episcopalian. Author: (with Edward E. Williams) Business Planning for the Entrepreneur: How to Write and Execute a Business Plan, 1983. Home: 4036 Ruskin St Houston TX 77005-4335 Office: Greater Houston Partnership 1100 Milam St Ste 25 Houston TX 77002-5508

MANZULLO, DONALD A, congressman, lawyer; b. Rockford, Ill., 1944; s. Frank A. Sr. and Kathryn M.; m. Freda Teslik; children: Neil, Noel, Katie. BA in Polit. Sci./Internat. Rels., American U., 1967; JD, Marquette U. Law Sch. Atty., 1970—; mem. 103th Congress from 16th Ill. Dist., 1993—; mem. House Com. on Internat. Rels., subcom. econ. policy, trade and environ., subcom. on Asia and the Pacific, House Com. on small bus., chmn. on subcom. on procurement exports and bus. opportunity, Joint Econ. Commn. Mem. No. Ill. Alliance for Arts, Friends of Severson Dells, Citizens Against Govt. Waste, Rep. Nat. Com. Recipient George Washington honor medal for excellence in pub. comm. Freedoms Found., Valley Forge, Pa., 1991. Mem. ABA, Ill. Bar Assn., Ogle County Bar Assn. (pres. 1971, 73), Nat. Legal Found., Acad. Polit. Sci., Ill. Press Assn., Ill. C. of C., Oregon City C. of C., Nat. Land Inst., Nat. Fedn. Ind. Bus., Ogle County Hist. Soc., Aircraft Owners and Pilots Assn., Ogle County Pilots Assn., Ill. Farm Bur., Ogle County Farm Bur. Office: US Ho of Reps 426 Cannon House Office Bld Washington DC 20515-1316

MAPEL, WILLIAM MARLEN RAINES, retired banking executive; b. Maryville, Mo., Sept. 17, 1931; s. William and Evelyn (Raines) M.; m. Gail Manchee, June 21, 1958; children: Daniel B., Susan L., Stephen W. B.A., Yale U., 1953. Indsl. relations asst. Union Carbide Corp., N.Y.C., 1953-57; with Citibank (N.A.), N.Y.C., 1957-88; asst. cashier Citibank (N.A.), 1959-62, asst. v.p., 1962-64, v.p., 1964-69, sr. v.p., 1969-88; chmn. Merc. and Gen. Reins. Co. Am.; bd. dirs. Merc. & Gen. Life Reassurance Co. Am., Brundage, Story & Rose Investment Trust, Churchill Ptnrs., Galey & Lord, NSC Corp., U.S. Life Income Fund, Inc., Atlantic Salmon Fedn., Que.-Labrador Found. Mem. U.S. Srs. Golf Assn., Woodway Country Club, Anglers Club, Pine Valley Golf Club, Links, Wolf's Head, Delta Kappa Epsilon. Home: 18 Stephanie Ln Darien CT 06820-2723

MAPES, GLYNN DEMPSEY, newspaper editor; b. N.Y.C., July 15, 1939; s. John George and Dorothy (Glynn) M.; m. Elizabeth Adlum, Apr. 13, 1963; children—Timothy Glynn, Susannah Glynn. B.A., Williams Coll., 1961. Reporter Wall St. Jour., San Francisco, 1965-67; bur. chief Wall St. Jour., Phila., 1967-70; fgn. editor Wall St. Jour., N.Y.C., 1970-71, bur. chief, 1971-75, Page One editor, 1975-88, Reports editor, 1988-89; bur. chief Wall St. Jour., London, 1989-93; money and investing editor Wall St. Jour., N.Y.C., 1993—. Served to lt. (j.g.) USN, 1961-65. Democrat. Club: Collegiate Chorale, London Concert Choir. Home: 570 1st St Brooklyn NY 11215-2353 Office: Wall St Jour 200 Liberty St New York NY 10281-1003

MAPES, JEFFREY ROBERT, journalist; b. San Francisco, Nov. 21, 1954; s. James Robert and Phyllis June (Bloemker) M.; m. Karen Jane Minkel, Aug. 20, 1978; children: Katharine, James. BA, San Jose State U., 1976. Reporter Napa (Calif.) Register, 1976-79; Washington corr. Scripps League Newspapers, 1979-83; reporter The Oregonian, Portland, 1984-87, chief polit. reporter, 1987—. Office: The Oregonian 1320 SW Broadway Portland OR 97201-3469

MAPES, PIERSON, television broadcasting company executive; m. Patricia Carlson. Grad. Norwich Univ. With NBC, 1963-72; account exec., sales mgr., v.p. Blair TV, 1972-79; v.p. NBC TV Network, 1979-82, now pres., NBC TV Network, NBC-TV, N.Y.C., 1982—; bd. dirs. Ramapo Land Co., Sloatsbury, N.Y.; bd. dirs. Broadcast Pioneers, Broadcast Pioneers Library. Trustee Norwich Univ. Capt. U.S. Army, 1959-63. Mem. Internat. Radio and TV Soc., Network TV Assn. (exec. com., bd. advt. coun.).

MAPLE, DONALD PAUL, military officer; b. Farmington, Minn., Nov. 9, 1946; s. Paul Harrison and Esther Arlene (Seefeldt) M.; m. Leslie Lynn Thompson, Aug. 19, 1967. BA, U. Ga., 1968; MA, U. Tex., 1977. Commd. U.S. Army, 1968—, advanced through grades to col.; rifle platoon leader 101st Airborne Divsn., Vietnam, 1971; comdr. Co. D 4th Brigade, Ft. Jackson, S.C., 1972-74; asst. prof. journalism Def. Info. Sch., Indpls., 1977-80; dir. pub. affairs 7th Army Tng. Command, Grafenwoehr, Germany, 1980-83; media officer Army Pub. Affairs/Pentagon, Washington, 1983-86; dep. dir. pub. affairs U.S. European Command, Stuttgart, Germany, 1991-93; chief pub. comm. Dept. of Army/Pentagon, Washington, 1994—. Editor-in-chief Soldiers mag., 1987-90. Decorated Legion of Merit, Bronze Star medals (2). Mem. Phi Kappa Phi. Home: 13604 Post Oak Ct Chantilly VA 22021 Office: Public Communications HQDA The Pentagon Washington DC 20310

MAPLE, JOHN E., protective services official; b. N.Y.C., Sept. 23, 1952; s. George and Grace (Cassedla) M.; children: Jaqueline, Brendan. Police officer N.Y.C. Transit Police, detective, patrol supr., detective supr., detective squad commdr., spl. asst. for ops. to chief of dept.; spl. asst. to police commr. Boston Police Dept.; dep. police commr. for crime control strategies N.Y.C. Police Dept. Recipient Disting. Svc. award N.Y. Shields, 1994. Mem. N.Y. Police Dept. Honor Legion, N.Y. Transit Police Dept. Honor Legion. Avocations: fishing, military strategy. Office: New York City Police Dept 1 Police Plz New York NY 10038-1403

MAPLES, WILLIAM ROSS, anthropology educator, consultant; b. Dallas, Tex., Aug. 7, 1937; s. William Hunter and Agnes Ross (Bliss) M.; m. Margaret Jane Kelley, Dec. 20, 1958; children: Lisa Linda, Cynthia Lynn. BA, U. Tex., 1959, MA, 1962, PhD, 1967. Diplomate Am. Bd. Forensic Anthropology. With Darajani (Kenya East Africa) Primate Rsch. Sta., 1962-63; teaching asst. U. Tex., Austin, 1963-64; mgr. S.W. Primate Rsch. Ctr., Nairobi, Kenya, East Africa, 1964-66; asst. prof. Western Mich. U., Kalamazoo, 1966-68; from asst. prof. to prof. anthropology U. Fla., Gainesville, 1968—; with Fla. Mus. Natural History, Gainesville, 1972-78, chmn. dept. social scis., 1973-87, curator in charge human indentificaion lab., 1986—; Disting. Svc. prof. Fla. Mus. Natural History, 1994—; cons. Armed Forces Graves Registration Office, Honolulu, 1986—, Armed Forces Inst. Pathology, 1989, N.Y. State Police Forensic Unit, Albany, 1987—; cons. in residence U.S. Army Ctrl. Identification Lab., Honolulu, 1986-87; post mortem examination in hist. cases includes: Don Francisco Pizarro, Lima, Peru, The Elephant Man, Joseph Merrick, London, Pres. Zachary Taylor, Louisville, Czar Nicholas II and family, Ekaterinburg, Russia. Author: (with Michael Browning) Dead Men Do Tell Tales, 1994; contbr. articles to profl. jours. Recipient Disting. Tchr. Cert., U. Fla., 1973, Cert. of Honor, City of Lima, Peru, 1985. Fellow Am. Anthropol. Assn., Am. Assn. Physics Anthropologists; mem. Am. Acad. Forensic Scis (v.p. 1986-87, bd. dirs. 1989-93, Phys. Anthropology Sect. award 1996), Forensic Scis. Found. (trustee, treas. 1988-95), Am. Bd. Forensic Anthropology (treas. 1984-87, pres. 1987-89). Avocations: photography, sailing. Office: U Florida Florida Museum Natural History Gainesville FL 32611

MAPOTHER, TOM CRUISE, IV See CRUISE, TOM

MAPP, ALF JOHNSON, JR., writer, historian; b. Portsmouth, Va., Feb. 17, 1925; s. Alf Johnson and Lorraine (Carney) M.; m. Hartley Lockhart, Mar. 28, 1953; 1 son, Alf Johnson III; m. Ramona Hartley Hamby, Aug. 1, 1971. A.A., Coll. William and Mary, 1945, A.B. summa cum laude, 1961. Editorial writer Portsmouth Star, 1945-46, assoc. editor, 1946-48, editorial chief, 1948-54; news editor, editorial writer Virginian-Pilot, Norfolk, 1954-58; free-lance writer, 1958—; lectr. Old Dominion U., 1961-62, instr., 1962-67, asst. prof. English and history, 1967-73, asso prof. English, journalism, creative writing, history, 1973-79, prof., 1979-82, eminent prof., 1982-89, eminent scholar, 1989-92, eminent scholar emeritus, 1992—, Louis I. Jaffe prof. English, 1990-92; Louis I. Jaffe prof. emeritus, 1992—; profl. lectr., 1984—. Host TV series Jamestown to Yorktown, 1975-77; author: The Virginia Experiment, 1975, 3d edit., 1987, Frock Coats and Epaulets, 1963, 5th edit., 1996, America Creates Its Own Literature, 1965, Just One Man, 1968, The Golden Dragon: Alfred the Great and His Times, 1974, 4th edit., 1990, Thoms Jefferson: A Strange Case of Mistaken Identity, 1987, 3d edit., 1989 (Book-of-Month Club feature selection 1987), Thomas Jefferson: Passionate Pilgrim, 1991, 3d edit., 1993 (Book-of-Month Club feature selection 1991), (novel) Bed of Honor, 1995; co-author: Chesapeake Bay in the Revolution, 1981, Portsmouth: A Pictorial History, 1989, Constitutionalism: Founding and Future, 1989, Constitutionalism and Human Rights, 1991, Great American Presidents, 1995; mem. editl. bd. Jamestown Found., 1967—. Mem. Portsmouth-Norfolk County Savs. Bond Com, 1948-51, Va. Com. on Libr. Devel., 1949-50; mem. publs. com. 350th Anniversary of Rep. Govt. in the Western World, 1966-69, War of Independence Commn., 1967-83; chmn. Portsmouth Revolutionary Bicentennial Com., 1968-81; chmn. awards jury Baruch award United Daus. Confederacy-Columbia U., 1976, mem., 1980; chmn. Portsmouth Mus. and Fine Arts Commn., 1983-85, Southeastern Va. Anglo-Am. Friendship Day, 1976, Bicentennial Commemoration of Cornwallis' Embarkation for Yorktown, 1981, World Premiere of Mary Rose Marine Archeol. Exhibit, 1985; mem. grant rev. com. Va. Commn. for the Arts, 1986-87; bd. dirs. Portsmouth Pub. Libr., 1948-58, v.p., 1954-56; bd. dirs. Va. Symphony, 1986-87, trustee, 1987—; mem. taxes and mandates com. City of Portsmouth, 1982-86; mem. adv. com. City Mgr. of Norfolk, 1988-94; bd. dirs. Portsmouth Area Cmty Chest, 1948-52, Va. YMCA Youth and Govt. Found., 1950-52; mem. All-Am. cities com. for award-winning city Nat. League Municipalities, 1976; bd. advisors Ctr. Study Interactive Learning, Pasadena, Calif., 1993—; mem. steering com. Old Dominion U. Friends of the Libr., 1994-95, dir., 1995—; trustee Coun. for Am.'s First Freedom, 1994—. Named Portsmouth Young Man of Year, 1951; recipient honor medal Freedoms Found., 1951, Disting. Rsch. award Old Dominion U., 1987, Great Citizen award Hampton Roads 8 Cities, 1987, Notable Citizen award Portsmouth, Va., 1987; English award Old Dominion Coll., 1961; Troubadour, Great Tchrs. award, 1969; Outstanding Am. Educator award, 1972, 74; Nat. Bicentennial medal Am. Revolution Bicentennial Adminstrsn., 1976; medal Comité Francais du Bicentenaire de l'Independence des Etats-Unis, France, 1976; (with Ramona Mapp) Nat. Family Svc. award Family Found. Am., 1980; Laureate award Commonwealth of Va., 1981; Disting. Alumnus award Old Dominion U., 1982; Liberty Bell award Portsmouth Bar Assn., 1985; Old Dominion U. Triennial Phi Kappa Phi Scholar award, 1986, 91; History medal Nat. Soc. Daus. Am. Revolution; Portsmouth Downtown Merchants award, 1984, 85, Nat. Founders and Patriots award, 1995; Old Dominion U. Outstanding Achievement award, 1995; Gladstone Hill Friend of the Arts award (with Ramona H. Mapp), 1995; named to Order of the Crown of Charlemagne, 1993. Mem. Am. Hist. Assn., Va. Hist. Soc., Portsmouth Hist. Soc. (historiographer 1975-82, v.p. 1982-84es. 1985), Norfolk Hist. Soc. (dir. 1965-72), No. Neck Hist. Soc., Hist. Socs. Eastern Va. (dir. 1971—), SAR, Am. Assn. U. Profs., Authors Guild, Va. Library Assn. (legislative com. 1950-51), Poetry Soc. Va. (pres. 1974-75, adv. com. 1976—), Va. Writers Club, Assn. Preservation of Va. Antiquities, Order of Cape Henry (dir. 1970—, nat. pres. 1975-76), Jamestowne Soc. (chief historian 1975-77, internat. sec. state 1978-79), English Speaking Union (dir. 1976-77), Modern Lang. Assn., Order of First Families Va. 1607-1624, Nat. Historians Circle, Phi Theta Kappa, Delta Phi Omega (chpt. pres. 1961), Phi Kappa Phi. Baptist. Home: Willow Oaks 2901 Tanbark Ln Portsmouth VA 23703-4828 *Reared in an intellectual family with high ethical standards, enthusiasm for the arts, and firm belief in hard work, I also had impressed on me that advantages conferred obligations. In an historic environment, I became aware of my generation's responsibility to those that had preceded it (to preserve the good they had created) and to those that would follow (to create things that would enrich their lives). This concept, with personal ambition, imbues my professional life.*

MAPP, KENNETH E., lieutenant governor. Lt. gov. St. Thomas, V.I. Office: Kogens Glade Saint Thomas VI 00802*

MAQUET, JACQUES JEROME PIERRE, anthropologist, writer; b. Brussels, Belgium, Aug. 4, 1919; came to U.S., 1967, naturalized, 1974; s. Jerome and Jeanne (Lemoine) M.; m. Emma de Longrée, June 17, 1946; children: Bernard, Denis; m. Gisèle Cambresier, Nov. 13, 1970. JD, U. Louvain, Belgium, 1946, D.Phil., 1948; student, Harvard, 1946-48; PhD, U. London, Eng., 1952; Dr. ès-lettres, Sorbonne, France, 1973. Field anthropologist Inst. Sci. Research in Central Africa, 1949-51; head Inst. Sci. Research in Central Africa (Social Scis. Center), 1951-57; prof. State U. of Congo, Elisabethville, 1957-60; research dir. Ecole pratique des Hautes Etudes, U. Paris, 1961-68; prof. anthropology Case Western Res. U., 1968-71; prof. UCLA, 1971-91, chmn. dept. anthropology, 1978-83, prof. emeritus anthropology, 1991—; vis. prof. Northwestern U., 1956, Harvard, 1964, U. Montreal, 1965, U. Pitts., 1967; extraordinary prof. U. Brussels, 1963-68. Author: The Sociology of Knowledge, 1951, Aide-mémoire d'ethnologie africaine, 1954, Ruanda, 1957, (with others) Elections en Société féodale, 1957, The Premise of Inequality in Ruanda, 1961, Power and Society in Africa, 1971, Civilizations of Black Africa, 1972, Africanity, The Cultural Unity of Black Africa, 1972, Introduction to Aesthetic Anthropology, 1979, The Aesthetic Experience, 1986; co-editor: (with others) Dictionary of Black African Civilization, 1974. Recipient Waxweiler award Royal Acad. Belgium, 1961; First World Festival of Negro Arts award Dakar, 1966. Mem. Am. Anthrop. Assn., Internat. Assn. Buddhist Studies, Pali Text Soc., AAUP, Fedn. Am. Scientists. Office: UCLA Dept Anthropology Los Angeles CA 90095-1553

MARA, JOHN K., professional sports team executive. Exec. v.p., gen. counsel N.Y. Giants, East Rutherford, N.J. Office: NY Giants Giants Stadium East Rutherford NJ 07073

MARA, JOHN LAWRENCE, veterinarian, consultant; b. Whitesboro, N.Y., May 17, 1924; s. William Edward and Olive Pearl (Brakefield) M.; m. Kathleen Keefe, 1946 (div. 1958); children: William, Michael, Daniel, Patrick; m. Patricia Louise Paulk, 1970 (div. 1994); children: Jennifer Lee, Kennon. DVM, Cornell U., 1951. Diplomate Am. Coll. Vet. Nutrition. Intern N.Y. State Coll. Vet. Medicine, Cornell U., Ithaca, 1951-52; assoc. veterinarian L.W. Goodman Animal Hosp., Manhasset, N.Y., 1952-55; owner, pres. Mara Animal Hosp., Huntington, N.Y., 1955-79; profl. rep. Hills Pet Products, Topeka, Kans., 1979-80, mgr. profl. rels., 1980-81, dir. profl. affairs, 1981-88, dir. vet. affairs, 1988-94, sr. fellow profl. and acad. affairs, 1994—. V.p. Huntington United Fund; chmn. Huntington Taxpayers Party, 1968-78, Ch. in the Garden, Garden City, N.Y., 1975-77, trustee, 1975-77. Sgt. U.S. Army, 1943-45, ETO. Recipient Disting. Svc. award We. Vet. Conf., 1988; named hon. alumnus Coll. Vet. Medicine, Wash. State U. Mem. AVMA (Pres.'s award), L.I. Vet. Medicine Assn., N.Y. State Vet. Medicine Assn., Am. Animal Hosp. Assn., Kans. Vet. Medicine Assn. Republican. Baptist. Avocations: gardening, swimming, reading. Home: 6439 SW Castle Ln Topeka KS 66614-4392

MARA, VINCENT JOSEPH, college president; b. Worcester, Mass., Sept. 19, 1930; s. Edward Stephan and Mary Stephanie (Kavanaugh) M.; m. Clare Owens, Feb. 15, 1958; children: John, Kevin, Maryellen, Thomas, Clare. BS in Edn., Worcester State Coll.; EdM, U. Conn.; PhD. Asst. prof., then assoc. prof. Framingham (Mass.) State Coll., 1960-63, dir. admissions, 1963-69, acad. dean, 1969-76; acting pres. Salem (Mass.) State Coll., 1974-75; pres. Fitchburg (Mass.) State Coll., 1976-95, prof. emeritus, 1995—; corporator Fitchburg Savs. Bank, 1976-85; mem. Montachusett Region Pvt. Industry Coun., 1983—; dir. Safety Fund Nat. Bank. Contbr. articles to profl. jours. Trustee Notre Dame Prep. Sch., Fitchburg, 1985-86; trustee Worcester Pub. Libr., 1967-70, pres. bd. trustees, 1970; bd. dirs Fitchburg Civic Ctr., 1977-80, Cushing Acad., 1978-80, North Ctrl. Mass. Mental Health Assn., 1979-81, United Way, 1981-87, Montachusett Region Pvt. Industry Coun., 1983-93; bd. dirs. Thayer Symphony Orch., 1987-90, pres., 1994-95; mem. Mass. Commn. Edn. Telecomm., 1983-90, Fitchburg Bd. Health, 1982-93. With U.S. Army, 1952-53. Named Outstanding Young Man of Yr. Worcester C. of C., 1960; recipient Disting. Citizen award City of Fitchburg, 1989. Mem. NEA, Am. Conf. Acad. Deans, Am. Assn. State Colls. and Univs., N.Am. C. of C. (bd. dirs. 1984-91), Fitchburg C. of C. (bd. dirs. 1977-83), Fay Club, Phi Delta Kappa, Kappa Delta Pi. Democrat. Roman Catholic. Home: 242 Pearl Hill Rd Fitchburg MA 01420-2019 Office: Fitchburg State Coll 160 Pearl St Fitchburg MA 01420-2631

MARA, WELLINGTON T., professional football team executive; b. Aug. 8, 1916. Pres. N.Y. Giants, East Rutherford, N.J., also co-chief exec. officer. Office: NY Giants Giants Stadium East Rutherford NJ 07073 also: Nat Football League 410 Park Ave New York NY 10022-4407

MARABLE, JUDY VIRGINIA GORDON, insurance company supervisor; b. Roberta, Ga., Jan. 1, 1947; d. Barney Wesley and Bessie Pauline (Averett) Gordon; m. Clifton Ronnie Marable, June 1, 1971; 1 child, Clifton Ronnie II. Cert. assoc. in automation mgmt., assoc. in ins. svcs., underwriting Ins. Inst. Am., profl. ins. woman;cert. gen. ins. Asst. supr. Cigna P&C Ins., Macon, Ga., 1965-76, supr., 1976-80, personal lines underwriter, 1980-90; supr. Cigna Info. Svcs., Macon, 1990-94. Vol. United Way, 1991; pres. Crawford City Hist. Soc., Roberta, Ga., 1988-89; cubmaster Cub Scouts Pack 264, Roberta, 1984-87. Recipient Edn. award Profl. Ins. Agents, 1992. Mem. Nat. Assn. Ins. Women (treas. 1993-94, Ga. state dir. 1991-93, chmn. Ga. membership 1990-91, rep. regional nominating com. 1991, 94, Region III Ins. Profl. of Yr. 1994, Region III Individual Edn. Achievement Award 1993, Region III T.J. Mims Award of Excellence 1992, Nat. Ins. Profl. Yr. 1994), Ins. Women of Macon (Pres. award 1988, 90, 91, Ins. Woman of Yr. 1990, 91, pres.-pres.-elect 1987-89, bd. dirs. 1989-95, 10 various offices, chair 23 coms. 1987-95), Postal Customer Coun. (sec. 1991-92), United Daus. of Confederacy (pres. 1991—), Ctrl. Ga. Geneal. Soc. (pres. 1991-92). Avocations: antiques, doll collecting, pottery. Home: RR 1 Box 2460 Roberta GA 31078-9612 Office: 620 Bass Rd Macon GA 31210-7303

MARABLE, SIDNEY THOMAS, lawyer; b. Henderson, N.C., Dec. 4, 1954; s. Nathaniel and Julia M. (Vann) M.; m. Frances J. Marable; 1 child, Marcus Latham. BA in Polit. Sci., N.C. Agrl. & Tech. State U., 1976; JD, U. N.C., 1979. Bar: N.C. 1979, Ariz. 1983, U.S. Supreme Ct. 1979. Assoc. Castro, Zipf & Rogers, Phoenix, 1983-87, ptnr., 1987-92; pvt. practice Phoenix, 1992—; mem. Civil Practice Procedure Com., Phoenix, 1994—, Maricopa County Bench/Bar Com., Phoenix, 1994—, Fed. Dist. Ct. Local Rules Com., Phoenix, 1995—. Bd. dirs. Ctrl. Ariz. Arthritis Found., Phoenix, 1987-88; mem. Mayor's Profl. Sports Adv. Com., Phoenix, 1988-91, Bus. Ptnrs. of Phoenix Symphony, 1993-95. Capt. JAG, USAF, 1979-83. Master Sandra Day O'Connor Inn of Ct.; mem. ABA, Ariz. State Bar Assn., Fed. Bar Assn., Maricopa County Bar Assn. (mem. pub. rels. com. 1993-95, chair 1995—). Avocations: flying, camping, skiing, sailing, hiking. Office: Law Offices Sidney T Marable 3030 N Central Ave Ste 1000 Phoenix AZ 85012

MARADUDIN, ALEXEI A., physics educator; b. San Francisco, Dec. 14, 1931. BS, Stanford U., 1953, MS, 1954; PhD in Physics, Bristol U., 1956. Rsch. assoc. physics U. Md., 1956-57, rsch. asst. prof., 1957-58; asst. rsch. prof. Inst. Fluid Dynamics & Applied Math., 1958-60; physicist Westinghouse Rsch. Labs., 1960-65; cons. semiconductor br. U.S. Naval Rsch. Lab., 1958-60, Los Alamos Sci. Lab., 1965-67, 83—, Gen. Atomic Divsn. Gen. Dynamics Corp., 1965-71; chmn. dept. U. Calif., Irvine, 1968-71, prof. physics, 1965—. Recipient Alexander von Humboldt U.S. sr. scientist award, 1980-81. Fellow Am. Phys. Soc.; mem. Optical Soc. Am., Sigma Xi. Office: U Cal Irvine Inst Surface & Interface Sci Physical Scis Bldg 2 Rm 2172 Irvine CA 92717*

MARAFINO, VINCENT NORMAN, aerospace company executive; b. Boston, June 8, 1930; m. Doris Marilyn Vernall, June 15, 1958; children: Marli Ann, Sheri Louise, Wendi Joan. A.B. in Acctg. and Econs., San Jose State Coll., 1951; M.B.A., Santa Clara U., 1964. Chief acct. Am. Standard Advance Tech. Lab., Mountain View, Calif., 1956-59; with Lockheed Missiles & Space Co., Sunnyvale, Calif., 1959-70, asst. dir. fin. ops., 1968-70; asst. controller Lockheed Corp., Burbank, Calif., 1970-71, v.p., controller, 1971-77, sr. v.p. fin., 1977-83, exec. v.p., chief fin. and administrv. officer, 1983-88, vice chmn. bd., chief fin. and adminstrv. officer, 1988—, also dir.; bd. dirs. Lockheed Missiles & Space Co., Inc.; chmn. bd. dirs. Lockheed Fin. Corp. Trustee Holy Cross Med. Ctr., Mission Hills, Calif. Served with USAF, 1953-55. Mem. Fin. Execs. Inst., AICPAs, North Ranch Country Club. Office: Lockheed Corp 4500 Park Granada Calabasas CA 91399-0001

MARALDO, ANGELA MARIE, project engineer; b. Grosse Pointe, Mich., Sept. 26, 1966; d. Mario Victor and Judith Ann (Raether) M. BSCE, Mich. Tech. U., 1989. Registered profl. engr. Mich. Project engr. City of Monroe (Mich.), 1989—. Mem. on-site selection com. Monroe County Habitat for Humanity. Mem. ASCE, Mich. Soc. Profl. Engrs. Avocations: travel, four wheeling. Office: City of Monroe 120 E 1st Monroe MI 48161

MARAM, BARRY S., lawyer; b. Chgo., Mar. 21, 1946. BA, U. Ill., 1967; MA with honors, U. Chgo., 1985; JD, Ill. Inst. Tech., 1971. Bar: Ill. 1971, Fla. 1973, U.S. Dist. Ct. (no. dist.) Ill. 1971, U.S. Dist. Ct. (so. dist.) Fla. 1974. Ptnr. Winston & Strawn, Chgo., 1994, Sonnenschein, Nath, Rosenthal; instrs. bus. law Triton Coll., 1983-85; assoc. dir. Ill. Dept. Health, 1985; exec. dir. Ill. Health Facilities Authority, 1986-89. Pub. Policy fellow. Mem. Ill. State Bar Assn., Fla. Bar. Office: Sonnenschein Nath Rosenthal 237 S Wacker Dr Chicago IL 60601*

MARAMOROSCH, KARL, virologist, educator; b. Vienna, Austria, Jan. 16, 1915; came to U.S., 1947, naturalized, 1952; s. Jacob and Stefanie Olga (Schlesinger) M.; m. Irene Ludwinowska, Nov. 15, 1938; 1 dau., Lydia Ann. M.S. magna cum laude in Entomology, Agrl. U., Warsaw, Poland, 1938; student, Poly. U. Bucharest, Rumania, 1944-46; fellow, Bklyn. Bot. Garden, 1947-48; Ph.D. (predoctoral fellow Am. Cancer Soc. 1948-49), Columbia, 1949. Civilian internee in Rumania, 1939-46; asst., then assoc. Rockefeller Inst., N.Y.C., 1949-61; sr. entomologist Boyce Thompson Inst., Yonkers, N.Y., 1961-74, program dir. virology and insect physiology, 1962-74; prof. microbiology Waksman Inst., Rutgers U., New Brunswick, N.J., 1974-85; prof. entomology Cook Coll., Rutgers U., New Brunswick, 1985—, Robert L. Starkey prof., 1983—; vis. prof. agr. U. Wageningen, Netherlands, 1953, Cornell U., 1957, Rutgers U., 1967-68, Fordham U., 1973, Sapporo U., Japan, 1980, Justus Liebig U., Giessen, Ger., 1983; Mendel lectr. St. Peters Coll., Jersey City, 1963; virologist FAO to Philippines, 1960; Disting. Vis. prof. Fudan U., Shanghai, 1982; cons. FAO-UN, World-wide survey, 1963; chmn. U.S.-Japan Coop. Seminar, 1965, 74, 85; mem. panel food and fiber Nat. Acad. Scis., 1966; cons. rice virus diseases AID-IRRI, Hyderabad, India, 1971; cons. UNDP, Bangalore, India, 1978-79; virologist FAO/UNDP, Sri Lanka, 1981, 82, 83, Mauritius, 1985; AIBS lectr., 1970-72, Found. Microbiology Nat. lectr., 1972-73, Fulbright Disting. prof., Yugoslavia, 1972, 78; mem. tropical medicine and parasitology study sect. NIH, 1972-76; chmn. 1st-3d Internat. Confs. Comparative Virology, 1969, 73, 76. Author: Comparative Symptomatology of Coconut Diseases of Unknown Etiology, 1964; editor: Biological Transmission of Disease Agents, 1962, Insect Viruses, 1968, Viruses, Vectors and Vegetation, 1969, Comparative Virology, 1971, Mycoplasma Diseases, 1973, Viruses, Evolution and Cancer, 1974, Invertebrate Immunity, 1975, Legume Diseases in the Tropics, 1975, Invertebrate Tissue Culture: Research Applications, 1976, Invertebrate Tissue Culture: Applications in Medicine, Biology and Agriculture, 1976, Aphids as Virus Vectors, 1977, Insect and Plant Viruses: An Atlas, 1977, Viruses and Environment, 1978, Practical Tissue Culture Applications, 1979, Leafhopper Vectors and Plant Disease Agents, 1979, Vectors of Plant Pathogens, 1980, Invertebrate Systems in Vitro, 1980, Vectors of Disease Agents, 1981, Mycoplasma Diseases of Trees and Shrubs, 1981, Mycoplasma and Allied Pathogens of Plants, Animals and Human Beings, 1981, Plant Diseases and Vectors: Ecology and Epidemiology, 1981, Invertebrate Cell Culture Applications, 1982, Pathogens, Vectors and Plant Diseases: Approaches to Control, 1982, Subviral Pathogens of Plants and Animals, 1985, Viral Insecticides for Biological Control, 1985, Biotechnology Advances in Insect Pathology and Cell Culture, 1987, Mycoplasma Diseases of Crops, 1988, Invertebrate and Fish Tissues Culture, 1988, Biotechnology for Biological Controls of Pests and Vectors, 1991, Viroids and Satellites: Molecular Parasites at the Frontier of Life, 1991, Plant Diseases of Uncertain Etiology, 1992, Insect Cell Biotechnology, 1994, Arthropod Cell Culture Systems, 1994, Forest Trees and Palms: Diseases and Control, 1996; Methods in Virology, 1964—, Advances in Virus Research, 1972—, Archives of Virology, 1973-78, Intervirology, 1973-77, Advances in Cell Culture, 1979—; editor in chief Jour. N.Y. Entomol. Soc, 1972-84; assoc. editor: Virology, 1964-68, 75-79. Recipient Sr. Research award Lalor Found., 1957; Nat. Ciba-Geigy award in agr., 1976; Wolf prize in agr., 1980; Jurzykowski prize in biology, 1980; Disting. Service award Am. Inst. Biol. Scis., 1983. Fellow AAAS (Campbell award 1958), Entomol. Soc. Am., N.Y. Acad. Scis. (A. Cressy Morrison prize natural sci. 1951, chmn. div. microbiology 1956-60, rec. sec. 1960-61, v.p. 1962-63), Nat. Acad. Scis. India (hon.); mem. Harvey Soc., Growth Soc., Pytopath. Soc., Indian, Japan, Can. phytopath. socs., Leopoldina Acad., Internat. Com. Virus Nomenclature, Electron Microscope Soc., Am. Soc. Microbiology (Waksman award 1978), Tissue Culture Assn. (pres. N.E. br. 1978-81, pres. history br. 1988-90), Soc. Invertebrate Pathology (founder's lectr., Adelaide 1990), Internat. Assn. Medicinal Forest Plants (pres. 1989—), Sigma Xi (pres. Rugers chpt. 1978). Home: 17 Black Birch Ln Scarsdale NY 10583-7456 Office: Rutgers U Dept Entomology New Brunswick NJ 08903

MARAN, STEPHEN PAUL, astronomer; b. Bklyn., Dec. 25, 1938; s. Alexander P. and Clara F. (Schoenfeld) M.; m. Sally Ann Scott, Feb. 14, 1971; children: Michael Scott, Enid Rebecca, Elissa Jean. B.S., Bklyn. Coll., 1959; M.A., U. Mich., 1961, Ph.D., 1964. Astronomer Kitt Peak Nat. Obs., Tucson, 1964-69; project scientist for orbiting solar observatories NASA-Goddard Space Flight Center, Greenbelt, Md., 1969-75; head advanced systems and ground observations br. NASA-Goddard Space Flight Ctr., 1970-77, mgr. Operation Kohoutek, 1973-74, sr. staff scientist Lab. for Astronomy and Solar Physics, 1977-95; asst. dir. Space Scis. for Info. and Outreach, 1995—; Cons. Westinghouse Rsch. Labs., 1966; vis. lectr. U. Md., College Park, 1969-70; sr. lectr. UCLA, 1976; A. Dixon Johnson lectr. in sci. communication, Pa. State U., 1990; lectr. on astronomy cruises and eclipse tours. Author: (with John C. Brandt) New Horizons in Astronomy, 1972, 2d edit., 1979, Arabic edit., 1979, The Gems of Hubble, 1993; editor: Physics of Nonthermal Radio Sources, 1964, The Gum Nebula and Related Problems, 1971, Possible Relations Between Solar Activity and Meteorological Phenomena, 1975, New Astronomy and Space Science Reader, 1977, A Meeting with the Universe, 1981, Astrophysics of Brown Dwarfs, 1986, The Astronomy and Astrophysics Encyclopedia, 1991; assoc. editor: Earth, Extraterrestrial Scis, 1969-79; editor: Astrophys. Letters, 1974-77, assoc. editor, 1977-85; contbg. editor Air & Space/Smithsonian, 1990—; contbr. articles on astronomy, space to popular mags. Named Disting. Visitor Boston U., 1970; recipient Group Achievement awards NASA, 1969, 74, Exceptional Achievement medal, 1991. Fellow AAAS; mem. Internat. Astron. Union (editor daily newspaper 1988), Am. Astron. Soc. (Harlow Shapley vis. lectr. 1981—), press. officer 1985—), Royal Astron. Soc., Am. Phys. Soc., Am. Geophys. Union. Office: Code 600 NASA Goddard Space Flight Ctr Greenbelt MD 20771

MARANDA, GUY, oral maxillofacial surgeon, Canadian health facility executive, educator; b. Paris, May 9, 1936; arrived in Canada, 1937; s. Emilien and Lucille (Fortin) M.; married; children: Lucille, Jean, Isabelle. BA, U. Ottawa, Ont., Can., 1957; DDs, U. Montreal, Can., 1962; cert. oral surgeon, U. Pa., 1965. Pvt. practice Quebec, 1965-70; mem. faculty U. Laval, Ste. Foy, Que., Can., 1970—, asst. prof., 1987-94, prof., 1995—; bd. dirs. Ordre Dentistes du Québec; pres. Quebec Assn. Oral Surgeons, 1985; cons. Quebec Health Bd., Assurance Auto Quebec, various law firms. Mem. Royal coll. Dentists Can. (diplomate, pres. 1991), Internat. Assn. Oral Surgeons, Can. Assn. Oral Surgeons, Am. Assn. Oral Surgeons, Can. Dental Assn. Ordre Dentistes Que. Roman Catholic. Home: 822 Bellevue, Sainte Foy, PQ Canada G1V 2R5 Office: U Laval, Faculty Dental Medicine, Sainte Foy, PQ Canada G1V 7P4

MARANDA, PIERRE JEAN, anthropologist, writer; b. Quebec, Que., Can., Mar. 27, 1930; s. Lucien and Marie Alma (Rochette) M.; m. Elli Köngäs, Mar. 12, 1963 (dec.); children: Erik Pierre, Nicolas Martin. B.A., U. Laval, Quebec, 1949; M.A., U. Montreal, Que., 1953; Ph.D., Harvard U., 1966; Dr. honoris causa, Meml. U. Nfld., 1984. Asst. prof. anthropology U. Laval, 1955-58, research prof., 1975—, prof., 1976—, dept. head, 1989—; tutor Harvard U., 1964-65, research fellow, 1966-70; dir. studies Ecole Pratique des Hautes Etudes, 6th Sect., Paris, 1968-69; assoc. prof. U. B.C. (Can.), Vancouver, 1969-73; prof. U. B.C. (Can.), 1973-75; prof. étranger College de France, Paris, 1975; bd. dirs. several internat. research insts.; vis. prof. Universidade Federal, Rio de Janeiro, 1983. Author: (with Köngäs Maranda) books, including Structural Models in Folklore and Transformational Essays, 1962, 2d rev. edit., 1970, Introduction to Anthropology: A Self-Guide, 1972, French Kinship: Structure and History, 1974, Soviet Structural Folkloristics, 1974, Dialogue Conjugal, 1985; DiscAn: A Computer System for Contents and Discourse Analysis, 1989, (with Fidèle Nze-Guema) L'Unité culturelle dans la diversité: Une Geste bantu, 1994; contbr. numerous articles to profl. jours. Pres. Comité des Citoyens de Belvedere, Que., 1976-83. Recipient Medaille du College de France, 1975. Fellow Royal Soc. Can., Am. Anthrop. Assn.; mem. Internat. Semiotics Assn., Internat. Center Linguistics and Semiotics, Can. Inst. Advanced Research (council), Can. Ethnol. Soc. (former pres.), Can. Anthropology and Sociology Assn. (former pres.), Can. Semiotics Research Assn. (bd. dirs.), Can. Folklore Studies Assn.

MARANGI, VITO ANTHONY, SR., claim adminstrator; b. Utica, N.Y., Jan. 1, 1932; s. Mary Margaret Lokey, Apr. 10, 1960 (div. July 1973); children: Vito Anthony Jr., Vanetta Gayle, Gregory Alan; m. Diann Louise Bunch, Apr. 11, 1987. BS, SUNY, Potsdam, 1958. Asst. regional claims mgr. Hartford Ins. Group, Fresno, Calif., 1958-67; supervising adjuster Underwriters Adjusting Co., Fresno, 1967-70; home office claim supr. Meritplan Ins. Co., Newport Beach, Calif., 1970-71; appeals referee State of Nev., Reno and Carson City, 1971-73, 76-79; br. mgr. Brown Bros. Adjusters, Reno,

1974-87; ind. ins. adjuster Tony Marangi, Adjuster, Carson City, 1987—; vice chmn., bd. trustees Carson-Tahoe Hosp., 1991-96. Scout master Boy Scouts Am., Utica, N.Y., Fresno, Calif., Carson City, 1953-85. With USN, 1949-53. Mem. Nev. State Claims Assn. (pres., v.p., treas., sec.), No. Nev. Claims Assn. (pres., v.p., treas., sec.), Nat. Assn. of Adminstrv. Law Judges, Internat. Assn. of Arson Investigators (Nev. chpt.), Carson City Elks Lodge, VFW, Carson City C. of C. (bus. edn. com. 1987—, transp. com. 1987—). Avocations: photographer, bowling, dancing, classic car owner, musician. Home: PO Box 843 Carson City NV 89702-0843 Office: Carson Tahoe Hosp PO Box 2168 Carson City NV 89702-2168

MARANISS, DAVID, reporter; b. 1949. Reporter, now staff writer The Washington Post. Author: First in His Class: A Biography of Bill Clinton, 1995. Recipient Pulitzer Prize for nat. reporting, 1993. Office: Washington Post 1150 15th St NW Washington DC 20071-0001

MARANO, ANTHONY JOSEPH, cardiologist; b. White Plains, N.Y., Apr. 14, 1934; s. Anthony Joseph and Mary Antoinette (Perrotta) M.; m. Mary Regina Marbach, Aug. 23, 1958; children—Thomas, Kathryn, Michele. B.A., Williams Coll., 1956; M.D., Cornell Med. Coll., 1960. Diplomate Am. Bd. Internal Medicine, Am. Bd. Cardiovascular Disease. Intern Bellevue Hosp., N.Y.C., 1960-61; resident St. Luke's Hosp., N.Y.C., 1961-63; NIH fellow in cardiology Mt. Sinai Hosp., N.Y.C., 1963-64, research assoc., 1964-75; clin. assoc. in medicine Coll. Physicians and Surgeons, N.Y.C., 1970-86; pres. med. staff White Plains Hosp., 1984-86, chief cardiology, 1985-91, chief cardiology emeritus, 1991—, bd. dirs., 1983-88; cons. in cardiology Burke Rehab. Ctr.; med. dir., founder Paramedic Ambulance, White Plains, 1976-82. Contbr. articles to med. jours. Trustee Pace U., N.Y.C., 1975—, Home Savs. Bank, White Plains, 1973-90; bd. dirs. YMCA, White Plains, 1978-82 ; team physician White Plains High Sch., 1967—; cons. physician Dept. Pub. Safety, White Plains, 1968—; cons. physician City of White Plains Sch. System, 1994—; bd. dirs. Westchester County Sports Hall of Fame, 1993—; alumni trustee Tyng Found., Williams Coll., 1994—. Tyng scholar Williams Coll., 1952-59; recipient Outstanding Achievement award Emergency Med. Services Council, 1982. Fellow ACP, Am. Coll. Cardiology; mem. AMA, Am. Coll. Sports Medicine, Am. Heart Assn., N.Y. State Heart Assn. (bd. dirs. 1982-85), Westchester Heart Assn. (v.p. 1983-86, pres. 1987-90), Phi Beta Kappa. Clubs: University (White Plains) (pres. 1970-71); Westchester Country (Harrison, N.Y.). Avocations: tennis, skiing, gardening. Home: 9 Fairway Dr White Plains NY 10605-4107 Office: 20 Old Mamaroneck Rd White Plains NY 10605-2060

MARANO, RICHARD MICHAEL, lawyer; b. Waterbury, Conn., June 22, 1960; s. Albert Nicholas and Angeline Domenica (Viotti) M.; m. Eileen N. Barry. BA, Fairfield U., 1982; JD, Seton Hall U., 1985. Bar: Conn. 1985, U.S. Dist. Ct. Conn. 1985, U.S. Tax Ct. 1986, U.S. Supreme Ct. 1990, U.S. Ct. Appeals (2d cir.) 1991. Assoc. Moynahan, Ruskin, Mascolo & Mariani, Waterbury, 1985-87; ptnr. Marano & Diamond, Waterbury, 1987—; alderman City of Waterbury 1988-90. Author: History of the Order Sons of Italy of Waterbury, Connecticut, 1995; co-editor: Counsel for the Defense, 1991-93, editor, 1993—; contbr. law articles to Conn. Bar Jour. Bd. dirs. Italian-Am. Dem. Club, Waterbury, 1988—, Ctrl. Naugatuck Valley HELP, 1992—, Anderson Boys Club, 1989—, Waterbury Housing Police Fund, 1992-94, Waterbury Crime Stoppers Inc., 1994—; pres. Conn. Young Dems., 1981-82; state coord. McGovern for U.S. Presdl. campaign, 1983-84; campaign mgr. Orman for Congress, 1984; commr. Waterbury Pub. Assistance, 1986-88; justice of the peace, Waterbury, 1989—; gen. counsel Waterbury Dem. Town Com., 1990—; trustee Our Lady of Lourdes Ch., 1993—. Mem. ABA, ATLA, KC, Conn. Bar Assn., Nat. Assn. Criminal Def. Lawyers, Conn. Criminal Def. Lawyers Assn. (sec. 1994-96, v.p. 1996—), Conn. Italian-Am. Bar Assn. (pres. 1993-95), Conn. Trial Lawyers Assn., Waterbury Bar Assn. (bd. dirs. 1993—), New Haven County Bar Assn., Nat. Italian-Am. Bar Assn., Sons of Italy (pres. lodge # 66 1994—), Unico Club, Elks, Alpha Mu Gamma, Pi Sigma Alpha. Roman Catholic. Home: 22 Stephana Ln Waterbury CT 06710-1126 Office: Marano & Diamond 61 Field St Waterbury CT 06702-1907 *Notable cases include: State vs. Rafael Molina Jud. dist. Waterbury, CR4-145496, acquittal on a first degree sexual assault charge; Davis vs. Alaska 415 U.S. 308, 1974; State vs. Dawn Marotta, Jud. Dist. Waterbury Crs-18353, State's evidence of cocaine was suppressed; Petruzzi vs. Sterling, Jud. dist. Waterbury, 87-792347, violation of Conn. statutes pertaining to prescription and dispensing of drugs.*

MARANS, J. EUGENE, lawyer; b. Butte, Mont., May 26, 1940; s. Edward and Florence M.; m. Anne Marie Borger, Sept. 3, 1978; children: Julia C., John E. A.B., Harvard U., 1962, LL.B., 1965. Bar: N.Y. 1966, D.C. 1971. Law clk. to Judge John M. Wisdom U.S. Ct. Appeals (5th cir.), New Orleans, 1965-66; assoc. Cleary, Gottlieb, Steen & Hamilton, N.Y.C., 1966-70, Paris, 1970-71; assoc. Cleary, Gottlieb, Steen & Hamilton, Washington, 1971-74, ptnr., 1975-90, 93—; ptnr. Cleary, Gottlieb, Steen & Hamilton, Hong Kong, 1990-93; mem. N.Y. State adv. com. U.S. Commn. Civil Rights, 1969-70; mem. nat. eval. com. on. simplified method of determining eligibility in pub. assistance HEW, 1969-70; sec., counsel Bipartisan Com. on Absentee Voting, 1973—. Contbr. articles to legal jours. Bd. dirs. New Leadership Fund, chmn. 1977-79; mem. Sabre Found., pres. 1990. Mem. Assn. Ams. Resident Overseas, Ripon Soc. (nat. governing bd. 1962—, chmn. 1969-70), Council on Fgn. Relations, ABA, D.C. Bar (chmn. internat. sect. 1978-79), Assn. of Bar of City of N.Y., Am. Soc. Internat. Law, Union Internat. des Avocats, Washington Fgn. Law Soc. (pres. 1985-86), Am. Law Inst. Office: 1752 N St NW Washington DC 20036-2806

MARANS, ROBERT WARREN, architect, planner; b. Detroit, Aug. 3, 1934; s. Albert and Anne Rose (Siegel) M.; m. Judith Ann Bloomfield, Jan. 24, 1956; children: Gayl Elizabeth, Pamela Jo. BArch, U. Mich., 1957; M in Urban Planning, Wayne State U., 1961; PhD, U. Mich., 1971. Reg. architect, Mich. Archtl. engr., planner Detroit City Planning Comn., 1957-61; planning cons. Blair & Stein Assocs., Providence, 1961-64; architect-urban designer Artur Glikson, Architect, Tel Aviv, Israel, 1964-65; regional planner Detroit Area Transp. Land Use Study, 1965-67; asst. prof. Fla. State U., Talahassee, 1967; rsch. assoc., sr. study dir. Inst. Social Rsch., Ann Arbor, Mich., 1968-74, program dir., 1974—; from lectr. to assoc. prof. Coll. Architecture Urban Planning, Ann Arbor, 1971-78; prof. architecture and urban planning U. Mich., Ann Arbor, 1978—; cons. TVA, 1972, UN, 1974; chmn. urban and regional planning program, 1987—. Co-author: Planned Residential Environments, 1970, Quality of NonMetropolitan Living, 1978, Evaluating Built Environments, 1981, Retirement Communities: An American Original, 1984; co-editor: Methods of Environmental and Behavioral Research, 1987, Advanced Monograph Series on Environment, Behavior and Design, 1990, Environmental Simulation: Research and Policy Perspectives, 1993; contbr. articles to profl. jours. and tech. reports. Sec. Washtenaw County Parks Recreation Commn., Ann Arbor, 1972—; chmn. Huron-Clinton Met. Parks Authority, Brighton, Mich., 1986—. Recipient fellow Social Sci. Rsch. Coun., 1969-70; Fulbright Rsch. award Coun. Internat. Exchange Scholars, Israel, 1977; Progressive Architecture Applied Rsch. award Progressive Architecture Mag., 1982; Design Rsch. Recognition award Nat. Endowment for Arts, 1983. Mem. Am. Planning Assn., Nat. Recreation Pk. Assn., Environ. Design Rsch. Assn. Avocations: swimming, stamp collecting. Office: U Mich Coll Arch and Urban Planning Ann Arbor MI 48109

MARANZANO, MIGUEL FRANSCISCO, design engineer; b. Buenos Aires, Argentina, Aug. 14, 1941; came to U.S., 1977; s. Miguel and Nelida (Pizzini) M.; m. Ana Isabel Carranza, Mar. 25, 1978; children: Cynthia, Rossana, Giancarlo, Gabriel. BS, SUNY, 1982; MS, Rensselaer Poly., 1985. Field engr. Johnson Controls, Phila., 1978-82; sr. rsch. engr. Hi-G Rsch., Bloomfield, Conn., 1979-82; engr. mgr. Locknetics, Hamden, Conn., 1982-85; group leader Superior Elec., Bristol, Conn., 1985-86; mgr. elec. testing Springborn Labs., Enfield, Conn., 1986-88; sr. product engr. Skinner Valve, New Britain, Conn., 1988-89, Kip, Inc., Farmington, Conn., 1989-95; sr. design engr. Peter Paul Electronics, New Britain, Conn., 1995—; mem. adj. faculty dept. math. and sci. Manchester C.C., 1986-88; presenter 39th internat. conf. Nat. Assn. Relay Mfrs. Contbr. articles to profl. jours. Mem. Hispanic-Am. Cultural Coun., New Britain, Conn., 1990. Achievements include patent on electronic game and solenoid valve. Home: 110 Pheasant Run Bristol CT 06010-4891 Office: Peter Paul Electronics 480 John Downey Dr New Britain CT 06050

MARASH, STANLEY ALBERT, consulting company executive; b. Bklyn., Dec. 18, 1938; s. Albert Samuel and Esther (Cunio) M.; m. Muriel Sylvia Sutchin, June 24, 1961; children: Judith Ilene, Alan Scott. Student, Bklyn. Coll., 1956-58; BBA, CCNY, 1961; student, U. Idaho, 1962-63, Boston U., 1964-66; MBA, Baruch Coll., 1970, PhD, 1995. Registered profl. engr., Calif.; cert. quality engr., reliability engr. Statistician Electric Boat Gen. Dynamics, Groton, Conn., 1961-62; statistician Idaho Nat. Energy Lab. Electric Boat Gen. Dynamics, Idaho Falls, 1962-63; mgr. quality assurance memory product ops. RCA, Needham, Mass., 1963-65; cons. engr. astroelectronics div. RCA, Princeton, N.J., 1965-66; corp. mgr. quality assurance Ideal Corp., Bklyn., 1966-68; mgr. quality assurance Gen. Instrument, Signalite, Neptune, N.J., 1968; pres. STAT-A-MATRIX, Inc., Edison, N.J., 1968-90; chmn. bd. STAT-A-MATRIX Inst., Edison, N.J., 1975—; chmn., CEO STAT-A-MATRIX Group, Edison, N.J., 1990-94, The SAM Group - STAT-A-MATRIX, Edison, N.J., 1994—; trustee Ellis R. Ott Found., Edison, 1982-95; chmn. Quality N.J., 1989-94, chmn. emeritus, 1994—; advisor quality tech. Middlesex County Coll., Edison, 1970-94; vis. prof. U. Sao Paulo, Brazil, 1974, 75, 77, Madrid Poly. U., 1976; expert cons. Internat. Atomic Energy Agy., Vienna, 1974-77; cons. various govt. agys. and pub. and pvt. cos., 1972—; mem. indsl. adv. com. dept. stats. Rutgers U., 1977-78; mem. exec. stds. coun. Am. Nat. Stds. Inst., N.Y.C., 1979-80. Author: (tng. manual) Statistically Aided Management: What Every Executive Needs to Know, 1987; contbr. numerous articles, manuals and tng. texts. Examiner Malcolm Baldridge Nat. Quality Award, 1990, 91. Fellow Am. Soc. Quality Control (chmn. met. sect. 1966-68, Ellis R. Ott award 1981, chmn. internat. cooperation com. 1989—); mem. IEEE (sr.), ASTM, ASME, Am. Statis. Assn., Am. Soc. Tng. Devel., Am. Nuclear Soc. Office: The SAM Group/Stat-A-Matrix One Quality Pl Edison NJ 08820-1059

MARAYNES, ALLAN LAWRENCE, filmmaker, television producer; b. N.Y.C., Apr. 26, 1950; s. Harry and Dorothy (Kaufman) M.; m. Bitsy Healy, Oct. 14, 1978; children: Sean, Megan, Matthew. BA, Queens Coll., 1972; MA, Loyola U., L.A., 1974. Assoc. producer CBS News, N.Y.C., 1976-77; producer CBS News-60 Minutes, N.Y.C., 1974-88; pres. Northern Films, N.Y.C., 1988—; exec. producer ABC "SST" program, 1989; producer 20/20 ABC News, N.Y.C., 1990-93; sr. investigative prodr. ABC News 20/20, 1994—; lectr. New Sch., N.Y.C., 1979, Columbia U., N.Y.C. Writer, dir. CBS News, 60 Minutes, 1976-88; author: (play) A Straight Line to the Market Place, 1975, (screenplay) Warp, 1991. Recipient Emmy award NATAS, 1981, 85, 89, 91, 93, George Foster Peabody award, 1989. Mem. NATAS, Writers Guild Am. Avocations: N.Y. Yankees. Office: ABC News 157 Columbus Ave New York NY 10023-5907

MARAZITA, MARY LOUISE, genetics researcher; b. Cheboygan, Mich., June 13, 1954; m. Richard T. McCoy, 1984; 3 children. BS, Mich. State U., 1976; PhD in Genetics, U. N.C., 1980. Fellow U. So. Calif., 1980-82; statistician, instr. UCLA, 1982-86; asst. prof. human genetics Med. Coll. Va., 1986-93; dir. Cleft Palate-craniofacial Ctr. U. Pitts., 1993—; instr. biomath. U. Calif., 1984-86; asst. prof. dentistry Med. Coll. Va., 1992-93; assoc. prof. human genetics and oral maxillofacial surgery U. Pitts., 1993—. Fellow Am. Coll. Med. Genetics, Am. Cleft Palate Assn., Am. Soc. Human Genetics, Internat. Genetic Epidemiol. Soc., Internat. Assn. Dental Rsch. Achievements include research in genetics of cleft lip, cleft palate and other craniofacial anomalies, including statistical genetic analysis and gene mapping studies. Office: U Pitts Cleft Palate-Craniofac Ctr 317 Salk Hall Pittsburgh PA 15261-1931*

MARBACH, DIANE, food service executive; b. N.Y.C., Mar. 7, 1932; d. Charles Saul and Anne Helen (Leighter) Nusbaum; widowed; children: Barbara Dorset, Edward. BFA, New Sch. for Social Rsch.; student, Pratt Inst. Chmn., owner JAMAC Frozen Food Corp., Jersey City, N.J., 1959—. Contbr. articles to profl. jours. Named Woman of Yr. Food and Beverage Am., 1993; recipient Moderator-Spkr. award for Food Svc. Industry. Mem. Food Svc. Execs. (pres. 1962-64), Soc. Food Mgmt., Hosp. Food Mgmt. Assn. Republican.

MARBLE, DUANE FRANCIS, geography educator, researcher; b. Seattle, Dec. 10, 1931; s. Francis Augustus and Beulah Belle (Simmons) M.; m. Jacquelynne Hardester, Aug. 18, 1957; children: Kimberley Eileen, Douglas Craig. BA, U. Wash., 1953, MA, 1956, PhD, 1959. Asst. prof. real estate U. Oreg., Eugene, 1959; asst. prof. regional sci. U. Pa., Phila., 1960-63; from assoc. prof. geography to prof. geography Northwestern U., Evanston, Ill., 1963-73, assoc. dir. Transp. Ctr., 1966-73; prof. geography and computer sci. SUNY at Buffalo, Amherst, N.Y., 1973-87; prof. geography and natural resources Ohio State U., Columbus, 1987—; chmn. com. on geog. data sensing and processing Internat. Geog. Union, 1980-88; bd. dirs. Castlereagh Enterprises, Phoenix; founder Internat. Symposium Spatial Data Handling; cons. on GIS to U.S. Bur. Census, UN, also pvt. orgns. Editor: Intro Readings in GIS, 1990, Taylor & Francis, 1990-95; author computer program (best software award Assn. Am. Geogs. 1990). Mem. AAAS, Assn. Am. Geographers (honors 1993), IEEE Computer Soc. Home: 1310 Langston Dr Upr Arlington OH 43220-3900 Office: Dept Geography Ohio State Univ Columbus OH 43210-1361

MARBLE, MELINDA SMITH, writer, editor; b. Ponca City, Okla., June 17, 1960; d. Monte Gene and Dorothy Worthington Smith; m. Sanford Marble. BA with high hons., spl. hons. English, U. Tex., 1984. Mktg. Data Base Publs., Austin, Tex., 1986-87; assoc. editor Austin Area Bus. Women Directory, 1987-88; asst. pub. Travelers' Times, Austin, 1988-89; assoc. editor Tex. Bar Jour., Austin, 1989-95; freelance editor, Austin, 1989-95, novelist, freelance journalist, Morristown, N.J., 1995—. Contbr. articles to newspapers and profl. jours. Recipient Gold Quill award of merit Internat. Assn. Bus. Communicators, 1993, Gold Quill Excellence award for First Person Articles, 1995; Best of Austin 4 Color Mag. award, 1993, 2 awards of merit, 1995, Presdl. Citation, State Bar of Tex., 1993, Nat. Assn. Govt. Communicators award of Honor 4 Color Mag., 1994, Best of Austin Feature Writing award, 1995, Best of Austin Advocacy Writing award, 1995. Avocations: reading, writing, traveling, skiing.

MARBURGER, JOHN HARMEN, III, university president, physics educator; b. S.I., N.Y., Feb. 8, 1941; s. John H., Jr. and Virginia A. (Smith) M.; m. Carol Preston Godfrey, June 12, 1965; children: John Harmen, Alexander Godfrey. B.A. in Physics magna cum laude, Princeton U., 1962; Ph.D. in Applied Physics (NASA trainee), Stanford U., 1967. Physicist Goddard Space Flight Center, NASA, 1962-63; asst. prof. physics and elec. engring. U. So. Calif., Los Angeles, 1966-69, assoc. prof., 1969-75, prof., 1975-80, chmn. physics dept., 1972-75, interim dean Coll. Letters, Arts and Scis., 1976-77, dean Coll. Letters, Arts and Scis., 1977-80; prof. physics and elec. engring., pres. SUNY, Stony Brook, 1980-94; cons. laser fusion program Lawrence Livermore Labs., 1972-75; chmn. N.Y. State fact finding panel on Shoreham Nuclear Power Facility, 1983; chmn. bd. trustees Universities Rsch. Assn., 1988-94; co-chair NASULGC Bd. on Oceans and Atmosphere, 1992-93; bd. dirs. N.Y. State Edn. and Rsch. Network, Inc., 1986-88, L.I. Rsch. Inst., 1992, L.I. High Tech. Incubator Corp., 1990—. Contbr. articles to tech. publs. Bd. dirs. Mus. at Stony Brook, 1980-92, L.I. Assn., Inc., 1983-93, Action Com. for L.I., 1980-83, L.I. Forum for Tech., Inc., 1980—, Rsch. Found. SUNY, 1990—; bd. trustees Princeton U., 1985-89; chmn. N.Y. State Energy Office Rev. Commn., 1980-81, Suffolk County (N.Y.) Task Force on Priorities in Fin., 1980-81; campaign chmn. United Way of L.I., 1991-92. Recipient Shuichi Kusaka Meml. Prize Princeton U., 1962. Mem. Assn. of Colls. and Univs. State of N.Y. (pres. 1988-89), Coleman Chamber Music Assn. (bd. dirs. 1969-80). Office: SUNY Office of Pres Stony Brook NY 11794-0701

MARBURY, RITCHEY MCGUIRE, III, engineering executive, surveyor; b. Albany, Ga., May 18, 1938; s. Ritchey McGuire and Shirley Kathryn (VanHouten) M.; m. Fonda Gayle Starnes, June 16, 1962; children: Mary Kathryn, Ritchey McGuire IV. BCE, Ga. Tech. Inst., 1960, M in City Planning, 1966. Registered profl. engr., Ga., Fla., Idaho, Ala.; land surveyor, Ga. V.p. Marbury Engring. Co., Albany, Ga., 1965-78, pres., chmn. bd., 1981—; pres. Marbury, Ritter, Scott & Turner, Inc., Albany, 1970-78, 81-92, Marbury Assocs., Inc., 1991—, Idaho Boise Mission of Latter-day Saints Ch., 1978-81; presenter seminars on total quality mgmt. to nat. convs. of Am. Cons. Engrs. Coun., Design Constrn. Quality Inst., Sml. Firm Coalition of Cons. Engrs., Assn. for Project Mgrs. Exec. bd. Boy Scouts Am., Southwest Ga., 1982—. Served to 1st lt. U.S. Army, 1963-65. Mem. NSPE (South Ga. chpt. pres. 1993-95), Am. Cons. Engrs. Coun., Surveying and Mapping Soc. of Ga. (bd. dirs. 1966-78), Ga. Planning Assn., Home Builders Assn. (bd. dirs. 1985-86), Rotary. Mem. LDS Ch. Avocations: fishing, writing, music, computer, golf. Home: 1824 Green Valley Dr Albany GA 31707-3116 Office: 2334 Lake Park Dr Albany GA 31707-3132 *Always be a role model of Christlike behavior and do those things that make a significant differenc for good. Do what's right simply because it's the right thing to do. The greatest results come through kindness.*

MARBUT, ROBERT GORDON, communications and broadcast executive; b. Athens, Ga., Apr. 11, 1935; s. Robert Smith and Laura Gordon (Powers) M.; m. Margo Susan Spitz, Sept. 24, 1989; children: Robert Gordon, Laura Dodd, Michael Powers, Marcy Lizbeth. B Indsl. Engring., Ga. Inst. Tech., 1957; MBA with distinction, Harvard U., 1963. Registered profl. engr., Calif. Engr. Esso Standard Oil Co., Baton Rouge, 1957; corp. dir. engring. and plans Copley Press, La Jolla, Calif., 1963-70; v.p. named changed to Harte-Hanks Newspapers, Inc., San Antonio, 1970-71; pres., CEO named changed to Harte-Hanks Comm., Inc., San Antonio, 1971-91, also dir., 1971-91, vice chmn. bd. dirs., 1991; founder, chmn., CEO Argyle Comm., Inc, San Antonio, 1992—; founder, CEO, dir. Argyle TV Holding, Inc., San Antonio, 1993-95; co-founder, chmn., CEO Argyle TV, Inc., San Antonio, 1994—; dir. AP, 1979-88, vice chmn. 1987-88; chmn. Newspaper Advt. Bur., 1988-90, exec. com. dir. 1974-80, 82-90; bd. dirs Tupperware, Inc., Diamond Shamrock, Inc., Tracor, Inc., Katz Media Group; pres. adv. bd. U Ga. Henry W. Grady Sch. Journalism, 1975—, mem. adv. Found. for Comm. Sch. U. Tex., 1975—; bd. dirs. Tex. Rsch. League, 1975—, Salzburg Inst. Am. Studies, 1978-81; mem. adv. bd. Ga. Tech., 1978-81; founding mem. Am. Bus. Conf., 1981-89; mem. U. Tex. Centennial commn., 1981-83; pres. adv. coun. U. Tex. Coll. Comm., 1982-83; bd. dirs. Up With People, 1983—, exec. com., 1984—; instr. Armstrong Coll., 1951, Calif. State, Los Angeles, 1964, Woodbury Coll., 1964. Author: (with Healy, Henderson and others) Creative Collective Bargaining, 1965; also articles in mags., jours.; frequent spkr. Coordinating chmn. San Antonio Target 90 commn., 1983-84; campaign chmn. United Way, San Antonio, 1985, chmn. bd. dirs., 1988-89; vice chmn. Tex. select com. on Tax Equity, 1987-89; mem select com. Tex. Revenues, 1991-92; mem. Tex. World Trade Coun., 1986-87. Served with USAF, 1958-61. Recipient Isaiah Thomas award Rochester Inst. Tech., 1980, EXCEL award in comm., 1987, People of Vision award, 1991; selected to Acad. Disting. Engring. Alumni Ga. Tech., 1995. Mem. Am. Newspaper Pubs. Assn. Rsch. Inst. (exec. com. 1973—), Am. Newspaper Publs. Assn. (chmn. task group on future, chmn. telecomm. com. 1974—, bd. dirs. 1976—, chmn. future task group), So. Newspaper Pubs. Assn. (pres. 1979-80, dir. 1975-81, treas. 1977, chmn. bus. and adminstrn. com. 1976), Am. Newspaper Pubs. Assn. Found. (trustee 1976—), Tex. Daily Newspaper Assn. (pres. 1979, Tex. Newspaper Leader of Yr., 1981), Greater San Antonio C. of C. (chmn. long range planning task force, dir. 1979—, exec. com. 1981—, chmn., 1984), Delta Tau Delta, Omicron Delta Kappa, Phi Eta Sigma. Protestant. Club: San Antonio Country, Argyle. Office: Argyle Communications 200 Concord Plz Ste 700 San Antonio TX 78216

MARCEAU, MARCEL, pantomimist, actor, director, painter, poet; b. Strasbourg, France, Mar. 22, 1923; s. Charles and Anne (Werzberg) Mangel. Student, Sch. Dramatic Art, Sarah Bernhardt Theatre, Paris, 1946; D (hon.), Linfield Coll., Princeton U., U. Mich. Dir. artistique Ecole De Mimodrame de Paris Marcel Marceau. Performer role of Arlequin, pantomime Baptiste; Praxitele and the Golden Fish, Sarah Bernhardt Theatre; creator character Bip, 1947; performer Maggio Musicale in Florence and Edinburgh festivals; organizer, Pantomime Co., Paris; producer: The Overcoat, The Three Wigs, 14th of July, The Pawn Shop, Pierrot de Montmartre,Paris qui rit Paris qui pleure, Don Juan; performer extensive tours U.S., S.Am., Africa, Australia, China, Japan, South East Asia, Russia, Europe, 1950—; performer worldwide TV shows; appeared in motion pictures: Barbarella, 1967, Shanks, 1974, Silent Movie, 1976; appeared as Scrooge in TV film A Christmas Carol, 1973; author, illustrator: The Story of Bip, Pimporello; lithographer The 7 Deadly Sins, The Third Eye. Decorated Officier Legion d'Honneur; comdr. Order Arts and Letters; Commandeur of Merit (France); recipient Emmy awards, 1956, 68, Medaille Vermeil de la ville de Paris, 1978. Mem. Acad. Fine Arts Berlin, Acad. Fine Arts Munich, Academie Des Beaux Arts France. Office: Ecole Internat Mimodrame Paris, 17 Rue Rene Boulanger, 75010 Paris France

MARCEAU, YVONNE, ballroom dancer. Ballet dancer Ballet West; ptnr. with Pierre Dulaine, 1976; founder, artistic dir. Am. Ballroom Theatre, N.Y.C., 1984—; guest tchr. Sch. Am. Ballet, N.Y.C.; tchr. ballroom dancing Juilliard Sch. Appearances include The Smithsonian Inst., JFK Ctr. for Performing Arts, N.Y. State Theater, N.Y.C., Sadlers Wells, London, (Broadway and London show) Grand Hotel, 1989-92; toured with Pierre Dulaine and Am. Ballroom Theatre worldwide. Recipient Brit. Theatrical Arts Championships 4 times, Spl. Astaire award, Dance Educator awards, Outstanding Achievement in Dance award Nat. Coun. Dance Am., 1992, Dance Mag. award, 1993. Office: Am Ballroom Theatre 129 W 27th St No 705 New York NY 10001*

MARCELLUS, JOHN ROBERT, III, trombonist, educator; b. Overton, Tex., Sept. 17, 1939; s. John Robert and Grace (Stockman) M.; children: Robert Gray, John Frederick. B.S., U. Md., 1964; Mus.M., Catholic U. Am., 1970, D.Mus. Arts, 1972. Adj. prof. trombone Cath. U. Am., dir. trombone choir and brass ensembles, 1966-78; prof. N.C. Sch. Arts, 1965-68; mem. rotating faculty Inst. Advanced Mus. Studies, Montreux, Switzerland, 1974, Am. U., 1970-78; prof. trombone Eastman Sch. Music, Rochester, N.Y., 1978—, acting chmn. woodwind, brass and percussion, 1981, dir. internat. trombone workshop, 1991; co-dir. Ea. Trombone Workshop, Towson, Md., 1974-80, Internat. Trombone Workshop, 1991; guest condr. Chautauqua Symphony Orch., Penfield Symphony Orch., Chautauqua Wind Ensemble, U.S. Naval Acad. Band, Nat. Music Camp, Interlochen. Trombonist USN Band, Washington, 1960-64, Balt. Symphony, 1964-65; trombonist Nat. Symphony, Washington, 1965-78, prin. trombone, 1970-78; prin. trombone Chautauqua Symphony Orch., 1978; mem. Eastman Brass Quintet; clinician, soloist King Benge Mus. Instruments; solo tours to Scandinavia, Japan, Germany, Australia, England, France; performer with Art Mooney, Ray Eberle, Charlie Spivak, Vaughn Monroe, Henry Mancini Orchs.; music dir. Brighton Symphony Orch., 1980—; contbr. articles to Music Educators Jour., Instrumentalist, Accent, Internat. Trombone Assn. Jour. Mem. Internat. Trombone Assn. (founder, bd. dirs., pres. 1988-90), Am. Fedn. Musicians, Nat. Assn. Wind and Percussion Instruments, Music Educators Nat. Conf., Phi Mu Alpha. Office: Eastman Sch Music 26 Gibbs St Rochester NY 14604-2505 *Dedication, drive and determination to the art of music has been center front on my career in music.*

MARCH, BERYL ELIZABETH, animal scientist, educator; b. Port Hammond, B.C., Can., Aug. 30, 1920; d. James Roy and Sarah Catherine (Wilson) Warrack; m. John Algot March, Aug. 31, 1946; 1 dau., Laurel Allison. B.A., U. B.C., Vancouver, 1942, M.S.A., 1962; D.Sc., U. B.C., 1988. Mem. indsl. research staff Can. Fishing Co. Ltd., 1942-47; mem. research staff, faculty U. B.C., 1947—, prof. animal sci., 1970—. Recipient Poultry Sci. Assn.-Am. Feed Mfrs. award, 1969, Queen's Jubilee medal, 1977, Earle Willard McHenry award Can. Soc. Nutritional Sci., 1986, 125th Can. Confederation Annv. medal, 1993. Fellow Agrl. Inst. Can., Royal Soc. Can., Poultry Sci. Assn.; mem. Profl. Agrologists, Agr. Inst. Can., Can. Soc. Nutritional Sci., Poultry Sci. Assn., Am. Soc. Exptl. Biology and Medicine, Am. Inst. Nutrition, Can. Soc. Animal Sci., Aquaculture Assn. Can. Avocation: researching poultry and fish nutrition and physiology. Office: U BC Dept Animal Sci, Vancouver, BC Canada V6T 2A2

MARCH, JACQUELINE FRONT, retired chemist; b. Wheeling, W.Va.; m. A.W. March (dec.); children: Wayne Front, Gail March Cohen. BS, Case Western Res. U., 1937, MA, 1939; postgrad. U. Chgo., U. Pitts. (1942-45), Ohio State U. Clin. chemist, Mt. Sinai Hosp., Cleve.; med. rsch. chemist U. Chgo.; rsch. analyst Koppers Co., also info. scientist Union Carbide Corp., Carnegie-Mellon U., Pitts.; propr. March Med. Rsch. Lab., etiology of diabetes, Dayton, Ohio; guest scientist Kettering Found., Yellow Springs, Ohio; Dayton Found. fellow Miami Valley Hosp. Rsch. Inst.; mem. chemistry faculty U. Dayton, computer/chem. info. scientist Rsch. Inst. U. Dayton; on-base prin. investigator Air Force Info. Ctr. Wright-Patterson AFB, 1969-79; chem. info. specialist Nat. Inst. Occupl. Safety and Health, Cin., 1979-90; propr. JFM Cons., Ft. Myers, Fla., 1990-93; ret., 1993;

designer info. sys., spkr. in field. Contbr. articles to profl. publs. Active Retired & Sr. Vol. Program Lee County Sch. Dist., 1992-93, Lee County Hosp. Med. Libr., Rutenberg County Libr., Wyeth Gastrointestinal fellow med. rsch. U. Chgo., 1940-42. Mem. AAUP (exec. bd. 1978-79), Am. Soc. Info. Sci. (treas. South Ohio chpt. 1973-75), Am. Chem. Soc. (emeritus, Fla. chpt., pres. Dayton 1977), Dayton Engring. Soc. (hon.), Soc. Advancement Materials & Process Engring. (Fla. chpt., pres. Midwest chpt. 1977-78), Dayton Affiliated Tech. Socs. (Outstanding Scientist and Engr. award 1978), Sigma Xi (emeritus, Fla. chpt., pres. Cin. fed. environ. chpt. 1986-87). Home: 1301 SW 10th Ave F-203 Delray Beach FL 33444-1280

MARCH, JAMES GARDNER, social scientist, educator; b. Cleve., Jan. 15, 1928; s. James Herbert and Mildred (MacCorkle) M.; m. Jayne Mary Dohr, Sept. 23, 1947; children: Kathryn Sue, Gary Clifton, James Christopher, Roderic Gunn. BA, U. Wis., 1949; MA, Yale U., 1950, PhD, 1953; hon. doctorate, Copenhagen Sch. Econs., 1978, Swedish Sch. Econs., 1979, U. Wis., Milw., 1980, U. Bergen, 1980, Uppsala U., 1987, Helsinki Sch. Econs., 1991, Dublin City U., 1994. From asst. prof. to prof. Carnegie Inst. Tech., 1953-64; prof., dean Sch. Social Scis. U. Calif., Irvine, 1964-70; prof. mgmt., higher edn., polit. sci. and sociology Stanford (Calif.) U., 1970-95, prof. emeritus, 1995—; cons. in field, 1954—; Mem. Nat. Council Ednl. Research, 1975-78; mem. Nat. Sci. Bd., 1968-74; mem. sociol.-social psychology panel NSF, 1964-66; social sci. tng. com. NIMH, 1967-68; mem. math. social sci. com. Social Sci. Research Council, 1958-60; mem. Assembly Behavioral and Social Sci., NRC, 1973-79, chmn. com. on aging, 1977-82, chmn. com. on math., sci., tech. edn., 1984-86. Author: (with H.A. Simon) Organizations, 1958, 2nd edit., 1993, (with R.M. Cyert) A Behavioral Theory of the Firm, 1963, 2nd edit., 1992, Handbook of Organizations, 1965, (with B.R. Gelbaum) Mathematics for the Social and Behavioral Sciences, 1969, (with M.D. Cohen) Leadership and Ambiguity, 1974, 2nd edit., 1986, Academic Notes, 1974, (with C.E. Lave) An Introduction to Models in the Social Sciences, 1975, (with J.P. Olsen) Ambiguity and Choice in Organizations, 1976, Aged Wisconsin, 1977, Autonomy as a Factor in Group Organization, 1980, Pleasures of the Process, 1980, Slow Learner, 1985, (with R. Weissinger-Baylon) Ambiguity and Command, 1986, Decisions and Organizations, 1988, (with J.P. Olsen) Rediscovering Institutions, 1989, Minor Memos, 1990, A Primer on Decision Making, 1994, Fornuft og Forandring, 1995, (with J.P. Olsen) Democratic Governance, 1995; contbr. articles to profl. jour. Fellow Ctr. Advanced Study in Behavioral Scis., 1955-56, 73-74; recipient Wilbur Lucius Cross medal Yale U., 1968; named knight 1st class Royal Norwegian Order of Merit, 1995. Mem. NAS, Nat. Acad. Edn., Accademia Italiana di Economia Aziendale, Royal Swedish Acad. Scis., Norwegian Acad. of Sci. and Letters, Am. Acad. Arts and Scis., Am. Econ. Assn., Am. Polit. Sci. Assn. (v.p. 1983-84), Am. Psychol. Assn., Am. Sociol. Assn., Acad. Mgmt., Russell Sage Found. (trustee 1985-94, chmn. 1990-93), Finnish Soc. Scis. and Letters, Phi Beta Kappa, Sigma Xi. Home: 837 Tolman Dr Stanford CA 94305-1025 Office: Stanford U Dept Sociology 509 Ceras Stanford CA 94305-3084

MARCH, MARION D., writer, astrologer, consultant; b. Nürnberg, Germany, Feb. 10, 1923; came to the U.S., 1941; d. Franz and Grete Dispeker; m. Nico D. March, Sept. 1, 1948; children: Michele, Nico F. Diploma, Ecole de Commerce, Lausanne; attended, Columbia U. Cons. astrologer L.A., 1970—; founder, pres., tchr. Aquarius Workshops, L.A., 1975—; internat. lectr. in field, 1976—; chmn. bd. dirs., convention dir. United Astrology Congress, 1986, 89, 92; co-founder, mem. bd. dirs. Assn. for Astrological Networking; cons. in astrology to psychology profls. Author: (books) (with Joan McEvers) The Only Way To... Learn Astrology, 1981-94 (6 vol. series), Astrology: Old Theme, New Thoughts, 1984; editor (mag.) ASPECTS, 1976-93; contbr. numerous articles to jours. in field. Recipient Regulus award for edn. United Astology Congress, 1989, for community svc., 1992, PAI Annual award Profl. Astrologers, Inc., 1990, Syotisha Ratna award Syotish Samsthan of Bombay, India, 1986, Robert Carl Jansky Astrology Leadership award, 1994. Mem. Nat. Coun. for Geocosmic Rsch. (mem. adv. bd.), Internat. Soc. Astrological Rsch., Profl. Astrologers Inc., Astrological Assn. Great Britain. Avocations: reading, gardening, music, skiing, travelling. Office: c/o Publisher ACS PO Box 34487 San Diego CA 92163-4487

MARCH, RALPH BURTON, retired entomology educator; b. Oshkosh, Wis., Aug. 5, 1919; s. Albert Harold and Vanita Ida Cora (Siewert) M.; m. Robinetta Tompkin, Dec. 26, 1942; children: John S., Janice A., Susan E. Student, Oshkosh State Tchrs. Coll., 1937-38; B.A., U. Ill., 1941, M.A. (Grad. scholar 1941-42), 1946, Ph.D. (Grad. fellow 1947-48), 1948. Faculty U. Calif. at Riverside, 1948—, entomologist, 1957—, prof. entomology, 1961-83, prof. entomology emeritus, 1983—, dean grad. div., 1961-68, head div. toxicology and physiology dept. entomology, 1968-72, chmn. dept. entomology, 1978-83. Served with USAAF, 1942-46. Mem. Entomol. Soc. Am., Am. Chem. Soc., AAAS, Phi Beta Kappa, Sigma Xi, Phi Kappa Phi, Phi Sigma. Home: 300 Deer Valley Rd # 4A San Rafael CA 94903-5514

MARCHAK, MAUREEN PATRICIA, anthropology and sociology educator; b. Lethbridge, Alta., Can., June 22, 1936; d. Adrian Ebenezer and Wilhelmina Rankin (Hamilton) Russell; m. William Marchak, Dec. 31, 1956; children: Geordon Eric, Lauren Craig. BA, U. B.C., Vancouver, Can., 1958, PhD, 1970. Asst. prof. U. B.C., Vancouver, 1972-75, assoc. prof., 1975-80, prof., 1980—, head dept. anthropology and sociology, 1987-90, dean faculty arts, 1990-96. Author: Ideological Perspectives on Canada, 1975, 2d edit., 1981, 3d edit., 1988, In Whose Interests, 1979, Green Gold, 1983 (John Porter award 1985), The Integrated Circus, The New Right and The Restructuring of Global Markets, 1991, Logging The Globe, 1995; author, co-editor: Uncommon Property, 1987; mem. editorial bd. Can. Rev. Sociology and Anthropology, Montreal, Que., 1971-74, Studies in Polit. Economy, Ottawa, Ont., Can., 1980-87, Current Sociology, 1980-86, Can. Jour. Sociology, 1986-90, B.C. Studies, 1988-90. Bd. dirs. U. B.C. Hosp., 1992-93; chairperson ethics com. Cedar Lodge Trust Soc., 1989-92; mem. adv. coun. Ecotrust, 1992-93, bd. dirs., 1993—; chmn. bd. dirs. B.C. Bldgs. Corp., 1992-95; mem. B.C. Forest Appeals Commn., 1996—. Fellow Royal Soc. Can. (v.p. Acad. II 1994-95); mem. Can. Sociology and Anthropology Assn. (pres. 1979-80, other offices), Internat. Sociol. Assn., Can. Polit. Sci. Assn., Assn. for Can. Studies, Forest History Soc. (mem. exec. com. 1991-92). Mem. New Dem. Party (Can.). Avocations: hiking, swimming, travelling. Home: 4455 W 1st Ave, Vancouver, BC Canada V6R 4H9 Office: U BC Faculty Arts Office of Dean, 1866 Main Mall, Vancouver, BC Canada V6T 1Z1

MARCHAND, J. C. DE MONTIGNY, Canadian public servant; b. St. Jérome, Qué., Can., Mar. 19, 1936; s. Jean-Charles and Françoise (Magnan) M.; children—Julie, Charles, Emmanuelle. B.A., U. Montré, Que., Can., 1955; LL.L., U. Montreal, 1959; postgrad. Sch. Comm., Boston U. Bar: Que. 1960; cr. Q.C. 1978. Asst. to dir. pub. rels. U. Montreal, 1960-64, asst. to sec. gen., 1964-65, exec. asst. to pres., 1965-67, sec. gen., 1967-69; dir. research, co-sec. telecommission Dept. Comm., Can., 1969-71; asst. dep. min. (ops.) Dept. Comm., 1971-74, sr. asst. dep. min. (policy), 1974-75; dep. sec. to cabinet (ops.) Privy Council Office, Can., 1975-79; on spl. assignment to Western Europe Can. govt., Paris, 1979-80; assoc. under-sec. of state for external affairs Dept. External Affairs, Can., 1980-82; dep. min. polit. affairs Dept. External Affairs, 1982-85; dep. min. comm. Dept. Comm., Ottawa, Ont., Can., 1985; dep. min. Dept. Energy, Mines & Resources, Can., 1985-86; sr. advisor Privy Coun. Office, Can., 1986-87; amb., permanent rep. to UN, Geneva, 1987-90; rep. Conf. on Disarmament, Geneva, 1987-90; under-sec. Dept. External Affairs, Can., 1990-91; amb. to Italy with additional accreditation to Malta and San Marino Can. Govt., 1991—; head Can. del. to Third Plenary Session Intelsat, Washington, 1971, World Adminstrn. Radio Conf. on Space Communications, Geneva, 1971, Fourth, Fifth and Sixth Session UN Working Group Direct Broadcasting by Satellite, N.Y. and Geneva, 1972, 73, 74; dep. head Can. del. to ITU Plenipotentiary Conf., Malaga-Torremolinos, 1973; pres. Inst. canadien des Affaires publiques, 1967-68; dir. Canadian Overseas Telecomm. Corp., 1971-75, Uranium Canada Ltd., 1975-79. Bd. dirs. Nat. Film Bd., 1978-79, 82-85; bd. govs. U. Ottawa, 1980-83; personal rep. to P.M. for preparation of Versailles Summit, 1982, Williamsburg Summit, 1983, London Summit, 1984; chmn. bd. Internat. Energy Agy., 1986-87. Club: Five Lakes Fishing. Avocations: fishing; tennis; reading. Home: Via di Porta Latina 11, 00179 Rome Italy Office: The Candian Embassy, Via G.B. de Rossi 27, 00161 Rome Italy

MARCHAND, LESLIE ALEXIS, language educator, writer; b. Bridgeport, Wash., Feb. 13, 1900; s. Alexis and Clara Adele (Buckingham) M.; m. Marion Knill Hendrix, July 8, 1950. B.A., U. Wash., 1922, M.A., 1923; Ph.D., Columbia U., 1940; postgrad., Sorbonne, Paris, 1927-28, U. Munich, Germany, summer 1932; L.H.D. hon., U. Alaska, 1976; Litt.D. (hon.), Rutgers U., 1981. Asst. in English U. Wash., Seattle, 1920-23; instr., summer U. Wash., 1924, vis. prof., 1925, 58; prof. English and French Alaska Agrl. Coll. and Sch. Mines (now U. Alaska), 1923-27, 34-35; extension tchr. English Columbia U., 1928-34, instr., summers 1929-31, vis. prof., summers 1945-46, 65; lectr. Columbia U. (Coll. Pharmacy), 1936-37; instr. Rutgers U., 1937-42, asst. prof., 1942-46, asso. prof., 1946-53, prof., 1953-66, emeritus, 1966—; Fulbright prof. U. Athens, Greece, 1958-59; lectr. English Hunter Coll., 1960-62; Berg vis. prof. N.Y. U., 1962-63; vis. prof. Ariz. State U., 1966-67; Adams chair English Hofstra U., 1967-68; vis. prof. U. Calif. at Los Angeles, summer 1949, U. Ill., summer 1954, Harvard U., summer 1969. Author: The Athenaeum: A Mirror of Victorian Culture, 1941, Byron: A Biography, 1957, Byron's Poetry: A Critical Introduction, 1965, Byron: A Portrait, 1970; editor: Letters of Thomas Hood, 1945, Selected Poetry of Lord Byron, 1951, Lord Byron: Don Juan, 1958, Byrons's Letters and Jours., Vols. 1-12, 1973-82, supplementary vol., 1994, Lord Byron: Selected Letters and Jours., 1982; editl. bd.: Keats-Shelley Jour.; contbr. articles to profl. jours. Recipient Ivan Sandrof award Nat. Book Critics Circle, 1982; Guggenheim fellow, 1968-69, 79-80; Nat. Endowment for Humanities grantee, 1972-73, 74-75, 76-79. Fellow Royal Soc. Lit. (Eng.); mem. PEN, MLA (James Russell Lowell prize), Keats-Shelley Assn. Am. (dir.), Byron Soc., Phi Beta Kappa. Home: 570 Foxwood Blvd Englewood FL 34223-6100

MARCHAND, RUSSELL DAVID, II, fire chief; b. Lafayette, Ind., May 14, 1950; s. Russell David and Mable My (Gean) M.; m. Sandra Green, June 12, 1951 (div. Nov. 1986); 1 child, Russell David III; m. Carol Bella Flashenburg, May 31, 1987 (div. Feb., 1996). AA in Fire Sci., Clark County Community Coll., Las Vegas, Nev., 1979. Cert. fire service instr., supr. instr. Firefighter North Las Vegas Fire Dept., 1973-78, engr., 1978-82, capt., 1982-95, divsn. chief, officer-in-charge bldg. and constrn., 1990—; pres. Local 1607 Internat. Assn. Fire Fighters, Las Vegas, 1980— (v.p. 1976-80); instr. N. Las Vegas Fire Dept., 1986. Chmn. N. Las Vegas Firefighters Polit. Action Com., 1980—, Muscular Dystrophy Assn., 1980-83, 85. Sgt. USMC, 1968-72, South Vietnam. Named Fireman of Yr., Optimist Club, 1981, Lions Club Nev., 1989, Profl. Ins. Agts. of Am.; received citation of merit Muscular Dystrophy Assn., 1982, commendation City of N. Las Vegas, 1980, 83, 85. Mem. Fed. Firefighters Nev. (received commendation 1982), Internat. Assn. Fire Fighters (local 1607 pres. emeritus 1990). Avocations: sailing, computers. Office: 2626 E Carey Ave North Las Vegas NV 89030-6215

MARCHANT, DAVID J., lawyer; b. Oakland, Calif., Jan. 12, 1939; s. Luther Brusie and Mariam Hand (Fisher) M.; m. Susan Robbins (div. 1980); children: Michael Hilton, Robbins Fisher, Lauren Payton. BA, U. Calif., Berkeley, 1961; JD, U. Calif., San Francisco, 1967. Bar: Calif. Atty. Calif. Pub. Utilities Commn., San Francisco, 1967-68; ptnr. Graham & James, San Francisco, 1968—. Mem. ABA (pub. utility law sect.), Bohemian Club. Office: Graham & James 1 Maritime Plz Ste 300 San Francisco CA 94111-3406*

MARCHANT, MAURICE PETERSON, librarian, educator; b. Peoa, Utah, Apr. 20, 1927; s. Stephen C. and Beatrice (Peterson) M.; m. Gerda VaLoy Hansen, June 3, 1949; children: Catherine, Barrie, Alan, Roxanne, Claudia, David, Theresa. BA, U. Utah, 1949, MS, 1953; AM in Libr. Sci., U. Mich., 1966, MA, 1968, Ph.D., 1970. Tchr. area h.s. Altamont, Utah, 1949-50; libr. area h.s. Salt Lake City and Preston, Idaho, 1950-53; chief tech. libr. Dugway (Utah) Proving Ground, 1953-58; libr. Carnegie Free Libr., Ogden, Utah, 1958-66; mem. faculty Brigham Young U., Provo, Utah, 1969-92, prof. libr. and info. scis., 1976-92, dir. Sch. Libr. and Info. Scis., 1975-82; prof. emeritus libr. and info. scis. Brigham Young U. (Sch. Library and Info. Scis.), Provo, Utah, 1992—; exec. dir. Nat. Libr. Week, Utah, 1961-62. Author: Participative Management in Academic Libraries, 1976, SPSS as a Library Research Tool, 1977, Books That Made a Difference in Provo, 1989, Why Adults Use the Public Library, 1994, also articles. Served with USN, 1945-46. Mid-career fellow Coun. Libr. Resources, 1972. Mem. AAUP, ALA (rsch. paper award Libr. Rsch. Round Table 1975), Utah Libr. Assn. (pres. 1964-65, Disting. Svc. award 1986). Address: 2877 N 220 E Provo UT 84604-3906 *Man has the potential of learning to love or exploit, to become wise or remain ignorant. God intends us to become charitable and wise, preparing us to contribute to human progress. My measure of success as a librarian and educator must reflect my commitment to lifelong learning and to honest respect of others.*

MARCHANT, TRELAWNEY ESTON, retired national guard officer, lawyer; b. Columbia, S.C., Dec. 9, 1921; s. Trelawney Eston and Lila (Cave) M.; m. Caroline Melton Bristow, Nov. 10, 1951; children—Trelawney Eston, III, Walter Bristow, Caroline M., Nancy Lila. B.S., U. S.C., 1942, LL.B., 1947; grad. various USMC and U.S. Army schs. Bar: S.C. 1947. Pvt. practice Columbia, 1948-78; mem. S.C. N.G., 1947-95, maj. gen., 1979; comdr. Palmetto Mil. Acad., 1968-71; adj. gen. State of S.C., 1978-95. Mem. bd. visitors The Citadel, Charleston, S.C., 1979-95; trustee U. S.C., 1965-70, chmn., 1970-78, mem. devel. adv. coun., 1963-77; chmn. Nat. Found., 1953-60; v.p. U. S.C. Ednl. Found., 1957-77; chmn. Richland County Dem. Party, 1964-68. Served as officer USMCR, 1942-46. Mem. ABA, Am. Judicature Soc., 4th Cir. Jud. Conf., Adjs. Gen. Assn. U.S. (pres. 1989-91), Acad. Polit. Sci., S.C. Bar Assn., Richland County Bar Assn. (pres. 1970-71), Mil. Order World Wars (past chpt. pres.), Am. Legion, N.G. Assn. S.C. (past pres.), U. S.C. Alumni Assn. (past pres.), Order of Palmetto (S. Carolinian of Yr. 1990), Sigma Nu, Omicron Delta Kappa. Episcopalian. Clubs: Columbia Cotillion (pres. 1991-92), Columbia Ball, Tarantella, Summit, Forest Lake. Home: 5046 Courtney Rd Columbia SC 29206-2909

MARCHELLO, JOSEPH MAURICE, mathematics and physical science educator; b. East Moline, Ill., Oct. 6, 1933; s. Anton Joseph and Katherine Margaret (Scavarda) M.; m. Mary Louise Coulson, Jan. 27, 1960; children—Sara Leigh, Katherine C. B.S. in Chem. Engring, U. Ill., 1955; Ph.D., Carnegie-Mellon U., 1959. Asst. prof. chem. engring. Okla. State U., 1959-61; asst. prof. U. Md., 1961-62, assoc. prof., 1962-66, prof., 1966-78, chmn. dept. chem. engring., 1967-73, provost div. math. and phys. scis. and engring., 1973-78; chancellor U. Mo.-, Rolla, 1978-85; pres. Old Dominion U., Norfolk, Va., 1985-88; prof., 1985—; Pres. Mo. Council Pub. Higher Edn., 1981-82. Author: Control of Air Pollution Sources, 1976; editor: (with John J. Kelly) Gas Cleaning for Air Pollution Control, 1975, (with Albert Gomezplata) Gas-Solids Handling in the Process Industry, 1976; contbr. numerous articles to profl. jours. Mem. Md. Air Quality Control Adv. Council, 1966-78, chmn., 1971-78; mem. Md. Adv. Commn. on Atomic Energy, 1973-78; chmn. Md. Power Plant Siting Com., 1978. Mem. AAAS, NSPE, Air Pollution Control Assn., Am. Inst. Chem. Engrs., Am. Chem. Soc., Mo. Soc. Profl. Engrs., N.Y. Acad. Sci., Mo. Acad. Sci., Cosmos Club. Presbyterian. Home: 6 Rhoda Ct Hampton VA 23664-1769 Office: Coll Engring Old Dominion Norfolk VA 23508

MARCHESANO, JOHN EDWARD, electro-optical engineer; b. N.Y.C., Aug. 20, 1927; s. John R. and Maria J. (Mollino) M.; divorced; children: Pamela, Debra, Scott, Neal. BEE, CCNY, 1951; postgrad., U. Pa., 1954-56. Project engr. Philco Rsch., Pa., 1951-56; sr. engr. Am. Bosch Arma, Garden City, N.Y., 1956-60; pres. Automation Labs. Inc., Mineola, N.Y., 1960-66; pres., CEO Decilog, Inc., Melville, N.Y., 1966—. Achievements include development and design of wide angle lens for aircraft collision avoidance, of modulation transfer system for low light level TV evaluation, long wavelength infared missile research. Office: Decilog Inc 555 Broadhollow Rd Melville NY 11747-5001

MARCHESE, MICHAEL JAMES, JR., radiation oncologist; b. N.Y.C., Mar. 9, 1955; s. Michael James Sr. and Mabel Gladys (Rosero) M.; m. Kathryn Allen, Aug. 7, 1982 (div. May 1993); 1 child, Michael James III. BA magna cum laude, NYU, 1976; MD, Baylor Coll. Medicine, 1979. Diplomate Am. Bd. Radiology. Intern Monmouth Med. Ctr., Hahnemann Med. Coll., Long Branch, N.J., Phila., 1979-80; resident and chief resident radiation therapy Presbyn. Hosp., Columbia U. Coll. Physicians and Surgeons, N.Y.C., 1980-83, asst. attending physician radiation oncology, 1983-87; resident brachytherapy svc. Meml. Hosp. Cancer & Allied Diseases, Cornell U. Med. Coll., N.Y.C., 1982; asst. clin. prof. radiation oncology Columbia U. Coll. Physicians & Surgeons, N.Y.C., 1983-84, asst. prof. radiation oncology, 1984-87; attending staff radiology/radiation oncology Cmty. Med. Ctr., Toms River, N.J., 1987-96, Kimball Med. Ctr., Lakewood, N.J., 1994—, Med. Ctr. Ocean County, Brick, N.J., 1996—; investigator Nat. Cancer Inst., 1983-87, investigator radiation therapy oncology group, 1983-87, 95—, physician surveyor, 1983-85, investigator cancer and leukemia group B, 1986-87, investigator Ea. Coop. Oncology Group, 1995—; physician surveyor practice accreditation program Am. Coll. Radiology, 1986-87. Author: (with others) Radiation Therapy of Gynecological Cancers, 1987, Frontiers of Radiation Therapy and Oncology, vol. 22, 1988; contbr. articles to profl. jours. Bd. dirs. Am. Cancer Soc., Ocean County, N.J., 1993—, v.p., 1993-94, pres., 1994—. Recipient Resident/Fellow award Am. Radium Soc., Travel award European Soc. Therapeutic Radiology and Oncology, Clin. Oncology Career Devel. award Am. Cancer Soc. Mem. Am. Coll. Radiology, Am. Soc. Therapeutic Radiology and Oncology, Am. Soc. Clin. Oncology, Acad. Medicine N.J., Radiation Rsch. Soc., N.Y. Acad. Sci., Ocean County Med. Soc., Med. Soc. N.J. Roman Catholic. Home: 44 Lake Shore Dr Red Bank NJ 07701-5840 Office: Ocean Radiation Therapy Ctr 19 Mule Rd Toms River NJ 08755-6423

MARCHESE, RONALD THOMAS, ancient history and archaeology educator; b. Fresno, Calif., Mar. 17, 1947; s. John Anthony and Julie Rita (Ferrarese) M.; m. Marcia Lynn Schneider, Apr. 6, 1974 (div. Apr. 1980); children: Stephanie Jo, Kayla Marie. BA summa cum laude, Calif. State U., Fresno, 1970; MA, N.Y.U., 1972, PhD with distinction, 1976; postgrad., Columbia U., 1972-73. Asst. prof. Va. Poly. Inst., Blacksburg, 1976-77; asst. to assoc. prof. ancient history and archaeology U. Minn., Duluth, 1977-87, prof., 1987—; rsch. assoc. dept. classics NYU, 1972-74; evaluator grant proposals NEH, HSF; excavator numerous sites in Israel and Turkey; lectr. in field. Author 4 books; contbr. articles to profl. jours. Recipient Fulbright-Hays Sr. Research fellowship, Turkey, 1984-85, 91-92, The Am. Council Learned Socs. fellowship, 1977-78, NDEA Title VI Fgn. Languages fellowship, 1972-75, Spl. Commendation for Excellence award Phi Alpha Theta, 1979; grantee NEH, 1978, 80, nat. Geographic Soc., 1974, Andrew Mellon Found., NSF, Ford Found., 1971-72, U. Minn., others. Mem. NEH, Nat. Assn. Scholars, Coun. for Internat. Exchange, Am. Coun. Learned Socs., Fulbright Alumni Assn., Phi Alpha Theta, Sigma Xi. Roman Catholic. Avocations: tennis, golf, dressage. Home: 5789 220th St N Forest Lake MN 55025-9677

MARCHESI, VINCENT T., biochemist, educator; b. N.Y.C., Sept. 4, 1935; married, 1959; three children. BA, Yale U., 1957, MD, 1963; PhD in Pathology, Oxford (Eng.) U., Eng., 1961. Intern, resident in pathology Wash. U., Bethesda, Md., 1963-65; rsch. assoc. cell biology Rockefeller U., New Haven, 1965-66; staff assoc. Nat. Cancer Inst., 1966-68; chief sect. chem. pathology Nat. Inst. Arthritis, Metabolism & Digestive Disorders, 1968-77; Anthony N. Brady prof. pathology Sch. Medicine Yale U., 1977—; dir. Boyer Ctr. Molecular Medicine Yale U., New Haven, 1987—; cons. Miles Pharm., West Haven, Conn., 1982—. Bd. dirs. Am. Cyanamid, N.J., 1992-94. Lt. comdr. USPHS, 1966-72. Mem. Inst. Medicine-NAS, Histochem. Soc., N.Y. Acad. Sci., Am. Soc. Cell Biology. Avocations: tennis, history. Office: Yale U Sch Medicine Dept Pathology Brady Meml Lab New Haven CT 06520 Office: Boyer Ctr Molecular Medicine 205 Congress Ave New Haven CT 06519*

MARCHETTI, MARILYN H., lawyer; b. Whiting, Ind., Mar. 10, 1947; d. Stephen D. and Helen F. (Ajinovich) Hrpka; m. George Arthur Marchetti, Aug. 21, 1976; 1 child, Christine Stephanie. BA in English, Ind. U., 1969; JD, IIT, 1979. Bar: Ill. 1980. Tchr. jr. high school North Easton (Mass.) schs., 1969-70; social worker Ind. Dept. Pub. Welfare, Gary, 1970-74; medicaid specialist U.S. Dept. Health, Edn., Welfare, Chgo., 1974-78; law clk. to Justice Thomas Moran Ill. Supreme Ct., Waukegan, 1979-81; assoc. Mayer, Brown & Platt, Chgo., 1982-84; ptnr. Keck, Mahin & Cate, Chgo., 1984-94, Oppenheimer, Wolff & Donnelly, Chgo., 1994—; guest lectr. Harvard U.; cons. USSR marine industry privatization, 1990-91; speaker The Employee Stock Ownership Plan Assn. Paris Internat., London, 1991, 92; mem. U.S. del. promoting concept of employee ownership, to China, 1994, to Zimbabwe, 1995. Contbr. articles to profl. jours., chpts. to books. Asst. troop leader Girl Scouts U.S., Western Springs, Ill., 1990—; mem. parish coun. St. John of the Cross Ch., Western Springs, 1991-92; fundraiser Carol Mosely Braun Campaign, Chgo., 1992; founder Girls' Cir., 1994—. Mem. Employee Stock Ownership Plan Assn. (bd. dirs., adminstrv. com. 1989—, legis. com. 1990—, founder, sec., treas. Ill. chpt.), Nat. Assn. of Women Bus. Owners, Nat. Ctr. Employee Ownership, Women in Employee Benefits (steering com. 1987). Avocations: golf, bridge, writing. Office: Oppenheimer Wolff & Donnelly Two Prudential Plz 180 N Stetson Ave Chicago IL 60601

MARCHI, JON, cattle rancher, exporter, former investment brokerage executive; b. Ann Arbor, Mich., Aug. 6, 1946; s. John Robert and Joan Trimble (Toole) M.; m. Mary Stewart Sale, Aug. 12, 1972; children: Aphia Jessica, Jon Jacob. Student Claremont Men's Coll., 1964-65; BS, U. Mont., 1968, MS, 1972. Sec., treas. Marchi, Marchi & Marchi, Inc., Morris, Ill., 1968-69; account exec. D. A. Davidson & Co., Billings, Mont., 1972-75, asst. v.p., office mgr., 1976-77, v.p. mktg. and adminstrn., Great Falls, Mont., 1977—; sec., dir., v.p. fin. svcs. and exec. devel., D. A. Davidson Realty Corp., Great Falls, 1978-85, chmn. rsch. com., 1980; cattle rancher, Polson, Mont., 1985—; bd. dirs. Big Sky Airlines, Billings, Mont., chmn. bd. dirs., 1995; bd. dirs. Energy Overthrust Found., Mansfield Found., Mont. Beverages, Mont. Venture Capital Network, Direct Advantage, Inc., Hamilton, Mont., Mont. Naturals Internat., Inc., Eclipse Techs., Inc., Mont. Small Bus. Investment Corp.; chmn., dir. Devel. Corp. Mont., Helena, 1995. Chmn. Mont. Gov.'s Subcom. for Venture Capital Devel., Mont. Cmty. Fin. Corp., Helena; chmn. investment com., State of Mont. Sci. and Tech. Alliance, 1985—; chmn. seed capital com. State of Mont., bd. dirs. job svc. com. Mem. Mont. Peoples Action; sec.-treas. Valley View Assn., 1987—; trustee sch. dist. # 35, Polson, Mont., 1990—, chmn., 1991—; bd. dirs. Mont. Entrepreneurship Ctr., Missoula, Mont., 1990—; pres., dir., sec./treas. Mont. Pvt. Capital Network, Bozeman, Mont., 1990—, pres., 1992—; chmn., dir. Mont. Naturals Interant., Inc., 1991; dir. Mont. State Rural Devel. Coun., 1992, Mont. SBA Adv. Coun., 1992; dir. Ctr. Econ. Renewal and Tech. Transfer Mont. State U., Bozeman, 1994—; del. to White House Conf. on Small Bus., Washington, 1994-95. With U.S. Army, 1969-71. Mem. Nat. Cattlemen's Assn. (fgn. trade com.), Am. Wagyu Assn., Can. Wagyu Assn., Polson C. of C. (bd. dirs.), Valley View Assn. (bd. dirs.), Mont. Cattle Feeders Assn., Montana Angus Assn., Am. Angus Assn., Western Mont. Stockgrowers Assn., Securities Industry Assn., Mont. Stock Growers Assn., Mont. Ambassadors (dir. 1995), Polson C. of C. (dir.), Leadership Great Falls Club, Ski Club, Mont. Club, Helena Wilderness Riders Club, Rotary. Episcopalian. Home: 7783 Valley View Rd Polson MT 59860-9302 Office: Marchi Angus Ranches 7783 Valley View Rd Polson MT 59860-9302

MARCHI, LORRAINE JUNE, association executive; b. San Francisco, June 5, 1923; d. Leopold Pulverman and Josephine Lillian (Trieber) Heiman; m. Gene Marchi, Apr. 10, 1943 (div. 1973); children: Gene, Jeffrey, Debra, Beth; m. Robert L. Fastie, Oct. 21, 1973. Student Stanford U., 1941-42, U. Calif.-Berkeley, 1942-43. Founder Com. To Aid Visually Handicapped Children, San Francisco, 1954-57; pres. Aid to Visually Handicapped, San Francisco, 1957-59; founder, exec. dir. Nat. Assn. for Visually Handicapped, San Francisco, 1972—; sec. Calif. Conf. for Exceptional and Rehab. Needs, San Francisco, 1955-66; chmn. bd. Langley Porter Neuropsychiat. Inst., San Francisco, 1966-73. Recipient spl. svc. award Los Angeles County Soc. Ophthalmology, 1971; honor award Am. Acad. Ophthalmology and Otolaryngology, 1971, Lifetime Achievement award Nat. Assn. for Visually Handicapped, 1989; cert. of appreciation Am. Acad. Ophthalmology, 1978; named Woman of Yr. San Francisco sect. Nat. Council Jewish Women, 1957, one of Ten Disting. Women San Francisco Examiner Bay Area, 1959. Home: 305 E 24th St New York NY 10010-4011

MARCHI, SERGIO SISTO, Canadian government official; b. Buenos Aires, May 12, 1956; s. Ottavio and Luisa (D'Agostinis) M.; m. Laureen Storozuk, Oct. 1, 1983. BA with honors, York U., Toronto, 1979. Exec. asst. to Ron Irwin and Hon. Jim Flemming, 1980-82; alderman City of North York, 1982-84; M.P. from York West dist. Ho. of Commons, Ottawa, 1984—, min. citizenship and immigration, 1993-96; min. of environment

Canada, 1996. Vice chmn. North York Planning Bd., Toronto, 1982-84, Standing Com. on Transport, Ottawa, 1990-93; chmn. Nat. Liberal Caucus, Ottawa, 1990-93. Mem. Liberal Party. Roman Catholic. Avocations: reading, walking, fishing, skiing. Office: Environment, 10 Wellington St 28th Fl, Hull, PQ Canada K1A 0H3*

MARCHIBRODA, TED (THEODORE JOSEPH MARCHIBRODA), professional football coach; b. Mar. 15, 1931; m. Henrietta Marchibroda; children: Jodi, Teddy, Lonni, Robert. Student, St. Bonaventure Coll., 1950-51, U. Detroit, 1952. Football player Pitts. Steelers, 1953-54, 55-56, Chgo. Cardinals, 1957-58; asst. coach Washington Redskins, 1961-65, offensive coord., 1971-74; asst. coach L.A. Rams, 1966-70; head coach Balt. Colts, 1975-79; offensive coord., quarterbacks coach Chgo. Bears, 1981; offensive coord. Detroit Lions, 1982-83; offensive coord., quarterbacks coach Phila. Eagles, 1984-85; quarterbacks coach Buffalo Bills, 1987-88, offensive coord., 1989-92; head coach Indpls. Colts, 1992-95, Balt. Ravens, 1996—. Served with U.S. Army, 1954-55. Office: Baltimore Ravens 11001 Owings Mills Blvd Owings Mills MD 21117*

MARCHIDO, WILLIAM F., finance executive, accountant; b. Muskegon, Mich., Nov. 7, 1950; s. Fabian William and Ila Belle (Deater) M.; m. Nancy May Steele, Aug. 22, 1970; 1 child, Mary Lynn. ABA in Acctg., Davenport Bus. Coll., 1976; BBS in Acctg. and Fin., Grand Valley U., 1978, MBA in Fin. and Econs., 1984. Cost acctg. Kelvinator, Inc., Grand Rapids, Mich., 1972-76; cost acctg. Lescoa, Inc., Grand Rapids, 1976-78, cost mgr., 1978-79; acctg. mgr. Haven-Busch Corp., Grandville, Mich., 1979-82, controller, 1982-85, v.p. fin., 1985-88; controller Rapistan Corp., Grand Rapids, 1988, v.p. fin., 1988—. Project div. tchr. Jr. Achievement, Grand Rapids, 1986-87. USNG, 1971-77. Mem. Cert. Mgmt. Accts. Republican. Roman Catholic. Office: Rapistan Corp 507 Plymouth Ave NE Grand Rapids MI 49505-6029*

MARCHUK, DOUGLAS ALAN, medical educator; b. Cleve., July 17, 1956. BS in Biology cum laude, U. Dayton, 1978; MS in Microbiology, U. Conn., 1980; PhD in Molecualr Genetics and Cell Biol., U. Chgo., 1985. Postdoctoral U. Mich. Med. Sch., Ann Arbor, 1987-91, asst. rsch. scientist, 1991-93; asst. prof. genetics Duke U. Med. Ctr., Durham, N.C., 1993—; vis. asst. prof. biology Hope Coll., Holland, Mich., 1985-87; lectr. in field. Mem. editorial bd. jour. Genome Rsch., 1993—; ad hoc reviewer jours.; contbr. chpts. to books and numerous articles to profl. jours. Mem. med. adv. bd. Hereditary Hemorrhagic Telengietasis Found., 1992—. Baxter Found. scholar, 1983—; grantee NIH, 1992—, Share Found., 1992-93, Am. Heart Assn., 1995—, Sandoz Pharms. Corp., 1995, Baxter Found., 1993—. Mem. Alpha Sigma Tau. Office: Duke U Med Ctr Rm 265 CARL Bldg Box 3175 Reseachr Dr Durham NC 27710*

MARCIALIS, ROBERT LOUIS, planetary astronomer; b. N.Y.C., Sept. 14, 1956; s. Louis Angelo and Joan Regina (Dippolito) M. SB in Aero. and Astronautical Engring., MIT, 1978, SB in Earth and Planetary Scis., 1980; MS in Physics and Astronomy, Vanderbilt U., 1983; PhD in Planetary Scis., U. Ariz., 1990. Teaching asst. dept. earth and planetary scis. MIT, Cambridge, 1976-80; lab. instr. dept. physics and astronomy Vanderbilt U., Nashville, 1981, 82-83, rsch. asst. Arthur J. Dyer Obs., 1981-82; rsch. asst. Lunar and Planetary Lab. U. Ariz., Tucson, 1983-86, rsch. assoc., 1986-90; JPL postdoctoral fellow Jet Propulsion Lab., Pasadena, Calif., 1990-92; adj. faculty Pima C.C., Tucson, 1992—; founding mem. Pluto/Charon Mut. Eclipse Season Campaign. Contbr. articles to Nature, Bull. Am. Astron. Soc., Astron. Jour., Minor Planet Circular, Lunar and Planetary Sci., Sci., Jour. Brit. Astron. Assn., Astrophys. Jour., Icarus, also others. Instr. water safety ARC, 1981-82; ednl. counselor MIT, 1983—; fastpitch softball umpire, 1975—. Rsch. fellow NASA, 1986-89. Mem. AAAS, Am. Astron. Soc., Am. Geophys. Union, Astron. Soc. Pacific, Internat. Occultation Timing Assn., Sigma Pi Sigma. Roman Catholic. Achievements include discovery of water ice on surface of Pluto's moon Charon; construction of an albedo map for surface of Pluto; research on Pluto, Charon and Triton, icy satellites, outer solar system formation and evolution, solar system photometry, occultation astronomy, RS Canum Venaticorum binary stars. Office: U Ariz Lunar and Planetary Lab Tucson AZ 85716

MARCIANO, MAURICE, apparel executive. CEO Guess?, L.A. Office: Guess Inc 1444 S Alameda St Los Angeles CA 90021-2448

MARCIANO, RICHARD ALFRED, research executive; b. Providence, Apr. 9, 1934; s. Eugene and Venera (Stramondo) M.; children: Melissa, Cristina. Student Brown U., 1951-52; BA, Syracuse U., 1970. Computer programmer RAND Corp., Santa Monica, Calif., 1956-58; computer scientist, mgr. System Devel. Corp., Santa Monica, 1958-65; sr. staff SRI Internat., Menlo Park, Calif., 1965-76, dir. edn. rsch., 1976-81, asst. to pres., 1981-93, v.p. technology commercialization, 1983-87, v.p. commercialization and ventures, 1987-93; founder, pres. The Agrari Group, San Francisco, 1993—; dir. TGV Software Inc. Santa Cruz, Calif.; mem., chmn. bd. dirs., Confirma Tech. Corp., Menlo Park. Mem. Assn. Computing Machinery, Ops. Rsch. Soc. Am., Inst. Mgmt. Scis., Assn. Univ. Tech. Mgrs., Licensing Execs. Soc. Office: The Agrari Group 1221 Jones St Ste D4 San Francisco CA 94109

MARCIL, WILLIAM CHRIST, SR., publisher, broadcast executive; b. Rolette, N.D., Mar. 9, 1936; s. Max L. and Ida (Fuerst) M.; m. Jane Black, Oct. 15, 1960; children: Debora Jane, William Christ Jr. BSBA, U. N.D., 1958. Br. mgr. Community Credit Co., Mpls., 1959-61; with Forum Comms. Co., Fargo, N.D., 1961—, pres., pub., CEO, 1969—. Pres. Forum Comm. Found.; past bd. dirs. North Ctrl. region Boy Scouts Am. With U.S. Army, 1958-59. Mem. Inland Newspaper Press Assn., N.D. Press Assn., Am. Newspaper Pubs. Assn. (past dir., chmn.), Fargo and Moorhead C. of C., N.D. State C. of C. (past pres.), U.S. C. of C. (past chmn.), Sigma Delta Chi, Lambda Chi Alpha. Republican. Lodges: Masons, Shriners, Elks, Rotary. Home: 1618 8th St S Fargo ND 58103-4240 Office: Forum Comm Co 101 Fifth St N Fargo ND 58102-4826

MARCINEK, MARGARET ANN, nursing educator; b. Uniontown, Pa., Sept. 29, 1948; d. Joseph Hugh and Evelyn (Bailey) Boyle; m. Bernard Francis Marcinek, Aug. 11, 1973; 1 dau., Cara Ann. R.N., Uniontown Hosp., 1969; B.S. in Nursing, Pa. State U., 1970; M.S.N., U. Md., 1973; Ed.D., W.Va. U., 1983. Staff nurse Presbyn. U., Pitts., 1970-71; instr. nursing W.Va. U., Morgantown, 1973-77, asst. prof., 1977-80, assoc. prof., 1980-83; assoc. prof. California U. of Pa., 1983-87, prof., 1987—, dept. chmn., 1985—. Contbg. author: Critical Care Nursing. Contbr. articles to profl. jours. Mem. adv. coun. In Home Health, Inc.; mem. adv. coun. Albert Gallatin VNA. Mem. Am. Nurses Assn., Am. Assn. Critical Care Nurses, Nat. League for Nurses, Sigma Theta Tau, Phi Kappa Phi.

MARCO, GUY ANTHONY, librarian, educator; b. N.Y.C., Oct. 4, 1927; s. Gaetano Mongelluzzo and Evelyn Capobianco; m. Karen Csontos, July 23, 1949; 1 son, Howard William. Student, DePaul U., 1947-50; B.Mus., Am. Conservatory Music, Chgo., 1951; M.A. in Music, U. Chgo., 1952, M.L.S., 1955, Ph.D. in Musicology, 1956. Librarian, instr. musicology Chgo. Mus. Coll., 1953-54; asst. classics library U. Chgo., 1954; asst. librarian, instr. music Wright Jr. Coll., Chgo., 1954-56; librarian, instr. music Amundsen Jr. Coll., Chgo., 1957-60; asso. prof. library sci., chmn. dept. Kent State U., 1960-66; prof., dean Kent State U. (Sch. Library Sci.), 1966-77; chief gen. reference and bibliography div. Library of Congress, Washington, 1977-78; dir. for N.Am., Library Devel. Cons.'s, London, 1979-81; prof., dir. div. library sci. San Jose State U., 1981-83; exec. dir. Global Research Services, Washington, 1984-85; chief libr. activities U.S. Army, Ft. Dix, N.J., 1985-89; sr. fellow, adj. prof. libr. sci., editor Third World Librs. Rosary Coll., River Forest, Ill., 1989—; vis. lectr. library sci. U. Wis., summer 1955; reference librarian Chgo. Tchrs. Coll., summer 1957; vis. prof. library sci. N.Y. State Coll. Tchrs., Albany, summer 1956, 58; guest lectr. library sci. U. Denver, summer 1959; vis. prof. U. Okla., summer 1960, Coll. Librarianship, Wales, summer 1974, 76, 77, U. Md., summer 1978. Author: The Earliest Music Printers of Continental Europe, 1962, An Appraisal of Favorability in Current Book Reviewing, 1959, (with Claude Palisca) The Art of Counterpoint, 1968, Information on Music, vol. I, 1975, vol. II, 1977, vol. III, 1984, Opera: A Research and Information Guide, 1984, Ency. of Recorded Sound in the United States, 1993; contbr. 150 articles to profl. jours., also book revs. Served with AUS, 1946-47. Mem. ALA, Am. Musicological Soc. Home: 3450 N Lake Shore Dr Apt 3508 Chicago IL 60657-2864 Office: Rosary Coll Libr Sch River Forest IL 60305

MARCOCCIA, LOUIS GARY, accountant, university administrator; b. Syracuse, N.Y., Nov. 6, 1946; s. George A. and Rose J. (Misita) M.; m. Susan Evelyn Miller, June 21, 1974; 1 child: Rachel Kathryn. BS, Syracuse U., 1968, MS, 1969. CPA, N.Y. Acct. Price Waterhouse & Co., Syracuse, N.Y., 1969-75; dir. internal audit Syracuse U., 1975-76, comptroller, 1976-82, v.p., controller, 1985-95, sr. v.p. bus., fin. and adminstrv. svcs., 1985-95, 1995—; bd. dirs. Syracuse Bd. Chase Lincoln First Bank N.A., Univ. Hill Corp.; speaker Harvard U. Inst. Ednl. Mgmt., 1984-88, 90-91. Pres. parish coun. St. Michael's Ch., Syracuse, 1985-88, Syracuse U. Theatre Corp., 1987—; bd. dirs. Friends of Burnet Park Zoo, 1987-93, Syracuse U. Press., 1982—, Syracuse Sports Corp., 1990-91. Mem. AICPA, N.Y. Soc. CPAs, Nat. Assn. Accts., Fin. Execs. Inst., Inst. Internal Auditors. Republican. Roman Catholic. Clubs: Drumlins (pres. 1976—); Century. Avocations: swimming, golf. Home: Hedge Ln Cazenovia NY 13035 Office: Syracuse U Off of VP Bus Fin Adminstrv Svc Skytop Rd Syracuse NY 13244

MARCOPOULOS, GEORGE JOHN, history educator; b. Salem, Mass., June 30, 1931; s. John George and Urania Christou (Moustakis) M. BA, Bowdoin Coll., 1953; MA, Harvard U., 1955, PhD, 1966. Instr. Tufts U., Medford, Mass., 1961-66, asst. prof., 1966-71, assoc. prof., 1971-92, prof., 1992—. Contbr. articles to profl. jours. and Am. Ann. yearbooks. Bd. dirs., treas. Gerondelis Found., Inc., Lynn, Mass., 1987—. Recipient Mellon Faculty Devel. grant Tufts U., 1983. Mem. AAUP, Am. Assn. Advancement Slavic Studies, Am. Hist. Assn., New Eng. Hist. Assn., Danforth Assocs. New Eng., Modern Greek Studies Assn., Phi Beta Kappa. Greek Orthodox. Avocations: music, films, reading, performing arts, excursions. Office: Tufts U Dept History East Hall Medford MA 02155

MARCOSSON, THOMAS I., service company executive; b. N.Y.C., Jan. 31, 1936; s. Mark and Mollie (Schreiber) M.; m. Carla F. Hunt, May 15, 1988; children: Mark, Susan, Samuel, Jill. Student, Union Coll., Schenectady, 1953-55; B.S., NYU, 1959. CPA, N.Y. Mgr. Touche Ross & Co., N.Y.C., 1959-63; v.p. fin., dir. Superior Surg. Mfg. Co., Inc., Huntington, N.Y., 1964-66; div. pres., gen. mgr. OEI div., Vernitron Corp., Great Neck, N.Y., 1967-71; controller Allied Maintenance Corp., N.Y.C., 1972-75; v.p. fin. Allied Maintenance Corp., 1975-82; chief fin. officer Remco Maintenance Corp., N.Y.C., 1982-84; exec. v.p., chief operating officer Remco Maintenance Corp., 1984-88; pres. MBW Advt. Network Inc., N.Y.C., 1988-89; founder, pres. Dunmarc Assocs., Inc., N.Y.C., 1989—; exec. v.p. Greater Talent Network, Inc., 1991—. Office: 150 Fifth Ave Ste 900 New York NY 10011-4311

MARCOUX, CARL HENRY, former insurance executive, writer, historian; b. San Francisco, Jan. 6, 1927; s. Henry Roderick and Margaret (Carlin) M.; m. Ana Virginia Penate-Melara, Nov. 11, 1967; children: Eric Henry, Grant Reynold. B.A., Stanford U., 1950; M.B.A., Golden Gate U., San Francisco, 1958; M.A. in Latin Am. History, U. Calif., Irvine, 1988; PhD in Latin Am. History, U. Calif., Riverside, 1994. Gen. mgr. Nat. Union Ins. Co., Pitts., 1953-68; exec. v.p. Transam. Ins. Co., 1968-85. Served with U.S. Mcht. Marine, 1944-46; USAF, 1951-53. Mem. Stanford Alumni Assn. Republican. Home: 1967 Port Cardigan Pl Newport Beach CA 92660-5347

MARCOUX, JULES EDOUARD, physicist, educator, writer; b. Charny, Que., Can., Jan. 26, 1924; s. Romeo Joseph and Atala (Fontaine); m. Hermina Manz, July 2, 1955; children: Daniel, Edouard, Elise, Vincent, Pierre, Paul. B.A., Laval U., 1946, B.S., 1952; M.A., Toronto U., 1952, Ph.D. (Burton fellow), 1956. Research assoc. U. Montreal, Que., 1957; assoc. prof. physics U. Laval, Quebec, Que., 1962-64; prof. physics Royal Mil. Coll., St.-Jean, Que., 1958-62, 64-90, ret., 1990. Author in French: (with A. Ares) Physics Textbook, 6 vols, 1970-76, Astronauts and Astronautics, 1975, Energy: Its Sources, Its Future, 1982, Mechanics for Engineers, 1983; contbr. articles to profl. publs. Exec. com. bd. dirs. College de St.-Jean-sur-Richelieu, Que., 1981—. Postdoctoral fellow NRC Can., 1957. Mem. Am. Assn. Physics Tchrs., Can. Assn. Univ. Tchrs., Can. Mil. Colls. Faculty Assn. (pres. 1980-82). Home: 29 rue de Tilleuls, Saint Luc, PQ Canada J2W 1B4

MARCOUX, JULIA A., midwife; b. St. Helens, England, Aug. 7, 1928; d. Robert Patrick and Margaret Mary Theresa (White) Ashall; m. Albert Marcoux, Apr. 23, 1955; children: Stephen, Ann Marie, Richard, Michael, Maureen, Patrick, Margaret, Julie. Diploma, Withington Hosp., Manchester, England, 1950; grad., Cowley Hill Hosp., St. Helens, England, 1952; BS in Pub. Adminstrn., St. Joseph's Coll. RN, Conn.; lic. midwife, Conn. Nurse, labor, delivery rm. and nursery Day Kimbal Hosp., Putnam, Conn.; sch. nurse Marianapolis Prep. Sch., Thompson, Conn.; occupational nurse U.S. Post Office, Hartford, Conn.; pvt. duty and gerontology nurse Conn. Contbr. articles to profl. jours. Named Internat. Cath. Family of Yr., 1982.

MARCOUX, WILLIAM JOSEPH, lawyer; b. Detroit, Jan. 20, 1927; s. Lona J. and Anna (Ransom) C.; m. Kae Marie Sanborn, Aug. 23, 1952; children: Ann K., William C. B.A., U. Mich., 1949, LL.B., 1952. Bar: Mich. 1953. Pvt. practice Pontiac, Mich., 1953; assoc. McKone, Badgley, Domke and Kline, Jackson, Mich., 1953-65, ptnr., 1965-75; dir. Marcoux, Allen, Abbott, Schomer & Bower, P.C., Jackson, Mich., 1975-93. Mem. exec. bd. Great Sauk Trail council Boy Scouts Am., pres., 1965-66; bd. dirs. Jackson County United Way, pres., 1983-84. Served with USNR, 1945-46. Recipient Silver Beaver award Boy Scouts Am., 1969, Disting. Citizen award Land O'Lakes coun. Boy Scouts Am., 1991. Fellow Am. Coll. Trial Lawyers; mem. Mich. Bar Assn., Jackson County Bar Assn. (pres. 1979-80). Methodist (chmn. adminstrv. bd., chmn. bd. trustees 1976-78, chmn. fin. com. 1986-89). Clubs: Rotarian (pres. 1963-64), Country, Clark Lake Yacht (hon. mem.; commodore 1959). Home: 1745 Malvern Dr Jackson MI 49203-5378 Office: Marcoux Allen Abbott Schomer & Bower PC 145 S Jackson St Jackson MI 49201-2211

MARCOUX, YVON, financial executive, lawyer; b. St. Lambert, Que., Can., Mar. 26, 1941; s. Henry Marcoux and Irène Simard; m. Odette Marcoux, Sept. 5, 1964; children: Stéphane, Sylvain, Sébastien, Valérie. BA, Université Laval, Que., Can., 1960, LL.L., 1963, postgrad., 1966; LL.M., U. Toronto, Can., 1965. Prof. Université Laval, Faculty Law, 1966-70; asst. sec. treasury bd., asst. dep. min. mcpl. affairs Govt. Que., 1970-78; v.p., sec. Nat. Bank Can., Montréal, 1978-81; sr. v.p. adminstrn. Laurentian Bank, Montréal, 1981-86; pres., chief exec. officer Trust La Laurentienne, Montréal, 1985-86; chmn., chief exec. officer Groupe SGF, Montréal, 1986-88; exec. v.p. adminstrn. Provigo, Montreal, 1988—; bd. dirs. Groupe LGS, Montreal, Corp. d'assurance de personnes La Laurentienne. Pres. Inst. for Pub. Adminstrn. Can., 1977-78, Found. U. Laval, 1991-93, 93-94, Que. C. of C., 1992-93, Montreal C. of C., 1985-86; bd. dirs. La Fondation Jean Duceppe, Inst. de design de Montrèal, Found. Paul Gèrin-Lajoie, Can. Coun. of Grocery Distbrs. Mem. Can. Bar Assn., Bar Que., Club St. Denis. Office: Provigo, 1611 Crémazie Blvd E, Montreal, PQ Canada H2M 2R9

MARCOVICH, MIROSLAV, classics educator; b. Belgrade, Yugoslavia, Mar. 18, 1919; came to U.S., 1969; s. Svetozar and Mila (Sakich) M.; m. Verica Tosich, May 30, 1948; 1 son, Dragoslav. B.A., U. Belgrade, 1942; DLitt (hon.), U. Ill., 1994. Lectr. in classics U. Belgrade, 1946-55; prof. Los Andes U., Merida, Venezuela, 1955-69; prof. classics U. Ill., Urbana, 1969-89, chmn. dept., 1973-77, lectr. humanities, 1987. Author: M. Maruli Davidias, 1957, Fr. Natalis Carmina, 1958, Bhagavadgita, 1958, Heraclitus Elenchos, 1986, Studies in Choticism, 1988, Alcestis Barchinonesis, 1988, Prosper of Aquitaine, De Providentia Dei, 1989. Athenagoras, Legatio pro Christianis, 1990, Ps.-Justin, Cohortatio, 1990, Studies in Greek Poetry, 1991, Theodorus Prodromus, Rhodanthe and Dosicles, 1992, Justin Martyr, Apologies, 1994, Tatian, Oratio, 1994, Theophilus, Ad Autolycum, 1995, Clementis Alexandrini Protrepticus, 1995, Justin Martyr, Dialogues cum Tryphone, 1996, others; founder, editor Illinois Classical Studies, 1976—; contbr. numerous articles to profl. jours. Guggenheim fellow, 1980, NEH, 1990; U. Ill. scholar, 1973, sr. scholar, 1986, Sackler scholar Te. Aviv U., 1990-91; recipient Premio Sesquicentenario Gold medal Venezuela, 1962, 64, Silver Cross Mt. Athos, Greece, 1963, Bechman award, 1991, 93, 94. Mem. Am. Philol. Assn. (mem. adv. com. Thesaurus Linguae Graecae 1973-80). Home: 2114 S Vine St Urbana IL 61801-6616

MARCOVITZ, LEONARD EDWARD, retail executive; b. Bismarck, N.D., Sept. 6, 1934; s. Jacob and Frieda M. Asst. mgr. Greengard's Clothing, Mandan, N.D., 1955-58; mgr. K-G Men's Stores, Inc., Bismarck, 1958-61, Billings, Mont., 1961-69; v.p. store ops. K-G Men's Stores, Inc., 1969-73; pres. Leonard's Men's Stores, Yakima, Wash. and Billings, Mont., 1973-77; chief exec. officer K-G Retail div. Chromalloy Am. Corp., Englewood, Colo., 1977-81; pres. DeMarcos Men's Clothing, Casper, Wyo., 1982—, Idaho Falls, Idaho, 1984—, Billings, Mont., 1986—. Mem. Menswear Retailers Am. (past dir.), Billings Petroleum Club, Order of Demolay (Degree of Chevalier 1952, Internat. Master Councilor 1953, Demolay Dad 1959), Elks. Home: PO Box 23344 Billings MT 59104-3344

MARCUCCIO, PHYLLIS ROSE, association executive, editor; b. Hackensack, N.J., Aug. 25, 1933; d. Filippo and Rose (Henry) M. AB, Bucknell U., 1955; MA, George Washington U., 1976. Trainee Time, Inc., 1956-57; art prodn. for mags. of Med. Econs., Inc., 1958-60; mem. staff Nat. Sci. Tchrs. Assn., Washington, 1961—; assoc. editor Sci. and Children, 1963-65, editor, 1965—, dir. div. elem. edn., 1974-78, dir. div. program devel. and continuing edn., 1978-83; dir. publs. Nat. Sci. Tchrs. Assn., 1983—, assoc. exec. dir., 1990—; lectr., cons. in field. Author, photographer, illustrator numerous articles; co-author: Investigation in Ecology, 1972; editor: Science Fun, 1977, 2d edit., 94; illustrator: Selected Readings for Students of English as a Second Language, 1966; compiler: Opportunities for Summer Studies in Elementary Science, 1968, 2d edit., 1969. Apptd. commr. Rockville (Md.) Housing Authority, 1981-91, chairperson, 1984-86; bd. dirs. Nat. Sci Resource Ctr., Nat. Acad. Sci., 1986—, Hands on Sci. Outreach, Inc., 1988—. Recipient Citizenship medal DAR, 1951; hon. life mem. Ohio Council Elem. Sch. Sci., 1974. Life mem. Nat. Sci. Tchrs. Assn.; mem. Council Elem. Sci. Internat. (Internat. award outstanding contbns. sci. edn. 1971, 72, 86, 94), Am. Nature Study Soc., Soil Conservation Soc. Am., Nat. Free Lance Photographers Assn., Photog. Soc. Am., Nat. Wildlife Fedn., Nat. Audubon Soc., Nat. Geog. Soc., Wilderness Soc., AAAS, Washington Edn. Press Assn. (treas. 1966-67, pres. 1975-76), Ednl. Press Assn. Am. (regional dir. 1969-71, sec. 1979—, Disting. Achievement award 1969, 71-74, 76, 77, 80, 88, 93, 95, Eleanor Fishburn award 1978), Sci. Teaching Assn. N.Y. (Outstanding Service to Sci. Edn. award 1987), Nat. Assn. Industry Edn. Coop. (bd. dirs. 1980-86), Pocono Environ. Edn. Ctr. (bd. dirs. 1989—), Nat. Press Club, Theta Alpha Phi, Phi Delta Gamma, Phi Delta Kappa., Sigma Delta Chi. Home: 406 S Horners Ln Rockville MD 20850-1556 Office: Nat Sci Tchrs Assn 1840 Wilson Blvd Arlington VA 22201-3000

MARCUM, DEANNA BOWLING, library administrator; b. Salem, Ind., Aug. 5, 1946; d. Anderson and Ruby (Mobley) Bowling; m. Thomas P. Marcum, June 13, 1974; 1 child, Ursula. BA, U. Ill., 1967; MA, So. Ill. U., 1969; MLS, U. Ky., 1971; PhD, U. Md., 1991. Tchr. Deland-Weldon (Ill.) High Sch., 1967-68; instr. English U. Ky., Lexington, 1969-70, cataloging librarian, 1970-73, asst. to dir., 1973-74; asst. dir. pub. svcs. Joint U. Librs., Nashville, 1974-77; mgmt. tng. specialist Assn. Rsch. Librs., Washington, 1977-80; sr. cons. Info. Systems Cons., Inc., Washington, 1980-81; v.p. Coun. on Libr. Resources, Washington, 1981-89; dean Sch. Libr. and Info. Sch. Cath. U., Washington, 1989-92; dir. pub. svcs. and collections mgmt. Libr. of Congress, Washington, 1993-95; pres. Coun. on Libr. Resources, Washington, 1995—; adv. bd. So. Edn. Found., Atlanta, 1986-91; chmn. grants com. Coun. on Libr. resources, Washington, 1990-94. Author: Good Books in a Country Home, 1993; co-author: (with Richard Boss) The Library Catalog, 1980, On-Line Acquisitions Systems, 1981; contbr. articles to profl. jours. Pres., Commn. on Preservation and Access, 1995—. Mem. ALA, Am. Studies Assn., Orgn. Am. Historians, Am. Antiquarian Soc. (adv. bd. 1989—), Beta Phi Mu, Phi Kappa Phi. Home: 3315 Wake Dr Kensington MD 20895 Office: Coun on Libr Resources 1400 16th St NW Ste 715 Washington DC 20036-2217

MARCUM, JOSEPH LARUE, insurance company executive; b. Hamilton, Ohio, July 2, 1923; s. Glen F. and Helen A. (Stout) M.; m. Sarah Jane Sloneker, Mar. 7, 1944; children: Catharine Ann Marcum Lowe, Joseph Timothy (dec.), Mary Christina Marcum Manchester, Sarah Jennifer Marcum Shuffield, Stephen Sloneker. B.A., Antioch Coll., 1947; M.B.A. in Fin, Miami U., 1965. With Ohio Casualty Ins. Co. and affiliates, 1947—, now chmn. bd., also bd. dirs.; bd. dirs. First Nat. Bank S.W. Ohio; bd. dirs., chmn. exec. com. First Fin. Bancorp., Monroe, Ohio. Chmn. bd. trustees Miami U., Oxford, Ohio. Capt., inf. U.S. Army. Mem. Soc. CPCU, Queen City Club, Bankers Club, Princeton Club N.Y., Little Harbor club, Walloon Lake Country Club, Mill Reef Club. Presbyterian. Home: 475 Oakwood Dr Hamilton OH 45013-3466 Office: Ohio Casualty Corp 136 N 3rd St Hamilton OH 45025-0002

MARCUM, WALTER PHILLIP, manufacturing company executive; b. Bemidji, Minn., Mar. 1, 1944; s. John Phillip and Johnnye Evelyn (Edmiston) M.; m. Barbara Lynn Maloof, Apr. 17, 1976. BBA, Tex. Tech U., 1967. Researcher Collins Securities, Denver, 1968-70, Hanifin Imhoff, Denver, 1970-71; cons. Marcum-Spillane, Denver, 1971-76; with MGF Oil Corp., Midland, Tex., 1976-87, sr. v.p., 1978, exec. v.p., 1979-83, pres., chief exec. officer, 1983-87; sr. v.p. corp. fin. Boettcher & Co., Denver, 1987-90; pres., chief exec. officer Marcum Natural Gas Svcs., Inc., Denver, 1991—; dir. Homefree Village Resorts, Hydrologic Inc., Asheville, N.C., Well Tech., Inc., Houston. Republican. Presbyterian. Home: 676 Monroe St Denver CO 80206-4451 Office: 1675 Broadway Ste 2200 Denver CO 80202-4622

MARCUS, ALAN C., public relations consultant; b. N.Y.C., Feb. 26, 1947; s. Percy and Rose (Fox) M.; m. Judith Lamel, June 21, 1979; 1 child, Allison. Student Hun Sch., Princeton, 1966. Dir. pub. relations Bergen County Rep. Com., Hackensack, N.J., 1968; clk. N.J. Gen. Assembly, Trenton, 1969, sec. to majority party of assembly, 1970; pres. The Marcus Group, Inc., Secaucus, 1971—; adj. prof. Rutgers U. Grad. Sch., 1986-88. Trustee Nat. Leukemia Assn., 1976-82, Hun Sch. of Princeton, 1977-88, Passaic River Coalition, 1980-82. Recipient Youth Enterprise award Jim Walter Corp., 1972. Mem. Pub. Relations Soc. Am. (N.J. chpt. pres.'s award 1975, past pres. and bd. dirs. N.J. chpt. 1976-77), N.J. C. of C., N.J. Bus. and Industry Assn., N.J. Press Assn., Apple Ridge Country Club, Capitol Hill Club, Fed. City Club (Washington). Office: 500 Plaza Dr PO Box 3309 Secaucus NJ 07096-3309 also: 50 W State St Trenton NJ 08608-1220 also: 370 Lexington Ave New York NY 10017-6503

MARCUS, BARRY PHILIP, lawyer; b. Mount Vernon, N.Y., July 25, 1953; m. Jean Kytt Jacobs, Sept. 4, 1977. BA, Cornell U., 1974; JD, U. Va., 1977. Bar: N.Y. 1978. Assoc. Debevoise & Plimpton, N.Y.C., 1977-80; assoc., ptnr. Kaye, Scholer, Fierman, Hays & Handler, N.Y.C., 1980—. Mem. ABA, N.Y.C. Bar Assn. Home: 420 E 72nd St New York NY 10021-4615 Office: Kaye Scholer Fierman Hays & Handler 425 Park Ave New York NY 10022-3506*

MARCUS, BERNARD, lawyer; b. Wilkes-Barre, Pa., Mar. 10, 1924; m. Frances Frank; children: Kate, Aaron, Charles, Mary. Student, U. Pa., 1941-43, Carnegie-Mellon U., 1943-44; LL.B., Harvard U., 1948; postgrad., Loyola U. of South, New Orleans, 1958. Bar: D.C. 1949, La. 1958. Atty. legis. reference service Library of Congress, 1949-50; acting counsel small bus. com. Ho. of Reps., 1950; atty. NLRB, Washington, Cin., Buffalo and New Orleans, 1950-57; assoc. Deutsch, Kerrigan & Stiles, New Orleans, 1957-58; ptnr. Deutsch, Kerrigan & Stiles, 1958-95, mng. ptnr., 1985-89, emeritus ptnr., 1995—; cons. Dept. State, 1965-69; labor arbitrator Am. Arbitration Assn., Fed. Mediation and Conciliation Svc., USDA, U.S. Dept. Def., U.S. Dept. Transp., City of Houston, Fla. Power and Light, Internat. Paper Co., Celotex, Mead Paper, ADM Corp., GTE, SW Bell, Ingalals Shipbldg., Gulf States Utilities, PPG Industries, Ga. Pacific Corp., Westvaco, Hertz, Memphis Comml. Appeal, Schering Plough, Chevvron, Bryan Foods, also others. Author: Congress and the Monopoly Problem, 1950; contbr. to casebooks. Pres. New Orleans Jewish Community Center, 1973-75; mem. Nat. Jewish Welfare Bd., 1974-83; bd. dirs. New Orleans Jewish Welfare Bd., Jewish Family and Children's Service, New Orleans, Communal Hebrew Sch.; v.p. New Orleans Home for Jewish Aged, 1978-80, Florence Heller Rsch. Found. Served US Army, 1943-46. Mem. ABA, Fed. Bar Assn., La. Bar Assn., New Orleans Bar Assn. (exec. com. 1971-74), D.C. Bar Assn. Home: 630 Burdette St New Orleans LA 70118-3937 Office: 755 Magazine St New Orleans LA 70130-3629

MARCUS, BERNARD, retail executive; b. 1929; married. BS, Rutgers U., 1954. V.p. Vornado Inc., 1952-68; pres. Odell Inc., 1968-70; v.p. Daylin Inc., 1970-73; with Handy Dan Home Improvement, Los Angeles, 1972-78; with Home Depot Inc., Atlanta, 1978—, now chmn., chief exec. officer, sec., also bd. dirs. Office: Home Depot Inc 2727 Paces Ferry Rd NW Atlanta GA 30339-4053*

MARCUS, BETH E., religious organization administrator. Moderator Gen. Synod Council of the Reformed Ch. in Am., N.Y.C. Office: Reformed Church in Am 475 Riverside Dr Ste 1811 New York NY 10115-0122

MARCUS, CLAUDE, advertising executive; b. Paris, Aug. 28, 1924; s. Jacques and Louise (Bleustein) M.; m. Claudine Pohl, May 27, 1948; children: Michele, Pierre, Anne-Marie, Isabelle. Diploma in Econs., U. Paris, 1947; Lic., Paris Law Sch., 1947. Sec. gen. Publicis, Paris, 1948-55, dir. comml. to dir. gen. adjoint, 1961, dir. gen., 1962-68; mng. dir. Publicis Conseil, Paris, 1968-83; pres. Publicis Internat., Paris, 1984-88; vice-chmn. Publicis Communication, Paris, 1988—, Publicis FCB Communication, Paris, 1989; dir. Publicis SA, Paris, 1988—; chmn. Publicis N.Y., 1986-93; chmn. supervisory bd. FCA, Paris; vice chmn. Metrobus Publicities, Paris, 1994. Decorated Chevalier de la Legion d'Honneur, 1970. Mem. Conseil Nat. de la Cosommation, Bur. de Verification de la Publicite (vice chmn.), Racing Club (France). Home: 12 Rue Felicien David, 75016 Paris France Office: Publicis, 133 Champs Elysees, 45008 Paris France also: 304 E 45th St New York NY 10017-3425

MARCUS, CRAIG BRIAN, lawyer; b. Boise, Idaho, May 30, 1939; s. Claude Virgil and Marie Louise M.; m. Lynne Merryweather, Sept. 3, 1960; children: Shawn, Brian, Trent. Student, Boise Jr. Coll., 1958, U. Pa., 1958-59, Mexico City Coll., 1959-60; JD, U. Idaho, 1963. Bar: Idaho 1963, U.S. Dist. Ct. Idaho 1963. Ptnr. Marcus, Merrick & Montgomery, predecessors, Boise, 1963—. Ada County dir. Rep. Congl. Campaigns, Boise, 1964-66; Ada County coord. Rep. Senatorial Campaigns, 1969; chmn. jud. campaign Idaho Ct. of Appeals, 1984, 90. Mem. ABA, Idaho Bar Assn. (peer rev. com. 1971-73), 4th Dist. Bar Assn. (treas. 1967-68, ct. trial porcedural rules com. 1973-74), Lincoln Day Banquet Assn. (pres. 1975), Elks. Avocations: fishing, hunting, golf, skiing, trap shooting. Home: 7711 Apache Way Boise ID 83703-1903 Office: Marcus Merrick & Montgomery 737 N 7th St Boise ID 83702-5504

MARCUS, DEVRA JOY COHEN, internist; b. Bronx, N.Y., Sept. 5, 1940; d. Benjamin and Gertrude (Siegel) Cohen; m. Robert A. Marcus, Apr. 1963 (div. 1974); children: Rachel, Adam; m. Michael J. Horowitz, Mar. 2, 1975; 1 child, Naomi. BA, Brandeis U., 1961; MD, Stanford U., 1966. Diplomate Am. Bd. Internal Medicine. Intern in internal medicine Stanford U., 1966-67, resident, 1967-68; gen. internist D.C. Dept. Pub. Health, 1968-69, Cardozo Neighborhood Health Ctr., Washington, 1969-73; med. dir. East of the River Health Assn., Washington, 1973-75; fellow in infectious disease Washington Hosp. Ctr., 1975-77; gen. internist Police and Fire Clinic, Washington, 1977-78; gen. internist, pvt. practice Washington, 1977—; assoc. clin. prof. medicine George Washington U. Med Ctr., Washington, 1978—; gen. internist World Bank, Washington, 1978-81; ptnr. Traveller's Med. Svc. D.C., 1980-82; gen. internist Community of Good Hope Med. Clinic, Washington, 1984-85; assoc. clin. prof. medicine Georgetown U. Med. Ctr., Washington, 1987—; preceptor Georgetown U. Hosp., 1986—. Contbr. articles to profl. jours. Exec. com. Woodley Park Citizen's Assn., 1979-80; chair mayor's adv. com. on prevention, 1982-83; bd. dirs. Exodus Youth Svcs., 1987-89. Fellow ACP; mem. AMA (Physicians Recognition award, 1981, 84, 87, 90, 93), Med. Soc. D.C. (credentials com., communicable disease com., founder com. on women 1983, pres. 1985-87, med. ethics and judiciary com. 1987-91, judiciary coun. 1992-96). Home: 1205 Crest Ln Mc Lean VA 22101-1837 Office: 2021 K St NW Washington DC 20006

MARCUS, DONALD HOWARD, advertising agency executive; b. Cleve., May 16, 1916; s. Joseph and Sarah (Schmitman) M.; m. Helen Olen Weiss, Feb. 12, 1959; children: Laurel Kathy Heifetz, Carol Susan Greene, James Randall (dec.), Jonathan Anthony. Student, Fenn Coll., 1934-35. Mem. publicity dept. Warner Bros. Pictures, Cleve., 1935-37; mem. advt. dept. RKO Pictures, Cleve., 1937-40; mem. sales dept. Monogram Pictures, Cleve., 1940-42; pres. Marcus Advt. Inc., Cleve., 1946-85, chmn., 1986—. Mem. Ohio Democratic exec. com., 1969-70, del. nat. conv., 1968; vice-chmn. communication div. Jewish Welfare Fund Appeal Cleve., 1964-70, chmn., 1971-72; trustee Jewish Community Fedn., 1973-74; trustee Cleve. Jewish News, 1974—, v.p., 1983-85; trustee No. Ohio regional office Anti Defamation League of B'nai B'rith, 1986—, Jewish Community Ctr., 1988-90; bd. dirs. Cuyahoga County unit Am. Cancer Soc., 1979—, Cleve. State U. Devel. Found., 1987—, Achievement Ctr. for Children, 1991—. Served to 1st lt. USAAF, 1942-46. Mem. Nat. Acad. TV Arts and Scis. (Silver Circle award 1994), Ohio Commodores, Cleve. Advt. Club (elected to Hall of Fame), Cleve. Growth Assn., Mensa, Union Club of Cleve., Beechmont Country Club (past pres.). Jewish (temple trustee). Home: 22449 Shelburne Rd Cleveland OH 44122-2053 Office: Marcus Advt Inc 25700 Science Park Dr Cleveland OH 44122-7312

MARCUS, EDWARD, economist, educator; b. Bklyn., Apr. 29, 1918; s. Herman and Rose (Marayna) M.; m. Mildred Rendl, Aug. 10, 1956. B.S., Harvard, 1939, M.B.A., 1941; student, King's Coll., Cambridge (Eng.) U., 1946-47; Ph.D., Princeton, 1950. Economist Fed. Res. Bd., 1950-52; prof. econs. Bklyn. Coll., 1952-81, chmn. dept., 1966-79; cons. Nat. Acad. Scis., 1959, UN Conf. Trade and Devel., 1966; dir. Syracuse U. Maxwell Sch. Nigerian Project, 1961; participant Internat. Econometrics Assn., Amsterdam, Holland, 1968. Author: Canada and the International Business Cycle, 1927-1938, 1954, (with Mildred Rendl Marcus) Investment and Development Possibilities in Tropical Africa, 1960, International Trade and Finance, 1965, Monetary and Banking Theory, 1965, Economic Progress and the Developing World, 1971, Economics, 1978. Served with AUS, 1941-42; Served with USCGR, 1942-46. Grantee Merrill Found., 1953. Mem. Am. Econ. Assn., Canadian Econ. Assn., N.Y. Met. Econ. Assn. (pres. 1966-67), Am. Finance Assn., Royal Econ. Soc., Econ. Soc. S. Africa, Am. Assn. U. Profs., New Canaan Hist. Soc. Treas. 1983—), Phi Beta Kappa. Home: PO Box 814 New Canaan CT 06840-0814

MARCUS, ERIC PETER, lawyer; b. Newark, Aug. 31, 1950; s. John J. and Alice M. (Zeldin) M.; m. Terry R. Toll, Oct. 9, 1983. BA, Brown U., 1972; JD, Stanford U., 1976. Bar: N.Y. 1977, N.J. 1977. Assoc. Kaye, Scholer, Fierman, Hays & Handler, N.Y.C., 1976-84, ptnr., 1985—. Contbr. articles to profl. jours. Mem. Phi Beta Kappa. Office: Kaye Scholer Fierman Hays & Handler 425 Park Ave New York NY 10022-3506

MARCUS, ERIC ROBERT, psychiatrist; b. N.Y.C., Feb. 16, 1944; s. Victor and Pearl (Maddow) M.; m. Eslee Samberg, Nov. 24, 1985; children: Max, Pia. AB, Columbia U., 1965; MD, U. Wis., 1969. Diplomate Am. Bd. Psychiatry and Neurology. Intern NYU Med. Ctr. Bellevue Hosp., 1969-70; resident Columbia Presbyn. Med. Ctr.-N.Y. State Psychiatric Inst., 1972-75; dir. St. Marks Free Clinic, N.Y.C., 1971-75; from co-dir. to dir. neuropsychiatric/diagnostic treatment unit Columbia-Presbyn. Med. Ctr., N.Y.C., 1975-84; dir. med. student edn. in psychiatry Columbia U. Coll. Physicians and Surgeons, N.Y.C., 1981—; supervising-tng. analyst Ctr. for Psychoanalytic Tng.-Rsch. Columbia U. Ctr. for Psychoanalytic Tng.-Rsch., N.Y.C., 1995—; clin. prof. psychiatry and social medicine Columbia U. Coll. Physicians and Surgeons, N.Y.C., 1995—; clin. prof. psychiatry and social medicine Columbia U. Coll. Physicians and Surgeons, 1995—; bd. govs. student health Columbia U., 1986—. Author: Psychosis and Near Psychosis, 1992; mem. editorial bd. The Psychoanalytic Study of Society, 1989-94; contbr. articles to profl. jours. Recipient Weber rsch. award Columbia U. Psychoanalytic Ctr., 1991, O'Connor Teaching award, 1995. Fellow Am. Psychiat. Assn. (Roeske award 1991), Am. Psychoanalytic Assn., Am. Coll. Psychoanalysts, N.Y. Acad. Medicine. Avocations: classical music, photography, swimming, reading. Office: Columbia U Dept Psychiatry 722 W 168th St New York NY 10032-2603

MARCUS, FRANK, biochemist; b. Berlin, July 27, 1933; came to U.S., 1974; s. Heinz and Feiga (Wolf) M.; m. Marietta Munoz, Sept. 12, 1959; children: Claudio, Daniel, Andres. Pharm. chemist, U. Chile, 1958. Rockefeller Found. postdoctoral fellow dept. biochemistry Australian Nat. U., 1962-63, U. Wis, 1964; asst. prof. biochemistry U. Chile, Santiago, 1965-68; prof. biochemistry and chmn. Inst. Biochemistry Southern U., Valdivia, Chile, 1968-74; vis. prof. Inst. Enzyme Research U. Wis., Madison, 1974-77; assoc. prof. biochemistry Univ. Health Scis. Chgo. Med. Sch., 1977-81, prof. biochemistry, 1981-87, vice chmn. Dept. Biol. Chemistry and Structure, U. Health Scis., 1982-87; dir. protein chemistry Chiron Corp., Emeryville, Calif., 1988-94, sr. dir. vaccine protein purification, analytical devel., 1994-95, protein chemistry and protein purification cons., 1995—. Contbr. articles to profl. jours. Recipient Morris L. Parker rsch. award Chgo. Med. Sch., 1982; Fulbright travel awardee, 1968; grantee NIH, 1977-89, USDA, 1983-89. Mem. AAAS, Am. Soc. Biol. Chemists, Protein Soc., Alpha Omega Alpha. Home: 43 Remington Ct Danville CA 94526-3730 Office: Chiron Corp 4560 Horton St Emeryville CA 94608-2916

MARCUS, FRANK ISADORE, physician, educator; b. Haverstraw, N.Y., Mar. 23, 1928; s. Samuel and Edith (Sattler) M.; m. Janet Geller, June 30, 1957; children: Ann, Steve, Lynn. BA, Columbia U., 1948; MS, Tufts U., 1951; MD cum laude, Boston U., 1953. Diplomate Am. Bd. Internal Medicine, subspecialty cardiovascular diseases. Intern Peter Bent Brigham Hosp., Boston, 1953-54; asst. resident Peter Bent Brigham Hosp., 1956-57, research fellow in cardiology, 1957-58; clin. fellow in cardiology Georgetown U. Hosp., 1958-59, chief med. resident, 1959-60; chief of cardiology Georgetown U. Med. Service, D.C. Gen. Hosp., Washington, 1960-68; instr. medicine Georgetown U. Sch. Medicine, 1960-63, asst. prof., 1963-68, assoc. prof., 1968; prof. medicine, chief cardiology sect. U. Ariz. Coll. Medicine, Tucson, 1969-82, disting. prof. internal medicine (cardiology), 1982—, dir. electrophysiology, 1982—; cons. cardiology VA Hosp., Tucson, 1969, USAF Regional Hosp., Davis-Monthan AFB, Tucson, 1969; mem. courtesy staffs Tucson Med. Ctr., St. Mary's Hosp., Tucson.; mem. panel drug efficacy study, panel on cardiovascular drugs Nat. Acad. Scis.-NRC, 1967-68; chmn. undergrad. cardiovascular tng. grant com. HEW-NIH, 1970. Editor: Modern Concepts of Cardiovascular Disease, 1982-84; mem. editl. bd.: Circulation, 1976-81, Current Problems in Cardiology, 1976-80, Cardiovascular Drugs and Therapy, 1986—, New Trends in Arrythmias, 1984—, Jour. Am. Coll. Cardiology, 1984-87, 96—, Am. Jour. Cardiology, 1984—, Jour. Cardiovasc. Drugs and Therapy, 1994—, Jour. Cardiovasc. Pharmacology and Therapeutics, 1994—, Pacing and Clin. Electrophysiology, 1995—; contbr. numerous articles to med. jours. Chmn. Washington Heart Assn. High Sch. Heart Program, 1966-68. Served to capt. USAF, 1954-56. Recipient Career Devel. award NIH, 1965, Student AMA Golden Apple award Georgetown U. Sch. Medicine, 1968; Mass. Heart Assn. fellow, 1957-58; John and Mary Markle scholar, 1960-65. Fellow Coun. on Clin. Cardiology Am. Heart Assn., ACP (Ariz. laureate award 1987), Am. Coll. Cardiology (bd. govs. Ariz. 1984-87, asst. sec. 1987-89, trustee); mem. Am. Fedn. Clin. Rsch., Am. Soc. Pharm. and Exptl. Therapeutics, Assn. Univ. Cardiologists, Inc. (v.p. 1989-90, pres. 1990-91), Ariz. Heart Assn. (dir. 1970, v.p. 1972-73, chmn. rsch. com. 1970-72), So. Ariz. Heart Assn. (dir. 1969), N.Am. Soc. for Pacing and Electrophysiology, Alpha Omega Alpha. Home: 4949 E Glenn St Tucson AZ 85712-1212 Office: U Ariz Univ Med Ctr 1501 N Campbell Ave Tucson AZ 85724-0001

MARCUS, GREIL GERSTLEY, critic; b. San Francisco, June 19, 1945; s. Gerald Dodd and Eleanore (Hyman) M.; m. Jenelle Bernstein, June 26, 1966; children: Emily Rose, Cecily Helen. BA, U. Calif., Berkeley, 1967, MA, 1968. Record editor Rolling Stone mag., San Francisco and N.Y.C., 1969-70; book columnist Rolling Stone mag., 1975-80, Calif. Mag., L.A., 1982-83, 88-90; pop music columnist Music Mag., Tokyo, 1978-94, New West mag., L.A., 1978-82, Artforum mag., N.Y.C., 1983-87, 90—, Village Voice newspaper, N.Y.C., 1986-90, Interview Mag., N.Y.C., 1992—; dir. Pagnol et Cie, operators Chez Panisse restaurant, Berkeley. Author: Mystery Train: Images of America in Rock 'n Roll Music, 1975, U.S. rev. , 1982, 90 (Brit., German, Greek, Dutch and Japanese edits.), Real Life Rock (Japanese), 1984, Lipstick Traces: A Secret History of the 20th Century, 1989 (Brit., Italian, Spanish and German edits.), Dead Elvis: A Chronicle of a Cultural Obsession, 1991 (Brit., Japanese and German edits.), Ranters and Crowd Pleasers: Punk in Pop Music, 1977-92, 93, In The Fascist Bathroom: Writings on Punk (Brit. and German edits.), The Dustbin of History (Brit. edit.), 1995; editor: Stranded, 1979, rev. 1996, Psychotic Reactions and Carburetor Dung (Lester Bangs), 1987; contbr. criticism to publs. including N.Y. Times, N.Y. Times Book Rev., Creem, New Yorker, Express-Times, Triquar., Boston Phoenix, New Mus. Express, Another Room, L.A. Times, Newsday, IT, New Formations, RAW, Rock and Roll Confidential, Threepenny Rev., South Atlantic Quar., Common Knowledge.

MARCUS, HARRIS LEON, mechanical engineering and materials science educator; b. Ellenville, N.Y., July 5, 1931; s. David and Bertha (Messite) M.; m. Leona Gorker, Aug. 29, 1962; children: Leland, M'Risa. BS, Purdue U., 1963; PhD, Northwestern U., 1966. Registered profl. engr., Tex. Tech. staff Tex. Instruments, Dallas, 1966-68; tech. staff Rockwell Sci. Ctr., 1968-70, group leader, 1971-75; prof. mech. engring. U. Tex., Austin, 1975-79, Harry L. Kent Jr. prof. mech. engring., 1979-90, Cullen Found. prof., 1990-95, dir. ctr. for Materials Sci. and Engring., dir. program, 1979-95; prof. metallurgy and materials engring., dir. Inst. for Material Sci., U. Conn., 1995—; cons. numerous orgns. Contbr. numerous articles to profl. publs. Recipient U. Tex. faculty U. Tex. Engring. Found., 1983; Krengel lectr. Technion, Israel, 1983; Alumni Merit medal Northwestern U., 1988, Disting. Purdue Univ. Engring. Alumnus award, 1994. Fellow Am. Soc. Metals; mem. ASTM, ACS, AIME (bd. dirs. Metall. Soc. 1976-78, 84-86), Materials Rsch. Soc. Achievements include 15 patents. Home: 48 Dog Ln Storrs Mansfield CT 06268 Office: Univ Conn Inst Materials Scis U-136 Storrs Mansfield CT 06269

MARCUS, HYMAN, business executive; b. Roumania, May 3, 1914; s. Morris and Fannie M.; m. Sydelle Allen, June 29, 1935; children: Beverly Faith, Carole Ann. BA, Columbia U., 1932; MA, CCNY, 1993. Math instr., 1932-39; pres. Empire Designing Corp., 1939-46, Manhattan Capital Co., 1946-54; pres., chmn. U.S. Hoffman Machinery Corp., 1954-58; ptnr. Van Alstyne Noel & Co., 1956-59; chmn. bd. Artloom Industries, 1958—, pres., 1959—; chmn. bd. Hoffman Internat., 1957-59; pres., chmn. bd. Trans-United Industries, 1958; chmn. First Capital Corp., 1968—, Maralco Enterprises Inc., 1969—. Chmn. planning commn. Village of Atlantic Beach; trustee Riverside Sch., Jewish Meml. Hosp. Home: 159 W 53rd St New York NY 10019-6050 Office: 200 W 51st St New York NY 10019-6202

MARCUS, JAMES STEWART, investment banker; b. N.Y.C., Dec. 15, 1929; s. Bernard Kent and Libby (Phillips) M.; m. Barbara Ellen Silver, July 18, 1962 (dec. Nov. 1970); m. Ellen Mary Friedman, June 21, 1974. AB magna cum laude, Harvard U., 1951, MBA with distinction, 1953. Assoc. Goldman, Sachs and Co., N.Y.C., 1956-64, gen. ptnr., 1964-82, ltd. ptnr., 1982—; bd. dirs. Kellwood Co., St. Louis, Am. Bilrite Inc., Wellesley, Mass. Bd. dirs. Met. Opera Assn., N.Y.C., 1973—, chmn., 1986-93, Met. Opera Guild, Met. Opera Club; mem. exec. com. Lincoln Ctr. for the Performing Arts, N.Y.C., 1982-93; trustee Lenox Hill Hosp., N.Y.C., 1985—, chmn. bd. dirs., 1993—, Guild Hall, East Hampton, N.Y., 1977—, Am. Composers Orch., N.Y.C., 1984—, WNET Channel 13, Regenstrief Found., Alex Hillman Family Found., Animal Med. Ctr., Manhattan Theatre Club, The Juilliard Sch.; former trustee Nat. Opera Inst., Brazilian Cultural Found. Served with U.S. Army, 1953-55. Recipient U.S. Presdl. Recognition award, 1986. Mem. Century Assn., Phi Beta Kappa. Republican. Jewish. Office: Goldman Sachs & Co 85 Broad St New York NY 10004-2434

MARCUS, JOSEPH, child psychiatrist; b. Cleve., Feb. 27, 1928; s. William and Sarah (Marcus) Schwartz; m. Cilla Furmanovitz, Oct. 3, 1951; children: Oren, Alon. B.Sc., Western Res. U., 1963; M.D., Hebrew U., 1958. Intern Tel Hashomer Govt. Hosp., Israel, 1956-57; resident in psychiatry and child psychiatry Ministry of Health, Govt. of Israel, 1958-61; acting head dept. child psychiatry Ness Ziona Rehab. Ctr., 1961-62; sr. psychiatrist Lasker dept. child psychiatry Hadassah U. Hosp., 1962-64; research asso. Israel Inst. Applied Social Research, 1966-69; practice medicine specializing in psychiatry Jerusalem, 1966-72; assoc. dir. devel. neuropsychiatry Jerusalem Infant and Child Devel. Ctr., 1969-70; dept. head Eytanim Hosp., 1970-72; cons. child psychiatrist for Jerusalem Ministry of Health, 1970-72; dir. dept. child psychiatry and devel. Jerusalem Mental Health Ctr., 1972-75; prof. child psychiatry, dir. unit for research in child psychiatry and devel. U. Chgo., 1975-85, prof. emeritus, co-dir. unit for research in child psychiatry and devel., 1986—; vis. research psychiatrist UCLA Dept. Psychiatry, 1987—. Chief editor: Early Child Devel. and Care, 1972-76; mem. editorial bd.: Israel Annals of Psychiatry and Related Disciplines, 1965-70, Internat. Yearbook of Child Psychiatry and Allied Professions, 1968-74; contbr. articles to med. jours. Mem. Am. Acad. Child Psychiatry (com. on research, com. on psychiat. aspects of infancy), Soc. Research in Child Devel., Internat. Assn. Child Psychiatry and Allied Professions (asst. gen. sec. 1966-74), European Union Paedopsychiatry (hon.), World, Israel psychiat. assns., Internat. Coll. Psychosomatic Medicine, Israel Center Psychobiology. Home: 910 Chelham Way Santa Barbara CA 93108-1049 Office: 5841 S Maryland Ave # 30077 Chicago IL 60637-1463

MARCUS, KAREN MELISSA, foreign language educator; b. Vancouver, B.C., Feb. 28, 1956; came to the U.S., 1962; d. Marvin Marcus and Arlen Ingrid (Sahlman) Bishop; m. Jorge Esteban Mezei, Jan. 7, 1984 (div. Mar. 1987). BA in French, BA in Polit. Sci., U. Calif., Santa Barbara, 1978, MA in Polit. Sci., 1981; MA in French, Stanford U., 1984, PhD in French, 1990. Lectr. in French Stanford (Calif.) U., 1989-90; asst. prof. French No. Ariz. U., Flagstaff, 1990—; cons. Houghton Mifflin, 1993, Grand Canyon (Ariz.) Natural History Soc., 1994. Vol., letter writer Amnesty Internat. Urgent Action Network, 1991—; vol. No. Ariz. Aids Outreach Orgn., Flagstaff, 1994—. Recipient medal for outstanding achievement in French, Alliance Francaise, Santa Barbara, 1978; named Scholarship Exch. Student, U. Geneva, Switzerland, 1979-80; doctoral fellow Stanford (Calif.) U., 1981-85. Mem. MLA, Am. Assn. Tchrs. French, Am. Coun. on the Tchg. Fgn. Langs., Am. Literary Translators Assn., Women in French, Coordination Internat. des Chercheurs Sur Les Litteratures Maghrebines, Phi Beta Kappa, Pi Delta Phi, Alpha Lambda Delta. Democrat. Jewish. Avocations: walking, yoga, reading, writing short stories. Office: No Ariz Univ Modern Lang Dept Box 6004 Flagstaff AZ 86011

MARCUS, LAURENCE RICHARD, education policy and planning educator; b. Brookline, Mass., July 23, 1947; s. Herbert M. and Joyce (Chaban) M.; m. Maureen Flanagan; children: Yvette, Christina Ann. BA in Polit. Sci. and Am. Govt., U. Mass., Amherst, 1969; MEd, 1972, EdD, 1976. Staff asst. U. Mass., Amherst, 1970-76; asst. to v.p. acad. affairs Stockton State Coll., Pomona, N.J., 1976-79, interim dean gen. studies, 1977; asst. to chancellor N.J. Dept. Higher Edn., Trenton, 1979-81, dir. state colls., 1981-87; dir. N.J. Fund for Improvement of Collegiate Edn., 1984-87, Div. Faculty Devel. and Ednl. Policy, 1987-89, dep. asst. chancellor, 1989-91, asst. chancellor for academic and fiscal affairs, 1991-94; prof. ednl. leadership and policy Rowan Coll. of N.J., Glassboro, 1994—. tchr. U. Mass., Stockton State Coll.; cons. race relations, ednl. administrn. and leadership; trustee Glassboro State Coll., 1986-87, Trenton State Coll, 1986-87, 89-94, Montclair State Coll., 1989-91, Kean Coll. of N.J., 1990-94; trustee, N.J. Marine Scis. Consortium, 1990-94, exec. com., 1990-94. Mem. Amherst Town Meeting, 1971-73, Franklin-Hampshire Concil for Children, 1974-76, N.J. Commn. Future of State Colls., 1982-84; adv. Commn. on Investing in State Colls., 1993-94. Mem. Assn. Study of Higher Edn., Am. Ednl. Research Assn. (chair div. J govt. relations com., 1986-88, chair div. J comm. on publs. 1988-89, chair spl. interst group futures rsch. and strategic planning 1995—), Am. Polit. Sci. Assn., Policy Studies Orgn., Adelphia (past pres.). Co-author: (with Benjamin D. Stickney) Race and Education: The Unending Controversy, 1981; (with A. Leone, E. Goldberg) The Path to Excellence, 1983; (with Benjamin D. Stickney) The Great Education Debate-Washington and the Schools, 1984, (Choice's award as Outstanding Academic Book, 1985-86), (with Janet Johnson) Blue Ribbon Commissions and Higher Education: Changing Academe from the Outside, 1986, (with Benjamin D. Stickney) Politics and Policy in the Age of Education, 1990. Fighting Words: The Politics of Hateful Speech, 1996; mem. editorial bd. Review of Higher Edn., 1991-95, On the Horizon, 1994—; consulting editor: ASHE/ERIC Higher Edn. Report Series, 1994—; contbr. numerous articles to profl. jours. Home: 33 Forest Ave Medford NJ 08055-3447 Office: Rowan Coll NJ Dept Ednl Adminstrn Glassboro NJ 08028-1701

MARCUS, LEONARD, retail company executive. Sr. v.p. Abraham & Strauss, Bklyn.; pres. COO Abraham & Strauss, Cincinnati, Ohio, 1993—. Office: Abraham & Straus 7 W 7th St Cincinnati OH 45202-2405*

MARCUS, LOLA ELEANOR, elementary and secondary education educator; b. Mass., Apr. 8, 1934; d. Wendel Phillip and Janice Eleanor (Padan) Shedd; m. Bruce Richard Marcus, May 30, 1953; children: Robert Bruce, Craig Donald, Brian Phillip. BS in Edn., Ohio State U., 1962; MA in Econs. Edn., Ohio U., 1982. Tchr. Columbus (Ohio) Pub. Schs., 1962—; dir., cons. Sylvan Learning Ctr., Reynoldsburg, Ohio, 1984—. Elder Blvd. Presbyn. Ch., Columbus, 1990-93. Martha Holden Jennings Found. scholar, 1977-78. Mem. Columbus Edn. Assn. (bldg. rep. 1976), Order of Eastern Star, Alpha Delta Kappa Hon. Educators Sorority, Zeta Phi Eta, Alpha Chi Omega. Presbyterian. Home: 1177 Lincoln Rd Columbus OH 43212-3237

MARCUS, MARIA LENHOFF, lawyer, law educator; b. Vienna, Austria, June 23, 1933; came to U.S., 1938, naturalized, 1944; d. Arthur and Clara (Gruber) Lenhoff; m. Norman Marcus, Dec. 23, 1956; children: Valerie, Nicole, Eric. BA, Oberlin Coll., 1954; JD, Yale Law Sch., 1957. Bar: N.Y. 1961, U.S. Dist. Ct. (so. and ea. dists.) N.Y. 1962, U.S. Ct. Appeals (2d cir.) 1962, U.S. Supreme Ct. 1964. Assoc. counsel NAACP, N.Y.C., 1961-67; asst. atty. gen. N.Y. State, N.Y.C., 1967-78; chief litigation bur. Atty. Gen. N.Y. State, 1976-78; adj. assoc. prof., Law Sch. NYU, 1976-78; assoc. prof. law Fordham Law Sch., N.Y.C., 1978-86, prof. law, 1986—; arbitrator Nat. Assn. Securities Dealers; chair subcom. interrogatories U.S. Dist. Ct. (so. dist.) N.Y., 1983-85. Contbr. articles to profl. jours. Fellow N.Y. Bar Found.; mem. Assn. Bar City of N.Y. (v.p. 1995-96, exec. com. 1976-80, com. audit 1988-95, labor com. 1981-84, judiciary com. 1975-76, chmn. civil rights com. 1972-75), N.Y. State Bar Assn. (exec. com. 1979-81, ho. dels. 1978-81, com. constitution and by-laws 1984-93). Office: Fordham Law Sch 140 W 62d St New York NY 10023

MARCUS, MARIANO NAKAMURA, secondary school principal; b. Weno Chuuk, Federated States Micronesia, Sept. 5, 1961; s. Teruo Ignacio and Machko Ursula (Nakamura) M.; m. Marcelly Kantito, Feb. 28, 1987; children: Antinina, Antinisi, Anter, Anterina, Ancher, Mariano, Mark Metek. BSW, U. Guam, Mangilao, 1986. Registrar Xavier H.S., Weno Chuuk, 1979-80, dean students, 1981-83; rschr. Micronesian Seminar, Weno Chuuk, 1986-87; health educator Dept. Health, Weno Chuuk, 1987-89, mental health counselor, 1989-90; prin. Saramen Chuuk Acad., Weno Chuuk, 1990—; mem. rsch./devel. cadre Pacific Regional Ednl. Lab., Honolulu, 1992—. Sec.-treas. Mechitiw Village, Weno Chuuk, 1990—; chmn. Youth Commn., Weno Chuuk, 1992-94; bd. consultors Xavier H.S., Weno, 1992—; chmn. non-pub. schs., Weno, 1993—; mem. Close Up Washington Program, 1992-94. Mem. ASCD, Nat. Cath. Edn. Assn., Cath. Sch. Adminstrs. Roman Catholic. Home: PO Box 633 Chuuk FM 96942 Office: Saramen Chuuk Academy PO Box 96942 Chuuk FM 96942

MARCUS, NORMAN, lawyer; b. N.Y.C., Aug. 31, 1932; s. David and Evelyn (Freed) M.; m. Maria Eleanor Lenhoff, Dec. 23, 1956; children: Valerie, Nicole, Eric. BA, Columbia U., 1953; LLB, Yale U., 1957. Bar: N.Y. 1958, U.S. Dist. Ct. (so. dist.) 1960, U.S. Supreme Ct. 1964. Assoc. LaPorte & Meyers, N.Y.C., 1957-61; assoc. counsel Stanley Warner Corp., N.Y.C., 1961-63; gen. counsel N.Y.C. Planning Commn. and Dept. of City Planning, 1963-85; ptnr. Finley, Kumble, Wagner, Heine, Underberg, Manley, Myerson & Casey, N.Y.C., 1985-87; counsel Bachner, Tally, Polevoy & Misher, N.Y.C., 1987—; adj. prof. Pratt Inst., Bklyn., 1965-85, NYU Law Sch., 1977—, Benjamin N. Cardozo Sch. Law, N.Y.C., 1983-85, NYU Wagner Sch. Pub. Svc., 1986—, Princeton (N.J.) U. Sch. Architecture, 1990-91. Contbr. articles to profl. jours. Recipient Meritorious Achievement award Am. Planning Assn., 1986. Mem. N.Y. State Bar Assn., Assn. of Bar of City of N.Y., N.Y. County Lawyers Assn. (bd. dirs., chmn. com. on urban devel. and land use), Am. Coll. Real Estate Lawyers, The Fine Arts Fedn. N.Y. (v.p.), Century Club. Avocations: antique books, swimming, drama criticism. Home: 91 Central Park W New York NY 10023-4600 Office: Bachner Tally Polevoy & Misher 380 Madison Ave New York NY 10017-2513 *Solve problems and you leave the world a better place.*

MARCUS, PAUL, lawyer, educator; b. N.Y.C., Dec. 8, 1946; s. Edward and Lillian (Rubin) M.; m. Rebecca Nimmer, Dec. 22, 1968; children: Emily, Beth, Daniel. AB, UCLA, 1968, JD, 1971. Bar: Calif. 1971, U.S. Dist. Ct. (cen. dist.) Calif. 1972, U.S. Ct. Appeals (D.C. cir.) 1972, U.S. Ct. Appeals (7th cir.) 1976. Law clk. U.S. Ct. Appeals (D.C. cir.), 1971-72; assoc. Loeb

& Loeb, L.A., 1972-74; prof. law U. Ill., Urbana, 1974-83; dean Coll. Law U. Ariz., Tucson, 1983-88, prof., 1988-92; Haynes prof. law Coll. William and Mary, Williamsburg, Va., 1992—; reporter, cons. Fed. Jud. Ctr. Commn. Author: The Entrapment Defense, 1989, 2d edit., 1995, The Prosecution and Defense of Criminal Conspiracy, 1978, 3d edit., 1992, Gilbert Law Summary, 1982, 5th edit., 1995, Criminal Law: Cases and Materials, 1982, 3d edit., 1995; nat. reporter on criminal law Internat. of Comparative Law, 1978-94. Mem. accreditatio com. Am. Assn. Law Schs., 1978-81; nat. reporter on criminal law Internat. of Comparative Law, 1978-94. Office: Coll of William and Mary Williamsburg VA 85721

MARCUS, RICHARD ALAN, lawyer, distribution company executive; b. N.Y.C., Aug. 25, 1933; s. Berthold and Dorothy (Kerstin) M.; m. Davys Kay Weisberg, June 4, 1961 (dec. 1992); children: Barbara Jo, Kimberly Ellen, Scott Arak. B.A., CCNY, 1954; J.D., U. Va., 1959. Bar: Va. 1959, N.Y. 1960, Fla. 1960, Minn. bar 1962. Asso. Bernard C. Fuller, Miami Beach, Fla., 1960-62; asso. firm Robbins, Davis, Lyons, Mpls., 1962-64; gen. counsel Napco Internat., Inc., Hopkins, Minn., 1964-86, 68-88, sr. v.p., 1968-86; sec. Napco Internat., Inc., 1980-86; dir. Napco Internat. Ltd.; dir., officer Inter-Ad Inc., Internat. Aircraft Sales and Support, Inc., Ordnance Corp. Am., Napco Export Corp., Napco Internat. (S.A.), Belgium, GmgH, W. Ger.; bd. govs., exec. com. Am. League for Export and Security Assistance, now ret. Pres., dir. Sea Ranch Club Condominium Assn. Inc. Served with AUS, 1954-56. Mem. Am. Soc. Corp. Secs., Nat. Soc. Corp. Planning, Am. Mgmt. Assn., Am. Bar Assn., Sigma Nu Phi, Pi Delta Epsilon. Club: Mpls. LaCrosse. Home: 4900 N Ocean Blvd Apt 621 Fort Lauderdale FL 33308-2932

MARCUS, ROBERT, aluminum company executive; b. Arlington, Mass., Feb. 24, 1925; s. Hymen David and Etta (Arbetter) M.; m. Emily Patricia Ulrich, 1988; children: Lawrence Brian, Janie Sue, Clifford Scott, Emily. AB, Harvard U., 1947; MBA, U. Mich., 1949; MEd, Tufts U., 1950. Market analyst Govt. Commodity Exch., N.Y.C., 1952-54; market rsch. analyst Gen. Electric Co., 1954-55; corp. market analyst Amax Inc., N.Y.C., 1955-62, staff market mgr. aluminum group, 1962-65, pres. internat. aluminum div., 1965-70, v.p., 1970-71; exec. v.p. Amax Pacific Corp., San Mateo, Calif., 1971-72; exec. v.p., dir. Alumax Inc., San Mateo, 1973-82, pres., chief exec. officer, dir., 1982-86; ptnr. Am. Indsl. Ptnrs., San Francisco, 1987-92; dir. Saybrook Inst., 1992—; dir. Domtar, Montreal, 1984-90, Kaiser Aluminum Corp., 1990—. Trustee Mex. Mus., 1988-93. With USN, 1943-46. Mem. Japan Soc. (bd. dirs.). Clubs: Harvard (N.Y.C.); University, Commonwealth, (San Francisco). Home: 2700 Scott St San Francisco CA 94123-4637

MARCUS, ROBERT D., historian, educator; b. Bklyn., Jan. 14, 1936; s. Leonard Roger and Dorothy (Zimmerman) M.; m. Deborah Irene Weisstein, Aug. 13, 1961 (div. 1970); children: Anthony Allen, Elizabeth Sarah; m. Grania Bolton, Mar. 14, 1971 (div. 1989); children: Abigail Whitney, Benjamin Luke; m. Jill Gussow, Dec. 3, 1989; 1 child, Zora Marcus Gussow. B.A., Columbia U., 1957, M.A., 1963; postgrad., Oriel Coll., Oxford U., 1957-58; Ph.D., Northwestern U., 1967. Lectr. in history Ind. U., Bloomington, 1964-67; asst. prof. history SUNY-Stony Brook, 1967-71, assoc. prof., 1971-80, dean undergrad. studies, 1974-80; v.p. acad. affairs Rollins Coll., Winter Park, Fla., 1980-83; v.p. acad. affairs SUNY-Brockport, 1983-92, prof. history, 1992—. Author: Grand Old Party, 1971, A Giant's Strength, 1971, A Brief History of the United States Since 1945, 1975, (with others) America: A Portrait in History, 1978, American Voices, 1992, American Firsthand, 3d edit., 1994. Social Sci. Research Council Faculty Research fellow, 1970; NEH grantee, 1969; Euretta J. Kellett fellow, 1957-58. Mem. Am. Hist. Assn., Orgn. Am. Historians, Phi Beta Kappa. Democrat. Office: State Coll Dept History Brockport NY 14420

MARCUS, RUDOLPH ARTHUR, chemist, educator; b. Montreal, Que., Can., July 21, 1923; came to U.S., 1949, naturalized, 1958; s. Myer and Esther (Cohen) M.; m. Laura Hearne, Aug. 27, 1949; children: Alan Rudolph, Kenneth Hearne, Raymond Arthur. BS in Chemistry, McGill U., 1943, PhD in Chemistry, 1946, DSc (hon.), 1988; DSc (hon.), U. Chgo., 1983, Poly. U., 1986, U. Göteborg, Sweden, 1987, U. N.B., Can., 1993, Queens U., Can., 1993, U. Oxford, Eng., 1995, Yokohama Nat. U., 1996. Rsch. staff mem. RDX Project, Montreal, 1944-46; postdoctoral rsch. assoc. NRC of Can., Ottawa, Ont., 1946-49, U. N.C., 1949-51; asst. prof. Poly. Inst. Bklyn., 1951-54, assoc. prof., 1954-58, prof., 1958-64; prof. U. Ill., Urbana, 1964-78; Arthur Amos Noyes prof. chemistry Calif. Inst. Tech., Pasadena, 1978—; Baker lectr. Cornell U., Ithaca, N.Y., 1991; hon. prof. Fudan U., Shanghai, China, 1994—; hon prof. Inst. Chemistry Chinese Acad. Scis., Beijing, China, 1995—; hon. fellow University Coll., Oxford, England, 1995—; mem. Courant Inst. Math. Scis., NYU, 1960-61; trustee Gordon Rsch. Confs., 1966-69, chmn. bd., 1968-69, mem. coun., 1965-68; mem. rev. panel Argonne Nat. Lab., 1966-72, chmn., 1967-68; mem. rev. panel Brookhaven Nat. Lab., 1971-74; mem. rev. com. Radiation Lab., U. Notre Dame, 1975-80; mem. panel on atmospheric chemistry climatic impact com. NAS-NRC, 1975-78, mem. com. kinetics of chem. reactions, 1973-77, chmn., 1975-77, mem. com. chem. scis., 1977-79, mem. com. to survey opportunities in chem. scis., 1982-86; adv. com. for chemistry NSF, 1977-80, external adv. bd. NSF ctr. Photoinduced Charge Transfer, 1990—; advisor Ctr. for Molecular Scis., Chinese Acad. Scis. and State Key Lab. for Structural Chemistry of Unstable and Stable Species, Beijing, 1995—; vis. prof. theoretical chemistry U. Oxford, Eng., IBM, 1975-76; also professorial fellow Univ. Coll. Former mem. editl. bd. Jour. Chem. Physics, Ann. Rev. Phys. Chemistry, Jour. Phys. Chemistry, Accounts Chem. Rsch., Internat. Jour. Chem. Kinetics Molecular Physics, Theoretica Chimica Acta, Chem. Physics Letters, Faraday Trans., Jour. Chem. Soc.; mem. editl. bd. Laser Chemistry, 1982—, Advances in Chem. Physics, 1984—, World Sci. Pub., 1987—, Internat. Revs. in Phys. Chemistry, 1988—, Progress in Physics, Chemistry and Mechanics (China), 1989—, Perkins Transactions 2, Jour. Chem. Soc., 1992—, Chem. Physics Rsch. (India), 1992—, Trends in Chem. Physics Rsch. (India), 1992—; hon. editor Internat. Jour. Quantum Chemistry, 1996—. Treas. L.A. Cen. City Assn., 1995. Alfred P. Sloan fellow, 1960-61, sr. postdoctoral fellow NSF, 1960-61; sr. Fulbright-Hays scholar, 1972; recipient Sr. U.S. Scientist award Alexander von Humboldt-Stiftung, 1976, Electrochem. Soc. Lecture award Electrochem. Soc., 1979, Robinson medal Faraday divsn. Royal Soc. Chemistry, 1982, Centenary medal Faraday divsn., 1988, Chandler medal, Columbia U., 1983, Wolf prize in Chemistry, 1985, Nat. Medal of Sci., 1989, Evans award Ohio State U., 1990, Nobel prize in Chemistry, 1992, Hirshfelder prize in Theoretical Chemistry, U. Wis., 1993, Golden Plate award Am. Acad. Achievement, 1993, Lavoisier medal French Chem. Soc., 1994; named Hon. Citizen, City of Winnipeg, 1994, Treasure of L.A., Ctrl. City Assn., 1995. Fellow AAAS, Am. Acad. Arts and Scis. (hon., exec. com. western sect., co-chmn. 1981-84, rsch. and planning com. 1989-91), Am. Phys. Soc., Internat. Soc. Electrochemistry (hon.), Royal Soc. Chemistry (hon.), Royal Soc. London (hon.), Internat. Acad. Quantum Molecular Sci. (hon.), Royal Soc. Can. (hon.); mem. NAS (hon.), Am. Philos. Soc. (hon.), Am. Chem. Soc. (past divsn. chmn., mem. exec. com., mem. adv. bd. petroleum rsch. fund, Irving Langmuir award in chem. physics 1978, Pter Debye award in phys. chemistry 1988, Willard Gibbs medal Chgo. sect. 1988, S.C. Lind Lecture, East Tenn. sect. 1988, Theodore William Richards medal Northwestern sect. 1990, Edgar Fahs Smith award Phila. sect. 1991, Ira Remsen Meml. award Md. sect. 1991medal Portland, Oreg., and Puget Sound sect. 1991), Internat. Acad. Quantum Molecular Sci. (hon.). Achievements include responsibility for the Marcus Theory of electron transfer reactions in chemical systems and RRKM theory of unimolecular reactions. Home: 331 S Hill Ave Pasadena CA 91106-3405

MARCUS, RUTH BARCAN, philosopher, educator, writer, lecturer; b. N.Y.C.; d. Samuel and Rose (Post) Barcan; divorced; children: James Spencer, Peter Webb, Katherine Hollister, Elizabeth Post. BA, NYU, 1941; MA, Yale U., 1942, PhD, 1946; LHD (hon.), U. Ill., 1995. Rsch. assoc. in anthropology Inst. for Human Relations, Yale U., New Haven, Conn., 1945-47; AAUW fellow, 1947-48; vis. prof. (intermittently) Northwestern U., 1950-57, Guggenheim fellow, 1953-54; asst. prof., assoc. prof. Roosevelt U., Chgo., 1957-63; NSF fellow, 1963-64; prof. philosophy U. Ill. at Chgo., 1964-70, head philosophy dept., 1963-69; fellow U. Ill. Center for Advanced Study, 1968-69; prof. philosophy Northwestern U., 1970-73; Reuben Post Halleck prof. philosophy Yale U., 1973-93; sr. rsch. scholar, 1994—; fellow Ctr. Advanced Study in Behavioral Sci., Stanford, Calif., 1979; vis. fellow Inst. Advanced Study, U. Edinburgh, 1983, Wolfson Coll., Oxford U., 1985, 86; vis. fellow Clare Hall, Cambridge U., 1988, lifetime mem. common room, 1989—; past or present mem. adv. coms. Princeton U., MIT, Calif. Inst. Tech., Cornell U. Humanities Ctr., Columbia U., UCLA, others. Author: Modalities, 1993; editor: The Logical Enterprise, 1975, Logic Methodology and Philosophy of Science VII, 1986; mem. editorial bd. Past or Present Metaphilosophy, Monist, Philos. Studies, Signs, Jour. Symbolic Logic, The Philosophers Annual; editor, contbr. to profl. jours. and books. Recipient Machette prize for contbn. to profession; Medal, College de France, 1986; Mellon sr. fellow Nat. Humanities Ctr., 1992-93; vis. disting. prof. U. Calif., Irvine, 1994; fellow Conn. Acad. Arts & Scis. Fellow Am. Acad. Arts and Scis.; mem. Coun. on Philos. Studies (pres. 1988—), Assn. for Symbolic Logic (past exec. coun., exec. com. 1973-83, v.p. 1980-82, coun. 1980-85, pres. 1982-84), Am. Philos. Assn. (past sec., treas., nat. bd. dirs. 1967-83, pres. ctrl. divsn. 1975-78, chmn. nat. bd. officers 1977-85), Philosophy of Sci. Assn., Inst. Internat. Philosophie (past exec. com., v.p. 1983-86, pres. 1990-93, hon. pres. 1994—), Fedn. Internat. Philosophy (exec. com., steering com. 1985—), Elizabethan Club (v.p. 1989, pres. 1989-90), Phi Beta Kappa (professorial lectr. 1993). Office: Yale U Dept Philosophy PO Box 208306 New Haven CT 06525-0650

MARCUS, SHELDON, social sciences educator; b. N.Y.C., Aug. 4, 1937; s. Manny and Sarah (Lande) M.; m. Phyllis Knight; children: Beth, Jonathan, Evan. B.A., CCNY, 1959, M.S., 1960; Ed.D., Yeshiva U., 1970. Tchr. N.Y.C. Pub. Schs., 1959-68; lectr. social sci. CUNY, 1965-68; mem. faculty Fordham U., N.Y.C., 1968-70, chmn. div. urban edn., 1970-76, assoc. dean grad. edn. Tarrytown campus, 1976-93, prof., 1993—; mem. exec. bd. tchr. corps program U.S. Office Edn., 1974-82; trustee Doctoral Assn. N.Y., 1973-82; co-dir. Fordham Inst. for Rsch. on Supervision and Tchg., 1992-94, Fordham U./N.Y.C. Supts. Network, 1995—. Author or co-author: Conflicts in Urban Education, 1970; Urban Education: Crisis or Opportunity?, 1972; Father Coughlin: The Tumultuous Life of the Priest of the Little Flower, 1973, (nominated for Pulitzer Prize); The Urban In-Service Education Experience, 1977; Administrative Decision Making in Schools: A Case Study Approach to Strategic Planning, 1986, Strategic Planning: A Case Study Approach to Administrative Decision Making. Case Teaching Notes, 1987; contbr. articles to profl. jours. Recipient Scanlon award for contbns. to edn., 1992, Adminstr. of Yr. award Phi Delta Kappa, 1993. Mem. Am. Ednl. Rsch. Assn. (proposal reviewer 1992—). Home: 36 Pocantico River Rd Pleasantville NY 10570-3510 Office: Fordham U Sch Edn Tarrytown Campus Tarrytown NY 10591

MARCUS, STANLEY, federal judge; b. 1946. BA, CUNY, 1967; JD, Harvard U., 1971. Assoc. Botein, Hays, Sklar & Herzberg, N.Y.C., 1974-75; asst. atty. U.S. Dist. Ct. (ea. dist.) N.Y., 1975-78; spl. atty., dep. chief U.S. organized crime sect. Detroit Strike Force, 1978-79, chief U.S. organized crime sect., 1980-82; U.S. atty. So. Dist. of Fla., Miami, 1982-85; judge U.S. Dist. Ct. (so. dist.) Fla., Miami, 1985—. Office: US Dist Ct 301 N Miami Ave Miami FL 33128-7702*

MARCUS, STEPHEN A., lawyer; b. Chgo., Nov. 25, 1943. BS, U. Ill., 1965; JD, Northwestern U., 1968. Bar: Ill. 1968. Ptnr. Holleb & Coff, Chgo. Mem. ABA (mem. bus. law sect.), Chgo. Bar Assn. (mem. securities law com.), Chgo. Coun. Lawyers. Office: Holleb & Coff 55 E Monroe St Ste 3900 Chicago IL 60603-5803*

MARCUS, STEPHEN HOWARD, hospitality and entertainment company executive; b. Mpls., May 31, 1935; s. Ben D. and Celia Marcus; m. Joan Glasspiegel, Nov. 3, 1962; children: Greg, David, Andrew. B.B.A., U. Wis., Madison, 1957; LL.B., U. Mich., 1960. Bar: Wis. 1960. V.p. Pfister Hotel Corp., Milw., 1963-69; exec. v.p. Pfister Hotel Corp., 1969-75; pres. Marcus Hotel Corp., Milw., 1975-91; chmn., chief oper. officer Marcus Corp., Milw., 1980—; chief oper. officer Marcus Corp., 1988, also dir., CEO; exec. v.p. Marc Plaza Corp.; v.p. Wis. Big Boy Corp., Marcus Theatres Corp.; dir. Med. Coll. Wis., 1986—; dir. Preferred Hotels Assn., 1972—, chmn. bd., 1979; dir. Bank One N.A. Pres. Milw. Conv. and Visitors Bur., 1970-71, bd. dirs., mem. exec. com., 1968—; chmn. Wis. Gov.'s Adv. Council on Tourism, 1976-81; bd. dirs. Multiple Sclerosis Soc. Milw., 1965-67, Milw. Jewish Fedn., 1968-76, Milw. Jewish Chronicle, 1973-76, Children's Hosp. Found., Inc., Competitive Wis.; asso. chmn. bus. div. United Fund Campaign, Milw., 1971; co-chmn. spl. gifts com. United Performing Arts Fund, Milw., 1972-74, bd. dirs., 1973-81, chmn. maj. gifts, 1982, co-chmn., 1983—; bd. dirs. Friends of Art, Milw., 1973-74; pres. Summerfest, 1975; bd. dirs. MECCA, Milw., 1975-82, mem. exec. com., 1977; bd. dirs. Jr. Achievement, Milw., 1976—; trustee Mt. Sinai Med. Center, 1977—, Nat. Symphony Orchestra, 1985; bd. govs. Jewish Community Campus; co-chmn. Ann. Freedom Fund Dinner, NAACP, 1980-81; chmn. Icebreaker Festival, 1989. Served with U.S. Army, 1960-61. Recipient Ben Nickoll award Milw. Jewish Fedn., 1969, Headliner award Milw. Press Club, 1986, Humanitarian award NCCJ, 1988, Lamplighter award Greater Milw. Conv. and Visitors Bur., 1991. Mem. Am. Hotel and Motel Assn. (dir. 1976-79, exec. com. 1978-79), Greater Milw. Hotel and Motel Assn. (pres. 1967-68), Wis. Innkeepers Assn. (pres. 1972-73), Variety Club, Milw. Assn. Commerce (bd. dirs. 1982-85), Downtown Assn., Young Pres.'s Orgn., Wis. Assn. Mfrs. and Commerce (dir. 1978-82), Greater Milw. Com. (dir. 1981). Office: The Marcus Corporation 250 E Wisconsin Ave Ste 1700 Milwaukee WI 53202-4208*

MARCUS, STEPHEN HOWARD, lawyer; b. N.Y.C., June 30, 1945; s. Jacob and Mildren (Cohen) M.; m. Carol Sylvia Beatrice, June 11, 1967; children: Joshua David, Rebecca Lynn, Daniel Benjamin. BME, MIT, 1967; JD, Harvard U., 1970. Bar: Calif. 1971, U.S. Dist. Ct. (cen. dist.) Calif. 1971, U.S. Dist. Ct. (so. dist.) Calif. 1974, U.S. Dist. Ct. (so. dist.) Calif. 1975, U.S. Ct. Appeals (9th cir.) 1980. Assoc. Mitchell, Silberberg & Knopp, L.A., 1971-72, Greenberg, Bernhard, Weis & Karma, L.A., 1972-76; ptnr. Greenberg, Bernhard, Weiss & Rosin, L.A., 1976-85; assoc. Frandzel & Share, L.A., 1985-87, ptnr., 1987—; judge pro tem L.A. Mcpl. Ct., 1976-83. Editor Harvard Law Rev., 1970. Mem. Los Angeles County Bar Assn. (arbitrator client rels. com. 1982—), Century City Bar Assn. (bd. govs. 1985—), MIT Club So. Calif. (pres. 1978-79, bd. govs. 1979—), Sigma Xi, Tau Beta Pi. Democrat. Jewish. Avocations: senior soccer, skiing, square dancing. Office: Frandzel & Share 6500 Wilshire Blvd Los Angeles CA 90048

MARCUS, STEVEN, dean, English educator; b. N.Y.C., Dec. 13, 1928; s. Nathan and Adeline Muriel (Gordon) M.; m. Gertrud Lenzer, Jan. 20, 1966; 1 son, John Nathaniel. Ph.D., Columbia U., 1961; D.H.L. (hon.), Clark U., 1985. Prof. English Columbia U., 1966—, George Delacorte prof. humanities, 1976—, chmn. dept. English and comparative lit., 1977-80, 85-90; v.p. Sch. of Arts and Scis., 1993-95; dean Columbia Coll., 1993-95; dir. planning Nat. Humanities Center, 1974-76; chmn. exec. com. bd. dirs. Nat. Humanities Ctr., 1976-80, 96—, also bd. dirs.; chmn. Lionel Trilling Seminars, 1976-80. Author: Dickens: From Pickwick to Dombey, 1965, The Other Victorians, 1966, Engels, Manchester and the Working Class, 1974, Representations, 1976, Doing Good, 1978, Freud and The Culture of Psychoanalysis, 1984; Assoc. editor: Partisan Rev. Co-dir. Heyman Ctr. for the Humanities. With AUS, 1954-56. Guggenheim Found. fellow, 1967-68; Nat. Humanities Ctr. fellow, 1980-82; Rockefeller Found. fellow in humanities, 1980-81; fellow Ctr. Advanced Studies in the Behavioral Scis., 1972-73. Fellow Am. Acad. Arts and Scis., Acad. Lit. Studies; mem. Columbia Soc. Fellows in Humanities (co-chmn.), Am. Psychoanalytic Assn. (hon.), Inst. for Psychoanalytic Tng. and Rsch. (hon.), Am. Acad. Psychoanalysis (sci. assoc.). Home: 39 Claremont Ave New York NY 10027-6824

MARCUS, STEVEN IRL, electrical engineering educator; b. St. Louis, Apr. 2, 1949; s. Herbert A. and Peggy L. (Polishuk) M.; m. Jeanne M. Wilde, June 4, 1978; children: Jeremy A., Tobin L. BA, Rice U., 1971; SM, MIT, 1972, PhD, 1975. Research engr. The Analytic Scis. Corp., Reading, Mass., 1973; asst. prof. U. Tex., Austin, 1975-80, assoc. prof., 1980-84, prof., 1984-91, assoc. chmn., dept. elec. and computer engring., 1984-89, L.B. Meaders prof. engring., 1987-91; prof. elec. engring., dir. Inst. for Systems Rsch. U. Md., College Park, 1991—; cons. Tracor Inc., Austin, 1977, 90. Assoc. editor Math. of Control Signals and Systems, 1987—, Jour. on Discrete Event Dynamic Systems, 1990, Acta Applicandae Mathematicae, 1983—. NSF fellow, 1971-74; Werner W. Dornberger Centennial Teaching fellowship in engring., U. Tex., Austin, 1982-84. Fellow IEEE (prize paper awards com. 1985-88, field awards com. 1989-90, assoc. editor Transactions Info. Theory 1990-92), IEEE Control Systems Soc. (bd. govs. 1985-90, chmn. conf. on decision and control program com. 1983, chmn. working group on stochastic control and estimation 1984-87, assoc. editor Transactions Automatic Control 1980-81); mem. Am. Math. Soc., Soc. Indsl. and Applied Math. (editor Jour. Control and Optimization 1990—), Acta Applicandae Math., 1983—, Eta Kappa Nu, Tau Beta Pi. Home: 9516 Thornhill Rd Silver Spring MD 20901-4836 Office: U Md Inst for Systems Rsch 2167 Av Williams Bldg 115 College Park MD 20742

MARCUS, WILLIAM MICHAEL, rubber and vinyl products manufacturing company executive; b. Boston, Jan. 31, 1938; s. Richard and Diana (Litch) M.; m. Cynthia Steinman, Dec. 9, 1962; children: Melanie, Daniel, Richard. B.S. in Bus. Adminstrn., Babson Inst., 1959. With Am. Biltrite Inc., Wellesley Hills, Mass., 1960—; exec. v.p., treas. Am. Biltrite Inc., 1983—, also dir.; bd. dirs. Reebok Internat. Inc., Congoleum Corp. Served with U.S. Army, 1960-61. Office: Am Biltrite Inc 57 River St Wellesley MA 02181-2006

MARCUSA, FRED HAYE, lawyer; b. Paterson, N.J., Jan. 31, 1946; s. Harry and Alice Marcusa; m. Andrea Disario, Jun. 28, 1986; children: Michael, Daniel. A.B., Dartmouth Coll., 1967; J.D., U. Pa., 1970. Bar: N.Y. 1971. Assoc. Davis, Polk & Wardwell, N.Y.C., 1970-79; v.p., gen. counsel The Coca-Cola Bottling Co. of N.Y., Inc., N.Y.C., 1979-81; ptnr. Kaye, Scholer, Fierman, Hays & Handler, N.Y.C., 1981—. Office: Kaye Scholer Fierman Hays & Handler 425 Park Ave New York NY 10022-3506

MARCUSE, ADRIAN GREGORY, academic administrator; b. N.Y.C., Mar. 25, 1922; s. Maxwell Frederick and Mildred Ann (Hitter) M.; m. Janet Constance Radlo, Oct. 28, 1945 (dec. Mar. 22, 1980); children: Nancy Ruth Marcuse Marshall, Sally Ann Marcuse Crawford, Elizabeth Susan Marcuse Peterman; m. Betty Jane Lieberman Rossman, Jan. 11, 1985; 1 stepchild, Amy Beth Rossman Schurtz. BS, MIT, 1942, MS, 1946; LLD (hon.), Lab Inst. Merchandising, 1992. Registered profl. engr. N.Y., Fla. Rsch. assoc. MIT, Cambridge, Mass., 1945-46; rsch. scientist United Aircraft Co., E. Hartford, Conn., 1946-47; application engr. Westinghouse Electric Corp., Boston, N.Y.C., 1947-60; consulting engr. pvt. practice, N.Y.C., 1955-62; v.p. mktg. and sales Corrosion Control Corp., N.Y.C., 1960-62; sales & merchandising mgr. B. Altman & Co., N.Y.C., 1962; v.p., chief operating officer Lab. Inst. of Merchandising, N.Y.C., 1962-72, pres., chief exec. officer, 1972—; pres. LIM Fashion Edn. Found., N.Y.C., 1978—; chmn. Assn. Regionally Accredited Prvt. Colls. and Univs., Washington, 1990-93. Charter commr. City of Glen Cove, N.Y., 1964, chmn. bd. engrs., 1964-68, mem. planning bd., 1980-87; past treas. Community Concert Assn., Glen Cove; past trustee and budget chmn. North Country Reform Temple, Glen Cove; past mem. YMCA Fund-Raising Coun., Glen Cove. 1st lt. USAAF, 1942-45, PTO. Mem. Am. Assn. Higher Edn., Nat. Assn. Coll. Admissions Counselors, Assn. Proprietary Colls. (former pres., chmn.), N.Y. State Assn. Two-Yr. Colls., N.Y. State Counselors Assn., Soc. Sigma Xi. Republican. Avocations: sailing, bicycling, travel, theater. Office: Lab Inst of Merchandising 12 E 53rd St New York NY 10022-5208

MARCUSE, DIETRICH, retired physicist; b. Koenigsberg, East Prussia, Germany, Feb. 27, 1929; came to U.S., 1957; s. Richard and Gertrud (Solty) M.; m. Haide Schwarz, Jan. 13, 1959; children: Christina, Mikel. Diplom Physiker, Freie Universität, Berlin, 1954; Doktor Ingenieur, Karlsruhe Universität, 1962. Mem. tech. staff Siemens and Halske, Berlin, 1954-57; mem. tech. staff AT&T Bell Labs., Holmdel, N.J., 1957-94, dist. mem. tech. staff, 1982-94; ret., 1994. Author: Principles of Quantum-Electronics, 2d edit., 1980, Light Transmission Optics, 2d edit., 1982, Theory of Dielectric Optical Wave-guides, 1972, 2nd edit.,1991, Principles of Optical Fiber Measurements, 1981; also over 200 articles. Fellow IEEE (Quantum Electronics award 1981), Optical Soc. Am. (Max Born award 1989).

MARCUSS, STANLEY JOSEPH, lawyer; b. Hartford, Conn., Jan. 24, 1942; s. Stanley Joseph and Anne Sutton (Leone) M.; m. Rosemary Daly, July 6, 1968; children: Elena Daly, Aidan Stanley. BA, Trinity Coll., 1963, Cambridge U., 1965; MA, Cambridge U., 1968; JD, Harvard U., 1968. Bar: D.C., N.Y., Conn., U.S. Supreme Ct. Staff atty. office of gen. counsel HUD, Washington, 1968; atty. firm Hogan and Hartson, Washington, 1968-73; counsel to internat. fin. subcom. U.S. Senate Com. on Banking, Housing and Urban Affairs, 1973-77; dep. asst. sec. for trade regulation Dept. Commerce, Washington, 1977-78; sr. dep. asst. sec. for industry and trade Dept. Commerce, 1978-79, acting asst. sec. for industry and trade, 1979-80, acting asst. sec. for trade regulation, 1980; mem. firm Milbank, Tweed, Hadley & McCloy, Washington, 1980-93, Bryan Cave, 1993—; former adj. prof. Am. U. Law Sch. Author: Effective Washington Representation, 1983; mem. bd. overseers U. Calif. Berkeley Law Jour.; contbr. articles to profl. jours. Former trustee Trinity Coll., Hartford. Marshall scholar. Mem. ABA, D.C. Bar (former chmn., steering com. internat. law div.), Phi Beta Kappa. Home: 4616 29th Pl NW Washington DC 20008-2105

MARCUVITZ, NATHAN, electrophysics educator; b. Bklyn., Dec. 29, 1913; s. Samuel and Rebecca (Feiner) M.; m. Muriel Spanier, June 30, 1946; children—Andrew, Karen. B.E.E., Poly. Inst. Bklyn., 1935, M.E.E., 1941, D.E.E., 1947; Laurea Honoris Causa, Politecnico Di Torino, 1993. Engr. RCA Labs., 1936-40; research asso. Radiation Lab., Mass. Inst. Tech., 1941-46; asst. prof. elec. engring. Poly. Inst. Bklyn., 1946-49, asso. prof., 1949-51, prof., 1951-65; dir. Poly. Inst. Bklyn. (Microwave Research Inst.), 1957-61; v.p. research, acting dean Poly. Inst. Bklyn. (Grad. Center), 1961-63, prof. electrophysics, 1961-66, dean research, dean, 1964-65; asst. dir. def. research and engring. Dept. Def., Washington, 1963-64; prof. applied physics N.Y.U., 1966-73; prof. electrophysics Poly. Inst. N.Y., 1973—, prof. emeritus, 1978—; vis. prof. Harvard U., spring 1971. Author: Waveguide Handbook, Vol. 10, 1951, (with L. Felsen) Radiation and Scattering of Waves, 1973; also numerous articles. Recipient Microwave Career award IEEE Microwave Theory and Techniques Soc., 1985. Fellow IEEE (Heinrich Hertz medal 1989); mem. Nat. Acad. Engring., Am. Phys. Soc., Sigma Xi, Tau Beta Pi, Eta Kappa Nu. Home: 7 Ridge Dr E Great Neck NY 11021-2806 Office: Polytech U Rt 110 Farmingdale NY 11735

MARCY, CHARLES FREDERICK, food products company executive; b. Buffalo, Aug. 25, 1950; s. Charles and Mary Jane (Frederick) M.; m. Helen Jean Shank, May 6, 1972 (div. Dec. 1986); children: Michelle Catherine, Adam Charles; m. Cynthia Louise Shockey, June 17, 1989; 1 child, Brooke Allison. BA, Washington and Jefferson Coll., Washington, Pa., 1972; MBA, Harvard U., 1974. Various mktg. and strategic planning positions Gen. Foods Corp., White Plains, N.Y., 1974-84; v.p. mktg. Sara Lee Bakery, Deerfield, Ill., 1984-86; v.p., gen. mgr. Wolferman's Inc., (Divsn. of Sara Lee Corp.), Lenexa, Kans., 1987-89; v.p. strategy and mktg. Kraft Gen. Foods Frozen Products, Glenview, Ill., 1989-90; pres. Kraft Gen. Foods Nat. Dairy Products Corp., Phila., 1991-92, Golden Grain Co., Pleasanton, Calif., 1993—. Bd. dirs. Phila. Police Athletic League, 1991-92, Boys and Girls Club of Kansas City, Mo., 1987-90, Lake Forest (Ill.) Symphony, 1984-87. Office: Golden Grain Co 4576 Willow Rd Pleasanton CA 94588-2708*

MARD, MICHAEL JOSEPH, business appraiser; b. St. Louis, July 30, 1947; s. Joseph Raymond and Geneva (Plumlee) M.; m. Pamela Louise Johnston, June 28, 1985; 1 child, Michael Seph. BS in Acctg., U. South Fla., 1974, M in Acctg., 1977. Fin. and operational auditor Peat, Marwick, Mitchell & Co., 1974-78; sec., treas., supervising sr. auditor Kemper Group of Ins. Cos., 1978-83; v.p. Valtec Assocs., Inc., 1983-85; pres. The Fin. Valuation Group, Tampa, Fla., 1985—. Contbr. articles to profl. jours. Served with USN, 1971. Mem. AICPA, Am. Soc. Appraisers (accredited sr.; program chair internat. appraisal conf. 1991-92, bus. valuation com. 1993—), Inst. Bus. Appraisers, Fla. Inst. CPAs (chmn. bus. valuation ad hoc subcom. of litigation com. 1992, chmn. litigation svcs. com. 1994—), Inst. Mgmt. Accts., Tampa Bay Estate Planning Coun., The ESOP Assn., Nat. Ctr. for Employee Ownership, Assn. Eminent Domain Profls., Tampa C. of C. Office: The Fin Valuation Group 8074 N 56th St Tampa FL 33617-7620

MARDAR, DIANNA, reporter; b. Phila., May 1, 1948. BA in Journalism summa cum laude, Temple U., 1984. Reporter city desk The Philadelphia Inquirer, 1985—; instr. Temple U., Phila., 1992. Recipient George Polk award Long Island U., 1990, Nat. Headliners award Atlantic City Press Assn., investigative, 1990, Investigative Editors and Reporters award reporting call, 1990. Office: Phila Inquirer 400 N Broad St Philadelphia PA 19130-4015

MARDEN, ANNE ELLIOTT ROBERTS, estates and trust specialist; b. N.Y.C., Dec. 17, 1935; d. James Ragan and Jane Ziegler (Elliott) Roberts; m. George Linn Davis, May 29, 1955 (div. Aug. 1967); children: James Roberts, Elliott Britton, George Linn Jr., William Vaughn (dec.); m. Robert Gray Peck III, Oct. 24, 1969 (div. April 1993); children: Andrew Adams, Matthew Canfield Roberts; m. John Newcomb Marden, June 26, 1993. BA in English with honors, Wellesley Coll., 1957; MA in English and Comparative Lit. with honors, Columbia U., 1966; postgrad. in law Villanova U., 1978-80, U. Bridgeport, 1988; Bus. Law and Corp. Fin. diploma, The Phila. Inst., 1988. Contbg. editor Newsfront mag., 1960-63; English tchr. The Masters Sch., Dobbs Ferry, N.Y., 1963-65; sports feature writer Westchester-Rockland newspapers, Reporter Dispatch, Gannett chain, White Plains, N.Y., 1969-70; corr., weekly column Knickerbocker News-Union Star, Schenectady Gazette, Capital Newspapers, Hearst chain, Albany and Schenectady, N.Y., 1971-73; on-screen TV panel moderator "Access", Channel 17, Albany, 1971-73; pub. and exec. tax preparer H & R Block, Inc., Wayne, Pa., 1976-79; sr. estate planning trust officer Provident Nat. Bank-Trust div. PNC Bank, Phila., 1981-86; asst. v.p., trust officer estate planning dept., trusts and investments div. Mellon Bank (East) N.A., 1986-87; asst v.p., trust officer People's Bank, Stamford, Conn., 1987-88; estates and trusts paralegal estates dept. Pepper, Hamilton and Scheetz, Berwyn, Pa., 1988-89; pres., ptnr. ChoirMaster, Inc., 1988—; estate and trusts paralegal adminstr. Blank, Rome, Comisky and McCauley, Phila., 1989—. Mem. Mus. Art and Sci. acquisitions com., Schenectady, N.Y., 1960-68; asst. producer "Poetry", Channel 25-TV, N.Y.C.; bd. dirs., legis. chmn. Greenacres Sch. PTA, 1967-69; pub. rels. chmn. Planned Parenthood League, Schenectady; sec., parliamentarian N.Y. State Legis. Forum, 1971-73; pres., founder TheCareer Group, Phila., 1983-85; editorcongregation directory St. David's Episcopal Ch., 1976, mem. exec. com. every-member canvass, 1977; ann. fair gates-keeper, Episcopal Diocese Phila., 1974-80, rep. Merion Deanery; lector St. James the Less Ch., Scarsdale, N.Y., 1995—; maj. gift solicitor Planned Parenthood Southeastern Pa., 1975-76; mem. plant sale exec. com. and Merry Mart com. Haverford Sch., 1976, 77; Rep. pollchecker Tredyffrin Twp., 1978, 79; majority insp. of elections Tredyffrin Twp. E-2, 1980—; mem. ARC; vol. Armed Svcs. to Mil. Families and Vets. and Emergency Svcs., Phila., Major Gifts Campaign, White Plains, N.Y., 1994-95, Hospice of Westchester, Inc. (diploma), 1994. Recipient prize Coll. Bd. Contest Mademoiselle mag., 1954, Prix de Paris, Vogue mag., 1957. Mem. DAR (bd. mgrs.-pub. rels. Phila. chpt., treas. 1983) Phila. Bicentennial Celebration com. 1976), AAUW (bd. dir. Schenectady 1971-73, legis. chmn. Valley Forge br., Albany-Schenectady br.), Schenectady County Mus. of Arts and Sci., N.Y. State Women's Press Club (Capital dist. br.), Jr. League Phila. (sustainer, pub. affairs com., art com., edn. com., child abuse ctr. com., Bicentennial Cookbook com., Waterworks Restoration com., 1984, bd. dirs. 1960-61), Schenectady Curling Club, Valley Forge Coun. Rep. Women, Mohawk Golf Club (Schenectady), Shenorock Shore Club (Rye, N.Y.), The Merion Cricket Club (Haverford, Pa.), Acorn Club (Phila.), Little Acorns Investment Club, Career Group W. in P. (founder, chair 1983-85), Nat. Soc. Daus. Am. Revolution, Jeptha Abbott Chap (Bryn Mawr), Wellesley Alumnae (Phila.), Phila. Assn. Paralegals, Phila. Bar Assn. (probate and trust law sect., non-lawyer assoc.), Phila. Estate Planning Coun., Chester County Estate Planning Coun., Little Egg Harbor Yacht Club (Beach Haven, N.J.), Jr. League of Phila. (sustainer, waterworks restoration com., pub. affairs com.). Republican. Episcopalian.

MARDEN, JOHN NEWCOMB, lawyer; b. N.Y.C., Feb. 14, 1935; s. Orison S. and Virginia (McAvoy) M.; children: Cynthia, Elizabeth; m. Anne Roberts. BA, Yale U., 1957; LLB, Cornell U., 1960. Bar: N.Y. 1960. Assoc. Curtis, Mallet Prevost Colt & Mosle, N.Y.C., 1960-69, ptnr., 1969—. Republican. Office: Curtis Mallet Prevost Colt & Mosle 101 Park Ave New York NY 10178

MARDEN, KENNETH ALLEN, advertising executive; b. Englewood, N.J., Dec. 12, 1928; s. Allen H. and Doris (Littlefield) M.; m. Julia Lee Black, June 11, 1949; children—Priscilla Anne, Emily Gage. B.A., U. Maine, 1950. Hosp. salesman Johnson & Johnson, New Brunswick, N.J., 1959-61, product dir. hosp. div., 1962-68, advt., pub. relations mgr. hosp. div., 1969-71, group product dir., patient care div., 1972-74, advt. dir. patient care div., 1974-78; v.p. F.J. Axelrod, Inc., N.Y.C., 1978-80; v.p. account mgmt. Vicom/FCB, Phila., 1980-87; pres. Am. Kennel Club, N.Y., 1987-90, cons. on dog legislation, 1990—, also bd. dirs.; pres. Crossing Creek Comm., 1991—; bd. dirs. The Dog Mus., 1995—. 1st lt. U.S. Army, 1951-53. Mem. DogWriters Assn. Am. Republican. Episcopalian. Clubs: German Shorthaired Pointer of Am. (del. 1976—, v.p. 1985-86), Eastern German Shorthaired Pointer (pres. 1972-74, 95-96), Jersey Rag Racers (pres. 1994-96), Kennel Club Phila. (bd. dirs.), Hunterdon Hills Kennel, Nat. Animal Interest Alliance (bd. dirs. 1994—), Nat. Breed Clubs Alliance (v.p. 1996—). Home: Crossing Creek Farm 53 Nedsland Ave Titusville NJ 08560-1715 Office: Crossing Creek Communications 53 Nedsland Ave Titusville NJ 08560-1715

MARDEN, PHILIP AYER, physician, educator; b. Newport, N.H., Oct. 31, 1911; s. Albion Sullivan and Laura Isobel (McEchern) M.; m. Magdalen Rekus, Aug. 5, 1950. A.B., Dartmouth, 1933; student, Med. Sch., 1933-34; M.D., U. Pa., 1936. Intern Presbyn. Hosp., Phila., 1936-38; chief resident Delaware County Hosp., Drexel Hill, Pa., 1938-39; fellow otolaryngology U. Pa. Hosp., 1939-40, chief otolaryngology, 1959-72; mem. faculty U. Pa. Med. Sch., 1940—, prof. dept. otolaryngology, 1959—; chief otolaryngology, div. A Phila. Gen. Hosp., 1959-94; emeritus prof. dept. otolaryngology U. Pa. Med. Sch., 1994—; cons. Presbyn. Hosp., Phila., VA Hosp., Phila., Phila. Gen. Hosp. Served to maj., M.C. AUS, 1942-46, CBI. Mem. AMA, Am. Acad. Ophthalmology and Otolaryngology, A.C.S., Coll. Physicians Phila., Phi Beta Kappa, Sigma Xi. Home: 163 Vassar Rd Bala Cynwyd PA 19004-2135

MARDENBOROUGH, LESLIE A., newspaper publishing company executive. V.p. human resources The New York Times Co. Office: The New York Times Co 229 W 43rd St New York NY 10036-3913

MARDER, AMY RUTH, medical educator; b. N.Y.C., Dec. 20, 1952. BA in Biology & Ethology magna cum laude, U. Pa., 1973, DVM magna cum laude, 1979. Intern in medicine and surgery Grand Ave Pet Hosp, 1980; residency in animal behavior U. Pa., 1985; clin. asst prof. dept. medicine Tufts U. Sch. Vet. Medicine, 1985—; animal behavior cons.; part-time assoc. vet. Somerville (Mass.) Animal Clinic, 1987—, Wellesley-Natick Vet. Hosp., Natick, Mass., 1986-88. Author: Your Healthy Pet, 1994; writer and cons. Prevention Mag., 1987—; staff writer Animals Mag. MSPCA, Boston, 1992—; contbr. articles to profl. pubs. including Vet. Clinic of N.Am., Pet Veterinarian, others. Mem. Am. Vet. Soc. Animal Behavior (pres.-elect 1984-86, pres. 1986-88), Am. Vet. Med. Assn., Animal Behavior Soc., The Delta Soc., Mass. Vet. Med. Assn. Home: 46 Madison Ave Cambridge MA 02140

MARDER, JOHN G., real estate investor, marketing consultant, corporate director; b. N.Y.C., Dec. 27, 1926; s. Joseph T. and Rhea (Greenspun) M.; m. Barbara Sand, 1956 (div. 1971); children; Jonathan Allen, Susan Beth, Jane Alison; m. Joan Kron, 1971. Student, Cornell, 1944-45; B.S., Columbia U. Sch. Bus., 1950. Merchandising exec. Macy's, N.Y.C., 1951-56; exec. v.p. Grey Advt. Inc., N.Y.C., 1956-86; real estate investor-developer Miami Beach, Anguilla B.W.I., 1986—; bd. dirs. several profit, not-for-profit and ednl. corps. Served as radio officer U.S. Maritime Service, U.S. Army Transport Service, 1945-46; 2d Lt. Q.M.C. U.S. Army, 1951-53. Home: 205 E 63rd St New York NY 10021-7425 also: 18 Hedges Banks Dr East Hampton NY 11937-3505

MARDER, MICHAEL ZACHARY, dentist, researcher, educator; b. N.Y.C., Aug. 30, 1938; s. Jospeh Theodore and Rhea (Greenspun) M.; (widowed); children: Sherri Ellen, Robert Whitney. Student, Tufts U., 1959; D.D.S., Columbia U., 1963. Diplomate: Am. Bd. Oral Medicine. Practice dentistry N.Y.C., 1963-66, 68—; asst. Sch. Dental and Oral Surgery, Columbia U., N.Y.C., 1963-66, instr., 1968, asst. clin. prof., 1968-72, assoc. clin. prof., 1972-76, clin. prof. dentistry, 1976—, researcher, 1963—; dir. oral medicine, 1972-84, dir. clin. cancer tng., 1993—; asst. attending dental surgeon Presbyn. Hosp., 1972-76; assoc. attending dentist, 1976-82, attending dentist, 1982—; cons. Good Samaritan Hosp., Suffern, N.Y.; lectr. in field. Author 2 textbooks in dental medicine; contbr. chpts. to med. and dental textbooks, articles to profl. jours. Served to capt. U.S. Army, 1966-68. Recipient Cert. of Achievement U.S. Army, 1968. Fellow N.Y. Acad. Dentistry; mem. ADA, Internat. Assn. Dental Rsch., Am. Acad. Oral Medicine, Frist Dist. Dental Soc. N.Y., Omicron Kappa Upsilon, Sigma Xi. Office: 119 W 57th St New York NY 10019-2303

MARDIAN, DANIEL, construction company director; b. Pasadena, Calif., Apr. 10, 1917; s. Samuel and Akabe (Lekerian) M.; m. Katherine Evkhanian, Jan. 30, 1942; children: Daniel Jr., Tom, John, Paul, Scott. Student, Pasadena City Coll., 1937; diploma, U.S. Army Engring. Sch., Ft. Belvoir, Va., 1944, U.S. Army Command and Gen. Staff Coll., 1961. Commd. U.S. Army, 1942, advances through grades to lt. col., 1962, ret., 1970; ptnr. Mardian Constrn. Co., Phoenix, 1945-47, exec. v.p., 1947-66, pres., 1966-78, also bd. dirs.; past chmn., mem. Nat. Joint Apprenticeship/Tng. Commn. Oper. Engrs., Washington, 1975-78; mem. adv. bd. constrn. programs Ariz. State U., Tempe, 1957—, mem. adv. bd. coll. engring., 1957—; bd. dirs. Citibank, Phoenix, 1962-87. Pres. Am. Coun. Constrn. Edn., Monroe, La., 1991-93; past pres., bd. dirs. Fiesta Bowl, Tempe, 1986-92; gen. campaign chmn. United Way, Phoenix, 1967; pres. Met. Phoenix C. of C., 1967-68. Capt. C.E., U.S. Army, 1942-46, PTO, 1970—. Recipient Hall of Fame award Ariz. State U., 1990, medallion of merit, 1984, Excellence in Constrn. award Am. Subcontractors Assn., 1988, Hall of Fame award Nat. Football Found., 1987, Brotherhood award Ariz. chpt. NCCJ, 1981, Fellow award Am. Inst. Constructors, 1996. Mem. Associated Gen. Contractors Am. (life bd. dirs., chmn. yr. award 1970, mem. workforce devel. com., mem. laborers tng. com., 1969—), Sun Angel Found. (chmn. 1989-91), Ariz. Acad., Phoenix Country Club (bd. dirs., pres. 1985-86), Phoenix Kiwanis Club (past dir.). Republican. Mem. United Ch. Christ. Avocations: golfing, fishing. Home: 7215 N 3rd St Phoenix AZ 85020-4904 Office: Perini Building Co 360 E Coronado Rd Phoenix AZ 85004-1524

MARDIN, ARIF, musician; b. Istanbul, Turkey, 1932. Grad., Istanbul U.; postgrad., London Sch. Econs., Berklee Coll. Music; D (hon.), Berklee Coll. Music. V.p. Atlantic Records, 1969, sr. v.p. Prodr. The Young Rascals, Dusty Springfield, Aretha Franklin, Roberta Flack, Donny Hathaway, Hall & Oates, John Prine, Willie Nelson, The Average White Band, , the Bee Gees, Phil Collins, Bette Midler, Judy Collins, Carly Simon, Laura Nyro, Dionne Warwick, Culture Club, Howard Jones, George Benson, Melissa Manchester, CHaka Kahn. Recipient Man of Yr. award Assembly Turkish Am. Assns., 1990, Shofar of Peace award Sephardic Hebrew Acad., 1992, Best Musical Show Album Grammy award, 1996, inducted into Nat. Acad. Record Arts & Scis. Hall of Fame, 1990; Quincy Jones scholar, 1958. Office: Atlantic Records 75 Rockefeller Plz New York NY 10019*

MAREADY, WILLIAM FRANK, lawyer; b. Mullins, S.C., Sept. 13, 1932; s. Jesse Frank and Vera (Sellers) M.; m. Brenda McCanless, Nov. 3, 1979. AB, U. N.C., 1955, JD with honors, 1958. Bar: N.C. 1958, U.S. Dist. Ct. N.C. 1960, U.S. Ct. Appeals (4th cir.) 1962, U.S. Supreme Ct. 1968. Assoc. Mudge, Stern, Baldwin & Todd, N.Y.C., 1958-60, Hudson, Ferrell, Carter, Petree & Stockton, Winston-Salem, N.C., 1960-65; ptnr. Petree, Stockton & Robinson, Winston-Salem, 1965-92, Robinson, Maready, Lawing & Comerford, 1992—; N.C. chmn. Winston-Salem/Forsyth County Bd. Edn., 1968-70, chmn., bd. dirs. and mem. exec. com. N.C. State Port Authority, 1984—. Served with Green Berets, U.S. Army, 1952-54. Recipient Disting. Svc. award N.C. Sch. Bds. Assn. Fellow Am. Coll. Trial Lawyers, Am. Bar Found.; mem. ABA (chmn. standing com. on aero. law 1979-82, chmn. forum com. on air and space law 1982-86), N.C. Bar Assn. (chmn. litigation sect. 1981-82, adminstrn. of justice com. 1981-82), Nat. Parent Tchr. Assn. (life), Order of Coif, Phi Delta Phi, Phi Beta Kappa. Republican. Methodist. Clubs: Forsyth County. Lodge: Rotary of Winston Salem. Office: 370 Knollwood St Ste 600 Winston Salem NC 27103-1835

MAREE, WENDY, painter, sculptor; b. Windsor, Eng., Feb. 10, 1938. Student, Windsor & Maidenhead Coll., 1959; studied with Vasco Lazzlo, London, 1959-62. Exhibited in group shows at Windsor Arts Festival, San Bernardino (Calif.) Mus.; one-woman shows include Lake Arrowhead (Calif.) Libr., 1989, Amnesty Internat., Washington, 1990, Phyllis Morris Gallery, Many Horses Gallery, L.A., 1990, Nelson Rockefeller, Palm Springs, Calif., 1992, 94, Stewart Gallery, Rancho Palos Verdes, Calif., Petropavlovsk (Russia) Cultural Mus., Kamchatka, Russia, 1993, Coyle-Coyle Gallery, Blue Jay, Calif., 1995, La Quinta Sculpture Park, Calif., 1995, Avante-Garde Gallery, Palm Springs, 1996; others; represented in pvt. collections His Royal Highness Prince Faisal, Saudi Arabia, Gena Rowlands, L.A., John Cassavetes, L.A., Nicky Blairs, L.A., Guilford Glazer, Beverly Hills, Calif., June Allyson, Ojai, Calif., Amnesty Internat., Washington. Recipient award San Bernardino County Mus., 1988, Gov. Kamchatka of Russia, 1993. Mem. Artist Guild of Lake Arrowhead. Address: 246 Saturmino Dr Palm Springs CA 92262

MAREK, VLADIMIR, ballet director, educator; b. Uzhorod, Czechoslovakia, Sept. 26, 1928; came to U.S., 1969; s. Jaroslav and Julia (Valkova) Sourek. Student Bus. Acad., Czechoslovakia, ballet schs., Czechoslovakia, 1945-47. Soloist Nat. Theater Ballet, Prague, Czechoslovakia, 1947-50, prin. dancer, Bratislava, Czechoslovakia, 1950-69, ballet master, 1958-68; ballet tchr. Our Lady of Lake U., San Antonio, 1970-78; owner, tchr. V. Marek Ballet Acad., San Antonio, 1970—; founder, artistic dir. San Antonio Ballet, 1970—. Home: 212 E Mulberry Ave San Antonio TX 78212 Office: San Antonio Ballet 212 E Mulberry Ave San Antonio TX 78212-3041

MARELLA, PHILIP DANIEL, broadcasting company executive; b. Italy, Sept. 9, 1929; came to U.S., 1930; s. T. Joseph and Julia (Santolina) M.; m. Lucinda Minor, Dec. 30, 1955; children: Philip Daniel, Laura Ann, William Scott. BS, Calif. State U., 1955; MS, Syracuse U., 1956. Account exec. WGR-TV, Buffalo, 1956-57; account exec., sales mgr. WIIC-TV, Pitts., 1957-66; gen. mgr. WCHS-TV, Charleston, W.Va., 1966-68; v.p. radio and television Rollins, Inc., Atlanta, 1968-70; pres. WAVY-TV, Inc., Tidewater, Va., 1970—; v.p. ops. Lin Broadcasting, Inc., N.Y.C.; also dir.; pres., owner WMGC-TV, Binghamton, N.Y., 1978-86; CEO, pres. Pinnacle Comm., Inc., 1987—; CEO Pinnacle Broadcasting Co., 1987; owner radio stas. WFXC-FM, WDUR, WFXX, Raleigh, N.C., WRNS-AM-FM, Coastal, N.C., WYAV-FM, Myrtle Beach, S.C., KLLL-AM-FM, Lubbock, Tex., WYNG-FM, Evansville, Ind., WSOY-AM-FM, Decatur, Ill. Bd. dirs. Salvation Army, 1966-68; bd. dirs., v.p. United Fund; bd. dirs. Portsmouth chpt. ARC, Tidewater Regional Health and Planning Commn.; bd. dirs., v.p. Binghamton Symphony. Served with USMC, 1948-49, 50-52. Mem. Nat. Assn. Broadcasters (v.p.), Va. Assn. Broadcasters, N.C. Broadcasters Assn., Variety Club Pitts., Radio and TV Club, Portsmouth C. of C. (pres.-elect), Norfolk C. of C., Newport News C. of C., Cavalier Golf and Yacht Club (Virginia Beach, Va.), N.Y. Athletic Club, Binghamton Country Club. Home: 2073 Cheshire Rd Binghamton NY 13903-3199 also: Central Pk Pl 301 W 57th St Apt 43C New York NY 10019-3180 Office: 331 W 57th St Ste 288 New York NY 10019-3101

MARELLI, SISTER M. ANTHONY, secondary school principal. Prin. Boylan Ctrl. Cath. High Sch., Rockford, Ill. Recipient Blue Ribbon Sch. award U.S. Dept. Edn., 1990-91. Office: Boylan Ctrl Cath High Sch 4000 Saint Francis Dr Rockford IL 61103-1661

MARES, MICHAEL ALLEN, ecologist, educator; b. Albuquerque, Mar. 11, 1945; s. Ernesto Gustavo and Rebecca Gabriela (Devine) M.; m. Lynn Ann Brusin, Aug. 27, 1966; children: Gabriel Andres, Daniel Alejandro. BS in Biology, U. N.Mex., 1967; MS, Ft. Hays Kans. State U., 1969; PhD, U. Tex.-Austin, 1973. Adj. prof. U. Nacional de Cordoba, Argentina, 1971-72; adj. prof. U. Nacional de Tucuman, Argentina, 1972, vis. prof., 1974; from asst. to assoc. prof. U. Pitts., 1973-81; vis. scientist U. Ariz., Tucson, 1980-81; assoc. prof., curator mammals U. Okla., Norman, 1981-83, dir. Okla. Mus. Nat. Hist., 1983—, assoc. prof. zoology, 1983-85, prof., 1985—; NUS cons., Venezuela, 1980-81; cons. Argentine Nat. Sci. Found., Inst. Arid Zone Research, Mendoza, 1983; World Wildlife Fund cons., Brazil, 1986; mem. Council Internat. Exchange of Scholars, Am. Republics Bd., Fulbright Commn., 1983-86, 88-91; bd. dirs. Coun. Internat. Exchange of Scholars, 1988-91; Okla. rep. to U.S. Fish and Wildlife Service Endangered Mammal Species Commn., 1987-95; co-chair Internat. Programs Com. Systematics 2000, 1991-94; sci. cons. interim working group White House Biodiversity, Ecology, and Ecosystems, 1992-94; apptd. adv. bd. Ctr. Biol. Diversity, Dept. Interior; mem. Commn. on Future of Smithsonian Instns., 1993-95. NSF grantee, 1974-79, 82-93; Nat. Fulbright research fellow, 1976; Nat. Geog. Soc. grantee, 1992-95. Active Chicano Council on Higher Edn. rsch. fellow, 1978; Ford Found. Minority Rsch. fellow, 1980-81; Brazilian Nat. Acad. Sci. rsch. award, 1975-78. Mem. AAAS (Western Hemispheric coop. com. 1989-93), Am. Soc. Mammalogists (1st v.p. 1990-94), Am. Ecol. Soc., Interam. Assn. Advancement Sci., Am. Inst. Biol. Sci., Am. Soc. Naturalists, Soc. Study of Evolution, Southwestern Assn. Naturalists (Donald W. Tinkle rsch. excellence award), Paleontol. Soc., Sigma Xi, Phi Kappa Phi, Beta Beta Beta. Contbr. articles to profl. jours. Home: 3930 Charing Cross Ct Norman OK 73072-3201 Office: U Okla Mus Natural History 1335 Asp Ave Norman OK 73019-0606

MARESH, ALICE MARCELLA, retired educational administrator; b. Chgo., Sept. 17, 1922; d. Joseph Anton and Barbara Magdalene (Slad) M. BEd, Chgo. Tchrs. Coll., 1944; MEd, Loyola U., Chgo., 1962. Chemist Best Foods, Inc., Chgo., 1944-54; tchr. Chgo. Bd. Edn., 1954-65, counselor, 1965-67, asst. prin., 1967-69, prin., 1969-93; retired, 1993. Recipient Outstanding and Dedicated Svc. award Puerto Rican Congress, 1975, Those Who Excel award Ill. Bd. Edn., 1978, Whitman award for excellence in ednl. mgmt. Whitman Acad., Chgo., 1990, Outstanding Svc. to Edn. in Chgo. award Nat. Coun. Negro Women, 1992. Mem. Chgo. Prins. Assn., Chgo. Area Reading Assn., Aquin Guild (Dedicated Svc. award 1976), Delta Kappa Gamma (pres. 1976-78), Phi Delta Kappa, Pi Lambda Theta (sec. 1995—). Democrat. Roman Catholic. Avocations: music, travel, calligraphy, theater. Home: 3850 W Bryn Mawr Ave #308 Chicago IL 60659-3135

MARGARITIS, JOHN PAUL, public relations executive; b. N.Y.C., June 8, 1949; s. George H. and Mary (Liakos) M.; m. Charlene Corenman, Feb. 21, 1982. BA in English, Washington and Jefferson Coll., 1971; MA in Media Studies, New Sch. Social Rsch., 1977. Account exec. Hank Boerner & Assocs., Uniondale, N.Y., 1974-76; account exec. Manning, Selvage & Lee, N.Y.C., 1976-77; account supr. Gen. Electric Co., N.Y.C., 1977-79, Burson-Marsteller, Inc., Chgo., 1979-80; v.p., dir. client services Burson-Marsteller, Inc., Los Angeles, 1980-82; exec. v.p., gen. mgr., sr. ptnr. Fleishman-Hillard, Inc., Los Angeles, 1982-88; chmn., chief exec. officer Ogilvy & Mather Pub. Relations, N.Y.C., 1988-92; pres., COO Ogilvy Adams and Rinehart, N.Y.C., 1992-94, pres., CEO, 1994—; also bd. dirs. Ogilvy Adams and Rinehart; bd. dirs. Rsch. Am., Young Pres. Orgn., Arthur Ashe Found. 2nd lt. U.S. Army, 1972-74. Mem. Pub. Rels. Soc. Am. (hons. and awards com. 1986-89, counselors acad. 1985—), Alpine Country Club. Republican. Greek Orthodox. Home: 38 Hidden Ledge Rd Englewood NJ 07631-5125 Office: Ogilvy Adams and Rinehart 708 3rd Ave New York NY 10017*

MARGE, MICHAEL, disability prevention specialist; b. Albany, N.Y., Oct. 26, 1928; s. Charles and Victoria (Arwady) M.; m. Dorothy Kunsevilch, July 9, 1960; children: Lisa Ann, Michael Charles. BA, Emerson Coll., 1952; MAT, Harvard U., 1953, EdD, 1959. Dir. speech therapy project N.Y. State Assn. for Crippled Children, Glens Falls, 1953-55; dir. speech therapy Glens Falls and Hudson Falls (N.Y.) Pub. Schs., 1955-57; co-chmn. speech and hearing grad. program Seton Hall U., South Orange, N.J., 1960-64; program specialist Office Edn. Dept. HEW, Washington, 1964-68, dep. asst. sec. Office Edn., 1968-71; dep. bur. chief Office Edn. Bur. Internat. Studies, Washington, 1971-74; dean Coll. for Human Devel. Syracuse (N.Y.) U., 1974-79, prof. spl. edn. and rehab., 1979—, dir. Ctr. for the Prevention of Disabilities, 1985—; cons. Orgn. Am. States, Washington, 1976—; intergovtl. profl. cons. Ctrs. for Disease Control, Atlanta, 1994-95; disabilities prevention scientist ctrs. for disease control and prevention Dept. of Health and Human Svcs., Atlanta, 1994-95; mem. Nat. Coun. on Disability, Washington, 1982-87, cons., 1987-92; expert UN Devel. Program, N.Y.C., 1977—; rsch. prof. dept. phys. medicine and rehab., SUNY Med. Coll., Syracuse, 1995—. Co-author: Principles of Childhood Language Disabilities, 1972; creator in field. Mem. interagy. com. HHS, Washington, 1986-89, Nat. Coun. on the Handicapped, Washington, 1982-87; mem. prevention task force N.Y. State Devel. Disabilities Planning Coun., Albany, 1986, Disability Prevention Coun., N.Y. State Dept. Health, Albany, 1989—; bd. dirs. Laubach Literacy Inc., Syracuse, 1986, Eye Rsch. Inst. Cen. N.Y., Syracuse, 1988-91; mem. com. on transp. disadvantaged Transport. Rsch. Bd. NAS, Washington, 1989-92; mem. adv. bd. on prevention Minorities Health Professions Found., 1993—; mem. citizens adv. com. Town of Dewitt, N.Y., 1995—. Cpl. U.S. Army, 1946-48. Recipient Nat. Eagle award Nat. Coun. on Disability, 1987; J.M. Found. grantee, 1985. Fellow Am. Speech-Lang.-Hearing Assn. (exec. bd. 1968-70, Cert. Appreciation 1975, 85); mem. Am. Psychol. Assn., Am. Pub. Health Assn., N.Y. State Speech-Lang.-Hearing Assn., N.J. Speech and Hearing Assn. (Honor of the Assn. 1965), Am. Disability Prevention and Wellness Assn. (pres. 1994—), Nat. Rehab. Assn. (Mary E. Switzer fellow 1980), Harvard Club (Syracuse, admissions com. 1984-87). Club: Harvard (Syracuse, admissions com. 1984-87). Avocations: bicycling, hiking, classical music. Office: Syracuse U 805 S Crouse Ave Syracuse NY 13210-1714

MARGERISON, RICHARD WAYNE, diversified industrial company executive; b. Phila., Nov. 5, 1948; s. Kenneth Hilton and Edythe (Helmuth) M.; m. Leah Blythe Creed, July 18, 1970; children: Andrew Kenneth, Ashley Creed. BA in Econs., U. N.C., 1970; MBA with distinction, Harvard U., 1977. Mgr. So. Bell Telephone Co., Greensboro, N.C., 1972-75; mgr. sub. liaison Atlas Powder Co. subs. Tyler Corp., Dallas, 1978-79, dir. mktg. svcs., 1979-80; exec. v.p. Micro-Term, Inc., St. Louis, 1980-83, pres., chief exec. officer, 1983-85; mgr. acquisitions Tyler Corp., Dallas, 1977-78, v.p., 1985-88, sr. v.p., 1988-89, exec. v.p., 1989-94, pres., COO, 1994—, also bd. dirs. Mem. Northway Christian Ch., Dallas, 1985—; coach Youth Soccer, Dallas, 1987—; advisor YMCA Indian Princess and Indian Guides, 1987-89; adult leader Boy Scouts Am., 1988-93; mem. Dallas Citizens Coun.; active Dallas United Way, 1990. Love fellow Harvard Grad. Sch. Bus., 1975-77. Mem. Harvard Bus. Sch. Club of Dallas, Lakewood Country Club, Order of Old Well, Phi Beta Kappa. Avocations: golf, youth soccer, running. Office: Tyler Corp 2121 San Jacinto St Ste 3200 Dallas TX 75201-6704

MARGERUM, DALE WILLIAM, chemistry educator; b. St. Louis, Oct. 20, 1929; s. Donald C. and Ida Lee (Nunley) M.; m. Sonya Lora Pedersen, May 16, 1953; children: Lawrence Donald, Eric William, Richard Dale. BA, S.E. Mo. State U., 1950; PhD, Iowa State U., 1955. Research chemist Ames Lab., AEC, Iowa, 1952-53; instr. Purdue U., West Lafayette, Ind., 1954-57; asst. prof. Purdue U., 1957-61, assoc. prof., 1961-65, prof., 1965—, head dept. chemistry, 1978-83; inorganic-analytical chemist, vis. scientist Max Planck Inst., 1963, 70; vis. prof. U. Kent, Canterbury, Eng., 1970; mem. med. chem. study sect. NIH, 1965-69; mem. adv. com. Research Corp., 1973-78; mem. chemistry evaluation panel Air Force Office Sci. Research, 1978-82. Cons. editor McGraw Hill, 1962-72; mem. editorial bd. Jour. Coordination Chemistry, 1971-81, Analytical Chemistry, 1967-69, Inorganic Chemistry, 1985-88. Recipient Grad. Rsch. award Phi Lambda Upsilon, 1954, Alumni Merit award S.E. Mo. State U., 1991, Sagamore of the Wabash, State of Ind., 1994; NSF sr. postdoctoral fellow, 1963-64. Fellow AAAS; mem. AAUP, Am. Chem. Soc. (chmn. Purdue sect. 1965-66, com. on profl. tng. 1993—, Disting. Svc. award in advancement of inorganic chemistry 1996), Sigma Xi, Phi Lambda Upsilon. Office: Dept Chemistry Purdue U West Lafayette IN 47907

MARGERUM, J(OHN) DAVID, chemist; b. St. Louis, Oct. 20, 1929; s. Donald Cameron and Ida Lee (Nunley) M.; m. Virginia Bolen, June 5, 1954; children: John Steven, Kris Alan, Julie Ellen. A.B., S.E. Mo. State Coll., 1950; Ph.D., Northwestern U., 1956. Rsch. chemist Shell Oil Co., Wood River, Ill., 1954-55; chief spectroscopy sect. U.S. Army QMR&E Center, Natick, Mass., 1957-59; research specialist Sundstrand Corp., Pacoima, Calif., 1959-62; with Hughes Research Labs., Malibu, Calif., 1962—, sr. scientist, head chemistry sect., 1967—, head material scis. sect., 1988—, asst. dept. mgr. exploratory studies dept., 1989—, mgr. dept. materials sci., lab. chief scientist, 1991—; prin. rsch. scientist, 1993—. Contbr. articles to profl. jours.; patentee in field. Served with U.S. Army, 1955-57. Recipient Holley medal ASME, 1977. Fellow AAAS; mem. Am. Chem. Soc., Electrochem. Soc., Soc. Info. Display, Inter-Am. Photochem. Soc., Internat. Liquid Crystal Soc., Sigma Xi. Democrat. Unitarian. Home: 5433 Rozie Ave Woodland Hills CA 91367-5760 Office: 3011 Malibu Canyon Rd Malibu CA 90265-4737

MARGESSON, MAXINE EDGE, professor; b. Cordele, Ga., Aug. 29, 1933; d. Bryant Peak and Maxie (Grantham) Edge; m. Burland Drake

Margesson, June 24, 1956; children: Anda Margesson Foxwell, Risa Margesson Carpenter. BS, Bob Jones U., 1958; MEd, SUNY, Buffalo, 1971; EdD, Western Mich. U., 1983. Elem. tchr. Cheektowaga (N.Y.) Cen. Sch. Dist., 1965-72; elem. prin. Grand Rapids (Mich.) Bapt. Acad., 1972-85; reading rsch. Wake Forest U., Winston-Salem, N.C., 1987-90; prof. Piedmont Bible Coll., Winston-Salem, 1985-90; reading specialist Randolph (N.Y.) Ctrl. Sch. Dist., 1990—; bd. dirs. Salem Day Sch., Winston-Salem. Mem. Forsyth County Coalition for Literacy Com. Mem. Assn. for Supervision and Curriculum Devel., Assn. Christian Schs. Internat. Republican. Baptist. Avocations: travel, reading, sewing. Office: Randolph Ctrl Sch Randolph NY 14772

MARGETON, STEPHEN GEORGE, law librarian; b. Elizabeth, N.J., Mar. 22, 1945; s. Louis George and Josephine A. (Bednarik) M.; m. Margaret Mary Salter, May 14, 1977; children: Catherine Ann, Elizabeth Ann. AB, Mt. St. Mary's Coll., 1967; JD, George Washington U., 1970; MLS, Cath. U., 1973. Reference librarian Am.-Brit. law div. Library of Congress, Washington, 1968-72; law libr. Steptoe & Johnson, Washington, 1972-85; librarian Supreme Ct. of U.S., Washington, 1985-88; dir. Judge Kathryn J. DuFour Law Libr. The Cath. Univ. Am., 1988—; instr. George Mason Law Sch., Arlington, Va., 1977-80. Mem. Am. Assn. Law Libraries, Internat. Assn. Law Libraries. Office: Cath U Am Kathryn J DuFour Law Libr 3600 John McCormack Rd NE Washington DC 20064-8206

MARGETTS, W. THOMAS, automobile parts company executive, lawyer; b. Passaic, N.J., May 16, 1936; s. Walter T. Jr. and Josephine (Sharon) M.; m. Donna D. Ditman, July 21, 1962; children: Melissa, Sharon, Robert, James. AB, Dartmouth Coll., 1959; LLB, U. Va., 1962; LLM, George Washington U., 1964. Bar: N.Y., N.J., Va. Assoc. Lord Day & Lord, N.Y.C., 1965-67; atty. Standard Brands, N.Y.C., 1967-70; counsel Purolator Courier Corp., Basking Ridge, N.J., 1970-71, sec. counsel, 1971-80, v.p., 1980-83, sr. v.p., 1983-88; adminstrn. sr. v.p. Stant Inc., Richmond, Ind., 1988—; of counsel Crummy, Del Deo, Dolan, Griffinger & Vecchione, Newark, 1988-92; dir. Komline-Sanderson Engring. Corp.; trustee N.J. Delta Dental Plan, Inc., Parsippany, 1985—. Bd. dirs. Kessler Assisted Living Ctrs., L.L.C.; mem. twp. com. Harting Twp., N.J., 1972-83, mayor, 1976-83; trustee, chmn. County Coll. of Morris; trustee, v.p Morris Mus., 1992-95, N.J. Camp for Blind Children, 1992—. 1st lt. U.S. Army. Home: PO Box 18 New Vernon NJ 07976-0018

MARGILETH, ANDREW MENGES, physician, former naval officer; b. Cin., July 17, 1920; s. Elmer C. and Bertha (Menges) M.; m. Catherine Lanier, Oct. 31, 1994; children: R. Lynn, Andrew C., Elle C., David Lanier. B.A., Washington and Jefferson Coll., 1943; B.S., Mass. Inst. Tech., 1944; M.D., U. Cin., 1947. Diplomate Am. Bd. Pediatrics. Commd. ensign USN, 1943, advanced through grades to capt., 1963; intern, resident pediatrics Nat. Naval Med. Center, 1947-49; resident pediatrics Johns Hopkins Hosp., 1949-50; chief pediatrics U.S. Naval Hosps., Corona, Calif., 1953-57, Chelsea, Mass., 1957-63, Bethesda, Md., 1963-67; prof. pediatrics Uniformed Svcs. U. Health Scis., 1979-90; clin. prof. pediatrics U. Va. Health Scis. Ctr., 1990-95, Mercer Univ. Sch. Medicine, 1995—; council mem. Nat. Inst. Child Health and Human Devel., 1963-67; sr. attending physician Childrens Hosp., Washington; assoc. clin. prof. pediatrics Med. Sch., Howard U.; adj. prof. pediatrics Med. Sch., George Washington U. Contbr. chpt. to Current Peidatric Therapy, 1970, 72, 74, 76, 80, 83, 85, 90, 93, 95; contbr.: (textbooks) Neonatology, 1975, 81, 86, 94, Pediatrics, 1977, 81, 86, 91, 95, 96, Medicine, 1978, 82, 86, 88, 91, Current Therapy Medicine, 1996, Pediatric Dermatology, 1978, 86, 88, also 150 articles to profl. jours.; co-editor Clin. Procs. of Children's Hosp. Nat. Med. Ctr., 1970-79. Fellow Am. Acad. Pediatrics, ACP; mem. Assn. Mil. Surgeons, Am. Pediatric Soc., Soc. Pediatric Dermatologists, Soc. Pediatric Infectious Diseases, Alpha Omega Alpha. Address: 20 Kingston Rd Hilton Head Island SC 29928

MARGIOTTA, MARY-LOU ANN, software engineer; b. Waterbury, Conn., June 14, 1956; d. Rocco Donato and Louise Antoinette (Carosella) M. AS in Gen. Edn., Mattatuck Community Coll., Waterbury, 1982; BS in Bus. Mgmt., Teikyo Post U., 1983; MS in Computer Sci., Rensselaer Polytech. Inst., 1989. Programmer analyst Travelers Ins. Co., Hartford, Conn., 1985-87; sr. programmer analyst Conn. Bank and Trust Co., East Hartford, Conn., 1987-88; programmer analyst Ingersoll-Rand Corp., Torrington, Conn., 1990-91; sr. programmer analyst Orion Capital Cos. Inc., Farmington, Conn., 1991-92; pres., prin. A.M. Consultants, New Britain, Conn., 1992-95; project leader Travelers Ins. Co., Hartford, 1995—; pres. C Spl. Interest Group; bd. dirs. Conn. Object Oriented Users Group. Mem. social action com. St. Helena's Parish, West Hartford, Conn., 1988-95; advisor Jr. Achievement, Waterbury, 1981-83; tutor Traveler's Ins. Co. Tutorial Program, West Hartford, 1986-87; trainer CPR, ARC, Hartford, 1986-87. Clayborn Pell grantee Post Coll., 1982-83, State of Conn. grantee, 1982-83; recipient Citation, Jr. Achievement, 1982; Bd. Trustees scholar Post Coll., 1982-83. Mem. IEEE, Assn. for Systems Mgmt., Assn. Computing Machinery, Toastmasters Internat., Tau Alpha, Beta Gamma. Roman Catholic. Avocations: European travel, gourmet cooking, reading, tennis, golf. Home: 210 Brittany Farms Rd Ste E New Britain CT 06053-1282

MARGO, KATHERINE LANE, physician; b. Buffalo, June 3, 1952; d. Warren Wilson and Virginia (Penney) Lane; m. Geoffrey Myles Margo, Apr. 20, 1980; 1 child, Benjamin; stepchildren: Jenny, Judy. BA, Swarthmore Coll., 1974; MD, SUNY Health Sci. Ctr., Syracuse, 1978. Resident physician St. Joseph's Hosp., Syracuse, 1979-82; attending physician Health Svcs. Assn., Syracuse, 1982-90, asst. med. dir. for quality assurance, 1985-90; asst. prof. family medicine SUNY-HSC at Syracuse, 1990-94; residency faculty Harrisburg (Pa.) Hosp., 1994—. Contbr. articles to profl. jours. Bd. of trustees Pt. Choice, Syracuse, 1993-94, Planned Parenthood, Syracuse, 1984-94, Friends of Chamber Music, Syracuse, 1985-94. Mem. Soc. Tchrs. of Family Medicine, Am. Acad. of Family Practitioners (v.p. Syracuse chpt.), Am. Acad. Ortho. Medicine. Home: 4705 Maple Shade Dr Harrisburg PA 17110-3217

MARGOL, IRVING, personnel consultant; b. St. Louis, May 28, 1930; s. William and Dora (Karsh) M.; m. Myrna Levy, Dec., 1959; children—Bradley, Lisa, Cynthia. B.A., Washington U., St. Louis, 1951, M.A., 1952. Employment mgr. Am. Car & Foundry div. ACF, St. Louis, 1955-59; asst. personnel dir. Vickers Inc. div. Sperry-Rand, St. Louis, 1959-60; instr. personnel mgmt. Washington U. (St. Louis), 1960-62; personnel dir. Energy Controls div. Bendix Corp., South Bend, Ind., 1962-69; exec. v.p. community/employee affairs group, community rels. dept., employee assistance program Security Pacific Nat. Bank, L.A., 1969-92; mng. dir. Southern Calif. Jannotta, Bray & Assocs., Inc., 1992—; pres. Security Pacific Found., L.A., 1989-94; mng. dir. Jannotta Bray & Assocs., L.A., 19092-94, Right and Assocs., L.A., 1995—; instr. UCLA Extension Div., Los Angeles; Grad. Sch. Banking, Rutgers U., Notre Dame U. Bd. dirs. L.A. chpt. ARC, Am. Heart Assn., Am. Cancer Soc., Nat. Conf. Christians & Jews, Braille Inst.; bd. overseers Southwestern U. Law. Mem. Am. Bankers Assn. (exec. com. 1979—), Am. Soc. Tng. and Devel., Am. Soc. Personnel Adminstrs., Am. Inst. Banking, Washington U. Alumni Assn. Democrat. Jewish. Office: Right and Assocs 5320 Pacific Councourse Dr Los Angeles CA 90045

MARGOLIASH, EMANUEL, biochemist, educator; b. Cairo, Feb. 10, 1920; s. Wolf and Bertha (Kotler) M.; m. Sima Beshkin, Aug. 22, 1944; children: Reuben, Daniel. BA, Am. U., Beirut, 1940, MA, 1942, MD, 1945. Rsch. fellow, lectr., acting head cancer rsch. labs. Hebrew U., Jerusalem, 1945-58; rsch. fellow Molteno Inst. Cambridge (Eng.) U., 1951-53; Dazian fellow Nobel Inst., 1958; rsch. assoc. U. Utah, Salt Lake City, 1958-60, McGill U., Montreal, Que., Can., 1960-62; rsch. fellow Abbott Labs., North Chicago, Ill., 1962-69, sr. rsch. fellow Abbott Labs., 1969-71, head protein sect., 1962-71; prof. biochemistry and molecular biology Northwestern U., Evanston, Ill., 1971-90, prof. chemistry, 1985-90, Owen L. Coon prof. molecular biology, 1988-90, Owen L. Coon prof. molecular biology emeritus, 1990—; prof. biol. scis. U. Ill., Chgo., 1989—, coord. lab. for molecular biology, 1990-93; mem. com. on cytochrome nomenclature Internat. Union Biochemistry, 1962—; mem. adv. com. Plant Research Lab., Mich. State U./AEC, 1967-72; co-chmn. Gordon Research Conf. on Proteins, 1967. Editl. bd. Jour. Biol. Chemistry, 1966-72, Biochem. Genetics, 1966-80, Jour. Molecular Evolution, 1971-82, Biochemistry and Molecular Biology Internat., 1981—, Jour. Protein Chemistry, 1982-86, Chemtracts, Biochem. Molecular Biology, 1990—; contbr. over 275 articles and revs. to sci. jours. Rudi Lemberg fellow Australian Acad. Sci., 1981; Guggenheim fellow, 1983. Fellow Am. Acad. Arts and Scis., Am. Acad. Microbiology; mem. Nat. Acad. Scis., Biochem. Soc. (Keilin Meml. lectr. 1970), Harvey Soc. (lectr. 1970-71), Am. Soc. Biochem. Molecular Biology (publs. com. 1973-76), Am. Chem. Soc., Can. Biochem. Soc., Soc. Devel. Biology, Biophys. Soc. (exec. com. U.S. bioenergetics group 1980-83), N.Y. Acad. Sci., Ill. Acad. Sci., Am. Soc. Naturalists, Sigma Xi (nat. lectr. 1972-73, 74-77). Home: 353 Madison Ave Glencoe IL 60022-1809 Office: Univ Ill Chgo Dept Bio-Scis 845 W Taylor St Chicago IL 60607-7060

MARGOLIN, ARTHUR STANLEY, distillery company executive; b. N.Y.C., Aug. 7, 1936; s. Samuel and Belle (Gelb) M.; m. Barbara Jane Lester, June 27, 1965; children: Sarah Jennifer, Julie Ellen, Carolyn Leigh. BA in Econs., NYU, 1957, postgrad. in bus., 1961. Analyst, sr. analyst Asch Market Research (div. JES), N.Y.C., 1961-63; field asst. to eastern div. mgr. Calvert Distillers, N.Y.C., 1963-64, asst. to asst. and met. N.Y. mgr., 1964-72, asst. to exec. v.p. sales, asst. to pres., 1972-78; exec. asst. to pres. House of Seagram, N.Y.C., 1978-80; dir. U.S. ops. Seagram Europe, London, 1980-82; asst. to pres. Seagram Internat. Joseph E. Seagram & Sons Inc., N.Y.C., 1982, asst. to office of chmn. and pres., 1982-85, v.p. spl. asst. to office of chmn. and pres., 1985—; bd. dirs. Forhan Forwarding and Handling Co., N.V., Antwerp, Belgium. Mng. editor Heights Daily News, 1956-57. Bd. dirs. Fifth Ave. Assn., N.Y.C., 1987—, USO of Metro N.Y., 1994—. Republican. Jewish. Avocations: collecting stamps and coins, baseball. Office: Joseph E Seagram & Sons Inc 375 Park Ave New York NY 10152

MARGOLIN, HAROLD, metallurgical educator; b. Hartford, Conn., July 12, 1922; s. Aaron David and Sonia (Krupnikoff) M.; m. Elaine Marjorie Rose, July 4, 1946; children: Shelley, Deborah, Amy. B in Engring., Yale U., 1943; M in Engring., Yale Univ., 1947, DEng, 1950. Rsch. assoc./scientist divsn. rsch. NYU, N.Y.C., 1949-56, assoc. prof. metall. engring., 1956-62, prof., 1962-73; prof. phys. metallurgy Poly. U. N.Y., Bklyn., 1973-93, disting. rsch. prof., 1993-96; ret. U. N.Y., Bklyn., 1995; cons. in field. Contbg. author books; contbr. articles to profl. publs. With USNR, 1944-46. Named Theodore W. Krengel vis. prof. Technion, Haifa, Israel, 1983. Fellow Am. Soc. Metals (edn. award N.Y. chpt. 1967); mem. Metall. Soc. (honoree symposium in his name San Francisco 1994), Am. Soc. Materials, TMS. Democrat. Jewish. Patentee in field. Home: 19 Crescent Rd Larchmont NY 10538-1733 *Achievement, work, and refusal to accept defeat are intimately intertwined.*

MARGOLIS, BERNARD ALLEN, library administrator, antique book merchant and appraiser; b. Greenwich, Conn., Oct. 2, 1948; s. Sidney S. and Rose (Birkenfeld) M.; m. Amanda Batey, Nov. 2, 1973. BA in Polit. Sci., U. Denver, 1970, MLS, 1973. Cert. libr., Mich. Libr. asst. Denver Pub. Libr., 1970-72; br. head Virginia Village Libr., Denver Pub. Libr., 1972-73; dep. dir. Monroe County Libr. Sys., Mich., 1973-75; dir. Raisin Valley Libr. Sys., Monroe, 1976-78, S.E. Mich. Regional Film Libr., Monroe, 1976-88, Monroe County Libr. Sys., 1976-88, Pikes Peak Libr. Dist., Colorado Springs, Colo., 1988—; pres. Colo. Ctr. for Books, 1989-92, Colo. Ctr. for the Book, 1993—; cons. in libr. pub. rels., 1976—; founding trustee United Colo. Investment Trust, 1993-95; chmn. Colo. Gov.'s Conf. on Libr. and Info. Svcs., 1990; lectr. Western Mich. U., Kalamazoo, 1978-81; appraiser rare books, Monroe, Colorado Springs, 1970—. Contbr. articles to profl. jours; mem. editl. bd. Bottom Line Mag. Fin. Mgmt. for Librs., 1986—. Bd. dirs. Monroe Sen. Citizens Ctr., 1976-80, Monroe Fine Arts Coun., 1978-81, Am. the Beautiful Centennial Celebration, Inc., 1993, The Libr. Consortium, 1993—, Downtown Colo. Springs, Inc., 1994—, Care & Share, Inc., sec., 1994—, vice chmn., 1995, chmn., 1995—; chmn. Blue Cross-Blue Shield Consumer Coun., Detroit, 1984-88; mem. adv. bd. Access Colo. Libr. and Info. Network (ACLIN), 1991—, Mercy Meml. Hosp., Monroe, 1984-86, 5th Congl. Art Competition Com., 1992—; Dem. candidate for Mich. Senate, 1986; mem. allocations com. Pikes Peak United Way, 1988-91, chmn., 1990-91, bd. dirs., 1990-91, 94—; chmn. Great Pikes Peak Cowboy Poetry Gathering, 1990, 91, 92, 94, 95; del. White House Conf. on Libr. and Info. Scis.; mem. El Paso County, Colo. Retirement Bd., 1995—. Recipient Mayoral Cert. Commendation award Denver, 1972, 73; named Mich. Libr. of Yr., 1985, Colo. Libr. of Yr., 1990; commendation John F. Kennedy Ctr. for Performing Arts, 1993. Mem. ALA (governing coun. 1986—, endowment trustee 1989-93, sr. endowment trustee 1993—, chmn. resolutions com. 1991-92, cons. ann. swap and shop 1979-84, John Cotton Dana award 1977, 91, Libr. Awareness Idea Search award Washington 1982), Colo. Libr. Assn. (mem. legis. com., Intellectual Freedom award 1993), Libr. Adminstrv. Mgmt. Assn., Pub. Libr. Assn. Democrat. Jewish. Home: 10640 Hungate Rd Colorado Springs CO 80908-4380 Office: Pikes Peak Libr Dist PO Box 1579 5550 N Union Blvd Colorado Springs CO 80901-1579

MARGOLIS, DANIEL HERBERT, lawyer; b. Montgomery, W.Va., Feb. 11, 1926; s. Morris Abraham and Miriam (Finkelstein) M.; m. Anabel Tendler, Dec. 23, 1951 (dec.); children—Peter, Beth, Laura, James; m. Sidney Millman Moore, Feb. 5, 1983. B.A., Johns Hopkins U., 1948; LL.B., Harvard U., 1951. Bar: D.C. 1951, U.S. Supreme Ct. 1959. Atty adv. Office Price Stblzn., Washington, 1951-52; trial atty. Antitrust div. Dept. Justice, Washington, 1952-56; sr. ptnr. Bergson, Borkland, Margolis & Adler, Washington, 1956-86; ptnr. McGuire, Woods, Battle & Boothe, 1986-89, Patton, Boggs L.L.P., 1989—. Contbr. articles to profl. jours. Mem. adv. bd. Internat. Human Rights Law Group, 1989—. Served with USN, 1945-46, PTO. Fellow ABA (chmn. spl. com. on jury comprehension, litigation sect. 1983-90), Washington Lawyers for Civil Rights. Democrat. Avocations: sailing; skiing. Office: Patton Boggs LLP 2550 M St NW Washington DC 20037-1301

MARGOLIS, DAVID I(SRAEL), corporate executive; b. N.Y.C., Jan. 24, 1930; s. Benjamin and Celia (Kosofsky) M.; m. Barbara Schneider, Sept. 7, 1958; children: Brian, Robert, Peter, Nancy. BA, CCNY, 1950, MBA, 1952; postgrad., NYU, 1952-55. Security analyst Josephthal Co., 1952-56; asst. treas. Raytheon Co., 1956-59; treas. IT&T, N.Y.C., 1959-62; with Coltec Industries Inc., N.Y.C., 1962-95, pres., 1968-91, CEO, 1984-95, chmn. bd. dirs., 1985-95; chmn. exec. com., 1995—; bd. dirs. Burlington Industries, Ft. Howard Corp., Offitbank. Mem. bd. trustees Presbyn. Hosp. City N.Y.; bd. overseers NYU Stern Sch. Bus. Mem. Coun. Fgn. Rels. Office: Coltec Industries Inc 430 Park Ave New York NY 10022-3505

MARGOLIS, EMANUEL, lawyer, educator; b. Bklyn., Mar. 18, 1926; s. Abraham and Esther (Levin) M.; m. Edith Cushing; m. Estelle Thompson, Mar. 1, 1959; children: Elizabeth Margolis-Pineo, Catherine, Abby Margolis Newman, Joshua, Sarah. BA, U. N.C., 1947; MA, Harvard U., 1948, PhD, 1951; JD, Yale U., 1956. Bar: Conn. 1957, U.S. Dist. Ct. Conn. 1958, U.S. Sup. Ct. 1969. Instr. dept. govt. U. Conn. 1951-53; assoc. Silberberg & Silverstein, Ansonia, Conn. 1956-60; assoc. Wofsey Rosen Kweskin & Kuriansky Stamford, Conn. 1960-66, ptnr. 1966—; arbitrator State of Conn., 1984-85; trial referee, 1985—; spl. master fed. cts., 1987—; adj. prof. Quinnipiac Coll. Sch. Law, 1986—. Sr. editor Conn. Bar Jour., 1971-80, 83—, editor-in-chief, 1980-83; contbr. to legal jours. Mem. nat. bd. ACLU, 1975-79; mem. Westport (Conn.) Planning & Zoning Commn., 1971-75; chmn. Conn. CLU, 1988-95, legal advisor, 1995—. Served with U.S. Army, 1944-46. Decorated Purple Heart; recipient First Award for Disting. Service to Conn. Bar, Conn. Law Tribune, 1987. Mem. ABA, Conn. Bar Assn. (chmn. human rights sect. 1970-73), Nat. Assn. Criminal Def. Lawyers. Home: 72 Myrtle Ave Westport CT 06880-3512 Office: 600 Summer St Stamford CT 06901-1403

MARGOLIS, EUGENE, lawyer, government official; b. Bronx, N.Y., Dec. 19, 1935; s. Louis and Minnie (Kaplan) M.; m. Sally Fay Gellman, Sept. 22, 1962; children—Judith Miriam, Linda Aileen, Aaron Keith, Pamela June. BME, Rensselaer Poly. Inst., 1957; JD, Georgetown U., 1960, M in Patent Law, 1962. Bar: N.Y. 1961, U.S. Supreme Ct. 1969; cert. exec. U.S. Office Personnel Mgmt., 1983. Patent examiner U.S. Patent Office, Washington, 1957-60; trial atty. antitrust div. U.S. Dept. Justice, Washington, 1960-66, N.Y.C., 1966-67; chief consumer protection div. N.Y.C. Dept. Law, 1967-71; gen. counsel Mayor's Interdeptl. Com. on Pub. Utilities, N.Y.C., 1972-73; spl. counsel to commr. N.Y.C. Dept. Gen. Services, 1974-79; dir. N.Y.C. Office of Energy Conservation, 1975-79; sr. legal adviser U.S. Dept. Energy, Washington, 1979-95, dep. asst. gen. counsel, 1995—; adj. prof. Cooper Union, 1978-79; adj. assoc. prof. Grad. Sch., CUNY, 1974-80. Mem. editorial bd. Georgetown Law Jour., 1958-60. Chmn. govtl. relations and grants com. Village of Larchmont, N.Y., 1977-79, mem. cable TV com., 1977-79, mem. tax base com., 1974-79; chmn. Larchmont Democratic Com., 1976-77; vice chmn. Mamaroneck Dem. Com., 1979; mem. Westchester County Dem. Com., 1975-77, 79; bd. dirs. Jewish Community Coun. Greater Washington, 1986-94; mem. adv. bd. Dept. Volunteerism, Commonwealth Va., 1987-91; mem. pub. social policy com. United Jewish Appeal-Fedn. Greater Washington, 1988—, mem. No. Va. leadership coun. 1990—; bd. govs. B'nai Brith Internat., 1992-94, 95—, internat. coun., 1992-94, Hillel com., 1991-94, mem. nat. fund raising cabinet, 1987-90, com. on community vol. svcs., 1985-89, pres. dist. 5, 1993-94, pres. Va. State Assn., 1986-87, pres. Va. Hillel Found., 1985-86. Recipient Cert. of Appreciation U.S. Dept. Energy, 1984, Sec. of Energy's Award, Outstanding Community Svc. Vol., 1990, Gov. Va.'s Cmty. Svc. and Volunteerism award, 1995. Mem. N.Y. State Bar Assn., ASME, Phi Delta Phi, Pi Delta Epsilon, Tau Epsilon Phi. Jewish. Clubs: Rensselaer Alumni (sec. chpt. 1976-77), U. Va. Fund Parents, Town and Village Synagogue Men's (pres. 1970-71). Lodge: B'nai Brith (pres. Mcpl. lodge 1976-78, Larchmont-Mamaroneck lodge 1978-80, Masada lodge 1984-85, Internat. Lodge Col. Elliot A. Niles Community Svc. award 1984, Dist. 5 Outstanding Ben Brith award 1988, Outstanding State Pres. award 1987, Hillel award 1986, Community Vol. Svc. award 1984, Va. State Assn. Herman G. Koplen Meml. award 1987, Sherry B. Rose Leadership award 1984). Home: 6504 Sparrow Point Ct Mc Lean VA 22101-1638 Office: US Dept Energy Forrestal Bldg 1000 Independence Ave SE Washington DC 20585-0001

MARGOLIS, GERALD, museum director; b. Montreal, Quebec, Can., Mar. 8, 1944; came to U.S., 1963; s. Samuel and Ida (Lebner) M.; m. Lila Sara Cymet; children: David Seth, Jessica Simone. BA, U. Calif., 1968, MA, 1970, PhD in English, 1977. Cert. Comty. Coll. supr., Comty. Coll. adminstrv. officer, Calif. Lectr. in English U. Calif., Santa Barbara, 1970-79; dean Kerem Coll., Santa Clara, Calif., 1979-82; dir. acad. devel. Yeshiva U. of L.A., 1982-83; dir. Simon Wiesenthal Ctr., L.A., 1983—, Mus. of Tolerance, L.A., 1992—; mem. State of Calif. Commn. on Prevention of Hate Violence, 1991—, Hate Violence Response Alliance, Human Rels. Commn., L.A., 1992—. Editor: (film guides) Resource guide to The Inheritors, 1985, Tchr.'s guide to Genocide, 1987; author, designer (mus. exhibit) The Courage to Remember, 1988; contbr. op-ed essays to L.A. Times, Miami Herald, Newsday, L.A. Herald Examiner, Dallas Times Herald, Cleve. Plain Dealer, Star and Tribune; cons. (TV series, films) War and Remembrance, 1985-88, The Execution,1985, Wallenberg: A Hero's Story, 1985, Shoah, 1986; editor (annual) Simon Wiesenthal Ctr., 1984-88. Mem. MLA, Am. Assn. Mus., Internat. Coun. Mus., Am. Hist. Assn., Assn. of Holacaust Orgns., Internat. Acad. Adv. Bd. Simon Wiesenthal Ctr. Office: Mus of Tolerance 9786 W Pico Blvd Los Angeles CA 90035

MARGOLIS, GERALD JOSEPH, psychiatrist, psychoanalyst; b. Bronx, N.Y., May 7, 1935; s. Max and Sophie (Siegel) M.; A.B., U. Rochester, 1957; M.D., U. Chgo., 1960; postgrad. Inst. Phila. Assn. Psychoanalysis, 1972; m. June Edelman Greenspan, July 13, 1976; children: David J., Peter S., Steven J. Intern, psychiat. resident, Upstate Med. Center, SUNY, Syracuse, 1960-64, instr. psychiatry, 1966-67; from instr. to clin. prof. psychiatry Med. Sch., U. Pa., Phila., 1967—; practice medicine specializing in psychiatry and psychoanalysis, Cherry Hill, N.J.; tng. and supervising analyst Inst. of Phila. Assn. for Psychoanalysis. Served with M.C., USAF, 1964-66. Diplomate Am. Bd. Psychiatry and Neurology. Mem. Am. Psychoanalytic Assn. (cert.), Am. Psychiat. Assn., AMA, Phila. Assn. for Psychoanalysis (tng. and supervising analyst), Phi Beta Kappa. Club: B'nai B'rith. Contbr. articles to profl. publs. Home: 408 Park Ln Moorestown NJ 08057-2000 Office: One Cherry Hill One Mall Dr Ste 930 Cherry Hill NJ 08002-2194

MARGOLIS, HAROLD STEPHEN, epidemiologist; b. Tucson, Ariz., Feb. 22, 1946; s. Maurice H. and Helen (Letz) M.; m. Susan Helen Quinn, July 3, 1971; children: Ellis, Leah, Amber. BS, U. Ariz., 1968, MD, 1972. Diplomate Am. Bd. Med. Examiners. Resident in pediatrics U. Colo. Health Scis. Ctr., Denver, 1972-75; med. epidemiologist Ctrs. for Disease Control, Anchorage, 1975-79, Phoenix, Ariz., 1981-83; dep. chief hepatitis br. Ctrs. for Disease Control, Atlanta, 1983-87; chief hepatitis br., 1995—; chief Ctrs. for Disease Control, Atlanta, 1987—; rsch. fellow Nat. Jewish Hosp., Denver, 1979-81; dir. WHO Collaborative Ctr. for Rsch. and Reference in Viral Hepatitis, Atlanta, 1987—; cons. WHO, 1988, 89, Agy. for Internat. Devel.; guest advisor Inst. Medicine, 1989, 92. Editor: Viral Hepatitis and Liver Disease, 1991; contbr. articles to profl. jours. Capt. USPHS, 1975—. Fellow Am. Acad. Pediats., Infectious Disease Soc. Am.; mem. Alpha Omega Alpha, Sigma Xi. Achievements include development of strategies to prevent viral hepatitis through immunization; research in characterization of hepatitis A viruses and molecular pathogenesis of viral hepatitis. Office: Nat Ctr for Infectious Diseases Hepatitis Branch 1600 Clifton Rd NE Atlanta GA 30329-4018*

MARGOLIS, JULIUS, economist, educator; b. N.Y.C., Sept. 26, 1920; s. Sam and Fannie (Weiner) M.; m. Doris Lubetsky, Oct. 30, 1942; children—Jane S., Carl W. B.S.S., City Coll. N.Y., 1941; Ph.M. in Econs, U. Wis., 1943; M.P.A. in Econs, Harvard, 1947, Ph.D., 1949. Instr. econs. Tufts Coll., 1947-48; asst. prof. econs. and planning U. Chgo., 1948-51; asst. prof. econs. Stanford, 1951-54; prof. bus adminstrn. U. Calif. at Berkeley, 1954-64; prof. econs. and engring. econ. systems Stanford, 1964-69; prof., dir. Fels Center of Govt., U. Pa., 1969-76; prof. econs. U. Calif. at Irvine, 1976—; dir. Ctr. on Global Peace and Conflict Studies, 1985—; cons. to govt. and industry, 1958—. Author: (with others) The Public Economy of Urban Communities, 1965, The Northern California's Water Industry, 1966, Public Economics, 1969, Public Expenditure and Policy Analysis, 1984; also articles. Served with AUS, 1943-46. Mem. Am. Econ. Assn., Royal Econ. Soc. Home: 45 Whitman Ct Irvine CA 92715-4059 Office: U Calif Dept Econ Irvine CA 92717

MARGOLIS, LAWRENCE STANLEY, federal judge; b. Phila., Mar. 13, 1935; s. Reuben and Mollie (Manus) M.; m. Doris May Rosenberg, Jan. 30, 1960; children: Mary Aleta, Paul Oliver. BSME, Drexel U., 1957; JD, George Washington U., 1961. Bar: D.C. 1963. Patent examiner U. S. Patent Office, Washington, 1957-62; patent counsel Naval Ordnance Lab., White Oak, Md., 1962-63; asst. corp. counsel D.C., 1963-66; atty. criminal div., spl. asst. U.S. atty. Dept. of Justice, Washington, 1966-68; asst. U.S. atty. for D.C., 1968-71; U.S. magistrate judge U.S. Dist. Ct., Washington, 1971-82; judge U.S. Ct. Fed. Claims, Washington, 1982—; chmn. task force on discovery reform U.S. Claims Ct., Washington, chmn. alt. dispute resolution; mem. faculty Fed. Jud. Ctr. Editor-in-chief The Young Lawyer, 1965-66, D.C. Bar Jour., 1967-73; bd. editors The Dist. Lawyer, 1978-82. Trustee Drexel U., 1983-89; bd. govs. George Washington U. Alumni Assn., 1978-85, 93—. Recipient Contbn. award D.C. Jaycees, 1966, Svc. award Boy Scouts Am., 1970, Alumni Svc. award George Washington U., 1976, Disting. Alumni Achievement award George Washington U., 1985, Disting. Alumni Achievement award Drexel U., 1988, Drexel 100 award, 1992, Alt. Dispute Resolution award Ctr. for Pub. Resources, 1988, Alumni Recognition award George Washington U., 1996. Fellow Inst. Jud. Adminstrn., Am. Bar Found.; mem. ABA (chmn. jud. adminstrn. divsn., Disting. Svc. award 1981), ABA Nat. Conf. Spl. Ct. Judges (chmn., Disting. Svc. award 1978), D.C. Jud. Conf., Bar Assn. D.C. (bd. dirs. 1970-72, jour. editor-in-chief, Contbn. award young lawyers sect. 1983), Fed. Bar Assn., George Washington U. Nat. Law Assn. (pres. D.C. chpt. 1974-76, pres. 1983-84), Univ. Club, Rotary (bd. dirs. Washington 1984-90, pres. 1988-89, dist. gov. 1991-92, Rotarian of Yr. 1984), Charles Fahy Am. Inn of Ct. Office: US Ct Fed Claims 717 Madison Pl NW Ste 703 Washington DC 20005-1011

MARGOLIS, LEO, marine biologist; b. Montreal, Que., Can., Dec. 18, 1927; m. Ruth Anne Lall; children: Rhonda Lee, Robert Allan, Murray Howard, Conrad Anton. B.Sc., McGill U., 1948, M.Sc., 1950, Ph.D., 1952. Rsch. scientist Pacific Biol. Sta., Can. Dept. Fish and Oceans, Nanaimo, B.C., 1952-67, head various rsch. divs., 1967-81, head fish health and parasitology sect., 1981-90, sr. scientist, 1990—; co-chmn. Can. Com. on Fish Diseases, 1970-73; mem. com. on biology and rsch. Internat. North Pacific Fisheries Commn., 1971-93, sr. Can. scientist, 1976-93, advisor Can. sect., 1976-93; advisor Fed.-Provincial Fish Com., 1969, 70, 78; mem. Can. Del. North Pacific Anadromous Fish Commn., 1993—, chmn. com. sci. rsch. and stats., 1993-95; mem. editl. referees com. Bull. Internat. North Pacific Fisheries Commn., 1976-84; mem. adv. bd. sci. info. and publs. Fisheries and

Oceans Can., 1979-83; mem. aquatic sci. rsch. evaluation com. Sci. Coun. B.C., 1979-88, chmn., 1986-88; adj. prof. Simon Fraser U., 1983—; cons. Internat. Devel. Rsch. Ctr., 1986; mem. nat. tech. com. Can. Fish Health Protection Regulations, 1990—; mem. sci. adv. com. N.B. Aquaculture Consortium, 1991—; mem. external adv. com. BSc in Biology program Malaspina Coll., 1992—. Assoc. editor Can. Jour. Zoology, 1971-81, Jour. World Aquaculture Soc., 1986—; mem. editl. bd., editl. cons. Jour. of Parasitology, 1977-93; mem. adv. bd. Amphipacifica, Jour. of Systematic Biology, 1993—; editl. advisor Diseases of Aquatic Organisms Jour., 1994—; author 3 books; editor 6 books; contbr. articles on parasites and diseases of fishes and other aquatic animals, and on biology of salmon to various profl. jours. Pres. B.C. Amateur Hockey Assn., 1963-66, hon. v.p., 1968-88, life mem. 1988—, Diamond Stick award, 1989, Can. Amateur Hockey Assn. Order of Merit, 1990. Decorated officer Order of Can.; recipient Commemorative medal 125th Anniversary Confedn. Can., 1992, Gold medal Profl. Inst. Pub. Svc. of Can., 1995. Fellow Royal Soc. Can.; mem. Can. Soc. Zoologists (coun. mem. parasitology sect. 1977-78, recognition com. 1985-88, 93-95, 2d v.p. 1988-89, 1st. v.p. 1989-90, pres. 1990-91, recognition com. 1991-94, chmn. 1991-93, bd. trustees Zool. Edn. Trust 1988-93, chmn. 1990-91, R.A. Wardle lectr. award 1982), Atlantic Can. Soc. Parasitologists (hon.), Am. Soc. Parasitologists (in memoriam com. 1982, pub. responsibilities com. 1988, chmn. nominating com. 1992-93, coun. 1994—, Disting. Svc. award 1995), Can. Fedn. Biol. Socs. (bd. dirs. 1990-91), Am. Fisheries Soc. (awards com. 1975-76), Wildlife Disease Assn., Aquaculture Assn. Can., World Aquaculture Soc., Asian Fisheries Soc., Brit. Soc. for Parasitology (hon.). Office: Pacific Biol Sta, Nanaimo, BC Canada V9R 5K6

MARGOLIS, PHILIP MARCUS, psychiatrist, educator; b. Lima, Ohio, July 7, 1925; s. Harry Sterling and Clara (Brunner) M.; m. Nancy Nupuf, July 26, 1959; children: Cynthia, Marc, David, Laurence. B.A. magna cum laude, U. Minn., 1945, M.D., 1948. Diplomate Am. Bd. Psychiatry and Neurology (examiner 1973—). Intern Milw. County Hosp., 1948-49; resident VA Hosp. and U. Minn., 1949-52, Mass. Gen. Hosp. and Harvard U., Boston, 1952-54; instr. U. Minn., Milw., 1953-55; asst. prof. dept. psychiatry Med. Sch., U. Chgo., 1955-60, assoc. prof., 1960-66; prof. psychiatry Med. Sch. U. Mich., 1966—, prof. cmty. mental health, 1968—, mem. civil liberties bd., 1995—, chair civil liberties bd., 1996—; chief psychiat. inpatient service U. Chgo. Hosps. and Clinics, 1956-66; cons. Forensic Psychiat. Ctr., State of Mich., 1972—, coord. med. student edn. program, 1975-78, dir., 1978-82; cons. Turner Geriatric Clin., 1978-86, cons. Breast Cancer Clinic, 1988, Powertrain subs. Gen. Motors, 1984—, Dept. Mental Health, U.S. Dept. Justice; assoc. chief clin. affairs U. Mich. Hosps., 1981-85, chmn. ethics com.; bd. dirs., mem. profl. rev. com. PSRO Area VII, 1982-86; mem. Mich. State Bd. Medicine, 1986-94, chmn. 1992-94, senate adv. com. Univ. Affairs., 1986-89; bd. dirs. Fedn. of State Med. Bds., 1994—, Mich. del., 1988—, FLEX Com. Nat. Bd. Med. Examiners. Author: Guide for Mental Health Workers, 1970, Patient Power: The Development of a Therapeutic Community in a General Hospital, 1974; also articles.; cons. editor: Community Mental Health jour, 1967—. Recipient Commonwealth Fund fellow award, 1964, Career Svc. award, 1992, Resident Appreciation award, 1991. Fellow Am. Coll. Psychiatrists, Am. Psychiat. Assn. (life, chmn. membership com. 1979-83, cons. ethics com. 1983-86, trustee 1985-88, sec. 1989-91, cons. steering com. on practical guidelines, 1991—, mem. assembly 1992—, coun. med. edn. and career devel. 1993—, budget com. 1991—, chmn. ethics appeals bd. 1989—, pres. Lifers 1994—); mem. Washtenaw County Med. Soc. (exec. coun. 1982—, chmn. ethics com. 1983-87, pres. 1987-88, editl. bd. 1995—), Mich. Psychiat. Soc. (pres. 1980-81, chmn. ethics com. 1983-86), Mich. State Med. Soc. (bioethics com., 1989—, com. on med. licensure and discipline, 1995—, legis. and regulations com., 1995—, mental health liaison com., 1995—, Internat. Assn. Social Psychiatry, World Fedn. Mental Health, Am. Acad. Psychoanalysis, Am. Acad. Psychiatry and Law (com. on psychoanalytic edn. 1995—). Home: 228 Riverview Dr Ann Arbor MI 48104-1846 Office: 900 Wall St Ann Arbor MI 48105-1910

MARGOLIS, RICHARD MARTIN, photographer, educator; b. Lorain, Ohio, June 10, 1943; s. Harold and Claudine (Martin) M.; m. Sherry Lynn Phillips. BS, Kent State U., 1969; MFA, Rochester Inst. Tech, 1978. Asst. prof. SUNY-Brockport, 1981-88; presenter Bridge Project, Stories about Bridges, Soc. for Indsl. Archeology Nat. Conf., 1995; delivered 1995 Barbara L. Bush Meml. Lectr., Longwood Coll., Farmville, Va. Exhibitor over 70 one-person shows, including Foto, N.Y.C., 1976, 79, 81, 83, Carpenter Ctr., Harvard u., 1978, George Eastman House, Rochester, N.Y., 1978, Camden Arts Ctr., London, 1981, NAS, Washington, 1990, Magic Powers, Rochester, 1991, Bridges: Symbols of Progress, catalog and exhbn. on nat. tour, 1991-94, Rochester's Landmarks Airport Art Project Permanent Insallation; group shows 130 Yrs. of Ohio Photography, Columbus, 1978, Contemporary Expression, Catskill Ctr. for Photography, Woodstock, N.Y., 1979; curator (exhbns.), 1980, 82; curator: Photography Art of State, 1983, Computers and Photography, 1989; contbr. Contemporary Photographers, 3rd edit., 1995, Photographers Encyclopedia International, 1939 to the Present, 1985, Photographic Artists and Innovators, 1983. Creative Artists Pub. Svc. Found. grantee N.Y. State Coun. on Arts, 1977-78; N.Y. State Coun. on Arts grantee to photograph N.Y. bridges, 1985, 90; SUNY Rsch. Found. incentive grantee, 1983; Lift grantee, 1989; recipient Individual Artist award Rochester N.Y. Arts and Cultural Alliance, 1994. Mem. Soc. for Photog. Edn. (chmn. 1982-83), Photog. Heritage Assn. (founder, steering com.), Soc. for Indsl. Archaeology. Studio: 250 North Goodman St Rochester NY 14607

MARGOLIS, SIDNEY O., textile and apparel company executive; b. Boston, Dec. 13, 1925; s. Joseph and Lillian (Frank) M.; m. Phyllis Teichberg, June 24, 1950; children: Jonathan S., Dean F., Brian B. BS in Indsl. Engring., Ohio State U., 1949. Indsl. engr. ACME Backing Corp., Bklyn., 1949-53; purchasing agt. Flexible Barriers Inc., Stamford, Conn., 1953-57; office mgr. United Mchts. and Mfrs. Inc., N.Y.C., 1957-69, comptroller merchandising, 1970-77, v.p. adminstrn., 1977-80, sr. v.p. adminstrn., 1980—, exec. v.p. adminstrn., 1984—, also bd. dirs.; bd. dirs. 10 West 86th Street Corp., N.Y.C. Cpl. USAAF, 1943-44. Mem. Inst. Indsl. Engrs. (recipient 25 yr. disting. svc. award N.Y.C. chpt. 1985), Am. Inst. Indsl. Engrs. (Svc. award 1984), Adminstrv. Mgmt. Soc., Textile Distbrs. Assn., Am. Textile Mfrs. Inst. Avocations: sports, travel, reading, water skiing, tennis. Office: United Mchts & Mfrs Inc 1650 Palisade Ave Teaneck NJ 07666-3630

MARGOLIS, SYLVIA GANZ, retired secondary education educator; b. Norfolk, Va., Aug. 6, 1910; d. Morris Louis and Pauline (Buch) Margolius; m. Irving H. Ganz, Feb. 23, 1941 (dec. Sept. 1969); 1 child, Marshall Louis; m. Morris D. Margolis, Mar. 30, 1974 (dec. May 1977). AB, Coll. William and Mary, 1932; postgrad., UCLA, Calif. State U., Fresno, U. Calif., Long Beach, Sorbonne, Paris. Cert. tchr., Calif., Va. English tchr. YWCA, Richmond, Va., 1937-40; substitute tchr. Am. Dependents' Schs., Germany, 1946-49; tchr. Fresno City Schs., 1951-53, Kern County Schs., Richland, Calif., 1953-66, L.A. Unified Sch. Dist., 1966-76; mem. State Com., Sacramento, 1964-65; del. Nat. Edn. Assn. to World Conf. of Educators, West Berlin, 1975; lectr. numerous orgns. Bd. mem. YWCA, Bay City, Mich., 1943-46; chair United Nations Day, Bakersfield, Calif., 1960; bd. mem. Jewish Fedn. Coun. L.A., 1968-74; vol. tchr. at local C.C., Northridge, Calif., 1980-81; mem. com. Judaic studies at Coll. William and Mary, Williamsburg, Va., 1983-87. Recipient cert. appreciation Girl Scout Coun., Johnstown, Pa., 1942; Fed. Dept. Edn. grantee Univ. Pitts., 1962. Mem. AAUW (edn. rep. 1978-80, San Fernando Valley br. bd. mem. 1979-84, del. to UN Conf. on Women in Copenhagen 1980), Anti-Defamation League, Hadassah (bd. mem. 1978-85), Bridges for Peace (Am.), Coll. William and Mary Alumni Assn. (mem. com. on Judaic studies 1980s), B'nai Brith Women, Phi Kappa Phi, Tau Kappa Alpha. Democrat. Jewish. Avocations: reading, writing poetry, participating in study and discussion groups, traveling. Home: 18627 Victory Blvd Reseda CA 91335-6442

MARGOLIUS, HARRY STEPHEN, pharmacologist, physician; b. Albany, N.Y., Jan. 29, 1938; s. Irving Robert and Betty (Zweig) M.; m. Francine Rockwood, May 22, 1964; children: Elizabeth Anne, Craig Matthew. BS, Union U., 1959, PhD, 1963; MD, U. Cin., 1968. Diplomate Nat. Bd. Med. Examiners, 1969, chmn. pharmacology test com., 1990-94. Intern, resident Harvard Med. Svc. Boston City Hosp., 1968-70, pharmcology rsch. assoc., 1970-72; sr. clin. investigator NHLBI NIH, Bethesda, 1972-74; assoc. prof. pharmacology, asst. prof. medicine Med. U. S.C., Charleston, 1974-77, prof. pharmacology, assoc. prof. medicine, 1977-80, prof. pharmacology, prof. medicine, 1980—, chmn. pharmacology, 1989—; cons. NIH, FDA, VA, NSF, Washington, Bethesda, 1975—; mem. editorial bd. Am. Heart Assn., Dallas, 1980—. Editor: Kinins IV, 1986, Renal Function, Hypertension and Kallikrein-Kinin System, 1988; contbr. numerous articles to profl. jours. Commdr. USPHS, 1967-74. Recipient S.C. Gov.'s award for sci. S.C. Acad. Scis., 1988; Burroughs-Wellcome scholar, 1976; vis. scholar U. Cambridge, Eng., 1980-81; sr. fellow Fitzwilliam Coll., 1996; NIH grantee, 1975—; named Theodore Cooper Meml. Lectr., 1995. Fellow Coun. for High Blood Pressure Rsch., Am. Heart Assn.; mem. Am. Soc. for Pharmacology and Exptl. Therapeutics, Am. Soc. for Clin. Investigation and 10 additional med., sci. socs. Jewish. Achievements include studies of the role of kallikreins and kinins in human and animal forms of hypertension; discovery of abnormalities which signify roles in causing high blood pressure. Office: Medical Univ of SC College of Medicine 171 Ashley Ave Charleston SC 29425-0001

MARGON, BRUCE HENRY, astrophysicist, educator; b. N.Y.C., Jan. 7, 1948; s. Leon and Maxine E. (Margon) Siegelbaum; m. Carolyn J. Bloom, May 8, 1976; 1 dau., Pamela. A.B., Columbia U., 1968; M.A., U. Calif.-Berkeley, 1971, Ph.d., 1973. Asst. rsch. astronomer U. Calif.-Berkeley, 1973-76; assoc. prof. astronomy UCLA, 1976-80; prof. astronomy U. Wash., Seattle, 1980—, chmn., 1981-87, 90-95; bd. govs. Astrophys. Rsch. Consortium, Inc., Seattle; chmn. bd. dirs. AURA, Inc., Washington; co-investigator Hubble space telescope NASA, Washington, 1977—. NATO postdoctoral fellow, 1973-74; Sloan Found. research fellow, 1979-83. Fellow AAAS, Am. Phys. Soc.; mem. Internat. Astron. Union, Am. Astron. Soc. (Pierce Prize 1981), Royal Astron. Soc. Office: Univ Wash Box 351580 Astronomy Dept Seattle WA 98195-1580

MARGRAVE, JOHN LEE, chemist, educator, university administrator; b. Kansas City, Kans., Apr. 13, 1924; s. Orville Frank and Bernice J. (Hamilton) M.; m. Mary Lou Davis, June 11, 1950; children: David Russell, Karen Sue. B.S. in Engring. Physics, U. Kans., 1948, Ph.D. in Chemistry, 1950. AEC postdoctoral fellow U. Calif. at Berkeley, 1951-52; from instr. to prof. chemistry U. Wis., Madison, 1952-63; prof. chemistry Rice U., 1963—, E.D. Butcher chair, 1986—, chmn. dept., 1967-72, dean advanced studies and research, 1972-80, v.p., 1980-86; v.p. for research Houston Advanced Research Ctr., 1986-89, chief sci. officer, 1989—; dir. Materials Sci. Ctr., 1986-93; vis. prof. chem. Tex. So. U., 1993—; dir. Council for Chem. Research, 1985-88; Reilly lectr. Notre Dame, 1968, Phi Lambda Upsilon lectr. Kans. State U., 1995; vis. distinguished prof. U. Wis., 1968, U. Iowa, 1969, U. Colo., 1975, Ga. Inst. Tech., 1978, U. Tex. at Austin, 1978, U. Utah, 1982; Seydel-Wooley lectr. Ga. Inst. Tech., 1970; Dupont lectr. U. S.C., 1971; Abbott lectr. U. N.D., 1972; Cyanamid lectr. U. Conn., 1973; Sandia lectr. U. N.Mex., 1981; R.A. Welch lectr., 1985; NSF-Japan Joint Thermophys. Properties Symposium, 1983; chmn. com. on chem. processes in severe nuclear accidents NRC, 1987-88; mem. Wilhelm und Else Heraeus Stiffung Found. Symposium on Alkali Metal Reactions, Fed. Republic Germany, 1988; various nat. and internat. confs. on chem. vapor deposition of thin diamond films, 1989-95; orgnl. com. First, Second Third and Fourth World Superconductivity Congresses, 1989, 90, 92, 94, NATO Conf. on Supercooled Metals, Il Ciocio, Italy, 1993; mem. adv. coms. chem., materials sci., rsch. U. Tenn. Knoxville, Ohio State U., Tex. So. U., La. Bd. Regents, sci. adv. bd. SI Diamond Tech., 1992—, BioNumerik, 1993—, Intrepid Tech., 1994—; cons. to govt. and industry, 1954—; pres. Mar Chem., Inc., 1970—, High Temperature Sci., Inc., 1976—; dir. Rice Design Center, Houston Area Research Ctr.; U. Kans. Research Found., Gulf Univs. Research Consortium, Energy Research and Edn. Found., Spectroscopic Assocs., World Congress on Superconductivity; advisor NROTC Assn., 1984—. Editor: Modern High Temperature Sci., 1984; contbg. editor Characterization of High Temperature Vapors, 1967, Mass. Spectrometry in Inorganic Chemistry, 1968; editor High Temperature Sci., 1969—, Procs. XXIII and XXIV Confs. on Mass Spectrometry, 1975, 76; author: (with others) Bibliography of Matrix Isolation Spectroscopy, 1950-85, 87; contbr. articles to profl. jours. Served with AUS, 1943-46; capt. Res. ret. Sloan research fellow, 1957-58; Guggenheim fellow, 1960; recipient Kiekhofer Teaching award U. Wis., 1957; IR-100 award for CFX lubricant powder, 1970, IR-100 award for Cryolink, 1986; Tex. Honor Scroll award, 1978; Disting. Alumni citation U. Kans., 1981, Sci. and Tech. award North Harris Montgomery Cmty. Coll., 1994. Fellow AAAS, Am. Inst. Chemists, Am. Phys. Soc., Tex. Acad. Sci.; mem. AAUP, NAS, Am. Chem. Soc. (Inorganic Chemistry award 1967, S.W. Regional award 1978, Fluorine Chemistry award 1980, S.E. Tex. Sect. award 1993, chem. edn. com. 1968-70, publs. com. 1973-74, patents and related matters com. 1994—), Am. Ceramic Soc., Am. Soc. Mass Spectrometry (dir.), Am. Soc. Metals, Electrochem. Soc., Chem. Soc. London, Tex. Philos. Soc., Materials Rsch. Soc., Sigma Xi (Disting. Svc. award 1994), Omicron Delta Kappa, Sigma Tau, Tau Beta Pi, Alpha Chi Sigma. Methodist. Patentee in field. Home: 5012 Tangle Ln Houston TX 77056-2114 Office: Rice University PO Box 1892 6100 South Main Houston TX 77005

MARGULIES, JULIANNA, actress. Actress (film) Out for Justice, 1991 (TV) Murder, She Wrote, Law and Order, Homicide, ER, 1994—(Emmy award for supporting actress Drama, 1995). Office: The Gersh Agy Inc 232 N Canon Dr Beverly Hills CA 90210*

MARGULIES, JAMES HOWARD, editorial cartoonist; b. Bklyn., Oct. 8, 1951; s. Henry Norman and Miriam Margulies; m. Martha Anne Golub, May 21, 1978; children: Elana, David. BFA, Carnegie-Mellon U., 1973. Editorial cartoonist Jour. Newspapers, Springfield, Va., 1980-84, Houston Post, 1984-90, The Record, Hackensack, N.J., 1990—; syndicated cartoonist various newspapers, 1985—. Author: My Husband is Not a Wimp, 1988; contbr. columns to profl. jours.; cartoons featured on TV programs. Mem. leadership com. Jewish Community Ctr., Houston, 1987, 88. Recipient Best Cartoon award Population Inst., 1985, Global Media award, 1985, 2d Place Editl. award Pavillion of Humor, 1985, Judges award World Hunger Media awards, 1986, Katie award Press Club of Dallas, 1989, Best Black and White Illustration in Advt. and Graphic Arts Addy award Houston Advt. Fedn., 1990, John Peter Zenger award N.Y. State Bar Assn., 1992, Nat. Headliner award for editl. cartoons; named one of Texans Who Made the Eighties winter Ultra Mag., 1990. Mem. Assn. Am. Editorial Cartoonists. Avocation: running. Office: The Record 150 River St Hackensack NJ 07601-7110

MARGULIES, JEFFREY J., lawyer; b. Sioux Falls, S.D., 1946. BA magna cum laude, U. Iowa, 1968, JD with high distinction, 1973. Bar: Ohio 1973. Ptnr. Squire, Sanders & Dempsey, Cleve. Mem. ABA, Ohio Bar Assn., Cleve. Bar Assn. Office: Squire Sanders & Dempsey 4900 Society Ct 127 Public Sq Cleveland OH 44114-1216*

MARGULIES, LAURA JACOBS, lawyer; b. Bklyn., Feb. 5, 1956; d. David and Marcia (Reichman) Jacobs; children: Moshe, Yaakov, Miriam, Yehuda, Shira. BS in Edn., HTD, Yeshiva U., 1977; JD, U. Balt., 1988. Bar: Md. 1988, D.C. 1990. Jud. intern to Hon. James F. Schneider U.S. Bankruptcy Ct., Balt., 1986; law clk. Shawe & Rosenthal, Balt., 1987-88; law clk. to Hon. Paul E. Alpert Md. Ct. Spl. Appeals, Towson, 1988-89; assoc. Semmes, Bowen & Semmes, Balt., 1989-92, Shaw, Pittman, Potts & Trowbridge, Washington, 1992-93; pvt. practice Rockville, Md., 1993—; adj. prof. U. Md. U. Coll., College Park, 1993—; civil mediator Cir. Ct. of Balt. City, 1991-93. Editor U. Balt. Law Review, 1986-88. Recipient David Gann scholarship U. Balt. Sch. Law, 1987. Mem. Bankruptcy Bar Assn. for Dist. of Md. (so. div. co-chmn. 1994-95, chmn. 1995-96), Md. State Bar Assn., D.C. Bar Assn. Avocations; walking, reading, swimming. Office: 1 Church St Ste 802 Rockville MD 20850

MARGULIES, LEE, newspaper editor. Television editor Los Angeles Times, Calif. Office: Los Angeles Times Times Mirror Sq Los Angeles CA 90053

MARGULIES, MARTIN B., lawyer, educator; b. N.Y.C., Oct. 6, 1940; s. Max N. and Mae (Cohen) M.; m. Beth Ellen Zeldes, July 26, 1981; children: Max Zeldes, Adam Zeldes. AB, Columbia Coll., 1961; LLB, Harvard U., 1964; LLM, NYU, 1966. Bar: N.D. 1968, N.Y. 1974, Mass. 1977, U.S. Dist. Ct. Mass. 1977, U.S. Ct. Appeals (2d cir.) 1984, Conn. 1988. Asst. prof. law U. N.D., Grand Forks, 1966-69; editor-in-chief Columbia Coll. Today, Columbia U., N.Y.C., 1969-71; assoc. editor Parade Mag., N.Y.C., 1971-72; assoc. prof. law Western New Eng. Law Sch., Springfield, Mass., 1973-76; Bernard Hersher prof. law U. Bridgeport, Conn., 1977-92; prof. law Quinnipiac Coll., 1992—. Author: The Early Life of Sean O'Casey, 1970. Contbr. articles to profl. jours. Cooperating atty. Conn. Civil Liberties Union, Hartford, 1979—, bd. dirs., 1982-94; bd. dirs. Conn. Attys. for Progressive Legislature, New Haven, 1982—; bd. dirs. ACLU, 1987-94, mem. free speech-assn. and poverty constitutional rights com. 1988-94; chmn. bd. dirs. Fairfield County Civil Liberties Union, 1982-87, Hampden County Civil Liberties Union, 1976-78; bd. dirs. Civil Liberties Union Mass., Boston, 1975-78, Greater Springfield Urban League, 1976-78, Conn. Civil Liberties Union, 1982-94, ACLU, 1987-94. Ctr. for First Amendment Rights, Inc., 1993—. Recipient Media award N.Y. State Bar Assn., 1972, Gavel award ABA, 1973, Outstanding Tchr. award U. Bridgeport Law Sch., 1986, 87. Mem. Mass. Bar Assn., N.Y. State Bar Assn. Jewish. Home: 79 High Rock Rd Sandy Hook CT 06482-1623 Office: Quinnipiac Coll Sch Law 275 Mt Carmel Ave Hamden CT 06518-1947

MARGULIS, ALEXANDER RAFAILO, physician, educator; b. Belgrade, Yugoslavia, Mar. 21, 1921; came to U.S., 1946; s. Rafailo and Olga (Weiss-Belic) M.; m. Hedvig Hricak, Feb. 26, 1983; 1 son, Peter Hricak-Margulis. Student, U. Belgrade, 1939-41, 45-46; MD, Harvard U., 1950; hon. doctorates, Aix-Marseille U. Sch. Medicine, 1980, Med. Coll. Wis., 1986, Cath. U. Louvain, 1986, Karolinska Inst., Stockholm, 1986, U. Munich, 1987, U. Toulouse, 1987, U. Montpellier, 1993. Diplomate Am. Bd. Radiology. Intern Henry Ford Hosp., Detroit, 1950-51; resident in radiology U. Mich. Hosps., 1951-53; jr. clin. instr. U. Mich., 1953-54; instr., then asst. prof. U. Minn., 1954-59; asst. prof. sch. medicine Washington U., St. Louis, 1959-60, assoc. prof. to prof., 1960-63; prof. radiology, chmn. dept. U. Calif., San Francisco, 1963-89, dir. magnetic resonance Sci. Ctr., assoc. chancellor spl. projects, 1989-93; spl. cons. to vice chancellor U. Calif.; radiologist in chief U. Calif. Hosps., 1963-89; cons. VA Hosp., Letterman Gen. Hosp., San Francisco, U.S. Naval Hosp., Oakland, Calif.; cons. in radiology Office Surgeon Gen., 1967-71. Author (with others) Roentgen Diagnosis of Abdominal Tumors in Childhood, 1957; co-editor Alimentary Tract Roentgenology; editorial bd. Calif. Medicine, 1964-74, Radiology, 1975-93; assoc. editor Investigative Radiology, 1980-89; editor Opinion in Radiiology, 1988-91. Served to capt. AUS, 1957-59. Recipient J.P. Allyn medal P. Roberts Rsch. Inst., 1989. Fellow Faculty Radiologists (hon.); sr. mem. Nat. Acad. Scis.-Inst. Medicine; mem. AMA (cons. drugs 1961—), Royal Coll. Radiologists, Roentgen Ray Soc., Assn. Univ. Radiologists (pres. 1966-67, chmn. adv. com. acad. radiology 1971), Am. Gastroenterology Assn., Soc. Chmn. Acad. Radiology Depts. (pres. 1968-69), Radiol. Soc. N.Am., San Francisco Radiol. Soc. (pres. 1973-74), Rocky Mountain Radiol. Soc. (hon.), Calif. Acad. Medicine (pres. 1978), Soc. Magnetic Resonance in Medicine (pres. 1983), Serbian Acad. Scis. (fgn.), Russian Acad. Med. Scis. (fgn.). Home: 8 Tara Hill Rd Belvedere Tiburon CA 94920-1554 Office: Univ Calif 3333 California St Ste 16 San Francisco CA 94118-1944

MARGULIS, LES, advertising executive; b. Granite City, Ill., July 13, 1948; s. Manuel and Fay (Taylor) M.; m. Deborah Margulis. BS, U. of the Pacific, 1970; MS, Syracuse U., 1975. Asst. media mgr. Young & Rubicam, N.Y.C., 1975-76; media planner DMB&B, N.Y.C., 1976-77; media supr. BBDO, N.Y.C., 1977-83, v.p., 1983-88, sr. v.p., 1988—; advisor Newhouse Sch. Comm., Syracuse U., 1992—. Recipient Creative Media award Advertising Age Mag., 1986, Media award Media Week, 1990. Mem. Internat. Advt. Assn. (pres. U.S. chpt. 1991-93, v.p. N.Am. chpt. 1994—), Internat. Radio and TV Soc. Avocations: cooking, traveling. Office: BBDO NY 1285 Avenue Of The Americas New York NY 10019-6028

MARGULOIS, DAVID See MERRICK, DAVID

MARHIC, MICHEL EDMOND, engineering educator, entrepreneur, consultant; b. Ivry, Seine, France, June 25, 1945; came to U.S., 1968; s. Jean-Marie and Yvonne Marie (Nenez) M. Ingenieur, Ecole Sup. D'Electricite, Paris, 1968; MS, Case Western Res. U., 1970; PhD, UCLA, 1974. Asst. prof. Northwestern U., Evanston, Ill., 1974-79, assoc. prof., 1980-84, prof., 1985—; vis. asst. prof. U. So. Calif., L.A., 1979-80; vis. prof. Stanford U., 1984-85, 93-94; bd. dirs. Holicon Corp., Evanston, Holographic Industries, Lincolnshire, Ill. Contbr. and co-contbr. over 130 jour. articles and conf. publs.; holographic portrait Ronald Reagan, 1991. Mem. IEEE (sr.), Optical Soc. Am., Tau Beta Pi. Achievements include 8 patents in field. Office: Northwestern U Dept Elec Engring 2145 Sheridan Rd Evanston IL 60208-0834

MARIE, LINDA, artist, photographer; b. Cheverly, Md., Nov. 8, 1960; d. Thomas Grason Jr. and Rosalinda (Wepf) McWilliams; 1 child, Ann Marie. AA with honors, Cecil C.C., North East, Md., 1991. One-woman shows include Franklin Hall Arts Ctr., Chesapeake City, Md., 1993, Humanities and Arts Gallery-Essex (Md.) C.C., 1993, Widner Art Mus., Chester, Pa., 1996; group exhbns. include Del. Ctr. Contemporary Art, Wilmington, 1991, Md. Fedn. Art, Annapolis, 1991-93, Acad. of Arts, Easton, Md., 1992, Elkton (Md.) Arts Ctr., 1990-92, Md. Gallery East, Havre de Grace, 1992, Chautaqua (N.Y.) Inst., 1992, Washington Project for Arts, 1992, Ward-Nasse Gallery, N.Y.C., 1994, Sinclair C.C., Dayton, Ohio, 1994, AAAS, Washington, 1994-95, ACP, College Park, Md., 1994, B.A.I., Barcelona, Spain, 1996; represented in permanent collections at AAAS, Cecil C.C. Mem. Del. Ctr. Contemporary Arts, Md. Fedn. Art, Cecil County Arts Coun., Alpha Alpha Theta. Home and Studio: 6 Walnut St North East MD 21901

MARIELLA, RAYMOND P., chemistry educator, consultant; b. Phila., Sept. 5, 1919; s. Angelo Raphael and Sophia (Peel) M.; m. Miriam Margaret McMahon, Nov. 26, 1943; children: Miriam Margaret, Raymond P., Anne Marie, Patricia Sue. B.S., U. Pa., 1941; M.S., Carnegie Inst. Tech., 1942, D.Sc., 1945; postdoctoral fellow, U. Wis., 1946. Instr., then asst. prof. chemistry Northwestern U., 1946-51; mem. faculty Loyola U., Chgo., 1951-77; prof. chem. Loyola U., 1955-77, chmn. dept., 1951-70; asso. dean Loyola U. (Grad. Sch.), dir. grad. sci. programs, 1968-69, dean, 1969-77, sci. cons. indsl. orgns., 1951-77; assoc. exec. dir. Am. Chem. Soc., 1977, exec. dir., 1978-82; Sec.-treas. Midwestern Assn. Grad. Schs., 1972-77; exec. com. Council of Grad. Schs., 1972-74; Sci. adviser to gov. Ill. Producer, performer sci. TV shows Chgo. networks, 1956-65; Author: Laboratory Manual of Organic Chemistry and Biochemistry, 1953, Inorganic Qualitative Analysis, (with J. L. Huston), 1958, Chemistry of Life Processes, (with Rose Blau), 1968, Selected Laboratory Experiments for Chemistry of Life Processes, 1968, also articles. Recipient McCormack Freud Hon. lectr. award chemistry and chem. engring. Omicron chpt. Phi Lambda Upsilon, 1961; Merit award Chgo. Tech. Socs. Council, 1962. Mem. Am. Chem. Soc. (chmn. Chgo. 1960-61, nat. councilor 1956-82, chmn. bd. com. on profl. relations 1974-75, cons. to chmn. bd.), AAAS, N.Y. Acad. Scis., Sigma Xi (pres. Loyola chpt. 1956-57), Phi Kappa Phi, Alpha Chi Sigma, Phi Lambda Upsilon, Lambda Chi Sigma, Sigma Delta. Home and Office: 21215 N 123rd Dr Sun City West AZ 85375-1944

MARIENTHAL, GEORGE, telecommunications company executive; b. Kansas City, Mo., Nov. 15, 1938; s. George and Sadie (James) M.; children: Shawn Ann Capon, Patrick James, Shannon Lee Van Winter. B.S., U.S. Naval Acad., 1962; M.S., Stanford U., 1963; M.B.A., Am. U., 1974. Sr. rsch. assoc. Logistics Mgmt. Inst., Washington, 1967-71; dir. regional ops. EPA, 1971-75, dir. water policy, 1984-85; dep. asst. sec. def. Dept. Def., Washington, 1975-81; v.p. Survival Tech., Inc., Bethesda, Md., 1981-84; dep. asst. sec. agr. Dept. Agr., Washington, 1985-86; dep. adv. programs Titan Systems, Inc., 1986-87; mgr. mktg. Computer Scis. Corp., Falls Church, Va., 1987-89; exec. mgr. nat. accounts MCI Communications Corp., McLean, Va., 1989—; bd. dirs. 1st Security Fed. Savs. Bank. Served with USAF, 1962-67. Mem. Inst. Indsl. Engrs., Am. Def. Preparedness Assn., Armed Forces Communications and Electronics Assn., Internat. Telephone Pioneers Assn. Republican. Episcopalian. Club: Masons. Home: 10202 Parkwood Dr Kensington MD 20895-4130

MARIMOW, WILLIAM KALMON, journalist; b. Phila., Aug. 4, 1947; s. Jay and Helen Alma (Gitnig) M.; m. Diane K. Macomb, Oct. 18, 1969; children: Ann Esther, Scott Macomb. BA, Trinity Coll., Conn., 1969. Asst. editor Comml. Car Jour., Chilton Co., Bala Cynwyd, Pa., 1969-70; asst. to econ. columnist Phila. Bull., 1970-72; staff writer Phila. Inquirer, 1972—, city hall bur. chief, 1979-81, editor Main Line Neighbors, 1986-87, N.J. editor, 1987-89, city editor, 1989-91; city editor, asst. to pub. Phila. Inquirer and Daily News, 1991-93; met. editor Balt. Sun, 1993, assoc. mng. editor,

1993-95, mng. editor, 1995—; instr. urban studies U. Pa., 1979; instr. English Rutgers U., Camden, N.J., 1981; mem. nominating jury Pulitzer Prize, 1991-92. Recipient 1st pl. award for team reporting Phila. Press Assn., 1977, 1st pl. award for deadline reporting AP Mng. Editors of Pa., 1977, Pub. Svc. awards, 1978, 85, Nat. Pub. Svc. award Sigma Delta Chi, 1978, 1st pl. award for best news story Sigma Delta Chi Phila., 1977, 2nd pl. award for deadline reporting, 1980, Pub. Svc. awards, 1978, 85, Pub. Svc. awards Sigma Delta Chi N.J., 1978, Pulitzer prize for disting. pub. svc., 1978, Pulitzer prize for investigative reporting, 1985, Silver Gavel award ABA, 1978, 82, Roy W. Howard Pub. Svc. award Scripps-Howard Found., 1978, Robert F. Kennedy Journalism award, 1978, 2nd pl. award for investigative reporting Keystone Press Assn., 1978, 85, 1st pl. award for best news story, 1982, Media Achievement award Phila. Bar Assn., 1982, William Schnader award Pa. Bar Assn., 1982, Nat. Headliners award, 1985, Trinity Coll. Alumni Achievement award, 1984; Nieman fellow Harvard U., 1982-83. Mem. Pen and Pencil Club, Investigative Reporters and Editors, Inc. Home: 1025 Winding Way Baltimore MD 21210-1232 Office: The Baltimore Sun PO Box 1377 501 N Calvert St Baltimore MD 21202-3604

MARIN, CHEECH (RICHARD ANTHONY MARIN), actor, writer, director; b. L.A., July 13, 1946; s. Oscar and Elsa Meza M.; m. Patti Heid, Apr. 1, 1986. BS, Calif. State U., Northridge. Co-founder improvisational group, City Works, Vancouver; formed comedy duo with Tommy Chong called Cheech and Chong; appeared in clubs throughout U.S., Can., Europe and Australia including Carnegie Hall, JFK Ctr.; recs. include Sleeping Beauty, Cheech and Chong, Big Bamba, Los Cochinos (Grammy award best comedy), The Wedding Album, Get Out of My Room, Born in East L.A., (films) Up in Smoke, 1978, Cheech & Chong's Next Movie, 1980, Nice Dreams, 1981, It Came from Hollywood, 1982, Yellow Beard, 1983, Things Are Tough All Over, 1982, Still Smokin', 1983, The Corsican Brothers, 1984, After Hours, 1984 (Best Film award Havanna Film Festival 1987, Best Screenplay), Echo Park, 1985, Fatal Beauty, 1987, Rude Awakening, 1988, Oliver and Company (voice only), 1988, Troop Beverly Hills, 1989, Ghost Busters II, 1989, Shrimp on the Barbie, 1990, Fern Gully: The Last Rainforest (voice only), 1993, The Lion King (voice only), 1994, A Million to Juan, 1994, Ring of the Muscateers, 1994, Mr. Payback, 1995, Desperado, 1995, Dusk til Dawn, 1995, Tin Cup, 1995, Great White Hype, 1995, Santa Bugito (voice only), 1995; (video) Get Out of My Room, 1986 (Gold Cert. award); writer, dir., star (movie) Born in East L.A., 1987 (Grammy nomination 1986, Best Art Direction); co-writer title song Up in Smoke; producer, writer, actor, dir. (TV series) Culture Clash, 1991; actor: Golden Palace, 1992, (TV movie) The Cisco Kid, 1994—; concerts USA, Can., Europe and Australia. Recipient Grammy award for Los Cochinos, Best Comedy Rec., 1973. Office: CAA 9830 Wilshire Blvd Beverly Hills CA 90212-1804*

MARINACCIO, CHARLES LINDBERGH, lawyer; b. Stratford, Conn., Dec. 10, 1933. BA, U. Conn., 1957; JD with honors, George Washington U., 1962. Bar: Conn. 1962, D.C. 1982. Trial lawyer U.S. Dept. Justice, Washington, 1963-69; advisor supervisory and regulation div. Fed. Res. Bd., Washington, 1969-73; dir., exec. sec. law enforcement assistance adminstrn. U.S. Dept. Justice, Washington, 1973-75; gen. counsel banking housing and urban affairs com. U.S. Senate, Washington, 1975-84; commr. SEC, Washington, 1984-85; ptnr. Kelley, Drye & Warren, Washington, 1985-94; ind. cons. Washington, 1995—; apptd. by Pres. Clinton to bd. dirs. Securities Investor Protection Corp. Home and Office: 4911 Massachusetts Ave NW Washington DC 20016-4310

MARINACCIO, PAUL JOHN, JR., marketing professional; b. Oceanside, N.J., Sept. 1, 1957; s. Paul J. and Jeanette (Romanescu) M. AB, Rutgers U., 1979. Polit. writer The N.J. Herald, Newton, 1979-82; reporter, bur. chief The Star Ledger, Newark, 1982-85; staff writer Newsday, Melville, N.Y., 1985-87; nat. econs. writer, bus. writer Newsday, N.Y. Newsday, N.Y.C., 1987-91; exec. dir. Econ. Policy Mktg. Group City of N.Y., 1991-94; mktg. exec. Deloitte and Touche, Wilton, Conn., 1994-95, dir. bus. devel., 1995—; dir. bus. devel. Deloitte and Touche, Wilton; contbg. editor N.J. Monthly, Princeton, N.J., 1979-82; cons. Ctr. for Capital Studies CUNY, N.Y.C., 1994. Editor: New York City 1991: the World's Capital in Transition, 1991, Strong Economy, Strong City: Jobs for New Yorkers, 1993. Recipient 1st place award for deadline reporting Press Club L.I., 1986, for bus. writing N.Y. State AP, 1988, for labor reporting Newspaper Guild N.Y., 1989, Golden Quill award Garden State Scholastic Press Assn., 1991; Davenport fellow U. Mo. Sch. Journalism, 1990.

MARINAKOS, PLATO ANTHONY, medical center administrator; b. Pitts., Dec. 26, 1935; m. Vaselia Pecunis; children—Plato, Constantine, Theodore, Alexia. B.S., U. Pitts., M.S. in Hosp. Adminstrn. with honors; postgrad. Sch. Law, Duquesne U. Adminstrv. asst. Homestead Gen. Hosp., Pa., 1960-61; asst. exec. dir. Allegheny Gen. Hosp., Pitts., 1961-65, assoc. exec. dir., 1965-68, exec. dir., 1968-73; pres. Conemaugh Valley Meml. Hosp., Johnstown, Pa., 1973-77; exec. v.p. Mercy Catholic Med. Ctr., Phila., 1977—; chmn. planning bd. Eastern Mercy Health Systems, Phila., 1983—. Contbr. articles to profl. jours. Bd. dirs. YMCA, Pitts., 1975-78, Better Bus. Bur. of S.E. Pa., Phila., 1977, Pa. Trauma Systems Found., 1985—; bd. dirs., mem. exec. com. West Phila. Corp., 1981—, Delaware Valley Hosp. Council, 1984—. Mem. Am. Hosp. Assn. (ho. of dels. 1984—), Assn. Am. Med. Colls., Hosp. Assn. Pa. (bd. dirs. 1984—). Republican. Greek Orthodox. Avocations: reading; skiing. Home: 1116 Beech Rd Bryn Mawr PA 19010-1648 Office: Mercy Health Corp SE PA 1 Bala Plz Ste 402 Bala Cynwyd PA 19004-1401*

MARINARI, DONALD J., advertising executive; b. 1944. With BCE Telecom Corp., Montreal, Que., Can., 1964-92; with Nat. Telephone Directory, Somerset, N.J., 1993—, now pres. Office: Nat Telephone Directory 3 Executive Dr Somerset NJ 08873-4004*

MARINARO, EDWARD FRANCIS, actor; b. Mar. 31, 1950; s. Louis John and Rose Marie (Errico) M. B.S., Cornell U. Football player Minn. Vikings; football player N.Y. Jets, N.Y.C., Seattle Seahawks. Television appearences include (TV series) Laverne and Shirley, Hill Street Blues, 1980-86, Sisters, 1991—; (TV guest appearances) Falcon Crest; (films) Mace, 1987, Tonight's the Night, 1987, Sharing Richard, 1987, Amy Fisher: My Story, 1992, The Diamond Trap, 1988. Avocations: golf; racquetball; cooking; traveling. *

MARINE, CLYDE LOCKWOOD, agricultural business consultant; b. Knoxville, Tenn., Dec. 25, 1936; s. Harry H. and Idelle (Larue) M.; m. Eleanor Harb, Aug. 9, 1958; children: Cathleen, Sharon. B.S. in Agr., U. Tenn., 1958; M.S. in Agrl. Econs., U. Ill., 1959; Ph.D. in Agrl. Econs., Mich. State U., 1963. Sr. market analyst Pet Milk Co., St. Louis, 1963-64; mgr. market planning agr. chems. div. Mobile Chem. Co., Richmond, Va., 1964-67; mgr. ingredient purchasing Central Soya Co., Ft. Wayne, Ind., 1970-73, corp. economist, 1967-70, v.p. ingredient purchasing, 1973-75, sr. v.p., 1975-90; pres. Marine Assocs., Ft. Wayne, 1991—; bd. dirs. SCAN, 1992—; mem. agrl. policy adv. com. U.S.D.A. Bd. dirs. Ft. Wayne Fine Arts Found., 1976-79; bd. dirs. Ft. Wayne Pub. Transp. Corp., 1975-83; v.p. Ft. Wayne Philharm., 1974-76. Served with U.S. Army, 1959-60. Mem. Nat. Soybean Processors Assn. (chmn.), U.S. C. of C., Am. Agrl. Econs. Assn., Am. Feed Mfrs. Assn. (chmn. purchasing coun.). Episcopalian. Club: Ft. Wayne Country. Office: Marine Assocs 4646 W Jefferson Blvd Fort Wayne IN 46804-6832

MARINELLI, LYNN M., county official; b. Akron, Ohio, Aug. 4, 1962; d. Michael and Christine (Golonka) Madden; divorced; 1 child, Jessica. BA in English, Daemen Coll., 1985. Pub. rels. coord. Bison Baseball Inc., Buffalo, 1985-86; exec. asst. to Assemblyman William B. Hoyt N.Y. State Assembly, Buffalo, 1986-92; exec. dir. Erie County Commn. on Status of Women, Buffalo, 1992—; chair Erie County Coalition Against Family Violence, 1992-95; co-chair domestic violence com. Multidisciplinary Coordinating Coun., 1992—; mem. adv. bd. Dept. Social Svcs., Erie County, 1992—. Sec. dem. com. Town of Tonawanda, 1991—; active Dem. Jud. Adv. Com. Erie County, 1990—, Reapportionment Com., Erie County, 1991, Ct. Care Project, 1992—, Compass House, Erie County, 1993—, Women for Downtown, 1993—, Citizens Com. on Rape and Sex Assault, 1993—, Leadership Buffalo, 1994, United Way Family Support and Safety, 1994—. Recipient Disting. Svc. award Coalition Against Family Violence, 1992; named Young Careerist, Bus. and Profl. Women, 1991; named to 40 Under Forty list, Bus. First, 1993. Roman Catholic. Avocations: skiing, reading. Office: Erie County Commission on Women 95 Franklin St Rm 1655 Buffalo NY 14202-3904

MARINETTI, GUIDO V., biochemistry educator; b. Rochester, N.Y., June 26, 1918; s. Michael and Nancy (Lippa) M.; m. Antoinette F. Francione, Sept. 19, 1942; children: Timothy D., Hope L. B.S., U. Rochester, 1950, Ph.D., 1953. Research biochemist Western Regional Lab., Albany, Calif., 1953-54; instr. U. Rochester, N.Y., 1954-57; asst. prof. U. Rochester, 1957-60, assoc. prof., 1960-66, prof. sch. medicine and dentistry, 1966—; cons. Eastman Kodak, 1978, Rochester Gas & Electric, 1979. Author: Disorders of Lipid Metabolism, 1990; editor: Lipid Chromatographic Analysis, 3 vols., 1969, 2nd edit., 1976; contbr. 160 pub. articles in sci. jours. Served with USAAF, 1942-46. Recipient Nat. Infantile Paralysis award, 1952; recipient Glycerine Research award, 1957; NSF grantee, 1953; recipient Lederle Med. Faculty award, 1955, 56. Mem. Am. Soc. Biol. Chemists, Am. Chem. Soc., AAAS, Sigma Xi, Phi Beta Kappa. Rsch. area: membrane structure and function, biochemistry of phospholipids, phosphatidylinositol metabolism in isolated synaptomsomes. Office: Univ Rochester Med Ctr 601 Elmwood Ave Rochester NY 14642-0001

MARINI, FRANK NICHOLAS, political science and public administration educator; b. Melrose Park, Ill., June 18, 1935; s. Joseph and Lillian Lee (Stuart) M.; m. Elsie B. Adams; children: Lisa M., Katherine D. B.A., Ariz. State U., 1960, M.A., 1961; Ph.D., U. Calif., Berkeley, 1966. Instr. U. Mo., Columbia, 1963-64; asst. prof. polit. sci. U. Ky., 1966-67; asst. prof. Syracuse U., 1967-70; assoc. prof., assoc. dean Syracuse U. (Maxwell Sch.), dir. public adminstrn. programs, 1970-73; dean Coll. Arts and Letters, San Diego State U., 1973-80; provost, v.p. acad. affairs Calif. State U., Fullerton, 1980-84; sr. adviser chancellor's office Calif. State U., 1984-85; sr. v.p., provost U. Akron, Ohio, 1985-90, prof. pub. adminstrn., urban studies, polit. sci., 1990—. Author pamphlets; contbr. numerous articles to profl. jours.; editor: Toward a New Public Administration, 1971; mng. editor: Public Administrn. Rev, 1967-77; editor-in-chief Jour. Pub. Adminstrn. Edn., 1994—. Served with USAF, 1954-58. Mem. Am. Soc. Pub. Adminstrn., Am. Polit. Sci. Assn. Office: U Akron Dept Pub Adminstrn Urban St Akron OH 44325-7904

MARINI, JOHN JOSEPH, medical scientist, educator, physician; b. Syracuse, N.Y., Oct. 6, 1946; s. Warren John and Theresa Josephine (Palermo) M.; m. Margaret Elizabeth Mooney, June 13, 1970. B in Engring. Sci., Johns Hopkins U., 1969, MD, 1973. Intern internal med. U. Wash., Seattle, 1973-74, resident internal med., 1974-76, fellow respiratory diseases, 1976-78, asst. prof., assoc. prof. medicine, 1978-83; assoc. prof. medicine Vanderbilt U., Nashville, 1983-89; prof. medicine U. Minn., Mpls., St. Paul, 1989—; dir. pulmonary and critical care medicine St. Paul-Ramsey Med. Ctr., 1989—; chmn. critical care section Am. Thoracic Soc., 1989-90; mem. policy and exam writing com. Am. Bd. Internal Medicine, 1991—; disting. Simmons lectr. UCLA, 1991; Eagan Sci. lectr. Am. Assn. for Respiratory Care, 1992. Author 6 books on pulmonary and intensive care; mem. editl. bds. 4 profl. jours.; contbr. numerous articles to profl. jours. Named one of Outstanding Pulmonologists/Critical Care Physicians in U.S., Town & Country, 1989, 95, One of Best Doctors in Am. Woodward Whyte, 1995. Fellow Am. Coll. Chest Physicians (Cecil Lehman Mayer award 1980, 86), Am. Bd. Internal Medicine; mem. European Soc. Intensive Care, European Respiratory Soc., Am. Thoracic Soc., Soc. Critical Care Medicine. Avocations: skiing, tennis, foreign languages, computer science. Office: St Paul-Ramsey Med Ctr 640 Jackson St Saint Paul MN 55101-2595

MARINI, ROBERT CHARLES, environmental engineering executive; b. Quincy, Mass., Sept. 29, 1931; s. Larry and Millie (Cirillo) M.; m. Myrna Lydia Pellegrini, June 26, 1955 (dec. June 1994); children: Debra, Robert Charles, Larry; m. B. Anne Jones, May 27, 1995. B.S.C.E. with honors, Northeastern U., 1954; S.M.S.E., Harvard U., 1955, postgrad. Advanced Mgmt. Program, 1985. Registered profl. engr., Mass., N.Y., Maine, R.I., N.H., Conn., Vt., Calif., N.C., Wash., Colo., Mich., Fla., Wis., Tenn., La., Ariz., Ohio, Ill., Va. Jr. engr. Camp Dresser & McKee Inc., Boston, 1955-56, project engr., 1958-64, assoc., 1964-67, ptnr., sr. v.p., 1967-77, pres. environ. engring. div., 1977-82, exec. v.p., 1982-84, pres., 1984-90, chief exec. officer, 1989—, also chmn. bd. dirs.; mem. civil engring. adv. com. Worcester (Mass.) Poly. Inst., 1985-90, U. Mass., 1986-90, U. Tex., Austin, 1989-91, chmn., 1991-92, mem. engring. found. adv. coun., 1991—. Contbr. articles to profl. jours. Dir. nat. coun. Northeastern U., Boston, 1983—, mem. corp. bd., 1983—, bd. overseers, 1985-89, trustee, 1989—; chmn. Leadership Phase Century II Fund, 1989-91, chmn. devel. com., 1991—; corporator Weymouth Savs. Bank, 1988—, trustee, 1991—; bd. dirs. Mass. Bus. Round Table, 1991—, vice chmn., 1995—. Recipient Disting. Eagle Scout award Boy Scouts Am., 1986, W. Erwin Story award, 1991, Outstanding Civil Engring. Alumni award Northeastern U., 1992, Outstanding Alumni award, 1993. Fellow ASCE, NAE, Instn. Engrs. Australia; mem. Am. Pub. Works Assn. (Man of the Yr. award New Eng. chpt. 1981), Am. Water Works Assn., Mass. Soc. Profl. Engrs. (Young Engr. of Yr. award 1966), Am. Acad. Environ. Engrs. (diplomate, trustee at large 1989-92, v.p. 1992-93, pres.-elect 1993-94, pres. 1994-95, Stanley E. Kappe award 1992), Water Environment Fedn. (hon.), Internat. Assn. Water Pollution Rsch. and Control, Engring. Soc. New Eng. (New Eng. award 1994), Tau Beta Pi, Phi Kappa Phi. Roman Catholic. Home: 1 Nevin Rd Weymouth MA 02190-1610 Office: Camp Dresser & McKee Inc 1 Cambridge Ctr Cambridge MA 02142-1601

MARINIS, THOMAS PAUL, JR., lawyer; b. Jacksonville, Tex., May 31, 1943; s. Thomas Paul and Betty Sue (Garner) M.; m. Lucinda Cruse, June 25, 1969; children—Courtney, Kathryn, Megan. B.A., Yale U., 1965; LL.B., U. Tex., 1968. Bar: Tex. Assoc. Vinson & Elkins, Houston, 1969-76, ptnr., 1977—. Served with USAF, 1968-74. Fellow Tex. Bar Found; mem. ABA (sec. taxation sect. 1984-85), Tex. Bar Assn. (chmn. taxation sect. 1986-87). Clubs: Houston Country, Houston Ctr., Coronado.

MARINO, ANN DOZIER, real estate agent; b. Durham, N.C., Apr. 22, 1944; d. Walter Joseph and Ellen G. (Cheek) Dozier; m. John Harrison Marino, Oct. 15, 1966 (div. Jan. 1981); children: John Harrison Jr., Ann Southerlyn. BA, Salem Coll., 1966. Sales assoc. Rector Assocs. Realtors, Alexandria, Va., 1984—. Vol. Jr. League, Chgo., 1970-74; bd. dirs. Jr. League, Washington, 1979-95, Vol. Clearing House, Washington, Project Open Rd., Chgo., Fire and Burn Inst., Washington; mem. parents coun. Burgundy Farm Sch., 1983; mem. parish coun. St. Mary's, Oldtown, 1977-80. Recipient Rookie of Yr. award No. Va. Bd. Realtors, 1985, Lifetime Top Producer award, Million Dollar Club, No. Va. Bd. Realtors, 1985-94. Mem. Salem Coll. Alumnae Club (pres. Chgo. chpt. 1970-73), Million Dollar Club (life). Republican. Roman Catholic. Office: Rector Assocs 211 N Union St Ste 250 Alexandria VA 22314-2643

MARINO, DANIEL CONSTANTINE, JR., professional football player; b. Pittsburg, Sept. 15, 1961. BA, communications, U. Pitts., 1983. Profl. football player Miami Dolphins, NFL, 1983—. Named All-America team quarterback, The Sporting News, 1981; Rookie of the Year, The Sporting News, 1983, NFL All-Pro team, The Sporting News, 1984-86, MVP, Nat. Football League, 1984-85; named to Pro Bowl Team, 1983-87, 91-92. NFL career record for most games (12) with 400 or more yards passing; NFL records for most seasons (6) with 4,000 or more yards passing, most seasons (9) with 3,000 or more yards passing, 1984-1992, most consecutive games (4) with four or more touchdown passes, 1984; NFL record for lowest percentage (2.03) of passes intercepted by a rookie, 1983; NFL record for most games (17) with four or more touchdown passes, 1984. Office: care Miami Dolphins Joe Robbie Stadium 2269 NW 199th St Opa Locka FL 33056-2600*

MARINO, EUGENE LOUIS, publishing company executive; b. N.Y.C., Jan. 7, 1929; s. Salvatore A. and Florence M. (Casabona) M.; student Columbia U., 1945-48; m. Patricia Ryan, Mar. 11, 1948; children—Jeanette, Anthony, John, Eugene III. Credit mgr. Sears, Roebuck Inc., L.I., N.Y., 1951-60; gen. credit mgr. Davison-Paxon div. R.H. Macy, Inc., Atlanta, 1960-63, Grand-Way div. Grand Union Co., N.Y.C., 1963-66; v.p., gen. credit mgr. Consumer Products div. Singer Co., N.Y.C., 1966-75, Grolier, Inc., Danbury, Conn., 1975-90, ret.; officer, v.p., gen. credit mgr., dir. numerous subsidiaries. Recipient Quarter Century cert. Internat. Consumer Credit Assn., 1981. Mem. Mchts. Research Council, Internat. Consumer Credit Assn., Nat. Assn. Credit Mgmt., Alpha Sigma Phi. Home: 4858 Tivoli Ct Sarasota FL 34235-3653

MARINO, IGNAZIO ROBERTO, transplant surgeon, researcher; b. Genova, Italy, Mar. 10, 1955; s. Pietro Rosario and Valeria (Mazzanti) M.; m. Rossana Parisen-Toldin, Sept. 15, 1990; 1 child, Stefania Valeria. Maturità-Classica, Coll. of Merode, Rome, 1973; MD, Cath. U., Rome, 1979. Diplomate Nat. Bd. Gen. Surgery, Nat. Bd. Vascular Surgery. Intern, then resident Gemelli U. Hosp., Rome, 1979-84; temp. asst. dept. surgery Cath. U., Rome, 1981, asst. prof. surgery, 1983-92; asst. prof. surgery Transplantation Inst., U. Pitts., 1991-95; assoc. prof. surgery Transplantation Inst./U. Pitts., 1995—; prof. surgery postgrad. Sch. Microsurgery, Exptl. Surgery U. Milan, 1994—; prof.surgery Sch. Medicine U. Perugia, 1994—; attending surgeon U. Pitts. Med. Ctr., Pitts., 1991—; assoc. dir. transplant divsn. VA Med. Ctr., Pitts., 1992—; attending surgeon Children's Hosp. Pitts., 1993—; mem. surg. team 1st and 2d baboon to human liver transplants U. Pitts. Med. Ctr., 1992, 93, dir. European med. divsn., 1995—; sci. journalist Agenzia Nazionale Stampa Associata, 1992—; mem. nat. ad hoc donations com. United Network for Organ Sharing, 1995—. Author: New Technique in Extracorporeal Circulation, 1985 (Ann. prize Italian Soc. Surgery 1986), New Technique in Liver Transplantation, 1986 (De Angelis award 1986); contbr. more than 300 articles to profl. jours. Mem. Italian Ordine Giornalisti, 1994—. Grantee Italian Nat. Coun. Rsch., 1979, 86, 87, 88, 89-93, Gastroenterology Soc., 1988; recipient award Instituto Nazionale Previdenze Dirigenti Aziende Industriali, 1982. Mem. ACS, Am. Soc. Transplantation Surgeons, Am. Soc. Transplant Physicians, Italian Soc. Surgery, Transplantation Soc. (grant 1988), European Soc. for Organ Transplantation, Soc. Surgeons Under 40 (Ann. prize 1986), Cell Transplant Soc. (founding mem.), Acad. Surg. Rsch., Soc. Critical Care Medicine, Internat. Liver Transplantation Soc., Assn. Italian Correspondents in N.Am. (assoc.), Xenotransplantation Club (founding mem.). Avocations: reading (history books), sailing, Annibale (pet cat). Home: Corso Italia 29, Rome 00198, Italy Office: Univ Pitts Transplant Inst 4 Falk Clinic 3601 5th Ave Pittsburgh PA 15213-3403

MARINO, JOSEPH ANTHONY, retired publishing executive; b. Geneva, N.Y., Apr. 1, 1932; s. Anthony Rocco and Antoinette (DePalma) M.; m. Catherine Colville, Dec. 18, 1953; children: Joseph, Michael, Paul. B.S., Tri-State U., 1959; M.B.A., Mich. State U., 1960. Mgr. Gillette Co., Boston, 1960-82; pres., chief exec. officer Liquid Paper Corp. div. Gillette, Dallas, 1979-82, Western Pub. Co., Inc., Racine, Wis, 1982-89; mem. adv. bd. Heritage Bank, Racine, 1983—; bd. dirs. Wickes Furniture Co., Aerosol Svcs. Co., Inc. Mem. bus. alumni adv. bd. Mich. State U., 1987. Served with USAF, 1951-54. Recipient award of Honor Fedn. Jewish Philanthropies, 1973. Mem. Racine Country Club (Wis.).

MARINO, MICHAEL, church administrator. Asst. gen. overseer Christian Ch. of N. Am. Office: Christian Church of North Am 25595 Chardon Rd Mayfield Heights OH 44143

MARINO, MICHAEL FRANK, lawyer; b. Little Falls, N.Y., Feb. 19, 1948; s. Michael Frank and Betty (Roberts) M.; m. Catherine Viladesau, Aug. 31, 1970; children: Michael John, Lisa Kathryn, Matthew Christopher. BS, Cornell U., 1971; JD, Syracuse U., 1974; LLM, Georgetown U., 1982. Bar: D.C. 1975, U.S. Dist. Ct. D.C. 1975, U.S. Ct. Mil. Appeals 1975, N.Y. 1976, U.S. Dist. Ct. (ea. and we. dists.) Va. 1977, U.S. Dist. Ct. Md. 1980, U.S. Ct. Appeals (4th cir.) 1982, Va. 1982, U.S. Ct. Appeals (9th cir.) 1994. Civilian employee head rels. br. Office of the Judge Adv. of the Navy, Washington, 1975-76; spl. asst. to the gen. counsel Office of Sec. of Navy, Washington, 1977; asst. gen. counsel labor and employment Office of the Gen. Counsel of the Navy, Washington, 1978; assoc. Pierson, Ball & Dowd, Washington, 1978-81; ptnr. Boothe, Prichard & Dudley, Fairfax and Mc Lean, Va., 1981-87, McGuire, Woods, Battle & Boothe, Mc Lean, 1987-89, Reed, Smith, Shaw & McClay, Mc Lean, 1989—; labor group head, Washington, Va.; mng. ptnr. McLean Office. Author: Virginia Employer's Guide to Labor Law, 1982; co-author: New York Employer's Guide, 1989, 92-94, Fla. Labor and Employment Law, 1994, Labor Employment Law in Pa., 1994. Mem. planning com. SMU Multi State labor Law Conf., Dallas; chmn. Arlington (Va.) Chamber Employee Rels. Com.; bd. dirs. Arlington Chamber Bd. of Dirs.; mem. Va. Chamber Mgmt. Rels. Com. Richmond, 1980—. Capt. USMC, 1971-78. Named Best Lawyer in Am., 1986-95. Mem. ABA (labor law com. 1974—), D.C. Bar Assn. (labor law com. 1974—), Va. Bar Assn. (labor law com. 1974—, sec.-treas. labor law sect. 1995), N.Y. Bar Assn. (labor law com. 1974—), Westwood Country Club. Roman Catholic. Avocations: jogging, fitness, hunting, fishing. Office: Reed Smith Shaw & McClay 8251 Greensboro Dr Ste 1100 Mc Lean VA 22102-3809

MARINO, RAUL, JR., neurosurgeon; b. São Paulo, Brazil, Mar. 22, 1936; s. Raul and Brigida Quartim (de Albuquerque) M.; m. Angela Zacarelli; children: Ricardo, Rodolfo. MD, U. São Paulo Med. Sch., 1961. Medical Diplomate. Resident Lahey Clinic, Boston, 1964-65; rsch. fellow Harvard Med. Sch., Boston, 1965-66; resident McGill U., Can., 1966-67; vis. scientist NIH, Bethesda, 1967-68; neurosurgeon, founder functional neurosurgery divsn. U. São Paulo, 1970-90; prof., chmn. divsn. neurosurgery Hosp. das Clinicas/U. São Paulo Med. Sch., 1990—. Author: The Japanese Brain, 1990; editor: Functional Neurosurgery, 1979. Med. lt. Brazilian Army, 1961. Mem. São Paulo Acad. Medicine (pres. 1993-95). Avocations: philosophy, theology, history of medicine. Office: S Paulo Neurol Inst, Rua Maestro Cardim 808, 01323001 São Paulo Brazil

MARINO, RICHARD J., publishing executive. With Harcourt/Brace/Jovanovich; sr. v.p. advtg. and mktg. ABC Cap Cities Pub. Corp.; assoc. pub. PC World Communications, 1990-92, pub.; pres., COO, 1994—. Office: 501 2d St San Francisco CA 94107

MARINO, SHEILA BURRIS, education educator; b. Knoxville, Nov. 24, 1947; d. David Paul and Lucille Cora (Maupin) Burris; m. Louis John Marino, Dec. 19, 1969; children: Sheila Noelle, Heather Michelle. BS, U. Tenn., 1969, MS, 1971, EdD, 1976; postgrad., W.Va. U., Europe. Elem./early childhood tchr. Knoxville City Schs., 1969-71; cooperating tchr. U. Tenn., Knoxville, 1969-71; dir. early childhood edn./tchr. Glenville (W.Va.) State Coll., 1971-72, Colo. Women's Coll., Denver, 1972-73; asst. prof. edn. Lander U., Greenwood, S.C., 1973-75; instr., spl. asst. coordinator of elem./early childhood edn. U. Tenn., 1975-76; prof. edn., dir. clin. experiences, asst. dean Sch. Edn. Lander U., 1976-95, dean sch. edn., 1993-94; cons. in field; dir. Creative Activities Prog. for Children, Lander U., 1979—; mem. W.Va. Gov.'s Early Childhood Adv. Bd., 1971-72, Gov.'s Team of Higher Edn. Profls. on Comprehensive Plan for S.C. Early Childhood Edn., 1982; moderator Presbytery of Southeast, 1995—. Contbr. articles to profl. jours.; author: International Children's Literature, 1989. Bd. dirs. Greenwood Lit. Coun., v.p., 1990, pres., 1991; bd. dirs. St. Nicholas Speech and Hearing Ctr., Greenwood, pres., 1992; bd. dirs. Old Ninety-Six coun. Girl Scouts U.S.A., 1987-92; vol. March of Dimes Program, Greenwood, 1987. Mem. AAUW (pres. 1990—), AAUP, SNEA (state advisor 1981-88), S.C. Student Edn. Assn., Piedmont Assn. Children and Adults with Learning Disabilities (pres. 1986—, exec. bd.), Learning Disabilities Assn. S.C. (pres. 1990-94), S.C. Edn. Assn., S. C. Assn. for Children Under Six, So. Assn. for Children under Six, S.C. Assn. Tchr. Educators, Piedmont Reading Coun. (v.p. 1985-86, 90-91, pres. 1986-88, 91-92), S.C. Coun. Internat. Reading Assn. (exec. bd. 1986-88, 91—), Delta Kappa Gamma (pres. Epsilon chpt. 1984-88, 92-94, mem. exec. bd.), Pi Lambda Theta, Kappa Delta Pi (pres. U. Tenn. chpt. 1974-75), Phi Delta Kappa (v.p. 1988-90, pres. Lander U. chpt. 1990-91, 94—). Democrat. Presbyterian. Avocations: reading, gardening, swimming, music, arts and crafts. Home: 103 Essex Ct Greenwood SC 29649-9561 Office: Lander U Stanley Avenue Greenwood SC 29649

MARINO ANGSTADT, MARLENE, fine artist, artist agent; b. N.Y.C., Jan. 1, 1947; d. Michael John and Anne (Bisogno) Marino; m. Robert David Angstadt, Dec. 29, 1972. Student, Caldwell Coll., 1965-66; BA, So. Ill. U., 1966-69, Teaching Cert., 1970. Free-lance art dir. J. Walter Thompson; Foote, Cone & Belding; Michael Marino & Assocs., N.Y.C., 1970-72; art dir. Sun Printing Corp., Naperville, Ill., 1973-79; art dir./prodn. mgr. New World Pub. Co., Chgo., 1980-86; pres., owner FDM Prdons., Inc./Marlene Marino Mktng. and Creative Svcs., Chgo., 1986—; lectr. career seminar North Cen. Coll., Naperville, 1978; pvt. tutor art creativity, Chgo. area, 1985—; tchr. Columbia Coll., Chgo., 1992. Mem. The Art Inst. of Chgo.,

Nat. Mus. of Women in the Arts, Am. Craft Coun. Avocations: appreciation of all forms of visual arts and music; painting, gardening, travel. Office: FDM Prodns Inc 75 E Wacker Dr STe 2500 Chicago IL 60601

MARINOVICH, GREG, photojournalist. Freelance photographer AP. Recipient Pulitzer prize for spot news photography, 1991. Office: The Associated Press 50 Rockefeller Plz New York NY 10020-1605*

MARIO, ERNEST, pharmaceutical company executive; b. Clifton, N.J., June 12, 1938; s. Jerry and Edith (Meijer) M.; m. Mildred Martha Daume, Dec. 10, 1961; children: Christopher Bradley, Gregory Gerald, Jeremy Konrad. B.S. in Pharmacy, Rutgers U., 1961; M.S. in Phys. Scis., U. RI., 1963, Ph.D. in Phys. Scis., 1965. Registered pharmacist, R.I., N.Y. Vice pres. mfg. Smith Kline Corp., Phila., 1975-77; v.p. mfg. ops. U.S. Pharm. Co. (divsn. E. R. Squibb), New Brunswick, N.J., 1977-79; v.p., gen. mgr. chem. div. E. R. Squibb, Princeton, N.J., 1979-81; pres. chem. and engring. div., sr. v.p. Squibb Corp., Princeton, 1981-84; v.p. Squibb Corp., 1984-86; pres., COO Glaxo Inc., 1986-88, chmn., CEO, 1988, chmn., 1989-91; CEO Glaxo Holdings plc, 1989-93, dep. chmn., 1991-93; co-chmn., CEO, Alza Corp., Palo Alto, Calif., 1993—; grad. asst., instr. U. R.I., Kingston, 1961-66; research fellow Inst. Neurol. Diseases, Bethesda, Md., 1963-65. Contbr. articles to profl. jours. Trustee Duke U., Rockefeller U., U. R.I. Found.; mem. pres.'s coun. U. R.I.; chmn. Am. Found. for Pharm. Edn.; bd. dirs. Nat. Found. Infectious Diseases, Antigenics, Pharm. Product Devel., Stanford Health Svcs., Tech. Mus. Innovation; mem. Calif. gov.'s coun. on biotech. Office: Alza Corp 950 Page Mill Rd Palo Alto CA 94304-1012

MARION, GAIL ELAINE, reference librarian; b. Bloomington, Ill., May 31, 1952; d. Ralph Herbert and Norma Mae (Crump) Nyberg; m. David Louis Marion, May 13, 1972 (div. Apr. 1983). AA in Liberal Arts, Fla. Jr. Coll., 1976; BA in U.S. History, U. North Fla., 1978; MS in Libr. and Info. Sci., Fla. State U., 1985. Law libr., legal rschr. Mathews Osborne et al, Jacksonville, Fla., 1979-82; reference libr. City of Jacksonville-Pub. Librs., 1982—. With U.S. Army, 1970-72, maj. U.S. Army Res., 1978—, with Fla. Army N.G., 1974-78. Named to Outstanding Young Women of Am., 1985; N.G. Officers Assn. scholar, 1980. Mem. ALA, WAC Vets. Assn., Adj. Gen. Regimental Corps, Res. Officers Assn., Fla. Libr. Assn., Fla. Paleontol. Soc., Jacksonville Gem and Mineral Soc. Republican. Methodist. Avocations: art, history, photography, reading, rock hounding. Home: 3200 Hartley Rd Apt 70 Jacksonville FL 32257-6719 Office: Jacksonville Pub Librs 122 N Ocean St Jacksonville FL 32202-3314

MARION, JOHN LOUIS, fine arts auctioneer and appraiser; b. N.Y.C., Nov. 27, 1933; s. Louis John and Florence Adelaide (Winters) M.; children: John L., Deborah Mary, Therese Marie, Michelle Marie; m. Anne Burnett Windfohr, May 26, 1988. BS, Fordham U., 1956; postgrad., Columbia U., 1960-61. With Sotheby Parke Bernet Inc., N.Y.C., 1960—, dir., 1965—, v.p., 1966-70, exec. v.p., 1970-72, pres., 1972-87; chmn. bd. Sotheby's Inc., N.Y.C., 1975—, now hon. chmn.; bd. dirs. Sotheby Holdings Inc., London. Chmn. fine arts N.Y.C. div. Am. Cancer Soc., 1983—; vice chmn. bldg. steering com. Dobbs Ferry (N.Y.) Hosp., 1975; bd. dirs. Internat. Found. Art Research, Ctr. for Hope. Served as lt. (j.g.) USN, 1956-60. Mem. Appraisers Assn. Am., Lotos Club, Eldorado Club, Shady Oaks, Vintage Club. Home: 1400 Shady Oaks Ln Fort Worth TX 76107-3538 Office: Sotheby's Inc 1334 York Ave New York NY 10021-4806*

MARION, JOHN MARTIN, academic administrator; b. Fitchburg, Mass., Jan. 11, 1947; s. Don Louis and Violet Pearl (Richard) M.; m. Joann Elizabeth Trzcinski, Aug. 8, 1970; children: Benjamin Andrew, Jessica Noelle. BS in Edn., Fitchburg State Coll., 1969, M in Edn., 1971; postgrad. in Computer Edn., Lesley Coll. Tchr. Groton (Mass.) Dunstable Regional Schs., 1969-84; computer tchr. Littleton (Mass.) Pub. Schs., 1985-86; computer coord. K-12th grades Newburyport (Mass.) Pub. Schs., 1986-90; chair Acad. Computing Endicott Coll., Beverly, Mass., 1990—; instr. Merrimack Edn. Ctr., Chelmsford, Mass., 1980-90; trainer, cons. Logo Computer Sys., Inc., N.Y.C., 1984-90; tchr. trainer Lego-Decta, Lego Sys., Inc., Enfield, Conn., 1987-90; mem. adv. bd. Claris Software Co.; bd. dirs. Mass. Computer Using Educator, 1989-90. Fulbright scholar tchr. exch., Southampton, Eng., 1973-74. Mem. Internat. Soc. Tech. in Edn., Boston Computer Soc. Home: 123 Chestnut St Pepperell MA 01463-1019 Office: Endicott Coll 376 Hale St Beverly MA 01915-2096

MARION, MARJORIE ANNE, English educator; b. Winterset, Iowa, May 6, 1935; d. Virgil Arthur and Marilyn Ruth (Sandy) Hammon; m. Robert H. Marion, Dec. 20, 1964; 1 dau., Kathryn Ruth. BA, Colo. Coll., 1958; MA, Purdue U., 1969; postgrad., Inst. Mgmt. Lifelong Edn. Harvard U., 1981. Chairperson English dept. Lincoln-Way High Sch., New Lenox, Ill., 1964-68; dir. pub. rels. Coll. St. Francis, Joliet, Ill., 1968-70, chairperson English dept., 1971-75, chairperson div. humanities and fine arts, 1975-79, coord. instructional devel., 1979-80, dir. continuing edn., 1980-84, acting v.p. for acad. affairs, 1984-85, dean of faculty, 1985-89, assoc. prof. English, 1989—; dir. Freshman Core Program, 1993-95; dir. Writing Ctr., 1996; mem. vis. team North Cen. Assn., Joliet & Lockport, Ill, 1975-79; lectr. at ednl. workshops and insts.; TV and radio appearances regarding lifelong edn., Chgo., St. Louis, Albuquerque, Pheonix, 1982-85. Drama critic Joliet Herald News, 1970-82. Recipient Pres.'s award Coll. St. Francis, 1975. Mem. Am. Assn. Higher Edn., Nat. Coun. Tchrs. of English. Roman Catholic.

MARION, MILDRED RUTH, honor society executive; b. St. Louis, Nov. 3, 1904; d. Charles G. and Cora B. (Sutton) Bryan; m. Leroy B. Bale, Mary 29, 1930 (div. May 1, 1940); m. Eugene H. Marion, Dec. 24, 1941 (dec.). PhB, U. Chgo., 1928; MBA, Northwestern U., 1953, postgrad., 1976-90. CPCU. Underwriter Liberty Mut. Ins. Co., Chgo., 1929-69; ret., 1969; exec. sec., editor newsletter, del. Delta Mu Delta Honor Soc., Chgo., 1970—; counsellor Chgo. Campus, Northwestern U., 1958-69. Mem. Northwestern U. Guild (chmn. bylaws 1983-85), Fedn. Bus. Honor Socs. (bd. govs. 1991), Assn. Coll. Honor Socs. (chmn. ins. com.), Woman's Club Evanston (membership com. 1974-76, corr. sec. 1991-92, chmn. printing, chmn. elections), Order Ea. Star (worth matron 1974-76), Phi Chi theta (nat. pres. 1964-66, chmn. bylaws alumni chpt. 1984-90, Cert. 1989, Gold Key award 1991), Delta Mu Delta (nat. pres. 1962-64, rep., spl. plaque Beta chpt. 1969, nat. spl. plaque 1986, 91). Republican. Avocations: sewing, reading, music, art.

MARIONI, TOM, artist; b. Cin., May 21, 1937; s. John D. and Jennie (Geiss) M.; m. Kathan Brown, June 14, 1983; children by previous marriage: Marino, Anthony, Miles. MFA, Cin. Art Acad., 1959. Curator, Richmond Art Ctr. (Calif.), 1968-71; founding dir. Mus. Conceptual Art, San Francisco, 1970-84. Exhibited one-man shows: Galeria Foksal, Warsaw, Poland, 1975, DeYoung Mus., San Francisco, 1977, Modern Art Gallery, Vienna, Austria, 1979, Crown Point Press, San Francisco, 1993, Margarete Roeder Gallery, N.Y.C., 1994; group shows include: Tate Gallery, London, 1982, Belca House, Kyoto, Japan, 1982, Mus. Contemporary Art, L.A., 1995; editor, designer Vision, 1975-81. Mem. tech. assistance com. San Francisco Redevel. Agy., 1982—. Served with U.S. Army, 1960-63. W.Ger. Nat. Endowment Arts grantee, 1980; Guggenheim Found. fellow, 1981; Awards in Visual Arts grantee, 1984. Address: 657 Howard St San Francisco CA 94105

MARIOTTI, JAY ANTHONY, journalist; b. Ellwood City, Pa., June 22, 1959; s. Geno Anthony and Dolores Virginia (Lordi) M.; m. Dana Lynne Barnard, Apr. 19, 1985; children: Karina, Allison. Student, Ohio U., 1976-80. Sports writer The Detroit News, 1980-85; sports columnist The Cin. Post, 1985-87, The Rocky Mountain News, Denver, 1987-89, The Denver Post, 1989-90, The Nat. Sports Daily, N.Y.C., 1990-91, The Chgo. Sun-Times, 1991—. Recipient AP Sports Editors award, 1987, 1993, Crain's Forty under 40 award Crain's Chgo. Bus., 1992, Peter Lisagor award Chgo. Headline Club, 1992. Avocations: reading, tennis, golf, travel. Office: Chicago Sun-Times 401 N Wabash Ave Chicago IL 60611-3532

MARIS, STEPHEN S., lawyer, educator; b. Dallas, Dec. 19, 1949; m. Bronwyn Holmes; children: Shane, Kara. BS, Stephen F. Austin State, 1971; JD, So. Meth. U., 1975. Bar: U.S. Dist. Ct. (no. dist.) Tex. 1975, U.S. Dist. Ct. (ea. dist.) Tex. 1986, U.S. Dist. Ct. (so. dist.) Tex. 1992, U.S. Ct. Appeals (5th cir.) 1980, U.S. Ct. Appeals (11th cir.) 1981, U.S. Supreme Ct. Tex. 1975. Assoc. Passman & Jones, Dallas, 1975-80, ptnr., 1980-87; ptnr. Fulbright & Jaworski, Dallas, 1987—; prof. So. Ill. U., 1979-80, So. Meth. U., Dallas, 1980—; mem. faculty Nat. Inst. Trial Advocacy, 1980—. Editor: Southwest Law Journal, 1973-75. Mem. ABA, State Bar Tex., Dallas Bar Assn., Barristers, Order Coif, Phi Delta Phi. Office: Fulbright & Jaworski 2200 Ross Ave Ste 2800 Dallas TX 75201-6773

MARISOL (MARISOL ESCOBAR), sculptor; b. Paris. Ed., Ecole des Beaux-Arts, Paris, 1949, Art Students League, N.Y.C., 1950, New Sch. for Social Research, 1951-54, Hans Hofmann Sch., N.Y.C., 1951-54; DFA (hon.), Moore Coll. Arts, Phila., 1969, R.I. Sch. Design, 1986, SUNY, Buffalo, 1992. One-woman shows include Leo Castelli Gallery, 1958, Stable Gallery, 1962, 64, Sidney Janis Gallery, N.Y.C., 1966, 67, 73, 75, 81, 84, 89, Hanover Gallery, London, 1967, Moore Coll. Art, Phila., 1970, Worcester (Mass.) Art Mus., 1971, N.Y. Cultural Center, 1973, Columbus (Ohio) Gallery of Fine Arts, 1974, Makler Gallery, Phila., 1982, Boca Raton Mus. Art, Fla., 1988, Galerie Tokoro, Tokyo, 1989, Hasagawa Gallery, Tokyo, 1989, Nat. Portrait Gallery, Washington, 1991, Marlborough Gallery, 1995, Hakone Open Air Mus., Kanagawa, Japan, 1995, Mus. Modern Art, Shiga, Japan, 1995, Iwai City Art Mus., Fukushima, Japan, 1995, Kagoshima City (Japan) Mus. Art, 1995, numerous others; exhibited in group shows including Painting of a Decade, Tate Gallery, London, 1964, New Realism, Municipal Mus., The Hague, 1964, Carnegie Internat., Pitts., 1964, Art of the U.S.A, 1670-1966, Whitney Mus. Am. Art, N.Y.C., 1966, American Sculpture of the Sixties, Mus. of Art, Los Angeles, 1967, Biennale, Venice, 1968, Art Inst. Chgo., 1968, Boymans-van Beuningen Mus., Rotterdam, The Netherlands, 1968, Inst. Contemporary Art, London, 1968, Fondation Maeght, Paris, 1970, Hirshhorn Mus. and Sculpture Garden, 1984, Nat. Portrait Gallery, Washington, 1987, Heckscher Mus., Huntington, N.Y., 1987, Whitney Mus. at Philip Morris, N.Y.C., 1988, Rose Art Mus., Waltham, Mass., 1990, Nat. Portrait Gallery, London, 1993; represented in permanent collections at Mus. Modern Art, N.Y.C., Whitney Mus. Am. Art, Albright-Knox Gallery, Buffalo, Hakone Open Air Mus., Tokyo, Nat. Portrait Gallery, Washington, Harry N. Abrams Collection, N.Y.C., Yale U. Art Gallery, Art Inst. Chgo., Met. Mus., N.Y.C., numerous others; pub. installation Am. Mcht. Mariner's Meml., Promenade Battery Pk. Pier A., Port of N.Y., N.Y.C. Mem. Am. Acad. and Inst. Arts and Letters (v.p. art 1984-87). Address: Marlborough Gallery 40 W 57th St New York NY 10019-4001

MARITZ, WILLIAM E., communications company executive; b. St. Louis; m. Phyllis Mesker; 4 children. Grad., Princeton U., 1950. With Maritz Inc., St. Louis, now pres., chmn. bd. Bd. dirs. Community Sch., John Burroughs Sch., Princeton U., Sta. KETC, Mo. Bot. Garden, St. Luke's Hosp., Washington U., Brown Group, Am. Youth Found., Camping and Edn. Found., Cystic Fibrosis, others; founder, chmn. bd. Laclede's Landing Devel. Corp., St. Louis; chmn. bd. VP Fair Found. Recipient Levee Stone award Downtown St. Louis; Right Arm of St. Louis award, Regional Commerce and Growth Assn. Served with USN. Home: 10 Upper Ladue Rd Saint Louis MO 63124-1630 Office: Maritz Inc 1375 N Highway Dr Fenton MO 63099*

MARK, ALAN SAMUEL, lawyer; b. N.Y.C., Mar. 13, 1947; s. Stanley M. and Miriam (Gordon) M.; m. Paula Calimafde, Oct. 14, 1978; children: Ilana, Clifford, Clayton. Student, Johns Hopkins U., 1965-66; BA, NYU, 1969; JD cum laude, Am. U., 1973; LLM in Taxation, George Washington U., 1977. Bar: D.C. 1973, Maryland 1979. Ptnr. Verner, Liipfert, Bernhard, McPherson, Washington, 1982-85, Finley, Kumble, Wagner et al, Washington, 1986-88, Perito & Dubuc, Washington, 1988-91; sr. counsel Paley, Rothman Goldstein, Rosenberg & Cooper Chtd., Bethesda, Md., 1991—; adj. prof. law Georgetown Law Sch., Am. U. Washington Coll. Law. With U.S. Army, 1969-75. Mem. ABA. Avocation: tennis.

MARK, HANS MICHAEL, aerospace engineering educator, physicist; b. Mannheim, Germany, June 17, 1929; came to U.S., 1940, naturalized, 1945; s. Herman Francis and Maria (Schramek) M.; m. Marion G. Thorpe, Jan. 28, 1951; children: Jane H., James P. A.B. in Physics, U. Calif. at Berkeley, 1951; Ph.D., MIT, 1954; Sc.D. (hon.), Fla. Inst. Tech., 1978; D. Eng. (hon.), Poly. U. N.Y., 1982; DEng (hon.), Milw. Sch. Engring., 1991; LHD (hon.), St. Edward's U., 1993. Research assoc. MIT, 1954-55, asst. prof., 1958-60; research physicist Lawrence Radiation Lab., U. Calif. at Livermore, 1955-58, 60-69, exptl. physics div. leader, 1960-64; assoc. prof. nuclear engring. U. Calif. at Berkeley, 1960-66, prof., 1966-69, chmn. dept. nuclear engring., 1964-69; lectr. dept. applied sci. U. Calif. at Davis, 1969-73; cons. prof. engring. Stanford, 1973-84; dir. NASA-Ames Research Center, 1969-77; undersec. Air Force, Washington, 1977-79; sec. Air Force, 1979-81; dep. adminstr. NASA, Washington, 1981-84; chancellor U. Tex. System, Austin, 1984-92; prof. aerospace engring. and engring. mechanics U. Tex., Austin, 1988—; mem. Pres.'s Adv. Group Sci. and Tech., 1975-76; bd. dirs. BDM Internat. Corp., Astronautics Corp. Am., MAC Equipment Co., Arrowsmith Techs., Inc.; trustee Poly. U., 1984—. Author: (with N.T. Olson) Experiments in Modern Physics, 1966 (with E. Teller and J.S. Foster, Jr.) Power and Security, 1976, (with A. Levine) The Management of Research Institutions, 1983, The Space Station-A Personal Journey, 1987; also numerous articles.; Editor: (with S. Fernbach) Properties of Matter Under Unusual Conditions, 1969, (with Lowell Wood) Energy in Physics, War and Peace, 1988. Recipient Disting. Svc. medal NASA, 1972, 77, medal for exceptional engring. achievement, 1984, Exceptional Civilian Svc. award USAF, 1979, Disting. Pub. Svc, medal, Dept. Def., 1981. Fellow AIAA (Von Karman lectr. astronautics 1992), Am. Phys. Soc.; mem. Nat. Acad. Engring., Am. Nuclear Soc., Am. Geophys. Union, Coun. Fgn. Rels., Cosmos Club. Achievements include research on nuclear energy levels, nuclear reactions, applications, nuclear energy for practical purposes, atomic flourescence yields, measurement X-rays above atmosphere, spacecraft and experimental aircraft design. Office: U Tex Dept Aerospace Engring & Engring Mechs Austin TX 78712-1085

MARK, HENRY ALLEN, lawyer; b. Bklyn., May 16, 1909; s. Henry Adam and Mary Clyde (McCarroll) M.; m. Isobel Ross Arnold, June 26, 1940; BA, Williams Coll., 1932; JD, Cornell U., 1935. Bars: N.Y. 1936, Conn. 1981, U.S. Dist. Ct. (so. dist.) N.Y. 1943. Assoc. firm Allin & Tucker, N.Y.C., 1935-40; mng. atty. Indemnity Ins. Co. of N.Am., N.Y.C., 1940-43; assoc. firm Mudge, Stern, Williams & Tucker, N.Y.C., 1943-50, Cadwalder, Wickersham & Taft, N.Y.C., 1950-53; ptnr. Cadwalader, Wickersham & Taft, 1953-74; lectr. Practicing Law Inst., N.Y.C., 1955-68. Mem. adv. com. zoning Village of Garden City (N.Y.), 1952-54, planning commn., 1957-59, zoning bd. appeals, 1959-61, trustee, 1961-65, mayor, 1965-67; chmn. planning commn. Town of Washington (Conn.), 1980-84; trustee The Gunnery Sch., Washington, Conn., 1980-86; mem. adv. com. on continuing care State of Conn., 1996—. Recipient Disting. Alumnus award Cornell U., 1983. Mem. ABA, N.Y. Bar Assn., Assn. Bar City of N.Y., Conn. Bar Assn., Hartford County Bar Assn., Cornell Law Assn. (pres. 1971-73), Bar Assn. Nassau County (grievance com. 1974-77), St. Andrew's Soc., Phi Beta Kappa. Republican. Congregationalist. Lodge: Masons. Address: 80 Loeffler Rd # G405 Bloomfield CT 06002-2274

MARK, JAMES B. D., surgeon; b. Nashville, June 26, 1929; s. Julius and Margaret (Baer) M.; m. Jean Rambar, Feb. 5, 1957; children: Jonathan, Michael, Margaret, Elizabeth, Katherine. B.A., Vanderbilt U., 1950, M.D., 1953. Intern, resident in gen. and thoracic surgery Yale-New Haven Hosp., 1953-60; instr. to asst. prof. surgery Yale U., 1960-65; asso. prof. surgery Stanford U., 1965-69, prof., 1969—, Johnson and Johnson prof. surgery, 1978—, head div. thoracic surgery, 1972—, assoc. dean clin. affairs, 1988-92; chief staff Stanford U. Hosp., 1988-92; governing bd. Health Systems Agy., Santa Clara County, 1978-80; sr. Fulbright-Hays fellow, vis. prof. surgery U. Dar es Salaam, Tanzania, 1972-73. Mem. editl. bd.: Jour. Thoracic and Cardiovasc. Surgery, 1986-94, World Jour. Surgery, 1995—; contbr. numerous articles to sci. jours. Bd. dirs. Stanford U. Hosp., 1992-94. With USPHS, 1955-57. Fellow ACS (pres. No. Calif. chpt. 1980-81), Am. Coll. Chest Physicians (pres. 1994-95); mem. Am. Assn. Thoracic Surgery, Am. Surg. Assn., Western Surg. Assn., Pacific Coast Surg. Assn., Halsted Soc. (pres. 1984), Western Thoracic Surg. Assn. (pres. 1992-93), Calif. Acad. Medicine (pres. 1978), Santa Clara County Med. Soc. (pres. 1976-77). Home: 921 Casanueva Pl Stanford CA 94305-1001 Office: Stanford U Med Ctr CVRB Stanford CA 94305

MARK, JOHN, film company executive. With John Mark Film Co., L.A., 1971—; chmn., ceo John Mark Film Co., Beverly Hills, Calif., 1992—. Office: John Mark Film Corp 421 N Rodeo Dr # 1500 Beverly Hills CA 90210-4500

MARK, LAURENCE MAURICE, film producer; b. N.Y.C., Nov. 22; s. James Mark and Marion Lorraine (Huebner) Green. BA, Wesleyan U., 1971; MA, NYU, 1973. Exec. dir., publicity Paramount Pictures, N.Y.C., 1978-80; v.p., West Coast mktg. Paramount Pictures, L.A., 1980-82, v.p., prodn., 1982-84; exec. v.p., prodn. Twentieth Century Fox, L.A., 1984-86; pres. Laurence Mark Prodns., L.A., 1986—. Exec. prodr.: (films) Black Widow, 1987, My Stepcother is an Alien, 1988, Working Girl, 1988, Mr. Destiny, 1990, Sister Act 2: Back in the Habit, 1993, (TV) Sweet Bird of Youth, 1989; prodr.: (films) Cookie, 1989, True Colors, 1991, One Good Cop, 1991, The Adventures of Huck Finn, 1993, Cutthroat Island, 1995, Tom and Huck, 1995, Jerry Maguire, 1996. Mem. Acad. Motion Pictures Arts and Scis. Home: 7888 Woodrow Wilson Dr West Hollywood CA 90046-1256 Office: Hollywood Pictures Walt Disney Studios 500 S Buena Vista St Burbank CA 91521-0001

MARK, MARSHA YVONNE ISMAILOFF, artistic director; b. Bridgeport, Conn., Mar. 15, 1938; d. Nicholas and Louba (Foullon) Ismailoff; m. Robert Louis Mark, June 25, 1960; children: Robert, William, Staci. Ballet tng. with, George Balanchine, 1946-50, George Volodine, 1945-60, 65-69; student, Skidmore Coll., 1978-80, Vaganova Method Sch., Minsk, USSR, 1983, U. of the Arts, 1990. Founder Marsha Imailoff Mark Sch. of Ballet, Newtown, Conn., 1969—; artistic dir. Com. for Ballet Miniatures, Newtown, Conn., 1974—, Malenkee Ballet Repertoire Co., Newtown, Conn., 1980—; v.p. Cmty. Arts Project Ext., Newtown, 1987-91; artistic dir. Danbury (Conn.) Music Ctr., 1989; instr. for neurologically impaired Ripton Sch., Shelton, Conn., 1992; choreographed section of Nutcracker Ballet for Special Children; toured Russia with Malenkee Ballet Repertoire Co. Choreographer including original works: Mademoiselle Angot, 1974, Circus, 1975, Haydn Concerto, 1976, Evening at the Zoo, 1977, Match Girl, 1978, The Four Seasons, 1979, Malenkee Waltz, 1980, Magic Key, 1981, Midsummer Night's Dream, 1982, Macbeth A Witches Haunt, 1983, Etudes, 1984, Toy Boutique, Etudes, 1985, Under the Sea, 1986, Nutcracker, 1987, 88, 89, 90, 91, 92, 93, 94, 95, Mere, Mere, Mere, 1988, Ellis Island Memoirs, 1991, Moonlight Etudes, 1992, Echoes of Soft Thunder, 1995; premiered in Baku USSR. Hostess for artists from Russia, translator UN Hostess Com., N.Y.C., 1988; Russian translator Friends of Music, Newtown, 1990, Sacred Heart U., Fairfield, Conn., 1994. Home: 57 Mount Pleasant Rd Newtown CT 06470-1530

MARK, MELVIN, consulting mechanical engineer, educator; b. St. Paul, Nov. 15, 1922; s. Isadore William and Fannye (Abrahamson) M.; m. Elizabeth J. Wyner, Sept. 9, 1951; children: Jonathan S., David W., Peter B. B.M.E., U. Minn., 1943, M.S., 1946; Sc.D. (Teaching, Research fellow), Harvard, 1950. Registered profl. engr., Mass., Minn. Instr. N.D. State U., 1943-44, U. Minn., 1945-47; project mgr. Gen. Electric Co., Lynn., Mass., 1950-52; mgr. Raytheon Co., Wayland, Mass., 1952-56; cons. engr., 1956—; prof. Lowell Technol. Inst., 1957-59, dean faculty, 1959-62; prof. mech. engring. Northeastern U., Boston, 1963-84; dean engring. Northeastern U., 1968-79, provost, sr. v.p. for acad. affairs, 1979-84; vis. lectr. Mass. Inst. Tech., 1955, Brandeis U., 1958; vis. prof. U. Mass., 1984-86; mem. Mass. Bd. Registration of Profl. Engrs. and Land Surveyors, 1990—. Author: Thermodynamics: An Auto-Instructional Text, 1967, Concepts of Thermodynamics, 1975, Thermodynamics: Principles and Applications, 1979, Engineering Thermodynamics, 1985. Contbr. articles to profl. jours. Served with USAAF, 1944-45. Recipient prize Lincoln Arc Welding Found., 1947. Hon. fellow ASME (fellow 1948-50); mem. Am. Soc. Engring. Edn., Sigma Xi, Tau Beta Pi, Pi Tau Sigma, Phi Kappa Phi. Patentee in field. Home: 17 Larch Rd Newton MA 02168-1413 Office: 93 Union St Suite 400 Newton Center MA 02159

MARK, MICHAEL LAURENCE, music educator; b. Schenectady, N.Y., Dec. 1, 1936; s. David and Ruth (Garbowitz) M.; m. Lois Nitekman, Jan. 28, 1942; children: Michelle, Diana. BM, The Cath. U. of Am., 1958, DMA, 1969; MA, George Washington U., 1960; M in Music Edn., U. Mich., 1962. Tchr. Prince George's County, Md. Pub. Schs., 1958-60, 61-66; assoc. prof. music Morgan State U., Balt., 1966-70; supr. music Auburn (N.Y.) Enlarged Sch. Dist., 1970-72; dir. music Elmira (N.Y.) Enlarged Sch. Dist., 1972-73; assoc. prof., sch. music Cath. U. Am., Washington, 1973-81; dean grad. sch., prof. music Towson (Md.) State U., 1981-95, prof. music, 1995—; Edtl. com. five jours. in field. Author: Contemporary Music Education, 1978, 3rd rev. edit., 1996, Source Readings in Music Education Histor, 1982; co-author: A History of American Music Education, 1992. Mem. Music Educators Nat. Conf. (numerous coms.), Coll. Music Soc. Avocations: travel, woodworking. Office: Music Dept Towson State U Towson MD 21204

MARK, PETER, director, conductor; b. N.Y.C., Oct. 31, 1940; s. Irving and Edna M.; m. Thea Musgrave, Oct. 2, 1971. BA (Woodrow Wilson fellow), Columbia U., 1961; MS, Juilliard Sch. Music, 1963. Prof. music and dramatic art U. Calif., Santa Barbara, 1965-94; fellow Creative Arts Inst., U. Calif., 1968-69, 71-72; guest condr. Wolf Trap Orch., 1979, N.Y.C. Opera, 1981, L.A. Opera Theater, 1981, Royal Opera House, London, 1982, Hong Kong Philharm. Orch., 1984, Jerusalem Symphony Orch., 1988, Tulsa Opera, 1988, Compania Nacional de Opera, Mexico City, 1989, 92, N.Y. Pops, Carnegie Hall, 1991. Concert violist U.S., S.Am., Europe, 1961-67; artistic dir., condr. Va. Opera, Norfolk, 1975—, gen. dir., 1978—; condr.: Am. premier of Mary, Queen of Scots (Musgrave), 1978; World premier of A Christmas Carol (Musgrave), 1979, of Harriet, the Woman Called Moses (Musgrave), 1985, of Simon Bolivar (Musgrave), 1984, Porgy and Bess, Buenos Aires, Mexico City and São Paulo, 1992, Orlando Opera co., 1993, Richmond Symphony, 1993, Krakow Opera, 1995, Pacific Opera Victoria (Can.), 1996, Cleve. Opera, 1996, Festival Pucciniano-Torre del Lago, Italy, 1996. Recipient Elias Lifchey viola award Juilliard Sch. Music, 1963; named hon. citizen of Norfolk (Va.). Mem. Musicians Union, Phi Beta Kappa. Office: Va Opera PO Box 2580 Norfolk VA 23501-2580

MARK, REUBEN, consumer products company executive; b. Jersey City, N.J., Jan. 21, 1939; s. Edward and Libbie (Berman) M.; m. Arlene Slobzian, Jan. 10, 1964; children: Lisa, Peter, Stephen. AB, Middlebury Coll., 1960; MBA, Harvard U., 1963. With Colgate-Palmolive Co., N.Y.C., 1963—; pres., gen. mgr. Colgate-Palmolive Co., Venezuela, 1972-73, Can., 1973-74; v.p., gen. mgr. Far East div. Colgate-Palmolive Co., 1974-75, v.p., gen. mgr. household products div., 1975-79, group v.p. domestic ops., 1979-81, exec. v.p., 1981-83, chief operating officer, 1983-84, pres., 1983—, chief exec. officer, 1984—, chmn. bd., 1986—; lectr. Sch. Bus. Adminstrn., U. Conn., 1977. Served with U.S. Army, 1961. Mem. Soap and Detergent Assn. (bd. dirs.), Grocery Mfrs. Am. (dir.), Nat. Exec. Service Corp. Office: Colgate-Palmolive Co 300 Park Ave New York NY 10022-7402*

MARK, SHELLEY MUIN, economist, educator, government official; b. China, Sept. 9, 1922; came to U.S., 1923, naturalized, 1944; s. Hing D. and S. (Wong) M.; m. Janet Chong, Sept. 14, 1946 (dec. Mar. 1977); children—Philip, Diane, Paul, Peter, Steven; m. Tung Chow, July 8, 1978. B.A., U. Wash., 1943, Ph.D., 1956; M.S., Columbia, 1944; postgrad. (Ford Found. fellow), Harvard, 1959-60. Fgn. news reporter CBS, N.Y., 1945-46; instr. U. Wash., 1946-48; asst. prof. Ariz. State Coll., 1948-51; territorial economist OPS, Honolulu, 1951-53; prof. econs. U. Hawaii, 1953-62, dir. econ. rsch. ctr., 1959-62; dir. planning and econ. devel. State of Hawaii, 1962-74, state land use commr., 1962-74, state energy coord., 1973-74; dir. Office Land Use Coordination EPA, Washington, 1975-77; prof. econs. U. Hawaii, 1978—; rsch. fellow East-West Ctr., Inst. Econ. Devel. and Policy, 1984-94; Asian advisor Internat. Ctr. Econ. Growth, 1992—; sr. advisor Dept. Bus., Econ. Devel. and Tourism, Hawaii, 1995—; vis. scholar Harvard U., 1986; vis. faculty Grad. Sch. People's Bank of China, 1988; also econ. cons. Philippines Inst. Devel. Studies, Devel. Rsch. Ctr. State Coun., China, also other orgns.; mem. Gov.'s Adv. Com. Sci. and Tech., 1963-74, Oahu Transp. Policy Com., 1964-74, Regional Export Expansion Coun., 1964-74;. Author: Economics in Action, 4th edit., 1969, Macroeconomic Performance of Asia-Pacific Region, 1985, Development Economics and Developing Economies, 1990, Aspects of Chinese Economic Development, 1991; editor: Economic Interdependence and Cooperation in Asia-Pacific, 1993, Asian Transitional Economies, 1996; contbr. articles to profl. jours. Bd. dirs. U. Hawaii Rsch.

Corp.; bd. dirs. Coun. State Planning Agys., pres., 1973-74, hon. mem., 1975—; governing bd. Coun. State Govts., 1972-74. Recipient Sackett Meml. award Columbia, 1944. Mem. Hawaii Govt. Employees Assn. (pres. univ. chpt., dir. 1958-59), Am. Econ. Assn., Royal Econ. Soc., Western Regional Sci. Assn. (pres. 1974-75, dir.), Phi Beta Kappa, Sigma Delta Chi. Mem. United Ch. of Christ. Home: 2036 Keeaumoku St Honolulu HI 96822-2526

MARK, SHEW-KUEY TOMMY, physics educator; b. Canton, China, Aug. 8, 1936; emigrated to Can., 1952, naturalized, 1952; s. Yook Sue and Nuey (Fong) M.; m. Yan Chu Woo, Sept. 9, 1961; children: Bethany Mark, Terence Mark. BSc, McGill U., 1960, MSc, 1962, PhD, 1965. Postdoctoral fellow NRC of Can., U. Man., 1965-66; asst. prof. McGill U., Montreal, 1966-70; assoc. prof. McGill U., 1970-75, prof. physics, 1975—; dir. McGill U. (Foster Radiation Lab.), 1971-79; chmn. dept. physics McGill U., 1982-90. Contbr. articles to profl. jours. Grantee Natural Scis. and Engring. Rsch. Coun. of Can., 1965—, DOE of U.S., 1990—. Mem. Canadian Assn. Physicists, Am. Phys. Soc., Canadian Assn. Univ. Tchrs. Home: 660 Victoria Ave, Westmount, PQ Canada H3Y 2R9 Office: 3600 University St, Montreal, PQ Canada H3A 2T8

MARK, WAYNE MICHAEL, technical education director; b. Rochester, N.Y., June 26, 1952; s. Henry S. and Mary (Bucci) M.; m. Peggy Halling, Apr. 1, 1971 (div. Apr. 1987); children: Crystal, Jonathan; m. Janet Louise Richards, Dec. 18, 1987; children: Michael, Christopher, Joshua. Grad. high sch., Rochester. Cert. automotive technician. Mgr. NAPA Auto Parts, Hollywood, Fla., 1970-73; mgr. NAPA Auto Parts, Canandaigua, N.Y., 1973-78, gen. mgr., 1978-80; sales rep. Echlin, Inc., Branford, Conn., 1980-83, tech. tng. specialist, 1983-88, dir. advanced tech. edn., 1988-93, mgr. spl. tng. svcs., 1994—; cons. Genuine Parts Co., Atlanta, 1991—, T.H. Pickens Tech. Ctr., Aurora, Colo., 1992—, Automotive Svc. Excellence, Hampton, Va., 1992—, Internat. Platform Assn., 1994—. Editor, dir, advisor: (video prodn.) Automotive Servicing, 1990, 92, Soc. of Automotive Engineers, 1995—; contbr. editorials to profl. publ. Roman Catholic. Avocations: model railroading, camping, auto restoration, gardening. Home: 1605 S Mobile St Aurora CO 80017-5168 Office: Echlin Inc 175 N Branford Rd Branford CT 06405-2810

MARKE, JULIUS JAY, law librarian, educator; b. N.Y.C., Jan. 12, 1913; s. Isidore and Anna (Taylor) M.; m. Sylvia Bolotin, Dec. 15, 1946; 1 child, Elisa Hope. BS, CCNY, 1934; LLB, NYU, 1937; BS in Lib. Sci., Columbia U., 1942. Bar: N.Y. 1938. Reference asst. N.Y. Pub. Libr., 1937-42; pvt. practice law N.Y.C., 1939-41; prof. law, law libr. NYU, 1949-83, prof. law emeritus, 1983—, interim dean of librs., 1975-77; Disting. Prof., dir. Law Libr. St. John's U. Sch. Law, 1983-95; disting. rsch. prof. law St. John's U. Sch. Law, Jamaica, N.Y., 1995—; lectr. Columbia Sch. Library Service, 1962-78, adj. prof., 1978-85; cons. Orientation Program Am. Law, 1965-68, Ford Found. Overseas Law Libraries Am. Law, 1968-79, copyright Ford Found., law libraries, Coun. Fgn. Rels., 1990—, Shubert Archives, 1991, others. Author: Vignettes of Legal History, 1965, 2d series, 1977, Copyright and Intellectual Property, 1967 (with R. Sloane) Legal Research and Law Library Management, rev. edit., 1990, 96; editor: Modern Legal Forms, 1953, The Holmes Reader, 1955, The Docket Series, 1955—, Bender's Legal Business Forms, 4 vols., 1962; compiler, editor: A Catalogue of the Law Collection at NYU with Selected Annotations, 1953, Dean's List of Recommended Reading for Pre-Law and Law Students, 1958, 84, and others; chmn. editl. bd. Oceana Group, 1977—, Index to Legal Periodicals, 1978—; columnist N.Y. Law Jour., 1970—; contbr. articles to profl. jours. Mem. publs. coun. N.Y.U., 1964-80. Sgt. AUS, 1943-45. Decorated Bronze Star. Mem. ABA, Am. Assn. Law Librs. (pres. 1962-63, Disting. Svc. award 1986), Assn. Am. Law Schs., Coun. of Nat. Libr. Assns. (exec. bd., v.p. 1959, 60), Law Libr. Assn. Greater N.Y. (pres. 1949, 50, chmn. joint com. on libr. edn. 1950-52, 60-61), NYU Law Alumni Assn. (Judge Edward Weinfeld award 1987, mem. exec. bd. 1988—), Columbia Sch. Libr. Svc. Alumni Assn. (pres. 1973-75), Order of Coif (pres. NYU Law Sch. br. 1970-83), NYU Faculty Club (pres. 1966-68), Field Inn, Phi Delta Phi. Home: 4 Peter Cooper Rd Apt 8F New York NY 10010-6746

MARKEE, KATHERINE MADIGAN, librarian, educator; b. Cleve., Feb. 24, 1931; d. Arthur Alexis and Margaret Elizabeth (Madigan) M. AB, Trinity Coll., Washington, 1953; MA, Columbia U., 1962; MLS, Case Western Res. U., 1968. Employment mgr., br. store tng. supr. The May Co., Cleve., 1965-67; assoc. prof. libr. sci., data bases libr. Purdue U. Libr., West Lafayette, Ind., 1968—. Contbr. articles to profl. jours. Mem. ALA, AAUP, Spl. Librs. Assn., Ind. Online Users Group, Sigma Xi (Rsch. Support award 1986). Avocations: photography, sailing, gardening. Office: Purdue U Libr West Lafayette IN 47907-1530

MARKEL, ROBERT THOMAS, mayor; b. Wilmington, Del., Apr. 4, 1943; s. Robert H. and Margaret T. (Dillon) M.; m. Mary C. Alby, Aug. 5, 1967; children: Robert J., Katharine C. BA, Notre Dame U., 1965, PhD, 1975. Assoc. prof. Am. Internat. Coll., Springfield, Mass., 1969-92; city councillor City of Springfield, 1978-92, mayor, 1992—; mem. Springfield Conservation Commn., 1976-78, Springfield Preservation Trust, 1982—, local govt. adv. commn. Commonwealth of Mass., Boston, 1982-90; bd. dirs. World Affairs Coun. Western Mass., 1979—, Mass. Mcpl. Assn., Boston, 1981-88; pres. Springfield City Coun., 1986. Bd. dirs. Stage West Resident Theatre, 1987—. Mem. Am. Polit. Sci. Assn. Democrat. Roman Catholic. Avocations: skiing, fishing, running. Home: 53 Florentine Gdns Springfield MA 01108-2507 Office: Office of Mayor Adminstrn Bldg 36 Court St Springfield MA 01103-1699

MARKELL, ALAN WILLIAM, linguistic company executive; b. Boston, June 6, 1933; s. Edward and Frances B. Markell; m. Carol Markell (div. Apr. 1978); children: Jennifer, Adam. AB, Bowdoin Coll., 1954; MBA, Columbia U., 1956. Fin. analyst RCA Corp., Camden, N.J. and N.Y.C., 1956-58; controller Jenkins Spirits Corp., Somerville, Mass., 1958-60, Marum Knitting Mills, Lawrence, Mass., 1960-63; pres. Norfolk Fluoridation Corp., Dedham, Mass., 1963-65, Car Mark Inc., Brookline, Mass., 1965-78; v.p. Linguistic Systems Inc., Cambridge, Mass., 1978-90, also bd. dirs.; pres. Cambridge Inst. Inc., Boston, 1979-86, instr. in mgmt.; ptnr. Moss Roberts and Co., Cambridge, 1978-90, bd. dirs. Bd. dirs. Miami Chamber Symphony, 1991—. Home: 200 Ocean Lane Dr Key Biscayne FL 33149-1461 Summer Address: 2145 Pinkham Point Rd Harpswell ME 04011

MARKEN, GIDEON ANDREW, III, advertising and public relations executive; b. Hampton, Iowa, June 24, 1940; s. Gideon Andrew Jr. and Cleone (Marie Riss) M.; m. Jeannine Gay Hill, Dec. 28, 1963; children: Tracy Lynn, Gideon Andrew. BS, Iowa State U., 1962; MBA, Hamilton Inst., 1967. Pub. relations mgr. Fairchild Instrumentation, Mountain View, Calif., 1967-68; pub. relations dir. Barnes-Hind Pharms., Sunnyvale, Calif., 1968-69; v.p. acct. supr. Hal Lawrence, Inc., Palo Alto, Calif., 1969-74, Bozell-Jacobs, Palo Alto, 1974-77; pres. Marken Communications, Sunnyvale, Calif., 1977—. Contbr. articles to profl. jours. Served as sgt. USAF, 1963-67. Mem. Pub. Relations Soc. of Am., Peninsula Mktg. Assn., Bus. Publishing Advt. Assn., Am. Mgmt. Assn., Am. Electronics Assn., Am. Med. Writers Assn. (pres. 1968-70, 72-74). Republican. Methodist. Club: San Rafael Yacht. Home: 1428 Bellingham Ave Sunnyvale CA 94087-3811 Office: Marken Comm 3375 Scott Blvd # 108 Santa Clara CA 95054

MARKEN, WILLIAM RILEY, magazine editor; b. San Jose, Calif., Sept. 2, 1942; s. Harry L. and Emma Catherine (Kraus) M.; m. Marilyn Tonascia, Aug. 30, 1964; children—Catherine, Elizabeth, Michael, Paul. Student, Occidental Coll., 1960-62; BA, U. Calif., Berkeley, 1964. From writer to editor-in-chief Sunset Mag., Menlo Park, Calif., 1964-96; editor-at-large Sunset Publ. Corp., Menlo Park, Calif., 1996—. Bd. dirs. Calif. Tomorrow, 1979-83; pres. League to Save Lake Tahoe, 1994-96. Avocations: tennis; skiing; basketball. Office: Sunset Mag 80 Willow Rd Menlo Park CA 94025-3661

MARKER, DAVID GEORGE, university president; b. Atlantic, Iowa, Mar. 20, 1937; s. Calburt D. and Vera (Smith) M.; children—Paul C., Elizabeth A. A.B., Grinnell Coll., 1959; M.S., Pa. State U., 1962, Ph.D., 1966; L.H.D. (hon.), Hope Coll., 1984; ScD (hon.), Grinnell Coll., 1993. Instr., asst. prof., assoc. prof., prof. physics Hope Coll., Holland, Mich., 1965-84, adminstrv. dir. Computer Ctr., 1969-74, chmn. dept. computer sci., 1973-79, assoc. dean acad. affairs, 1973-74, provost, 1974-84; pres. Cornell Coll., Mount Vernon, Iowa, 1984-94, U. of Osteo. Medicine and Health Scis., Des Moines, 1994—; bd. dirs. Des Moines Gen. Hosp., Firstar, Des Moines, Sci. Ctr. Iowa; cons. in field. Contbr. articles to profl. jours. Bd. dirs. St. Luke's Hosp., 1987-90; mem. adv. com. NSF Project Kaleidoscope, 1990-94. Recipient Bishop's Service Cross. Mem. NCAA (pres. commn. 1989-93), Nat. Assn. Colls. and Univs. (chmn. commn. on policy analysis 1991), Iowa Assn. Ind. Colls. and Univs. (exec. com. 1986-93, chmn. 1991-92), Iowa Coll. Found. (exec. com. 1987-92, chmn. 1990-91), Rotary, Phi Beta Kappa, Sigma Xi. Episcopalian. Avocations: cycling; music; photography. Home: Apt 601 3131 Fleur Dr Des Moines IA 50321 Office: Univ Osteo Medicine Health 3200 Grand Ave Des Moines IA 50312-4104

MARKER, MARC LINTHACUM, lawyer, investor; b. Los Angeles, July 19, 1941; s. Clifford Harry and Voris (Linthacum) M.; m. Sandra Yocom, Aug. 29, 1965; children: Victor, Gwendolyn. BA in Econs. and Geography, U. Calif.-Riverside, 1964; JD, U. So. Calif., 1967. Asst. v.p., asst. sec. Security Pacific Nat. Bank, L.A., 1970-73; sr. v.p., chief counsel, sec. Security Pacific Leasing Corp., San Francisco, 1973-92; pres. Security Pacific Leasing Svcs. Corp., San Francisco, 1977-85, dir., 1977-92; bd. dirs., sec. Voris, Inc., 1973-86; bd. dirs. Refiners Petroleum Corp., 1977-81, Security Pacific Leasing Singapore Ltd., 1983-85, Security Pacific Leasing Can. Ltd., 1989-92; lectr. in field. Served to comdr. USCGR. Mem. ABA, Calif. Bar Assn., D.C. Bar Assn., Am. Assn. Equipment Lessors. Republican. Lutheran. Club: Univ. (L.A.). Office: 471 Magnolia Ave # B Larkspur CA 94939-2034

MARKER, ROBERT SYDNEY, management consultant; b. Nashville, July 27, 1922; s. Forest M. and Lassie (Weatherford) M.; m. Elizabeth Davis, Oct. 27, 1943; children—Christopher, Andrew. B.A., Emory U., 1946. Account exec. Griswold-Eshleman, 1949-51; advt. mgr. B.F. Goodrich Co., 1947-49; copy group head Maxon, Inc., 1951-56; sr. v.p., dir. creative services McManus, John & Adams, 1956-63; v.p. McCann-Erickson, Inc., 1963-64, sr. v.p., 1964-67; mgr. McCann-Erickson, Inc. (Detroit office), 1964-68; exec. v.p. McCann-Erickson, Inc. (Detroit office), N.Y.C., 1967-68; pres. McCann-Erickson, Inc. (Detroit office), 1968-71, chmn. bd., chief exec. officer, 1971-74, also bd. dirs., mem. exec. com.; chmn. exec. com. Needham, Harper & Steers, Inc., 1975-80; mng. ptnr. Robert S. Marker, Inc., Tequesta, Fla. and N.Y.C., 1980-90; Bd. dirs. Am. Assn. Advt. Agys., Detroit Adcraft Club, 1965, Detroit Advt. Assn., 1965, N.Y. Bd. Trade. Mem. Mayor's Council on Environment. Served with USAAC, 1943-46. Recipient Creative Advt. awards N.Y. Art Dirs. Club, Creative Advt. awards Detroit Advt. Club, Creative Advt. awards Chgo. Copy Club, Creative Advt. awards Alpha Delta Sigma. Mem. Am. Assn. Advt. Agys. (dir., chmn. Eastern region), Alpha Delta Sigma, Sigma Delta Chi. Clubs: Turtle Creek (Fla.); Winged Foot (Mamaroneck, N.Y.). Home: Apt 101 10555 SE Terrapin Pl Jupiter FL 33469-1582

MARKERT, CLEMENT LAWRENCE, biology educator; b. Las Animas, Colo., Apr. 11, 1917; s. Edwin John and Sarah (Norman) M.; m. Margaret Rempfer, July 29, 1940; children—Alan Ray, Robert Edwin, Betsy Jean. B.A. summa cum laude, U. Colo., 1940; M.A., UCLA, 1942; Ph.D., Johns Hopkins U., 1948. Merck-NRC fellow Calif. Inst. Tech., 1948-50; asst. prof. zoology U. Mich., 1950-56, assoc. prof., 1956-57; prof. biology Johns Hopkins, 1957-65; chmn. dept. biology Yale U., 1965-71, prof. biology, 1965-86, dir. Center for Reproductive Biology, 1974-86; Disting. Univ. Research prof. N.C. State U., 1986-93, disting. univ. prof. emeritus, 1993—; panelist NSF, 1959-63; panelist subcom. on marine biology President's Sci. Adv. Com., 1965-66; mem. council Am. Cancer So., 1976-78; co-chmn. devel. biology interdisciplinary cluster Pres.' Biomed. Research Panel, 1975; mem. com. on animal models and genetic stocks NRC, 1979-85; trustee Bermuda Biol. Sta. for Research, 1959-83, life trustee, 1983—; bd. sci. advisers La Jolla Cancer Research Found.; mem. bd. sci. advs. Jane Coffin Childs Meml. Fund for Med. Research, 1979-86; chmn. bd. trustees BIOSIS, 1981, mem., 1976-81. Editor Prentice-Hall Series in Developmental Biology, Procs. 3d, 5th, 6th, 7th Internat. Congress Isozymes, 1974, 86, 89, 92; assoc. editor The Physiology of Reproduction; mng. editor Jour. Exptl. Zoology, 1963-85; mem. editl. bd. Archives of Biochemistry and Biophysics, 1963-81, Sci. mag., 1979-83, Differentiation, 1973—, Developmental Genetics, 1979-92, Cancer Rsch., 1982-85, Tansgenics, 1993—; mem. spl. adv. bd. Jour. Reprodn. and Devel., 1992—. Served with Internat. Brigades, 1938, Spain; with Mcht. Marine, 1944-45. Mem. Am. Inst. Biol. Scis. (pres. 1965), NAS (governing council 1970-71, 77-80), Inst. Medicine, Am. Soc. Biochemistry and Molecular Biology, Internat. Soc. Developmental Biologists, Am. Soc. Developmental Biology (pres. 1963-64), Soc. Study of Reprodn., Am. Acad. Arts and Scis. (governing council 1980-84), Am. Genetic Assn. (pres. 1980), Am. Soc. Naturalists (v.p. 1967), Am. Soc. Zoologists (pres. 1967), Genetics Soc. Am., Am. Soc. Animal Sci., Phi Beta Kappa, Sigma Xi. Home: 4005 Wakefield Dr Colorado Springs CO 80906-4324

MARKESBERY, WILLIAM R., neurology and pathology educator, physician; b. Florence, Ky., Sept. 30, 1932; s. William M. and Sarah E. (Tanner) M.; m. Barbara A. Abram, Sept. 5, 1958; children—Susanne Hartley, Catherine Kendall, Elizabeth Allison. B.A., U. Ky., 1960; M.D. with distinction, U. Ky. Med. Coll., 1964. Diplomate Am. Bd. Neurology and Psychiatry Diplomate Am. Bd. Pathology. Intern U. Hosp., Lexington, KY, 1964-65; resident neurology Presbyn. Hosp., N.Y.C., 1965-67; fellow neuropathology Coll. Physicians and Surgeons, Columbia U., N.Y.C., 1967—; asst. prof. pathology, neurology U. Rochester, N.Y., 1969-72; assoc. prof. pathology, neurology U. Ky., Lexington, 1972-77, prof. neurology, pathology, anatomy, 1977—, dir. Ctr. on Aging, 1979—, prof. neurology, pathology, dir., 1977—; mem. pathology study sect. NIH, Washington, 1982-85, nat. adv. coun. NIH, 1990-94; chmn. Med. Sci. Adv. Bd., Chgo., 1989-94, Nat. Alzheimer's Assn., Chgo., 1985-86, adv. panel on dementia U.S. Congress of Tech., Washington, 1985-86; dir. Alzheimer's Disease Research Ctr., 1985—, Alzheimer's Diseases Program Project Grant, 1984—. Mem. editorial bd. Jour. Neuropathology and Exptl. Neurology, 1983-86, 89—, Neurobiology of Aging, 1986—, Ann. Neurology, 1990—; contbr. numerous articles to profl. jours. With U.S. Army, 1954-56. Recipient Disting. Achievement award Ky. Research Found., Lexington, 1978; named U. Ky. Disting. Alumni prof., 1985, Disting. Research prof., U. Ky., 1977, Disting. Alumni U. Ky. Coll. Medicine, 1993; inductee U. Ky. Disting Alumni, 1989; prin. investigator NIH, Washington, 1977—. Mem. Am. Acad. Neurology, Am. Assn. Neuropathologists (exec. com. 1984-86, pres1991—), Soc. Neurosci., Am. Neurol. Assn., Alpha Omega Alpha. Home: 1555 Tates Creek Rd Lexington KY 40502-2229 Office: U Ky Coll Med Dept Neurology & Pathology 800 Rose St Lexington KY 40536-0001*

MARKEY, EDWARD JOHN, congressman; b. Malden, Mass., July 11, 1946; s. John E. and Christine M. (Courtney) M. B.A., Boston Coll., 1968, J.D., 1972. Bar: Mass. Mem. Mass. Ho. of Reps., 1973-76, 94th-104th Congresses from 7th Mass. Dist., 1975—, New Eng. Congl. Caucus, N.E.-Midwest Econ. Advancement Coalition, Dem. Study Group, Environ. Study Conf. Freshman Caucus, now chmn. subcom. telecomm. and fin.; ranking minority mem., mem. commerce subcom. on telecomm. and fin. Mem. editorial staff: Boston Coll. Law Rev. Served with USAR, 1968-73. Mem. Mass. Bar Assn. (Mass. Legislator of Year 1975). Club: K.C. Home: 7 Townsend St Malden MA 02148-6322 Office: US Ho of Reps 2133 Rayburn HOB Washington DC 20515-2107*

MARKEY, ROBERT GUY, lawyer; b. Cleve., Feb. 25, 1939; s. Nate and Rhoda (Gross) M.; children: Robert Jr., Randolph; m. Nanci Louise Brooks, Aug. 25, 1990. AB, Brown U., 1961; JD, Case Western Res., 1964. Bar: Ohio 1964. Assoc., ptnr. Kahn and Kleinman, Cleve., 1964-75; ptnr. Arter & Hadden, Cleve., 1975-83, Baker & Hostetler, Cleve., 1983—; dir., sec. Blue Coral, Inc., Cleve.; bd. dirs. Matrix Essentials, Inc., Cleve., McKay Chem. Co., L.A. Chmn. attys. div. United Way Svcs., Cleve., 1978; trustee Fedn. Community Planning, Cleve., 1980-87, Cleve. Ctr. Contemporary Art, 1993—, pres. 1995—. Mem. ABA, Cleve. Bar Assn. (chmn. securities law com. 1974-75), Ohio State Bar Assn., Union Club, Chagrin Valley Hunt Club. Republican. Jewish. Office: Baker & Hostetler 3200 National City Ctr 1900 E 9th St Cleveland OH 44114-3401

MARKEY, WILLIAM ALAN, health care administrator; b. Cleve., Dec. 29, 1927; s. Oscar Bennett and Claire (Feldman) M.; m. Irene Nelson, Oct. 31, 1954; children—Janet Ellen Markey-Hisakawa, Suzanne Katherine Markey-Johnson. Student, Case Inst. Tech., 1945-48; BA, U. Mich., 1950; MS, Yale U., 1954. Resident hosp. adminstrn. Beth Israel Hosp., Boston, 1953-54; asst. dir. Montefiore Hosp., Pitts., 1954-56; asst. adminstr. City of Hope Med. Ctr., Duarte, Calif., 1956-57; adminstrv. dir. City of Hope Med. Ctr., 1957-66; assoc. dir. cancer hosp. project, instr. pub. health U. So. Calif. Sch. Medicine, 1966-67, asst. clin. prof. pub. health and community medicine, 1968-70, asst. prof., 1970-75, dep. dir. regional med. programs, 1967-71; adminstr. Health Care Agy., County of San Diego, 1971-74; health services cons. Health Care Agy., 1974-75; dir. Maricopa County Dept. Health Services, Phoenix, 1975-79; cons. Maricopa County Dept. Health Services, 1979-80; adminstr. Sonoma Valley Hosp., Calif., 1980-83;; lectr. pub. health Sch. Pub. Health, UCLA, 1969-74; lectr. community medicine Sch. Medicine, U. Calif.-San Diego, 1973-75; cons. L.A. County Dept. Hosps., 1966-71, cons. Hosp./Health Svcs., 1983—; CEO Chinese Hosp., San Francisco, 1985-86, 90-91; adj. instr. Golden Gate U., 1992—. Mem. bd. edn. Duarte Unified Sch. Dist., 1967-72, pres., 1970-72; bd. dirs. Hosp. Coun. So. Calif., 1963-67, sec. 1966-67; bd. dirs. Duarte Pub. Libr. Assn., 1965-72, Duarte-Bradbury chpt. Am. Field Svc., 1965-72, Duarte-Bradbury Cmty. Chest, 1961-68, Cen. Ariz. Health Svcs. Agy., 1975-80, Vis. Nurse Assn. The Redwoods, Santa Rosa, Calif., 1985-86, Sonoma Greens Homeowners Assn., 1990-91, Sonoma City Opera, 1987, 93, United Way, Sonoma, 1995—; com. chmn. Sonoma County Bd. Realtors, 1990-92; active Sonoma County Multiple Listing Svc., 1987—. Served with AUS, 1950-52. Fellow Am. Coll. Health Care Execs. (life); mem. Am. Hosp. Assn. (life), Am. Pub. Health Assn., Royal Soc. Health, Calif. Hosp. Assn. (trustee 1966-69, dir. 1966-69), Internat. Fedn. Hosps., Hosp. Coun. No. Calif. (dir. 1981-83), Kiwanis, Rotary (past pres. Duarte). Home: 866 Princeton Dr Sonoma CA 95476-4186 Office: PO Box F Sonoma CA 95476-0370

MARKEY, WINSTON ROSCOE, aeronautical engineering educator; b. Buffalo, Sept. 20, 1929; s. Roscoe Irvin and Catherine L. (Higgins) M.; m. Phoebe Anne Sproule, Sept. 10, 1955; children: Karl Richard, Katherine Ilse, Kristina Anne. BS, MIT, 1951, Sc.D., 1956. Engr. MIT, 1951-57, asst. prof., 1957-62, assoc. prof., 1962-66, prof., 1966—, chmn. undergrad. com., 1988—, dir. Measurement Systems Lab., 1961-89; chief scientist USAF, 1964-65, mem. sci. adv. bd., 1966-69. Author: (with J. Hovorka) The Mechanics of Inertial Position and Heading Indication, 1961; Assoc. editor: AIAA Jour, 1963-66. Recipient Exceptional Civilian Service award USAF, 1965. Mem. Sigma Xi, Tau Beta Pi, Gamma Alpha Rho. Home: 11 Edgewood Rd Lexington MA 02173-3501 Office: MIT Bldg 33-208 Cambridge MA 02139

MARKGRAF, J(OHN) HODGE, chemist, educator; b. Cin., Mar. 16, 1930; s. Carl A. and Elizabeth (Hodge) M.; m. Nancy Hart, Apr. 4, 1957; children: Carrie G., Sarah T. A.B., Williams Coll., 1952; M.Sc., Yale U., 1954, Ph.D., 1957; postgrad., U. Munich, W. Ger., 1956-57. Research chemist Procter & Gamble Co., Cin., 1958-59; asst. prof. chemistry Williams Coll., Williamstown, Mass., 1959-65; assoc. prof. Williams Coll., Williamstown, 1965-69, prof., 1969—, Ebenezer Fitch prof. chemistry, 1977-85, 94—, provost, 1980-83, v.p. for alumni relations and devel., 1985-94, coll. marshal, 1995—; vis. prof. U. Calif., Berkeley, 1964-65, 68-69, 76-77, Duke U., 1983-84. Contbr. articles to profl. jours. NSF fellow; Sci. Faculty fellow; grantee NSF; grantee Am. Chem. Soc. Petroleum Research Fund; grantee Research Corp.; grantee Merck & Co. Mem. Am. Chem. Soc., Phi Beta Kappa, Sigma Xi. Patentee in field. Home: 104 Forest Rd Williamstown MA 01267-2029 Office: Williams College Dept Chemistry Williamstown MA 02167-2692

MARKHAM, CHARLES BUCHANAN, lawyer; b. Durham, N.C., Sept. 15, 1926; s. Charles Blackwell and Sadie Helen (Hackney) M. A.B., Duke U., Durham, N.C., 1945; postgrad., U. N.C. Law Sch., Chapel Hill, 1945-46; LL.B., George Washington U., Washington, 1951. Bar: D.C. 1951, N.Y. 1961, N.C. 1980, U.S. Ct. Appeals (2d cir.) 1962, U.S. Ct. Appeals (D.C. cir.) 1955, U.S. Supreme Ct. 1964. Reporter Durham Sun, N.C., 1945; asst. state editor, editorial writer Charlotte News, N.C., 1947-48; dir. publicity and research Young Democratic Clubs Am., Washington, 1948-49, exec. sec., 1949-50; polit. analyst Dem. Senatorial Campaign Com., Washington, 1950-51; spl. atty. IRS, Washington and N.Y.C., 1952-60; assoc. Battle, Fowler, Stokes and Kheel, N.Y.C., 1960-65; dir. research U.S. Equal Employment Opportunity Commn., Washington, 1965-68; dep. asst. sec. U.S. Dept. Housing and Urban Devel., Washington, 1969-72; asst. dean Rutgers U. Law Sch., Newark, 1974-76; assoc. prof. law N.C. Central U., Durham, 1976-81, prof. law, 1981-83; mayor City of Durham, N.C., 1981-85; ptnr. Markham and Wickham, Durham, 1984-86; Trustee Hist. Preservation Soc. Durham, 1982-86; bd. dirs. Stagville Ctr., 1984-86; mem. Gov.'s Crime Commn., Raleigh, 1985; dep. commr. N.C. Indsl. Commn., Raleigh, 1986-93. Editor: Jobs, Men and Machines: The Problems of Automation, 1964. Mem. Carolina Club, Phi Beta Kappa, Omicron Delta Kappa, Phi Delta Phi, Phi Delta Theta. Republican. Episcopalian. Home: 204 N Dillard St Durham NC 27701-3404

MARKHAM, JESSE WILLIAM, economist; b. Richmond, Va., Apr. 21, 1916; s. John James and Edith (Luttrell) M.; AB, U. Richmond, 1941; postgrad. Johns Hopkins U., 1941-42, U.S. Fgn. Service Sch., 1945; MA, Harvard U., 1947, PhD, 1949; m. Penelope Jane Anton, Oct. 15, 1944; children: Elizabeth Anton Markham McLean, John James, Jesse William. Accountant, E.I. duPont de Nemours Co., Richmond, 1935-38; teaching fellow Harvard U., 1946-48; asst. prof. Vanderbilt U., 1948-52, asso. prof., 1952-53; chief economist FTC, Washington, 1953-55; asso. prof. Princeton U., 1955-57, prof. econs., 1957-68; prof. Harvard Grad. Sch. Bus. Adminstrn., 1968-72, Charles Edward Wilson prof., 1972-82, prof. emeritus, 1982—; prof. Harvard U. Extension Svcs., 1984—; vis. prof. Columbia U., 1958; Ford Found. vis. prof. Harvard Grad. Sch. Bus. Adminstrn., 1965-66; rsch. prof. Law and Econs. Ctr., Emory U., 1982-84; rsch. staff, mem. bd. editors Patent Trademark Copyright Rsch. Inst., George Washington U., 1955-70; econs. editor Houghton Mifflin Co., 1961-71; U.S. del. comm. experts on bus. practices European Productivity Agy., OEEC, 1956, 57, 58, 59, 61; vis. prof. Harvard U., 1961-62; dir. Ford Found. Seminar Region II, 1961; adv. com. mktg. to sec. commerce, 1967-71; mem. Am. Bar Assn. Commn. to study FTC, 1969. Del. People to People Diplomacy Mission to USSR, 1989; active Boy Scouts Am.; chmn. Harvard Parents Com., 1969-72. Served as lt. USNR, World War II. Ford Found. research prof., 1958-59. Mem. Am. Econ. Assn., U.S. C. of C. (econ. policy com.), Harvard Club (N.Y.C., Sarasota, Fla.), The Cedars Club. Episcopalian. Author: Competition in the Rayon Industry, 1952; The Fertilizer Industry: Study of an Imperfect Market, 1958; The American Economy, 1963; (with Charles Fiero and Howard Piquet) The European Common Market: Friend or Competitor, 1964; (with Gustav Papanek) Industrial Organization and Economic Development, 1970; Conglomerate Enterprise and Public Policy, 1973 (with Paul Teplitz) Baseball Economics and Public Policy, 1982; sect. on oligopoly Internat. Ency. Social Scis.; contbr. articles to econ. jours. Mem. Phi Beta Kappa. Home: 663 Martin Rd Friendship ME 04547 Office: Harvard U Grad Sch Bus Adminstrn 300 Cumnock Boston MA 02163

MARKHAM, JORDAN J., physicist, retired educator; b. Samokov, Bulgaria, Dec. 25, 1916; s. Reuben Henry and Mary (Gall) M.; m. Lillian Cagnon, Feb. 6, 1943; children—Linda C., Roger H. B.S., Beloit (Wis.) Coll., 1938; M.S., Syracuse U., 1940; Ph.D., Brown U., 1946. With div. war research Columbia U., 1942-45; trainee Clinton Lab., Oak Ridge, 1946-47; instr. physics U. Pa., 1947-48; asst. prof. Brown U., 1948-50; physicist Applied Physics Lab., Johns Hopkins U., 1950-53; research lab. Zenith Radio Corp., 1953-60; sci. adv. Armour Research Found., 1960-62; prof. physics Ill. Inst. Tech., 1962-81, ret., 1981; vis. prof. Phys. Inst., U. Frankfurt, Germany, summer 1965; sabbatical leave U. Reading, Eng., 1977. Author: F-centers in Alkali Halides, 1966, also articles. Home and Office: Villa 128 Carolina Meadows Chapel Hill NC 27514

MARKHAM, REED B., education educator, consultant; b. Alhambra, Calif., Feb. 14, 1957; s. John F. and Reeda (Bjarason) M. BA, Brigham Young U., 1982, MA, 1982; BS, Regents Coll., 1981, MA, 1982; MPA, U. So. Calif., 1983; MA, UCLA, 1989; PhD, Columbia Pacific U., 1991. Mem. faculty Brigham Young U., Provo, Utah, 1984; mem. faculty Calif. State U., Fullerton and Long Beach, 1984, Northridge, 1985; mem. faculty El Camino Coll., Torrance, Calif., 1986, Orange Coast Coll., Costa Mesa, Calif., 1986, Pasadena (Calif.) Coll., 1986, Fullerton (Calif.) Community Coll., 1986; instr., mem. pub. rels. com. Chaffey (Calif.) Coll., 1986-87; prof., CARES dir. Calif. State Poly. U., Pomona, 1987—; adj. prof. Calif. State U., L.A., 1992-93, dir. Ctr. for Student Retention, 1995—; rsch. asst. to pres. Ctr. for the Study of Cmty. Coll., 1985; mem. faculty Riverside (Calif.) Coll., 1989-90,

Rio Hondo (Calif.) Coll., 1989-90, English Lang. Inst., 1994, Calif. Poly Summer Bridge, 1989-95, East L.A. Coll.; speechwriter U.S. Supreme Ct., Washington, 1980; cons. gifted children program Johns Hopkins U./Scripps Coll., Claremont, Calif., 1987-88. Author: Power Speechwriting, 1983, Power Speaking, 1990, Public Opinion, 1990, Advances in Public Speaking, 1991, Leadership 2000: Success Skills for University Students, 1995; co-author: Student Retention: Success Models in Higher Education, 1996; editor Trojan in Govt., U. So. Calif., 1983; editl. bd. mem. Edn. Digest, Speaker and Gavel, Innovative Higher Edn., Pub. Rels. Rev., Nat. Forensic Jour., The Forensic Educator, Clearinghouse for the Contemporary Educator, Hispanic Am. Family Mag.; writer N.Y. Times, Christian Sci. Monitor; ednl. columnist San Bernardino (Calif.) Sun., 1992-95. Pres. bd. trustees Regents Coll., 1986. Mem. Doctorate Assn. N.Y. Scholars, Nat. Assn. Pvt. Non-traditional Colls. (accrediting com. 1989—), Pub. Rels. Soc. Am. (dir.-at-large inland empire 1992-93, faculty advisor). LDS. Home: 801 E Alosta Ave # T-307 Azusa CA 91702-2744 Office: Calif Polytech U Communications Dept 3801 W Temple Ave Pomona CA 91768-2557

MARKHAM, RICHARD GLOVER, research executive; b. Pasadena, Calif., June 18, 1925; s. Fred Smith and Maziebelle (Glover) M.; m. Jonne Louise Pearson, Apr. 29, 1950; children: Janet B., Fred S., Charles R., Richard G., Marilyn A. Student, Stanford U., 1943; BS, Calif. Inst. Tech., Pasadena, 1945; MS, Stanford U., 1947. Pres., owner Aquarium Pump Supply, Prescott, Ariz., 1957-78; 1st v.p., dir. Bank of Prescott, 1981-87; also v.p., bd. dirs. Oxycal Labs., Prescott, 1981—. Mem. Ariz. Dept. Econ. Planning and Devel., 1967-72; treas. Ariz. State Rep. Com., 1970-72; active Ariz. Acad., 1974—; trustee Orme Sch., Mayer, Ariz., 1970-83, Prescott Coll., 1979-83. Office: Oxycal Labs 533 Madison Ave Prescott AZ 86301-2432

MARKHAM, RICHARD LAWRENCE, chemist; b. Texarkana, Ark., July 31, 1940; s. Andre Lawrence and Elizabeth Ella (Beck) M.; m. Judith Lynn Roberts, Aug. 5, 1972. BS, Okla. State U., 1962; MS, U. Ariz., 1969. Rsch. scientist Celanese Plastics Co., Summit, N.J., 1969-72; narcotics analyst U.S. Army Crime Lab., Frankfurt, Germany, 1973-74; from plant chemist to mfg. mgr. Amerace Corp., Kehlen, Luxembourg, Butler, NJ, Johnson City, Tenn., 1974-79; from project mgr. to product mgr. Battelle Meml. Inst., Columbus, Ohio, 1979-90, bus. devel. mgr., 1991—; adv. bd. Plastics Cons. Dir., Tucson, 1990—. Author, editor: Identification of Major Developments in Polymer Blends, 1987, Reactive Processing of Polymeric Materials, 1988, Compatibilization of Polymer Blends, 1994; contbr. articles to profl. jours. Founder, pres. East. Tenn. chpt. St. Jude Rsch. Hosp., Johnson City, 1977, 78, 79; pres., trustee Lakeside Forest Homeowners Assn., Westerville, Ohio, 1993-94. Mem. Am. Chem. Soc. (polymer chem. div., polymeric materials sci. & engring. div.), Sigma Xi. Patentee in field. Avocations: fastpitch softball, racquetball, photography. Home: 420 Hickory Ln Westerville OH 43081-3004 Office: Battelle Meml Inst 505 King Ave Columbus OH 43201-2696

MARKHAM, WILLIAM E., timber and logging company owner; b. Chehalis, Wash., Oct. 9, 1922; s. John Howard and Grace (Young) M.; m. L. Jean Eddins, Sept. 25, 1943; children: William Jr., Michael, Patrick. BS in Bus., U. Wash., 1946. Owner Markham & Son Lumber Co., Riddle, Oreg., 1947-93; mem. Oreg. Legis., Riddle, 1969—, speaker pro tem, 1990—; bd. dirs. Douglas Nat. Bank, Rosebury, Oreg., Pacific State Bank, Reedsport, Oreg. Bd. dirs. Umpqua Coll., Rosebury, 1964-88. Lt. USAF, 1942-45. Mem. Lions, VFW, Am. Legion, Masons, Elks. Republican. Episcopalian. Avocation: hunting. Home: PO Box 300 Riddle OR 97469-0300

MARKIEWICZ, ALFRED JOHN, bishop; b. Bklyn., May 17, 1928. Student, St. Francis Coll., Bklyn., Immaculate Conception Sem., Huntington, N.Y. Ordained priest Roman Cath. Ch., 1953, ordained titular bishop of Afufenia and aux. bishop of Rockville Centre, N.Y., 1986. Ordained priest Brooklyn, 1953; ordained titular bishop of Afufenia and aux. bishop New York, 1986—; vicar for Nassau Diocese of Rockville Centre. Office: St Joseph's Villa 215 N Westnedge Ave Kalamazoo MI 49007-3718

MARKIN, DAVID ROBERT, motor company executive; b. N.Y.C., Feb. 16, 1931; s. Morris and Bessie (Markham) M.; children: Sara, John, Christopher, Meredith. B.S., Bradley U., 1953. Foreman Checker Motors Corp., Kalamazoo, 1955-57, factory mgr., 1957-62, v.p. sales, 1962-70, pres., 1970—, dir.; bd. dirs. Jackpot Inc. Trustee Kalamazoo Coll. Served to 1st lt. USAF, 1953-55. Mem. Alpha Epsilon Pi. Clubs: Standard (Chgo.); Park (Kalamazoo). Home: 2121 Winchell Ave Kalamazoo MI 49008-2205 Office: Internat Controls Corp 2016 N Pitcher St Kalamazoo MI 49007-1869*

MARKINSON, MARTIN, theatre owner, producer; b. Bklyn., Dec. 23, 1931; s. Abraham and Dora (Rosenthal) M.; m. Arlene Francis Gelfand, Apr. 15, 1962; children: Brett, Keith, Sydney. Owner, operator Helen Hayes Theatre, N.Y.C.; bd. govs. Am. League of Theatre and Producers, N.Y.C. Producer Broadway plays including: Poor Murderer, Some of My Best Friends, Cheaters, Whoopee, Ned and Jack, Snoopy, Torch Song Trilogy (Tony award 1983), Passion, And a Nightingale Sang, Corpse, Dusky Sally, Last Minstral Show and Daddy Goodness. Sgt. USAF, 1951-53, Korea.

MARKLAND, FRANCIS SWABY, JR., biochemist, educator; b. Phila., Jan. 15, 1936; s. Francis Swaby Sr. and Willie Lawrence (Averritt) M.; m. Barbara Blake, June 27, 1959; children: Cathleen Blake, Francis Swaby IV. B.S., Pa. State U., 1957; Ph.D., Johns Hopkins U., 1964. Postdoctoral fellow UCLA, 1964-66, asst. prof. biochemistry, 1966-73; vis. asst. prof. U. So. Calif., Los Angeles, 1973-74, assoc. prof., 1974-83, prof., 1983—, acting chmn. dept. biochemistry, 1986-88, vice-chmn., 1988-92; cons. Clin. Lab. Med. Group, L.A., 1977-88, Cortech, Inc., Denver, 1983-88.; mem. biochem., endocrinology study sect. NIH, 1986-90. Editorial bd. Toxicon., Internat. Jour. of Toxinology; contbr. articles, chpts. and abstracts to profl. publs.; patentee in field. Mem. Angeles Choral, Northridge, Calif. Served to capt. USNR. Recipeint NIH rsch. career devel. award USPHS, NIH, 1968-73; rsch. grantee Nat. Cancer Inst., 1979-86, 91-93, Nat. Heart Lung and Blood Inst., 1984-88, 95-96. Mem. Am. Soc. Biochem. and Molecular Biology, Am. Chem. Soc., Internat. Soc. on Toxinology, Internat. Soc. on Thrombosis and Haemostasis (subcom. exogenous hemostatic factors, chair 1994-96), Am. Assn. Cancer Rsch., Am. Soc. Hematology, Protein Soc., Sigma Xi, Alpha Zeta. Avocations: singing, skiing, aerobics. Office: U So Calif Sch Medicine Cancer Rsch Lab Rm 106 1303 N Mission Rd Los Angeles CA 90033-1020

MARKLE, CHERI VIRGINIA CUMMINS, nurse; b. N.Y.C., Nov. 22, 1936; d. Brainard Lyle and Mildred (Schwab) Cummins; m. John Markle, Aug. 26, 1961 (dec. 1962); 1 child, Kellianne. RN, Ind. State U. and Union Hosp., 1959; BS in Rehab. Edn., Wright State U., 1975; BSN, Capital U., 1987; postgrad. in nursing adminstrn., Wright State U., 1987-89; MS, Calif. Coll. Health Sci. Administration, 1994; postgrad., Columbia Pacific U., 1995—. Cert. clin. hypnotherapist Nat. Guild Hypnotherapists. Coordinator Dayton (Ohio) Children's Psychiat. Hosp., 1962-75; dir. nursing Stillwater Health Ctr., Dayton, 1975-76; rehab. cons. Fairborn, Ohio, 1976-91; sr. supr. VA, Dayton, 1977-85, nurse coord. alcohol rehab., 1985-86; DON Odd Fellows, Springfield, Ohio, 1987-88, Miami Christel Manor, Miamisburg, Ohio, 1988—; DON, rehab. cons. NMS Tng. Sys., Dayton, 1989-91; psychiat. unit nurse VA Med. Ctr., N.Y. Rheab., 1991, mem. com. women vets., 1991-93; advisor Calif. Coll. Health Sci. Newspaper columnist Golden Times, Clark County. Bd. dirs. Temple Universal Judaism. 1st lt. USAF, 1959-61. Mem. ANA (cert. adminstrn. 1983, cert. gerontology 1984), NAFE, AAUW, Nat. Rehab. Nursing Soc., Nurse Mgrs. Assembly, Gerontol. Nurse Assembly, Rehab. Soc., Nat. Guild Hypnotherapists, Internat. Assn. Counselors and Therapists, Wright State U. Alumni Assn., Am. Legion, Women's City Club N.Y., Gilbert & Sullivan Soc., Internat. Consortium Prise Scholars, Alpha Sigma Alpha, Sigma Theta Tau. International Scholars, advisor Calif. Coll. Health Science. Democrat. Jewish. Avocations: cats, reading, music, needlework, swimming. Office: VA Med Ctr 423 E 23rd St New York NY 10010-5050 *Reach beyond what you think is possible. Grow and learn throughout your life. Help those you meet to do the same.*

MARKLE, DAVID A., optical engineer. With Ultratech Stepper, San Jose, Calif. Recipient David Richardson medal Optical Soc. Am., 1994. Office: Ultratech Stepper 3050 Zanker Rd San Jose CA 95134

MARKLE, GEORGE BUSHAR, IV, surgeon; b. Hazleton, Pa., Oct. 29, 1921; s. Alvan and Gladys (Jones) M.; m. Mildred Donna Umstead, July 3, 1944; children: Donna Markle Partee, Melanie Jones Markle, George Bushar, Christian; m. Teresa Damm, Mar. 31, 1996. B.S., Yale U., 1943; M.D., U. Pa., 1946. Diplomate Am. Bd. Surgery. Intern Geisinger Med. Ctr., Danville, Pa., 1946-47, resident, 1947-49; surg. fellow Mayo Clinic, Rochester, Minn., 1949-52; chief surgery U.S. Army Hosp., Ft. Monroe, Va., 1952-54; practice gen. surgery Carlsbad, N.Mex., 1954-94; surg. staff Carlsbad Regional Med. Ctr., 1954-77, Guadalupe Med. Ctr., 1977-94; ret., 1994; panelist Voice of Am. Author: Ill Health and Other Foolishness, 1966, How to Stay Healthy All Your Life, 1968, The Teka Stone, 1983, How to Be Healthy, Wealthy and Wise, 1991, Donna's Story, 1991; contbr. articles to profl. jours., radio health series. Mem. Eddy County Ctrl. Rep. Com.; candidate N.Mex. Ho. of Reps., 1996. With M.C., U.S. Army, 1952-54. Recipient Distinguished Service award Jr. C. of C., 1956. Fellow Internat. Coll. Surgeons (regent, Regent of Yr. 1991), Southwestern Surg. Congress, Priestley surg. Soc., Western Surg. Assn.; mem. Eddy County Med. Soc., Ogden Surg. Soc., Kiwanis. Presbyterian. Home: 1003 N Shore Dr Carlsbad NM 88220-4635 Office: 911 N Canal St Carlsbad NM 88220-5109 *Those blest in family and fortune, things not of their own making, ought, I believe, to strive, as they are able, to deserve those blessings through service to God and Man. Even the least of us has some power to influence others through our examples and attitudes, and through each we influence, for good or bad, we may affect sequentially many others, like ever widening ripples on the water.*

MARKLE, JOHN, JR., lawyer; b. Allentown, Pa., July 20, 1931; s. John Markle II and Pauline (Powers) Mulligan; m. Mary B. McLean, Apr. 19, 1952 (div. Apr. 1990); children: Ellen, John III, Patricia, Stephen, Mary; m. Kathryn E. Wheeler, July 14, 1990. Grad., The Hill Sch., Pottstown, Pa., 1949; BA, Yale U., 1953; LLB, Harvard Law Sch., 1958. Assoc. Drinker Biddle & Reath, Phila., 1958-64, ptnr., 1964—; mem. Pa. Labor Rels. Bd., 1996—. Contbg. editor: The Developing Labor Law, 1976—. Bd. dirs. Main Line Health Sys., Inc., Radnor, Pa., 1987—, The Hill Sch., 1970—; treas., bd. dirs. Paoli (Pa.) Meml. Hosp., 1982—, The Found. at Paoli, 1995—. Lt. col. USMCR, 1951-73. Named Most Outstanding Young Rep. (Pa.), 1966. Mem. ABA, Pa. Bar Assn., Am. Arbitration Assn. Republican. Clubs: Union League of Phila., Yale of Phila., Merion Golf. Avocations: golf, photography. Home: 205 Cambridge Chase Exton PA 19341-3137 Office: Drinker Biddle & Reath 1000 Westlakes Dr Ste 300 Berwyn PA 19312-2409

MARKLE, ROGER A(LLAN), retired oil company executive; b. Sidney, Mont., Dec. 12, 1933; s. Forrest William and Mary Elizabeth (Hartley) M.; m. Mary Elizabeth Thompson, Jan. 13, 1967. B.S. in Mining Engring, U. Alaska, 1959; M.S., Stanford U., 1965; M.B.A., U. Chgo., 1972. Mgr. mine devel. Amoco Minerals, Inc., Chgo., 1973-74; pres. western div. Valley Camp Coal Co., Salt Lake City, 1974-78; pres., chief exec. officer Valley Camp Coal Co., Cleve., 1979-82; pres. Quaker State Corp., Oil City, Pa., 1982-86, chief operating officer, 1986-88, also bd. dirs.; vice chmn. Quaker State Corp., Oil City, 1988-89; pres. Nerco Oil & Gas, Vancouver, Wash., 1990-92; dir. U.S. Bur. Mines, Washington, 1978-79. Served with USN, 1951-54. Mem. AIME.

MARKMAN, HOWARD J., psychology educator; b. Oct. 27, 1950; s. Arnold J. and Claire (Fox) M.; m. Fran Dickson, June 29, 1980; children: Mathew Lee, Leah Deborah. BA, Rutgers U., 1972; MA in Clin. Psychology, Ind. U., 1976, PhD in Clin. Psychology, 1977. Lic. clin. psychologist, Colo. Assoc. instr. psychology Ind. U., 1973-75; psychology trainee, consultation team Monroe County Community Mental Health Ctr., Bloomington, Ind., 1975-76; clin./community psychology intern U. Colo. Sch. Medicine, Denver, 1976-77; asst. prof. psychology Bowling Green (Ohio) U., 1977-80, U. Denver, 1980-83; dir. Denver Ctr. for Marital and Family Studies, U. Denver, 1980—; dir. clin. tng. U. Denver, 1983-86, assoc. prof. psychology, 1983-89, prof. psychology, 1989—; presenter in field. Author: Couples' Guide to Communication, 1976, Prevention and Relationship Enhancement Program, 1980, We Can Work it Out, Fighting for your Marriage; mem. editorial bd. Jour. Consulting and Clin. Psychology, 1988-90, Behavioral Assessment, Jour. Family Psychology, Contemporary Psychology, Am. Assn. for Marriage and Family Therapy, Am. Jour. Family Therapy; guest assoc. editor Behavioral Assessment, 1989, Human Communication Rsch.; contbr. articles and reviews to profl. jours. Bd. dirs. Assn. Children and Youth, Boulder, Colo., 1985-86. NIMH grantee, 1980-82. Fellow APA; mem. NIMH (adhoc reviewer 1980—), NSF (adhoc reviewer 1980—), APA, Internat. Soc. Social and Personal Relationships (world conf. planning com. 1990—), Colo. Psychol. Assn. (co-chmn. 1990—), Nat. Coun. on Family Rels., Am. Assn. Marriage and Family Therapy (clin. mem.), Rocky Mountain Conf. Family Rels. (bd. dirs.). Democrat. Jewish. Avocations: softball, photography, tennis, hockey, skiing. Office: Univ of Denver Ctr Marital & Family Studies Dept of Psychology Denver CO 80208

MARKMAN, RONALD, artist, educator; b. Bronx, N.Y., May 29, 1931; s. Julius and Mildred (Berkowitz) M.; m. Barbara Miller, Sept. 12, 1959; 1 dau., Ericka Elizabeth. B.F.A., Yale U., 1957, M.F.A., 1959. Instr. Art Inst. Chgo., 1960-64; prof. fine arts Ind. U., 1964—; color cons. Hallmark Card Co., 1959-60. One-man shows Kanegis Gallery, 1959, Reed Coll., 1966, Terry Dintenfass Gallery, 1965, 66, 68, 70, 76, 79, 82, 85, The Gallery, Bloomington, Ind., 1972, 79, Indpls. Mus., 1974, Tyler Sch. Art, Phila., 1976, Franklin Coll., 1980, Dart Gallery, Chgo., 1981, Patrick King Gallery, Indpls., 1983, 86, John Heron Gallery, Indpls., 1985, New Harmony Gallery, 1985; two-man show Dintenfass Gallery, 1984; group shows include Kanegis Gallery, Boston, 1958, 60, 61, Boston Arts Festival, 1959, 60, Mus. Modern Art, 1959, 66, Whitney Mus., N.Y.C., 1960, Art Inst. Chgo., 1964, Gallery 99, Miami, Fla., 1966, Ball State Coll., 1966, Butler Inst., 1967, Indpls. Mus., 1968, 69, 72, 74, Phoenix Gallery, N.Y.C., 1970, Harvard U., 1974, Skidmore Coll., 1975, Am. Acad. Arts and Letters, 1977, 89, Tuthill-Gimprich Gallery, N.Y.C., 1980, Patrick King Gallery, 1988, numerous others; represented in permanent collections Met. Mus. Art, Mus. Modern Art, Art Inst. Chgo., Library of Congress, Cin. Art Mus., Bklyn. Mus., Ark. Art Center, others; commns. include 5 murals Riley Children's Hosp., Indpls., 1986; installation Evanston (Ill.) Art Ctr., 1989, 2-part installation Ortho Child Care Ctr., Raritan, N.J., 1991; illustrator Acid and Basics-A Guide to Acid-Base Physiology, 1992. Served with U.S. Army, 1952-54. Recipient Ind. Arts Commn. award, 1990, 93; Fulbright grantee, Italy, 1962, grantee Ctr. for New TV, Chgo., 1992; Lilly Endowment fellow, 1989, honorable mention, Ohio Film Festival, 1995. Home: 719 S Jordan Ave Bloomington IN 47401-5123 Office: Ind U Dept Fine Arts Bloomington IN 47401

MARKMAN, SHERMAN, investment banker, venture capital investor, corporate financier; b. Denver, Aug. 21, 1920; s. Abe and Julia (Rosen) M.; m. Paula Elaine Henderson. Student So. Meth. U., 1962-64; children: S. Michael, Joan, Lori. V.p. Lester's, Inc., Oklahoma City, 1940-59; exec. v.p. Besco Enterprises, San Francisco, 1960-61; sr. v.p. Zale Corp., Dallas, 1962-69; pres., chief exec. officer Leased Jewelry div., 1965-69, pres. Designcraft Industries, N.Y.C., 1969-75, chief exec. officer, 1969-75; pres. Tex. Internat. Export Co., Dallas, 1975—, CAC Fin. Group (Tex.), Dallas, 1975—; fin. advisor Vocational Video, Huntington, N.Y., Consolidated Transplant Network, Saint Rose, La., Thera-Test Diagnostic Labs., Chgo., Kemper Mil. Acad., Boonville, Mo., Soft-Trac Info. Systems, Jasper, Ala., client referal arrangement The Dai-ichi Kangyo Bank, Ltd.; former bd. dir. Pipelife Svc. Corp., Chem. Applicators, Lafayette, La., Coverage Cons., N.Y.C., Transworld Ins. Intermediaries, Ltd.; former cons. Homecare Mgmt., Ronkonkoma, N.Y., Credicorp, Chgo., The Windy City Group, Chgo.; charter mem. N.Y. Ins. Exch.; guest lectr. fin. risk confs., 1982—; pres., chief exec. officer The Myers Fin. Orgn., N.Y., 1975-86, The Markman Fin. Orgn., Dallas, 1975—. Contbr. articles to profl. jours. Vol. social worker Presbyn. Hosp., Dallas; mem. Dallas Coun. World Affairs, 1962—; active NCCJ. With USMCR, 1942-45; PTO. Clubs: Press, City (Dallas); India Temple (Oklahoma City); L.A. Athletic. Office: Rural Route 1 Box 1236 Keswick VA 22947

MARKO, ANDREW PAUL, school system administrator; b. Kingston, Pa., Aug. 16, 1936; s. Andrew Paul and Anna (Stragis) M.; m. Janet Thimm, Aug. 10, 1988; 1 child, Danielle. BA, Kings Coll., Wilkes-Barre, Pa., 1962; MA, Scranton U., 1968, prin.'s cert., 1971; postgrad., Oxford (Eng.) U., 1988, Lehigh U., 1991, Widener U., 1991—. Cert. tchr., secondary prin., supt.'s letter of eligibility, Pa. Elem. tchr. Dundalk Elem. Sch., Balt., 1963-64; English tchr. Kingston (Pa.) High Sch., 1964-66; English tchr. Wyoming Valley West High Sch., Plymouth, Pa., 1966-90, vice prin., 1980, 89; secondary curriculum adminstr. Wyoming Valley West Sch. Dist., Kingston, 1990, dir. instrnl. svcs. and pupil svcs., 1991-95, apptd. supt., 1995—; wrestling coach Kingston High Sch., 1964-69; jr.-sr. class advisor Wyoming Valley West High Sch., Plymouth, 1968-88, newspaper advisor, 1970-90, literary mag. advisor, 1970-90, publs. bus. mgr., 1988-90. Councilman Kingston Borough Coun., 1969-77; pres. Holy Name Soc.; ward capt. Heart Fund and March of Dimes. With USN, 1954-57. Mem. ASCD, Pa. Assn. Student Assistance Profls., Pa. Assn. for Supervision and Curriculum Devel., Pa. Assn. Pupil Svcs. Adminstrs., Nat. Assn. Pupil Svcs. Adminstrs., Pa. Staff Devel. Coun., Nat. Mid. Sch. Assn., Ptnrs. for Quality Learning, VFW, Am. Legion, KC. Democrat. Roman Catholic. Avocations: sports, gardening, building, reading. Home: 6 Halowich Rd Harveys Lake PA 18618-0108 Office: Wyoming Valley West Sch Dist 450 N Maple Ave Kingston PA 18704-3630

MARKO, HAROLD MEYRON, diversified industry executive; b. Detroit, Oct. 29, 1925; s. Louis Meyron and Mae (Goldberg) M.; m. Barbara Soss, July 2, 1951; children—Clifford S., Neil L., Matthew P. B.A., U. Mich., 1948. Salesman Core Industries Inc (formerly SOS Consol. Inc.), Bloomfield Hills, Mich., 1951-57; v.p. sales Core Industries Inc (formerly SOS Consol. Inc.), 1957-60, pres., 1960-91; chmn. emeritus, chmn. exec. com. Core Industries Inc. (formerly SOS Consol. Inc.), 1991—; also dir. Core Industries Inc (formerly SOS Consol. Inc.), chmn. bd. dirs., chief exec. officer, 1986. Editorial adv. bd. Fin. World mag.; contbr. chpt. to book. Mem. Founders' Soc., Detroit Inst. Arts; trustee Nat. Jewish Hosp., Denver, Mich. Opera Theatre; bd. dirs. Detroit Symphony Orch.; mem. adv. bd. Greater Detroit Round Table; bd. govs. Cranbrook Acad. Art. Served with AUS, 1943-45. Club: Bloomfield Open Hunt. Home: 1132 Woburn Grn Bloomfield Hills MI 48302-2300 Office: Core Industries Inc 500 N Woodward Ave Bloomfield Hills MI 48304-2961

MARKOE, FRANK, JR., lawyer, business and hospital executive; b. Balt., Sept. 5, 1923; s. Frank and Margaret (Smith) M.; m. Margaret McCormack (div.); children: Andrée Markoe Caldwell, Ritchie Harrison Markoe Scribner. AB, Washington and Lee U., 1947; LLB, U. Md., 1950. Bar: Md. 1950. Pntr. Karl F. Steinmann, Balt., 1948-50, 50-53, Cable & McDaniel, Balt., 1954-55; gen. counsel, dir. Emerson Drug Co., Balt., 1955-56; adminstrv. v.p. Emerson Drug Co., 1957-58; v.p., sec., dir., gen. counsel Warner-Lambert Pharm. Co., 1958-67, exec. com., sr. v.p., dir., gen. counsel, sec., 1967-69, exec. asst. chmn. bd., 1970-71, sr. v.p., 1971-73; exec. v.p. Warner-Lambert Co., Morris Plains, N.J., 1973-77; vice chmn. bd. Warner-Lambert Co., 1977-81; vice chmn. adv. bd. N.Y. Hosp.-Cornell Med. Ctr., 1987—, also chmn. major gifts com. Capital Campaign; hon. holder Alfred E. Driscoll chair Fairleigh Dickinson U. Trustee Morristown Meml. Hosp., Morris County Soc. for Crippled Children and Adults; bd. dirs. N.J. Coll. Medicine and Dentistry, Bd. Internat. Broadcasting, Radio Free Europe/Radio Liberty, Kips Bay Boys; bd. dirs., exec. com., pres. N.J. Ballet. With USAAF, 1942-45, PTO. Mem. U.S. C. of C., Proprietary Assn. (chmn., bd. dir., exec. com.), Pharm. Mfrs. Assn. (bd. dir., exec. com.), N.J. State C. of C. (bd. dir.), Phi Beta Kappa. Home and Office: 201 Grenville Rd Hobe Sound FL 33455-2414 also: Peacock Point Locust Valley NY 00001

MARKOFF, BRAD STEVEN, lawyer; b. N.Y.C., July 29, 1957; s. Daniel and Geri (Skitol) M.; m. Danna Kay Schmidt, May 17, 1980; children: Andrew David, Paul Steven. AB, Duke U., 1979; JD, Washington U., St. Louis, 1982. Bar: Mo. 1982, U.S. Tax Ct. 1984, N.C. 1985. Assoc. Stolar Partnership, St. Louis, 1982-84; assoc., ptnr. Moore & Van Allen, Raleigh, N.C., 1984-92; ptnr. Smith Helms Mulliss & Moore, Raleigh, 1992—; bd. dirs. Coun. for Entreprenurial Devel., Research Triangle Park, N.C.; spl. coun. apptd. by N.C. Gov. N.C. R.R. Study Group, 1992-93. Contbr. articles to profl. jours. Mem. ABA, Nat. Assn. Bond Lawyers, Mo. Bar Assn., N.C. Bar Assn. Avocations: golf, astronomy. Office: Smith Helms Mulliss & Moore 316 W Edenton St Raleigh NC 27603-1747

MARKOFF, STEVEN C., finance company executive. CEO A. Mark Fin. Office: A-Mark Financial 100 Wilshire Blvd 3rd Floor Santa Monica CA 90401 Office: 100 Wilshire Blvd 3rd Fl Santa Monica CA 90401

MARKOPOULOS, ANDREW JOHN, retail executive; b. Toledo, Mar. 23, 1931; s. John G. and Maria (Paraskevopoulos) M.; m. Joanne Valassis; children: Maria, Nicole. Diploma, Woodward High Sch., Toledo. With Macy's, Toledo and Kansas City, Mo., 1953-73, Gimbels, Phila., 1973-80; sr. v.p. visual merchandising and design Dayton Hudson Dept. Store Co., Mpls., 1980—; guest lectr. Drexel U., U. Wis. Bd. dirs. Friends of Goldstein Gallery, U. Minn. Cpl. U.S. Army, 1951-53. Recipient Markopoulos Design award, 1996. Mem. Nat. Retail Merchants Assn. (chmn. bd. dirs. 1983-84, Silver Plaque 1986, Visual Merchandiser of Yr. award 1981), Soc. Visual Merchandisers (bd. dirs.), Nat. Assn. Display Industries (Hall of Fame 1980), Western Assn. Visual Merchandising (adv. bd.), Am. Hellenic Ednl. Progressive Assn. Republican. Greek Orthodox. Home: 10950 Spoon Rdg Eden Prairie MN 55347-2956 Office: Dayton Hudson Corp Dept Store Divsn 700 On The Mall Minneapolis MN 55402-2065

MARKOS, CHRIS, real estate company executive; b. Cleve., Nov. 25, 1926; s. George and Bessie (Papathatou) M.; m. Alice Zaharopoulos, Dec. 11, 1949; children: Marilyn, Irene, Betsy. BA, Case Western Reserve, Cleve., 1960; LLB, LaSalle U., Chgo., 1964. Cert. gen. real estate appraiser, Ohio. Vice-pres. Herbert Laronge Inc., Cleve., 1963-76; v.p. Calabrese, Racek and Markos Inc., Cleve., 1976-83; v.p. Herbert Laronge Inc., Cleve., 1983-87, pres., 1987-88; v.p. Cragin Lang, Inc., Cleve., 1989-91; sr. cons. Grubb & Ellis, Cleve., 1991-93; sr. v.p. Realty One Appraisal Divsn., Independence, Ohio, 1993—; pres. Alcrimar Inc., 1989—. Co-author: Ohio Supplement to Modern Real Estate Practice, 5th-7th edits.; cons. editor, co-author: Modern Real Estate Practice in Ohio, 1st-3d edits. Bd. dirs. David N. Meyers Coll., Cleve., 1984—. With U.S. Army, 1945-46. Named Realtor of the Year, Cleve. Bd Realtors, 1976. Mem. Am. Soc. Appraisers (sr., pres. 1973, state dir. 1976), Cleve. Bd. Realtors (pres. 1974, Realtor of Yr. 1976). Republican. Greek Orthodox. Home: 6731 Hidden Lake Trail Brecksville OH 44141-3189 Office: Realty One 6000 Rockside Woods Blvd Cleveland OH 44131-2330 *Everyone's life has a beginning and an ending. It is what happens between these two points that makes up the essence of a person.*

MARKOSKI, JOSEPH PETER, lawyer; b. Floral Park, N.Y., Nov. 7, 1948; s. Stephen Nicholas and Josephine Veronica (Lapkofsky) M.; m. Julie Ann Angus, June 30, 1979; children: Katherine, Caroline, Peter. BSFS, Georgetown U., 1970, JD, 1973. Bar: D.C. 1973. Law clk. Hon. Thomas A. Flannery U.S. Dist. Ct., Washington, 1973-74; assoc. Wilkinson, Cragun & Barker, Washington, 1975-80, ptnr., 1980-82; ptnr. Squire, Sanders & Dempsey, Washington, 1982—, mng. ptnr., 1991—; co-chmn. task force on open network initiatives Strategic Planning Group of .S. CCITT Nat. Com., 1988-92; bd. dirs. Comty. Lodgings, Inc. Author: (with others) Internat. Telecommunications Handbook, 1986; contbr. articles to profl. jours. Active Fed. City Coun. Capt., USAR, 1970-78. Mem. ABA (vice-chmn. common carrier com. sci. and tech. sect. 1986-88, internat. common carrier project 1980-86), Fed. Commn. Bar Assn. (com. common carrier practice and procedure 1980—), Computer Law Assn. (bd. dirs., chmn. telecomm. bar liaison com. 1994—), Econ. Club Washington. Democrat. Roman Catholic. Office: Squire Sanders & Dempsey 1201 Pennsylvania Ave NW PO Box 407 Washington DC 20044

MARKOU, PETER JOHN, economic developer; b. Keene, N.H., Apr. 11, 1940; s. Peter John and Zoe Nicholas (Kussku) M.; m. Ann Corcoran Gibbons, June 25, 1983; 1 child, Justin Peter. BSBA cum laude, Suffolk U., 1964, MSBA, 1965; cert. in taxation, U. Hartford, 1977; PhD in Econ. Devel., Am. U. London, 1993. Purchasing agt. Fed. Prison Industries, Danbury, Conn., 1965; instr. Becker Jr. Coll., Worcester, Mass., 1967-70; assoc. prof. Post Coll., Waterbury, Conn., 1976-77; asst. prof. bus. North Adams (Mass.) State Coll., 1970-76, assoc. prof., 1977-84, prof., 1984-94; exec. dir. Green Mountain Econ. Devel. Corp., White River Junction, Vt., 1994—. Contbr. articles to small bus. and econ. devel. proc. Pres. North Adams Community Devel. Corp., 1985-91, Hardman Indsl. Pk. Corp., North Adams, 1989-91; mem. North Adams Mgmt. Improvement Com., 1987-88; mem., sec. Mass.

Mus. Contemporary Art Cultural Commn., North Adams, 1988—; bd. dirs. No. Berkshire Community Action, North Adams, 1989-91; mem. adv. bd. Salvation Army, North Adams, 1988-90. Recipient Mass. Pride in Performance award Commonwealth of Mass., 1989. Mem. Nat. Soc. Pub. Accts. (educator mem.), Am. Econ. Devel. Coun. (mem. bd. dirs.), N.E. Indsl. Developers Assn. Home: 34 Deerfield Dr Montpelier VT 05602-2129 Office: Green Mountain Econ Devel Corp Gates-Briggs Bldg White River Junction VT 05001

MARKOVCHICK, VINCENT J., surgeon; b. Hazleton, Pa., 1944. MD, Temple U., 1970. Intern Presbyn. Med. Ctr., Denver, 1970-71; resident emergency medicine U. Chgo. Hosps.-Clinics, 1974-76; mem. staff Denver Gen. Hosp.; assoc. prof. U.Colo. Health Sci. Ctr. Mem. Am. Coll. Emergency Physicians, Colo. Med. Soc., STEM. Office: Denver Gen Hosp Emergency Medicine Dept 777 Bannock St Denver CO 80204-4507*

MARKOVICH, PATRICIA, economist; b. Oakland, Calif.; d. Patrick Joseph and Helen Emily (Prydz) Markovich; BA in Econs., MS in Econs., U. Calif.-Berkeley; postgrad. (Lilly Found. grantee) Stanford U., (NSF grantee) Oreg. Grad. Rsch. Ctr.; children: Michael Sean Treece, Bryan Jeffry Treece, Tiffany Helene Treece. Cert. Emergency Mgmt. Planner. pub. rels. Pettler Advt., Inc.; pvt. practice polit. and econs. cons.; aide to majority whip Oreg. Ho. of Reps.; lectr., instr., various Calif. instns., Chemeketa (Oreg.) Coll., Portland (Oreg.) State U.; commr. City of Oakland (Calif.), 1970-74; chairperson, bd. dirs. Cable Sta. KCOM; mem. gen. plan commn. City of Piedmont, Calif.; mem. Oakland Mus. Archives of Calif. Artists. Mem. Internat. Soc. Philos. Enquiry, Mensa (officer San Francisco region), Bay Area Artists Assn. (coord., founding mem.), Berkeley Art Ctr. Assn., San Francisco Arts Commn. File, Calif. Index for Contemporary Arts, Pro Arts, YLEM: Artists Using Sci. and Tech., NAFE, No. Calif. Pub. Ednl. and Govt. Access Cable TV Com. (founding), Triple Nine Soc., Nat. Coord. Coun. Emergency Mgmt., Am. Econs. Assn., Allied Social Scis. Assn.

MARKOWICZ, VICTOR, video company executive; b. Tynda, USSR, July 6, 1944; s. Szymon and Gustawa (Goldstain) M.; m. Monica A. Minkiewicz, July 10, 1971; children: Clara, Daniela. Student, U. Warsaw, Poland, 1962-64; BS in Maths., Technion U., Haifa, Israel, 1966. Software mgr. Elbit Computers, Ltd., Haifa, 1966-69; tech. dir., co-founder System Ops., Inc., Princeton, N.J., 1970-76; pres., co-founder Gaming Dimensions, Providence, 1976-78; v.p. Datatrol Inc., Hudson, Mass., 1978-80; chmn., dir., co-founder GTech Corp., Providence, 1981—; bd. dirs. Intervoice, Dallas, Nat. TV Network Mgmt., Pasadena. Designer of state lottery games, 1970—; exec. producer (movie) South of Reno, 1987. Jewish. Avocations: bridge, skiing, tennis. Office: Gtech Corp 55 Technology Way West Greenwich RI 02817-1711

MARKOWITZ, HARRY M., finance and economics educator; b. Chicago, Ill., Aug. 24, 1927; s. Morris and Mildred (Gruber) M.; m. Barbara Gay. PhB, U. Chgo., 1947, MA, 1950, PhD, 1954. With research staff Rand Corp., Santa Monica, Calif., 1952-60, 61-63; tech. dir. Consol. Analysis Ctrs., Inc., Santa Monica, 1963-68; prof. UCLA, Westwood, 1968-69; pres. Arbitrage Mgmt. Co., N.Y.C., 1969-72; pvt. practice cons. N.Y.C., 1972-74; with research staff T.J. Watson Research Ctr. IBM, Yorktown Hills, N.Y., 1974-83; Speiser prof. fin. Baruch Coll. CUNY, N.Y.C., 1982—; dir. rsch. Daiwa Securities Trust Co, Jersey City, N.J., 1990—; v.p. Inst. Mgmt. Sci., 1960-62. Author: Portfolio Selection: Efficient Diversification of Investments, 1959, Mean-Variance Analysis in Portfolio Choice, 1987; co-author: SIMSCRIPT Simulation Programming Language, 1963; co-editor: Process Analysis of Economic Capabilities, 1963. Recipient John von Neumann Theory prize Ops. Rsch. Soc. Am. and Inst. Mgmt. Sci., 1989, Nobel Prize in Econs., 1990. Fellow Econometric Soc., Am. Acad. Arts and Scis.; mem. Am. Fin. Assn. (pres. 1982—). Office: CUNY Baruch Coll Bus Sch 155 E 24th St New York NY 10010-3727 also: Daiwa Securities 1 Evertrust Plz Jersey City NJ 07302-3051

MARKOWITZ, SAMUEL SOLOMON, chemistry educator; b. Bklyn., Oct. 31, 1931; s. Max and Florence Ethel (Goldman) M.; children: Michael, Daniel, Jonah; m. 2d Lydia de Antonis, Oct. 31, 1993. BS in Chemistry, Rensselaer Poly. Inst., 1953; MA, Princeton U., 1955, PhD, 1957; postgrad. Brookhaven Nat. Lab., 1955-57. Asst. prof. chemistry U. Calif.-Berkeley, 1958-64, assoc. prof., 1964-72, prof., 1972—; faculty sr. scientist Lawrence Berkeley Lab., 1958—; vis. prof. nuclear physics Weizmann Inst. Sci., Rehovot, Israel, 1973-74. Mem. Bd. Edn. of Berkeley Unified Sch. Dist., 1969-73, pres. bd., 1971-72. Recipient Elizabeth McFeely D'Urso Meml. Pub. Ofcl. award Alameda County Edn. Assn., 1973; LeRoy McKay fellow Princeton U., 1955; Charlotte Elizabeth Proctor fellow Princeton U., 1956; NSF postdoctoral fellow U. Birmingham, Eng., 1957-58; NSF sr. postdoctoral fellow Faculte des Scis. de L'Universite de Paris a Orsay, Laboratoire Joliot-Curie de Physique Nucleaire, 1964-65. Fellow AAAS; mem. Am. Chem. Soc. (bd. dirs. Calif. sect., chmn. 1991, 93-94), Am. Phys. Soc., Am. Inst. Chemists, N.Y. Acad. Scis., Calif. Inst. Chemists, Sigma Xi. Home: 317 Tideway Dr Alameda CA 94501-3540 Office: U Calif Dept Chemistry Berkeley CA 94720

MARKOWSKA, ALICJA LIDIA, neuroscientist, researcher; b. Warsaw, Poland, Aug. 22, 1948; came to U.S., 1986; d. Marian Boleslaw and Eugenia Krystyna (Wodzynska) Pawlak; m. Janusz Jozef Markowski, Oct. 23, 1971; children: Marta Agnieszka, Michal Jacek. BA, MSc, Warsaw U., 1971; PhD, Nencki Inst., Warsaw, 1979. Postdoctoral fellow Nencki Inst., 1979-81, asst. prof., 1981-86; assoc. rschr. Johns Hopkins U., Balt., 1987-91, rsch. scientist, 1991-92, prin. rsch. sci., prof., 1992-94, head of neuromnemonic lab., 1994—; vis. fellow Czechoslovak Acad. Sci., Prague, 1981; rschr., lectr. U. Bergen, Norway, 1983; vis. faculty Johns Hopkins U., 1986-87; cons. Sigma Tau & Otsuka Co., Italy, Japan, 1990-92. Reviewer Neurobiology of Aging, 1992—, Behavioral Brain Rsch., 1992—' contbr. chpts. to Preoperative Events, 1989, Prospective on Cognitive Neuroscience, 1990, Encyclopedia of Memory, 1992, Neuropsychology of Memory, 1992, Methods in Behavioral Pharmacology, 1993. Grantee Nat. Inst. Age, 1993—, NSF, 1990-93, NIH, 1992—. Mem. AAAS, Soc. for Neuroscience, Internat. Brain Rsch., N.Y. Acad. Sci. Achievements include first evidence that pharmacological interventions with cholinergic against, oxotremorine, through intracranial stimulation of the septohippocampal system can alleviate age-related mnemonic impairments, research has focused on an importance of the septohippocampal cholinergic system in memory function, brain mechanisms involved in different kinds of memory and sensorimotor skills and their relations to aging, amnesia, and dementia, animal models to examine the effect of nerve growth factor treatment. Home: 1301 Kingsbury Rd Owings Mills MD 21117-1343 Office: Johns Hopkins U 34th Charles St Baltimore MD 21218

MARKS, ANDREW H., lawyer; b. N.Y.C., May 5, 1951; s. Theodore and Rosalie Ruth (Goldman) M.; m. Susan G. Esserman, Aug. 3, 1975; children: Stephen Matthew, Clifford Michael, Michael David. AB, Harvard Coll., 1973; JD, U. Mich., 1976. Law clerk for Hon. Charles R. Richey U.S. Dist. Ct. D.C., Washington, 1976-78; exec. asst. to personal rep. of Pres. to Middle East Peace negotiations, Washington, 1979-81; assoc. Shea & Gardner, Washington, 1978-79, 81-84, ptnr., 1984-86; ptnr. Crowell & Moring, Washington, 1986—. Mem. D.C. Bar (gen. counsel 1987-89, bd. govs. 1989-95, chmn. task force civility in the profession 1993—), Harvard Club Washington (pres. 1994—). Office: Crowell & Moring 1001 Pennsylvania Ave NW Washington DC 20004-2505

MARKS, ARNOLD, journalist; b. Phila., Aug. 4, 1912; s. Morris M. and Esther (Joel) M.; m. Isabelle Ruppert, Oct. 3, 1942 (dec.); 1 son, Rupert William Joel (dec.); m. Emi Seligman Simon. B.A., U. Wash., 1935; M.S., Columbia U., 1939. Editor Pasco (Wash.) Herald, 1946; with Oreg. Jour., Portland, 1946-78; drama, TV, entertainment editor Oreg. Jour., 1948-58, entertainment editor, 1958-78, ret., 1978, freelance writer. Served with AUS, 1942-46. Mem. Sigma Delta Chi, Sigma Alpha Mu. Club: University (Portland). Home: PO Box 590 Gleneden Beach OR 97388-0590 also: 2393 SW Park Pl Portland OR 97205-1056 *In retrospect, there is great satisfaction in the thought that the years seem more loaded with heartwarming memories than with disappointments.*

MARKS, ARTHUR, prosthodontist, educator; b. N.Y.C., June 5, 1920; s. Louis and Elizabeth (Levine) M.; AB, NYU, 1942, DDS, 1944; m. Ruth Flamberg, July 18, 1948; children: Pauline, Deborah, Frances. Practice dentistry, N.Y.C., 1947—; assoc. vis. oral surgeon Sydenham Hosp., N.Y.C., 1947-75; mem. speakers bur. N.Y. Oral Hygiene Com.; dental rep. interprofl. socs. adv. com. on Medicaid to commr. health N.Y.C.; asst. clin. prof. removable prosthodontics, asst. clin. prof. dept. family practice NYU Coll. Dentistry, 1981-87, assoc. clin. prof. prosthodontics and occlusion, comprehensive care and practice adminstrn., 1987—. Hon. asst. chmn. Democratic State Conv., N.Y., 1966; mem. New Rochelle Dem. City Com.; mem. New Rochelle Columbus Day Com., 1981, 82. Served with Dental Corps, AUS, 1944-47. Recipient N.Y. U. Alumni Meritorious Service award, 1976. Fellow Am. Coll. Dentists, Acad. Gen. Practice, Am. Endodontic Soc., Internat. Coll. Dentists; mem. Am. Acad. Prosthodontics, ADA, Am. Soc. Advancement Gen. Anesthesia in Dentistry, Am. Soc. Childrens Dentistry, Am. Dental Soc. Anaesthesiology, N.Y. Inst. Clin. Oral Pathology, Alumni Assn. N.Y. U. Dental Sch. (dir. 1961—, chmn. installation dinner 1963-64, 65, 67, chmn. constl. by-laws com. 1964-66, sec. 1968-69, pres. elect 1970-71, pres. 1971-72), Alumni Fedn. N.Y. U. (past pres., dir., Great Teacher award 1990), N.Y. Hort. Soc., Am. Acad. Polit. and Social Sci., Eastern Dental Soc. (pres. 1978), First Dist. Dental Soc. (dir., chmn. govt. funded health care com.), Empire Dental Polit. Action Com. (sec. 1976-77), Sydenham Hosp. Dental Clin. Soc. (pres. 1971-72), Grand St. Boys Assn., Assn. Mil. Surgeons, Thomas Paine Hist. Soc. Democrat. Club: N.Y. University College of Dentistry Century (organizing com. N.Y.C., dir. 1961-66). Home: 85 Hillary Cir New Rochelle NY 10804-1805 Office: 601 W 139th St New York NY 10031-7312

MARKS, BERNARD BAILIN, lawyer; b. Sioux City, Iowa, Sept. 6, 1917; s. Meyer A. and Beulah (Bailin) M.;m. Betty L. Marks; 1 child, Susan E. BA, Harvard U., 1939, JD, 1942. Bar: Iowa 1942. With firm Shull, Marshall & Marks, Sioux City, 1946-85, ptnr., 1949-85; ptnr. Marks & Madsen, Sioux City, 1985—; sec., asst. treas., dir. Flavorland Industries, Inc. (formerly Needham Packing Co., Inc.), Sioux City, 1962-81; sec., dir. KTIV-TV Co., Sioux City, 1965-74; bd. dirs. First Nat. Bank, Firstar Bank, Sioux City, 1963-91. Bd. dirs. Iowa Heart Assn., 1960, Woodbury County chpt., 1958-64, pres., 1962-64; bd. dirs. Sioux City Art Center, 1952-54, Sioux City United Fund, 1965-71, Sioux City Community Appeals Bd., 1965-68; trustee Briar Cliff Coll., Sioux City, 1968-74. Served with USAAF, 1942-46. Fellow Iowa Bar Assn. Found.; mem. ABA, Iowa Bar Assn., Woodbury County Bar Assn. (prews. 1958), Am. Coll. Trust and Estate Counsel, Sioux City C. of C. (bd. dirs. 1964-67, treas. 1965-66), Sioux City Lawyers Club (pres. 1951), Sioux City Country Club (bd. dirs. 1963-64). Clubs: Sioux City Lawyers (pres. 1951), Sioux City Country (bd. dirs. 1963-64). Office: Marks & Madsen 303 Piper Jaffray Bldg PO Box 3226 Sioux City IA 51102

MARKS, BRUCE, artistic director, choreographer; b. N.Y.C., Jan. 23, 1937; s. Albert and Helen (Kosersky) M.; m. Toni Pihl Petersen, Jan. 27, 1966 (dec. May 1985); children: Erik Antony, Adam Christopher, Kenneth Rikard. Student, Brandeis U., 1954-55, Juilliard Sch., 1955-56; DFA (hon.), Wheaton Coll., 1986, Franklin Pierce Coll., 1990, U. Mass., 1995, Juilliard Sch., 1996. Prof. U. Utah, 1981, 84-86; now artistic dir. Boston Ballet Co., 1985—; mem. dance adv. panel Nat. Endowment for Arts, 1979, chmn. internat. selection com., 1979, chmn. dance adv. panel, 1981, mem. nat. adv. bd. on arts and edn., 1989; bd. dirs., mem. exec. com., Dance/USA 1989, 92—, chmn., 1990-92, chmn. govt. affairs, 1992—; mem. U.S.-USSR Commn. on Dance and Theatre Studies, Am. Coun. Learned Socs./IREX; mem. jury Internat. Moscow Internat. Ballet Competition, 1989. Prin. dancer Met. Opera, 1956-6l, Am. Ballet Theatre, 196l-72, Royal Swedish Ballet, 1963, Festival Ballet, London, 1965, Royal Danish Ballet, 197l-76; artistic dir. Ballet West, Salt Lake City, 1976-85; choreographer Eliot Feld Ballet Co., 1970, Royal Danish Ballet, 1972-73, Netherlands Dance Theatre, 1974, Ballet West, 1976-85; artistic fellow Aspen Inst. for Humanistic Studies, 1979—. Bd. dirs. Am. Arts Alliance, 1983-85, Am. Coun. for Arts, 1985—; bd. dirs. Dance U.S.A., 1988-94, chmn., 1990-92; chmn. U.S.A. Internat. Ballet Competition, Jackson, Micc., 1990—, vice chair jury Helsinki, Finland, 1991, judge Helsinki Ballet Competition 1995; mem. nat. adv. bd. on arts and edn. NEA, 1989-91; mem. internat. jury 1st Japan Internat. Ballet Competition, Hagoya, Japan, 1993, Am. jury for Prix de Lausanne, 1994; mem. Brandeis Creative Arts Awards Commn., 1993, chmn. Brandeis Creative Arts Awards Dance, 1994; chair Grants to Dance Cos. panel NEA, 1993, overview panel, 1994. Recipient Disting. Svc. award for artistic prodn. Nat. Govs. Assn., 1994, Capezio award Balletmakers, Inc., 1995, Hon. Doctorate Fine Arts, Julliard, 1996. Office: Boston Ballet 19 Clarendon St Boston MA 02116-6107

MARKS, CHARLES CALDWELL, retired investment banker, retired industrial distribution company executive; b. Birmingham, Ala., June 1, 1921; s. Charles Pollard and Isabel (Caldwell) M.; m. Jeanne Vigeant, Jan. 12, 1945; children: Randolph C., Margaret Marks Porter, Charles P. Student, Birmingham U., 1930-38; BS in Physics, U. of South, 1942; grad. mgmt. seminar, Harvard U., 1957; DCL (hon.), U. of the South, 1989; LLD (hon.), U. Ala., Birmingham, 1990. With Owen-Richards Co. (name changed to Motion Industries, Inc. 1970), Birmingham, 1946—; chmn. bd. Owen-Richards Co. (name changed to Motion Industries, Inc. 1970), 1952-73, pres., 1973-83; vice chmn. bd. Porter White & Yardley Cos., Inc., 1984-92, ret., 1992; bd. dirs. emeritus Genuine Parts Co., BE & K Inc.; bd. dirs., chmn. Birmingham br. Fed. Res. Bank of Atlanta. Bd. dirs. So. Rsch. Inst., exec. com., 1987-95, dir. emeritus, 1995—; bd. govs. Indian Springs Sch., dir. emeritus, 1995—; pres., bd. dirs. Workshop for Blind, Birmingham, 1958-61, Children's Aid Soc. Birmingham, 1962; chmn. Com. of 100, Birmingham, 1963; co-chmn. United Appeals of Jefferson County, 1963; trustee, regent U. of South; pres. St. Vincent's Found., 1987; bd. dirs. U. Ala.-Birmingham Rsch. Found., Exec. Svcs. Corps. of Birmingham, 1984—. Lt. USNR, WWII, ATO, MTO. Mem. Navy League, The Club, Redstone Club, John's Island Club, Mountain Brook Club, Willow Point Club, Ala. Newcomen Soc., Blue Key, Phi Beta Kappa, Sigma Alpha Epsilon. Episcopalian. Home: 2828 Cherokee Rd Birmingham AL 35223-2607 Office: 2160 Highland Ave Suite 301 Birmingham AL 35205

MARKS, CHARLES DENNERY, insurance salesman; b. New Orleans, Nov. 22, 1935; s. Sidney Leroy Marks and Melanie Dennery; m. Gillian E. Otter, Sept. 1, 1963; children: Elizabeth Dennery, Richard Dennery. BA, Yale U., 1957. CLU, ChFC. With Charles Dennery, Inc., 1959-63; sales rep. Prudential Ins. Co., New Orleans, 1964—; v.p. Mgmt. Compensation Group, New Orleans, 1985—. Past bd. dirs. Boys Club Greater New Orleans, Big Bros. Greater New Orleans, United Way; past pres. Goodwill Rehab. Ctr.; vice chmn. Jr. Achievement; active Temple Sinai Synagogue. 1st lt. U.S. Army, 1957-59. Recipient award Volunteer Activist, 1983. Mem. Am. Soc. CLU and ChFC (pres. New Orleans chpt. 1984-85), Assn. Advanced Life Underwriting, Life Underwriters Pol. Action Com. (diplomat, sec./treas. 1982-87), La. Assn. Life Underwriters (Life Underwriter of Yr. 1985, 87, pres. 1986-87), New Orleans Estate Planning Coun. (pres. 1986-87), New Orleans Life Underwriters Assn. (Life Underwriter of Yr. 1981, pres. 1982-83), Million Dollar Round Table (Top of the Table 1986-89, exec. com. 1990-94, pres. 1993) Nat. Assn. Life Underwriters (vice chmn. fin. com. 1993—), Life and Health Found. for Edn. (life, chmn. 1996—). Republican. Home: 1525 Eleonore St New Orleans LA 70115-4242 Office: Mgmt Compensation Group 1250 Poydras St Ste 325 New Orleans LA 70113-1804

MARKS, CRAIG, management educator, consultant, engineer; b. Salt Lake City, Oct. 9, 1929; s. Elmer Lester and Louie Thelma (Marks) M.; m. Lois Marie Brinkman, June 11, 1950 (div. 1972); children—Gary C., Diane Marks White, Marian Marks Deming; m. Anne Mary Crowe, Oct. 28, 1972. B.S.M.E., Calif. Inst. Tech., 1950, M.S.M.E., 1951, Ph.D. in Mech. Engring., 1955. Instr. Calif. Inst. Tech., Pasadena, 1953-55; supr. Ford Motor Co., Detroit, 1955-56, Gen. Motors Research Labs., Warren, Mich., 1956-57; asst. engr.-in-charge engring. staff Gen. Motors Corp., Warren, 1957-67; engr.-in-charge Gen. Motors Corp., 1967-72, exec. asst. to v.p., 1972-79, exec. dir. environ. activity staff, 1979-83; v.p. engring. and tech. TRW Inc., Cleve., Ohio, 1983-88; v.p. tech. and productivity Allied Signal Inc., Southfield, Mich., 1988-91; prof. U. Mich., 1991—; pres. CMS-Creative Mgmt. Solutions, Bloomfield Hills, Mich., 1991—; co-dir. Tauber Mfg. Inst. U. Mich., 1995—. Contbr. articles to profl. jours.; patentee in field. Speaker civic leaders meetings Gen. Motors Corp., 1977-82. Fellow Soc. Automotive Engrs. (bd. dirs.); mem. NAE, ASME, Engring. Soc. Detroit (bd. dirs.), Sigma Xi, Tau Beta Pi. Christian Scientist. Avocations: flying; tennis; golf. Home and Office: 174 Kirkwood Ct Bloomfield Hills MI 48304-2926

MARKS, DAVID BRUCE, control systems engineer; b. Dallas, Jan. 11, 1960; s. William Carl and Eula Belle (Casey) M.; m. Hui Chong Mun, Oct. 17, 1991. BS, Tex. A&M U., 1982, MS, 1985. Profl. engr., Tex. Sr. engr. M.W. Kellogg, Houston, 1985—. Mem. AIChE, Am. Chem. Soc., Instrument Soc. Am. Avocations: travel, jogging, hunting, camping. Home: 8146 San Leandro Dr Dallas TX 75218-4403

MARKS, EDWARD B., international social service administrator; b. N.Y.C., Apr. 22, 1911; s. Edward B. and Miriam (Chuck) M.; m. Margaret Levi (dec. 1980); 2 children; m. Vera J. Barad, 1987. BA cum laude, Dartmouth Coll., 1932; MA in Sociology, Columbia U., 1938. Assoc. editor Am. Wine and Liquor Jour., N.Y.C., 1933-36; mng. editor Better Times mag. Welfare Coun. N.Y.C., 1937-38; dir. div. for social and cultural adjustment Nat. Refugee Svc., N.Y.C., 1938-42; refugee program officer War Relocation Authority, Dept. Interior, Washington, 1942-46; chief of mission for Greece UN Internat. Refugee Orgn., Geneva and Athens, 1947-50; chief of mission successively for Greece, N.Y., and Yugoslavia Internat. Migration Orgn., 1951-58; exec. dir. U.S. Com. for Refugees, N.Y.C., 1958-62; dep. chief office cen. African affairs AID, Washington, 1962-65; asst. dir. for relief and rehab., Vietnam AID, 1965-66, aid coordination officer, Am. Embassy, U.K., 1966-68, asst. dir. for relief and rehab., Nigeria, 1969-71, voluntary agy. liaison officer for Asia, 1973-75; various emergency and liaison assignments UNICEF, N.Y.C., Paris, Geneva, 1971-73; dep. dir. secretariat Internat. Yr. of Child UNICEF, N.Y.C., 1976-80, liaison rep. for UN Yr. for Disabled, 1981-82, internat. cons., 1983-85; interim pres. U.S. Com. for UNICEF, N.Y.C., 1985, bd. dirs., mem. exec. com., chmn. nominating com., 1986-92; pres. then chmn. Immigration and Refugee Svcs. Am., 1985—; instr. Boston U. Sch. Social Work, 1988, 89. Author: A World of Art--The United Nations Collection, 1996; contbr. articles to The New Yorker, N.Y. Times Mag., other jours. Recipient 1st Disting. Career award AID, 1976; Nat. Endowment for Arts grantee, 1994. Address: 333 E 46th St New York NY 10017-7401 also: 4 Channing St Cambridge MA 02138-4714

MARKS, EDWIN S., investment company executive; b. N.Y.C., June 3, 1926; s. Carl and Edith R. (Smith) M.; m. Nancy Lucille Abeles, June 21, 1949; children: Carolyn Gail, Linda Beth, Constance Ann. Student, Princeton U., 1944-45; BS, U.S. Mil. Acad., 1949. V.p. Carl Marks & Co., Inc., N.Y.C., 1958-61, pres., 1961—, also bd. dirs.; dir., exec. v.p. CMNY Capital Co. Inc., 1962—. Author: What I Know about Foreign Securities, 1958. Trustee Lincoln Ctr. Fund, 1966-77, Hofstra U., 1974-79, Sarah Lawrence Coll., 1979-81, North Shore Univ. Hosp., Manhasset, N.Y.; chmn. bd. overseers Rsch. Lab., North Shore Univ. Hosp.; bd. dirs. Chief Execs. Orgn. Cold Spring Harbor Labs., 1992, Smith New Court PLC, London, 1988-94; bd. dirs., exec. com. Lincoln Ctr. for the Performing Arts. Mem. West Point Soc., N.Y. Bd. Trade, Harmonie Club. Office: Carl Marks & Co Inc 135 E 57th St New York NY 10022-2009

MARKS, ELAINE, French language educator; b. N.Y.C., Nov. 13, 1930; d. Harry and Ruth (Elin) M. BA, Bryn Mawr Coll., 1952; MA, U. Pa., 1953; PhD, NYU, 1958. Asst. prof. French NYU, N.Y.C., 1958-60; assoc. prof. U. Wis., Milw., 1963-65; prof. U. Wis., Madison, 1967-68, prof. French, Italian and women's studies, 1980—; prof. French U. Mass., Amherst, 1965-66; dir. Women's Studies Rsch. Ctr., 1977-85. Author: Colette, 1960, 2d edit., 1981, Simone de Beauvoir: Encounters with Death, 1973, Marrano as Metaphor: the Jewish Presence in French Writing, 1996; co-editor: Homosexualities and French Literature, 1979, 2d edit., 1990, New French Feminisms, 1980, 81; editor: Critical Essays on Simone de Beauvoir, 1987. Decorated officier Ordre Palmes Académiques (France), 1994; recipient Disting. Alumni award NYU Grad. Sch. Arts and Sci. Alumni Assn., 1994; Wis. Alumni Rsch. Found. U. House Professorship, 1988; Fulbright fellow, France, 1956-57, Guggenheim fellow, 1992. Mem. MLA (pres. 1993), Midwest MLA, Am. Assn. Tchrs. French, Nat. Women's Studies Assn. Home: 2040 Field St Madison WI 53713-1159

MARKS, ESTHER L., metals company executive; b. Canton, Ohio, Oct. 3, 1927; d. Jacob and Ella (Wisman) Rosky; m. Irwin Alfred Marks, June 29, 1947; children: Jules, Howard, Marilyn. Student, Ohio State U., 1945-46, Youngstown State U., 1946-47. V.p. Steel City Iron & Metal, Inc., Youngstown, Ohio. Pres. Jr. Hadassah, Youngstown, 1943-45, Pioneer Women, Youngstown, 1951, Anshe Emeth Sisterhood, Youngstown, Broadway Theatre League, Youngstown, 1958, B'nai B'rith Women, Youngstown, 1962, Dist. 2 B'nai B'rith Women, Cleve., 1969-70, Jewish Cmty. Ctr., Youngstown, Youngstown Area Jewish Fedn., 1988-90; v.p. United Way, Youngstown, 1991, chmn., 1996; grad. Leadership Youngstown, 1991; bd. Akiva Acad. Commn. for Jewish Edn., Temple El Emeth, Stambaugh Auditorium. Named Guardian of the Menorah B'nai B'rith, Youngstown, 1978; recipient BBG Alumna award B'nai B'rith Girls, Washington, 1989. Mem. LMV, YWCA, Ohio Hist. Soc. Democrat. Jewish. Avocations: knitting, organizational work. Home: 3511 5th Ave Youngstown OH 44505-1907 Office: 703 Wilson Ave Youngstown OH 44506-1445

MARKS, FLORENCE CARLIN ELLIOTT, nursing informaticist; b. Louisville, Ky., Oct. 15, 1928; d. David Carlin and Anna Marie (Lance) Elliott; m. George Edward Marks, Mar. 18, 1961; children: Mary Ellen Marks Fox, Ruth Ann, Charles Douglas. BS in Chemistry, Zoology, U. Cin., 1949; BSN, U. Minn., 1953, M of Nursing Adminstrn., 1956. RN, Minn. From staff nurse to asst. head nurse U. Minn. Hosps., Mpls., 1953-54; staff nurse Marseilisbog Hosp., Aarhaus, Denmark, 1954-55; nursing supr. U. Minn. Hosps., Mpls., 1956-61, spl. asst. to dir. of nursing svc., 1962; rsch. asst. Hill Family Found. Nursing Rsch. Project, Mpls., 1966-69; writer U. Minn. Sch. of Nursing, Mpls., 1976; cons. U. Minn. Sch. of Nursing, 1976, 1978; nursing program specialist Hennepin County Med. Ctr., Mpls., 1978-84, nursing info. systems dir., cons., 1987—; nursing utilization system coord. U. Minn. Hosps., Mpls., 1984-87; cons. Creative Nursing Mgmt., 1992—; speaker, lectr. various nursing confs. in U.S. Contbr. articles to profl. pubis., chpts. to profl. books, posters, abstracts; co-author: (with Joan Williams) (TV series) TLC, 1953 (McCall's award 1954); editor: Tomorrow's Nurse, 1960-62; Minn. Nursing Accent (commemorative issue 60th anniversary) May, 1965. Prin. flutist St. Anthony Civic Orch., 1975—, bd. dirs., 1988-92, adminstrv. bd. Hennepin Ave. United Meth. Ch., 1974-77, tchr., 1966-83 intermittently, cmty. outreach ministry, chair adv. com., 1992-95; mem. U. Minn. Sch. Nursing Densford Recognition Com., 1992-96; troop leader Mpls. coun. Girl Scouts USA, 1971-85, bd. dirs., 1977-79, svc. unit mgr., 1973-77; den leader Cub Scouts Webelo den, Viking coun. Boy Scouts Am., 1977-79; v.p. Wilshire Park PTSA, 1975-76, pres., 1976-77. Recipient Thanks Badge Greater Mpls. Girl Scout Coun. Mem. Minn. Nurses Assn. (various coms., bd. dirs. 1959-61), Minn. League for Nursing, Minn. Heart Assn. (profl. edn. com. 1959-61), Nursing Info. Discussion Group (chmn. Twin City program com. 1985-91, 95—), U. Minn. Sch. Nursing Alumni Assn. (bd. dirs. 1963-67, pres. 1965-66), Mortar Bd., Zeta Tau Alpha, Tau Beta Sigma, Sigma Theta Tau (bd. dirs. Zeta chpt. 1969-73, 89-91, pres. 1972-73, heritage com. 1990). Home: 3424 Silver Lake Rd NE Minneapolis MN 55418-1605

MARKS, HERBERT EDWARD, lawyer; b. Dayton, Ohio, Nov. 3, 1935; s. I.M. and Sarah S. M.; m. Marcia Frager; children: Jennifer L., Susan E. A.B. with high distinction, U. Mich., 1957; J.D., Yale U., 1960; postgrad., George Washington U. Law Sch., 1965-67. Bar: Ohio 1960, D.C. 1964, U.S. Supreme Ct. 1965. Law clk. to chief judge U.S. Ct. Claims, 1964-65; assoc. Wilkinson, Cragun & Barker, Washington, 1965-69, ptnr., 1969-82; ptnr. Squire, Sanders & Dempsey, Washington, 1982—; assoc. gen. counsel Presdl. Inaugural Coms., 1969, 73, 81; chmn. U.S. State Dept. Adv. Panel on Internat. Telecomm. Law, 1987-91; mem. adv. com. on internat. comm. and info. policy U.S. State Dept., 1988-91; mem. U.S. del. ITU European Telecomm. Devel. Conf., 1991. Contbr. articles to legal jours. Served to capt. JAG USAF, 1960-64. Mem. ABA (chair sci. and tech. sect. 1990-91, chmn. communications div. 1986-88), D.C. Bar Assn., Computer Law Assn. (pres. 1975-77, bd. dirs. 1972-85, adv. bd. 1985—), Fed. Communications Bar Assn., Cosmos Club, Kenwood Golf & Country Club, Phi Beta Kappa. Office: Squire Sanders & Dempsey 1201 Pennsylvania Ave NW PO Box 407 Washington DC 20004 also: 5317 Cardinal Ct Bethesda MD 20816-2908

MARKS, IDA RENAE, psychological counselor; b. Merced, Calif., Aug. 13, 1954; d. Samuel Joseph and Laudine Francess (Carter) Marks; divorced; children: Isaiah, Charity, Angela. BAS, Stephen F. Austin State U., 1980;

MA, Chapman U., 1986; AA, U. S.D., 1989. Edn. counselor Civil Svc., Offutt AFB, Nebr., 1985-86; coord. job placement program ARC, Omaha, 1987-88; vocat. rehab. counselor Dept. Edn. State of Nebr., Omaha, 1989-91; vocat. rehab. specialist Heartland Rehab., Omaha, 1991-92; cons. Am. Ins. Health and Reahb. Svcs., Omaha, 1992; coord. of counseling and testing U. Tex., Tyler, 1993—. With USAF, 1973, Res. Decorated Mil. Commendation medal. Mem. Am. Counseling Assn. Avocations: aerobics, reading, walking. Office: U Tex 3900 University Blvd Tyler TX 75799

MARKS, JAMES S., public health service administrator; b. May 13, 1948. AB cum laude, Williams Coll., 1969; MD, SUNY, Buffalo, 1973; MPH, Yale U., 1980. Diplomate Am. Bd. Pediatrics. Intern in pediat. U. Calif., San Francisco, 1973-74, resident in pediat., 1974-75, chief resident pediatric outpatient dept., 1975-76; resident in preventive medicine Ctrs. for Disease Control, Atlanta, 1977-78; fellow Robert Wood Johnson Clin. Scholars Program Yale U., New Haven, Conn., 1978-80; resident in preventive medicine Ctrs. for Disease Control, Atlanta, 1981-82, chief epidemiology and rsch. br., nutrition divsn., 1982-84, asst. dir. preventive medicine residency program, 1985-87, dir. divsn. reproductive health, 1987, coord. for chronic disease control activities, 1987-88, acting dir. divsn. diabetes transl., 1988-89, acting dir. divsn. chronic disease control, 1990-91, dir. divsn. reproductive health, 1992-95, dir. Nat. Ctr. Chronic Disease Prevention/Health Promotion, 1995—; adj. assoc. prof. Emory U. Sch. Pub. Health, Atlanta, 1990—; editor Chronic Disease Notes and Reports, 1989-92; clinic physician Planned Parenthood of San Francisco Teen Clinic, San Francisco, 1975-76; cons. physician Ohio Dept. Health Bur. Preventive Medicine, 1978-79; cons. PAHO Consultative Group on Perinatal Care, Washington, 1982, WHO Malaysia Ministry of Health, 1982, 83, WHO Maternal and Child Health Unit Geneva, 1983, World Bank China Program Third Health Project, 1988, 1991, World Bank Poland, Health Promotion/Chronic Disease Prevention, 1992, World Bank China, Seventh Health Project, 1993. Contbr. articles to profl. jours, chpts. to books. Exec. sec. Diabetes Tech. Adv. com., 1989-92; liaison mem. Nat. Diabetes Adv. Bd., 1988-89; mem. Diabetes Mellitus Interagy. Coording. com., 1988-89; mem. subcom. adult edn., Am. Cancer Soc., 1987-92; staff White House Task Force on Infant Mortality, 1989; presenter in field. Epidemic Intelligence Svc. Officer USPHS Field Svcs. Divsn., 1976-78. Recipient Alexander D. Langmuir award, 1978, CDC Group award, 1984, Commendation Medal USPHS, 1984, and many other awards and citations. Fellow Am. Coll. Epidemiology; mem. APHA (active in com. work), Am. Epidemiol. Soc., Soc. Epidemiol. Rsch., Am. Acad. Pediat. (com. pediatric rsch. 1994-95), Internat. Epidemiol. Assn., Physicians for Social Responsibility, Soc. on Med. Decision Making, Epidemic Intelligence Svc. Alumni Assn., Sigma Xi. Home: 3158 Kings Arms Court Atlanta GA 30345 Office: Ctrs for Disease Control Ctr Chronic Disease Prevtn Atlanta GA 30333*

MARKS, JEROME, lawyer; b. N.Y.C., June 24, 1931; m. Margarita A. Marks; children: Susan Marks Schmetterer, David J., Ilyse Marks Kelly, Laurence K. BA, Northwestern U., 1952, JD summa cum laude, 1955. Bar: Ill. 1955. Assoc. Friedman & Koven, Chgo., 1956-63, ptnr., 1963-86; ptnr. Rudnick & Wolfe, Chgo., 1986—. Asst. editor-in-chief Northwestern U. Law Rev., 1954-55. Co-chmn. No. Suburbs div. Operation Breadbasket, Chgo. and Highland Park (Ill.), 1968-72. Mem. Chgo. Bar Assn., Chgo. Coun. Lawyers, Order of Coif. Democrat. Avocations: walking, swimming, horse racing. Office: Rudnick & Wolfe 203 N La Salle St Ste 1800 Chicago IL 60601-1210

MARKS, JOHN HENRY, Near Eastern studies educator; b. Denver, Aug. 6, 1923; s. Ira and Clara E. (Dralle) M.; m. E. Aminta Willis, July 21, 1951; children: Peter A., Fleur A., John B. B.A., U. Denver, 1946; B.D. (O.T. fellow), Princeton Theol. Sem., 1949; Th.D., U. Basel, (Switzerland), 1953. Instr. Princeton Theol. Sem., 1953-54; instr. Princeton U., 1954-55, asst. prof. to assoc. prof. Near Eastern studies, 1955-61, prof., 1979-93; dir. Am. Schs. Oriental Research, Jerusalem, 1966-67; pres. Am. Ctr. Oriental Research, Amman, Jordan, 1969-79; trustee Am. Schs. Oriental Research, Phila, 1971-86 ; Acting dean Princeton U. Chapel, 1980. Author: Der Textkritische Wert des Psalterium Hieronymi iuxta Hebraeos, 1956, Visions of One World, Legacy of Alexander, 1985; also translator. Pres. Sch. Bd. Princeton, 1969-71; mem. Planning-Zoning Bds. Princeton, 1964-66. Served with U.S. Army, 1943-45. Mem. Soc. Bibl. Lit. Democrat. Presbyterian. Home: 107 Moore St Princeton NJ 08540-3308 Office: 110 Jones Dr Princeton NJ 08540

MARKS, LAWRENCE EDWARD, psychologist; b. N.Y.C., Dec. 28, 1941; s. Milton and Anne (Parnes) M.; m. Joya Ellen Cazes, Dec. 24, 1963; children: Liza, Laura. AB, Hunter Coll., N.Y.C., 1962; PhD, Harvard U., Cambridge, Mass., 1965; PhD honoris causa, Stockholm U., 1994. Rsch.-assoc. prof. Yale U., New Haven, 1966-84; asst.-assoc. fellow John B. Pierce Lab., New Haven, 1966-84; prof. psychology Yale U., New Haven, 1984—; fellow John B. Pierce Lab., New Haven, 1984—. Author: Sensory Processes: The New Psychophysics, 1974, The Unity of the Senses, 1978. Named to Hall of Fame, Hunter Coll., N.Y.C., 1985; recipient Jacob Javits award NIH, Washington, 1987. Fellow AAAS, Am. Psychol. Assn., Am. Psychol. Soc., N.Y. Acad. Sci. Democrat. Jewish. Achievements include elucidation of common principles underlying sensory processes in various sense modalities; development of validational scheme for quantifying magnitudes of sensory experience; indication of role of cross-modal (synesthetic) perception in relation to language and literature. Home: 48 Maplevale Dr Woodbridge CT 06525-1118 Office: John B Pierce Lab 290 Congress Ave New Haven CT 06519-1403

MARKS, LEONARD, JR., retired corporate executive; b. N.Y.C., May 22, 1921; s. Leonard M. and Laura (Colegrove) Rose; m. Antonia Saldaña Riley, July 19, 1986; children from previous marriage: Linda, Patricia Anne, Peter K. A.B. in Econs., Drew U., 1942; M.B.A., Harvard U., 1948, D.B.A., 1961. Asst. prof. bus. adminstrn. Harvard U., 1949-55; prof. fin. Stanford U., 1955-64; asst. sec. USAF, Washington, 1964-68; v.p. corp. devel. Times Mirror Co., Los Angeles, 1968-69; sr. v.p. Wells Fargo Bank, San Francisco, 1969-72; exec. v.p. Castle & Cooke Inc., San Francisco, 1972-85; gen. ptnr. Marks-Hoffman Assocs., Venture Capital, 1985-92; ind. corp. dir., 1992—; bd. dirs. Airlease Mgmt. Svcs., Alexion Pharm. Inc., No. Trust Bank of Ariz. Co-author: Case Problems in Commercial Bank Management, 1962; contbg.: Credit Management Handbook, 1958. Capt. AUS, 1942-46, ret. brig. gen. USAFR.

MARKS, LEONARD HAROLD, lawyer; b. Pitts., Mar. 5, 1916; s. Samuel and Ida (Levine) M.; m. Dorothy Ames, June 3, 1948; children: Stephen Ames, Robert Evan. B.A., U. Pitts., 1935, LL.B., 1938. Bar: Pa. 1938, D.C. 1946. Asst. prof. law U. Pitts. Law Sch., 1938-42; prof. law Nat. U., 1943-55; asst. to gen. counsel FCC, 1942-46, ops. counsel, 1986—; ptnr. Cohn & Marks, Washington, 1946-65, 69-86; chmn. exec. com. Nat. Savs. and Trust Co., 1977-85; chmn. Internat. Conf. on Comm. Satellites, 1968-69; Am. del. Internat. Broadcasting Confs., 1948-69; pres. Internat. Rescue Com., 1973-79, Honor Am. Com., 1977-86; chmn. U.S. Adv. Commn. on Internat. Ednl. and Cultural Affairs, 1973-78; chmn. Fgn. Policy Assn., 1981-87, exec. com., 1987-96; head U.S. del. Internat. Telecom. Union, 1983, 87; chmn. U.S. del. to London Info. Forum, Commn. on Security and Cooperation in Europe, 1989. Mem. ABA (ho. of dels. 1962-64), Fed. Communications Bar Assn. (pres. 1959-60), Bar Assn. D.C., World Affairs Council Washington (chmn.), Phi Beta Kappa, Order of Coif, Omicron Delta Kappa, Sigma Delta Chi. Clubs: Cosmos, Metropolitan, Federal City, Broadcasters, (pres. 1957-59), Alfalfa (Washington). Home: Shoreham West Apt 714 2700 Calvert St NW Washington DC 20008 Office: 1333 New Hampshire Ave NW Washington DC 20036-1511

MARKS, MARTHA ALFORD, author; b. Oxford, Miss., July 27, 1946; d. Truman and Margaret Alford; m. Bernard L. Marks, Jan. 27, 1968. BA, Centenary Coll., 1968; MA, Northwestern U., 1972, PhD, 1978. Tchr. Notre Dame High Sch. for Boys, Niles, Ill., 1969-74; teaching asst. Northwestern U., Evanston, Ill., 1974-78, lectr., lang. coord., 1978-83; asst. prof. Kalamazoo (Mich.) Coll., 1983-85; writer Riverwoods, Ill., 1985—; cons. WGBH Edn. Found., Boston, 1988-91, Am. Coun. on the Tchg. of Fgn. Langs., 1981-92, Ednl. Testing Svcs., 1988-90, Peace Corps., 1993. Co-author: Destinos: An Introduction to Spanish, 1991, Al corriente, 1989, 93, Que tal?, 1986, 90; author: (workbook) Al corriente, 1989, 93; contbr. articles to profl. jours. Mem. Lake County (Ill.) Bd., Forest Preserve Commn., 1992—, Lake County Conservation Alliance; vice chmn. Friends of Ryerson Conservation Area Bd.; co-founder Reps. for Environ. Protection. Mem. AAUW. Home: 2940 Cherokee Ln Riverwoods IL 60015-1609 Office: County Bd Office County Bldg Rm 1001 18 N County St Waukegan IL 60085-4304

MARKS, MERTON ELEAZER, lawyer; b. Chgo., Oct. 16, 1932; s. Alfred Tobias and Helene Fannie (Rosner) M.; m. Radee Maiden Feiler, May 20, 1966; children: Sheldon, Elise Marks Vazelakis, Alan, Elaine Marks Ianchiou. BS, Northwestern U., 1954, JD, 1956. Bar: Ill. 1956, U.S. Ct. Mil. Appeals 1957, Ariz. 1958, U.S. Dist. Ct. Ariz. 1960, U.S. Ct. Appeals (9th cir.) 1962, U.S. Supreme Ct. 1970. Assoc. Moser, Compere & Emerson, Chgo., 1956-57; ptnr. Morgan, Marks & Rogers, Tucson, 1960-62; asst. atty. gen. State of Ariz., Phoenix, 1962-64, counsel indsl. commn., 1964-65; assoc., then ptnr. Shimmel, Hill, Bishop & Greunder, Phoenix, 1965-74; ptnr. Lewis & Roca, Phoenix, 1974—; lectr. on pharm., health care, product liability, ins. and employers' liability subjects; Judge Pro Tempore Ariz. Ct. Appeals, 1994. Contbr. more than 35 articles to profl. jours. Capt. JAGC, USAR, 1957-64. Mem. ABA (tort and ins. practice sect., chmn. spl. com. on fed. asbestos legis. 1987-89, chmn. workers compensation and employers liability law com. 1983-84), Am. Bd. Trial Advocates, Am. Coll. Legal Medicine, Internat. Bar Assn., Internat. Assn. for Ins. Law, Internat. Assn. Lawyers, Drug Info. Assn., Am. Soc. Pharmacy Law, State Bar Ariz. (chmn. workers compensation sect. 1969-73), Nat. Coun. Self Insurers, Ariz. Self Insurers Assn., Fedn. Ins. and Corp. Counsel (chmn. pharm. litig. sect. 1989-91, chmn. workers compensation sect. 1977-79, v.p. 1978-79, 81, bd. dirs. 1981-89), Internat. Assn. Def. Counsel, Ariz. Assn. Def. Counsel (pres. 1976-77), Maricopa County Bar Assn., Def. Rsch. Inst. (drug and device com., chmn. workers compensation com. 1977-78). Office: Lewis & Roca 40 N Central Ave Phoenix AZ 85004-4424

MARKS, MICHAEL J., lawyer, corporate executive; b. 1938. AB, Cornell U., 1960; JD, U. Chgo., 1963. Assoc. Stroock & Stroock & Lavan, 1964-70, Chun, Kerr & Dodd, 1970-72; counsel Kelso, Spencer, Snyder & Stirling, 1972-75; asst. gen. counsel Alexander & Baldwin Inc., Honolulu, 1975-80, v.p., gen. counsel, 1980-84, v.p., gen. counsel, sec., 1984-85, sr. v.p., gen. counsel, sec., 1985—. Office: Alexander & Baldwin Inc 822 Bishop St Honolulu HI 96813-3924

MARKS, PAUL ALAN, oncologist, cell biologist, educator; b. N.Y.C., Aug. 16, 1926; s. Robert R. and Sarah (Bohorad) M.; m. Joan Harriet Rosen, Nov. 28, 1953; children: Andrew Robert, Elizabeth Susan Marks Ostrer, Matthew Stuart. AB with gen. honors, Columbia U., 1945, MD, 1949; D in Biol. Sci. (hon.), U. Urbino, Italy, 1982; PhD (hon.), Hebrew U., Jerusalem, Israel, 1987, U. Tel Aviv, 1992. Fellow Columbia U. Coll. Physicians and Surgeons, 1952-53, assoc., 1955-56, mem. faculty, 1956-82, dir. hematology tng., 1961-74, prof. medicine, 1967-82, prof. human genetics and devel., 1969-82, dean faculty of medicine, v.p. med. affairs, 1970-73, dir. Comprehensive Cancer Ctr., 1972-80, v.p. health scis., 1973-80, Frode Jensen prof. medicine, 1974-80; prof. medicine and genetics Cornell U. Coll. Medicine, N.Y.C., 1982—, prof. medicine Grad. Sch. Med. Scis., 1983—; instr. Sch. Medicine, George Washington U., 1954-55; cons. VA Hosp., N.Y.C., 1962-66; attending physician Presbyn. Hosp., N.Y.C., 1967-82; pres., CEO Meml. Sloan-Kettering Cancer Ctr., 1980—; attending physician Meml. Hosp. for Cancer and Allied Diseases, 1980—; mem. Sloan-Kettering Inst. for Cancer Rsch., 1980—; adj. prof. Rockefeller U., 1980—; vis. physician Rockefeller U. Hosp., 1980—; hon. staff N.Y. Hosp., 1981—; bd. sci. counselors divsn. cancer treatment Nat. Cancer Inst., 1980-83; mem. steering com. Frederick Cancer Rsch. Facility Nat. Cancer Inst., 1982-86; chmn. program adv. com. Robert Wood Johnson Found., 1983-89; mem. Gov.'s Commn. on Shoreham Nuclear Plant, 1983; mem. Mayor's Commn. Sci. and Tech. City of N.Y., 1984-87; mem. adv. com. on NIH to Sec. HHS, 1989-90, 93—, external adv. com. Intramural Rsch. Program Rev. NIH; mem. coun. biol. scis. Pritzker Sch. Medicine U. Chgo., 1977-88; first lectr. Nakasone Program for Cancer Control U. Tokyo, 1984; Ayrey fellow, vis. prof. Royal Postgrad. Med. Sch. U. London, 1985; William Dameshek vis. prof. hematology Mt. Sinai Med. Ctr., 1985; nat. vis. com. CUNY Med. Sch., 1986-89; trustee Feinberg Grad. Sch. Weizmann Inst. Sci., Rehovot, Israel, 1986—; William H. Resnick lectr. in medicine Stamford Hosp., 1986; disting. faculty lectr. M.D. Anderson Hosp. U. Tex., 1986; Maurice C. Pincoffs lectr. U. Md., Balt., 1987; Japan Soc. Hematology Disting. lectr., 1989; vis. prof. Coll. de France, 1988; Alpha Omega Alpha vis. prof. N.Y. Med. Coll., 1990; Mario A. Baldini vis. prof. Harvard Med. Sch., 1991; mem. sci. adv. bd. City of Hope Nat. Med. Ctr., Duarte, Calif., 1987-92, Raymond and Beverly Sackler Found., Inc., 1989, Jefferson Cancer Inst., Phila., 1989, Hong Kong Cancer Inst., U. Hong Kong, 1994; mem. Found. Biomed. Rsch., 1989—; advisor Third World Acad. Sci.; mem. sci. adv. com. Imperial Cancer Rsch. Fund, 1994; mem. bd. govs. Friends of Sheba Med. Ctr., Tel Hashomer. Editor: Monographs in Human Biology, 1963; author 9 books; contbr. over 350 articles to profl. jours.; mem. editl. bd. Blood, 1964-71, assoc. editor, 1976-77, editor-in-chief, 1978-82; assoc. editor Jour. Clin. Investigation, 1967-17; mem. editl. bd. Cancer Treatment Revs., 1981—, Cancer Preventions, 1989, Sci., 1990; guest editl. bd. Japanese Jour. Cancer Rsch., 1985—; assoc. editor Molecular Reprodn. and Devel., 1988—; expert analyst Chemistry and Molecular Biology edit. of Chemtracts, 1990-92; mem. adv. bd. Internat. Jour. Hematology, 1992, Stem Cells; bd. contbr. editors Blood Cells, Molecules and Diseases, 1994, Comite des Sages, 1994. Trustee St. Luke's Hosp., 1970-80, Roosevelt Hosp., 1970-80, Presbyn. Hosp., 1972-80, Metpath Inst. Med. Edn., 1977-79; mem. jury Albert Lasker awards, 1974-82; bd. govs. Weizmann Inst., 1976—; bd. dirs. Revson Found., 1976-91, Am. Found. for Basic Res. Israel, Israel Acd. Scis., 1991; mem. tech. bd. Milbank Meml. Fund, 1978-85; bd. govs. Friends of Sheba Med. Ctr., Tel Hashomer. Recipient Charles Janeway prize Columbia U., 1949, Joseph Mather Smith prize, 1959, Stevens Triennial prize, 1960, Swiss-Am. Found. award in medColumbia U. Coll. Physicians and Surgeons Disting. Achievement medal, 1980, Centenary medal Inst. Pasteur, 1987, Disting. Oncologist award Hipple Cancer Ctr. and Kettering Ctr., 1987, Found. for Promotion of Cancer Rsch. medal, 1984 (Japan), Disting. Svc. medal Robert Wood Johnson Found., 1989, Outstanding Achievement award in hematopoiesis U. Innsbruck, 1991, Pres.'s Nat. Medal Sci., 1991, Gold medal for Disting. Acad. Accomplishments, Coll. Physicians and Surgeons, 1994, Joseph Mather Smith prize Columbia U., 1995, Japan Found. for Cancer Rsch. award 1995, John Jay award for Disting. Profl. Achievement, Columbia Coll., N.Y., 1996; Commonwealth Fund fellow Pasteur Inst., 1961-61. Master ACP, Coll. Phys. Surgeons; fellow AAAS, Royal Soc. Medicine, Am. Acad. Arts and Scis., Pasteur Inst. Paris; mem. NAS (chmn. sect. med. genetics, hematology and oncology 1980-83, chmn. Acad. Forum Adv. Com. 1980-81, mem. coun. 1984-87, del. biol. warfare com. Internat. Security and Arms Control 1986-89), Royal Soc. Medicine (London), Inst. Medicine (mem. coun. 1973-76, chmn. com. study resources clin. investigation with NAS 1988), Red Cell Club (past chmn.), Am. Fedn. Clin. Rsch. (past councillor Ea. dist.), Am. Soc. Clin. Investigation (pres. 1972-73), Am. Soc. Biol. Chemists, Am. Soc. Human Genetics (past mem. program com.), Am. Assn. Cancer Rsch., Assn. Am. Cancer Insts. (bd. dirs. 1983-88), Soc. Cell Biology, Am. Soc. Hematology (pres.-elect 1983, pres. 1984, chmn. adv. bd. 1985), Assn. Am. Physicians, Econ. Club (n.y.C.), Harvey Soc. (pres. 1973-74), Internat. Soc. Devel. Biologists, Italian Assn. Cell Biology and Differentiation (hon.), Chinese Anti-Cancer Assn. (hon.), Soc. for Devel. Biology, Japanese Cancer Assn. (hon.), Japan Soc. Hematology (Disting. lectr. 1989), Internat. Leadership Ctr. on Longevity and Soc. Interurban Clin. Club, Soc. for Study Devel. and Growth, Third World Acad. Scis., Sci. Adv. Hong Kong Cancer Inst., U. Hong Kong, Weizmann Inst. Sci. (gov. emeritus, Israel), Health Scis. Adv. Coun. Columbia U., Century Assn., Econ. Club, N.Y.C., Univ. Club N.Y.C., Alpha Omega Alpha. Office: Meml Sloan-Kettering Cancer Ctr 1275 York Ave New York NY 10021

MARKS, RICHARD, film editor; b. N.Y.C., Nov. 10, 1943; s. Ben and Irene (Epstein) Marks; m. Barbara Joan Fallick, Jan. 15, 1967; 1 child, Leslie Sharon. Student, NYU; BA, CCNY. Freelance film editor N.Y.C. and Los Angeles, 1964—. Mem. Motion Picture Acad. Arts and Scis., American Cinema Editors.

MARKS, RICHARD DANIEL, lawyer; b. N.Y.C., June 21, 1944; s. Morris Andrew and Dorothy (Schill) M.; m. Cheryl L. Hoffman, Nov. 13, 1971. BA, U. Va., 1966; JD, Yale U., 1969. Bar: D.C., U.S. Ct. Appeals (3rd, 4th, 8th, 11th and D.C. cir.), U.S. Supreme Ct. Assoc. Dow, Lohnes & Albertson, Washington, 1972-78, ptnr., 1978—. Co-author: Legal Problems in Broadcasting, 1974. Capt. U.S. Army, 1970-72. Mem. ABA (chmn. contracting for computer com., sect. for sci. and tech., computer law div., chmn. computer law div. 1994), Fed. Comms. Bar Assn., Capital Area Assn. Flight Instrs. (pres. 1989-90), UVA Club of Washington (pres. 1991-92). Avocations: aviation, skiing. Office: Dow Lohnes & Albertson LLC Ste 800 1200 New Hampshire Ave NW Washington DC 20036-6802

MARKS, ROBERT E., advertising executive; b. Bklyn., Apr. 27, 1950; s. Herbert and Florence Sadie (Mintz) M.; m. Lynn Susan Eisenberg, Dec. 24, 1973; children: Dana Maris, Heather Leigh. BS in Mgmt., SUNY, Buffalo, 1972; MBA in Mktg., NYU, 1975. Mktg. exec. Newspaper Advt. Bur., N.Y.C., 1972-73; account exec. Doyle, Dane, Berbach Advt., N.Y.C., 1973-77; account supr., v.p. Young & Rubicam Advt., N.Y.C., 1977-81; mgmt. supr., sr. v.p. Geers Gross Advt., N.Y.C., 1981-84; group account dir., sr. v.p. Ephron, Raboy, Tsao, and Kurnit Advt., N.Y.C., 1984-88; dir. account svcs., sr. v.p. Berenter, Greenhouse & Webster Advt., N.Y.C., 1988—. Democrat. Jewish. Avocations: tennis, photography, music. Office: Berenter Greenhouse Webster 233 Park Ave S New York NY 10003-1606

MARKS, ROBERT HUTCHINSON, publishing executive; b. Bklyn., May 2, 1926; s. Robert John and Martha Jean (Hutchinson) M.; m. Dorothy Beatrice Alexander, Feb. 3, 1951 (dec. Feb. 1974); m. 2d, Joyce Marie Goodwin, July 23, 1983. BS in Civil Engring., MIT, 1947. Application engr. Permutit Co., N.Y.C., 1948-56, dist. mgr., 1960-62; assoc. editor Power Mag., McGraw-Hill, Inc., N.Y.C., 1956-60, mng. editor 1962-69; mgr. pub. relations Michel-Cather, Inc., N.Y.C., 1969-70; assoc. dir. pub. Am. Inst. Physics, N.Y.C., 1970-84, dir. pub., 1985-88. dir. pub. div. Am. Chem. Soc., 1988—. Cons., Carnegie Found., N.Y.C., 1979—; treas., dir. Nat. Fedn. of Abstracting and Info. Svcs., Phila., 1980-83, pres. 1984-85; pres. Masonic Assn. for Charity, Bklyn., 1981; trustee Hanson Pl. Cen. United Meth. Ch., Bklyn., 1970-87, Engring. Info., Inc., 1976-82. Served to lt. USNR, 1944-46. Mem. Coun. Engring. and Sci. Soc. Execs., Soc. Scholarly Pub., AAAS, Am. Chem. Soc., Am. Inst. Chem. Engrs., ASME, ASCE, Am. Waterworks Assn., Nat. Assn. Corrosion Engrs. Republican. Methodist. Lodge: Masons. Home: 1200 N Nash St Apt 214 Arlington VA 22209-3613 Office: American Chemical Soc 1155 16th St NE Washington DC 20002-2901

MARKS, RUSSELL EDWARD, JR., management consultant; b. Sparrows Point, Md., July 6, 1932; s. Russell Edward and Edna Elizabeth (Johnson) M.; m. Patricia Mary Hunt, June 12, 1954; children—Tamara Elizabeth, Melissa. A.B., Princeton U., 1954; P.M.D., Harvard U., 1969. With W.R. Grace & Co., 1954-70; mem. staff W.R. Grace & Co., Bolivia, 1957-58, Peru, 1960-68; v.p. Latin Am. Group W.R. Grace & Co., N.Y.C., 1969-70; exec. v.p. Marine Internat. Corp., 1971-72; with Phelps Dodge Internat. Corp., N.Y.C., 1973-78; v.p., group v.p. Phelps Dodge Internat. Corp., Coral Gables, Fla., 1978-81, sr. v.p., pres., dir.; sr. v.p. Haley Assocs. Inc., N.Y.C., 1985-87, exec. v.p., 1988; v.p. A.T. Kearney Inc., 1988-90; mng. dir. Webb, Johnson & Klemmer Assoc., 1990—; dir. Coun. of the Ams., N.Y.C., 1978-85, pres., 1981-85; dir. Ctr. for Inter-Am. Rels., N.Y.C., 1980-85, pres., 1981-85; dir., pres. Ams. Soc., N.Y.C.; pres., dir. Pan Am. Soc. , N.Y.C., 1981-85; pres., dir. Caribbean/Cen. Am. Action, Washington, 1984-85; mem. U.S. del. to observe elections, El Salvador, 1982. Dir. Accion Internat., Boston, 1983-86, Bolivarian Soc., N.Y.C., 1982-85, Fla. Philharm. Orch., Miami, 1979; trustee Am. Acad. Dramatic Arts, N.Y., 1985-90; mem. adv. bd. internat. internship program James Madison U., 1989-90; mem. Princeton U. Alumni Coun., 1987-92, exec. com. 1991-92. With U.S. Army, 1955-57. Mem. Coun. on Fgn. Rels.

MARKS, STANLEY J., international legal and business consultant, historian, lecturer; b. Chgo., Apr. 26, 1914; s. Samuel and Sarah Marks; m. Ethel Milgrom, Aug. 1, 1936; 1 child, Roberta E. AB, U. Ill., 1934; LLB, JD, John Marshall Law Sch., Chgo., 1937. Bar: Ill. 1939. Pres., chmn. bd. Beauti-Dor, Inc., Chgo., from 1939, Glamour Glass Door, Inc., Chgo., from 1939; legal and bus. practice Calif., from 1964; internat. and nat. legal and bus. cons. L.A., 1964—; lectr. on polit. and social/econ. events worldwide. Author: (with Ethel Marks) The Bear That Walks Like a Man, 1943, Murder Most Foul, 1967, Two Days of Infamy, 1969, Coup d'Etat!, 1970, Through Distorted Mirrors, 1974, Judaism Looks at Christianity, 1986, A Year in the Lives of the Damned, Reagn, REaganism, 1986, The 1991 U.S. Consumer Market, 1991, Yes, Americans, A Conspiracy Murdered JFK!, 1992, Jews, Judaism and the U.S., 1992, Civilization's Last Hope-Judaism, 1996, If This Be Treason!, 1996, Justice For Whom?, 1996, others; playwright: Two Days of Judgement, 1984; pub. weekly polit. newsletter Diogenes, 1984, 88. Writer Dem. Nat. Com., 1936, 40, 48, 52, 60, 91. With AUS, 1944-46. Recipient various Army decorations. Mem. Am. Acad. Polit. and Social Scis., Soc. Am. Mil. Engrs., Authors League Am., Libr. of Congress Assn., Dramatists Guild (life) Masons, Shriners. Home: 1530 S Saltair Ave Los Angeles CA 90025-2613

MARKUS, KENT RICHARD, lawyer; b. Cleve., Feb. 1, 1959; s. Richard and Carol (Slater) M.; m. Susan Mary Gilles, Apr. 15, 1987. BS, Northwestern U., 1981; JD with honors, Harvard U., 1984. Bar: Ohio 1984, U.S. Dist. Ct. (no. dist.) Ohio 1984, U.S. Ct. Appeals (6th cir.) 1986. Jud. clk. to Hon. Alvin I. Krenzler U.S. Dist. Ct. (no. dist.) Ohio, Cleve., 1984-86; litigation assoc. Gold, Rotatori, Schwartz & Gibbons, Cleve., 1986-89; transition dir. Ohio Atty. Gen. Office, Colombus, Ohio, 1990-91, first asst. atty. gen., chief of staff, 1991-93; counsel to dep. atty. gen. U.S. Dept. Justice, Washington, 1994, dep. assoc. atty. gen., 1994-95, acting asst. atty. gen., 1995—, chair counsel legal affairs, 1995-96, youth violence counselor to atty. gen, 1996—; adj. prof. law Cleveland-Marshall Coll. Law, 1987-88. Co-editor: Trial Handbook for Ohio Lawyers, 2nd edit., 1988; contbn. editor for law Webster's New World Dictionary, 3d edit., 1988. Bd. dirs., former legis. chair Handgun Control Fedn. of Ohio, 1984—; mem. adv. coun. Northwestern U. Sch. Speech, 1985—; spl. projects dir. Celeste for Gov. Com., Cleve., 1986; campaign mgr. Lee Fisher for Atty. Gen., Cleve. and Colombus, 1989-90; bd. dirs., trustee Cleve. NAACP, 1986-87; chief of staff Dem. Nat. Com., Washington, 1993-94. Named Rising Star of Dem. Party, Campaigns and Elections mag., 1991. Mem. ATLA, Cleve. Bar Assn., Ohio State Bar Assn. (former chair young lawyers divsn.), Ohio Legal Needs Implementation Com. (former chair fin. resources subcom.), Cuyahoga County Bar Assn. (mem. grievance com.). Home: 7215 MacArthur Blvd Bethesda MD 20816 Office: US Dept Justice Rm 5131 10th & Constitution Ave NW Washington DC 20530

MARKUS, LAWRENCE, retired mathematics educator; b. Hibbing, Minn., Oct. 13, 1922; s. Benjamin and Ruby (Friedman) M.; m. Lois Shoemaker, Dec. 9, 1950; children: Sylvia, Andrew. BS, U. Chgo., 1942, MS, 1946; PhD, Harvard U., 1951. Instr. meteorology U. Chgo., 1942-44; rsch. meteorologist Atomic Project, Hanford, 1944; instr. math. Harvard U., 1951-52; instr. Yale U., 1952-55; lectr. Princeton U., 1955-57; asst. prof. U. Minn., Mpls., 1957-58, assoc. prof., 1958-60, prof. math., 1960-93, assoc. chmn. dept. math., 1961-63, dir. control scis., 1964-73, Regents' prof. math., 1980-93, Regents' prof. emeritus, 1993—; dir. Control Sci. and Dynamical Systems Ctr. U. Minn., 1980-89; Leverhulme prof. control theory, dir. control theory centre U. Warwick, Eng., 1970-73, Nuffield prof. math., 1970-85, hon. prof., 1985—; regional conf. lectr. NSF, 1969; vis. prof. Yale U., Columbia U., U. Calif., U. Warsaw, 1980, Tech. Inst. Zurich, 1983, Peking U. (China), 1983; dir. conf. Internat. Centre Math., Trieste, 1974; lectr. Internat. Math. Congress, 1974, Iranian Math. Soc., 1975, Brit. Math. Soc., 1976, Japan Soc. for Promotion Sci., 1976, Royal Instn., London, 1982, U. Beer Sheva, Israel, 1983; vis. prof. U. Tokyo, 1976, Tech. U., Denmark, 1979; mem. panel Internat. Congress Mathematicians, Helsinki, 1978; sr. vis. fellow Sci. Rsch. Coun., Imperial Coll., London, 1978; mem. UNESCO sci. adv. com. Control Symposium, U. Strasbourg, France, 1980; IEEE Plenary lectr., Orlando, Fla., 1982; Sci. and Engring. Rsch. Coun. vis. prof. U. Warwick, Eng., 1982-90; Neustadt meml. lectr. U. So. Calif., 1985, prin. lectr. symposium U. Minn., 1988, dir. NSF workshop, 1989; mem. adv. bd. Office Naval Rsch., Air Force Office Sci. Rsch. Author: Flat Lorentz Manifolds, 1959, Flows on Homogeneous Spaces, 1963, Foundations of Optimal Control Theory, 1967, rev. edit., 1985, Lectures on Differentiable Dynamics, 1971, rev. edit., 1980, Generic Hamiltonian Dynamical Systems, 1974, Distributed Parameter Control System, 1991; editor Internat. Jour. Nonlinear Mechanics, 1965-73, Jour. Control, 1963-67; mem. editorial bd. Proc. Georgian Acad. Sci. Math., 1993—; contbr. articles to profl. jours. Lt. (j.g.) USNR, 1944-46. Recipient Rsch. prize Internat. Conf. Nonlinear Oscillations, Ukrainian Acad. Sci., Kiev, 1969, Festschrift volume, 1993; Fulbright fellow Paris, 1950; Guggenheim fellow Lausanne, Switzerland, 1963. Mem. Am. Math. Soc. (past mem. nat. coun.), Am. Geophys. Soc., Soc. Indsl. and Applied Math. (past nat. lectr.), Phi Beta Kappa, Sigma Xi. Office: U Minn Math Dept 127 Vincent Hall Minneapolis MN 55455

MARKUS, RICHARD M., lawyer; b. Evanston, Ill., Apr. 16, 1930; s. Benjamin and Ruby M.; m. Carol Joanne Slater, July 26, 1952; children: Linda, Scott, Kent. BS magna cum laude, Northwestern U., 1951; JD cum laude, Harvard U., 1954. Bar: D.C. 1954, Ohio 1956, Fla. 1994. Appellate atty., civil div. Dept. Justice, Washington, 1954-56; ptnr. civil litigation law firms Cleve., 1956-76, 89—; judge Cuyahoga County (Ohio) Common Pleas Ct., 1976-80, Ohio Ct. Appeals, 1981-88; instr. M.I.T., 1952-54; adj. prof. Case Western Res. U. Law Sch., 1972-78, 84-87, Cleve. State U. Law Sch., 1960-80; prof. Harvard Law Sch., 1980-81; mem. Nat. Commn. on Med. Malpractice, 1971-73; chmn. Nat. Inst. Trial Advocacy, 1978-81, trustee 1971—. Author: Trial Handbook for Ohio Lawyers, 1973, 3d edit., 1991; contbr. articles to profl. jours.; editor Harvard U. Law Rev, 1952-54. Republican nominee Justice of Ohio Supreme Ct., 1978; co-founder Nat. Advocacy Coll., 1970; bd. dirs. Lutheran Coun. Greater Cleve., 1979-81, Fairview Luth., Hosp., 1985—. Mem. Ohio State Bar Assn. (pres. 1991-92), Cuyahoga County Bar Assn., Greater Cleve. Bar Assn. (trustee 1967-70, 85-90), Assn. Trial Lawyers Am. (nat. pres. 1970-71), Ohio Acad. Trial Lawyers (pres. 1965-66), Phi Beta Kappa, Pi Mu Epsilon, Delta Sigma Rho, Phi Alpha Delta. Home: 3903 N Valley Dr Cleveland OH 44126-1716 Office: Porter Wright Morris & Arthur 925 Euclid Ave Cleveland OH 44115-1408

MARKUS, ROBERT MICHAEL, journalist; b. Chgo., Jan. 30, 1934; s. David White and Anna (Tonkonogy) M.; m. Leslie Winnifred Ator, Aug. 25, 1962; children—Catherine Mary, Patricia Anne, Michael Hughes. B.J., U. Mo., 1955. Gen. assignment reporter Moline (Ill.) Dispatch, 1955-59; successively copy editor, sports columnist, feature writer, baseball writer, coll. sports writer, hockey writer Chgo. Tribune, 1959—. Mem. Northbrook (Ill.) Caucus, 1967. Served with U.S. Army, 1956-58. Recipient Nat. Headliner award as best columnist, 1973; named Ill. Sports Writer of Year, 1970, 71, 72. Mem. Football Writers Assn. Am., Baseball Writers Assn. Am., Am. Auto Racing Writers and Broadcasters Assn., Hockey Writers Assn. Home: 402 Willow Rd Winnetka IL 60093-4132 Office: Chgo Tribune PO Box 25340 Chicago IL 60625-0340

MARKWARDT, KENNETH MARVIN, former chemical company executive; b. St. Paul, Mar. 6, 1928; s. Rudy A. and Kathryn M. (Thell) M.; m. Bernice M. Kimmel, Aug. 5, 1950; children: Ronald, Mary Ellen, Gary, Thomas, Jean. BBA, Coll. St. Thomas, 1950. With Ecolab, Inc., St. Paul, 1951-83, contr., 1961-69, v.p., contr., 1968-73, v.p., treas., sr. v.p. fin., 1973-83, also bd. dirs.; bd. advisors 1st Trust Co., St. Paul. Treas. St. Patrick's Guild, bd. dirs., 1951—; bd. dirs., sec. Health East, St. Paul. Served with AUS, 1946-47. Mem. Cath. Athletic Assn. (pres. 1956-57, dir. 1953-80, trustee 1980—), Tax Execs. (pres. Minn. chpt. 1962-63), K.C. Home: 100 Imperial Dr W Apt 304 West Saint Paul MN 55118

MARKWART, PAUL MARTIN, architect; b. Buffalo, Feb. 4, 1942; s. Herbert Martin and Irene Josephine (Pawlak) M.; m. Nancy Ott, June 29, 1964; children: Anton Martin, Heather Elizabeth. BS in Bldg. Sci., Rensselaer Poly. Inst., 1964. Registered architect, N.Y. Ohio, Pa. Draftsman Cannon Partnership, Niagara Falls, N.Y., 1966-67; office mgr. Highland & Highland Architects, Buffalo, 1967-72; dir. design Caldwell Devel. Corp., Williamsville, N.Y., 1972-74; dir. planning and design McIntosh & McIntosh P.C., Lockport, N.Y., 1974-76; chmn. Trautman Assocs., Buffalo, 1976—. Prin. works include Chem. Loading Facility, 1978. House designer Habitat for Humanity, Buffalo, 1989—. 1st lt. U.S. Army Corps Engrs., 1964-66. Mem. AIA (dir. Buffalo Western N.Y. chpt. 1976—), N.Y. State Assn. Architects, Buffalo Canoe Club, Western N.Y. Preservation Coalition. Democrat. Presbyterian. Avocation: sailing. Home: 53 Berkley Pl Buffalo NY 14209-1001 Office: Trautman Assocs 470 Franklin St Buffalo NY 14202-1302

MARKWOOD, SANDRA REINSEL, human services administrator; b. Washington, Aug. 27, 1955; d. Francis Eugene and Delores Jean (Horning) Reinsel-Kahn; m. James Scott Markwood, Aug. 4, 1984; children: Christopher Scott, Anne Meredith. BA with distinction, U. Va., 1977, M in Urban and Environ. Planning, 1979. Sr. rsch. asst. Nat. League of Cities, Washington, 1979-80; rsch. assoc./ project dir. Nat. Assn. Counties, Washington, 1980-84; asst. to county exec. Albemarle County, Charlottesville, Va., 1984-86; sr. rsch. assoc./ project dir. Nat. Assn. Counties, Washington, 1986—; exec. sec. Nat. Assn. County Aging Programs, Washington, 1986—; co-staff dir. Local Collaboration for Children and Youth; com. co-chair Generations United, Washington, 1988-90; intergovtl. liaison Nat. Hwy. Traffic Safety Adminstrn., Washington, 1989-91; chair Aging Needs Assessment Com., Charlottesville, 1985-86. Author: (handbook) Local Officials Guide to Urban Recreation, 1980, (guide) Building Support for Traffic Safety Programs, 1991; co-author: (guide) Graying of Suburbia, 1988; editor: Counties and Volunteers, Partners in Service, 1992-95; co-author: Counties Care for Kids: Programs That Work. Vol. tchr. St. Louis Cath. Sch., Alexandria, Va., 1980-83, St. Rita's Cath. Sch., Alexandria, 1987-89; vol. Jr. Friends of Campaign Ctr., Alexandria; coord. Sister Cities Exch. Program, Charlottesville, 1985. Recipient Cert. of Appreciation, Nat. Hwy. Traffic Safety Adminstrn., 1991. Mem. Women's Transp. Seminar, Smithsonian Assocs., Generations United. Roman. Catholic. Avocations: reading, jogging, walking, sailing. Home: 3106 Lot A Russell Rd Alexandria VA 22305-1742

MARLAND, ALKIS JOSEPH, leasing company executive, computer science educator, financial planner; b. Athens, Greece, Mar. 8, 1943; came to U.S., 1961, naturalized, 1974; s. Basil and Maria (Pervanides) Mouradoglou; m. Anita Louise Malone, Dec. 19, 1970; children: Andrea, Alyssa. BS, Southwestern U., 1963; MA, U. Tex., Austin, 1967; MS in Engring. Adminstrn., So. Meth. U., 1971. Cert. in data processing, enrolled agt., fund specialist, ChFC, CLU, CFP, RFC, CTP. With Sun Co., Richardson, Tex., 1968-71, Phila., 1971-76; mgr. planning and acquisitions Sun Info. Svcs. subs. Sun Co., Dallas, 1976-78; v.p. Helios Capital Corp. subs. Sun Co., Radnor, Pa., 1978-83; pres. ALKAN Leasing Corp., Wayne, Pa., 1983—, bd. dirs., 1983—; prof. dept. computer scis. and bus. adminstrn. Eastern Coll., St. David's, Pa., 1985-87; prof. math. Villanova (Pa.) U., 1987-89. Bd. dirs. Radnor Twp. Sch. Dist., 1987-91, Delaware County Intermediate Unit, 1988-91, Phila. Fin. Assn., 1989-92, Delaware Valley Soc. ICFP, 1993—. Mem. IEEE, Assn. Computing Machinery, Data Processing Mgmt. Assn., Internat. Assn. Fin. Planners, Am. Soc. CLUs and ChFC, Am. Assn. Equipment Lessors, Inst. Cert. Fin. Planners (bd. dirs. Del. Valley Soc. 1993—, v.p. mem. 1994-95, treas. 1995—), Nat. Assn. Enrolled Agts., Nat. Assn. Tax Practitioners, Nat. Assn. Pub. Accts., Fin. Analysts Phila., Phila. Fin. Assn. (sec. 1989-92, mem. award 1988, bd. dirs. 1989-92), Fgn. Policy Rsch. Inst., World Affairs Coun. Phila., Phila. Union League, Main Line C. of C., Assn. Investment Mgmt. and Rsch., Rotary (pres. Wayne club 1989-90, gov.'s rep. dist. 7450, 1990-91, 93-94), Masons (32 degree). Republican. Home: 736 Brooke Rd Wayne PA 19087-4709 Office: PO Box 8301 Radnor PA 19087-8301

MARLAS, JAMES CONSTANTINE, holding company executive; b. Chgo., Aug. 22, 1937; s. Constantine J. and Helen (Cotsirilos) M.; m. Kendra S. Graham, 1968 (div. 1971); m. Glenn Close, 1984 (div. 1987); m. Marie Nugent-Head, 1993. A.B. cum laude, Harvard U., 1959; M.A. in Jurisprudence, Oxford (Eng.) U., 1961; J.D., U. Chgo., 1963. Bar: Ill. 1963, N.Y. 1966. Assoc. firm Baker & McKenzie, London and N.Y.C., 1963-66; exec. v.p. South East Commodity Corp., N.Y.C., 1967-68; chmn. bd. Union Capital Corp., N.Y.C., 1968—; vice chmn. bd. Mickelberry's Food Products Co., N.Y.C., 1970-71; pres., dir. Mickelberry Comm. Corp., N.Y.C., 1972—; chief exec. officer Mickelberry Comm. Corp., 1973—; chmn. bd. Mickleberry Commn. Corp., 1984—; chmn. bd., CEO Newcourt Industries, Inc., 1976—; chmn. bd. dirs. Bowmar Instrument Corp., chmn. exec. com., 1983-92. Co-editor: Univ. Chgo. Law Rev, 1962-63; Contbr. articles to profl. jours. Bd. dirs. N.Y.C. Opera, Commanderie de Bordeaux, Brasenose Coll. Charitable Found. Mem. Am. Fgn. Law Assn., Young Pres.'s Orgn. Clubs: Boodle's (London); Racquet and Tennis (N.Y.C.). Office: Mickelberry Comm Corp 405 Park Ave New York NY 10022-4405

MARLATT, JERRY RONALD, lawyer; b. Vancouver, B.C., Can., Apr. 13, 1942; s. Edgerton Myron and Marion Christina (MacLeod) M.; m. Linda Susan Vaughn, Nov. 25, 1972 (div. 1985); children: Catherine Anne, Lindsey Alexandra, Christopher David. BA, U. So. Calif., 1967; JD, Southwestern U., 1977. Bar: Calif. 1977, D.C. 1979, N.Y. 1985. Systems analyst U. So. Calif., Los Angeles, 1964-72; City of Los Angeles, 1972-73, Rand Corp., Santa Monica, Calif., 1973-78; staff atty. SEC, Washington, 1978-81, spl. counsel, 1981, legal asst. to commr. P.A. Loomis, 1981-82, to commr. J.C. Treadway, 1982-84, asst. gen. counsel, 1984, assoc. Seward & Kissel, N.Y.C., 1984-87; assoc. Skadden, Arps, Slate, Meagher & Flom, N.Y.C., 1987-88; ptnr. Hunton & Williams, N.Y.C., 1988—. Assoc. editor Law Rev., 1976-77. Mem. ABA, Assn. Bar City of New York.

MARLEAU, DIANE, Canadian government official; b. Kirkland Lake, Ont., Can., June 21, 1943; d. Jean-Paul and Yvonne (Desjardins) LeBel; m. Paul C. Marleau, Aug. 3, 1963; children: Brigitte, Donald, Stéphane. Student, U. Ottawa, Ont., 1960-63; BA in Econs., Laurentian U., Sudbury, Ont., 1976. With Donald Jean Acctg. Svcs., Sudbury, 1971-75; receiver mgr. Thorne Riddell, Sudbury, 1975-76; treas. No. Regional Residential Treatment Program for Women, Sudbury, 1976-80, Com. for the Industry and Labour Adjustment Program, Sudbury, 1983; mem. transition team Ont. Premier's Office, Toronto, 1985; firm adminstr. Collins Barrow-Maheu Noiseux, Sudbury, 1985-88; M.P. from Sudbury House of Commons, Ottawa, 1988—; minister of health for Can., 1993-96; min. of public works Canada, 1996; councilor Regional Municipality of Sudbury, 1980-85, chair fin. com., 1981; alderman City of Sudbury, 1980-85; mem. No. Devel. Coun., Sudbury, 1986-88; vice chair Nat. Liberal Standing Com. on Policy, 1989; chair Ont. Liberal Caucus, 1990; apptd. nat. exec. Liberal Party Can., 1990, assoc. critic Govt. Ops., 1990, Dep. Opposition Whip, 1991, assoc. critic Fin., 1992; vice chair standing com. fin., 1992. Chmn. fund-raising Canadian Cancer Soc., Sudbury, 1987-88; co-chmn. Laurentian Hosp. Cancer Care Svcs. fund-raising campaign, Sudbury, 1988; chair bd. govs. Cambrian Coll., 1987-88, bd. govs., 1983-88; mem. Sudbury and Dist. Health Unit Bd., 1981-82; mem. fin. com., bd. dirs. Laurentian Hosp., 1981-85; chair Can. Games for the Physically Disabled, 1983; apptd. Ont. Adv. Coun. Women's Issues, 1984. Mem. Sudbury Bus. and Profl. Women Club. (named Woman of the Day 1989). Avocations: playing piano, gardening, cooking. Office: Pubilc Works & Gov't Serv, 18A1 Place du Portage Phs III11 Laurier, Hull, PQ Canada K1A 0S5 also: 36 Elgin St, Sudbury, ON Canada P3C 5B4*

MARLEAU, ROBERT, parliamentary clerk; b. Cornwall, Ont., Can., Apr. 27, 1948; m. Ann Spilsbury; children: Stéphane, Kristian. Grad., Cornwall Classic Coll., 1967, U. Ottawa, 1969. French high sch. tchr., 1969-70; com. clk. Coms. and Pvt. Legis. Br., 1970-74, prin. clk., 1981-83; dep. sec. gen., Parliamentary Relations Secretariat Can. Ho. Commons, Ottawa, 1974-81, clk. asst., 1983-87, clk., 1987—; adv. bd. faculty of adminstrn. U. Ottawa. Decorated comdr. Ordre de la Pléiade. Mem. Can. Study Parliament Group, Can. Soc. Clks. at the Table, Assemblée Sec. Gén. Parlements Membres l'Assemblée Internationale des Parlementaires de Langue Française, Ordre de la Pléiade (comdr.), Sovereign Mil. Order Malta (knight magistral grace), Forum for Young Canadians (dir., 125th medal 1992). Office: Ho of Commons, Ottawa, ON Canada K1A 0A6

MARLEN, JAMES S., chemical-plastics-building materials manufacturing company executive; b. Santiago, Chile, Mar. 14, 1941; came to U.S., 1961; grad. in Chem. Engring. (tennis athletic scholar), U. Ala., 1965; MBA, U. Akron, 1971; m. Carolyn S. Shields, Jan. 23, 1965; children: James, Andrew, John. With GenCorp., Akron, Ohio, 1965-93, engring., marketing and gen. mgmt. positions domestic and internat. ops., 1965-76; divsn. pres. GTR Coated Fabrics Co., 1977-80, group pres. 1980-87; pres., GenCorp Polymer Products, Akron, Ohio, 1988—, v.p., GenCorp, Akron, 1988-93; pres., CEO Ameron, Inc., Pasadena, Calif., 1993—, bd. dirs., Ameron, Inc., chmn. bd. dirs., pres. and CEO, 1995—, A. Schulman, Inc., Tamco Steel, Gifford-Hill, gen., hon. chmn. Nat. Inventors Hall of Fame Induction, 1993. Bd. dirs. YMCA Met. L.A., The Employers Group of Calif., Town Hall of L.A., gov.; mem. The Beavers; mem. L.A. Sports Coun. Mem. Am. Mgmt. Assn. (mem. pres. assn.), Chem. Mfrs. Assn. (past pres.), Assocs. Caltech, Calif. C. of C., L.A. C. of C. (dir.), Portage Country Club (Akron, Ohio), Calif. Club. (L.A.), Annandale Golf Club (Pasadena). Office: Ameron Inc 245 S Los Robles Ave Pasadena CA 91101-2820

MARLER, ADDIE KAREN, elementary school educator; b. Dothan, Ala., Nov. 5, 1950; d. James Luther and Beulah Lee (Clenney) Savell; m. Thomas Franklin Marler, June 15, 1967; children: Jeffery, Jamie, Pamela. AA, Pasco Hernado C.C., 1981; BA, St. Leo Coll., 1985; postgrad., U. South Fla. 6th and 7th grade lang. arts tchr. Moore Mickens Mid. Sch., Dade City, Fla., 1985-86, 7th grade gifted class tchr., 1985-86; developmental kindergarten tchr. Pasco Elem. Sch., Dade City, 1986-88, tchr. 6th grade self-contained class, 1988-89, 1st grade tchr., 1989-90, 1st/2d grade tchr., 1990-91, primary house K-2d grade tchr., 1991-93, intermediate house 3d-5th grade tchr., 1993-94; migrant lead tchr. Pasco Elem. Sch., 1990-92, ESL tchr., 1994-95, ESOL resource tchr., 1994-96; dist. curriculum writer Pasco County Schs., 1991-93; ednl. cons., 1990—. Mem. adv. bd. Fla. League of Tchrs./Fla. Dept. Edn.; mem. Heritage Arts Assn., Dade City. Named 20th Anniversary Ambassador, Edn. Ctr. N.C., 1993-94. Mem. Fla. Assn. Childhood Edn., Alpha Delta Kappa (historian, scholarship chmn. 1990-93 Alpha Phi chpt.). Republican. Baptist. Avocations: interior decorating, shopping, audio books, elderly advocacy. Office: Pasco Elem 37350 Florida Ave Dade City FL 33525-4041

MARLETT, DE OTIS LORING, retired management consultant; b. Indpls., Apr. 19, 1911; s. Peter Loring and Edna Grace (Lombard) M.; m. Ruth Irene Pillar, Apr. 10, 1932 (dec. Feb., 1969); children: De Otis Neal, Marilynn Ruth; m. Marie Manning Ostrander, May 1, 1970 (dec. Apr. 1982); m. Peggie P. Whittlesey, Jan. 15, 1983 (dec. Oct., 1993); m. Estelle B. Brewer, Sept. 23, 1994. B.A., M.A., U. Wis., 1934; postgrad., Northwestern U., (part time), 1934-39, Harvard U.; postgrad. (Littauer fellow in econs. and govt.), 1946-47. CPA, Wis., 1935. Staff mem. Ill. Commerce Commn., 1934-39; lectr. in econs. and pub. utilities Northwestern U., (part time), 1936-39; staff mem. Bonneville Power Adminstrn., U.S. Dept. Interior, 1939-45, asst. adminstr., 1945-52; acting adminstr. Def. Electric Power Adminstrn., 1950-51; asst. to v.p., gen. mgr. Dicalite and Perlite divs. Great Lakes Carbon Corp., 1952-53; v.p., also gen. mgr. Dicalite, Perlite, Mining and Minerals divs. Gt. Lakes Carbon Corp., 1953-62, v.p. property investment dept., 1962-81; pres., chief exec. officer Great Lakes Properties, Inc., 1981-83, ret., 1983; past pres., dir. Rancho Palos Verdes Corp., G.L.C. Bldg. Corp., Del Amo Energy Co., Torrance Energy Co.; former mem. L.A. arbitration panel N.Y. Stock Exch. Contbr. articles and reports on public utility regulation, operation and mgmt. to profl. jours. Past bd. dirs. United Cerebral Palsy Assn. Los Angeles County; bd. dirs., past co-chmn. So. Calif. region NCCJ, mem. nat. trustee, mem. nat. exec. bd., nat. protestant co-chmn., 1987-90; past mem. Orthopaedic Hosp. Adv. Coun.; past trustee City of Hope; past pres., dir. Los Angeles area coun., past chmn. relationships com., past pres. Sunshine area, pres. Western region Boy Scouts Am., 1978-81, nat. exec. bd., 1978-88, past mem. nat. exec. com., past chmn. properties com., chmn. logistics for world jamboree delegation to Australia, 1987-88; past trustee Nat. Scouting Mus.; mem. internat. com. Baden Powell fellow World Scouting Found., 1984; past mem. Western Govs. Mining Adv. Coun., Calif. State Mining Bd.; bd. govs. Western div. Am. Mining Congress, chmn., 1962-63; incorporator, past pres., dir. Torrance Meml. Med. Center Health Care Found.; region III dir., mem. corp. adminstrn. and fin. com., Los Angeles United Way. Recipient Disting. Service medal U.S. Dept. Interior, 1952; named knight Order of Crown Belgium; commd. Ky. Col.; recipient Silver Beaver, Silver Antelope, Silver Buffalo awards Boy Scouts Am., 1984. Mem. AIME, AICPA, Fin. Execs. Inst., L.A. World Affairs Coun., Wis. Alumni Assn., Perlit Inst. (past pres., dir.), L.A. C. of C. (past dir., chmn. mining com.), Mining Assn. So. Calif. (past pres., dir.), Calif. Mine Operators Assn. (past dir.), Bldg. Industry Assn. So. Calif., Calif. Club, Portuguese Bend Club (past pres.), Palos Verdes Bay Club (past v.p.), Phi Kappa Phi, Beta Gamma Sigma, Phi Beta Kappa, Beta Alpha Psi, Lambda Alpha Internat. Democrat. Home: 32759 Seagate Dr Apt 204 Rancho Palos Verdes CA 90275

MARLETT, JUDITH ANN, nutritional sciences educatr, researcher; b. Toledo. BS, Miami U., Oxford, Ohio, 1965; PhD, U. Minn., 1972; postgrad., Harvard U., 1973-74. Registered dietitian. Therapeutic and metabolic unit dietitian VA Hosp., Mpls., 1966-67; spl. instr. in nutrition Simmons Coll., Boston, 1973-74; asst. prof. U. Wis., Madison, 1975-80, assoc. prof. dept. nutritional scis., 1981-84, prof. dept. nutritional scis., 1984—; cons. U.S. AID, Leyte, Philippines, 1983; acting dir. dietetic program dept. Nutritional Scis. U. Wis., 1977-78, dir., 1985-89; cons. grain, drug and food cos., 1985—, adv. bd. U. Ariz. Clin. Cancer Ctr., 1987-95; sci. bd. advisors Am. Health Found., 1988—; reviewer NIH, 1982—. Mem. editl. bd. Jour. Sci. of Food and Agrl., 1989—, Jour. Food Composition and Analysis, 1994—; contbr. articles to profl. jours. Mem. AAAS, NIH (Diabetes amd Digestive and Kidney Disease spl. grant rev. com. 1992-96), Am. Inst. Nutrition, Am. Dietetic Assn., Am. Soc. Clin. Nutrition, Inst. Food Technologists, Am. Assn. Cereal Chemists. Achievements include research and international speaker on human nutrition and disease, dietary fiber and gastrointestinal function. Office: U Wis Dept Nutritional Sci 1415 Linden Dr Madison WI 53706-1527

MARLETTE, DOUGLAS NIGEL, editorial cartoonist, comic strip creator; b. Greensboro, N.C., Dec. 6, 1949; m. Melinda Hartley; 1 child, Jackson Douglas. Student, Fla. State U. Editorial cartoonist The Charlotte (N.C.) Observer, 1972-87, The Atlanta Constn., 1987-89, N.Y. Newsday, N.Y.C., 1989—; syndicated to over 200 newspapers through Creators Syndicate, Inc., L.A., 1988—. Creator syndicated comic strip Kudzu; works reproduced in Time, Newsweek, Christian Century, Rolling Stone, Der Spiegel, Esquire mags., also textbooks and encys.; author: The Emperor Has No Clothes, If You Can't Say Something Nice, Drawing Blood, Kudzu, 1982, Preacher, The Wit and Wisdom of Will B. Dunn, 1984, Just A Simple Country Preacher, 1985, It's a Dirty Job But Somebody Has To Do It, There's No Business Like Soul Business, 1987, Chocolate is My Life, Shred This Book, I Am Not a Televangelist, Doublewide with a View, 1989, In Your Face, A Cartoonist At Work, 1991, (children's book) The Before and After Book, Even White Boys Get the Blues, 1992, Gone With the Kudzu, 1995; co-wrote screenplay "EX"; TV appearances include ABC's Nightline, Good Morning Am., Today Show, CBS Morning News, Nat. Pub. Radio's Morning Edition; syndicated animated editorial cartoons NBC Today Show. Nieman fellow, 1st for editorial cartoonist, Harvard U.; recipient Nat. Headliners award 1983, 88, Robert F. Kennedy Meml. award 1984, Sigma Delta Chi Disting. Service award 1986, First Amendment award, 1986, 1st Pl. award John Fischetti Editorial Cartoon Competition, 1986, The Golden Plate Acad. of Achievement award, 1991; named to Register of Men and Women Who Are Changing Am., Esquire Mag., 1984; recipient Pulitzer Prize for editorial cartooning Newsday, 1988; 1st Prize, John Fischetti Editorial Cartoon Competition, 1992. Office: NY Newsday 2 Park Ave New York NY 10016-5603 also: care Creators Syndicate Inc 5777 W Century Blvd Ste 700 Los Angeles CA 90045-5677

MARLEY, EVERETT ARMISTEAD, JR., lawyer; b. Memphis, June 15, 1933; s. Everett Armistead and Elizabeth (Alexander) M.; m. Carolyn Marie McKay, June 21, 1958; children: Elizabeth Ann, Jill Marie. B.A. in Econs., Rice Inst., 1955; LL.B., U. Tex.-Austin, 1959. Bar: Tex.; cert. specialist in estate planning State Bar of Tex., 1977. C.P.A., Tex. Assoc. Butler & Binion L.L.P., Houston, 1959-68; ptnr. Butler & Binion, L.L.P., 1968—. Trustee Schreiner Coll., Kerrville, Tex., 1980-88, San Francisco Theol. Sem., San Anselmo, Calif., 1991—; elder St. Philip Presbyn. Ch., Houston. Fellow Am. Coll. Trust and Estate Counsel; mem. ABA. Presbyterian. Avocation: bass fishing. Office: Butler & Binion LLP 1600 First Interstate Bank Pl Houston TX 77002

MARLIN, ALICE TEPPER, research organization administrator; b. Long Branch, N.J., Aug. 10, 1944; d. Walter L. and Grace A. (Comins) Tepper; m. John Tepper Marlin, Sept. 25, 1971; children—John Joseph, Caroline. Ed. The Baldwin Sch., 1962; B.A., in Econs., Wellesley Coll., 1966; postgrad. in Bus. Adminstrn., N.Y.U. Securities analyst Drexel Burnham, N.Y.C., 1966-68; scheduler, advance planner McCarthy for Pres. Campaign, 1968; fin. analyst T. O'Connel Mgmt. and Research, N.Y.C., 1968-69; exec. dir. Council on Econ. Priorities, N.Y.C., 1969—; bd. dirs. Gathering Internat. Families Together, N.Y.C., 1982—; chmn. investment com. fund for Constl. Govt., Washington, 1983—; trustee Winston Found., N.Y.C., 1985—; v.p. Social Investment Forum. Author: Good Business: Shopping for a Better World, 1986. Editor: (monthly) Council Econ. Priorities Newsletter; editor more than 30 books. Contbr. articles to profl. jours. Mem., Com. for Nat. Security, Club of Rome, Women's Forum. Recipient Inventory of Hope award Saturday Review, disting. alumnae award The Baldwin Sch.; named woman of Yr., Mademoiselle mag.; Point fellow, 1972; Japan Soc. Leadership fellow, 1985-86. Democrat. Unitarian. Club: Harvard (N.Y.C.). Avocations: tennis; gardening. Address: Council on Econ Priorities 30 Irving Pl New York NY 10003-2303

MARLIN, KENNETH BRIAN, information and software company executive; b. N.Y.C., Feb. 2, 1955; s. Elmer David and Edith Barbara (Stern) M.; m. Marcia A. Levis, Dec. 15, 1988; 1 child, Victoria Rae. BA, U. Calif., Irvine, 1977; MBA, UCLA, 1979; advanced profl. cert., NYU, 1981. Mgr. Dun & Bradstreet Corp., N.Y.C., 1981-85; v.p. Dun & Bradstreet Internat., N.Y.C., 1985-88; sr. v.p. fin. info. group Dun & Bradstreet Corp., N.Y.C., 1988-92; pres. Telekurs (N.Am.), Inc., Stamford, Conn., 1992-95; pres., CEO Telesphere Corp., N.Y.C., 1995—. Trustee Hurricane Island Outward Bound Sch., Rockland, Maine, 1990—; bd. mem., vice chmn. N.Y. chpt. Red Cross of Greater N.Y., N.Y.C., 1991—. Office: Telesphere Corp One State St Plz New York NY 10004

MARLIN, RICHARD, lawyer; b. N.Y.C., June 1, 1933; s. Edward and Lillian (Milstein) M.; m. Merrel Pincus, June 12, 1955 (div. 1972); children: John F., Elizabeth; m. Jenesta Rutherford, July 29, 1974 (div. 1981); m. Caroline Mary Hirsch Magnus, Nov. 1, 1981. BA magna cum laude, Yale U., 1955, LLB, 1958; LLM, NYU, 1964. Bar: N.Y. 1959, Fla. 1978. Law clk. to presiding justice U.S. Dist. Ct. Conn., New Haven, 1958-59; assoc. Cleary, Gottlieb, Steen & Hamilton, N.Y.C., 1959-62, Wien Lane & Klein, N.Y.C., 1962-64; ptnr. Mnuchin Moss & Marlin, N.Y.C., 1964-66, Marshall, Bratter, Greene, Allison & Tucker, N.Y.C., 1966-79; sr. ptnr. Kramer, Levin, Naftalis, Nessen, Kamin & Frankel, N.Y.C., 1979—. Bd. editors Yale Law Jour. Mem. ABA, N.Y. State Bar Assn., Assn. Bar City N.Y. (corp. law com., chmn. subcom.), N.Y. County Lawyers' Assn., Glen Oaks Club (Old Westbury, N.Y.) (bd. govs. 1979-85, 92-94), Phi Beta Kappa. Office: Kramer Levin Naftalis et al 919 3rd Ave New York NY 10022

MARLIN, STERLING, professional race car driver. Winner Daytona 500, 1994, 1995. Office: NASCAR PO Box 2875 Daytona Beach FL 32120-2875*

MARLING, LYNWOOD BRADLEY, lawyer; b. Cin., Apr. 17, 1944; s. John Bertron Marling and Florence Mary (Kelly) Lyman;m. Patricia Lynne Coté, June 13, 1981; children: Burke, Brady, Dustin. B Ceramic Engring., Ga. Inst. Tech., 1967; MBA, Stanford U., 1969; JD, Tex. Tech U., 1976. Bar: Tex. 1976, U.S. Dist. Ct. (no. dist.) Tex. 1977; cert. in family law Tex. Bd. Legal Specialization. Distbn. cons. Jos. Schlitz Brewing Co., Milw., 1969-71; pres., owner Marling Industries, Lubbock, Tex., 1971-74; pvt. practice, Hurst, 1981-88; ptnr. Caston and Marling, Hurst, Tex., 1976-81, 88—; legal cons. St. John the Apostle Sch., Ft. Worth, 1982—. Contbr. articles to legal jours. Mem. St. John the Apostle Sch. Bd., 1982-84; campaign mgr. Robert Caston for State Rep., Tarrant County, Tex., 1980, Rick Barton for Mayor, Bedford, Tex., 1992. Recipient svc. award St. John the Apostle Sch., 1988. Mem. ABA, State Bar Tex. (coll. 1987—), Tarrant County Bar Assn., N.E. Tarrant County Bar Assn. (pres. 1990-92), Soto Grande Tennis Club (Outstanding Mem. award 1980). Avocations: snow skiing, tennis, officiating high school football, public speaking. Office: 1848 Norwood Plaza Ct Ste 214 Hurst TX 76054-3752

MARLOW, JAMES ALLEN, lawyer; b. Crossville, Tenn., May 23, 1955; s. Dewey Harold and Anna Marie (Hinch) M.; m. Sabine Klein, June 9, 1987; children: Lucas Allen, Eric Justin. BA, U. Tenn., 1976, JD, 1979; postgrad., Air War Coll., Maxwell AFB, Ala., 1990-91, Internat. Studienzentrum, Heidelberg, Fed. Republic Germany, 1985-86. Bar: Ga. 1979, D.C. 1980, Tenn. 1980, U.S. Dist. Ct. (mid. dist.) Tenn. 1984, U.S. Ct. Fed. Claims 1987, U.S. Ct. Internat. Trade 1988, U.S. Tax Ct. 1987, U.S. Ct. Mil. Appeals 1980, U.S. Ct. Appeals (fed. cir.) 1987, U.S. Supreme Ct. 1987. Assoc. Carter & Assocs., Frankfurt, Fed. Republic Germany, 1984-85; chief internat. law USAF, Sembach AFB, Fed. Republic Germany, 1986—; adj. prof. Embry-Riddle Aero. U., Kaiserslauten, Fed. Republic Germany,

1985—; judge advocate USAFR, Ramstein Air Base, Fed. Republic Germany, 1984—. Capt. USAF, 1980-84. Mem. Phi Beta Kappa. Avocations: genealogy, basketball, chess, German and Spanish languages. Home: RR 8 Box 385 Crossville TN 38555-9058 Office: 17 AF/JA Unit 4065 APO AE 09136-4065

MARLOWE, EDWARD, research company executive; b. N.Y.C., May 5, 1935; children: Shari Marlowe Kasten, Steven Richard. B.S., Columbia U., 1956, M.S., 1958; Ph.D., U. Md.-Balt., 1962. Research assoc. Merck, Sharp & Dohme Research Lab., West Point, Pa., 1962-64; sr. scientist Ortho Pharm. Corp. div. Johnson & Johnson, Raritan, N.J., 1964-67; dir. research and devel. Whitehall Labs. div. Am. Home Products Corp., Hammonton, N.J., 1967-72; v.p. research and devel. Plough Products div. Schering-Plough Corp., Memphis, 1972-81; v.p. research and devel., consumer products group Warner-Lambert Co., Morris Plains, N.J., 1981-83, pres. consumer products div. rsch. and devel., 1983-91, v.p., 1984-91, v.p. parent Co.; v.p. R&D Clairol Inc., Stamford, Conn., 1992—. Contbr. articles to profl. publs. Bd. dirs. Lowenstein Found., Overlook Hosp., 1985-94. Recipient award Skin Cancer Found., 1979; Pfizer fellow, 1958; Robert Lincoln McNeil fellow, 1961. Mem. Am. Pharm. Assn., Acad. Pharm. Scis., Soc. Cosmetic Chemists, Indsl. Rsch. Inst., Cosmetic, Fragrance and Toiletry Assn. (sci. affairs com. 1976-79), Non-Prescription Drug Mfrs. Assn. (sci. affairs com. 1976-91, policy planning subcom. 1977-91, bd. dirs. 1981-83), N.Y. Acad. Sci., Sigma Xi, Rho Chi. Home: 56 Kean Rd Short Hills NJ 07078-1430 Office: Clairol Inc 2 Blachley Rd Stamford CT 06902-4149

MARLOWE, MARY LOUISE, lawyer; b. Pasadena, Calif., Sept. 3, 1957; d. Robert Emmet and Mary Louise (Gelera) Coughlan); m. Daniel Robert Marlowe, Aug. 16, 1986; children: Benjamin, Marisa. BS, James Madison U., 1979; JD, George Mason U., 1983. Bar: N.Mex. 1984. Law clerk tax div. Dept. Justice, Washington, 1979-81, Nat. Assn. Mfrs., Washington, 1982-83; assoc. producer The McLaughlin Group, Washington, 1983-84; asst. atty. gen. N.Mex. Atty. Gen's Office, Santa Fe, 1984-87; ptnr. Marlowe & Marlowe, Taos, N.Mex., 1987-90; gen. counsel Securities Div. State of N.Mex., Santa Fe, 1990; ptnr. The Marlowe Law Firm, Santa Fe, 1990—. Mem. ABA, N.Mex. State Bar Assn. Democrat. Roman Catholic. Avocations: mountain biking. Office: Marlowe Law Firm 200 W Marcy St Ste 216 Santa Fe NM 87501-2033

MARMADUKE, JOHN H., retail executive; b. Amarillo, Tex., May 6, 1947; m. Martha Ann Harter, July 29, 1975; children: Margaret, Owen, Samuel. Student, Amarillo Coll., 1965-67; BBA in Fin., U. Tex., Austin, 1969. Advt. mgr., salesman Western Merchandisers, Inc., Amarillo, 1969-73; pres., dir., chief exec. officer Western Merchandisers, Inc., 1982-94; v.p. Hastings Books & Records, Inc., Amarillo, 1973-76; pres., dir., chief exec. officer Hastings Books & Records, Inc., 1976—; pres., Gift of Music Found., 1982-84. Past bd. dirs. Amarillo Art Ctr.; bd. dirs. Ctr. for Non-Profit Mgmt., Amarillo, 1988—, Amarillo Area Found., 1989; chmn. Don & Sybil Harrington Cancer Ctr., Amarillo, 1988-91. Recipient spl. merit award, Internat. Music Industry Conf., Berlin, 1982, Golden Nail award, Amarillo, 1987; named Vol. of Yr., Panhandle chpt. Tex. Multiple Sclerosis assn., 1988. Mem. Nat. Assn. Recording Merchandisers (pres. 1981-82). Republican. Roman Catholic. Avocations: skiing, fly fishing, cooking, travel, racquetball. Office: Hastings Books Music & Video Inc PO Box 35350 Amarillo TX 79120-5350

MARMARELIS, VASILIS ZISSIS, engineering educator, author, consultant; b. Mytilini, Greece, Nov. 16, 1949; came to U.S., 1972; s. Zissis P. and Elpis V. (Galinos) M. Diploma in elec. and mech. engring., Nat. Tech. U. of Athens, Greece, 1972; MS in Info. Sci., Calif. Inst. Tech., 1973, PhD in Engring. Sci., 1976. Rsch. fellow Calif. Inst. Tech., Pasadena, 1976-78; asst. prof. U. So. Calif., L.A., 1978-83, assoc. prof., 1983-88, prof., 1988—, also dir. biomed. simulations resource, 1985—, chmn. dept. biomed. engring., 1990—; pres. Multispec Corp., L.A., 1986—. Author: Analysis of Physiological Systems, 1978, translated in Russian 1981, translated in Chinese 1990; Advanced Methods of Physiological Systems Modeling, vol. I, 1987, vol. II, 1989, vol. III, 1994; editor: Annals of Biomed. Engring.; contbr. numerous articles to profl. jours. Mem. AAAS, IEEE, Internat. Fedn. Automatic Control, N.Y. Acad. Scis., Biomed. Engring. Soc., Neural Networks Soc. Office: U So Calif OHE 500 Los Angeles CA 90089-1451

MARMAS, JAMES GUST, retired businees educator, retired college dean; b. Virginia, Minn., July 11, 1929; s. Gust George and Angela (Fatili) M.; m. Ruth Phyllis Leinonen, May 23, 1952; children—James Matthew, Lynn Marie, Brenda Kay. B.S., St. Cloud (Minn.) State Coll., 1951; M.A., U. Minn., 1956; Ed.D., Stanford, 1961. Tchr. bus. Littlefork (Minn.) High Sch., 1951-53, Lake City (Minn.) High Sch., 1953-55, Austin (Minn.) High Sch., 1955-59; asst. prof. bus. edn. Los Angeles State Coll., 1961-62; chmn. dept. bus. edn., dir. Center Econ. Edn., St. Cloud State Coll., 1962-66; dean Coll. of Bus. St. Cloud State Coll. (Sch. Bus.), 1966-87; bd. dirs. Ins. and Savs. and Loan. Author articles in field. Bd. dirs., mem. exec. com. Minn. Council Econ. Edn.; bd. dirs. St. Cloud (Minn.) Econ. Devel. Ptnrship., chmn. research and planning com. (sec., bd. dirs.). Mem. Nat. Bus. Edn. Assn., Minn. Bus. Edn. Assn., N. Central Bus. Edn. Assn. (2d v.p.), Midwest Bus. Adminstrn. Assn., St. Cloud C. of C., Phi Delta Kappa, Delta Pi Epsilon (nat. research com.), Beta Gamma Sigma. Club: Rotary (pres. St. Cloud). Home: 13215 County Road 4 N Nisswa MN 56468-8514

MARMER, NANCY, editor; b. N.Y.C., Nov. 19, 1932; d. Carl and Frances Marmer; m. Gerald Jay Goldberg, Jan. 23, 1954; 1 child, Robert. BA magna cum laude, Queens Coll., 1954; postgrad., U. Minn., 1954-57, UCLA, 1968-71. L.A. corr. Art Internat., 1965-67; West Coast editor Artforum, 1976-77; sr. editor Art in America, N.Y.C., 1979-81, exec. editor, 1981-83, book rev. editor, 1983—, mng. editor, 1983—; lectr. Mellon seminar R.I. Sch. Design, 1983; lectr. art criticism Visual Arts dept. U. Calif., San Diego, 1978; faculty expository writing Dept. English, U. Minn., 1954-57. Author: The Modern Critical Spectrum, 1962; contbr. numerous articles to profl. jours.; art critic/reviewer for Art in America, Art Internat., Artforum, L.A. Times. Recipient Samuel Kress Found. Award in Art History; Nat. endowment for the Arts fellow in art criticism. Mem. Phi Beta Kappa. Office: Art in America 575 Broadway New York NY 10012

MARMET, PAUL, physicist; b. Levis, Que., Can., May 20, 1932; s. Albert and Corinne (Filteau) M.; m. Jacqueline Cote, June 6, 1959; children—Louis, Marie, Nicolas, Frederic. B.Sc., Laval U., Quebec, Que., 1956, D.Sc., 1960. Research asst. Commonwealth Sci. and Inds. Research Orgn., Melbourne, Australia, 1960-61; asst. prof. physics Laval U., 1961-66, assoc. prof., 1966-70, prof., 1970-84; sr. research officer Herzberg Inst. Astrophysics, 1984-91; prof. physics dept. U. Ottawa, 1991—; vis. prof. U. Liège, Belgium, 1967; com. mem. NRC Can.; bd. dirs. Atomic Energy Control Bd. of Can., 1979-84. Author: (with others) Case Studies in Atomic Physics I, 1969, A New Non-Doppler Redshift, 1981, Absurdities in Modern Physics: A Solution, 1993; contbr. (with others) numerous articles to internat. sci. jours. Recipient Sci. prize Province Que., 1962; Royal Soc. Can. Rutherford Meml. fellow Melbourne, 1960; decorated officer Order of Can. Fellow Royal Soc. Can.; mem. AAAS, Can. Assn. Physicists (pres. 1981-82, Herzberg medal 1971), Am. Phys. Soc., Royal Astron. Soc. Can. (Svc. award 1977), Assn. canadienne-francaise pour l'avancement des scis. (Parizeau medal 1976). Patentee energy analyser of charged particules. Office: Univ Ottawa, Physics Dept, Ottawa, ON Canada K1N 6N5

MARMION, WILLIAM HENRY, retired bishop; b. Houston, Oct. 8, 1907; s. Charles Gresham and Katherine (Rankin) M.; m. Mabel Dougherty Nall, Dec. 28, 1935; children: William Henry, Roger Mills Nall. B.A., Rice U., 1929; M.Div., Va. Theol. Sem., 1932, D.D. (hon.), 1954. Ordained to ministry Episc. Ch., 1932. Priest-in-charge St. James, Taylor, Tex., and Grace Ch., Georgetown, Tex., 1932-35; asso. rector St. Mark's Ch., San Antonio, 1935-38; rector St. Mary's-on-the-Highlands, Birmingham, Ala., 1938-50, St. Andrew's Ch., Wilmington, Del., 1950-54; bishop Episcopal Diocese of Southwestern Va., Roanoke, 1954-79, ret., 1979; Former dir. diocesan camps for young people in Tex. and Ala., headed diocesan youth work, several yrs; dep. to Gen. Conv. Episcopal Ch., 1943, 46, alternate dep., 1949, 52; del. to Provincial Synod; mem. exec. council Episcopal Ch., 1963-69; chmn. Ala. Com. on Interracial Cooperation, 4 yrs. Trustee Va. Theol. Sem., Va. Episc. Sch., St. Paul's Coll.; pres. Appalachian Peoples Svc. Orgn.; interim warden Coll. of Preachers, 1981-82, diocesan coord. of pastoral ministry to retired clergy and families, 1990—. Home: 2730 Avenham Ave SW Roanoke VA 24014-1527

MARMOR, JUDD, psychiatrist, educator; b. London, May 1, 1910; came to U.S., 1911, naturalized, 1916; s. Clement K. and Sarah (Levene) M.; m. Katherine Stern, May 1, 1938; 1 son, Michael Franklin. AB, Columbia U., 1930, MD, 1933; DHL, Hebrew Union Coll., 1972. Diplomate: Am. Bd. Psychiatry and Neurology, Nat. Bd. Med. Examiners. Intern St. Elizabeth Hosp., Washington, 1933-35; resident neurologist Montefiore Hosp., N.Y.C., 1935-37; psychiatrist Bklyn. State Hosp., 1937; psychoanalytic tng. N.Y. Psychoanalytic Inst., N.Y.C., 1937-41; pvt. practice psychiatry, psychoanalysis and neurology N.Y.C., 1937-46, L.A., 1946—; instr. assoc. in neurology Columbia Coll. Physicians and Surgeons, 1938-40; adj. neurologist, neurologist-in-charge clinic Mt. Sinai Hosp., N.Y.C., 1939-46; lectr. New Sch. Social Rsch., N.Y.C., 1942-43; instr. Am. Inst. Psychoanalysis, N.Y.C., 1943; lectr. psychiatry N.Y. Med. Coll., 1944-46; lectr. social welfare UCLA, 1948-49, vis. prof. social welfare, 1949-64, clin. prof. psychiatry sch. medicine, 1953-80, adj. prof. psychiatry, 1980—; vis. prof. psychology U. So. Calif., 1946-49; tng. analyst, also pres. So. Calif. Psychoanalytic Inst., 1955-57; sr. attending psychiatrist L.A. County Gen. Hosp., 1954—; dir. divs. psychiatry Cedars-Sinai Med. Ctr., L.A., 1965-72; Franz Alexander prof. psychiatry U. So. Calif. Sch. Medicine, 1972-80, emeritus, 1980—; sr. cons. regional office social svc. VA, L.A., 1946-50; cons. psychiatry Brentwood VA Hosp., Calif., 1955-65; mem. Coun. Mental Health of Western Interstate Commn. Higher Edn., 1966-72. Editor: Sexual Inversion-The Multiple Roots of Homosexuality, Modern Psychoanalysis: New Directions and Perspectives, Psychiatry in Transition: Selected Papers of Judd Marmor, Homosexual Behavior: A Modern Reappraisal; (with S. Woods) The Interface Between the Psychodynamic and Behavioral Therapies, Psychiatrists & Their Patients: A National Study of Private Office Practice; (with S. Eisenstein and N.A. Levy) The Diadic Transaction: An Investigation into the Nature of the Psychotherapeutic Process; (with P. Nardi and D. Sanders) Growing Up Before Stonewall; mem. editl. bd. Am. Jour. Psychoanalysis, Contemporary Psychoanalysis, Archives Sexual Behavior; contbr. articles in field to profl. jours. Served as sr. attending surgeon USPHS USNR, 1944-45. Fellow Am. Psychiat. Assn. (life mem., pres. 1975-76), N.Y. Acad. Medicine (life mem.), Am. Acad. Psychoanalysis (pres. 1965-66), Am. Orthopsychiat. Assn. (dir. 1968-71), AAAS, Am. Coll. Psychiatrists; mem. AMA, Calif. Med. Assn., Group for Advancement Psychiatry (dir. 1968-70, pres. 1973-75), Am. Fund for Psychiatry (dir. 1955-57), So. Calif. Psychiat. Soc., So. Calif. Psychoanalytic Soc. (pres. 1960-61), Am. Psychoanalytic Assn., Los Angeles County Med. Soc., Phi Beta Kappa, Alpha Omega Alpha. Home: 655 Sarbonne Rd Los Angeles CA 90077-3214 Office: 1100 Glendon Ave Ste 921 Los Angeles CA 90024-3513

MARMOR, MICHAEL FRANKLIN, ophthalmologist, educator; b. N.Y.C., Aug. 10, 1941; s. Judd and Katherine (Stern) M.; m. C. Jane Breeden, Dec. 20, 1968; children: Andrea K., David J. AB, Harvard U., 1962, MD, 1966. Diplomate Am. Bd. Ophthalmology. Med. intern UCLA Med. Ctr., 1967; resident in ophthalmology Mass. Eye and Ear Infirmary, Boston, 1970-73; asst. prof. ophthalmology U. Calif. Sch. Medicine, San Francisco, 1973-74; asst. prof. surgery (ophthalmology) Stanford (Calif.) U. Sch. Medicine, 1974-80, assoc. prof., 1980-86, prof., 1986—, head. div. ophthalmalogy, 1984-88, chmn. dept., 1988-92, dir. Basic Sci. Course Ophthalmology, 1993—; mem. assoc. faculty program in human biology Stanford U., 1982—; chief ophthalmology sect. VA Med. Ctr., Palo Alto, Calif., 1974-84; mem. sci. adv. bd. No. Calif. Soc. to Prevent Blindness, 1984-92, Calif. Med. Assn., 1984-92, Nat. Retinitis Pigmentosa Found., 1985-95. Author: The Eye of the Artist, 1996; editor: The Retinal Pigment Epithelium, 1975, The Effects of Aging and Environment on Vision, 1991; editor-in-chief Doc. Ophthalmologica, 1995—; editl. bd. Healthline, Lasers and Light in Ophthalmology; contbr. more than 175 articles to sci. jours., 25 chpts. to books. Mem. affirmative action com. Stanford U. Sch. Medicine, 1984—. Sr. asst. surgeon USPHS, 1967-70. Recipient Svc. award Nat. Retinitis Pigmentosa Found., Balt., 1981, Rsch. award Alcon Rsch. Found., Houston, 1989; rsch. grantee Nat. Eye. Inst., Bethesda, Md., 1974-94. Fellow Am. Acad. Ophthalmology (bd. councillors 1982-85, pub. health com. 1990-93, rep. to NAS com. on vision 1991-93, Honor award 1984); mem. Internat. Soc. Clin. Electrophysiology of Vision (v.p. 1990—), Assn. Rsch. in Vision and Ophthalmology, Internat. Soc. for Eye Rsch., Macula Soc. (rsch. com.), Retina Soc. Democrat. Avocations: tennis, race-walking, chamber music (clarinet), art, medical history. Office: Stanford U Sch Medcine Dept Ophthalmology Stanford CA 94305

MARMOR, THEODORE RICHARD, political science and public management educator; b. Bklyn., Feb. 24, 1939; s. James and Mira Bernice (Karpf) M.; m. Jan Schmidt, Oct. 20, 1961; children—Laura Carleton, Sarah Rogers. BA, Harvard U., 1960, PhD, 1966; postgrad., Wadham Coll., Oxford U., Eng., 1961-62. Asst. and assoc. prof. polit. sci. U. Wis.-Madison, 1967-69; assoc. prof. pub. affairs U. Minn.-Mpls., 1970-73; prof. U. Chgo., 1973-79; prof. polit. sci. Yale U., New Haven, 1979—, chmn. Ctr. Health Studies, 1979-85, pf. pub. mgmt. Sch. Orgn. and Mgmt., 1983—; vis. fellow Russell Sage Found., 1987-88; cons., lectr. in field. Author: The Politics of Medicare, 1973, Political Analysis and American Medical Care, 1983, Understanding Health Care Reform, 1994; co-author: Health Care Policy, 1982, America's Misunderstood Welfare State, 1992; editor: Poverty Policy, 1971, National Health Insurance, 1980, Social Security: Beyond the Rhetoric of Crisis, 1988, Why Some People Are Healthy and Others Not, 1994, Jour. Health Politics Policy and Law, 1980-84; contbr. articles to profl. jours. Mem. Council on Fgn. Relations, N.Y.C., 1979-80, Pres.' Commn. on 1980s, 1980; social policy adviser Walter Mondale Presdl. Campaign, 1984. Can. Inst. Advanced Rsch. fellow, 1987—; fellow Adlai Stevenson Inst., J.F.K. Inst. Politics. Fellow Inst. Medicine, Nat. Acad. Social Ins.; mem. U.S. Squash Racquets Assn. (bd. dirs. 1983—), Century Assn. (N.Y.C.), United Oxford and Cambridge Club (London), Lawn Club. Democrat. Jewish. Home: 139 Armory St Hamden CT 06517-4005 Office: Yale Univ Sch of Mgmt 135 Prospect St New Haven CT 06511-3729

MARNEY, SAMUEL ROWE, physician, educator; b. Bristol, Va., Feb. 15, 1934; m. Elizabeth Ann Bingham, Oct. 1, 1966; children: Samuel Rowe III, Annis Morison. BA in Chemistry, U. Va., 1955, MD, 1960. Staff physician VA Hosp., Nashville, 1968-69, clin. assoc., 1969-71, clin. investigator, 1971-74, staff physician, infectious disease and allergy cons., 1974—; asst. prof. medicine Med. Ctr. Vanderbilt U., Nashville, 1971-76, assoc. prof., 1976—, dir. allergy and immunology, 1974—; vis. investigator Scripps Clinic and Rsch. Found., La Jolla, Calif., 1973-74. Capt. USAF, 1962-64, Korea. Fellow ACP, Am. Acad. Allergy and Immunology, Am. Coll. Allergy and Immunology; mem. Southeastern Allergy Assn. (pres. 1986-87, Hal M. Davison Meml. award, 1981), Tenn. Soc. Allergy and Immunology. Home: 4340 Sneed Rd Nashville TN 37215-3242 Office: Vanderbilt U Med Ctr All&Im 1500 21st Ave S Ste 3500 Nashville TN 37212

MAROCKIE, HENRY R., state school system administrator. Instr., rsch. assoc., asst. to dean W.V. Univ., Morgantown, 1968; asst. supt. Fin., Secondary Schs., Parkersburg, W.V., 1971; supt. Ohio County Schs., Wheeling, W.V., 1972-89; state supt. schs. Charleston, W.V., 1989—; chair Nat. gov. bd. Project Use It, W.V. Literacy Coun.; co-chair Learning Techs. com. Coun. Chief State Sch. Officers; pres. W.V. Sch/ Bldg. Authority; exec. com. mem. W.V. Edn. Fund; past officer W.V. Bd. Edn.; dir. reorgn. W.V. Dept. Edn., new evaluation systems tchrs., adminstrs.; launched Tobacco Control Policy W.V. schs.; est. Student, Tchr. Code Conduct, policies to modernize curriculum to State Bd., Gov's, Am. 2000 goals. Contbr. articles to profl. jours. Officer W.Va. Bd. Dirs., W.Va. Bd. Trustees, W.Va. Gov.'s Honors Acad., W.Va. Profl. Devel. Ctr., W.Va. Joint Commn. Vocat., Tech., Occupational Edn. Recipient W.Va. Supt. Yr. award, W.Va. Leader Learning award Dept. Edn., 1984, Supt. Yr. award W.Va. Assn. Music Educators, 1986, Leadership award Coll. Human Resources and Edn., W.Va. U., 1988, Alumni Achievement award West Liberty State Coll., 1985, citation edn. excellence W.Va. Ho. of Dels., 1982, Disting. Svc. award Nat. Alliance Health/Phys. Edn. Mem. W.V. Bd. Pub. Works, Ednl. Broadcasting Authority, Labor Mgmt. Coun., Tchrs. Retirement Bd., Drug Control Policy Bd., State Job Tng. Coord. Coun., Private Ind. Coun. W.V. Inc. Office: State Dept Edn 1900 Kanawha Blvd E Charleston WV 25305-0002*

MAROLDA, ANTHONY JOSEPH, management consulting company executive; b. Winthrop, Mass., Sept. 7, 1939; s. Daniel Arthur and Rose Marie (Pagliarulo) M.; m. Maria Theresa Rizzo, Oct. 10, 1970; children: Matthew, Ria. BS in Physics, Northeastern U., 1962; MS in Physics, Northeaster U., 1968; MBA, Harvard U., 1970. Rsch. physicist High Voltage Engring. Corp., Burlington, Mass., 1962-65; sr. scientist E.G. & G. Inc., Wellsley, Mass., 1965-68; v.p. Arthur D. Little, Inc., Cambridge, Mass., 1970-85; pres. The Winbridge Group, Inc., Cambridge, Mass., 1985—; bd. dirs. Daetwyler N.Am., Burlington, N.J., Altdorf, Switzerland. Inventor Apparatus High Density Plasma, 1965; co-author: Business Problem Solving, 1980, Modern Marketing, 1986. Adv. Waterbury-Leningrad. Intersport, Waterbury, Conn., 1988-92. Recipient Hayden Meml. Scholarship, Northeastern U., 1957. Mem. Harvard Club, Harvard Bus. Sch. Alumni Assn. Republican. Roman Catholic. Avocations: hiking, sailing, tennis. Office: The Winbridge Group Inc University Place 124 Mount Auburn St Cambridge MA 02138-5758

MARON, MELVIN EARL, engineer, philosopher, educator; b. Bloomfield, N.J., Jan. 23, 1924; s. Hyman and Florence (Goldman) M.; m. Dorothy Elizabeth Mastin, Aug. 16, 1948; children—Nadia, John. B.S. in Mech. Engring, U. Nebr., 1945, B.A. in Physics, 1947; Ph.D. in Philosophy, U. Calif. at Los Angeles, 1951. Lectr. philosophy UCLA, 1951-52; tech. engr. IBM Corp., San Jose, Calif., 1952-55; mem. tech. staff Ramo-Wooldridge Corp., 1955-59; mem. sr. staff, computer scis. dept. RAND Corp., 1959-66; prof. Sch. Libr. and Info. Studies U. Calif., Berkeley. Served with AUS, 1943-46. Fellow AAAS; mem. Assn. Computing Machinery, Am. Soc. Info. Sci., Philosophy Sci. Assn. Home: 63 Ardilla Rd Orinda CA 94563-2201 Office: U Calif Sch Libr & Info Studies Berkeley CA 94720

MARONDE, ROBERT FRANCIS, internist, clinical pharmacologist, educator; b. Monterey Park, Calif., Jan. 13, 1920; s. John August and Emma Florence (Palmer) M.; m. Yolanda Cerda, Apr. 15, 1970; children—Robert George, Donna F. Maronde Varnau, James Augustus, Craig DeWald. B.A., U. So. Calif., 1941, M.D., 1944. Diplomate: Am. Bd. Internal Medicine. Intern L.A. County-U. So. Calif. Med. Ctr., 1943-44, resident, 1944-45, 47-48; asst. prof. physiology U. So. Calif., L.A., 1948-49, asst. clin. prof. medicine, 1949-60, assoc. clin. prof. medicine, 1960-65, assoc. prof. medicine and pharmacology, 1965-67, prof. medicine and pharmacology, 1968-90, emeritus, 1990—, prof. emeritus, 1990—; spl. asst. v.p. for health affairs, 1990—; cons. FDA, 1973, Medco Containment Co. Inc., 1991—, State of Calif. Dept. Health Svcs., 1993. Served to lt. (j.g.) USNR, 1945-47. Fellow ACP; mem. Am. Soc. Clin. Pharmacology and Therapeutics, Alpha Omega Alpha. Home: 785 Ridgecrest St Monterey Park CA 91754-3759 Office: U So Calif 2025 Zonal Ave Los Angeles CA 90033-4526 *Scientific integrity, objectivity, concern for the quality of life and adherence to the ethics of Nuremberg are ingredients for the evaluation of therapy for human illness. This is the ultimate objective of the practice of medicine.*

MARONI, DONNA FAROLINO, biologist, researcher; b. Buffalo, Feb. 27, 1938; d. Enrico Victor and Eleanor (Redlinska) Farolino; m. Gustavo Primo Maroni, Dec. 16, 1974. BS, U. Wis., 1960, PhD, 1969. Project assoc. U. Wis., Madison, 1960-63, 68-74; Alexander von Humboldt fellow Inst. Genetics U. Cologne, Fed. Republic Germany, 1974-75; Hargitt fellow Duke U., Durham, N.C., 1975-76, rsch. assoc., 1976-83, rsch. assoc. prof., 1983-87; sr. program specialist N.C. Biotech. Ctr., Research Triangle Park, 1987-88, dir. sci. programs div., 1988-92, v.p. for sci. programs, 1992-94, ret., 1995; mem. adv. com. MICROMED at Bowman Gray Sch. Medicine, Winston-Salem, N.C., 1988—, Minority Sci. Improvement Alliance for Instrn. and Rsch. in Biotech. Ala. A & M U., Normal, 1990-91. Contbr. over 20 articles and revs. to profl. jours. Grantee NSF, 1977-79, NIH, 1979-82, 79-83, 82-87. Mem. Am. Soc. Cell Biology, Genetics Soc. Am., N.C. Acad. Sci., Inc. (bd. dirs. 1983-86), Sigma Xi (mem. exec. com. Duke U. chpt. 1989-90). Achievements include research in electron microscopy, evolution of chromosomes, chromosome structure, evolution of mitosis, and mitosis and fungal phylogeny.

MARONI, PAUL L., finance executive; b. Scranton, Pa., June 20, 1947; s. L. Paul and Mary M. (Manzo) M.; m. Margaret Garretson Bronner, Apr. 27, 1985; 1 child, Emily Garretson. BA, U. Scranton, 1969; MLS, Rutgers U., 1972; MBA, Cornell U., 1980. Reference libr. SUNY Coll., Oneonta, 1972-78; fin. analyst Continental Grain Co., N.Y.C., 1980-82; asst. treas. Newmont Mining Corp., N.Y.C., 1982-88; treas. Newmont Mining/ Newmont Gold, N.Y.C., Denver (Colo.), 1988-93; v.p. Newmont Mining/ Newmont Gold, Denver, 1990-91, sr. v.p., chief fin. officer, 1991-93; sr. v.p. fin. Consolidated Hydro, Inc., Greenwich, Conn., 1994—. Mem. Fin. Execs. Inst., Nat. Assn. Corp. Treas. Office: Consolidated Hydro Inc 1 Greenwich Plz Greenwich CT 06830-6352

MAROON, MICKEY, clinical social worker; b. Flint, Mich., July 20, 1948; d. Harold Clifford and Dorothy Ruth (Fuller) McDaniel; m. Michael Martin Maroon, Aug. 22, 1970. BA, Bradley U., 1970; MSW, Denver U., 1975. Lic. clin. social worker, Colo.; bd. cert. diplomate. Social worker Ill. Dept. Children and Family Svcs., Peoria, Ill., 1970-73; clin. social worker Adams County Social Svcs., Westminster, Colo., 1975-77, Bethesda Hosp., Denver, 1977-84; pvt. practice Denver, 1979—; clin. cons. Human Svcs., Inc., Denver, 1988-91; vol. faculty Health Sci. Ctr. U. Colo., Denver, 1987—; chair attending social work staff West Pines Hosp., Wheat Ridge, Colo., 1988-89. Mem. NASW (pres. Colo. chpt. 1994—), Colo. Soc. Clin. Social Work (Denver chpt. pres. 1992, state pres. 1993).

MAROONE, MICHAEL E., car and truck sales executive; b. 1962. CEO Maroone Car & Truck Sales, Pembroke Pines, Fla.; bd. dirs. Intercontinental Bank; chmn. South Fla. Internat. Auto Show, 1995. Bd. dirs. Dan Marino Found., Boys and Girls Club of Broward County, Children Cancer Caring Ctr., Police Athletic League. Named Humanitarian of Yr. Transflorida Bank, Forbes mag. Top 500 Cos., 1994. Mem. South Fla. Auto Truck Dealers Assn. (pres. 1994), South Fla. Chevrolet Dealers Mktg. Assn. (pres. 1994), Fla. Automotive Dealers Assn. (bd. dirs.). Office: Maroone Auto Plz 8600 Pines Blvd Pembroke FL 33024

MAROTTA, JOSEPH THOMAS, medical educator; b. Niagara Falls, N.Y., May 28, 1926; emigrated to Can., 1930; s. Alfred and Mary (Montemuro) M.; m. Margaret Hughes, Aug. 31, 1953; children: Maureen, Patricia, Margaret, Fred, Thomas, Jo Anne, Michael, Martha, John, Virginia. M.D., U. Toronto, 1949. Trainee in internal medicine U. Toronto, 1949-52; trainee in neurology Presbyn. Hosp., N.Y.C., 1952-55, U. London, Eng., 1955-56; mem. faculty U. Toronto, 1956—, prof. medicine, 1969—; former assoc. dean clin. affairs U. Toronto (Faculty of Medicine), 1981-89; hon. prof. of neurology U. Western Ontario, 1990—; consulting staff Dept. of Neurol. Scis. Victoria Hosp., U. Hosp., London. Fellow Royal Coll. Physicians (Can.); mem. Acad. Medicine (Toronto), Alpha Omega Alpha, Phi Chi. Home and Office: 46 Carnforth Rd, London, ON Canada M6G 4P6

MAROVICH, GEORGE M., federal judge; b. 1931. AA, Thornton Community Coll., 1950; BS, U. Ill., 1952, JD, 1954. Atty. Chgo. Title & Trust Co., 1954-59; mem. firm Jacobs & Marovich, South Holland, Ill., 1959-66; v.p., trust officer South Holland Trust & Savs. Bank, 1966-76; judge Cir. Ct. Cook County, Ill., 1976-88; dist. judge U.S. Dist. Ct. (no. dist.) Ill., Chgo., 1988—; adj. instr. Thornton Community Coll., 1977-88. Mem. Ill. Judges Assn., Ill. Jud. Conf., Chgo. Bar Assn., South Suburban Bar Assn. Office: US Dist Ct Chambers 1956 219 S Dearborn St Chicago IL 60604-7206*

MAROVITZ, ABRAHAM LINCOLN, judge; b. Oshkosh, Wis., Aug. 10, 1905; s. Joseph and Rachel (Glowitz) M. JD, Chgo.-Kent Coll. Law, 1925; LHD, Lincoln (Ill.) Coll., 1956; LLD, Winston Churchill Coll., 1968; HHD, Chgo. Med. Sch., 1984; LLD (hon.), Ill. Inst. Tech., 1988, Roosevelt U., 1989, Nat.-Louis U., 1991. Bar: Ill. bar 1927. Asst. state's atty. Cook County, Ill., 1927-33; practiced in Chgo., 1933-50; judge Superior Ct. Cook County, 1950-63; chief justice Cook County Criminal Ct., 1958-59; U.S. judge No. dist. Ill., 1963-75, sr. judge, 1975-89; ret., 1989; chmn. bd. Lincoln Nat. Bank, 1946-63; past nat. chmn. Nat. Conf. State Ct. Trial Judges; past mem. lawyer's adv. council U. Ill. Law Forum. Mem. Ill. Senate, 1938-50; Bd. dirs. Hebrew Theol. Coll.; mem. adv. bd. YMCA Met. Chgo.; trustee Chgo.-Kent Coll. Law, Chgo. Med. Sch.; former trustee Ill. Hist. Library; past mem. Jewish Bd. Edn. Served to sgt. maj. USMCR, 1943-46. Named Outstanding Legislator, Ind. Voters Ill., 1949; named to Wisdom Hall of Fame, 1979; recipient Founders' Day award Loyola U. in Chgo., 1967, awards Chgo. Press Club, Chgo. Press Photographers Assn., 1968, Man of

Yr. award Jewish Nat. Fund, Israel Bond Orgn., 1973, Horatio Alger award, 1979, Na. Americanism medal DAR, 1980, Citizens' award Chgo. Police Dept., 1982, Lincoln The Lawyer award, 1985, Chgo. Park Dist. Sr. Citizen of Yr. award, 1985, Spirit of Lincoln award Anti-Defamation League, 1985, Celtic Man of Yr. award Celtic Legal Soc. Chgo., 1989, Disting. Pub. Svc. award Union League Club, 1990, Jack Robbins award Boys Brotherhood Republic Alumni Assn., 1990, Excellence in Pub. Svc. award North Shore Retirement award, 1990, Recognition award B'nai B;rith Sports Lodge, 1990, award Immigration and Naturalization Svc., 1993, Sr. medal of honor Cook County Sheriff, 1994, plaque Intellectual Property Law Assn., 1994, Profl. Achievement award Chgo. Kent Law Sch., 1995, Making History award Chgo. Hist. Soc., 1995; named to Chgo. Jewish Sports Hall of Fame, 1994; Judge Abraham Lincoln Marovitz Ct. in Chgo. named in his honor, 1992, Judge Abraham Lincoln Marovitz Courtroom at Chgo. Kent Law Sch. named in his honor, 1992, Chgo. chpt. Am. Inns. of Ct. named in his honor, 1994. Mem. ABA, Ill. State Bar Assn., Chgo. Bar Assn. (past mgr., Exemplary Svc. award 1987), Internat. Assn. Jewish Lawyers & Jurists, Decalogue Soc. of Lawyers (ann. merit award 1968), Jewish War Vets. U.S. (past dept. comdr., Man of Yr. 1994), Am. Legion (past comdr. Marine post Chgo.). Jewish (bd. dirs. synagogue). Home: 3260 N Lake Shore Dr Apt 8A Chicago IL 60657-3955 Office: U S Dist Ct 219 S Dearborn St Apt 1900 Chicago IL 60604-1801

MAROVITZ, JAMES LEE, lawyer; b. Chgo., Feb. 21, 1939; s. Harold and Gertrude (Luster) M.; m. Gail Helene Florsheim, June 17, 1962; children: Andrew, Scott. BS, Northwestern U., 1960, JD, 1963. Bar: Ill. 1963, U.S. Dist. Ct. (no. dist.) Ill. 1963, U.S. Ct. Appeals (7th cir.) 1990. Assoc. Leibman, Williams, Bennett, Baird & Minow, Chgo., 1963-70, ptnr., 1970-72; ptnr. Sidley & Austin, Chgo., 1972—; bd. dirs. Cobra Elec. Corp., Chgo. Plan commr. Village of Deerfield, Ill., 1972-79, trustee, 1983-93. Mem. ABA, Ill. Bar Assn., Chgo. Bar Assn. Club: Univ. (Chgo.). Office: Sidley & Austin 1 First Nat Plz Chicago IL 60603

MAROZSAN, JOHN ROBERT, publishing company executive; b. Trenton, N.J., Oct. 25, 1941; s. John Nichols and Anna Mary (Lacko) M.; m. Anne Marie Gousha, Mar. 18, 1983; children—Andre J., Marc J., Carl B. A.S., Trenton Jr. Coll., 1965; B.A., Trenton State Coll., 1967; M.A., Harvard U., 1969. Tchr. Princeton Pub. Sch., N.J., 1967-68; coordinator secondary pub. Ginn and Co., Boston, 1969-72; program mgr. Ginn and Co., Lexington, Mass., 1972-75; v.p., editor-in-chief Aspen Publishers, Inc., Rockville, Md., 1975-80, sr. v.p. pub., 1980-85; pres. Aspen Pubs., Inc., Gaithersburg, 1986—. Bd. dirs. Hospice Caring, Wolters Klumen U.S.; bd. examiners Henry B. Betts Found.; bd. govs. WUSA One and Only Award. With USAF, 1959-63. Recipient Sci. award NSF, 1968. Mem. Newsletter Assn. Am., Rotary. Home: 9713 Lookout Pl Gaithersburg MD 20879-2158 Office: Aspen Pubs Inc 200 Orchard Ridge Dr Gaithersburg MD 20878-1978

MARPLE, DOROTHY JANE, retired church executive; b. Abington, Pa., Nov. 24, 1926; d. John Stanley and Jennie (Stetler) M. A.B., Ursinus Coll., 1948; M.A., Syracuse U., 1950; Ed.D., Columbia U. Tchrs. Coll., 1969; L.H.D., Thiel Coll., 1965, Gettysburg Coll., 1979, Ursinus Coll., 1981; D. Humanitarian Services, Newberry Coll., 1977; DD, Trinity Luth. Sem., 1987. Counselor, asst., office dean undergrad. women Women's Coll., Duke, 1950-53; dean women, fgn. student adv. Thiel Coll., 1953-61; asst. social dir. Whittier Hall, Columbia Tchrs. Coll., 1961-62; exec. dir. Luth. Ch. Women, Luth. Ch. Am., Phila., 1962-75; asst. to bishop Luth. Ch. Am., 1975-85; coord. Transition Office Evang. Luth. Ch. Am., 1986-87; asst. gen. sec. ops. Nat. Coun. Chs. of Christ in U.S., N.Y.C., 1987-89; coordinator Luth. Ch. in Am. commn. on function and structure, 1970-72. Home: 8018 Anderson St Philadelphia PA 19118-2936

MARPLE, GARY ANDRE, management consultant; b. Mt. Pleasant, Iowa, Feb. 22, 1937; s. Kenneth Lowry and Truma Janice (Cook) M.; m. Ellen I. Metcalf, May 29, 1971 (div. 1981); m. Meredith Ann Rutter, July 23, 1988; children: Brian Edward, Stephen Lowry. BS, Drake U., 1959; MBA, Mich. State U., 1962, DBA, 1963. Postdoctoral fellow mgmt. MIT, 1963; cons. Arthur D. Little Inc., Cambridge, Mass., 1963-82; pres. Commonwealth Strategies, Inc., Acton, Mass., 1982—; Oceanus Holding, Ltd., S.W., Harbor, Maine, 1985—; treas. Bramar, Inc., Stow, Mass., 1988—. Editor, author: Grocery Manufacturing in the U.S., 1968; contbr. to Conquering Government Regulation, 1982. Mem. Arthur D. Little Alumni Assn. (bd. dirs., past pres. Lexington, Mass. 1992—).

MARPLE, STANLEY LAWRENCE, JR., electrical engineer, signal processing researcher; b. Tulsa, Sept. 7, 1947; s. Stanley Lawrence and Geraldine Doris (Van Duyne) M.; m. Suzanne Eileen Stevens, Aug. 31, 1974; children: Darci Leah, Rebecca Anne, Matthew Lawrence. BA, Rice U., 1969, MEE, 1970; DEng, Stanford U., 1976. Staff engr. Argo Systems, Inc., Sunnyvale, Calif., 1972-78; sr. staff engr. Advent Systems, Inc., Mountain View, Calif., 1978-79, The Analytic Scis. Corp., Mc Lean, Va., 1980-82; sr. devel. engr. Schlumberger Well Svcs., Houston, 1983-85; mgr., devel. engr. Martin Marietta Aero & Naval Systems, Balt., 1986-88; chief scientist Orincon Corp., San Diego, 1989-93, Acuson Corp., Mountain View, Calif., 1993—. Author: Digital Spectral Analysis, 1987, Digital Time, Frequency, and Space Analysis, 1996. Capt. Signal Corps, U.S. Army, 1972-80. Fellow IEEE; mem. IEEE Signal Processing Soc. (editor Trans. on Signal Processing 1982-86, Sr. Paper award 1984, adminstrv. com. 1985-88, chmn. spectral estimation and array processing com. 1989-91). Avocations: stamp collecting, hiking, writing. Office: Acuson Corp 1220 Charleston Rd Mountain View CA 94043-1330

MARQUARD, WILLIAM ALBERT, diversified manufacturing company executive; b. Pitts., Mar. 6, 1920; s. William Albert and Anne (Wild) M.; m. Margaret Thoben, Aug. 13, 1942; children: Pamela, Suzanne, Stephen. BS, U. Pa., 1940; HHD (hon.), U. Puebla (Mex.). With Westinghouse Electric Corp., Pitts. and Mexico City, 1940-52; with Mosler Safe Co., Hamilton, Ohio, 1952-67, sr. v.p., 1961-67, pres., 1967-70; with Am. Standard, Inc., N.Y.C., 1967—, sr. exec. v.p., 1970, pres., chief exec. officer, 1971-85, also chmn., 1971-86, chmn. exec. com., from 1985; now chmn. Am. Standard, Inc. subs. ASI Holding Corp., N.Y.C.; bd. dirs. Chem. N.Y. Corp., Chem. Bank, N.Y. Life Ins. Co., Shell Oil Co., N.L. Industries, Inc., Allied Stores; chmn., bd. dirs. Arkansas Best Corp. Trustee U. Pa., N.Y.C. Citizens Budget Commn., N.Y. Infirmary-Beekman Downtown Hosp., Washington Opera, Found. of U. Ams., Com. Econ. Devel.; bd. overseers Wharton Sch. Bus., Bus. Com. for Arts, Brit.-N. Am. Com.; mem. Com. Corp. Support Pvt. Univs.; bd. dirs. Nat. Minority Purchasing Council. Mem. Conf. Bd. (sr.). Address: Ark Best Corp 1000 S 21st St Fort Smith AR 72901-4008*

MARQUARDT, CHRISTEL ELISABETH, lawyer; b. Chgo., Aug. 26, 1935; d. Herman Albert and Christine Marie (Geringer) Trolenberg; children: Eric, Philip, Andrew, Joel. BS in Edn., Mo. Western Coll., 1970; JD with honors, Washburn U., 1974. Bar: Kans. 1974, Mo. 1992, U.S. Dist. Ct. Kans. 1974, U.S. Dist. Ct. (we. dist.) Mo. 1992. Tchr. St. John's Ch., Tigerton, Wis., 1955-56; pers. asst. Columbia Records, L.A., 1958-59; ptnr. Cosgrove, Webb & Oman, Topeka, 1974-86, Palmer & Marquardt, Topeka, 1986-91, Levy and Craig P.C., Overland Park, Kans., 1991-94; sr. ptnr. Marquardt and Assocs., L.L.C., Fairway, Kans., 1994—; judge Kans. Ct. Appeals, 1995—; mem. atty. bd. discipline Kans. Supreme Ct., 1984-86. Mem. editorial adv. bd. Kans. Lawyers Weekly, 1992—; contbr. articles to legal jours. Bd. dirs. Topeka Symphony, 1983-92, Arts and Humanities Assn. Johnson County, 1992—, Brown Found., 1988-90; hearing examiner Human Rels. Com., Topeka, 1974-76; local advisor Boy Scouts Am., 1973-74; bd. dirs., mem. nominating com. YWCA, Topeka, 1979-81; bd. govs. Washburn U. Law Sch., 1987—, v.p., 1994-95; mem. dist. bd. adjudication Mo. Synod Luth. Ch., Kans., 1982-88. Names Woman of Yr., Mayor, City of Topeka, 1982; Obee scholar Washburn U., 1972-74. Fellow Am. Bar Found., Kans. Bar Found. (trustee 1987-89); mem. ABA (labor law, family and litigation sects., mem. ho. dels. 1988—, state del. 1995—, specilization com. 1987-93, chmn. 1989-93, lawyer referral com. 1993—, bar svcs. and activities, 1995—), Kans. Bar Assn. (sec., treas. 1981-82, 83-85, v.p. 1985-86, pres. 1987-88, bd. dirs.), Kans. Trial Lawyers Assn. (bd. govs. 1982-86, lectr.), Topeka Bar Assn., Am. Bus. Women's Assn. (lectr., corr. sec. 1983-84, pres. career chpt. 1986-87, named one of Top 10 Bus. Women of Yr., 1985). Home: 8572 Hauser Ct Lenexa KS 66215-4546 Office: 4330 Shawnee Mission Pky Fairway KS 66205-2522

MARQUARDT, KATHLEEN PATRICIA, association executive; b. Kalispell, Mont., June 6, 1944; d. Dean King and Lorraine Camille (Buckmaster) Marquardt; m. William Wewer, Dec. 6, 1987; children: Shane Elizabeth, Montana Quinn. Purser, Pan Am. World Airways, Washington, 1968-75; info. specialist Capital Systems Group, Kensington, Md., 1979-81; dir. pub. affairs Subscription TV Assn., Washington, 1981-83, exec. dir., 1983-86; pres. Internat. Policy Studies Orgn., 1983-90; pres., designer Elizabeth Quinn Couture; lectr. in field. Chmn. bd. Friends of Freedom, 1982-90, Putting People First, 1990—, Mont. Matters, 1996—; v.p. Am. Policy Ctr., 1996—; treas. Mont. Tax Reduction Movement. Author: Animal Scam-The Beastly Abuse of Human Rights, 1993, (national newpaper column) From the Trenches; contbr. articles to syndicated newspapers and mags.; host Grass Roots radio. Recipient Citizen Achievement award Ctr. fo Def. Free Enterprise, 1992, Gold Medal award Pa. State Fish and Game Protective Assn., 1993. Mem. Outdoor Writers Assn. Am. Home: 533 5th Ave Helena MT 59601-4359 Office: Putting People First 21 N Last Chance Gulch Helena MT 59601

MARQUARDT, SANDRA MARY, activist, lobbyist, researcher; b. Dhahran, Saudi Arabia, Mar. 5, 1959; parents Am. citizens; d. Donald Edward and Mary Eleanor (Lindsay-Rea) M. BA, U. Wis., 1982. Editor, organizer Nat. Coalition Against the Misuse of Pesticides, Washington, 1983-87; rschr., author Environ. Policy Inst., Washington, 1987-88; organizer, lobbyist Greenpeace, Washington, 1988-95; rschr. Consumer's Union., 1995—; mem. steering com., former chmn. Pesticide Action Network, San Francisco, 1984-89, 92—. Author reports on pesticide exports, bottled water, organic cotton. Avocation: bicycling, frisbee (ultimate), running, stained glass, photography. Office: Consumers Union Ste 310 1666 Connecticut Ave NW Washington DC 20009

MARQUARDT, STEVE ROBERT, library director; b. St. Paul, Sept. 7, 1943; s. Robert Thomas and Dorothy Jean (Kane) M.; m. Judy G. Brown, Aug. 4, 1968; 1 child, Sarah. BA in History, Macalester Coll., 1966; MA in History, U. Minn., 1970, MLS, 1973, PhD in History, 1978. History instr. Macalester Coll., St. Paul, 1968-69; original monographic cataloger N.Mex. State U. Libr., Las Cruces, 1973-75; acting univ. archivist, acting dir. Rio Grande Hist. Collections N. Mex. State U. Libr., Las Cruces, 1973-74; acquisitions librarian Western Ill. U. Libr., Macomb, 1976-77, head cataloger, Online Computer Libr. Ctr. coord., 1977-79; asst. dir. resources & tech. svcs. Ohio U. Libr., Athens, 1979-81; dir. librs. U. Wis., Eau Claire, 1981-89; dir. univ. librs. No. Ill. U., DeKalb, 1989-90; dir. librs. U. Wis., Eau Claire, 1990-96; dean of librs. S.D. State U., Brookings, 1996—. Editor Jour. Rio Grande History, 1974; contbr. articles to profl. jours. Coord. Amnesty Internat. Adoption Group 275, Eau Claire, 1985-88; pres. Chippewa Valley Free-net, 1994-96. Mem. ALA, Assn. Coll. and Rsch. Librs. (chmn. performance measures in acad. librs. com. 1985-89). Lutheran. Avocations: tennis, bicycling. Office: SD State U Briggs Libr Box 2201 Brookings SD 57007-2098

MARQUEZ, ALFREDO C., federal judge; b. 1922; m. Linda Nowobilsky. B.S., U. Ariz., 1948, J.D., 1950. Bar: Ariz. Practice law Mesch Marquez & Rothschild, 1957-80; asst. atty. gen. State of Ariz., 1951-52; asst. county atty. Pima County, Ariz., 1953-54; adminstrv. asst. to Congressman Stewart Udall, 1955; judge U.S. Dist. Ct. Ariz., Tucson, 1980—. Served with USN, 1942-45. Office: US Dist Ct US Courthouse Rm 327 55 E Broadway Blvd Tucson AZ 85701-1719

MARQUEZ, HOPE, school system worker, educator; b. Winters, Tex., Sept. 12, 1948; d. Richard Ruiz and Candelaria (Medrano) Palomo; m. Arthur G. Marquez Jr.; children: Beverly Ruth Gonzales, Lytha Maria Mendoza, Hope. Bus driver, office asst., safety officer Ft. Worth Ind. Sch. Dist., 1977-90; ops.mgr., in charge bus driver tng. and cert. Ednl. Svc. Ctr., Ft. Worth, 1990—, coord., 1994. Vol. Ft. Worth Fire Dept. Relief, 1987, sec., 1991. Mem. Tex. Assn. for Pupil Transp. (region XI reporter 1995, 96, chmn. poster contest 1995). Office: Edn Svc Ctr Region XI 3001 North Fwy Fort Worth TX 76106-6526

MARQUEZ, JOAQUIN ALFREDO, lawyer; b. Humacao, P.R., Aug. 1, 1942; s. Joaquin and Emelina (Tudela) M.; m. Jocelyn Christiansen, Mar. 27, 1967; children: Joaquin A. Jr., Julian A. BS in Econs., U. Pa., 1964; LLB, U. P.R., 1967; LLM in Taxation, Georgetown U., 1974. Bar: P.R. 1967, U.S. Dist. Ct. P.R. 1968, U.S. Ct. Appeals (lst cir.) 1968, D.C. 1972, U.S. Dist. Ct. D.C. 1972. Assoc. Goldman, Antonetti & Subira, San Juan, P.R., 1967-68; adminstrv. asst. to resident commr. for P.R. Washington, 1971-72, 77-78; sr. atty.-advisor AID U.S. Dept. State, Washington, 1973-76; dir. P.R. Fed. Affairs Adminstrn., Washington, 1978-81; ptnr. Hopkins & Sutter, Washington, 1981-94, Drinker, Biddle & Reath, Washington, 1994—; mem. P.R. Export Promotions Coun., San Juan, 1979-81; staff dir. So. Govs.' Assn., Washington, 1980-81. Capt. U.S. Army, 1968-70, Vietnam. Decorated Bronze Star. Mem. ABA, P.R. Bar Assn., D.C. Bar Assn. Republican. Roman Catholic. Avocations: sailing, reading. Office: Drinker Biddle & Reath 901 15th St NW Washington DC 20005-2327

MARQUIS, BARBARA S., maternal, women's health nurse; b. Benton, Ill., Nov. 11, 1937; d. Haskell C. and Zetta Ruth (Martin) Boaz; m. Paul R. Marquis, Sept. 6, 1958; children: Michael, Carol, Lisa. Diploma, DePaul Hosp., St. Louis, 1958; BS, Coll. of St. Francis, Joliet, Ill., 1980. Nursing positions, 1958-60; staff nurse, relief evening supr. Franklin Hosp., Benton, Ill., 1961-62; staff nurse labor and delivery U.S. Naval Hosp., Camp Lejeune, N.C., 1963-67; staff nurse/relief charge nurse labor and delivery St. Joseph's Hosp., Orange, Calif., 1968-69; staff nurse labor and delivery U.S. Naval Hosp., Camp Lejeune, 1971-73; from night staff nurse to night charge nurse labor/delivery Maricopa Med. ctr., Phoenix, 1973-75, night supr., 1975-77, head nurse labor and delivery, ob-gyn. surgery, 1977-83; from. maternal transport nurse to head nurse labor/delivery St. Joseph's Hosp. and Med. Ctr., Phoenix, 1984-89; home perinatal nurse CareLink Corp., Phoenix, 1989-90; MCH coord. Health Choice Ariz., Phoenix, 1990-94, prior authorization case mgmt. mgr. Health Choice Ariz., 1994—; cons. in field; expert witness, case reviewer for legal profls. in field of obstetrics. Mem. Nurses Assn. of Am. Coll. Obstetricians and Gynecologists (publicity chmn. conf. dist. VIII 1976, vice chmn. Ariz. sect. 1979-80, chmn. Ariz. sect. 1981-83, vice chmn. dist. VIII 1985—), Ariz. Nursing Network, Healthy Mothers, Healthy Babies of Ariz. (adv. bd.). Home: 3922 W Orchid Ln Phoenix AZ 85051-4661

MARQUIS, CHRISTOPHER HOLLIDAY, newspaper correspondent; b. Kentfield, Calif., Nov. 13, 1961; s. Harold H. and Nancy J. Marquis. Student, U. Seville, Spain, 1981-82; BA in Comparative Lit., U. Calif., Berkeley, 1984; MS in Journalism, Columbia U., 1985. Freelance journalist Pitts., 1985-86; city desk reporter The Miami Herald, 1987-90, Latin Am. corr., 1989-90, diplomatic corr., 1991—. Recipient Citation for Excellence, Overseas Press Club, 1991, Pedro Joaquin Chamorro award Inter-Am. Press Assn., 1992, Green Eyeshade award, 1995; fellow Inter-Am. Press Assn., 1986; scholar Scripps-Howard Found., 1984. Office: 700 National Press Building Washington DC 20045-1701

MARQUIS, ROLLIN PARK, retired librarian; b. Badin, N.C., Nov. 29, 1925; s. Rollin Howard and Carmen (Park) M.; m. Marian Horton Bonstein, Aug. 21, 1954 (dec. Aug. 1995); children: Rollin Hilary, Jeffrey Perrin, Anne-Louise. B.A., Columbia, 1948; postgrad. linguistics, St. Catherines Soc. U. Oxford, 1948-50; painting, Art Students League N.Y., 1950-52; M.L.S., Carnegie Inst. Tech., 1958. Catalog asst. Columbia Med. Library, 1952-53; adminstrv. asst. Nat. Council Chs. Christ in U.S.A., N.Y.C., 1953-56, Friends Com. on Nat. Legislation, Washington, 1956-57; reference asst. Carnegie Library, Pitts., 1957-58; dir. Citizens Library, Washington, Pa., 1958-59, River Edge (N.J.) Free Pub. Library, 1959-63, Allegany County Library, Cumberland, Md., 1963-64; city librarian Dearborn (Mich.) Dept. Libraries, 1964-89, ret., 1989. Active Fine Arts Assocs., U. Mich., Dearborn. With AUS, 1944-46. Mem. ALA, Better Edn. thru Simplified Spelling, Dearborn Orchestral Soc., Fair Lane Music Guild, Schoolcraft Coll. Cmty. Choir, Torch Club (Detroit), Rotary. Democrat. Mem. Soc. of Friends. Home: 16351 Rotunda Apt 349 Dearborn MI 48120 *The things obtained through cooperation, sharing and mutual goodwill are the achievements which satisfy—as significantly for public and business life, as for private life.*

MARR, CARMEL CARRINGTON, retired lawyer, retired state official; b. Bklyn.; d. William Preston and Gertrude Clementine (Lewis) Carrington; BA, Hunter Coll., 1945; JD, Columbia U., 1948; m. Warren Marr, II, Apr. 11, 1948; children: Charles Carrington, Warren Quincy III. Bar: N.Y. 1948, U.S. Dist. Ct. (ea. dist.) N.Y. 1950, U.S. Dist. Ct. (so. dist.) N.Y. 1951; clk. Dyer & Stevens, N.Y.C., 1948-49; pvt. practice, N.Y.C., 1949-53; adviser legal affairs U.S. mission to UN, N.Y.C., 1953-67, sr. legal officer Office Legal Affairs, UN Secretariat, 1967-68; mem. N.Y. State Human Rights Appeal Bd., 1968-71; mem. N.Y. State Pub. Svc. Commn., 1971-86; cons. Gas Rsch. Inst., 1987-91; lectr. N.Y. Police Acad., 1963-67. Contbr. articles to profl. jours. Mem. N.Y. Gov.'s Com. Edn. and Employment of Women, 1963-64; mem. Nat. Gen. Svcs. Pub. Adv. Council, 1969-71; mem., former chmn. adv. coun. Gas Rsch. Inst.; mem., chmn. tech. pipeline safety standards com. Dept. Transp., 1979-85; former mem. task force Fed. Energy Regulatory Commn. and EPA to examine PCBs in gas supply system; past chmn. gas com. Nat. Assn. Regulatory Utility Commrs.; past pres. Great Lakes Conf. Pub. Utilities Commrs., mem. exec. com.; mem. UN Devel. Corp., 1969-72; bd. dirs. Amistad Rsch. Ctr., New Orleans, 1970—, chmn. bd. dirs., 1981-94; bd. dirs. Bklyn. Soc. Prevention Cruelty to Children, Nat. Arts Stblzn. Fund, 1984-93, Prospect Park Alliance, 1987—; bd. visitors N.Y. State Sch. Girls, Hudson, 1964-71; mem. exec. bd. Plays for Living, N.Y.C., 1968-75; pres. bd. dirs. Billie Holiday Theatre, 1972-80; mem. nat. adv. coun. Hampshire Coll.; pres.'s. coun. Tulane U., 1988-95. Mem. Phi Beta Kappa, Alpha Chi Alpha, Alpha Kappa Alpha. Republican. Episcopalian.

MARR, DAVID FRANCIS, television announcer, former professional golfer, journalist; b. Houston, Dec. 27, 1933; s. David Francis and Grace Anne (Darnell) M.; m. Caroline Elizabeth Dawson, Sept. 25, 1972; children by previous marriage: Elizabeth S., David Francis III, Anthony J. Student, Rice U., 1950-51, U. Houston, 1951-52. Profl. golfer, 1953—, tour player, 1960-72, part-time tour player, 1973—; golf announcer ABC Sports, 1970-91, BBC Sports, 1992—; dir. Nabisco-Dinah Shore Tournament, 1981-86. Elected to Coll. golf Hall of Fame, 1981, Tex. Golf Hall of Fame, 1981; named to Ryder Cup Team, 1965. Mem. Profl. Golfers Assn. (nat. champion 1965, Player of Year 1965), AFTRA. Roman Catholic. Clubs: Lochinvar Golf (Houston); Houston City; Champions Golf (Houston); Brae-Burn Country. Capt. Ryder Cup Team, 1981. Office: care Riviere-Marr 2100 West Loop S Ste 800 Houston TX 77027-3509 also: care Hans Kramer IMG 1 Erieview Plz Ste 1300 Cleveland OH 44114-1715

MARR, DIANE DEMPSEY, counselor, school psychologist, educator; b. San Francisco, Oct. 31, 1954; d. Robert Harold and Emma Delia (Bianchi) Dempsey; m. Dargan Howell Marr, July 26, 1985; children: Dina Marie, Jacob Reese. BA, San Jose State U., 1976; MA, EdS in Sch. Psychology, U. Idaho, 1982, PhD, 1991. Lic. profl. counselor; nat. cert. sch. psychologist. Pvt. practice counseling and sch. psychology various cities, Idaho, 1981-85, Naphtali Psychol. Svcs., Cape Girardeau, Mo., 1993—; sch. psychologist Tri-Dist. Spl. Svcs., St. Anthony, Idaho, 1984-85, Coos Edn. Svc. Dist., Coos Bay, Oreg., 1985-89; instr./grad. asst. U. Idaho, Moscow, 1989-91; sch. psychologist Moscow Sch. Dist., 1991-92; asst. prof. counseling S.E. Mo. Stte U., Cape Girardeau, 1992—; cons. in field. Author: Gender Specific Treatment: A Program for Chemically Dependent Women in Recovery, 1994. Mem. Children's Caring Coun., Cape Girardeau, 1992—. Mem. Am. Counseling Assn., Am. Counselor Educators, Mo. Counseling Assn., Nat. Assn. Sch. Psychologists, S.E. Mo. Sch. Counselors Assn. Avocations: songwriting, creative writing. Office: SE Missouri State Univ One University Pla Cape Girardeau MO 63701

MARR, JACK WAYNE, lawyer; b. Ft. Worth, Aug. 19, 1949; s. Norman L. and Florence (Mohn) M.; m. Sharon Lee Hutto, Jan. 2, 1971; children: Justin, Dallas. BBA, Tex. Tech. U., 1971, JD, 1974. Bar: Tex. 1994. Briefing counsel 13th Ct. Civil Appeals, Corpus Christi, Tex., 1974-75; assoc. Guittard & Henderson, Victoria, Tex., 1975-79; ptnr. Lewis & Kelly, Victoria, 1979-81, Kelly, Stephenson & Marr, Victoria, 1981-91, Kelly, Marr, Meier & Hartman, Victoria, 1991-93, Marr, Meier & Hartman, Victoria, 1993—. Contbr. articles to profl. jours. Pres. Southwest Little League, Victoria, 1991-92. Mem. State Bar Tex. (family law coun., legis. com., practice manual com.), Tex. Acad. Family Law Specialists (pres. 1994-95).

MARR, LUTHER REESE, communications executive, lawyer; b. Kansas City, June 23, 1925; s. Luther Dow and Aileen (Shimfessel) M.; m. Christelle Lois Taylor, July 12, 1956; children—Michelle Lois, Stephen Luther, Christelle Elizabeth. A.B., U. Calif. at Los Angeles, 1946; J.D., U. So. Calif., 1950. Bar: Calif. 1951. With firm Hasbrouck & Melby, Glendale, 1952-54; atty. The Walt Disney Co., Burbank, Calif., 1954-92; corp. sec. The Walt Disney Co., 1957-78, v.p. corp. and shareholder affairs, 1978-87, v.p. shareholder svc., 1987-92. Trustee Le Lycée Français de Los Angeles. Served with USNR, 1946-47. Mem. Am. Soc. Corp. Secs., Calif., Los Angeles Bar Assns., Phi Beta Kappa, Phi Alpha Delta. Republican. Methodist. Home: 1785 Cielito Dr Glendale CA 91207-1023

MARR, ROBERT BRUCE, physicist, educator; b. Quincy, Mass., Mar. 25, 1932; s. Ralph George and Ethel (Beals) M.; m. Nancy Rosa Parkes, June 12, 1954; children: Richard, Jonathan, Rebecca. B.S., MIT, 1953; M.A., Harvard U., 1955, Ph.D., 1959. Research asso. Brookhaven Nat. Lab., Upton, N.Y., 1959-61; asso. physicist Brookhaven Nat. Lab., 1961-64, physicist, 1964-68, sr. physicist, 1968-95, assoc. chmn. applied math. dept., 1974-75, 83-88, chmn., 1975-78; ret., 1995; adj. assoc. prof. Columbia U., 1969; lectr. SUNY at Stony Brook, 1969-70, vis. prof. dept. computer sci., 1979; guest mathematician U. Colo., 1970; vis. mathematician Lawrence Berkeley Lab., 1978; cons. NSF, NIH, 1969—. Contbr. articles to profl. jours. Served with U.S. Army, 1958-59. NSF grantee, 1974. Mem. Soc. for Magnetic Resonance in Medicine (trustee 1982-87, sec.-treas. 1984-86, treas. 1986-87). Home: 368 Private Rd Patchogue NY 11772-5827 Office: Brookhaven Nat Lab Applied Sci Dept Upton NY 11973

MARRETT, CORA B., science foundation administrator, science educator; b. Richmond, Va., June 15, 1942; d. Horace Sterling and Clora Ann (Boswell) Bagley; m. Louis Everard Marrett, Dec. 24, 1968. BA, Va. Union U., 1963; MS, U. Wis., 1965, PhD, 1968. Asst. prof. U. N.C., Chapel Hill, 1968-69; from asst. to assoc. prof. Western Mich. U., Kalamazoo, Mich., 1969-73; from assoc. prof. to full prof. U. Wis., Madison, 1973—; asst. dir. NSF, Arlington, Va., 1992—; mem. sci. adv. panel U.S. Army, Washington, 1976-77; mem. Naval Rsch. Adv. Com., Washington, 1978-81, Pres. Commn. on the Accident at Three Mile Island, 1979; bd. govs. Argonne (Ill.) Nat. Lab., 1983-90. Editor: Research in Race and Ethnic Relations, 1988, Gender and Classroom Interaction, 1990. Resident fellow NAS, 1973-74; fellow Ctr. for Advanced Study in Behavioral Scis., 1976-77. Mem. AAAS, ASA, Phi Kappa Phi. Avocations: reading, travel, film appreciation. Home: 4545 Connecticut Ave NW # 207 Washington DC 20008 Office: NSF 4201 Wilson Blvd Arlington VA 22230

MARRINER, SIR NEVILLE, orchestra conductor; b. Lincoln, Eng., Apr. 15, 1924; s. Herbert Henry and Ethel May (Roberts) M.; m. Elizabeth Sims, Dec. 20, 1957; children: Susan Frances, Andrew Stephen. Ed., Royal Coll. Music, Paris Conservatory. Violinist Martin String Quartet, 1946-53, Virtuoso String Trio, 1950, Jacobean Ensemble, 1952, London Symphony Orch., from 1956; condr. L.A. Chamber Orch., 1969-77; music dir. Minn. Orch., 1979-86, Stuttgart (Germany) Symphony Orch., 1986-89; dir. South Bank Festival Music, 1975-78, Meadow Brook Festival, Detroit, 1979-84. Condr. Béatrice et Bénédict, Festival Hall, 1989; recs. include CDs of Dvořák Serenades, Haydn Violin Concerto in C, Mozart Serenade K361, Il Barbiere di Siviglia, Schubert 4th and 5th Symphonies, Baroque Favourites, with Yehudi Menuhin, The English Connection (Vaughan Williams The Lark Ascending, Elgar Serenade and Tippett Corelli Fantasia), Trumpet Concertos, with Håkan Hardenberger, Mendelssohn Piano Works with Murray Perahia, Mozart Haffner Serenade, 200 other recordings include Bach Concertos, Suites and Die Kunst der Fuge, Vivaldi, The Four Seasons and other concertos, Concerti Grossi by Corelli, Geminiani, Torelli, Locatelli and Manfredini, Mozart Symphonies, Concertos, Serenades and Divertimenti, Handel Messiah, Opera overtures and Water and Fireworks music, Die Zauberflöte, Handel Arias with Kathleen Battle, Il Turco in Italia and Don Giovanni. Bd. dirs., founder Acad. of St. Martin-in-the Fields, 1959—. Decorated Comdr. of Brit. Empire, KBE; recipient Grand Prix du Disque, Edison award, Mozart Gemeinde prize, Tagore prize, Grammy award, Shakespeare prize, KT of Polar Star, others. Fellow Royal Coll. Music, Royal Acad. Music. Office: Acad St Martin Fields Raine House, Raine St, London E1 9RG, England

MARRINGA, JACQUES LOUIS, manufacturing company executive; b. Rotterdam, The Netherlands, Aug. 8, 1928; came to U.S., 1965; s. Jakob and Christine Antoinette (Vandervalk) M.; m. Joan Kathryn Potter, Oct. 23, 1965; children—Jack, Bob, Katy. student, Erasmus U., Rotterdam, 1946-49, Doctors in Econs., 1954, Advanced Mgmt. Program Harvard U., 1984. Rsch. asst. Chem. Projects, N.Y.C., 1955; product mgr. Philips,N.V., Eindhoven, Netherlands, 1956-61; product line mgr. ITT, Brussels and N.Y.C., 1961-70; v.p. Elco Corp., Willow Grove, Pa., 1970-72, v.p. Crouse-Hinds, Syracuse, N.Y., 1972-77; group v.p. Sta-Rite Industries, Milw., 1977-94; pres. Marringa Internat. Corp, 1994—; bd. dirs. Marlo Inc., Racine, Wis. Mem. Milw. Country Club, Rotary (Milw.). Home: 2520 W Dean Rd Milwaukee WI 53217-2019

MARRINGTON, BERNARD HARVEY, retired automotive company executive; b. Vancouver, B.C., Can., Nov. 9, 1928; s. Fredrick George and Constance Marie (hall) M.; m. Patricia Grace Hall, Sept. 3, 1953 (div. 1993); children: Jodie Lynn, Stacey Lee. Student, U. Pitts., 1982, Bethany Coll., W.Va., 1983; BS in Mktg. Mgmt., Pacific Western U., 1985. V.p., sales mgr. W & L of La Mesa, Calif., 1960-66; pres., gen. mgr. W & L of La Mesa, 1966-68; regional mgr. PPG Industries, Inc., L.A., 1977-88, regional mgr. profit ctr., 1988-91; cons. L.A. Unified Sch. Dist., 1972, South Coast Air Quality Mgmt. Dist., El Monte, Calif., 1987-91; adv. com. So. Calif. Regional Occupational Ctr., Torrance, 1978-91. Contbr. articles to profl. jours. Sustaining sponsor Ronald Reagan Presdl. Found., Simi, 1987—; sustaining mem. Rep. Nat. Com., L.A., 1985-92, Rep. Presdl. Legion of Merit, 1986-94; del. Rep. Platform Planning com., L.A., 1992; charter mem. Nat. Tax Limitation Com., Washington, 1988, Jarvis Gann Taxpayers Assn., L.A., 1979-94; sponsor Reagan Presdl. Libr., 1986. Recipient Award for Outstanding Community Support, So. Calif. Regional Occupational Ctr., 1986. Episcopalian. Avocations: rose gardening, circus culture, golf, sailing, classical music.

MARRIOT, SALIMA SILER, state legislator, social work educator; b. Batl., Dec. 5, 1940; d. Jesse James and Cordie Susie (Ayers) Silver; m. David Small Mariott, Sept. 24, 1964 (div. 1972); children: Terrez Siler, Patrice Kenyatta. BS, Morgan State Coll., 1964; M in Social Work, U. Md., 1972; D in Social Work, Howard U., 1988. Tchr. Balt. City Pub. Sch., 1964-65; social worker N.Y.C. Social Svcs., 1965-67, Balt. City Social Svcs., 1968-72; instr., asst. prof. Morgan State U., Balt., 1972—; now also mem. Md. Ho. of Dels.; chair Park Heights Devel. Corp., Balt., 1976-92, Nat. Black Women's Health Project, 1993-94. Co-editor: U.S. Policy Toward Southern Africa, 1984. Cons. Balt. City Head Start, 1985-94; del. Dem. Conv., Atlanta, 1988; active Md. Dem. Ctrl. Com., 1988-90; sec. Nat. Rainbow Coalition; exec. bd. Nat. Black Caucus of State Legislators; vice chmn. Md. Legis. Black Caucus. Flemming fellow, 1995. Mem. Delta Sigma Theta. Office: Md House of Dels 4515 Homer Ave Baltimore MD 21215-6302

MARRIOTT, ALICE SHEETS (MRS. JOHN WILLARD MARRIOTT), restaurant chain executive; b. Salt Lake City, Oct. 19, 1907; d. Edwin Spencer and Alice (Taylor) Sheets; m. John Willard Marriott, June 9, 1927; children—John Willard, Richard Edwin. AB, U. Utah, 1927, LHD (hon.), 1974; LHD (hon.), Mt. Vernon Coll., 1980. Ptnr. Marriott Corp. (formerly Marriott-Hot Shoppes, Inc.), Washington, 1927, v.p., dir., 1929. Chmn. adv. com. on arts John F. Kennedy Center For Performing Arts, 1970-76; mem. adv. com. Nat. Com. Child Abuse, 1976—; mem. adv. council Nat. Arthritis and Musculoskeletal and Skin Diseases NIH, 1987—; bd. dirs. Washington Ballet Guild, Washington Home Rule Com., Arthritis and Rheumatism Found. of Met. Washington; trustee John F. Kennedy Center, 1972—; hon. trustee Nat. Arthritis Found., 1987—; mem. exec. com., vice chmn. Rep. Nat. Com., 1965-76, mem., officer numerous state coms.; treas. Rep. Nat. Conv., 1964, 68, 72, mem. Arrangements com., 1960, 64, 68, 72; mem. coord. com. Women's Nat. Rep. Club. Recipient 1st ann. Marriott Lifetime Achievement award Arthritis Found. Med. Washington Area, 1987. Mem. League Rep. Women D.C. (treas. 1955-57, v.p. 1957-59), Nat. Symphony Orch. Assn., Am. Newspaper Womens Club (asso. mem.), Capitol Speakers Club (membership chmn.), Welcome to Washington Internat. Clubs (treas., dir.), Chi Omega (Women of Achievement award 1989), Phi Kappa Phi. Mem. Ch. of Jesus Christ of Latter-Day Saints. Clubs: Washington, Capitol Hill, 1925 F Street. Home: 4500 Garfield St NW Washington DC 20007-1131 Office: Marriott Dr Washington DC 20058

MARRIOTT, DAVID M., public relations executive; b. Port Townsend, Wash., Oct. 1, 1943. BA in Radio and TV Comm., U. Wash., 1966. Reporter Sta. KVI, Seattle, 1966-68; gen. assignment and city hall reporter Sta. KIRO-TV, Seattle, 1968-72; press sec. Mayor of Seattle, 1972-77; dir. corp. comm. Alaska Airlines, 1977-82; area dir. Sheraton Corp. N.Am., 1982-84; v.p. Corp. Comm., Inc., 1984-86; ptnr. Bean/Marriott Pub. Rels., 1986; eec. v.p., gen. mgr. Evans/Kraft/Bean Pub. Rels., 1986-90; sr. v.p., mng. dir. pub. rels. Elgin Syferd, 1990-95; pres. Elgin Syferd Pub. Rels., Seattle, 1995—. Office: Elgin Syferd Pub Rels 1008 Western Ave Ste 601 Seattle WA 98104

MARRIOTT, JOHN WILLARD, JR., hotel and food service chain executive; b. Washington, Mar. 25, 1932; s. John Willard and Alice (Sheets) M.; m. Donna Garff, June 29, 1955; children: Deborah, Stephen Garff, John Willard, David Sheets. B.S. in Banking and Fin, U. Utah, 1954. V.p. Marriott Hot Shoppes Inc., 1959-64, exec. v.p., bd. dirs., 1964; pres. Marriott Corp., 1964—, chief exec. officer, 1972—, chmn. bd., 1985—; bd. dirs. Outboard Marine Corp., Waukegan, Ill., GM, U.S.-Russia Bus. Coun., Host Marriott Corp. (formerly Marriott Corp.). Trustee Mayo Found., Nat. Geog. Soc., Eisenhower Med. Ctr., Exec. Coun. on Fgn. Diplomats; mem. nat. adv. bd. Boy Scouts Am.; mem. conf. bd. Bus. Coun., Bus. Roundtable. Lt. USNR, 1954-56. Recipient Bus. Leader of Yr. award, Georgetown U. Sch. Bus. Adminstrn., 1984, Svc. Above Self award, Rotary Club at JFK Internat. Airport, 1985, Am. Mgr. of Yr. award, Nat. Mgmt. Assn., 1985, Golden Chain award, Nations's Restaurant News, 1985, Hall of Fame award, Consumer Digest Mag., 1985, Citizen of Yr. award, Boy Scouts of Am., 1986, Restaurant Bus. Leadership award, Restaurant Bus. Mag., 1986, Gold Plate award, Am. Acad. Achievement, 1986, Hall of Fame, Am. Hotel and Motel Assn., 1986, Hall of Fame award, Culinary Inst. of Am., 1987, Hospitality Exec. of Yr. award, Pa. State U., 1987, Bronze winner in Fin. World's Chief Exec. Officers award, 1988, Silver Plate award Lodging Hospitality Mag., 1988, Chief Exec. Officer of Yr. Chief Exec. Officer Mag., 1988, Signature award CA chpt. Nat. Multiple Scelerosis, 1988; named Outstanding Mktg. Exec. Gallagher Report, 1988. Mem. Conf. Bd., U.S. C. of C., Sigma Chi. Mem. LDS Ch. Clubs: Burning Tree (Washington), Met. (Washington). Office: Marriott Hotels Resorts & Suites Marriott Dr Washington DC 20058*

MARRO, ANTHONY JAMES, newspaper editor; b. Middlebury, Vt., Feb. 10, 1942; s. Francis James and Esther Martha (Butterfield) M.; m. Jacqueline Helen Cleary, June 5, 1965; 1 child, Alexandria. B.A. in History, U. Vt., 1965; M.S. in Journalism, Columbia U., 1968. Reporter Rutland (Vt.) Herald, 1964-67; Reporter Newsday, L.I., N.Y., 1968-74, chief Washington bur., 1979-81, mng. editor, 1981-86, exec. editor, 1986-87, editor, 1987—; reporter Newsweek, Washington, 1974-76, N.Y. Times, Washington, 1976-79. Co-recipient Pulitzer prizes for Pub. Service Reporting, 1970, 74. Office: Newsday 235 Pinelawn Rd Melville NY 11747-4226

MARRON, DONALD BAIRD, investment banker; b. Goshen, N.Y., July 21, 1934; m. Catherine D. Calligar. Student, Baruch Sch. Bus., 1949-51, 55-57. Investment analyst N.Y. Trust Co., N.Y.C., 1951-56, Lionel D. Edie Co., N.Y.C., 1956-58; mgr. research dept. George O'Neill & Co., 1958-59; pres. D.B. Marron & Co. Inc., N.Y.C., 1959-65; pres. Mitchell Hutchins & Co. Inc. (merger with D.B. Marron & Co. Inc. 1965), N.Y.C., 1965-69, pres., chief exec. officer, 1969-77; pres. PaineWebber Inc. (merger with Mitchell Hutchins & Co. Inc. 1977), N.Y.C., 1977-88, chief exec. officer, 1980—, chmn. bd., 1981—, also bd. dirs.; co-founder, former chmn. Data Resources, Inc.; former dir. N.Y. Stock Exchange. Vice chmn. bd. trustees Mus. of Modern Art; bd. overseers and mgrs. Meml. Sloan-Kettering; trustee for cultural resources N.Y.C., trustee Dana Found.; bd. dirs. N.Y.C. Partnership; bd. dirs. Bus. Com. for the Arts, Inc.; mem. Govs.'s Sch. and Bus. Alliance Task Force, N.Y.; mem. Coun. on Fgn. Rels., Inc.; mem. pres.'s com. on The Arts and The Humanities, Inc. Office: PaineWebber Group Inc 1285 Avenue Of The Americas New York NY 10019-6028 also: Mus Modern Art 11 W 53rd St New York NY 10019-5401*

MARROW, TRACY See ICE-T

MARRS, JAMES F. (JIM), JR., author, journalist, educator; b. Ft. Worth, Dec. 5, 1943; s. James Marrs; m. Carol Ann Worcester, May 25, 1968; children: Cathryn Nova Ayn, Jayme Alistar. BA in Journalism, North Tex. State U., 1966; postgrad., Tex. Tech. Coll., 1967-68. Editor/owner Magpie Mag., 1963-64; sports/news writer, cartoonist Denton (Tex.) Record Chronicle, 1965-66; reporter, copy editor, cartoonist and photographer Lubbock (Tex.) Avalanche-Jour., 1967-68; news and feature writer, cartoonist, photographer Lubbock Sentinel, 1968; reporter, feature writer, photographer, cartoonist Ft. Worth Star-Telegram, 1968-80; prodr. "Texas Roundup" Sammons Cable TV, Ft. Worth, 1982-83; scriptwriter Spindletop Prodns., Dallas, 1982-83; pub. rels. cons. The Mktg. Group, Dallas, 1982-83; pubr., co-owner The Springtown (Tex.) Current, 1983-84; comm. dir. Continental State Bank, Springtown, 1985—; editl. page editor Campus Chat, North Tex. State U., 1965-66; part-time copywriter, pub. rels. dir., cartoonist Jerre R. Todd & Assocs., 1972-74, dir. spl. projects, account exec., pub. rels. dir., 1980-81; editor/pub. and co-owner Cowtown Trails, Ft. Worth, 1983-84; faculty Office Continuing Edn. U. Tex., Arlington, 1976—; comm. dir. N.E. HealthCare Ctr., Hurst, Tex., 1985-86. Contbr. articles to profl. jours.; author: Crossfire: The Plot That Killed Kennedy, 1992; scriptwriter, dir. video: Fake, 1991, The Many Faces of Lee Harvey Oswald, 1992; author: The Enigma Files: The True Story of America's Psychic Warfare Program, 1995. Prodr. Tex. Gridiron Show, Ft. Worth, 1978-79, dir., 1980; chmn. pub. info. subcom. Ft. Worth Mayor's Com. on Employment of Handicapped, 1979-82; co-chmn. Springtown Centennial Com., 1984; workshop tchr. Operation CLASP, Neighborhood Adv. Coun., Community Devel. Block Grant, City of Ft. Worth, 1984; community rels. cons. All Church Home for Children, Ft. Worth, 1984—. With USAR, 1969-70. Recipient White Helmet award Ft. Worth Fire dept., 1969, 71, Assoc. Press writing awards, 1969-76, Nat. Writing award Aviation/Aerospace Writers Assn., 1972, Human Rights Leadership award Freedom Mag., 1993; named Arts and Entertainment Newsmaker of the Yr., Tex. Gridiron Club, Soc. Profl. Journalists, 1991. Mem. Tex. Mil. Hist. Soc., Springtown Optimist Club, Delta Sigma Phi, Sigma Delta Chi. Libertarian. Methodist. Avocation: civil war reenactor. Home and Office: Wise Comms PO Box 189 Springtown TX 76082-0189

MARRS, RICHARD PRESTON, gynecologist, obstetrician; b. Paducah, Tex., Dec. 6, 1947; s. Benjamin Verne and Mary Angela (Mattei) M., m. Joyce Marie Vargyas, Nov. 1, 1980 (div.); children: Ashley Marie, Austen Michael. AA, Schreiner Inst., Kerrville, Tex., 1968; BA, U. Tex., Austin, 1970; MD, U. Tex., Galveston, 1974. Lic. MD Tex, 1974, Calif., 1977; diplomate Am. Bd. Ob-Gyn, Am. Bd. Reproductive Endocrinology. Resident in Ob-Gyn U. Tex. Med. Br., Galveston, 1974-77, asst. prof., 1979-82; fellow in reproductive endocrinology U. So. Calif. Sch. Medicine, L.A., 1977-79, clin. instr. dept Ob-Gyn, 1977-79, from asst. to assoc. prof. dept. Ob-Gyn, 1979-86; dir. div. reproductive endocrinology and infertility Cedars-Sinai Med. Ctr., L.A., 1986-88; prof. dept. Ob-Gyn UCLA Sch. Medicine, 1986-88; dir. inst. for reproductive rsch. Hosp. Good Samaritan, L.A., 1988-92; pres. Marrs/Vargyas Corp., 1983-93; mem. sci. adv. bd. IVF Australia, 1988-92, Serono Pharm., 1989-94; mem. physician's adv. bd. Resolve, Inc., 1989—. Mem. editorial bd. Jour. In Vitro Fertilization and Embryo Transfer, Jour. Clin. Endocrinology and Metabolism; contbr. over 75 articles to med. jours.; contbr. chpts. to books. Recipient Squibb prize Pacific Coast Fertility Soc., 1979, Sci. Exhibit award Am. Coll. Ob-Gyn, 1980, Mem. Found. award 49th Ann. Mtg. Pacific Coast Ob-Gyn Coc., 1982, sr. residents award for excellence in teaching, 1980. Fellow Am. Coll. Obstetrics and Gynecology, Jeanne Kemper Found.; mem. In Vitro Fertilization Spl. Interest Group (chmn. 1986-88, pres. 1987-88), Los Angeles Obstetrics and Gynecology Soc., Salerni Collegium, AMA, Soc. for Gynecol. Investigation, Endocrine Soc., Soc. for Study of Reproduction, Am. Inst. Ultrasound In Medicine. Avocations: tennis, racquetball, horseback riding. Office: Marrs/Vargyas Corp 1245 16th St Ste 220 Santa Monica CA 90404-1240

MARRS, STEVEN D., advertising executive; b. Landstuhl, Platinate, Germany, Mar. 11, 1967; came to U.S., 1968; s. Cecil D. and Cynthia (Head) M.; m. Karol Ann Zeno, Aug. 9, 1992. BS in Advt., U. Fla., 1992. Account exec. McCabe and Co., N.Y.C., 1992; mktg. cons. MTV Networks, N.Y.C., 1992; account dir., dir. bus. devel. Frankfort Balkind Advt., N.Y.C., 1993—. Com. mem. Commn. Blind and Visually Handicapped, N.Y.C., 1994—. Mem. Am. Mktg. Assn. (Effie Judging Awards Honor, 1995), Advt. Club N.Y. (chmn. Pub. Svc. Com.), N.Y. New Media Assn. Office: Frankfort Balkind Partners 244 E 58th St New York NY 10022

MARS, FORREST E., SR., candy company executive; s. Frank and Ethel Mars; children: Forrest Jr., John, Jacqueline. Chmn. Mars Inc., McLean, Va. Office: Mars Inc 6885 Elm St Mc Lean VA 22101-3810

MARS, FORREST E., JR., candy company executive; s. Forrest Mars Sr.; married. Grad., Yale U., 1953. Co-pres., CEO Mars Inc. Office: Mars Inc 6885 Elm St Mc Lean VA 22101-3810*

MARS, JOHN F., candy company executive; b. 1935; married. Student, Yale U., 1957. Chmn. Kal Kan Foods Inc.; co-pres., CEO Mars Inc., 1973—. Office: Mars Inc 6885 Elm St Mc Lean VA 22101-3810*

MARSALIS, BRANFORD, musician; b. New Orleans, Aug. 26, 1960; s. Ellis Marsalis. Student, So. U., 1978, Berklee Coll. Music, 1979-81. Mem. Art Blakey Group, 1981, Wynton Marsalis Quintet, 1982; ind. saxophonist, 1983—; bandleader The Tonight Show, L.A., 1992-95. Rec. Artist: (with Wynton Marsalis) Wynton Marsalis, Think of One, Hot House Flowers, Black Codes (From the Underground), (with Art Blakey) Keystone 3, (with Kevin Eubanks) Opening Nights, (with Dizzy Gillespie) New Faces, Closer to the Source, (with Andy Jaffe) Manhattan Projects, (with Sting) Dream of the Blue Turtles, Bring on the Night; (solo albums) Romances for Saxophone, 1986, Royal Garden Blues, 1986, Renaissance, 1987, Random Abstract, 1988, Tio Jeepy, 1989, Crazy People Music, 1990, The Beautiful Ones Are Not Yet Born, 1991, Bloomington, 1993, Scenes in the City, I Heard You Twice the First Time, (Guru) Jazzmatazz, 1993; composer various pieces including No Backstage Pass, Solstice, Waiting for Rain, (video) David and Goliath, 1993, (film) Mo' Better Blues, 1990. Winner Down Beat magazine's readers' poll, best soprano sax player, 1991-92; Grammy award, Best Pop Instrumental 1994 for "Barcelona Mona" with Bruce Hornsby. also: PO Box 55398 Washington DC 20040-5398

MARSALIS, WYNTON, musician; b. New Orleans, Oct. 18, 1961; s. Ellis and Dolores Marsalis. Studied with John Longo; student, New Orleans Ctr. for Performing Arts, Berkshire Music Ctr., Juilliard Sch. Music, 1979-81. Trumpet soloist with New Orleans Philharm. Orch., 1975; recitalist with New Orleans Ctr. for Creative Arts, 1979; played with various New Orleans and N.Y.C. orchs.; with Art Blakey's Jazz Messengers, 1980-81, Herbie Hancock's V.S.O.P. quartet; formed own group, 1981; albums include Fathers and Sons, 1982, Hummel/Haydn/L. Mozart Trumpet Concertos, 1983 (Grammy award), Wynton Marsalis (Best Jazz Record, Downbeat readers' poll 1982), Think of One, 1983 (Grammy award), Handel, purcell, Torelli, Fasch, Moler (Grammy award), Trumpet Concertos, 1983, Hot House Flowers, 1984, Black Codes from the Underground, 1985 (2 Grammy awards), J Mood, 1986, Carnaval, 1987, Marsalis Standard Time, Vol. 1, 1987 (Grammy award), Majesty of the Blues, 1989, Standard Time, Vol. 3, 1990, Intimacy Calling Standard Time, Soul Gestures in Southern Blue, Vols. 1, 2, 3, 1991, Blue Interlude, 1992, Citi Movement, 1993, In This House, On This Morning, 1994. Named Jazz Musician of Yr., Downbeat readers' poll, 1982, 84-86, 89, Best Trumpet Player, Downbeat critics' poll, 1984, Acoustic Jazz Group of Yr., 1984, Best Trumpet Player, Downbeat readers' poll, 1985; recipient Grammy award for best solo jazz instrumental, 1983-85, Grammy award for best solo classical performance with orch., 1984-85, Grammy award for best jazz instrumental performance with group, 1985, 87; musician of the Year, Down Beat Readers' poll, 1992. Office: care Agy for Performing Arts 9000 W Sunset Blvd West Hollywood CA 90069-5801

MARSAN, JEAN-CLAUDE, architect, urban planner, educator; b. St-Eustache, Que., Can., Oct. 7, 1938; s. Aimè and Gertrude (Bolduc) M.; children: Jean-Sèbastien, Marc-Aurèle. BA, U. Montreal, Que., 1960, BArch, 1965; MSc in Urban Planning, U. Edinburgh, Scotland, 1968, PhD in Urban Planning, 1975. Assoc. prof. Sch. Architecture U. Montreal, 1975-84, prof., 1984—, dean Faculté de L'Amènagement, 1984-93, dir. Sch. Architecture, 1975-79; rsch. prof. Inst. quèbècois de recherche sur la culture, 1980-82; pres. Com. to Study the Future of Olympic Installations, Montreal, 1977. Author: Montrèal en èvolution, 1974, Montrèal une esquisse du futur, 1983, Sauver Montrèal, 1990; contbr. articles to profl. jours. and newspapers, chpts. to books. Founding mem. Save Montreal, 1973-78, Mcpl. Action Group, 1978; pres. Heritage Montreal, 1983-88; bd. dirs. Mus. Fine Arts Montreal, 1975-87, v.p., 1978-87, Hô tel Dien Hospital Montrèal, 1996—, Commn. de la Capital Nationale Du Quebec, 1995—. Mem. Ordre des Architectes du Que. (Priz Paul-Henri Lapoint 1984, 85, 87, Prix Gérard Morisset 1992, govt. of Que.), Royal Soc. Can., Ordre des Urbanistes du Què, Officier de L'Ordre du Can. Office: U Montreal Box 6128 Sta A, Faculté de l'Aménagement, Montreal, PQ Canada H3C 3J7

MARSCHER, FRAN HEYWARD (FRAN SMITH), editor; b. Charleston, S.C., Dec. 10, 1941; d. Daniel H. Jr. and Margaret (Zorn) Hegward; m. Elmer Hainesworth Smith Jr., July 30, 1961 (div. Feb. 1987); children: Georgia Leigh Smith Horan, Margaret Daniel Smith McCarthy; m. William Frederick Marscher, Nov. 26, 1994. BA in Journalism, U. S.C., 1963. Feature writer Savannah (Ga.) News Press, 1963-65; English tchr. Bluffton (S.C.) H.S., 1968-70; reporter The Island Packet, Hilton Head Island, S.C., 1978-80, 81-85, assoc. editor, 1985-87, editor, 1987—; reporter Daily News Sun, Sun City, Ariz., 1980-81; workshop chmn. S.C. Press Assn., Columbia, 1991-92, mem. com., 1987-91. Bd. dirs. Vol. Action Ctr., Hilton Head Island, 1988-90, Literacy Vols., Hilton Head Island, 1988-92; founding bd. dirs. Bluffton (S.C.) Libr., 1985-88, Hilton Head Mus., 1985-87. Recipient 1st place Pub. Svc. award S.C. Press Assn., 1991-92, 1st place award Inst. for So. Studies, 1991-92, Harry Hampton award for Journalism, S.C. Wildlife Fedn., 1983. Mem. S.C. Coastal Conservation League. Episcopalian. Avocations: reading, gardening, birdwatching, music. Home: 23 Big Oak St Hilton Head Island SC 29926 Office: The Island Packet 1 Pope Ave Park Hilton Head Island SC 29928

MARSCHING, RONALD LIONEL, lawyer, former precision instrument company executive; b. N.Y.C., Mar. 30, 1927; m. Marjory Fleming Duncan, Dec. 31, 1964; children: Christine, Jane. BA cum laude, Princeton U., 1950; JD, Harvard U., 1953. Bar: N.Y. 1954. Assoc. White & Case, N.Y.C.; vice chmn., gen. counsel Timex Corp., Waterbury, Conn., 1967-86, also bd. dirs. Served with U.S. Army, 1953-55. Mem. ABA, Nat. Assn. Dirs., University Club (N.Y.C. chpt.). Home: 41 E Hill Rd Woodbury CT 06798-3017

MARSDEN, BRIAN GEOFFREY, astronomer; b. Cambridge, Eng., Aug. 5, 1937; came to U.S., 1959; s. Thomas and Eileen (West) M.; m. Nancy Lou Zissell, Dec. 26, 1964; children: Cynthia Louise, Jonathan Brian. BA, Oxford U., U.K., 1959, MA, 1963; PhD, Yale U., 1965. Rsch. asst. Yale U., New Haven, 1959-65; lectr. astronomy Harvard U., Cambridge, Mass., 1966-83; astronomer Smithsonian Astrophys. Obs., Cambridge, 1965-86; assoc. dir. planetary scis. Harvard-Smithsonian Ctr. for Astrophysics, Cambridge, 1987—; dir. Cen. Bur. Astron. Telegrams, 1968—, Minor Planet Ctr. Internat. Astron. Union, 1978—. Editor: The Earth-Moon System, 1966, The Motion, Evolution of Orbits and Origin of Comets, 1972, Catalogue of Cometary Orbits, 1996, Catalogue of Orbits of Unnumbered Minor Planets, 1996. Recipient Merlin medal Brit. Astron. Assn., 1965, Goodacre medal, 1979; Van Biesbroeck award U. Ariz., 1989, Camus-Waitz prize Societé astronomique de France, 1993. Dirk Brouwer award Am. Astron. Soc., 1995. Fellow Royal Astron. Soc.; mem. Am. Astron. Soc. (chmn. div. on dynamical astronomy 1976-78), Internat. Astron. Union (pres. commn. 1976-79), Astron. Soc. Pacific, Sigma Xi. Office: Harvard-Smithsonian Ctr Astrophysics 60 Garden St Cambridge MA 02138-1596

MARSDEN, CHARLES JOSEPH, financial executive; b. N.Y.C., Dec. 18, 1940; s. David Joseph and Louise (Noell) M.; m. Marilyn Weber, Nov. 12, 1988 ; children from previous marriage: Anne Brewer, George David. A.B. cum laude, Amherst Coll., 1962; M.B.A. with distinction, Harvard U., 1965. Credit analyst Irving Trust Co., N.Y.C., 1962-63; with W.R. Grace & Co., 1965-81; treas. Polyfibron Div. W.R. Grace & Co., Cambridge, Mass., 1969-72; v.p. fin. adminstrn. Cryovac Div. W.R. Grace & Co., Duncan, S.C., 1972-78; v.p. fin. Indsl. Chems. Group W.R. Grace & Co., N.Y.C., 1978-81; exec. v.p., chief fin. officer The Grand Union Co., Elmwood Park, N.J., 1981-83; also dir. The Grand Union Co.; v.p. fin. Pan Am. World Airways, Inc., 1984-85; v.p. fin., chief fin. officer Crompton & Knowles Corp., 1985—, also dir. Mem. Harvard Club. Office: Crompton & Knowles Corp 1 Station Pl Stamford CT 06902-6800

MARSDEN, HERCI IVANA, classical ballet artistic director; b. Omis-Split, Croatia, Dec. 2, 1937; came to U.S., 1958; d. Ante and Magda (Smith) Munitic; m. Myles Marsden, Aug. 10, 1957 (div. 1976); children—Ana, Richard, Mark; m. Dujko Radovnikovic, Aug. 27, 1977; 1 child, Dujko. Student, Internat. Ballet Sch., 1955. Mem. corps de ballet Nat. Theatre, Split, 1954-58; founder Braecrest Sch. Ballet, Lincoln, R.I., 1958—; founder State Ballet of R.I., Lincoln, 1960—, artistic dir., 1976—; artistic dir. U. R.I. Classical Ballet, Kingston, 1966—, lectr., 1966—.

MARSDEN, LAWRENCE ALBERT, retired textile company executive; b. Mpls., May 28, 1919; s. Lawrence N. and Carrie Elizabeth (Ross) M.; m. Millicent Irene Snyder, Mar. 24, 1941; children: Millicent Carrie, Andrea Leigh, Lawrence Stewart, John Daniel. B.S. in Law, U. Minn., 1941; LL.B., George Washington U., 1946. Bar: D.C. 1946. Ptnr. Onion, Marsden & New, Washington, 1947-48; pres. Marsden-Slate, Inc., High Point, N.C., 1949-68; v.p. Guilford Mills, Inc., Greensboro, N.C., 1968-72, sr. v.p., 1973-84; chmn. Marcor, Inc., High Point, 1980—; ptnr. SPM Investments; pres. Fabrilux Products, Inc., High Point, 1995—. Served to lt. comdr. USN, 1941-46, PTO. Mem. Am. Assn. Textile Chemists and Colorists, Sportsman Pilots Assn. (past pres.), Aircraft Owners and Pilots Assn., Rolls Royce Owner's Club, Quiet Birdmen, High Point Country Club, Willow Creek Golf Club (High Point), Isla Del Sol Yacht and Country Club (St. Petersburg, Fla.), Phi Delta Phi, Phi Delta Theta. Republican. Home: 1706 Maryfield Ct High Point NC 27260-2684

MARSDEN, WILLIAM, government official; b. Cambridge, Eng., Sept. 15, 1940; s. Christopher Alexander Marsden and Ruth Kershaw; m. Kaia Collingham, Sept. 9, 1964; children: Inge, Thomas. BSc in Econs., London U., 1973; MA, Cambridge U., 1962. 3d sec. U.K. Del. to NATO, Paris, 1964-66; 2d sec. Brit. Embassy, Rome, 1966-70; 1st sec. Brit. Embassy, Moscow, 1976-78; min. trade Brit. Embassy, Washington, 1992-94; 1st sec. sci. and tech. Fgn. Office, London, 1971-75, asst. head European community dept., 1978-81, head African dept., commr. Brit. Indian Ocean Ter., 1985-89, amb. to Costa Rica and Nicaragua, 1989-92, asst. under sec. of state For the Americas, 1994—; counsellor U.K. Representation to EEC, Brussels, 1981-85. Named Companion of Order St. Michael and St. George by Her Majesty the Queen. Mem. Brit. Inst. Mgmt., The City London (freeman), The Grocers' Co. London (freeman), The Univ. Club, The Lansdowne Club. Office: Under Sec For the Americas, Fgn Office, London SW1A 2AH, England

MARSEE, STUART (EARL), educational consultant, retired; b. Gardener, Oreg., Sept. 30, 1917; s. William and Clare (Grimes) M.; m. Audrey Belfield, June 1, 1940; children: Frederic, Jeffrey, Wayne. BS, U. Oreg., 1939, MS, 1942; EdD, U. So. Calif., 1947; LLD, Pepperdine U., 1977. Asst. supt. for bus. Pasadena City Schs., Calif., 1949-57, acting supt., 1957-58, asst. supt., 1949-58; pres. El Camino Coll., 1958-82, cons., 1982—; lectr. UCLA, 1965, U. So. Calif., 1956-57; adj. prof. Pepperdine U., 1978-79. Author: History of the Rotary Club of Torrance, 1962-74, 1974; contbr. articles to profl. jours. Recipient Disting. Service award Los Angeles County Bd. Suprs., 1958, Disting. Service Leadership award Kiwanis Internat., 1970; named Citizen of Yr., Torrance, Calif., 1981, Redondo Beach, Calif., 1986. Mem. Am. Assn. Cmty. and Jr. Colls. (pres. 1968), Nat. Commn. Accrediting (dir. 1970-74), Coun. Postsecondary Accreditation (dir. 1974-78), Western Coll. Assn. (mem. exec. com. 1978-81). Office: 358 Camino De Las Colinas Redondo Beach CA 90277-6435

MARSEE, SUSANNE IRENE, lyric mezzo-soprano; b. San Diego, Nov. 26, 1941; d. Warren Jefferson and Irene Rose (Wills) Dowell; m. Mark J. Weinstein, May, 1987; 1 child, Zachary. Student, Santa Monica City Coll., 1961; BA in History, UCLA, 1964. Mem. voice faculty Am. Mus. and Dramatic Acad., N.Y.C., 1994—; assoc. prof. La State U. Appeared with numerous U.S. opera cos., 1970—, including N.Y.C. Opera, San Francisco Opera, Boston Opera, Houston Grand Opera; appeared with fgn. cos., festivals, Mexico City Bellas Artes, 1973, 78, Canary Islands Co., 1976, Opera Metropolitana, Caracas, Venezuela, 1977, Spoleto (Italy) Festival, 1977, Aix en Provence Festival, France, 1977, Calgary, Alta., Can., 1986; recorded Tales of Hoffman, ABC/Dunhill Records; TV appearances include Live from Lincoln Center, Turk in Italy, Cenerentola, 1980, Live from Wolftrap, Roberto Devereux's Rigoletto, 1988, A Little Night Music, 1990, Marriage of Figaro, 1991, (PBS TV) Rachel, La Cubana; recs. and CDs Anna Bolena with Ramey, Scotto, Roberto Devereux with Beverly Sills, Roberto Devereux with Monserat Caballé, Tales of Hoffmann with Beverly Sills, Rigoletto with Quilico and Carreras; videotape Roberto Devereux with Beverly Sills. Recipient 2d place award Met. Opera Regional Auditions, 1968, San Francisco Opera Regional Auditions 1968; named winner Liederkranz Club Contest, 1970; Gladys Turk Found. grantee, 1968-69; Corbett Found. grantee, 1969-73; Martha Baird Rockefeller grantee, 1969-70, 71-72. Mem. AFTRA, Am. Guild Mus. Artists (past bd. dirs.), Nat. Assn. Tchrs. of Singing (bd. dirs. for N.Y.). Democrat.

MARSEL, ROBERT STEVEN, lawyer, legal educator, mediator, arbitrator; b. N.Y.C., July 23, 1947; s. Bernard and Vivian (Gilbert) M. J.D., U. Calif., 1971. Bar: N.Y., D.C., U.S. Supreme Ct. Fellow Worcester Coll., Oxford, Eng.; vis. lectr. Faculty Law, U. Auckland N.Z.; spl. asst. U.S. atty., San Francisco; legal officer U.S. Supreme Ct., Washington; vis. asst. prof. law U. Miami, 1983-84; prof. South Tex. Coll. Law, Houston, 1984—; chmn. com. on privacy and confidentiality U.S. Dept. Commerce, 1973-75; trainer, lectr. on mediation; mediator pro bono Houston Dispute Resolution Ctr.; faculty mem. Ctr. for Legal Responsibility. U. Calif. hon. traveling fellow, 1971-72. Fellow Houston Bar Found.; mem. Am. Arbitration Assn., Tex. Assn. Mediators, State Bar Tex. (mem. alternative dispute resolution section), Tex. Accts. and Lawyers for the Arts (mediation com.), Soc. Profls. in Dispute Resolution. Office: South Texas Coll of Law 1303 San Jacinto St Houston TX 77002-7013

MARSELLA, ANTHONY J., psychologist, educator; b. Cleve., Sept. 12, 1940; m. Joy Anne Marsella, June 22, 1963; children: Laura Joy, Gianna Malia. BA in Psychology with honors, Baldwin-Wallace Coll., 1962; PhD in Clin. Psychology, Pa. State U., 1968. Lic. psychologist, Hawaii. Intern Worcester (Mass.) State Hosp., 1966-67; Fulbright rsch. scholar Alteneo de Manila U., Quezon City, The Philippines, 1967-68; postdoctoral rsch. scholar NIMH Culture-Mental Health Program, East-West Ctr., Honolulu, 1968-69; prof. psychology, dir. clin. studies program U. Hawaii, Honolulu, 1969—; dir. WHO Psychiat. Rsch. Ctr., Honolulu; cons. Inst. Stress Rsch. of Karolinska Inst., Stockholm, Divsn. Mental Health, WHO, Geneva; mem. Substance Abuse, Alcoholism and Mental Health Adminstrn. Health Mental Health Grant Review Panel for Ctr. for Mental Health Svcs.; v.p. acad. affairs U. Hawaii, 1985-89; vis. prof. Melbourne U., Monash U., Korea U., King George Med. Coll., India, Shanghai Psychiat. Inst., Ateneo de Manila U., Johns Hopkins U., Balt.; lectr. in field. Author 10 books and over 100 articles to profl. jours.; assoc. editor: Encyclopedia of Psychology; jour. reviewer. Fellow APA; mem. Hawaii Psychol. Assn., Internat. Assn. for Cross-Cultural Psychology, Soc. for Study of Culture and Psychiatry, World Fedn. Mental Health, Amnesty Internat., Psi Chi, Omicron Delta Kappa, Sigma Xi. Home: 1429 Laamia St Honolulu HI 96821

MARSH, BENJAMIN FRANKLIN, lawyer; b. Toledo, Apr. 30, 1927; s. Lester Randall and Alice (Smith) M.; m. Martha Kirkpatrick, July 12, 1952; children: Samuel, Elizabeth. BA, Ohio Wesleyan U., 1950; JD, George Washington U., 1954. Bar: Ohio 1955. Pvt. practice law Toledo, 1955-88, Maumee, Ohio, 1988—; assoc., ptnr. Doyle, Lewis & Warner, Toledo, 1955-71; ptnr. Ritter, Boesel, Robinson & Marsh, Toledo, 1971-88, Marsh & McAdams, Maumee, 1988—; personnel officer AEC, 1950-54; asst. atty. gen. State of Ohio, 1969-71; asst. solicitor City of Maumee, 1959-63, solicitor, 1963-92; mem. U.S. Fgn. Claims Settlement Commn., Washington, 1990-94; counsel N.W. Ohio Mayors and Mgrs. Assn., 1993—; mem. regional bd. rev. Indsl. Commn. Ohio, Toledo, 1993-94; mem. Ohio Dental Bd. U.S. rep. with rank spl. amb. to 10th Anniversary Independence of Botswana, 1976; past pres. Toledo and Lucas County Tb Soc., citizens for metro pks.; past mem. Judges Com. Notaries Pub.; formerly mem. Lucas County Bd. Elections; former chmn. bldg. commn. Riverside Hosp., Toledo; past trustee Com. on Rels. with Toledo, Spain; past chmn. bd. trustee Med. Coll., Ohio; past treas. Coglin Meml. Inst.; chmn. Lucas County Rep. Exec. Com., 1973-74; precinct commiteeman, Maumee, 1959-73; legal counsel, bd. dirs. Nat. Coun. Rep. Workshops, 1960-65; pres. Rep. Workshops, Ohio, 1960-64; alt. del. Rep. Nat. Conv., 1964; candidate 9th dist. U.S. Ho. of Reps., 1968; adminstrv. asst. to Rep. state chmn. Ray C. Bliss, 1954; chmn. Lucas County Bush for Pres., 1980; co-chmn. Reagan-Bush Com. for Northwestern Ohio, 1980, vice chmn. fin. com. Bush-Quayle, 1992; co-chmn. Ohio steering com. Bush for Pres., mem. nat. steering com., 1988; del. Rep. Nat. Conv., 1988; past bd. dirs. Ohio Tb and Respiratory Disease Assn.; apptd. Ohio chmn. UN Day, 1980, 81, 82; adminstrv. asst. Legis. Svc. Commn., Columbus, 1954-55; mem. Lucas County Charter Commn., Toledo, 1959-60; vice-chmn. U.S. Nat. Commn. for UNESCO, mem. legal com., del. 17th gen. conf., Paris, 1972, U.S. observer meeting of nat. commns., Africa, 1974, Addis Ababa, Ethiopia; past mem. industry functional adv. com. on standards trade policy matters; mem. nat. def. exec. res. Dept. Commerce; active Am. Bicentennial Presdl. Inauguration, Diplomatic Adv. Com. With USNR, 1945-46. Named Outstanding Young Man of Toledo, 1962. Mem. ABA, Maumee C. of C. (trustee), Ohio Bar Assn., Toledo Bar Assn., Nat. Inst. Mcpl. Law Officers, Ohio Mpcl. League (past pres.), Am. Legion, Maumee Valley Hist. Soc. (trustee), George Washington Law Assn., Internat. Inst. Toledo, Ohio Mcpl. Attys. Assn. (past pres.), Ohio Hist. Soc., Am. Canal Soc., Canal Soc. Ohio, Toledo Mus. Art, Ohio Wesleyan U. Alumni Assn. (past pres.), Toledo C. of C., Ohio State Bar Found., Rotary, Laurel Hill Swim and Tennis Club, Faculty Club Med. Coll., Toledo Country Club, Press Club, Omicron Delta Kappa, Delta Sigma Rho, Theta Alpha Phi, Phi Delta Phi. Presbyterian. Home: 124 W Harrison St Maumee OH 43537-2119 Office: 312 Conant St Maumee OH 43537-3358

MARSH, BRUCE DAVID, geology educator; b. Munising, Mich., Jan. 4, 1947; s. William Roland and Audrey Jane (Steinhoff) M.; m. Judith Anne Congdon, Jan. 24, 1970; children: Hannah Eyre, William Noah. BS, Mich. State U., 1969; MS, U. Ariz., 1971; PhD, U. Calif.-Berkeley, 1974. Geologist, geophysicist Anaconda Co., Tucson, 1969-71; asst. prof. dept. earth/planet sci. Johns Hopkins U., Balt., 1974-78, assoc. prof., 1978-81, prof., 1981—; chmn., 1989-93; vis. prof. Calif. Inst. Tech., Pasadena, 1985, U. Maine, 1992-93; co-chmn. Gordon Rsch. Conf. on Inorganic Geochemistry, Holderness, N.H., 1983-84; advisor NASA, Washington, 1975-84, NSF, Washington, 1978-90, NRC, 1985-91; Hallimond lectr. Mineral. Soc. Great Britain and Ireland, 1995. Assoc. editor Geology, 1981-83, Jour. Volcanology and Geothermal Rsch., 1978—, Jour. Petrology, 1986—. Fellow Geol. Soc. Am. (assoc. editor Bulletin 1986-92), Royal Astron. Soc.; Fellow Am. Geophys. Union (sec. sect. on volcanology, geochemistry and petrology 1984-86, pres. elect 1988-90, pres. 1990-92, Bowen award 1993); mem. Model A Ford Club Am. Office: Johns Hopkins U Dept Earth & Planetary Scis 322 Olin Hall Baltimore MD 21218

MARSH, CARYL AMSTERDAM, museum exhibitions curator, psychologist; b. N.Y.C., Mar. 9, 1923; d. Louis and Kitty (Weitz) Amsterdam; m. Michael Marsh, Sept. 3, 1942; children: Susan E., Anna L. B.A., Bklyn. Coll., 1942; M.A., Columbia U., 1946; Ph.D., George Washington U., 1978. Lic. psychologist, D.C. Asst. cultural attache Am. Embassy, Paris, 1946-48; psychologist D.C. Recreation Dept., 1957-69; spl. asst. Smithsonian Instn., Washington, 1966-73; curator exhbns. Nat. Archives, Washington, 1978-85, sr. exhbns. specialist, 1985-86; dir. traveling psychology exhbn. Am. Psychol. Assn., 1986-93, sr. advisor, 1993-95; chair humanities seminars in sci. mus. Assn. Sci. Tech. Ctrs., 1994—; rsch. fellow exptl. gallery Smithsonian Instn., 1992; rsch. cons. Nat. Zoo, 1981-92, Smithsonian Folk Life Festival, Nat. Mus. Am. History, 1977-78; organizer Discovery Room Nat. Mus. Natural History, 1969-73; cons. Meyer Found., 1964-66. Editor: Exhibition: The American Image, 1979. Organizer Anacostia Neighborhood Mus., Washington, 1967, bd. dirs., 1974—, v.p. 1993; sec. D.C. Commn. on Arts and Humanities, 1969-72; pres. Pre-Sch. Parents Coun., Washington, 1956-57. Fellow Nat. Mus. Am. Art, 1975-77; vis. scholar Nat. Mus. Am. Art, 1978—; grad. fellow CUNY, 1945-46; scholar George Washington U.; noted for Disting. Contbn. to Pub. Understanding of Psychology, APA, 1993. Mem. AAAS, APA (Outstanding Svc. award 1992, Disting. Contbn. to Pub. Understanding of Psychology award 1993), D.C. Psychol. Assn., Am. Assn. Mus., Mus. Edn. Roundtable (bd. dirs. 1983-87). Home and Office: 3701 Grant Rd NW Washington DC 20016-1819

MARSH, CARYL GLENN, career officer; b. Ky., Oct. 12, 1939; m. Claire Boudrias, Sept. 11, 1961; children: Jeffrey, Regina, John. BS in Agr., U. Ky., 1961; MPA, Auburn U., 1973. Commd. 2d lt. U.S. Army, 1962, advanced through grades to lt. gen., 1994; ops. officer, then dep. brigade comdr. Berlin Brigade, 1979-81, brigade comdr., 1987-89; div. chief staff 9th Inf. Divsn. Inf. Div., Ft. Lewis, Wash., 1981-82, brigade comddr., 1982-84; chief staff I Corps, Ft. Lewis, 1984-85; asst. div. comdr. Air Assault Div., Ft. Campbell, Ky., 1985-87; comdg. gen. 2d Inf. Div., Camp Casey, Republic of Korea, 1989-91; dep. comdr.-in-chief, chief staff Hdqrs. Forces Command, Ft. McPherson, Ga., 1991-94; comdr. I Corps and Ft. Lewis (Wash.), 1994—. Mem. Kiwanis. Roman Catholic. Avocation: hunting. Office: I Corps & Ft Lewis Fort Lewis WA 98433*

MARSH, CHERYL LEPPERT, marketing professional; b. Upper Darby, Pa., July 24, 1946; d. Edward Franklin and Jeanne Isabelle (Stults) Leppert; m. John Nicholas Marsh III, July 24, 1972; children: Barnaby, Jessica, Wellesley, Brooks, Forbes. Student, Art Inst./Carnegie Tech., 1968, Barnes Found., 1972. Advt. and sales promotion mgr. Binney and Smith Inc., N.Y.C., 1974-75; advt. and sales promotion dir. consumer and indsl. products Carborundum Corp., N.Y.C., 1972-74, Union Carbide Corp., N.Y.C., 1968-72; sr. planner IV State of Alaska, Anchorage, 1982-83; mktg. and art svcs. staff Mkt. Rsch. and Design Assocs., N.Y.C., 1975-78; pres. Epicurean Delights, Cambridge, Mass. Recipient Senatorial scholarship Art Inst/Carnegie Tech., 1968. Mem. NAFE, Am. Mgmt. Assn., Art Dirs. Club. Home: 462 Apple Dr Exton PA 19341-3148 Office: Market Rsch & Design 200 Park Ave New York NY 10166-0005 also: Box 1215 Harvard Sq Cambridge MA 02238

MARSH, DAVE RODNEY, writer, publisher, editor; b. Pontiac, Mich., Mar. 1, 1950; s. Oliver Kenneth and Mary A. (Evon) M.; m. Barbara E. Carr, July 21, 1979; stepchildren: Sasha J. Carr, Kristen A. Carr (dec.). Student, Wayne State U., 1968-69. Editor Creem Mag., Detroit and Birmingham, Mich., 1969-73; music critic Newsday, Garden City, N.Y., 1973, 74-75; assoc. editor Rolling Stone Mag., N.Y.C., 1975-78, contbg. editor, 1978-85; contbg. editor The Record, N.Y.C., 1982-84; editor, pub. Rock & Rap Confidential, L.A., 1983—; music critic Playboy, 1985—, Rock Today (syndicated radio), 1987-92; contbg. editor Entertainment Weekly, 1991-93. Author: Born to Run: The Bruce Springsteen Story, 1979, The Book of Rock Lists, 1981, Elvis, 1982, Before I Get Old, 1983, Fortunate Son, 1985, Michael Jackson and the Crossover Dream, 1985, Glory Days: Bruce Springsteen in the 1980s, 1987; The Heart of Rock and Soul, 1989, 50 Ways to Fight Censorship, 1991, Louie, Louie, 1993, Merry Christmas Baby, 1993, The New Book of Rock Lists, 1994; editor: Rolling Stone Record Guide, 1979, The First Rock and Roll Confidential Report, 1985, Pastures of Plenty (Woody Guthrie, Harper and Row), 1990, (with Don Henley) Heaven Is Under Our Feet: Essays for Walden Woods, 1991, Mid-Life Confidential: The Rock Bottom Remainders Tour America, 1994; host Radio Mafia, Finland, 1990—. Trustee Kristen Ann Carr Fund; active The Critics Chorus, Rock Bottom Remainders, 1992-95. Office: Rock & Rap Confidential PO Box 341305 Los Angeles CA 90034-9305

MARSH, DONALD JAY, college dean, medical educator; b. N.Y.C., Aug. 5, 1934; m. Wendy G. Clough; 2 children. AB, U. Calif., Berkeley, 1955; MD, U. Calif., San Francisco, 1958. Intern in medicine UCLA Hosp., 1958-59; postdoctoral fellow dept. physiology NYU, 1959-60, instr. dept. physiology, 1960-61, asst. prof. physiology and biophysics, 1963-67, assoc. prof. physiology and biophysics, 1967-71; prof. biomed. engrng. U. So. Calif., 1971-92, prof., chmn. dept. physiology and biophysics, 1978-92, prof. medicine, 1982-92, rsch. prof. physiology and biophysics, 1992—; prof. physiology Brown U., Providence, 1992—, dean medicine and biol. scis., 1992—, Frank L. Day prof. biology, 1995—; mem. engrng. in medicine and biology tng. com. NIH, 1973, cardiovascular renal study sect., 1983-86, ad hoc mem. med. lab. scis. rev. com., 1976, inst. gen. med. scis. adv. com., 1982; ad hoc reviewer NSF; mem. rsch. com. Am. Heart Assn., 1979-82, rev. coms. for grants-in-aid, pub. affairs com., 1986-88; cons. com. interdisciplinary rsch. Nat. Rsch. Coun.- Inst. of Medicine, 1989; mem. med. schs. sect. task force AMA, 1994—; lectr. in field. Mem. editorial bd. Annals of Biomed. Engrng., 1972-74, mng. editor, 1974-78; mem. editorial bd. Am. Jour. Physiology and Jour. of Applied Physiology, 1972-76, Am. Jour. Physiology: Regulatory, Integrative and Comparative Physiology, 1977-79, Am. Jour. Physiology: Renal, Fluid and Electrolyte Physiology, 1977-82, 88-94, Am. Jour. Physiology: Modelling Methodology Forum, 1984-91; guest reviewer Biophys. Jour., Circulation Rsch., Jour. Clin. Investigation, Jour Theoretical Biology, Kidney Internat., Sci., Pfluegers Archiv European Jour. Physiology; contbr. articles to profl. jours., chpts. to books. Named Career Scientist, Health Rsch. Coun. N.Y., 1964-71; Spl. fellow NIH, 1970-71, grantee, 1990-94, 91—. Fellow AAAS; mem. Assn. Am. Med. Colls. (coun. of deans), Am. Soc. Nephrology, Am. Physiol. Soc. (com. on coms. 1980-83, chmn. renal sect. 1982-83, long range planning com. 1990-93), Biophys. Soc., Microvascular Soc., Soc. Gen. Physiologists, Soc. Math. Biology (nominating com. 1983, publs. com. 1984-85, bd. dirs. 1986-88), Alpha Omega Alpha. Home: 148 Pratt St Providence RI 02906-1411 Office: Brown U Sch of Medicine Box G-A1 Providence RI 02912

MARSH, FRANK (IRVING), former state official; b. Norfolk, Nebr., Apr. 27, 1924; s. Frank and Delia (Andrews) M.; m. Shirley Mac McVicker, Mar. 5, 1943; children: Sherry Anne Marsh Tupper, Corwin Frank, Stephen Alan (dec.), Mitchell Edward, Dory Michael, Melissa Lou. BS, U. Nebr., 1950; hon. degree in commerce and bus., Lincoln Sch. Commerce, 1975. Builder, businessman, part-time instr. Lincoln Sch. System, 1946-52; sec. of state State of Nebr., Lincoln, 1953-71, lt. gov., 1971-75, state treas., 1975-81, 87-91; state dir. Farmers Home Adminstrn., Lincoln, 1981-85; with Tabitha, Inc., Lincoln, 1986; ptnr. Lincoln Landscaping and Landscape Interiors Inc., 1983—; organizer, CEO Lincoln FoodNet, Inc. Ops., 1985—; U.S. State Dept. escort, interpreter, cons. Ctr. Continuing Edn., U. Nebr., 1986-87; mem. Foodchain Assn. (prepared perishable food rescue programs); bd. dirs. Ultras Pharmaceuticals; founder/CEO Agates Etc. Bd. dirs. Lincoln Mayor's Com. Internat. Friendship, 1967—; affiliate mem., past pres. Nat. Coun. Internat. Visitors, Washington, 1967; bd. dirs. Nebraskaland Found., Inc., Lincoln, 1970—, Lincoln-Lancaster Food and Hunger Coalition, Good Neighbor Ctr.; hunger coord. Lincoln Dist. United Meth. Ch.; port insp., past fleet adm. Soc. Nebr. Adms. With AUS, 1943-46, ETO. Recipient Gov.'s Citation, State of Nebr., 1984, Outstanding Svc. award U.S. Info. Agy., 1990, Lincoln Parks and Recreation award, 1991, Mayor's Waste and Recycling award, 1993, Lincoln Dist. Outstanding Laity award United Meth. Ch., 1993, Citation of Achievement Nebr. Game and Parks Commn., 1993, Unsung Hero award United Way, 1996. Mem. VFW (life), Internat. Livestock Identification Assn. (life), Am. Legion, Disabled Am. Vets. (life), Nebr. Alumni Assn. (Outstanding Alumni award 1975, life), Nebr. Nut Growers Assn., Nebr. Hist. Soc. (life), Alpha Phi Omega (life), Sertoma (past pres. Gateway Club). Republican. Methodist. Home: 2701 S 34th St Lincoln NE 68506-3211 Office: 1911 R St Lincoln NE 68503-2931

MARSH, HARRY DEAN, journalism educator; b. Marfa, Tex., Feb. 28, 1928; s. Samuel Ferguson and Susanna Flora (Martie) M.; m. Ellie Elizabeth Bruton, Sept. 3, 1967; children: William Lawrence, Marti Christian. BA, Baylor U., 1949; MS, Columbia U., 1957; PhD, U. Tex., 1974. Reporter, news editor Hillsboro (Tex.) Evening Mirror, 1949-51, Delta Democrat-Times, Greenville, Miss., 1954-60; Miss. correspondent Birmingham (Ala.) News, 1960-61; asst. to editorial page editor N.Y. Herald Tribune, N.Y.C., 1961-66; telegraph desk staff N.Y. News, N.Y.C., 1966-67; asst. to assoc. prof. journalism Baylor U., Waco, Tex., 1967-75; chmn. dept. journalism U. Ark., Fayetteville, 1975-80; head. dept. journalism and mass communication Kans. State U., Manhattan, 1980-86, prof. journalism, 1986—. Author: Creating Tomorrow's Mass Media, 1995; co-author: Excellence in Reporting, 1987. Pres. SW Journalism Congress, Waco, 1973-74. Served with U.S. Army, 1951-53. Recipient Advanced Internat. Reporting fellowship Columbia U., N.Y.C., 1966-67. Mem. Soc. Profl. Journalists, Assn. Edn. in Journalsim and Mass Communication, Kappa Tau Alpha. Democrat. Presbyterian. Avocation: photography. Home: 1739 Fairchild Ave Manhattan KS 66502-4037 Office: Kans State U Dept of Journalism 104 Kenzie Hall Manhattan KS 66506-1500

MARSH, JAMES C., JR., secondary school principal. Headmaster Westminster Christian Acad., St. Louis. Recipient Blue Ribbon Sch. award U.S. Dept. of Edn., 1990-91. Office: Westminster Christian Acad 10900 Ladue Rd Saint Louis MO 63141-8425

MARSH, JEAN LYNDSEY TORREN, actress, writer; b. London, July 1, 1934; d. Henry Charles John and Emmeline Susannah Nightingale Poppy (Bexley) M.; m. Jon Devon Roland Pertwee, Apr. 2, 1955 (div. 1960). Student in dance, voice and mime; DHL (hon.), Marymount Coll. Whotographers' model; with repertory cos.; Broadway debut in Much Ado About Nothing, 1959; other theatrical appearances include Travesties, The Importance of Being Earnest, 1977, Too True to Be Good, 1977, My Fat Friend, Whose Life Is It Anyway?, 1979, Hamlet, Blithe Spirit, Habeas Corpus, Uncle Vanya, Pygmalion, The Chalk Garden; movie appearances include Cleopatra, 1963, Frenzy, 1972, Dark Places, The Eagle Has Landed, 1977, The Limbo Line, 1969, The Changeling, 1980, Return to Oz, Willow, 1988; artistic dir. Adelphi U. Theatre, 1981; co-creator, story cons., starred in I.T.V. series Upstairs, Downstairs, 1974-77, The House of Elliott, 1992, also starred The Grover Monster/Jean Marsh Cartoon Special, 1975, A State Dinner for Queen Elizabeth II, 1976, Mad About the Boy: Noel Coward--A Celebration, 1976; other TV appearances include The Ring, The Rory Bremner Show, The Alexei Sayle Show, (series) Nine to Five, (film) Jane Eyre, Master of the Game, Act of Will, A Connecticut Yankee at the Court of King Arthur, Dr. Who, Tomorrow People, Adam Bede, Carlton Lives, Fatherland (HBO); author: (novel) House of Elliott. Named Most Outstanding New Actress of 1972; Recipient Emmy award, 1975. Office: Fifi Oscard Agy Inc 24 W 40th St New York NY 10018-3904

MARSH, JEANNE CAY, social welfare educator, researcher; b. Madison, Wis., July 9, 1948; d. Herbert Louis and Helen Irene (Moeckly) M.; m. Steven King Shevell, Oct. 3, 1976; children: Lee Catherine Marsh, Lauren Elisabeth Marsh. BA, Mich. State U., 1969; MSW, U. Mich., 1972, PhD, 1975. Postdoctoral fellow Inst. for Social Rsch., U. Mich., Ann Arbor, 1975-77; asst. prof. Sch. Social Svc. Adminstrn., U. Chgo., 1978-83, assoc. prof., 1983-88, prof., dean, 1988—; acad. vis. London (Eng.) Sch. Econ.; vis. fellow Clare Hall U. Cambridge, Eng., 1987-88. Author: (with N. Caplan and A. Geist) Rape and the Limits of Law Reform, 1982, (with S. Berlin) Informing Practice Decisions, 1993; editor (with others) spl. issues of Jour. Social Issues, 1982, Evaluation and Program Planning, 1991; chair editorial bd. Social Svc. Rev., 1988—; mem. editorial bd. Social Work Rsch. and Abstracts, 1982-92, Internat. Applied Social Svc. Index, 1988—. Trustee Chgo. Theol. Sem., 1988—. Recipient Disting. Alumna award Sch. Social Work, U. Mich., 1987; Leadership Greater Chgo. fellow, 1985-86. Mem. NASW, Am. Psychol. Assn., Am. Evaluation Assn., Leadership Fellows Assn., Phi Beta Kappa. Office: U Chgo Sch Social Svc Adminstrn 969 E 60th St Chicago IL 60637-2640

MARSH, JOHN S., JR., newspaper editor; b. Niagara Falls, N.Y., Apr. 23, 1949; s. John S. and Muriel (MacLaren) M.; m. Elizabeth Poreda, July 10, 1971; children: Beth, Colleen. BA in Gov., Baldwin-Wallace Coll., 1971. Reporter, then various editing positions Times-Union, Rochester, N.Y., 1971-82; mng. editor Daily Press, Utica, N.Y., 1982-84; exec. editor Observer-Dispatch, Utica, 1984-91; pub., pres. Daily Jour., Vineland, N.J., 1991-92; exec. editor Argus Leader, Sioux Falls, S.D., 1992—. Bd. dirs. Forward Sioux Falls. Mem. Am. Soc. Newspaper Editors, AP Mng. Editors, S.D. Assn. Press Mng. Editors Assn. (pres. 1994-95), Rotary. Office: Argus Leader PO Box 5034 Sioux Falls SD 57117-5034

MARSH, JOSEPH FRANKLIN, JR., emeritus college president, educational consultant; b. Charleston, W.Va., Feb. 24, 1925; s. Joseph Franklin and Florence (Keller) M. Student, Concord Coll., 1941-42; W.Va. U., 1942-43; A.B., Dartmouth Coll., 1947; student, Nat. Inst. Pub. Affairs, Washington, 1947-48; M.P.A., Harvard U., 1949; LL.D., Davis and Elkins Coll., 1968; L.H.D., Alderson-Broaddus Coll., 1982. Cons. Hoover Commn., Washington, 1948; instr. in gt. issues Dartmouth, 1952-54, instr. econs., 1953-55, asst. prof., 1955-59; pres. Concord Coll., Athens, W.Va., 1959-73, pres. emeritus, 1985—; ednl. cons., 1973-74; pres. Waynesburg (Pa.) Coll., 1974-83, pres. emeritus, 1983—; v.p. The Armand Hammer United World Coll. of the Am. West, Montezuma, N. Mex., 1984-85; pres. Marsh Edn Cons., Athens, W.Va., 1985—; Dir. One Valley Bank of Mercer County. Author articles. Mem. State Dept. Ednl. Mission to U.A.R., 1964, Mercer County (W.Va.) Planning Commn., 1964-74, 83-94, hon., 1994—; vice chmn. W.Va. Com. for Constnl. Amendments, 1966; mem. regional coun. Internat. Edn. Study Mission to Europe, 1970; bd. dirs. Am. Assn. State Colls. and Univs., 1972-73, Regional Coun. for Internat. Edn., 1973, Hospice Care Mercer County, W.Va., 1987-91, Faculty Merit Found. W.Va., 1990—; bd. dirs. Pa. Assn. Colls. and Univs., 1974-83, exec. com., 1980-82; bd. dirs. Pa. Commn. for Ind. Colls. and Univs., 1974-83, sec.-treas., 1976-77, vice chmn., 1977-80, chmn., 1980-82; trustee Found. Ind. Colls. Pa., 1974-83, mem. exec. com., 1979-82; bd. visitors Midway Coll., Ky., 1979-93; adv. com. Pa. State Coun. Higher Edn., 1980-82; trustee Concord Coll. Found., 1986, bd. dirs., 1987—; active Town of Athens Planning Commn., 1986-94, pres. commn. 1987-94; vice chmn. bd. trustees, Princeton (W.Va.) Cmty. Hosp. Found., 1989—; Gov's. appointee to bd. dirs. State Coll. System W.Va., 1989-96, chmn. adminstrv. com., 1990-91, vice chmn. of bd., 1991-95, chmn., 1995-96. Served as gunnery officer USNR, 1943-46. Named Outstanding Young Man, W.Va. Jr. C. of C., 1960; recipient Alumnus of Yr. award Concord Coll., 1973, Golden Alumnus award, 1992; Outstanding Citizen award Athens Woman's Club, 1992; Rotary fellow Oxford (Eng.) U., 1950-52. Mem. AAUP, Am. Assn. Univ. Adminstrs., Am. Econ. Assn., Royal Inst. Pub. Adminstrn., Oxford Union Debating Soc. (life), Oxford Soc. (life), Pa. Soc., Duquesne Club (Pitts.), Univ. Club (Bluefield), Masons, Rotary (dist. gov. 1992-93), Phi Beta Kappa, Phi Tau, Phi Delta Pi, Phi Sigma Kappa, Alpha Kappa Psi (hon.). Methodist. Home: 106 First Ave Athens WV 24712 Office: PO Box 734 Athens WV 24712-0734

MARSH, MALCOLM F., federal judge; b. 1928. BS, U. Oreg., 1952, LLB, 1954, JD, 1971. Ptnr. Clark & Marsh, Lindauer & McClinton (and predecessors), Salem, Oreg., 1958-87; judge U.S. Dist. Ct. Oreg., Portland, 1987—. With U.S. Army, 1946-47. Fellow Am. Coll. Trial Lawyers; mem. ABA. Office: US Dist Ct 114 US Courthouse 620 SW Main St Portland OR 97205-3037*

MARSH, MICHAEL, track and field athlete. Olympic runner Barcelona, Spain, 1992. Recipient 200m Track and Field Gold medal Olympics, Barcelona, 1992. Office: US Olympic Com 1750 E Boulder St Colorado Springs CO 80909-5724*

MARSH, OWEN ROBERT, education educator; b. Springfield, Ill., Oct. 4, 1935; s. Owen Rainey and Dorothea Nell (Frutiger) M.; m. Evelyn Joyce Mathews, Aug. 19, 1958; children: Jeffrey, John, Thomas. BS in Edn., Ill. State Normal U., 1957, MS in Edn., 1958; EdD, Ill. State U., Normal, 1967. Tchr. Galesburg (Ill.) Pub. Schs., 1958-61; instr. edn. Western Ill. U., Macomb, 1962-64, Ill. State U., Normal, 1967; rsch. assoc. Ill. Bd. Higher Edn., Springfield, 1967-69; registrar U. Ill., Springfield, 1969-72; dean of admissions and records Tex. Ea. U., Tyler, 1972-80; registrar U. Tex., Tyler, 1980-89, assoc. prof., 1989—. Author: Illinois Board of Higher Education, 1969; contbr. articles to mags. Pres. Springfield Lions Club, 1967-72, Tyler Evening Lions, 1979-80, 86-87; treas. Assn. of Retarded Citizens, Springfield, 1971-72; mem. Human Rights Com., Tyler, 1992—. Served with USAF, 1961-62. Recipient Roy A. Clark scholarship Ill. State U., 1967. Mem. St. Louis Performance Coun., Kappa Delta Pi (counselor 1992—). Methodist. Avocation: camping. Home: 3613 Glendale Dr Tyler TX 75701-8642 Office: Univ Tex Tyler 3900 University Blvd Tyler TX 75799

MARSH, QUINTON NEELY, banker; b. Omaha, July 1, 1915; s. Arthur J. and Rose L. (Baysel) M.; m. Thelma May Beck, Nov. 24, 1944. B.C.S., Benjamin Franklin U., Washington, 1949, M.C.S., 1950; student, Am. U., 1950-51; diploma, Sch. Bank Adminstrn., U. Wis., 1959. Chartered bank auditor; cert. internal auditor; cert. protection profl. V.p., gen. auditor Am.

Security & Trust Co., Washington, 1972, sr. officer auditing and security, 1972-77; sr. v.p., cashier Bank of Columbia N.A., Washington, 1977-79; sr. v.p. United Nat. Bank of Washington, 1979-80. Mem. Bank Adminstrn. Inst. (pres. D.C. 1966-67, auditing commn. 1968-70), Inst. Internal Auditors (pres. D.C. 1962-63), Am. Soc. Indsl. Security. Lodges: Masons, Shriners. Home: # 312 4801 Connecticut Ave Washington DC 20008-2203

MARSH, RICHARD J., strategic management consultant; b. Bklyn., Dec. 7, 1933; s. Thomas and Claire (Mangi) M.; m. Catherine Monahan, Sept. 24, 1960; children: Amy E., Jamie P. B.S. in Bus., U. Conn., 1955; M.S. in Human Resources, U. Bridgeport, 1974. Regional mgr. Student Mktg. Inst., N.Y.C., 1955-58; project mgr. bus. devel. Harvey Research Co., Rochester, N.Y., 1958-60; account exec. Rumrill-Hoyt Mktg./Advt., Inc., N.Y.C. and Rochester, N.Y., 1960-67; dir. mktg. services Burlington Hosiery Co., 1967-71; v.p. Innotech Corp., Trumbull, Conn., 1972-78; mng. dir. Nordic ops. Innotech, 1978-81; cons., founder Strategic Bus. Devel. Services Internat., Mount Kisco, N.Y., and Hillsboro, N.H., 1981—; course leader Am. Mgmt. Assn., 1976—; lectr. Tech-Transfer Conf., Hanover, Germany, 1994, Innovatin Processes and Foucsin, Luxembourg. Contbr. articles to profl. jours. Pres. PTA, Bedford, N.Y., 1976-77; bd. dirs. Property Owners Assn. Hillsboro, N.H., 1977-78. Mem. Am. Mktg. Assn., Licensing Execs. Soc., Comml. Devel. Assn., Internat. Soc. Product Innovation (v.p.). Republican. Clubs: American (Stockholm); Chemists (N.Y.C.), Royal Commonwealth (U.K.), Tech. Innovation and Info. (Luxembourgh). Avocations: skiing; canoeing; touring. Office: Strategic Bus Devel Svcs Internat 367 Bog Rd PO Box 567 Hillsboro NH 03244-0657

MARSH, ROBERT BUFORD, chemical engineer, consultant; b. Chgo., Nov. 16, 1946; s. Ivar Buford and Blanche Julien (Morrisette) M.; m. Claudia Ann Werner, Feb. 14, 1970; children: Julie Ann, Kristy Louise. BS in chem. engr., Mich. Tech. U., 1968. Registered profl. engr., Mass. Engr. 1 design engr. Chevron Rsch., Richmond, Calif., 1968-70, tech. svc. engr., 1970-73; lustrex supr. Monsanto, Long Beach, Calif., 1973-78; mfg. supr. Monsanto, Everett, Mass., 1978-83, environ. engr., 1984-85, mfg. tech. specialist, 1986-91; worldwide plasticizer tech. expert engring. specialist Monsanto, Everett, Indian Orchard, Mass., 1992-93; pres. Marsh Engr., Inc., Andover, Mass., 1992—; environ. instr., U. Mass., 1994; cons. Mass. Dept. Environ. Protection, Lowell, 1993-94; cons. EPA Rsch. grant, 1994; speaker in field. Adv., co. leady Jr. Achievement, Long Beach, 1975-77; vol. Andover Sch. System, 1983-84, Chicopee River Watershed Assn., Springfield, Mass., 1993, Shawsheen River Watershed Assn., Tewksbury, Mass., 1994; election com. & tech. adv. State Senator O'Brien com., 1994-95. Mem. Nat. Soc. Profl. Engrs., AICHE. Democrat. Methodist. Achievements include orginal research and published a Chevron Report on Ammonia-Hydrogen Sulfide Equilibrium in the 10-50% range. Avocations: reading, camping, tennis, swimming, stock market. Home: 8 Mulberry Cir Andover MA 01810 Office: Marsh Engring Inc PO Box 3232 Andover MA 01810

MARSH, ROBERT CHARLES, writer, music critic; b. Columbus, Ohio, Aug. 5, 1924; s. Charles L. and Jane A. (Beckett) M.; m. Kathleen C. Moscrop, July 4, 1956 (div. 1985); m. Ann Noren, Feb. 25, 1987; 1 child, James MacArtain. BS, Northwestern U., 1945, AM, 1946; postgrad., U. Chgo., 1948; EdD, Harvard U., 1951; postgrad., Oxford U., 1952-53, Cambridge U., 1953-56. Instr. social sci. U. Ill., 1947-49; lectr. humanities Chgo. City Jr. Coll., 1950-51; asst. prof. edn. U. Kansas City, 1951-52; vis. prof. edn. SUNY, 1953-54; humanities staff U. Chgo., 1956-58, lectr. in social thought, 1976; music critic Chgo. Sun-Times, 1956-91; dir. Chgo. Opera Project, Newberry Libr., 1983—. Author: Toscanini and the Art of Orchestral Performance, 1956, rev. edit., 1962, The Cleveland Orchestra, 1967, Ravinia, 1987, James Levine at Ravinia, 1993; editor: Logic and Knowledge, 1956. Co-recipient Peabody award for ednl. broadcasting, 1976; Ford Found. fellow, 1965-66. Mem. Harvard U. Faculty Club. Roman Catholic. Home and Office: 1001 7th St New Glarus WI 53574-0790

MARSH, ROBERT MORTIMER, sociologist, educator; b. Everett, Mass., Jan. 22, 1931; s. Henry Warren and Ruth (Dunbar) M.; children: Eleanor L., Christopher S.H., Diana E. Student, Boston U., 1948-50; A.B., U. Chgo., 1952; M.A., Columbia, 1953, Ph.D., 1959. Fellow Ford Found., Japan, Taiwan, Hong Kong, 1956-58; instr. sociology U. Mich., 1958-61; asst. prof. sociology Cornell U., 1961-65; asso. prof. Duke, 1965-67; mem. faculty Brown U., 1967—, prof. sociology, 1968—, chmn. dept., 1971-75; manpower personnel and tng. rsch. prof. U.S. Naval Acad., Annapolis, 1987-88; vis. prof. Nat. Tsing Hua U., Taiwan, 1991. Author: The Mandarins: The Circulation of Elites in China, 1961, Comparative Sociology: A Codification of Cross-Societal Analysis, 1967; (with H. Mannari) Modernization and the Japanese Factory, 1976, Organizational Change in Japanese Factories, 1988, The Great Transformation: Social Change in Taipei, Taiwan Since the 1960s, 1996; also articles; assoc. editor Adminstrv. Sci. Quar., 1963-67, Jour. Comparative Family Studies, 1970-74; co-editor: (with J. Michael Armer) Comparative Sociological Research in the 1960s and 1970s. East Asian Inst. summer fellow Chinese Columbia, 1955; Ford Found. and Guggenheim Found. fellow Japan, 1969-70; Japan Soc. Promotion Sci. fellow, 1976, 83; Chiang Ching Kuo Found. and Nat. Sci. Coun. fellow (Taiwan, Republic of China). 1991-93. Mem. Am. Sociol. Assn., Ea. Sociol. Assn., Assn. Asian Studies, Internat. Studies Assn. (exec. com. comparative interdisciplinary studies sect. 1971-76), Japan Human Rels. Assn. (councilor 1970—). Office: Dept Sociology Brown Univ Providence RI 02912

MARSH, ROBERT THOMAS, corporate executive, retired air force general; b. Logansport, Ind., Jan. 3, 1925; m. Joan Spears, June 7, 1949; children: Kathy, Teri, Debi. Student, Wabash Coll., 1943; B.S., U.S. Mil. Acad., 1949; M.S. in Engring, U. Mich., 1956; postgrad., Air Command and Staff Coll., 1960, Air War Coll., 1965. Commd. 2d lt. USAF, 1949, promoted to gen., 1970; space systems project officer, Hdqrs. Space Systems div. Los Angeles Air Force Sta., USAF, Calif., 1960-64; staff officer Directorate of Reconnaissance & Electronic Warfare, USAF; chief Projects Div., Directorate of Space, Office of Dep. Chief of Staff for Research and Devel., Hdqrs. USAF, Washington, 1965-67; exec. officer to dep. chief of staff Research & Devel., Hdqrs. USAF, Washington, 1967-69; dep. for reconnaissance, strike and electronics warfare Aero. Systems Div., Wright-Patterson AFB, Ohio, 1969-73; dep. chief of staff, devel. plans Hdqrs. Air Force Systems Command, Andrews AFB, Md., 1973, dep. chief of staff, Systems, 1973-75, vice comdr., 1975-77; comdr. Electronic Systems Div., Hanscom AFB, Mass., 1977-81, Air Force Systems Command, Andrews AFB, 1981-84; ret., 1984; exec. dir. Air Force Aid Soc.; bd. dirs. Teknowledge Corp., CAE-Electronics Corp., ITHACO Inc., Comverse Govt. Sys. Corp.; trustee Mitre Inc. Served with U.S. Army, 1943-45. Decorated Legion of Merit, Disting. Service medal with 2 oak leaf clusters. Office: Air Force Aid Soc 1745 Jefferson Davis Hwy Arlington VA 22202 *I realized early in my military career some 40 plus years ago that all jobs—no matter how small—should be handled with equal determination, persistence, and dedication. Just as important to doing a job well is the need for leadership. That means professionally—able to stand alone with decision-making responsibility; and organizationally—being sensitive to the needs of one's people and motivating them toward getting the job done.*

MARSH, ROBERTA REYNOLDS, elementary education educator, consultant; b. Kokomo, Ind., June 2, 1939; d. Elwood Bert and Mildred Bell (Wolford) Reynolds; m. Ronald Dean Marsh Sr., Apr. 5, 1958; children: Ronald Jr., Bryan William, Joel Allen. BEd, Ind. U., Kokomo, 1970; MEd, Ind. U., Bloomington, 1971. Cert. tchr., spl. edn. tchr., Ind., Ariz. Tchr. spl. edn. Kokomo Ctr. Schs., 1970-77; tchr. spl. edn. Tempe (Ariz.) Elem. Dist. #3, 1978-86, tchr. civics, geography, English/lit., 1986—. Local dir. Spl. Olympics, Kokomo, 1974-77, Tempe Assn. Retarded Citizens, 1978-88; den mother Boy Scouts Am., Kokomo, 1967-73; leader 4-H Club, Kokomo, 1974-77. Recipient Excellence in Edn. award Tempe Diablo, 1991. Mem. Coun. for Exceptional Children (state pres. 1986-87, Tempe chpt. pres. 1994-95, Outstanding Leader 1985, Outstanding Regular Tchr. of Yr. Tempe coun.), Internat. Reading Assn., Assn. for Children with Learning Disabilities, Ind. U. Alumni Assn., Alpha Delta Kappa (corr. sec. 1986-88, Theta pres. 1990-92). Democrat. Avocations: bridge, traveling, reading, collecting apples and bells. Home: 4113 E Emelita Cir Mesa AZ 85206-5109 Office: Hudson Sch 1325 E Malibu Dr Tempe AZ 85282-5742

MARSH, SUE ANN, special education educator; b. Marshall, Tex., Dec. 5, 1949; d. Orman and Della Florence (Floyd) M. BS in Edn., Stephen F. Austin State U., Nacogdoches, Tex., 1971, MEd, 1975. Cert. elem. tchr., reading tchr., spl. edn. in mental retardation, Tex. Tchr. Title 45 Dickinson (Tex.) Ind. Sch. Dist., 1971, tchr. Title I, 1971-72; tchr. trainable mentally retarded Conroe (Tex.) Ind. Sch. Dist., 1972-85, tchr. Option III, 1985—; coach, asst. coach Vol. Spl. Olympics, Conroe, 1973—, advt. chmn for golf tournament, 1989-90. Editor: Almost Reader Series. Leader for mentally retarded boys and girls Boy Scouts Am., Conroe, 1990—; chmn. Crockett Cougars Year Book Advertisement 50th Anniversary Edit. Named Crockett Intermediate Tchr. of Yr., 1992; recipient Sam Houston Disting. Scouting award of merit, 1993; co-recipient State Centennial Farm award, Career Ladder, 1984-93. Mem. Assn. Tex. Profl. Educators (bldg. rep. 1983—), Classroom Tchrs. Assn. (bldg. rep. 1975-78), Floyd Family Assn. (sec.-treas. Plantersville, Tex.), River Plantation Lions (camp chmn. 1990—, chmn. attendance 1990-91, bd. dirs. 1990—, 3rd v.p. 1992-93, 2nd v.p. 1993-94, v.p. 1994-95, pres. 1995-96). Democrat. Baptist. Avocations: travel, needlecrafts, plays, concerts. Office: Wash Intermediate Sch 507 Ave K Conroe TX 77301

MARSH, TERENCE, production designer. Prodn. designer: (films) (with John Box) Doctor Zhivago, 1965 (Academy award best art direction 1965), (with Box) A Man for All Seasons, 1966, (with Wallis Smith) The Wild Affair, 1966, (with Box) Oliver!, 1968 (Academy award best art direction 1968), (with Robert Laing) Perfect Friday, 1970, The Looking Glass War, 1970, (with Robert Cartwright) Scrooge, 1970, (with Cartwright) Mary, Queen of Scots, 1971 (Academy award nomination best art direction 1971), (with Cartwright) The Public Eye, 1972, Follow Me!, 1972, (with Alan Tomkins) The Mackintosh Man, 1973, (with Tomkins) A Touch of Class, 1973, (with Tomkins) Juggernaut, 1974, The Abdication, 1974, The Adventures of Sherlock Holmes' Smarter Brother, 1975, (with Tomkins) Royal Flash, 1975, A Bridge Too Far, 1977, (with Robert Lawrence) Magic, 1978, (with Marvin March) The Frisco Kid, 1979, (with others) Sunday Lovers, 1980, Absence of Malice, 1981, (with Peter Lamont and Gil Parrondo) Sphinx, 1981, (with J. Dennis Washington) To Be or Not to Be, 1983, (with Tomkins) Haunted Honeymoon, 1986, (with Fernando Ramirez, El Polo, George Richardson, and Craig Edgar) Miracles, 1987, (with Harold Michelson) Spaceballs, 1987, (with Dianne Wager) Bert Rigby, You're a Fool, 1989, (with Richardson) Havana, 1990, (with Wager, Donald Woodruff, and William Cruse) The Hunt for Red October, 1990, Basic Instinct, 1992, The Shawshank Redemption, 1994, Forget Paris, 1995, (TV movies) Great Expectations, 1974; prodn. designer, prodr.: (films) (with Steve Sardanis) The World's Greatest Lover, 1977; prodn. designer, co-prodr. (with Washington), co-screenwriter (with Ronny Graham and Charles Dennis): (films) Finders Keepers, 1984. Office: Sandra Marsh Mgt 9150 Wilshire Blvd Ste 220 Beverly Hills CA 90212-3429

MARSH, WILLIAM LAURENCE, retired research pathology executive; b. Cardiff, Wales, Great Britain, Apr. 21, 1926; came to U.S., 1969; s. William and Violet (Hill) M.; m. Jean Beryl Margaret Hill, June 6, 1952; children: Christine Margaret, Nicholas John. Fellow, Inst. Med. Lab. Sci., London, 1954, Inst. Biology, London, 1969; PhD, Columbia Pacific U., 1968; fellow, Royal Coll. Pathologists, London, 1985. Lab. chief Regional Blood Transfusion Ctr., Brentwood, Eng., 1955-69; assoc. investigator N.Y. Blood Ctr., N.Y.C., 1969-79, investigator, 1980-83, sr. investigator, 1984-87; sr. v.p. rsch. Lindsley Kimball Rsch. Inst. of N.Y. Blood Ctr., N.Y.C., 1987-94; ret.; editorial bd. Transfusion jour., 1979-91, Blood Transfusion and Immunohematology jour., 1980-86; sci. reviewer various jours. Author chpts. on human blood groups in textbooks, 1965-91; contbr. over 250 articles to profl. jours. Recipient Blood Donors award of merit Blood Donor Assn., Eng., 1961. Fellow Inst. Med. Lab. Sci. (Race prize 1976), Inst. Biology, Royal Coll. Pathologists; mem. Internat. Soc. Blood Tranfusion, Am. Assn. Blood Banks (Dunsford Meml. award 1975, Emily Cooley award 1988, Grove-Rasmussen award 1990, Karl Landsteiner award 1995), Am. Soc. Clin. Pathologists (Philip Levine Outstanding Rsch. award 1993), Brit. Soc. Hematology, Brit. Soc. Blood Transfusion. Avocations: sailing, flying, photography. Home: 101 Hillcrest Dr Moneta VA 24121-3003 Office: NY Blood Ctr S310 E 67th St New York NY 10021-6204

MARSHAK, ALAN HOWARD, electrical engineer, educator; b. Miami Beach, Fla., Mar. 21, 1938; s. Jerome and Yetta (Feiner) M.; children: Jerry Brian. B.Sc.E.E., U. Miami, 1960; M.S., La. State U., 1962; Ph.D., U. Ariz., 1969. Asst. prof. elec. engring. La. State U., Baton Rouge, 1969-73; assoc. prof. La. State U., 1973-78, prof., 1978—, chmn. dept. elec. and computer engring., 1983—; vis. prof. Electron Device Rsch. Ctr., U. Fla., Gainesville, 1979-80; tech. reviewer NSF, 1976—, panelist, 1993—; panelist NRC, 1993; mem. Southeastern Ctr. Elec. Engring. Edn., 1984—, chmn., CEO, 1992—; spkr. profl. confs. Tech. referee various jours. including Solid-State Electronics, Jour. Applied Physics; assoc. editor IEEE Trans. Electron Devices, 1991—; author: (with D. J. Hamilton and F. A. Lindholm) Principles and Applications of Semiconductor Device Modeling, 1971, Basic Experiments in Electronics: A Laboratory Manual, 1978, also tech. papers. NSF grad. trainee, 1967-69; grantee, 1970, 73, 75, 78; named F.H. Coughlin/CLECO prof. of elec. engring., 1993. Fellow IEEE; mem. Electron Devices Soc., Sigma Xi, Eta Kappa Nu. Home: 320 Misty Creek Dr Baton Rouge LA 70808-8174 Office: La State U Elec And Computer Dept Baton Rouge LA 70803

MARSHAK, MARVIN LLOYD, physicist, educator; b. Buffalo, Mar. 11, 1946; s. Kalman and Goldie (Hait) M.; m. Anita Sue Kolman, Sept. 24, 1972; children: Rachel Kolman, Adam Kolman. AB in Physics, Cornell U., 1967; MS in Physics, U. Mich., PhD in Physics, 1970. Rsch. assoc. U. Minn., Mpls., 1970-74, asst. prof., 1974-78, assoc. prof., 1978-83, prof. physics, 1983—, dir. grad. studies in physics, 1983-86, prin. investigator high energy physics, 1982-86, head sch. of physics and astronomy, 1986—. Contbr. articles to profl. jours. Trustee Children's Theater Co., 1989-94. Mem. Am. Phys. Soc. Home: 2855 Ottawa Ave S Minneapolis MN 55416-1946 Office: U Minn Dept Physics 116 Church St SE Minneapolis MN 55455-0149

MARSHAK, ROBERT REUBEN, former university dean, medical educator, veterinarian; b. N.Y.C., Feb. 23, 1923; s. David and Edith (Youselovsky) M.; m. Ruth Emilie Lyons, Dec. 4, 1948; children: William Lyons, John Ball, Richard Best; m. Margo Post Marshall, June 25, 1983. Student, U. Wis., 1940-41; D.V.M., Cornell U., 1945; D.V.M. (hon.), U. Bern, 1968; M.A. (hon.), U. Pa., 1971. Diplomate: Am. Coll. Vet. Internal Medicine (charter). Practice vet. medicine Springfield, Vt., 1945-56; prof., chmn. dept. medicine Sch. Vet. Medicine, U. Pa., Phila., 1956-58; prof. medicine Grad. Sch. Medicine, 1957-64; chmn. dept. clin. studies Sch. Vet. Medicine, 1958-73; dir. Bovine Leukemia Research Center, 1965-73; dean Sch. Vet. Medicine, 1973-87; co-dir. Center on Interactions Animals and Soc., 1975-79, also mem. grad. group com. in comparative med. scis.; prof. medicine, chief sect. epidemiology and pub. health Sch. Vet. Medicine U. Pa., 1990-93, prof. medicine emeritus, 1993—; mem. adv. bd. Pa. Dept. Agr., 1973-87; chmn. Gov.'s Study Group on Horse Racing Industry in Pa., 1979; mem. del. to evaluate vet. med. and rsch. Chinese Ministry Agr.; mem. adv. com. Stroud Water Rsch. Ctr., 1992—; mem. adv. coun. Coll. Vet. Medicine, Cornell U., 1993—. Sr. co-editor Advances in Veterinary Science and Comparative Medicine; contbr. numerous articles to sci. jours. Bd. dirs. Humane Soc. U.S., 1978-82, Bide-a-wee Home Assn., 1980-85; sci. adv. bd. mem. Sch. Vet. Medicine The Hebrew U., Jerusalem, 1984—; chmn. external com. Sch. Vet. Medicine Tuskegee U.; trustee Upland Country Day Sch., 1988-91; mem. animal adv. com. City of Phila., 1989-93. Served with AUS, 1943-44. Recipient Disting. Veterinarian award Pa. Vet. Med. Assn., 1984, Barnraiser award Pa. Farmers Assn., 1987. Fellow Phila. Coll. Physicians; mem. AAAS, John Morgan Soc. (pres. 1967-68), Am. Assn. Cancer Rsch., Am. Vet. Med. Assn., Pa. Vet. Med. Assn., NAS Inst. Medicine (sr.), Pa. Livestock Assn. (dir.), Westminster Kennel Club, James A. Baker Inst. for Animal Health (mem. adv. coun. 1977—), Phila. Soc. for Promoting Agr., Pa. Friends of Agr. Found., Phila. Zool. Soc. (bd. dirs. 1986-87), Sigma Xi, Phi Zeta.

MARSHALEK, EUGENE RICHARD, physics educator; b. N.Y.C., Jan. 17, 1936; s. Frank M. and Sophie (Weg) M.; m. Sonja E. M. Lennhart, Dec. 8, 1962; children: Thomas, Frank. BS, Queens Coll., 1957; PhD, U. Calif., Berkeley, 1962. NSF postdoctoral fellow Niels Bohr Inst., Copenhagen, Denmark, 1962-63; rsch. assoc. Brookhaven Nat. Lab., Upton, N.Y., 1963-65; asst. prof. U. Notre Dame, Ind., 1965-69, assoc. prof., 1969-78, prof., 1978—. Contbr. articles to profl. jours. Recipient Alexander von Humboldt sr. scientist award, 1985. Mem. AAAS, Am. Phys. Soc., Sigma Xi. Office: U Notre Dame Dept Physics Notre Dame IN 46556

MARSHALL, ALAN GEORGE, chemistry and biochemistry educator; b. Bluffton, Ohio, May 26, 1944; s. Herbert Boyer Marshall Jr. and Cecile (Mogil) Rosser; m. Marilyn Gard, June 13, 1965; children: Gwendolyn Scott, Brian George. BA in Chemistry with honors, Northwestern U., 1965; PhD in Phys. Chemistry, Stanford U., 1970. Instr. II U. B.C., Vancouver, Can., 1969-71, asst. prof., 1971-76, assoc. prof., 1976-80; prof. chemistry and biochemistry Ohio State U., Columbus, 1980-93; prof. chemistry Fla. State U., Tallahassee, 1993—; cons. Extrel FTMS, Madison, Wis., 1989-92, Oak Ridge (Tenn.) Nat. Lab., 1990—; dir. Ion Cyclotron Resonance Program Nat. High Magnetic Field Lab., 1993—. Author: Biophysical Chemistry, 1978, Fourier Transforms in Spectroscopy, 1990; editor ICR/ION Trap newsletter, 1986—; N.Am. editor Rapid Comm. on Mass Spectrometry, 1988—; mem. editorial bd. Analytical Chemistry, 1990-92, Internat. Jour. Mass Ion Procs., 1987—, Jour. Am. Soc. Mass Spectrometry, 1989—, Mass Spectrometry Rev., 1994—, Jour. Magnetic Resonance, 1995—; contbr. more than 220 articles to profl. jours. Recipient Disting. Scholar award Ohio State U. Fellow AAAS, Am. Phys. Soc.; mem. Am. Chem. Soc. (award in chem. instrumentation, Akron sect. award, award in analytical chemistry Ea. Analytical Symposium 1991, Frank H. Field and Joe L. Franklin award 1995), Soc. Applied Spectroscopy (chmn. local sect. 1990-91), Am. Soc. Mass Spectroscopy (bd. dirs. 1991-92). Office: Fla State Univ Nat High Magnetic Field Lab 1800 East Paul Dirac Dr Tallahassee FL 32310

MARSHALL, ALTON GARWOOD, real estate counselor; b. Flint, Mich., Sept. 19, 1921; s. William Robert and Lela Christine (Brabon) M.; m. Mary Lee Golden, June 22, 1945 (div. July 1971); children: William A., Stephen B., Bruce S., Mary Ann Marshall Trebian, John L.; m. Sarah Elizabeth DeLand, Sept. 4, 1971; 1 child, Sarah Graham. BA, Hillsdale Coll., 1942; MS, Syracuse U., 1948, LLD (hon.), 1974; D Pub. Service & Bus. Adminstrn. (hon.), Hillsdale Coll., 1980. Sec. utility regulations pub. svc. commn. N.Y. State, Albany, 1953-61, dep. dir. div. budget, 1961-65, exec. officer, then sec. to gov., Office of Gov., 1965-70; pres., bd. dirs. Rockefeller Ctr., N.Y.C., 1971-81; pres. A.G. Marshall Assocs., N.Y.C., 1981—; chmn., pres., chief exec. officer Lincoln Savs. Bank, N.Y.C., 1984-88, chmn., chief exec. officer, 1988-91, also bd. dirs.; mem. exec. com. Nat. Realty Com., Washington, 1970—; bd. dirs. N.Y. State Electric & Gas Corp., 1971—; ind. gen. ptnr. Equitable Capital Ptnrs. and Equitable Capital Ptnrs. Retirement Fund, 1989—; bd. dirs. Equitable Life Assurance Soc., N.Y. Prism and Equitable Trusts, 1977-91; trustee Hudson River Trust, 1991—. Mem. exec. com., steering com. Assn. for a Better N.Y., 1971—; mem. exec., landmarks and polit. action coms. Real Estate Bd. N.Y., sec. bd. dirs., 1973—; chmn. Nat. Assn. on Drug Abuse Problems, 1990-92. Sr. fellow The Nelson A. Rockefeller Inst. Govt., 1991-94. Mem. Am. Soc. Real Estate Counselors. Office: Alton G Marshall Assocs Inc 136 E 79th St New York NY 10021-0328

MARSHALL, ANNETTE, special education educator; b. Winchester, Mass., Dec. 4, 1942; d. Laurence Fredrick and Agnes Estelle (Hannegan) Sanford; m. Patrick Henry Marshall, Aug. 14, 1965; children: Peter Randolph, Natalie Jean, Daniel Patrick, Michael Laurence Cavins. BS in Elem. Edn., St. Joseph's Coll., 1964; MEd, Rivier Coll., 1992. Cert. tchr., spl. tchr., learning disabilities tchr. Grade 4 tchr. St. Mary's Elem. Sch., Waco, Tex., 1964-65; grade 6 tchr. Orlando, Fla., 1965-66; grade 4 tchr. St. Monica Elem. Sch., Indpls., 1969-71; vol. work sch. and cmty., 1971-85; substitute tchr. Hudson, N.H., 1985-89, para-profl. behavior modification class, 1989-91; spl. needs tchr. 3rd and 4th grades Nottingham West Elem. Sch., Hudson, N.H., 1992—. Recipient award Children and Adults with Attention Deficit So. N.H., 1995. Mem. Internat. Reading Assn. (Granite State literary award 1993). Roman Catholic. Avocations: reading, sewing, craft projects. Home: 5 Beaver Path Hudson NH 03051-5101 Office: Nottingham West Elem Sch 10 Pelham Rd Hudson NH 03051-4830

MARSHALL, ARTHUR K., lawyer, judge, arbitrator, educator, writer; b. N.Y.C., Oct. 7, 1911. BS, CUNY, 1933; LLB, St. John's U., N.Y.C., 1936; LL.M., U. So. Calif., 1952. Bar: N.Y. State 1937, Calif. 1947. Practice law N.Y.C., 1937-43, Los Angeles, 1947-50; atty. VA, Los Angeles, 1947-50; tax counsel Calif. Bd. Equalization, Sacramento, 1950-51; inheritance tax atty. State Controller, Los Angeles, 1951-53; commr. Superior Ct. Los Angeles County, 1953-62; judge Municipal Ct., Los Angeles jud. dist., 1962-63, Superior Ct., Los Angeles, 1963-81; supervising judge probate dept. Superior Ct., 1968-69, appellate dept., 1973-77; presiding judge Appellate Dept., 1976-77; pvt. practice arbitrator, mediator, judge pro tem, 1981—; acting asst. prof. law UCLA, 1954-59; grad. faculty U. So. Calif., 1955-75; lectr. Continuing Edn. of the Bar; mem. Calif. Law Revision Commn., 1984—, chmn., 1986-87, 92-93; chmn. com. on efficiency and econs. Conf. Calif. Judges, past chmn. spl. action com. on ct. improvement; past chmn. probate law cons. group Calif. Bd. Legal Specialization. Author: Joint Tenancy Taxwise and Otherwise, 1953, Branch Courts, 1959, California State and Local Taxation Text, 2 vols., 1962, rev. edit., 1969, supplement, 1979, 2d edito., 1981, Triple Choice Method, 1964, California State and Local Taxation Forms, 2 vols., 1961-75, rev. edit., 1979, California Probate Procedure, 1961, 5th rev. edit., 1994, Guide to Procedure Before Trial, 1975; contbr. articles to profl. jours. Mem. Town Hall. With AUS, 1943-46; lt. col. JAGC, USAR ret. Named Judge of Yr. Lawyers Club L.A. County, 1975; first recipient Arthur K. Marshall award established by estate planning, trust and probate sect. L.A. Bar Assn., 1981, Disting. Jud. Career award L.A. Lawyers Club, award L.A. County Bd. Suprs., 1981. Fellow Am. Bar Found.; mem. ABA (probate litigation com. real property, probate and trust sect.), Am. Arbitration Assn. (mem. nat. panel of arbitrators), Internat. Acad. Estate and Trust Law (academician, founder, 1st pres., now chancellor), Calif. State Bar (advisor to exec. com. real property, probate and trust sect. 1970-83), Santa Monica Bar Assn. (pres. 1960), Westwood Bar Assn. (pres. 1959), L.A. Bar Assn., Am. Legion (comdr. 1971-72), U. So. Calif. Law Alumni Assn. (pres. 1969-70), Phi Alpha Delta (1st justice alumni chpt.). Office: 300 S Grand Ave Fl 28 Los Angeles CA 90071-3109

MARSHALL, BRIAN LAURENCE, trade association executive; b. Kingston-on-Thames, England, Apr. 6, 1941; came to U.S., 1949; s. John and Marguerite Elizabeth (Sandele) M. BA in European History, U. N.C., 1963; MS in Internat. Mgmt., Am. Grad. Sch. Internat. Mgmt., Glendale, Ariz., 1973. Commd. 2d lt. USAF, 1964, advanced through grades to capt., 1972; instr. Armed Forces Air Intelligence Tng. Ctr., Denver, 1965-68; intelligence analyst Task Force Alpha, Nakhon Phanom, Thailand, 1968-69; intelligence systems analyst Headquarters Tactical Air Command, Langley AFB, Va., 1969-72, resigned, 1972; cons. Gen. Research Corp., McLean, Va., 1974; systems analyst Computer Scis. Corp., Falls Ch., Va., 1974-87; dir. U.S. membership and pubs. U.S.-Mexico C. of C., Washington, 1987-91; v.p. pub. affairs, bd. dirs. N.Am. Free Trade Assn., Washington, 1991—; v.p. internat. N.Am. Trade and Investment Group, Washington, 1991—, also bd. dirs.; contract team leader, strategic planning studies and analyses U.S. Dept. Defense, Joint Chiefs of Staff, Washington, 1976-82. Contbr. articles to booklets and newsletters. Vol. Pres. Ford Com., Washington, 1976; bd. dirs. Columbia Plaza Tenants Assn., Washington, 1981-84; sustaining mem. Rep. Nat. Com., Washington, 1978-88. Mem. Assn. Former Intelligence Officers, World Affairs Coun., Fgn. Policy Assn. (group leader discussion program), Thunderbird Alumni Assn. (pres. Washington chpt. 1980-87), Washington Mgmt. and Bus. Assn. (vice chmn. 1981-83, treas. 1987—). Republican. Lodge: Hash House Harriers. Avocations: jogging, tennis, travel, discussion groups, reading. Home: 5304 Albemarle St Bethesda MD 20816-1827 Office: N Am Free Trade Assn 1130 Connecticut Ave NW Ste 500 Washington DC 20036-3904

MARSHALL, BRYAN EDWARD, anesthesiologist, educator; b. London, Oct. 24, 1935; came to U.S., 1965, naturalized, 1979; m. Carol Davies, Sept. 1957; children—Leisa, David. M.D., Leeds U., 1959. Diplomate: Am. Bd. Anesthesiology. Rotating intern Hereford (Eng.) Gen. Hosps., 1959-60; sr. house officer anesthesia Taunton Gen. Hosps., Cambridge, Eng., 1960-61; registrar anesthesia United Cambridge Hosps., 1961-63; research scholar Cambridge U., 1963-65; research fellow U. Pa. Med. Sch., 1965-66, mem. faculty, 1966—, prof. anesthesia, 1972—; prof. comparative anesthesia U. Pa. Vet. Sch., 1973—, Horatio C. Wood prof. research in anesthesia, dir. anesthesia research, 1982; vis. prof., U.S., Can., Europe, Asia, Australia; lectr. throughout, U.S.; mem. merit rev. bd. VA; study sect. NIH. Author textbooks and numerous articles in field.; editor: Anesthesiology, 1975—,

Circulatory Shock; mem. editorial bds. profl. jours. Recipient Career Devel. award NIH, 1971-76. Fellow Am. Coll. Anesthesiologists, Royal Coll. Physicians; mem. AAUP, AAAS, Assn. Univ. Anesthesiologists (Rsch. Excellence award 1995), Am. Physiol. Soc. Am., Soc. Exptl. Biology and Medicine, Assn. Anesthesiologists Gt. Britain and Ireland (Rsch. prize 1964), Anesthesia Rsch. Group Gt. Britain, Shock Soc., Phila. Med. Sco., Pa. Soc. Anesthesiologists, Phila. Physiol. Soc., Pa. Thoracic Soc., Laennec Soc. Phila., Circanes Soc., John Morgan Soc., Sigma Chi. Home: 119 Adrienne Ln Wynnewood PA 19096-1205 Office: Hosp U Pa 773 Dudley St Bldg Philadelphia PA 19148-2423

MARSHALL, BURKE, law educator; b. Plainfield, N.J., Oct. 1, 1922. A.B., Yale U., 1944, LL.B., 1951, M.A., 1970. Bar: D.C. bar 1952. Assoc., then partner firm Covington and Burlington, Washington, 1951-61; asst. atty. gen. U.S., 1961-65; gen. counsel IBM Corp., Armonk, N.Y., 1965-69; sr. v.p. IBM Corp., 1969-70; prof. law Yale U. Law Sch., 1970—, Nicholas deB. Katzenbach prof. emeritus; chmn. Nat. Adv. Commn. SSS, 1967; bd. dirs. State Farm Mut. Author: Federalism and Civil Rights, 1965; co-author: The Mylai Massacre and Its Cover-up, 1975; editor: The Supreme Court and Human Rights, 1982, A Workable Government?, 1989; contbr. articles, revs. to legal publs. Bd. dirs. Ctr. Community Change, Washington, 1968—, Robert F. Kennedy Meml., 1969—, Vera Inst. Justice, N.Y.C., 1965—. Home: Castle Meadow Rd Newtown CT 06470 Office: Yale U Sch Law 127 Wall St New Haven CT 06511-6636

MARSHALL, C. TRAVIS, manufacturing executive, government relations specialist; b. Apalachicola, Fla., Jan. 31, 1926; s. John and Estelle (Marks) M.; m. Katherine Rose Lepine; children: Melanie, Monica, Katharine. BS, U. Notre Dame, 1948. Chief clk. Firestone Tire & Rubber Co., Detroit, 1948-51; gen. sales mgr. The Hallicrafters, Chgo., 1952-65; v.p. mktg. E. F. Johnson, Waseca, Minn., 1965-70; v.p. mktg. ops. Motorola, Inc., Schaumburg, Ill., 1970-72, dir., govt. relations, communications div., 1972-74; v.p., dir. govt. relations Motorola, Inc., Washington, 1974-85, sr. v.p., dir., gov. relations, 1985-92; telecomm. cons., 1992—; bd. dirs. Iridium, Inc. Appointed amb. by Pres. Bush to Internat. Telecomm. Union Conf.; trustee Md. Youth Symphony Orch. Recipient Disting. Service award Electronics Industries Assn., Washington, 1987. Mem. Electronics Industries Assn. (treas. 1982-92, treas. emeritus 1992—, v.p. 1975-88), Burning Tree Country Club (Bethesda), Columbia Country Club (Chevy Chase), Met. Club (Washington), Crystal Downs Country Club (Frankfort, Mich.). Republican. Roman Catholic. Avocations: sailing, golf. Office: Motorola Inc 1350 I St NW Washington DC 20005-3305

MARSHALL, CAROLYN ANN M., church official, consultant; b. Springfield, Ill., July 18, 1935; d. Hayward Thomas and Isabelle Bernice (Hayer) McMurray; m. John Alan Marshall, July 14, 1956 (dec. Sept. 1990); children: Margaret Marshall Bushman, Cynthia Marshall Kyrouac, Clinton, Carol. Student, De Pauw U., 1952-54; BSBA, Drake U., 1956; D of Pub. Svc. (hon.), De Pauw U., 1983; LHD (hon.), U. Indpls., 1990. Corp. sec. Marshall Studios, Inc., Veedersburg, Ind., 1956-89, exec. cons., 1989-93; sec. Gen. Conf., lay leader South Ind. conf. United Meth. Ch., 1988—; Carolyn M. Marshall chair in women studies Bennett Coll., Greensboro, N.C., 1988; fin. cons. Lucille Raines Residence, Inpls., 1977—. Pres. Fountain Ctrl. Band Boosters, Veedersburg, 1975-77; del. Gen. Conf., United Meth. Ch., 1980, 84, 88, 92, 96, pres. women's divsn. gen. bd. global ministries, 1984-88; bd. dirs. Franklin (Ind.) United Meth. Ch. Home: 204 N Newlin St Veedersburg IN 47987-1358

MARSHALL, CHARLES, communications company executive; b. Vandalia, Ill., Apr. 21, 1929; s. William Forman and Ruth (Corson) M.; m. Millicent Bruner, Jan. 2, 1953; children: Ruth Ann, Marcia Marshall Rinek, William Forman, Charles Tedrick. B.S. in Agr., U. Ill., 1951. With Ill. Bell Telephone Co., 1953-59, 61-64, 65-70, 71-72, 77-81; pres., chief exec. officer Ill. Bell Telephone Co., Chgo., 1977-81; with AT&T, 1959-61, 64-65, 70-71, 76-77, 81-89; chmn., chief exec. officer Am. Bell, Morristown, N.J., 1983-84, AT&T Info. Systems, 1984-85; vice chmn. AT&T, N.Y.C., 1985-89; bd. dirs. Ceridian, GATX, Sundstrand, Sonat, Hartmarx; trustee U. Ill. Found. Served to 1st lt. USAF, 1951-53. Mem. Econ. Club Chgo., Comml. Club Chgo., Club of Pelican Bay, Tavern Club, Chgo. Club. Avocations: fishing, golfing, reading. Home: Ph-B 6001 Pelican Bay Blvd Naples FL 33963-8166

MARSHALL, CHARLES BURTON, political science consultant; b. Catskill, N.Y., Mar. 25, 1908; s. Caleb Carey and Alice (Beeman) M.; m. Betty Louise O'Brien, Aug. 1, 1958 (dec. July, 1991); children (by previous marriage) Charles Richard, Jean Marshall Vickery. BA, U. Tex., 1931, MA, 1932; PhD, Harvard U., 1939; LHD, Johns Hopkins U., 1987. With newspapers in El Paso and Austin, Tex., 1925-31; With newspapers in Detroit, 1934-38; instr., tutor govt. Harvard U. and Radcliffe Coll., 1938-42; vis. lectr. Harvard U., summer 1963; cons. Intergovtl. Com. Refugees, 1946-47; staff cons. com. fgn. affairs U.S. Ho. of Reps., 1947-50; mem. policy planning staff State Dept., 1950-53; adviser to prime minister Pakistan, 1955-57; research assoc. Washington Center Fgn. Policy Research, 1957-74, acting dir., 1969-70; vis. prof. Sch. Advanced Internat. Studies, Johns Hopkins, 1965-66, prof., 1966-67, Paul H. Nitze prof. internat. politics, 1967-75; Alumni prof. internat. studies U. N.C., 1960-61; Centennial vis. prof. Tex. A&M U., 1976; cons. in field, 1961—; U.S. govt. rep. XIV Conf. Internat. Red Cross, Toronto, Can., 1952; mem. Gen. Adv. Com. Arms Control and Disarmament, 1982-92. Author: The Limits of Foreign Policy, 1954, The Exercise of Sovereignty, 1965, The Cold War: A Concise History, 1965, Crisis Over Rhodesia: A Skeptical View, 1967; Cons. editor: New Republic, 1959-64; contbg. editor: Nat. Rev, 1979-83. Served to lt. col. AUS, 1942-46. Fellow Carnegie Endowment Internat. Peace, 1934-35; vis. scholar, 1958-59. Mem. Coun. Fgn. Rels., Washington Inst. Fgn. Affairs, Cosmos Club. Home: 4106 N Randolph St Arlington VA 22207-4808

MARSHALL, CHARLES NOBLE, railroad consultant; b. Phila., Feb. 18, 1942; s. Donnell and Cornelia Lansdale (Brooke) M.; m. Ann Shaw Donovan, Jan. 12, 1971; children—Elizabeth, Caroline, Cornelia, Edward. B.S. in Engring., Princeton U., 1963; J.D., U. Mich., 1967. Bar: Md. 1967, D.C. 1975, Pa. 1978. Atty. Balt. & Ohio R.R., Balt. and Cleve., 1967-73; gen. atty. So. Ry., Washington, 1973-78; gen. counsel commerce Conrail, Phila., 1978-83, v.p. mktg., 1983-85, sr. v.p. mktg. and sales, 1985-89, sr. v.p. devel., 1989-95; bd. dirs. Phila. Reg. Port Authority, Pa. Chamber, Inc. Republican. Episcopalian.

MARSHALL, CLIFFORD WALLACE, mathematics educator; b. N.Y.C., Mar. 11, 1928; s. Clifford Wallace and Virginia (Roe) M.; m. Adele Kentoffio, Nov. 21, 1955; children: Wallace F., James A. B.A., Hofstra U., 1949; M.A., Syracuse U., 1950; M.S., Poly. Inst. Bklyn., 1954; Ph.D., Columbia U., 1961. Staff mem. Inst. Def. Analyses, Washington, 1958; prin. engr. Inst. Def. Analyses, 1959-60, cons. summer staff mem., 1965-68; specialist operations analyst Republic Aviation Corp., Farmingdale, N.Y., 1963; cons. USN Strategic Systems Project Office, Washington, 1968-69; assoc. prof. math. Polytechnic U., Brooklyn, 1963-68, prof. math., 1968-95, adj. prof. computer sci., 1995—; Cons. Urban Inst., 1971-77, U.S. Dept. Energy, 1977-80, U.S. Dept. Energy (Simulation Systems Div., Gould Inc.), 1976-80. Author: Applied Graph Theory, 1971; assoc. editor Naval Rsch. Logistics, 1977—. Mem. Math. Assn. Am., Am. Math. Soc., Sigma Xi. Home: 264 N Ocean Ave Patchogue NY 11772-2010 Office: Rt 110 Farmingdale NY 11735

MARSHALL, CODY, bishop. Bishop No. Ill. Ch. of God in Christ, Chgo. Office: Ch of God in Christ 8050 Revell Ct Orland Park IL 60462-6100

MARSHALL, CONRAD JOSEPH, entrepreneur; b. Detroit, Dec. 23, 1934; s. Edward Louis Fedak and Maria Magdalena Berzsenyi; m. Dorothy Genieve Karnafil, Dec. 1, 1956 (div. 1963); children: Conrad Joseph Jr., Kevin Conrad, Lisa Marie; m. Beryle Elizabeth Callahan, June 15, 1965 (div. 1972); children: Brent Jasmer, Farah Elizabeth. Diploma, Naval Air Tech. Tng. Ctr., Norman, Okla., 1952; student, Wayne State U., 1956-59; Diploma, L.A. Police Acad., 1961. Dir. mktg. Gulf Devel., Torrance, Calif., 1980-83; sales mgr. Baldwin Piano Co., Santa Monica, Calif., 1977-80; dir. mktg., v.p. Western Hose, Inc., L.A., 1971-76; city letter carrier U.S. Post Office, L.A., 1969-71; writer freelance L.A., 1966—; police officer L.A. Police Dept., 1961-66; asst. sales mgr. Wesson Oil Co., Detroit, 1958-60; agt. Life Ins. Co. of Va., Wayne, Mich., 1956-58; pres. Am. Vision Mktg., L.A., 1990—, Con-Mar Prodns., L.A., 1983—; sr. v.p. Pacific Acquisition Group, 1992—, Invest. Admin. HealthCom., Int., 1993—; pres. Midway TV Co., 1994—; tech. advisor Lion's Gate Films, Westwood, Calif., 1970-74, Medicine Wheel Prodns., Hollywood, Calif., 1965-75; mng. gen. ptnr. Encino Wireless #1, 1994—; CEO Midway TV Inc., 1995. Author: (series) "Dial Hot Line", 1967, (screenplay) "Heads Across the Border", 1968, "The Fool Card", 1970, "Probable Cause", 1972; co-author: The Fedak File, 1995; albums include Song Shark, 1992, Conrad Marshall Quintet, 1991. Campaign vol. Dem. Ctrl. Com., L.A., 1976, Rep. Ctrl. Com., 1994. Mem. Screen Actors Guild, Internat. Platform Assn. Avocations: poetry, song writing, club singing, philosophy, theology. Home: 11853 Kling Ste 17 Valley Village CA 91607 Office: Con-Mar Prodns 2026 Holly Hill Ter Hollywood CA 90068

MARSHALL, CONSUELO BLAND, federal judge; b. Knoxville, Tenn., Sept. 28, 1936; d. Clyde Theodore and Annie (Brown) Arnold; m. George Edward Marshall, Aug. 30, 1959; children: Michael Edward, Laurie Ann. A.A., Los Angeles City Coll., 1956; B.A., Howard U., 1958, LL.B., 1961. Bar: Calif. 1962. Dep. atty. City of L.A., 1962-67; assoc. Cochran & Atkins, L.A., 1968-70; commr. L.A. Superior Ct., 1971-76; judge Inglewood Mcpl. Ct., 1976-77, L.A. Superior Ct., 1977-80, U.S. Dist. Ct. Central Dist. Calif., L.A., 1980—; lectr. U.S. Information Agy. in Yugoslavia, Greece and Italy, 1984, in Nigeria and Ghana, 1991, in Ghana, 1992. Contbr. articles to profl. jours.; notes editor Law Jour. Howard U. Mem. adv. bd. Richstone Child Abuse Center. Recipient Judicial Excellence award Criminal Cts. Bar Assn., 1992; research fellow Howard U. Law Sch., 1959-60;. Mem. State Bar Calif., Calif. Women Lawyers Assn., Calif. Assn. Black Lawyers, Calif. Judges Assn., Black Women Lawyers Assn., Los Angeles County Bar Assn., Nat. Assn. Women Judges, NAACP, Urban League, Beta Phi Sigma. Office: US Dist Ct 312 N Spring St Los Angeles CA 90012-4701*

MARSHALL, DALE ROGERS, college president, political scientist, educator; b. Mar. 22, 1937; m. Donald J. Marshall; children: Jessica, Cynthia, Clayton. BA in Govt., Cornell U., 1959; MA in Polit. Sci., U. Calif., Berkeley, 1960; PhD in Polit. Sci. with distinction, UCLA, 1969. Lectr. in polit. sci. UCLA, 1969-70, U. Calif., Berkeley, 1970-72; from asst. prof. to prof. U. Calif., Davis, 1972-86, faculty asst. to vice chancellor acad. affairs, 1980-82, assoc. dean Coll. Letters and Scis., 1983-86; acting pres. Wellesley (Mass.) Coll., 1987-88, dean of coll., prof. polit. sci., 1986-92, pres., 1992—; mem.e xec. bd. Calif. Assembly Fellowship Program, 1980-86; bd. trustees, bd. overseers Newton-Wellesley Hosp., 1989-93; bd. trustees Cornell U., Ithaca, N.Y., 1983-93, chair Cornell Fund, co-chair Coll. Arts and Scis. Capital Campaign, 1990-93; bd. trustees New Eng. Zenith Fund, New Eng. Mut. Life Ins. Co., 1995—; bd. dirs. Am. Student Assistance Guarantor, Am. Student Assistance Corp, 1994—. Author: (with John C. Bollens) Guide to Participation: Field Work, Role Playing Cases and Other Forms, 1973, (with Roger Montgomery) Housing Policy for the 80's, 1980, (with Rufus P. Browning and David H. Tabb) Protest is Not Enough: The Struggle of Blacks and Hispanics for Eqaulity in Urban Politics, 1984 (APSA Ralph J. Bunche award for best book on ethnic rels. 1985, Gladys Kammerer award for best book in Am. policy 1985); editor: Urban Policy Making, 1979, (with David K. Leonard) Institutions of Rural Development for the Poor: Decentralization and Organizatonal Linkages, 1982, (with Rufus P. Browning and David H. Tabb, co-editor), Racial Politics in merican Cities, 1990; mem. editl. bd. Am. Polit. Sci. Rev., 1972-76, Pub. Adminstrn. Rev., 1985-86; contbr. articles to profl. jours. Woodrow Wilson fellow, 1959-60, Calif. Regents fellow, 1966-67, 67-68; NSF grantee, 1976-78, 79-80; recipient Disting. Teaching award Significant Contbn. to Status of Women citation Chancellor's Com. on Status of Women at U. Calif. at Davis, 1978. Mem. Am. Polit. Sci. Assn. (mem. exec. coun. 1974-76, v.p. 1985-86, mem. nominating com. 1988-90), Western Polit. Sci. Assn. (mem. exec. coun. 1973-75, pres. 1984-85), Nat. Acad. Pub. Adminstrn., Mortar Bd., Phi Beta Kappa, Phi Kappa Phi. Office: Wheaton Coll Office of Pres Norton MA 02766

MARSHALL, DANIEL STUART, advertising executive; b. London, Eng., Nov. 14, 1930; came to U.S., 1964; s. Leslie Stuart and Jessie (Morrison) M.; m. Solange Goohier, Sept. 2, 1985. Student, St. Johns Coll., Hassocks, Eng., 1944. Dir. art J. Walter Thompson, Santiago, Chile, 1958-61, San Paulo, Brazil, 1961-64, N.Y.C., 1964-75; exec. v.p., creative dir. Marshall Jacomma & Mitchell, N.Y.C., 1978—. Artist, designer (book) The Dream Theatre, 1975, In a Monastery Kitchen, 1975. Office: Marshall Jacomma & Mitchell 41 Madison Ave New York NY 10010-2202

MARSHALL, DONALD GLENN, English language and literature educator; b. Long Beach, Calif., Sept. 9, 1943; s. Albert Louis and Margaret Corinne (Morrison) M.; m. Kathleen Bonann, June 21, 1975; children—Stephanie Deborah, Zachary Louis. A.B. summa cum laude, Harvard U., 1965; M.Phil., Yale U., 1969, Ph.D., 1971. Asst. prof. English UCLA, 1969-75; assoc. prof. English U. Iowa, Iowa City, 1975-79; prof. English U. Iowa, 1979-90, honors dir. Coll. Liberal Arts, 1981-85; prof., head English dept. U. Ill., Chgo., 1990—. Editor: Philosophy as Literature/Literature as Philosophy, 1986; compiler: Contemporary Critical Theory: A Selective Bibliography, 1993; translator: (with Joel Weinsheimer) Truth and Method by Hans-Georg Gadamer, 1989; contbr. articles and revs. to profl. jours. Recipient Bell prize Harvard U., 1965, Webster prize Yale U., 1967; NEH Younger Humanist fellow, 1973-74; grantee UCLA, U. Iowa. Mem. MLA, Internat. Assn. Philosophy and Lit., Soc. Values in Higher Edn., Ill. Humanities Coun. (bd. dirs. 1994—). Democrat. Roman Catholic. Office: U Ill Dept English Univ Hall 601 S Morgan St Chicago IL 60607-7100

MARSHALL, DONALD STEWART, computer systems company executive; b. Saskatoon, Sask., Can., Nov. 18, 1938; s. Arthur Stewart and Helen Margaret (Pederson) M.; children: Douglas Stewart, Andrew Christopher. B Applied Sci. in Civil Engring., Queen's U., Kingston, Ont., Can., 1962. Registered profl. engr., Ont. Progressed from computer systems analyst to branch mgr. Honeywell, IBM and AGT Data Systems, 1962-71; pres. Ventek Ltd., London, 1971-80; v.p. CDC Data Systems Ltd., Toronto, Ont., 1980-83; exec. v.p. Meridian Techs. Inc., Toronto, 1983-93; pres. Nextest Ltd (formerly Atelco Ltd.), Markham, Ont., 1993—; bd. dirs. Incontext Sys. Inc., Halozone Tech. Inc., Nextest Ltd. Mem. Assn. Profl. Engrs. Ont. Avocations: golf, squash, tennis. Home: 54 Anderson Ave, Toronto, ON Canada M5P 1H7 Office: Nextest Ltd, Ste 241, 50 McIntosh Dr, Markham, ON Canada L4B 3H6

MARSHALL, DONALD TOMPKINS, industrial distribution executive; b. Schenectady, N.Y., Oct. 29, 1933; s. Allen Donald and Margaret (Leahy) M.; m. Susan Fisher, July 25, 1959; m. Anna Marie Pikes O'Brien, Feb. 14, 1987; children: Amy, Scott, Jennifer. BS in Math., St. Lawrence U., 1956; BS in Mech. Engring., Columbia U., 1957. With Union Carbide Corp., N.Y.C., 1958-70; pres. airco cryo plants div. Air Reduction Corp., Murray Hill, N.J., 1970-76; pres. Gen. Energy Corp., Willingboro, N.J., 1976-78; v.p. Sun Distbrs. div. Sun Co., Phila., 1978-82, pres., 1982-86; chmn., chief exec. officer Sun Distbrs. Co.- N.Y. Stock Exch., Phila., 1986—. Mem. ASME, Riverton Golf Club (treas. 1979-85), Seabrook Island Club, Pine Valley Golf Club. Avocations: golf, hunting, fishing. Office: Sun Distbrs Inc 1 Logan Sq Philadelphia PA 19103-6933*

MARSHALL, E. G., actor; b. Owatonna, Minn., June 18, 1910; s. Charles G. and Hazel Irene (Cobb) M.; m. Helen Wolf, Apr. 26, 1939 (div. 1953); children: Jill, Degen. Student, Carlton Coll., 1930, U. Minn., 1932. Began profl. career on radio stas. St. Paul, Mpls., Chgo., 1932. Featured on radio program Eugene O'Neill's The Iceman Cometh, Theatre Guild on the Air, 1946-47; actor: (films) including Bachelor Party, 1957, House on 92d Street, 13 Rue Madeleine, Swamp Angel, Caine Mutiny, 1954, Pushover, 1954, Bamboo Prison, 1954, Broken Lance, 1954, Silver Chalice, 1954, Left Hand of God, 1955, Scarlet Hour, 1956, Call Northside 777, Twelve Angry Men, 1957, Compulsion, 1959, The Journey, 1959, Town Without Pity, 1961, The Chase, 1966, The Bridge at Remagen, 1969, Tora! Tora! Tora!, 1970, Pursuit of Happiness, 1971, Interiors, 1978, Superman II, 1980, Creepshow, 1982, Power, 1986, My Chauffer, 1986, La Gran Fiesta, 1987, National Lampoon's Christmas Vacation, 1989, Two Evil Eyes (The Black Cat), 1991, Consenting Adults, 1991, (plays) The Gang's All Here, 1959, The Crucible, Red Roses for Me, Waiting for Godot, (TV movies) Vampire, 1979, Disaster on the Coastliner, 1979, The Phoenix, 1981, John Steinbeck's The Winter of Our Discontent, 1983, Under Siege, 1986, At Mother's Request, 1987, Emma, Queen of the South seas, 1988, The Hijacking of the Achille Lauro, 1989, Ironclads, 1991, Stephen King's The Tommyknockers, 1993, (TV miniseries) Eleanor: First Lady of the World, 1982, Kennedy, 1983, At Mother's Request, 1987, Ike, 1987, Oldest Living Confederate Widow Tells All, 1994, (TV series) The Defenders, 1961-65 (2 Emmy awards), The Bold Ones (The Doctors), 1969-73, Chicago Hope, 1994. Recipient Emmy award for best actor in Defenders series, 1961, 62. Office: Paradigm Talent Agy 10100 Santa Monica Blvd 125th Flr Los Angeles CA 90067*

MARSHALL, ELLEN RUTH, lawyer; b. N.Y.C., Apr. 23, 1949; d. Louis and Faith (Gladstone) M. AB, Yale U., 1971; JD, Harvard U., 1974. Bar: Calif. 1975, D.C. 1981, N.Y. 1989. Assoc. McKenna & Fitting, Los Angeles, 1975-80; ptnr. McKenna, Conner & Cuneo, Los Angeles and Orange County, Calif., 1980-88, Morrison & Foerster, Orange County, Calif., 1988—. Mem. ABA (bus. law sect., savs. inst. com., asset securitization com., tax sect., employee benefits com.), Orange County Bar Assn. Club: Center (Costa Mesa, Calif.). Office: Morrison & Foerster 19900 Macarthur Blvd Irvine CA 92715-2445

MARSHALL, F. RAY, public affairs educator. BA, Millsaps Coll., 1949; MA, La. State U., 1950; PhD, U. Calif., Berkeley, 1954. Pres. Indsl. Rels. Rsch. Assn., 1976-77; U.S. sec. of labor, 1977-81; pres. Internat. Labor Rights Rsch. and Edn. Fund; Audre and Bernard Rapoport Centennial chair in econs. and pub. affairs, Lyndon B. Johnson Sch. Pub. Affairs U. Tex., Austin; bd. dirs. German Marshall Fund, Aurora Nat. Life Assurance, USX Corp., Nat. Ctr. on Edn. and Economy, Inst. for the Future; mem. Coun. on Fgn. Rels. Office: U Tex Sch of Pub Affairs Austin TX 78713-7450

MARSHALL, FRANCIS JOSEPH, aerospace engineer; b. N.Y.C., Sept. 5, 1923; s. Francis Joseph and Mary Gertrude (Leary) M.; m. Joan Eager, June 14, 1952; children—Peter, Colin, Stephen, Dana. B.S. in Mech. Engring, CCNY, 1948; M.S., Rensselaer Poly. Inst., 1950; Dr. Eng. Sci., N.Y. U., 1955. Engr. Western Union Co., N.Y.C., 1948, Gen. Electric Co., Schenectady, 1948-50; engr. Wright-Aero Corp., Woodridge, N.J., 1950-52; group leader Lab. for Applied Scis., U. Chgo., 1955-60; instr. Ill. Inst. Tech., 1957-59; prof. Sch. Aeros. and Astronautics, Purdue U., West Lafayette, Ind., 1960—; engr. U.S. Naval Underseas Warfare Center, Pasadena, Calif., 1966-68; faculty fellow NASA-Langley, 1969-70; vis. prof. Inst. Tech. Mara-Midwest Univs. Consortium for Internat. Activities, Malayasia, 1989. Contbr. articles to profl. jours. Served with U.S. Army, 1943-46. Decorated Combat Inf. badge.; NASA research grantee, 1970-76; Fulbright scholar, Turkey, 1988-89. Asso. fellow AIAA; mem. Am. Soc. Engring. Edn., AAUP. Home: 120 Leslie Ave West Lafayette IN 47906-2410 Office: Sch Aeros and Astronautics Purdue U West Lafayette IN 47907

MARSHALL, FRANK W., film producer, director. Student, UCLA. Location mgr.: The Last Picture Show, 1971, What's Up Doc?, 1972; assoc. prodr.: Paper Moon, 1973, Daisy Miller, 1974, At Long Last Love, 1975. Nickelodeon, 1976, The Driver, 1978; line prodr.: Orson Welles' The Other Side of the Wind (unreleased), Marin Scorsese's The Last Waltz, 1977; prodr.: (films) Raiders of the Lost Ark, 1981 (Academy award nomination for best picture 1981), Noises Off, 1992; (with Steven Spielberg) Poltergeist, 1982; (with Spielberg, Quincy Jones, and Kathleen Kennedy) The Color Purple, 1985 (Academy award nomination for best picture 1985), (with Kathleen Kennedy and Kane Startz) Indian in a Cupboard; (with Spielberg and Kennedy) Empire of the Sun, 1987, Always, 1989; (with Robert Watts) Who Framed Roger Rabbit, 1988; (with Kennedy and Gerald R. Molen) Hook, 1991; (with Kennedy) Milk Money, 1994; exec. prodr.: (films) The Warriors, 1979, Twilight Zone-The Movie, 1983; (with George Lucas) Indiana Jones and the Temple of Doom, 1984; (with Kennedy and Spielberg) Gremlins, 1984, The Goonies, 1985, Back to the Future, 1985, Young Sherlock Holmes, 1985, *batteries not included, 1987, Dad, 1989, Back to the Future Part II, 1989, Gremlins 2: The New Batch, 1990, Back to the Future Part III, 1990, Joe Versus the Volcano, 1990, Cape Fear, 1991, We're Back! A Dinosaur's Story, 1993; (with Kennedy) Fandango, 1985; (with Kennedy, Spielberg, and David Kirschner) An American Tail, 1986; (with Kennedy and Art Levinson) The Money Pit, 1986; (with Kennedy, Spielberg, Peter Guber, and Jon Peters) Innerspace, 1987; (with Kennedy, Lucas, and Spielberg) The Land Before Time, 1988; (with Kennedy and Lucas) Indiana Jones and the Last Crusade, 1989; (with Kennedy and Kirschner) An American Tail: Fievel Goes West, 1991; (with Chris Meledandri) Swing Kids, 1993; (with Kennedy and Molen) A Far Off Place, 1993; exec. prodr. (with Spielberg, Robert W. Cort, and Ted Field), dir.: Arachnophobia, 1990; dir.: Alive, 1993, Congo, 1995; exec. producer: TV Roger Rabbit and the Secret of Toontown; prodr., dir. TV Johnny Bago. Office: Kennedy/Marshall Co Clinton # 100 650 N Bronson Ave Los Angeles CA 90004-1404

MARSHALL, GARLAND ROSS, biochemist, biophysicist, medical educator; b. San Angelo, Tex., Apr. 16, 1940; s. Garland Ross and Jewel Wayne (Gray) M.; m. Suzanne Russell, Dec. 26, 1959; children: Chris, Keith, Melissa, Lee. BS, Calif. Inst. Tech., 1962; PhD, Rockefeller U., 1966; DSc (hon.), Politechnika, Lodz, Poland, 1993. Instr. Washington U., St. Louis, 1966-67, asst. prof., 1967-72, assoc. prof., 1972-76, prof. biochemistry, 1976—, prof. pharmacology, 1985—, dir. Ctr. for Molecular Design, 1988—; vis. prof. Massey U., Palmerston North, New Zealand, 1975; vis. prof. chemistry U. Florence, Italy, 1991; pres. Tripos Assocs., Inc., St. Louis, 1979-87; chmn. 10th An. Peptide Symposium, St. Louis, 1986-88; councilor Am. Peptide Soc., 1990-93; established investigator Am. Heart Assn., Washington, 1970-75. Editor: Peptides: Chemistry and Biology, 1988, Peptides: Chemistry, Structure and Biology, 1990; editor-in-chief Jour. Computer-Aided Molecular Design, 1986—. Recipient medal XL-Lecia Tech. U., Lodz, Poland, 1987, Vincent de Vigneaud award Am. Peptide Soc., 1994. Mem. Am. Chem. Soc. (Medicinal Chemistry award 1988), Am. Soc. for Biochemistry and Molecular Biology, Am. Soc. for Pharmacology and Exptl. Therapeutics, Biophys. Soc., Am. Peptide Soc. (Vincent du Vigneaud award 1994). Office: Washington U Ctr for Molecular Design One Brookings Dr Saint Louis MO 63130-4899

MARSHALL, GARRY, film producer, director, writer; b. N.Y.C., Nov. 13, 1934. B.S., Northwestern U. Writer I Spy, Jack Paar Show, Joey Bishop Show, Danny Thomas Show, Lucy Show, Dick Van Dyke Show; writer, creator Hey Landlord; exec. producer The Odd Couple, 1968; creator, exec. producer Evil Roy Slade, 1972, Happy Days, Laverne and Shirley, Mork and Mindy, Angie, Joanie Loves Chachi; writer, producer films, How Sweet It Is, 1968, The Grasshopper, 1970; dir. Young Doctors in Love, 1982; screenwriter, dir. Flamingo Kid, 1984; dir. films Nothing in Common, 1987, Overboard, 1987, Beaches, 1988, Pretty Woman, 1990, Frankie & Johnny, 1991, Exit to Eden, 1994; film appearance includes Psych-out, 1968, Lost in America, 1985, Soapdish, 1991, A League of Their Own, 1992, Hocus Pocus, 1993.

MARSHALL, GEOFFREY, academic administrator; b. Lancaster, Pa., Feb. 6, 1938; s. Ray Ardell and Mary (Elsen) M.; m. Mary Gale Beckwith, June 17, 1961; children: Eden Elizabeth, Erin Elizabeth. BA, Franklin and Marshall Coll., 1959; MA, Rice U., 1961, PhD, 1965; LHD (hon.), Mansfield State Coll., 1980, Ursinus Coll., 1990. Assoc. prof. English U. Okla., Norman, 1964-74; asst. provost U.Okla., Norman, 1973-74; dir. div. state programs Nat. Endowment for Humanities, Washington, 1974-78, dir. div. edn. programs, 1978-80, dep. chmn., 1981-85; assoc. provost and dean for acad. affairs Grad. Sch. CUNY, 1985-92, acting provost and v.p. for acad. affairs, 1992-94, provost, sr. v.p., 1994—; bd. dirs. Ursinus Coll., 1986—. Author: Restoration Serious Drama, 1975; contbr. articles to profl. jours. Trustee Norman Pub. Library, 1970-74; chmn. Okla. Humanities Com., 1971-74; mem. Norman Human Rights Commn., 1972-73. Assoc. Danforth Found., 1968-74; recipient Couch Scholars award for excellence in undergrad. edn. U. Okla., 1967. Mem. MLA, Nat. Council Tchrs. English, Am. Soc. 18th Century Studies, Nat. Collegiate Honors Council (exec. com. 1972-74). Home: 125 Cypress Dr Hightstown NJ 08520-2315 Office: CUNY Grad Sch and Univ Ctr 33 W 42rd St New York NY 10036

MARSHALL, GEORGE DWIRE, supermarket chain executive; b. Washington, Feb. 7, 1940; s. Joseph Paull and Jane Schouler (Dwire) M.; m. Sharon Ruth Carter, Nov. 17, 1968; children: Sarah Dwire, Benjamin Carter. BA, Amherst Coll., 1962; JD, U. Calif., Berkeley, 1965. Bar: Calif. 1966. Atty., then sr. atty. legal div. Safeway Inc., Oakland, Calif., 1970-79, v.p., mgr. labor rels. divsn., 1979—; employer trustee UFCW Internat. Union-Industry Pension Fund, 1980—. Served to lt. USNR, 1966-70,

Korea, Vietnam. Mem. State Bar Calif., Bar Assn. San Francisco, Psi Upsilon, Phi Delta Phi. Republican. Presbyterian. Office: Safeway Inc 201 4th St Oakland CA 94607-4311

MARSHALL, GERALD FRANCIS, optical engineer, consultant, physicist; b. Seven Kings, Eng., Feb. 26, 1929. BSc in Physics, London U., 1952. Physicist Morganite Internat., London, 1954-59; sr. research devel. engr. Ferranti Ltd., Edinburgh, Scotland, 1959-67; project mgr. Diffraction Limited Inc., Bedford, Mass., 1967-69; dir. engring. Medical Lasers, Inc., Burlington, Mass., 1969-71; staff cons. Speedring Systems, Troy, Mich., 1971-76; dir. optical engring. Energy Conversion Devices, Inc., Troy, Mich., 1976-87; sr. tech. staff specialist Kaiser Electronics, San Jose, Calif., 1987-89; cons. in optics design and engring., 1989—. Editor, contbg. author: Laser Beam Scanning, 1985, Optical Scanning, 1991; patentee in field. Fellow Inst. Physics, Internat. Soc. Optical Engring. (syymposia chair 1990), bd. dirs. 1991-93, exec. chair Internat. Symposium on Electronic Imaging Device Engring., Munich 1993); mem. Optical Soc. Am. (program chair 1979-80, pres. Detroit sect. 1980-81, bd. dirs. No. Calif. sect. 1990-92).

MARSHALL, GORDON BRUCE, construction company executive; b. Hamilton, Ont., Can., Sept. 26, 1943; s. J. Gordon and Mae J. (Tucker) M.; m. Rita J. Penca, Apr. 22, 1979. BSBA, Northwestern U., 1965; MBA, U. Chgo., 1970; AAS, Coll. Lake County, 1975. CPA, Mo., Ill. Comptrollership trainee Continental Ill. Nat. Bank, Chgo., 1967-68; profit analyst Morton Salt Co., Chgo., 1968-70; sr. fin. specialist Abbott Labs., North Chicago, Ill., 1970-76; treas. Pott Industries Inc., St. Louis, 1976-81; v.p. fin. and adminstrn. Pepper Constrn. Co., Chgo., 1981-84; v.p. fin., chief fin. officer The Pepper Cos. Inc., Chgo., 1985-89, v.p. fin., treas., 1989—; instr. Coll. Lake County, Grayslake, Ill., 1975-76; pres. Blue Jay Ventures Inc., West Dundee, Ill., 1988—. Served to lt. (j.g.) USNR, 1965-67. Recipient Eagle Scout honor Boy Scouts Am. Mem. AICPA, Ill. CPA Soc., Constrn. Fin. Mgmt. Assn. (bd. dirs., pres. 1987-88), Nat. Constrn. Industry Coun. (bd. dirs. 1987-88), Am. Coun. for Constrn. Edn. (trustee 1989—, treas. 1991-93, v.p. 1993-95, pres. 1995—). Office: The Pepper Cos Inc 411 Lake Zurich Rd Barrington IL 60010-3141

MARSHALL, HAROLD D., leasing and financial services company executive; b. 1936; married. Student, U. Fla., Nat. Installment Banking Sch., U. Colo. Mgmt. trainee Family Fin., 1959-61; with Assocs. Corp. N.Am., 1961—, regional v.p. N.W. zone, 1969-73, sr. v.p. Ea. ops., 1973-74, sr. v.p., 1974-79, past exec. v.p., now vice chmn., 1979—, then sr. exec. v.p., now vice chmn.; exec. v.p. Assocs. Comml. Corp., 1976-79, past sr. exec. v.p., now vice chmn., 1979—. With USAR, 1959-65. Office: Assocs Comml Corp PO Box 650363 Dallas TX 75265-0363*

MARSHALL, HERBERT A., lawyer; b. Clinton, Ill., Aug. 20, 1917; s. Harry A. and Andrea (Pederson) M.; m. Helen Christman, May 3, 1941; children—James A., Thomas O., Mary (Mrs. William Nichols). A.B., Washburn U., 1940, LL.B., J.D., 1943. Bar: Kans. bar 1943. Law clk. U.S. Ct. Appeals, 1943-44; asst. county atty. Shawnee County, Kans., 1944-50; practiced in Topeka, 1944—; instr. practice ct. Washburn U. Law Sch., 1963—; mem. Kans. Supreme Ct. Nominating Commn., 1968-79. Trustee, elder Presbyn. Ch. Fellow Am. Bar Found. (life), Kans. Bar Found. (life), Am. Coll. Trial Lawyers; mem. ABA, Kans. Bar Assn. (exec. council 1968—, v.p. 1977, pres. 1979), Am. Judicature Soc., Topeka Bar Assn. (pres. 1968), Topeka C. of C., Optimist Club, Masons, Elks. Home: 4722 SW Brentwood Rd Topeka KS 66606-2204

MARSHALL, HOWARD LOWEN, music educator, musicologist; b. Nokesville, Va., July 21, 1931; s. Howard Hampton and Florence Annie (Nash) M.; m. Doris Mae Rosencranz, July 14, 1962. B of Music Edn., Shenandoah U., 1952; MusM, U. Cin., 1958; PhD, U. Rochester, 1968. Asst. prof. music Lake Forest (Ill.) Coll., 1966-73; Charles B. Thompson prof. music, chmn. music dept. Mercer U., Macon, Ga., 1974—. Author: The Four-Voice Motets of Thomas Crecquillon, Symbolism in Schubert's Winterreise in Studies in Romanticism, The Motets of Georg Prenner. Lt. comdr. USNR, ret. Mem. Am. Musicological Soc., AAUP, Phi Mu Alpha, Phi Kappa Lambda. Avocation: photography. Home: 1324 Maplewood Dr Macon GA 31210-3106 Office: Mercer U Music Dept 1400 Coleman Ave Macon GA 31207-1000

MARSHALL, IRL HOUSTON, JR., residential and commercial cleaning company executive; b. Evanston, Ill., Feb. 28, 1929; s. Irl H. and Marjorie (Greenleaf) M.; m. Barbara Favill, Nov. 5, 1949; children: Alice Marshall Vogler, Irl Houston III, Carol Marshall Allen. AB, Dartmouth Coll., 1949; MBA, U. Chgo., 1968; cert. franchise exec., La. State U., 1991. Gen. mgr. Duraclean Internat., Deerfield, Ill., 1949-61; mgr. Montgomery Ward, Chgo., 1961-77; pres., chief exec. officer Duraclean Internat., 1977—. Inventor/patentee in field. Pres. Cliff Dwellers, Chgo., 1977; exec. com., treas., dir. Highland Park Hosp., 1971-80; dir. Continental Ill. Bank Deerfield, 1982-90; bd. dirs. Better Bus. Bur. Chgo. & No. Ill., Chgo., 1988—. Mem. Internat. Franchise Assn. (bd. dirs. 1981-90, pres. 1985, chmn. 1985-86), Econ. Club Chgo., Exmoor Country Club, Univ. Club Chgo. Presbyterian. Home: 1248 Ridgewood Dr Northbrook IL 60062-3725

MARSHALL, JAMES JOHN, publishing executive; b. Fall River, Mass., Apr. 15, 1930; s. John and Florence (Carr) M.; m. Kathleen Seibert, Apr. 14, 1967 (dec. Jan. 1988); children: Kathleen C., Mary E. BS, Providence Coll., 1953; MS, Columbia U., 1954. Reporter Providence Jour., 1954-55, 57-60; seminarian Maryknoll, Ossining, N.Y., 1960-62; press sec. Office of R.I. Gov. John H. Chafee, Providence, 1962-67; pub. affairs dir. Rep. Govs. Assn., Washington, 1967-69, Citizens Com. for Postal Reform, Washington, 1969-70; pres. Govt. Info. Svcs., Arlington, Va., 1971—, Edn. Fund Rsch. Coun., Arlington, 1971—; pres. Newsletter Press of New Eng., East Providence, R.I., 1976—, Internat. Law Libr., Arlington, 1994—; bd. dirs. Manisses Comms., Providence. With USN, 1955-57. Mem. Newsletter Pubs. Assn. (founding mem., bd. dirs. 1977-87, pres. 1984), Newsletter Pubs. Found., Ind. Newsletter Assn. (pres. 1976), Nat. Press Club. Roman Catholic. Home: 10906 Quimby Point Ln Reston VA 22091 Office: Govt Info Svcs 4301 N Fairfax Dr # 875 Arlington VA 22203

MARSHALL, JANE PRETZER, newspaper editor; b. Chase County, Kans.; married; 2 children. BS in Home Econs. and Journalism, Kans. State U., 1967; student, Tex. A&M, U. Mo., Tex. Christian U., Brite Divinity Sch. Asst. editor dept. agr. info. Tex. Agrl. Ext. Sta. Tex. A&M U., College Station, 1967-70; staff writer Gazette-Telegraph, Colorado Springs, Colo., 1970-72; editor corporate publ. Colorado Interstate, Colorado Springs, 1972-75; co-editor The Pampa (Tex.) News, 1975-78; exec. features editor Ft. Worth Star-Telegram, 1978-84; features editor Denver Post, 1984-88, Houston Chronicle, 1988—. Recipient 1st place for feature writing Tex. AP Mng. Editors Assn., 1978. Mem. Am. Assn. Sunday and Features Editors (bd. dirs., founding chairperson Features First), Women's Found. Health Edn. and Rsch. (bd. dirs.), Journalism and Women Symposium (1st pres.). Office: Houston Chronicle 801 Texas St Houston TX 77002-2906

MARSHALL, JEAN MCELROY, physiologist; b. Chambersburg, Pa., Dec. 31, 1922; d. Frank Lester and Florence (McElroy) M. A.B., Wilson Coll., 1944; M.A., Mt. Holyoke Coll., 1946; Ph.D., U. Rochester, 1951. Instr. Johns Hopkins U. Med. Sch., Balt., 1951-56; asst. prof. Johns Hopkins U. Med. Sch., 1956-60; research postdoctoral fellow Oxford (Eng.) U., 1954-55; asst. prof. Harvard U. Med. Sch., Boston, 1960-66; asso. prof. physiology Brown U., Providence, 1966-69; prof. Brown U., 1969-88, prof. emerita, 1988, E. Brintzenhof Prof. Med. Sci., 1987—; mem. physiology study sect. NIH, 1967-71, mem. tng. com. engring. in biology and medicine, 1971-74, mem. tng. com. lab. medicine, 1976-77; physiol. test com. Nat. Bd. Med. Examiners, 1972-76, neurobiology adv. com., 1977-80. Editor: The Initiation of Labor, 1964; mem. editorial bd. Jour. Pharmacology and Exptl. Therapeutics, 1963-69, Am. Jour. Physiology, 1969-73, Circulation Research, 1973-81; contbr. articles to profl. jours. Mem. Am. Physiol. Soc., Am. Pharmacol. Soc., N.Y. Acad. Scis., Soc. Reproductive Biology, Soc. Gen. Physiologists, Phi Beta Kappa, Sigma Xi. Home: 14 Aberdeen Rd Weston MA 02193-1733 Office: R I Hosp/Brown Univ Dept Medicine Providence RI 02903

MARSHALL, JEFFREY SCOTT, mechanical engineer, educator; b. Cin., Feb. 10, 1961; s. James C. and Norma E. (Everett) M.; m. Marilyn Jane Patterson, July 16, 1983; children: Judith K., Eric G., Emily J. BS summa cum laude, UCLA, 1983, MS, 1984; PhD, U. Calif., Berkeley, 1987. Asst. rsch. engr. U. Calif., Berkeley, 1988; engr. Creare, Inc., Hanover, N.H., 1988-89; from asst. to assoc. prof. dept. ocean engring. Fla. Atlantic U., 1989-93; assoc. prof. dept. mech. engring., rsch. scientist Iowa Inst. Hydraulic Rsch. U. Iowa, Iowa City, 1993—. Contbr. articles to profl. jours. Rsch. grantee Am. Soc. Engring. Edn./USN Summer Faculty Rsch. Programs, 1991-94. ARO Young Investigator Program, 1992-95. Mem. ASME (assoc., Henry Hess award 1992), Am. Phys. Soc., Tau Beta Pi. Achievements include research in fluid mechanics, three-dimensional vortex dynamics and geophysical flows. Office: U Iowa Iowa Inst Hydraulic Rsch Dept Mech Engring Iowa City IA 52242

MARSHALL, JIM, religious organization leader. Co-chair Ecumenical Coalition for Econ. Justice, 1995—. Office: Ecumenical Coalition for Econ Justice, 402-77 Charles St W, Toronto, ON Canada M5S 1K5

MARSHALL, JOHN, professional society administrator; b. Sandwich, Mass., June 30, 1917; s. Walton H. and Vira F. (Stowe) M.; m. Anna Silk, May 11, 1961. BA cum laude, Williams Coll., 1939; Diploma, Sorbonne U., Paris. Trainee Am. Tobacco C., Va., 1939-41; asst. to sr. v.p. European dept. Singer Sewing Machine Co., Europe, Near East and Africa, 1946-56; past pres. Amateur Astronomers Assn., CEO; lectr. in field. Contbr. articles to profl. jours. Lt. comdr. USN, 1941-45, ETO. Recipient Excellence in French Studies award Govt. of France, 1939, Amateur Astronomers medal, 1985. Mem. N.Y. Acad. Scis. Home: 1 Gracie Ter New York NY 10028-7955*

MARSHALL, JOHN ALOYSIUS, bishop; b. Worcester, Mass., Apr. 26, 1928; s. John A. and Katherine T. (Redican) M. A.B. cum laude, Holy Cross Coll., Worcester, 1949; postgrad., Sem. de Philosophie, Montreal, Can., 1949-50; S.T.L., Pontifical Gregorian U., Rome, 1954; M.A. in Guidance and Psychology, Assumption Coll., Worcester, 1964. Ordained priest Roman Catholic Ch., 1953, consecrated bishop, 1972; parish priest in Mass., 1954-57; asst. vice rector Pontifical N. Am. Coll., 1957-61; instr. Acad. Sacred Heart, Worcester, 1961-62, St. Vincent Hosp. Sch. Nursing, Worcester, 1961-62; headmaster St. Stephen Cath. High Sch., Worcester, 1962-68; spiritual dir. Pontifical N. Am. Coll., 1968-71, bus. mgr., 1969-71; bishop of Burlington Vt., 1972-91; bishop Diocese of Springfield, Springfield, Mass., 1992—; chmn. com. priestly formation Nat. Conf. Cath. Bishops, 1975-78. Bd. dirs. Champlain Coll., Burlington, from 1974, Wadhams Hall, Ogdensburg, N.Y., from 1974. Office: PO Box 1730 76 Elliott St Springfield MA 01101

MARSHALL, JOHN CROOK, internal medicine educator, researcher; b. Blackburn, Lancashire, Eng., Feb. 28, 1941; came to U.S., 1976; s. Albert Acey and Marion Miller (Crook) M.; m. Marilyn Dallas Parry, Sept. 20, 1969; children—Samantha Jane, Susannah Crook. B.S., Victoria U., Manchester, Eng., 1962, M.B., Ch.B., 1965, M.D., 1973. Diplomate Am. Bd. Internal Medicine, Am. Bd. Endocrinology and Metabolism. Intern Manchester Royal Infirmary, 1965-66; resident Brompton Hosp., Nat. Heart Hosp., London, 1966-69; resident Hammersmith Hosp., 1966-69, research fellow, London, 1969-72; lectr. U. Birmingham, Eng. 1972-76; assoc. prof. internal medicine U. Mich., Ann Arbor, 1976-79, prof., 1979—; chief endominology and metabolism, 1987—; sci. counselor NIH, Bethesda, Md., 1983—. Editor Endocrinology Jour., 1979-83. Contbr. articles to profl. jours. NIH grantee 1977-87. Fellow Royal Coll. Physicians, Royal Soc. Medicine, ACP; mem. Central Soc. for Clin. Research (council 1983—), Assn. Am. Physicians, Am. Soc. for Clin. Investigation. Anglican. Avocations: vintage racing cars; golf; tennis.

MARSHALL, JOHN DAVID, lawyer; b. Chgo., May 19, 1940; s. John Howard and Sophie (Brezenk) M.; m. Marcia A. Podlasinski, Aug. 26, 1961; children: Jacquelyn, David, Jason, Patricia, Brian, Denise, Michael, Catherine. BS in Acctg., U. Ill., 1961; JD, Ill. Inst. Tech., 1965. Bar: Ill. 1965, U.S. Tax Ct. 1968, U.S. Dist. Ct. (no. dist.) Ill. 1971; CPA, Ill. Ptnr. Mayer, Brown & Platt, Chgo., 1961—. Bd. dirs. Levinson Ctr. for Handicapped Children, Chgo., 1970-75. Fellow Am. Coll. Probate Counsel; mem. Ill. Bar Assn., Chgo. Bar Assn. (agribus. com. 1978—, trust law com. 1969—, probate practice com. 1969—, com. on coms. 1983—, vice chmn. 1988-89, chmn. 1989-90, legis. com. of probate practice com. 1983—, chmn. and vice chmn. legis. com. of probate practice com. 1983-84, chmn. exec. com. probate practice com. 1982-83, vice chmn. exec. com. 1981-82, sec. exec. com. 1980-81, div. chmn. 78-79, div. vice chmn. 1977-78, div. sec. 1976-77, Appreciation award 1982-83), Chgo. Estate Planning Council. Roman Catholic. Club: Union League (Chgo.). Home: 429 Willow Wood Dr Palatine IL 60067-3831 Office: Mayer Brown & Platt 190 S La Salle St Chicago IL 60603-3410

MARSHALL, JOHN ELBERT, III, foundation executive; b. Providence, July 2, 1942; s. John Elbert Jr. and Millicent Edna (Paige) M.; m. Diana M. Healy, Aug. 16, 1968; children: Nelson John, Priscilla Anne. B.A., Brown U., 1964. Advt. mgr. U.N. Alloy Steel Corp., Boston, 1968-70; assoc. dir. devel. Brown U., 1970-74; exec. dir. R.I. Found., Providence, 1974-79; v.p. Kresge Found., Troy, Mich., 1979-82, exec. v.p., 1982-87, pres., 1987—, trustee, 1991—; CEO, 1993—; bd. dirs., former chmn. Coun. Mich. Founds.; chmn. Mich. Cmty. Found. Youth Project. Bd. dirs. United Way Cmty. Svcs., Detroit Symphony Orch. Hall, Mich. Campus Compact, Greater Downtown Partnership; former bd. dirs., vice chmn. Family Svc. Detroit and Wayne County; past pres. Bloomfield Village Assn.; former trustee Coun. on Founds., Washington. Office: Kresge Found PO Box 3151 Troy MI 48007-3151

MARSHALL, JOHN HARRIS, JR., geologist, oil company executive; b. Dallas, Mar. 12, 1924; s. John Harris and Jessie Elizabeth (Mosley) M.; BA in Geology, U. Mo., 1949, MA in Geology, 1950; m. Betty Eugenia Zarecor, Aug. 9, 1947; children: John Harris III, George Z., Jacqueline Anne Marshall Leibach. Geologist, Magnolia Oil Co., Jackson, Miss., 1950-59, assoc. geologist Magnolia/Mobil Oil, Oklahoma City, 1959-63, dist. and div. geologist Mobil Oil Corp., L.A. and Santa Fe Springs, Calif., 1963-69, div. geologist, L.A. and Anchorage, 1969-71, exploration supt., Anchorage, 1971-72, western region geologist, Denver, 1972-76, internat. and offshore geol. mgr., Dallas, 1976-78, chief geologist Mobil Oil Corp., N.Y.C., 1978-81, gen. mgr. exploration for Western Hemisphere, 1981-82; chmn. Marshall Energetics, Inc., Dallas, 1982—; dir. exploration Anschutz, 1985-91; pres. Madera Prodn. Co., 1992—, Summit Oil and Gas Worldwide, 1993-96; CEO Marshall Energetics Ltd., 1994—; active Geology Devel. Bd. U. Mo., 1982—. Councilman, City of Warr Acres (Okla.), 1962-63; various positions Meth. Ch., 1951—, Boy Scouts Am., 1960-68; Manhattan adv. bd. Salvation Army, 1980-82; trustee The Sci. Place., Dallas, 1995—. Served with U.S. Army, 1943-46. Recipient U. Mo. Bd. Curators medal, ROTC Most Outstanding Student, 1949; registered geologist, Calif., Wyo., Ky. Mem. Am. Assn. Petroleum Geologists (Pacific sect.), Am. Geol. Inst., Petroleum Exploration Soc. N.Y., Dallas Geol. Soc., Rocky Mountain Assn. Geologists, Alaska Geol. Soc., Oklahoma City Geol. Soc., N.Y. Acad. Sci., L.A. Basin Geol. Soc. (pres. 1969-70)., Am. Sci. Affiliation, Assn. Christian Geologists, Meth. Men Club, Denver Petroleum Club, Sigma Xi. Democrat. Office: Marshall Energetics Inc 12720 Hillcrest Rd Ste 105 Dallas TX 75230

MARSHALL, JOHN L., III, construction company executive; b. 1934. Grad., Brown U., 1957. With Marshall Contractors, Inc., Rumford, R.I., 1957-63, pres., treas., 1963—. Office: Marshall Contractors Inc 75 Newman Ave Rumford RI 02916-1945*

MARSHALL, JOHN PATRICK, lawyer; b. Bklyn., July 3, 1950; s. Harry W. and Mary Margaret (Kelly) M.; m. Cheryl J. Garvey, Aug. 10, 1975; children: Kelly Blake, Logan Brooke. BA, Rutgers U., 1972; JD cum laude, N.Y. Law Sch., 1976. Bar: N.Y. 1977, N.J. 1977, U.S. Dist. Ct. N.J. 1977, U.S. Dist. Ct. (so. and ea. dists.) N.Y. 1978, U.S. Ct. Appeals (3rd cir.) 1982, U.S. Dist Ct. (no. dist.) N.Y. 1991. Assoc. Kelley Drye & Warren, N.Y.C., 1976-84; ptnr. Kelley Drye & Warren, N.Y.C. and Parsippany, 1985—; bd. dirs. Am. Foreign Shipping Co., Inc., Westfield, N.J. Editorial bd. N.Y. Law Sch. Law Rev., 1975-76, staff mem., 1974-75; contbr. articles to profl. jours. Mem. jud. screening com. N.Y. Dem. Com., N.Y. New Dem. Coalition, 1988; exec. v.p. Humanitarian Found. for Nicaragua, 1991; mem., sec. Respect for Law Found., 1996; mem. Southern Dist. N.Y. Mediation Panel, 1994—. Fellow Am. Bar Found.; mem. ABA, N.Y. State Bar Assn. (sec. com. on cts. and the cmty. 1993-95), N.Y. County Lawyers' Assn. (sec. 1984-87, mem. com. on Supreme Ct. 1984-94, mem. legal edn., admission to bar and lawyer placement com. 1983-93), Am. Arbitration Assn. (mem. nat. panel arbitrators N.Y. and N.J. regions 1991—, mem. corp. counsel com. 1993—), Assn. of Bar of City of N.Y. (sec. judiciary com. 1989-92, mem. com. on arbitration 1994—, sec. coun. on judical adminstrn. 1996—). Office: Kelley Drye & Warren 101 Park Ave New York NY 10178 also: 5 Sylvan Way Parsippany NJ 07054-3805

MARSHALL, JOHN PAUL, broadcast engineer; came to U.S., 1967; Degree, U. Grenoble, France, 1963; student, U. Munich, 1964-65, San Francisco State, 1969-71, John O'Connell Tech. Inst., 1973-74. Mem. faculty law and econ. scis. U. Grenoble, 1963-64; mem. Expo '67 staff City of Montreal, Que., Can., 1967; filmmaker Cinemalab, San Francisco, 1970; engr. film and TV Able Studios, San Francisco, 1971-73; radio and TV engr. Sta. KALW-FM (Nat. Pub. Radio), San Francisco, 1973-74; broadcast engr. Sta. KRON-TV (NBC), San Francisco, 1974-91; intern Centre d'Informatique et de Maintenance Automatisme, Tunisia, 1993; founder Marshall U.S.A., San Francisco, 1994; freelance broadcast engr. KPIX-TV (CBS), KGO-Radio (ABC), KSFO-Radio (ABC), San Francisco, 1995—; freelance audio visual tech. advisor, San Francisco area, 1975—, lectr. radio, TV, motion pictures, 1975—, cons. customized electronic effects; freelance worker KPIX, San Francisco, 1995—, KGD, San Francisco, 1995—; tech. advisor, assoc. Broadkast Skills Bank. Translator tech. pubs. and manuals, 1975—. Mus. dir., participant in theater prodns., 1950-59; active Boy Scouts Am. Govt. of France scholar, 1960-63. Mem. Rolls Royce Owners Club Found. (life), Internet Soc. Avocations: classical pianist, polyglot, world traveler. Office: 298 4th Ave Ste 419 San Francisco CA 94118-2468 *Personal philosophy: (French proverb) Aide toi, le ciel t'aidera--Use your own resources and you will always receive a helping hand from heaven.*

MARSHALL, JOHN STEVEN, artist, educator, museum administrator; b. Oct. 20, 1957. Spl. studies, U. of the South, 1979-80; AA, Motlow State Community Coll., Tullahoma, Tenn., 1981; BFA, Middle Tenn. State U., 1983; MFA, U. N.C., 1985. Registrar, curatorial asst. Weatherspoon Art Gallery, U. N.C., Greensboro, 1983-85, asst. curator, lectr., 1985, acting curator, 1986; instr./curator Meridian C.C., 1986—; dir. Meridian Mus. Art, 1986-89; represented by Artworks Gallery Laurel, Miss.; represented by Gen. Art and Frame Gallery, Meridian, Miss.; Artworks Gallery, Laurel, Miss.; lectr. art various Tenn. and Miss. orgns.; curator, jury mem. various exhbns. One-man shows include Meridian Mus. Art, 1989, Miss. State U., 1990, 92, Miss. U. for Women, 1990, Tusculum Coll., 1992, Gen. Art Gallery, Miss., 1993, Coleman Art Ctr., Ala., 1995, Meridian C.C., 1995, Lauderdale Cmty. Gallery, 1995, Meridian Underground Gallery, 1996, Arts in the Park, 1996; 2-person show Winfield Gallery, 1991; exhibited in group shows Elliot U. Ctr. Gallery, Brentwood and Nashville, 1984, Weatherspoon Art Gallery, Greensboro, 1985, 86, Waterworks Gallery, Winston-Salem, N.C., 1985, Meridian Mus. Art, 1987, 89, Casteel Art Gallery, Meridian, 1987, U. So. Miss., 1988, Greenville Art Gallery, 1988, Space-One-Eleven Gallery, 1990, Birmingham-So. Coll., 1990, Winfield Gallery, 1991; represented in pvt. collections. Named Arts Educator of the Yr., Meridian, Miss., 1996. Office: Meridian Community Coll 910 Highway 19 N Meridian MS 39307-5801

MARSHALL, JOHN TREUTLEN, lawyer; b. Macon, Ga., Nov. 1, 1934; s. Hubert and Gladys (Lucas) M.; m. Katrine White, May 1, 1959; children: Allison, Rebecca, Paul, Mary Anne. BA, Vanderbilt U., 1956; LLB, Yale U., 1962. Bar: Ga. 1962, U.S. Dist. Ct. (no., mid. and so. dists.) Ga. 1962, U.S. Ct. Appeals (5th cir.) 1962, U.S. Supreme Ct. 1978, U.S. Ct. Appeals (11th cir.) 1982. Ptnr. Powell, Goldstein, Frazer & Murphy, Atlanta, 1962—; adj. prof. law Emory U. Sch. Law, 1968-86, mem. coun.; chmn. No. Dist. Ga. Bar Coun., 1989; chmn. Ga. State Commn. on Continuing Lawyer Competency, 1991-93. Bd. editors: Yale Law Jour. Bd. dirs. Atlanta Legal Aid, 1972-73; trustee Ga. Inst. Continuing Legal Edn., 1983-90, chmn. adv. bd. Atlanta Vol. Lawyers Found. Recipient S. Phillip Heiner award Atlanta Vol. Lawyers Assn., 1992, A. Gus cleveland award Ga. Commn. on Continuing Edn., Tradition of Excellence award State Bar Ga., 1995. Fellow Am. Coll. Trial Lawyers (state chmn. 1985-86), Am. Acad. Appellate Lawyers, Am. Bar Found., Ga. Bar Found.; mem. ABA (ho. of dels. 1976-86, Harrison Tweed award 1986), Atlanta Bar Assn. (pres. 197475, Charles E. Watkins Jr. award 1988), Ga. Inst. Trial Advocacy (chmn. 1982-830, Cherokee Town and Country Club, 191 Club, Layers Club. Office: Powell Goldstein Frazer & Murphy 191 Peachtree St NE 16th Fl Atlanta GA 30303-1741

MARSHALL, JOSEPH FRANK, electronic engineer; b. Wyoming, Pa., Mar. 2, 1917; s. Anthony Marchel and Mary (Moosic) M.; m. Margaret Mary Kennedy, June 17, 1961. BSEE, Pa. State Coll., 1941; MSEE, Harvard U., 1951. Registered profl. engr., Mass., N.J. Devel. engr., project mgr. Stromberg Carlson Co., Rochester, N.Y., 1941-49; design engr., staff engr. Bell Aircraft Corp., Buffalo, 1952-60; fellow engr. Electronics div. Westinghouse, Balt., 1961-62; sr. staff engr. Avco Corp., Wilmington, Mass., 1962-64; rsch. electrical engr. Cornell Lab., Buffalo, 1964-65; systems engr. Radio div. Bendix, Balt., 1966-67, Raytheon Corp., Sudbury, Mass., 1967-69, Astro Electronics div. RCA, Princeton, N.J., 1969-72; broadcast engr. N.J. Pub. TV, Princeton, 1972-74; sr. staff engr. Office of Engring. Tech. FCC, Washington, 1974-92; with Luthier Acoustic Rsch., Pittsford, N.Y.; IRE subcom. mem. Industry Audio Amplifier Standards, 1944-46; served on EIA TR-8 ad hoc com. Nationwide Cellular Mobile Radio Standards, 1979-80. Violinist Pa. State Coll. Symphony Orch., 1937-40. Fellow Radio Club of Am., Inc.; mem. Inst. Elec./Electronics Inc. (life), Radio Club of Washington, Violin Soc. Am., Catgut Acoustical Soc. Inc., Harvard Club of Rochester, Eta Kappa Nu, Sigma Tau, Tau Beta Pi, Pi Mu Epsilon. Democrat. Roman Catholic. Achievements include patents for selective tuning and damping of partials of rods and method of clamping tunable rods for electronic carillons, for critical components employed in a Navy secure missile command guidance system. Home: 9 Kimberly Rd Pittsford NY 14534-1505

MARSHALL, J(ULIAN) HOWARD, JR., lawyer; b. Balt., Apr. 18, 1922; s. Julian Howard and Eleanor (Jones) M.; m. Penelope Stewart Spurr, Apr. 11, 1953; children: Edward A., Clinton S., Julia H., Margaret B., Alexander S. AB, Princeton U., 1943; JD, Harvard U., 1949. Bar: Md. 1949, N.Y. 1949. Assoc. Root, Ballantine, Harlan, Bushby & Palmer, N.Y.C., 1949-55; assoc. Wickes, Riddell, Bloomer, Jacobi & McGuire, N.Y.C., 1955-58, ptnr., 1958-78; ptnr. Morgan, Lewis & Bockius, N.Y.C., 1979-88, ret., 1988. Chmn. Irvington (N.Y.) Planning Bd., 1966-89. Served to capt. arty. U.S. Army, 1943-45, PTO. Mem. ABA, N.Y. State Bar Assn., Assn. of Bar of City of N.Y., Internat. Bar Assn. Republican. Episcopalian. Home: Pond House N Broadway PO Box 317 Irvington NY 10533-0317

MARSHALL, JULIE W. GREGOVICH, engineering executive; b. Pasadena, Calif., Mar. 3, 1953; d. Gibson Marr and Anna Grace (Peterson) Wolfe; m. Michael Roy Gregovich Dec. 18, 1976 (div. June 1994); children: Christianna, Kerry Leigh; m. Robert Brandon Marshall, Aug. 6, 1994. BA magna cum laude, Randolph-Macon Woman's Coll., 1975; MBA, Pepperdine U., 1983. cert. tchr. K-12, Calif. Test engr. Westinghouse Hanford, Richland, Wash., 1975-76; startup engr. Bechtel Power Corp., Norwalk, Calif., 1976-77; test engr. Wash. Pub. Power, Richland, 1978-80; from mgr. to v.p. Sun Tech. Svcs., Mission Viejo, Calif., 1983-93; cons. Mission Energy Co., Irvine, Calif., 1993-94; owner, CEO, pres. Key Employee Svcs., Inc., Key Largo, Fla., 1994—. contbr. article to jour. Named Young Career Woman of the Yr. Wash. Pub. Power Supply System, 1979. Mem. Am. Nuc. Soc. (mem. bd. trustees pub. edn. program 1992—), Phi Beta Kappa.

MARSHALL, KATHRYN SUE, lawyer; b. Decatur, Ill., Sept. 12, 1942; d. Edward Elda and Frances M. (Minor) Lahniers; m. Robert S. Marshall, Sept. 5, 1964 (div. Apr. 1984); m. Robert J. Arndt, June 25, 1988; children: Stephen Edward, Christine Elizabeth. BA, Lake Forest Coll., 1964; JD, John Marshall Law Sch., Chgo., 1976. Intern U.S. Atty.'s Office, Chgo., 1974-76; mng. ptnr. Marshall and Marshall Ltd., Waukegan, Ill., 1976-84; pvt. practice Waukegan, 1984-93. Contbr. articles to profl. jours. Cert. jud. candidate Dem. party, Lake County, Ill.; bd. mem. Camerata Soc., Lake Forest; bd. mem., v.p. Lake Forest (Ill.) Fine Arts Ensemble. Fellow ABA (gov. 1993—, Ill. State Bar Assn., Coll. Law Practice Mgmt.; mem. Navy League (life). Avocations: boating, reading, travel.

MARSHALL, KERRY JAMES, artist; b. Birmingham, Ala., Oct. 17, 1955. BFA, Otis Art Inst., L.A., 1978. Prodn. designer Praise House & Hendrix Project, 1991; art instr. L.A. City Coll., 1980-83; art faculty L.A. S.W. Coll., 1981-85; adj. asst. prof. Sch. Art and Design, U. Ill., Chgo., 1993-94. One man exhibits include L.A. S.W. Coll. Calif., 1981, James Turcotte Gallery, L.A., 1983, Pepperdine U., Malibu, 1984, Koplin Gallery, 1985, 91, Studio Mus. Harlem, 1986, Terra Incognito, Chgo. Cultural Ctr., 1992, Jack Shainmen Gallery, N.Y.C., 1993, Koplin Gallery, Santa Monica, Calif., 1993, Cleveland Ctr. Contemporary ARts, 1994, Drawings III, Kopline Gallery, Santa Monica, 1993, Markts of Resistance, White Columns Gallery, N.Y.C. 1993, 43rd Biennial of Contemporary Am. Painting, Corcoran Gallery ARt, Washington, 1993, Bridges and Boundaries: Chicago Crossings, Spertus Mus., Chgo., 1994, Saddlebrook Coll. ARt Gallery, Mission Viejo, Calif., 1994; contbr. articles to profl. jours. Fellowship Nat. Endowment Arts Visual Art, 1991; visual arts grant Ill. Arts Coun., 1992; grantee Tiffany Found., 1993. Mem. Ill. Arts Coun. Office: 4122 S Calument Ave Chicago IL 60653*

MARSHALL, L. B., clinical lab scientist; b. Chgo., Feb. 10; s. Gillman and Ethel (Robinson) M.; m. Esther Wood, Sept. 28, 1961; children: Lester B. III, Kiti B., Lelani. Student, San Francisco State U., 1950; AA, City Coll. San Francisco, 1957; BS in Podiatric Medicine, U. Puget Sound, 1961; ScD, London Inst., Eng., 1972. Pres., Med. Offices Health Svcs. Group Inc., San Francisco, 1964—. Mem. NAACP. With U.S. Army, 1947-53. Decorated Bronze Star, Med. Combat Badge; recipient Cert. Appreciation Pres. Nixon, 1973, Urban League, 1973, Calif. Dept. Human Resources, 1973. Mem. Am. Calif. Assns. Med. Technologists, Calif. State Sheriff's Assn. (assoc.), Oyster Point Yacht Club, Press Club, Commonwealth Club (San Francisco).

MARSHALL, LEE DOUGLAS, entertainment company executive; b. Pitts., Sept. 23, 1956; s. Joseph Samuel and Lois Jean (Mickey) M.; m. Karen Lynne Drumm, Mar. 17, 1984; children: Jessica Lee, Lauren Lee. B in Communication, Ohio U., 1978. Account exec. Energy Talent Agy., Beachwood, Ohio, 1978-81; v.p. Magic Promotions & Theatricals, Inc., Aurora, Ohio, 1984—; pres. S. and S. Mgmt., Inc., Beachwood, 1981-84; The Touring Artists Group, 1992—; mgr. Boxcar Willie and Tony Perez. Prodr.: The Magic of David Copperfield, South Pacific, Elvis, An American Musica, Jesus Christ Superstar, Man of La Mancha, Hello Dolly (starring Carol Channing), The Phantom of the Opera (with Ken Hill), Aint Misbehavin' A Chorus Line (starring the Pointer Sisters), Nutcracker on Ice (starring Oksana Baiul, Brian Boitano and Viktor Petrenko), others. Mem. League of Am. Theatres and Producers. Mem. League of Am. Theatres and Prodrs. Avocations: boating, golfing, snow skiing. Office: Magic Promotions Inc 199 E Garfield Rd Aurora OH 44202

MARSHALL, LINDA KAYE, judge; b. Batesville, Ark.; d. Lucy Ellen (Westerfield) McDoniel. BS in Bus., U. Ark., Little Rock, 1977; MS in Ops. Mgmt., U. Ark., 1982; JD, U. Ark., Little Rock, 1987. Bar: Ark. 1987. EEO officer Ark. Power & Light Co., Little Rock, 1978-88; dep. prosecuting atty. Pulaski County Prosecuting Atty., Little Rock, 1988-90; atty. Gail Laster Law Firm, Little Rock, 1990-91; legal advisor Ark. Workers' Compensation Com., Little Rock, 1991-93, chief legal advisor, 1993-95, adminstrv. law judge, 1995—; state grievance appeal panel mem. State of Ark., Little Rock, 1993-95. Bd. dirs. Super Speech, Little Rock, 1984-88; active Big Bros./Big Sisters, Little Rock, 1988-90; vol., selection com. mem. Habitat for Humanity, Little Rock, 1994—, Carti Auxiliary, 1995. Mem. Ark. Bar Assn., Pulaski County Bar Assn. Home: 1301 Hunters Cove Little Rock AR 72211 Office: Ark Workers Compensation PO Box 950 Little Rock AR 72203

MARSHALL, LORETTA, elementary education educator; b. Pensacola, Fla., Aug. 20, 1957; d. Leon and Nettie Lucile (Franklin) M.; (div.); 1 child, Matthew Teliferro Smith Jr. BE, Tuskegee U., 1979; BS in Elem. Edn., U. Ga., 1980; student, Ga. State U., 1982; MEd, Ft. Valley (Ga.) State Coll., 1991. Cert. elem. tchr., Ga., Ala. 3rd grade tchr. Walker Park Sch., Monroe, Ga., 1979-81; 3rd grade tchr. Monroe Primary Sch., 1982-87, 2d grade tchr., 1987-95, 1st and 2nd grade Chpt. I and math. tchr., 1995—; staff devel. coord., Monroe Primary Sch., 1983-87, 93—, student support team chairperson, 1987-90, sch. data collector and support tchr., 1982-90, textbook adoption com. mem., 1991-92. Mem. PTO, Monroe, 1991, PTA, Bogart, Ga., 1993. Mem. ASCD, NEA, Ga. Assn. Educators, Walton Assn. Educators (v.p., pres. 1984-86), Delta Sigma Theta (sec. 1981-82). Democrat. Seventh Day Adventist. Avocations: travel, music, reading. Home: 200 Crane Dr # 12 Bogart GA 30622 Office: Monroe Primary School 109 Blaine St Monroe GA 30655-2403

MARSHALL, MARGARET DELORES, securities trader, marketing professional; b. Kingston, Jamaica, West Indies, Mar. 20, 1935; came to U.S., 1959; d. Vincent and Jeslyn Ianthy (Nunez) Brown; m. Frances Ustace Marshall, Oct. 30, 1957 (dec. Feb. 1988); children: Christopher, Stephen, Kimberly. BS, NYU, 1963. Registered securities-ins. broker, Okla. Mktg. assoc. Hudson Pulp & Paper, N.Y.C., 1963-65; regional sales mgr. Celebrity Gems, N.Y.C., 1975-83; regional v.p. A.L. Williams Ins. Co., Atlanta, 1983-84; tng. dir. Pre-Paid Legal Svcs., Inc., Ada, Okla., 1985-88, dir., 1991—; regional v.p. U.S. Legal Protection Co., Clearwater, Fla., 1989-91. Vol. coord. Miracle Children's Network, Atlanta, 1989, Atlanta Womens Polit. Caucus, Atlanta, 1990. Fellow: Leads & Contact (asst. dir. 1987-90), Ind. Order Foresters (dep. 1989-90), Ga. Crime Prevention Assn. Avocations: music, theater, reading. Office: Direct Marketing Cons 6065 Roswell Rd NE Ste 1172 Atlanta GA 30328-4011

MARSHALL, MARGARET HILARY, lawyer; b. Newcastle, Natal, South Africa, Sept. 1, 1944; came to U.S., 1968; d. Bernard Charles and Hilary A.D. (Anderton) M; m. Samuel Shapiro, Dec. 14, 1968 (div. Apr. 1982); m. Anthony Lewis, Sept. 23, 1984. BA, Witwatersrand U., Johannesburg, 1966; MEd, Harvard U., 1969; JD, Yale U., 1976; LHD (hon.), Regis Coll., 1993. Bar: Mass. 1977, U.S. Dist. Ct. Mass., U.S. Dist. Ct. N.H., U.S. Dist. Ct. D.C., U.S. Dist. Ct. (ea. dist.) Mich., U.S. Tax Ct., U.S. Ct. Appeals (1st, 11th and D.C. cirs.), U.S. Supreme Ct. Assoc. Csaplar & Bok, Boston, 1976-83, ptnr., 1983-89; ptnr. Choate, Hall & Stewart, Boston, 1989-92; v.p., gen. counsel Harvard U., Cambridge, Mass., 1992—; mem. jud. nominating coun., 1987-90, 92; chairperson ct. rules subcom. Alternative Dispute Resolution Working Group, 1985-87; mem. fed. appts. commn., 1993; mem. adv. com. Supreme Judicial Ct., 1989-92, mem. gender equality com., 1989-94; mem. civil justice adv. group U.S. Dist. Ct. Mass., 1991-93; spl. counsel Jud. Conduct Commn., 1988-92; trustee Mass. Continuing Legal Edn., Inc., 1990-92. Trustee Africa News, Africa Fund, Regis Coll., 1993-95; bd. dirs. Internat. Design Conf., Aspen, 1986-92, Boston Mcpl. Res. Bur., 1990—, Supreme Judicial Ct. Hist. Soc., 1990-94, sec., 1990-94. Fellow Am. Bar Found. (Mass. state chair); mem. Boston Bar Assn. (treas. 1988-89, v.p. 1989-90, pres.-elect 1990-91, pres. 1991-92), Internat. Women's Forum, Mass. Women's Forum, Boston Club, Phi Beta Kappa (hon.). Home: 8 Lowell St Cambridge MA 02138-4726 Office: Harvard U Massachusetts Hall Cambridge MA 02138

MARSHALL, MARGO, artistic director; b. Louisville, Nov. 3, 1934; d. Irving Robert and Elizabeth (Greenleaf) Lisbony; m. Jay C. Marshall, 1952 (div. 1971); 1 child, Dennis. BA, U. Houston, 1953. Pvt. tchr. dance Houston, 1950-58, owner, operator pvt. dance sch., 1958—; guest tchr. Joffrey Sch., N.Y., Internat. Acad. Dance, Portugal, Louisville Ballet, Boston Ballet's Summer Workshops, 1981-85, The Place, London, and others; part-time faculty mem. High Sch. for the Performing and Visual Arts, Houston; tchr. dance U. Houston, Sam Houston State U. Artistic dir. City Ballet Houston, 1967—; mem. dance panel Cultural Arts Coun. Houston; advisor Tex. Commn. on the Arts. Recipient Adjudicator award Mid-States Regional Ballet Assn., 1986. Mem. Southwestern Regional Ballet Assn. (officer 1965—). Office: City Ballet 9902 Long Point Rd Houston TX 77055-4116

MARSHALL, MARTIN VIVAN, business administration educator, business consultant; b. Kansas City, July 22, 1922; s. Vivan Dean and Marie (Church) M.; m. Rosanne Borden, Sept. 5, 1951 (dec. Feb. 8, 1986); children: Martin Dean, Michael Borden, Neil McNair; m. Hildegard Meyer, June 24, 1988. A.B., U. Mo., 1943; M.B.A., Harvard U., 1947, D.C.S., 1953. Instr. mktg. and advt. U. Kans., 1947-48; mem. faculty Harvard U., 1948—, Henry R. Byers prof. bus. adminstrn., 1960—, chmn. mktg. area faculty, 1962-66, chmn. Smaller Co. Mgmt. Program, 1981-84; chmn. Owner/Pres. Mgmt. Program, 1985-94; mem. faculty Inst. Ednl. Mgmt. Harvard U., 1981-90; cons. U.S. and internat. bus., 1950—; dir. ann. seminar mktg. and advt. Am. Advt. Fedn., 1958-78; vis. prof. mktg. IMEDE Mgmt. Inst., Lausanne, 1965-66; sr. prof., ednl. dir. Internat. Mktg. Inst., 1967-71; vis. prof. Indian Inst. Mgmt., Agra, 1968, IPADE, Mexico City, 1969, U. Melbourne, Australia, 1977, 79; bd. dirs. Western Stone & Metal. Author: Automatic Merchandising, 1954, (with N.H. Borden) Advertising Management, 1960, Notes on Marketing, 1983, 88, 90, 92, 93. Bd. dirs. Youth Svcs. Internat., Inc., 1994—. Served to lt. (s.g.) USNR, 1943-46. Home: 130 Mount Auburn St Apt 309 Cambridge MA 02138-5779 Office: Harvard U Cumnock Hall Boston MA 02163

MARSHALL, MARY JONES, civic worker; b. Billings, Mont.; d. Leroy Nathaniel and Janet (Currie) Dailey; m. Harvey Bradley Jones, Nov. 15, 1952 (dec. 1989); children: Dailey, Janet Currie, Ellis Bradley; m. Boyd T. Marshall, June 27, 1990. Student, Carleton Coll., 1943-44, U. Mont., 1944-46, UCLA, 1959. Owner Mary Jones Interiors. Founder, treas. Jr. Art Council, L.A. County Mus., 1953-55, v.p., 1955-56; mem. costume council Pasadena (Calif.) Philharm.; co-founder Art Rental Gallery, 1953, chmn. art and architecture tour, 1955; founding mem., sec. Art Alliance, Pasadena Art Mus., 1955-56; benefit chmn. Pasadena Girls Club, 1959, bd. dirs., 1958-60; chmn. L.A. Tennis Patron's Assn. Benefit, 1965; sustaining Jr. League Pasadena; mem. docent council L.A. County Mus.; mem. costume council L.A. County Mus. Art., program chmn. 20th Century Greatest Designers; mem. blue ribbon com. L.A. Music Ctr.; benefit chmn. Venice com. Internat. Fund for Monuments, 1971; bd. dirs. Art Ctr. 100, Pasadena, 1988—; pres. The Pres.'s L.A. Children's Bur., 1989; co-chmn. benefit Harvard Coll. Scholarship Fund, 1974, steering com. benefit, 1987, Otis Art Inst., 1975, 90th Anniversary of Children's Bureau of L.A., 1994; mem. Harvard-Radcliffe scholarship dinner com., 1985; mem. adv. bd. Estelle Doheny Eye Found., 1976, chmn. benefit, 1980; adv. bd. Loyola U. Sch. Fine Arts, L.A., Art Ctr. Sch. Design, Pasadena, Calif., 1987—; patron chmn. Benefit Achievement Rewards for Coll. Scientists, 1988; chmn. com. Sch. Am. Ballet Benefit, 1988, N.Y.C.; bd. dirs. Founders Music Ctr., L.A., 1977-81; mem. nat. adv. council Sch. Am. Ballet, N.Y.C., nat. co-chmn. gala, 1980; adv. council on fine arts Loyola-Marymount U.; mem. L.A. Olympic Com., 1984, The Colleagues; founding mem. Mus. Contemporary Art, 1986; chmn. The Pres.'s Benefit L.A. Children's Bur., 1990; exec. com. L.A. Alive for L.A. Music Ctr., 1992; mem. exec. com. Children's Bur. of L.A. Found., 1992; chmn. award dinner Phoenix House, 1994, 96; bd. dirs. Andrews Sch. Gerontology, U. So. Calif., 1996—, Leakey Found., 1996—; bd. regents Children's Hosp. L.A., 1996—. Mem. Am. Parkinson Disease Assn. (steering com. 1991), Valley Hunt Club (Pasadena), Calif. Club (L.A.), Kappa Alpha Theta. Home: 10375 Wilshire Blvd Apt 8B Los Angeles CA 90024-4728

MARSHALL, NANCY HAIG, library administrator; b. Stamford, Conn., Nov. 3, 1932; d. Harry Percival and Dorothy Charlotte (Price) Haig; m. William Hubert Marshall, Dec. 28, 1953; children—Bruce Davis, Gregg Price, Lisa Reynolds, Jeanine Haig. B.A., Ohio Wesleyan U., 1953; M.A.L.S., U. Wis., 1972. Dir. Wis. Inter Libr. Svcs., Madison, 1972-79; Reference librarian U. Wis., Madison, 1972, assoc. dir. univ. libraries, 1979-86; dean univ. librs. Coll. William and Mary, Williamsburg, Va., 1986—; mem. adv. com. Copyright Office, Washington, 1978-82; dir. USBE, Inc., Washington, 1983-86; trustee OCLC, Inc., Dublin, Ohio, 1982-88. Contbr. articles to profl. jours. Mem. ALA (coun. 1980-88, 90-93), Wis. Libr. Assn. (Libr. of the Yr. award 1982), Va. Libr. Assn., Beta Phi Mu. Office: Coll William and Mary E G Swem Libr Williamsburg VA 23185

MARSHALL, NANCY JEAN, women's health nurse; b. Randall, W.Va., Feb. 23, 1935; d. William Samuel and Elizabeth Lee (Mance) Gardner; m. Charles Henry Marshall, July 2, 1955; children: Charles Keith, Barbara Kim, Thomas Kevin. Diploma, Upshur County Sch. Nursing, 1985. Staff nurse Stonewall Jackson Meml. Hosp., Weston, W.Va., 1985—; adv. bd. mem. Fred Eberle Sch. Practical Nursing, Buckhannon, W.Va., 1988—. Mem. Nat. Assn. Practical Nursing Edn. and Svcs., LPN W.Va. (newsletter chairperson 1985—), Dist. #19 LPN (sec. 1986—), Concerned Nurses W.Va. (bd. dirs. 1988—), Nat. League Nursing, Fedn. and Nursing Edn. Licensure. Republican. Avocations: reading, camping, continuing education. Home: 359 First St Weston WV 26452

MARSHALL, NATALIE JUNEMANN, economics educator; b. Milw., June 13, 1929; d. Harold E. and Myrtle (Findlay) Junemann; m. Howard D. Marshall, Aug. 7, 1954 (dec. 1972); children: Frederick S., Alison B.; m. Phillip Shatz, May 27, 1988. AB, Vassar Coll., 1951; MA, Columbia U., 1952, PhD, 1963, JD, 1994. Instr. Vassar Coll., Poughkeepsie, N.Y., 1952-54, 59, 59-60, 63, dean studies, prof. econs., 1973-75, v.p. for student affairs, 1975-80, v.p. for adminstrn. and student services and prof. econs., 1980-91, prof. econs., 1991-94; teaching fellow Wesleyan U., Middletown, Conn., 1955-56; from asst. prof. to prof. SUNY, New Paltz, 1964-73; prof. econs. Vassar Coll., Poughkeepsie, N.Y., 1973-94; of counsel Anderson, Banks, Curran and Donoghue, Mt. Kisco, N.Y., 1994—. Editor: (with Howard Marshall) The History of Economic Thought, 1968; Keynes, Updated or Outdated, 1970; author: (with Howard Marshall) Collective Bargaining, 1971. Trustee St. Francis Hosp., 1979-88, Area Fund Dutchess County, 1981-87, Coll. New Rochelle, 1994—, Hudson Valley Philharm., 1985-92, pers., 1989-91. Mem. AAUP, Am. Assn. Higher Edn., Am. Econ. Assn., AAUW (v.p. N.Y. State div. 1964-66), Poughkeepsie Vassar Club (pres. 1965-67). Home: PO Box 2470 Poughkeepsie NY 12603-8470

MARSHALL, NATHALIE, artist, writer, educator; b. Pitts., Nov. 10, 1932; d. Clifford Benjamin and Clarice (Stille) Marshall; m. Robert Alfred Van Buren, May 1, 1952 (div. June 1965); children: Christine Van Buren Popovic, Clifford Marshall Van Buren, Jennifer Van Buren Lake; m. David Arthur Nadel, Dec. 30, 1976 (div. Sept. 1996). AFA, Silvermine Coll. Art, New Canaan, Conn., 1967; BFA, U. Miami, Coral Gables, 1977, MA, 1982, PhD in English and Fine Art, 1982. Instr. humanities Miami Ednl. Consortium, Miami Shores, Fla., 1977-79, Barry U., Miami Shores, 1979-81, U. Miami, Coral Gables, 1977-81; sr. lectr. Nova U., Ft. Lauderdale, Fla., 1981-84, assoc. prof. humanities, 1985-86; prof. art, chair dept. art. Old Coll., Reno, Nev., 1986-88; chief artist Rockefeller U., N.Y.C., 1973-75; asst. registrar Lowe Art Mus., Coral Gables, 1976-78; co-founder, dir. The Bakehouse Art Complex, Miami, 1984-86; advisor, bd. mem. NAH YAH EE (Indian children's art exhibits), Weimar, Calif., 1984—; mem. adv. bd. New World Sch. Arts, Miami, 1985-86. One-woman shows include Silvermine Coll. Art, New Canaan, Conn., 1968, Ingber Gallery, Greenwich, 1969, Capricorn Gallery, N.Y.C., 1969, Pierson Coll. at Yale U., New Haven, 1970, The Art Barn, Greenwich, 1972, Art Unltd., N.Y.C., 1973, Benevy Gallery, N.Y.C., 1974, Richter Libr., U. Miami, 1985, Nova U., Ft. Lauderdale, 1985, Ward Nasse Gallery, N.Y.C., 1985, Old Coll., Reno, 1986, Washoe County Libr., Reno, 1987, Sabal Palms Gallery, Gulfport, Fla., 1992, Ambiance Gallery, St. Petersburg, 1995, 96; group shows include: Capricorn Gallery, N.Y.C., 1968, Ingber Gallery, Greenwich, 1968, Compass Gallery, N.Y.C., 1970, Optimums Gallery, Westport, Conn., 1970, Finch Coll. Mus., N.Y.C., 1971, Town Hall Art Gallery, Stamford, Conn., 1973, 74, Jewish Community Ctr., Miami Beach, 1981, Continuum Gallery, Miami Beach, 1982, South Fla. Art Inst., Hollywood, Fla., 1984, Met. Mus., Coral Gables, Fla., 1985, Ward Nasse Gallery, N.Y.C., 1985, Brunnier Mus., Iowa State U., Ames, 1986, Nat. Mus. of Women in The Arts Libr., Washington, 1987, 89, U.S. Art in Embassies Program, 1987-88, UN World Conf. Women, Nairobi, 1987, Raymond James Invitational, St. Petersburg, Fla., 1989-92, Arts Ctr., St. Petersburg, 1990, 91, 92, Global Gallery, Tampa, Fla., 1990, 91, Sabal Palms Gallery, Gulfport, Fla., 1992, No. Nat. Nicolet Coll., Rhineland, Wis., 1992, Internat. Biennale, Bordeaux, France, 1993, Salon de Vieux Colombier, Paris, 1993, Synchronicity Space, N.Y.C., 1993, Women's 1st Internat. Biennal of Women Artists, Stockholm, 1994-95 (gold medal), Tampa Arts Forum, Fla., 1995, 96, Salon Internat. des Seigneurs de l'Art, Aix-en-Provence, France, 1995 (silver medal), World's Women Online Internet Installation Ariz. State U. 1995-96, UN 4th Conf. on Women, Beijing, 1995-96, Artemisa Gallery, Chgo., 1995-96; author, artist: Vibrations on Revelations, 1973, The Firebird, 1982, Homage to John Donne's Holy Sonnets 10 & 13, 1987, Tidepool, 1995; numerous artist books, 1968—; author: Be Organized for College, 1980; artist: (children's book) The Desert: What Lives There?, 1972; editor, designer: Court Theaters of Europe, 1982; writer, dir. T.V. programs Moutain Mandala: Autumn, Mountain Mandala: Winter, The Unexpected, 1992; contbr. poems to poetry mags., articles to profl. jours. Recipient Sponsor's award for Painting Greenwich Art Soc., 1967; Steven Buffton Meml. award Am. Bus. Women's Assn., 1980; grantee Poets & Writers, 1993; one of 300 global artists in Internat. Hope and Optimism Portfolio, Oxford. Mem. MLA, Coll. Art Assn., Nat. Women's Studies Assn., Women's Caucus for Art (nat. adv. bd. 1983-88, pres. Miami chpt. 1984-86, southeast regional v.p. 1986). Address: 5444 1/2 30th Ave S # 5C Gulfport FL 33707-5207

MARSHALL, NINA COLLEEN CLUBB, elementary school educator; b. Beaumont, Tex., Apr. 11, 1960; d. Thomas Joseph and Ella Lucille (Garvin) Clubb; m. David Louis Marshall, June 21, 1986; children: Sarah Lynn, Aaron Thomas. BS, Lamar U., 1981, M in Elem. Edn., 1988. Cert. elem., kindergarten, early childhood and math. tchr. Elem. tchr. East Chambers Ind. Sch. Dist., Winnie, Tex., 1982-85; middle sch. tchr. Conroe (Tex.) Ind. Sch. Dist., 1985-86, Nederland (Tex.) Ind. Sch. Dist., 1986-87, Port Arthur (Tex.) Ind. Sch. Dist., 1987-93, Hamshire-Fannett Ind. Sch. Dist., 1994—. Mem. ASCD, Nat. Coun. Tchrs. Math., Tex. Math. & Sci. Coaches Assn., Tex. State Tchrs. Assn., Tex. Classroom Tchrs. Home: RR 2 Box 2548 Beaumont TX 77705-9755

MARSHALL, ODESSA JOSEPHINE, mental health nurse; b. Arkadelphia, Ark., Jan. 4, 1933; d. Ulysses S. Grant and Augusta Marion (Balch) Cummings; m. Charles Clarence Marshall, Apr. 13, 1958; children: Gregory Douglas, Kathy Lynn Marshall Carter. AA, Penn Valley C.C., Kansas City, Mo., 1971, ASN, 1984; BS in Edn., Ctrl. Mo. State U., Warrensburg, 1975, MS, 1981; BSN, Webster U., 1990. RN, Mo.; ANA cert. psychiatric nursing. Nurse mgr. intermediate care, weekend house supr. Rockhill Nursing Home, Kans. City, Mo., 1984-85; charge nurse med./surgical V.A. Med. Ctr., Kans. City, Mo., 1985-88, charge nurse psychiatry, 1988—; nursing home adminstr., Hawthorne House, Sedalia, Mo., 1989-91, geriatric cons., 1991-92; geriatric cons. Harvest Home, Kans. City, Mo., 1991-92; clin. instr. in med./surgical nursing Penn Valley C.C., Kans. City, Mo., 1991—; supr. ch. nurses Friendship Bapt. Ch., Kans. City, Mo., 1991-95. Fellow Am. Bd. Disability Analysts (cert. disability analyst); mem. Black Nurses Assn. Democrat. Baptist. Avocations: sewing, reading, bowling.

MARSHALL, PAUL MACKLIN, oil company executive; b. Toronto, Ont., Can., Sept. 21, 1923; s. Griffith Macklin and Josephine Angela (Hodgson) M.; m. Carol Ann Dickie; children: Blake, Gregory, Jonathan, Kirk. B.C.L., McGill U., Montreal, Que., Can., 1949. Bar: called to bar Que. 1949. Legal asst. Sun Life Assurance Co., Montreal, 1949-52; exec. asst. to Canadian minister nat. def., Ottawa, Ont., 1952-54; with Canadian Chem. & Cellulose Co. Ltd., Montreal, 1955-69; v.p. Canadian Chem. & Cellulose Co. Ltd., 1958-59; v.p., sec.-treas. Chemcell Ltd., 1959-67, chmn. bd., 1967-69; v.p., treas. Columbia Cellulose Co. Ltd., 1959-62, pres., chief exec. officer, 1962-66; v.p., treas. Can. Chem. Co. Ltd., Celgar Ltd., 1959-62; v.p. Hamilton Bros. Petroleum Corp., 1969-72; pres. Hamilton Bros. Exploration Co., Denver, 1972; exec. v.p. Hamilton Bros. Oil Co., 1972; pres. Canadian Hydrocarbons Ltd., Calgary, Alta., 1972-77, Westmin Resources Ltd., 1978-90; vice chmn. Brascan Ltd., 1987—; pres., dir. Brascade Resources, Inc.; dir. Brascan Ltd., Journey's End Corp. Lt. Royal Can. Army, 1943-45. Office: Brascan Ltd, BCE Pl, Ste 4400 181 Bay St PO Box 762, Toronto, ON Canada M5J 2T3

MARSHALL, (C.) PENNY, actress, director; b. N.Y.C., Oct. 15, 1943; d. Anthony W. and Marjorie Irene (Ward) M.; m. Michael Henry (div.); 1 child, Tracy Lee; m. Robert Reiner, Apr. 10, 1971 (div. 1979). Student, U. N.Mex., 1961-64. Appeared on numerous television shows, including The Odd Couple, 1972-74, Friends and Lovers (co-star), 1974, Let's Switch, 1974, Wives (pilot), 1975, Chico and the Man, 1975, Mary Tyler Moore, 1975, Heaven Help Us, 1975, Saturday Night Live, 1975-77, Happy Days, 1975, Battle of Network Stars (ABC special), 1976, Barry Manilow special, 1976, The Tonight Show, 1976-77, Dinah, 1976-77, Mike Douglas Show, 1975-77, Merv Griffin Show, 1976-77, Blansky's Beauties, 1977, Network Battle of the Sexes, 1977, Laverne and Shirley (co-star), 1976-83; TV films More Than Friends, 1978, Love Thy Neighbor, 1984; appeared in motion pictures How Sweet It Is, 1967, The Savage Seven, 1968, The Grasshopper, 1970, 1941, 1979, Movers and Shakers, 1985, The Hard Way, 1991, Hocus Pocus, 1993; dir. films: Jumpin' Jack Flash, 1986, Big, 1988, Awakenings, 1990, A League of Their Own, 1992, Renaissance Man, 1994; co-exec. prodr. TV series A League of Their Own, 1993 (also dir. pilot). Office: care CAA/Todd Smith 9830 Wilshire Blvd Beverly Hills CA 90212-1804*

MARSHALL, PHILIPS WILLIAMSON, insurance agency executive; b. Orange, N.J., Aug. 28, 1935; s. Herbert Jr. and Evelyn Lenore (Philips) M.; m. Sandra Richards Vose, Mar. 29, 1958; children: Tracy Anne Marshall Santa Florentina, Laurie Williamson Marshall Holbrook. BS in Econs., U. Pa., 1957. Enlisted U.S. Army, 1958, advanced through grades to capt., 1964, resigned, 1970; underwriter Continental Ins. Co., N.Y.C., 1957-60; salesman A.W. Marshall & Co., Newark, 1960-65; spl. agt. Aetna Ins. Co., Millburn, N.J., 1965-66; v.p. Woodward & Williamson, Jersey City, 1966-88; pres. Woodward & Williamson, 1988—; pres. Ind. Ins. Agts. Hudson County, Jersey City, 1979-80. Chmn. ARC-Millburn (N.J.)-Short Hills, 1971-74, Harriman Div. coun. ARC, N.Y.C., 1976-77; chief Millburn Aux. Police, Millburn, 1976-81. Mem. Ind. Ins. Agts. N.J. (exec. com. 1982-86, Presdl. Citation 1986), Ducks Unltd. (chmn. State of N.J. 1990-92), Short Hills Club. Republican. Episcopalian. Avocations: tennis, fishing, hunting. Home: 24 Meadowview Ln Berkeley Heights NJ 07922-1370 Office: Woodward & Williamson 25A Hanover Rd Florham Park NJ 07932-0165

MARSHALL, PRENTICE H., JR., lawyer; b. Oak Park, Ill., Sept. 5, 1952. BA, U. Ill., 1974; JD magna cum laude, U. Iowa, 1977. Bar: Ill. 1977, U.S. Ct. Appeals (7th cir.) 1978, U.S. Dist. Ct. (no. dist.) Ill. 1978. Law clk. to Hon. Philip W. Tone U.S. Ct. Appeals (7th cir.), 1977-78; ptnr. Sidley & Austin, Chgo.; adj. prof. law John Marshall Law Sch., 1979-82, ITT, Chgo., 1985-88. Office: Sidley & Austin 1 First Nat Plz Chicago IL 60603

MARSHALL, RICHARD, art historian, curator; b. L.A., 1947. B.A., Calif. State U., Long Beach, 1969; postgrad. U. Calif., Irvine, 1969-70. Advisor Mus. Modern Art, N.Y., 1974-77, Whitney Mus. Am. Art, curator, 1974-93. Art editor Paris Rev. mag., 1977-94; ind. curator, 1995—.

MARSHALL, RICHARD TREEGER, lawyer; b. N.Y.C., May 17, 1925; s. Edward and Sydney (Treeger) M.; m. Dorothy M. Goodman, June 4, 1950; children—Abigail Ruth Marshall Bergerson, Daniel Brooks; m. 2d, Sylvia J. Kelley, June 10, 1979. B.S., Cornell U., 1948; J.D., Yale U., 1951. Bar: Tex. 1952, U.S. Ct. Appeals (5th cir.) 1966, U.S. Ct. Appeals (10th cir.) 1980, U.S. Supreme Ct., 1959. Sole practice, El Paso, Tex., 1952-59, 61-79; assoc. Fryer & Milstead, El Paso, 1952; sr. ptnr. Marshall & Wendorf, El Paso, 1959-61; sr. ptnr. Marshall & Volk, El Paso, 1979-81; sr. atty. Richard T. Marshall & Assocs., P.C., El Paso, 1981-85; sr. ptnr. Marshall, Thomas & Winters, El Paso, 1985-87, sr. atty. Marshall & Winters, 1987-88; sr. atty. Marshall, Sherrod & Winters, 1988-90, pvt. practice law, 1990—; instr. polit. sci. U. Tex., El Paso, 1961-62; instr. ins. law C.L.U. tng. course Am. Coll.; officer, dir. Advance Funding, Inc., El Paso. Mem. ABA, Coll. State Bar Tex., El Paso Bar Assn., El Paso Trial Lawyers Assn. (pres. 1965-66), Tex. Trial Lawyers Assn., Assn. Trial Lawyers Am. (sec. personal injury law sect. 1967-68, nat. sec. 1969-70, sec.-treas. environ. law sect. 1970-71, vice chmn. family law litigation sect. 1971-72); Roscoe Pound-Am. Trial Lawyers Found. (Commn. on Profl. Responsibility 1979-82). Editor: El Paso Trial Lawyers Rev., 1973-80; contbr. articles to legal jours. Office: 6070 Gateway Blvd E Ste 508 El Paso TX 79905-2031

MARSHALL, ROBERT CHARLES, computer company executive; b. Berwyn, Ill., June 19, 1931; s. Joseph H. and Rose M.; m. Sarane Virruso, Aug. 1, 1954; children—Joseph, Lisa, Jim. B.S.E.E., Heald Engring. Coll., 1956; M.B.A., Pepperdine U., 1976. Engr. Lawrence Radiation Lab., Livermore, Calif., 1956-64; systems engr. Electronics Assos., Palo Alto, Calif., 1964-69; v.p. mfg. Diablo Systems, Hayward, Calif., 1969-75; with Tandem Computers, Inc., Cupertino, Calif., 1975—; sr. v.p., chief operating officer, dir. Tandem Computers, Inc., 1979-96; pres., CEO Info Gear, 1996—. Served with U.S. Army, 1952-54.

MARSHALL, ROBERT GERALD, language educator; b. Houston, Feb. 19, 1919; s. Luther Pierce and Nancy (May) M.; m. Kathryn Keller, Aug. 27, 1949; children—Christoph Patton, Ann Patterson, Philip Sanburn. B.A., Rice U., 1941, M.A., 1946; Ph.D., Yale, 1950; diploma, U. Siena, Italy, 1954. Asst., then instr. French Yale, 1947-49; asst. prof. fgn. langs. Tex. Women's U., 1949-51; mem. faculty Wells Coll., Aurora, N.Y., 1951—; prof. Romance langs. Wells Coll., 1958—, chmn. dept., 1956-72, coordinator summer programs, 1963-67; dir. NDEA Inst. Advanced Study French, 1963-67; prof.-in-charge Sweet Briar Coll. Jr. Year In Paris, France, 1967-68; dir. Jr. Year in France, 1972-84. Contbr. to profl. jours.; editor-in-chief: Catalogue of 16th Century Italian Books in American Libraries, 1970; editor: (with F. C. St. Aubyn) Les Mouches (Sartre), 1963, Trois Pièces Surréalistes, 1969, Abraham de Vermeil in Textes et Contexts, 1986, American, French, Italian Relationships in Mélanges André Bordeaux, 1988; contbr. to Columbia Dictionary of Modern European Lit., 18th Century Bibliography. Commr., Historic Area Commn., St. Michaels, Historic Preservation Commn., Talbot County, Md. Served to capt. AUS, 1942-46. Decorated chevalier dans L'Ordre des Palmes Academiques France); R.G. Marshall scholarship named in his honor Sweet Briar Coll.; grantee Am. Council Learned Socs., 1953; Fulbright research grantee Rome, Italy, 1959-60. Mem. Am. Assn. Tchrs. French (v.p. Central N.Y. chpt. 1965-67, pres. Va. chpt. 1979-84), South Atlantic Modern Lang. Assn., Soc. Profs. français à l'Etranger. Episcopalian. Home: PO Box 1059 Saint Michaels MD 21663-1059

MARSHALL, ROBERT HERMAN, economics educator; b. Harrisburg, Pa., Dec. 6, 1929; s. Mathias and Mary (Bubich) M.; m. Billie Marie Sullivan, May 31, 1958; children: Mellisa Frances, Howard Hylton, Robert Charles. A.B. magna cum laude, Franklin and Marshall Coll., 1951; M.A., Ohio State U., 1952, Ph.D., 1957. Teaching asst. Ohio State U., 1952-57; mem. faculty, then prof. econs. U. Ariz., Tucson, 1957-95, prof. emeritus, 1995; dir. Internat. Bus. Studies Project, 1969-71; research observer Sci.-Industry Program, Hughes Aircraft Co., Tucson, summer 1959. Author: Commercial Banking in Arizona: Structure and Performance Since World War II, 1966, (with others) The Monetary Process, 2d edit, 1980. Bd. dirs. Com. for Econ. Opportunity, Tucson, 1968-69. Faculty fellow Pacific Coast Banking Sch., summer 1974. Mem. Am. Econ. Assn., Phi Beta Kappa, Beta Gamma Sigma, Pi Gamma Mu, Phi Kappa Phi, Delta Sigma Pi. Democrat. Roman Catholic. Home: 6700 N Abington Rd Tucson AZ 85743-9795

MARSHALL, ROBERT LEWIS, musicologist, educator; b. N.Y.C., Oct. 12, 1939; s. Saul and Pearl (Shapiro) M.; m. Traute Maass, Sept. 9, 1966; children—Eric, Brenda. A.B., Columbia U., 1960; M.F.A., Princeton U., 1962, Ph.D., 1968; postgrad., U. Hamburg, W. Ger., 1965. Instr. dept. music U. Chgo., 1966-68, asst. prof., 1968-71, assoc. prof., chmn. dept., 1972-78, prof., 1978-83; prof. Brandeis U., 1983—, chmn. dept., 1985-93, incumbent endowed chair Louis, Frances and Jeffrey Sachar prof. music, 1986—; vis. assoc. prof. Princeton U., 1971-72; endowed prof. Univ. Ala., 1994; mem. rev. bd. rsch. materials program NEH, 1982, rev. bd. edits., 1991. Author: The Compositional Process of J.S. Bach, 2 vols., 1972, The Music of Johan Sebastian Bach: The Sources; The Style; The Significance, 1989, Mozart Speaks: View on Music, Musicians and the World, 1991, Dennis Brain on Record: A Comprehensive Discography of His Solo, Chamber, and Orchestral Recordings, 1996; editor New Bach Edit., Eighteenth Century Keyboard Music, 1994; contbr. articles to musical jours. in U.S., Gt. Brit., Germany. Mem. music adv. bd. Ill. Arts Council, 1977-79. Recipient Deems Taylor award ASCAP, 1990; NEH fellow, 1978-79; Hon. Harold Spivacke consultantship Library of Congress. Mem. Am. Musicol. Soc. (bd. dirs. 1974-75, v.p. 1985-86, editl. bd. jour. 1975-80, rev. editor 1986-89, chmn. publs. com. 1991-94, Otto Kinkeldey prize 1974), New Bach Soc. (chmn. Am. chpt. 1977-80), Phi Beta Kappa. Home: 100 Chestnut St Newton MA 02165-2538 Office: Music Dept Brandeis U Waltham MA 02254

MARSHALL, RUSSELL FRANK, research company executive; b. Fort Madison, Iowa, Sept. 10, 1941; s. William Frank and Dorothy Eleanor (Mikels) M.; m. Mary Jean Bailey, June 19, 1966; children: William Russell, Robert Scott, Gregory Howard. AB, Monmouth Coll., 1963; MS, U. Ill., 1965, PhD, 1971. Rsch. engr. Materials Rsch. Lab, Urbana, Ill., 1970-75; mgr. acad. computing Drake U., Des Moines, 1975-80; v.p. GMI Ltd., Des Moines, 1980-83; sr. v.p., treas. Communication Devel. Co., West Des Moines, 1983—. Contbr. articles to profl. jours. Active Boy Scouts Am., 1982—; mem. Des Moines Coummunity Theatre. Grantee AEC, 1964-71. Mem. Assn. Computing Machinery, Am. Phys. Soc., Assn. for Systems Mgmt., Sigma Xi. Presbyterian. Avocations: music, reading. Home: 1625 19th St West Des Moines IA 50265-1622

MARSHALL, SHARON BOWERS, nursing educator, director clinical trials; b. Alameda, Calif.; d. Stanley Jay and Rosalie Kathryn (Soldati) Bowers; m. Lawrence F. Marshall; children: Derek, Kathryn, Samantha. BS in Nursing, San Francisco State U., 1970. Charge nurse med./surg. unit Mt. Zion Hosp., San Francisco, 1970-73, charge nurse med./surg. ICU, 1973-75; clin. nurse U. Calif. San Diego Med. Ctr., 1975-78, coordinator neurotrauma study, 1978-79, project coordinator Nat. Traumatic Coma Data Bank, 1979-88, project mgr. Comprehensive Cen. Nervous System Injury Ctr., 1979-86, mgr. neurotrauma research, 1984-91; asst. clin. prof. neurol. surg. U. Calif. San Diego Sch. Medicine, 1992—; dir. study Internat. Tirilazad Study, 1991—; prin. investigator Internat. Selfotel Trial, 1994—. Author: Head Injury, 1981; Neuroscience Critical Care: Pathophysiology and Patient Management, 1990; contbr. articles to profl. jours. Mem. Internat. Soc. Study of Traumatic Brain Injury, Am. Assn. Neurosci. Nursing. Avocations: skiing, traveling. Office: 1899 Mckee St Ste 200 San Diego CA 92110-1976

MARSHALL, SHEILA HERMES, lawyer; b. N.Y.C., Jan. 17, 1934; d. Paul Milton and Julia Angela (Meagher) Hermes; m. James Josiah Marshall, Sept. 30, 1967; 1 child, James J.H. BA, St. John's U., N.Y.C., 1959; JD, NYU, 1963. Bar: N.Y. 1964, U.S. Ct. Appeals (2d, 3d, 5th and D.C. cirs.), U.S. Supreme Ct. 1970. Assoc. LeBoeuf, Lamb, Greene & MacRae, N.Y.C., 1963-72, ptnr., 1973—; specialist in field. Mem. ABA, N.Y. State Bar Assn., Assn. of Bar of City of N.Y. Republican. Home: 1035 Park Ave New York NY 10028-0912 Office: LeBoeuf Lamb Greene & MacRae 125 W 55th St New York NY 10019-5369

MARSHALL, SHERRIE, newspaper editor. Metro editor Star Tribune, Mpls. Office: Star Tribune 425 Portland Ave Minneapolis MN 55488-0001

MARSHALL, STANLEY, former educator, business executive; b. Cheswick, Pa., Jan. 27, 1923; s. Walter W. and Mildred (Crawford) M.; m. Ruth Cratty, June 10, 1944 (div. 1966); children: David, Sue, John; m. Shirley Ann Slade, Sept. 10, 1966; children: Kimberly, James Andrew. B.S., Slippery Rock (Pa.) State Tchrs. Coll., 1947; M.S., Syracuse U., 1950, Ph.D., 1956. Tchr. sci. Mynderse Acad., Seneca Falls, N.Y., 1947-52; asst. prof. sci. State U. N.Y. Coll. Edn., Cortland, 1953-55; asso. prof. State U. N.Y. Coll. Edn., 1956-57, prof., 1957-58; instr. Syracuse U., 1955-56; prof., head dept. sci. edn. Fla. State U., Tallahassee, 1958; asso. dean Fla. State U. (Sch. Edn.), 1965-67; dean Fla. State U. (Coll. Edn.), 1967-69, pres., 1969-76; pres. Sonitrol of Tallahassee, Inc., 1978-87, COMSAFE Inc., 1981-84; pres. James Madison Inst. for Pub. Policy Studies, 1987-90, chmn. bd. dirs., 1990—; pres. Marshall Land Co., 1989—; pres. So. Scholarship and Research Found., 1968-69. Author: (with E. Burkman) Current Trends in Science Education, 1966, (with I. Podendorf and C. Swartz) The Basic Science Program, 1965; Editor: Jour. of Research in Sci. Teaching, 1962-66; Mem. editorial bd.: Science World, 1962-65; Contbr. articles to profl. jours. Mem. U.S. Navy Sec.'s adv. bd. edn. and tng. U.S. Army adv. panel ROTC, 1975-79; bd. regents Nat. Libr. Medicine, 1970-75; bd. dirs. Tallahassee Meml. Regional Med. Ctr., 1980-86; mem. Citizens Commn. on the Fla. Cabinet, 1995—; trustee Bethune Cookman Coll., 1993—. Fellow AAAS; mem. Am. Inst. Physics, Nat. Sci. Tchrs. Assn., Fla. Acad. Scis., Fla. Assn. Sci. Tchrs., So. Assn. State Univs. and Land-Grant Colls (pres. 1971-72), Nat. Assn. Research Sci. Teaching, NEA, Fla. Edn. Assn., Sigma Xi, Phi Delta Kappa, Kappa Delta Pi. Home: 5000 Brill Pt Tallahassee FL 32312-5600

MARSHALL, SUSAN, artistic director; b. Hershey, Pa.. Student, Julliard Sch. Founder, artistic dir. Susan Marshall & Co., N.Y.C., 1982—. Recipient Dance Mag. award, 1995. Office: 280 Broadway Ste 412 New York NY 10007

MARSHALL, THOM, columnist. Columnist The Houston Chronicle, Tex. Office: Houston Chronicle 801 Texas St Houston TX 77002-2906

MARSHALL, THOMAS, chemical company executive; b. Pitts., 1929. Grad., U. Pitts., 1957. With USX Corp., 1949-86, pres. U.S. Diversified Group, 1986; chmn., chief exec. officer Aristech Chem. Corp., Pitts., 1986-95, also bd. dirs.; ret. Aristech Chem. Corp., 1995. With USN, 1946-49.

MARSHALL, THOMAS CARLISLE, applied physics educator; b. Cleveland, Ohio, Jan. 29, 1935; s. Stephen Irby and Bertha Marie (Bieger) M.; children—Julian, John. B.Sc., Case Inst. Tech., 1957; M.Sc., U. Ill., 1958, Ph.D., 1960. Asst. prof. elec. engring. U. Ill., 1961-62; mem. faculty Columbia U., 1962—, asst. prof. elec. engring., 1962-65, assoc. prof., 1965-70, prof. engring. sci., 1970-78, prof. applied physics, 1978—. Author: Free Electron Lasers, 1985, Book of the Toade, 1992; contbr. over 100 articles to profl. jours. Research grantee Dept. Energy, Office Naval Research, NSF. Fellow Am. Phys. Soc. (study group on directed energy weapons 1985-87), Free Election Lasers and Accelerator Physics. Office: Columbia U 213 Mudd Bldg New York NY 10027

MARSHALL, THOMAS OLIVER, JR., lawyer; b. Americus, Ga., June 24, 1920; s. Thomas Oliver and Mattie Louise (Hunter) M.; m. Angie Ellen Fitts, Dec. 20, 1946; children: Ellen Irwin Marshall Beard, Anne Hunter Marshall Peagler, Mary Olivia Marshall Hodges. BS in Engring., U.S. Naval Acad., 1941; JD, U. Ga., 1948. Bar: Ga. 1947. Pvt. practice law Americus, Ga., 1948-60; judge S.W. Judicial Circuit, Americus, 1960-74, Ga. Ct. Appeals, Atlanta, 1974-77; justice Ga. Supreme Ct., Atlanta, 1977-86, chief justice, 1986-89; pvt. practice Atlanta, 1989—; chmn. bd. visitors U. Ga. Law Sch., 1970. Trustee Andrew Coll., So. Ga. Meth. Home for Aged; active ARC, 1948-60, United Givers Fund, 1948-54. Served with USN, World War II, Korean War. Decorated Bronze Star; named Young Man of Yr. Americus, 1953. Mem. ABA, Ga. Bar Assn. (bd. govs. 1958-60), Atlanta Bar Assn., State Bar Ga., Am. Judicature Soc., Nat. Jud. Coll., Jud. Coll. Ga., VFW, Am. Legion. Methodist. Lodges: Kiwanis, Masons, Shriners. Home: 238 15th St NE Apt 3 Atlanta GA 30309-3594 Office: 230 Peachtree St NW Ste 1100 Atlanta GA 30303-1513

MARSHALL, TREVOR JOHN, engineering professional; b. Faversham, Kent, U.K., Jan. 5, 1954; came to U.S., 1992; s. John Rodney and Margaret (Hutchinson) M.; m. Kathleen Patricia Keenan, May 22, 1994. B of Chemistry, Leicester U., 1975. Rsch. chemist Ever Ready Batteries, London, 1975-80; tech. devel. coord. Ever Ready Batteries, Oxford, U.K., 1981-83; project mgr. Renata Batteries, Sissach, Switzerland, 1983-84; tech. coord. Alupower, Inc., Bernardsville, N.J., 1985-86; battery devel. cons. UKAEA (Lithium Batteries), Harwell, U.K., 1987-88; industry mgr. Freudenberg, Halifax, U.K., 1988-92; product engr. mgr. Seatronics, Inc., Hatboro, Pa., 1992—; cons. Piles Wonder, Paris, 1984, Gold Peak Industries, Hong Kong, 1984. Mem. Internat. Battery Data Registry. Avocation: indsl. archaeology. Office: Seatronics Co Inc 3235 Sunset Ln Hatboro PA 19040-4528

MARSHALL, VICTOR FRAY, physician, educator; b. Culpeper, Va., Sept. 1, 1913; s. Otis and Marie Josephine (Riton) M.; m. Barbara Walsh, Dec. 11, 1943; children—Fray F., Victor R., Philip S. M.D., U. Va., 1937; D.Sc., Washington and Lee U., 1975. Diplomate: Am. Bd. Urology (past pres.). Intern N.Y. Hosp., 1937-38; tng. in gen. surgery and urology Cornell U. Med. Coll.-N.Y. Hosp., 1938-43, staff mem., 1943-88; attending-in-charge urology James Buchanan Brady Found., 1949-78; faculty Med. Coll., Cornell U., 1938-81, asso. prof. clin. surgery urology, 1947-57, prof. clin. surgery (urology), 1957-78, James J. Colt prof. urology in surgery, 1970-78, head service urology, 1946-78, emeritus, 1978-88; prof. urology U. Va., Charlottesville, 1979-83; cons., 1983-88, ret., 1988; asst. attending surgeon Meml. Center for Cancer and Allied Diseases, 1943-52, assoc. attending, 1952-67, attending surgeon, 1967-83, emeritus, 1983—. Contbr. articles to med. jours. Fellow ACS, N.Y. Acad. Medicine (Valentine medal 1974); mem. AAAS, N.Y. Urol. Soc. (past pres.), Am. Urol. Assn. (Guiteras award 1975), N.Y. Cancer Soc. (past pres.), Soc. Pelvic Surgeons (past pres.), Mexican Acad. Surgery, Am. Surg. Assn., Am. Acad. Pediatrics, Soc. Pediatric Urology, Clin. Soc. Genito-Urinary Surgeons (pres. 1976), Surg. Soc. Venezuela, Mexican Urol. Soc., Brit. Assn. Urol. Surgeons, Venezuelan Soc. Urology, Am. Assn. Genito-Urinary Surgeons (Barringer medal 1970, Keyes medal 1994), Canadian Urol. Assn. (hon.), Royal Coll. Surgeons Ireland (hon.), Alpha Omega Alpha, Pi Kappa Alpha, Nu Sigma Nu. Home: The Colonades C8 2600 Barracks Rd Charlottesville VA 22901-2100

MARSHALL, VINCENT DE PAUL, industrial microbiologist, researcher; b. Washington, Apr. 5, 1943; s. Vincent de Paul Sr. and Mary Frances (Bach) M.; m. Sylvia Ann Kieffer, Nov. 15, 1986; children from previous marriage: Vincent de Paul III, Amy. BS, Northeastern State Coll., Tahlequah, Okla., 1965; MS, U. Okla. Health Sci. Ctr., Oklahoma City, 1967, PhD, 1970. Rsch. assoc. U. Ill., Urbana, 1970, postdoctoral fellow, 1971-73; rsch. scientist The Upjohn Co., Kalamazoo, Mich., 1973-74, rsch. head, 1975, sr. rsch. scientist, 1976-91, sr. scientist, 1991—. Mem. editorial bd. Jour. of Antibiotics, 1990—, Jour. Indsl. Microbiology, 1989—, Devels. in Indsl. Microbiology, 1990; contbr. numerous articles to profl. jours., chpts. to books; patentee in field. Served with U.S. Army Nat. Guard, 1960-65. NIH predoctoral fellow, 1967-70; NIH postdoctoral fellow, 1971-73. Fellow Am. Acad. Microbiology; mem. Soc. for Indsl. Microbiology (membership com. 1988-90, co-chair edn. com. 1989-93, local sects. com. 1991—, chair nominating com. 1993-94, co-chair program com. 1993-94, dir. 1994-96, pres. Ind. sect. 1992-95), Am. Soc. Microbiology, Am. Soc. Biochemistry and Molecular Biology, Internat. Soc. for Antimicrobial Activity of Non-Antibiotics (sci. adv. bd.), Sigma Xi. Republican. Episcopalian. Home: 203 Paisley Ct Kalamazoo MI 49006-4359 Office: Pharmacia and Upjohn Inc Chem & Biol Screening 7000 Portage Rd Kalamazoo MI 49007-4940

MARSHALL, WALTER, special education educator; b. Wadesboro, N.C., Feb. 15, 1942; s. Andrew and Sarah (Lomax) M.; m. Paulette L. Gwyn, Feb. 12, 1966; children: Krista Colette, Malcolm Taussaint. BS in Health and Phys. Edn., Winston-Salem State U., 1965; MA in Intermediate Edn., Aant State U., 1976. Cert. special edn. tchr., N.C. Phys. edn. and social studies tchr. Lee County Schs., Sanford, N.C., 1965-69; spl. edn. tchr. High Point (N.C.) City Schs., 1969-92; case mgr. Guilford County Schs., High Point, 1993—. Mem. Winston-Salem Forsyth County Sch. Bd., 1992—; mem. ednl. legal adv. bd. NAACP, 1990-92; chmn. state edn. com. N.C. NAACP, 1988-91; bd. pres. Winston-Salem NAACP, 1986-92; exec. bd. N.C. Dem. Ctrl. Com., 1984-90, del. conv., San Francisco, 1984. Recipient Human Rel. award N.C. Assn. Educators, 1989, Disting. Alumni award Nat. Assn. for Equal Opportunity in Higher Edn., 1990. Mem. Assn. Classroom Tchrs. (pres. 1970-71), N.C. Assn. Classroom Tchrs. (dist. v.p. 1970-71), Coun. for Exceptional Children. Baptist. Home: 3246 Kittering Ln Winston Salem NC 27105-6923

MARSHALL, WAYNE KEITH, anesthesiology educator; b. Richmond, Va., Feb. 9, 1948; s. Chester Truman and Lois Ann (Tiller) M.; m. Dale Claire Reynolds, June 18, 1977; children: Meredith Reynolds, Catherine Truman, Whitney Wood. BS in Biology, Va. Poly. Inst. and State U., 1970; MD, Va. Commonwealth U., 1974. Diplomate Am. Bd. Anesthesiology, Nat. Bd. Med. Examiners; bd. cert. in pain mgmt. Surg. intern U. Cin., 1974-75, resident in surgery, 1975-77; resident in anesthesiology U. Va. Coll. Medicine, Charlottesville, 1977-79, rsch. fellow, 1979-80; asst. prof. anesthesia Pa. State U. Coll. Medicine, Hershey, 1980-86, assoc. prof., 1986-95, assoc. clin. dir. oper. rm., 1982-95, dir. pain mgmt. svc., 1984-95, chief divsn. pain mgmt., 1992-95; prof., chmn. dept. anesthesiology Med. Coll. Va., Richmond, 1995—; moderator nat. meetings. Mem. editorial bd. Anesthesiology Rev., 1987—, Jour. Neurosurg. Anesthesiology, 1988—; contbr. articles and abstracts to med. jours. Recipient Antarctic Svc. medal NSF, 1980. Mem. AMA, Soc. Neurosurg. Anesthesia and Critical Care (sec.-treas. 1985-87, v.p. 1987-88, pres. 1989-90, bd. dirs. 1985-91), Assn. Univ. Anesthetists, Am. Soc. Anesthesiologists (del. ASA ho. of dels. 1990-92), Internat. Anesthesia Rsch. Soc., Pa. Soc. Anesthesiology. Republican. Baptist. Office: VCU Med Coll Va Dept Anesthesiology PO Box 980695 Richmond VA 23298-0695

MARSHALL, WILLIAM, III, think tank executive; b. Norfolk, Va., 1952; m. Katryn S. Nicolai; children: Olivia, William. BA in English and History, U. Va., 1975. Reporter Richmond Times-Dispatch; various positions on Capitol Hill and electoral politics; policy dir. Dem. Leadership Coun., 1985—; pres. Progressive Found.; pres., founder Progressive Policy Inst., Washington, 1989—; Sr. editor 1984 House Dem. Caucus policy, Renewing America's Promise; participant in drafting nat. legis., including a demonstration project for vol. nat. svc. Nat. Cmty. Svc. Act of 1990; press sec., spokesman, speechwriter for 1984 U.S. Senate campaign of current N.C. Gov. Jim Hunt; speechwriter, policy analyst for late U.S. Rep. Gillis Long of La., chmn. of House Dem. Caucus; spokesman, speechwriter 1982 U.S. Senate campaign of former Va. Lt. Gov. Dick Davis. Co-editor: Mandate for Change, 1992; contbr. articles to profl. jours. Office: Progressive Policy Inst 316 Pennsylvania Ave SE Ste 55 Washington DC 20003-1146

MARSHALL, WILLIAM EDWARD, historical association executive; b. St. Paul, Apr. 19, 1925; s. William Edward and Louise (White) M.; m. Ruth Marie Winner, Sept. 3, 1947 (div.); children: Michael Scott, Terry Lee, Sharon; m. Loretta E. Slota, Nov. 6, 1976; children: Marc William, Matthew Ryan. B.A., Mont. State U., 1950; B.F.A., Wittenberg U., 1951; postgrad., Ohio State U., 1951-52. Owner, operator Public Library Public Relations Service, 1952-55, Specialized Press, 1952-60; graphic and exhibits designer Ohio Hist. Soc., 1952-60, State Historic Soc. Colo., Denver, 1960-61; dep. exec. dir. State Historic Soc. Colo., 1961-63, exec. dir., 1963-79; cons. to hist. agys., author, 1979—; founding mem. Little Kingdom Hist. Found.; condr. historic interpretation seminars and workshops. Author historic TV and film prodns., books, fiction and non-fiction in nat. publs.; editor: Humboldt Historian, 1990-91, CEO MediFacts, 1992—; illustrator, photographer books and periodicals; contbr. articles to profl. jours. Bd. dirs. Rocky Mountain Center on Environment, 1967-72, Trinidad Mus. Soc., 1986-89; chmn. Colo. Humanities Program Com., 1971, 75. With USMCR, 1943-45. Mem. Am. Assn. Museums (exec. com. 1973-74, mus. accreditation evaluator), Am. Assn. State and Local History (mem. council 1966-72, awards com. 1966-80, com. on fed. programs in history), Orgn. Am. Historians (hist. sites com. 1974-75). Presbyterian. Home: Moonstone Heights 719 Driver Rd Trinidad CA 95570-9722

MARSHALL, WILLIAM EMMETT, biotechnology company executive, biochemistry researcher; b. Chgo., July 21, 1935; s. William E. and Margaret (Fitzgerald) M.; m. Bonnie M. Dallman, June 10, 1961; children: Elizabeth, Stephanie, William. BS, U. Ill., 1957, MS, 1959, PhD, 1961. Asst. prof. U. Minn. Med. Sch., Mpls., 1961-67; dir. tech. devel. Gen. Foods Corp., White Plains, N.Y., 1967-83; pres. Microbial Genetics div. Pioneer Hi-Bred Internat. Inc., Johnston, Iowa, 1983-91, pres. Microbial Environ. Svcs. div., 1989-91; pres. Immunom Techs. Inc., Bedford Hills, N.Y., 1991—; mem. Grace Commn. U.S. Govt., 1982-83; chmn. adv. bd. Nat. Agrl. Research and Extension Users, Washington, 1983-88; mem. panel on new devel. in biotech. Office of Tech. Assessment, Washington, 1986-90; vice-chmn bd. dirs. Rodale Inst., Emmaus, Pa., Keystone (Colo.) Adv. Panel on Biotech.; mem. adv. com. on intellectual property matters to Gen. Agreement on Trade and Tariffs; mem. adv. bd. NSF Ctr. for Microbial Ecology, Mich. State U., 1990—; adj. assoc. prof. dept. microbiology N.Y. Med. Coll., Valhalla, 1992—. Contbr. articles to profl. jours.; patentee in field. Recipient award of Merit U. Ill., 1994. Mem. AAAS, Iowa Acad. Sci. (awards and recognition com.). Club: Univ. (Washington). Office: NY Med Coll Dept Microbiology & Immunology Valhalla NY 10507

MARSHALL-NOLT, SYLVIA JANE, rehabilitation nurse; b. Greensboro, N.C., Nov. 21, 1953; d. Troy and Audrey (Southard) Marshall; m. Glenn Nolt, Dec. 19, 1992. BSBA, High Point U., 1976; ASN, Valencia C.C., 1987. RN, Fla.; cert. rehab. nurse. Apparel mgr. K-Mart Corp., Orlando, Fla., 1976-82; sales rep. EGP, Orlando, Fla., 1982-83; acctg. SJM Bus. Svcs., Orlando, Fla., 1983-87; rehab. clin. evaluator Fla. Hosp. Rehab. Ctr., Orlando, 1987—. Mem. Nat. Assn. Rehab. Nurses, Fla. State Assn. Rehab. Nurses (bd. dirs. 1994), Ctrl. Fla. Assn. Rehab. Nurses (nominating com. 1991, scholar com. 1992, treas. 1992, pres. elect 1993, pres. 1994), Heart Fla. Civitan Club (bd. dirs. 1992, sec. 1992), Valencia C.C. Alumni Assn. (bd. dirs. 1990-94, sec. 1992), N.C. 4H Honor Club, Phi Beta Kappa, Delta Mu Delta. Republican. Methodist. Avocations: tennis, bowling, cross-stitch, reading. Home: 349 Silver Pine Dr Lake Mary FL 32746-4831 Office: Fla Hosp Rehab Ctr 601 E Rollins St Orlando FL 32803-1248

MARSIK, FREDERIC JOHN, microbiologist; b. Camden, N.J., June 22, 1943; s. Ferdinand Vincent and Helen (Reidl) M.; children: Terri Jean, Kristi Ann Marsik McCann. BA, Lebanon Valley Coll., 1965; MS, U. Mo., 1970, PhD, 1973. Diplomate Am. Bd. Med. Microbiology. Asst. prof. Sch. Medicine, U. Va., Charlottesville, 1976-80; tech. dir. microbiology and serology Children's Hosp. Wis., Milw., 1980-84; assoc. prof. microbiology and internal medicine Sch. Medicine, Oral Roberts U., Tulsa, 1984-87; dir. microbiology Crozer-Chester Med. Ctr., Upland, Pa., 1987-88; dir. rsch. and devel. media tech. Becton Dickinson Microbiology Systems, Cockeysville, Md., 1988—; mem. adv. com. Milw. Area Tech. Coll., Milw., 1983-84, Tulsa Jr. Coll., 1985-87; mem. rev. bd. Clin. Lab. Sci. Publ., Washington, 1990—. Contbr. chpts. to textbooks. Treas. Rose Fire Co. and Ambulance Svc., New Freedom, Pa., 1989—; bd. govs. New Freedom Community Ctr., 1989—; mem. adult edn. com. So. York County Sch. Dist., Glen Rock, Pa., 1989—. Lt. col. USAR. Recipient Best Rsch. Project award S.W. Assn. for Clin. Microbiology, 1984. Mem. Am. Soc. Microbiology (mem. lab. practices com. 1990—), Am. Soc. Med. Tech., N.Y. Acad. Scis. Congregationalist. Avocations: fishing, camping, basketball. Home: 6 Keesey Rd New Freedom PA 17349-9638 Office: Becton Dickinson 250 Schilling Cir Cockeysville MD 21031-1103

MARSOLAIS, HAROLD RAYMOND, trade association administrator; b. Troy, N.Y., Mar. 10, 1942; s. Harold George and Viola Marie (Chamberlain) M.; m. Susan Lemieux, Jul. 5, 1964; children: Michelle, Harold R. BS, U. So. Miss., 1974; MS, Webster Coll., 1979. Officer US Army, 1961-82; CEO Minn. Dak. Hardware Assn., Mpls., 1982-84, Penn. ATL. Sbd. Hardware Assn., Harrisburg, Pa., 1984-87; v.p. sales Natl. Retail Hardware Assn., Indpls., Ind., 1987-89; CEO Nat. Retail Hardware Assn., Indpls., 1989-94; pres. Marsolais & Assoc., 1995—; exec. dir. Russell Mueller Found. 1989, Home Center Inst. 1987. Author: Guide to FAA Reg., 1971, In Store Merchandising, 1987, Doing the Right Thing: An Environmental Guide, 1994. Dir. Jr. Chamber, Hattiesburg, Pa., Rotary Intl., Harrisburg, Pa. Recipient W.B. Harlan Business award U. So. Miss., 1974, Outstanding Young Man Jaycees, Hattiesburg, 1974. Decorated Distinguished Flying Cross. Mem. Am. Soc. Assn. Exec. Avocations: golf, boating, flying. Office: Marsolais and Assocs 115 S Lake Cir Saint Augustine FL 32095

MARSTERS, GERALD FREDERICK, retired aerospace science and technology executive; b. Summerville, N.S., Can., Dec. 18, 1932; s. Ralpha Roland and Madge Thelma (Harvey) M.; m. Lorena May Gunter, Oct. 23, 1954; children: Mariko Collette, Cynthia Denise. BS, Queens U., Kingston, Ont., Can., 1962; PhD, Cornell U., 1967. Registered profl. engr., Ont., Can. Prof. mech. engring. Queen's U., 1967-82; dir. airworthiness Dept. of Transport, Ottawa, 1982-87; dir. gen. Inst. for Aerospace Rsch., Nat. Rsch. Coun., Ottawa, 1987-94; ret., 1994; proprietor, cons. AeroVations: Aerospace Tech. Specialists; nat. del. adv. group Aerospace Rsch. (NATO), Paris, 1987-94. Flying officer Royal Can. Airforce, 1953-58. Recipient Gold medal for Extraordinary Svc. FAA, 1986. Fellow AIAA, Can. Aero. and Space Inst. (past pres. 1992-93), Can. Acad. Engring., Can. Soc. for Mech. Engring.; mem. SAE (aerospace coun. 1985). Avocations: recreational flying, model railroads. Home: 39 Westpark Dr, Gloucester, ON Canada K1B 3G6

MARSTON, EDGAR JEAN, III, lawyer; b. Houston, July 5, 1939; s. Edgar Jr. and Jean (White) M.; m. Graeme Meyers, June 21, 1961; children: Christopher Graham, Jonathan Andrew. BA, Brown U., 1961; JD, U. Tex., 1964. Bar: Tex. 1964. Law clk. to presiding justice Supreme Ct. Tex., Austin, 1964-65; assoc. Baker & Botts, Houston, 1965-71; ptnr. Bracewell & Patterson, Houston, 1971-89, of counsel, 1990—, now ptnr.; exec. v.p., gen. counsel Southdown, Inc., Houston, 1987—, also bd. dirs. Mem. ABA, Tex. Bar Assn., Tex. Bar Found., Houston Bar Assn., Houston Country Club, Coronado Club. Episcopalian. Avocations: hunting, fishing, philately, reading. Office: Bracewell & Patterson 711 Louisiana Ste 2900 Houston TX 77002-4401*

MARSTON, MICHAEL, urban economist, asset management executive; b. Oakland, Calif., Dec. 4, 1936; s. Lester Woodbury and Josephine (Janovic) M.; m. Alexandra Lynn Geyer, Apr. 30, 1966; children: John, Elizabeth. BA, U. Calif., Berkeley, 1959; postgrad. London Sch. Econs., 1961-63. V.p. Larry Smith & Co., San Francisco, 1969-72, exec. v.p. urban econ. divsn., 1969-72; chmn. bd. Keyser Marston Assocs., Inc., San Francisco, 1973-87; gen. ptnr. The Sequoia Partnership, 1979-91; pres. Marston Vineyard and Winery, 1982—, Marston Assocs., Inc., 1982—, The Ctr. for Individual and Instnl. Renewal, 1996—. Cert. rev. appraiser Nat. Assn. Rev. Appraisers and Mortgage Underwriters, 1984—. Chmn., San Francisco Waterfront Com., 1969-86; chmn. fin. com., bd. dirs., mem. exec. com., treas. San Francisco Planning and Urban Rsch. Assn., 1976-87, Napa Valley Vintners, 1986—, mem. gov. affairs com.; trustee Cathedral Sch. for Boys, 1981-82, Marin Country Day Sch., 1984-90; v.p. St. Luke's Sch., 1986-91; pres. Presidio Heights Assn. of Neighbors, 1983-84; chmn. Presidio Com. 1991—; v.p., bd. dirs., mem. exec. com. People for Open Space, 1972-87; mem. Gov.'s Issue Analysis Com. and Speakers Bur., 1966; mem. speakers bur. Am. Embassy, London, 1961-63; v.p., bd. dirs. Dem. Forum, 1968-72; v.p., trustee Youth for Service. Served to lt. USNR. Mem. Napa Valley Vintners, Urban Land Inst., World Congress Land Policy (paper in field), Order of Golden Bear, Chevalier du Tastevin, Bohemian Club, Pacific Union Club, Lambda Alpha. Contbr. articles to profl. jours. Home: 3375 Jackson St San Francisco CA 94118-2018 *Personal philosophy: Success is what you do with what you have not what others think or what is in vogue.*

MARSTON, ROBERT ANDREW, public relations executive; b. Astoria, N.Y., Aug. 6, 1937; s. Frank and Lena (DiDomenico) M.; m. Maryann Doherty, Sept. 23, 1990; 1 child, Robert Brendan. BA, Hofstra U., 1959. Sr. v.p. Rowland Co., N.Y.C., 1959-68, Rogers & Cowen, Inc., N.Y.C., 1968-70; founder, chmn., CEO Robert Marston And Assocs., Inc., N.Y.C., 1970—. Contbr. articles and photographs to profl. jours. and popular mags. Mem. Pub. Rels. Soc. Am. (counselors sect.), Marco Polo Club, Doubles Club, Southampton Bath & Tennis Club. Roman Catholic. Home: 570 Park Ave New York NY 10021-7370 also: 130 Captains Neck Ln Southampton NY 11968-4561 Office: 485 Madison Ave New York NY 10022-5803

MARSTON, ROBERT QUARLES, university president; b. Toano, Va., Feb. 12, 1923; s. Warren and Helen (Smith) M.; m. Ann Carter Garnett, Dec. 21, 1946; children: Ann, Robert, Wesley. B.S., Va. Mil. Inst., 1943; M.D., Med. Coll. Va., 1947; B.Sc. (Rhodes scholar 1947-49), Oxford (Eng.) U., 1949; B.Sc. 6 hon. degrees. Intern Johns Hopkins Hosp., 1949-50; resident Vanderbilt U. Hosp., 1950-51; resident Med. Coll. Va., 1953-54, asst. prof. medicine, 1954; asst. prof. bacteriology and immunology U. Minn., 1958-59; asso. prof. medicine, asst. dean charge student affairs Med. Coll. Va., 1959-61; dean U. Miss. Sch. Medicine, 1961-66; dir. U. Miss. Sch. Medicine (Med. Center), 1961-65, vice chancellor, 1965-66; asso. dir. div. regional med. programs NIH, 1966-68; adminstr. Fed. Health Services and Mental Health Adminstrn., 1968; dir. NIH, Bethesda, Md., 1968-73; scholar in residence U. Va., Charlottesville, 1973-74; Disting. fellow Inst. of Medicine, Nat. Acad. Scis., 1973-74; pres. U. Fla., 1974-84, pres. emeritus, emeritus prof. medicine, emeritus prof. fish and aquaculture; bd. dirs. Johnson and Johnson, Nat. Bank Alachua, Wackenhut Corp.; chmn. bd. dirs. Cordis Corp.; chmn., mem. Fla. Marine Fisheries Commn. Author articles in field. Chmn. Commn. on Med. Edn. for Robert Wood Found.; chmn. Safety Adv. Bd. Three Mile Island; chmn. adv. com. med. implications of nuclear war NAS; exec. coun. Assn. Am. Med. Coll., 1964-67; past chmn. exec. com. Nat. Assn. State Univs. and Land Grant Colls., chmn., 1982. 1st lt. AUS, 1951-53. Decorated Knight of North Star (Sweden); Markle scholar, 1954-59; hon. fellow Lincoln Coll. Oxford U. Fellow Am. Pub. Health Assn.; mem. Inst. Medicine of NAS, AAAS, Am. Hosp. Assn. (hon.), Nat. Med. Assn. (hon.), Assn. Am. Rhodes Scholars, Assn. Am. Physicians, Assn. Am. Med. Colls. (disting. mem.), Am. Clin. and Climatol. Assn., Soc. Scholars Johns Hopkins, Alpha Omega Alpha. Episcopalian. Home: 19810 Old Bellamy Rd Alachua FL 32615

MARSTON-SCOTT, MARY VESTA, nurse, educator; b. St. Stephen, N.B., Can., Apr. 5, 1924; d. George Frank and Betsey Mildred (Babb) M.; m. John Paul Scott, June 30, 1979. B.A., U. Maine, 1946; M.N., Yale U., 1951; M.P.H., Harvard U., 1957; M.A., Boston U., 1964, Ph.D., 1969. Research asst. Roscoe B. Jackson Meml. Lab., Bar Harbor, Maine, 1946-48; nurse, 1952-54; instr. Yale U. Sch. Nursing, 1955-56; nurse cons. Div. Nursing, Washington, 1957-62; asso. prof. Frances Payne Bolton Sch. Nursing, Case-Western Res. U., Cleve., 1969-74; prof. grad. program community health nursing Boston U., 1974-86; assoc. prof. Coll. Nursing U. Ill., Chgo., 1986-94, assoc. prof. emerita, 1994—; cons. in field. Contbr. articles to profl. jours. Served with USPHS, 1957-62. Fellow Am. Acad. Nursing; mem. Am. Psychol. Assn., Am. Public Health Assn., Am. Nurses Assn., Sigma Theta Tau. Home: 1052 Pinewood Ct Bowling Green OH 43402-2173 Office: U Ill Coll Nursing 845 S Damen Ave Chicago IL 60612-7350

MARTEAU, KIMBERLY K., federal agency administrator; b. L.A., Feb. 22, 1959; d. Donald S. Mart and Roberta Blank; m. John B. Emerson, Sept. 15, 1990. BA magna cum laude, UCLA, 1981; JD, U. Calif., Hastings, 1984. Practicing atty. Tuttle & Taylor, 1986-88; mem. nat. adv. staff Dukakis for Pres. Com., 1988; dir. internat. devel. and distbn. Patchett-Kaufman Entertainment, 1989-90; mgmt. assoc. Sony Pictures Entertainment, 1990-92; v.p. Motion Pictures, Savoy Pictures, Entertainment, 1992-93; dir. office of pub. liaison U.S. Info. Agy., 1993—. Editor Hastings Law Review, 1984-85. Grantee Edn. Abroad Program, 1979; fellow Rotary Club, 1984-85. Avocations: politics, snow skiing, films, French cuisine, dance. Office: Public Liaison US Info Agy 301 4th St SW Rm 602 Washington DC 20547-0009

MARTEKA, VINCENT JAMES, JR., magazine editor, writer; b. Uxbridge, Mass., Jan. 29, 1936; s. Vincent James and Genevieve (Ramian) M.; m. Janet Littler, May 26, 1962; children: Andrew, Peter, Katherine. B.S. in Geology, U. Mass., 1958; M.S., Rensselaer Poly. Inst., 1959. Editor U.S. Geol. Survey, Washington, 1959-60; sci. writer, news editor Sci. Service, Washington, 1961-63; sci. editor My Weekly Reader, children's newspaper, Middletown, Conn., 1964-65; editor Current Sci., sci. mag. jr. high sch. students, Middletown, 1966-95. Author: Bionics, 1965, Mushrooms: Wild and Edible, 1980, also numerous articles (writing awards Edn. Press Assn.); series editor: Our Living World, 12 books, 1993-94. Served with AUS, 1960. Mem. Nat. Assn. Sci. Writers, Mycological Soc. Am., N.Am. Mycological Assn., Nat. Audubon Soc., Mattabeseck Audubon Soc. (pres. 1976). Home: 239 Jobs Pond Rd Portland CT 06480-1712 Office: Weekly Reader Corp 245 Long Hill Rd Middletown CT 06457-4063

MARTEL, JACQUES G., engineer, adminstrator. BA, Coll. Jean-de-Bréboeuf, Montreal, 1964; BScA in Engring. Physics, U. Montreal, 1968; PhD in Nuclear Engring., MIT, 1971. Dir. Gen. Indsl. Materials Inst. Nat. Rsch. Coun. Can., Boucherville, PQ, Canada. Office: Indsl Materials Rsch Inst, 75 De Mortagne Blvd, Boucherville, PQ Canada J4B 6Y4

MARTEL, WILLIAM, radiologist, educator; b. N.Y.C., Oct. 1, 1927; s. Hyman and Fanny M.; m. Rhoda Kaplan, Oct. 9, 1956; children: Lisa, Pamela, Caryn, Jonathan, David. M.D., NYU, 1953. Intern, Kings County Hosp., N.Y., 1953-54; resident in radiology Mt. Sinai Hosp., N.Y.C., 1954-57; instr. radiology U. Mich., 1957-60, asst. prof., 1960-63, assoc. prof., 1963-67, prof., 1967—, Fred Jenner Hodges prof., 1984—, chmn. dept. radiology, 1981-92, dir. skeletal radiology, 1970-81. Contbr. articles to Radiol. Diagnoses of Arthritic Diseases. Served with USAAF, 1945-46. Recipient Amoco U. Mich. Outstanding Teaching award, 1980. Mem. Radiol. Soc. N.Am., Am. Roentgen Ray Soc., Assn. Univ. Radiologists. Home: 2972 Parkridge Dr Ann Arbor MI 48103-1737 Office: Univ Mich Hosps Dept Radiology 1500 E Med Ctr Dr Ann Arbor MI 48109

MARTELL, ARTHUR EARL, chemistry educator; b. Natick, Mass., Oct. 18, 1916; s. Ambrose and Dorina (Lamoureaux) M.; m. Norma June Saunders, Sept. 2, 1944; children: Stuart A., Edward S., Janet E., Judith S., Jon V., Elaine C.; m. Mary Austin, 1965; children: Helen E., Kathryn A. B.S., Worcester Poly. Inst., 1938, D.Sc. (hon.), 1962; Ph.D., NYU 1941. Instr. Worcester Poly. Inst., 1941-42; mem. faculty Clark U., 1942-61, prof. chemistry, 1951-61, chmn. dept., 1959-61; prof. chemistry, chmn. dept. Ill. Inst. Tech., 1960-66; prof. chemistry Tex. A&M U., College Station, 1966—; Disting. prof. Tex. A&M U., 1973—, dept. head, 1966-80, adv. to pres., 1980-82; rsch. on chem equilibria, kinetics, catalysis, metal chelate compounds in solution. Author: (with M. Calvin) Chemistry of the Metal Chelate Compounds, 1952, (with S. Chaberek, Jr.) Organic Sequestering Agents, 1959, (with L.G. Sillen) Stability Constants, 1964; supplement, 1971, (with M.M. Taqui Khan) Homogeneous Catalysis by Metal Complexex, 2 vols., 1973, (with R.M. Smith) Critical Stability Constants, Vol. 1, 1974, Vol. 2, 1975, Vol. 3, 1977, Vol. 4, 1976, Vol. 5, 1982, Vol. 6, 1989, (with R.J. Motekaitis) Determination and Use of Stability Constants, 1989, 2nd edit., 1992, (with R.D. Hancock) Metal Complexes in Aqueous Solutions, 1996; editor: ACS Monograph on Coordination Chemistry, Vol. 1, 1973, Vol. 2, 1978, ACS Symposium Series 140, inorganic Chemistry in Biology and Medicine, 1980, Jour. Coordination Chemistry, 1970-80; mem. editl. bd. Bioinorganic Chemistry, Jour. Inorganic and Nuclear Chemistry, Inorganic Chemisty; contbr. articles to profl. jours. Mem. sch. bd. Northborough, Mass., 1958-61, chmn., 1959-61. Research fellow U. Calif. at Berkeley, 1949-50; Guggenheim fellow U. Zurich, Switzerland, 1954-55; NSF sr. postdoctoral fellow, also fellow Sch. Advanced Studies Mass. Inst. Tech., 1959-60; NIH Spl. fellow U. Calif. at Berkeley, 1964-65. Fellow N.Y. Acad. Scis. (hon. life); mem. AAAS, Am. Chem. Soc. (chmn. ctrl. Mass. sect. 1957-58, chmn. Tex. A&M sect. 1990-91, S.W. Regional award 1976, Nat. award for Disting. Svc. 1980, Patterson-Crane award 1995), Am. Acad. Arts and Scis., Japan Soc. for Analytical Chemistry (hon.), Sigma Xi, Phi Lambda Upsilon (hon.). Home: 9742 Myrtle Dr College Station TX 77845-6786

MARTELL, DENISE MILLS, lay worker; b. Newberry, S.C., Apr. 8, 1965; d. Wyman Harman and Evangeline (Berry) Mills; m. Marty Martell, FEb. 29, 1992. Grad., Newberry High Sch., 1983. Tchr. Vacation Bible Sch., Newberry, 1984—, Sun. Sch., Newberry, 1989-92; dir. Bapt. Young Women, Newberry, 1989-92; sec. Sunday Sch. Bapt. Ch., Newberry, S.C., 1993-95, Sun. Sch. tchr. 1-3 grades, 1995—; tchr. mission trips, various locations, 1987-89; tchr. Mission Friends, Newberry, 1987-96, mem. choir, 1986—, mem. Newberry Cmty. choir, 1992-95, tchr. children's choir, 1993-95; leader Weekday Bible Club, 1990-92, missionary to Bolivia, South Am., 1996. Active March of Dimes Walk Am., Am. Diabetes Assn. Bike-a-thon. Home: 8769 Monticelle Rd Columbia SC 29203-9708 Office: Shakespeare E and F Newberry SC 29108 *We are to be an encourager to share Christ love with all we meet. There is no task we can not handle. What ever God calls us to do, He has already equipped us to handle—standing faithful and firm in Christ to be a light in this world.*

MARTEN, GORDON CORNELIUS, research agronomist, educator, federal agency administrator; b. Wittenberg, Wis., Sept. 14, 1935; s. Clarence George and Cora Levina (Verpoorten) M.; m. Lynette Joy Hanson, Sept. 9, 1961; 1 dau., Kimberly Joy. BS, U. Wis., 1957; MS, U. Minn., 1959, PhD, 1961; postgrad., Purdue U., 1962. Rsch. agronomist U.S. Dept. Agr., U. Minn., St. Paul, 1961-72, supervisory rsch. agronomist, rsch. leader, 1972-89; adj. prof. agronomy U. Minn., St. Paul, 1971-95; assoc. dir. USDA-Agr. Rsch. Svc., Beltsville, Md., 1989-96; ret., 1996; mem. governing body and U.S. rep. to OECD Biol. Resource Mgmt. Program, Paris, 1990-96; adminstrv. coun. USDA Sustainable Agrl. Rsch. and Edn. Program, 1993-95. Assoc. editor: Crop Sci., 1972-74; sr. editor USDA Handbook Near Infrared Reflectance Spectroscopy: Analysis of Forage Quality, 1985, rev. edit., 1989; mem. edit. bd. Sci. of Food and Agriculture, 1985-90; contbr. numerous articles to profl. jours. Recipient Merit award Am. Forage and Grassland Coun., 1976, Outstanding Svc. award, 1981, Civil Servant of Yr. award Twin Cities, Minn., 1976; NSF grad. fellow, 1959-61; numerous cert. merit USDA Agrl. Rsch. Svc., Northrup King Faculty Outstanding Performance award U. Minn., 1986, Superior Svc. award USDA, 1987. Fellow Am. Soc. Agronomy, Crop Sci. Soc. Am. (bd. dirs. 1975-77); mem. Am. Forage and Grassland Coun. (bd. dirs. 1977-80), Coun. Agr. Sci. and Tecch. (bd. dirs. 1985-90), Agronomicc Sci. Found. (trustee 1984-89), Biol. Club, Sigma Xi, Gamma Sigma Delta (Adminstrn. award of merit/Nat. Capital Area 1994), Alpha Zeta, Delta Theta Sigma. Lutheran. Home: 1312 Willow Cir Roseville MN 55113

MARTENS, HELEN EILEEN, elementary school educator; b. Atkinson, Nebr., Jan. 13, 1926; d. Robert McKinley and Minnie Viola (Alfs) M. BS, Dana Coll., 1971; postgrad., U. Nebr., 1971-94, Wayne (Nebr.) U., 1971-94. Cert. tchr., Nebr. Rural sch. tchr. Dist. 231, Atkinson, Nebr., 1943-44, Dist. 77, Atkinson, Nebr., 1944-45, Dist. 119, Atkinson, Nebr., 1945-47; tchr. Emmet (Nebr.) Pub. Sch., 1947-59, O'Neill (Nebr.) Pub. Sch., 1959-96; mgr. Saddle Horn Ranch for Youth. Mem. Holt County 4-H Coun., 1986-90, leader, 1946—; mem. youth edn. com. Holt County Cancer Soc., 1976-94; activity sec. Dr. Boots and Saddle Club, Holt County, 1969-95; demonstration tchr. Nebr. Tchrs. Help Mobile. Recipient Good Neighbor citation Knights of Aksarben, 1986, Amb. award O'Neill C. of C., 1986, Tchr. of Yr. World Herald Newspaper, 1986, Outstanding Elem. Tchr. Nebr. Rural Cmty. Schs., 1994; named Grand Marshall O'Neill St. Patrick's Parade, 1986. Mem. NEA, Nebr. Edn. Assn., O'Neill Edn. (sec., v.p., pres. 1960-94), Order Eastern Star, Alpha Delta Kappa, Delta Kappa Gamma (sec., v.p. 1959-94). Republican. Methodist. Avocation: ranching. Home: HC 69 Box 41 Atkinson NE 68713-9615

MARTENS, LYLE CHARLES, state education administrator; b. Wausau, Wis., June 22, 1935; s. Norman Theodore and Eloise Loretta (Kreger) M.; m. Darlene Carrol Pyatt, Dec. 22, 1956; children: William Lyle, Robert Michael. BS in Indsl. Edn., Stout State U., 1957, MS in Indsl. Tech., 1962. Tchr. indsl. arts Mercer (Wis.) Pub. Schs., 1957-62; high sch. prin. Seymour (Wis.) Community Schs., 1962-65, supt. schs., 1965-87; supt. schs. Green Bay (Wis.) Area Pub. Schs., 1987-89; asst. state supt. State Dept. Edn., Madison, Wis., 1989-90, dep. state supt., 1990-93; coord. sch.-to-work Cesa 7, Green Bay, Wis., 1993—. Chair United Way Edn. Fund Dr., Brown County, Wis., 1989; mem. bd.dirs. Green Bay C. of C., Good Shepherd Nursing Home, Seymour, Wis., 1975-87; mem. Econ. Devel. Corp., Outagamie County, Wis., 1985-86; founder Fallen Timber's Environment Ctr., 1972. Recipient Martens Praire Honor, 1995. Mem. Am. Assn. Sch. Dist. Adminstrs., Wis. Assn. Sch. Dist. Adminstrs. (pres. 1978-79), Assn. Svc./Curriculum Devel., North Cen. Regional Ednl. Lab., Fox Valley Tech. Inst., Masons, Phi Delta Kappa. Lutheran. Avocations: fishing, hunting, flying, woodworking, raising and showing dogs. Home: 6504 County Road R Denmark WI 54208-9729 Office: Cesa 7 595 Baeten Rd Green Bay WI 54304

MARTENS, PATRICIA FRANCES, adult education educator; b. St. Louis, Nov. 27, 1943; d. John William and Mary Ruth (Bolds) Martens; m. George Joseph Miller, Aug. 7, 1965 (div.); children: Nicolette, George Jr., Jeffrey. BS in Psychology, So. Ill. U., 1975; MA in Counseling, St. Louis U., 1990, PhD in Psychol. Founds., 1996. Cert. sexuality educator. Primary, intermediate tchr. St. Hedwig Sch., St. Louis, 1961-66; jr. high tchr. Assumption Sch., St. Louis, 1976-81; tchr. trainer grad. students Paul VI Cathechetical Inst., St. Louis, 1986-88; nat. tchr. trainer St. Louis, 1989—; cons. Archdiocese L.A., Archdiocese St. Louis, Nat. Coun. Cath. Bishops, 1991; del. Nat. Cath. Ednl. Del. to Russia and Lithuania, 1993; frequent spkr. and presenter at schs., parishes ednl. confs., nat. and internat. religious edn. mtgs.; TV appearances on ABC and CTNA; nat. ednl. cons. Tabor Pub. Author: (videos) In God's Image: Make and Female, 1989, God Doesn't Make Junk, 1989 (Cath. Audio Visual Educators award 1991), (books) Parent to Parent, 1989, Sex Is Not A Four-Letter Word!, 1994. Recipient Award Cath. Press Assn., 1995. Mem. AACD, Nat. Cath. Educators Assn., Am. Assn. Sex Educators, Counselors, Therapists, Assn. for Religious Values in Counseling, Am. Sch. Counselor Assn., Am. Coll. Personnel Assn., Soc. for Sci. Study of Sex, Pi Lambda Theta. Avocations: travel, swimming, biking, movies, sharing youth activities. Home and Office: 8061 Daytona Dr Apt 1E Saint Louis MO 63105-2549

MARTENSON, EDWARD ALLEN, theater manager; b. Paris, Ky., May 4, 1949; s. Milton A. and Bettye (Hudnall) M.; m. Gina Franz, Mar. 18, 1979; children: Benn, Hallie. AB, Princeton U., 1971. Mgr. McCarter Theater, Princeton, N.J., 1973-79; mng. dir. Yale Repertory Theater, New Haven, 1979-82; dir. theater program NEA, Washington, 1982-86; exec. dir. Guthrie Theater, Mpls., 1986—; adj. assoc. prof. Sch. Drama Yale U., New Haven, 1979-82, co-chmn. adminstrn., 1979-82. Home: 102 Farmdale Rd W Hopkins MN 55343-7183 Office: Guthrie Theater 725 Vineland Pl Minneapolis MN 55403-1139

MARTH, ELMER HERMAN, bacteriologist, educator; b. Jackson, Wis., Sept. 11, 1927; s. William F. and Irma A. (Bublitz) M.; m. Phyllis E. Menge, Aug. 10, 1957. BS, U. Wis., 1950, MS, 1952, PhD, 1954. Registered sanitarian, Wis. Teaching asst. bacteriology U. Wis., Madison, 1949-51; research asst. U. Wis., 1951-54, project asso., 1954-55, instr. bacteriology, 1955-57, assoc. prof.food sci., bacteriology and food microbiology and toxicology, 1966-71, prof., 1971-90, prof. emeritus, 1990—; vis. prof. Swiss Fed. Inst. Tech., Zurich, 1981; with Kraft Foods, Inc., Glenview, Ill., 1957-66, rsch. bacteriologist, 1957-61, sr. rsch. bacteriologist, 1961-63, group leader microbiology, 1963-66, assoc. mgr. microbiology, 1966; mem. Intersoc. Coun. on Std. Methods for Exam. Dairy Products, 1968-84, chmn., 1972-78. Contbg. author books; editor: Jour. Milk and Food Tech, 1967-76, Jour. Food Protection, 1977-87; contbr. articles to profl. publs. Sec. Luth. Acad. Scholarship, 1961-71; WHO travel fellow, 1975. Recipient Nordica award for rsch. Am. Cultured Dairy Products Inst., 1979, Meritorious Svc. award APHA, 1977, 83, Sanitarian of Yr. award Wis. Assn. Milk and Food Sanitarians, 1983, Meritorious Svc. award Nat. Confectioners Assn., 1987, Joseph Mityas Meml. Laboratorian of Yr. award Wis. Lab. Assn., 1989, Quality of Comm. award Am. Agrl. Econs. Assn., 1992. Fellow Inst. Food Technologists (Nicholas Appert award 1987, Babcock-Hart award 1989); mem. Am. Soc. Microbiology, Am. Dairy Sci. Assn. (Pfizer rsch. award 1975, Dairy Rsch. Found. award 1980, Borden award 1986, Kraft Inc. teaching award 1988), Internat. Assn. Milk, Food, and Environ. Sanitarians (hon. life, Educator award for rsch. and teaching food hygiene 1977, citation award 1984), Coun. Biology Editors, Inst. Food Technologists, Sigma Xi, Alpha Zeta, Kappa Eta Kappa, Phi Sigma, Phi Tau Sigma, Delta Theta Sigma, Gamma Sigma Delta, Gamma Alpha. Patentee in field. Office: U Wis Dept Food Sci 1605 Linden Dr Madison WI 53706-1519

MARTI, ERWIN ERNST, physicochemist, researcher; b. Basel, Switzerland, Dec. 27, 1932; s. Ernst and Marta (Kistler) M.; m. Alice Magrit Stieger, Jan. 18, 1936; children: Dominik, Barbara, Florian. PhD, U. Basel, 1963. Postdoctoral fellow U. Calif., Berkeley, 1966-68; with mgmt. Ciba-Geigy Ltd., Basel, 1968—, sci. expert, 1978—, rsch. group leader, 1984—; head sci. project team Swiss Fed. Office of Oecology, Incineration of Dioxin containing waste from Seveso, 1983-87; chmn. organizing com. European Symposium Thermal Analysis and Calorimetry 3, Interlaken, Switzerland, 1984; sci. chmn. Symposium Pharmacy and Thermal Analysis, Freiburg, Germany, 1993, Geneva, 1995, Monte Verita, Switzerland, 1997. Mem. editl. bd. Thermochimica Acta, 1994; regional editor Jour. Thermal Analysis, 1995; patentee in field. Bd. dirs. Free Dem. Party of Canton Basel-Stadt, 1986—; active Guild of Heaven, Basel, 1968—. Mem. Swiss Soc. Thermal Analysis and Calorimetry (pres.), European Soc. Thermal Analysis, Calorimetry, Thermodynamics and Chem. Reactivity (pres.). Avocations: hiking, downhill skiing. Home: Im Langen Loh 181, CH-4054 Basel Switzerland Office: Ciba-Geigy Ltd, Klybeckstrasse, CH-4002 Basel Switzerland

MARTIN, AGNES, artist; b. Maklin, Sask., Can., 1912; came to U.S., 1932, naturalized, 1950; Student, Western Wash. State Coll., 1935-38; BS, Columbia U., 1942, MFA, 1952. One-woman shows include Betty Parsons Gallery, N.Y.C., 1958, 59, 61, Robert Elkon Gallery, N.Y.C., 1961, 63, 72, 76, Nicolas Wilder Gallery, Los Angeles, 1963-66, 67, Visual Arts Ctr., N.Y.C., 1971, Kunstraum, Munich, 1973, Inst. Contemporary Art U. Pa., Phila., 1973, Pace Gallery, N.Y.C., 1975, 76, 77, 78, 79, 80-81, 81, 83, 84, 85, 86, 89, 91, 92, Mayor Gallery, London, 1978, 84, Galerie Rudolf Zwirner, Cologne, Fed. Republic Germany, 1978, Harcus/Krakow Gallery, Boston, 1978, Margo Leavin Gallery, Los Angeles, 1979, 85, Mus. N.Mex., Santa Fe, 1979, Richard Gray Gallery, Chgo., 1981, Garry Anderson Gallery, Sydney, Australia, 1986, Waddington Galleries Ltd., London, 1986, Stedelijk Mus., Amsterdam, 1991, Whitney Mus. Am. Art, N.Y.C., 1992; exhibited in group shows at Carnegie Inst., Pitts., 1961, Whitney Mus. Am. Art, N.Y.C., 1962, 66, 67, 74, 77, 92, Tooth Gallery, London, 1962, Gallery Modern Art, Washington, 1963, Wadsworth Atheneum, Hartford, Conn., 1963, Solomon R. Guggenheim Mus., N.Y.C., 1965, 66, 76, Mead Corp., 1965-67, Mus. Modern Art, N.Y.C., 1967, 76, 85, Inst. Contemporary Art, Phila., 1967, Detroit Inst. Art, 1967, Corcoran Gallery Art, Washington, 1967, 81, Finch Mus., N.Y., 1968, Phila. Mus., 1968, Zurich Art Mus., Switzerland, 1969, Ill. Bell Telephone Co., Chgo., 1970, Mus. Contemporary Art, Chgo., 1971, Inst. Contemporary Art U. Pa., Phila., 1972, Randolph-Macon Coll., N.C., 1972, Kassel, Fed. Republic Germany, 1972, Stedelijk Mus., Amsterdam, 1975, U. Mass., Amherst, 1976, Venice Biennale, Italy, 1976, 80, Cleve. Mus. Art, 1978, Albright-Knox Gallery, Buffalo, 1978, Inst. Contemporary Art, Boston, 1979, Art Inst. Chgo., 1979, San Francisco Mus. Modern Art, 1980, ROSC Internat. Art Exhbn., Dublin, Ireland, 1980, Marilyn Pearl Gallery, N.Y.C., 1983, Kemper Gallery, Kansas City Art Inst., 1985, Am. Acad. and Inst. Arts and Letters, N.Y.C., 1985, Charles Cowles Gallery, N.Y.C., 1986, Moody Gallery Art U. Ala., Birmingham, 1986, Butler Inst. Am. Art, 1986, Art Gallery Western Australia, Perth, 1986, Mus. Contemporary Art, Los Angeles, 1986, Boston Fine Arts Mus., 1989; represented in permanent collections Mus. of Modern Art, N.Y.C., Albright-Knox Gallery, Aldrich Mus., Ridgefield, Conn., Art Gallery Ont., Can., Australian Nat. Gallery, Canberra, Grey Art Gallery and Study Ctr., N.Y.C., Solomon R. Guggenheim Mus., High Mus. Art, Atlanta, Hirshhorn Mus. and Sculpture Garden, Washington, Israel Mus., Jerusalem, La Jolla (Calif.) Mus. Contemporary Art, Los Angeles County Mus. Art, Mus. Art R.I. Sch. Design, Providence, Mus. Modern Art, Neuegalerie der Stadt, Aachen, Fed. Republic Germany, Norton Simon Mus. Art at Pasadena, Calif., Stedelijk Mus., Amsterdam, The Netherlands, 1992, Mus. Modern Art, paris, 1992, Tate Gallery, London, Wadsworth Atheneum, Walker Art Ctr., Mpls., Whitney Mus. Am. Art, 1993, Sofia, Madrid, 1993, Huosten, 1993, Worcester (Mass.) Art Mus., Yale U. Art Gallery, New Haven; subject of various articles. Office: care The Pace Gallery 32 E 57th St New York NY 10022-2513

MARTIN, ALBERT CAREY, architect; b. Los Angeles, Aug. 3, 1913; s. Albert Carey and Carolyn Elizabeth (Borchard) M.; m. Dorothy Virginia Dolde, Nov. 15, 1937; children—Albert Cary III, David Charles, Mary Martin Marquardt, Claire, Charles Dolde. B.Arch. cum laude, U. So. Calif., 1936. Registered architect, Calif. Architect Albert C. Martin and Assocs., Los Angeles, 1937-42; ptnr. Albert C. Martin and Assocs., 1942—; dir. Rancho Los Alamitos Found. Prin. works include Los Angeles Dept. Water and Power, ARCO Twin Towers, St. Basil's Ch., Union Bank Sq. Trustee Los Angeles Orthopaedic Hosp.; bd. dirs. Long Beach Mus. Art Found. Recipient Annual Spirit of Los Angeles award Los Angeles Hdqrs. City Assn., 1980, Brotherhood award NCCJ, 1980, Asa V. Call Achievement award U. So. Calif. Alumni Assn., 1984, Boy Scouts Am. Good Scout award L.A. Area Coun., 1989; named Constrn. Man of Yr. Los Angeles C. of C., 1971. Fellow AIA (past dir., pres. So. Calif. chpt., past v.p. Calif. Coun.); mem. U. So. Calif. Archtl. Guild (advisor, disting. alumnus 1990), L.A. C. of C. (past pres.), Calif. C. of C. (past dir.), Lambda Alpha, Automobile Club of So. Calif. Republican. Roman Catholic. Clubs: California, Jonathan (Los Angeles). Avocation: sailing. Office: Albert C Martin and Assocs 811 W 7th St Los Angeles CA 90017-3408

MARTIN, ALBERT CHARLES, manufacturing executive, lawyer; b. San Lucido, Italy, Sept. 20, 1928; s. Joseph and Carmela M.; m. Jean Perrin, Aug. 22, 1953; children: Lynne, Ken. B.S., Mich. State U., 1952; M.S., U. Mich., 1953; J.D., Detroit Coll. Law, 1962. Bar: Mich. 1962. Corp. counsel, sec. Udylite Corp., Detroit, 1963-68; corp. counsel Hooker Chem. Corp., N.Y.C., 1968-70, Grow Chem. Co., N.Y.C., 1970-71; group v.p. Leeds & Northrup Internat., North Wales, Pa., 1971-79, pres., 1979—. Served with U.S. Army, 1946-48. Mem. Mich. Bar Assn.

MARTIN, ALLEN, lawyer; b. Manchester, Conn., Aug. 12, 1937; s. Richard and Ruth Palmer (Smith) M.; m. Bonnie Reid, Sept. 8, 1979; children: Elizabeth Palmer, Samuel Bates. B.A., Williams Coll., 1960, Oxford U., 1962; LL.B., Harvard U., 1965. Ptnr. firm Downs, Rachlin and Martin, Burlington, Brattleboro and St. Johnsbury, Vt., 1971—; chmn. bd. dirs. Elcon Inc., 1991—; bd. dirs., chmn. fin. com. Union Mut. Ins. Co., New Eng. Guaranty Ins. Co.; mem. Vt. Jud. Responsibility Bd., vice-chmn., 1978-80. Chmn. Vt. Bd. Edn., 1978-83; chmn. Vt. Rep. Party, 1991-95; mem. Rep. Nat. Com., 1991-95. Mem. Am. Law Inst., Am., Vt. bar assns. Republican. Home: 283 S Union St Burlington VT 05401-5507 Office: PO Box 190 199 Main St Burlington VT 05402-0190

MARTIN, ALVIN CHARLES, lawyer; b. Bklyn., Oct. 25, 1933; s. George and Dora (Gitlin) M.; m. Susan Goldman, Sept. 3, 1959 (div. Jan. 1980); children: Robert, Peter; m. Gail Leichtman, Oct. 25, 1985; stepchildren:

Hilary Macht, Timothy Macht. BBA, CCNY, 1954; JD, Harvard U., 1957; LLM in Taxation, NYU, 1963. Bar: N.Y. 1958, N.J. 1977, Fla. 1991. Pvt. practice N.Y.C., 1958-76, Newark and Morristown, N.J., 1977—; with Office of Regional Counsel, IRS, 1959-64; assoc. Curtis Mallet-Prevost Colt & Mosle, 1964-66; ptnr. Zissu, Halper & Martin, 1966-76; ptnr. Shanley & Fisher, 1977-88, counsel, 1988—; of counsel Ruden, McClosky, Smith, Schuster & Russell P.A., Ft. Lauderdale, Fla., 1990—; sec. Vornado, Inc., 1966-79, exec. v.p., asst. to chmn. bd., 1971-76, also bd. dirs.; adj. prof. taxation NYU, 1972-86; mem. taxation faculty Pace Coll. Grad. Sch. Bus. Adminstrn., 1964-70, Baruch Sch. Bus. and Pub. Adminstrn., 1959-62. Author: New Jersey Estate Planning, Will Drafting and Estate Administration Forms, 1988, 95. Bd. dirs. Met. Jewish Geriatric Ctr., 1980-84. With U.S. Army, 1957. Fellow Am. Coll. Trust and Estate Counsel. Clubs: Boca West (Fla.). Home: 20179 Fairfax Dr Boca Raton FL 33434-3235 Office: 131 Madison Ave Morristown NJ 07960-6086 also: 200 E Broward Blvd Fort Lauderdale FL 33301-1963

MARTIN, ANDREA LOUISE, actress, comedienne, writer; b. Portland, Md., Jan. 15, 1947. Grad., Emerson Coll. Appearances include (plays) Hard Shell, 1980 (off-Broadway debut), Sorrows of Stephen, 1980, What's a Nice Country Like You Doing in a State Like This?, 1974, She Loves Me, My Favorite Year, 1993 (Tony award, Featured Actress in a Musical), (films) Cannibal Girls, 1973, Black Christmas, 1974, Wholly Moses!, 1980, Soup for One, 1982, Club Paradise, 1986, Innerspace, 1987, Martha Ruth and Eddie, 1988, Worth Winning, 1989, Boris and Natasha, 1989, Rude Awakening, 1989, Too Much Sun, 1991, Stepping Out, 1991, All I Want for Christmas, 1991; (TV) Second City TV, 1977-81, That Thing on ABC, 1978, Torn Between Two Lovers, 1979, The Robert Klein Show, 1981, Kate and Allie, 1982, The Comedy Zone, 1984, Late Night Film Festival, 1985, Second City Twenty-Fifth Anniversary, 1985, Martin Short Concert for the North Americas, 1985, The Smothers Brothers Comedy Hour, 1988, Poison, 1988, and numerous others; TV host Women of the Night II, 1988, Second City Fifteen Anniversary Special, 1988, Andrea Martin: Together Again, 1989; actress/writer: TV series SCTV Network 90, 1981-83 (2 Emmy awards 1982, 83), TV pilot From Cleveland, 1980; also The Completely Mental Misadventures of Ed Grimley, 1988-90 (voice of Mrs. Freebus). Office: care William Morris Agy 1325 Avenue Of The Americas New York NY 10019-4702*

MARTIN, ANDREW AYERS, lawyer, educator; b. Toccoa, Ga., Aug. 18, 1958; s. Wallace Ford and Dorothy LaTranquil (Ayers) M. BA, Emory U., Atlanta, 1980, MD, 1984; JD, Duke U., 1988. Bar: Calif. 1989, La. 1990, D.C. 1991; diplomate Am. Bd. Pathology, Nat. Bd. Med. Examiners; lic. physician, La. Intern in pediatrics Emory U./Grady Meml. Hosp., Atlanta, 1984; intern Tulane U./Charity Hosp., New Orleans, 1989-90, resident in anatomic and clin. pathology, 1990-94; law clk. Ogletree, Deakins, Smoak, Stewart, Greenville, S.C., summer 1986, Thelen Marrin Johnson Bridges, L.A., summer 1987, Duke Hosp. Risk Mgmt., 1987-88; assoc. Haight Brown Bonesteel, Santa Monica, Calif., 1988; pvt. practice L.A., 1989; physician/atty. Tulane Med. Ctr./Charity Hosp., New Orleans, 1989-94, Baylor Coll. Medicine/Tex. Med. Ctr., Houston, 1994-95; lab. dir., sr. ptnr. King's Daus. Hosp., Greenville, Miss., 1995—; bd. dirs. Martin Bldrs., Inc., Toccoa; mem. AIDS Legis. Task Force for La.; case cons. Office of tech. Assessment, Washington; tech. cons. and autopsy extra Oliver Stone's "JFK". Contbr. articles to profl. jours.; author: Reflections on Rusted Chrome (book of poetry). Fellow Coll. Am. Pathologists, Coll. Legal Medicine, La. State Med. Soc. (del. meeting 1992-93). Home: 8300 El Mundo #612 Houston TX 77054 Office: Kings Daughters Hosp PO Box 1857 Greenville MS 38702-1857

MARTIN, ANN MATTHEWS, writer, juvenile; b. Princeton, N.J., Aug. 12, 1955; d. Henry R. and Edith Aiken (Matthews) M. BA cum laude, Smith Coll., 1977. Elem. sch. tchr. Plumfield Sch., Noroton, Conn., 1977-78; editorial asst. Simon & Schuster, N.Y.C., 1978-80; copywriter Teenage Book Club, Scholastic Books, Inc., N.Y.C., 1980-81; assoc. editor Scholastic Books, Inc., N.Y.C., 1981-83, editor, 1983; sr. editor Bantam Books, N.Y.C., 1983-85; free lance writer, editor N.Y.C., 1985—. Author: (novels) Bummer Summer, 1983, Just You and Me, 1983, Inside Out, 1984, Stage Fright, 1984, Me and Katie (the Pest), 1985, With You and Without You, 1986, Missing Since Monday, 1986, Just a Summer Romance, 1987, Slam Book, 1987, Yours Turly, Shirley, 1988, Ten Kids, No Pets, 1988, Fancy Dance in Feather Town, 1988, Ma and Pa Dracula, 1989, Moving Day in Feather Town, 1989, Eleven Kids, One Summer, 1991, Rachel Parker, Kindergarten Show-Off, 1992, (novels in series) The Baby-sitters Club, Baby-sitters Little Sister, Baby-sitters Club Mysteries, The Kids in Ms. Colman's Class. Mem. PEN, Authors Guild, Soc. Children's Book Writers and Illustrators. Democrat. Avocations: sewing, needlework. Office: c/o Scholastic Inc 555 Broadway New York NY 10012-3919

MARTIN, ARTHUR MEAD, lawyer; b. Cleveland Heights, Ohio, Mar. 29, 1942; s. Bernard P. and Winifred (Mead) M. AB, Princeton U., 1963; LLB, Harvard U., 1966. Bar: Ill. 1966, U.S. Dist. Ct. (no. dist.) Ill. 1969, U.S. Ct. Appeals (7th cir.) 1970, U.S. Supreme Ct. 1980. Instr. law U. Wis., Madison, 1966-68; assoc. Jenner & Block, Chgo., 1968-74, ptnr., 1975—; co-trustee Dille Family Trust, 1982—; bd. dirs. Sleepeck Printing Co. Author: Historical and Practice Notes to the Illinois Civil Practice Act and Illinois Supreme Court Rules, 1968-88. Trustee 4th Presbyn. Ch., Chgo. Mem. ABA, Am. Law Inst., Ill. Bar Assn., Chgo. Bar Assn. (bd. editors 1972-86), Am. Arbitration Assn. (panel), Lake Mich. Fedn. (bd. dirs. 1993—, exec. com. 1994—), Law CLub Chgo., Legal Club Chgo. Office: Jenner & Block 1 E Ibm Plz Chicago IL 60611

MARTIN, BARBARA ANN, secondary education educator; b. Lexington, Ky., Apr. 11, 1946; d. Robert Newton and Juanita June (Karrick) M. AA, Beckley Coll., 1966; BS in Edn., Concord Coll., 1969; MA, Western Ky. U., 1974, rank I, 1982. Standard teaching cert., adminstrn., secondary edn., Ky. Tchr. Daviess County Mid. Sch., Owensboro, Ky., 1969—; inservice speaker Daviess County Schs., Owensboro, 1969—; acad. writer Ky. Acad. Assn., Frankfort, 1992—. Author: Social Studies for Gifted Student, 1977; contbr.: (game) National Geographic Global Pursuit, 1988. Ky. rep. tchr. adv. coun. Nat. Rep. Party, Washington, 1993—; exec. com. Daviess County Rep. Party, 1987—. Named Outstanding Young Woman, 1978, Outstanding Social Studies Tchr., Ky. Coun. for Social Studies, 1978; recipient Outstanding Comty. Svc. award Owensboro (Ky.) City Commn. and Mayor, 1982. Mem. NEA (del., mid-atlantic coord. women's caucus 1969—), Ky. Edn. Assn. (del., legis. com. 1969—), 2d Dist. Assn. (del., pres. 1969—), Daviess County Edn. Assn. (del., pres. 1969—). Presbyterian. Avocations: writing, photography, gardening, family history, Ky. Wildcat basketball. Home: 4325 Fischer Rd Owensboro KY 42301-8109 Office: Daviess County Mid Sch 1415 E 4th St Owensboro KY 42303-0134

MARTIN, BARBARA JEAN, elementary education educator; b. St. Louis, May 20, 1949; d. Robert Clarke and Ruth Eloise (Baseler) M. BS in Elem. Edn., N.E. Mo. State U., 1971; MA in Elem. Edn., Maryville U., 1991. Classroom instr. Hazelwood (Mo.) Sch. Dist., 1971—; mem. curriculum revision com., Hazelwood Sch. Dist., 1974-94, profl. devel. Com., 1992-94, steering com. 1993-94; advisor/cons. Hazelwood Sch. Dist. Early Childhood Parents and Staff, 1985—. Mem. chmn. PTA, Russell Sch., 1989—; tchr., musician Bermuda Bible Hall Ch., St. Louis, 1965—; asst. dir., sec., musician, tchr. Hickory Cove Bible Camp, Hickory, N.C., 1975—. Recipient Disting. Vol. award Christian Camping Internat., 1986; recipient Robert D. Elsea scholarship St. Louis Cooperating Sch. Dist., St. Louis County, 1989. Mem. Assn. for Edn. of Young Children (pres. seminar 1994), Christian Educators Assn., Sigma Alpha Iota (pres. 1978-81, v.p. 1976-78, scholarship chmn. 1981—, Sword of Honor 1981, Rose of Honor 1996). Avocations: music, sewing, ch. youth activities. Home: 18 Buckeye Dr Ferguson MO 63135-1515 Office: Russell Sch 7350 Howdershell Rd Hazelwood MO 63042-1306

MARTIN, BENJAMIN GAUFMAN, ophthalmologist; b. Louisville, Aug. 18, 1937; s. Benjamin and Catherine L. Martin; m. Caroline Sue Martin, May 25, 1975; children: Benjamin, Lori, Tamara, Farrell, Steven, David. BME, U. Louisville, 1954, M. Engring., 1973; MD, U. So. Calif., 1964. Design engr. Philco/Ford, Palo Alto, Calif., 1957-60; rsch. engr. N.Am./Rockwell, Inglewood, Calif., 1961-63; intern Wright-Patterson Med. Ctr., Dayton, Ohio, 1964-65; ophthalmology resident Wilford Hall Med. Ctr., San Antonio, 1968-71; commd. USAF, 1963, advanced through grades to col., ret., 1980; CEO Cape Coral (Fla.) Eye Ctr., 1980—. With USN, 1954-57. Decorated Legion of Merit, DFC, Bronze Star, Air medal. Mem. Daedalions, Masons, Shriner. Republican. Lutheran. Office: Cape Coral Eye Ctr 4120 Del Prado Blvd S Cape Coral FL 33904-7165

MARTIN, BERNARD LEE, former college dean; b. Dayton, Ohio, May 29, 1923; s. Harley L. and Clare (Murphy) M.; m. Mary Patricia McDonald, Nov. 23, 1950; children: Joseph, Mary, David, Patrick, Paul, Timothy, Michael, Christopher. B.A., Athenaeum of Ohio, 1941-45; M.A. in History, Xavier U., 1950, M.B.A., 1955; Ph.D. in Econs, U. Cin., 1963; Ph.D. honoris causa, Canisius Coll., 1978. Mem. faculty Xavier U., Cin., 1948-65; asst. prof. bus. adminstrn. Xavier U., 1955-62, assoc. prof. mktg., 1962-65, chmn. mktg. dept., 1961; chmn., prof. mktg. Eastern Mich. U., Ypsilanti, 1965-66; dean Sch. Bus. Adminstrn. Canisius Coll., Buffalo, 1966-71, 1973-78, acting acad. v.p. of coll., 1971-73; dean McLaren Coll. Bus. Adminstrn., U. San Francisco, 1978-86, prof. mktg., 1986-91; prof. emeritus U. San Francisco, 1992. Author: (with others) Contemporary Economic Problems and Issues, 3d edit, 1973. Ford Found. grantee Harvard, 1964. Mem. Am. Mktg. Assn., Am. Econ. Assn. Home: 1062 Cherry Ave San Jose CA 95125

MARTIN, BERNARD MURRAY, painter, educator; b. Ferrum, Va., June 21, 1935. Student, Wake Forest Coll.; BFA, Richmond Profl. Inst.; MA, Hunter Coll. Assoc. prof. painting Winston-Salem (Mass.) Univ., 1961—; represented by Gallery K, Washington. One-man shows include Gallery K, Washington, 1978, 80, Gallery Contemporary Art, Winston-Salem, Mass., 1972; exhibited in Am. Fedn. Arts Traveling Exhibit, 1968, Va. Mus. Fine Art, 1970, Corcoran Gallery, Washington, 1971; represented in permanent collections Va. Mus. Fine Arts, Walter Rawls Mus., Chrysler Mus., Nat. Collection, First & Merchants Nat. Bank. Recipient Certificate of Distinction, Va. Mus. Fine Arts, 1964, 66, 68, 70; first prize Gallery Contemporary Art, 1970, 71. Address: 1015 Francisco Rd Richmond VA 23229*

MARTIN, BETTY CAROLYN, library director; b. Louisville, Nov. 2, 1933; d. Earl Francis and Marie Dorothy (Baertich) Snyder; m. Charles Frank Martin, Aug. 18, 1956. BS, Ind. U., 1956, MLS, 1982. Sch. libr. Decatur Twp. Schs., Indpls., 1955-57; tchr. Indpls. Schs., 1957-58; libr., libr. dir. Vigo County Pub. Libr., Terre Haute, Ind., 1958—; exec. bd. Ind. State Libr. Adv. Coun., Indpls., 1989-94. Contbr. articles to profl. jours. Bd. dirs. State Student Assistance Commn., Indpls., 1991—, United Way Wabash County, Terre Haute, 1989-95, Alliance for Growth and Progress, sec., 1989; bd. dirs. LWC, pres., 1980; bd. dirs. Pres. Adv. Bd. St. Mary of Woods Coll., Salvation Army, pres., 1990-92; sec. bd. dirs. Work Force Devel. Commn. Western Ind., Terre Haute, 1990—. Recipient Louise Maxwell award SLIS-IU Alumni Assn., Bloomington, Ind., 1991; named Outstanding Woman of COmmunity, Bus. & Profl. Womens Club, Terre Haute, 1990. Mem. ALA, Ind. Libr. Fedn. (bd. dirs., pres. 1989-90, Assn. Leadership award 1990), Ind. U. Libr. Sch. Alumni (pres. 1992-94), C.of C. (Terre award 1989). Democrat. Roman Catholic. Avocations: reading, travel, gardening. Home: 5351 N 13th St Terre Haute IN 47805-1613 Office: Vigo County Public Lib 1 Library Sq Terre Haute IN 47807-3609

MARTIN, BETTY J., speech, language pathologist; b. East St. Louis, Ill., Nov. 2, 1950; d. Nathaniel and Minnie Mae (Long) Gause; m. Leander Martin, Jr.; children: Leander III, Lavell, Kenneth. BS, So. Ill. Univ., 1978, MS, 1980. Cert. speech-lang. pathologist.. Bd. sec. State C.C., East St. Louis, 1970-75; speech-lang. pathologist East. St. Louis Sch. Dist. 189, 1980—. site coord. Educom, St. Peter's, Mo., 1993. Tutor Project Love, East St. Louis, 1990; tchr. Vacation Bible Sch., East St. Louis, 1994, 95; sec. Steward BBd. #2, East St. Louis, 1994. Mem. Am. Speech Hearing Lang. Assn. (cert.), Ill. Speech Hearing Assn., So. Ill. Speech Hearing Assn. Methodist. Home: 520 Green Haven Dr Belleville IL 62221 Office: Miles Davis Elem Sch East Saint Louis IL 62201

MARTIN, BILL, artist, art educator; b. South San Francisco, Calif., Jan. 22, 1943; s. Gordon and Zelia (Sonderman) M.; m. Shelley Persistence Balaban, Feb. 22, 1975. B.F.A., San Francisco Art Inst., 1968, M.F.A., 1970. instr. Acad. Art, San Francisco, 1970-71, U. Calif., Berkeley, 1972, San Francisco Art Inst., 1972, Calif. State U., San Jose, 1973, Coll. Marin, Kentfield, Calif., 1975-78, Coll. of the Redwoods, Mendocino, Calif., 1983—. One-man shows, San Francisco Mus. Art, 1973, Nancy Hoffman Gallery, N.Y.C., 1977, 79, 82, Zara Gallery, San Francisco, 1978, 80, Joseph Chowning Gallery, 1983, 85, 87, 89, 92, 94, U. Nev., 1988, Clatsop Coll., Oreg., 1989, Joseph Chwoning Gallery, San Francisco, 1989, Chabot Coll., Hayward, Calif., 1990, Kabutoya Gallery, Tokyo, 1991; Joseph Chowning Gallery, San Francisco, 1992, Atrium Galley, San Francisco, 1992; group shows include, San Francisco Art Inst., 1966, 68, 70, 71, Unicorn Gallery, San Francisco, 1969, Sun Gallery, San Francisco, 1969, Richmond (Calif.) Art Center, 1970, Pioneer Mus., Stockton, Calif., 1970, U. So. Calif., Los Angeles, 1971, Whitney Mus. Am. Art, N.Y.C., 1972-73, U. Pa., 1972, Calif. State U., San Jose, 1973, Nancy Hoffman Gallery, N.Y.C., 1974, State U. Albany, 1974, Milw. Arts Center, 1974, Chgo. Art Inst., 1974, Mus. Modern Art, Paris, 1975, Tri-Ann. Invitational of India, 1978, European traveling exhbn. organized by New Mus., N.Y.C., 1979-81, Zara Gallery, 1979, 80, Western Assn. Arts Mus., 1980-81, Joseph Chowning Gallery, 1983, 85, 87, Mendocino (Calif.) Art Gallery, 1987, Cheney Cowles Mus., Spokane, Wash., 1988, Humbolt State Univ., 1988, Muscarelle Mus. Art Coll. William & Mary Coll., 1988, Salt Lake City, 1988, Mus. of Rockies, Bozeman, Mont., 1988, Lancaster (Calif.) Mus., 1988, Humboldt State U., Arcata, Calif. 1988, City Coll. San Francisco, 1988, Medocino (Calif.) Art Ctr., 1989, So. Utah State U., 1989, Springfield (Mo.) Art Mus., 1989, From the Studio: Recent Painting and Sculpture by 20 California Artists, Oakland (Calif.) Mus., 1992; painting and sculptures represented in permanent collections, Neue Gallerie der Stadt Acchen, Germany, AT&T, San Francisco Internat. Airport, Oakland Mus., Calif., Owens Corning, Vesti Corp., Boston, Varney Collection, San Francisco, Ohio, Capital Group Inc., Los Angeles, McDermott, Will & Emery, N.Y.C., Clayton E. Michael CPA., San Fancisco, Police Data Systems, Dublin, Calif., John F. Kennedy U., Orinda, Calif., Madison (Wis.) Art Ctr.; author: Visions, Bill Martin Paintings 1969-1979, Composition In Painting Drawing, Joy of Drawing, Lost Legends, 1995, (videotape series) Principles of Painting. Home: PO Box 511 Albion CA 95410-0511

MARTIN, BOE WILLIS, lawyer; b. Texarkana, Ark., Oct. 6, 1940; s. E. H. and Dorothy Annette (Willis) M.; m. Carol J. Edwards, June 12, 1965; children—Stephanie Diane, Scott Andrew. B.A., Tex. A&M U., 1962; LL.B., U. Tex., 1964; LL.M., George Washington U., 1970. Bar: Tex. 1964. Law clk. Tex. Supreme Ct. 1966-67; assoc. Snakard, Brown & Gambill, Fort Worth, 1967-69; asst. counsel U.S. Senate Labor and Pub. Welfare Com., 1969; legis. asst. U.S. Senator Ralph W. Yarborough, 1969-71; assoc., ptnr. Snakard, Brown & Gambill, Fort Worth, 1971-72; assoc., ptnr. Stalcup & Johnson, Dallas, 1972-77; assoc., ptnr. Coke & Coke, Dallas, 1977-80; ptnr., shareholder Johnson & Gibbs, Dallas, 1981-95, Hutcheson & Grundy, LLP, 1995—; vis. prof. law So. Meth. U. Sch. Law, 1972, 73, 75, 88, 89, U. Tex. Sch. Law, 1977, 79. Mem. Carter-Mondale Campaign staff, 1976, 1980; cons. to Vice-Pres. of U.S., 1977-80; cons. Mondale for Pres. Campaign, 1983-84, Dukakis for Pres. campaign, 1988, State of Minn., for visit of Pres. Mikhail Gorbachev, 1990. Served to capt. U.S. Army, 1964-69. Mem. ABA, Tex. Bar Assn., Dallas Bar Assn. Democrat. Methodist. Contbr. articles to legal jours. Home: 4435 Arcady Ave Dallas TX 75205-3604 Office: Hutcheson & Grundy 901 Main St Ste 6200 Dallas TX 75202

MARTIN, BOYCE FICKLEN, JR., federal judge; b. Boston, Oct. 23, 1935; s. Boyce Ficklen and Helen Artt M.; m. Mavin Hamilton Brown, July 8, 1961; children: Mary V. H., Julia H.C., Boyce Ficklen III, Robert C. G. II. AB, Davidson Coll., 1957; JD, U. Va., 1963. Bar: Ky. 1963. Law clk. to Shackelford Miller, Jr., chief judge U.S. Ct. Appeals for 6th Circuit, Cin., 1963-64; asst. U.S. atty. Western Dist. Ky., Louisville, 1964; U.S. atty. Western Dist. Ky., 1965; pvt. practice law Louisville, 1966-74; judge Jefferson Circuit Ct., Louisville, 1974-76; chief judge Ct. Appeals Ky., Louisville, 1976-79; judge U.S. Ct. Appeals (6th cir.), Cin. and Louisville, 1979—. Mem. vestry St. Francis in the Fields Episcopal Ch., Harrods Creek, Ky., 1979-83; bd. visitors Davidson (N.C.) Coll., 1980-86, trustee, 1994—; trustee Isaac W. Bernheim Found., Louisville, 1981—, chmn., 1982-95; trustee Blackacre Found., Inc., Louisville, 1983-94, chmn., 1986-94; trustee Hanover (Ind.) Coll., 1983—, vice chmn., 1992—; mem. exec. bd. Old Ky. Home coun. Boy Scouts of Am., 1968-72; pres. Louisville Zool. Commn., 1971-74. Capt. JAGC U.S. Army, 1958-66. Fellow Am. Bar Found.; mem. Inst. Jud. Adminstrn., Am. Judicature Soc., Fed Bar Assn., ABA (com. effective appellate advocacy Conf. Appellate Judges), Ky. Bar Assn., Louisville Bar Assn. Office: US Ct Appeals 209 US Courthouse 601 W Broadway Louisville KY 40202-2227

MARTIN, BOYD ARCHER, political science educator emeritus; b. Cottonwood, Idaho, Mar. 3, 1911; s. Archer Olmstead and Norah Claudine (Imbler) M.; m. Grace Charlotte Swingler, Dec. 29, 1933; children: Michael Archer, William Archer. Student, U. Idaho, 1929-30, 35-36, B.S., 1936; student, Pasadena Jr. Coll., 1931-32, U. Calif. at Los Angeles, summer 1934; A.M., Stanford, 1937, Ph.D., 1943. Rsch. asst. Stanford U., 1936-37, teaching asst., 1937-38; instr. polit. sci. U. Idaho, 1938-39; acting instr. polit. sci. Stanford U., 1939-40; John M. Switzer fellow, summer 1939-40; chief personnel officer Walter Butler Constrn. Co., Farragut Naval Tng. Center, summer 1942; instr. polit. sci. U. Idaho, 1940-43, asst. prof. polit. sci., 1943-44, asso. prof. polit. sci., 1944-47; prof., head dept. social sci., asst. dean coll. letters and sci. U. Idaho, 1947-55, dean, 1955-70, Borah Distinguished prof. polit. sci., 1970-73, prof., dean emeritus, 1973—; vis. prof. Stanford U., summer 1946, spring 1952, U. Calif., 1962-63; affiliate Center for Study Higher Edn., Berkeley, 1962-63; mem. steering com. N.W. Conf. on Higher Edn., 1960-67, pres. conf., 1966-67; mem. bd. Am. Assn. of Partners of Alliance for Progress; chmn. Idaho Adv. Coun. on Higher Edn.; del. Gt. Plains UNESCO Conf., Denver, 1947; chmn. bd. William E. Borah Found. on Causes of War and Conditions of Peace, 1947-55; mem. Commn. to Study Orgn. Peace; dir. Bur. Pub. Affair Rsch., 1959-73, dir. emeritus, 1973—; dir. Martin Peace Inst., 1970—. Author: The Direct Primary in Idaho, 1947, (with others) Introduction to Political Science, 1950, (with other) Western Politics, 1968, Politics in the American West, 1969, (with Sydney Duncombe) Recent Elections in Idaho (1964-70), 1972, Idaho Voting Trends: Party Realignment and Percentage of Voters for Candidates, Parties and Elections, 1890-1974, 1975, In Search of Peace: Starting From October 19, 1980, 1980, Why the Democrats Lost in 1980, 1980, On Understanding the Soviet Union, 1987; editor: The Responsibilities of Colleges and Universities, 1967; contbr. to: Ency. Britannica, 1990, 91; also articles. Mem. Am. Polit. Sci. Assn. (exec. council 1952-53), Nat. Municipal League, Am. Soc. Pub. Adminstrn., Fgn. Policy Assn., UN Assn., AAUP, Western Polit. Sci. Assn. (pres. 1950), Phi Beta Kappa, Pi Gamma Mu, Kappa Delta Pi, Pi Sigma Alpha. Home: 516 N Eisenhower St Moscow ID 83843-9596 *Attempt to contribute to society to the maximum of your ability. Assume responsibility in positions commensurate with the obligations and accountability of the position. In making decisions, first gather all factual data, interpret it fairly, make the decision, and assume responsibility for the decision. In dealing with people, whether family, friends, professionals, or adversaries, try to remember the sensitivity of personal feelings and personal pride. Commend people who achieve and contribute. Be completely honest; when you don't know, admit it.*

MARTIN, BRUCE DOUGLAS, university official, chemist; b. Rochester, N.Y., Apr. 8, 1934; s. Frederic and Harriet Emily (Krieger) M.; m. Geraldine Ann Coughlin, July 6, 1957 (div. 1980); children: James Scott, Robert Douglas; m. Marilyn Frances Harris, Aug. 15, 1984. B.S. in Pharmacy, Albany Coll. Pharmacy, 1955; M.S. in Pharm. Chemistry, U. Ill., 1959, Ph.D., 1962. Asst. prof. Sch. Pharmacy, Duquesne U., 1961-64, asso. prof., 1964-68, prof., chmn. dept. pharm. chemistry, 1968-71, dean, 1971-81, acting dean health professions, 1979-80, acting v.p. acad. affairs, 1981-82, assoc. v.p. acad. affairs, 1982—; acting dean Grad. Sch., Duquesne U., 1984-86; state dir. Pa. Sci. Talent Search, 1989-96. Fulbright lectr. U. Sci. and Tech. Kumasi, Ghana, 1968-69. Mem. Pa. Pharm. Assn., Allegheny County Pharm. Assn. (exec. bd. 1970—), Am. Pharm. Assn., Am. Chem. Soc., Pa. Acad. Sci. (pres. 1980-82), Inst. for German-Am. Rels. (founder, chmn. bd. dirs. 1990—), AAUP, Sigma Xi, Kappa Psi, Rho Chi, Sigma Pi Sigma, Alpha Epsilon Delta, Phi Delta Chi, Omicron Delta Kappa, Phi Lambda Sigma, Phi Kappa Phi. Home: 5340 Pocussett St Pittsburgh PA 15217-1909 Office: Duquesne U 502 Adminstrn Bldg Pittsburgh PA 15282

MARTIN, BRUCE JAMES, newspaper editor; b. Pontiac, Mich., Sept. 2, 1956; s. James Patrick and Patricia Ann (Taylor) M.; m. Elizabeth Hartley Nutting, July 30, 1988. BJ, U. Mo., 1982. Reporter Spinal Col. Newsweekly, Union Lake, Mich., 1982; sports editor Northville (Mich.) Record/Novi News, 1982-85; news editor Novi News, Northville, 1984-85; copy editor Kalamazoo Gazette, 1985-89; copy editor Ann Arbor (Mich.) News, 1989-91, homes editor, 1991, arts and entertainment editor, 1991—. Recipient 1st Place in Sports Writing in Circulation Category, Mich. Press Assn., 1993. Avocations: songwriting, playing piano and guitar. Office: Ann Arbor News 340 E Huron St Ann Arbor MI 48104-1909

MARTIN, BRYAN LESLIE, allergist, immunologist; b. Macomb, Ill., June 25, 1954; s. George Albert and Vernal Louise (Stutsman) M.; m. Deborah Ann Schettig, June 22, 1979; children: Emily, Stephanie, Scott. BA, St. Vincent Coll., 1976; postgrad., Ohio U., 1976-79; DO, U. Osteo. Medicine/Hlth. Scis., 1984; M of Mil. Art and Sci., Command & Staff Officer Coll., 1994. Diplomate Am. Bd. Internal Medicine, Am. Bd. Allergy and Immunology, Nat. Bd. Osteo. Med. Examiners. Commd. 2d lt. U.S. Army, 1980, advanced through grades to maj., 1990—, comdr. med. troop 3d armored cavalry regiment, 1990-91; resident in internal medicine William Beaumont Army Med. Ctr., 1987-90, chief med. resident, 1990-91; with U.S. Army Command and Gen. Staff Coll., 1993-94. Student body pres. U. Osteopathic Medicine and Health Scis., Des Moines, 1981-82. Allergy/immunology fellow Fitzsimons Army Med. Ctr., Aurora, Colo., 1991-93; Health Professions scholar U.S. Army, 1980-84; decorated Bronze star. Fellow Am. Coll. Allergy, Asthma and Immunology (fellow-in-tng. rep. to bd. regents 1991-93, chmn. fellow-in-tng. sect. 1992-93); mem. ACP, AMA (del. resident physicians sect. 1991-93, young physicians sect. 1993—), Am. Acad. Allergy and Immunology, Am. Osteo. Assn. (del. 1981-83), Dustoff Assn., Nat. Med. Vets. Soc., Sigma Sigma Phi. Avocations: mountain biking, photography, model railroading, computers. Office: Chief Allergy/Immunology Ireland Army Cmty Hosp Fort Knox KY 40121-5520

MARTIN, BURCHARD V., lawyer; b. Millville, N.J., May 9, 1933; s. William J. and Helen (Mullane) M.; m. Elizabeth Del Rossi, June 11, 1955; children: Doris, Burchard S., William J., Thomas O. BS in Econs., Villanova (Pa.) U., 1954, LLB, 1958. Bar: N.J. 1960, U.S. Dist. Ct. N.J. 1960, U.S. Ct. Appeals (3d cir.), U.S. Supreme Ct. 1976. Assoc. Carroll, Taylor & Bischoff, Camden, N.J., 1960-63; ptnr. Taylor, Bischoff, Neutze & Williams, Camden, 1963-70, Taylor, Bischoff, Williams & Martin, Camden, 1970-72, Martin, Crawshaw & Mayfield, Haddonfield-Westmont, N.J., 1972-91, Martin, Gunn & Martin, Westmont, 1991—. Bd. cons. Villanova Law Sch., 1983—. Recipient Trial Bar award, Trial Attys. of N.J., 1987. Fellow Am. Coll. Trial Lawyers (state chmn. 1982-83); mem. ABA, N.J. Bar Assn., Camden County Bar Assn. (bd. dirs., Peter J. Devine award 1981). Avocation: golf. Office: Martin Gunn & Martin PA 216 Haddon Ave Apt 420 Collingswood NJ 08108-2812

MARTIN, C. D., lawyer; b. Seminole, Okla., Mar. 24, 1943. BS, U. North Tex., 1964; LLB, U. Tex., 1967. Bar: Tex. 1967, N.Mex. 1967, U.S. Dist. Ct. N.Mex., U.S. Dist. Ct. (we. and no. dists.) Tex. Mem., mng. ptnr. Hinkle, Cox, Eaton, Coffield & Hensley, P.L.L.C., Midland, Tex. Mem. Midland Planning and Zoning Commn., 1979-82, chmn., 1982; mem. adv. coun. Sch. Arts & Scis., U. Tex. at Permian Basin; bd. trustees Permian Basin Petroleum Mus.; past dir. U. Tex. Law Sch. Found. Fellow Tex. Bar Found. (life), N.Mex. Bar Found.; mem. ABA, State Bar Tex., State Bar N.Mex., Midland County Bar Assn. (pres. 1984-85), Phi Delta Phi. Office: Hinkle Cox Eaton Coffield & Hens PLLC PO Box 3580 Midland TX 79702

MARTIN, CAROL JACQUELYN, educator, artist; b. Ft. Worth, Tex., Oct. 6, 1943; d. John Warren and Dorothy Lorene (Coffman) Edwards; m. Boe Willis Martin, Oct. 6, 1940; children: Stephanie Diane, Scott Andrew. BA summa cum laude, U. N. Tex., 1965; MA, U. Tex., El Paso, 1967. Tchr. Edgemere Elem. Sch., El Paso, Tex., 1965-66, Fulmore Jr. H.S., Austin, 1966-67, Monnig Jr. H.S., Ft. Worth, 1967-68, Paschal H.S., Ft. Worth, 1968-69; instr. Tarrant County Jr. Coll., Ft. Worth, 1968-69, 71-72; press sec. U.S. Sen. Gaylord Nelson, Washington, 1969-71; instr. Eastfield C.C., Dallas, 1981, Richland C.C. Dist., 1982. Editor The Avesta Mag., 1964-65; exhibited in group shows at City of Richardson's Cottonwood Park, 1970-86, Students of Ann Cushing Gantz, 1973-85, Art About Town, 1979,

80, shows by Tarrant County and Dallas County art assns. Active Dallas Symphony Orch. League, Easter Seal Soc., Dallas Hist. Soc., Women's Bd. of the Dallas Opera, Dallas Arboretum and Garden Club, Dallas County Heritage Soc. Mem. Internat. Platform Assn., Mortar Bd., Alpha Chi, Sigma Tau Delta, Kappa Delta Pi, Delta Gamma. Democrat. Methodist. Avocations: travel, photography, snow skiing, oil painting. Address: 4435 Arcady Ave Dallas TX 75205-3604

MARTIN, CATHERINE ELIZABETH, anthropology educator; b. N.Y.C., Feb. 14, 1943; d. Walter Charles and Ruth (Crucet) Strodt; children: Kai Stuart, Armin Wade. BA, Reed Coll., 1965; MA, UCLA, 1967, PhD, 1971. Cert. C.C. tchr., Calif. From asst. to full prof. anthropology Calif. State U., L.A., 1970—, coord. women's studies, 1979-88, acting dir. acad. advisement, 1992-93, dir. Can. studies, 1991, advisement coord., 1996—. Contbr. chpts. to books and poetry to profl. publs. Cubmaster, den mother Boy Scouts Am., L.A. and Pasadena, 1982-85; leader Tiger Cubs, Boy Scouts Am., 1983. Recipient Outstanding Tiger Cub Leader award Boy Scouts Am., L.A., 1983, Cub Scout Growth award Boy Scouts Am., L.A., 1984. Mem. Am. Anthropol. Assn., Southwestern Anthropol. Assn., Soc. Applied Anthropology. Avocations: reading, traveling, new experiences. Office: Calif State U LA Dept Anthropology 5151 State University Dr Los Angeles CA 90032

MARTIN, CHARLES NEIL, JR., health care management company executive; b. Florence, Ala., Dec. 11, 1942; s. Charles Neil Sr. and Hazel Lucy (Hawkins) M. BS, So. Coll., Chattanooga, 1964. Adminstr. El Reposo Nursing Home, Florence, 1964-66, Parkwood Convalescent Ctr., Chattanooga, 1966-67; project dir. Tenn. Hosp. Assn., Nashville, 1967-68, asst. dir., 1968-69; v.p. Gen. Care Corp., Nashville, 1969-76, exec. v.p., 1976-79, pres., chief operating officer, 1979-80; sr. v.p. HCA, Nashville, 1980-85, exec. v.p., 1985-87, also bd. dirs.; pres., chief operating officer HealthTrust, Inc. - The Hosp. Co., Nashville, 1987—; bd. dirs. Equicor, Nashville, 1986—. Bd. dirs. Cystic Fibrosis Found., Nashville, 1987. Office: Ornda Healthcorp 3401 W End Ave Ste 700 Nashville TN 37203-1070*

MARTIN, CHARLES WALLACE, travel executive, retired university administrator; b. Columbia, S.C., Feb. 1, 1916; s. Earle Purkerson and Caroline Louise (Keenan) M.; m. Nancy Miles Chisolm, Sept. 30, 1944; children: Nancy Miles, Charles Wallace, Louise Elizabeth. B.A., U. S.C., 1936. Br. office employee N.Y. Life Ins. Co., Columbia, 1936-38; mgr. Palmetto Theatre Co., Columbia, 1938-42, Reamer Appliance Co., Columbia, 1946-47; local sales mgr. WIS Radio, Columbia, 1947-50; pres., gen. mgr. WMSC Radio, Columbia, 1950-60; dir. devel. U. S.C., Columbia, 1960-66; exec. dir. ednl. found. U. S.C., 1960-77, v.p. for devel., 1966-77, instr. English, 1948-52; chmn. Carolina V.I.P. Tours, 1977—; adv. bd. Bankers Trust S.C., Columbia, 1960-78. Chmn. United Way Columbia, 1954; pres. Columbia Philharm. Orch., 1967-68; commr. Columbia Housing Authority, 1971-76, chmn., 1974-76; bd. dirs. Bus. Ptnrs. Found., 1969-77, Providence Hosp. Found., 1977-82; trustee Columbia Mus. Arts and Sci., 1977-80, 88-94, life mem.; co-chmn. S.C. Gov.'s Mansion Found., 1979-83; vestryman Trinity Cathedral, Columbia; chmn. Trinity Found. Lt. USNR, 1942-45. Named Young Man of Year Columbia, 1951. Mem. Columbia Stage Soc. (dir. 1947-59, 66-69), Greater Columbia C. of C. (pres. 1959), S.C. Broadcasters Assn. (pres. 1954), Am. Coll. Pub. Relations Assn. (dir., treas. Mason-Dixon dist. 1967-72), English-Speaking Union U.S. (pres. Columbia br. 1973-75, nat. dir. 1972-75), Sigma Nu, Omicron Delta Kappa, Pi Gamma Mu. Episcopalian. Clubs: Kiwanian (pres. 1957), Forest Lake, Pine Tree Hunt (pres. 1985-86) Centurion Soc., Columbia Ball (pres. 1959), Forum (pres. 1989-90), Palmetto. Home: 1718 Madison Rd Columbia SC 29204

MARTIN, CHESTER Y., sculptor, painter; b. Chattanooga, Nov. 2, 1934; s. Woodfin Ballenger and Mabel Willett (Young) M.; m. Patricia Ann Parnell, Aug. 15, 1963; 1 child, Sharon Elizabeth (Mrs. Christopher Pruitt). Student, U. Chattanooga, 1952-55, 60-61, Internat. Medallic Workshop-Pa. State U., 1984. Freelance artist Chattanooga, 1967-86; sculptor, engraver U.S. Mint, Phila., 1986-92. One-man shows include Hunter Mus. Art, Chattanooga, 1979; group shows: Kottler Galleries, N.Y.C., 1966; Internat. Exposition Contemporary Medals, Italy, 1983, Sweden, 1985, Finland, 1990; U.S. Dept. State, 1984, Nat. Sculpture Soc., N.Y.C., 1984, 85, Cast Iron Gallery, N.Y.C., 1992, Internat. Exhbn. of Contemporary Medals, Brit. Mus., London, 1992, Hungarian Nat. Gallery, Budapest, 1994, Neuchatel, 1996, numerous others; permanent collections: British Mus., London; Smithsonian Instn.; Food and Agrl. Orgn., Rome; Am. Numismatic Soc., N.Y.C.; Julius Wile Sons and Co., N.Y.C.; Brookgreen Gardens, S.C., U.S. Mint, Phila.; major comms.: World Food Day Medal, UN, 1984, others; other major works: History of Chattanooga Mural, 1974; Centennial Mural for Chattem Inc., Chattanooga, 1980; sculptured Congl. Bicentennial Silver Dollar, 1989, Eisenhower Centennial Dollar reverse, Mt. Rushmore Dollar obverse, 1991; designer Andrew Wyeth Congl. medal, 1989, George Bush Presdl. medal reverse; designer Yosemite Nat. Park Centennial Congressional Medal, 1991, Gen. Colin L. Powell Congressional Medal, 1992, White House Bicentennial Dollar reverse, 1992. Served with USAF, 1956-60. Recipient numerous art awards, most recent being Purchase award Benedictine Art Competition, 1975, Medallic Sculpture award Am. Numismatic Assn., 1993. Mem. Fedn. Internationale de la Medaille (Am. del.), Am. Medallic Sculpture Assn. (v.p. 1987). Methodist. Avocations: modern languages. Mailing Address: 4110 Sunbury Ave Chattanooga TN 37411-5232

MARTIN, CHRYS ANNE, lawyer; b. Portland, Oreg., June 18, 1953; d. Richard Keith and Doris Glenna (Osborne) M.; m. Jack Pessia, Oct. 18, 1987. BA with honors, Oreg. State U., 1975; JD cum laude, Northwestern U., Portland, 1981. Bar: Oreg. 1981, U.S. Dist. Ct. (we. dist.) Oreg. 1981. Adminstrv. asst. City of Portland, 1975-76, Multnomah County Dist. Atty., Portland, 1976-80; assoc. Bullivant, Houser, Bailey, Pendergrass & Hoffman, Portland, 1981-86, shareholder, 1987—. Contbr. articles to profl. jours. Mem. ABA (chair com. on health ins. 1992-93, vice chair employee benefits com, sect. labor and employment law 1985—), Def. Rsch. Inst. (chair life, health and disability com. 1990-93, chair employment law com., 1995—, mem. law inst.), Oreg. State Bar (chair affirmative action com. 1988, chair civil rights sect. 1989), Inst. Managerial and Profl. Women (pres. 1983-85). Democrat. Avocations: snow and water skiing. Office: Bullivant Houser Bailey Pendergrass & Hoffman 300 Pioneer Tower 888 SW 5th Ave Portland OR 97204-2012

MARTIN, CLAUDE RAYMOND, JR., marketing consultant, educator; b. Harrisburg, Pa., May 11, 1932; s. Claude R. and Marie Teresa (Stapf) M.; m. Marie Frances Culkin, Nov. 16, 1957; children: Elizabeth Ann, David Jude, Nancy Marie, William Jude, Patrick Jude, Cecelia Marie. B.S., U. Scranton, 1954, M.B.A, 1963; Ph.D., Columbia U., 1969. Newsman Sta. WILK-TV, Wilkes-Barre, Pa., 1953-55; news dir. Sta. WNEP-TV, Scranton, Pa., 1955-60; dir. systems Blue Cross & Blue Shield Ins., Wilkes-Barre, 1960-63; lectr. mktg. St. Francis Coll., Bklyn., 1964, U. Mich., Ann Arbor, 1965-68; asst. prof. U. Mich., 1968-73, asso. prof., 1973-77, prof., 1977-80, Isadore and Leon Winkelman prof. retail mktg., 1980—, chmn. mktg. dept., 1986-90; bd. dirs. Perry Drug Stores, cons. mktg., 1983-89; spl. cons. on rsch. changes in U.S. currency Fed. Res. Sys., 1978—; pub. mem. Nat. Advt. Rev. Bd., 1989-94. Contbr. articles on mktg. analysis, consumer research to profl. publs. Trustee U. Scranton, 1996—. Served with USNR, 1955-57. Mem. Acad. Mktg. Sci., Am. Mktg. Assn., S.W. Mktg. Assn., Bank Mktg. Assn., Assn. Consumer Research, Am. Collegiate Retailing Assn., Am. Acad. Advt. Roman Catholic. Home: 1116 Aberdeen Dr Ann Arbor MI 48104-2812

MARTIN, CLYDE VERNE, psychiatrist; b. Coffeyville, Kans., Apr. 7, 1933; s. Howard Verne and Elfrieda Louise (Moehn) M.; m. Barbara Jean McNeilly, June 24, 1956; children: Kent Clyde, Kristin Claire, Kerry Constance, Kyle Curtis. Student Coffeyville Coll., 1951-52; AB, U. Kans., 1955; MD, 1958; MA, Webster Coll., St. Louis, 1977; JD, Thomas Jefferson Coll. Law, Los Angeles, 1985. Diplomate Am. Bd. Psychiatry and Neurology. Intern, Lewis Gale Hosp., Roanoke, Va., 1958-59; resident in psychiatry U. Kans. Med. Ctr., Kansas City, 1959-62, Fresno br. U. Calif.-San Francisco, 1978; staff psychiatrist Neurol. Hosp., Kansas City, 1962; practice medicine specializing in psychiatry, Kansas City, Mo., 1964-84; founder, med. dir., pres. bd. dirs. Mid-Continent Psychiat. Hosp., Olathe, Kans., 1972-84; adj. prof. psychology Baker U., Baldwin City, Kans., 1969-84; staff psychiatrist Atascadero State Hosp., Calif., 1984-85; clin. prof. psychiatry U. Calif., San Francisco, 1985—; chief psychiatrist Calif. Med. Facility, Vacaville, 1985-87; pres., editor Corrective and Social Psychiatry, Olathe, 1970-84, Atascadero, 1984-85, Fairfield, 1985—. Contbr. articles to profl. jours. Bd. dirs. Meth. Youthville, Newton, Kans. 1965-75, Spofford Home, Kansas City, 1974-78. Served to capt. USAF, 1962-64, ret. col. USAFR. Oxford Law & Soc. scholar, 1993. Fellow Am. Psychiat. Assn., Royal Soc. Health, Am. Assn. Mental Health Profls. in Corrections, World Assn. Social Psychiatry, Am. Orthopsychiat. Assn.; mem. AMA, Assn. for Advancement Psychotherapy, Am. Assn. Sex Educators, Counselors and Therapists (cert.), Assn. Mental Health Adminstrs. (cert.), Kansas City Club, Masons, Phi Beta Pi, Pi Kappa Alpha. Methodist (del. Kans. East Conf. 1972-80, bd. global ministries 1974-80). Office: PO Box 3365 Fairfield CA 94533-0587

MARTIN, CRAIG LEE, engineering company executive; b. Dodge City, Kans., Nov. 23, 1949; s. Ray N. and Nadia C. Martin; m. Diane E. Hensley, Mar. 19, 1977. BS in Civil Engring., U. Kans., 1971; MBA, U. Denver, 1982. Project mgr. Martin K. Eby Constrn. Co., Wichita, Kans., 1972-83; exec. v.p., COO CRSS Constructors, Inc., Denver, 1983-89; exec. v.p. CRSS Comml. Group, Houston, 1989-90; sr. v.p. CRSS Capital, Houston, 1990-92, CRSS Inc., Houston, 1992-94; pres. CRSS Architects, Inc., Houston, 1992-94; sr. v.p. ops. Jacobs Engring. Group Inc., 1994-95; pres. Jacobs Constructors, Inc., 1994-95; sr. v.p. gen. sales and mktg. Jacobs Engring. Group, Inc., 1995—; mem. adv. bd. Constrn. Bus. Rev., 1993—; bd. dirs. Meridian Engrs. Mem. ASCE, Am. Mgmt. Assn. Avocations: golf, clay shooting, fishing. Home: 930 S El Molino Pasadena CA 91106 Office: Jacobs Engring Group Inc 251 S Lake Ave Pasadena CA 91101

MARTIN, CURTIS, professional football player; b. Pitts., May 1, 1973. Student, U. Pitts. Running back New Eng. Patriots, Foxboro, Mass., 1995—. Selected to Pro Bowl, 1995.

MARTIN, D. JOE, accountant; b. Greenville, Ohio, May 19, 1947; s. Stanley E. and Mildred E. (Ford) M.; m. Kathleen Brosmer, Dec. 22, 1991. BS in Acctg., Capital U., 1969. CPA, Ohio. Staff acct. Peat Marwick & Mitchell & Co., Columbus, Ohio, 1969-71; audit supr. First Banc Group of Ohio, Columbus, 1971-74; asst. treas. First Trust Co. of Ohio, Columbus, 1974-76; v.p. fin. Buckeye Fin. Corp., Columbus, 1976-80; prin., ptnr., owner D. Joe Martin Co., CPAs, Columbus, 1979—; treas., dir. So. Fin. Holding Corp., West Palm Beach, Fla., 1984-85; vice chair, corp. sec., dir. Ravenna Savs. Bank, Columbus, 1987—; pres., CEO Sterling Fin. Holdings, Inc., West Palm Beach, fla., 1995—. Mem. AICPA, Ohio Soc. CPAs. Republican. Lutheran. Avocations: tennis, skiing. Home: 663 Overbrook Dr Columbus OH 43214-3130 Office: D Joe Martin Co CPAs 380 E Town St Columbus OH 43215-6700

MARTIN, DANIEL RICHARD, pharmaceutical company executive; b. Lima, Peru, June 9, 1937; s. James Marion and Clemmy Caroline (Valencia) M.; m. Barbara Artemis Cyrus, June 23, 1962; children: Daniel Richard Jr., John Alexander, Christopher Andrew. BA, Cornell U., 1958; MS, Columbia U., N.Y.C., 1959. Area sales supr. Schering Corp., Bloomfield, N.J., 1960-64; assoc. McKinsey & Co., N.Y.C., 1964-69; treas. Harper & Row, Pubs., N.Y.C., 1969-72; mng. dir. Merck & Co., Rahway, N.J., 1972-77; group v.p. Bell & Howell Co., Chgo., 1977-80; pres. Howland Martin Corp., N.Y.C., 1980-85; pres. Sterling Europe, Middle East, Africa Sterling Drug, Inc., N.Y.C., 1986-89; pres., CEO E-Z-EM, Inc., Westbury, N.Y., 1990—; adj. prof. mgmt. Pace U., N.Y.C., 1996—. Co-chmn. Accion Internat., Cambridge, Mass., 1988—; trustee Bangor (Maine) Theol. Sem., 1991—; dir. Americas Found.; bd. dirs., fin. com. White Plains (N.Y.) Hosp. Decorated Order of Merit (Ecuador). Mem. Coun. on Fgn. Rels., Americas Soc., Univ. Club (N.Y.C., Chgo.), Cornell Club (N.Y.C.). Republican. Congregationalist. Home: 2 Dolma Rd Scarsdale NY 10583-4506 Office: E-Z-EM Inc 717 Main St Westbury NY 11590-5021

MARTIN, DANIEL WILLIAM, acoustical physicist; b. Georgetown, Ky., Nov. 18, 1918; s. Dean William and Ethel (Weigle) M.; m. Martha Elizabeth Parker, June 9, 1941; children: Mary Elizabeth, David William, Nancy Jane, Donald Warren. A.B., Georgetown Coll., 1937, Sc.D., 1981; M.S., U. Ill., 1939, Ph.D., 1941. Asst. physics U. Ill. at Urbana, 1937-41; with RCA, 1941-49, tech. coordinator, 1946-49; acoustical research supr. Baldwin Piano Co., Cin., 1949-57; research dir. D.H. Baldwin Co., Cin., 1957-70, 74-83; chief engr. D.H. Baldwin Co., 1970-74; acoustical cons., 1983—; extension instr. math. Purdue U., 1941-46; asst. prof. mus. acoustics U. Cin., 1964-73, assoc. prof., 1973-75. Author; Editor: I.R.E. Trans. on Audio, 1953-55; assoc. editor: Sound, 1961-63; patent reviewer Jour. Acoustical Soc. Am, 1950—, assoc. editor, 1977-85, editor-in-chief, 1985—. Trustee Pikeville Coll., 1976-82; mem. theology and worship ministry unit Presbyn. Ch. (U.S.A.), 1987-93, vice-chair, 1987-89, 91-92, vice-chmn. Presbyn. Assn. for Sci., Tech. and Christian Faith, 1992—. Recipient Ohio Engr. of Yr. award Nat. Soc. Profl. Engrs., 1972. Fellow Acoustical Soc. Am. (exec. council 1957-60, pres.-elect 1983-84, pres. 1984-85), Audio Engring. Soc. (pres. 1964-65), IEEE (nat. chmn. audio group 1956-57); mem. Engring. Soc. Cin. (dir. 1964-67, pres. 1969-70), Tech. and Sci. Socs. Council Cin. (pres. 1967-68, Cin. Engr. Year 1972), Nat. Council Presbyn. Men (pres. 1977). Republican. Patentee in field. Home and Office: 7349 Clough Pike Cincinnati OH 45244-3745 *A Christian home, economic need, and early choice of profession gave me momentum. Generous personal assistance and teaching, professional opportunity and family stability sustained my efforts. The byproducts of striving for goals are just as valuable as the realization of goals. Building bridges between disciplines is difficult but intellectually stimulating. Great are the rewards of service to profession, people and the church.*

MARTIN, DAVID ALAN, law educator, government official; b. Indpls., July 23, 1948; s. C. Wendell and Elizabeth Bowman (Meeker) M.; m. Cynthia Jo Lorman, June 13, 1970; children: Amy Lynn, Jeffrey David. BA, DePauw U., 1970; JD, Yale U., 1975. Bar: D.C. Law clk. Hon. J. Skelly Wright U.S. Ct. Appeals (D.C. cir.), 1975-76; law clk. Hon. Lewis F. Powell U.S. Supreme Ct., Washington, 1976-77; assoc. Rogovin, Stern & Huge, Washington, 1977-78; spl. asst. bur. human rights and humanitarian affairs U.S. State Dept., Washington, 1978-80; from asst. prof. to assoc. prof. U. Va. Sch. Law, Charlottesville, 1980-86, prof., 1986-91, Henry L. & Grace Doherty prof. law, 1991—, F. Palmer Weber Rsch. prof. civil liberties and human rights, 1992-95; on leave U.S. Immigration and Naturalization Svc., Washington, 1995—; cons. Adminstrv. Conf. U.S., Washington, 1988-89, 91-92, U.S. Dept. Justice, 1993-95; gen. counsel U.S. Immigration and Naturalization Svc., 1995—. Author: Immigration: Process and Policy, 1985, 2d edit., 1991, 3d edit., 1995, Asylum Case Law Sourcebook, 1994, The Endless Quest: Helping America's Farm Workers, 1994; editor: The New Asylum Seekers, 1988; contbr. numerous articles to profl. jours. Mem. nat. governing bd. Common Cause, Washington, 1972-75; elder Westminster Presbyn. Ch., Charlottesville, 1982-84, 89-92. German Marshall Fund Rsch. Fellow, Geneva, 1984-85. Mem. Am. Soc. Internat. Law (ann. book award 1986), Internat. Law Assn. Democrat. Office: Immign & Naturaliz Svc Rm 6100 425 I St NW Washington DC 20536

MARTIN, DAVID BRITON HADDEN, JR., lawyer; b. Beverly, Mass., Dec. 9, 1946; s. David Briton Hadden and Mary Louise (Ward) M.; m. Martha Bacon, June 21, 1969; children: Charlotte, Jessica, Benjamin Ward. BA, Yale U., 1969; JD, U. Va., 1976. Bar: Va. 1976, D.C. 1977. Assoc. Dunnells, Duvall, Bennett & Porter, Washington, 1976-79, Dickstein, Shapiro & Morin, Washington, 1979-80; spl. counsel SEC, Washington, 1980-84, spl. counsel to chmn., 1984-85; assoc. Hogan & Hartson, Washington, 1985-87, ptnr., 1987—. Mng. editor U. Va. Law Review, 1975-76. Chair The Washington Revels, 1993—; mem. adv. bd. Jubilee Jobs, 1993—; bd. dirs. First Night Alexandria, Va., 1995—, Alexandria Indsl. Devel., 1980-82. Mem. Metro. Club. Office: Hogan & Hartson 555 13th St NW Washington DC 20004-1109

MARTIN, DAVID EDWARD, health sciences educator; b. Green Bay, Wis., Oct. 1, 1939; s. Edward Henry and Lillie (Luckman) M. B.S., U. Wis., 1961, M.S., 1963, Ph.D., 1970. Ford Found. research trainee Wis. Regional Primate Ctr., Madison, 1967-70; asst. prof. health scis. Ga. State U., Atlanta, 1970-74, assoc. prof., 1974-80, prof., 1980-91, regents prof., 1992—; affiliate scientist Yerkes Primate Rsch. Ctr., Emory U., Atlanta, 1970—; U.S. rep. to Internat. Olympic Acad., 1978; sports medicine rsch. assoc. U.S. Olympic Com., 1981-84; chmn. sports scis. U.S.A. Track and Field; mem. coaching staff U.S. teams to world championships in distance running, Rome, 1982, Gateshead, Eng., 1983, Budapest, Hungary, 1994, head coach, Paris, 1980, Madrid, 1984, Hiroshima, Japan, 1985, Warsaw, Poland, 1987, Antwerp, Belgium, 1991; mem. Olympic med. support group Atlanta Olympic Games. Author: Laboratory Experiments in Human Physiology, 4th edit., 1980, The Marathon Footrace, 1979, La Corsa Di Maratona, 1982, The High Jump Book, 1982, 2d edit., 1987, Respiratory Anatomy and Physiology, 1987, Training Distance Runners, 1991, German edit., 1992, Spanish edit., 1995; contbr. articles to profl. jours. Trustee Ga. Found. for Athletic Excellence. Recipient fed. and univ. grants for physiol. research; named Disting. prof. Ga. State U., 1975, 81, 85. Fellow Am. Coll. Sports Medicine; mem. Internat. Soc. Olympic Historians, Am. Physiol. Soc., Atlanta Track Club. Home: 510 Coventry Rd Apt 13A Decatur GA 30030-5038 Office: Ga State U Dept Cardiopulmonary S Atlanta GA 30303

MARTIN, DAVID HUBERT, physician, educator; b. Detroit, Mar. 24, 1943; s. Hubert Cillis and Mable Anita (Stewart) M.; m. Jane Ellen Schlichtemeier, Nov. 22, 1970; children: Jennifer, Jason. BA with distinction, U. Kans., 1965; MD cum laude, Harvard Coll., 1969. Diplomate Nat. Bd. Med. Examiners, Am. Bd. Internal Medicine, Infectious Disease Subspecialty Bd. Am. Bd. Internal Medicine. Intern Bronx (N.Y.) Mcpl. Hosp. Ctr., 1969-70; staff assoc. Nat. Inst. Allergy and Infectious Diseases, Mid. Am. Rsch. Unit, NIH, Panama Canal Zone, 1970-73; med. resident U. Wash. Affiliated Hosps., 1973-75; sr. fellow in infectious diseases U. Wash., 1976-78; chief resident in medicine USPHS Hosp., Seattle, 1975-76, staff internal medicine clinic, 1975, attending physician internal medicine, 1976-78; staff dept. internal medicine USPHS Hosp., New Orleans, 1979-81; staff Hotel Dieu Hosp., New Orleans, 1982-94; clin. asst. prof. medicine La. State U. Med. Sch., New Orleans, 1979-81, asst. prof. medicine divsn. infectious diseases, 1981-82, assoc. prof. medicine divsn. infectious diseases, 1982-88, assoc. prof. microbiology, 1986-88, prof. internal medicine and microbiology, 1988, asst. chief sect. infectious diseases, 1988-89, chief sect. infectious diseases, 1990—, Harry E. Dascomb M.D. prof. of medicine, 1990—; instr. dept. medicine U. Wash. Sch. Medicine, Seattle, 1975-78, acting asst. prof. medicine, 1978-79; chmn. infection control com., chmn. instnl. rev. bd. human rsch. com., chmn. antibiotic utilization com., sec. rsch. and editl. com., sec. animal welfare com. USPHS Hosp., New Orleans, 1979-81, dep. chief clin. rsch. dept., 1979-81, chmn. credentials com., 1980-81; mem. infection control com. Hotel Dieu Hosp., New Orleans, 1983-84, chmn. pharmacy and therapeutics com., 1988-94, mem. infection control com., 1990-94; vis. physician Charity Hosp. (now Med. Ctr. of La. at New Orleans), New Orleans, 1982—, chmn. antiobiotics com., 1982—, dir. infection control program, 1993—, chmn. infection control com., 1993—, vice chmn. pharmacy and therapeutics com., 1995—; cons. sexually transmitted diseases control program Dept. Health and Human Resources, State of La., 1985—; staff physician Jefferson Parish Venereal Disease Clinic, 1986-90, New Orleans (La.) Sexually Transmitted Disease Clinic, 1992—; cons. pharmacy and therapeutics com. Mercy Hosp., New Orleans, 1989-91; cons. La. AIDS Cmty. Rsch. Project, 1989-92; chmn. comprehensive medicine head search com. La. State U. Med. Sch., 1989-90, dept. medicine faculty promotion com., 1988—, AIDS policy com., 1992; mem. La. State Labs. Adv. Bd., 1993—, State La. Pub. Health Lab. Adv. Com., 1994—, U.S. Pub. Health Region 6 Infertility Prevention Adv. Com., 1995—; lectr., workshop presenter and rschr. in field; others. Peer reviewer various jours. including Sexually Transmitted Diseases, The Jour. of Infectious Diseases, The Am. Jour. of the Med. Scis., Archives of Internal Medicine, Clin. Infectious Diseases, New Eng. Jour. Medicine, Annals Internal Medicine, Jour. AMA; contbr. chpts. to books and articles to profl. jours. With USPHS, 1970-82. Achievements include established the first chlamydia laboratory in the Gulf South. Fellow ACP (La. chpt. program chmn. 1994-95), Infectious Diseases Soc. Am.; mem. Internat. Soc. for Sexually Transmitted Disease Rsch. (bd. dirs. 1991—, chmn. 1995 meeting organizing com. 1993-95), Am. Fedn. for Clin. Rsch., Am. Venereal Disease Assn. (v.p. 1992-94, pres. 1994—), Am. Soc. for Microbiology, European Soc. for Clin. Microbiology and Infectious Diseases, So. Soc. for Clin. Investigation, La. Miss. Infectious Diseases Soc. (bd. dirs., sci. program chmn. 1993), Phi Beta Kappa. Achievements include research in the effect of sexually transmitted microorganisms on pregnancy outcome; antibiotic treatment of sexually transmitted diseases and in particular C. trachomatis; the epidemiology of C. trachomatis in normal populations; Chancroid and other genital ulcer diseases. Office: Sch 1542 Tulane Ave New Orleans LA 70112-2825

MARTIN, DAVID HUGH, private investigator, business executive, writer; b. Ft. Worth, Mar. 24, 1952; s. Joesph Morgan Jr. and Jane Maurine (Harriss) M.; children: David Christian, Thomas Joshua, Michael Morgan. Ordained to ministry Meth. Ch., 1979; lic. pvt. investigator, Tex. CEO Woodland West Corp., Houston, 1977-84; owner D. H. Martin & Assocs. Investigations, Austin, Tex., 1980—; fin. mgr. The Williams Trust, Austin, 1982—; chmn. Biologic, Inc., Austin, 1983—; exec. dir. Grace Ministries, Austin, 1980—. Author: Rain Music, 1990; albums include Voice of a Child, 1987. Recipient Prism award Nat. Homebuilders Assn., 1979, 80, 82. Mem. MENSA, SAG, Tex. Assn. Lic. Investigators, Tex. Assn. Nurserymen, Rep. Nat. Com. Avocations: deep sea fishing, coin and relic hunting. Office: DH Martin & Assocs PO Box 5581 Austin TX 78763-5581

MARTIN, DAVID MACCOY, lawyer; b. Springfield, Ohio, Feb. 23, 1944; s. Oscar Thaddeus II and Dorothy (Traquair) M.; m. Judith Reed, Aug. 2, 1975; 1 child, Scott David. AB cum laude, Princeton U., 1971; JD, U. Denver, 1974. Bar: Ohio 1975, U.S. Supreme Ct. 1978, U.S. Tax Ct. 1976. Pvt. practice Springfield, 1975—. Served USAF, 1964-68. Mem. ABA, Ohio State Bar Assn. (mem. banking, comml. and bankruptcy law com. 1982—), Clark County Bar Assn., Am. Judicature Soc., Phi Alpha Delta. Home: 1776 Appian Way Springfield OH 45503 Office: David M Martin Co LPA 4 W Main St Ste 707 Springfield OH 45502

MARTIN, DAVID S., educator, administrator; b. N.Y.C., May 14, 1941; s. Perry Johnson and Polly Edith (Shedlov) M.; m. Florence E. Martin, Jan. 14, 1989; children: Drew M:chael, Amy Davida. BA, Adelphi Coll., 1962, MA, 1966; profl. cert., Hofstra U., 1969. Cert. secondary tchr., sch. dist. adminstr., N.Y. Adj. assoc. prof. Pace U., White Plains, N.Y., 1978—; tchr., computer coord. Jericho (N.Y.) Pub. Schs., 1962—. Author: Teachers Manual for Introduction to Pascal; co-author: How To Prepare for SAT II: Physics, 6th edit.; also author other books; contbr. articles to profl. jours. Fulbright-Hays grantee, 1967-68; recipient Grand award L.I. Sci. Congress, 1958, Disting Achievement award Electronic Learning, 1983, Outstanding Accomplishment award RITEC, 1984. Mem. IEEE (sr.), Internat. Soc. for Technology in Edn., Am. Assn. Physics Tchrs., Assn. Computing Machinery, Authors Guild, Jericho Tchrs. Assn., N.Y. State United Tchrs., Flambeau, Phi Delta Kappa, Sigma Pi Sigma. Home: 16 Elm Pl Sea Cliff NY 11579-1634 Office: Jericho Pub Schs Cedar Swamp Rd Jericho NY 11753

MARTIN, DEANNA COLEMAN, university director; b. Kansas City, Mo., Feb. 6, 1939; d. Olaf Arthur and Dolores Augustine (Judd) Coleman; m. Robert Allan Blanc, Apr. 28, 1982; children: Chris Robert Martin, Coleman O'Brian Martin. BA in English, U. Kansas City, 1960; MA in Reading Edn., U. Mo., Kansas City, 1974, PhD in Reading Edn., 1976. Cert. tchr., Mo. Tchr. Raytown (Mo.) H.S., 1964-74, Lee's Summit (Mo.) H.S., 1964-74; coord. learning resources U. Mo., Kansas City, 1974, dir. student learning ctr., 1975, dir. ctr. for acad. devel., 1980—, assoc. prof. sch. edn., 1987—; cons., presenter in field. Cons. editor Unit. for Rsch. into Higher Edn.--Ctr. for Sci. Devel. of the South African Human Scis. Rsch. Coun.; co-author: Supplemental Instruction: A Guide to Student Retention, 1983, Study Guide and Readings for Abnormal Psychology: Current Perspectives, 1984, Supplemental Instruction: Improving First-Year Student Success in High Risk Courses, 1992, Supplemental Instruction: Increasing Student Achievement and Persistence, 1994, also book chpts., monographs; contbr. articles to profl. publs. Trustee Multi-Media Network Trust, Johannesburg, South Africa. Grantee HEW, 1976, 81, Kansas City Assn. Trusts and Founds., 1977, 84, 85, U. Mo.-Kansas City, 1978, 79, 80, Nat. Basic Skills Improvement Schs. Program, 1980, Nat. Assn. State Univs. and Land-Grant Colls., 1984-85, Ctr. Sch. Dist., 1994, Sch. Dist. of City of Independence, Mo., Ft. Osage Sch. Dist., 1984, Consol. Sch. Dist. Raytown, 1984, Kansas City Pub. Sch. Dist., 1984, Coalition of 100 Black Women, 1985, U.S. Dept. Edn., 1989—, Nat. Diffusion Network, Office Edn., 1984—; recipient Retention Excellence award Noel/Levitz Nat. Ctr. for Student Retention, 1990, Cert. of REcognition, Nat. Assn. of Student Pers. Adminstrs., 1981. Mem. Nat. Assn. for Developmental Edn., Am. Assn. for Higher Edn.

Avocations: hiking, biking. Office: U Mo Kansas City Ctr Acad Devel 5100 Rockhill Rd Kansas City MO 64110-2446

MARTIN, DEBRA MICHELE, nurse; b. Hagerstown, Md., Sept. 19, 1950; d. James Kingsley and Mary Madalan (Bultman) Noel; m. David Richard Rawls, June 9, 1973 (div. June 1981); children: Derek Joseph, Dayna Noel; m. Sydney Lee Martin, June 25, 1982 (div. Oct. 1988). RN, Sinai Hosp., Balt., 1971. RN, Pa., Md.; cert. ACLS, CPR, CEN, BTLS, PALS, emergency vehicle operators course, hazardous materials tng. Asst. head RN Sinai Hosp., Balt., 1971-73, postpartum charge RN, 1975-77; ob-gyn. office RN Scher, Muher & Lowen, PA, Balt., 1973-74; emergency dept. RN Meml. Hosp., York, Pa., 1978-80, advance life charge RN, 1980—; teaching EMT's and paramedics Harrisburg (Pa.) Area C.C., 1984—, St. Joseph's Hosp., Lancaster, Pa., 1984—. Health profl. Pa. Dept. of Health, Harrisburg, 1988—. Named ALS Provider of Yr., Emergency Med. Svcs. Assn. of York County, 1990. Mem. Emergency Health Sys. Fedn. (RN adv. bd. 1986—), Emergency Nurses Assn. Democrat. Roman Catholic. Avocations: motorcycle riding, skiing, self-improvement, golf, hiking. Home: 123 S Main St Shrewsbury PA 17361-1528

MARTIN, DON P., lawyer; b. Roanoke, Va., Jan. 9, 1949. BA with distinction, U. Va., 1972, JD, 1975. Bar: Ariz. 1975, Nev. 1992. Ptnr. Streich Lang, Phoenix, 1975—. Echols scholar, Dupont scholar. Office: Streich Lang Renaissance One Two N Central Ave Phoenix AZ 85004-2391*

MARTIN, DONALD WILLIAM, psychiatrist; b. Columbus, Ohio, Aug. 13, 1921; s. Olin R. and Clara (Jahraus) M.; m. Clara Jane Jones, June 23, 1951; children: Jennifer Christine, David Lawrence. B.A., Ohio State U., 1942, M.D., 1944. Diplomate: Am. Bd. Psychiatry and Neurology. Intern Met. Hosp., N.Y.C., 1944-45; resident psychiatrist Kings Park (N.Y.) State Hosp., 1945-46, sr. psychiatrist, 1948-49; supervising psychiatrist Central Islip (N.Y.) State Hosp., 1950-56; staff psychiatrist Summit County Receiving Hosp. (name now Fallsview Psy. Hosp.), Cuyahoga Falls, Ohio, 1956-59; supt. Summit County Receiving Hosp. (name now Fallsview Psy. Hosp.), 1959-63; dir. Pontiac (Mich.) State Hosp. (name now Clinton Valley Center), 1963-79; pvt. practice cons. psychiatry, 1979-90, ret., 1990. Served from 1st lt. to capt. M.C., U.S. Army, 1946-48. Fellow Am. Psychiat. Assn. (life). Home: 608 Millwright Ct # 21 Millersville MD 21108 *My experiences over the years have only strengthened my belief that our happiness and growth as human beings derives above all else from our relationships with others. The life's theme I have evolved is: becoming and being a loving person.*

MARTIN, DONNA LEE, publishing company executive; b. Detroit, Aug. 7, 1935; d. David M. Paul and Lillian (Paul); m. Rex Martin, June 5, 1956; children: Justin, Andrew. B.A., Rice U., 1957. Mng. editor trade dept. Appleton-Century-Crofts Co., N.Y.C., 1961-62; dir. publs. Lycoming Coll., Williamsport, Pa., 1966-68; editor Univ. Press of Kans., Lawrence, 1971-74; mng. editor Andrews & McMeel, Kansas City, Mo., 1974-80, v.p., editorial dir., 1980-95, v.p., editor-at-large, 1995; v.p. Universal Press Syndicate, Kansas City, 1980—; lectr. U. Mo., Kansas City. Author: (adaptation) Charles Dickens' A Christmas Carol: Adapted for Theatre; contbr. articles to profl. jours. Named Disting. Alumna Rice U., 1990. Mem. Women in Comms., The Groucho Club (London), Phi Beta Kappa. Office: Universal Press Syndicate 4900 Main St Fl 9 Kansas City MO 64112-2630

MARTIN, EDGAR THOMAS, telecommunications consultant, lawyer; b. Princeton, W.Va., May 1, 1918; s. Edgar Frank and Delia Florence (Nowlin) M.; m. Hannelore Elisabeth Trucksaess, Jan. 12, 1952. BS, Va. Poly. Inst., 1938, MS, 1953; grad., Royal Air Force Coll., Cranwell, 1941; MA, Am. U., 1957; JD, George Washington U., 1957, M of Forensic Sci., 1977; LLM, Georgetown U., 1959; grad., U.S. Army Command and Gen. Staff Coll., 1963, Indsl. Coll. Armed Forces, 1963. Bar: Va. 1958, U.S. Ct. Mil. Appeals 1959; registered profl. engr., Va., 1939. Chief lab. technician Va. Poly. Inst. Elec. Engring. Dept., 1938-40; elec. engr. Radford Ordnance Works, 1940-41, chief radio sect., 1946-48, chief telecommunications br., 1948-49; office of mil. govt. for Germany; communications specialist Office High Commr., Germany, 1949-52; chief cen. frequency staff, 1952-54, chief engr., 1954-58; engring mgr., Broadcasting Svc. (Voice of Am.) USIA, 1958-75; telecomm. cons., 1975—. 2d lt. USAR, 1940, U.S. Army, 1941-46, lt. col. USAR, 1946, col. USAR, 1961, col. AUS ret. 1978. Fellow IEEE; mem. ABA, Am. Acad. Forensic Sci., Am. Soc. Internat. Law, Va. Trial Lawyers Assn., Soc. Bibl. Lit., Am. Soc. for Legal History, Soc. for Mil. History, U.S. Commn. on Mil. History, Nat. Lawyers Club, Army Navy Club, Am. Fgn. Svc. Assn., Nat. Mil. Intelligence Assn. Home: 922 26th Pl S Arlington VA 22202-2412

MARTIN, EDWARD BRIAN, electrical engineer; b. Lawrence, Kans., Feb. 9, 1936; s. Edward Brian and Dorothy Irene (Dowers) M.; m. Sharon Anne Zimmerman, Dec. 21, 1955; children: Terry Brian, Ricky Lynn, Mindy Anne, Timothy Alan. BSEE, U. Kans., 1958; MSEE, St. Louis U., 1969. Registered profl. engr., Mo. Program mgr. McDonnell Douglas, St. Louis, 1980-85, mgr. avionics, 1985-86, dir. engring., 1986-88, dir. electronics, 1988-89, sr. dir. tech. processes, 1989-91, sr. dir. avionics tech., 1991-92, dir. advanced missile systems, 1992-95, dir. advanced weapon systems, 1995—; chmn. bd. dirs. Martin Internat., Ltd. Contbr. numerous articles to profl. jours. Pres. PTA, St. Louis, 1972; founder Martin Family Found. Mem. AIAA. Avocations: running, mountain climbing, writing. Home: 5 Baron Ct Florissant MO 63034-1203

MARTIN, EDWARD CURTIS, JR., landscape architect, educator; b. Albany, Ga., Aug. 21, 1928; s. Edward Curtis and Mildred Lee (Tyler) M.; m. Roberta Inman Parker, Mar. 18, 1967; children: Edward Curtis III, Andrew Parker. BFA, U. Ga., 1950, M of Landscape Architecture, 1969. Registered landscape architect, Miss. Landscape architect Norman C. Butts Landscape Contractor, Atlanta, 1950; M.T. Brooks Office of Landscape Architecture, Birmingham, Ala., 1950-56; univ. landscape architect, horticulturalist Miss. State U., Mississippi State, 1956-70, prof. landscape architecture, 1970-92, Disting. prof., 1988, prof. emeritus, 1992—, part-time prof., 1992—; originator, chmn. Miss. Landscape Design Sch., Mississippi State, 1957—; guest lectr. U. San Luis Potosi, Mex., 1990, U. Mexico, Mex. City, 1991, La. State U., 1990, 91, 92, 94, Biendenharn Found., Monroe, La., 1991, Longue Vue Found., New Orleans, 1991, So. Garden Symposium, 1993, St. Francisville, La., 1993, Southern Regional Meeting Garden Writers Assn. Am., Memphis, 1993, Rotary Internat. Dist. Conf., Memphis, 1993, Deep S. Regional Conf. Nat. Coun. State Garden Clubs, Lafayette, La., 1993; guest instr. Nat. Landscape Design Study Courses Nat. Coun. State Garden Clubs, Inc., U.S., Mex., 1960—, Guatemala first study course, 1995; originator, lectr. Garden Design Workshops, Miss. State U., 1988—; host Flower and Garden Tour of British Isles, Southland Travel Svcs., 1985, Flower and Garden Tour of Europe, 1981, 82; photographic landscape architecture rsch. study: Europe, 1958, 66, 74, 85, S.Am., 1960, Israel, 1993; vis. prof. La. State U., 1990-93, vis. landscape architecture prof., 1994; host, lectr. historic southern gardens on Miss. River, New Orleans to Vicksburg, Delta Queen Steamboat; host Chelsea Flower Show and English Gardens Tour, 1994, Nat. Coun. State Garden Clubs, 1994, Fla. Wild Flower Conf. Fla. Fedn. Garden Clubs, Inc., 1994; instr. ecology tour Copper Canyon, Mex., 1994. Author: Landscape Plants in Design, A Photographic Guide, 1983; co-author: Home Landscapes, Planting Design and Management, 1994; invited to participate in Attingham Summer Program in Historic Preservation (English country houses and gardens) Eng., 1985; author/photographer of 80-captioned slide series, one on Home Landscapes, another on Urban Landscape Design for use by Nat. Coun. State Garden Clubs, Inc., 1994. Mem. Miss. State Bd. Landscape Architects for Profl. Registration, 1973-74; mem. Starkville (Miss.) Park and Recreation Bd., 1973-79. Recipient Silver Seal award Nat. Coun. State Garden Clubs 1969, honoree 1995; recipient Landscape Heritage award Fraser Found. Calif. 1986. Fellow Am. Soc. Landscape Architects (chmn. edn. com. 1960-61, pres. Miss. sect. S.W. chpt. 1975, chmn. S.W. chpt. ann. awards com. 1976, trustee Miss. chpt. 1977-81); mem. Nat. Trust for Historic Preservation, So. Garden History Soc., Coun. of Educators in Landscape Architecture, Nat. Coun. State Garden Clubs (chmn. landscape design 1993—), Garden Clubs Miss. (bd. dirs. 1958—, Silver Trophy 1961, Spl. Silver award 1980, Gold trophy 1993). Presbyterian. Home: 1335 Ridgewood Rd Starkville MS 39759-9177 Office: Dept Landscape Architecture Box 9725 Mississippi State MS 39762

MARTIN, EDWIN J(OHN), psychologist; b. Washington, Mar. 14, 1934; s. Richard Edwin and Florence (Johnson) M.; m. Helen Onis Tilley, Aug. 22, 1959; children—Theresa, John Charles. B.S. in Math, N.Mex. State U., 1960; Ph.D. in Psychology, U. Iowa, 1963. Mem. faculty dept. psychology U. Mich., Ann Arbor, 1963-74; asso. prof. U. Mich., 1967-71, prof., 1971-74; prof. dept. psychology U. Kans., Lawrence, 1974—, chmn. dept., 1989-93. Editor: Jour. Verbal Learning and Verbal Behavior, 1972-76, (with A.W. Melton) Coding Processes in Human Memory, 1972. Served with USN, 1953-57. Fellow AAAS, APA, Am. Psychol. Soc.; mem. Psychonomic Soc., Sigma Xi. Home: 848 E 1259 Road Lawrence KS 66047

MARTIN, EDYTHE LOUVIERE, business educator; b. Breaux Bridge, La., Dec. 30, 1940; d. James Ivy and Volna Mary (Landry) L.; m. James Henry Martin, Aug. 23, 1969; 1 child, Lois Elizabeth. BS in Bus. Edn., U. Southwestern La., 1972; MEd in Supervision, La. State U., 1977, Specialist Degree in Ednl. Adminstrn., 1988, postgrad studies in Ednl. Adminstrn., 1989—. Geol. sec. Sohio Petroleum Co., Lafayette, La., 1960-67, Bintliff Oil & Gas Co., Lafayette, 1967-69; bus. tchr. Cottonport (La.) H.S., 1972-74; bus. instr. Acadian Tech. Coll., Crowley, La., 1975—; team leader, mem. accrediting teams So. Assn. Colls. and Schs., 1978—, chmn. of steering com. for Acadian Tech. evaluation, 1991; speaker, presenter at meetings and seminars of educators. Publicity chairperson Miss Eunice (La.) Pageant, 1981-88; chairperson Eunice Lady of Yr. award, 1982; organizer chairperson, St. Jude Children's Hosp., Fund Raiser, Memphis, Eunice, 1985-91; PTC sec. St. Edmund Sch., Eunice, 1982-84; vol. March of Dimes, 1995. Mem. Office Occupations Assn., La. Vocat. Assn. Inc., La. Vocat. Assn. (trade and indsl. divsn.). Democrat Roman Catholic. Avocations: collecting, travel. Home: 750 Viola St Eunice LA 70535-4340 Office: Acadian Tech Coll 1933 W Hutchinson Ave Crowley LA 70526-3215

MARTIN, ELLIOT EDWARDS, theatrical producer; b. Denver, Feb. 25, 1924; s. William Harrison and Elma Abigale (Harvey) M.; m. Marjorie Cuesta, Oct. 7, 1949; children: Richard, Linda Lisa. Student, U. Denver, 1943-46. Actor, singer, stage mgr., assoc. producer Theatre Guild, N.Y.C. and London, 1947-53; prodn. stage mgr. 20 Broadway plays and musicals, 1953-61; theatrical producer Never Too Late, Nobody Loves an Albatross, N.Y.C., 1962-66; theatre producer London, 1963; mng. dir. Center Theatre Group, Music Ctr., Los Angeles, 1966-71; producer Elliot Martin Prodns., N.Y.C., 1972—; mem. exec. bd. Nat. Theatre of the Deaf, Chester, Conn., 1981—, Westport-Weston Arts Council, 1976—. Prodns. on Broadway include: Dinner at Eight, 1966, More Stately Mansions, 1967, Abelard and Heloise, 1971, Emperor Henry IV, 1973, A Moon for the Misbegotten, 1973 (spl. Tony award), When You Comin' Back, Red Rider, 1974 (Outer Critics award), Of Mice and Men, 1975, Touch of the Poet, 1976, Dirty Linen and New Found Land, 1977, Caesar and Cleopatra, 1977, Kingfisher, 1979, Clothes for a Summer Hotel, 1980, Kingdoms, 1981, American Buffalo, 1981, Angels Fall, 1983, Glengarry Glen Ross, 1984 (Pulitzer prize), Woza Albert, 1984, American Buffalo, 1984, Harrigan 'n' Hart, 1985, Arsenic and Old Lace (Broadway and nat. tour), 1986-87, Joe Turner's Come and Gone (7 Tony nominations, N.Y. Drama Critic's award best play), 1988, Steel Magnolias (nat. tour), 1989, The Circle, 1989-90, Shadowlands, 1990-91, Breaking Legs, 1991-92, She Loves Me (9 Tony noms.). Mem. bd. assocs. U. Bridgeport, 1978-83. Recipient Tony award for most innovative revival, 1977-78, Larry Tajiri award for outstanding contbn. to arts Denver Post, 1970, Congl. commendation, 1970, Profl. Achievement award U. Denver, 1987. Mem. Platform Speakers Am., League N.Y. Theatres and Producers. Republican. Club: N.Y. Athletic (N.Y.C.). Office: Elliot Martin Prodns 152 W 58th St New York NY 10019-2139

MARTIN, ERNEST LEE, academic administrator, historian, theologian, writer; b. Meeker, Okla., Apr. 20, 1932; s. Joel Chester and Lula Mae (Quinn) M.; m. Helen Rose Smith, Aug. 26, 1957 (div. 1980); children: Kathryn, Phyllis, Samuel; m. Ramona Jean Kinsey, June 27, 1987. BA, Ambassador U., 1958, MA, 1960, PhD, 1966. Dean faculty Ambassador U., St. Albans, Eng., 1965-72; chmn. dept. theology Ambassador U., Pasadena, Calif., 1972-74; dir. Found. for Bibl. Rsch., Pasadena, 1974-84, Acad. for Scriptural Knowledge, Portland, 1985—; dir. 450 coll. students Herodian Temple archaeol. excavations, Jerusalem, 1969-74. Author: Birth of Christ Recalculated, 1978, 2d edit., 1980, The Original Bible Restored, 1984, Secrets of Golgotha, 1987, 2d edit., 1996, The Star That Astonished the World, 1991, 101 Bible Secrets That Christians Do Not Know, 1993, The People That History Forgot, 1993, The Place of the New Third Temple, 1994, Restoring the Original Bible, 1994, The Biblical Manual, 1995. Tech. sgt. USAF, 1950-54. Mem. SBL (advisor to original Bible project), Planetarium Soc. Home: PO Box 25000 Portland OR 97225-0990 Office: Acad for Scriptural Knowledge 4804 SW Scholls Ferry Rd Portland OR 97225-1668 *Christianity is the teaching that all humanity is destined to be reconciled to God, and that is my prime philosophical belief.*

MARTIN, FRANK BURKE, statistics consultant; b. Cleve., Mar. 21, 1937. BA, St. Mary's Coll., Minn., 1958; MS, Iowa State U., 1966, PhD in Stats., 1968. Instr. math. St. Mary's Coll., Minn., 1960-63; teaching asst. stats. Iowa State U., Ames, 1963-65, rsch. assoc., 1965-67; asst. prof. to assoc. prof. U. Minn., St. Paul, 1967-78, statistician Exptl. Sta., 1967-78; cons. statistician Dept. Statistics U. Minn., Mpls., 1978—. Mem. Biometrical Soc., Am. Statis. Assn. Office: U Minn Statis Ctr/ 1994 Buford Ave 352 Classroom Office Bldg Saint Paul MN 55108*

MARTIN, FRED, artist, college administrator; b. San Francisco, June 13, 1927; s. Ernest Thomas and Leona (Richey) M.; m. Genevieve Catherine Fisette, Jan. 29, 1950 (dec.); children: T. Demian, Fredericka C., Anthony J.; m. Stephanie Zuperko Dudek, 1992. B.A., U. Calif.-Berkeley, 1949, M.A., 1954; postgrad. Calif. Sch. Fine Arts, 1949-50. Registrar Oakland (Calif.) Art Mus., 1955-58; dir. exhbns. San Francisco Art Inst., 1958-65, dir. coll., 1965-75, dean acad. affairs, 1983-92; dean acad. affairs emeritus. Exhibited one man shows, Zoe Dusanne Gallery, Seattle, 1952, M.H. deYoung Meml. Mus., San Francisco, 1954, 64, Oakland Art Mus., 1958, San Francisco Mus. Modern Art, 1958, 73, Dilexi Gallery, San Francisco, 1961, Minami Gallery, Tokyo, 1963, Royal Marks Gallery, N.Y.C., 1965-70, Hansen Fuller Gallery, San Francisco, 1974, 75, 76, Quay Gallery, San Francisco, 1979, 81, 84, Natsoulas Gallery, Davis, Calif., 1991, Belcher Studios Gallery, San Francisco, 1994, Frederick Spratt Gallery, San Jose, 1996; represented in permanent collections, Mus. Modern Art, N.Y.C., San Francisco Mus. Modern Art, Oakland Art Mus., Whitney Mus., Fogg Mus.; author: Beulah Land, 1966, Log of the Sun Ship, 1969, Liber Studiorum, 1973, A Travel Book, 1976, From an Antique Land, 1979; Bay area corr.: Art Internat.; contbg. editor Art Week, 1976-93. Recipient prizes Oakland Art Mus., 1951, 58, prizes San Francisco Mus. Art, 1957, 58, prizes Richmond (Calif.) Art Center, 1962, prizes Nat. Found. for Arts, 1970. Home: 232 Monte Vista Ave Oakland CA 94611-4922 Office: San Francisco Art Inst 800 Chestnut St San Francisco CA 94133-2206

MARTIN, FRED, retired municipal official; b. Detroit, Oct. 21, 1925; s. Fred McKinley and Eva Irene (Agnew) M.; m. Ernestine Robinson, Sept. 20, 1947 (div. 1980); children: Robin K. Turner, Keith R. BA, Wayne State U., 1953, MEd, 1954, postgrad., 1970-74. Tchr. Detroit Schs., 1953-61, asst. prin., 1961-63, personnel adminstr., 1963-67, asst. to supt., 1967-74, exec. dir. pers., 1974-78, pers. dir., dep. supt., 1978-81; pers. dir. City of Detroit, 1981-82, chief exec. asst. to mayor, 1981-92, personnel dir., 1992-94; instr. Wayne State U., 1968-75, U. Mich., Detroit, 1972; cons. U. Detroit, 1968. Author: Corrective Discipline - Management Grade, 1978. Bd. dirs. Greater Detroit Resource Recovery Authority, 1985, Detroit Sci. Ctr., 1987; pres. Northwest Activities Ctr., Detroit, 1987-94; mem. libr. commn. Detroit Pub. Libr., 1987; trustee Detroit Med. Ctr. With U.S. Army, 1944-46, ETO, PTO. Mem. Forum Black Pub. Adminstrs. (bd. dirs. 1984—), Your Heritage House, Detroit Inst. Arts. (Founders Soc.), Kappa Alpha Psi. Democrat. Baptist. Avocations: reading, music, sports. Home: 1300 E Lafayette St Apt 1401 Detroit MI 48207-2921

MARTIN, FREDERICK NOEL, audiology educator; b. N.Y.C., July 24, 1931; s. Philip and Mildred Ruth (Austin) M.; m. Mary Catherine Robinson, Apr. 4, 1954; children: David C., Leslie Anne. B.A., Bklyn. Coll., 1957, M.A., 1958; Ph.D., CUNY, 1968. Audiologist, Lenox Hill Hosp., N.Y.C., 1957-58; Audiologist Ark. Sch. for the Deaf, Little Rock, 1958-60; dir. audiology Bailey Ear Clinic, Little Rock, 1960-66; mem. faculty Bklyn. Coll., 1966-68; mem. faculty U. Tex., Austin, 1968—, endowed prof. audiology, 1982—. Author: Introduction to Audiology, 1975, 5th edit., 1994, Pediatric Audiology, 1978, Medical Audiology, 1981, Basic Audiometry, 1986; editor: Remediation of Communication Disorders, Vol. 10, 1978, Hearing Disorders in Children, 1986, Effective Counseling in Audiology, 1994, Hearing Care for Children, 1996; contbr. over 100 articles to profl. jours. Served with USAF, 1951-55. Fellow Am. Speech-Language Hearing Assn., Am. Acad. Audiology; mem. Tex. Speech-Lang.-Hearing Assn., Am. Auditory Soc. Home: 8613 Silver Ridge Dr Austin TX 78759-8144 Office: U of Tex Austin TX 78712

MARTIN, GARY JOSEPH, medical educator; b. Chgo., Mar. 12, 1952; m. Helen Gartner; children: Daniel T., David G. BA in Psychology, U. Ill., 1974, MD, 1978. Diplomate Am. Bd. Internal Medicine, Am. Bd. Cardiovascular Disease, Nat. Bd. Med. Examiners; lic. physician, Ill. Intern, resident internal medicine Northwestern U. Med. Sch., Chgo., 1978-81, instr. medicine, 1981-82, asst. prof. medicine, 1984-90, assoc. prof., 1990—, divsn. chief, divsn. gen. internal medicine, 1988—; cardiology fellow Loyola U. Med. Ctr., 1982-84; attending physician Northwestern Meml. Hosp./ Northwestern Med. Faculty Found., Chgo., 1984—; chief med. resident, attending physician Northwestern Meml. Hosp., Chgo., 1981-82; faculty and course dir. Nat. Ctr. for Advanced Med. Edn., 1984—; chmn. outpatient utilization rev. and quality assurance com., 1985—; chmn. Northwestern Meml. Hosp./Lakeside VA Rsch. Com., 1988-91; dir. tng. gen. internal medicine residency program, 1985—; bd. dirs. com. Northwestern Med. Faculty Found., 1993—; cons. health care divsn. Ernst & Young, 1991—; peer reviewer Faculty Devel. Rev. Com. Panel 1, 1994. Contbr. articles to profl. jours. Fellow Buehler Ctr. on Aging. Fellow Am. Coll. Cardiology; mem. ACP, Am. Fedn. Clin. Rsch., Soc. Gen. Internal Medicine, Am. Heart Assn., Soc. Med. Decision Making. Home: 215 N Home Park Ridge IL 60068-3029 Office: Northwestern U Med Sch Divsn Gen Internal Medicine 303 E Ohio Ste 300 Chicago IL 60611

MARTIN, GARY O., film company executive; b. Santa Monica, Calif., Aug. 14, 1944; s. Ivan C. and Helen M. (Werner) M.; m. Susan Alden Seaton, Sept. 2, 1967; 1 child, Sean Robert. Student, Calif. State U., Northridge, 1962-65. V.p. prodn. Columbia Pictures, Burbank, Calif., 1984-86, exec. v.p. prodn., exec. prodn. mgr., 1986-88; pres. prodn. adminstrn. Columbia Pictures and Tri Star Pictures, Culver City, Calif., 1988-95; pres. product adminstrn. Columbia Tri Star Motion Picture Cos., Culver City, 1995—. Mem. Motion Picture Acad. Arts and Scis., Dirs. Guild. Republican. Home: 8605 Amestoy Ave Northridge CA 91325-3405 Office: Columbia Pictures 10202 Washington Blvd Culver City CA 90232-3195

MARTIN, GARY WAYNE, lawyer; b. Cin., Feb. 14, 1946; s. Elmer DeForrest and Nellie May (Hughes) M.; m. Debra Lynn Goldsmith, June 25, 1982; children: Christopher, Jeremy, Joie, Casey. BA, Wilmington Coll., 1967; JD, U. Cin., 1974. Bar: Fla. 1974. Head casualty dept. Fowler White Gillen Boggs Villareal & Banker, Tampa, Fla., 1974—, also bd. dirs. Lt. USNR, 1967-71. Mem. The Tampa Club, Harbour Island Athletic Club. Republican. Presbyterian. Avocation: tennis. Office: Fowler White Gillen Boggs Villareal & Banker 501 E Kennedy Blvd Ste 1600 Tampa FL 33602-5200

MARTIN, GEORGE COLEMAN, aeronautical engineer; b. Everett, Wash., May 16, 1910; s. Walter Franklin and Minnie (Coleman) M.; m. Mary Sturart Patrick, June 29, 1935; children: Marian Coleman, Edith Patrick. B.S. cum laude, U. Wash., 1931. With Boeing Airplane Co., Seattle, 1931—; successively chief of stress, staff engr. stress and power plant, XB-47 project engr., preliminary design chief, B-47 project engr., chief project eng Boeing Airplane Co., 1951-53; chief engr. Boeing Airplane Co. (Seattle div.), 1953-58, v.p., 1958-64, v.p. engring., 1964-72, cons., 1972—. Recipient Disting. Alumnus award Dept. Aeros. and Astronautics, Coll. of Engring. of U Wash., 1983, Pathfinders award Mus. of Flight, 1987. Fellow Am. Inst. Aeros. and Astronautics; mem. Aerospace Industries Assn. (chmn. aerospace tech. council 1969), Phi Beta Kappa, Tau Beta Pi. Club: Seattle Yacht. Home: 900 University St Apt 5P Seattle WA 98101-2728

MARTIN, GEORGE CONNER, pomology educator; b. San Francisco, Sept. 15, 1933; s. Henry B. and Doris E. (Brockman) M.; m. C. Patricia Thayer, June 28, 1953; children: Steven P., Pamela J. MS, Purdue U., 1960, PhD, 1962. Plant physiologist USDA, Wenatchee, Wash., 1962-67; assoc. prof. dept. pomology U. Calif., Davis, 1967-73, prof. dept. pomology, 1973-94; ret., 1994. Contbr. over 245 articles to scholarly and profl. jours. 1st lt. USMC, 1955-58. Fellow Am. Soc. Hort. Sci. (pres. 1989-90, chmn. bd. 1990-91, Gourley award 1971, Membership award 1976, 81, 83, 85, Stark award 1980, Miller award 1981, Popenoe award 1982, Rschr. of Yr. award 1987, Fruit Publ. award 1992).

MARTIN, GEORGE FRANCIS, lawyer; b. Yuba City, Calif., July 7, 1944; s. John Severd and Albaina Marie M.; m. Linda Louise D'Aoust, Mar. 17, 1968; children: Brandon, Bry. BA in Govt., Calif. State U., Sacramento, 1968; JD, U. Calif., Davis, 1971. Bar: Calif. Adminstr. asst. Assemblyman E. Richard Barnes, Sacramento, 1967-68; with Borton, Petrini & Conron, Bakersfield, Calif., 1971—; mng. gen. ptnr. Borton, Petrini & Conron, Bakersfield, 1977—; holdings numerous ventures, partnerships including Golden Empire Land and Devel., Inc.; lectr. in field; founder, owner theatrical bus. Mgmt. by Martin, Inc., Shower of Stars, Frantic Records, 1962-67. Editor-in-chief Verdict Jour. of Law, Calif. Def. Mag.; newspaper reporter Appeal Democrat, Marysville, Calif., 1959-62. Former vice chmn. Kern County Rep. Ctrl. Com.; past pres. So. Calif. Def. Counsel; past chmn. Ctrl. Calif. Heart Inst.; bd. dirs. Calif. State U. at Bakersfield Found., Kern County Food Bank, Calif. Coun. Partnerships, Bakersfield Meml. Hosp., Kern Hospice, Kern Econ. Devel. Corp. Mem. Greater Bakersfield C. of C. (bd. dirs., past pres.). Offic: Borton Petrini & Conron 1600 Truxtun Ave Bakersfield CA 93301-5104

MARTIN, GEORGE J., JR., lawyer; b. Port Chester, N.Y., June 7, 1942; s. George J. and Eileen Ann (Buckley) M.; m. Joanne L. Frost, Aug. 21, 1965 (div. May 1986); children: Amy Anne, Ryan Frost; m. Anna Marie Cipriati, June 21, 1986; children: Marissa McCreay, Jill McCreay. BA, Georgetown U., 1964, JD, 1967. Bar: N.Y. 1969; conseil juridique, France, 1977. From assoc. to ptnr. Mudge Rose Guthrie Alexander & Ferdon, N.Y.C., 1967-95; ptnr. Coudert Bros., N.Y.C., 1995—. Mem. Friends Vieilles Maisons Francaises Inc. (dir.-sec.). Roman Catholic. Home: 165 State St Brooklyn NY 11201-5609 Office: Coudert Bros. 1114 Avenue of Americas New York NY 10036

MARTIN, GEORGE M., pathologist, gerontologist, educator; b. N.Y.C., June 30, 1927; s. Barnett J. and Estelle (Weiss) M.; m. Julaine Ruth Miller, Dec. 2, 1952; children: Peter C., Kelsey C., Thomas M., Andrew C. BS, U. Wash., 1949, MD, 1953. Diplomate Am. Bd. Pathology, Am. Bd. Med. Genetics. Intern Montreal Gen. Hosp., Quebec, Can., 1953-54; resident-instr. U. Chgo., 1954-57; instr.-prof. U. Wash., Seattle, 1957—; vis. scientist Dept. Genetics Albert Einstein Coll., N.Y.C., 1964; chmn. Gordon Confs. Molecular Pathology, Biology of Aging, 1974-79; chmn., nat. res. Plan on Aging Nat. Inst. on Aging, Bethesda, Md., 1985-89; dir. Alzheimer's Disease Rsch. Ctr. U. Wash., 1985—. Editor Werner's Syndrome and Human Aging, 1985, Molecular Aspects of Aging, 1995; contbr. articles in field to profl jours. Active Fedn. Am. Scientists. With USN, 1945-46. Recipient Allied Signal award in Aging, 1991, Rsch. medal Am. Agy. Assn., 1992, Kleemeier award, 1994; named Disting. Alumnus, U. Wash. Sch. Medicine, 1987; USPHS rsch. fellow dept. genetics, Glasgow U., 1961-62; Eleanor Roosvelt Inst. Cancer Rsch. fellow Inst. de Biologie, PHysiologie, Chimie, Paris, 1968-69; Josiah Macy faculty scholar Sir William Din Sch. Pathology, Oxford (Eng.) U., 1978-79, Humboldt Disting. scientist dept. genetics U. Wurzburg, Germany, 1991. Fellow AAAS, Gerontol. Soc. Am. (chmn. Biol. Sci. 1979, Brookdale award 1981), Tissue Culture Assn. (pres. 1986-88); mem. Inst. Medicine, Am. Assn. Univ. Pathologists (emeritus), Am. Soc. Human Genetics, Am. Soc. Investigative Pathology. Democrat. Avocations: internat. travel, jazz music, biography. Home: 2223 E Howe St Seattle WA 98112-2931 Office: U Wash Sch Medicine Dept Pathology Sm # 30 Seattle WA 98195

MARTIN, GEORGE (WHITNEY), writer; b. N.Y.C., Jan. 25, 1926; s. George Whitney and Agnes Wharton (Hutchinson) M. B.A., Harvard U., 1948; student, Trinity Coll., Cambridge (Eng.) U., 1950; LL.B., U. Va., 1953.

Bar: N.Y. 1955. With firm Emmet, Marvin & Martin, N.Y.C., 1955-59; engaged in writing, 1959—. Author: The Opera Companion, A Guide for the Casual Operagoer, 1961, 4th edit., 1994, The Battle of the Frogs and Mice, An Homeric Fable, 1962, 2d edit., 1987, Verdi, His Music, Life and Times, 1963, 4th edit., 1992, The Red Shirt and The Cross of Savoy, The Story of Italy's Risorgimento, 1748-1871, 1969, Causes and Conflicts, The Centennial History of the Association of the Bar of the City of New York, 1870-1970, 1970, Madam Secretary: Frances Perkins, 1976, The Companion to Twentieth Century Opera, 1979, 3d edit., 1989, The Damrosch Dynasty, America's First Family of Music, 1983, Aspects of Verdi, 1988, 2nd edit., 1993, Verdi at the Golden Gate, San Francisco in the Golden Years, 1993; contbr. articles to profl. jours., mags. Home: 21 Ingleton Cir Kennett Square PA 19348-2000

MARTIN, GEORGE WILBUR, trade association administrator; b. Oklahoma City, Aug. 24, 1930; s. Jeff Frank and George Mullineaux (Bullard) M.; m. Maryellen Brokaw, June 20, 1953; 1 son, Michael Blake. Student, Okla. A&M Coll., 1951. Real estate salesman Washington, 1955-59; jr. analyst CIA, Washington, 1953-55; advt. mgr. Guns and Ammo Mag., Petersen Pub. Co., Los Angeles, 1959-66; editor Guns and Ammo Mag., Petersen Pub. Co., 1967-73; pub. Petersen's Hunting, Guns and Ammo and shooting splty. books, 1974-78; exec. dir. publs. NRA, Washington, 1978-93, exec. dir. industry rels., 1993-95; publishing cons., 1995—; cons. White House Com. Firearms Legis., 1971—. Served with USAF, 1951-52. Named hon. lt. gov. State of Okla.; recipient Anschutz-Precision Sales Internat. Outstanding Writer award, 1988. Mem. NRA (endowment mem.), Internat. Profl. Hunters Assn., Alaska Profl. Hunters Assn., Hunting Hall of Fame Found. (charter, life), Am. Handgunner Awards Orgn. (endowment), Outdoor Writers Assn. Am., Wildflower Assn. Scotland. Home: 1593 Paiute Rd Saint George UT 84790

MARTIN, GERALD WAYNE, professional football player; b. Forest City, Ark., Oct. 26, 1965. Degree in Criminal Justice, U. Ark., 1990. Defensive end New Orleans Saints, 1989—. Named to The Sporting News coll. All-Am. 1st team, 1988; selected to Pro Bowl, 1994. Office: New Orleans Saints 1500 Poydras New Orleans LA 70112

MARTIN, GORDON MATHER, physician, educator, administrator; b. Brookline, Mass., Mar. 2, 1915; s. Harry O. and Mary Alice (Mather) M.; m. Neva M. Cocklin, June 14, 1940; children—Richard, Lawrence, Douglas. Student, U. N.H., 1932-34; A.B., Nebr. Wesleyan U., 1936; M.D., U. Nebr., 1940; M.S. (fellow in phys. medicine Mayo Found.), U. Minn., 1944. Diplomate Am. Bd. Phys. Medicine and Rehab. (asst. sec. 1974-77, exec. sec.-treas. 1977-85, exec. dir. 1985-92, asst. exec. dir. 1992-95, historian 1993—). Intern U. Nebr. Hosp., Omaha, 1940-41; 1st asst. phys. medicine Mayo Clinic, 1943-44, cons. phys. medicine and rehab., 1947-65, chmn. dept. phys. medicine and rehab., 1965-73, sr. cons., 1973-81, emeritus cons., 1981—; asst. prof. phys. medicine, dir. dept. U. Kans. Sch. Medicine, 1944-47, dir. sch. phys. therapy, 1944-47; asso. prof. phys. med. and rehab. Mayo Grad. Sch. Med., U. Minn. Grad. Sch.; prof. Mayo Med. Sch., 1973-81, prof. emeritus, 1981—; chmn. sub-com. phys. medicine and rehab. Gov.'s Adv. Council Mental Health for Minn., 1956-60; cons. chronic diseases program USPHS, 1959-62; chmn. residency rev. com. phys. medicine and rehab., 1975-81, ex-officio, 1981—. Author chpts. to med. books. Recipient Alumni Achievement award Nebr. Wesleyan U., 1957. Fellow ACP; mem. AAAS, AMA (sec. phys. medicine and rehab. sect., coun. 1963-69, chmn. 1970-76, Nat. Rehab. Assn., Am. Congress Rehab. Medicine (pres. 1955-56, exec. coun., Gold Key award 1985), Am. Bd. Med. Specialties, Am. Acad. Phys. Medicine and Rehab. (v.p., disting. mem. award 1994), Am. Coll. Rheumatology, Minn. Rehab. Assn. (pres. 1970), Assn. Acad. Physiatrists, Internat. Rehab. Med. Assn., Am. Guild of Organists, Rochesters C. of C., Sigma Xi, Alpha Omega Alpha. Home: Charter House 211 2d St NW Apt 2116 Rochester MN 55901-3101 Office: Mayo Clinic 200 1st St SW Rochester MN 55905-0001

MARTIN, GUY, lawyer; b. Los Angeles, Jan. 22, 1911; s. I.G. and Mary Pearl (Howe) M.; m. Edith Kingdon Gould, Oct. 12, 1946; children—Guy III, Jason Gould, Christopher Kingdon, Edith Maria Theodosia Burr. A.B., Occidental Coll., 1931; B.A. (1st class hons.), Oxford U., 1934, M.A., 1944; LL.B., Yale, 1937. Bar: N.Y. 1938, D.C. 1947. Practiced with Donovan, Leisure, Newton & Lumbard, N.Y.C., 1938-41; gen. counsel All Am. Aviation, Inc., 1942, Am. Mexican Claims Commn., U.S. Dept. State, 1945-47; ptnr. Martin, Whitfield, Smith & Bebchick (and predecessors), Washington, 1952-80; counsel Martin and Smith (and predecessors), 1981-86; pres., vice chmn. bd., dep. chief exec. officer Internat. Bank, 1981-86; with Law Office of Saltzstein & Martin, 1988—. Served with USN; sea duty 1942-45. Mem. ABA, Assn. of Bar of City of N.Y., Bar Assn. D.C, Phi Beta Kappa, Sigma Alpha Epsilon. Episcopalian. Clubs: Yale, Brook, Knickerbocker (N.Y.C.); Metropolitan, City Tavern (Washington). Home: 3300 O St NW Washington DC 20007-2813

MARTIN, HAROLD CLARK, humanities educator; b. Raymond, Pa., Jan. 12, 1917; s. Henry Floyd and Anna May (Clark) M.; m. Elma Hicks, Dec. 21, 1939; children—Thomas, Joel, Ann, Rebecca. A.B., Hartwick Coll., Oneonta, N.Y., 1937, LL.D. (hon.), 1965; A.M., U. Mich., 1941; Ph.D., Harvard, 1954; student, U. Wis., 1936, Columbia, 1941; L.H.D. (hon.), Elmira Coll., 1967, Siena Coll., 1968, Concord Coll., 1968; D.H.L. (hon.), Trinity Coll., Conn., 1970; Litt.D. (hon.), Skidmore Coll., 1974; L.H.D. (hon.), Coll. St. Rose, 1974, Union Coll., 1975. High sch. tchr. English and French langs. Adams, N.Y., 1937-39; high sch. tchr. English Goshen, N.Y., 1939-44; prin. high sch., 1944-49; mem. faculty Harvard U., 1951-65, dir. gen. edn., 1951-63, lectr. comparative lit., 1954-65; chancellor Union U.; also pres. Union Coll., Schenectady, 1965-74; pres. Am. Acad., Rome, Italy, 1974-76; Margaret Bundy Scott prof. Williams Coll., 1977; Charles A. Dana prof. humanities Trinity Coll., Conn., 1977-82, prof. emeritus, 1982—, sr. lectr. humanities, 1982—. Author: Logic and Rhetoric of Exposition, 1958, Spanning Three Centuries, 1984, Outlasting Marble and Brass, 1986. Editor: Inquiry and Expression (with Richard Ohmann), 1958, Style in Prose Fiction, 1959. Chmn. Mass. Com. Fulbright Awards, 1955-65, Coll. Bd. Com. English, 1959-64; Trustee Hartwick Coll., Siena Coll., Franklin Coll., Switzerland, Wenner-Gren Found. Served with USNR, 1945-46. Home: 1317 W Meadowlark Ln Corrales NM 87048-9691

MARTIN, HAROLD EUGENE, publishing executive, consultant; b. Cullman, Ala., Oct. 4, 1923; s. Rufus John and Emma (Meadows) M.; m. Jean Elizabeth Wilson, Nov. 25, 1945; children: Brian, Anita. B.A. in History with honors, Howard Coll., Birmingham, Ala., 1954; M.A. in Journalism, Syracuse U., 1956. Asst. gen. mgr. Birmingham News Newhouse Newspapers, 1960-63, asst. prodn. mgr. St. Louis Globe-Democrat, 1958-60, asst. bus. mgr. Syracuse Herald Jour., 1957-58; pub. Montgomery Advertiser and Ala. Jour., Ala., 1963-70; pres. Multimedia Newspapers, editor and pub. Montgomery Advertiser and Ala. Jour. Multimedia, Inc., 1970-78, v.p., mem. mgmt. bd., 1973-78, also corp. dir.; exec. v.p., chief exec. officer So. Baptist Radio and TV Commn., Ft. Worth, 1979; pres. Jefferson Pilot Publs., Inc., Beaumont, Tex., 1980-85; pres., pub. Beaumont Enterprise, 1981-85; owner, pub. Herald Citizen daily newspaper, Cookeville, Tenn., 1970-78, News-Observer, Crossett, Ark., 1970-78; co-owner, pub Baxter Bull., Mountain Home, Ark., 1970-78; disting. vis. prof. Sch. Journalism, U. Fla., 1979-80; adj. prof. Samford U., 1961; juror Pulitzer Prize, 1971-72; dir. exec. Svc. Corp. of Ft. Worth. Contbr. articles to newspapers. Bd. dirs. Billy Graham Evangelistic Assn., Mpls.; coun. Samford U. Study Ctr., London. Recipient awards for articles; recipient citation Howard Coll, 1965, award of Outstanding Merit Ala. Dental Assn., 1966, Community Service award AP Assn., 1969, 72, 73, Pulitzer prize, 1970, First Place Newswriting award AP, 1971, Newswriting award for Best Stories of Yr. by Ala. Reporters AP, 1974, 75, Canon award, 1972, Ann. award for outstanding contbn. to health care Ala. State Nurse's Assn., 1973, News award Ala. State Nurses' Assn., 1976, Ala. Bapt. Communications award Ala. Bapt. State Conv., 1975; named Alumnus of Yr. Samford U., 1970. Mem. Alumni Assn. Samford U. (pres. 1967, 92, 93, adv. bd. Samford London Centre), Sigma Delta Chi (Green Eye Shade citation for Reporting 1969). Baptist. Home: 4958 Overton Woods Ct Fort Worth TX 76109-2433

MARTIN, HARRY CORPENING, educator, retired state supreme court justice; b. Lenoir, N.C., Jan. 13, 1920; s. Hal C. and Johnsie Harshaw (Nelson) M.; m. Nancy Robiou Dallam, Apr. 16, 1955; children: John, Matthew, Mary. A.B., U. N.C., 1942; LL.B., Harvard U., 1948; LL.M., U. Va., 1982. Bar: N.C. 1948. Sole practice Asheville, N.C., 1948-62; judge N.C. Superior Ct., Asheville, 1962-78, N.C. Ct. Appeals, Raleigh, 1978-82; justice N.C. Supreme Ct., 1982-92; ptnr. Martin & Martin, Attys., Hilllsborough, N.C., 1992—; adj. prof. U. N.C. Law Sch., 1983-92, Dan K. Moore disting. vis. prof., 1992—; sr. conf. atty. U.S. Ct. Appeals for 4th Cir., 1994—; adj. prof. Duke U., 1990-91. Served with U.S. Army, 1942-45, South Pacific. Mem. U.S. Supreme Ct. Hist. Soc., N.C. Supreme Ct. Hist. Soc. (pres.). Democrat. Episcopalian. Home: 702 E Franklin St Chapel Hill NC 27514-3823 Office: U NC Law Sch Van Hecke-Wettach Hall Chapel Hill NC 27599

MARTIN, HENRY ALAN, lawyer; b. Nashville, Sept. 5, 1949; s. James Alvin and Mary Elizabeth (Long) M.; m. Gloria B. Ballard, May 9, 1975; children: Nathan Daniel, Anna Elizabeth. BA, Vanderbilt U., 1971, JD, 1974. Bar: Tenn. 1975, U.S. Dist. Ct. (mid. dist.) Tenn. 1975, U.S. Ct. Appeals (6th cir.) 1976, U.S. Supreme Ct. 1979. Pvt. practice Nashville, 1975-76; ptnr. Haile & Martin, P.A., Nashville, 1976-82; assoc. firm Barrett & Ray, P.C., Nashville, 1982-85; fed. pub. defender U.S. Dist. Ct. (mid. dist.) Tenn., Nashville, 1985—; mem. adv. com. on rules criminal procedure U.S. Judicial Conf., 1994—. CO-author, co-editor trial manual, Tools for the Ultimate Trial, 1985, 2d edit., 1988; contbr. articles to profl. jours. Del., Witness for Peace, Managua, Nicaragua, 1987. Mem. ABA (coun. criminal justice sect. 1993—), NACDL, Nat. Lawyers Guild, Assn. Fed. Defenders (pres. 1995—), Nashville Bar Assn., Napier Looby Bar Assn., Nat. Legal Aid and Def. Assn., Tenn. Assn. Criminal Def. Lawyers (bd. dirs. 1978-94, pres. 1984-85, President's award 1984). Democrat. Avocations: jogging, swimming. Home: 3802 Whitland Ave Nashville TN 37205-2432 Office: Fed Pub Defender 810 Broadway Ste 200 Nashville TN 37203-3805

MARTIN, J. LANDIS, manufacturing company executive, lawyer; b. Grand Island, Nebr., Nov. 5, 1945; s. John Charles and Lucile (Cooley) M.; m. Sharon Penn Smith, Sept. 23, 1978; children: Mary Frances, Sarah Landis, Emily Penn. BS in Bus. Adminstrn., Northwestern U., 1968, JD cum laude, 1973. Bar: Ill. 1974, D.C. 1978, Colo. 1982. Assoc. Kirkland & Ellis, Chgo., 1973-77; ptnr. Kirkland & Ellis, Washington, 1978-81; mng. ptnr. Kirkland & Ellis, Denver, 1981-87, firm com. mem., Chgo., 1983-87; pres., CEO NL Industries Inc., Houston, 1987—; also bd. dirs. NL Industries Inc.; chmn., CEO Baroid Corp., Houston, 1987-94; chmn. bd., pres., CEO Tremont Corp., 1990—, also bd. dirs.; dir. Dresser Industries, Dallas, Aimco. Editor-in-chief: Exchange Act Guide to SEC Rule 144, 1973; articles editor Northwestern U. Law Rev., 1972-73. Pres Ctrl. City Opera House Assn., Denver, 1986-88, chmn. 1987; pres. Ctrl. City Opera House Endowment Fund, 1992—; vis. com. Northwestern U. Sch. Law, 1987—; mem. exec. com. Houston Grand Opera, 1991—, sr. v.p. devel. 1992—, pres. 1993-95, chmn. 1995—; bd. trustees Denver Art Mus., 1994—, Graland Country Day Sch., 1992—. With U.S. Army, 1969-71. Mem. ABA, Ill. Bar Assn., Colo. Bar Assn., D.C. Bar Assn. Clubs: Chevy Chase (Md.), John Evans (Evanston, Ill.), Denver, Denver Country, Castle Pines Golf. Office: NL Industries Inc 16825 Northchase Dr Ste 1200 Houston TX 77060-2544

MARTIN, JAMES ALFRED, JR., religious studies educator; b. Lumberton, N.C., Mar. 18, 1917; s. James Alfred and Mary (Jones) M.; m. Ann Bradsher, June 1, 1936 (dec. 1982); m. Nell Gifford, Jan. 6, 1984. AB, Wake Forest Coll., 1937, LittD, 1965; MA, Duke U., 1938; PhD, Columbia U., 1944; student, Union Theol. Sem., 1940-43; M.A. (hon.), Amherst Coll., 1950. Ordained to ministry Bapt. Ch., 1944; asst. pastor Roxboro (N.C.) Ch., 1937-38; instr. philosophy and psychology Wake Forest Coll., 1938-40; asst. philosophy religion Union Theol. Sem., N.Y.C., 1941-44; Danforth prof. religion in higher edn. Union Theol. Sem., 1960-67, adj. prof. philosophy religion, 1967-82; prof. religion Columbia U., 1967-82, prof. emeritus, 1982—, chmn. dept., 1968-77; asst. prof. religion Amherst Coll., 1946-47, asso. prof., 1947-50, prof., 1950-54, Marquand and Stone prof., 1954-57, Crosby prof. religion, 1957-60; ordained deacon P.E. Ch., 1953; vis. prof. Cornell U., summer 1948, Mt. Holyoke Coll., 1949-50, 52-53, 59-60, State U. Iowa, summer 1959, U. N.C., summer 1964; Univ. prof. Wake Forest U., 1984—; vis. prof. religious studies U. Va., 1984; asso. mem. East-West Philosophers Conf., U. Hawaii, 1949. Author: Empirical Philosophies of Religion, 1944, (with J.A. Hutchison) Ways of Faith, 1953, rev., 1960, Fact, Fiction, and Faith, 1960, The New Dialogue between Philosophy and Theology, 1966, Beauty and Holiness, 1990; contbr. articles to profl. jours. and encys., chpts. to books. Chmn. bd. visitors Wake Forest Coll., 1981-83. Served as lt. chaplain USNR, 1944-46, PTO. Recipient Disting. Alumnus award Wake Forest U., 1971, Nat. Faculty award Assn. of Grad. Liberal Studies Programs, 1995. Mem. Soc. Values in Higher Edn. (Kent fellow, pres. 1964-69), Am. Theol. Soc. (v.p. 1981-82, pres. 1982), Soc. Theol. Discussion, Soc. Philosophy of Religion, Phi Beta Kappa, Omicron Delta Kappa, Pi Kappa Alpha. Home: PO Box 6746 Winston Salem NC 27109-6746 *My experience of life has increasingly underscored the central importance of honesty-in understanding of oneself, and in perceptions of and relations to others. The quest for honesty entails a relentless and often painful search for truth. Acceptance of truth, and of others as they truly are, requires grace. The goal is to speak the truth in love.*

MARTIN, JAMES FRANCIS, state legislator, lawyer; b. Atlanta, Aug. 22, 1945; s. Joseph Grant and Helen (Hester) M.; m. Joan Vohryzek, Jan. 30, 1970; children: Morgan, Rebecca, James, Frank. AB, U. Ga., 1967, JD, 1969, LLM, 1972; MBA, Ga. State U., 1980. Bar: Ga. 1972. Asst. legis. counsel Ga. Gen. Assembly, Atlanta, 1972-77; staff atty. Atlanta Legal Aid and Ga. Legal Svc. Programs, 1977-80; ptnr. Martin and McDuffie, 1980-86; of counsel Martin and Wilkes, 1986—, Martin Bros. P.C., 1986—; mem. Ga. Ho. of Reps., 1983—. Chmn. Ethics Com., 1993—. 1st lt. U.S. Army, 1969-71, Vietnam. Democrat. Presbyterian. Office: State Capitol Rm 132 Atlanta GA 30334

MARTIN, JAMES GILBERT, university provost emeritus; b. Paris, Ill., Dec. 10, 1926; s. James and Ruth Ann (Gilbert) M.; m. Doris E. Edmonson, Aug. 23, 1969; children—Bradley Keith, Philip Roger. B.A., Ind. State Coll., 1952, M.A., 1953; Ph.D., Ind. U., 1957. Instr. Ind. State Coll., Terre Haute, 1952-53; lectr. Ind. U., Bloomington, 1953-56; instr. sociology Okla. U., Norman, 1956-57; asst. prof. sociology No. Ill. U., DeKalb, 1957-65; asso. prof. No. Ill. U., 1959-64; asst. dean Coll. Arts and Scis., Ohio State U., Columbus, 1965-68; asso. dean Coll. Arts and Scis., Ohio State U. (Coll. Social and Behavioral Scis.), 1968-70, acting dean, 1970-71; v.p., provost U. No. Iowa, Cedar Falls, 1971-89, provost emeritus, 1989—; intern academic adminstrn. E.L. Phillips Found., 1963-64. Author: The Tolerant Personality, 1964, Minority Group Relations, 1973. Mem. Iowa Peace Inst. Bd., 1989-92. With AUS, 1945-48. Home: 749 Hidden Cir Dayton OH 45458-3317

MARTIN, JAMES GRUBBS, medical research executive, former governor; b. Savannah, Ga., Dec. 11, 1935; s. Arthur Morrison and Mary Julia (Grubbs) M.; m. Dorothy Ann McAulay, June 1, 1957; children: James Grubbs, Emily Wood, Arthur Benson. BS, Davidson Coll., 1957; PhD, Princeton U., 1960. Assoc. prof. chemistry Davidson (N.C.) Coll., 1960-72; mem. 93d to 98th Congresses from N.C., 1973-85; gov. State of N.C., 1985-92; chmn. James G. Cannon Med. Rsch. Ctr., Charlotte, N.C., 1993—; mem. Mecklenburg (N.C.) Bd. County Commrs., 1966-72, chmn., 1967-68, 70-71; v.p. Nat. Assn. Regional Couns., 1971-72; pres. N.C. Assn. County Commrs., 1970-71; mem., tuba player Charlotte Symphony, 1961-66. Danforth fellow, 1957-60. Mem. Beta Theta Pi (v.p., trustee 1966-69, pres. 1975-78), Masons (33 deg.), Shriners. Presbyterian. Office: PO Box 32861 Charlotte NC 28232-2861

MARTIN, JAMES HARBERT, school administrator, retired Air Force officer; b. Sparta, Tenn., Jan. 5, 1941; s. Harbert Rogers and Monia Gladys (Grissom) M.; m. Madoline Carter, Sept. 14, 1963; children: Erin Dawn, Ann Farley, John Harbert. MSBA, Tenn. Tech. U., 1963; MBA, Auburn U., 1975. CPA; cert. profl. logistician. Commd. USAF, 1963, advanced through ranks to col., 1983; dep. program mgr. B1B System Program Office, 1982-84; dir. logistics Aero. Systems Div., Wright-Patterson AFB, Ohio, 1984-86; dep. comdr. resources Incirlik Air Base, Adana, Turkey, 1986-88; comdr. Tyndall AFB, Panama City, Fla., 1988-90; vice comdr. Air Force Engring. and Svcs. Ctr., Tyndall AFB, 1990; ret., 1990; exec. dir. Lookout Mountain (Ga.) Golf Club, 1991-94; CFO Riverside Mil. Acad., Gainesville, Ga., 1994—. Mem. exec. bd. Gulf Coast coun. Boy Scouts Am., Pensacola, Fla., 1989-92; chmn. Bay County WalkAmerica (March of Dimes), Panama City, 1990. Decorated Legion of Merit (2). Mem. Air Force Assn., Masons. Republican. Methodist. Office: Riverside Mil Acad Box 565 2001 Riverside Dr Gainesville GA 30501

MARTIN, JAMES JOHN, JR., retired consulting research firm executive, systems analyst; b. Paterson, N.J., Feb. 3, 1936; s. James John and Lillian (Lea) M.; m. Lydia Elizabeth Bent, June 11, 1954; children: David, Peter, Laura, Daniel, Lucas. B.A., U. Wis.-Madison, 1955; postgrad., Div. Sch., Harvard U., 1955-57; M.S., Navy Postgrad. Sch., 1963; Ph.D., MIT, 1965. Commd. ensign USN, 1957, advanced through grades to comdr., 1971, ret., 1977; sector v.p. Sci. Applications Internat. Corp., La Jolla, Calif., 1977-95. Author: Bayesian Decision Problems and Markov Chains, 1967; editor: On Not Confusing Ourselves, 1991; author articles on nat. security. Bd. dirs. Mil. Conflict Inst., 1986-92. Decorated Legion of Merit; recipient Superior Svc. medal Dept. Def. Mem. Internat. Inst. Strategic Studies, Ops. Research Soc. Am., Mil. Ops. Research Soc. (bd. dirs. 1974-77). Republican. Avocation: cooking. Home: 6603 Aranda Ave La Jolla CA 92037-6216

MARTIN, JAMES KIRBY, historian, educator; b. Akron, Ohio, May 26, 1943; s. Paul Elmo and Dorothy Marie (Garrett) M.; m. Karen Wierwille, Aug. 7, 1965; children: Darcy Elizabeth, Sarah Marie, Joelle Kathryn Garrett. B.A. summa cum laude, Hiram Coll., 1965; M.A., U. Wis., 1967, Ph.D., 1969. Asst. prof. history Rutgers U., New Brunswick, N.J., 1969-73, assoc. prof., 1973-79, prof., 1979-80, asst. provost, 1972-74, v.p. acad. affairs, 1977-79; vis. prof. Rutgers Ctr. of Alcohol Studies, 1978-88; prof. history U. Houston, 1980—, chmn. dept., 1980-83; vis. prof. history Rice U, 1992; chmn. bd. sponsors Papers of Thomas Edison Project, 1977-80; mem. editorial adv. bd. Papers of William Livingston Project, 1973-80. Author: Men in Rebellion, 1973, In the Course of Human Events, 1979, (with M.E. Lender) A Respectable Army: The Military Origins of the Republic, 1982 (contemporary mil. reading lists), Drinking in America: A History, 1982, rev. edit. 1987, (with others) America and Its People, 1989, 2d edit., 1993, concise edit. 1995; editor: Interpreting Colonial America, 1973, 2d edit. 1978, The Human Dimensions of Nation Making (with K. Stubaus) The America Revolution, Whose Revolution?, 1977, 81 (with M.E. Lender) Citizen-Soldier: The Revolutionary War Journal of Joseph Bloomfield, 1982 (R.P. McCormick prize), Ordinary Courage: The Revolutionary War Adventures of Joseph Plum Martin, 1993; mem. bd. editors Houston Rev., 1981, N.J. History, 1986, Conversations with the Past Series, 1993-95; gen. editor Am. Social Experience Series, 1983—. Recipient N.J. Soc. of the Cin. prize for Disting. Achievement in Am. History, 1995, Hiram Coll. Alumni Achievement award, 1996. Mem. Tex. Assn. for Advancement History (bd. dirs. 1981-93, v.p. 1986-90), Inst. for Internat. Bus. Analysis (adv. coun. 1982-86), Am. Hist. Assn. (Beveridge-Dunning prize com. 1990-93), Orgn. Am. Historians, So. Hist. Assn., Soc. Historians Early Am. Republic (adv. coun. 1985-88), Phi Beta Kappa, Phi Kappa Phi, Pi Gamma Mu, Omicron Delta Kappa, Phi Alpha Theta. Office: U Houston Dept History 4800 Calhoun Rd Houston TX 77204-3785

MARTIN, JAMES ROBERT, identification company executive; b. Indpls., Mar. 31, 1943; s. Walter and Helen (Snider) M.; m. Jan. 24, 1970 (div. Dec. 1990); children: Julia, Justin; m. Tamara Hicks, Dec. 21, 1991; stepchildren: Hunter Hoskins, Laura Hoskins. BA, DePauw U., 1965; MBA, Ind. U., 1967. Bus. analyst TRW, Inc., Redondo Beach, Calif., 1967-70; fin. analyst Internat. Industries, Beverly Hills, Calif., 1970; v.p. fin., treas. A & E Plastik Pak Co., Inc., Industry, Calif., 1970-75; pres. Plasti-Line, Inc., Knoxville, Tenn., 1975-92, chmn., CEO, 1992—; bd. dirs. 1st Am. Corp., Nashville, Signal Thread Co., Chattanooga, Tenn. Bd. dirs. Knoxville Symphony Soc., 1976, Fort Sanders Health System, Knoxville United Way; bd. dirs., vice-chmn. Am. Symphony Orch. League, Washington, Webb Sch., Knoxville, 1986; bd. dirs., chmn. fin. com. Thompson Cancer Survival Ctr., Knoxville, 1985; bd. mem. Knoxville Mus. Art. Mem. Chief Execs. Orgn., Club LeConte (bd. dirs.), East Tenn. Automobile Club (bd. dirs.), St. Francis Yacht Club, Cherokee Country Club. Republican. Episcopalian. Home: 1029 Scenic Dr Knoxville TN 37919-7641 Office: Plasti-Line Inc PO Box 59043 Knoxville TN 37950-9043

MARTIN, JAMES RUSSELL, lawyer; b. Columbus, Ohio, June 24, 1947; s. Robert Wells and Gwendolyn (Collins) M.; m. Susan Virginia Jarman, Aug. 4, 1973; children: James Russell Jr., Elizabeth Collins. BA in History, Denison U., 1969; JD, U. Denver, 1972. Bar: Colo. 1972, U.S. Dist. Ct. Colo. 1972. Sole practice Denver, 1972-74, 76-78, 1983-85; asst. atty. gen. State of Colo., Denver, 1974-76; v.p. Butterwick Enterprises Ltd., Denver, 1978-81, pres., 1981-83; ptnr. Baker & Hostetler, Denver, 1985—. Mem. ABA, Colo. Bar Assn., Denver Bar Assn. Club: Hiwan Golf (Evergreen, Colo.). Avocations: skiing, tennis, golf, cycling. Office: Baker & Hostetler 303 E 17th Ave Ste 1100 Denver CO 80203-1264*

MARTIN, JAY HERBERT, psychoanalysis and English educator; b. Newark, Oct. 30, 1935; s. Sylvester K. and Ada M. (Smith) M.; m. Helen Bernadette Saldini, June 9, 1956; children: Helen E., Laura A., Jay Herbert. AB with honors, Columbia U., 1956; MA, Ohio State U., 1957, PhD, 1960; PhD in Psychoanalysis, So. Calif. Psychoanalytic Inst., 1983. Instr. English Pa. State U., 1957-58; instr., then asst. to assoc. prof. English and Am. Studies Yale U., New Haven, Conn., 1960-68; prof. English and comparative culture U. Calif., Irvine, 1968-79; asst. prof. psychiatry and human behavior, clin. supr. residency program Calif. Coll. Medicine Calif. Coll. Medicine U. Calif., Irvine, 1978-96; Leo S. Bing prof. English and Am. lit. U. So. Calif., Irvine, 1979-96, dir. undergrad. program in Am. studies, 1968-69, dir. program in comparative culture, 1969-71, dir. edn. abroad program, 1971-75, dir. grad. studies dept. English, 1980-83; chaired prof. of govt. and humanities Claremont McKenna Coll., 1996—; instr. psychoanalysis So. Calif. Psychoanalytic Inst., 1984-96; Bicentennial prof. Am. lit. and culture Moscow State U., USSR, 1976; vis. Parmenter lectr. Children's Hosp., San Francisco, 1989, Ann. William Faulkner Lecture, 1991, Herman Serota Found. lecture, 1992; cons. to pub. houses; lectr. USSR, Poland, Norway, France, Costa Rica, Fed. Republic Germany, Brazil, Can., U. London, Hebrew U., Jerusalem, Seoul, Rep. Korea, Bergen, Norway; dir. NEH summer sems., 1976, 77; mem. evaluation com. dept. pvt. post-secondary edn. State of Calif., 1986; cons. numerous univs., pubs., NEA, NEA, J.S. Guggenheim Found., Calif. Coun. for Humanities and Pub. Policy, U.S. Congress Com. on Edn. and Labor; faculty assoc. Coun. Internat. Exch. of Scholars; frequent speaker profl. orgns. and sems., univs., confs., hosps. Author: (criticism and biography) Conrad Aiken: A Life of His Art, 1962, Harvests of Change: American Literature 1865-1914, 1967, Nathanael West: The Art of His Life, 1970 (U. Calif. Friends Libr. award), Robert Lowell, 1970, Always Merry and Bright. The Life of Henry Miller, 1978, (U. Calif. Friends of Libr. award, Phi Kappa Phi Best Faculty Publ. prize U. So. Calif., transl. in French, Japanese and German), (fiction) Winter Dreams: An American in Moscow, 1979, Who Am I This Time, Uncovering the Fictive Personality, 1988 (Burlington No. Found. award 1989); Swallowing Tigers Whole, 1996, a Corresponding Leap of Love: Henry Miller, 1996; and Henry Miller Dream Song, author one hour radio drama, William Faulkner. Sound Portraits of Twentieth-Century Humanists, starring Tennessee Williams, Glenn Close, Colleen Dewhurst, Nat. Pub. Radio, 1980; author sects. 24 books including most recently American Writing Today, vol. I, 1982, The Haunted Dusk: American Supernatural Fiction, 1820-1902, 1983, Frontiers of Infant Psychiatry, vol.II, 1986, Centenary Essays on Huckleberry Finn, 1985, Robert Lowell: Essays on the Poetry, 1987, William Faulkner: The Best from American Literature, 1989, The Homosexualities: Reality, Fantasy and the Arts, 1991, Life Guidance Through Literature, 1992, Biography and Source Studies, 1995, William Faulkner and Psychology, 1995, Psychotherapy East and West, 1996; contbr. numerous articles and revs. to profl. jours., bulls., L.A. Times Book Rev., Partisan Rev., N.Y. Times Book Rev., Internat. Rev. Psycho-Analysis, Am. Lit., London Times Lit. Supplement; editor: Winfield Townley Scott (Yale series recorded poets), 1962, Twentieth Century Interpretations of the Waste Land: A Collection of Critical Essays, 1968, Twentieth Century Views of Nathanael West, 1972, A Singer in the Dawn: Reinterpretations of Paul Laurence Dunbar (with intro.), 1975, Economic Depression and American Humor (with intro.), 1986, The Theory and Practice of the Contemporary American Short Story, 1996; mem. editl. bd. Am. Lit., 1978-81, Humanities in Society, 1979-1983; editor-in-chief Psychoanalytic Edn., 1984-89; appearances on TV and radio including Connie Martinson Talks Books Barbara Brunner Nightline, Sonya Live in L.A., Oprah Winfrey Show, 1988-89. Pres. Friends of Irvine Pub. Libr., 1974-75; mem. Com. for Freud Mus. Recipient Fritz Schmidl Meml. prize for rsch. applied psychoanalysis Seattle Assn. Psychoanalysis, 1982,

Marie H. Briehl prize for child psychoanalysis, 1982, Franz Alexander prize in psychoanalysis, 1984; Morse rsch. fellow, 1963-64, Am. Philos. Soc. fellow, 1966, J.S. Guggenheim fellow, 1966-67, Rockefeller Found.humanities sr. fellow, 1975-76, Rsch. Clin. fellow So. Calif. Psychoanalytic Soc. 1977-81, Rockefeller fellow, Bellagio, Italy, 1983, NEH sr. fellow, 1983-84. Mem. So. Calif. Am. Studies Assn. (pres. 1969-71), Am. Studies Assn. (exec. bd. 1969-71, del. to MLA Assembly 1974, chmn. Ralph Gabriel prize com. 1975-77), MLA (chmn. prize com. Jay B. Hubbell Silver medal in Am. lit. 1978-84), Nat. Assn. Arts and Letters (prize com. 1987-88), Nat. Humanities Faculty (advisor to Valhalla High Sch., El Cajon, Calif. 1979-81), Nat. Am. Studies Faculty, Internat. Psychoanalytic Assn., Internat. Assn. Empirical Aesthetics, Internat. Assn. U. Profs. English, Internat. Karen Horney Soc., Phi Beta Kappa. Home: 18651 Via Palatino Irvine CA 92715-3445

MARTIN, JEFFREY ALLEN, anesthesiologist; b. Sacramento, Dec. 3, 1956; s. Edward and Doris Ester (Marsch) M.; m. Sherry Lee Kroll, Oct. 16, 1993. BA in Psychology cum laude, Washington and Jefferson Coll., 1978; M of Med. Sci., Emory U., 1983; MD, Med. Coll. Ga., 1991. Diplomate Nat. Bd. Med. Examiners, Am. Bd. Anesthesiology; lic. physician asst., Ga., lic. physician, Pa. Physician asst. dept. anesthesiology divsn. cardiothoracic anesthesia Emory U. Hosp., Atlanta, 1983-91, mem. sci. staff, 1983-91, chief anesthetist cardiac transplant team, 1985-87; intern in medicine Nat. Naval Med. Ctr., Bethesda, Md., 1991-92, resident in anesthesiology, 1992-95, chief resident in anesthesiology, 1995; clin. scholar in anesthesiology Yale U., 1995-96; asst. dept. head Naval Hosp. Submarine Base, Groton, Conn., 1995-96, attending anesthesiologist, 1995—; clin. instr. cardiothoracic anesthesia, Emory U. Sch. Medicine, Atlanta, 1983-91; tng. cardiothoracic anesthesia Yale New Haven Hosp.; attending anesthesiologist Yale New Haven Hosp. Yale U. Contbr. articles to profl. jours. Lt. Cmdr. 1991-95. Mem. AMA, Am. Soc. Anesthesiologists, Am. Acad. Anesthesia Assocs. (v.p. 1985, pres. 1986), Undersea and Hyperbaric Med. Soc., Pa. Med. Soc., Wayne Pike Med. Soc., Navy Anesthesia Soc., Soc. Air Force Physicians, Ducks Unltd., Delta Tau Delta (Outstanding Young Am. award 1977). Republican. Avocations: skiing, scuba, hunting, fishing, martial arts. Home: 33 Mott Ave New London CT 06320-2841 Office: Naval Hosp Submarine Base Groton CT 06322

MARTIN, JENNIFER KAYE, artist, educator; b. Pearisburg, Va., Dec. 13, 1947; d. Arthur Paul and Lorraine (Porterfield) M.; m. Danny L. Evans, Sept. 6, 1967 (div. Jan. 1985); 1 child, Paul Edward Evans. BA cum laude, Va. Polytech. Inst., 1991, MFA, 1994. Prototype electronic tech. model shop Electro-Tec Corp. KDI, Blacksburg, Va., 1971-83; supr., coord. electronic prodn. Internat. Sci. Industries, Christiansburg, Va., 1983-85; electronic tech., supr., coord. tech. staff Va. Polytech. Inst., Blacksburg, 1985-88, electronic tech., physics cons., 1988-92; artist, cons. Blacksburg, 1992—; physics cons. AMY rsch. detector in supercollider, Ibaraki, Japan. Group shows include Artlink Contemporary Art Space, Fort Wayne, Ind., 1986 (purchase award 1986), Ariel Gallery, N.Y.C., 1988, Art Gallery Fells Point, Balt., 1988 (Best in show award 1988), Davidson County Art Guild, Lexington, N.C., 1988 (Best in Graphics Category 1988). Mem. Golden Key Nat. Honor Soc., Phi Kappa Phi, Tau Sigma Delta (life). Avocation: painting nature. Home and Studio: 411 W Main St Christiansburg VA 24073-3312

MARTIN, JERRI WHAN, public relations executive; b. Aurora, Ill., Oct. 21, 1931; d. Forest Livings and Geraldeane Jeanette (Cutler) Whan; m. Charles L. Martin (div.); children: Vicki, Bill, Erica, Kevin. BMus, Wichita State U., 1952. Co-owner Sta. KCNY, San Marcos, Tex., 1957-70; correspondent Austin Am.-Statesman, 1959-85; co-owner Sta. KWFT, Wichita Falls, Kans., 1965-96; cons. U.S. Office Econ. Opportunity, Austin, 1966-68, Tex. Ednl. Found., Inc., San Marcos, 1975—. Pres. Hays County Women's Polit. Caucus, Tex., 1985-89; officer Tex. Women's Polit. Caucus, 1990; del. State Dem. Convs., Dallas, Houston, 1982, 84, 96; bd. dirs. Ctrl. Tex. Higher Edn. Authority, San Marcos, 1982-87, Scheib Opportunity Ctr., San Marcos, 1983-90; bd. dirs., chm. Edwards Underground Water Dist., San Antonio, 1985-96; trustee Tex. Ednl. Found., Inc., 1991—. Named Outstanding Reporter in Tex., Tex. Legis., 1960; inducted into San Marcos Hall of Fame, 1993; recipient Extraordinary Svc. award Trust for Pub. Land, 1994. Mem. San Marcos C. of C., LWV, Hays Women's Ctr. Office: Tex Ednl Found Inc PO Box 1108 San Marcos TX 78667-1108

MARTIN, JERRY C., oil company executive; b. Indpls., May 10, 1932; s. Joel C. and Blanche J. (Traubel) M.; m. Marilyn L. Brock, Sept. 7, 1952 (div. 1976); children: Cathy J., Kiefer, Douglas E.; m. Connie B. Young, May 8, 1979 (div. 1988); m. Rachel M. Fulgieri, Aug. 22, 1990. BS in Acctg., Butler U., 1953. Acct. Allison div. Gen. Motors, Indpls., 1953-57; acctng. and budget mgr. Standard Oil, Indpls., 1957-60; budget dir. Inland Container Corp., Indpls., 1960-71; corp. controller Storm Drilling and Marine Co., Chgo., 1971-75; v.p. Scottsman Norwood, Houston, 1975-76; corp. controller Internat Systems and Controls, Houston, 1976-79; v.p., controller Global Marine Drilling Co., Houston, 1979-85; sr. v.p., chief fin. officer Global Marine, Inc., Houston, 1985—. Bd. dirs. Global Marine Inc., 1993—. Mem. Fin. Execs. Inst., Mensa, Westlake Club, Westside Tennis Club, Houstonian Club. Republican. Avocation: tennis. Office: Global Marine Inc 777 N Eldridge Pky Houston TX 77079-4425

MARTIN, JERRY LEE, organization executive, philosophy educator; b. Turkey, Tex., Oct. 16, 1941. Student, San Diego State Coll., 1961; BA in Polit. Sci., U. Calif., Riverside, 1963; MA in Philosophy and Polit. Sci., U. Chgo., 1966; PhD in Philosophy, Northwestern U., 1970. Asst. prof. U. Colo., Boulder, 1967-74, chmn. dept. philosophy, 1979-81, assoc. prof., 1974-84, adjunct prof., 1984—; rsch. analyst House Rep. Rsch. Com., 1982-87; legis. asst. Congressman Hank Brown, 1982-87; dir. divisn. edn. programs NEH, Washington, 1987-88, asst. chmn. studies and evaluation, 1988-89, asst. chmn. programs and policy, 1989—, acting chmn., 1993; adj. prof. Georgetown U., 1993—; adj. scholar Am. Enterprise Inst.; dir. Ctr. Study Values and Social Policy, U. Colo., Boulder, 1981-82; founding mem. organized rsch. program State of Colo., 1981-82; mem. exec. com. faculty adv. coun. Colo. Commn. Higher Edn., 1980-82; pres. Nat. Alumni Forum, 1995—; spkr. in field, frequent guest on radio and TV. Contbr. articles to profl. jours. Andrew W. Mellon Found. Congl. fellow, 1992-93. Mem. AAUP (state pres. 1977-79), Am. Philos. Assn., Soc. Historians Early Am. Republic, Am. Polit. Sci. Assn., Soc. Social, Polit. and Legal Philosophy. Avocations: tennis, baseball, hist. tours. Home: 5902 Mount Eagle Dr Apt 108 Alexandria VA 22303-2514 Office: Nat Alumni Forum 1625 K St NW Ste 310 Washington DC 20006

MARTIN, JIM G., church renewal consultant; b. Mannington, W.Va., Nov. 16, 1933; s. Jacob Calvin and Dona Marie (Edgel) M.; m. R. Carolyn Holdman, Dec. 28, 1957; children: Susan Diane Martin Fenker, Stephen Glen. Pastor Bloom Ctr. Ch. of God, Bloomdale, Ohio, 1955-57, Esther (Mo.) Ch. of God, 1957-61, Silver Creek Ch. of God, Silver Lake, Ind., 1961-69, Oak Grove Ch. of God, Columbia City, Ind., 1969-77, Enola (Pa.) Ch. of God, 1977-81; sr. pastor Chambersburg (Pa.) Ch. of God, 1985-92; renewal assoc. Chs. of God Gen. Conf., Findlay, Ohio, 1992—. Office: Churches of God PO Box 926 700 E Melrose Ave Findlay OH 45840-4417

MARTIN, JOAN CALLAHAM, psychologist, educator; b. N.Y.C., June 9, 1930; d. Jack Alfred and Mary Louise (Williams) Callaham; m. Donald Charles Martin, Aug. 15, 1959; children: Walter Michael, Steven Raymond. B.A., U. Fla., 1959; M.S., Fla. State U., 1962, Ph.D., 1965. Postdoctoral trainee Duke U. Med. Center, Durham, N.C., 1965-67; postdoctoral fellow Duke U. Med. Center (Center for Aging and Human Devel.), 1967-69, asst. prof. psychiatry and research asso. anatomy, 1969-71; adminstrv. fellow NIH, Bethesda, Md., 1971-72; asso. prof. psychiatry and behavioral sci. U. Wash., Seattle, 1972-79; asso. dean U. Wash. (Grad. Sch.), 1977-80, prof./research coordinator psychiatry and behavioral scis., 1979—; clinical psychologist, 1990—; mem. gen. research support review com., div. research resources NIH, 1980—; cons. Nat. Cancer Inst., NIH, 1971-79; lectr. Mem. editorial bd. Neurobehavioral Toxicology and Teratology; contbr. articles to profl. jours.; referee: Sci., Physiology and Behavior, Pharm. Biochem. and Behavioral Psychopharmacology. Mem. Am. Psychol. Assn., N.Y. Acad. Sci., Teratology Soc., Psychonomic Soc., Assn. Women in Sci., Am. Assn. Univ. Profs. (pres. 1993-95), Sigma Xi. Office: U Wash Dept Psychiatry & Behavioral Sci Seattle WA 98195

MARTIN, JOANNE, business educator; b. Salem, Mass., Sept. 25, 1946; d. Richard Drake and Nathalie (Ashton) M.; m. Beaumont A. Sheil, July 9, 1977; 1 child, Beaumont Martin Sheil. BA, Smith Coll., 1968; PhD in Social Psychology, Harvard U., 1977. Assoc. cons. McBer & Co. (formerly Behavior Sci. Ctr. of Sterling Inst.), 1968-70, dir. govt. mktg., 1970-72; asst. prof. orgnl. behavior and sociology Grad. Sch. Bus., Stanford (Calif.) U., 1977-80; assoc. prof. grad. sch. bus. Stanford (Calif.) U., 1980-91, prof. grad. sch. bus., 1991—, dir. doctoral programs, grad. sch. bus., 1991-95, Fred H. Merrill prof. orgn. behavior and sociology, 1996—, mem. univ. adv. bd., 1995—; vis. scholar Australian Grad. Sch. of Mgmt., U. N.S.W., Dept. Psychology, Sydney (Australia) U., 1989-90; Ruffin fellow bus. ethics Darden Grad. Sch. of Bus. Adminstrn., U. Va., 1990. Author/co-author four books; contbr. over four dozen articles to profl. jours. Lena Lake Forrest Rsch. fellowship Bus. and Profl. Women's Found., 1978, James and Doris McNamara Faculty fellowship Grad. Sch. of Bus., Stanford U., 1990-91. Fellow APA (dissertation award), Acad. of Mgmt. (western divsn. promising young scholar award 1982, rep.-at-large 1983-85, divsn. program chair 1985-87, divsn. chair 1987-89, nat. bd. govts. 1992-95), Am. Psychol. Soc.; mem. Cons. Psychologists Press (bd. dirs.). Office: Stanford U Grad Sch Bus Stanford CA 94305

MARTIN, JOEL JEROME, physics educator; b. Jamestown, N.D., Mar. 27, 1939; s. Clarence and Marian (Stelter) M. BS in Physics, S.D. State U., 1961, MS in Physics, 1962; PhD in Physics, Iowa State U., 1967. Postdoctoral fellow Ames Lab. Iowa State U., Ames, 1967-69; asst. prof. Okla. State U., Stillwater, 1969-73, assoc. prof., 1973-79, prof., 1979—. Contbr. articles to profl. jours. Mem. Am. Phys. Soc., Am. Assn. Physics Tchrs., Am. Assn. for Crystal Growth. Office: Okla State U Dept Physics Stillwater OK 74078*

MARTIN, JOHN BRUCE, chemical engineer; b. Auburn, Ala., Feb. 2, 1922; s. Herbert Marshall and Lannie (Steadham) M.; m. Mildred Jane Foster, Aug. 7, 1943 (dec. Nov. 1960); children—Shirlie Martin Briggs, John Bruce; m. 2d, Phyllis Barbara Rodgers, June 25, 1963; 1 child, Richard Kipp. B.S., Ala. Poly. Inst., 1943; M.Sc., Ohio State U., 1947, Ph.D., 1949. Registered profl. engr., Ohio. With Procter & Gamble Co., Cin., 1949-82, coordinator orgn. devel., research and devel., 1967-77, mgr. indsl. chem. market research, 1977-82; sr. assoc. Indumar Inc., Cin., 1982-86, sr. v.p., 1986-87; lectr. U. Cin., 1982-88; adj. assoc. prof. Auburn U., 1983-88. Contbr. articles to profl. jours.; patentee in field. Served with AUS, 1943-46. Decorated Air Medal, Bronze Star with oak leaf cluster; recipient Disting. Alumnus award Coll. Engring., Ohio State U., 1970, Disting. Engr. award Tech. Socs. Council Cin., 1982. Fellow AIChE (bd. dirs. 1968-70, chmn. mktg. divsn. 1985, Mktg. Hall of Fame 1988, Chem. Engr. of Yr. award Ohio Valley 1971); mem. Am. Chem. Soc., Am. Soc. Engring. Edn., Engring. Soc. Cin. (pres. 1972-73), Tech. and Sci. Socs. Cin. (pres. 1972-73), Chem. Mgmt. and Resources Assn., Sigma Xi, Tau Beta Pi, Phi Kappa Phi, Phi Lambda Upsilon. Republican. Mem. Disciples of Christ Ch. Home: 644 Doepke Ln Cincinnati OH 45231-5045

MARTIN, J(OHN) EDWARD, architectural engineer; b. L.A., Oct. 23, 1916; s. Albert C. and Carolyn Elizabeth (Borchard) M.; m. Elizabeth Jane Hines, May 27, 1944; children: Nicolas Edward, Peter Hines, Sara Jane McKinley Reed, Christopher Carey, Elizabeth Margaret Ferguson. Student, U. So. Calif., 1934-36; BS in Archtl. Engring., U. Ill., 1939. Registered profl. engr., Calif., Ill. Structural engr. Albert C. Martin & Assocs., L.A., 1939-42, ptnr., 1945-75, mng. ptnr., 1975-86. Founding mem. bd. trustees Thomas Aquinas Coll., Santa Paula, Calif., 1971—. Lt. USNR, 1942-45. Fellow ASCE; mem. Structural Engrs. Assn. Calif., Cons. Engrs. Assn. Calif., Jonathan Club (bd. dirs. 1978-81), Calif. Club (Ranchero Visitadores), Valley Hunt Club, Flintridge Riding Club, West Hills Hunt Club (Master of Fox Hounds 1975-88), Saddle & Sirloin Club, Rep. Assn. L.A., Heritage Found., Traditional Mass Soc. (founder). Republican. Roman Catholic. Avocation: horsemanship. Office: Albert C Martin & Assocs 811 W 7th St Los Angeles CA 90017-3408

MARTIN, JOHN GUSTIN, investment banker; b. Bay Port, Mich., Dec. 25, 1928; s. Rig and Phoebe (Ballard) M.; m. Patricia Jean Martell, Nov. 16, 1957; children: James Martell, John Douglas. BA, Mich. State Coll., 1952; student, U. Detroit Law Sch., 1952-54. With First of Mich. Corp., Detroit, 1952—; sr. v.p. First of Mich. Corp., 1966-69, exec. v.p., 1969, pres., 1970—, dir., 1966—; trustee Renaissance Assets Trust; mem. regional firms adv. com. N.Y. Stock Exch. Chmn. bd. Bon Secours Health System Found., Grosse Pointe, Mich. Mem. Bond Club Detroit (pres. 1961), Security Traders Detroit (pres. 1963), Investment Bankers Am. (nat. com. 1969—), Nat. Assn. Security Dealers (nat. com. 1973), Security Industry Assn. (bd. dirs. 1986-89), Mich. State U. Bus. Alumni Assn. (dir., recipient Outstanding Alumni award 1974). Clubs: Detroit, Grosse Pointe Yacht, Renaissance. Home: 794 N Saint Joseph St #44 Suttons Bay MI 49682-9755 Office: First of Michigan Corp 100 Renaissance Ctr Fl 26 Detroit MI 48243-1003

MARTIN, JOHN HUGH, lawyer, retired; b. Los Angeles, Apr. 19, 1918; s. John Hume and Carrie Suzanne (Hatcher) M.; m. Jean Morrison Park, Sept. 17, 1945; 1 dau., Suzanne L. B.S., Monmouth Coll., 1939; J.D., U. Chgo., 1942. Bar: Ill. 1943, Calif. 1962. Practice law Chgo., 1943-52; sec., gen. counsel Am. Community Builders, Park Forest, Ill., 1952-54; dep. counsel Bur. Aero., Dept. Navy, Washington, 1954-57; with Lockheed Aircraft Corp., Burbank, Calif., 1957-79; European counsel Lockheed Aircraft Corp., 1960-61, div. counsel, 1961-71, asst. sec., chief counsel, 1971-77, corp. adv., 1977-79; pvt. practice law, 1980-94, retired, 1994. Mem. Am., Fed., Internat., Los Angeles County bar assns., Phi Alpha Delta. Democrat. Episcopalian. Club: Legal (Chgo.);. Home: 1611 Arboles Dr Glendale CA 91207-1127

MARTIN, JOHN JOSEPH, journalist; b. N.Y.C., Dec. 3, 1938; s. John and Marie Agnes (Jacobsen) M.; children from previous marriage: Sophie Suzanne, Claire Catherine; m. Katherine Fitzhugh, Feb. 14, 1987. BA in Journalism, San Diego State U., 1995. Copy editor, reporter San Diego Union, 1958-62; copy editor Augusta (Ga.) Chronicle, 1963, N.Y. Times Internat. Edit., Paris, 1964-65; editorial asst. Temple Fielding Publs., Mallorca, Spain, 1965-66; reporter, producer Sta. KCRA-TV News, Sacramento, 1966-75; corr. ABC-TV News, 1975—. Served with U.S. Army, 1962-64. Recipient Nat. Headliner awards, 1980, 89, NSPE award, 1982, Nat. Assn. Home Care award, 1992, Emmy award, 1993, George Polk award, 1994, DuPont-Columbia U. Gold baton. Mem. AFTRA, U.S. Tennis Assn., Coffee House Club N.Y.C., Nat. Press Club. Office: 1717 Desales St NW Washington DC 20036-4401

MARTIN, JOHN L., state legislator; b. Eagle Lake, Maine, June 5, 1941; s. Frank and Edwidge (Raymond) M. BA in History and Govt., U. Maine, 1963, postgrad., 1963-64. Tchr. Am. govt. and history Ft. Kent (Maine) Community High Sch., 1966-72; instr. U. Maine, Ft. Kent, 1972—; asst. prof. U. Maine, 1989—; mem. from Eagle Lake and St. Francis dist. Maine Ho. of Reps., 1964—, minority fl. leader, 1970-74, speaker of ho., 1975-94, chmn. com. on energy & natural resources, 1994-95; adj. lectr.; mem. intergovtl. rels. com. Nat. Legis. Conf., 1970—; chmn. Maine Land Use Regulation Commn., 1972-73, Maine Bur. Human Rels., 1972, State Legis. Leaders Found., 1979—; mem. exec. bd. Nat. Conf. State Legislatures, chmn. state-fed. assembly, 1985-86, chair task force on reapportionment, 1987-88, vice chmn. budget, fiscal and rules com., 1986-87, v.p., 1988-89, pres.-elect, 1989-90, pres., 1990-91, immediate past pres., 1991-92; mem. exec. com. New Eng. Caucus of State Legislatures, 1978-95, chmn., 1982; mem. regional exec. com. Nat. Dem. State Legis. Leaders Assn., 1991-95, chmn., 1987—; bd. dirs. Found. for State Legislatures, 1988—; mem. exec. com. Dem. Nat. Com., 1991-94. Trustee Eagle Lake Water and Sewer Dist., 1966—, No. Maine Gen. Hosp., Ft. Kent, Ea. Maine Health Care, 1991—; mem. rural health steering com. Nat. Acad. for State Health Policy; advisor White House Task Force on Health Care Reform; dir. intergovtl. affairs Nat. Health Care Campaign, 1994. Mem. New Eng. Polit. Sci. Assn. Home: PO Box 250 Eagle Lake ME 04739-0250 Office: Maine Ho of Reps State House Augusta ME 04333

MARTIN, JOHN S., JR., federal judge; b. Bklyn., May 31, 1935. BA, Manhattan Coll., 1957; LLB, Columbia U., 1961. Law clk. to Hon. Leonard P. Moore U.S. Ct. Appeals (2d cir.), 1961-62; asst. U.S. atty. U.S. Dist. Ct. (so. dist.) N.Y., 1962-66; ptnr. Johnson, Hekker & Martin, Nyack, N.Y., 1966-67; asst. to solicitor gen., 1967-69, sole practitioner, 1969-72; ptnr. Martin, Obermaier & Morvillo, 1972-79, Schulte, Roth & Zabel, 1979-80; U.S. atty. U.S. Dist. Ct. for So. Dist. N.Y., N.Y.C., 1980-83; ptnr. Schulte, Roth & Zabel, 1983-90; judge U.S. Dist. Ct. for So. Dist. N.Y., N.Y.C., 1990—. Fellow Am. Coll. Trial Lawyers; mem. Assn. Bar City N.Y. Office: US Dist Ct So Dist NY 500 Pearl St New York NY 10007

MARTIN, JOHN WILLIAM, JR., lawyer, automotive industry executive; b. Evergreen Park, Ill., Sept. 1, 1936; s. John William and Frances (Hayes) M.; m. Joanne Cross, July 2, 1966; children: Amanda Hayes, Bartholomew McGuire. AB in History, DePaul U., 1958, JD, 1961. Bar: Ill. 1961, D.C. 1962, N.Y. 1964, Mich. 1970. Antitrust trial atty. Dept. Justice, Washington, 1961-62; assoc. Donovan, Leisure, Newton & Irvine, N.Y.C., 1962-70; sr. atty. Ford Motor Co., Dearborn, Mich., 1970-72, assoc. counsel, 1972-74, counsel, 1974-76, asst. gen. counsel, 1976-77, assoc. gen. counsel, 1977-89, v.p., gen. counsel, 1989—; trustee Ford Motor Co. Fund, 1989—; bd. dirs. Ctr. Social Gerontology, Inc., Nat. Women's Law Ctr. Contbr. articles to profl. jours. Mem. Assn. Gen. Counsel, Am. Law Inst. Coun., Nat. Legal Aid and Defender Assn. (bd. dirs.), Little Traverse Yacht Club. Republican. Roman Catholic. Office: Ford Motor Co The American Rd Dearborn MI 48124

MARTIN, JOSEPH, JR., lawyer, former ambassador; b. San Francisco, May 21, 1915; m. Ellen Chamberlain Martin, July 5, 1946; children: Luther Greene, Ellen Myers. AB, Yale U., 1936, LLB, 1939. Assoc. Cadwalader, Wickersham & Taft, N.Y.C., 1939-41; ptnr. Wallace, Garrison, Norton & Ray, San Francisco, 1946-55, Pettit & Martin, San Francisco, 1955-70, 73-95; gen. counsel FTC, Washington, 1970-71; ambassador, U.S. rep. Disarmament Conf., Geneva, 1971-76; mem. Pres.'s Adv. Com. for Arms Control and Disarmament, 1974-78; bd. dirs. Astec Industries, Inc. Pres. Pub. Utilities Commn., San Francisco, 1956-60; Rep. nat. committeeman for Calif., 1960-64; treas. Rep. Party Calif., 1956-58; bd. dirs. Patrons of Art and Music, Calif. Palace of Legion of Honor, 1958-70, pres., 1963-68; bd. dirs. Arms Control Assn., 1977-84; pres. Friends of Legal Assistance to Elderly, 1983-87. Lt. comdr. USNR, 1941-46. Recipient Ofcl. commendation for Outstanding Service as Gen. Counsel FTC, 1973, Distinguished Honor award U.S. ACDA, 1973, Lifetime Achievement award Legal Assistance to the Elderly, 1981. Fellow Am. Bar Found. Clubs: Burlingame Country, Pacific Union. Home: 2879 Woodside Rd Woodside CA 94062-2441 Office: 3 Embarcadero Ctr #2280 San Francisco CA 94111

MARTIN, JOSEPH BOYD, neurologist, educator; b. Bassano, Alta., Can., Oct. 20, 1938; s. Joseph Bruce and Ruth Elizabeth (Ramer) M.; m. Rachel Ann Wenger, June 18, 1960; children: Bradley, Melanie, Douglas, Neil. BSc, Eastern Mennonite Coll., Harrisonburg, Va., 1959; MD, U. Alta., 1962; PhD, U. Rochester, N.Y., 1971; MA (hon.), Harvard U., 1978; ScD (hon.), McGill U., 1994, U. Rochester, 1996. Resident in internal medicine Univ. Hosp., Edmonton, Alta., 1962-64; resident in neurology Case-Western Res. U. Hosps., 1964-67; rsch. fellow U. Rochester, N.Y., 1967-70; mem. faculty McGill U. Faculty Medicine, Montreal, Que., Can., 1970-78; prof. medicine and neurology, neurologist-in-chief Montreal Neurol. Inst., 1976-78; chmn. dept. neurology Mass. Gen. Hosp., Boston, also Dorn prof. neurology Harvard U. Med. Sch., 1978-89; dean Sch. Medicine U. Calif., San Francisco, 1989-93; chancellor U. Calif., San Francisco, 1993—; mem. med. adv. bd. Gairdner Found., Toronto, 1978-83; adv. council neurol. disorders program Nat. Inst. Neurol., Communicative Disorders and Stroke, 1979-82. Co-author: Clinical Neuroendocrinology, 1977, The Hypothalmamus, 1978, Clinical Neuroendocrinology: A Pathophysiological Approach, 1979, Neurosecretion and Brain Peptides: Implications for Brain Functions and Neurological Disease, 1981, Brain Peptides, 1983; editor Harrison's Principles of Internal Medicine, Clin. Neuroendocrinology 2d edit., 1987. Recipient Moshier Meml. gold medal U. Alta. Faculty Medicine, 1962, John W. Scott gold med. award, 1962; Med. Research Council Can. scholar, 1970-75. Mem. NAS, Internat. Soc. Neuroendocrinology (coun. 1980—), Am. Neurol. Assn. (pres. 1990), Am. Physiol. Soc. (Bowditch lectr. 1978), Royal Coll. Phys. and Surg. Can., Endocrine Soc., Soc. Neurosci., Am. Soc. Clin. Investigation, Assn. Am. Physicians, Am. Acad. Arts and Scis., Inst. of Medicine, Nat. Adv. Coun., Nat. Inst. Aging. Office: U Calif 513 Parnassus Ave Ste 126 San Francisco CA 94122-2722

MARTIN, JOSEPH PATRICK, lawyer; b. Detroit, Apr. 19, 1938; s. Joseph A. and Kathleen G. (Rich) M.; m. Denise Taylor, June 27, 1964; children: Timothy J., Julie D. Martin Digiovanni. AB magna cum laude, U. Notre Dame, 1960; JD with distinction, U. Mich., 1963; postgrad., London Sch. Econs., 1964. Bar: Mich. 1963, U.S. Dist. Ct. (ea. dist.) Mich. 1963, U.S. Ct. Appeals (6th cir.) 1967, U.S. Supreme Ct. 1979, U.S. Dist. Ct. (we. dist.) Mich. 1981. Spl. asst. to gen. counsel Ford Motor Co., Dearborn, Mich., 1962; assoc. Dykema, Wheat, Spenceer et al, Detroit, 1963-66; assoc., then ptnr. Poole Littell Sutherland, Detroit, 1966-76; sr. atty., ptnr., shareholder Butzel Long, Detroit and Birmingham, Mich., 1976-94; sr. atty., shareholder Dykema, Wheat, Spencer et al, Bingham Farms, Mich., 1994-96, Gourwitz and Barr, P.C., Southfield, Mich., 1996—; settlement moderator Mich. Ct. Appeals, 1995—; adj. prof. law U. Detroit Law Sch., 1989-92, CLE lectr., 1992—; arbitrator Am. Arbitration Assn., Southfield, 1986—, Nat. Assn. Security Dealers, 1988—, N.Y. Stock Exch., 1991—; mediator, facilitator Oak County Cir. Ct., Pontiac, Mich., 1985—, Lex Mundi Coll. Mediators, Dallas, 1992—, Mediation Tribunal Assn., Wayne County, Mich., 1995—; moderator Mich. Ct. Appeals, 1995—; spl. regional and nat. panelist large complex case program Am. Arbitration Assn., 1992—, mediation trainer, 1995—. author, editor: Laches-Oak County Bar Assn. Legal Jour., 1984, 92, 96, Real Property Rev., 1989-90, Mich. Law Weekly, 1990. Scholar Cook Found., Ford Found., London, 1963-64. Mem. ABA, Mich. Bar Assn., Detroit Bar Assn., Oakland County Bar Assn. Roman Catholic. Avocations: gardening, golf, platform tennis, walking, bridge. Home: 1663 Hoit Tower Dr Bloomfield Hills MI 48302-2630 Office: Gourwitz and Barr PC 2000 Town Center Ste 1400 Southfield MI 48075-1147

MARTIN, JOSEPH PAUL, university department director; b. Liverpool, Eng., June 28, 1936; s. Joseph and Winifred (Austin) M.; m. Roberta Martin, Aug. 7, 1971; children: Christopher, Elizabeth. PhL, Angelicum, Rome, 1960, STL, 1964; PhD, Columbia U., 1973. Cert. comparative and internat. edn. Missionary Oblate Fathers, Lesotho, 1964-67; dir. Earl Hall Ctr. Columbia U., N.Y.C., 1972-86, exec. dir. ctr. study of human rights, 1977—. Lt. Brit. Artillery, 1954-56. Mem.ACLU (ch.-state com. 1987—), African Studies Assn., Amnesty Internat. Office: Columbia U Ctr Human Rights 1108 International Affairs Bldg New York NY 10027

MARTIN, JOSEPH RAMSEY, retired philosophy educator; b. Paducah, Ky., Oct. 15, 1930; s. J. Ramsey and Mary Terry (Burnett) M.; m. Barbara Bench, Sept. 17, 1955 (dec. Jan. 1992); children: Joseph Ramsey III, Mary Case; m. Joan Garland, Oct. 8, 1993. B.A., U. Va., 1952, M.A., 1958, Ph.D., 1967. Master, head lower sch. Brooks Sch., North Andover, Mass., 1958-62; asst. prof. Transylvania Coll., Lexington, Ky., 1967-68; prof. philosophy Washington and Lee U., Lexington, Va., 1968-96, ret., 1996. Mem. Piedmont Environ. Coun., Warrenton, Va., 1973-76; bd. dirs. Va. Found. for Humanities and Pub. Policy, Charlottesville, 1982-89. Lt. USN, 1952-56. Mem. Am. Philos. Assn., Va. Philos. Assn., Airplane Owners and Pilots Assn. Home: PO Box 285 Ivy VA 22945-0285 Office: Washington and Lee U Dept Philosophy Lexington VA 24450

MARTIN, JUDITH SYLVIA, journalist, author; b. Washington, Sept. 13, 1938; d. Jacob and Helen (Aronson) Perlman; m. Robert Martin, Jan. 30, 1960; children: Nicholas Ivor, Jacobina Helen. BA, Wellesley Coll., 1959; DHL (hon.), York Coll., 1985, Adelphi U., 1991. Reporter-critic, columnist Washington Post, 1960-83; syndicated columnist United Feature Syndicate, N.Y.C., 1978—; critic-at-large Vanity Fair, 1983-84. Author: The Name on the White House Floor, 1972, Miss Manners' Guide to Excruciatingly Correct Behavior, 1982, Gilbert, 1982, Minn Manners' Guide to Rearing Perfect Children, 1984, Common Courtesy, 1985, Style and Substance, 1986, Miss Manners' Guide for the Turn-of-the-Millennium, 1989, Miss Manners on (Painfully Proper) Weddings, 1996, Miss Manners Rescues Civilization, 1996; mem. editl. bd. The American Scholar. Bd. dirs. Washington Concert Opera; mem. nat. adv. coun. Inst. Govtl. Studies, U. Calif., Berkeley. Mem. Cosmos Club (bd. mgmt.). Office: United Feature Syndicate 200 Madison Ave New York NY 10016

MARTIN, JUDSON PHILLIPS, retired education educator; b. Butler, Wis., Feb. 4, 1921; s. Darwin H. and Emma (Phillips) M.; m. June Ruth Elletson, June 19, 1948 (div.); children: Christopher Alan, Karen Marie; m. Mary Belle Jepson, Sept. 23, 1973 (dec. Apr. 1995); stepchildren: Stephen, Susan, Sandra, Christopher; m. Kathryn L. Tompkins, Feb. 17, 1996; stepchildren: David, Dale. BS, U. Wis., 1942, MA, 1946, PhD, 1955. Registrar, acad. dean Bemidji (Minn.) State U., 1946-68; dean grad. study, prof. edn. N.E. Mo. State U., 1968-71, prof. edn., 1971-80, 82-85, head div. edn. and head tchr. edn., 1980-82; substitute tchr. Seminole County, Fla., 1990—. Dist. officer Minn. Boy Scouts Am.; mem. Bemidji City Coun., 1951; pres. Red Barn Cmty. Arts Coun.; sch. vol. Seminole County, Fla., 1994—; newspaper reader for the blind Sta. WMFE, Orlando, Fla. With AUS, 1942-45. Decorated Bronze Star; Croix de Guerre (France) avec etoille. Mem. NEA, Am. Legion, Minn. Edn. Assn. (past pres. higher edn. sect.), Mo. Edn. Assn., Am. Assn. Higher Edn., Mo. Fiber Artists Assn., Weavers of Orlando, Handweavers of Am. Tropical Weavers of Fla., Masons, K.T., Elks, Kiwanis (dist. lt. gov. 1974-75), Phi Delta Kappa. Methodist. Home: 802 Live Oak Ln Oviedo FL 32765-9533

MARTIN, JUDY BRACKIN HEREFORD, higher education administrator; b. York, Ala., May 25, 1943; d. Julian Byron and Willie Lee (Aiken) B.; m. Roy Nichols Hereford, Jr., Apr. 1, 1962 (dec. Mar. 1988); children: Leanne, Roy Nichols III, Rachel, Samantha; m. John Lawrence Martin Sr., Nov. 23, 1988. BA, Judson Coll., 1964. Co-owner, ptnr. Hereford Haven Farms, Faunsdale, Ala., 1962-93; ptnr. The Mustard Seed, Demopolis, Ala., 1974-76; ptnr., sales mgr. Hereford & Assocs. Auction Co., Faunsdale, Ala., 1967-91; alumnae dir., dir. admissions Judson Coll., Marion, Ala., 1988-90, asst. to pres., 1990-94, interim v.p. for instnl. advancement, 1996—; exec. sec.-treas. Ala. Women's Hall of Fame, Judson Coll., Marion, 1991—; exec. dir. Ala. Rural Heritage Found., Thomaston, 1991-95. Officer Marengo County Red. Cross, 1987-88; mem. Marengo County Hist. Soc., Econ. Devel. Assn. Ala., 1991—; com. mem. Marengo Dem. Exec. Com.; bd. dirs. Dept. Human Resources, Marengo County, 1987-95, Marengo County Farmers Fedn. Bd., 1985-95; mem. So. Arts Fedn. Adv. Coun., 1994-95; mem. steering com. Leadership Marengo, 1994; chmn. bd. Faunsdale United Meth. Ch., 1989-91. Mem. Blackbelt Tourism Coun. (bd. dirs. 1991), Judson Coll. Alumnae Assn. (treas. 1992-96). Methodist. Avocations: cattle farming, sewing, painting.

MARTIN, JUNE JOHNSON CALDWELL, journalist; b. Toledo, Oct. 6; d. John Franklin and Eunice Imogene (Fish) Johnson; m. Erskine Caldwell, Dec. 21, 1942 (div. Dec. 1955); 1 child, Jay Erskine; m. Keith Martin, May 5, 1966. AA, Phoenix Jr. Coll., 1939-41; BA, U. Ariz., 1941-43, 53-59; student Ariz. State U., 1939, 40. Free-lance writer, 1944—; columnist Ariz. Daily Star, 1956-59; editor Ariz. Alumnus mag., Tucson, 1959-70; book reviewer, columnist Ariz. Daily Star, Tucson, 1970-94; ind. book reviewer and audio tape columnist, Tucson, 1994—; panelist, co-producer TV news show Tucson Press Club, 1954-55, pres., 1958; co-founder Ariz. Daily Star Ann. Book & Author Event. Contbg. author: Rocky Mountain Cities, 1949; contbr. articles to World Book Ency., and various mags. Mem. Tucson CD Com., 1961; vol. campaigns of Samuel Goddard, U.S. Rep. Morris Udall, U.S. ambassador and Ariz. gov. Raul Castro. Recipient award Nat. Headliners Club, 1959, Ariz. Press Club award, 1957-59, 96, Am. Alumni Council, 1966, 70. Mem. Nat. Book Critics Circle, Jr. League of Tucson, Tucson Urban League, PEN U.S.A. West, Planned Parenthood of So. Ariz., Pi Beta Phi. Democrat. Methodist. Club: Tucson Press. Home: Desert Foothills Sta PO Box 65388 Tucson AZ 85728

MARTIN, KATHLEEN MINDER, lawyer; b. Ludlow, Mass., Mar. 16, 1957; d. Norbert F. and Gladys Minder; m. Thomas O. Martin, May 21, 1982; children: Matthew Thomas, Andrew William. BA, U. Minn., 1978, JD cum laude, 1981. Bar: Minn., 1981, U.S. Dist. Ct. Minn. 1981, U.S. Ct. Appeals (8th cir.) 1982, U.S. Supreme Ct. 1995. Ptnr. Malkerson Gilliland Martin LLP, Mpls., 1996—. Mem. ABA, Minn. Bar Assn., Hennepin County Bar Assn., Mpls. Women's Rotary (pres. 1986—, v.p. 1985-86), Mpls. Club. Home: 440 Pheasant Ridge Rd Wayzata MN 55391-9581 Office: Malkerson Gilliland Martin 1500 AT&T Tower 901 Marquette Ave Minneapolis MN 55402-3205

MARTIN, KEITH, lawyer; b. Mpls., May 5, 1953; s. L. John and Lois Ann (Henze) M.; m. Linda Harvill, 1977 (div. 1985). BA, Wesleyan, 1974; JD, George Washington U., 1977; MSc, London Sch. Econs., 1978. Bar: D.C. 1978, N.Y. 1985. Legis. asst. Sen. Henry M. Jackson Washington, 1974-77, legis. counsel Sen. Daniel Patrick Moynihan, 1979-82; ptnr. Chadbourne & Parke, Washington, 1983—, mng. ptnr., 1989-93. Democrat. Office: Chadbourne & Parke 1101 Vermont Ave NW Washington DC 20005-3521

MARTIN, KEN, insurance executive. Pres. Sedgwick Noble Lowndes. Office: 1285 Ave of Americas New York NY 10019

MARTIN, KEVIN JOHN, nephrologist, educator; b. Dublin, Ireland, Jan. 18, 1948; came to U.S., 1973; s. John Martin and Maura (Tighe) M.; m. Grania E. O'Connor, Nov. 16, 1972; children: Alan, John, Ciara, Audrey. MB BCh, Univ. Coll. Dublin, 1971. Diplomate Am. Bd. Internal Medicine, Am. Bd. Nephrology. Intern St. Vincent's Hosp., Dublin, 1971-72, resident, 1972-73; resident Barnes Hosp., St. Louis, 1973-74, fellow, 1974-77; asst. prof. Washington U., St. Louis, 1977-84, assoc. prof., 1984-89; prof., dir. div. nephrology St. Louis U., 1989—. Contbr. numerous articles to med. jours. Office: Saint Louis Univ Med Ctr 3635 Vista Ave Saint Louis MO 63110-2539

MARTIN, LE ROY, accounting firm executive; b. 1941. With Mc Gladrey & Pullen, Mpls., 1962—, now mng. ptnr., CEO. Office: Mc Gladrey & Pullen 800 MArquette Ave Ste 1300 Minneapolis MN 55402*

MARTIN, LEE, mechanical engineer; b. Elkhart, Ind., Feb. 7, 1920; s. Ross and Esther Lee (Schweitzer) M.; m. Geraldine Faith Fitzgarrald, July 20, 1945; children: Jennifer L., Casper, Rex, Elizabeth L. SBME, SMME, MIT, 1943. With GE, 1940-42; with NIBCO Inc., Elkhart, 1943—, pres., 1957-76, chmn., 1975—. Chmn. Samaritan Inst., Denver, 1980-86; dir. Interlochen (Mich.) Ctr. for Arts, 1983-94; trustee Tri-State U., Angola, Ind., 1973-88. Mem. Union League Club (Chgo.).

MARTIN, LELAND MORRIS (PAPPY MARTIN), history educator; b. Patrick Springs, Va., Aug. 8, 1930; s. Rufus Wesley and Mary Hilda (Biggs) M.; m. Mildred Greer, May 12, 1956; children: Lee Ann Martin Powell, Mitzi Jo. AB, Berea Coll., 1953; MS, U. Tenn., 1954; grad., Air War Coll., Maxwell AFB, Ala., 1978; MA in History, U Tex. Pan-Am., 1993. Enlisted USAF, 1954, advanced through grades to col., 1977; comdr. RAF, Greenham Common, Welford, 1974-76; comdt., comdr. Mil. Airlift Command Noncommisioned Officers Acad., McGuire AFB, N.J., 1976-79; vice comdr., comdr. RAF Mildenhall and RAF Chicksands, Eng., 1979-83; chief staff 21st Air Force, McGuire AFB, 1983-84; pres. Air Force Phys. Evaluation Bd., Randolph AFB, N.J., 1984-86; ret., 1986; dep. exec. dir. Confederate Air Force, Harlingen, Tex., 1986-88; exec. dir. Am. Airpower Heritage Found., Harlingen, 1986-88; tchg. asst., lectr. in history Pan Am. dept. U. Tex., Edinburg, 1989-93; adj. prof. history Tex. State Tech. Coll., Harlingen, 1994—; co-chair (with Sir Douglas Bader) 1976 Internat. Air Tatoo at RAF Greenham Common; chair Air Fete 80 and 81, RAF Mildenhall, Eng. Co-editor: History of Military Assistance Command, Vietnam, 1970. Decorated Legion of Merit with two oak leaf clusters, Bronze Star; Cross of Gallantry (Vietnam); recipient Amb.'s award Ct. St. James, London, 1974, 83. Mem. Air Force Assn., Airlift Assn., Am. Watchmakers Inst., Nat. Assn. Watch and Clock Collectors, Brit. Officers Club Phila. (hon.), Rotary (gov. internat. dist. 5930 1995-96), Order of Daedalians, Phi Alpha Theta, Phi Kappa Phi. Republican. Presbyterian. Avocations: clock repairs, photography, golf, fishing. Home: 3001 Emerald Lake Dr Harlingen TX 78550-8621 Office: Tex State Tech Coll Dept History Harlingen TX 78550-3697

MARTIN, LEROY E., finance company executive; b. Mpls., Apr. 9, 1941; m. Gayle Martin; children: Lisa, Michelle, Bradley. BSBA in Acctg., U. Minn., 1963. CPA, Minn. Mem. client svc. staff, ptnr. McGladrey & Pullen, Mpls., 1962-74, dir. audit, acctg. and SEC practice, 1974-76, ptnr. in charge St. Paul office, 1976-79, coord. audit and acctg., 1979-83, regional mng. ptnr., 1983-89, mng. ptnr., 1989—; mem. SEC Practice Sect. Exec. Com., chmn. Group B adv. com.; past mem. Auditing Standards Exec. Com. Fin. Acctg. Standards Adv. Coun.; chmn. RSM Internat. Mem. AICPA, Minn. Soc. CPAs, Accts. Liability Assurance Co. Ltd. (bd. dirs.). *

MARTIN, LESLIE EARL, III, marketing executive; b. Madison, Wis., Sept. 19, 1955; s. Leslie Earl Jr. and Dorothy Mae (Clark) M. BBA, U. Wis., 1978. Agt. Conn. Mut. Life Ins. Co., Madison, Wis., 1978-81; dir. mktg. Strand Assocs., Inc., Madison, Wis., 1981-85; bus. devel. Balcor/Am. Express, San Francisco, 1985-86; v.p. sales QualiCorp. Fin., Inc., Tampa, Fla., 1986-88, Calvert Group, Bethesda, Md., 1988-91; v.p. mktg. SRI Group, Inc., Atlanta, 1991, IDEX Mut. Funds, Clearwater, Fla., 1992—. Mem. Internat. Assn. Fin. Planning (chmn. 1993-94). Avocations: automobile racing, running, travel. Office: IDEX/Western Reserve Life 201 Highland Ave Largo FL 34640

MARTIN, LINDA GAYE, demographer, economist; b. Paris, Ark., Dec. 17, 1947; d. Leslie Paul and Margie LaVerne (Thomas) M. BA in Math., Harvard U., 1970; MPA, Princeton U., 1972, PhD in Econs., 1978. Dir. mgmt. info. bur. purchased social svcs. for adults City of N.Y., 1972-74; rsch. assoc., rsch. dir. U.S. Ho. of Reps. Select Com. on Population, Washington, 1977-79; rsch. assoc. East-West Population Inst., Honolulu, 1979-89, asst. dir., 1982-84; asst. prof. econs. U. Hawaii, Honolulu, 1979-81, assoc. prof., 1981-89, prof., 1989; dir. com. on population Nat. Acad. Scis., Washington, 1989-93; dir. domestic rsch. divsn., v.p. RAND, Santa Monica, Calif., 1993-95, v.p. for rsch. devel., 1995—; mem. neurosci. behavior and sociology of aging rev. com. Nat. Inst. on Aging, Bethesda, 1991-95; chair panel on aging in developing countries NAS, Washington, 1987, mem. com. on population , 1993—. Editor: The ASEAN Success Story, 1987; co-editor: Demographic Change in Sub-Saharan Africa, 1993, Demographic Effects of Economic Reversals in Sub-Saharan Africa, 1993, The Demography of Aging, 1994; author: (monograph) The Graying of Japan, 1989; contbr. articles to profl. jours. Recipient Fulbright Faculty Rsch. award Coun. for Internat. Exch. of Scholars, 1988. Mem. Gerontol. Soc. Am., Internat. Union for Scientific Study Population, Population Assn. Am. (bd. dirs. 1991-93), Japan Am. Soc. So. Calif. (bd. dirs. 1994—). Democrat. Office: Rand PO Box 2138 Santa Monica CA 90407-2138

MARTIN, LINDA SUE, minister of pastoral care; b. Fort Wayne, Ind., Oct. 3, 1953; d. Myron Lee and Helen Louetta (Hughes) M. BS, Manchester Coll., 1976; MS, Saint Francis Coll., Fort Wayne, Ind., 1984; Cert. of Gerontology, Ind. U., 1988. Cert. art educator. Art instr. Met. Sch. Dist., Wabash County, Ind., 1977-78; arts and crafts coord. Sr. Citizens Ctr., Fort Wayne, Ind., 1978-90; minister of pastoral care Saint Joseph United Meth. Ch., Fort Wayne, Ind., 1990—; owner Down Home Designs, Ft. Wayne, 1978—; tchr., cons. Very Spl. Arts Ind., Ft. Wayne, 1989—. Freelance artist including logo design for Am. Lawyers Aux., 1986; contbg. author: (poetry) At The Crossroads, 1988. Sec. bd. dirs. Arthritis Found., Allen County, Ind., 1984-94, bd. dirs. Ind. chpt., 1990-94; mem. St. Joseph United Meth. Ch., Ft. Wayne, 1984—; sr. PAC chair, bd. dirs. Jr. League Ft. Wayne, 1991-93; vol. aux. Turnstone Ctr. for the Disabled, 1996—. Recipient "Food Hero" award Community Harvest Foodbank, 1992, Artist Recognition award Johnny Appleseed Festival, 1988. Mem. Am. Bus. Women's Assn. (mem. ways and means chair 1989-91). Methodist. Avocations: creative arts, swimming. Office: Saint Joseph United Meth Ch 6004 Reed Rd Fort Wayne IN 46835-2215

MARTIN, LOUIS EDWARD, retired library director; b. Detroit, Sept. 16, 1928; s. Emerick G. and Irene Rose (Fuhrman) M.; m. Barbara Hilda Heinrich, Apr. 7, 1951; children: Paul Emerique, Clare Ellen, Ann Maureen. PhB, U. Detroit, 1951, MA, 1954; MLS, U. Mich., 1960. Instr. in English U. Detroit, 1953-58, circulation librarian, 1958-60; asst. librarian Oakland U., Rochester, Mich., 1960-62; asst. dir. libraries U. Rochester, N.Y., 1962-65, assoc. dir. libraries, assoc. prof. bibliography, 1965-68; assoc. exec. dir. Assn. Research Libraries, 1968-72; librarian Harvard Coll., Cambridge, Mass., 1972-79; univ. librarian Cornell U., Ithaca, N.Y., 1979-85; dir. Linda Hall Library, Kansas City, Mo., 1985-93; cons. library bldgs. and mgmt. Served with USMCR.

MARTIN, LUCY Z., public relations executive; b. Alton, Ill., July 8, 1941; d. Fred and Lucille J. M. BA, Northwestern U., 1963. Adminstrv. asst., copywriter Batz-Hodgson-Neuwoehner, Inc., St. Louis, 1963-64; news reporter, Midwest fashion editor Fairchild Publs., St. Louis, 1964-66; account exec. Milici Advt. Agy., Honolulu, 1967; publs. dir. Barnes Med. Ctr., St. Louis, 1968-69; communications cons. Fleishman-Hillard, St. Louis, 1970-74; communications cons., chief exec. officer, pres. Lucy Z. Martin & Assocs., Portland, Oreg., 1974—; spkr. Healthcare Assn. Hawaii, 1993, Oreg. Assn. Healthcare, 1992, Healthcare Fin. Mgmt. Assn., 1993, Healthcare Communicators Oreg., 1994, Pub. Rels. Soc. Am. (Coe River chpt.), 1996. Featured in Entrepreneurial Woman mag.; contbr. articles to profl. jours. Chmn. women's adv. com. Reed Coll., Portland, 1977-79; mem. Oreg. Commn. for Women, 1984-87; bd. dirs. Ronald McDonald House Oreg., 1986, Oreg. Sch. Arts and Crafts, 1989—, Inst. Managerial and Profl. Women, 1992—, Northwestern U. Alumni Coun., 1992—; chmn. bd. Good Samaritan Hosp. Assocs., 1991-96; mem. pub. policy com. YMCA, 1993-95; mem. adv. bd. Jr. League, 1994—. Recipient MacEachern Citation Acad. Hosp. Pub. Relations, 1978, Rosey awards Portland Advt. Fedn., 1979, Achievement award Soc. Tech. Communications, 1982, Disting. Tech. Communication award, 1982, Exceptional Achievement award Council for Advancement and Support Edn., 1983, Monsoon award Internat. Graphics, Inc., 1984; named Woman of Achievement Daily Jour. Commerce, 1980. Mem. Pub. Rels. Soc. Am. (pres. Columbia River chpt. 1984, chmn. bd. 1980-84, Oreg. del. 1984-86, judicial panel N. Pacific dist 1985-86, exec. bd. health care sect. 1986-87, mem. Counselors Acad., Spotlight awards 1985, 86, 87, 88, nat. exec. com. 1987-91), Portland Pub. Rels. Roundtable (chmn. 1985, bd. dirs. 1983-85), Assn. Western Hosps. (editorial adv. bd. 1984-85), Best of West awards 1978, 80, 83, 87), Oreg. Hosp. Pub. Relations Orgn. (pres. 1981, chmn. bd. 1982, bd. dirs. 1992-93), Acad. Health Service Mktg., Am. Hosp. Assn., Am. Mktg. Assn. (Oreg. chpt. bd. dirs. 1992-93), Am. Soc. Hosp. Mktg. & Pub. Relations, Healthcare Communicators Oreg. (conf. keynote speaker 1994), Internat. Assn. Bus. Communicators (18 awards 1981-87), Oreg. Assn. Hosps. (keynote speaker for trustee, 1991, speaker, 1993, bd. dirs. 1992-93), Oreg. Press Women, Nat. and Oreg. Soc. Healthcare Planning and Mktg., Women in Communications (Matrix award 1977), Inst. Managerial and Profl. Women (bd. dirs. 1992—), City Club Portland. Office: 1881 SW Edgewood Rd Portland OR 97201-2235

MARTIN, MALCOLM ELLIOT, lawyer; b. Buffalo, Dec. 11, 1935; s. Carl Edward and Pearl Maude (Elliot) M.; m. Judith Hill Harley, June 27, 1964; children: Jennifer, Elizabeth, Christina, Katherine. AB, U. Mich., Ann Arbor, 1958, JD, 1962. Bar: N.Y. 1963, U.S. Ct. Appeals (2d cir.) 1966, U.S. Supreme Ct. 1967. Assoc., Chadbourne, Parke, Whiteside & Wolff, N.Y.C., 1962-73, ptnr., 1974—, now Chadbourne & Parke LLP, 1986; dir., sec. Carl and Dorothy Bennett Found., Inc.; sec., counsel Copper Devel. Assn., Inc.; sec., treas. Jute Carpet Backing Council, Inc., Burlap and Jute Assn. Served with U.S. Army, 1958-60. Mem. ABA, N.Y. State Bar Assn., Assn. Bar City N.Y., St. Andrew's Soc. of State of N.Y., Met. Opera Guild. Clubs: Oratamin (Blauvelt, N.Y.), Nyack Boat, Rockefeller Center, Copper (N.Y.C.). Home: 74 S Highland Ave Nyack NY 10960-3602 Office: Chadbourne & Parke LLP 30 Rockefeller Plz New York NY 10112

MARTIN, MARGARET ANNE See STEELE, ANITA MARTIN

MARTIN, MARILYN JOAN, library director; b. Golden Meadow, La., Jan. 17, 1940; d. Marion Francis Mobley and Audrey Virna (Goza) Sapaugh; m. James Reginald Martin, Dec. 16, 1958; children: James Michael, Linda Jill Michaels. BA in History, U. Wash., 1975, MLS, 1976; MA in Pub. History, U. Ark., 1992; PhD in Libr. Sci., Tex. Woman's U., 1993. Cataloger, reference libr. St. Martin's Coll., Lacey, Wash., 1976-78; asst. reference libr. Pacific Luth. U., Tacoma, 1978-85; serials libr. Henderson State U., Arkadelphia, Ark., 1985-86, collection devel. libr., 1987-88, dir. learning resources, 1989-95; dean libr. svcs. Rowan Coll. of N.J., Glassboro, 1995—. Contbr. articles to profl. jours. Pres. Ark. United Meth. Hist. Soc., 1994—, also bd. dirs.; chmn. Little Rock Conf., Commn. on Archives and History, United Meth. Ch., 1993—, sec., mem. exec. bd. Gen. Commn. on Archives and History, 1984-92. Mem. ALA (rsch. com. 1993-94, stds. com. 1994-95), Assn. Coll. and Rsch. Librs., Ark. Libr. Assn. (chmn. future conf. site com. 1993-94), Ark. Hist. Assn. (awards com. 1992-940. Republican. Avocations: walking, reading, collecting names. Office: Library Rowan Coll of NJ Glassboro NJ 08028-1701

MARTIN, MARSHA PYLE, federal agency administrator; married; 2 children. BA, Tex. Woman's U.; MS, Tex. A&M U. Sr. officer Fed. Intermediate Credit Bank Tex., 1970-94; apptd. chmn. Farm Credit Adminstrn. Bd., 1994—; bd. dirs. Farm Credit Sys. Ins. Corp. Office: Farm Credit Adminstrn 1501 Farm Credit Dr McLean VA 22102-5090

MARTIN, MARY, secondary education educator; b. Detroit, Mich., May 17, 1954; d. Enos and Sara (Evans) M. AS, Highland Park C.C., 1975; BA, Wayne State U., 1975, MA in Teaching, 1981; postgrad., So. Calif. Sch. Ministry, Detroit, 1992—. Dietary aide Allan Dee Nursing Home, Detroit, 1972; dietary aide Harper Hosp., Detroit, 1973, 74, nurse aide, 1974-75, respiratory technician, 1975-80; respiratory technician Dr.'s Hosp., Detroit, 1980; head cook, supr. Focus Hope, Detroit, 1981; substitute tchr. Detroit Bd. Edn., 1984-90, tchr. adult edn., 1990-93, tchr., 1993—; interim advisor student coun. Wayne State U., Detroit, 1985. Sunday sch. teaching trainer People's Missionary Bapt. Ch., Detroit, 1986, del., 1984-87, mem. All Aid, 1984-87, mem. choir, 1984, usher, 1984; precinct del. 13th Congl. Dist., 1986-88, 90-92, model, 1985. Recipient Spirit of Detroit award Detroit City Coun., 1993, Spl. Congl. cert. Hon. Barbara Rose Collins, 1994, Proclamation, Wayne County Commr. George Cushingberry, 1994. Mem. Nat. Sociol. Honor Soc. Democrat. Avocations: reading, shopping, movies, golf, driving.

MARTIN, MARY COATES, genealogist, writer, volunteer; b. Gloucester County, N.J.; d. Raymond and Emily (Johnson) Coates; m. Lawrence O. Kupillas (dec.); m. Clyde Davis Martin (dec.); 1 child, William Raymond. Contbg. editor Md. & Del. Genealogist, St. Michaels, Md., 1985—. Author: The House of John Johnson (1731-1802) Salem County, N.J. and His Descendants, 1979, Fifty Year History of Daughters of Colonial Wars in the State of New York, 1980, 350 Years of American Ancestors: 38 Families: 1630-1989, 1989, Colonial Families: Martin and Bell Families and Their Kin: 1657-1992, Clifton--Coates Kinfolk and 316 Allied Families, 1995. Pres. Washington Hdqrs. Assn., 1970-73, bd. dirs., 1962—; Centennial pres. Sorosis, Inc., 1966-68; bd. dirs. Soldiers Sailors Airmen's Club, N.Y.C., 1976-81, Yorkville Youth Coun., N.Y.C., 1954-60; co-chmn. Colonial Ball, N.Y.C., 1965-67; rec. sec. Parents League of N.Y., Inc., 1954-57; mem. com. Internat. Debutante Ball, N.Y.C., 1977-81; mem. Am. Flag Inst., N.Y.C., 1963-72. Mem. Hereditary Order of Descendants of Colonial Govs. (gov. gen. 1981-83), Nat. Soc. Colonial Dames of Seventeenth Century (N.Y. State pres. 1977-79, parlimentarian 1979-81), Nat. Soc. Daus. of Colonial Wars (N.Y. State pres. 1977-80), Nat. Soc. DAR (regent 1962-65, pres. roundtable 1964-65, N.Y. State chaplain 1968-71, parliamentarian 1980-83, nat. platform com. 1970-76, certificate of award 1971, nat. vice chmn. lineage rsch. com. 1977-80, geneal. com. 1980-83), Nat. Soc. New Eng. Women (dir. gen. 1972-77, nat. vice chmn. helping hand disbursing fund 1968-71), Order of Crown of Charlemagne U.S.A. (corr. sec. gen. 1985-88, 3rd v.p. 1988-89, 2nd v.p. 1989-91), Nat. Soc. Children Am. Revolution, Nicasius de Sille Soc. (pres. 1960-62), Order Ams. of Armorial Ancestry (1st v.p. gen. 1985-88, councillor gen. 1988—), Nat. Gavel Soc., Nat. Soc. Magna Carta Dames, Descendants of Soc. of Colonial Clergy, Huguenot Soc. Am., Descendants of a Knight of Most Noble Order Garter, Nat. Soc. Daus. Am. Colonists, Nat. Soc. U.S. Daus. 1812, Order of Descendants of Colonial Physicians and Chirurgiens, Plantagenet Soc., Vt. Soc. Colonial Dames, Del. Geneal. Soc., Huguenot Hist. Soc., DuBois Family Assn. (1st v.p.), Cumberland County N.J. Hist. Soc., Gloucester County N.J. Hist. Soc., Md. Hist. Soc., Hist. Soc. Del., Salem County N.J. Hist. Soc., Woodstown-Pilesgrove N.J. Hist. Soc., Hereditary Order First Families of Mass., Inc. Avocation: travel. Home: Hague Towers # 1815 330 W Brambleton Ave Norfolk VA 23510-1307

MARTIN, MARY LOIS, nursing director, critical care nurse; b. Greensburg, Ky., June 19, 1954; d. John Will and Nellie Gertrude (Akin) M.; 1 child, Amanda. ADN, Midway (Ky.) Coll., 1974. RN, Ky.; CCRN; cert. BLS, ACLS and pediatric advanced life support provider and instr., affiliate faculty ACLS, Am. Heart Assn. Med. surg. staff nurse Ctrl. Bapt. Hosp., Lexington, Ky., 1974-75, 76-77; med. surg. staff nurse Taylor County Hosp., Campbellsville, Ky., 1975-76, house shift supr., 1978-79, staff nurs ICU and med.- surg. unit, 1979-84, emergency room ICU coord., 1984-89, ICU nursing dir., 1989-90, 92—, ICU, emergency rm. nursing dir., 1991-92. Mem. AACN, Greater Louisville chpt. AACN. Democrat. Baptist. Avocation: reading. Home: 101 Churchill Dr Campbellsville KY 42718-2129 Office: Taylor County Hosp 1700 Old Lebanon Rd Campbellsville KY 42718-9662

MARTIN, MARY-ANNE, art gallery owner; b. Hoboken, N.J., Apr. 26, 1943; d. Thomas Philipp and Ruth (Kelley) M.; m. Henry S. Berman, June 9, 1963 (div. 1976); 1 child, Julia Berman. Student, Smith Coll., 1961-63; BA, Barnard Coll., 1965; MA, NYU, 1967. Head dept. painting Sotheby Parke Bernet, N.Y.C., 1971-78; sr. v.p. Sotheby's, N.Y.C., 1978-82; pres. Mary-Anne Martin, Fine Art, N.Y.C., 1982—; founder Latin Am. dept. Sotheby's, 1977. Mem. Art Dealers Assn. Am. (v.p., bd. dirs.). Avocations: art collecting, scuba diving. Office: 23 E 73rd St New York NY 10021-3522

MARTIN, MAURICE JOHN, psychiatrist; b. Tuscola, Ill., July 6, 1929; s. Daniel Ambrose and Mary Alta (Payne) M.; m. Ada Himma, Aug. 15, 1953; children: Daniel, Mark, Matthew, Tina, Lisa. BS, U. Ill., 1951, MD, 1954; MS, U. Minn., 1960. Diplomate Am. Bd. Internal Medicine, Am. Bd. Psychiatry and Neurology (bd. dirs. 1984-92, treas. 1988-90, v.p. 1991), Am. Bd. Emergency Medicine (bd. dirs. 1990-94), Am. Bd. Med. Spltys. (v.p. 1992, pres. elect 1993, pres. 1994-96), Am. Bd. Med. Spltys. Edn. Rsch. Found. (pres. 1992-94). Intern Presbyn. Hosp., Chgo., 1954-55; resident Mayo Grad. Sch. Medicine, Rochester, Minn., 1955-57, 59-62; cons. in adult psychiatry Mayo Clinic, Rochester, 1962—; head adult psychiatry Mayo Clinic, 1968-74, sr. cons. adult psychiatry, 1985—; chmn. dept. psychiatry and psychology Mayo Clinic and Mayo Med. Sch., 1974-85, asst. prof. psychiatry and psychology, 1965-70, assoc. prof., 1970-75, prof., 1975—; pres. staff Mayo Clinic, 1981-82; mem. Minn. Bd. Med. Practice, 1989, v.p., 1995, pres., 1996; pres., pres. exec. com. ABMS, USMLE Step 3 Com., 1995—. Contbr. articles on psychiatry and psychosomatic medicine to profl. jours. Served to col., M.C. USAR, 1955-95. Decorated Order Mil. Med. Merit; recipient H.V. Jones award Mayo Found., 1960, Burlingame award Inst. of Living, 1994. Fellow Am. Psychiat. Assn. (life), Am. Coll. Psychiatrists (regent 1980-83, v.p. 1986-89, pres.-elect 1988, pres. 1989-90, sec. gen. 1993—, Bowls award 1992), Acad. Psychosomatic Medicine (pres. 1974-75, Prestigious Achievement award 1986), Fedn. State Med. Bds. (exam com. 1992-95); mem. Minn. Psychiat. Soc. (pres. 1977-79), Benjamin Rush Soc. (sec.-treas. 1993-96, v. pres. 1996—), Minn. Med. Assn. (Pres. award 1994), Sigma Xi (chpt. pres. 1981-82), Alpha Omega Alpha. Home: 914 Sierra Ln NE Rochester MN 55906-4227 Office: 200 1st St SW Rochester MN 55905-0001 *Diligence, perseverance, and hard work —all virtues learned on the farm in Illinois, along with a strong desire for excellence in the altruistic service of sick patients have led to accomplishment. The jump from horse-drawn farm equipment to professor and chairman of a large department of psychiatry in 25 years required the above factors in addition to being in the right place at the right time.*

MARTIN, MELISSA CAROL, radiological physicist; b. Muskogee, Okla., Feb. 7, 1951; d. Carl Leroy and Helen Shirley (Hicks) Paden; m. Donald Ray Martin, Feb. 14, 1970; 1 child, Christina Gail. BS, Okla. State U., 1971; MS, UCLA, 1975. Cert. radiol. physicist, Am. Bd. Radiology, radiation oncology, Am. Bd. Med. Physics. Asst. radiation physicist Hosp. of the Good Samaritan, L.A., 1975-80; radiol. physicist Meml. Med. Ctr., Long Beach, Calif., 1980-83, St. Joseph Hosp., Orange, Calif., 1983-92, Therapy Physics, Inc., Bellflower, Calif., 1993—; cons. in field. Editor: (book) Current Regulatory Issues in Medical Physics, 1992. Fund raising campaign div. mgr. YMCA, Torrance, Calif., 1988-92; dir. AWANA Youth Club-Guards Group, Manhattan Beach, Calif., 1984—. Named Dir. of Symposium, Am. Coll. Med. Physics, 1992. Fellow Am. Coll. Med. Physics (chancellor western region 1992-95); mem. Am. Assn. Physicists in Medicine (profl. coun. 1990-95), Am. Coll. Radiology (econs. com. 1992-95), Calif. Med. Physics Soc. (treas. 1991-95), Am. Soc. for Therapeutic Radiology and Oncology, Health Physics Soc. (pres. So. Calif. chpt. 1992-93), Am. Brachytherapy Soc.

Baptist. Avocations: Christian youth group dir. Home: 507 Susana Ave Redondo Beach CA 90277-3953 Office: Therapy Physics Inc 9156 Rose St Bellflower CA 90706-6420

MARTIN, MICHAEL LEE, orthotist; b. Long Beach, Calif., May 30, 1947; s. Troy Lee and Ruth Elizabeth (Hummer) M.; m. Sharon Lee Johnson, Aug. 23, 1969; 1 child, Tanya Lee. Student, Northwestern U., 1973; AA, Cerritos (Calif.) Coll., 1976; student, UCLA, 1976. Diplomate Am. Bd. Orthotists and Prosthetist. Cable splicer Gen. Telephone, Dairy Valley, Calif., 1965-66; orthotic technician Johnson's Orthopedic, Santa Ana, Calif., 1969-73, orthotist, 1974—; pres. Johnson's Orthopedic, Orange, Calif., 1989—; rsch. orthotist Rancho Los Amigos Hosp., Downey, 1973; mem. rsch. adv. bd. Rancho Los Amigos Hosp. Mem. rsch. adv. com. on tech. for children Rancho Los Amigos Hosp., Downey. With U.S. Army, 1966-68, Vietnam. Mem. Am. Acad. Orthotists and Prosthetists (sec., pres. So. Calif. chpt. 1976-79, sec., pres. Region IX 1979-87, bd. dirs. 1994—, Practitioner of Yr. award 1992), Orthotic and Prosthetic Provider Network (pres. Calif. chpt. 1988—), Internat. Soc. for Prosthetics and Orthotics. Democrat. Avocations: fishing, golf, surfing. Home: 19 Fontaire Coto De Caza CA 92679-4717 Office: Johnson's Orthopedic 1920 E Katella Ave Ste G Orange CA 92667-5146

MARTIN, MICHAEL TOWNSEND, racing horse stable executive, sports marketing executive; b. N.Y.C., Nov. 21, 1941; s. Townsend Bradley and Irene (Redmond) M.; m. Jennifer Johnston, Nov. 7, 1964 (div. Jan. 1977); children: Ryan Bradley, Christopher Townsend; m. Jean Kathleen Meyer, Mar. 1, 1980. Grad., The Choate Sch., 1960; student, Rutgers U., 1961-62. Asst. gen. mgr. N.Y. Jets Football Club, N.Y.C., 1968-74; v.p. NAMANCO Prodns., N.Y.C., 1975-76; v.p., gen. mgr. Cosmos Soccer Club, N.Y.C., 1976-77; exec. asst. Warner Communications, N.Y.C., 1978-84; owner, operator Martin Racing Stable, N.Y.C., 1983—; pres. Sports Mark, Inc., N.Y.C., 1990—; ptnr. Halstead Property Co., N.Y.C., 1987—; bd. dirs. Juilliard Sch., VVZV Rsch. Found., Inc., Night Kitchen, N.Y. Thoroughbred Horsemen's Assn., Inc., also v.p. Bd. dirs. Very Spl. Arts, 1982—, Phipps Houses, 1986—; chmn. Mote Marine Lab., Sarasota, Fla., 1989—; bd. trustees Pennington Sch. Mem. Athletics Congress (life, cert. official 1984—), U.S. Tennis Assn. (life), Internat. Oceanographic Found. (Miami life mem.), Thoroughbred Horsemens Assn. (pres. 1995), Fla. Thoroughbred Breeders Assn., Quogue Field Club, The Union Club. Republican. Episcopalian. Avocation: collecting Inuit (Eskimo) art. Home: 131 E 69th St Apt 11A New York NY 10021-5158 Office: 575 Madison Ave Ste 1006 New York NY 10022-2511

MARTIN, MURRAY SIMPSON, librarian, writer, consultant; b. Lower Hutt, N.Z., July 21, 1928; came to U.S., 1966, naturalized, 1974; s. Francis Roy and Sarah Isabel (Mitchell) M.; m. Noelene Phyllis Ax, Aug. 28, 1954. B.A., U. New Zealand, Auckland, 1948; M.A., U. New Zealand, 1949; B.Comm., U. New Zealand, Auckland and Wellington, 1958; Diploma, New Zealand Library Sch., Wellington, 1950. Cert. pub. acct., N.Z. With New Zealand Nat. Library Service, Wellington, 1951-63; br. serials librarian U. Sask., Saskatoon, Can., 1963-66; acquisitions-collections devel. librarian Pa. State U., University Park, 1967-73; assoc. dean librs. Pa. State U., 1973-81; univ. librarian, prof. library sci. Tufts U., Medford, Mass., 1981-89, prof. libr. sci. emeritus, univ. libr. emeritus, 1990—, spl. asst. to provost for libr. planning and devel., 1989-90; sr. acad. library planner Aaron Cohen Assocs., 1990-91; interim exec. sec. Coll. and Univ. Librs. Assn., 1990-92; treas. Universal Serials and Book Exchange Washington, 1979-80, 82-84, v.p., 1985, pres., 1986; pres. Pitts. Regional Library Ctr., 1980-81, Boston Library Consortium, 1984-85; mem. adj. faculty Simmons Coll., 1989—. Author: Budgetary Control in Academic Libraries, 1979, Issues in Personnel Management in Academic Libraries, 1981, Academic Library Budgets, 1993, Collection Development and Finance, 1995; editor: Financial Planning in Libraries, 1983, Library Finance: New Needs, New Models, 1994, Issues in Collection Management, 1995; assoc. editor: Bottom Line, 1990—, Guide to Reference Books, 1993-94; column editor: Technicalities, 1995—; mng. editor: Advances in Library and Information Science, JAI Press, Inc., 1990—; contbr. articles and revs. to profl. and lib. publs. Mem. ALA, MLA, Can. Libr. Assn., New Zealand Libr. Assn. (chmn. fiction com. 1960-63, assoc.), Am. Comparative Lit. Assn., Am. Assn. Australian Lit. Studies, N.E. MLA, soc. for Scholarly Pub. Democrat. Avocations: bird-watching; stamp-collecting; conservation; travel.

MARTIN, NATHANIEL FRIZELL GRAFTON, mathematician, educator; b. Wichita Falls, Tex., Oct. 10, 1928; s. James Thelbert and Ethel Elizabeth (Nycum) M.; m. Joan Bowman, Apr. 10, 1954; children: Nathaniel Grafton, Jonathan Bowman. BS, North Tex. State U., 1948, MS, 1950; PhD, Iowa State U., 1958. Instr. Midwestern U., Wichita Falls, 1950-52; teaching asst. Iowa State U., Ames, 1955-59; from instr. to prof. math. U. Va., Charlottesville, 1959-96, prof. emeritus math., 1996, assoc. dean Grad. Sch. Arts and Scis., 1976-82; rsch. assoc. U. Calif., Berkeley, 1965-66; guest lectr. U. Copenhagen, 1969-70; rsch. assoc. U. Warwick, Coventry, Eng., 1982; vis. mem. MSRI, Berkeley, 1992; vis. faculty Univ. Coll., London, 1992. Author: Mathematical Theory of Entropy, 1981; editor: McGraw-Hill Dictionary of Physics & Math, 1978, Sci. & Tech. Terms, 1974. Lt. USNR, 1952-55. Mem. Am. Math. Soc., Math. Assn. Am., Sigma Xi, Pi Mu Epsilon. Office: U Va Dept Math Dept Math Kerchof Hall Charlottesville VA 22903

MARTIN, NED HAROLD, chemistry educator; b. New Brunswick, N.J., May 18, 1945; s. Harold and Gertrude (Link) M.; m. Lynda Susan Blackadar, June 14, 1980; 1 child, Tara Elizabeth. BA, Denison U., 1967; PhD, Duke U., 1972. NDEA trainee Duke U., Durham, N.C., 1967-69; rsch. chemist Research Triangle Inst., Research Triangle Park, N.C., 1969-70; rsch. asst. Duke U., Durham, 1970-72, lectr., 1971-72; asst. prof. U. N.C., Wilmington, 1972-77, assoc. prof., 1977-82, prof., 1982—, chair chemistry dept., 1992—, Will S. DeLoach prof. chemistry, 1996—; cons. Corning Glass, Wilmington, 1979-80, LaQue Ctr. for Corrosion Tech., Wrightsville Beach, N.C., 1983-87, Condux, Inc., Newark, Del., 1989-90, Trinity Mfg., Inc., 1991; postdoctorate researcher U. Geneva, 1980-81. Co-author: Organic Chemistry Lab Manual with Waste Management and Molecular Modeling, 1993, Chemistry 211/212 Lab Manual, 1987. Mem. N.C. Acad. Sci. (v.p. 1988-90, pres.-elect 1989-90, pres. 1990-91, past pres. 1991-92), Am. Chem. Soc., Sigma Xi (assoc.), Phi Beta Kappa, Omicron Delta Kappa, Phi Soc., Phi Eta Sigma, Phi Lambda Upsilon. Office: UNCW 601 S College Rd Wilmington NC 28403-3297

MARTIN, NOEL, graphic design consultant, educator; b. Syracuse, Ohio, Apr. 19, 1922; s. Harry Ross and Lula (Van Meter) M.; m. Coletta Ruchty, Aug. 29, 1942; children—Dana, Reid. Cert. in Fine Arts, Art Acad. Cin., Doctorate (hon.), 1994. Designer Cin. Art Mus., 1947-93, asst. to dir., 1947-55; freelance designer for various ednl., cultural and indsl. orgns., 1947—; instr. Art Acad. Cin., 1951-57, artist-in-residence, 1993—; design cons. Champion Internat., 1959-82, Xomox Corp., 1961—, Federated Dept. Stores, 1962-83, Hebrew Union Coll., 1969—; designer-in-residence U. Cin., 1968-71, adj. prof., 1968-73; mem. adv. bd. Carnegie-Mellon U., R.I. Sch. Design, Cin. Symphony Orch., Am. Inst. Graphic Arts; lectr. Smithsonian Instn., Libr. of Congress, Am. Inst. Graphic Arts, Aspen Design Conf., various additional schs. and orgns. nationally. One man shows include Contemporary Arts Ctr., Cin., 1954, 71, Addison Gallery Am. Art, 1955, R.I. Sch. Design, 1955, Soc. Typographic Arts, Chgo., 1956, White Mus. of Cornell U., 1956, Cooper & Beatty, Toronto, Ont., Can., 1958, Am. Inst. Graphic Arts, 1958, Ind. U., 1958, Ohio State U., 1971; exhibited in group shows at Mus. Modern Art, N.Y.C., Library of Congress, Musee d'Art Moderne, Paris, Grafiska Inst., Stockholm, Carpenter Ctr., Cambridge, Gutenberg Mus., Mainz, U.S. info. exhbns. In Europe, South America and USSR; represented in permanent collections Mus. Modern Art, Stedelijk Mus., Amsterdam, Cin. Art Mus., Boston Mus. Fine Arts, Cin. Hist. Soc., Library of Congress; contbr. to various publs. Served to sgt. U.S. Air Force, 1942-45. Recipient Art Directors medal, Phila., 1957, Sachs award, Cin., 1973, Lifetime Achievement award Cin. Art Dirs., 1989.

MARTIN, PARKER, accountant, financial consultant; b. Barbourville, Ky., Dec. 6, 1947; s. Stanley Chester Martin and Georgia Thelma (Bullock) Lofgren. BS in Acctg., Calif. State U., Los Angeles, 1976. CPA, Calif. Acctg. mgr. Coca Cola, Los Angeles, 1970-76; staff acct. Tilles and Gest, CPA's, Beverly Hills, Calif., 1977-86; owner Parker Martin, CPA, Burbank, Calif., 1986—. Co-author: The Mansions of Beverly Hills, 1967. Mem. Am. Inst. CPA's, Calif. Soc. CPA's. Republican. Club: Valley Bus. Alliance (Burbank). Avocations: reading, swimming. Home: 733 E Grinnell Dr Burbank CA 91501-1719 Office: 1178 Hartford St Cambria CA 93428-2908

MARTIN, PATRICIA ANN, music educator; b. Salinas, Calif., Mar. 11, 1939; d. Kenneth Duane and Hazel Gertrude (Setser) Lowe; m. Raymond Dalton Martin, Aug. 22, 1959; children: William Dalton, Brian David. BA, Calif. State U., 1965. Choir accompanist Salinas Christian Ch., 1954-57; choir accompanist North Fresno Christian Ch., Fresno, Calif., 1957-93, organist, 1965—, choir dir., 1968-70; tchr. music pvt. lessons Fresno, 1962—; tchr. music Mountain View Christian Sch., Fresno, 1992-93; organist for weddings, various chs., Fresno, 1962—; dir. bell choir North Fresno Christian Ch., 1985-86, dir. ministry, 1989-90. Composer songs, piano teaching pieces, 1974—; contbr. poetry to anthologies, 1981—. Mem. AAUW, Am. Guild Organists (sec. 1978-79), Calif. Fedn. Music Clubs (pres. 1988-91), Music Tchrs. Assn. Calif. (state chmn. Cal-Plan 1981-83, pres. 1983-85, condr. workshops 1978—, dir. pianorama 1976-88), Jr. Music Festival (pres. 1987-91, performer in New Wrinkles Sr. Theatre 1993—). Republican.

MARTIN, PATRICK, business equipment company executive; b. N.Y.C., Mar. 16, 1941; s. Michael and Theresa (Devaney) M.; children: Julia, Margaret, Brendan, Patrick, Sean Patrick; m. Donna Knutson, 1995. BS in Math., Iona Coll., 1962; MS in Math., George Washington U., 1965, PhD in Elec. Engring. and Computer Sci., 1971. Sr. scientist Research Analysis Corp., 1962-64; sr. mgr. Informatics Inc., 1964-66; pres. NCS Computing Corp., 1966-72; assoc. prof. George Washington U., 1966-77; dep. asst. sec. USDA, 1972-77; v.p., gen. mgr. China bus. devel. Xerox Corp., Rochester, N.Y., 1977-91; pres., gen. mgr. Am. Customer Ops., Stamford, Conn., 1991—. Contbr. numerous articles and research papers in computer sci. and mgmt. jours. Avocations: squash, skiing, reading, ethnic dances. Home: 14 Creekside Ln Rochester NY 14618 Office: Xerox Corp 800 Long Ridge Rd Stamford CT 06904

MARTIN, PAUL, Canadian government official; b. Windsor, Ont., Can., Aug. 28, 1938; s. Paul Joseph and Eleanor (Adams) M.; m. Sheila Ann Cowan, Sept. 11, 1965; children—Paul William James, Robert James Edward, David Patrick Anthony. BA in Philosophy and History, U. Toronto, Can., 1962, LLB, 1965; LLB, U. Toronto, Can., 1965. Bar: Ont. 1966. Exec. asst. to pres. Power Corp. Can. Ltd., 1966-69, v.p., 1969-71; v.p. spl. projects Consol.-Bathurst Ltd., 1971-73; v.p. planning and devel. Power Corp., Can., 1973-74; pres. Can. S.S. Lines Ltd., Montreal, 1974-80, chief exec. officer, 1976-80; pres., chief exec. officer CSL Group Inc., 1980-88; M.P. Ho. of Commons, 1988-93; min. of finance Dept. of Finance Canada, 1993—; former min. for fed. office of regional devel. Can. Govt., 1993-95. Former mem. C.D. Howe Inst. Policy Analysis Com., Birt, N.Am. Com., Ctr. Rsch. Action on Race Rels.; former bd. dirs. Can. Coun. Christians and Jews; founding dir. emeritus North-South Inst., Can., Coun. Native Bus.; bd. govs. Concordia U., coun., v.p., past mem. bd. advisors. Liberal. Avocations: sports, reading. Office: Dept of Finance Canada, 140 O'Connor St, Ottawa, ON Canada K1A 0G5*

MARTIN, PAUL CECIL, physicist, educator; b. Bklyn., Jan. 31, 1931; s. Harry and Helen (Salzberger) M.; m. Ann Wallace Bradley, Aug. 7, 1957; children: Peter, Stephanie Glennon, Daniel. A.B., Harvard U., 1952, Ph.D., 1954. Mem. faculty Harvard U., Cambridge, Mass., 1957—, prof. physics, 1964-82, J. H. VanVleck prof. pure and applied physics, 1982—, chmn. dept. physics, 1972-75, dean div. applied scis., 1977—, assoc. dean Faculty Arts and Scis., 1981—; vis. prof. Ecole Normale Superieure, Paris, 1963, 66, U. Paris, Orsay, 1971; mem. materials rsch. adv. coun. NSF, 1986-89; bd. dirs. Mass. Tech. Pk. Corp., 1990—, exec. com., 1992—. Bd. editors: Jour. Math Physics, 1965-68, Annals of Physics, 1968-82, Jour. Statis. Physics, 1975-80. Bd. dirs. Assoc. Univs. for Rsch. in Astronomy, 1979-85; trustee Assoc. Univs., Inc., 1981—, exec. com., 1986-90, 92-94. NSF postdoctoral fellow, 1955; Sloan Found. fellow, 1959-62; Guggenheim fellow, 1966, 71. Fellow AAAS (chair physics sect. 1986), NAS, Am. Acad. Arts and Scis., Am. Phys. Soc. (councillor-at-large 1982-84, panel on pub. affairs 1983-86, chmn. nominating com. 1994), N.Y. Acad. Scis. Office: Harvard U Dept Physics Cambridge MA 02138

MARTIN, PAUL EDWARD, retired insurance company executive; b. Santa Claus, Ind., Sept. 10, 1914; s. James F. and Anna (Singer) M.; m. Pauline Peva, Dec. 22, 1939 (dec. Feb. 1982); 1 child, Peter McDowell; m. Ann Parker, Oct. 14, 1983. B.A., Hanover Coll., 1936. With actuarial dept. State Life Ins. Co., Indpls., 1936-42; asst. actuary Ohio Nat. Life Ins. Co., Cin., 1946-48; asso. actuary Ohio Nat. Life Ins. Co., 1948-49, actuary, 1949-55, actuarial v.p., 1955-56, adminstrv. v.p., 1956-67, sr. v.p. ins. adminstrn., 1967-71, pres., 1971-72, chmn. bd., chief exec. officer, 1972-79, also dir. Trustee Hanover (Ind.) Coll. Served to maj. F.A. AUS, 1942-46, PTO. Fellow Soc. Actuaries, Acad. Actuaries; mem. Comml. Club, Skyline Club, Masons, Shriners, Gamma Sigma Pi, Beta Theta Pi. Presbyterian. Home: 7146 N Finger Rock Pl Tucson AZ 85718-1406

MARTIN, PAUL JOSEPH, biomedical engineer, cardiology researcher, educator, consultant; b. Hammond, Ind., May 22, 1936; s. Joseph Edwin and Verna Catherine (Heidgerken) M.; m. Jeanne Therese Oubre, Sept. 10, 1960 (div. 1992); children: Mary Kay, Barry James, Craig Anthony, Colleen Therese; m. Marjie Anne Prentice, June 19, 1993. BSEE, U. Tex., 1960; MS in Biomed. Engring., Drexel U., 1961; PhD in Biomed. Engring., Case Western Res. U., 1967. Rsch. fellow Latter Day Sts. Hosp., Salt Lake City, 1961-62; biomed. rsch. engr. Tech., Inc., Dayton, Ohio, 1962-63; rsch. assoc. Mt. Sinai Med. Ctr., Cleve., 1967-75, head bioengring. sect., div. investigative medicine, 1975-89, assoc. chief, div. investigative medicine, 1989—, chmn. instl. rev. bd., 1973—; asst. prof. physiology, biophysics and biomed. engring. Case Western Res. U. Sch. Medicine and Engring., Cleve., 1967-76, assoc. prof., 1976-83, prof., 1983—; physiology cons. Artificial Heart Program of Cleve. Clinic, 1963-70; computer cons. Acad. Medicine of Cleve., 1987-92; cons. various rsch. labs.; mem. study sect. NIH, NSF, EPA, Washington, 1973—; treas. G & R Sports, Inc. Contbr. numerous articles, book chpts. to profl. publs.; assoc. editor Am. Jour. Physiology, Heart and Circulatory Physiology, 1976-81; mem. editorial bd. Circulation Rsch., 1979-80. Mem. campaign com. Cleveland Heights Dems., 1970-84. With USN, 1954-57. NIH Spl. fellow, Bethesda, Md., 1961-62, 64-67; rsch. grantee Am. Heart Assn., Cleve., 1966-74, NIH, 1979—. Fellow Am. Heart Assn. (chmn. rsch. study sect. N.E. Ohio 1975-79), Am. Physiol. Soc.; mem. IEEE (sr.), Biomed. Engring. Soc. (sr.), Royal Scottish Country, Dance Soc. (treas. 1988-93). Avocations: woodworking, hammered dulcimer, classical guitar, Scottish country dancing. Home: 3611 Runnymede Blvd Cleveland Hts OH 44121-1333 Office: Mt Sinai Med Ctr University Circle Cleveland OH 44106

MARTIN, PAUL ROSS, editor; b. Lancaster, Pa., May 14, 1932; s. Paul Rupp and Amanda (Minnich) M.; m. Julia Ibbotson, June 5, 1954 (div. Apr. 1979); children: Monica Martin Goble, Julia, Paul Jr., Barbara, Drew, Eric. BA, Dartmouth Coll., 1954. Reporter, wire editor Lancaster New Era, Lancaster Newspapers Inc., 1954-60; copyreader, makeup man Wall St. Jour. divsn. Dow Jones & Co., N.Y.C., 1960-63, copy editor nat. news, 1963-69, editor bus. and fin. column, 1969-72, nat. copydesk chief, 1972-75, page one sr. spl. writer, 1975-90, asst. to mng. editor, 1990-93, asst. mng. editor, 1993—. Editor: The Possible Dream, 1978, Retirement Without Fear, 1981, Wall Street Journal Style Book, 1981, 2d edit., 1987, 3d edit., 1992, 4th edit., 1995; co-author, editor: American Dynasties Today, 1983. Bd. dirs. Community Bd. 1, S.I., N.Y., 1976-84. Mem. N.Y. Fin. Writers Assn. (past officer). Avocations: basketball, tennis, travel. Office: Wall St Jour 200 Liberty St New York NY 10281-1003

MARTIN, PEDRO A., lawyer; b. Camaguey, Cuba, Jan. 27, 1949. BSIE, U. Fla., 1971, JD with honors, 1978; MBA, Rollin Coll., 1974. Bar: Fla. 1978, U.S. Dist. Ct. (so. dist.) Fla.1979, U.S. Ct. Appeals (11th cir.) 1981. Mem. Greenberg, Traurig, Miami. Apptd. by Gov. Bob Martinez to State of Fla. Hispanic Commn., 1987-91. Mem. ABA, Nat. Hispanic Bar Assn., Cuban Am. Bar Assn., Fla. Bar (sects. real property, probate and trust law, environ. law), Dade County Bar Assn., Order of Coif, Phi Kappa Phi. Office: Greenberg Traurig 1221 Brickel Ave Ste 2100 Miami FL 33131

MARTIN, PETER ROBERT, psychiatrist, pharmacologist; b. Budapest, Hungary, Sept. 6, 1949; came to U.S.,1980; s. Nicholas M. and Eva (Horvat) M.; m. Barbara Bradford, Dec. 23, 1985; 1 child, Alexander Bradford. BSc with honors, McGill U., Montreal, Que., Can., 1971, MD, CM, 1975; MSc, U. Toronto (Ont., Can.), 1978. Diplomate Am. Bd. Psychiatry and Neurology, Psychiatry, Addiction Psychiatry. Resident Dept. Medicine U. Toronto, Can., 1975-76, Psychiatry, U. Toronto, 1978-80; fellow Clin. Pharmacology Addiction Rsch. Found., Toronto, 1976-78; chief Sect. Clin. Sci., Nat. Inst. on Alcohol Abuse & Alcoholism, Bethesda, 1983-86; assoc. prof. Vanderbilt U. Sch. Medicine, Nashville, 1986-92, prof., 1992—; dir. Addiction Rsch. Ctr. Vanderbilt U., Nashville, 1994—, chief psychiatrist Vanderbilt Addiction Care Ctr., 1995—; vis. scientist Lab. of Clin. Sci., NIMH, Bethesda, Md., 1980-83; investigator John F. Kennedy Ctr. for Rsch. on Human Devel., Nashville, 1993—. Fellow Royal Coll. Physicians (Can.), Am. Psychiatric Assn.; mem. AAAS, Am. Soc. Clin. Pharmacology and Therapeutics, Am. Acad. Addiction Psychiatry, Am. Coll. Psychiatrists, Rsch. Soc. on Alcoholism, Internat. Soc. Biomed. Rsch. in Alcoholism. Office: Vanderbilt U Sch Medicine Dept Psychiatry MCN A2205 Nashville TN 37232

MARTIN, PETER WILLIAM, lawyer, educator; b. Cin., Apr. 11, 1939; s. Wilfred Samuel and Elizabeth (Myers) M.; m. Ann Wadsworth, Nov. 28, 1964; children: Leah, Elliot, Isaac. B.A., Cornell U., 1961; J.D., Harvard U., 1964. Bar: Ohio 1964. Atty. AF Gen. Counsel's Office, 1964-67; asso. prof. law U. Minn., 1967-71; vis. asso. prof. law Cornell U., 1971-72, prof. law, 1972—, dean, 1980-88, Edward Cornell prof. law, 1989-92, Jane Foster prof. law, 1992—; co-dir. Legal Info. Inst., 1992—; pres. Ctr. for Computer Assisted Legal Instrn., 1986-88; cons. Adminstrv. Conf. U.S., 1977-79; reporter Am. Bar Assn. Task Force on Lawyer Competency and the Role of the Law Schs. Author: The Ill-Housed, 1971, (with others) Social Welfare and the Individual, 1971, Cases and Materials on Property, 1974, 3d edit., 1992, Social Security Law, 1990, Basic Legal Citation, 1992, Social Security Plus, 1994; editor Jour. Legal Edn., 1985. Chmn. Ithaca Bd. Zoning Appeals, 1974-79. Served to capt. USAF, 1964-67. Mem. ABA (task force on law schs. and legal profession 1990-92), Am. Bar Found. (vis. com.), Am. Assn. Law Schs. (chmn. law and computers sect. 1987-88, 93-94). Office: Cornell U Law Sch Myron Taylor Hall Ithaca NY 14853

MARTIN, PHILLIP HAMMOND, lawyer; b. Tucson, Jan. 4, 1940; s. William P. and Harriet (Hammond) M.; m. Sandra S. Chandler, June 17, 1961 (div. Mar. 1989); children: Lisa, Craig, Wade, Ryan; m. Erika Zetty, May 9, 1990. BA, U. Minn., 1961, JD, 1964. Bar: Minn. 1964, U.S. Tax Ct. 1967, U.S. Dist. Ct. Minn. 1968, U.S. Ct. Appeals (8th cir.) 1973, U.S. Supreme Ct. 1981, U.S. Claims Ct. 1983, U.S. Ct. Appeals (fed. cir.) 1988, U.S. Ct. Appeals (7th cir.) 1989. Assoc. Dorsey & Whitney, Mpls., 1964-69, ptnr., 1970—. Home: 487 Portland Ave Saint Paul MN 55102-2216 Office: Dorsey & Whitney 220 S 6th St Minneapolis MN 55402-1498

MARTIN, PRESTON, financial services executive; b. L.A., Dec. 5, 1923; s. Oscar and Gaynell (Horne) M.; 1 child, Pier Preston. BS in Fin., U. So. Calif., 1947, MBA, 1948; PhD in Monetary Econs., U. Ind., 1952. Prof. fin. Grad. Sch. Bus. Adminstrn. U. So. Calif., 1950-60; prin. in housebldg. firm, 1952-56; with mortgage fin. and consumer fin. instns., 1954-57; commr. savs. and loan State of Calif., 1967-69; chmn. Fed. Home Loan Bank Bd., Washington, 1969-72; founder, CEO PMI Mortgage Ins. Co., 1972-80; chmn., CEO Seraco Group subs. Sears, Roebuck & Co., 1980-81, also bd. dirs. parent co.; chmn., CEO WestFed Holdings Inc., L.A., 1986-92, SoCal Holdings, Inc., L.A., 1987-93, H.F. Holdings, Inc., San Francisco, 1986-92; vice-chmn. Fed. Res. Bd., Washington, 1982-86; founder Fed. Home Loan Mortgage Corp.; prof. bus. econ. and fin. Inst. per lo Studio Organizitzatione Aziendale, Italy; bd. dirs. So. Calif. Savs., Beverly Hills, Calif., USA/ROC Econ. Coun. Author: Principles and Practices of Real Estate, 1959. Mem. President's Commn. on Housing, 1980-81; prin. Coun. Excellence in Govt., Washington. Recipient House and Home award, 1969, award Engring. News Record, 1971, Turntable award Nat. Assn. Home Builders, 1973. Mem. Lambda Chi Alpha. Presbyterian.

MARTIN, QUINN WILLIAM, lawyer; b. Fond du Lac, Wis., Mar. 12, 1948; s. Quinn W. and Marcia E. (Petrie) M.; m. Jane E. Nehmer; children: Quinn W., William J. BSME, Purdue U., 1969; postgrad., U. Santa Clara, 1969-70; JD, U. Mich., 1973. Bar: Wis. 1973, U.S. Dist. Ct. (ea. dist.) Wis. 1973, U.S. Ct. Appeals (7th cir.) 1973. Sales support mgr. Hewlett-Packard, Palo Alto, Calif., 1969-70; assoc. Quarles & Brady, Milw., 1973-80, ptnr., 1980—; bd. dirs. Associated Bank Milw., U-Line Corp., Altim, Inc., Tomahawk, Wis., Martin Comm., Inc., Kaukauna, Wis., ALTIM, Inc., Tomahawk, Wis., Gen. Timber and Land, Inc., Fond du Lac. Active McCallum for Lt. Gov., Wis., U. Mich. Law Sch. Fund; bd. dirs. Milw. Zool. Soc., Found. for Wildlife Conservation. Mem. ABA, Wis. Bar Assn., Milw. Bar Assn., Milw. Club, Ozaukee Country Club, Chaine des Rottiseurs, Delta Upsilon (sec.), Milw. Alumni Club. Office: Quarles & Brady 411 E Wisconsin Ave Milwaukee WI 53202-4409

MARTIN, R. EDEN, lawyer; b. Sullivan, Ill., May 17, 1940. BA, U. Ill., 1962; MA, Harvard U., 1964, LLB, 1967. Bar: Ill. 1967, U.S. Supreme Ct. 1972, D.C. 1982. Ptnr. Sidley & Austin, Chgo. Office: Sidley & Austin 1 First Nat Plz Chicago IL 60603

MARTIN, R. KEITH, business and information systems educator, consultant; b. Seattle, Sept. 5, 1933; s. Jerome Milton and Winifred (Gifford) M.; m. Carolyn Joanne Carosella, June 15, 1957; children: Jefferson, Sean, Jennifer, Katherine. AB, Whitman Coll., 1955; MBA with high honors, CCNY, 1965; PhD, U. Wash., 1973. Registered, lic. profl. engr.; cert. data processing, cert. systems profl., cert. computer profl. Div. mgr. Campus Merchandising Bur., Inc., N.Y.C., 1955-56; sales rep IBM, Seattle, 1956, Service Bur. Corp. subs. IBM, N.Y.C., 1957-58; specialist mgmt. adv. services Price Waterhouse & Co., N.Y.C., 1959-65; specialist mgmt. adv. services Price Waterhouse & Co., Seattle, 1965-66, mgr., 1966-67; dir. mgmt. systems dept. U. Wash., 1967-71, lectr. dept. acctg. Sch. Bus. Adminstrn, 1971-73; asst. prof. dept. accountancy Baruch Coll., CUNY, 1973-76, assoc. prof., 1977-79; prof. acctg. and info. systems Fairfield U., 1979-94, assoc. dean Sch. Bus., 1980-82, dean, 1982-93, acting dean grad. Sch. of Communications, 1988-90, prof. info. systems, 1994—; v.p. Eastalco Systems, 1971-72; faculty fin. div. Am. Mgmt. Assn., 1963-64; part-time lectr. Bellevue Community Coll., 1967-69, Shoreline Community Coll., 1968-72, Seattle U., 1971-72. Co-author: Management Control of Electronic Data Processing, 1965; author: Management Information Systems in Higher Education: Case Studies at Three Universities, 1973, Effective Business Communications, 1976, 79, 91, Systems Development and Computer Concepts, 1977; assoc. editor: Industry Guides for Accountants and Auditors, 2 vols., 1980; mem. editorial rev. bd. Dickenson Pub. Co., 1974-75, Prentice-Hall, Inc., 1977-78, 87-88, 90-91, Reston Pub. Co., 1977-78, Jour. Acctg. Edn., 1981-83; contbr. monographs and articles. Mem. Citizens' Legis. Rev. Com., 1968-69; mem. City of Seattle EDP Adv. Com., 1968-71, chmn., 1968-69; vice chmn. subcom. Citizens Adv. Com. Licensing and Consumer Affairs, 1970-73; chmn. indsl. engring. adv. com. Shoreline C.C., 1968-72; mem. mgmt. info. systems data element task force Western Interstate Commn. Higher Edn., 1968-70, adv. council, 1969-71; mem. com. for non-partisan nomination and election of Bronxville Sch. Bd. Trustees, 1976-78, chmn., 1977, chmn. mgmt. policies and procedures com., 1981-82, mem. fin. com., chmn. audit subcom., 1985-86; cons. to Urban Acad., City N.Y., 1974-78; chmn., pres. Loft Film and Theatre Ctr., Inc., 1977-78, mem. adv. bd., 1982-83; v.p. Normandy Homeowners Assn., 1978-80, pres., 1983, treas., 1989-91; sec.-treas. governing mem., mem. of policy com. The Com. on Developing American Capitalism, 1982—; bd. dirs. Intelligent Communications Network, 1982-86, chmn. audit com., 1983-86, mem. compensation com., 1982-86; trustee Conn. Joint Council Econ. Edn., 1982-93; trustee Ctr. Fin. Studies, 1983-95, vice chmn. audit com., 1983-95, mem. exec. com., 1985-94; cons. examiner and mem. com. bus. Charter Oak Coll., 1984-92, co-chmn., 1987-91, com. on degrees, 1987-92, core curriculum com., 1989-91, vice chmn., 1991-92; bd. advisers Econ. Club of Conn., Nat. Assn. Economists, 1985-86; mem. adv. com. regional vocat. mgmt. program, City of Bridgeport, 1987-87; mem. adv. bd. So. Conn. Bus. Jour., 1987-88; mem. Am. Assembly of Collegiate Schs. of Bus. Task Force on Faculty Renewal, 1985-87, nominating com., 1989-90; adv. bd. So. Conn. Bus. Jour., 1987-88; mem. bd. edn. Village of Bronxville, 1987-90, mem. fin. com., 1987-88, v.p., 1989-90, chmn. pers. com., 1988-90; acad. policy and stds. com. Inst. for Fin. Planning, 1987-92, sec.-treas., 1988-90; exec. com. Deans of Jesuit Schs. of Bus., 1987-91, sec.-treas., 1988-89, v.p., 1989-90, pres., 1990-91; cons. TRI Corp., 1991-95. Recipient cert. of appreciation Am. Mgmt. Assn., 1966, cert. of merit for disting. service to

Mgmt. Scis., 1969, for disting. service to info. systems profession, 1973; Merit award Assn. Systems Mgmt., 1971, Achievement award, 1972; cert. for service City of Seattle, 1973; named Outstanding You Man Am., 1970, One of 300 Outstanding Alumni, Whitman Coll., 1979; Kellogg fellow, 1971-72, Price Waterhouse faculty fellow, 1976. Mem. Am. Inst. Indsl. Engrs. (dir. Seattle chpt. 1967-70, chmn. regional conf. 1969), Inst. Mgmt. Accts. (assoc. dir. N.Y. chpt. 1963-64, 75-85 Seattle chpt. 1967-70), Assn. Systems Mgmt. (sec. 1968-69, v.p. 1969-70, pres. Pacific N.W. chpt. 1970-71), Data Processing Mgmt. Assn., Assn. Computing Machinery, Soc. Cert. Data Processors, NSPE, N.Y. Soc. Profl. Engrs., Soc. Mgmt. Info. Systems, AAUP, Am. Acctg. Assn., Phi Delta Theta (province pres. 1986-87), Mu Gamma Tau, Phi Delta Kappa, Beta Alpha Psi. Club: Bronxville Field. Home: 2 Normandy Rd Bronxville NY 10708-4808

MARTIN, RALPH GUY, writer; b. Chgo., Mar. 4, 1920; s. Herman and Tillie (Charno) M.; m. Marjorie Jean Pastel, June 17, 1944; children: Maurice Joseph, Elizabeth, Tina. B.J., U. Mo., 1941. Reporter, mng. editor Box Elder News Jour., Brigham, Utah, 1940-41; contbr. mags. including Sunday N.Y. Times, Look, Harpers mag., 1945-53; assoc. editor New Republic mag., 1945-48; assoc. editor charge spl. reports Newsweek mag., 1953-55; exec. editor House Beautiful mag., 1955-57; pub., pres. Bandwagon, Inc. Author: Boy From Nebraska, 1946, The Best is None Too Good, 1948, Ballots and Bandwagons: Five Key Conventions since 1900, 1964, Skin Deep, 1964, The Bosses, 1964, President from Missouri, 1964, Wizard of Wall Street, 1965, World War II, Pearl Harbor to V-J Day, 1966, The GI War, 1967, A Man for All People, 1968, Jennie: The Life of Lady Randolph Churchill, The Romantic Years, 1969, vol. II, The Dramatic Years, 1971, Lincoln Center for the Performing Arts, 1971, The Woman He Loved: The Story of the Duke and Duchess of Windsor, 1974, Cissy, The Extraordinary Life of Eleanor Medill Patterson, 1979; A Hero For Our Time, An Intimate Study of the Kennedy Years, 1983, Charles and Diana, 1985, Golda, Golda Meir: The Romantic Years, 1988, Henry and Clare: An Intimate Portrait of the Luces, 1991, Seeds of Destruction: Joe Kennedy and His Sons; co-author: Stevenson Speeches, 1952, Eleanor Roosevelt: Her Life in Pictures, 1958, The Human Side of FDR, 1960, Front Runner, Dark Horse, 1960, Money, Money, Money, 1960, Man of Destiny: Charles DeGaulle, 1961, Man of the Century: Winston Churchill, 1961, The Three Lives of Helen Keller, 1962, World War II: From D-Day to VE-Day, 1962; Contbr. to: Yank The GI History of The War, Social Problems in America, 1955, Democracy in Action, 1962, others. Dep. dir. pub. relations Nat. Vols. for Stevenson-Kefauver, 1956; mem. Dem. Nat. Campaign Com. Combat corr. Stars and Stripes, Yank mag., 1941-45. Mem. Author's League Am., Author's Guild, English-Speaking Union, Tenn. Squires, Dramatist's Guild. Clubs: Century, Overseas Press. Home: 135 Harbor Rd Westport CT 06880-6918

MARTIN, RANDI CHRISTINE, psychology educator; b. Salem, Oreg., May 24, 1949; d. Harold Raymond and Maxine Constance (Torgeson) M.; m. Lawrence P. Chan, Aug. 30, 1974. BA, U. Oreg., 1971; MA, Johns Hopkins U., 1977, PhD, 1979. Lectr. U. Calif., Santa Cruz, 1979-80; assoc. rsch. scientist Johns Hopkins U., Balt., 1980-82; asst. prof. Rice U., Houston, 1982-87, assoc. prof., 1987-93, prof., 1993—. Assoc. editor Psychonomic Bulletin & Rev., Austin, Tex., 1995—; editl. bd. mem. Cognitive Neuropsychology, London, 1994—, Jour. Neurolinguistics, Cambridge, Eng., 1994—; contbr. articles to profl. jours. Recipient Claude Pepper award NIH Deafness and Comm. Disorders Inst., 1995—. Mem. APA, Psychonomic Soc. (sec./treas. 1993-95), Acad. Aphasia (program com. 1990-93). Achievements include research in short term memory deficits in brain damaged patients. Office: Rice U Psychology Dept 6100 Main St Houston TX 77005-1827

MARTIN, RAY, banker; b. Nogales, AZ, 1936. With Coast Savs. and Loan Assn. (now Coast Fed. Bank), L.A., 1959—, pres., 1980-84, pres., chief exec. officer, from 1984, now chmn. bd., chief exec. officer, also bd. dirs. Office: Coast Svgs Fin Inc 1000 Wilshire Blvd Los Angeles CA 90017-2457*

MARTIN, REBECCA REIST, librarian; b. Princeton, N.J., Mar. 2, 1952; d. Benjamin A. and Harriet (Nold) Reist; 1 child, Benjamin R. BA, U. Calif., Santa Cruz, 1973; MA, San Jose State U., 1975; DPA, U. So. Calif., 1992. Med. libr. VA Med. Ctr., San Francisco, 1975-77, chief libr. svc., 1977-81; head biology libr. U. Calif., Berkeley, 1981-85; assoc. libr. dir. San Jose (Calif.) State U., 1985-90; dean of librs. U. Vt., Burlington, 1990—. Author: Libraries and the Changing Face of Academia, 1994; contbr. articles to profl. jours., chpts. in books. Mem. Libr. Commn. San Jose, 1989-90. Mem. ALA, New England Libr. Assn., Am. Soc. Pub. Adminstrn., Am. Assn. Coll. and Rsch. Librs., Libr. Adminstrn. and Mgmt. Assn. (bd. dirs. 1987-89), NELINET (bd. dirs. 1995—). Office: U Vt Bailey/Howe Libr Burlington VT 05405

MARTIN, REX, manufacturing executive. CEO Nibco, Elkhart, Ind. Office: Nibco Inc 500 Simpson Ave PO Box 1167 Elkhart IN 46516*

MARTIN, RICHARD HARRISON, curator, art historian; b. Bryn Mawr, Pa., Dec. 4, 1946; s. Frank Harrison and Margaret Dever M. BA, Swarthmore Coll., 1967; MA, Columbia U., 1969, M.Phil., 1971. Instr. William Paterson Coll. of N.J., Wayne, 1972-73; editor Arts Mag., N.Y.C., 1974-88; prof. Fashion Inst. Tech., SUNY, N.Y.C., 1973-93, Ednl. Found. for the Fashion Industries, 1991-93; exec. dir. Shirley Goodman Resource Center, 1980-93; critic-in-residence Md. Inst. Coll. Art, 1985-87; editor, pub. Textile & Text, 1989-93; curator The Costume Inst., Met. Mus. Art, N.Y.C., 1993—; adj. faculty Sch. Visual Arts, N.Y.C., 1975-80, 93—; adj. prof. NYU, 1977—, Columbia U., 1987-89, 95—, Vt. Coll., 1991-93. Author: Fashion and Surrealism, 1987, Jocks and Nerds, 1989, The Historical Mode, 1989, The New Urban Landscape, 1990, Giorgio Armani: Images of Man, 1990, Flair: Fashion Collected by Tina Chow, 1992, Infra-Apparel, 1993, Diana Vreeland: Immoderate Style, 1993, Waist Not, 1994, Madame Grès, 1994, Orientalism: Visions of the East in Western Dress, 1994, Bloom, 1995, Contemporary Fashion, 1995, Haute Couture, 1995. Mem. Coll. Art Assn. Am., Victorian Soc. Am. (dir. 1980-84, chpt. dir. 1981-83), Soc. Archtl. Historians, Am. Soc. for Aesthetics, Art Libraries Soc. N.Am., N.Y. Hist. Soc., Soc. for History of Tech., Costume Soc. Am. (dir. 1983-89, Region II pres. 1984-87). Home: 225 E 79th St New York NY 10021-0855 Office: Met Mus Art The Costume Inst 1000 5th Ave New York NY 10028-0198

MARTIN, RICHARD JAY, medical educator; b. Detroit, May 16, 1946; s. Peter Aaron and Tillie Jean (Munch) M.; m. Helene Iris Horowitz, Dec. 23, 1967; children: Elizabeth Hope, David Evan. BS, U. Mich., 1967, MD, 1971. Diplomate Am. Bd. Internal Medicine and Pulmonary Disease. Intern Ariz., 1971-72; resident Tulane U., New Orleans, 1974-76; asst. prof. medicine U. Okla., Okla. City, 1978-80; asst. prof. medicine U. Colo., Denver, 1980-85, assoc. prof., 1985-92, prof., 1992—; dir. Cardiorespiratory Sleep Rsch., Nat. Jewish Ctr. for Immunology and Respiratory Medicine, Denver, 1980-89, staff physician, 1980—, head divsn. pulmonary medicine, 1993—. Author: Cardiorespiratory Disorders During Sleep, 1984, 2d edit., 1990, (with others) Current Therapy in Internal Medicine, 1984, Clinical Pharmacology and Therapeutics in Nursing, 1985, Interdisciplinary Rehabilitation of Multiple Sclerosis and Neuromuscular Disorders, 1984, Drugs for the Respiratory System, 1985, Current Therapy in Pulmonary Medicine, 1985, Abnormalities of Respiration During Sleep, 1986, Mitchell's Synopis of Pulmonary Medicine, 1987, Pulmonary Grand Rounds, 1990, Asthma and Rhinitis, 1994, The High Risk Patient: Management of the Critically Ill, 1995, Manual of Asthma Management, 1995, Sever Asthma: Pathsyenesis and Clinical Management, 1995, Curret Pulmonology, 1995, Pulmonary and Respiratory Therapy Secrets, 1996; editor: Nocturnal Asthma: Mechanisms and Interventions, 1993; author, editor: Nocturnal Asthma: Mechanisms and Treatment, 1993; mem. editl. bd.: (jour.) Am. Jour. of Respiratory and Critical Care Medicine, 1994—, Bronchial Asthma: Index and Review, 1996—; assoc. editor: Clinical Care for Asthma, 1995—; contbr. articles, reviews, reports on respiratory and neuromuscular diseases to profl. jours. Pres. Congregation Rodef Shalom, Denver, 1984-85; regional v.p. United Synagogues of Am., Denver, 1988-89. Pulmonary fellow Am. Lung Assn., 1977-79; James F. Hammarsten Outstanding fellow U. Okla. Health Scis. Ctr., 1978; grantee Purdue-Frederick Co., Winthrop-Breon Labs. Inc., Werner-lambert Co., VA, U. Okla. Lung Assn., NIH, Parker B. Francis Found.; recipient Best Paper in Internal Medicine award Okla. Soc. Interna. Medicine, 1977, 78, U. Okla. Gastroenterology sect, 1977. Mem. Am. Thoracic Soc., Am. Fedn. for Clin. Rsch., Am. Coll. Chest Physicians (rep. to Young Pulmonary Physician Conf., St. Charles, Ill. 1979), ACP, Colo. Trudeau Soc., Western Soc. Clin. Investigation. Avocations: biking, golf, karate. Office: Nat Jewish Ctr Immunology & Respiratory Medicine 1400 Jackson St Denver CO 80206-2762

MARTIN, RICHARD KELLEY, lawyer; b. Tulsa, June 30, 1952; s. Richard Loye and Maxine (Kelley) M.; m. Reba Lawson, June 12, 1993; children from previous marriage: R. Kyle, Andrew J. BA, Westminster Coll., 1974; JD, So. Meth. U., 1977. Bar: Tex. 1977, U.S. Tax Ct. 1979. Ptnr. Akin, Gump, Strauss, Hauer & Feld, LLP, Dallas, 1977-95; prnt. Haynes and Boone LLP, Dallas, 1995—. Bd. dirs. Goodwill Industries, Dallas, 1986—, v.p., 1986-91; bd. dirs. Greater Dallas Youth Orchs., 1987-90; bd. dirs., v.p., pres. Big Bros. and Sisters Met. Dallas, 1988-91; bd. dirs. Tejas coun. Girl Scouts U.S. Mem. Tex. Bar Assn., Salesmanship Club Dallas. Republican. Methodist. Office: Haynes and Boone LLP 3100 NationsBank Plz 901 Main St Dallas TX 75202-3714

MARTIN, RICHARD L., insurance executive; b. Franklin, N.J., Feb. 2, 1932; s. Richard Lewis and Elizabeth (Roe) M.; m. Susan Mazuy, June 20, 1970; children: David Cory, Scott Mazuy. BEd, U. Miami, 1958; MA, Columbia U., 1963. Chartered Property Casualty Underwriter. Educator Franklin (N.J.) Sch. Dist., 1958-60; mng. dir. Sparta (N.J.) Sch. Dist., 1960-66; adminstr. Orange (N.J.) Sch. System, 1966-71; chief exec. officer Montague (N.J.) Sch. Dist., 1971-72, Stanhope (N.J.) Sch. System, 1972-73; v.p. Selective Ins. Group, Branchville, N.J., 1973-87; pres., chief exec. officer Med. Malpractice Ins. Assn., N.Y.C., 1987—; chmn. N.J. Anti-Car Theft Com., Trenton, 1980-87; treas. N.J. Ins. News Svc., Newark, 1982-87; chmn. AIA-N.J. State Conf., Trenton, 1983-87. Contbr. several articles to mags. With USMC, 1952-54. Mem. CPCU, Am. Mgmt. Assn., Soc. Ins. Research, Soc. for Corp. Planning, City Midday, Newton Country, Branchville Rotary, Sons of Am. Revolution, Mayflower Soc. Presbyterian. Avocations: golf, hunting. Home: Two Plains Rd Augusta NJ 07822 Office: Med Malpractice Ins Assn 110 William St New York NY 10038-3901

MARTIN, ROBERT BRUCE, chemistry educator; b. Chgo., Apr. 29, 1929; s. Robert Frank and Helen (Woelffer) M.; m. Frances May Young, June 7, 1953. B.S., Northwestern U., 1950; Ph.D., U. Rochester, 1953. Asst. prof. chemistry Am. U., Beirut, Lebanon, 1953-56; research fellow Calif. Inst. Tech., 1956-57, Harvard U., 1957-59; asst. prof. chemistry U. Va., Charlottesville, 1959-61, assoc. prof., 1961-65, prof., 1965—, chmn. dept., 1968-71; spl. fellow Oxford U., 1961-62; Program dir. Molecular Biology Sect., NSF, 1965-66. Author: Introduction to Biophysical Chemistry, 1964. Fellow AAAS; mem. Am. Chem. Soc. Office: Univ Va Dept Chemistry Charlottesville VA 22901

MARTIN, ROBERT DAVID, judge, educator; b. Iowa City, Oct. 7, 1944; s. Murray and G'Ann (Holmgren) M.; m. Ruth A. Haberman, Aug. 21, 1966; children: Jacob, Matthew, David. A.B., Cornell Coll., Mt. Vernon, Iowa, 1966; J.D., U. Chgo., 1969. Bar: Wis. 1969, U.S. Dist. Ct. (we. dist.) Wis. 1969, U.S. Dist. Ct. (ea. dist.) Wis. 1974, U.S. Supreme Ct. 1973. Assoc., Ross & Stevens, S.C., Madison, Wis., 1969-72, ptnr., 1973-78; chief judge U.S. Bankruptcy Ct. We. Dist. Wis., 1978—; instr. gen. practice course U. Wis. Law Sch., 1974, 76, 77, 80, lectr. debtor/creditor course, 1981-82, 83, 85, 87, farm credit seminar, 1985, advanced bankruptcy problems, 1989; co-chmn. faculty Am. Law Inst.-ABA Fin. and Bus. Planning for Agr., Stanford U., 1979; faculty mem. Fed. Jud. Ctr. Schs. for New Bankruptcy Judges, 1985-93; chmn. Ann. Continuing Legal Edn. Wis. Debtor Creditor Conf., 1981—. Author: Bankruptcy: Annotated Forms, 1989; co-author: Secured Transactions Handbook for Wisconsin Lawyers and Lenders, Bankruptcy-Text Statutes Rules and Forms, 1992, Ginsberg and Martin on Bankruptcy, 4th edit., 1996. Bd. dirs., exec. com. Luth. Social Svcs. for Wis. and Upper Mich. Mem. Wis. State Bar, Am. Coll. Bankruptcy, Am. Judicature Soc., Nat. Conf. Bankruptcy Judges (bd. govs. 1989-91, sec. 1993-94, v.p. 1994-95, pres. 1995-96), Nat. Bankruptcy Conf. Office: 120 N Henry Rm 340 PO Box 548 Madison WI 53701-0548

MARTIN, ROBERT EDWARD, architect; b. Dodge City, Kans., Mar. 17, 1928; s. Emry and Alice Jane (Boyce) M.; m. Billie Jo Lange, Aug. 16, 1952 (div. Feb. 1970); m. Kathryn M. Arvanitis, June 26, 1971; children: Lynn, Amy, Blaine. Student, McPherson Coll., 1946-48; BArch, U. Cin., 1954. Registered architect, Ohio. Architect Samborn, Steketee, Otis & Evans, Inc., Toledo, 1956-58; prin. Schauder & Martin, Toledo, 1958-72, The Collaborative, Inc., Toledo, 1972-93; mem. Bd. Examiners Archs., Ohio, 1985—, pres., 1989-94; bd. examiners Nat. Coun. Archtl. Registration Bds., 1986—, edn. com., 1992; chmn. site design divsn. Archtl. Registration Exam., 1989, 90, 91; mem. Nat. Coun. Archtl. Registration Bds. Grading, 1987-94; chmn. study of Toledo Fire & Rescue Dept., Corp. for Effective Govt., 1994. Artist numerous paintings. Mem. Toledo Planning Commn., 1971-74, Toledo Zoning Appeals Bd., 1973, Toledo Bd. Bldg. Stds., 1967-84, Citizens Fire Adv. Commn., 1974-80, Citizens Urban Area Adv. Commn., 1962, Toledo Area Coun. Govts., 1977-80, Com. of 100, Toledo, 1987-89, Spectrum Friends Fine Arts, Inc., Toledo; chmn. bd. Toledo Area Govtl. Rsch. Assn., 1981-90; chmn. Corp. for Effective Govt., Study of Toledo Fire and Rescue Dept., 1994; chmn. Cystic Fibrosis, Toledo. 1985. Seved to capt. USAF, 1954-56. Recipient numerous watercolor awards. Fellow AIA (pres. Toledo chpt. 1966, Arch. of Yr. 1993), Archs. Soc. Ohio (pres. 1975), Ohio Watercolor Soc., N.W. Ohio Watercolor Soc., Toledo Fedn. Art Socs. (pres. 1989, 90), Spectrum, Tile Club, Toledo Artists Club, Toledo Artists Club, Sylvania Country Club, Rotary, Masons, Shriners, Jesters. Mem. Ch. of Brethren. Avocation: painting. Home: 5119 Regency Dr Toledo OH 43615-2946 Office: 1700 N Reynolds Rd Toledo OH 43615-3628

MARTIN, ROBERT FINLAY, JR., retired judge; b. Akron, O., May 4, 1925; s. Robert Finlay and Olive (Dexter) M.; m. Eleanor A. Gunn, Sept. 3, 1948; children—Roberta C. (Mrs. Bobby P. Grimes), Craig J., Scott D. B.A., Kent State U., 1949; J.D., U. Akron, 1954. Bar: Ohio bar 1955, Okla. bar 1963, U.S. Supreme Ct. bar 1974, Supreme Ct. Okla. bar 1963, Supreme Ct. Ohio bar 1955, U.S. Dist. Ct. Northeastern Dist. Okla. bar 1971. Claims atty. Ohio Farmers Ins. Cos., LeRoy, 1951-59; claims supr. Selman & Co., Tulsa, 1959-63; practiced in Tulsa, 1963-66; judge Common Pleas Ct., Tulsa, 1967-69, Dist. Ct., Tulsa, 1969-88. City solicitor City of Seville, Ohio, 1958-59; Trustee Bd. Pub. Affairs, LeRoy, 1957-59, Ct. Fund Trustees Tulsa County, 1971-74. Served with USNR, 1943-46. Lodge: Masons. Home: 2315 S Fulton Pl Tulsa OK 74114-3746

MARTIN, ROBERT LESLIE, physician; b. Abilene, Tex., Oct. 28, 1934; s. Leslie Resa and Garnet Iva (Brown) M.; m. Henrietta Montgomery, 1956; children: Randal, Christopher. BA, U. Kans., 1956, MD, 1960. Diplomate in clin. pathology Am. Bd. Pathology; diplomate Nat. Bd. Med. Examiners; lic. physician, Calif., Fla. Intern U. Kans., 1960-61, resident and fellow in pathology, 1964-67; asst. prof. pathology Case We. Res. U., Cleve., 1967-78; dir. clin. labs. Univ. Hosps. of Cleve., 1972-76; assoc. prof. pathology U. South Fla., Tampa, 1978-82; chief clin. pathology James A. Haley Vets. Hosp., Tampa, 1978-82; project mgr. Scott Sci. & Tech., Albequerque, N.Mex., 1982-83; physician advisor Profl. Found. for Health Care Inc., Tampa, 1984-89; primary care physician Tampa, Fla., 1986—. Contbr. articles to profl. jours. Fellow Coll. Am. Pathologists; Alpha Omega Alpha, Phi Gamma Delta. Republican. Episcopalian. Home: 15840 Sanctuary Dr Tampa FL 33647-1075

MARTIN, ROBERT RICHARD, emeritus college president, former senator; b. McKinney, Ky., Dec. 27, 1910; s. Henry Franklin and Annie Frances (Peek) M.; m. Anne French Hoge, May 31, 1952. AB, Eastern Ky. U., 1934; MA, U. Ky., 1940; EdD, Columbia U., 1951. Tchr., prin. pub. schs. Mason and Lee counties, Ky., 1935-48; with Ky. Dept. Edn., 1948-59, beginning as auditor, successively dir. finance, head bur. adminstrn. and finance, 1948-55, supt. pub. instrn., 1955-59; commr. finance Commonwealth Ky., 1959-60; pres. Eastern Ky. U., Richmond, 1960-76; pres. emeritus Eastern Ky. U., 1976—; mem. Ky. Senate, 1977-86; chmn. health and welfare com.; assisted devel. found. program for financing of edn. in Ky.; bd. dirs. Bank One; chmn. health and welfare com.; assisted devel. found. program for financing edn. in Ky. Bd. dirs. Pattie A. Clay Hosp., Telford Community Center, Ky. Diabetes Assn.; mem. Ky. Cancer Commn.; bd. dirs. Jud. Form Retirement; hon. chmn. United Way Madison County, 1978—; trustee, elder Presbyn. ch. Tech. sgt. USAAF, 1942-46; meteorologist. Recipient Outstanding Alumnus award Eastern Ky. State Coll., 1956; named Kentuckian of Yr. Ky. Press Assn., 1964; recipient Service award Joint Alumni Council Ky., 1970, Civilian Service award Dept. Army, 1971; Danforth Found. grantee, 1971. Mem. NEA, Am. Assn. Sch. Adminstrs., English-Speaking Union, Civil War Roundtable (bd. dirs.), Ky. Hist. Soc. (pres. 1974—), Ky. Edn. Assn., Am. Assn. State Colls. and Univs. (pres. 1971-72), Phi Delta Kappa, Kappa Delta Pi. Democrat. Presbyterian. Lodge: Masons (Shriners), Rotary, Filson. Home: 300 Summit St Richmond KY 40475-2134

MARTIN, ROBERT WILLIAM, retired corporate executive; b. Toronto, Ont., Can., June 7, 1936; s. William George and Evelyn Irene (Phillips) M.; m. Patricia Lorraine Norris, June 27, 1959; children: Stephen Gregory, Robert Scott, Adrienne Christine Teron. B.A.Sc., U. Toronto, 1958. V.p. ops. Consumers Gas, Toronto, 1973-80, pres., dir., 1981-92, CEO, ret., 1992; chmn. Silcorp. Ltd.; bd. dirs. IPL Energy Inc., Cara Ops. Ltd., Peoples Jewellers Ltd., ACC TeleEnterprises Ltd., Reed Stenhouse Cos., Goldfarb Corp. Bd. dirs. York U.; campaign chmn. United Way Toronto, 1988; chmn. Toronto Symphony Orch.; pres. West Park Hosp. Found. Recipient Meritorious Svc. award U. Toronto, 1983, Arbor award. Mem. Assn. Profl. Engrs. Ont., Can. Gas Assn. (past chmn.), Ont. Natural Gas Assn. (past pres.), Mad River Golf Club, Mississauga Golf and Country Club, Toronto Club. Home: 118 Farnham Ave, Toronto, ON Canada MHW 1HH

MARTIN, ROBLEE BOETTCHER, retired cement manufacturing executive; b. St. Louis, Apr. 21, 1922; s. Henry W. and Esther (Boettcher) M.; m. Lillian Seegraves, July 15, 1940; children: Mary Katherine, Bruce Daniel, Amy Lee. B.S. in Chem. Engring., Columbia U., 1943, M.S. in Chem. Engring., 1947; D.Sc. in Bus. Adminstrn. (hon.), Cleary Coll., 1962. Prodn. supr. Monsanto Chem. Co., St. Louis, 1946-49; dir. research and devel. Miss. Lime Co., Ste. Genevieve, Mo., 1949-59; pres. Dundee Cement Co., Mich., 1959-69; v.p. Fruehauf Corp.; gen. mgr. (Fruehauf Bldgs. div.), Detroit, 1969-72; pres. Presidents Assn. div. Am. Mgmt. Assn., N.Y.C., 1972-74; pres. insulation div. Keene Corp., Princeton, N.J., 1974-76; chmn., chief exec. officer Keystone Cement Co., Bath, Pa., 1976-89, Giant Cement Co., Harleyville, S.C., 1985-89; sr. v.p., dir. Giant Group Ltd., Beverly Hills, Calif., 1985-89. Served to lt. (j.g.) USNR, 1944-46, PTO. Mem. Sigma Xi, Tau Beta Pi, Phi Lambda Upsilon. Baptist. Home: 2151 Palermo Pl Charleston SC 29406-9231

MARTIN, ROGER BOND, landscape architect, educator; b. Virginia, Minn., Nov. 23, 1936; s. Thomas George and Audrey (Bond) M.; m. Janis Ann Kloss, Aug. 11, 1962; children: Thomas, Stephen, Jonathan. BS with high distinction, U. Minn., 1958; M. Landscape Arch., Harvard U., 1961. Asst. prof. U. Calif.-Berkeley, 1964-66; assoc. prof. U. Minn., Mpls., 1966, prof., 1968—, chmn. dept. landscape architecture, 1966-77, 83-87, dir. grad. studies in landscape architecture, 1983-84, dir. undergrad. studies, 1987-94, dir. profl. studies, 1994—; owner Roger Martin & Assoc., site planners and landscape architects, Mpls., 1966-68; prin. InterDesign, Inc., Mpls., 1968-84, Martin & Pitz Assocs., Inc., 1984—; vis. prof. U. Melbourne, 1979-80. Prin. works include Minn. Zool. Gardens, 1978 (merit award Am. Soc. Landscape Archs. 1978), Mpls. Pky. Restorations, 1972-87 (merit award 1978, Minn. Classic award Am. Soc. Landscape Archs. 1994), South St. Paul Ctrl. Sq., 1978 (merit award 1978), Festival Park, Chisholm, Minn., 1986, Miss. Wildlife Refuge (visual image assessment merit award 1985), Nicollet Island Park (merit award 1989), Hennepin Avenue Master Plan, 1995 (merit award 1995). Recipient Fredrick Mann award for svc. to edn. U. Minn., 1990, Disting. Educator award Sigma Lambda Alpha, 1990; fellow Am. Acad. in Rome, 1962-64. Fellow Am. Soc. Landscape Archs. (pres. Minn. chpt. 1970-72, trustee 1980-84, nat. pres. 1987, chmn.-elect coun. fellows 1991, chmn. 1992-94, past chmn. 1994-96, Pub. Svc. award 1985); mem. Nat. Coun. Instrs. Landscape Architecture (pres. 1973-74), Can. Soc. Landscape Archs. (hon.). Home: 2912 45th Ave S Minneapolis MN 55406-1829 Office: Martin & Pitz Assocs Inc 1409 Willow St Minneapolis MN 55403-2249

MARTIN, ROGER HARRY, college president; b. N.Y.C., June 26, 1943; s. Edwin Diller and Emma (Neuenburg) M.; m. Susan Bradford, Aug. 29, 1970; children: Katherine R., Emily G. BA, Drew U., 1965; BD, Yale U., 1968, STM, 1969; DPhil, Oxford (Eng.) U., 1974. Program officer Edn. Incentive Program, N.Y.C., 1969-70; devel. officer NYU, 1970-71, 75-76; asst. dir. devel. Rensselaer Polytech Inst., Troy, N.Y., 1974-75; asst. prof. history, exec. asst. to pres. Middlebury (Vt.) Coll., 1976-80; assoc. dean Harvard Div. Sch., Cambridge, Mass., 1980-86; prof. history, pres. Moravian Coll., Bethlehem, Pa., 1986—. Author: Evangelicals United: Ecumenical Stirrings in Pre-Victorian Britain, 1795-1830, 1983. Chmn. bd. assocs. Yale Divinity Sch.; trustee Moravian Acad. Mem. Harvard Club (N.Y.C.), Saucon Valley Country Club. Mem. Soc. of Friends. Avocations: skiing, running. Home: Frueauff House 79 W Church St Bethlehem PA 18018-5821 Office: Moravian Coll Office of President 1200 Main St Bethlehem PA 18018-6614

MARTIN, ROGER JOHN, computer scientist, computer systems analyst; b. Ft. Atkinson, Iowa, Sept. 11, 1947; s. Raymond Charles and Linda R. (Kuennen) M.; m. Jane Degnan, Nov. 21, 1970; children: John, Kathryn, Susan, Jacquelyn. BS in Computer Sci., Iowa State U., 1969, MS in Computer Sci., 1971. Computer specialist Naval Ship R & D Ctr., Bethesda, Md., 1971-76; supervisory systems analyst Exec. Office of Pres., Washington, 1976-82; computer scientist, mgr. software engring. group Inst. for Computer Scis. and Tech., Nat. Inst. Standards and Tech., Washington, 1982-92, chief System and Software Technology Divsn., 1993-95, mgr. Software Methods, 1995—, program co-chmn. Conf. on Software Maintenance, 1985, gen. chair, 1987; gen. chair Computer Standards Conf. 1988. Coach soccer Montgomery County Recreation Dept., Rockville, Md., 1979-83; treas., del. Mill Creek Towne Elem. Sch. PTA, Rockville, 1981-84, pres. 1986-87; Magruder cluster PTA coordinator, 1984-86; leader Cub Scouts, Rockville, 1983-84, asst. scoutmaster troop, 1984-92. Recipient Outstanding Performance award Naval Ship R & D Ctr., 1976; Outstanding Performance award Exec. Office of Pres., 1979, Spl. Achievement award, 1981, Interagency Com. on Info. Resources Mgmt. award for Tech. Excellence, 1989, Fed. Computer Week award, 1992; cert. of recognition Nat. Bur. Standards, 1983; Dept. Commerce Bronze medal award, 1984, Silver Medal award, 1989, . Mem. Assn. for Computing Machinery, IEEE Computer Soc. (chmn. working group on test methods for POSIX 1986-93, chmn. tech. com. on operating system steering com. on conformance testing 1989—, cert. recognition 1987, tech. com. on operating system project mgmt. com. 1991-93, Meritorious Svc. award 1991, Standards Medallion, 1992). Home: 7413 Cliffbourne Ct Rockville MD 20855-1101 Office: NIST/CSL NN820/ m5509 Gaithersburg MD 20899

MARTIN, RON, newspaper editor in chief. Editor Atlanta Journal-Constitution, Ga. Office: Atlanta Jour-Constn 72 Marietta St PO Box 4689 Atlanta GA 30302-5501

MARTIN, ROY BUTLER, JR., museum director, retired broker; b. Norfolk, Va., May 13, 1921; s. Roy Butler and Anne (Holman) M.; m. Louise Eggleston, Apr. 17, 1948; children: Roy Butler III, Anne Beverly Martin Sessoms. Student, William and Mary Coll., Norfolk, 1939-40; BS in Commerce, U. Va., 1943. Chmn. bd. Commonwealth Brokers Inc., 1955-88; mayor City of Norfolk, 1962-74; pres. Chrysler Mus., Norfolk, 1989—; pres. U.S. Conf. Mayors, Washington, 1973-74; trustee Sentara Health System. Chmn. Douglas MacArthur Found., 1963—, Civic Facilities Commn., Norfolk, 1986—; bd. dirs. Norfolk Forum; exec. com., pres. Va. Mcpl. League, 1968-69; past mem. Va. State Water Control Bd.; past mem. exec. com., adv. bd. Nat. League of Cities, com. on community devel., U.S. Conf. Mayors, Southeastern Va. Planning Dist. Commn; chmn. Southeastern Tidewater Area Manpower Planning System, Mayor's Youth Commn.; Gov.'s Com. on Youth; past bd. dirs. Norfolk Urban Coalition; past mem. VALC Zoning Procedures Com.; past bd. dirs. Norfolk Symphony Orch., Boys Club Norfolk, Old Dominion U. Edns. Found.; past mem. Norfolk Cerebral Palsy Tng. Ctr., vestry Ch. of Good Shepherd, Norfolk. Lt. USNR, 1943-46, USNR, 1948-52. Decorated officer in Order of the Crown (Belgium); recipient Outstanding Alumni award Old Dominion U., 1964, Sales of Yr. award Sales and Mktg. Club Tidewater, 1971, Meritorious Pub. Svc. Citation Dept. Navy, 1974, Cmty. Svc. award Jewish Cmty. Ctr., 1974, Cert. Appreciation Va. Food Dealers Assn., 1974, Fall Guy award Saints and Sinners, 1974, Brotherhood award NCCJ, 1976, First Citizen award City of Norfolk, 1974. Mem. Norfolk Yacht and Country Club (pres. 1990-92),

Va. Club (bd. dirs. 1991-93), Chi Phi, Alpha Kappa Psi. Episcopalian. Home: 1519 Commonwealth Ave Norfolk VA 23505-1719

MARTIN, SAM See MOSKOWITZ, SAM

MARTIN, SIVA, lawyer; b. Chgo., Oct. 26, 1925; s. Leon and Goldie (Baronian) M.; m. Mary Kaprelian, Aug. 12, 1952; children: Robert, Jack. BS, Loyola U., 1950; MA, Northwestern U., 1951; JD, DePaul U., 1953. Bar: Ill. 1953. Loan officer Nat. Blvd. Bank, Chgo., 1955-62; v.p. Ill. State Bank, Chgo., 1962-73; sole practice Chgo., 1973—. Dist. chmn. Boy Scouts Am., Chgo., 1957; pres. Chgo. Chpt. Armenian Gen. Benevolent Union, 1978-80. Mem. ABA, Ill. State Bar Assn., Chgo. Bar Assn., Chgo. Mortgage Attys., Northwest Real Estate Bd. Democrat. Mem. Apostolic Ch. Club: Lions. Home: 6550 N Kenton Ave Chicago IL 60646-3433 Office: 5860 W Higgins Ave Chicago IL 60630-2036

MARTIN, STANLEY A., lawyer; b. Logansport, Ind., Apr. 9, 1955; s. Richard James and Helen Elizabeth (Newburn) M.; m. Kellie Lea McCabe, Aug. 14, 1988. BS, MIT, 1977; JD, Boston Coll., 1984. Bar: Mass. 1985, U.S. Dist. Ct. Mass. 1985, U.S. Ct. Appeals (1st cir.) 1985, N.H. 1986, U.S. Dist. Ct. N.H. 1987. Prin. Stan Martin, Designer/Builder, Andover, Mass., 1977-84; assoc. Gadsby & Hannah, Boston, 1984-91, ptnr., 1992—; lectr. Northeastern Univ., Boston, 1989—. Author: Mechanic's Liens, Performance and Payment Bonds under Massachusetts Law, 1989, 7th rev. edit., 1996; co-author: Architect-Engineer Liability Under Massachusetts Law, 1985, 5th rev. edit., 1990, Wiley Construction Law Update Annual; contbr. articles to profl. jours. Bd. dirs. Andover Com./A Better Chance-ABC, 1981-84. Mem. ABA (pub. contract sect., chair region I 1990—), Am. Arbitration Assn. Constrn. Industry Panel, Mass. Bar Assn. (chair pub. law sect. 1993-94), Internat. Bar Assn., N.H. Bar Assn. Home: 13 Brown St Andover MA 01810-5302 Office: Gadsby & Hannah 125 Summer St Ste 1500 Boston MA 02110-1616

MARTIN, STEPHEN JAMES, lawyer; b. Montclair, N.J., Mar. 20, 1930; s. Willis Elwin and Katherine Elizabeth M.; m. Kathleen Ellen Lyons, May 10, 1958; children: Christopher John, Therese Marie. Ph.B., U. Notre Dame, 1951; J.D., U. Mich., 1954; LL.M., NYU, 1959. Bar: Mich. 1954, Calif. 1960; diplomate: C.P.A., Calif. Mem. pub. acctg. staff Touche, Ross, Bailey & Smart, Detroit, 1954-58; assoc. Pillsbury, Madison & Sutro, San Francisco, 1959-66, ptnr., 1965—. Contbr. articles to profl. jours. Mem. ABA (sect. taxation council 1981-83), State Bar Calif., Am. Bar Found., Am. Coll. Tax Counsel, Am. Inst. C.P.A.s, Calif. Soc. C.P.A.s. Clubs: San Francisco (sec.-treas.) (1982-83); World Trade (San Francisco), Bankers (San Francisco). Home: 60 Denise Dr Burlingame CA 94010-7150 Office: Pillsbury Madison & Sutro 225 Bush St San Francisco CA 94104-4207

MARTIN, STEVE, comedian, actor; b. Waco, Tex., 1945; s. Glenn and Mary Lee Martin; m. Victoria Tennant, Nov. 20, 1986 (div. 1994). Student, Long Beach State Coll., UCLA. Exec. prodr. TV show Domestic Life, 1984. TV writer for Smothers Bros. (co-winner Emmy award 1969), Sonny and Cher, Pat Paulsen, Ray Stevens, Dick Van Dyke, John Denver, Glen Campbell; nightclub comedian; guest and host appearances NBC's Saturday Night Live, Tonight Show; appeared on Carol Burnett Show; starred in TV spls. Steve Martin: A Wild and Crazy Guy, 1978, Comedy is Not Pretty, 1980, Steve Martin's Best Show Ever, 1981; rec. comedy albums Let's Get Small, 1977 (Grammy award 1977), A Wild and Crazy Guy, 1978 (Grammy award 1978), Comedy is Not Pretty, 1979, The Steve Martin Brothers, 1982; actor, screenwriter (films) The Absent Minded Waiter, 1977 (Academy award nomination best short film 1977), The Jerk, 1979, Pennies From Heaven, 1981, Dead Men Don't Wear Plaid, 1982, The Man With Two Brains, 1983, All of Me, 1984 (Nat. Soc. Film Critics award best actor 1984, New York Film Critics' Circle award best actor 1984), Three Amigos, 1986, Roxanne, 1987, (Nat. Soc. Film Critics award best actor 1988, Los Angeles Film Critics' award best actor 1988), L.A. Story, 1991; actor (films) Sergeant Pepper's Lonely Hearts Club Band, 1978, The Muppet Movie, 1979, The Kids Are Alright, 1979, The Lonely Guy, 1984, Little Shop of Horrors, 1986, Planes, Trains and Automobiles, 1987, Dirty Rotten Scoundrels, 1988, Parenthood, 1989, My Blue Heaven, 1990, Father of the Bride, 1991, Grand Canyon, 1991, Housesitter, 1992, Leap of Faith, 1993, Mixed Nuts, 1994, Twist of Fate, 1994; (theatre) Waiting For Godot, 1988; (television) And the Band Played On, 1993; screenwriter (films) Easy Money, 1983; author Cruel Shoes, 1977; playwright Picasso at the Lapin Agile, 1993. Recipient Georgie award Am. Guild Variety Artists 1977, 78; Grammy award 1978. Office: care ICM 8942 Wilshire Blvd Beverly Hills CA 90211 also: Rogers & Cowan c/o Michelle Bega 1888 Century Park E # 500 Los Angeles CA 90067

MARTIN, SUSAN KATHERINE, librarian; b. Cambridge, Eng., Nov. 14, 1942; came to U.S., 1950, naturalized, 1961; d. Egon and Jolan (Schonfeld) Orowan; m. David S. Martin, June 30, 1962. BA with honors, Tufts U., 1963; MS, Simmons Coll., 1965; PhD, U. Calif., Berkeley, 1983. Intern libr. Harvard U., Cambridge, Mass., 1963-65, systems libr., 1965-73; head systems office gen. libr. U. Calif., Berkeley, 1973-79; dir. Milton S. Eisenhower Libr. Johns Hopkins U., Balt., 1979-88, exec. dir. Nat. Commn. on Libraries and Info. Sci., 1988-90; univ. libr. Georgetown U., Washington, 1990—; mem. libr. adv. com. Princeton (N.J.) U., 1987—; mem. vis. com. Harvard U. Libr., 1987-93, 94—; bd. overseers for univ. libr. Tufts U., 1986—; mem. libr. adv. com. Hong Kong U. Sci. Tech., 1988—; mem. acad. libr. adv. group U. Md. Sch. Librs. and Info. Sci., 1994-96; cons. to various librs. and info. cos., 1975—; mem. adv. bd. ERIC, 1990-92, History Assocs., Inc., 1990-92. Author: Library Networks; Libraries in Partnership, 1986-87; editor; Jour. Libr. Automation, 1972-77; mem. editorial bd. Advanced Tech./Librs., 1973-93, Jour. Libr. Adminstrn., 1986—, Libr. Hi-Tech., 1989-93, Jour. Acad. Librarianship, 1994—; contbr. articles to profl. jours. Trustee Phila. Area Libr. Network, 1980-81; bd. dirs. Universal Serials and Book Exch., 1981-82, v.p., 1983, pres., 1984; trustee Capital Consortium, 1992-95; mem. bd. Potomac Internet, 1995—. Recipient Simmons Coll. Disting. Alumni award, 1977; Council on Library Resources fellow, 1973. Mem. ALA (coun. 1988-92), Rsch. Librs. Group (gov., exec. com. 1985-87), Libr. and Info. Tech. Assn. (pres. 1978-79), Assn. Rsch. Librs., Libr. of Congress (optical disk pilot project adv. com. 1985-89), Coalition for Networked Info. (leader working group 1990-92), Assn. Coll. and Rsch. Librs. (pres. 1994-95), Internat. Fedn. Libr. Assns. (com. mem. 1995—), Cosmos Club, Grolier Club, Phi Beta Kappa. Home: 4709 Blagden Ter NW Washington DC 20011-3719 Office: Georgetown U Lauinger Libr Washington DC 20057

MARTIN, SUSAN TAYLOR, newspaper editor; b. N.Y.C., Aug. 3, 1949; d. Lewis Randolph and Carolyn Emmons (Douthat) Taylor; m. James Addison Martin Jr., Nov. 15, 1975; 1 child, Steven Randolph. BA in Polit. Sci., Duke U., 1971. Reporter Ft. Myers (Fla.) News Press, 1972-75, Tampa (Fla.) Tribune, 1975-77, Associated Press, Detroit, 1977-78; bur. chief Detroit News, 1978-81; asst. city editor Orlando (Fla.) Sentinel, 1981-82; exec. bus. editor St. Petersburg (Fla.) Times, 1982-86, city editor, 1986-87, nat. corr., 1987-91, asst. mng. editor, 1991-93, dep. mng. editor, 1993—. Trustee Poynter Fund, St. Petersburg, 1992—. Recipient Non-Deadline Reporting award Soc. Profl. Journalists, 1990, Investigative Reporting award, 1991, Feature, Depth Reporting award Fla. Soc. Newspaper Editors, 1990, Depth Reporting award, 1991. Mem. Suncoast Figure Skating Club. Democrat. Episcopalian. Avocations: figure skating, travel, antiques, reading. Home: 1312 51st Ave NE Saint Petersburg FL 33703-3209 Office: St Petersburg Times 490 1st Ave S Saint Petersburg FL 33731

MARTIN, SUZANNE CAROLE, health facility administrator; b. Columbus, Ohio, Aug. 29, 1945; d. John Fredrick and Clairmae (Kelley) Belknap; m. Daniel C. Martin, Mar. 16, 1968 (div. Apr. 1974); m. Richard Wayne Shadburn, Sept. 10, 1986. Diploma in nursing, Mount Carmel Sch. Nursing, Columbus, Ohio, 1977; BA in Sociology, Ohio Dominican Coll., 1976; JD cum laude, Capital U., 1983. Bar: Ohio 1983. From staff nurse to unit dir., med. dir. medicine Mount Carmel Med. Ctr., Columbus, 1966-77; dir. nursing McNamara-Mercy Hosp., Fairplay, Colo., 1977-78; staff nurse Nurse Pro Nurses Registry, San Diego, 1978-80; from dir. ambulatory care to asst. v.p., quality assurance to v.p. quality, utilization and risk mgmt. to v.p. patient care svcs. Mount Carmel Med. Ctr., Columbus, 1981-92; sr. cons. Deloitte & Touche, 1992-93; v.p. patient care svcs. Santa Rosa Health Care, San Antonio, 1993—; bd. dirs. United Ostomy Assn. Ctrl. Ohio, Columbus; com. mem. Franklinton Health Ctr., Columbus, 1985-92; mem. ethics com. Cath. Conf., Columbus, 1989-92; lectr. various group and orgns. on nursing and legal aspects. Mem. Columbus Zoo, 1990-93, Friends of Sta. WOSU, Columbus, 1990-93. Mem. Am. Acad. Hosp. Attys., Am. Soc. Hosp. Risk Mgrs., Am. Orgn. Nurse Execs., Ohio Soc. Nurse Execs., Ohio Soc. Risk Mgrs., Wilderness Soc., Mount Carmel Alumni Assn., Capital U. Alumni Assn. Roman Catholic. Home: 20210 Bat Cave Rd Garden Ridge TX 78266-2300 Office: Santa Rosa Health Care 519 W Houston St San Antonio TX 78207-3108

MARTIN, TERESA ANN, special education educator; b. Kingsport, Tenn., May 16, 1959; d. Bryan Hagan and Patsy Ruth (Owens) Hilbert; m. Harold Tony Martin, June 10, 1989. BS in Spl. Edn., Tenn. Tech. U., 1982, MA in Spl. Edn., 1983. Spl. edn. tchr. Gunnings Sch., Blountville, Tenn., 1984-85, S.E. H.S., Dalton, Ga., 1985-89, Murray County H.S., Chatsworth, Ga., 1989-94, N.W. H.S., Tunnel Hill, Ga., 1994—. Mem. Coun. for Exceptional Children, Delta Kappa Gamma (pres. 1994—). Baptist. Avocations: reading, collecting Norman Rockwell memorabilia, needle work. Home: 100 Sims Dr Ringgold GA 30736 Office: Northwest Whitfield HS 1651 Tunnel Hill Varnell Rd Tunnel Hill GA 30755-9247

MARTIN, THEODORE KRINN, former university administrator (deceased); b. Blue Mountain, Miss., Jan. 2, 1915; s. Thomas Theodore and Ivy (Manning) M.; m. Lorene Garrison, Sept. 6, 1947; children: Glenn Krinn, Mary Ann, Janet Kay. A.B., Georgetown (Ky.) Coll., 1935; M.A., La. State U., 1941; Ph.D., George Peabody Coll., 1949. Tchr. Consol. Sch., Dumas, Miss., 1935-36; prin. Mississippi Heights Acad., 1936-39; tchr. Murphy High Sch., Mobile, Ala., 1940-41; registrar Miss. State U., 1949-53, registrar, adminstrv. asst. to pres., 1953-56, dean Sch. Edn., 1956-61, exec. asst. to pres., 1961-66, v.p., 1966-85, dir. Summer Sch., 1956-70, ret., 1985. Served as capt. AUS, 1941-46. Mem. Masons, Kappa Alpha, Phi Kappa Phi, Omicron Delta Kappa, Kappa Delta Pi, Phi Delta Kappa. Home: 1151 East Dr Starkville MS 39759-9216

MARTIN, THOMAS E., motel chain executive; b. Jackson, Mich., Apr. 13, 1942; s. Clarence A. and Olive Martin; m. Maureen D. Hunt, Feb. 7, 1975; 1 child, Anne Marie; children by previous marriage: Julie, Laurie, Kathy, Cindy. BS in Acctg., Mich. State U., 1964; MBA, Western Mich. U., 1971. Cert. mgmt. acct. Jr. acct. Ernst & Ernst, Grand Rapids, Mich., 1964; various acctg. positions Consumers Power Co., Jackson, 1965-69, mgr. acctg., 1969-73; dir. acctg. Ramada Inns, Inc., Phoenix, 1973-75, domestic controller, 1975-76, v.p., controller, 1976-79, sr. v.p., chief fin. officer, 1979-82, exec. v.p. fin. and adminstrn., from 1982, now exec. v.p. restaurants, 1979-90, also dir., until 1990; pres., dir. Elsinore Corp., Las Vegas, 1990—; pres. Four Queens Inc., Las Vegas, 1993—. Mem. minority relations com. Dean's Council of 100, Ariz. State U.; bd. dirs., mem. fin. and long range planning coms. Ariz. Zool. Soc. Mem. Nat. Assn. Accts., Am. Mgmt. Assn., Inst. Mgmt. Acctg. (bd. regents, chmn. examination policy com.), Fin. Execs. Inst., Beta Alpha Psi. Office: Four Queens Inc 202 Fremont St Las Vegas NV 89101-5606*

MARTIN, THOMAS HOWARD, pastor; b. Clovis, N.Mex., Aug. 22, 1952; s. Howard Venson and Gertrude Ernestine (Winkler); children: Tara Catherine, Aubrey Lynn, Andrew Thomas; m. Kathryn Ann Brinson, May 19, 1984. BBA, Eastern N.Mex. U., 1974; MDiv, Southwestern Bapt. Theol. Sem., 1978; D.Min., New Orleans Bapt. Theol. Sem., 1986. Lic. to Preach, 1975; ordained to Min., 1977. Pastor Hilltop Bapt. Ch., Fort Worth, 1976-77, Pioneer Drive Bapt. Ch., Irving, Tex., 1977-80, Buckner Terr. Bapt. Ch., Dallas, 1980-83; v.p. DBC Found. Dallas Bapt. Coll., 1983-84; stewardship cons. Resource Svcs., Inc., Dallas, 1984-85; minister with single adults Pioneer Drive Bapt. Ch., Abilene, Tex., 1985-87; v.p. advancement Howard Payne U., Brownwood, Tex., 1987-88; dir. client rels. Community Svc. Bur., Inc., Dallas, 1988-89; pastor Sandia Bapt. Ch., Clovis, N.Mex., 1989-93, First Bapt. Ch., Hobbs, N.Mex., 1993—. Contbr. articles to profl. jours. Named Outstanding Young Men Am., 1981, 86, 88. Mem. Bapt. Convention of N.Mex. (vice chmn exec. bd.). Baptist. Avocations: golf, reading. Home: 100 W Wolfcamp Dr Hobbs NM 88240-1911 Office: First Bapt Ch 300 E Cain St Hobbs NM 88240

MARTIN, THOMAS LYLE, JR., university president; b. Memphis, Sept. 26, 1921; s. Thomas Lyle and Malvina (Rucks) M.; m. Helene Hartley, June 12, 1943 (dec. Sept. 1983); children: Michele Marie, Thomas Lyle; m. Mildred L. Moore, June 5, 1984. B.E.E., Rensselaer Poly. Inst., 1942, M.E.E., 1948, D.Eng., 1967; Ph.D., Stanford U., 1951. Prof. elec. engring. U. N.Mex., 1948-53; prof. engring. U. Ariz., 1953-63, dean engring., 1958-63; dean engring. U. Fla., Gainesville, 1963-66, So. Meth. U., Dallas, 1966-74; pres. Ill. Inst. Tech., Chgo., 1974-87, pres. emeritus, 1987—; bd. dirs. Cherry Corp. Capt. Signal Corps AUS, 1943-46. Fellow IEEE; mem. Nat. Acad. Engring. Home and Office: PO Box 167845 Irving TX 75016-7845

MARTIN, THOMAS STEPHEN, lawyer; b. N.Y.C., Aug. 31, 1946; s. Stephen Paul and Kathleen Mary (Redmond) M.; m. Lynne Kathryn Mallory, Oct. 2, 1968; children: Laura Kathryn, Mallory Anne. B.A. maxima cum laude, King's Coll., 1968; J.D., U. Chgo., 1972. Bar: D.C. 1973. Assoc. Steptoe & Johnson, Washington, 1972-75; spl. asst. to asst. atty. gen., civil div. Dept. Justice, Washington, 1975-76, asst. to solicitor gen., 1976-78, dep. asst. atty. gen. civil div., 1978-80, acting asst. atty. gen. civil div., 1981-82; ptnr. Venable, Baetjer, Howard & Civiletti, Washington, 1982-83, Jenner & Block, Washington, 1983-90, Shearman & Sterling, Washington, 1990—; mem. adv. com. fed. rules of civil procedure, 1980-84; chmn. com. admissions and grievances U.S. Ct. Appeals (D.C. cir.), 1991—. Comment editor: U. Chgo. Law Rev, 1971-72. Mem. D.C. Bar Assn., Am. Law Inst. *

MARTIN, TODD, professional tennis player; b. Hinsdale, Ill., July 8, 1970. Student, Northwestern U. Profl. tennis player, 1990—. Moved into world's top ten in tennis 1994; 3 pro singles titles 1993, 94 (2). Office: US Tennis Assn 1212 Ave of Americas New York NY 10036

MARTIN, ULRIKE BALK, laboratory analyst; b. Kelheim, Germany, Oct. 28, 1965; d. Gunther Anton and Elfriede Babette (Eiser) Balk; m. Kent Daniel Martin, May 1, 1988. BS summa cum laude, Stephen F. Austin State U., Nacogdoches, Tex., 1992; MS, 1994. Lab. analyst Eastman Chem. Co., Longview, Tex., 1994—. Author: An Analysis of Heavy Metals on Forest Stream Ecosystems Receiving Run Off from an Oil Field, 1992. Mem. Tex. Acad. Sci., Sigma Xi. Home: 3019 B Tryon Rd Longview TX 75605

MARTIN, VERNON EMIL, librarian; b. Guthrie, Okla., Dec. 15, 1929; s. Vernon E. Sr. and Marian (Brandon) M.; m. Arlan Stone, June 30, 1956 (div. 1977); children: Vernon Martin III, Jeffrey Martin; m. Elizabeth Jean Chapin, June 16, 1979; 1 child, Amy Chapin Hathaway. MA in Music, Columbia U., 1959, MS in Libr., 1965. Libr. Lincoln Ctr. Libr. Mus., N.Y.C., 1964-66; music libr. North Tex. State U., Denton, 1966-70; libr. dir. Morningside Coll., Sioux City, Iowa, 1970-74; head art dept. Hartford (Conn.) Pub. Libr., 1974-93, ret., 1993. Composer operas including Ladies Voices, 1956, Waiting For the Barbarians, 1956, Fables By Thurber, 1986. CHmn. Cultural Affairs Commn., Hartford, 1984-86. Mem. ASCAP (Standard award 1969-72). Home: 7 Tamarack Dr Bloomfield CT 06002-1792

MARTIN, VINCENT GEORGE, management consultant; b. N.Y.C., Feb. 9, 1922; s. Joseph R. and Mae B. (Mulligan) M.; m. Alice Ann McGovern, June 8, 1946; children—Kathleen (Mrs. Michael Greiner), Joseph F. Student, Pace Coll., 1948-49, Am. Internat. Coll., 1950. Salesman Lavigna Jewels, N.Y.C., 1945-47; indsl. engr. Barton Watchcase Mfg., N.Y.C., 1948-49; office procedures Local Loan Co., N.Y.C., 1950-51; sr. time study engr. Perkins Machine & Gear Co., West Springfield, Mass., 1951-52; with Milton Bradley Co., East Longmeadow, Mass., 1952-79; mgr. mfg. Milton Bradley Co., 1962-64, v.p. mfg., 1964-69, exec. v.p., 1969—, dir., 1971—, gen. mgr., 1972-79; with Vincent G. Martin Assos. (Mgmt. Consultants), 1979—; trustee Springfield Inst. for Savs., 1978-81; dir. Armoury Corp., Stockbridge Corp., 1978-80. Past pres. Springfield Speech and Hearing Center; mem. East Longmeadow Indsl. Park Steering Com.; gen. campaign chmn. United Fund Pioneer Valley, 1976; bd. dirs. Springfield Symphony Orch.; corporate Springfield Coll., 1976-79, Wesson Meml. Hosp., 1976-80. Served with AUS, 1942-45. Decorated Bronze Star. Mem. Soc. Advancement Mgmt. (pres. Western Mass. chpt. 1954-56), Am. Mgmt. Assn., Toy Mfrs. Am. (dir. 1973-75), Springfield C. of C. (dir. 1974-78), Newcomen Soc. N.Am., East Longmeadow C. of C. (pres., dir. 1965-68). Club: Rotarian (dir. 1970-72). Home: 3555 John Anderson Dr Ormond Beach FL 32176-2176 Office: 8 Flume Ave PO Box 505 Marstons Mills MA 02648

MARTIN, VINCENT LIONEL, manufacturing company executive; b. Los Angles, June 29, 1939; s. Arthur Seymon and Alice Maria (Miller) M.; m. Janet Ann Dowler, Mar. 25, 1961; children: Jennifer Lynn, Karen Arlene, Timothy Paul. B.S., Stanford U., 1960; M.B.A., Harvard U., 1963. Various staff positions FMC Corp, Chgo, 1966-74; gen. mgr. Crane and Excavator div. FMC Corp, Cedar Rapids, Iowa, 1974-79; pres. Equipment Systems div. AMCA Internat. Corp., Houston, 1979-81; group v.p. AMCA Internat. Corp., Brookfield, Wis., 1981-85; pres. Jason Inc., Milw., 1986—. Mem. Phi Beta Kappa, Tau Beta Pi. Republican. Presbyterian. Home: 2601 W Cedar Ln Milwaukee WI 53217-2861 Office: Jason Inc 411 E Wisconsin Ave Milwaukee WI 53202-4409

MARTIN, WALTER EDWIN, biology educator; b. DeKalb, Ill., Jan. 14, 1908; s. Walter Sylvester and Tillie Lula (Secora) M.; m. Ruth Virginia Butler, June 16, 1934; children: Carol Ann, John Walter, Judith Kathryn, David Butler. B.E., No. Ill. State Tchrs. Coll., 1930; M.S., Purdue U., 1932, Ph.D., 1937. Asst. Purdue U., 1930-34, instr., 1934-37; instr. No. Ill. State Tchrs. Coll., summers 1930-31; mem. sci. expdn. Honduras, summer 1934; mem. staff Marine Biol. Lab., summers 1935-42; asst. prof. DePauw U., 1937-41, assoc. prof., 1941-46, prof., 1946-47; assoc. prof. U. So. Calif., 1947-48, prof., 1948—, head zoology dept., 1948-54, head biology dept., 1954-58; naval technician to, Egypt, summer 1953, 55, Japan, Taiwan and Philippines, 1957; sabbatical leave Marine Lab., U. Hawaii, 1956-57; sabbatical year Neuchatel, Switzerland, 1963-64, U. Queensland, Brisbane, Australia, 1970-71. Fellow Ind. Acad. Sci., AAAS, So. Calif. Acad. Sci.; mem. Am. Soc. Zoologists, Am. Soc. Parasitologists, Am. Micros. Soc., Western Soc. Naturalists, Phi Sigma, Alpha Epsilon Delta. Home: 2185 Warmouth St San Pedro CA 90732-4530 Office: U of Southern California Dept Bio Los Angeles CA 90007

MARTIN, WILFRED WESLEY FINNY, psychologist, property owner and manager; b. Rock Lake, N.D., Dec. 3, 1917; s. William Isaac and Anna Liisa (Hendrickson-Juntunen) M.; m. Stella Helland, Sept. 25, 1943; children: Sydney Wayne, William Allan. BA, Jamestown Coll., 1940; army specialized tng. program, Hamilton Coll., 1944; MS, EdD, U. So. Calif., 1956. Highsch. prin., coach pub. sch., Nekoma, N.D., 1940-42; contact rep., psychologist VA, L.A., 1946-49, psychologist, chief rehab., 1972-77; from intern to resident Fargo (N.D.) VA Hosp., 1953-58; guidance dir., instr. Concordia Coll., Moorhead, Minn., 1951-53; psychologist VA, Fargo, N.D., 1953-57; assoc. Sci. Rsch. Assoc./IBM, Boulder, Colo., 1957-65; regional dir. Sci. Rsch. Assoc./IBM, L.A., 1966-72; owner, mgr. Martin Investments, Huntington Beach, Calif., 1977—; adjutant U. Miss., Oxford, 1942; trustee Wilfred W. and Stella Martin Trust, Huntington Beach, 1991. Author: Veterans Administration Work Simplification, 1948, 57. Charter mem. Rep. Presdl. Task Force, 1980; adv. sr. ptnrs. bd. dirs. U. Calif. Med. Sch., Irvine, 1990; donor Dr. and Mrs. W.W. Martin Endowment, Jamestown Coll., N.D., 1985. With U.S. Army, 1942-45. Mem. Am. Psychol. Assn., Cardinal & Gold U. So. Calif., Jamestown Coll. Heritage Circle (charter), Suomi Coll. Second Century Soc., Elks. Republican. Lutheran. Avocations: reading, Finnish heritage, swimming, sports, card playing. Home: PO Box 5445 Huntington Beach CA 92615 *The dominant force in my life is described by the Finnish word SISU, which means perseverence, determination, competitiveness, and tenacity toward goal-oriented achievements. Due to SISU, faith, and hard work I enjoy an active successful life.*

MARTIN, WILLIAM AUBERT, law association executive, lawyer, retired air force officer; b. Warren, Ark., Dec. 7, 1931; s. Aubert and Anna Christine (Joiner) M.; m. Mary Lou Mauderly, Mar. 31, 1963; children: Kathryn G. Gutierrez, Karen E. Caster, Michael W. J.D., U. Ark., 1955; M.B.A., Ariz. State U., 1969. Bar: Ark. 1955. Commd. 2d lt. U.S. Air Force, 1955, advanced through grades to col.; chief claims and tort litigation div., U.S. Air Force Hdqrs., Washington, 1973-77; staff judge adv. Oklahoma City Air Logistics Ctr., Tinker AFB, Okla., 1977-79, Hdqrs. 5th Air Force, Yokota AFB, Tokyo, 1979-81, Hdqrs. Air Tng. Command, Randolph AFB, Tex., 1981-83; ret., 1983; exec. dir. Ark. Bar Assn., Little Rock, 1983—. Treas. Ark. Iolta Found., Inc.; trustee Nat. Conf. Bar Founds. Mem. ABA, Ark. Bar Assn., Fed. Bar Assn., Pulaski County Bar Assn., Judge Advocates Assn, Am. Soc. Assn. Execs., Ark. Alumni Assn. (treas. capital chpt.), Rotary. Methodist. Office: Ark Bar Assn 400 W Markham St Little Rock AR 72201-1408

MARTIN, WILLIAM BRYAN, college president, clergyman; b. Lexington, Ky., Apr. 11, 1938; s. William Stone and Alice Bryan (Spiers) Martin; m. Mary Ellen Matson, Aug. 11, 1973; children: Chanley Morgan, Matson Bryan, Evan Andrew. AB, Transylvania U., 1960; JD, U. Ky., 1964; LLM, Georgetown U., Washington, 1965; MDiv summa cum laude, Emory U., 1979. Bar: Ky. 1964, D.C. 1964; ordained to ministry Christian Ch. (Disciples of Christ), 1981. Legal intern Pub. Defender, Washingotn, 1964-65; asst. U.S. atty. Western Dist. Ky., 1965-67; assoc. McElwain, Denning, Clarke and Winstead, Louisville, 1967-69; asst. atty. gen. Commonwealth of Ky., 1969-70; prof. U. Louisville Sch. Law, 1970-81; dean Oklahoma City U. Sch. Law, 1982-83; pres. Franklin Coll. Ind., 1983—; bd. dirs. Coun. Ind. Colls., Washington, 1990-94; mem. Commn. on Pub. Rels. Nat. Assn. Ind. Colls. and Univs., 1992—; bd. dirs. Ind. Colls. Ind. Found., 1983—, 1st vice chmn., 1992—, chmn., 1993—, mem. spl. study com. and strategic planning com., mem. transition task force, 1991—; mem. Ind. Colls. Ind., Ind. Conf. Higher Edn., 1983—; sec. Am. Bapt. Assn. Colls. and Univs., 1989—; cons.-evaluator North Ctrl. Assn., Commn. on Instns. Higher Edn., 1985. Columnist Scripps Howard News Svc., 1991—; contbr. articles to profl. jours. Mem. adv. bd. Heartland Film Festival, 1995—; bd. regents Ind. Acad., 1988—, chair nominating com.; bd. trustees Christian Theol. Sem., 1986—, past mem. investment com., chair ednl. policies com.; bd. dirs., exec. com. Historic Landmarks Found. Ind., 1987-91, adv. coun., 1991—; first chmn. coun. pres. Ind. Collegiate Athletic Conf., 1987-90; elder Tabernacle Christian Ch., Franklin, 1983-91, North Christian Ch., Columbus, 1994—; mem. Progress Forum Johnson County, 1987-92; mem. adv. bd. Greater Johnson County Cmty. Found., inc., 1992—; mem. Historic Preservation Task Force, Divsn. Historic Preservation and Archaeology, Ind. Dept. Natural Resources; mem. Nat. Environ. Task Force.ship com., tchr. family life class Douglass Blvd. Christian Ch.; deacon Crown Heights Christian Ch., Okla. Recipient Svc. award Franklin Heritage, 1986, Man of Yr. award Franklin C. of C., 1986, Disting. Svc. cert. Transylvania U., 1987. Mem. Ben Franklin Soc., Ind. Soc. Chgo., Econ. Club Indpls., Junto Club Indpls., Columbia Club Indpls., Rotary of Franklin, Hillview Country Club, Alpha Soc. Home: Pres Residence & Reception 253 S Forsythe Franklin IN 46131 Office: Franklin Coll Ind 501 E Monroe St Franklin IN 46131

MARTIN, WILLIAM C., sociology educator, writer; b. San Antonio, Dec. 31, 1937; s. Lowell Curtis and Joe Bailey (Brite) M.; m. Patricia Dale Summerlin, Dec. 31, 1957; children: Rex Martin, Jeff Martin, Elisabeth Dale Martin Thomas. BA, Abilene Christian U., 1958, MA, 1960; BD, Harvard Divinity Sch., 1963; PhD, Harvard U., 1969. Instr. history Dana Hall Sch., Wellesley, Mass., 1965-68; instr. sociology Rice U., Houston, 1968-69, asst. prof. sociology, 1969-73, assoc. prof. sociology, 1973-79, prof. sociology, 1979—, master Sid W. Richardson Coll., 1976-81, chair dept. sociology, 1983-86, 89-94; cons. films and TV documentaries; speaker in field. Author: These Were God's People, 1966, Christians in Conflict, 1972, A Prophet With Honor: Billy Graham Story, 1991 (Christianity Today's Critic's Choice award 1992), My Prostate and Me: Dealing With Prostate Cancer, 1994; contbg. editor Tex. Monthly (Nat. Headliner award 1982); contbr. numerous articles to profl. jours. and pop mags.; numerous radio and TV appearances. Dir. House of the Carpenter, Inc., inner-city youth program, Boston, 1963-66, pres. and bd. dirs. non-profit housing corp.; bd. dirs. Fellowship Racial and Econ. Equality, 1970-71; mem. exec. com. Houston Coun. Human Rels. Recipient Nicholas Salgo Outstanding Tchr. award Rice U., 1971, 93, Brown Coll. award for Teaching in the Humanities Rice U., 1974, 76, George R. Brown Award for Superior Teaching, alumni Rice U., 1974, 76, 77, 84, for Excellence in Teaching, 1975, 82, Life Honor award, 1985; grantee Am. Coun. Learned Socs. and Am. Philos. Soc., 1974. Mem. Am. Sociol. Assn., Soc. Scientific Study Religion, Religious Rsch. Assn., Tex. Inst. Letters (J.

Frank Dobie/Paisano fellowship 1980). Democrat. Protestant. Avocations: bicycling, squash. Home: 2148 Addison Rd Houston TX 77030-1222 Office: Rice U Dept Sociology 6100 Main St Houston TX 77005-1827

MARTIN, WILLIAM COLLIER, hospital administrator; b. Atlanta, Aug. 16, 1926; s. William Henry and Lillian (Collier) M.; BS, U. Ga., 1950; diploma Charlotte Meml. Hosp., 1952; postgrad. U. Okla., 1969; m. Alice Elizabeth Nickle, Jan. 12, 1952; children: Mary Anne, Patricia Jean, William Collier, Nancy Lee. Operating room technician Athens (Ga.) Gen. Hosp., 1949-50; hosp. adminstrn. intern/resident Charlotte (N.C.) Meml. Hosp., 1950-52; hosp. adminstr. Rockmart-Aragon Hosp., Rockmart, Ga., 1952-54; asst. hosp. adminstr. St. Agnes Hosp., Raleigh, N.C., 1954-56; hosp. adminstr. Florence-Darlington Tb. Sanitorium, Florence, S.C., 1956-58; commd. 1st lt. MSC, U.S. Army, 1959, advanced through grades to lt. col.; adj. U.S. Army Hosp., Ft. Campbell Ky., 1959; comdg. officer med. co. U.S. Army Hosp., 1959-61; comdg. officer U.S. Army Med. Service Detachment, Ft. Gulick, C.Z., 1961-64; exec. officer 5th Evacuation Hosp., Ft. Bragg, N.C., 1964, comdg. officer, 1964-65; adj. personnel officer 55th Med. Group, Ft. Bragg, 1965-66, Qui Nhon, Republic Vietnam, 1966-67; comdg. officer 47th Gen. Hosp., Fitzsimons Gen. Hosp., Denver, 1967-68; exec. officer Evans Health Care Facility, Ft. Buckner, Okinawa, 1968-69; dir. security plans and ops. U.S. Army Med. Center, Camp Kue, Okinawa, 1969-71; med. ops. officer VII Corps, Moehringen, W.Ger., 1971-73; chief tng., exercises and readiness U.S. Army Med. Command, Europe, Heidelberg, W.Ger., 1973-74; dir. security plans and tng. Fitzsimons Army Med. Center, 1974-77, ret., 1977; guest lectr. health care adminstrn. U.S. Army Med. Command in Europe, 1973-74; exec. dir. Thomas Rehab. Hosp., Asheville, N.C., 1977-78; chmn. Pub. Health Trust of Escambia County, Pensacola, Fla., 1979-86; guest lectr. to profl. assns., civic orgns. and mil. units, 1965—; mem. N.C. Gov.'s Adv. Com. on Rehab. Centers, 1977-78; mem. regional Hospice Program for NW Fla., Inc., 1979-80, chmn., bd. dirs., 1980-83, exec. dir., 1983-85; mgmt. cons. Pensacola (Fla.) Habatat for Humanity, Inc., 1986-88, Niceville (Fla.) Mktg. Resources, 1986-87, Dan Laumpking Mgmt. Cons., Fairhope, Ala., 1986-87. Mem. Pres.'s Com. on Employment of the Handicapped, 1978; sec. United Meth. Bd. Pastoral Care and Counseling, 1988-90; mem., v.p., bd. ministries Pensecola Dist. United Meth. Ch., Inc., 1988—; dir. lay speaking, bd. laity, council on ministries Ala.- West Fla. Conf. United Meth. Ch., 1988—; mem. Health and Human Services task force of citizens goals for Pensacola, 1981-86; vice chmn. adminstrv. bd. Pine Forest United Meth. Ch., Pensacola, 1979-86; mem. fin. com., 1979-86; dir. for lay speaking Pensacola Dist. United Meth. Ch., 1985-88; bd. dirs. Hispanic Minorities, Inc., 1986-93, Meth. Homes for the Aging, Inc., 1988—, Pastoral Counseling, Care and Tng., Inc., 1990-95. Served with USN, 1944-46. Decorated Legion of Merit, Bronze Star; Vietnam Royal Cross of Gallantry with bronze palm; cert. lay speaker of United Meth. Ch. Fellow Am. Acad. Med. Adminstrs.; mem. Am. Soc. Tng. and Devel. (dir. 1977-78), Ret. Officers Assn., Assn. of U.S. Army (dir. Denver-Centennial chpt. 1974-77, Greater Gulf Coast chpt. 1979-86), U.S. Power Squadrons, V.F.W., Phi Delta Theta. Democrat. Club: Masons.

MARTIN, WILLIAM EDWIN, government official; b. Bowling Green, Ky., Oct. 16, 1943; s. John Edwin and Bess Carolyn (Matherly) M.; children: Anne Whitson, William Whitson; m. Jean Clinton Nelson, Aug. 1, 1981. BA, Vanderbilt U., 1965, JD, 1968. Bar: Tenn. 1968. Ptnr. Waller Lansden Dortch & Davis, Nashville, 1968-75; sr. ptnr. Harwell Martin & Stegall, Nashville, 1975-93; dep. asst. sec. for internat. affairs U.S. Dept. Commerce-NOAA, Washington, 1993—. Contbr. articles to newspapers and law revs. Dir. polar programs Wilderness Soc., Washington, 1990-92; pres. Environ. Action Fund, Nashville, 1982; bd. dirs. Tenn. Environ. Coun., Nashville, 1992, So. Appalachian Highland Conservancy, Johnson City, Tenn., 1988-90. Mem. Nashville Bar Assn. (bd. dirs. 1979-80). Democrat. Episcopalian. Avocations: mountain climbing, photography, running, tennis. Office: Nat Oceanic and Atmospheric Admn 14th & Constitution Ave NW Washington DC 20230*

MARTIN, WILLIAM GIESE, lawyer; b. Canton, Ohio, Nov. 4, 1934; s. George Denman and Emily (Giese) M.; m. Martha Justice, June 14, 1958; children: William E.J., Peter J.D., George F.D. BA, Yale U., 1956; LLB, Harvard U., 1959. Bar: Ohio 1959, U.S. Dist. Ct. (so. dist.) Ohio 1963. Assoc. Porter, Stanley, Treffinger & Platt, Columbus, Ohio, 1963-68; ptnr. Porter, Wright, Morris & Arthur, Columbus, 1968—. Lt. USNR, 1959-63. Mem. ABA, Ohio State Bar Assn., Columbus Bar Assn., Capital Club, Rocky Fork Hunt and Country Club, Yale Club of N.Y. Home: 6169 Havens Corners Rd Blacklick OH 43004-9676 Office: Porter Wright Morris & Arthur 41 S High St Columbus OH 43215-6101

MARTIN, WILLIAM ROYALL, JR., association executive; b. Raleigh, N.C., Sept. 3, 1926; s. William Royall and Edith Ruth (Crocker) M.; m. Betty Anne Rader, June 14, 1952; children: Sallie Rader martin Busby, Amy Kemp Martin Lewis. AB, U. N.C., 1948, MBA, 1964; BS, N.C. State U., 1952. Chemist Stamford (Conn.) rsch. labs. Am. Cyanamid Co., 1952-54; chemist Dan River Mills, Danville, Va., 1954-56, Union Carbide Corp., South Charleston, W.Va., 1956-59; rsch. assoc. Sch. Textiles N.C. State U., 1959-63; tech. dir. Am. Assn. Textile Chemists and Colorists, Research Triangle Park, N.C., 1963-73, exec. dir., 1974-96; adj. asst. prof. Coll. Textiles, N.C. State U., 1966-88, adj. assoc. prof., 1989—; del. Internat. Orgn. Standardization, Pan Am. Standards Commn. With USNR, 1944-46. Fellow Am. Inst. Chemists, Soc. Dyers and Colourists, Textile Inst.; mem. Am. Chem. Soc., Coun. Engring. and Sci. Soc. Execs. (past pres. 1992-93), Fiber Soc., Am. Assn. Textile Chemists and Colorists, Masons, Rotary, Phi Kappa Phi, Phi Gamma Delta. Methodist. Home and Office: 224 Briarcliff Ln Cary NC 27511-3901

MARTIN, WILLIAM RUSSELL, nuclear engineering educator; b. Flint, Mich., June 2, 1945; s. Carl Marcus and Audrey Winifred (Rosene) M.; m. Patricia Ann Williams, Aug. 13, 1967; children: Amy Leigh, Jonathn William. B.S.E. in Engring. Physics, U. Mich., 1967; MS in Physics, U. Wis., 1968; M.S.E. in Nuclear Engring., U. Mich., 1975, PhD in Nuclear Engring., 1976. Prin. physicist Combustion Engring., Inc., Windsor, Conn., 1976-77; asst. prof. nuclear engring. U. Mich., Ann Arbor, 1977-81, assoc. prof. nuclear engring., 1981-88, prof. nuclear engring., 1988—, dir. lab. for sci. computation, 1986—, chmn. nuclear engring., 1990-94, assoc. dean for acad. affairs Coll. Engring., 1994—; cons. Lawrence Livermore Nat. Lab., Livermore, Calif., 1982—, Los Alamos (N.Mex.) Nat. Lab., 1980-89, IBM, Inc., Kingston, N.Y., 1984, Rockwell Internat., Pitts., 1985. Author: Transport Theory, 1979; author tech. and conf. papers. Recipient Glenn Murphy award Am. Soc. for Engring. Edn., 1993; Disting. scholar U. Mich. Coll. Engring., 1967; vis. fellow Royal Soc., London, 1989. Mem. Am. Nuclear Soc., Am. Phys. Soc., Soc. for Indsl. and Applied Math., IEEE. Avocations: running, reading, skiing, sailing. Home: 1701 Crestland St Ann Arbor MI 48104-6329 Office: U Mich Dept Nuclear Engring Ann Arbor MI 48109

MARTIN, WILLIAM TRUETT, oral surgeon, state legislature; b. Throckmorton, Tex., Oct. 23, 1924; s. Olin O. and Marie (Gautier) M.; m. C. Maxine Almond, Aug. 31, 1946; children: Dawne, Sally, William C. BS, North Tex. State U., 1947; DDS, U. Mo., Kansas City, 1952; MS in Oral Surgery, U. Iowa, 1959. Diplomate Am. Bd. Oral and Maxillofacial Surgery. Pvt. practice, Warrensburg, Mo., 1952-56; resident in oral surgery U. Iowa, Iowa City, 1956-59; pvt. practice oral surgery, Colorado Springs, Colo., 1959-88; mem. Colo. Ho. of Reps., Denver, 1988—. 1st lt., pilot USAAF, 1942-45. Fellow Am. Assn. Oral and Maxillofacial Surgeons, Am. Coll. Dentists, Internat. Coll. Dentists; mem. ADA, Colo. Dental Assn. (pres. 1984). Republican. Avocations: golf, tennis, flying, fishing. Office: Colo Ho of Reps State Capital Denver CO 80203

MARTIN, WILLIE PAULINE, elementary school educator, illustrator; b. Pendleton, Tex., May 27, 1920; d. Lester B. and Stella (Smith) M.; m. Charles M., June 23, 1946; 1 child, Charles Jr. BS, Middle Tenn. State U., Murfreesboro, 1944; MS, U. Tenn., 1965; postgrad., U. Ga., 1980. Cert. tchr., Tenn., Tex., Ga. Elem. tchr. Bd. Edn., Sparta, Tenn., 1940-44; home econs. tchr. Bd. Edn., Salado, Tex., 1944-46; rsch. technician Oak Ridge (Tenn.) Nat. Lab., 1946-50; art, gen. sci. tchr. Bd. Edn., State of Tenn., 1965-69; art, reading, elem. tchr. Bd. Edn., State of Ga., 1970-83; elem. tchr. Bd. Edn., Augusta, Ga., 1984-86; tchr. aerospace edn. workshop Middle Tenn. State U., 1969; spkr. in field. Contbr. articles in field to profl. jours. Exhibitor Oak Ridge (Tenn.) Festival. Mem. Nat. Art Edn. Assn. (del. conv. Washington 1989, Balt. 1994), Ga. Art Edn. Assn. (del. state conv., dist. pres. 1974, del. conv. Savannah 1986, Augusta 1993, del. state conv. Athens 1994), Tenn. Edn. Assn. Methodist. Avocations: art, crafts, music, singing, reading. Home: 1406 Flowing Wells Rd Augusta GA 30909-9767

MARTIN-BOWEN, (CAROLE) LINDSEY, freelance writer; b. Kansas City, Kans., Aug. 4, 1949; d. Lawrence Richard and V. Marie (Schaffer) Pickett; m. Frederick E. Nicholson, July 3, 1971 (div. 1977); 1 child, Aaron Frederick; m. Edwin L. Martin, June 18, 1980 (div. 1987); 1 child, Ki Elise; m. Michael L. Bowen, Dec. 23, 1988. BA in English Lit., U. Mo., Kansas City, 1972, MA in English and Creative Writing, 1988, postgrad., 1991-94; postgrad., U. Mo. Kansas City Sch. Law, Kansas City, 1995—. Tech. editor Office Hearings and Appeals, U.S. Dept. Interior, Washington, 1976-77; reporter, photographer Louisville Times, 1982-83; reporter, features editor Sun Newspapers, Overland Park, Kans., 1983-84; assoc. editor Modern Jeweler, Overland Park and N.Y.C., 1984-85; writer Coll. Blvd. News, Overland Park, 1985-89, KC View, Kansas City, Mo., 1988-89; editor Number One, Kansas City, Mo., 1986-88, cons., 1988-89; copywriter Sta KXEO/KWWR Radio, Mexico, Mo., 1989; editorial asst. New Letters, 1985—; features writer, columnist The Squire, Prairie Village, Kans., 1990-95; instr. English U. Mo., Kansas City, 1986-88, Johnson County C.C., 1988-95; tchr. English and fiction Longview C.C., 1988-95; instr. writing and mass comm. Webster U., 1990—; instr. world lit., Am. lit., women in lit., creative writing Penn Valley C.C., 1993—, faculty sponsor The Penn; owner, writer Paladin Freelance Writing Svc., Kansas City, 1988—; prodn. editor Nat. Paralegal Reporter, 1992-95, editor 1994—; staff writer, editor Nat. Fedn. Paralegal Assns., Inc. books and pubs.; writing contest judge New Letters, 1987—. Author: (novel) The Dark Horse Waits in Boulder, 1985, (poetry) Waiting for the Wake-Up Call, 1990, Second Touch, 1990, (fiction) Cicada Grove and Other Stories, 1992; contbr. poems, book revs., features, cartoon artwork, and photographs to numerous publs. including New Letters, Lip Service and Contemporary Lit. Criticism. Campaigner McGovern for Pres. Campaign, Kansas City, 1971-72. Regents scholar, 1967; GAF fellow, 1986. Mem. U. Mo.-Kansas City Alumni Assn. (media com. 1983-84), Phi Kappa Phi. Roman Catholic. Avocations: acrylic and oil painting, downhill skiing, music, Greek cooking, paralegal work. Home: 7109 Pennsylvania Ave Kansas City MO 64114-1316 Office: Nat Paralegal Reporter Hdqs. 32 W Bridlespur Ter. Kansas City MO 64114

MARTINDALE, LARRY, hotel executive. BS in Bus. Adminstrn., U. Miss. Divsn. mgr. Waffle House Restaurants, Inc.; with W.B. Johnson Properties, 1976-78; pres. Northlake Foods subs W.B. Johnson Properties, 1978-84, J.P. Hotels subs W.B. Johnson Properties, 1984-86; exec. v.p., Coo Ritz Carlton Hotel Co. subs. W.B. Johnson Properties, 1986-88, vice chmn., 1988—, asst. v.p. With USMC. Office: The Ritz-Carlton Hotel Co 3414 Peachtree Rd NE Atlanta GA 30326-1113*

MARTINEN, JOHN A., travel company executive; b. Sault St. Marie, Mich., June 26, 1938; s. John Albert and Ina Helia (Jarvi) M.; BS with highest honors, Mich. State U., 1960; LLB, NYU, 1963. With Grace Line, N.Y.C., 1963-69; cons. Empresa Turistica Internat., Galapagos Cruises, Quito, Ecuador, 1969-70; regional mgr. Globus & Cosmos (Group Voyagers Inc.), N.Y.C., 1971-73, v.p., 1974-76, exec. v.p., 1977-78, pres., CEO, 1979-92, Littleton, Colo., 1993—. Mem. U.S. Tour Operators Assn. (bd. dirs.), Am. Soc. Travel Agts., Tour Operator Plan Com. (bd. dirs.), Denver Acad. Travel & Tourism, Lotos, Sky and Wings Club (N.Y.), Columbine Country Club, Denver Athletic Club. Democrat. Home: 1450 Wynkoop St Denver CO 80202-1116 Office: 5301 S Federal Cir Littleton CO 80123-2980

MARTINES, LAURO, historian, writer; b. Chgo., Nov. 22, 1927; m. Julia O'Faolain, Nov. 20, 1957; 1 child, Lucien. A.B., Drake U., 1950; Ph.D., Harvard, 1960. Asst. prof. history Reed Coll., 1958-62; fellow Villa I Tatti, Harvard Center for Italian Renaissance Studies, Florence, Italy, 1962-65; prof. history UCLA, 1966-92; vis. prof. Warburg Inst., U. London, 1985; vis. dir. studies Ecole des Hautes Etudes en Sces Sociales, Paris, spring 1992, 94. Author: The Social World of the Florentine Humanists, 1963, Lawyers and Statecraft in Renaissance Florence, 1968, Power and Imagination: City-States in Renaissance Italy, 1979, Society and History in English Renaissance Verse, 1985, An Italian Renaissance Sextet: Six Tales in Historical Context, 1994; co-author: Not in God's Image: Women in Western Civilization, 1973; Editor: Violence and Civil Disorder in Italian Cities 1200-1500, 1972, Riti e rituali melle societa medievali, 1994. Served with AUS, 1945-47. Fellowships include Am. Council Learned Socs., 1962-63, Harvard U. Ctr. Italian Renaissance Studies, Villa i Tatti, Florence, Italy, 1962-65, Guggenheim Meml. Found., 1964-65;, sr. fellow Nat. Endowment for Humanities, 1971, 78-79; resident fellow Rockefeller Found. Bellagio Ctr., Italy, 1990. Fellow Mediaeval Acad. Am., Italian Deputation for History Tuscany (fgn.); mem. Am. Hist. Assn., Renaissance Soc. Am. Home: 8 Gloucester Crescent, London NW1 7DS, England

MARTINETTI, RONALD ANTHONY, lawyer; b. N.Y.C., Aug. 13, 1945; s. Alfred Joseph and Frances Ann (Battipaglia) M. Student, U. Chgo., 1981-82; JD, U. So. Calif., 1982. Bar: Calif. 1982; U.S. Dist. Ct. (cen. and no. dists.) Calif. 1982, U.S. Dist. Ct. Ariz., 1992; U.S. Ct. Appeals (9th cir.) 1982. Ptnr. Kazanjian & Martinetti, Glendale, Calif., 1986—. Author: James Dean Story, 1995. Vol. trial lawyer Bet Tzedek Legal Svcs., 1987—; judge pro tem L.A. Superior Ct., 1994—. Mem. Calif. Bar Assn. Roman Catholic. Office: Kazanjian & Martinetti 520 E Wilson Ave Glendale CA 91206-4374

MARTINEZ, AL, journalist, screenwriter; b. Oakland, Calif., July 21, 1929; s. Alfredo Martinez and Mary (Larragoite) Lehmann; m. Joanne Cinelli, July 30, 1949; children: Cinthia, Linda, Allen. Student, San Francisco State U., 1949-50, U. Calif., Berkeley, 1952-53, Contra Costa Jr. Coll., Walnut Creek, Calif., 1953-54. Reporter, feature writer Richmond (Calif.) Ind ., 1952-55; reporter, feature writer Oakland Tribune, 1955-71, columnist, 1963-71; profilist, feature writer L.A. Times, 1972-84, columnist, 1984—; screenwriter CBS, ABC, NBC, L.A., 1975—; tech. advisor Lou Grant TV Series, CBS, Los Angeles, 1979-80. Author: Rising Voices, 1974, Jigsaw John, 1976, Ashes in the Rain, 1989, Dancing Under the Moon, 1992, Rising Voices: A New Generation, 1993, City of Angles, 1995; screenwriter TV movie That Secret Sunday, 1988, Out on the Edge, 1990 (nominated for Emmy Best Screenplay 1990), other TV movies, pilots, 1975—. Recipient Nat. Headliner award Atlantic City Press Club, 1987, 88, Best Columnist award Nat. Soc. News Columnist, St. Louis, 1986, Pulitzer prize (shared Gold medal to L.A. Times) Columbia U., 1984, Nat. Ernie Pyle award, 1991. Mem. PEN, Writers Guild Am. Office: Los Angeles Times Editorial Dept Times Mirror Sq Los Angeles CA 90053

MARTINEZ, ANDREW TREDWAY, lawyer; b. New Orleans, Oct. 24, 1930; s. Andrew Richmond and Mary Leslie (Tredway) M.; m. Margaret Leslie Buchan, June 7, 1952; children: Andrew, Leslie, Margaret. BA, Tulane U., 1952, LLB, 1956. Bar: La. 1956, U.S. Dist. Ct. (ea. dist.) La. 1956, U.S. Ct. Appeals (5th cir.) 1962, U.S. Supreme Ct. 1971. Ptnr. Terriberry, Carroll and Yancey, New Orleans, 1956—. Assoc. editor Am. Maritime Cases, 1989—; adv. editor Tulane Maritime Jour., 1976—. Lt. (j.g.) USN, 1952-54. Mem. ABA, Maritime Law Assn. U.S., Assn. Average Adjusters U.S., La. Bar Assn., New Orleans Bar Assn. Home: 1500 Jefferson Ave New Orleans LA 70115-4121 Office: Terriberry Carroll Yancey 3100 Energy Ctr New Orleans LA 70163

MARTINEZ, ARTHUR C., retail company executive; b. N.Y.C., Sept. 25, 1939; s. Arthur F. and Agnes (Caulfield) M.; m. Elizabeth Rusch, July 30, 1966; children: Lauren, Gregory. BSME, Polytech. U., 1960; MBA, Harvard U., 1965. Dir. planning Internat. Paper Co., N.Y.C., 1967-69; asst. to pres. Talley Industries, Mesa, Ariz., 1969-70; dir. fin. RCA Corp., N.Y.C., 1970-73, v.p., 1973-80; sr. v.p., CFO Saks Fifth Ave., N.Y.C., 1980-84, exec. v.p., 1984-87, vice chmn., 1990-92; sr. v.p. and group chief exec. Batus Inc., Louisville, 1987-90; chmn., CEO Sears Merchandise Group, Chgo., 1992-95; chmn., ceo Sears, Roebuck and Co., 1995—; bd. dirs. Sears, Roebuck and Co., Sprout Venture Capital Group, N.Y.C., Ameritech, Defenders of Wildlife and Sprout Venture Capital Group; trustee Polytechnic U., Northwestern U., chmn. Nat. Minority Supplier Devel. Coun., Inc. Bd. dirs. Defenders of Wildlife, 1992—; chmn. bd. trustees Polytech. U., 1990—, chmn. devel. com. 1st lt. U.S. Army, 1961-63. Mem. Nat. Retail Fedn. (bd. dirs.). Avocations: tennis, golf, gardening. Office: Sears Roebuck and Co 3333 Beverly Rd Hoffman Estates IL 60179-0002

MARTINEZ, ARTURO, newspaper editor. Entertainment editor The Star-Ledger, Newark. Office: The Star-Ledger One Star Ledger Plz Newark NJ 07102-1200

MARTINEZ, EDGAR, professional baseball player; b. N.Y.C., Jan. 2, 1963. Student, American Coll., Puerto Rico. Baseball player Seattle Mariners, 1982—. Named. to Am. League All-Star Team, 1992, Am. League Silver Slugger Team, 1992. Am. League Batting Champion, 1992. Office: Seattle Mariners PO Box 4100 411 1st Ave S Seattle WA 98104

MARTINEZ, GUILLERMO BILL, administrator; b. Fort Worth, Oct. 22, 1944; s. Marion and Clara (Macias) M.; m. Olivia Villegas, Feb. 4, 1966; children: Elisa Ann, Leticia Marie. B of Music Edn., U. Tex., Arlington, 1972; M in Guidance Counseling, Tex. Christian U., 1975; postgrad., U. North Tex., 1980. Cert. adminstr., cert. supr., Novell adminstr. Tutoring supr. Tarrant County Jr. Coll., Fort Worth, 1972-75; prodn. supr. Bilingual Materials Devel. Ctr., Fort Worth, 1975-80; sr. programmer analyst Dallas Ind. Sch. Dist., 1980-82, assessment/evaluation specialist, 1982-84, tech. specialist, 1984-87, interim dir. instrnl. tech., 1987-89, dir. instrnl. tech., 1989-93; data processing supr. Bus. Magnet Ctr. Dallas Ind. Sch. Dist., 1993—; adv. mem. Tex. Assessment of Acad. Skills, Austin, 1992-93, Technology Task Force, Dallas Sch. Dist., 1989-93; com. chair Electronic Sch. of the Future, Dallas Ind. Sch. Dist., 1989-93; adv. mem. Richland Jr. Coll., 1987, State Bd. of Edn. Tech. Stds., 1991. Evaluator (bilingual textbook) Estampas Historicas de los Estados Unidos, 1975-80. Pres. St. Andrew's Mex. Am. Coun., Fort Worth; v.p. St. Andrew's Sch. Bd., Fort Worth; bd. dirs., officer U. of Tex. Band Alumni, Arlington. With U.S. Army, 1966-69. Mem. Tex. Computer Edn. Assn. (pres. 1991, v.p. 1990, Plaque 1991, 92), Inst. for the Trans. Tech., Tex. Ctr. for Ednl. Tech. (bd. dirs., Plaque 1992), Nat. Assn. of Bilingual Edn. Roman Catholic. Avocations: photography, outside sports, fishing, camping, snorkeling. Office: Dallas Sch Dist 3700 Ross Ave Dallas TX 75201-2602

MARTINEZ, GUSTAVE *See* **SOLOMONS, GUS, JR.**

MARTINEZ, HERMINIA S., economist, banker; b. Havana, Cuba; came to U.S., 1960, naturalized, 1972; d. Carlos and Amelia (Santana) Martinez Sanchez; m. Mario Aguilar, 1982; children: Mario Aguilar, Carlos Aguilar; BA in Econs. cum laude, Am. U., 1965; MS in Fgn. Svc. (Univ. fellow), MS in Econs., Georgetown U., 1967, PhD in Econs., 1969; postgrad. Nat. U. Mex. Instr. econs. George Mason Coll., U. Va., Fairfax, 1967-68; researcher World Bank, 1967-69, indsl. economist, industrialization div., 1969-71, loan officer, Central Am., 1971-79, loan officer, economist, Mex., 1973-74, Venezuela and Ecuador, 1973-77, sr. loan officer in charge of Panama and Dominican Republic, Washington, 1977-81, sr. loan officer for Middle East and North Africa, 1981-84, sr. loan officer for Western Africa region, 1985-87, sr. economist Africa Region, 1988-91, prin. ops. officer Africa region, 1991—. Mid-Career fellow Princeton U., 1988-89. Mem. Am. Econ. Assn., Soc. Internat. Devel., Brookings Inst. Latin Am. Study Group. Roman Catholic. Contbg. author: The Economic Growth of Colombia: Problems and Prospects, 1973, Central American Financial Integration, 1975. Home: 5145 Yuma St NW Washington DC 20016-4336 Office: World Bank 1818 H St NW Washington DC 20433

MARTINEZ, JULIO J., chemical company executive; b. 1932; came to U.S., 1961; With Chemtex Inc., Old Greenwich, Conn., 1961-89; with Chemtex Internat., N.Y.C., 1989—, pres., CEO. Office: Chemtex Internat Inc 560 Lexington Ave New York NY 10022-6828

MARTÍNEZ, LUÍS OSVALDO, radiologist, educator; b. Havana, Cuba, Nov. 27, 1927; came to U.S., 1962, naturalized, 1967; s. Osvaldo and Felicita (Farinas) M.; children: María Elena, Luís Osvaldo, Alberto Luis; m. Nydia M. Ceballos. MD, U. Havana, 1954. Intern Calixto García Hosp., Havana, 1954-55; resident in radiology Jackson Meml. Hosp., Miami, Fla., 1963-65, fellow in cardiovascular radiology, 1965-67; instr. radiology U. Miami, 1965-68, asst. prof., 1968, clin. asst. prof., 1968-70, assoc. prof., 1970-76, prof., 1976-91, clin. prof., 1991-94; chief radiol. svcs. VA Med. Ctr., 1991—; assoc. dir. dept. radiology Mt. Sinai Med. Ctr., Miami Beach, Fla., 1969-91, chief div. diagnostic radiology, 1970-91, dir. residency program in diagnostic radiology; dir. Spanish Radiology Seminar. Reviewer Am. Jour. Radiology, Radium Therapy and Nuclear Medicine, 1978; contbr. articles to profl. jours. Former pres. League Against Cancer. Recipient Medaille Antoine Beclere ICR-89, 1989, Carlos J. Finlay Gold medal Cuban Med. Congress in Exile, 1990. Mem. AMA, AAUP, Radiol. Soc. France (hon. 1991), Internat. Soc. Lymphology, Interam. Coll. Radiology (pres.), Internat. Coll. Surgeons, Internat. Coll. Angiology, Internat. Soc. Radiology, Interam. Coll. Radiology (Gold medal 1975), Cuban Med. Assn. in Exile, Am. Coll. Chest Physicians (assoc.), Radiol. Soc. N.Am., Am. Coll. Radiology, Am. Roentgen Ray Soc., Am. Assn. Fgn. Med. Grads., Am. Profl. Practice Assn., Am. Thoracic Soc., Pan Am. Med. Assn., Am. Assn. Univ. Radiologists, Brit. Inst. Radiology, Am. Heart Assn. (mem. council cardiovascular radiology), Faculty Radiologists, Soc. Gastrointestinal Radiologists, Am. Geriatrics Soc., Am. Coll. Angiology, Royal Coll. Radiologists, Am. Soc. Therapeutic Radiologists, Assn. Hosp. Med. Edn., Am. Coll. Med. Imaging, Interasma, So. Med. Assn., N.Y. Acad. Scis., Fla. Thoracic Soc., Fla. Radiol. Soc., Dade County Med. Assn., Greater Miami Radiol. Soc., Cuban Radiol. Soc. (sec.), Can. Assn. Radiologists, Soc. Thoracic Radiologists (founding mem.), Emeritus mem., Am. Coll. of Angiology, 1989, Emeritus mem., Am. Heart Assn., 1992; hon. mem. numerous med. socs. of Mex., Cen. and S.Am. Roman Catholic. Office: 1201 NW 16th St Miami FL 33125-1624

MARTINEZ, MARIA DOLORES, pediatrician; b. Cifuentes, Cuba, Mar. 16, 1959; d. Demetrio and Alba Silvia (Perez) M.; m. James David Marple, Apr. 25, 1992. MD, U. Navarra, Pamplona, Spain, 1984. Med. diplomate. Resident in pediatrics Moses Cone Hosp., Greensboro, N.C., 1986-89; pvt. practice Charlotte, N.C., 1989-93, Mooresville, N.C., 1993—. Mem. AMA, Am. Acad. Pediatrics, N.C. Med. Soc., Mecklenburg County Med. Soc. Republican. Roman Catholic. Avocations: horseback riding, travel. Office: Salisbury Rowan Med Ctr 401 Mocksville Ave Salisbury NC 28144

MARTINEZ, MATTHEW GILBERT, congressman; b. Walsenburg, Colo., Feb. 14, 1929; children: Matthew, Diane, Susan, Michael, Carol Ann. Cert of competence, Los Angeles Trade Tech. Sch., 1959. Small businessman and bldg. contractor; mem. 97th-103rd Congresses from 30th (now 31st) Calif. dist., 1982—; mem. edn. and labor com., fgn. affairs com. Mem. Monterey Park Planning Commn., 1971-74; mayor City of Monterey Park, 1974-75; mem. Monterey Park City Council, 1974-80, Calif. State Assembly, 1980-82; bd. dirs. San Gabriel Valley YMCA. Served with USMC, 1947-50. Mem. Congl. Hispanic Caucus, Hispanic Am. Democrats, Nat. Assn. Latino Elected and Apptd. Ofcls., Communications Workers Am., VFW, Am. Legion, Latin Bus. Assn., Monterey Park C. of C., Navy League (dir.). Democrat. Lodge: Rotary. Office: US Ho of Reps 2239 Rayburn Bldg Ofc Washington DC 20515-0005*

MARTINEZ, PEDRO JAIME, professional baseball player; b. Manoquayabo, Dominican Republic, July 25, 1971. With L.A. Dodgers, 1992-93; pitcher Montreal Expos, 1994—. Named Minor League Player Sporting News, 1991. Office: Montreal Expos, 4549 Pierre de Coubertin, Montreal, PQ Canada H1V 3N7*

MARTINEZ, PETE R., beverage company executive; b. San Antonio, July 8, 1937; m. Aurora Valadez; children: Shirley Jeanne, Peter Roland, Frieda Ann, Ruben Jay and Lynn Virginia (twins). A in Mgmt., San Antonio Coll., 1974. Various positions Coca-Cola Bottling Co. of S.W., San Antonio, 1952-79, v.p., 1979, BEVTEX gen. mgr., 1979-84, spl. events/concessions/youth market depts. mgr., 1984-86, spl. events/concessions/ice/youth market/cold drink telephone sales and cooler depts. mgr., 1986-87, v.p. govt. and cmty. rels., 1987—; chmn. U.S. Hispanic Bus. Bilateral Commn. on Free Trade Agreement, 1990—. Vol. United Way San Antonio, 1979, bd. dirs. 1989-96; mem. adv. com. San Antonio Coll. Mgmt., 1984-91; bd. dirs. Leukemia Soc. Am., 1985, v.p., 1986, pres. S.W. Tex. chpt., 1987, 88, 89; chmn. nat. hispanic leukemia televent, 1990, treas., 1990-91, nat. bd. trustee class A, 1988-92; bd. dirs. Goodwill Industries of San Antonio, 1985-90, vice chmn., 1991-94, bd. chmn., 1995-96; bd. dirs. Jr. Achievement South Tex., 1985-94, chmn., 1995, Keep San Antonio Beautiful, 1987-94, chmn. legis. com., 1990; chmn. found. bd. dirs. Alamo Cmty. Coll. Dist., 1985, 94, vice chmn., 1986-95; commr. San Antonio Fiesta Commn./Ann. Fiesta Week, 1986-91, v.p., chmn. pub. rels. com., 1989, mem. exec. bd. presdl. appointee, 1990, mem. exec. bd. treas. and chmn. finance com., 1991, mem. exec. bd. sr. v.p.-chmn., 1992, mem. pers. com., pres. 1993, mem. exec. bd. cmty. rels. and nominating com., 1994; mem. distribution com. San Antonio Area Found., 1985-92, treas. exec. com., 1994-95; so. sector task force chmn. City of San Antonio, 1985-86, bd. dirs. Citizens for Dome, 1988-89, bd. dirs. Inst. Ams.; mem. fgn. trade and transp. com. San Antonio Target Commn. 1983-84; mem. awards selection panel J.C. Penny Golden Rule Awards, Bexar County, Tex., 1988, 89; bd. dirs. North San Antonio Chamber, 1988-91, vice chmn. cmty. devel., 1989, 91, YMCA of San Antonio & Hill Country, 1989-90, vice chmn. pub. policy 1990, vice chmn. bd. devel., 1991, vice chmn. ptnrs. in youth 1992-94, bd. chmn. 1993, 94; mem. pub. policy com. YMCA of Tex., 1989-94, bd. dirs. YMCA of U.S.A., 1994-96; Assumption Sem. Press area chmn. Papal Visit Pope John Paul II, 1989; mem. corporate adv. coun. to sch. bd. Ursuline Acad., 1989-91. Recipient Leadership award Jr. Achievement San Antonio, 1989, Corporate Sponsor of Yr. award Keep San Antonio Beautiful, 1989. Mem. Tex. Soft Drink Assn., San Antonio Mex.-Am. Profl. Men's Assn. (bd. dirs. 1985, 86, v.p. 1987), U.S. Hispanic C. of C. (bd. dirs. 1980, mem. adv. bd. 1981, Member of Yr. award 1984, Corp. Adv. of Yr. award 1990), Tex. Assn. Mex. C. of C. (San Antonio rep. 1976-92, chmn. conv. 1980, 92, state chmn. bd. dirs. 1980-81, 86-87, 87-88, spl. advisor to chmn. 1989-92, Pres. award 1980), San Antonio Hispanic C. of C. (bd. dirs. 1975-77, 81, 82, 84, 1st v.p. 1978, 3d v.p. 1979, 2d v.p. 1980, co-chmn. conv. 1985, 86, adv. to chmn. bd. dirs. 1987-91, bd. historian 1992, bd. chair advisor 1996), Greater San Antonio C. of C. (mem. Internat./Mex. Day Stock Show com. 1976-93, chmn. com. 1980-85, mem. steering com. econ. devel. coun. 1980, 81), San Antonio Downtown Rotary. Office: Coca-Cola Bottling Co SW 1 Coca Cola Pl San Antonio TX 78219-3712

MARTINEZ, RAUL L., mayor, publisher; b. Santiago, Oriente, Cuba, Mar. 6, 1949; came to U.S., 1960; s. Chin and Aida Martinez; m. Angela Callava, Jan. 10, 1970; children—Aida, Raul. AA, Miami Dade Coll.; BS in Criminal Justice, Fla. Internat. U., Miami. Pub., founder El Sol de Hialeah, Fla., 1969—; pres. Martex Realty, Fla., 1975—; mem. city council City of Hialeah, 1977-81, mayor, 1981—; Mem. Dem. Policy Commn.'s Roundtable on Defense and Fgn. Policy, State Comprehensive Plan Com., Dade Clean Inc.; past vice chmn. Beacon Council; chmn. Dade County Council Mayors, So. Fla. Employment and Tng. Consortium, Hialeah Dade Devel. Inc.; bd. dirs. Hialeah Pk. racecourse; mem. franchise and environ. rev. com. High Speed Rail, 1987; mem. Gov.'s Commn. on Statewide Prosecution Function, 1984-85, Fla. State Commn. on Hispanic Affairs, 1979-82;pres. Fla. League of Cities. Mem. Dade County Assn. Chiefs Police, Little Havana Nutrition and Activities Ctr., State Fla. Planning Commn., United Way of Dade County (community devel. com.), Little Havana Activity Ctrs. Commn., St. John Home Health Care Inc.; adv. bd. Barry U.; hon. adviser Miami Dade Community Coll., North Campus-Hialeah Ctr. Fedn. Hispanic Students; chmn. So. Mcpl. Conf.; bd. dirs. Nat. League of Cities; former pres. Fla. League of Cities. Recipient Legion of Honor award, 1977, Citizen Involvement award Crime Commn. of Greater Miami, 1977, Over the Top award Hialeah-Miami Springs YMCA, 1979, Pub. Adminstr. of Yr. award South Fla. chpt. Am. Soc. Pub. Adminstrn., 1984. Mem. U.S. Conf. of Mayors, Hialeah-Miami Springs-N.W. Dade Area C. of C., Nat. League Cities, Fla. League Cities (pres.), Dade County League (past. pres.), Hialeah Latin C. of C., Kiwanis. Lodge: Kiwanis. Office: City of Hialeah 501 Palm Ave Hialeah FL 33010-4719

MARTINEZ, RICARDO, federal agency administrator; m. Robin Rosser. MD, La. State U. Sch. Medicine, 1980. Intern Lafayette (La.) Charity Hosp., 1980-81; resident Charity Hosp., New Orleans, 1983-85; vis. fellow accident rsch. unit Ctr. Automotive Engring./U. Birmingham, U.K., 1989; adminstr. Nat. Hwy. Traffic Safety Adminstrn, Washington; assoc. prof. emergency medicine Emory U. Sch. Medicine, Atlanta, assoc. dir. Ctr. for Injury Control. Home: 1218 Dartmouth Rd Alexandria VA 22314

MARTINEZ, ROMAN, IV, financial executive; b. Santiago, Cuba, Dec. 29, 1947; came to U.S., 1960, naturalized, 1971; s. Roman and Virginia G. (Gomez) M.; B.S., Boston Coll., 1969; MBA, U. Pa., 1971; m. Helena Hackley, Dec. 20, 1974; children—Roman, Helena Catalina. Asso., Kuhn Loeb & Co., N.Y.C., 1971-73, v.p., 1974-77; corp. v.p. Lehman Bros. Kuhn Loeb Inc., N.Y.C., 1977, mng. dir., 1978-84; mng. dir. Lehman Bros. (formerly Shearson Lehman Bros. Inc.), N.Y.C., 1984—. Republican. Roman Catholic. Clubs: Racquet and Tennis, Links, River, Piping Rock. Home: 555 Park Ave New York NY 10021-8166 Office: Lehman Bros 3 World Fin Ctr New York NY 10285

MARTINEZ, VERONICA, special education educator; b. Ft. Worth, June 21, 1959; d. Joe and Helen (Guereca) M.; divorced. BS, Tex. Wesleyan U., 1981; MEd, U. North Tex., 1986. Cert. elem. tchr., Tex. Spl. Edn. resource tchr. Ft. Worth Ind. Sch. Dist., 1981—. Active Learning Disabilities Assn. Ft. Worth Coun. Reading. Mem. NEA, Internat. Reading Assn., Nat. Coun. Tchrs. English, Tex. State Tchrs. Assn., Delta Kappa Gamma.

MARTINEZ, WALTER BALDOMERO, architect; b. Havana, Cuba, Sept. 21, 1937; came to U.S., 1961; s. Baldomerò and Maria J. Amparo (Rodriguez) M.; m. Olga Justa Sardina, July 23, 1961; children: Teresita Maria, Gabriel Jose. Cert. in civil constrn., Arts and Craft Vocat. Sch., Havana, 1957; student, U. Havana, 1958-60; student Sch. Architecture, U. Miami, 1963-64, cert. fallout shelter analyst, 1970. Registered architect, Fla.; cert. gen. contractor, Fla. Job capt. Tony Sherman Architect, Miami, Fla., 1961-63; project mgr. Ken Miller Architect, Miami, 1968-69; designer, project mgr. Russell-Melton & Assocs., Miami, 1969-70; head archtl. dept. Sanders & Thomas, Miami, 1971-72; assoc. Russell-Wooster & Assoc., Miami, 1973-77; prin. Russell-Martinez & Holt, Miami, 1977-84; prin., pres. The Russell Partnership, Miami, 1985—. Contbr. articles to Constrn. mag. Bd. dirs. Biscayne Nature Ctr., Miami, 1982—; vice chmn. Latin Quarters Rev. Bd., Miami, 1989, 95. Fellow AIA (nat. chmn. minority resources com. 1985, pres. Miami chpt. 1982, Silver medal 1981); mem. Nat. Assn. Cuban Archs. (bd. dirs. Miami chpt. 1986-87, Gold medal 1984), Latin Builders Assn., Fla. Bd. Archs. (chmn. 1991), NCARB, Greater Miami C. of C. (Hispanic affairs com. 1988-93, chmn. affordable housing com. 1989), Nat. Arch. Accrediting Bd., Inc. (accreditation team mem. 1992-95). Republican. Roman Catholic. Avocations: boating, photography. Home: 223 Grand Canal Dr Miami FL 33144-2529 Office: Russell Partnership Inc 2733 SW 3rd Ave Miami FL 33129-2330

MARTINEZ-CARRION, MARINO, biochemist, educator; b. Felix, Almeria, Spain, Dec. 2, 1936; came to U.S., 1957; naturalized, 1961.; s. Juan Martinez and Maria Carrion; m. Ana J. Iriarte, Apr. 20, 1987; children: Victoria, Marino Juan. BA, U. Calif, Berkeley, 1959, MA, 1961, PhD, 1964. NIH postdoctoral fellow U. Rome, 1964-65; asst. prof. U. Notre Dame, Ind., 1965-68, 1968-74, prof., 1974-77; chmn. Va. Commonwealth U., Richmond, 1977-86; dean Sch. Biol. Sci. U. Mo., Kansas City, 1986—; dir. Ctr. for Innovative Tech. Inst. Biotech., Richmond, 1984-86; chmn. biophys. chemistry study sect. NIH, Washington, 1977-82; mem. cell neurobiol. panel NSF, Washington, 1985-89. Contbr. numerous articles on biochem. subjects to profl. jours.; mem. Jour. Protein Chemistry; mem. editorial bd. Archives Biochemistry and Biophysics, Jour. Biol. Chemistry. Rsch. grantee NIH, 1965—, NSF, 1974—, Am. Heart Assn., 1974-77, career devel. grantee NIH, 1972-77. Fellow N.Y. Acad. Scis.; mem. Am. Chem. Soc., Am. Soc. Biochemistry and Molecular Biology, Pan Am. Assn. Biochem. Socs. (treas. 1987-90, vice chmn. 1990-93, chmn. 1993—), Internat. Soc. Neurochemistry, Biophys. Soc. Democrat. Roman Catholic. Office: U Mo Sch Biol Scis Kansas City MO 64110

MARTINEZ DE LA ESCALERA, GONZALO, neuroendocrinologist; b. Montevideo, Uruguay, Jan. 1, 1956; arrived in Mex., 1969; s. Fernando and Raquel (Lorenzo) M.; m. Carmen Clapp, June 19, 1980; children: Daniela, Lucia. BS, Met. U. Mex., 1978; PhD, Nat. U. Mex., 1984. Rsch. asst. Biomed. Rsch. Inst., Mex., 1977-81, asst. prof., 1982-85, assoc. prof., 1988-90, prof., 1991-94; prof. Neurobiology Ctr., Mex., 1994—; vis. scientist U. Calif., San Francisco, 1989, 90, 91-92, 93. Editor: Neuroendocrine Communication: Molecular and Cellular Bases, 1993; editl. bd. Neuroendocrinology, 1994—; contbr. articles to profl. jours. Recipient Syntex Found. award, 1995, Sci. Rsch. Acad. award, 1995, Young Scientist award Nat. U. Mex., 1995; fellow U. Calif., San Francisco, 1985-88, Andrew William Mellon Found. fellow, N.Y., 1985, Rockefeller Found. fellow, N.Y., 1988, 92, John Simon Guggenheim Meml. Found. fellow, N.Y., 1993. Mem. The Endocrine Soc., Soc. Neuroscis., Internat. Soc. Neuroendocrinology. Home: Ingenio de Zacatepec 68, 14330 Mexico City Mexico Office: Ciudad U Neurobiology Ctr, PO Box 70228, 04510 Mexico City Mexico

MARTINEZ-LÓPEZ, ENRIQUE, Spanish educator; b. Granada, Spain, Aug. 18, 1928; came to the U.S., 1959, naturalized 1967; s. Francisco and Amparo (Lopez Mesa) M.; m. Maria Teresa Leal, Feb. 10, 1954 (div. 1965); children: Maria Teresa, Maria Isabel, Enrique; m. Natalie Louise Campbell, Nov. 10, 1966. BA, U. Granada, 1947; MA in Romance Philology, U. Madrid, 1952, PhD, 1964. Instr. SPanish and Hispanic Lit. U. da Paraiba, João Pessoa, Brazil, 1954-56, U. do Recife, Brazil, 1956-59; asst. prof. Spanish U. Houston, 1959-63; asst. prof. Spanish U. Calif., Santa Barbara, 1963-66, assoc. prof., 1966-72, chmn. dept. Spanish and Portuguese, 1970-74, prof., 1972—; vis. lectr. U. Wis., Madison, 1966, 67; fellow, rschr. Cervantes INst. Consejo Superior de Investigaciones Cientificas, Madrid, 1952-54; conf. organizer III Ann. So. Calif. Cervantes Symposium, Santa Barbara, 1992. Author: Granada, Paraiso Cerrado, 1971, 89; editor: Camoniana Californiana, 1985; editor: Ency. Britannica Editores, 1962-64. Chair intercultural com. YWCA, Houston, 1960-62; chair com. on culture Alianza Cultural Mexicana, Santa Barbara, 1973-75. 2d lt. Spanish Army, 1953-54. Recipient award Cruz de Caballero, Orden del Merito Civil Govt. of Spain, 1955; grantee Am. Philos. Soc. Inst. Humanities, 1966, 71, 74. Mem. MLA, Am. Assn. Tchrs. Spanish and Portuguese, Internat. Assn. Hispanists, Internat. Inst. Iberoam. Lit., Am. Soc. Sephardic Studies, Internat. Assn. Golden Age Studies, Inst. Brasileiro de Cultura Hispanica (pres. 1956-58). Democrat. Roman Catholic. Home: 503 Miramonte Dr Santa Barbara CA 93109-1400 Office: U Calif Dept Spanish and Portuguese Santa Barbara CA 93106-4150

MARTINEZ-MALDONADO, MANUEL, medical service administrator, physician; b. Yauco, P.R., Aug. 25, 1937; s. Manuel Martinez and Josefa Maldonado; m. Nivia Elena Rivera, Dec. 18, 1959; children: Manuel, David, Ricardo, Pablo. BS, U. P.R., 1957; MD, Temple U., 1961. Diplomate Am. Bd. Internal Medicine (assoc. mem. nephrology com. 1982-86), Am. Bd. Nephrology. Intern St. Charles Hosp., Toledo, 1961-62; resident VA Hosp., San Juan, PR, 1962-65, chief resident, 1964-65; instr. U. Tex. Southwestern Med. Sch., Dallas, 1967-68; asst. prof. medicine Baylor Coll. Medicine, Houston, 1968-71, assoc. prof. medicine, 1971-73, prof. medicine, dir. renal sect., 1973; prof. medicine U. P.R. Sch. Medicine, 1973-90, prof. physiology, 1974-90; prof. medicine U. Caribbean, Bayamon, P.R., 1980-90; chief med. services VA Hosp., San Juan, P.R., 1973-90; dir. renal metabolic lab VA Hosp., San Juan, PR, 1973-90; prof., vice chmn. dept. medicine Emory U. Sch. Medicine, 1990—; chief med. svcs., assoc. chief of staff for ambulance care Atlanta VA Med. Ctr.; chief, med. svcs., assoc. chief of staff Ambulance Care VA Med. Ctr., Atlanta; mem. nat. adv. bd. gen. medicine, B study sect. Nat. Inst. Arthritis, Metabolism and Digestive Diseases NIH; mem. bd. sci. counselors, sci. advisors com. Nat. Heart, Lung and Blood Inst., Nat. Insts. Health. Author: La Voz Sostenida, 1984, Palm Beach Blues, 1986, Por Amor al Arte, 189; film critic for El Reportero, 1983-86, El Mundo, 1987-90; contbr. over 200 med. rsch. articles to sci. jours.; editor or co-editor of 11 books on renal phamacology, nephrology, physiology; mem. editl. bd. U. P.R. Press, numerous profl. jours.; editor-in-chief Am. Jour. of Med. Scis., 1994-97. Mem. health com. Poplar Dem. Com., P.R., 1982-84; mem. Com. 500th Anniversary of Discovery Am., P.R., 1987-92; mem. com. on human rights Inst. of Medicine, Washington, 1987-92. Recipient Lederle Internat. award, 1966-67, Scholar award Macy Faculty, 1979-80, Grand Mobil prize medicine Mobil Oil Corp., 1981, Disting. Alumnus award Temple Med. Sch., 1988, Presdl. award Nat. Kidney Found, 1988, Donald W. Seldin medal 1994, Disting. Physician award P.R. Hosps. Assn., 1988, Orden del Cafetal award Municipality of Yauco, 1989; named one of Outstanding Med (medicine) P.R. C. of C., 1976, Fed. Supr. Employee of Yr., Fed. Execs. Assn., P.R., 1977. Fellow ACP, AAAS, Coun. for High Blood Pressure Rsch., Am. Heart Assn. (hypertension rsch. coun.; mem. Inst. Medicine NAS, Am. Soc. Nephrology (legis. liaison com., chmn. audit com. 1988), So. Soc. Clin. Investigation (sec.-treas. 1983-85, pres. 1985-86, Founders medal 1990), Am. Soc. for Clin. Investigation, Nat. Kidney Found. (chmn. sci. adv. bd. 1987-89, Donald W. Seldin medal, chmn. pub. policy com. 1992-94, pub. svc. medal), Latin Am. Soc. Nephrology (v.p. 1987-91, pres. elect 1991-94, pres. 1994—), Inter-Am. Soc. Hypertension Assn. (bd. govs., chmn. 8th Sci. Congress 1989), U.S. Pharmacopeial Convention Cardio Renal Drugs Com., Assn. Am. Physicians, Inst. Medicine, Alpha Omega Alpha. Achievements include contributions in field of kidney physiology and pathophysiology; contributions in treatment of clinical disturbances of blood composition, clinical use of diuretics, mechanisms of the development of hypertension. Office: VAMC Med Svc 1670 Clairmont Rd Decatur GA 30033-4004

MARTING, MICHAEL G., lawyer; b. Cleve., Nov. 5, 1948. BA summa cum laude, Yale U., 1971, JD, 1974. Bar: Ohio 1974. Assoc. Jones, Day, Reavis & Pogue, Cleve., 1974-83, ptnr., 1984—. Mem. ABA, Union Club, Cleve. Racquet Club, Kirtland Country Club, Tavern Club (treas., sec., trustee local chpt. 1985-88). Avocations: fly fishing, birdshooting, big game hunting, squash, golf. Office: Jones Day Reavis & Pogue N Point 901 Lakeside Ave E Cleveland OH 44114-1116

MARTINI, ROBERT EDWARD, wholesale pharmaceutical and medical supplies company executive; b. Hackensack, N.J., 1932. BS, Ohio State U., 1954. With Bergen Brunswig Corp., Orange, Calif., 1956-92, v.p., 1962-69, exec. v.p., 1969-81, pres., 1981-92, CEO, 1990—; chmn. Bergen Brunswig Corp., Orange, 1992—; chmn. exec. com. Bergen Brunswig Corp. Capt. USAF, 1954. *

MARTINI, WILLIAM J., congressman; b. Passaic, N.J.; m. Gloria Martini; children: William Jr., Marissa. Degree, Villanova U., 1968; JD, Rutgers U., 1972. Elected mem. City Coun. of Clifton, N.J., Passaic County Bd. Chosen Freeholders, U.S. House of Reps., 1994—. Pres. Nicholas Martini Found.; trustee United Way of Passaic County, Ctr. Italian Am. Culture, Passaic Valley Coun. Boys Scouts of Am. Office: US House Reps 1513 Longworth House Office Bldg Washington DC 20515-3008*

MARTINO, CHERYL DERBY, insurance company executive; b. Paterson, N.J., Jan. 19, 1946; d. Elles Mayo and Sarah Emma (Steele) D.; m. Leonard D. Martino, Nov. 4, 1995. BA, Elmira Coll., 1967; MBA, NYU, 1982. Tchr. Ramsey (N.J.) High Sch., 1967-70; contbns. analyst Met. Life Ins. Co., N.Y.C., 1970-83, fin. writer investments dept., 1983-93, asst. sec., 1994—. Bd. trustees United Meth. Ch. of Waldwick, N.J., v.p., 1989-91, pres., 1992-93. Fellow Life Mgmt. Inst. (bd. dirs. Greater N.Y. chpt. 1984-91, pres. 1986, edn. coun. 1990-93), Life Mgmt. Inst. Edn. Coun. (nat. adminstrv. com. chmn. 1990-92, mktg. subcom. 1985-93), Nat. Orchestral Assn. (bd. dirs. 1990-92); mem. Elmira Coll. Alumni Club N.J. (exec. bd. 1982-87). Methodist. Office: Met Life 1 Madison Ave New York NY 10010-3603

MARTINO, DONALD JAMES, composer, educator; b. Plainfield, N.J., May 16, 1931; s. James Edward and Alma Ida (Renz) M.; m. Mari Rice, Sept. 5, 1953 (div. June 1968); 1 child, Anna Maria; m. Lora Harvey, June 5, 1969; 1 child, Christopher James. B.Mus., Syracuse U., 1952; M.F.A., Princeton, 1954; MA (hon), Harvard U., 1983. Instr. music Princeton, 1957-59; asst. prof. theory music Yale, 1959-66, assoc. prof., 1966-69; chmn. dept. composition New Eng. Conservatory Music, Boston, 1969-80; Irving Fine prof. music Brandeis U., 1980-82; prof. music Harvard U., 1983—, Walter Bigelow Rosen prof. music, 1989-93; Walter Bigelow Rosen prof. emeritus, 1993—; tchr. composition and theory Yale Summer Sch. of Music and Art, summers 1960-63; tchr. composition Berkshire Music Ctr., summers, 1965-67, 69; composer in residence Berkshire Music Ctr., 1973; vis. lectr. Harvard U., 1971; composer in residence Composers' Conf., Johnson, Vt., summer 1979, May in Miami, 1994; Maurice Abravanel vis. disting. composer U. Utah, 1994, Mary Duke Biddle disting. composer Duke U., 1995. Composer: Separate Songs, 1951; for high voice and piano, Sonata for Clarinet and Piano, 1951, The Bad Child's Book of Beasts, 1952, Suite of Variations on Medieval Melodies, 1952; cello solo, A Set for Clarinet, 1954, Quodlibets for Flute, 1954, Three Songs, 1955, Portraits; a secular cantata for chorus, soloists and orch., 1955, Sette Canoni Enigmatici, 1956, Contemplations for Orch. (commd. by Paderewski Fund), 1956, 24 Tin Pan Alley Tunes, 1956, Quartet for Clarinet and Strings, 1957, Canon Ball, Three Way, MacFugal, Cathy, Lover Come Bach, 1957, Piano Fantasy, 1958, Trio for violin, clarinet and piano, 1959, Cinque Frammenti, 1961, Two Rilke Songs, 1961, Fantasy-Variations for violin, 1962, Concerto for Wind Quintet (commd. by Fromm Found. and Berkshire Music Center), 1964, Parisonatina Al'Dodecafonia; for cello solo, 1964, Concerto for Piano and Orch. (commd. by New Haven Symphony), 1965, B, a, b, b, it, t; for clarinet, 1966, Strata; for bass clarinet, 1966, Mosaic for grand orch. (commd. by U. Chgo.), 1967, Pianississimo; sonata for piano, 1970, Seven Pious Pieces, 1971, Concerto for Violoncello and Orch., 1972, Augenmusik, 1972, Notturno, 1973 (Naumburg Chamber Music award commn., Pulitzer prize in music 1974), Paradiso Choruses for Chorus, Soloists, Orch. and Tape, 1974 (Paderewski Fund commn., Classical Critics citation Record World mag. 1976), Ritorno for Orch. (Plainfield Symphony commn.), 1975, Triple Concerto for Clarinet, Bass Clarinet and Contrabass Clarinet with Chamber Ensemble (N.Y. State Council on Arts and Andrew W. Mellon Found. commn.), 1977, Impromptu for Roger; piano solo, 1977, Quodlibets II; flute solo, 1980, Fantasies and Impromptus, piano solo (Koussevitzky Found. commn.), 1981, Divertissements for Youth Orch. (Groton, Mass. Arts Ctr. Commn.), 1981, Suite in Old Form, piano solo, 1982, String Quartet (Elizabeth Sprague Coolidge Commn., winner 1st prize Kennedy Ctr. Friedheim Awards 1985), 1983, Canzone e Tarantella, clarinet and cello, 1984, The White Island, for chorus and chamber orchestra (Boston Symphony Centennial Commn.), 1985, Concerto for Alto Saxophone and Chamber Orch. (Nat. Endowment Consortium commn.), 1987, From the Other Side, Divertimento for Flute, Cello, Percussion and Piano (commd. by Flederman New Music Ensemble for the Australian Bicentennial, 1988), 12 Preludes (commd. Meet the Composer-Readers Digest), 1990, 15, 5, '92 AB for Carinet solo, 1992, Three Sad Songs, 1993, Viola and Piano (Elizabeth Sprague Coolidge commn.); numerous others; contbr. articles to prof. jours. Recipient BMI Student Composer awards, 1952, 53; Bonsall fellow, 1953-54; Kosciuszko scholar, 1953-54; Nat. Fedn. Music Clubs award, 1953; Kate Neal Kinley fellow U. Ill., 1954-55; Fulbright grantee Florence, Italy, 1954-56; Pacifica Found. award, 1961; Creative Arts citation Brandeis U., 1963; Morse Acad. fellow, 1965; Nat. Inst. Arts and Letters grantee, 1967; Guggenheim fellow, 1967-68, 73-74, 82-83; Nat. Endowment on Arts grantee, 1973, 76, 79, 89; Mass. Council on Arts grantee, 1973, 79, 89; Pulitzer prize in music, 1974; recipient Kennedy Ctr. Friedheim Awards 1st prize, 1985, Mark M. Horblit award Boston Symphony Orch., 1987, Paul Revere award for mus. autography Music Publ. Assn., 1990, 91, 92. Mem. AAAS, AAAL, Coll. Music Soc., Am. Composers Alliance, Broadcast Music Inc., Am. Music Ctr., Internat. Soc. Contemporary Music (a founder New Haven chpt. 1964, dir. U.S. sect. 1961-64), Am. Soc. U. Composers (founding mem., exec. com. 1965-66, trustee 1965—), Internat. Clarinet Soc. (bd. dirs.). Office: Harvard U Dept Music Cambridge MA 02138

MARTINO, FRANK DOMINIC, union executive; b. Albany, N.Y., Apr. 9, 1919; s. Benedetto and Rosina (Esposita) M.; m. Phyllis E. Higgins, June 15, 1963; children—Michael M., Lisa R. Student, Rutgers U., Cornell U., Oxford U. Timekeeper N.Y.C. R.R., 1937-41; chem. operator Sterling Drug Co., 1946-56; internat. rep. Internat. Chem. Workers Union, Akron, Ohio, 1956-70; internat. v.p. Internat. Chem. Workers Union, 1970-72, sec.-treas., 1972-75, internat. pres., 1975—, Washington rep., dir., 1962-70. Served with USAF, 1941-45. Democrat. Roman Catholic. Office: Internat Chem Workers Union 1655 W Market St Akron OH 44313-7004

MARTINO, JOSEPH PAUL, research scientist; b. Warren, Ohio, July 16, 1931; s. Joseph and Anna Elizabeth (Kubina) M.; m. Mary Lou Bouquot, May 18, 1957; children: Theresa, Anthony, Michael. A.B., Miami U., Ohio, 1953; M.S., Purdue U., 1955; Ph.D., Ohio State U., 1961. Commd. 2d lt. USAF, 1953, advanced through grades to col., 1973; project engr. armament lab. USAF, Wright-Patterson AFB, Ohio, 1955-58; mathematician Office Sci. Rsch. USAF, Washington, 1961-62; staff scientist Avionics Lab. USAF, Wright-Patterson AFB, 1972-73; dir. engring. standardization Def. Electronics Supply Ctr. USAF, Dayton, Ohio, 1973-75; ret. USAF, 1975; sr. scientist, rsch. inst. U. Dayton, 1975-93. Author: Technological Forecasting for Decisionmaking, 1972, rev. edit., 1983, 3d edit., 1992, A Fighting Chance-The Moral Use of Nuclear Weapons, 1988, Science Funding: Politics and Porkbarrel, 1992, Research and Development Project Selection, 1995; assoc. editor: Tech. Forecasting and Social Change Jour., 1968—. Fellow IEEE, AAAS, AIAA (assoc.); mem. Inst. for Ops. Rsch. and Mgmt. Sci., Am. Soc. Engring. Mgmt. Roman Catholic. Office: U Dayton Rsch Inst 300 College Park Ave Dayton OH 45469-0120

MARTINO, MICHAEL CHARLES, entertainer, musician; b. Philadelphia, Pa., Sept. 10, 1950; s. Salvatore Joseph and Marie Angela (Langone) M. Grad. high sch., Upper Darby, Pa. Spokesperson/rep. Petosa Accordion Co., Seattle, 1979—; featured TV entertainer Mike Martino Show, Delaware County, Pa., 1987-89; accordion tchr. Drexel Hill, Pa., 1989—; entertainer/host/producer St. Jude's Children's Hosp. Marathon, King of Prussia, Pa., 1973; opening act comedian Morty Gunty Downingtown, Pa., 1973, opening act comedian Morty Gunty, 1973, Pat Cooper, Phila., 1981; guest artist/entertainer Internat. Platform Assn. Conv., Washington, 1979; nite club performer Glen Mills, Pa., 1989; actor TV commls., Elkton, Md., 1979, Halloween Spl. KYW-TV, Phila., 1986; performed radio contest jingle Sta. KISS 100 radio, Media, Pa., 1992. Author: (movie script) Forever Fiftys, 1990; composer popular songs; directed, produced, starred video Forever Fiftys; composed theme song Forever Fiftys, (movie theme) That First September; creator, performer Suspended Triple Bellows Shake Technique for the Accordion, 1994; composer (ballad) Through the Music, Through the Words I Sing, 1995. Recipient citation U.S. Ho. Reps., 1989, Proclamation Mike Martino Day Mayor Ward, Del. County, 1988, Danny Thomas Hon. award St. Jude's Hosp., Del. County, 1973, Mayor's Svc. award Upper Darby, Pa., 1994. Roman Catholic. Avocations: antique cars, dogs. Home: 2530 Stoneybrook Ln Drexel Hill PA 19026-1610

MARTINO, ROBERT LOUIS, computational scientist and engineer, researcher; b. Derby, Conn.; s. Pasquale Theodore and Louise Mary (Bartomioli) M.; m. Alfreda Helen Guarente, Aug. 28, 1971. BS, Northeastern U., 1971; MS, U. Md., 1973, PhD, 1982. Elec. engr. Goddard Space Flight Ctr., NASA, Greenbelt, Md., 1970-71; electronics engr. NIH, Bethesda, Md., 1973-89; mem. adj. grad. sch. faculty Johns Hopkins U., Balt., 1982—; chief computational sci. and engring. sect. NIH, 1989-93, chief computational bioscience and engring. lab., 1993—; mem. computer sci. program com. Johns Hopkins U., 1985—; NIH rep. Nat., Multi-Agy. High-Performance Computing and Comm. Program, Bethesda, 1992—; mem. program com. Symposium on Frontiers of Massively Parallel Computing, 1993-95. Author: (with others) High Performance Computational Methods for Biological Sequence Analysis, 1996, Parallel and Distributed Computing Handbook, 1995; contbr. articles to profl. jours. Recipient Disting Svc. award HHS, 1994; Grad. fellow U. Md., 1971-73. Mem. IEEE, Sigma Xi, Tau Beta Pi, Eta Kappa Nu. Achievements include the adaptation of high-performance parallel supercomputing to computationally intensive problems in basic and clinical biomedical research; application of concepts and technology of computer science and electrical engineering to biomedical applications for the advancement and understanding of the fundamentals of biological systems and medical practices and for the development of new and improved methods of health care. Home: 7996 Aladdin Dr Laurel MD 20723 Office: NIH Bldg 12A Rm 2033 12 South Dr MSC 5624 Bethesda MD 20892-5624

MARTINO, ROBERT SALVATORE, orthopedic surgeon; b. Clarksburg, W.Va., May 31, 1931; s. Leonard L. and Sarafina (Foglia) M.; m. Jenna Cappellanti, May 22, 1954; children: Robert S. Jr., Leslie F. Reckyiegal. AB, W.Va. U., 1953, postgrad., 1955-56, BS in Medicine, 1958; MD, Northwestern U., 1960. Diplomate Am. Bd. Orthopaedic Surgery; lic. Ill., Calif., Ind. Intern Chgo. Wesley, 1960-61; resident dept. orthopaedic surgery Northwestern U., 1961-65, Chgo. Wesley Meml., 1961-62, Am. Legion Hosp. for Crippled Children, 1962-63, Cook County Hosp., Chgo., 1964, 64-65; orthopaedic surgeon Gary, Ind., 1965-67; orthopaedic surgeon Merrillville, Ind., 1967—; fellow Nat. Found. Infantile Parralysis, 1956, Office of Vocat. Rehab., Hand Surgery, 1965; chief of staff St. Mary Med. Ctr., 1976, chief of surgery, 1974-85; chief of staff Gary Treatment Ctr./Ind. Crippled Children's Svcs., 1974-84; adj. asst. prof. anatomy Ind. U., 1978, clin. asst. prof. orthopaedic surgery, 1980, others; mem. Zoning Bd., 1989-90. Chmn. Planning Bd. Town of Dune Acres, 1992-96; bd. dirs. United Steel Workers Union Health Plan, 1994—, St. Mary's Med. Ctr., Hobart, Ind.; com. on

Health Care Reform. Capt. U.S. Army, 1953-56. Mem. Ind. Med. Soc., Ill. Med. Soc., Chgo. Med. Soc., Lake County Med. Soc., AMA, Ill. Orthopaedic Soc., Ind. Orthopaedic Soc., Mid-Am. Orthopaedic Assn., Tri-State Orthopedic Soc., Clin. Orthopaedic Soc. Home: 22 Oak Dr Chesterton IN 46304-1016

MARTINO, ROCCO LEONARD, computer systems executive; b. Toronto, Ont., Can., June 25, 1929; s. Domenic and Josephine (DiGiulio) M. BSc, U. Toronto, 1951, MA, 1952; PhD, Inst. Aerospace Studies, 1955, DSc, Neumann Coll., 1993; m. Barbara L. D'Iorio, Sept. 2, 1961; children: Peter Domenic, Joseph Alfred, Paul Gerard, John Francis. Dir., Univac Computing Svc. Ctr., Toronto, 1956-59; pres. Mauchly Assos. Can. Ltd., Toronto, 1959-62, v.p. Mauchly Assocs., Inc., Ft. Washington, Pa., 1959-61; mgr. advanced systems Olin Mathieson Chem. Corp., N.Y.C., 1962-64; dir. advanced computer systems Booz, Allen & Hamilton, N.Y.C., 1965-70; pres., chmn. bd. Info. Industries, Inc. and subs.'s, Wayne, Pa., 1965-70; chmn. bd., chief exec. officer XRT, Inc., Wayne, Pa., 1970—; chmn. bd. MBF Computer Ctr. for Handicapped Children; mem. bd. St. Joseph's U., Phila., Gregorian U. Found., N.Y., vice chmn. bd., 1990—; mem. exec. com. Gregorian U., N.Y. and Rome, 1987—, bd. dirs. 1984—, pontifical circle, 1985—, active, 1982—; assoc. prof. math. U. Waterloo, 1959-62, prof. engring., dir. Inst. Systems and Mgmt. Engring., 1964-65; adj. assoc. prof. NYU, 1963-64, adj. prof. math., 1964-65, 66; lectr. on computers mgmt.; chmn. Gov. Ill. Task Force, 1970-71, Ill. Bd. Higher Edn. Task Force, 1971-72, Computer-Use Task Force FCC, 1972-73, Computer-Use Planning Task Force U.S. Postal Svc., 1973-74. Trustee Gregorian Found., N.Y.C. and Rome, 1984—; bd. dirs. St. Joseph's U., 1987—, Cath. League Religious and Civil Rights, 1988-91; chmn. bd. dirs. MBF Ctr. Disabled Children, 1985—; founder Vatican Observatory, 1988—, bd. dirs. Tucson, Rome, 1990—. Mem. Assn. Computing Machinery, Ops. Rsch. Soc. Am., Nat. Italian Am. Found. (bd. dirs. 1991—), Profl. Engrs. Ont., Computing Soc. Can., ITEST (bd. dirs.), Union League Phila., Lions, Overbrook Golf and Country Club, Yacht of Sea Isle City Club (commodore 1973-74, trustee 1975-86, chmn. 1983-86), Commodores Club, Mid-Atlantic Yacht Racing Assn. (commodore 1979-81, sec. 1981-83, officer 1983—), Order St. Gregory the Great (papal knight 1991—), Legatus (bd. dirs. 1988, ea. regional v.p. 1992), Equestrian Order Holy Sepulchre (knight 1986, knight comdr. 1989), KC, Order of Malta, Knights of Malta (knight 1988, knight commdr. 1989), Cath. Campaign for Am. (nat. coun. 1992). Author: Resources Management, 1968, Dynamic Costing, 1968, Project Management, 1968, Information Management: The Dynamics of MIS, 1968, MIS-Management Information Systems, 1969, Decision Patterns, 1969, Methodology of MIS, 1969, Personnel Information Systems, 1969, Integrated Manufacturing Systems, 1972, APG-Virtual Application Systems, 1981; contbr. numerous articles on mgmt., computers and planning in profl. publs.; designer, developer Application Program Generator computer system, 1974-75, integrated treasury systems; developer cash mgmt. and on-line internat. trading systems, 1984, local area network systems fault tolerant and disaster tolerant systems for real-time fin. transactions, comml. paper trading systems for global networks.

MARTINS, HEITOR MIRANDA, foreign language educator; b. Belo Horizonte, Brazil, July 22, 1933; came to U.S., 1960; s. Joaquim Pedro and Emilia (Miranda) M.; m. Teresomja Alves Pereira, Nov. 1, 1958 (div. 1977); children—Luzia Pereira, Emilia Pereira; m. Marlene Andrade, Jan. 11, 1984. A.B., U. Federal de Minas Gerais, 1959; Ph.D., U. Federal de Minas Gerais, 1962. Instr. U. N.M., Albuquerque, 1960-62; asst. prof. Tulane U., New Orleans, 1962-66; assoc. prof. Tulane U., 1966-68; prof. dept. Spanish and Portuguese Ind. U., Bloomington, 1968—; chmn. dept. Ind. U., 1972-76; vis. prof. U. Tex., Austin, 1963, Stanford U. 1968. Author: poetry Sirgo nos Cabelos, 1961; essay Manuel de Galhegos, 1964; essays Oswald de Andrade e Outros, 1973; critical anthology Neoclassicismo, 1982; Essays Do Barroco a Guimarães Rosa, 1983; editor: essays Luso-Brazilian Literary Studies. Social Sci. Research Council grantee, 1965; Fulbright-Hays Commn. grantee, 1966; Ford Found. grantee, 1970, 71. Mem. MLA, Renaissance Soc. Am., Am. Comparative Lit. Assn., Am. Assn. for 18th Century Studies. Home: 1316 S Nancy St Bloomington IN 47401-6050 Office: Indiana U Dept Spanish and Portuguese Bloomington IN 47405

MARTINS, NELSON, physics educator; b. Santos, Brazil, Oct. 18, 1930; s. Aniceto and Angelica Martins; m. Maria Lucia, Jan. 8, 1959 (div. Sept. 1983); children: Flavia, Paulo. BS in Physics, Mackenzie U., São Paulo, Brazil, 1958; D in Physics, Pontifica U., Campinas, Brazil, 1977. Cert. physicist. Dir. engring. Mackenzie U., 1971-73, dir. Exact Sci., 1983-90; gen. dir. Ednl. Found., Barretos, Brazil, 1973-76; chief physics dep. Engring. Sch., Araraquara, Brazil, 1991; chief physics dept. U. Santo Amaro, São Paulo, 1990-92; dir. CCET Ctr. Exact Scis. and Tech., São Paulo, 1992-95. Author: (with others) Electriciy and Magnetism, 1973, Dimensional Analysis, 1980, Dynamics, 1982. Mem. Am. Assn. Physics Tcrhs., Brazil Soc. Physics. Office: UNISA, Prof Enéas Siqueira Neto, 04829300 São Paulo SP, Brazil

MARTINS, NILAS, dancer; b. Copenhagen, 1967. Tng., Royal Danish Ballet Sch. Featured in ballets (John Neumaier) Romeo and Juliet, (August Bournonville) Conservatoriet, A Folk Tale, Napoli, (Glen Tetley) Firebird, (Robbins) The Concert, Conservatoriet, Dances at a Gathering, Fanfare, The Four Seasons, Glass Pieces, The Goldberg Variations, Mother Goose, Opus 19, The Dreamer, Robbins with Twyla Tharp) Brahms/ Handel, (Balanchine) Cortege Hongrois, Who Cares?, Apollo, Chaconne, Coppelia, Divertimento No. 15, Duo Concertant, The Four Temperaments, Haieff Divertimento, Jewels, A Midsummer Night's Dream, The Nutcracker, Scotch Symphony, Serenade, Sonatina, La Sonnambula, Stars and Stripes, Stravinsky Violin Concerto, Swan Lake, Symphony in Three Movements, Tschaikovsky Suite No. 3, Union Jack, Vienna Waltzes, Western Symphony, Orpheus, (Martins) Delight of the Muses, Fearful Symmetries, Jazz, Jeu de Cartes, Sleeping Beauty, Tanzspiel, The Waltz Project, X-Ray; also appeared in Ray Charles in Concert with the N.Y.C. Ballet, N.Y.C. Ballet's Balanchine Celebration, 1993. Office: New York City Ballet NY State Theater Lincoln Ctr Plz New York NY 10023

MARTINS, PETER, ballet master, choreographer, dancer; b. Copenhagen, Oct. 27, 1946; came to U.S., 1967, naturalized, 1970; m. Lise La Cour (div. 1973); 1 child, Nilas; m. Darci Kistler, 1991. Pupil of Vera Volkova and Stanley Williams with Royal Danish Ballet. With N.Y.C. Ballet, 1967—, tchr., 1975, ballet master, 1981-83, co-ballet master-in-chief, 1983-89; ballet master-in-chief, 1989—; Tchr. Sch. Am. Ballet, 1975; artistic adviser Pa. Ballet, 1982—. Mem. Royal Danish Ballet, 1965-67, prin. dancer (including Bournonville repertory), 1967; guest artist N.Y.C. Ballet, 1967-70, prin. dancer, 1970-83; guest artist regional ballet cos. U.S., also Nat. Ballet Can., Royal Ballet, London, Grand Theatre Geneva, Paris Opera, Vienna State Opera, Munich State Opera, London Festival Ballet, Ballet Internat., Royal Danish Ballet; TV appearance in series of Balanchine works, 1974; also has appeared on PBS Dance in America series including A Choreographer's Notebook: Stravinsky Piano Ballets by Peter Martins, 1984; choreographed Broadway musicals including Dream of the Twins (co-choreographer) 1982, On Your Toes, 1982, Song and Dance, 1985; works choreographed include Calcium Light Night, 1977, Tricolore (Pas de Basque sect.), 1978, Rossini Pas de Deux, 1978, Tango-Tango (ice ballet), 1978, Dido and Aeneas, 1979, Sonate di Scarlatti, 1979, Eight Easy Pieces, 1980, Lille Suite, 1980, Suite from Histoire du Soldat, 1981, Capricio Italien, 1981, The Magic Flute, 1981, Symphony No. 1, 1981, Delibes Divertissement, 1982, Piano-Rag-Music, 1982, Concerto for Two Solo Pianos, 1982, Waltzes, 1983, Rossini Quartets, 1983, Tango, 1983, A Schubertiad, 1984, Mozart Violin Concerto, 1984, Poulenc Sonata, 1985, La Sylphide, 1985, Valse Triste, 1985, Eight More, 1985, We Are the World, 1985, Eight Miniatures, 1985, Ecstatic Orange, Tanzspiel, 1988, Jazz, 1993, Symphonic Dances, 1994, Barber Violin Concerto, 1994, Mozart Paino Concerto (No. 17), 1994, X-Ray, 1995; author: (autobiography) Far from Denmark, 1982. Recipient Dance mag. award 1977, Cue's Golden Apple award 1977, award of merit Phila. Art Alliance, 1985, Liberty award N.Y.C., 1986, H.C. Andersen Ballet prize, Royal Danish Theatre, 1988. Office: NY State Theater NYC Ballet Lincoln Ctr Plz New York NY 10023

MARTINSON, CONSTANCE FRYE, television program hostess, producer; b. Boston, Apr. 11, 1932; d. Edward and Rosalind Helen (Sperber) Frye; m. Leslie Herbert Martinson, Sept. 24, 1955; 1 child, Julianna Martinson Carner. BA in English Lit., Wellesley Coll., 1953. Dir. pub. relations Coro Found., Los Angeles, 1974-79; producer/host KHJ Dimensions, Los Angeles, 1979-81, Connie Martinson Talks Books, Los Angeles, 1981—; instr. dept. humanities UCLA, 1981—; moderator, instr. Univ. Judaism; celebrity advisor Book Fair-Music Ctr., L.A., 1986; advisor, moderator L.A. Times Festival of Books, 1996; bd. dirs. Friends of English UCLA; TV rep. L.A. Pub. Libr. L.A. Cityview, Sta. WNYE, Channel Am. Author Dramatization of Wellesley After Images, 1974; book editor, columnist Calif. Press Bur. Syndicate, 1986—. Pres. Mayor's adv. council on volunteerism, Los Angeles, 1981-82; chmn. community affairs dept. Town Hall of Calif., Los Angeles, 1981-85; bd. dirs. legal def. fund NAACP, Los Angeles, 1981-84. Mem. Women in Cable, Am. Film Inst., Jewish TV Network (bd. dirs. 1985-87), PEN, Nat. Book Critics Assn., Wellesley Coll. Club (pres. 1979-81), Mulholland Tennis Club. Democrat. Jewish. Avocations: tennis, theater, reading. Home and Office: 2288 Coldwater Canyon Dr Beverly Hills CA 90210-1756

MARTINSON, IDA MARIE, nursing educator, nurse, physiologist; b. Mentor, Minn., Nov. 8, 1936; d. Oscar and Marvel (Nelson) Sather; m. Paul Varo Martinson, Mar. 31, 1962; children—Anna Marie, Peter. Diploma, St. Luke's Hosp. Sch. Nursing, 1957; B.S., U. Minn., 1960, M.N.A., 1962; Ph.D., U. Ill., Chgo., 1972. Instr. Coll. St. Scholastica and St. Luke's Sch. Nursing, 1957-58, Thornton Jr. Coll., 1967-69; lab. asst. U. Ill. at Med. Ctr., 1970-72; lectr. dept. physiology U. Minn., St. Paul, 1972-82; asst. prof. Sch. Nursing U. Minn., 1972-74, assoc. prof. rsch., 1974-77, prof., dir. rsch., 1977-82; prof. dept. family health care U. Calif., San Francisco, 1982—, chmn. dept., 1982-90; vis. rsch. prof. Nat. Taiwan U., Def. Med. Ctr., 1981; vis. prof. nursing Sun Yat-Sen U. Med. Scis., Guang Zhou, Republic of China, Ewha Women's U., Seoul, Korea; vis. prof. nursing Frances Payne Bolton Sch. Nursing, Case Western Res. U., Cleve., 1994—; chair, prof. dept. health scis. Hong Kong Poly. U., 1996—. Author: Mathematics for the Health Science Student, 1977; editor: Home Care for the Dying Child, 1976, Women in Stress, 1979, Women in Health and Illness, 1986, The Child and Family Facing Life Threatening Illness, 1987, Family Nursing, 1989, Home Health Care Nursing, 1989; contbr. chpts. to books, articles to profl. jours. Active Am. Cancer Soc. Recipient Book of Yr. award Am. Jour. Nursing, 1977, 80, 87, 90, Children's Hospice Internat. award, 1988, Humanitarian award for pediatric nursing, 1993; Fulbright fellow, 1991. Mem. ANA, Coun. Nurse Rschrs., Am. Acad. Nursing, Inst. Medicine, Sigma Xi, Sigma Theta Tau. Lutheran. Office: U Calif Family Health Care Nursing San Francisco CA 94143-0606 *The challenge of quality health care to all of society and the critical role nursing has to play in order to achieve this goal has motivated me throughout my professional life. The richness of talent in this country spurs me on.*

MARTINSON, JACOB CHRISTIAN, JR., academic administrator; b. Menomonie, Wis., Apr. 15, 1933; s. Jacob Christian and Matilda Kate (Wisner) M.; m. Elizabeth Smathers, Apr. 29, 1962; children—Elizabeth Anne, Kirsten Kate. BA, Huntingdon Coll., Ala., 1954, LLD (hon.), 1993; MDiv, Duke U., 1957; DDiv, Vanderbilt U., 1972; grad., Inst. Ednl. Mgmt., Harvard U., 1981. Ordained elder United Methodist Ch. Minister Trinity United Meth. Ch., Lighthouse Point, Fla., 1960-67; sr. minister First United Meth. Ch., Winter Park, Fla., 1967-71; supervising instr. Vanderbilt U. Div. Sch., Nashville, 1971-72; pres. Andrew Coll., Cuthbert, Ga., 1972-76, Brevard Coll., N.C., 1976-85, High Point (N.C.) U., 1985—; bd. dirs. First Union Nat. Bank, High Point, chmn. 1989; lectr. St. Mary's Theol. Soc., U. St. Andrews, Scotland. Bd. advisors Uwharrie coun. Boy Scouts Am. Glen Slough scholar Vanderbilt U., 1971; Z. Smith Reynolds grantee Harvard U. Inst. Ednl. Mgmt., 1981; hon. fellow Westminster Coll., Oxford, Eng., 1994. Mem. Nat. Assn. Schs. and Colls. United Meth. Ch. (bd. dirs. 1982-85, 87-90, chmn. fin. com.), So. Assn. Colls. and Schs. (commn. on colls.), Ind. Coll. Fund. N.C. (trustee), N.C. Ctr. Ind. Higher Edn. (bd. dirs.) Brevard C. of C. (pres. 1979), High Point C. of C. (chmn. 1992), Piedmont Ind. Coll. Assn. (chmn. 1991-93), Carolinas Intercollegiate Athletic Conf. (pres. 1991-93), Rotary, Phi Theta Kappa. Methodist. Avocation: mountain hiking. Home: 1109 Rockford Rd High Point NC 27262-3607 Office: High Point U Office of Pres High Point NC 27262-3598

MARTINUZZI, LEO SERGIO, JR., banker; b. Newton, Mass., Aug. 1, 1928; s. Leo Sergio and Jessica (Stewart) M.; m. Helen Renfrew Gibson, Oct. 26, 1957; children: John James, Georgiana Gibson, Samuel Stewart. B.A., Harvard U., 1950; B.Litt., Oxford U., 1952. With Chase Manhattan Bank, N.Y.C., 1956-81; asst. treas. Chase Manhattan Bank, 1960, asst. v.p. Japanese brs., 1961-64, v.p. Japanese brs., 1964-68, marketing exec. internat. staff, 1968-72, sr. v.p., 1971-81; corporate devel. officer Chase Manhattan Corp., 1972-75, group exec. info. services, 1975-81; chmn. Chase Econometric Assocs. Inc., 1975-80; sr. v.p. strategic planning Squibb Corp., 1981-87, cons., 1988-91; chmn. Strategic Dimensions, Inc., 1990—. Trustee Internat. Found. for St. Catherine's Coll., Oxford. Lt. (j.g.) USNR, 1952-56. Mem. Coun. on Fgn. Rels. Home: 336 Galleon Dr Naples FL 33940-7638

MARTLAND, THOMAS RODOLPHE, philosophy educator; b. Port Chester, N.Y., May 29, 1926; s. Thomas Rodolphe and Anne Elizabeth (Newbury) M.; BS magna cum laude, Fordham U., 1951; MA, Columbia U., 1955, PhD, 1959; m. Agatha Murphy, Apr. 3, 1952; children: David Allen, Luke Thomas. Asst. prof. Lafayette Coll., Easton, Pa., 1959-65; assoc. prof. So. Ill. U., Carbondale, 1965-66; assoc. prof. philosophy SUNY-Albany, 1966-84, prof., 1984—, dir. religious studies program, 1980-87; dir. philosophy grad. studies program, 1988-91; disting. Jeannette K. Watson vis. prof. of religion, Syracuse U., 1987; dir. Master of Arts in Liberal Studies Program, 1995—; Served to lt. (s.g.) USN, 1944-47, 51-53. Faculty Exchange Guest scholar 1976-77, rsch. fellow, 1967, 68, 71, 87; Jones Fund award Lafayette Coll., 1962-63, Signum Laudis award for excellence in tchg. and rsch., 1986. Mem. Am. Philos. Assn., Am. Soc. Aesthetics (steering com. 1985-88), Internat. Assn. Philosophy and Lit. (exec. com. 1976-81). Author: Religion as Art: An Interpretation, 1981; The Metaphysics of William James and John Dewey, 1969; editorial bd. Jour. Comparative Lit. & Aesthetics, 1982-91; guest editor Annals of Scholarship, 1982. Home: RR # 1 Box 33 East Ryegate VT 05042 Office: SUNY/Albany Dept Philosophy Albany NY 12222

MARTO, PAUL JAMES, mechanical engineering educator, researcher; b. Flushing, N.Y., Aug. 15, 1938; s. Peter Joseph and Natalie Janet (Verrinoldi) M.; m. Mary Virginia Indence, June 10, 1961; children: Terese V. Marto Sanders, Paul J. Jr., Wayne T., Laura C. BS, U. Notre Dame, 1960; SM, MIT, 1962, ScD, 1965. Disting. prof. Naval Postgrad. Sch., Monterey, Calif., 1965-69, assoc. prof., 1969-77, prof., 1977-85, disting. prof., 1985-96, chmn. dept. mech. engring., 1978-86, dean rsch., 1990-96, disting. prof. emeritus, 1996—; cons. Modine Mfg. Co., Racine, Wis., 1986—. Editor: Power Condenser Heat, 1981; regional editor N.Am. Jour. of Enhanced Heat Transfer, 1993—; contbr. articles to profl. jours. Lt. USN, 1965-67. Recipient Rear Adm. John J. Schieffelin award Naval Postgrad. Sch., 1976, Alexander von Humboldt U.S. Sr. Scientist award Humboldt Stiftung, Fed. Republic Germany, 1989-90, Disting. Civilian Svc. award Sec. of Navy, 1996. Fellow ASME (assoc. tech. editor Jour. of Heat Transfer 1984-90); mem. Am. Soc. Naval Engrs., Am. Soc. for Engring. Edn., Sigma Xi. Avocations: walking, tennis, music. Office: Naval Postgrad Sch Dept Mechanical Engring Code ME/MX Monterey CA 93943

MARTOCCHIO, LOUIS JOSEPH, lawyer, educator; b. Hartford, Conn., May 12, 1966; s. Louis Joseph and Mary Noel (Higgins) M.; m. Jodie Meheran, Jan. 4, 1991. BS in Bus. Econs., So. Conn. State U., 1988; JD, U. Bridgeport, 1991. Bar: Conn. 1991. Atty. Carswell Law OFfices, Bridgeport, Conn., 1991-92, Moynahan, Ruskin, Mascolo, Minnella & Crozier, Waterbury, Conn., 1993—; prof. Morse Sch. Bus., Hartford, Conn., 1992—; bd. dirs. Camelot Property, South Windsor; legal cons. Lobo Enterprises, Southington, Conn., 1994—. Recipient Univ. award U. Bridgeport, 1991. Mem. ABA, Conn. Bar Assn., Conn. Trial Lawyers Assn., Hartford Bar Assn.

MARTON, EVA, opera singer; b. Budapest, Hungary, June 18, 1943; m. Zoltan Marton; children: Zoltan, Diana. Student, Liszt Acad., Budapest. Debut Budapest State Opera, 1968-72; performed with Frankfurt Opera, 1972-77, Hambrug State Opera, 1977-80, Maggio Musicale Fiorentino, Vienna State Opera, La Scala Milan, Met. Opera, N.Y., Lyric Opera, Chgo., Grand Opera, Houston, San Francisco Opera, Convent Garden, London, Teatro Liceo, Barcelona, Munich State Opera, Berlin, Paris, Sydney, Teatro Colon Buenos Aires, Bayreuth Festival, Salzburg Festival, Area of Verona, others; roles include Manon Lescaut, Tosca, Turandot, Aida Elisabetta in Don Carlo, Leonora in Forza del destino and in Il Trovatore, Fedora, Maddalena in A Chenire, Wally, Gioconda, Leonore in Fidelio, Salome, Ariadne, Helene in Agyptische Helene, Chrysothemis in Electra, Empress in Die Frau ohne Schatten, Vensu and Elisabeth in Tannhäuser, Elsa and Ortrud in Lohengrin, Sieglinde and Brüünnhilde in the Ring, Isolde, others; rec. include Turandot, Tosca, La Fanciulla del West, A Chenier, Fedora, La Gioconda, Violanta, Tiefland, La Wally, Semirama, Bluebeards Castle, Mefistofele, Electra, Salome, Die Walkuere, Siegfrid, Götterdämmerung, Gurrelider, Forza del destino, Tristan und Isolde, Puccini Arias, Wagner arias, Songs by Bartok and Liszt, others. Office: Orgn Int Opera et Concert, 19 rue Vignon, F-75008 Paris France

MARTON, LAURENCE JAY, clinical pathologist, educator, researcher; b. Bklyn., Jan. 14, 1944; s. Bernard Dov and Sylvia (Silberstein) M.; m. Marlene Lesser, June 27, 1967; 1 child, Eric Nolan. BA, Yeshiva U., 1965, DSc (hon.), 1993; MD, Albert Einstein Coll. Medicine, 1969. Intern Los Angeles County-Harbor Gen. Hosp., 1969-70; resident in neurosurgery U. Calif.-San Francisco, 1970-71, resident in lab. medicine, 1973-75, asst. research biochemist, 1973-74, asst. clin. prof. depts. lab. medicine and neurosurgery, 1974-75, asst. prof., 1975-78, assoc. prof., 1978-79, prof., 1979-92, asst. dir. div. clin. chemistry, dept. lab. medicine, 1974-75, dir. div., 1975-79, acting chmn. dept., 1978-79, chmn. dept., 1979-92; dean med. sch. U. Wis., 1992-95, prof. pathology and lab. medicine and oncology, 1992—; prof. dept. human oncology U. Wis., Madison, 1993-95. Co-editor: Polyamines in Biology and Medicine, 1981; Liquid Chromatography in Clinical Analysis, 1981; Clinical Liquid Chromatography, vol. 1, 1984, vol. 2, 1984. Served with USPHS, NIH, 1971-73. Recipient Rsch. Career Devel. award Nat. Cancer Inst., Disting. Alumnus award Albert Einstein Coll. Medicine, 1992. Mem. Am. Assn. Cancer Rsch., AAAS, Acad. Clin. Lab. Physicians and Scientists, Am. Investigative Pathology, Am. Soc. Clin. Pathologists, Soc. Analytical Cytology, Alpha Omega Alpha. Jewish. Avocations: photography, art, music, travel. Home: 5810 Tree Line Dr Fitchburg WI 53711-5826 Office: U Wis Med Sch McArdle Lab Cancer Rsch 1400 University Ave Madison WI 53706

MARTONE, JEANETTE RACHELE, artist; b. Mineola, N.Y., June 5, 1956; d. John and Mildred Cecilia (Loehr) M. BFA, SUNY, Purchase, 1978. One woman shows include Ariel Gallery, N.Y.C., 1990, La Mantia Gallery, Northport, N.Y., 1994-96; exhibited in group shows from 1980 to 1996 including Harbor Gallery, Cold Spring Harbor, 1980, Huntington coun. Arts, 1986, Pindar Gallery, N.Y.C., 1987, Mills Pond House, Smithtown, N.Y., 1987, Suffolk County Exec. Offices, Hauppage, N.Y., 1988, La Mantia Gallery, Northport, N.Y., 1990, Nassau County Office Cultural Affairs, 1991, Ward-Nasse. Gallery, N.Y.C., 1991, Monsterrat Gallery, N.Y.C., 1991, Priscilla Redfield Roe Gallery, Bellport, N.Y., 1991, L.I. U., Brookville, 1992, Northport B.J. Spoke Gallery, Huntington, N.Y., 1992, Fischetti Gallery, N.Y., 1992, Artists Space, N.Y.C., 1992, N.Y. Botanical Gardens, Bronx, N.Y., 1993, Visions Gallery, Albany, L.I. U., Brookville, N.Y., 1994, Goodman Gallery, Southampton, N.Y., 1994, B.J. Spoke Gallery, Huntington, N.Y., 1994-95, Islip Art Mus., East Islip, N.Y., 1994, L.I. MacArthur Airport, Ronkonkoma, N.Y., 1995. Recipient Award of Excellence Gold medal Art League of Nassau County, 1993, Best in Show award Nat. League Am. PEN Women Artists, 1990, 92, Windsor and Newton award for oil Arts Coun. East Islip, N.Y., 1989, award of excellence Art League of Nassau County, 1987, 88, many best in shows, Supervisor's award Babylyon Citizens Coun. Arts Juried Exhbn., 1994, Bob Jones Glad Hand Press award Stamford Art Assn., 1995, Faber Biren Nat. Color award Stamford Art Assn., 1995. Mem. Catherine Lorillard Wolfe Art Club (Frank B. and Mary Anderson Cassidy Meml. award 1992, Award for Oil 1987), Allied Artists of Am. (John Young Hunter Meml. award 1993, Antonio Cerino Meml. award 1990), Hudson valley Art Assn., Knickerbock Artists of Am., Nat. Art League. Avocations: travel, reading, volunteer work. Home: 47 Summerfield Ct Deer Park NY 11729-5642

MARTONE, PATRICIA ANN, lawyer; b. Bklyn., Apr. 28, 1947; d. David Andrew and Rita Mary (Dullmeyer) M. BA in Chemistry, NYU, 1968, JD, 1973; MA in Phys. Chemistry, Johns Hopkins U., 1969. Bar: N.Y. 1974, U.S. Dist. Ct. (so. and ea. dists.) N.Y. 1975, U.S. Ct. Appeals (2d cir.) 1975, U.S. Ct. Appeals (1st cir.) 1981, U.S. Ct. Appeals (fed. cir.) 1984, U.S. Patent and Trademark Office 1983, U.S. Supreme Ct. 1984, U.S. Dist. Ct. (ea. dist.) Mich. 1985, U.S. Dist. Ct. (no. dist.) Calif. 1995. Tech. rep. computer timesharing On-Line Systems, Inc., N.Y.C., 1969-70; assoc. Kelley Drye & Warren, N.Y.C., 1973-77; assoc. Fish & Neave, N.Y.C., 1977-82, ptnr., 1983—; adj. prof. NYU Sch. Law, 1990—; participating atty. Cmty. Law Offices, N.Y.C., 1974-78; atty. Pro Bono Panel U.S. Dist. Ct. (so. dist.) N.Y., 1982-84; lectr. Practising Law Inst., N.Y.C., 1995, Aspen Law & Bus., 1990-95, Franklin Pierce Law Sch., 1992—; Lic. Exec. Soc., 1995; mem. panel arbitration Am. Arbitration Assn.; dir. N.Y. Lawyers for the Pub. Interest, 1987—, exec. com., 1989—, treas., 1992-94; dir. Legal Svcs. N.Y.C., 1991-95. Mng. editor NYU Law Sch. Rev. Law and Social Change, 1972-73. Contbr. articles to profl. jours. Recipient Founder's Day award NYU Sch. Law, 1973; NSF grad. trainee John Hopkins U., 1968-69; NYU scholar, 1964-68. Mem. ABA, Assn. Bar City N.Y. (mem. environ. law com. 1978-83, trademarks, unfair competition com. 1983-86), Fed. Bar Council, Fed. Cir. Bar Assn., Am. Chem. Soc., Licensing Execs. Soc., Intellectual Property Law Assn., N.Y. University Club. Office: Fish & Neave 1251 Avenue Of The Americas New York NY 10020-1104

MARTONOSI, ANTHONY NICHOLAS, biochemistry educator, researcher; b. Szeged, Hungary, Nov. 7, 1928; came to U.S., 1957; s. Antal and Anna (Zsoter) M.; m. Mary Alice Gouvea, May 2, 1959; children: Mary Anne, Anthony, Margaret, Susan. MD, U. Med. Sch., Szeged, 1953. Asst. prof. dept. physiology Med. Sch., Szeged, 1955-57; rsch. fellow Mass. Gen. Hosp., Boston, 1957-59; rsch. assoc. Retina Found., Boston, 1959-62, asst. dir. dept. muscle rsch., 1962-65; assoc. prof. biochemistry St. Louis U. Sch. Medicine, 1965-69, prof., 1969-79; prof. biochemistry SUNY Health Sci. Ctr., Syracuse, 1979—; Albert Szent-Gyorgyi Prof., U. Med. Sch., Szeged, Hungary, 1994; adj. prof. Kwangju Inst. of Sci. and Tech., Korea, 1995—; vis. scientist dept. biochemistry U. Birmingham, Eng., 1963-64. Editor: The Enzymes of Biological Membranes, Vols. 1-4, 1976, 2d edit., 1985; Membranes and Transport, Vols. 1-2, 1982; contbr. over 180 articles to sci. publs.; mem. editorial adv. bd. Jour. Muscle Rsch. and Cell Motility, 1980—, Biochimica et Biophysica Acta, 1988—. Recipient Established Investigator award Am. Heart Assn., 1961-66; rsch. grantee USPHS, NIH, 1959—, NSF, 1963—, Muscular Dystrophy Assn., 1975—. Mem. Am. Soc. Biochemists and Molecular Biologists, Biophys. Soc. Roman Catholic. Home: 110 Stanwood Ln Manlius NY 13104-1412 Office: SUNY Health Sci Ctr 766 Irving Ave Syracuse NY 13210-1605

MARTORANA, BARBARA JOAN, secondary education educator; b. N.Y.C., Oct. 18, 1942; d. Samuel and Joan Renee (Costello) M. BA, St. John's U., Jamaica, N.Y., 1970, MS in English Edn., 1972; advanced cert. computers in edn., L.I. U., 1988, profl. diploma in edn. adminstrn., 1990. Cert. sch. dist. adminstr., sch. adminstr. and supr., tchr. English grades 7-12, N.Y. Exec. sec. Am. Petroleum Inst., N.Y.C., 1960-65; exec. asst. to v.p. Goldring, Inc., N.Y.C., 1965-67; exec. asst. Rsch. Inst. for Cath. Edn., N.Y.C., 1967-69; English tchr. St. Martin of Tours Sch., Amityville, N.Y., 1970-77, Oceanside (N.Y.) Jr. H.S., 1977-78, Freeport (N.Y.) H.S., 1979—; rec. sec. Freeport (N.Y.) Tchr. Ctr. Policy Bd., 1986-89; co-chair Middle States Steering Com., Freeport, 1988-90; chair Freeport (N.Y.) H.S. Shared Decision Team, 1992-93; workshop facilitator L.I. Writing Project, Garden City, N.Y., 1993—, co-leader Summer Insts. Co-author: (textbooks) Writing Competency Practice, 1980, Writing Competency Practice-Revised and Expanded, 1989. With Seaford (N.Y.) Rep. Club, 1975—. Mem. ASCD, Nat. Coun. Tchrs. English (conf. on English edn.), N.Y. State English Coun., L.I. Writing Project. Avocations: reading, writing, traveling. Office: Freeport HS 50 S Brookside Ave Freeport NY 11520-3144

MARTORANA, SEBASTIAN VINCENT, educator, educational consultant; b. Farnham, N.Y., Jan. 7, 1919; s. Francis and Jennie (Mancuso) M.; m. Carrie Mae Stephenson, Sept. 20, 1947; children: Vincenne (Mrs. Alfred Kirmss), Francis Stephen, John Charles. B.S., N.Y. State Coll. at Buffalo, 1939; postgrad., U. Buffalo, 1940; M.A., U. Chgo., 1946, Ph.D., 1948. Prof. Wash. State Coll., 1948-53; dean Ferris State Inst., 1953-55; specialist community colls. U.S. Office Edn., Washington, 1955-57; chief state and regional orgns. U.S. Office Edn., 1957-63; asst. commr. for higher edn. planning N.Y. State Bd. Regents, 1963-65; vice-chancellor for community colls., provost tech. edn. SUNY, 1965-72; sr. rsch. assoc. Ctr. Study Higher Edn., prof. higher edn. Pa. State U., 1972-89, prof. emeritus, 1989; mem. nat. bd. inservice edn. project Edn. Commn. States, 1976-82; pres., chmn. bd. Assoc. Cons. in Edn., 1976-94; lectr. in field. Author: (with D Grant Morrison) Criteria for Establishing Two Year Colleges, 1961, State Formulas for the Support of Public Two Year Colleges, 1962, (with E. Hollis) State Boards Responsible for Higher Education, 1960, College Board of Trustees, 1963, (with C. Blocker, L. Bender) The Political Terrain of American Postsecondary Education, 1975, (with E. Kuhns) Managing Academic Change, 1975, (with Gary McGuire) State Legislation Relating to Community and Junior Colleges, 1975, (with L. Nespoli), 1976, Regionalism in American Postsecondary Education: Concepts and Practices, 1978, Regionalism: Study, Talk, and Action, 1978, (with E. Kuhns) Quality Beyond the Campus, 1983, (with W. D. Smutz) State Legislation Relating to Community and Junior Colleges, 1979, (with W. Piland) Designing Programs for Community Groups, 1984; editor: (with W. Toombs, D. Breneman) Graduate Education and Community Colleges, 1976, (with E. Kuhns) Qualitative Methods for Institutional Research, 1982, (with J. Broomall) State Legislation on Affecting Community, Jr. and 2-Year Technical Colleges, 1981, (with P. Corbett) State Legislation Affecting Community, Jr. and 2-Year Technical Colleges, 1982, (with P. Garland) State Legislation Affecting Community, Jr. and Two-Year Technical Colleges, 1985, 86, 87, 88, 89, (with T. Kelley and L.A. Nespoli) Politics, Law and Economics of Higher Education, 1987; mem. editorial bd. Community Coll. Rev., 1972-86; mem. editorial adv. bd. Jour. Edn. Finance, 1972-86. Pres. Wakefield Forest Civic Assn., Annandale, Va., 1958-59, Pearse Rd. Civic Assn., Schenectady, 1966-67; Trustee Coll. Entrance Exam. Bd., 1966-70, Washington Internat. Coll., 1974-80; lay adv. bd. Notre Dame High Sch., Schenectady, 1968-72; bd. human resources Nat. Acad. Scis., 1971-72; mem. Pres. Nat. Adv. Commn. on Higher Edn., 1969. Served with USAAF, 1942-45. Decorated Legion of Merit; recipient Distinguished Alumnus award State U. N.Y. Coll. at Buffalo, 1959, Distinguished Service award HEW, 1960, Award of Merit N.Y.S. Jr. Coll. Assn., 1972, Outstanding Reservist, Air Univ., 1974, Outstanding Publ. award Nat. Council Univ. and Coll. Profs./Am. Assn. Community and Jr. Colls., 1982, 86, Disting. Svc. award Nat. Coun. Univ. and Coll. Profs./Am. Assn. Community and Jr. Coll Assn., 1985; named to Community Coll. Founders Hall of Fame, 1984. Danforth Found. grantee, 1974; Ford Found. grantee, 1978; grantee Fund for Improvement of Postsecondary Edn., 1982. Mem. NEA, Nat. Coun. State Dirs. Comty. and Jr. Colls. (founding mem., pres. 1968, 72), Am. Assn. Higher Edn., Am. Ednl. Rsch. Assn., Assn. Instnl. Rsch., Am. Assn. Comty. and Jr. Colls. (dir. 1977-80, Nat. Leadership award 1988), Nat. Soc. Study Edn., Nat. Assn. Coll. and Univ. Attys. (founding mem.), Nat. Coun. Coll. and Univ. Profs. Comty. and Jr. Colls. (pres. 1979, bd. dirs. 1987-89), Pa. Higher Edn. Assn., Res. Officers Assn., Air Force Assn., KC, Sons of Italy, Italic Studies Inst. (adv. coun. mem.), Ret. Officers Assn., Phi Delta Kappa. Home: Box 256 Rural Delivery 1 Centre Hall PA 16828 Office: 400 Charlotte Bldg University Park PA 16802-6107

MARTORI, JOSEPH PETER, lawyer; b. N.Y.C., Aug. 19, 1941; s. Joseph and Teresa Susan (Fezza) M. BS summa cum laude, NYU, 1964, MBA, 1968; JD cum laude U. Notre Dame, 1967. Bar: D.C. 1968, U.S. Dist. Ct. D.C. 1968, U.S. Dist. Ct. Ariz. 1968, U.S. Ct. Appeals (9th cir.) 1969, U.S. Supreme Ct. 1977. Assoc. Sullivan & Cromwell, N.Y.C., 1967-68, Snell & Wilmer, Phoenix, 1968-69; pres. Goldmar Inc., Phoenix, 1969-71; ptnr. Martori, Meyer, Hendricks & Victor, P.A., Phoenix, 1971-85; ptnr. Brown & Bain, P.A., Phoenix, 1985-94, chmn. corp. banking & real estate dept.; bd. dirs. Firstar, Met. Bank, Phoenix, Red Rock Collection Inc., Phoenix; chmn. ILX Inc., Varsity Clubs Am. Inc. Author: Street Fights, 1987; also articles, 1966-70. Bd. dirs. Men's Arts Coun., Phoenix, 1972—; trustee Boys' Clubs Met. Phoenix, 1974—; consul for Govt. of Italy, State of Ariz., 1987—. Mem. ABA, State Bar Ariz., Maricopa County Bar Assn., Lawyers Com. for Civil Rights Under Law (trustee 1976—), Phoenix Country Club, Plaza Club (founding bd. govs. 1979-90). Republican. Roman Catholic. Office: ILX Inc 2777 E Camelback Rd Phoenix AZ 85016-4302

MARTUZA, ROBERT L., neurosurgeon; b. Wilkes-Barre, Pa., July 1, 1948. BA, Bucknell U., Lewisburg, Pa., 1969; MD, Harvard U., 1973. Diplomate Am. Bd. Neurol. Surgery. Instr. surgery Harvard Med. Sch., Boston, 1980-81, asst. prof., 1981-86, assoc. prof., 1986-91; prof., chmn. dept neurosurgery Georgetown U., Washington, 1991—; Dir. Georgetown Brain Tumor Ctr., Washington, 1993—, Mass. Gen. Hosp. Neurofibromatosis Clinic, Boston, 1990-91; chair Decade of the Brain Task Force, Chgo., 1994—. Contbr. articles to profl. jours. Recipient Von Recklinghanson award Nat. NF Found., N.Y.C., 1989. Mem. Am. Acad. Neurol. Surgeons, Soc. Neurol. Surgery (Grass award), Am. Assn. Neurol. Surgeons, Congress Neurol. Surgeons. Achievements include development of genetically engineered viruses for brain tumor therapy; first development of replication-competent viral vectors for tumor therapy; localization of NF2 gene defects to chromosome 22. Office: Georgetown U Dept Neurosurgery 3800 Reservoir Rd NW Washington DC 20007

MARTY, JOHN, state senator, writer; b. Evanston, Ill., Nov. 1, 1956; s. Martin E. and Elsa Louise (Schumacher) M.; m. Connie Jaarsma, Nov. 29, 1980; children: Elsa, Micah. BA in Ethics, St. Olaf Coll., 1978. Researcher Minn. Ho. of Reps., St. Paul, 1980-82, com. adminstr. com. criminal justice, 1982-84; corp. found. grant adminstr., 1984-86; mem. Minn. State Senate, St. Paul, 1987—. Dem. Farm Labor gubernatorial candidate, 1994.

MARTY, LAWRENCE A., magistrate; b. Leigh, Nebr., June 17, 1926. Student Wayne State U., 1944-46, Creighton Sch. Law, 1946-48; J.D., U.Wyo., 1954. Bar: Wyo. 1954. Sole practice, Green River, Wyo., 1954-67; ptnr. Marty & Clark, Green River, 1967-74; ptnr. Marty & Ragsdale, Green River, 1975—; judge Green River Mcpl. Ct., 1956-58; U.S. Magistrate Dist. Wyo., 1958—. Alt. del. Rep. Nat. Conv., 1964. Mem. ABA, Wyo. Bar Assn., Sweetwater County Bar Assn. Office: 20 E Flaming Gorge Way Green River WY 82935-4210

MARTY, MARTIN EMIL, religion educator, editor; b. West Point, Nebr., Feb. 5, 1928; s. Emil A. and Anne Louise (Wuerdemann) M.; m. Elsa Schumacher, 1952 (dec. 1981); children: Frances, Joel, John, Peter, James, Micah, Ursula; m. Harriet Lindemann, 1982. MDiv, Concordia Sem., 1952; STM, Luth. Sch. Theology, Chgo., 1954; PhD in Am. Religious and Intellectual History, U. Chgo., 1956; LittD (hon.), Thiel Coll., 1964; LHD (hon.), W.Va. Wesleyan Coll., 1967, Marian Coll., 1967, Providence Coll., 1967; DD (hon.), Muhlenberg Coll., 1967; LittD (hon.), Thomas More Coll., 1968; DD (hon.), Bethany Sem., 1969; LLD (hon.), Keuka Coll., 1972; LHD (hon.), Willamette U., 1974; DD (hon.), Wabash Coll., 1977; LLD (hon.), U. So. Calif., 1977, Valparaiso U., 1978; LHD (hon.), St. Olaf Coll., 1978, De Paul U., 1979; DD (hon.), Christ Sem.-Seminex, 1979, Capital U., 1980; LHD (hon.), Colo. Coll., 1980; DD (hon.), Maryville Coll., 1980, North Park Coll. Sem., 1982; LittD (hon.), Wittenberg U., 1983; LHD, Rosary Coll., 1984; LHD (hon.), Rockford Coll., 1984; DD (hon.), Va. Theol. Sem., 1984; LHD (hon.), Hamilton Coll., 1985, Loyola U., 1986; LLD (hon.), U. Notre Dame, 1987; LHD (hon.), Roanoke Coll., 1987, Mercer U., 1987, Ill. Wesleyan Coll., 1987, Roosevelt U., 1988, Aquinas Coll., 1988; LittD (hon.), Franklin Coll., 1988, U. Nebr., 1993; LHD (hon.), No. Mich. U., 1989, Muskingum Coll., Coe Coll., Lehigh U., 1989, Hebrew Union Coll. and Governors State U., 1990, Whittier Coll., 1991; Calif. Luth. U., 1993; DD (hon.), St. Xavier Coll. and Colgate U., 1990, Mt. Union Coll., 1991, Tex. Luth. Coll., 1991, Aurora U., 1991, Baker U., 1992; LittD (hon.), U. Nebr., 1993; LHD (hon.), Luth. U., 1993; Litt.D, U. Nebr., 1993; LHD, Calif. Luth. U., 1993, Midland Luth. Coll., 1995; DD, Hope Coll., 1993, Northwestern Coll., 1993; LHD (hon.), George Fox Coll., 1994, Drake U., 1994, Centre Coll., 1994; DD, Yale U., 1995, Yale U., 1995. Ordained to ministry Luth. Ch., 1952. Pastor Washington, 1950-51; asst. pastor River Forest, Ill., 1952-56; pastor Elk Grove Village, Ill., 1956-63; prof. history of modern Christianity Div. Sch. U. Chgo., 1963—, Fairfax M. Cone Disting. Service prof., 1978—; assoc. editor Christian Century mag., Chgo., 1956-85, sr. editor, 1985—; co-editor Ch. History mag., 1963—; pres. Park Ridge (Ill.) Ctr.: An Inst. for Study of Health, Faith and Ethics, 1985-89; dir. fundamentalism project Am. Acad. Arts & Scis., 1988—. Author: A Short History of Christianity, 1959, The New Shape of American Relicion, 1959, The Improper Opinion, 1961, The Infidel, 1961, Baptism, 1962, The Hidden Discipline, 1963, Second Chance for American Protestants, 1963, Church Unity and Church Mission, 1964, Varieties of Unbelief, 1964, The Search for a Usable Future, 1969, The Modern Schism, 1969, Righteous Empire, 1970 (Nat. Book award 1971), Protestantism, 1972, You Are Promise, 1973, The Fire We Can Light, 1973, The Pro and Con Book of Religious America, 1975, A Nation of Behavers, 1976, Religion, Awakening and Revolution, 1978, Friendship, 1980, By Way of Response, 1981, The Public Church, 1981, A Cry of Absence, 1983, Health and Medicine in the Lutheran Tradition, 1983, Pilgrims in Their Own Land, 1984, Protestantism in the United States, 1985, Modern American Religion, The Irony of it All, Vol. 1, 1986, An Invitation to American Catholic History, 1986, Religion and Republic, 1987, Modern American Religion. The Noise of Conflict, Vol. 2, 1991, (with R. Scott Appleby) The Glory and the Power, 1992; editor: (with Jerald C. Brauer) The Unrelieved Paradox: Studies in the Theology of Franz Bibfeldt, 1994; editor (jours.) Context, 1969—, Second Opinion, 1990; sr. editor The Christian Century, 1956—; contbr. articles to religious publs. Chmn. bd. regents St. Olaf Coll. Sr. scholar-in-residence The Park Ridge Ctr., 1989—. Fellow Am. Acad. Arts and Scis. (dir. fundamentalism project 1988-94), Soc. Am. Historians; mem. Am. Phil. Soc., Am. Soc. Ch. History (pres. 1971), Am. Cath. Hist(pres. 1981), Am. Acad. Religion (pres. 1987-88), Am. Antiquarian Soc. Home: 239 Scottswood Rd Riverside IL 60546-2223

MARTYAK, JOSEPH J., lawyer; b. Hazleton, Pa.; s. Gabriel S. and Catherine A. (Cranston) M.; m. Vicki Jean Love, July 12, 1980; children: J. Winston, Marisa Love. B.A. cum laude, Georgetown U.; student, Institut d'Etudes Europeennes, Paris; J.D., Georgetown U. Bar: Pa. 1975, D.C. 1975. Legis. asst. to Rep. Daniel Flood, Pa., 1973-75; legis. asst. House Com. on Interstate and Fgn. Commerce, 1975-77; legis. rep. AGA, 1977-79; sr. Washington rep. Union Carbide Corp., 1979-85; prin. dep. under sec. Dept. Interior, Washington, 1985-87; v.p. corp. affairs Rhone-Poulenc Inc., Washington, 1987-96; v.p. public affairs ICI Americas, Washington, 1996—. Mem. ABA, Pa. Bar Assn., D.C. Bar Assn., Club at Franklin Sq., Pisces Club, Capitol Hill Club, Congl. Country Club. Office: ICI Americas Inc 1300 Connecticut Ave NW Ste 901 Washington DC 30036

MARTYL (MRS. ALEXANDER LANGSDORF, JR.), artist; b. St. Louis, Mar. 16, 1918; d. Martin and Aimee (Goldstone) Schweig; m. Alexander Langsdorf, Jr., Dec. 31, 1941; children: Suzanne, Alexandra. A.B., Washington U., St. Louis, 1938. instr. art dept. U. Chgo.; artist in residence Tamarind Inst., U. N.Mex., Albuquerque, 1974. One-man shows include, Calif. Palace of Legion of Honor, 1956, Chgo. Art Inst., 1949, 76, Feingarten Galleries, N.Y.C., Beverly Hills and Chgo., 1961, 62, 63, St. Louis, 1962, Feingarten Gallery, N.Y.C., 1963, Los Angeles, 1964, Kovler Gallery, Chgo., 1967, Washington U., St. Louis, 1967, U. Chgo. Oriental Inst. Mus., 1970, Deson&Zaks Gallery, 1973, Fairweather-Hardin Gallery, 1977, 81, 83, Ill. State Mus., 1978, Fermilab, 1985, 91, Bklyn. Mus., 1986, Oriental Inst. Mus., 1987, Gibbes Art Mus., Charleston, S.C., 1988, Fairweather-Hardin Gallery, 1988, Tokyo Internat. Art Expo, 1990, State of Ill. Art Gallery, Chgo., 1990, Expo Navy Pier, Chgo., 1993, Printworks Gallery Ltd., Chgo., 1995; represented in permanent collections, Met. Mus. Art, Chgo. Art Inst., Pa. Acad. Fine Arts, Ill. State Mus., Bklyn. Mus., DuSable Mus., Chgo., Los Angeles County Mus., Whitney Mus. Am. Art, Davenport (Iowa) Municipal Mus., St. Louis Art Mus., Washington U., U. Ariz., Arnot Gallery, Elmira, N.Y., Greenville (S.C.) Mus., Nat. Coll. Fine Arts, Hirshhorn Mus. and Sculpture Gallery, Rockford (Ill.) Mus. Recipient 1st prize City Art Mus., St. Louis, 1943, 44; Armstrong prize Chgo. Art Inst., 1947; William H. Bartels award, 1953; Frank Logan medal and prize, 1950; Walt Disney purchase award Los Angeles Museum; purchase prize Portrait of America competition, Colo. Springs Fine Arts Center, 1961; honor award for mural AIA, 1962, Outstanding Achievement award in the Arts YWCA, 1986; named Artist of Year Am. Fedn. Arts, 1958. Mem. Chgo. Network, Arts Club (Chgo.), Quadrangle Club (Chgo.). Unitarian. *To be an artist means devoting a lifetime to an intensely difficult activity—one that requires concentration and skill. I've spent my time learning the power of color, line, shape and meaning. I like to think that I have opened out experiences people cannot reveal by themselves.*

MARTZ, JOHN ROGER, lawyer; b. Buffalo, June 13, 1937; s. George Albert and Dorothy (Dinsbier) M.; m. Charlotte Gail Lemberes, July 22, 1966; children: Teresa Gail, Nicole Jackie. BS, U.S. Mil. Acad., 1960; MS in Engring., Purdue U., 1964; JD, U. San Francisco, 1980. Bar: Nev. 1980. Commd. 2d lt. U.S. Army, 1960; nuclear engr. Army Nuclear Power Program, 1964-66; with Spl. Forces in Okinawa, Vietnam, Thailand, Korea, Taiwan,, Philippines, 1966-72; elec. engr. Armed Forces Radiobiology Rsch. Inst. and Def. Nuclear Agy., 1972-75; advisor N.G., Calif. and Nev., 1975-80; ret. U.S. Army, 1980; atty. Henderson & Nelson, Reno, 1980-85; pvt. practice Reno, 1985—. Decorated Bronze Star, Combat Inf. badge; recipient Joint Svc. Commendation medal U.S. Dept. Def., 1975. Mem. Nev. State Bar Assn., Washoe County Bar Assn. Avocations: running, hiking, fishing, motorcycling. Office: 440 Ridge St Reno NV 89501-1718

MARTZ, LAWRENCE STANNARD, periodical editor; b. Bklyn., Apr. 2, 1933; s. Lawrence Stannard Martz and Jean Lee Bailey; m. Anne-Sophie Uldall, May 28, 1955; children: Geoffrey Stannard, Jenny-Anne Horst-Martz. AB, Dartmouth Coll., 1954; postgrad., U. Edinburgh, 1955. Reporter The Pontiac (Mich.) Press, 1955-56, The Detroit News, 1956-59; copy editor The Wall St. Jour., N.Y.C., 1959-60; bus. writer/editor to asst mng. editor, editor internat. editions Newsweek Mag., N.Y.C., 1961-93; editor World Press Rev. Mag., 1993—. Co-author: Ministry of Greed, 1988; author: Making Schools Better, 1992. Recipient J.C. Penney-Mo. award for bus. writing, U. Mo. Sch. of Journalism, 1969, Silver Gavel award ABA, 1990, Media award N.Y. State Bar Assn., 1986. Mem. Am. Soc. Mag. Editors, Overseas Press Club of Am. (bd. dirs. 1994—). Office: World Press Rev 200 Madison Ave New York NY 10016-3903

MARTZ, LOUIS LOHR, English literature educator; b. Berwick, Pa., Sept. 27, 1913; s. Isaiah Louis Bower and Ruth Alverna (Lohr) M.; m. Edwine Montague, June 30, 1941 (dec. 1985); children: Frederick, Louis, Ruth Anne; m. Barbara Stuart, May 5, 1990; children: Olivia, Andrew. AB, Lafayette Coll., 1935, LittD (hon.), 1960; PhD, Yale U., 1939; LHD (hon.), De Pauw U., 1983; LittD (hon.), Siena Coll., 1984. Instr. English Yale U., 1938-44, asst. prof., 1944-48, assoc. prof., 1948-54, prof., 1954-57, Douglas Tracy Smith prof. English and Am. lit., 1957-71, Sterling prof. English, 1971-84, prof. emeritus, 1984—, chmn. dept., 1956-62, 64-65, dir. div. humanities, 1959-62, 80, dir. Beinecke Rare Book and Manuscript Libr., 1972-77, acting master Saybrook Coll., 1978-79, chmn. coll. seminar program, 1968-71, acting dir. Ctr. Brit. Art, 1981; vis. prof. English Georgetown U., 1985-91; vis. prof. English Emory U., 1986-88. Author: The Later Career of Tobias Smollett, 1942, The Poetry of Meditation, 1954, The Paradise Within, 1964, The Poem of the Mind, 1966, The Wit of Love, 1969, Poet of Exile (Milton), 1980, Thomas More: The Search for the Inner Man, 1990, From Renaissance to Baroque: Essays on Literature and Art, 1991; editor: Pilgrim's Progress, 1949, The Meditative Poem, 1963, Milton: Critical Essays, 1966, Anchor Anthology of 17th Century Verse, Vol. I, 1969, (with R. Sylvester) Thomas More's Prayer Book, 1969, Marlowe's Hero and Leander, 1972, (with F. Manley) Thomas More's Dialogue of Comfort, 1976, (with Aubrey Williams) The Author in His Work, 1978, H.D. (Hilda Doolittle) Collected Poems, 1912-1944, 1983, George Herbert and Henry Vaughan, 1986, H.D. Selected Poems, 1988, George Herbert, 1994, Quetzacoatl (D.H. Lawrence), 1995, Henry Vaughan, 1995; mem. editl. bd. Yale Editl. Prose works of John Milton; chmn. Yale Editl. Works of Thomas More; contbr. articles, revs. to Brit. and Am. jours. Recipient Christian Gauss prize, 1955; Guggenheim fellow, 1948-49, 81, Rockefeller fellow, 1966-67, NEH fellow, 1977-78. Mem. Am. Acad. Arts and Scis., Amici Thomae Mori, Renaissance Soc. Am., Brit. Acad., Elizabethan Club, Yale Club (N.Y.C.), Athenaeum Club (London), Phi Beta Kappa, Kappa Delta Rho. Home: 60 Old Quarry Rd Guilford CT 06437-3707 Office: 200994 Yale Sta New Haven CT 06520

MARUMOTO, WILLIAM HIDEO, management consultant; b. L.A., Dec. 16, 1934; s. Harry Y. and Midori Mary (Koyama) M.; m. Jean Masako Morishige, June 14, 1959; children: Wendy H. Vlahos, Todd M., Lani M. Moore, J. Tamiko Smith. BA, Whittier Coll., 1957; postgrad., U. Oreg., 1957-58. Dir. alumni rels. Whittier (Calif.) Coll., 1958-65; assoc. dir. alumni and devel. UCLA, 1965-68; v.p. planning and devel. Calif. Inst. of the Arts, L.A., 1968-69; sr. cons. Peat, Marwick & Mitchell, L.A., 1969; asst. to sec. HEW, Washington, 1969; spl. asst. Pres. of U.S., Washington, 1970-73; pres. The Interface Group Ltd./Boyden, Washington, 1973-89, chmn., 1989—; lectr. on career strategy, planning and diversity, 1973—; mem. White House Pers. Task Force, 1981-88, White House Conf. on Small Bus., 1986. Trustee Whittier Coll., 1978—, Japanese Am. Nat. Mus., 1989—, Mex. Am. Legal Def. and Ednl. Fund, 1989-93, Wolf Trap Found. for Performing Arts, 1995—, Coun. for Advancement and Support Edn., 1980-84; chmn. Nat. Japanese Am. Meml. Found., 1994—, chmn., 1995—; chmn. Leadership Edn. for Asian Pacifics, Inc., 1994—. Named one of Am.'s Top 150 Exec. Recruiters, Harper & Rowe Pubs., 1990, 92, 94. Mem. Assn. Exec. Search Cons. (bd. dirs. 1994—), U.S. Nat. Assn. Corp. and Profl. Recruiters, Employment Mgmt. Assn., Congl. Country Club. Republican. Methodist. Home: 8808 Brook Rd McLean VA 22102-1509 Office: The Interface Group Ltd/ Boyden 2828 Pennsylvania Ave NW Washington DC 20007-3719

MARUOKA, JO ANN ELIZABETH, information systems manager; b. Monrovia, Calif., Jan. 1, 1945; d. John Constantine and Pearl (Macovei) Gotsinas; m. Lester Hideo Maruoka, Nov. 8, 1973 (div. Aug. 1992); stepchildren: Les Scott Kaleohano, Lee Stuart Keola. BA with honors, UCLA, 1966; MBA, U. Hawaii, 1971. Office mgr. and asst. R. Wenkam, Photographer, Honolulu, 1966-69; computer mgmt. intern and sys. analyst Army Computer Sys. Command, Honolulu, 1969-78; reservations mgr. Hale Koa Hotel, Honolulu, 1978-79; equal employment opportunity specialist U.S. Army Pacific Hdqs., Honolulu, 1979-80, computer specialist, 1980-87, supervisory info. sys. mgr., chief plans and programs, 1987—; bd. dirs. High Performance Computing and Comm. Coun., Tiverton, R.I.; pacific v.p. Fedn. Govt. Info. Processing Couns., Washington, 1992-95. Mem. Nat. and Hawaii Women's Polit. Caucus, Honolulu, 1987—; advisor Fed. Women's Coun. Hawaii, Honolulu, 1977—. Mem. NAFE, Nat. Women's Polit. Caucus, AAUW, LWV, Armed Forces Comm.-Electronics Assn. (Hawaii chpt., Internat. award for IRM excellence 1992), Assn. U.S. Army (Pacific Fed. Mgr. award 1990), Federally Employed Women (advisor Aloha and Rainbow chpts. 1977—), Army Signal Corps Regimental Assn., Hawaii Intergovt. Info. Processing Coun. (pres. 1988-89, Svc. award 1989, Fed. 100 of 1996). Democrat. Avocations: travel, reading, tai chi, support of performing arts. Office: APIM-PR US Army Pacific Hdqrs Fort Shafter HI 96858

MARUVADA, PERESWARA SARMA, engineering executive, researcher; b. Rajahmundry, India, Jan. 1, 1938; emigrated to Can., 1964; s. Ramakrishnamma and Meenakshi (Karra) M.; m. Kamakshi Karra, Nov. 28, 1963; children: Venkata Rao, Siva Prasad. B.E. with honors, Coll. Engring., Kakinada, India, 1958; M.E. with distinction, Indian Inst. Sci. (Bangalore), 1959; M.A.Sc., U. Toronto, 1966, Ph.D., 1968. Sr. teaching fellow Indian Inst. Tech., Kharagpur, India, 1959-61; lectr. M.A. Coll. Tech., Bhopal, India, 1961-64; researcher Institute de Recherche d'Hydro-Que., Varennes, Que., 1969-75, program mgr., 1975-81, group mgr., 1981-83, research mgr., 1983-87, sr. researcher, 1987—. Contbr. articles to profl. jours.; patentee in field. Recipient Platinum Jubilee Alumni award Indian Inst. Sci., 1985. Fellow IEEE (exec. chmn. 1996 IEEE/PES Transmission and Distbn. Conf.); mem. Internat. Conf. on Large High Voltage Electric Systems (chmn. study com. 36 on power sys. electromagnetic compatibility), Que. Order Engrs. Home: 817 de Serigny, Boucherville, PQ Canada J4B 5C5 Office: Institut de Recherche d'Hydro-Que, 1800 Montee Sainte-Julie, Varennes, PQ Canada J3X 1S1

MARVEL, L. PAIGE, lawyer; b. Easton, Md., Dec. 6, 1949; d. E. Warner Marvel and Louise Harrington Harrison; m. Robert H. Dyer, Jr., Aug. 9, 1975; children: Alex W. Dyer, Kelly E. Dyer. BA magna cum laude, Notre Dame Coll., 1971; JD with honors, U. Md., 1974. Bar: Md. 1974, U.S. Dist. Ct. Md. 1974, U.S. Tax Ct. 1975, U.S. Ct. Appeals (4th cir.) 1977, U.S. Supreme Ct. 1980, U.S. Ct. Claims 1981, D.C. 1985. Assoc. atty. Gabris & Schwait, Balt., 1974-76; shareholder Garbis & Schwait, Balt., 1976-85, Garbis, Marvel & Junghans, Balt., 1985-86, Melnicove, Kaufman, Weiner, Smouse & Garbis, Balt., 1986-88; ptnr. Venable, Baetjer and Howard LLP, Balt., 1988—; bd. dirs. IRS Commr.'s Rev. Panel on IRS Integrity Controls, Washington, 1989-91, Commn. to Revise Annotated Code of Md.; mem. U. Md. Bd. Vis., 1995—; mem. adv. com. U.S. Dist. Ct. Md., 1991-93. Co-editor procedure dept. Jour. Taxation, 1989—; contbr. chpts. to books, articles to profl. jours. Active Women's Law Ctr., 1974-85, Md. Dept. Econ. and Community Devel. Adv. Comm., 1978-80. Recipient Recognition award Balt. is Best Program, 1981,. Fellow Am. Bar Found., Am. Coll. Tax Counsel (regent); mem. ABA (sect. taxation coun. dir. 1989-92, vice-chair com. ops. 1993-95, Disting. Svc. award), Md. Bar Assn. (taxation sect. chair 1982-83, Disting. Svc. award), Md. Bar Found., Balt. Bar Assn. (mem.-at-large exec. coun.), J. Edgar Murdock Am. Inns of Ct., Serjeant's Inn, Rule Day Club. Avocations: golf, music, travel. Home: 7109 Sheffield Rd Baltimore MD 21212-1628 Office: Venable Baetjer & Howard LLP 2 Hopkins Plz Baltimore MD 21201-2930

MARVEL, THOMAS STAHL, architect; b. Newburgh, N.Y., Mar. 15, 1935; s. Gordon Simis and Madelyn Emigh (Jova) M.; m. Lucilla Wellington Fuller, Apr. 19, 1958; children—Deacon Simis, Jonathan Jova, Thomas Stahl. A.B., Dartmouth Coll., 1956; M.Arch., Harvard U., 1962. Registered architect, N.C., P.R., Mass., N.Y. Designer Synergetics, Inc., Raleigh, N.C., 1958; designer IBEC Housing, N.Y.C., 1959; ptnr.-architect Torres-Beauchamp-Marvel, San Juan, P.R., 1960-85, Marvel-Flores-Cobian, San Juan, P.R., 1985—; prof. Sch. Architecture, U. P.R., Rio Piedras, 1967-89. Author: Antonin Nechodoma, Architect, 1994; co-author: Parish Churches of Puerto Rico, 1984. Works include Am. Embassy, Guatemala, 1973, U.S. Courthouse and Fed. Office Bldg., V.I., 1976, City Hall, Bayamon, P.R., 1978, Mcpl. Baseball Stadium, Bayamon, 1975, Am. Embassy, Costa Rica, 1986. Bd. dirs. St. John's Sch., San Juan, 1976-93. Recipient 1st award for regional coll. design U. P.R., Utuado, 1983; Harvard Grad. Sch. Design Julia Amory Appleton travelling fellow, 1962, Henry Klumb prize, 1991. Fellow AIA (awards for design Fla. Caribbean region 1981, 84-85, 90-91); mem. P.R. Coll. Architects, Acad. Arts and Scis. Roman Catholic. Club: Harvard (N.Y.C.). Home: Del Valle 450 San Juan PR 00915 Office: Marvel-Flores-Cobian 1555 Calle Francia Santurce San Juan PR 00911-1979

MARVIN, CHARLES RODNEY, JR., lawyer; b. Elizabeth, N.J., Feb. 26, 1953; s. Charles Rodney Sr. and Doris Marie (Richards) M.; m. Carol Ann Welteroth, Aug. 30, 1975; children: Kathryn, Kristin, Cynthia, Gregory. BA in Econs., Mich. State U., 1975; JD, Boston U., 1978; LLM in Mil. Law, Judge Advocate Gen. Sch., 1987; LLM in Govt. Contracts, George Washington U., 1995. Bar: N.J. 1982, U.S. Dist. Ct. N.J. 1982, U.S. Ct. Mil. Appeals 1982, U.S. Ct. Appeals (fed. cir.) 1994. Officer nuclear missile U.S. Army, Schwaebisch, Germany, 1979-82; mil. prosecutor U.S. Army, Fort Sill, Okla., 1983-86; sr. def. counsel U.S. Army Tr. Def. Svc., Ft. Polk, La., 1987-89; trial counsel, chief protest br. U.S. Army Contract Appeals Divsn., Arlington, Va., 1990-94; of counsel Venable, Baetjer, Howard & Civiletti, Washington, 1994—. Mem. ABA (vice-chair, bid protest com., pub. contract law sect. 1992-93), Bd. Contract Appeals Bar Assn. (bd. govs. 1993-96), Fed. Cir. Bar Assn., FBA. Roman Catholic. Avocations: musical composing, adult education, golf, woodworking. Office: Venable Baetjer et al # 1000 1201 New York Ave NW Washington DC 20005-3917

MARVIN, DAVID KEITH, international relations educator; b. Lincoln, Nebr., Apr. 8, 1921; s. Henry Howard and Alma (Wright) M.; m. Frances Parks Cash, Dec. 14, 1946; children: Margaret Elaine, Keith Wright, Martha Jean. B.A., U. Nebr., 1943; M.A., Northwestern U., 1955, Ph.D., 1957. Mem. UNRRA, Austrian Mission, 1946; vice consul Am. Fgn. Service, Peiping, 1947-50; 2d sec. London, 1950-53; consul Dar-es-Salaam, 1953; Ford Found. fellow Tanganyika, 1956-58; vis. asst. prof. Northwestern U., 1958; asst. prof. San Francisco State U., 1958-62, assoc. prof., 1962-67, prof., 1967—, asst. chmn. social sci. div., 1960-64, chmn. dept. internat. relations, 1964-70, 77-78, 80-84, prof. emeritus, 1986—; vis. prof. U. Calif. at Berkeley, 1967. Author: Emerging Africa in World Affairs, 1965. Chmn. North Coastside Community Council, 1962-64; Bd. dirs. Diablo Valley Edn. Project. Served with inf. AUS, 1943-46. Fellow African Studies Assn.; mem. Phi Beta Kappa. Office: 467 Urbano Dr San Francisco CA 94127-2862

MARVIN, DOUGLAS RAYMOND, lawyer; b. E. Stroudsburg, Pa., Aug. 20, 1947; s. Lester Daniel and Merle Catherine (Loeb) M.; m. Judith Ann; children: Douglas R. Jr., Drew, Carrie, Jill. A.B., Lafayette Coll., 1969; J.D., U. Va., 1972. Bar: Va. 1972, Pa. 1972, D.C. 1977, U.S. Supreme Ct. 1977. Atty.-adv. office of legal counsel U.S. Dept. Justice, Washington, 1972-74; counsel subcom. on criminal laws and procedure Senate Jud. Com., U.S. Senate, Washington, 1974; counsel Senate Jud. Com., 1974; counselor to

Atty. Gen. U.S., 1975-77; ptnr. firm Williams & Connolly, Washington, 1977—. Bd. dirs. Braddock Rd. Youth Club. Recipient spl. commendation for outstanding service Atty. Gen., Dept. Justice, 1973. Mem. Am. Law Inst., Am. Bar Assn. (litigation sect.), Va. Bar Assn., Pa. Bar Assn., D.C. Bar Assn., Order of Coif. Home: 4501 Demby Dr Fairfax VA 22032-1728 Office: 839 17th St NW Washington DC 20006-3902

MARVIN, JAMES CONWAY, librarian, consultant; b. Warroad, Minn., Aug. 3, 1927; s. William C. and Isabel (Carlquist) M.; m. Patricia Katharine Moe, Sept. 8, 1947; children: Heidi C., James Conway, Jill C., Jack C. B.A., U. Minn., 1950, M.A., 1966. City librarian Kaukauna, Wis., 1952-54; chief librarian Eau Claire, Wis., 1954-56; dir. Cedar Rapids (Iowa) Pub. Library, 1956-67, Topeka Pub. Library, 1967-92; Am. Library Assn.-Rockefeller Found. vis. prof. Inst. Library Sci. U. Philippines, 1964-65; vis. lectr. dept. librarianship Emporia (Kans.) State U., 1970-80; chmn. Kans. del. to White House Conf. on Libraries and Info. Services, Gov.'s Com. on Library Resources, 1980-81; mem. Kans. State Libr. Adv. Commn., 1992—. Served with USNR, 1945-46. Mem. ALA, Iowa Libr. Assn. (past pres.), Kans. Libr. Assn., Philippine Libr. Assn. (life), Mountain Plains Libr. Assn. Home: 40 SW Pepper Tree Ln Topeka KS 66611-2055

MARVIN, OSCAR MCDOWELL, retired hospital administrator; b. Statesville, N.C., Apr. 12, 1924; s. Oscar McDowell and Gladys (Early) M.; m. Jane Everitt Krauss, June 16, 1951 (div. 1975); children: Frederick McDowell, Elizabeth Anne, Robert Doyle; m. Marcia Ann Benefiel Jackson, Dec. 2, 1977; children: Jonathan Paul, Katherine Susanne. A.B., U. N.C., 1948; M.B.A., U. Chgo., 1953; M.S., U. Louisville, 1971. Foreman Hanes Dye & Finishing Co., Winston-Salem, N.C., 1948-51; adminstrv. resident N.C. Bapt. Hosp., Winston-Salem, 1952-53; asst. adminstr. City Meml. Hosp., Winston-Salem, 1953-55, N.C. Med. Care Commn., Raleigh, 1955-57; hosp. adminstr., missionary Bd. World Missions, Presbyn. Ch. U.S., Yodogawa Christian Hosp., Osaka, Japan, 1957-60; asst. adminstr. City Memphis Hosp., 1960-62, adminstr., 1962-68; exec. dir. Louisville Med. Ctr., Inc., 1968-93, Med. Ctr. Commn. Jefferson County, 1982-93; lectr. dept. preventive medicine U. Tenn., 1963-68; assoc. prof. Coll. Pharmacy, 1965-68; organizer N.C. chpt. Hosp. Accts., 1954, pres., 1955-56; treas. Memphis Hosp. Coun., 1963, v.p., 1964, pres., 1965; sec. Memphis Inst. Medicine and Religion, 1966-68; sec.-treas. Assn. Coop. Hosp. Laundries, 1970-71; bd. dirs. Nat. Assn. Hosp. Hospitality Houses, Inc., 1986-93, v.p., 1990-91; sec., bd. dirs. Louisville Med. Ctr. Fed. Credit Union, 1974-92, Med. Ctr. Hospitality House, Inc., 1988-93. Contbr. articles to profl. jours. Mem. Memphis Mayor's Com. to Employ Handicapped, 1963; chmn. hosp. divsn. Shelby United Neighbors, Memphis, 1965; trustee Med. Benevolence Found., 1971; pres. Jefferson County Assn. Children with Learning Disabilities, 1973-74, Ky. Assn. Children with Learning Disabilities, 1974-78; sec., bd. dirs. Butchertown Neighborhood Assn., 1992—. Served with AUS, 1942-45. Mem. Am. Coll. Health Care Execs., Sigma Nu. Presbyterian (deacon, elder). Clubs: Rotary, Belles 'n Beau's Square Dance (pres. 1983-84). Home: 225 Bramton Rd Louisville KY 40207-3419

MARVIN, ROY MACK, foundry executive; b. Aberdeen, Wash., May 4, 1931; s. Merrill McKinley and Jennie Marie (Larsen) M.; B.S., Lewis and Clark Coll., 1954; A.S., Grays Harbor Coll., 1951; m. Diane Valeri MacKenzie, Nov. 26, 1955. Acct., Pope, Loback & Co., Portland, Oreg., 1953-54, 56-59; controller Ranch Homes, Inc., Beaverton, Oreg., 1959-61; controller, Precision Castparts Corp., Portland, Oreg., 1961-70, treas., 1967-93, dir., 1967—, v.p. fin., 1970-80, v.p. adminstrn., 1980—, sec., 1983—, dir. Physicians Assn. Clackamas County, Providence, Milwaukie, Oreg. Bd. dirs. Dwyer Hosp., 1970-79, 84-86; mem. exec. com. Greater Portland Bus. Group on Health; mem. Clackamas County Econ. Devel. Commn., 1984-91, dep. Oreg. Bus. Coun., 1982-90; bd. dirs Boys and Girls Aid Soc. Oreg., 1990—. Served with U.S. Army, 1954-56. C.P.A., Oreg. Mem. Nat. Assn. Accts. (past pres. Portland chpt.), Planning Execs. Inst. (past pres. Portland chpt.), AICPA, Fin. Execs. Inst., Oreg. Soc. C.P.A.s, Associated Oreg. Industries (bd. dirs., vice chmn. 1992-94), Assoc. Oreg. Indus. Pol. Action Com., (pres. 1991, trustee), North Clackamas C. of C. (pres. 1973), Oreg. Metals Industry Coun. (pres. 1991-94). Republican. Presbyterian. Club: Multnomah Athletic. Office: Precision Castparts Corp 4600 SE Harney Dr Portland OR 97206-0825

MARVIN, WILLIAM GLENN, JR., former foreign service officer; b. Dobbs Ferry, N.Y., Oct. 30, 1920; s. William Glenn and Charlotte (Linden) M.; m. Sheila Wells, June 6, 1945 (dec.); children: Sally Marvin Lockhart, William Glenn III (dec.), Wells.; m. Suzanne Franzon, Oct. 16, 1982. Student, U. Calif., Berkeley, 1938-40; B.S., Harvard U., 1942; M.A., Stanford U., 1948. European rep. Hoover Instn., 1948-49; polit. scientist Stanford Research Inst., 1949-52; commd. fgn. service officer Dept. State, 1952; vice consul Algiers, 1952-55; consul Berlin, 1955-60; consul, prin. officer Fort de France, Martinique, 1964-66; econ. sec. CENTO, Ankara, Turkey, 1974-76; consul gen. Bordeaux, France, 1977-80; ret., 1980. Served to capt. U.S. Army, 1942-46. Mem. U.S. Fgn. Service Assn., Assn. Bordeaux-L.A. Clubs: Connetablie de Guyenne, Ordre de Tursan.

MARVIT, ROBERT CHARLES, psychiatrist; b. Lynn, Mass., Jan. 23, 1938. BS summa cum laude, Mass. Coll. Pharmacy, 1960; MD, Tufts U., 1964; M.Sc., Harvard U., 1970. Intern New Eng. Med. Ctr., Pratt Diag. Hosp., 1964-65; resident in psychiatry, neuropsychol. medicine Mass. Gen. Hosp., Boston, 1967-70; pvt. practice medicine, specializing psychiatry Honolulu, 1970—; prof. pub. health U. Hawaii, Honolulu, 1974-78, adj. prof. Sch. Pub. Health, 1978—; forensic advisor Hawaii Mental Health Div., 1977—; dir. Health Info. Sys. Office, Dept. Health, 1976-80; cons. in field; lectr. in field. Contbr. articles to profl. jours. Served with USPHS, 1965-67 to lt. comdr. Recipient Alpha Omega Alpha Research award Tufts U., 1963. Fellow Am. Coll. Preventive Medicine, Internat. Soc. Social Psychiatry of Am. Pub. Health Assn., Am. Psychiat. Soc.; mem. Am. Acad. Psychiatry and the Law, Hawaii Psychiat. Soc., AAAS, Harvard Med. Soc., Boston Soc. Neurology and Psychiatry, Hawaii Neurol. Soc., Internat. Soc. Neurosci., Am. Acad. Forensic Psychiatry, Alpha Omega Alpha. Home: 929 Pueo St Honolulu HI 96816-5234 Office: 1314 S King St Ste 759 Honolulu HI 96814-1942

MARWEDEL, WARREN JOHN, lawyer; b. Chgo., July 3, 1944; s. August Frank and Eleanor (Wolgamot) M.; m. Marilyn Baran, Apr. 12, 1975. BS in Marine Engring., U.S. Merchant Marine Acad., 1966; JD, Loyola U., Chgo., 1972. Bar: Ill. 1972, U.S. Dist. Ct. (no. dist.) Ill. 1972, U.S. Supreme Ct. 1974. With U.S. Merchant Marines, 1966-70; ptnr. Keck, Mahin & Cate, Chgo. Served to lt. (j.g.) USNR. Mem. ABA (Ho. of Dels. 1989—), Ill. Bar Assn., Chgo. Bar Assn., Maritime Law Assn. Club: Propellor (Chgo.) (pres. 1982). Avocations: boating, reading, history. Office: Keck Mahin & Cate 77 W Wacker Dr Chicago IL 60601-1629

MARWELL, GERALD, sociology educator, research consultant; b. NYC, Feb. 12, 1937; s. Hilton M. and Pearl (Berman) M.; m. Barbara Epstein, June 16, 1957. B.S., MIT, 1957; M.A., NYU, 1959, Ph.D., 1964. Asst. prof. U. Wis., Madison, Wis., 1963-68, assoc. prof., 1968-71, prof., 1971—, chmn. dept. sociology, 1982-85; vis. rsch. assoc. Internat. Peace Rsch. Inst., Oslo, 1969-70; vis. prof. U. Oslo, 1970, U. Essex, Colchester, Eng., 1978-79, Columbia U., 1989; chief cons. radio programs Sound Studies in Sociology, 1982-84 (recipient Ohio State award 1985). Author: Dynamics of Idealism, 1971; Cooperation: An Experimental Analysis, 1975, Self-Esteem: Its Conceptualization and Measurement, 1976, The Critical Mass in Collective Action, 1993; editor Am. Sociol. Rev., 1990-93; contbr. articles to profl. jours. Vol. cons. Madison Metro Sch. System, 1984; coach Madison Youth Soccer Assn. Avocation: fantasy baseball. Home: 3509 Blackhawk Dr Madison WI 53705-1477 Office: U Wis Sociology Dept 1180 Observatory Dr Madison WI 53706-1320 Office: Am Sociological Assn Am Sociological Review 1722 N St NW Washington DC 20036-2983

MARX, ANNE (MRS. FREDERICK E. MARX), poet; came to U.S., 1936, naturalized, 1938; d. Jacob and Susan (Weinberg) Loewenstein; m. Frederick E. Marx, Feb. 12, 1937; children: Thomas J., Stephen L. Student, U. Heidelberg, U. Berlin. mem. staffs N.Y.C. Writers Conf., 1965, Iona Coll., 1964, 65, 70, Wagner Coll., 1965, Poetry Workshop, Fairleigh Dickinson U., 1962, 63, 64, Poetry Soc. Am. Workshop, 1970-71, 78-79; Bronxville Adult Sch. Lecture Series, 1972; bd. dir. poetry series Donnell Library Ctr. (N.Y. Pub. Library), 1970-74; poetry day chmn. Westchester County, 1959—; Poetry Day Workshop, Ark., 1966, 70, Ark. Writers Conf., 1971, South and West Conf., Okla., 1972; vis. poet So. U., 1979; tchr., poetry readings, Jakarta, Indonesia, summer 1979; poetry workshop leader Scarsdale Cultural Ctr., 1981-82; conv. speaker Nat. Fedn. State Poetry Socs., 1974, 81, 82; condr. symposium Immigrant Voices, Pa. State U., 1986; judge Chapbook Award, 1994; judge various nat. poetry contests. Poet; more than 1500 poems published in nat. mags., anthologies, lit. jours. and newspapers; Author: Ein Buechlein, 1935, Into the Wind of Waking, 1960, The Second Voice, 1963, By Grace of Pain, 1966, By Way of People, 1970, A Time to Mend; selected poems, 1973; A Conversation with Anne Marx; 2 hour talking book for blind, 1974; Hear of Israel and Other Poems, 1975, 40 Love Poems for 40 Years, 1977, Face Lifts for All Seasons, 1980, 45 Love Poems for 45 Years, 1982, Holocaust: Hurts to Healings, 1984, German edit. Wunden und Narben, 1986; A Further Semester, 1985, Love in Late Season (New Poems by Anne Marx), 1993; co-editor: Pegasus in the Seventies, 1973; contbr. to American Women Poets Discuss Their Craft, 1983, The Courage to Grow Old, 1989, A Collection of Essays by Ballantine Books, 1989; nat. editor poetry recs., Lamont Library at Harvard, stas. WFAS, WRNW, WEVD, WRVR, Voice of Am., The Pen Woman, 1986-88, Christian Sci. Monitor Anthology of Poems, 1989, Canadian Anthology, 1991, Irish Anthology, 1991. Recipient Am. Weave Chapbook award 1960, Nat. Sonnet 1959, 67, 81, award World Order Narrative Poets, 1981-85 1959, 67, prizes Nat. Fedn. Women's Clubs 1959, 60, Nat. Fedn. State Poetry Socs. 1962, 65, 66, 73, 80-83, South and West Publn. award 1965, Greenwood prize Eng. 1966, 2d Ann. Viola Hayes Parsons award 1977, award Delbrook Center Advanced Studies 1978, 1st prize Nat. Essay Competition, 1990, N.Y. State Outstanding Writer award, 1991; named Poet of the Year N.Y. Poetry Forum, 1981; winner Chapbook competition Crossroads Press, 1984, Ann. Writer's Digest award, 1983-90. Mem. Poetry Soc. Am. (life, exec. bd. 1965-70, v.p. 1971-72, 2 fellowships, Cecil Hemley Meml. award 1974), Poetry Soc. Gt. Britain, Nat. League Am. Pen Women (pres. Westchester county br. 1962-64, North Atlantic regional chmn. 1964-66, nat. letters bd. 1972-74, biennial poetry workshop leader, nat. poetry editor 1974-78, N.Y. State lit. chmn. 1979-80, N.Y. State pres. 1982-84, 2d nat. v.p. 1984-86, nat. editor Pen Woman mag. 1986-88, contbg. editor 1990—, Biennial Book award 1976, Biennial awards (4), 1982, (2), 1984, Writer of Yr. 1991, N.Y. State Poetry award 1995), Acad. Am. Poets, Poet Soc. Pa., Composers, Authors and Artists Am., Inc. (poetry editor mag. 1973-78), Poets and Writers, Inc., N.Y. Poetry Forum (life). Subject of story "An American by Choice, A Poet's Credo" pub. in The PEN Woman mag., Nov. 1988, The Courage to Grow Old, 1989, N.Y. Times interview "Finding Poetry in All of Life's Events," 1993; collected works N.Y. Pub. Libr.: Anne Marx Archives, 1992, early German material added to collection, 1994. *To be undeterred is the key to any achievement that is important to our lives. Undeterred by detractors asserting that one's goal is impossible to reach. Undeterred by blame or praise. Undeterred by demands of custom and fashion. Undeterred by all but the most essential bonds of family and friends. Undeterred even by the knowledge that there will be no greatness at the end of the long climb - only the satisfaction that we have tried to bring out the best that is in us, that we have added to our years that special ingredient we needed most to add zest to existence.*

MARX, ARTHUR, author, playwright, director; b. N.Y.C., July 21, 1921; s. Groucho and Ruth (Johnson) M.; m. Irene Kahn, Feb. 27, 1943 (div. 1960); children: Steve, Andy; m. Lois Goldberg, June 27, 1961. Student, U. So. Calif., 1939-40. Copywriter Hal Horne Agy., 1941. Radio comedy writer Milton Berle Show, 1942, Sealtest Show, 1942, Edgar Bergen Show, 1948; writer: (films) Blondie in the Dough, 1947, Pete Smith Specialties, 1949-50 (MGM one real short subjects), A Global Affair, 1964, I'll Take Sweden, 1965, Eight on the Lam, 1967, Cancel My Reservation, 1972; free-lance mag. writer for Parade, N.Y. Times Mag., Sports Illustrated, Cosmopolitan, L.A. Mag., Cigar Aficionado, others; Broadway playwright: The Impossible Years, 1965, Minnie's Boys, 1970, My Daughter's Rated X, 1971, Groucho: A Life in Review, 1986; mus. adaptation of the Ghost and Mrs. Muir, 1987; dir.: Groucho: A Life in Review; author: (books) The Ordeal of Willie Brown, 1950, Life With Groucho, 1954, Not as a Crocodile, 1958, Son of Groucho, 1972, Everybody Loves Somebody Sometime, 1974, Goldwyn, 1976, Red Skelton, 1979, The Nine Lives of Mickey Rooney, 1986, My Life With Groucho, 1988, Set to Kill, 1993, The Secret Life of Bob Hope, 1993; exec story editor, writer (TV series) Alice, 1977-81, TV segments All in the Family, McHale's Navy, Life With Lucy. Served with USCG, 1942-45, PTO. Mem. Dramatists Guild, Authors Guild, Writers Guild Am., West, Acad. Motion Picture Arts and Scis., Internat. Assn. Crime Writers. Jewish. U.S. Intercollegiate Freshman Tennis Champion, 1940. Office: c/o Scovil Chichak & Galen Ste 1020 381 Park Ave S New York NY 10016

MARX, DAVID, JR., lawyer; b. Chgo., Nov. 15, 1950. BA cum laude, Amherst Coll., 1972; JD, Syracuse U., 1975. Bar: N.Y. 1976, Ill. 1986. Ptnr. McDermott, Will & Emery, Chgo. Mem. ABA, Chgo. Bar Assn. Office: McDermott Will & Emery 227 W Monroe St 31st Fl Chicago IL 60606-5016*

MARX, GERTIE FLORENTINE, anesthesiologist; b. Frankfurt am Main, Germany, Feb. 13, 1912; came to U.S., 1937, naturalized, 1943; d. Joseph and Elsa (Scheuer) M.; m. Eric P. Reiss, Sept. 26, 1940 (dec. 1968). Student, U. Frankfurt, Germany, 1931-36; M.D., U. Bern, Switzerland, 1937. Diplomate: Nat. Bd. Med. Examiners, Am. Bd. Anesthesiology. Intern, resident in anesthesiology Beth Israel Hosp., N.Y.C., 1939-43; adj. anesthesiologist Beth Israel Hosp., 1943-50, assoc. anesthesiologist, 1950-55; attending anesthesiologist Bronx Municipal Hosp. Center, 1955-95; attending anesthesiologist Bronx VA Hosp., 1966-72, cons., 1972-84; asst. prof. anesthesiology Albert Einstein Coll. Medicine, 1955-60, assoc. prof., 1960-70, prof., 1970-95, prof. emeritus, 1995—. Author: (with Orkin) Physiology of Obstetric Anesthesia, 1969; assoc. editor: Survey Anesthesiology, 1957-83; editor: Parturition and Perinatology, 1973, Clinical Management of Mother and Newborn, 1979, (with G. M. Bassell) Obstetric Analgesia and Anesthesia, 1980, Obstetric Anesthesia Digest, 1981—; cons. editor Internat. Jour. Obstetric Anesthesia, 1991—; contbr. articles to profl. jours. Recipient Nils Lofgren award, 1990, Coll. medal Royal Coll. Anaesthetists, 1993. Fellow Am. Coll. Anesthesiology, N.Y. Acad. Medicine, Am. Coll. Obstetricians and Gynecologists; mem. AMA, Am. Soc. Anesthesiologists (Disting. Svc. award 1988), N.Y. State Soc. Anesthesiologists, Am. Soc. Regional Anesthesia (Disting. Svc. award 1990), Bronx County Med. Soc., N.Y. Acad. Scis. Home: 642A Heritage Vlg Southbury CT 06488-1551 Office: Albert Einstein Coll Medicine Dept Anesthesiology Bronx NY 10461 *I have devoted my professional life to easing the discomfort of childbirth and dare to hope that my efforts have helped to improve the outcome of pregnancy for mother and baby.*

MARX, KATHRYN, photographer, author; b. N.Y.C., June 4, 1950; d. Arthur and Emilie (Hyman) M. Freelance journalist, photographer N.Y. Newsday, N.Y. Daily News, Village Voice, Soho News, 1974-82, Infinito Mag., Italy, 1986; photographer Photo-Reporter, Paris, 1986, Editions Paris-Musées, 1992. Photography exhbns. include Le Grand Palais, Paris, 1991, U.S. Embassy, Brussels, 1990, Carnavalet Mus., Paris, 1992, N.Y. Pub. Libr., 1992, Mus. Modern Art, Paris, 1994, exhbn. of mobiles Galerie Monde de L'Art, 1996; author: Photography for the Art Market, 1988, Right Brain/Left Brain Photography, 1994; collaborator (with author Michael S. Lasky) The Complete Junkfood Book, 1974-76; contbr. articles to profl. jours. Rape crisis counselor St. Vincents Hosp., N.Y.C., 1981-83; active ACLU, N.Y.C., 1974-76; mem. Plan Internat. Foster Program, R.I., 1992—. Grantee Acad. Am. Poets, 1982, Eastman Kodak Co., Paris, N.Y., 1992-96, Fuji Film France, Paris, 1991-94, Sernam Corp., Paris, 1992-97. Mem. Author's Guild, Author's League of Am. Democrat. Avocations: painting, sculpture, yoga, birds, philosophy. Home: 61 Jane St New York NY 10014-5107 Office: 77 rue Notre Dame Des Champs, 75006 Paris France

MARX, MORRIS LEON, academic administrator; b. New Orleans, May 21, 1937. BS in Math., Tulane U., 1959, MS in Math., 1963, PhD, 1964. Asst. prof. math. Vanderbilt U., 1966-69, assoc. prof., 1969-77, dir. grad. studies in math., 1970-72; prof. math., chmn. dept. U. Okla., 1977-81, assoc. dean coll. of arts and scis., 1981-84, interim dean coll. of arts and scis., 1984-85; vice chancellor acad. affairs, prof. math. U. Miss., 1985-88; pres., prof. math. U. West Fla., Pensacola, 1988—. 1st lt. U.S. Army, 1964-65, capt., 1965-66. Office: U West Fla Office of President Pensacola FL 32514-0101

MARX, NICKI DIANE, sculptor, painter; b. L.A., Oct. 3, 1943; d. Donald F. and Ruth H. (Ungar) M. Undergrad., U. Calif., Riverside, 1965, U. Calif., Santa Cruz, 1973. Represented by Tally Richards Gallery, Taos, N.Mex., Lumina Gallery, Taos, N.Mex., Fred Kline Gallery, Santa Fe, N.Mex. One-woman shows include Palm Springs Desert Mus., 1977, Julie Artisans Gallery, N.Y.C., 1975, Phoenix Art Mus., 1975, Weston Gallery, Carmel, Calif., 1981, Kirk de Gooyer Gallery, L.A., 1982, Rocklands Gallery, Monterey, Calif., 1983, Fetish Gallery, Taos, 1988, Fenix Gallery, Taos, 1991, Earthworks, 1993, Lamberts, 1994, Stables Gallery, Taos, 1995, Fred Kline, 1995, others; group exhbns. include E.P. Smith Gallery, Santa Cruz, 1994, Lumina Gallery, Taos, 1994, Cafe Gallery, Albuquerque, 1991, Bareiss Gallery, Taos, 1990, Ctr. for Contemporary Art, Santa Fe, 1989, Jordan Gallery, Taos, N.Mex., 1988, 89, Stables Art Gallery, Taos, 1988, 94, Albuquerque State Fair Grounds, 1986, San Francisco Mus. Modern Art, 1977, 78, The Elements Gallery, Greenwich, Conn., 1977, Pacific Design Ctr., L.A., 1976, Lester Gallery, Inverness, Calif., 1976, numerous others; work included in sixteen invitational shows; represented in pub. collections IBM, Milford, Conn., N.Y.C., San Jose, Calif., Bank of Am., San Francisco, The Continental Group, Inc., Stamford, Conn., Cedars-Sinai Hosp., L.A., Farm Bur. Fedn., Sacramento, Calif., Sherman Fairchild Sci. Ctr., Stanford, Calif., Palm Springs (Calif.) Desert Mus., Univ. Mus., Ariz. State U. at Tempe, Mills Coll. Art Gallery, Berkeley, Calif.; exhibited in pvt. collections of Estate of Eugene Klein, Estate of Louise Nevelson, Estate of Georgia O'Keeffe, Fritz Scholder, Ray Graham, Bunny Horowitz, Sue and Otto Meyer, Burt Sugarman, Craig Moody, Paul Pletka, others; subject of numerous articles in jours. and mags. MacDowell Colony fellow, 1975; recipient Adolph and Esther Gottleib Found. grant, 1985. Studio: PO Box 1135 Ranchos De Taos NM 87557-1135

MARX, OWEN COX, lawyer; b. Grosse Pointe, Mich., Oct. 17, 1947; s. Leo A. and Anne (Cox) M.; m. Patricia Windschill, Aug. 14, 1971; children: Patrick Cox, Molly Simser, Anne Windschill. BA, Coll. of St. Thomas, St. Paul, 1969; JD, Cath. U., Washington, 1972. Bar: Minn. 1972, N.Y. 1973. Law clk. to presiding justice Minn. Supreme Ct., St. Paul, 1972-73; assoc. Mudge, Rose, Guthrie & Alexander, N.Y.C., 1973-75; assoc. Dorsey & Whitney, Mpls., 1975-78, ptnr., 1979-86; ptnr., head London office Dorsey & Whitney, 1986-90; ptnr. Dorsey & Whitney, N.Y.C., 1990—; bd. dirs. Bush Mfg. Co., Detroit, Off Site Tech. Inc., Detroit, OFLA Receivables Corp., San Diego. Mem. Internat. Bar Assn., Minn. Bar Assn., Mpls. Athletic Club, N.Y. Athletic Club. Republican. Roman Catholic. Home: 136 E 79th St New York NY 10021-0328 Office: Dorsey & Whitney 350 Park Ave New York NY 10022-6022

MARX, PAUL BENNO, author, social service administrator, missionary; b. Saint Michael, Minn., May 8, 1920; s. George and Elizabeth Marx. PhD in Family Sociology, Cath. U. Am., 1957. Ordained priest Roman Cath. Ch., 1947. Worldwide prolife missionary; founder, exec. dir. Human Life Ctr., 1972-80; founder, chmn. bd., pres. Human Life Internat., 1980—; prof. sociology S. John's U., Collegeville, Minn., 1957-80. Author: Virgil Michel and the Liturgical Movement, 1957, The Mercy Killers, 1971, The Death Peddlers: War on the Unborn, 1972, Japanese edit., 1972, Spanish edit., 1973, Death without Dignity: Killing for Mercy, 1983, And Now Euthanasia. . ., 1985, Confessions of a Prolife Missionary, 1988, Fighting for Life, 1989, The Flying Monk, 1991; contbr. numerous chpts. to books and articles to jours.; founder (quars.) The Internat. Rev. Natural Family Planning, Human Life Issues, Sorrow's Reward, (bi-monthlies) Escoge la Vida!, Seminarians for Life International; (monthly) Pro-Family Parish Notes. Mem. Internat. Fedn. for Family Life Promotion, Japan Found. for Family Life Promotion. Home: 7845 Airpark Rd Gaithersburg MD 20879-4124

MARX, SHARON ROSE, health facility administrator; b. Ferndale, Mich., Dec. 11, 1951; d. William Bernard and Evelyn Grace (Culbert) M. Student, U. Mich., 1970-72; BSN, U. Tex., Galveston, 1975; MS, U. Colo., Denver, 1984. RNC, cert. ob/gyn. nurse practitioner. Staff nurse John Sealy Hosp., Galveston, 1975, Harper Grace Hosp., Detroit, 1975-77, Hutzel Hosp., Detroit, 1977-79; office nurse Sellers & Sanders Clinic, New Orleans, 1979-82; clin. mgr. Rocky Mountain Hosp., Denver, 1982-83; clin. nurse specialist William Beaumont Hosp., Royal Oak, Mich., 1985-89; dir. maternal, child health Botsford Gen. Hosp., Farmington Hills, Mich., 1989-92; dir. women's and children's svcs. McLaren Regional Med. Ctr., Flint, Mich., 1992—; rsch. coord. maternal child health demonstration project Mich. Dept. Pub. Health, Royal Oak, 1985. Bd. dirs. March of Dimes, Flint, 1993—, Children's Wish Fund, Flint, 1992—; mem. task force on children Flint Focus Coun./Focus on Children, 1994. March of Dimes ednl. grantee, 1993. Mem. Mich. Orgn. Nurse Execs., Perinatal Assn. of Mich. (bd. dirs. 1985-86), Assn. Women's Health, Obstetric and Neonatal Nursing (membership coord. Mich. sect. 1993-95, chpt. coord. Detroit 1986-88). Avocations: gardening, fishing. Home: 6036 W Dodge Rd Clio MI 48420-8508 Office: McLaren Regional Med Ctr 401 S Ballenger Hwy Flint MI 48532-3638

MARX, THOMAS GEORGE, economist; b. Trenton, N.J., Oct. 25, 1943; s. George Thomas and Ann (Szymanski) M.; m. Arlene May Varga, Aug. 23, 1969; children: Melissa Ann, Thomas Jeffrey, Jeffrey Alan. BS summa cum laude, Rider Coll., 1969; PhD, U. Pa., 1973. Fin. analyst Am. Cyanamid Co., Trenton, 1968; economist FTC, Washington, 1973; econ. cons. Foster Assocs. Inc., Washington, 1974-77; sr. economist GM, Detroit, 1977-79, mgr. indsl. econs., 1980-81, dir. econs. policy studies, 1981-83; dir. corp. strategic planning group GM, 1984-86, gen. dir. market analysis and forecasting, 1986-88, gen. dir. econ. analysis, 1988-90, gen. dir. issues mgmt. on industry govt. rels. staff, 1990-96; dir. econ. issues and analysis corp. affairs staff GM, Detroit, 1996—; mem. faculty Temple U., 1972-73, U. Pa., 1972-73; adj. prof. Wayne State U., 1981—, U. Detroit, 1988—. Assoc. editor Bus. Econs., 1980—; mem. editorial bd. Akron Jour. Bus. and Econs., 1981-90; contbr. articles to profl. jours. Served with USAF, 1961-65. Mem. Nat. Econs. Club, Am. Econ. Assn., Nat. Assn. Bus. Economists, Detroit Area Bus. Economists (v.p.), Econ. Soc. Mich., So. Econ. Assn., Western Econ. Assn., Planning Forum, Assn. Pub. Policy Analysts, Pi Gamma Mu, Beta Gamma Sigma. Roman Catholic. Home: 3312 Bloomfield Park Dr West Bloomfield MI 48323-3514 Office: GM Corp 3044 W Grand Blvd Detroit MI 48202-3091

MARZETTI, LORETTA A., government agency executive, policy analyst; b. N.Y., Mar. 13, 1943; d. Lawrence Arthur and Josephine (Palazzo) M.; m. Gerald Oren Miller, July 12, 1986. AB in Sociology, Cath. U. Am., 1965. Chief info. svcs. br., OARM EPA, Washington, 1985-88, dir. comms., analysis and budget divsn. Office Solid Waste, 1988-95; dir. comms., info., resources mgt. divsn. Office Solid Waste, 1995—. Avocations: aerobics, exercise, walking, European travel. Home: 3088 S Woodrow St Arlington VA 22206-2115 Office: EPA Solid Waste 5305W 401 M St SW Washington DC 20460

MARZIO, PETER CORT, museum director; b. Governor's Island, N.Y., May 8, 1943; s. Francis and Katherine (Mastroberte) M.; m. Frances Ann Parker, July 2, 1979; children: Sara Lon, Steven Arnold. B.A. (Neva Miller scholar), Juniata Coll., Huntingdon, Pa., 1965; M.A., U. Chgo., 1966, Ph.D. (univ. fellow, Smithsonian Instn. fellow), 1969. Research asst. to dir., then historian Nat. Mus. History and Tech., Smithsonian Instn., 1969-73, asso. curator prints, 1977-78, chmn. dept. cultural history, 1978; dir., chief exec. officer Corcoran Gallery Art, Washington, 1978-82; dir. Mus. Fine Arts, Houston, 1982—; instr. Roosevelt U., Chgo., 1966-68; assoc. prof. U. Md., 1976-77u; adv. coun. Anthrop. Film Ctr., Archives Am. Art; mem. adv. bd. Smithsonian Inst. Press; bd. dirs. First Interstate Bank of Tex. Author: Rube Goldberg: His Life and Works, 1973, The Art Crusade, 1976, The Democratic Art: An Introduction to the History of Chromolithography in America, 1979; editor: A Nation of Nations, 1976. Mem. adv. council Dumbarton Oaks, 1979-86; trustee, mem. exec. com., pres. Texart 150, Tex. Commn. on the Arts, Tex. Assn. for Promotion of Art, 1990-91. Sr. Fulbright fellow Italy, 1973-74. Mem. Print Council Am., Am. Print Council, Dunlap Soc., Assn. Art Mus. Dirs. (pres. 1988-89), Am. Assn. Mus. (exec. com.), Am. Fedn. of the Arts (trustee), Young Pres. Orgn. Club: Cosmos (Washington). Home: 101 Westcott St Houston TX 77007 Office: Mus Fine Arts PO Box 6826 1001 Bissonet St Houston TX 77005

MARZLUF, GEORGE AUSTIN, biochemistry educator; b. Columbus, Ohio, Sept. 29, 1935; s. Paul Bayhan and Opal Faun (Simmons) M.; children: Bruce, Julie, Philip, Glenn. BS, Ohio State U., 1957, MS, 1960; PhD, Johns

Hopkins U., 1964. Postdoctoral fellow U. Wis., Madison, 1964-66; asst. prof. biochemistry Marquette U., Milw., 1966-70; assoc. prof. Ohio State U., Columbus, 1970-75, prof., 1975—, chmn. dept. biochemistry, 1985—. Contbr. articles to profl. jours. Mem. Genetics Soc. Am., Am. Soc. Microbiology, AAAS, Am. Soc. Biochemists and Molecular Biologists. Office: Ohio State U Dept of Biochemistry 484 W 12th Ave Columbus OH 43210-1214

MARZLUFF, WILLIAM F., medical educator; b. Washington, May 7, 1945. BA in Chemistry magna cum laude, Harvard Coll., 1967; PhD in Biochemistry, Duke U., 1971; postdoc. student in Biology, Johns Hopkins U., 1971-74. From asst. prof. to prof. chemistry Fla. State U., Tallahassee, 1974-84, prof. chemistry, 1984-91; prof., dir. program molecular biology, biotech. U. N.C., Chapel Hill, 1991—; cons. physiology course MBL, Woods Hole, 1976; istr. sci. summer and math. camp Fla. State U., 1985, dir. program molecular biophysics, 1986-91; acting chmn. dept. biochem. and biophysics, U. N.C., 1994—; mem. rsch. com. Fla. Divsn. Am. Cancer Soc., 1977-91, chmn. summer rsch. fellowship subcom., 1979-83, 90-91; mem. site visit team NIH, 1980-88, ad hoc mem. molecular cytology study sect., 1982-85, ad hoc mem. molecular biology study sect., 1982-83, 86, 88, 89, mem. molecular biology study sect., 1989-91, chmn. molecular biology study sect., 1991-93; mem. cell biology panel NSF, 1987-89, mem. rev. panel biological ctrs., 1987-90; lectr. in field. Co-editor: Histone Genes: Organization and Expression, 1984; mem. editl. bd. Gene Expression; contbr. over 80 articles to profl. pubs. MBL fellow, 1975, NIH fellow; recipient Career Devel. award USPHS, 1975-80, tchg. award Program Med. Scis., 1978. address: 5116 Green Meadows Rd Hillsborough NC 27278*

MARZULLA, ROGER JOSEPH, lawyer; b. Glendale, Calif., Aug. 12, 1947; m. Nancie George. Student, U. Calif., Berkeley, 1964-66; BA in Polit. Sci., U. Santa Clara, 1968, JD magna cum laude, 1971. Bar: Calif. 1971, U.S. Dist. Ct. (no. dist.) Calif. 1971, U.S. Ct. Apls. (9th cir.) 1971, U.S. Supreme Ct. 1975, U.S. Ct. Apls. (10th cir.) 1981, Colo. 1982, U.S. Dist. Ct. Colo. 1982, U.S. Ct. Apls. (D.C. cir.) 1982, D.C. 1985. Assoc. Mager and Matthews, San Jose, Calif., 1971-74; ptnr. Matthews & Marzulla, San Jose, 1974-81; pres. Mountain States Legal Found., Denver, 1981-82; spl. litigation counsel Land and Natural Resources div. U.S. Dept. Justice, Washington, 1983-84, dep. asst. atty. gen., 1984-87, asst. atty. gen., 1987-89; instr. internat. law San Jose State U., 1975; instr. real estate law San Jose City Coll., 1976-81; judge pro tem Calif. Mcpl. Ct., 1978-81, Superior Ct., 1978-81. Named Jaycees Young Man Yr. 1982. Mem. ABA, State Bar Calif., State Bar Colo., D.C. Bar Assn. Presbyterian. Office: Akin Gump et al Ste 400 1333 New Hampshire Ave NW Washington DC 20036-1511

MARZULLI, JOHN ANTHONY, JR., lawyer; b. Orange, N.J., Jan. 3, 1953; s. John Anthony Sr. and Ruth Eileen (Dyer) M.; m. Penelope Bennett, Dec. 13, 1986; children: Emily Mooers, John A. III, Peter Bennett. BA magna cum laude, Middlebury Coll., 1975; JD, NYU, 1978. Bar: N.J. 1978, N.Y. 1979. Law clk. to chief judge U.S. Dist. Ct., N.J., 1978-80; assoc. atty. Shearman & Sterling, N.Y.C., 1980-87, pntr., 1988—. Contbg. author: Corporate Restructuring, 1990, European Corporate Finance Law, 1990. Mem. ABA, N.Y. State Bar Assn., N.J. Bar Assn., Order of Coif, Phi Beta Kappa. also: Shearman & Sterling, 199 Bishopsgate, London EC2M 3TY, England

MASAI, MITSUO, chemical engineer, educator; b. Kobe, Hyogo, Japan, Sept. 30, 1932; s. Ei-ichi and Fumiko (Kimoto) M.; m. Rei Yamamura, May 1960; 1 child, Yohsuke. BS, Osaka U., 1956; PhD, Tokyo Inst. Tech., 1969. Researcher Showa Oil Co., Ltd., Tokyo, 1956-62; rsch. assoc. Tokyo Inst. Tech., 1962-69; from assoc. prof. to prof. catalysis Kobe U., 1969-96, emeritus prof., 1996—; prof. Fukui U. Tech., 1996—. Contbr. articles to profl. jours. Mem. Chem. Soc. Japan, Catalysis Soc. Japan (achievement award 1991), Japan Petroleum Inst., Soc. Chem. Engrs., Surface Sci. Soc. Japan, Camerata Muti Club, Nippon Gi-in Club. Avocations: classical music, audio, photography, visiting art museums. Home: Rokken-cho 2-2-406, Nishinomiya 662, Japan Office: Kobe U/Faculty Engring, Rokkodai Nada, Kobe 657, Japan

MASCARA, FRANK, congressman; b. Belle Vernon, Pa., Jan. 19, 1930; married; 4 children. BS, Calif. U. Pa., 1972. Pub. acct., 1956-75; contr. Washington County, 1974-79; chmn. Wash. Bd. County Commrs., 1980-94; mem. 104th Congress 20th Pa. dist., 1995—. Office: US House Reps 1531 Longworth HOB Washington DC 20515-3820

MASCETTA, JOSEPH ANTHONY, principal; b. Canonsburg, Pa., Sept. 2, 1931; s. Joseph Alphonso and Amalia (Ciavarra) M.; m. Jean Verrone, June 18, 1960; children: Lisa Marie, Linda Jo, Lori Jean. BS, U. Pitts., 1954; MS, U. Pa., 1963; cert. advanced study, Harvard U., 1970. Cert. tchr. math., phys. scis., adminstr. secondary sch., Pa. Tchr. chemistry Canonsburg High Sch., 1956-59; tchr. chemistry Mt. Lebanon High Sch., Pitts., 1959-75, chair sci. dept., 1967-75; coord. secondary curriculum Mt. Lebanon Sch. Dist., Pitts., 1975-81; prin. Mt. Lebanon Sr. High Sch., Pitts., 1981-91; ret., 1991; vis. team mem. Mid. States Assn. Colls. and Schs., Phila., 1967-78, chair vis. teams, 1981—, Pa. state adv. com., 1988-91; mem. sch. bd. and edn. commn. St. Patrick Sch., Canonsburg, 1972-85; regional dir. Pa. Jr. Acad. Sci., Pitts., 1976-82. Author: Modern Chemistry Review, 1968, Chemistry the Easy Way, 1989, revised, 1995, Barron's SAT II, Chemistry, 1994; contbg. author: (ency.) Barron's Student Concise Ency., 1988, rev. 1994, Barron's New Student's Concise Ency., 1993. Recipient Outstanding Tchr. award Spectroscopy Soc., 1973; grantee NSF, 1961, 62-63, 63, 67, 69-70, 73; sci. fellow GE, 1959. Mem. ASCD, Nat. Assn. Secondary Sch. Prins. (cert. recognition 1991), Pa. Assn. Curriculum & Supervision (exec. bd. dirs. 1985-87, regional pres. 1987), Western Pa. Assn. Curriculum & Supervision (v.p. 1983-85, pres. 1985-87, exec. bd. dirs. 1989—), Phi Delta Kappa. Roman Catholic. Avocations: painting, writing. Home: 451 Mcclelland Rd Canonsburg PA 15317-2258

MASCHO, GEORGE LEROY, education educator emeritus; b. Warsaw, N.Y., Feb. 5, 1925; s. Clayton Leroy and Dorothy Emma (Bailey) M. B.Ed., SUNY, Geneseo, 1948; M.A., Stanford U., 1950; Ed.D., Ind. U., 1961. Tchr. Ontario (N.Y.) Jr. High Sch., 1948-49, Burris Lab. Sch., Muncie, Ind., 1950-61; mem. faculty Ball State U., Muncie, 1961-85; prof. edn. Ball State U., 1967-85, prof. emeritus, 1985—. Contbr. articles to profl. jours. Bd. dirs., treas. United Day Care Center, 1977—; mem. nat. com. developing Head Start program, 1965-66; vol. tutor Hui Malama Adult Literacy Svcs., 1988—; corr. sec. Maui Sr. Citizen Planning and Coordinating Coun., 1987-88; chmn. community ctr. planning com. Pukalani Community Assn., 1989. With inf. U.S. Army, 1943-46. Mem. Nat. Assn. Edn. Young Children, Ind. Assn. Edn. Young Children (chmn. legis. com. 1968-70), Assn. Childhood Edn., Hawaii State Ret. Tchrs. Assn. (chmn. planning com. conv. 1991), Maui Ret. Tchrs. Assn. (dir. 1985—, v.p. 1987-88, 88-89), Maui Sr. Citizen Planning/Coordinating Coun. (corr. sec. 1987-89), AARP, Hawaii, Hawaii State Ret. Tchrs. Assn. (Maui rep. 1989-90), Ind. Arabian Horse Assn. (dir. 1968-73), Am. Contract Bridge League, Pukalani Bridge Club (treas. 1993—), Phi Delta Kappa. Home: 2792 Aina Lani Dr Makawao HI 96768-8404 *To educate is to work with the future. All educators attempt to motivate, provide stimulating environments, prod and inspire students to reach just a bit higher than they would have reached had such contact not been made. If I attain that goal, my life is worthwhile.*

MASCI, JOSEPH RICHARD, medical educator, physician; b. New Brunswick, N.J., Nov. 27, 1950; s. Joseph Nicholas and Delfina (Musa) M.; m. Elizabeth Bass, May 21, 1993; 1 child, Jonathan Samuel. BA, Cornell U., 1972; MD, NYU, 1976. Diplomate Am. Bd. Internal Medicine, Am. Bd. Infectious Diseases. Instr. medicine Boston U. Sch. Medicine, 1979-80; instr. medicine Mt. Sinai Sch. Medicine, N.Y.C., 1982-84, asst. prof. clin. medicine, 1984-88, asst. prof. medicine, 1988-90, assoc. prof. medicine, 1990—; assoc. dir. medicine Elmhurst (N.Y.) Hosp. Ctr., 1987—; peer reviewer NIH, 1994—. Author: Primary and Ambulatory Care of the HIV-Infected Adult, 1992, Outpatient Management of HIV-Infection, 1996. Fellow Am. Coll. Angiology, Am. Coll. Chest Physicians; mem. ACP, Am. Soc. Microbiology, Assn. Program Dirs. Internal Medicine. Office: Elmhurst Hosp Ctr 79-01 Broadway Elmhurst NY 11373-1329

MASCITELLI, JOEL, oil industry executive. With Ultramar Group, Tarrytown, N.Y., 1978-1989; sr. v.p.-operations Ultramar Inc., Hanford, Calif., 1989—; sr. v.p. operations Ultramar Inc., Long Beach, C.A. Office: Can Ultramar Ltd, 1 Valleybrook Dr, Don Mills, ON Canada M3B 2S8 Office: Ultramar Inc 111 W Ocean Blvd Ste 1400 14th-15th Fl Long Beach CA 90802*

MASELLI, JOHN ANTHONY, food products company executive; b. N.Y.C., Feb. 18, 1929; s. Anthony and Livia M.; m. Brigitta Degenkolb, Dec. 26, 1948; children: Elisa, John A. Jr. BS in Chemistry, CCNY, 1947; MS in Chemistry, Fordham U., 1949, PhD in Chemistry, 1952. Dir. research and devel. Standard Brands, Stamford, Conn., 1952-64; mgr. product devel. M&M/Mars, Hackettstown, N.J., 1964-67; pres. OZ Food Corp., Chgo., 1967-79; v.p. tech. Nabisco Brands, East Hanover, N.J., 1979-85; v.p. corp. research and devel. RJR Nabisco, Winston-Salem, N.C., 1985-87; sr. v.p. tech. Planters LifeSavers Co., Winston-Salem, 1987-91, cons., 1991—; bd. dirs. Cultor U.S., Xyrofin (Finland), N.C. Biotech. Ctr., Sci-Works, Winston Salem. Patentee in field. Bd. dirs. Chgo. Boy's Club, 1975-79, YMCA, Wilton, Conn, 1980-84. Mem. AAAS, ACS, Inst. Food Tech., Am. Soc. Bakery Engrs., Indsl. Biotechnology Assn., Indsl. Research Inst. Republican. Avocations: sailing, photography, music. Home: 529 Knob View Pl Winston Salem NC 27104-5107

MASER, DOUGLAS JAMES, lawyer; b. Canton, Ohio, Nov. 21, 1951; s. David James and Mardell Margaret (Getz) M.;m. Kristy Leigh Kable, June 14, 1975; 1 child, Cortney Leigh. BA, Ohio State U.; JD, Capital U., Columbus, Ohio. Bar: Ohio 1976, U.S. Dist. Ct. (so. dist.) Ohio 1977. Asst. pros. atty. Franklin County Pros. Attys. Office, Columbus, 1975-80; assoc. Janes and Jack Law Offices, Columbus, 1980-85; pvt. practice Columbus, 1985-88; ptnr. Day, Ketterer, Raley, Wright & Rybolt, Columbus, 1988-95; dep. adminstr. med. mgmt. & cost containment Ohio Bur. Worker's Compensation, Columbus, 1995—; legis. cons. Ohio Assn. Chiefs Police, Columbus, 1983-1886, Franklin County Bd. Mental Health, Columbus, 1988-90, Ohio Fire Chiefs Assn., Columbus, 1985-90. Dir. Upper Arlington (Ohio) Civic Assn., 1994; mem. Bd. Social Concern, Upper Arlington Luth. Ch., 1993-94; col. Ohio Army Nat. Guard/112 Med. Brigade, 1994-95. 1st lt. U.S. Army, 1977. Mem. ABA, Ohio State Bar Assn., Columbus Bar Assn., Athletic Club Columbus. Republican. Avocations: computer simulations, war gaming, bicycling, hiking, swimming. Office: Ohio Bur Workers Comp Rybolt 30 W Spring St Columbus OH 43266-1508

MASER, FREDERICK ERNEST, clergyman; b. Rochester, N.Y., Feb. 26, 1908; s. Herman A. and Clara (Krumm) M.; m. Anne S. Spangeberg, Aug. 3, 1933; m. Mary L. Jarden, Dec. 25, 1959. AB, Union Coll., Schenectady, N.Y., 1930; MA, Princeton U., 1933; MDiv, Princeton Theol. Sem., 1933; DD, Dickinson Coll., 1957; LL.D. (hon.), McKendree Coll., 1964. Ordained to ministry Methodist Ch., 1933. Pastor Alice Focht Meml. Ch., Birdsboro, Pa., 1933-38, Central Ch., Frankford, Phila., 1938-45, St. James Ch., Olney, Phila., 1945-53; dist. supt. Northwest dist. Phila. Meth. Ann. Conf., 1953-58; pastor Old St. George's Ch., Phila., 1958-67; on sabbatical leave Europe, 1967-68; acting dean students Conwell Sch. Theology, 1968-69; dir. pub. relations Eastern Pa. Conf. United Meth. Ch., 1969-72; exec. sec. World Meth. Hist. Soc., 1971-74; cons. commn. on archives and history United Meth. Ch., 1974—; Tipple lectr. Drew U., Madison, N.J., 1977; spl. lectr. N.Am. sect. World Meth. Hist. Soc., Ashbury Sem., Wilmore, Ky., 1984—; rep. from Northeast Jurisdiction to TV Radio and Film Commn. Meth. Ch., 1952-60; exec. com. Am. Hist. Socs. of Meth. Ch., 1952-68; vice chmn. N.E. Jurisdictional Hist. Socs., 1948; chmn. div. evangelism Pa. Council Chs., 1953-58; mem.-at-large TV, Radio and Film Commn. Meth. Ch., 1960-64; del. Phila. Ann. Conf. to Jurisdictional Conf. of Meth. Ch., 1952; leader ministerial del. to Gen. Conf. Meth. Ch., Mpls., 1956; del. 9th World Conf. of Methodism, Lake Junaluska, 1956, 10th Conf., Oslo, 1961, 12th Conf., Denver, 1971, 13th Conf., Dublin, 1976, 14th Conf., Hawaii, 1981; dir. pub. relations Phila. Meth. ann. conf., 1961-68; exec. sec. World Meth. Hist. Soc., 1971-74. Author: The Dramatic Story of Early American Methodism, 1965, The History of Methodism in Central Pennsylvania, 1971, The Human Side of the Mother of Methodism, 1973, Challenge of Change: The Story of a City's Central Church, 1982, Robert Strawbridge, First American Methodist Circuit Rider, 1983, The Story of John Wesley's Sisters or Seven Sisters in Search of Love, 1988, The Wesley Sisters, 1990, Unfolding the Secret of History, 1991, Theories of the Atonement and the Final Solution, 1993, Sara Teasdale, A Returning Comet, 1993, John Wesley and the Indians of Georgia, 1995, The Little Known Appearances of Jesus, 1996; co-author: Proclaiming Grace and Freedom, 1984, Christina Rossetti, 1991, United Methodism in America, A Compact History, 1992; mem. editorial bd. Meth. History, 1971-75; editor in chief Jour. Joseph Pilmore, 1968; mem. editorial bd., author History American Methodism, 1964, Ency. World Methodism, 1974, Second Thoughts on John Wesley, 1977, Affectionately, your Brother, 1994, The Little Known Appearences of Jesus-A Fantasy, 1996; contbr. articles to religious jours. Trustee George Ruck Trust, 1958-82; mem. adv. council Wesley Theol. Sem., Washington, 1960-72. Recipient St. George's Gold medal award for disting. svc. to Meth. Ch., 1967, Citation Temple U., 1971, (with Mary L. Maser) Phyllis Goodhart award Bryn Mawr Coll. Libr., 1988, cert. appreciation for disting. contbns. to field of Meth. history Commn. on Archives and History of United Meth. Ch., honoree for life-long commitment to Wesley studies The Charles Wesley Soc., 1992. Mem. Pa. Acad. Fine Arts, Colonial Phila. Hist. Soc. (bd. dirs. 1956-64), Ch. History Soc., Union League, Wesley Soc. (life, honored for disting. contbn. in field of rsch.), Philobiblon Club, Princeton Club, Phi Beta, Phi Alpha. Home: Heritage Towers Apt 634 200 Veterans Ln Doylestown PA 18901-3450 *Life offers many honors but the older I grow, the more I realize that the highest honor is to have one's name written in the Lamb's Book of Life.*

MASEY, JACK, exhibition designer; b. N.Y.C., June 10, 1924; s. Max and Anna Masey; m. Mary Lou Leach, Dec. 27, 1959. Student, Cooper Union, 1941-43; B.F.A., Yale, 1950. Pres. MetaForm Inc., N.Y.C., 1979—; co. project mgr. for design of La. Pavilion, World Expo., New Orleans, 1984, Statue of Liberty Exhibit, N.Y.C., 1986; project mgr. for design Johnstown (Pa.) Flood Mus., 1988, Ellis Island Immigration Mus., N.Y.C., 1990; co. project mgr. for design of Nat. D-Day Mus., New Orleans, 1994, Harry S. Truman Mus., Independence, Mo., 1994; lectr. Sch. Art and Architecture, Yale U., 1968-69. Cartoonist Esquire mag, 1946; exhibits officer, USIS, New Delhi, 1951-55; designer U.S. Pavilion, Kabul Internat. Fair, 1956; dir. design Am. Nat. Exhbn., Moscow, 1959, chief, East-West exhibits br. USIA, Washington, 1960-67; chief design U.S. Pavilion, Montreal (Que., Can.) World's Fair, 1967, dep. commr. gen. for planning and design Osaka (Japan) World Expn., 1970; dir. design Am. Revolution Bicentennial Commn., Washington, 1971-73; dir. design and exhbns. Am. Revolution Bicentennial Adminstrn., 1974-77, design dir. Internat. Communication Agy., Washington, 1977—; designer: Medicine-U.S.A. exhbn. for, USSR exchange program, 1962, Tech.-Books exhbns., 1963. Served with AUS, 1943-45, ETO. Recipient Meritorious Service award USIA, 1959, Superior Service award, 1964, Superior Honor award, 1967, 75; award of excellence Fed. Design Council, 1975; Outstanding Achievement award, 1979; award of excellence Soc. Fed. Artists and Designers, 1971; Gold medal Art Dirs. Club, 1965; cert. of excellence Am. Inst. Graphic Arts, 1964; two Fed. Design Achievement awards for Contributions to Excellence in Design, U.S. Govt., 1984, Presdl. awards for Statue of Liberty Exhibit, 1986, for Ellis Island Immigration Mus., 1990. Home: 131 E 66th St Apt 3A New York NY 10021-6129 Office: 15 E 26th St New York NY 10010-1505

MASH, DONALD J., college president; b. Oct. 12, 1942; m. Julia Larson; children: Maria, Christina, Donnie (dec.). BS in Edn., Ind. U. Pa., 1960; MA in Geography, U. Pitts., 1966; PhD, Ohio State U., 1974. Teaching fellow U. Pitts., 1964-65; instr. geography U. Pitts.-Bradford, 1965-68; dean for student svcs. Ohio Dominican Coll., 1968-75; v.p. for student affairs George Mason U., Fairfax, Va., 1975-85, exec. v.p. adminstrn., 1985-88; pres. Wayne (Nebr.) State Coll., 1988—. Office: Wayne State Coll Office of Pres Wayne NE 68787

MASHAW, JERRY L., lawyer, educator; b. 1941. B.A., Tulane U., 1962, LL.B., 1964; Ph.D., U. Edinburgh, 1969. Bar: La. 1964, Va. 1975. Asst. prof. Tulane U., 1966-68; asst. prof. U. Va., 1968-69, assoc. prof., 1969-72, prof., 1972-76; prof. Yale U. Law Sch., 1976—, William Nelson Cromwell prof., 1983—; cons. Ctr. Adminstrn. Justice. Mem. Order of Coif, Phi Beta Kappa. Author: (with Merrill) Introduction to the American Public Law System, 1975; (with others) Social Security Hearings and Appeals, 1978, Bureaucratic Justice, 1983, Due Process in the Adminstrative State, 1985; past editor-in-chief Tulane Law Rev. Office: Yale U Law Sch PO Box 208-215 New Haven CT 06520-0401*

MASHBERG, GREGG M., lawyer; b. Peekskill, N.Y., Dec. 4, 1951; s. edward and Mildred (Weinstein) M.; m. Amy Lee Garfinkel, Aug. 1, 1976; children: Jenny, Emily. BA, Case Western Res. U., 1973; JD, NYU, 1977. Bar: N.Y. 1978, U.S. Dist. Ct. (so. and ea. dists.) N.Y. 1978, U.S. Ct. Appeals (2nd cir.) 1979, U.S. Supreme ct. 1988. Asst. corp. counsel Law Dept., City of N.Y., 1978-83; assoc./ptnr. Schwartz Klink & Schreiber, P.C., N.Y.C., 1983-87; ptnr. Proskauer Rose Goetz & Mendelsohn, N.Y.C., 1987—. Bd. dirs. Children's Day Treatment Ctr. and Sch., N.Y.C., 1987—; founder, mem. New Rochelle (N.Y.) Coalition for Excellence in Pub. Schs., 1992. Mem. Assn. Bar City of N.Y. (Award for Excellence Com. on Mcpl. Affairs 1981), N.Y. Bar Assn., Anti-Defamation League (nat. com. legal affairs). Avocations: jogging, skiing, clarinet. Home: 21 Arbor Dr New Rochelle NY 10804-1101 Office: Proskauer Rose Goetz et al 1585 Broadway New York NY 10036-8200*

MASHECK, JOSEPH DANIEL, art critic, educator; b. N.Y.C., Jan. 19, 1942; s. Joseph Anthony and Dorothy Anna (Cahill) M. A.B., Columbia U., 1963, M.A., 1965, Ph.D., 1973. Editorial researcher Bollingen Found.-Princeton U. Press, 1967-69; lectr. liberal studies Maidstone Coll. Art, Kent, Eng., 1968-69; preceptor in art history Columbia U., 1970-71; instr. art history Barnard Coll., 1971-73, asst. prof., 1973-82; lectr. visual and environ. studies Harvard U., Cambridge, Mass., 1983-86; assoc. prof. art history Hofstra U., Hempstead, N.Y., 1987-94, prof., 1994—; coord. grad. program in humanities, curatorial cons. Hofstra Mus., Hempstead, N.Y. Author: Historical Present: Essays of the 1970s, 1984, Smart Art (Point 1), 1984, Modernites: Art-Matters in the Present, 1993, Building-Art: Modern Architecture Under Cultural Construction, 1993; editor: Marcel Duchamp in Perspective 1975, Van Gogh 100, 1996. Bd. dirs. Crosby St. Project, N.Y., 1995—. Nat. Endowment Arts fellow, 1972-73, 75-76; Guggenheim fellow, 1977-78. Mem. AAUP, Coll. Art Assn., Internat. Assn. Art Critics, United Arts Club (Dublin). Roman Catholic. Democrat. Office: Hofstra U Dept. Fine Arts and Art History Calkins Hall Hempstead NY 11550-1090

MASHIN, JACQUELINE ANN COOK, medical sciences consultant; b. Chgo., May 11, 1941; d. William Hermann and Ann (Smidt) Cook; m. Fredric John Mashin, June 7, 1970; children: Joseph Glenn, Alison Robin. BS, U. Md., 1984. Cert. realtor. Adminstrv. asst. CIA, Washington, 1963-66; asst. to mng. dir. Aerospace Edn. Found., Washington, 1966-74; exec. asst. to asst exec. dir. Air Force Assn., Washington, 1974-79; v.p., ptnrship. owner Discount Linen Store, Silver Spring, Md., 1979-81; asst. regional polit. dir. Office of Pres.-elect, Washington, 1980-81; confidential asst. to dir. Office of Personnel Mgmt. (US), Washington, 1981-83; spl. asst. to dep. dir. Office of Mgmt. and Budget, Washington, 1983-86; dir. internat. communications and spl. asst. to commr. Dept. of the Interior, Washington, 1986-89, cons., 1989—. Pres. Layhill Civic Assn., Silver Spring, Md., 1980; state chmn. Md.'s Reagan Youth Delegation, Annapolis, Md., 1980; state treas., office mgr. Reagan-Bush State Hdqrs. of Md., Silver Spring, 1980; mem. Women's Com. Nat. Symphony Orch. Mem. Air Force Assn. (life), Aux. Salvation Army (life), Am. League Lobbyists, Internat. Platform Assn., U.S. Capital Hist. Soc., Women's Nat. Rep. Club (N.Y.C.), Indian Springs Country Club. Republican. Avocations: golf, horseback riding, collecting wine glasses, Hibel plates, lithos and Lalique crystal. Home and Office: 2429 White Horse Ln Silver Spring MD 20906-2243

MASI, DALE A., research company executive, social work educator; b. N.Y.C.; d. Alphonse E. and Vera Avella; children: Eric, Renee, Robin. BS, Coll. Mt. St. Vincent; MSW, U. Ill.; D Social Work, Cath. U. Lectr. Sch. Social Svcs., Ipswitch, Eng., 1970-72; project dir. occupational substance abuse program, asso. prof. Boston Coll. Grad. Sch. Social Work, 1972-79; dir. Office Employee Counseling Svc., Dept. Health/Human Svcs., Washington, 1979-84; pres. Masi Research Cons., Inc.., 1984—; prof. U. Md. Grad. Sch. Social Work, 1980—; adj. prof. U. Md. Coll. Bus. and Mgmt., 1980—; mem. IBM Mental Health Adv. Bd., 1990—; cons. IBM, Toyota, Mobil Chem., The Washington Post, U.S. Ho. Reps., White House, WHO, Bechtel Corp., other orgns. in pub. and pvt. sector; bd. advisors Employee Assistance mag. and Nat. Security Inst.; USIA AmPart lectr. on alcohol, drugs and AIDS in the workplace. Author: Human Services in Industry, Organizing for Women, Designing Employee Assistance Programs, Drug Free Workplace, AIDS Issues in the Workplace: A Response Model for Human Resource Management, The AMA Handbook for Developing Employee Assistance and Counseling Programs, Evaluating Your Employee Assistance and Managed Behavioral Care Program; also over 40 articles. Fulbright fellow, 1969-70; AAUW postdoctoral fellow; NIMH fellow, 1962-64; recipient award Employee Assistance Program Digest; named to Employee Assistance Program Hall of Fame. Mem. AAUW, NASW (Internat. Rhoda G. Sarnat award 1993), Acad. Cert. Social Workers, Employee Assistance Profls. Assn. (nat. individual achievement award 1983), Fulbright Assn. (nat. bd.). Democrat. Roman Catholic. Office: 500 23d St NW Ste 202 Washington DC 20037-2801

MASI, EDWARD A., computer company executive; b. Medford, Mass., May 7, 1947; s. Joseph Carl and Rita Olivine (Metras) M.; m. Kristine Ann Lauderbach Masi, Jan. 24, 1970. BSME, Tufts U., 1969. Mktg. sales IBM, Boston, 1969-76; commercial analysis IBM, Westchester, N.Y., 1976-78; mktg. mgr. IBM, Bethesda, Md., 1978-80; region mgr. mktg. sales Cray Rsch., Calverton, Md., 1980-87; exec. v.p. mktg. Mpls., 1988-92; corp. v.p. and pres. Intel Corp., Beaverton, Oreg., 1992. Mem. Am. Electronics Assn. (vice chair 1991-92). Avocations: tennis, scuba diving. Office: Intel Scalable Systems Divsn 5200 NE Elam Young Pkwy Beaverton OR 97124*

MASIELLO, ANTHONY M. (TONY MASIELLO), mayor; b. 1947; s. Dan and Bridget M.; married; 1 child, Kimberly; m. Kathleen McCue; 1 child, Ariel Lynn. BS, Canisius Coll.; LHD (hon.), Medaille Coll. Mem. North Dist. Buffalo Common Coun., councilman-at-large, coun. majority leader; mem. N.Y. State Senate, 1980—; mayor City of Buffalo. Office: Office of the Mayor 201 City Hall 65 Niagara Sq Buffalo NY 14202*

MASIELLO, ROCCO JOSEPH, airlines and aerospace manufacturing executive; b. N.Y.C., Jan. 9, 1922; s. Joseph and Armanda (Mansueti) M.; m. Rita Elizabeth Amoruso, Feb. 19, 1945; children: Richard, Robin, Janet. Student, CCNY, 1946-48, Hofstra U., 1951-54. Registered profl. engr., Maine. With Pan. Am. World Airways, N.Y.C., 1950-59; v.p. maintenance and engring. U.S. Air Group, Pitts., 1959-72, Am. Airlines, Tulsa, 1973-82; sr. v.p. ops. Am. Airlines, Dallas, 1982-86; founder, exec. v.p. USAfrica Airways, 1990-94, also bd. dirs; founder The Reston Group; aerospace cons., prin. R.J. Masiello and Assocs. Mem. Soc. Automotive Engr., Royal Aero. Soc. Roman Catholic.

MASIN, MICHAEL TERRY, lawyer; b. Montreal, Jan. 28, 1945; came to U.S., 1954; s. Frank J. and Sonia (Ellmann) M.; m. Joanne Elizabeth Combé, June 4, 1966; 1 child, Courtney. BA, Dartmouth U., 1966; JD, UCLA, 1969. Bar: Calif. 1969, D.C. 1970. Assoc. O'Melveny & Myers, Los Angeles, 1969-76; ptnr. O'Melveny & Myers, Washington, 1976-91; mng. ptnr. O'Melveny & Myers, N.Y.C., 1991—; bd. dirs. Trust Co. West, L.A., GTE Corp., Stamford, Conn., vice chmn., 1993-95, vice chmn., pres. internat., 1995; bd. dirs. Compana Anonima Nacional Telefonos de Venezuela, Brit. Columbia Telephone. Mem. bus. com. bd. trustees Mus. Modern Art; trustee Carnegie Hall; mem. dean's adv. com. Dartmouth Coll., U.S.-Can. Pvt. Sector Adv. Coun. of Inter-Am. Devel.; bd. mem. China Am. Soc. Mem. ABA, Coun. on Fgn. Rels., The Brook, Calif. Club. Republican. Methodist. Office: GTE Corp 1 STamford Forum Stamford CT 06904

MASINTER, EDGAR MARTIN, investment banker; b. Huntington, W.Va., Jan. 2, 1931; s. Ralph Leon and Gazella (Schlossberg) M.; m. Margery Flocks, July 8, 1962; children: Robert Andrew, Catherine Diane. BA, Princeton U., 1952; LLB, Harvard U., 1955. Bar: D.C. 1955, N.Y. 1958. Assoc. Simpson Thacher & Bartlett, N.Y.C., 1957-65, ptnr., 1966-95; ptnr. The Bridgeford Group, N.Y.C., 1996—; bd. dirs. IBJ Schroder Bank & Trust Co.; spl. advisor Princeton U. Investment Co., Nassau Capital. V.p. bd. dirs. Grand St. Settlement, N.Y.C.; mem. bd. regents The Mercersburg (Pa.) Acad.; mem. ethics com. Whitney Mus. Am. Art. With U.S. Army, 1955-57. Mem. ABA, Assn. of Bar of City of N.Y. Office: The Bridgeford Group 280 Park Ave New York NY 10017

MASKE, MONICA, newspaper editor. Religion editor The Star Ledger, Newark. Office: The Star-Ledger 1 Star Ledger Plz Newark NJ 07102-1200

MASKELL, DONALD ANDREW, contracts administrator; b. San Bernadino, Calif., June 22, 1963; s. Howard Andrew Maskell and Gloria Evelyn (Iglesias) White. BA, U. Puget Sound, 1985. Adminstrv. asst. State of Wash., Kent, 1986-87; data analyst Boeing Co., Seattle, 1987-93, engring. contract requirements coord., 1993—, requirements support specialist. Mem. Elks. Republican. Presbyterian. Avocations: travel, computers, golf, theater, history.

MASKET, EDWARD SEYMOUR, television executive; b. N.Y.C., Mar. 3, 1923; s. Isadore and Jennie (Bernstein) M.; m. Frances Ellen Rees, June 11, 1958 (div.); children: Joel Daniel, Johanna Rees Ettaeib, Kate Isobel Smiley. BS, CCNY, 1942; LLB, JD, Harvard U., 1949. Bar: N.Y. 1949. Atty., dir. bus. affairs, v.p. bus. affairs ABC, 1951-68; v.p. to exec. v.p. Columbia Pictures TV, Burbank, Calif., 1968-81; sr. v.p. adminstrn. Universal TV, 1982-86, exec. v.p. adminstrn., 1986-90; exec. v.p. adminstrn. MCA TV Group, 1990-93; TV cons., 1993—. Served as 2d lt. AUS, 1942-46, PTO. Mem. Motion Picture Pioneers, Phi Beta Kappa. Avocation: tennis, golf. Office: Paramont Pictures Corp 5535 Melrose Ave Hollywood CA 90038-3197

MASKIN, ARVIN, lawyer; b. Bklyn., Mar. 27, 1954; s. Robert and Clair (Diamond) M.; m. Debra Ann, 1979; children: Daniel Chase, Andrew Noah, Sophie Leah. BA, Georgetown U., 1975, JD, 1978. Bar: N.Y. 1978, Pa. 1984, D.C., U.S. Ct. Appeals (2d, 3d and fed. cirs.), U.S. Supreme Ct. Dep. atty. gen. Office of Atty. Gen. Pa., Dept. Justice, Phila., 1978-82; trial atty. civil div. U.S. Dept Justice, Washington, 1982-86; assoc. Weil, Gotshal & Manges, N.Y.C., 1987-88, counsel, 1988-90, ptnr., 1990—; bd. dirs. Civil Trial Manual, Bureau Nat. Affairs, Toxics Law Report, reporter Product Safety and Liability; lectr. Yale U., Columbia U., Fordham U. Founder, editor-in-chief Product Liability Perspective; contbr. articles to profl. jours. Mem. ABA (nat. inst. subcom., torts and ins. com., litigation com.), U.S. C. of C. (mass tort task force). Jewish. Office: Weil Gotshal & Manges 767 5th Ave New York NY 10153*

MASK-MONROE, ROSE MARIA, reading specialist, educator; b. Newport News, Va., Nov. 1, 1955; d. Curtis Van and Mary Ella (Pearson) Mask; m. Marke A. Monroe, Sept. 6, 1986 (div. May 1993); children: Monteece C., Jamila T. BA, Utica Coll. Syracuse U., 1976; MS, Morgan State U., 1984. Asst. Liberty Street Day Care, Newburgh, N.Y., 1969; jr. counselor Neighborhood Youth Corps, Newburgh, 1974; tutor, counselor Higher Edn. Opportunity Program, Utica, N.Y., 1976; tchr. English Balt. Pub. Schs., 1977-79; agt. Balt. Police Dept., 1979-88; instr. Bowie (Md.) State U., 1988-91; assoc. prof. Balt. City C.C., 1991—; tutor reading Utica (N.Y.) Free Acad., 1975; tutor English, Utica Coll., 1976; reading clinician Towson (Md.) State U., 1984; instr. Reading Community Coll. Balt., 1987-91. Counselor Utica YWCA, 1974. Recipient Merit Sonitrol Security Systems award, 1983; grantee Ottawa Found., 1973, Utica Coll. Higher Edn. Opportunity Program, 1973. Mem. Vanguard Justice Soc. (sec. 1980-82), Alpha Kappa Alpha. Democrat. Baptist. Avocations: reading, singing, traveling. Office: 2901 Liberty Heights Ave Baltimore MD 21215-7807

MASLACH, CHRISTINA, psychology educator; b. San Francisco, Jan. 21, 1946; d. George James and Doris Ann (Cuneo) M.; m. Philip George Zimbardo, Aug. 10, 1972; children: Zara, Tanya. B.A., Harvard-Radcliffe Coll., 1967; Ph.D., Stanford U., 1971. Prof. psychology U. Calif.-Berkeley, 1971—. Author: Burnout: The Cost of Caring, 1982; co-author: Influencing Attitudes and Changing Behaviour, 1977, Maslach Burnout Inventory (rsch. scale), 1981, 2d edit., 1986, 3d edit., 1996, Experiencing Social Psychology, 1979, 2d edit., 1984, 3d edit., 1993, Professional Burnout, 1993. Recipient Disting. Teaching award, 1987, Best Paper award Jour. Orgnl. Behavior, 1994. Fellow AAAS, APA, Am. Psychol. Soc., Soc. Clin. and Exptl. Hypnosis (Henry Guze rsch. award 1980), We. Psychol. Assn. (pres. 1989); mem. Soc. Exptl. Social Psychology. Democrat. Office: U Calif Dept Psychology Tolman Hall # 1650 Berkeley CA 94720-1650

MASLACH, GEORGE JAMES, former university official; b. San Francisco, May 4, 1920; s. Michael J. and Anna (Pszczolkowska) M.; m. Doris Anne Cuneo, Mar. 12, 1943; children: Christina, James, Steven. A.A., San Francisco Jr. Coll., 1939; B.S., U. Calif., 1942. Staff mem. radiation lab. Mass. Inst. Tech., 1942-45, Gen. Precision Labs., 1945-49; research engr. Inst. Engring. Research, 1949-52, asst. dir., 1956-58; assoc. prof. U. Calif., Berkeley, 1952-58, prof., 1959-72, dean Coll. Engring., 1963-72, provost profl. schools and colls., 1972-81, vice-chancellor research and acad. services, 1981-83; internat. cons. edn. and econ. devel., 1982—; adv. aeros. research and devel. NATO, 1960-78, U.S. Naval Acad. Rev. Bd., 1966-75, Dept. Commerce Tech. Adv. Bd., 1964-69, Ford Found. and Am. Soc. Engring. Edn., 1966-78. Mem. ASME, AAAS, Sigma Xi. Home: 265 Panoramic Way Berkeley CA 94704-1831

MASLAND, LYNNE S., university official; b. Boston, Nov. 18, 1940; d. Keith Arnold and Camilla (Puleston) Shangraw; m. Edwin Grant Masland, Sept. 19, 1960 (div. 1975); children: Mary Conklin, Molly Allison; m. Steven Alan Mayo, July 1, 1995. Student, Mt. Holyoke Coll., South Hadley, Mass., 1958-60; BA, U. Calif., Riverside, 1970; MA, U. Calif., 1971; PhD, U. B.C., Vancouver, Can., 1994. Asst. pub. rels. dir. Inter-Am. U., San German, P.R., 1963-64; asst. to dir. elem. edn. Govt. of Am. Samoa, Pago Pago, 1966-68; project dir., cons. Wash. Commn. for Humanities, Seattle, 1976-80; exec. editor N.W. Happenings Mag., Greenbank, Wash., 1980-84; media specialist Western Wash. U., Bellingham, 1984-88; dir. pub. info. Western Wash. U., 1988—; asst. prof. Fairhaven Coll., 1995—; cons. William O. Douglas Inst., Seattle, 1984, Whatcom Mus. History and Art, Bellingham, 1977; instr. U. Nebr., Omaha, 1972-86, Western Wash. U., 1972-86. Editor: The Human Touch: Folklore of the Northwest Corner, 1979, Proceedings: The Art in Living, 1980, Reports to the Mayor on the State of the Arts in Bellingham, 1980-81; contbr. numerous articles to profl. jours. Pres. LWV, Whatcom County, Bellingham, 1977-79; bd. dirs. N.W. Concert Assn., 1981-83, Wash. State Folklife Coun., 1985-90; docent Nat. Gallery, Washington, 1969; bd. dirs. Sta. KZAZ, nat. pub. radio, Bellingham, 1992-93. Univ. grad. fellow U. B.C., 1990-94. Mem. Am. Comparative Lit. Assn., Nat. Assn. Presswomen, Wash. Press Assn. (pres. 4th Corner chpt. 1987-88, Superior Performance award 1986), Can. Comparative Lit. Assn., Internat. Comparative Lit. Assn., Philological Assn. of Pacific Coast, Coun. for Advancement and Support Edn. (Case Dist. VIII Gold award for Media Rels.), Rotary (bd. dirs. 1992-94). Episcopalian. Avocations: boating, gardening, travel, piano. Office: Western Wash U High St Bellingham WA 98225

MASLANSKY, CAROL JEANNE, toxicologist; b. N.Y.C., Mar. 3, 1949; d. Paul Jeremiah and Jeanne Marie (Filiatrault) Lane; m. Steven Paul Maslansky, May 28, 1973. BA, SUNY, 1971; PhD, N.Y. Med. Coll., 1983. Diplomate Am. Bd. Toxicology; cert. gen. toxicology. Asst. entomologist N.Y. State Dept. Health, White Plains, 1973-74; sr. biologist Am. Health Found., Valhalla, N.Y., 1974-76; rsch. fellow N.Y. Med. Coll., Valhalla, 1977-83, Albert Einstein Coll. Medicine, Bronx, N.Y., 1983; copr. toxicologist Texaco, Inc., Beacon, N.Y., 1984-85; prin. GeoEnviron. Cons., Inc., White Plains, N.Y., 1982—; lectr. in entomology Westchester County Parks and Preserves, 1973—, lectr. toxicology and hazardous materials, 1985—. Author: Air Monitoring Instrumentation, 1993, (with others) Training for Hazardous Materials Team Members, 1991 (manual, video) The Poison Control Response to Chemical Emergencies, 1993. Mem. Harrison (N.Y.) Vol. Ambulance Corps., 1986-91, Westchester County (N.Y.) Hazardous Materials Response Team, 1987—. Monsanto Fund Fellowship in Toxicology, 1988-90; grad. fellowship N.Y. Med. Coll., 1977-83. Mem. AAAS, Nat. Environ. Health Assn., N.Y. Acad. Sci., Am. Coll. Toxicology, Am. Indsl. Hygiene Assn., Environ. Mutagen Soc. Achievements include participation in development of genetic toxicity assays to identify potential carcinogens; rsch. on air monitoring instrumentation at hazardous materials sites, health and safety for hazardous waste site workers, environmental and chemical toxicology, genetic toxicology. Home: 8500 Buchanan Dr Prescott AZ 86301

MASLIN, HARVEY LAWRENCE, staffing service company executive; b. Chgo., Oct. 22, 1939; s. Jack and Shirley Maslin; m. Marcia Silberman, Aug. 21, 1960; children: Elaine, Shelley, Bonnie. BS, U. Ariz., 1961, JD, 1964. Bar: Ariz., 1964, Calif., 1966, U.S. Dist. Ct., 1964, 66. Ptnr. Maslin, Rotundo & Maslin, Sherman Oaks, Calif., 1966-67; gen. counsel Western Temporary Svcs., Inc., San Francisco, 1967-71, v.p., 1972-78, sr. v.p., sec., 1979-84; pres., chief oper. officer Western Staff Svcs., Inc., Walnut Creek, Calif., 1985-95, vice chmn. bd. dirs., chief adminstrv. officer, 1996—; dir. Western Staff Svcs., USA, Western Staff Svcs., U.K. Ltd., London, Western Staff Svcs. Pty Ltd., Melbourne, Australia, Western Staff Svcs. (N.Z.) Ltd., Auckland, Western Svc. A/S, Copenhagen, Denmark, Western Svc./Kontorsvc. A/S Oslo, Western Svc., Inc., Zurich, Western Video Images, Inc., San Francisco. Mem. Rep. Presidential Task Force, Washington, 1981. Mem. Nat. Assn. Temporary and Staffing Svcs. (bd. dirs.), Calif. Bar Assn., Ariz. Bar Assn., World Trade Club, Phi Alpha Delta. Office: Western Staff Svcs Inc Exec Offices 301 Lennon Ln Walnut Creek CA 94598

MASLIN, JANET, film critic; b. N.Y.C., Aug. 12, 1949; d. Paul and Lucille (Becker) M.; m. Benjamin Cheever; children: John, Andrew. BA in Math., U. Rochester, 1970. Film and music critic The Boston Phoenix, 1972-76; film critic Newsweek, N.Y.C., 1976-77; dep. film critic The N.Y. Times, N.Y.C., 1977-93, chief film critic, 1993—. Office: The NY Times 229 W 43rd St New York NY 10036-3913

MASLOW, WILL, lawyer, association executive; b. Kiev, Russia, Sept. 27, 1907; came to U.S., 1911, naturalized, 1924; s. Saul and Raeesa (Moonves) M.; m. Beatrice Greenfield, Dec. 21, 1933; children: Laura, Catha. A.B., Cornell U., 1929; J.D., Columbia U., 1931. Bar: N.Y. 1932, U.S. Supreme Ct. 1932. Reporter N.Y. Times, 1929-31; assoc. Arthur Garfield Hays, 1931-34; assoc. counsel Dept. Investigation, N.Y.C., 1934-36; trial atty., trial examiner NLRB, 1937-43; dir. field operations Pres.'s Com. Fair Employment Practice, 1943-45; gen. counsel Am. Jewish Congress, 1945—, exec. dir., 1960-72; Faculty N.Y. Sch. Social Research, 1948-60; adj. prof. Coll. City N.Y., 1965-84. Editor: Boycott Report, 1977-94, Radical Islamic Fundamentalism Update, 1995—. Trustee Meml. Found. for Jewish Culture; bd. dirs. Interracial Council for Bus. Opportunity, A. Philip Randolph Inst. Mem. World Jewish Congress (exec. com.), ACLU (dir. 1963-72), Am. Jewish Congress (Stephen Wise laureate 1972), Phi Beta Kappa. Home: 401 E 86th St New York NY 10028-6403 Office: 15 E 84th St New York NY 10028-0458

MASNARI, NINO ANTONIO, electrical engineer, educator; b. Three Rivers, Mich., Sept. 20, 1935; s. Antonio and Giovanna (Lupato) M.; m. Judy E. Guild, June 29, 1957; children: Michael A., Jeffrey P., Maria L. BSEE, U. Mich., 1958, MSEE, 1959, PhD, 1964. Lectr., rsch. assoc. U. Mich., Ann Arbor, 1964-67; electronics engr. R&D ctr. GE, Schenectady, N.Y., 1967-69; assoc. prof. elec. engring. U. Mich., 1969-76, prof., 1976-79, dir. elec. physics lab., 1975-79; prof. elec. engring. N.C. State U., Raleigh, 1979—; dept. head N.C. State U., 1979-88, dir. AEMP Ctr., 1988—; cons. in field. Raytheon predoctoral fellow 1962. Fellow IEEE; mem. Am. Soc. Engring. Edn., Matl. Rsch. Soc., Sigma Xi, Phi Kappa Phi, Tau Beta Pi, Eta Kappa Nu. Achievements include patent for Process for Manufacturing Inertial Confinement Fusion Targets and Resulting Product.

MASO, MICHAEL HARVEY, managing director; b. N.Y.C., Aug. 9, 1951; s. James and Goldie (Aronowitz) M.; m. Lisa Marie Coady, Sept. 13, 1987; children: Alexander Peter, Graham Emanuel. BA, SUNY, Stony Brook, 1972; postgrad., Cornell U., 1973-76. Gen. mgr. Roundabout Theatre Co., N.Y.C., 1972-73; bus. mgr. P.A.F. Playhouse, Huntington, N.Y., 1976-78; pres. Taos (N.Mex.) Arts Mgmt., 1978-80; mng. dir. Ala. Shakespeare Festival, Anniston, 1980-82, Huntington Theatre Co., Boston, 1982—; sec. League of Resident Theatres, 1985-89, v.p., 1988-93; trustee, treas. StageSource, Boston, 1986-95; trustee Mass. Advocates for Arts, Scis. and Humanities, Boston, 1992—; trustee Arts Boston, 1995—. Chair theater advancement panel NEA, Washington, 1988, panelist/challenge grant, 1989; chair Cultural & Sci. Dirs. Group, Boston, 1993—; trustee Arts Boston, 1995—. Avocations: reading, running. Office: Huntington Theatre Co 264 Huntington Ave Boston MA 02115-4606

MASON, ANTHONY GEORGE DOUGLAS, professional basketball player; b. Miami, Fla., Dec. 14, 1966; s. Mary Mason; 1 child, Antoine. G-rad., Tenn. State U., 1988. Basketball player, forward N.J. Nets, 1989-90, Tulsa Fast Breakers, 1990-91, Denver Nuggers, 1990, L.I. Surf, 1991, N.Y. Knickerbockers, 1991—. Recipinet Miller Genuine Draft NBA 6th Man award, 1995. Office: NY Knickerbockers Madison Sq Garden Two Pennsylvania Plz New York NY 10121-0091

MASON, BARBARA E. SUGGS, educator; b. Champaign, Ill., July 9, 1952; d. Raymond Eugene and Hester Barbara (Nelson) Suggs; m. Frederick A. Mason, May 7, 1988. B of Music Edn., Northwestern U., 1974; MS in Music Edn., U. Ill., 1976, M of Music, 1985. Cert. music tchr. K-12, supervisory endorsement, voice performance and lit., Ill. Gen. music specialist Oak Park (Ill.) Sch. Dist. 97, 1976-82; tchr. for the gifted performing arts unit Champaign Community Schs., 1985-86; choral dir. Evanston (Ill.) Twp. H.S., 1986-87, dist. curriculum leader for gen. music, 1990-95; coord. for mid. level edn. Oak Park Sch. Dist. 97, 1995—; adj. instr. Elmhurst Coll., 1990-95; curriculum cons. Office of Cath. Edn. Black History Com., Chgo., 1992—; acad. task team mem. Quigley Preparatory Sem., Chgo, 1993; curriculum cons., presenter Dept. of Mus. Edn., Art Inst. of Chgo., 1992; chmn. dist. comprehensive arts grant com. Dist. 97, Oak Park, 1992—. Bd. dirs. Oak Park and River Forest Children's Chorus, 1991-95; mem. arts fund com. Oak Park Area Arts Coun., 1993-95. Grad. coll. fellowship U. Ill., 1984-85; recipient Award of Merit Those Who Excel Program Ill. State Bd. of Edn., 1993. Mem. NEA, ASCD, Nat. Middle Sch. Assn., Music Educators Nat. Conf., Ill. Alliance for Arts Edn. (svc. award selection com. 1993), In-and-About Chgo. Music Educators Club, Mu Phi Epsilon, Phi Delta Kappa. Roman Catholic. Office: Oak Park Sch Dist 97 970 Madison St Oak Park IL 60302-4430

MASON, BARRY JEAN, retired banker; b. Big Spring, Tex., June 3, 1930; s. Vernon E. and Irene E. (Owen) M.; m. Alexana Petroff, Aug. 31, 1958; children: Scott Alexander, Lydia Claire. B.S., U. Tex., 1957; B.F.T., Am. Inst. Fgn. Trade, 1958; postgrad., Advanced Mgmt. Program Harvard, Auspices U. Hawaii, 1968. Trainee First Nat. City Bank, N.Y., Hong Kong, 1959-60; asst. accountant First Nat. City Bank, N.Y., Toyko, Japan, 1960-63; asst. mgr. First Nat. City Bank, N.Y., 1963-66; mgr. First Nat. City Bank, N.Y., Hong Kong, 1966-67; resident v.p. First Nat. City Bank, N.Y., 1967-68, Tokyo, 1968-69; v.p. First Nat. City Bank, N.Y., Japan, Korea, Okinawa, 1969; v.p. Republic Nat. Bank Dallas, 1969-70, sr. v.p., 1970-72, exec. v.p., 1972-83; chmn., chief exec. officer Republic Bank Las Colinas, 1983-87; sr. advisor Sumitomo Trust and Banking Co. Ltd., 1989-91; mem. adv. bd. PEFCO. Trustee Am. Sch. Japan; bd. advisers Internat. Sch. Hong Kong. Served with AUS, 1948-49; Served with USNR, 1952-53; Served with USMCR, 1953-55. Mem. Bankers Assn. for Fgn. Trade (past dir.), Am. Bankers Assn. Clubs: Hong Kong, T Bar M Racquet. Home: 7730 Yamini Dr Dallas TX 75230-3231

MASON, BERT E., podiatrist; b. Ryderwood, Wash., Mar. 17, 1944; s. Jean Grenette and Bette Evelyn (Phillips) M.; m. Rachel Nell Hall, May 17, 1991. BA with honors, U. Calif., San Diego, 1971; B in Basic Med. Sci., Calif. Coll. Podiatric Medicine, 1975; D Podiatric Medicine, Calif. Coll. Podiatric Med., 1977. Diplomate Am. Bd. Podiatric Surgery, Am. Bd. Podiatric Orthopedics, Am. Acad. Pain Mgmt. Pvt. practice Fairfield, Calif., 1977-79; chief podiatry sect., dir. podiatric residency VA Med. Ctr., Huntington, W.Va., 1983-87; pvt. practice San Diego, 1987-89; chief podiatry svc., dir. podiatric residency program VA Med. Ctr., Huntington, W.Va., 1993—; asst. prof. podiatric surgery Ohio Coll. Podiatric Medicine, Cleve., 1984-87, 1993—; asst. prof. dept. surgery and community medicine Marshall U. Sch. Medicine, Huntington, 1985-87; v.p. Smith Hanna Med. Group; assoc. prof. of podiatric medicine, Coll. of Podiatric Medicine, Osteo. U. and Health Scis., De Moines, 1993—. Alumni mem. scholarship com., U. Calif., San Diego, 1988—. Maj. U.S. Army, 1979—, chief Podiatry Sect. Ft. Knox, Ky., Ireland Army Hosp. 1980-83, Individual Augmentee Health Svcs. Command, 1983—. Luth. Hosp. Soc. scholar, 1968. Fellow Am. Coll. Foot Surgeons, Am. Coll. Foot Orthopedics, Am. Assn. Hosp. Podiatrists; mem. AAAS, Am. Podiatric Med. Assn., Am. Acad. Pain Mgmt. (diplomate), West. Va. Podiatry Group (pres.), U. Calif. San Diego Alumni Assn. (bd. dirs.). Republican. Avocations: mountain climbing, golf. Home: 350 Grand Blvd Huntington WV 25705-3612 Office: VA Med Ctr Dept Podiatry Huntington WV 25704

MASON, BETTY ROSE, elementary school educator; b. Emporia, Kans., Oct. 4, 1940; d. Virgil Roosevelt and Flora Rose (Leffler) Shellenberger; m. Donnie Lee Mason, Mar. 24, 1961; 1 child, Jeffry Lee. BS, Emporia State U., 1962, postgrad., 1978-79; postgrad., Hays State U., 1967, Pittsburg (Kans.) State U., 1970, Wichita State U., 1971-72, 77-79, 82-83, 89-91, Holy Name Coll., 1974, Friends U., 1992-93. Cert. tchr. K-8 elem., K-9 reading specialist, 7-9 social studies and composition, 7-9 English, Kans. Tchr. 2d grade Kingman/Norwich Sch./Unified Sch. Dist. #331, Kingman, Kans., 1962—, profl. devel. chair, 1983—, profl. devel. records sec. for bd. edn., 1983—; presenter numerous state devel. convs.; supr. student tchrs. state colls. Vol. Meals on Wheels Program, Kingman, 1973—; adminstr. Alice Ann Woodson Children's Fund, Unified Sch. Dist. # 331, Kingman, 1989—; mem. OES Dist. AIDS Assn. Kans., 1985—; sch. coord. learning for life program Boy Scouts Am. Unified Sch. Dist. # 331 Local Dist. Tech. grantee, 1983; recipient 25 Yr. Tchg. award U. Kans., 1987. Mem. Assn. Supervision and Curriculum Devel., Nat. Edn. Assn., Nat. Staff Devel. Coun., Kans. Staff Devel. Coun. (bd. dirs. 1992—), Kans. Edn. Assn., Ednl. Svcs. and Staff Devel. Assn. Ctrl. Kans. (mem. coun. 1987—), Order Ea. Star (Martha 1972-73, 79-92, assoc. conductress 1975, conductress 1976, Della chpt. assoc. matron 1977, Worthy Matron 1978), Mid Century Club (pres. 1989), Kans. Assn. Supervision and Curriculum Devel., Kans. Nat. Edn. Assn. Republican. Methodist. Avocations: collecting carved elephants, glass birds, raising birds, house and car restoration. Home: 120 East Ave F Kingman KS 67068 Office: Unified Sch Dist #331 Kingman-Norwich 115 N Main St Kingman KS 67068-1333

MASON, BOBBIE ANN, novelist, short story writer; b. Mayfield, Ky., May 1, 1940; d. Wilburn A. and Christianna (Lee) M.; m. Roger B. Rawlings, April 12, 1969. BA, U. Ky., 1962; MA, SUNY, Binghamton, 1966; PhD, U. Conn., 1972. Asst. prof. English Mansfield (Pa.) State Coll., 1972-79. Author: Nabokov's Garden, 1974, The Girl Sleuth: A Feminist Guide to the Bobbsey Twins, Nancy Drew and Their Sisters, 1976, 2d edit., 1995, Shiloh and Other Stories, 1976 (Ernest Hemingway award Nat. Book Critic's Circle award nominee, Am. Book award nominee, PEN Faulkner award nominee), In Country, 1985, Spence Lila, 1988, Love Life, 1989, Feather Crowns, 1993 (Nat. Book Critic's Circle award nominee, So. Book award); contbr. regularly to the New Yorker, 1980—; contbr. fiction to the Atlantic, Redbook, Paris Rev., Mother Jones, Harpers, N.Am. Rev., Va. Quar. Rev., Story, Ploughshares, So. Rev., Crazyhorse; contbr. works Best American Short Stories, 1981, The Pushcart Prize; Best of the Small Presses, 1983, Best American Short Stories, 1983. Recipient O. Henry Anthology awards, 1986, 88; grantee Pa. Arts Coun., 1983, 89, Nat. Endowment Arts, 1983, Am. Acad. and Inst. Arts and Letters, 1984; Guggenheim fellow, 1984. Address: care Amanda Urban Internat Creative Mgmt PO Box 518 Lawrenceburg KY 40342

MASON, BRIAN HAROLD, geologist, curator; b. N.Z., Apr. 18, 1917; came to U.S., 1947, naturalized, 1953; s. George Harold and Catherine (Fairweather) M. M.Sc., U. New Zealand, 1938; Ph.D., U. Stockholm, 1943. Lectr. geology Canterbury Coll., N.Z., 1944-47; prof. mineralogy Ind. U., 1947-53; chmn. dept. mineralogy Am. Mus. Natural History, N.Y.C., 1953-65; research curator Dept. Mineral Scis. Smithsonian Instn., Washington, 1965—. Author: Principles of Geochemistry, 3d edit, 1967, Meteorites, 1962, The Literature of Geology, 1958, (with L. G. Berry) Mineralogy, 1959, (with W.G. Melson) The Lunar Rocks, 1970, Victor Moritz Goldschmidt: Father of Modern Geochemistry, 1992. Fellow Mineral. Soc. Am., Geol. Soc. Am.; mem. Geochem. Soc., Royal Soc. N.Z., Swedish Geol. Soc. Office: Dept Mineral Scis Smithsonian Instn Washington DC 20560

MASON, CARTER GREGG, government employee; b. Fresno, Calif., Feb. 18, 1935; s. Morley Jack Mason and Viola Louise (Carter) Densmore; m. Betty Jean Manly, 1964 (div. 1973); 1 child, Denver Morley; m. Beverly Ann Libbon, Oct. 19, 1974; children: Michael Dean Libonati, Nicholas Gregg. B in Sociology, Stanislaus State Coll., 1970; MPA, U. So. Calif., L.A., 1974. Asst. mgr. Standard Stas., Yosemite, Calif., 1953-54; mgr. Standard Stas., Yosemite, 1959-61; correctional officer Calif. Dept. Corrections, Jamestown, Calif., 1961-69; parole agt. Calif. Dept. Corrections, San Jose, Calif., 1970-89; spl. agt. Dept. Def., Santa Clara, Calif., 1989—. V.p. Affirmative Action Com. for Dept. of Corrections, So. Calif., 1972-73; spl. liaison Ventura (Calif.) County Corrections, 1973-74; planning commr. Planning Comm., Santa Maria, Calif., 1980-84. 2d class petty officer USN, 1953-59, master chief petty officer USCGR, 1977-95. Mem. Loyal Order Elks, E Clampus Vitus. Republican. Roman Catholic. Avocations: competetive pistol shooting, archaeology, back packing, wing shooting. Home: 1031 Crestview Dr Apt 116 Mountain View CA 94040-3401

MASON, CHARLES ELLIS, III, magazine editor; b. Boston, Oct. 31, 1938; s. Charles Ellis, Jr. and Ada Brooks (Trafford) M. B.A., Yale U., 1960. Loan officer State St. Bank, Boston, 1963-68; asso. editor Sail mag., Boston, 1968-74; exec. editor Sail mag., 1974—. Author: (with Buddy Melges) Sailing Smart, 1983; editor: Best of Sail Trim, 1976, Best of SAIL Navigation, 1981. Mem. exec. com. Sierra Club Greater Boston Group, 1992. Served with USNR, 1960-62. Home: 16 Joy St Boston MA 02114-4140 Office: Sail Publs 84 State St Boston MA 02109

MASON, CHERYL WHITE, lawyer; b. Champaign, Ill., Jan. 16, 1952; d. John Russell and Lucille (Birden) White; m. Robert L. Mason, Oct. 9, 1972; children: Robert L. II and Daniel G. BA, Purdue U., 1972; JD, U. Chgo., 1976. Bar: Calif. 19767. Assoc. O'Melveny & Myers, L.A., 1976-81, 84-86, ptnr., 1987—; exec. dir. Public Counsel, L.A., 1981-84; bd. dirs. Calif. Pub. Policy Inst. Chmn. State Bar, Legal Svcs. Trust Fund, 1987; trustee L.A. County Bar, 1985-88; bd. dirs. Challengers Boys and Girls Club, L.A., 1990—, Western Ctr. Law and Poverty, L.a., 1991-94. Mem. ABA (co-chair environ. litigation commn. 1992-94, lawyer rep. 9th cir. jud. conf. 1993-94), Calif. Women Lawyers, L.A. County Bar Assn., Women Lawyers L.A., Black Women Lawyers L.A., Langston Bar Assn. Democrat. Office: O'Melveny & Myers 400 S Hope St Los Angeles CA 90071-2801

MASON, DAVID DICKENSON, statistics educator; b. Abingdon, Va., Jan. 22, 1917; s. William Thomas and Eva (Dorton) M.; m. Virginia Louise Pendleton, Oct. 28, 1944; children: Marjorie F., David P. B.A., King Coll., 1936; M.S. (Acad. Merit fellow), Va. Poly. Inst., 1938; postgrad., Ohio State U., 1939-40; Ph.D., N.C. State U., 1948. Asst. soil scientist Va. Poly. Inst., 1938-39; asst. prof. soils Ohio State U., 1947-49; prin. biometrician Dept. Agr., Beltsville, Md., 1949-53; prof. stats. N.C. State U., 1953-62, prof., head dept. stats., 1962-81, emeritus prof. and head, 1981—; head Inst. Stats., 1962-81, emeritus head, 1981—; Sr. cons. United Fruit Co., Boston, 1957-71. Contbr. articles to profl. jours. Instl. rep. So. Regional Edn. Bd. com. statistics, 1963-81, chmn., 1973-75; Bd. dirs. Triangle Univs. Computation Center Corp., chmn., 1968-70. Served with AUS, 1941-45. Fellow Am. Statis. Assn., Am. Soc. Agronomy, Soil Sci. Soc. Am.; mem. Biometric Soc., Sigma Xi, Phi Kappa Phi, Gamma Sigma Delta. Presbyn. (elder, deacon). Club: Rotarian. Home: 4212 Arbutus Dr Raleigh NC 27612-3702 Office: Inst Stats PO Box 8203 Raleigh NC 27695

MASON, DEAN TOWLE, cardiologist; b. Berkeley, Calif., Sept. 20, 1932; s. Ira Jenckes and Florence Mabel (Towle) M.; m. Maureen O'Brien, June 22, 1957; children: Kathleen, Alison. BA in Chemistry, Duke U., 1954, MD, 1958. Diplomate Am. Bd. Internal Medicine, Am. Bd. Cardiovasc. Diseases, Nat. Bd. Med. Examiners. Intern, then resident in medicine Johns Hopkins Hosp., 1958-61; clin. assoc. cardiology br., sr. asst. surgeon USPHS, Nat. Heart Inst., NIH, 1961-63, asst. sect. dir. cardiovascular diagnosis, attending physician, sr. investigator cardiology br., 1963-68; prof. medicine, prof. physiology, chief cardiovascular medicine U. Calif. Med. Sch., Davis-Sacramento Med. Center, 1968-82; dir. cardiac ctr. Cedars Med. Ctr., Miami, Fla., 1982-83; physician-in chief Western Heart Inst., San Francisco, 1983—; chmn. dept. cardiovascular medicine St. Mary's Med. Ctr., San Francisco, 1986—; co-chmn. cardiovascular-renal drugs U.S. Pharmacopeia Com. Revision, 1970-75; mem. life scis. com. NASA; med. rsch. rev. bd. VA, NIH; vis. prof. numerous univs., cons. in field; mem. Am. Cardiovascular Splty. Cert. Bd., 1970-78. Editor-in-chief Am. Heart Jour., 1980—; contbr. numerous articles to med. jours. Recipient Research award Am. Therapeutic Soc., 1965; Theodore and Susan B. Cummings Humanitarian award State

Dept.-Am. Coll. Cardiology, 1972, 73, 75, 78; Skylab Achievement award NASA, 1974; U. Calif. Faculty Research award, 1978; named Outstanding Prof. U. Calif. Med. Sch., Davis, 1972. Fellow Am. Coll. Cardiology (pres. 1977-78), A.C.P., Am. Heart Assn., Am. Coll. Chest Physicians, Royal Soc. Medicine; mem. Am. Soc. Clin. Investigation, Am. Physiol. Soc., Am. Soc. Pharmacology and Exptl. Therapeutics (Exptl. Therapeutics award 1973), Am. Fedn. Clin. Research, N.Y. Acad. Scis., Am. Assn. U. Cardiologists, Am. Soc. Clin. Pharmacology and Therapeutics, Western Assn. Physicians, AAUP, Western Soc. Clin. Research (past pres.), Phi Beta Kappa, Alpha Omega Alpha. Republican. Methodist. Club: El Marcero Country. Home: 44725 Country Club Dr El Macero CA 95618-1047 Office: Western Heart Inst St Mary's Med Ctr 450 Stanyan St San Francisco CA 94117-1079

MASON, DOUGLAS MICHAEL, environmental scientist; b. Phila., Apr. 20, 1950; s. Clayton Douglas and Veronica Mary (Doyle) M.; m. Peng Keokamsorn, Apr. 1, 1973 (div. 1983); children: Frank, Penny; m. Josephine Ruth Joliet, June 30, 1990 (div. 1993); children: Wendy, Jonathan, Kimberly. BS, Del. Valley Coll., 1978; M in Agr., Pa. State U., 1982; PhD, U. Pa., 1993. Lab. asst. Community Coll., Phila., 1973-77; soil conservationist USDA Soil Conservation Svc., Somerset, Pa., 1977-79; rsch. asst. Pa. State U. Dept. of Agronomy, State Coll., 1979-82; soil scientist Pa. Dept. Environ. Resources, Norristown, 1982-87; agronomist/soil scientist Nat. Ctr. for Appropriate Tech., Memphis, 1987-88; soil scientist Ozark Soil Svcs., Inc., Springfield, Mo., 1988-89; dir. pollution prevention Hoosier Environ. Coun., Indpls., 1989-92; soil scientist Hoosier Soil Svcs., Inc., Indpls., 1992-93, Ind. Dept. Environ. Mgmt., Indpls., 1993-94; exec. dir. Hoosier UNCED Watch, Indpls., 1994—; environ. sci. Specialty Sys. Hazardous Waste, Inc., Indpls., 1995—; bd. dirs., Found. for Global Sustainability, Knoxville, Tenn., 1987-92, Hoosier Alliance for Consumer Rights, Indpls., 1989-92, Citizens Action Coalition, Indpls., 1990-91, Indpls. Peace and Justice Ctr., 1994—. Contbr. articles to profl. jours. Candidate, U.S. Ho. Reps., State Coll., Pa., 1980; environ. rep., Fin. AssuranceBd., Indpls., 1992; lobbyist, Hoosier Environ. Coun., Indpls., 1989-92. Sgt. USAF,1969-73. Mem. Am. Soc. Agronomy, Crop Sci. Soc. Am., Soil Sci. Soc. Am., Internat. Soc. Soil Sci., World Assn. Soil & Water Conservation, Soil & Water Conservation Soc.,Am. Registry of Cert. Profls. in Agronomy, Crops & Soils. Roman Catholic. Avocations: peace and justice advocacy, environmentalist, harmonica, nature, photography. Office: SSHW Inc Hoosier UNCED Watch 310 S State St Indianapolis IN 46201

MASON, EARL LEONARD, steel company executive; b. Jersey City, July 12, 1947; s. Herman E. and Marguerite (Rondeau) M.; m. Patricia Fladung (div. 1976); children: Holly Ann, Wendy Lynn; m. Bonita L. Blair, Dec. 11, 1976. BS, Fairleigh Dickinson U., 1969, MBA, 1984. With AT&T, N.J., 1969-79, dir. mktg., 1979-81; corp. contr. ATT Info. Systems, 1981-85; dir. fin. mgmt. and planning AT&T, N.J., 1985-87; controller mfg. Digital Equipment Corp., Maynard, Mass., 1987-91; European CFO Digital Equipment Corp., Geneva, 1991—; v.p. fin., CFO Inland Steel Industries, Chgo., 1991—, now sr. v.p.; dir. Family Inn, Boston, 1992—. dir. Family Inn, Boston, 1992—, State of Ill. Mem. Am. Iron and Steel Inst., Fin. Execs. Inst., Univ. Club, East Bank Club, City of Chgo. C. of C. (bd. dirs.). Avocations: squash, racquetball, tennis, golf, boating. Office: 30 W Monroe St Chicago IL 60603-2401*

MASON, EDWARD EATON, surgeon; b. Boise, Idaho, Oct. 16, 1920; s. Edward Files and Dora Bell (Eaton) M.; m. Dordana Fairman, June 18, 1944; children—Daniel Edward, Rose Mary, Richard Eaton, Charles Henry. B.A., U. Iowa, 1943, M.D., 1945; Ph.D. in Surgery, U. Minn., 1953. Intern, resident in surgery Univ. Hosps., Mpls., 1945-52; asst. prof. surgery U. Iowa, 1953-55, asso. prof., 1956-60, prof., 1961-91, prof. emeritus, 1991—, chmn. gen. surgery, 1978-91; cons. VA Hosp.; trainee Nat. Cancer Inst., 1949-52. Author: Computer Applications in Medicine, 1964, Fluid, Electrolyte and Nutrient Therapy in Surgery, 1974, Surgical Treatment of Obesity, 1981; developer gastric bypass and gastroplasty for treatment of obesity; contbr. articles profl. jours. Served to lt. (j.g.) USNR, 1945-47. Fellow ACS; mem. AMA, Am. Surg. Assn., Western Surg. Assn., Soc. Univ. Surgeons, Internat. Soc. Surgery, Ctrl. Surg. Assn., Soc. Surgery Alimentary Tract, Am. Thyroid Assn., Am. Soc. Bariatric Surgery, Sigma Xi, Alpha Omega Alpha. Republican. Presbyterian. Home: 5 Melrose Cir Iowa City IA 52246-2013 Office: Dept of Surgery University Hospitals Iowa City IA 52242 *Continuity of interest and planning weaves the daily decisions into a whole cloth that does more than cover one's imperfections.*

MASON, ELLSWORTH GOODWIN, librarian; b. Waterbury, Conn., Aug. 25, 1917; s. Frederick William and Kathryn Loretta (Watkins) M.; m. Rose Ellen Maloy, May 13, 1951 (div. Oct. 1961); children: Kay Iris, Joyce Iris; m. Joan Lou Shinew, Aug. 16, 1964; 1 son, Sean David. B.A., Yale U., 1938, M.A., 1942, Ph.D., 1948; L.H.D., Hofstra U., 1973. Cert. Inst. Children's Lit., 1996. Reference asst. Yale Library, 1938-42; export license officer Bd. Econ. Warfare, 1942-43; instr. English Williams Coll., 1948-50; instr. humanities div. Marlboro (Vt.) Coll., 1951-52; serials libr. U. Wyo. Libr., 1952-54; reference libr. Colo. Coll. Libr., Colorado Springs, 1954-58; lectr., libr. Colo. Coll., 1958-63; prof., dir. libr. svcs. Hofstra U., Hempstead, N.Y., 1963-72; prof., dir. U. Colo. Librs., Boulder, 1972-76; freelance writer children's lit., 1995—; adj. prof. U. Ill., Urbana, 1968; pres. Mason Assocs., Ltd., 1977—; rsch. assoc. U. Calif.-Berkeley, 1965; vis. lectr. Northwestern U., 1961, Colo. Coll., 1965, Syracuse U., 1965-68, Elmira Coll., 1966, Columbia U., 1966-68, U. Ill., 1972, Lincoln U., 1969, U. B.C. (Can.), 1969, U. Toronto, 1970, U. Tulsa, 1971, 76, Rutgers U., 1971, Colgate U., 1972, Simmons Coll., 1972, U. Oreg., 1973, Hofstra U., 1974, U. N.C., 1976, U. Ala., 1976, Ball State U., 1977, U. Lethbrige, Can., 1977, U. Ariz., 1981, Ariz. State U., 1981, Victoria U., New Zealand, 1983, U. Canterbury, New Zealand, 1983, U. Nev. Las Vegas, 1992, Remember Pearl Harbor Assn., 1993, 94; libr. cons., 1958—, libr. value engr., 1992—. Editor: (with Stanislaus Joyce) The Early Joyce, 1955, Xerox U.M. edit., 1964, (with Richard Ellmann) The Critical Writings of James Joyce, 1959, 2d edit., 1989, Critical Commentary on A Portrait of the Artist as a Young Man, 1966; translator: Recollections of James Joyce (S. Joyce), 1950, Essais de J. Joyce, 1966, Escritos Criticos de James Joyce, (Portuguese edit.), 1967, (Spanish edit.), 1973, 75, James Joyce's Ulysses and Vico's Cycle, 1973, Kritische Schriften v. James Joyce, 1975, Mason on Library Buildings, 1980, (with Walter and Jean Shine) A MacDonald Potpourri, 1988, The University of Colorado Library and Its Makers, 1876-1972, 1994; contbr. Contemporary Authors, 1988—; editor: Colorado College Studies, 1959-62; editor and compiler: Focus on Robert Graves, 1972-88; adv. editor: Focus on Robert Graves and His Contemporaries, 1988—; editor: The Booklover's Bounty, 1977—; mem. editorial bd. Serial Slants, 1957-59, The Serials Librarian, 1977—, Choice, 1962-65, Coll. and Rsch. Librs., 1969-72. Mem. exec. bd. U. Ky. Libr. Assocs., 1991—. Served with USNR, 1943-46. Recipient Harry Bailly spkr.'s award Assn. Colls. of Midwest, 1975; fellow Coun. on Libr. Resources, 1969-70; grantee Am. Coun. Learned Socs., Edn. Facilities Labs., Hofstra U., U. Colo.; named Ky. Col., 1993. Mem. ALA (councillor-at-large 1961-65), Colo. Libr. Assn. (pres. so. dist. 1960-61), Bibliog. Soc. Am., Libr. Assn. (London), N.Z. Libr. Assn., MLA, Pvt. Librs. Assn., Alcuin Soc. Vancouver, Conf. Editors Learned Journs., N.Z. Royal Forest and Bird Protection Soc., Colo. Book Collectors (founder, pres. 1975—), Inst. Vico Studies, James Joyce Found. (chmn. sect. on translation from Joyce, 2d Internat. James Joyce Symposium, Dublin 1969), Black America's PAC, Caxton Club, Archons of Colophon, Ghost Town Club, Alpha Sigma Lambda, Sigma Kappa Alpha (pres. 1969-70). Home: 736 Providence Rd Lexington KY 40502-2267 also: 39 Discovery Dr, Whitby New Zealand

MASON, FRANK HENRY, III, automobile company executive, leasing company executive; b. Paris, Tenn., Nov. 16, 1936; s. Frank H. and Dorothy (Carter) M.; children—Robert C., William C. B.E.E., Vanderbilt U., 1958; M.S. in Indsl. Mgmt., MIT, 1965. With Ford Motor Co., 1965-71, asst. controller Ford Brazil, Sao Paulo, Brazil, 1971-74, mgr. overseas financing dept., Dearborn, Mich., 1974-76, asst. controller engine div., 1976-78, mgr. facilities and mgmt. services, 1978-81; controller Ford Motor Credit Co., Dearborn, 1981-87; dir. finance Ford Fin. Services Group, Dearborn, 1987-89; exec. v.p., chief fin. officer U.S. Leasing, Internat., San Francisco, 1989-92; ret. 1992. Served to lt. USN, 1958-63.

MASON, FRANKLIN ROGERS, automotive executive; b. Washington, June 16, 1936; s. Franklin Allison and Jeannette Morgan (Rogers) M.; m. Aileen Joan Larson, July 29, 1961; children: William Rogers, Elisa Ellen. BS in Engring, Princeton U., 1958; MBA, Northwestern U., 1960. With Ford Motor Co., 1960-75, finance mgr., Portugal, 1969-72; fin. analysis mgr. Ford subs. Richier S.A., France, 1972-75; sr. v.p. finance Raymond Internat. Inc., Houston, 1975-86; chief fin. officer Quanex Corp., Houston, 1986-87; group v.p., chief fin. officer Gulf States Toyota, Inc., Houston, 1987—. With arty. U.S. Army, 1960. Mem. Princeton U. Alumni Assn., Univ. Club, Racquet Club. Republican. Episcopalian. Home: 5765 Indian Cir Houston TX 77057-1302 Office: Gulf States Toyota Inc 7701 Wilshire Place Dr Houston TX 77040-5346 *Business is people, and success is dependent on good communication with people. Effective communication must be accompanied by fairness, consistency, patience, and a willingness to compromise.*

MASON, GEORGE H., business educator, consultant; b. Chgo., Sept. 11, 1929; s. Robert De Main and Dorothy Wills (Belden) M.; m. Constance Eleanor Wolcott, May 14, 1960. AB, Kenyon Coll., 1955; MBA, Cornell U., 1957; MF, Duke U., 1983. CFA. Investment officer Travelers Ins. Co., Hartford, Conn., 1957-88; exec.-in-residence U. Hartford, West Hartford, 1989—; mng. dir. Heaphy Trust Group, Springfield, Mass.; mem. bus. bd. adv. Sustainable Forest Sys. Corp., Incline Village, Nev.; vis. prof. Jagiellonian U., Cracow, Poland, spring 1996. Co-author: Timberland Investments, 1992. Mem. Assn. Investment Mgmt. & Rsch., Soc. Am. Foresters, Hartford Soc. Fin. Analysts, Cornell Club. Republican. Avocations: skiing, golf, writing. Office: U Hartford 200 Bloomfield Ave Hartford CT 06117

MASON, GEORGE ROBERT, surgeon, educator; b. Rochester, N.Y., June 10, 1932; s. George Mitchell and Marjorie Louise (Hooper) M.; m. Grace Louise Bransfield, Feb. 4, 1956; children: Douglas Richard, Marcia Jean, David William. BA, Oberlin Coll., 1955; MD with honors, U. Chgo., 1957; PhD in Physiology, Stanford U., 1968. Diplomate: Am. Bd. Surgery (examiner 1977-80, dir. 1980-86), Bd. Thoracic Surgery. Teaching asst. pathology U. Chgo., 1954-56; rotating intern U. Chgo. Clinics, 1957-58; tchg. asst. surgery, NIH postdoctoral fellow, USPHS fellow surgery Stanford U., 1960-62; from asst. resident in surgery to sr. and chief resident in surgery Stanford U. Hosps., 1962-66; mem. faculty Stanford Med. Sch., 1965-71, assoc. prof., 1970-71; prof., chmn. dept. surgery U. Md. Med. Sch., Balt., 1971-80; also prof. physiology; prof., chmn. dept. surgery U. Calif., Irvine, 1980-89; chief surgical svc. Hines (Ill.) VA Hosp., 1990-95; prof. surgery and thoracic cardiovascular surgery Loyola U. Med. Ctr., 1990—; chmn. dept. thoracic and cardiovasc. surgery Loyola U. Med. Ctr., Maywood, Ill., 1995—; mem. residency review com. for surgery, 1981-87. Contbr. to profl. jours., med. textbooks. Served to capt. M.C., USAF, 1958-60. Giannini fellow Stanford U., 1966-67; recipient Markle scholarship in acad. medicine, 1968-74. Mem. ACS, Am. Assn. Thoracic Surgeons, Am. Coll. Chest Physicians, Am. Physiol. Soc., Am. Gastroent. Assn., Pacific Coast Surg. Assn., Assn. Acad. Surgery, Ctrl. Surg. Soc., So. Surg. Soc., Chgo. Surg. Soc., Am. Surg. Assn., Western Surg. Assn., Soc. Thoracic Surgeons, Ill. Thoracic Surg. Soc. (pres. 1994-95), Halsted Soc., Chesapeake Vascular Soc., Soc. Internat. Chirurgie, Soc. Clin. Surgery, Soc. for Surgery Alimentary Tract, Soc. Univ. Surgeons. Home: PO Box 3877 Oak Brook IL 60522-3877 Office: Rm 6240 EMS LUMC Rm 6240 Bldg 110 2160 S First Ave Maywood IL 60153

MASON, GREGORY WESLEY, JR., secondary education educator; b. Chgo., Jan. 21, 1963; s. Gregory Wesley and Diana (Burton) M.; m. LaTanya Yvonne Brown, June 8, 1991; 1 child, Gregory Arthur. BS, Ill. State U., 1986. Cert. secondary tchr., Ill. Instr. City Coll. Chgo., 1986-89; instr. project alert Roosevelt U., Chgo., 1989-91, counselor project upward bound, 1991-93; tchr. math. Bowen High Sch., Chgo., 1993—, chmn. profl. planning adv. com., 1994—; tchr. math. Whitney M. Young Magnet H.S., Chgo., 1995—; instr. Ill. Math. and Sci. Acad., Aurora, summers 1993—. Named Outstanding Young Men of Am., 1985. Mem. ASCD, Nat. Coun. Tchrs. Maths., Ill. Coun. Tchrs. Maths., Ill. Coun. for Coll. Attendance (bd. dirs. 1993—), Benjamin Banneker Assn., Phi Delta Kappa. Avocations: swimming, chess, reading, stock trading, computers. Home: 2729 W 84th St Chicago IL 60652 Office: Whitney M Young Magnet HS 211 S Laflin Ave Chicago IL 60607

MASON, HENRY LLOYD, political science educator; b. Berlin, Germany, Nov. 4, 1921; came to U.S., 1940, naturalized, 1943; s. Hugo L. and Maria (Werner) M.; m. Mathilde Jessé, Jan. 23, 1946; children—Monica (Mrs. Robert Mimeles), Paul. B.A., Johns Hopkins, 1942; Ph.D., Columbia, 1951. Mem. faculty Tulane U., New Orleans, 1952—, prof. polit. sci., 1961—, chmn. dept., 1966-75, 87-88; vis. assoc. prof. Columbia, 1958; Fulbright prof. U. Innsbruck, 1958-59, Free U. Berlin, 1965; vis. prof. U. Amsterdam, 1973-74. Author: The Purge of Dutch Quislings, 1952, The European Coal and Steel Community, 1955, Toynbee's Approach to World Politics, 1959, Mass Demonstrations Against Foreign Regimes, 1966, University Government, 1972. Bd. dirs. Urban League Greater New Orleans, 1961-69. Served to 1st lt., M.I. AUS, 1942-46, ETO. Mem. AAUP (mem. nat. council 1966-69 1st nat. v.p. 1984-86), Internat. Studies Assn. (pres. so. region 1972-73), So. Polit. Sci. Assn. (mem. exec. council 1973-76). Home: 1821 Upperline St New Orleans LA 70115-5547

MASON, HENRY LOWELL, III, lawyer; b. Boston, Feb. 10, 1941; s. Henry Lowell and Fanny Crowninshield (Homans) M.; m. Elaine Bobrowicz, June 7, 1969. AB, Harvard U., 1963, LLB, 1967. Bar: Ill. 1967. Assoc. Leibman, Williams, Bennett, Baird & Minow, Chgo., 1967-72; assoc. Sidley & Austin, 1972-73, ptnr., 1973—. Republican. Office: Sidley & Austin 1 First Nat Plz Chicago IL 60603

MASON, HERBERT WARREN, JR., religion and history educator, author; b. Wilmington, Del., Apr. 20, 1932; s. Herbert Warren and Mildred Jane (Noyes) M.; m. Jeanine Young, June 25, 1982; children from previous marriage: Cathleen, Paul, Sarah. AB, Harvard U., 1955, AM, 1965, PhD, 1969. English tchr. Am. Sch. Paris, 1959-60; asst. prof. St. Joseph's Coll., Gorham, Maine, 1960-62; vis. lectr. Simmons Coll., Boston, 1962-63; vis. lectr. in Islamic Hist. Tufts U., Medford, Mass., 1965-66; teaching fellow in English Harvard U., Cambridge, Mass., 1962-66, teaching fellow in Islamic Hist., 1966-67; translator Bollingen Found., N.Y.C., 1968-72; prof. History and Religion Boston U., 1972—. Author: Reflections on the Middle East Crisis, 1970, Two Statesmen of Medieval Islam, 1971, Gilgamesh, 1971 (Nat. Book award nomination), The Death of al-Hallaj, 1979, Moments in Passage, 1979, (novel) Summer Light, 1980; translator: La Passion d'al-Hallaj, 4 vols., Bollingen Series (Louis Massignon), 1983, abridged 1 vol., 1994, A Legend of Alexander, 1986, Memoir of a Friend: Louis Massignon, 1988, Testimonies and Reflections, 1989, al-Hallaj, 1995; co-editor Humaniora Islamica; contbr. articles, essays, reviews, fiction, reviews and poetry to popular fiction mags. Sec. Inter-racial Riverside Assn., Cambridge, Mass., 1965-67; trustee Bd. Charity of Edward Hopkins, Boston Athenaeum. Fellow Soc. for Values in Higher Edn.; mem. PEN (bd. dirs. Delos chpt.), Medieval Acad. Am., Am. Oriental Soc., Am. Acad. Religion, Mark Twain Soc., Inst. Internat. des Recherches Louis Massignon in Paris (dir. edn.). Home: 30 The Common Phillipston MA 01331-9735 Office: Boston U 745 Commonwealth Ave Boston MA 02215-1401

MASON, JACKIE, comedian, actor; b. Sheboygan, Wis., June 9, 1934. Stand-up comedian; performances include (theater) A Teaspoon Every Four Hours, 1969, The World According to Me! (one man show, Tony, Emmy and Ace awards 1987), Brand New, Politically Incorrect, 1994; (films) Operation Delilah, 1966, The Stoolie, 1972, The Jerk, 1979, History of the World Part I, 1981, The Perils of P.K., 1986, Caddyshack II, 1988; TV appearances in Steve Allen, Ed Sullivan, Jack Paar, Garry Moore, Perry Como and Merv Griffin Shows, Johnny Carson, Arsenio Hall, Late Night with David Letterman; (TV series) Chicken Soup, The Jackie Mason Show; (TV movies) The Best of Times; (TV specials) Jackie Mason on Broadway (Emmy award for writing in a variety or music program 1988); records include The World According to Me!, Brand New. Recipient special Tony award, 1987, Emmy award for The Simpsons, 1991. Office: csre William Morris Agy 1350 Avenue Of The Americas New York NY 10019-4702

MASON, JAMES ALBERT, museum director, university dean; b. Eureka, Utah, 1929; married, 1956; 3 children. BA, Brigham Young U., 1955, MA, 1957; EdD, Ariz. State U., 1970. Cons., clinician in fine arts, 1955—; former chmn. dept. music Brigham Young U., Provo, dean Coll. Fine Arts and Communications, 1982-93; now dir. Mus. of Art Brigham Young U., 1993—; vis. prof., lectr. Ind. U., Northwestern U., Cin. Coll.-Conservatory, U. Tex., Central Conservatory, Beijing, Internat. Soc. Music Edn., Warsaw; chmn. nat. symposium Applications of Psychology to the Teaching and Learning of Music; chmn., bd. dirs. The Barlow Endowment for Music Composition; co-founder, 1st pres. Utah Valley Symphony Orch.; past condr. Utah Valley Youth Orch.; bd. trustees Utah Opera Co.; commr. Utah Centennial of Statehood. Editor: The Instrumentalist, Orch. News, Utah Music Educator, Research News column, Jour. Research in Music Edn. Bd. dirs. Presser Found. Mem. Music Educators Nat. Conf. (past nat. pres., council), Nat. Music Council (past bd. dirs.), Am. Music Conf. (past bd. dirs.). Office: Brigham Young U Art Mus Provo UT 84602-1026

MASON, JAMES OSTERMANN, public health administrator; b. Salt Lake City, June 19, 1930; s. Ambrose Stanton and Neoma (Thorup) M.; m. Lydia Maria Smith, Dec. 29, 1952; children: James, Susan, Bruce, Ralph, Samuel, Sara, Benjamin. BA, U. Utah, 1954, MD, 1958; MPH, Harvard U., 1963, DPH, 1967. Diplomate Am. Bd. Preventive Medicine. Intern Johns Hopkins Hosp., Balt., 1958-59; resident in internal medicine Peter Bent Brigham Hosp.-Harvard Med. Service, Boston, 1961-62; chief infectious diseases Latter-day Saints Hosp., Salt Lake City, 1968-69; commr. Health Services Corp., Ch. of Jesus Christ of Latter-day Saints, 1970-76; dep. dir. health Utah Div. Health, 1976-78, exec. dir., 1979-83; chief epidemic intelligence service Ctr. Disease Control, Atlanta, 1959, chief hepatitis surveillance unit epidemiology br., 1960, chief surveillance sect. epidemiology br., 1961, dep. dir. bur. labs., 1964-68, dep. dir. of Ctr., 1969-70; dir. Ctrs. for Disease Control, Atlanta; adminstr. Agy. for Toxic Substances and Disease Registry, 1983-89; acting asst. sec. health HHS, Washington, 1985, asst. sec. for health, acting surgeon gen., 1989-90, asst. sec. for health, 1990-93; asst. prof. dept. medicine and preventive medicine U. Utah, Salt Lake City, 1968-69; assoc. prof., chmn. div. community medicine, dept. family and community medicine U. Utah, 1978-79; v.p. planning, devel., prof. preventive medicine and biometrics Uniformed Svcs. U. Health Scis., 1993-94; 2nd quorum of Seventy LDS Ch., 1994—; physician, cons. to med. services Salt Lake VA Hosp., 1977-83; clin. prof. dept. family and community medicine, U. Utah. Coll. Medicine, 1979-83, clin. prof. dept. pathology, 1980-83; clin. prof. community health Emory U. Sch. Medicine, 1984-86; chmn. joint residency com. in preventive medicine and pub. health Utah Coll. Medicine, 1975-80; mem. Utah Cancer Registry Research Adv. Com., 1976-83; mem. adv. com. Utah Ctr. Health Stats., 1977-79; chmn. bd. Hosp. Coop. Utah, 1977-79; chmn. exec. com. Utah Health Planning and Resource Devel. Adv. Group, 1977-79; chmn. Utah Gov.'s Adv. Com. for Comprehensive Health Planning, 1975-77; mem. recombinant DNA adv. com. NIH, 1979-83; mem. Gov.'s Nuclear Waste Repository Task Force, 1980-83, chmn., 1980-82; bd. dirs. Utah Health Cost Mgmt. Found., 1980-83; mem. adv. com. for programs and policies Ctrs. for Disease Control, 1980; mem. com. on future of local health depts., Inst. Medicine, 1980-82; mem. exec. com., chmn. tech. adv. com. Thrasher Research Found., 1980-89; mem. Robert Wood Johnson Found. Program for Hosp. Initiatives in Long-Term Care, 1982-84; mem. sci. and tech. adv. com. UNDP-World Bank-WHO Spl. Programme for Research and Tng. in Tropical Diseases, 1984-89; mem. Utah Resource for Genetic and Epidemiologic Research, 1982-85, chmn. bd., 1982-83; U.S. rep. WHO Exec. Bd., 1990-93. Author: (with H.L. Bodily and E.L. Updyke) Diagnostic Procedures for Bacterial, Mycotic and Parasitic Infections, 5th edit., 1970; (with M.H. Maxell, K.H. Bousfield and D.A. Ostler) Funding Water Quality Control in Utah, Procs. for Lincoln Inst., 1982; contbr. articles to profl. jours. Mem. nat. scouting com. Boy Scouts Am., 1974-78. Recipient Roche award U. Utah, 1957, Wintrobe award U. Utah, 1958, Disting. Alumni award U. Utah, 1973, Adminstr. of Yr. award Brigham U., 1980, spl. award for outstanding pub. svc. Am. Soc. Pub. Adminstrn. 1984, Disting. Svc. medal USPHS, 1988, LDS Hosp. Deseret Found. Legacy of Life award, 1992, Gorgas Medal and Scroll, 1993. Mem. Inst. Medicine of NAS, AMA, Am. Pub. Health Assn. (task force for credentialing of lab. personnel 1976-78, program devel. bd. 1979-81), Utah State Med. Assn. (trustee 1979-83), Utah Acad. Preventive Medicine (pres. 1982-83), Utah Pub. Health Assn. (pres. 1980-82, Beatty award 1979), Sigma Xi, Alpha Epsilon Delta, Phi Kappa Phi, Alpha Omega Alpha, Delta Omega. Mem. LDS Ch. Lodge: Rotary. Office: LDS ChThe 70 47 E South Temple St Salt Lake City UT 84150 also: Africa Area Adminstrv Office, POBox 1218, Lonehill 2062, South Africa

MASON, JAMES TATE, surgeon; b. Seattle, June 17, 1913; s. James Tate and Laura (Whittlesey) M.; m. Margaret Elisabeth Thomas, Jan. 10, 1942; children—Laura Mason Foster, Anne Mason Curti, James Tate, Mary Mason, Paul. Student, U. Wash., 1936; M.D., U. Va., 1940. Diplomate: Am. Bd. Urology (trustee 1974-80, pres. 1979-80, exec. sec. 1980-84). Intern Bellevue Hosp., N.Y.C., 1940-41; resident Lahey Clinic, Boston, 1942-43, U. Mich., 1946-49; practice medicine, specializing in urologic surgery Seattle, 1949-83; staff Mason Clinic, Virginia Mason, Univ., Harborview hosps., all Seattle; clin. prof. urology U. Wash., Seattle, 1974-83, emeritus clin. prof., 1983—. Contbr. articles to profl. jours. Bd. dirs. Virginia Mason Hosp., 1956-79, pres., 1975-78; trustee Virginia Mason Research Found., Seattle, 1960-79, King County (Wash.) chpt. Boys' Clubs Am., 1965-76, Seattle Art Mus., 1978-88, Seattle Hist. Soc., 1979-86. Served to comdr. M.C., USNR, 1941-46. Fellow A.C.S.; Mem. Am. Urol. Assn. (pres. Western sect. 1968-69, exec. com. assn. 1973-76, nat. pres. 1984-85), Am. Assn. Clin. Urologists, AMA, Am. Assn. Genitourinary Surgeons, Pacific Coast Surg. Assn., SAR (pres. chpt. 1957-58). Clubs: University, Seattle Tennis. Home: 3825 E Mcgraw St Seattle WA 98112-2428 Office: U Wash Med Sch Seattle WA 98195 *Family and friends are the greatest treasures a person may have. One must try in every way to live up to their expectations.*

MASON, JOHN LATIMER, engineering executive; b. Los Angeles, Nov. 8, 1923; s. Zene Upham and Edna Ella (Watkins) M.; m. Frances Howe Draeger, Sept. 1, 1950 (dec. June 1951); m. Mary Josephine Schulte, Nov. 26, 1954; children: Andrew, Peter, Mary Anne, John Edward. B.S. in Meteorology, U. Chgo., 1944; B.S. in Applied Chemistry, Calif. Inst. Tech., 1947, M.S. in Chem. Engring., 1948, Ph.D., 1950. Registered profl. engr., Calif. Engr. AiResearch Mfg. Co., Los Angeles, 1950-60; dir. engring. AiResearch Mfg. Co. div. Garrett Corp., Los Angeles, 1960-72; v.p. engring. Garrett Corp., Los Angeles, 1972-87; v.p. engring. and tech. Allied-Signal Aerospace Co., Los Angeles, 1987-88, cons., 1989—; chmn. tech. adv. com. Indsl. Turbines Internat., Inc., Los Angeles, 1972-81, bd. dirs., 1980-88; adj. prof. engring. Calif. State U., Long Beach, 1992—; mem. tech. adv. bd. Tex. Ctr. for Superconductivity, U. Houston, 1989—; chair Calif. Coun. Sci. and Tech. Panel on Transp. R&D Ctr., 1993-94; bd. dirs. San Juan Capistrano Rsch. Inst.; cons. Capstone Turbine Corp., 1994—. Patentee in field. Chmn. energy and environment com. FISITA Coun., 1990-94. 1st lt. USAAF, 1943-45, PTO. Fellow AIAA (assoc.). Soc. Automotive Engrs. (bd. dirs. 1984-87, 90-93, pres.-elect 1989-90, pres. 1990-91), Performance Rev. Inst. (chmn. 1990-91, bd. dirs. 1992-93); mem. AAAS, NAS (com. on alternative energy R&D strategies 1989-90), Office Sci. and Tech. Policy (Nat. Critical Techs. panel 1992-93), Inst. Medicine of NAS (com. on health effects of indoor allergens 1992-93), Nat. Acad. Engring., U.S. Advanced Ceramics Assn. (chmn. tech. com., bd. dirs. 1985-88), Am. Chem. Soc., Am. Ceramic Soc., Caltech Assocs., Sigma Xi. Office: Allied Signal Automotive 3201 Lomita Blvd Torrance CA 90505-5015

MASON, JOHN MILTON (JACK MASON), judge; b. Mankato, Minn., Oct. 31, 1938; s. Milton Donald and Marion (Dailey) M.; m. Vivian McFerran, Aug. 25, 1962; children: Kathleen, Peter, Michael. BA cum laude, Macalester Coll., 1960; JD, Harvard U., 1963. Bar: Minn. 1963, U.S. Supreme Ct. 1970. Assoc. Dorsey & Whitney, Mpls., 1963-68, ptnr., 1969-71, 73-95; solicitor gen. State of Minn., St. Paul, 1971, chief dep. atty. gen., 1972-73; U.S. magistrate judge Dist. of Minn., St. Paul, 1995—. Bd. dirs. Macalester Coll., St. Paul, 1971-77, St. Paul Chamber Orch., 1979-88, U. Minn. Hosps. and Clinics, St. Paul, 1979-83, Mpls. Bd. Edn., 1973-80, Minn. Chorale, 1990-95, MacPhail Ctr. for Arts, 1990—, Ordway Music Theatre, 1991—; mem. nat. adv. bd. Concordia U. Lang. Villages, 1996—. With USAF, 1957, with Res., 1957-65. Mem. Harvard Law Sch. Assn. (pres. Minn. sect. 1980-81). Avocations: classical piano, bicycling, accordion, German, French and Italian languages. Home: 2849 Burnham Blvd Minneapolis MN 55416-4331 Office: 610 Federal Cts Bldg 316 N Robert St Saint Paul MN 55401

MASON, JOSEPH See BUSHINSKY, JAY

MASON, LEON VERNE, financial planner; b. Lawrence, Kans., Jan. 13, 1933; s. Thomas Samuel and Mabel Edith (Hyre) M.; divorced; children: Mark Verne, Kirk Matthew, Erik Andrew. BS in Engring. with honors, U. Kans., 1955; MS in Mgmt. with honors, U. Colo., 1970. Engr., Pittsburg Des Moines Steel Co., 1955-56; with IBM, 1958—, sr. engr., San Jose, Calif., 1975-77, Boulder, Colo., 1977—; sr. engr. on loan, dir. capital campaign Vols. of Am., 1980-81; with exec. mgmt. IBM, 1985-87, cons. 1988—. Pres., Boulder Interfaith Housing; dir. Golden West Manor, 1978-84, pres., 1983-84; dir. Ret. Sr. Vol. Program, 1979-86; chmn. elders 1st Christian Ch., Boulder, 1977-79. Served with USAF, 1955-57; col. Res. Cert. fin. planner; registered profl. engr.; chmn. trustees 1st Christian Ch., 1989, 93; supervisory faculty Regis U., 1988—, pres. Mason & Assoc. Bus. Cons., 1988—. Mem. Internat. Assn. Fin. Planners, Am. Soc. Quality Control, Soc. Mfg. Engrs. Club: Kiwanis. Home: 5577 N Fork Ct Boulder CO 80301-3548

MASON, MARILYN GELL, library administrator, writer, consultant; b. Chickasha, Okla., Aug. 23, 1944; d. Emmett D. and Dorothy (O'Bar) Killebrew; m. Carl L. Gell, Dec. 29 1965 (div. Oct. 1978); 1 son, Charles E.; m. Robert M. Mason, July 17, 1981. B.A., U. Dallas, 1966; M.L.S., N. Tex. State U., Denton, 1968; M.P.A., Harvard U., 1978. Libr. N.J. State Libr., Trenton, 1968-69; head dept. Arlington County Pub. Libr., Va., 1969-73; chief libr. program Metro Washington Coun. Govts., 1973-77; dir. White House Conf. on Librs. and Info. Svcs., Washington, 1979-80; exec. v.p. Metrics Rsch. Corp., Atlanta, 1981-82; dir. Atlanta-Fulton Pub. Libr., Atlanta, 1982-86, Cleve. Pub. Libr., 1986—; trustee Online Computer Library Ctr., 1984—; Evalene Parsons Jackson lectr. div. librarianship Emory U., 1981. Author: The Federal Role in Library and Information Services, 1983; editor: Survey of Library Automation in the Washington Area, 1977; project dir.: book Information for the 1980's, 1980. Bd. visitors Sch. Info. Studies, Syracuse U., 1981-85, Sch. of Libr. and Info. Sci., U. Tenn.-Knoxville, 1983-85; trustee Coun. on Libr. Resources, Atlant, 1992—. Recipient Disting. Alumna award N. Tex. State U., 1979. Mem. ALA (mem. council 1986—), Am. Assn. Info. Sci., Ohio Library Assn., D.C. Library Assn. (pres. 1976-77). Home: 12427 Fairhill Rd Cleveland OH 44120-1015 Office: Cleve Pub Libr 325 Superior Ave E Cleveland OH 44114-1205

MASON, MARSHA, actress, director, writer; b. St. Louis; d. James and Jacqueline M.; m. Gary Campbell, 1965 (div.); m. Neil Simon, Oct. 25, 1973 (div.). Grad., Webster (Mo.) Coll. Performances include cast Broadway and nat. tour Cactus Flower, 1968; other stage appearances include The Deer Park, 1967, The Indian Wants the Bronx, 1968, Happy Birthday, Wanda June, 1970, Private Lives, 1971, You Can't Take It With You, 1972, Cyrano de Bergerac, 1972, A Doll's House, 1972, The Crucible, 1972, The Good Doctor, 1973, King Richard III, 1974, The Heiress, 1975, Mary Stuart, 1982, Amazing Grace, 1995, Night of the Iguana, 1996; one-woman show off-Broadway, The Big Love, Perry St. Theatre, 1988, Lake No Bottom, Second Stage, 1990, Escape From Happiness, With the Naked Angels, 1994; film appearances include Blume in Love, 1973, Cinderella Liberty, 1973 (recipient Golden Globe award 1974, Acad. award nominee), Audrey Rose, 1977, The Goodbye Girl, 1977 (recipient Golden Globe award 1978, Acad. award nominee), The Cheap Detective, 1978, Promises in the Dark, 1979, Chapter Two, 1979 (Acad. award nominee), Only When I Laugh, 1981 (Acad. award nominee), Max Dugan Returns, 1982, Heartbreak Ridge, 1986, Stella, 1988, Drop Dead Fred, 1990, I Love Trouble, 1994; TV appearances include PBS series Cyrano de Bergerac, 1974, The Good Doctor, 1978, Lois Gibbs and the Love Canal, 1981, Surviving, 1985, Trapped in Silence, 1986, The Clinic, 1987, Dinner At Eight, 1989, The Image, 1990, Broken Trust, 1994, series Sibs, 1991; dir. (plays) Juno's Swans, 1987, Heaven Can Wait; dir. ABC Afternoon Spl. Little Miss Perfect, 1988. Office: care Internat Creative Mgmt 8942 Wilshire Blvd Beverly Hills CA 90211-1934

MASON, MARSHALL W., theater director; b. Amarillo, Tex., Feb. 24, 1940; s. Marvin Marshall and Lorine (Chrisman) M. B.S. in Speech, Northwestern U., 1961. Prof. Ariz. State U., 1994—; chief drama critic New Times, Phoenix, 1994—. Founder, artistic dir. Circle Repertory Co., 1969-87, guest artistic dir., Ctr. Theater Group, 1988; dir. Broadway prodns. Redwood Curtain, 1993, The Seagull, 1992, Solitary Confinement, 1992, Burn This, 1987, As Is, 1985 (Drama Desk award, Tony nomination), Passion, 1983, Angels Fall, 1983 (Tony nomination), Fifth of July, 1981 (Tony nomination), Talley's Folly, 1980, (Pulitzer Prize, N.Y. Drama Critics Circle award, Tony nomination), Murder at the Howard Johnsons, 1979, Gemini, 1977, Knock Knock, 1976 (Tony nomination); Off-Broadway prodns. A Poster of the Cosmos/The Moonshot Tape, 1994, The Destiny of Me, 1992, Sunshine, 1989, Talley and Son, 1985, Childe Byron, 1980, Hamlet, 1979, Serenading Louie, 1976 (Obie award), Knock Knock, 1976 (Obie award), The Mound Builders, 1975 (Obie award), Battle of Angeles, 1974 (Obie award), The Sea Hourse, 1974, The Hot L Baltimore, 1973 (Obie award); dir. numerous prodns. including Who's Afraid of Virginia Woolf?, Tokyo, 1985, Talley's Folly, 1982, London, Home Free! and The Madness of Lady Bright, 1968, London, Nat. Tour Sleuth, 1988, Summer and Smoke, 1988, Whisper in the Mind, 1990; dir. numerous TV prodns. including Picnic, 1986, Kennedy's Children, 1982, The Fifth of July, 1983. Recipient Vernon Rice award, 1975, Drama Desk award, 1977, Margo Jones award, 1977, Outer Critics Circle award, 1978, Theatre World award, 1979, Shubert's Vaughan award, 1980, Obie award for Sustained Achievement, 1983, Inge Festival award for lifetime achievement, 1990, Last Frontier award, 1994, Erwin Piscator award, 1996. Mem. Soc. Stage Dirs. and Choreographers (pres. 1983-85), Dirs. Guild Am., Actors Equity Assn. Address: 1948 E Ellis Circle Mesa AZ 85203

MASON, NANCY TOLMAN, state agency director; b. Buxton, Maine, Mar. 14, 1933; d. Ansel Robert and Kate Douglas (Libby) M. Grad., Bryant Coll., Providence, R.I., 1952; BA, U. Mass., Boston, 1977; postgrad., Inst. Governmental Services, Boston, 1985, The Auditor's Inst., 1988. Asst. to chief justice Mass. Superior Ct., Boston, 1964-68; community liaison Action for Boston Community Devel., Boston, 1968-73; mgmt. cons. East Boston Community Devel. Assn., Boston, 1973-78; asst. dir. Mass. Office of Deafness, Boston, 1978-86; dir. of contracts Mass. Rehab. Commn., Boston, 1986—; cons. Jos. A Ryan Assocs., Boston and Orleans, Mass., 1981-86, Radio Sta. WFCC, Chatham, Mass., 1987-91. Author: Bromley-Heath Security Patrols, 1974, Reorganization of East Boston Community Development Corporation, 1976, How to Start Your Own Small Business, 1981. Bd. dirs. Deaf-Blind Contact Ctr., Boston, 1988-91; vol. Am. Cancer Soc., Winchester, Mass., 1986-93, Tax Equity Alliance Mass., 1994. Recipient Good Citizen award DAR, 1950, Community Svc. award Northeastern U., 1986, Gov.'s citation for outstanding performance, 1993; named to Outstanding Young Women of Am., 1965. Mem. NOW, NAFE, Mass. State Assn. Deaf, MRC Statewide Cen. Office Dirs. (chair 1995-96). Democrat. Episcopalian. Avocations: reading, music, bridge, swimming, sign language. Office: Mass Rehab Commn 27-43 Wormwood St Boston MA 02210

MASON, PERRY CARTER, philosophy educator; b. Houston, Sept. 24, 1939; s. Lloyd Vernon and Lorraine (Carter) M.; m. Judith Jane Fredrick, June 11, 1960; children—Gregory Charles, Nicole Elizabeth. B.A., Baylor U., Waco, Tex., 1961; B.D., Harvard U., 1964; M.A., Yale U., 1966, Ph.D., 1968. Asst. prof. philosophy Carleton Coll., Northfield, Minn., 1968-73, assoc. prof. philosophy, 1973-80, prof. philosophy, 1980—, v.p. for planning and devel., 1988-89, v.p. for external rels., 1989-91. Contbr. articles to profl. publs. Fellow Soc. for Values in Higher Edn.; mem. Minn. Philos. Soc., Am. Philos. Assn. Democrat. Home: 8629 Hall Ave Northfield MN 55057-4884 Office: Carleton College One North College St Northfield MN 55057

MASON, PHILLIP HOWARD, aircraft company executive, retired army officer; b. Cash, Va., Mar. 13, 1932; s. Phillip Howard and Mary Armisted (Hogg) M.; m. Frances Murray Gallogly, Mar. 3, 1962 (dec. 1996); children: Mary Catherine, Patrick Howard, Susan Frances, Sheryl Ann. B.S. in B.A., magna cum laude, St. Benedicts, 1966; M.B.A., Shippensburg State Coll., 1976; postgrad., U.S. Army Command and Gen. Staff Coll., 1965-66, U.S. Army War Coll., 1975-76. Enlisted in U.S. Army, 1948, advanced through grades to brig. gen., 1980; bn. comdr. 1st Bn., 1st ADA U.S. Army, Ger., 1971-73, sec. gen. staff 32d Army Air Def. Command, 1974; systems coordinator ODCSRDA, Dept Army U.S. Army, Washington, 1975; project mgr. AD Command and Control Redstone Arsenal, Ala., 1976-78; comdr. 11th ADA Bde Fort Bliss, Tex., 1978-79; project mgr. STINGER Redstone Arsenal, 1979-83; dir. combat support system ODCSRDA, Dept. Army Washington; ret. U.S. Army, 1983; v.p. bus. devel. Sanders Assocs., Nashua, N.H., 1984-90; project mgr. Hughes Aircraft Co., 1990—. Decorated Disting. Svc. medal, Legion of Merit with oak leaf cluster, Bronze star, Meritorious Svc. medal with two oak leaf clusters, Joint Svcs. Commendation medal, Army Commendation medal. Home: 20 Winterberry Dr Amherst NH 03031-1605 Office: 1100 Wilson Blvd Ste 2000 Arlington VA 22209-2297

MASON, RAYMOND ADAMS, brokerage company executive; b. Lynchburg, Va., Sept. 28, 1936; s. Raymond Watsi and Marion (Adams) M.; married; children: Paige Adams, Pamela Ann, Carter Meade, Morgan Rand. BA in Econs., Coll. William and Mary, 1959. Rep. Mason & Lee Inc., Richmond, Va., 1960-62; founder, pres. Mason & Co. Inc., Newport News, Va., 1962-70; pres. Legg, Mason & Co., Inc., Washington, 1970-73; pres. Legg, Mason Wood Walker, Inc., Balt., 1978—, chmn. bd. dirs.; pres., chmn., chief exec. officer Legg Mason, Inc., 1981—; bd. dirs. Environ. Elements Corp.; chmn. regional firms com. N.Y. Stock Exchange, 1978-81; bd. dirs. Legg Mason Value Trust, Howard Weil Fin., Western Asset Mgmt. Trustee emeritus Endowment Assn., Coll. William and Mary; bd. dirs. emeritus William and Mary Sch. Bus. Adminstrn. Sponsors, Inc.; former trustee Balt. Mus. Art; former bd. dirs. Nat. Aquarium, Balt.; bd. dirs., exec. com., chair fin. com. Johns Hopkins Hosp.; mem. exec. com., chair endowment funds, fin. com. Johns Hopkins U.; former chmn. bd. sponsors Sch. Bus. & Mgmt. Loyola Coll., Balt., 1980-88; bd. dirs. Greater Balt. Com., 1982—, chmn., 1987-89; chmn. United Way Ctrl. Md. Mem. Nat. Assn. Securities Dealers (bd. govs. 1971-75, chmn. bd. govs. 1974-75), Securities Industry Assn. (bd. dirs. 1982—, chmn. 1985-86, bd. govs. 1984-88, chmn. bd. govs. 1987). Clubs: Ctr., Md., Balt. Country, L'Hirondelle, Caves Valley, New Orleans Country Club. Home: 1832 Circle Rd Baltimore MD 21204-6415 Office: Legg Mason Inc 111 S Calvert St Baltimore MD 21202-6174

MASON, ROBERT JOSEPH, automotive parts company executive; b. Muskegon, Mich., Nov. 17, 1918; s. Robert J. and Delora (Houle) M.; m. Kathleen Carr, June 24, 1944 (dec. Nov. 1965); children: Marcia (Mrs. Richard Dwyer), Eileen A. (Mrs. Thomas Wilhelm); m. Carol F. Fales, Jan. 31, 1967. M.B.A., U. Chgo., 1941. Accounting analyst Carnegie-Ill. Steel Corp., Gary, Ind., 1941-45; with Sealed Power Corp., Muskegon, 1945-83; sec.-treas. Sealed Power Corp., 1959-70, v.p. finance, 1970-83, dir., 1972-92. Bd. dirs. Muskegon County United Appeal, Muskegon Area C. of C.; adv. bd. Mercy Hosp. Mem. C. of C., Fin. Execs. Inst., Am. Soc. Corp. Secs. Clubs: Century (pres., dir.), Muskegon Country (past bd. dirs.). Home: 320 W Circle Dr Muskegon MI 49445

MASON, ROBERT MCSPADDEN, technology management educator, consultant; b. Sweetwater, Tenn., Jan. 16, 1941; s. Paul Rankin and Ruby May (McSpadden) M.; m. Betty Ann Durrence (div. 1980); children: Michael Dean, Donald Robert; m. Marilyn Killebrew Gell, July 17, 1981. SB, MIT, 1963, SM, 1965; PhD, Ga. Inst. Tech., 1973. Tech. staff mem. Sandia Labs., Livermore, Calif., 1965-68; rsch. scientist Ga. Inst. Tech., Atlanta, 1971-75, sr. rsch. scientist, 1975; prin. Metrics, Inc., Atlanta, 1975-80; pres. Metrics Rsch. Corp., Atlanta, 1980-86, Cleve., 1986—; adj. prof. Weatherhead Sch. Mgmt. Case Western U., 1987-88, vis. prof., 1988-91, prof. for practice of tech. mgmt., 1991—; dir. Ctr. Mgmt. Sci. and Tech., 1988-96. Co-author: Library Micro Consumer, 1986; co-editor: Information Services: Economics, Management, and Technology, 1981, Management of Technology V: Technology Management in a Changing World, 1996; co-author: The Impact of Office Automation on Clerical Employment, 1985-2000, 1985; Am. editor Technovation, 1994—; contbr. article series "Mason on Micros" to Libr. Jour., 1983-86, articles to various profl. publs. Mem. Internat. Assn. for Tech. Mgmt. (newsletter editor 1992-93, program chair internat. conf., 1994-96, pres.). Republican. Presbyterian. Avocations: flying, skiing, sailing, scuba diving, photography. Home: 12427 Fairhill Rd Cleveland OH 44120-1015 Office: Ctr Mgmt Sci & Tech Weatherhead Sch Mgmt Case Western Res U Cleveland OH 44106-7235

MASON, SCOTT AIKEN, management consultant; b. Boston, May 23, 1951; s. Ward Sherman and Ursula (Aiken) M. BS, Duke U., 1973; MPA, Pa. State U., 1975; DPA, George Washington U., 1981. Adminstrv. rschr. Milton S. Hershey Med. Ctr., Hershey, Pa., 1974-75; systems analyst Health Svcs. Systems Devel. Project, Harrisburg, Pa., 1975-76; cons. Booz Allen & Hamilton, Washington, 1976-77; staff specialist Am. Hosp. Assn., Washington, 1978-79; corp. dir. Samaritan Health Svcs., Phoenix, 1979-81; mng. ptnr. Nat. Health Advisors, McLean, Va., 1981—. Author: Multihospital Arrangements: Public Policy Implications, 1979; contbr. articles to profl. jours. Active Potomac Presbyn. Ch. Fellow Am. Coll. Healthcare Execs., Am. Assn. Healthcare Cons. (bd. dirs.); mem. TPC at Avenel, Pi Alpa Alpha. Republican. Office: Nat Health Advisors Ltd 8201 Greensboro Dr Ste 817 Mc Lean VA 22102-3810

MASON, SCOTT MACGREGOR, entrepreneur, inventor, consultant; b. N.Y.C., Feb. 11, 1923; s. Gregory Mason and Mary Louise Turner; m. Mildred Davidson, Mar. 13, 1949 (div. 1970); children: Alan Gregory, Phoebe Louise, Caleb; m. Virginia Frances Perkins, May 5, 1970 (dec. 1990). AB, Princeton U., 1943; MS, NYU, 1947. Control chemist Firestone Tire & Rubber Co., Akron, Ohio, 1943-44; R & D chemist Am. Cyanamid Co. Rsch. Labs., Stamford, Conn., 1948-52; mgr. stearate dept. Warwick Chem. div. Sun Chem. Corp., Wood River Junction, R.I., 1952-58; cons., Stonington, Conn., 1958-59; instr. Williams Meml. Inst., New London, Conn., 1959-63; NSF fellow Brown U., Providence, 1963-64; tchr. Moses Brown Sch., Providence, 1964-70; owner, mgr. Innoventures, Wakefield, R.I., 1970—; cons. Greene Plastics Corp., Canonchet, R.I., 1972-80, Dorette Inc., Pawtucket, R.I., 1982-83. Patentee in field. Trustee Pine Point Sch., Stonington, 1956-62, pres. bd., 1959-61. With AUS, 1944-46, ETO. Named Tchr. of Week, Sta. WICE, Providence, 1967; summer rsch. fellow NSF, U. R.I., 1960. Mem. AAAS, N.Y. Acad. Scis. Avocations: tennis, fishing, snorkeling, photography, music. Office: Innoventures PO Box 369 Wakefield RI 02880-0369

MASON, STACY, editor-in-chief; b. Washington, Sept. 19, 1963; d. Paul Joseph and Zena (Sapperstein) M.; m. Tod H. Cohen, May 28, 1989; 1 child, Max Hunter Cohen. BA, Tufts U., Medford, Mass., 1985; MSJ, Northwestern U., Evanston, Ill., 1986. Asst. editor Roll Call, Washington, 1987-88, mng. editor, 1988-93, editor-in-chief, 1993—. Office: Roll Call 900 2d St NE Washington DC 20002

MASON, STEPHEN OLIN, academic administrator; b. Fresno, Calif., July 11, 1952; s. Olin James and Mary Edna (Moyer) M. BA, Bridgewater (Va.) Coll., 1974; MEd, James Madison U., 1979; PhD, Loyola U., Chgo., 1991. Asst. to the dir. student ctr. Bridgewater Coll., 1974-76; guidance counselor Woodlawn Elem. Sch., Sebring, Fla., 1976-77; asst. dean for student devel. Bridgewater Coll., 1977-81; dir. student life Roger Williams Coll., Bristol, R.I., 1981-83; assoc. dean for residential svcs. Dickinson Coll., Carlisle, Pa., 1983-84; v.p., dean student affairs Westmar Coll., LeMars, Iowa, 1984; rsch. assoc. to pres. Elmhurst (Ill.) Coll., 1986-87; v.p. student affairs Felician Coll., Chgo., 1987-88; dean students Huntingdon Coll., Montgomery, Ala., 1988-90; dir. devel. McPherson (Kans.) Coll., 1990-94, v.p. fin. svcs., 1994—. Participant ARC Blood Drive, 1978-79; mem. allocations com. United Way, Carlisle, 1984; mem. adv. bd. LeMars chpt. Siouxland Coun. for Alcoholism and Drug Abuse, 1984; site coord. for coat drive Mental Health Greater Chgo., 1985; dir-at-large Bridgewater Coll. Alumni Bd., 1987-90; v.p. McPherson Habitat for Humanity, 1993, 94, bd. dirs., 1993-96, pres., 1994; bd. dirs. McPherson Mus. and Arts Found., 1992-94, Assn. Brethren Caregivers, 1993—. Mem. Am. Assn. for Higher Edn., Assn. for Study of Higher Edn., Coun. for Advancement and Support of Edn. Avocations: calligraphy, community theatre, barbershop singing, spelunking. Home: 1502 E Sharp St Mc Pherson KS 67460-3851 Office: McPherson Coll 1600 E Euclid St Mc Pherson KS 67460-3847

MASON, STEVEN CHARLES, forest products company executive; b. Sarnia, Ont., Can., Feb. 22, 1936. B.S., MIT, 1957. Pres. div. Mead Corp., Dayton, Ohio, 1978-79, group v.p., 1979-82, sr. v.p. ops., 1982, pres., chief oper. exec., 1990-92, vice chmn., 1992—, chmn., CEO, 1992—. Office: Mead Corp Courthouse Plz NE Dayton OH 45463

MASON, STEVEN JUDE, wholesale and insurance companies executive; b. New Orleans, Mar. 4, 1944; s. Henry Lee and Mildred (Griffin) M.; m. Linda Lauve; children: Steven Jr., Michael, David. BA, La. State U., 1966; JD, Loyola U., New Orleans, 1969. Bar: La. 1969, Tenn. 1981. Atty. FTC, New Orleans, 1969-70, Ingram Corp., New Orleans, 1970-78; v.p., gen. counsel Ingram Industries Inc., Nashville, 1978-83; pres. Ingram Book Co., La Vergne, Tenn., 1983—, 1989—, vice chmn., 1990-95; pres., CEO, Permanent Gen. Assurance Co., Nashville, 1995—; bd. dirs. So. Festival of Books. Bd. dirs. Nashville Opera Assn., 1985—, Nashville Juvenile Diabetess Assn. Recipient Am. Legion Award, New Orleans, 1962. Mem. La. State Bar Assn., Tenn. Bar Assn. Home: 1318 Chickering Rd Nashville TN 37215-4522 Office: Ingram Book Co 1125 Heil Quaker Blvd La Vergne TN 37086-3610 also: Permanent Gen Assurance Co 301 Plus Pk Nashville TN 37219

MASON, THEODORE W., lawyer; b. June 17, 1943. AB, Yale U., 1965; JD, U. Pa., 1972. Bar: Pa. 1972, Fla. 1987. Ptnr. Morgan, Lewis & Bockius LLP, Phila. Mem. Nat. Assn. Bond Lawyers (steering com. workshop, enforcement com.). Office: Morgan Lewis & Bockius LLP 2000 One Logan Sq Philadelphia PA 19103

MASON, THOMAS ALBERT, lawyer; b. Cleve., May 4, 1936; s. Victor Lewis and Frances (Speidel) M.; m. Elisabeth Gun Sward, Sept. 25, 1965; children: Thomas Lewis, Robert Albert. AB, Kenyon Coll., 1958; LLB, Case-Western Res. U., 1961. Bar: Ohio 1961. Assoc. Thompson, Hine and Flory, Cleve., 1965-73, ptnr., 1973—. Trustee Cleve. YMCA, 1975-94. Capt. USMCR, 1962-65. Mem. ABA, Am. Coll. Real Estate Lawyers, Am. Land Title Assn. (lender's counsel group), Mortgage Bankers Assn. of Met. Cleve., Ohio Bar Assn., Cleve. Bar Assn., Am. Coll. Mortgage Attys., Nat. Assn. Indsl. and Office Pks., The Country Club, Union Club of Cleve. Republican. Episcopalian. Avocations: tennis; golf. Home: 23375 Duffield Rd Cleveland OH 44122-3101 Office: Thompson Hine & Flory PLL 3900 Society Ctr 127 Public Sq Cleveland OH 44114-1216

MASON, VIVIAN LEE CONWAY, elementary education educator; b. Richmond, Va., Jan. 16, 1942; d. Edward Gordon and Raconia (Boyd) Conway; m. Eugene Albertis Mason Jr., June 30, 1962; children: Eugene Albertis III, Yevette Matrease. BS, Va. Commonwealth U., 1976; postgrad., U. Richmond, 1979, Va. Union U., 1982, Hampton U., 1985. Cert. collegiate profl., Va. Tchr. Richmond (Va.) Pub. Schs., 1976—; chairperson Am. Bus. Women's Assn., Richmond, 1990-91; trainer, cons. Project Head Start, 1987-89. Mem. Richmond Dem. Party, 1991-92, Alpha Kappa Alpha Sorority, Richmond, 1986-92. Mem. NEA, AAUP, Va. Edn. Assn., Richmond Edn. Assn. (bd. dirs. 1993, 95-97), NEA Women's Caucus, Am. Bus. Women's Assn. (Inner Circle award 1992, founder Edward Daniel McCreary Jr. Scholarship Fund 1994). Democrat. Avocations: writing children's literature, painting, jogging, working with youth and families. Home: 6319 Windcroft Rd Richmond VA 23225-6842 Office: Richmond Pub Schs 301 S 9th St Richmond VA 23219-3913

MASON, WILLIAM A(LVIN), psychologist, educator, researcher; b. Mountain View, Calif., Mar. 28, 1926; s. Alvin Frank and Ruth Sabina (Erwin) M.; m. Virginia Joan Carmichael, June 27, 1948; children: Todd, Paula, Nicole, Hunter. B.A., Stanford U., 1950, M.S., 1952, Ph.D., 1954. Asst. prof. U. Wis.-Madison, 1954-59; research assoc. Yerkes Labs. Primate Biology, Orange Park, Fla., 1959-63; head dept. behavioral sci. Delta Primate Research Ctr., Tulane U., Covington, La., 1963-71; prof. psychology, research psychologist U. Calif., Davis, 1971—, leader behavioral biology unit Calif. Primate Rsch. Ctr., 1972-96; bd. dirs. Jane Goodall Inst., 1978-92, Karisoke Rsch. Ctr., 1980-86. Mem. Editorial bd. Animal Learning and Behavior, 1973-76, Internat. Jour. Devel. Psychobiology, 1980-92, Internat. Jour. Primatology, 1980-90; contbr. numerous articles to profl. jours., chpts. to books. With USMC, 1944-46. USPHS spl. fellow, 1963-64. Fellow AAAS, APA (pres. divsn. 6 1982, disting. sci. contbn. award 1995), Am. Psychol. Soc., Animal Behavior Soc.; mem. Internat. Primatological Soc. (pres. 1976-80, 81-84), Am. Soc. Primatologists (pres. 1988-90, disting. primatologist award), Internat. Soc. Devel. Psychobiology (pres. 1971-72, Best Paper of Yr. award 1976), Sigma Xi. Home: 2809 Anza Ave Davis CA 95616-0257 Office: U Calif Regional Primate Rsch Ctr Davis CA 95616

MASON, WILLIAM CORDELL, III, hospital administrator; b. Montgomery, Ala., June 7, 1938; s. William C. and Sibyl (Evans) M.; m. Mona Holloway, Jan. 5, 1957 (div. June 1992); children: Michael C., Rebecca Mason Malone, Stephen E., Holly M.; m. Juliette Baldwin Woodruff, Apr. 17, 1993. B.S., U. Southwestern La., 1961; M. Hospital and Health Care, Trinity U., 1971. Hosp. rep. Eaton Labs., Norwich, N.Y., 1962-66; fgn. service officer U.S. Dept. State, Manila and Saigon, 1966-69; chief exec. officer Bapt. Hosp. of East Africa, Mbeya, Tanzania, 1971-74, Bapt. Hosp., Bangalore, India, 1974-78; chief operating officer Bapt. Med. Ctr., Jacksonville, Fla., 1978-84, vice chmn., CEO, 1984-95; pres., CEO Bapt./St. Vincent's Health Sys. Inc., Jacksonville, Fla., 1995—; mem. adj. faculty U. No Fla. Jacksonville, 1985—; cons. So. Bapt. Fgn. Mission Bd., Richmond, Va., 1980-85; bd. dirs. Sun Bank of North Fla., N.A., SunHealth Corp., sec. exec. com., 1990-94. Contbr. articles to profl. jours. Chmn. deacons Hendricks Ave. Bapt. Ch., Jacksonville, 1984-85, Calvary Bapt. Ch., Bangalore, 1976-77; treas. Karnataka State Bapt. Conv., Bangalore, 1975-77; trustee Jacksonville Symphony Orch.; bd. dirs. U. No. Fla.Assn. Vol. Hosps., 1986, Med. Assistance Program Internat., 1986-87, United Way, 1990; chmn. Greater Jacksonville Area Hosp. Coun., 1985, Mayor's Health Econ. Devel. Coun., 1986-87, Greater Jacksonville U.S. Savs. Bond Campaign, 1987; mem. adv. coun. Jacksonville U. Sch. Bus., 1986-88; chmn. area devel. coun. So. Bapt. Fgn. Mission Bd., 1987-91. Fellow Am. Coll. Hosp. Execs.; mem. Am. Hosp. Assn., Fla. Hosp. Assn. (trustee 1982, 83-85, 86), Fla. Hosp. Assn. (chmn. 1992-93, trustee 1994—), Healthcare Exec. Study Soc., Jacksonville C. of C. (vice chmn. exec. com. 1988-89, chmn. health econ. devel. 1992-95, chmn. cornerstone econ. devel. initiative), Epping Forest Yacht Club (bd. govs. 1990—), Beta Sigma Gamma, Rotary. Avocations: golf, boating, reading. Home: 947 Greenridge Rd Jacksonville FL 32207-5203 Office: Bapt/St Vincent's Health Sys Inc 800 Prudential Dr Jacksonville FL 32207-8203

MASONER, PAUL HENRY, counseling educator; b. Middletown, Ohio, Mar. 25, 1908; s. Paul and Emma Martha (Hayes) M.; m. Lorraine Carr, 1983; children: Paul, David, Linda; stepchildren: Elisabeth Carr-Jones, Phillip Carr, Jr. Student, Capital U., 1926-28; B.A. in English, Ohio State U., 1930, M.A. in Sociology, 1931; postgrad., Wilmington Coll., summer 1931; Ph.D. in Counseling, U. Pitts., 1949; postgrad., U. London, Eng., summers 1964, 66; D.Litt. (hon.), Hanyang U., Seoul, Korea, 1978. Tchr. English Central High Sch., Uhrichsville, Ohio, 1930-32; tchr. social scis. Bellevue High Sch., Pitts., 1932-34; counselor, vice prin. Bellevue High Sch., 1934-43, acting prin., 1943-44; adminstrv. head Engring. and Sci. Mgmt. War Tng. Center, Bellevue, Pa., 1942-44; sr. analyst Nat. Def. Research Com., U. Pa., 1944-45; counselor, lectr. psychology Vets. Counseling Center, U. Pitts., 1945-46; instr. Vets. Counseling Center, U. Pitts. (Sch. Edn.), 1946-48, asst. prof., 1948-50, assoc. prof., 1950-51, prof., 1953—, asst. dean, 1952-54, acting dean, 1954, dean, 1955-73, dean emeritus, 1973—, Univ. prof., 1973—; Mem. adv. com. Learning Research and Devel. Center, Pitts., 1965-73; cons. scholarship aid programs; ednl. cons. to sch. systems, colls., univs., ednl. orgns., govt. agys., others; mem. accreditation teams Middle States Assn. and Nat. Council for Accreditation of Tchr. Edn., 1954-75; mem. adv. com. Pa. Grad. Tchr. Edn., 1964-70; mem. Pa. Curriculum Commn., 1964-70, Com. of One Hundred Citizens for Better Edn., 1963-67; mem. council Nat. Council Accreditation Tchr. Edn., 1968-70; mem. Nat. Adv. Council Edn. Professions Devel., 1970-73; mem. exec. bd. Nat. Reading Center, Washington, 1970-73; Extensive fgn. travel and study. Contbg. author: Standards for the 60's, 1962, Counseling: Selected Readings, 1962, Changes in Teacher Education: An Appraisal, 1964; author: Design for Teacher Education, 1964, An Imperative: A National Policy for Teacher Education, 1972, Evaluación de Sistemas de Communicación Educativa, 1980. Bd. dirs. Falk Elementary Sch., Pitts., 1955-73, Westminster Found., 1964-66, Pitts. Council of Chs., 1964-66; pres. bd. trustees Robert Morris Coll. Recipient Outstanding Service to Edn. award Commonwealth of Pa., 1962, Effective Leadership to Tchr. Edn. award, 1964. Fellow Coll. Preceptors (hon., Eng.); mem. NEA, AAUP, AAAS, We. Pa. Scholarship Assn. (exec. sec. 1950-70), Pa. State Edn. Assn. (exec. coun. 1966-68), We. Pa. Edn. Conf. (chmn. 1955-70), Pa. Schoolman's Club (pres. 1963), Pa. Assn. Liberal Arts Colls. for

Advancement of Tchg. (pres. 1959), Am. Pers. and Guidance Assn., Nat. Vocat. Guidance Assn. (profl.), Am. Assn. Sch. Adminstrs. (profl.), Internat. Coun. Edn. for Tchg. (trestee 1973-76, pres. 1976-86), Am. Assn. Colls. Tchr. Edn. (pres. 1970-71), Civic Club Allegheny County (Pa.), Allegheny Roundtable (pres. 1964-70), Omicron Delta Kappa, Delta Pi Epsilon (hon.), Iota Lambda Sigma (hon.), Phi Delta Kappa, Kappa Phi Kappa. Conglist. Clubs: Cosmos (Washington); University (Pitts.). Office: 44 Oxford Ct Pittsburgh PA 15237-4501

MASORO, EDWARD JOSEPH, JR., physiology educator; b. Oakland, Calif., Dec. 28, 1924; s. Edward Joseph and Louise Elizabeth (DePaoli) M.; m. Barbara Weikel, June 25, 1947. AB, U. Calif., Berkeley, 1947, PhD, 1950. Asst. prof. physiology Queen's U., Kingston, Ont., Can., 1950-52; asst. prof., then asso. prof. Tufts U. Sch. Medicine, 1952-62; research asso. prof., then research prof. physiology and biophysics U. Wash., 1962-64; prof. physiology and biophysics, chmn. dept. Med. Coll. Pa., 1964-73; prof. physiology, chmn. dept. U. Tex. Health Sci. Center, San Antonio, 1973-91, prof., 1991—; dir. Aging Rsch. and Edn. Ctr., 1992—; cons. coun. basic sci. Am. Heart Assn., 1965-67; chmn. metabolic discussion group Fed. Am. Soc. Exptl. Biology, 1969-73; mem. aging rev. com. Nat. Inst. on Aging, 1981-84, chmn. bd. sci. counselors, 1985-89; chmn. Gordon Conf. on Biology of Aging, 1983; mem. bd. sci. advisors Human Nutrition Inst., Internat. Life Sci. Inst., 1989-92; mem. rsch. com. Am. Fedn. Aging Rsch., 1988—; vis. prof. U. Pisa, 1993; Wellcome vis. prof. basic med. scis., 1992-93. Author: Physiological Chemistry of Lippids in Mammals, 1967; co-author: Acid-Base Regulation: Its Physiology and Pathophysiology, 1971, 2d edit., 1977; editor sct. 24 Internat. Ency. Pharmacology and Therapeutics, 1974; mem. editorial bd. Jour. Lipid Rsch., 1967-83, Jour. Gerontology, 1979-91, Exptl. Gerontology, 1984—, Proc. Soc. Exptl. Biol. Medicine, 1986-92, Physiol. Rev., 1988-94; editor Jour. Gerontology: Biol. Scis., 1991-95, Handbook Physiol. Aging, 1995; editor for biol. scis. Exptl. Aging Rsch., 1980-88; co-editor Aging: Clinical and Experimental Research, 1989—; contbr. articles to profl. jours. Served with USNR, 1943-46. Recipient Christian R. and Mary F. Lindback Disting. Teaching award Med. Coll. Pa., 1967, Golden Apple award Student Am. Med. Assn., 1966, 71, Achievement award Allied Signal, 1989, Rsch. Achievements in Gerontology, U. Pisa, 1991, Irving Wright award Am. Fedn. Aging Rsch., 1995, Glenn Found. award, 1995. Fellow AAAS (coun. 1970—), Gerontol. Soc. Am. (chmn. biol. sci. sect. 1978-79, v.p. 1978-79, Kleemeir award 1990, pres.-elect 1992-93, pres. 1994-95); mem. AAUP, Am. Physiol. Soc. (chmn. endocrinology and metabolism sect. 1981-82), Soc. Exptl. Biology and Medicine (coun. 1987-91), Am. Soc. Biochemistry and Molecular Biology, N.Y. Acad. Scis., Phila. Physiol. Soc. (pres. 1966-67). Office: U Tex Dept Physiology Health Sci Ctr San Antonio TX 78284

MASOTTI, LOUIS HENRY, management educator, consultant; b. N.Y.C., May 16, 1934; s. Henry and Angela Catherine (Turi) M.; m. Iris Patricia Leonard, Aug. 28, 1958 (div. 1981); children: Laura Lynn, Andrea Anne; m. Ann Randel Humm, Mar. 5, 1988. AB, Princeton U., 1956; MA, Northwestern U., 1961, PhD, 1964. Fellow Nat. Ctr. Edn. in Politics, 1962; asst. prof. polit. sci. Case Western Res. U., Cleve., 1963-67, assoc. prof., 1967-69, dir. Civil Violence Rsch. Ctr., 1968-69; sr. Fulbright lectr. Johns Hopkins U. Ctr. Advanced Internat. Studies, Bologna, Italy, 1969-70; assoc. prof. Northwestern U., Evanston, Ill., 1970-72, prof. polit. sci. and urban affairs, 1972-83, dir. Ctr. Urban Affairs, 1971-80, dir. Program in Pub. and Not-for-Profit Mgmt., Kellogg Sch. Mgmt., 1979-80, prof. mgmt. and urban devel. Kellogg Sch. Mgmt., 1983-94, dir. Real Estate Research Ctr., 1986-88; cons. to numerous publs., govt. agys., real estate devels., and corps.; vis. assoc. prof. U. Wash. summer 1969; exec. dir. Mayor Jane Byrne Transition Com., Chgo., 1979; vis. prof. Stanford Sch. Bus., 1989-92, UCLA Sch. Mgmt., 1989-92; prof., dir. real estate mgmt. program U. Calif. Grad. Sch. Mgmt., Irvine, 1992—, bd. dirs. MHC, Inc., Tucker Properties Corp., Facilities Mgmt. Internat. Author: Education and Politics in Suburbia, 1967, Shootout in Cleveland, 1969, A Time to Burn?, 1969, Suburbia in Transition, 1973, The New Urban Politics, 1976, The City in Comparative Perspective, 1976, co-editor: Metropolis in Crisis, 1968, 2d edit., 1971, Riots and Rebellion, 1968, The Urbanization of the Suburbs, 1973, After Daley: Chicago Politics in Transition, 1981, Downtown Development, 1985, 2d edit., 1987; editor Edn. and Urban Soc., 1968-71, Urban Affairs Quar., 1973-80; sr. editor Econ. Devel. Quar., 1986-92; vice chmn. bd. Illinois Issues jour., 1986-92. Rsch. dir. Carl Stokes for Mayor of Cleve., 1967; mem. Cleveland Heights Bd. Edn., 1967-69; devel. coordinator for high tech. State of Ill.-City Chgo., 1982-83; advisor to various congl., gubernatorial and mayoral campaigns, Ohio, Ill., N.J., Calif.; cons. urban devel. issues Corps. developers, govt. agys. and news media. Lt. USNR, 1956-59. Fellow Homer Hoyt Inst. for Advanced Real Estate Studies; recipient Disting. Service award Cleve. Jaycees, 1967; numerous fed. and found. research grants, 1963—. Mem. Urban Land Inst., Nat. Coun. Urban Econ. Devel., Internat. Assn. Corp. Real Estate Execs., Internat. Devel. Rsch. Coun., Nat. Assn. Indsl. Office Properties (bd. dirs.), Lambda Alpha Internat. Home: 2810 Villa Way Newport Beach CA 92663-3729

MASOVER, GERALD KENNETH, microbiologist; b. Chgo., May 12, 1935; s. Morris H. and Lillian (Perelgut) M.; m. Bonnie Blumenthal, Mar. 30, 1958 (dec. 1992); children: Steven, Laurie, David; m. Lee H. Tower, Mar. 25, 1995. BS, U. Ill., Chgo., 1957, MS, 1970; PhD, Stanford U., 1973. Registered pharmacist, Calif., Ill. Owner, operator Ropert Pharmacy, Chgo., 1960-68; rsch. assoc. Stanford U. Med. Sch., Palo Alto, Calif., 1974-80; assoc. rsch. cell biologist Children's Hosp., Oakland, Calif., 1980-83; rsch. microbiologist Hana Biologics, Berkeley, Calif., 1983-86; pharmacist various locations, 1970—; quality control sect. head Genentech, Inc., South San Francisco, 1986-90, quality control sr. microbiologist, 1990—. Contbr. articles to profl. jours., chpts. to books. 1st Lt. USAR, 1957-66. NSF predoctoral fellow, 1970-73; NIH rsch. grantee, 1974-78. Mem. Soc. In Vitro Biology, Internat. Orgn. for Mycoplasmology, Parenteral Drug Assn., Am. Soc. Microbiology, Sigma Xi. Jewish. Achievements include patents on triphasic mycoplasmatales detection method; triphasic mycoplasmatales detection device. Home: 4472 24th St San Francisco CA 94114 Office: Genentech Inc 460 Point San Bruno Blvd South San Francisco CA 94080-4918

MASRI, MERLE SID, biochemist, consultant; b. Jerusalem, Palestine, Sept. 12, 1927; came to U.S., 1947; s. Said Rajab and Fatima (Muneimné) M.; m. Maryjean Loretta Anderson, June 28, 1952 (div. 1974); children: Kristin Corinne, Allan Eric, Wendy Joan, Heather Anderson. BA in Physiology, U. Calif., Berkeley, 1950; PhD in Mammalian Physiology and Biochemistry, U. Calif. Berkeley, 1953. Rsch. asst. Dept. Physiology, Univ. Calif., Berkeley, 1950-53; predoctoral fellow Baxter Labs., Berkeley, 1952-53; rsch. assoc. hematology Med. Rsch. Inst., Michael Reese Hosp., Chgo., 1954-56; sr. rsch. biochemist Agrl. Rsch. Svc., USDA, Berkeley, 1956-87; supervisory rsch. scientist Agrl. Rsch. Svc., USDA, N.D. State U. Sta., Fargo, N.D., 1987-89; pvt. practice as cons. Emeryville, Calif., 1989—; lectr. numerous confs. Contbr. articles to profl. jours. and books. Recipient Spl. Svc. and Merit awards USDA, 1966, 76, 77, Superior Svc. award USDA, 1977. Mem. AAAS, Am. Chem. Soc., Am. Oil Chemists Soc., Am. Assn. Cereal Chemists, N.Y. Acad. Scis., Inst. Food Technologists, Commonwealth Club Calif., Internat. Platform Assn., Sigma Xi. Achievements include patents for detoxification of aflatoxin in agricultural crops, new closed-circuit raw wool scouring technology to conserve water and energy and control pollution, synthesis and use of polymers for wastewater treatment, and for enzyme immobilization, toxic heavy metals removal and textile finishing treatment, non-polluting new technology for scouring raw wool in a closed circuit with water recycling and re-use and waste effluent control; discovered new methods and reagents for protein and amino acid residue modification and analysis, new metabolic pathways; developed other non-polluting textile finishing treatments; improved dyeability of cotton fabrics and reduced dye and electrolyte discharge in plant effluent. Home: 9 Commodore Dr Emeryville CA 94608-1652

MASRI, SAMI F(AIZ), civil and mechanical engineering educator, consultant; b. Beirut, Dec. 9, 1939; came to U.S., 1956; B.S. in Aerospace Engring., U. Tex., 1960, M.S. in Aerospace Engring., 1961; M.S. in Mech. Engring., Calif. Inst. Tech., 1962, Ph.D. in Mech. Engring., 1965. Research fellow Calif. Inst. Tech., Pasadena, 1965-66; asst. prof. civil and mech. engring. U. So. Calif., Los Angeles, 1966-69; assoc. prof. U. So. Calif., 1969-76, prof., 1976—. Contbr. articles to profl. jours. Research grantee NSF, NASA, NRC. Mem. AIAA, ASME, ASCE, IEEE, AAAS, Sigma Xi. Office: U So Calif Dept Civil Engring Mc # 2531 Los Angeles CA 90089

MASS, M. F., allergist, immunologist; b. Phila., Feb. 24, 1945; s. Edward I. and Pearl (Markovitz) M.; m. Marilyn Halpern, June 12, 1966; children: Ellis, David. Student, U. Fla., 1963; BA, Brandeis U., 1966; MD, U. Fla., 1970; postgrad., U. Colo., Albany, N.Y., 1972, U. Colo., Denver, 1975. Intern Albany (N.Y.) Med. Ctr., 1970-71, residency, 1971-72; sr. residency U. Colo. Med. Ctr., Denver, 1972-73, postgrad. fellow/allergy-immunology, 1973-75; assoc. clin. professor of medicine U. Fla., Jacksonville, Fla., 1977—; dir. Osteoporosis Diagnostic Lab. Meml. Med. Ctr., Jacksonville; chmn. Duval County Environ. Protection Bd., 1995-97; past chmn. dept. medicine Meml. Med. Ctr., Jacksonville; sec. S.E. Regional Am. Coll. Rheumatology; v.p. Duval County Med. Soc. Inventor skin chamber. Maj. USAF, 1975-77. Health Professions scholar U. Fla. Fellow Am. Coll. Physicians, Am. Acad. Allergy and Immunology, Am. Coll. Allergy; mem. Am. Coll. Rheumatology (sec. S.E. region), N.E. Fla. Arthritis Found. (bd. dirs., past pres.). Office: 3636 University Blvd S Ste B2 Jacksonville FL 32216-4223 also: 1895 Kingsley Ave Ste 401 Orange Park FL 32073-4453

MASSA, CONRAD HARRY, religious studies educator; b. Bklyn., Oct. 27, 1927; s. Harry Frederick and Josephine W. (Lepold) M.; m. Anna W. Rossi, Aug. 19, 1951; children: Stephen Mark, Barbara Ann. A.B. with honors, Columbia U., 1951; M.Div., Princeton Theol. Sem., 1954, Ph.D., 1960; HHD, Lafayette Coll., 1987. Ordained to ministry Presbyn. Ch., 1954. Pastor Elmwood Presbyn. Ch., East Orange, N.J., 1954-57; asst. prof. homiletics Princeton Theol. Sem., 1957-61; sr. pastor Old First Ch., Newark, 1961-66, Third Presbyn. Ch., Rochester, N.Y., 1966-78; dean acad. affairs Princeton Theol. Sem., 1978-94, dean emeritus, 1994—, Charlotte W. Newcombe prof., 1978-95, Charlotte W. Newcombe prof. emeritus, 1995—; 1st moderator Synod of the Northeast, United Presbyn. Ch.; vis. prof. St. Bernard's Roman Cath. Sem., Rochester, 1968-70; keynote speaker 11th ann. conf. Inst. Theology, Yonsei U., Seoul, Republic of Korea, 1991. Author articles and book revs. Trustee Lafayette Coll., Easton, Pa., 1982-93. Served with U.S. Army, 1946-47. Mem. Acad. Homiletics, Am. Acad. Religion. Home: 14691 Blackbird Ln Fort Myers FL 33919 *I have learned to try to understand all events and persons in terms of their relationships to other things, persons and events. While it is sometimes fruitful to isolate a particular and study it in its solitude, nothing and no one really exists in such isolation. This has become a guiding principle in my continued research and growth in those areas of greatest interest - religion, education and society.*

MASSA, PAUL PETER, publisher; b. Hammond, Ind., Aug. 20, 1940; s. Paul Peter and Frances (Ferrara) M.; m. Susan W. Olsgard, Sept. 13, 1969; children: Katherine Alice, Karen Elizabeth. B.S., Ind. U., 1962, postgrad., 1962. Instr. Ind. U. Lab. Sch., 1962, 64-65; with Harcourt Brace Jovanovich Inc., 1965-73; bus. mgr. sch. div. Harcourt Brace Jovanovich Inc., N.Y.C., 1969-73; v.p., gen. mgr., dir. Congl. Quar. Inc., Washington, 1973-80; exec. v.p., chief oper. officer, bd. dirs. Congl. Info. Svc., Inc., Washington, 1980-81, pres., chief exec. officer, bd. dirs., 1981—; chmn. Elsevier Realty Info., Inc., 1988—, also bd. dirs.; chmn. Greenwood Pub. Group, Inc., 1985-91, also bd. dirs.; pres. Elsevier Investment Corp., 1987-88, also bd. dirs.; mem. info. industry adv. coun. GPO. Mem. bd. visitors Sch. Edn. Ind. U., 1987—, adv. panel for assessment of tech., pub. policy and changing nature of fed. info. dissemination U.S. Congress Office of Tech. Assessment; mem. Friends of the Law Libr. of Congress. 1st lt. USAR, 1962-64, Korea. Mem. ALA (mem. commn. freedom and equality of access to info.), Info. Industry Assn. (dir. 1993—), Assn. Am. Pubs., Soc. Scholarly Pub., Washington Pubs. Assn., Nat. Press Club. Office: Congressional Info Service 4520 E West Hwy Bethesda MD 20814-3319*

MASSA, SALVATORE PETER, psychologist; b. Queens, N.Y., Aug. 5, 1955; s. Joseph and Marie Massa; AAS, Orange County Community Coll., 1975; BA in Psychology, Queens Coll., 1977; MA, St. John's U., 1978, profl. diploma, 1979, PhD, 1985; m. Patricia Louise Kathryn Kelley, Mar. 12, 1979; children: Kathryn Kelley, Kristopher Kelley, KayLynn Kelley, Patrick Kelley, Grace Kelley. Lic. psychologist, N.Y.; nat. cert. sch. psychologist. Intern psychologist Sagamore Children's Psychiat. Hosp., Melville, N.Y., 1978-79; habilitation supr. Suffolk Child Devel. Center, Smithtown, N.Y., 1979; staff psychologist Cumberland Mental Health Center, Bklyn., 1979-81; asst. program dir., dir. clin. services Rhinebeck (N.Y.) Country Sch., 1981-87; cons. psychologist Brookwood Ctr., 1985-86, Anderson Sch., 1987-89, Renssalaer Columbia Greene BOCES, 1987—; chmn. Com. on Spl. Edn., 1991—, Com. on Presch. Edn., 1991—; sch. psychologist Red Hook Cen. Sch. Dist., cons. psychologist Rhinebeck Cen. Sch. Dist., 1986-90, chmn. profl. conf. com., 1986-87, Anderson Sch., 1987-88; cons. Columbia County Assn. for Retarded Citizens, Rehab. Programs, Inc., 1989; adj. prof. Marist Coll., Poughkeepsie, N.Y., 1989—. Head football coach YMCA winter league, 1979-81; asst. football coach Rhinebeck Country Sch., 1982; coach Germantown Little League, Germantown Winter Basketball League. Recipient public service award for vol. work Middletown State Hosp., 1975; spl. recognition award Internat. Council Psychology, 1981; cert. sch. psychology, N.Y. Mem. Am. Psychol. Assn. (divs. pediatric psychology, psychotherapy, sch. psychology, neuropsychology), Eastern Psychol. Assn., Internat. Council Psychologists, Hudson Valley Psychol. Assn., Nat. Assn. Sch. Psychologists, Nat. Soc. Autistic Children. Democrat. Roman Catholic. Contbr. papers to profl. confs.; co-author study on relaxation tng. in residential treatment.

MASSAD, STEPHEN ALBERT, lawyer; b. Wewoka, Okla., Dec. 20, 1950; s. Alexander Hamilton and Delores Jean (Razook) M.; m. Amy S. Massad, Jan. 13, 1979; children: Caroline, Sarah, Margaret. AB, Princeton U., 1972; JD, Harvard U., 1975. Bar: Tex. 1975. Assoc. Baker & Botts, Houston, 1975-82, ptnr., 1983—. Office: Baker & Botts 3000 One Shell Plz 910 Louisiana St Houston TX 77002

MASSALSKI, THADDEUS BRONISLAW, material scientist, educator; b. Warsaw, Poland, June 29, 1926; came to U.S., 1959; s. Piotr and Stanislawa (Andrukaniec) M.; m. Sheila Joan Harris, Sept. 19, 1953; children: Irena, Peter, Christopher. B.Sc., Birmingham (Eng.) U., 1952, Ph.D., 1954, D.Sc., 1964; fellow, Inst. Study Metals, U. Chgo., 1954-56; D.Sc. (h.c.), Warsaw (Poland) U., 1973. Lectr. Birmingham U., 1956-59; head. metal physics group Mellon Inst., Pitts., 1959-75; staff fellow Mellon Inst., 1961—; prof. metal physics and materials sci. Carnegie-Mellon U., 1968—; vis. prof. U. Buenos Aires, 1962, Calif. Inst. Tech., 1962, Stanford, 1963, U. Calif., 1964, 66, Inst. Physics, Bariloche Argentina, 1966, 70, Harvard, 1969; exchange prof. Krakow (Poland) U., 1968; vis. scientist Nat. Bur. Standards, 1980-81; NAVSEA prof. Naval Postgrad. Sch., Monterey, Calif; chmn. bd. govs. Acta Metallurgica, Inc., 1992—. Co-author: Structure of Metals, 3d edit, 1966, Advanced Physical Metallurgy, 1965; co-editor Progress in Materials Science, 1969—, Metall. Transactions, 1991—; editor-in-chief ASM/NIST Phase Diagram Program, 1980—; author papers and articles on alloy theory, crystallography, metal physics, meteorites. Guggenheim fellow Oxford U., 1965-66; recipient Alexander von Humboldt prise, 1991. Fellow Am. Soc. Metals (gold medal 1993), Am. Phys. Soc., The Metals Soc. (gold medal 1995), Brit. Inst. Metals, Brit. Inst. Physics, AIME (Hume-Rotherly prize 1989); mem. Polish Acad. Sci. (fgn.), German Acad. Sci. (fgn.), Phys. Soc. Home: 900 Field Club Rd Pittsburgh PA 15238-2127 Office: Carnegie Mellon U 3303 Wean Hall Pittsburgh PA 15213

MASSÉ, LAURENCE RAYMOND, personnel search firm executive; b. Holland, Mich., July 27, 1926; s. Lawrence Joseph and Gladys Lucille (Tidd) M.; m. Barbara Anne Kranendonk, Dec. 23, 1948 (div. 1970); children: Laurel, Babette; m. Pamela Bateman, Feb. 3, 1982; children: Heather, Edward. BA in English, Hope Coll., 1950. Tchr. Pub. Sch. System, Holland, 1950-53; cons. Gen. Motors Corp., Flint, Detroit, Mich., 1953-56; dir. personnel Gen. Foods Corp., White Plains (N.Y.), London, Paris, 1956-66; dir. adminstrn. & personnel Internat. Telephone & Telegraph Co., Brussels, 1966-68; cons. Heidrick & Struggles, N.Y.C., 1968-69; v.p. indsl. relations REA Express Inc., N.Y.C., 1969-72; sr. ptnr. Ward Howell Internat., N.Y.C., Chgo., 1972—; chmn. Ward Howell Internat. Group, 1991-95. Dir. Ridgefield (Conn.) Community Ctr., 1960-63. With U.S. Navy, 1945-46. Mem. AMA, Chgo. Council Fgn. Relations, Nat. Indsl. Conf. Bd., U.S. C. of C. Republican. Presbyterian. Avocations: reading, music, gardening, swimming, antique collecting. Office: Ward Howell Internat Inc 1300 S Grove Ave Ste 100 Barrington IL 60010-5246

MASSÉ, MARCEL, Canadian government official; b. Montreal, June 23, 1940; m. Josee M'Baye; 4 children. BA, U. Montreal, 1958; LLB, McGill U., 1961; PhB in Econs., Oxford U., 1966; Diploma in Internat. Law, U. Warsaw, Poland, 1962; Diplomas in Internat. Affairs, Econs., Spanish, German and Italian, École des hautes études commerciales de Montréal. Econ. adviser Privy Coun. Office, Ottawa, ON, Can., 1971-73; dep. minister fin. Province of N.B., Fredericton, Can., 1973-74, chmn. Cabinet Secretariat, 1974-77; dep. sec. to Cabinet Fed.-Provincial Rels., Ottawa, 1977-79; dep. sec. to Cabinet Privy Coun. Office, Ottawa, 1979, sec. to Cabinet and clk., 1979-80; pres. Can. Internat. Devel. Agy., Hull, 1980-82, 89-93; undersec. state for external affairs Ottawa, 1982-85; sec. to Cabinet Intergovtl. Affairs, Ottawa, 1993; pres. Queen's privy coun. for Can., min. intergovtl. affairs, min. pub. svc. renewal Govt. of Can., Ottawa, 1993-96; pres. Treasury Bd. of Can., min. infrastructure, Ottawa; bd. dirs. for Can. IMF, Washington, 1985-89; mem. Parliament Hull-Aylmer Constituency, 1993—. World Univ. Service scholar in internat. law, 1961; Rhodes scholar, 1963; Nuffield Coll. scholar in econs. Oxford U., 1966. Office: 140 O'Connor St 9th Fl East Tower, Ottawa, ON Canada K1A 0R5

MASSENGALE, MARTIN ANDREW, agronomist, university president; b. Monticello, Ky., Oct. 25, 1933; s. Elbert G. and Orpha (Conn) M.; m. Ruth Audrey Klingelhofer, July 11, 1959; children: Alan Ross, Jennifer Lynn. BS, Western Ky. U., 1952; MS, U. Wis., 1954, PhD, 1956; LHD (hon.), Nebr. Wesleyan U., 1987; DS (hon.), Senshu U., Tokyo, 1995. Cert. profl. agronomist, profl. crop scientist. Research asst. agronomy U. Wis., 1952-56; asst. prof., asst. agronomist U. Ariz., 1958-62, assoc. prof., assoc. agronomist, 1962-65, prof., agronomist, 1965-76, head dept., 1966-74, assoc. dean Coll. Agr. assoc. dir. Ariz. Agr. Expt. Sta., 1974-76; vice chancellor for agr. and natural resources U. Nebr., 1976-81; chancellor U. Nebr.-Lincoln, 1981-91, interim pres., 1989-91; pres. U. Nebr., 1991-94, pres. emeritus, 1994, found. prof. and dir. Ctr. for Grassland Studies, 1994—; chmn. pure seed adv. com. Ariz. Agrl. Expt. Sta.; past chmn. bd., pres. Mid-Am. Internat. Agrl. Consortium; coord. com. environ. quality EPA-Dept. Agrl. Land Grand U.; past chmn. bd. dirs. Am. Registry Cert. Profls. in Agronomy, Crops and Soils; bd. dirs. Ctr. for Human Nutrition, Agronomic Sci. Found., U. Nebr. Found.; mem. exec. com. U. Nebr. Tech. Park, LLC. Chmn. NCAA Pres.'s Commn., 1988-91; distbn. revenue com., standing com. on appointments North Ctrl. Assn. Commn. on Insts. Higher Edn., 1991; trustee Nebr. State Hist. Soc.; bd. govs. Nebr. Sci. and Math. Initiative; active Knight Found. Commn. on Intercollegiate Athletics. Named Midlands Man of Yr., 1982, to We. Ky. U. Hall of Disting. Alumni, 1992, Outstanding Educator of Am., 1970; recipient faculty recognition award Tucson Trade Bur., 1971, Ak-Sar-Ben Agrl. Achievement award, 1986, Agrl. Builders Nebr. award, 1986, Walter K. Beggs award, 1986, hon. state farmer degrees Ky., Ariz., Nebr. Future Farmers of Am. Assns. Fellow AAAS (sect. chmn.), Crop Sci. Soc. Am. (past dir., pres. 1972-73, past assoc. editor), Am. Soc. Agronomy (past dir., vis. scientist program, past assoc. editor Agronomy Jour., past chmn. bd. dirs., Disting. Svc. award 1984); mem. Am. Grassland Coun., Ariz. Crop Improvement Assn. (bd. dirs.), Am. Soc. Plant Physiology, Nat. Assn. Colls. and Tchrs. Agr., Soil and Water Conservation Soc. Am., Ariz. Acad. Sci., Nebr. Acad. Sci., Agrl. Coun. Am. (bd. dirs., issues com.), Coun. Agrl. Sci. and Tech. (bd. dirs. 1979-82, 94—), Nat. Assn. State Colls. and Land Grant Univs. (chmn. com. on info. tech. 1987-94, exec. com. 1990-92, bd. dirs. 1992-94), Edn. Engring. Professions (mem. commn.), Coll. Football Assn. (chmn., bd. dirs. 1986-88), Am. Assn. State Coll. and Univs. (task force instl. resource allocation), Assn. Am. Univs. Rsch. Librs. (steering com. 1992-94), Nebr. C. of C. and Industry, Nebr. C.C. Assn. (hon.), Lincoln C. of C., Nebr. Vet. Med. Assn. (hon.), Sigma Xi, Phi Kappa Phi, Gamma Sigma Delta, Alpha Zeta, Phi Sigma, Gamma Alpha, Alpha Gamma Rho, Phi Beta Delta, Golden Key Nat. Honor Soc. Office: U Nebr 220 Keim Hall Lincoln NE 68583

MASSENGILL, ALAN DURWOOD, lawyer; b. Four Oaks, N.C., Feb. 16, 1937; s. Percy Bryant and Bettie Pearl (Parker) M.; children: Skip, Alan, Brian, Craig; m. Barbara Ann Berdner, Dec. 20, 1974. BS in Econs., U. Md., 1964, JD, 1966. Bar: Md. 1966, U.S. Ct. Appeals (4th cir.) 1968, U.S. Supreme Ct. 1972, U.S. Dist. Ct. D.C. 1979. Law clk. 6th Jud. Ct., Rockville, Md., 1966-67; pvt. practice Gaithersburg, Md., 1967—. Contbr. articles to profl. jours. Mem. ABA (mediation arbitration com. 1981-95), Md. Bar Assn. (spl. com. on alternative dispute resolution 1993-95), Md. Trial Lawyers Assn., Montgomery County Bar Assn. (mediation subcom. 1980-83, coms.), Frederick County Bar Assn. Avocations: writing, carving, guitar, birding, hiking. Office: 2 Professional Dr Ste 239 Gaithersburg MD 20879-3422

MASSEY, ANDREW JOHN, conductor, composer; b. Nottingham, Eng., May 1, 1946; came to U.S., 1978; s. Henry Louis Johnson and Margaret (Park) M.; m. Sabra Ann Todd, May 29, 1982; children: Colin Sebastian, Robin Elizabeth. BA, Oxford U., 1968, MA, 1981; MA, Nottingham U., 1969. Asst. condr. The Cleve. Orch., 1978-80; assoc. condr. New Orleans Symphony, 1980-86, San Francisco Symphony, 1985-88; music dir. Fresno (Calif.) Philharmonic, 1986-93, R.I. Philharmonic, Providence, 1986-91; music dir. Toledo Symphony Orch., 1991—, also condr.; vis. scholar Brown U., Providence, 1986—. Composer incidental music (stage prodns.) Murder in the Cathedral, 1968, King Lear, 1971, A Midsummer Night's Dream, 1972. Avocations: trees, computers, astrology, philosophy of Karl Popper. Office: care Toledo Symphony Two Maritime Plz Toledo OH 43604-1868

MASSEY, CHARLES KNOX, JR., advertising agency executive; b. Durham, N.C., Jan. 16, 1936; s. Charles Knox and Louise (Southerl) M.; m. Mary Ann Keith, Aug. 27, 1960; children: Elizabeth, Knox, Louise. BS in Bus. Adminstrn. U. N.C., 1959. Vice pres. C. Knox Massey & Assoc., Inc., advt. agy., Durham, N.C., 1959-64; account exec. Tucker Wayne & Co., advt. agy., Atlanta, 1964-78; pres. Tucker Wayne & Co., advt. agy., 1978-88; pres. Tucker Wayne/Luckie & Co., Atlanta, 1988-93, chmn., CEO, 1994—. Trustee The Lovett Sch., Atlanta, Inst. for the Arts and Scis., U. N.C., Chapel Hill. Mem. Piedmont Driving Club (pres. 1990-92), Coral Beach and Tennis Club (Bermuda), Highlands (N.C.) Country Club. Episcopalian. Home: 67 Brighton Rd NE Atlanta GA 30309-1518 Office: Tucker Wayne & Co 1100 Peachtree St NE Ste 1800 Atlanta GA 30309-4518

MASSEY, DONALD E., automotive executive. CEO Don Massey Cadillac. Office: Don Massey Cadillac Inc 40475 Ann Arbor Rd E Plymouth MI 48170-4576 Office: 40475 Ann Arbor Rd Plymouth MI 48170

MASSEY, DONALD WAYNE, microfilm consultant, small business owner; b. Durham, N.C., Mar. 7, 1938; s. Gordon Davis and Lucille Alma (Gregory) M.; m. Violet Sue McIlvain, Nov. 2, 1958; children: Kimberly Shan (dec.), Leon Dale, Don Krichele, Anthony Donn Prestarri. Student, U. Hawaii, 1959, U. Ky., 1965, 66, U. Va., 1970, Piedmont C.C., 1982. Head microfilm sect. Ky. Hist. Soc., Frankfort, 1961; dir. microfilm ctr. U. Ky., Lexington, 1962-67; dir. photog. svcs. and graphics U. Va., Charlottesville, 1967-73; pres. Micrographics II, Charlottesville, Va. & Charleston, S.C., 1973—; owner Roseraie Nursery Ctr., 1988—; instr. U. Va. Sch. Continuing Edn., 1971-72, Central Va. Piedmont Community Coll., 1976; cons. Microform Systems and Copying Centers; owner Massland Farm, Shadwell, Va.; basketball coach Rock Hill Acad., 1975-77; chaplain Cedars Nursing Home, Charlottesville, 1992-94; chaplain Colonnades Charlottesville, Va., 1994—. Pub.: Micropublishing Series, 18th Century Sources for Study of English Lit. and Culture, Women Authors 18th and 19th Centuries, 1993, Va. Colonial History, 1994—, Theology in the 18th and 19th Centuries, 1995; author: Episcopal Churches in the Diocese of Virginia, 1989, A Catechism for Children, 1995, A Guide to Colonial Churches in Virginia, 1996, The Christian Philosophy of Patrick Henry, In Memoriam to the Rt. Rev. William Meade, Third Bishop of Virginia, 1996, Jamestown, the Beginning of the Church in Virginia, 1996, Christ Episcopal Church, Monticello Parish, Charlottesville, Va. The First 100 years, 1924-1924, 1996. Chmn. bd. dirs. Park St. Christian Ch., 1970, 75; pres., Rock Hill Acad. Aux., 1975-76; pres. bd. Workshop V for handicapped, Charlottesville, Va., 1972-73; bd. chmn. Park St. Christ Ch., 1969-73; mem. Emmanuel Episc. Ch., Greenwood, Va., Grace Episc. Ch., Cismont, Va.; pres. region XV Episc. Diocese of Va.; chalice bearer St. Luke's Chapel Simeon, Va., Christ Ch., Charlottesville, 1992, lay eucharistic min., 1993—; lay reader eucharistic minister Christ Episcopal Ch., Charlottesville, Va.; chaplain Cedars Nursing Home, Charlottesville, 1991—; rep. Senatorial Inner Circle, 1990, George Bush Rep. Task Force, 1990; eucharistic min. Grace Episc. Ch., Cismont, 1995—. With

USMCR, 1957-63. Named Ky. Col.; recipient Key award Workshop V. Mem. Am. Libr. Assn., Va. Libr. Assn. Soc. Reprodn. Engrs., Nat. Microfilm Assn. (libr. rels. com. 1973—), Va. Microfilm Assn. (pres. 1971-72, v.p. 1973-74, program chmn. ann. conf. 1974, Pioneer award 1973, Fellow award 1976), Ky. Microfilm Assn. (Outstanding award 1967, pres. 1964-67), Assn. for Info. and Image Mgmt., Va. Gamebird Assn., Thoroughbred Owners and Breeders Assn., Am. Rose Soc., Thomas Jefferson Rose Soc. (charter), Nat. Rifle Assn. Contbg. editor Va. Librarian, 1970-71, Micro-News Va. Microfilm Assn., 1970-71, Plant & Print Jour., 1983-85; contbr. articles to profl. publs. Home and Office: RR 2 Box 44 Keswick VA 22947-9317

MASSEY, GWENDOLYN INEZ, nurse, counselor; b. Greensboro, Ala., Oct. 12, 1929; d. Judson Lyons Kilpatrick and Rubye Hill Kilpatrick-Jacobs; m. James Earl Massey, Aug. 4, 1951. BSN, Wayne State U., 1952; MA, Ball State U., 1978. Sr. pub. health nurse Dept. Pub. Health Nursing, Detroit; supr. patient care and edn., clin. instr. pub. health nsg. Henry Ford Hosp., Detroit; coord. of refugee and relief svcs. Missionary Bd. of Ch. of God, Anderson, Ind. Contbr. articles to profl. jours. Recipient Distikng. Svc. award, Commn. on Social Concerns, Ch. of God. Mem. Am. Nursing Assn., Am. Assn. Counseling and Devel. Home: 201 Mill Stream Ln Anderson IN 46011-1916

MASSEY, IKE, newspaper publishing executive; b. San Angelo, Tex.. Staff and mgmt. positions in adv., circulation, prodn., editorial, bur. chief Odessa, Tex. San Angelo Standard-Times, to 1978; pub. Tulsa (Okla.) Suburban Newspapers Park Newspapers, Inc., 1979-85, head Western Divsn., 1983-85; v.p. MediaNews Group, 1986-88; pres., chief oper. officer DTH Media, Inc., Dallas, 1988-91; pub., chief exec. officer Houston Post, 1991—. Dir. Better Bus. Bur., Sam Houston Area Coun. Boy Scouts Am., Houston Symphony, Houston Bus. Com. Ednl. Excellence; trustee United Way Tex. Gulf Coast; mem. adv. coun. Sch. Comm. U. Houston, adv. com. Lombardi Award, adv. bd. Houston Proud, Houston Livestock Show and Rodeo, life. Recipient 3 Mng. Editor awards Tex. AP, 1978; honored Outstanding Tex. leader John Ben Shepperd Leadership Found. LBJ Sch. Pub. Affairs, Austin, 1988. Mem. Tex. Daily Newspaper Assn., Forum Club, Houston Rotary Club. Office: The Houston Post PO Box 4747 Houston TX 77210

MASSEY, JAMES EARL, clergyman, educator; b. Ferndale, Mich., Jan. 4, 1930; s. George Wilson and Elizabeth (Shelton) M.; m. Gwendolyn Inez Kilpatrick, Aug. 4, 1951. Student U. Detroit, 1949-50, 55-57; BTh, BRE, Detroit Bible Coll., 1961; AM, Oberlin Grad. Sch. Theology, 1964; postgrad. U. Mich., 1967-69; DD, Asbury Theol. Sem., 1972, Ashland Theol. Sem., 1991, Huntington Coll., 1994; Hum. D. Tuskegee U., 1995; DD Warner Pacific Coll., 1995; LittD Anderson U., 1995; postgrad. Pacific Sch. Religion, 1972, Boston Coll., 1982-83. Ordained to ministry Church of God, 1951. Assoc. minister Ch. of God, Detroit, 1951-53; sr. pastor Met. Church of God, Detroit, 1954-76, pastor-at-large, 1976; speaker Christian Brotherhood Hour, 1977-82; prin. Jamaica Sch. Theology, Kingston, 1963-66; campus minister Anderson Coll., Ind., 1969-77, asst. prof. religious studies, 1969-75, assoc. prof., 1975-80, prof. N.T. and homiletics, 1981-84; dean of chapel and univ., prof. religion and society Tuskegee U., Ala., 1984-89; dean, prof. preaching and bibl. studies Anderson (Ind.) Sch. of Theology, 1989-95, dean emeritus and disting. prof.-at-large, 1995—; chmn. Commn. on Higher Edn. in the Ch. of God, 1968-71; vice chmn. bd. publs. Ch. of God, 1968-78; dir. Warner Press, Inc. Author: When Thou Prayest, 1960; The Worshipping Church, 1961; Raymond S. Jackson, A Portrait, 1967; The Soul Under Siege, 1970; The Church of God and the Negro, 1971; The Hidden Disciplines, 1972; The Responsible Pulpit, 1973; Temples of the Spirit, 1974; The Sermon in Perspective, 1976; Concerning Christian Unity, 1979; gen. editor: Christian Brotherhood Hour Study Bible, 1979; Designing the Sermon, 1980; co-editor Interpreting God's Word for Today, 1982; editor Educating for Service, 1984; The Spiritual Disciplines, 1985, The Bridge Between, 1988, Preaching From Hebrews, 1992, The Burdensome Joy of Preaching, 1996; mem. editl. bd. The Christian Scholar's Rev. Leadership mag.; mem. editorial bd., contbg. editor Vol. I New Interpreter's Bible, 1990—; contbg. editor Preaching mag.; sr. editor Christianity Today Mag. Mem. Corp. Inter-Varsity Christian Fellowship; bd. dirs. World Vision. Served with AUS, 1951-53. Rsch. scholar Christianity Today Inst. Mem. Nat. Assn. Coll. and Univ. Chaplains, Nat. Com. Black Churchmen, Nat. Negro Evang. Assn. (bd. dirs. 1969-86). Office: 201 Mill Stream Ln Anderson IN 46011-1916

MASSEY, LEON R., professional society administrator; b. Grand Island, Nebr., Jan. 16, 1930; s. James Moore and Iva Pearl (Richardson) M.; m. Jean M. Nielsen, June 17, 1951; children: Dean R., Maureen L. Student, U. Colo., 1948-49; BA, U. Nebr., 1955; postgrad., N.Y. Inst. Fin., 1963. Salesman consumer products Union Carbide Corp., Memphis, 1956-57, Greenville, Miss., 1957-58, Albuquerque, 1958-61, Dallas, 1962-63; regional sales mgr. GC Electric div. Textron Corp., Dayton, Ohio, 1963-64; account exec. Merrill Turben Co., Dayton, 1964-66; with Nat. Electric Contractors Assn., Dayton, 1967-72, Denver, 1972-83, exec. sec., 1967-83, also bd. dirs. Rocky Mountain chpt.; pres. RLM's Assocs., Englewood, Colo., 1983—; instr. adult edn. Wayne State U., Dayton, 1964-66. City councilman City of Greenwood Village, Colo., 1986-90; pres. Cherry Creek Civic Assn., 1979-80, bd. dirs. 1973-74; bd. dirs. Assn. Operating Rm. Nurses, Cherry Creek Village Water Dist., 1992-95; bd. dirs. Goldsmith Gulch Sanitation Dist., 1990—, pres., 1992—; active Dem. Party, 1960. With USAF, 1950-54, Korea. Mem. Am. Soc. Assn. Execs. (cert., bd. dirs.), Colo. Soc. Assn. Execs. (life, pres. 1979), Civitan Club, Masons, Phi Kappa Psi. Office: RLM Assocs 4935 E Greenwich Ln Highlands Ranch CO 80126

MASSEY, LEWIS, state official; b. Gainesville, Ga.; s. Abit and Kayanne M.; m. Amy Massey; children: Chandler, Cameryn. BBA in Finance, U. Ga. Mem. campaign staff Ct. Appeals Judge Robert Benham; mgr. reelection campaign Gov. Joe Frank Harris; dir. election campaigns various first time candidates apptd. by Gov. Joe Frank Harris; spl. asst. Gov. Joe Frank Harris; campaign mgr. Pierre Howard for Lt. Gov.; chief of staff Lt. Gov. Pierre Howard; v.p. Bank South Securities Corp.; apptd. sec. of state. State of Ga., 1996—. Elder Peachtree Presbyn. Ch.; mem. bd. dirs. Am. Cancer Soc., Eagle Ranch Home For Boys. Recipient Blue Key ALumnus of the Yr. award U. Ga., Outstanding Young Alumnus Bus. Sch. U. Ga. Office: Office of Sec of State State Capitol Rm 214 Atlanta GA 30334

MASSEY, RAYMOND LEE, lawyer; b. Macon, Ga., Sept. 25, 1948; s. Ford B. and Juanita (Sapp) M.; m. Lynn Ann Thielmeier, Aug. 23, 1967; children: Daniel, Caroline. BA, U. Mo., St. Louis, 1971; JD, U. Louisville, 1974. Bar: Mo. 1974, Ill. 1976, U.S. Dist. Ct. (ea. and we. dists.) Mo. 1974, U.S. Dist. Ct. (so. dist.) Ill. 1976. Assoc. Thompson & Mitchell, St. Louis, 1974-79, ptnr., 1979—. Mem. Maritime Law Assn. of U.S. (bd. dirs., chmn. ocean and river towing). Home: 3 Wild Rose Dr Saint Louis MO 63124-1465 Office: Thompson & Mitchell 1 Mercantile Ctr Ste 3300 Saint Louis MO 63101-1643

MASSEY, RICHARD WALTER, JR., investment counselor; b. Birmingham, Ala., May 19, 1917; s. Richard Walter and Elizabeth (Spencer) M.; m. Ann Hinkle, Sept. 4, 1959; children—Richard Walter, Dale Elizabeth. B.S., U. Va., 1939; M.A., Birmingham-So. Coll., 1954; Ph.D., Vanderbilt U., 1960. Owner, mgr. Massey Bus. Coll., Birmingham, Ala., 1946-56; asst. to chancellor Vanderbilt U., 1959-60; chmn. dept. econs. Birmingham-So. Coll., 1960-66; investment trust officer 1st Nat. Bank of Birmingham, 1966-67; prof. econs. U. Ala., Tuscaloosa, 1967-68; v.p., dir. investment rsch. Sterne, Agee & Leach, Inc., Birmingham, 1968-75; pres. Richard W. Massey & Co., Inc., Investment Counsel, Birmingham, 1975—. Served to maj. U.S. Army, 1941-46. Mem. Country Club of Birmingham. Home and Office: 1304 Kingsway Ln Birmingham AL 35243-2174

MASSEY, ROBERT UNRUH, physician, university dean; b. Detroit, Feb. 23, 1922; s. Emil Laverne and Esther Elisabeth (Unruh) M.; m. June Charlene Collins, May 28, 1943; children: Robert Scott, Janet Charlene. Student, Oberlin Coll., 1939-42, U. Mich. Med. Sch., 1942-43; M.D., Wayne State U., 1946. Intern, resident in internal medicine Henry Ford Hosp., Detroit, 1946-50; assoc. Lovelace Clinic, Albuquerque, 1950-68; chmn. dept. medicine Lovelace Clinic, 1958-68, bd. govs., 1957-68; dir. med. edn. Lovelace Found. for Med. Edn. and Research, 1960-68; clin. assoc. U. N.Mex. Sch. Medicine, 1961-68; prof. medicine U. Conn. Sch. Medicine, Farmington, 1968—; assoc. dean for grad edn. U. Conn. Sch. Medicine, 1968-71, dean Sch. Medicine, 1971-84, currently prof. emeritus dept. community medicine and health care, acting univ. v.p. for health affairs, 1975-76; chief staff Newington (Conn.) VA Hosp., 1968-71; trustee Am. Assn. Med. Clinics, 1966-68; exec. com., regional adv. group Conn. Regional Med. Program, 1971-76; trustee, v.p. Capitol Area Health Consortium, 1974-78, pres., 1980-81. Editor-in-chief Conn. Medicine, 1986—; editor Jour. of the History of Medicine and Allied Scis., 1987-91. Bd. dirs. Health Planning Coun., Inc., 1974-76; bd. dirs. Hartford Inst. for Criminal and Social Justice, 1976-80, Conn. Easter Seal Soc., 1977-85, Hospice Inst. Edn., Tng. and Rsch., 1979-81. With AUS, 1955-57; maj. Res. Fellow ACP; mem. Am. Group Practice Assn. (accreditation commn. 1968-78), Assn. Am. Med. Colls., Am. Assn. History of Medicine, Hartford County Med. Assn., AMA, Conn., Hartford med. socs., Am. Osler Soc., Beaumont Med. Club, Soc. Med. Adminstrs., Twilight Club (Hartford), Sigma Xi, Alpha Omega Alpha. Roman Catholic. Office: U Conn Sch Medicine Farmington CT 06032

MASSEY, STEPHEN CHARLES, auctioneer; b. London, May 9, 1946; s. Charles Dudley and Sheila Florence (Browne) M.; divorced; 1 child, Sarah Louise. Grad. high sch., U.K. Cataloguer books and manuscripts Christie's, London, 1964-75; sr. dir. rare books and manuscripts dept. Christie's, N.Y.C., 1975—. Fellow Pierpont Morgan Libr.; mem. The Grolier Club, The Old Book Table. Avocations: cinema, reading, running, music, forestry. Office: Christie's Internat Inc 502 Park Ave New York NY 10022-1108

MASSEY, THOMAS BENJAMIN, academic administrator; b. Charlotte, N.C., Sept. 5, 1926; s. William Everard and Sarah (Corley) M.; m. Bylee Hunnicutt Massey, July 10, 1968; children: Pamela Ann, Caroline Forest. A.B., Duke U., 1948; M.S., N.C. State U., 1953; Ph.D., Cambridge U., 1968. Assoc. dean students Ga. Inst. Tech., Atlanta, 1950-58; lectr. U. Md. Univ. Coll., 1960-66, asst. dir. London, 1966-69, dir. Toyko, 1969-71, dir. Heidelberg (Fed. Republic of Germany), 1971-76, vice chancellor, 1976-78, chancellor, 1978-88, pres., 1988—; bd. dirs. Internat. Univ. Consortium for Telecommunications in Learning, 1983—. Served with USN, 1943-46. Mem. Am. Assn. Adult and Continuin Edn., Soc. Rsch. in Higher Edn., Nat. Univ. Continuing Edn. Assn., Am. Psychol. Assn., Am. Assn. Higher Edn., Internat. Confs. on Improving Univ. Teaching (chmn. 1975—). Office: U Md Univ Coll University Blvd at Adelphi Rd College Park MD 20742-1600

MASSEY, VINCENT, biochemist, educator; b. Berkeley, New South Wales, Australia, Nov. 28, 1926; s. Walter and Mary Ann (Mark) M.; m. Margot Grunewald, Mar. 4, 1950; children: Charlotte, Andrew, Rachel. BSc with honors, U. Sydney, Australia, 1947; PhD, U. Cambridge, Eng., 1953; DSc (hon.), U. Tokushima, 1994. Mem. research staff Henry Ford Hosp., Detroit, 1955-57; lectr. to sr. lectr. U. Sheffield, 1957-63; prof. Med. Sch. U. Mich., Ann Arbor, 1963-95, J. Lawrence Oncley Disting. U. prof., 1995—; mem. biochemistry-biophysics rev. panel NSF, 1980-84; mem. fellowship rev. panel NIH, 1965-69, mem. biochemistry study sect. NIH, 1972-76, chmn. 1974-76. Contbg. author numerous books.; co-editor Flavins and Flavoproteins, 1982; contbr. numerous articles, chiefly on oxidative enzymology, to profl. jours. Recipient Alexander von Humboldt U.S. Sr. Scientist award, 1973-74, 86; Imperial Chem. Industries Research fellow, 1953-55. Fellow Royal Soc. London; mem. NAS, Biochem. Soc., Am. Soc. Biochemistry and Molecular Biology (membership com. 1970, nominating com. 1978-80, chmn. 1979-80, chmn. program com. 1992-93), Am. Chem. Soc. (exec. bd. divsn. biol. chemistry 1975-77). Home: 2536 Bedford Rd Ann Arbor MI 48104-4008 Office: U Mich Med Sch Dept Biol Chemistry Ann Arbor MI 48109

MASSEY, WALTER EUGENE, physicist, science foundation administrator; b. Hattiesburg, Miss., Apr. 5, 1938; s. Almor and Essie (Nelson) M.; m. Shirley Streeter, Oct. 25, 1969; children: Keith Anthony, Eric Eugene. BS, Morehouse Coll., 1958; MA, Washington U., St. Louis, 1966, PhD, 1966. Physicist Argonne (Ill.) Nat. Lab., 1966-68; asst. prof. physics U. Ill., Urbana, 1968-70; assoc. prof. Brown U., Providence, 1970-75, prof., dean of Coll., 1975-79; prof. physics U. Chgo., 1979-93; dir. Argonne Nat. Lab., 1979-84; v.p. for rsch. and for Argonne Nat. Lab. U. Chgo., 1984-91; dir. NSF, Washington, 1991-93; sr. v.p. acad. affairs U. Calif. System, 1993-95; mem. NSB, 1978-84; cons. NAS, 1973-76. Contbr. articles on sci. edn. in secondary schs. and in theory of quantum fluids to profl. jours. Bd. fellows Brown U., 1980-90, Mus. Sci. and Industry, Chgo., 1980-89, Ill. Math. and Sci. Acad., 1985-88; bd. dirs. Urban League R.I., 1973-75. NAS fellow, 1961, NDEA fellow, 1959-60, AAAS fellow, 1962. Mem. AAAS (bd. dirs. 1981-85, pres.-elect 1987-88, pres. 1988-89, chmn. 1989-90), Am. Phys. Soc. (councillor-at-large 1980-83, v.p. 1990), Sigma Xi. Office: Morehouse Coll 830 Westview Dr SW Atlanta GA 30314

MASSEY, WILLIAM LLOYD, federal agency administrator, lawyer; b. Malvern, Ark., Oct. 19, 1948. BA cum laude, Ouachita Bapt. U., 1970; JD, U. Ark., 1973; ML, Georgetown U., 1985. Bar: Ark. 1973, D.C. 1992, U.S. Supreme Ct. 1985, U.S. Ct. Appeals (8th cir.) 1973, U.S. Ct. Appeals (D.C. cirs. 1985), U.S. Dist. Ct. (ea. and we. dists.) Ark. 1973. Assoc. Youngdahl & Larrison, Little Rock, 1973-76; chief atty. Ctrl. Ark. Legal Svcs., Little Rock, 1976-77, dir., 1977-78; law clk. to Hon. Richard S. Arnold U.S. Ct. Appeals (8th cir.), 1978-80; legis. asst. U.S. Senator Dale Bumpers, Washington, 1980-81, chief counsel, legis. dir., 1989-91; ptnr. Mayer, Brown & Platt, Washington, 1991-93; commr. FERC, Washington, 1993—. Contbr. articles to profl. publs. Mem. ABA, D.C. Bar Assn., Ark. Bar Assn., Fed. Energy Bar Assn. Democrat. Presbyterian. Office: Commr FERC 888 1st St NE Washington DC 20002-4232*

MASSEY, WILLIAM S., mathematician, educator; b. Granville, Ill., Aug. 23, 1920; s. Robert R. and Alma (Schumacher) M.; m. Ethel Heap, Mar. 14, 1953; children—Eleanor, Alexander, Joan. Student, Bradley U., 1937-39; B.S., U. Chgo., 1941, M.S., 1942; Ph.D., Princeton, 1948. Mem. research dept. Princeton, 1948-50; from asst. prof. to prof. Brown U., 1950-60; prof. math. Yale, 1960—, Erastus L. Deforest prof. math, 1964-82, Eugene Higgins prof. math., 1983-91, Eugene Higgins prof. math. emeritus, 1991—, chmn. dept. math., 1968-71. Author: Algebraic Topology: An Introduction, 1967, Homology and Cohomology Theory, 1978, Singular Homology Theory, 1980, A Basic Course in Algebraic Topology, 1991; mem. editorial staff math. jours. Served as officer USNR, 1942-46. Fellow Am. Acad. Arts and Scis.; mem. Am. Math. Soc. Achievements include research in algebraic topology, differential topology, homotopy theory, fibre bundles. Home: 64 N Lake Dr Hamden CT 06517-2420 Office: Yale U Math Dept PO Box 208283 New Haven CT 06520-8283

MASSEY, WILLIAM WALTER, JR., sales executive; b. Lawrenceburg, Tenn., Sept. 21, 1928; s. William Walter and Bess Ann (Brian) M.; m. Virginia Claire Smith, Aug. 16, 1952; children: William Walter III, Laura Ann, Lynn Smith, Lisa Claire. BBA, U. Miami, Fla., 1949; BFA, U. Fla., 1969. Exec. v.p., dir. Massey Motors, Inc., Jacksonville, Fla., 1950—; v.p., dir. Atlantic Discount Co. Inc., Jacksonville, 1954-64; pres. Owners Surety Corp., Jacksonville, 1959—, General Svcs. Corp., Jacksonville, 1960-69, Owners Guaranty Life, Phoenix, Ariz., 1960-64, Securities Guaranty Life, Phoenix, Ariz., 1961-64, Fla. Properties, Inc., Jacksonville, 1961-66, Chi-Cha, Inc., Jacksonville, 1965-70, Univ. Square Properties, Jacksonville, 1969-80; v.p., bd. dir. Southside Country Day School, Jacksonville, 1963-68; bd. dirs. Southside Atlantic Bank, Jacksonville, 1965-93. Exhibited in group shows at Internat., N.Y., 1970, Ball State U., 1972. Lt. USAF, 1950-1952. Mem. Ponte Vedra Club, River Club, Epping Forest Club, Sigma Chi. Methodist. Avocations: music, painting, writing.

MASSIE, ANN MACLEAN, law educator; b. South Bend, Ind., Sept. 17, 1943; d. John Allan and Gladys Sherill (Wilkie) MacLean; m. Kent Belmore Massie, Aug. 25, 1973; children: Allan Barksdale, Laura Sherrill. BA, Duke U., 1966; MA in English, U. Mich., 1967; JD, U. Va., 1971. Bar: Ga. 1971. Assoc. Alston, Miller & Gaines, Atlanta, 1971-73, Long and Aldridge, Atlanta, 1974-76; staff atty. regional office FTC, Atlanta, 1973-74; law clk. to Hon. J. Harvie Wilkinson III U.S. Ct. Appeals (4th cir.), Charlottesville, Va., 1984-85; adj. prof. law Washington & Lee U., Lexington, Va., 1985-88, asst. prof. law, 1988-93; assoc. prof. law Washington & Lee U., Lexington, 1993—. Contbr. articles to law jours. Deacon Waynesboro (Va.) Presbyn. Ch., 1986-88; bd. dirs., v.p. Hosp. Aux., Waynesboro, 1986-88; elder Lexington Presbyn. Ch., 1995—. Named Prof. of Yr., Women Law Students Orgn., 1993. Mem. Am. Soc. Law, Medicine and Ethics, Hastings Ctr., Choice in Dying. Avocations: reading, walking, swimming, skiing, cultural events. Home: PO Box 1076 Lexington VA 24450-1076 Office: Washington and Lee U Sch of Law Lexington VA 24450

MASSIE, ANNE ADAMS ROBERTSON, artist; b. Lynchburg, Va., May 30, 1931; d. Douglas Alexander and Annie Scott (Harris) Robertson; m. William McKinnon Massie, Apr. 30, 1960; children: Anne Harris, William McKinnon, Jr. Grad., St. Mary's Coll., Raleigh, N.C., 1950; BA in English, Randolph Macon Woman's Coll., 1952. Tchr. English E.C. Glass High Sch., Lynchburg, 1955-60. Bd. dirs. Lynchburg Hist. Found., 1968-81, 91-95, pres., 1978-81; bd. dirs. Lynchburg Fine Arts Ctr., 1992—; trustee Va. Episcopal Sch., Lynchburg, 1983-89. Mem. Am. Watercolor Soc. (signature, Dolphin fellow 1993, Gold medal Honor 1993), Nat. Watercolor Soc. (signature, Artist's Mag. award), Nat. League Am. Pen Women (pres. 1987, Best in Show 1994), Knickerbocker Artists (signature, Silver medal Watercolor 1993), Watercolor USA Honor Soc., Watercolor West (signature), Catharine Lorrilard Wolfe Art Club (signature), Southern Watercolor Soc (signature), Va. Watercolor Soc. (artist mem., Best in Show 1992, chmn. exhbns. 1986, pres. 1995-96), Colonial Dames Am. (chmn. 1987-90), Hillside Garden Club (pres. 1974-76), Jr. League (editor 1953-72), Lynchburg Art Club (bd. dirs. 1995—, chmn. 1981-84), Antiquarian Club. Episcopalian. Avocations: book club, gardening, tennis, skiing. Home: 3204 Rivermont Ave Lynchburg VA 24503-2028

MASSIE, BETSY MCPHERSON, clergywoman; b. Oakland, Calif., Feb. 18, 1949; d. Andrew Harper and Elizabeth (Wright) M.; m. James Carl Bauder, June 12, 1976; children: Carl Bauder, Simon Massie. AB, Goucher Coll., 1971; MDiv, McCormick Sem., Chgo., 1975. Ordained to ministry Presbyn. Ch., 1975. Asst. pastor 1st Presbyn. Ch., Sioux City, Iowa, 1975-77; pastor Portalhurst Presbyn. Ch., San Francisco, 1977-95; stated clk. San Francisco Presbytery, Berkeley, Calif., 1992—; adj. prof. San Francisco Theol. Sem., San Anselmo, Calif., 1980-86; lectr. com., San Francisco State U., 1983-85; mem. U.S. Racquetball Team, 1981. Pres. Laguna Salada Parent Coun., Pacifica and San Bruno, Calif., 1993-95, Pacifica Dems., 1995; mem. sch. bd. Laguna Salada Union Sch. Dist., Pacifica and San Bruno, 1994—; rep. Calif. Sch. Bd. Del. Assembly, 1995. Recipient Elena Flynn vol. award Laguna Salada Parent Coun., 1994, vol. award City of Pacifica, 1995. Mem. Stated Clk. Assn. (exec. com. 1994—). Avocation: racquetball (nat. champion 1981). Office: San Francisco Presbytery 2024 Durant Ave Berkeley CA 94704

MASSIE, M.A., physics/optics researcher, engineering executive; b. Inglewood, Calif., Jan. 4, 1944. PhD, UCLA, 1974. Project engr. Rockwell Internat., 1975-83; dept. mgr. Western Res., 1983-86; project mgr. Lawrence Livermore Nat. Lab., 1986-93; CEO MRL Inc., San Ramon, Calif., 1993—. Mem. Am. Physics Soc., Optical Soc. Am., Med. Inst. Ophthalmology, Internat. Soc. Optical Engrs. Office: Pacific Advanced Tech Solvang CA 94550*

MASSIE, NOEL DAVID, lawyer; b. Bessemer, Mich., Sept. 23, 1949; s. Leo Oliver and Ann Matilda (Salmi) M.; m. Diane Soubly, June 16, 1978; 1 child, Courtney Alimine. BS, Mich. State U., 1970; JD, U. Mich., 1978. Bar: Mich. 1978, U.S. Ct. Appeals (6th cir.) 1982. Rsch. atty. Mich. Ct. Appeals, Lansing, 1978-79; law clk. Mich. Supreme Ct., Lansing, 1979-81; assoc. Dickinson, Wright, Moon, Van Dusen & Freeman, Detroit, 1981-84, ptnr., 1985—. Mem. State Bar Mich., Ctr. for Pub. Resources (com. on employment dispute resolution 1992—). Office: Dickinson Wright MoonVan Dusen & Freeman 500 Woodward Ave Ste 4000 Detroit MI 48226-3423

MASSIE, ROBERT JOSEPH, publishing company executive; b. N.Y.C., Mar. 19, 1949; s. Franklin Joseph and Genevieve Helen (Savarese) M.; m. Barbara Ellen Batchelder, Apr. 16, 1982; children—David Chance, Caroline Courtenay, Laura Brett. B.A., Yale U., 1970; M.B.A., Columbia U., 1974, J.D., 1974; Diploma, U. d'Aix en Provence, France, 1969. Bar: D.C. 1974. Assoc. Covington & Burling, Washington, 1975-79; mgmt. cons. McKinsey & Co., N.Y.C., 1979-82; v.p. Harlequin Enterprises, Toronto, Ont., Can., 1982-84, exec. v.p. overseas div., 1984-89; exec. v.p. Direct Mktg., 1989-90; pres., chief exec. officer Gale Rsch., Inc., Detroit, 1990-92; dir. Chem. Abstracts Svc., Columbus, Ohio, 1992—; chmn. bd. dirs. Harlequin Mondadori, Milan, Italy, 1985-88; bd. dirs. Harlequin Hachette, Paris, Cora Verlag, Hamburg, Fed. Republic Germany, Mills & Boon, Sydney, Australia, Harlenik Ltd., Athens, Greece. Contbr. articles to law jours. Bd. dirs. Columbus Symphony Orch., Ctr. of Sci. and Industry, Columbus. Harlan Fiske Stone scholar, 1974. Office: Am Chem Soc Chem Abstracts Srvcs PO Box 3012 Columbus OH 43210-0012

MASSIE, ROBERT KINLOCH, author; b. Lexington, Ky., Jan. 5, 1929; s. Robert K. and Mary (Kimball) M.; m. Suzanne L. Rohrbach, 1954 (div. 1990); children: Robert Kinloch, Susanna, Elizabeth; m. Deborah L. Karl, 1992; 1 child, Christopher. BA, Yale U., 1950; BA (Rhodes scholar), Oxford U., 1952. Reporter Collier's mag., N.Y.C., 1955-56; writer, corr. Newsweek mag., N.Y.C., 1956-62; writer USA-1 mag., N.Y.C., 1962, Sat. Eve. Post, N.Y.C., 1962-65; Ferris prof. journalism Princeton U., 1977, 85; Mellon prof. humanities Tulane U., 1981. Author: Nicholas and Alexandra, 1967, Journey, 1975 (Christopher award 1976), Peter the Great: His Life and World, 1980 (Am. Book award nomination 1981, Pulitzer Prize for biography 1981), Dreadnought: Britain, Germany, and the Coming of the Great War, 1991, The Romanovs: The Final Chapter, 1995. Served to lt. (j.g.) USNR, 1952-55. Mem. PEN, Authors Guild Am. (v.p. 1985-87, pres. 1987-91), Soc. Am. Historians. Address: 52 W Clinton Ave Irvington NY 10533

MASSIER, PAUL FERDINAND, mechanical engineer; b. Pocatello, Idaho, July 22, 1923; s. John and Kathryn (Arki) M.; m. Miriam Parks, May 1, 1948 (dec. Aug. 1975); children: Marilyn Massier Schwegler, Paulette Massier Holden; m. Dorothy Hedlund Wright, Sept. 12, 1978. Cert. engring., U. Idaho (so. br.), 1943; BSME, U. Colo., 1948; MSME, MIT, 1949. Engr. Pan-Am. Refining Corp., Texas City, Tex., 1948; design engr. Maytag Co., Newton, Iowa, 1949-50; research engr. Boeing Co., Seattle, 1951-55; sr. research engr. and supr. dep. sect. mgr. Jet Propulsion Lab. Calif. Inst. Tech., Pasadena, 1955-84, task mgr., 1984-88, mem. tech. staff, 1989-94. Contbr. articles to profl. jours. Mem. Arcadia High Sch. Music Club, 1966-71. Served with U.S. Army, 1943-46. Recipient Apollo Achievement award NASA, 1969, Basic Noise Rsch. award NASA, 1980, Life Mem. Svc. award Calif. PTA, 1970, Layman of Yr. award Arcadia Congl. Ch., 1971, Mil. Unit Citation award, 1946. Fellow AIAA (assoc., Sustained Svc. award 1980-81), Am. Biog. Inst. Rsch. Assn., Internat. Biographical Assn.; mem. N.Y. Acad. Scis., Planetary Soc., Sigma Xi, Tau Beta Pi, Pi Tau Sigma, Sigma Tau. Congregationalist. Achievements include reduction of cooling requirements for rocket engines, experimental evaluation of heat transfer from thermally ionized gases, design of supersonic diffusers for rocket engine testing, reduction of noise from aircraft jet engines. Avocations: travelog and documentary film production and presentations, genealogy and history research, antiques, collecting sheet music. Home: 1000 N First Ave Arcadia CA 91006

MASSIMINO, ROLAND V., former university basketball coach; b. Hillside, N.J., Nov. 13, 1934; s. Salvatore and Grace (Alberti) M.; m. Mary Jane Reid, Aug. 13, 1958; children—Thomas, Lee Ann, Michele, R.C., Andrew. Degree in Bus., U. Vt., 1956; M.P.E., Rutgers U., 1959; guidance cert., Tufts U., 1969. Asst. coach Cranford High Sch., N.J., 1956-59; coach Hillside High Sch., N.J., 1959-63; Lexington High Sch., Mass., 1963-69; head coach SUNY-Stony Brook, 1969-71; asst. coach U. Pa., 1971-73; head coach Villanova U., Pa., 1973-92, U. Nev., Las Vegas, 1992-95. Winning coach NCAA Nat. Basketball Championship, 1985; named Coach of Yr., Phila. Big 5, 1975-76, 77-78, 81-82, 82-83, 84-85, Eastern Athletic Assn., 1976-77, Eastern 8 Conf., 1978-79, 79-80, Widmer Cup Eastern Coach of Yr., 1981-82, Coach of Yr., Big East Conf., 1981-82, Eastern Basketball Eastern Coach of Yr., 1984-85, Harry Latwick/Herb Good Phila. Mem. Nat. Assn. Basketball Coaches. *

MASSION, WALTER HERBERT, anesthesiologist, educator; b. Eitorf, Ger., June 4, 1923; came to U.S., 1954; s. Rudolf and Margarethe (Polch) M.; m. Rose Marie Kumin, July 15, 1956; children: Birgit, Stuart, Iris. BS, U. Cologne, Ger., 1948; MD, U. Heidelberg, 1951, U. Bonn, 1951. Diplomate German Bd. Anesthesiology. Intern U. Zurich Hosps., 1951-52; trainee WHO Anesthesiology Centre, Copenhagen, 1952-53; asst. prof. physiology

U. Basel, Switzerland, 1953-54; postdoctoral fellow U.S. Nat. Acad. Sci., Rochester, N.Y., 1954-56; asst. prof. anesthesiology U. Okla. Med. Ctr., Oklahoma City, 1957-61, assoc. prof., 1961-67; prof. anesthesiology, physiology and biophysics U. Okla. Health Sci. Ctr., Oklahoma City, 1967-88, prof. emeritus, 1988; prin. investigator NATO Collaborative Rsch. Project, Oklahoma Cityand Homburg, 1988-95. Editor: Hemorrhage/Anesth. Requirements, 1974, Multiple Trauma, 1984, Critical Care Cardiology, 1988; contbr. over 125 articles to profl. jours. Hon. consul Fed. Republic Germany, Oklahoma City, 1980-95. Grantee WHO, 1953, U.S. Nat. Acad. Scis., 1954, NIH, 1959-88; Fulbright scholar, 1985; named Newsmaker of the Yr., Okla. Press Assn., 1964, Alexander von Humboldt prize, 1974; decorated Order of Merit 1st class Fed. Republic Germany, 1990. Avocations: gardening, chamber music, travel. Office: Univ Okla Health Sci Ctr PO Box 26901 Oklahoma City OK 73126

MASSLER, HOWARD ARNOLD, lawyer, corporate executive; b. Newark, July 22, 1946; s. Abraham I. and Sylvia (Botwin) M.; m. Randee Elyce Karch, July 1, 1977; children: Justin Scott, Jeremy Ross. BA, U. Pa., 1969; JD, Rutgers U., 1973; LLM in Taxation, NYU, 1977. Bar: N.J. 1974, U.S. Dist. Ct. N.J. 1974, D.C. 1975, U.S. Ct. Appeals (D.C. cir.) 1975, N.Y. 1977, U.S. Dist. Ct. (we. dist.) N.Y. 1977, U.S. Tax Ct. 1977. Counsel house banking, currency and housing com., chmn. sub-com. U.S. Ho. Reps., Washington, 1974-76; tax atty. Lipsitz, Green, Fahringer, Roll, Schuller & James, N.Y.C. and Buffalo, 1977-79; pvt. practice Mountainside, N.J., 1979-89; pres. Bestway Products Inc., A.A. Records Inc., Servor Corp., 1979-85; pres., chief exec. officer, chmn. bd. Bestway Group Inc., Dover, Del., 1985-91; gen. ptnr. 26/27 Law Drive Assocs., 1988—; ptnr. Shonageri, Pearce & Massler, Hackensack, N.J., 1989-90, Mott, Pearce, Williams & Lee, Hackensack and Washington, 1990-91, Pearce & Massler, Hackensack, N.J., 1991—; prodn. staff asst. DECCA House Ltd., London, 1968; chief exec. officer Basura Pub., Inc. (affiliated with BMI), 1974-80; arbitrator U.S. Dist. Ct. N.J., 1985—; adj. prof. law Seton Hall U., Newark, N.J., 1988-89, N.J. Inst. for Continuing Legal Edn., 1986; lectr. N.J. Inst. for Continuing Legal Edn., 1986—; assoc. dir. United Jersey Bank/Franklin State Bank, 1987—; del. adv. com. on indsl. trade and econ. devel. U.S./China Joint Sessions, Beijing, People's Republic of China, 1988. Author: QDROs (Tax and Drafting Considerations), 1986, 2nd. ed., 1987; contbr. West's Legal Forms, Vol. 7., 2d edit., 1987, 3d edit., Domestic Relations with Tax Analysis, Contemporary Matrimonial Law Issues: A Guide to Divorce Economics and Practice; tax author: Matthew Bender, NYCP-Matrimonial Actions and Equitable Distribution Actions, 1988; tax author, tax editor: Matthew Bender, Alimony, Child Support & Counsel Fees-Award, Modification and Enforcement, 1988, 2d edit., 1989, 3d edit., 1991, Matthew Bender, Valuation & Distribution of Marital Property, 1988, 89, 91, 92, 94, 95; contbg. author: How to Make Legal Fees Tax Deductible, 1988, Closely Held Corporations, Forms and Checklists, Buy-Sell Agreement Forms with Tax Analysis, 1988, The Encyclopedia of Matrimonial Practice, 1991, 4th edit., 1995; author: New York Practice Guide: Negligence, Tax Law of Compensation for Sickness and Injury, 2d edit., 1992; contbg. editor Pensions and Ins. Problems, 1984—, Taxation, 1984—, Fair$hare, 1984—, Law & Bus., Inc., 1984—; staff contbr., N.J. Law Jour., 1986—; contbr. articles to law revs. and profl. jours. Bd. dirs., legal counsel western N.Y. chpt. Nat. Handicapped Sports and Recreation Assn., 1977-79; counsel Union County, N.J., 1984-85; candidate Springfield (N.J.) Twp. Commn., 1986. Mem. ABA, N.J. Bar Assn. (vice chmn. taxation comm. family law section 1987—), N.Y. Bar Assn. (taxation com., subcom. on criminal and civil penalties), D.C. Bar Assn., Erie County Bar Assn. (sec. taxation com. 1977-79, continuing edn. lectr. taxation 1977—), Essex County Bar Assn. (tax com. 1981—), Union County Bar Assn. (chmn. tax com. 1984—). Republican. Avocation: Sports Car Club Am. formula Ford racing. Home: 4 Overlook Dr Warren NJ 07059-5144 Office: 25 Main St Hackensack NJ 07601-7025

MASSMAN, RICHARD ALLAN, lawyer; b. Beaumont, Tex., Aug. 19, 1943; s. Irwin Massman and Sylvia (Schmidt) Schwartz; m. Barbara Elaine Kessler; children: Jason Todd, Karen Faye. BS cum laude, U. Pa., 1965; JD cum laude, Harvard U., 1968. Bar: Tex. 1968; cert. in taxation, Tex. Bd. Legal Specialization. Assoc. Coke & Coke, Dallas, 1968-70; assoc. Johnson & Wortley, P.C. (formerly Johnson & Gibbs, P.C.), Dallas, 1970-71, ptnr., 1971-88, shareholder, 1988-94; of counsel Johnson & Wortley P.C., Dallas, 1994-95; sr. v.p., gen. counsel Hunt Consolidated, Inc., Dallas, 1994—; lectr. So. Meth. U., Dallas, 1973. Bd. dirs. Martin Luther King Jr. Community Ctr., Dallas, 1979-81, Jewish Fedn. Greater Dallas, 1980-83, 89—; mem. exec. com. Dallas regional bd. Anti-Defamation League, 1979—, chmn., 1990-92; chmn. Dallas Civil Svc. Bd., 1983; trustee Greenhill Sch., Dallas, 1985-92, vice chmn., 1990-92. Mem. Tex. State Bar (chmn., sec. taxation 1983-84), Dallas Bar Assn. (chmn., sec. taxation 1978), Dallas Petroleum Club, Columbian Club. Office: Hunt Consolidated Inc Fountain Pl 20th Fl 1445 Ross Ave Dallas TX 75202-2785

MASSOF, ROBERT WILLIAM, neuroscientist, educator; b. Minn., Jan. 2, 1948; m. Darcy Rood; children: Eric, Allison. BA, Hamline U., 1970; PhD, Ind. U., 1975. Postdoctoral fellow in ophthalmology Johns Hopkins U. Sch. Medicine, Balt., 1975-76, instr. ophthalmology, 1976-78, asst. to assoc. prof. ophthalmology, 1978-91, prof. ophthalmology, 1991—, prof. neurosci., 1994—, prof. computer sci., 1994—; vis. prof. Taiwan U., Taipei, 1983, Warsaw Acad. Medicine, Poland, 1987, Robert Y. Garrett Meml. Lecture, Lancaster, Pa., 1988, Albert Einstein Coll. Medicine, N.Y.C., 1989, Ohio State U., Columbus, 1991, Mayo Clinic, Rochester, Minn., 1993; guest lectr. in field. Mem. editorial bd. Clin. Vision Scis., N.Y.C., 1985—, Eye Care Technology/Computers in Eye Care, Folsom, Calif., 1992—; patentee in field (3); contbr. articles to profl. jours. Recipient Manpower award, 1989, Technology Transfer award NASA, 1993, Popular Mechanics Design and Engring. award, 1994, EyeCare Lifetime Acheivement award, 1995, Richard E. Hoover Svc. award, 1995. Fellow Optical Soc. Am. (chmn. edn. coun. 1993-95, bd. dirs. 1993-95), Am. Acad. Optometry; mem. Assn. Rsch. in Vision and Ophthalmology. Office: Johns Hopkins Univ Lions Vision Ctr 550 N Broadway Fl 6 Baltimore MD 21205-2020

MASSOLO, ARTHUR JAMES, banker; b. N.Y.C., July 21, 1942; s. Silvio Libro and Josephine Louise (Oneto) M.; A.B., Hamilton Coll., 1964; J.D., U. Chgo., 1967; m. Karen Irene Clasen, Mar. 7, 1970; 1 son, Arthur Reab. Vol. Peace Corps, 1967-68; with 1st Nat. Bank of Chgo., 1969—, beginning as trainee, sucessively rep. in Indonesia, gen. mgr. Italy, area head Latin Am. in Panama, sr. v.p. and head corp. personnel, 1979-81, sr. v.p., head Internat. Banking div., 1981-85; pres., chief exec. officer Banco Denasa de Investimento S.A., Brazil, 1985-87; also bd. dirs.; sr. v.p. Internat. Asset Enhancement, 1987-89, corp. sr. v.p. asset mgmt., 1990-94, corp. sr. v.p. of Latin Am., 1995-96; head of the Northea. United States For First Chgo. NBD Corp., 1996—; founding dir. Banco Latino Americano de Exportaciones Panama; chmn., bd. dirs. Link Unlimited. Past trustee Hamilton Coll. Mem. Ill. Bar Assn., Phi Beta Kappa. Office: 153 W 51st St New York NY 10019

MASSON, GAYL ANGELA, airline pilot; b. L.A., Feb. 5, 1951; d. Jack Watson and Margaret Jean (Evans) M.; 1 child, Athena. BFA, U. So. Calif., 1970, MA, 1972, MPA, 1975, PhD, 1976. Lic. airline transport, seaplane, glider pilot, flight instr., flight engr. Pilot Antelope Valley Land Investment Co., Century City, Calif., 1972; ROTC flight instr. Claire Walters Flight Acad., Santa Monica, Calif., 1973; flight instr. Golden West Airways, Santa Monica, 1974; co-pilot Express Airways, LaMoore Naval Air Sta., Calif., 1975-76; charter pilot, instr. Shaw Airmotive, Orange County Airport, Calif., 1976; flight engr. Am. Airlines, Dallas, 1976-79, co-pilot, 1979-86, capt., 1986—; accident prevention counselor FAA, 1993—. Contbr. articles to profl. publs. Participant Powder Puff Derby, Angel Derby, Pacific Air Race and others. First woman type-rated on Boeing 747, also type-rated on DC-10, DC-9, Boeing 767, Boeing 757, Airbus-310. Mem. Airline Pilots Assn., Internat. Soc. Women Airline Pilots (charter), Ninety-Nines (past v.p. Smo Bay chpt.), Aerospace Med. Assn., Aerospace Human Factors Assn. Avocations: oil paint, viticulture.

MASSON, ROBERT HENRY, paper company executive; b. Boston, June 27, 1935; s. Robert Louis and Henrietta Hill (Worrell) M.; m. Virginia Lee Morton, Dec. 28, 1957; children: Linda Anne, Kenneth Morton, Robert Louis, II. B.A. in Econs. (Travis and Woods award), Amherst Coll., 1957; M.B.A., Harvard U., 1964. Fin. staff Ford Motor Co., Dearborn, Mich., 1964-68; mktg. services div. controller Ford Motor Co., 1968-70; pres. Knutson Constrn. Co., Mpls., 1970-72; v.p. fin., treas. Ellerbe, Inc., Bloomington, Minn., 1972-77; fin. dir. CirTech, Inc., Mpls., 1973-77; v.p. fin. transp. div. PepsiCo., Inc., Tulsa, 1977; corp. v.p., treas. PepsiCo., Inc., Purchase, N.Y., 1978-80; v.p., treas. Combustion Engring., Inc., Stamford, Conn., 1981-86, v.p. fin. and venture devel., 1986-87, v.p. venture fin. and internat. ops., 1988-90; v.p., CFO Parsons & Whittemore, Inc., Rye Brook, N.Y., 1990—; adv. bd. Shawmut Bank, 1988—. Author: (with others) The Management of Racial Integration in Business, 1964. Pres. North Georgtown Homeowner's Assn., Birmingham, Mich., 1968-70, U.S. Presdl. Advance Man, 1972-76; trustee Naval Aviation Mus. Found., 1987—, Hebron Acad., 1993—; elder Presbyn. Ch. of Old Greenwich, 1992—. Served to lt. USN, 1957-62; lt. comdr. Res. Mem. Am. Forest and Paper Assn. (fin. com. 1991—), Fin. Execs. Inst. (com. on corp. fin. 1981—), Fairchester Treas. Group (pres. 1986), Lucas Point Homeowner's Assn. (pres. 1986-87), Theta Delta Chi. Clubs: Wayzata Yacht (dir.-treas. 1973-77), Riverside Yacht (asst. treas. 1985-87). Office: Parsons & Whittemore Inc 4 International Dr Rye Brook NY 10573-1065

MASSURA, EDWARD ANTHONY, accountant; b. Chgo., July 1, 1938; s. Edward Matthew and Wilma C. (Kussy) M.; m. Carol A. Barber, June 23, 1962; children: Edward J., Beth Ann, John B. BS, St. Joseph's Coll., Rensselaer, Ind., 1960; JD, DePaul U., 1963. Bar. Ill. 1963; CPA, Mich., Ill., others. Tax acct. Arthur Andersen & Co., Chgo., 1963—, ptnr., 1973—; dir. tax div. Arthur Andersen & Co., Detroit, 1974-84, dep., co-dir. internat. tax, 1983-84, ptnr.-in-charge internat. trade customs practice, 1983-88. Co-author: West's Legal Forms, 2d. edit., 1984; contbr. numerous articles to bus. jours. Bd. dirs. Arts Found. of Mich., Detroit, 1982-95, treas., 1982-93; bd. dirs. Ctr. for Internat. Bus. Edn. and Rsch., Wayne State U. Mem. AICPA, Internat. Fiscal Assn. (v.p. Eastern Gt. Lakes region), Assn. for Corp. Growth, Mich. Assn. CPAs, Mich. Dist. Export Coun. (chmn. 1985-92), Detroit Internat. Tax Group (founder,co-moderator), Licensing Exec. Soc., World Trade Club of Detroit, Bus. Assn. Mexico and Mich, Inc., Orchard Lake Country Club, Renaissance Club Detroit, Skyline Club, Fairlane Club. Office: Arthur Andersen & Co 500 Woodward Ave Detroit MI 48226-3423

MASSY, WILLIAM FRANCIS, education educator, academic administrator; b. Milw., Mar. 26, 1934; s. Willard Francis and Ardys Dorothy (Digman) M.; m. Sally Vaughn Miller, July 21, 1984; children by previous marriage: Willard Francis, Elizabeth. BS, Yale U., 1956; SM, MIT, 1958, PhD in Indsl. Econs., 1960. Asst. prof. indsl. mgmt. MIT, Cambridge, 1960-62; from asst. prof. to prof. bus. adminstrn. Stanford U., Calif., 1962—, assoc. dean Grad. Sch. Bus., 1971, vice provost for research, 1971-77, v.p. for bus. and fin., 1977-88, v.p. fin., 1988-91; prof. edn., dir. Stanford Inst. Higher Edn. Research, Calif., 1988—; sr. v.p. P.R. Taylor Assocs., 1995—; cons. assoc. Coopers & Lybrand L.L.P., 1995—; bd. dirs. Diebold, Inc., Bijur Lubricating Corp., 1979-95; mem. univ. grants com. Hong Kong, 1990—; mem. coun. Yale U., 1980-95; mgmt. cons.; mem. Stanford Mgmt. Co., 1991-93. Author: Stochastic Models of Buying Behavior, 1970, Marketing Management, 1972, Market Segmentation, 1972, Planning Models for Colleges and Universities, 1981, Endowment, 1991, Resource Allocation in Higher Education, 1996; mem. editl. bd. Jour. Mktg. Rsch., 1964-70, Harcourt, Brace Jovanovich, 1965-71; contbr. articles to profl. jours. Bd. dirs. Palo Alto-Stanford chpt. United Way, 1978-80, Stanford U. Hosp., 1980-91, MAC, Inc., 1969-84, EDUCOM, 1983-86. Ford Found. faculty research fellow, 1966-67. Mem. Am. Mktg. Assn. (bd. dirs. 1971-73, v.p. edn. 1976-77), Inst. Mgmt. Scis. Office: Stanford U PO Box 5156 Stanford CA 94309

MAST, FREDERICK WILLIAM, construction company executive; b. Quincy, Ill., Jan. 3, 1910; s. Christian Charles and Jessie Minnie (Pape) M.; B.S., U. Ill., 1933; m. Kathryn Mary Boekenhoff, Sept. 15, 1932 (dec. Jan. 17, 1975); children—Robert Frederick, Janet (Mrs. James Austin Jones), Susan (Mrs. Edward Hoskins Wilson), Linda (Mrs. William Frederick Bohlen), Teresa Ann (Mrs. Charles Edward Connell); m. 2d, Elaine Ellen Thies Driver, Feb. 14, 1976. Hwy. engr. Adams County (Ill.) Hwy. Dept., Quincy, 1929-33; jr. engr. Ill. Div. Hwys. Rd. Office, Springfield, 1933-35, asst. hwys. architect, 1935-39; estimator Jens Olesen & Sons Constrn. Co., Waterloo, Iowa, 1939-41, v.p., 1941-54, exec. v.p., 1954-65, pres., 1965-76, chmn. bd., 1970-80; owner Frederick W. Mast & Assos., Waterloo, 1946-60; pres. Broadway Bldg. Co., 1951—, Kimball Shopping Center, Inc., 1964-78; dir. First Fed. Savs. Bank of Waterloo, 1957-78, Nat. Bank of Waterloo, 1958-79. Mem. Council Constrn. Employers, Washington, 1968-72, chmn., 1969; ofcl. U.S. del. to Soviet Union under U.S./USSR Exchanges Agreement, 1968-69; del. 8th and 9th sessions bldg., civil engring. and public works com. ILO, Geneva, 1971, 77; sr. builder specialist Tech. for the Am. Home Exhibit USIA, USSR, 1975; mem. Nat. Def. Exec. Res., assigned to Fed. Emergency Mgmt. Agy., 1969-89. Mem. Iowa Bldg. Code Council, Des Moines, 1947-50; mem. Bd. Zoning Adjustment, Waterloo, 1947-59; mem. City Plan and Zoning Commn., Waterloo, 1955-78; chmn. Community Devel. Bd., City of Waterloo, 1959-70; fin. chmn. Black Hawk County Republican Central Com., 1958-60; chmn. Waterloo-Cedar Falls Symphony Orch. endowment fund dr., 1977-79, St. Francis Health Care Found., 1980-86; chmn. bd. dirs. St. Francis Hosp., 1976-78; chmn. contractors adv. com. Iowa Coll. Found., 1972-73. Served to col., C.E., AUS, 1941-46. Decorated Legion of Merit; recipient Disting. Service award Waterloo C. of C., 1962; Ky. Col. Registered architect, Ill., Iowa. Mem. Asso. Gen. Contractors Am. (dir. 1956—, mem. exec. com. 1959-62, 66-72, nat. pres. 1968, SIR award Nev. chpt. 1970), Master Builders Iowa (pres. 1952, hon. mem. 1981), Am. Inst. Constructors, Contractors Mut. Assn. Washington (dir. 1971-83, chmn. exec. com. 1971-73), Iowa Engring. Soc., Nat. Soc. Profl. Engrs., Soc. Am. Mil. Engrs., Waterloo Tech. Soc., Amvets, Am. Legion, Phi Eta Sigma, Sigma Phi Epsilon, Tau Beta Pi, Tau Nu Tau, Theta Tau. Roman Catholic. Clubs: Sunnyside Country. Lodges: Elks, Kiwanis. Home: 3309 Inverness Rd Apt F Waterloo IA 50701-4650 Office: PO Box 575 Waterloo IA 50704-0575

MAST, STEWART DALE, retired airport manager; b. Kalamazoo, May 10, 1924; s. Virgil S. and S. Louise (Rippey) M.; m. Judy Jo Bolton; children: Peter S., Frances Ann Mast Adams; m. May 20, 1979. Student, U. Mich., 1942-43; grad., Spartan Sch. Aerospace, Tulsa, 1946, Argubright Bus. Coll., Battle Creek, Mich., 1947. Mgr. Mcpl. Airport, Battle Creek, 1948-60; airport dir. Mitchell Field, Milw., 1961-66; mgr. Tampa (Fla.) Internat. Airport, 1966-89, ret.; pres. Mich. Assn. Airport Mgrs., 1958; bd. dirs. The Summit Ministries, Inc., Manitou Springs, Colo. Past mem. aviation coun. Milw. . of C.; past mem. bd. rev. Boy Scouts Am., Milw.; bd. dirs. Sun'n Fun Aviation Found., Inc., Lakeland, Fla., 1992—, Sun'n Fun EAA Fly-in, Inc., Lakeland, Fla., 1994—. 1st lt. USAAF, 1943-45. Recipient Community Leadership award Greater Tampa C. of C., 1979. Mem. Am. Assn. Airport Execs. (past bd. dirs., pres.'s award 1979), Southeastern Airport Mgrs. Assn., Fla. Assn. Airport Mgrs. Avocations: antique/classic aircraft, photography.

MASTANDREA, LINDA LEE, lawyer; b. Chgo., June 10, 1964; d. Robert Anthony and Dorothy Jean (Kilpatrick) M. BA in Speech Comm., U. Ill., 1986; JD, IIT, 1994. Bar: Ill. 1995. Account rep. Health Chgo. HMO, Lisle, Ill., 1986-87; peer counselor Peninsula Ctr. Ind. Living, Newport News, Va., 1988-89; program mgr. Progress Ctr. Ind. Living, Oak Park, Ill., 1990-91; ind. legal rschr., writer Ill., 1994—; pub. spkr., Ill., 1991—. Athlete rep. Atlanta Paralympics, 1994—; v.p. athlete's adv. com. Rehab. Inst. Chgo., 1992—. Named Athlete of Yr. Colo. Sports Coun., Denver, 1994, Outstanding Woman in Sports YWCA DuPage Dist., DuPage County, Ill., 1995; recipient IOC Pres. Disabled Athlete award U.S. Sports Acad., Mobile, Ala., 1995. Mem. U.S. Cerebral Palsy Athletic Assn. (v.p. 1994—), Nat. Italian Bar Assn., Justinian Soc. Lawyers, Chgo. Bar Assn., DuPage County Bar Assn. Avocation: wheelchair track world-record holder 100, 200, 400, 800 and 1500 meters. Home: 266 Michigan St Elmhurst IL 60126

MASTEN, CHARLES C., federal agency administrator; b. Albany, Ga., Apr. 20, 1943; s. Charles C. and Sophia L. (Wynn) M.; m. Betty Dodson, June 25, 1966; children: Deborah Denise, Mia Tereon, Kelle Marie, Stephan John. BS Bus. Adminstrn., Albany State Coll., 1965; MBA, U. Ark., 1976; degree mgmt. law enforcement execs., FBI Exec. Devel. Inst., 1991. Asst. nat. bank examiner comtroller of currency U.S. Treasury, Atlanta, 1969-71; cashier Citizens Trust Bank, Atlanta, 1971-72; spl. agt. FBI, Memphis, 1973-77; supervisory spl. agent FBI, Little Rock, 1978-85; supervisory spl. agent FBI, Washington, 1985-87, unit chief, 1987-91; dep. inspector gen. U.S. Dept. Labor, Washington, 1991-94, inspector gen., 1994—. Lt. USN, 1966-69, Vietnam. Mem. Assn. Govt. Accts. Roman Catholic. Avocations: jogging, gardening. Office: Dept of Labor Office of the Inspector General 200 Constitution Ave NW Ste S Washington DC 20210-0001*

MASTER-KARNIK, PAUL JOSEPH, art museum director; b. N.Y.C., Nov. 20, 1948; s. Charles Oldrich and Evelyn Theresa (Donnelly) K.; m. Susan Irene Master, Aug. 19, 1973. BA, Rutgers U., 1970, MA, 1971, PhD, 1978. Cert. in mus. studies, 1979. Faculty Rutgers U., New Brunswick, N.J., 1974-78; art critic Newhouse Publs., N.Y.C., 1976-80; faculty NYU, N.Y.C., 1980-83; dir. N.J. Ctr. for Visual Arts, Summit, 1981-84, DeCordova Mus. & Sculpture Pk., Lincoln, Mass., 1984—; bd. dirs. UrbanArts, Inc., Boston, 1988—, Mus. Coun. of N.J., Trenton, 1982-84; adv. bd. Archives of Am. Art, Boston, 1985—; vis. com. Sch. Mus. Fine Arts, Boston, 1987-90. Author: Exhibition Catalogues, 1982—. Recipient Outstanding Svc. award Inst. Mus. Svcs., 1988; Art Critic fellow NEA, 1980, Burns-Marvin fellow Rutgers U., 1971-73. Mem. Assn. Art Mus. Dirs. Office: DeCordova Mus & Sculpture 51 Sandy Pond Rd Lincoln MA 01773-2600

MASTERMAN, JACK VERNER, insurance company executive; b. Calgary, Alta., Can., Aug. 8, 1930; s. Lawrence Arthur and Mary F.G. (Robinson) M.; m. Isabel Christine Kaitting, June 25, 1954 (dec. 1990); children: Christine, Lawrence, Sheila, Keith. B.Com. with honors, U. Man., Can., 1953. With Mut. Life Assurance Co. Can., Waterloo, Ont., 1953—, v.p. ops., 1972-75, v.p. individual ins. and annuities, 1975-78, exec. v.p., 1978-82, pres., chief operating officer, 1982-85, pres., chief exec. officer, 1985-89, chmn., chief exec. officer, 1989-92, also bd. dirs., 1980—. Mem. United Ch. of Can. Office: Mut Life Assurance Co Can, 227 King St S, Waterloo, ON Canada N2J 4C5*

MASTERS, BEDA M., elementary educator; b. McComb, Miss., Feb. 14, 1942; d. Robert C. and Selma Doris (Barksdale) Moak; m. Terry Labe Masters Sr., Oct. 12, 1940; children: Terry Labe Jr., Karen Denise Masters Ishee. AS, S.W. Miss. Jr. Coll., 1971; BS, U. So. Miss., 1975; M in Edn., William Carey Coll., 1981. Cert. elem. educator, Miss. Teller 1st Nat. Bank, McComb, 1971-72, Laurel, Miss., 1972-73; tchr. Jones County Schs., Laurel, 1975—; presenter at reading confs. Mem. Internat. Reading Coun., Miss. Reading Coun., Laurel-Jones County Reading Coun. (pres. 1980-81, membership dir. 1988-89), Assn. for Excellence in Edn., PhiTheta Kappa, Phi Kappa Phi, Kappa Delta Pi, Delta Kappa Gamma (corr. sec. state Zeta Mu chpt. 1986-88, chmn. world fellowship 1990-92). Baptist. Avocations: swimming, sewing, cooking, travel, interior design. Home: 43 Jennings Masters Rd Laurel MS 39440-8401

MASTERS, CHARLES DAY, geologist; b. Pawhuska, Okla., Aug. 4, 1929; s. Alan Dunning and Maxine Lueretta (Day) M.; m. Anna Ruth Sandin, June 6, 1953; children—Cynthia Ruth, Eric Alan, Carolyn Frances. B.S., Yale U., 1951, Ph.D., 1965; M.S., Colo. U., 1957. Exploration geologist Pan Am. Petroleum Corp., Denver, 1957-62, 65-68; research geologist Pan Am. Petroleum Corp., Tulsa, 1968-70; chmn. div. sci. and math., asso. prof. geology W. Ga. Coll., Carrollton, 1970-73; chief Office Energy Resources; also acting chief Office Marine Geology, Geol. Div., U.S. Geol. Survey, Reston, Va., 1973-80; pub. law research scientist branch of petroleum geology, chief The World Energy Resources Program, 1980-95; ret., 1995; Pecora fellow in U.S. Geol. Survey for continued world energy studies. Activities chmn. Tulsa YMCA, 1968-70; founder pres. W. Ga. chpt. Ga. Conservancy, 1971-73. Served with USNR, 1951-55. Fellow Geol. Soc. Am.; mem. Am. Assn. Petroleum Geologists, Sigma Xi. Democrat. Unitarian. Home: 1028 Walker Rd Great Falls VA 22066-1928

MASTERS, EDWARD E., association executive, former foreign service officer; b. Columbus, Ohio, June 21, 1924; s. George Henry and Ethel Verena (Shaw) M.; m. Allene Mary Roche, Apr. 2, 1956; children: Julie Allene, Edward Ralston. Student, Denison U., 1942-43; BA with distinction, George Washington U., 1948; MA, Fletcher Sch. Law and Diplomacy, 1949. Joined U.S. Fgn. Service, 1950; intelligence research analyst Near East Dept. State, 1949-50; resident officer Heidelberg, Germany, 1950-52; polit. officer embassy Karachi, Pakistan, 1952-54; Hindustani lang. and area tng. U. Pa., 1954-55; consul, polit. officer Madras, India, 1955-58; intelligence research specialist South Asia Dept. State, 1958-60; chief Indonesia-Malaya br. Dept. State (Office Research Asia), 1960-61, officer-in-charge Thailand affairs, 1961-63; grad. Nat. War Coll., 1964; counselor for polit. affairs Am. embassy, Djakarta, 1964-68; country dir. for Indonesia Dept. State, 1968-70; dir. Office East Asian Regional Affairs, 1970-71; minister Am. embassy, Bangkok, Thailand, 1971-75; ambassador to Bangladesh, 1976-77, to Indonesia, 1977-81; adj. prof. diplomacy Fletcher Sch. Law and Diplomacy, 1981-82; sr. v.p. Natomas Co., 1982-84; pres. Nat. Planning Assn., 1985-92, Edward Masters & Assocs., Washington, 1992—, U.S.-Indonesia Soc., 1994—. Mem. Am. Fgn. Svc. Assn., Phi Beta Kappa, Omicron Delta Kappa, Pi Gamma Mu, Delta Phi Epsilon, Cosmos Club. Home: 4525 Garfield St NW Washington DC 20007-1165

MASTERS, JOHN CHRISTOPHER, psychologist, educator, writer; b. Terre Haute, Ind., Oct. 25, 1941; s. Robert William and Lillian Virginia (Decker) M.; m. Mary Jayne Capps, June 6, 1970; children—Blair Christopher, Kyle Alexander. A.B., Harvard Coll., 1963; Ph.D., Stanford U., 1967. Asst. prof. Ariz. State U., Tempe, 1968-69; from asst. prof. to prof. U. Minn., Mpls., 1969-79; assoc. dir. Inst. Child Devel., 1974-79; Luce prof. pub. policy and the family, prof. psychology Vanderbilt U., Nashville, 1979-87, interim chair dept. psychology, 1986-88; pres. Profl. Mgmt. Group, Inc., 1991—; dir. Master Ventures, 1989—, Master Travel, 1989—. Assoc. editor: Child Development, 1973-76, Behavior Therapy: Techniques and Empirical Findings, 1974, 79, 88; editor: Psychol. Bull., 1987-89. Fellow Am. Psychol. Assn.; mem. Soc. for Research in Child Devel., Internat. Soc. for Study of Behavioral Devel., Assn. for Public Policy and Mgmt. Home: 555 Crosswinds Dr Mount Juliet TN 37122-5064

MASTERS, JON JOSEPH, lawyer; b. N.Y.C., June 20, 1937; s. Arthur Edward and Esther (Shady) M.; m. Rosemary Dunaway Cox, June 16, 1962; children: Brooke Alison, Blake Edward. B.A., Princeton U., 1958; J.D., Harvard U., 1964. Bar: N.Y. 1965, U.S. Dist. Ct. (so. dist.) N.Y. 1965, U.S. Ct. Appeals (2d cir.) 1965. Cons. asst. to under sec. Dept. Army, 1961; mem. policy planning staff asst. sec. for internat. security affairs Dept. Def. Washington, 1962; mem. Pres. Johnson's Spl. Polit. Research Staff, Washington, 1964; assoc. Shearman & Sterling, N.Y.C., 1965-68, 69; mem. staff Bedford-Stuyvesant D & S Corp., Bklyn., 1968-69; v.p., sec., gen. counsel, dir. Baker, Weeks & Co., Inc., N.Y.C., 1969-76; ptnr. Christy & Viener, N.Y.C., 1976—; prin. Lear, Yavitz & Assocs., N.Y.C., 1996—; mem. SEC adv. com. broker-dealer compliance, 1972-74; legal advisor NACD Blue Ribbon Commn. on CEO and Dir. Performance Evaluation, 1994; chmn. bd. Clear and Present Prodns., 1992-93; bd. dirs. Harris & Harris Group Inc., 1992—. Mem. implementation com. Econ. Devel. Task Force of N.Y. Urban Coalition, 1968; mem. bd. Internat. Social Service, Am. Br., Inc., 1978-83, pres., 1979-83; bd. dirs. The Arts Connection, 1979-85; mem. steering com. N.Y. Lawyers Alliance for Nuclear Arms Control, 1983—. Served with USN, 1958-61. Mem. ABA, Assn. Bar City N.Y. (com. mcpl. affairs 1977-80), N.Y. State Bar Assn. Home: 530 E 86th St New York NY 10028-7535 Office: 620 5th Ave New York NY 10020-2402

MASTERS, LEE, broadcast executive; married; 2 children. Student, Temple U. Various positions including programmer, sta. mgr., owner radio stas.; exec. v.p., gen. mgr. MTV; pres., CEO E! Entertainment TV, 1990—; conf. co-chair CTAM '96. Mem. Nat. Cable TV Assn. (Vanguard award for programmers 1995, pub. affairs com., co-chair state and local govt. com.). Office: E! Entertainment TV Inc 5670 Wilshire Blvd Los Angeles CA 90036-3709

MASTERS, ROGER DAVIS, government educator; b. Boston, June 8, 1933; s. Maurice and S. Grace (Davis) M.; m. Judith Ann Rubin, June 6, 1956 (div. 1984); children—Seth J., William A., Katherine R.; m. Susanne R. Putnam, Aug. 25, 1984. B.A., Harvard U., 1955; M.A., U. Chgo., 1958, Ph.D., 1961; M.A. (hon.), Dartmouth Coll., 1974. Instr. dept. polit. sci. Yale U., 1961-62, asst. prof., 1962-67; assoc. prof. dept. govt. Dartmouth

Coll., Hanover, N.H., 1967-73; prof. Dartmouth Coll., 1973—, John Sloan Dickey Third Century prof., 1980-85, chmn. dept., 1986-89, Nelson A. Rockefeller prof., 1991—; cultural attache Am. Embassy, Paris, 1969-71; chmn. France-Am. Commn. Ednl. and Cultural Exch., 1969-71; vis. lectr. Yale U. Law Sch., 1988-89, Vt. Law Sch., 1993, 94; sect. editor Social Sci., Info., 1971; chmn. exec. com. Gruter Inst. Law and Behavioral Rsch., 1995—. Author; The Nation Is Burdened, 1967, The Political Philosophy of Rousseau, 1968, The Nature of Politics, 1989, Beyond Relativism, 1993, Machiavelli, Leonardo, and the Science of Power, 1996; editor: Rousseau's Discourses, 1964, Rousseau's Social Contract, 1978; co-editor: Ostracism: A Social and Biological Phenomenon, 1986, Collected Writings of J.J. Rousseau, 1990—, Primate Politics, 1991, The Sense of Justice, 1992, The Neurotransmitter Revolution, 1994; editor Gruter Inst. Reader in Biology, Law, and Human Social Behavior, 1992—. Served with AUS, 1955-57. Fulbright fellow Institut d'Etudes Politiques, Paris, 1958-59; joint Yale U.-Social Sci. Rsch. Coun. fellow, 1964-65; Guggenheim fellow, 1967-68; fellow Hastings Ctr. for Ethics and Life Scis., 1973-78. Mem. AAAS, Am. Polit. Sci. Assn., Assn. Polit. and Life Sci. (coun.), Am. Soc. for Legal and Polit. Philosophy, Gruter Inst. for Law and Behavioral Rsch. (adv. bd.), Internat. Soc. Human Ethology, Human Behavior Evolution Soc. Home: PO Box 113 South Woodstock VT 05071-0113 Office: Dartmouth Coll Dept Govt Hanover NH 03755

MASTERS, WILLIAM HOWELL, physician, educator; b. Cleve., Dec. 27, 1915; s. Francis Wynne and Estabrooks (Taylor) M.; children: Sarah Worthington, William Howell III. BS, Hamilton Coll., 1938, ScD (hon.), 1973; MD, U. Rochester, 1943; ScD (hon.), 1975. Diplomate Am. Bd. Obstetricians and Gynecologists; cert. Am. Assn. Sex Educators, Counselors and Therapists. Intern obstetrics and gynecology St. Louis Maternity and Barnes Hosp., 1943, asst. resident, 1944; intern pathology Washington U. Sch. Medicine, St. Louis, 1944; asst. resident gynecology Barnes Hosp., 1944, intern internal medicine, 1945, resident gynecology, 1945-46; resident obstetrics St. Louis Maternity Hosp., 1946-47; mem. faculty Washington U. Sch. Medicine, 1947—, assoc prof. clin. obstetrics and gynecology, 1964-69, prof., 1969—; dir. Reproductive Biology Research Found., 1964-73; co-dir. Masters & Johnson Inst. (formerly Reproductive Biology Research Found.), 1973-80, chmn. bd., 1981—; asso. physician St. Louis Maternity Barnes and St. Louis Children's hosps.; asso. physician Washington U. Clinics; asst. attending physician Jewish Hosp., St. Louis. Meml. Hosp. Author: (with Virginia E. Johnson) Human Sexual Response, 1966, Human Sexual Inadequacy, 1970, The Pleasure Bond, 1975, Homosexuality in Perspective, 1979, (with Kolodny et al) Textbook of Sexual Medicine; editor: (with V.E. Johnson and R.C. Kolodny) Ethical Issues in Sex Therapy and Research, Vol. 1, 1977, Vol. 2, 1980. Bd. dirs. St. Louis Family and Childrens Service, Planned Parenthood Assn., St. Louis Health and Welfare Council. Served to lt. (j.g.) USNR, 1942-43. Recipient Paul H. Hoch award Am. Psychopathol. Assn., 1971, award SECUS, 1972, Disting. Svc. award Am. Assn. Marriage and Family Counselors, 1976, award fo rdisting. achievement N=Modern Medicine, 1977, award Am. Assn. Sex. Educators, Counselors and Therapists, 1978; Paul Harris fellow, 1976. Mem. Gerontol. Soc., Am. Fertility Soc., Internat. Fertility Assn., Endocrine Soc., Am. Coll. Obstetricians and Gynecologists, N.Y. Acad. Sci., Soc. Sci. Study Sex, AAAS, Comprehensive Med. Soc., Pan Am. Med. Assn., Internat. Soc. for Research in Biology Reprodn., Am. Geriatric Soc., Am. Soc. Cytology, Soc. for Study Reprodn., AMA, Eastern Mo. Psychiat. Soc. (hon.), Authors Guild, Alpha Omega Alpha, Alpha Delta Phi. Episcopalian. Address: 4970 E Oakmont Pl Tucson AZ 85718-1730

MASTERSON, CARLIN See GLYNN, CARLIN

MASTERSON, CHARLES FRANCIS, retired social scientist; b. N.Y.C., Nov. 3, 1917; s. Frank Joseph and Harriett Geneva (Whittaker) M.; m. Vivian Ethel Reppke, May 8, 1954; children by previous marriage: Michael Charles, Susan Masterson Forrest. A.B., L.I. U., 1938; M.A., Columbia U., 1939, Ph.D., 1952. Dir. pub. relations Poly. Prep., Bklyn., 1946-49, Bklyn. C. of C., 1949-50, N.Y.C. Mission Soc., 1950-53; spl. asst. White House, Washington, 1953-56, Rumbough Co., N.Y., 1957-60, Nat. Safety Council, 1960-62; exec. dir. Office of Trustees, 1962-77; sr. assoc. Clark, Phipps, Clark & Harris, 1978-80; now ret. Author: World History, 1949, History of Asia, 1950. Mem. Pub. Rels. Soc. Am., Nat. Inst. Social Scis., N.Y.C. Mission Soc. (bd. dirs.), U.S. Com. for UN (bd. dirs.), Phi Delta Kappa. Presbyterian (elder). Club: Internat. Lawn Tennis. Home: 9801 Shore Rd Brooklyn NY 11209-7655

MASTERSON, JAMES FRANCIS, psychiatrist; b. Phila., Mar. 25, 1926; s. James Francis and Evangeline (O'Boyle) M.; m. Patricia Cooke, Jan. 28, 1950; children: James F., Richard K., Nancy. BS, U. Notre Dame, 1947; MD, Jefferson Med. Sch., Phila., 1951. Diplomate Am. Bd. Psychiatry, Am. Bd. Neurology. Intern Phila. Gen. Hosp., 1951-52; resident in psychiatry Payne Whitney Clinic, N.Y. Hosp., N.Y.C., 1952-55, chief resident, 1955-56, dir. adolescent OPD, 1956-66, head adolescent program, 1968-75, asst. attending psychiatrist, 1956-60, assoc. attending psychiatrist, 1960-70, attending psychiatrist, 1970—, dir. The Symptomatic Adolescent Research Project, 1957-67; dir. Masterson Group, P.C. for Study and Treatment Personality Disorders, N.Y.C., 1977—. Author: Psychotherapy of the Borderline Adolescent, Psychotherapy of the Borderline Adult, Countertransference, Narcissistic Personality Disorder, The Real Self, The Psychiatric Dilemma of Adolescence, The Test of Time: From Borderline Adolescent to Functioning Adult; contbr. articles to profl. jours. Fellow Am. Psychiat. Assn., Am. Coll. Psychoanalysts; mem. AMA, Am. Coll. Psychoanalysis, N.Y. Soc. Adolescent Psychiatry (founder, past pres.), N.Y. County Med. Soc. Office: 60 Sutton Pl S New York NY 10022-4168

MASTERSON, JOHN PATRICK, retired English language educator; b. Chgo., Mar. 15, 1925; s. Michael Joseph and Delia Frances (Dolan) M.; m. Jean Frances Wegrzyn, Aug. 18, 1956; children: Mary Beth, Michael, Maureen, Laura. B.A., St. Mary of the Lake, 1947; M.A., De Paul U., 1952; Ph.D., U. Ill., 1961. Chmn. English dept. De Paul U., Chgo., 1964-67, head humanities div., 1967-70, prof. English, 1970, dean Coll. Liberal Arts and Scis., 1970-76, prof. mgmt., 1976-80, 82-87, prof. emeritus, 1988—, dean Grad. Sch., 1980-82; cons. in field. Recipient award Shell Oil Co., 1968, Via Sapientiae award De Paul U., 1987; fellow adminstrn. program Am. Coun. Edn. Roman Catholic. Home: 1922 Belleview Ave Westchester IL 60154-4345

MASTERSON, KLEBER SANDLIN, former organization executive, retired naval officer; b. San Jon, N.Mex., July 12, 1908; s. John Patrick and Lela (Johnson) M.; m. Charlotte Elizabeth Parker, Oct. 3, 1931 (dec. 1986); 1 son, Kleber Sandlin, Jr. Student, U. N.Mex., 1925-26; B.S., U.S. Naval Acad., 1930; grad., U.S. Naval Postgrad. Sch., 1939, Naval War Coll., 1953. Commd. ensign U.S. Navy, 1930, advanced through grades to vice adm., 1964; assigned various ships, 1930-41; main battery asst. U.S.S. Arizona, Pearl Harbor; gunnery officer U.S.S. Pennsylvania, to 1944; staff research and devel. div., bur. ordnance Navy Dept., Wash., 1944-46; mem. staff CINCLANT FLT, 1946-47; comdr. Destroyer Div. 102, 1947-48; head ammunition br. Bur. Naval Ordnance, 1950-52; comdg. officer U.S.S. Lenawee, 1953-54; comdr. Naval Adminstrv. Unit, also asst. comdr. operations, field command Armed Forces Spl. Weapons Project, 1954-56; comdg. officer U.S.S. Boston, 1956-57; dir. guided missile div. Office Chief Naval Operations, exec. mem. navy ballistic missile com., 1958-60; comdr. Cruiser Div. 1, 1960-61; asst. chief naval operations devel. Office Chief Naval Operations, 1961; dep. chief Bur. Naval Weapons, 1961-62, chief, 1962-64; comdr. 2d Fleet and comdr. Striking Fleet Atlantic, 1964-66; dir. Weapons Systems Evaluation Group. Office of Sec. of Def., Washington, 1966-69; ret. Weapons Systems Evaluation Group. Office of Sec. of Def., 1969; pres. Navy Relief Soc., 1969-73. Decorated D.S.M., Legion of Merit, Navy Commendation; commandeur del'Ordre National du Mérite (France). Mem. U.S. Naval Acad. Alumni Assn., U.S. Naval Inst. Navy Hist. Found. Club: Army Navy Country (Arlington, Va.). Home: 3440 S Jefferson St Apt 915 Falls Church VA 22041-3128

MASTERSON, KLEBER SANLIN, JR., physicist; b. San Diego, Sept. 26, 1932; s. Kleber Sandlin and Charlotte Elizabeth (Parker) M.; m. Sara Ann Cooper, Dec. 21, 1957; children: Thomas Marshall, John Cooper. BS in Engring., U.S. Naval Acad., 1954; MS in Physics, USN Postgrad. Sch., 1960; PhD in Physics, U. Calif., San Diego, 1963; student Advanced Mgmt. Programs, Harvard Bus. Sch., 1981-82. Commd. ensign USN, 1954, advanced through grades to rear adm., 1979; comdg. officer USS Preble, Pearl Harbor, Hawaii, 1969-71; mgr. antiship missile def. project USN, Washington, 1974-77, exec. asst. to sec. of Navy, 1977-79, asst. dep. comdr. Naval Sea Systems Command, 1979-81, chief Studies, Analyses and Gaming Agy., 1981-82; ret. USN, 1982; prin. Booz, Allen and Hamilton, Inc., Arlington, Va., 1982-87; v.p. Booz, Allen and Hamilton, Inc., Arlington, 1987-92; sr. v.p. Sci. Applications Internat. Corp., 1992-94; pres. The Riverside Group, Ltd., 1994—; Washington area mgr. The Nettleship Group Inc., 1995—; bd. control U.S. Naval Inst., Annapolis, Md., 1971-82; bd. dirs. Mil. Ops. Rsch. Soc., 1984-90, pres., 1988-89. Editor: Book of Navy Songs, 1954; contbr. articles on plasma and theoretical nuclear physics, computer science, radars, ops. rsch. to profl. publs. Mem. Am. Phys. Soc., U.S. Naval Acad. Alumni Assn. (pres. Washington chpt. 1989-90), U.S. Naval Acad. Found. (trustee 1991—), Sigma Xi. Achievements include development of NELIAC computer program and Strategic Simulation Methodology. Home: 101 Pommander Walk Alexandria VA 22314-3844 Office: The Riverside Group Ltd 101 Pommander Walk Alexandria VA 22314-3844

MASTERSON, MARY STUART, actress; b. N.Y.C., June 29, 1966; d. Peter and Carlin Glynn Masterson. Theatre appearances include Alice in Wonderland, 1982, Been Taken, 1985, The Lucky Spot, 1987, Lily Dale, 1987; TV movies include Love Lives On, 1985, City in Fear; films: The Stepford Wives, 1975, Heaven Help Us, 1984, At Close Range, 1985, My Little Girl, 1986, Gardens of Stone, 1987, Some Kind of Wonderful, 1987, Mr. North, 1988, Chances Are, 1989, Immediate Family, 1989, Funny About Love, 1990, Fried Green Tomatoes, 1991, Married To It, 1993, Benny and Joon, 1993, Bad Girls, 1994, Radioland Murders, 1994, Heaven's Prisoners, 1994. Office: Creative Artists Agency 9830 Wilshire Blvd Beverly Hills CA 90212*

MASTERSON, MICHAEL RUE, journalist, educator, editor; b. Harrison, Ark., Dec. 10, 1946; s. Rue B. and Elaine H. (Hammerschmidt) M.; m. Ruthie Louette Laws; children: Brandon Lee, Anna Kathleen. Student, U. N.Mex., 1965-68; BA, U. Cen. Ark., 1971. Editor The Daily Independent, Newport, Ark., 1971-73; exec. editor Sentinel-Record, Hot Springs, Ark., 1973-80; staff writer L.A. Times, 1980; investigative reporter Chgo. Sun-Times, 1981; spl. projects editor WEHCO Media (daily newspapers), Little Rock, 1982-86; investigative team leader Ariz. Republic, 1986-89; Kiplinger Program chair, prof. journalism Ohio State U., Columbus, 1989-94; investigative projects editor The Asbury Park (N.J.) Press, 1994—; isntr. journalism Garland Community Coll., 1974-75. Co-author: (text) Excellence in Reporting, 1987; contbg. editor, cons. Two River Times, Monmouth, N.J., 1993—. With USCGR, 1968-73. Recipient Nat. Headliner awards Press Club Atlantic City, 1971, 89, Robert F. Kennedy awards, 1972, 74, 77, 80, Freedom of Info. and Investigative Reporting awards Ark. chpt. Soc. Profl. Journalists, 1974, honor awards, 1975, award for editorial Freedom Found. Valley Forge, 1974, Mass Media Gold Medallion NCCJ, 1974, Paul Tobenkin Meml. awards Columbia Grad. Sch. Journalism, 1975, 85, 88, 89, Disting. Svc. awards Sch. Journalism U. Ark. Little Rock, ann. 1979-84, citation Roy Howard Pub. Svc. Awards, 1978, Cert. of Merit ABA, 1980, 84, Nat. Assn. Black Journalists reporting prize, 1985, Don Bolles award for outstanding investigative reporting, 1987, 88, Best of West Journalism awards, 1987, 88, Congl. Achievement award Nat. Congress Am. Indians, 1987, Clarion journalism award, 1988, George Polk award for nat. reporting, 1989, Heywood Broun Meml. awards, 1984, 87, hon. mention, 1975; finalist Pulitzer Prize Nat. Reporting 1988, Specialized Reporting 89; named one of Outstanding Young Men Am., 1973, Ark. Journalist of Yr., 1986; Alicia Patterson journalism fellow, 1976-77; teaching fellow Poynter Inst. Media Studies, 1993; finalist First Journalist in Space Program, 1986. Mem. Investigative Reporters and Editors (Nat. Journalism awards 1979, 82, IRE Bronze Medallion 1979, Disting. Teaching honors Ohio State 1994, bd. dirs. 1982-87), Sigma Delta Chi, Nat. Headliners Club. Home: 242 W 18th Ave Columbus OH 43210-1107 Office: Ohio State U Dept Journalism Columbus OH 43210 *To call attention to the events, predicaments and inequities in the neighborhood in hopes at least one person who follows will somehow benefit from my having once been here.*

MASTERSON, PETER, actor, director; b. Houston, June 1, 1934; s. Carlos Bee and Josephine Yeager (Smith) M.; m. Carlin Glynn, Dec. 29, 1960; children: Carlin Alexandra, Mary Stuart, Peter Carlos. BA in History, Rice U., 1957. Appeared in Broadway plays Marathon '33, 1963, Blues for Mr. Charlies, 1964; title role in Trial of Lee Harvey Oswald, 1967; appeared in The Great White Hope, 1968, That Championship Season, 1974, The Poison Tree, 1975, (films) The Exorcist, 1972, Man on a Swing, 1973, The Stepford Wives, 1974; playwright The Best Little Whorehouse in Tecas, 1978; dir. Broadway prodns. The Best Little Whorehouse in Texas, 1978 (Drama Desk award for Best Dir. of Musical 1978); co-dir., co-writer The Best Little Whorehouse Goes Public, 1994; dir. off-Broadway prodns. The Cover of Life, 1994, The Young Man from Atlanta (Pulitzer prize 1995); screenwriter The Best Little Whorehouse in Texas, 1980; prodr. (TV film) City in Fear, 1980; dir. films The Trip to Bountiful, 1985, Blood Red, 1986, Full Moon in Blue Water, 1987, Night Game, 1988, Convicts, 1989, Arctic Blue, 1993, Lily Dale, 1996. Mem. AFTRA, SAG, Actors Equity Assn., Soc. Stage Dirs. and Choreographers, Writers Guild Am., Actors Studio, Dirs. Guild Am., Seawanhaka Club, Corinthian Yacht Club, Tex. Corinthian Yacht Club.

MASTERSON, THOMAS A., lawyer; b. Phila., Dec. 10, 1927; s. James F. and Evangeline O. Masterson; m. Louise M., Apr. 27, 1982. A.B. magna cum laude, Harvard U., 1949; LL.B. cum laude, U. Pa., 1952. Bar: Pa. 1953, U.S. Dist. Ct. Pa., U.S. Ct. Appeals (3d cir.) 1953. Asst. dist. atty., 1954-56; dep. city solicitor City of Phila., 1956-60; ptnr. Morgan, Lewis & Bockius, Phila., 1960-67, 1973—; judge U.S. Dist. Ct. Eastern Dist. Pa., 1967-73. Mem. Phila. Human Relations Commn., 1960-64; mem. Phila. Sch. Bd., 1964-67. Mem. Am. Coll. Trial Lawyers, ABA.

MASTNY-FOX, CATHERINE LOUISE, administrator, consultant; b. New Rochelle, N.Y., June 4, 1939; d. Louis Francis and Catherine Marie (Haage) Kacmarynski; m. Vojtech Mastny, July 25, 1964 (div. Oct. 1987); m. Richard K. Fox, Oct. 10, 1993; children: Catherine Paula (dec.), John Adalbert (dec.), Elizabeth Louise. BA magna cum laude, Coll. New Rochelle, 1961; MA, Columbia U., 1963, PhD, 1968. Lectr. in history various colls., N.Y. and Calif., 1968-71; researcher, writer H. W. Wilson Co., N.Y.C., 1971-81; contbg. editor Columbia U. Press, N.Y.C., 1972-74; v.p., exec. dir. Internat. Mgmt. and Devel. Inst., Washington, 1978-84, exec. dir., spl. asst. to chmn., 1986-91; v.p. Meridian House Internat., Washington, 1984-85; dir. corp. devel. Washington Music Ensemble, 1991—, also bd. dirs.; cons. in field; panelist NEH, Washington, 1983; internat. advisor Global Nomads, Washington, 1990—. Contbg. author: The American Book of Days, 1978, World Authors, 1970-1971, 1980; contbg. editor: Columbia Ency., 3d edit., 1975. Fulbright Found. grantee, 1961-62; fellow Woodrow Wilson Found., 1962-63, Walter L. Dorn, 1963-64, Konrad Adenauer fellow, 1965-66. Democrat. Roman Catholic. Avocations: travel, classical music, hiking, art collecting, gardening. Home: 5102 Wyoming Rd Bethesda MD 20816-2267

MASTRANTONIO, MARY ELIZABETH, actress; b. Lombard, Ill., Nov. 17, 1958; d. Frank A. and Mary D. (Pagone) M. Student, U. Ill., 1976-78. Actress: (stage prodns.) Copperfield, 1981, Oh, Brother, 1981, Amadeus, 1982, Sunday in the Park with George, 1983, The Human Comedy, 1984, Henry V, 1984, Measure for Measure, 1985, The Knife, 1987, Twelfth Night, (feature films) Scarface, 1983, The Color of Money, 1986 (Acad. award nomination 1986), The January Man, 1989, The Abyss, 1989, Fools of Fortune, 1990, Class Action, 1991, Robin Hood: Prince of Thieves, 1991, Consenting Adults, 1992, White Sands, 1992, Three Wishes, 1995; (TV movie) Mussolini: The Untold Story, 1985. Office: Internat Creative Mgmt 8942 Wilshire Blvd Beverly Hills CA 90211-1934*

MASTRION, GUY, secondary school principal. Prin. Longwood Mid. Sch., Middle Island, N.Y. Recipient Blue Ribbon Sch. award U.S. Dept. Edn., 1990-91. Office: Longwood Mid Sch Middle Island-Yaphank Rd Middle Island NY 11953

MASTROIANNI, LUIGI, JR., physician, educator; b. New Haven, Nov. 8, 1925; s. Marion (Dallas) M.; m. Elaine Catherine Pierson, Nov. 4, 1957; children: John James, Anna Catherine, Robert Luigi. AB, Yale U., 1946; MD, Boston U., 1950, DSc (hon.), 1973; MA (hon.), U. Pa., 1970. Diplomate Am. Bd. Ob-gyn. and Reproductive Endocrinology and Infertility. Intern, then resident ob.-gyn. Met. Hosp. N.Y., 1950-54; fellow rsch. Harvard Med. Sch. and Free Hosp. for Women, Boston, 1954-55; instr. dept. ob-gyn. Sch. of Medicine Yale U., New Haven, 1955-56, asst. prof. ob.-gyn. dept., 1956-61; prof. U. Calif., L.A., 1961-65; chief ob-gyn Harbor Gen. Hosp., L.A., 1961-65; William Goodell prof. ob.-gyn., chmn. dept. U. Pa. Sch. of Medicine, Phila., 1965-87, William Goodell prof. ob.-gyn. dept., dir. human reproduction div., 1987—. Contbr. numerous articles to profl. jours. Recipient Squibb prize Pacific Coast Fertility Soc., 1965, Christian R. and Mary Lindback award, 1969, Gold medal Barren Found., 1977, King Faisal prize in medicine, 1989, Pub. Recognition award Assn. Profls. of Gynecology and Obstets., 1990, Disting. Svc. award Soc. Study Reproduction, 1992, Axel Munthe award, 1996. Mem. ACS, Am. Gyneol. and Obstet. Soc., Am. Gynecol. Club, Am. Soc. for Reproductive Medicine, Am. Physiol. Soc., Am. Coll. Obs.-Gyns., Inst. Medicine of NAS, Soc. Gynecology Investigation, Soc. for Exptl. Biology and Medicine, Endocrine Soc., Soc. for Study Reproduction (Disting. Svc. award 1992), Pacific Coast Fertility Soc. (hon.), Cen. Assn. Ob-Gyns. (hon.), Tex. Assn. Ob.-Gyns. (hon.), N.C. Gynecol. Soc. (hon.), Assn. Profs. Ob-Gyns., Brazilian Fertility Soc. (hon.), Italian Soc. Ob-Gyns. (hon.). Argentina Fertility Soc. (hon.), Peruvian Fertility Soc. (hon.), Sociedad Espanola de Fertilidad (hon.), Israel Soc. Ob-Gyn. (hon.), Uruguan Soc. Sterility and Fertility (hon.), Inst. Medicine, Sigma Xi, Alpha Omega Alpha. Home: 561 Ferndale Ln Haverford PA 19041-1614 Office: Hosp U Pa 3400 Spruce St Philadelphia PA 19104

MASTROIANNI, MARCELLO, actor; b. Fontana Liri, Italy, Sept. 28, 1924; s. Ottone and Ida (Irolle) M.; ed. U. Rome; m. Flora Carabella, 1950; 1 child, Barbara; 1 child with Catherine Deneuve, Chiara. Cashier, Eagle Lion Films, Rome, 1944; debut U. Rome stage prodn. Angelica, 1948; appeared in films including: Una Domenica d'Agosto, 1949, Le Notti Bianche, 1957, I Soliti Ignoti, 1958, Beli' Antonio, 1960, La Dolce Vita, 1960, La Notte, 1961, A Very Private Affair, 1961, Divorce—Italian Style, 1961, 8 1/2, 1963, Family Diary, 1963, Yesterday, Today and Tomorrow, 1964, Fantasmi a Roma, 1964, Casanova 70, 1965, Marriage-Italian Style, 1965, The Organizer, 1965, The 10th Victim, 1965, Ciao Rudy, 1966, Lo Straniera, 1967, Viaggio di G. Mastorna, 1967, Shout Louder, I Don't Understand, L'Etranger, 1967, The Man with the Balloons, 1968, Diamonds for Breakfast, 1968, Leo the Last, 1970, The Priest's Wife, 1970, Drama of Jealousy, (prize for best actor Cannes 1970), 1970, Sunflower, 1970, The Pizza Triangle, 1970, What?, 1972, La Grande Bouffe, 1973, Salut L'Artiste, 1973, Massacre in Rome, 1973, Tuche Pas la Femme Blanche, 1974, Allonsanfan, 1975, Gangster Doll, 1975, Down the Ancient Stairs, 1975, The Sunday Woman, 1976, A Special Day, 1977, Bye Bye Monkey, 1978, Stay as You Are, 1979, La Cite des Femmes, 1979, Blood Feud, 1981, The New World, 1981, Gabriella, 1982, Nuit de Varennes, 1983, Allonsanfan, 1985, Macasoni, 1985, Ginger and Fred, 1986, Dark Eyes (best actor Cannes Film Fest.), 1987, Intervista, 1987, The Beekeeper, 1988, The Two Lives of Martin Pascal, Splendor, 1989, What's the Time (Best Actor Venice Film Festival), 1989, The Hesitant Step of the Stork, 1991, Everybody's Fine, 1991, A Fine Romance, Used People, 1992, The Beekeeper, 1993, The Children Thief, 1994, I Don't Want To Talk About It, 1994, Ready to Wear (Prêt-à-Porter), 1994. Recipient Silver ribbon Italian Film Critics, 1958, 61, European Film award, 1988.*

MASUDA, GOHTA, physician, educator; b. Tokyo, Nov. 21, 1940; s. Ryota and Chiyo (Ikeuchi) M.; m. Mitsuko Taguchi, May 14, 1983. MD, Keio U., 1966, PhD, 1977. Intern, Keio Univ. Hosp., Tokyo, 1966-67; instr. Keio U., Tokyo, 1967-74, 76-78; asst. prof. Kitasato U., Kanagawa-Ken, Japan, 1974-76; chief dept. infectious diseases Tokyo Met. Komagome Hosp., 1978-95; dir. dept. infectious diseases Tokyo Met. Komagome Hosp., 1995—; asst. prof. Toho U., Tokyo, 1985—, Keio U., 1986—, Gunma U., 1989—, Juntendo U., 1995—. Contbr. articles to profl. jours. Mem. Japanese Assn. for Infectious Diseases, Japan Soc. Chemotherapy, Am. Soc. Microbiology, Brit. Soc. for Antimicrobial Chemotherapy. Buddhist. Home: 1-14-12-305 Komagome, Toshima-ku 170 Tokyo Japan Office: Tokyo Met Komagome Hosp Dept Infectious Diseases, 3-18-22 Honkomagome, Bunkyo-ku 113 Tokyo Japan

MASUR, KURT, conductor; b. Brieg, Silesia, Germany, July 18, 1927. Grad., Nat. Music Schule, Breslau, Germany, 1944, Leipzig Conservatory, 1946-48; hon. degree, U. Mich., Cleve. Inst. Music, Leipzig U., Westminster Choir Coll., Hamilton Coll. Repetiteur and conductor Halle Nat. Theatre, 1948-51; conductor Erfurt City Theatre, 1951-53, Leipzig City Theatre, 1953-55, Dresden Philharm., 1955-58; gen. music dir. Mecklenburg Staatstheater, 1958-60; mus. dir. Komische Oper Berlin, 1960-64; chief conductor Dresden Philharm., 1967-72; conductor Leipzig Gewandhaus Orch., since 1970; mus. dir. New York Philharmonic, N.Y.C., since 1991; conductor London Philharm. Orch., 1989-92; prof. Leipzig Acad. Music, 1975—; hon. guest conductor The Israel Philharm. Orch., 1992. Tours include Europe, South Am., Japan, U.S., Can., Middle East; recordings include: Symphonies by Mendelssohn, Brahms, Bruckner, Beethoven, Schumann, Tchaikovsky, Prokofiev's Piano Concertos, Beethoven's Missa Solemnis. Office: care NY Philharmonic Avery Fischer Hall 10 Lincoln Ctr Plz New York NY 10023-6973 also: Gewandhaus zu Leipzig, Augustusplatz 8, O-7010 Leipzig Germany

MASYS, DANIEL RICHARD, medical school director; b. Columbus, Ohio, Mar. 6, 1949; s. Paul John and Jane Marie (Mollenauer) M.; m. Linda Suzanne Bross, June 2, 1974; 1 child, Christopher. AB in Biochemistry, Princeton U., 1971; MD, Ohio State U., 1974. Diplomate Am. Bd. Internal Medicine. Staff hematologist, oncologist U.S. Naval Hosp., San Diego, 1980-84; chief ICRDB br. NIH, Bethesda, Md., 1984-86; dir. Lister Hill Nat. Ctr. Nat. Libr. Medicine, Bethesda, Md., 1986-94; dir. informatics and assoc. clin. prof. Sch. Medicine U. Calif., San Diego, 1994—. Assoc. editor Acad. Medicine jour., 1988-91. Mem. high performance computing White House Office of Sci., Washington, 1991-94; rep. Fed. Networking Coun., Washington, 1991-94. Capt. USPHS, 1984-94. Fellow ACP, Am. Coll. Med. Informatics (exec. com. 1989-92); mem. Am. Med. Informatics Assn. (bd. dirs. 1992-95, assoc. editor jour. 1993—, Pres.'s award 1992), Alpha Omega Alpha. Office: Univ of Calif San Diego Sch of Medicine 9500 Gilman Dr Rm 1317 La Jolla CA 92093-0602

MATALON, NORMA, travel and public relations executive; b. N.Y.C., Jan. 20, 1949; d. Albert and Suzanne Matalon. BA, Skidmore Coll., 1970. Cert. market mgmt., fin. mgmt. Am. Mgmt. Assn., computer automation. Cons., regional sales mgr. Revlon, N.Y.C., 1970-76; dir. sales, mktg. Diane Von Furstenberg Inc., N.Y.C., 1976-78; pres. Norma Matalon Cosmetic Cons., N.Y.C., 1978—, Norma Matalon Internat. Ltd., N.Y.C., 1982—; cons. to overseas cosmetic and fragrance cos., 1986—. Patentee in field. Com. mem., April in Paris Charities, 1976—, Project Hope, 1986—, United World Coll. Schs., 1983—, Northwood Inst., 1978—, Internat. Debutante Found. Charities, 1976—, Princess Grace Found. for Arts U.S., 1984—, Am. Cancer Soc., 1976—, raffle chmn., 1985, 86, 87. Recipient Outstanding Performance award Revlon, N.Y.C., 1972. Mem. Foreign Policy Assn., N.Y.C. (Nat. Adv. Bd. 1985—), The Fragrance Found., Am. Mgmt. Assn., The Foragers of Am., Newport Preservation Soc., Royal Oak Found., Royal Acad. Art, Royal Acad. Music, Met. Mus. Art, Mus. Modern Art, Whitney Mus. Unitarian. Clubs: The Lansdowne (London), The American (London); Cosmopolitan (N.Y.C.), St. Anthony (N.Y.C.), New Eng. (N.Y.C.), Regency Whist (N.Y.C.), The Tuxedo of N.Y., Annabel's (London). Avocations: travel, vol. fundraising, foreign languages. Home: 445 E 77th St New York NY 10021-2318

MATALON, VIVIAN, theatrical director; b. Manchester, Eng., Oct. 11, 1929; came to U.S., 1977; s. Moses and Rose (Tawil) M. Student, Munro Coll., Jamaica (W.I.) Coll., Neighborhood Playhouse, N.Y.C. Prof. acting Brandeis U., 1977-78; prof. acting and direction SUNY, Stony Brook, 1985-86. Dir. Broadway prodns. After the Rain, Noel Coward in Two Keys, P.S. Your Cat is Dead, Morning's at Seven (Tony award, Drama Desk award 1980), Brigadoon, The American Clock, The Corn is Green, The Tap Dance Kid (Tony nomination 1984); London West End Prodns. include Season of Goodwill, The Chinese Prime Minister, The Glass Menagerie, Suite in Three Keys, After the Rain, Two Cities, Girlfriend, I Never Sang for My Father, Small Craft Warnings, The Gingerbread Lady, Bus Stop, Morning's at Seven; dir. Ah Wilderness, Stratford (Ont., Can.) Festival, The Heiress,

Chichester (Eng.) Festival; television prodns. Private Contentment, Am. Playhouse, Morning's at Seven, Showtime.

MATARAZZO, JOSEPH DOMINIC, psychologist; b. Caiazzo, Italy, Nov. 12, 1925; (parents Am. citizens); s. Nicholas and Adeline (Mastroianni) M.; m. Ruth Wood Gadbois, Mar. 26, 1949; children: Harris, Elizabeth, Sara. Student, Columbia U., 1944; BA, Brown U., 1946; MS, Northwestern U., 1950, PhD, 1952. Fellow in med. psychology Washington U. Sch. Medicine, 1950-51; instr. Washington U., 1951-53, asst. prof., 1953-55; research assoc. Harvard Med. Sch., assoc. psychologist Mass. Gen. Hosp., 1955-57; prof., head med. psychol. dept. Oreg. Health Scis. U., Portland, 1957—; Mem. nursing rsch. and patient care study sect., behavioral medicine study sect. NIH, nat. mental health adv. coun. NIMH; mem. bd. regents Uniformed Svcs. U. Health Scis., 1974-80. Author: Wechsler's Measurement and Appraisal of Adult Intelligence, 5th edit., 1972, (with A.N. Wiens) The Interview: Research on its Anatomy and Structure, 1972, (with Harper and Wiens) Nonverbal Communication, 1978; editor: Behavioral Health: A Handbook of Health Enhancement and Disease Prevention, 1984; editorial bd.: Jour. Clin. Psychology, 1962—; cons. editor: Contemporary Psychology, 1962-70, 80—, Jour. Community Psychology, 1974-81, Behavior Modification, 1976-91, Intelligence: An Interdisciplinary Jour, 1976-90, Jour. Behavioral Medicine, 1977—, Profl. Psychology, 1978—, Jour. Cons. and Clin. Psychology, 1978-85; editor: Psychology series Aldine Pub. Co, 1964-74; psychology editor: Williams & Wilkins Co, 1974-77; contbr. articles to psychol. jours. Ensign USNR, 1943-47; capt. Res. Recipient Hofheimer prize Am. Psychiat. Assn., 1962. Fellow AAAS, APA (pres. 1989-90, divsn. health psychology 1978-89, Coun. Reps. 1982-91, bd. dirs. 1986-90); mem. Western Psychol. Assn., Oreg. Psychol. Assn., Am. Assn. State Psychology Bds. (pres. 1963-64), Nat. Assn. Mental Health (bd. dirs.), Oreg. Mental Health Assn. (bd. dirs., pres. 1962-63), Internat. Coun. Psychologists (bd. dirs. 1972-74, pres. 1976-77), Assn. Advancement of Psychology (trustee 1980-84, chmn. bd. trustees 1983-85). Home: 1934 SW Vista Ave Portland OR 97201-2455 Office: Oreg Health Scis U Sch Medicine 3181 SW Sam Jackson Park Rd Portland OR 97201-3011

MATARAZZO, RUTH GADBOIS, psychology educator; b. New London, Conn., Nov. 9, 1926; d. John Stuart and Elizabeth (Wood) Gadbois; m. Joseph D. Matarazzo, Mar. 26, 1949; children: Harris, Elizabeth, Sara. A.B., Brown U., 1948; M.A., Washington U., St. Louis, 1952, Ph.D., 1955. Diplomate in clin. psychology and clin. neuropsychology Am. Bd. Examiners in Profl. Psychology. Rsch. fellow pediatrics Washington U. Med. Sch., 1954-55; rsch. fellow psychology Harvard U. Med. Sch., 1955-57; asst. prof. med. psychology Oreg. Health Scis. U., Portland, 1957-63, assoc. prof., 1963-68, prof., 1968—; woman liaison officer to Assn. Am. Med. Colls., 1979-90. Author: (with E. Greif) Behavioral Approaches to Rehabilitation: Coping with Change, 1982; contbr. chpts. to books and articles to profl. jours. Fellow Am. Psychol. Assn. (bd. ednl. affairs, del. to coun. reps., vice chair accreditation com., chmn. accreditation task force, chair membership com.); mem. AAAS, Western Psychol. Assn. (bd. dirs.), Oreg. Psychol. Assn. (past pres.), Portland Psychol. Assn. (past pres.), Sigma Xi. Home: 1934 SW Vista Ave Portland OR 97201-2455

MATARÉ, HERBERT F., physicist, consultant; b. Aachen, Germany, Sept. 22, 1912; came to U.S., 1953; s. Josef P. and Paula (Broicher) M.; m. Ursula Krenzien, Dec. 1939; children: Felicitas, Vitus; m. Elise Walbert, Dec. 1983; 1 child, Victor B. BS in Physics, Chemistry and Math., Aachen U. Geneva, 1933; MS in Tech. Physics, U. Aachen, 1939; PhD in Electronics, Tech. U. Berlin, 1942; PhD in Solid State Physics summa cum laude, Ecole Normale Supérieure, Paris, 1950. Asst. prof. physics & electronics Tech. U. Aachen, 1936-45; head of microwave receiver lab. Telefunken, A.G., Berlin, 1939-46; mgr. semicondr. lab. Westinghouse, Paris, 1946-52; founder, pres. Intermetall Corp., Düsseldorf, Fed. Republic Germany, 1952-56; head semincondr. R & D, corp. rsch. labs. Gen. Telephone & Electronics Co., N.Y.C., 1956-59; dir. rsch. semicondr. dept. Tekade, Nürnberg, Fed. Republic Germany, 1959-61; head quantum physics dept. rsch. labs. Bendix Corp., Southfield, Mich., 1961-64; tech. dir., acting mgr. hybrid microelectronics rsch. labs. Lear Siegler, Santa Monica, Calif., 1963-64; asst. chief engr. advance electronics dept. Douglas Aircraft Co., Santa Monica, 1964-66; tech. dir. McDonnell Douglas Missile Div., 1964-69; sci. advisor to solid state electronics group Autonetics (Rockwell Internat.), Anaheim, Calif., 1966-69; pres. Internat. Solid State Electronics Cons., L.A., 1973—; prof. electronics U. Buenos Aires, 1953-54; vis. prof. UCLA, 1968-69, Calif. State U., Fullerton, 1969-70; dir. Compound Crystals Ltd., London, 1989—; cons. UN Indsl. Devel. Orgn. to 15 Indian insts. and semiconductor cos. with conf. talks at India Inst. Tech., New Delhi and Bombay, 1978. Author: Receiver Sensitivity in the UHF, 1951, Defect Electronics in Semiconductors, 1971, Conscientious Evolution, 1978, Energy, Facts and Future, 1989, (with P. Faber) Renewable Energies, 1993; patentee first European transistor, first vacuum growth of silicon crystals with levitation, growth of bicrystals, first low temperature transistor with bicrystals, optical heterodyning with bicrystals, first crystal TV transmission link, first color TV transmission over fiber with LEDs and bicrystals, liquid phase epitaxy for LEDs and batch process for III-V-solar cells; contbr. over 100 articles to profl. jours. Fellow IEEE (life); mem. AAAS, IEEE Nuclear Plasma Scis. Soc., IEEE Power Engring. Soc., Inst. for Advancement of Man (hon.), Am. Phys. Soc. (solid state div.), Electrochem. Soc., Am. Vacuum Soc. (thin film div.), Materials Rsch. Soc., N.Y. Acad. Scis. (emeritus). Avocations: astrophysics, biology, classical music, piano. Home: 23901 Civic Center Way Apt 130 Malibu CA 90265-4883 Office: ISSEC PO Box 2661 Malibu CA 90265-7661

MATASAR, ANN B., former dean, business and political science educator; b. N.Y.C., June 27, 1940; d. Harry and Tillie (Simon) Bergman; m. Robert Matasar, June 9, 1962; children—Seth Gideon, Toby Rachel. AB, Vassar Coll., 1962; MA, Columbia U., 1964, PhD, 1968; M of Mgmt. in Fin., Northwestern U., 1977. Assoc. prof. Mundelein Coll., Chgo., 1965-78; prof., dir. Ctr. for Bus. and Econ. Elmhurst Coll., Elmhurst, Ill., 1978-84; dean Roosevelt U., Chgo., 1984-92; prof. Internat. Bus. and Fin. Walter E. Heller Coll. Bus. Adminstrn. Roosevelt U., 1992—; dir. Corp. Responsibility Group, Chgo., 1978-84; chmn. long range planning Ill. Bar Assn., 1982-83; mem. edn. com. Ill. Commn. on the Status of Women, 1978-81. Author: Corporate PACS and Federal Campaign Financing Laws: Use or Abuse of Power?, 1986; (with others) Research Guide to Women's Studies, 1974. Contbr. articles to profl. jours. Dem. candidate 1st legis. dist. Ill. State Senate, no. suburbs Chgo., 1972; mem. Dem. exec. com. New Trier Twp., Ill., 1972-76; rsch. dir., acad. advisor Congressman Abner Mikva, Ill., 1974-76; bd. dirs. Ctr. Ethics and Corp. Policy, 1985-90. Named Chgo. Woman of Achievement Mayor of Chgo., 1978. Fellow AAUW (trustee ednl. found. 1992—, v.p. fin.); mem. Am. Polit. Sci. Assn., Midwest Bus. Adminstrn. Assn., Acad. Mgmt., Women's Caucus for Polit. Sci. (pres. 1980-81), John Howard Assn. (bd. dirs. 1986-90), Am. Assembly of Coll. Schs. of Bus. (bd. dirs. 1989-92, chair com. on diversity in mgmt. edn. 1991-92), North Ctrl. Assn. (commr. 1994—), Beta Gamma Sigma. Democrat. Jewish. Avocations: jogging, biking, tennis, opera, crosswords. Office: Roosevelt U Coll Bus Adminstrn Dept Fin 430 S Michigan Ave Chicago IL 60605-1301

MATAXIS, THEODORE CHRISTOPHER, consultant, lecturer, writer, retired army officer, educator; b. Seattle, Aug. 17, 1917; s. Chris P. and Edla (Osterdahl) M.; m. Helma Mary Jensen, Aug. 27, 1940; children: Shirley Jeanne (Mrs. J. L. Slack), Theodore Christopher, Kaye Louise (Mrs. Vernon P. Isaacs, Jr.). B.A., U. Wash., 1940; student, Def. Services Staff Coll., India, 1950-51, Army War Coll., 1957-58; M.A. in Internat. Relations, George Washington U., 1965. Commd. 2d lt. U.S. Army, 1940, advanced through grades to brig. gen., 1967; inf. bn. comdr. Europe, World War II; regt. comdr. Korea, 1952-53; mem. Gov. Harriman's Presdl. Mission to Establish Mil. Aid Program India, 1962; mil. asst., speech writer for chmn. Joint Chiefs of Staff, 1962-64; sr. adviser II Vietnamese Army Corps. Pleiku, 1964-65; dep. comdr. 1st Brigade, 101st Airborne Div., 1966, asst. div. comdr. 82d Airborne Div., 1967; chief army sect. Army Mission/MAAG Iran, 1968-70; asst., acting div. comdr. Americal Div. Vietnam, 1970; chief mil. equipment delivery team Cambodia, 1971-72; ret., 1972; ednl. and systems mgmt. cons. Republic of Singapore, 1972-74; asst. supt., comdt. cadets Valley Forge Mil. Acad., Wayne, Pa., 1975-83; dir. AZED Assocs., Ltd., Southern Pines, N.C., 1983—; faculty Am. Mil. U., 1993—. Author: (with Seymour Goldberg) Nuclear Tactics, 1958, (chpt.) International Affairs in South West Asia, 1984, American Military Encyclopedia; also numerous mil. and hist. articles. Mem. adv. council Com. for Free Afghanistan. Decorated D.S.M., Silver Star, D.F.C., Bronze Star with 3 oak leaf clusters with V, Commendation medal with 3 oak leaf clusters and V, Joint Services Commendation medal, Purple Heart with oak leaf cluster, Legion of Merit with 2 oak leaf clusters, Air medal with V and 30 oak leaf clusters, Combat Inf. Badge with 2 stars (U.S.); Nat. Order 5th class; Distinguished Service Order; 4 Gallantry crosses; Honor medal 1st class; Air medal Vietnam; Def. medal Order of Republic Cambodia; Chapel of Four Chaplains-Legion of Honor. Mem. Oral History Assn., Soc. Study Mil. History, U.S. Commn. on Mil. History, Mil. Order World Wars (life), Am. Coun. for Study Islamic Socs., The Federalist Rsch. Inst. (bd. dirs.), Am. Legion, VFW, Airborne Assn. (life), 70th Divsn. Assn. (life), Assn. U.S. Army, Nat. Rifle Assn. (endowment mem.), 82d Airborne Divsn. Life Assn. (life), Am. Security Coun. (spkrs. bur.), Ends of the Earth, Scabbard and Blade (adv. coun. nat. soc.), Freedom Medicine (adv. bd.), Def. Policy Coun., Nat. Policy Forum, Am. Immigration Control (mem. adv. bd.). Clubs: Elks (Southern Pines), Army Navy (Washington); Tanglin (Singapore). Office: AZED Assocs Ltd PO Box 1643 Southern Pines NC 28388-1643

MATCHETT, JANET REEDY, psychologist; b. Chgo., Sept. 2, 1926; d. Joseph Franklin and Minnie Mae (Burr) Reedy; m. Russell W. Kemerer, Jan. 20, 1949 (div. Aug. 1974); children: Brian Lee, Pamela Ann, Patricia Lynn, Bruce Reed, Bryce Jason; m. Charles Ernest Matchett, Nov. 17, 1984. BS summa cum laude, U. Pitts., 1974; MEd, Indiana U. of Pa., 1977, Ednl. Specialist, 1978; postgrad., U. Akron, U. Pitts., Pa. State U. Lic. psychologist; cert. sch. psychologist, Pa., Ohio, W.Va., nationally. Tchr. adult edn. Greensburg (Pa.)-Salem Sch., 1963-70; tchr. cons. Peterson Sys., Inc., Greensburg, 1967-75, Ednl. Self-Devel., Inc., Greensburg, 1975-78; sch. psychologist Columbiana Bd. Edn., Lisbon, Ohio, 1979, Struthers (Ohio) City Schs., 1979-80; instr. Monroeville (Pa.) Sch. Bus., 1983; sch. psychologist Cmty. Mental Health Ctr. Beaver County, Rochester, Pa., 1983-84, South Side Area Sch. Dist., Hookstown, Pa., 1984-87, Blackhawk Sch. Dist., Beaver Falls, Pa., 1984—; instr. Pa. State U., New Kensington, 1984-86; substitute tchr. Greensburg (Pa.)-Salem Sch. Dist., 1975-83, long range planning com. 1981-82; cons. Allegheny East Mental Health/Mental Retardation Ctr., Monroeville, Pa., 1981-83, Westmoreland County Community Coll, Youngwood, Pa., 1981-83; sch. psychologist Wetzel County Schs., New Martinsville, W.Va., 1981; com. action team, strategic planning com. Blackhawk Sch. Dist., Beaver Falls, 1991—. Vol. Adelphi House, 1978; chmn. drug/alcohol abuse prevention program, City of Greensburg, 1981; troop leader Girl Scouts Am.; asst. den mother Boy Scouts Am.; ch. sch. tchr. United Meth. Ch., Greensburg; Bible sch. program vol. United Ch. of Christ, Greensburg; chmn. PTO, Greensburg. Mem. NEA, NASP, Assn. Sch. Psychologists Pa., Western Pa. Assn. Sch. Psychologists, Beaver County Sch. Psychologists Assn., Blackhawk Edn. Assn., Alpha Sigma Lambda. Republican. Avocations: reading, swimming, sewing, hiking, motorcycling, lecturing. Home: 48 W Manilla Ave Pittsburgh PA 15220-2838 Office: Blackhawk Sch Dist 635 Shenango Rd Beaver Falls PA 15010-1660

MATCHETT, WILLIAM H(ENRY), English literature educator; b. Chgo., Mar. 5, 1923; s. James Chapman and Lucy H. (Jipson) M.; m. Judith Wright, June 11, 1949; children: David H., Katherine C., Stephen C. BA with highest honors, Swarthmore Coll., 1949; MA, Harvard U., 1950, PhD, 1957. Teaching fellow Harvard U., Cambridge, Mass., 1953-54; instr. English lit. U. Wash., Seattle, 1954-56, asst. prof., 1956-61, assoc. prof., 1961-66, prof., 1966-82, prof. emeritus, 1982—. Author: The Phoenix and the Turtle, 1965, Fireweed, 1980; numerous poems; co-author: Poetry: From Statement to Meaning, 1965; editor: Modern Lang. Quar., Seattle, 1964-82. Mem. Soc. Friends. Home: 1017 Minor Ave Apt 702 Seattle WA 98104-1303

MATE, MARTIN, bishop; b. Port Rexton, Nfld., Can., Nov. 12, 1929; s. John and Hilda (Toope) M.; m. Florence Mabel Hooper, Nov. 12, 1962; children: Carolyn, Elizabeth, Phyllis, John, Carl. L.Th., Queens Coll., St. John's Nfld., 1953; B.A. with honors, Bishop's U., Que., 1966, M.A. with honors, 1967. Ordained deacon Anglican Ch. of Can., 1952, priest, 1953, elected bishop, 1980, consecrated, 1980. Curate Anglican Cathedral, St. John's, 1952-53; rector Pushthrough Parish, Nfld., 1953-58; incumbent St. Anthony Mission, Nfld., 1958-64; rector Cookshire Parish, Que., 1964-67, Catalina Parish, Nfld., 1967-72, Pouch Cove Parish, Nfld., 1972-76; treas. Diocese of Eastern Nfld. and Labrador, St. John's, 1976-80; bishop Diocese of Eastern Nfld. and Labrador, St. John's, 1980—; mem. liturgical, programme, exec. and fin. coms. Anglican Diocese of Nfld. and Diocese of Eastern Nfld. and Labrador, 1972—; mem. provincial synod and provincial council Anglican Province of Can., 1975—; mem. gen. synod, nat. exec and adminstrn. and fin. com. Anglican Ch. of Can., 1975—. Office: Diocese of Eastern Nfld, 19 Kings Bridge Rd, Saint John's, NF Canada A1C 3K4

MATEJKOVIC, EDWARD MICHAEL, athletic director, coach; b. Coatesville, Pa., July 19, 1947; s. Edward Michael and Helen Theresa (Kowalczyk) M.; m. Judith Ann Mento, Feb. 6, 1970; children: Jennifer lynn, Leigh Allison, Jude Michael. BS, West Chester State U., 1969, MEd, 1975; EdD, Temple U., 1983. Tchr., coach Gt. Valley Sch. Dist., Malvern, Pa., 1970-82; asst. facilities dir. Temple U., Phila., 1982-83; athletic dir., football coach SUNY, Brockport, 1984-95; athletic dir. West Chester U., 1995—; cons. Ednl. Cons., Inc., Brockport, 1985—; mem. Ea. Collegiate Athletic Conf. Contbr. articles to profl. jours. Mem. Games for the Physically Challenged, Brockport, 1986-90. Mem. AAHPERD, Am. Football Coaches Assn., Nat. Assn. Coll. Dirs. Athletes. Republican. Roman Catholic. Avocations: weight lifting, golfing, furniture refinishing, camping. Home: 54 Sherwood Dr Brockport NY 14420-1440 Office: West Chester U Rm 205 South Campus Field House West Chester PA 19383

MATEJU, JOSEPH FRANK, hospital administrator; b. Cedar Rapids, Iowa, Oct. 18, 1927; s. Joseph Frank and Adeline (Smid) M. B.A., U. N.Mex., 1951; M.A., N.Mex. State U., 1957. Sr. juvenile probation officer San Diego County, 1958-64; adminstr. Villa Solano State Sch., Hagerman, N.Mex., 1965-67; state coordinator on mental retardation planning N.Mex. Dept. Hosps. and Instns., Santa Fe, 1969-70; adminstr. Los Lunas (N.Mex.) Hosp. and Tng. Sch., 1968-69, 70-85. Bd. dirs. Mountain-Plains region Deaf-Blind Program. Served with USAAF, 1946-47. Fellow Am. Assn. Mental Deficiency; fellow Am. Coll. Nursing Home Adminstrs.; mem. Nat. Assn. Supts. Residential Facilities for Mentally Retarded, Assn. Mental Health Adminstrs., Am. Assn. Retarded Children, Albuquerque Assn. Retarded Citizens (1st v.p.), N.Mex. Hosp. Assn., Pi Gamma Mu. Home: 405 Fontana Pl NE Albuquerque NM 87108-1168 Office: PO Box 1269 Los Lunas NM 87031-1269

MATEKER, EMIL JOSEPH, JR., geophysicist; b. St. Louis, Apr. 25, 1931; s. Emil Joseph and Lillian (Broz) M.; m. Lolita Ann Winter, Nov. 25, 1954; children: Mark Steven, Anne Marie, John David. BS in Geophys. Engring., St. Louis U., 1956, MS in Rsch. Geophysics, 1959, PhD in Seismology, 1964. Registered geologist and geophysicist, Calif. Assoc. prof. geophysics Washington U., St. Louis, 1966-69; mgr. geophys. rsch. Western Geophys. Co. of Am., Houston, 1969-70; v.p. R & D Western Geophys. Co. of Am., 1970-74; pres. Litton Resources Sys., Houston, 1977, Litton Westrex, Houston, 1974-79; pres. Aero Svc. div. Western Geophys. Co. of Am., 1974-87, v.p., 1974-90; v.p. Western Atlas Internat., Inc., Houston, 1987—; pres. Aero Svc. div. Western Atlas Internat., Inc., Houston, 1987-90; v.p. tech. Western Geophys. div. Western Atlas Internat., Inc., Houston, 1990-93; pres. Western Atlas Software Divsn. Western Atlas Internat. Inc., Houston, 1993-94; sr. v.p. tech. Western Atlas Internat. Inc., 1994—; mem. State of Calif. Bd. Registration for Geophysicists, Sacramento, 1974—, State of Calif. Bd. Registration for Geologists, Sacramento, 1974—. Author: A Treatise on Modern Exploration Seismology, 2 vols., 1965; contbr. articles to profl. jours.; asst. editor Geophysica, 1969-70. Baseball mgr. Westchester High Sch., 1969-74; soccer coach Spring Forest Jr. High Sch., Houston, 1974; bd. dirs. St. Agnes Acad., Houston, 1977-82; pres. Strake Jesuits Booster Club, Houston, 1977-78. 2nd lt. U.S. Army, 1951-54. Recipient St. Louis U. Alumni award, 1976. Mem. AAAS, Am. Geophys. Union, Seismological Soc. Am., Geophys. Soc. Houston, European Assn. Exploration Geophysicists, Soc. Exploration Geophysicists (chmn. 1974). Roman Catholic. Avocations: racquetball, golf, literature, running, fishing. Home: 419 Hickory Post Ln Houston TX 77079-7430 Office: Div Western Atlas Internat 10205 Westheimer Rd Houston TX 77042-3115

MATELAN, MATHEW NICHOLAS, software engineer; b. Stephenville, Tex., Aug. 21, 1945; s. Mathew Albert and Mary Frances (Hardwick) M.; m. Lois Margaret Waguespack, Apr. 5, 1975; children: Evelyn Nicole, Eleanor Gillian. BS in Physics, U. Tex., Arlington, 1969; MS in Computer Engring., So. Meth. U., 1973, PhD in Computer Sci., 1976. Sr. aerospace engr. Gen. Dynamics, Ft. Worth, 1969-75; sys. engr. Lawrence Livermore (Calif.) Labs., 1975-76; group mgr. Gen. Dynamics, Ft. Worth, 1976-78; computer R&D mgr. United Techs./Mostek, Carrollton, Tex., 1978-82; chief sys. arch. Honeywell Comm., Dallas, 1982-83; pres., CEO, chmn., co-founder Flexible Computer Corp., Dallas, 1983-90; chief arch. Matelan Software Sys., Dallas, 1991-94; chief engr. Expertware, Santa Clara, Calif., 1991-94; chief tech. officer Learn Techs. Interactive, N.Y.C., 1994—; cons. Bendix Flight Controls Divsn., Teterboro, N.J., 1974-75; founding dir. Picture Telephone, Boston, 1984-86, Spectrum Digital, Washington, 1984-86; adv. bd. Axavision, N.Y.C., 1993—. Contbr. articles to profl. jours. Libr. automation bd. So. Meth. U., Dallas, 1985-86. Devel. grantee U.S. Energy Dept., 1975, NASA, 1985. Mem. IEEE (sr. mem.), Assn. for Computing Machinery. Avocations: traveling, music, skiing, aviation. Home: 3969 Courtshire Dr Dallas TX 75229 Office: Learn Techs Interactive 3530 Forest Ln S 61 Dallas TX 75234

MATELES, RICHARD ISAAC, biotechnologist; b. N.Y.C., Sept. 11, 1935; s. Simon and Jean (Phillips) M.; m. Roslyn C. Fish, Sept. 2, 1956; children: Naomi, Susan, Sarah. BS, MIT, 1956, MS, 1957, DSc, 1959. USPHS fellow Laboratorium voor Microbiologie, Technische Hogeschool, Delft, The Netherlands, 1959-60; mem. faculty MIT, 1960-70, assoc. prof. biochem. engring., 1965-68; dir. fermentation unit Jerusalem, 1968-77; prof. applied microbiology Hebrew U., Hadassah Med. Sch., Jerusalem, 1968-80; vis. prof. dept. chem. engring. U. Pa., Phila., 1978-79; asst. dir. rsch. Stauffer Chem. Co., Westport, Conn., 1980, dir. rsch., 1980-81, v.p. rsch., 1981-88; sr. v.p. applied scis. IIT Rsch. Inst., Chgo., 1988-90; proprietor Candida Corp., Chgo., 1990—. Editor: Biochemistry of Some Foodborne Microbial Toxins, 1967, Single Cell Protein, 1968, Jour. Chem. Tech. and Biotech., 1972—; contbr. articles to profl. jours. Mem. Conn. Acad. Sci. Engring., 1981—; mem. vis. com., dept. applied biol. sci. MIT, 1980-88; mem. exec. com. Coun. on Chem. Rsch., 1981-85. Fellow Am. Inst. Med. and Biol. Engring.; mem. AICE, AAAS, SAR, Am. Chem. Soc., Am. Soc. Microbiology, Soc. for Gen. Microbiology U.K., Inst. Food Technologists, Soc. Chem. Ind. (U.K.) Union League, Sigma Xi. Home: 150 W Eugenie St # 46 Chicago IL 60614-5839 Office: 175 W Jackson Blvd Chicago IL 60604-2601

MATELIC, CANDACE TANGORRA, museum studies educator, consultant, museum director; b. Detroit, Aug. 21, 1952; d. Paul Eugene and Madeline Marie (Tangora) M.; m. Steven Joseph Mrozek, Sept. 17, 1983 (div. Sept. 1987); 1 child, Madeline Rose. BA, U. Mich., 1974; MA, SUNY, Oneonta, 1977; postgrad., SUNY, Albany. Interpretive specialist Living History Farms, Des Moines, 1978-80; mgr. adult edn. Henry Ford Mus./Greenfield Village, Dearborn, Mich., 1981-82, mgr. interpretive tng., 1982-84; dir., prof. mus. studies Cooperstown grad. program SUNY, Oneonta, 1986-94; exec. dir. Mission Houses Mus., Honolulu, 1994—; cons. history mus., 1979—; lectr., tchr. nat. and regional confs., workshops, seminars, 1979—; grant reviewer Nat. Endowment for the Humanities and Inst. for Mus. Svc., Washington, 1982—. Author: (with others) Exhibition Reader, 1992; co-author: A Pictorial History of Food in Iowa, 1980, Survey of 1200-Plus Museum Studies Graduates, 1988; contbr. articles and videos on mus. interpretation and tng., 1979—; author conf. proceedings. Trustee Motown Hist. Mus., 1989—. Mem. Am. Assn. State and Local History (sec., bd. dirs. 1988-93, program chmn. ann meeting 1988, mem. edn. com. 1996—, co-chair task force on edn. and tng. 1994-96), Assn. Living Hist. Farms and Agrl. Mus. (bd. dirs. 1980-88, pres. 1985), Midwest Open Air Mus. Coordinating Coun. (founder, bd. dirs., pres. 1978-80), Am. Assn. Museums (mus. studies com. 1986-94), Internat. Coun. Museums, Nat. Trust for Hist. Preservation, Hawaii Museums Assn. (bd. dirs.), Honolulu Rotary. Democrat. Roman Catholic. Office: Mission Houses Mus 553 S King St Honolulu HI 96813

MATER, GENE P., communications consultant; b. N.Y.C., Nov. 27, 1926; s. Albert and Anne (Lande) M.; m. Jeanne M. Blanc, Mar. 7, 1947; children: Richard L., Gene A., Philip E. Student, Bklyn. Poly. Inst., 1943-44. Editor news agy., various newspapers Fed. Republic of Germany, 1946-48; reporter, county editor, city editor San Bernardino (Calif.) Sun-Telegram, 1949-53; copy editor, makeup editor, asst. night editor, news editor N.Y. World-Telegram & Sun, N.Y.C., 1953-59; news dir. Radio Free Europe, Munich, 1959-65; exec. v.p., sec. Radio Free Europe Fund, Inc., N.Y.C., 1965-70; spl. asst. to pres. Broadcast Group, CBS, Inc., N.Y.C., 1970-72, v.p., asst. to pres., 1972-80, sr. v.p., 1981-83; sr. v.p. CBS News, N.Y.C., 1983-84, v.p. internat. affairs, 1984-85; spl. asst. to dir. Commn. Bicentennial U.S. Constn., 1986; v.p. broadcasting Internat. Media Fund, 1990-95; exec. v.p. John Adams Assocs., 1996—; cons. comms. The Freedom Forum, Internat. Rsch. & Exchs. Bd., Williamsburg Charter Found., 1987—; guest columnist on comms. issues Washington Journalism Rev., others pubs.; mem. U.S. Commn. on Broadcasting to the People's Republic of China, 1992. Mem. adv. bd. World Press Freedom Com., Ohio State Awards, Ctr. for the Book, Libr. of Congress, 1981-85; trustee Radio and Television News Dirs. Found. With AUS, 1944-46. Home: 4001 9th St N Apt 708 Arlington VA 22203-1960 Office: John Adams Assocs 655 National Press Bldg Washington DC 20045

MATERA, FRANCES LORINE, elementary educator; b. Eustis, Nebr., June 28, 1926; d. Frank Daniel and Marie Mathilda (Hess) Daiss; m. Daniel Matera, Dec. 27, 1973; children: Richard William Post, Mary Jane Post Craig. BS in Edn., Concordia Tchrs. Coll., Seward, Nebr., 1956; MEd, U. Oreg., 1963; Luth. tchrs. diploma, Concordia Tchrs. Coll., Seward, 1947. Elementary tchr. Our Savior's Luth. Ch., Colorado Springs, Colo., 1954-57; tchr. 5th grade Monterey (Calif.) Pub. Schs., 1957-59; tchr. 1st grade Roseburg (Oreg.) Schs., 1959-60; tchr. several schs. Palm Springs (Calif.) Unified Sch. Dist., 1960-73; tchr. 3rd grade Vista del Monte Sch., Palm Springs, Calif., 1973-93; ret., 1993. Named Tchr. of the Yr., Palm Springs Unified Schs. Mem. Kappa Kappa Iota (chpt. and state pres.).

MATERA, RICHARD ERNEST, minister; b. Hartford, Conn., July 13, 1925; s. Charles Carlo and Philomena Antoinette Cecile (Liberatore) M.; m. Marylynn Olga Beuth, Sept. 3, 1949; children: Thomas Charles, Nancy Jean Matera Dye. Student, Trinity Coll., Hartford, 1943, Biarritz Am. U., France, 1945; BA magna cum laude, Colgate U., 1949; MDiv, Andover Newton Theol. Sch., 1953; DD, Calif. Christian U., 1981. Ordained to ministry Bapt. Ch., 1952. Dir. youth work Quincy Point (Mass.) Congl. Ch., 1949-50; pastor, dir. vacation ch. sch. Panton and Addison (Vt.) chs., 1950; min. Thompson (Conn.) Hill Ch., 1950-51, Waldo Congl. Ch., Brockton, Mass., 1951-54, Cen. Congl. Ch., Orange, Mass., 1954-59; sr. min. 1st Congl. United Ch. of Christ, Berea, Ohio, 1959-71, St. Paul Community Ch., Homewood, Ill., 1971-76; interim min. United Ch. Christ, Chgo., 1978—; pres. Millers River Coun. Chs., 1957-58; mem. dept. ch. world responsibility Mass. Coun. Chs., 1957-59; chmn. internat. affairs com. of state social action com. United Ch. of Christ, 1962-63, del. Gen. Synod, Chgo., mem. peace priority task force Western Res. Assn., 1967-70, mem. commn. on ch. and ministry Ohio conf., 1968-71, chmn. dept. ch. and community Western Res. Assn. Coun., Cleve., 1969-70, mem. peace and internat. rels. com., 1973; mem. ad hoc com. on Vietnam Greater Cleve. Coun. of Chs. of Christ, 1966-68; probation officer DuPage County Probation Dept., Wheaton, Ill., 1985-86; interim min. Chgo. area, 1978—, Sauk Village United Ch. of Christ, 1978-80, Steger 1st Congregation, 1981-83, Forest Park, 1986-88, River Grove Grace, 1989-91, Mont Clare Congregation, 1990-92, St. Nicolai, 1992—. Contbr. poetry to anthologies including Tears of Fire, 1994, A Break in the Clouds, 1994. Capt. Cleve. United Fund, 1961-63, Colgate Fund Dr., 1963; trustee Cleve. Union, 1961-63, Berea United Fund, 1963-69; mem. Berea Coun. on Human Rels., 1965-71, U.S. com. Christian Peace Conf., Prague, Czechoslovakia, 1967—, Nat. Arbor Day Found.; del. Action Conf. on Nat. Priorities, Washington, 1969; bd. dirs., mem. ecumenical mission com. Community Renewal Soc., Chgo., 1972-76; bd. dirs. Respond Now, Chicago Heights, Ill., 1972-78; mem. Pres.'s Coun., Chgo. Theol. Sem., 1973-81; pres. Mended Hearts Inc., Downers Grove, Ill., 1989-90. With U.S. Army Med. Corps., 1943-46, ETO. Austen Colgate scholar, 1946-49; recipient Harvard Book prize, 1942; name inscribed on The Wall of Liberty, Battle of Normandy Found., Normandy, France, 1994. Fellow Profl. Assn. Clergy, Acad. Parish Clergy; mem. Smithsonian Instn., Audubon Soc., Internat. Fellowship of Reconciliation, Internat. Soc. Poets, Nat. Libr.Poetry, Steinway Soc. Chgo., Planetary Soc., Jacques Cousteau Soc., Antique Automobile Club, Hupmobile Club, Cadillac Club, Phi Beta Kappa, Beta

Theta Pi. Democrat. Avocations: drawing, poetry, astronomy, piano, working out at health club. Home and Office: 5 E Memorial Rd Bensenville IL 60106-2541 *From world philosophers, I have gleaned this: While borders stand, we are in prehistory. When all borders are gone, human history will begin.-Yevtushenko A person only has the right to do that which he agrees should become universal law.-Kant Do to others as you want them to do to you.-Hebrew tchg. The human race is now capable of and ready for the above.*

MATERNA, JOSEPH ANTHONY, lawyer; b. Passaic, N.J., June 13, 1947; s. Anthony E. and Peggy Ann Materna; m. Dolores Corio, Dec. 14, 1975; children: Jodi, Jennifer, Janine. BA, Columbia U., 1969, JD, 1973. Bar: N.Y. 1975, Fla. 1977, U.S. Dist. Ct. (ea. and so. dists.) N.Y. 1977, U.S. Supreme Ct. 1977. Trusts and estates atty. Chadbourne Parke Whiteside & Wolff, N.Y.C., 1973-76, Dreyer & Traub, N.Y.C., 1976-80, Finley Kumble Wagner Heine Underberg & Casey, N.Y.C., 1980-85; ptnr., head trusts and estates dept. Newman Tannenbaum Helpern Syracuse & Hirschtritt, N.Y.C., 1985-90, Shapiro Beilly Rosenberg Albert & Fox, N.Y.C., 1990—; lectr. in field. Contbr. articles to profl. jours. Chmn. planned giving com., mem. bd. govs. Arthritis Found. N.Y. Chpt., N.Y.C., 1980—; mem. bd. trustees Cath. Interracial Coun., N.Y.C., 1992—; mem. bequests and planned gifts com. Cath. Archdiocese of N.Y., N.Y.C., 1988—. Recipient Planned Giving award Arthritis Found.-N.Y. Chpt., N.Y.C., 1994, Discovery Alliance award Arthritis Found.-N.Y. Chpt., N.Y.C., 1995; named Accredited Estate Planner, Nat. Assn. Estate Planners, Marietta, Ga., 1995. Mem. Fla. Bar (trusts and estate com.), N.Y. State Bar Assn. (com. on estates and trusts), Bar Assn. of the City of N.Y. (com. on surrogate's ct.), N.Y.C. Estate Planning Coun. (lectr., author), N.Y. County Lawyers Assn. (mem. com. on trusts and estates 1979—), Queen County Bar Assn. (mem. com. trusts and estates 1990—), Richmond County Bar Assn. (com. on surrogates ct.), Columbia Coll. Alumni Assn. of Columbia U. (class pres. 1969—). Republican. Roman Catholic. Home: 155 Johanna Ln Staten Island NY 10309 Office: Shapiro Beilly Rosenberg Albert & Fox 225 Broadway New York NY 10007

MATERNA, THOMAS WALTER, ophthalmologist; b. Passaic, N.J., Oct. 24, 1944; s. Anthony and Ann (Popowich) M.; m. Jorunn Pauline Aronsen, Aug. 18, 1973; children: Richard C., Barbara L. BA, Coll. Holy Cross, Worcester, Mass., 1966; MD, SUNY, N.Y.C., 1971; MBA, Rutgers U., Newark, 1990. Diplomate Am. Bd. Ophthalmology. Intern N.Y. Hosp.-Cornell U. Med. Ctr., N.Y.C., 1971-72; resident N.Y. Eye and Ear Infirmary, N.Y.C., 1975-78; pvt. practice ophthalmology San Francisco, 1986; ophthalmologist N.J. Eye Physicians & Surgeons, Newark; pres., CEO, US Try Zub Ent., Inc., Newark, Bizmore Internat., Inc., Luiv, Ukraine. Com. mem. N.J. Sch. for the Arts, Montclair, 1991—. Lt. USN, 1972-74, comdr. USNR, 1974—. Fellow ACS, Am. Acad. Ophthalmology; mem. Rotary, Army-Navy Club. Democrat. Roman Catholic. Avocations: coin collecting, rare document collecting, tennis, art history. Home: 87 Lorraine Ave Montclair NJ 07043-2304 Office: NJ Eye Physicians and Surgeons 20 Ferry St Newark NJ 07105-1420

MATEUS, LOIS, manufacturing executive; b. 1946. Grad., U. Ky., 1968. Asst. mgr. advt. Begley Drug, 1969-70; staff writer Commonwealth of Ky., 1970-72; dir. pub. rels. Ky. Dem. Party, 1973-75; exec. dir. Hist. Events Celebration Commn., 1976; free-lance writer, 1977-79; press sec., various other adminstrv. positions Gov. John Y. Brown of Ky., 1979-82; sr. v.p. corp. communications and corp. svcs. Brown-Forman Corp., Louisville, 1982—. Office: Brown-Forman Corp 850 Dixie Hwy Louisville KY 40210-1038*

MATHAI-DAVIS, PREMA ANNA, association executive; b. Thiruvalla, Kerala, India, Oct. 28, 1950; came to U.S., 1974; d. Stephen and Susy (Kovoor) Mathai; m. Wallace Mathai-Davis, Oct. 15, 1978; children: Stephen, Lisa, Tara. BS, Delhi U., 1970, MS, 1972; EdD, Harvard U., 1979. Family and child care specialist Grail Internat., New Delhi, 1972-73; instr. Samoa Coll., Western Samoa, 1973-74; project dir., rsch. assoc. Grad. Sch. Edn. Harvard U., Cambridge, Mass., 1978-79; dir. Gerontology Ctr. Mt. Sinai-Hunter Coll., N.Y.C., 1979-81; dir. S.I. social svc. programs Cmty. Svc. Soc., N.Y.C., 1981-85; pres., CEO Cmty. Agy. for Sr. Citizens, Inc., S.I., 1985-90; commr. City of N.Y. Dept. Aging, 1990-94; nat. exec. dir. YWCA of U.S., N.Y.C., 1994—; bd. dirs. Health Sys. Agy. of N.Y.C., 1990-94; vis. lectr. Sch. Social Sci. Bhopal U., India, 1972-73; mem. adv. coun. N.Y. State Assembly Com. on Aging; chair policy com. N.Y. State Assn. of Area Agencies on Aging; vis. fellow New Sch. Social Rsch.. Bd. dirs. Met. Transp. Authority State of N.Y., N.Y.C., 1991-95. Recipient Staten Island Borough medallion, 1995, numerous other awards; named Woman of Yr., Ms. mag., 1995. Fellow N.Y. Acad. Medicine; mem. Asian Am. Forum of N.Y. (bd. dirs.), Women's Forum. Episcopalian. Office: YWCA of the USA 726 Broadway New York NY 10003-9511

MATHAY, JOHN PRESTON, elementary education educator; b. Youngstown, Ohio, Jan. 27, 1942; s. Howard Ellsworth and Mary Clara (Siple) M.; m. Sandra Elizabeth Rhoades, June 9, 1973 (div. Jan. 1986); children: Elizabeth Anne, Sarah Susannah; m. Judith Anne Matthy, June 19, 1988; 1 child, Andrew Micah. B History, Va. Mil. Inst., Lexington, 1964; Cert. Teaching, Cleve. State U., 1972; postgrad., Mich. State U., 1964-65; MEd, Westminster Coll., New Wilmington, 1986. Cert. asst. supt., elem. tchr., elem. prin., high sch. prin. Cabinet maker Artisian Cabinet, Orwig Cabinets, Cleve. and Howland, Ohio, 1970-72; tchr. Urban Community Sch., Cleve., 1972-73, Pymatuning Valley Schs., Andover, Ohio, 1973—; cross country coach, 7th and 8th grade track coach, Andover. Bd. mem. Badger Sch. Bd., Kinsman, Ohio; trustee Kinsman Libr.; trustee, elder Kinsman Presbyn. Ch. Capt. U.S. Army Res., 1966-69. Martha Holden Jennings Found. scholar, Cleve., 1976. Mem. ASCD, Pymatuning Valley Edn. Assn. (pres. 1975-76, 91-92, 94-95), Ohio Edn. Assn., Am. Legion, Rotary (pres. 1991-92, sec. 1992-93, Paul Harris fellow), Masons (jr. deacon 1984-85, 32d deg., York Rite commandery), Ashtabula County Antique Engine Club, Phi Delta Kappa. Republican. Presbyterian. Avocations: sailing, skating, ham radio, fishing, reading. Home: 8424 Main St Kinsman OH 44428-9409 Office: Pymatuning Valley Schs W Main St Andover OH 44003

MATHAY, MARY FRANCES, marketing executive; b. Youngstown, Ohio, July 26, 1944; d. Howard E. and Mary C. (Siple) M.; m. Thomas Stone Withgott, Dec. 20, 1969 (div. June 1973). BA in English Lit. and Composition, Queens Coll., 1967; grad. in bus., Katharine Gibbs Sch., 1968. Corp. mktg. mgr., assoc. Odell Assocs., Inc., Charlotte, N.C., 1973-90; dir. pub. rels. and spl. events Charlotte (N.C.)-Mecklenburg Arts and Sci. Coun., 1990-92; pres. Mathay Comm., Inc., Charlotte, 1992—; speakers bur. chmn. Hospice at Charlotte, Inc., 1980-83; pub. rels. and advt. dir. "Chemical People" program PBS, Charlotte, 1983-84. Author: Legacy of Architecture, 1988; editor: Mint Mus. Antiques Show Mag., 1980, editorial advisor Crier, 1987-92; producer Charlotte's Web, 1977. Bd. dirs. Jr. League of Charlotte, Inc., 1978-79, mem. 1968—; bd. dirs. ECO, Inc., Charlotte, 1979-86, Queens Coll. Alumni, Charlotte, 1984-87, Learning How, Inc., Charlotte, 1988-91; bd. dirs. on adolescent pregnancy Mecklenburg County Coun., 1986-88; vol. tchr. ABLE Cen. Piedmont C.C., 1987-90; comm. com. vol. Am. Cancer Soc., 1994—, Charlotte-Mecklenburg Edn. Found., 1992-94, Charlotte-Mecklenburg Sr. Ctrs., 1994—. Mem. Pub. Rels. Soc. Am. (bd. dirs. 1989—, pres. 1995), Charlotte Pub. Rels. Soc. (bd. dirs. 1986-89, 92-93), Olde Providence Racquet Club, Tower Club. Republican. Presbyterian. Avocations: fgn. travel, tennis.

MATHENY, ADAM PENCE, JR., child psychologist, educator, consultant, researcher; b. Stanford, Ky., Sept. 6, 1932; s. Adam Pence and Dorotha (Steele) M.; m. Ute I. Debus, July 10, 1962 (div.); m. Mary P. Tolbert, June 24, 1967 (div.); children—Laura Steele, Jason Gaverick. B.S., Columbia U., 1958; Ph.D., Vanderbilt U., 1962. Sr. human factors engr. Martin Aerospace div., Balt., 1962-63; instr. Johns Hopkins U. Med. Sch., 1963-65; staff fellow Nat. Inst. Child Health and Human Devel., 1965-67; from asst. prof. to prof. pediatrics U. Louisville Med. Sch., 1967-86, assoc. dir. to dir. Louisville Twin Study, 1986—. mem. review panel NIH, 1991-95. Served with USN, 1951-55. Fellow Internat. Soc. Twin Research, Am. Psychol. Assn., Am. Psychol. Soc.; mem. Soc. Research Child Devel., AAAS, Behavior Genetics Assn., Internat. Soc. Behavior Devel., Internat. Soc. Infant Study, Phi Beta Kappa, Sigma Xi. Co-author: Genetics and Counseling in Medical Practice, 1969; contbr. articles to profl. jours.

MATHENY, CHARLES WOODBURN, JR., retired army officer, retired civil engineer, former city official; b. Sarasota, Fla., Aug. 7, 1914; s. Charles Woodburn Sr. and Virginia (Yates) M.; m. Jeanne Felkel, July 12, 1942; children: Virginia Ann, Nancy Caroline, Charles Woodburn III. BSCE, U. Fla., 1936; grad., Army Command and Gen. Staff Coll., 1944. Lic. comml. pilot. Sanitary engr. Ga. State Dept. Health, 1937-39; civil engr. Fla. East Coast Ry., 1939-41; commd. 2d lt. F.A., USAR, 1936, 2d lt. F.A. U.S. Army, 1942, advanced through grades to col., 1955; comdr. 351st Field Arty. Bn., 1946, 33rd Field Arty. Bn., 1st Inf. Divsn., 1946, staff officer, 1947; gen. staff G-3 Plans Dept. Army, 1948-51; qualified Air Force liaison pilot, 1951; qualified Army aviator, 1952; aviation officer 25th Inf. Div., Korea, 1952-53; sr. Army aviation advisor Korean Army, 1953; dep. commdt., dir. combat devel. Army Aviation Sch., 1954-55; dep. dir. research, dep. dir. dept. tactics Arty. Sch., 1955-57; aviation officer 7th U.S. Army, Germany, 1957-58; Munich sub area comdr. So. Area Command, Europe, 1958-59, qualified sr. army aviator, 1959, dep. chief staff for info. So. Area Command, 1960; Mich. sector comdr. VI Army Corps, 1961-62; ret., 1962; asst. dir. Tampa (Fla.), Dept. Pub. Works 1963-77, asst. to dir., 1977-81, ret., 1981. Initiator tact. use of helicopters in Army and army warrant officer aviator program, 1949, army combat units equipped with helicopter mobility, 1950; pilot 1st combat observation mission in army helicopter, Korea, 1952; organizer, comdr., helicopter pilot 1st Army combat ops. using helicopter mobility to support inf. and engr. front line units 25th Inf. Div., Korea, 1952; pilot 100 combat observation missions, Korea, 1952-53; author 1st state legis. to establish profl. sch. civil engring. for state of Fla., 1974. Contbr. numerous articles on tactical use of helicopter aerial vehicles to mags. Mem. troop com. Boy Scouts Am., 1965-73; active various community and ch. activities; patron Tampa Art Mus., 1965-83, Tampa Community Concert Series, 1979-82; bd. dirs. Tampa YMCA, 1967-71, Fla. Easter Seal Soc., 1978, Easter Seal Soc. Hillsborough County, 1971-84, hon. bd. dirs. 1984—, treas., 1973-76, pres., 1977. Decorated Bronze Star with oak leaf cluster, Air medal with three oak leaf clusters; named to U. Fla. Student Hall of Fame, 1936. Mem. ASCE (pres. West Coach br., dir. Fla. sect. 1973, Engr. of Yr. award West Coast br. Fla. sect. 1979, life mem. 1980), Am. Soc. Profl. Engrs., Fla. Engring. Soc., Am. Pub. Works Assn. (pres. West Coast br. Fla. chpt. 1972, exec. com. Fla. chpt. 1972-77, v.p. 1977, pres. 1978), Ret. Officers Assn., Army Aviation Assn., SAR, Fla. Blue Key, Alpha Tau Omega. Episcopalian. Lodge: Kiwanis. Home: 4802 W Beachway Dr Tampa FL 33609-4836

MATHENY, EDWARD TAYLOR, JR., lawyer; b. Chgo., July 15, 1923; s. Edward Taylor and Lina (Pinnell) M.; m. Marion Elizabeth Shields, Sept. 10, 1947; children: Nancy Elizabeth, Edward Taylor III.; m. Ann Spears, Jan. 14, 1984. B.A., U. Mo., 1944; J.D., Harvard, 1949. Bar: Mo. 1949. Pvt. practice Kansas City, 1949-91; ptnr. firm Blackwell, Sanders, Matheny, Weary & Lombardi, 1954-91, of counsel, 1992—; pres. St. Luke's Hosp., Kansas City, 1980-95. Pres. Cmty. Svc. Broadcasting of Mid-Am., Inc., 1971-72; chmn. Citizens Assn. Kansas City, 1958; chmn. bd. dirs. St. Luke's Found., Kansas City, 1980-95; trustee U. Kansas City, 1980—, Kansas City Cmty. Found., 1983-94, Eye Found., Kansas City, 1990—, H&R Block Found., Kansas City, 1996—, Jacob L. and Ella C. Loose Found., Kansas City, 1996—. Mem. Kansas City Bar Assn., Mo. Bar, River Club, Mission Hills Country Club, Phi Beta Kappa, Sigma Chi (Balfour Nat. award 1944). Episcopalian (chancellor Diocese West Mo. 1971-89). Home: 2510 Grand Blvd Kansas City MO 64108-2678 Office: 2300 Main St Kansas City MO 64108-2415

MATHENY, ELIZABETH ANN, special education educator; b. South Bend, Ind., Jan. 31, 1954; d. Walter Lee and Josephine Mary (Hickey) M. BS in Spl. Edn., Tenn. Tech. U., 1978; MEd in Spl. Edn., West Ga. Coll., 1987; postgrad., Troy State U., 1991-92. Cert. spl. edn. tchr. Tchr. spl. edn. Hi-Hope Tng. Ctr., Lawrenceville, Ga., 1978; trainer Sunshine Sheltered workshop Assn. for Retarded Citizens, Knoxville, Tenn., 1979; tchr. spl. edn. Roopville (Ga.) Elem. Sch., 1979-83, Berkeley Lake Elem. Sch., Duluth, Ga., 1983-84, Baker H.S., Columbus, Ga., 1984-91, Spencer H.S., Columbus, 1991—. Mem.-at-large adv. bd. Muscogee County Spl. Olympics. Mem. NEA, Alpha Delta Kappa (Rho chpt. pres. 1994-96, pres.-elect 1992-94, rec. sec. 1990-92). Republican. Baptist. Avocations: arts and crafts, gardening, home renovating, walking, swimming. Home: 3615 Walton St Columbus GA 31907-2550 Office: Muscogee County Sch Dist Spencer H S Columbus GA 31903

MATHENY, ROBERT LAVESCO, history educator, former university president; b. Lubbock, Tex., Jan. 15, 1933; s. Samuel Worth and Elsie Jane (Jones) M.; m. Sandra Hansen, July 6, 1973; children: Nelda, Monica, Cali. B.A., Eastern N.Mex. U., 1961, M.A., 1962; Ph.D., U. Ariz., 1975. Asst. prof. Eastern N.Mex. U., Portales, 1968-72, assoc. prof., 1972-76, v.p. Clovis campus, 1977-80, exec. v.p., 1981-83, pres., 1983-89, prof. dept. history, 1989—, dir. devel. and govt. rels., 1989—; dean continuing edn. Ft. Hays State U., Hays, Kans., 1980-81. Rockfellow Found. fellow, 1967-68. Mem. Western History Assn. Club: N.Mex. Amigos. Lodge: Rotary (Portales). Office: Ea NMex Univ Office Devel Portales NM 88130

MATHENY, RUTH ANN, editor; b. Fargo, N.D., Jan. 17, 1918; d. Jasper Gordon and Mary Elizabeth (Carey) Wheelock; m. Charles Edward Matheny, Oct. 24, 1960. B.E., Mankato State Coll., 1938; M.A., U. Minn., 1955; postgrad., Universidad Autonoma de Guadalajara, Mex., summer 1956, Georgetown U., summer, 1960. Tchr. in U.S. and S.Am., 1938-61; asso. editor Charles E. Merrill Pub. Co., Columbus, Ohio, 1963-66; tchr. Confraternity Christian Doctrine, Washington Court House, Ohio, 1969-70; assoc. editor Jr. Cath. Messenger, Dayton, Ohio, 1966-68; editor Witness Intermediate, Dayton, 1968-70; editor in chief, assoc. pub. Today's Cath. Tchr., Dayton, 1970—; editor in chief Catechist, Dayton, 1976-89, Ednl. Dealer, Dayton, 1976-80; v.p. Peter Li, Inc., Dayton, 1980—. Editorial collaborator: Dimensions of Personality series, 1969—; co-author: At Ease in the Classroom; author: Why a Catholic School?, Scripture Stories for Today: Why Religious Education?. Mem. Bd. Friends Ormond Beach Library. Mem. Nat. League Am. Pen Women, Nat. Coun. Cath. Women, Cath. Press Assn., Nat. Cath. Ednl. Assn., 3d Order St. Francis (eucharistic minister 1990—). Home: 26 Reynolds Ave Ormond Beach FL 32174-7043 Office: Peter Li Inc 330 Progress Rd Dayton OH 45449-2322 *In a world that is constantly changing, a strong religious faith is a dependable compass through which we are able to stay on a positive, forward course.*

MATHENY, TOM HARRELL, lawyer; b. Houston; s. Whitman and Lorene (Harrell) M. BA, Southeastern La. U., 1954; JD, Tulane U., 1957; LLD (hon.), Centenary Coll., 1979, DePauw U.; LHD (hon.), Oklahoma City U. Bar: La. 1957. Ptnr. Matheny & Pierson, Hammond, La., 1957—; gen. counsel First Guaranty Bank, 1960-83; trust counsel, chmn. bd. 1st Guaranty Bank, Hammond; v.p. Edwards & Assocs., So. Brick Supply, Inc.; faculty Southeastern La. U., Holy Cross Coll., New Orleans; lectr. Union Theol. Sem., Law Sci. Acad.; mem. com. on conciliation and mediation of disputes World Peace through Law Ctr. Chmn. advancement com. Boy Scouts Am., Hammond, 1960-64, mem. dist. coun., 1957-66, mem. exec. bd. Istrouma coun., 1966—, adv. com. to dist. area coun.; past pres. Tangipahoa Parish Mental Health Assn.; pres. La. Mental Health Assn., 1989—; mem. La. Mental Health Advocacy Svc.; co-chmn. La. Mental Health Advocacy Bd.; sec. Chep Morrison Scholarship Found.; mem. men's com. Japan Internat. Christian U. Found; chmn. speakers com., mem. com. on community action and crime prevention, La. Commn. on Law Enforcement and Adminstrn. Criminal Justice; campaign mgr. for Dem. gov. La., 1959-60, 63-64; bd. dirs. La. Moral and Civic Found., Tangipahoa Parish ARC, 1957-67, Hammond United Givers Fund, 1957-68, La. Coun. Chs., Southeastern Devel. Found., La. Mental Health Assn.; bd. dirs. Wesley Found., La. State U., 1965-68, 70—, chmn. bd.; trustee Centenary Coll., 1964-70, Scarritt Coll., 1975-81; pres., bd. trustees Lallie Kemp Hosp. Found., 1994—; hon. trustee John F. Kennedy Coll.; del. world conf. Nat. Assn. Conf. Lay Leaders, London, 1966, Denver, 1971, Dublin, 1976, Hawaii, 1981, del. to gen. confs., 1968, 70, 72; mem. Common Cause. Recipient Man of Yr. award Hammond, 1961, 64, also La. Jaycees, 1964, Layman of Yr. award La. Ann. Conf. United Meth. Ch., 1966, 73, Disting. Alumnus award Southeastern La. U., 1981, W.L. "Bill" May Outstanding Christian Bus. award La. Moral and Civic Found., 1986. Fellow Harry S. Truman Libr. Inst (hon.); mem. ABA (com. on probate), La. Bar Assn. (past gen. chmn. com. on legal aid, com. prison reform), 21st Jud. Dist. Bar Assn. (past sec.-treas., v.p. 1967-68, 71), Comml. Law League Am. (past mem. com. on ethics), La. Alumni Coun. (pres. 1963-65), Acad. Religion and Mental Health, La. Assn. Claimant Compensation Attys., Southeastern La. U. Alumni Assn. (dir., pres. 1961-62, dir. spl. fund 1959-62, dir. Tongipahoa chpt.), Tulane Sch. Law Alumni Assn., Am. Assn. for Family and Marriage Therapy, Internat. Soc. Barristers, Internat. Soc. Valuers, Assn. Trial Lawyers Am., Am. Judicature Soc., Law-Sci. Inst., World Peace Through Law Acad. (com. on conciliation), Acad. Polit. Sci., Am. Acad. Polit. and Social Sci., Internat. Acad. Law and Sci., Internat. Platform Assn., UN Assn. Am. Trial Lawyers Assn., La. Hist. Assn., Friends of Cabildo, Gideons Internat., Hammond Assn. Commerce (dir. 1960-65), Intern Soc. Barristers, Intern Assn. Valuers, La. Mental Health Assn. (pres.-elect), Masons (33 degree), La. Lawyers' Club, Demolay (dist. dep. to supreme coun. 1964—, Legion of Honor), Kiwanis (v.p., dir., Layman of Yr. award 1972), Rotary, Phi Delta Phi, Phi Alpha Delta. Democrat. Methodist. Lodges: Masons, Scottish Rite (33 degree), Demolay (dist. dep. to supreme council 1964—, Legion of Honor), Kiwanis (v.p., dir., Layman of Yr. award for La., Miss. and West Tenn. 1972), Rotary. Home: PO Box 221 Hammond LA 70404-0221 Office: PO Box 1598 401 E Thomas St Hammond LA 70404

MATHER, ALLEN FREDERICK, lawyer; b. Kansas City, Mo., Apr. 28, 1922; s. William Frederick and Alberta (Stephenson) M.; m. Patricia T. Mitchell, June 23, 1972; children—Allen Frederick, Nathaniel J., J. Miles Mitchell. A.B., Colgate U., 1943; LL.B., Harvard, 1949. Bar: Calif. bar 1953. With Agrl. Council of Calif., Sacramento, 1950-57; exec. sec. Agrl. Council of Calif., 1954-57; gen. counsel Sunkist Growers, Los Angeles, 1958-66; pres. Sun-Maid Raisin Growers of Calif., Kingsburg, 1966-72, Sunland Marketing, Inc., Menlo Park, Calif., 1971-72, First Nat. Bank Fresno, Calif., 1973-77; mem. firm Wild, Carter, Tipton & Oliver, 1977-84; mng. partner Agribus. Group, 1977—. Mem. Calif. Industry and World Trade Commn., 1969—; pres. Sequoia council Boy Scouts Am., 1969—. Served with USNR, 1943-46. Mem. Dried Fruit Assn. (dir.), Fresno C. of C. (dir.). Club: Sunnyside Country (Fresno). Home & Office: 5962 E Hamilton Ave Fresno CA 93727-6228

MATHER, BETTY BANG, musician, educator; b. Emporia, Kans., Aug. 7, 1927; d. Read Robinson and Shirley (Smith) Bang; m. Roger Mather, Aug. 3, 1973. MusB, Oberlin Conservatory, 1949; MA, Columbia U., 1951. Instr. U. Iowa, Iowa City, 1953-58, asst. prof., 1959-65, assoc. prof., 1965-73, prof., 1973-96; editor Romney Press; vis. instr. U. Iowa, Iowa City, 1952-53. Rec. artist; author: Interpretation of French Music from 1675-1775, 1973, (with David Lasocki) Free Ornamentation for Woodwind Instruments from 1700-1775, 1976 (with David Lasocki) The Classical Woodwind Cadenza, 1978, The Art of Preluding, 1984 (with Dean Karns) Dance Rhythmns of the French Baroque, 1987, (with Gail Gavin) The French Noel, 1996. Mem. Nat. Flute Assn. (v.p. 1986-87, pres. 1987-88, chmn. bd. dirs. 1988-89). Home: 308 4th Ave Iowa City IA 52245-4613

MATHER, BRYANT, research administrator; b. Balt., Dec. 27, 1916; s. Leon Bryant and Julia (Ferguson) M.; m. Katharine Selden Kniskern, Mar. 27, 1940 (dec. Feb. 1991). Grad., Balt. City Coll., 1934; A.B. in Geology, Johns Hopkins, 1936, postgrad., 1936-38; postgrad., Am. U., 1938-39; D.Sc. (hon.), Clarkson U., 1978. Curator mineralogy Field Mus. Natural History, 1939-41; with U.S. Army Corps Engrs., 1941—; geologist Central Concrete Lab., U.S. Mil. Acad., 1941-42, Mt. Vernon, N.Y., 1942-43; supervisory research civil engr., chief engring. scis. br., concrete lab. (Waterways Expt. Sta.), Vicksburg, Miss., 1946-65; asst. chief concrete lab. (Waterways Expt. Sta.), 1965-66, chief, 1966-76, acting chief structures lab., 1978-80, chief lab., 1980-92, dir. structures lab., 1992—; rsch. assoc. Fla. Dept. Agr. and Consumer Svcs., Gainesville, 1968—; Miss. Mus. Natural Scis., 1979—, Miss. Ent. Mus. Miss. State U., 1985—, Am. Mus. Natural History, N.Y.C., 1979—; mem. Sr. Exec. Assn., 1980—; mem. U.S. Com. of Internat. Commn. Large Dams, 1959—; lectr. Purdue U., 1961, Old Master lectr., 1991; lectr. U. Notre Dame, 1964, MIT, 1966, Clemson U., 1967; Henry M. Shaw lectr. N.C. State U., 1967, U. Wis., 1978—, U.Tex., 1987, Okla. State U., 1987, Johns Hopkins U., 1991, Utah State U., 1995; Stanton Walker lectr. U. Md., 1969; Edgar Marburg lectr. ASTM, 1970; mem. 4th, 5th, 6th and 7th Internat. Symposia Chemistry Cement, Internat. Symposium Movement Water in Porous Bodies, Paris, 1964. Co-author: Butterflies of Mississippi, 1958; Editor: Handbook for Concrete and Cement, 1942, 49, also quar. supplements, 1949—. Recipient Meritorious Civilian Svc. award, 1965, Exceptional Civilian Svc. award, 1968, with laurel-leaf cluster, 1991, Civilian of Yr. award C.E., 1992, Disting. Rsch. award Aggregates Found. for Tech., Rsch. and Engring., 1995. Fellow AAAS, ASTM (sec. com. C-9 1952-60, chmn. 1960-66, chmn. com. C-1 1968-74, chmn. com. E-39 1973-75, dir. 1970-73, v.p. 1973-75, pres. 1975-76, Award of Merit 1959, Sanford E. Thompson award 1961, Frank E. Richart award 1972, William T. Cavanaugh award 1990), Transp. Rsch. Bd., NAS-NRC (chmn. concrete divsn. 1963-69, chmn. curing com. 1970-76, hon. mem. concrete divsn. and concrete coms. 1987, Roy W. Crum Disting. Svc. award 1966, 2d Disting. Lectr. 1993), Inst. Concrete Technologists (Eng., hon. 1982); mem. NAE, ASCE (hon. mem. 1988), Entomol. Soc. Am., Am. Concrete Inst. (pres. 1964, Henry C. Turner medal 1973, Charles S. Whitney medal 1974, Robert E. Philleo award 1992, Delmar L. Bloem award 1990, hon. mem.), Entomol. Soc. Md., Mich. Entomol. Soc., Meteoritical Soc., Natural Hist. Soc. Md., Orleans County (Vt.) Hist. Soc., Lepidopterists Soc., Miss. Acad. Sci., Miss. Gem and Mineral Soc., Am. Mus. Natural History (hon. mem. 1968, hon. patron 1974), So. Lepidopterists Soc., Soc. Ky. Lepidopterists, Mining Metall. and Petroleum Engrs. (Legion of Honor), Mencken Soc., Phi Beta Kappa, Sigma Xi. Home: 213 Mount Salus Dr Clinton MS 39056-5007 Office: US Army Engr Waterways Expt Sta Structures Lab 3909 Halls Ferry Rd Vicksburg MS 39180-6133 *The production of hydraulic-cement concrete—a synthetic sedimentary rock, may be the human race's most successful attempt to reproduce an activity previously engaged in only by God; and we have done it better; there are more varieties and there is better uniformity.*

MATHER, ELIZABETH VIVIAN, health care executive; b. Richmond, Ind., Sept. 19, 1941; d. Willie Samuel and Lillie Mae (Harper) Fuqua; m. Roland Donald Mather, Dec. 26, 1966. BS, Maryville (Tenn.) Coll., 1963; postgrad., Columbia U., 1965-66. Tchr. Richmond Community Schs., 1963-67, Indpls. Pub. Schs., 1967-68; systems analyst Ind. Blue Cross Blue Shield, Indpls., 1968-71, Ind. Nat. Bank, Indpls., 1971; med. cons. Ind. State Dept. Pub. Welfare, Indpls., 1971-78, cons. supr., 1978-86; systems analyst Ky. Blue Cross Blue Shield, Louisville, 1988-89; contracts specialist Humana Corp., Louisville, 1989—. Active Rep. Cen. Com. Montgomery County, Crawfordsville, 1976-86, Centenary Meth. Ch., adminstrv. bd., 1990. Mem. DAR (treas. 1963-66, sec. 1978-86). Avocations: designing and sewing clothes. Home: 6106 Partridge Pl Floyds Knob IN 47119 Office: Humana Corp 500 W Main St Louisville KY 40201-1438

MATHER, JOHN CROMWELL, astrophysicist; b. Roanoke, Va., Aug. 7, 1946; s. Robert Eugene and Martha Belle (Cromwell) M.; m. Jane Anne Hauser, Nov. 22, 1980. BA, Swarthmore (Pa.) Coll., 1968; PhD, U. Calif., Berkeley, 1974; DSc (hon.), Swarthmore Coll., 1994. NAS/NRC rsch. assoc. NASA/Goddard Inst. for Space Studies, N.Y.C., 1974-76; lectr. in astronomy Columbia U., N.Y.C., 1975-76; astrophysicist NASA/Goddard Space Flight Ctr., Greenbelt, Md., 1976—, head infrared astrophysics br., 1988-89, 90-93, sr. scientist, 1989-90, 93—, study scientist Cosmic Background Explorer Satellite,, 1976-82, project scientist COBE, 1982—, prin. investigator FIRAS on COBE, 1976—; chmn. external adv. bd. Ctr. for Astrophys. Rsch. in the Antarctic, U. Chgo., 1992—; mem. lunar astrophysics mgmt. ops. working group NASA Hdqrs., Washington, 1992; study scientist Next Generation Space Telescope, 1995—. Contbr. over 50 articles to profl. jours. Recipient Nat. Space Achievement award Rotary, 1991, Laurels award Aviation Week and Space Tech., 1992, Space Sci. award AIAA, 1993, John Scott award City of Phila., 1995, Rumford prize Am. Acad. Arts and Scis., 1996; Goddard fellow, 1994—. Mem. Am. Astron. Soc. (Dannie Heineman prize astrophysics 1993), Am. Phys. Soc., Internat. Astron. Union, Sigma Xi. Democrat. Unitarian. Achievements include proposed Cosmic Background Explorer Satellite, led team to successful launch in 1989, measured spectrum of cosmic microwave background radiation to unprecedented accuracy. Office: NASA/Goddard Space Flight Code G85 Greenbelt MD 20771

MATHER, JOHN RUSSELL, climatologist, educator; b. Boston, Oct. 9, 1923; s. John and Mabelle (Russell) M.; m. Amy L. Nelson, 1946; children: Susan, Thomas, Ellen. BA, Williams Coll., 1945; BS in Meteorology, MIT, 1947, M.S., 1948; Ph.D. in Geography-Climatology, Johns Hopkins U.,

1951. Rsch. assoc., climatologist Lab. Climatology, Seabrook, N.J., 1948-54; prin. rsch. scientist Lab. Climatology, Centerton, N.J., 1954-63; pres. Lab. Climatology, C.W. Thornthwaite Assoc., Centerton, 1963-72; asst. prof. Johns Hopkins U., 1951-53; assoc. prof. climatology Drexel Inst. Tech., Phila., 1957-60; prof. geography U. Del., Newark, 1963—; chmn. dept. geography U. Del., 1966-89; state climatologist Del., 1978-92; vis. lectr. geography U. Chgo., 1957-61; vis. prof. U.S. Mil. Acad., 1989. Author 2 books on applied climatology, 1 book on water resources; co-author biography of C.W. Thornthwaite; U.S. editor joint U.S.-USSR book on global change; contbr. numerous articles to tech. jours. Fellow AAAS; mem. Am. Meteorol. Soc., Assn. Am. Geographers (v.p. 1990-91, pres. 1991-92), Am. Geog. Soc. (councilor 1981—, sec. 1982—), Am. Water Resources Assn., Tau Beta Pi, Phi Kappa Phi. Contributed to concept of potential evapotranspiration, its measurement, use in climatic water balance; moisture factor in climate; application of climatic water balance to studies in agr., hydrology, applied climatology. Home: 378 Daretown Rd Elmer NJ 08318-2728 Office: U Del Dept Geography Newark DE 19716

MATHER, MILDRED EUNICE, retired archivist; b. Washington, Iowa, July 25, 1922; d. Hollis John and Delpha Irene (Cummings) Whiting; m. Stewart Elbert Mather, Aug. 7, 1955; children: Julie Marie, Thomas Stewart (dec.). Cert. bus sch., Burlington and Des Moines (Iowa), 1941, 1947; cert., Stenotype Inst., 1948. Typist Burlington Willow-Weave, 1941-42, Burlington Basket Co., 1942; clk. typist U.S. Dept. War, Washington, 1942-43; supr. internat. conf. Dept. State, Washington, 1949-52; bookkeeper Iowa Wesleyan Coll., Mt. Pleasant, 1952-55; clk. typist Herbert Hoover Presdl. Libr., West Branch, Iowa, 1964-69; archives technician Herbert Hoover Presdl. Libr., West Branch, 1964-72, archivist, libr., 1972-92. WAC, 1943-46. Mem. Order of Eastern Star (worthy matron). Republican. Home: 79 Eisenhower St West Branch IA 52358-9403

MATHER, RICHARD BURROUGHS, retired Chinese language and literature educator; b. Baoding, Hebei, China, Nov. 11, 1913; s. William Arnot and Grace (Burroughs) M.; m. Virginia Marjorie Temple, June 3, 1939; 1 dau., Elizabeth Temple. B.A., Princeton U., 1935; B.Th., Princeton Theol. Sem., 1939; Ph.D. in Oriental Langs. U. Calif., Berkeley, 1949. Ordained to ministry United Presbyterian Ch. U.S., 1939; pastor Belle Haven (Va.) Presbyterian Ch., 1939-41; asst. prof. Chinese U. Minn., Mpls., 1949-57; assoc. prof. Chinese U. Minn., 1957-64, prof., 1964-84; mem. Am. Council Learned Socs. Com. on Study of Chinese Civilization, 1979-81. Author: Shih-shuo hsin-yu, A New Account of Tales of the World, 1976, The Poet Shen Yueh (441-513), the Reticent Marquis, 1988; contbr. articles on medieval Chinese lit. and religion. Guggenheim fellow, 1956-57; Fulbright Hays grantee, 1956-57, 63-64; Am. Council Learned Socs. grantee, 1963-64. Mem. Am. Oriental Soc. (pres. 1980-81), Assn. Asian Studies, Chinese Lang. Tchrs. Assn. Democrat. Home: 2091 Dudley Ave Saint Paul MN 55108-1415

MATHER, ROGER FREDERICK, music educator, freelance technical writer; b. London, England, May 27, 1917; came to U.S., 1938; s. Richard and Marie Louise (Schultze) M.; m. Dorothea Meinen, Sept. 11, 1943 (div. Sept. 1971); children: Arielle Diane, Christopher Richard; m. Betty Louise Bang, Aug. 3, 1973. BA with honors, Cambridge U., 1938; MSc, MIT, 1940; MA in Metallurgy, U. Cambridge, 1941. Registered profl. engr., Ohio, Mich., Pa. Rsch. metallurgist Inland Steel Co., East Chicago, Ind., 1940-42; chief metallurgist Willys-Overland Motors, Toledo, 1942-46, Kaiser-Frazer Corp., Willow Run, Mich., 1946-50; project mgr. U.S. Steel Corp., Pitts., 1950-61; dir. rsch. engring. Mine Safety Appliances Co., Pitts., 1961-62; rsch. staff Du Pont Co., Wilmington, Del., 1962-63; chief nuclear power tech. br. NASA, Cleve., 1963-73; adj. prof. music U. Iowa, Iowa City, 1973-96; instr. pub. speaking and stage fright U. Iowa, 1983-85, Kirkwood C.C., Iowa City, 1983-85; cons. Miyazawa Flutes, U.S.A., Coralville, Iowa, 1985-90; lectr. U. Toledo; Mich. state examiner Registration of Profl. Engrs.; condr. numerous workshops, clinics, classes, and flute recitals regionally, nationally, and abroad. Author: The Art of Playing the Flute, 1980, 2d vol., 1981; author chpts. in Woodwind Anthology and Fluting and Dancing; pub., exec. editor The Romney Press, 1980—; contbr. numerous articles to sci. and music jours. Mem. Nat. Flute Assn. (life, coms.), Nat. Assn. Coll. Wind and Percussion Instrs., Am. Mus. Instrument Soc., Nat. Assn. Mus. Instruments Techs., Am. Recorder Soc., Galpin Soc., Brit. Flute Soc., Soc. Automotive Engrs., AIME, Am. Soc. Metals, ASTM, ASME, AIAA, Soc. Experimental Stress Analysis, Air Force Assn., Army Ordnance Assn., NAM (rsch. com.), The Pa. Assn., Mensa. Episcopalian. Avocations: high fidelity sound reproduction, photography, poetry composition. Home: 308 4th Ave Iowa City IA 52245-4613 Office: U Iowa Sch Music Iowa City IA 52242

MATHER, ROLAND DONALD, administrative law judge; b. New Albany, Ind., Oct. 1, 1939; s. Howard Milton and Elizabeth Ann (Fisher) M.; m. Elizabeth Vivian Fuqua, Dec. 26, 1966. BS, Ind. State U., 1963; MA, Ball State U., 1967; JD, Ind. U., 1972; postgrad., Nat. Jud. Coll., 1977-92; grad., Ind. Jud. Coll., 1981. Bar: Ind. 1972, U.S. Dist. Ct. 1972. Tchr. Richmond (Ind.) Community Schs., 1963-67, Indpls. Pub. Schs., 1967-68; asst. dir. consumer protection div. Ind. Atty. Gen., Indpls., 1970-72, asst. atty. gen., dir. consumer protection div., 1972-75; county judge Montgomery County, Crawfordsville, Ind., 1976-84; U.S. adminstrv. law judge Office of Hearing and Appeals, Pitts., 1986-88, Louisville, 1988—. Mem. ABA, Ind. Bar Assn., Assn. Adminstrv. Law Judges. Republican. Methodist. Home: 6106 Partridge Pl Floyds Knobs IN 47119-9427 Office: Office Hearing Appeals 332 W Broadway St 1402 Louisville KY 40202-2119

MATHER, STEPHANIE J., lawyer; b. Kansas City, Mo., Dec. 5, 1952; d. Edward Wayne and H. June (Kunkel) M.; m. Miles Christopher Zimmerman, Sept. 23, 1988. BA magna cum laude, Okla. City U., 1975, JD with honors, 1980. Lawyer Pierce, Couch, Hendrickson, Johnston & Baysinger, Okla. City, Okla., 1980-88, Manchester, Hiltgen & Healy, P.C., Okla. City, 1989-90; sr. staff counsel Nat. Am. Ins. Co., Chandler, Okla., 1990—; asst. v.p. Lagere & Walkingstick Ins. Agy., Inc., Chandler, Okla., 1993—. Co-chair Lincoln County Dem. Party, 1991-92, 95—; v.p. Lincoln County Dem. Women, 1992-95, pres., 1995—; bd. dirs. Lincoln County Partnership for Chidlren, 1994—, Gateway to Prevention and Recovery, 1996—. Mem. Okla. Bar Assn. (editor, bd. editors 1992—), Lincoln County Bar Assn. (mem. libr. bd. 1990—), Lincoln County Profl. Women, Alpha Phi. Democrat. Avocations: reading, geneology, ranching, cooking. Home: PO Box 246 Chandler OK 74834-0246 Office: Nat Am Ins Co PO Box 9 Chandler OK 74834-0009

MATHERLEE, THOMAS RAY, health care consultant; b. Dayton, Ohio, Sept. 18, 1934; s. Dennis R. and Eleanor E. Matherlee; BS in Bus. Adminstrn. Findlay Coll., 1958; MBA, U. Chgo., 1960; m. Ann Deverka; children: Michael, Jennifer, Craig, Brent, Brian. Adminstrv. resident Shannon Hosp., San Angelo, Tex., 1959-60; asst. adminstr. Richland Meml. Hosp., Olney, Ill., 1960-61; adminstrv. asst., then adminstr. Forsyth Meml. Hosp., Winston-Salem, N.C., 1961-68; exec. dir. Gaston County (N.C.) Hosp., 1968-70; exec. dir. Gaston Meml. Hosp., Inc., Gastonia, 1970-80, pres., 1981-85; sr. v.p. Vol. Hosps. of Am. Inc., Washington, 1986-87, exec. v.p., Irving, Tex., 1987-90; pres. AMA Svcs., Inc., 1990-94; sr. v.p. The Hunter Group, 1994—; cons. Sch. Pastoral Care N.C. Bapt. Hosp., Winston-Salem, 1967-68; mem. sub-area adv. coun. Health Systems Agy., 1975-80; adj. faculty Sch. Community and Allied Health, U. Ala.-Birmingham, 1980-85; bd. dirs. Joint Commn. on Accreditation of Healthcare Orgns., 1994-98, treas., audit and fin. com. chmn., mem. exec. com. Dir. Olney Ill. CD, 1960-61; mem. fin. com. Piedmont coun. Boy Scouts Am., 1970; mem. adv. bd. Gastonia Wesleyan Youth Chorus, 1972; mem. joint com. nursing edn. N.C. State Bd. Edn. and Bd. Higher Edn., 1969-71; mem. adminstrv. bd. First United Meth. Ch., Gastonia, 1972-74; bd. dirs. Gaston County Heart Assn., 1968-70, Forsyth County Cancer Soc., 1964-65; trustee N.C. Hosp. Edn. and Research Found., 1966-71, pres., 1970-71; trustee N.C. Blue Cross and Blue Shield, Inc., 1971-77, Southeastern Hosp. Conf., 1971-72, 73-81, mem. edn. com., 1978—, mem. program com., 1975-76. Named Boss of Yr., Nat. Secs. Assn., 1970-71. Fellow Am. Coll. Healthcare Execs.; mem. MGMA, N.C. Hosp. Assn. (life; trustee 1966-72, pres. 1970-71, chmn. council govt. liaison 1978-81, Disting. Service award 1985), N.C. League Nursing, Am. Hosp. Assn. (ho. of dels. 1973-78, 83-85, speaker ho. of dels. 1985, trustee 1975-78, 83-85, chmn. bd. trustees 1984), Gastonia C. of C. (health affairs com. 1969-72). Lodge: Kiwanis. Contbr. articles on hosp. adminstrn. to profl. jours.

MATHERN, TIM, state senator, social worker; b. Edgeley, N.D., Apr. 19, 1950; s. John J. and Christina (Wolf) M.; m. Lorene Randall Mathern, Feb. 12, 1971; children: Rebecca, Tonya, Joshua, Zachary. BA, N.D. State U., 1971; MSW, U. Nebr., Omaha, 1980. Dir. of devel. Cath. Family Svc., Fargo, N.D., 1972—; mem. N.D. State Senate, Bismarck, 1986—, chmn. health and comms. com., 1993-95, mem. legis. mgmt. com., 1993—, asst. minority leader, 1993-95, 95—; mem. political subdivsn. com., N.D., 1995—. Mem. Fargo-Cass County Econ. Devel. Corp., 1993—, Nat. Family Life Ministries; asst. minority leader N.D. Senate, 1992—, Judicial Standards Com. Named Legislator of Yr., Red River Valley Mental Health Assn., 1989, 91, Legislator of Yr., N.D. Children's Caucus, 1993. Mem. NASW (Social Worker of Yr. award 1987), Mental Health Assn. Democrat. Roman Catholic. Home: 406 Elmwood Fargo ND 58103-4315 Office: 2537 S University Fargo ND 58103-5736

MATHERS, THOMAS NESBIT, financial consultant; b. Bloomington, Ind., Apr. 22, 1914; s. Frank Curry and Maud Esther (Bowser) M.; m. Helen M. Curtis, Oct. 23, 1943 (dec.); children: Mary, Abigail. A.B., Ind. U., 1936, LL.B., 1939; M.B.A., Harvard U., 1941. Bar: Ind. 1939. Research asst. No. Trust Co., 1941-43; legal asst. Chgo. Ordnance Dist., 1943-44; employee to ptnr. Woodruff Hays & Co., Chgo., 1944-51; pres. Security Counselors, Inc., Chgo., 1951-62; pres. Mathers & Co., Chgo., 1962-75, chmn. bd., 1975-85, vice chmn., 1985-91; bd. dirs. Lincoln Income Fund, 1978—, Lincoln Convertible Securities Fund, 1986—; pres. Mathers Fund, 1965-75, chmn. bd., 1975-85, vice chmn., 1985-91; v.p., bd. dirs. OFC Corp. Meadowood Project, 1991—. Trustee Beloit Coll., 1970—. Recipient Disting. Alumni Service award Ind. U., 1979. Mem. Ind. U. Disting. Alumni Assn. (past pres.). Republican. Presbyterian. Clubs: Union League, Econ. of Chgo, Westmoreland Country, Mich. Shores, Investment Analysts Chgo. (past pres.). Home: 115 Bertling Ln Winnetka IL 60093-4202

MATHERS, WILLIAM HARRIS, lawyer; b. Newport, R.I., Aug. 27, 1914; s. Howard and Margaret I. (Harris) M.; m. Myra T. Martin, Jan. 17, 1942; children: William Martin, Michael Harris, John Grinnell, Myra Tutt, Ursula Fraser. A.B., Dartmouth Coll., 1935; J.D., Yale U., 1938. Bar: N.Y. 1940. With Milbank, Tweed & Hope, 1938-48; mem. Milbank, Tweed, Hope & Hadley, 1948-57; v.p., sec., dir. Yale & Towne Mfg. Co., Stamford, Conn., 1957-60; ptnr. Chadbourne & Parke, 1960-75, counsel, 1983—; exec. v.p., gen. counsel, sec., dir. United Brands Co., 1975-82. Mayor, trustee Village of Cove Neck, N.Y., 1950-82; trustee Barnard Coll., 1958-69. Served as pvt. to maj. U.S. Army, 1942-46. Mem. ABA, N.Y. State Bar Assn., Nassau County Bar Assn., Assn. of Bar of City of N.Y., New Eng. Soc. in City of N.Y., Casque and Gauntlet, Corbey Court, Piping Rock Club, Seminole Golf Club, N.Y. Yacht Club, Cold Spring Harbor Beach Club, Phi Beta Kappa, Psi Upsilon. Home: Gordon Farm RR 1 Box 83 Sutton VT 05867-9721 Office: 30 Rockefeller Plz New York NY 10112

MATHES, STEPHEN JOHN, plastic and reconstructive surgeon, educator; b. New Orleans, Aug. 17, 1943; s. John Ernest and Norma (Deutsch) M.; m. Jennifer Tandy Woodbridge, Nov. 26, 1966; children: David, Brian, Edward. BS, La. State U., 1964; MD, La. State U., New Orleans, 1968. Diplomate Am. Bd. Surgery, Am. Bd. Plastic Surgery (dir. 1993—). Asst. prof. surgery Wash. U., St. Louis, 1977-78; assoc. prof. U. Calif., San Francisco, 1978-84, prof. surgery, 1984, prof. surgery, anatomy and cell biology, 1984-85, also bd. dirs. craniofacial anomalies; head plastic surgery sect. U. Mich., Ann Arbor, 1984-85, prof. surgery, 1984-85; prof. surgery, head plastic and reconstructive surgery div. U. Calif., San Francisco, 1985—. Author: (textbook) Clinical Applications for Muscle and Musculocutaneous Flaps, 1983 (Best Med. Book award Physician's category, Am. Med. Writer's Assn., 1983); contbr. articles to profl. jours. Recipient 1st prize plastic surgery scholarship contest, Plastic Surgery Edn. Found., 1981, 83, 84, 86; grantee NIH, 1982-85, 86—. Fellow ACS; mem. Am. Assn. Plastic Surgery, Plastic Surgery Research Council (pres.-elect 1986), Am. Soc. Surgery of Hand, Soc. Univ. Surgeons. Republican. Episcopalian. Avocations: gardening, tennis. Home: 30 Trophy Ct Burlingame CA 94010-7434 Office: U Calif San Francisco Dept Surgery San Francisco CA 94143-0932

MATHES, STEPHEN JON, lawyer; b. N.Y.C., Mar. 18, 1945; s. Joseph and Beatrice M.; m. Michele Marshall, Oct. 22, 1972 (div. 1992); children: Aaron, Benjamin; m. Maria McGarry, Dec. 19, 1992. BA, U. Pa., 1967, JD, 1970. Bar: N.Y. 1971, Pa. 1972, U.S. Dist. Ct. (ea. dist.) Pa. 1971, U.S. Ct. Appeals (3d cir.) 1972, U.S. Ct. Appeals (5th cir.) 1985, U.S. Ct. Appeals (4th cir.) 1985, U.S. Supreme Ct. 1978. Law clk. U.S. Ct. Appeals (3d cir.), Phila., 1970-71; asst. dist. atty. Office of Phil. Dist. Atty., Phila., 1975; assoc. Dilworth, Paxson, Kalish & Kauffman, Phila., 1971-74, 76-77, sr. ptnr., 1977-91, mem. exec. com., 1987-90, co-chmn. litigation dept., 1987-91; ptnr., mem. mng. com. Hoyle, Morris & Kerr, Phila., 1992—; bd. dirs. The Levitt Found., 1990—, sec., 1991—. Bd. dirs. Acad. Vocal Arts, 1993—. Mem. ABA, Pa. Bar Assn., Phila. Bar Assn. (arbitrator), Thanatopsis Soc., Racquet Club, Germantown Cricket Club. Home: 199 Lynnebrook Ln Philadelphia PA 19118-2706 Office: Holye Morris & Kerr One Liberty Pl Ste 4900 Philadelphia PA 19103

MATHESIUS, MICHELLE, performance company executive. Dir. dance N.Y.C. H.S. for Performing Arts; founding artistic dir. Denishawn Repertory Dancers. Mem. N.J. State Arts Coun.

MATHESON, ALAN ADAMS, law educator; b. Cedar City, Utah, Feb. 2, 1932; s. Scott Milne and Adele (Adams) M.; m. Milicent Holbrook, Aug. 15, 1960; children—Alan, David Scott, John Robert. B.A., U. Utah, 1953, M.S., 1957, J.D., 1959; postgrad. asso. in law, Columbia U. Bar: Utah 1960, Ariz. 1975. Asst. to pres. Utah State U., 1961-67; mem. faculty Ariz. State U., Tempe, 1967—; prof. law Ariz. State U., 1970—, dean, 1978-84; bd. dirs. Ariz. Center Law in Public Interest, 1979-81; bd. dirs. DNA Navajo Legal Services, 1984—. Pres. Tri-City Mental Health Citizens Bd., 1973-74. Served with AUS, 1953-55. Mem. Utah Bar Assn., Ariz. Bar Assn., Maricopa County Bar Assn., Phi Beta Kappa, Order of Coif. Democrat. Mormon. Home: 720 E Geneva Dr Tempe AZ 85282-3737 Office: Coll Law Ariz State U Tempe AZ 85287

MATHESON, KENT D., school system administrator. Supt. Highline Sch. Dist. 401, Seattle. Named state finalist Nat. Supt. of Yr. award, 1992. Office: Highline Sch Dist 401 15675 Ambaum Blvd SW Seattle WA 98166-2523

MATHESON, NINA W., medical researcher. Prof., dir. William H. Welch Med. Libr., Balt., 1985-94; prof. emeritus Jouns Hopkins U., Balt., 1994—. Named Disting. prof. nursing Vanderbilt Sch. Nursing, 1976-82. Office: John Hopkins Univ William H. Welch Medical Libr 720 Rutland Ave Baltimore MD 21205-2109*

MATHESON, WILLIAM LYON, lawyer, farmer; b. Coeburn, Va., Dec. 5, 1924; s. Julius Daniel and Ruth Steele Lyon M.; m. Katrina B. Hickox; children: Katherine, William Lyon, Alline, Thornton; m. Marjorie H. Anderson, Nov. 26, 1977. Student, Emory U., 1946-47; AB, Mercer U., 1944; LLB, U. Va., 1950. Bar: N.Y. 1951. Assoc. firm Patterson, Belknap & Webb, N.Y.C., 1950-57; assoc. Wertheim & Co. (investments), N.Y.C., 1957-58; ptnr. Webster & Sheffield, N.Y.C., 1959-65; pvt. practice N.Y.C., 1965-92; chmn. bd. Mich. Energy Resources Co., Monroe, 1959-89, Mercom Inc. (cable TV), 1984-91. Bd. dirs. Madison Sq. Boys' Club, N.Y.C., 1958-76, assoc. mem. bd. dirs., 1977-91; trustee Police Athletic League, N.Y.C., 1962—. Served to lt. (j.g.) USN, 1942-46. Mem. Links Club (N.Y.C.), Piping Rock Club (Locust Valley, N.Y.), Meadow Brook Club (Jericho, N.Y.), Seminole Golf (North Palm Beach, Fla.), Island Club (Hobe Sound, Fla.). Democrat. Home: 430 S Beach Rd Hobe Sound FL 33455-2702 also: Sunset Hill Heather Ln Mill Neck NY 11765

MATHEU, FEDERICO MANUEL, university chancellor; b. Humacao, P.R., Mar. 17, 1941; s. Federico Matheu-Baez and Matilde Delgado-Vazquez; m. Myrna Delgado-Miranda, May 30, 1963; children: Federico Antonio, Rosa Myrna, Alfredo Javier, David Reinaldo. B.S. in Chem. Engring, U. P.R., 1962; Ph.D. in Phys. Chemistry, U. Pitts., 1971. Chem. engr. Commonwealth Oil Refining Co., 1962-63; mem. adminstrv. staff and faculty U. P.R., 1963-78, dir. Humacao Coll., 1976-78; chancellor San German campus Inter Am. U. P.R., 1978-91; exec. dir., gen. coun. on edn. Commonwealth of P.R., Hato Rey, 1991—; cons. in field. Author papers, reports in field. Named Disting. Educator P.R. Jaycees, 1974. Mem. Colegio de Quimicos P.R., Am. Chem. Soc., Sci. Tchrs. Assn. P.R. (pres. 1975-76), P.R. Acad. Arts and Scis., Phi Delta Kappa, Phi Tau Sigma. Home: Parque de Villa Caparra Zuania St G-4 Guaynabo PR 00966 Office: Gen Coun on Edn PO Box 5429 San Juan PR 00906-5429

MATHEWS, ANNE JONES, consultant, library educator and administrator; b. Phila.; d. Edmond Fulton and Anne Ruth (Reichner) Jones; m. Frank Samuel Mathews, June 16, 1951; children: Lisa Anne Mathews-Bingham, David Morgan, Lynne Elizabeth Bietenhader-Mathews, Alison Fulton Sawyer. AB, Wheaton Coll., 1949; MA, U. Denver, 1965, PhD, 1977. Mem. field staff Intervarsity Christian Fellowship, Chgo., 1949-51; interviewer supr. Colo. Market Rsch. Svcs., Denver, 1952-64; reference libr. Oreg. State U., Corvallis, 1965-67; program dir. Ctrl. Colo. Libr. Sys., Denver, 1969-70; inst. dir. U.S. Office of Edn., Inst. Grant, 1979; dir. pub. rels. Grad. Sch. Librarianship and Info. Mgmt. U. Denver, 1970-76, dir. continuing edn., 1977-80, assoc. prof., 1977-79, prof., 1979-85; dir. Office Libr. Programs, Office Ednl. Rsch., Improvement U.S. Dept. Edn., Washington, 1986-91; dir. Nat. Libr. Edn., Washington, 1992-94; cons. Acad. Ednl. Devel., Washington, 1994—; vis. lectr. Simmons Coll. Sch. Libr. Sci., Boston, 1977; cons. USIA, 1984-85, mem. book and libr. adv. com., 1981-91; faculty assoc. Danforth Found., 1974-84; speaker in field; mem. secondary sch. curriculum com. Jefferson County Pub. Schs., Colo., 1976-78; mem. adv. com. Golden H.S., 1973-77; mem. adv. coun. White House Conf. on Librs. and Info. Svcs., 1991; del. Internat. Fedn. Libr. Assn., 1984-93. Author, editor 6 books; contbr. articles to profl. jours., numerous chpts. to books. Mem. rural librs. and humanities program Colo. planning and resource bd. NEH, 1982-83; bd. mgrs. Friends Found. of Denver Pub. Libr., 1976-82; pres. Faculty Women's Club, Colo. Sch. Mines, 1963-64. Mem. ALA (visionary leaders com. 1987-89, coun. mem. 1979-83, com on accreditation 1984-85, orientation com. 1974-77, 83-84, pub. rels. com.), Am. Soc. Info. Sci. (pub. rels. chmn. 1971), Mountain Plains Libr. Assn. (profl. devel. com. 1979-80, pub. rels. and publs. com. 1973-75, continuing edn. com. 1973-76), Colo. Libr. Assn. (pres. 1974, bd. dirs. 1973-75, continuing edn. com. 1976-80), Assn. Libr. & Info. Sci. Edn. (communication com. 1978-80, program com. 1977-78), Cosmos Club (Washington). Avocations: travel, reading, antique collecting, mus. & gallery activities. Home: 492 Mount Evans Rd Golden CO 80401-9626

MATHEWS, BARBARA EDITH, gynecologist; b. Santa Barbara, Calif., Oct. 5, 1946; d. Joseph Chesley and Pearl (Cieri) Mathews; AB, U. Calif., 1969; MD, Tufts U., 1972. Diplomate Am. Bd. Ob-Gyn. Intern, Cottage Hosp., Santa Barbara, 1972-73, Santa Barbara Gen. Hosp., 1972-73; resident in ob-gyn Beth Israel Hosp., Boston, 1973-77; clin. fellow in ob-gyn Harvard U., 1973-76, instr., 1976-77; gynecologist Sansum Med. Clinic, Santa Barbara, 1977—; faculty mem. ann. postgrad. course Harvard Med. Sch.; bd. dirs. Sansum Med. Clinic, vice chmn. bd. dirs., 1994-96; dir. ann. postgrad course UCLA Med. Sch. Bd. dirs. Meml. Rehab. Found., Santa Barbara, Channel City Club, Santa Barbara, Music Acad. of the West, Santa Barbara; mem. citizen's continuing edn. adv. council Santa Barbara C.C.; moderator Santa Barbara Cottage Hosp. Cmty. Health Forum. Fellow ACS, Am. Coll. Ob-gyn.; mem. AMA, Am. Soc. Colposcopy and Cervical Pathology (dir. 1982-84), Harvard U. Alumni Assn., Tri-counties Obstet. and Gynecol. Soc. (pres. 1981-82), Phi Beta Kappa. Clubs: Birnam Wood Golf (Santa Barbara). Author: (with L. Burke) Colposcopy in Clinical Practice, 1977; contbg. author Manual of Ambulatory Surgery, 1982. Home: 2105 Anacapa St Santa Barbara CA 93105-3503 Office: 317 W Pueblo St Santa Barbara CA 93105-4355

MATHEWS, DAVID, foundation executive; b. Grove Hill, Ala., Dec. 6, 1935; s. Forrest Lee and Doris (Pearson) M.; m. Mary Chapman, Jan. 24, 1960; children: Lee Ann Mathews Hester, Lucy Mathews Heegaard. A.B., U. Ala., 1958; Ph.D., Columbia U., 1965; LL.D., U. Ala., 1969, Mercer U., 1976; L.H.D., William and Mary Coll., 1976, Med. U. S.C., 1976, Samford U., 1978, Transylvania U., 1978, Stillman Coll., 1980, Miami U., 1982; H.H.D., Birmingham-So. Coll., 1976, Wash. U., St. Louis, 1984; L.H.D., Ctr. Coll., 1985; L.L.D., Ohio Wesleyan U., 1987, Lynchburg Coll., 1987; L.H.D., U. New Eng., 1988. Exec. v.p. U. Ala., 1968-69, pres., 1969-80, prof. history, 1977-81; pres., chief exec. officer Charles F. Kettering Found., Dayton, Ohio, 1981—; sec. HEW, Washington, 1975-77; dir. Birmingham br. Fed. Res. Bank of Atlanta, 1970-72, chmn., 1973-75; mem. council SRI Internat., 1978-85; chmn. Council Public Policy Edn., 1980—. Contbr. articles to profl. jours. Trustee Judson Coll., 1968-75, Am. Univs. Field Staff, 1969-80; bd. dirs. Birmingham Festival of Arts Assn., Inc., 1969-75; mem. Nat. Programming Council for Public TV, 1970-73, So. Regional Edn. Bd., 1969-75, Ala. Council on Humanities, 1973-75; vice chmn. Commn. on Future of South, 1974; mem. So. Growth Policies Bd., 1974-75; mem. nat. adv. council Am. Revolution Bicentennial Adminstrn., 1975; mem. Ala. State Oil and Gas Bd., 1975, 77-79; bd. dirs. Acad. Ednl. Devel., 1975—, Ind. Sector, 1982-88, ; chmn. Pres.'s Com. on Mental Retardation, 1975-77; chmn. income security com. aging com. Health Ins. Com. of Domestic Council, 1975-77; bd. govs. nat. ARC, 1975-77; bd. govs., bd. visitors Washington Coll., 1982-86 ; trustee John F. Kennedy Center for Performing Arts, 1975-77, Woodrow Wilson Internat. Center for Scholars, 1975-77; fed. trustee Fed. City Council, 1975-77; bd. dirs. A Presdl. Classroom for Young Americans, Inc., 1975-76; trustee Tchrs. Coll., Columbia U., 1977—, Nat. Found. March of Dimes, 1977-83, Coun. om Learning, 1977-84, Miles Coll., 1978—; mem. nat. adv. bd. Nat. Inst. on Mgmt. Lifelong Edn., 1979-84; mem. Ala. 2000, 1980—; spl. adviser Aspen Inst., 1980-84; mem. bd. trustees Gerald R. Ford Found., 1988—, bd. visitors Mershon Ctr. Ohio State U., 1988-91. Served with U.S. Army, 1959-60. Recipient Nicholas Murray Butler medal Columbia U., 1976, Ala. Adminstr. of Year award Am. Assn. Univ. Adminstrs., 1976, Educator of Year award Ala. Conf. Black Mayors, 1977, Brotherhood award NCCJ, 1979. Mem. Newcomen Soc. Am., Phi Beta Kappa, Phi Alpha Theta, Omicron Delta Kappa, Delta Theta Phi. Home: 6050 Mad River Rd Dayton OH 45459-1508 Office: Charles F Kettering Found 200 Commons Rd Dayton OH 45459-2788*

MATHEWS, EDWARD HENRY, engineering educator; b. Lichtenburg, Western Transvaal, South Africa, Apr. 12, 1957; s. Edward Henry and Wilhelmina Hendrika (Kemp) M.; m. Cornelia Zwarts, Oct. 2, 1982; children: George Edward, Marc John, Ian. BEng with honors, U. Stellenbosch, South Africa, 1981, MEng, 1983; DEng, Potchefstroom U., South Africa, 1985. Registered profl. engr. Sr. rschr Nat. Inst. for Aeros. and Sys. Tech., Coun. for Sci. and Indsl. Rsch, Pretoria, South Africa, 1982; chief rschr. Nat. Bldg. Rsch. Inst. Coun. for Sci. and Indsl. Rsch, Pretoria, 1982-85; asst. prof. U. Pretoria, 1986-88, prof., 1988—; chmn. Transfer Energy Momentum and Mass, Internat. (Pty.) Ltd., Pretoria, 1991—; head Ctr. for Exptl. and Numerical Thermoflow, Pretoria, 1988. Contbr. articles to profl. jours. Recipient Austin Whiller award South African Solar Energy Soc., 1987, 89, energy efficiency design award Electricity Supply Commn., 1991, President's award Found. for Rsch. Devel., 1992. Mem. ASHRAE, South African Inst. for Aeronautical Engring. (coun. 1981-93, Best Project award 1981), South African Inst. for Aerospace Engring. Avocations: reading, jogging, paper airplane designs. Office: U Pretoria Dept Mech & Aeronautical Engring, Lynnwood Rd, Pretoria Transvaal 0002, South Africa

MATHEWS, HARRY BURCHELL, poet, novelist, educator; b. N.Y.C., Feb. 14, 1930; s. Edward James and Mary (Burchell) M.; m. Niki de Saint Phalle, June 6, 1949 (div. 1964); 2 children; m. Marie Chaix, July 29, 1992. BA cum laude, Harvard Coll., 1952. Faculty Bennington (Vt.) Coll., 1978-80; vis. lectr. Hamilton Coll., Clinton, N.Y., 1979, Columbia U., N.Y.C., 1982-83; vis. writer Brown U., Providence, R.I., 1988, Temple U., Phila., 1990, Magdalene Coll., Cambridge, U.K., 1992; founding dir. Shakespeare & Co., Lenox, Mass.; lectr. in field, nat., internat. colls, art ctrs., instns. Author: The Conversions, 1962, Tlooth, 1964, The Sinking of the Odradek Stadium, 1975, Country Cooking and Other Stories, 1980, Cigarettes, 1987, 20 Lines A Day, 1988, The Orchard, 1988, The Way Home, 1988,, The American Experience, 1991, Singular Pleasures, 1993, The Journalist, 1994; (poetry) The Ring, Poems 1956-69, 1970, The Planisphere, 1974, Trial Impressions, 1977, Selected Declarations of Dependence, 1977, Armenian Papers: Poems 1954-84, 1987, Out of Bounds, 1989, A Mid-Season Sky: Poems 1954-89, 1991, (in French) Le savoir des rois: poèmes à perverbes, 1976, Ecrits français, 1990; (essays) Immeasurable Distances: The Collected Essays, 1981; trans.: A Man in a Dream (Georges Perec) 1975, The Laurels of Lake Constance (Marie Chaix) 1977, The Life: Memoirs of a

French Hooker (Jeanne Cordelier), 1978, Blue of Noon (Georges Bataille), 1978, Chronicles of Ellis Island (Georges Perec) 1981, The Dust of Suns (Raymond Roussel) 1991, various jour. articles; pub., co-editor Locus Solus, 1960-62; Paris editor The Paris Review, 1989—; contbr. poems, stories to anthologies, articles, criticisms, reviews to profl. jours. Recipient award Fiction Writing Am. Acad. Inst. Arts and Letters, N.Y., 1991; grantee Deutsche Akademische Austausch Dienst, Berlin, 1991; fiction writing grantee NEA, 1982. Mem. Ouvroir de Littérature Potentielle (Paris). Avocations: music making, back-country skiing, hiking, cooking.

MATHEWS, JACK WAYNE, journalist, film critic; b. L.A., Dec. 2, 1939; s. Walter Edwin and Dorothy Helen (Friley) M.; m. Lucinda Lucille Herbert, Nov. 5, 1971; children: Darren Brady, Shelby Kay. BA, San Jose (Calif.) State Coll., 1965; MS, UCLA, 1966. Reporter Riverside (Calif.) Press, 1967-69; mktg. exec. Riverside Raceway, 1969-75; columnist, editor Rochester (N.Y.) Democrat & Chronicle, 1975-78; columnist, film critic Detroit Free Press, 1978-82, USA Today, L.A., 1982-85; columnist L.A. Times, 1985-89, film editor, 1989-91; film critic Newsday, L.I., 1991—; co-host Cinema, PBS, 1995—; juror Montreal World Film Festival, 1993. Author: The Battle of Brazil, 1987. Mem. N.Y. Film Critics Cir. Democrat. Office: NY Newsday 2 Park Ave New York NY 10016-5603 also: Newsday Inc 235 Pinelawn Rd Melville NY 11747-4226

MATHEWS, JESSICA TUCHMAN, policy researcher, columnist; b. N.Y.C., July 4, 1946; d. Lester Reginald and Barbara (Wertheim) Tuchman; m. Colin D. Mathews, Feb. 25, 1978; children: Oliver Max Tuchman, Jordan Henry Morgenthau; stepchildren: Zachary Chase, Hilary Dustin. AB magna cum laude, Radcliffe Coll., 1967; PhD, Calif. Inst. Tech., 1973. Congrl. sci. fellow AAAS, 1973-74; profl. staff mem. Ho. Interior Com. on Energy and Environment, Washington, 1974-75; dir. issues and rsch. Udall Presdl. campaign, 1975-76; dir. Office of Global Issues NSC staff, Washington, 1977-79; mem. editorial bd. The Washington Post, 1980-82; v.p., dir. rsch. The World Resources Inst., Washington, 1982-92; dep. to undersec. for global affairs U.S. Dept. State, Washington, 1993; sr. fellow Coun. on Fgn. Rels., Washington, 1993—; columnist Washington Post, 1991—; mem. numerous adv. panels Office Tech. Assessment, NAS, AAAS, EPA; bd. dirs. Population Ref. Bur., Washington, 1988-93; adv. com. Air Products Corp. Bd. dirs., Joyce Found., Chgo., 1984-91, Inter-Am. Dialogue, 1991—, Radcliffe Coll., 1992—, Carnegie Endowment for Internat. Peace, Washington, 1992—, Rockefeller Bros Fund, N.Y.C., 1992—, Brookings Instn., Washington, 1995—, Surface Transportation Policy Project. Named Disting. fellow Aspen Inst. Mem. Coun. Fgn. Rels., Fedn. Am. Scientists (bd. dirs. 1985-87, 88-92, trilateral commn.), Inst. for Internat. Econs. (adv. com.). Democrat. Jewish. Office: Council on Fgn Relations 2400 N St NW Washington DC 20037-1153

MATHEWS, JOHN DAVID, electrical engineering educator, research director, consultant; b. Kenton, Ohio, Apr. 3, 1947; s. John Joseph and Mary (Long) M.; m. Monica Susan Mathews; children: John Todd, Debra Juanita, Alex David. BS in Physics with honors, Case Western Res. U., 1969, MS in Elec. Engring. and Applied Physics, 1972, PhD in Elec. Engring. and Applied Physics, 1972. Lectr. dept. elec. engring. and applied physics Case Western Res. U., Cleve., 1969-72, asst. prof., 1975-79, assoc. prof., 1979-85, prof., 1985-87; prof. dept. elec. engring. Pa. State U., University Park, 1987—, dir. Communications and Space Scis. Lab. Coll. Engring., 1988-94; dir. Comm. & Space Scis. Lab. Ctr. of Excellence, Coll. Engring., University Park, Pa., 1994—; vis. scientist Nat. Astronomy and Ionosphere Ctr., Case Western Res. U., Arecibo, P.R., 1972-75; adj. asst. prof. dept. elec. engring. Pa. State U., 1978-86, dir. artist-in-residence program Coll. Engring., 1990-92; mem. Arecibo adv. bd. and visiting com. Cornell U., 1989-92, chmn., 1991-92; cons. to engring. svc. group and laser engring. group Lawrence Livermore Nat. Labs., 1979-87; cons. Nat. Astronomy and Ionosphere Ctr. Arecibo Obs., 1980—; cons. engr., 1975—; presenter, speaker numerous profl. meetings. Contbr. articles to profl. jours. including Jour. Atmos. Terr. Physics, Jour. Geophys. Rsch., Radio Sci., Leonardo, Icarus, and others. Fulbright scholar, Sweden, 1996-97. Achievements include research on observations of narrow sodium and narrow ionization layers using both lidar and incoherent scatter radar techniqes, on tides and acoustic-gravity waves as observed in the motions of ionospheric E region meteoric ion layers, on electron concentration configurations during geomagnetic storms, and on detection and correction of coherent interference in incoherent scatter radar data processing, UHF radar meteor observations, and meteor physics. Office: Pa State U Communications & Space Scis Lab 316 Electrical Engineering E University Park PA 16802-2707

MATHEWS, KENNETH PINE, physician, educator; b. Schenectady, N.Y., Apr. 1, 1921; s. Raymond and Marguerite Elizabeth (Pine) M.; m. Alice Jean Elliott, Jan. 26, 1952 (dec.); children: Susan Kay, Ronald Elliott, Robert Pine; m. Winona Beatrice Rosenburg, Nov. 8, 1975. A.B., U. Mich., 1941, M.D., 1943. Diplomate Am. Bd. Internal Medicine, Am. Bd. Allergy and Immunology (past. sec.). Intern, asst. resident, resident in medicine Univ. Hosp., Ann Arbor, Mich., 1943-45, 48-50; mem. faculty dept. medicine med. sch. U. Mich., 1950—, assoc. prof. internal medicine, 1956-61, prof., 1961-86, prof. emeritus, 1986—, head div. allergy, 1967-83; adj. mem. Scripps Clinic and Research Found., La Jolla, Calif., 1986—; past chmn. residency rev. com. for allergy and immunology, past chmn. allergy and immunology rsch. com. NIH. Co-author: A Manual of Clinical Allergy, 2d edit, 1967; editor: Jour. Allergy and Clin. Immunology, 1968-72; contbr. numerous articles in field to profl. jours. Served to capt. M.C. AUS, 1946-48. Recipient Disting. Service award Am. Acad. Allergy, 1976; Faculty Disting. Achievement award U. Mich., 1984. Fellow Am. Acad. Allergy (past pres.), A.C.P. (emeritus); mem. Am. Assn. Immunologists (emeritus), Ctrl. Soc. Clin. Rsch. (emeritus), Am. Fedn. Clin. Rsch., Alpha Omega Alpha, Phi Beta Kappa. Home: 7080 Caminito Estrada La Jolla CA 92037-5714

MATHEWS, LINDA MCVEIGH, newspaper editor; b. Redlands, Calif., Mar. 14, 1946; d. Glenard Ralph and Edith Lorene (Humphrey) McVeigh; m. Thomas Jay Mathews, June 15, 1967; children—Joseph, Peter, Katherine. B.A., Radcliffe Coll., 1967; J.D., Harvard U., 1972. Gen. assignment reporter Los Angeles Times, 1967-69, Supreme Ct. corr., 1972-76, corr., Hong Kong, 1977-79, China corr., Peking, 1979-80, op-ed page editor, 1980-81, dep. nat. editor, 1981-84, dep. fgn. editor, 1985-88, editorial writer, 1988-89, editor L.A. Times mag., 1989-92; sr. producer ABC News, 1992-93; nat. editor N.Y. Times, 1993—; corr. Wall St. Jour., Hong Kong, 1976-77; lectr.; freelance writer. Author: (with others) Journey Into China, 1982; One Billion: A China Chronicle, 1983. Mem. Women's Legal Def. Fund, 1972-76; co-founder, pres. Hong Kong Montessori Sch., 1977-79; bd. dirs. Ctr. for Childhood. Mem. Fgn. Corrs. Club Hong Kong. Office: NY Times 229 W 43rd St New York NY 10036-3913

MATHEWS, MICHAEL STONE, investment banker; b. Ohio, Oct. 23, 1940; s. Robert Green and Dallas Victoria (Stone) M.; m. Cecilia Aall, May 13, 1967; children: Brandon, Mark, Alexander. AB, Princeton U., 1962; JD, U. Mich., 1965. Bar: N.Y. 1966. Assoc. White & Case, N.Y.C., 1965-69; v.p. Smith Barney Harris Upham & Co., N.Y.C., 1969-77; sr. v.p. Scandinavian Securities Corp., N.Y.C., 1977-79; sr. v.p. DNC Am. Banking Corp., N.Y.C., 1979-89; pres. DNC Capital Corp., 1986-89; ptnr. Bradford Assocs., 1989-92; mng. dir. Westgate Capital Co., 1993—; bd. dirs. Petroleum Geo-Svcs., Holo Pak Technols., Inc. Mem. Coun. Fgn. Rels., Univ. Club, Nassau Club, Pretty Brook Tennis Club. Home: 193 Elm Rd Princeton NJ 08540-2520 Office: 41 E 57th St New York NY 10022-1908

MATHEWS, PAUL JOSEPH, allied health educator; b. Washington, Aug. 17, 1944; s. Paul Joseph and Ruth Irene (O'Malley) M.; m. Loretta Jeanne Calvo; children: Heather Marie, Amy Elizabeth, Timothy Hunter. AS, Quinnipiac Coll., 1971, BS, 1975; MPA, U. Hartford, 1978; EdS, U. Mo., Kansas City, 1989. Registered respiratory therapist; lic. respiratory therapist, Kans. Instr., clin. coord. New Britain (Conn.) Gen. Hosp., 1971-74; instr. Quinnipiac Coll., Hamden, Conn., 1974-76; chief respiratory therapy dept. Providence Hosp., Holyoke, Mass., 1974-80, dir. cardiology/neurology, 1977-80, asst. dir. planning, 1980-81; asst. prof. U. Kans. Sch. Allied Health, Kansas City, 1981-88, assoc. prof. respiratory care edn., 1988—, chmn. dept. respiratory care edn., 1981-93, assoc. prof. phys. therapy Grad. Sch., 1992—; U. Kans.; adj. assoc. prof. Ctr. on Aging U. Kans. Med. Ctr., 1987—; hon. prof. U. Costa Rica, San Jose, 1987—; cons. FDA, 1988, NIH, 1988, 89, SUNY, Stony Brook, 1990, USPHS, 1994, 95. Mem. editl. bd. Nursing, 1989—, Neonatal Intensive Care, 1990, Jour. Respiratory Care Edn., 1993—, Respiratory Therapy, 1988, Respiratory Therapy Intern, 1991; author audio tapes in field; contbr. articles to profl. jours., chpts. to books. Recipient Creative Achievement award Puritan-Bennett Corp., 1984, 85, A. Gerald Shapiro award N.J. Soc. for Respiratory Care, 1990; internat. fellow Project HOPE, 1987, 92. Mem. Am. Assn. Respiratory Care (bd. dirs. 1984-87, v.p. 1987, pres.-elect 1988, pres. 1989), Am. Coll. Chest Physicians, Sigma Xi, Lambda Beta, Phi Lambda Theta. Avocations: scuba diving, reading, travel. Home: 8844 Hemlock Dr Overland Park KS 66212-2946 Office: U Kans 39th and Rainbow Blvd Kansas City KS 66103

MATHEWS, ROBERT C.H., state agency executive. Chmn. Metro. Nashville Airport Auth. Office: Metro Nashville Airport Authority 1 Terminal Dr Ste 501 Nashville TN 37214-4114*

MATHEWS, RODERICK BELL, lawyer; b. Lawton, Okla., Mar. 12, 1941; s. James Malcolm and Sallie Lee (Bell) M.; m. Karla Kurbjin, Apr. 26, 1980; children: Roderick Bell Jr., Andrew Crittenden, Malcolm Timothy. BA, Hampden Syndey Coll., 1963; LLB, U. Richmond, 1966; postgrad., U. Mich., 1991. Bar: Va. 1966. Assoc. Christian, Barton, Parker, Epps & Brent, Richmond, Va., 1966-72; ptnr. Christian, Barton, Epps, Brent & Chappell, Richmond, 1972-88; sr. v.p., corp. legal and govt. affairs officer Trigon Blue Cross & Blue Shield, 1989—. Trustee, mem. exec. com. Children's Hosp., Richmond, 1980—. Mem. ABA (ho. of dels. 1984-88, state del. Va. 1988-93, bd. govs. 1993-96, exec. com. 1995-96), Am. Bar Found., Am. Bar Endowment (bd. dirs.), Am. Judicature Soc. (bd. dirs.), Va. Bar Found., Va. State Bar (pres. 1987-88). Avocations: travel, fly fishing, photography, skiing. Office: Mail Drop 02H 2015 Staples Mill Rd Richmond VA 23230

MATHEWS, SHARON WALKER, artistic director, secondary school educator; b. Shreveport, La., Feb. 1, 1947; d. Arthur Delmar and Nona (Frye) Walker; m. John William (Bill) Mathews, Aug. 14, 1971; children: Rebecca, Elizabeth, Anna. BS, La. State U., 1969, MS, 1971. Dance grad. asst. La. State U., Baton Rouge, 1969-71, choreographer, 1975-76; 6th grade tchr. East Baton Rouge Parish, 1971-72, health phys. edn. tchr., 1972-74; dance instr. Magnet High Sch., Baton Rouge, 1975—; artistic dir. Baton Rouge Ballet Theatre, 1975—; dance dir. Dancers' Workshop, Baton Rouge, 1971—; choreographer Baton Rouge Opera, 1989-94. Named Dance Educator of Yr., La. Alliance for Health, Physical Edn., Recreation and Dance, 1986-87. Mem. Southwestern Regional Ballet Assn. (bd. dirs. 1981—, treas., exec. bd. dirs. 1989-92), La. Assn. for Health, Phys. Edn., Recreation and Dance (dance chairperson 1995). Republican. Baptist. Office: Baton Rouge Ballet Theater 10689 Perkins Rd Ste C Baton Rouge LA 70810-1608

MATHEWS, W. GARRET, columnist; b. Covington, Va., Sept. 23, 1949; s. Kenneth G. and Betsy (Waid) M.; m. MaryAnne, June 24, 1978; children: Colin, Evan. BS in Econs., Va. Poly. Inst. and State U., 1971. News editor/columnist Daily Telegraph, Bluefield, W.Va., 1972-87; columnist Evansville (Ind.) Courier, 1987—. Author: Folks I, 1979, Folks II, 1984. With U.S. Army, 1971-77. Avocations: juggling, coaching boys baseball. Home: 7954 Elna Kay Dr Evansville IN 47715-6210 Office: Evansville Courier 300 E Walnut St Evansville IN 47702-0268

MATHEWS, WILLIAM EDWARD, neurological surgeon, educator; b. Indpls., July 12, 1934; s. Ples Leo and Roxie Elizabeth (Allen) M.; m. Eleanor Jayne Comer, Aug. 24, 1956 (div. 1976); children: Valerie, Clarissa, Marie, Blair; m. Carol Ann. Koza, Sept. 12, 1987; 1 child, William Kyle. BS, Ball State U., 1958; DO, Kriksville Coll. Osteopathic Medicine, 1961; MD, U. Calif., L.A., 1962; student, Armed Forces Trauma Sch., Ft. Sam Houston, Tex., 1967-68. Diplomate Am. Bd. Neurol. and Orthopedic Surgery, Am. Bd. Pain Mgmt., Am. Bd. Indsl. Medicine, Am. Bd. Spinal Surgeons (v.p. 1990-92). Intern Kirksville (Mo.) Osteopathic Hosp., 1961-62; resident neurosurgery Los Angeles County Gen. Hosp., 1962-67; with Brookes Army Hosp., Ft. Sam Houston, 1967-68; with 8th field hosp. U.S. Army Neurosurgeon C.O. & 933 Med. Corp, Vietnam, 1968-69; chief neurosurgery Kaiser Med. Group, Walnut Creek, Calif., 1969-77; staff neurosurgeon Mt. Diablo Med. Ctr., Concord, Calif., 1977—; chief resident neurosurgery Los Angeles County Gen. Hosp., 1962-67; chief neurosurgery Kaiser Permanente Med. Group, Walnut Creek, 1969-77; comdg. officer 933d Med. Detachment Vietnam R.V.N., 1968-69; asst. prof. Kriksvelle Coll. Osteopathic Medicine, 1958-62; asst. lecturing prof. Neuroanatomy U. Calif. Coll. of Medicine, 1962-65. Author: (jour./book) Intracerebral Missile Injuries, 1972, Early Return to Work Following Cervical Disc Surgery, 1991; contbr. articles to profl. jours. Mem. adv. com. Rep. Presdl. Selection Com.Maj. U.S. Army, 1967-69, Vietnam. Recipient Disting. Svc. award Internat. Biography, 1987; scholar Psi Sigma Alpha, 1989. Fellow Congress Neurol. Surgeons (joint sect. on neurotrauma), Royal Coll. Medicine, Am. Acad. Neurologic and Orthopedic Surgeons (pres. 1981-82); mem. AMA, Calif. Med. Assn., San Francisco Neurologic, Contra Costa County Med. Soc. Roman Catholic. Avocations: pin and ink art, golf, gardening.

MATHEWSON, CHRISTOPHER COLVILLE, engineering geologist, educator; b. Plainfield, N.J., Aug. 12, 1941; s. George Anderson and Elsa Rae (Shrimpton) M.; m. Janet Marie Olmsted, Nov. 2, 1968; children: Heather Alexis, Glenn George Anderson. BSCE, Case Inst. Tech., 1963; MS in Geol. Engring., U. Ariz., 1965, PhD in Geol. Engring., 1971. Registered profl. engr., Tex., Ariz., geologist, Oreg., Alaska. Officer, lt. Nat. Ocean Survey, 1965-71; prof. Tex. A&M U., College Station, 1981—; cons., speaker in field. Author: Engineering Geology, 1981 (C.P. Holdredge award); contbr. articles to profl. publs. Chmn. College Station Planning and Zoning Commn., 1973-81. Fellow Geol. Soc. Am. (chmn. engring. geology divsn. 1986-87, Meritorious Svc. award 1991); mem. Assn. Engring. Geologists (editor bull. 1981-88, pres. 1988-89, C.P. Holdredge award 1981, F.T. Johnston Svc. award 1995), Am. Geol. Inst. (pres. 1991-92), Nat. Coal Coun., Internat. Assn. Engring. Geologists (chmn. U.S. nat. com. 1995—). Office: Tex A&M Univ Dept Geol College Station TX 77843-3115 *Commitment and dedication to the mission will lead to its successful completion regardless of the odds.*

MATHEWSON, DORIS MAY, nurse; b. Providence; d. Hugh Edward and Nellie May (Smith) Massey; m. Donald Walter Mathewson, May 25, 1946; 1 child, Susan Elaine. Diploma, R.I. Hosp. Sch. Nursing, 1944; BS in Nurse-Tchr. Edn., R.I. Coll., 1974; MS in Health Svcs. Adminstrs., Salve Regina Coll., 1986. From staff nurse to head nurse R.I. Hosp., Providence, 1961-67, coord., supr., 1967-69, nurse leader orthopedics, 1969-71, nurse leader med., 1971-81, asst. dir. nursing, 1981-86; primary nurse, chmn. edn. Hospice Care R.I., Providence, 1986-91; parish nurse Beneficent Congl. Ch., Providence, 1992—; mem. human and health svcs. task force R.I. Conf. U.C.C., Providence, 1990—; bd. dirs. Lucy Ayres Residence for Nurses, Providence; mem. Interfaith Counseling Ctr. Bd., Providence, 1991—. Del. Religious Adminstrs. Exch. U.S-USSR, Moscow, 1991; v.p., bd. dirs. Beneficent Congl. Ch., 1990-96, pres., 1996—; mem. R.I. State Coun. Chs.; mem. adv. bd. Cranston (R.I.) Adult Sr. Svcs., 1989-95. Mem. ANA, R.I. State Nurses Assn. (govt. affairs com.), West Cranston Garden Club (pres. 1994-96), R.I. Hosp. Nurses Alumni Assn. (bd. dirs. 1987—), R.I. Coll. Alumni, Salve Regina Coll. Alumni. Avocations: travel, gardening, cooking. Home: 44 Forsythia Ln Cranston RI 02921-2315

MATHEWSON, GEORGE ATTERBURY, lawyer; b. Paterson, N.J., Mar. 31, 1935; s. Joseph B. and Christina A. (Atterbury) M.; m. Ann Elizabeth, July 31, 1975; 1 child, James Lemuel. AB cum laude, Amherst Coll., 1957; LLB, Cornell U., 1960; LLM, U. Mich., 1961. Bar: N.Y. 1963. Atty. office spl. legal assts., trial atty. FTC, Washington, 1963-65; regional atty. N.Y. State Dept. Environ. Conservation, Liverpool, 1972-73; pvt. practice, Syracuse, N.Y., 1967-72, 73—; adj. instr. bus. law Onondaga Community Coll., Syracuse, 1979-84. Bd. dirs. South Side Businessmen, 1971-72, 88-91, v.p., 1992, pres., 1993; elder Onondaga Hill Presbn. Ch., 1979, 82-85; dir. Manlius C. of C., 1995. Mem. ABA, ATLA, Fed. Bar Assn., N.Y. State Bar Assn. (state and county bar assn. coms.), Kiwanis (bd. dirs. Onondaga club 1988-89, v.p. 1989, pres. 1989-91). Patentee safety device for disabled airplanes. Office: 4302 S Salina St Syracuse NY 13205-2065 also: 224 Fayette St Manlius NY 13104-1804

MATHEWSON, HUGH SPALDING, anesthesiologist, educator; b. Washington, Sept. 20, 1921; s. Walter Eldridge and Jennie Lind (Jones) M.; m. Dorothy Ann Gordon, 1943 (div. 1952); 1 child, Jane Mathewson Holcombe; m. Hazel M. Jones, 1953 (div. 1978); children: Geoffrey K., Brian E., Catherine E. Brock, Jennifer A. Jehle; m. Judith Ann Mahoney, 1979 (div. 1990). Student, Washburn U., 1938-39; A.B., U. Kans., 1942, M.D., 1944. Intern Wesley Hosp., Wichita, Kans., 1944-45; resident anesthesiology U. Kans. Med. Ctr., Kansas City, 1946-48; pvt. practice specializing in anesthesiology Kansas City, Mo., 1948-69; chief anesthesiologist St. Luke's Hosp., Kansas City, 1953-69; med. dir., sect. respiratory therapy U. Kans. Med. Ctr., 1969-92, assoc. prof., 1969-92, prof., 1975-92, prof. anesthesiology emeritus, respiratory care edn., 1992—; examiner schs. respiratory therapy, 1975—; oral examiner Nat. Bd. Respiratory Therapy; mem. Coun. Nurse Anesthesia Practice, 1974-78; prof. phys. therapy edn., 1993—. Author: Structural Forms of Anesthetic Compounds, 1961, Respiratory Therapy in Critical Care, 1976, Pharmacology for Respiratory Therapists, 1977; contbr. articles to profl. publs.; mem. editorial bd. Anesthesia Staff News, 1975-84; assoc. editor: Respiratory Care, 1980—, cons. editor, 1980—, editor-in-chief Respiratory Mgmt., 1989-92. Trustee Kansas City Mus., Kansas City Conservatory of Music, 1993—. Served to lt. comdr. USNR, 1956. Recipient Bird Lit. prize Am. Assn. Respiratory Therapists, 1976. Mem. Mo. Soc. Anesthesiologists (pres. 1963), Kans. Soc. Anesthesiologists (pres. 1974-77), Kans. Med. Soc. (council), Phi Beta Kappa, Sigma Xi, Lambda Beta (hon.). Office: Kans Med Ctr 39th and Rainbow Blvd Kansas City KS 66103

MATHEWSON, JUDITH JEANNE, special education educator; b. Normandy, Mo., May 4, 1954; d. Robert Edward and Jeanne Eileen (Parcels) M. AA, Kansas City C.C., 1974; BS in Psychology (Secondary Edn.) and Journalism, Kans. State U., 1976; MS in Psychology and Spl. Edn., Emporia State U., 1979. Cert. secondary tchr., Alaska, Kans. Spl. edn. tchr. Wichita Pub. Schs., 1978-79; tchr. severely emotionally disturbed students Whaley Ctr., Anchorage, 1979-83; tchr. Clark Jr. H.S., Anchorage, 1983-86, King Career Ctr., Anchorage, 1986-91; spl. edn. vocat. tchr. Chugiak H.S., Eagle River, 1994—; adj. faculty Def. Equal Opportunity Mgmt. Inst., Patrick AFB, Fla., 1989-91; lead instr., cons. Youth Corps Challenge Program Alaska Nat. Guard, Ft. Richardson, 1993-95; evening H.S. tchr. Anchorage Sch. Dist., 1991. Contbr. articles to newspapers and newsletters. Active Eagle River (Alaska) Boys and Girls Club, 1991-94; v.p. Alaska Coun. on Prevention Drug and Alcohol Abuse, Inc., Anchorage, 1986-93; usher Alaska Ctr. for Performing Arts, Anchorage, 1989—; diversity trainer Anchorage Sch. Dist., 1989—, tchr. rep., 1990. Capt. Alaska ANG, 1986—. Decorated Air Force Commendation medal, Achievement medal, Alaska Cmty. Svc. award, 1994. Mem. Holy Fools Clowning Group (treas. 1986—), Anchorage Woman's Club, Coun. for Exceptional Children (v.p. 1976—), Alaska NG Officers Assn. Roman Catholic. Avocations: computers, travel, teaching, skiing, bicycling. Home: 1762 Morningtide Ct Anchorage AK 99501

MATHIAS, CHARLES MCCURDY, lawyer, former senator; b. Frederick, Md., July 24, 1922; s. Charles McCurdy and Theresa McElfresh (Trail) M.; m. Ann Hickling Bradford, Nov. 8, 1958; children: Charles Bradford, Robert Fiske. B.A., Haverford Coll., 1944; student, Yale U., 1943-44; LL.B., U. Md., 1949. Bar: Md. 1949, U.S. Supreme Ct. 1954. Asst. atty. gen. of Md., 1953-54; city atty. City of Frederick, 1954-59; mem. Md. Ho. of Dels., 1958, 87th-90th Congresses from 6th Dist. Md., U.S. Senate from Md., 1969-87; ptnr. Jones Day Reavis and Pogue, Washington, 1987-93; chmn. bd. First Am. Bankshares, 1993—; Milton Eisenhower vis. prof. Johns Hopkins U., 1987—. Served from seaman to capt. USNR. Decorated Order of Merit (Federal Republic of Germany), Legion of Honor (France), Order of Orange Nassau (The Netherlands), Order of Brit. Empire (Eng.). Republican. Episcopalian. Office: 1450 G St NW Ste 700 Washington DC 20005-2088

MATHIAS, CHRISTOPHER JOSEPH, physician, educator, researcher, consultant; b. Mangalore, India, Mar. 16, 1949; arrived in the U.K., 1972; s. Elias Salvadore and Hilda Frances (Lobo) M.; m. Rosalind Margaret Jolleys, July 31, 1977; children: Sarah, James, Timothy. MB, BChir, Bangalore U., India, 1972; PhD, U. Oxford, Eng., 1976; DSc, U. London, 1995. Lic. Royal Coll Physicians and Surgeons. Hon. rsch. officer, registrar Dept. Neurology, Oxford, 1972-76; sr. house officer dept. medicine Royal Postgrad. Med. Sch., London, 1976-77; registrar dept. medicine, Portsmouth and renal unit Southampton (Eng.) U., 1977-79; Wellcome Trust sr. clin. rsch. fellow St. Mary's Hosp. and Med. Sch., London, 1979-84; Wellcome Trust sr. lectr. St. Mary's Hosp. Med. Ctr. and Nat. Hosp. Inst. Neurology, London, 1984-91; prof. neurovascular medicine St. Mary's/Imperial Coll., Nat. Hosp., U. Coll. London, 1991—; Nimmo vis. prof. U. Adelaide, Australia, 1996; mem. Sci. Ctr., Internat. Spinal Rsch. Trust, 1995; chmn. Rsch. Ctr. World Fedn. Neurology on Autonomic Disorders, 1993; chmn. sci. panel European Fedn. Neurological Soc., 1994; guest lectr. Thailand Neurological Soc., 1995. Co-editor (with M. Weber) Book on Mild Hypertension, 1984, (with P. Sever) Concepts in Hypertension, 1989, (with Sir Roger Bannister) Autonomic Failure: A Textbook of Clinical Disorders of the Autonomic Nervous System, 1992; contbr. chpts to books and articles to profl. jours.; found. editor-in-chief Clin. Autonomic Rsch., Jour. Am. Autonomic Soc., Brit. Clin. Autonomic Rsch. Soc., 1991—; mem. editl. bd. various internat. med./sci. jours. Mem. sci. com. Internat. Spinal Rsch. Trust, 1996—; chmn. sci. bd. European Fedn. Neurol. Soc., 1994—. Named Rhodes scholar U. Oxford, 1972-75, Dr. J. Thomas lectr. St. Johns Med. Coll., U. Bangalore, 1988, Lord Florey Meml. lectr. U. Adelaide, 1991; recipient Prof. Ruitinga award and vis. professorship U. Amsterdam, The Netherlands, 1988. n. Fellow Royal Coll. Physicians (Brit. Petroleum lectr. 1992), Royal Soc. Medicine; mem. Royal Coll. Physicians & Surgeons (licensed in Glasgow and Edinburgh 1974), Assn. Physicians Gt. Britain, Physiol. Soc., Assn. Brit. Neurologists, Brit. Pharm. Soc., Clin. Antonomic Rsch. Soc. (chmn. 1987-90, found. sec. 1982-86), Clin. Antonomic Rsch. Soc. of Great Britain (editor-in-chief Jour.). Avocations: gardening, watching cricket and football, observing human and canine behavior. Home: Meadowcroft West End Ln, Stoke Poges Bucks SL2 4NE, England Office: St Marys Hosp Imperial Coll Sci Tech Med, Pickering Unit Praed St, London W2 1NY, England

MATHIAS, EDWARD JOSEPH, merchant banker; b. Camden, N.J., Nov. 11, 1941; s. Edward Joseph and Zelma (Pollack) M.; m. Ann Robyn Rafferty, Aug. 3, 1968; 1 child, Ellen Susannah. BA, U. Pa., 1964; MBA, Harvard U., 1971. Mng. dir. T. Rowe Price Assocs., Inc., Balt., 1971-93; mng. dir., co-founder Carlyle Group Merchant Bank, Washington, 1994—; bd. dirs. Fresh Fields, Ovation, Inc. U.S. Office Supply Pathogenesis, SIRROM Capital; spl. ltd. ptnr. Trident Capital. Bd. overseers Sch. Arts and Scis. U. Pa.; chmn. bd. visitors Kogod Sch. Bus. Adminstrn., Am. Univ. Lt. USN, 1964-69. Mem. Harvard Club, Univ. Club (N.Y.C.), Columbia Country Club (Chevy Chase, Md.), Robert Trent Jones Golf Club (Manassas, Va.), Coral Beach Club (Bermuda), The Brook (N.Y.C.), Ctr. club (Balt.), Met. Club. Republican. Home: 5120 Cammack Dr Bethesda MD 20816-2902 Office: The Carlyle Group 1001 Pennsylvania Ave NW Washington DC 20004-2505

MATHIAS, JOHN JOSEPH, federal administrative law judge; b. Frostburg, Md., July 13, 1929; s. James Maxwell and Mary Genevieve (McGuire) M.; m. Rosemary Povanda, May 30, 1959; children: John Joseph, Terese, Susan. BS, Georgetown U., 1951, JD, 1953. Bar: Md. 1954, D.C. 1954. Ptnr. Lippel & Mathias, Cumberland, Md., 1960-62; adminstrv. law judge CAB, Washington, 1978-79; trial atty. U.S. FTC, Washington, 1956-60, 1962-78, adminstrv. law judge, 1979-84; adminstrv. law judge U.S. Internat. Trade Commn., Washington, 1984-90; chief adminstrv. law judge U.S. Dept. Transp., Washington, 1990—. With U.S. Army, 1954-56. Home: 8812 Connecticut Ave Chevy Chase MD 20815-6737 Office: US Dept Transp 400 7th St SW Washington DC 20590-0001

MATHIAS, JOSEPH SIMON, metallurgical engineer, consultant; b. Bombay, India, Oct. 28, 1925; came to U.S., 1948, naturalized, 1954; s. Pascal Lawrence and Dulcine Applina (De Souza) M.; m. Anna Katherine Elliott, Nov. 10, 1956. BS, U. Bombay, 1944, BA, 1946; PhD, Lehigh U., Bethlehem, Pa., 1954; M in Engring., U. Calif., Berkeley, 1951. Rsch. assoc. Lehigh U., 1951-54; chief metallurgist Superior Metals, Inc., Bethlehem, Pa., 1954-56; mgr. process metall. rsch. Foote Mineral Co., Easton, Pa., 1956-59; mgr. materials rsch., then group mgr. physics and materials Sperry Univac Co., Blue Bell, Pa., 1959-67; dir. rsch. Sperry Univac Co., 1967-79, dir. mfg. and systems hardware rsch., 1979-86, v.p. rsch. and tech., 1986-93; program dir. NSF, Washington; cons. Nat. Inst. Stds. and Tech./Advanced Tech. Program, Gaithersburg, Md., 1993—; mem. program com. Internat.

Magnetic Conf., 1969, 70; cons. in field. Author. Fellow Am. Inst. Chemists, N.Y. Acad. Scis.; mem. IEEE (sr.), Coun. Arts and Sci. Franklin Inst., Riverton Country Club, Rotary (bd. dirs.), Sigma Xi. Club: Riverton Country. Lodge: Rotary (dir.). Patentee in field. Home: 105 Thomas Ave Riverton NJ 08077-1134 Office: NIST/ATP Bldg A 101 Rm 309 Gaithersburg MD 20899

MATHIAS, LESLIE MICHAEL, electronic manufacturing company executive; b. Bombay, Dec. 17, 1935; came to U.S., 1957; s. Paschal Lawrence and Dulcine (D'Souza) M.; m. Vivian Mae Doolittle, Dec. 16, 1962. BSc, U. Bombay, 1957; BS, San Jose (Calif.) State U., 1961. Elec. engr. Indian Standard Metal, Bombay, 1957; sales engr. Bleisch Enging. and Tool, Mt. View, Calif., 1958-60; gen. mgr. Meadows Terminal Bds., Cupertino, Calif., 1961-63; prodn. mgr. Sharidon Corp., Menlo Park, Calif., 1963-67, Videx Corp., Sunnyvale, Calif., 1967-68, Data Tech. Corp., Mt. View, 1968-69; pres. L.G.M. Mfg., Inc., Mt. View, 1969-83; pvt. practice plating cons. Los Altos, Calif., 1983-87; materials mgr. Excel Cirs., Santa Clara, Calif., 1987-91, 93—, acct. mgr., 1991-93, materials mgr., 1993—. Social chmn. Internat. Students, San Jose, 1958-59. Mem. Nat. Fedn. Ind. Bus., Calif. Cirs. Assn., Better Bus. Bur., Purchasing Assn., U.S. C. of C. Roman Catholic. Avocations: computer hacker, electronics, reading, med. jours. Home: 20664 Mapletree Pl Cupertino CA 95014-0449

MATHIAS, REUBEN VICTOR (VIC MATHIAS), real estate executive, investor; b. Copperas Cove, Tex., Mar. 5, 1926; s. Alvin E. and Ella L. (Teinert) M.; m. Helen I. Thoresen, Jan. 28, 1950; children: Mona, Mark, Matt. B.B.A., U. Tex., 1950. Cert. Chamber Exec. Dist. mgr. W.A. Shaeffer Pen Co., Youngstown, Ohio, 1950-51; mgr. Cen-Tex Fair, Temple, Tex., 1951-52; dir. info. Tex. Assn. Soil Conservation Suprs., Temple, 1952-53; mgr. membership dept. Austin (Tex.) C. of C., 1953-56, chief exec. officer, 1956-82; dir. corp. devel. Hardin Corp., Austin, 1983-86; real estate and investments, 1987-92; pres. Tex. Travel Industry Assn., Austin, 1992—; v.p. Austin Tours, Inc.; sec. Longhorn Caverns, Inc.; chmn. bd., instr. Inst. for Orgn. Mgmt., U. Houston. Contbr. monthly editorial Thoughts While Thinking to Austin Mag., 1961-82. Pres. Austin USO Council, 1958-59; v.p. Beautify Tex. Council, 1975-77; founding pres. Discover Tex. Assn., 1969-70; chmn. Central Tex. Blood Donor Fund, 1979. Served with U.S. Army, 1944-46. Mem. Am. C. of C. Execs., Tex. C. of C. Execs. (pres. 1965), Rotary (pres. Austin 1985-86). Lutheran. Home: 3100 Mistywood Cir Austin TX 78746-7861 Office: 400 W 15th St Ste 711 Austin TX 78701-1648 *You can find happiness only by giving it to others. Much of my life has been devoted to community building through voluntary action. The fact that my career has allowed me to stay in one community has made it possible for me to make and carry out long-term plans, both for the community and personally.*

MATHIAS, SEAN GERARD, author, director; b. Swansea, South Wales, U.K., Mar. 14, 1956; s. John Frederick and Anne Josephine (Harding) M. Author: (plays) Cowardice, 1983, Infidelities, 1985, A Prayer for Wings, 1985, Poor Nanny, 1989, Swansea Boys, 1990, Language, 1991, (film) The Lost Language of Cranes, 1990, (novel) Manhattan Mourning, 1988; dir. (plays) Exceptions, 1988, Bent, 1990, Talking Heads, 1991, Noel and Gertie, 1991, Uncle Varya, 1991, Indiscretions, 1995 (Tony nomination - Direction of a Play). Bd. mem. West End Cares, 1990; trustee Ian Charleson Trust, London, 1990. Recipient Gold medal Lamda, 1972, Fringe First award Edinburgh Festival, 1985. Office: Jonathan Altaras Assocs Ltd, 2, Goodwins Ct, London WC2 4LL, England

MATHIES, ALLEN WRAY, JR., physician, hospital administrator; b. Colorado Springs, Colo., Sept. 23, 1930; s. Allen W. and Esther S. (Norton) M.; m. Lewise Austin, Aug. 23, 1956; children: William A., John N. BA, Colo. Coll., 1952; MS, Columbia U., 1956, PhD., 1958; MD, U. Vt., 1961. Rsch. assoc. U. Vt., Burlington, 1957-61; intern L.A. County Hosp., 1961-62; resident in pediatrics L.A. Gen. Hosp., 1962-64; asst. prof. pediatrics U. So. Calif., L.A., 1964-68, assoc. prof., 1968-71, prof., 1971—, assoc. dean, 1969-74, interim dean, 1974-75, dean, 1975-85, head physician Communicable Disease Svc., 1964-75; pres., CEO Huntington Meml. Hosp., Pasadena, Calif., 1985-94; pres., CEO So. Calif. Healthcare Sys., Pasadena, 1992-95, pres. emeritus, 1995—; bd. dirs. Pacific Mut. Contbr. articles to med. jours. Bd. dirs. Occidental Coll. With U.S. Army, 1953-55. Mem. Am. Acad. Pediatrics, Infectious Disease Soc. Am., Am. Pediatric Soc., Soc. Pediatric Rsch. Republican. Episcopalian. Home: 314 Arroyo Dr South Pasadena CA 91030-1623 Office: Huntington Meml Hosp PO Box 7013 Pasadena CA 91109-7013

MATHIESON, ANDREW WRAY, investment management executive; b. Pitts., June 11, 1928; s. Andrew Russell and Margaret (Wray) M.; m. Helen Fricke, Dec. 5, 1953; children—Margaret Adele Conver, Andrew Fricke, Peter Ferris. B.S. in Mech. Enging, Bucknell U., 1950; M.S. in Indsl. Adminstrn, Carnegie-Mellon U., 1952. With elevator div. Westinghouse Electric Corp., 1955-63; dist. mgr. Westinghouse Electric Corp., Cleve., 1960-62; asst. group v.p. constrn. group Westinghouse Electric Corp., Pitts., 1962-63; with T. Mellon and Sons., Pitts., 1963-71; v.p., gov. T. Mellon and Sons., 1967-71; v.p. Richard K. Mellon and Sons, Pitts., 1971-78; exec. v.p. Richard K. Mellon and Sons, 1978—; dir. Gen. Re Corp, Gen. Re Europe Ltd., Mellon Nat. Corp. Trustee, vice-chmn. Richard King Mellon Found., R.K. Mellon Family Found.; bd. dirs. St. Margaret Meml. Hosp., Pitts., 1966—, pres., 1976-81; exec. com. Allegheny Conf. Cmty. Devel., 1976. With USNR, 1952-55. Episcopalian. Clubs: Duquesne (Pitts.) (bd. dirs. 1986, pres. 1989), Fox Chapel Golf (Pitts.) (dir. 1974); Laurel Valley Golf (Ligonier, Pa.), Rolling Rock (Ligonier, Pa.) (v.p., gov.); University (N.Y.C.). Home: 14 The Trillium Pittsburgh PA 15238-1929 Office: Richard K Mellon & Sons 500 Grant St Ste 4106 Pittsburgh PA 15219-2502

MATHIEU, HELEN M., state legislator; b. Newport, R.I., May 8, 1940; m. Roger E. Mathieu, 1964. Grad., Salve Regina Coll. Mem. R.I. State Senate, dist. 46. Mem. Kappa Gamma Pi. Democrat. Roman Catholic. Home: 160 Lawrence Dr Portsmouth RI 02871-4063 Office: R I State Senate State Capitol Providence RI 02903

MATHIEU, HENRI DONAT See SAINT LAURENT, YVES

MATHIEU, MARY MARTHA, accountant, consultant; b. Shreveport, La., Oct. 2, 1952; d. Clyde Benjamin and Mary Frances (Cornelius) Phillips; m. Reese Alfred Mathieu III, Dec. 28, 1974; children: Mary Charlotte, Sarah Elizabeth, Reese Alfred IV. BBA in Acctg. summa cum laude, Tex. Christian U., 1975. CPA, Tex.; cert. mgmt. acct. Budget mgr. Arco Exploration Co., Dallas, 1984, mgr. internal control, 1985; various acctg. positions Arco Oil and Gas Co., Dallas, 1975-78, coord. acctg. devel., 1979, supr. cost acctg., 1980-81, cons. planning, 1985, cons. property sales, 1986, mgr. land and mktg. systems, 1987-91, transition mgr., 1992—; Arco Oil and Gas Co. recruiter Tex. Christian U., 1981-88; presenter oil industry conf. IBM, Monterey, Calif., 1990; mem. steering com. Arco-Haliburton Strategic Alliance, Houston, 1992. Editor: (tng. manual) Natural Gas Marketing System, 1990; author, editor publs. in field for Arco Oil and Gas Co. Chmn. Arco United Way campaign, Dallas and Plano, Tex., 1988; mem. Arco Civic Action Program, 1978—. Recipient recognition for mgmt. support El Centro Coll., Dallas, 1991. Mem. Tex. Soc. CPAs, Dallas chpt. Tex. Soc. CPAs, Inst. Mgmt. Accts., Am. Petroleum Inst., Tex. Christian U. Alumnae Assn. (student body treas. 1974-75, scholar 1975), Dallas County Med. Soc. Alliance, Assn. Baby Boomers, Delta Delta Delta. Presbyterian. Avocations: softball playing and coaching, water skiing, snow skiing.

MATHIEU, MICHELLE ELISE, lawyer; b. Detroit, Aug. 14, 1956; d. Kenneth G. and Geraldine M. (O'Rourke) M. BA, U. Mich., 1978; JD, Detroit Coll. Law, 1982. Bar: Mich. 1982, U.S. Dist. Ct. (ea. dist.) Mich. 1982, U.S. Ct. Appeals (6th cir.) 1991, U.S. Fed. Ct. (ea. dist.) Mich. Law clk. Joselyn, Rowe, Grinnan, Hayes & Callahan, Detroit, 1980-81; assoc. Joselyn, Rowe, Grinnan & Feldman, Detroit, 1982-88; ptnr. Joselyn & Keelean, P.C., Detroit, 1988-91; assoc., head appeal dept. Still, Nemier, Tolari & Landry, P.C., Farmington Hills, Mich., 1991—. Mem. Fed. Bar Assn. Office: Still Nemier et al 37000 Grand River Ave Farmington Hills MI 48335

MATHILE, CLAYTON LEE, corporate executive; b. Portage, Ohio, Jan. 11, 1941; s. Wilbert and Helen (Good) M.; m. Mary Ann Maas, July 7, 1962; children: Cathy, Tim, Mike, Tina, Jennie. BA, Ohio No. U., 1962, DBA (hon.), 1991; postgrad., Bowling Green State U., 1964. Acct. GM, Napoleon, Ohio, 1962-63; acct. Campbell Soup Co., Napoleon, 1963-65, buyer, 1965-67, purchasing agt., 1967-70; gen. mgr. The Iams Co., Dayton, Ohio, 1970-75, v.p., 1975-80, chief exec. officer, 1980-90, chmn., chief exec. officer, 1990—, also dir.; mem. Pet Food Inst.; bd. dirs. Midwest Group, Cin., Bush Bros. Co., Knoxville, Tenn. Author: A Business Owner's Perspective on Outside Boards. Trustee Chaminade-Julienne High Sch., Dayton, 1987—, U. Dayton; mem. adv. bd. coll. bus. Ohio No. U., Ada, 1987—, also trustee. Named Best of Best Ctr. for Values Rsch., Houston, 1987. Mem. Am. Mgmt. Assn., Am. Agt. Assn. Roman Catholic. Avocations: traveling, swimming, golf. Officer: The Iams Company 7250 Poe Ave Dayton OH 45414-2572*

MATHIS, BRUCE J., sports association executive. Competition mgr. adminstrv. sect. boxing competition Olympic Games, L.A., 1984; chmn. tournament orgn. and adminstrn. com. U.S. Amateur Boxing, Inc., Colorado Springs, nat. governing body's assoc. exec. dir., 1985—, interim exec. dir., 1993-94, exec. dir., 1994—. Pres. Wis. Amateur Boxing Fedn., 1979-85; regional coord. Jr. Olympic boxing program. Office: US Amateur Boxing Inc One Olympic Plz Colorado Springs CO 80909-5776

MATHIS, DAVID B., insurance company executive; b. Atlanta, Ga.. BA, Lake Forest Coll., 1960. Chmn. Kemper Corp., Long Grove, Ill., 1992-96; chmn., pres., CEO Kemper Nat. Ins. Cos., Long Grove, Ill., 1996—; also bd. dirs. Kemper Corp. Office: Kemper Nat Ins Cos 1 Kemper Dr Long Grove IL 60049

MATHIS, JACK DAVID, advertising executive; b. La Porte, Ind. Nov. 27, 1931; s. George Anthony and Bernice (Bennethum) M.; student U. Mo., 1950-52; BS, Fla. State U., 1955; m. Phyllis Dene Hoffman, Dec. 24, 1971; children: Kane Cameron, Jana Dene. With Benton & Bowles, Inc., 1955-56; owner Jack Mathis Advt., 1956—; cons. films, including That's Action!, 1977, Great Movie Stunts: Raiders of the Lost Ark, 1981, The Making of Raiders of the Lost Ark, 1981, An American Legend: The Lone Ranger, 1981; Heroes and Sidekicks: Indiana Jones and the Temple of Doom, 1984, The Republic Pictures Story, 1991, The Making of The Quiet Man, 1992, Roy Rogers: King of the Cowboys, 1992, Cliffhangers: Adventures from the Thrill Factory, 1993, The Making of Sands of Iwo Jima, 1993, Gene Autry: Melody of the West, 1994. Mem. U.S. Olympic Basketball Com. Recipient citation Mktg. Research Council N.Y., inducted Ill. Basketball Hall of Fame. Mem. Alpha Delta Sigma. Author: Valley of the Cliffhangers, Republic Confidential, Valley of the Cliffhangers Supplement. Office: PO Box 3580 Barrington IL 60011-3580

MATHIS, JOHN PRENTISS, lawyer; b. New Orleans, Feb. 10, 1944; s. Robert Prentiss and Lena (Horton) M.; m. Karen Elizabeth McHugh, May 31, 1966; children: Lisa Lynne, Andrew P. BA magna cum laude, So. Meth. U., Dallas, 1966; JD cum laude, Harvard U., 1969. Bar: Calif. 1970, D.C. 1975, U.S. Ct. Appeals (D.C. cir.) 1972, U.S. Ct. Appeals (5th cir.) 1975, U.S. Ct. Appeals (3rd cir.) 1980, U.S. Supreme Ct. 1982. Assoc. Latham & Watkins, Los Angeles, 1969-71; spl. asst. to gen. counsel, FPC, Washington, 1971-72; gen. counsel Calif. Pub. Utilities Commn., San Francisco, 1972-74; assoc. Baker & Botts, Washington, 1974-76, ptnr., 1976-92; ptnr. Hogan & Hartson, Washington, 1992—. Mem. ABA (litigation sect., chmn. energy litigation com. 1985-89, div. dir. 1989-90, chmn. legis. com. 1990-94, rep. to coord. group energy law 1992—), Fed. Energy Bar Assn., Harvard U. Law Sch. Assn. D.C. (past pres.). Republican. Methodist. Clubs: Harvard U., Congl. Country, Met. (Washington). Home: 9400 Turnberry Dr Potomac MD 20854 Office: Hogan & Hartson 555 13th St NW Ste 1200W Washington DC 20004-1109

MATHIS, JOHNNY, singer; b. San Francisco, Sept. 30, 1935; s. Clem and Mildred Mathis. Student, San Francisco State Coll. Recordings include It's Not for Me to Say, Chances Are, Someone, Twelfth of Never, There Goes My Heart, My One and Only Love, Let Me Love You; albums include Johnny Mathis, 1956, Wonderful, Wonderful, 1957, Warm, 1957, Good Night, Dear Lord, 1958, Johnny's Greatest Hits, 1958, Swing Softly, 1958, Merry Christmas, 1958, Open Fire, Two Guitars, 1959, More Johnny's Greatest Hits, 1959, Heavenly, 1959, Faithfully, 1960, The Rhythms and Ballads of Broadway, 1960, Johnny's Mood, 1960, I'll Buy You a Star, 1961, Portrait of Johnny, 1961, Live It Up, 1962, Rapture, 1962, Johnny's Newest Hits, 1963, Johnny, 1963, Romantically, 1963, I'll Search My Heart, 1964, Tender is the Night, 1965, The Wonderful World of Make Believe, 1965, This is Love, 1966, Ole, 1966, The Sweetheart Tree, 1967, Up, Up and Away, 1967, Love is Blue, 1968, Those Were the Days, 1968, People, 1969, The Impossible Dream, 1969, Raindrops Keep Fallin' On My Head, 1970, Close To You, 1970, Bacharach & Kaempfert, 1970, Love Story, 1970, You've Got a Friend, 1971, The First Time Ever I Saw Your Face, 1972, Song Sung Blue, 1972, Me and Mrs. Jones, 1973, Killing Me Softly With Her Song, 1973, I'm Coming Home, 1973, The Heart of a Woman, 1974, Feelings, 1975, I Only Have Eyes for You, 1976, Hold Me, Thrill Me, Kiss Me, 1977, You Light Up My Life, 1978, Mathis Magic, 1979, Different Kinda Different, 1980, Friends in Love, 1982, A Special Part of Me, 1984, Johnny Mathis Live, 1984, Right From the Heart, 1985, Christmas Eve With Johnny Mathis, 1986, In The Still of the Night, 1989, In a Sentimental Mood: Mathis Sings Ellington, 1990, Better Together, 1991, How do you Keep the Music Playing, 1992, Music of Johnny Mathis: A Personal Collection, 1993; appeared in films Lizzie, 1957, A Certain Smile, 1958; tours of Europe, Africa, Australia, S.Am., Orient, Can.; rec. artist, Columbia Records, Mercury Records, 1964-67. Avocations: cooking, golf. Office: care Rojon Prodns Inc PO Box 2066 Burbank CA 91507-2066

MATHIS, LARRY LEE, health care administrator; b. Lincoln, Nebr., May 29, 1943; s. Henry William George and Berneta Lucille (Van Laningham) M.; children—Julie, Jennifer. B.A. in Social Scis., Pittsburg State U., Kans., 1965; M.H.A., Washington U., St. Louis, 1972; postgrad. health systems mgmt., Harvard U., 1978, advanced mgmt. program, 1982. Adminstrv. resident Meth. Hosp., Houston, 1971-72, adminstrv. asst., 1972, asst. to pres., 1972-74, v.p., 1974-78, sr. v.p., 1978-80, exec. v.p., chief operating officer, 1980-83, pres., CEO, 1983—. Contbr. articles to profl. jours. Health svcs. chair U.S. Savs. Bond Vol. Com. Gulf Coast, Diagnostic Ctr. Hosp., Am. Hosp. Istanbul; mem. various coms. St. Luke's United Meth. Ch., Houston, 1972—; mem. bd. global ministries Tex. Conf. United Meth. Ch., 1984—; chmn., bd. dirs. Greater Houston Hosp. Coun. Rsch. and Edn. Found., 1985—. Capt. U.S. Army, 1965-70, Vietnam. Decorated Bronze Star, Vietnamese Cross of Gallantry; recipient Alumni Meritorious Achievement award Pittsburg State U., 1984. Fellow Am. Coll. Healthcare Execs. (gov. 1990-94); mem. Am. Hosp. Assn. (chmn. 1993, spkr. Ho. Dels. 1994), Healthcare Execs. Study Soc., Assn. Univ. Programs in Health Adminstrn., Assn. Am. Med. Colls. (various coms. coun. on tchg. hosps.), Tex. Hosp. Assn. (trustee 1984-90, chmn. 1988-89), Washington U. alumni Assn. (pres. 1988-90), Houston C. of C., Greater Houston Hosp. Coun. (chmn. bd. dirs. 1983-84), Petroleum Club, Ramada Club, Drs. Club, Harvard Bus. (bd. dirs. 1986-87), Houston City. Avocations: sailing; reading; hunting; traveling. Home: 3037 Reba Dr Houston TX 77019-6203 Office: Meth Hosp Sys 6565 Fannin St D-200 Houston TX 77030-2704*

MATHIS, LUSTER DOYLE, college administrator, political scientist; b. Gainesville, Ga., May 5, 1936; s. Luster and Fay Selena (Wingo) M.; m. Rheba Burch, June 5, 1958; children—Douglas James, Deborah Jane. A.B., Berry Coll., 1958; M.A., U. Ga., 1958, Ph.D. (Univ. Alumni Found. fellow), 1966. Asst. prof. polit. sci. Brenau Coll., Gainesville, 1960-61; asso. prof. Calif. Baptist Coll., 1961-62, Belmont Coll., Nashville, 1962-64; asso. prof., head dept. polit. sci. W.Ga. Coll., Carrollton, 1965-68; prof. W.Ga. Coll., 1969-75, head dept., 1969-71, chmn. div. grad. studies, 1970-73; assoc. dean, 1972-75; research asso., asst. editor Papers of Thomas Jefferson Princeton U., 1968-69; v.p., dean of coll. Berry Coll., Mt. Berry, Ga., 1975-93, v.p. acad. affairs, 1993—; cons. Citizens Com. on Ga. Gen. Assembly. Co-author: Courts as Political Instruments, 1970. Mem. Ga. Democratic Charter Commn., 1974-75; mem. consumer adv. com. Floyd Med. Center, 1978-80. Nat. Hist. Publs. Commn. fellow, 1968-69. Mem. Am. Assn. Higher Edn., Am. Conf. Acad. Deans, Ga. Polit. Sci. Assn. (pres. 1968-69), Conf. Acad. Deans of the So. States, Kiwanis. Democrat. Baptist. Office: Berry Coll Dept Acad Affairs Mount Berry GA 30149

MATHIS, MARK JAY, lawyer; b. N.Y.C., Aug. 25, 1947; s. Meyer and Beulah (Nechemias) M.; m. Marylin Gail Goodman, Aug. 14, 1971; children: Alison Leigh, Brian Todd. BS, MIT, 1969; JD, U. Pa., 1972. Bar: D.C. 1973. Assoc. Arent, Fox, Kintner, Plotkin & Kahn, Washington, 1972-75; minority counsel Com. on D.C. U.S. Ho. of Reps., 1975-76; atty. Chesapeake & Potomac Telephone Cos., Washington, 1977-81, gen. atty., 1982-83, v.p., gen. counsel, 1984-89; v.p., assoc. gen. counsel Bell Atlantic Network Svcs., Washington, 1988-89, v.p., gen. counsel, 1990-91; v.p., dep. gen. counsel, sec. Bell Atlantic Corp., Phila., 1992; v.p., gen. counsel Bell Atlantic NSI, Arlington, Va., 1993—. Office: Bell Atlantic NSI 8th Fl 1320 N Court House Rd Arlington VA 22201

MATHIS, SHARON BELL, author, elementary educator, librarian; b. Atlantic City, Feb. 26, 1937; d. John Willie and Alice Mary (Frazier) Bell; m. Leroy F. Mathis, July 11, 1957 (div. Jan. 1979); children: Sherie, Stacy, Stephanie. B.A., Morgan State Coll., 1958; M.L.S., Catholic U. Am., 1975. Interviewer Children's Hosp. of D.C., Washington, 1958-59; tchr. Holy Redeemer Elementary Sch., Washington, 1959-65, Charles Hart Jr. High Sch., Washington, 1965-72; spl. edn. tchr. Stuart Jr. High Sch., Washington, 1972-74; librarian Benning Elementary Sch., Washington, 1975-76; librarian Friendship Ednl. Center, 1976-95, ret., 1995; writer-in-charge children's lit. div. D.C. Black Writers Workshop; writer-in-residence Howard U., 1972-73. Author: Brooklyn Story, 1970, Sidewalk Story, 1971 (Council on Interracial Books for Children award 1970), Teacup Full of Roses, 1972 (Outstanding Book of Yr. award New York Times 1972), Ray Charles, 1973 (Coretta Scott King award 1974), Listen for the Fig Tree, 1974, The Hundred Penny Box, 1975 (Boston Globe-Horn Book Honor book 1975, Newberry Honor Book 1976), Cartwheels, 1977, Red Dog Blue Fly: Football Poems, 1991 (Children's Book of Yr. award Bank St. Coll. 1992), Red Dog Blue Fly: An American Bookseller (Pick of the List 1995). Mem. bd. advisers lawyers com. D.C. Commn. on Arts, 1972. Nominated Books for Brotherhood list NCCJ, 1970; recipient D.C. Assn. Sch. Librs. award 1976, Arts and Humanities award Archdiocese of Washington Black Secretariat, 1978; Weekly Reader Book Club fellow Bread Loaf Writers Conf., 1970, MacDowell Colony fellow, 1978. Roman Catholic. *My success is due to the glorious African blood which flows throughout my body—and to the dignity, intelligence, strength, pride, efforts, and faith of my very creative parents—and all other Black people who have helped me.*

MATHIS, TERANCE, professional football player; b. Detroit, June 7, 1967. Student, U. N.Mex. Wide receiver, kick returner N.Y. Jets, 1990-93, Atlanta Falcons, 1994—. Named to Sporting News Coll. All-Am. 1st Team, 1989; selected to Pro Bowl, 1994. Office: c/o Atlanta Falcons 2745 Burnett Rd Sewanee GA 30174*

MATHIS, WILLIAM LOWREY, lawyer; b. Jackson, Tenn., Dec. 19, 1926; s. Harry Fletcher and Syrene (Lowrey) M.; m. Marilyn Jayne Cason, Sept. 10, 1949; children—Amanda Jayne, Amy Susan, Peter Andrew, Perry Alexander, Anne Lowrey. B.M.E., Duke U., 1947; J.D., George Washington U., 1951. Bar: D.C. bar 1951, Fla. bar 1972, Va. bar 1977. Examiner U.S. Patent Office, 1947-52; mem. firm Swecker & Mathis, Washington, 1952-61, Burns, Doane, Swecker & Mathis, Alexandria, Va., 1961—; adj. prof. law Georgetown U. Law Center, 1974—. Co-author: Trademark Litigation in the Trademark Office and Federal Courts, 1977; also chpt. in Handbook of Modern Marketing, 2d edit., 1986. Mem. Am., D.C. bar assns., Am. Intellectual Property Law Assn., Order of Coif. Roman Catholic. Home: 3709 Chanel Rd Annandale VA 22003-2024 Office: George Mason Bldg Washington and Prince Sts Alexandria VA 22313

MATHISON, IAN WILLIAM, chemistry educator, academic dean; b. Liverpool, Eng., Apr. 17, 1938; came to U.S., 1963; s. William and Grace (Almond) M.; m. Mary Ann Gordon, July 20, 1968; children: Mark W., Lisa A. B. Pharm., U. London, 1960, Ph.D., 1963, D. Sci., 1976. Lic. pharmacist, Gt. Britain. Research assoc. U. Tenn. Ctr. for Health Scis., Memphis, 1963-65, asst. prof., 1965-68, assoc. prof., 1968-72, prof., 1972-76; medicinal chemistry prof. Ferris State U., Big Rapids, Mich., 1977—, dean, prof., 1977—; external examiner U. Sci., Malaysia, 1978-79; mem. Mich. dept. Mental Health Pharmacy Facilities Rev. Panel, Lansing, 1978-90, Quality Assurance Commn., 1979-90; cons. in field. Mem. editorial bd.: Jour. Pharm. Sci., 1981-86 ; contbr. articles to profl. jours.; sr. inventor, patentee in field. Marion Labs. awardee, 1965-74; NSF grantee, 1968-72; Beecham Co. grantee, 1974-79. Fellow Royal Inst. Chemistry, Royal Soc. Chemistry; mem. Am. Pharm. Soc., Am. Chem. Soc., Am. Assn. Coll. Pharmacy (bd. dirs. 1988-90), Nat. Assn. Retail Druggists (edn. adv. com. 1989-94), Royal Pharm. Soc. Gt. Britain, Nat. Assn. Chain Drug Stores (ednl. adv. com. 1993—). Home: 820 Osborn Cir Big Rapids MI 49307-2536 Office: Ferris State U 901 S State St Big Rapids MI 49307-2251

MATHOG, ROBERT HENRY, otolaryngologist, educator; b. New Haven, Apr. 13, 1939; s. William and Tiby (Gans) M.; m. Deena Jane Rabinowitz, June 14, 1964; children: Tiby, Heather, Lauren, Jason. AB, Dartmouth Coll., 1960; MD, NYU, 1964. Diplomate Am. Bd. Facial Plastic and Reconstructive Surgery. Intern Duke Hosp., Durham, N.C., 1964-65; resident surgery Duke Hosp., 1965-66, resident otolaryngology, 1966-69; practice medicine, specializing in otolaryngology Mpls., 1971-77, Detroit, 1977—; chief of otolaryngology Hennepin County Med. Center, Mpls., 1972-77; asst. prof. U. Minn., 1971-74, asso. prof., 1974-77; prof., chmn. dept. otolaryngology Wayne State U. Sch. Medicine, 1977—; chief otolaryngology Hennepin County Hosp., Mpls., 1972-77, Harper-Grace Hosps., Detroit, 1977—, Detroit Receiving Hosp., 1977-92; cons. staff VA Hosp., Allen Park, Minn., 1977—, Children's Hosp., Detroit, 1977—, Hutzel Hosp., Detroit, 1966; mem. adv. coun. Nat. Inst. Deaf and Other Communicable Disorders NIH, 1992—; chief otolaryngology, head and neck surgery June Hosp., 1994-95. Author: Otolaryngology Clinics of North America, 1976, Textbook of Maxillofacial Trauma, 1983; editor in chief Videomed. Edn. Systems, 1972-75; editor: Atlas of Craniofacial Trauma, 1992; contbr. articles to med. jours. Bd. dirs. Bexer County Hearing Soc., 1969-71; adv. coun. WIDCB, 1993. Maj. USAF, 1969-71. Recipient Valentine Mott medal for proficiency in anatomy, 1961, Recognition award Wayne State Bd. Govs. Faculty, 1993; Deafness Rsch. Found. grantee, 1979-81, NIH grantee, 1986, 92. Fellow ACS, Am. Acad. Otolaryngology, Head and Neck Surgery (Cert. award 1976, Cert. of Appreciation 1978), Am. Soc. Head and Neck Surgery, Triological Soc. (v.p. 1995—), Am. Otol. Soc., Am. Acad. Facial Plastic and Reconstructive Surgery (v.p. 1980), Am. Neurotology Soc.; mem. AMA, Am. Laryngol. Soc. (coun. 1994—), Am. Laryngol. Assn., Mich. Med. Soc., Am. Head and Neck Soc., Soc. Univ. Otolaryngologists (pres.-elect 1994), Assn. Acad. Depts. Otolaryngology, Assn. Rsch. Otolaryngology (pres. 1981), Soc. U. Otolaryngology-Head Neck Surgery (pres. 1995—). Home: 27115 Wellington Rd Franklin MI 48025-1329 Office: Otolaryngology 27177 Lahser Rd Ste 203 Southfield MI 48034-8468 Office: Wayne State U Sch Medicine 540 E Canfield St Detroit MI 48201-1928

MATHUES, THOMAS OLIVER, retired automobile company executive; b. Dayton, Ohio, Jan. 26, 1923; s. John Leslie and Florence (Killen) M.; m. Patricia McFarland, May 20, 1944 (dec. Feb. 1992); children: Thomas P., Rebecca, John, Jennifer; m. Mary Nell Galloway, Apr. 15, 1993. Student, Grove City Coll., 1944-45, U. Ill., 1945-46; B.M.E., Gen. Motors Inst., 1947; postgrad., Harvard U. Bus. Sch., 1976. With Inland div. Gen. Motors Corp., Dayton, 1940-78; gen. mgr. Inland div. Gen. Motors Corp., 1966-78; v.p. mfg. staff Gen. Motors, Warren, Mich., 1978-81, v.p. current engring. and mfg. services staff, 1981-85. Served with USNR, 1944-46. Mem. Soc. Automotive Engrs., Commonwealth Yacht Club (Grand Rivers, Ky.), Country Club of Paducah (Ky.), Phi Gamma Delta. Mem. Christian Ch. (Disciples of Christ). Patentee in field. Home: 1930 Sledd Creek Rd Gilbertsville KY 42044-8814

MATHUR, RUPA AJWANI, state official, risk management consultant; b. Khairpur, Sind, India, Nov. 2, 1939; came to U.S., 1980; d. Menghraj Lalchand and Giani Ajwani; m. Ramesh Saran Mathur, Mar. 2, 1967; children: Sanjay Saran, Seema. BA with honors, Bombay U., 1962, LLB, 1965. CPCU. Lawyer High Ct., Bombay; with GM, U.K., Lindus & Horton, U.K.; welfare staff Brit. High Commn., Africa, 1977-78; English tchr. Thailand, 1978-80; ins. specialist, analyst Met. Transit Authority, Houston, 1980-83; ins. analyst Coastal Corp., Houston, 1983-84; dir. ins. and employee benefits Houston Ind. Sch. Dist., 1984-88; dir. risk mgmt. and benefits Harris County, Houston, 1988-94; dir. State Risk Mgmt., Austin, 1994—;

bd. dirs. Surplus Line; owner Health Environ. and Risk Mgmt. Co. (HER Inc.); team leader risk mgmt. del. People to People, Ea. Europe and Russia, 1993, China, 1994; instr. CPCU and accredited advisor ins. courses U. Houston Sch. Inst. Mktg. and Fin., 1985-88; speaker in field. Author: Managing Occupational Injury Costs, 1993; contbr. articles to profl. jours. Chmn. Multi Cultural Soc., Ft. Bend County, Tex., 1992, Indian Cmty.-Equal Opportunity, Houston, 1990; bd. dirs. Children at Risk, Ft. Bend Sch. Dist., 1990, mem. task force Multi Culture Ctr., 1993; co-founder Internat. Gourmet Club, 1976; sec.-treas. Internat. Ladies Club, 1976; tchr. English, YMCA, Thailand, 1976; founder Indian Am. Orgn. for Equal Opportunity; bd. dirs. India Culture Ctr., 1993-94. Recipient Honor award Tex. Safety Assn., 1993, Woman on the Move award Houston Post and KPRC/Channel 2, 1993. Mem. Profl. Women in Govt., Risk and Ins. Mgrs. Soc. (com.), Pub. Risk and Ins. Mgmt. Assn. (past pres. Tex. chpt., mem. internat. com.), World Safety Orgn. (cert. safety exec., appreciation award 1991, Concerned Safety Profl. award 1993), CPCU's (edn. com.), State and Local Govt. Benefits Assn., Nat. Safety Coun. (safety awards), Profl. Devel. Inst. (past officer), Internat. Hospitality Coun. (bd. dirs.), People to People Orgn. (Austin chpt.). M. Avocations: travel, reading, writing, painting, fishing. Home: 3400 Pace Bend Rd Spicewood TX 78669

MATHWICH, DALE F., insurance company executive; b. 1934. Student, U. Wis., 1954. With Am. Family Mutual Ins. Co., Madison, Wis., 1955—; state dir. Am. Family Mutual Ins. Co., Rockford, Ill., 1970-79; mktg. dir. Am. Family Mutual Ins. Co., 1979-82, v.p. mktg., 1982-85, exec. v.p., 1985-86, pres., chief oper. officer, from 1986, now chmn. bd., CEO. Office: Am Family Ins Group 6000 American Pky Madison WI 53783

MATIA, PAUL RAMON, federal judge; b. Cleve., Oct. 2, 1937; s. Leo Clemens and Irene Elizabeth (Linkert) M.; m. Nancy Arch Van Meter, Jan. 2, 1993. BA, Case Western Res. U., 1959; JD, Harvard U., 1962. Bar: Ohio 1962, U.S. Dist. Ct. (no. dist.) Ohio 1969. Law clk. Common Pleas Ct. of Cuyahoga County, Cleve., 1963-66, judge, 1985-91; asst. atty. gen. State of Ohio, Cleve., 1966-69; adminstrv. ast. to atty. gen. State of Ohio, Columbus, 1969-70; senator Ohio State Senate, Columbus, 1971-75, 79-83; ptnr. Hadley, Matia, Mills & MacLean Co., L.P.A., Cleve., 1975-84; judge U.S. Dist. Ct. (no. dist.) Ohio, 1991—. Candidate Lt. Gov. Rep. Primary, 1982, Ohio Supreme Ct., 1988; vice chmn. exec. com. Cuyahoga County Rep. Orgn., Cleve., 1971-84. Named Outstanding Legislator, Ohio Assn. for Retarded Citizens, 1974, Watchdog of Ohio Treasury, United Conservatives of Ohio, 1979; recipient Heritage award Polonia Found., 1988. Mem. FBA, Am. Judicature Soc., Ohio Bar Assn., Cleve. Bar Assn. (President's award 1988), Cuyahoga County Bar Assn., Athletic Club Columbus, Club at Society Ctr. Avocations: skiing, gardening, travel. Office: US Dist Ct 201 Superior Ave E Cleveland OH 44114-1204

MATIAS, PATRICIA TREJO, Spanish educator; b. Havana, Cuba; came to U.S., 1967; d. Juan Mario and Maria (Rexach) Trejo; m. Miguel Matias, Mar. 20, 1972; children: Michael George, Mark Patrick. BA in French/Spanish, Ga. Coll., 1973; MAT in Spanish Edn., Ga. State U., 1985, EdS in Fgn. Lang. Edn., 1991. Cert. Spanish tchr., Ga. Spanish lead tchr. Wheeler High Sch., Marietta, Ga., 1980—; mem. adv. bd. So. Conf. Lang. Teaching, Ga., 1987—; part-time instr. Kennesaw State Coll., 1991—. VIP guest svc. goodwill amb. Olympics Games Com., Atlanta, 1995—. Mem. AAUW, ASCD, Am. Assn. Tchrs. Spanish and Portuguese, Profl. Assn. Ga. Educators, Fgn. Lang. Assn. Ga., Kappa Delta Pi, Sigma Delta Pi (hon.). Avocations: golf, travel, gardening, tennis. Office: Wheeler High Sch 375 Holt Rd Marietta GA 30068-3560

MATICH, MATTHEW P., secondary school English educator; b. San Pedro, Calif., June 30, 1962. B Fine and Comm. Arts, Loyola Marymount U., 1985; MEd, Nat. U., 1995; grad., Am. Sch. X-Ray, L.A., 1992. Cert. secondary sch. English tchr., Calif. Records retention clk. Starkist Foods, Terminal Island, Calif., 1979-83; producer, newswriter KMET Radio, Hollywood, Calif., 1981-83, 85-86; news dir., broadcaster KXLU Radio, L.A., 1983-87; instr., counselor Columbia Sch. Broadcasting, Hollywood, 1985-88; radio reporter KRTH Radio, L.A., 1987-88; radio producer Transtar Radio Network, Hollywood, 1987-88; deck crew/customer svc. Catalina Island (Calif.) Express, Avalon, 1989-91; substitute tchr. L.A. Unified Sch. Dist., 1989-92; English tchr., head coach football and track San Pedro (Calif.) H.S., 1992—, head coach freshman/sophomore football and track coach, 1993—; founder, mem. adv. bd. Acad. Athletes (now Extracurricular Academics), San Pedro, 1994—; founder local ethnic tribute/holiday Burrito Day in L.A., 1983—. Writer, prodr. radio program The Bluez Shift, 1983-87. Mem. San Pedro Pirate Boosters, 1987. Mem. United Tchrs. L.A., Am. Fedn. Tchrs., Nat. Coun. Tchrs. English, Calif. Assn. Tchrs. English, Dalmation Am. Club, Elks Club (scholarship com. 1990). Avocations: travel. Home: 2731 S Averill Ave San Pedro CA 90731-5632 Office: San Pedro HS 1001 W 15th St San Pedro CA 90731-3925

MATIJEVIC, EGON, chemistry educator,; b. Otocac, Croatia, Apr. 27, 1922; came to U.S., 1957; s. Grgur and Stefica (Spiegel) M.; m. Bozica Biscan, Feb. 27, 1947. Diploma in chem. engring., U. Zagreb, 1944, PhD in Chemistry, 1948, Dr. Habil. in Phys. Chemistry, 1952; DSc (hon.), Lehigh U., 1977, M. Curie-Sklodowska U., Lublin, Poland, 1990; DSc. (hon.), Clarkson U., 1992. Instr. chemistry U. Zagreb, Yugoslavia, 1944-47; sr. instr. phys. chemistry U. Zagreb, 1949-52, privat dozent in colloid chemistry, 1952-54, dozent in phys. and colloid chemistry, 1955-56, on leave, 1956-59; rsch. assoc. Inst. Cinematography, Zagreb, 1948; rsch. fellow dept. colloid sci. U. Cambridge, Eng., 1956-57; vis. prof. Clarkson Coll. Tech., Potsdam, N.Y., 1957-59; assoc. prof. chemistry Clarkson Coll. Tech., Postdam, N.Y., 1960-62; prof. Clarkson U., Postdam, 1962-86, disting. univ. prof., 1986—; assoc. dir. Inst. Colloid and Surface Sci. Clarkson Coll. Tech., 1966-68; dir. inst., 1968-81, chmn. dept. chemistry, 1981-87; vis. prof. Japan Soc. for Promotion Sci., 1973, U. Melbourne, Australia, 1976, Sci. U. Tokyo, 1979, 84; vis. scientist U. Leningrad, USSR, 1977; Internat. Atomic Energy Agy. adviser Buenos Aires, Argentina, 1978, 80; fgn. guest Inst. Colloid and Interface Sci. Sci. U. Tokyo, 1982; lectr. in field; mem. adv. com. Univs. and Space Research Assn.; referee NATO Advanced Study Inst. Author: (with M. Kesler) General and Inorganic Chemsitry for Senior High Schools, 11 edits., including Croatian, Macedonian, Hungarian, Italian, 1943-63; translator: Einfuhrung in die Stochiometrie (Nylen and Wigern), 1948; editor: (with Alter J. Weber) Adsorption from Aqueous Solution, 1968, Surface and Colloid Science, vols. 1-15, 1969-92; contbr. numerous articles to profl. publs. Recipient Gold medal Am. Electroplaters Soc., 1976; guest of honor 56th and 63rd Colloid and Surface Sci. Symposiums, Blacksburg, Va., 1982, Seattle, 1989. Mem. Am. Chem. Soc. (councilor div. colloid and surface chemistry 1982-87, chmn. 1969-70, Kendall award 1972, Langmuir Disting. Lectureship award 1985, Ralph K. Iler award 1993), Kolloid Gesellschaft (hon. life, Thomas Graham award 1985), Internat. Assn. Colloid Interface Sci. (pres. 1985-87), Chem. Soc. Japan, Inst. Colloid and Interface Sci. of Sci. of Tokyo (hon.), Phalanx Soc., Croatian Acad. Scis. and Arts (fgn.), Am. Ceramic Soc. (hon.), Materials Rsch. Soc. Japan (hon.), Acad. Ceramics (Italy), Croatian Chem. Soc. (Bozo Tezak medal 1991), Sigma Xi (Clarkson Coll. Tech. chpt. award 1972, nat. lectr. 1987-89). Roman Catholic. Office: Ctr Advanced Materials Proc Clarkson U Dept Chem Potsdam NY 13699-5814

MATIN, ABDUL, microbiology educator, consultant; b. Delhi, India, May 8, 1941; came to U.S., 1964, naturalized, 1983; s. Mohammed and Zohra (Begum) Said; m. Mimi Keyhan, June 21, 1968. BS, U. Karachi, Pakistan, 1960, MS, 1962; PhD, UCLA, 1969. Lectr. St. Joseph's Coll., Karachi, 1962-64; research assoc. UCLA, 1964-71; sci. officer U. Groningen, Kerklaan, The Netherlands, 1971-75; from asst. prof. to full prof. microbiology and immunology Stanford U., Calif., 1975—; prof. Western Hazardous Substances Rsch. Ctr. Stanford U., 1981—; cons. Engenics, 1982-84, Monsanto, 1984-86, Chlorox, 1992-93; chmn. Stanford Recombinant DNA panel; mem. Accreditation Bd. for Engring. and Tech.; mem. panel Yucca Mountain Microbial Activity, Dept. of Energy, mem. study sect.; participant DOE, NABIR program draft panel; convenor of microbiol. workshop and confs. Mem. editl. bd. Jour. Bacteriology, Ann. Rev. Microbiol.; reviewer NSF and other grants; contbr. numerous publs. to sci. jours. Fellow Fulbright Found., 1964, NSF, 1981-92, Ctr. for Biotech. Rsch., 1981-85, EPA, 1981—, NIH, 1989-92, Coll. BioTech., U.N. Tokten, 1987, DOE, 1993—, Dept. Agrl., 1995—. Mem. AAAS, AAUP, Am Soc. for Microbiology (Found. lectr. 1991-93), Soc. Gen. Microbiology, Soc. Indsl. Microbiology, No. Soc. Indsl. Microbiology (bd. dirs.), Biophys. Soc., Am. Chem. Soc. Avocations: reading, music, walking. Home: 690 Coronado Ave Stanford CA 94305-1039 Office: Stanford U Dept Microbiology and Immunology Fairchild Sci Bldg Stanford CA 94305-5402

MATIS, NINA B., lawyer; b. N.Y.C., June 23, 1947. AB cum laude, Smith Coll., 1969; JD, NYU, 1972. Bar: Ill. 1973. Ptnr. Katten Muchin & Zavis, Chgo.; adj. prof. law Northwestern U., 1984-87. Mem. Am. Coll. Lawyers, Urban Land Inst. Office: Katten Muchin & Zavis 525 W Monroe St Ste 1600 Chicago IL 60661-3629*

MATISOFF, SUSAN, cultural research organization administrator. Dir. Ctr. East-Asian Studies, Stanford U., Calif. Office: Stanford Univ/Ctr E Asian Stud Asian Lang Dept Bldg 250 300 Lasuen St Stanford CA 94305-8311*

MATJASKO, JANE, anesthesiologist; b. Harrison Twp., Pa., 1942. MD, Med. Coll. Pa., 1968. Resident in anesthesiology Md. Hosp., Balt., 1968-72; anesthesiologist U. Md. Hosp., Balt.; prof., chmn. anesthesiology U. Md. Office: U Md Hosp Dept Anesthesiology 22 S Greene St Baltimore MD 21201-1544*

MATKOWSKY, BERNARD JUDAH, applied mathematician, educator; b. N.Y.C., Aug. 19, 1939; s. Morris N. and Ethel H. M.; m. Florence Knobel, Apr. 11, 1965; children: David, Daniel, Devorah. B.S., CCNY, 1960; M.E.E., NYU, 1961, M.S., 1963, Ph.D., 1966. Fellow Courant Inst. Math. Scis., NYU, 1961-66; mem. faculty dept. math. Rensselaer Poly. Inst., 1966-77; John Evans prof. applied math., mech. engring. & math. Northwestern U., Evanston, Ill., 1977—, chmn. engring. sci. and applied math. dept., 1993—; vis. prof. Tel Aviv U., 1972-73; vis. scientist Weizmann Inst. Sci., Israel, summer 1976, summer 1980, Tel Aviv U., summer 1980; cons. Argonne Nat. Lab., Sandia Labs., Lawrence Livermore Nat. Lab., Exxon Research and Engring. Co. Editor Wave Motion-An Internat. Jour., 1979—, Applied Math. Letters, 1987—, SIAM Jour. Applied Math., 1989-96, Random and Computational Dynamics, 1991—, Internat. Jour. SHS, 1992—, Jour. Materials Synthesis and Processing, 1992—; mem. editl. adv. bd. Springer Verlag Applied Math. Scis. Series; contbr. chpts. to books, articles to profl. jours. Fulbright grantee, 1972-73; Guggenheim fellow, 1982-83. Fellow Am. Acad. Mechanics; mem. AAAS, Soc. Indsl. and Applied Math., Am. Math. Soc., Combustion Inst., Am. Phys. Soc., Am. Assn. Combustion Synthesis, Conf. Bd. Math. Scis. (coun., com. human rights of math. scientists), Com. Concerned Scientists, Soc. Natural Philosophy, Sigma Xi, Eta Kappa Nu. Home: 3704 Davis St Skokie IL 60076-1745 Office: Northwestern U Technological Institut Evanston IL 60208

MATLACK, GEORGE MILLER, radiochemist; b. Pitts., June 14, 1921; s. Allyn Wolcott and Mildred Narcissa (Miller) M.; m. Meredith Mildred Madsen, Sept. 4, 1943; children—Nancy, Christine, Martin, Allyn. AB, Grinnell Coll., 1943; MS, State U. Iowa, 1947, PhD, 1949. Prin. chemist Iowa Geol. Survey, Iowa City, 1943-46; rsch. asst. State U. Iowa, 1946-49; sect. leader, analytical chemistry Los Alamos (N.Mex.) Nat. Lab., 1949-82, assoc. group leader analytical chemistry div., 1983-90, mem. team for devel. remote sensing of dinosaur bones by radiometric methods, 1988-95, sr. adv. analytical chemistry divsn., 1990-95. Contbr. articles to profl. jours. Pres., Los Alamos Choral Soc., 1961-62, Los Alamos Sinfonietta, 1967-69. Fellow Am. Inst. Chemists, AAAS; mem. Am. Chem. Soc., Am. Nuclear Soc., N.Y. Acad. Scis., Iowa Acad. Scis., Four-Fifths Mus. Soc. Lodges: Masons, Eastern Star. Home: 254 San Juan St Los Alamos NM 87544-2635 Office: Los Alamos Nat Lab Chemistry Div MS-G740 PO Box 1663 Los Alamos NM 87545-0001

MATLEY, BENVENUTO GILBERT (BEN MATLEY), computer engineer, educator, consultant; b. Monroe, La., Sept. 8, 1930; s. Welcome Gilbert and Lucette Marie (Renaud) M.; m. Patricia Jean McWilliams, June 21, 1959; children: Elizabeth, Katherine, John, Stephen, Richard, David. AB, San Diego State U., 1960; MBA, U. So. Calif., 1964; EdD, Nova U., 1980. Cert. data processor. Mathematician, engr. various data processing and computing firms, San Diego and L.A., 1956-64; sr. computer systems engr. Nortronics div. Northrop Corp., Hawthorne, Calif., 1964-69; prof. data processing and math. Ventura (Calif.) Coll., 1969—; lectr. in mgmt. and computer sci. West Coast U., L.A., 1982—; software cons, ednl. cons., Ventura, 1972—. Author: Principles of Elementary Algebra: A Language and Equations Approach, 1991; sr. author: National Computer Policies, 1988; contbr. chpts. to books, articles to profl. jours. Active Ventura County coun. Boy Scouts Am., 1979-82; cons. Calif. Luth. U., Thousand Oaks, Calif., 1989. Lt. (j.g.) USNR, 1952-55, Europe. Mem. IEEE Computer Soc. (Disting Visitor 1988-91), Assn. for Computing Machinery, Math. Assn. Am. Avocation: writing. Office: Ventura Coll 4667 Telegraph Rd Ventura CA 93003-3872

MATLIN, MARLEE, actress; b. Morton Grove, Ill., Aug. 24, 1965; m. Kevin Grandalski, Aug. 29, 1993. Attended William Rainey Harper Coll. Appeared in films Children of a Lesser God (Acad. award for best actress), 1986, Walker, 1987, Linguini Incident, 1990, The Player, 1992, Hear No Evli, 1993; TV film: Bridge to Silence, 1989, Against Her Will: The Carrie Buck Sotry, 1994; TV series: Reasonable Doubts, 1991-93; guest of Picket Fences, 1993 (Emmy nomination, Guest Actress-Drama Series, 1994), Seinfeld, 1993 (Emmy nomination Guest Actress-Comedy Series, 1994). Recipient Golden Globe award Hollywood Fgn. Press Assn., 1987, named Best Actress. Office: care ICM 8942 Wilshire Blvd Beverly Hills CA 90211-1934*

MATLOCK, CLIFFORD CHARLES, retired foreign service officer; b. Whittier, Cal., Nov. 6, 1909; s. William Holl and Clara Louisa (Wallace) M.; m. Nina Stolypin, Nov. 6, 1934 (dec. Dec. 1969); m. Elisabeth Thompson Scobey, May 3, 1971. A.B., Stanford U., 1932; A.M., Harvard U., 1940, certificate pub. adminstrn. (Littauer fellow), 1940. Economist USDA, 1938-41, U.S. Treasury, 1941-42; economist, adminstr. Bd. Econ. Warfare, Fgn. Econ. Adminstrn., 1942-45; econ., polit. officer Dept. State, 1946-62; polit. adviser European coordinating com. Dept. State, London, 1949-50; polit. officer U.S. delegation North Atlantic Council, London, 1950-52; polit. officer, then dir. plans and policy staff Office U.S. spl. rep. in Europe, Paris, 1952-53; spl. asst. Am. ambassador, Tehran, 1955-57; spl. asst. econ. affairs asst. sec. state for Far Eastern affairs, also alternate to Dep. Asst. Sec., 1959-62, ret.; acting dep. asst. Sec. of State, 1959; spl. asst. for polit. and econ. affairs to asst. adminstr. East Asia AID, Dept. of State, 1962-68, dir. East Asia tech. adv. staff, 1966-68, cons. Bur. for East Asia, 1968-71; coordinator interdisciplinary Devel. Cycles Research Project, 1971-76, prin., 1977-84; U.S. del. Econ. Commn. for Asia and Far East (UN), Tokyo, Japan, 1962; U.S. del. to devel. assistance com. Orgn. for Economic Cooperation and Devel., Paris, France, 1962; Member U.S. delegation Colombo Plan Consultative Com., Seattle, 1958, London, 1964; Member Development Assistance Group, Orgn. Econ. Coop. and Development, Washington, 1960; U.S. alternate rep. UN Econ. Commn. for Asia and Far East, Bangkok, 1960; adviser, mem. U.S. del. bds. govs. Internat. Monetary Fund, Internat. Bank for Reconstrn. and Devel., Tokyo, Japan, 1964; exec. com. SE Asia Devel. Adv. Group, 1965-70. Author: Man and Cosmos: A Theory of Endeavor Rhythms, 1977; draftsman of American Credo (in support of Truman Doctrine, now in U.S. Archives, H.S. Truman Libr.), 1947. Recipient Superior Honor award AID, 1968. Mem. Fgn. Service Assn., Diplomatic and Consular Officers Ret., Phi Beta Kappa. Clubs: Metropolitan (Washington), Harvard (Washington); Harvard of Western N.C. Home: Rte 1 Box 388 Lowry Rd Balsam Heights Waynesville NC 28786

MATLOCK, (LEE) HUDSON, civil engineer, educator; b. Floresville, Tex., Dec. 9, 1919; s. Lee Hudson Sr. and Charlie Mary (Stevenson) M.; m. Harriett Nadine Kidder, Nov. 28, 1942 (dec. Jan. 1996); children: John Hudson, David Kidder. BSCE, U. Tex., 1947, MSCE, 1950. Registered profl. engr., Tex. From instr. to prof. U. Tex., Austin, 1948-78, chmn. dept. civil engring., 1972-76, prof. emeritus civil engring., 1995—; v.p. R & D Earth Tech. Corp., Long Beach, Calif., 1978-85; civil engring. cons. Kerrville, Tex., 1985—; cons. Shell, Mobil, Chevron, Conoco and others, 1958—. Contbr. numerous tech. papers and sponsored rsch. reports to profl. publs. 1st lt. AC, U.S. Army, 1941-45. Recipient Disting. Achievement award Offshore Tech. Conf., Houston, 1985; named Disting. Engring. Grad. Coll. Engring. U. Tex.-Austin, 1986. Fellow ASCE (J. James R. Croes medal 1968), Tau Beta Pi; mem. NAE. Methodist. Avocations: flying, fishing, gardening. Home and Office: HC 5 Box 574-655 Kerrville TX 78028-9034

MATLOCK, JACK FOUST, JR., diplomat; b. Greensboro, N.C., Oct. 1, 1929; s. Jack Foust and Nellie (McSwain) M.; m. Rebecca Burrum, Sept. 2, 1949; children: James, Hugh, Nell, David, Joseph. A.B. summa cum laude, Duke U., 1950; M.A., Columbia U., 1952; cert., Russian Inst., 1952; LLD (hon.), Greensboro Coll., 1989, Albright Coll., 1992, Conn. Coll., 1993. Instr. Dartmouth, 1953-56; fgn. service officer Dept. State, 1956-91; assigned Washington, 1956-58, Am. Embassy, Vienna, Austria, 1958-60; Am. consul. gen. Munich, Germany, 1960-61; assigned Am. Embassy, Moscow, 1961-63, Accra, Ghana, 1963-66; assigned Am. Consulate, Zanzibar, 1967-69, Am. Embassy, Dar es Salaam, Tanzania, 1969-70, Sr. Seminar in Fgn. Policy, Dept. State, 1970-71; country dir. for USSR State Dept., 1971-74; minister-counselor, dep. chief mission Am. Embassy, Moscow, 1974-78; diplomat-in-residence Vanderbilt U., Nashville, 1978-79; dep. dir. Fgn. Service Inst., Washington, 1979-80; chargé d'affaires ad interim Am. Embassy, Moscow, 1981; ambassador to Czechoslovakia, 1981-83; spl. asst. to pres., sr. dir. European and Soviet Affairs Nat. Security Council, 1983-87; U.S. ambassador to the Soviet Union, Moscow, 1987-91; sr. rsch. fellow Columbia U., N.Y.C., 1991-93, Kathryn and Shelby Collum Davis prof. Practice Internat. Diplomacy, 1993-96; George F. Kennan prof. history Inst. for Advanced Study, Princeton, N.J., 1996—. Author: Autopsy on an Empire: The American Ambassador's Account of the Collapse of the Soviet Union, 1995; compiler, editor: Index to J.V. Stalin's Works, 2d edit., 1971. Mem. Am. Acad. Diplomacy, Coun. on Fgn. Rels., Century Assn. N.Y. Home: 2913 P St NW Washington DC 20007-3069 also: 63 Battle Rd Princeton NJ 08540 Office: Inst for Advanced Study Princeton NJ 08540

MATLOCK, JOHN HUDSON, science administrator, materials engineer; b. San Angelo, Tex., Nov. 23, 1944; s. Lee Hudson Jr. and Harriett (Kidder) M.; m. Kathe Lynne Reep, Sept. 3, 1966; children: Michelle, Joseph. B. Engring. Sci., U. Tex., 1967, MSME, 1969, PhD in Material Sci. and Engring., 1970; MBA, So. Ill. U., Edwardsville, 1976. Registered profl. engr., Mo., Wash., Oreg. Sr. rsch. engr. Monsanto Co., St. Peters, Mo., 1970-72, rsch. specialist, 1972-74, supt. tech. svcs., 1974-79; sr. staff engr. Mostek Corp., Carrollton, Tex., 1979-80, mgr. material tech. group, 1980-83; v.p. tech. SEH Am., Inc., Vancouver, Wash., 1983-90, exec. v.p., 1990—; bd. dirs. Wash. Tech. Ctr., 1991—; mem. vis. com. Engring. Coll., U. Wash., Seattle, 1985-94, mem. indsl. adv. bd. Material Sci. and Engring., 1988—; mem. engring. adv. bd. Wash. State U., Pullman, 1984—, adj. lectr., 1985; bd. dirs. Wash. Higher Edn. Telecomms., 1985-90; adj. prof. mech. engring., mem. grad. faculty Oreg. State U., Corvallis, 1985-90; adj. asst. prof. physics So. Ill. U., Edwardsville, 1973-76. Contbr. approximately 40 articles on silicon crystal growing and the effect of silicon properties on electronic devic performance to profl. and trade jours. Mem. bd. trustees 1st Ch. of God, Vancouver, 1988-91, tchr. adult ch. sch., 1986-91; mem. sch. bd. Kingsway Christian Sch., Vancouver, 1990-91. Mem. Electrochem. Soc., Metall. Soc., AIME, Am. Soc. for Materials, Materials Rsch. Soc., ASTM, Tau Beta Pi, Pi Tau Sigma, Phi Kappa Phi, Beta Gamma Sigma. Home: 10916 NE 30th Ave Vancouver WA 98686-4346 Office: SEH Am Inc 4111 NE 112th Ave Vancouver WA 98682-6776

MATLOCK, KENNETH JEROME, building materials company executive; b. Oak Park, Ill., May 30, 1928; s. Harvey and Lillian (Sivertsen) Samuelson; m. Dorothy Belowski, Nov. 3, 1956; children—Geoffrey, Barbara, Gail, Paul. Student, James Millikin U., 1946-48; B.S. in Accountancy, U. Ill., 1950; postgrad., Northwestern U. Inst. Mgmt., summer 1963. C.P.A., Ill., Fla. Sr. audit mgr. Price Waterhouse & Co., Chgo., 1950-64; with Celotex Corp., Chgo., 1964-65; v.p. fin. ops. Celotex Corp., Tampa, Fla., 1965-74; asst. to v.p. Jim Walter Corp., Tampa, 1966-69, controller, 1970-72, v.p., 1972-74, v.p., chief acctg. officer, 1974-88, sr. v.p., CFO, 1987-91; v.p., CFO Walter Industries, Inc., Tampa, 1987-88; Walter Industries, Inc.; exec. v.p., bd. dirs. Walter Industries, Inc., Tampa, 1991—; exec. v.p., CFO, also bd. dirs. Walter Industries, Inc. Adviser Jr. Achievement, Chgo., 1958-60; active Heart Fund, United Fund, 1956-58. Served with USNR, 1945-46. Mem. AICPA, Ill. Soc. CPAs. Fla. Soc. CPAs, Fin. Execs. Inst. Home: 1401 87th Ave N Saint Petersburg FL 33702-2931 Office: Walter Industries Inc 1500 N Dale Mabry Hwy Tampa FL 33607-2551

MATOIAN, JOHN, broadcasting company executive. Dir. devel. Highgate Pictures/Learning Corp. Am., 1979-84; v.p. devel. Scholastic Prodns., 1984-86; head made-for-TV movies CBS, 1986-88; v.p. internat. program devel. CBS Entertainment, 1988-92, sr. v.p. motion pictures for TV and mini-series, 1992-94; pres. Fox Entertainment Group Fox Broadcasting Co., 1994—. Office: Fox Broadcasting Co PO Box 900 Beverly Hills CA 90213*

MATON, ANTHEA, education consultant; b. Burnley, Lancashire, England, Feb. 1, 1944; d. William Douglas Newton-Dawson and Beatrice Joan (Simpson) Bateman; m. K.F. Edward Asprey, Nov. 13, 1965 (div. 1978); children: George William Edward, Mariana Alexandra Beatrice; m. Paul Nicholas Maton, Mar. 23, 1978; 1 child, Petra Beatrice Suzanne. Tchg. cert., higher diploma, tchg. diploma; postgrad., U. Okla. Clin. instr. radiotherapy Hammersmith Hosp., London, 1970-75; prin. sch. radiotherapy Royal Free Hosp., London, 1977-80, acting supt., 1979-80; head of careers Putney High Sch. for Girls, London, 1981-83; head of physics St. Andrews Episc. High Sch., Bethesda, Md., 1984-88; vis. fellow Am. Assn. Physics Tchrs., 1988-89; nat. coord. project scope, sequence, and coordination Nat. Sci. Tchrs. Assn., 1989-91; exec. dir. Edn. Commections, Oklahoma City, 1991—, dir. exhbn. on art and physics, 1994—; vis. faculty physics Western Wash. U., 1995; vis. faculty Okla. Sch. Sci. and Math. 1995—; organizer U.S.-Soviet H.S. Physics Student Exch. and Visit, 1989; conducted numerous workshops on sci. curriculum reform and assessment reform, 1987—; faculty USA Physics Olympiad Team, 1986, 89; physics tchr. St. Andrews Episc. H.S., 1984-88, Putney H.S. for Girls, 1980-83, tchr. med. ethics, 1982-83; tchr. physics, anatomy and physiology, radiobiology Royal Free Hosp., 1977-80, contemporary physics edn. project, 1989—. Lead author Prentice Hall Sci., 1993; contbr. articles to profl. jours. Mem. Nat. Mus. Women Arts (charter), Women's Philharm. (charter); apptd. to scientific adv. bd. OMNIPLEX Sci. Mus., Okla. City; cons. Sta. WGBH, Boston, Smithsonian, Am. Mus. of Moving Image, UCLA, Del. Edn. Dept., Ark. Project Advise, Newcastle (Del.) Sch. Dist. Named one of Today's Leaders Okla. Edn. Equity Roundtable, 1992. Mem. NAFE, ASCD, AAUW (pub. policy chair 1995-96), NOW (coord. metro chpt. 1992-95, treas. Okla. state chpt. 1993-95), Nat. Sci. Tchrs. Assn., Am. Assn. Physics Tchrs., N.Y. Acad. Scis., Assn. for Sci. Edn., Soc. Radiographers U.K., Soc. Radiographers Radiotherapy. Avocations: gender and science, drawing, writing poetry, singing, making wood cuts. Home and Office: 1804 Dorchester Dr Oklahoma City OK 73120-4706

MATORY, W(ILLIAM) EARLE, JR., plastic surgeon, educator; b. Richmond, Va., Nov. 20, 1950; s. William Earle Sr. and Deborah L. (Love) M.; m. Yvonne Marie, Nov. 17, 1948; 1 child, William Earle III. BS, Yale U., 1972; MD, Howard U., 1976. Fellow Lahey Clinic, Boston, U. Calif., San Francisco; fellow U. Calif., San Francisco; from. asst. to assoc. prof. U. Mass. Med. Ctr. Author: Ethnic Considerations in Facial Aesthetic Surgery, 1995, Evolving Strategies in the Management of Breast Disease, 1995. Bd. dirs. Youth at Risk Breakthrough Found., San Francisco, 1993. Recipient Distinction award Nat. Med. Assn., 1991, Surg. Sect. award, Arthur L. Gaines award Columbia U., Edw. J. Mason award. Mem. ACS, Am. Soc. Plastic and Reconstructive Surgeons, Am. Soc. Aesthetic Plastic Surgeons (bd. dirs.), Am. Assn. Plastic Surgery. Avocations: racquetball, fishing. Office: A New You 250 E Yale Loop Ste A Irvine CA 92714

MATOS, CRUZ ALFONSO, environmental consultant; b. N.Y.C., Mar. 6, 1929; s. José and Gertrudes (Manzanares) M.; m. Aurelia Santos, Dec. 13, 1963; children: Miguel, Veronica, Monica, Angélica. B in Engring. Sci., Oxford U., 1957, M in Engring. Sci., 1958; DSc (honoris causa) U. Met., P.R., 1995. Pres., CEO Fischer & Porter de P.R., 1964-69; asst. sec. dept. pub. works Govt. of P.R., 1969-70, exec. dir. Environ. Quality Bd., 1970-73, sec. dept. natural resources, 1973-75, cabinet mem., 1970-75; UN chief tech., dir. Inst. Marine Affairs, Trinidad and Tobago, 1975-79; UN Devel. Program regional rep. Trinidad and Tobago, Barbados, Surinam and Dutch West Indies, 1978-80, UN chief tech. adviser South Pacific, dir. CCOP/SOPAC, Suva, Fiji, 1980-89, ret.; advisor to pres. P.R. Senate for natural resources, the environ. and energy, 1993—; advisor to exec. dir. UN Environ. Program for L.Am. and Caribbean, 1994—; mem. various adv. panels and overseas mission U.S. NAS; mem. U.S. Nat. Commn. on Environment, Consejo Consultive Recursos Naturales y Ambientales (apptd. Gov. P.R.), Consejo Consultivo del Programa de Patrimonio Natural de Puerto Rico, Com. Sobre Politica Publica Energetica P.R., Consejo Asesor Sobre Energia. Contbr. articles to sci. jours. and mags. Trustee, Conservation Found., U.S., bd. dirs., World Wildlife Fund-U.S.A.; mem. bd. dirs. Caribbean Environment and Devel. Inst., Caribbean Natural Resources Inst. Served with U.S. Army, 1952-54. Recipient Boriquen Conservation award, 1971. Office: PO Box 7627 Playa Cerro Gordo Vega Alta PR 00692

MATOY, ELIZABETH ANNE, personnel executive; b. Stillwater, Okla., Sept. 11, 1946; d. Ray Roland and Helen Louise (Springer) Matoy; m. Michael D. Banks; children: Heather Anne, Kirsten Sue, Aaron Christian, Kendra Jeanne Carlson. BA, U. Ill., Chgo., 1968; MSM, Frostburg (Md.) State Coll., 1975. Publs. mgr. Forum Press, Stillwater, Okla., 1982-84; editor centennial histories project Okla. State U., 1984-88, assoc. pers. dir., 1988-91, pers. dir., 1991—; owner, pub. Prairie Imprints, Stillwater, 1985-92; cons. Active Corps of Execs., Frostburg, Md., 1975-77. Editor: DAC in Oklahoma, 1984; also editor for Payne County (Okla.) Historical Soc., 1980-90. Pres. LaVale (Md.) Vol. Fire Dept. Aux., 1972-77; bd. dirs. Morgantown, W.Va. Shawnee Girl Scouts Council, 1975-77; mem. allocations com. Cumberland, Md. United Way, 1975-77; bus. mgr. Stillwater Sylvia Stapley Day Camp Girl Scouts, 1982-84. Recipient Bronze Pelican award Archdiocese of Tulsa, 1990, Sr. Profl. Human Resources award Human Resources Cert. Inst., 1992. Mem. Payne County Hist. Soc. (sec. 1980-82, historian 1986), Okla. Colls. Univs. Pers. Assn., Stillwater Rotary Club. Republican. Methodist. Home: 210 E Greenvale Ct Stillwater OK 74075-1662 Office: Okla State U Dept Pers Stillwater OK 74076-0481

MATRINEZ, RAMON JAIME, professional baseball player; b. Santo Domingo, Dominican Rep., Mar. 22, 1968. Grad. high sch., Dominican Rep. Pitcher L.A. Dodgers, 1988—. Achievements include mem. Dominican Rep. Olympic Baseball Team, 1988. Office: LA Dodgers 1000 Elysian Port Ave Los Angeles CA 90012

MATSCH, RICHARD P., judge; b. Burlington, Iowa, June 8, 1930. A.B., U. Mich., 1951, J.D., 1953. Bar: Colo. Asst. U.S. atty. Colo., 1959-61; dep. city atty. City and County of Denver, 1961-63; judge U.S. Bankruptcy Ct., Colo., 1965-74; judge U.S. Dist. Ct. for Colo., 1974-94, chief judge, 1994—; mem. Judicial Conf. of the U.S., 1991-94, mem. com. on criminal law, 1988-94; mem. bd. dirs. Fed. Judicial Ctr., 1995—. Served with U.S. Army, 1953-55. Mem. ABA, Am. Judicature Soc. Office: Byron White Court House 1823 Stout St Denver CO 80257*

MATSCHULLAT, DALE LEWIS, lawyer; b. Ft. Sill, Okla., May 1, 1945; s. Wayne Emil and Harriet Jane (Bowman) M.; m. Eileen Joanne Davidson, Aug. 26, 1967; children—Robert Charles, Stephen Francis. A.B., Stanford U., 1967, J.D., 1970. Bar: N.Y., Wis. Law clk. U.S. Dist. Ct. (ea. dist.) N.Y., Bklyn., 1970-71; assoc. firm Davis, Polk & Wardwell, Manhattan, N.Y., 1972-77; former sector counsel Allis Chalmers Corp., Milw., from 1977; former gen. counsel Allis Chalmers Corp.; now gen. counsel Newell Co., Freeport, Ill. Roman Catholic. Office: Newell Co 29 E Stephenson St Freeport IL 61032-4235

MATSEN, FREDERICK ALBERT, III, orthopedic educator; b. Austin, Tex., Feb. 5, 1944; s. Frederick Albert II and Cecilia (Kirkegaard) M.; m. Anne Lovell, Dec. 24, 1966; children: Susanna Lovell, Frederick A. IV, Laura Jane Megan. BA, U. Tex., Austin, 1964; MD, Baylor U., 1968. Intern Johns Hopkins U., Balt., 1971; resident in orthopaedics U. Wash., Seattle, 1971-74, acting instr. orthopaedics, 1974, asst. prof. orthopaedics, 1975-79, assoc. prof. orthopaedics, 1979-82, prof., 1982-85, 86—, adjunct prof. Ctr. Bioengring., 1985—, dir. residency program orthopaedics, 1978-81, vice chmn. dept. orthopaedics, 1982-85, acting chmn. dept. orthopaedics, 1983-84, prof., chmn. dept. orthopaedics, 1981—; mem. Orthopaedic Residency Rev. Com., Chgo., 1981-86. Author: Compartmental Syndromes, 1980; editor: The Shoulder, 1990; contbr. articles to profl. jours., chpts. to textbooks; assoc. editor Clin. Orthopaedics, Jour. Orthopaedic Rsch., 1981—. Lt. comdr. USPHS, 1969-71. Recipient Traveling fellowship Am. Orthopaedic Assn., 1983, Nicholas Andry award Assn. Bone and Joint Surgery, 1979, Henry Meyerding Essay award Am. Fracture Assn., 1974. Mem. Am. Shoulder and Elbow Surgeons (founding, pres. 1991—), Am. Acad. Orthopaedic Surgeons (bd. dirs. 1984-85), Orthopaedic Rsch. Soc., Western Orthopaedic Assn., Phi Beta Kappa. Office: U Wash Dept Orthopaedics RK-10 1959 NE Pacific St Seattle WA 98195-0004

MATSLER, FRANKLIN GILES, higher education educator; b. Glendive, Mont., Dec. 27, 1922; s. Edmund Russell and Florence Edna (Giles) M.; m. Lois Josephine Hoyt, June 12, 1949; children—Linda, Jeanne, David, Winfield. B.S., Mont. State U., Bozeman, 1948; M.A., U. Mont., Missoula, 1952; Ph.D., U. Calif. at Berkeley, 1959. Tchr. Missoula County (Mont.) High Sch., 1949-51, Tracy (Calif.) Sr. Elem. Schs., 1952-53, San Benito County (Calif.) High Sch. and Jr. Coll., 1953-55; grad. asst. U. Calif. at Berkeley, 1955-58; asst. prof. Humboldt State Coll., Arcata, Calif., 1958-62; asso. prof. Humboldt State Coll., 1962-63, asst. exec. dean, 1958-63; chief specialist higher edn. Calif. Coordinating Council for Higher Edn., Sacramento, 1963-68; exec. dir. Ill. Bd. Regents, Springfield, 1968-84; prof. higher edn. Ill. State U., Normal, 1968—, Regency prof. higher edn., 1984—; chancellor Ill. Bd. Regents, 1995—. Bd. dirs. Ill. Edn. Consortium, 1972-76; bd. dirs. Central Ill. Health Planning Agy., 1970-76, Springfield Symphony Orch. Assn.; pres. Bloomington/Normal Symphony Soc., 1988-90. Served to 1st lt. AUS, 1943-46. Mem. Nat. Assn. Sys. Heads (exec. v.p. 1985-92), Am. Assn. State Colls. and Univs. Assn. for Instl. Rsch., Phi Delta Kappa, Lambda Chi Alpha. Home: 2005 Woodfield Rd Bloomington IL 61704-2427 Office: Illinois State U 539 DeGarmo Hall Normal IL 61761

MATSON, PAMELA ANNE, environmental science educator; b. Eau Claire, Wis., Aug. 3, 1953. BS, U. Wis., 1975; MS, Ind. U., 1980; PhD, Oreg. State U., 1983. Prof. U. Calif., Berkeley, 1993—. MacArthur fellow, 1995. Mem. Am. Acad. Arts & Scis., Nat. Acad. Sci. Specializes in the interactions between the biosphere and the atmosphere; pioneered research into the role of land-use changes on global warming, analyzing the effects of greenhouse gas emissions resulting from tropical deforestization; investigating the effects of intensive agriculture on the atmosphere, especially the effects of tropical agriculture and cattle ranching, and is finding ways in which agricultural productivity can be expanded without increasing the level of greenhouse gasses. Office: U Calif Dept Sci Policy and Mgmt Dept Environ Science Berkeley CA 94720-3110

MATSON, ROBERT EDWARD, educator, leadership consultant; b. Chauncey, Ohio, Dec. 2, 1930; s. William I. and Mary Royal (Rivers) M.; m. Mary Athearn, June 27, 1954; children—Laurie, Jeanne, Scott. B.S., Ohio U., 1956, M.Ed., 1957; Ed.D., Ind. U., 1961. Dean of Men Carroll Coll., Wis., 1961-65; v.p. student affairs Kent State U, Ohio, 1965-70; pres. Ricker Coll., 1970-74; sr. prof. Fed. Exec. Inst., Charlottesville, Va., 1974-80, acad. dean, 1980-82, dir., 1982-87, sr. prof., dir. emeritus, 1987-89; prof. dir. leadership edn. program Ctr. Pub. Svc. U. Va., 1989—, dir. Inst. Govt., 1994—. Served to 1st. lt. U.S. Army, 1953-55; Korea. Mem. Am. Soc. Pub. Adminstrn., Am. Assn. Higher Edn., Internat. City/County Mgrs. Assn. (Sweeney Acad. award 1993), Am. Personnel and Guidance Assn.. Methodist. Office: Ctr for Pub Svc 918 Emmet St N Charlottesville VA 22903-4832

MATSON, VIRGINIA MAE FREEBERG (MRS. EDWARD J. MATSON), retired special education educator, author; b. Chgo., Aug. 25, 1914; d. Axel George and Mae (Dalrymple) Freeberg; m. Edward John Matson, Oct. 18, 1941; children: Karin (Mrs. Donald H. Skadden), Sara M. Drake, Edward Robert, Laurence D., David O. BA, U. Ky., 1934; MA, Northwestern U., 1941. Spl. edn. tchr. area high schs., Chgo., 1934-42, Ridge Farm, 1944-45; tchr. high schs. Lake County (Ill.) Pub. Schs., 1956-59; founder Grove Sch., Lake Forest, Ill., 1958-87, ret., 1987; instr. evening sch. Carthage Coll., 1965-66. Author: Shadow on the Lost Rock, 1958, Saul, the King, 1968, Abba Father, 1970 (Friends Lit. Fiction award 1972), Buried Alive, 1970, A School for Peter, 1974, A Home for Peter, 1983, Letters to Lauren, A History of the Methodist Campgrounds, Des Plaines; contbr. many articles to profl. publs. Mem. Friends of Lit. Dem. Recipient Humanitarian award Ill. Med. Soc. Aux. Home: 4133 Mockingbird Ln Suffolk VA 23434-7186

MATSON, WESLEY JENNINGS, educational administrator; b. Svea, Minn., June 25, 1924; s. James and Ettie (Mattson) M.; m. Doris Cragg; 1 child, James Jennings. BS with distinction, U. Minn., 1948; MA, U. Calif., Berkeley, 1954; EdD, Columbia U., 1960. High sch. tchr. Santa Barbara County Pub. Schs., Santa Maria, Calif., 1948-50; instr. U. Calif., Berkeley, 1950-54, Columbia U., N.Y.C., 1954-55; lectr. Fordham U., N.Y.C., 1955-56; asst. prof. U. Md., College Park, 1956-59; prof., asst. dean U. Wis., Milw., 1959-72; dean emeritus Winona (Minn.) State U., 1972-88; vis. prof. U. P.R., Rio Peidras, Western Wash. U., Bellingham, San Diego State U., U. Minn., Mpls., U. Hawaii; adj. faculty St. Olaf Coll., Northfield, Minn., 1990-95; cons. U.S. Dept. Edn., Washington, Ill., Wis.; bd. regents Wis. Dept. Pub. Instruction; examiner Nat. Coun. Accreditation Tchr. Edn., North Ctrl. Assn., Chgo. Editorial bd.: Jour. Instructional Psychology; contbr. articles to profl. jours. Exec. com. Minn. Alliance of the Arts, Mpls.; mem. Minn. Com. Certification Stds., St. Paul; bd. dirs. Ft. Snelling Meml. Chapel Found. Served to capt. USAAF, 1943-46, ETO. Decorated Bronze star; recipient Disting. Service award Wis. Assn. Tchr. Edn., 1972. Mem. Minn. Assn. Colls. for Tchr. Edn. (pres. 1983-85, hon. life award of merit 1985), Nat. Assn. Tchr. Educators (exec. com. 1970-72), Nat. Edn. Assn. (life), Assn. Higher Edn., Minn. Edn. Assn., Minn. Hist. Soc., U. Minn. Alumni Soc. (Outstanding Educator award 1984), Rotary, Phi Delta Kappa, Kappa Delta Pi, Alpha Sigma Phi. Home: 6615 Lake Shore Dr S Minneapolis MN 55423-2273

MATSUDA, FUJIO, retired educational administrator; b. Honolulu, Oct. 18, 1924; s. Yoshio and Shimo (Iwasaki) M.; m. Amy M. Saiki, June 11, 1949; children: Bailey Koki, Thomas Junji, Sherry Noriko, Joan Yuuko, Ann Mitsuyo, Richard Hideo. BSCE, Rose Poly. Inst., 1949; DSc, MIT, 1952; DEng (hon.), Rose Hulman Inst. Tech., 1975. Rsch. engr. MIT, 1952-54; rsch. asst. prof. engring. U. Ill., Urbana, 1954-55; asst. prof. engring. U. Hawaii, Honolulu, 1955-57; assoc. prof. U. Hawaii, 1957-62, chmn. dept. civil engring., 1960-63, prof., 1962-65, 74-84, dir. engring. expt. sta., 1962-63, v.p. bus. affairs, 1973-74, pres., 1974-84, exec. dir. Rsch. Corp., 1984-94; pres. Japan-Am. Inst. Mgmt. Sci., Honolulu, 1994-96, also bd. dirs., ret., 1996; dir. Hawaii Dept. Transp., Honolulu, 1963-73; v.p. Park & Lee, Ltd., Honolulu, 1956-58; pres. SMS & Assocs., Inc., 1960-63; pvt. practice structural engring., 1958-60; bd. dirs. C. Brewer & Co., Ltd., First Hawaiian Bank, First Hawaiian, Inc., Pacific Internat. Ctr. for High Tech. Rsch., Rehab. Hosp. of Pacific, Kuakini Health Sys., Japanese Cultural Ctr. of Hawaii; mem. Airport Ops. Coun. Internat., 1968-73; pres. Pacific Coast Assn. Port Authorities, 1969; mem. sci. bd. Dept. Army, 1978-80; mem. U.S. Army Civilian Adv. Group, 1978—; mem. exec. com. on sponsored rsch. MIT, 1991-94; mem. Rose-Hulman Inst. Tech. Com. on the Future, 1992-94. Bd. dirs. Aloha United Way, 1973-76, Kuakini Med. Ctr., 1987-89; trustee Kuakini Health Sys., 1984-86, bd. dirs., 1986-89; trustee Nature Conservancy, 1984-89, Hawaiian Cmty. Found. Recipient Honor Alumnus award Rose Poly. Inst., 1971, Disting. Svc. award Airport Ops. Coun. Internat., 1973, Disting. Alumnus award U. Hawaii, 1974, 91; named Hawaii Engr. of Yr., 1972. Mem. NAE, NSPE, ASCE (Parcel-Sverdrup Engring. Mgmt. award 1986), Social Sci. Assn., Western Coll. Assn. (exec. com. 1977-84, pres. 1980-82), Japan-Am. Soc. Honolulu (trustee 1976-84, adv. council 1984—), Japan-Hawaii Econ. Coun., World Sustainable Agr. Assn., Beta Gamma Sigma, Sigma Xi, Tau Beta Pi.

MATSUI, DOROTHY NOBUKO, elementary education educator; b. Honolulu, Jan. 9, 1954; d. Katsura and Tamiko (Sakai) M. Student, U. Hawaii, Honolulu, 1972-76, postgrad., 1982; BEd, U. Alaska, Anchorage, 1979, MEd in Spl. Edn., 1986. Clerical asst. U. Hawaii Manoa Disbursing Office, Anchorage, 1974-76; passenger service agt. Japan Air Lines, Anchorage, 1980; bilingual tutor Anchorage Sch. Dist., 1980, elem. sch. tchr., 1980—; facilitator for juvenile justice courses Anchorage Sch. Dist., Anchorage Police Dept., Alaska Pacific U., 1992-93; mem. adv. bd. Anchorage Law-Related Edn. Advancement Project. Vol. Providence Hosp., Anchorage, 1986, Humana Hosp., Anchorage, 1984, Spl. Olympics, Anchorage, 1981, Municipality Anchorage, 1978, Easter Seal Soc. Hawaii, 1975. Mem. NAFE, NEA, Alaska Edn. Assn., Smithsonian Nat. Assoc. Program, Nat. Space Soc., Smithsonian Air and Space Assn., World Aerospace Edn. Orgn., Internat. Platform Assn., Nat. Trust for Hist. Preservation, Nat. Audubon Soc., Planetary Soc., Cousteau Soc., Alaska Coun. for the Social Studies, Alaska Coun. Tchrs. Math., World Inst. Achievment, U.S. Olympic Soc., Women's Inner Circle Achievement, U. Alaska Alumni Assn., World Wildlife Fund, Japanese-Am. Nat. Mus., Alpha Delta Kappa (treas. Alpha chpt. 1988-92, corr. sec. 1993-96, sgt. at arms 1996—). Avocations: reading, sports, psychology. Office: Anchorage Sch Dist 7001 Cranberry St Anchorage AK 99502-7145

MATSUI, JIRO, importer, wholesaler, small business owner; b. Honolulu, Hawaii, Apr. 5, 1919; s. Juro and Tsuta (Murai) M.; m. Barbara Toshiko Tanji; children: Kenneth Jiro, Alan Kiyoshi, Carol Ritsu. BA, U. Hawaii, 1949. Owner Honolulu Aquarium and Pet Supply, Honolulu, 1946-77, Bird House, Honolulu, 1957-61; owner, pres., chmn. Petland, Inc., Honolulu, 1961—, Pets Pacifica, Inc., Honolulu, 1977—, Global Pet Industries, Honolulu, 1975—; organizer, coord. first Pet Consumer Show in U.S., 1979, pres. 1979-82; first Internat. Pet Show; cons. Japan Pet Product Mfr. Assn. Fair, Japan, 1981—. Pres. Waikiki Vets. Club, Kapahulu, Oahu, Hawaii, 1948-66, Waiawa (Oahu) Farmers, 1948-88; sr. adv. com. plants and animals State of Hawaii, 1974—. Sgt. U.S. Army, 1941-46. Decorated with Bronze Star, U.S. Army, 1947. Mem. Am. Pet Soc. (pres. 1979-82, chmn. 1989-92), World Wide Pet Supply Assn. (bd. dirs. 1974-93, pres. 1989-90, Edward B. Price award 1982), Honolulu C. of C. (bd. dirs. 1974—). Avocations: fishing, gardening,. Office: Pets Pacifica Inc 94-486 Ukee St Waipahu HI 96797-4211

MATSUI, ROBERT TAKEO, congressman; b. Sacramento, Sept. 17, 1941; s. Yasuji and Alice (Nagata) M.; m. Doris Kazue Okada, Sept. 17, 1966; 1 child, Brian Robert. AB in Polit. Sci, U. Calif., Berkeley, 1963; JD, U. Calif., San Francisco, 1966. Bar: Calif. 1967. Practiced law Sacramento, 1967-78; mem. Sacramento City Council, 1971-78, vice mayor, 1977; mem. 96th-104d Congresses from 5th Calif. dist., 1979—; ranking minority mem., mem. ways and means subcom. on oversight; dep. chair Dem. Nat. Com., 1995—; chmn. profl. bus. forum Dem. Congl. Campaign Com.; congl. liaison nat. fin. council Dem. Nat. Com.; mem. adv. council on fiscal policy Am. Enterprise Inst. chmn. Profl. Bus. Forum of the Dem. Congl. Co. and Com.; congl. liaison Nat. Fin. Council, Dem. Nat. Com.; mem. Am. Enterprise Inst. Adv. Council on Fiscal Policy. Named Young Man of Yr. Jr. C. of C., 1973; recipient Disting. Service award, 1973. Mem. Sacramento Japanese Am. Citizens League (pres. 1969), Sacramento Met. C. of C. (dir. 1976). Democrat. Clubs: 20-30 (Sacramento) (pres. 1972), Rotary (Sacramento). Office: US Ho of Reps 2311 Rayburn HOB Washington DC 20515-0505

MATSUMOTO, GEORGE, architect; b. San Francisco, July 16, 1922; s. Manroku F. and Ise (Nakagawa) M.; m. Kimi Nao, Dec. 15, 1951; children—Mari-Jane, Kiyo-Ann, Kei-Ellen, Kenneth Manroku, Miye-Eileen. Student, U. Calif. at Berkeley, 1938-42; B.Arch., Washington U., 1944; M.Arch., Cranbrook Acad. Art, 1945. Designer Heathers Garden Devel. Co., Calif., 1941-42; designer with George F. Keck, Chgo., 1943-44; sr. designer, planner Saarinen & Swanson, Birmingham, Mich., 1945-46; sr. designer Skidmore, Owings & Merrill, Chgo., 1948; partner Runnells, Clark, Waugh, Matsumoto, Kansas City, Mo., 1946-47; practice architecture Okla., N.C., 1948-61, San Francisco, 1962-92; pres. George Matsumoto and assocs., San Francisco, 1992-93; retired, 1993; instr. U. Okla., 1947-48; prof. N.C. State Coll., 1948-61, U. Calif. at Berkeley, 1961-67. Important works include libraries, office bldgs., schs., recreation ctrs., chs., govt. bldgs., pvt. residences, med. research labs. and offices. Bd. dirs. Young Audiences, Oakland Mus. Assn., Oakland Arts Coun., Friends of Oakland Park and Recreation, East Bay Agy. for Children. Recipient over 50 archtl. awards and prizes. Fellow AIA (dir. chpt.), Internat. Inst. Arts and Letters; mem. Mich. Soc. Architects, Assn. Coll. Sch. Architecture, Raleigh Council Architects, San Francisco Planning and Urban Renewal Assn., Nat. Council Archtl. Registration Bds., Calif. Assn. Architects, Bldg. Research Inst., Japanese-Am. Citizens League. Home: 1170 Glencourt Dr Oakland CA 94611-1405

MATSUMOTO, TERUO, surgeon, educator; b. Fukuoka City, Japan, Jan. 2, 1929; came to U.S., 1956, naturalized, 1964; s. Yoshinari and Fumie (Hayashi) M.; m. Mary L. Cousino, July 29, 1961; children: Louisa Michi, Maria Chieko, Monica Mieko, Nelson Tateru. M.D., Kyushu U., 1953, Ph.D., 1956. Diplomate: Am. Bd. Surgery, Am. Bd. Gen. Vascular Surgery. Intern Cook County Hosp., Chgo., 1956-57; surg. resident Med. Coll. Ohio, Toledo, 1957-61; commd. capt. U.S. Army, 1961, advanced through grades to lt. col., 1965; gen. surgeon U.S. Army Camp Zama Hosp., Japan, 1961-65; chief surg. service U.S. Army Camp Zama Hosp., 1962-65, chief gen. surgery sect., 1962-65; chief dept. exptl. surgery Walter Reed Army Inst. Research, 1965-68, dir. U.S. Army Surg. Research, Pacific, 1968; assoc. prof. surgery Hahnemann Med. Coll. and Hosp., Phila., 1969-72; prof. surgery Hahnemann U., Phila., 1973—; chmn. dept. surgery Hahnemann U., 1975-90, dir. divsn. vascular surgery, 1990—; pres. med. staff Hahnemann Med. Coll. and Hosp., 1979-81; mem. sci. rev. com. NIH, cons. field reader for Office of Orphan Products Devel., FDA, 1986. Editor Emergency Surgery, Jour. Internat. Surgery, Jour. Critical Care Medicine, Jour. Internat. Cardiovascular Surgery; contbr. to profl. jours. and books. Recipient Sir Henry Wellcome medal and prize, 1965, gold medal Southeastern Surg. Congress, 1968, Outstanding Achievement award U.S. Army Sci. Conf., 1969, Golden Apple award Student AMA, 1972. Fellow Southeastern Surg. Congress, ACS, Am. Coll. Angiology, Am. Assn. for Surgery of Trauma, Pan Am. Med. Assn., Assn. Surgery for Alimentary Tract, AMA, Japanese Coll. Surgeons, Internat. Cardiovascular Surgery, Soc. Vascular Surgery, AOA, Phila. Acad. Surgery, Pan Pacific Surg. Congress, Soc. Surg. Chairmen; mem. Council Cardiovascular Surgery, Soc. Surg. Oncology. Home: 1116 Sandringham Rd Bala Cynwyd PA 19004-2023 Office: Hahnemann U Med Sch Philadelphia PA 19102

MATSUMURA, KENNETH N., biomedical scientist, physician; b. Bangkok, Thailand, May 15, 1945; s. Jiro and Vera Yoshi (Tanaka) M.; m. Molleen Stark, Aug. 20, 1977; 1 child, Miriam Ellen Miriko. BS, U. Calif., Berkeley, 1966; MD, U. Calif., San Francisco, 1970. Diplomate Am. Coll. Angiology, Am. Bd. Sexology. Dir. rsch. and devel. Immunity Rsch. Lab., 1977-87; dir., coord. bio-artificial liver project, global devel. Alin Found., Berkeley, 1970—, dir. div. sci. and tech. devel., 1987—; chief urgent care West Oakland (Calif.) Ctr., 1975-79; pres. West Oakland Health Group, 1983—; chmn. People Together Telecomm. Network, 1993—; cons. to chancellor U. Calif., Berkeley, 1974-75. Author: After Fifteen Years: Artificial Liver and Pancreas, 1977, Heterosexual AIDS: Myth or Fact?, 1987; inventor bio-artificial liver and pancreas, drug removing side effects of cancer and AIDS chemotherapy, heart attack monitor wristwatch. Fellow N.Y. Acad. Scis., AAAS, Am. Coll. Angiology, Calif. Med. Assn.

MATTA, RAM KUMAR, aeronautical engineer; b. Karachi, India, May 9, 1946; came to U.S., 1967, naturalized, 1976; s. Madhavdas Lalchand and Damyanti (Ahuja) M.; m. Renee M. Verhoff, Dec. 1988. B.Tech., Indian Inst. Tech., New Delhi, 1967; M.S., U. Minn., 1969, Ph.D., 1973. Grad. asst. mechanics U. Minn., Mpls., 1967-68, research asst., 1968, teaching assoc., 1968-69, research assoc., 1969, research fellow, 1969-73; acoustics engr. advanced engring. and tech. program dept. engring. div. Aircraft Engine Group, Gen. Electric Co., Evendale, Ohio, 1973-75, mgr. turbomachinery acoustics, 1975-76, mgr. component tech., 1976-77, sr. engr. cycle systems analysis, 1977-78; bus. interface Gen. Electric Corp. R & D, Evendale, Ohio, 1979-80; mgr. new engine design support Aircraft Engine Group, Gen. Electric Co., Evendale, Ohio, 1980-83, mgr. advanced programs, 1983-84, mgr. CFM56-5 systems engring. and product improvements, 1984-87, gen. mgr. CFM56-5C and advanced programs, 1988-92; program gen. mgr. GE45/CFMXX, dir. CFM advanced programs Gen. Electric Co., Evendale, Ohio, 1992-93; bus. interface Gen. Electric Corp. Rsch. and Devel., 1993—. Contbr. articles to profl. publs.; patentee in field. Exec. mem., vol. Minn. Internat. Ctr., Mpls., 1970-72; chmn. Citizens Com. for Community Devel., Forest Park, Ohio, 1975-76. Recipient Pres.'s Gold medal Indian Inst. Tech., 1967, Profl. Performance award, 1975, Mgmt. award, 1979; Merit scholar Indian Inst. Tech., 1967; Sloan fellow Stanford U., 1987-88. Mem. AIAA, Sigma Gamma Tau. Home: 1010 Lamplighter Rd Schenectady NY 12309-1159 Office: GE CR&D MD KW-D281 PO Box 8 Schenectady NY 12301-0008

MATTAMMAL, MICHAEL BAPPO, biochemist; b. Kerala, India, Aug. 8, 1940; came to U.S., 1963; s. Augustine and Ann Mattammal; m. Mary Louise Wierschem, Aug. 12, 1971; children: Augustine, Maria, Michael, William. BS, St. Alberts Coll., India, 1960; MS, Creighton U., 1968; PhD, St. Louis U., 1975. Postdoctoral St. Louis U., 1975-77; rsch. chemist Dept. Vet. Affairs, St. Louis, 1977—; prof. medicine St. Louis U., 1990—. Contbr. over 50 articles to profl. jours. Mo. Alzheimer's grantee Mo. Alzheimer's and Related Disorders, 1990-91, VA Med. Rsch. Svc. grantee, 1995—. Mem. Nat. Registry in Clin. Chemistry (cert. clin. chemist), Am. Assn. Clin. Pathologists, Sigma Xi. Roman Catholic. Achievements include research in neurodegenerative diseases and mechanistic approach for neurodegeneration. Home: 3532 Magnolia Ave Saint Louis MO 63118-1134

MATTAR, PHILIP, institute director, editor; b. Haifa, Palestine, Jan. 21, 1944; came to U.S. 1961; m. Evelyn Ann Keith, June 20, 1971; 1 child, Christina. MPhil, Columbia U., 1977, PhD, 1981. Exec. dir. Inst. for Palestine Studies, Washington, 1984—; assoc. editor Jour. Palestine Studies, Washington, 1985—; adj. lectr. history Yale U., 1981; adj. prof. history Georgetown U., 1990, 91, 94. Author: Mufti of Jerusalem, 1988, 2d edit., 1991; contbr. articles to profl. jours., including Fgn. Policy, Middle East Jour., Middle Ea. Studies. Mem. adv. com. Human Rights Watch/Middle East. Vis. scholar Columbia U., 1984; Fulbright-Hays Rsch. fellow, 1978. Mem. Middle East Studies Assn., Middle East Inst. Avocations: jogging, chess, reading, travel. Office: Inst for Palestine Studies 3501 M St NW Washington DC 20007-2624

MATTAUCH, ROBERT JOSEPH, electrical engineering educator; b. Rochester, Pa., May 30, 1940; s. Henry Paul and Anna Marie (Mlinarcik) M.; m. Frances Sabo, Dec. 29, 1962; children: Lori Ann, Thomas J. BS, Carnegie Inst. Tech., Pitts., 1962; MEE, N.C. State U., Raleigh, 1963, PhD, 1967. Asst. prof. elec. engring. U. Va., Charlottesville, 1966-70, assoc. prof. elec. engring., 1970-76, prof. elec. engring., 1976-83, Wilson prof. elec. engring., 1983-86, Standard Oil Co. prof. sci. and tech., 1986-89, chmn. dept. elect. engring., 1987-95, BP Am. prof. sci. and tech., 1989-95; Commonwealth prof., chair dept. elec. engring. Va. Commonwealth U., Richmond, 1995—; cons. The Rochester Corp., Culpeper, Va., 1983-88, Milltech Corp., Deerfield, Mass., 1985. Patentee: infrared detector; solid state switching capacitor; thin wire pointing method, whiskerless Schottby diode, controlled in-situ etch back growth technique. Bd. dirs. U. Va. Patent Found. Recipient Excellence in Instruction of Engring. Students award Western Electric, 1980. Fellow IEEE (Centennial medal 1984); mem. Eta Kappa Nu (recipient Oustanding Prof. in Elec. Engring. 1975), Sigma Xi, Tau Beta Pi. Office: Va Commonwealth U Dept Elec Engring PO Box 843072 Richmond VA 23284-3072

MATTAUSCH, THOMAS EDWARD, public relations consultant, business owner; b. Davenport, Iowa, Dec. 4, 1944; s. Carl Henry and Luverna Ann (Koch) M.; B.A. in Journalism, U. Iowa, 1967; M.A. in Social Psychology Ball State U., 1974; children—Jason Paul, Laura Anne. Asst. to dir. public relations Gen. Telephone Co. Midwest, Grinnell, Iowa, 1968-71; mgr. public relations Midwestern div. Am. Water Works Service Co., Inc., Richmond, Ind., 1971-74; with IBM, 1974-82, sr. communications specialist, White Plains and Armonk, N.Y., 1974-79, mgr. communications and community relations IBM Info. Systems Center, Sterling Forest, N.Y., 1979-82; dir. communication programs, communication products group GTE, Stamford, Conn., 1982-84, dir. communication programs, diversified products and services group, 1984-87, dir. communication programs Products and Systems group, 1987-89; dir. pub. rels. svcs. corp. hdqrs., 1989-92; prin. T.E. Mattausch Pub. Rels. and Communications, 1993—; owner Serenities, 1994—. Mem. Iowa adv. com. to U.S. Commn. on Civil Rights, 1969-71; bd. dirs. Orange County (N.Y.) C. of C., 1979-82, Central Orange County United Way, 1979-82, Metro Pool, Inc., Stamford, Ct., 1992-93. Served with USNR, 1967-68. Mem. Public Relations Soc. Am. (dir. tech. sect.), Am. Mgmt. Assn., Am. Assn. Counseling and Devel., Internat. Communications Assn., Internat. Platform Assn., Internat. Assn. Bus. Communicators (dir. Iowa chpt. 1969-70, chpt. Best Employee Newsletter award 1970), Internat. Assn. of Bus. Communications ACE award of merit for annual report design, 1990, IABC ACE award of merit for Crisis Communications, 1990, Spl. Publs., 1991, Pub. rels. soc. of Am. (N.Y. chpt.), Big Apple award for annual reports, 1992, Ridgefield C. of C. Office: 23 Danbury Rd Ridgefield CT 06877-4001

MATTEA, KATHY, vocalist, songwriter; m. Jon Vezner, Feb. 14, 1988. Student, W.Va. U. Former mem. bluegrass band. Albums include Walk the Way the Wind Blows, 1986, Untasted Honey, 1987, Willow in the Wind, 1989, Kathy Mattea: A Collection of Hits, 1990, Time Passes By, 1991 (Best country video award Houston Internat. Film Festival 1991), Lonesome Standard Time, 1992, Good News, 1993 (Grammy award, Best Southern Gospel, Country Gospel or Bluegrass Gospel album, 1994), Walking Away a Winner, 1994. Recipient Best Single award, 1988 (Eighteen Wheels and a Dozen Roses), Song of the Yr. award, 1988 (Eighteen Wheels and a Dozen Roses), Top Female Vocalist award, 1989, Song of the Yr. award., 1989 (Where've You Been) Acad. Country Music, Best Female Vocalist award Country Music Assn., 1989, 90, Best Female Vocalist Radio & Records Country Readers Poll, 1990, Song of the Yr. award (Where've You Been) Country Music Assn., 1990, Best Country Vocal Female Grammy award, 1991, Grammy nomination, Best Country Vocal Collaboration for "Romeo" with Dolly Parton, Tanya Tucker, Billy Ray Cyrus, Pam Tillis & Mary-Chapin Carpenter, 1994. Address: care Robert R Titley 706 18th Ave S Nashville TN 37203-3215

MATTER, EDITH ANN, religion educator; b. Ft. Smith, Ark., Dec. 29, 1949; d. Robert Allen and Faye Bert (Overton) M. AB, Oberlin Coll., 1971; MA in Religious Studies, Yale U., 1975, PhD, 1976. R. Jean Brownlee term prof. religious studies U. Pa., Phila., 1976—. Author: The Voice of My Beloved: The Song of Songs in Western and Medieval Christianity, 1990; editor: De Partu Virginis, 1985; co-editor: Creative Women in Medieval and Early Modern Italy, 1994. Tchr., lectr. Pa. Humanities Coun., 1984. Faculty fellow Van Pelt Coll. House, 1981-86, summer rsch. fellow ACLS, 1978, rsch. fellow NEH, 1979, 88; John Simon Guggenheim Meml. Found. fellow, 1996; grantee Am. Philos. Soc., 1977, 81, 84; recipient Lindback award for tchg., 1982, Coll. Alumni Soc. tchg. award, 1995. Mem. Medieval Acad. Am., Am. Acad. Religion, Delaware Valley Medieval Assn. Democrat. Home: 941 Annin St Philadelphia PA 19147-4612 Office: U Pa Dept Religious Studies PO Box 36ch Philadelphia PA 19104

MATTERN, DONALD EUGENE, retired association executive; b. Mapleton Depot, Pa., Feb. 11, 1930; s. John Franklin and Lizzie May (Fiss) M.; m. Anna Mae Bard, Nov. 24, 1951; children: Debra Jeanne, Cynthia Ann, James Franklin. BA, Pa. State U., 1951; MBA, U. Pa., 1955. Exec. trainee Fed. Res. Bank Phila., 1953-55; from asst. cashier to cashier Cumberland County Nat. Bank, New Cumberland, Pa., 1955-63; v.p. 1st Nat. Bank State Coll., Pa., 1963-64; asst. v.p., v.p., sr. v.p., sec. Hamilton Bank, Lancaster, Pa., 1964-86; sec., v.p. Nat. Cen. Fin. Corp., 1972-83; exec. dir. Mfr.'s Assn. Berks County, 1986-95; mem. adv. bd. Berks campus Pa. State U., 1987-92. Treas., bd. dirs. Reading-Berks Human Rels. Coun., 1967-70; v.p. bd. dirs. local chpts. Ams. Competitive Enterprise Sys., 1970-92; past bd. dirs., past pres., gen. campaign chmn. United Way Berks County; trustee, former chmn. bd. Comty. Gen. Hosp., Reading, 1967—; bd. dirs. Nat. Coun. on Alcoholism, 1967-68, Reading Ctr. City Devel. Fund, 1976—, Greater Berks Devel. Fund, 1984-89, Reading Mus. Found., 1985—, Luth. Home Topton, 1990-96, Berkshire Health Plan, 1992—, Highlands at Wyomissing, 1995—, Congregation Coun. Advent Luth. Ch., Reading New Futures Project, Inc., 1988-91, Pub. Edn. Found. for Berks County, 1991-96; mem. exec. bd. Hawk Mountain coun. Boy Scouts Am., 1970—; mem. N.E. Pa. Synod Endowment Investment Fund Com., 1985—, treas., bd. dirs. Housing Opportunities, in Met. Environment, 1968-73. 1st lt. USAF, 1951-53. Mem. Masons, Shriners. Republican. Lutheran. Home: 20 Birchwood Rd Reading PA 19610-1908

MATTERN, VICTORIA LYNN, editor, writer; b. Bellefonte, Pa., Oct. 31, 1954; d. Thomas William and Colletta June (Bear) Krebs; m. Scott Keith Mattern, Sept. 8, 1973 (div. 1982); children: Joel Scott, Christopher Benjamin. BA in English, Kutztown U., 1984; postgrad., Allentown Coll., 1995. Rschr. Rodale Press., Emmaus, Pa., 1984-88, editl. asst., 1988, asst. editor, 1989-90, assoc. editor, 1990-91, sr. editor, 1991-95, mng. editor, 1995—. Contbg. editor: Best of Organic Gardening, 1995; contbr. articles to organic gardening mags. Active Lehigh County Hist. Soc., Allentown, Pa., 1993—, Nat. Trust Hist. Preservation, 1994—, Borough Parks and Recreation Commn., Emmaus, 1994-95. Mem. Garden Writers Am. Assn. Democrat. United Ch. Christ. Avocations: the arts, gardening, historic preservation. Office: Rodale Press 33 E Minor St Emmaus PA 18098

MATTERS, CLYDE BURNS, former college president; b. Fargo, N.D., Nov. 10, 1924; s. Lester H. and Pearl Lila (Burns) M.; m. Anna R. Skeels, Mar. 24, 1948; children—Cynthia (Mrs. Charles V. Carroll), Richard B. B.S., Whitworth Coll., Spokane, Wash., 1950, M.Ed., 1951; Ph.D., U. Wash., 1960; L.H.D. (hon.), Hastings Coll., 1985. Tchr. Spokane Pub. Schs., 1950-51; prof. Whitworth Coll., 1950-57, 70-72; research assoc. U. Wash., 1957-60; asst. supt. schs. King County, Wash., 1960-63; program adviser Ford Found., West Africa, 1963-70; pres. Hastings (Nebr.) Coll., 1972-85; pres. Nebr. Ind. Coll. Found.; mem. nexus com. Presbyn. Coll. Union; pres. Assn. Ind. Colls. and Univs. Nebr. Resident camp dir. Spokane YMCA, 1952-57, bd. dirs., 1970-72; bd. dirs. United Good Neighbors, Spokane County, 1969-70; trustee Synod of Alaska N.W. Found., 1995—. With AUS, 1943-46. Decorated Bronze Star. Mem. Assn. Ind. Colls. and Univs. (pres. Nebr. 1979-80), Phi Delta Kappa. Presbyterian (elder). Lodge: Kiwanis. Home: 4415 E 51st Ln # 3 Spokane WA 99223-7888

MATTERSON, JOAN MCDEVITT, physical therapist; b. Bryn Mawr, Pa., Feb. 24, 1949; d. William J. and Wanda Jean (Edwards) McD.; children: Brian, Jennie, Kira. BS in Biology, St. Joseph's U., Phila., 1973; cert. in phys. therapy, U. Pa., 1974. Assoc. pharmacologist, researcher immunology and arthritis Progressive Phys. Therapy, P.A., Wilmington, Del., 1976-93, pediatric phys. therapist, 1974-81, pres., 1976-95; rehab. dir. Achievement Rehab.; phys. therapist Liberty Home Health, 1995—; rehab. dir. Office of Joan Matterson, 1995—, Integrated Health Svcs.- Kent, Smyrna, Del., 1996—; lectr. in field of low level laser therapy. Dep. gov. Am. Biog. Rsch. Inst.; mem. adv. bd. Internat. Biographical Rsch. Inst., Cambridge, England. Mem. Am. Soc. Laser Medicine and Surgery, Internat. Platform Assn., Am. Phys. Therapy Assn., Am. Acad. Pain (assoc.), Inst. Noetic Sci., Am. Bd. Forensic Examiners. Avocations: dancing, skiing, cooking.

MATTES, MARTIN ANTHONY, lawyer; b. San Francisco, June 18, 1946; s. Hans Adam and Marion Jane (Burge) M.; m. Catherine Elvira Garzio, May 26, 1984; children: Nicholas Anthony, Daniel Joseph, Thomas George. BA, Stanford U., 1968; postgrad., U. Chgo., 1968-69, U. Bonn, Fed. Republic Germany, 1971; JD, U. Calif., Berkeley, 1974. Bar: Calif. 1974, U.S. Ct. Appeals (D.C., 5th and 9th cirs.) 1978, U.S. Dist. Ct. (no. dist.) Calif. 1979, U.S. Dist. Ct. (ea. dist.) Calif. 1991. Asst. legal officer Internat. Union Conservation of Nature and Natural Resources, Bonn, 1974-76; staff counsel Calif. Pub. Utilities Commn., San Francisco, 1976-79, legal advisor to pres., 1979-82, adminstrv. law judge, 1983, asst. chief adminstrv. law judge, 1983-86; ptnr. Graham & James, San Francisco, 1986—; mem. adv. group. to Calif. Senate Subcom. on Pub. Utilities Commn. Procedural Reform, 1994. Mng. editor Ecology Law Quar., 1973-74; contbr. articles to profl. publs. Mem. Conf. Calif. Pub. Utility Counsel (treas. 1988-90, v.p. 1990-91, pres. 1991-92), Internat. Coun. Environ. Law, San Francisco Bar Assn. Office: Graham & James 1 Maritime Plz Ste 300 San Francisco CA 94111-3406

MATTESON, CLARICE CHRIS, artist, educator; b. Winnipeg, Man., Can., Sept. 2, 1918; came to U.S., 1922; d. Sergis and Nina (Balter) Alberts; m. D.C. Matteson, 1956 (dec. 1976); children: Kemmer, Gretchen. BA, Met. State U., 1976; MA in Liberal Studies, Hamline U., 1986; PhD in Humanities, LaSalle U., 1995. Mem. Orson Welles' staff, Hollywood, Calif., 1945-46; owner Hilde-Gardes Co., L.A., 1947-56; instr. art North Hennepin C.C., Brooklyn Park, Minn., 1975-81; prodr., host Accent on Art TV Program, St. Paul, 1979—; instr. art Lakewood C.C., U. Minn., Normandale C.C., Bloomington (Minn.) Sch. Dist., Mpls. Sch. Dist., St. Paul Sch. Dist., 1981—. Exhibited in group shows at Mpls. Inst. Art, 1994-95, Govs. 1006 Soc., 1994-96; represented in permanent collections Richard James Gallery, Mpls., Gallery 416, Mpls.; corr. Schaumburg (Ill.) Newspapers, 1962-68; prodr., host TV series Kids Art, Mpls.-St. Paul, 1995; patentee plastic products. Active Minn. Orch. (WAMSO), Mpls., 1972—, vol. Recipient award for creative leadership Minn. Assn. for Continuing Adult Edn., 1977, Gold Cup award Bloomington Cable, 1989; Park Cable TV grantee, 1982, Minn. Humanities Commn. grantee, 1985. Mem. ASCAP, AAUW (dir. arts com. 1989-90, bd. dirs. 1990-92), Am. Pen Women (v.p. Minn. chpt. 1994-96), Minn. Artists Assn., Minn. Composers Forum, Minn. Territorial Pioneers (bd. dirs. 1995—, producer, host Kids' Art, Accent on Art), Internat. Alliance for Women in Music, St. Paul Neighborhood Network, N.Y. Neighborhood Network. Avocations: tennis, dancing, writing children's books, composing music. Home and Office: 2119 Sargent Ave Saint Paul MN 55105-1126

MATTESON, THOMAS T., academic administrator; s. Ruth (Cole) M.; m. Dorothy Johnston, Apr. 10, 1965; children: Juliet M., Jeffrey C. BS, U.S. Coast Guard Acad., 1957; MS, Naval Post Grad. Coll., 1969; postgrad., Air War Coll., 1976-77. Tng. officer USCG Air Sta., Miami, Fla., 1962-63; RCC contr. 9th dist. U.S. Coast Guard Acad., Cleve., 1963-65; asst. ops. officer air sta. U.S. Coast Guard Acad., Port Angeles, Wash., 1965-68; exec. officer Aviation Tng. Ctr. hdqrs. USCG, Washington, 1973-76; commdg. officer air sta. USCG, Borinquen, P.R., 1977-79; chief aviation br. hdqrs. USCG, Washington, 1979-81, chief, officer pers. divsn. hdqrs., 1981-82; chief ops. divsn. 8th dist. USCG, New Orleans, 1982-84; chief staff 8th dist. U.S. Coast Guard Acad., New Orleans, 1984-85, chief pub. and congl. affairs office of boating safety hdqrs., 1985-87, chief office pers. hdqrs., 1987-89; supt. U.S. Coast Guard Acad., New London, Conn., 1989-93, U.S. Merchant Marine Acad., Kings Point, N.Y., 1993—. Office: Dept Transp Merchant Marine Acad Kings Point NY 11024-1699

MATTESON, WILLIAM BLEECKER, lawyer; b. N.Y.C., Oct. 20, 1928; s. Leonard Jerome and Mary Jo (Harwell) M.; m. Marilee Brill, Aug. 26, 1950; children: Lynn, Sandra, Holly. B.A., Yale U., 1950; J.D., Harvard U., 1953. Bar: N.Y. 1954. Clk. to judge Augustus N. Hand U.S. Ct. Appeals, 1953-54; clk. to U.S. Supreme Ct. Justice Harold H. Burton, 1954-55; asso. firm Debevoise & Plimpton (and predecessors), N.Y.C., 1955-61; partner Debevoise & Plimpton (and predecessors), 1961—, Debevoise & Plimpton (European office), Paris, 1973-78; presiding ptnr., 1988-93; lectr. Columbia U. Law Sch., 1972-73, 78-80. Trustee Peddie Sch., Hightstown, N.J., 1968-73, Kalamazoo Coll., 1972-77, Miss Porter's Sch., Farmington, Conn., 1977-83, N.Y. Inst. Spl. Edn., 1981—, Salk Inst., La Jolla, Calif., 1994—, vice-chair, 1994—, Statue of Liberty Ellis Island Found., 1996—; chmn. USA Bus. and Industry Adv. Com. to the Orgn. for Econ. Coop. and Devel., Paris, 1986—; chmn. Worldwide Bus. and Industry Adv. Com., 1994—; vice chmn. U.S. Coun. for Internat. Bus., 1990—. Mem. ABA, FBA, Internat. Bar Assn., N.Y. State Bar Assn., Assn. of Bar of City of N.Y. (chmn. securities regulation com. 1968-71), Harvard U. Law Sch. Assn. N.Y.C. (trustee 1968-73), Coun. Fgn. Rels., Union Club, River Club, Sky Club, Links Club, Sankaty Head Club. Home: 201 E 62nd St New York NY 10021-7627 Office: Debevoise & Plimpton 875 3rd Ave New York NY 10022-6225

MATTESSICH, RICHARD VICTOR (ALVARUS), business administration educator; b. Trieste, Venezia-Julia, Italy, Aug. 9, 1922; s. Victor and Gertrude (Pfaundler) M.; m. Hermine Auguste Mattessich, Apr. 12, 1952. Mech. engr., Engring. Coll., Vienna, Austria, 1940; Diplomkaufmann, Hochschule für Welthandel, Vienna, 1944; Dr.rer.pol., Hochschule für Welthandel, 1945; Accademico Ordinario, Accademia Italiana di Economia Aziendale, Bologna, 1980—, Austrian Acad. Scis., Vienna, 1984—. Research fellow Austrian Inst. Econ. Research, Vienna, 1945-47; instr. Rosenberg Coll., St. Gallen, 1947-52; dep. head Mt. Allison U., Sackville, Can., 1953-59; assoc. prof. U. Calif.-Berkeley, 1958-67; prof. econs. Ruhr U., Bochum, W. Ger., 1966-67; prof. indsl. adminstrn. U. Tech., Vienna, 1976-78; prof. bus. adminstrn. U. B.C., Vancouver, 1967-87, Arthur Andersen & Co. Disting. chair, 1980-87, prof. emeritus, 1988—; Vis. prof. Free U., Berlin, 1965, U. Social Scis., St. Gallen, Switzerland, 1965-66, U. Canterbury, 1970, Austrian Acad. Mgmt., 1971, 73; mem. bd. nominations Acctg. Hall of Fame, Columbus, Ohio, 1978-87; bd. govs. Sch. Chartered Accountancy, Vancouver, 1981-82; bd. dirs. Can. Cert. Gen. Accts. Research Found., 1984-90; internat. adv. bd. CGA Rsch. Found., 1993—. Author: Accounting and Analytical Methods, 1964, Simulation of the Firm Through a Budget Computer Program, 1964, Instrumental Reasoning and Systems Methodology, 1978, Critique of Accounting, 1995, Foundational Research in Accounting: Professional Memoirs and Beyond, 1995; editor: Modern Accounting Research History, Survey and Guide, 1984, 89, 92, Accounting Research in the 1980s and Its Future Influence, 1991, French transl., 1993, others; mem. editl. bd. Theory and Decision Libr., Jour. Bus. Adminstrn., Economia Azlendale, Praziology, Acctg., Bus. and Fin. History. Sec.-treas. Internat. House, U. B.C., 1969-70; bd. dirs. Can. Cert. Gen. Accts. Research Found., 1984-90. Served to lt. Orgn. Todt., 1944-45. Recipient Gold medal and Lit. award AICPA, 1972, Haim Falk award Can. Acad. Acctg. Assn., 1991;Ford Found. fellow, 1961-62; Disting. Erskine fellow U. Canterbury, 1970; Killam sr. fellow U. B.C., 1971-72. Fellow Accademia Italiana di Economia Aziendale (accademico ordinario 1980—); mem. Inst. Chartered Accts., Am. Acctg. Assn. (lit. award 1972, 73), Schmalenbach Gesellschaft, Verb. d. Hochschullehrer für Betriebswirtschaft (exec. adv. council 1976-78), Inst. Chartered Accts. of B.C. (bd. of govs. 1981-82), Austrian Acad. Scis. (corr.), Acad. Acctg. Historians (life). Office: U BC, Dept Bus Adminstrn, Vancouver, BC Canada V6T 1Z2 *Cautious optimism is the best long-run optimization strategy.*

MATTEUCCI, DOMINICK VINCENT, real estate developer; b. Trenton, N.J., Oct. 19, 1924; s. Vincent Joseph and Anna Marie (Zoda) M.; BS, Coll. of William and Mary, 1948; BS, Mass. Inst. Tech., 1950. Registered profl. engr., Calif.; lic. gen. bldg. contractor, real estate broker; m. Emma Irene DeGuia, Mar. 2, 1968; children: Felisa Anna, Vincent Eriberto. Owner, Matteucci Devel. Co., Newport Beach, Calif.; pres. Nat. Investment Brokerage Co., Newport Beach. Home: 2104 Felipe Newport Beach CA 92660-4040 Office: PO Box 10474 Newport Beach CA 92658-0474

MATTHAU, WALTER, actor; b. N.Y.C., Oct. 1, 1920; s. Milton and Rose (Berolsky) M.; m. Carol Grace Marcus, Aug. 21, 1959; children—David, Jenny, Charles. Ed. pub. schs., N.Y.C. Broadway appearances include: Anne of a Thousand Days, 1948, The Liar, 1949, Season in the Sun, 1950, Fancy Meeting You Again, 1951, Twilight Walk, 1951 (N.Y. Drama Critics award), One Bright Day, 1951, In Any Language, 1952, The Grey-Eyed People, 1952, The Ladies of the Corridor, 1953, Will Success Spoil Rock Hunter, 1955, Once More with Feeling, 1958 (N.Y. Drama Critics award), Once There Was a Russian, 1960, A Shot in the Dark, 1961 (Antoinette Perry award), My Mother, My Father and Me, 1963, The Odd Couple, 1964 (Antoinette Perry award); motion pictures include A Guide for the Married Man, Secret Life of An American Wife, Mirage, Charade, The Kentuckian, 1955, The Indian Fighter, 1955, Slaughter on Tenth Avenue, 1957, Ride A Crooked Trail, A Face in the Crowd, 1957, No Power on Earth, Middle of the Street, Onion Head, 1958, Voice in the Mirror, 1958, Bigger Than Life, King Creole, 1958, Island of Love, Strangers When We Meet, 1960, The Gangster Story, 1960, Where's The Action, 1962, Lonely Are the Brave (Film Daily award), 1962, Fail-Safe, 1964, Goodbye Charlie, 1964, The Odd Couple, 1966, The Fortune Cookie (Academy award), 1966, Candy, 1968, Hello Dolly!, 1968, Cactus Flower, 1969, A New Leaf, Plaza Suite, Kotch, 1971, Pete 'n Tillie, 1972, Charley Varrick, Laughing Policeman, The Front Page, The Sunshine Boys, 1975, The Bad News Bears, The Taking of Pelham, One Two Three, California Suite, 1978, Casey's Shadow, 1978, House Calls, 1978, I Ought To Be In Pictures, Little Miss Marker, 1979, Hopscotch, 1979, First Monday in October, 1981, Buddy Buddy, 1981, The Survivors, Movers and Shakers, 1984, Pirates, 1986, Couch Trip, 1987, The Little Devil, 1988, J.F.K., 1991, Dennis the Menace, 1993, Grumpy Old Men, 1993, I.Q., 1994; TV films include: Incident in a Small Town, 1994. Served with USAAF, 1941-45, ETO. Office: care Ernst & Young 1999 Avenue Of The Stars Los Angeles CA 90067-6024

MATTHEI, EDWARD HODGE, architect; b. Chgo., Dec. 21, 1927; s. Henry Reinhold and Myra Beth (Hodge) M.; m. Mary Nina Hoffmann, June 30, 1951; children: Edward Hodge, Suzanne Marie, Christie Ann, Laura Jean, John William. B.S. in Archtl. Engring, U. Ill., 1951. Registered architect, Ariz., Fla., Ill., Mich., N.Y., Wis. Dir. health facilities planning and constrn. Child & Smith (architects and engrs.), Chgo., 1951-60; sr. v.p. health facilities planning Perkins & Will, Chgo., 1960-74; ptnr. firm Matthei & Colin Assoc., Chgo., 1974-96; planning and archtl. design cons. Chgo., 1996—; com. chmn. Am. Nat. Standards Inst., 1983-89; lectr. 1st Internat. Conf. on Rehab. of Handicapped, Beijing, 1986, Design USA, Novosbirsk and Moscow, USSR, 1990. Editor: Inland Architect, 1956-58; prin. works health facilities projects, med. ctr. master plans including Augustana Hosp. and Health Care Ctr., Chgo., Mercy Hosp., Davenport, Iowa, Westlake Cmty. Hosp., Chgo., Highland Park (Ill.) Hosp., Ctrl. DuPage Hosp., Winfield, Ill., Nebr. Meth. Hosp., Omaha, Rockford (Ill.) Meml. Hosp., U. Ala. Med. Ctr., Birmingham, U. Calif. Sch. Medicine, Irvine, Kent Hall, U. Chgo., Holy Cross Hosp., Md., West Mich. Cancer Ctr. Second v.p. Nat. Easter Seal Soc., 1978; mem. bd. dirs. St. Scholastica H.S., Chgo., 1973-83, 86-96; mem. Welfare Coun. Greater Met. Chgo., 1965-72; chair profl. adv. coun. Nat. Easter Seal Soc., 1988-89. With AUS, 1946-47. Recipient Leon Chatelain award for barrier-free environ. Nat. Easter Seals Soc., 1979, Disting. Svc. award, 1990, Am. Nat. Standards Inst., 1987, Speedy award Paralyzed Vets. Am., 1993. Fellow AIA (Disting. Svc. award Chgo. chpt. 1988); mem. Am. Hosp. Assn., Am. Assn. Hosp. Planning, Internat. Hosp. Fedn., Nat. Center Barrier Free Environ. (dir.), Builders Assn. Chgo., Chgo. Assn. Commerce and Industry. Home: 1437 W Glenlake Ave Chicago IL 60660-1801 Office: Matthei & Colin Assocs 332 S Michigan Ave Chicago IL 60604-4301

MATTHES, GERALD STEPHEN, advertising agency executive; b. Hamburg, Germany, Aug. 31, 1938; Brit. subject; came to U.S., 1964, naturalized 1977; s. Stanley Rutter and Gerda Elena (Spiro) M.; m. Betsy Durkin (div. 1981); 1 child, Peter Charlton; m. Margaret Emily Secher; children: Christopher Stanley, Lydia Janet. Undergrad. edn., Gt. Britain; M. in Communications, Advt. and Mktg., London Coll., 1963. Acct. exec. Press and Gen. Publicity, Ltd., London, 1959-61, Dudley, Turner and Vincent, Ltd., London, 1961-64; v.p., mgmt. supr. Doyle, Dane, Bernbach, N.Y.C., 1964-79; sr. v.p. internat. Bozell, N.Y.C., 1980—; cons. Robert P. Gersin Assoc., 1979. Contbr. articles to profl. jours. Recipient Gold Medal award Direct Mail Assn. Great Britain, 1963. Democrat. Episcopalian. Home: 709 Kensington Ln Bloomfield Hills MI 48304-3743 Office: Bozell Worldwide Inc 1000 Town Ctr Ste 1500 Southfield MI 48075-1241

MATTHEW, KATHRYN KAHRS, museum director; b. Charleston, S.C.. BA, Mt. Holyoke Coll., 1976; PhD, U. Pa., 1981; MBA, U. Minn., 1988. Collection asst., mgr. Acad. Natural Scis., Phila., 1979-82; curator sci. Cranbrook Inst. of Sci., Bloomfield Hills, Mich., 1983-85; asst. dir. Santa Barbara (Calif.) Mus. Natural History, 1988-89; dep. dir. Va. Mus. Natural History, Martinsville, 1989-91; dir. N.Mex. Mus. Natural History, Albuquerque, 1991—; prin. sci. adviser Omnimax film Sci. Mus. Minn., Mpls., 1988-92. Bd. dirs. Albuquerque Conv. and Visitors Bur., 1992—; mem. steering com. Magnifico Arts Festival, 1992; mem. govs. coun. Advance Math and Sci. Edn., 1992—; mem. rsch. com. N.Mex. First, 1992—. Mem. N.Mex. Women's Forum. Office: NM Mus Natural History & Sci 1801 Mountain Rd NW Albuquerque NM 87104-1375

MATTHEWS, BETTY PARKER, special education educator; b. Port Arthur, Tex., Dec. 9, 1929; d. Clarence G. and Florence (Sudduth) Parker; m. Paul A. Matthews, Mar. 25, 1955; children: Michael A., Scott P., Lisa M. Alexander. BS, La. Coll., 1975; MEd, Northwestern U., 1981. Specialist in edn. La., 1984; cert. elem. tchr., mentally retarded, learning disabled, ednl. cons., generic mild/moderate, assessment tchr., ednl. diagnostician, child search coord., La. 3d grade tchr. Rapides Parish Sch. Bd., Alexandria, La., 1975-76, tchr. spl. edn., 1976-81, assessment tchr., 1981-93; ednl. diagnostician Rapides Parish Sch. Bd., Alexandria, 1993—; ednl. cons. Briarwood Psychiatric Hosp., Alexandria, La., 1986-93, Crossroads Psychiat. Hosp., Alexandria, La., 1993-96; adj. prof. La. State U., Alexandria, 1990—. Dir. children's Bible study 1st Bapt. Ch., Pineville, La., 1985—. Mem. La. Ednl. Diagnosticians Assn. (regional rep. 1987-88, treas. 1988-90, Pres.'s Svc. award 1990-91, La. Assessment Tchr. of Yr. 1993), Coun. Exceptional Children, Reading Coun., Alpha Delta Kappa, Phi Delta Kappa, Epsilon Sigma Alpha (state pres., regional sec.). Home: 3050 Rigolette Rd Pineville LA 71360-7219

MATTHEWS, BRIAN W., molecular biology educator; b. Mount Barker, Australia, May 25, 1938; came to U.S., 1967; s. Lionel A. and Ethlinda L. (Harris) M.; m. Helen F. Denley, Sept. 7, 1963; children: Susan, Kristine. BS, U. Adelaide, Australia, 1959, BS with honors, 1960, PhD, 1964, DSc, 1986. Mem. staff Med. Rsch. Coun., Cambridge, Eng., 1963-66; vis. assoc. NIH, Bethesda, Md., 1967-69; prof. molecular biology U. Oreg., Eugene, 1969—, chmn. dept. physics, 1985-86, dir. Inst. Molecular Biology, 1980-83, 90-92; Drummond lectr. U. Calgary (Can.), 1995; advisor NSF, Washington, 1975-77; investigator Howard Hughes Med. Inst., 1989—; mem. U.S. Nat. Commn. for Crystallography, Washington, 1980-86, 88-90. Rsch. fellow Alfred P. Sloan Found., 1971, Guggenheim fellow, 1977; recipient Career Devel. award NIH, 1973, Faculty Excellence award Oreg. Bd. Edn., 1984, Discovery award Med. Rsch. Found. Oreg., 1987, Reed Coll. Vollum award, 1994. Mem. NAS, AAAS, Crystallographic Assn., Am. Chem. Soc., Protein Soc. (pres. 1995—). Office: U Oreg/HHMI Inst Molecular Biology Eugene OR 97403

MATTHEWS, BRUCE RANKIN, professional football player; b. Arcadia, Calif., Aug. 8, 1961. BS in Indsl. Engring., U. So. Calif., 1983. Center, guard Houston Oilers, 1983—. Named NFL All-Pro Team Guard by Sporting News, 1988-90, 92, Leader, 1993. Played in Pro Bowl, 1988-93. Office: Houston Oilers 6910 Fannin St Fl 3 Houston TX 77030-3806

MATTHEWS, CHARLES SEDWICK, petroleum engineering consultant, research advisor; b. Houston, Mar. 27, 1920; s. Charles James and Zadoc Coleman (Sedwick) M.; m. Miriam Loraine Ormerod, June 2, 1945; children—Joan Gail, Wendy Loraine. B.S. in Chem. Engring., Rice U., 1941, M.S. in Chem. Engring., 1943, Ph.D. in Chemistry, 1944. Registered profl. engr., Tex. Engr. Shell Devel. Co., San Francisco, 1944-48; research engr. Shell Devel. Co., Houston, 1948-56; dir. research Shell Devel. Co., 1967-72; chief reservoir engr. Shell Oil Co., Houston, 1965; mgr. engring. Shell Oil Co., 1972-73, sr. petroleum engring. cons., 1973-89; mem. engring. adv. com. Rice U., Houston, 1973-77; cons. Dept. Energy, Washington, 1974-78, mem. adv. com., 1975-79; spl. asst. Nat. Petroleum Council, Washington, 1981-83; mem. reserves com. Am. Petroleum Inst. Author: Pressure Buildup and Flow Tests in Wells, 1967; contbr. articles to profl. jours.; patentee in field. Chmn. Tex. Engrs. for Conservation, Houston, 1973. Recipient Disting. Alumnus award Rice U., 1994. Mem. NAE, Soc. Petroleum Engrs. (hon. mem., Lester Uren award 1975, disting. author, disting. lectr. 1968, Disting. lectr. emeritus 1986), Phi Beta Kappa, Sigma Xi, Tau Beta Pi, Phi Lambda Upsilon. Republican. Methodist. Clubs: Houston, Meyerland (treas. 1982-85). Avocations: swimming; fishing. Home: 5307 S Braeswood Blvd Houston TX 77096-4149

MATTHEWS, CHRIS, finance company executive; b. 1943. With The Hay Co., Toronto, 1968-90, Hay Acquisition Co., Inc., Phila., 1990—; chmn., CEO Hay Group, Inc., Phila. Office: The Hay Group 229 S 18th St Ste 6 Philadelphia PA 19103*

MATTHEWS, CLARK J(IO), II, retail executive, lawyer; b. Arkansas City, Kans., Oct. 1, 1936; s. Clark J. and Betty Elizabeth (Stewart) M.; children: Patricia Eleanor, Pamela Elaine, Catherine Joy. B.A., So. Meth. U., 1959, J.D., 1961. Bar: Tex. 1961. Trial atty. Ft. Worth Regional Office, SEC, 1961-63; law clk. to chief U.S. dist. judge No. Dist. Tex., Dallas, 1963-65; atty. Southland Corp., Dallas, 1965-73; v.p., gen. counsel Southland Corp., 1973-79, exec. v.p., chief fin. officer, 1979-83, sr. exec. v.p., chief fin. officer, 1983-87, exec. v.p., chief fin. officer, 1987-91, pres., chief exec. officer, 1991—. Mem. ABA, Tex., Dallas, Bar Assns., Am. Judicature Soc., Alpha Tau Omega, Pi Alpha Delta. Methodist. Club: DeMolay. Home: 7005 Stefani Dr Dallas TX 75225-1747 Office: Southland Corp 2711 N Haskell Ave Dallas TX 75204-2911

MATTHEWS, CRAIG GERARD, gas company executive; b. Bklyn., Mar. 8, 1943; m. Carol O. Olsen, Sept. 10, 1971; children: Kenneth C., Bradford P., Melinda M. BCE, Rutgers U., 1965; MS in Indsl. Mgmt., Polytech. Inst. Bklyn., 1971. Trainee Bklyn. Union Gas Co., 1965, exec. v.p., 1988—. Bd. dirs. Bklyn. Philharm., Salvation Army, Inform, Prospect Park Alliance, Regional Planning Assn., Greater Jamaica Devel. Corp., Pub. Utility Reports, Neighborhood Housing Svcs. Mem. Bklyn. C. of C. (bd. dirs., chmn.), Am. Gas Assn. (bd. dirs.). Republican. Presbyterian. Home: 17 Wynwood Rd Chatham NJ 07928-1755 Office: Bklyn Union Gas Co 1 Metrotech Ctr Brooklyn NY 11201-3602

MATTHEWS, DAN GUS, lawyer; b. Jacksonville, Tex., Feb. 6, 1939; s. Agustus Newcomb and Charlie (Morton) M.; m. Mary Ellen Whittredge, Dec. 12, 1959; children: Mark Henderson, Daniel William. BS in History and English, Stephen F. Austin U., 1960; LLB, U. Houston, 1964. Bar: Tex. 1964, U.S. Dist. Ct. (so. dist.) Tex. 1964, U.S. Ct. Appeals (5th cir.) 1965, U.S. Ct. Appeals (11th cir.) 1981, U.S. Supreme Ct. 1967, U.S. Dist. Ct. (ea. dist.) Tex. 1990. Briefing clk. Fed. Judge Ben C. Connally, Houston, 1964-66; assoc. firm Fulbright & Jaworski, Houston, 1966-73; ptnr. Fulbright & Jaworski, Houston and San Antonio, 1973—. Bd. dirs., exec. com., chmn. membership com. Los Compadres de San Antonio, Missions Nat. Hist. Pk., 1988—; deacon, elder Presbyn. Ch. Mem. ABA, State Bar Tex., Houston Bar Assn., San Antonio Bar Assn. Avocations: hunting, fishing. Office: Fulbright & Jaworski 300 Convent St Ste 2200 San Antonio TX 78205-3723*

MATTHEWS, DAVID, clergyman; b. Indianola, Miss., Jan. 29, 1920; s. Albert and Bertha (Henderson) M.; m. Lillian Pearl Banks, Aug. 28, 1951; 1 dau., Denise. A.B., Morehouse Coll., Atlanta, 1950; student, Atlanta U., 1950, Memphis Theol. Sem., 1965, Delta State U., Cleveland, Miss., 1969, 71, 72; D.D. (hon.), Natchez (Miss.) Jr. Coll., 1973, Morris Booker Meml. Coll., 1988. Ordained minister Nat. Baptist Conv. U.S.A., 1946; pastor chs. in Miss., 1951—, Bell Grove Baptist Ch., Indianola, 1951—, Strangers Home, Greenwood, 1958—; tchr., chmn. dept. social sci. Gentry H.S., Indianola, 1958-83; moderator Sunflower Bapt. Assn., 1957—; v.p. Gen. Bapt. Conv. Miss., 1958—, former lectr., conv. congress religious edn.; v.p. Nat. Bapt. Conv. U.S.A., 1971-94; del. to Nat. Coun. Chs., 1960, supr. oratorial contest, 1976; pres. Gen. Missionary Bapt. State Conv. Miss., 1974—. Mem. Sunflower County Anti-Poverty Bd., 1965-71, Indianola Bi-Racial Com., 1965—; mem. Gov.'s Advisory Com.; col. on staff Gov. Finch, 1976-80; mem. budget com. Indianola United Fund, 1971—; chmn. bd. Indianola FHA, 1971—; trustee Natchez Jr. Coll.; mem. Miss. Gov.'s Research and Devel. Council, 1984—; apptd. mem. So. Govs. Ecumenical Coun. Infant Mortality, 1987. Served with U.S. Army, 1942-45, PTO. Recipient citation Morehouse Coll., 1950, citation Miss. Valley State Coll., 1956; J.H. Jackson Preaching award Midwestern Baptist Laymen Fellowship, 1974; Gov.'s Merit award, 1975. Mem. NEA, Miss., Indianola Tchrs. Assns., Am. Bible Soc. (adv. coun. 1991—, student reform theol. sem. centennial edn. 1990—). Democrat. Home: PO Box 627 Indianola MS 38751-0627 *I have learned not to seek honors and success but to become so involved in worthwhile works that I lose myself and by such actions success and honors have come.*

MATTHEWS, DAVID FORT, military weapon system acquisition specialist; b. Lancaster, N.H., Sept. 25, 1944; s. Clinton Fort and Mabel Sawin (Oaks) M.; m. Eva Mae Horton, Nov. 10, 1990. BA, Vanderbilt U., 1966; MA, Mid. Tenn. U., 1973. Cert. acquisition mgr. Rsch. and devel. officer U.S. Army Rsch. Inst., Washington, 1974-77; exec. officer 194th Maintenence Battalion-Camp Humphreys, Korea, 1978-79; career program mgr. U.S. Army Mil. Pers. Ctr., Washington, 1979-82; logistics staff officer Dep. Chief of Staff Logistics, Washington, 1982-83; team chief Chief of Staff Army Study Group, Washington, 1983-85; logistics div. chief Multiple Launch Rocket System Project Office, Huntsville, Ala., 1985-88; comdr. Ordanance Program Div., Riyadh, Saudi Arabia, 1988-90; project mgr. Army Tactical Missile System, Huntsville, 1990-94; sr. lectr. weapon systems acquisition Naval Postgrad. Sch., Monterey, Calif., 1994—. Decorated Legion of Merit, Bronze Star; recipient award as project mgr. of yr. Sec. of Army, 1991. Mem. Am. Ordinance Assn., Am. Def. Prepardness Assn., Assn. U.S. Army. Avocations: spectator sports, water skiing, reading. Home: 83 High Meadow Ln Carmel CA 93923 Office: Naval Postgrad Sch Monterey CA 93943

MATTHEWS, DONALD ROWE, political scientist, educator; b. Cin., Sept. 14, 1925; s. William Procter and Janet Burch (Williams) M.; m. Margie C. Richmond, June 28, 1947 (div.); children: Mary, Jonathan; m. Carmen J. Onstad, July 7, 1970 (div.); children: Christopher, Amy. Student, Kenyon Coll., 1943, Purdue U., 1944-45; A.B. with high honors, Princeton, 1948, M.A., 1951, Ph.D., 1953; Dr. hon. causa, U. Bergen, 1985. Instr. Smith Coll., Northampton, Mass., 1951-53; asst. prof. govt. Smith Coll., 1953-57; lectr. polit. sci. U. N.C., Chapel Hill, 1957-58; assoc. prof. U. N.C., 1958-63, prof., 1963-70; research prof. Inst. for Research in Social Sci., 1963-70; sr. fellow in govtl. studies Brookings Instn., Washington, 1970-73; prof. polit. sci. and research assoc. Inst. for Research in Social Sci., U. Mich., Ann Arbor, 1973-76; prof. polit. sci. U. Wash., Seattle, 1976—, chmn. dept. polit. sci., 1976-83; guest prof. U. Bergen, Norway, 1980-81, 93; fellow Ctr. for Advanced Study in the Behavioral Scis., 1964-65; cons. to U.S. Commn. on Civil Rights, 1958-60, NBC News, 1966-68, Ford Found., 1967-68, U.S. Ho. of Reps., 1970-72, others; faculty lectr. U. Wash., 1989. Author: The Social Background of Political Decision-Makers, 1954, U.S. Senators and Their World, 1960, (with James Prothro) Negroes and the New Southern Politics, 1966, Perspectives on Presidential Selection, 1973, (with William Keech) The Party's Choice, 1976, (with James Stimson) Yeas and Nays: A Theory of Decision-Making in the U.S. House of Representatives, 1975; Contbr. articles to profl. jours. Served with USNR, 1943-46. Recipient Sr. Award for Research in Govtl. Affairs Social Sci. Research Council, 1962; Ford Found. fellow, 1969-70; Guggenheim fellow, 1980-81. Fellow Am. Acad. Arts and Scis.; mem. Am. Polit. Sci. Assn. (treas. 1970-72, v.p. 1985-86), Pacific N.W. Polit. Sci. Assn. (pres. 1977-78), Western Polit. Sci. Assn. (pres. 1979-80), So. Polit. Sci. Assn., Midwestern Polit. Sci. Assn., Inter-Univ. Consortium for Polit. Research (exec. com. 1970-72). Democrat. Home: Houseboat B 3125 Fairview Ave E Seattle WA 98102-3063 Office: U Wash Polit Sci Do # 30 Seattle WA 98195

MATTHEWS, EDWARD E., insurance company executive; b. 1931. AB, Princeton U., 1953; MBA, Harvard U., 1957. With Morgan Stanley & Co., 1957-73; exec. v.p. fin., vice chmn. bd. dirs. Am. Internat. Group, Inc., N.Y.C., from 1973, now vice chmn. bd. dirs. With U.S. Army, 1953-55. Office: Am Internat Group Inc 70 Pine St New York NY 10270-0002*

MATTHEWS, EDWIN SPENCER, JR., lawyer; b. Spokane, Wash., May 31, 1934; s. Edwin Spencer and Dorothy Chace (Ehrhardt) M.; m. Marie-Claude Paris, Dec. 19, 1959 (div. 1982); children: Nadia, Sylvie, Clarissa; m. Patricia L. Sills Barnes, Dec. 22, 1983; children: Paxton, Gillian. AB magna cum laude, Harvard U., 1956; Diplome d'Etudes Francaises, Institut de Tourraine, Tours, France, 1958; LLB, Yale U., 1962. Bar: N.Y. 1963, Calif. 1979, U.S. Supreme Ct. 1992; Conseil Juridique (France) 1965-79. Assoc. Coudert Bros., N.Y.C., 1962-65; assoc. Coudert Freres, Paris, 1965-69, ptnr., 1969-79; ptnr. Coudert Bros., San Francisco, 1979-80, N.Y.C., 1980—. Trustee Sierra Club Legal Def. Fund, San Francisco, 1984—; bd. dirs. Friends of Earth Found., N.Y.C., 1979-85; bd. dirs. Friends of Earth Inc., Washington, 1970-85, pres., 1979-80. With U.S. Army, 1957-58. Mem. Assn. of Bar of City of N.Y. (com. on housing and urban devel. 1964-65, com. on capital representation), Am. Alpine Club, Harvard Club, N.Y. Athletic Club. Democrat. Avocations: ocean sailing, carpentry, mountain climbing, sculling. Home: 11 Harrison St New York NY 10013-2837 also: PO Box 493 Washington Depot CT 06794-0493 Office: Coudert Brothers 1114 Avenue Of The Americas New York NY 10036-7703

MATTHEWS, ELIZABETH WOODFIN, law librarian, law educator; b. Ashland, Va., July 30, 1927; d. Edwin Clifton and Elizabeth Frances (Luck) Woodfin; m. Sidney E. Matthews, Dec. 20, 1947; 1 child, Sarah Elizabeth Matthews Wiley. BA, Randolph-Macon Coll., 1948, LLD (hon.), 1989; MS in Libr. Sci., U. Ill., 1952; PhD, So. Ill. U., 1972; LLD, Randolph-Macon Coll., 1989. Cert. law libr., med. libr., med. libr. III. Libr. Ohio State U., Columbus, 1952-59; libr., instr. U. Ill., Urbana, 1962-63, lectr. Grad. Sch. Libr. Sci., 1964; libr., instr. Morris Libr. So. Ill. U., Carbondale, 1964-67, classroom instr. Coll. Edn., 1967-70, med. libr., asst. prof. Morris Libr., 1972-74, law libr., asst. prof., 1974-79, law libr., assoc. prof., 1979-85, law libr., prof., 1985-93; prof. emerita, 1993—. Author: Access Points to Law Libraries, 1984, 17th Century English Law Reports, 1986, Law Library Reference Shelf, 1988, 2d edit., 1992, 3d edit., 1996, Pages and Missing Pages, 1983, 2d edit., 1989, Lincoln as a Lawyer: An Annotated Bibliography, 1991. Mem. AAUW (pres. 1976-78, corp. rep. 1978-88), Am. Assn. Law Librs., Mid Am. Assn. Law Librs., Beta Phi Mu, Phi Kappa Phi. Methodist. Home: 811 S Skyline Dr Carbondale IL 62901-2405 Office: So Ill U Law Libr Carbondale IL 62901

MATTHEWS, ESTHER ELIZABETH, education educator, consultant; b. Princeton, Mass., June 20, 1918; d. Ralph Edgar and Julia Ellen (Cronin) M. BS in Edn., Worcester State Coll., 1940; EdM, Harvard U., 1943, EdD, 1960. Tchr. various Mass. schs., 1942-47; guidance dir. Holden (Mass.) Pub. Schs., 1947-53, Wareham (Mass.) Pub. Schs., 1954-57; counselor Newton (Mass.) High Sch., 1957-60, head counselor, 1960-66; assoc. prof. edn. U. Oreg., 1966-70, prof. edn., 1970-80, prof. emerita, 1980—; vis. prof. U. Toronto, Ont., Can., summer 1971; lectr. on edn. Harvard U., 1963-66; cons. in field; lectr. various colls. and univs. Author book chpts.; contbr. numerous articles to profl. jours. and papers to conf. proc. Mem. ACD (Recognition for Contbn. to Promote Human Rights 1987), World Future Soc., Nat. Vocat. Guidance Assn. (pres. 1974-75, chair nat. com. 1966-67, sec. 1967-68, bd. trustees 1968-71, editl. bd. Vocat. Guidance Quar. 1966-68), Oreg. Pers. and Guidance Assn. (Leona Tyler award 1973, Disting. Svc. award 1979), Oreg. Career Devel. Assn. (Disting. Svc. award 1987, Esther E. Matthews Ann. award for outstanding contbn. to career devel. in Oreg. established in her honor 1993). Home: 832 Lariat Dr Eugene OR 97401-6438

MATTHEWS, EUGENE EDWARD, artist; b. Davenport, Iowa, Mar. 22, 1931; s. Nickolas Arthur and Velma (Schroeder) M.; m. Wanda Lee Miller, Sept. 14, 1952; children: Anthony Lee, Daniel Nickolas. Student, Bradley U., 1948-51; BFA, U. Iowa, 1953, MFA, 1957. Prof. fine arts grad. faculty U. Colo., Boulder, 1961—, dir. vis. artists program, 1985—; vis. artist Am. Acad. Rome, 1989. One-man shows include U. Wis., Milw., 1960, Brena Gallery, Denver, 1963, 65, 67, 70, 74, 76, 78, 80, 83, 88, Colorado Springs Fine Arts Ctr., 1967, Sheldon Art Gallery, U. Nebr., 1968, Denver Art Mus., 1972, James Yu Gallery, N.Y.C., 1973, 77, Dubins Gallery, L.A., 1981, Galeria Rysunku, Poznan, 1983, CU. Art Galleries, U. Colo., Boulder, 1996; exhibited in numerous group shows U.S., Europe, Africa, Asia; internat. watercolor exhbn. New Orleans, 1983, Louvre, Paris, Met. Mus. of Art, N.Y.C., Internat. Art Ctr., Kyoto, Japan, Mus. of Modern Art, Rijeka, Yugoslavia, Taipei Fine Arts Mus., Taiwan, Republic of China; represented in permanent collections Nat. Mus. Am. Art, Washington, Denver Art Mus., Butler Inst. Am. Art, Chrysler Art Mus., others. Recipient Penello d'Argento award Acitrezza Internazionale, 1958, S.P.Q.R. Cup of Rome, Roma Olimpionica Internazionale, 1959, Gold medal of honor Nat. Arts Club, N.Y.C., 1969, Bicentennial award Rocky Mountain Nat. Watercolor Exhbn., 1976, Am. Drawings IV Purchase award, 1982, others; fellow in painting Am. Acad. Rome, 1957-60, U. Colo. Creative Rsch. fellow, 1966-67. Mem. Watercolor U.S.A. Honor Soc. (charter). Home: 720 Hawthorn Ave Boulder CO 80304-2140

MATTHEWS, FRANCIS RICHARD, lawyer; b. Calgary, Alta., Can., Aug. 19, 1920; s. Charles Curtice and Grace (Cathro) M.; m. Joyce Winter Jarvis, Nov. 10, 1944; children: James Richard, Frances Elizabeth, Michael John. B.Com., U. Alta., 1941, LL.B., 1948. Bar: Called to Alta. bar 1949, created Queen's Counsel 1963. Assoc. firm Mackimmie, Matthews, Calgary, 1949-54; ptnr. Mackimmie, Matthews, 1954-87, of counsel, 1987—; dir. Murphy Oil Co. Ltd., Ranger Oil Ltd. Served to lt. Royal Canadian Naval Vol. Res., 1941-45. Mem. Calgary Philharmonic Orchestra Soc. (bd. govs., pres. 1955-56, 61-62), Calgary C. of C., Can., Alberta bar assns., Soaring Assn. Can., Delta Kappa Epsilon. Mem. Anglican Ch. Clubs: Calgary Petroleum, Ranchmen's. Home: 720 13th Ave SW Apt 1810, Calgary, AB Canada T2R 1M5 Office: Gulf Canada Sq 7th Fl, Calgary, AB Canada T2P 2M2

MATTHEWS, GEORGE TENNYSON, history educator; b. Bklyn., May 27, 1917; s. George Tennyson and Olive Beulah (Richardson) M.; m. Mildred G. Byars (dec. 1962); m. Margie R. Kresge, Sept. 1989; 1 child, Mildred; 1 stepchild, Christopher J. Kresge. AB, Columbia U., 1939, MA, 1941, PhD, 1953. Instr., then asst. prof. history Columbia U., 1946-59, chmn. contemporary civilization staff, 1953-59, asst. to dean Columbia Coll., 1951-59; mem. faculty Oakland U., Rochester, Mich., 1959—; prof. history Oakland U., 1960-85, prof. emeritus, 1985—, dist. prof. emeritus, 1988—, chmn. dept., 1960-62, assoc. dean humanities, then dean Coll. Arts and Scis., 1962-73, vice provost, 1973-79, pres., 1979-81; dir. honors coll. Oakland U., Rochester, Mich., 1991; Hill Family Found. lectr. MacAlister Coll., St. Paul, 1954. Author: Royal General Farms in 18th Century France, 1958, News and Rumor in Renaissance Europe, 1959; also articles, revs.; Editor: Man in Contemporary Society, 2 vols, 1957, Contemporary Civilization in the West, 2 vols, 1956. With USAAF, 1941-45. Mem. Soc. French Hist. Studies (treas. 1967-74), Am. Hist. Assn., Phi Beta Kappa (past chpt. treas.). Democrat. Home and Office: 2900 Heidelberg Dr Rochester Hills MI 48309

MATTHEWS, GILBERT ELLIOTT, investment banker; b. Brookline, Mass., Apr. 24, 1930; s. Martin W. and Charlotte (Cohen) M.; m. Anne Lisbeth Barnett, Apr. 20, 1958 (div. 1975); children: Lisa Joan, Diana Kory (dec. 1995); m. Elaine Rita Siegal Pulitzer, Jan. 2, 1978; 1 child, Jennifer Rachel. AB, Harvard U., 1951; MBA, Columbia U., 1953. Chartered fin. analyst. Dept. mgr. Bloomingdale's, N.Y.C., 1953, 56-60; security analyst Merrill Lynch, N.Y.C., 1960; investment banker Bear, Stearns & Co., N.Y.C., 1960-95, gen. ptnr., 1979-85; mng. dir. Bear, Stearns & Co. Inc., 1985-86, sr. mng. dir., 1986-95; sr. mng. dir. Sutter Securities Inc., San Francisco, 1995—; bd. dirs. Oak Industries, Inc., Waltham, Mass. Served as lt. (j.g.) USN, 1953-56. Mem. N.Y. Soc. Security Analysts. Democrat. Jewish. Home: 3362 Clay St San Francisco CA 94118 Office: Sutter Securities Inc One Sansome St Ste 3950 San Francisco CA 94104

MATTHEWS, JACK (JOHN HAROLD MATTHEWS), English educator, writer; b. Columbus, Ohio, July 22, 1925; s. John Harold and Lulu Emma (Grover) M.; m. Barbara Jane Reese, Sept. 16, 1947; children: Cynthia Ann Matthews Warnock, Barbara Ellen Matthews, John Harold. B.A., Ohio State U., 1949, M.A., 1954. Clk. U.S. Post Office, Columbus, 1950-59; prof. English Urbana Coll., Ohio, 1959-64; prof. English Ohio U., Athens, 1964-77, disting. prof., 1977—. Author: Bitter Knowledge, 1964 (Ohioana fiction award 1964), Hanger Stout, Awake!, 1967, The Charisma Campaigns, 1972 (nominee NBA Fiction award), Sassafras, 1983, Crazy Women, 1985, Booking in the Heartland, 1986 (Ohioana non-fiction award 1986), Ghostly Populations, 1986, Memoirs of a Bookman, 1989, Dirty Tricks, 1990, On The Shore of That Beautiful Shore (play), 1991, An Interview with the Sphinx (play), 1992, Storyhood As We Know It and Other Tales (stories), 1993, Booking Pleasures, 1996, others. Served with USCG, 1943-45. Recipient numerous ind. artist awards Ohio Art Council, Major Artist award, 1989-90; Guggenheim fellow, 1974-75. Mem. Phi Beta Kappa. Home: 4314 Fisher Rd Athens OH 45701-9333 Office: Ohio U Dept English Athens OH 45701

MATTHEWS, JACK, psychologist, speech pathologist, educator; b. Winnipeg, Man., Can., June 17, 1917; s. Samuel and Ellen (Walker) M.; m. Hannah Miriam Polster, Aug. 16, 1942; children: Rachel Sophia, Rebecca. A.B., Heidelberg Coll., 1938, D.Sc., 1976; M.A., Ohio U., 1940; Ph.D., Ohio State U., 1946; student, Vanderbilt U., 1942-43. Asst. dir. speech clinic Purdue U., 1946-48; dir. speech clinic, asst. prof. psychology and speech U. Pitts., 1948-55, dir. speech clinic, dir. div. psychol. services, asso. prof. psychology, 1950-55, prof., chmn. speech dept., 1955—, dean humanities, 1967-68, pres. univ. senate, 1969-72; bd. dirs. Community Hearing Coun., Pitts. Hearing Soc.; pres. Am. Bd. Examiners Speech Pathology and Audiology, 1966-67; sec. Speech and Hearing Found., 1964-68; mem. Edn. Commn. States, Nat. Adv. Com. on Handicapped Children; bd. trustees City Theatre, 1985—, Western Pa. Sch. for Deaf, 1980—, v.p. 1982-92. Asst. editor: Jour. Speech and Hearing Disorders, 1952-54; editorial bd., 1965-69, Speech Monographs, 1951-53, 56-55, Jour. Communications, 1961-64, Deafness, Speech and Hearing pubs.; cons. editor: Today's Speech, 1968-70, ERIC, 1975—; Contbr. articles to profl. jours. Served as sgt. AC Psychol. Research Unit USAAF, 1942-45. Mem. AAAS, APA, AAUP, Am. Speech and Hearing Assn. (pres. 1963-64, assoc. editor jours. 1959-62), Am. Assn. Cleft Palate Rehab. (pres. 1957-59), Speech Assn. (adminstrv. coun., rsch. bd. 1966-69, chmn. 1967-69), Am. Assn. Mental Deficiency, Soc. Psychol. Study Social Issues, Pa. Speech Assn. (pres. 1959-60), Assn. for Comm. Adminstrn. (exec. com. 1978-81), Sigma Xi, Pi Kappa Delta, Alpha Psi Omega, Tau Kappa Alpha, Sigma Alpha Eta. Home: Longwood at Oakmount Ch 53 500 Route 909 Verona PA 15147-3851

MATTHEWS, JAMES B., III, lawyer; b. Cordele, Ga., Aug. 31, 1957; s. James B. and Ruth (Mixon) M.; m. Lynn Bridges, June 18, 1983; children: Walker, Charles, Mary. BS in Econs., Ga. So. U., 1980; JD, U. Ga., 1983. Bar: Ga. 1983, U.S. Dist. Ct. (so. and no. dist.) Ga. 1983, U.S. Supreme Ct. 1993, U.S. Dist. Ct. (mid. dist.) Ga. 1984, U.S. Ct. Appeals (11th cir.) 1985, Ct. Appeals Ga. 1983; registered athlete agt., Ga. Assoc. Bouhan, Williams and Levy, Savannah, Ga., 1983-86; shareholder Blasingame, Burch, Garrard & Bryant, P.C., Athens, Ga., 1986-91; ptnr. Blackwood & Matthews, Atlanta, 1991-95, Blackwood, Matthews & Steel, Atlanta, 1995—. Recipient Award of Honor, Am. Baseball Coaches Assn., 1993. Mem. Assn. Trial Lawyers Am., Ga. Trial Lawyers Assn., Def. Rsch. Inst., Am. Judicature Soc. Office: Blackwood Matthews & Steel 2695 Buford Hwy Ste 100 Atlanta GA 30324

MATTHEWS, JAMES SHADLEY, lawyer; b. Omaha, Nov. 24, 1951; s. Donald E. and Lois Jean (Shadley) M.; m. Mary Kvaal, May 3, 1991; 1 child, Katherine. BA cum laude, St. Olaf Coll., 1973; JD, U. Ill., 1976; MBA, U. Denver, 1977. Bar: Minn. 1976, U.S. Dist. Ct. Minn. 1978. With Northwestern Nat. Life Ins. Co., Mpls., 1978-89; v.p., asst. gen. counsel Northwestern Nat. Life Ins. Co., 1985-89; ptnr. Lindquist & Venum, Mpls., 1990—; sr. v.p., gen. counsel Washington Square Capital, Inc., 1989; bd. dirs., sec. NWNL Health Network, Inc., St. Paul, 1987-89; pub. dir. Minn. Health Reins. Assn., 1992-94; speaker to profl. orgns., 1984—. Chmn. benevolence com. Colonial Congl. Ch., Edina, Minn., 1981-82. Mem. ABA, Nat. Health Lawyers Assn., Am. Acad. Hosp. Attys., Minn. Bar Assn. (chmn. health law sect. 1986-87). Office: Lindquist & Vennum 4200 IDS Ctr 80 S 8th St Minneapolis MN 55402-2100

MATTHEWS, JAY ARLON, JR., publisher, editor; b. St. Louis, Apr. 13, 1918; s. Jay Arlon and Mary (Long) M.; student San Jose State Coll., 1939-41, U. Tex., 1946-47; BLS St. Edward's U., 1994; m. May Clark McLemore, Jan. 16, 1944; children—Jay Arlon III, Emily Cochrane, Sally McLemore. Asst. dir. personnel Adj. Gen.'s Dept. Tex., 1947-53, dept. adj., 1957-65, mil. support plans officer, 1965-69, chief emergency operations, 1965-71; pub. Presidial Press, Mil. History Press. Past Dir. Civil Def., Austin; mem. adv. bd. Confed. Research Center, Hill Jr. Coll.; mil. historian 65th Legislature, Tex., 1977-78. Served with AGC, Tex. N.G., 1946—, brig. gen. ret., 1973. Named to Tex. Nat. Guard Hall of Honor, 1990. Fellow Co. Mil. Historians (gov. 1981-84); mem. Austin (state v.p. 1951-52), U.S. Jaycees (chmn. nat. security com. 1952-53), N.G. Assn. U.S. (chmn. publicity 81st Gen. Conf.), Instituto Internationale de Historia Militar (hon. life), Mil. Order World Wars (comdr. Austin chpt. 1980). Episcopalian. Club: Exchange (pres. Austin chpt. 1982-83). Editor: Mil. History of Tex. and S.W. Quar., 1961-88; editor emeritus Mil. Hist. of the West, 1989. Home: 1807 Stamford Ln Austin TX 78703-2939 also: PO Box 5248 Austin TX 78763-5248

MATTHEWS, JEFFREY ALAN, physicist; b. Lansdale, Pa., Apr. 1, 1962; s. Gerald and Idella Laura (Camburn) M. BS in Physics cum laude, Ursinus Coll., 1984. Teaching asst. physics dept. U. Del., Newark, 1984-85; physicist Army Material Systems Analysis Activity, Aberdeen Proving Ground, Md., 1986—. Disaster capt. ARC, Harford County, Md., 1992-95, alt. disaster coord., 1994-95, disaster coord., 1995—; EMT-A Abingdon (Md.) Vol. Fire Co., 1992-94. Recipient Red Cross Svc. award, 1992, 95. Mem. Sigma Xi, Sigma Pi Sigma. Avocations: model railroading, writing, poetry, playing guitar. Home: 1426 Saint Michael Ct Edgewood MD 21040-2197

MATTHEWS, JOHN FLOYD, writer, educator; b. Cin., Apr. 8, 1919; s. Floyd L. and Helen (Orth) M.; m. Maurine Zollman, Mar. 4, 1945 (dec. 1959); children—Lauralee Alice, Caroline Elaine (dec.); m. Brenda Martin, Aug. 27, 1966. Student, Wooster Coll., 1935-37, Northwestern U., 1937; B.A., U. Cin., 1940, postgrad., 1940-41; postgrad., Columbia U., 1943, New Sch. for Social Research, 1944-45. Lectr. New Sch. for Social Research, 1948-50; lectr., chmn. faculty Dramatic Workshop and Tech. Inst., N.Y.C., 1950-52; lectr. in playwriting CCNY, 1947-63; asst. prof. dramatic lit. and history Brandeis U., 1952-59, assoc. prof., 1959-67, Schulman prof., 1967-71, chmn. dept. theatre, 1955-58, prof. Am. studies, 1971—, chmn. dept. Am. studies, 1973-74, Richter prof. Am. Civilization and Instns., 1972-84, prof. emeritus, 1984—; vis. critic Yale Sch. Drama, 1965; mem. Seminar in Am. Studies, Circle Cultural de Royaumont, France, 1965; founding mem. Brandeis Creative Arts Awards Commn. Network radio actor, writer, producer, 1939-45, screenwriter, Warner Bros., 1945; author: plays, including The Scapegoat, 1950, Michael and Lavinia, 1956, Barnum, 1962; books The Old Vic In America, 1946, El Greco, 1952, Shaw's Dramatic Criticism, 1959, George Bernard Shaw, 1969, Reflections on Abortion, 1976; contbr. fiction to lit. mags.; cons., play doctor for script and prodn. problems of numerous Broadway and off-Broadway plays and musicals including Anastasia, The First Gentleman, others; TV scriptwriter for maj. networks, 1955-64; screenwriter, MGM, United Artists, Asso. Screen Prodns., Toronto, Ont., Can., 1958-64; Contbg. editor: Library of Living Painters, 1949-51, Dictionary of the Arts, 1946, Ency. World Biography, 1970. Mem. Westport (Conn.) Democratic Town Com., 1959-64; mem. Newton (Mass.) Republican City Com., 1977—, Mass. Rep. Platform Com., 1978; bd. dirs. Newton Taxpayers Assn., 1979-81, 86-91. Recipient Arts of the Theatre Found. award, 1950. Mem. Brit. Drama League, The Nat. Trust, English Speaking Union, Trustees of Reservations. Episcopalian. Home: 5 Tudor Close, Dean Court Rd, Rottingdean BN1 7DF, England

MATTHEWS, JULIE, performing arts company director; b. Cleve., Mar. 3, 1957; d. Daniel Louis Harb and Diane Louise (Salem) Mack; m. Guo Ming, Dec. 24, 1993. Student, Cuyahoga C.C., Cleve., 1975-77, HB Studio, N.Y.C., 1977, Lee Strassberg Actors Studio, N.Y.C., 1977. Acting coach Huntington Playhouse, Cleve., 1978-82; children's theatre dir. Chagrin Valley Little Theatre, Cleve., 1978-82; acting coach Independence Theatre, Cleve., 1982; host, dir. pub. rels. Cleveland Rocks TV Show, 1986-91; dir. on-camera casting/agt. Powers Internat., Cleve., 1991-92; casting dir. Motion Picture/"Babe Ruth", 1991; acting coach, casting dir., talent scout, founder/dir. Am. Performing Arts Network, Cleve., 1992—; cons. in field, 60 Minutes, Australian TV, 1994, Sally Jesse Raphael, CBS TV, 1994, Danny Bonaduce, Loop Radio/Chgo., 1994. Author: (manual) How to Get Into Show Business . . . The Right Way, 1993; film credits include: A Christmas Story, Major League, The Light of Day, Bob Roberts; leading stage role credits include: South Pacific, Cinderella, Fiddler on the Roof, Grease; studio vocalist various recording artists. Recipient Emmy for PSA comml., Am. Fedn. TV Arts and Scis., Cleve., 1974. Home: 17113 Neff Rd Cleveland OH 44119 Office: Am Performing Arts Network 3130 Mayfield Rd Cleveland OH 44118

MATTHEWS, KATHLEEN SHIVE, biochemistry educator; b. Austin, Tex., Aug. 30, 1945; d. William and Gwyn Shive; m. Randall Matthews. BS in Chemistry, U. Tex., 1966; PhD in Biochemistry, U. Calif., Berkeley, 1970. Post doctoral fellow Stanford (Calif.) U., 1970-72; mem. faculty Rice U., Houston, 1972—, chair dept., 1987-95, Wiess prof., 1989—; mem. BBCB study sect. NIH, Bethesda, Md., 1980-84, 86-88, BRSG adv. com., 1992-94; mem. adv. com. on rsch. programs Tex. Higher Edn. Coord. Bd., Austin, 1987-92; mem. undergrad. edn. initiative rev. panel Howard Hughes Rsch. Inst., Bethesda, 1991, mem. rsch. resources rev. panel, 1995. Mem. edit. bd. Jour. Biol. Chemistry, 1988-93, assoc. editor, 1994—; contbr. 130 reviewed papers. Mem. Am. Soc. Biochemistry and Molecular Biology (nominating com. 1993-94, 96-97), Phi Beta Kappa. Office: Rice Univ Dept Biochemistry & Cell Biology PO Box 1892 Houston TX 77251

MATTHEWS, KEVIN MICHAEL, architecture educator, researcher; b. Eugene, Oreg., Jan. 5, 1959; s. Herbert Maurice and Jennifer (Saunders) M.; m. Donna Marie Meredith. BA, U.Calif., 1982; MArch, U. Calif., 1988. Intern Esherick, Homsey, Dodge, Davis, San Francisco, 1987; lectr. U. Calif., Berkeley, 1988-89; prin. Matthews Assoc., Berkeley, 1985-90; CAD coord. Superconducting Super Collider, Dallas, 1989; asst. prof. dept. arch. U. Oreg., Eugene, Oreg., 1990—; dir. Design Integration Lab., Eugene, Oreg., 1992—; pres. Artifice, Inc., Eugene, Oreg., 1993—; CAD cons. SSC Central Design Group, Berkeley, 1987-88. Author: The Great Buildings Collection, 1994, DesignWorkshop, 1993. Recipient Rsch. grant Apple Computer Inc., 1991, 92, Curriculum Devel. grant., 1992. Mem. Am. Inst. Arch. (assoc.), Assn. Computing Machinery, Soc. Arch. Historians, Assn.

Collegiate Schs. Arch. Avocations: sailing, backpacking, traditional blacksmithing. Office: Design Integration Lab 204 Pacific Hall Eugene OR 97403-1206

MATTHEWS, L. WHITE, III, railroad executive; b. Ashland, Ky., Oct. 5, 1945; s. L. White and Virginia Carolyn (Chandler) M.; m. Mary Jane Hanser, Dec. 30, 1972; children: Courtney Chandler, Brian Whittlesey. BS in Econs, Hampden-Sydney Coll., 1967; MBA in Fin. and Gen. Mgmt, U. Va., 1970. Cons. fin. Chem. Bank, N.Y.C., 1970-72, asst. sec., 1972-74, asst. v.p., 1974-75, v.p., 1976-77; treas. Mo. Pacific Corp., St. Louis, 1977-82; v.p. fin. Mo. Pacific R.R. Co. subs. Mo. Pacific Corp., St. Louis, 1979-82; v.p., treas. Union Pacific Corp. and Union Pacific R.R. Co., N.Y.C., 1982-87; sr. v.p. fin. Union Pacific corp., Bethlehem, Pa., 1987-92, exec. v.p. fin., 1992—; mem. coun. of fin. execs. The Conf. Bd.; mem. nat. adv. bd. Chem. Bank of N.Y.; bd. dirs. Union Pacific Corp., Bethlehem, Pa. Trustee Pilot Funds, St. Louis; bd. dirs. Moravian Coll., Bethlehem, Pa.

MATTHEWS, LARRYL KENT, mechanical engineering educator; b. Lubbock, Tex., Sept. 18, 1951; s. Morrison Arliss and Juanita Ruby (Parr) M.; m. Marie Elizabeth Twist, May 15, 1972. MS, N.Mex. State U., 1975; PhD, Purdue U., 1982. Test engr. Sandia Nat. Labs., Albuquerque, 1976-81; rsch. dir., educator N.Mex. State U., Las Cruces, 1982—, assoc. dean for rsch.; cons. Sandia Nat. Labs., 1985-89, ISOTEC, Santa Fe, N.Mex., 1986-88; bd. dirs. Waste-Mgmt. Edn. Rsch. Consortium, Las Cruces, 1990—; mem. mgmt. bd. Ctr. for Space Power. Author: (with Gabe Garcia) Laser and Eye Safety in the Laboratory, 1994; contbr. articles to Jour. Solar Energy, Internat. Jour. Exptl. Heat Transfer, ASME Jour. Solar Engring., Internat. Jour. Heat and Mass Transfer, Intech mag., Jour. Quantitative Specifications and Radiol. Transfer. Mem. AAAS, ASME, Am. Astron. Soc., Soc. de Ingenieros (founder), Pi Tau Sigma. Democrat. Methodist. Achievements include develoment of multiple-head radiometer for large pool-fire environments, of CSMP (Circum Solar Measurement Package) for contentrating solar applications, and the LODS (Laser Optical Displacements System) for measuring large and small 2-D structural displacements. Office: NMex State U Engring Rsch Ctr PO Box 30001 Las Cruces NM 88003-3449

MATTHEWS, LEONARD SARVER, advertising executive, consultant; b. Glendean, Ky., Jan. 6, 1922; s. Clell and Zetta Price (Sarver) M.; m. Dorothy Lucille Fessler; children: Nancy, James, Douglas. B.S. summa cum laude, Northwestern U., 1948. With Leo Burnett Co., Inc., Chgo., 1948-75; v.p., dir. Leo Burnett Co., Inc., 1958-59, v.p. charge mktg. services, 1959-61, exec. v.p., 1961-69, pres., 1970-75; asst. sec. commerce for domestic and internat. bus., 1976; pres., exec. com., dir. Young and Rubicam, 1977-78; pres. Am. Assn. Advt. Agys., 1979-89; co-founder Matthews & Johnston, Stamford, Conn., 1989-92; chmn. Next Century Media, 1992—; bd. dirs. Digital Gen. Systems, San Francisco; adv. bds. Adcom, Carlsbad, Calif., Ambient Capital, Beverly Hills, Calif. Served as ensign USCGR, 1942-46. Mem. Advt. Coun. (bd. dirs.), Sky Club (N.Y.C.), Pine Valley Golf Club (N.J.), Rancho Santa Fe Golf (Calif.), Georgetown Club (Washington), Delta Sigma Pi, Beta Gamma Sigma. Republican. Lutheran. Office: PO Box 2629 Rancho Santa Fe CA 92067-2036

MATTHEWS, MILDRED SHAPLEY, scientific editor, freelance writer; b. Pasadena, Calif., Feb. 15, 1915; d. Harlow and Martha (Betz) Shapley; m. Ralph Vernon Matthews, Sept. 25, 1937; children:: June Lorrain, Bruce Shapley, Melvin Lloyd, Martha Alys. AB, U. Mich., 1936. Rsch. asst. Calif. Inst. Tech., Pasadena, 1950-61; bilingual editor, rsch. asst. Astron. Obs. Merate-Milan and Trieste, Italy, 1960-70; rsch. asst. Lunar-Planetary Lab., editor space sci. series U. Ariz., Tucson, 1970—. Contbr. articles to Sky and Telescope, Astronomia. Recipient Masursky Meritorious Svc. award div. planetary sci. Am. Astron. Soc., 1993. Avocation: classical music concerts, especially opera. Home: 1600 Milvia St Berkeley CA 94709 Office: U Ariz Lunar & Planetary Lab Tucson AZ 85721

MATTHEWS, NORMAN STUART, department store executive; b. Boston, Jan. 13, 1933; s. Martin W. and Charlotte (Cohen) M.; m. Joanne Banks, June 11, 1956; children: Gary S., Jeffrey B., Patricia A. B.A., Princeton U.; M.B.A., Harvard U. Ptnr. Beacon Mktg. and Advt. Assocs., N.Y.C., 1956-71; sr. v.p. Broyhill Furniture Co., Lenoir, N.C., 1971-73, E.J. Korvettes, N.Y.C., 1973-78; chmn., chief exec. officer Gold Circle Stores, Columbus, Ohio, 1978-82; vice chmn. Federated Dept. Stores, Cin., from 1982, pres., chief oper. officer, 1987-88, retail cons., 1988—; dir. Progressive Corp., Cleve., Loehmann's, N.Y.C., Finlay Fine Jewelry, N.Y.C., Lechters Inc., N.J., Toys 'R' Us, Paramus, N.J. Office: 650 Madison Ave New York NY 10022-1029

MATTHEWS, PATRICK JOHN, consumer products company executive; b. Winnipeg, Manitoba, Can., Mar. 17, 1942; m. Clarice Marie Carstens; children: Brian, Richard. B of Commerce, U. Manitoba, 1968. Chartered acct., Manitoba. Various positions Peat, Marwick, Mitchell & Co., Winnipeg, Manitoba, 1968-75, ptnr., 1975-79; v.p. corp. planning Gendis Inc., Winnipeg, Manitoba, 1979-82, v.p. fin., 1982—; dir. Chauvco Resources Ltd. Mem. Inst. Chartered Accts. Manitoba, Fin. Exec. Inst. Office: Gendis Inc, 1370 Sony Pl PO Box 9400, Winnipeg, MB Canada R3C 3C3

MATTHEWS, ROGER HARDIN, lawyer; b. Greensboro, N.C., Sept. 16, 1948; s. Shuford Roger and Jacqueline (Hardin) M.; m. Jane Elizabeth Dougan, Aug. 7, 1982; children: Christopher Hardin, Marielle Aimée. AB, Harvard U., 1970, JD, 1974. Bar: Mass. 1974. Assoc. Ropes & Gray, Boston, 1974-84, ptnr., 1984—. Mem. ABA (employee benefits com., tax sect.), Boston Bar Assn. (co-chmn. Employee Retirement Income Security Act com. 1985-88). Avocation: piano. Office: Ropes & Gray One International Place Boston MA 02110-2624

MATTHEWS, ROSALIND M., systems manager; b. Reading, Pa., Mar. 6, 1943; d. William Wilson and Jessye Long; m. Jackie L. Matthews, Aug. 9, 1965 (div. 1977); children: Kym, Derek, Darryl. BS, Kutztown U., 1966; MS, Pratt Inst., 1970. Asst. v.p. ABN/AMRO Svcs. Corp., Uniondale, N.Y., 1974—; systems analyst Savs. Banks Trust, N.Y.C., 1970-74, Anchor Savs. Bank, Bay Ridge, N.Y., 1969-70; systems engr. IBM, N.Y.C., 1966-69; programmer Berks County Trust, Reading, Pa., 1963-66; adj. prof. LaGuardia C.C., L.I. City, N.Y., 1983—, Adelphie U., Garden City, N.Y., 1990—. Mentor N.Y. State Mentoring Program, Uniondale, N.Y., 1993. Named Balck Achiever in Industry, Harlem YMCA, N.Y.C., 1983. Mem. Delta Sigma Theta. Democrat. Methodist. Avocations: sewing, reading, computer hacking. Office: EAB Plaza Uniondale NY 11555

MATTHEWS, ROWENA GREEN, biological chemistry educator; b. Cambridge, Eng., Aug. 20, 1938 (father Am. citizen); d. David E. and Doris (Cribb) Green; m. Larry Stanford Matthews, June 18, 1960; children: Brian Stanford, Keith David. BA, Radcliffe Coll., 1960; PhD, U. Mich., 1969. Instr. U. S.C., Columbia, 1964-65; postdoctoral fellow U. Mich., Ann Arbor, 1970-75, asst. prof., 1975-81, assoc. prof. biol. chemistry, 1981-86, prof. 1986—, assoc. chmn., 1988-92, G. Robert Greenberg disting. prof., 1995—; mem. phys. biochemistry study sect. NIH, 1982-86; mem. adv. coun. Nat. Inst. Gen. Med. Scis., NIH, 1991-94; adv. bd. NATO, 1994—. mem. editorial adv. bd. Biochem. Jour., 1984-92, Arch. Biochemistry, Biophysics, 1992—, Biochemistry, 1993—, Jour. Bacteriology, 1995—. Contbr. articles to profl. jours. Recipient Faculty Recognition award U. Mich., 1984, Merit award Nat. Inst. Gen. Med. Scis., 1991; NIH grantee, 1978—; NSF grantee, 1992—. Mem. AAAS, Am. Soc. Biochemical & Molecular Biol. (program chair 1995), Am. Chem. Soc. (program chmn. biochemistry div. 1985, sec. biochemistry div. 1990-92, chair elect 1992-94, chair 1994—), Phi Beta Kappa, Sigma Xi. Avocations: bicycling, snorkeling, cross country skiing, cooking. Home: 1609 S University Ave Ann Arbor MI 48104-2620 Office: U Mich Biophysics Rsch Divsn 4024 Chemistry 930 N University Ave Ann Arbor MI 48109-1055

MATTHEWS, ROY S., management consultant; b. 1945. BS, Lewis U., 1967; MBA, No. Ill. U., 1971. With Regis Paper Co., Chgo., 1967-68, Continental Ill. Nat. Bank, Chgo., 1968-69; instr. acctg. Marquette U., Milw., 1971-72; asst. dean Lewis U. Coll. Bus., Romeoville, Ill., 1972-78; mgr. Peat, Marwick, Mitchell & Co., Chgo., 1978-84; with George S. May Internat. Co., Park Ridge, Ill., 1984—, now v.p. fin., sec.-treas. With USAR, 1968-74. Office: George S. May International Co 303 S Northwest Hwy Park Ridge IL 60068-4232

MATTHEWS, STEVE ALLEN, lawyer; b. Columbia, S.C., Oct. 11, 1955; s. Philip Garland and Vernecia Neely (Wilson) M.; m. Caroline Elizabeth FitzSimons, Sept. 26, 1987; children: Philip Garland II, Nathalie FitzSimons. BA in History, U. S.C., 1977; JD, Yale U., 1980. Bar: S.C. 1980, D.C. 1982. Assoc. Boyd, Knowlton, Tate & Finlay, Columbia, 1980-81, Dewey, Ballantine, Bushby, Palmer & Wood, Washington, 1981-85; spl. counsel to asst. atty. gen. Civil Rights Div. U.S. Dept. Justice, Washington, 1985-86, dep. asst. atty. gen. for jud. selection, Office of Legal Policy, 1986-88; exec. asst. to U.S. Atty. Gen., 1988; mem. Sinkler & Boyd P.A., Columbia, 1988—. Mem. Federalist Soc., Party of the Right, Euphradian Soc., Nat. Assn. Bond Lawyers (bd. dirs.), Am. Coll. Bond Counsel (bd. dirs.), Collegiate Network, Inc. (chmn. bd. dirs.). Office: Sinkler & Boyd PA 1426 Main St Columbia SC 29201-2834

MATTHEWS, SIR STUART, aviation industry executive; b. London, May 5, 1936; came to U.S., 1974; s. Bernard De Lides and Daisy Vera (Woodcock) M.; student, Hatfield Coll. Advanced Tech., 1958; m. Kathleen Hilary Adams, Jan. 12, 1974; children: Anthony, Caroline, Joanna. Apprentice, de Havilland Aircraft Ltd., Hatfield, 1952-53; aircraft project design engr. Hawker Siddeley Aviation Ltd., Hatfield, 1953-64; with mktg. dept. Brit. Aircraft Co., Bristol, 1964-67; gen. mgr. planning Brit. Caledonian Airways, London, 1967-74; v.p. N.Am. div. Fokker-VFW Internat., Washington, 1974-80; pres., chief exec. officer Fokker Aircraft USA, Alexandria, Va., 1980-93, chmn. 1993-94, Aircraft Fin. and Trade, Alexandria, 1984-94; pres., CEO Flight Safety Found., Arlington, Va., 1994—; chmn. asso. mem. group Commuter Airlines Assn. Am., 1979-80. Chmn. Flight Safety Found.; mem. adv. bd. Am. Security Bank. Fellow Royal Aero. Soc. (chartered engr.), Inst. Transp. (charter); mem. AIAA, Royal Order of Orange Nassau (The Netherlands) (knight), Netherlands/Am. C. of C. (bd. dirs.), Alexandria C. of C. (bd. dirs.). Clubs: Aero, Nat. Aviation (Washington); Wings (N.Y.C., mem. bd. govs.); Lions (pres. Engleside, Va. 1977-78); Rotary Internat. Home: 9439 Mt Vernon Cir Alexandria VA 22309-3221 Office: Flight Safety Found 601 Madison St Alexandria VA 22314

MATTHEWS, THOMAS MICHAEL, energy company executive; b. Luling, Tex., May 20, 1943; s. Chester Raymond and Mary Lucille (Stutts) M.; m. Sherry Dianne Klein, May 25, 1968; children: Stephanie Dianne, Leslie Michelle. BSCE, Tex. A & M U., 1965; postgrad., U. Okla., 1967, UCLA, 1975, Stanford U., 1988, Columbia U., 1993. Staff engr. Exxon Co. USA, Houston, New Orleans, 1965-69; project engr. Exxon Co. USA, L.A., 1974-76; div. engr. Exxon Co. USA, Houston, 1969-74; engring. mgr. Exxon Co. USA, Anchorage, 1976-78; v.p. Exxon Gas, Houston, 1978-81, Tenn. Gas/Tenneco, Houston, 1981-86; pres. Tenn. Gas/Tenneco, 1986-89; v.p., gen. mgr. Texaco USA, Houston, 1989—; pres. Texaco Gas, 1990-93; pres., CEO Texaco Refining & Mktg., Inc.; v.p. Texaco, Inc.; dir. Offshore Tech. Ctr., Tex. A & M U., 1987-89, adv. coun.; bd. dirs. Inroads, Inc. Contbr. articles to profl. jours.; inventor in field. Pres., chmn. Ponderosa Forest Community Council, Houston, 1980-85; mem. PTO, Scenic Pk. Sch., Anchorage, 1976-78. Mem. NSPE (bd. dirs.), Soc. Petroleum Engrs., Soc. Ga. Assn., Am. Petroleum Inst., Natural Gas Supply Assn., Gas Rsch. Inst., Petroleum Club, Northgate Forest Country Club. Republican. Lutheran. Avocations: snow skiing, golf, reading, running, singing. Home: 17402 Ridge Top Dr Houston TX 77090-2021 Office: Texaco USA 1111 Bagby St Houston TX 77002-2551

MATTHEWS, VINCENT, III, oil company executive; b. Knoxville, Tenn., July 23, 1942; s. Vincent Jr. and Margaret Virginia (Kent) M.; m. Cissy Cullen, Aug. 16, 1965 (div. Nov. 1984); children: Vincent IV, Thompson; m. Susan Dawn Burdick, Jan. 26, 1985. BS in Geology, U. Ga., 1965, MS in Geology, 1967; PhD in Geology, U. Calif., Santa Cruz, 1973. Geologist Pan Am. Petroleum Corp., New Orleans, 1967-69; lectr. U. Calif., Santa Cruz, 1969-71; assoc. prof. U. No. Colo., Greeley, 1971-76; exploration mgr. Amoco Prodn. Co., Denver, 1977-81; divsn. mgr. Lear Exploration, Denver, 1981-85; v.p., regional mgr. Union Pacific Resources, Houston, 1985-89; pres. Penn Virginia Resources Corp., Duffield, Va., 1989—. Author: Wrench Fault Tectonics, 1989; editor: Laramide Folding in the Western U.S., 1978. Dir. found. S.W. Va. Pub. Edn. Consortium, Wise, 1993—; mem. adv. bd. Clinch Valley Coll. U. Va., Wise, 1993—; dir. at large Wise County C. of C., Norton, Va., 1994; vice chmn. of bd. Powell River Project Va. Tech., Blacksburg, 1993—. Danforth teaching fellow, 1970-71; recipient Outstanding Alumnus award Bd. Earth Sci. U. Calif.-Santa Cruz, 1987. Fellow Geol. Soc. Am.; mem. Am. Assn. Petroleum Geologists (trustee assoc., del.), Rocky Mountain Assn. Geologists (councillor), Soc. Petroleum Engrs., Assn. Women Geologists (found. dir. 1989-92). Avocations: reading, family newsletter, backpacking. Office: 999 Executive Park Blvd # 300 Kingsport TN 37660-4649

MATTHEWS, WANDA MILLER, artist; b. Barry, Ill., Sept. 15, 1930; d. Harry Leonard and Gladys (Smith) Miller; m. Eugene Edward Matthews, Sept. 14, 1952; children: Anthony Lee, Daniel Nicholas. BFA, Bradley U., Peoria, Ill., 1952; MFA, U. Iowa, 1957. Spl. services artist U.S. Army, Ft. Riley, Kans., 1954-55; research asst. printmaking U. Iowa, 1956-57; travel Italy and Europe, 1957-60. Producing, and exhibiting printmaker, Boulder, Colo., 1961—; one-woman exhbns. include, Lehigh U., Bethlehem, Pa., 1973, Gettysburg (Pa.) Coll., 1973, U. Colo., 1976, U. N.D., 1976, Jane Haslem Gallery, Washington, 1982, Am. Ctr. Gallery, Belgrade, Yugoslavia, 1982, Oxford Gallery (Eng.), 1982, U. Colo., Boulder, 1985, U. Northern Colo., Greeley, 1985, The Printerly Image: Wanda Miller Matthews 1951-1991, Arvada (Colo.) Ctr. for the Arts and Humanities, 1991, Jane Haslem Gallery, Washington, 1990, Barry (Ill.) Pub. Libr., 1995; group exhbns. include USIS Gallery, Naples, Italy, 1960; Nat. Invitational Print Exhbn., Otis Art Inst., L.A., 1962, 63, Brit. Internat. Print Biennale, Bradford, Eng., 1970, 79, Invitational Graphics, Minot (N.D.) State Coll., 1972, Printmaking Now, W. Tex. Mus., Lubbock, 1973, ColorPrint U.S.A., Tex. Tech U., Lubbock, 1974, 78, Nat. Invitational Print Show, Central Wash. State Coll., Ellensburg, 1975, 11th Internat. Exhbn. Graphic Art, Ljubljana, Yugoslavia, 1975, 6th, 7th, 8th, 10th Internat. Print Biennales, Cracow, Poland, 1976, 78, 80, 84, Internat. Book Fair, Leipzig, E.Ger., 1977, New Talent in Printmaking, 1980, Associated Am. Artists, N.Y.C. and Phila., 1980, Rockford Internat. Biennale, Ill., 1985, Western States Invitational, Portland Art Mus., Oreg., 1985, 40th Am. Colorprint Soc. Exhbn., Jenkintown, Pa., 1985, Premio Internzionale Biella per l'incisione, Italy, 1976, 80, 87, Small Graphic Forms, Poland, 1987, 4X4X4: Sixteen Contemporary Printmakers from the Four Corner States, Utah State U., 1987, 3d Internat. Biennial Print Exhbt.: 1987, Taipei, Taiwan, 1987-88, CSP Exch. Show, Brandts Klaedefabrik, Odense, Denmark, 1989, Am. Self Portraits in Prints (traveling exhbn.) Ind. U., Bloomington, 1990, Am. Prints: Last Half of 20th Century Jane Haslem Gallery, Washington, 1993, Juniper Gallery, Napa, Calif., 1993, Boston Archtl. Ctr., 1994, Am. Inst. Architecture, Washington, 1994, U. N.H., 1994, others; represented in permanent collections, Portland Art Mus. (Oreg.); Boston Pub. Library, Bytow Nat. Museum (Poland), L.A. County Mus., Nat. Collection Fine Arts, Washington, Phila. Mus. Art, Library of Congress, Coll. Bd. Collection of Prints by Am. Artists, N.Y.C., Honolulu Acad. Art, others. Recipient numerous awards including: Purchase prize Prints 1962 Nat. Exhbn., State U. Coll., Potsdam, N.Y., 1962, Prints 10th ann. print exhbn., 1970; purchase prize Dublin Nat. Print and Drawing competition Dulin Gallery Art, Knoxville, Tenn., 1968, 81, 22d ann. nat. exhbn. Boston Printmakers, 1970; recipient purchase award Graphics '71, Nat. Print and Drawing Exhbn., Western N.Mex. U., Silver City, 1971, Soc. Am. Graphic Artists, Nat. Exhbn., N.Y.C., 1979, Benton Spruance prize Print Club Phila., 1971, Am. Colorprint Soc. Drabkin Meml. award medallion, 1981, 1st Pl. in Color Prints Ybor Nat. Print Competition, 1985, Leila Sawyer Meml. award 97th ann. exhbn. Nat. Assn. Women Artists, 1986, Cash award Nat. Print Biennial, Silvermine Guild Arts Ctr., 1996; Tiffany grantee, 1957-58, 58-59. Mem. Calif. Soc. Printmakers, Print Club Phila., Soc. Am. Graphic Artists, The Boston Printmakers. Home: 720 Hawthorn Ave Boulder CO 80304-2140

MATTHEWS, WESTINA L., finance and banking executive; b. Chillicothe, Ohio, Nov. 8, 1948; d. Wesley Smith and Ruth (Fields) M. BS, U. Dayton, 1970, MS, 1974; PhD, U. Chgo., 1980. Tchr. Mills Lawn Elem. Sch., Yellow Springs, Ohio, 1970-75; program officer The Chgo. Community Trust, sr. program officer, 1983-85; v.p. philanthropic programs, sec. Merrill Lynch Found., N.Y.C., 1985—, trustee, 1993—. Bd. dirs. Arthur Ashe Inst.; trustee N.Y. Theol. Sem., Wilberforce U. Postdoctoral fellow Northwestern U., 1980-81, U. Wis., 1981-82. Office: Merrill Lynch & Co 225 Liberty St New York NY 10281-1008

MATTHEWS, WILLIAM D(OTY), lawyer, consumer products manufacturing company executive; b. Oneida, N.Y., Aug. 25, 1934; s. William L. and Marjorie L. (Doty) M.; m. Ann M. Morse, Aug. 4, 1956; children: Judith Anne, Thomas John. A.B., Union Coll., 1956; LL.B., Cornell U., 1960. Bar: N.Y. 1960, D.C. 1962. Atty. div. corp. fin. SEC, Washington, 1960-62; assoc. Whitlock, Markey & Tait, Washington, 1962-69; gen. counsel Oneida (N.Y.) Ltd., 1973-86, v.p., 1977-78, sr. v.p., 1978-86, exec. v.p., 1986, also dir., chmn., chief exec. officer, 1986—; bd. dirs. N.Y. State Bus. Coun. Alderman City of Oneida, 1972-79; mem. Madison County Bd. Suprs., 1984-86. Presbyterian. Home: 621 Patio Circle Dr Oneida NY 13421-1820 Office: Oneida Ltd Adminstrn Bldg Kenwood Station Oneida NY 13421-2808

MATTHEWS, WILLIAM EDMUND, newspaper and travel magazine publisher; b. Shelbyville, Ky., Apr. 30, 1930; s. Robert Foster and Zerelda Tribble (Baxter) M.; m. Else Vivien Bender Jorgensen, June 13, 1952; children: Lisa Gaines, William E. II, Ellen Matthews Oetinger, Bland Ballard. BA, U. Mich., 1952. Info. specialist C.I.A., Washington, 1953-61; owner, pubr. The Shelby Sentinel, Shelbyville, Ky., 1961-68; pres., gen. mgr. Newspapers Inc., Shelbyville, Ky., 1968-73; pres. Landmark Community Newspapers, Shelbyville, Ky., 1973-76; pubr./gen. mgr. Scripps Howard Community News, Cin., 1976-82; v.p., editor Mid-Continent Devel. & Tourism, Huntingburg, Ind., 1982-93, pres., editor, 1993—; editor The Huntingburg Press, 1987—, pub., 1993—. Editor/pubr.: The Relentless Reds, 1976, The Royal Reds, 1977. 2d lt. U.S. Army, 1952. Mem. Ky. Press Assn. (pres. 1977), Ky. Weekly Newspaper Assn. (pres. 1975), Rotary. Christian Ch. (Disciples of Christ). Avocation: gardening. Home: 467 Cove Rd Shelbyville KY 40065-8924 Office: The Huntingburg Press 423 E 4th St Huntingburg IN 47542-1339

MATTHEWS, WILLIAM L., diversified financial service company executive; b. 1939. Mng. ptnr. Plante and Moran, Southfield, Mich., 1961—. Office: Plante and Moran Inc PO Box 307 Southfield MI 48037*

MATTHEWS, WILLIAM PROCTER, English educator; b. Cin., Nov. 11, 1942; s. William P. and Mary Elizabeth (Sather) M.; m. Marie Murray Harris, May 4, 1963 (div. 1973); children: William, Sebastian. B.A., Yale U., 1965; M.A., U. N.C., Chapel Hill, 1966. Instr. English Wells Colls., Aurora, N.Y., 1968-69; asst. prof. Cornell U., 1969-74; asso. prof. U. Colo., 1974-78; prof. English U. Wash., Seattle, 1978-83, CCNY, 1983—; bd. dirs. Asso. Writing Programs, 1977-80, pres., 1979-80; mem. lit. panel Nat. Endowment Arts, 1976-79, chmn., 1978-79. Author: Ruining the New Road, 1970, Sleek For the Long Flight, 1972, Sticks and Stones, 1975, Rising and Falling, 1979, Flood, 1982, A Happy Childhood, 1984, Foreseeable Futures, 1987, Blues If You Want, 1989, Curosities, 1989, Selected Poems and Translations, 1992, Time and Money, 1995 (Nat. Book Critics' Cir. award 1995), The Mortal City: 100 Epigrams of Martial, 1995. Fellow Nat. Endowment Arts, 1974, 83, Guggenheim Found., 1980-81. Mem. Poetry Soc. Am. Office: CCNY Dept English New York NY 10038

MATTHEWS, WYHOMME S., music educator, college administrator; b. Battle Creek, Mich., July 22, 1948; d. Woodrow R. and LouLease (Graham) Sellers; m. Edward L. Matthews, Apr. 29, 1972; children: Channing DuVall, Triston Curran, Landon Edward, Brandon Graham. AA, Kellogg C.C., 1968; MusB, Mich. State U., 1970, MA, 1972, MusM, 1972. Cert. elem. and secondary tchr., Mich. Tchr., vocal music dir. Benton Harbor (Mich.) Pub. Schs., 1971-72, dir. vocal music, 1972; dir. edn. head start program Burlington (N.J.) County, 1972-73; pvt. music tchr., 1973-89; tchr. Southeastern Jr. H.S., 1986-87, W.K. Kellogg Jr. H.S., 1987-89; chair visual and performing arts dept. Kellogg C.C., Battle Creek, Mich., 1989—; 1972; part-time instr. Kellogg C.C., 1973-89, dir. Eclectic Chorale, 1994—, dir., organizer Kellogg C.C. Eclectic Chorale Sacred Cultural Festival, 1979—, judge various contests; presenter in field. Pres. Dudley Elem. Sch., 1981-85; active Battle Creek Pub. Schs. PTA, Pennfield Pub. Schs. PTA, Mt. Zion African Meth. Episc. Ch. Mich. State U. fellow, 1971; recipient Outstanding Cmty. Svc. award, 1975. Mem. Mich. Music Tchr. Assn., Nat. Music Tchrs. Assn., Battle Creek Music Tchrs. Assn., Battle Creek Morning Music Club (bd. dirs.), Nat. Leadership Acad., Battle Creek Cmty. Concert Assn. Home: 466 Alton Ave Battle Creek MI 49017-3212 Office: Kellogg CC 450 North Ave Battle Creek MI 49017-3397

MATTHIAS, JOHN EDWARD, English literature educator; b. Columbus, Ohio, Sept. 5, 1941; s. John Marshall and Lois (Kirkpatrick) M.; m. Diana Clare Jocelyn, Dec. 27, 1967; children—Cynouai, Laura. BA, Ohio State U., 1963; MA, Stanford U., 1966; postgrad., U. London, 1967. Asst. prof. dept. English U. Notre Dame, Ind., 1966-73, assoc. prof., 1973-80, prof., 1980—; vis. fellow Clare Hall, Cambridge U., 1966-77, assoc., 1977—; vis. prof. dept. English, Skidmore Coll., Saratoga Springs, N.Y., 1975, U. Chgo., 1980. Author: Bucyrus, 1971, Turns, 1975, Crossing, 1979, Five American Poets, 1980, Introducing David Jones, 1980, Contemporary Swedish Poetry, 1980, Bathory and Lermontov, 1980, Northern Summer, New and Selected Poems, 1984, The Battle of Kosovo, 1987, David Jones: Man and Poet: A Gathering of Ways, 1991, Reading Old Friends, 1991, Swimming at Midnight, 1995, Beltane at Aphelion, 1995. Recipient Columbia U. Transl. award, 1978, Swedish Inst. award, 1981, Poetry award Soc. Midland Authors, 1984, Ingram Merrill Found. award, 1984, 90; Woodrow Wilson fellow, 1963, Lily Endowment fellow, 1993; Fulbright grantee, 1966. Mem. AAUP, PEN, Poets and Writers, Poetry Soc. Am. (George Bogin Meml. award 1990), London Poetry Secretariat. Office: U Notre Dame Dept English Notre Dame IN 46556

MATTHIES, FREDERICK JOHN, architectural engineer; b. Omaha, Oct. 4, 1925; s. Fred. J. and Charlotte Leota (Metz) M.; m. Carol Mae Dean, Sept. 14, 1947; children—John Frederick, Jane Carolyn Matthies Godding. BSCE, Cornell U., 1947; postgrad., U. Nebr., 1952-53. Diplomate Am. Acad. Environ. Engrs.; registered profl. engr., Iowa, Nebr. Civil engr. Henningson, Durham & Richardson, Omaha, 1947-50, 52-54; sr. v.p. devel. Leo A. Daly Co., Omaha, 1954-90; cons. engr., 1990—; lectr. in field; mem. dist. export coun. U.S. Dept. Commerce, 1981-83. Contbr. articles to profl. publs. Mem. Douglas County Rep. Cen. Com., Nebr., 1968-72; bd. regents Augustana Coll., Sioux Falls., S.D., 1976-89; bd. dirs. Orange County Luth. Hosp. Assn., Anaheim, Calif., 1961-62, Nebr. Humanities Coun., 1988—, Omaha-Shizuoka City (Japan) Sister City Orgn.; trustee Luth. Med. Ctr., Omaha, 1978-82; mem. adv. bd. Marine Mil. Acad., Harlingen, Tex. 1st lt. USMCR, 1943-46, 50-52, Korea. Fellow ASCE, Instn. Civil Engrs. (London, Euro Engr. European Econ. Commn.); mem. NSPE, Am. Water Works Assn. (life), Air Force Assn., Am. Legion, VFW, The Omaha Club. Lutheran. Home: 337 S 127th St Omaha NE 68154-2309

MATTHIESEN, LEROY THEODORE, bishop; b. Olfen, Tex., June 11, 1921; s. Joseph A. and Rosa (Englert) M. BA, Josephinum Coll., Columbus, Ohio, 1942; MA, Cath. U., Washington, 1961; LittD, Register Sch. Journalism., Denver, 1962. Ordained priest Roman Cath. Ch., 1946. Editor West Tex. Cath., Amarillo diocese, from 1948; prin. Alamo Cath. High Sch, from 1969; pastor St. Francis parish, from 1972; ordained bishop of Amarillo, Tex., 1980—. Office: 1800 N Spring St PO Box 5644 Amarillo TX 79117-5644*

MATTHIESSEN, PETER, author; b. N.Y.C., May 22, 1927; s. Erard A. and Elizabeth (Carey) M.; m. Patricia Southgate, Feb. 8, 1951 (div.); m. Deborah Love, May 8, 1963 (dec. Jan. 1972); children: Lucas C., Sara C., Rue, Alexander F.L.; m. Maria Eckhart, Nov. 28, 1980. Student, The Sorbonne, Paris, 1948-49; B.A., Yale U., 1950. Author: Race Rock, 1954, Partisans, 1955, Wildlife in America, 1959, Raditzer, 1960, The Cloud Forest, 1961, Under the Mountain Wall, 1963, At Play in the Fields of the Lord, 1965, The Shorebirds of North America, 1967, Oomingmak: The Expedition to the Musk Ox Island in the Bering Sea, 1967, Sal Si Puedes, 1969, Blue Meridian, 1971, The Tree Where Man Was Born, 1972, Far Tortuga, 1975, The Snow Leopard, 1978 (nat. book award), Sand Rivers, 1981 (John Burroughs medal), In the Spirit of Crazy Horse, 1983, Indian Country, 1984, Nine-Headed Dragon River, 1986, Men's Lives, 1986, On the River Styx and Other Stories, 1989, Killing Mister Watson, 1990, African Silences, 1992,

Baikal: Sacred Sea of Siberia, 1992, Shadows of Africa, 1992. Trustee N.Y. Zool. Soc., 1965-78. AAAL grantee, 1963. Mem. AAAS, Am. Acad. Arts and Letters.

MATTIA, FRANK J., secondary school principal. Prin. Incarnation Cath. Sch., Centerville, Ohio. Recipient Elem. Sch. Recognition award U.S. Dept. Edn., 1989-90. Office: Incarnation Cath Sch 45 Williamsburg Ln Centerville OH 45459-4218

MATTICE, HOWARD LEROY, education educator; b. Roxbury, N.Y., Sept. 23, 1935; s. Charles Pierce and Loretta Jane (Ellis) M.; m. Elaine Grace Potts, Feb. 4, 1956; children: Kevin, Stephen. BA, King's Coll., 1960; MA, L.I. U., 1965, NYU, 1969; cert., CUNY, 1972; EdD, NYU, 1978. Cert. tchr. N.Y., clin. educators trainer, Fla. Dept. Edn. Social studies tchr. N.Y.C. Bd. Edn., 1961-90, mid. and jr. H.S. asst. prin., 1970-72, 73-75; assoc. prof. edn. and history Clearwater (Fla.) Christian Coll., 1990-92, chmn. divsn. of edn., prof. edn. and history, 1992—; adj. lectr. history S.I. C.C., CUNY, 1969-75; curriculum writer N.Y.C. Bd. Edn., 1985; program reviewer Fla. Dept. Edn., Tallahassee, 1994—; item writer GED Testing Svc., Washington, 1988-92; mem. So. Assn. Colls. and Schs. Accreditation Team H.S., 1995—. Chmn. bd. New Dorp Christian Acad., S.I., 1973-90; chmn. bd. deacons New Dorp. Bapt. Ch., S.I., 1981-90. Mem. ASCD, Assn. Tchr. Educators, Nat. Coun. Social Studies, So. Assn. Colls. and Schs. (h.s. accreditation review team 1995—). Avocations: reading, traveling, gardening. Office: Clearwater Christian Coll 3400 Gulf To Bay Blvd Clearwater FL 34619-4514

MATTILA, MARY JO KALSEM, elementary and art educator; b. Canton, Ill., Oct. 26, 1944; d. Joseph Nelson and Bernice Nora (Milbauer) Kalsem; m. John Peter Mattila, Jan. 27, 1968. BS in Art, U. Wis., 1966; student, Ohio State U., 1972, Drake U., 1981; MS in Ednl. Adminstrn., Iowa State U., 1988. Cert. tchr., prin., supr., adminstr., art tchr., secondary tchr., Iowa. Tchr. 2d grade McHenry (Ill.) Pub. Schs., 1966-67, Wisconsin Hts. Schs., Black Earth, Wis., 1967-69; substitute tchr. Columbus (Ohio) City Schs., 1969-70; elem. art tchr. Southwestern City Schs., Columbus, 1972-73; adminstrv. intern Ames, Iowa, 1984-86; lead tchr. at Roosevelt Sch. Ames Cmty. Schs., 1986-87, art vertical curriculum chair, 1983-89, art educator, elem. and spl. edn., 1973—. Author articles. Active LWV, Ames, 1982—; fundraiser Altrusa, Ames, 1992—. Recipient Very Spl. Svc. award for Disting. Svc. in Very Spl. Arts, Gov. of Iowa, 1984. Mem. ASCD, NEA, Nat. Assn. Elem. Sch. Prins., Nat. Art Edn. Assn. Avocations: collecting old stoneware jugs, growing orchids, reading. Home: 2822 Duff Ave Ames IA 50010-4710 Office: Ames Cmty Schs 120 S Kellogg Ave Ames IA 50010-6719

MATTINGLY, DONALD ARTHUR, professional baseball player; b. Evansville, Ind., Apr. 20, 1961; m. Kim Sexton; children: Taylor Patrick, Preston Michael. Baseball player N.Y. Yankees, 1979—. Named Most Valuable Player South Atlantic League, 1980, Am. League Most Valuable Player, Baseball Writer's Assn., 1985, Am. League Player of Yr., Sporting News, 1984-86, All-Star Team, 1984-89, Major League Player of the Yr. Sporting News, 1985; recipient Gold Glove award, 1985-89, 91-94, Silver Slugger award, 1985-87, Am. League batting champion, 1984. Office: NY Yankees Yankee Stadium Bronx NY 10451

MATTINGLY, J. VIRGIL, JR., federal lawyer; b. Leonardtown, Md., Oct. 18, 1944. BBA in Acctg., George Washington U., JD. Sr. atty. Fed. Res. Bd., Washington, 1974-79, asst. gen. counsel, 1979-81, assoc. gen. counsel, 1981-85, dep. gen. counsel, 1985-89, gen. counsel, 1989—. With JAGC, U.S. Army, 1970-74. Office: Fed Res Bd Bd Govs 20th & C Sts NW Washington DC 20551*

MATTINGLY, MACK F., former ambassador, former senator, entrepreneur; b. Anderson, Ind., Jan. 7, 1931; m. Carolyn Longcamp, 1957; children: Jane, Anne. BS, Ind. U., 1957. Acct. supr. IND, Arvin, Ind., 1957-59; mktg. mgr. IBM Corp., Ga., 1959-79; owner, pres. M's Inc., Ga., 1975-80; U.S. senator from Ga., 1981-87; asst. sec. gen. def. support NATO, Brussels, 1987-90; amb. to Seychelles Dept. State, 1992-93; spkr./author econ., def., fgn. policy, entrepreneur, 1990-92; mem. U.S. Senate Com. Appropriations, chmn. legis and mil. constrn. subcoms.; mem. energy and water devel., agt. rural devel., treasury, postal svc. and gen. govt., mil. constrn. legis. subcoms., U.S. Senate com. Banking, Housing and Urban Affairs, chmn. rural housing, econ. policy subcoms.; mem. select com. ethics, 1981-83, joint econ. com., 1983-87; chmn. Rep. Com. on Coms., mem. Rep. Senate Leadership, 1985-87,, Holocaust Commn.; U.S. del. GATT, Geneva, 1982. Author 40 U.S. Sen. Bills, Amendments and Resolutions. Del. Atl. Sgt.-at-Arms, Rep. Nat. Convs., Del. Georgian Rep. Party Convs., 1964-90; chmn. 8th Dist. Goldwater for Pres., 1964, Ga. 8th Congl. Dist., Cand. U.S. Congress, 8th Dist., 1966; mem. Ga. Rep. Party State Ctrl. Com., State Exec. Com., vice chmn. state party, 1968-75, chmn. Ga. Rep. Party, 1975-77; elected 1st Rep. U.S. Senator from Ga. since 1871, 1980; bd. dirs. U.S. Nat. Chamber Found., 1990, Bus. Leadership Coun., Color Graphics, Inc., First Fed. Savs. Bank; hon. mem. bd. dirs. M.L. King Jr. Fed. Holiday Commn. With USAF, 1951-55. Recipient Southeast Father of Yr. award 1984, Ga. Wildlife Fed. Conservationist of Yr. award 1985, Selective Svc. System Dist. Svc. Gold medal 1985, Watchdog of Treasury award 1981-86, Nat. Taxpayers Union Taxpayers Best Friend award 1981-86, NFIB's Guardian of Small Bus. award 1981-86, Am. Security Coun. award 1981-86, Sec. Def. medal for Outstanding Pub. Svc. 1988. Mem. Brunswick Golden Isle C. of C., Am. Legion. Episcopalian.

MATTINGLY, WILLIAM EARL, lawyer; b. Decatur, Ill., Mar. 6, 1948; s. Woodrow W. and Lena (Dayhuff) M.; children: Claire, Henry, Grace. BS in Indsl. Engring., Purdue U., 1971, MSE, 1972; JD cum laude, Ind. U., Indpls., 1975. Bar: Ind. 1975, Ill. 1978, Okla. 1980. Assoc. Sonnenschein, Carlin, Nath & Rosenthal, Chgo., 1978-80, Hall, Estill, et al, Tulsa, 1980-83; sr. ptnr. employee benefits dept. Katten, Muchin & Zavis, Chgo., 1984—; lectr. tax inst. conf. U. So. Calif., 1985, U. Ill. Conf. on Employee Stock Ownership Plans, 1987, Inst. for Health Law Loyola U., Chgo., 1987. Contbr. articles to profl. jours. Mem. ABA (chmn. 2 subcoms. banking and bus. law sects.), Chgo. Bar Assn., Ill. State Bar Assn. *

MATTIS, LOUIS PRICE, pharmaceutical and consumer products company executive; b. Balt., Dec. 12, 1941; s. Louis Wadsworth and Sara Helene (Myers) M.; m. Patricia Diane Brown, Nov. 29, 1963; children—Louis Wadsworth, Deborah Cook. A.B. in Internat. Affairs, Lafayette Coll., Easton, Pa., 1962; M.B.A., Tulane U., 1964. V.p., gen. mgr. Warner Lambert Co., Manila, 1971-74; regional dir. Warner Lambert Co., Hong Kong, 1974-76; region pres. Warner Lambert Co., Sydney, Australia, 1976-79; exec. v.p. Americas-Far East Richardson-Vicks, Inc., 1979-81, pres. Americas-Far East, 1981-84, exec. v.p., 1985-87; group v.p. Sterling Winthrop Inc., N.Y.C., 1987-88, chmn., pres., CEO, 1988-94; dir. Solomon Bros. Fund, 1992—. Mem. Gov. Ctr. for Creative Leadership, 1989—. Mem. New Canaan Country Club (Conn.), Sea Island Golf Club (Ga.), Shek-o Golf Club, Turnberry Golf Club, Ocean Forest Golf Club, Snowmass Club. Avocations: skiing, golf, woodworking. Home: Cottage 221 Sea Island GA 31561 Office: Sterling Winthrop Inc PO Box 31073 Sea Island GA 31561-1073

MATTISON, DONALD ROGER, dean, physician, military officer; b. Mpls., Apr. 28, 1944; s. Milford Zachary and Elizabeth Ruth (Davey) M.; m. Margaret Rose Libby, Jan. 28, 1967; children: Jon, Amy. BA cum laude in Chemistry and Math., Augsburg Coll., Mpls., 1966; MS in Chemistry, MIT, 1968; MD, Columbia U., 1973. Resident in ob-gyn Presbyn. Hosp., N.Y.C., 1973-75, 77-78; commd. rsch. assoc. USPHS, 1975, advanced through grades to comdr., 1984; rsch. assoc. Nat. Inst. Child Health and Human Devel., NIH, Bethesda, Md., 1975-77, med. officer then chief pregnancy rsch. br., 1978-84; assoc. prof. ob-gyn. U. Ark., Little Rock, 1984-87; prof. U. Pitts., 1987-90, assoc. prof. toxicology, 1984-88, prof., 1988-90, dean Grad. Sch. Pub. Health, prof., 1990—; mem. Bd. Environ. Studies and Toxicology, NRC, NAS, 1988—; mem. sci. adv. bd. Hawaii Heptachlor Edn. and Rsch. Found., 1987—; mem. sci. adv. panel Semicondr. Industry Assn., 1987—; mem. portfolio team United Way Allegheny County and Western Pa., 1990—; mem. pre-screening com. Magee-Women's Hosp., Pitts., 1990—; mem. steering com. Pa. Dept. Health, Harrisburg, 1990—; mem. com. Inst. Medicine, NAS, 1989-91; cons. Women's Vietnam Health Study Protocol Devel., New England Rsch. Inst., 1986-90. Mem. editorial bd. Pediatric Pharmacology, 1980-87, Reproductive Toxicology, 1987—, Devel. Pharmacology and Therapeutics, Switzerland, 1987—, Reproductive Scis., The Info. Netork, 1989—, Methods in Toxicology, 1989—; guest editor Jour. Symposium on Reproductive Toxicology, Am. Jour. Indsl. Medicine, 1983; contbr. numerous articles, abstracts, letters and editorials to profl. publs. Recipient Am. Chem. Soc. medal Minn. sect. Am. Chem. Soc., 1966, Assn. Am. Publs. award, 1983. Mem. APHA, Soc. Risk Analysis (editorial bd. jour. 1988—), Pitts. chpt. Soc. Risk Analysis, Am. Assn. Cancer Rsch., N.Y. Acad. Sci., Am. Coll. Toxicology, Am. Fertility Soc., Soc. Gynecologic Investigation, Soc. Toxicology. Avocations: photography, computer sciences, house restoration, cross country skiing. Office: U Pitts Grad Sch Pub Health 130 Desoto St Pittsburgh PA 15213-2535

MATTOCH, IAN L., lawyer. BA, Occidental Coll., 1965; JD, Northwestern U., 1968. Prin. Law Offices Ian L. Mattoch, Honolulu; instr. law and soc. Punahou Sch., 1970-92; lectr. in field. Editor-in-chief Hawaii Bar Journal, 1970-72; contbr. articles to profl. jours. Bd. dirs. PREVENT Child Abuse Hawaii, Make-A-Wish Hawaii, past pres. Fellow Consumer Lawyers of Hawaii (founding mem., bd. govs.); mem. ABA, Assn. Trial Lawyers Am., Hawaii State Bar Assn., Nebr. Bar Assn. Office: 737 Bishop St Ste 1835 Honolulu HI 96813-3209 also: 586 Kanoelehua Ave Ste 200 Hilo HI 96720 also: 75-170 Hualalai Rd Ste D211 Kailua Kona HI 96740-1737 also: Spencer House Kamuela HI 96743 also: 45-781 Kamehameha Hwy Kaneohe HI 96744-2949

MATTOON, HENRY AMASA, JR., advertising and marketing consultant, writer; b. Waterbury, Conn., Jan. 14, 1914; s. Henry A. and Sarah Currie (Hallock) M.; m. Dorothy Ann Teeter, Sept. 13, 1934; children: Ann Brooks Wofford, David Scott, Sara Halsey, Judith Scott Conn. BS, Yale U., 1935. Mail boy, then copywriter, copy supr. Compton Advt. Inc., N.Y.C., 1935-44; v.p., creative dir. Compton Advt. Inc., 1944-50; v.p., chmn. plans bd. Ruthrauff & Ryan, Inc., 1950-52; v.p., creative dir. Dancer-Fitzgerald-Sample, Inc., 1952-54; pres., dir. Reach, Yates & Mattoon, Inc., 1954-56; chmn. mktg. plans bd. McCann-Erickson, Inc., 1956-57, v.p., assoc. creative dir., 1957-62; v.p., gen. mgr. McCann-Erickson, Inc., Los Angeles, 1962-65; sr. v.p. and mgr. McCann-Erickson, Inc., Houston, 1965-68; v.p., dir. advt., pub. relations and sales promotion Yardley of London, Inc., 1968-69; ptnr. Walter Weintz & Co., Inc., Stamford, Conn., 1969-70; prin. Otto Man Assocs., Inc., Weston, Conn., 1970-93; exec. v.p. Mktg. Lab, Inc., Danbury, Conn., 1985—, also bd. dirs. Contbr., columnist profl. jours. and mags. Mem. Yale Club of N.Y., Crow Canyon Country Club, Knights of Malta, Chi Phi. Republican. Episcopalian. Home: 675 Doral Dr Danville CA 94526-6206

MATTOON, PETER MILLS, lawyer; b. Bryn Mawr, Pa., Oct. 22, 1931; s. Harold Gleason and Marguerite Jeanette (Mills) M.; m. Mary Joan Henley, June 27, 1953; children: Pamela M. Zisselman, R. Stephen, Peter H., Philip P. AB, Dartmouth Coll., 1953; LLB, Harvard U., 1959. Bar: Pa. 1960. Assoc. Ballard Spahr Andrews & Ingersdoll, Phila., 1959-67, ptnr., 1967—; mem. adv. bd. PNC Bank, Phila. Emeritus trustee The Episcopal Acad., Merion, Pa., 1970—, former chmn.; trustee, v.p. Widener Meml. Found., Lafayette Hill, Pa., 1972—; trustee, vice chmn. Widener U., Chester, Pa., 1984—; trustee Thomas Jefferson U., Phila, 1989—; chmn., overseer Widener U. Law Sch., Wilmington, 1979—. Served to lt USN, 1953-56. Mem. Greater Phila. C. of C. (dir.). Office: Ballard Spahr Andrews & Ingersoll 1735 Market St Ste 51 Philadelphia PA 19103-7501

MATTOS NETO, SEBASTIAO DE SOUZA, lawyer; b. San Paulo, Brazil, Apr. 29, 1951. LLB, Facultad de Direito da Universidade, San Paulo, Brazil, 1974; MCL, U. Ill., 1976; JD, Chgo. Kent Coll. Law, 1980. Bar: Brazil 1974, Ill. 1980, Portugal 1989. Ptnr. Baker & McKenzie, San Paulo, 1984-85, Chgo. Mem. adv. bd. Coun. Ams., N.Y.C. Office: Baker & McKenzie One Prudential Plz 130 E Randolph St Chicago IL 60601

MATTOX, KENNETH LEON, surgeon, educator, medical scientist; b. Ozark, Ark., Oct. 25, 1938. BS, Wayland Coll., 1960; MD, Baylor U., 1964. Diplomate Am. Bd. Surgery, Am. Bd. Thoracic Surgery. Intern surgery VA Hosp., Houston, 1964-65; resident in gen. surgery, asst. instr. Baylor U., Houston, 1967-71, resident in thoracic surgery, 1971-72, asst. instr. thoracic surgery, 1971-73, instr. surgery, 1973-74, asst. prof. surgery, 1974-78, assoc. prof. surgery, 1978-84, prof. surgery, 1984—; aeromed. cons. Dept. Army, Natick (Mass.) Labs., 1967-70; dep. surgeon in chief, dir. emergency surg. services, chief thoracic surgery service Ben Taub Gen. Hosp., Houston, 1973-90, chief surgery 1990—, surg. tech. adv. bd. 1982—, physician com. 1984—, chief of staff, 1990—; surg. cons. Tex. Inst. for Research and Rehab., Houston, 1973—; attending surgeon VA Hosp., Houston, 1973—, active staff Meth. Hosp., Houston, 1973—, Women's Hosp., Houston, 1973-82; courtesy staff St. Luke's Hosp., Houston, 1973—, Tex. Children's Hosp., Houston, 1973—; clin. prof. Uniformed Services U. for the Health Scis., Bethesda, Md., 1983—; sr. cardiac surgeon Baylor heart team King Faisal Specialist Hosp. and Research Ctr., Riyadh, Saudi Arabia, 1979, 80, 81, 83; active various coms. Baylor Coll. Medicine, Houston, vice chmn. dept. surgery; operating room com., profl. activities tng. fund com., critical care com., others Harris County Hosp. Dist., 1979—; adv. com. regional emergency med. services tng. program Health Sci. Ctr., U. Tex., 1978—; Curtis Artz Meml. lectr. Am. Coll. Surgeons, 1985; emergency med. services adv. council Tex. Dept. Health, 1983—; mem. task force for state health coordinating council for regionalization specialized health services State of Tex., 1985-86; chmn. categorization subcom. emergency med. services com. Houston-Galveston Area Council, 1978-82. Sr. editor Trauma, 1987; editor Complications in Trauma, 1993; edtl. cons. Chest, Med. Instrumentation, JAMA, Jour. Trauma; edtl. adv. bd. Emergency Medicine, 1975-92, Emergency Medicine Ann., Emergency Dept. News; assoc. editor thoracic trauma Current Concepts in Trauma Care, 1975-87; edtl. com. Tex. Medicine; reviewer Ann. Surgery, Ann. Thoracic Surgery, Am. Jour. Surgery; referee Med. Principles & Practice, contbr. over 400 sci. articles, chpts. and editorials to med. books and jours. Disaster physician Harris County Sheriff's Dept., 1973-82; pres. Emergency Medicine Found., 1982-83; mem. Houston area disaster and emergency med. system com. Greater Houston Hosp. Council, 1985—; trustee Wayland Bapt. U., 1984—; bd. dirs. Child Abuse Prevention Ctr., 1982-85. Served to capt. U.S. Army, 1965-67. Named one of Outstanding Young Men of Am., 1968; recipient Disting. Alumni award Wayland Bapt. U., 1986. Mem. Am. Assn. for the Surgery Trauma (bd. mgrs. 1985—, recorder, program chmn. 1990-93, pres.-elect 1995, pres. 1995-96), Am. Assn. Thoracic Surgery, Am. Coll. Cardiology (chmn. tech. exhibitor 1979-80), Am. Coll. Chest Physicians (bd. govs. 1986-90, gov. from Tex. 1986-91, Most Outstanding Motion Picture 1975, pulmonary surgery com. 1978, postgrad. med. edn. com. 1979—), Am. Coll. Emergency Physicians (bd. dirs. Tex. div. 1973-78, Cert. Appreciation 1975), Am. Coll. Surgeons (med. device com. 1980-85, chmn. 1983-85, com. on trauma 1983-89, bd. govs. 1985-91, others), AMA (Physician Recognition award 1972, 73), Am. Surg. Assn., Am. Trauma Soc. (founder, sec. 1974, v.p. 1975, Harris unit pres. Tex. div. 1975-76, state bd. dirs., nat. bd. dirs. 1973-82, 1988—, others), Assn. for Acad. Surgery, Assn. for Advancement Med. Instrumentation (bd. dirs. 1980-86, chmn. bd. stds. 1979-84, pres. elect 1987-88, pres. 1988-89), Am. Nat. Stds. Inst. (rep. med. device stds. bd.), Harris County Med. Soc. (alt. del. Tex. Med. Assn. 1982—, emergency med. svcs. com. 1973—, chmn. hosp. subcom. 1973-75, disaster subcom. 1973-78), Houston Surg. Soc. (pres.-elect 1995-96), Internat. Cardiovascular Soc., Internat. Coll. AneBakey Internat. Surg. Soc. (program chmn. 1980, 82, 84, bd. dirs. 1978—, sec.-treas. 1987—, others), Pan Am. Med. Assn. (v.p. trauma sect.), Pan Pacific Surg. Assn., Soc. Thoracic Surgery, Soc. Univ. Surgeons, Soc. Vascular Surgery, So. Surg. Assn., So. Thoracic Surg. Assn., Am. Coll. Surgeons (1st v.p. south Tex. chpt. 1983-84, pres. 1984-85), SW Surg. Congress (budget and fin. com. 1976-80), Tex. Med. Assn. (trauma com. 1975—, interspecialty com. 1985—, alt. del. 1982—), Tex. Surg. Soc., Univ. Assn. for Emergency Medicine (program. chmn. 1976-79, pres. 1979-80, exec. com. 1976-83, pres. 1979-80, emergency dept. design and function 1974-75, James Mackenzie award 1980), Tex. Collegiate Acad. Sci., Tex. Acad. Sci., Aerospace Med. Assn., Tex. Inst. Rehabilitation and Research (utilization rev. com.), TexPac (Harris County Med. Soc. exec. com. 1983), Alpha Chi, Sigma Tau Delta. Office: 1 Baylor Plz Houston TX 77030-3411

MATTRAN, DONALD ALBERT, management consultant, educator; b. Chgo., July 8, 1934; s. George Charles and Lucille Alice (Boule) M.; m. Betty Elena Flores, July 18, 1953 (div. Mar. 1988); children: Donald, Julie, Kimberly, Guy, Christy; m. Rose Lynn Castellano, May, 1988. B.Mus., U. Mich., 1957, M.Mus., 1960. Tchr. Van Buren Schs., Belleville, Mich., 1957-61; asst. prof. U. N.H., Durham, 1961-65, Boston U., 1965-66; assoc. prof. Hartt Sch. Music, West Hartford, Conn., 1966-82, dean, 1971-80; dir. Syracuse U. Sch. Music, N.Y., 1982-83; dean Sch. Fine and Performing Arts Montclair State Coll, Upper Montclair, N.J., 1983-87; pres. Sales Consultants of Sarasota (Fla.) Inc., 1987—; cons. Music div. Kaman Corp., Bloomfield, Conn.; cons., evaluator Nat. Assn. Schs. of Music and Joint Commn. Theater and Dance Accreditation; guest condr. Hartford Symphony Orch., Hartt Opera Theatre, All-State Festivals, 1976-83, Soc. New Music, Syracuse, N.J. Sch. Arts Orch., 1985-87. Co-author: (with Mary Rasmussen) A Teacher's Guide to the Literature of Woodwind Instruments, 1966; condr.: rec. Concerto for Cello and Jazz Band, 1972. Chmn. adv. com. Prodigy Inc., Syracuse, 1982-86; trustee Conn. Opera Assn., 1977-80; bd. advs. Watkinson Sch. Creative Arts Program, Hartford, 1977-80; mem. humanities adv. com. N.J. Dept. Higher Edn., 1984—; mem. multi-disciplinary panel N.J. State Council on Arts, 1985-87; mem. adv. com. on auditions Met. Opera Nat. Council, 1984-87; mem. adv. com. Frank and Lydia Bergen Found., 1986-87. Mem. Nat. Assn. Schs. Music (exec. bd., sec. 1978-81). Home: Apt 204 888 Boulevard Of The Arts Sarasota FL 34236-4827 Office: 1343 Main St Ste 600 Sarasota FL 34236-5630

MATTSON, FRANCIS OSCAR, retired librarian and rare books curator; b. Boston, Aug. 17, 1931; s. Frans Oscar and Catherine (Carr) M. BA, Boston U., 1957, MA, 1959; MS, Sch. Library Sci., Simmons Coll., 1967. Cert. librarian. Teaching fellow Boston U., 1958-60; instr. Tufts U., Medford, Mass., 1960-64, State Coll. at Salem, Mass., 1964-65; librarian Boston Pub. Library, 1965-68, N.Y. Pub. Library, N.Y.C., 1969-95; curator rare books N.Y. Pub. Library, 1981-88, chief spl. collections cataloging unit, 1988-93, curator Berg Collection of English and Am. Lit., 1991-95; mem. adv. com. Small Press Ctr., 1984-88; mem. adv. bd. Biblion, 1990—. Book rev. editor Printing History, 1983-86, contbg. editor Am. Book Collector, 1984-88. Staff sgt. USAF, 1952-56. Mem. ALA, Bibliog. Soc. Am., Bibliog. Soc. (London), Bibliog. Soc. of U. Va. (life), Printing Hist. Soc., Am. Printing History Assn. (program chmn. ann. confs. 1983, 84, bd. dirs. 1985-90), Manuscript Soc. (trustee 1977-80, 83-86), Am. Coll. and Research Libraries (rare books and manuscripts sect.), Assn. Internationale de Bibliophilie, Browning Inst. (sec. bd. dirs. 1975-90), Soc. for Preservation New Eng. Antiquities (life), Grolier Club. Home: PO Box 515 Midtown Sta New York NY 10018

MATTSON, JAMES STEWART, lawyer, environmental scientist, educator; b. Providence, July 22, 1945; s. Irving Carl and Virginia (Lutey) M.; m. Carol Sandry, Aug. 15, 1964 (div. 1979); children: James, Birgitta; m. Rana A. Fine, Jan. 5, 1983. BS in Chemistry, U. Mich., 1966, MS, 1969, PhD, 1970; JD, George Washington U., 1979. Bar: D.C. 1979, Fla. 1983, U.S. Dist. Ct. D.C. 1979, U.S. Dist. Ct. (so. dist.) Fla. 1984, U.S. Ct. Appeals (D.C. cir.) 1979, U.S. Ct. Claims 1985, U.S. Supreme Ct. 1985, U.S. Ct. Appeals (11th cir.) 1985, U.S. Ct. Appeals (5th cir.) 1987, U.S. Ct. Appeals (fed. cir.) 1990. Staff scientist Gulf Gen. Atomic Co., San Diego, 1970-71; dir. R & D Ouachita Industries, Inc., Monroe, La., 1971-72; asst. prof. chem. oceanography Rosenstiel Sch. Marine & Atmospheric Sci., U. Miami (Fla.), 1972-76; phys. scientist NOAA, Washington, 1976-78; mem. profl. staff & congl. liaison Nat. Adv. Commn. on Oceans and Atmosphere, 1978-80; ptnr. Mattson & Pave, Washington, Miami and Key Largo, Fla., 1980-86, Mattson & Tobin, Key Largo, 1987—; adj. prof. law U. Miami, 1983-93; cons. Alaska Dept. Environ. Conservation, 1981-91. Author: (with H.B. Mark) Activated Carbon: Surface Chemistry and Adsorption from Solution, 1971; editor (with others): Computers in Chemistry and Instrumentation, 8 vols., 1972-76; The Argo Merchant Oil Spill: A Preliminary Scientific Report, 1977, (with H.B. Mark) Water Quality Measurement: Modern Analytical Techniques, 1981; contbr. articles to profl. jours. Candidate dist. 120 Fla. Ho. of Reps., 1994. Fellow Fed. Water Pollution Control Adminstrn., 1967-68; recipient Spl. Achievement award U.S. Dept. Commerce, 1976-77; Regents Alumni scholar U. Mich., 1963. Mem. ABA, Am. Chem. Soc. (chmn. Symposium on Oil Spill Indentification 1971), Am. Trial Lawyers Assn., Order of Coif. Office: Mattson & Tobin PO Box 586 Key Largo FL 33037-0586

MATTSON, JOY LOUISE, oncological nurse; b. Moline, Ill., Feb. 1, 1956; d. Norman O. and Jeannette (Squier) M.; m. Duncan F. Crannell, Sept. 9, 1988. BA magna cum laude, Bates Coll., 1977; MTS, Harvard U., 1982; BSN magna cum laude, Rutgers U., Newark, 1988; MLS, Rutgers U., 1993. RN, N.J. Staff nurse oncology Muhlenberg Reg. Med. Ctr., Plainfield, N.J., 1987-88; staff nurse St. Lawrence Rehab. Ctr., Lawrenceville, N.J., 1988-89; clin. rsch. asst. G.H. Besselaar Assocs., Princeton, N.J., 1990-91; med. writer Convatec, Skillman, N.J., 1991-92, G.H. Besselaar Assocs., Princeton, N.J., 1992-94; clin. safety assoc. Pfizer Inc., N.Y.C., 1994—. Mem. Phi Beta Kappa. Home: 5 Tudor City Pl Apt 508 New York NY 10017

MATTSON, MARLIN ROY ALBIN, health facility administrator, psychiatry educator; b. Bellingham, Wash., Apr. 25, 1939; s. Conrad Roy and Ruth Viola (Thompson) M. BA, U. Wash., 1961, MD, 1965. Diplomate Am. Bd. Psychiatry and Neurology. Intern and resident in medicine Cornell U. program at Bellevue and Meml. Hosps., N.Y.C., 1965-67; resident in psychiatry Payne Whitney Clin. The N.Y. Hosp., N.Y.C., 1969-72, chief resident in psychiatry, 1972-73, asst. med. dir., 1973-89, assoc. med. dir., 1989—; asst. med. dir. quality assurance Westchester Div. The N.Y. Hosp., White Plains, 1979-89, assoc. med. dir. quality assurance, 1989-93; head of quality assurance program Dept. Psychiatry The N.Y. Hosp., N.Y.C., 1979-94; asst. prof. psychiatry Cornell U. Med. Coll., N.Y.C., 1973-79, assoc. prof. clin. psychiatry, 1979—; bd. visitors Manhattan Psychiat. Ctr., 1991—; bd. dirs. N.Y. County Health Svcs. Rev. Orgn., N.Y.C., 1983-95. Editor Manual of Psychiat. Quality Assurance, 1992; contbr. numerous articles to profl. jours. Capt. U.S. Army Med. Corp., 1967-69, Korea. Fellow Am. Psychiat. Assn. (mem. nat. com. on quality assurance 1988-95, chmn. 1992-95, mem. com. campus peer rev. program 1984-86, sec. N.Y. County dist. br. 1987-91, pres.-elect 1991-92, pres. 1992-93, co-pres. 1995-96, assembly rep. 1996—), N.Y. Acad. Medicine (com. pub. health 1984-92, sec. sect. on psychiatry 1993-94, chmn. 1994-95); mem. N.Y. State Psychiat. Assn. (chmn. peer rev. com. 1982-95, mem. com. econ. affairs 1995—). Republican. Episcopalian. Avocations: piano, European travel, theater, Swedish-American organizations. Home: 501 E 87th St Apt 4J New York NY 10128-7609 Office: NY Hosp Payne Whitney Psychiat Clinic 525 E 68th St New York NY 10021-4873

MATTSON, STEPHEN JOSEPH, lawyer; b. Abilene, Tex., Oct. 11, 1943; s. Joseph Martin and Dorothy Irene (Doyle) M.; m. Lynn Louise Mitchell, Mar. 13, 1965; children: Eric, Laura. BA (hon.), U. Ill., 1965, JD (hon.), 1970. Bar: Ill., 1970, U.S. Dist. Ct. (no. dist.) Ill. 1970. Assoc. Mayer, Brown & Platt, Chgo., 1970-77, ptnr., 1978—. Mem. ABA, Ill. State Bar Assn., Chgo. Bar Assn., Fed. Energy Bar Assn., Order of Coif. Office: Mayer Brown & Platt 190 S La Salle St Chicago IL 60603-3410

MATTSON, WILLIAM ROYCE, JR., health care consulting company executive; b. Decatur, Ill., Nov. 24, 1946; s. William Royce Sr. and Mary Carolyn (Olsen) M.; m. Carol Sue Eichel, June 8, 1968; children: Todd Kennedy, Nicole Maureen. BS in Acctg., Bradley U., 1968; MBA in Mktg., Loyola U., Chgo., 1972. Mgr. fin. analysis Abbott U.S.A., Chgo., 1970-74; bus. devel. mgr. Abbott Internat., Chgo., 1974-76; dir. mktg. Abbott Philippines, Manila, 1976-77; gen. mgr. Abbott Iran, Teheran, 1977-79; dir. internat. div. Abbott Labs., Chgo., 1979-82, group dir. hosp. products, 1982-83; dir. mktg. Monsanto, St. Louis, 1983-85; area v.p. G.D. Searle, Chgo., 1985-86; pres. Mattson Jack Group, St. Louis, 1986—; chief exec. officer Medstrategy, Inc., St. Louis, 1986—. Author: Thrombolytic Therapy to the Year 2000, 1986; producer film The Misconception, 1981 (5 film festival awards). With USAF, 1968-69. Mem. Licensing Execs. Soc., Fgn. Rels. Coun. St. Louis, Midwest Pharm. Advt. Coun., Biomed. Mktg. Soc., Washington U. Sch. Medicine Nat. Coun. Republican. Lutheran. Office: Mattson Jack Group Ste 180 11960 Westline Industrial Saint Louis MO 63146

MATTSSON, AKE, psychiatrist, physician; b. Stockholm, May 30, 1929; came to U.S., 1956, naturalized, 1964; s. Erik H. and Thyra (Bergsson) M.; m. Margareta Fürst, Jan. 5, 1953; children: Erik, Peter, Nicholas. B.M., Karolinska Inst., Stockholm, 1950, M.D., 1955. Intern Vanderbilt U. Med.

Sch., Nashville, 1955-56; resident in pediatrics and child psychiatry Karolinska Hosp., Stockholm, 1958-60; fellow in child devel. Case Western Res. U. Med. Sch., 1957-58, resident in psychiatry and child psychiatry, 1960-64, asst. prof. psychiatry, 1964-70; prof. psychiatry and pediatrics U. Va. Med. Sch., 1970-77, U. Pitts Med. Sch., 1977-78; prof. psychiatry and pediatrics, dir. div. child and adolescent psychiatry N.Y. U. Med. Sch., 1978-85, rsch. prof. psychiatry, 1985—; prof. psychiatry U. Va. Med. Sch., 1985-91; prof. psychiatry and pediatrics, dir. div. child and adolescent psychiatry Med. Sch., East Carolina U., Greenville, N.C., 1991—. Contbr. numerous articles to med. jours. Served with Swedish Navy, 1948-59. Fulbright-Hays grantee, 1975. Mem. Am. Psychiat. Assn., Am. Psychoanalytical Assn., Am. Psychosomatic Soc., N.Y. Psychiat. Soc., Am. Soc. Adolescent Psychiatry, Am. Acad. Child Adolescent Psychiatry, N.Y. Acad. Scis. Office: East Carolina U Med Sch Dept Psychiatry Greenville NC 27858

MATUG, ALEXANDER PETER, lawyer; b. Chgo., May 25, 1946; s. Alexander J. and Marianne (Paszek) M.; m. Jeanne Marie Buker, Aug. 16, 1969; children: Alexander W., Krista E., Thomas E. BA, St. Mary's Coll., Minn., 1968; JD, Loyola U., Chgo., 1972. Bar: Ill. 1972, U.S. Dist. Ct. (no. dist.) Ill. 1972. Pvt. practice, Palos Heights, Ill., 1972—. Bd. dirs. Am. Heritage, Sertoma, Palos Heights, 1991—; profl. adv. bd. Sertoma Speech and Hearing Ctr., Palos Hills, Ill., 1991—. Mem. Ill. Bar Assn., S.W. Suburban Bar Assn. Roman Catholic. Office: 7110 W 127th St Ste 250 Palos Heights IL 60463

MATULA, RICHARD A(LLAN), academic administrator; b. Chgo., Aug. 22, 1939; s. Ludvig A. and Leone O. (Dufeck) M.; m. Brenda C. Mather, Sept. 5, 1959; children: Scott, Kristopher, Daniel, Tiffiny. BS, Purdue U., 1961, MS, 1962, PhD, 1964. Instr. Purdue U., 1963-64; asst. prof. mech. engring. U. Calif., Santa Barbara, 1964-66, U. Mich., 1966-68; assoc. prof. mech. engring. Drexel U., Phila., 1968-70; prof. Drexel U., 1970-76, chmn. thermal and fluid sci. advanced study group, 1969-72; chmn. Drexel U. (Environ. Studies Inst.), 1972-73, chmn. dept. mech. engring. and mechanics, 1973-76; dean Coll. Engring.; prof. mech. engring. La. State U., Baton Rouge, after 1976; pres. Inst. Paper Chemistry, Appleton, Wis., 1986-89, Inst. Paper Sci. and Tech., Atlanta, 1989—. Contbr. articles to profl. jours. Treas., bd. dirs. Wexford Leas Swim and Racquet Club, Inc., 1968-73; v.p. Wexford Leas Civic Assn., 1969-71. Mem. Air Pollution Control Assn., Am. Soc. Engring. Edn., ASME, AAAS, Combustion Inst., Soc. Automotive Engrs., Sigma Xi, Pi Kappa Phi, Pi Tau Sigma, Sigma Pi Sigma, Tau Beta Pi. Roman Catholic. Home: 3143 St Ives Country Club Pky Duluth GA 30136-2001 Office: Inst Paper Sci and Tech 500 10th St NW Atlanta GA 30318-5714

MATULEF, GIZELLE TERESE, secondary education educator; b. Budapest, Jan. 17, 1945; came to the U.S., 1948; d. Louis and Gizelle Beke; m. Gary Matulef, Mar. 21, 1975; 1 child, Maryam. AA in Bus., Phoenix (Ariz.) Coll., 1964; BS in Edn., No. Ariz. U., 1966; MA, Ind. U., 1970, PhD in Comparative Lit., 1983. Cert. secondary teaching credential, Calif., C.C. instr. credential, Calif. Bus. instr. Drake Bus. Coll., N.Y.C., 1973, Cerro Coso Coll., Ridgecrest, Calif., 1973-74; English and bus. instr. Sawyer Bus. Coll., Westwood, Calif., 1974-75; bus. instr. Sierra Sands Adult Sch., Ridgecrest, 1975-82; Indian edn. dir. Sierra Sands Unifed Sch. Dist., Ridgecrest, 1980-82; sch. improvement program dir. Murray Jr. High Sch., Ridgecrest, 1982-89; English and econs. instr. Trona (Calif.) High Sch., 1989-92; tng. dir. High Desert Experience Unlimited Career Counseling, Ridgecrest, 1991-92; substitute tchr. Sierra Sands Unified Sch. Dist., Ridgecrest, 1993-96; archives asst. Albert Michelson Mus., Naval Weapons Ctr., China Lake, Calif., 1976-77, editorial asst. Tech. Info. Dept., 1977-78. Contbr. articles to profl. jours. Active PTA, Ridgecrest Schs., 1983-93, Music Parents Assn., Ridgecrest, 1985-93. Recipient fellowship Ind. U., Bloomington, 1966-69. Mem. AAUW (pres. China Lake/Ridgecrest br. 1992-96), NEA. Avocations: Hungarian culture, drama, classical music, cinema history. Home: PO Box 1041 Ridgecrest CA 93556-1041

MATUS, WAYNE CHARLES, lawyer; b. N.Y.C., Mar. 10, 1950; s. Eli and Alma (Platt) M.; m. Marsha Rothblum, Jan. 16, 1982; children: Marshall Scott, Scott Adam. BA, Johns Hopkins U., 1972; JD, NYU, 1975. Law clk. Superior Ct. D.C., 1975-76; assoc. Marshall, Bratter, Greene, Allison and Tucker, N.Y.C., 1976-79; assoc. Christy & Viener, N.Y.C., 1979-83, ptnr., 1984—; faculty ABA-Am. Law Inst., 1988; neutral mediator Supreme Ct. comml. divsn. 1st jud. dist. State of N.Y. Unified Ct. Sys. Mem. Assn. Bar City of N.Y. (com. on computer law 1985-88, chmn. com. on state cts., subcom. on motion practice 1982-84, com. product liability 1994—), N.Y. State Bar Assn. (comml. and fed. litigation sect., com. on complex civil litigation 1990—), N.Y. Litigators Club (steering com. 1985—), Johns Hopkins U. Alumni Assn. (bd. dirs. met. N.Y. chpt. 1987—, v.p. 1988—, mem. nat. alumni coun. 1996—). Office: Christy & Viener 620 Fifth Ave New York NY 10020-2402

MATUSKA, JOHN E., hospital administrator; b. Elizabeth, N.J., May 22, 1945; married. B, Seton Hall U., 1968; M, NYU, 1977. Dir. fin. svcs. Perth Amboy (N.J.) Gen. Hosp., 1971-77; v.p. fin., treas. St. Peter's Med. Ctr., New Brunswick, N.J., 1977-83, sr. v.p., treas., 1983-86, exec. v.p., 1986-89, pres., 1989—. Home: 833 Clawson Ave Neshanic Station NJ 08853-3313 Office: St Peter's Med Ctr PO Box 591 New Brunswick NJ 08903-0591*

MATUSZAK, ALICE JEAN BOYER, pharmacy educator; b. Newark, Ohio, June 22, 1935; d. James Emery and Elizabeth Hawthorne (Irvine) Boyer; m. Charles Alan Matuszak, Aug. 27, 1955; children: Matthew, James. BS summa cum laude, Ohio State U., 1958, MS, 1959; postgrad., U. Wis., 1959-60; PhD, U. Kans., 1963. Registered pharmacist, Ohio, Calif. Apprentice pharmacist Arensberg Pharmacy, Newark, 1953-58; rsch. asst. Ohio State U., Columbus, 1958, lab. asst., 1958-59; rsch. asst. U. Wis., Madison, 1959-60, U. Kans., Lawrence, 1960-63; asst. prof. U. of the Pacific, Stockton, Calif., 1963-67, assoc. prof., 1971-78, prof., 1978—; vis. fgn. prof. Kobe-Gakuin U., Japan, 1992. Contbr. articles to profl. jours. Recipient Disting. Alumna award Ohio State U. Coll. Pharmacy, 1994; NIH grantee, 1965-66. Fellow Am. Pharm. Assn. (chmn. basic scis. 1990); mem. Am. Assn. Colls. of Pharmacy (chmn. chemistry sect. 1979-80, bd. dirs. 1993-95), Am. Inst. History of Pharmacy (exec. coun. 1984-88, 90-92, 92-95, chmn. contributed papers 1990-92, pres.-elect 1995—), Cert. of Commendation 1990), Am. Chem. Soc., Internat. Fedn. Pharmacy, Acad. Pharm. Rsch. Sci. (pres. 1993-94), Coun. Sci. Soc. Pres., U.S. Adopted Names Coun. U.S. Pharmacopeial Conv., Sigma Xi, Rho Chi, Phi Kappa Phi, Kappa Epsilon (Unicorn award, award of merit 1995), Lambda Kappa Sigma, Delta Zeta. Democrat. Episcopalian. Avocation: collecting historical pharmacy artifacts. Home: 1130 W Mariposa Ave Stockton CA 95204-3021 Office: U of the Pacific Sch of Pharmacy Stockton CA 95211

MATUSZKO, ANTHONY JOSEPH, research chemist, administrator; b. Hadley, Mass., Jan. 31, 1926; s. Joseph Anthony and Katherine (Narog) M.; m. Anita Colley, Oct. 26, 1956; children—Martha, Mary, Stephen, Richard. BA, Amherst Coll., 1946; MS in Chemistry, U. Mass., 1951; PhD in Chemistry, McGill U., 1953. Demonstrator in chemistry McGill U., Montreal, Que., Can., 1950-52; from instr. to assoc. prof. chemistry Lafayette Coll., Easton, Pa., 1952-58; head fundamental process div. Naval Propellant Lab., Indian Head, Md., 1958-62; program mgr. in chemistry Air Force Office Sci. Research, Washington, 1962-89; cons., Annandale, Va., 1989—. Contbr. articles to tech. jours. Patentee in field. Pres. Forest Heights PTA, Md., 1967. Served with U.S. Army, 1946-48. Named Hon. Fellow in Chemistry, U. Wis.-Madison, 1967-68, recipient Superior Performance award USAF, Outstanding Career Svc. award U.S. Govt. Fellow AAAS, Am. Inst. Chemists (life); mem. Am. Chem. Soc., Cosmos Club, Sigma Xi. Home: 4210 Elizabeth Ln Annandale VA 22003-3654

MATYJASZEWSKI, KRZYSZTOF, chemist, educator; b. Konstantynow, Poland, Apr. 8, 1950; came to U.S., 1985; s. Henryk and Antonina (Styss) M.; m. Malgorzata Kowalska, July 15, 1972; children: Antoni, Maria. BS, MS, Tech. U., Moscow, 1972; PhD, Polish Acad. Scis., Lodz, 1976; DSc, Lodz Poly., 1985. Postdoctoral fellow U. Fla., 1977-78; rsch. assoc. Polish Acad. Scis., 1978-84, CNRS, France, 1984-85; asst. prof. chemistry Carnegie Mellon U., Pitts., 1985-89, assoc. prof., 1989-93, prof., 1993—, head dept. chemistry, 1994—; invited prof. U. Paris, 1985; vis. prof. U. Freiburg, 1988, U. Paris, 1990, U. Bayreuth, 1991, U. Strasbourg, 1992, U. Bordeaux, 1996; cons. Dow Corning, Midland, Mich., 1988-89, Arco, Phila., 1990-92, GE, Schenectady, 1992—, Amoco, Naperville, Ill., 1994—, Reilly Ind., Indpls., 1994—, Air Products, Allentown, Pa., 1994—. Author 3 books; mem. editorial bd. Macromolecules, Macromolecular Synthesis, Jour. Polymer Sci., Jour. Macromolecular Sci.-Pure and Applied Chemistry, Jour. Inorganic and Organometallic Polymers, Macromolecular Reports; contbr. chpts. to books, more than 200 articles to profl. jours.; patentee in field. Recipient award Polish Acad. Sci., 1981, Presdl. Yount Investigator award NSF, 1989. Mem. Am. Chem. Soc. (Carl S. Marvel award 1995), Internat. Union of Pure and Applied Chemistry (corr. mem. polymer nomenclature). Achievements include research in synthesis of well defined macromolecules via living and controlled polymerizations; organometallic polymers. Home: 9 Queens Ct Pittsburgh PA 15238 Office: Carnegie Mellon U 4400 5th Ave Pittsburgh PA 15213-2617

MATYSTIK, WALTER FRANCIS, engineering researcher; b. Yonkers, N.Y., Mar. 20, 1950; s. Walter F. Sr. and Orvilla F. (Collins) M.; m. Deborah J. DeBlassis, Oct. 18, 1975; children: Matthew M., Jennifer J. B of Engring., Manhattan Coll., 1972, M of Engring., 1974; JD, N.Y. Law Sch., 1981. Bar: N.Y. 1982, U.S. Dist. Ct. (so. dist.) N.Y. 1984. Project engr. Manhattan Coll., Riverdale, N.Y., 1974-77; rsch. project mgr. Manhattan Coll., Riverdale, 1978-83, dir. rsch., 1984—; atty. pvt. practice, 1982—. Bd. dirs. Mt. Pleasant Cen. Sch. Dist., Thornwood, N.Y., 1981-93, pres., 1984, 90, 91; dist. leader Mt. Pleasant Dem. Com., Hawthorne, N.Y., 1989—. Mem. ABA, ASCE, AAAS, CAUSE, Soc. Rsch. Adminstrs., Nat. coun. Univ. Rsch. Adminstrn., Internat. Assn. for Gt. Lakes Rsch., Westchester County Bar Assn., Sigma Xi (sec. Manhattan Coll. chpt. 1995—). Democrat. Roman Catholic. Office: Manhattan Coll 203RLC 4513 Manhattan College Pky Bronx NY 10471-4005

MATZ, KENNETH H., JR., newscaster; b. Phila., Oct. 25, 1945; s. Kenneth H. and Kathryn (Beddall) M.; m. Phyllis Ann Walton, Mar. 9, 1991; 1 child, Justin T. BBA, Lebanon Valley Coll., 1969. Radio news anchor WIBG, KYW, Phila., 1969-77; TV news anchor WITI-TV, Milw., 1977-79, KGO-TV/ABC, San Francisco, 1979-81, KTTV-TV/Metromedia, L.A., 1981-84, WMAR-TV, Balt., 1984-89, WCIX-TV/CBS, Miami, Fla., 1989-92, WCAU-TV/NBC, Phila., 1992—. Vol. host Muscular Dystrophy Assn. Telethon, Milw., 1978-80, Children's Miracle Network Telethon, Balt., 1984-89; hon. bd. dirs. Nazareth Hosp., 1995—; bd. dirs. Pa. AP Broadcasters Assn., 1975-77. With USAR, 1969-76. Recipient award Am. Heart Assn., March of Dimes, Nat. Kidney Found. Mem. NATAS (Emmy award for Investigative Report 1991, for Best Regularly Scheduled Daily News Program 1983, 84, Emmy award nomination for Outstanding News Feature Series, 1992, 94, for Outstanding Pub. Affairs Program, 1994, for Outstanding Individual Achievement, 1995). Avocations: scuba diving, wine, tennis. Home: 1311 Rutland Ln Wynnewood PA 19096 Office: WCAU-TV City at Monument Philadelphia PA 19131

MATZ, ROBERT, physician, educator; b. N.Y.C., Aug. 5, 1931; s. Milton and Celia (Wachovsky) M.; m. Lita Selma Freed, Dec. 24, 1955 (dec. July 1982); children: Jessica, Jonathan, Daniel; m. Bette Lynn Becker, Aug. 4, 1983. BA cum laude, NYU, 1952, MD, 1956. Diplomate Am. Bd. Internal Medicine. Intern Bronx (N.Y.) Mcpl. Hosp. Ctr., 1956-57, resident, 1957-60; assoc. dir. medicine Morrisania Hosp., Bronx, 1964-77; dir. medicine North Cen. Bronx Hosp., 1977-91, pres. med. bd., 1987-89, med. dir., 1989-91; med. dir. quality assurance and risk mgmt. Mt. Sinai Med. Ctr., N.Y.C., 1991—; attending physician St. Sinai Med. Ctr., N.Y.C., 1991—; prof. medicine Mt. Sinai Sch. Medicine, N.Y.C., 1991—; asst. prof. Albert Einstein Coll. Medicine, Bronx, 1967-71, assoc. prof., 1971-79, prof., 1979-91; cons. N.Y.C. Health and Hosp. Corp., 1983-91; mem. health adv. com. to pres. Borough of Bronx, 1987-91. Dept. editor Cardiovascular Revs. and Reports, 1985—; contbr. articles to med. jours., chpts. to books. Mem. physicians action network Amnesty Internat., 1979—. Capt. M.C., U.S. Army, 1960-62, Korea. Fellow ACP; mem. AMA, N.Y. Heart Assn., N.Y. Diabetes Assn. (v.p. 1977-83), Soc. Urban Physicians, Am. Diabetes Assn. (pres. elect chpt. 1987-89, pres. N.Y. downstate affiliate 1989-91), Harvey Soc., Hastings Hist. Soc., Phi Beta Kappa, Beta Lambda Sigma. Democrat. Jewish. Avocations: collecting antique postcards, coins, philately, travel. Home: 32 Buena Vista Dr Hastings On Hudson NY 10706-1104 Office: Mt Sinai Hosp 19 E 98th St New York NY 10029-6501

MATZEDER, JEAN MARIE ZNIDARSIC, lawyer; b. Kansas City, Mo., Jan. 27, 1948; d. August J. and Cecelia (Frick) Znidarsic; m. John August Matzeder, June 12, 1971; 1 child, Melanie. BA, St. Mary Coll., Leavenworth, Kans., 1970; JD, U. Mo., 1980. Bar: Mo. 1980, Tex. 1982. Assoc. Stinson Mag & Fizzell, Kansas City, 1980-81, Vinson & Elkins, Houston, 1981-85; asst. regulatory counsel C.E., Kansas City, 1985-88; assoc. Craft Fridkin Shaffer & Rhyne, Kansas City, 1988-90, Polsinelli, White Vardeman & Shalton, Kansas City, 1991-94; ptnr. Shaffer, Spies & Matzeder, P.C., Kansas City, Mo., 1994-96, Hardwick Law Firm, PC, Kansas City, 1996—. Treas. Sion Alliance, Kansas City, 1990-91; mem. MENSA. Mem. ABA, Mo. Bar Assn., Tex. Bar Assn., Assn. Women Lawyers, Bench and Robe Soc. Home: 200 NW Hemlock St Lees Summit MO 64064-1444 Office: Hardwick Law Firm PC 1044 Main St Ste 500 Kansas City MO 64105

MATZEK, RICHARD ALLAN, library director; b. Milw., Nov. 18, 1937; s. Robert Edward and Alice Elizabeth (Mudroch) M.; m. Ann Lynne Erickson, Aug. 24, 1963; 1 child, John Kensel. BA, Marquette Univ., 1959; MALS, U. Wis., 1960. Asst. libr. Marquette U., Milw., 1962-63; asst. libr. dir. Sacred Heart Univ., Bridgeport, Conn., 1963-66, libr. dir., 1966-77; libr. dir. Nazareth Coll., Rochester, N.Y., 1977—. Editor (book rev. sect.) Religious Book Rev., 1968-80, (publ. series) Libr. Adminstrn. and Mgmt. Assn., 1988-92; contbr. articles to profl. jours. Bd. trustees St. Bernard's Inst., Rochester, 1989—. Fellow Rotary Internat., 1974; recipient Cert. Spl. Thanks Libr. Adminstn. and Mgmt. Assn., 1992. Mem. ALA, N.Y. Libr. Assn. (councilor-at-large, Spirit of Librarianship award 1994), Rochester Regional Libr. Coun. (chair, coun. 2000). Avocations: golf, tennis, bridge, travel. Office: Nazareth Coll of Rochester 4245 East Ave Rochester NY 14618-0950

MATZICK, KENNETH JOHN, hospital administrator; b. Chgo., May 31, 1943; married. B, U. Iowa, 1965, MHA, 1967. Adminstrv. resident VA Med. Ctr., Iowa City, 1966; adminstrv. resident Morristown (N.J.) Meml. Hosp., 1967-68, asst. to exec. v.p., 1968-69; asst. dir. William Beaumont Hosp., Royal Oak, Mich., 1969-76; dir. William Beaumont Hosp., Troy, Mich., 1976-83; v.p., hosp. dir. William Beaumont Hosp., Royal Oak, 1983—. Home: 1204 Shore Club Dr Saint Clair Shores MI 48080-1565 Office: William Beaumont Hosp 3601 W 13 Mile Rd Royal Oak MI 48073-6712*

MATZKE, FRANK J., architect, consultant; b. Akron, Ohio, Jan. 28, 1922; s. Frank G. and Erna (Weibel) M.; m. Shirley Elizabeth Hall, Nov. 27, 1952 (div. Dec. 1966); children: Kim Elizabeth, Karla Jo. Student, State Tchrs. Coll. at Buffalo, 1940-41; B.Arch., Rensselaer Poly. Inst., 1951. Registered architect, N.Y., Md. Field rep., project architect W. Parker Dodge Assos., Rensselaer, N.Y., 1951-54; sr. architect div. architecture N.Y. State Dept. Pub. Works, Albany, 1954-58; assoc. architect State U. N.Y., Albany, 1958-62; dep. mgr. planning State U. Constrn. Fund, Albany, 1962-68; dep. gen. mgr. State U. Constrn. Fund, 1968-72; assoc. commr. for project mgmt. Pub. Bldgs. Service, GSA, Washington, 1972-75; acting asst. commr. for constrn. mgmt. Pub. Bldgs. Service, GSA, 1974-75; exec. dir. Ill. Capital Devel. Bd., 1975-76; v.p. for tech. and programs Nat. Inst. Bldg. Scis., Washington, 1978-83; mem. Bldg. Research Adv. Bd., Washington, 1976-79; chmn. Mgmt. Resource Council, 1974-75; cons. to pub. agys., colls. and univs. on methods to expedite design and constrn. of phys. facilities. Contbr. articles to profl. jours. Chmn. Johnsburg Planning Bd., 1962-65; nat. ski patrolman, 1953-73, past patrol leader O.C. Ski Club Ski Patrol; bd. dirs. Bldg Rsch. Inst., 1973-75, Town Ctr. Coop., Inc., 1980-82. 1st lt. inf., AUS, 1942-46, PTO. Decorated Bronze Star. Fellow AIA (pres. Ea. N.Y.. chpt 1959-60, dir. 1960-63, mem. nat. commn. on architecture for education 1966-72, chmn. nat. com. on architects in govt. 1975, medal for excellence 1951), N.Y. State Assn. Architects (dir. 1966-69); mem. VFW, Wilderness Soc., Sierra Club, Smithsonian Assocs., Natural Resources Def. Coun., Am. Rivers, Nature Conservancy, Environ. Def. Fund, Mil. Order of Caraboa, Nat. Order of Battlefield Commissions, 31st Inf. "Dixie" Divsn. Soc., 124th Inf. Rgt. Assn., Am. Legion, North Fla. Cruising Club, Sigma Xi (ret. assoc.), Tau Beta Pi, Sigma Phi Epsilon. Address: 24 Andalusia Ct Saint Augustine FL 32086-7647

MATZKE, GARY ROGER, pharmacist; b. Sturgeon Bay, Wis., July 13, 1950; s. Erwin Walter and Alice (Logerquist) M.; m. Cindy Claire Boxwell, Apr. 11, 1981; children: Megan, Jonathon, Jason, Christina, Alicia. BS in Pharmacy, U. Wis., 1973; PharmD, U. Minn., 1977. Asst. prof. Wayne State U. Sch. Pharmacy, Detroit, 1977-80; asst. prof. U. Minn., Mpls., 1980-84, assoc. prof., 1984-87, prof., 1987-89; prof., vice chmn. U. N.C., Chapel Hill, 1989-91; prof., dir. clin. scientist program Sch. of Pharmacy U. Pitts., 1991—; co-dir. The Drug Evaluation Unit, Mpls., 1981-89. Editor: Pharmacotherapy: A Pathophysiologic Approach, Pharmacotherapy: A Patient Focused Approach; contbr. over 150 articles to profl. jours. Fellow Am. Coll. Clin. Pharmacy, Am. Coll. Clin. Pharmacology; mem. Am. Soc. for Clin. Pharmacology and Therapeutics, Am. Soc. Nephrology, Internat. Soc. Nephrology, Internat. Soc. for Study of Xenobiotics. Avocations: golf, running. Office: U Pitts Sch Pharmacy 724 Salk Hall Pittsburgh PA 15261-1910

MATZKE, SUSAN MARIE, psychotherapist; b. Milw., Sept. 4, 1946; d. Harold T. and Fern M. (Bergman) Wardius; m. Robert F. Matzke, Feb. 10, 1973; children: Thad, Andrea, Kirstin, Ronald, Rob. AA, U. Wis., Janesville, 1980; BA in Psychology summa cum laude, U. Wis., Whitewater, 1982, MS in Guidance and Counseling, 1984. Cert. profl. counselor, Wis. Pres., clin. dir. Genesis Counseling Svcs., Ltd., Janesville, Wis., 1988—; cons. Dist. Com. on Ordained Ministry, Salem, Wis., 1993—. staff mem. Cargill United Meth. Ch., Janesville, 1990—. Mem. ACA, Rock County Mental Health Assn., Phi Kappa Phi, Psi Chi. Methodist. Avocations: photography, travel. Office: Genesis Counseling Svcs 2020 E Milwaukee St Janesville WI 53545-2600

MAU, WILLIAM KOON-HEE, financier; b. Honolulu, Apr. 25, 1913; s. Wah Hop and Mau (Ho Shee) M.; m. Jean Lau, Oct. 17, 1936; children—Milton, Cynthia, Lynette, Leighton, Letitia. Ed. pub. schs., Hawaii; LL.D., Pacific U., 1969. Chmn. bd., chief exec. officer Am. Security Bank, Honolulu, 1958-69; pres. Tropical Enterprises, Ltd. and Ambassador Hotel of Waikiki, Honolulu, Top of Waikiki Revolving Restaurant, Honolulu, 1955—; owner, developer Waikiki Bus. Plaza, Waikiki Shopping Plaza, Aloha Motors Properties; pres. Empress Ltd., Hong Kong, 1962-70, Aloha Motors, Inc. Vice chmn. Hawaii Bd. Land Natural Resources, 1959-63; Bd. dirs. Chinese Cultural Found., Hawaii, 1960—, Aloha United Fund, 1966—, Am. Nat. Red Cross, 1965—; past mem. exec. bd. Boy Scouts Am.; trustee Kauikeolani Children's Hosp., 1959-61. Recipient Golden Plate award Am. Acad. Achievement Bd. Govs., 1969; Wisdom Hall of Fame award of honor, 1969; named Bus. Man of Year Hawaii Bus. and Industry mag., 1966. Mem. Am., Hawaii bank assns., Newcomen Soc. N.Am., Am. Bd. Arbitration, Downtown Improvement Assn., United Chinese Soc., Tsung Tsin Assn., Hawaii Visitors Bur., Hawaii Islanders, Hawaii Pub. Links Golf Assn., Chinese C. of C. (dir., auditor 1959-62). Home: 3938 Monterey Pl Honolulu HI 96816-3922 Office: Waikiki Bus Plaza 2270 Kalakaua Ave Honolulu HI 96815-2519

MAUCH, ROBERT CARL, gas industry executive; b. Cleve., Dec. 7, 1939; s. Otto Herman and Clara (Lapple) M.; m. Rita Marie Szucs, Aug. 25, 1964 (div. Jan. 1980); children: David Otto, Martin Leslie, Karolyn Leigh; m. Drusilla Ann Tesch, Feb. 18, 1989. AMP, Harvard U., 1983; MS, U. Calif., Berkeley, 1965; BSChemE, Cleve. State U., 1962. V.p., gen. mgr., LP gas divsn. Amerigas Inc., Valley Forge, Pa., 1978-83; v.p. UGI Corp., Valley Forge, 1978-87, sr. v.p., 1987-90; dir. Ansutech, Inc., Valley Forge, 1981-82, Matheson Gas Products, Inc., Valley Forge, 1981-82; pres., dir. AP Propane Inc., Valley Forge, 1983-90, Amerigas Propane, Valley Forge, 1983—; pres., CEO, dir. AmeriGas Inc., Valley Forge, 1991—, Petrolane, Inc., Valley Forge, 1993—, Amerigas, Inc. subs. UGI Corp., Valley Forge, 1990—, AmeriGas Propane Inc. (gen. ptnr. AmeriGas Ptnrs. L.P.). Bd. govs. Pa. Economy League, Phila., 1985-91; mem. World Affairs Coun., Phila., 1980-95. Mem. Nat. Propane Gas Assn. (bd. dirs., exec. com., pres. 1978-95), Waynesborough C. of C., Propane Vehicle Coun. (chmn. 1994—). Lutheran. Avocations: tennis, reading, skiing, hunting, weight training. Office: Amerigas Inc PO Box 965 Valley Forge PA 19482-0965

MAUCK, HENRY PAGE, JR., medical and pediatrics educator; b. Richmond, Va., Feb. 3, 1926; s. Henry Page and Harriet Hutcheson (Morrison) M.; m. Janet Garrett Horsley, May 14, 1955; children—Henry Page III, John Waller. B.A., U. Va., 1950, M.D., 1952. Diplomate: Am. Bd. Internal Medicine. Intern Henry Ford Hosp., Detroit, 1952-53; resident Med. Coll. Va., Richmond, 1953-56; asst. prof. medicine and pediatrics Med. Coll. Va., 1961-66, assoc. prof., 1966-72, prof., 1972—; fellow in cardiology Am. Heart Assn., 1956-57; cons. cardiology Langley Field Air Force Hosp., Hampton, Va., McGuire's VA Hosp., Richmond. Contbr.: chpt. to Autonomic Control of Cardiovascular System, 1972; contbr. articles to sci. jours. Served with U.S. Army, 1944-46. Fellow ACP, Am. Coll. Cardiology (former gov. Va.); mem. Am. Physiol. Soc., So. Soc. Clin. Investigation, Am. Fedn. Clin. Research, So. Soc. Clin. Research. Presbyterian. Home: 113 Oxford Cir W Richmond VA 23221-3224 Office: Med Coll Va PO Box 281 Richmond VA 23202-0281

MAUCK, WILLIAM M., JR., executive recruiter, small business owner; b. Cleve., Mar. 30, 1938; s. William M. and Elizabeth Louise (Stone) M.; m. Paula Jean Mauck, Aug. 15, 1969 (div. Mar. 1983); children: Brian, David; m. Jeanne Lee Mauck, May 21, 1987. BS in Bus., Ind. U., 1961. Sales engr. Inland Container Corp., Louisville, 1961-69; sales mgr. Dixie Container Corp., Knoxville, Tenn., 1969-70, gen. mgr., 1970-75; v.p., ptnr. Heidrick & Struggles, Inc., Houston, 1975-81; pres. Booker & Mauck, Inc., Houston, 1981-85; ptnr. Ward Howell Internat. Inc., Houston, 1985-88; prin. William M. Mauck, Jr., Houston, 1988—; owner Pepe Engring., Inc., Houston, 1990—; mem. adv. bd. Women's Sports Found., N.Y.C., 1985—. Mem. Plaza Club (Houston) (chmn. bd. govs. 1987-88), Sertoma Club (Knoxville 1972-75) (pres. 1974-75). Republican. Methodist. Home: 5203 Norborne Ln Houston TX 77069-1537 Office: 9950 Cypresswood Dr Ste 300 Houston TX 77070-3400

MAUCKER, EARL ROBERT, newspaper editor, newspaper executive; b. St. Louis, Sept. 20, 1947; s. Robert Buffem and Linette (Meloy) M.; m. Betsy Ann Johnson, May 21, 1977; children: Eric Robert, Michael Earl. BA in Mass Communications, So. Ill. U., 1972. Reporter Alton (Ill.) Telegraph, 1969-73; reporter, city editor, news editor, asst. mng. editor Rockford (Ill.) Morning Star, 1973-79; mng. editor Springfield (Mo.) Daily News, 1979-80; mng. editor Ft. Lauderdale (Fla.) Sun-Sentinel, 1990-95, v.p. editorial, 1995—. Sgt. SUAF, 1966-69. Mem. Am. Soc. Newspapers Editors, Fla. Soc. Newspapers Editors, Associated Press Mng. Editors Assn. (bd. dirs. 1989-93). Home: 11160 SW 1st St Coral Springs FL 33071-8175 Office: Sun-Sentinel 200 E Las Olas Blvd Fort Lauderdale FL 33301-2248

MAUDERLY, JOE LLOYD, pulmonary toxicologist; b. Strong City, Kans., Aug. 31, 1943; s. Joseph Park and Violet May (Cox) M.; m. Cheryl Gaines, Jan. 31, 1965; children: Laurie Jean, Jameson Lynn. BS, Kans. State U., 1965, DVM, 1967. Respiratory physiologist Inhalation Toxicology Research Inst., Albuquerque, 1967-89, supr. pathophysiology group, 1976-89, dir., 1989—; rsch. prof. medicine U. N.Mex., Albuquerque, 1988—, clin. prof. pharmacy, 1990—; cons. in field. Assoc. editor Fundamental Applied Toxicology, 1989-94; contbr. articles to profl. jours., chpts. to books. Served to capt. USAF, 1967-69. Mem. Am. Thoracic Soc. (chmn. assembly of environ. and occupational health 1991-93, long-range planning com. 1991-94, sci. adv. com. 1993—, editl. bds., inhalation toxicology and exptl. lung rsch.), Am. Physiol. Soc., Am. Vet. Med. Assn., N.Mex. Vet. Med. Assn., Soc. of Toxicology, Exptl. Aircraft Assn. Republican. Home: 4517 Banff Dr NE Albuquerque NM 87111-2829 Office: Inhalation Toxicology Rsch Inst PO Box 5890 Albuquerque NM 87185-5890

MAUDLIN, ROBERT V., economics and government affairs consultant; b. Washington, June 8, 1927; s. Cecil V. and Eva Jane (Wright) M.; m. Carole M. Jackson, Sept. 3, 1949; children: Lynda C., David V., Tim W.E. Student, MIT, 1945; BS, Am. U., 1951. Ptnr. C.V. & R.V. Maudlin, Washington, 1952-72, owner, 1972—; mng. dir. Bur. Applied Econs., Washington, 1960—; sec. Nat. Assn. Scissors and Shears Mfrs., 1970—; exec. dir. Joint Govt. Liaison Com., 1973-81; mem. Industry Sector Adv. Com. U.S. Dept.

Commerce and U.S. Trade Rep., Washingotn, 1975—. Author econ. and statis. reports. Pres. Forest Hills Citizens Assn., Washington, 1964; chmn. Boy Scouts Am., Washington, 1972. Served to 2d lt. C.E., AUS, 1945-47. Republican. Home: 2906 Ellicott Ter NW Washington DC 20008-1023 Office: CV & RV Maudlin 1511 K St NW Washington DC 20005-1401

MAUER, ALVIN MARX, physician, medical educator; b. LeMars, Iowa, Jan. 10, 1928; s. Alvin Milton and Bertha Elizabeth (Marx) M.; m. Theresa Ann McGivern, Dec. 2, 1950; children: Stephen James, Timothy John, Daria Maureen, Elizabeth Claire. B.A., State U. Iowa, 1950, M.D., 1953. Intern Cin. Gen. Hosp., 1953-54; resident in pediatrics Children's Hosp. Cin., 1954-56; fellow in hematology dept. medicine U. Utah, Salt Lake City, 1956-59; dir. div. hematology Children's Hosp. Cin., prof. dept. hematology, 1959-73; prof. dept. pediatrics U. Cin. Coll. Medicine, 1959-73; prof. pediatrics U. Tenn. Coll. Medicine, Memphis, 1973—, prof. medicine, 1983—, chief med. oncology/hematology; dir. cancer program U. Tenn. Coll. Health Scis.; dir. St. Jude Children's Research Hosp., Memphis, 1973-83; mem. hematology study sect. NIH; mem. clin. cancer investigation rev. com. Nat. Cancer Inst.; mem. com. on maternal and infant nutrition NRC. Author: Pediatric Hematology, 1969; editor: The Biology of Human Leukemia, 1990. Served with U.S. Army, 1946. Mem. Am. Soc. Hematology (pres. 1980-81), Assn. Am. Cancer Insts. (pres. 1980), am. Acad. Pediatrics (com. on nutrition), Am. Assn. Cancer Edn., Am. Soc. Clin. Investigation, Am. Fedn. Clin. Rsch., Assn. Am. Physicians, Am. Pediatric Soc., Cen. Soc. Clin. Investigation, Cen. Soc. Clin. Rsch., Internat. Soc. Hematology (pres. 1988-90, chmn. 1992—, bd. councilors 1992—), Am. Cancer Soc. (pres. Tenn. divsn. 1992-93), Midwest Soc. Pediat. Rsch., N.Y. Acad. Scis., Soc. Pediat. Rsch., Am. Assn. Cancer Rsch., Phi Beta Kappa, Sigma Xi, Alpha Omega Alpha. Democrat. Roman Catholic. Office: U Tenn Memphis Cancer Ctr N327 Van Vleet Bldg 3 S Dunlap St Memphis TN 38103-4907

MAUER, ELIZABETH BANGEL, stockbroker; b. N.Y.C.; d. Arthur Benjamin and Millicent Sara (Hancles) Bangel; m. David Mauer, May 21, 1972 (div. 1991); children: Beth, Carolyn, Amanda. BA, SUNY, Stony Brook, 1970; MEd, U. Cin., 1974; postgrad., U. Bridgeport, Conn., 1978-79, U. Cin., 1991—. Trainee Lehman Bros., N.Y.C., 1971-72; head reading dept. Cin. Country Day Sch., 1973-77; cons. GTITC Corp., Cin., 1984-85, Little People Workshop, Cin., 1991; stockbroker Gradison & Co., Cin., 1992—. Bd. dirs. Cin. Ballet, 1990—, Coll. Conservatory of Music, Cin., 1989—, Children's Psychiat. Ctr., Cin., 1989-91, AHRC; mem. govt. rels. bd. Cin. Fine Arts Inst., 1992; v.p. exec. bd. dirs. Nat. Coun. Jewish Women, Cin., 1984-91. Mem. Town Club (chmn. events 1990—), Losantiville Country Club (chmn. events 1989), Met. Club (charter mem.), Univ. Club. Avocations: tennis, art, antiques, painting, writing. Home: 2861 Fair Acres Dr Cincinnati OH 45213-1015 Office: Gradison & Co 580 Walnut St Cincinnati OH 45202-3110

MAUGHAN, DERYCK C., investment banker. Degree earned, King's Coll., Univ. of London, 1969. With Treasury Dept., United Kingdom, from 1970, Salomon Bros. Inc., 1983—; mng. dir. Salomon Bros. Inc, 1985-91, Tokyo, until 1991; chief oper. officer Salomon Bros. Inc, N.Y.C., 1991-92, chmn., chief exec. officer, 1992—. Office: Salomon Bros Inc 7 World Trade Ctr New York NY 10048-1102*

MAUGHAN, WILLARD ZINN, dermatologist; b. Riverside, Calif., Apr. 21, 1944; s. Franklin David and Martha Charlotte (Zinn) M.; m. Rona Lee Wilcox, Aug. 20, 1968; children: Julie Anne, Kathryn Anita, Willard Wilcox, Christopher Keith. Student, Johns Hopkins U., Balt., 1962-64; BS, U. Utah, 1968, MD, 1972. Diplomate Am. Bd. Dermatology. Intern Walter Reed Army Med. Ctr., Washington, 1972-73; fellow Mayo Clinic, Rochester, Minn., 1976-79; pvt. practice Ogden, Utah, 1979—. Contbr. articles to profl. jours. Commr. Boy Scouts Am., Weber County, Utah, 1980-84, dist. chmn., 1993-94, assoc. mem. bd. dirs. Trapper Trails coun., 1995—; pres. Am. Cancer Soc., Weber County, 1985-86. Maj. U.S. Army, 1971-76. Recipient Dist. award of merit Boy Scouts Am., 1985, Silver Beaver award 1994. Fellow ACP, Am. Acad. Dermatology, Royal Soc. Medicine (London); mem. N.Y. Acad. Scis., Kiwanis Club. Republican. Mormon. Avocations: woodcarving, camping. Home: 2486 W 4550 S Roy UT 84067-1944 Office: 3860 Jackson Ave Ogden UT 84403-1956

MAUKE, OTTO RUSSELL, retired college president; b. Webster, Mass., Jan. 26, 1924; s. Otto G. and Florence (Giroux) M.; m. Leah Louison, June 18, 1950. A.B., Clark U., 1947, A.M., 1948; Ph.D. (Kellogg fellow), U. Tex., 1965. Tchr. history, acad. dean Endicott Jr. Coll., Beverly, Mass., 1948-65; acad. dean Cumberland County Coll., Vineland, N.J., 1966-67; pres. Camden County Coll., Blackwood, N.J., 1967-87, pres. emeritus. Served with U.S. Army, 1943-46, PTO. Home: 2119 E Lakeview Dr Sebastian FL 32958-8519

MAUKSCH, INGEBORG GROSSER, nursing educator; d. Frederick and Claire (Tauber) G.; children from previous marriage: Lawrence Bernard, Valerie. Ph.D., U. Chgo., 1969; D.Sc. (hon.), Syracuse U., 1979. Valere Potter disting. svc. prof. nursing Vanderbilt U. Sch. Nursing, Nashville; sr. program cons. Robert Wood Johnson nurse faculty fellowships in primary care program Vanderbilt U. Sch. Nursing, 1976—; mem. Presdl. Com. on Nat. Health Inst. Author: (with M. Miller) Implementing Change in Nursing, 1981, Systematic Patient Medication Record Review, 1980; mem. editorial bd.: Nursing Outlook, Nurse Educator. Mem. U.S. Holocaust Meml. Council. Recipient Alumni Achievement award Columbia U., 1979. Mem. Am. Nurses Assn. (hon.), Am. Acad. Nursing, Nat. Acad. Scis., Tenn. Nurses Assn. Office: Vanderbilt U Sch Nursing Nashville TN 37240

MAUL, MARGARET ELEANOR, financial planner; b. Fresno, Calif., Aug. 2, 1943. BBA magna cum laude, Calif. State U., Fresno, 1979; attended, U. Pa., 1991, 92, 94. CFP. Sr. acct. exec. Merrill Lynch, 1979-84; sr. v.p. investments Prudential Securities, Nev., 1984—; created Maul Fin. within Prudential Securities, 1994, chmn.'s coun., 1985—, equity coun.; spkr. fin. issues; leader fin. seminars. Guest, expert Sta. KVBC-TV News, Las Vegas; contbg. writer Fin. Planning on Wall St.; host Focus on Finance News 3 FM, Las Vegas. Bd. dirs. San Joaquin Valley Health Consortium, 1982; mem., corp. patron, corp. coun. Fresno Art Mus., 1993—; mem. fund raising com. Mus. Soc. Fresno Met. Mus., 1990-92; mem. steering com. Leon S. Peters Bldg. Campaign Calif. State U., 1986-94; mem. St. Regis Assn., 1995. Named Woman of Yr. by Fresno Bus. and Profl. Women. Mem. Inst. CFPs, Internat. Assn. Fin. Planning. Office: Prudential Securities 3763 Howard Hughes Pky Ste 330 Las Vegas NV 89109-0939

MAULDEN, JERRY L., utility company executive; b. North Little Rock, Ark., 1936; married. B.S., U. Ark., Little Rock, 1963. Acct. Dyke & Assocs., Inc., 1959-61; sr. auditor Madigan James & Co., C.P.A.'s, 1961-62; asst. controller Dillard Dept. Stores, Inc., 1962-65; asst. to treas. Ark. Power & Light Co. a company of Middle South Utilities, Inc., Little Rock, 1965-68, asst. controller, 1968-71; controller, asst. sec., asst. treas. and later spl. asst. to pres. Ark. Power & Light Co., Little Rock, 1971-73, sec.-treas., 1973-75, v.p. fin. svcs., sec., treas., 1975-79, pres., chief exec. officer, 1979-89, chmn. bd., chief exec. officer, 1989—, also dir.; former sr. v.p. Entergy Corp., Little Rock; now pres., chief operating officer Entergy Corp., New Orleans; sr. v.p. Mid. South Utilities, 1990; chmn., chief exec. officer Miss. Power & Light, also dir. Office: Ark Power & Light PO Box 551 Little Rock AR 72203-0551 Office: Entergy Corp 225 Baronne St New Orleans LA 70112-1704*

MAULDIN, JEAN ANN, controller; b. Ft. Chaffee, Ark., Oct. 12, 1957; d. Lawrence Ray and Antoinette Marie (Tusa) Mitchell; 1 child, Michele L. Carter. BBA in Acctg., U. Ctrl. Ark., 1979, MBA, 1985. Cost acct. FMC Automotive Svc. Divsn., Conway, Ark., 1979-82, mgr. cost acctg., 1982-85, divsnl. fin. analyst, 1985, plant contr., 1985-86, divsn. contr., 1986-88; mgr. cost acctg. Columbian Chems. Co., Atlanta, 1988-90, dir. field acctg., 1990-92, No. Am. contr., 1992-93, corporate controller, 1993-94; v.p., CFO Accuride Corp., Henderson, Ky., 1995—. Recipient Young Career Woman award Bus. and Profl. Women, 1986. Mem. Inst. Mgmt. Accts. (cert., v.p. adminstrn. 1993-94). Republican. Roman Catholic. Avocations: art, antiques, doll collecting.

MAULDIN, JEAN HUMPHRIES, aviation company executive; b. Gordonville, Tex., Aug. 16, 1923; d. James Wiley and Lena Leota (Noel-Crain) Humphries; B.S., Hardin Simmons U., 1943; M.S., U. So. Calif., 1961; postgrad. Westfield Coll., U. London, 1977-78, Warnborough Coll., Oxford, Eng., 1977-78; m. William Henry Mauldin, Feb. 28, 1942; children—Bruce Patrick, William Timothy III. Psychol. counselor social services 1st Baptist Ch., 1953-57; pres. Mauldin and Staff, public relations, Los Angeles, 1957-78; pres. Stardust Aviation, Inc., Santa Ana, Calif., 1962—. Mem. Calif. Democratic Council, 1953-83; rep. 69th Assembly Dist. Caucus to Calif. Dem. State Central com. exec. bd., 1957—, Orange County Dem. Central Com., 1960—; mem. U.S. Congl. Peace Adv. Bd., 1981—; del. Dem. Nat. Conv., 1974, 78, Dem. Mid-Term Conv., 1976, 78, 82, 86, Dem. Nat. Issues Conf.; mem. nat. advisor U.S. Congl. Adv. Bd. Am. Security Council; pres. Santa Ana Friends of Public Library, 1973-76, McFadden Friends of Library, Santa Ana, 1976-80; chmn. cancer crusade Am. Cancer Soc., Orange County, 1974; mem. exec. bd. Lisa Hist. Preservation Soc., 1970—; lay leader Protestant Episcopal Ch. Am., Trinity Ch., Tustin, Calif. Named Woman of Yr., Key Woman in Politics, Calif. Dem. Party, 1960-80. Am. Mgmt. Assn. (pres.'s club), Bus. and Profl. Women Am., Exptl. Aircraft and Pilots Assn., Nat. Women's Polit. Caucus, Dem. Coalition Central Coms., Calif. Friends of Library (life), Women's Missionary Soc. (chmn.), LWV, Nat. Fedn. Dem. Women, Calif. Fedn. County Central Com. Mems., Internat. Platform Assn., Peace Through Strength, Oceanic Soc., Nat. Audubon Soc., Sierra Club, Nat. Wildlife Fedn., Internat. Amnesty Assn., Am. Security Council, Nat. Women's Pilot. Club: U. So. Calif. Ski, Town Hall of Calif. Author: Cliff Winters, The Pilot, The Man, 1961; The consummate Barnstormer, 1962; The Daredevil Clown, 1965. Home: 1013 S Elliott Pl Santa Ana CA 92704 also: 102 E 45th St Savannah GA 31405-2115 Office: 16542 Mount Kibby St Fountain Valley CA 92708

MAULDIN, ROBERT RAY, banker; b. China Grove, N.C., Jan. 15, 1935; s. Raymond Ray and Hazel Inez (Luther) M.; m. Patricia Crain Jarman, Aug. 29, 1959; children—John Clayton, Patricia Crain, Elizabeth Jarman, Anne Luther, Katherine Purnell. Student, N.C. State U., 1953-54; B.S., U. N.C., 1959. Trainee, asst. trust officer Nations Bank, Charlotte, 1959-62; cashier Bank of York, S.C., 1962-65; v.p. Colonial Am. Nat. Bank, Roanoke, Va., 1965-69; exec. v.p. Peoples Bank & Trust Co., Rocky Mount, N.C., 1969-81; pres. Peoples Bank & Trust Co., 1981-85, chmn., chief exec. officer, 1985-90; chmn., CEO Centura Banks Inc., 1993—. Pres. Rocky Mount United Cmty. Svcs., 1974-75; mem. Rocky Mount City Schs. Bd., 1979-83, Commn. for Competitive N.C., 1994—; trustee N.C. Wesleyan Coll., 1993—, Va. Episc. Sch., 1993—; bd. dirs. N.C. Citizens Assn., N.C. Pub. TV Found., Global Tranpark Found., N.C. Partnerships for Children, N.C. Cmty. Found., Carolinas Gateway Partnership; mem. adv. bd. Kenan Flaglar Bus. Sch. U. N.C., 1994—. Mem. Am. Inst. Banking, N.C. Young Bankers (pres. 1974-75), N.C. Bankers Assn. (dir. 1984-95), Robert Morris Assocs., Rocky Mount C. of C. (dir. 1975-80, pres. 1978-79), Kiwanis (pres. Rocky Mount 1976-77), Chi Phi. Presbyn. Home: 109 Essex Ct Rocky Mount NC 27803-1207 Office: Centura Bank 134 N Church St Rocky Mount NC 27804-5401

MAULDIN, THAD, museum director. Exec. dir. The U.S. Space and Rocket Ctr., Huntsville, Ala. Office: US Space & Rocket Ctr PO Box 070015 Huntsville AL 35807-7015

MAULDIN, WILLIAM HENRY (BILL MAULDIN), cartoonist; b. Mountain Park, N.Mex., Oct. 29, 1921; s. Sidney Albert and Edith Katrina (Bemis) M.; m. Norma Jean Humphries, Feb. 28, 1942 (div. 1946); children—Bruce Patrick, Timothy; m. Natalie Sarah Evans, June 27, 1947 (dec. Aug. 1971); children—Andrew, David, John, Nathaniel; m. Christine Ruth Lund, July 29, 1972; children: Kaja Lisa, Samuel Lund. Ed. pub. schs. and high schs., N.Mex. and Ariz.; studied art, Chicago Acad. of Fine Arts; M.A. (hon.), Conn. Wesleyan U., 1946; Litt.D. (hon.), Albion Coll., 1970, N.Mex. State U., Las Cruces, 1972; L.H.D. (hon.), Lincoln Coll., 1970, Wash. U., St. Louis, 1984, Coll. of Santa Fe, 1986. Cartoonist St. Louis Post-Dispatch, until 1962, Chgo. Sun-Times, 1962-91. Tech. adviser, actor film Teresa, 1950; actor film The Red Badge of Courage, 1950; author or cartoonist: Star Spangle Banter, 1941, Sicily Sketch Book, 1943, Mud, Mules and Mountains, 1943, This Damn Tree Leaks, 1945, Up Front (Book of the Month selection), 1945, Back Home (Book of the Month seleaction), 1947, A Sort of a Saga, 1949, Bill Mauldin's Army, 1951, Bill Mauldin in Korea, 1952, What's Got Your Back Up?, 1961, I've Decided I Want My Seat Back, 1965, The Brass Ring, 1971 (Book of Month Club selection), Mud and Guts, 1978: Let's Declare Ourselves Winners and Get the Hell Out, 1985; illustrator: Bradley: A Soldier's Story, 1978; author, illustrator numerous articles Sports Illus., Life, Collier's. Served with U.S. Army, 1940-45, 45th Inf. Div. and Stars and Stripes; campaigns Sicily, Italy, France, Germany. Decorated Purple Heart, Legion of Merit; recipient Pulitzer prize for cartoons 1944, 59, Sigma Delta Chi award for cartoons 1963, 69, 72; Prix Charles Huard de dessin de presse Fondation pour l'Art et la Recherche Paris, 1974, Walter Cronkite award for journalistic excellence Ariz. State U., 1985. Fellow Sigma Delta Chi. Home: Watkins-Loomis Agy 133 E 35th New York City NY 10016

MAULDING, BARRY CLIFFORD, lawyer; b. McMinnville, Oreg., Sept. 3, 1945; s. Clifford L. and Mildred (Fisher) M.; m. Reva J. Zachow, Dec. 27, 1965; children: Phillip B., John C. BA in Psychology, U. Oreg., 1967, JD, 1970. Bar: Oreg. 1970. Sec., gen. counsel Alaska Continental Devel. Corp., Portland, also Seattle, 1970-75; gen. counsel Alaska Airlines, Seattle, 1975-84; dir. legal services, corp. sec. Univar Corp., Seattle, 1984-91; v.p., gen. counsel, corp. sec. Prime Source Corp., Seattle, 1991—; dir. Alaska N.W. Properties, Inc., Seattle. Mem. editorial bd. Oreg. Law Rev. Trustee Good Neighbor Found., Seattle. Republican.

MAULIK, NILANJANA, medical educator; b. Dec. 22, 1960. BS in Chemistry, St. Xavier's Coll., 1981; MS in Biochemistry, U. Coll. Sci., 1983, PhD in Biochemistry, 1990. Asst. prof. dept. surgery U. Conn. Sch. Medicine, Farmington, 1994—; lectr. in field. Jr. Rsch. fellow U. coll. Sci., Calcutta, India, 1983-85, Sr. Rsch. fellow, 1985-90, Postdoctoral fellow U. Conn. Sch. Medicine, 1992-92, Am. Heart fellow, 1992—; Nat. Merit scholar, 1978; recipient Young Investigator award Am. Coll. ANgiology, 1982, Internat. Soc. Angiology, 1994. Mem. Am. Soc. Biochemistry amd Molecular Biology, Am. Heart Assn. (cardiovascular coun.), N.Y. Acad. Sci. Internat. Soc. Heart Rsch., Soc. Biol. Chemists, Indian Sci. Congress Assn. (life). Office: U Conn Sch Medicine Dept Surgery Farmington CT 06030-1110

MAULL, GEORGE MARRINER, music director, conductor; b. Phila., Oct. 14, 1947; s. Frederick Dunlap and Helen Norbury (Jordan) M.; m. Marcia Eileen Korn, Aug. 13, 1984. MusB, U. Louisville, 1970, MusM, 1972; postgrad., Julliard Sch. Music, 1976-78. Condr. Louisville Ballet Co., 1971-75; asst. condr. Opera Orch. N.Y., N.Y.C., 1976-78, N.J. Symphony Orch., Newark, 1979-80; music dir., condr. Bloomingdale Chamber Orch., N.Y.C., 1980-83, N.J. Youth Symphony, Summit, 1980—, Philharm. Orch. N.J., Warren, 1987—. Conducting debut Carnegie Hall, N.Y.C., 1989; condr. in Eng., Belgium, The Netherlands, Poland, Romania, Hungary, Germany; featured in WNET mini-documentary Art Effects: Young and Noteworthy, 1988. Named Disting. Alumnus, U. Louisville, 1994. Mem. Am. Fedn. Musicians, Am. Symphony Orch. League (conducting fellow 1978, Nat. Cert. Merit 1980), Condr's. Guild. Episcopalian. Home: 79 Stone Run Rd Bedminster NJ 07921-1711 Office: Philharm Orch of NJ PO Box 4064 Warren NJ 07059-0064

MAULSBY, ALLEN FARISH, lawyer; b. Balt., May 21, 1922. A.B., Williams Coll., Williamstown, Mass., 1944; LL.B., U. Va., 1946. Bar: Md. 1947, N.Y. 1950. Law clk. to judge U.S. Circuit Ct. Appeals 4th Circuit, 1946-47; assoc. firm Cravath Swaine & Moore, N.Y.C., 1947-57; partner Cravath Swaine & Moore, 1958—. Vestryman St. James' Episcopal Ch., N.Y.C., 1962-68, 80-85, warden, 1986-87; trustee Greer-Woodycrest Child Care, 1961-82; bd. dirs. Episc. Ch. Found., 1973-86. Mem. Am. Bar Found., N.Y. Bar Found., Am. Coll. Trial Lawyers, Am. Bar Assn., N.Y. State Bar Assn., Fed. Bar Assn., Assn. Bar City N.Y., N.Y. County Lawyers Assn. Office: Cravath Swaine & Moore Worldwide Pla 825 8th Ave New York NY 10019-7475

MAUN, MARY ELLEN, computer consultant; b. N.Y.C., Dec. 18, 1951; d. Emmet Joseph and Mary Alice (McMahon) M. BA, CUNY, 1977, MBA, 1988. Sales rep. N.Y. Telephone Co., N.Y.C., 1970-76, comml. rep., 1977-83, programmer, 1984-86; systems analyst Telesector Resources Group, N.Y.C., 1987-89, sr. systems analyst, 1990-95; pres. Sleepy Hollow Techs., Inc., North Tarrytown, N.Y., 1995—. Corp. chmn. United Way of Tri-State Area, N.Y.C., 1985; recreation activities vol. Pioneers Am., N.Y.C., 1982—; active Sleepy Hollow Hist. Soc. Recipient Outstanding Community Service award, Calvary Hosp., Bronx, N.Y., 1984. Mem. N.Y. Health and Racquet Club, Road Runners. Democrat. Avocations: antique restoration, classical music, skiing, running. Home: 3 Farrington Ave North Tarrytown NY 10591-1302 Office: Sleepy Hollow Techs Inc 3 Farrington Ave North Tarrytown NY 10591-1302

MAUNDER, ADDISON BRUCE, agronomic research company executive; b. Holdrege, Nebr., May 13, 1934; s. Addison Haynes and Marie Sophia (Luebs) M.; m. Katherina Marlene Blum, Sept. 8, 1978; children: Lynda Diane, Christopher Allen. B.Sc., U. Nebr., 1956; M.Sc., Purdue U., 1958, Ph.D., 1960; DSc (hon., U. Nebr., 1991. With DeKalb AgResearch, Inc., Lubbock, Tex., 1960—, sorghum breeder, 1960-61, dir. sorghum research, 1961-76, v.p. sorghum research, 1976-78; v.p. rsch. AgResearch, Inc., Lubbock, Tex., 1978-82; v.p. DeKalb-Pfizer Genetics, DeKalb, Ill., 1982-89; v.p. agronomic research DeKalb Plant Genetics, DeKalb, Ill., 1989-91; sr. v.p. DeKalb Genetics Corp., DeKalb, Ill., 1991—; bd. dirs. Diversity Mag., Washington, 1984-95; adj. prof. Tex. Tech. U., 1992—. Contbr. 11 chpts. to books and more than 72 articles to profl. jours. Mem. deans adv. com. Tex. Tech. U., Lubbock, 1983-86; chmn. external rev. INTSORMIL of AID, Lincoln, Nebr., 1980—; bd. dirs. Tex. Tech. U. Rsch. Found., 1986-92; mem. Nat. Plant Genetic Resources Bd., 1991-92, Nat.t Plant Variety Protection Bd., 1991-94. Recipient Gerald Thomas award Tex. Tech. U., 1974, Prodn. award Grain Sorghum Producers Assn., 1985, Genetics and Plant Breeding award for Industry, 1987, Indsl. Agronomy award, 1988. Fellow AAAS, Am. Soc. Agronomy (bd. dirs. 1991-92), Crop Sci. Soc. Am. (bd. dirs. 1991-92, pres. 1995-96); mem. Sigma Xi, Alpha Zeta. Republican. Achievements include development of plant products (130 hybrids) emphasizing improved drought and insect resistence as well as nutritional quality. Office: DeKalb RR 2 Box 56 Lubbock TX 79415-9717

MAUPIN, ARMISTEAD JONES, lawyer; b. Raleigh, N.C., Nov. 10, 1914; s. Alfred McGhee and Mary Armistead (Jones) M.; m. Diana Jane Barton, May 16, 1942 (dec.); children: Armistead Jones, Anthony Westwood, Jane Stuart; m. Cheryl Leigh Erhard, July 31, 1982. A.B., U. N.C., 1936; J.D., George Washington U., 1940. Bar: N.C. 1939. Ptnr. Maupin, Taylor & Ellis., Raleigh. Pres. Occoneechee coun. Boy Scouts Am., 1962-64; pres. Carolina Charter Corp., 1976-80, 93—; former chancellor Episcopal Diocese of N.C.; former sr. warden Christ Ch. Parish; vice chmn. Am. Battle Monuments Commn., 1981-90. Comdr. USNR, WWII, PTO. Decorated chevalier French Legion of Honor. Fellow Am. Bar Found.; mem. ABA (ho. of dels. 1960-72), N.C. State Bar (coun. 1955-60, pres. 1959-60), Soc. of Cincinnati (v.p. gen. 1968-70, pres. gen. 1971-74, pres. N.C. soc. 1964-67), Carolina Country Club, Circle Club, Triangle Fox Hounds Club. Republican. Episcopalian. Home: 2005 Banbury Rd Raleigh NC 27608-1121 Office: Highwoods Tower One 3200 Beech Leaf Ct Raleigh NC 27604-1064

MAUPIN, ARMISTEAD JONES, JR., writer; b. Washington, May 13, 1944; s. Armistead Jones and Diana Jane (Barton) M. BA, U. N.C., 1966. Reporter News and Courier, Charleston, S.C., 1970-71, AP, San Francisco, 1971-72; account exec. Lowry Russom and Leeper, Pub. Rels., San Francisco, 1973; columnist Pacific Sun mag., San Francisco, 1974; publicist San Francisco Opera, 1975; serialist San Francisco Chronicle, 1976-77, 81, 83; commentator Sta. KRON-TV, San Francisco, 1979; serialist San Francisco Examiner, 1986. Author: (novels) Tales of the City, 1978, More Tales of the City, 1980, Further Tales of the City, 1982, Babycakes, 1984, Significant Others, 1987, Sure of You, 1989, (omnibus) 28 Barbary Lane, 1990, (omnibus) Back to Barbary Lane, 1991, Maybe the Moon, 1992; librettist musical Heart's Desire, 1990; exec. prodr. (TV program) Armistead Maupin's Tales of the City, 1993; contbr. articles to N.Y. Times, L.A. Times, others. Lt. (j.g.) USN, 1967-70, Vietnam. Recipient Freedom Leadership award Freedoms Found., Valley Forge, Pa., 1972, Comms. award Met. Elections Com. L.A., 1989, Exceptional Achievement award ALA, 1990, Best Dramatic Serial award Royal TV Soc., 1994, Peabody award 1994, Outstanding Miniseries award, Gay and Lesbian Alliance Against Defamation, 1994, Best Miniseries award Nat. Bd. of Rev., 1994. Office: Harper Collins 10 E 53rd St New York NY 10022-5244

MAUPIN, ELIZABETH THATCHER, theater critic; b. Cleve., Oct. 21, 1951; d. Addison and Margaret (Thatcher) M. BA in English, Wellesley (Mass.) Coll., 1973; M in Journalism, U. Calif., Berkeley, 1976. Editorial asst. Houghton-Mifflin Co., Boston, 1973-74; intern Washington bureau McClatchy Newspapers, 1975; reporter, movie critic Times-Standard, Eureka, Calif., 1976-78; theater and movie critic Chronicle-Telegram, Elyria, Ohio, 1978-79; movie and restaurant critic Ledger-Star, Norfolk, Va., 1979-82; feature writer Va.-Pilot and Ledger-Star, Norfolk, 1982-83; sr. theater critic Orlando (Fla.) Sentinel, 1983—. Fellow Nat. Arts Journalism program Columbia U., 1995—. Fellow Nat. Critics Inst.; mem. Am. Theatre Critics Assn. (exec. com. 1993—). Office: Orlando Sentinel 633 N Orange Ave Orlando FL 32801-1300

MAURER, ADAH ELECTRA, psychologist; b. Chgo., Oct. 26, 1905; d. Frank Ulysses and Mary Louise (Meng) Bass; m. Harry Andrew Maurer, June 14, 1937 (div. 1947); children: Douglas, Helen. BS, U. Wis., 1927; MA, U. Chgo., 1957; PhD, Union Inst., 1976. Lic. sch. psychologist, Calif. Tchr. pub. schs. Chgo., 1927-61; psychologist pub. schs. Calif., 1962-71; pvt. practice marriage, family and child counselor Berkeley, Calif., 1965-75; organizer, chief exec. officer End Violence Against the Next Generation, Inc., Berkeley, 1972—; lectr. U. Calif., Davis, 1965-68; bd. dirs. Nat. Ctr. for Study Cpl. Punishment & Alternatives in Schs. Temple U., Phila.; liaison People Opposed to Paddling Students, Houston, 1981—; v.p. Nat. Coalition to Abolish Cpl. Punishment in Schs., Columbus, Ohio, 1987—; cons. Calif. State Dept. Social Svcs., 1988. Author: Paddles Away, 1981, 1001 Alternatives, 1984, (with others) The Bible and the Rod, 1983, Think Twice, 1985; editor: (newsletter) The Last? Resort, 1972—; contbr. numerous articles to profl. jours. Sponsor End Phys. Punishment of Children Worldwide. Recipient Disting. Humanitarian award Calif. State Psychol. Assn., Presdl. award Nat. Assn. Sch. Psychologists, 1988, Donna Stone award Nat. Commn. for Prevention of Child Abuse, 1988, commendation Giraffe Project, 1988, award in recognition of pioneering efforts in banning corporal punishment in nation's schs. Nat. Coalition to Abolish Corporal Punishment in Schs., Achievement award Child, Youth and Family Svcs. Am. Psychol. Assn., 1994. Fellow Am. Psychol. Assn. (Lifetime Career Achievement award 1995); mem. Hemlock Soc. Avocations: hiking, gardening. Home and Office: 977 Keeler Ave Berkeley CA 94708-1440

MAURER, BARBARA GLEE, educational administrator; b. Coopeville, Wash., May 21, 1945; d. James Clifton and Roberta Margaret (Torrison) Lawrence; m. Paul Gerry Maurer, June 3, 1984; children: Karl Norsen, Curtis Norsen. BS in Edn., U. Idaho, 1967; MA in Edn. Adminstrn., U. Wash., 1982. Cert. tchr. K-12, Wash. Tchr. Seattle Pub. Schs., 1968-70, 76-78, 85-86, program mgr., 1978-83, curriculum specialist, 1983-85; curriculum specialist Highline Sch. Dist., Seattle, 1986-87, curriculum coord., 1988—; curriculum cons. Sch. Dists., Seattle, 1980—; bd. dirs., sec. Wash. Coun. Honors and Advanced Placement, 1990—; cons. MacMillan McGraw Hill, N.Y.C., 1992-93; editor newsletter Gifted Unltd., 1985-88; cert. trainer Lead Devel. Project; liaison adminstr. Project Leadership; adj. prof. Seattle Pacific U. Contbr. articles to profl. jours. Precinct com. chmn. Rep. Party, 1980-85. Recipient Outstanding Project award Nat. Diffusion Network, 1981, Project Leadership award Wash. Assn. Sch. Adminstrs., 1992, Leadership in Profl. Devel. Award Wash. State ASCD, 1992. Mem. ASCD, Nat. Assn. Social Studies, Nat. Assn. for Gifted, Nat. Coun. Tchrs. English, Wash. Assn. Edn. Talented and Gifted (award 1990, Outstanding Leader award 1995), Wash. Coalition for Gifted and Talented (sec. 1991-92), Rotary (bd. dirs., pres. 1996). Avocations: sailing, skiing, gardening, cooking. Office: Highline Sch Dist 15675 Ambaum Blvd SW Seattle WA 98166-2523

MAURER, CHRISTOPHER HERMAN, foreign language educator; b. Abington, Pa., Oct. 21, 1949; s. Herman H. and Neva (Kerr) M.; m. Maria Estrella Iglesias, Mar. 2, 1977; children: Daniel, Pablo. BA, Columbia U., 1977; MA, U. Pa., 1980, PhD, 1982. Tchg. fellow Spanish U. Pa., 1977-82; asst. prof. Spanish Harvard U., Cambridge, Mass., 1982-85; assoc. prof. Spanish Harvard U., Cambridge, 1985-90; prof. Spanish, chair dept. Spanish and Portuguese Vanderbilt U., Nashville, 1990—. Author: Obra y vida de

Francisco de Figueroa, 1988; co-author: (textbook) Temas: Invitación a la literatura hispánica, 1993; editor, translator: The Poetical Works of Federico Garcia Lorca, 1988-95, The Art of Worldly Wisdom, 1991, A Pocket Mirror for Heroes, 1996; editor: Epistolario, 1995; mem. editl. bd. FGL Boletin de la Fundación Federico Garcia Lorca, 1988—, Cuadernos Cervantes, 1994—; contbr. articles to profl. jours. Fellow Fulbright Commn., Madrid, Spain, 1981-82; annual rsch. grantee Clark Fund, Harvard U., 1982-90; rsch. grantee Com. on Cultural Cooperation Between Spain's Ministry of Culture and U.S. Univs., 1988; grantee Gen. Book and Libr. Divsn. of the Spanish Ministry of Culture and from Whitehead Found., 1990; Univ. Rsch. Coun. grantee Vanderbilt U., 1993; Travel to Collections grantee NEH, summer 1993, others. Mem. MLA. Democrat. Roman Catholic. Avocation; music. Home: 1102 Graybar Ln Nashville TN 37204 Office: Vanderbilt Univ Dept Spanish & Portuguese Box 1617B Nashville TN 37235

MAURER, DAVID L., lawyer; b. Evansville, Ind., Oct. 31, 1945; s. John G. Jr. and Mildred M. (Lintzenich) M.; m. Diane M. Kaput, Aug. 11, 1973; children: Eric W., Kathryn A. BA magna cum laude, U. Detroit, 1967, Cert. in Teaching, 1971; JD, Wayne State U., 1975. Bar: Mich., U.S. Dist. Ct. (ea. and we. dist.) Mich., U.S. Ct. Appeals (6th cir.) Cin. Law clk. Mich. Ct. Appeals, Detroit, 1976, Supreme Ct. Mich., Lansing, 1977-78; asst. U.S. atty. civil div. U.S. Dept. Justice, Detroit, 1978-81; assoc. to ptnr. Butzel, Long, Gust, Klein & Van Zile, Detroit, 1981-85; ptnr. Pepper, Hamilton & Scheetz, Detroit, 1986—; guest lectr. Practicing Law Inst., 1988—, Nat. Bus. Inst., 1989—, U. Mich. Law Sch., U. Detroit Law Sch., 1990, Hazardous Waste Super Conf., 1986-87. Co-author: Michigan Environmental Law Deskbook, 1992; contbr. articles to profl. jours. and chpts. in books. Mem. Energy & Environ. Policy Com., 1988—, chairperson, 1989-90; mem. Great Lakes Water Resources Commn., 1986. Mem. State Bar Mich. (environ. couns. 1986-91, sec., treas., chairperson-elect, chairperson 1991-93). Office: Pepper Hamilton & Scheetz 100 Renaissance Ctr Ste 3600 Detroit MI 48243-1101

MAURER, GERNANT ELMER, metallurgical executive, consultant; b. Sayre, Pa., May 5, 1949; s. Elmer L. and Joyce F. (Fox) M.; m. Suzanne Walker Berry, Aug. 19, 1972. BES, Johns Hopkins U., 1971; PhD, Rensselear Poly. Inst., 1976. Materials engr. Spl. Metals Corp., New Hartford, N.Y., 1976-80, mgr. R & D, 1981-84, dir. R & D, 1985-87, v.p. tech., 1987—; founding v.p. Splty. Metals Processing Consortium, pres., 1992-93; chmn. Internat. Symposium on Superalloys, 1984-88; mem. adv. com. for materials engring. Wash. State U., 1993—. Co-editor: Superalloys, 1980, 2d edit., 1988; contbr. tech. papers to profl. jours.; inventor various superalloys. Dir. devel. com. Munson William Proctor Inst., Utica, N.Y., 1988-89. Fellow Am. Soc. for Metals (trustee 1992-95); mem. The Metall. Soc., Am. Vacuum Soc. (bd. dirs. metall. div. 1988), Utica Area C. of C. (bd. dirs. 1986-89), Wash. State U. (adv. materials engring. adv. bd. 1993—), Yahnundasis Club. Avocations: golf, fly fishing, art, photography, metal working. Home: 27 Sherman Cir Utica NY 13501-5808 Office: Spl Metals Corp Middle Settlement Rd New Hartford NY 13413

MAURER, GILBERT CHARLES, media company executive; b. N.Y.C., May 24, 1928; s. Charles and Mildred (Petite) M.; m. Ann D'Espinosa. A.B., St. Lawrence U., 1950; M.B.A., Harvard U., 1952. With Cowles Communications, Inc., N.Y.C., 1952-71, Look Mag., 1952-62; pub. Venture mag., 1963-67; pres. Family Circle mag., 1967-69, v.p., dir. corporate planning, exec. com., 1969-71, also dir.; sr. v.p., dir. F.A.S. Internat., Inc., 1971-73; v.p. mag. div. Hearst Corp., 1973-74, exec. v.p., 1974-76, pres. mag. div., 1976-90, also dir.; exec. v.p. The Hearst Corp., 1985—, chief operating officer, 1990—. Mem. N.Y. adv. bd. Salvation Army, 1979—; trustee Whitney Mus. Am. Art, 11983—, pres., 1994—; mem. vis. com. Medill Sch. Journalism Northwestern U., 1985-94, chmn., 1989-94; bd. dirs. Boys and Girls Club Am., 1986—; mem. bd. mgrs. N.Y. Bot. Garden, 1989. Mem. Mag. Pubs. Assn. (bd. dirs., chmn. 1979-81). Clubs: Harvard (N.Y.C.), Metropolitan (N.Y.C.). Office: The Hearst Corp 959 8th Ave New York NY 10019-3767

MAURER, HAROLD MAURICE, pediatrician; b. N.Y.C., Sept. 10, 1936; s. Isador and Sarah (Rothkowitz) M.; m. Beverly Bennett, June 12, 1960; children: Ann Louise, Wendy Sue. A.B., N.Y. U., 1957; M.D., SUNY, Bklyn., 1961. Diplomate Am. Bd. Pediatrics, Am. Bd. Pediatric Hematology-Oncology. Intern pediatrics Kings County Hosp., N.Y.C., 1961-62; resident in pediatrics Babies Hosp., Columbia-Presbyn. Med. Center, N.Y.C., 1962-64; fellow in pediatric hematology/oncology Columbia-Presbyn. Med. Center, 1966-68; asst. prof. pediatrics Med. Coll. Va., Richmond, 1968-71; asso. prof. Med. Coll. Va., 1971-75, prof., 1975—, chmn. dept. pediatrics, 1976-93; dean U. Neb. Coll. Medicine, Omaha, 1993—; chmn. Intergroup Rhabdomyosarcoma Study; exec. com. Pediatric Oncology Group; mem. cancer clin. investigation rev. com. NIH. Editor: pediatrics, 1983, Rhabdomyosarcoma and Related Tumors in Children and Adolescence, 1991; mem. editorial bd. Am. Jour. Hematology, Journal Pediatric Hematology and Oncology, Medical and Pediatric Oncology, 1984—; contbr. articles to profl. jours. Mem. Youth Health Task Force, City of Richmond., Gov.'s Adv. Com. on Handicapped.; mem. nat. com. on childhood cancer Am. Cancer Soc., bd. dirs. Va. div. Served to lt. comdr. USPHS, 1964-66. NIH grantee, 1974—. Mem. Am. Acad. Pediatrics (com. oncology-hematology), Am. Soc. Hematology, Soc. Pediatric Rsch., Am. Pediatric Soc., Va. Pediatric Sic. (exec. com.), Assn. Med. Sch. Pediatric Dept. Chmn., Internat. Soc. Pediatric Oncology, Am. Soc. Clin. Oncology, Va. Hematology Soc., Am. Assn. Cancer Rsch., Am. Cancer Soc., Am. Soc. Pediatric Hematology (v.p. 1990-91, pres. 1991-93), Sigma Xi, Coun. Deans AAMC, Gov.'s Blue Ribbon Commn., Alpha Omega Alpha. Republican. Jewish. Home: 9822 Ascot Dr Omaha NE 68114-3848 Office: U Neb Coll Medicine 600 S 42nd St Omaha NE 68105-1002

MAURER, JEFFREY STUART, finance executive; b. N.Y.C., July 9, 1947; s. Herbert and Phoebe Maurer; m. Wendy S. Newman. BA, Alfred U., 1969; MBA, NYU, 1975; JD, St. John's U., 1976. With U.S. Trust Co. N.Y., 1970—, pres., 1990; COO U.S. Trust Co., N.Y.C., 1994—. Trustee Alfred (N.Y.) U., 1984; mem. adv. bd. Salvation Army Greater N.Y., 1987; bd. dirs., treas. Children's Health Fund, N.Y.C., 1988; bd. dirs. Hebrew Home Aged, Riverdale, N.Y., 1992; mem. Citizens Budget Commn. and Bankers Roundtable. Mem. ABA, N.Y. State Bar Assn., Nassau County Bar Assn., N.Y. State Bankers Assn. (chmn. trust div. 1987-88), Am. Bankers Assn. (chmn. trust div. 1992-93), Glen Head Country Club. Jewish. Avocations: skiing, golf. Office: US Trust Co NY 114 W 47th St New York NY 10036-1510

MAURER, JOHAN FREDRIK, religious denomination administrator; b. Oslo, Mar. 23, 1953; came to U.S., 1957; s. Harald and Erika Elfreide (Schmitz) M.; m. Judith Marshall Van Wyck, Aug. 9, 1980; children: Luke Van Wyck, Eliot Heyerdahl. BA in Russian, Carleton U., Ottawa, Ont., Can., 1976; postgrad., Earlham Coll., 1983—. Asst. dir., dir. Beacon Hill Friends House, Boston, 1977-80; field sec. Friends World Com. for Consultation, Wilmington, Ohio, Richmond, Ind., 1983-93; coord. Right Sharing of World Resources, Wilmington and Richmond, 1986-93; gen. sec. Friends United Meeting, Richmond, 1993—; mem. Europe com. Nat. Coun. Chs., N.Y.C., 1985—; recorded min. Ind. Yearly Meeting of Friends, Muncie, 1989—; mem. U.S. Ch. Leaders, Chgo., 1993—; mem. bd. advisors Earlham Coll. Sch. Religion, Richmond, 1993—; keynote speaker numerous denominational events, 1982—. Editor Quaker Life, 1994—; contbr. numerous articles to religious publs. Mem., mem. steering com. Social Action Ministries Greater Boston, 1978-80; mem. Boston 350 Com., 1979-80; bilingual vol. Jewish Family and Children's Svcs., Boston, 1978-80. Mem. Quaker U.S.-USSR Com., Soc. for Internat. Devel., Bible Assn. Friends, World Hunger Edn. Svc. (assoc.), Richmond Ministerial Assn., Evangs. for Social Action. Avocations: correspondence, computers, reading, walking. Office: Friends United Meeting 101 Quaker Hill Dr Richmond IN 47374-1926

MAURER, LAWRENCE MICHAEL, acting school administrator, educator; b. Bklyn., Oct. 2, 1935; s. Charles and Ethel (Ryan) M.; married Mar. 20, 1970 (div. 1971); 1 child, Lalaine; m. Carol Schneider, July 27, 1971. B of Vocat. Edn., San Diego State U., 1976; MS in Sch. Adminstrn., Nat. U., 1981. Cert. sch. adminstr., tchr., c.c. educator, Calif. Commd. ensign USN, 1953; advanced through grades to chief, 1969, ret., 1972; tchr. San Diego County Office Edn., 1972—, acting vice prin., 1989—; bd. dirs. Multi-cultural Affairs Com., San Diego, 1991—, Self Esteem Devel. C.C., San Diego, 1990—, Vocat. Edn. Commn., San Diego, 1986—; cons. Vocat. Edn. in Ct. Schs., San Diego, 1986—; adj. prof. U. Calif., San Diego. Organizer Dem. party. Named Excellent Tchr. of Yr. Corp. for Excellence in Pub. Edn., 1992; vocat. grantee, 1988. Mem. ASCD (bd. dirs.), Nat. Vocat. Educators, Calif. Reading Assn., Calif. Ct. Sch. Adminstrs. Avocation: civil rights activist. Home: 98-80 Magnolia Ave Santee CA 92071 Office: San Diego County Office Edn 6401 Linda Vista Rd San Diego CA 92111-7319

MAURER, MARC MORGAN, federation administrator, lawyer; b. Des Moines, June 3, 1951; s. Fred V. and June Jeraldine (Davis) M.; m. Patricia Ann Schaaf; children: David Patrick, Dianna Marie. Student, Orientation and Ajdustment Ctr. of Iowa Commn. Blind; grad. cum laude, U. Notre Dame, 1974; JD, U. Ind., 1977. Bar: Ind. 1977, Ohio 1978, Iowa 1978, Md. 1979, U.S. Supreme Ct. 1981. Former auto mechanic; dir. sr. legal assistance project Advocates for Basic Legal Equality, Toledo, Ohio, 1977-78; lawyer rates and routes div. Office of Gen. Counsel CAB, Washington, 1978-81; pvt. practice Balt., 1981—; v.p. Nat. Fedn. of the Blind Ind., 1971, elected pres., 1973, 75, Nat. Fedn. of the Blind Md., 1984-86; pres. Nat. Fedn. of the Blind, 1986—. Bd. dirs. various tenants and community assns. Avocations: oenology, books, barbecue. Office: Nat Fedn Blind 1800 Johnson St Baltimore MD 21230-4940

MAURER, PAUL HERBERT, biochemist, educator; b. N.Y.C., June 29, 1923; s. Joseph and Clara (Vogel) M.; m. Miriam Esther Merdinger, June 27, 1948; children—Susan Gail, David Mark, Philip Mitchell. B.S., City Coll. N.Y., 1944; Ph.D., Columbia, 1950. Research biochemist Gen. Foods Corp., Hoboken, N.J., 1944-46; instr. City Coll., N.Y., 1946-51; research asso. Coll. Phys. and Surg., Columbia, 1950-51; asst. research prof. Sch. Medicine, U. Pitts., 1951-54, asso. prof. immunochemistry, 1954-60; asso. prof. microbiology Seton Hall Coll. Medicine, 1960-62; prof. microbiology N.J. Coll. Medicine, 1962-66; prof., chmn. dept. biochemistry Jefferson Med. Coll., Phila., 1966-93, prof. pathology, biochemistry and molecular biology emeritus, 1993—; mem. allergy and infectious diseases tng. grant com. NIH, 1961-66; mem. commn. on albumin Protein Fedn.; mem. NRC com. on plasma; chmn. Transplantation Biology and Immunology Com. NIAID, 1986—. Asso. editor: Immunochemistry, 1964, Science, 1966; Contbr. profl. jours. Served with USNR 1946-48. Recipient Research Career award Nat. Inst. Allergy and Infectious Diseases, 1962-66, Chemistry medal City Coll. N.Y., 1944. Mem. Am. Chem. Soc., N.Y. Acad. Scis., Biochem. Soc. (London), Harvey Soc., Am. Assn. Immunologists, Am. Soc. Biol. Chemistry, AAAS, Societe de Chimie Biologique (France), Soc. Exptl. Biology and Medicine, Sigma Xi. Home: 8470 Limekiln Pike Apt B517 Wyncote PA 19095-2712 Office: Jefferson Med Coll Dept Pathology 1020 Locust St Philadelphia PA 19107-6731

MAURER, RICHARD MICHAEL, investment company executive; b. Bethlehem, Pa., June 4, 1948; s. Richard Thomas and Anna Theresa (Bold) M.; m. Karen Coe, June 13, 1970; children: Christopher Coe, Mark Emerson. Student, Pa. State U., 1966-68; BS, Point Park Coll., 1971; MBA, U. Pitts., 1982. CPA Pa. Staff acct. Price Waterhouse, Pitts., 1972-74, tac acct., 1974, sr. tax acct., 1974-77, tax mgr., 1977-78; dir. taxes The Hillman Co., Pitts., 1978-85; pres. Maurer Ross & Co., Inc., Pitts., 1985—; co-mng. ptnr. Wesmar Ptnrs,, Pitts., 1985—; bd. dirs. Gateway Additive Co., Inc., Pitt Penn Oil Co., Pitt Penn Distbn. Co., Springdale Splty. Plastics, Inc., M & R Distbn. Co., Am. Home Improvement Products, Inc., S2 Golf Inc., Maurer Ross & Co., Inc., Maurer & Ross, Inc. With U.S. Army, 1970-76. Mem. AICPA, Assn. Corp. Growth, Pa. Inst. CPAs, Rotary (past dir., past pres.), Oakmont Country Club, Duquesne Club, Lake Nona Golf Club, Rivers Club. Office: Three Gateway Ctr Pittsburgh PA 15222

MAURER, ROBERT DISTLER, retired industrial physicist; b. St. Louis, July 20, 1924; s. John and Elizabeth J. (Distler) M.; m. Barbara A. Mansfield, June 9, 1951; children: Robert M., James B., Janet L. B.S., U. Ark., 1948, LL.D., 1980; Ph.D., MIT, 1951. Mem. staff MIT, 1951-52; with Corning Glass Works, N.Y., 1952-89; mgr. physics research Corning Glass Works, 1963-78, research fellow, 1978-89. Contbr. articles to profl. jours., chpts. to books. Served with U.S. Army, 1943-46. Recipient Indsl. Physics prize Am. Inst. Physics, 1978, L.M. Ericsson Internat. prize in telecommunications, 1979, Indsl. Rsch. Inst. Achievement award, 1988, Optical Soc. Am./IEEE Leos Tyndall award, 1987, Disting. Alumni award U. Ark, 1994, Am. Innovator award U.S. Dept. Commerce, 1995. Fellow IEEE (Moris N. Liebmann award 1978), Am. Ceramic Soc. (George W. Morey award 1976); mem. NAE, Am. Phys. Soc. (New Materials prize 1989), Nat. Inventors Hall of Fame. Patentee in field. Home: 6 Roche Dr Painted Post NY 14870-1225 Office: Corning Inc Sullivan Park Corning NY 14830

MAURICE, DON, personal care industry executive; b. Peoria, Ill., Aug. 29, 1932; s. Imajean (Webster) Crayton; m. Cindalu Jackson, Aug. 31, 1990. Student, Loma Linda U., 1984-86; cert. paralegal studies, Calif. State U., San Bernardino, 1994. Lic. hair stylist, skin therapist; cert. paralegal, notary pub. Owner 2 schs. in advanced hair designs, San Diego, 1962-64, D & M Enterprises, Advt. Agy., 1964-78; now cons. D&M Enterprises Advt. Agy.; dist. mgr. AqRo Matic Co. Water Purification Systems, San Diego, 1972-75; profl. sales educator Staypower Industries, San Diego, 1972-76, 3d v.p., 1975-76; regional bus. cons. Estheticians Pharmacology Rsch., Garden Grove, Calif., 1975-81; owner, operator Don Maurice Hair Designs, Hemet, Calif., 1980-83; dir., operator Hair Sytles by Maurice, Loma Linda, Calif., 1984-88; owner, pres. Grooming Dynamics, Redlands, Calif., 1988—; bus. cons. Yogurt Place, Paradise Valley, Ariz., 1978-79, others; regular guest Channel 6/Channel 8, San Diego, 1968-78; cons. infomercial Pre-Paid Legal Svcs., Inc., 1994—. Author: The New Look For Men, 1967, The Art of Men's Hair Styling, 1968 (accepted by Library of Congress), Baldness, To Be or Not To Be, 1989. Promoter Spl. Olympics, Hemet, 1981. Sgt. U.S. Army, 1950-53, Korea. Decorated Purple Heart, 1952; named Leading Businessman in His Profession, Union and Evening Tribune, 1969. Mem. Internat. Platform Assn., Christian Businessmen's Assn. Avocations: writing, sculpting, art, sports, music. Office: Grooming Dynamics PO Box 1279 Loma Linda CA 92354-1279

MAURO, RICHARD FRANK, lawyer, investment manager; b. Hawthorne, Nev., July 21, 1945; s. Frank Joseph and Dolores D. (Kreimeyer) M.; m. LaVonne M. Madden, Aug. 28, 1965; 1 child, Lindsay Anne. AB, Brown U., 1967; JD summa cum laude, U. Denver, 1970. Bar: Colo. 1970. Assoc. Dawson, Nagel, Sherman & Howard, Denver, 1970-72; assoc. Van Cise, Freeman, Tooley & McClearn, Denver, 1972-73, ptnr., 1973-74; ptnr. Hall & Evans, Denver, 1974-81, Morrison & Forester, Denver, 1981-84; of counsel Parcel, Mauro, Hultin & Spaanstra, P.C., Denver, 1984—, pres., 1988-90, of counsel, 1992—; pres. Sundance Oil Exploration Co., 1985-88; exec. v.p. Castle Group, Inc., 1992—; adj. prof. U. Denver Coll. Law, 1981-84. Symposium editor: Denver Law Jour., 1969-70; editor: Colorado Corporation Manual; contbr. articles to legal jours. Pres. Colo. Open Space Coun., 1974; mem. law alumni coun. U. Denver Coll. Law, 1988-91. Francis Wayland scholar, 1967; recipient various Am. jurisprudence awards. Mem. ABA, Colo. Bar Assn., Denver Bar Assn., Colo. Assn. Corp. Counsel. (pres. 1974-75), Am. Arbitration Assn. (comml. arbitrator), Order St. Ives, Denver Athletic Club (bd. dirs. 1986-89). Home: 2552 E Alameda Ave No 128 Denver CO 80209-3320 Office: 475 17th St Ste 750 Denver CO 80202-4017

MAUS, RODGER, film production designer. Films include 10, 1979, Herbie Goes Bananas, 1980, S.O.B., 1981, Victor/Victoria, 1982, Trench Coat, 1983, The Man Who Loved Women, 1983, The Buddy System, 1984, Micki & Maude, 1984, A Fine Mess, 1986, Blind Date, 1987, Spellbinder, 1988, Sunset, 1988, Skin Deep, 1989, Switch, 1991; TV films include Fire! Trapped on the 37th Floor, 1991, Scarlett, 1994 (Emmy award for outstanding individual achievement in art direction for a miniseries of spl.). Office: Paul Gerard Agy care Steve England 4254 Bellingham Ave Studio City CA 91604

MAUSEL, PAUL WARNER, geography educator; b. Mpls., Jan. 2, 1936; s. Paul George and Esther Victoria (Sundstrom) M.; m. Jean Frances Kias, July 2, 1966; children: Paul Brandon, Catherine Suzanne, Justin Thomas. BA in Chemistry and Geography, U. Minn., 1958, MA in Geography, 1961; PhD, U. N.C., 1966. Asst. prof. geography Eastern Ill. U., Charleston, 1965-70, assoc. prof., 1970-71; assoc. prof. geography Ind. State U., Terre Haute, 1971-75, prof., 1975—, dir. Remote Sensing Lab., 1975-89, Geog. Inf. Systems, 1989—; rsch. geographer Lab. Applications of Remote Sensing Purdue U., West Lafayette, Ind., 1972-73; soils geographer cons. U. Mo. at Columbia, summer 1974; lectr. in field; grants, contracts with EPA, NSF, Nat. Park Svc., Dept. Energy, Stnnis Space Ctr./ITD, Oak Ridge Nat. Lab., U.S. Forest Svc., NASA, USDA, USFWS, The Nature Conservancy. Contbr. articles to profl. jours., Chpts. to textbooks. NSF fellow, 1978; recipient research award Ind. State U., 1983. Mem. Assn. Am. Geographers, Am. Soc. Photogrammetry and Remote Sensing (Meritorious Svc. award 1988, 96). Home: 7400 E Old Maple Ave Terre Haute IN 47803-9627

MAUSKOPF, SEYMOUR HAROLD, history educator; b. Cleve., Nov. 11, 1938; s. Philip and Dora (Trompeter) M.; m. Josephine Mary Album, Aug. 9, 1964; children: Deborah, Philip, Alice. A.B., Cornell U., 1960; Ph.D., Princeton U., 1966. Instr. history Duke U., Durham, N.C., 1964-66, asst. prof., 1966-72, assoc. prof., 1972-80, prof., 1980—, dir. program in sci. tech. and human values, 1979-84. Author: Crystals and Compounds, Molecular Structure and Composition in Nineteenth Century French Science, 1976, (with M.R. McVaugh) The Elusive Science; Origins of Experimental Physical Research, 1915-1940, 1980; editor: The Reception of Unconventional Science by the Scientific Community, 1979, Chemical Sciences in th e Modern World, 1993. NSF postdoctoral fellow, 1971-72; NSF grantee, 1974, 92-93; Am. Philos. Soc. travel grantee, 1979; Nat. Endowment for Humanities summer stipend, 1982; Edelstein internat. fellow in history chem. scis. and tech. Beckman Ctr. U. Pa. and Hebrew Univ., Jerusalem, 1988-89. Mem. History Sci. Soc. (exec. com. treas. 1979-83, coun. 1993-95). Jewish. Office: Duke U PO Box 90719 Bldg Durham NC 27708-0719

MAUTZ, EDWARD JOHN, professor, public information officer; b. Inglewood, Calif., Aug. 21, 1942; s. Ferdinand Ludwig and Myrtle Margaret (Gillaspie) M.; m. Donna June Kunz, Feb. 2, 1963; children: Felicia Lucette, Edward John II. BA in Pub. Svc. Mgmt., U. Redlands, 1978; MPA, U. San Francisco, 1982; D of Pub. Adminstrn., U. La Verne, 1995. Sgt. L.A. Police Dept., L.A., 1968-93; assoc. dept. Pub. Adminstrn. U. La Verne (Calif.), 1989—; instr. El Camino C.C., Torrance, Calif., 1981-91, L.A. Trade Tech. Coll., 1985-92; lectr. El Camino Coll., 1981-91, L.A. Trade Tech. Coll., 1985-92, U. La Verne, 1989—. Scout master, asst. scout master Boy Scouts Am., L.A., 1977—. Mem. Acad. Criminal Justice Sci., Assn. Pub. Policy and Mgmt., Acad. Polit. Sci., Am. Soc. Law Enforcement Trainers, Am. Soc. Pub. Adminstrs., Internat. City Mgrs. Assn., Internat. Soc. for Gen. Semantics, The Inst. of Mgmt. Sci., Operation Rescue Soc. Am., West & Pacific Assn. Criminal Justice Edn. Republican. Avocations: backpacking, bicycling, traveling. Office: U La Verne 2220 3rd St La Verne CA 91750-4917

MAUTZ, KARL EMERSON, engineering executive; b. Columbia, Mo., Sept. 30, 1957; s. Wayne Albert Mautz and Imogene (Embrey) Whitten; m. Pamela Dawn Quillen, Mar. 12, 1988; children: Alyssa Mae, Brandon Tyler. BS in Chemistry, U. Tex., El Paso, 1979, BS in Geology, 1983; MS in Chemistry, Ariz. State U., 1985, PhD, 1987. Process engr. Motorola, Inc., Mesa, Ariz., 1980-87; mem. tech. staff Motorola, Inc., Austin, Tex., 1988—; cons. Motif, Inc., Portland, Oreg., 1994. Contbr. articles to profl. jours. Mem. recycling com. Homeowners Assn., Austin, 1992. Mem. Electrochem. Soc., Am. Chem. Soc. Achievements include patents for semiconductor processes; two patents pending. Office: Motorola Inc 1 Tex Ctr Ste 1050 505 Barton Springs Rd Austin TX 78704

MAUTZ, ROBERT BARBEAU, lawyer, educator; b. Marion, Ohio, Jan. 22, 1915; s. Albert Edward and Bessie (Barbeau) M.; m. Esther Guthery, Feb. 22, 1947 (dec. Sept. 1993). BA, Miami U., Oxford, Ohio, 1937; JD, Yale U., 1940; postgrad., 1949-50; hon. degrees, U. Miami, U. Fla., Miami U., Oxford U., Jacksonville U., Fla. Inst. Tech., U. South Fla., Flagler Coll. Bar: N.Y. 1941. Assoc. Root, Clark, Buckner & Ballantine, N.Y.C., 1940-41; atty. Pan Am. Airways, Brit. W. Africa, 1941-42; exec. officer legal div. Office Mil. Govt., Berlin, 1945-48; dep. legal dir. Hesse, 1948-49; prof. law, asst. dean U. Fla., Gainesville, 1950-58, dean acad. affairs, 1958-63, v.p. acad. affairs, 1963-68; chancellor State Univ. System of Fla., 1968-75; Regent's prof., dir. Inst. Learned Scholars, Gainesville, 1975-80; spl. advisor for higher edn. Fla. Commr. of Edn., 1981-83; mem. Post-Secondary Edn. Planning Commn. of Fla., 1983—. Author legal and other articles. Former commr. Edn. Commn. of States; mem. exec. bd. So. Regional Edn. Bd.; bd. dirs. Am. Coll. Testing Program, Nat. Ctr. for Higher Edn. Mgmt. Systems; adv. coun. Nat. Ctr. for Edn. Stats, Def. Systems Mgmt. Coll.; exec. com. Yale Law Sch. Served to col. USAAF, 1942-45; maj. gen. USAF, ret. Decorated D.S.M.; chevalier Swedish Royal Order North Star; Star of Yugoslavia with gold wreaths; named Man of Yr. by several orgns. Mem. Phi Beta Kappa, Beta Theta Pi, Omicron Delta Kappa, Phi Alpha Delta, Order of Coif. Home: 5027 SW 9th Ln Gainesville FL 32607-3869 Office: U Fla 401 Seagle Bldg Gainesville FL 32611

MAUZ, HENRY HERRWARD, JR., retired naval officer; b. Lynchburg, Va., May 4, 1936; s. Henry Herrward and Rene C. (Ball) M.; m. Margaret Catherine O'Neill, June 6, 1959; children: Sheila, David, Lynn, Daniel. BS, U.S. Naval Acad., 1959; BSEE, U.S. Naval Postgrad. Sch., 1965; MBA, Auburn U., 1970. Commd. ensign USN, 1959, advanced through grades to adm., 1992, various ships and shore duty assignments, 1977-80; strategy and concepts officer Office of Chief Naval Ops. Washington, 1980-82; comdg. officer USS England, San Diego, 1980-82, chief of staff Carrier Group One, 1982-83; ops./readiness officer SHAPE Belgium, 1983-85; comdr. Cruiser/Destroyer Group 12 Mayport, Fla., 1985-86; ops./plans officer to comdr. in chief Pacific Fleet, Pearl Harbor, Hawaii, 1986-88; comdr. Seventh Fleet Yokosuka, Japan, 1988-90; dep. chief Office Naval Ops., Washington, 1991-92; comdr. in chief U.S. Atlantic Fleet, 1992-94; ret. USN, 1994. Decorated D.S.M. with four gold stars, Def. Superior Svc. medal, Legion of Merit, Bronze Star with combat V device. Mem. U.S. Naval Inst., U.S. Naval War Coll. Found., Naval Hist. Found., Monterey Peninsula Country Club, Army-Navy Country Club. Avocations: golfing, skiing. Home: 1608 Viscaino Rd Pebble Beach CA 93953

MAUZERALL, DAVID CHARLES, biophysics educator, research scientist; b. Sanford, Maine, July 22, 1929; s. David James and Jeannette (Morin) M.; m. Miriam I. Jacob, July 31, 1959; children—Denise, Michele. B.S., St. Michael's Coll., 1951; Ph.D. (NSF fellow), U. Chgo., 1954. Mem. faculty Rockefeller U., N.Y.C., 1954-65, 67-69, 69—; prof. biophysics Rockefeller U.; vis. assoc. prof. U. Calif.-San Diego, 1966, now adj. prof. Guggenheim fellow, 1966. Mem. Am. Soc. Biol. Chemists, Biophys. Soc., Am. Chem. Soc. Home: 36 Belden Ave Dobbs Ferry NY 10522-1102 Office: Rockefeller U 1230 York Ave New York NY 10021-6307

MAUZY, MICHAEL PHILIP, environmental consultant, chemical engineer; b. Keyser, W.Va., Nov. 14, 1928; s. Frank and Margery Ola (Nelson) M.; m. Nancy Shepherd Watson, Mar. 27, 1949; children: Michael P. Jr., Jeffrey A., Rebecca A. BSChemE, Va. Poly. Inst., 1950; MSChemE, U. Tenn., 1951. Registered profl. engr., Va., Ill. With Monsanto Co., St. Louis, 1951-71, dir. engring. and mfg., 1968-71; mgr. coml. devel. Kummer Corp., Creve Coeur, Mo., 1971-72; mgr. labs. Ill. EPA, Springfield, 1972-73, mgr. water pollution control, 1973-74, mgr. environ. programs, 1974-77, dir., 1977-81; v.p. Roy F. Weston, Inc., West Chester, Pa., 1981-88, Vernon Hills, Ill., 1988-93, Albuquerque, 1993—; also bd. dirs. Roy F. Weston, Inc., West Chester, Pa.; bd. dirs. DeTox Internat. Corp., St. Charles, Ill.; provider Congl. testimony, 1974-81; presenter various workshops, symposia and seminars, 1974—. Contbr. articles on environ. mgmt. to profl. publs., 1974—. Mem. Ohio River Valley Water Sanitary Commn., Cin., 1976-81. 1st lt. U.S. Army, 1951-53. Recipient Environ. Quality award Region V, U.S. EPA, Chgo., 1976, Disting. Svc. award Cons. Engrs. Coun. of Ill., 1978, Ill. award Ill. Assn. Sanitary Dists., 1979, Clarence W. Klassen award Ill. Assn. Water Pollution Control Ops., 1984. Mem. Am. Pub. Works Assn., Am. Inst. Chem. Engring., Water Pollution Control Assn., Am. Mgmt. Assn. Avocations: reading, travel, home improvements.

MAUZY, OSCAR HOLCOMBE, lawyer, retired state supreme court justice; b. Houston, Nov. 9, 1926; s. Harry Lincoln and Mildred Eva (Kincaid) M.; m. Anne Rogers; children: Catherine Anne, Charles Fred, James Stephen. BBA, U. Tex., 1950, JD, 1952. Bar: Tex. 1951. Practiced in Dallas, 1952-87; pres. Mullinax, Wells, Mauzy & Baab, Inc. (P.C.), 1970-78; mem. Tex. Senate from 23d Dist., 1967-87, chmn. edn. com., 1971-81, chmn. jurisprudence com., 1981-87, pres. pro tempore, 1973; justice Tex. Supreme Ct., 1987-93; pvt. practice Austin, 1993—; Mem. Tex. Adv. Commn. Intergovtl. Relations, Nat. Conf. State Legislators, Edn. Commn. of the States,

Am. Edn. Finance Assn., 1971-87. Vice chmn. judiciary com. Tex. Constl. Conv., 1974; nat. committeeman Young Democrats, 1954. Served with USNR, 1944-46. Home: 5000 Crestway Dr Austin TX 78731-5404

MAVES, MICHAEL DONALD, medical association executive; b. East St. Louis, Ill., Oct. 14, 1948. BS, U. Toledo, 1970; MD, Ohio State U., 1973; MBA, U. Iowa, 1988. Lic. physician, Iowa, Mo., Ill., D.C.; diplomate Am. Bd. Otolaryngology. Rsch. fellow Ohio State U. Coll. Medicine, Columbus, 1977; fellow head and neck surgery Columbia-Presbyn. Med. Ctr., N.Y.C., 1978, U. Iowa Hosps. and Clinics, Iowa City, 1980-81; asst. prof. otolaryngology, head and neck surgery Ind. U. Sch. Medicine, Indpls., 1981-84; asst. prof. otolaryngology, head and neck surgery U. Iowa Hosps. and Clinics, Iowa City, 1984-87, assoc. prof., 1987-88; chmn. dept. otolaryngology St. Louis U. Sch. Medicine, St. Louis, 1988-94; exec. v.p. Am. Acad. Otolaryngology, Head and Neck Surgery, Alexandria, Va., 1994—; lectr. in field. Contbr. articles to profl. jours. Capt. U.S. Army, 1974-76. Recipient numerous awards including Honor award and Pres.'s award Am. Acad. Otolaryngology-Head and Neck Surgery; named one of Best 1000 Physicians in U.S., 1992, 94, One of Best 400 Cancer Doctors in Am., Good Housekeeping, 1992. Fellow ACS; mem. AMA (RBRVS update com.), Am. Cancer Soc., Am. Dermatologic Soc., Mo. Med. Assn., others. Office: Am Acad Otolaryngology One Prince St Alexandria VA 22314

MAWARDI, OSMAN KAMEL, plasma physicist; b. Cairo, Dec. 12, 1917; came to U.S., 1946, naturalized, 1952; s. Kamel Ibrahim and Marie (Wienig) M.; m. Betty Louise Hosmer, Nov. 23, 1950. B.S., Cairo U., 1940, M.S., 1945; A.M., Harvard U., 1947, Ph.D., 1948. Lectr. physics Cairo U., 1940-45; asst. prof. Mass Inst. Tech., 1951-56, asso. prof., 1956-60; prof. engring., dir. plasma research program Case Inst. Tech., Cleve., 1960-88; dir. Energy Research Office, Case Western Res. U., 1977-82; pres. Collaborative Planners, Inc.; mem. Inst. Advanced Study, 1969-70; also cons. Contbr. articles to profl. jours. Trustee Print Club Cleve., Cleve. Inst. Art. Recipient Biennial award Acoustical Soc. Am., 1952; CECON medal of achievement, 1979. Fellow AAAS, Acoustical Soc. Am., Am. Phys. Soc., IEEE (Edison lectr. 1968-69, Centennial award 1984, Cleve. sect. Engr. of Yr. 1994); mem. N.Y. Acad. Scis., Sigma Xi, Eta Kappa Nu. Home: 15 Mornington Ln Cleveland OH 44106 Office: 2490 Lee Rd Cleveland OH 44118-4125 *I never cease to be amazed that the goals I really believe in invariably materialize.*

MAWBY, RUSSELL GEORGE, retired foundation executive; b. Grand Rapids, Mich., Feb. 23, 1928; s. Wesley G. and Ruby (Finch) M.; m. Ruth E. Edison, Dec. 16, 1950; children: Douglas, David, Karen. B.S. in Horticulture, Mich. State U., 1949, Ph.D. in Agrl. Econs., 1959, LL.D. (hon.), 1972; M.S. in Agrl. Econs, Purdue U., 1951, D.Agr. (hon.), 1973; L.H.D. (hon.), Luther Coll., Decorah, Iowa, 1972, Alma (Mich.) Coll., 1975, Nazareth Coll., 1976, Madonna Coll., 1983, N.C. Central U., 1986; LL.D. (hon.), N.C. A&T State U., Greensboro, 1974, Tuskegee Inst., 1978, Kalamazoo Coll., 1980; D.P.A. (hon.), Albion Coll., 1976; D.C.L. (hon.), U. Newcastle, Eng., 1977; D.Sc. (hon.), Nat. U. Ireland, 1980; D.Pub. Service (hon.), No. Mich. U., 1981; D.H.L. (hon.), So. Utah State Coll., 1983; HHD (hon.), Grand Valley State U., 1988; ScD (hon.), Calif. State U., 1989; LLD (hon.), Adrian Coll., 1990; LittD (hon.), Olivet Coll., 1991. Ext. specialist Mich. State U., East Lansing, 1952-56; asst. dir. coop. ext. svc. Mich. State U., 1956-65; dir. div. agr. W.K. Kellogg Found., Battle Creek, Mich., 1965-66; mem., trustee W.K. Kellogg Found., 1967—, v.p. programs, 1966-70, pres., 1970-82, chmn., CEO, 1982-95, chmn. emeritus, 1995—; bd. dirs. Detroit br. Fed. Res. Bank Chgo., 1980-85, J.M. Smucker Co., 1983—; fellow Inst. for Children, Youth and Families Mich. State U., 1993; hon. fellow Kellog Coll., U. Oxford, Eng., 1990; mem. chancellor's ct. of benefactors U. Oxford, Eng., 1991. Trustee Arabian Horse Trust, 1978-90 (emeritus 1990—), Starr Commonwealth, 1987— (chmn. bd. trustees 1993-95), Found. Ctr., 1988-94 (chmn. bd. trustees 1989-94), Mich. Non-profit Assn., 1990-94 (chmn. bd. trustees 1990-94, emeritus 1994—), Mich. State U., 1992 (chmn. bd. trustees 1995); bd. dirs. Coun. on Founds., 1978-84, Mich.'s Children, 1995—; mem. Joint Coun. on Food and Agrl. Scis., USDA, 1984-88; mem. Com. on Agrl. Edn. in Secondary Schs., NRC, 1985-88, Gov.'s Task Force on Revitalization of Agr. Through Rsch. and Edn., 1986; mem. rural bus. partnership adv. bd. Mich. Dept. Commerce, 1989-90, Mich. Coop. Ext. Svc. Study Com., 1989; mem. pres.'s adv. coun. Clemson U., 1987-95; mem. policy bd. Calhoun County Cmtys. in Schs., 1995—; mem. Lt. Gov.'s Children's Commn., State of Mich., 1995—; mem. leadership adv. coun. Olivet Coll., 1995—; With AUS, 1953-55. Decorated knight 1st class Royal Order St. Olaf Norway; knight's cross Order of Dannebrog 1st class Denmark; comdr.'s medal Order of Finnish Lion Finland; recipient Disting. Service award U.S. Dept. Agr., 1963, Disting. Alumni award Mich. State U., 1971, Nat. Alumni award 4-H Clubs, 1972, Disting. Eagle Scout award Boy Scouts Am., 1973, Meritorious Achievement award Fla. A&M U., 1973, Nat. Ptnr. in 4-H award Dept. Agr. Ext. Svc., 1976; named hon. fellow Spring Arbor (Mich.) Coll., 1972; recipient Walter F. Patenge medal for pub. service Coll. Osteo. Medicine, Mich. State U., 1977, Disting. Service award Coll. Agr. and Natural Resources, 1980, Seaman A. Knapp Meml. lectr. U.S. Dept. Agr., 1983; recipient George award for cmty. svc. City of Battle Creek, 1986, Disting. Service award Rural Sociol. Soc., 1986, Centennial Alumnus award for Mich. State U. Nat. Assn. State Univs. and Land Grant Colls., 1988, Pres.'s award Clemson U., 1989, Disting. Citizen award Southwest Mich. Coun. Boy Scouts Am., 1989, Disting. Svc. award 1890 Land-Grant Colls. and Univs., 1990, Vol. of Yr. award Clemson U., 1990, Disting. Grantmaker award Coun. on Founds., 1992, Disting. Svc. award Nat. Assn. Homes and Svcs. for Children, 1992, Merit award Nat. Soc. Fund Raising Execs. West Mich. chpt., 1992, Red Rose award Rotary Club of Battle Creek, 1993, George W. Romney award Nat. Soc. Fund Raising Execs. Greater Detroit chpt., 1993, Director's award Arabian Horse Assn. of Mich., 1994, Disting. Svc. award Mich. Hort. Soc., 1994, Michiganian of Yr. The Detroit News, 1995, Gerald G. Hicks Child Welfare Leadership award Mich. Fedn. Private Child and Family Agys., 19 Bradley Humanitarian for Youth award No. Area Assn., Detroit, 1995, award of Honor Am. Hosp. Assn., 1995. Mem. Mich. Soc. Architects (hon.), Am. Agrl. Econ. Assn., Mich. State U. Alumni Assn. (bd. dirs. 1984-88), Alpha Gamma Rho (dir. 1976-82, grand pres. 1980-82, Man of Year Chgo. Alumni chpt. 1976, Hall of Fame 1986), Alpha Zeta, Phi Kappa Phi (Disting. Mem. award Mich. State U. 1978), Epsilon Sigma Phi (certificate of recognition 1974, Nat. Friend of Ext. 1982), Gamma Sigma Delta, Delta Sigma Pi (hon. mem., 1995). Home: 8400 N 39th St Augusta MI 49012-9713 Office: Heritage Tower 25 W Michigan Ave Ste 1701 Battle Creek MI 49017

MAX, CLAIRE ELLEN, physicist; b. Boston, Sept. 29, 1946; d. Louis William and Pearl (Bernstein) M.; m. Jonathan Arons, Dec. 22, 1974; 1 child, Samuel. AB, Harvard U., 1968; PhD, Princeton U., 1972. Postdoctoral researcher U. Calif., Berkeley, 1972-74; physicist Lawrence Livermore (Calif.) Nat. Lab., 1974—; dir. Livermore br. Inst. Geophysics and Planetary Physics, 1984-93; mem. Math.-Sci. Network Mills Coll., Oakland, Calif.; mem. com. on fusion hybrid reactors NRC, 1986, mem. com. on internat. security and arms control NAS, 1986-89, mem. com. on phys. sci., math. and applications NRC, 1991-94, mem. policy and computational astgrophys. panels, astron. and astgrophys. survey NRC, 1989-91. Editor: Particle Acceleration Mechanisms in Astrophysics, 1979; contbr. numerous articles to sci. jours. Fellow AAAS, Am. Phys. Soc. (exec. com. div. plasma physics 1977, 81-82); mem. Am. Astron. Soc. (exec. com. div. high energy astrophysics 1975-76), Am. Geophys. Union, Internat. Astron. Union, Phi Beta Kappa, Sigma Xi. Rsch. interests include adaptive optics and laser guide stars for astronomy; astrophys. plasmas. Avocations: violin, skiing. Office: Lawrence Livermore Nat Lab PO Box 808 7000 East Ave L-413 Livermore CA 94550-9900

MAX, HERBERT B., lawyer; b. Newark, May 24, 1931; children: Adam, Eric, Daniel. BA, Columbia U., 1952, LLB, 1954. Bar: N.Y. 1958. Assoc. Delson & Gordon, N.Y.C., 1959-65; pvt. practice N.Y.C., 1965-85; ptnr. Mayer, Brown & Platt, N.Y.C., 1985-89; of counsel Spengler, Carlson, N.Y.C., 1989-92, Reid & Priest, N.Y.C., 1992—. Author: Raising Capital: Private Placement Forms and Techniques, 2nd edit. 1987; assoc. editor N.Y. State Legislative Annual, 1958-59. With USN, 1955-57. Mem. ABA, N.Y. State Bar Assn., Assn. of Bar of City of N.Y. Office: Reid & Priest 40 W 57th St New York NY 10019-4001

MAX, THEODORE CONRAD, surgeon; b. Langhorne, Pa., Apr. 29, 1929; s. Theodore Louis and Marian (Smith) M.; m. Melva Sholenberg, June 17, 1950; children: Christopher, Steven, Melva, Theodore, Erica. BS, Hobart Coll., 1950; MD, U. Rochester, 1954. Diplomate Am. Bd. Surgery. Resident in surgery Strong Meml. Hosp., Rochester, N.Y., 1954-60; instr. surgery U. Rochester Sch. Medicine, 1961-63; pvt. practice gen. and vascular surgery Utica, N.Y., 1963—; chief surgery, pres. med. staff St. Luke's Meml. Hosp., Utica; chief surgery, pres. med. staff St. Elizabeth Hosp., Utica, dir. surgery family practice residency program, 1976—; mem. bd. profl. conduct N.Y. State Dept. Health, 1978-86; dir. Med. Liability Ins. Co., N.Y.C., 1986—. Dir., chpt. pres. Am. Heart. Assn., 1976-78. Capt. USAF, 1957-59. Fellow Am. Coll. Surgeons (pres. chpt. 1977-78, gov. 1982-88); mem. N.Y. Soc. Surgeons (pres. 1974-76), Med. Soc. State of N.Y. (del. for surgery 1974-94). Home: 238 W Main St Holland Patent NY 13354 Office: 2206 Genesee St Utica NY 13502-5829

MAXA, RUDOLPH JOSEPH, JR., journalist; b. Cleve., Sept. 25, 1949; s. Rudolph Joseph and Christine Marie (Kimpel) M.; m. Kathleen Ann Zolciak, June 19, 1971 (div. 1988); children: Sarah Lynn, Alexander. BS in Journalism cum laude, Ohio U., 1971. Reporter Washington Post, 1971-82; sr. writer The Washingtonian, 1983-92; daily commentator Cable News Network, 1980-82; chief Washington bur. Spy mag., 1992-94; talk show host Sta. WRC; lectr. on journalism; travel commentator Pub. Radio Internat. marketplace, 1990—; columnist Ocean Drive mag., 1993—. Contbg. editor Worth Mag., 1995—. Recipient John Hancock award for excellence in bus. and fin. writing, 1972, writing excellence 1st place award for best regular column Fla. Mag. Assn., 1995. Office: 1746 N St NW Washington DC 20036-2907

MAXEINER, CLARENCE WILLIAM, lawyer, construction company executive; b. Sioux City, Iowa, Mar. 24, 1914; s. Frank A. and Dora A. (Olson) M.; m. Julie Frazer, Sept. 8, 1937; children: Martha Ann, Jay Frank, Mary Katherine, Nancy Carol; m. Rosalie F. Steele, May 29, 1974. Student, Columbia Coll., 1933-34, Columbia U. Law Sch., 1938-39; A.B., Grinnell Coll., 1936; J.D., U. Calif.-Berkeley, 1941. Bar: Calif. 1941. Ptnr. Thelen, Marrin, Johnson & Bridges, San Francisco and Los Angeles, 1941-60; sr. v.p., gen. counsel, dir. J.H. Pomeroy & Co., Inc. (and affiliated cos.), San Francisco, 1959-65; v.p., gen. counsel Dillingham Corp. (and affiliated cos.), Honolulu, 1966—; sr. v.p., gen. counsel, sec., dir., mem. exec. com. Dillingham Corp. (and affiliated cos.), 1968-71, spl. counsel, 1971—. Chmn. equipment fund com. Sonoma State Hosp., 1956-65; bd. overseers Grinnell Coll., 1964; bd. dirs. Del Monte Forest Found., Calif. Autism Found. Mem. ABA, San Francisco Bar Assn., State Bar Calif., Am. Judicature Soc., Hawaii State Bar (assoc.), Columbia, U. Calif. law schs. assns., Phi Beta Kappa, Phi Delta Phi. Congregationalist. Clubs: Commonwealth of Calif. (San Francisco), The Family (San Francisco). Home: 4071 Sunset Ln Pebble Beach CA 93953-3049

MAXEY, DAVID WALKER, lawyer; b. Scranton, Pa., May 17, 1934; s. Paul Harold and Margaret (Walker) M.; m. Catharine Eglin, June 6, 1968; children: Paul Eglin, Margaret Wilson. AB, Harvard U., 1956, LLB cum laude, 1960. Bar: Pa. 1961, U. S. Dist. Ct. (ea. dist.) Pa. 1961, U.S. Ct. Appeals (3d cir.) 1963. Assoc. Drinker Biddle and Reath, Phila., 1960-66, ptnr., 1967—, chmn. real estate dept., 1970-88, mng. ptnr., 1977-91, co-chmn., 1988-91; bd. dirs. Ikea Property, Inc., Plymouth Meeting, Pa.; vis. faculty mem. Villanova (Pa.) U. Law Sch., 1987—. Contbr. articles to profl. jours. Sec., bd. dirs. Greater Phila. Internat. Network, 1981-94; bd. dirs. Young Audiences Ea. Pa., Phila., 1985—, Libr. Co., Phila., 1993—; chmn. bd. dirs. Hist. Soc. Pa., Phila., 1991-93; chmn. internat. adv. com. Greater Phila. First; bd. dirs. Gladwyne (Pa.) Libr., 1991—, pres., 1996—. Recipient Hughes-Gossett award U.S. Supreme Ct. Hist. Soc., Washington, 1991. Mem. ABA, Pa. Bar Assn., Phila. Bar Assn., Am. Coll. Real Estate Lawyers, Harvard Club Phila. (pres. 1970-72), Franklin Inn Club, Merion Cricket Club, Sunday Breakfast Club (mem. steering com.). Avocation: historical research and publication. Home: 829 Black Road Rd Gladwyne PA 19035 Office: Phila Nat Bank Bldg 1345 Chestnut St Philadelphia PA 19107-3426

MAXFIELD, GUY BUDD, lawyer, educator; b. Galesburg, Ill., May 4, 1933; s. Guy W. and Isabelle B. Maxfield; m. Carol Tunick, Dec. 27, 1970; children—Susan, Stephen, Kim. A.B. summa cum laude, Augustana Coll., 1955; J.D., U. Mich., 1958. Bar: N.Y. 1959. Assoc. White & Case, N.Y.C., 1958-63; prof. law NYU, 1963—. Mem. ABA, Am. Law Inst., N.Y. State Bar Assn. Author: Tennessee Will and Trust Manual, 1982, Federal Estate and Gift Taxation, 6th edit. 1990, Florida Will and Trust Manual 1984, Tax Planning for Professionals, 1986; contbr. articles to profl. jours. Trustee Acomb Found., Newark, 1974—. Served with U.S. Army, 1958-64. Fellow Am. Coll. Tax Counsel; mem. ABA, Am. Law Inst., N.Y. State Bar Assn., Phi Beta Kappa, Order of Coif. Office: NYU Sch Law 40 Washington Sq S New York NY 10012-1005

MAXFIELD, JOHN EDWARD, retired university dean; b. Los Angeles, Mar. 17, 1927; s. Chauncey George and Rena Lucile (Cain) M.; m. Margaret Alice Waugh, Nov. 24, 1948; children—Frederick George (dec.), David Glen, Elaine Rebecca, Nancy Catherine, Daniel John. B.S., Mass. Inst. Tech., 1947; M.S., U. Wis., 1949; Ph.D., U. Oreg., 1951. Instr. U. Oreg., 1950-51; mathmatician U.S. Naval Ordnance Test Sta., China Lake, Calif., 1949-56, head computing br., 1956-57, head math. div., 1957-60; lectr. UCLA, 1951-60; head prof. dept. math. U. Fla., 1960-67; prof., chmn. dept. math. Kans. State U., 1967-81; dean Grad. Sch. and univ. research La. Tech. U., 1981-92, dean emeritus, 1992—; ret. La. Tech. U., 1992. Mem. Am. Math. Soc., Math. Assn. Am., Soc. Indsl. and Applied Math., Sigma Xi. Home: 209 E Louisiana Ave Ruston LA 71270-4471

MAXFIELD, KENNETH WAYNE, transportation company executive; b. Leo, Ind., Oct. 26, 1924; m. Beverly Maxfield; 2 children. Student, Loyola U., Chgo., 1946-48; LL.B., De Paul U., 1950. Bar: Ind., Ill. bars 1950. With North Am. Van Lines Inc., Ft. Wayne, Ind., 1950-89, exec. v.p. corp. world hdqrs., 1966-77, pres., chief oper. officer, chmn. bd., 1977-89, ret.; chmn. Am. Movers Conf., 1989; vice chmn. litigation sect. Am. Trans. Assn., 1987-89. Pres. bd. Jr. Achievement, Ft. Wayne, 1976-77. Served with U.S. Army, 1943-46. Mem. Ft. Wayne C. of C. (pres. 1974).

MAXFIELD, MICHAEL GERALD, venture capitalist; b. Pontiac, Mich., Feb. 27, 1954; s. Gerald E.L. and Mildred (Lewis) M. BS, Mich. State U., 1973, MBA, 1975. CPA, Mich. Mgr. Deloitte, Haskins & Sells, Detroit and Grand Rapids, Mich., 1975-86; exec. v.p. Universal Cos., Inc., Grand Rapids, 1986-94, treas., 1986-89; pres. Enterprise Capital, Grand Rapids, 1994—. Treas. Kent County Rep. Com., Grand Rapids, 1984-92, chmn., 1992-94, 5th dist. fin. chmn.; bd. dirs. Kent Cmty. Hosp., 1988-92, 95—. Mem. AICPA, Mich. Assn. CPAs, Grand Rapids C. of C. (chmn. 1984-88), Fin. Execs. Inst. Republican. Home: 2965 E Fulton Grand Rapids MI 49506-9999 Address: 201 W Fulton St Apt 1416 Grand Rapids MI 49503-2678

MAXFIELD, PETER C., state legislator, law educator, lawyer; b. 1941. AB, Regis Coll., 1963; JD, U. Denver, 1966; LLM, Harvard U., 1968. Bar: Colo. 1966, Wyo. 1969. Trial atty. Dept. Justice, 1966-67; assoc. Hindry, Erickson & Meyer, Denver, 1968-69; asst. prof. U. Wyo. Coll. Law, 1969-72, assoc. prof., 1972-76, prof., 1976—, dean, 1979-87; vis. assoc. prof. U. N.Mex., 1972-73; Raymond F. Rice Disting. prof. U. Kans., 1984; Chapman Vis. Disting. prof., U. Tulsa, 1987; vis. prof. U. Utah, 1992. Coord. Wyo. State Planning, 1988-89; spl. asst. Gov. Wyo. 1989-90; Dem. nominee U.S. Ho. Reps., 1990; mem. Wyo. Environ. Quality Coun., 1991-93; mem. Wyo. Senate, Laramie, 1993—. Mem. Order St. Ives, Omicron Delta Kappa, Pi Delta Phi. Author: (with Bloomenthal) Cases and Materials on the Federal Income Taxation of Natural Resources, 1971, 72, 77; (with Houghton) Taxation of Mining Operations, 1973, 76; (with Trelease and Dietrich) Natural Resources Law on American Indian Lands, 1977. Home: 3501 Grays Gable Rd Laramie WY 82070 Office: U Wyo Coll Law PO Box 3035 Laramie WY 82071-3035

MAXFIELD, THOMAS H., lawyer; b. Scottsbluff, Nebr., Feb. 20, 1944. BA, U. Wyo., 1966, JD, 1970; LLM, NYU, 1971. Bar: Wyo. 1970, Colo. 1971. Ptnr. Baker & Hostetler, Denver. Mem. ABA, Colo. Bar Assn., Denver Bar Assn., Wyo. State Bar. Office: Baker & Hostetler 303 E 17th Ave Ste 1100 Denver CO 80203-1264*

MAXHEIM, JOHN HOWARD, utility executive; b. Clinton, Iowa, Oct. 4, 1934; s. Vincent J. and Dorothy F. M. B.S. in Indsl. Engring., Iowa State U., 1958. Indsl. sales engr. Mobil Oil Co., Chgo., 1958-59; indsl. sales engr. and mgr. Milw. Gas Light Co., 1959-62; asst. to pres. United Cities Gas Co., Nashville, 1962-65, v.p., 1965-66, exec. v.p., 1966-70, pres., chief exec. officer, 1970-78, also bd. dirs., 1970-78; pres., chief operating officer Piedmont Natural Gas Co., Inc., Charlotte, N.C., 1978-80, also bd. dirs., 1979—, chief exec. officer, chmn., 1980—, now also pres.; dir. Wachovia Bank & Trust Co., Univ. Research Park. Past chmn. Charlotte Auditorium-Coliseum Conv. Ctr. Authority; trustee Inst. Gas Tech., N.Y. Mercantile Exchange; mem. Nat. Gas Adv. Com.; adv. bd. Fuqua Sch. Bus., Duke U.; trustee Ind. Coll. Fund N.C. ; bd. visitors Johnson C. Smith U.; U. N.C., Charlotte; bd. dirs. Found. U. N.C. Mem. Am. Gas Assn. (bd. dirs.), So. Gas Assn. (past chmn.), Southeastern Gas Assn. (past dir.), Tenn. Gas Assn. (past pres.), Greater Charlotte C. of C. (bd. dirs.), Nashville City Club, Carolina Ambassadors, Capital City Club, Quail Hollow Country Club. Home: 4100 Beresford Rd Charlotte NC 28211-3810 Office: Piedmont Natural Gas Co Inc PO box 33068 1915 Rexford Rd Charlotte NC 28233

MAXIMOS (MAXIMOS DEMETRIOS AGHIORGOUSSIS), bishop; b. Callimassia, Chios, Greece, Mar. 5, 1935; s. Evanghelos G. and Lemonia G. (Rythianou) A. Licentiate, Patriarchal Sch. Theology, Halki, 1957; Baccalaureate, U. Louvain, Belgium, 1964, Th.D., 1964. Ordained to ministry Greek Orthodox Ch., 1957; chaplain U. Louvain, 1957-64; pastor chs. Brussels, Rome, Brookline, Mass., Manchester and Newport, N.H., 1960-78; observer-del. II Vatican Council, 1964-65; chaplain Holy Cross Sem., Brookline, 1967-76; prof. systematic theology Holy Cross Sch. Theology, Brookline, 1967-79, Christ Savior Sem., Johnstown, Pa., from 1979; bishop Greek Orthodox Diocese Pitts., 1979—; mem. Orthodox-Roman Cath. Consultation, from 1967; v.p. Nat. Council Chs. Christ U.S., 1979-81; ecumenical officer Greek Orthodox Archdiocese N. and S. Am., 1978-79, chmn. synodal coms. ecumenical affairs, spiritual renewal and youth, from 1979. Author articles in field. Mem. Orthodox Theol. Soc. Am., AAUP, Christian Assos. Pitts., Pa. Council Chs., W.Va. Council Chs., Helicon Cultural Soc. Office: Greek Orthodox Diocese Pittsburgh 5201 Ellsworth Ave Pittsburgh PA 15232-1421 *My ministry is such that it requires a total commitment to its goals, but first of all a total commitment to Christ. In my childhood, I was fortunate to be guided by excellent parents and grandparents, who gave me not only the necessary security and stability, but also the inspiration to imitate their personal commitment to the Lord. I fully trust in the grace of the Lord, but I also have always accepted my responsibility for everything I have done.*

MAXMAN, SUSAN ABEL, architect; b. Columbus, Ohio, Dec. 30, 1938; d. Richard Jack Abel and Gussie (Brenner) Seiden; children: Andrew Frankel, Thomas Frankel, Elizabeth Frankel; m. William H. Maxman; children: Melissa, Abby, William Jr. Student, Smith Coll., 1960; MArch., U. Pa., 1977; HHD, Ball State U., 1993. Registered profl. architect, Pa., Ohio, N.J., N.Y., Md., W.Va., Va. Project designer Kopple Sheward & Day, Phila., 1978-80; ptnr. Maxman & Sutphin, Phila., 1980-83; prin. Susan Maxman Architects, Phila., 1984—; bd. overseers Grad. Sch. Fine Arts U. Pa.; bd. dirs. Found. Arch. Works include design of Women's Humane Soc. Animal Shelter, Bensalem, Pa. (Northeastern Sustainable Energy Assn.'s Comml. Bldg. award, 1994, Metal Constrn. Assn. award 1995), Camp Tweedale-Freedom Valley, Girl Scouts USA (AIA honor award, 1991), restoration Vernon House (honorable mention Remodeling Mag.), Germantown, Robert Lewis House (McArthur award 1985), Phila., Restoration Pennock Farmstead (Grand Prize Nat. Trust Historic Preservation 1995), Julia DeBurgos Biligual Middle Sch., Phila., Feasibility Study and renovations Old Main Complex, Kutztown U., Pa., Chestnut Hill Nat. Bank, Phila. Mem. Eco-Efficiency Task Force Pres. Coun. Sustainable Devel.; bd. dirs. Alliance to Save Energy, Phila. Hist. Preservation Corp. Recipient Disting. Dau. Pa. award Gov. Tom Ridge, 1995, Excellence citation Engring. News Record, Shattering the Glass Ceiling award Women's Nat. Dem. Club, Mayor's commendation City Phila., citation Pa. Ho. Reps. Mem. AIA (nat. pres. 1993), Pa. Women's Forum, FOrum Exec. Women, Carpenter's Co. Phila. Avocations: swimming, gardening. Office: 123 S 22nd St Philadelphia PA 19103-4335

MAXON, DON CARLTON, construction company executive, mining company executive; b. Downers Grove, Ill., Dec. 23, 1914; s. Norman T. and Agnes M. (Matteson) M.; m. Mary T. Quirk, June 14, 1941; children: Maureen, Don, Paul, Anne, Lee; m. Ella Luanne Roy, Dec. 10, 1971; 1 stepchild, Tom Roy. Student pub. schs., Barrington, Ill. Founder, pres. Maxon Constrn. Co., Barrington, 1936, Gen. Mining & Devel. Co., Santa Fe, N.Mex., 1967—, U.S. Communities S.A. Panama, 1974, Taipei, Taiwan, 1986—, Carson City, NA, 1989—, Bonanza Mines Internat., Carson City, NA, 1987; rancher; internat. fin. cons. Fiduciary Banks, London, Paris, Geneva, mem. pres.'s club. Pres. Johnson and Kennedy; mem. Pockets of Poverty Commn.; founder City of Streamwood, Ill., 1954, City of Green Valley, Ariz., 1963. With Seabees, USN, 1942-45. Recipient awards for designing family communities of Streamwood, Barrington Woods, Ill. and Trout Valley, Ill., Parents' mag., 1953, 59, 60; Tenn. Squire. Mem. Nat. Assn. Home Builders (Nat. Homes Pres.'s Land Planning first place award 1954), Gov.'s Club Ariz. Democrat. Roman Catholic. Rsh. on methods for testing and extracting gold from complex ores and rsch. to create the finest possible environment for quality of life and sci. applications of all disciplines needed for a self contained city of 150,000 population; builder U.S. Gypsum Co. Rsch. Village, Barrington. Home: 2586 E Avenida De Maria Tucson AZ 85718-3056

MAXSON, LINDA ELLEN, biologist, educator; b. N.Y.C., Apr. 24, 1943; d. Albert and Ruth (Rosenfeld) Resnick; m. Richard Dey Maxson, June 13, 1964; 1 child, Kevin. BS in Zoology, San Diego State U., 1964, MA in Biology, 1966; PhD in Genetics, U. Calif. and San Diego State U., 1973. Instr. biology San Diego State U., 1966-68; tchr. gen. sci. San Diego Unified Sch. Dist., 1968-69; instr. biochemistry U. Calif., Berkeley, 1974; asst. prof. zoology, dept. genetics and devel. U. Ill., Urbana-Champaign, 1974-76, asst. prof. dept. genetics, devel. and ecology, ethology & evolution, 1976-79, assoc. prof., 1979-84, prof., 1984-87, prof. ecology, ethology and evolution, 1987-88; prof., head dept. biology Pa. State U., State College, 1988-94; assoc. vice-chancellor acad. affairs/dean undergrad. acad. affairs, prof. ecology and evolutionary biology U. Tenn., Knoxville, 1995—; exec. officer biology programs Sch. Life Scis., U. Ill., 1981-86, assoc. dir. acad. affairs, 1984-86, dir. campus honors program, 1985-88; vis. prof. ecology and evolutionary biology U. Calif., Irvine, 1988; mem. adv. panel rsch. tng. groups behavioral biol. scis. NSF, 1990-94. Author: Genetics: A Human Perspective, 3d edit., 1992; edtl. bd. Molecular Biology Evolution, Amphibia/Reptilia; exec. editor Biochem. Sys. & Ecology, 1993—; contbr. numerous articles to scientific jours. Recipient Disting. Alumni award San Diego State U., 1989, Disting. Herpetologist award Herpetologists' League, 1993. Fellow AAAS (disting. herpetologist award 1993); mem. Am. Men and Women in Sci., Am. Genetics Assn. (coun. 1994—), Soc. for Study of Amphibians and Reptiles (pres. 1991), Internat. Herpetol. Com., Soc. Study Evolution, Soc. Systematic Biology, Soc. Molecular Biology and Evolution (sec. 1992-95, treas. 1992-94), Am. Soc. Ichthyologists and Herpetologists, Am. Soc. Zoologists, Herpetologists League, Soc. Europea Herpetologica, European Soc. Evolutionary Biology. Home: 409 Boxwood Sq Knoxville TN 37919 Office: U Tenn 505 Andy Holt Twr Knoxville TN 37996-0154

MAXSON, M. FINLEY, lawyer; b. Toledo, Ohio, Aug. 9, 1934. AB, Duke U., 1956; LLB, Harvard U., 1962. Bar: Ill. 1962. Ptnr. Winston & Strawn, Chgo. Mem. ABA, Ill. State Bar Assn., Chgo. Bar Assn. Office: Winston & Strawn 35 W Wacker Dr Chicago IL 60601-1614*

MAXTED, WILLIAM C., dean; b. Rome, N.Y., Oct. 12, 1928; m. Claire Cody Maxted (wid. 1995); children: William C., Jr., Ann Marie, Gerard Edward. BS cum laude, Georgetown U., 1950; MD cum laude, Georgetown U. Sch. of Medicine, 1954. Diplomate Am. Bd. Urology. Intern Mercy Hosp., Buffalo, N.Y., 1954-55; asst. resident in pediatrics Georgetown Med. Ctr., Washington, 1957-58, resident in urology, 1958-61, instr. in surgery, 1961-65, asst. prof. of surgery, 1965, assoc. prof. of surgery, 1969-79, prof. surgery, 1979—, dir. divsn. urology, 1976-89, chief of urology, 1976-89, acad. dean, 1989—; cons. for urology to chief, Aeromed. Stds. Divsn., Office of

Aviation Medicina, FAA, 1972-90; cons. FDA, 1979-90, VA, 1976—, Dept. of Army, Walter Reed Army Hosp., 1979-80, Dept. of Navy, Nat. Naval Med. Ctr., Bethesda, Md., 1979-90, others; numerous coms., speaker. Mem. Georgetown Clin. Soc. (sec.-treas., v.p. and pres. 1971-75), Washington Urology Soc. (pres. 1978-79), Am. Urologic Assn., Mid-Atlantic Sect. of Am. Urologic Assn., Am. Coll. Surgeons, Soc. Univ. Urologists, Alpha Omega Alpha, others. Office: Office of Acad Dean Georgetown U Sch Medicine Washington DC

MAXWELL, ANDERS JOHN, corporate executive; b. San Francisco, Oct. 3, 1946; s. John L. and Deborah A. M.; divorced; children: Lauren A., Colin A., Ian W., Erin C., Ryan S. BArch, U. Calif.-Berkeley, 1969; MBA, U. Pa., 1971. Analyst Gen. Electric Co., 1971-73; v.p. Gen. Electric Credit Corp., Stamford, Conn., 1973-83; mng. dir. Dean Witter Reynolds Inc., N.Y.C., 1983-87; v.p. Kidder Peabody & Co., Inc., N.Y.C., 1987-88; prin. L.F. Rothschild & Co., N.Y.C., 1988; v.p. Smith Barney, Harris Upham & Co., Inc., 1989-91, Lazard Frères & Co., N.Y.C., 1991-92; ptnr. Benedetto, Gartland & Greene, N.Y.C., 1992-94; v.p., gen. mgr. GE Capital Corp., Stamford, Conn., 1994—. Served to capt. U.S Army, 1971. Office: GE Capital Corp 260 Long Ridge Rd Stamford CT 06927-1600

MAXWELL, ARTHUR EUGENE, oceanographer, marine geophysicist, educator; b. Maywood, Calif., Apr. 11, 1925; s. John Henry and Nelle Irene (Arnold) M.; m. Colleen O'Leary, July 1, 1988; children: Delle, Eric, Lynn, Brett, Gregory, Sam Wade, Henry Wade. BS in Physics with honors, N.Mex. State U., 1949; MS in Oceanography, Scripps Instn. Oceanography, 1952, PhD in Oceanography, 1959. Jr. rsch. geophysicist Scripps Instn. Oceanography, La Jolla, Calif., 1950-55; head oceanographer Office Naval Rsch., Washington, 1955-59, head br. geophysics, 1959-65; assoc. dir. Woods Hole (Mass.) Oceanographic Instn., 1965-69, dir. rsch., 1969-71, provost, 1971-81; prof. dept. geol. scis., dir. Inst. Geophysics U. Tex., Austin, 1982-94, prof. emeritus dept. geol. sci., 1994—; bd. dirs. Palisades Geophys. Inst. Corp; chmn. bd. govs. Joint Oceanographic Instns., 1985-86, chmn. planning com. deep earth sampling, 1968-70, chmn. exec. com. deep earth sampling, 1971-72, 78-79, 91-92; mem. joint U.S./USSR com. for coop. studies of the world ocean NAS/NRC, 1973-80, chmn. U.S. nat. com. to Internat. Union Geodesy and Geophysics, 1976-80, vice chmn. outer continental shelf/environ. studies rev. com., 1986-93; chmn. U.S. nat. com. on geology NAS, 1979-83, chmn. geophysics rsch. bd. geophysics study com., 1982-87; nat. sea grant review panel NOAA, 1982-85, 90—; mem. vis. com. Rosenstiel Sch. Marine and Atmospheric Studies U. Miami, 1982-86, dept. physics N.Mex. State U., 1986-94; acad. adv. com. Com. Exchanges CIA, 1983—; mem. Gulf of Mexico Regional Marine Rsch. Bd., 1992—. Editor: The Sea, Vol. 4, Parts I and II, 1970; editorial adv. bd. Oceanus, 1981-92; contbr. articles to profl. jours. Chmn. tech. adv. com. Navy Thresher Search, 1963; mem. Mass. Gov's. Adv. Com. on Sci. and Tech., 1965-71. With USN, 1942-46, PTO. Recipient Meritorious Civilian Svc. award Chief Naval Rsch., 1958, Albatross award AMSOC, 1959, Superior Civilian Svc. award Assn. Sec. of Navy, 1963, Disting. Civilian Svc. award Sec. of Navy, 1964, Disting. Alumni award N.Mex. State U., 1965, Bruun Meml. Lecture award Intergovtl. Oceanographic Commn., 1969, Outstanding Centennial Alumnus award N. Mex. State U., 1988. Fellow Am. Geophys. Union (pres. 1976-78, pres. oceanography sect. 1970-72); mem. Marine Tech. Soc. (charter, pres. 1981-82), Cosmos Club. Achievements include research in heat flow through the ocean floor, in structure and tectonics of the sea floor. Home: 8115 Two Coves Dr Austin TX 78730-3122 Office: U Tex Inst for Geophysics 8701 N Mo Pac Expy Austin TX 78759-8345

MAXWELL, BRYCE, engineer,educator; b. Glen Cove, N.Y., July 26, 1919; s. Howard W. and Helen (Young) W.; m. Margurite Kulsar, June 5, 1953 (dec. 1974); children: Bryce Jr., Margaret H., Stephen H. B.S. in Engring, Princeton, 1943, M.S. in Engring, 1948. Rsch. assoc. Princeton U., 1948-53, asst. prof., 1953-57, assoc. prof., 1957-66, asst. dean Sch. Engring., 1962-66, prof. chem. engring. Sch. Engring., 1966-68, prof. chem. engring. for polymer studies, chmn. polymer materials program, 1968-85, prof. emeritus, 1985—; pres. Maxwell Instrument Inc., 1992—; bd. dirs. U.S. Rubber Reclaiming Co., Inc., Vicksburg, Miss., 1962-80; cons. several chem. cos. Trustee Plastics Inst. Am. Served with USNR, 1943-46. Recipient Honor Scroll N.J. Inst. Chemists, 1981. Mem. ASME (life), ASTM, Soc. Rheology, Soc. Plastics Engrs. (gold medal and internat. award in plastics sci. and engring. 1976, fellow 1992), Sigma Xi. Achievements include research and publication in polymer viscoelastic behavior, polymer melt rheology; inventor elastic melt extruder, orthogonal rheometer, melt elasticity tester, 12 U.S. patents, 14 foreign patents. Home: Rossmoor 686A Yarborough Way Jamesburg NJ 08831-2012

MAXWELL, CARLA LENA, dancer, choreographer, educator; b. Glendale, Calif., Oct. 25, 1945; d. Robert and Victoria (Carbone) M. Student, Bennington Coll., 1963-64; B.S., Juilliard Sch. Music, 1967. Mem. Jose Limón Dance Co., N.Y.C., 1965; prin. dancer José Limón Dance Co., 1969—, acting artistic dir., 1977-78, artistic dir., 1978—; lectr., tchr. in field. Soloist, Louis Falco Dance Co., 1967-71, Harkness Festival at N.Y.C. Delacorte Theater, from 1964, artist-in-residence, Gettysburg Coll., 1970, Luther Coll., Decorah, Iowa, 1971, U. Idaho, 1973, guest tchr., performer, Centre Internat. de la Danse, Vichy, France, 1976; choreographer: Function, 1970, Improvisations on a Dream, 1970, A Suite of Psalms, 1973, Homage to José Linón, Place Spirit, 1975, Aadvark Brothers; Schwartz and Columbo Present Please Don't Stone The Clowns, 1975, Blue Warrier, 1975, Sonata, 1980, Keeping Stil, Mountain, 1987; featured in Carlota, Dances For Isadora, La Malinche, Comedy, The Moor's Pavane, The Winged, There Is A Time, The Shakers, Brandenburg Concerto No. 4, Trnaslucence, Caviar, Missa Brevis, Day on Earth, Two Ecstatic Themes, A Choreographic Offering, The Exiles, Sacred Conversations; toured East and West Africa, 1969. N.Y. State Cultural Council grantee, 1971; recipient Dance Mag. award, 1995. Home: 7 Great Jones St New York NY 10012-1135 Office: Jose Limon Dance Ctr 611 Broadway Fl 9 New York NY 10012-2617*

MAXWELL, CYNTHIA NEAGLE, food products executive; b. Charlotte, N.C., July 15, 1953; d. Emmett Orr and Nettie Prue (McCaslin) Neagle; m. L.A. Waggoner III, Apr. 30, 1977 (div. Aug. 1987); 1 child, Margaret "Rett" Emma Waggoner; m. Kirby Ben Maxwell, June 19, 1991; stepchildren: Rachel Meredith, Jennifer Lauren Maxwell. BA in Psychology, U. N.C., 1975. Health care techician II, asst. recreational therapist Gaston-Lincoln Area Mental Health, Gastonia, N.C., 1975-77; social worker I Mecklenburg County Mental Health Svcs., Charlotte, N.C., 1978; vol. svcs. coord. Mecklenburg County Mental Health Svcs., Charlotte, 1978-79, dir. community rels., 1979-81; exec. dir. Heart Soc. Gaston County, Inc., Gastonia, N.C., 1983-85; product rep. Perma-Bound, Jacksonville, Fla., 1984-86; dist. adminstr. Guardian Ad Litem Program, Gastonia, N.C., 1985-91; v.p., food products exec. Maxwell Assocs., 1991—; criminal law mitigation expert; jury selection specialist. Author: Volunteer Manual, 1979; author, editor: Gaston County Bar Assn., 1993. bd. dirs., chmn., exec. com., personnel com., search com., pub. rels. com., sec., program com., fin. com., by laws com., Gaston-Lincoln Area Mental Health, Mental retardation and Substance Abuse Program, 1978-87; search com., by laws com., rep., pres. bd. dirs., 1983-87; co-chair, chair, exec. by laws chair, Jr. League Gaston County, N.C., 1980-91; CPR instr. Gaston County Red Cross, 1985—; mem. devel. chair. Civitans, 1986-90; mem. planning and zoning bd., Belmont, N.C., 1994—; dir. Alliance Healthier Babies. Named Vol. of Yr. Gaston County C. of C., 1982, Gaston County Mental Health Assn., 1983; N.C. Col. of Yr. N.C. Coun. of Community Mental health Programs, 1983. Mem. Gaston County C. of C., United Meth. Women, Humane Soc. Gaston County, Gaston County Commn. of Family. Democrat. Methodist. Avocations: water sports, needlework, sewing, pets, houseplants, gardening, landscaping, crafts, furniture refinishing, calligraphy. Office: 426 Breezewood Dr Belmont NC 28012-8649

MAXWELL, D. MALCOLM, college president, minister; b. Watford, Eng., Apr. 6, 1934; s. Arthur S. and Rachel Elizabeth (Jouce) M.; m. Eileen J. Bolander, Aug. 25, 1955; children: Wendy E. Maxwell Henderson, D. Kevin. BA in Theology and Biblical Langs., Pacific Union Coll., 1956; MA in Systematic Theology, Andrews U., 1958; PhD in Biblical Studies New Testament, Drew U., 1968. Ordained to ministry Seventh-Day Adventists Ch., 1960. Pastor No. Calif. Conf. Seventh-Day Adventists, Oakland, Calif., 1956-64; instr. in religion Union Coll., Lincoln, Nebr., 1964-65; prof. in religion Walla Walla Coll., College Place, Wash., 1965-78, v.p. acad. affairs, 1978-83; pres. Pacific Union Coll., Angwin, Calif., 1983—. Bd. trustees St. Helena Hosp., Deer Park, Calif., 1983—, Rio Lindo Acad., Healdsburg, Calif., 1983—; bd. dirs., membership com. Adventist Health Sys./West, Roseville, Calif., 1983—. Rockefeller fellow, 1967-68; Drew U. scholar, 1967-68; named Tchr. of Yr., Wash. State Auto Assn., 1971. Mem. Soc. Biblical Lit., Rotary. Avocations: golf, boatings, gardening. Office: Pacific Union Coll 1 Angwin Ave Angwin CA 94508

MAXWELL, DAVID E., academic executive, educator; b. N.Y.C., Dec. 2, 1944; s. James Kendrick and Gertrude Sarah (Bernstein) M.; children: Justin Kendrick, Stephen Edward. BA, Grinnell Coll., 1966; MA, Brown U., 1968, PhD, 1974. Instr. Tufts U., Medford, Mass., 1971-74, asst. prof., 1974-78, assoc. prof. Russian lang. and lit., 1978-89, dean undergrad. studies, 1981-89; pres. Whitman Coll., Walla Walla, Wash., 1989-93; dir. Nat. Fgn. Lang. Ctr., Washington, 1993—; chmn. steering com. Coop. Russian Lang. Program, Leningrad, USSR, 1981-86, chmn. 1986-90; cons. Coun. Internat. Ednl. Exchange, 1974—, bd. dirs., 1988-92, 93-94, vice chair, 1991-92, cons. Internat. Rsch. Exchanges, 1976—; mem. adv. bd. Israeli Lang. Policy Inst. Contbr. articles to scholarly jours. Fulbright fellow, 1970-71, Brown U., 1966-67, NDEA Title IV, 1967-70; recipient Lillian Leibner award Tufts U., 1979; citation Grad. Sch. Arts & Scis., Brown U., 1991. Mem. MLA, Am. Coun. Edn. (commn. on internat. edn., pres.'s coun. on internat. edn.), Am. Assn. Advancement of Slavic Studies, Am. Assn. Tchrs. Slavic and E. European Langs., Assn. Am. Colls., Am. Assn. Higher Edn., Am. Coun. Tchg. Fgn. Langs., Brown U. Alumni Assn. Democrat. Avocations: tennis, running, music. Office: Nat Fgn Lang Ctr 1619 Massachusetts Ave NW Washington DC 20036-2213

MAXWELL, DAVID OGDEN, former government official and financial executive; b. Phila., May 16, 1930; s. David Farrow and Emily Ogden (Nelson) M.; m. Joan Clark Paddock, Dec. 14, 1968. BA, Yale U., 1952; LLB, Harvard U., 1955. Bar: Pa. 1955, D.C. 1955. Assoc. Obermayer, Rebmann, Maxwell & Hippel, Phila., 1959-67, ptnr., 1963-67; ins. commr. State of Pa., 1967-69, adminstrn. and budget sec., 1969-70; gen. counsel HUD, Washington, 1970-73; pres., CEO Ticor Mortgage Ins. Co., 1973-81; CEO Fed. Nat. Mortgage Assn., Washington, 1981-91; bd. dirs. Corp. Ptnrs., L.P., Fin Security Assurance Holdings, Ltd., Hechinger Co., Potomac Electric Power Co., Salomon, Inc., SunAm., Inc.; trustee Enterprise Found., European Inst., Irban Inst., Brookings Instn. Bd. dirs. Sta. WETA-TV; mem. trustees coun. Nat. Gallery Art. With USNR, 1955-59. Home: 3525 Springland Ln NW Washington DC 20008-3119 Office: 5335 Wisconsin Ave NW Ste 440 Washington DC 20015-2030

MAXWELL, DIANA KATHLEEN, early childhood education educator; b. Seminole, Okla., Dec. 16, 1949; d. William Hunter and ImoJean (Mahurin) Rivers; m. Clarence Estel Maxwell, Jly 3, 1969; children: Amanda Hunter, Alexandra Jane. BS, U. Md., 1972; M of Secondary Edn., Boston U., 1974; PhD, U. Md., 1980. Cert. tchr., counselor, Tex. Tchr. Child Garden Presch., Adelphi, Md., 1969-71; tchr., dir. PREP Edn. Ctr., Heidelberg, Germany, 1972-74; tchr. N.E. Ind. Schs. Larkspur, San Antonio, 1974-77, 89-90, Headstart, Boyds, Md., 1978; dir., founder First Bapt. Child Devel. Ctr., Bryan, Tex., 1982-84; instr. English lang. Yonsei Med. Ctr., Seoul, Republic of Korea, 1985-87; asst. prof. Incarnate Word Coll., San Antonio, 1987-89; tchr. kindergarten Fairfax County Pub. Schs., Kings Park, Va., 1990-94; tchr. Encino Park, San Antonio, Tex., 1994-95; lectr. U. Tex., San Antonio, 1995—; cons. Sugar N'Spice Child Devel. Ctr., Kilgore, Tex., 1980-90; bd. dirs. Metro Area Assn. for Childhood Edn. Internat., 1991-93. Author: (book revs.) Childhood Education, 1979, 80, 92. Block chairperson March of Dimes, 1991, 92, 93, Am. Heart Assn., Fairfax, Fa., 1991, 92, Am. Diabetes Assn., Fairfax, 1992; judge speaking com. Burke Optomists, 1992, 931 judge writing competition N.E. Ind. Sch. Dist., 1996; sec. Cole H.S. Cougar Club, Ft. Sam Houston, San Antonio, 1996-97; Bible tchr. 1st Bapt. Ch., Alexandria, Va., 1992-94; tchr. kindergarten Trinity Bapt. Ch., San Antonio, 1995—. Named one of Outstanding Young Women of Am., 1983; Md. fellow State of Md., 1978, 79; grantee San Antonio, 1990, Springfield, 1991. Mem. ASCD, Internat. Reading Assn., Assn. Profl. Tchr. Educators, Edn. Internat., Assn. for Childhood Edn. Internat. (v.p., pres.-elect), Tex. Assn. Childhood Edn., Bexar County and Surrounding Areas Assn. Childhood Edn. Avocations: oriental brush painting, singing, collecting butterflies, children/teacher advocate. Home: 106 Artillery Post Rd San Antonio TX 78234 Office: U Tex Divsn Edn 6900 North Loop 1604 San Antonio TX 78249-0616

MAXWELL, DONALD POWER, JR., ophthalmologist, physician, educator; b. Lawton, Okla., Aug. 13, 1955; s. Donald Power and Beverly Sue (Schilling) M.; m. Karen Sue Carringer, May 14, 1982. BS, U. Okla., 1977, MD, 1982. Diplomate Am. Bd. Ophthalmology, Nat. Bd. Med. Examiners. Intern U. Okla. Tulsa Med. Br., 1982-83; resident in ophthalmology U. Kans., Kansas City, 1983-86; vitreo-retinal fellow Tulane Med. Ctr., New Orleans, 1986-88, clin. instr., 1986-88, asst. prof., 1988-92, assoc. prof., 1992—; adv. mem. curriculum com. Tulane Med. Ctr., 1993—, mem. admissions com., 1993—. Contbr. articles to profl. jours. Fellow ACS, Am. Acad. Ophthalmology; mem. AMA (physician's recognition award 1986—), Retina Soc. Vitreous Society, Am. Acad. Opthalmology-Honor Award-1996, Comm. on Ophthalmic Procedure Assessment-Retina Panel Chmn., SAR, Soc. of Cincinnati, Soc. Colonial Wars; Sons of revolution, Soc. War 1812, Col. Soc. Americans Royal Descent, Order of American Armorial Ancestry, Col. Order of the Crown, Internal. Soc. of Charlemagne. Office: Tulane Med Ctr 1430 Tulane Ave New Orleans LA 70112-2699

MAXWELL, DONALD STANLEY, publishing executive; b. L.A., May 30, 1930; s. Harold Stanley and Margaret (Trenam) M.; m. Martha Helen Winn, Dec. 5, 1952; children: Sylvia Louise, Cynthia Lynn, Bruce Stanley, Bradley Erl, Walter James, Wesley Richard, Amy Bernice. Student, Long Beach City Coll., 1948-50; BBA, Woodbury Coll., 1956; D of Bus. Adminstrn. (hon.), Woodbury U., 1991. CPA. Ptnr. Robert McDavid & Co. (CPAs), L.A., 1955-61; controller Petersen Pub. Co., L.A., 1961-68; v.p. fin. Petersen Pub. Co., 1969; controller L.A. Times, 1969-79; v.p. Los Angeles Times, 1977-79, v.p. fin., 1979-81; asst. treas. Times Mirror Co., 1971-82, v.p., controller, 1982-87, v.p., chief acctg. officer, 1987-93, v.p., 1993, exec. dir. fin. program, 1993-95; ret., 1995. Trustee Woodbury U., 1981—, chmn. bd. trustees, 1984-87. Served with AUS, 1950-52. Mem. Fin. Execs. Inst. (dir. 1979-82, pres. L.A. chpt. 1973-74), Internat. Newspaper Fin. Execs. (dir. 1978-82, pres. 1980-81), Am. Inst. CPAs, Calif. Soc. CPAs, Am. Horse Council, Internat. Arabian Horse Assn., Arabian Horse Assn. So. Calif., Friendly Hills Country Club. Republican. Baptist. Home: 2160 Le Flore Dr La Habra CA 90631

MAXWELL, HAMISH, diversified consumer products company executive; b. 1926. BA, Cambridge U., Eng., 1949. With Thomas Cook Sons & Co., 1949-54, Philip Morris, Inc., 1954-85; salesman Philip Morris, Inc., Richmond, Va., 1954-69; v.p. Philip Morris, Inc., 1969-76, sr. v.p., 1976-78, exec. v.p., 1978-83, pres., chief operating officer, 1983-84, chmn., chief exec. officer, 1984-85, also bd. dirs.; with Philip Morris Internat., 1961-83, advt. dir., 1961-63, v.p. mktg., 1963-65, regional v.p., Asia/Pacific region, 1965-73, exec. v.p. Canadian & Asia/Pacific regions, 1973-75, exec. v.p. Can./Asia & Europe/Middle East/Asia regions, 1975-78, pres., chief exec. officer, 1978-85; chmn., chief exec. officer Philip Morris Cos. Inc., 1985-91, chmn. exec. com., 1991—, also bd. dirs., 1985—. Served with RAF, 1944-47. Office: Philip Morris Cos Inc 120 Park Ave New York NY 10017-5523

MAXWELL, J. DOUGLAS, JR., chemical service company executive; b. Glen Cove, N.Y., Sept. 26, 1941; s. John Douglas M. and Marie Elise (Powers) Cummings; m. Hanne Agnete Kristensen, June 6, 1970; children: Scott Rogers, Samuel Douglas, Whitney Bodil. BA, Williams Coll., 1963; MBA, L.I.U., 1970. With Photocircuits Corp., Glen Cove, 1963-70; mgr. epuipment mktg. Chemco Techs., Inc., Glen Cove, 1970-76, treas., 1976-79, mng. dir., 1979-84, pres., 1984-89, also bd. dirs.; chmn. bd. dirs., chief exec. officer Empower Inc., Glen Cove, 1990—; dir. Kellmorgen Corp., Stamford, Conn., Slater Electric Corp., Glen Cove, First Nat. Bank L.I., Glen Head. Bd. dirs., v.p. Glen Cove Boys & Girls Club, 1970; bd. dirs., treas. L.I. Coun. on Alcoholism, Mineola, 1980; trustee Green Wood Cemetery, Bklyn., 1984, Green Vale Sch., Glen Head, 1986. Home: Cherry Ln Glen Head NY 11545-2216 Office: Chemco Tech Inc Charles St Glen Cove NY 11542-2957

MAXWELL, JACK ERWIN, manufacturing company executive; b. Cleve., July 17, 1926; s. Fred A. and Gertrude F. (Haug) M.; m. Martha Jane Miller, Dec. 28, 1966; children by previous marriage: Laura Jane, Fredric, Elizabeth Grant, Carla Moore, Linda Hanson. B.S., Case Inst. Tech., 1949; M.B.A., Harvard U., 1952. Indsl. engr. Lincoln Electric Co., Cleve., 1952-53; mr. purchase analysis Ford Motor Co., Dearborn, Mich., 1953-57; v.p. Booz, Allen & Hamilton, Inc., Detroit, 1957-69; v.p. corp. devel. Am. Motors Corp., Detroit, 1969-71; v.p. adminstrn. Am. Motors Corp., 1971-76, v.p. non-automotive subsidiaries, 1976-79, v.p. diversified ops., 1979-80; chmn., pres. Wheel Horse Products, Inc., South Bend, Ind., 1974-80; chmn. Ingersoll Products Corp., Chgo., 1980-86; pres. Wellmax, Inc., 1976—. Served with USNR, 1944-46. Mem. Case Inst. Tech. Alumni Assn., Harvard Bus. Sch. Alumni Assn., Tau Beta Pi, Theta Tau. Clubs: Detroit Athletic, Economics, Chicago, Old Club. Home: 3541 Bradway Blvd Bloomfield Hills MI 48301-2409 Office: 6905 Telegraph Rd Ste 330 Bloomfield Hills MI 48301-3160

MAXWELL, J.B., financial and marketing consultant; b. Clarksburg, W.Va., Sept. 30, 1944; s. J.B. and Martha (Hornor) M.; m. Valerie Ronson, Oct. 13, 1983; 1 child, Jennifer. BS, Salem (W.Va.) Coll., 1967; M of Mktg., Harvard U., 1970. Lic. in real estate sales, ins., secutities; registered commodity rep.; accredited mgmt. cons. and fin. planner; registered fin. planner, investment adv. Exec. v.p. Textron Inc., Providence, 1968-71; pres. Martech Inc. and 6 other cos., Portland, Maine, 1968—; v.p. E.F. Hutton Co., Portland, 1976-83; 1st v.p. fin. planning Dean Witter Reymonds, Boston, 1983-90; pres. Planning Svcs. Corp., Boston, 1990-92; 1st v.p. Gruntal & Co., Inc., Boston, 1992—; Author handbooks, booklets and articles. Contbr. Portland Coll. Art, 1980-93. Bd. dirs. Wellness Inst., Boston, 1990-91. Recipient Bronze award Nat. Acad. Scis., 1962. Mem. Internat. Assn. for Fin. Planning, Am. Mgmt. Assns., Am. Mktg. Assn., Inst. Mgmt. Cons., World Affairs Coun., Nat. Assn. Security Dealers (formerly br. office mgr.), Boston C. of C., Rotary Internat. Avocations: golf, woodworking, travel, literature. Home: 9279 McCormack Sta Boston MA 02209-9279 Office: Gruntal & Co Inc One Post Office Sq Boston MA 02109-3400

MAXWELL, JOE, state senator; b. Kirksville, Mo., Mar. 17, 1957; s. Robert E. and Molly B. Maxwell; m. Sarah Maxwell; children: Megan, Elizabeth, Shannen Lee. BS in Secondary Edn., Social Studies, U. Mo., 1986, JD, 1990. Farmer Rush Hill, Mo., 1976-78; ptnr., operator Maxwell Svc., Laddonia, Mo., 1978-84; rural mail carrier U.S. Postal Svc., Rush Hill, 1980-84; outstate field coord. Travis Morrison's Campaign for State Auditor, Mo., 1986; Mo. state field coord. Richard Gephardt for Pres., 1986-87; atty. Mexico, Mo., 1992—; state senator State of Mo., 1991-94, 1994—; mem. Senate Appropriations, Commerce and Environment, Edn., Judiciary, Labor and Indsl. Rels., Pub. Health and Welfare coms.; vice chair Elections, Pensions and Vet.'s Affairs coms. Assoc. editor-in-chief Mo. Jour. of Dispute Resolution, 1989, candidate, 1988. Mem. Am. Legion, 1982—, adj. Post 510, 1982-84; mem. Young Dem. Clubs Mo., 1982—, jud. coun. Young Dems. Am., 1985, pres., 1984-87, 9th Congl. Dist. chmn., 1982; mem. Laddonia Bapt. Ch., 1975—, Sunday Sch. tchr., 1990-91, pulpit com.; bd. dirs. Handi-Shop Inc., Mexico, 1981-84, chmn. mfg. and mktg. com., 1982-84; bd. dirs. Boy Scouts Am. Troop 94, 1980-82. Recipient St. Louis Globe Dem. award for outstanding achievement, 1979, Cert. of Appreciation, Troop 94, Boy Scouts Am., 1982, Mo.'s Outstanding Male Young Dem. award, 1987, George B. Freeman award for outstanding svc., 1987, Appreciation award Mo. Bar, 1992, Mo. Ho. of Reps. Resolution # 624 for exceptional svc. Mo., 1987, Mo. State Senate Resolution # 382 for exceptional svc. Mo., 1987; named one of Outstanding Young Men of Am., 1983, 85. Mem. Moose, Jaycees (Laddonia chpt. pres. 1978-79, coord. Laddonia Area Blood Drive, coord. Laddonia City Clean-up Day, chmn. Mexico Soybean Festival 1989, chmn. Lenten Breakfast 1990, Presdl. award of honor 1979), Kappa Delta Pi, Golden Key Nat. Honor Soc. Office: State Senate Rm 329 Capitol Bldg Jefferson City MO 65101

MAXWELL, JOHN RAYMOND, artist; b. Rochester, N.Y., Nov. 3, 1909; s. Herbert F. and Esther Helen (Donovan) M.; m. Phyllis Mitchell Custer, Sept. 9, 1968. Student, Rochester Inst. Tech., U. Rochester, Provincetown Workshop; studied with nationally known artists including V. Candell, L. Manso, C. Peters, and A. Clements. Past pres. Nat. Advt. Agy., Phila., N.Y.C., L.A. Arts in oil, watercolor, acrylic. Exhbns. include Nat. Acad. of Design, Am. Watercolor Soc., Toledo Mus., Ohio, Richmond Mus., Va., Norfolk Mus., Va., Smithsonian Instn., Art Inst. Chgo., Lehigh U., San Francisco Palace Legion Honor, Corcoran Gallery, Rutgers U., U. Pa., William Penn Mus., Harrisburg, Pa.; represented in permanent collections Phila. Mus. Art, Nat. Acad. Design, Butler Inst. Am. Art, Wichita State U., Allentown (Pa.) Art Mus., U. Pa. Sci. Ctr., Lehigh U., Am. Coll., Phila., Woodmere Mus., Phila.; represented in pvt. collections in U.S., Can. and abroad; work featured in several books on contemporary painting; works reviewed in newspapers and jours.; contbr. articles on art and artists to nat. mags. Recipient Dana medals Pa. Acad. Fine Arts, Soc. Painters Casein and Acrylic, Purchase prizes Butler Inst. Am. Art, Woodmere Mus. Mem. NAD (Altman prize), Am. Watercolor Soc. (silver and bronze honor medals, other prizes), Audubon Artists, Allied Artists Am., Nat. Soc. Painters in Watercolor & Acrylic, Phila. Sketch Club (Gold medals). Studio: 234 Sunset Rd Strafford PA 19087

MAXWELL, MARILYN JULIA, elementary education educator; b. Flint, Mich., Apr. 3, 1933; d. Clement Daniel and Gwendoline Mae (Evans) Rushlow; m. Dewey Theodore Maxwell, Apr. 22, 1965; 1 child, Bruce Dewey. Student, Baldwin-Wallace Coll., 1951-53; BS, U. Tenn., 1954-56, MEd, 1962. Cert. elem. edn. tchr.; lang. devel. specialist. Elem. tchr. Guy Selby Sch., Flint, Mich., 1956-58, Henry L. Barger Sch., Chattanooga, 1958-63, Dept. of Def. Sch., Seville, Spain, 1963-65, Loma Vista Elem. Sch., Lompoc, Calif., 1965-66, Crestview Elem. Sch., Lompoc, 1966-68, LaHonda Elem. Sch., Lompoc, 1969—; lang. arts mentor tchr. Lompoc Unified Schs., 1985-86. Mem. Internat. Reading Assn., Nat. Coun. Tchrs. of Math., Calif. Tchrs. of English to Speakers of Other Langs., Nat. Trust for Hist. Preservation, Am. Fedn. Tchrs. Home: 4219 Centaur St Lompoc CA 93436-1229 Office: LaHonda Elem Sch 1213 N A St Lompoc CA 93436-3514

MAXWELL, NEAL A., church official; m. Colleen Hinckley; four children. B in Polit. Sci., M in Polit. Sci., U. Utah, LLD (hon.); LLD (hon.), Brigham Young U.; LittD (hon.), Westminster Coll.; HHD (hon.), Utah State U., Ricks Coll. Legis. asst. U.S. sen. Wallace F. Bennett, Utah; exec. v.p. U. Utah, Salt Lake City; various ch. positions including bishop Salt Lake City's Univ. Sixth Ward, mem. gen. bd. youth orgn., adult correlation com. and one of first Regional Reps. of the Twelve; elder Ch. Jesus Christ Latter Day Sts., Asst. to the Council of Twelve, 1974-76, mem. of Presidency of First Quorum of the Seventy, 1976-81, mem. Coun. of Twelve Apostles, 1981—. Mem. Quorum of the Twelve Ch. of Jesus Christ of Latter-Day Saints, Salt Lake City. Recipient Liberty Bell award Utah State Bar, 1967; named Pub. Adminstr. of Yr. Inst. Govt. Service Brigham Young U., 1973. Office: LDS Church Quorum of the Twelve 47 E South Temple Salt Lake City UT 84150

MAXWELL, RAYMOND ROGER, accountant; b. Parmer County, Tex., Jan. 7, 1918; s. Frederick W. and Hazel Belle (Rogers) M.; m. Jeanne Hollarn, June 16, 1945 (dec. Dec. 1987); children: Donald R., Bruce Edward, Sabrina G. Spiering Warren Kleinecke. Ed.B., Western Ill. State Tchrs Coll., 1941; MBA in Acctg., U. Fla., 1949; postgrad., UCLA, 1965-68. CPA, Fla., Calif. Asst. to bus. mgr. Western Ill. State Tchrs. Coll., Macomb, 1939-41; apprentice acct. Charles H. Lindfors, CPA, Ft. Lauderdale, Fla., 1946-48; acct./auditor Frederic Dunn-Rankin & Co. CPA, Miami, Fla., 1948-49; CPA staff Charles Costar, CPA, Miami, 1951; resident auditor/CPA prin. Raymond R. Maxwell CPA, Ft. Lauderdale, 1951-56; supt. pub. instrn. Broward County, Ft. Lauderdale, 1956-61; staff asst. in fin. North Am. Aviation, Inc., El Segundo, Calif., 1961-65; tchr. Calif. Polytechnic, 1967; acctg. prin. Raymond R. Maxwell, CPA, Whittier, Calif., 1968—; tchr. Calif. State U., Fullerton, 1989; part-time rsch. asst. UCLA, 1965, teaching asst., 1966, 67; instr. Calif. Poly., 1967. Active precinct election bds., Whittier, L.A. County, 1989; 1st reader First Ch. of Christ, Scientist, Whittier, 1990-92, exec. bd., 1989, exec. bd. chmn., 1993, participant Bible Explorations, 1991-92. 1st lt. USAAF, 1942-46. Republican. Avocations: dancing, swimming, computers. Office: 8235 Painter Ave Whittier CA 90602 *One, with God, is a majority.*

MAXWELL, RICHARD CALLENDER, lawyer, educator; b. Mpls., Oct. 7, 1919; s. Bertram Wayburn and Blossom (Callender) M.; m. Frances Lida McKay, Jan 27, 1942; children—Richard Callender, John McKay. B.S.L., U. Minn., 1941, LL.B., 1947; LL.D. (hon.), Calif. Western U., 1983; LLD (hon.), Southwestern U., 1993. Assoc. prof. U. N.D., 1947-49; assoc. prof. U. Tex., 1949-51, prof., 1951-53; counsel Amerada Petroleum Corp., 1952-53; prof. UCLA, 1953-81; dean UCLA (Sch. Law), 1959-69, Connell prof., 1979-81, Connell prof. emeritus, 1981—; Chadwick prof. Duke U. Sch. Law, 1981-89, Chadwick prof. emeritus, 1989—; vis. prof. Columbia U., 1955; vis. Alumni prof. U. Minn., 1970-71; Fulbright lectr. Queen's U., No. Ireland, 1970; vis. Ford Found. prof. U. Singapore, 1971; Thompson prof. U. Colo., 1982; vis. prof. Hastings Coll. Law, 1976, Duke U., 1979-80, U. Tex., 1985; pres. Minn. Law Rev., 1946; chmn. Council Legal Edn. Opportunity, 1971-72; pres. Assn. Am. Law Schs., 1972; chmn. adv. com. law Fulbright Program, 1971-74, chmn. adv. com. U.K., 1974-77; mem. com. on gas prodn. opportunities NRC, 1977-78; mem. law sch. editorial and adv. bd. West Pub. Co., 1971-94. Author: (with S. A. Riesenfeld) Cases and Materials on Modern Social Legislation, 1950, (with H.R. Williams and C.J. Meyers) Cases on Oil and Gas Law, 1956, 6th edit., (with Stephen F. Williams, Patrick H. Martin, Bruce M. Kramer), 1992, (with S. A. Riesenfeld) California Cases on Security Transactions, 1957, 4th edit. (with S.A. Riesenfeld, J.R. Hetland, W.D. Warren), 1991; West Coast editor Oil and Gas Reporter, 1953—. Mem. Los Angeles Employee Relations Bd., 1971-74; bd. dirs. Constl. Rights Found., 1963-81; trustee Calif. Western U., 1979-81; bd. visitors Duke U. Sch. Law, 1973-79, chmn. bd. Pvt. Adjudication Ctr., 1984-89; bd. visitors Southwestern U. Sch. Law, 1981—. Served to lt. comdr. USNR, 1941-46. Recipient Disting. Tchg. award UCLA, 1977, Duke Law Sch., 1986, UCLA medal, 1982, Clyde O. Martz Tchg. award Rocky Mountain Mineral Law Found., 1994. Mem. ABA (com. on youth edn. for citizenship 1975-79, spl. com. on public understanding about the law 1979-84), Order of Coif. (nat. exec. com. 1980-86). Office: Duke U Sch Law Durham NC 27708-0362

MAXWELL, ROBERT EARL, federal judge; b. Elkins, W.Va., Mar. 15, 1924; s. Earl L. and Nellie E. (Rexstrew) M.; m. Ann Marie Grabowski, Mar. 29, 1948; children—Mary Ann, Carol Lynn, Ellen Lindsay, Earl Wilson. Student, Davis and Elkins Coll., LLD (hon.), 1984; LL.B., W.Va. U., 1949; LLD (hon.), Davis and Elkins Coll., 1984. Bar: W.Va. 1949. Practiced in Randolph County, 1949, pros. atty., 1952-61; U.S. atty. for No. Dist. W.Va., 1961-64; judge U.S. Dist. Ct. (no. dist.) W.Va., Elkins, 1965—, Temp. Emergency Ct. of Appeals, 1980-89; past chmn. budget com. Jud. Conf. U.S.; former mem. exec. com. Nat. Conf. Fed. Trial Judges; former mem. adv. bd. W.Va. U. Mem. bd. advisors W.Va. U., past chmn.; bd. advisors Mary Babb Randolph Cancer Ctr. Recipient Alumni Disting. Svc. award Davis and Elkins Coll., 1969, Religious Heritage Am. award, 1979, Outstanding Trial Judge award W.Va. Trial Lawyers Assn., 1988, Order of Valdalia award W.Va. U., Outstanding Alumnus award, 1992, Tenured Faculty Mem. Recognition award Bd. Govs., Def. Trial Coun., W.Va., 1992, Cert. of Merit, W.Va. State Bar, 1994, Justitia Officium award Coll. of Law, W.Va. U., 1994. Mem. Nat. Conf. Federal Trial Judges, Dist. Judges Assn. 4th Cir. (past pres.), Moose (life), Lions (life), Beta Alpha Beta (merit award), Elkins-Randolph County C. of C. (citizen of yr. 1994). Office: US Dist Ct No Dist PO Box 1275 Elkins WV 26241-1275

MAXWELL, ROBERT HAWORTH, agriculture educator, university administrator; b. Earlham, Iowa, Oct. 8, 1927; s. Charles Erich and Mildred Grace M.; m. Betty Ruth Michener, Dec. 24, 1950; children: Robert Steven, Daniel Guy, Timothy Charles, Kristen Kimuli. Student, Earlham Coll., 1946-48; BS in Farm Ops., Iowa State U., 1950, MS in Agrl. Edn., 1964; PhD in Agrl. Edn., Cornell U., 1970. Cert. tchr., Iowa. Farm operator Iowa, 1952-60; instr. Earlham Coll., Richmond, Ind., 1960-62; tchr. vocat. agr. Earlham (Iowa) Community Sch., 1963-64; asst. prof. agrl. edn. W.Va. U., Morgantown, 1964-68, assoc. prof. agrl. edn., 1970-75, prof. agrl. edn., 1975-79, asst. dean coll. agr. & forestry, acting chmn. divsn. animal & vet. scis., 1980, assoc. dean coll. agr. & forestry, chmn. divsn. internat. agr. & forestry, 1980-84, interim dean coll. agr. & forestry, interim dir. W.Va. agrl. & forestry experiment sta., 1984-85, dean coll. agr. & forestry, dir. W.Va. agrl. & forestry experiment sta., 1985-93; prof. agr., coord. internat. agr. U. W.Va., Morgantown, 1994-95, assoc. provost for ext. and pub. svc., dir. coop. ext. svc., 1995—; vocat. agr. tchr. Dexfield Community Schs., Redfield, Iowa, 1958-60; grad. asst. dept. edn. Cornell U., 1969-70; contract AID agrl. edn. advisor Kenya Ministry Edn., 1960-62, 64-68, spl. asst. dir. manpower devel. divsn. Tanzania Ministry Agr., 1975-79; dir. Allegheny Highlands Project, 1970-75; bd. dirs. Northeast Regional Ctr. Rural Devel., W.Va. U. Rsch. Corp.; lectr. in field. Author: (with others) Agriculture for Primary School series, 1979, 82, 85; editor Empire State Vo-Ag Teacher Jour., 1969-70; pub. papers and reports; contbr. articles to profl. jours. Unit leader United Way, Elkins, W.Va., 1970-75, Morgantown, 1979-93. With U.S. Army, 1950-52. Named Disting. West Virginian Gov. W.Va., 1993; recipient Commemorative medal U. Agr., Nitra, Slovakia, 1993; named to W.Va. Agriculture and Forestry Hall of Fame, 1995. Mem. AAAS, Am. Assn. Agrl. Edn., Am. Farmland Trust (life), Am. Soc. Agrl. Conss. (Meritorious Svc. award 1994), Am. Soc. Agrl. Conss. Internat. (cert., bd. dirs.), Nat. Assn. Colls. and Tchrs. Agr., Nat. Peace Inst., World Future Soc., Soc. Internat. Devel., Assn. Internat. Agrl. and Extension Educators (pres.-elect, pres. 1994, Outstanding Svc. 1991), Assn. Internat. Agr. and Rural Devel. (Outstanding Svc. 1992), Coun. Agrl. Sci. and Tech., Northeast Regional Assn. Agrl. Experiment Sta. Dirs. (Svc. Commendation 1993), UN Assn. of the USA, Soil and Water Conservation Soc. (life), Kenya Assn. Tchrs. Agr. (life), Tanzanian Soc. Agr. Edn. and Extension (life), W.Va. Shepherd's Fedn., W.Va. Poultry Assn., W.Va. Cattlemen's Assn., W.Va. Farm Bur., Iowa Farm Bur., W.Va. Grassland Coun., W.Va. Horticultural Soc., Agriculture and Forestry Hall of Fame Found. W.Va. (past pres.), Upshur Livestock Assn. (life), Morgantown Rotary Club, Iowa State U. Alumni Assn. (life), Cornell U. Alumni Assn. (life), W.Va. U. Alumni Assn. (life), FFA Alumni Assn. (life), Phi Delta Kappa, Gamma Sigma Delta, Alpha Zeta, Phi Mu Alpha (life). Mem. Soc. of Friends. Home: 4009 Cedar Ct Morgantown WV 26505-2823 Office: W Va Univ Coll Agriculture & Forestry Evansdale Campus PO Box 6108 Morgantown WV 26506-6108

MAXWELL, ROBERT OLIVER, insurance company executive; b. Sioux City, Iowa, Sept. 23, 1940; s. Lyle Charles and Corinne Zenobia (Knudson) M.; m. Carol Marie Lejchar, June 23, 1973; 1 child, Todd Robert. BS in Mktg., Drake U., 1962. Office mgr. Occidental Life Ins. Co., L.A., 1962-68; sales rep. William Volker & Co., L.A., 1968-70; mgr. sales office State Farm Ins. Co., Palos Verdes, Calif., 1970-71; pres., CEO Congress Life Ins. Co., Mpls., 1971—; also bd. dirs. Congress Life Ins. Co.; pres., CEO Security Ins. Co., Mpls., 1971—; also bd. dirs. Security Ins. Co. With U.S. Army, 1963-69. Mem. Hazeltine Golf Club. Republican. Lutheran. Home: 15034 Boulder Pointe Rd Eden Prairie MN 55347-2410 Office: Security Life Ins Co 10901 Red Circle Dr Minnetonka MN 55343-9304

MAXWELL, ROBERT WALLACE, II, lawyer; b. Waynesburg, Pa., Sept. 6, 1943; s. Robert Wallace and Margaret M.; m. Mamie Lee Payne, June 18, 1966; children—Virginia, Robert William. B.S. magna cum laude, Hampden-Sydney Coll., 1965; J.D. with honors, Duke U., 1968. Bar: Ohio 1968. Assoc. Taft, Stettinius & Hollister, Cin., 1968-75, ptnr., 1975-88; ptnr. Keating, Muething & Klekamp, 1988— ; part-time instr. U. Cin. Sch. Law, 1975-76. Bd. dirs. Contemporary Arts Ctr. of Cin; bd. dirs. Cin. Ballet Co.; elder Wyoming First Presbyterian Ch. Mem. ABA, Am. Assn. Mus. Trustees. Republican. Home: 535 Larchmont Dr Cincinnati OH 45215-4215 Office: Keating Muething & Klekamp 1 E 4th St Cincinnati OH 45202-3717

MAXWELL, SANDRA ELAINE, guidance counselor; b. Memphis, Jan. 8, 1959; d. Nathaniel and Corine (Sims) Stevenson; m. Clyde Maxwell, Dec. 19, 1981; 1 child, Ryan. BS, Memphis State U., 1980, MS, 1985, postgrad., 1992. Cert. sch. counselor, spl. edn. tchr., cert. in adminstrn. and supervision, Tenn. Guidance counselor Memphis City Schs., 1981—. Mem. NEA, West Tenn. Counselor's Assn., Assn. Am. Sch. Counselors, Memphis Edn. Assn., Tenn. Edn. Assn. Home: 4552 Melwood St Memphis TN 38109-5253

MAXWELL, SARA ELIZABETH, counseling and developmental psychologist, educator, speech & language pathologist, learning consultant, psychoeducational examiner; b. DuQuoin, Ill., Jan. 23; d. Jean A. (Patterson) Green; m. David Lowell Maxwell, Dec. 27, 1960 (div. Mar. 1990); children: Lisa Marina, David Scott. BS, So. Ill. U., 1963, MS, 1964, MSEd, 1965; MEd, Boston Coll., 1982; attended, Harvard U., 1983; PhD, Boston Coll., 1992. Cert. and lic. speech/lang. pathologist, early childhood specialist, guidance counselor, sch. adjustment counselor, EMT. Clin. supr. Clin. Ctr. So. Ill. U., Carbondale, 1964-65, grad. clin. instr., 1965-66; speech/lang. pathologist, sch. adjustment counselor Westwood (Mass.) Pub. Schs., 1967-93; grad. faculty Emerson Coll., Boston, 1979-81; cons. Mass. Dept. Mental Health, Boston, 1979-82; grad. clin. supr. Robbins Speech/Hearing Ctr., Emerson Coll., Boston, 1979-82; cons. Westwood Nursery Preschs., 1986-93; devel. and clin. staff psychologist S. Shore Mental Health Ctr., Hingham and Quincy, Mass., 1989-93; emergency svcs. team and respite house manager S. Shore Mental Health Ctr., Quincy, Mass., 1990-93; pvt. practice Twin Oaks Clin. Assocs., Westwood, Mass, 1986-88, S. Coast Counseling Assocs., Quincy, 1989-93; cons. local collaboratives and preschs., Westwood, 1980-93; profl. workshops presenter Head Start, 1980; predoctoral intern in clin. psychology S. Shore Mental Health Ctr., Quincy, 1985-86; program specialist speech and lang. learning Broward County (Fla.) Schs., 1993—; adj. prof. grad. dept. sch. psychology Nova Southeastern U., 1995—; presenter Head Start, ASHA, CEC, APSC, IALP, and other profl. nat. and state confs., 1980-93; invited del. to Sino-Am. Conf. on Exceptionality Beijing U., 1995. Contbr. articles to profl. jours., chpts. to textbooks. Mem. adv. coun. Westwood Bd. Health, 1977-80; emergency med. technician Westwood Pub. Schs. Athletic Dept., 1981. Vocat. Rehab. fellow So. Ill. U., 1964; Merit scholar Perry County, Ill., 1959-64, Gloria Credi Meml. scholar So. Ill. U., 1964. Mem. APA, Am. Speech and Hearing Assn. (nat. schs. com., nat. chairperson Pub. Sch. Caucus 1985-87), Assn. Psychiat. Svcs. for Children, Coun. Exceptional Children, Internat. Assn. of Logopedics, Rio Vista Civic Assn., Boston Coll. Alumni Assn., Harvard Club, Sigma Kappa. Episcopalian. Avocations: squash, sailing, skiing. Office: Nova Southeastern U 3301 College Ave Fort Lauderdale FL 33314-7721

MAXWELL, W(ILBUR) RICHARD, management consultant; b. Troy, Ohio, June 20, 1920; s. Wilbur D. and Gertrude (McDowell) M.; m. Roberta Mae Kennedy, June 29, 1942; children: Douglas R., Jean Ann. Student, Ohio Wesleyan U., 1938-41; BS, Richmond Profl. Inst. of Coll. William and Mary, 1955. Sec. Troy C. of C., 1948-50, Va. C. of C., 1950-55; asst. to pres./chmn. bd. Reynolds Metals Co., 1955-64; v.p., dir. Reynolds Fgn. Sales Inc., 1964-68; pres. Nat. Better Bus. Bur., 1968-70; pres., chief exec. officer Jr. Achievement, Inc., Stamford, Conn., 1970-82; instr. Richmond Profl. Inst., part-time 1955-57; sponsor-trustee U. Va. Grad. Bus. Sch., 1963-72. Pres. Lancaster County Libr., 1984-85, Rappahannock Gen. Hosp. Found., 1988-90, Northern Neck Vocat.-Tech. Edn. Ctr., 1991-93; bd. dirs. Rappahannock Gen. Hosp., 1988-90, Richmond (Va.) Cmty. H.S., 1989-91; chmn. Northumberland County (Va.) Econ. Devel. Commn., 1994—. Civilian specialist USAAF, USN, 1942-46. Recipient Albert Schweitzer award Hugh O'Brien Youth Fedn., 1982; inducted Jr. Achievement Profl. Hall of Fame, 1986. Mem. Indian Creek Yacht and Country Club (v.p., 1991-93, bd. dirs. 1991-93). Home: PO Box 1090 Kilmarnock VA 22482-1090

MAXWELL, WILLIAM HALL CHRISTIE, civil engineering educator; b. Coleraine, County Londonderry, Northern Ireland, Jan. 25, 1936; came to U.S., 1958, naturalized, 1967; s. William Robert and Catherine Dempsey (Christie) M.; m. Mary Carolyn McLaughlin, Sept. 28, 1960; children: Katrina, Kevin, Wendy, Liam. B.Sc., Queen's U., Belfast, No. Ireland, 1956; M.Sc., Queen's U., Kingston, Ont., Can., 1958; Ph.D., U. Minn., 1964. Registered profl. engr., Ill. Site engr. Motor Columbus AG, Baden, Switzerland, 1956; teaching asst. Queen's U., 1956-58; research asst. to instr. U. Minn., Mpls., 1959-64; asst. prof. civil engring. U. Ill., Urbana, 1964-70, assoc. prof., 1970-82, prof., 1982—; chmn. program com. First Internat. Conf. on New/ Emerging Concepts for Rivers, Chgo., 1996. Editor: Water Resources Management in Industrial Areas, 1982; Water for Human Consumption, Man and His Environment, 1983; Frontiers in Hydrology, 1984. Vestryman, Emmanuel Meml. Episcopal Ch., Champaign, Ill., 1977-80. State exhibitor Ministry Edn., Stormont, No. Ireland, 1953-56; Queen's U. Found. scholar, Belfast, 1954-56; R.S. McLaughlin travelling fellow Queen's U., 1958-59. Fellow ASCE (com. chmn. 1982-83), Internat. Water Resources Assn. (editor-in-chief Water Internat. 1986-93, sr. editor 1994—, mem. publs. com. 1980—, v.p. U.S. geog. com. 1986-91, chmn. awards com. 1995—, bd. dirs. 1995—, Editl. award 1994); mem. Internat. Assn. for Hydraulic Research, Am. Geophys. Union. Avocations: camping, fishing, home construction, oil painting. Home: 1210 Devonshire Dr Champaign IL 61821-6527 Office: U Ill Dept Civil Engring 205 N Mathews Ave Urbana IL 61801-2352

MAXWELL, WILLIAM LAUGHLIN, industrial engineering educator; b. Phila., July 11, 1934; s. William Henry and Elizabeth (Laughlin) M.; m. Judith Behrens, July 5, 1969; children: Deborah, William, Judith, Keely. BMechE, Cornell U., 1957, PhD, 1961. Andrew Schultz Jr. prof. dept. indsl. engring. Cornell U., Ithaca, N.Y., 1961—. Author: Theory of Scheduling, 1967. Recipient Disting. Teaching award Cornell Soc. Engrs., 1968. Fellow Inst. Indsl. Engrs.; mem. Ops. Rsch. Soc., Soc. Mfg. Engrs. Home: 106 Lake Ave Ithaca NY 14850-3537 Office: Cornell U Dept Indsl Engring Ithaca NY 14850

MAXWELL, WILLIAM STIRLING, retired lawyer; b. Chgo., May 2, 1922; s. W. Stirling and Ethel (Bowes) Maxwell Reineke. A.B. with distinction, U. Mich., 1947, postgrad., 1946-49, J.D., 1949. Bar: Ill. 1949, U.S. Ct. Mil. Appeals 1951, U.S. Supreme Ct. 1952. Assoc. Sidley & Austin, Chgo., 1949-60, 61, ptnr., 1962-84; now ret.; sr. legis. counsel U.S. Treasury, Washington, 1960-61. Trustee Mid-North Animal Shelter Found., Chgo., 1971—. Mem. Order of Coif, Phi Beta Kappa. Republican. Episcopalian. Clubs: Law, Legal (Chgo.). Home: PO Box 1776 Brookings OR 97415-0058

MAXWORTHY, TONY, mechanical and aerospace engineering educator; b. London, May 21, 1933; came to U.S., 1954, naturalized, 1961; s. Ernest Charles and Gladys May (Butson) M.; m. Emily Jean Parkinson, June 20, 1956 (div. 1974); children: Kirsten, Kara; m. Anna Barbara Parks, May 21, 1979. BS in Engring., U. London, 1954; MSE, Princeton U., 1955; PhD, Harvard U., 1959. Research asst. Harvard U., Cambridge, Mass., 1955-59; sr. scientist, group supr. Jet Propulsion Lab., Pasadena, Calif., 1960-67, cons., 1968—; assoc. prof. U. So. Calif., Los Angeles, 1967-70, prof., 1970—, Smith Internat. prof. mech. and aero. engring., 1988—, chmn. dept. mech. engring., 1979-89; cons. BBC Rsch. Ctr., Baden, Switzerland, 1972—, J.P.L., Pasadena, Calif., 1968—; lectr. Woods Hole Oceanographic Inst., Mass., summers 1965, 70, 72, 83; Forman vis. prof. aeronautics Technion Haifa, 1986; vis. prof. U. Poly., Madrid, 1988, Inst. Sup. Tech., Lisbon, 1988, Swiss Fed. Inst. Tech., Zurich, 1989, E.P.F., Lausanne, 1989—; assoc. prof. IMG, U. Joseph Fourier, Grenoble, 1980—, Higher Sch. Physics and Indsl. Chemistry, Paris, 1995; Shimizu vis. prof. Stanford U., 1996. Mem. editorial bd. Geophys. Fluid Dynamics, 1973-79, 88—, Dynamic Atmospheric Oceans, 1976-83, Phys. Fluids, 1978-81, Zeitschrift fuer Angewandte Mathematik und Physik, 1987—; contbr. articles to profl. jours. Recipient Humboldt sr. scientist award, 1981-93; fellow Cambridge U., 1974, 93-95, Australian Nat. U., 1978, Nat. Ctr. Atmospheric Rsch., 1976; Glennon fellow U. Western Australia, 1990, F.W. Mosey fellow, 1993; sr. Queen's fellow in marine scis. Commonwealth of Australia, 1984. Fellow Am. Phys. Soc. (chmn. exec. com. fluid dynamics divsn. 1974-79, Otto Laporte award 1990); Mem. NAE, ASME, Am. Meteorol. Soc., Am. Geophys. Union, European Geophys. Soc. Office: U So Calif Dept Mech Engring Exposition Park Los Angeles CA 90089-1453

MAY, ADOLF DARLINGTON, civil engineering educator; b. Little Rock, Mar. 25, 1927; s. Adolf Darlington and Inez (Shelton) M.; m. Margaret Folsom, Dec. 23, 1948; children—Dolf, Barbara, David, Larry. B.Sc. in Civil Engring, So. Meth. U., 1949; M.Sc., Iowa State U., 1950; Ph.D., Purdue U., 1955. Asst. prof., then assoc. prof. Clarkson Coll. Tech., 1952-56; assoc. prof. Mich. State U., 1956-59; research engr. Thompson-Ramo Wooldridge, 1959-62; project dir. Ill. Div. Hwys., 1962-65; mem. faculty U. Calif., Berkeley, 1965—, prof. civil engring., 1965-91, prof. emeritus, 1991—; guest prof. numerous univs., 1965—, cons. to industry, 1965—. Contbr. to profl. jours., books. Served with USNR, 1944-47. Recipient Disting. Engring. Alumnus award Purdue U., 1978, Transp. Sci. and Ethics Internat. award, 1995; Fulbright scholar to Netherlands, 1977; German Humboldt scholar, 1980. Mem. ASCE (Turner award 1994), Transp. Rsch. Bd. (Disting. Lectr. award 1994), Nat. Acad. Engring. (Matson Transp. Rsch. award 1992), Am. Soc. Engring. Edn. (hon.), Inst. Traffic Engrs. (award 1995), Sigma Xi, Tau Beta Pi. Home: 1645 Julian Dr El Cerrito CA 94530-2011 Office: U Calif Dept of Civil Engring 114 McLaughlin Hall Berkeley CA 94720

MAY, ARTHUR W., university president; b. St. John's, Nfld., Can., June 29, 1937; s. William J. and Florence (Dawe), M.; m. Sonia Susan Streeter, Aug. 18, 1958; children—Stephen J., Heather E., Maria S., Douglas W. BSc with honors, Meml. U., St. John's, 1958; MSc, Meml. U., 1964; PhD, McGill U., Montreal, Que., Can., 1966; D of Univ. (hon.), U. Ottawa, 1988; DSc (hon.), Meml. U. Nfld., 1989; LLD (hon.), Brock U., 1992. Sci. adviser internat. fisheries Dept. Fisheries, Ottawa, Ont., Can., 1971-73; dir. Nfld. biol. sta. Dept. Fisheries, St. John's, 1973-75; dir. gen. resource services Dept. Fisheries, Ottawa, 1975-78; asst. dep. minister Atlantic Dept. Fisheries and Oceans, Ottawa, 1978-82; dep. minister Dept. Fisheries and Oceans, 1982-86; pres. Natural Sci. and Engring. Rsch. Coun. Canada, 1986-90; pres., vice chancellor Meml. U. Nfld., St. Johns, 1990—; v.p. Internat. Coun. for Exploration of Seas, Copenhagen, 1977-79; mem. Task Force on Atlantic Fisheries, Ottawa, 1982, Nat. Adv. Bd. Sci. and Tech., 1988-90, 94-95; Canadian rep. to NATO Sci. Conf., 1990—. Contbr. articles to profl. jours. Served to sub. lt. Can. Navy, 1955-58. Decorated officer Order of Can.; recipient Gov.-Gen.'s medal Nfld. Dept. Edn., 1954, Meml. U. Nfld., 1958; named Alumnus of Yr., Meml. U. Nfld., 1983. Mem. N.W. Atlantic Fisheries Orgn. (pres. 1977-80). Anglican. Avocations: gardening; philately. Home: 20 Baker St, Saint John's, NF Canada A1A 5A7 Office: Meml Univ Nfld, Saint John's, NF Canada A1C 5S7

MAY, BEVERLY, elementary school educator; b. Marshall, Tex., Sept. 11, 1939; d. Carl Glendon and Omie Louise (Berry) Brewster; m. William Raymond May, Sept. 19, 1958; children: William Jr., Karri, David. BS in Elem. Edn., U. Houston, 1969, MEd, 1978. Cert. elem. tchr., profl. reading specialist, profl. supr., Tex. Ednl. materials rep. World Book/Childcraft, Houston, 1975-90; reading cons. Region IV Edn. Svc. Ctr., Houston, 1977-83; supr. reading lab. downtown campus U. Houston, 1985; clk. sec. Houston Ind. Sch. Dist., 1957-64, tchr. grades two, three, seven Elem. Reading Ctr., 1969-90; pvt. reading skills and study skills specialist, 1975—; cons., presenter workshops in field. clerical/secretarial (1957-90). gr 2,3,7, elem. reading center, 1969-90. Participant TV-Radio broadcast ministries workshop 1st Bapt. Ch., Houston, 1988.all organizations are current. Mem. Inspirational Writers Alive, Soc. Children's Book Writers and Illustrators, Internat. Reading Assn., Greater Houston Area Reading Coun. Home: 2102 Du Barry Ln Houston TX 77018-5060

MAY, CECIL RICHARD, JR., academic adminstrator; b. Memphis, June 13, 1932. BA in biblical langs. magna cum laude, Harding U., MA in New Testament, MTh; LLD (hon.), Freed-Hardeman U., 1984. Min. Holly Springs, Miss., 1954-57, Ripley, Miss., 1957-59; min. Pine Bluff Ch., Ctrl. Acad. Ch., Miss., 1959-60; dist. scout exec. Yocona Area Coun. Boy Scouts Am., Oxford, Miss., 1959-60; min. Ashland, Miss., 1961, Fulton, Miss., 1962-67; min. Eastside Campus Ch., Portland, Oreg., 1967-69; Bible tchr. Columbia Christian Coll., Portland, 1967-69; min. Vicksburg, Miss., 1969-76; dean Internat. Bible Coll., Florence, Ala., 1977-80; pres. Magnolia Bible Coll., Kosciusko, Miss., 1980—; lectr. in field. Editor: Preacher Talk; assoc. editor: Magnolia Messenger; contbr. articles to profl. jours. Elder Vicksburg (Miss.) Ch., 1971-76, South Huntington St. Ch., Kosciusko, 1981—; active Boy Scouts Am., 1954-76; com. chair Kosciusko-Attala County C. of C., 1992; bd. dirs. Am. Cancer Soc., 1971-74, fin. campaign chmn., 1971; bd. dirs. Miss. Econ. Coun., 1985-86, 89-92, area vice-chmn., 1991-92; chmn. Attala County Med. Study Task Force, 1991-92. Mem. Nat. Assn. Ind. Coll. and Univs., Miss. Assn. Ind. Colls. (bd. dirs.), Evang. Theol. Soc., Miss. Assn. Colls., Rotary Club (bd. dirs. 1983-85, pres. 1985-86). Office: Magnolia Bible Coll PO Box 1109 Kosciusko MS 39090-1109

MAY, CHARLES KENT, lawyer; b. Pitts., Nov. 28, 1939; s. Charles Leroy and Nora Margaret (Brown) M.; m. Valerie Lynne Harrell, May 18, 1981; children: C. Kent, Kerry Elizabeth, Kathryn Lynn, Andrew John, James Davis, Grant Stevens. BA, Dickinson Coll., 1961; LLB, U. Pitts., 1964. Bar: Pa. 1965, U.S. Dist. Ct. (we. dist.) Pa. 1965. Assoc. Eckert Seamans Cherin & Mellott, Pitts., 1964-70, ptnr., 1971—, chmn. corp. bus. dept., 1986-91, mng. ptnr., 1991-95; chmn. Western Pa. Better Bus. Bur., 1992-93; dir. Western Pa. BBB, 1991-93, chmn., 1992-93; bd. dirs., v.p. The Pilot Group co., Ltd.; bd. dirs. Consumers Packaging Inc., Fabrica de Envases de Vidrio S.A. de C., Main St. Capital Holdings, L.L.C., The Stiffel co. Bd. dirs., mem. exec. com. Pitts. Pub. Theatre; bd. dirs. Mendelssohn Choir, Main St. Capital, Children's Home Pitts., 1978-79. Mem. ABA, Pa. Bar Assn., Allegheny County Bar Assn., Duquesne Club. Republican. Home: 137 Old Mill Rd Pittsburgh PA 15238-1941 Office: Eckert Seamans Cherin & Mellott 600 Grant St Pittsburgh PA 15219-2702

MAY, CLIFFORD DANIEL, newspaper editor, journalist; m. Lou Ann Brunwasser; children: Miranda Rose, Evan Phillip Barr. Cert. in Russian lang. and lit., U. Leningrad, 1972; BA, Sarah Lawrence Coll., 1973; M Journalism, Columbia U., 1975, M Internat. Affairs, 1975. Assoc. editor Newsweek, 1975-78; roving fgn. corr. Hearst Newpapers, 1978-79; sr. editor Am. edit. Geo mag., 1979-80; gen. editor Sunday Mag., Washington corr. N.Y. Times, 1980-89; chief West Africa bur. N.Y. Times, Abidjan, Ivory Coast, 1984; assoc. editor Rocky Mountain News, Denver, 1989—; spl. corr. CBS Radio News, Bill Moyers' Jour./Internat. Report-PBS-TV, 1970's; host, prodr. Roundtable, Sta. KRMA, Colo.; freelance writer, 1979-89. Contbg. editor World Press Rev. Mag.; host, prodr. roundtable Sta. KRMA, Denver, 1994—; host Race for the Presidency TCI News, 1995-96. Avocations: downhill skiing, outdoor activities. Office: Rocky Mountain News 400 W Colfax Ave Denver CO 80204-2607

MAY, DAVID A., protective services official, public official; b. Buffalo, N.Y., May 23, 1947; s. Arthur F. M.; m. Mary E. Beer, Oct. 6, 1973; children: Jordan D., Jared R. AAS in Bus. Adminstrn., Niagara County C.C., Sanborn, N.Y., 1983; BS in Pub. Adminstrn., Empire State Coll., 1988; MA in Orgn. Mgmt., U. Phoenix, 1996. V.p. Simpson Security, Inc., Niagara Falls, N.Y., 1973-78; lt. Niagara Falls (N.Y.) Police Dept., 1986—. Bd. mem. Nat. Conf. Christians and Jews, 1984-90, ARC, 1986-89, Music Sch. of Niagara, 1987-90, Niagara Falls Little Theatre, chmn., 1994; pres. Niagara Cmty. Ctr., Niagara Falls, 1987, Niagara Falls (N.Y.) Sch. Bd., 1988, Niagara Falls (N.Y.) Meml. Day Assn., 1990, 91, 93; lt. gov. N.Y. State Kiwanis, 1989; mem. Niagara Co. Lrgis., 1994. Recipient Svc. award Fellowship House Found., Niagara Falls, 1986; named Civic Leader of Yr., Niagara Cmty. Ctr., Niagara Falls, 1990. Mem. Kiwanis Club North Niagara Falls (pres. 1987, Kiwanian of the Yr. 1991), Lasalle Am. Legion (vice commdr. 1975), Lasalle Sportsmens Club (fin. sec. 1989). Avocations: playing tennis, golfing, amateur historian. Home: 3024 Macklem Ave Niagara Falls NY 14305-1832

MAY, DONALD ROBERT LEE, ophthalmologist, retina and vitreous surgeon, educator, academic administrator; b. Spring Valley, Ill., Nov. 26, 1945; s. Reo Georg and Edna Antoinette (Klein) M.; m. Jane N. Sakauye, Nov. 12, 1988. BS in Liberal Arts and Scis. with high honors, U. Ill., 1968, MD, 1972. Diplomate Am. Bd. Ophthalmology, Nat. Bd. Med. Examiners. Med. student rsch. fellow Dept. Ophthalmology U. Ill. Eye and Ear Infirmary, Chgo., 1971-72; intern rotating internal medicine Northwestern U. Sch. Medicine Meml. Hosps., Chgo., 1972-73; resident Ophthalmology U. Ill. Eye and Ear Infirmary, Chgo., 1973-76, instr. dept. Ophthalmology, 1974-77, attending surgeon dept. Ophthalmology, 1976-77; fellow in Diabetic Retinopathy study, Diabetic Retinopathy Vitrectomy study, and Retina and Vitreous Surgery U. Ill. Eye and Ear Infirmary, 1976-77; founder and dir. Retina/Vitreous/Ocular Trauma Svc. of the USAF dept. Ophthalmology, Wilford Hall USAF Medical Ctr., Lackland AFB, Tex., 1977-79; asst. prof. Ophthalmology, founder, dir. Retina/Vitreous/Ocular Trauma Svc. U. Calif. Davis Sch. Medicine, Calif., 1979-81; assoc. prof. of Ophthalmology, dir. Retina/Vitreous/Ocular Trauma Svc. U. Calif. Sch. Medicine, Davis, 1981-84; prof. Ophthalmology Tulane U. Sch. Medicine, New Orleans, 1984-89, dir. med. student edn., dept. of Ophthalmology, 1985-89; dir. Ophthalmology Tulane U. Sch. Medicine div., Charity Hosp., New Orleans, 1985-89; prof. Tex. Tech. U. Health Scis. Ctr., Lubbock, Tex., 1989—; chmn. dept. ophthalmology and visual scis. Tex. Tech. U. Health Scis. Ctr., Lubbock, 1989-94; prof. dept. health orgn. mgmt. Tex. Tech U. Health Scis. Ctr., Lubbock, 1993—, assoc. dean Sch. Medicine, 1994—; co-investigator in the Intraocular Gentamicin Prophylaxis Study, Govt. Erskine Hosp., Madurai, So. India, 1975, Dept. Ophthalmology, Audie Murphy VA Hosp., San Antonio, 1977-79, Martinez VA Hosp., Calif., 1979-84, VA Hosp., New Orleans, 1984-89, VA Med. Ctr., Alexandria, La., 1985-89, VA Med. Ctr., Big Spring, Tex., 1989-93, VA Ctr., Lubbock, Tex., 1989-92; cons. People's

Republic China, 1980, 82, 85, 96, Japan, 1982, 83, 85; vis. prof. Germany, 1984, Switzerland, 1987; 1st v.p. U.S. Eye Injury Registry, 1990-92, pres.-elect, 1992-94, pres. 1994-96; founder, med. dir. Tex. Eye Injury Registry. Contbg. editor Ocutome/Fragmatome Newsletter, 1978-81; assoc. editor Vitreoretinal Surgery and Tech., 1989—; mem. editl. bd. Jour. Eye Trauma, 1996—; contbr. articles to profl. jours.; appeared in numerous TV and radio programs. Mem. coms. Sch. Medicine, U. Calif., Davis, Tulane U. Sch. Medicine, New Orleans, Am. Acad. Ophthalmology, San. Francisco, Sch. Medicine Tex. Tech. U. Health Scis. Ctr.; U. Med. Ctr., Lubbock. Maj. USAF, 1973-80. Decorated Air Force Commendation medal. Mem. ACS, AMA, Am. Acad. Ophthalmology, Assn. Rsch. in Vision and Ophthalmology, Chinese Am. Ophthal. Soc. (charter mem.), Christian Med. Soc., So. Med. Assn. (vice chmn. sec. ophthalmology 1995-96), So. Retina Study Group (steering com. 1987-89), Tex. Med. Assn. (com. continuing edn. 1993—), Tex. Ophthal. Assn. (chair edn. com. 1990-93, coun. 1990-93, nominating com. 1991-93), Tex. Tech. Rsch. Found. (bd. dirs. 1993—), The Pan-Am. Assn. Ophthalmology, The Retina Soc., The Vitreous Soc. (charter mem.), World Eye Found. (bd. dirs. 1982—), Soc. Med. Cons. to Armed Forces, Sigma Xi (sec. Tex. Tech. chpt. 1990-91). Republican. Lutheran. Avocations: farming, travel, photography, cycling, hiking. Home: PO Box 1678 Lubbock TX 79408-1678 Office: Tex Tech U Health Scis Ctr Sch Medicine Office of Dean Lubbock TX 79430 *If we are to survive as a free society, we must each accept responsibility. The individual must function on the premise that personal rewards come with the investment of hard, honest work and not as a right mediated by government at the expense of others. Our legislative bodies must enact laws for the common good and not for individual self-interest. Our judicial systems must provide for the just enforcement of our laws. Our leadership must be the watchdog to ensure the indivdual has the opportunity to life without unreasonable danger, the freedom to follow one's dreams, and the ability to pursue happiness through individual achievement. Security comes with the contribution of all who are able.*

MAY, EDGAR, former state legislator, nonprofit administrator; b. Zurich, Switzerland, June 27, 1929; came to U.S., 1940, naturalized, 1954; s. Ferdinand and Renee (Bloch) M. B.J. with highest distinction, Northwestern U., 1957. Reporter, acting editor Bellows Falls (Vt.) Times, 1951-53; reporter Fitchburg (Mass.) Sentinel, 1953; part time reporter Chgo. Tribune, 1955-57; reporter Buffalo Evening News, 1958-61; dir. pub. welfare projects State Charities Aid Assn., 1962-64; mem. President's Task Force on War Against Poverty, 1964; spl. asst. to dir., asst. dir. Office Econ. Opportunity, 1964; spl. adviser to Ambassador Sargent Shriver, 1968-70; cons. Ford Found., 1970-75; mem. Vt. Ho. of Reps., 1975-82; mem. Vt. Senate, 1983-91, chmn. com. appropriations; project dir. Vt. Jud. Mgmt. Study, 1992; COO Spl. Olympics Internat., Washington, 1993—. Author: The Wasted Americans, 1964. With AUS, 1953-55. Recipient Page One award Buffalo Newspaper Guild, 1959, Walter O. Bingham award, 1959; Pulitzer prize for local reporting, 1961; Merit award Northwestern U. Alumni Assn., 1962. Office: 1325 G St NW Washington DC 20005

MAY, EILEEN MARIE, elementary education educator; b. Bklyn., Aug. 10, 1945; d. Leo John and Helen Agnes (McGowan) Kelly; m. Albert William May, Aug. 16, 1975; children: Michael Raymond, James Leo. BA in Econs., Coll. of St. Elizabeth, 1967; cert. elem. edn., William Paterson Coll. N.J., 1983. Various retail mgmt. positions N.J., 1967-77; tchr. St. Joseph's Sch., Maplewood, N.J., 1977-79, Sacred Heart Sch., Dover, N.J., 1979-82; tchr. compensatory edn. Lenape Valley H.S., Stanhope, N.J., 1987-90; tchr. Rev. George Brown Sch., Sparta, N.J., 1990—. Grantee A Plus for Kids, 1992. Mem. Nat. Cath. Edn. Assn., Nat. Coun. Tchrs. Math., Assn. of Math. Tchrs. N.J., N.J. Math. Coalition. Home: 127 Marne Rd Hopatcong NJ 07843-1843

MAY, ELAINE, actress, theatre and film director; b. Phila., Apr. 21, 1932; d. Jack Berlin; m. Marvin May (div.); 1 child, Jeannie Berlin; m. Sheldon Harnick, Mar. 25, 1962 (div. May 1963). Ed. high sch., studied Stanislavsky method of acting withMarie Ouspenskaya. Stage and radio appearances as child actor; performed with Playwright's Theatre, in student performance Miss Julie, U. Chgo.; appeared with improvisational theatre group in night club The Compass, Chgo., 1954-1957, (with Mike Nichols) appeared N.Y. supper clubs, Village Vanguard, Blue Angel, also night clubs other cities; TV debut on Jack Paar Show, 1957; also appeared in Omnibus, 1958, Dinah Shore Show, Perry Como Show, Laugh Line, Laugh-In, TV spls.; comedy albums include Improvisations to Music, An Evening with Mike Nichols and Elaine May, Mike Nichols and Elaine May Examine Doctors; weekly appearance NBC radio show Nightline; appeared (with Mike Nichols) NBC radio show, N.Y. Town Hall, 1959, An Evening with Mike Nichols and Elaine May, Golden Theatre, N.Y.C., 1960-61; theater appearances include The Office, N.Y.C., 1966, Who's Afraid of Virginia Woolf?, Long Wharf Theatre, New Haven, Conn., 1980; dir. plays The Third Ear, N.Y.C., 1964, The Goodbye People, Berkshire Theater Festival, Stockbridge, Mass., 1971, various plays at Goodman Theatre, Chgo., 1983; dir., author screenplay, actress film A New Leaf, 1972; dir. films The Heartbreak Kid, 1973, Mikey and Nicky, 1976 (writer, dir. remake 1985), Ishtar, 1987 (also writer); appeared in films Luv, 1967, California Suite, 1978 (Acad. award Best Supporting Actress 1978), In The Spirit, 1990; co-author screenplay Heaven Can Wait, 1978, Birdcage, 1996; author plays A Matter of Position, 1962, Not Enough Rope, 1962, Adaptation, 1969, Hot Line, 1983, Better Part of Valor, 1983, Mr. Gogol and Mr. Preen, 1991, (one act) Death Defying Acts, 1995; stage revue: (with Mike Nichols) Telephone, 1984; co-recipient (with Mike Nichols) Grammy award for comedy performance, Nat. Acad. Recording Arts & Scis., 1961. Office: care Julian Schlossberg Castle Hill Productions 1414 Ave of the Americas New York NY 10019*

MAY, ERNEST MAX, charitable organization official; b. Newark, July 24, 1913; s. Otto Bernard and Eugenie (Morgenstern) M.; m. Harriet Elizabeth Dewey, Oct. 12, 1940; children: Ernest Dewey, James Northrup, Susan Elizabeth. BA, Princeton, 1934, MA, 1935; PhD in Organic Chemistry, U. Chgo., 1938; LittD (hon.), Montclair State Coll., 1989. With Otto B. May, Inc., Newark, 1938-73; successively chemist, gen. mgr. Otto B. May, Inc., 1938-52, pres., 1952-73; trustee Youth Consultation Service Diocese of Newark, 1952-59, 61-66, 68—; pres., 1971-75; dir. Cone Mills Corp., 1961-73, mem. exec. com., 1968-71; tech. adviser to spl. rep. trade negotiations, 1964-67. Councilman, Summit, N.J., 1963-70; mem. Summit Environ. Com., 1971-75, chmn., 1974-75; pres. Family Svc. Assn. Summit, 1959-61, Mental Health Assn. Summit, 1964, Summit Coun. Chs. Christ, 1962-63; mem. exec. com. Christ Hosp., Jersey City, 1971—, v.p., chmn., 1974—; chmn. Summit Hwy. Adv. Com., 1976-94; trustee, organizer Summer Organic Chemistry Inst., Choate Sch., Wallingford, Conn.; mem. Union County Mental Health Bd., 1973-76; bd. dirs. N.J. Mental Health Assn., 1974-81; trustee Montclair (N.J.) State Univ., 1975-85, vice-chmn., 1976-80, chmn., 1980-83; adviser applied prof. psychology Rutgers U., 1976—; mem. Nat. commn. on Nursing, 1980-83; adviser dept. music Princeton U.; trustee Assn. for Children in N.J., 1975—, Citizen's Com. on Biomed. Ethics in N.J., 1984-95, N.J. Health Decisions, 1995—; advisor Nat. Exec. Svcs. Corps Health Care Consulting Group, 1994—. Fellow Am. Inst. Chemists; mem. Am. Chem. Soc., Sweiss Chem. Soc., German Chem. Soc., Synthetic Organic Chem. Mfrs. Assn. (bd. govs. 1952-54, 63-70, v.p. 1966-68, chmn. internat. comml. rels. com. 1968-73, hon. mem.), Vol. Trustees Not-for-Profit Hosps. (trustee 1986-88, 94—), Met. Opera (N.Y.), Chemists Club (N.Y.), Beacon Hill Club (Summit, N.J.), Nassau Club (Princeton), N.J. Hosp. Assn. (coun. on edn. 1990-91), Sigma Xi. Republican. Episcopalian (vestry 1950-60). Home: 57 Colt Rd Summit NJ 07901-3004 also: State Rd Chilmark MA 02535 *To live right and help others live right too, each in his own way.*

MAY, ERNEST RICHARD, historian, educator; b. Ft. Worth, Tex., Nov. 19, 1928; s. Ernest and Rachel (Garza) M.; m. Nancy Caughey, Dec. 15, 1950 (div. Feb. 1982); children: John Ernest, Susan Rachel, Donna LaRee; m. Susan B. Wood, June 22, 1988. A.B., UCLA, 1948, M.A. (Native Sons of Golden West fellow in history), 1949, Ph.D. (Univ. fellow), 1951; M.A. (hon.), Harvard U., 1959. Lectr. history Los Angeles State Coll., 1950; mem. hist. sect. Joint Chiefs of Staff, 1952-54; instr. history Harvard U., 1954-56, asst. prof., 1956-59, assoc. prof., 1959-63, prof., 1963—, Charles Warren prof. history, 1981—; Allston Burr sr. tutor Harvard U. (Kirkland House), 1960-66; mem. Harvard U. (Inst. Politics), 1967—, dir. inst., 1971-74, dean of coll., 1969-71, assoc. dean faculty arts & scis., 1970-71; mem. Council on Fgn. Relations. Author: The World War and American Isolation, 1914-17, 1959, The Ultimate Decision, The President as Commander in Chief, 1960, Imperial Democracy, The Emergence of America as a Great Power, 1961, The American Image, 4 vols, 1963, (with John W. Caughey) A History of the United States, 1964, (with editors of Life) The Progressive Era, 1964, War, Boom and Bust, 1964, From Isolation to Imperialism, 1898-1919, 1964, (with John W. Caughey and John Hope Franklin) Land of the Free, 1966, American Imperialism; A Speculative Essay, 1968, Lessons of the Past: The Use and Misuse of History in American Foreign Policy, 1973, The Making of The Monroe Doctrine, 1975, (with Dorothy G. Blaney) Careers for Humanists, 1981; author: A Proud Nation, 1983, Knowing One's Enemies: Intelligence Assessment before the Two World Wars, 1984, (with Richard E. Neustadt) Thinking in Time; The Uses of History for Decision Making, 1986 (Gravemeyer prize 1987), American Cold War Strategy: NSC 69, 1994; author also numerous articles. Chmn. bd. control John Anson Kittredge Trust. Served as lt. (j.g.) USNR, 1951-54. Guggenheim fellow, 1958-59; faculty research fellow Social Sci. Research Council, 1959-61; fellow Center for Advanced Study Behavioral Scis., 1963-64; fellow Woodrow Wilson Internat. Center, 1983. Mem. Mass. Hist. Soc., Am. Hist. Assn., Soc. Historians Am. Fgn. Relations (pres. 1982-83), AAUP, Am. Acad. Arts and Scis. Episcopalian. Club: Belmont Hill. Office: History Dept Harvard U Cambridge MA 02138

MAY, FELTON EDWIN, bishop; b. Chgo., Apr. 23, 1935; s. James Albert May and Florine C. (Felton) May Caruthers; m. Phyllis Elizabeth Henry, June 22, 1963; children: Daphne Endrea, Felton Edwin II. B.A., Judson Coll., 1962; M.Div., Crozer Theol. Sem., 1970; DD, Lycoming Coll., 1989, Lebanon Valley Coll., 1989, Wesley Coll., Dover, Del., 1990, Rust Coll., 1996. Ordained deacon United Meth. Ch., 1962, elder, 1970. Asst. pastor St. James Meth. Ch., Chgo., 1961-63; pastor Maple Park United Meth. Ch., Chgo., 1963-68; assoc. exec. dir. Meth. Action Program, Wilmington, Del., 1968-70, Ezion-Mt. Carmel United Meth. Ch., Wilmington, 1970-75; dist. supt. Peninsula Conf., United Meth. Ch., Easton, Md., 1975-81; coun. dir. Peninsula Conf., United Meth. Ch., Dover, 1981-84; bishop United Meth. Ch., Harrisburg, Pa., 1984-90; spl. assignment Coun. of Bishops, Washington, 1990-91; bishop United Meth. Ch., Harrisburg, 1991—; chairperson United Meth. Shalom Communities Com., 1992, Pan Meth. Commn., 1993; co-chair Coalition of Religious Leaders, Harrisburg, Pa. Author: Developmental Evangelism (workbook), 1979; co-contbr. articles to mags.; co-author church sch. curriculum. Mem. Atty.'s Grievance Com., Annapolis, 1979-81; bd. govs. Wesley Sem., Washington, 1975—; bd. dirs. Boy Scouts Am., Dover, 1981-83, Wesley Coll., 1972-83, Wilmington Parking Authority, 1974, Del. Health and Social Svc. Commn., Dover, 1972; mem. Del. Civil Rights Com., Wilmington, 1970; trustee Lycoming Coll., Lebanon Valley Coll., Camp David Chapel; com. Camp David, Md. With U.S. Army, 1957-59. Avocations: oil painting; tennis; plants; travel. Home: PO Box 239 Harrisburg PA 17108-0239 Office: United Meth Ch Harrisburg Area 900 S Arlington Ave Harrisburg PA 17109-5024

MAY, FRANCIS HART, JR., retired building materials manufacturing executive; b. Dunkirk, Ind., Apr. 2, 1917; s. Francis Hart and Agnes (Elabarger) M.; m. June Breen, Aug. 31, 1940; children: Francis Hart, John Joseph, Marcia Ann. A.B., U. Notre Dame, 1938; M.B.A., Harvard, 1940. Mgr. war contracts div. Owens-Ill. Glass Co., Toledo, 1940-44; v.p., sec. Glass Fibers Inc., Toledo, 1946-54; v.p., sec., treas. L-O-F Glass Fibers Co., Toledo, 1955-58; v.p., gen. mgr. Johns-Manville Fiber Glass, Inc., 1959-60; asst. v.p. finance Johns-Manville Corp., N.Y.C., 1960-61; v.p. fin., dir. Johns-Manville Corp., 1962-70, exec. v.p. fin. and adminstrn., 1971-79, vice-chmn. bd., 1979-80, spl. projects, 1980-82, ret., 1982. Served with inf. AUS, 1944-46. Mem. Fin. Execs. Ins., Dolphin Head Golf Club (Hilton Head Island, S.C.). Home: 8330 E Quincy Ave J-103 Denver CO 80237 Home (summer): PO Box 955 Cooperstown NY 13326-5955 Home (winter): 29 China Cockle Ln Hilton Head Island SC 29926-1908

MAY, GERALD WILLIAM, university administrator, educator, civil engineering consultant; b. Kenya, Jan. 2, 1941; s. William and Ruth (Koch) M.; m. Mary Joyce Pool, July 27, 1963; children: Erica Ruth, Christian William, Heidi Clara. B.S., Bradley U., 1962; M.S., U. Colo., 1964, Ph.D., 1967. Registered profl. engr., N.Mex. Civil engr. Ill. Hwy. Dept., Peoria, summer 1959-63; instr. U. Colo., Boulder, 1964-67; from asst. to prof. engring. U. N.Mex., Albuquerque, 1967-77, prof. of civil engring, 1977—; dean Coll. Engring., U. N.Mex., Albuquerque, 1980-86; pres. U. N.Mex., Albuquerque, 1986-90; dir. accident study program, Albuquerque, 1970-75, cons. to corps., govtl. agys. Contbr. articles to profl. jours., chpts. to books. Recipient Borden Freshman award Bradley U., 1958. Mem. ASCE (pres. N.Mex. sect. 1982-83), Am. Soc. Engring. Edn. (Outstanding Young Faculty award 1973), Nat. Soc. Profl. Engrs., Sigma Xi, Chi Epsilon, Tau Beta Pi, Phi Eta Sigma. Office: Univ N Mex Civil Engring Dept Albuquerque NM 87131

MAY, GITA, French language and literature educator; b. Brussels, Sept. 16, 1929; came to U.S., 1947, naturalized, 1950; d. Albert and Blima (Sieradska) Jochimek; m. Irving May, Dec. 21, 1947. BA magna cum laude, CUNY-Hunter Coll., 1953; MA, Columbia U., 1954, PhD, 1957. Lectr. French CUNY-Hunter Coll., 1953-56; instr. Columbia U., 1956-58, asst. prof., 1958-61, assoc. prof., 1961-68, prof., 1968—, chmn., 1983-93, mem. senate, 1979-83, 86-88, chmn. Seminar on 18th Century Culture, 1986-89; lecture tour English univs., 1965. Author: Dederot et Baudelaire, critiques d'art, 1957, De Jean-Jacques Rousseau a Madame Roland: essai sur la sensibilitia preromantique et revolutionaire, 1964, Madame Roland and the Age of Revolution, 1970 (Van Amringe Disting. Book award), Stendhal and the Age of Napoleon, 1977; co-editor: Diderot Studies III, 1961; mem. editl. bd. 18th Century Studies, 1975-78, French Rev., 1975-86, Romanic Rev., 1959—; contbg. editor: Deuvres completes de Diderot, 1984, 95; gen. editor: The Age of Revolution and Romanticism: Interdisciplinary Studies, 1980—; contbr. articles and revs. to profl. jours. Decorated chevalier and officer Ordre des Palmes Acad.; recipient award Am. Coun. Learned Socs., 1961, award for outstanding achievement CUNY-Hunter Coll., 1963; Fulbright rsch. grantee, 1964-65; Guggenheim fellow, 1964-65, NEH fellow, 1971-72. Mem. AAUP, MLA (del. assembly 1973-75, mem. com. rsch. activities 1975-78, mem. exec. coun. 1980-83), Am. Assn. Tchrs. of French, Am. Soc. 18th Century Studies (pres. 1985-86, 2nd v.p. 1983-84, 1st v.p. 1984-85), Soc. Française d'Etude du Dix-Huitième Siècle, Soc. Diderot, Am. Soc. French Acad. Palms, Phi Beta Kappa. Home: 404 W 116th St New York NY 10027-7202

MAY, GREGORY EVERS, lawyer; b. Harrisonburg, Va., Sept. 17, 1953; s. Russell J. and Arlene Virginia (Ringgold) M. AB, Coll. of William and Mary, 1975; JD, Harvard U., 1978. Bar: Va. 1978, U.S. Dist. Ct. (ea. dist.) Va. 1979, U.S. Ct. Appeals (4th cir.) 1979, U.S. Claims Ct. 1981, U.S. Tax Ct. 1981, D.C. 1985, N.Y. 1988. Law clk. to Judge Butzner U.S. Ct. Appeals (4th cir.), Richmond, Va., 1978-79; law clk. to Justice Powell U.S. Supreme Ct., Washington, 1979-80; assoc. Hunton & Williams, Richmond, 1980-83; assoc. Hunton & Williams, Washington, 1984-86, ptnr., 1986-89; ptnr. Milbank, Tweed, Hadley & McCloy, Washington, 1989—. Articles editor Harvard Law Rev., 1977-78. Mem. ABA, Va. State Bar, D.C. Bar, N.Y. State Bar. Office: Milbank Tweed Hadley & McCloy 1825 I St NW Ste 1100 Washington DC 20006-5492

MAY, HAROLD EDWARD, chemical company executive; b. N.Y.C., Oct. 18, 1920; s. Charles Edward and Mollie (Flax) M.; m. Margaret June Hochman, June 27, 1943; children: Charles S., Michael E., Suzanne E. A.B., Columbia U., 1941, B.S. in Mech. Engring, 1942. With E.I. duPont de Nemours & Co., Inc., 1942—; v.p. materials and logistics E.I. duPont de Nemours & Co., Inc., Wilmington, Del., 1977-82, sr. v.p. corp. staff, 1982-85; ret. E.I. duPont de Nemours & Co., Inc., 1985. Recipient Illig medal Columbia U., 1942. Mem. Phi Beta Kappa, Tau Beta Pi. Jewish. Home: 36 Southridge Dr Kennett Square PA 19348-2714

MAY, J. PETER, mathematics educator; b. N.Y.C., Sept. 16, 1939; s. Siegmund Henry and Jane (Polachek) M.; m. Maija Bajars, June 8, 1963; children: Anthony D., Andrew D. BA, Swarthmore Coll., 1960; PhD, Princeton U., 1964. Instr. Yale U., New Haven, 1964-65, asst. prof., 1965-67; assoc. prof. U. Chgo., 1967-70, prof., 1970—, chmn. dept. math., 1985-91, chmn. coun. on teaching, 1991—; mem. Inst. Advanced Study, Princeton, 1966; vis. prof. Cambridge U., Eng., 1971-72, 1977. Author: Simplicial Objects in Algebraic Topology, 1967, The Geometry of Iterated Loop Spaces, 1972, E-infinity Ring Spaces and E-infinity Ring Spectra, 1977, Equivariant Homotopy and Cohomology Theory, 1996; co-author: The Homology of Iterated Loop Spaces, 1976, H-infinity Ring Spectra and Their Applications, 1986, Equivariant Stable Homotopy Theory, 1986; also numerous articles and monographs. NSF grantee, 1967—; Fulbright fellow, 1971-72; fellow Nat. Research Council, Eng., 1977. Mem. AAUP, Am. Math. Soc. Office: U Chgo Dept Math 5734 S University Ave Chicago IL 60637-1514

MAY, JAMES L(EROY), psychologist; b. Rupert, Idaho, May 22, 1939; s. LeRoy L. and Dale (Gibson) M.; BA, Idaho State U., 1967; MS (NDEA fellow 1970-73), Kans. State U., 1972, PhD, 1974; m. Sharon Lee Aherin, Nov. 8, 1968; children: Nathan Andrew, Erica Jane. Social caseworker Idaho Dept. Public Assistance, Idaho, 1967-70, county dir., Mountain Home, 1970; mem. faculty North Adams (Mass.) State Coll., 1974—, assoc. prof. psychology, 1978-87, prof., 1987—, chmn. dept., 1981-85. 91-93; coord. profl. devel. NASC, 1993—; cons. in field, 1982-83; pres. bd. dirs. No. Berkshire Mental Health Assn., North Adams. Served with USAR, 1961-63. Mem. Am. Psychol. Assn., Soc. Advancement Social Psychology, New Eng. Social Psychology Assn., Midwestern Psychol. Assn., N.Y. Acad. Scis. Mem. Ch. of Jesus Christ of Latter-day Saints. Author articles in field. Office: Murdock Hall North Adams State Coll Adams MA 02147

MAY, JAMES WARREN, JR., plastic surgeon, medical association executive; b. Lexington, Ky., 1943. MD, Northwestern U., 1969. Intern Mass. Gen. Hosp., Boston, 1969-70, resident, 1970-75, resident plastic surgeon, 1975—; fellow U. Louisville, 1975; assoc. prof. clin. surgery Harvard Med. Sch., Boston; chmn. Am. Bd. Plastic Surgery. Office: Harvard Med Sch Mass Gen Hosp 15 Parkman St Fl 453 Care Boston MA 02114-3117*

MAY, JERRY RUSSELL, psychologist; b. Seattle, Apr. 24, 1942; s. Harold Russell May and Anne Margret (Jones) DeGolier; m. Carolyn Marlene May; children: Darin, Christopher, Laurel. Student, Sorbonne U., Paris, 1961-62; BA, Western Wash. U., 1966; PhD, Bowling Green State U., 1974. Prof. psychiatry sch. medicine U. Nev., Reno, 1974-90, dean admissions and student affairs sch. medicine, 1977—; cons. VA Med. Ctr., Reno, 1974-90, U.S. Olympic Sports Medicine Program, Colorado Springs, Colo., 1977—; pvt. practice clin. psychology, mgmt. cons., Reno, 1977—; team psychologist U.S. Ski Team, Park City, Utah, 1977-92; chmn. U.S. Olympic Psychology Com., Colorado Springs, 1985-92; mem. U.S. Olympic Sports Medicine Coun., Colorado Springs, 1985-92; team psychologist U.S. Sailing Team, 1992—. Author/editor: Sports Psychology: The Psychological Health of the Athlete, 1987; contbr. articles to profl. jours., chpts. to books. Pres. West Coast Group on Student Affairs, 1981-82. Served to lt. USN, 1968-71. Recipient Disting. Alumni award Western Wash. U., 1993, Bowling Green State U., 1995. Fellow APA; mem. No. Nev. Assn. Cert. Psychologists (pres. 1979-82), Am. Assn. Med. Colls., Western Psychol. Assn., Nev. Psychol. Assn. Office: U Nev Sch Medicine Reno NV 89557

MAY, JOHN ANDREW, petrophysicist, geologist; b. Lawrence, Kans., July 4, 1952; s. Donald Lawrence and Marie Jean (McCartney) M.; m. Aurelia Angela Szyfer, Nov. 23, 1988; children: Sean, Thomas, Daniel, Krystyna. BS in Geology, U. Kans., 1974. Sr. geologist Cities Svc. Oil Co., Tulsa, 1974-80; div. geologist Exxon, Denver, 1980-85; mgr. exploration systems Sci. Software-Intercomp, Denver, 1985-88; sr. staff geologist Kerr-McGee, Oklahoma City, 1985—; mem. quality assurance com. Internat. MWD Soc., Houston, 1994—. Mem. Am. Assn. Petroleum Geologists (cert., Cert. of Merit award 1993), Soc. Petroleum Engrs., Soc. Profl. Well L.A. (publs. com. 1995—), Okla. SPWLA (pres. 1993-94, v.p. tech. 1994-95). Democrat. Roman Catholic. Achievements include mapping of Natuna D-Alpha Reef complex in South China Sea; development of Environ and Calc numerical petrophysical models. Avocations: computers, travel, camping. Home: 403 Hunters Ct Edmond OK 73034 Office: Kerr McGee 123 Robert S Kerr Oklahoma City OK 73102

MAY, JOSEPH LESERMAN (JACK), lawyer; b. Nashville, May 27, 1929; s. Daniel and Dorothy (Fishel) M.; m. Natalie McCuaig, Apr. 12, 1957 (dec. May 1990); children: Benjamin, Andrew, Joshua, Maria; m. Lynn Hewes Lance, June 10, 1994. BA, Yale U., 1951; JD, NYU, 1958; postgrad., Harvard Bus. Sch., 1969. Bar: Tenn. 1959. Prodr. Candied Yam Jackson Show, 1947-51; with CIA, 1951-55; pres. Nuweave Socks, Inc., N.Y.C., 1955-59, May Hosiery Mills, Nashville, 1960-83, Athens Hosiery Mills, Tenn., 1966-83; v.p. Wayne-Gossard Corp., Chattanooga, 1972-83; pvt. practice law Nashville, 1984—; bd. dirs. Convertible Holdings, Princeton, N.J., World Income Fund, Princeton, Merrill Lynch Growth Fund; adv. group Civil Justice Reform Act U.S. Dist. Ct., 1991; adv. bd. Asian Strategies Group, 1994. Bd. dirs. Vanderbilt Cancer Ctr., 1994—; pres. Jewish Cmty. Ctr., 1969; chmn. Guardianship and Trust Corp., 1994; trustee Tenn. Hist. Soc., 1996—. With USN, 1947-53, U.S. Army, 1954. Mem. Tenn. Bar Assn., Nashville Bar Assn., Eagle Scout Assn., Shamus Club, Old Oak Club, Yale Club N.Y., Rotary (pres. Nashville 1971). Home: 2136 Golf Club Ln Nashville TN 37215-1224 Office: Box 190628 424 Church St Ste 2000 Nashville TN 37219-0628

MAY, KENNETH NATHANIEL, food industry consultant; b. Livingston, La., Dec. 24, 1930; s. Robert William and Mary Hulda (Caraway) M.; m. Patsy Jean Farr, Aug. 4, 1953; children: Sherry Alison (dec.), Nathan Elliott. BS in Poultry Sci., La. State U., 1952, MS in Poultry Sci., 1955; PhD in Food Tech., Purdue U., 1959, DAgr, 1988. Asst. prof. U. Ga., Athens, 1958-64, assoc. prof., 1964-67, prof., 1967-68; prof. Miss. State U., State College, 1968-70; dir. rsch. Holly Farms Poultry, Wilkesboro, N.C., 1970-73, v.p., 1973-85, pres., 1985-88, chmn., CEO, 1989; bd. dirs. Hudson Foods, Inc., Embrex, Inc., Alcide Corp.; adj. prof. N.C. State U., 1975. Contbr. over 60 articles to profl. jours.; patentee treatment of cooked poultry. Bd. trustees Appalachian State U., 1987-94, chmn., 1989-90. Recipient Industry Service award Poultry and Egg Inst. Am., 1971, Meritorious Service award, Ga. Egg Commn., 1964, Disting. Service award Agribus. N.C., 1986; named to Am. Poultry Hall of Fame, 1992. Fellow Poultry Sci. Assn.; mem. Nat. Poultry Hist. Soc. (bd. dirs. 1982-83), Inst. Food Technologists. Methodist. Avocations: reading, stained glass.

MAY, LINDA KAREN CARDIFF, safety engineer, nurse; b. San Mateo, Calif., Oct. 26, 1948; d. Leon Davis and Jane Vivian (Gallow) Cardiff; m. Donald William May, Dec. 7, 1969 (div. Feb. 1988); children: Charles David, Andrew William. Student in nursing So. Ill. U., 1969, Ill Wesleyan U., 1989; AAS, Parkland Coll., 1977; BS in Pub. Health and Safety Engring. with honors, U. Ill., Urbana, 1987; RN, BSN, Lakeview Coll., 1990. RN, Ill., Ind., Mo., N.Mex., Tex., Wis.; registered profl. nurse; nat. registered EMT, Ill.; OSHA accredited instr. constrn. safety and health. Indsl. nurse C.S. Johnson Co., Champaign, Ill., 1978-79; safety dir. Solo Cup Co., Urbana, Ill., 1979-84; safety engr. Clinton Nuclear Power Plant, Ill. Power Co., 1984-86, occupational safety and health specialist Danville Vet.'s Med. Ctr., 1986—; with LKM Health and Safety Cons., Inc., Champaign, Ill. Mem. Champaign County Crime Prevention Coun., 1978-83, bd. dirs., 1980-82; active Champaign County Task Force on Arson, 1981—, Mercy Hosp. Aux., Covenant Hosp Auxiliary, 1977—. Ill. State Gen. Assembly scholar, 1967. Mem. AACN, APHA (mem. occupational health and safety sect.), Am. Soc. Safety Engrs. (vice chair Ctrl. Ill. sect. 1985-86), Am. Nuclear Soc. (mem. biology and medicine divsn., mem. radiopharm. and isotope product stds. com.), Am. Assn. Occupational Health Nurses, Nat. Registery EMT, Ill. Environ. Health Assn., Ill. Soc. Pub. Health Educators, Associated Ill. Milk, Food and Environ. Sanitarians, Pre-Hosp. Care Providers Ill., Ill. EMTs Assn., N.Y. Acad. Sci, U. Ill. Alumni Assn. (life), Parkland Coll. Almuni Assn. (life, bd. dirs. 1987—, v.p. 1992—), Parkland Coll. Found. Bd. (alumni assn. liason bd. dirs. 1993), Ill. Wesleyan U. Alumni Assn., Lakeview Coll. Nursing Alumni Assn., Eta Sigma Gamma. Methodist. Home: PO Box 3954 Champaign IL 61826-3954

MAY, MARGRETHE, allied health educator; b. Tucson, Ariz., Oct. 6, 1943; d. Robert A. and Margrethe (Holm) M. BS in Human Biology, U. Mich., 1970, MS in Anatomy, 1986. Cert. surg. technologist. Surg. technologist Hartford (Conn.) Hosp., 1965-68, U. Mich. Hosps., Ann Arbor, 1968-70; asst. operating room supr. U. Ariz. Med. Ctr., Tucson, 1971-72; coord. operating room tech. program Pima Coll., Tucson, 1971-76; prof., coord. surg. tech. and surg. first asst. programs Delta Coll., University Center, Mich., 1978—; commr. Commn. on Accreditation of Allied Health Ednl. Programs, Chgo., 1994—, Coun. Accreditation and Unit Recognition, 1994—. Editor: Core Curriculum for Surgical Technology, 3d edit., 1990,

Core Curriculum for Surgical First Assisting, 1993; contbr. articles to profl. jours. Mem. Assn. Surg. Technologists (bd. dirs. 1987-89, pres.-elect 1989-90, pres. 1990-91, on-site visitor program accreditation 1974—, chmn. exam writing com. 1981, liaison coun. on cert. co-chmn. 1977, chmn. 1978, sec.-treas. 1979, chmn. accreditation review com for edn. in surg. tech. 1994—), Am. Soc. Law, Medicine and Ethics, Mich. Assn. Allied Health Professions (sec. 1994—), Nat. Network Health Career Programs in Two-Year Colls. Avocations: international health care issues and allied health education. Home: 2506 Abbott Rd Apt P-2 Midland MI 48642-4876 Office: Delta Coll Dept Surgery University Center MI 48710

MAY, MELANIE ANN, theologian; b. Washington, Jan. 6, 1955; d. Russell Junior and Arlene Virginia (Ringgold) May. AB, Manchester Coll., 1976; MDiv., Harvard U., 1979, AM, 1982, PhD, 1986. Teaching fellow div. sch. Harvard U., Cambridge, Mass., 1981-83, asst. head tutor, 1983-84; staff program for women Ch. Brethren Gen. Bd., Elgin, Ill., 1985-87, ecumenical officer, 1985-91, assoc. gen. sec. human resources, 1987-91; adj. faculty Bethany Theol. Sem., Oak Brook, Ill., 1986-92, Garrett-Evang. Theol. Sem., 1991-92; dean program in the study of women and gender in ch. and soc., prof. theology Colgate Rochester Div. Sch., Bexley Hall, Crozer, 1992—. Author: Bonds of Unity, Women, Theology and Worldwide Church, 1989, Women and Church: A Challenge of Solidarity in an Age of Alienation, 1991, For All The Saints: The Practice of Ministry in the Church, 1990, A Body Knows: A Theopoetics of Death and Resurrection, 1995; assoc. editor Jour. Ecumenical Studies. Quality Ministerial candidates, 1987—, chmn. commn. Faith and Order, Nat. Council, N.Y., 1988; mem. standing commn. Faith and Order, World Coun. Chs., 1991—. Mem. N.Am. Acad. Economists, Am. Acad. Religion. Avocations: reading, gardening, swimming. Home: 309 Rugby Ave Rochester NY 14619-1219

MAY, MELVIN ARTHUR, computer software company executive; b. Cortez, Colo., Oct. 22, 1940; s. Everett James and Viola Christina (Lair) M.; m. Dale Charlene Kelly, Oct. 3, 1963; children: Diana, Michael. A.A., Pueblo Coll., 1959; B.S., U. Colo., 1961. Accountant Haskins & Sells (C.P.A.'s), San Diego, Denver, and Colorado Springs, Colo., 1961-68; asst. to v.p., treas. Holly Sugar Corp., Colorado Springs, 1968-69, asst. treas., 1970-71, treas., 1972-82, v.p., 1977-82; v.p. fin. Cibar, Inc., Colorado Springs, 1982-86, chief operating officer, 1983-86, sr. v.p. fin., 1986-87; ret., 1987. Served with USMCR, 1963-64. Mem. NRA. Home: 637 Dexter St Colorado Springs CO 80911-2539

MAY, NORMA BUTLER, reading educator; b. Cairo, Ill., Sept. 6, 1940; d. John William and Irene Virginia (Cartwright) Butler; m. Willie L. May, July 4, 1964; children: Kristian, Karen. AS, Vincennes U., 1960; BS, Ind. State U., 1961, MS, 1966. Kindergarten tchr. Sch. Dist. 130, Blue Island, Ill., 1961-70; subs. tchr. Chgo. Bd. Edn., 1974-76; reading specialist Evanston Twp. H.S., Ill., 1976—. Recipient internat. teaching award Delores Kohl Found., 1994. Mem. NEA, ASCD, Nat. Coun. Tchrs. English, AAUW (presenter Title I IASA statewide conf. 1995), NAACP, Internat. Reading Assn., Ill. Edn. Assn., Jack & Jill of Am., U. Ill. Mothers Assn. (2d v.p. 1992-93, pres. 1993-94). Methodist. Avocations: reading, walking, theater, spectator sports, music. Home: 8333 S Dorchester Ave Chicago IL 60619-6401 Office: Evanston Twp HS 1600 Dodge Ave Evanston IL 60201-3449

MAY, PETER WILLIAM, business executive; b. N.Y.C., Dec. 11, 1942; s. Samuel D. and Isabel (Meyer) M.; m. Leni Finkelstein, Aug. 16, 1964; children: Jonathan Paul, Leslie Ann. AB, U. Chgo., 1964, MBA, 1965. CPA, N.Y. Mgr. Peat, Marwick, Mitchell & Co., N.Y.C., 1965-72; exec. v.p. Flagstaff Corp., N.Y.C., 1972-78; pres., chief operating officer Trian Group. L.P. (formerly Triangle Industries, Inc.), N.Y.C., 1978—, also bd. dirs.; pres., COO Triar Cos., Inc., N.Y.C. Trustee Mt. Sinai Hosp., N.Y.C., exec. com., founding mem. Laura Rosenberg Meml. Fund for Pediatric Leukemia Rsch.; alumni dir. U. Chgo. Grad. Sh. Bus.; bd. dirs. 92d St. YMCA, United Jewish Appeal, Operation Exodus campaign. Mem. Am. Inst. CPA's, N.Y. Soc. of CPA's. *

MAY, PHILIP ALAN, sociology educator; b. Bethesda, Md., Nov. 6, 1947; s. Everette Lee and Marie (Lee) M.; m. Doreen Ann Garcia, Sept. 5, 1972; children: Katrina Ruth, Marie Ann. BA in Sociology, Catawba Coll., 1969; MA in Sociology, Wake Forest U., 1971; PhD in Sociology, U. Mont., 1976. NIMH predoctoral fellow U. Mont., Missoula, 1973-76; dir. health statistics and rsch. Navajo Health Authority, Window Rock, Ariz., 1976-78; asst. prof. U. N.Mex., Albuquerque, 1978-82, assoc. prof., 1982-89, prof., 1989—, dir. Ctr. on Alcoholism, Substance Abuse and Addictions, 1990—; mem. fetal alcohol syndrome study com., Inst. of Medicine/Nat. Acad. Scis., 1994-95; cons. various govt. agys., 1976—; dir. Nat. Indian Fetal Alcohol Syndrome Prevention Program, Albuquerque, 1979-85; mem. adv. bd. Nat. Orgn. on Fetal Alcohol Syndrome, Washington, 1990—; rsch. assoc. Nat. Ctr. for Am. Indian and Alaska Native Mental Health Rsch., 1986—. Contbr. chpts. to books and articles to profl. jours. Mem. Ctrl. United Meth. Ch., Albuquerque, 1980-90, First United Meth. Ch., Albuquerque, 1990—. Lt. USPHS, 1970-73. Recipient Spl. Recognition award U.S. Indian Health Svc., 1992, award Navajo Tribe and U.S. Indian Health Svc., 1992, Human Rights Promotion award UN Assn., 1994. Mem. APHA, Am. Sociol. Assn., Population Ref. Bur., Coll. on Problems of Drug Dependence. Home: 4610 Idlewilde Ln SE Albuquerque NM 87108-3422 Office: U NMex CASAA 2350 Alamo Ave SE Albuquerque NM 87106-3202

MAY, PHYLLIS JEAN, financial executive; b. Flint, Mich., May 31, 1932; d. Bert A. and Alice C. (Rushton) Irvine; m. John May, Apr. 24, 1971. Grad. Dorsey Sch. Bus., 1957; cert. Internat. Corr. Schs., 1959, Nat. Tax Inst., 1978; MBA, Mich. U., 1970. Registered real estate agt; lic. life, auto and home ins. agent. Office mgr. Comml. Constrn. Co., Flint, 1962-68; bus. mgr. new and used car dealership, Flint, 1968-70; contr. various corps., Flint, 1970-75; fiscal dir. Rubicon Odyssey Inc., Detroit, 1976-87, Wayne County Treas.'s Office, 1987-93; exec. fin. office Grosse Pointe Meml. Ch., 1993—; acad. cons. acctg. Detroit Inst. Commerce, 1980-81; pres. small bus. specializing in adminstrv. cons. and acctg., 1982—; supr. mobile svc. sta., upholstery and home improvement businesses; owner retail bus. Pieces and Things. Pres. PTA Westwood Heights Schs., 1972; vol. Fedn. of Blind, 1974-76, Probate Ct., 1974-76; mem. citizens adv. bd. Northville Regional Psychiat. Hosp., 1988, sec. 1989-90. Recipient Meritorious Svc. award Genesee County for Youth, 1976, Excellent Performance and High Achievement award Odyssey Inc., 1981. Mem. NAFE (bd. dirs.), Am. Bus. Women's Assn. (treas. 1981, rec. sec. 1982, v.p. 1982-83, Woman of Yr. 1982), Womens Assn. Dearborn Orch. Soc., Dearborn Community Art Ctr., Mich. Mental Health Assn., Internat. Platform Assn., Guild of Carillonneurs in N.Am., Pi Omicron (officer 1984-85). Baptist.

MAY, RICHARD EDWARD, lawyer; b. Austin, Tex., Feb. 5, 1946; s. Howard Curtis and Gertrude E. (Wallace) M.; m. Tracey C. May; 1 child, Elynor Lee. AB, U. Md., 1967; JD, Georgetown U., 1973. Bar: D.C. 1973, Va. 1984. Assoc. Steptoe & Johnson, Washington, 1973-79; spl. asst. to chief counsel IRS, Washington, 1979-81; ptnr. Jenkens & Gilchrist, Dallas, 1981-83, Hunton & Williams, Washington, 1983—. Served to lt. USN, 1968-71. Mem. ABA (taxation sect., chmn. reorganization subcom. 1981-83, vice chmn. corp. stockholder relationships com. 1983-85, chmn. 1985-87, tax sect. asst. sec. 1988-89, tax sect. sec. 1989-91, coun. dir. 1991—). Episcopalian. Clubs: Metropolitan (Washington); Commonwealth (Richmond). Office: Hunton & Williams PO Box 19230 2000 Pennsylvania Ave NW Washington DC 20006-1812*

MAY, ROBERT GEORGE, dean, accounting educator; b. Detroit, Nov. 11, 1943; s. George Joseph and Winifred Marie (Donnelly) M.; m. Carol Ann Rogers, June 18, 1965; children: Gregory Charles, Lynn Marie. B.B.A., Mich. State U., 1965, Ph.D., 1970. Asst. prof. U. Wash., Seattle, 1970-73, assoc. prof., 1973-79; prof. acctg. U. Tex., Austin, 1979—, chmn. dept. acctg., 1988-92, assoc. dean, 1992-95, interim dean, 1995—; vis. asst. prof. Stanford U., 1972-73; dir. Fedn. Schs. Accountancy, Athens, Ga., 1982. Co-author: Accounting, 1995, Financial Accounting, 1995, Managerial Accounting, 1995, Corporate Financial Accounting, 1995; assoc. editor: the Accounting Review. Recipient Notable Contbn. to Acctg. Lit. award AICPAs, 1976; named Outstanding Alumnus, Mich. State U. Dept. Acctg., 1995. Mem. Am. Acctg. Assn. (chmn. audit sect. 1988-89, pres., adminstrs. of acctg. programs 1993-94, Innovation in Acctg. Edn. award 1991, 93). Home: 7137 Valburn Dr Austin TX 78731-1812 Office: U Tex Dept Acctg Austin TX 78712

MAY, RONALD ALAN, lawyer; b. Waterloo, Iowa, Sept. 8, 1928; s. John W. and Elsie (Finlayson) M.; m. Naomi Gray, Aug. 18, 1950 (div. Feb. 1974); children: Sarah, Jonathan, Andrew, Rachel; m. Susan East Gray, May 9, 1975. B.A., U. Iowa, 1950; LL.B., Vanderbilt U., 1953. Bar: Ark. 1953. Atty. Daggett & Daggett, Marianna, 1953-57, Wright, Lindsey & Jennings, Little Rock, 1957-84; sr. ptnr. Wright, Lindsey & Jennings, 1986-96, of counsel, 1996—; Editor: Automated Law Research, 1972, Sense and Systems in Automated Law Research, 1975; contbg. editor Fifty State Construction Lien and Bond Law, 1992, Fifty State Public Construction Contracting, 1996; assoc. editor Jour. Irreproducible Results. Editor: Automated Law Research, 1972, Sense and Systems in Automated Law Research, 1975; contbg. editor Fifty State Construction Lien and Bond Law, 1992; assoc. editor: Jour. Irreproducible Results. Pres. Spl. Com. on Pub. Edn., Ark. Assn. for Mental Health, Friends of Library, Central Ark. Radiation Therapy Inst.; chmn. Ark. Cancer Research Ctr., 1990-92; bd. dirs. Nat. Assn. for Mental Health, Ark. State Hosp., Gaines House, State Bd. Architects; bd. dirs. State Bd. Bar Examiners, chmn. 1987-88, Ark. ethics com., 1991-93; trustee Mus. Sci. and Natural History, Little Rock, chmn., 1973; mem. profl. adv. bd. sch. architecture U. Ark., 1990—, mem. profl. adv. bd. sch. urban studies and design, 1993—. Served with AUS, 1946-47. Mem. ABA (chmn. sci. and tech. sect. 1975-76), Ark., Pulaski County Bar Assns., Internat. Assn. Def. Counsel, Am. Inns of Ct. (Master of the Bench), Assn. for Computing Machinery, Order of Coif, Phi Beta Kappa. Republican. Episcopalian. Clubs: Capital, Little Rock Country. Home: 821 N Ash St Little Rock AR 72205-2051 Office: Wright Lindsey & Jennings 200 West Capital Ste 2200 Little Rock AR 72201

MAY, STEPHEN, writer, former government official; b. Rochester, N.Y., July 30, 1931; s. Arthur J. and Hilda (Jones) M. Grad., Wesleyan U., 1953; LL.B., Georgetown U., 1961. Bar: N.Y. 1963. Exec. asst. to Rep. and Senator Kenneth B. Keating, 1955-64; asso., mem., then ptnr. Branch, Turner & Wise, Rochester, 1965-81; city councilman-at-large Rochester, 1966-73; mayor, 1970-73; chmn. and commr. N.Y. State Bd. Elections, Albany, 1975-79; asst. sec. for legis. and Congl. relations Dept. Housing and Urban Devel., 1981-88; lectr. and freelance writer for newspapers and mags., 1988—; Vice chmn. Temporary State Commn. on Powers of Local Govt., 1970-73; mem. 20th Century Fund Task Force on Future of N.Y.C., 1979, Nat. Adv. Commn. Higher Edn. for Police Officers, 1977-79, Joint Com. Assn. Bar City N.Y. and Drug Abuse Council on N.Y. Drug Law Evaluation, 1977-78; chmn. Rochester Interfaith Com. on Israel, 1973-81; del.-at-large Republican Nat. Conv., 1972; mem. N.Y. State Crime Control Planning Bd., 1970-73. Contbr. numerous articles on Am. art, culture and hist. preservation to newspapers and periodicals. Bd. dirs. Police Found., 1970-81, Nat. Com. for Labor Israel, 1977-81, Empire State Report, 1974-81, Inst. Mediation and Conflict Resolution, 1973-81. Served with U.S. Army, 1953-55. Mem. Phi Beta Kappa. Home and Office: 4101 Cathedral Ave NW Washington DC 20016-3585

MAY, TIMOTHY JAMES, lawyer; b. Denver, Aug. 3, 1932; s. Thomas Henry and Helen Frances (O'Conner) M.; m. Monica Anita Gross, Aug. 24, 1957; children: Stephanie, Maureen, Cynthia, Timothy, Anthony. BA, Cath. U. Am., 1954; LLB, Georgetown U., 1957, LLM, 1960. Bar: D.C. 1957, U.S. Supreme Ct. 1961. Law clk. to judge U.S. Ct. Appeals, D.C. Cir., 1957-58; assoc. Covington & Burling, Washington, 1958-61; cons. Exec. Office of Pres. U.S., Washington, 1961-62; chief counsel subcom. on stockpile Armed Svcs. Com., U.S. Senate, Washington, 1962-63; mng. dir. Fed. Maritime Commn., Washington, 1963-66; gen. counsel U.S. Post Office Dept., Washington, 1966-69; mng. ptnr. Patton Boggs, L.L.P., Washington, 1969—. Bd. dirs. Legal Aid Soc. D.C., 1984—, Coun. for Ct. Excellence, Washington, 1985—; chmn. bd. regents Cath. U. Am., 1988-93, trustee, 1993—. Fellow Am. Bar Found.; mem. ABA (House of Dels.), Fed. Bar Assn., Bar Assn. of D.C. (pres. 1991-92), Congl. Country Club (bd. govs. 1992—, sec. 1994—), Met. Club, Indian Creek Country Club, Bal Harbour Club, Knight of Malta. Democrat. Roman Catholic. Home: 3828 52nd St NW Washington DC 20016-1924 Office: Patton Boggs LLP 2550 M St NW Washington DC 20037

MAY, WALTER GRANT, chemical engineer; b. Saskatoon, Sask., Can., Nov. 28, 1918; came to U.S., 1946, naturalized, 1954; s. George Alfred and Abigail Almira (Robson) M.; m. Mary Louise Stockan, Sept. 26, 1945 (dec. 1977); children: John R., Douglas W., Caroline O; m. Helen Dickerson, 1988. B.Sc., U. Sask., Saskatoon, 1939, M.Sc., 1942; Sc.D., M.I.T., 1948. Registered profl. engr., Ill. Chemist British Am. Oil Co., Moose Jaw, Sask., 1939-40; asst. prof. U. Sask., 1943-46; with Exxon Research & Engring. Co., Linden, N.J., 1948-83; sr. sci. adv., 1976-83; prof. U. Ill., 1983-90, prof. emeritus, 1990—; with Advanced Research Projects Agy., Dept. Def., 1959-60; industry based prof. Stevens Inst. Tech., 1968-74, Rensselaer Poly. Inst., 1975-77. Recipient Process Indsl. Div. award ASME, 1972. Fellow Am. Inst. Chem. Engrs.; mem. Am. Inst. Chem. Engrs. (Chem. Engring. Practice award 1989), Nat. Acad. Engring. Home: 916 W Clark St Champaign IL 61821-3328 Office: U Ill Dept Chem Engring 1209 W California Ave Urbana IL 61801-3705

MAY, WILLIAM FREDERICK, manufacturing executive; b. Chgo., Oct. 25, 1915; s. Arthur W. and Florence (Hartwick) M.; m. Kathleen Thompson, June 14, 1947; children: Katherine Hartwick (Mrs. Edward W. Bickford), Elizabeth Shaw. BS, U. Rochester, 1937; grad. Advanced Mgmt. Program, Harvard, 1950; D in Engring., Clarkson U.; LLD, Okla. Christian Coll.; LHD, Livingstone U.; LLD, Lafayette U. Research worker E.I. Du Pont de Nemours Co., 1937-38; with Am. Can Co., 1940-80, mgr., 1957-58, v.p., 1958-64, exec. v.p., 1964-65, vice chmn. bd. dirs., 1965, chmn. bd. dirs., chief exec. officer, 1965-80; mem. exec. com. Am. Can Co., Greenwich, Conn., 1960—; bd. dirs. U.S. Surgical & Catalyst Energy Corp., Phibro-Salomon Corp.; dean Grad. Sch. Bus. Adminstrn., NYU, 1980-84; chmn. and chief exec. officer Statue of Liberty Found., 1984—. Bd. dirs. Lincoln Ctr.; trustee Am. Ditchley Found., Am. Mus. Natural History, Taft Inst. Govt., Columbia-Presbyn. Hosp., U. Rochester; mem. corp. Poly. Inst. N.Y.; chmn. pub. policy council Advt. Council. Mem. Nat. Order of Merit (France, officier), River Club, Econ. Club, Round Hill Club, Meganticook Golf Club, Golf Phi Beta Kappa, Alpha Delta Phi. Episcopalian. Home: 35 Lauder Ln Greenwich CT 06831-3707 Office: Statue of Liberty Found 52 Vanderbilt Ave New York NY 10017-3808

MAYALI, LAURENT, law educator; b. 1956. LLB, 1976, DEA, 1978, habilitation, 1985; doctorat d'Etat, U. Montpellier, France, 1985. Prof. legal history Roman and comparative law U. Calif., Berkeley, 1989—; dir. Robbins Religious and Civil Law Collection. Office: U Calif Sch Law Boalt Hall Berkeley CA 94720

MAYBAY, DUANE CHARLES, recycling systems executive; b. Ft. Dodge, Iowa, Oct. 5, 1922; s. John H. and Florabel (Hibbard) Lungren; m. Mary Tribble Parrish, Dec. 18, 1947 (div. Oct. 1972); children: Tina Biggs, Karen Woodward. BA in Mktg., U. Wis., 1948. Product engr. Gates Rubber Co., Denver, 1948-50; asst. dir. sales & mktg. Hi-C divsn. Hi-C and Snow Crop Divsn. Minute Maid Corp., N.Y.C., 1951-63; mktg. dir. Knudsen Foods, L.A., 1963-70; owner Mountain Foods, Altadena, Calif., 1970-76, Maybay Recycling Sys., Irvine, Calif., 1976-84; ptnr. Resource Recovery Sys., Irvine, 1984—. Served to lt. col. U.S. Army Air Corps, 1943-45, Italy. Avocation: antiques. Home: 104 Pergola Irvine CA 92715-1704 Office: Resource Recovery Sys PO Box 17426 Irvine CA 92713-7426

MAYBERRY, JULIUS EUGENE, realty company owner, investor; b. Qulin, Mo., July 3, 1935; s. Julius E. and Mabel L. (Gunnells) M.; m. Nettie Sue Burden, Dec. 8, 1953; children: Michael Eugene, Cynthia E. Copeland, Karen Sue Mayberry-Lee. AS, Ga. Mil. Acad., 1973; postgrad., Augusta Coll., 1976. Enlisted U.S. Army, 1957, advanced through grades to first sgt., 1973, ret., 1979; salesperson TIPS Realty Co., Augusta, Ga., 1979—, owner, broker, 1984—. Scoutmaster Boy Scouts of Am., Ft. Gordon, Ga., 1961-67. Decorated Bronze medal, Purple Heart. Mem. Augusta Bd. Realtors, Multiple Listing Service Augusta. Republican. Baptist. Lodge: Optimist (v.p. 1987). Avocation: golf. Home: 2327 Lumpkin Ct Augusta GA 30906-3090 Office: TIPS Realty Co 2327 Lumpkin Ct Augusta GA 30906-3090

MAYBERRY, WILLIAM EUGENE, retired physician; b. Cookeville, Tenn., Aug. 22, 1929; s. Henry Eugene and Beatrice Lucille (Maynard) M.; m. Jane G. Foster, Dec. 29, 1953; children: Ann Graves, Paul Foster. Student, Tenn. Tech. U., 1947-49; M.D., U. Tenn., 1953; M.S. in Medicine, U. Minn., 1959; D.H.L. (hon.), Jacksonville U., 1983. Diplomate Am. Bd. Internal Medicine. Intern U.S. Naval Hosp., Phila., 1953-54; resident Mayo Grad. Sch. Medicine, Rochester, Minn., 1956-59; mem. staff New Eng. Med. Ctr., Boston, 1959-60, Nat. Inst. Arthritis and Metabolic Diseases, 1962-64; cons. internal medicine, endocrine research and lab. medicine, chmn. dept. lab. medicine Mayo Clinic, Rochester, 1971-75, bd. govs., 1971-87, vice chmn., 1974-75, chmn., chief exec. officer, 1976-87, prof. lab. medicine, 1971—, prof. medicine, 1983-92; asst. in medicine Tufts U. Med. Sch., 1959-60; mem. faculty Mayo Grad. Sch. Medicine and Mayo Med. Sch., 1960-92; trustee Mayo Found., 1971-87, vice chmn., 1974-85, pres. 1986-87, chmn. bd. devel. 1988—; trustee Minn. Mut. Life Ins., 1983-92; bd. dirs. George A. Hormel & Co., 1986-92. Mem. editorial bd. (Jour. of Clin. Endocrinology and Metabolism), 1971-73; contbr. articles to profl. jours. Trustee Mpls. Soc. Fine Arts, 1983-91, Cumberland U., 1984-86, Twin Cities Pub. TV, Inc., 1991-92, trustee, 1991-92; bd. overseers Mpls. Coll. Art and Design, 1983-86, U. Minn. Sch. Mgmt., 1985-88; bd. dirs. Greater Rochester Area Univ. Ctr., 1986-87, Minn. Acad. Excellence Found., 1986-87, U.S. West-Minn. Exec. Bd., 1988-92; rep. Congl. Dist. I State of Minn. Compensation Council, 1986; chmn. Presdl. Commn. on Human Immunodeficiency Virus Epidemic, 1987. Recipient Disting. Alumni award Tenn. Technol. U., 1976, chair of excellence in bus. adminstrn. named in his honor, 1989; recipient Outstanding Alumni award U. Tenn., 1982, Med. Exec. Award Am. Coll. Med. Group Adminstrs., 1986; rsch. fellow NIH, 1959-60, Am. Cancer Soc., 1962-64; NIH research grantee, 1965-71. Fellow ACP; mem. Inst. Medicine of NAS, Am. Thyroid Assn., Am. Clin. and Climatological Soc., Endocrine Soc., Soc. Med. Adminstrs., Am. Acad. Med. Dirs., Am. Coll. Physician Execs. (bd. regents 1983, vice chmn. 1985-86), Sigma Xi. Clubs: Mpls. Club, Rochester Golf & Country, The Club at Pelican Bay (Naples, Fla.). Home: 826 Rue De Vl Naples FL 33963-8531 Office: Emeritus Siebens 9 200 1st St SW Rochester MN 55905-0001

MAYCOCK, IAN DAVID, oil executive; b. St. Helens, Lancashire, Eng., Dec. 8, 1935; s. Joseph and Lilian (Hewitt) M.; m. Katherine Ella Bennett, May, 1968; children: Alison, Fiona, Colin, Andrew. BSc in Geology with honors, St. Andrews (Scotland) U., 1957; MSc in Geology, Queens U., Kingston, Ont., Can., 1959; PhD in Geology, Reading (Eng.) U., 1962. Field geologist Ont. Dept. Mines, 1957, Texaco Can., 1958-59; subsurface rsch. geologist Sask. (Can.) Dept. Mineral Resources, 1962-64; geologist Conoco, U.K., U.S., Middle East, 1964-73; exploration mgr. Zapata Exploration, London, 1973-80; pres. Hunt United, London, 1980-86; v.p. exploration Yemen Hunt Oil Co., Dallas, 1986-88; sr. v.p. exploration Hunt Oil Co., Dallas, 1989—. Queens/St. Andrews exchange scholar St. Andrews U., 1957; Thayer Linsdley rsch. fellow Queens U., 1958. Mem. Am. Assn. Petroleum Geologist, Soc. Econ. Paleontologists and Mineralogists, Dallas Petroleum Club. Avocations: fishing, photography. Office: Hunt Oil Co Fountain Pl 1445 Ross Ave Dallas TX 75202-2812

MAYCOCK, JOSEPH FARWELL, JR., lawyer; b. Buffalo, June 8, 1930; s. Joseph Farwell and Annie (Richmond) M.; m. Margaret Shaw, May 25, 1968; children—Suzannah, Mary, John. B.A., Hamilton Coll., 1952; J.D., U. Mich. Law Sch., 1955. Bar: Mich. Assoc. Miller, Canfield, Paddock & Stone, Detroit, 1958-68, ptnr., 1968—. Contbr. articles to profl. jours. Trustee Greater Detroit Soc. for Blind, 1984—; mem. adv. bd. Small Bus. Council of Am., Columbia Ga., Washington, 1983—. Served with U.S. Army, 1955-57. Mem. ABA, Mich. Bar Assn., Detroit Bar Assn., Mich. Employee Benefits. Republican. Episcopalian. Clubs: Country of Detroit. Office: Miller Canfield Paddock & Stone 150 W Jefferson Ave Detroit MI 48226-4415

MAYDA, JARO, lawyer, educator, author, consultant; b. Brno, Czechoslovakia; came to U.S., 1949, naturalized, 1955; s. Francis and Maria (Hornova) M.; m. Maruja del Castillo, 1967; children by previous marriage: Jaro II, Maria Raquel, Pavel. Dr. Juris Utriusque, Masaryk U., Brno, 1945; J.D. (Rockefeller fellow 1955-56), U. Chgo., 1957. Legal counsel export div. Skodaworks, Pilsen-Prague, 1946-48; vis. prof. polit. sci. Denison U., Granville, Ohio, 1949-50, Ohio State U., Columbus, 1950-51; asst. prof. law and polit. sci. U. Wis.-Madison, 1951-56; mem. faculty U. P.R., Rio Piedras, 1957—; prof. law and public policy U. P.R., 1958-85, research prof., 1985-89; dir. Inst. Policy Studies and Law, 1972-75, spl. asst. to pres., 1972; Fulbright research prof. Inst. Comparative Law, U. Paris, 1967-68; fellow Woodrow Wilson Internat. Ctr. for Scholars (Smithsonian Instn.), 1971; Bailey lectr. La. State U., 1969; lectr. Am. specialist program Dept. State, 1960, Fed. Office of Environ., Berlin, 1983, UN Ctr. for Formation in Environ. Scis., Madrid, 1983, Grad. Sch. Bus. Adminstn., IESA, Caracas, Venezuela, 1987, U.S. Info. Agy. (German Democratic Republic, Czechoslovakia, Poland), 1988; Fulbright prof. Sch. Applied Econs., Dakar, Senegal, 1980; dep. sec. gen. 42d Conf. Internat. Law Assn., 1947; cons. Internat. Assn. Legal Sci., UNESCO, 1972—, FAO, 1974—, UN Environ. Program, 1977—, UN Econ. and Social Commn. for Asia and Pacific, 1977-78, UN Econ. Commn. for Europe, 1981, World Bank, 1994; mem. adv. com. Govt. of Columbia, 1974, Govt. of Honduras, 1977, Govt. of St. Vincent and the Grenadines, 1983, AID, Haiti, 1985, Mozambique, Guinea-Bissau, 1991, Chile, 1992, China, 1993, São Tomé & Principe, 1994; mem., policy adv. Gov.'s Study Group P.R. and Sea, 1972; research assoc. Ctr. Energy and Environ. Research, U. P.R.-U.S. Dept. Energy, 1977-88; adviser P.R. Environ. Quality Bd., 1984-86; mem. com. environ. policy and law Internat. Union Conservation Nature, 1972-78; mem. adv. com. Internat. Juridicial Orgn., Rome, 1991—; adv. panel on Ecosystem Data Handbook, NSF, 1976-77; mem. Internat. Council Environ. Law, Bonn, Ger., 1974—; U.S. rapporteur X Internat. Congress Comparative Law, Budapest, 1978; reporter on comparative legislation Congress on Forest Mgmt. and Environment, Madrid, 1984, Environ. Penal Law Internat. Symposium, San Juan, P.R., 1991, Globalization and Environment Conf. on Wider Caribbean, San Juan, 1994, NATO Advanced Rsch. Workshop on integrated assessment , Durham, N.C., 1995; lectr. Academia Istropolitana, U. Bratislava, 1994, Internat. Seminar on Environ. Impact Assessment, Moscow, 1995. Author: Introduction to Law, 1959, 74, Environment and Resources: From Conservation to Ecomanagement, 1967, Francois Geny and Modern Jurisprudence, 1978, Policy Research and Development: Outline of a Methodology, 1979, UNEP Manual on Environ. Legis., 1979; also articles, manuals; translator: law treatises; mem. editorial bd.: Am. Jour. Comparative Law, 1958-78; dir.: U. P.R. Law Rev, 1958-62; contbr. to Ency. Environ. Law, Berlin, 1987, 93. Home: R Pedro de Ornelas 12-B, P-9050 Funchal Madeira, Portugal

MAYDEN, BARBARA MENDEL, lawyer; b. Chattanooga, Sept. 18, 1951; d. Eugene Lester Mendel and Blanche (Krugman) Rosenberg; m. Martin Ted Mayden, Sept. 14, 1986. AB, Ind. U., 1973; JD, U. Ga., 1976. Bar: Ga. 1976, N.Y. 1980. Assoc. King & Spalding, Atlanta, 1976-79, Willkie Farr & Gallagher, N.Y.C., 1980, Morgan Lewis & Bockius, N.Y.C., 1980-82, White & Case, N.Y.C., 1982-89; spl. counsel Skadden, Arps, Slate, Meagher & Flom, N.Y.C., 1989-95; lectr. Vanderbilt U. Sch. Law, Nashville, 1995—. Mem. U. Ga. Bd. Visitors, Athens, 1986-89. Fellow Am. Bar Found. (life); mem. ABA (chairperson young lawyers div. 1985-86, house of dels. 1986—, commr. commn. on women 1987-91, commr. commn. opportunities for minorities in profession 1986-87, chmn. assembly resolutions com. 1990-91, select com. of the house 1989-91, membership com of the house 1991-92, bd. govs. 1991-94, chair bd. govs. ops. com., exec. com. 1993-94, mem. task force long range fin. planning 1993—), Nat. Assn. Bond Lawyers (bd. dirs. 1985-86), Bond Attys.' Workshop (chmn. 1986), N.Y. State Bar Assn. (mem. ho. of dels. 1993—), Assn. of Bar of City of N.Y. (internat. human rights com. 1986-89, 2d century com. 1986-90, com. women in the profession, 1989-92), N.Y. County Lawyers Assn. (com. spl. projects, chair com. rels with other bars). Democrat. Jewish. Home: 4414 Herbert Pl Nashville TN 37215 Office: Vanderbilt U Sch Law Nashville TN 37245

MAYEKAWA, MARY MARGARET, education counselor; b. Neptune, N.J., Nov. 13, 1941; d. Willis Gilbert and Thelma Anita Virginia (Anderson) Bills; m. Jackie Toshio Mayekawa, Nov. 28, 1970; 1 child, Leland Willis Magokichi. BA, Western Ky. U., 1965; postgrad., U. Va., 1966-68; MEd in Counseling, Coll. of William and Mary, 1971. Educator Fairfax County Schs., Annandale, Va., 1965-68; project transition counselor U.S. Army, Ft. Hood, Tex., 1971-73; student officer wives liason U.S. Army Transp. Sch.,

Ft. Eustis, Va., 1980-83; guidance counselor U.S. Army Japan IX Corp, Japan, 1983-87, 2nd Infantry Divsn., Korea, 1987-89, USAF, Reese AFB, Tex., 1989—. Vol. Edn. Divsn. Tex. Tech. Mus., Lubbock, 1990—, mem. women's coun., 1990—; vestry Episcopal Ch., Okinawa and Sagamihara City, Japan, 1974, 76, 84-86; counselor Camp Blue Yonder, Reese AFB, Tex., 1989—. Capt. U.S. Army, 1968-71. Mem. Am. Counselor Assn., Mil. Educator Counselor Assn., Tex. Assn. for Counseling and Devel., Tex. Career Guidance Assn. Avocations: Japanese flower arranging, Japanese dollmaking, church activities, reading. Home: PO Box 434 Reese Air Force Base TX 79489-0001

MAYER, ALLAN, magazine editor; b. N.Y.C., Mar. 15, 1950; s. Theodore H. and Phyllis (Zwick) M. BA, Cornell U., 1971. Staff reporter Wall Street Jour., N.Y.C., 1972-73; assoc. editor, gen. editor Newsweek mag., N.Y.C., 1973-77; fgn. corr. Newsweek mag., London, 1977-80; sr. editor Newsweek mag., N.Y.C., 1980-82; editl. dir. Arbor House Pub., N.Y.C., 1986-88; sr. editor Simon & Schuster, N.Y.C., 1988-89; editor-in-chief Buzz mag., L.A., 1990-95, editor-in-chief, pub., 1996—. Author: Madam Prime Minister, 1980, Gaston's War, 1987. Recipient award Overseas Press Club, 1974, nat. mag. award Am. Soc. Mag. Editors, 1978, William Allen White award City and Regional Mag. Assn., 1995-96. Mem. Writers Guild Am. Office: Buzz Mag 11835 W Olympic Blvd Los Angeles CA 90064

MAYER, ARNO JOSEPH, history educator; b. Luxembourg, June 19, 1926; came to U.S., 1941, naturalized, 1944; s. Frank J. and Ida (Lieben) M.; m. Nancy Grant, June 19, 1955 (div. Dec. 1965); children: Carl, Daniel. BBA, CCNY, 1949; MA, Yale U., 1950, PhD, 1953. Asst. prof. politics Brandeis U., 1954-58; asst. prof. history Harvard U., 1958-61; prof. history Princeton U., 1961—; vis. prof. Columbia U., 1966-71, NYU, 1971-72; research assoc. Ecole Pratiques des Hautes Études, Paris, 1973. Author: Political Origins of the New Diplomacy, 1959, Politics and Diplomacy of Peacemaking, 1967, Dynamics of Counterrevolution, 1971, The Persistence of the Old Regime, 1981; Why Did the Heavens Not Darken?, 1988. With intelligence service AUS, 1944-46. Recipient Herbert Baxter Adams prize Am. Hist. Assn., 1968, Isaac Deutscher prize, 1991; fellow Am. Coun. Learned Socs., 1960-61, Soc. Sci. Rsch. Coun., 1961-62, Rockefeller Found., 1963-64, Guggenheim Found., 1967-68, rsch. fellow Inst. War and Peace Columbia, 1971-72, Lehrman Inst., 1976-77. Fellow PEN, Am. Acad. Arts and Scis. Home: 58 Battle Rd Princeton NJ 08540-4902

MAYER, CARL JOSEPH, lawyer, town official; b. Boston, Apr. 23, 1959; s. Arno Joseph and Nancy Sue (Grant) M. AB magna cum laude, Princeton U., 1981; JD, U. of Chgo., 1986; LLM, Harvard U., 1988. Bar: N.J. 1986, Mass. 1988, N.Y. 1989, D.C. 1989. Writer for Ralph Nader Washington, 1981-83; law clk. to presiding justice U.S. Dist. Ct., Wilmington, Del., 1986-87; asst. prof. Hofstra Law Sch., Hempstead, N.Y., 1989-94; atty. Milberg, Weiss, Bershad, Hynes and Lerach, N.Y.C., 1995—; cons. U.S. Senate Com., Washington, 1988-89. Co-author: Public Domain, Private Dominion, 1985; contbr. articles to profl. jours. Town committeeman, Princeton, N.J. NYU fellow, 1988-89. Mem. ABA, N.Y. Bar Assn., N.J. Bar Assn., Mass. Bar Assn. Avocations: marathon running, squash, tennis. Home: 58 Battle Rd Princeton NJ 08540-4902 Office: Milberg Weiss Bershad Hynes & Lerach One Pennsylvania Plz New York NY 10019

MAYER, DENNIS THOMAS, biochemist, educator; b. Lexington, Mo., Jan. 3, 1901; s. August John and Agatha (Gavin) M.; m. Virginia Louise Miller, May 8, 1937; children—Dennis T., David R., Michael J. Student, U. Ill., 1923-25; A.B., U. Mo., 1931, M.A., 1933, Ph.D., 1938. Agt. U.S. Dept. Agr., 1937-42; mem. faculty U. Mo. at Columbia, 1937—, prof. agrl. biochemistry, 1952—, dir. research in physiology and biochemistry reprodn., 1942—, dir. interdisciplinary reproductive biology tng. program, 1966, chmn. dept. agrl. chemistry, dir. grad. studies, 1966-71, prof. emeritus, 1971—. Contbr. articles to profl. jours. Mayer lecture series designated by U. Mo. in his honor, 1987. Mem. Am. Soc. Biol. Chemists, Soc. for Exptl. Biology and Medicine, Am. Soc. Animal Sci., N.Y. Acad. Scis., Mo. Acad. Sci., Phi Beta Kappa, Sigma Xi, Gamma Sigma Delta. Home: 3812 Cedar Ln Columbia MO 65201-6502

MAYER, ELIZABETH BILLMIRE, educational administrator; B.Ed., Nat. Coll. Edn., Evanston, Ill., 1953; M.A. in Liberal Studies, Wesleyan U., 1979. Teaching asst. Hull House, Chgo., 1950-51; teaching scholar Nat. Coll. Edn. Demonstration Sch., 1952-53; pre-sch. tchr. St. Matthew's Sch., Pacific Palisades, Calif., 1959-63, tchr. 2d grade, 1963-67; librarian Chandler Sch., Pasadena, Calif., 1971-72, tchr. 4th grade, 1972-80, curriculum coordinator 1st-8th grades, 1979-80; tchr. 4th-6th grades Inst. for Experimentation in Tchr. Edn., SUNY-Cortland, 1980; asst. prof. edn. SUNY-Cortland, 1980-82; founder, headmistress The Mayer Sch., Ithaca, N.Y., 1982-92, Ariz. State U., Tempe, 1992—, Coll. Edn., 1992-94, faculty liaison Acad. Affairs, 1994—. Mem. Nat. Council Tchrs. Math., Nat. Council Tchrs. English, Nat. Sci. Tchrs. Assn., Rotary Internat. (mem. bd. dirs. 1994-96), Phi Delta Kappa (officer 1980-81, 92-96), Mem. Leadership America, class of 1995. Office: Ariz State U MS 3N21 Box 870101 Tempe AZ 85287

MAYER, FOSTER LEE, JR., toxicologist; b. Fletcher, Okla., Nov. 17, 1942; s. Foster Lee Sr. and Annis Lucille (Edwards) M.; m. Anita June Poarch, Aug. 31, 1962 (div. Nov. 1981); children: Sunie K., Carolyn Elizabeth; m. Kathleen Joyce Stecher, July 14, 1983. BS in Biology and Chemistry, Southwestern Okla. State U., 1965; MS in Wildlife Biology, Utah State U., 1967, PhD in Toxicology, 1970. Instr. Utah State U., Logan, 1969-70; research sect. leader U.S. Fish and Wildlife Service Columbia (Mo.) Fish Research Lab., 1970-73, asst. chief biologist, 1973-74, chief biologist, 1974-80, research scientist, 1980-84; sect. chief U.S. EPA, Gulf Breeze, Fla., 1984-85; br. chief EPA, Gulf Breeze, Fla., 1985-91, sr. rsch. scientist, 1991—; expert witness U.S. Fish and Wildlife Service, 1973-84. Author: Manual of Acute Toxicity-Freshwater, 1986, Acute Toxicity Handbook-Estuarine, 1987, also book chpts.; editor: Aquatic Toxicity and Hazard Evaluation, 1977; contbr. numerous articles to profl. jours. Instr. 4-H Club, Columbia, Mo., 1978-80. Mem. Am. Chem. Soc., Am. Fisheries Soc. (chpt. pres. 1976, sect. pres. 1979), Soc. Environ. Toxicology and Chemistry (editor 1982-87, bd. dirs. 1985-88), Soc. Toxicology (editl. bd. 1981-90, 95—), Am. Inst. Fishery Rsch. Biologists, ASTM, NRA, Sigma Xi. Republican. Baptist. Avocations: hunting, fishing, boating, wood carving, scrimshawing. Office: EPA Sabine Island Gulf Breeze FL 32561

MAYER, FRANK D., JR., lawyer; b. Dec. 23, 1933. BA, Amherst Coll., 1955; student, Cambridge U.; JD, U. Chgo., 1959. Bar: Ill. 1959. Ptnr. Mayer, Brown & Platt, Chgo. Mem. ABA, Chgo. Bar Assn., Order of Coif, Phi Beta Kappa. Office: Mayer Brown & Platt 190 S La Salle St Chicago IL 60603-3410

MAYER, HALDANE ROBERT, federal judge; b. Buffalo, N.Y., Feb. 21, 1941; s. Haldane Rupert and Myrtle Kathleen (Gaude) M.; m. Mary Anne McCurdy, Aug. 13, 1966; children: Anne Christian, Rebecca Paige. B.S., U.S. Mil. Acad., 1963; J.D., Coll. William and Mary, 1971. Bar: Va. 1971, U.S. Ct. Appeals (4th cir.) 1972, U.S. Dist. Ct. (ea. dist.) Va. 1972, U.S. Ct. Mil. Appeals, U.S. Army Ct. Mil. Rev. 1973, D.C. 1980, U.S. Supreme Ct. 1977, U.S. Ct. Claims 1984. Law clk. U.S. Ct. Appeals (4th cir.), Richmond, Va., 1971-72; atty. McGuire Woods & Battle, Charlottesville, Va., 1975-77; spl. asst. to chief justice U.S. Supreme Ct., Washington, 1977-80; atty. Baker & McKenzie, Washington, 1980-81; acting spl. counsel U.S. Merit Systems Protection Bd., Washington, 1981-82; judge U.S. Claims Ct., Washington, 1982-87, U.S. Ct. Appeals (Fed. cir.), Washington, 1987—; adj. prof. U. Va. Sch. Law, 1975-77, 92-94, George Washington U. Law Sch., 1992—. Bd. dirs. William and Mary Law Sch. Assn., 1979-85. Served to maj. AUS, 1963-75, lt. col. res. ret. Decorated Bronze Star, two Army Commendation medals, Meritorious Service medal. Mem. West Point Assn. Grads., Army Athletic Assn., West Point Soc. D.C., Omicron Delta Kappa. Office: US Ct Appeals for Fed Cir 717 Madison Pl NW Washington DC 20439-0001

MAYER, HENRY MICHAEL, mass transit consultant; b. Wauwatosa, Wis., Oct. 20, 1922; s. Henry and Rose (Daas) M.; m. Colleen C. Reisner, July 25, 1944; children: Michael, Michele, David, Jennifer. B.S. in Bus. Adminstrn., Marquette U., 1947. With Milw. Transit System, 1947-83, exec. asst., 1959-67, v.p., gen. mgr., 1967-75; pres., mng. dir. Milw. Transport Services, Inc., 1975-83; cons., 1983—; lectr., cons., author, mass transit. Lt. USNR, 1943-46, PTO. Named to Pub. Transit Hall of Fame. Mem. Inst. Transp. Engrs., Alpha Sigma Nu. Originator bus service using pvt. shopping centers as park-ride lots for freeway express service to downtown. Home: 9995 W North Ave #350 Milwaukee WI 02504-6940

MAYER, HERBERT CARLETON, JR., computer consultant; b. Newton, Mass., Aug. 2, 1922; s. Herbert Carleton and Elsie Marie (Hauser) M.; m. Maryetta Brodkord, Aug. 21, 1948; children: Judith Marie, Christine Louise. BS, Parsons Coll., 1943; MS, U. Iowa, 1947; PhD, U. So. Calif., 1975. Instr. math. U. Idaho, Moscow, 1947-48, U. Utah, Salt Lake City, 1949-51; edn. adminstr. Gen. Electric co., Richland, Wash., 1951-59; systems engr., univ. industry specialist IBM, Chgo., 1959-81; assoc. prof. mgmt. info. systems Wash. State U., Pullman, 1980-82; assoc. prof. U. Wis.-Parkside, Kenosha, 1982-85, Eastern Wash. U., Cheney, 1985-90; adj. prof. mgmt. U. Tex., El Paso, 1976-78. Pres. Tri-City Heights Assn., Kennewick, Wash., 1956-58, PTA, Kennewick, 1957-58; v.p. Kennewick Sch. Bd., 1958-59, pres., 1959. Mem. Math. Assn. Am., Internat. Assn. Computing in Edn., Am. Soc. Engring. Edn., Data Processing Mgmt. Assn. (bd. dirs., sec. Spokane chpt. 1988, v.p. edn. Spokane chpt. 1989, v.p. student chpt. 1990), Phi Delta Kappa (found. chmn. Spokane chpt. 1992-94). Home: 3334 S Bernard St Spokane WA 99203-1636

MAYER, JAMES HOCK, mediator, lawyer; b. Neptune City, N.J., Nov. 1, 1935; s. J. Kenneth and Marie Ruth (Hock) M.; m. Carol I. Keating, Sept. 20, 1958 (div. Feb. 1981); children: Craig, Jeffrey; m. Patrisha Renk, Mar. 28, 1981. AB with distinction, Dartmouth Coll., 1957; JD, Harvard U., 1964. Bar: Calif. 1965, U.S. Dist. Ct (no. dist., so. dist.) Calif. 1965, U.S. Ct. Appeals (9th cir.) 1965, U.S. Supreme Ct. 1974. Assoc. Pillsbury, Madison & Sutro, San Francisco, 1964-72, ptnr., 1973—; ind. mediator, 1992—. Rear adm. USNR, 1957-93. Rufus Choate scholar Dartmouth Coll., 1956-57. Mem. Newcomen Soc., Navy League, Naval Order of U.S., Harvard Club. Office: 101 W Broadway Ste 1800 San Diego CA 92101-8219

MAYER, JAMES JOSEPH, retired corporate lawyer; b. Cin., Nov. 27, 1938; s. Cletus Joseph and Berna Mae (Schroeder) M.; m. Margaret Ann Hobbs, Oct. 24, 1964; children: Kimberly, Susanne, Terri. BEE, U. Cin., 1961; JD, No. Ky. U., 1969. Registered profl. engr., Ohio. Bar: Ohio 1969, Ky. 1975. Engr. Cin. Gas & Electric Co., 1961-69, atty., 1969-85, gen. counsel, 1986-91, v.p., gen. counsel, 1991-95, ret., 1995; of counsel Taft, Stetinius & Hollister, Cin., 1995—. Served with USAFR, 1961-64. Mem. Ohio Bar Assn., Ky. Bar Assn., Cin. Bar Assn. Republican. Roman Catholic. Club: Bankers. Avocations: home remodeling, sports, golf.

MAYER, JAMES WALTER, materials science educator; b. Chgo., Apr. 24, 1930; s. James Leo and Kathleen (Engels) M.; m. Elizabeth Billmire, June 27, 1952; children: James Leo, John William, Frank Charles, Helen Kathleen, William Andrew. BSME, Purdue U., 1952, PhD in Physics, 1960; DSc (hon.), SUNY, Albany, 1988. Tech. staff Hughes Research Lab., Malibu, Calif., 1959-67; prof. Calif. Inst. Tech., Pasadena, 1967-80; master of student houses Calif. Inst. Tech., 1975-80; F. Norwood Bard prof. materials sci. Cornell U., Ithaca, N.Y., 1980-92, Bard prof. emeritus, 1992—; dir. Ctr. for Solid State Sci., Regents' prof. Ariz. State U., Tempe, 1992—; scuba instr. Nat. Assn. Underwater Instrs. 1970-80. Author: Backscattering Spectrometry, 1978, Ion Implantation in Semiconductors, 1970, Materials Analysis by Ion Channeling, 1982, Fundamentals of Surface and Thin Film Analysis, 1986, Electronic Materials Science, 1990, Electronic Thin Film Science, 1992; editor: Laser Annealing of Semiconductors, 1982. Served to 1st lt. U.S. Army, 1952-54. Recipient Von Hippel award, Materials Research Soc., Boston, 1981, Silver Medal of U. Catania, Italy, 1986. Fellow Am. Phys. Soc., IEEE; mem. Bohmische Physical Soc., Am. Vacuum Soc., Nat. Acad. Engring. Home: 3355 N Valencia Ln Phoenix AZ 85018-6610 Office: Ariz State U Box 871704 Ctr for Solid State Sci Tempe AZ 85287-1704

MAYER, JOHN, lawyer; b. Beatrice, Nebr., Aug. 25, 1948; m. Kathleen A. Slaydon, Mar. 8, 1986; children: Amelia, Holly. BA, U. N.Mex., 1970; JD, U. Tex., 1973. Bar: Tex. 1973; cert. Tex. Bd. Civil Trial Advocacy. Assoc. Ross, Banks, May, Cron & Cavin, Houston, 1973-80, ptnr., 1980—. Mem. Assn. Trial Lawyers Am., Tex. Assn. Bank Counsel, Comml. Law League Am. Home: 725 E Creekside Dr Houston TX 77024-3239 Office: Ross Banks May Cron & Cavin 2 Riverway Ste 700 Houston TX 77056-1912

MAYER, MARGERY WEIL, publishing executive; b. Beaufort, S.C., Feb. 11, 1952; d. Warren Burke Weil and Elise Jean (Schiff) Rubel; m. Theodore Van Huysen Mayer, Dec. 28, 1975; children: Lily, Henry. BA, Middlebury Coll., 1974; MS, MIT, 1976. Planning analyst Digital Equipment Corp., Maynard, Mass., 1976-77; editor-in-chief sch. pub. sect. Holt, Rinehart & Winston, N.Y.C., 1977-87; pres. Ginn div. Silver, Burdett & Ginn, Needham, Mass., 1987-90; exec. v.p. Scholastic Inc., N.Y.C., 1990—. Editor Sloan Mgmt. Rev., 1975-76. Trustee program Read With Me, Dedham, Mass., 1989; mem. rev. panel U.S. Dept. Edn. Sch. Recognition Program. Mem. Phi Beta Kappa. Office: Scholastic Inc 555 Broadway New York NY 10012-3919*

MAYER, MARILYN GOODER, steel company executive; b. Chgo.; d. Seth MacDonald and Jean (McMullen) Gooder; m. William Anthony Mayer, Nov. 14, 1959; children—William Anthony Jr., Robert MacDonald. grad. Career Inst. Chgo., 1941; student Lake Forest Coll., Ill., 1942. Adminstrv. asst. Needham, Louis & Brorby, Chgo., 1949-53; v.p. RMB Corp., Chgo., 1963-71, Mayer Motors, Ft. Lauderdale, Fla., 1965-74, Gooder-Henrichsen, Chicago Heights, Ill., 1975—; dir. Barnett Bank, West Palm Beach, Fla. Trustee Gulf Stream (Fla.) Sch., St. Andrew's Sch., Boca Raton, Fla.; bd. dirs. Bethesda Hosp. Assn., Boynton Beach, Fla., pres. 1981-82; bd. dirs. Gulf Stream Civic Assn. Mem. Soc. Four Arts. Republican. Episcopalian. Clubs: Little, Gulf Stream Bath and Tennis. Avocation: travel. Home: 2925 Polo Dr Delray Beach FL 33483-7331

MAYER, MORRIS LEHMAN, marketing educator; b. Demopolis, Ala., Dec. 14, 1925; s. Lehman M. and Anne (Rochotsh) M.; m. Judith Marian Morton, Dec. 22, 1957; children: Susan Morton, Elizabeth Anne. B.S. in Bus. Adminstrn, U. Ala., 1949, DHL (hon.), 1994; M.S. in Retailing, N.Y. U., 1950; Ph.D. in Bus. Orgn. Ohio State U., 1961. Buyer Goldblatts Dept. Store, Chgo., 1951-55; mem. faculty U. Ala., 1955—, prof., 1960—, chmn. dept. mktg., 1969-74, dir. Hess Inst. Retailing, 1985-92, Bruno prof. mktg., 1986-92; Bruno prof. mktg. emeritus, 1992—; instr. Ohio State U., Columbus, 1956-60; cons. Mgmt. Horizons Co., Columbus, 1966-70, N.C.R. Co., Dayton, Ohio, 1967-75. Co-author: Modern Retailing, 1978, 6th edit., 1993, Retailing, 1981, 5th edit., 1993. Served with AUS, 1944-46, 50-51. Recipient Teaching Excellence award Burlington No. Found., 1986; Ford Found. fellow, 1962-63, So. Mktg. fellow, 1986; named to U. Ala. Bus. Faculty Hall of Fame, 1995, Retail Patronage Acad. Hall of Fame, 1995; Morris Mayer Endowed scholarship established 1992; Morris L. Mayer award established U. Ala., 1993; Morris L. Mayer Outstanding Sutdent award established Sales and Mktg. Execs., 1993, others. Mem. Am. Mktg. Assn. (Morris L. Mayer Outstanding Mem. award estab. Birmingham chpt. 1993), So. Mktg. Assn. (pres.), Ala. Retail Assn. (bd. dirs.), Am. Coll. Retail Assn. (pres., Hall of Fame 1992, Mortar Bd., Beta Gamma Sigma, Eta Mu Pi, Pi Sigma Epsilon, Omicron Delta Kappa, Zeta Beta Tau (chpt. trustee). Jewish (temple trustee). Home: 1321 Montclair Cir Tuscaloosa AL 35404-4241 Office: U Ala PO Box 870225 Tuscaloosa AL 35487-0225

MAYER, NANCY J., state official; b. Phila., June 9, 1937; d. Benjamin and Florence Hannah (Altshuler) Rosenstein; m. Edward C. Leand, Sept. 6, 1958 (div. 1970); children: Judith, Marjorie; m. William L. Mayer, June 16, 1971. BA in Am. Hist., Barnard Coll., 1958; MAT in Am. Hist., Brown U., 1972; JD, Northeastern U., 1982. Assoc. firm Tillinghast, Collins & Graham, Providence, 1982-84; chief legal cunsel R.I. Dept. Bus. Regulation, Providence, 1986-92; treas., general treas. State of R.I., 1992—; candidate R.I. Senate, 1978, 80. Mem. R.I. adv. com. U.S. Commn. on Civil Rights; mem. R.I. Partnership of Sci. and Tech.; mem. AGing 2000 Health Care for Srs. Com., adv. com. U.S. Com. on Civil Rights (R.I. Chpt.). Mem. Nat. Assn. State Treas. (v.p.). Republican. Jewish. Avocations: tennis (former nationally and regionally ranked player), cycling, jogging, writing, duplicate bridge. Office: Treasury Dept 102 State St Providence RI 02908-5021*

MAYER, PATRICIA JAYNE, financial officer, management accountant; b. Chgo., Apr. 27, 1950; d. Arthur and Ruth (Greenberger) Hersh; m. William A. Mayer Jr., Apr. 30, 1971. AA, Diablo Valley Coll., 1970; BSBA, Calif. State U., Hayward, 1975. Cert. mgmt. acct. Staff acct., auditor Elmer Fox Westheimer and Co., Oakland, Calif., 1976; supervising auditor Auditor's Office County of Alameda, Oakland, 1976-78; asst. acctg. mgr. CBS Retail Stores doing bus. as Pacific Stereo, Emeryville, Calif., 1978-79; contr. Oakland Unified Sch. Dist., 1979-84; v.p. fin., CFO YMCA, San Francisco, 1984-96; v.p. fin. customer segments Charles Schwab & Co., San Francisco, 1996—; instr. acctg. to staff YMCA, San Francisco, 1984-96, CBS Retail Stores, 1978-79. Draft counselor Mt. Diablo Peace Ctr., Walnut Creek, Calif., 1970-72; dep. registrar of voters Contra Costa County Registrar's Office, Martinez, Calif., 1972-77. Mem. Fin. Execs. Inst. (bd. dirs. San Francisco chpt.), Inst. Mgmt. Accts. (pres.-elect Diablo Valley chpt. 1995—, pres. 1995-96), Dalmatian Club No. Calif., Dalmatian Club Am. Democrat. Jewish. Avocations: showing and breeding Dalmatians, playing Tex. Hold 'Em poker tournaments. Office: Charles Schwab & Co 101 Montgomery st San Francisco CA 94104

MAYER, PATRICIA LYNN SORCI, mental health nurse, educator; b. Chgo., July 22, 1942; d. Ben and Adonia (Grenier) Sorci; 1 child, Christopher David Mayer. AGS with high honors, Pima Community Coll., Tucson, 1983; BSN with honors, U. Ariz., 1986, MS in Nursing, 1987. RN, Ariz.; cert. addictions counselor, chem. dependency therapist; lic. pvt. pilot. Nurse educator Tucson. Contbr. articles to profl. jours. Mem. Nat. Nurses Soc. on Addictions, Phi Kappa Phi, Sigma Theta Tau, Pi Lambda Theta, Golden Key.

MAYER, PETER, publisher; b. London, 1936. Grad., Columbia Coll., Oxford U., Eng. CEO Penguin Books, London, N.Y.C., 1978—; now chmn. Penguin USA, N.Y.C. Recipient grad. fellowship Ind. Univ.; Fulbright scholar Univ. Berlin. Office: Penguin Books Ltd, 27 Wrights Ln, London W8 5TZ, England also: Penguin USA 375 Hudson St New York NY 10014-3658

MAYER, RAYMOND RICHARD, business administration educator; b. Chgo., Aug. 31, 1924; s. Adam and Mary (Bogdala) M.; m. Helen Lakowski, Jan. 30, 1954; children: Mark, John, Mary, Jane. B.S., Ill. Inst. Tech., 1948, M.S., 1954, Ph.D., 1957. Indsl. engr. Standard Oil Co., Whiting, Ind., 1948-51; orgn. analyst Ford Motor Co., Chgo., 1951-53; instr. Ill. Inst. Tech., Chgo., 1953-56; asso. prof. Ill. Inst. Tech., 1958-60; asst. prof. U. Chgo., 1956-58; Walter F. Mullady prof. bus. adminstrn. Loyola U., Chgo., 1960—. Author: Financial Analysis of Investment Alternatives, 1966, Production Management, 1962, rev. edit., 1968, Production and Operations Management, 1975, rev. edit., 1982, Capital Expenditure Analysis, 1978. Served with USNR, 1944-46. Ingersoll Found. fellow, 1955-56; Machinery and Allied Products Inst. fellow, 1954-55; Ford Found. fellow, 1962. Mem. Acad. Mgmt., Am. Econ. Assn., Am. Statis. Assn., Am. Inst. for Decision Scis., Nat. Assn. Purchasing Mgmt., Polish Inst. Arts and Scis. in Am., Alpha Iota Delta, Alpha Kappa Psi, Beta Gamma Sigma. Home: 730 Green Bay Rd Winnetka IL 60093-1912 Office: 820 N Michigan Ave Chicago IL 60611-2103

MAYER, RICHARD DEAN, mathematics educator; b. Ft. Wayne, Ind., May 26, 1930; s. Lester Blyle and Velma Lucille (Maulsby) M.; m. Patsy Jean Hartwell, Aug. 31, 1952; children—Susan, Joann, John. B.S., Purdue U., 1952, M.S., 1954; Ph.D., U. Wash., 1959. Teaching asst. Purdue U., 1952-54, U. Wash., 1954-59; asst. prof. math. Idaho State U., 1959-61, assoc. prof. math., chmn. dept., 1961-67; prof. math. SUNY, Oswego, 1967-91, prof. math. emeritus, 1991—, chmn. dept., 1967-74; rsch. engr. Boeing Airplane Co., Seattle, summer, 1959, Carter Oil Co., Billings, Mont., summer, 1960. Mem. The Planetary Soc., Math. Assn. Am., Am. Math. Soc., Sigma Xi, Sigma Pi Sigma, Delta Rho Kappa, Pi Mu Epsilon, Kappa Mu Epsilon. Avocations: handball. Home: 23040 Chisholm Trl Bend OR 97702-9664

MAYER, RICHARD EDWIN, psychology educator; b. Chgo., Feb. 8, 1947; s. James S. and Bernis (Lowy) M.; m. Beverly Linn Pastor, Dec. 19, 1971; children: Kenneth Michael, David Mark, Sarah Ann. BA with honors, Miami U., Oxford, Ohio, 1969; MS in Psychology, U. Mich., 1971, PhD in Psychology, 1973. Vis. asst. prof. Ind. U., Bloomington, 1973-75; asst. prof. psychology U. Calif., Santa Barbara, 1975-80, assoc. prof., 1980-85, prof., 1985—, pres., chmn. dept., 1987-90; vis. scholar Learning Rsch. and Devel. Ctr., U. Pitts., 1979, Ctr. for Study of Reading, U. Ill., 1984. Author: Foundations of Learning and Memory, 1979, The Promise of Cognitive Psychology, 1981, Thinking, Problem Solving, Cognition, 1983, 2d edit., 1992, BASIC: A Short Course, 1985, Educational Psychology, 1987; editor: Human Reasoning, 1980, Teaching and Learning Computer Programming, 1988; editor jours. Instructional Sci., 1983-87, Educational Psychologist, 1983-89. Sch. bd. officer Goleta (Calif.) Union Sch. Dist., 1981—. NSF grantee, 1975-88. Fellow APA (divsn. 15 officer 1987—, G. Stanley Hall lectr. 1988), Am. Psychol. Soc.; mem. Am. Ednl. Rsch. Assn. (divsn. C officer 1986-88), Psychonomic Soc. Democrat. Jewish. Avocations: computers, hiking, bicycling, reading, dogs. Office: U Calif Dept Of Psychology Santa Barbara CA 93016

MAYER, RICHARD PHILIP, food executive; b. Bloomfield, N.J., Feb. 13, 1940; s. Richard R. and Margaret (Kernan) M.; m. Diane Marie Krouse; children: Margaret, Catherine. B.S., Rutgers U., 1962, M.B.A., 1965. Dir. group prodns. Gen. Foods Corp., 1962-72; dir. bus. devel. Heublein, Inc., Farmington, Conn., 1973-75; v.p. mktg. planning Heublein Grocery Prodn., Farmington, Conn., 1975-77; v.p. planning and program integration Kentucky Fried Chicken, Louisville, 1977-78, sr. v.p. mktg., planning and devel., 1978-79, pres., 1979-80, chmn., chief exec. officer, 1980-89; pres. Gen. Foods USA (divsn. Kraft Gen. Foods), White Plains, N.Y., 1989-91; chmn. bd., CEO Kraft Gen. Foods, Northfield, Ill., 1991-1995. Chmn. Louisville Fund for Arts, 1984-85; bd. dirs. Northwestern Meml. Hosp., Chgo., Lyrice Opera of Chgo., Nat. City Bank, Louisville, Brown-Forman Corp., Louisville. Served with U.S. Army, 1964-70. Recipient Gold Medal award Am. Mktg. Assn. Mem. First Ky. Nat. Corp. (bd. dirs.). Office: Kraft Gen Foods 3 Lakes Dr Northfield IL 60093*

MAYER, ROBERT ANTHONY, college president; b. N.Y.C., Oct. 30, 1933; s. Ernest John and Theresa Margaret (Mazura) M.; m. Laura Wiley Christ, Apr. 30, 1960. BA magna cum laude, Fairleigh Dickinson U., 1955; MA, NYU, 1967. With N.J. Bank and Trust Co., Paterson, 1955-61; mgr. advt. dept. N.J. Bank and Trust Co., 1959-61; program supr. advt. dept. Mobil Oil Co., N.Y.C., 1961-62; asst. to dir. Latin Am. program Ford Found., N.Y.C., 1963-65; asst. rep. Ford Found., Brazil, 1965-67; asst. to v.p. adminstrn., 1967-73; officer in charge logistical services Ford Found., 1968-73; asst. dir. programs N.Y. Community Trust, N.Y.C., 1973-76; exec. dir. N.Y. State Council on the Arts, N.Y.C., 1976-79; mgmt. cons. N.Y.C., 1979-80; dir. Internat. Mus. Photography, George Eastman House, Rochester, N.Y., 1980-89, mgmt. cons., 1989-90; pres. Cleve. Inst. of Art, 1990—. Mem. editorial adv. bd.: Grants mag., 1978-80; author: (plays) La Borgia, 1971; Alijandru, 1971, They'll Grow No Roses, 1975. Mem. state program adv. panel NEA, 1977-80; mem. Mayor's Com. on Cultural Policy, N.Y.C., 1974-75; mem. pres.'s adv. com. Bklyn. campus, L.I. U., 1978-79; bd. dirs. Fedn. Protestant Welfare Agys., N.Y.C., 1977-79, Arts for Greater Rochester, 1981-83, Garth Fagan's Dance Theatre, 1982-86; trustee Internat. Mus. Photography, 1981-89, Lacoste Sch. Arts, France, 1991—, sec., 1994—; mem. dean's adv. com. Grad. Sch. Social Welfare, Fordham U., 1976; mem. N.Y. State Motion Picure and TV Devel. Adv. Bd., 1984-87, N.Y. State Martin Luther King Jr. Commn., 1985-90, Cleve. Coun. Cultural Affairs, 1992-94; chmn. Greater Cleve. Regional Transit Authority Arts in Transit Com., 1992-95. Recipient Nat. award on advocacy for girls Girls Clubs Am., 1976. Mem. Nat. Assembly Art Agys. (bd. dirs. 1977-79, 1st vice chmn. 1978-79), Alliance Ind. Colls. Art (bd. dirs. 1983-91, vice chmn. 1986-87, sec. 1987-89), N.Y. State Assn. Museums (bd. councilors 1983-86, pres. 1986-89), Assn. Ind. Colls. Art and Design (bd. dirs. 1991—, exec. com. 1991-93). Home: 20201 N Park Blvd Apt 101 Shaker Heights OH 44118-5024 Office: Cleve Inst Art 11141 East Blvd Cleveland OH 44106-1710

MAYER, ROBERT WALLACE, emeritus finance educator; b. Mt. Pulaski, Ill., Apr. 17, 1909; s. Edward Otto and Minnie Laura (Clark) M.; m. Nella Coryell DeAtley, AUg. 2, 1933 (dec.); children: nancy (Mrs. Donald G. Wyatt), Anne (Mrs. Robert M. Shannon, dec.), Caroline (Mrs. Chester R.

Keller), Melinda (Mrs. Thomas Martinez). B.S., U. Ill., 1930, M.S., 1931, Ph.D., 1933. Cert. ofcl. U.S. Track and Field Fedn. Statistician Libby McNeill & Libby, Chgo., 1929, Commonwealth Edison Co., Chgo., 1930; from instr. to asst. prof. Lehigh U., 1933-42; sr. economist WPB, Washington, 1942-45; asso. prof. econs. U. Ill., Urbana, 1945-52; prof. U. Ill., 1952-57, prof. finance, 1957-77, prof. emeritus, 1977—, vice chmn. dept. econs., 1953-57; vis. prof. fin. Ill. State U., Normal, 1978-79; Exec. sec. Combined (Brit.-Am.) Steel Com., 1943-45; cons. Rand Corp., 1951-53. Author Stemma, 1984m Bios Didaskalos, 1991; contbr. articles to profl. jours. Mem. Am. Finance Assn, Midwest Finance Assn. (pres. 1967-68), Am. Econ. Assn., Chgo. Fin. Writers Assn., SAR, U. Ill. Varsity Assn. (hon.), Beta Gamma Sigma, Phi Kappa Phi, Alpha Kappa Psi, Tau Kappa Epsilon. Republican. Presbyterian. Club: Kiwanian (pres. 1969-70). Home: 17 Greencroft Dr Champaign IL 61821-5117 Office: U Ill Dept Econ Urbana IL 61801

MAYER, SUSAN MARTIN, art educator; b. Atlanta, Oct. 25, 1931; d. Paul McKeen and Ione (Garrett) Martin; m. Arthur James Mayer, Aug. 9, 1953; 1 child, Melinda Marilyn. Student, Am. U., 1949-50; BA, U. N.C., Greensboro, 1953; postgrad., U. Del., 1956-58; MA, Ariz. State U., 1966. Artist-in-residence Armed Forces Staff Coll., Norfolk, Va., 1968-69; coord. of edn. Huntington Art Gallery U. Tex., Austin, 1970—, mem. art faculty, 1971—. Co-editor: Museum Education: History, Theory and Practice, 1989; author various mus. publs.; contbr. articles to profl. jours. Recipient award Austin Ind. Sch. Bd., 1985. Mem. Nat. Art Edn. Assn. (bd. dirs. 1983-87, award 1987, 91), Tex. Art Edn. Assn. (mus. edn. chair 1982-83, legis. rep. 1988—, Mus. Educator of Yr. 1986), Tex. Assn. Mus. (mus. edn. chair), Austin Visual Arts Assn., Am. Assn. Mus. Office: U Tex Art/Art History Dept Austin TX 78712

MAYER, VICTOR JAMES, earth system science educator; b. Mayville, Wis., Mar. 25, 1933; s. Victor Charles and Phyllis (Bachhuber) M.; m. Mary Jo Anne White, Nov. 25, 1965; children: Gregory, Maribeth. BS in Geology, U. Wis., 1956; MS in Geology, U. Colo., 1960, PhD in Sci. Edn., 1966. Tchr. Colo. Pub. Schs., 1961-65; asst. prof. SUNY Coll., Oneonta, 1965-67; asst. prof. Ohio State U., Columbus, 1967-70, assoc. prof., 1970-75, prof. ednl. studies, geol. scis. and natural resources, 1975-95, prof. emeritus, 1995—, coord. earth sys. edn. program, 1991—, prof. emeritus, 1995—; co-organizer symposium at 29th Internat. Geol. Congress; internat. sci. edn. assistance to individuals and orgns. in Japan, Korea, Taiwan, Russia, and Venezuela; dir. NSF Insts., program for leadership Earth Sys. Edn., 1990-95; dir. Korean Sci. Tchrs. Insts., 1986-88, 95; keynote spkr. U.S.A. rep. Internat. Conf. on Geoscis. Edn., Southampton, Eng., 1993; co-convenor Second Internat. conf. on Geosci. Edn., Hila, Hawaii, 1997. Contbr. articles to profl. jours. Served with USAR. Named Disting. Investigator, Ohio Sea Grant Program, 1983. Fellow AAAS (chmn. edn. 1988-89), Ohio Acad. Sci. (v.p. 1978-79, exec. com. 1993-94, outstanding univ. educator 1995); mem. Nat. Sci. Tchrs. Assn. (bd. dirs. 1984-86), Sci. Edn. Coun. Ohio (pres. 1987-88), Sigma Xi, Phi Delta Kappa. Roman Catholic. Avocation: photography. Home: 111 W Dominion Blvd Columbus OH 43214-2607 Office: Ohio State U Coll of Edn 1945 N High St Columbus OH 43210-1120

MAYER, WALTER GEORG, physics educator; b. Silberbach, Bohemia, Czech Republic, Mar. 13, 1927; came to U.S., 1949; s. Karl and Berta *Guldan) M.; m. Gretl Anna König, Mar. 21, 1959. AB, Hope Coll., 1953; MS, Mich. State U., 1955, PhD, 1958. Rsch. scientist Siemens Corp., Erlangen, Germany, 1958-59; asst. rsch. prof. Mich. State U., East Lansing, 1959-65; asst. prof. Georgetown U., Washington, 1965-69, assoc. prof., 1969-72, prof. physics, 1972—, dir. Ultrasonics Rsch. Lab., 1988—; vis. prof. U. Saarbruecken, Germany, 1980-81, U. Solidstate, Paris, 1990. Editor Ultrasonics, 1989; contbr. articles to profl. jours. Recipient Humboldt prize Humboldt Found., 1980, Medaille d'Argent, Acoutsical Soc. France, 1990. Fellow Acoustical Soc. Am., Inst. Acoustics U.K. Office: Georgetown U Physics Dept 37th and O Sts NW Washington DC 20057

MAYER, WILLIAM DIXON, pathologist, educator; b. Beaver Falls, Pa., Oct. 5, 1928; s. Emil Leroy and Elizabeth (Townsend) M.; m. Donna S. Dashiell; children: Elizabeth Ann, David Dixon, William Dixon, Kathy Dashiell. A.B., Colgate U., 1951; M.D. with honor, U. Rochester, 1957; D.Sc. (hon.), U. Osteopathic Medicine and Health Scis., 1988. Intern, then resident pathology Strong Meml. Hosp., Rochester, N.Y., 1957-61; instr., mem. faculty U. Mo. Sch. Medicine, 1961-76, dir. Univ. Med. Center, 1967-74; dean U. Mo. Sch. Medicine (Sch. Medicine), 1967-74, prof. pathology, 1967-76; asst. chief med. dir. for acad. affairs VA, Washington, 1976-79; pres. Med. Coll. Hampton Roads, Norfolk, Va., 1979-87; assoc. dir. div. regional med. programs NIH, 1966-67; mem. exec. com. Nat. Bd. Med. Examiners, 1969-81, treas., 1975-79, vice-chmn., 1979-81, hon. mem., 1981—, fin. com., 1987-93; bd. regent Nat. Libr. of Medicine, 1980-84, chmn., 1982-84. Bd. dirs., 1st v.p. Future of Hampton Rds., 1983—; bd. dirs. Greater Norfolk Corp., 1987-91—, exec. v.p., 1989-90; founding mem. bd. dirs. Town Point Club, 1983-91. With USMC, 1946-48. Markle scholar acad. medicine, 1962-67. Fellow Coll. Am. Pathologists; mem. AMA, Assn. Am. Med. Colls. (Disting. Service mem.), C. of C. (bd. dirs. 1986-91), Sigma Xi, Alpha Omega Alpha. Episcopalian. Home: 223 Ocean Hills Rd Virginia Beach VA 23451-2601

MAYER, WILLIAM EMILIO, dean; b. N.Y.C., May 7, 1940; s. Emilio and Marie Mayer; m. Katherine Mayer, May 16, 1964; children: Kristen Elizabeth, William Franz. BS, U. Md., 1966, MBA, 1967. Pres., chief exec. officer First Boston Corp., N.Y.C., 1967-91; dean Coll. Bus. & Mgmt. U. Maryland, College Park, 1992—; bd. dirs. Am. Med. Internat., Inc., Chart House Enterprises, Inc., TechnoServe, Riverwood Interant., Hambrecht & Quist, Inc., Colonial Mut. Fund Group. Bd. dirs. U. Md. Found., College Park; bd. adminstrs. Tulane U.; trustee Cancer Rsch. Inst. 1st lt. USAF, 1961-65. Mem. Bond Club N.Y., Investment Assn. of N.Y., Annapolis Yacht Club, Manhasset Bay Club (N.Y.), Univ. Club (N.Y.C.), Mashomack Fish & Game Club. Home: 172 Long Neck Point Rd Darien CT 06820-5816 Office: U Maryland Coll Bus & Mgnt Van Munching Hall College Park MD 20742

MAYERI, BEVERLY, artist, ceramic sculptor, educator; b. N.Y.C., Nov. 2, 1944; d. Bernard and Cora (Wisoff) Howard; m. Earl Melchior Mayeri, Sept. 1, 1968; 1 child, Rachel Theresa. BA, U. Calif., Berkeley, 1967; MA in Art and Sculpture, San Francisco State U., 1976. tchr., seminar conductor, lectr. Dominican Coll., San Rafael, Calif., 1978, Sonoma State U., Rohnert Park, Calif., 1978, NYU, 1987, Calif. State U., 1989, Creative Growth, Oakland, Calif., 1990, Acad Art Coll., 1990, Foothill Coll., Los Altos Hills, 1990, Natsoulas Gallery, 1992, U. Minn., Mpls., 1993, Sonoma Stae U., Rohnert Park, Calif., 1994, Mendocino (Calif.) Art Ctr., 1995, Fresno State U., 1996. Artist: solo exhibitions include Palo Alto (Calif.) Cultural Ctr., 1979, Ivory/Kimpton Gallery, San Francisco, 1981, 83, Garth Clark Gallery, N.Y., 1985, 87, Esther Saks Gallery, Chgo., 1988, 90, Dorothy Weiss Gallery, San Francisco, 1990, 92, 94, 96, San Jose Inst. Contemporary Art, 1990, Robert Kidd Gallery, Birmingham, Mich., 1993; group exhibitions include San Francisco Mus. of Art, Northern Calif. Clay Routes: Sculpture Now, 1979, Smithsonian Instn., Renwick Gallery, 1981, Ivory Kimpton Gallery, San Francisco, 1982, Prieto Meml. Gallery, Mills Coll., Oakland, Calif. 1982, Crocker Art Mus., San Francisco, 1983, Euphrate Gallery, De Anza Coll., Cupertino, Calif., 1984, 88, Fisher Gallery, U. So. Calif., L.A., traveled to Pratt Inst., N.Y.C., 1984, Arts Commn. Gallery, San Francisco, 1984, Signet Arts Gallery, St. Louis (two person show), 1984, Garth Clark Gallery, N.Y., 1985, Robert L. Kidd Gallery, Birmingham, Mich., Animals Contemporary Vision, Major Concepts: Clay, 1986, Fresno (Calif.) Arts Ctr. and Mus., 1987, Canton (Ohio) Art Inst., 1991, Soc. for Contemporary Crafts, Pitts., 1992, Triton Mus. of Art, Santa Clara, Calif., 1992, Nat. Mus. of History Taipei, Taiwan, 1993, Lew Allen Gallery, Santa Fe, New Mex., 1993, Perimeter Gallery, 1995; works in pub. and private collections include: Nat. Mus. History, Taipei, Canton Art Inst., Long Beach (Calif.) Parks and Recreation, L.A. Arts Commn., Mr. and Mrs. Eric Lidow, L.A., Alfred Shands, Louisville, Mrs. Audrey Landy, Atlanta, Karen Johnson Boyd, Racine, Wis., Alan and Esther Saks, Chgo. Founder Marin Women Artists, Marin County, Calif., 1974-84. Recipient fellowship visual artist NEA, Washington, 1982, 88; grantee: Marin Arts Coun., 1987, Virgina A. Groot Found., 1991. Avocations: painting, hiking, skiing, gardening, environmentalist. Office: Dorothy Weiss Gallery 256 Sutter St San Francisco CA 94108

MAYERS, BARBARA W., lawyer; b. Chgo., Nov. 28, 1940. BA, Roosevelt U., 1970; JD magna cum laude, DePaul U., 1975. Bar: Ill. 1975. Ptnr. McDermott, Will & Emery, Chgo. Mem. Ill. State Bar Assn., Chgo. Bar Assn., Nat. Health Lawyer's Assn., Group Health Assn. Am. Office: McDermott Will & Emery 227 W Monroe St Chicago IL 60606-5016*

MAYERS, DANIEL KRIEGSMAN, lawyer; b. Scarsdale, N.Y., July 10, 1934; s. Chauncey Maurice and Helen P. (Kriegsman) M.; m. Karen E. Silverman, Sept. 30, 1956, children—Peter D., Leslie H. Shroyer. A.B., Harvard U., 1955, LL.B., 1960. Bar: D.C. 1961, U.S. Supreme Ct. 1961. Law clk. to Justice Felix Frankfurter, U.S. Supreme Ct., Washington, 1960-61; spl. asst. U.S. Dept. Justice, Washington, 1961-62; assoc. Wilmer Cutler & Pickering, Washington, 1962-65, ptnr., 1967—; exec. asst. to undersec. U.S. State Dept., Washington, 1965-66; mem. vis. com. Harvard Law Sch., Cambridge, Mass., 1982-89, chmn., 1986-89; bd. dirs. Legal Action Ctr., N.Y.C., 1982—; chmn. Washington Ednl. TV Assn., 1993—. Pres. Nat. Symphony Orch., Washington, 1987-89; chmn. Sidwell Friends Sch., Washington, 1979-81; mem. Ams. for Peace Now, 1991—, Fed. City Coun., Washington, 1981—; counsel, dir. Ctr. for Nat. Policy, Washington, 1984-93. With U.S. Army, 1955-57. Recipient Sears prize Harvard Law Sch., 1959. Mem. ABA, Met. Club, Woodstock Country Club. Democrat. Jewish. Avocations: tennis; fishing. Home: 3222 Woodland Dr NW Washington DC 20008-3547 Office: Wilmer Cutler & Pickering 2445 M St NW Washington DC 20037-1435

MAYERS, EUGENE DAVID, philosopher, educator; b. N.Y.C., July 30, 1915; s. Sylvester and Estelle (Weinstein) M.; m. Odette Julia Marguerite Gilchriest, Dec. 30, 1950; children: David Allan, Marilyn Anne, Judith Odette, Peter Michael. AB, Yale U., 1936, LLB, 1940; PhD, Columbia U., 1956. Bar: N.Y. State bar 1941. With Nat. Bur. Econ. Research, N.Y.C., 1941, Office Gen. Counsel, Navy Dept., 1946; mem. faculty Carleton Coll., Northfield, Minn., 1950-61, Columbia, 1959-60, Mills Coll., Oakland, Calif., 1961-63; prof. philosophy Calif. State U., Hayward, 1963-92, prof. emeritus, 1992—; chmn. dept. philosophy Calif. State U., 1963-73, acting head div. humanities, 1966-67; adj. prof. Calif. State U., 1996. Author: Some Modern Theories of Natural Law, 1957; Contbr. articles to profl. jours. Served to capt. AUS, 1941-46, 51-52; lt. col. USAR ret. Fellow Soc. Values in Higher Edn.; mem. AAUP, Am. Philos. Assn. (chmn. conf. dept. chmn. Pacific divsn. 1973-75, Pacific divsn. exec. com. 1976-80, chmn. exec. com. 1978-80), Am. Soc. Polit. and Legal Philosophy, Pacific Coast Theol. Soc. (sec. 1984-86), Internat. Assn. Philosophy Law and Social Philosophy, Am. Acad. Religion, Soc. Advancement Am. Philosophy, Soc. Study Process Philosophies (Pacific Coast rep. 1987—). Home: 3191 Frye St Oakland CA 94602-4040 Office: Calif State U Dept Philosophy Hayward CA 94542

MAYERS, JEAN, aeronautical engineering educator; b. N.Y.C., June 8, 1920; s. Lou and Ida (Edrich) M.; m. Reva Lee Bookbinder, May 20, 1945; children: Eileen, Laurence. B.Aero. Engring., Poly. Inst. Bklyn., 1942, M.Aero. Engring., 1948. Research asst. aero. engring. Poly. Inst. Bklyn., 1946-48; aero. research scientist, structures research div. NACA, Langley Field, Va., 1948-56; successively prin. engr., engring. sec. head, engring. dept. head Sperry Utah Co. div. Sperry Rand Corp., 1956-61; vis. asso. prof. Stanford U., 1961-63, mem. faculty, 1963—, prof. aero. engring., 1967-83, prof. emeritus, 1984—, vice chmn. dept. aero. and astronautics, 1966-71; vis. prof. Technion-Israel Inst. Tech., Haifa, 1970; Naval Air Systems Command Research prof. U.S. Naval Acad., 1978-79; Sci. adviser U.S. Army, 1962-74; cons. to govt. and industry, 1962—; mem. ad hoc vis. com. on aero. engring. curricula Engrs. Council for Profl. Devel., 1969-70. Author articles, reports in field. ARC vol. USN Hosp., Bethesda, Md., 1992—. Lt. comdr. USNR, 1942-46. Recipient U.S. Army Outstanding Civilian Service medal, 1972. Asso. fellow Am. Inst. Aero. and Astronautics (asso. editor jour. 1967-70); mem. Aircraft Owners and Pilots Assn., Naval Res. Assn., Ret. Officers Assn., Am. Soc. Engring. Edn., Sigma Xi. Home: 4550 N Park Ave Apt 909 Chevy Chase MD 20815-7238

MAYERS, ROY, publishing executive. Mgr. Globe Book Co., Inc., N.Y.C., 1962-66, asst. to pres., 1966-69, gen. mgr., 1969-71, v.p., gen. mgr., 1971-75; pres. Modern Curriculum Press divsn. Esquire, Inc., 1975-85, v.p., group exec., 1982-85; pres., founder Schoolhouse Press. divsn. Simon and Schuster, 1985; elementary group pres. Coronet Media, Ginn and Co., Modern Curriculum Press, Schoolhouse Press divsns., Simon and Schuster Internat. divsns. Simon and Schuster, Boston, 1985-86; group pres. numerous divsns. Simon and Schuster, 1986-87; pres., CEO Steck-Vaughn Co., Austin, 1987—; mem. found. adv. coun. U. Tex. Coll. Edn. Bd. dirs. Travis County Adult Literacy Coun. Mem. Internat. Reading Assn., Austin C. of C. Mem. Internat. Reading Assn., Austin C. of C. also: Berrent Pubs 1025 Northern Blvd Roslyn NY 11576-1506

MAYERS, STANLEY PENROSE, JR., public health educator; b. Phila., Nov. 9, 1926; s. Stanley Penrose and Margaret Amelia (Thorpe) M.; m. Virginia Lee Lytle, Aug. 25, 1951 (dec. Oct. 1990); children: Douglas Lytle, Kenneth Stanley, Daniel John, Andrew William; m. Patricia Ann Harne Hulsey, Mar. 6, 1993. BA, U. Pa., 1949, MD, 1953; MPH, Johns Hopkins U., 1958. Diplomate Am. Bd. Preventive Medicine. Intern Phila. Gen. Hosp., 1953-54; resident Arlington County Health Dept., Va., 1954-55; health dir. Henry-Martinsville-Patrick Health Dist., Martinsville, Va., 1955-57; regional dir. Va. State Health dept., Richmond, 1958-59; dist. state health officer N.J. State Dept. of Health, Trenton, 1959-62; asst. prof. and asst. dean Johns Hopkins Sch. Hygiene and Pub. Health, Balt., 1962-65; dir. Arlington County Dept. of Human Resources, Arlington, Va., 1965-71; prof. Health Planning and Adminstrn. Program Pa. State U., Univ. Pk., Pa., 1971-74, 88—; prof. in charge Pa. State U., Univ. Park, Pa., 1974-78; chmn. Pa. State U., Univ. Pk., Pa., 1979-88; assoc. dean undergrad. studies Coll. Health and Human Devel. Pa. State U., Univ. Pk., 1989-92, assoc. dean acad. studies Coll. Health and Human Devel., 1992-95; faculty assoc. Johns Hopkins U. Sch. Medicine, Balt., 1965-75; clin. assoc. prof. Georgetown U. Sch. Medicine, Washington, 1965-71; cons. VA, 1985—. Author numerous reports, articles and surveys on pub. health. Mem. Arlington Optimist Club, 1979-72, pres. 1970-71; bd. dirs. Centre County Family Planning Svcs., Bellefonte, Pa., 1972-79. With USN, 1945-46. Recipient Outstanding Achievement award Dept. Community Medicine, Georgetown U. Sch. Medicine, 1968, Saubel award Coll. of Human Devel., Pa. State U., 1985. Fellow Am. Coll. Preventive Med., Am. Pub. Health Assn. (chmn. membership com. health officer's sect. 1968-70, mem. nominating com. health adminstrn. sect. 1970-72, chmn. com. to draft a statement on local health agy. responsibilities 1973-74); mem. AMA, Arlington County Med. Soc. (Wellborn award 1971), Centre County Med. Soc. (pres. 1978), Med. Soc. Va., Met. Washington Health Officers Assn. (sec. 1967-71), Am. Assn. Pub. Health Physicians (pres. Va. chpt. 1970-71), Pa. Med. Soc. (mem. Ho. of Dels. for Centre County 1974-76, 81—, treas. 1973-74, 85—, sec. 1974-76, v.p. 1976, pres. elect 1977, pres. 1978), University Club (State College, Pa.), Phi Beta Kappa. Episcopalian. Avocations: fishing, boating, hiking. Home: 648 Wiltshire Dr State College PA 16803-1450 Office: Pa State U Human Devel Bldg Rm 201 University Park PA 16802 *Never attempt to promote something or someone that you do not believe in yourself.*

MAYERSON, HY, lawyer; b. Phila., June 29, 1937; s. Henry and Gertrude Mayerson; m. June 13, 1964 (div. 1973); children: Merrie Joy, Benjamin, Erin Megan, Stephnie Dawn; m. Colleen Koos. BS, Temple U., 1958, JD, 1961. Bar: Pa. 1961, Phila. Ct. Common Pleas 1962, Pa. Supreme Ct. 1968, U.S. Ct. Appeals (3d cir.) 1980, U.S. Ct. Appeals (4th cir.) 1986, U.S. Dist. Ct. (ea. dist.) Pa. Pvt. practice law Phila., 1961-65; sr. ptnr. Hy Mayerson Law Offices, 1965-81, Mayerson, Schniper & Gerasimowicz, Spring City, Pa., 1981-87, Mayerson, Gerasimowicz & Munsing, Spring City, 1987-91, Mayerson, Munsing, Corchin & Rosato, P.C., Spring City, 1991-95; pvt. practice law Mayerson Law Offices, Spring City, 1995—; coord. Nat. Forklift Litigation, 1978-91; lead counsel Agent Orange Product Liability Litigation. Contbr. articles to profl. jours. Mem. Am. Trial Lawyers (chmn. sect. on Indsl. & Agrl. Eqipment, Product Liability adv.bd.), Pa. Trial Lawyers Assn. Home: Sky Farm Birchrunville PA 19421 Office: RR 72 Spring City PA 19475

MAYERSON, PHILIP, classics educator; b. N.Y.C., May 20, 1918; s. Theodore and Clara (Fader) M.; m. Joy Gottesman Ungerleider, Nov. 25, 1976 (dec. Sept. 9, 1995); children: Miriam Mayerson, Clare Mayerson, Peter Ungerleider, Steven Ungerleider, Jeanne Ungerleider, Andrew Ungerleider. AB, NYU, 1947, PhD, 1956. With Puritan Fed. Clothing Stores, N.Y.C., 1935-42; instr. NYU, 1948-56, asst. prof., 1956-60, assoc. prof., 1960-66, prof. classics, 1966—, vice dean, 1969-71, acting dean, 1971-73, dean Washington Sq. and U. Coll. Arts and Scis., 1973-78. Author: The Ancient Agricultural Regime of Nessana and the Central Negeb, 1961, Classical Mythology in Literature, Art and Music, 1971, Monks, Martyrs, Soldiers and Saracens, 1994; contbr. articles in field to profl. jours. Served with USN, 1942-45. Rockefeller Found. grantee, 1956-57; Am. Council of Learned Socs. fellow, 1961-62. Mem. Am. Philological Assn., Am. Schs. of Oriental Rsch. Home: 4 Oak Ln Larchmont NY 10538-3917 Office: 100 Washington Sq E New York NY 10003-6656

MAYERSON, SANDRA ELAINE, lawyer; b. Dayton, Ohio, Feb. 8, 1952; d. Manuel David and Florence Louise (Tepper) M.; m. Scott Burns, May 29, 1977 (div. Oct. 1978); 1 child, Katy Joy. BA cum laude, Yale U., 1973; JD, Northwestern U., 1976. Bar: Ill. 1976, U.S. Ct. Appeals (7th cir.) 1976, U.S. Dist. Ct. (no. dist.) Ill. 1977, U.S. Dist. Ct. Md. 1989, U.S. Ct. Appeals (5th cir.) 1994. Assoc. gen. counsel JMB Realty Corp., Chgo., 1979-80; assoc. Chatz, Sugarman, Abrams et al, Chgo., 1980-81; ptnr. Pollack, Mayerson & Berman, Chgo., 1981-83; dep. gen. counsel AM Internat., Inc., Chgo., 1983-85; ptnr. Kirkland & Ellis, Chgo., 1985-87; ptnr., chmn. bankruptcy group Kelley Drye & Warren, N.Y.C., 1987-93; ptnr., chmn. N.Y. bankruptcy group McDermott, Will & Emery, N.Y.C., 1993—; examiner Interco chpt. II, 1991. Bd. dirs. Jr. Med. Rsch. Inst. coun. Michael Reese Hosp., Chgo., 1981-86; mem. met. div. Jewish Guild for Blind, 1990-92; mem. nat. legal afffairs com. Anti-Defamation League, 1990—. Fellow Branford Coll., Yale U., 1993—. Mem. ABA (bus. bankruptcy com. 1976—, sec. 1990-93, chair avoiding powers subcom. 1993—), Ill. State Bar Assn. (governing council corp. and securities sect. 1983-86), Chgo. Bar Assn. (current events chmn. corp. sect. 1980-81), 7th Cir. Bar Assn. Democrat. Jewish. Clubs: Yale (N.Y.C.), Metropolitan (Chgo.). Office: McDermott Will & Emery 1211 Avenue Of The Americas New York NY 10036*

MAYERSON CANNELLA, RENEE, lawyer; b. N.Y.C., June 3, 1965; d. Seymour Sheldon and Edi (Wellner) Mayerson; m. Anthony Joseph Cannella, Oct. 1, 1994. BA in Polit. Sci./Legal Studies, SUNY, Purchase, 1987; JD with honors, U. Conn., 1991. Bar: Conn. 1991, U.S. Dist. Ct. Conn. 1992, U.S. Dist. Ct. (so. dist.) N.Y. 1993. Atty. Casper & de Toledo, Stamford, Conn., 1991—; advocate Rape and Sexual Abuse Crisis Ctr., Stamford, 1993—. Contbr. article to profl. jour. Mem. ATLA, Conn. Bar Assn., Stamford/Norwalk Regional Bar Assn., Conn. Trial Lawyers Assn. Office: Casper & de Toledo 600 Summer St Stamford CT 06901-1403

MAYES, BERNARD DUNCAN, broadcast journalist, educator, dramatist; b. London, Oct. 10, 1929; came to U.S., 1957; s. Reginald Harry and Nellie (Drew) M. BA, Cambridge (Eng.) U., 1952, MA, 1954. Ordained to ministry Eng. Episc. Ch., 1958. Reporter BBC, London, 1954-79, Hollywood, Calif., 1965-70; reporter ABC, Sydney, Australia, 1970-84, CBC, Toronto, Ont., 1970-75, Radio New Zealand, Wellington, 1970-80; mem. summer faculty Stanford (Calif.) U., 1970-84; mgr. Sta. KQED-FM, San Francisco, 1969-71; founding chmn. Nat. Pub. Radio, Washington, 1969-71; exec. v.p. Sta. KQED-TV, San Francisco, 1971-73; pres. Trans Pacific Consortium, San Francisco, 1980-87; mem. faculty U. Va., 1984—; dir. U. Va. Ctr. Modern Media Studies, Charlottesville, 1987—; sr. cons. Corp. for Pub. Broadcasting, Washington, 1978-84. Author: Getting It Across, 1957, This is Bernard Mayes in San Francisco, 1986; audio dramatist The Odyssey, Agammemnon and Antigone; actor (audio drama prodns.) The Hobbit, Lord of the Rings; producer documentary USA 200. Founder Ctr. for Suicide Prevention, San Francisco, 1961-70, The Parsonage Episc. Study Ctr., San Francisco, 1981; chmn. media com. Campaign to End Homophobia, Boston, 1987; bd. dirs. Cerebral Palsy Assn., 1975-77, Heartland Project; mem. Lesbian and Gay Task Force. Recipient Scripts award Nat. Endowment for Arts., Washington, 1985. Fellow Brown Coll.; mem. Bay Area Suicide Prevention Assn. (pres. 1975-77). Democrat. Avocation: writing. Office: U Va Modern Media Studies Brown Coll Charlottesville VA 22903-3102 also: 217 South St Sausalito CA 94965-2530

MAYES, FRANK GORR, food company executive; b. Kellogg, Idaho, Nov. 27, 1930; s. Gilford H. and Rose (Gorr) M.; m. Pamela Ruth Healy, Apr. 20, 1968; 1 child, Matthew A. B.S., Northwestern U., 1952; M.S., NYU, 1953. Supr. mdse. engring. Marshall Field & Co., Chgo., 1953-58; product mgr. Topco Assocs., Inc., Skokie, Ill., 1959-66, dir. grocery, 1966-72, v.p. grocery, 1972-80, sr. v.p. non-perishables, 1980-88, sr. v.p., planning and devel., 1989—; lectr. mktg. Northwestern U., Chgo., 1956-73. Mem. Am. Mktg. Assn. Office: Topco Assocs Inc 7711 Gross Point Rd Skokie IL 60077-2615

MAYES, ILA LAVERNE, minister; b. Eldorado, Okla., Dec. 23, 1934; d. Thomas Floyd and Irene Elizabeth (Buchanan) Jordan; m. Forrest Clay Mayes, July 2, 1954; children: Barbara, Marian, Cynthia, Janice. BA, U. Tex., 1973; MSW, U. Mich., 1976; MDiv, Austin Presbyn. Sem., 1986. Ordained to ministry Presbyn. Ch. (U.S.A.), 1986; cert. social worker. Pastor First Presbyn. Ch., Childress, Tex., 1986—; med./social worker Childress Regional Med. Ctr., Tex., 1996—; mem. Austin Sem. Alumni Bd., 1991-94, Synod of the Sun Evangelism Com., Denton, 1990-93, Transition Coordinating Agy., 1991—. Chmn. ARC, Childress, 1990; bd. dirs. Am. Cancer Soc., Childress, 1988-89. Mem. AAUW, Mortarboard, Rotary Internat., Alpha Chi, Alpha Lambda Delta. Home: 309 Avenue B SE Childress TX 79201-5429 Office: First Presbyn Ch 311 Commerce St Childress TX 79201-4525 also: Childress Regional Med Ctr Hwy 83 N Childress TX 79201 *You and I live in a wonderful tension between the past and the future. As our Faith in God helps us to reinterpret the past and reshapes our future, we grow and change. I like that.*

MAYES, JAMES PAUL, lawyer, government official; b. Mar. 10, 1952; s. James and Hattie May (Parks) M.; m. Sharon Payne, June 23, 1973 (div. Nov. 1992); children: Khadejah, Zain, Rashid, Shehu; m. Minnie Battle, Feb. 21, 1993; 1 child, Maisa Hannah. BA, Princeton U., 1974; MA, Ohio State U., 1977; JD, U. Balt., 1991. Bar: Md. 1992, U.S. Dist. Ct. Md. 1992. Escort interpreter U.S. Dept. State, Washington, 1986—; budget analyst D.C. Dept. Corrections, Washington, 1986-87; staff atty. Md. Legal Aid Bur., Balt., 1991-93; pvt. practice, Md., 1993—; exec. dir. Kuumba Na Nia Dance and Theatre Troup, 1980. Bd. dirs. Nat. Assn. Neighborhoods, Washington, 1986-94, Rehab. Coun. Balt., 1991-93. Mem. ABA. Avocations: theatre, dance. Home: 5145 Autumncrest Dr Greensboro NC 27407

MAYES, PAUL EUGENE, engineering educator, technical consultant; b. Frederick, Okla., Dec. 21, 1928; s. Robert Franklin and Bertha Ellen (Walter) M.; m. Lola Mae Davis, June 4, 1950; children: Gwynne Ellen, Linda Kay, Stuart Franklin, Patricia Gail, Steven Lee, David Thomas. BS in Elec. Engring., U. Okla., 1950; MS in Elec. Engring., Northwestern U., 1952, PhD, 1955. Rsch. asst. Northwestern U., Evanston, Ill., 1950-54; asst. prof. U. Ill., Urbana, 1954-58, assoc. prof., 1958-63, prof., 1963-93, prof. emeritus, 1994—; tech. cons. TRW, Redondo Beach, Calif. Author: Electromagnetics for Engineers, 1965; contbr. articles to profl. jours.; inventor in field. Fellow IEEE. Avocations: woodworking, hiking, camping. Home: 1508 Waverly Dr Champaign IL 61821-5002 Office: U Ill 1406 W Green St Urbana IL 61801-2918

MAYES, WENDELL WISE, JR., broadcasting company executive; b. San Antonio, Mar. 2, 1924; s. Wendell Wise and Dorothy Lydia (Evans) M.; m. Mary Jane King, May 11, 1946; children: Cathey, Sarah, Wendell Wise, III. Student, Schreiner Inst., 1941-42, U. Tex. at Austin, 1942, Daniel Baker Coll., 1946; B.S., Tex. Tech. Coll., 1949. Program dir., sta. mgr. Sta. KBWD, Brownwood, Tex., 1949-57; mgr. Sta. KCRS, Midland, Tex., 1957-63; pres. Sta. KCRS, 1965-84, chmn., 1984—; pres. Sta. KNOW, Austin, Tex., 1970-81; pres. Stas. KVIC and KAMG, Victoria, Tex., 1970-84, chmn., 1984—; chmn. Sta. KCRS-FM, Midland, 1984—; pres. Sta. KCSW, San Marcos, 1976-81; sec.-treas. Sta. KSNY-AM-FM, Snyder, 1952-94; mem. bd. mgrs. Sta. KLBJ/KHHT-AM-FM, Austin, 1991—; lectr. Coll. Communications, U. Tex., Austin, 1978-81. Pres. Tex. Broadcast Edn. Found., 1973-76; chmn. bd. Am. Diabetes Assn., 1974-77; mem. Nat. Diabetes Adv. Bd., 1977-84; v.p. Internat. Diabetes Fedn., 1980-88, pres.-elect, 1988-91, pres., 1991-94; mem. Tex. Diabetes Coun., 1983-86, chmn., 1983-86; bd. regents Tex. Tech. U., 1985-91, chmn., 1987-88. With USNR, 1943-46. Recipient Addison B. Scoville award Am. Diabetes Assn., 1977, first Wendell Mayes Jr. award, 1986, Josiah K. Lilly award, 1991, Harold Rifkin award, 1994,

Masaji Takeda medal Kobe, Japan Colloquium Med. Sci., 1994; named to Tex. Tech. Mass Comm. Hall of Fame, 1978, Hall of Fame Tex. affiliate Am. Diabetes Assn., 1994; named Disting. Alumnus Tex. Tech. U., 1981, Disting. Engr., 1985. Mem. Tex. Assn. Broadcasters (pres. 1964, named Pioneer Broadcaster of Year 1978), Nat. Assn. Broadcasters (dir. 1969-72), Am. Council on Edn. in Journalism (dir. 1977-80), Broadcast Edn. Assn. (dir. 1973-77), AP Broadcasters (bd. dirs. 1988-91), Tex. Tech. Elec. Engring. Acad. Episcopalian (vestryman 1966-69, 86-88; sr. warden 1988). Home: 2834 Montebello Rd #1 Austin TX 78746 Office: Wendell Mayes Stas 1907 N Lamar Blvd Austin TX 78705-4900

MAYFIELD, CURTIS LEE, musician; b. Chgo., June 3, 1942; s. Kenneth and Marion (Washington) M.; children—Tracy, Curtis, Todd, Sharon, Tymphani, Kirk. co-pres. Curtom Records Inc. Performer with group Impressions, 1958-70; solo albums include Curtis, 1970, Curtis Live, Roots, 1971, Back to the World, 1973, Sweet Exorcist, 1974, America Today, 1975, Never Say You Can't Survive, 1977, Do It, We Came in Peace with a Message of Love, 1985, Give, Get, Take and Have, 1992; composer, arranger, performer soundtrack; also actor film Super Fly, 1972; now rec. artist, producer, songwriter film. Recipient: Nat. Acad. of Recording Arts & Sciences Lifetime Achievement Award, 1994. Office: care Epic Records 51 W 52nd St New York NY 10019-6119 Office: Curtom Records PO Box 724677 Atlanta GA 31139-1677

MAYFIELD, DAVID MERKLEY, genealogy director; b. Salt Lake City, Nov. 29, 1942; s. Orson Smith and Isabell (Merkley) M.; m. Judy Rae White, Dec. 17, 1965; children: Celeste, Melody, Michael, Paul, Nathan, Heather, Christopher, Benjamin. BA in German, U. Utah, 1967, MA in German, 1969; MLS, UCLA, 1971. Instr. Brigham Young U., Provo, Utah, 1971-72; mgr., dir. hist. dept., mem. and stats. records dept., info. systems dept. Ch. of Jesus Christ of Latter-day Saints, Salt Lake City, 1972-80; dir. family history library of Ch. of Jesus Christ of Latter-day Saints, Salt Lake City, 1980-92; dir., priesthood and area support, 1992—; v.p. Geneal. Soc. Utah, 1988—. Contbr. articles to profl. jours. Fellow NDEA, 1967, HEW Title II, 1970. Mem. Nat. Geneal. Soc., (nat. coun., 1992—), Fedn. Geneal. Socs. (adv. counc. 1988-91), Nat. Soc. Sons of Utah Pioneers (v.p. 1982-83), Phi Beta Kappa. Republican. Mormon. Office: Family History Dept 50 E North Temple Salt Lake City UT 84150-0001

MAYFIELD, RICHARD HEVERIN, lawyer; b. Washington, Sept. 29, 1921; s. Robert Edwin and Helen May (Benton) M.; m. Caroline C. Mayfield; children: Elinor D., Nancy L., Anne W. A.B., Swarthmore Coll., 1943; LL.B., Harvard U., 1948. Bar: D.C., Md. Asso. firm McKenney, Flannery & Craighill (name later changed to Craighill, Mayfield & Fenwick & Cromelin), Washington, 1948-54; partner McKenney, Flannery & Craighill (name later changed to Craighill, Mayfield, Fenwick & Cromelin), 1954—. Editor: Will Forms and Clauses, 1969, Trust Forms and Clauses, 1975. Bd. govs. Beauvoir Sch., 1961-67, chmn., 1967. Served with AUS, 1943-46. Fellow Am. Coll. Trust and Estates Counsel; mem. Washington Estate Planning Coun., Barrister Club (sec. 1959), Lawyers Club, Columbia Country Club, Farmington Country Club, Masons, Shriners. Home: 5 E Kirke St Bethesda MD 20815-4216 Office: 4910 Massachusetts Ave NW Washington DC 20016-4300

MAYFIELD, ROBERT CHARLES, university official, geography educator; b. Abilene, Tex., Oct. 15, 1928; s. Percy Anderson and Fay (Hicks) M.; m. Loraine Poindexter, Sept. 3, 1952; children: Julie Barnes, Jennifer Manley, Mark Stanley, Malcolm Randall. B.A., Tex. Christian U., 1952; M.S., Ind. U., 1953; Ph.D., U. Wash., 1961. Chmn. geography dept. Tex. Christian U., Ft. Worth, 1960-64, U. Tex., Austin, 1967-71; Chmn. geography dept. Boston U., 1972-77, acad. v.p. external programs, 1977-83, provost, 1979-84; cons. Coun. for Econ. Action, Boston, 1980—; adj. prof. U. Tex., Austin, 1987—; lectr. U.S. Info. Svc., Bangladesh, 1994; lectr. S.A.G.E., 1995-96. Editor, contbg. author: Man, Environment and Space, 1972. Served with USAF, 1946-49. Research fellow Nat. Acad. Sci. No. India, 1957-58; Fulbright-Hays fellow Office Edn., Bangalore, Mysore, India, 1966-67; research grantee Agrl. Devel. Council, 1968. Mem. Assn. Am. Geographers.

MAYFIELD, ROBIN S., surgeon, researcher; b. Pitts., Nov. 28, 1957; d. Lamont and Patricia Anne (Flaherty) S.; m. Chancey C. Mayfield; 1 child, Zoe Bryson Mayfield. BA, Swarthmore Coll., 1980; MD, Harvard U., 1990. Intern U. Calif., San Francisco, 1990-91, resident gen. surgery, 1991-93; rsch. fellow Mass. Gen. Hosp., Boston, 1993—. Resident scholar Am. Coll. Surgeons, 1994. Office: Mass Gen Hosp TBRC 149 13th St Boston MA 02129-2060

MAYFIELD, T. BRIENT, IV, media and computer executive; b. Athens, Tenn., Mar. 31, 1947; s. Thomas Brient III and Alma Ruth (Bolton) M.; m. N. Katherine Rodgers, Dec. 7, 1974 (div. Mar. 1984); children: Brittany Alexander, Blair Ashton, Katherine Thomas; m. Margaret L. Reeves, Oct. 3, 1987. BS, U. Tenn., 1969. Project mgr. Mayfield Dairy Farms, Athens, 1969-70; v.p. fin. 13-30 Corp., Knoxville, Tenn., 1970-72; exec. v.p. Computer Concepts Corp., Knoxville, 1970-77, pres., 1977-85; pres. Resource Optimization Inc., Knoxville, 1986—; co-founder Whittle Communications LP, Knoxville, 1970, v.p., pub., 1987-92. Bd. dirs. Results Edn. Fund, Washington,, 1990—. Republican. Avocations: flying, music. Home: 5108 Buckhead Trl Knoxville TN 37919-8903 Office: Resource Optimization Inc 531 S Gay St Ste 1212 Knoxville TN 37902-1520

MAYHEW, AUBREY, music business executive; b. Washington, Oct. 2, 1927; s. Aubrey and Verna June (Hall) M.; m. Carol de Onis, May 10, 1962 (div. 1971); children: Lawrence Aubrey, Michael Aubrey, Parris Mitchell, Casey Aran. Student, Wilson Tchs. Coll., 1948. Dir. Sta. WWVA, Wheeling, W.Va., 1947-54, Sta. WCOP, Boston, 1954-56; asst. to pres. MGM Records, N.Y.C., 1957-58; v.p. mktg. Capitol Records, Los Angeles, 1958-60; prodr., dir. Sta. KCAM-TV Prodns., Nashville, 1981—; pres., founder John F. Kennedy Meml. Ctr., 1968; authority on John F. Kennedy life and memorabilia. Author: (books) Commandants Marine Corps, 1953, World Tribute to John F. Kennedy, 1965; composer (music) Touch My Heart, 1966 (Broadcast Music, Inc. award, 1967); record producer, artist mgmt., 1947—; music pub., 1954—; developed careers numerous entertainers including Johnny Paycheck, Jeannie C. Riley, Bobby Helms. Served to cpl. U.S. Army Signal Corps, 1945-48. Named Govs. Aide, Nashville, 1978. Mem. Country Music Assn., Broadcast Music Inc., Manuscript Soc., N.Y. Numismatic Soc., Gospel Music Assn. Republican. Episcopalian. Avocations: collector, historian, author. Home: 827 Meridian St Nashville TN 37207-5856 Office: Amcorp Music Group 827 Meridian St Nashville TN 37207-5856

MAYHEW, CATHERINE CHAPIN, newspaper executive; b. Evanston, Ill., Apr. 28, 1952; d. Troy Albertus Jr. and Catherine Mayfield (Wiswell) Chapin; m. Mark Allen Mayhew, Apr. 14, 1990; 1 child, Noah Chapin. BA, Murray State U., 1974. Reporter, editor Tampa (Fla.) Tribune, 1974-77; reporter, columnist Charlotte (N.C.) Observer, 1977-83; anchor WBTV, Charlotte, 1983-84, prodr., 1984-86, exec. prodr., 1986-87, asst. news dir., 1987-89; features editor Reno (Nev.) Gazette Jour., 1989-93; mng. editor features The Tennessean, Nashville, 1993-95, asst. mng. editor news, 1995—. Vol. Nev. Women's Fund, Reno, 1990-94. Mem. Am. Assn. Sunday and Feature Editors (bd. dirs. 1993-95). Episcopal. Avocations: gourmet cooking, reading, needlework. Office: The Tennessean 1100 Broadway Nashville TN 37203

MAYHEW, DAVID RAYMOND, political educator; b. Putnam, Conn., May 18, 1937; s. Raymond William and Jeanie (Nicholson) M. B.A., Amherst Coll., 1958; Ph.D. (Delancey K. Jay dissertation prize 1964), Harvard U., 1964. Teaching fellow Harvard U., 1961-63; instr., then asst. prof. polit. sci. U. Mass., Amherst, 1963-67; vis. asst. prof. Amherst Coll., 1965-66; mem. faculty Yale U., 1968—, prof. polit. sci., 1977—, chmn. dept., 1979-82, Alfred Cowles prof. govt., 1982—. Author: Party Loyalty Among Congressmen, 1966, Congress: The Electoral Connection, 1974 (Washington Monthly ann. polit. book award 1974), Placing Parties in American Politics, 1986, Divided We Govern, 1991. Recipient Richard E. Neustadt prize 1992; Woodrow Wilson fellow, 1958-59, vis. fellow Nuffield Coll., Oxford, 1978, Guggenheim fellow, 1978-79, Hoover Nat. fellow, 1978-79, Sherman Fairchild fellow, 1990-91, fellow Ctr. for Advanced Study in Behavioral Scis., 1995-96. Fellow Am. Acad. Arts and Scis.; mem. Am. Polit. Sci. Assn. (nat. council 1976-78, Congl. fellow 1967-68), So. Polit. Sci. Assn., New Eng. Polit. Sci. Assn. Home: 100 York St Apt 5C New Haven CT 06511-5611 Office: Yale U Polit Sci Dept Box 208301 New Haven CT 06520-8301

MAYHEW, HARRY EUGENE, physician, educator; b. St. Clair, Mich., Apr. 16, 1933; s. Eugene Nelson and Viola Erma (Danneels) M; m. Eunice Yvonne Brown, June 23, 1950; children: Dawn Boers, Timothy, Stephen, Elise Couch, Betheny, Heidi Reimer. Student, Port Huron Jr. Coll., 1951-53; MD, U. Mich., 1958. Diplomate Am. Bd. Family Practice. Intern St. Joseph Hosp., Flint, Mich., 1958-59; pvt. practice St. Clair, Mich., 1959-73; asst. dir. family practice residency Sparrow Hosp., Lansing, Mich., 1974-76; asst. prof. dept. family practice Coll. Human Medicine, Mich. State U., 1974-76; prof., chmn. dept. family medicine Med. Coll. Ohio, Toledo, 1976—; cons. Residency Assistance Program Acad. Family Physicians, Kansas City, Mo., 1978-95; adv. bd. Salvation Army. Co-editor: Critical Issues in Family Practice: Cases and Commentaries, 1982, Basic Procedures in Family Practice, 1984, Genital Urinary Problems in the Male Patient, 1989. Mem. AMA, Soc. Tchrs. Family Medicine, Assn. Depts. Family Medicine, Coun. Acad. Socs., Assn. Depts. Family Medicine Bd., Coun. Acad. Soc. Bd., Toledo Country Club, Alpha Omega Alpha. Baptist. Office: Med Coll Ohio Dept Family Medicine PO Box 10008 Toledo OH 43699-0008

MAYHEW, KENNETH EDWIN, JR., transportation company executive; b. Shelby, N.C., Sept. 27, 1934; s. Kenneth Edwin and Evelyn Lee (Dellinger) M.; m. Frances Elaine Craft, Apr. 7, 1957; 1 dau., Catherine Lynn Prince. A.B., Duke U., 1956. CPA, N.C. Sr. auditor Arthur Andersen & Co., Atlanta, 1956-58, 60-63; controller Trendline, Inc., Hickory, N.C., 1963-66; with Carolina Freight Corp., Cherryville, 1966-93; treas., 1969-74; v.p. Carolina Freight Carriers Corp., Cherryville, 1971-72, exec. v.p., 1972-85, pres., chief oper. officer, 1985-89, dir., 1968-93, chmn., pres., CEO, 1989-93; pres., dir. Robo Auto Wash Shelby Inc., 1967-73, Robo Auto Wash Cherryville, Inc., 1968-73; dir. Cherryville Nat. Bank, Kenmar Bus. Group, Inc. Mem. Bus. Adv. Bd., Fuqua Sch. Bus., Duke U.; bd. dirs., vice-chmn. Gaston Meml. Hosp.; trustee Pfeiffer Coll. With AUS, 1958-60. Mem. AICPA, Am. Trucking Assn. (dir., v.p.), N.C. Trucking Assn. (dir., chmn.), Gaston County C. of C. (v.p. pub. affairs), Lions (pres. Cherryville 1972-73), Phi Beta Kappa, Omicron Delta Kappa, Phi Eta Sigma. Methodist. Home: 507 Spring St Cherryville NC 28021-3540

MAYHEW, WILLIAM A., judge; b. Pueblo, Colo., July 21, 1940; s. Wilbren D. and Dorothy L. (Holloway) M.; m. Marianne J., May 8, 1971; children: Lance, Kevin, Christie. AA, Modesto Jr. Coll., 1959; BS, UCLA, 1961, JD, 1964. Bar: Calif. 1965, U.S. Ct. Appeals (9th cir.) 1965, U.S. Dist. Ct. (no., ea. dists.) Calif. 1965. Dep. atty. gen. State Calif., 1964-67; ptnr., pvt. practice Thompson, Mayhew & Michel (now Thompson & Heller), 1968-82; prof. law Miss. Coll. Sch. Law, 1982-86; atty. Sarhad & Mayhew, Turlock, Calif., 1986-88; mng. ptnr. Borton, Petrini & Conron, Modesto, Calif., 1988-94; judge Stanislaw County Mcpl. Ct., Modesto, 1994-95, Stanislaw County Superior Ct., Modesto, 1995—; assoc. prof. Coll. Law U. Toledo, 1975-76; lecturer in field. Bd. editors UCLA Law Review; contbr. articles to profl. jours. Mem. Turlock H.S. Bd. Trustees, 1989-94, pres., 1992; usher, progress com. St. Francis Episcopal Ch.; mem. standing com. Episcopal Diocese San Joaquin Diocesan Conv., 1991; vice chancelor Episcopal Bishop of San Joaquin, 1990-94. Maj. JAGC, Calif. Army N.G., 1966-77. Mem. Am. Bd. Trial Advocates (nat. bd. dirs., advocate, chair western regional conf. 1987, Miss. chpt., sec.-treas. 1985), Turlock Rotary Club, Order of Coif. Republican. Office: Stanislaw County Superior Ct PO Box 1011 Modesto CA 95353-1011

MAYHUE, RICHARD LEE, dean, pastor, writer; b. Takoma Park, Md., Aug. 31, 1944; s. J. Richard Mayhue and Myrtle Lorraine (Hartsell) Lee; m. Lois Elaine Nettleingham, June 18, 1966; children: Lee, Wade. BS, Ohio State U., 1966; MDiv, Grace Theol. Seminary, Winona Lake, Ind., 1974, ThM, 1977, ThD, 1981. Ordained pastor. Asst. pastor Grace Brethren Ch. of Columbus (Ohio), 1975-77; asst. prof. New Testament & Greek Grace Theol. Seminary, Winona Lake, 1977-80; assoc. pastor Grace Cmty. Ch., Sun Valley, Calf., 1980-84, 89—; sr. pastor Grace Brethren Ch., Long Beach, Calif., 1984-89; sr. v.p., dean, prof. systematic theology and pastoral mins. The Master's Seminary, Sun Valley, 1989—; bd. dirs. Grace Theol. Sem., 1987-89. Author: (booklets) The Biblical Pattern for Divine Healing, 1979, Snatched Before the Storm, 1980, (books) Divine Healing Today, 1983, How to Interpret the Bible for Yourself, 1986, A Christian's Survival Guide, 1987, Unmasking Satan, 1988, Spiritual Intimacy, 1990, Spiritual Maturity, 1992, The Healing Promise, 1994, What Would Jesus Say About Your Church?, 1995; contbr., editor: Rediscovering Expository Preaching, 1992, Rediscovering Pastoral Ministry, 1994; contbr. New Am. Std. Study Bible, 1997; Old Testament editor MacArthur Study Bible, 1997; contbr. articles to profl. jours. Lt. USN, 1966-71, Vietnam. Recipient Bronze Star with Combat V USN, 1969. Mem. Evang. Theol. Soc., Nat. Fellowship Grace Brethren Ministers (pres. 1988), Far West Region Evang. Theol. Soc. (pres. 1995), Slavic Gospel Assn. (bd. dirs. 1993—). Avocation: N gauge model railroading. Office: The Master's Seminary 13248 Roscoe Blvd Sun Valley CA 91352-3739

MAYHUGH, JOEL OGDEN, JR., financial executive; b. Little Rock, Nov. 9, 1941; s. Joel Ogden Sr. and Jessie Olin (Hall) M.; m. Caroline Elizabeth Boellner, Nov. 5, 1966; 1 child, Katherine Elizabeth. BA in Social Scis., U. Little Rock, 1969. Sales rep. Kraft Foods, Little Rock, 1964-66, 68-72; sr. fin. cons. Merrill Lynch, Little Rock, 1972-92; asst. v.p. Merrill Lynch, Hot Springs, Ark., 1992—. Co-chmn. North Little Rock Port Authority, 1982; pres. Ark. affiliate Am. Diabetes Assn., Little Rock, 1980, North Little Rock Kiwanis Club, 1977; bd. dirs. YMCA, North Little Rock, 1983. With U.S. Army, 1966-68. Named Outstanding Kiwanian of Yr. Kiwanis Club, 1976, Outstanding Stock Broker in the U.S. Money Mag., 1987. Mem. Hot Springs Jazz Soc., Little Rock C. of C. (bd. dirs. 1977-78), Hot Springs C. of C., North Hills Country Club (greens com. 1975-76), Ark. State Golf Assn., Ark. Fly Fishing Assn., Ark. Wilde Life Assn., Ducks Unltd. Baptist. Avocations: golf, boating, cooking, fly fishing, duck hunting. Home: 1340 Rock Creek Rd Hot Springs National Park AR 71913-9283 Office: Merrill Lynch Inc PO Box 205 Hot Springs National Park AR 71951-0205

MAYLAND, KENNETH THEODORE, economist; b. Miami, Fla., Nov. 17, 1951; s. Herbert and Vera (Bob) M; m. Gail Fern Bassok, Apr. 14, 1984. BS, MIT, 1973; MS, U. Pa., 1976, PhD, 1979. Cons. economist Data Resources, Inc., Lexington, Mass., 1973; economist, then chief economist First Pa. Bank, Phila., 1973-89; sr. v.p., chief economist Soc. Nat. Bank, Cleve., 1989-94; sr. v.p., chief fin. economist Key Corp., Cleve., 1994-96, sr. v.p., chief economist, 1996—; econs. instr., Chartered Fin. Aanalysts Assn., Phila, 1984—; econ. adv. com. Phila. Econ. Devel. Coalition, 1984-86; chmn. econ. adv. com. Pa. Bankers Assn., Harrisburg, 1982-84; mem. Gov.'s Econ. Adv. Com., Ohio, 1989—. Contbr. semi-monthly periodical Money Markets, 1981-85, quar. periodical Regional Report, 1980-89, Econ. Viewpoint biweekly periodical, 1989—, Regional Rev. quarterly periodical, 1989—. Mem. curriculum adv. com. Widener U., 1986-89. Mem. Am. Bankers Assn. (econ. adv. com. 1990-93), Internat. Econ. Roundtable (vice chmn. 1987-88, chmn. 1988-90), Nat. Assn. Bus. Economists (New Face for the Eighties award 1979), Phila. Coun. Bus. Economists (pres. 1982-84), Cleve. Bus. Economist Club (sec.-treas. 1990-91, v.p. 1991-92, pres. 1992-93). Avocations: fishing, badminton, gardening, camping. Home: 3237 Fox Hollow Dr Cleveland OH 44124-5426 Office: Key Corp 127 Public Sq Cleveland OH 44114-1216

MAYNARD, CHARLES DOUGLAS, radiologist; b. Atlantic City, Sept. 11, 1934; m. Mary Anne Satterwhite; children—Charles D., Deanne, David. B.S., Wake Forest U., 1955, M.D., 1959. Diplomate Am. Bd. Radiology (trustee, sec.-treas., v.p. 1992-94, pres. 1994—). Intern U.S. Army Hosp., Honolulu, 1959-60; resident N.C. Baptist Hosp., 1963-66; dir. Nuclear Medicine Lab., 1966-77; asst. dean admissions Bowman Gray Sch. Medicine, 1966-71, asso. dean student affairs, 1971-75, prof. radiology, chmn. dept., 1977—; guest examiner Am. Bd. Radiology. Author: Clinical Nuclear Medicine, 1969; mem. editorial bd. Academic Radiology, Yearbook of Diagnostic Radiology, Contemporary Diagnostic Radiology. Mem. Leadership Winston-Salem, Triad Leadership Network; bd. dirs. Downtown Devel. Corp., 1995—, Winston-Salem Bus., Inc., 1995—. Mem. AMA, Soc. Nuclear Medicine (past pres.), Am. Coll. Radiology (past bd. chancellors, past chmn. commn. on nuclear medicine), Radiol. Soc. N.Am. (sec.-treas.), Assn. Univ. Radiologists, Soc. Chairmen Radiology Depts. (past pres.), Acad. Radiology Rsch. (bd. dirs. 1995—), Am. Bd. Radiology (bd. trustees 1987—, pres. 1994—), Am. Bd. Med. Specialists, Greater Winston-Salem C. of C. (bd. dirs.). Office: Medical Center Blvd Winston Salem NC 27157

MAYNARD, DANIEL DWIGHT, lawyer; b. Ft. Belvoir, Va., July 22, 1951; s. Luther Dwight and Dorothy Louise (Hester) M.; m. Susan Patricia Holm, Aug. 19, 1972; children: Katherine Phyllis, Jill Erin, Adam Daniel, Andrew Patrick. BA, U. Ala., Tuscaloosa, 1973, MA, 1975; JD, John Marshall Law Sch., Chgo., 1979. Bar: Ill. 1979, U.S. Dist. Ct. (no. dist.) Ill. 1980, U.S. Ct. Appeals (7th cir.) 1980, Ariz. 1983, U.S. Dist. Ct. Ariz. 1983, U.S. Ct. Appeals (4th cir.) 1984, U.S. Supreme Ct. 1985. Law clk. Supreme Ct. Ill., Springfield, 1979-80; assoc., then ptnr. Winston & Strawn, Chgo. and Phoenix, 1980-89; ptnr. Johnston Maynard Grant & Parker, Phoenix, 1989—. Editor John Marshall Law Jour., 1978-79. Bd. dirs. Am. Cancer Soc., Phoenix, 1987-94, Recreation Assn. Madison Meadows, Phoenix, 1987-94; chmn. Center Dance Emsemble, Phoenix, 1990-92. Named Vol. of Yr., Am. Cancer Soc., 1987. Mem. ABA, Ariz. Bar Assn. (Vol. of Month award 1992), Lukes Men (exec. bd., chmn. spl. events 1994-95). Home: 6233 N 4th Dr Phoenix AZ 85013-1369 Office: Johnston & Maynard et al 3200 N Central Ave Ste 2300 Phoenix AZ 85012-2443

MAYNARD, DONALD NELSON, horticulturist, educator; b. Hartford, Conn., June 22, 1932; s. Harry Ashley and Elsie Frances (Magnuson) M.; m. Adrienne A. Taylor; 1 child, David Nelson. BS, U. Conn., 1954; MS, N.C. State U., 1956; PhD, U. Mass., 1963. Instr. plant sci. U. Mass., Amherst, 1956-62, asst. prof., 1962-67, assoc. prof., 1967-72, prof., 1972-79, asst. dean, 1974-75, prof. emeritus, 1979—; prof. vegetable crops U. Fla., Gainesville, 1979—; chmn. dept. U. Fla., 1979-85; cons. Greenleaf, Inc., Hackensack, N.J., SRD Rsch., Logan, Utah. Assoc. editor Jour. Am. Soc. Hort. Sci., 1976-80, 89-91, HortSci, 1975-80, 89—. Recipient Aid to Edn. award Gulf Oil Corp., 1965. Fellow Am. Soc. for Hort. Sci. (Environ. Quality Rsch. award 1975, Marion W. Meadows award 1977, pres. 1996-97); mem. Sigma Xi, Phi Kappa Phi, Alpha Zeta, Phi Tau Sigma. Republican. Episcopalian. Home: 5551 Contento Dr Sarasota FL 34242-1836 Office: U Fla Gulf Coast Rsch Edn Ctr Bradenton FL 34203

MAYNARD, E. ROSE, retired school health services coordinator; b. Mosquero, N.Mex., Feb. 7, 1934; d. E.H. and Eudora M. (Freeland) McGlothlin; m. Bob Maynard, Aug. 2, 1952; children: Michael, Michele, Mark. BSN with hons., Calif. State U., L.A., 1971, MA, 1974. CPNP, RN, Calif. Sch. nurse ABC Unified Sch. Dist., Cerritos, Calif., 1970-86, pediatric nurse practitioner, 1977-86; dept. chmn. health svcs. Lancaster (Calif.) Sch. Dist., 1986-92, pediatric nurse practitioner, 1986-96, DATE coord., 1990-96, coord. health svcs., 1992-96; ret., 1996; presenter Ednl. Conf., Hawaii, 1982; PASS Project Replicator, CSNO and NASN, Calif., 1987-91; presenter Calif. Sch. Bd. Ann. State Conf., San Jose, 1994. Coord. Calif. State Contest, 1985. CPR/FA instr. ARC, Quartz Hill, Calif., 1986—; mem. Tobacco Task Force, Am. CA Soc., Palmdale, Calif., 1989—. Fellow Nat. Assn. Pediat. Nurses; mem. Calif. Sch. Nurses Assn. (bd. dirs. so. sect. 1991-93), Nat. Assn. Sch. Nurses, Assn. Calif. Sch. Adminstrs., Alpha Gamma Sigma. Republican. Avocations: travel, exercise, reading, family activities.

MAYNARD, JOHN RALPH, lawyer; b. Seattle, Mar. 5, 1942; s. John R. and Frances Jane (Mitchell) Maynard Kendryk; m. Meridee J. Sagadin, Sept. 10, 1995; children: Bryce James, Pamela Ann. BA, U. Wash., 1964; JD, Calif. Western U., San Diego, 1972; LLM, Harvard U., 1973. Bar: Calif. 1972, Wis. 1973. Assoc. Whyte & Hirschboeck, Milw., 1973-78, Minahan & Peterson, Milw., 1979-91, Quarles & Brady, Milw., 1991—. Bd. dirs. Am. Heart Assn., 1979-82. Mem. Wis. Adv. Coun. to U.S. SBA, 1987-89. Served to lt. USN, 1964-69. Mem. ABA, Harvard Club (Wis.), Yacht Club (Milw.). Republican. Home: 809 E Lake Forest Ave Milwaukee WI 53217-5377 Office: Quarles & Brady 411 E Wisconsin Ave Milwaukee WI 53202-4409

MAYNARD, JOHN ROGERS, English educator; b. Williamsville, N.Y., Oct. 6, 1941; s. Atherton Rogers and Olive (Fisher) M.; m. Florence Michelson, July 1, 1967 (div. 1980); 1 child, Alex Stevens; m. Ursula Krammer, Oct. 17, 1992 (div. 1995). BA, Harvard U., 1963, PhD, 1970. Asst. prof. Harvard U., Cambridge, Mass., 1969-74, NYU, N.Y.C., 1974-76, assoc. prof., 1976-84, prof. English, 1984—, chmn. English dept., 1983-89; chmn. Faculty Council NYU, 1983-84; vis. prof. U. Venice, Italy, 1991. Author: Brownings Youth, 1977 (Wilson prize 1977), Charlotte Bronte and Sexuality, 1984, Victorian Discourses on Sexuality and Religion, 1993; editor: (with Lockridge and Stone) Nineteenth Century Lives, 1989, (with Bloom) Shankman's Anne Thackeray Ritchie: Journals and Letters, (with Munich) Victorian Literature and Culture, 1991—. Organizer, Concord Sq. Assn., Boston, 1972-74. NEH grantee, 1972-73; Guggenheim fellow, 1979-80. Mem. MLA, PEN, Browning Inst. (bd. dirs.), Signet Soc., Andiron Club (pres. 1983-84). Democrat. Avocation: bicycling. Home: 39 Schermerhorn St Brooklyn NY 11201-4825 Office: NYU Dept of English 19 University Pl New York NY 10003-4501

MAYNARD, PARRISH, ballet dancer; b. Epernay, France. Student, San Francisco Ballet Sch., 1978-80. Dancer Am. Ballet Theatre II, N.Y.C., 1983-85; soloist Joffrey Ballet, N.Y.C., 1986-88; mem. corps de ballet Am. Ballet Theatre, N.Y.C., 1988-92, soloist, 1992—; guest artist Australian Nat. Ballet, 1993, English Nat. Ballet, 1993. Created role of narrator in Ulysses Dove's Serious Pleasures; performed in dances including (with Joffrey Ballet) The Clowns, A Midsummer Night's Dream, Monotones I, (with Am. Ballet Theatre) La Bayadere, Etudes, Drink to Me Only With Thine Eyes, Giselle, Romeo and Juliet, The Sleeping Beauty, Swan Lake, Symphonic Variations, Moondance, La Sylphide, The Nutcracker. Office: Am Ballet Theatre 890 Broadway New York NY 10003-1211

MAYNARD, ROBERT HOWELL, lawyer; b. San Antonio, Feb. 15, 1938; s. William Simpson Sr. and Lillian Isabel (Tappan) M.; m. Joan Marie Pearson, Jan. 6, 1962; children: Gregory Scott, Patricia Kathryn, Alicia Joan, Elizabeth Simms. BA, Baylor U., 1959, LLB, 1961; LLM, Georgetown U., 1965. Bar: Tex. 1961, D.C. 1969, Ohio 1973. Trial atty. gen. litigation sect. lands div. U.S. Dept. Justice, Washington, 1964-65; spl. asst. to solicitor U.S. Dept. Interior, Washington, 1965-69; legis. asst. U.S. Senate, Washington, 1969-73; ptnr., dept. head Smith & Schnacke, Dayton, Ohio, 1973-83; dir. Ohio EPA, Columbus, Ohio, 1983-85; ptnr., environ. policy and stategy devel., tech. law Vorys, Sater, Seymour and Pease, Columbus, 1985—. Trustee Ohio Found. for Entrepren. Edn., Business Technology Ctr., Episcopal Cmty. Svcs. Found. USNR, 1962-65. Episcopalian. Office: Vorys Sater Seymour & Pease PO Box 1008 52 E Gay St Columbus OH 43216-1008

MAYNARD, STEVEN HARRY, writer; b. San Diego, July 4, 1954; s. Harry Clark and Ruby Kristina (Odna). BA in Communications, U. Wash., 1976; MA in Theology, Fuller Theol. Seminary, 1979. Religion writer, gen. news reporter Walla Walla (Wash.) Union-Bulletin, 1979-84; religion writer Houston Chronicle, 1984-87; religion/ethics/values reporter The News Tribune, Tacoma, Wash., 1987—. Recipient Mng. Editors award Tex. Associated Press, 1984, Wilbur award Religious Pub. Relations Council, 1981. Mem. Religion Newswriters Assn. Office: 1950 S State St Tacoma WA 98405-2817

MAYNARD, TERRELL DENNIS, minister; b. Paducah, Ky., Dec. 10, 1944; s. Claude and Euda (Finley) M.; m. Mary Jacqueline Chappell, Sept. 3, 1965; children: Terrell Geoffrey, Christopher Dennis. BA, Bethel Coll., 1966; MDiv, Memphis Theol. Sem., 1969. Pastor Cumberland Presbyn. Ch., Searcy, Ark., 1969-72, Hohenwald, Tenn., 1972-76; pastor Swan Cumberland Presbyn. Ch., Centerville, Tenn., 1972-76, Elliottsville Presbyn. Ch., Alabaster, Ala., 1976-94, 1st Cumberland Presbyn. Ch., Jackson, Tenn., 1994—; pres. Bd. Christian Edn., Memphis, 1976-85; chair Gen. Assembly's Exec. Com., Memphis, 1987-93. Bd. dirs., pres. Shelby Emergency Assistance, Montevallo, Ala., 1990-94; bd. dirs. Developing Ala. Youth Found., Alabaster, 1989-94, Shelby County Hosp. Authority, Alabaster, 1993-94. Recipient Disting. Alumni award Bethel Coll., McKenzie, Tenn., 1992; named Outstanding Vol. Shelby County Chpt. ARC, Alabaster, 1989. Mem. Assn. Cumberland Presbyn. Ch. Educators. Avocations: fishing, golf, hunting, reading, college basketball. Home: 139 Paddock Pl Jackson TN 38305 Office: 1st Cumberland Presbyn Ch 1730 Us Highway 45 Byp Jackson TN 38305-4415

MAYNE, LUCILLE STRINGER, finance educator; b. Washington, June 6, 1924; d. Henry Edmond and Hattie Benham (Benson) Stringer; children: Patricia Anne, Christine Gail, Barbara Marie. BS, U. Md., 1946; MBA, Ohio State U., 1949; PhD, Northwestern U., 1966. Instr. fin. Utica Coll., 1949-50; lectr. fin. Roosevelt U., 1961-64; lectr. fin. Pa. State U., 1965-66, asst. prof., 1966-69, assoc. prof., 1969-70; assoc. prof. banking and fin. Case-Western Res. U., 1971-76, prof., 1976-94, prof. emerita, 1994—, grad. dean Sch. Grad. Studies, 1980-84; sr. economist, cons. FDIC, 1977-78; cons. Nat. Commn. Electronic Fund Transfer Sys., 1976; rsch. cons. Am. Bankers Assn., 1975, Fed. Res. Bank of Cleve., 1968-70, 73; cons. Pres.'s Commn. Fin. Structure and Regulation, 1971, staff economist, 1970-71; analytical statistician Air Materiel Command, Dayton, Ohio, 1950-52; asst. to promotion mgr. NBC, Washington, 1946-48; expert witness cases involving fin. instns.; bd. dirs. Cleve. Citywide Devel. Corp. Assoc. editor: Jour. Money, Credit and Banking, 1980-83, Bus. Econs., 1980-85; contbr. articles to profl. jours. Vol. Cleve. Soc. for Blind, 1979—, Benjamin Rose Inst., 1995—; mem. policyholders nominating com. Tchrs. Ins. and Annuity Assn./Coll. Retirement Equities Fund, 1982-84, chairperson com., 1984; bd. dirs. Women's Cmty. Found., 1994—. Grad. scholar Ohio State U., 1949; doctoral fellow Northwestern U., 1963-65. Mem. Midwest Fin. Assn. (pres. 1991-92, bd. dirs. 1975-79, officer 1988-93), Phi Kappa Phi, Beta Gamma Sigma. Episcopalian. Home: 3723 Normandy Rd Cleveland OH 44120-5246 Office: Case Western Res U Weatherhead Sch Mgmt U Circle Cleveland OH 44106-7235

MAYNE, WILEY EDWARD, lawyer; b. Sanborn, Iowa, Jan. 19, 1917; s. Earl W. and Gladys (Wiley) M.; m. Elizabeth Dodson, Jan. 5, 1942; children—Martha (Mrs. F.K. Smith), Wiley Edward, John. S.B. cum laude, Harvard, 1938; student, Law Sch., 1938-39; J.D., State U. Iowa, 1939-41. Bar: Iowa bar 1941. Practiced in Sioux City, 1946-66, 75—; mem. Shull, Marshall, Mayne, Marks & Vizintos, 1946-66, Mayne and Berenstein, 1975-87, Mayne & Mayne, 1988—; spl. agt. FBI, 1941-43; Mem. 90th-93d Congresses, 6th Dist. Iowa; mem. judiciary com., agr. com. Commr. from Iowa Nat. Conf. Commrs. Uniform State Laws, 1956-60; chmn. grievance commn. Iowa Supreme Ct., 1964-66; del. FAO, 1973; chmn. Woodbury County Compensation Bd., 1975-80. Chmn. Midwest Rhodes Scholar Selection Com., 1964-66; pres. Sioux City Symphony Orch. Assn., 1947-54, Sioux City Concert Course, 1982-85; vice chmn. Young Republican Nat. Fedn., 1948-50; bd. dirs. Iowa Bar Found., 1962-68. Served to lt. (j.g.) USNR, 1943-46. Fellow Am. Coll. Trial Lawyers; mem. ABA (ho. of dels. 1966-68), Iowa Bar Assn. (pres. 1963-64), Sioux City Bar Assn., Internat. Assn. Def. Counsel (exec. com. 1961-64), Harvard Club (N.Y.C.), Capitol Hill Club, Sioux City Country Club, Masons (Scottish Rite/33 deg.). Home: 2728 Jackson St Sioux City IA 51104-3623 Office: Pioneer Bank Bldg 701 Pierce St Ste 400 Sioux City IA 51101-1036

MAYNES, CHARLES WILLIAM, editor, former government official; b. Huron, S.D., Dec. 8, 1938; s. Charles William and Almira Rose (Summers) M.; m. Gretchen Schiele, July 17, 1965; children: Stacy Kathryn, Charles William. BA, Harvard U., 1960; MA, Oxford (Eng.) U., 1962. UN polit. affairs ofcl. Dept. State, Washington, 1962-65; chief monetary economist AID, Laos, 1965-67; econ. officer Am. Embassy, Moscow, 1968-70; sec. Carnegie Endowment Internat. Peace, 1971-76; sr. legis. asst. to Sen. Fred R. Harris, 1972; mem. issues Sargent Shriver's Vice-Presdl. campaign, 1972; mem. Carter-Mondale Transition team, 1976-77; asst. sec. for internat. orgn. affairs Dept. State, 1977-80; editor Fgn. Policy mag., 1980—; mem. Clinton-Gore Transition team, 1992-93; mem. Coun. Fgn. Rels., Internat. Inst. Strategic Studies, Washington Inst. Internat. Affairs, UN Assn., Overseas Devel. Coun., Nat. Acad. Pub. Adminstrn.; adv. com. European Inst., Lincoln U. Ctr. Pub. Policy and Diplomacy, Overseas Devel. Coun., Nat. Inst. Citizen Participation and Negotiation, U. Calif. Inst. Global Conflict and Cooperation, UN Assn., others. Contbr. articles to profl. jours. Recipient Meritorious Service award Dept. State; congl. fellow Rep. F. Bradford Morse, 1971, Sen. Fred R. Harris, 1971; Rhodes scholar. Mem. Phi Beta Kappa. Democrat. Office: Fgn Policy Mag 2400 N St NW Washington DC 20037-1153 Home: 3914 Leland St Chevy Chase MD 20815-5036

MAYO, BERNIER L., secondary school principal. Headmaster St. Johnsbury (Vt.) Acad. Recipient Blue Ribbon Sch. award U.S. Dept. Edn., 1990-91. Office: St Johnsbury Acad 7 Main St Saint Johnsbury VT 05819-2699

MAYO, CLYDE CALVIN, organizational psychologist, educator; b. Robstown, Tex., Feb. 2, 1940; s. Clyde Culberson and Velma (Oxford) M.; m. Jeanne Lynn McCain, Aug. 24, 1963; children: Brady Scott, Amber Camille. BA, Rice U., 1961; BS, U. Houston, 1964, PhD, 1972; MS, Trinity U., 1966. Lic. psychologist, Tex. Mgmt. engr. LWFW, Inc., Houston, 1966-72, sr. cons., 1972-78, prin., 1978-81; ptnr. Mayo, Thompson, Bigby, Houston, 1981-83, founder Mgmt. and Personnel Systems, Houston, 1983—; counselor Interface Counseling Ctr., Houston, 1976-79; dir. Mental Health HMO Group, 1985-87; instr. St. Thomas U., Houston, 1979—, U. Houston Downtown Sch., 1972, U. Houston-Clear Lake, 1983-88, U. Houston-Central Campus, 1984—; dir. mgmt. devel. insts. U. Houston Woodlands and West Houston, 1986-1991, adj. prof. U. Houston, 1991—. Author: Bi/Polar Inventory of Strengths, 1978, LWFW Annual Survey of Manufacturers, 1966-1981. Coach, mgr. Meyerland Little League, 1974-78, So. Belles Softball, 1979-80, S.W. Colt Baseball, 1982-83, Friends of Fondren Library of Rice U., 1988—; charter mem. Holocaust Mus. Mem. Soc. Indsl. Organizational Psychologists, Tex. Indsl. Orgnl. Psychologists (founder, bd. dirs. 1995—), Houston Psychol. Assn. (membership dir. 1978, sec. 1984), Tex. Psychol. Assn., Am. Psychol. Assn., Bus. Execs. for Nat. Security, Houston Area Indsl. Orgnl. Psychologists (bd. dirs. 1989-92), Forum Club. Methodist. Club: Meyerland (bd. dirs. 1988-92, pres. 1991). Home: 8723 Ferris Dr Houston TX 77096-1409 Office: Mgmt and Personnel Systems 4545 Bissonnet St Bellaire TX 77401

MAYO, ELIZABETH BROOM, lawyer; b. Jackson, Miss., Aug. 20, 1948; d. Harmon W. and Elizabeth (Kehoe) Broom; m. Gerald E. Mayo, Aug. 30, 1980; stepchildren: Sharon E. Parker, Gerald E. Jr. AB, Spring Hill Coll., 1970; JD, Washington U., 1973; LLM in Taxation, Capital U., 1989. Bar: Ohio 1973, S.C. 1995. Assoc. Schottenstein, Zox & Dunn, Columbus, Ohio, 1973-75, ptnr., 1982-89; 2d v.p. underwriting Midland Mut. Life Ins. Co., Columbus, 1975-80; dir. fin. svcs. Nationwide Ins. Cos., Columbus, 1980-82; ptnr. Porter, Wright, Morris & Arthur, Columbus, 1989—, mem. directing ptnrs. com., 1989-93, mem. compensation com., 1990-94, chair healthcare practice group; of counsel Norit, Scariminach & Williams P.A., Hilton Head Island, S.C., 1996—. Active Ohio Arts Coun., 1991—, vice chair, 1994—; active Franklin County Pvt. Industry Coun., Columbus, 1990-95, vice chair, 1994-95; active Recreation and Parks Commn., Columbus, 1990—, chmn., 1993-95; active Met. Human Svcs. Commn., Columbus, 1987-94, chmn., 1991-92. Fellow Am. Coll. Trusts and Estates Counsel; mem. ABA, S.C. Bar Assn., Ohio Bar Assn., Columbus Bar Assn., Nat. Health Lawyers Assn., Capital Club. Office: Porter Wright Morris & Arthur 41 S High St Columbus OH 43215-6101 also: Novit Scariminach Williams 52 New Orleans Rd Hilton Head Island SC 29928

MAYO, GEORGE WASHINGTON, JR., lawyer; b. Waycross, Ga., Dec. 23, 1946; s. George Washington Sr. and Perrie R. (Ling) M.; m. Katherine Louise Boland, Nov. 15, 1977; children—Regan L.B., Taylor L.B. A.B., Emory U., 1967; J.D., U. Va., 1973. Bar: Va. 1973, D.C. 1974. Assoc., Hogan & Hartson, Washington, 1973-80, ptnr., 1980—. Contbr. articles to prof. jours. Bd. dirs. Vietnam Vets. Meml. Fund, Inc., 1978—, Earth Conservation Corps., 1990—, dean's coun. Emory U., 1994—. Served to 1st lt., U.S. Army, 1969-71, Vietnam. Mem. ABA, D.C. Bar Assn., Order of Coif. Democrat. Methodist. Club: Met. (Washington), City (Washington). Home: 26 Holly Leaf Ct Bethesda MD 20817-2652 Office: Hogan & Hartson 555 13th St NW Washington DC 20004-1109

MAYO, J. HASKELL, JR., bishop. Bishop African Methodist Episcopal Church 4th Dist., Chgo. Office: African Methodist Episcopal Ch PO Box 53539 400 E 41st St Ste 114 Chicago IL 60653-2757

MAYO, JOAN BRADLEY, microbiologist, healthcare administrator; b. Ada, Okla., Oct. 24, 1942; d. Samuel S. and Norene (Parker) Bradley; m. Harry D. Mayo III, Sept. 30, 1967. BA, Drake U., 1964; MS in Microbiology, NYU, 1978; MBA in Mgmt., Fairleigh Dickinson U., 1989. RN. Technologist clin. labs. St. John's Episc. Hosp., Bklyn., 1964-66; supr. Med. Tech. Sch. Bklyn.-Cumberland Med. Ctr., 1966-71; clin. instr., technologist SUNY Downstate Med. Ctr., Bklyn., 1970-73; supr. bacteriology lab. Meml. Sloan-Kettering Cancer Ctr., N.Y.C., 1973-82, mgr. microbiology labs., 1982-87; dir. infection control svc. N.Y.C. Health and Hosp. Corp./Harlem Hosp. Ctr., 1987-95; mgr. infection control dept. Atlantic Health System/The Mountainside Hosp., Montclair, N.J., 1995—; mem. com. for prevention of bloodborne diseases N.Y.C. Health and hosp. Corp., 1990-95. Contbr. articles to profl. publs. Active Friends of Harlem Hosp., 1988—, North Bergen (N.J.) Action Group, 1987—. Mem. Am. Soc. Microbiology, Am. Pub. Health Assn., Assn. Practitioners in Infection Control, Delta Mu Delta, Alpha Kappa Alpha. Avocations: writing, travel, reading. Home: 7855 Boulevard E North Bergen NJ 07047-5938 Office: The Mountainside Hosp Bayand Highland Aves Montclair NJ 07047

MAYO, JOHN SULLIVAN, telecommunications company executive; b. Greenville, N.C., Feb. 26, 1930; s. William Louis and Mattie (Harris) M.; m. Lucille Dodgson, Apr. 1957; children: Mark Dodgson, David Thomas, Nancy Ann, Lynn Marie. BS, N.C. State U., 1952, MS, 1953, PhD, 1955. With AT&T Bell Labs., Murray Hill, N.J., 1955-95, exec. dir. toll electronic switching div., 1973-75, v.p. electronics tech., 1975-79, sr. v.p. network systems and network svcs., 1979-91, pres., 1991-95, pres. emeritus, 1995—; mem. adv. bd. Coll. Engring., U. Calif., Berkeley; mem. sci. adv. group House subcom. on renewing U.S. Sci. and Tech. Policy; bd. dirs. Johnson and Johnson, Found. for Nat. Medals of Sci. and Tech. Contbr. articles to profl. jours.; patentee in field. Trustee Polytech U., The Kenan Inst. for Engring., Tech. and Sci. at N.C. State U., Liberty Sci. Ctr.; mem. bd. overseers N.J. Inst. Tech.; mem. commn. on future of Smithsonian Instn. Recipient Indsl. Rsch. Inst. medal, 1992, Navy League N.Y. Coun. Roosevelts gold medal for sci., 1993, Engring. Mgr. of Yr. award Am. Soc. for Engring. Mgmt., 1992, N.J. Sci./Tech. medal, 1994; named Outstanding Engring. Alumnus N.C. State U., 1977; Internat. Engring. Consortium fellow, 1994. Fellow IEEE (Alexander Graham Bell award 1978, Simon Ramo medal 1988, C&C prize 1988, Nat. Medal of Tech. 1990), Internat. Engring. Consortium; mem. NAE, Royal Swedish Acad. Engring. Scis., Sigma Xi, Phi Kappa Phi. Baptist. Avocations: fishing, gardening, bicycling, jogging. Office: AT&T Bell Labs 600 Mountain Ave New Providence NJ 07974

MAYO, LOUIS ALLEN, corporation executive; b. Durham, N.C., Nov. 27, 1928; s. Louis Allen and Amy Earl (Overton) M.; student Calif. State Poly. Coll., 1948-50; BA in Criminology, Calif. State Coll., Fresno, 1952; MA in Pub. Adminstrn., Am. U., 1960, PhD in Pub. Adminstrn., 1983; postgrad. U. So. Calif., 1960-62; m. Emma Jean Minshew, Oct. 31, 1953 (div.); children: Louis Allen III, Robert Lawrence, Carolyn Jean; m. 2d, Myrna Ann Smith, Feb. 16, 1980 (div.). Spl. agt. U.S. Secret Svc., Treasury Dept., L.A., 1956-58, 60-63, White House, Washington, 1958-60, 63-66; program mgr. law enforcement Office Law Enforcement Assistance, Justice Dept., 1967-68; acting chief Rsch. Ctr., rsch. program mgr. Nat. Inst. Law Enforcement and Criminal Justice, 1968-74; alternate assoc. mem. Fed. Coun. on Sci. and Tech., White House, 1973-74; dir. tng. and testing div. Nat. Inst. Justice, 1975-87; pres. Murphy, Mayo & Assocs., Alexandria, Va., 1987—; lectr. criminology Armed Forces Inst. Tech., 1954-55; professorial lectr. Am. U., 1974-82; adj. prof. August Vollmer U., 1990—. 2d lt. to 1st lt. USAF, 1952-56. Mem. Internat. Assn. Chiefs of Police, Am. Soc. Pub. Adminstrn. (nat. chmn. sect. on criminal justice adminstrn. 1975-76), Acad. Criminal Justice Scis., Police Exec. Rsch. Forum, Soc. Police Futurists Internat., Pi Sigma Alpha. Methodist. Home and Office: 5200 Leeward Ln # 101 Alexandria VA 22315-3944

MAYO, ROBERT PORTER, banker; b. Seattle, Mar. 15, 1916; s. Carl Asa and Edna Alberta (Nelson) M.; m. Marian Aldridge Nicholson, Aug. 28, 1942; children: Margaret Alice, Richard Carl, Carolyn Ruth (Mrs. Gregory Brown), Robert Nelson. A.B. magna cum laude, U. Wash., 1937, M.B.A., 1938. Research asst., auditor Wash. State Tax Commn., 1938-41; economist U.S. Treasury, 1941-47, asst. dir. office of tech. staff, 1948-53, chief debt div. analysis staff, 1953-59; asst. to sec. Treasury Dept., 1959-60; v.p. Continental Ill. Nat. Bank & Trust Co. of Chgo., 1960-69; chmn. Boye Needle Co., 1963-67; staff dir. Pres. Commn. on Budget Concepts, 1967; dir. U.S. Bur. of Budget, 1969-70; counsellor to Pres. U.S., 1970; pres. Fed. Res. Bank of Chgo., 1970-81; trustee Instnl. Liquid Assets and Assoc. Goldman Sachs Funds, CNA Income Shares; dir. Chgo. Tokyo Bank, Duff and Phelps Utilities Income Fund. Trustee YMCA, Chgo.; bd. dirs. Exec. Svc. Corps, Chgo. Mem. Comml. Club Chgo., Econ. Club Chgo., Perico Bay (Fla.) Club, Bartlett-on-the-Greens Homeowner's Assn., Phi Beta Kappa. Presbyterian.

MAYOCK, ROBERT LEE, internist; b. Wilkes-Barre, Pa., Jan. 19, 1917; s. John F. and Mathilde M.; m. Constance M. Peruzzi, July 2, 1949; children: Robert Lee, Stephen Philip, Holly Peruzzi. B.S., Bucknell U., 1938; M.D., U. Pa., 1942. Diplomate Am. Bd. Internal Medicine. Intern Hosp. U. Pa., Phila., 1943-44; resident Hosp. U. Pa., 1944-45, chief med. resident, 1945-46, attending physician, 1946—; chief pulmonary disease Phila. Gen. Hosp., 1955-72, chief pulmonary disease sect., 1959-72, sr. cons. pulmonary disease sect., 1972—; asst. prof. clin. medicine U. Pa., 1949-59, assoc. prof., 1959-70, prof. medicine, 1970-87, prof. emeritus, 1987—; mem. med. adv. com. for Tb Commonwealth of Pa., 1965-74, mem. med. adv. com. on chronic respiratory disease, 1974-92, chmn. adv. com., 1981-90; mem. subsplty bd. pulmonary disease Am. Bd. Internal Medicine, 1965-76; nat. bd. dirs. Am. Lung Assn., 1983-92, local bd. dirs., 1961, local pres., 1966-69, dir. at large, 1983—. Contbr. articles in field to med. jours. Served to capt. U.S. Army, 1952-54. Fellow ACP, Am. Coll. Chest Physicians (regent 1972-79), Phila. Coll. Physicians; mem. AMA, Am. Thoracic Soc., Am. Fedn. Clin. Rsch., Am. Heart Assn., Pa. Lung Assn. (dir. 1976—), N.Y. Acad. Scis., Pa. Med. Soc., Phila. County Med. Soc., Physiology Soc. Phila., Laennec Soc. Phila., Merion Cricket Club, Westmoreland Club, Swiftwater Res., Sigma Xi. Home: 244 Gypsy Ln Wynnewood PA 19096-1113 Office: U Penn 3rd Fl Ste F Ravdin Bldg Philadelphia PA 19104

MAYOL, RICHARD THOMAS, advertising executive, political consultant; b. Springfield, Ill., Oct. 30, 1949; s. Richard McFaren and Marjorie (Maddex) M. AA, Springfield Coll., 1969; BS, U. Tulsa, 1972. Co-owner First Tuesday Inc., Phoenix, 1976-85; pres. Mayol and Assocs., Phoenix, 1985—; CEO New West Policy Group, Prescott, Ariz., 1993—; cons. Dem. candidates, Dem. candidates ballot issues, corp. pub. policy Western U.S., Mo. Udall for Congress, Tucson, Mayor Terry Goddard, Phoenix, Senator John Melcher, Mont. Mem. Phoenix Film Commn., 1985—. Mem. Am. Assn. Polit. Cons., Phoenix Grand Prix Commn. Avocations: photography, writing, horseback riding. Home and Office: 348 Moreland Cir Prescott AZ 86303-4035 also: 223 Union St Prescott AZ 86303-3813

MAYOR, ALFRED HYATT, editor; b. Boston, June 4, 1934; s. Alpheus Hyatt and Virginia (Sluder) M.; m. Brunhilde Hillmann, Feb. 16, 1966. AB, Harvard U., 1956, MA, 1957, PhD, 1961. Editorial asst. Newsweek mag., N.Y.C., 1961-62; sub-editor Reuters Ltd., London, 1962-64, Internat. Herald Tribune, Paris, 1964; sr. editor Holiday mag., N.Y.C., 1964-68; mng. editor Corinthian Editions, N.Y.C., 1968; assoc. editor Am. Heritage Press, N.Y.C., 1969-71; exec. editor Antiques mag., N.Y.C., 1972—. Author: (book) Parliament's Passport to London, 1968; mem. editorial bd. Sculpture Soc. Am., N.Y.C., 1984. Advisor Brookgreen Gardens, Murrells Inlet, S.C., 1984; trustee Hispanic Soc. Am., N.Y.C., 1986. Club: Century. Avocations: photography, small repair jobs. Office: Antiques Mag 575 Broadway New York NY 10012-3230

MAYOR, RICHARD BLAIR, lawyer; b. San Antonio, Mar. 27, 1934; s. E. Allan and Elizabeth Ann (Hastings) M.; m. Heather Donald, July 28, 1956; children: Diana Boyd, Philip Hastings. BA, Yale U., 1955; postgrad., Melbourne U., Australia, 1955-56; JD, Harvard U., 1959. Bar: Tex. 1960. Assoc. Butler and Binion, Houston, 1959-67, ptnr., 1967; founding, sr. ptnr. Mayor, Day, Caldwell & Keeton, L.L.P., Houston, 1982—; bd. dirs., founder Internat. Ctrs. Arbitration. Trustee, chmn. exec. com. Contemporary Arts Mus., Houston, 1972-78; trustee Houston Ballet Found., 1983-88. Fulbright scholar, 1955-56. Fellow Tex. Bar Found.; mem. ABA, Am. Law Inst., Tex. Bar Assn., Ramada Club, Houstonian Club, Houston Club, Phi Beta Kappa. Office: Mayor Day Caldwell & Keeton LLP 700 Louisiana St Ste 1900 Houston TX 77002

MAYORA-ALVARADO, EDUARDO RENE, lawyer, law educator; b. Guatemala, Guatemala, Apr. 20, 1957; s. Eduardo Alfredo Mayora-Dawe and Adelaida (Alvarado) De Mayora; m. Alicia Bascunana, June 18, 1983; children: Javier Eduardo, Santiago, Jose Andres, Sebastian. JD, U. Rafael Landivar, Guatemala, 1980; LLM, Georgetown U., U.S.A., 1982; Diploma (2) in Principles Econ. Sci., U. Francisco Marroquin, Guatemala, 1991. Bar: Guatemala, 1980; cert. notary. Assoc. Mayora & Mayora, Guatemala, 1980-81, ptnr., 1982—; prof. bus. law and principles of law U. Francisco Marroquin, Guatemala, 1984-87, prof. bus. law and principles of law Sch. of Econs., 1986-88, prof. constitutional law, dean Sch. of Law, 1989—, prof. principles of pvt. and pub. law, 1993; bd. dirs. Financiera De Inversion S.A., Guatemala; alternate dir. Seguros Alianza S.A., Guatemala; mem. bd. trustees U. Francisco Marroquin, 1989—; vis. prof. Pontificia U. Catolica, Porto Alegre, Brazil, 1994, Montpellier U. Sch. Law, Feance, 1995. Co-author: El Desafio Neoliberal, 1992; author: (essay) El Drama De La Arena Movedisa, 1993 (Charles Stillman award 1993); contbr. to profl. jours. Mem. Guatemala Bar Assn. (author articles Bar Law Jour. 1990—m v.p. ethics bd. 1985-86), Assn. De Amigos Del Pais, Fundacion Para La Cultura (v.p. 1994), Inst. Guatemalteco De Derecho Notarial, Rotary Club, Phi Delta Phi, Guatemala Country Club. Roman Catholic. Avocations: reading, sailing, golf. Office: Mayora & Mayora, Ruta 6, 9-21 4th Flr, Zona 4 01004 Guatemala City Guatemala also: PO Box 661447 Miami FL 33166

MAYORAS, DONALD EUGENE, corporate executive, speaker, consultant, educator; b. Danville, Ill., Aug. 25, 1939; s. Andrew John and Katherine Ann (Shelato) M.; m. JoAnna Marie Kacmer, June 9, 1962; children—Tyler, Stacie. B.S. in Edn., Purdue U., 1962; postgrad., Northwestern U., 1968-71; M.B.A., So. Ill. U., 1977. Regional mgr. Pacific Intermountain Express, Akron, Ohio, 1972-74; v.p. United Van Lines, Fenton, Mo., 1974-78; pres. Bekins Van Lines, L.A., 1978-83; pres., chief exec. officer Sun Carriers, Inc., Holliston, Mass., 1983-90, chmn. bd. dirs.; vice chmn., chief exec. officer Builders Transport, Camden, S.C., 1990-91; pres., CEO Truckload Holding Inc., Devon, Pa., 1995, Mau Trucking, Inc., Ida Grove, Iowa. Trustee Ross Ade Found., West Lafayette, Ind., 1962—. Capt. U.S. Army, 1962-68; Europe, Vietnam. Decorated Bronze Star. Mem. Am. Trucking Assn. (v.p. 1983-91, trustee Found. 1983-91), Nat. Spkrs. Assn., Nat. Coun. Logistics, Nat. Pvt. Truck Coun., Purdue U. Alumni Assn., Nat. Def. Transp. Assn., Aronomink Golf Club (Newton Sq., Pa.), Delta Nu Alpha, Beta Gamma Sigma, Omicron Delta Kappa. Republican. Roman Catholic. Avocations: golf, antiques, classic automobiles, tennis.

MAYPOLE, JOHN FLOYD, real estate holding company executive; b. Chgo., May 17, 1939; s. John James and Althea Floyd M.; m. Anne White, 1961; children: Cynthia, John, Kimberly. B.A. in Econs, Yale U., 1961. With Arthur Andersen & Co., 1961-62, 65-66; mgr. corp. acctg. Interpace Corp., 1966, asst. treas., 1967-68, treas., 1968-70, treas., controller, 1970-73, v.p. fin., 1973-77, sr. v.p., 1977-80, exec. v.p., 1980-81, pres., 1981-83; pres., chief operating officer Clevepak Corp., 1983-84; mng. ptnr. Peach State Real Estate Holding Co., Toccoa, Ga., 1984—; bd. dirs. Dan River Mills, Blodgett Corp., Briggs Industries Inc., Bell Atlantic Corp., Mass. Mut. Life Ins. Co., Davies, Turner & Co., Igloo Products Corp. Bd. adjustment Borough of Mountain Lakes, N.J., 1971-81, chmn., 1980-81. Served with USMC, 1962-65. Mem. Yale Club (N.Y.C.), Rockaway River Country Club, Laurel Oak Country Club. Republican. Office: PO Box 1223 Toccoa GA 30577

MAYR, ERNST, retired zoology educator, author; b. Kempten, Germany, July 5, 1904; came to U.S., 1931; s. Otto and Helene (Pusinelli) M.; m. Margarete Simon, May 4, 1935; children: Christa E., Susanne. Cand. med., U. Greifswald, 1925; Ph.D., U. Berlin, 1926; Ph.D. (hon.), Uppsala U., Sweden, 1957; D.Sc. (hon.), Yale U., 1959, U. Melbourne, 1959, Oxford U., 1966, U. Munich, 1968, U. Paris, 1974, Harvard U., 1980, Guelph U., U. Cambridge, 1982, U. Vt., 1984; DSc (hon.), U. Mass., 1993; PhD (hon.), U. Vienna, 1994; DPhil (hon.), U. Konstanz, 1994; DSc (hon.), U. Bologna, 1995. Asst. curator zool. mus. U. Berlin, 1926-32; mem. Rothschild expdn. to Dutch New Guinea, 1928, expdn. to Mandated Ty. of New Guinea, 1928-29, Whitney Expdn., 1929-30; research asso. Am. Mus. Natural History, N.Y.C., 1931-32; asso. curator Am. Mus. Natural History, 1932-44, curator, 1944-53; Jesup lectr. Columbia U., 1941; Alexander Agassiz prof. zoology Harvard U., 1953-75, emeritus, 1975—; dir. Mus. Comparative Zoology, Harvard U., 1961-70; Messenger lectr. Cornell U., 1985; Hitchcock prof. U. Calif., 1987; hon. fellow Ctr. for Philosophy of Sci., U. Pitts. Author: List of New Guinea Birds, 1941, Systematics and the Origin of Species, 1942, Birds of the Southwest Pacific, 1945, Birds of the Philippines, (with Jean Delacour), 1946, Methods and Principles of Systematic Zoology, (with E. G. Linsley and R. L. Usinger), 1953, Animal Species and Evolution, 1963, Principles of Systematic Zoology, 1969, Populations, Species and Evolution, 1970, Evolution and the Diversity of Life, 1976, (with W. Provine) Evolutionary Synthesis, 1980, Biologie de l'Evolution, 1981, The Growth of Biological Thought, 1982, Toward a New Philosophy of Biology, 1988, One Long Argument, 1991; editor: Evolution, 1947-49. Pres. XIII Internat. Ornith. Congress, 1962. Recipient Leidy medal, 1946, Wallace Darwin medal, 1958, Brewster medal Am. Ornithologists Union, 1965, Daniel Giraud Elliot medal, 1967, Nat. Medal of Sci., 1970, Molina prize Accademia delle Sci., Bologna, Italy, 1972, Linnean medal, 1977, Gregor Mendel medal, 1980, Balzan prize, 1983, Darwin medal Royal Soc., 1987, Disting. Scientist award UCLA, 1993, Galvin Godman medal, 1994, Japan prize, 1994, Benjamin Franklin medal 1995. Fellow Linnaean Soc. N.Y. (past sec. editor), Am. Ornithol. Union (pres. 1956-59), N.Y. Zool. Soc.; mem. NAS, Am. Philos. Soc., Am. Acad. Arts and Scis., Am. Soc. Zoologists, Soc. Systematic Zoology (pres. 1966), Soc. Study Evolution (sec. 1946, pres. 1950); hon. or corr. mem. Royal Soc., Royal Australian, Brit. ornithol. unions, Zool. Soc. London, Soc. Ornithol. France, Royal Soc. New Zealand, Bot. Gardens Indonesia, S. Africa Ornithol. Soc., Linnean Soc. London, Deutsche Akademie der naturforsch Leopoldina, Accad. Naz. dei Lincei, Royal Soc., Academie des Sci., Ctr. for Philosophy of Sci. (Pitts.), Russian Acad. Sci., Berlin - Brandenburgische Akademie. Office: Harvard U Mus Comparative Zoology 26 Oxford St Cambridge MA 02138

MAYR, LINDA HART, internal medicine nurse; b. Orange, Tex., July 15, 1951; d. Richard Gail and Gwendolyn (Condrey) Hart; m. Julius Charles Mayr, Nov. 20, 1987; children: Christopher Feazel, Keith Feazel, Kimberly Feazel, Christina Duke, Thomas Mayr. Diploma, North Harris County Coll., Houston, 1980. Newborn nursery and neonatal ICU nurse Houston N.W. Med. Ctr., 1980-81, 1982-84; pvt. nurse Frederick Hill, D.O., Houston, 1981-82; nurse FM 1960 Pediatric Ctr., Houston, 1984-85; nurse ob-gyn. Steven Zarzour, M.D., Houston, 1985-86; office mgr. Bert Williams, D.C., Houston, 1986-87; office nurse Ronald E. Sims, M.D., Houston, 1987—; allied health profl. Meth. Hosp., Houston, 1987—. Mem. Am. Assn. Office Nurses, Assn. Nurses AIDS Care, The Care Group, Inc. (profl. adv. com.). Home: 206 E Oak St Deer Park TX 77536-4104

MAYRON, MELANIE, actress, writer; b. Phila., Oct. 20, 1952. Ed., Am. Acad. Dramatic Arts, N.Y.C. Writer Tribeca Prodns. Appearences include (films) Harry and Tonto, 1974, Car Wash, 1976, The Great Smokey Road Block, 1976, Girl Friends (British Acad. award nomination), You Light Up My Life, 1977, Heart Beeps, 1981, Missing, 1982, Sticky Fingers (also co-writer, co-producer), 1988, Checking Out, 1989, My Blue Heaven, 1990, Drop Zone, 1994; (TV movies) Hustling, 1975, Katie: Portrait of a Centerfold, 1978, The Best Little Girl in the World, 1981, Will There Really Be a Morning?, 1983; (TV miniseries) Wallenberg: A Hero's Story, 1985, Playing for Time, The Boss's Wife, (TV series) thirtysomething (Emmy award for best supporting actress in a drama series, 1989), dir. 2 episodes; film dir.: The Baby-Sitters Club, 1995; author (anthology): Stepping Back. •

MAYS, GEORGE WALTER, JR., educational technology educator, consultant; b. Decatur, Ill., July 1, 1926; s. George Walter Sr. and Ida May (Lookabaugh) M.; children: Richard, Steven, John, James. BS in Edn., U. Ill., Champaign, 1950, MS in Edn., 1952; BSEE, U. md., 1960; cert., Calif. State U., Carson, 1987. Tchr. math. and physics Mahomet (Ill.) High Sch., 1950-52, prin., 1952-55; br. chief engring studies Nat. Security Agy., Ft. Meade, Md., 1955-62; sr. engr. Jet Propulsion Lab., Pasadena, Calif., 1962-71; tchr. math.-sci., chair Aviation High Sch., Redondo Beach, Calif., 1971-82; tchr. math. and physics, dept. chair Redondo Union High Sch., 1982-89; cons. edn. tech. Apple Valley, Calif., 1989—; math. coord. Sci. and Tech. Ctr., Apple Valley, Calif., 1990—; part-time instr. electronics Pasadena City

Coll., 1963-72, Pepperdine U., 1975-76, math. Victor Valley Coll., 1991—. Author: Educational Technology Application Notes, 1989-90. With USN, 1944-46. Recipient Appollo Achievement award NASA, 1969. Mem. IEEE (life), Calif. Tchrs. Assn. (WHO award 1988-89), Nat. Coun. Tchrs. of Math., Computer Using Educators, Apple Valley Country Club, Victor Valley Aero Club. Avocations: reading, sports, computer usage, flying. Home and Office: 14070 Seminole Rd PO Box 1930 Apple Valley CA 92307-0037

MAYS, GLENDA SUE, education educator; b. Freer, Tex., July 18, 1938; d. Archie Richard and Helen Hildred (Morgan) Cox; m. Dewey William Mays, Sept. 7, 1963; children: Rose Marie, Teresa Sue, Frank Dewey. BS, Tex. Tech. U., 1959, MA, 1961; PhD, North Tex. State U., 1969. Cert. tchr., supr., prin. Tchr. Lubbock (Tex.) Pub. Schs., 1959-61, Amarillo (Tex.) Pub. Schs., 1961-62, Austin (Tex.) Pub. Schs., 1962-63; curriculum intern/rsch. asst., elem. coord. U. Tex. at Austin, Hurst, Tex., 1963-65; asst. prof. McMurry U., Abilene, Tex., 1965-67; assoc. prof. Dallas Bapt. U., 1968-71; reading resource tchr., dept. chair Ft. Worth (Tex.) Ind. Sch. Dist., 1971-74, reading specialist, 1974-82, instructional specialist, 1982—; spkr. lang. acquisition and reading 7th World Congress in Reading, Hamburg, Germany, 1978. Advisor/writer (English textbook): McDouglas Littel Language, 1985-86; writer: Bilingual Stories for Ft. Worth Ind. Sch. Dist., 1979-80. Patron Kimbell Mus. Art, Ft. Worth, 1994—; mem. Nat. Cancer Soc., Ft. Worth, 1980—. Fulbright-Hays scholar, Kenya, Africa, 1970; grantee in fgn. langs. Nat. Endowment Arts U. Ark., 1987, Ft. Worth Ind. Sch. Dist. Study grantee U. London, 1978. Fellow ASCD, NEA, Tex. State Tchrs. Assn., Ft. Worth Edn. Assn., Internat. Reading Assn. (hostess 1st Tex. breakfast 1969), Nat. Geog. Soc., Smithsonian Instn., Libr. of Congress, Ft. Worth Reading Assn., Nat. Coun. for Social Studies spkr. social studies symposium N.Y.C. 1970, Tex. Elem. Prins. and Suprs. Assn. (sec. 1971-72). Avocations: travel, reading, music, writing, antique collecting. Home: 1225 Clara St Fort Worth TX 76110-1009

MAYS, JANICE ANN, lawyer; b. Waycross, Ga., Nov. 21, 1951; d. William H. and Jean (Bagley) M. AB (hon.), Wesleyan Coll., Macon, Ga., 1973; JD, U. Ga., 1975; LLM in Taxation, U. Georgetown, 1980. Bar: Ga. 1976. Tax counsel com. on ways and means U.S. Ho. Reps., Washington, 1975-88, chief tax counsel com. on ways and means, staff dir. subcom. select revenue measures, 1988-93, chief counsel, staff dir. com. on ways and means, 1993-95, minority chief counsel, staff dir. com. on ways and means, 1995—. Mem. Tax Coalition (past chair). Office: Ways & Means Com 1106 Longworth Office Bldg Washington DC 20515

MAYS, JOSEPH BARBER, JR., lawyer; b. Birmingham, Ala., Dec. 15, 1945; s. Joseph B. and Elizabeth (Tiller) M.; m. June Blackwell, June 13, 1970; 1 child, Mary-Elizabeth. BA, Tulane U., 1967; MA, Cornell U., 1969; JD, U. Ala., 1978. Bar: Ala. 1978, U.S. Ct. Appeals (5th, 4th, 6th, 11th cir.) Ala., U.S. Supreme Ct., U.S. Tax Ct. Ala. Tchr. Indian Springs Sch., Helena, Ala., 1969-75; assoc. Bradley, Arant, Rose & White, Birmingham, 1978-84, ptnr., 1984—; tchr. Birmingham Sch. Law, 1979—. Contbr. articles to profl. jours. Recipient Woodrow Wilson fellowship Woodrow Wilson Found., 1968-69. Mem. ABA, Nat. Assn. Criminal Def. Lawyers, Ala. State Bar Assn., Birmingham Bar Assn., Phi Beta Kappa. Episcopalian. Avocations: sailing, fly-fishing, photography. Home: 3514 Country Club Rd Birmingham AL 35213-2824 Office: Bradley Arant Rose & White 1400 Park Place Towers Birmingham AL 35203

MAYS, LESTER LOWRY, broadcast executive; b. Houston, July 24, 1935; s. Lester T. and Virginia (Lowry) M.; m. Peggy Pitman, July 29, 1959; children: Kathryn Mays Johnson, Linda Mays McCaul, Mark P., Randall T. BS in Petroleum Engring., Tex. A&M U., 1959; MBA, Harvard U., 1962. Comml. recorder San Antonio; with Sta. KTTU-TV, Tucson, Sta. KOKI/KTFO-TV, Tulsa, Sta. WMPI/WJTC-TV, Mobile and Pensacola, Okla., Sta. WAWS-TV, Jacksonville, Fla., Sta. KSAS-TV, Wichita, Kans., Sta. KLRT/KASN-TV, Little Rock, Sta. WFTC-TV, Mpls., Sta. WFTC-TV, WLMT/WMTU-TV, WLMT/WMTU TV, Memphis, Sta. WXXA, Albany, Sta. WQUE-AM-FM, New Orleans, Clear Channel Sports, Des Moines, Okla. News Network, Oklahoma City, Va. News Network, Stas. KJYO and KTOK, Oklahoma City, Sta. KEBC, Oklahoma City, Sta. WELI, New Haven, Sta. WKCI-WAVZ, New Haven, Sta. KPEZ, Austin, Tex., Stas. KHYS, KALO, KBXX, KMJQ, KPRC, KSEV and KYOK, Houston and Point Arthur, Tex., KMOD & KAKC, Tulsa, KTAM & KORA, Bryan and College Station, Tex., WHAS & WAMZ, Louisville; with radio and TV broadcasting WOAI, KQXT, and KAJA, San Antonio; pres., CEO Clear Channel Comms., Inc., San Antonio; past chmn. bd. CBS Radio Affiliates Bd. Bd. dirs., trustee Tex. Rsch. Pk.; bd. dirs., mem. exec. com. United Way; chmn. United Way San Antonio and Bexar County, 1995; regent emeritus Tex. A&M U. Sys.; trustee Tex. Rsch. and Tech. Found.; mem. deve. bd. U. Tex. Health Sci. Ctr.; adv. dir. Permanent Univ. Fund Tex. Mem. Nat. Assn. Broadcasters (past chmn. joint bd.), Greater San Antonio C. of C. (past chmn.), Rotary. Home: 400 Geneseo Rd San Antonio TX 78209-6127 Office: Clear Channel Comm PO Box 659512 San Antonio TX 78265-9512

MAYS, M. DOUGLAS, state legislator, financial consultant; b. Pittsburg, Kans., Aug. 18, 1950; s. Marion Edmund and Lilliemae Ruth (Norris) M.; m. Lena M. Krog, June 10, 1971; children: Jessica, Aaron. BFA, Pittsburg State U., 1972; postgrad., Washburn U., 1973—. Registered rep. Waddell & Reed, Inc., Topeka, 1981-83, Paine Webber Jackson & Curtis, Topeka, 1983-85, Columbian Securities, Topeka, 1985-87; commr. securities State of Kans., Topeka, 1987-91; pres. Mays & Assocs., Topeka, 1991—; mem. Kans. Ho. Reps., Topeka, 1993—; adminstrv. law judge various securities proceedings, 1987—; with securities and commodities fraud working group U.S. Dept. Justice, 1988-90; with penny stock task force SEC, 1988-90; del. Commonwealth Secretariat Symposium Comml. Crime, Cambridge, Eng., 1989; securities arbitrator, 1991—. Rep. precinct committeeman Shawnee County, Kans., 1976—, county chmn., 1978-82; mem. 2d Dist. Rep. State Com., Kans., 1976-86, 92—; mem. Kans. Rep. State Com., 1976-87; Senate steering com. Kassebaum for Senate campaign, 1978; chmn., mgr. Hoferer for Senate campaign, 1984; campaign coord., dir. fin. Hayden for Gov., 1986; mem. pub. bldg. commn. City of Topeka, 1985-86, bldg. and fire appeals bd., 1986-89, dep. mayor, 1987-88; mem. Topeka City Coun., 1985-89; exec. bd. Topeka/Shawnee County Interngovtl. Coun., 1986-89; adv. bd. Topeka Performing Arts Ctr., 1989-90; active Topeka/Shawnee County Met. Planning Commn., 1992—, chmn., 1994—. Mem. North Am. Securities Adminstrs. Assn. (chmn. enforcement sect. 1988-89, pres.-elect, bd. dirs. 1989-90, pres. 1990-91), Nat. Assn. Securities Dealers, Nat. Futures Assn. (bd. arbitrators), Internat. Orgn. Securites Commns. (inter-Am. activities consultative com. 1990, pres.'s com. 1990, del. 1990). Methodist. Home: 1920 SW Damon Ct Topeka KS 66611-1926 Office: Kans Ho Reps State Capitol Topeka KS 66612

MAYS, WILLIE HOWARD, JR. (SAY HEY KID), former professional baseball player; b. Westfield, Ala., May 6, 1931; s. William Howard and Ann M.; m. Mae Louise Allen, Nov. 27, 1971; 1 adopted son, Michael. Baseball player Birmingham Black Barons, 1948-50, Trenton Inter-State League, 1950-51, Mpls. Millers, Am. Assn., 1951, N.Y. Giants, 1951-57, San Francisco Giants, 1958-72, N.Y. Mets, 1972-73; with Bally's Park Place, Atlantic City, 1980—; pub. rels. exec. San Francisco Giants, 1986—. Author: Willie Mays: My Life In and Out of Baseball, 1966, Say Hey: The Autobiography of Willie Mays, 1988. Served with AUS, 1952-54. Named Most Valuable Player Nat. League, 1954, 65; named Player of Yr. Sporting News, 1954, Baseball Player of Decade Sporting News, 1970, Male Athlete of Yr. AP, 1954, Rookie of the Yr., 1951, Most Exciting Playin Sport Sporting News, 1954, All-Star Game, 1954-73; recipient Hickok belt, 1954, Golden Bat award to commemorate 600 home runs, Gold Glove award (12 times), 1st Commissioner's award, 1970, Golden Plate awarded to America's Captains of Achievement by Am. Acad. Achievement, 1976, Spirit of Life award City of Hope, 1988, Sportsman of Decade, Cong. Racial Equality, 1991, Legendary Star award HBO Video; inducted into Ala. Sports Hall of Fame, Baseball Hall of Fame, 1979, Black Hall of Fame, 1973, Calif. Sports Hall of Fame. Holder 3d place in major league homeruns (660); lifetime batting average of .302; signed lifetime pub. rels. contract with San Francisco Giants, 1993. Office: care San Francisco Giants Candlestick Park San Francisco CA 94124

MAYSENT, HAROLD WAYNE, hospital administrator; b. Tacoma, Wash., June 26, 1923; s. Wayne L. Shivley and Esther Pierce M.; m. Marjorie Ellen Hodges, June 13, 1953; children: Jeffrey, Nancy, Brian, Gregory. BA, U. Wash., 1950; MS in Hosp. Adminstrn. with distinction, Northwestern U., 1954. Adminstrv. resident Passavant Meml. Hosp., 1953-54, adminstrv. asst., 1954-55; research asso. hosp. adminstrn. Northwestern U., Evanston, Ill., 1954-55; with Lankenau Hosp., Phila., 1955-72; dir. Lankenau Hosp., 1963-67, exec. dir., 1967-72; exec. v.p. Rockford (Ill.) Meml. Hosp., 1972-75, pres., 1975-91; pres. Rockford Meml. Corp., 1983-91, pres. emeritus, 1991—; pres. The Rockford Group, 1983-91; tchg. assoc. Rockford Sch. Medicine, U. Ill., 1974-89, adj. assoc. prof., 1989-92; mem. Ill. Health Facility Planning Bd., 1980-92; chmn. bd. Ill. Hosp. Joint Ventures, Inc., 1977-78, Vol. Hosps. Am. Midwest Partnership, 1985-89. Contbr. articles to profl. jours. Chmn.-elect Coll. Healthcare Execs., 1988-89, chmn., 1989; coach, adminstr. Broomal (Pa.) Little League, 1962-72; bd. dirs. Community Health Assn., 1964-70, Rockford Med. Edn. Found., 1972-87, Tri State Hosp. Assembly, 1978-80, Rockford Coun. 100, 1987-91, exec. com. 1987-91. With AUS, 1942-46. Recipient Malcolm T. MacEachern award Northwestern U., 1954, Laura G. Jackson Alumni Assn. award, 198, Disting. Svc. award Ill. Hosp. Assn., 1989. Fellow Am. Coll. Hosp. Adminstrs. (Ill. regent 1979-84, dist. bd. govs. 1984-88, gov. 1984-88, chmn. elect 1988-89, chmn. 1989-90, past chmn. 1990-91); mem. Am. Hosp. Assn. (com. on vols. 1976-80, coun. patient svcs. 1980-82, ho. of dels. 1977-84, rep. Am. Acad. Pediatrics com. on hosp. care 1983-85), Pa. Hosp. Assn. (bd. dirs. 1965-68), Ill. Hosp. Assn. (trustee 1973-79, sec. 1974-76, chmn. elect 1977, chmn. bd. trustees 1978, named Outstanding Leader in Hosp. Industry 1978, Disting. Svc. award 1989). Office: Rockford Meml 2400 N Rockton Ave Rockford IL 61103-3655

MAYTHAM, THOMAS NORTHRUP, art and museum consultant; b. Buffalo, July 30, 1931; s. Thomas Edward and Margaret (Northrup) M.; m. Daphne Chace, Dec. 30, 1960 (div.); 1 child, T.F. Gifford; m. Gloria Maytham, June 11, 1994. BA in Art History, Williams Coll., Williamstown, Mass., 1954; MA in Art History, Yale U., 1956; cert. in German, Colby Coll., 1954. Intern Wadsworth Atheneum, 1955; rsch. asst. Yale U., 1956; head dept. paintings Boston Mus. Fine Arts, 1957-67; assoc. dir., acting dir. Seattle Art Mus., 1967-74; dir. Denver Art Mus., 1974-83; art cons., pub. Maytham & Assocs., Denver, 1983—; mus. accreditation program evaluator Am. Assn. Museums; past trustee, mem. exhbns. adv. com. Am. Fedn. Arts, N.Y.; past mem. mus. program panel, grants reviewer Nat. Endowment for Arts, Washington; reviewer Nat. Endowment for Humanities, Washington; mem. adv. panel, grants reviewer Nat. Mus. Act, Smithsonian Instn.; past mem. policy panel and adv. com., econ. impact of arts study Colo. Coun. Arts and Humanities; co-founder Consortium of Rocky Mountain Regional Conservation Ctr., U. Denver; founder dirs. assn. Denver cultural agys.; del. Inter-Am. Museums Conf., Oaxaca, Mexico; co-founder United Arts Fund, Seattle; mem. art adv. com. Airport Art Program, Port of Seattle; vis. faculty Leadership Denver program, Pres.'s Leadership class U. Colo.; cons. Aspen Ctr. Visual Arts, Sangre de Cristo Arts Ctr., Pueblo, Western States Arts Found., Santa Fe, BBHC, Cody, Wyo.; lectr. museums, colls., corporate groups and art assns. Exhbns. organized include Ernst Ludwig Kirchner Retrospective, Seattle, Pasadena and Boston museums, 1968-69, Am. Painting from the Boston and Met. Museums, Nat. Gallery, St. Louis and Seattle museums, 1970-71; contbr. articles to profl. jours.; presenter TV programs on collections and exhbns. Boston Pub. TV, WGBH-TV. Trustee Internat. Exhbns. Found., Washington. Recipient Gov.'s Arts award Seattle Airport Art Program, 1972, Denver Art mus., award Downtown Denver Inc., 1978. Mem. Assn Art Mus. Dirs. (officer, trustee, ops. com. sec., future directions. com. chmn.). Office: Maytham Art Cons Ltd 3882 S Newport Way Denver CO 80237

MAZA, MICHAEL WILLIAM, newspaper editor, columnist; b. Detroit, June 19, 1947; s. Frank Michael and Irene (Boiczuk) M.; m. Cynthia Jeanne Nash, Apr. 8, 1972 (div. Apr. 1985); 1 child, Lydia Anne; m. Jean Ann Zinsmaster, Mar. 1, 1987. BA, U. Detroit, 1969. Reporter, editor Detroit Free Press, 1969-70, Detroit News, 1970-77; film, theater critic, arts editor Ariz. Republic, Phoenix, 1979-87; assst. arts editor Dallas Morning News, 1987-89; book columnist "Help Yourself" Dallas Morning News/KRT Newswire, Dallas, Washington, 1989—; mng. editor Dallas Life Mag., 1989-95; mng.editor Guide, Dallas, 1995—; Ariz. corr. People weekly mag., N.Y.C., 1983-84; Detroit corr. New Times, mag., N.Y.C., 1974-75. Avocations: running, ceramics, travel. Office: Dallas Morning News 508 Young St Dallas TX 75202

MAZAIKA, ROBERT J., chemicals executive; b. 1934. BS in Chemistry, Boston U., 1956. With Uniroyal, Inc., Middlebury, Conn., 1956-85, Uniroyal Chem. Co., Inc., Middlebury, Conn., 1985—; with Uni Royal Chem. Corp., Middlebury, Conn., 1988—, now pres., CEO. Office: Uniroyal Chem Inc World Headquarters Benson Rd Middlebury CT 06749*

MAZANEC, GEORGE L., natural gas company executive; b. Chgo., May 30, 1936; s. Charles and Catherine (Traczyk) M.; m. Elsa Weiffenbach, Oct. 1, 1960; children: Robert A., John C. AB in Econs., DePauw U., 1958; MBA, Harvard U., 1960. Various positions Internorth Inc., 1964-82; exec. v.p., CFO Tex. Gas Resources Corp., Owensboro, Ky., 1982-85; CFO, v.p. fin. Duquesne Light Co., 1985-87; formerly sr. v.p. Tex. Ea. Corp.; formerly pres. TETCO; group v.p. Panhandle Ea. Corp., Houston, 1989-91, exec. v.p., 1991-93, vice chairman, 1993—; bd. dirs. Panhandle Ea. Corp., TEPPCO Ltd., Associated Electric Gas Ins. Svcs. Ltd. Mem. Am. Gas Assn. (bd. dirs.), Houston Mus. of Natural Sci. (bd. dirs.), Houston Grand Opera (bd. dirs.), Ramada Club, Houston Country Club, Old Baldy Club. Home: 302 Fall River Ct Houston TX 77024-5611 Office: Panhandle Ea Corp PO Box 1642 Houston TX 77251*

MAZANKOWSKI, DONALD FRANK, Canadian government official; b. Viking, Alta., Can., July 27, 1935; s. Frank and Dora (Lonowski) M.; m. Lorraine Poleschuk, Sept. 6, 1958; children: Gregory, Roger, Donald. Student, pub. schs., 1987; PhD in Engring (hon.), N.S. Inst. Tech.; LLD (hon.), U. Alta., 1993. MP Ho. of Commons, 1968—, chmn. com. transp., 1972-74, mem. com. govt. ops., 1976-77, mem. com. trans. and communication, 1977-79; min. of transp., min. responsible for Can. Wheat Bd. Govt. of Can., 1979-80, min. of transp. (re-drafted Nat. Transp. Act), 1984-86, dep. prime min., 1986—, govt. house leader, 1986-88, pres. Privy Coun., 1986-91, pres. Treas. Bd., 1987-88, min. responsible for privatization and regulatory affairs, 1988-91, min. of agriculture, 1988-91, min. of fin., 1991-93; mem. bd. govs. U. Alta; mem. bd. dirs. Gulf Can. Resources, Great West Life Assurance, The Investors Group, Can. Utilities Ltd., Shaw Comms. Inc., Weyerhaeuser Can. Ltd., Greyhound Lines of Can., Golden Star Resources, Equimar Capital Inc. Mem. Royal Can. Legion (life). Roman Catholic. Club: Vegreville Rotary (past dir.). Lodge: KC.

MAZE, THOMAS H., engineering educator; b. St. Paul, June 1, 1952; s. Robert O. and Viola A.E. (Schultz) M.; m. Leslie Foster Smith, Aug. 2, 1979; children: Lauren L. Simonds, Julie W. Simonds. BS in Civil Engring., Iowa State U., 1975; M of Engring., Urban and Pub. Systems, U. Calif., Berkeley, 1977; PhD in Civil Engring., Mich. State U., 1982. Asst. prof. dept. civil engring. Wayne State U., 1979-82; assoc. prof. sch. civil engring. and environ. sci. U. Okla., Norman, 1982-87; prof. dept. civil and construction engring. Iowa State U., Ames, 1988—, prof. in-charge transp. planning program, 1987—, dir. Iowa transp. ctr., ctr. transp. ext. and applied rsch., 1988—; assoc. dir. inst. urban transp., transp. rsch. ctr. Ind. U., Bloomington, 1987—; dir. Midwest Transp. Ctr., U.S. Dept. Transp.'s Univ. Transp. Ctr. Fed. Region VII, 1990—. Mem. ASCE, Am. Pub. Transit Assn., Its Am. (founding, instl. issues com., CVO com.), Am. Pub. Works Assn. (adj. workshop faculty mem. 1986-91, exec. coun. inst. equipment svcs. 1991—), Coun. Univ. Transp., Transp. Rsch. Bd. (mem. various coms., chair 8th equipment mgmt. conf. 1990), Inst. Transp. Engrs. (assoc. mem. dept. 6 standing com., chmn. various coms., pres. U. Fla. student chpt. 1976-79), Chi Epsilon (faculty advisor U. Okla. 1985-87), Sigma Xi. Office: Iowa State U Iowa Transp Ctr Ste 125 2521 Elwood Dr Ames IA 50010-8626 : Ctr Transp Rsch and Edn 2625 N Loop Dr Ste 2100 Ames IA 50010-8615

MAZEK, WARREN F(ELIX), academic administrator, economics educator; b. Pitts., Oct. 14, 1938; s. Felix Frank and Josephine Catherine (Sethner) M.; m. Nancy Lee Metcalfe, June 18, 1960 (div. Jan. 1982); children: Thomas W., Erika A., Laura J., Michael M.; m. Susan Chapman, Apr. 24, 1982; 1 child, Marissa C. AB, Washington and Jefferson Coll., 1960; MA, Ind. U., 1962; PhD, U. Pitts., 1965. Asst. prof. econs. Coll. Wooster, 1965-67; asst. prof. Fla. State U., 1967-70, assoc. prof., 1970-75, prof., 1975-86, dean coll. Social Scis., 1973-86; prof., asst. supt. acad. affairs U.S. Merchant Marine Acad., Kings Point, N.Y., 1986—. Cons. on econ. loss to legal firms, 1974—; vestryman Christ Ch., Manhasset, 1991—; chmn. Big Bend chpt. March of Dimes, Tallahassee, 1981-83. Recipient faculty research award Fla. State U., 1973-74; Resources of the Future dissertation fellow, 1964; Richard K. Mellon fellow Am. Council for Edn., 1975. Mem. Am. Assn. Higher Edn., Am. Econs. Assn., Regional Sci. Assn., Conf. Fed. Degree Granting Insts., Assn. Acad. Affairs Adminstrs. Episcopalian. Home and Office: US Merchant Marine Acad Kings Point NY 11024

MAZELIS, MENDEL, plant biochemist, educator, researcher; b. Chgo., Aug. 31, 1922; s. Jacob and Anna (Brvarnick) M.; m. Noreen Beimer, Mar. 24, 1969; 1 son, Jacob Russell. B.S., U. Calif.-Berkeley, 1943, Ph.D., 1954. Jr. research biochemist U. Calif.-Berkeley, 1954-55; research assoc., instr. U. Chgo., 1955-57; assoc. chemist Western Regional Research Lab., Albany, Calif., 1957-61; asst. prof. U. Calif.-Davis, 1961-64, assoc. prof., 1964-73, prof., 1973-91, prof. emeritus, 1991—. Served to lt. (j.g.) USN, 1943-46. Mem. Am. Soc. Plant Physiologists, Am. Soc. Biochemists and Molecular Biologists, Biochem. Soc. London, Phytochem. Soc. N.Am., Phytochem. Soc. Europe, Inst. Food Technologists. Office: U Calif Dept Food Sci/Tech Davis CA 95616

MAZER, NORMA FOX, writer; b. N.Y.C., May 15, 1931; d. Michael and Jean (Garlen) Fox; m. Harry Mazer, Feb. 12, 1950; children: Anne E., Joseph D., Susan R., Gina B. Author: I, Trissy, 1971, A Figure of Speech, 1973 (Nat. Book award nominee 1974); Saturday, the Twelfth of October, 1975 (Lewis Carroll Shelf award 1976); Dear Bill, Remember Me? and Other Stories, 1976 (N.Y. Times Notable Book 1976, ALA Notable Book 1976, Sch. Library Jour. Best Books of Yr. 1976, Christopher award 1976, Lewis Carroll Shelf award 1977); (with Harry Mazer) The Solid Gold Kid, 1978 (ALA Best Books for Young Adults 1978, Internat. Reading Assn. Children's Choice, 1979, ALA 100 Best of the Best award 1968-93); Up in Seth's Room, 1979 (ALA Best Books for Young Adults 1979, SLJ Best Books of Yr. 1979, ALA Best of the Best Books, 1970-83); Mrs. Fish, Ape and Me, The Dump Queen, 1980 (German Children's Literature prize 1982, List of Honor Austrian Children's Books 1983); Taking Terri Mueller, 1981 (Edgar award 1982, Calif. Young Readers' Medal 1985), Summer Girls, Love Boys and Other Short Stories, 1982, When We First Met, 1982 (Iowa Teen award 1985); Someone to Love, 1983 (ALA Best Books for Young Adults 1983), Downtown, 1984 (ALA Best Books for Young Adults 1984, N.Y. Times Notable Book 1984), Supergirl The Novel, 1984, Three Sisters, 1986, A, My Name Is Ami (Internat. Reading Assn. Children's Choice, 1987), 1986, B, My Name is Bunny, 1987, After the Rain, 1987 (Newbery Honor Book, ALA Notable Book, Sch. Library Jour. Best Books 1987, ALA Best Books for Young Adults 1987, Canadian Children's Book Coun. Choice 1988, Assn. Booksellers for Children Choice, 1988, Horn Book Fanfare Book 1988), Silver, 1988 (ALA Best Books for Young Adults, 1988, Iowa Teen award 1990-91, ALA 100 Best of the Best award 1968-93), (with Harry Mazer) Heartbeat, 1989 (Internat. Reading Assn. Children's Choice 1990, Literature prize ZDF Germany); editor: Waltzing on Water, 1989, C, My Name Is Cal, 1990, D, My Name Is Danita, 1991, Babyface, 1991 (Am. Booksellers pick of list 1991, Internat. Reading Assn. Tchr.'s Choice), E, My Name Is Emily, 1991, (with Harry Mazer) Bright Days, Stupid Nights, 1992 (Am. Bookseller Pick of List 1992), Out of Control, 1993 (Am. Booksellers Pick of the List 1993, ALA Best Books for Young Adults 1994); contbr. short stories and articles to numerous anthologies, collections and mags. including Redbook, Playgirl, Voice, Ingenue, English Jour., The Writer, Alan Review. Home: 7626 Brown Gulf Rd Jamesville NY 13078-9636

MAZLISH, BRUCE, historian, educator; b. N.Y.C., Sept. 15, 1923; s. Louis and Lee (Reuben) M.; m. Neva Goodwin, Nov. 22, 1988; children from previous marriage: Anthony, Jared, Cordelia, Peter. B.A., Columbia U., 1944, M.A., 1947, Ph.D., 1955. Instr. history U. Maine, 1946-48, Columbia U., 1949- 50, Mass. Inst. Tech., 1950-53; dir. Am. Sch. in Madrid, Spain, 1953-55; mem. faculty Mass. Inst. Tech., 1955—, prof. history, 1965—, chmn. history sect., 1965-70, head dept. humanities, 1974-79. Author: (with J. Bronowski) The Western Intellectual Tradition, 1960, The Riddle of History, 1966, In Search of Nixon, 1972, James and John Stuart Mill: Father and Son in the 19th Century, 1975, 2d edition, 1988, The Revolutionary Ascetic, 1976, Kissinger, The European Mind in American Policy, 1976, The Meaning of Karl Marx, 1984, A New Science: The Breakdown of Connections and the Birth of Sociology, 1989, The Leader, the Led and the Psyche, 1990, The Fourth Discontinuity: The Co-Evolution of Humans and Machines, 1993; Editor: Psychoanalysis and History, 1963, rev. edit., 1971, The Railroad and the Space Program: An Exploration in Historical Analogy, 1965, (with Ralph Bultjens) Conceptualizing Global History, 1993, (with Les Marx) Progress: Fact or Illusion, 1996. Bd. dirs. Rockefeller Family Fund, 1987—; v.p. Mount Desert Festival of Chamber Music, 1985—; bd. dirs. Toynbee Prize Found., 1992—. Served with inf. and OSS, AUS, 1943-45. Recipient Toynbee prize, 1986-87. Fellow Am. Acad. Arts and Scis. Clubs: Cambridge Tennis, Badminton and Tennis; Harbor (Seal Harbor, Maine). Home: 11 Lowell St Cambridge MA 02138-4725 Office: M.I.T. 77 Massachusetts Ave Cambridge MA 02139-4301

MAZO, MARK ELLIOTT, lawyer; b. Phila., Jan. 12, 1950; s. Earl and Rita (Vane) M.; m. Fern Rosalyn Litman, Aug. 19, 1973; children: Samantha Lauren, Dana Suzanne, Ross Elliott, Courtney Litman. AB, Princeton U., 1971; JD, Harvard U., 1974. Bar: D.C. 1975, U.S. Dist. Ct. D.C. 1975, U.S. Claims Ct. 1975, U.S. Ct. Appeals (D.C. cir.) 1976, U.S. Supreme Ct. 1979. Assoc. Jones, Day, Reavis & Pogue, Washington, 1974-79; assoc. Crowell & Moring, Washington, 1979-81, ptnr., 1981-90; ptnr. Hogan & Hartson, L.L.P., Washington and Paris, 1990—. Contbr. articles to profl. jours. White House intern Exec. Office of Pres., Washington, 1972. Capt. USAR, 1971-79. Mem. ABA, Harvard Law Sch. Assn., D.C. Bar Assn., Columbia Country Club, Princeton Club (N.Y.C.), Colonial Club, City Club, Phi Beta Kappa. Republican. Home: 3719 Cardiff Rd Chevy Chase MD 20815-5943 Office: Hogan & Hartson LLP 555 13th St NW Washington DC 20004-1109

MAZO, ROBERT MARC, chemistry educator, retired; b. Bklyn., Oct. 3, 1930; s. Nathan and Rose Marion (Mazo) M.; m. Joan Ruth Spector, Sept. 5, 1954; children: Ruth, Jeffrey, Daniel. B.A., Harvard U., 1952; M.S., Yale U., 1953, Ph.D., 1955. Research assoc. U. Chgo., 1956-58; asst. prof. Calif. Inst. Tech., 1958-62; assoc. prof. U. Oreg., Eugene, 1962-65; prof. chemistry U. Oreg., 1965-95; prof. emeritus, 1996; head chemistry dept. U. Oreg., 1978-81, dir. Inst. Theoretical Sci., 1964-67, 84-87, assoc. dean Grad. Sch., 1967-71; program dir NSF, 1977-78; Alfred P. Sloan fellow, NSF Sr. Postdoctoral fellow, vis. prof. U. Libre de Bruxelles, Belgium, 1968-69; vis. prof. Technische Hochschule Aachen, Weizmann Inst., Rehovoth, Israel, 1981-82, U. New South Wales, Australia, 1989. Author: Statistical Mechanical Theories of Transport Processes, 1967; also research articles. NSF Postdoctoral fellow U. Amsterdam, Netherlands, 1955-56. Mem. Am. Phys. Soc., AAAS, AAUP. Home: 2460 Charnelton St Eugene OR 97405-3214 Office: U Oreg Inst Theoretical Sci Eugene OR 97403

MAZRUI, ALI AL'AMIN, political science educator, researcher; b. Mombasa, Kenya, Feb. 24, 1933; came to U.S., 1960; s. Al'Amin Ali and Safia (Suleiman) M.; m. Molly Vickerman, 1962 (div. 1982); children: Jamal, Al'Amin, Kim Abubakar; m. Pauline Uti, Oct. 1991; children: Farid Chinedu, Harith Ekenechukwu. B.A. with distinction, U. Manchester, Eng., 1960; M.A., Columbia U., 1961; D.Phil., Oxford U., 1966. Lectr. Makerere U., Kampala, Uganda, 1963-65, prof. polit. sci., head dept. polit. sci., 1965-73; dean faculty social scis. Faculty Social Scis., Makerere U., Kampala, Uganda, 1967-69; prof. polit. sci. U. Mich., Ann Arbor, 1974-91, prof. Ctr. Afroam. and African Studies, dept. polit. sci., 1974-91; Andrew D. White prof.-at-large Cornell U., Ithaca, 1986-92; research prof. polit. sci. U. Jos, Nigeria, 1981-86; Albert Schweitzer prof. humanities SUNY, Binghamton, 1989—; Albert Luthuli prof.-at-large U. Jos (Nigeria), 1991—; sr. scholar, Andrew D. White prof.-at-large emeritus Cornell U, Ithaca, 1992—; dir. Inst. Global Cultural Studies SUNY, Binghamton, 1991—; Reith lectr. BBC, London, 1979; vis. prof. various univs. including U. London, U. Chgo., Oxford U., U. Pa., Ohio State U., Manchester U., Harvard U. Nairobi U., UCLA, Northwestern U., U. Singapore, Colgate Coll., U. Australia, U. Cairo, Sussex U., U. Leeds, 1965—; mem. bank's coun. African advisers

World Bank, Washington, 1988-91. Author: Towards A Pax Africana: A Study of Ideology and Ambition, 1967, The Anglo-African Commonwealth: Political Friction and Cultural Fusion, 1967, On Heroes and Uhuru-Worship: Essays on Independent Africa, 1967, Violence and Thought: Essays on Social Tensions in Africa, 1969, Cultural Engineering and Nation-Building in East Africa, 1972, World Culture and the Black Experience, 1974, The Political Sociology of the English Language: An African Perspective, 1975, Soldiers and Kinsmen in Uganda: The Making of a Military Ethnocracy, 1975; co-editor: (with Robert I. Rotberg) Protest and Power in Black Africa, 1970, (with Hasu Patel) Africa in World Affairs: The Next Thirty Years, 1973; editor: The Warrior Tradition in Modern Africa, 1978, Africa since 1935 Volume III Unesco General History of Africa, 1973-93, (with Alamin M. Mazrui) The Political Culture of Language Swahili, Society and the State, 1996—; sr. editor: (with T.K. Levine) The Africans: A Reader, 1986; author: The Trial of Christopher Okigbo, 1971, A World Federation of Cultures: An African Perspective, 1976; Africa's International Relations: The Diplomacy of Dependency and Change, 1977, Political Values and the Educated Class in Africa, 1978, The African Condition: A Political Diagnosis, 1980 (with Michael Tidy) Nationalism and New States in Africa, From About 1935 to the Present, 1984; narrator, presenter: The Africans: A Triple Heritage, 1986, Cultural Forces in World Politics, 1990; mem. editl. bd. various profl. jours., 1963—; contbr. articles to profl. publs. Fellow Ctr for Advanced Study in Behavioral Scis., Palo Alto, Calif., 1972-73; sr. fellow Hoover Instn. on War, Revolution and Peace, Stanford, Calif., 1973-74, Mich. Soc. Fellows, 1978-82. Fellow Internat. Assn. Mid. Ea. Studies, Ghana Acad. Arts and Scis. (hon.); mem. African Studies Assn. (exec. bd. 1975—, pres. 1978-79, Disting. Africans award 1995), Internat. Congress African Studies (v.p. 1978-85), Internat. Polit. Sci. Assn. (v.p. 1970-73), World Order Models Project (dir. African sect. 1968-83), Royal African Soc. (v.p.), Royal Commonwealth Soc., United Kenya Club (Nairobi), Athenaeum Club (London). Office: SUNY Inst Global Cultural Studies Off Schweitzer Chair PO Box 6000 Binghamton NY 13902-6000

MAZUMDER, JYOTIRMOY, mechanical and industrial engineering educator; b. Calcutta, India, July 9, 1951; came to U.S., 1978; s. Jitendra Mohan and Gouri (Sen) M.; m. Aparajita, June 17, 1982; children: Debashis, Debayan. B in Engring., Calcutta U., 1973; diploma, PhD, Imperial Coll., London U., 1978. Rsch. scientist U. So. Calif., L.A., 1978-80; asst. prof. mechanical and indsl. engring. U. Ill., Urbana, 1980-84, assoc. prof., 1984-88, prof., 1988—; co-dir. ctr. laser aided material processing U. Ill., 1990—; dir. Quantum Laser Corp., Edison, N.J., 1982-89; pres. Laser Scis., Inc., Urbana, 1988—; vis. scholar physics dept. Stanford (Calif.) U., 1990. Author: (with others) Laser Welding; co-editor: Laser Materials Processing, 1984, 88; contbr. numerous articles to profl. jours. Fellow Am. Soc. of Metals and Laser Inst. of Am. (life, sr. editor Jour. Laser Application); mem. Am. Inst. Metallurgical Engrs. (phys. mets. com. 1980—), Optical Soc. Am. Achievements include non-equilibrium synthesis of Ni-Cr-Al-Hf alloy by laser; patentee: weld pool visualization system for measurement of free surface deformation. Office: U Ill Dept Mech and Ind Engring 1206 W Green St Urbana IL 61801-2906

MAZUR, ALLAN CARL, sociologist, engineer, educator; b. Chgo., Mar. 20, 1939; s. Joseph and Esther (Markowitz) M.; m. Minnette Albrecht, Jan. 21, 1968; children—Julie Elizabeth, Rachel Lee. B.S., Ill. Inst. Tech., 1961; M.S., UCLA, 1964; Ph.D., Johns Hopkins U., 1969. Research engr. North Am. Aviation Co., Los Angeles, 1961-64; instr. polit. sci. Mass. Inst. Tech., 1966-67; ops. research analyst Lockheed Missile & Space Corp., Sunnyvale, Calif., 1967-68; asst. prof. sociology Stanford U., 1968-71; mem. faculty Syracuse U., N.Y., 1971—; prof. pub. affairs Syracuse U., 1992—. Author: Dynamics of Technical Controversy, 1981, Global Social Problems, 1991, Rashomon at Love Canal, 1996; co-author: Biology and Social Behavior, 1972; contbr. articles to profl. jours. Fellow AAAS; mem. Am. Sociol. Assn. Jewish. Home: 246 Scottholm Ter Syracuse NY 13224-1738 Office: Syracuse U Maxwell Sch Syracuse NY 13244

MAZUR, ERIC, physicist, educator; b. Amsterdam, The Netherlands, Nov. 14, 1954; came to U.S., 1982; s. Peter and Hèlène E.C. (Contamine) M.; m. Angela B.Romijn, July 14, 1984; children: Natalie I., Marc, Sophie B. BA in Physics and Astronomy, U. Leiden, 1975, MS in Physics, 1977, PhD, 1981. Research fellow Harvard U., Cambridge, Mass., 1982-84, asst. prof., 1984-88, assoc. prof., 1988-90; prof. physics and Gordon McKay prof. applied physics Harvard U., 1990—; cons. N.E. Rsch. Assocs., Woburn, Mass., 1985-89. Contbr. articles to profl. jours. Recipient Presidential Young Investigator award, 1988. Fellow. Am. Phys. Soc., Optical Soc. Am. Avocation: photography. Office: Harvard U 29 Oxford St Cambridge MA 02138-2901

MAZUR, JAY J., trade union official. BA in Indsl. Relations, CUNY, 1965; MA in Labor Studies, Rutgers U., 1977. Dir. orgn. local 40 Internat. Ladies Garment Workers Union, N.Y.C., 1955-59, dir. orgn. local 23, 1959-64, asst. mgr. local 23-25, 1964-77, mgr. sec. local 23-25, 1977-83, gen. sec.-treas., 1983-86; pres. Unite, N.Y.C., 1986—; v.p. exec. council AFL-CIO, Washington, 1986—, N.Y. State exec. council, Albany; mem. exec. council Indsl. Union Dept., Washington, 1984—; mem. exec. bd. Fiber, Fabric and Apparel Coalition, Washington, 1986—; bd. dirs. Occupational Health Legal Rights Fund, Washington. V.p. Nat. Immigration Refugee and Citizenship Forum, Washington; bd. dirs. Regional Plan Assn., N.Y.C., 1983, Spl. Contbn. Fund NAACP, Balt., 1987. Avocations: music, jogging, gardening. Office: Unite 1710 Broadway New York NY 10019-5254*

MAZUR, MICHAEL, artist; b. N.Y.C., Nov. 2, 1935; s. Burton Boris and Helen (Isaacs) M.; m. Gail Lewis Beckwith, Dec. 28, 1958; children: Daniel Isaac, Kathe Elizabeth. BA, Amherst Coll., 1958; BFA, Yale U., 1959, MFA, 1961. Asst. prof. fine arts Brandeis U., Waltham, Mass., 1965-76; instr. RISD, 1962-65; vis. prof. Yale U. Sch. Art and Arch., 1972, 81, Queens Coll., CUNY, 1973, U. Calif., Santa Barbara, 1974-75, Boston U., 1982; lectr. Mus. Fine Arts, Boston, Brown U., U. Calif., Berkeley, New Sch. for Social Rsch., Bennington Coll., U. Iowa, Boston U., 1994-95, Katonah Mus., N.Y. Studio Sch., 1994; vis. lectr. Carpenter Ctr., Harvard U., 1976, 78, 89, 92, 94, 95, others; illustrator The Inferno of Dante, Farrar, Strans & Giroux, 1994. Exhibited in one-man shows at Kornblee Gallery, N.Y.C., 1960, 63, 66, Boris Mirski, Boston, 1963, 65, Phila. Print Club, 1964, Silvermine Guild, 1964, Fla. State U., 1966, Shoemaker Gallery Juniata Coll., 1966, Alpha Gallery, Boston, 1967, 68, 74, OGL Gallery, Los Angeles, Calif., 1968, Rose Art Mus., Brandeis U., 1969, A.A.A. Gallery, 1969, Inst. Contemporary Art, Boston, 1970, Terry Dintenfass, N.Y.C., 1974, 76, Alpha Gallery, Boston, 1974, Picker Gallery, Colgate U., 1973, Trinity Coll., 1976, Ohio State U., 1975, Robert Miller Gallery, N.Y.C., 1977, 80, Harkus-Krakow, Boston, 1977, 79, 80, Pace Gallery, N.Y.C., 1980, John Stoller, Mpls., 1981, 85, 88, 91, William and Mary Coll., 1981, Ronald Greenberg, St. Louis, 1981, Janus Gallery, L.A., 1982, 84, 88, Barbara Mathes Gallery, N.Y.C., 1984, 86, Barbara Krakow Gallery, Boston, 1984, 86, 89, 91, 93, 95, Art Club Chgo., 1985, Beaver Coll., 1985, Joe Fawbush, N.Y., 1987, 88, Jan Turner Gallery, L.A., 1988, Butler Gallery, Houston, 1989, Mary Ryan Gallery, N.Y.C., 1990, 94, 95; exhibited group shows at, Mus. Modern Art, 1964, 75, Bklyn. Mus., 1960, 62, 64, 66, 76, 80, 84, 86, Fogg Art Mus., 1966, 76, 94, Art. Inst. Chgo., 1964, Pa. Acad., 1966, 93, Phila. Mus., 1966, 88, Boston Mus. Fine Arts., 1967, 68, 76, 77, 80, 88, 90-91, 92, DeCordova Mus., Lincoln, Mass., 1965-67, 75, 86, 87, Whitney Mus. Am. Art, 1965, 81, 90, 92, Nat. Inst. Arts and Letters, 1965, 74, 80, 86, Sivermine Guild, 1965, Print Biennial of Americas, Santiago, Chile, 1965, Paris Biennale, 1969, Venice Biennale, 1970, Finch Coll. Mus., 1971-72, 2d and 3d Biennial Graphic Art, Cali, Colombia, N.A.D. Ann., 1974, Butler Inst., Youngstown, Ohio, 1974, Ball State U., 1974, America-1976, Sense of Place, Met. Mus., N.Y.C., 1979, 80, Montreal Mus. Fine Arts, 1977, Palais Royale, Brussels, 1979, Claude Bernard, Paris, 1980, Alan Frumkin, N.Y.C., 1981, 82, Madison Art Ctr., 1989, Nat. Gallery of Art, Washington, 1990, Pratt Mus., N.Y.C., 1990; traveling exhbns. include, Bicentennial Exhbn., 1976, State Arts Councils, Iowa, Kans., Mo., Nebr., 1973, Am. Monotypes, Smithsonian Instn., 1977; represented in permanent collections, Met. Mus., N.Y.C., Mus. Modern Art, Smith Coll. Art Mus., Library Congress, Fogg Art Mus., Art Inst. Chgo., Whitney Mus., Los Angeles County Art Mus., Mus. R.I. Sch. Design, Oreg. Art Mus., U. Maine, Mpls. Inst., Pa. State U., Toledo Art Mus., Phila. Art Mus., U. Ohio Westminster Found., Boston Mus. Fine Arts, Boston Pub. Library, Bklyn. Mus., Addison Gallery, Andover Acad., Yale Art Gallery, Montreal Mus. Fine Arts; (Recipient 2d prize Soc. Am. Graphic Artists 1963, Nat. Inst. Arts and Letters award 1965). Co-founder Artists Against Racism and the War, 1968; bd. dirs. Artists Found., co-chair, 1995—; bd. dirs. Fine Arts Work Ctr., Provincetown, Mass.; mem. Mass. Coun. on Arts and Humanities; mem. Pennell com. Libr. of Congress, 1983-93; founder, dir. Art for Nuc. Weapons Freeze, 1983-84, New Provincetown Print Project, 1990-95. Grantee Tiffany Found., 1964, Tamarind Lithography Workshop, 1968; Guggenheim Found. fellow, 1964-65; winner numerous purchase awards. Home: 5 Walnut Ave Cambridge MA 02140-2706 also: 561 Commercial St Provincetown MA 02657-1724

MAZUR, PETER, cell physiologist, cryobiologist; b. N.Y.C., March 3, 1928; s. Paul M. and Adolphia (Kaske) M.; m. Drusilla Stevens, May 28, 1953 (dec. May 1982); 1 child, Timothy Stevens; m. Sara Jo Bolling, June 16, 1984. A.B. magna cum laude, Harvard U., 1949, Ph.D., 1953. NSF postdoctoral fellow, Princeton U., N.J., 1957-59; research staff biology div. Oak Ridge Nat. Lab., 1959—, group leader fundamental and applied cryobiology, 1966—, sci. dir. biophysics and cell physiology, biology div., 1974-75, corporate fellow, 1985; mem. vis. com. biology Harvard U. Bd. Overseers 1972-77; prof. U. Tenn.; mem. Space Sci. Bd. of Nat. Acad., 1975-77. Contbr. articles to prof. jours. Served to capt. USAF, 1953-57. Recipient Author of Yr. award Martin-Marietta Energy Systems, 1985, Disting. Svc. award Am. Assn. Tissue Banks, 1993, R & D 100 award R & D Mag., 1993; Lalor fellow Harvard U., 1952, John Harvard fellow, 1951. Sigma Xi Nat. lectr., 1980. Fellow AAAS; mem. Soc. for Cyrobiology (pres. 1973-74, bd. govs., 1979—), Phi Beta Kappa. Club: Cosmos (Washington). Current work: Cryobiology mechanisms of freezing injury in living cells and tissues. Subspecialties: Cell biology; Biophysics (biology). Home: 125 Westlook Cir Oak Ridge TN 37830-3856 Office: Oak Ridge Nat Lab Biology Divsn PO Box 2009 Oak Ridge TN 37831-8080

MAZUR, RHODA HIMMEL, social services association administrator; b. Bklyn., July 4, 1929; d. Morris and Gussie (Nadler) Himmel; m. Marvin Irwin Mazur, June 7, 1952; children: Jody, Amy, Leslie, Eric. Student, CCNY, CUNY. Pres. United Jewish Community Va. Peninsula Inc, Newport News, 1985-88, Friends of the Homeless, Inc., 1993—; chmn. Social Action Com. Rodef Sholom Temple, 1990-93 (com. mem. 1990—). bd. dirs. Anti-Defamation League Regional Bd., Richmond, 1985—, v.p., 1983-85, Newport News Social Svcs. Adv. Bd., 1979-84, Coun. Jewish Fedns., N.Y.C., 1985-87, Gov.'s Commn. Status Women, Richmond, 1981-84, Nat. Coun. Christians and Jews, 1985-89; mem. adv. bd. Friends of the Homeless, 1987—, Associated Marine Inst., 1988-92; active Newport News Task Force on Emergency Housing, 1984-85; chair fin. com. Peninsula Peace Edn. Ctr., Newport News, 1984-85; mem. social svcs. com. United Jewish Cmty. Va. Peninsula, 1995—. Recipient Young Leadership award Jewish Fedn. Newport News, 1968, Brotherhood citation Nat. Conf. Christians and Jews, 1984. Democrat. Avocations: hand crafts, reading, music, photography. Home: 114 James River Dr Newport News VA 23601-3604

MAZUREK, JOSEPH P., state attorney general, former state legislator; b. San Diego, July 27, 1948; B.A., U. Mont., 1970, J.D., 1975; m. Patty Mazurek; 3 children. Bar: Mont. 1975; atty. Gough, Shanahan, Johnson, and Waterman, Helena, Mont.; mem. Mont. Senate from 23d Dist., 1981-92; Senate pres., 1991-92; atty. gen., State of Mont., 1993—; mem. Revenue Oversight Com., 1983-92; chmn. Senate Judiciary Com.; assoc. editor Mont. Law Rev., 1974-75. Served with U.S. Army, 1970-72. Mem. ABA, Beta Gamma Sigma, Phi Delta Phi, Phi Delta Theta. Office: Justice Bldg PO Box 201401 215 N Sanders 3rd Fl Helena MT 59620*

MAZURSKY, PAUL, screenwriter, theatrical director and producer; b. Bklyn., Apr. 25, 1930; s. David and Jean (Gerson) M.; m. Betsy Purdy, Mar. 12, 1953; children—Meg, Jill. B.A., Bklyn. Coll., 1951. Actor, star, TV and Films, 1951—, including film Deathwatch, Miami Rhapsody, 1995; night club comedian, 1954-60; writer Danny Kaye Show, 1963-67; co-writer film I Love You, Alice B. Toklas, 1968; writer, dir. films Bob & Carol & Ted & Alice, 1969, Alex in Wonderland, 1970, Blume in Love, 1972, Harry & Tonto, 1973, Next Stop, Greenwich Village, 1976, An Unmarried Woman, 1977-78, Willie & Phil, 19679-80, Tempest, 1982, Moscow on the Hudson, 1984; writer, prodr., dir. films Down and Out in Beverly Hills, 1986, Moon Over Parador, 1988; co-scriptwriter, prodr., dir. film Enemies, A Love Story, 1989, Scenes From a Mall, 1990, The Pickle, 1992, Faithful, 1995.

MAZZA, LINDA MARIE, international flight attendant, purser; b. N.Y.C., Dec. 12, 1962; d. John and Marylin Ann (Eger) M. BS, Niagara U., 1984. Customer svc. rep. Capitol Air, N.Y.C., 1982, Command Airways, Poughkeepsie, N.Y., 1984-85; internatl sales rep. N.Y.-Tokyo Tours, N.Y.C., 1985; corp. travel counselor Thomas Cook Travel, N.Y.C., 1985-86; internat. flight attendant, purser Tower Air, N.Y.C., 1986—. Author: (booklet) Hairstyles for You, 1993. Mem. Hudson River Sloop: Clearwater, Newburgh, N.Y., 1992-93. Recipient Civilians of Desert Shield/Desert Storm award USAF, 1993, Cert. of Achievement for Contbn. to Desert Storm/Desert Shield, U.S. Army, 1993. Mem. NOW, Internat. Assn. Travel Agts. Presbyterian. Avocations: photography, keeping travel scrapbooks. Home: 13 Overlook Blf Marlboro NY 12542-6403

MAZZA, THOMAS CARMEN, lawyer; b. Erie, Pa., Feb. 14, 1940; s. Carmen J. and Helen (Fronius) M.; m. Lois Bigbie, June 12, 1993; children: Elizabeth Williamson Burnette, Thomas Denholm. BA, Yale U., 1961, LLB, 1964. Bar: N.Y. 1965; U.S. Ct. Appeals (2nd cir.) 1965, U.S. Dist. Ct. (so. and ea. dists.) N.Y. 1976, U.S. Ct. Appeals (11th cir.) 1980, U.S. Dist. Ct. (no. dist.) N.Y. 1982, U.S. Supreme Ct. 1982. Assoc. Dewey Ballantine, N.Y.C. and Brussels, 1964-72; ptnr. Dewey Ballantine, N.Y.C., 1972—. Vestryman Trinity Parish, N.Y.C., 1976-83, 86-93, 94—; bd. dirs. St. margaret's House Housing Corp., N.Y.C., 1994—. Fellow Am. Coll. Investment Counsel; mem. ABA, N.Y. State Bar Assn., Assn. Bar City of N.Y., Collectors Club N.Y. (gov. 1989—, pres. 1993—). Episcopalian. Avocations: music, philately. Office: Dewey Ballantine 1301 Avenue Of The Americas New York NY 10019-6022 also: The Collectors Club Inc 22 E 35th St New York NY 10016-3806

MAZZAFERRI, ERNEST LOUIS, physician, educator; b. Cleve., Sept. 27, 1936; s. Joseph and Nanetta (Marinelli) M.; m. Florence Mildred Marolt, Nov. 23, 1957; children: Patricia Marie Atchison, Michael Louis, Sharon Lynne Brown, Ernest Louis. BS cum laude, John Carroll U., 1958; MD, Ohio State U., 1962. Diplomate Am. Bd. Internal Medicine, Am. Bd. Endocrinology and Metabolism. Intern Ohio State U. Hosps., Columbus, 1962-63; resident Ohio State U. Hosps., 1963-64, 66-68; asst. prof. medicine Ohio State U., 1968-70, assoc. prof., 1973-76, prof., 1976-79, dir. div. endocrinology and metabolism, 1975-78; acting dean U. Nev., Reno, 1979-81; prof., chmn. dept. medicine U. Nev., 1978-84, prof. physiology, 1982-84; prof., chmn. dept. medicine, prof. physiology Ohio State U., Columbus, 1984—; pres. Dept. of Medicine Found., 1986—. Author: Endocrinology Case Studies, 3d edit., 1985, Internal Medicine Pearls, 1993; editor: Textbook of Endocrinology, 3d edit., 1986, Contemporary Internal Medicine, 1988, 3d edit., 1990, Advances in Endocrinology and Metabolism, Vol. 6, 1995, Endocrine Tumors, 1993; mem. sci. adv. bd. Western Jour. Medicine, 1993; mem. editl. bd. Jour. Lab. Clin. Medicine, 1987—, Hosp. Practice; contbr. articles to profl. jours. Chmn. Gov.'s Com. on Radiation Fallout in Nev., 1980-84, hosp. ethics com. Ohio State U.; mem. Sec. of Energy Dose Assessment Adv. Com., 1980-84, Agy. for Health Care Policy, Rsch. Cataract Guideline Com., 1991-92. Lt. col. USAF, 1964-72; col. USAR. Decorated Air Force Commendation medal, Meritorious Svc. medal. Fellow ACP (gov. for Nev. 1984-85, chmn. clin. efficacy assessment program com. 1992-95, mem. health and pub. policy com., edn. policy com.); mem. Am. Bd. Internal Medicine (Endocronology and Metabolism, 1996—), AMA, Am. Thyroid Assn., Am. Diabetes Assn. (pres. Ohio affiliate 1988-89), Endocrine Soc., Am. Clin. and Climatol. Assn., Ctrl. Soc. Clin. Rsch., Am. Coll. Clin. Endocrinology (bd. dirs. 1995—), Alpha Omega Alpha. Republican. Roman Catholic. Research in treatment thyroid cancer, gastric inhibitory polypeptide and diabetes mellitus. Home: 2481 Slate Run Rd Columbus OH 43220-2850 Office: Ohio State U Means Hall 1655 Upham Dr Columbus OH 43210-1251 *Success, like every other human experience, is relative, measured against shifting standards and subject to the scrutiny of time. One must strike a fine balance—self certainty against external review—that permits the full expression of new ideas enriched by the best and time-worn thoughts of others.*

MAZZARELLA, DAVID, newspaper editor; b. 1938. With AP, Lisbon, N.Y.C., Rome, 1962-70, Daily American, Rome, 1971-75, Gannett News, D.C., 1976-77, The Bridgewater, Bridgewater, N.J., 1977-83; now editor USA Today, Arlington, Va. Office: USA Today 1000 Wilson Blvd Arlington VA 22209-3901*

MAZZARELLA, JAMES KEVIN, business administration educator; b. Phila., Sept. 22, 1955; s. Samuel Charles and Rosemary C. (Queenan) M. BA, St. Joseph' U., 1977; MBA, La Salle U., 1981; MA, Temple U., 1987; PhD, Columbia-Pacific U., 1987; DBA, Pacific-Western U., 1988; cert. in acctg., Thomas Edison State Coll., 1994. Asst. mgr. Olney Oil & Burner Co., Phila., 1977-80; data processing Craig Fuel Co., Phila., 1980-84; supr. M. Kelley Son's Inc., Phila., 1984-86; adj. instr. Holy Family Coll., Phila., 1987-88, instr., 1989, asst. prof., 1989—; adj. instr. Phila. (Pa.) Coll. Textiles, 1984-86, La Salle U., Phila., 1985—, Rosemont (Pa.) Coll., 1988-91. Mem. Am. Econ. Assn., Am. Fin. Assn., Am. Statis. Assn., Nat. Assn. Bus. Econs., Math. Assn. Am., Fin. Mgmt. Assn., Prodn. and Ops. Mgmt. Soc., Midwest Fin. Assn., Western Econs. Assn. Internat., Ea. Econ. Assn., Ea. Fin. Assn., Am. Mgmt. Assn., So. Fin. Assn., Multinat. Fin. Soc., Am. Math. Soc., Am. Law and Econs. Assn. Roman Catholic. Home: 5101 N Fairhill St Philadelphia PA 19120-3126 Office: Holy Family College Grant & Frankford Ave Philadelphia PA 19114

MAZZE, EDWARD MARK, consultant, business educator; b. N.Y.C., Feb. 14, 1941; s. Harry Alan and Mollie (Schneider) M.; m. Sharon Sue Hastings, Sept. 7, 1967; children—Candace, Thomas. B.B.A., City U. N.Y., 1961, M.B.A., 1962; Ph.D., Pa. State U., 1966. Lectr. bus. adminstrn. CCNY, 1961-62; bus. cons., 1961—; pres., dir. JET Corp., East Orange, N.J., 1976-79; instr. bus. Pa. State U., 1963-66; assoc. prof. mktg. U. Detroit, 1966-68; assoc. prof., dir. spl. programs W.Va. U., 1968-70; prof. bus. adminstrn., coordinator mktg. program Va. Poly. Inst. and State U., Blacksburg, 1970-75; v.p. adminstrv. services, dean Sch. Bus., Seton Hall U., South Orange, N.J., 1975-79; dean sch. bus. adminstrn. Temple U., Phila., 1979-86, prof. mktg. and internat. bus., 1979-93; dean Belk Coll. Bus. Adminstrn., prof. mktg. U. N.C.-Charlotte, Charlotte, 1993—; chmn. bd. William Penn Bank, Phila., 1985-87; bd. dirs. Technitrol, Inc.; mem. dist. export coun. U.S. Dept. Commerce, 1978-80, 83-93; mem. panel trustees U.S. Bankruptcy Ct., 1984—. Author: International Business: Articles and Essays, 1963, Readings in Organization and Management, 1963, Marketing in Action, 1963, Case Histories in Sales Management, 1965, Sales Management: Theory and Practice, 1965, International Marketing Adminstration, 1967, Introduction to Marketing, 1970, Marketing in Turbulent Times: The Challenges and the Opportunities, 1975, Personal Selling: Choice Against Chance, 1976; mem. editorial bd. Jour. Econs. and Bus., 1976-80, Indsl. Mktg. Mgmt., 1977—, Jour. Internat. Bus. Studies, 1978-82, Jour. Acad. Mktg. Sci., 1980-91, Jour. Mktg. Edn., 1985-94, Jour. Global Mktg., 1987—; contbr. articles to profl. and trade jours. Trustee Phila. Home Care, 1984-89, Manor Coll., 1985-92, Thomas A. Edison State Coll. Found., 1987-89, Delaware Valley Coll. Sci. and Agr., 1991—, Pa. Inst. Tech., 1992-93; chmn. econ. devel. adv. com. Village South Orange, 1977-80; mem., vice-chmn. Bd. Suprs. Doylestown Twp., 1980-81. Ford. Found. fellow, 1962-63. Mem. Am. Mktg. Assn., Acad. Internat. Bus., Nat. Assn. Corp. Dirs., Acad. Mktg. Sci., City Club, Tower Club, Beta Gamma Sigma, Alpha Kappa Psi, Pi Sigma Epsilon, Pi Kappa Alpha. Home: 6805 Linkside Ct Charlotte NC 28277-0394 Office: Univ NC Charlotte NC 28223

MAZZE, ROGER STEVEN, medical educator, researcher; b. N.Y.C., May 14, 1943; s. Harry Alan and Mollie (Schneider) M.; m. Rochelle Linda March, Dec. 28, 1969; children—Aaron, Rebekkah. B.A., Queens Coll., 1965, M.A., 1967; Ph.D., U. Ill., 1971. Fellow in social psychiatry Brandeis U., Waltham, Mass., 1971; chmn. urban studies Fordham U., N.Y.C., 1970-75; from assoc. to full prof. epidemiololgy and social medicine Einstein Coll. Medicine, N.Y.C., 1975-87, exec. dir. Diabetes Research and Tng. Ctr., 1980-88; sr. v.p. research and devel. Internat. Diabetes Ctr., Mpls., 1988—; clin. prof. U. Minn. Med. Sch., 1988—; v.p. Inst. for Rsch. and Edn. HSM, Mpls., 1993—; adv. bd. Nat. Diabetes Info. Clearinghouse, Washington, 1980-84, Pa. Diabetes Acad., Harrisburg, 1982—; co-dir. WHO Coll. Ctr. in Diabetes Care, Edn. and Computer Sci., Mpls., 1988—. Author: Narcotics, Knowledge and Nonsense, 1977, Professional Education in Diabetes, 1983, Frontiers of Diabetes Research, 1990, Staged Diabetes Management, 1995; editor: Practical Diabetes, 1987-89; contbr. articles to profl. jours. Active Internat. Diabetes Fedn., European Assn. for Study of Diabetes; chmn. Am. Diabetes Assn. Named Disting. vis. Scientist CDC, 1983-84; Hoechst lectr. Australian Diabetes Soc., 1985, 87, Japanese Diabetes Assn., 1983, 88, 93, 94, Polish Diabetes Assn., 1993, 94, 95, 96; named Best Spkr. of Yr., Soc. for Clin. Chemistry, 1991, Minn. Med. Alley award for excellence in rsch. and devel., 1995; grantee NIH, 1977—, ADA, 1991—, Juvenile Diabetes Found., 1992—. Mem. Am. Diabetes Assn. (chmn.), Itnernat. Diabetes Fedn., European Assn. for Study Diabetes. Home: 5870 Boulder Bridge Ln Excelsior MN 55331-7969 Office: Internat Diabetes Ctr 3800 Park Nicollet Blvd Minneapolis MN 55416-2699

MAZZIA, VALENTINO DON BOSCO, physician, educator, lawyer; b. N.Y.C., Feb. 17, 1922; s. Alexander Lloret and Francesca M.; m. Rosana Sgarlata, Sept. 2, 1974; children: Lisa Mitchell, Donald Mitchell, Christopher Mitchell. B.S. cum laude, CCNY, 1943; M.D., NYU, 1950; postgrad., U. So. Calif. Sch. Law, 1973-74; J.D., U. Denver, 1978. Bar: Colo. 1978, U.S. Dist. Ct. Colo. 1978, Calif. 1979, U.S. Dist. Ct. (So. dist.) Calif. 1979, U.S. Supreme Ct. 1982, Ala. 1984, U.S. Dist. Ct. Ala. 1984, N.Y. 1987; diplomate: Am. Bd. Anesthesiology., Am. Bd. Law in Medicine. Intern Kings County Hosp., Bklyn., 1950-52; resident N.Y. Hosp., N.Y.C., 1952-54; asst. prof. Cornell U. Med. Coll., N.Y.C., 1952-61; prof. anesthesiology, chmn. dept. Coll. Medicine NYU, N.Y.C., 1961-72, prof. anesthesiology, chmn. dept. Postgrad. Med. Sch., 1961-72, prof. anesthesiology Coll. Dentistry, 1962-72; dir., attending anesthesiologist Univ. Hosp., N.Y.C., 1961-72; vis.-in-charge, dir. anesthesia service Bellevue Hosp. Center, N.Y.C., 1961-72; cons. N.Y. VA Hosp., Manhattan State Hosp., 1961-72; dir. anesthesiology Los Angeles County/Martin Luther King Jr. Gen. Hosp., 1971-73; chief anesthesiology Kern County Gen. Hosp., Bakersfield, Calif., 1973; practice medicine specializing in anesthesiology Bakersfield, Los Angeles; solo practice Las Vegas; staff 35 hosps., 1973-75; prof. anesthesiology U. Colo. Health Scis. Center and Dental Sch., Denver, 1976-83; clin. prof. U. Colo. Health Scis. Center and Dental Sch., 1984-88; clin. dir. operating room for anesthesiology Univ. Hosp., 1976-82; vis. prof., chmn. anesthesiology Charles R. Drew Post Grad. Med. Sch., Los Angeles, 1971-73; vis. prof. anesthesiology UCLA, 1972; asst. med. examiner, cons. forensic anesthesiology Office of Chief Med. Examiner, N.Y.C., 1962-73; dep. coroner, asst. med. examiner County Coroner's Office, Los Angeles, 1973-82; of counsel Cunningham Bounds Yance Crowder & Brown, Mobile, Ala. Co-author: Practical Anesthesiology, 1962—; contbr. chpts. to books, articles to profl. jours. Served with USAAF, 1943-45, to med. dir. USPHS Res., 1945-95. Fellow Am. Coll. Anesthesiology, N.Y. Acad. Medicine, Am. Coll. Chest Physicians, Am. Osteo. Coll. Anesthesiologists, Am. Coll. Legal Medicine; mem. Harvey Soc., Assn. Trial Lawyers Am., Ala. Trial Lawyers Assn., Phi Beta Kappa, Sigma Xi, Alpha Omega Alpha. Club: New York Athletic (life). Office: 120 E 87th St Apt P14D New York NY 10128-1101 Office: 1601 Dauphin St Mobile AL 36604 *When one's progress appears to be blocked by circumstances or people, change location or vocation. Persistence always wins.*

MAZZILLI, PAUL JOHN, investment banker; b. White Plains, N.Y., Dec. 4, 1948; s. Philip Joseph and Sara (Bialick) M.; m. Sharon Pickett, May 23, 1986; children: Meredith Paige, Nicholas Parker. BS in Indsl. Engring., Syracuse U., 1970; MBA, Columbia U., 1973. Lic. real estate agt., N.Y. Budget analyst The Pentagon, Washington, 1972; mgr. planning and analysis Xerox Corp., White Plains, 1973-75; mgr. planning and analysis Morgan Stanley & Co., Inc., N.Y.C., 1975-78, dir. planning and analysis, 1979-80, exec. asst. to oper. com., 1981-82, new product specialist, 1982-83, v.p. hedging products, 1984-85, prin. pension svcs. group, 1986-87, head stategy group for Employee Stock Ownership Plan, 1988-91, head of Equity Derivatives Corp. Svc. Group, 1992-93; prin. Equity Capital Markets Svcs., 1993—; pres. Wall St. Planning Group, N.Y.C., 1979-80; adj. prof. fin. Mercy Coll., Dobbs Ferry, N.Y., 1977-79; mem. tax rev. bd. Town of Greenburgh, N.Y., 1972-77. Coun. mem. Jr. Achievement N.Y., 1976-78; elected Westchester County Rep. Com., 1970-75. Capt. USAFR, 1970-76. Mem. Nat. Assn. Securities Dealers (registered rep.), Columbia U. Alumni Assn. (rep. 1979-80), Columbia Bus. Sch. Alumni Assn. (bd. dirs., v.p. 1978-81), Sleepy Hollow Country Club, Shattemuc Yacht Club (Ossining, N.Y.). Home:

Tower Hill Rd Scarborough NY 10510 Office: Morgan Stanley & Co Inc 1251 Ave Of The Americas New York NY 10020-1104

MAZZO, KAY, ballet dancer, educator; b. Evanston, Ill., Jan. 17, 1946; d. Frank Alfred and Catherine M. (Hengel) M.; m. Albert C. Bellas, 1978; children: Andrew, Kathryn. Student, Sch. Am. Ballet, 1959-61. Profl. debut in ballets U.S.A. 1961, touring Europe with co., performing for Pres. Kennedy at White House, 1961, joined N.Y.C. Ballet, 1962-80, soloist, 1965-69, prin. ballerina, 1969-80, prin. roles in world premiere of ballets including Tschaikowsky Suite No. #3, 1970, PAMTGG, 1971, Stravinsky Violin Concerto, 1972, Scherzo A La Russe, 1972, Duo Concertant, 1972, Sheherazade, 1975, Union Jack, 1976, Vienna Waltzes, 1977, Davidsbundlertanze, 1980; ballet tchr. Sch. Am. Ballet, 1980—; appeared as guest artist in leading roles with numerous cos. including Boston Ballet, Washington Ballet, Berlin Ballet, Geneva Ballet; appeared on TV in U.S., Can., Fed. Republic Germany. Recipient Mademoiselle Merit award 1970. Office: Sch Am Ballet 70 Lincoln Center Plz New York NY 10023-6548

MAZZOCCO, ANGELO, language educator; b. Cerreto di Vastogirardi, Isernia, Italy, May 13, 1936; came to U.S., 1954, naturalized, 1957; s. Giuseppe and Ida (Rotolo) M.; m. Elizabeth Hunt Davis, Oct. 7, 1990; children: Michael Ray, Marco Angelo. BS, BA, Ohio State U., 1959, MA, 1963; PhD in Romance Langs. and Lits., U. Calif., Berkeley, 1973. Instr. Spanish John Carroll U., Cleve., 1962-65; teaching asst. Italian U. Calif., Berkeley, 1966-69; asst. prof. Italian No. Ill. U., DeKalb, 1970-75; asst. prof. Spanish and Italian Mt. Holyoke Coll., South Hadley, Mass., 1975-78, assoc. prof., 1978-83, prof., 1983—, chair dept., 1981-84, 93—; chair romance langs. and lits., 1989-93; assoc. Columbia U. Renaissance Seminar. Author: Linguistic Theories in Dante/Humanists, 1993; contbr. chpts. in books and articles to profl. jours. Travel grantee Am. Coun. Learned Socs., 1985, Gladys Krieble Delmas Found. Rsch. grantee, 1993-94; Italian-Am. traveling fellow U. Calif., 1969-70, NEH Italian Humanism summer sem. fellow, 1981, NEH/NSF award, 1995-98. Mem. MLA (N.E. chpt., exec. com. Medieval and Renaissance Italian Lit. 1981-85, assembly del. a985-87), Am. Assn. Tchrs. Italian, Dante Soc. Am. (coun. assoc. 1985-90, coun. 1994—), Medieval Acad. Renaissance Soc. Am., Internat. Assn. Neo-Latin Studies, Internat. Assn. History Lang. Soc., Assn. Internat. Sudi di Lingua e Letteratura Italiana, Internat. Soc. Classical Tradition, Am. Boccaccio Assn. (v.p. 1982-83), Am. Assn. Italian Studies, Nat. Assn. Scholars. Office: Mt Holyoke Coll Dept Spanish Italian South Hadley MA 01075

MAZZOCCO, GAIL O'SULLIVAN, nursing educator; b. Bklyn., Aug. 5, 1942; d. John F. and Marie A. (Saleski) O'S.; m. Victor E. Mazzocco, Jan. 5, 1973; children: Victor, Diane, Denise, Michelle, Mark. Diploma, Mass. Gen. Hosp., 1963; BSN, U. Md., 1972, MS, 1974, EdD, 1988. Staff nurse Meml. Hosp., Cumberland, Md., 1964-67; area supr. Meml. Hosp., Cumberland, 1967-69; clin. specialist Sacred Heart Hosp., Cumberland, 1974-75; asst. prof. U. Md. Sch. Nursing, 1977—, acting chair RN to BSN program/acting dir. statewide program, 1994-95; coord. We. Md. Outreach Sites, 1995—; bd. dirs., pres. Allegany Cmty. Coll. Found. Contbr. chpt. to book. Mem. Md. Nurses Assn. (Dist. 1 Nurse of Yr. 1986, Nurse Educator of Yr. 1991), Nat. League for Nursing, Sigma Theta Tau, Phi Kappa Pi (Faculty Mentor award 1994). Home: 9 Warfield Pl Cumberland MD 21502-7433

MAZZOLA, ANTHONY THOMAS, editor, art consultant, designer; b. Passaic, N.J., June 13, 1923; s. Thomas and Jennie (Failla) M.; m. Michele Morgan, Nov. 18, 1967; children: Anthony Thomas II, Marc Eden, Alisa Morgan. Grad., Cooper Union Art Sch., N.Y.C., 1948. Art dir. Street & Smith Publs., N.Y.C., 1948, Town and Country mag. (pub. by Hearst Corp.), N.Y.C., 1948-65; editor-in-chief Town and Country mag. (pub. by Hearst Corp.), 1965-72, Harpers Bazaar, 1972-92; pres. Anthony Mazzola Design Corp., N.Y.C., 1963—; creative cons. Hearst Mags., 1992—; editorial dir. 125 Great Moments of Harper's Bazaar, 1991-94, Town & Country 150th Anniversary, 1994—; cons. designer United Nations Childrens' Fund, Assn. Jr. Leagues Am., Columbia Pictures Corp., Sells Spltys., Gen. Foods, Paramount Pictures, Princess Marcella Borghese, Inc., Huntington Hartford, Ltd., N.Y. World's Fair, 1965. Exhibited, Art Dirs. Club. N.Y., ann. exhbns., 1948—. Served with AUS, 1943-46. Decorated Bronze Star, Knight Officer of Order of Merit Italy; recipient Cert. of Merit awards N.Y. Art Dirs. Club; medal Art Dirs. Club N.Y.C., 1955. Office: Town & Country 150th Anniversary 1790 Broadway New York NY 10019-1412

MAZZOLA, JOHN WILLIAM, former performing arts center executive, consultant; b. Bayonne, N.J., Jan. 20, 1928; s. Roy Stephen and Eleanor Burnett (Davis) M.; m. Sylvia Drulie, Mar. 7, 1959; children: Alison, Amy. AB, Tufts U., 1949; LLD, Fordham U., 1952. Bar: N.Y. 1956. Mem. firm Milbank, Tweed, Hadley & McCloy, N.Y.C., 1952-64; sec., exec. v.p. Lincoln Center for Performing Arts, N.Y.C., 1964-68; gen. mgr., chief exec. officer Lincoln Center for Performing Arts, 1969-70, mng. dir., chief exec. officer, 1970-77, pres., chief exec. officer, 1977-84; cons. performing arts ctrs. in U.S. and abroad, also motion pictures, non-profit orgns. Bd. dirs. various charitable orgns.; mem. adv. bd. U. S.C. Koger Arts Ctr. With CIC, U.S. Army, 1953-55. Decorated cavaliere ufficiale Ordine al Merito della Repubblica Italiana; Ordre des Arts et des Lettres France; Benjamin Franklin fellow Royal Soc. Arts. Mem. Watch Hill Yacht Club, Misquamicut Club (R.I.). Episcopalian. Home: 12 Beekman Pl New York NY 10022-8059

MAZZONE, A. DAVID, federal judge; b. Everett, Mass., June 3, 1928; s. A. Marino and Philomena M.; m. Eleanor G. Stewart, May 10, 1951; children: Margaret Clark, Andrew David, John Stewart, Jan Eleanor, Martha Ann, Robert Joseph, Carolyn Cook. B.A., Harvard U., 1950; J.D., DePaul U., 1957. Bar: Ill. 1957, Mass. 1959, U.S. Supreme Ct. 1964. Asst. dist. atty. Middlesex County, Mass., 1961; asst. U.S. atty. Mass., 1961-65; partner firm Moulton, Looney & Mazzone, Boston, 1965-75; asso. justice Superior Ct., Boston, 1975-78; U.S. dist. judge, now sr. judge Boston, 1978—. Served with U.S. Army, 1951-52. Mem. ABA, Mass. Trial Lawyers Assn., Am. Law Inst., Mass. Bar Assn., Boston Bar Assn., Middlesex Bar Assn., Fed. Bar Assn. Democrat. Roman Catholic. Office: US Dist Ct 2001 US Courthouse Boston MA 02109*

MAZZOTTA, GIUSEPPE FRANCESCO, Italian language and literature educator; b. Curinga, Calabria, Italy, Jan. 1, 1942; s. Pasquale and Rosa (Anania) M.; m. Carol Carlson, Mar. 2, 1972; children: Rosanna, Antony, Paula. BA, U. Toronto, Can., 1965, MA, 1966; PhD, Cornell U., 1969. Asst. prof. dept. romance studies Cornell U., Ithaca, N.Y., 1969-70, assoc. prof. dept. romance studies, 1973-78, prof. romance langs., 1978-83; asst. prof. dept. romance studies Yale U., New Haven, 1970-72, prof. Italian lang. and lit., 1983—; assoc. prof. Medieval Inst. U. Toronto, 1972-73. Author: Dante, Poet of the Desert: History and Allegory in the Divine Comedy, 1979, 2d edit., 1987, The World of Play: A Study of Boccaccio's Decameron, 1986, Dante's Vision and the Circle of Knowledge, 1993, The Worlds of Petrarch, 1993; mem. editl. bd. Yale Italian Studies, Dante Studies, Yale Jour. Criticism, Yale Jour. Law and Humanities. NEH fellow Cornell U., 1977, Guggenheim Found. fellow Yale U., 1986-87. Fellow Am. Coun. Learned Soc., Soc. for the Humanities; mem. Dante Soc. Am. (assoc.). Roman Catholic. Avocations: basketball. Home: 152 Waite St Hamden CT 06517-2526 Office: Yale U 82-90 Wall St Fl 4 New Haven CT 06520

MCABEER, SARA CARITA, school administrator; b. Logan, Utah, Aug. 19, 1906; d. Edward Thomas and Carrie Estelle (Martin) Harris; m. Frederick Alexander McAbeer, Dec. 24, 1929 (div. 1971); 1 child, Winifred. BA, Iowa State Tchr., Cedar Falls, 1929; postgrad., Sacramento (Calif.) Coll., 1956. Cert. high sch. adminstr. Clk., bookkeeper Curtis Jewelry, Kemmerer, Wyo., 1923-24; tchr. Miles High Sch., Miles, Iowa, 1929-30, Salinas (Calif.) High Sch., 1930-32; sec. supervised teaching U. Calif., Berkeley., 1934-41; tchr. Vallejo (Calif.) Jr. High Sch., 1947-50, Napa (Calif.) Jr. High Sch., 1950-52; dean of girls Napa High Sch., 1952-72. Active mem. Napa County Dem. Party, 1950-52, St. Thomas Altar Guild, Napa, 1973—, Cmty. Projects, Inc., Napa, 1966-67, 77-94; mem., vol. tchr., bd. dirs. North Bay Suicide Prevention, Inc., Napa, 1972-91; leader Vallejo Girl Scouts, 1947-49; tchr. St. John's Cath. Ch., Napa, 1960-62. Recipient Vol. of Yr. North Bay Suicide Prevention Napa, 1986, Finalist continuing Svc. Vol. Ctr. Napa, 1988; Top Ten Ia. State Tchr. Cedar Falls scholar, 1929. Mem. AAUW, Delta Kappa Gamma. Democrat. Roman Catholic. Avocations: needlepointing, bridge, dancing.

MCADAM, PAUL EDWARD, library administrator; b. Balt., Jan. 30, 1934; s. Joseph Francis Jr. and Irene Cecile (Heineck) McA. BA in Romance Langs., Johns Hopkins U., 1955, MA, 1956; MLS, Drexel U., 1970. Libr. Free Libr. Phila., 1969-81; br. mgr. Phila. City. Inst. Libr., 1974-81; dir. Am. Libr., Paris, France, 1981-85; libr. collection devel., libr. tech. svcs. Catonsville (Md.) C.C., 1986-89; assoc. v.p. learning resources Carroll C.C., Westminster, Md., 1989—; mem. adv. bd. Coop. Librs. Ctrl. Md., Annapolis, 1992-96, State Libr. Resource Ctr., Balt., 1994-95, Renew, 1995—; del. Internat. Fedn. Libr. Assns., 1993, 95. Vol. MPT, Walters Art Gallery, Md. Fine Arts Festival. 1st lt. U.S. Army, 1956-58. Mem. ALA (mem. membership com. 1996—), Coll. Air Consortium, Congress Resource Dirs., Md. Libr. Assn. (membership chair 1993-96, awards chair 1996—), Consortium Md. C.C. Libr. Dirs. (treas. 1993—), Beta Phi Mu (Sigma chpt.). Democrat. Home: 524 Academy Rd Baltimore MD 21228-1814 Office: Carroll Cmty Coll 1601 Washington Rd Westminster MD 21157-6944

MCADAM, THOMAS ANTHONY, III, lawyer; b. Louisville, July 17, 1943; s. Thomas A. and Rita (Bowman) M.; m. Margaret Ann Logsdon, June 21, 1969; 1 child, Thomas A. IV. AB in Philosophy, Bellarmine Coll., 1966; JD, U. Louisville, 1976. Bar: Ky. 1976, U.S. Dist. Ct. (we. dist.) Ky. 1976, U.S. Ct. Appeals (6th cir.) 1978, U.S. Supreme Ct. 1984. Pvt. practice Louisville, 1976—; counsel Louisville Police Dept., 1983-91, Louisville and Jefferson County Human Rels. Com., 1991; spl. counsel Louisville Bd. Aldermen, 1993—. Bd. dirs. State Libr. Adv. Coun., Frankfort, Ky., 1991-95, Jefferson County Law Libr., Louisville, 1989—, Louisville Legal Aid Soc., 1983-91. Sgt. U.S. Army, 1968-70. Named Outstanding Vol. Lawyer Louisville Legal Aid Soc., 1990. Mem. Ky. Acad. Justice (pres. 1985). Democrat. Roman Catholic. Home: 3031 Wickland Rd Louisville KY 40205 Office: 235 S 5th St Louisville KY 40202

MCADAM, WILL, electronics consultant; b. Wheeling, W.Va., Oct. 22, 1921; s. Will and Elizabeth Margaret (Wickham) McA.; m. Evelyn Virginia Warren, Sept. 22, 1945; children: Elizabeth Ruth, Margaret Evelyn. BSEE, Case Inst. Tech., 1942; MSEE, U. Pa., 1959. Registered control engr., Calif. Rsch. technologist Leeds & Northrup Co., Phila., 1945-57; head elec. sect. R&D dept. Leeds & Northrup Co., North Wales, Pa., 1957-68, assoc. dir. rsch. ops., 1968-75, mgr. devel. and engring. adv. devel., 1977-79, prin. scientist rsch. dept., 1979-82, ret., 1982; cons. in electronics, 1982—. Contbr. articles to profl. jours., chpts. to handbooks; 30 patents in field. 1st lt. AUS, 1942-45, ETO. Decorated Bronze Star. Fellow IEEE (life; chmn. subcom. on elec. and high frequency measurements 1957-59, com. indsl. electronic and control instruments 1961-65, Prize Paper award 1958), Eta Kappa Nu, Tau Beta Pi. Republican. Presbyterian. Avocations: amateur radio, woodworking/cabinetmaking, hiking, bicycling. Home: PO Box 470 Worcester PA 19490-0470

MCADAMS, CHARLES ALAN, music educator; b. Memphis, June 3, 1958; s. Ernest Clinton and Jimmie Dee (Watson) McA.; m. Rebecca Carol Taylor, Aug. 9, 1980; children: James Alan, Kathryn Lynne. BS in Music Edn., Tenn. Technol. U., Cookeville, 1980; MS, U. Ill., 1981, EdD, 1988. Cert. tchr. K-12 instrumental music, Mo., Tenn. Dir. bands York Inst. H.S., Jamestown, Tenn., 1981-82, South Side H.S., Jackson, Tenn., 1982-83; assoc. prof. music (tuba/euphonium) Ctrl. Mo. State U., Warrensburg, 1983—; freelance music contest adjudicator, 1983—; curriculum cons. to various pub. schs.; presenter in field. Asst. editor/author: (reference) The Tuba Source Book, 1995; active recitalist in solo recitals and as soloist with bands througout the Midwest; contbr. articles to profl. jours. Mem. Tubists Universal Brotherhood Assn. (regional chpt. coord. 1988-93, pub. rels. coord. 1994-95), Mo. Soc. for Music Tchr. Edn. (state chair 1994), Music Educators Nat. Conf., Pi Kappa Lambda, Phi Kappa Phi. Home: 305 Birch St Warrensburg MO 64093-1988 Office: Ctrl Mo State U Dept Music Warrensburg MO 64093

MCADAMS, HERBERT HALL, II, banker; b. Jonesboro, Ark., June 6, 1915; s. Herbert Hall I and Stella (Patrick) McA.; children by previous marriage: Judith (Mrs. Walter A. DeRoeck), Sandra (Mrs. Robert C. Connor), Herbert Hall III, Penny (Mrs. Tim Hodges); m. Shelia Wallace, Nov. 27, 1970; 1 child, Nicole Patrick. BS, Northwestern U., Evanston, Ill., 1937; postgrad., Harvard U., 1937-38, Loyola U., Chgo., 1938-39; JD with honors, U. Ark., 1940; LLD (hon.), Ark. State U., 1984. Bar: Ark. 1940, U.S. Dist. Ct. Ark., U.S. Supreme Ct. 1944, U.S. Ct. Appeals (8th cir.) 1944, U.S. Ct. Claims 1944,. Chmn. bd., CEO Citizens Bank and Citizens Bancshares Corp., Jonesboro, 1958-95; chmn. bd. emeritus, chief exec. officer Union Nat. Bank, Little Rock, 1970-93, Union Ark. Corp., 1980-93; bd. dirs. Worthen Bank Corp., 1993-95; McAdams-Frierson chair bank mgmt. Ark. State U., 1987; bd. dirs. 1st Ark. Devel. Fin. Corp., Systematics, Inc. Pres. Jonesboro Sch. Dist., 1948-50, Bapt. Med. Ctr. Sys. Real Estate Corp., 1977—; state chmn. Citizen's Com. on Edn., 1950; mem. Ark. Indsl. Devel. Commn., 1965-73, chmn., 1967-72; trustee Ark. Children's Hosp., 1972-75, Bapt. Med. Ctr. Sys., 1975-77, Bapt. Found., 1975; bd. govs. Ark. State Fair and Livestock Show Assn., 1976; mem. Bapt. Med. Ctr. Sys. Corp., Fifty for Future; founder, chmn. bd. govs. Ark. State U. Found.; bd. dirs. Nat. Children's Eye Care Found., 1987—, numerous others. Decorated Purple Heart; recipient Rector Meml. award 50 for the Future, 1973-81; named outstanding alumnus U. Ark., 1984. Mem. ABA (uniform law coms. 1961-66, mem. tax sect. 1954—), Ark. Bar Assn., Ark. Coun. Econ. Edn., Craighead (Ark.) County Bar Assn. (past pres.), Pulaski (Ark.) County Bar Assn., Greater Little Rock C.of C. (dir.), Sales and Mktg. Execs. (top mgmt. honoree 1972), Sigma Nu. Methodist. Clubs: Country of Little Rock, Capital, Little Rock. Lodge: Rotary. Home: 47 Edgehill Rd Little Rock AR 72207-5461 Office: Union Nat Bldg 124 W Capitol Ave Ste 1700 Little Rock AR 72201-3737

MCADAMS, JAMES G. (), federal official. BA in Psychology, Davidson Coll., 1970; JD cum laude, U. Miami, 1981. Asst. U.S. atty. U.S. Attys. Office (so. dist.) Fla., Miami, 1982-88, chief narcotivs divsn., 1989-92, acting U.S. atty., 1992, mng. asst. U.S. atty., 1992-94; sr. litigation counsel U.S. Attys. Office (so. dist.) Fla., 1994-95; counsel for intelligence policy Dept. Justice, Washington, 1995—. Office: US Dept Justice Office Intelligence Policy 10th & Pennsylvania Ave NW Washington DC 20530

MCADAMS, JOHN P., lawyer; b. Phila., June 5, 1949; s. Eugene P. and Mary (Miller) McA.; m. Anne Christina Connelly, Sept. 5, 1970; children: Emily Lane, Anne Connelly. BA, U. N.C., 1971; JD, Wake Forest U., 1976. Bar: Fla. 1976, N.C. 1976, U.S. Dist. Ct. (mid. dist.) Fla. 1977. Assoc. Carlton, Fields, Ward, Emmanuel, Smith & Cutler, Tampa, Fla., 1976-82, ptnr., 1982—. Contbg. editor: The Developing Labor Law, 1983, Employee Duty of Loyalty, 1995; contbr. articles to profl. jours. Pres. Hillsborough Community Mental Health Ctr., Tampa, 1983; trustee City of Temple Ter. (Fla.) Pension Plan, 1985-89; pres. Hyde Park Preservation, Inc., Tampa, 1993. Mem. ABA, ABA Equal Rights & Responsibilities Com., Fla. Bar Assn. (exec. coun. labor sect. 1987-89). Republican. Episcopalian. Home: 820 S Delaware Ave Tampa FL 33606-2915 Office: Carlton Fields PO Box 3239 Tampa FL 33601-3239

MCADAMS, ROBERT, JR., electronics executive; b. San Francisco, July 10, 1939; s. Robert Sr. and Emily Dolores (Ragozzino) McA.; m. Frances Rose Heinrich, June 24, 1961; children: Michael, Kevin, Timothy, Darin. BS in Indsl. Mgmt., San Jose State U., 1963. Various fin. positions Ampex Corp., Redwood City, Calif., 1960-71, asst. corp. controller, 1971-74, v.p., controller, 1974-80, v.p. fin., 1980-83; sr. v.p. fin. and adminstrn. Measurex Corp., Cupertino, Calif., 1983-93, sr. v.p. oper. and info. svcs., 1993-94, exec. v.p., CFO, 1995—. Mem. Fin. Execs. Inst. (bd. dirs. 1978-81), Am. Electronics Assn. (chmn. acctg. and fin. com. 1986-91). Avocations: golf, coaching soccer. Office: Measurex Corp One Results Way Cupertino CA 95014

MCAFEE, JOHN GILMOUR, nuclear medicine physician; b. Toronto, Ontario, Can., June 11, 1926; came to U.S., 1952; s. Robert Duncan and Susan Jane (Damery) McA.; m. Joan Weber, Feb. 11, 1952 (dec. 1978); children: Paul Clifton, Carol Joan, David Robert. MD, U. Toronto, 1948. Rotating intern Victoria Hosp., London, Ont., Can., 1948-49; resident in radiology Victoria Hosp., London, Ont., 1950-51; resident in internal medicine Westminster Hosp., London, 1949-50; resident in radiology Johns Hopkins Hosp., Balt., 1951-52, fellow, 1952-53; instr. radiology Johns Hopkins Sch. Medicine, Balt., 1953-55, asst. prof. radiology, 1955-58, assoc. prof. radiology, 1958-65; prof., chmn. radiology SUNY Health Sci. Ctr., Syracuse, 1965-73, dir. div. nuclear medicine, 1973-78, dir. div. radiological scis., 1978-90; prof. div. nuclear medicine George Washington U. Med. Ctr., Washington, 1990-92; sect. chief, dept. nuclear medicine Clin. Ctr., NIH, Bethesda, Md., 1992-95; cons. in nuclear medicine, 1995—; chmn. radiology tng. com. NIH, Bethesda, Md., 1970-73; bd. dirs. Am. Bd. Nuclear Medicine, L.A., 1973-80; cons. editl. bd. Jour. Nuclear Medicine, N.Y.C., 1975—; chmn. subcom. nuclear medicine DOE, Gaithersburg, Md., 1987-88; trustee Rsch. and Edn. Fund, 1990-96; mem. radiopharms. adv. bd. U.S. Pharmacopeial Conv., 1990-95. Author, editor: (with others) Differential Diagnosis in Nuclear Medicine, 1984; assoc. editor: Year Book of Nuclear Medicine, 1993-95; contbr. articles to profl. jours. NIH grantee, 1961-92. Fellow Royal Coll. Physicians, Am. Coll. Nuclear Physicians; mem. Soc. Nuclear Medicine (Paul C. Aebersold award 1979, Georg Charles De Hevesy Nuclear Medicine Pioneer award 1989), Radiol. Soc. N.Am., Am. Roentgen Ray Soc., Assn. Univ. Radiologists. Avocations: sailing, jazz, organ, yachting, swimming. Home: 3203 Winnett Rd Bethesda MD 20815-3201

MC AFEE, MARILYN, ambassador; b. Portsmouth, N.H., Jan. 23, 1940; m. Joel William Febel. BA in History with honors, U. Pa., 1961; MA, Johns Hopkins U., 1962. Joined Fgn. Svc., Washington, 1968; served with U.S. Embassy, Guatemala, 1969-70, Nicaragua, 1970-72, Iran, 1972-77; served with Fgn. Svc., Dept. State, Washington, 1977-80; served with U.S. Embassy, Costa Rica, 1980-83, Venezuela, 1983-86, Chile, 1986-89; dep. chief of mission U.S. Embassy, Bolivia, 1989-92; amb. U.S. Embassy, Guatemala City, Guatemala, 1993-96; career min., 1996—. Ford Found. fellow; recipient 4 Meritorious Honor awards, 1 Superior Honor award, 1 Presdl. Meritorious Svc. award. Mem. Army Navy Country Club, Marsh Landing Country CLub. Office: Am Embassy Guatamala APO AA 34024-5000

MC AFEE, WILLIAM, government official; b. Port Royal, Jan. 25, 1910; s. French and Willietta (Anderson) McA. B.A., Coll. of Wooster, 1932; M.A. in Am. History, Pa. State U., 1941; student, Oxford, Eng., summer 1937. Wooster in India rep. on faculty Ewing Christian Coll., Allahabad, India, 1932-35; tchr. pub. high schs. and prep. sch. Pa., 1935-42; joined State Dept., 1946; country specialist (Office Chinese Affairs), 1946-50; coordinator current intelligence (Bur. Intelligence and Research), 1950-56, spl. asst. to dir., 1956-60, dir. ops. staff, 1960-66, asst. dep. dir. coordination, 1966-72, dep. dir. coordination, 1972-80, dep. asst. sec. intelligence coordination, 1980—; dir. (Office of Intelligence Liaison), 1981-86, ret.; adviser Griffin Econ. Aid Mission to S.E. Asia, 1950. Served to lt. col. AUS, 1942-46, CBI. Decorated Legion of Merit; Order Brit. Empire; Precious Tripod Chinese Nationalist Govt.; recipient Superior Honor award State Dept., 1964, Disting. Honor award, 1980. Mem. Am. Fgn. Service Assn., Delta Sigma Rho. Home: 4433 Brandywine St NW Washington DC 20016-4419

MCAHREN, ROBERT WILLARD, history educator; b. Sioux City, Iowa, Dec. 3, 1935; s. Willard Calvin and Winifred Mae (Small) McA. B.A., So. Meth. U., 1958; Ph.D., U. Tex.-Austin, 1967. Instr. history Washington & Lee U., Lexington, Va., 1966-67, asst. prof. history, 1967-70, assoc. prof. history, 1970-75, prof. history, 1975—, asst. dean coll., 1971-73, assoc. dean coll., 1973-77, head dept. history, 1988—. Editor (with David D. Van Tassel) document collection with interpretive introduction; European Origins of American Thought, 1969. Mem. Phi Beta Kappa. Democrat. Avocations: orchid growing; model railroading. Office: Washington and Lee U Dept Of History Lexington VA 24450

MC ALEECE, DONALD JOHN, mechanical engineering educator; b. Detroit, May 26, 1918; s. Joseph Patrick and Kathryn (DeLeeuw) McA.; m. Margaret Ann Mull, Nov. 25, 1954; children: Stephen, Donald, Michele Denise. Diploma, machinist-toolmaker apprentice program, Gen. Electric Co., 1940; BS, Purdue U., 1952; MA, Ball State U., 1968; postgrad., U. S.C., 1990, 91. With Gen. Electric Co., Fort Wayne, Ind., 1936-66; mem. faculty Purdue U., Ft. Wayne campus, 1966-88, prof. mech. engring. tech., 1966-88, prof. emeritus, 1988—; tchr. Ind. U.-Purdue U., Fort Wayne, Ind. Vocation Tech. Coll., Fort Wayne, fall 1988; vis. prof. U. Ark., Little Rock, 1989, Trident Tech. Coll., Charleston, S.C., 1989—; assisted devel. job tng. program and minority intro. to engring. and tech. ind. U.-Purdue U., Ft. Wayne, summer 1986, 87; design engr., advanced safety rsch. Ford Motor Co., Dearborn, Mich., 1972; Job placement cons. Outreach office Nat. Alliance Businessmen, Fort Wayne, 1968; indsl. engr. cons. Am. Hoist & Derric Co., Ft. Wayne, 1969; cons. Franklin Electric Co., 1970, Wayne Home Equipment divsn. Scott & Fetzer, 1979; intern Harvester Co., 1977; engring. cons. Dana Corp., Ft. Wayne, 1984; mem. Tech. Accreditation Commn., Accreditation Bd. Engring. and Tech., 1980-82, program evaluator, 1988; statis. process control cons. Gen. Motors Corp., Ft. Wayne, 1986. Mem. editorial cons. bd. Indsl. Press, Inc., 1982-84. Scout master, com. Boy Scouts Am. With AUS, 1946-47. Ednl. Profl. Devel. Act grantee, 1971; Soc. Mfg. Engrs. grantee, 1982; named Eagle Scout Boy Scouts Am. Mem. Am. Soc. Engring. Edn., Am. Tech. Edn. Assn., Soc. Auto Engrs., Inc. (faculty advisor student br. Trident Coll. 1991-95, elec. vehicle com. 1980-95, svc. award 1982, Ralph R. Teetor award 1972, outstanding faculty adv. svc. award 1974), Soc. Am. Mil. Engrs., ASME (life, chmn. program com. 1971-75), ASHRAE (nat. engring. coun. prof. devel. accreditation team), S.C. Tech. Edn. Assn. Robotics Internat. of Soc. Mfg. Engrs. (life cert.), GE Co. Quarter Century Club (Ft. Wayne), GE Apprentice Alumni Assn., Eagle Scout Assn. (scoutmaster, com. BSA 1968-72), Pi Tau Sigma. Baptist (deacon 1968-72). Lodges: Masons, Shriners. Home: Apt 8B 7930 Saint Ives Rd North Charleston SC 29418

MCALEER, JOHN JOSEPH, English literature educator; b. Cambridge, Mass., Aug. 29, 1923; s. Stephen Ambrose and Helen Louise (Collins) McA.; m. Ruth Ann Delaney, Dec. 28, 1957; children: Mary Alycia, Saragh Delaney, Seana Caithlin, John Joseph, Paul Bernard, Andrew Stephen. AB, Boston Coll., 1947, MA, 1949; PhD, Harvard U., 1955. Teaching fellow Boston Coll., 1947-48, English and Latin instr., 1948-50; Dexter fellow in Europe Harvard U., 1952, teaching fellow gen. edn., 1953-55; from asst. prof. to prof. Boston Coll., 1955—; vis. fellow Durham (Eng.) U., 1988-89. Author: Ballads and Songs Loyal to the Hanoverian Succession, 1962, Theodore Dreiser: A Biography, 1968, Artist and Citizen Thoreau, 1971, (with M. Tjader) Notes on Life: The Philosophical Writings of Theodore Dreiser, 1974, Rex Stout: A Biography, 1977, Justice Ends at Home: The Early Crime Fiction of Rex Stout, 1977, (with others) Rex Stout: An Annotated Primary and Secondary Bibliography, 1980, (with Billy Dickson) Unit Pride, 1981, Royal Decree: Conservations with Rex Stout, 1983, Ralph Waldo Emerson: Days of Encounter, 1984, Queens Counsel: Conversations with Ruth Stout, 1986, Coign of Vantage, 1988; editor-in-chief: Rex Stout Jour., 1979—, Thorndyke File, 1981-95, Best Sellers, 1965-85, Shakespeare newsletter, 1959-71, Armchair Detective, 1978-82; cons. editor: Dreiser Studies, 1971—. Mem. adv. bd. Walden Woods Project, 1990—, Parents Choice, 1980—. Sgt. U.S. Army, 1942-46. Recipient Cath. Press Assn. award, 1969, New Eng. Hist. Soc. award, 1985, Humanities award Boston Coll. Alumni Assn., 1991, Ignatian medal Boston Coll., 1995. Mem. Thoreau Soc. (pres., dir. 1971—), Mystery Writers Am. (v.p., dir. 1979-89, Edgar Allan Poe award 1978), R. Austen Freeman Soc. (pres. 1981—), Edith Wharton Soc., Jane Austen Soc. (Burke award 1991), Internat. Dreiser Soc. (founding mem. 1991—), Boston Authors Club (pres., dir. 1982-95), Tavern Club (Boston), Baker St. Irregulars. Democrat. Roman Catholic. Avocations: swimming, bibliopoly, genealogy, philately, gardening. Home: 121 Follen Rd Lexington MA 02173-5942 Office: Boston Coll Dept English McGuinn 530 Chestnut Hill MA 02167

MCALEER, WILLIAM HARRISON, software company executive; b. Pitts., Feb. 14, 1951; s. William Kearns and Helen (Harrison) McA.; m. Colleen McGinn, Aug. 9, 1975; children: William F., Lindsay J. BS, Cornell U., 1973, MBA, 1975. CPA, Wash. Sr. acct. KPMG-Peat Marwick, Seattle, 1975-78; v.p., controller Westin Hotels, Seattle, 1978-87; v.p. finance, CFO Ecova Corp., Seattle, 1987-88; v.p. fin., CFO, sec. Aldus Corp., Seattle, 1988-95; pres. E. Liance Ptnrs., Seattle, 1995—; bd. dirs. Truevision Corp., Four Gen Corp., Primus Comm. Corp. Pres., dir. Seattle Jr. C. of C., 1977-82; bd. dirs. Big Bros. King County, Seattle, 1994—. Mem. Fin. Execs. Ins., Software Pubs. Assn., Wash. Software Assn., Wash. Soc. CPAs, Cornell Alumni Club, Sand Point Country Club. Avocations: hiking, travel, golfing, boating, gardening. Home: 3530 W Laurelhurst Dr NE Seattle WA 98105-5358 Office: E Liance Ptnrs 1001 4th Ave Ste 3200 Seattle WA 98154

MCALESTER, ARCIE LEE, JR., geologist, educator; b. Dallas, Feb. 3, 1933; s. Arcie Lee and Alverta (Funderburk) McA.; m. Virginia Wallace Savage; children: Kirstie Martine, Archibald Keven. B.A., B.B.A., So. Methodist U., 1954; M.S., Yale U., 1957, Ph.D., 1960. Mem. faculty Yale U., 1959-74, prof. geology, 1966-74; curator invertebrate paleontology Peabody Mus., 1966-74; prof. geol. scis. So. Meth. U., Dallas, 1974—; dean Sch. Humanities and Scis. So. Meth. U., 1974-77. Author: The Earth, 1973, The History of Life, 1977, History of the Earth, 1980, Physical Geology, 1984, History of the Earth's Crust, 1984, (with V.S. McAlester) A Field Guide to American Houses, 1984, Discover Travel Guides, 1988—, Great American Houses, 1994; assoc. editor Am. Scientist, 1970-74; also articles. Served to 1st lt. USAF, 1954-56. Guggenheim fellow Glasgow U., Scotland, 1965. Office: So Meth U Dept Geol Scis Dallas TX 75275

MCALHANY, TONI ANNE, lawyer; b. Decatur, Ind., May 1, 1951; d. Robert Keith and Evelyn L. (Fisher) McA. BA, Ind. U., 1973; JD, Valparaiso U., 1976. Bar: Mich. 1976, Ind. 1982, Ill. 1986, U.S. Dist. Ct. (no. dist.) Ind. 1989. Asst. prosecutor Ottawa County Prosecutor's Office, Grand Haven, Mich., 1976-81; assoc. Hann, Doss & Persinger, Holland, Mich., 1981-82, Romero & Thonert, Auburn, Ind., 1982-85; ptnr. Dahlgren & McAlhany, Berwyn, Ill., 1985-88, Colbeck, McAlhany & Stewart, Angola, Ind. & Coldwater, Mich., 1988—; atty. Angola (Ind.) Housing Authority, 1989—. Bd. dirs. Child and Family Svcs., Ft. Wayne, Ind., 1983, Fillmore Ctr., Berwyn, 1986-88, Altrusa, Coldwater, 1989-92. Mem. ATLA, State Bar Mich., State Bar Ind., State Bar Ill., Branch County Bar Assn., Steuben County Bar Assn. Avocations: traveling, horseback riding. Office: McAlhany & Stewart 215 W Maumee Angola IN 46703

MC ALISTER, LINDA LOPEZ, educator, philosopher; b. Long Beach, Calif., Oct. 10, 1939; d. Manuel Lee and Elena Maria (Sherwood) McAlister; AB, Barnard Coll., 1962; postgrad. Coll. City N.Y., 1963-64; PhD, Cornell U., 1969. Mem. faculty, adminstr. Bklyn. Coll., 1968-77, CUNY. Grad. Center, 1970-77; prof. humanities, dean campus Imperial Valley campus San Diego State U., 1977-82; prof. philosophy, campus dean U. South Fla., Ft. Myers, 1982-85; spl. asst. to vice chancellor for acad. programs State Univ. System Fla., 1985-87; prof. Women's Studies and Philosophy U. South Fla., Tampa, 1987—, chair women's studies, 1996—; Fla. state coordinator Am. Council Edn. Nat. Identification Project, 1983-86. Franz Brentano Found. grantee, 1968-72; Fulbright-Hays research grantee, 1973-74. Mem. Am. Philos. Assn., Nat. Women's Studies Assn., Soc. Women in Philosophy, Internat. Assn. von Philosophinnen (founding). Author: The Development of Franz Brentano's Ethics, 1982; gen. editor Hypatia: A Journal of Feminist Philosophy, 1990—; editor Hypatia's Daughters: 1500 Years of Women Philsophers, 1996; contbr. articles to profl. jours. Editor and translator: Psychology From an Empirical Standpoint (Franz Brentano), 1973; Sensory and Noetic Consciousness (Franz Brentano), 1980; editor: The Philosophy of Brentano, 1976; translator: On Colour (Ludwig Wittgenstein), 1977, SWIP-L Electronic Mail Forum for Feminist Philosophy, 1992—, Film Criticism: Radio, Print and Electronic Media, 1990—. Office: U South Fla HMS 413 4202 E Fowler Ave Tampa FL 33620-9951

MCALISTER, MAURICE L., savings and loan association executive; b. 1925; married. Pres., dir. Downey Savs. and Loan, Newport Beach, Calif., 1957—, chmn. bd. Office: Downey Savs & Loan Assn PO Box 6000 3501 Jamboree Rd Newport Beach CA 92660-2939*

MCALISTER, MICHAEL HILLIS, architect; b. Bakersfield, Calif., May 22, 1945; s. Doyle R. and Mary E. McAlister. AA, Bakersfield Coll., 1967; BArch, Calif. Polytech. U., 1971. Planning technition Bakersfield City Hall, 1963; carpenter Del Webb Corp., Kern City, Calif., 1964; architectural draftsman Goss & Choy Architects, Bakersfield, 1965-67; architect, v.p. D.G.C. & Assocs., Bakersfield, 1971-80; dir. architecture, v.p. N.B.A. & Assocs., Architects, Bakersfield, 1980-83; architect, pres. Michael H. McAlister, A.I.A., Bakersfield, 1983—; nepthrology design cons. for various treatment groups and hosps., 1987—. Commr., architectural advisor Historic Preservation Commn., Bakersfield, 1986-87; bd. dirs. Camp Fire Coun., Kern County, Calif., 1980-84. Recipient Architectural Pub. Bldg. Hist. award Beautiful Bakersfield Com., City of Bakersfield's City Coun. and Hist. Preservation Commn., 1985, 87, Exterior Environ. Design Excellence Bakersfield C. of C., 1988, Comml. Design Excellence award, 1984, Design Excellence and Beautification award City of Taft, Calif., 1989, Design Excellence award State of Nev., 1992. Mem. AIA (Calif. Coun., Golden Empire chpt.). Avocations: horseback riding, art and sculpture. Office: 5030 Office Park Dr Ste B Bakersfield CA 93309-0612

MCALISTER, ROBERT BEATON, lawyer; b. N.Y.C., Oct. 5, 1932; s. Richard Charles and Martha Olive (Weisenbarger) McA.; widowed; children: Michael, Peter, Betsy. AB, Kenyon Coll., 1954; JD, U. Mich., 1957. Ptnr. Alexander, Ebinger, Fisher, McAlister & Lawrence, Columbus, Ohio, 1957-85; supt. Ohio Div. Savs. & Loan Assns., Columbus, 1985; ptnr. Baker & Hostetler, Columbus, 1985—, chmn. litigation dept., 1988-93. Exec. com. mem. Ohio Dem. Party, Columbus, 1967-74; active Dem. Nat. Com., Washington, 1972-76; counsel Gov. Richard F. Celeste, Columbus, 1982-90, Senator John Glenn, Washington, 1986-94. With USAF, 1968-64. Fellow Ohio Bar Found., Columbus Bar Found.; mem. Capital Club (Columbus). Democrat. Episcopalian. Home: 5571 Sutterton Ln Westerville OH 43081-5228 Office: Baker & Hostetler 65 E State St Columbus OH 43215-4213

MCALLISTER, DEE THERESA, elementary education educator; b. Islip, N.Y., Jan. 7, 1942; d. Joseph August and Victoria Harriet (Szczepaniak) Boesel. BS in Elem. Edn. and Spl. Edn., Marywood Coll., Scranton, Pa., 1963; postgrad., L.I.U., 1983-86. Cert. elem. tchr., N.Y., lic. real estate. Tchr. Our Lady of Good Counsel Parochial Sch., Inwood, N.Y., 1963-64, Elmont (N.Y.) Sch. Dist., 1964, Middle County Sch. Dist., Centereach, N.Y., 1968—; union rep. MCTA, Centereach, 1969-70. Mem. Audubon Soc., Mus. Nat. History, Nat. Geographic Soc., NCTM, Internat. Platform Assn., N.Y. State United Tchrs. Avocations: traveling, playing piano, reading, photography, bird watching, breeding English Budgies. Home: PO Box 407 Centereach NY 11720-0407 Office: Elem Sch North Coleman Rd Centereach NY 11720

MC ALLISTER, GERALD NICHOLAS, retired bishop, clergyman; b. San Antonio, Feb. 23, 1923; s. Walter Williams and Leonora Elizabeth (Alexander) McA.; m. Helen Earle Black, Oct. 2, 1953; children—Michael Lee, David Alexander, Stephen Williams, Elizabeth. Student, U. Tex., 1939-42, Va. Theol. Sem., 1948-51; D.D. (hon.), Va. Theol. Sem., 1977. Rancher, 1946-48; ordained deacon Episcopal Ch., 1953, priest, 1954; deacon, priest Ch. of Epiphany, Raymondville, Ch. of Incarnation, Corpus Christi, St. Francis Ch., Victoria, all Tex., 1951-63; 1st canon Diocese of W. Tex., 1963-70; rector St. David's Ch., San Antonio, 1970-76; consecrated Episcopal bishop of Okla., Oklahoma City, 1977-89, ret., 1989; bishop-in-residence Episcopal Theol. Sem., Austin, Tex., 1990-93; trustee Episcopal Theol. Sem. of S.W., 1961—, adv. bd., 1974—; mem. Case Commn. Bd. for Theol. Edn., 1981-82; pres. Tex. Council Chs., 1966-68, Okla. Conf. Chs., 1980-83; bd. dirs. Presiding Bishop's Fund for World Relief, 1972-77, Ch. Hist. Soc., 1976—; chmn. Nat. and World Mission Program Group, 1973-76; mem. Structure of Ch. Standing Commn., 1979, mem. standing com. on Steward-ship/Devel., 1979-85; founder Chaplaincy Program, Bexar County Jail, 1968; mem. governing bd. nat. council Ch. of Christ, 1982-85; chmn. standing commn. on stewardship Episcopal Ch., 1983-85; v.p., trustee The Episc., Episc. Theol. Sem. of Soutwest, 1987—, chmn. bd. trustees, 1993—. Author: What We Learned from What You Said, 1973, This Fragile Earth Our Island Home, 1980. Bd. dirs. Econ. Opportunity Devel. Corp., San Antonio, 1968-69; mem. exec. com. United Way, 1968-70, vice-chmn., 1970. Served with U.S. Mcht. Marines, 1942; to 1st lt. USAAF, 1942-45. Recipient Agudas Achim Brotherhood award, 1968. Address: 507 Bluffestates San Antonio TX 78216-7930

MCALLISTER, ROBERT JOSEPH, priest, publisher; b. Balt., Aug. 29, 1918; s. Robert Emory and Ann Gertrude (Doran) McA. BA, Loyola Coll., Balt., 1940; PhL, Gregorian U., Rome, 1945; STL, Gregorian U., 1952. Joined Soc. of Jesus, Roman Cath. Ch., 1940, ordained priest, 1951. From asst. pastor to pastor St. Ignatius Ch., Hill Top, Md., 1954-58; student counselor Gonzaga High Sch., Washington, 1958-64; asst. to nat. dir. Apostleship of Prayer, N.Y.C., 1964-70, nat. dir., 1970—; mem. adv. coun. Internat. Inst. of Heart of Jesus, 1972—, Apostolate for Family Consecration, 1975—, bd. sponsors Priestly Heart Program, 1976—. Home: 3 Stephan Ave New Hyde Park NY 11040-3130 Office: Apostleship of Prayer Inc 3 Stephan Ave New Hyde Park NY 11040-3130

MCALLISTER, WAYNE R., principal. Prin. Garrettford Elem. Sch., Drexel Hill, Pa. Recipient Elem. Sch. Recognition award U.S. Dept. of Edn., 1989-90. Office: Garrettford Elem Sch 3830 Garrett Rd Drexel Hill PA 19026-3502

MCALLISTER, WILLIAM ALEXANDER, JR., manufacturing company executive; b. Phila., Oct. 30, 1928; s. William Alexander and Evelyn Eunice (Kidd) McA.; m. Jean Carol Dungan, Apr. 22, 1950; children: Martha Jill, Margaret Louise, William Alexander III. AA, Ohio U., 1995. Salesman Del. Asbestos & Rubber Co., Phila., 1946-62; v.p. DAR Indsl. Products Inc., Phila., 1962-72, pres., 1972—; pres. DARCO So., Inc., Independence, Va., 1976—; treas. McAllister Mills, Inc., Independence, 1980—; bd. dirs. Thermofab, Inc., Toronto, Ont., Can. Chmn. bd. Twin County Regional Healthcare, Galax, Va., 1982—; bd. dirs. Wytheville (Va.) C.C., 1986-93. Mem. Fluid Sealing Assn. (past pres. and bd. dirs.). Avocation: golf. Home: 81 Sea March Rd Fernandina Beach FL 32034 Office: DARCO So Inc 253 DARCO Dr Independence VA 24348

MCALLISTER, WILLIAM HOWARD, III, newspaper reporter, columnist; b. Durham, N.C., Nov. 6, 1941; s. William Howard, Jr. and Dorothy Fisk (Tillett) McA.; m. Rena Catherine Farrell, June 13, 1965; children: William Howard IV, Christopher F., Jonathan T., Benjamin J. B.A. in Polit. Sci. U. N.C., Chapel Hill, 1964, M.A. in Journalism, 1966. Cecil Prince research asst. U. N.C., 1965; reporter The Virginian-Pilot, Norfolk, 1964-67; reporter, city editor Virginian-Pilot, 1972-75; reporter Wall St. Jour., San Francisco, 1968-72; reporter Washington Post, 1975-78, Va. editor, 1978-86, nat. reporter, 1986—, columnist stamp and coin sect., 1987—; TV cons. Ford Found., 1969-72. Capt. USNR, 1966-93. Decorated Navy Commendation medal, Meritorious Svc. medal, Gold Star; recipient Lidman prize for philatelic writing, 1990. Mem. Kappa Tau Alpha. Presbyterian. Home: 4140 Lenox Dr Fairfax VA 22032-1111 Office: 1150 15th St NW Washington DC 20071-5000

MCALPINE, ANDREW, production designer. Prodn. designer: (films) Sid and Nancy, 1986, Aria, 1987, Straight to Hell, 1987, High Season, 1988, Stormy Monday, 1988, For Queen and Country, 1989, The Rachel Papers, 1989, Slipstream, 1989, The Piano, 1993, The Tool Shed, 1993. Office: Sandra Marsh Mgt 9150 Wilshire Blvd Ste 220 Beverly Hills CA 90212-3429

MCALPINE, DONALD, cinematographer. Cinematographer: (films) The Adventures of Barry McKenzie, 1972, Don's Party, 1976, The Getting of Wisdom, 1977, The Odd Angry Shot, 1979, Patrick, 1979, Breaker Morant, 1979, My Brilliant Career, 1980, The Club, 1980, The Earthling, 1981, Money Movers, 1981, Don't Cry, It's Only Thunder, 1981, Tempest, 1982, Now and Forever, 1983, Puberty Blues, 1983, Blue Skies Again, 1983, Harry & Son, 1984, Moscow on the Hudson, 1984, King David, 1985, Down and Out in Beverly Hills, 1986, The Fringe Dwellers, 1987, Orphans, 1987, Predator, 1987, Moon Over Parador, 1988, Moving, 1988, Parenthood, 1989, See You in the Morning, 1989, Stanley & Iris, 1990, The Hard Way, 1991, Career Opportunities, 1991, Patriot Games, 1992, The Man Without a Face, 1993, Mrs. Doubtfire, 1993, Clear and Present Danger, 1994, Nine Months, 1995.

MCALPINE, PHYLLIS JEAN, genetics educator, researcher; b. Petrolia, Ont., Can., Aug. 29, 1941; d. Archie S. and Jessie Mae (Cran) McA. B.S. with honors, U. Western Ont., London, Can., 1963; M.A., U. Toronto, Ont., Can., 1966; Ph.D., U. London, U.K., 1970. Postdoctoral fellow Queen's U., Kingston, Ont., 1970-72; postdoctoral fellow Coll. Hosp. Med. Sch., London, Eng., 1972; research assoc. U. Man., Winnipeg, Can., 1972-74; from asst. to assoc. prof. genetics U. Man., 1974-84, acting dir. div. human genetics, 1982-84, prof., 1984—; mem. sci. staff Health Scis. Ctr., Winnipeg, 1975—. Contbr. articles to profl. jours. Pres. Manitoba Opera Assn. Guild, Winnipeg, 1976-78. Recipient Gold medal in Zoology U. Western Ontario, 1963. Fellow Can. Coll. Med. Geneticists; mem. Genetics Soc. Can., Am. Soc. Human Genetics, AAAS, Electrophoresis Soc. Avocation: performing arts. Office: U Manitoba, Dept of Human Genetics, Winnipeg, MB Canada R3E 0W3

MCAMIS, EDWIN EARL, lawyer; b. Cape Girardeau, Mo., Aug. 8, 1934; s. Zenas Earl and Anna Louise (Miller) McA.; m. Malin Eklof, May 31, 1959 (div. 1979); 1 child, Andrew Bruce. AB magna cum laude, Harvard U., 1956, LLB, 1959. Bar: N.Y. 1960, U.S. Dist. Ct. (so. dist.) N.Y. 1962, U.S. Supreme Ct. 1965, U.S. Ct. Appeals (2d and 3d cirs.) 1964, U.S. Ct. Appeals (D.C. cir.) 1981. Assoc. law firm Webster, Sheffield & Chrystie, N.Y.C., 1959-61, Regan Goldfarb Powell & Quinn, N.Y.C., 1962-65; assoc. law firm Lovejoy, Wasson, Lundgren & Ashton, N.Y.C., 1965-69, ptnr., 1969-77; ptnr. Skadden, Arps, Slate, Meagher & Flom, N.Y.C., 1977-90, spl. ptnr., pro bono, 1990-93; adj. prof. law Fordham U., 1984-85, Benjamin N. Cardozo Sch. Law, N.Y.C., 1985-90. Bd. dirs. Aston Magna Found. for Music, Inc., 1982-93, Cmty. Rsch. Initiative N.Y., 1988-89; mem. Lambda Legal and Edn. Fund, 1991-95. With U.S. Army, 1961-62. Mem. ABA, Selden Soc. Home: 4110 Kiaora St Coconut Grove FL 33133

MCANDREWS, JAMES PATRICK, retired lawyer; b. Carbondale, Pa., May 11, 1929; s. James Patrick and Mary Agnes (Walsh) McA.; m. Mona Marie Steinke, Sept. 4, 1954; children: James P., George A., Catherine McAndrews Lawlor, Joseph M., Anne Marie, Michael P., Edward R., Daniel P. B.S., U. Scranton, 1949; LL.B., Fordham U., 1952; grad., Real Estate Inst., NYU, 1972. Bar: N.Y. 1953, Ohio 1974. Assoc. James F. McManus, Levittown, N.Y., 1955; atty. Emigrant Savs. Bank, N.Y.C., 1955-68; counsel Tchrs. Ins. and Annuity Assn., 1968-73; assoc. Thompson, Hine & Flory, 1973-74; ptnr. Thompson, Hine & Flory, Cleve., 1974-84, Benesch, Friedlander, Coplan & Aronoff, Cleve., 1984-94; mem. law faculty Am. Inst. Banking, N.Y.C., 1968-69. 1st lt. USAF, 1952-54. Fellow Am. Bar Found. (life); mem. ABA (past chmn. real estate financing com. 1985-87), Am. Coll. Real Estate Lawyers (gov. 1983-86, treas. 1986-88, chmn. membership devel. com. 1985-87), Ohio Bar Assn., Bar Assn. Greater Cleve. (past chmn. real estate sect.). Roman Catholic. Home: 6638 Duneden Ave Cleveland OH 44139-4048

MCANIFF, EDWARD JOHN, lawyer; b. N.Y.C., June 29, 1934; s. John Edward and Josephine (Toomey); m. Jane Reiss, June 11, 1960; children: John E., Maura T., Anne T., Jane A., Peter J., Kathleen A. AB magna cum laude, Holy Cross Coll., 1956; LLB cum laude, NYU, 1961. Bar: N.Y. 1962, Calif. 1963, D.C. 1976. Law clk. to Justice A.T. Goodwin Supreme Ct. Oreg., Salem, 1961-62; assoc. then ptnr. O'Melveny & Myers, L.A., 1962—; lectr. Stanford U., 1974-75, 94—, Boalt Hall Law Sch., 1992—; fgn. law counsel Freehill, Hollingdale & Page, Sydney, 1981-82; bd. dirs. Mellon Bank Corp. Bd. dirs. L.A. Master Chorale, 1979-81, 87—, pres., 1992—; trustee Music Ctr. L.A. County, 1992—, mem. exec. com., 1992—; bd. dirs. Music Ctr. Found., 1992—. Capt. USNR, 1956-87. Mem. City Club, Valley Hunt Club. Republican. Home: 3315 San Pasqual St Pasadena CA 91107-5436 Office: O'Melveny & Myers 400 S Hope St Ste 1060 Los Angeles CA 90071*

MCANIFF, NORA P., publishing executive. BA, CUNY. Pub. People Weekly, N.Y.C., 1994—. Office: People Magazine Time Inc Rockfeller Ctr New York NY 10020-1393

MCANINCH, HAROLD D., college president; b. Leota, Mo., May 29, 1933; s. James Loyd and Essie L. McA.; m. Karyl Kay Woodbridge, May 25, 1956; children: Michele Kay, Michael Sean. B.S., S.W. Mo. State U., 1957; M.A., U. Ark., 1958; Ed.D., U. Mo., 1967; postgrad., Loyola U., Chgo., 1972-74; D.Hum. (hon.), Lewis U., 1974. Tchr. Smith Cotton High Sch., Sedalia, Mo., 1958-61; instr. U. Mo., Columbia, 1961-64; dean Jefferson Coll., Hillsboro, Mo., 1964-68; pres. Jackson (Mich.) Community Coll., 1968-71, Joliet (Ill.) Jr. Coll., 1971-79, Coll. of DuPage, Glen Ellyn, Ill., 1979—. Contbr. articles to profl. jours. Chmn. Will County Cancer Crusade; bd. dirs. United Crusade of Will County. Served with U.S. Army, 1950-53. Mem. Council North Central Community and Jrs. Colls. (pres. 1975), Ill. Council Public Community Coll. Presidents (vice chmn. 1976, pres. 1977, past chmn. fin. com.), North Central Assn. Colls. and Secondary Schs. (evaluator, commr.), Am. Assn. Community and Jr. Colls. (chmn. President's Acad. 1979, dir. 1980-84, vice chmn. 1982, chmn. 1983), Phi Delta Kappa. Lodge: Rotary. Office: Coll of DuPage 22nd and Lambert Rds Glen Ellyn IL 60137

MCANINCH, JACK WELDON, urological surgeon, educator; b. Merkel, Tex., Mar. 17, 1936; s. Weldon Thomas and Margaret (Canon) McA.; m. Barbara B. Buchanan, Dec. 29, 1960 (div. Aug. 1972); m. Burnet B. Sumner, Dec. 29, 1987; children: David A., Todd G., Brendan J. BS, Tex. Tech U., 1958; MS, U. Idaho, 1960; MD, U. Tex., 1964. Diplomate Am. Bd. Urology (trustee 1991—, pres. 1996—). Commd. capt. U.S. Army, 1964-66, advanced through grades to col., 1977, ret., 1977; col. USAR; intern then resident Letterman Army Med. Ctr., San Francisco, 1964-69; chief urol. surgery San Francisco Gen. Hosp., 1977—; prof. urol. surgery U. Calif., San Francisco, 1977—. Editor: Urogenital Trauma, 1985, Urologic Clinics of North America, 1989, Smith's General Urology, 1995; section editor: Early Care of the Injured Patient, 1990, Traumatic and Reconstructive Urology, 1996. Col. US Army, 1964-72. Recipient Disting. Alumnus award Tex. Tech U., 1994. Fellow ACS (gov. 1992—); mem. Am. Urol. Assn. (pres. we. sect. 1992-93, bd. dirs. 1990—, pres. 1996—), Genitourinary Reconstructive Surgeons (pres.), Am. Assn. Surgery Trauma (v.p.), Soc. Univ. Urologists, Am. Bd. Urology (pres. 1996—). Office: San Francisco Gen Hosp Dept Urology 1001 Potrero Ave San Francisco CA 94110-3518

MC ANINCH, ROBERT DANFORD, philosophy and government affairs educator; b. Wheeling, W.Va., May 21, 1942; s. Robert Danford and Dorothy Elizabeth (Goudy) McA.; 1 child, Robert Michael; m. Helen M. Perry, June 5, 1993. AB, West Liberty State Coll., 1969; MA, W.Va. U., 1970; MA, Morehead State U., 1975; postgrad. U. Hawaii, U. Ky. Engring. technician Hydro-Space Rsch., Inc., Rockville, Md., 1965-66; prof. govt., philosophy Prestonsburg (Ky.) Community Coll., 1970—; v.p. Calico Corner, Inc.; dir. Chase-Options, Inc., Medisin, Inc. Bd. dirs. Big Sandy Area Community Action Program, Inc., 1973-76; chmn. Floyd County Solid Waste, Inc.; mem. War on Drug Task Force. Served with AUS, 1962-65. Recipient Great Tchr. award Prestonsburg Community Coll., 1971; named Ky. col., 1977. Mem. Am. Polit. Sci. Assn., Am. Philos. Soc., Ky. Philosophy Assn., Ky. Assn. Colls. and Jr. Colls. Achievements include designed Cosmic ray chamber, artificial human circulatory system, Wilson type cloud chamber, TOTO 1, 2. Home: Bert Combs Dr Prestonsburg KY 41653

MCANUFF, DES, artistic director; b. Princeton, Ill., June 19, 1952; s. John Nelson and Ellen Boyd; m. Susan Berman, Jan. 1, 1984; 1 child, Julia Violet. Artistic dir. La Jolla Playhouse, until 1994; Founding mem. Dodger Prodns.; former faculty Julliard Sch.; now adj. prof. theatre U. Calif. San Diego. Dir.: (Broadway prodns.) Big River (Tony award 1985), A Walk in the Woods (San Diego Critics Circle award), Tommy (Tony award 1993), How to Succeed in Business Without Really Trying (Tony nomination 1995); (off-Broadway prodns.) Gimme Shelter (Soho Arts award 1979), The Crazy Locomotive, Chelsea Theatre Ctr., Mary Stuart, How It All Began, Henry IV Part One, The Death of Von Richthofen as Witnessed from Earth (Villager award 1982), N.Y. Shakespeare Festival, A Mad World My Masters, Romeo & Juliet, As You Like It (San Diego Critics Circle award), The Sea Gull, Shout Up A Morning, Gillette, The Matchmaker, Two Rooms, 80 Days, Down The Road, Macbeth, The Three Sisters, A Funny Thing Happened on the Way to the Forum, Twelfth Night, La Jolla Playhouse, Macbeth, Stratford Festival Can., others; prodr.: A Walk in the Woods, My Children! My Africa!; playwright Leave it to Beaver is Dead (Soho Arts award), The Death of Von Richthofen as Witnessed from Earth (Villager and Bay Area Circle Critics awards), Troll, A Lime in the Morning, Silent Edward; contbg. editor Am. Theatre Mag. Can. Council grantee, Rockefeller grantee. Mem. Theatre Communications Group (past bd. dirs.), Soc. of Stage Dirs. and Choreographers.

MC ANULTY, HENRY JOSEPH, university administrator; b. Pitts., Apr. 25, 1915; s. William J. and Catherine (Calpin) McA. BA, Duquesne U., 1936; BTh, St. Mary's Sem., Ferndale, Norwalk, Conn., 1941; LLD, Loyola U., Los Angeles, 1958; DEd, St. Vincent Coll., Latrobe, Pa., 1961; LHD, U. Pitts., Duquesne U., 1990. Joined Congregation of Holy Ghost, 1936; ordained priest Roman Catholic Ch., 1940; nat. sec., Pitts. Diocesan dir. Pontifical Assn. Holy Childhood, 1941-44; commd. 1st lt. chaplain USAAF, 1944; advanced through grades to lt. col. USAF, resigned, 1958; brig. gen. (Res.); asst. to pres. Duquesne U., 1958-59, pres., 1959-80. Bd. dirs. Pitts. Symphony Soc., Pitts. Regional Indsl. Devel. Corp., Pitts. Conv. and Visitors Bur., Allegheny Conf. for Community Devel. Mem. Am. Legion, K.C.

MCARDLE, JOHN, publishing company executive; b. Boston, 1928. Attended, Boston Coll., 1952, 70. Pres., chief exec. officer, dir. Fin. Pub. Co., Boston. Home: Box 201 19 Towne Hill Topsfield MA 01983 Office: Financial Pub Co 82 Brookline Ave Boston MA 02215-3905*

MCARDLE, RICHARD JOSEPH, academic administrator; b. Omaha, Mar. 10, 1934; s. William James and Abby Marie (Menzies) McA.; m. Katherine Ann McAndrew, Dec. 27, 1958; children: Bernard, Constance, Nancy, Susan, Richard. B.A., Creighton U., 1955, M.A., 1961; Ph.D., U. Nebr., 1969. Tchr. pub. high schs. Nebr., 1955-65; grad. asst. romance langs. U. Nebr., 1965-66, instr. fgn. lang. methods, 1966-69; chmn. dept. edn. Cleve. State U., 1969-70; chmn. dept. elem. and secondary edn. U. North Fla., 1971-75; dean Coll. Edn. Cleve. State U., 1975-87, prof. edn., 1987-89, spl. asst. to pres. for campus planning, 1989-91, vice provost for strategic planning, 1991-92, acting provost, v.p. for acad. affairs, 1992-94; vice provost for strategic planning, 1994—; cons. in field. Author articles related to issues in tchr. edn. Mem. World Future Soc., Soc. Coll. and Univ. Planning, Am. Assn. Higher Edn., Phi Delta Kappa. Office: Office of Provost Academic Affairs Cleve State U Cleveland OH 44115

MCARTHUR, ELDON DURANT, geneticist, researcher; b. Hurricane, Utah, Mar. 12, 1941; s. Eldon and Denise (Dalton) McA.; m. Virginia Johnson, Dec. 20, 1963; children: Curtis D., Monica McArthur Bennion, Denise, Ted O. AS with high honors, Dixie Coll., 1963; BS cum laude, U. Utah, 1965, MS, 1967, PhD, 1970. Postdoctoral rsch. fellow, dept. demonstrator Agrl. Rsch. Coun. Gt. Britain, Leeds, Eng., 1970-71; rsch. geneticist Intermountain Rsch. Sta. USDA Forest Svc., Ephraim, Utah, 1972-75; rsch. geneticist Shrub Scis. Lab., Intermountain Rsch. Sta. USDA Forest Svc., Provo, Utah, 1975-83, project leader, chief rsch. geneticist, 1983—; adj. prof. dept. botany and range sci. Brigham Young U., Provo, 1976—. Author over 250 rsch. papers; contbr. chpts. to books; editor symposium procs. Named USDA Forest Svc. Superior Scientist, 1990, Disting. Scientist, 1996; Sigma Xi grantee, 1970, NSF grantee, 1981, 85, 96, Coop. State Rsch., Svc. grantee, 1986, 91. Mem. Soc. Range Mgmt. (pres. Utah sect. 1987, Outstanding Achievement award 1992), Botan. Soc. Am., Soc. Study Evolution, Am. Genetic Assn., Shrub Rsch. Consortium (chmn. 1983—), Intermountain Consortium for Aridlands Rsch. (pres. 1991—). Mormon. Avocations: hiking, cycling, basketball. Home: 555 N 1200 E Orem UT 84057-4350 Office: USDA Forest Svc Shrub Scis Lab 735 N 500 E Provo UT 84606-1856

MC ARTHUR, GEORGE, journalist; b. Valdosta, Ga., July 15, 1924; s. George and Ann (Johnson) McA.; m. Eva Kim, Sept. 17, 1979. B.A. in Journalism, U. Ga., 1948. With AP, 1948-69; corr. AP, Korea, 1950-54, Paris, 1954-60; bur. chief AP, Cairo, 1960-63, Manila, 1963-65; corr. AP, Saigon, 1966-68; bur. chief AP, 1968-69; with Los Angeles Times, 1969-83; bur. chief Los Angeles Times, Saigon, 1970-75; corr. for Southeast Asia Los Angeles Times, Bangkok, 1975-79; diplomatic corr. U.S. News & World Report, 1983-85. Served with USNR, 1943-45. Recipient citation for fgn. reporting Overseas Press Club, 1973. Mem. Sigma Delta Chi. Clubs: Fgn. Corrs. (Hong Kong); Glen Arven Country (Thomasville, Ga.); River Bend Country (Gt. Falls, Va.). Address: 506 E Creek Ct Vienna VA 22180-3578

MC ARTHUR, JANET WARD, endocrinologist, educator; b. Bellingham, Wash., June 25, 1914; d. Hyland Donald and Alice Maria (Frost) McA. A.B., U. Wash., 1935, M.S., 1937; M.B., Northwestern U., 1941, M.D., 1942; ScD (hon.), Mt. Holyoke Coll., 1962. Diplomate: Am. Bd. Internal Medicine. Intern Cin. Gen. Hosp., 1941-42, asst. resident in medicine, 1942-43; asst. resident, rsch. fellow in medicine H.P. Walcott fellow clin. medicine Mass. Gen. Hosp., Boston, 1943-47, assoc. physician,

1959-84, assoc. children's svc., 1968-84; instr. Harvard U., 1955-57, asst. prof., 1960-64, assoc. prof., 1964-73, prof., 1973-84, prof. emeritus, 1984—; clin. prof. medicine Boston U. Sch. Medicine, 1984—; adj. prof. Sargent Coll. Allied Health Scis. Boston U., 1982—; mem. reproductive biology study sect. NIH, 1974-78, Com. on Population Studies, 1980-84; co-dir. Vincent Meml. Rsch. Lab., 1977-79; sr. scientist U. London, 1985-86. Author: (with others) Functional Endocrinology from Birth Through Adolescence, 1952; editor: (with Theodore Colton) Statistics in Endocrinology, 1970; contbr. articles to profl. jours. Fellow ACP; mem. AMA, AAAS, Endocrine Soc., Am. Soc. Reproductive Medicine, Am. Assn. Clinical Endocrinologists, Boston Obstetrical Soc., Phi Beta Kappa, Sigma Xi, Alpha Omega Alpha. Home: 19 Brimmer St Boston MA 02108-1025 Office: Boston U 635 Commonwealth Ave Fl 4 Boston MA 02215-1605

MCARTHUR, JOHN HECTOR, business educator; b. Vancouver, B.C., Can., Mar. 31, 1934; came to U.S., 1957; s. Hector and Elizabeth Lee (Whyte) McA.; m. Netilia Ewasiuk, Sept. 15, 1956; children: Jocelyn Natasha, Susan Patricia. B in Commerce, U. B.C., 1957; MBA, Harvard U., 1959, DBA, 1962; LLD (hon.), Simon Fraser U., 1982, Queens U., 1985, Middlebury Coll., 1988, U. Western Ont., 1992; hon. degree, U. Navarra, Spain, 1989. Prof. dean. Sch. Bus. Adminstrn. Harvard U., Cambridge, Mass., 1980—; bd. dirs. BCE, Inc., Chase Manhattan Corp., Rohm and Haas Co., Inc., Springs Industries, Inc., Cabot Corp., Glaxo Welcome Plc.; cons. numerous cos. and govt. agys. in Can., Europe and U.S. Chmn. bd. trustees Brigham and Women's Corp., 1986, Ptnrs. Health Sys., 1994. Home: 140 Old Connecticut Path Wayland MA 01778-3202 Office: Sch Bus Adminstrn Harvard U Boston MA 02163

MCATEE, PATRICIA ANNE ROONEY, medical educator; b. Denver, Apr. 20, 1931; d. Jerry F. and Edna E. (Hansen) Rooney; m. Darrell McAtee, Sept. 4, 1954; 1 son, Kevin Paul. BS, Loretto Heights Coll., 1953; MS, U. Colo., 1961; PhD, Union of Univs., 1976. Supr. St. Anthony Hosp., Denver, 1952-55; pub. health nurse, edn. dir. Tri-County Health Dept., Colo., 1956-58; adminstr. sch. health program Littleton (Colo.) Pub. Schs., 1958-60; asst. prof. community health, acad. adminstr. continuing edn. U. Colo., 1966-70; project dir. Western Interstate Commn. for Higher Edn., 1972-74; asst. prof. pediatrics, project co-dir. Sch. Medicine U. Colo., 1975—; mem. profl. svcs. staff Mead Johnson & Co., 1981—; cons. Colo. Safety Coun.; treas. Vista Nueva Assocs. Editor: Pediatric Nursing, 1975-77. Chmn. bd. dirs. Found. for Urban and Neighborhood Devel.; mem. Arapahoe Health Planning Coun. Mem. NAS, APHA, Inst. Medicine, Nat. Bd. Pediatric Nurse Practitioners and Assocs. (pres.), Nat. Assn. Pediatric Nurse Practitioners (v.p.), Am. Acad. Polit. and Social Scientist, Nat. League Nursing, Western Soc. Rsch., Am. Sch. Health Assn., Sigma Theta Tau. Home: 877 E Panama Dr Littleton CO 80121-2531 Office: 4200 E 9th Ave Box C-219 Denver CO 80262

MCATEER, J. DAVITT, federal agency administrator; m. Kathryn Grace Lough; 5 children. BA, Wheeling Coll., 1966; JD, W.Va. U., 1970. Solicitor of safety United Mine Workers Am., 1972-76; with Ctr. for Law and Social Policy, Washington, 1976-84; exec. dir. Occupl. Safety and Health Law Ctr., Sheperdstown, W.Va., 1984-94; asst. sec. of labor Mine Safety and Health Adminstrn., Arlington, Va., 1994—; acting solicitor of labor U.S. Dept. Labor, Washington, 1996—. Office: US Dept Labor 200 Constitution Ave Washington DC 20210

MCAULEY, SKEET, artist; b. Monahans, Tex., Mar. 7, 1951; s. George Clifford and Thelma Lee (Martin) McA.; m. Karen Suzanne Gee, June 25, 1994. BA, Sam Houston State U., 1976; MFA, Ohio U., 1978. Instr. photography Spring Hill Coll., Mobile, Ala., 1978-79, Tyler (Tex.) Jr. Coll., 1979-81; assoc. prof. photography U. N.Tex., Denton, 1981-93; featured in numerous articles and publs. One-person exhibits include Christopher Grimes Gallery, Santa Monica, Calif., 1995, Lowinsky Gallery, N.Y.C., 1993, U.S. Golf Assn. Mus., Far Hills, N.J., 1993, Dallas Mus. Art, 1992, Moody Gallery, Houston, 1992, Tyler Mus. of Art, 1992, The Heard Mus., Amherst, Mass., 1991, Calif. Mus. Photography, Riverside, 1991, Etherton/Stern Gallery, Tucson, Ariz., 1991, The Albuquerque Mus., 1990; group exhibits include Cleve. Mus. Art, 1994, Virginia Beach Ctr. for Arts, 1994, others; author: Sign Language: Contemporary Southwest Native Americans, 1989. Grantee Polaroid Copr., 1988, Nat. Endowment for the Arts Individual Artist fellowship, 1984, 86. Mem. Soc. Photographic Education (bd. dirs. 1990-93). Democrat. Office: 3516 Madera Ave Los Angeles CA 90039-1930

MCAULIFFE, CLAYTON DOYLE, chemist; b. Chappell, Nebr., Aug. 18, 1918; s. John F. and Emma Elizabeth (Stenger) McA.; m. Irene Opal Pickering, Sept. 5, 1943 (dec. Dec. 1988); children: Carol Ann McAuliffe Krenek, Clifford Andrew, Douglas Clayton, Thomas Frank; m. Wilma G. Long, Oct. 2, 1993. A.B., Nebr. Wesleyan U., 1941; M.A., U. Minn., 1942; Ph.D., Cornell U., 1948. Lab. asst. Nebr. Wesleyan U., 1939-41; research chemist Manhattan Project, 1943-46; cons. Dept. Agrl., 1947-48; research assoc. Cornell U., 1948-50; research assoc. prof. chemistry N.C. State U., 1950-56; sr. research chemist Chevron Oil Field Research Co., La Habra, Calif., 1956-67, sr. research assoc., 1967-86; pres. Clayton McAuliffe and Assocs., Inc., 1986-94; mem. steering com. petroleum in marine environ. Nat. Acad. Scis., 1972-75, com. energy and environ. 1974-76, com. dispersnat effectiveness, 1985-89; mem. Ocean Scis. Bd., 1975-77; cons. in field. Contbr. articles to profl. jours., chpts. to books; patentee in field. U. Minn. fellow, 1941-42; Cornell U. fellow, 1942-43, 46-48; NSF grantee; duPont Co. grantee; AEC grantee. Fellow AAAS; mem. Am. Chem. Soc., Soc. Petroleum Engrs., Am. Soc. Agronomy, Soil Sci. Soc. Am., Am. Assn. Petroleum Geologists. Republican. Methodist. Home and Office: 1220 Frances Ave Fullerton CA 92631-1807

MCAULIFFE, JANE DAMMEN, Middle Eastern and Islamic studies educator. BA in Classics and Philosophy, Trinity Coll., 1968; MA in Religious Studies, U. Toronto, 1979, PhD in Islamic Studies, 1984. Asst. prof. dept. religious studies U. Toronto, 1981-86, assoc. prof. dept. Middle East and Islamic studies, 1992—, chair dept. study of religion, dir. Ctr. Study of Religion, 1992—; from asst. prof. to assoc. prof. history of religions and Islamic studies Candler Sch. Theology Emory U., Atlanta, 1986-92, assoc. dean Candler Sch. Theology, 1990-92; appointed Vatican Commn. for Religious Rels. with Muslims, 1994. Author: Qur'anic Christians: An Analysis of Classical and Modern Exegesis, 1991, 'Abbasid Authority Affirmed: The Early Years of al-Mansur, vol. 28, 1995; contbr. articles to profl. jours. Danforth Found. fellow, 1976-80, NEH Summer fellow, 1979-80, Charles Gordon Heyd fellow, 1980-81, Social Scis. and Humanities Rsch. Coun. doctoral fellow, 1981-84, Postdoctoral fellow, 1984-86, CASA II fellow, 1986, NEH Summer Faculty Travel fellow, 1989, NEH Rsch. fellow, 1992, Mellon fellow, 1994, Guggenheim fellow, 1996. Mem. Am. Soc. Study of Religion, Am. Acad. Religion, Am. Oriental Soc., Can. Soc. Study of Religion, Mid. East Studies Assn. (Thesis award 1985), Oriental Club Toronto, Soc. Values in Higher Edn. Office: U Toronto Dept & Ctr Religion, 123 Saint George St, Toronto, ON Canada M5S 2E8

MC AULIFFE, MICHAEL F., bishop; b. Kansas City, Mo., Nov. 22, 1920. Student, St. Louis Prep. Sem., Cath. U. Ordained priest Roman Cath. Ch., 1945; consecrated bishop, 1969; bishop diocese of Jefferson City Jefferson City, Mo., 1969—. Office: Chancery Office 605 Clark Ave PO Box 417 Jefferson City MO 65101*

MCAULIFFE, RICHARD L., church official; m. Janet Bettinghaus; children: Brian, Andrea Stephenson. Student, Carleton Coll.; MBA, Harvard U. Exec. v.p., treas., CFO Harris Bankcorp, Harris Trust and Savs. Bank, 1960-90; mng. agt. Resolution Trust Corp., 1990—; treas. Evang. Luth. Ch. in Am., Chgo., 1992—; pres. Grace Luth. Ch., Glen Ellyn, Ill., Evang. Luth. Ch. Am. Ch. Coun.; treas. English Synod and Christ Sem.-Seminex, AELC; bd. dirs./com. mem. Christian Century Found., Luth. Gen. Healthcare Sys.; active Luth. Social Svcs. Ill. Office: Evang Luth Ch Am 8765 W Higgins Rd Chicago IL 60631-4101

MCAULIFFE, STEVEN JAMES, federal judge; b. 1948. BA, Va. Mil. Inst., 1970; JD, Georgetown U., 1973. Capt. appellate coun. U.S. Army Judge Advocate Gens. Corps, 1973-77; asst. atty. gen. Office N.H. Atty. Gen., 1977-80; ptnr. Gallagher, Callahan, Gartrell, P.A., Concord, N.H., 1980-92; fed. judge U.S. Dist. Ct. (N.H. dist.), Concord, 1992—. Trustee Univ. System of N.H., 1986-94; bd. dirs. N.H. Med. Malpractice Stabilication Res. Fund Trust, 1987-92, Office Pub. Guardian, 1980-92, Challenger Ctr. for Space Sci. Edn.; active N.H. Dem. Leadership Coun., 1988-92. Capt. U.S. Army, 1970-77, USAR, 1977-80, N.H. Army NG, 1980-88. Fellow N.H. Bar Found.; mem. ABA, N.H. Bar Assn. (pres. 1991-92, pres.-elect 1990-91, v.p. 1989-90, mem. ex-officio N.H. Supreme Ct. com. profl. conduct 1989-90, mem. ethics com. 1984-86), Nat. Conf. Bar Pres., Merrimack County Bar Assn., D.C. Bar Assn., U.S. Supreme Ct. Hist. Soc., N.H. Jud. Coun. (vice-chmn. 1991-92), Aircraft Owners and Pilots Assn., N.H. Hist. Soc., Concord Country Club. Office: US Dist Ct PO Box 1498 55 Pleasant St Concord NH 03301*

MCAVITY, JOHN GILLIS, museum director, association executive, museologist; b. St. John, N.B., Can., Oct. 30, 1950; s. J. Patrick H. and Catharine A. (McNeill) McA. B.A., U. N.B., 1972. Cert. assn. exec. Asst. curator Kings Landing Mus., Fredericton, N.B., Can., 1972-73; provincial mus. adviser N.B. Mus., St. John, Can., 1973-76; exec. dir. Ont. Mus. Assn., Toronto, Can., 1976-81, Can. Mus. Assn., Ottawa, Ont., Can., 1981—. V.p. St. John Heritage Trust, 1974-76; exec. com. Can. Club, St. John, 1975, English Speaking Union, St. John, 1974-76; vol. fundraiser Kidney Found., Can.; bd. dirs. Centretown Citizens Corp.; founding dir. Mus. Found. Can., 1994—. Mem. Am. Assn. Museums, Am. Assn. for State and Local History (awards com. 1981-84, nominations com. 1985), Mus. Found. Can. (founding dir. 1994—), Inst. Assn. Execs. (chmn. postal com., bd. dirs. Ottawa chpt., cert.), Assn. Cultural Execs. (bd. dirs. 1988-92, apptd. to senate 1995), Quaco Hist. and Libr. Soc. (hon. life), Tourism Industry Assn. Can. (bd. dirs.), Assn. Museums N.B. (founding mem.), Ont. Assn. Art Galleries (bd. dirs. 1986-90), Can. Soc. Copyright Consumers, Can. Soc. Assn. Execs. (bd. dirs. 1993—), Can. Art Mus. Dirs. Orgn., Shefford Heritage Co-op (membership com. 1992—). Anglican. Home: Apt 41, 300 Cooper St, Ottawa, ON Canada K2P 0G7

MCAVOY, BRUCE RONALD, scientist, consultant; b. Jamestown, N.Y., Jan. 30, 1933; s. George Harold and Agda Amelia (Martinson) McA. BS in Physics, U. Rochester, 1954. Jr. engr. Westinghouse Air Arm Div., Balt., 1956-57, assoc. engr., 1957-58; rsch. engr. Westinghouse Rsch. Ctr., Pitts., 1958-69; sr. rsch. engr. Westinghouse R & D Ctr., Pitts., 1969-78, fellow engr., 1978-84, adv. scientist, 1984—; adv. bd. mem. Nat. Ctr. Physical Acoustics, U. Miss., 1987-88. Editor spl. issue IEEE Trans. Microwave Theory Tech., Ultrasonics Symposium procs., 1976-93; mem. editl. bd. jour. Microwave and Guided Wave Letters, 1990. With U.S. Army, 1954-56. Fellow IEEE (awards and recognition com. 1989—, def. R&D policy com. 1989-91, Centennial medal 1984); mem. DAV (life), Ultrasonic, Rerroelectric and Frequency Control Soc. of IEEE (pres. 1986-87), Electromagnetics Acad., Microwave Theory and Techniques Soc. (chmn. microwave acoustics tech. com. 1988—). Republican. Lutheran. Home: 926 Ivy St Pittsburgh PA 15232-2651

MCAVOY, JOHN JOSEPH, lawyer; b. Worley, Idaho, June 28, 1933; s. Earl Francis and Florence Jewel (Mitchell) McA.; m. Joan Marjorie Zeldon, Sept. 20, 1964; children: Jason, Jon. B.A., U. Idaho, 1954, LL.B., 1958; LL.M., Yale U., 1959. Bar: Idaho 1958, U.S. Supreme Ct. 1962, N.Y. 1963, U.S. Tax Ct. 1969, D.C. 1976. Asst. prof. law George Washington U., Washington, 1959-62; staff atty. stockpile investigating subcom. Armed Forces Com. U.S. Senate, Washington, 1962; assoc. White & Case, N.Y.C., 1963-71, ptnr., 1972-95; of counsel Lukas, McGowan, Nace & Gutierrez, 1995—; adj. prof. Washington Coll. Law, Am. U., Washington, 1990. Bd. dirs. N.Y. Civil Liberties Union, 1975-77; chmn. due process com. ACLU, 1971-75. Served with U.S. Army, 1954-56. Mem. Assn. of Bar of City of N.Y., D.C. Bar Assn. (ethics com. 1982-88, vice chmn. 1986-87, chmn. 1987-88), Phi Beta Kappa, Phi Alpha Delta. Democrat. Avocations: swimming, bicycling, fgn. travel. Office: White & Case 1111 19th St NW Washington DC 20036

MCAVOY, THOMAS JAMES, federal judge; b. 1934. AB, Villanova U., 1960; JD, Union U., 1964. Bar: N.Y. 1964, U.S. Dist. Ct. (no. dist.) N.Y. 1964. Assoc. Hinman, Howard & Kattell, Binghamton, N.Y., 1964-69, Kramer, Wales, & McAvoy, Binghamton, 1969-84, McAvoy & Hickey, P.C., Binghamton, 1984-85; from judge to chief judge U.S. Dist. Ct. (no. dist.) N.Y., Binghamton, 1986—. With USMC, 1958. Office: US Dist Ct/No Dist NY 225 Fed Bldg 15 Henry St Binghamton NY 13901-2723*

MCAWARD, PATRICK JOSEPH, JR., architectural and engineering company executive; b. Flushing, N.Y., Feb. 13, 1934; s. Patrick Joseph and Lucy (Aufenanger) McA.; m. Jean Ann Schehr, Dec. 26, 1955; children: Patrick J., Michael J., Timothy J., Maura J., Kevin J. BSCE, U. Notre Dame, 1955; postgrad, CCNY, 1957. Registered profl. engr. in 17 states. With TAMS Consultants Inc., N.Y.C., 1955—; project engr. N.Y.C., 1965-68; assoc. and resident engr. Charleston, W.Va., 1968-71, head bridges and structures dept., 1968-71; project coord. for projects in Ethiopia, Kenya, Malawi, Botswana, Zaire, 1973-76; mgr. projects, Ga., N.J., Mass., N.Y., L.I., Tex., N.Y., 1977-80; head transp. divsn., 1976-81, ops. mgr., 1975-81; prin. N.Y.C., 1981—. Mem. ASCE, NSPE, Am. Pub. Transit Assn., Internat. Bridge, Tunnel and Turnpike Assn. (assoc.). Roman Catholic. Home: 135 Succabone Rd Bedford Hills NY 10507-2230 Office: TAMS Consultants Inc 655 3rd Ave New York NY 10017-5617

MCBAINE, JOHN NEYLAN, lawyer; b. San Francisco, Apr. 29, 1941; s. Turner H. and Jane Frances (Neylan) McB.; m. Alison Denny, Feb. 22, 1963 (div.); 1 child, Diana; m. Ariel Bybee, Nov. 24, 1972; 1 child, Neylan. B.A., Stanford U., 1962; J.D., U. Calif., 1967. Bar: D.C. 1968, Calif. 1970, N.Y. 1975. Assoc. law firm Covington & Burling, Washington, 1967-68; law clk. Hon. Gerhard A. Gesell U.S. Dist. Ct., D.C., 1968-69; assoc. law firm Pillsbury, Madison & Sutro, San Francisco, 1970-74; ptnr. Lord, Day & Lord, N.Y.C., 1975-86, Coudert Bros., N.Y.C., 1986—. Contbr. articles to profl. jours. Pres. Lincoln Plaza Tenants Corp., 1982-84, bd. dirs., 1982—; bd. visitors Brigham Young Law Sch., 1980-83. Served with AUS, 1963. Mem. ABA, Calif. Bar Assn., N.Y. Bar Assn. Mem. LDS Ch. Home: 44 W 62nd St New York NY 10023-7008 Office: Coudert Bros 1114 Avenue Of The Americas New York NY 10036-7703*

MCBATH, DONALD LINUS, osteopathic physician; b. Chgo., May 19, 1935; s. Earl and Phyllis (Michalski) McB.; m. Ruth Southerland, Jan. 18, 1956; children: Donald L. Jr., Donna Ruth McBath Bassett, Daniel P. BA in Polit. Sci., U. Fla., 1957, BS in Pre Med., 1962; DO, Kansas City (Mo.) Coll. Osteopathy and Surgery, 1969; MA, St. Leo Coll., 1981. Diplomate Nat. Bd. Examiners; cert. family practice Am. Osteo. Bd. Family Physicians, Correctional Health Prof. Med. Med. dir. various orgns., Dade City, Fla., 1971; chief of staff Jackson Meml. Hosp., Dade City, Fla., 1969—; past chief of staff, med. dir. East Pasco Med. Ctr., Zephyrills, Fla.; med. dir. Pasco County, Hernando County Prison Sys/.Fla.; bd. dirs. East Pasco med. Ctr., Zephrills; mem. adv. bd. Prudential Health Plan; trustee, pres., exe.c com. Fla. Osteo. Med. Assn.; sports physician Pasco Comprehensive H.S.; med. examiner FAA; Dade City grand marshall, past chmn. adv. coun.; pres., trustee East Pasco Med. Ctr. Found.; assoc. prof. clin. sci. Southeastern U. halth Scis., Miami, Fla.; mem. coun. predoctoral assn. AOA. Trustee St. Leo (Fla.) Coll.; adv. dir. First Union Nat. Bank Fla., Dade City; com. chmn. Hall of Fame Bowl, Pasco County, Fla., 1987. Recipient Pump Handle award Pasco County Health Authority, 1988, Outstanding Contbn. award H.R.S. Pasco County Pub. Health Unit, 1988, Outstanding Svc. award Fla. Interscholastic Athletic Adminstrs. Assn., 1994; named Gen. Practitioner of Yr., Fla. Acad. Gen. Practice, 1990-91. Fellow Am. Coll. Osteo. Family Physicians; mem. Am. Osteo. Assn. (nat. program conv. chmn., conv. com., exhibit adv. com., mem. ho. of dels., coun. on predoctoral edn.), Fla. Soc. Am. Coll. of Gen. Practitioners (nat. conv. com., bd. dirs. 1989-90, pres. 1991-92), Rotary (Dade City chpt. past pres., Paul Harris fellow). Roman Catholic. Avocation: sports. Home and Office: McBath Med Ctr 13925 17th St Dade City FL 33525-4603

MCBAY, ARTHUR JOHN, toxicologist, consultant; b. Medford, Mass., Jan. 6, 1919; s. Arthur and Virginia (Davito) McB.; m. Avis Louise Botsford, Aug. 24, 1946; children: John, Robert. BS, Mass. Coll. Pharmacy, 1940, MS, 1942; PhD, Purdue U., 1948. Diplomate Am. Bd. Forensic Toxicology; cert. toxicol. chemist Am. Bd. Clin. Chemistry; registered pharmacist, Mass. Asst. prof. chemistry Mass. Coll. Pharmacy, Boston, 1948-53, asst. in legal medicine, dept. legal medicine, 1953-63; lectr. legal medicine Harvard U.; toxicologist, criminalist, cons. Mass. State Police Chemistry Lab., 1955-63; instr. Northeastern U., 1962-63; assoc. prof. toxicology Law-Medicine Inst. Boston U., 1963-69, assoc. prof. pharmacology Med. Sch., 1963-69; supr. lab. Mass. Dept. Pub. Safety, Boston, 1963-69; assoc. prof. pathology and toxicology U. N.C., Chapel Hill, 1969-73, prof., 1973-89, prof. emeritus pharmacy and pathology, 1989—; chief toxicologist Office Chief Med. Examiner, Chapel Hill, 1969-89; mem. task force on alcohol, other drugs and transp. NRC; cons. toxicology resource com. Coll. Am. Pathologists, 1975-95, Bur. Med. Devices and Diagnostic Products, FDA, 1975-91, N.C. Drug Authority, 1971-75; dir. Mass. Alcohol Project, 1968-69. Mem. editl. bd. Jour. Forensic Scis., 1981-95; bd. editors Yearbook of Pathology, 1981-91; contbr. numerous articles on toxicology to profl. jours. Served to capt. USAAF, 1943-45. Fellow Am. Acad. Forensic Scis.; mem. Internat. Assn. Forensic Toxicologists, Nat. Safety Coun. (exec. bd. com. on alcohol and drugs 1981-91), Am. Pharm. Assn. (sec., treas. sci. sect. 1954-57), Soc. Forensic Toxicologists (dir. 1978), Am. Chem. Soc., Sigma Xi, Rho Chi, Phi Lambda Upsilon. Democrat. Roman Catholic. Home: V-306 Carolina Meadows Chapel Hill NC 27514

MCBEAN, SHARON ELIZABETH, church administrator; b. Chgo., July 15, 1937; d. Archibald Lewis Jr. and Mary Elizabeth (Rees) McBean; children: Debra Sue Sanders, Catherine Leigh Sanders Ferguson. BA cum laude, La Roche Coll., 1977; MS in Edn., Duquesne U., 1978. Cert. ch. bus. adminstr. Adminstrv. asst. 1st Presbyn. Ch., Santa Barbara, Calif., 1988-89, bus. mgr., 1989—; deacon 1st Presbyn. Ch., Santa Barbara, 1987-89. Mem. bd. mgrs. Valle Verde Retirement Comty., chair health svcs. com. Mem. Presbyn. Ch. Bus. Adminstrn. Assn., Nat. Assn. Ch. Bus. Adminstrs.

MCBEATH, ANDREW ALAN, orthopedic surgery educator; b. Milw., Mar. 4, 1936; s. Ivor Charles and Lida McBeath; m. Margaret McBeath; children: Craig Matthew, Drew Alan. BS, U. Wis., 1958, MD, 1961. Diplomate Am. Bd. Orthopaedic Surgery (oral examiner). Intern, resident Hartford (Conn.) Hosp., 1961-63; resident in orthopedic surgery U. Iowa, Iowa City, 1963-66; asst. prof. div. orthopedic surgery U. Wis., Madison, 1968-72, assoc. prof., 1972-79, prof., 1979—, Frederick J. Gaenslen prof., 1980, acting chmn. div., 1972-75, chmn. div., 1975—. Contbr. over 70 articles, chpt. to books. Capt. M.C., USAF, 1966-68. Mem. AMA, Am. Acad. Orthopaedic Surgeons, Orthopaedic Rsch. Soc., Am. Orthopaedic Assn., Hip Soc., Wis. Orthopaedic Soc., Rotary, Alpha Omega Alpha. Avocations: bicycling, skiing, reading. Office: U Wis Div Orthopedic Surg G5/361 600 Highland Ave # G5/361 Madison WI 53792-0001

MCBEATH, GERALD ALAN, political science educator, researcher; b. Mpls., Sept. 13, 1942; s. Gordon Stanley and Astrid Elvira (Hjelmeir) McB.; m. Jenifer Huang, June 7, 1970; children: Bowen, Rowena. BA, U. Chgo., 1963, MA, 1964; PhD, U. Calif., Berkeley, 1970. Vis. asst. prof. polit. sci. Rutgers Coll., New Brunswick, N.J., 1970-72; asst. prof. John Jay Coll., CUNY, N.Y.C., 1972-74, 75-76; assoc. prof. Nat. Chengchi U., Mucha, Taipei, Taiwan, 1974-75; prof. U. Alaska, Fairbanks, 1976—, acting dean coll. liberal arts, 1991-93, dir. faculty devel., 1990-92; cons. Inst. Social and Econ. Rsch., Anchorage, 1976-77; contract rschr. Alaska Dept. Natural Resources, Alaska Dept. Edn., Nat. Inst. Edn., others; staff dir. task force on internat. trade policy Rep. Conf., U.S. Senate. Sr. author: Dynamics of Alaska Native Self-Government, 1980; author monograph: North Slope Borough Government and Policymaking, 1981; jr. author: Alaska's Urban and Rural Governments, 1984; sr. editor Alaska State Government and Politics, 1987; co-author: Alaska Politics and Government, 1994 (Am. Assn. State & Local History Commendation cert. 1995); editor: Alaska's Rural Development, 1982. Mem. bd. edn. Fairbanks North Star Borough, 1986-95, pres. 1989-90, 93-94, treas., 1991-93. Recipient Emil Usibelli Disting. Svc. award 1993; Chiang Ching-Kuo Found. fellow, 1995—; named Outstanding Faculty Mem., Assn. Students U. Alaska, Fairbanks, 1979, Alumni Assn. U. Alaska, Fairbanks, 1981; grantee Nat. Inst. Edn., 1980-83, Alaska Coun. on Sci. and Tech., 1982-84, Spencer Found., 1987-88, Chiang Ching-Kuo Found., 1995—. Mem. Asian Studies on Pacific Coast (program chmn. 1983, bd. dirs. 1982-83), Assn. Asian Studies, Western Polit. Sci. Assn. (mem. editl. bd. Western Govtl. Rschr.), Am. Polit. Sci. Assn., Am. Soc. Pub. Adminstrn. (v.p. Alaskachpt.), Fairbanks N. Star Borough Bd. Edn. Democrat. Home: 1777 Red Fox Dr Fairbanks AK 99709-6625 Office: U Ala Dept Polit Sci Fairbanks AK 99775

MCBEE, FRANK WILKINS, JR., industrial manufacturing executive; b. Ridley Park, Pa., Jan. 22, 1920; s. Frank Wilkins and Ruth (Moulton) McB.; m. Sue U. Brandt, Apr. 10, 1943; children: Marilyn Moore, Robert Frank. BSME, U. Tex, 1947, MSME, 1950; PhD (hon.), St. Edward's U., Austin, 1986. Instr. to asst. prof. mech. engring. U. Tex., Austin, 1946-53, supr. mech. dept. Def. Research Lab., 1950-59; co-founder Tracor, Inc., Austin, 1955, treas., sr. v.p., 1955-67, exec. v.p., 1967-70, pres., 1970-86, chief exec. officer, 1970-88, chmn. bd., 1972-88, exec. cons., 1988-91; bd. dirs. MCorp, Dallas, Radian Corp., Austin, Rsch. Applications, Inc., Austin. Sr. active mem. adv. coun. U. Tex. Engring. Found.; mem. chancellor's coun. U. Tex.; bd. dirs. St. Edward's U.; mem. bd. dirs. Tex. Nature Conservancy, Audubon Soc., Smithsonian Instn.; chmn. adv. bd. Discovery Hall; devel. com. mem. U. Tex. Dept. Computer Scis.; hon. chmn. Allan Shivers Radiation Therapy Ctr.; past chmn. bd. trustees Laguna Gloria Art Mus.; fin. coun. Seton Med. Ctr., Seton N.W. Corp. Campaign; past chmn. Austin Area Rsch. Orgn.; trustee emeritus S.W. Tex. Pub. Broadcasting Coun.; sustaining mem. Friends of Archer M. Huntington Art Gallery, Austin; contbg. mem. N.Y. Met. Mus. Art; sr. advisor Tex. Lyceum; trustee Headliners Found.; chmn. Headliners Club; patron Ctr. for Battered Women, Austin; dir., chmn. bd. SW Rsch. Inst., San Antonio; past dir. Paramount Theatre for Performing Arts. Capt. USAAF, 1944-46. Recipient Benefactor award Austin Community Found., 1980, Spl. award Austin C. of C. Econ. Devel. Council, 1982, Clara Driscoll award Laguna Gloria Art Mus., 1987, Disting. Alumnus award U. Tex. Coll. Engring., 1978, Austinite of Yr. award Austin C. of C., 1986, Disting. Alumnus award U. Tex., 1988, Hist. Preservation awards 1964, 75, Walter Bremond House, 1990, Raymond Todd Civic award Austin Community Found., 1989, Allan Shivers Jr. award Bus. Com. for the Arts, Greater Austin C. of C., 1989, Brotherhood award Nat. Conf. Christians and Jews, 1981; named to Stephen F. Austin High Sch. Hall of Honor, 1981, Tex. Bus. Hall of Fame, 1990, Bus. Stateman of Yr. Harvard Bus. Sch. Club, 1990, Man of Yr. Air Force Assn. (Austin chpt.), 1977. Mem. NAE (life), NSPE, Tex. Soc. Profl. Engrs. (Outstanding Engr. of Yr. 1983), Tex. Assn. Bus., Tex. Taxpayers Assn. (bd. dirs.), Austin Heritage Soc. (life), Austin History Ctr. Assn. (founding), Nat. Trust for Hist. Preservation (sustaining mem.), Nat. Acad. Engring., Tex. Bus. Hall of Fame, U. Tex. Pres.'s Assocs., Austin C. of C., U. Tex. Ex-Students Assn. (life), 100 Club, Tau Beta Pi, Sigma Xi, Pi Tau Sigma, Austin Yacht Club (former commodore, vice chmn.). Office: 705 San Antonio St Austin TX 78701-2823

MCBEE, MARY LOUISE, state legislator, former academic administrator; b. Strawberry Plains, Tenn., June 15, 1924; d. John Wallace and Nina Aileen (Umbarger) McB. BS, East Tenn. State U., 1946; MA, Columbia U., 1951; PhD, Ohio State U., 1961. Tchr. East Tenn. State U., Johnson City, 1947-51; asst. dean of women, 1952-56, 57-60, dean of women, 1961-63; dean of women U. Ga., Athens, 1963-67; world campus afloat adminstr., 1966-67, assoc. dean of students, 1967-72, dean of students, 1972-74, asst. v.p. acad. affairs, 1974-76, assoc. v.p. acad. affairs, 1976-86, v.p. acad. affairs, 1986-88; now mem. Ga. Gen. Assembly; bd. dirs. Ga. Nat. Bank, Athens, 1989—. Author: College Responsibility for Values, 1980; co-author: The American Woman: Who Will She Be?, 1974, Essays, 1979,, 2d edit. 1981. Bd. dirs. Salvation Army, Athens, 1978—, United Way, Athens. Fulbright scholar, The Netherlands, 1956-57. Mem. Athens C. of C. (bd. dirs.). Democrat. Methodist. Avocations: gardening, tennis, hiking. Home: 145 Pine Valley Pl Athens GA 30606-4031 Office: GA House of Reps State Capitol Atlanta GA 30334

MCBEE, SUSANNA BARNES, journalist; b. Santa Fe, Mar. 28, 1935; d. Jess Stephen and Sybil Elizabeth (Barnes) McBee; m. Paul H. Recer, July 2, 1983. AB, U. So. Calif., 1956; MA, U. Chgo., 1962. Staff writer Washington Post, 1957-65, 73-74, 77-79, asst. nat. editor, 1974-77; asst. sec. for public affairs HEW, 1979; articles editor Washingtonian mag., 1980-81; assoc. editor U.S. News & World Report, 1981-86; news editor Washington Bur. of Hearst Newspapers, 1987-89, asst. bur. chief, 1990—; Washington corr. Life mag., 1965-69; Washington editor McCall's mag., 1970-72. Bd. dirs. Washington Press Club Found., 1992-95. Recipient Penney-Missouri mag. award, 1969, Hall of Fame award, Soc. Profl. Journalists 1996; Sigma Delta Chi Pub. Svc. award, 1969. Mem. Nat. Press Club, Cosmos Club. Home: 5190 Watson St NW Washington DC 20016-5329 Office: 1701 Pennsylvania Ave NW Washington DC 20006-5805

MCBIRNEY, BRUCE HENRY, lawyer; b. L.A., June 16, 1954; s. Bruce H. and Gretta (Doyle) McB.; m. Joanne Stillman McBirney, May 31, 1980; children: James Stillman, Esther Kathleen. BA summa cum laude, Loyola Marymount U., L.A., 1976; JD, U. Calif., Berkeley, 1979. Bar: Calif. 1979, U.S. Dist. Ct. (ctrl. dist.) 1979. Mem. Thorpe & Thorpe, L.A., 1979-95, mng. ptnr., 1991, pres., 1992-94, dir., 1992-95, v.p., 1994-95; shareholder, dir., v.p. McBirney & Chuck, L.A., 1995—. Named Scholar of Yr. Loyola Marymount U., L.A., 1976, assoc. editor Calif. Law Review, Berkeley, 1977-79, Eagle Scout Boy Scouts Am., 1968. Mem. Bldg. Owners and Mgrs. Assn., L.A. Serra Club, L.A. County Bar Assn., State Bar Calif. Office: McBirney & Chuck 611 W 6th St Ste 2500 Los Angeles CA 90017

MCBRAYER, LAURA JEAN H., school media specialist; b. Bremen, Ga., July 11, 1944; d. Robert Byron Holloman and Ruth Mildred (McGukin) McLaughlin; m. Dennis Durrett McBrayer; children: Keith, Dana, Scott, Leah. BA in English, West Ga. Coll., 1966, MEd, 1977, M in Media, 1982. Cert. media tchr., secondary English tchr., Ga. English tchr. Bremen (Ga.) H.S., 1966-72, Villa Rica (Ga.) H.S., 1974-75, Ctrl. H.S., Carrollton, Ga., 1975-78; libr., English tchr. Mt. Zion (Ga.) H.S., 1979-80; media specialist West Haralson Jr. H.S., Tallapoosa, Ga., 1980-86, Bremen H.S./Sewell Mid. Sch., Bremen, 1986—. Mem., past sec. West Ga. Regional Libr. Bd., 1988—; sec. Warren P. Sewell LIbr. Bd., Bremen, 1989—, Haralson County Libr. Bd., 1988—; mem. choir First Bapt. Ch., Bremen, 1987-92; mem. centennial com. Dem. Party, Haralson County, 1989—. Mem. ALA, Ga. Libr. Media Assn., Ga. Libr. Assn., Ga. Assn. for Instrnl. Tech., Phi Delta Kappa (Tchr. of Yr. 1977). Avocations: photography, reading, walking, movies, music. Home: 623 Laurel St Bremen GA 30110-2129 Office: Sewell Mid-Bremen HS Media Ctr 504 Laurel St Bremen GA 30110-2128

MCBRAYER, SANDRA L., educational director, homeless outreach educator. AA, San Diego Mesa Coll., 1981; BA in Applied Arts and Scis., San Diego State U., 1986, MA in Edn., 1990. Cert. presch.-kindergarten, grs. 1-12, adult edn., Calif. Tchr. asst. group homes Oz, The Bridge, Gatehouse, 1984-87; tchr. Hillcrest Receiving Home, 1987-88, Juvenile Hall, 1987-88, Comprehensive Adolescent Treatment Ctr., 1987-88; head tchr. Homeless Outreach Sch., 1988—; lectr., cons. Ctrs. Careers Edn., Sch. Tchr. Edn. San Diego State U., 1990—; collaborator sch. dists. State Dept. Edn., Equity/Homeless Office, 1992—; staff devel. tng. Recipient award Exceptional Vols. Svc. Family Care Ctr., 1988, San Diego's 10 Leadership award Sta. KGTV, 1991, Celebrate Literacy award Internat. Reading Assn., 1992, Women of Vision in Edn. award LWV San Diego, 1992, Disting. Alumna of Yr.-Edn. award San Diego State U., 1992, Golden Bell award Calif. Sch. Bds. Found., 1992; named San Diego County Tchr. of Yr. by San Diego County Office of Edn., 1993, Calif. Tchr. of Yr. by State Dept. Edn., 1993; Tech. Tchr. of Yr., Coun. on Tech. Tchr. Edn., 1994; Coun. of State Sch. Officers Nat. Tchr. of Yr. awd 1994; recognized by local and nat. news media. Mem. NEA, Calif. Tchrs. Assn., Assn. Educators, Nat. Dropout Prevention Network, Calif. Homeless Coalition, Phi Kappa Phi. Office: Homeless Outreach Sch Program 1245 Market St Ste A San Diego CA 92101-7311

MCBREEN, MAURA ANN, lawyer; b. N.Y.C., Aug. 18, 1953; d. Peter J. and Frances S. (McVeigh) McB. AB, Smith Coll., 1975; JD, Harvard U., 1978. Bar: Ill. 1978. Ptnr. Kirkland & Ellis, Chgo., 1978-86, Isham, Lincoln & Beale (merged with Reuben & Proctor), Chgo., 1986-88, Baker & McKenzie, Chgo., 1988—. Mem. ABA, Chgo. Bar Assn., Midwest Pension Conf. Office: Baker & McKenzie 1 Prudential Pla 130 E Randolph Dr Chicago IL 60601*

MCBRIDE, ANGELA BARRON, nursing educator; b. Balt., Jan. 16, 1941; d. John Stanley and Mary C. (Szcpepanska) Barron; m. William Leon McBride, June 12, 1965; children: Catherine, Kara. BS in Nursing, Georgetown U., 1962; LHD (hon.), 1993; MS in Nursing, Yale U., 1964; PhD, Purdue U., 1978; D of Pub. Svc. (hon.), U. Cin., 1983; LLD (hon.), Ea. Ky. U., 1991; DSc(hon.), Med. Coll. of Ohio, 1995. Asst. prof., rsch. asst. inst. Yale U., New Haven, 1964-73; assoc. prof., chairperson Ind. U. Sch. Nursing, Indpls., 1978-81, 80-84, prof., 1981-92, disting. prof., 1992—; assoc. dean rsch. Ind. U. Sch. Nursing, 1985-91, interim dean, 1991-92, univ. dean, 1992—. Author: The Growth and Development of Mothers, 1973, Living with Contradictions, A Married Feminist, 1976, How to Enjoy A Good Life With Your Teenager, 1987; editor: Psychiatric-Mental Health Nursing: Integrating the Behavioral and Biological Sciences, 1996 (Best Book award 1996). Recipient Disting. Alumna award Yale U., Disting. Alumna award Purdue U., Univ. Medallion, U. San Francisco, 1993; Kellog nat. fellow; Am. Nurses Found. scholar. Fellow APA (nursing and health psychology award divsn. 38 1995), Am. Acad. Nursing (past pres.), Nat. Acads. Practice; mem. Midwest Nursing Rsch. Soc. (Disting. Rsch. award 1985), Soc. for Rsch. in Child Devel., Inst. of Medicine, Nat. Acad. Scis., Sigma Theta Tau Internat. (past pres., mentor award 1993). Office: Ind U Sch Nursing 1111 Middle Dr Indianapolis IN 46202-5107

MCBRIDE, BARRY CLARKE, microbiology and oral biology educator, research microbiologist; b. Victoria, B.C., Can., June 22, 1940; s. Clarke Fyfe and Phyllis Frankie (Whitchelo) McB.; m. Barbara Elizabeth Insley, Oct. 12, 1963; children—Christopher, David. B.Sc., U. B.C., Vancouver, Can., 1963; M.Sc., U. B.C., 1965; Ph.D., U. Ill., 1970. Asst. prof. oral biology and microbiology U. B.C., 1970-75, assoc. prof., 1976-80, prof., head dept. oral biology, 1981-86, head dept. microbiology, 1986-89, dean faculty sci., 1990—; mem. Med. Research Council, 1973-79, vis. scientist, 1979, vis. prof., 1982-84; sci. officer Dental Scis. Grants Com., 1981-86. Assoc. editor Oral Microbiology and Immunology; contbr. articles to profl. jours. Rsch. grantee Med. Rsch. Coun., 1971—. Mem. Internat. Assn. Dental Research, Can. Assn. Dental Research (pres. 1990), Am. Soc. Microbiology, Sigma Xi. Avocations: mountaineering; kayaking; sailing. Office: U BC, Faculty of Sci, Vancouver, BC Canada V6T 1Z4

MC BRIDE, BEVERLEY BOOTH, psychologist; b. Richmond, Va., June 29, 1929; d. Edward Lee and Myrtle Grace (Woodlief) Booth; m. John William McBride; children: John David, William Stephen, Philip Anthony, James Andrew. Student Randolph-Macon Woman's Coll., 1949-51; BS, Va. Commonwealth U., 1951, postgrad., 1951-53; MS, Va. Poly. Inst. and State U., 1964; postgrad. Ohio U., 1969. Staff psychologist Mountain Empire Guidance Clinic, Radford, Va., 1959-67, acting dir., 1963-65; cons. psychologist Greenbrier Valley Mental Health Clinic, Lewisburg, W.Va., 1964-70, chief psychologist, 1970-89, clin. dir., 1976-79; dir. clin. services Seneca Mental Health/Mental Retardation Council, 1979-89; pvt. practice, Parkersburg, W.Va., 1967-69, Lewisburg, W.Va., 1989—; program cons. Headstart-Day Care Program, West Cen. W.Va. Community Action Assn., Parkersburg, 1967-70, dir. counseling unit Manpower Program, 1968-70; faculty Radford Coll., 1962-64, W.Va. U., Parkersburg, 1968-70; cons. psychologist Div. Vocat. Rehab., Richmond Area, 1953-58, Monroe County Bd. Edn., Union, W.Va., 1965-68, Greenbrier County Bd. Edn., Lewisburg, 1965-72, Monroe County Mental Health Clinic, Union, W.Va., 1970-73. Chmn. fine arts com. Radford Jr. Woman's Club, 1960-61, program chmn., 1961-62, v.p., 1962-63, pres., 1963-64; mem. Gov.'s Study Commn. on Youth, 1962-63, Gov.'s Study Commn. on Mental Health, 1964-65; chmn. Multicounty Interagy. Council, Radford, 1963-64; mem. Parkersburg Fine Arts Center, 1967-70; mem. adv. bd. Radford Fine Arts Council, 1963-65, Greenbrier Tng. Center, 1973-75; bd. dirs. Va. Thanksgiving Festival, Inc., 1983-86, 89—. Mem. Nat. Assn. Sch. Psychologists (del. 1971-73), W.Va. Assn. Sch. Psychologists (pres. 1975-76), W.Va. Psychol. Assn., Assn. Psychiat. Outpatient Centers Am. (sec. 1975-78), Assn. Rural Mental Health (vice-chmn. 1978-80, dir. 1977-82), Preservation Alliance of W.Va. (sec. 1992-96, publicity chmn. 1983-85), Lewisburg Hist. Landmark Commn. (chmn. 1990-94), W.Va. Hunanities Ctr. (adv. bd. 1990-94). Episcopalian. Home and Office: 409 E Washington St Lewisburg WV 24901-1701

MCBRIDE, DONNA JANNEAN, publisher; b. Kansas City, Kans., July 3, 1940; d. Donald Merle and Hazel Frances (Williams) McBride. AB, Central Coll., 1962; MLS, U. Mo.-Columbia, 1969. Tchr., Pilot Grove (Mo.) H.S., 1961-62; corr. Bus. Men's Assurance Co., Kansas City, Mo., 1962-66; acctg. clk. Prudential of Eng., Sydney, Australia, 1966-67; head tech. processes Kansas City Pub. Library (Mo.), 1967-77; customer rep. C.L. Systems, Inc., Newtonville, Mass., 1977-80; dir. support services Leon County Pub. Library, Tallahassee, 1980-82; v.p., CFO The Naiad Press, Inc., Tallahassee, 1982—; dir. The Naiad Press, 1976—, Sappho's Libr., 1983—. Mem. ALA, Nat. Gay Task Force, Am. Booksellers Assn., Nat. Women's Studies Assn., NOW. Home: RR 1 Box 3319 Havana FL 32333-9759 Office: The Naiad Press Inc PO Box 10543 Tallahassee FL 32302-2543

MC BRIDE, GUY THORNTON, JR., college president emeritus; b. Austin, Tex., Dec. 12, 1919; s. Guy Thornton and Imogene (Thrasher) McB.; m. Rebekah Jane Bush, Sept. 2, 1942; children: Rebekah Ann, William Howard, Ellen McBride McCarty. B.S. in Chem. Engring., U. Tex., 1940; Sc.D., MIT, 1948; D.P.S. (hon.), Regis Coll., 1979; D.Engring. (hon.), Colo. Sch. Mines, 1984. Registered profl. engr., Tex. La., N.Y., Colo. Instr. chem. engring. Mass. Inst. Tech., 1942-44, research assoc., 1946-48; job engr. Standard Oil Co. Calif., 1944-46; asst. prof. chem. engring Rice Inst., 1948-55, assoc. dean students, 1950-57, dean, 1957-58, assoc. prof., 1955-58; cons. Tex. Gulf Sulphur Co., 1950-58, asst. mgr. research dept., 1958-59, mgr., 1959-60, v.p., mgr. research, 1960-63; v.p. Tex. Gulf Sulphur Co. (Phosphate div.), 1963-70, gen. mgr., 1966-70; pres. Colo. Sch. Mines, Golden, 1970-84; ret.; dir. Halliburton Co., Kerr-McGee Corp., Hercules, Inc.; hon. dir. Tex-asgulf Inc. Fellow Am. Inst. Chem. Engrs.; mem. Am. Chem. Soc., Nat. Soc. Profl. Engrs., Sigma Xi, Phi Lambda Upsilon, Tau Beta Pi. Club: Mile High (Denver). Home: 2615 Oak Dr Apt 13 Lakewood CO 80215-7182

MCBRIDE, JONATHAN EVANS, executive search consultant; b. Washington, June 16, 1942; s. Gordon Williams and Martha Alice (Evans) McB.; BA, Yale U., 1964; m. Emilie Evans Dean, Sept. 5, 1970; children: Webster Dean, Morley Evans. Account exec. Merrill Lynch & Co., Washington, 1968-72; v.p. dept. mgr. Lionel D. Edie & Co., N.Y.C., 1972-76; v.p., exec. search cons. Simmons Assocs., Inc., Washington, 1976-79; pres. McBride Assocs., Inc., Washington, 1979—. Bd. dirs. Yale U. Alumni Fund, 1974-79. Served to lt. USNR, 1964-68. Clubs: Yale (N.Y.C.); Met. (Washington); Chevy Chase (Md.). Office: 1511 K St NW Washington DC 20005-1401

MCBRIDE, KAREN SUE, school guidance counselor; b. Hinton, W.Va., Dec. 31, 1953; d. Ira and Betty Ann (Simmons) Patrick; m. Charles Lynn Jones, Jul. 3, 1976 (div. June 1985); m. Arnett Dean McBride, Oct. 18, 1986. BS, Concord Coll., 1975; M, W.Va., 1987. Cert. early childhood edn., elem. edn. tchr. Learning disabilites tchr. Riverview Sch., Hinton, W.Va., 1975, first, second grade tchr., 1975-80; first grade tchr. Hinton Area Elem., Hinton, W.Va., 1980-89; sch. counselor Summers Co. Schs., 1989-92, Hinton Area Elem., Hinton, W.Va., 1992—; cons. W.Va. Dept. Edn., 1984—, coord. Summers County Drug Free Schs., Hinton, 1990-94; adv. bd. mem. Concord Coll. Head Start, Hinton, 1992—. Author: Let's Party, 1994, Developmental Guidance, 1994; co-creator Day Camp, 1991. Coach girls elem. basketball, Hinton, 1986-91; elem. cheerleader sponsor, Hinton, 1987, 88, 90, 91. Recipient Golden Apple award W.Va. Edn. Funds, 1983, Min-grant for classroom, 1983. Mem. W.Va. Edn. Assn. (chpt. pres., sec. 1975—), W.Va. Sch. Counselors Assn., Delta Kappa Gamma (chtp. treas. 1991—). Avocations: cross-stitch, quilting, reading science fiction. Home: HC 85 Box 322 Jumping Branch WV 25969-9500 Office: Summers County Bd Edn. 116 Main St Hinton WV 25951-2439

MCBRIDE, KENNETH EUGENE, lawyer, title company executive; b. Abilene, Tex., June 8, 1948; s. W. Eugene and I. Jean (Wright) McB.; m. Peggy Ann Waller, Aug. 7, 1969 (div. 1980); m. Katrina Lynne Small, June 1, 1985; children: Katherine Jean, Kellie Elizabeth. BA, Central State U., 1971; JD, Oklahoma City U., 1974. Bar: Okla. 1974. Assoc. Linn, Helms & Kirk, Oklahoma City, 1974-76; city atty. City of Edmond (Okla.), 1976-77; v.p., gen. counsel Am. First Land Title Ins., Oklahoma City, 1977-81; pres. Am. First Abstract Co., Norman, Okla., 1981-90, Lawyers Title of Oklahoma City, Inc., 1990—; CEO Am. Eagle Title Ins. Co., 1994—; pres. Okla. Land Title Assn., 1987-88; bd. dirs. Okla. Acad. for State Goals, 1994—, Okla City Met. Assn. Realtors, 1996—. Bd. dirs. Norman Bd. Adjustment, 1982-85, Leadership Okla., Inc., 1986-94, pres., 1989-90, 93-94. Fellow Okla. Bar Found.; mem. ABA, Okla. Bar Assn. (bd. dirs. Real Property Sect. 1992-94), Oklahoma County Bar Assn., Oklahoma City Met. Assn. Realtors, Oklahoma City Title Attys. Assn., Leadership Norman Alumni. Democrat. Presbyterian. Avocation: sailing. Office: Lawyers Title Oklahoma City Inc 1141 N Robinson Ave Oklahoma City OK 73103-4929

MCBRIDE, MICHAEL FLYNN, lawyer; b. Milw., Mar. 27, 1951; s. Raymond Edward and Mariam Dunne McBride; m. Kerin Ann O'Brien, Mar. 23, 1991. BS in Chem. and Biology, U. Wis., 1972, JD, 1976; MS in Environ. Engr. Sci., Calif. Inst. Tech., 1973. Bar: Wis. 1976, D.C. 1976. Assoc. LeBoeuf, Lamb, Greene & MacRae, Washington, 1976-84, ptnr., 1985—. Mem. Fed. Energy Bar Assn., Assn. Transp. Practitioners (v.p., energy tranps. law inst. com. 1990, co-chmn. 1991—, pres. 1994-95, editor ATP Jour.), Chantilly Nat. Golf and Country Club. Roman Catholic. Avocations: golf, reading, travel. Home: 6648 Byrns Pl McLean VA 22101-4419 Office: LeBoeuf Lamb Greene & MacRae LLP 1875 Connecticut Ave NW Washington DC 20009

MCBRIDE, MILFORD LAWRENCE, JR., lawyer; b. Grove City, Pa., July 16, 1923; s. Milford Lawrence and Elizabeth B. (Douthett) McB.; m. Madeleine Coulter, Aug. 6, 1947; children: Marta, Brenda, Trip, Randy, Barry. AB, Grove City Coll., 1944; BS, N.Y.U., 1944; JD, U. Pa., 1949. Bar: Pa. 1949, U.S. Dist. Ct. (we. dist.) Pa. U.S. Supreme Ct. Ptnr., McBride & McBride, Grove City, 1949-77, sr. ptnr., 1992—; ptnr. McBride and McNickle, Grove City, 1977-92; dir. Integra Fin. Corp., 1988-93. Served to 1st lt. USAAF, 1943-46. Mem. Mercer County Bar Assn. (state treas. 1970-77), ABA, Am. Bar Found. Republican. Clubs: Oakmont Country, University (Pitts.). Office: 211 S Center St Grove City PA 16127-1508

MCBRIDE, NANCY ALLYSON, child resource center administrator; b. Lakewood, Ohio, June 15, 1952; d. Harold Jackson and Mary Alice (Inman) McB. BA in Psychology magna cum laude, Oakland U., 1977. Program dir. Alternative Lifestyles, Inc., Pontiac, Mich., 1975-77; youth counselor Creative Outlooks Counseling Ctr., Pontiac, Mich., 1977-78; chief probation officer 47th Dist. Ct., Farmington Hills, Mich., 1978-80; exec. dir. Kids in Distress, inc., Wilton Manors, Fla., 1980-81; program coord. Adam Walsh Ctr., Ft. Lauderdale, Fla., 1981-87; regional trainer Home Box Office, Inc., Atlanta, 1987-90; exec. dir. Nat. Ctr. for Missing and Exploited Children/Fla. Br., Lake Park, Fla., 1990—; adj. instr. Nova U., Ft. Lauderdale, 1985-87, 90—, Broward C.C., Ft. Lauderdale, 1986-87; cons. 5 maj. TV prodns., Ft. Lauderdale, 1983-87; instr. Inst. for Nonprofit Orgn. and Mgmt., Denver, 1986-87; instr. victims svcs. cert. program Palm Beach Atlantic Coll., West Palm Beach, Fla., 1993-94. Author: (rsch. project) Child Abuse & Neglect: The Plight of the 2nd Class Citizen, 1977. Tutor Laubach Literacy Tng., Chgo., 1972; vol Erie Neighborhood House, Chgo., 1970, 72, student intern Macomb County Youth Svcs., Warren, Mich., 1977; family aide Family Focus, Birmingham, Mich., 1976-77. Recipient plaque 2d Conf. Missing Children, Chgo., 1987, Guardian Ad Litem Program, Ft. Lauderdale, 1982, Cmty. Svc. award Consortium for Human Devel., Troy, Mich., 1980, Spl. Plaque award John and Reve Walsh, 1992. Democrat. Avocations: swimming, reading, creative writing. Office: Nat Ctr - Florida Ste 100 9176 Alternate A1A Lake Park FL 33403-1452

MC BRIDE, RAYMOND ANDREW, pathologist, physician, administrator, educator; b. Houston, Dec. 27, 1927; s. Raymond Andrew and Rita (Mullane) McB.; m. Isabelle Shepherd Davis, May 10, 1958 (div. 1978); children: James Bradley, Elizabeth Conway, Christopher Ramsey, Andrew Gore. B.S., Tulane U., 1952, M.D., 1956. Diplomate: Am. Bd. Pathology. Surg. intern Jefferson Davis Hosp., Baylor U. Coll. Medicine, Houston, 1956-57; asst. in pathology Peter Bent Brigham Hosp., Boston, 1957-60; sr. resident pathologist Peter Bent Brigham Hosp., 1960-61; resident pathologist Free Hosp. for Women, Brookline, Mass., 1959; asst. resident pathologist Children's Hosp. Med. Center, Boston, 1960; teaching fellow pathology Harvard Med. Sch., Boston, 1958-61; research trainee Nat. Heart Inst., NIH, HEW, 1958-61; spl. postdoctoral fellow Nat. Cancer Inst., HEW, McIndoe Meml. Research unit Blond Labs., East Grimstead, Sussex, Eng., 1961-63; asst. attending pathologist Presbyn. Hosp., N.Y.C., 1963-65; asst. prof. pathology Coll. Physicians and Surgeons, Columbia U., 1963-65; research asso. Mt. Sinai Hosp., N.Y.C., 1965-68; assoc. prof. surgery and immunogenetics Mt. Sinai Sch. Medicine, N.Y.C., 1965-68; career scientist Health Research Council City N.Y., 1967-73; attending pathologist Flower and Fifth Ave. Hosps., N.Y.C., 1968-78, Met. Hosp. Center, N.Y.C., 1968-78; prof. pathology N.Y. Med. Coll., 1968-78; prof. pathology Baylor Coll. Medicine, Houston, 1978-96, emeritus prof. pathology, 1996—; attending pathologist Harris County Hosp. Dist., Ben Taub Gen. Hosp., Houston, 1978-96; chief pathology svcs. Harris County Hosp. Dist., 1988-96; assoc. staff Meth. Hosp., Houston, 1978-81, active staff to hon. emeritus, 1981-96, 96—; vis. grad. faculty Tex. A & M U., College Station, 1979—; clin. prof. pathology U. Tex. Grad. Sch. Biomed. Scis., Galveston, 1982—, U. Tex. Med. Br., Galveston, 1982—; prof. pathology Libero Istituto Universitario Campus Bio-Medico, Rome, 1993—; adj. prof. dept. stats. Rice U., Houston; mem. sci. com. Libero Istituto Universitario Campus Bio-Medico, Rome, 1991—; exec. dean N.Y. Med. Coll., Valhalla, 1973-75; exec. dir., COO, bd. dirs. Westchester Med. Ctr. Devel. Bd., Valhalla, 1974-76. Mem. editorial bd. Jour. Immunogenetics, Exptl. and Clin. Immunogenetics, European Jour. Immunogenetics; contbr. articles to profl. jours. Bd. dirs. Westchester Artificial Kidney Found., Inc., 1974-78, Westchester Med. Ctr. Libr., 1974-78, Westchester div. Am. Cancer Soc., 1973-78, Magnificat House, 1989-92, Found. for Life, Nat. Bd. Cath. Campaign for Am., 1989—, Tuxedo Libr., 1976-78; co-chmn. Westchester Burn Ctr. Task Force, 1975-76. Grantee Health Research Council, N.Y.C., 1963-73; Grantee Am. Cancer Soc., 1971-72; Grantee NIH, USPHS, 1964—; Grantee NSF, 1965-68. Fellow Royal Soc. Medicine; mem. Transplantation Soc., Soc. for Organ Sharing, Am. Soc. Extpl. Pathology, Reticuloendothelial Soc., AAAS, Am. Assn. Pathologists and Bacteriologists, Soc. for Investigative Pathology, Am. Assn. Immunologists, AAUP, AMA, Tex. Med. Assn., Harris County Med. Soc., Tex. Soc. Pathologists, Coll. Am. Pathologists, Am. Assn. Clin. Pathologists, Houston Acad. Medicine, Houston Soc. Clin. Pathologists, Assn. Am. Med. Colls., Fedn. Am. Scientists, Am., N.Y. cancer socs., Soc. Health and Human Values, Am. Acad. Med. Ethics, Alpha Omega Alpha (hon. med. soc.). Republican. Roman Catholic. Club: Tuxedo (Tuxedo Park, N.Y.). Achievements include research on relationship between genes of the major histocompatibility complex and the ability to regress tumors induced by different groups of avian sarcoma retroviruses; haptencarrier relationship between erythrocyte isoantigens providing a strategy for the production of antibodies to weakly immunogenic differentiation antigens; complementation of MHC and non-MHC genes in the ability to regress avian sarcoma retrovirus induced tumors; demonstration that the induction of skin graft tolerance in adult inbred mouse strains by means of parabiosis is accompanied by lymphoid cell chimerism; development of an assay for quantitation of isoimmune plaque forming cells in a non-hemolytic system. Home: 5001 Woodway Dr Apt 1404 Houston TX 77056-1719 Office: Baylor Coll Medicine Tex Med Ctr Dept Pathology One Baylor Plz Houston TX 77030 Address: via Lancellotti 18, Palazzo Lancellotti, 00186 Rome Italy also: Villa Marignoli, Via PO 2, 00186 Rome 00198, Italy also: Libero Instituto Universitario CBM, Via Longoni 83, 00155 Rome Italy

MC BRIDE, ROBERT DANA, steel company executive; b. Decatur, Ill., Nov. 5, 1927; s. Glen Clovis and Winifred Audrey (Spates) McB.; m. Gloria Jean Haefner, July 8, 1950; children: Scott, Dana, Kelly, Kitty. B.S., U.S. Mil. Acad., 1950; grad., Advanced Mgmt. Program, Harvard U., 1974. V.p. ops. Granite City Steel Co., Ill., from 1966; pres. Granite City Steel div. Nat. Steel Corp., 1976-77; pres. Great Lakes Steel div. Nat. Steel Corp., Detroit, 1977-82; pres. Nat. Steel Corp., Pitts., 1983-86; sr. cons. Genix Corp., Pitts., 1987-89; pres. Trebbi Cons., Washington, 1989-90; pres., CEO McLouth Steel, Trenton, Mich., 1991-92, chmn., CEO, 1993-94, chmn., 1995—, also bd. dirs.; bd. dirs. The Dreyfus/Laurel Funds, Pitts., Salem Corp., Pitts.; mem. bd. visitors Marine Biol. Lab., Woods Hole, Mass. Served with U.S. Army, 1950-56. Decorated Purple Heart, Silver Star, Bronze Star. Mem. Am. Iron and Steel Inst., Assn. Iron and Steel Engrs. (dir., past pres.). Roman Catholic. Home: 15 Waverly Ln Grosse Pointe MI 48236-3039

MCBRIDE, RODNEY LESTER, investment counselor; b. Denver, Sept. 1, 1941; s. Laurence Thomas and Harriet Alvina (Primmer) McB.; m. Nancy Faye Davenport, Mar. 21, 1964 (div. June 1984); children: Douglas L., Cheryl L.; m. Judy Winslow, Nov. 7, 1992; stepchildren: Mark P. Winslow, Scott C. Winslow. BS in Mktg., U. Colo., 1963; MBA, U. Calif., Berkeley, 1976. Chartered investment counselor Investment Counsel Assn. Am., Fin. Analyst Fedn. Indsl. salesman Fibreboard Corp., San Diego and San Francisco, 1963-66; investment counselor Shuman, Agnew & Co., San Francisco, 1966-71; investment counselor, co-founder capital counseling svc. Bank of Am., San Francisco, 1971-75; investment counselor Scudder, Stevens and Clark, San Francisco, 1975-76; sr. v.p., office mgr. Crocker Investment Mgmt. Corp., Los Angeles, 1977-84; sr. v.p., dir. portfolio mgmt., chmn. equity strategy com. Crocker Investment Mgmt. Corp., San Francisco, 1984-86; mng. dir., sr. portfolio mgr., chmn. equity strategy com., chmn. core equity com., chmn. internat. asset allocation com. Chancellor Capital Mgmt., Inc. (formerly Citicorp Investment Mgmt. Corp.), N.Y.C., 1986-94; mng. dir., sr. portfolio mgr., chmn. equity strategy com. Furman Selz Capital Mgmt., N.Y.C., 1994—. Pres., coach Palos Verdes (Calif.) Basketball Assn., 1982-83; mem. 2d Congregational Ch.; bd. dirs. Greater N.Y. couns. Boy Scouts Am. Mem. L.A. Soc. Fin. Analysts (sec., bd. dirs. 1984, treas. 1983, chmn. seminar com. 1982-83), N.Y. Soc. Fin. Analysts, Assn. Investment Mgmt. and Rsch. (chartered fin. analyst), Western Pension Conf., U. Colo. Alumni Assn., U. Calif. Alumni Assn., Stanwich Country Club, Round Hill Country Club, Alpha Kappa Psi (treas. 1963). Republican. Avocations: golf, tennis, volleyball, duck hunting, fishing. Home: 148 Clapboard Ridge Rd Greenwich CT 06831-3351 Office: Furman Selz Capital Mgmt 230 Park Ave New York NY 10169-0005

MCBRIDE, SANDRA TEAGUE, critical care nurse; b. Corinth, Miss., Sept. 13, 1958; d. Clarence R. and Alice (Ingram) T. AAS, Shelby State Community Coll., 1983; BSN, U. North Ala., 1987. RN, Miss., Tenn. Nurse supr. Alcorn County Care, Inc., Corinth, Miss., 1985-87; staff nurse Bolivar (Tenn.) Community Hosp., 1988-90; staff nurse West Tenn. High Security Facility Tenn. Dept. of Corrections, Ripley, 1990-91; staff nurse U.S. Med. Ctr. for Fed. Prisoners, Springfield, Mo., 1991-92, Western Mental Health Inst., Bolivar, 1992—.

MCBRIDE, THOMAS DWAYNE, mechanical engineer; b. Brownwood, Tex., Feb. 13, 1947; s. Thomas Alfred and Eula Faye (Harvey) McB.; m. Peggy Anne Kimbrough McBride, Oct. 14, 1967; children: Jeffery Dwayne, Stacy Anne. AS, Crowder Coll., Neosho, Mo., 1967; BS in Mech. Engring., U. Mo., Rolla, 1970; MBA in Mgmt., U. Akron, 1978. Engring. supr. Babcock & Wilcox, Barberton, Ohio, 1972-79; mgr. engring. Bendix Corp., South Beloit, Ill., 1979-83; mgr. sales engring. Bendix/Warner & Swasey, Worcester, Mass., 1983-84, mgr. Product Engring., 1984-86; program mgr. Design Tech. Corp., Billerica, Mass., 1986-87; mgr. engring. Netco, Inc., Haverhill, Mass., 1987-88; dir. engring. The Nelmor Co., North Uxbridge, Mass., 1988—; tech. and bus. cons. Micromation, Inc., Altoona, Pa., 1988-90. Inventor: Granulator Knife, 1991, 94, Bin Deflector, 1991; author: Society of Manufacturing Engineers, 1992. 1st lt. U.S. Army, 1970-72. Recipient Curator's scholarship U. Mo., 1967. Mem. Soc. Plastics Engrs., Environ. Industry Assn. (co-chairperson Wastec divsn. subcom. on safety standards for size reduction equipment 1995—). Mem. Trinity Ch. Avocations: golf, genealogy, religious history. Home: 36 Deerfield Rd Shrewsbury MA 01545-1530 Office: The Nelmor Co Rivulet St North Uxbridge MA 01538

MCBRIDE, THOMAS FRANCIS, machinery company executive; b. Essington, Pa., Oct. 22, 1935; s. Thomas F. and Margaret F. (Schuhay) McB.; B.S. in Acctg., Kings Coll., Pa., 1957; m. Marie E. Schultz, Feb. 7, 1959; children: Maureen, Thomas, Colleen, Mary Kathleen. Cost acct. Air Products Co., Allentown, Pa., 1957-59; mgr. cost acctg. Litton Industries, College Park, Md., 1961-64; mgr. ops. adminstrn. RCA, Eng., 1964-65, mgr. ops. analysis, N.J., 1965-68; v.p. fin. Singer Co., State College, Pa., 1968-71, v.p., group controller, N.Y.C., 1971-74; asst. comptroller Ingersoll-Rand, Woodcliff Lake, N.J., 1974-79, v.p., corp. comptroller, 1979-93, sr. v.p., CFO, 1993—. Bd. dirs. Bergen County council Boy Scouts Am. Served with USMC, 1959. Mem. Fin. Execs. Inst., Am. Mgmt. Assn. (fin. council). Roman Catholic. Club: KC. Office: Ingersoll-Rand Co Inc 200 Chestnut Ridge Rd Westwood NJ 07675

MC BRIDE, THOMAS FREDERICK, lawyer, former university dean, government official; b. Elgin, Ill., Feb. 8, 1929; s. Thomas Wallace and Sarah

Rosalie (Pierce) McB.; m. Catherine Higgs Milton, Aug. 23, 1975; children: Matthew (dec.), Elizabeth, John, Raphael, Luke. BA, NYU, 1952; LLB, Columbia U., 1956. Bar: N.Y. 1956, D.C. 1966, U.S. Supreme Ct. 1963, Calif. 1989. Asst. dist. atty. N.Y. County, 1956-59; trial atty. organized crime sect. Dept. Justice, 1961-65; adviser to Home Ministry, Govt. India, 1964; ofcl. Peace Corps, 1965-68; dep. chief counsel select com. on crime Ho. of Reps., 1969-70; assoc. dir., staff dir. Police Found., 1970-73; assoc. spl. prosecutor Watergate, 1973-75; dir. bur. enforcement CAB, 1975-77; insp. gen. U.S. Dept. Agr., Washington, 1977-81, U.S. Dept. Labor, Washington, 1981-82; assoc. dean Stanford Law Sch. (Calif.), 1982-89; mem. Pres.'s Commn. Organized Crime, 1983-86, Calif. Council on Mental Health, 1986-90; dir. environ. health and safety Stanford U., 1990-92; counselor U.S. Dept. Energy, Washington, 1993-95. Served with AUS, 1946-47. Mem. D.C. Bar Assn. Home and Office: 837 Cedro Way Stanford CA 94305-1034

MCBRIDE, WANDA LEE, psychiatric nurse; b. Dayton, Ohio, Dec. 13, 1931; d. Owen Francis Staup and Ruby Madonna (Campbell) Inscore; m. Richard H. McBride, July 28, 1951 (div. Mar. 1966); children: Kathleen Kerns, Kimberlee Haley. Diploma, Christ Hosp. Sch., Cin., 1953; student, U. Cin., 1954-55. Cert. psychiat. mental health nurse ANA. Various health-care positions, 1953-66; from supr. 4 acute male units to supr. outpatient dept. Cen. Ohio Psychiat. Hosp., Columbus, 1966-77; supr. hosp., head nurse urology and respiratory diseases flr. St. Anthony Hosp., Okla., 1977-83; shift supr. and coord. child program Willowview Hosp., Spencer, Okla., 1983-88; adminstrv. nursing supr. Grant Ctr. of Deering Hosp., Miami, 1988—, assessment specialist, 1995—; case mgr. Kemper Svcs., Plantation, Fla., 1996—. Mem. Gov.'s Com. for Mental Health and Retardation, 1963-66, Logan County Mental Health League, Ohio, 1963-66. Named Nurse of Yr., 1983-90. Mem. Nat. League for Nursing, Mental Health League (past pres.), Lioness Club (past pres.). Republican. Episcopalian. Avocations: orchid growing, classical music, cooking, fishing, camping. Home: 304 Lakeside Ct Fort Lauderdale FL 33326-2117

MCBRIDE, WILLIAM BERNARD, treasurer; b. N.Y.C., May 22, 1931; s. William and Nora (Hughes) McB.; m. Lorraine Barry, May 27, 1956; children: Mary, William, Stephen, Anne. BS, Fordham U., 1952; MBA, Baruch Sch., 1963. CPA, N.Y. Staff auditor Touche, Ross, Bailey & Smart (CPAs), N.Y.C., 1952-58; asst. v.p. Bankers Trust Co., N.Y.C., 1959-67; treas. Kidde, Inc., Saddle Brook, N.J., 1967-87; v.p. Kidde, Inc., 1974-87; cons. Hanson Industries, other cos., Iselin, N.J., 1987—. Mem. AICPA, N.Y. State Soc. CPAs. Home and Office: 243 Sunset Ave Ridgewood NJ 07450-2420

MC BRIDE, WILLIAM LEON, philosopher, educator; b. N.Y.C., Jan. 19, 1938; s. William Joseph and Irene May (Choffin) McB.; m. Angela Barron, July 12, 1965; children: Catherine, Kara. A.B., Georgetown U., 1959; postgrad. (Fulbright fellow), U. Lille, 1959-60; M.A. (Woodrow Wilson fellow), Yale U., 1962, Ph.D. (Social Sci. Research Council fellow), 1964. Instr. philosophy Yale U., New Haven, 1964-66, asst. prof., 1966-70, assoc. prof., 1970-73; lectr. Northwestern U., Evanston, Ill., summer 1972; assoc. prof. Purdue U., West Lafayette, Ind., 1973-76, prof., 1976—; lectr. Korcula Summer Sch., Yugoslavia, 1971, 73. Author: Fundamental Change in Law and Society, 1970, The Philosophy of Marx, 1977, Social Theory at a Crossroads, 1980, (with R.A. Dahl) Demokrati og Autoritet, 1980, Sartre's Political Theory, 1991, Social and Political Philosophy, 1994; editor: (with C.O. Schrag) Phenomenology in a Pluralistic Context, 1983. Mem. AAUP (pres. Purdue chpt. 1983-86, pres. Ind. conf. 1988-89), Am. Philos. Assn. (chmn. com. on internat. coop. 1992-95, bd. dirs. 1992-95), Am. Soc. Polit. and Legal Philosophy, Soc. Phenomenology and Existential Philosophy (exec. co-sec. 1977-80), Sartre Soc. N.Am. (chmn. bd. dirs. 1985-88, 91-93), Am. Soc. Philosophy in the French Lang. (pres. 1994-96). Home: 744 Cherokee Ave Lafayette IN 47905-1872 Office: Purdue U Dept Philosophy West Lafayette IN 47907-1360

MCBRIEN, RICHARD PETER, theology educator; b. Hartford, Conn., Aug. 19, 1936; s. Thomas Henry and Catherine Ann (Botticelli) McB. AA, St. Thomas Sem., 1956; BA, St. John Sem., 1958, MA, 1962; STD, Gregorian U., 1967. Assoc. pastor Our Lady of Victory Ch., West Haven, Conn., 1962-63; prof., dean of studies Pope John XXIII Nat. Sem., Weston, Mass., 1965-70; prof. theology Boston Coll., Newton, Mass., 1970-80, dir. inst. of religious edn. and pastoral ministry, 1975-80; prof. theology U. Notre Dame, Ind., 1980—, chmn. dept., 1980-91; cons. various dioceses and religious communities in the U.S. and Can., 1965—; vis. fellow John F. Kennedy Sch. Govt. Harvard U., Cambridge, 1976-77; mem. Council on Theol. Scholarship and Research Assn. of Theol. Schs., 1987-91. Author: Do We Need Church?, 1969, Catholicism, 2 vols., 1980, rev. edit., 1994 (Christopher award 1981), Caesar's Coin: Religion and Politics in America, 1987, Report on the Church: Catholicism after Vatican II, 1992, Responses to 101 Questions on the Church, 1996, Inside Catholicism, 1996; editor: Encyclopedia Religion, 1987, Harper Collins Encyclopedia of Catholicism, 1995. Recipient Best Syndicated Weekly Column award Cath. Press Assn. of U.S. and Can., 1975, 77, 78, 84. Mem. Cath. Theol. Soc. of Am. (pres. 1973-74, John Courtney Murray award 1976), Coll. Theology Soc., Am. Acad. Religion. Office: Univ of Notre Dame Dept of Theology Notre Dame IN 46556

MCBROOM, NANCY LEE, insurance executive; b. Tulsa, Nov. 7, 1925; d. Lee Webster and Dora Irene (Londigan) Adams; m. Robert B. McBroom, Jan. 22, 1945 (dec. Aug. 1969); children: Dacia Adams, Rene McBroom, Robert McBroom. Student, John Brown U., 1941-42, Little Rock Bus. Coll., 1941-42. Profl. horse trainer, judge, breeder N.C., Va. and Calif., 1955-75; owner Stombock's West, Inc., Del Mar, Calif., 1968-74; agt. Mut. Omaha Ins. Co., San Diego, 1978-84; owner, broker McBroom Ins. Svcs., San Diego, 1984—; dir. Dependent's Riding Program, USMC, Camp LeJeune, N.C., 1963-66. Author: Handbook for Riding Instructors, 1963. Mem. com. Civitan Fund Raiser for Spl. Olympics, 1986. Mem. Nat. Assn. Securities Dealers, Rancho Bernardo C. of C. (com. 1986). Republican. Lodge: Soroptimist Internat. (mem. com. Women Helping Women 1985-86). Avocations: music, tennis, swimming, horseback riding, hiking, travel. Home: 12093 Caminito Campana San Diego CA 92128-2061 Office: McBroom Ins Svcs 16776 Bernardo Ctr Dr Ste 203 San Diego CA 92128-2534

MCBROOM, THOMAS WILLIAM, SR., utility manager; b. Atlanta, Mar. 29, 1963; s. William Ralph and Ethel Irene (Bradley) McB. B in Mech. Engring., Ga. Tech., 1985, MS in Mech. Engring., 1987; JD, Ga. State U., 1992, MBA, 1992. Bar: Ga. 1993, D.C. 1994, U.S. Tax Ct. 1993; registered profl. engr., Ga.; lic. comml. pilot and flight instr. Mfg. engr. AT & T Techs., Norcross, Ga., 1985-86; energy systems engr. Atlanta Gas Light Co., 1987-89, sales engr., 1989-90, dir. power systems markets, 1991-94, sr. corp. planning analyst, 1994-95, mgr. maj. accounts, 1995—. Mem. Leadership Coweta, 1996. Mem. ASHRAE, Ga. Bar Assn., Ga. Soc. Profl. Engrs. (treas. 1990-91, sec. 1991-92, pres. 1992-93, Young Engr. of Yr. 1991), Newnan-Coweta C. of C. (transp. com. 1996), Toastmasters Internat. (treas. 1996—), Phi Delta Phi (exchequer 1991). Home: 15 Culpepper Way Newnan GA 30265-2217 Office: Atlanta Gas Light Co PO Box 4569 Atlanta GA 30302-4569

MCBRYDE, JOHN HENRY, federal judge; b. Jackson, Oct. 9, 1931; m. Betty Vinson; children: Rebecca McBryde Dippold, Jennifer, John Blake. BS in Commerce, Tex. Christian U., 1953; LLB, U. Tex., 1956. Bar: Tex. 1956, U.S. Ct. Appeals (5th cir.) 1958, U.S. Dist. Ct. (no. dist.) 1958, U.S. Dist. Ct. (ea. dist.) 1989, U.S. Supreme Ct. 1972. Assoc. Cantey, Hanger, Johnson, Scarborough & Gooch, Ft. Worth, 1956-62; ptnr. Cantey & Hanger and predecessor firm, Ft. Worth, 1962-69, McBryde, Bennett and predecessor firms, Ft. Worth, 1969-90; judge U.S. Dist. Ct. (no. dist.) Tex., Ft. Worth, 1990—. Fellow Am. Bar Found., Tex. Bar Found. (life), Am. Coll. Trial Lawyers. Office: US Dist Ct US Courthouse Rm 401 501 W 10th St Fort Worth TX 76102-3637

MCBRYDE, NEILL GREGORY, lawyer; b. Durham, N.C., Jan. 11, 1944; s. Angus M. and Priscilla (Gregory) McB., m. Margaret McPherson, Aug. 1, 1970; children: Margaret Courtauld, Neill Gregory Jr. AB cum laude, Davidson Coll., 1966; JD with high honors, U. N.C., 1969. Bar: N.C. 1969, Ga. 1972. Assoc. King & Spalding, Atlanta, 1971-76; ptnr. Fleming, Robinson, Bradshaw & Hinson, Charlotte, N.C., 1977-81, Helms, Mulliss & Johnston, Charlotte, 1981-86, Smith Helms Mulliss & Moore, Charlotte, 1986-90, Moore & Van Allen PLLC, Charlotte, 1990—; lectr. in field, conducter workshops in field. Author, editor: First Union National Bank of North Carolina Will Book, 1986; contbr. to profl. jours. Elder and Deacon Myers Park Presbyn. Ch., Charlotte, 1980-86, 92-95; dir. sec. Presbyn. Home for Aged, Charlotte, 1978-82; trustee Charlotte Latins Schs., Inc., 1980-86, 87-93. Fellow Am. Coll. Trust and Estate Counsel (mem. bd. regents, sec.), Am. Coll. Tax Counsel; mem. ABA, Ga. Bar Assn., N.C. Bar Assn. (probate and fiduciary law sect.), Order of Coif, Phi Beta Kappa, Omicron Delta Kappa. Republican. Avocations: tennis, golf, fishing. Office: Moore & Van Allen PLLC Nations Bank Corp Ctr 100 N Tryon St Fl 47 Charlotte NC 28202-4000

MCBRYDE, WILLIAM ARTHUR EVELYN, chemistry educator and researcher; b. Ottawa, Ont., Can., Oct. 20, 1917; married, 1949; 2 children. BA, U. Toronto, 1939, MA, 1940; PhD in Chemistry, U. Va., 1947. Asst. chemist U. Toronto, 1939-41; chemist Welland Chem. Works, 1942-44; asst. prof. chemistry U. Va., 1947-48; from asst. prof. to assoc. prof. U. Toronto, 1948-60; prof., chmn. dept. U. Waterloo, 1960-64; dean faculty sci. U. Waterloo, Ont., Can., 1961-69, chmn. dept., 1971-77, prof., 1971-86, prof. chemistry emeritus, 1986—; vis. fellow Australian Nat. U., 1969-70. Recipient Fisher Lectr. award Analysis chem., 1973. Mem. Chem. Inst. Can. (Chem. Edn. award 1967). Achievements include research in chemistry of precious metals; colorimetric analysis; coordination chemistry; history of chemistry. Office: Univ of Waterloo, Dept of Chemistry, Waterloo, ON Canada N2L 3G1*

MCBURNEY, GEORGE WILLIAM, lawyer; b. Ames, Iowa, Feb. 17, 1926; s. James William and Elfie Hazel (Jones) McB.; m. Georgianna Edwards, Aug. 28, 1949; children: Hollis Lynn, Jana Lee McBurney-Lin, John Edwards. B.A., State U. Iowa, 1950, J.D. with distinction, 1953. Bar: Iowa 1953, Ill. 1954, Calif. 1985. With Sidley & Austin and predecessor, Chgo., 1953—, ptnr., 1964-1993, counsel, 1994—; resident ptnr. Singapore, 1982-84. Editor-in-chief: Iowa Law Rev., 1952-53. Mem. Chgo. Crime Commn., 1966-84; trustee Iowa Law Sch. Found., 1988—, Old People's Home of City of Chgo., 1968-83, sec., 1967-69, exec. v.p., 1969-74, pres., 1974-82, hon. life trustee, 1983—; hon. life trustee Georgian, Evanston, Ill., trustee, counsel, 1976-82, v.p., 1980-82. Served with inf. AUS, 1944-46. Fellow Am. Coll. Trial Lawyers, Am. Bar Found. (life); mem. ABA, State Bar Calif., L.A. County Bar Assn., Fed. Bar Assn., Bar Assn. 7th Fed. Cir., Am. Judicature Soc., Am. Arbitration Assn. (panelist large complex dispute resolution program), Assn. Atty. Mediators (So. Calif. chpt.), Assn. Bus. Trial Lawyers, The Ctr. for Internat. Comml. Arbitration L.A. (bd. dirs., exec. v.p.), Nat. Coll. Edn. (bd. assocs. 1967-84), U.S. C. of C. (govt. and regulatory affairs com. on coun. on antitrust policy 1980-82), L.A. Complex Litigation Inn of Ct., Law Soc. Singapore (hon.), Western Ctr. on Law and Poverty (bd. dirs. 1992—), L.A. Union League Club (vet.), Mid-Day Club Chgo., Law Club (life), Legal Club Chgo., Am. Club, Cricket Club, Town Club Singapore, Phi Kappa Psi, Omicron Delta Kappa, Delta Sigma Rho, Phi Delta Phi. Republican. Presbyterian. Home: Malibu Pacifica 13 3601 Vista Pacifica Malibu CA 90265-4830 Office: Sidley & Austin 555 W 5th St Ste 4000 Los Angeles CA 90013-3000

MCBURNEY, MARGOT B., librarian; b. Lethbridge, Alta., Can.; d. Ronald Laurence Maness and R. Blanche (Lott) Hart; children: Margot Elisabeth McBurney Lane, James Ronald Gordon. B.A. with honours, Principia Coll., 1953; M.Sc. in L.S, U. Ill., 1969. Sec. Marshall Brooks Library, Principia Coll., Elsah, Ill., 1966-69; reference librarian Marshall Brooks Library, Principia Coll., 1969-70; systems analyst trainee in library systems U. Alta. Library, Edmonton, 1970-71; undergrad. reference librarian U. Alta. Library, 1971-72, editor periodicals holdings list, 1972-73, serials catalogue, 1973-74, head acquisitions div., 1974-77; chief librarian Queen's U. Library, Kingston, Ont., Can., 1977-90. Editor: Am. Soc. Info. Sci. Western Can. chpt. Proceedings, 1975, 76. Mem. ALA, Am. Soc. Info. Sci. (councilor-at-large 1976-79, past chmn. chpt.), Assn. Research Libraries (dir. 1978-81, chmn. task force on library edn. 1980-83), Can. Assn. Info. Sci., Can. Assn. Research Libraries, Can. Library Assn., Council on Library Resources (PETREL com. 1981-84), Phi Alpha Eta, Beta Phi Mu.

MCCABE, CHARLES LAW, retired manufacturing company executive, management consultant; b. Port Deposit, Md., Oct. 13, 1922; s. Joshua Burton and Adah (Law) McC.; m. Ingrid Alice Koebel, Dec. 21, 1949; children: Chad, Sigrid Christina, Ingrid Lisa. B.S., Dickinson Coll., 1943; M.S., Carnegie Mellon U., 1947, Sc.D., 1948. Mem. faculty Carnegie Mellon U., Pitts., 1951-65, prof., 1959-65; dean Grad. Studies, Carnegie Mellon U., 1962-65, v.p. research, 1964-65; pres. Koebel Diamond Tool Co., Detroit, 1966-70, Teledyne Firth Sterling, Pitts., 1970-75; gen. mgr. v.p. High Tech. Materials div. Cabot Corp., Kokomo, Ind., 1975-82; v.p. Cabot Corp., Boston, 1982-87; pres. High St. Assocs., Boston, 1988—. Author: (with C.L. Bauer) Metals, Atoms and Alloy, 1964. Past trustee Dickinson Coll.; active fund drives United Way. Served with AUS, 1945-46. Fellow Am. Soc. Metals (Pitts award 1961); mem. AIME, Grosse Pointe Club, Naples Yacht Club (dir. 1995—), Pt. Royal Club (Naples). Episcopalian.

MC CABE, GERARD BENEDICT, retired library administrator; b. N.Y.C., Jan. 22, 1930; s. Patrick Joseph and Margaret Irene (McDonald) McC.; m. Jacqueline L. Maloney, Aug. 3, 1963 (dec. 1987); children: Theresa Marie, Rebecca Mary. B.A. in English, Manhattan Coll., 1952; A.M. in Library Sci. (scholar), U. Mich., 1954; M.A. in English, Mich. State U., 1959. Asst. acquisitions dept. U. Nebr. Library, Lincoln, 1954-56; chief bibliog. acquisitions dept. Mich. State U. Library, East Lansing, 1956-58; librarian Inst. Community Devel. and Service, Mich. State U., 1958-59; acquisitions librarian U. S. Fla., Tampa, 1959-66; asst. dir. planning and devel. U. S. Fla., 1967-70; assoc. dir. U. Ark. Library, Fayetteville, 1966-67; dir. univ. libraries Va. Commonwealth U., Richmond, 1970-82; dir. libraries Clarion U. of Pa., 1982-95; ret., 1995; libr. cons., Wilmington, N.C., 1995—. Editor: The Smaller Academic Library: A Management Handbook, 1988, Operations Handbook for Small Academic Library, 1989, Academic Libraries in Urban and Metropolitan Areas, 1992; co-editor ann. pub. Advances in Libr. Adminstrn. and Orgn., vols. 1-12, Insider's Guide to Libr. Automation: Essays of Practical Experience, 1993, Acad. Librs.: Their Rationale and Role in Am. Higher Edn., 1995, Introducing and Managing Academic Library Automation Projects, 1996; contbr. articles to profl. jours. Mem. ALA, Southeastern Library Assn., Bibliog. Soc. Am. Home and Office: PO Box 4793 Wilmington NC 28406-1793 *Consideration for others is a guiding principle for my personal and professional behavior. I, as a librarian, must have concern for those I serve. Their needs are my first and only interest, not success, not notoriety, only their service and their satisfaction.*

MCCABE, JAMES J., lawyer; b. Phila., May 8, 1929; s. James J. and Marie D. (Seitz) McC.; m. Dolores A. Ruane, Sept.17, 1954 (dec.); children: Deirdre McCabe Affel, Judith Ann McCabe Jarvis, James. J. III; m. Rosemarie T. Smith, June 29, 1984. AB, LaSalle Coll., 1951; JD, Temple U., 1955. Bar: Pa. and fed. cts., 1956, U.S. Supreme Ct. 1971. Assoc., Duane, Morris & Heckscher, Phila., 1955-64, ptnr. 1964—; chmn. litigation dept., 1984—; lectr. med. and ins. law, trial technique Practicing Law Inst., N.Y. Law Jour. Seminars, Defense Rsch. Inst.; adj. prof. family medicine Thomas Jefferson U. Sch. Medicine, Phila. Trustee Phila. Bar Found., 1979-81; past pres. St. Thomas More Soc., Phila.; vol. in Miss. Lawyers' Com. for Civil Rights, 1968. Case note editor Temple Law Quar.; contbg. editor Med. Malpractice Law and Strategy. Fellow Am. Coll. Trial Lawyers, Am. Bd. Profl. Liability Attys., Pa. Bar Found. (life); mem. Pa. Bar Assn., Phila. Bar Assn., Am. Bd. Trial Advocates (founder Pa. chpt. 1982), Am. Coll. Legal Medicine, Assn. Def. Trial Attys., Assn. Def. Counsel Phila. (past pres.), Internat. Assn. Def. Counsel, Def. Rsch. Inst. Inc. (Pa. chmn. 1973-77, v.p. Atlantic region 1977-80, dir. 1980-83), Attys.' Liability Assurance Soc. Ltd. (bd. dirs.), Legatus (Phila. chpt.), Master of the Rolls, Temple Inn of Ct.

MCCABE, JAMES R., school system administrator. Supt. Lake County Sch. Dist. R-1, Leadville, Colo. State finalist Nat. Supt. Yr. award, 1992. Office: Lake County Sch Dist R-1 PO Box 977 107 Spruce Leadville CO 80461

MC CABE, JOHN CHARLES, III, writer; b. Detroit, Nov. 14, 1920; s. Charles John and Rosalie (Dropiewski) McC.; m. Vija Valda Zarina, Oct. 19, 1962 (dec. 1984); children—Linard Peter, Sean Cahal and Deirdre Rose (twins); m. Rosina Lawrence, June 8, 1987. Ph.B., U. Detroit, 1947; M.F.A. in Theatre, Fordham U., 1948; Ph.D. in English Lit, Shakespeare Inst., U. Birmingham, Eng., 1954. Instr. theatre Wayne State U., 1948-51, CCNY, 1955; mem. faculty N.Y. U., 1956-68, prof. dramatic art, chmn. dept., 1962-68; chmn. dept. drama and theatre arts Mackinac Coll., Mackinac Island, Mich., 1968-70; founder The Sons of the Desert (group devoted to works Laurel and Hardy), 1963. Profl. actor, 1928—, producer-dir., Milford (Pa.) Playhouse, summers, 1948-53, prodr., N.Y.U. Summer Theatre, Sterling Forest, N.Y., 1963-65, author-in-residence, Lake Superior State Coll., Sault Ste. Marie, Mich., 1970-86; author: Mr. Laurel and Mr. Hardy, 1961, rev. edit., 1986, George M. Cohan: The Man Who Owned Broadway, 1973, The Comedy World of Stan Laurel, 1974, Laurel & Hardy, 1975, (with G.B. Harrison) Proclaiming the Word, 1976, Charles Chaplin, 1978, Grand Hotel: Mackinac Island, 1987, Babe: The Life of Oliver Hardy, 1990, The High, 1992; ghostwriter of James Cagney's autobiography, Cagney by Cagney, 1976. Served with USAAF, 1943-45, ETO. Mem. Shakespeare Assn. Am., Actors Equity Assn., Catholic Actors Guild Am., Baker St. Irregulars. Clubs: The Players (N.Y.C.), The Lambs (N.Y.C.). Home: British Landing PO Box 363 Mackinac Island MI 49757-0363 *At fourteen I learned from the Jesuits that one who knows both the function and beauty of an English sentence will be blessed life-long.*

MCCABE, MICHAEL, broadcast executive; b. Toronto, 1938; divorced; 2 children. Honours degree Philosophy, English, U. Toronto. Exec. asst. fed. cabnet minister Ottawa, 1963-68; v.p. Helix Investments Ltd., 1968-70; dir.-gen. policy and program devel. citizenship br. Dept. State, Ottawa, 1970-74; chmn. policy and rsch. Can. Mortgage and Housing Corp., Ottawa, 1974-76; asst. dep. minister comsumer affairs Fed. Dept. Consumer and Corp. Affairs, Ottawa, 1976-78; exec. dir. Can. Film Devel. Corp. (now Telefilm Can.), Ottawa, 1978-80; pres. McCabe Comm. Ltd., Ottawa, 1981-88; pres.& CEO Can. Assn. Broadcasters, Ottawa, 1988—. Office: Can Assn Broadcasters, 350 Sparks St #306, PO Box 627 Stn B, Ottawa, ON Canada K1P 5S2

MCCABE, MICHAEL JAMES, art director; b. DeKalb, Ill., Apr. 2, 1954; s. Thomas Andrew and Mary Jean (Conlin) McC.; m. Nancy Jean McIlrath, Dec. 24, 1976; children: Erin Mary, Michaela. AA, Kishwaukee Community Coll., 1974; BA, Ill. State U., Normal, 1976, postgrad., 1976. Graphic designer Ad Pro, Sycamore, Ill., 1977-79; art dir. Ad Creation, DeKalb; art dir. Bader Rutter & Assocs., Brookfield, Wis., 1982-86, assoc. creative dir., 1986—; Freelance photographer Tony Stone Images, Chgo., 1986—. Recipient numerous awards Nat. Agri-Mktg. Assn., 1980-96; Bell award Bus. Profl. Advt. Assn., Milw., 1985, 86, Cert. of Excellence award Print Mag., N.Y.C., 1986, 93. Mem. Illustrators and Designers Club of Milw. Roman Catholic. Avocations: photography, boating, water skiing, landscaping. Office: Bader Rutter & Assocs 13555 Bishops Ct Brookfield WI 53005-6224

MCCABE, MONICA PETRAGLIA, lawyer; b. Bronx, N.Y., Jan. 11, 1959; d. John Francis and Eleanor Angela (Gengaro) Petraglia; m. Edward D. McCabe, May 27, 1984; 1 child, Eleanor Angela. BA summa cum laude, Fordham U., 1981; MA in Polit. Sci., U. of Chgo., 1984; JD cum laude, Georgetown U., 1985. Bar: N.Y. 1986, D.C. 1987, U.S. Dist. Ct. (so. dist.) N.Y. 1987, U.S. Dist. Ct. (ea. dist.) N.Y. 1988, U.S. Supreme Ct. 1991. Law clk. U.S. Dept. of State, Washington, 1984-85; jud. clk. to judge U.S. Dist. Ct. U.S. Dist. Ct., Washington, 1985-86; assoc. Simpson, Thacher & Bartlett, N.Y.C., 1986-89; assoc. Reid & Priest, N.Y.C., 1989-95, ptnr., 1995—; assoc. counsel gov.'s judicial screening com. First Judicial Dept., 1991—. Exec. editor Internat. Law Rev., 1988-91, editor-in-chief, 1991-94, mem. adv. bd., 1994—; editor Law Policy in Internat. Bus., 1985. Bd. dirs. Bay Street Landing Homeowners Corp. Mem. ABA, Internat. Bar Assn., N.Y. State Bar Assn., Assn. Bar City N.Y. (mem. fgn. and comparative law com. 1990-93, mem. internat. human rights com. 1993—), Women in Music, Women's Inner Cir. of Achievement (N.Am.), Phi Beta Kappa. Democrat. Roman Catholic. Home: 20 Bay Street Landing #BIJ Staten Island NY 10301-2534 Office: Reid & Priest 40 W 57th St New York NY 10019-4097

MCCABE, RICHARD LEE, real estate developer; b. Cheyenne, Wyo., June 9, 1943; s. Thomas Junior and Alice May (Vernon) McC.; m. Janet Ann Lefkow (div.); children: Bradley Samuel, Kevin Ira; m. Julianne Clements, Dec. 22, 1979; children: Thomas Durant, Claire Angela Kim. BArch., U. Colo., 1967. V.p., sec. McSan Enterprises, Inc., Boulder, 1968-72; pres. Boulder (Colo.) Design & Tool Group, Inc., 1972-74; pvt. practice R.L. McCabe & Assocs., Boulder, 1974-77; pres. R.L.M. Inc., Boulder, 1977-80, Cubit Corp., Boulder, 1980-84, Centermark Corp., Boulder, 1984-87, Cubit Constrn. Corp., Boulder, 1987-88, Core Corp., Boulder, 1988—; dir. Boulder Builders Group, 1988-89, Nat. Fastpitch Assn., Mpls., 1990—; pres. Boulder County Builders Assn., 1990-91. Co-author: (mcpl. legislation) Community Housing Assistance Plan, 1991. Mem. Affordable Housing Task Force, Boulder, 1989, Thistle Community Housing Corp., Boulder, 1991; mem. steering com. North Boulder Subcmty., 1994. Recipient Svc. award Assn. Student Chpts. of AIA, 1966, award of appreciation City Boulder Housing Authority, 1989, cert. award Dept. Housing and Human Svcs., Boulder, 1990, cert. appreciation Boulder County Safehouse, 1991. Mem. Boulder County Chpt. of the Met. Denver Home Builders Assn. (pres. 1991-92), Congress for New Urbanism. Avocations: sailing, fishing, camping, hiking, river floating. Home: 526 Arapahoe Ave Boulder CO 80302-5827 Office: Core Corp 2041 Broadway 2d Fl Boulder CO 80302

MCCABE, ROBERT HOWARD, educator, college president; b. Bklyn., Dec. 23, 1929; s. Joseph A. and Kathryn (Greer) McC.; m. Arva Moore Parks, June 1992. BEd, U. Miami (Fla.), 1952; MS, Appalachian State U., Boone, N.C., 1959; PhD, U. Tex., Austin, 1963; LLD (hon.), Barry U., 1986, U. Miami, 1990, Fla. Internat. U., 1990. Asst. to pres. Miami-Dade C.C. (Fla.), 1963-65, v.p., 1965-67, exec. v.p., 1969-80, pres., 1980-95 pres. Essex County Coll., Newark, 1967-69; sr. fellow League for Innovation in the C.C., 1995—; exec. com. So. Regional Edn. Bd., Atlanta, 1981-83; trustee Coll. Bd., chmn., 1988-90; vice chair The Miami Coalition for a Drug-Free Cmty., 1989-93. Recipient Disting. Svc. award Fla. Congl. Del., 1983, Spirit of Excellence award The Miami Herald, 1988, Harold W. McGraw Jr. prize in Edn., 1991, The Coll. Bd. medal, 1995; named Outstanding Grad., Coll. Edn., U. Tex., 1982, named one of the 18 Most Effective Chief Exec. Officer in Am. Higher Edn. Bowling Green U., 1988; Disting. Svc. award, Dade County, Fla., 1983; Kellogg fellow, 1962-63, MacArthur fellow John D. and Catherine T. MacArthur Found., 1992. Fellow League for Innovation in the C.C. (dir. exec. com. 1985—, disting. svc. award 1995); mem. Am. Assn. C.C. (bd. dirs. 1991—, disting. svc. award 1995), Am. Assn. Higher Edn. (dir. 1973-75), Am. Assn. for Environ. Edn. (pres. 1970-73), Am. Coun. on Edn., Commn. on Higher Edn. Issues, Higher Edn. Consortium, Am. Coun. Edn. (bd. dir. 1983-85, 92—), Southeast Fla. Edn. Consortium (chmn. bd. 1981-83). Episcopalian. Author: Man and Environment, 1971; contbr. articles to profl. jours.; editor Jour. Environ. Edn.; cons. editor Change Mag., 1980—. Home: 1601 S Miami Ave Miami FL 33129

MCCABE, SHARON, humanities and art educator; b. Flint, Mich., Sept. 6, 1947. AA, Pasco Hernando C.C., New Port Richey, Fla., 1988; BA in Art, U. South Fla., 1990, MA in Art, gifted endorsement, 1992, MLA in Humanities, 1996. Cert. gifted edn. tchr., Fla. Tchr. art Hernando County Schs., Spring Hill, Fla., 1990—; prof. humanities Pasco Hernando C.C., 1992—. Recipient numerous art awards, 1982—. Office: PHCC Humanities Dept 10230 Ridge Rd New Port Richey FL 34654

MCCABE, STEVEN LEE, structural engineer; b. Denver, July 11, 1950; s. John L. and M. Leora (Shaw) McC.; m. Ann McCabe, Aug. 10, 1974; 1 child, Stephanie A. BSME, Colo. State U., 1972, MSME, 1974; PhD in Civil Engring., U. Ill., 1987. Registered profl. engr., Colo., Kans., Okla. Engr. Pub. Svc. Co. of Colo., Denver, 1974-77; sr. engr. R.W. Beck and Assocs., Denver, 1977-78; engr., project engr. Black & Veatch Cons. Engrs., Kansas City, Mo., 1978-81; asst. prof. civil engring. U. Kans., Lawrence, 1985-91, assoc. prof., 1991—, tchg. fellow, 1994—; vis. prof. structural engring. Norwegian Inst. Tech., Trondheim, 1995-96. Contbr. articles to profl. jours. Named Fulbright scholar U.S. Govt. to Norway, 1995-96, Ill. fellow, 1981-82; grantee Am. Inst. Steel Constrn., 1990-91, NSF, 1989-91, 91—, Civil Engring. Rsch. Found., 1991—; recipient Mech. Coupler Industry Testing Consortium Funding, 1992-95, Structural Rsch. Paper award Am. Concrete Inst., 1996. Mem. ASME (pressure vessels and piping divsn. honor paper award 1989, cert. of recognition for svc. 1993), ASTM, ASCE (assoc. editor Jour. Structural Engring. 1992-94), ACI (pres. Kans. chpt. 1992),

IEEE Computer Soc., Am. Soc. Engring. Edn., Earthquake Engring. Rsch. Inst., European Assn. Concrete, Sigma Xi, Sigma Tau, Pi Tau Sigma, Phi Kappa Phi, Chi Epsilon. Republican. Roman Catholic. Achievements include development of improved damage mechanics techniques for prediction of earthquake effects on structures, seismic design criteria for power plants; research on inelastic cyclic behavior of reinforcing bars and mechanical couplers, on structural dynamics and earthquake engineering as well as computational mechanics, on the evaluation of response and damage and predictions of reserve capacity in structures and members subjected to earthquake strong ground motion, on use of finite element analysis for the response of structures and machines to various types of loading. Office: U Kans 2015 Learned Hall Lawrence KS 66045-2225

MCCAFFERTY, JAMES ARTHUR, sociologist; b. Columbus, Ohio, Jan. 1, 1926; s. James A. and Marjorie Agatha (Gilchrist) McC.; m. Jane Roush, June 13, 1948 (dec. Oct. 1984); children: Lucinda Jane Martin, James Stanley Thomas, Bridget Anne Roush Green; m. Carolyn Ring Bradley, Nov. 7, 1987 (div. Apr. 1992); m. Irma Mae Prosser Nicholson, May 28, 1993. BS, Ohio State U., 1948; MA, 1954; postgrad. Am. U. Social rsch. analyst Ohio State Dept. Pub. Welfare, 1948-51; criminologist U.S. Bur. Prisons, Washington, 1951-63; asst. chief div. info. systems Adminstrv. Office of U.S. Cts., Washington, 1963-77, chief statis. analysis and reports div., 1977-86, ret.; vis. lectr. American U., 1959, 62-64; adj. instr. Fordham U., 1978-89. Editor: Capital Punishment, 1972; contbr. articles on criminology to profl. jours. Life mem. Md. State PTA; past pres. Potomac area coun. Camp Fire Girls of U.S., 1966-67; v.p. Prince George's County (Md.) Coun. of PTAs, 1964-65; chmn. Prince George's County Youth Commn., 1970-72; past pres. Hypoglycemia Assn., 1991-93, past pres. Interfaith Cmty. Action Coun., Inc. Cpl. USAAF, 1944-46. Mem. AAUP, Md. Soc. SAR (past pres., trustee), Am. Sociol. Assn., Am. Correctional Assn. (life), Assn. Correctional Rsch. and Info. Mgmt., Am. Statis. Assn., Prince George's County Geneal. Soc. (past pres.), Ohio Geneal. Soc. (Nat. Capital Buckeye chpt., co-editor newsletter), Judicature Soc., Md. State Beekeepers Assn. (life), DAV (life), Sons of Union Vets. Civil War (camp comdr), Am. Legion. Presbyterian. Home: 613 Rosier Rd Fort Washington MD 20744-5554

MCCAFFREE, BURNHAM CLOUGH, JR., retired naval officer; b. San Diego, Sept. 28, 1931; s. Burnham Clough and Elisabeth Cory (Woodhull) McC.; m. Erlend Elizabeth Carlton, June 19, 1954; children: Elizabeth Anne McCaffree Antanitus, Debora Lynn McCaffree Hagwood. BS in Naval Engring., U.S. Naval. Acad., 1954. Commd. ensign USN, 1954, advanced through grades to rear adm., 1983, served on six ships, mem. staffs Atlantic Fleet and Pacific Fleet, until 1970; comdg. officer USS Johnston, U.S. Atlantic Fleet, Charleston, S.C., 1970-72; action officer, sr. navy planner Office Chief Naval Ops., Washington, 1972-76, dir. mobile logistic support forces, amphibious, mine and spl. warfare div., 1982-84, asst. dep. chief naval logistics, 1986-87, dir. logistics plans div., 1987-88; comdg. officer USS Shreveport, U.S. Atlantic Fleet, Norfolk, Va., 1976-78; chief staff, comdr. amphibious group 2 U.S. Atlantic Fleet, Norfolk, 1978-80, comdr. amphibious squadron 2, 1980-82; comdr. amphibious force U.S. 7th Fleet, Okinawa, Japan, 1984-86; ret., 1988; mem. adj. rsch. staff Inst. Def. Analyses, Alexandria, Va., Ctr. Naval Analyses, Alexandria, Va., 1989—. Decorated Legion of Merit with 4 gold stars, Meritorious Service Medal, others. Mem. U.S. Naval Inst., U.S. C. of C. (assoc.). Episcopalian. Home: 3620 Buckwood Ct Annandale VA 22003-1951

MCCAFFREY, ANNE INEZ, author; b. Cambridge, Mass., Apr. 1, 1926; d. George H. and Anne (McElroy) McC.; m. Wright Johnson, Jan. 14, 1950 (div. Aug. 1970); children: Alec Anthony, Todd, Georgeanne. B.A. cum laude, Radcliffe Coll., 1947; student, U. City of Dublin, 1970-71. Copywriter, layout designer Liberty Music Shops, N.Y.C., 1948-50; copywriter, sec. Helena Rubinstein, N.Y.C., 1950-52. Author: Restoree, 1967, Dragonflight, 1968, Decision at Doona, 1969, Ship Who Sang, 1969, Mark of Merlin, 1971, Dragonquest: Being the Further Adventures of the Dragonriders of Pern, 1971, Ring of Fear, 1971, To Ride Pegasus, 1973, Cooking Out Of This World, 1973, A Time When, 1975, Dragonsong, 1976, Kilternan Legacy, 1975, Dragonsinger, 1977, Dinosaur Planet, 1977, Get Off the Unicorn, 1977, White Dragon, 1978, Dragondrums, 1979, Crystal Singer, 1981, The Worlds of Anne McCaffrey, 1981, The Coelura, 1983, Moreta: Dragonlady of Pern, 1983, Dinosaur Planet Survivors, 1984, Stitch in Snow, 1984, Killashandra, 1985, The Girl Who Heard Dragons, 1985, The Year of the Lucy, 1986, Nerilka's Story, 1986, The Lady, 1987, People of Pern, 1988, Dragonsdown, 1988, Renegades of Pern, 1989, (with Jody-Lynn Nye) The Dragonlover's Guide to Pern, 1989, The Rowan, 1990, Pegasus in Flight, 1990, (with Elizabeth Moon) Sassinak, 1990, (with Nye) The Death of Sleep, 1990, All the Weyrs of Pern, 1991, Generation Warriors, 1991, Damia, 1991, (with Margaret Ball) The Partnership, 1991, (with Nye) Crisis at Doona, 1991, Damia, 1992, (with Mercedes Lackey) The City Who Fought, 1993, (with Elizabeth Ann Scarborough) Powers That Be, 1993, Chronicles of Pern: First Fall, 1993, Lyon's Pride, 1994, (with Nye) The Ship Who Won, 1994, (with Scarborough) Power Lines, 1994, Dolphins of Pern, 1994, (with Scarborough) Power Play, 1995, Freedom's Landing, 1995, Black Horses for The King, 1996, Red Star Rising, 1996; editor: Alchemy and Academe, 1970; anthology: The Girl Who Heard Dragons, 1991; dir. musical Brecks Mill Cronies, 1962-65. Recipient Hugo award, 1967, Nebula award, 1968, E.E. Smith award, 1975, Ditmar award, 1979, Gandalf award, 1979, Eurocon/Streso award, 1979, Balrog award, 1980, Golden PEN award, 1981, Sci. Fiction Book Club award, 1986, 89, 91, 92, 93, 94. Mem. PEN (Ireland), Sci. Fiction Writers Am. (sec.-treas. 1968-70), Authors' Guild. Office: Dragonhold Underhill, Timmore Ln, Newcastle, Wicklow Ireland

MCCAFFREY, BARRY RICHARD, federal official, retired army officer; b. Taunton, Mass., Nov. 17, 1942; s. William Joseph and Mary Veronica (Curtin) McC.; m. Jill Ann Faulkner, June 8, 1964; children: Sean, Tara, Amy. BS, U.S. Mil. Acad., 1964; MA, Am. U., 1971; postgrad., Command and Gen. Staff Coll., Ft. Leavenworth, Kans., 1976, Army War Coll., Carlisle Barracks, Pa., 1982. Commd. 2d lt. U.S. Army, 1964, advanced through grades to maj. gen., 1990; co. comdr. 1st Cav. Div., Vietnam, 1968-69; assoc. prof. dept. social sci. U.S. Mil. Acad., West Point, N.Y., 1972-75; bn. comdr. 3d Inf. Div., Germany, 1979-83; div. chief staff, then brigade comdr. 9th Inf. Div., Ft. Lewis, Wash., 1983-86; asst. comdt. U.S. Army Inf. Sch., Ft. Benning, Ga., 1986-88; dep. U.S. mil. rep. NATO, Brussels, 1988-89; dir. strategic plans policy Joint Staff, Washington, 1989-90; div. comdr. 24th Inf. Div., Ft. Stewart, Ga., 1990-95; dir. Nat. Drug Control Policy, Washington, DC, 1995—; mem. Pres. Cabinet, 1995—. Contbr. articles to mil. publs. Decorated D.S.C. with oak leaf cluster, Silver Star with oak leaf cluster, Purple Heart with two oak leaf clusters. Mem. Legion of Valor. Roman Catholic. Avocations: hunting, reading military history. Office: Office Nat Drug Control Policy 750 17th St NW Washington DC 20006*

MCCAFFREY, CARLYN SUNDBERG, lawyer; b. N.Y.C., Jan. 7, 1942; d. Carl Andrew Lawrence and Evelyn (Back) Sundberg; m. John P. McCaffrey, May 24, 1967; children: John C., Patrick, Jennifer, Kathleen. Student, Barnard Coll., 196.; AB in Econs., George Washington U., 1963; LLB cum laude, NYU, 1967, LLM in Taxation, 1970. Bar: N.Y. 1974. Law clk. to presiding justice Calif. Supreme Ct., 1967-68; teaching fellow law NYU, N.Y.C., 1968-70, asst. prof. law, 1970-74; assoc. Weil, Gotshal & Manges, N.Y.C., 1974-80, ptnr., 1980—; prof. in residence Rubin Hall NYU, 1971-75; adj. prof. law NYU, 1975—, U. Miami, 1979-81; lectr. in field. Contbr. articles to profl. jours. Mem. ABA (chmn. generation-skipping transfer tax 1979-81, 93—, real property probate and trust law sect.), N.Y. State Bar Assn. (exec. com. tax sect. 1979-80, chmn. estate and gift tax com. 1976-78, 95—, life ins. com. 1983-85, trusts and estates sect.), Assn. of Bar of City of N.Y. (matrimonial law com., chmn. tax subcom. 1984-86, ACTEC (bd. regents 1992—, mem. exec. com. 1995—). Home: 38 Sidney Pl Brooklyn NY 11201-4607 Office: Weil Gotshal & Manges 767 5th Ave New York NY 10153

MCCAFFREY, JUDITH ELIZABETH, lawyer; b. Providence, Apr. 26, 1944; d. Charles V. and Isadore Frances (Langford) McC.; m. Martin D. Minsker, Dec. 31, 1969 (div. May 1981); children: Ethan Hart Minsker, Natasha Langford Minsker. BA, Tufts U., 1966; JD, Boston U., 1970. Bar: Mass. 1970, D.C. 1972, Fla. 1991. Assoc. Sullivan & Worcester, Washington, 1970-76; atty. FDIC, Washington, 1976-78; assoc. Dechert, Price & Rhoads, Washington, 1978-82, McKenna, Conner & Cuneo, Washington, 1982-83; gen. counsel, corp. sec. Perpetual Savs. Bank, FSB, Alexandria, Va., 1983-91; ptnr. Powell, Goldstein, Frazer & Murphy, Washington, 1991-92, McCaffrey & Raimi, P.A., 1992—. Contbr. articles to profl. jours. Mem. edn. com. Bd. Trade, Washington, 1986-92. Mem. ABA (chairperson subcom. thrift instns. 1985-90), Fed. Bar Assn. (exec. com., banking law com. 1985-91), D.C. Bar Assn. (bd. govs. 1981-85), Women's Bar Assn. (pres. 1980-81), Zonta Club of Naples (dir. 1994—). Episcopalian. Avocations: golf, travel, tennis, sailing, reading. Home: PO Box 2081 Naples FL 33939-2081 Office: McCaffrey & Raimi PA Ste 206-A 5811 Pelican Bay Blvd Naples FL 33963

MCCAFFREY, R. MICHAEL, orthopedic company executive; b. Parkersburg, W.Va., Apr. 6, 1942; s. Robert James and Margaret Rita (McDermott) McC.; m. Penny Sue Weems McCaffrey, June 5, 1965; children: Molly, Katie. BS cum laude, Xavier U., 1964, MBA, 1965. Naval officer U.S. Navy, Newport, R.I., 1966-71; v.p. Johnson & Johnson, Somerville, N.J., 1971-84; pres. DePuy Inc., Warsaw, Ind., 1984—. Lt. U.S. Navy, 1966-71. Republican. Roman Catholic. Avocation: fishing. Home: 1904 Deer Trl Warsaw IN 46580-2105 Office: DePuy Inc 700 Orthopedic Dr Warsaw IN 46580*

MCCAFFREY, ROBERT HENRY, JR., retired manufacturing company executive; b. Syracuse, N.Y., Jan. 20, 1927; s. Robert Henry and May Ann (McGuire) McC.; m. Dorothy Anne Evers, Sept. 22, 1956; children: Michael Robert, Kathleen Mary. BS, Syracuse U., 1949. Sales asst. Sealright Corp., Fulton, N.Y., 1949-50; with TEK Hughes div. Johnson & Johnson, Metuchen, N.J., 1950-67, gen. sales mgr., 1958-59, v.p. sales, 1959-62, pres., 1962-67; gen. mgr. med. div. Howmet Corp., N.Y.C., 1967-70; group v.p. Howmedica, Inc., 1970-73, sr. v.p., 1973-74, exec. v.p., also bd. dirs., 1974-76; pres., CEO C.R. Bard, Inc., Murray Hill, N.J., 1976-78, chmn. bd. dirs., CEO, 1978-89, chmn. bd., 1989-91, also bd. dirs.; chmn. exec. com. C.R. Bard, Inc., Murray Hill, 1991—; bd. dirs. Summit and Elizabeth Trust, Summit Bancorp, Thomas & Betts Corp. Trustee Found. for Univ. Medicine and Dentistry N.J., 1987-90, Syracuse U., 1979—, chmn. corp. adv. council, 1974-75. With AUS, 1945-46. Mem. Orthopedic Surg. Mfrs. Assn., Health Industry Mfrs. Assn. (bd. dir., chmn. 1982-83), N.Y. Sales Execs. Club, Algonquin Club (Boston), Baltusrol Golf Club (Springfield, N.J.), Oyster Harbors Club (Osterville, Mass.), Sigma Chi. Republican. Roman Catholic. Avocations: reading, skiing, golf. Office: C R Bard Inc 1200 Technology Park Dr Billerica MA 01821-4139

MCCAFFREY, WILLIAM THOMAS, financial services company executive; b. N.Y.C., July 7, 1936; s. Daniel and Alice (Dineen) McC.; m. Mary Margaret Timms, June 25, 1960; children: Ann, William E., Christine. BS, NYU, 1970; MS in Bus., Columbia U., 1972. Dir. pub. The Equitable Fin. Cos., N.Y.C., 1968-71, asst. v.p. communications, 1972-74, v.p., office of the pres., 1975-77, v.p. corp. devel., 1977-79, v.p., personnel dir., 1980-84, sr. v.p. pers. and adminstrn., 1984-85, exec. v.p. corp., 1986-87, exec. v.p., chief adminstrv. officer, 1988—, chmn. benefits com., 1986—; bd. dirs. Equitable Variable Life Ins. Co., N.Y.C. Bd. dirs. Equitable Found., 1987—, Bronx-Lebanon Hosp.; project mgr. Grace Commn., Washington, 1982—; chmn. bd. trustees Xavier U., New Orleans, 1986—; chmn. bd. Deafness Rsch. Found., N.Y.C. Sgt. U.S. Army, 1957-58. Mem. West Side Tennis Club (Forest Hills, N.Y.) (gov. 1988—). Avocations: tennis, photography. Home: 89-25 63rd Ave Flushing NY 11374-2836 Office: Equitable 787 7th Ave New York NY 10019-6018*

MCCAGHY, CHARLES HENRY, sociology educator; b. Eau Claire, Wis., Apr. 29, 1934; s. Elmer and Anna Josephine (Soha) McC.; m. M. Dawn Ysebaert, June 10, 1961. B.B.A., U. Wis., 1956, M.S., 1962, Ph.D, 1966. Instr. sociology U. Conn., 1964-66; asst. prof. sociology Case Western Res. U., Cleve., 1966-70; assoc. prof. sociology Bowling Green State U., Ohio, 1970-76, prof., 1976-94, prof. emeritus, 1994—; vis. scholar Australian Inst. Criminology, 1984. Author: Deviant Behavior: Crime, Conflict and Interest Groups, 1976, 3d edit., 1994, Crime in American Society, 1980, 2d edit., 1987. Served to lt. (j.g.) USN, 1956-59. Mem. Am. Sociol. Assn., Am. Soc. Criminology (treas. 1978-82), Soc. for Sci. Study of Sex. Office: 221 Williams St Bowling Green OH 43402

MCCAHILL, BARRY WINSLOW, federal public affairs official; b. Glen Ridge, N.J., May 25, 1947; s. William Francis and Frances (Elliott) McC.; m. Margaret Anne Bonnes, Feb. 8, 1980; children: Jennifer, Kimberly, Erin, Meghan; 1 stepchild, Rob White. BA in English, U. Va., 1969, postgrad., 1974-76. USCG lic. master. Account exec. Whyte Berry Price, Advt. & Pub. Rels., Washington, 1967-69; publs. mgr. Nat. Telephone Coop. Assn., Washington, 1972-74; visual info. specialist U.S. Customs Svc., Washington, 1974-76; pub. affairs specialist IRS, Washington, 1976-79; mgr. radio and TV news Nat. Hwy. Traffic Safety Adminstrn., U.S. Dept. Transp., Washington, 1979-85, dep. dir. Office Pub. and Consumer Affairs, 1985—. Loaned exec. Combined Fed. Campaign United Way, Washington, 1983. 1st lt. U.S. Army, 1969-72. Recipient Blue Pencil award Nat. Assn. Govt. Communicators, 1975, 88, Adminstrs. award for exceptional achievement Nat. Hwy. Traffic Safety Adminstrn., 1983, Adminstr.'s Leadership award, 1995, Sec.'s Honor award Sec. of Treasury, 1983, Sec.'s award for meritorious achievement Sec. of Transp., 1985, Spl. Recognition award, 1995, Way To Go award, 1995. Mem. Old Dominion Morgan Horse Assn. (pres.), Cobbosseecontee Yacht Club (Manchester, Maine), Pi Kappa Alpha. Avocations: boating, morgan horses. Home: 4832 Heron Neck Ln Fairfax VA 22033-4406 Office: Nat Hwy Traffic Safety Adminstrn 400 7th St SW NOA-40 Washington DC 20590

MCCAIG, JEFFREY JAMES, transportation company executive; b. Moose Jaw, Sask., July 5, 1951; s. John Robert and Anne Shorrocks (Glass) McC.; m. Marilyn Graves, July 7, 1983; children: Robbert Angus, Scott Thomas, Christa Mae. Student, Can. Jr. Coll. Lausanne, Switzerland, 1970; AB, Harvard Coll., 1973; LLB, Osgoode Hall Law Sch., Can., 1976; MSc in Mgmt., Leland Stanford Jr. U., 1984. Assoc. MacKimmie Matthews, 1976-81; owner, sr. officer Jeffery J. McCaig Profl. Corp., 1981-83; v.p. planning and corp. devel. Trimac Ltd., Calgary, Alta., Can., 1983-87, exec. v.p., 1987-90; pres. Trimac Ltd., Clagary, Alta., Can., 1990-94, pres., CEO, 1994—; chmn. Bovar, Inc., Calgary, 1994—; bd. dirs. Bovar, Inc., chmn., bd. dirs. Trimac Ltd., Greyhound Lines Can. Ltd., Richland Petroleum Corp., Conf. Bd. Can., ATA Found.,. Mem. Law Soc. Alta., Young Pres.'s Orgn., Calgary Golf and Country Club, Calgary Petroleum Club, Glencoe Club, 400 Club. Home: 1201 Riverdale Ave SW, Calgary, AB Canada T2S 0Z1 Office: Trimac Ltd, 800 5 Ave SW Ste 2100, Calgary, AB Canada T2P 3T6

MCCAIG, JOHN ROBERT, transportation executive; b. Moose Jaw, Sask., Can., June 14, 1929; m. Ann McCaig; children: Jeffrey, JoAnn, Melanie. Grad. pub. sch., Moose Jaw. Various positions Maccam Transport Ltd., 1947-52, gen. mgr., 1952-60; pres. Trimac Transp. Ltd. and H.M. Trimble & Sons Ltd., 1961-68, Westburne Internat. Industries Ltd., 1969-70; chmn. Trimac Ltd., Calgary, Alta., Can., 1970-72, 80—; pres. Trimac Ltd., Calgary, Alta., 1972-80, CEO, 1972-94; chmn. Trimac Ltd., Calgary, 1994—; bd. dirs. Banister Found., Inc., Chauvco Resources Ltd., Computalog, Inc., Cameo Corp., Carena Devel. Ltd. Past pres. Jr. Achievement So. Alta, Calgary; campaign chmn. Western Orthopaedic and Arthritis Found., Calgary. Mem. Calgary Petroleum Club, Ranchmen's Club, Calgary Golf and Country Club, Glencoe Club. Avocations: golf, skiing. Office: Trimac Ltd, 800 5 Ave SW Ste 2100, Calgary, AB Canada T2P 3T6

MCCAIG, JOSEPH J., retail food chain executive; b. Bklyn., 1944. B.S., Seton Hall U., 1967. With The Grand Union Co., Elmwood Park, N.J., 1965—, gen. store mgr., 1967-68, resident trainer suburban div., 1968-69, supr. personnel, 1969-70, dist. mgr., 1970-72, supt. stores, 1972-73, asst. to sr. v.p. store ops., 1973-74, v.p. empire div. and v.p. no. region, 1974-78, v.p. no. region, 1978-80, sr. v.p., 1980-81; pres., chief operating officer The Grand Union Co, Wayne, N.J., 1981-89, 1989—. Office: Grand Union Co 201 Willowbrook Blvd Wayne NJ 07470*

MCCAIN, BETTY LANDON RAY (MRS. JOHN LEWIS MCCAIN), political party official, civic leader; b. Faison, N.C., Feb. 23, 1931; d. Horace Truman and Mary Howell (Perrett) Ray; student St. Marys Jr. Coll., 1948-50; AB in Music, U. N.C., Chapel Hill, 1952; MA, in Music Columbia U., 1953; m. John Lewis McCain, Nov. 19, 1955; children: Paul Pressly III, Mary Eloise. Courier, European tour guide Ednl. Travel Assocs., Plainfield, N.J., 1952-54; asst. dir. YWCA, U. N.C., Chapel Hill, 1953-55; chmn. N.C. Democratic Exec. Com., 1976-79 (1st woman); mem. Dem. Nat. Com., 1971-72, 76-79, 80-85, chmn. sustaining fund, N.C., 1981, 88-91, mem. com. on Presdl. nominations (Hunt Commn.), 1981-82, mem. rules com., 1982-85, mem. cabinet Gov. James B. Hunt, Jr., sec. dept. cultural resources 1993—; mem. Winograd Commn., 1977-78; pres. Dem. Women of N.C., 1971-72, dist. dir., 1969-72; pres. Wilson County Dem. Women, 1966-67; precinct chmn., 1972-76; del. Dem. Nat. Conv., 1972, 88; mem. Dem. Mid-term Confs., 1974, 78, mem. judicial council Dem. Nat. Com., 1985-89; dir. Carolina Tel. & Tel. Co., 1981— (1st woman). Sunday sch. tchr. First Presbyn. Ch., Wilson, 1970-71, 86-88, 90-92, mem. chancel choir, 1985—, deacon, 1986-92, elder, 1992-95, chmn. fin. com., 1990-91; treas. Wilson on the Move, 1990-92; mem. Council on State Goals and Policy, 1970-72, Gov.'s Task Force on Child Advocacy, 1969-71, Wilson Human Relations Commn., 1975-78, chmn. Wilson-Greene Morehead scholarship com., 1986-89; mem. career and personal counseling service adv. bd. St. Andrews Coll.; charter mem. Wilson Edn. Devel. Council; active Arts Council of Wilson, Inc., N.C. Art Soc., N.C. Lit. and Hist. Assn.; regional v.p., bd. dirs. N.C. Mental Health Assn.; pres., bd. dirs., legis. chmn. Wilson County Mental Health Assn.; bd. dirs. U. N.C. Ctr. Pub. TV, 1993—, Country Doctor Mus., 1968-93, Wilson United Fund; bd. govs. U. N.C., 195-81, personnel and tenure com., 1985-93, chmn. budgets and fin. com. 1991-93; bd. regents Barium Springs Home for Children; bd. dirs., pres. N.C. Mus. History Assocs., 1982-83, membership chair, 1987-88; co-chmn. Com. to Elect Jim Hunt Gov., 1976, 80, co-chmn. senatorial campaign, 1984; mem. N.C. Adv. Budget Com., 1981-85 (1st woman); chmn. State Employees Combined Campaign N.C., 1993; bd. visitors Peace Coll., Wake Forest U. Sch. Law, U. N.C., Chapel Hill; co-chmn. fund drive Wilson Community Theatre; state bd. dirs. N.C., Am. Lung Assn., 1985-88; bd. dirs. Roanoke Island Commn. 1994—, USS/NC Battleship Commn., 1993—. Recipient state awards N.C. Heart Assn., 1967, Easter Seal Soc., 1967, Community Service award Downtown Bus. Assocs., 1977, award N.C. Jaycees, 1979, 85, Women in Govt. award N.C. and U.S. Jaycettes, 1985, Flora Mac Donald Scottish Heritage award, 1995, Carpathian award N.C. Equity, 1995; named to Order of Old Well and Valkyries, U. N.C., 1952; named Dem. Woman of Yr., N.C., 1976, Disting. Alumna U. N.C., Chapel Hill, 1993. Mem. U. N.C. Chapel Hill Alumni Assn. (dir.), St. Marys Alumni Assn. (regional v.p.), AMA Aux. (dir., nat. vol. health services chmn., aux. liaison rep. Council on Mental Health, aux. rep. Council on Vol. Health Orgns.), N.C. (pres., dir., parliamentarian) med. auxs., UDC (historian John W. Dunham chpt.), DAR, N.C. Found. for Nursing (bd. dirs. 1989-92), N.C. Agency Pub. Telecoms.(bd. dirs. 1993—), Info. Resources Mgmt. Commn. N.C. (bd. dirs. 1993—), N.C. Symphony (bd. dirs. 1993—), N.C. Soc. Internal Medicine Aux. (pres., bd. dirs. N.C. Equity), N.C. Sch. Arts (bd. trustees 1993—), Pi Beta Phi. The Book Club (pres.), Little Book Club , Wilson Country Club. Contbg. editor History of N.C. Med. Soc. Home: 1134 Woodland Dr Wilson NC 27893-2122

MCCAIN, JOHN SIDNEY, III, senator; b. Panama Canal Zone, Aug. 29, 1936; s. John Sidney and Roberta (Wright) McC.; m. Cindy Hensley, May 17, 1980; children: Doug, Andy, Sidney, Meghan, Jack, Bridget. Grad. U.S. Naval Acad., 1958; grad., Nat. War Coll., 1973-74. Commd. ensign U.S. Navy, 1958, capt., navy pilot, 1977; prisoner of war Hanoi, Vietnam, 1967-73; dir. Navy Senate Liaison Office, Washington, 1977-81; mem. 98th-99th Congress from 1st Ariz. Dist.; U.S. senator from Ariz., 1987—. Bd. dirs. Community Assistance League, Phoenix, 1981-82. Decorated Legion of Merit; decorated Silver Star, Bronze Star, Purple Heart, D.F.C., Vietnamese Legion of Honor. Mem. Soc. of the Cin., Am. Legion, VFW. Republican. Episcopalian. Office: US Senate 241 Russell Senate Office Washington DC 20510*

MCCAIN, MARGARET, province official. Lt. gov. Govt. New Brunswick, Fredericton, Can. Office: Office of Lt Gov, 736 King St PO Box 6000, Fredericton, NB Canada E3B 5H1*

MCCALEB, GARY DAY, university administrator; b. Anson, Tex., Nov. 2, 1941; s. Victor Earl and Vivian (Day) McC.; m. Sylvia Ravanelli, June 5, 1964; children: Cara Lee Cranford, Bryan Day. BA, Abilene Christian Coll., 1964; MBA, Tex. A&M U., 1975, PhD, 1979. Asst. dir. alumni rels. Abilene (Tex.) Christian U., 1964-65, dir. alumni rels., 1965-69, dir. coll. rels., 1969-73, asst. acad. dean, 1978-80, v.p. pub. rels., 1980-83, v.p., dean campus life, 1983-91, v.p., 1991—; asst. dir. devel. Tex. A&M U., Bryan, 1973-75; leader internat. travel and goodwill groups. Coun. mem. City of Abilene, 1985-90, mayor, 1990—; bd. dirs. Taylor County Am. Cancer Soc., 1972-73; mem. adv. bd. United Way of Abilene, 1979-83, dir. pub. svc. divsn., 1987, chmn. consortium on drug and alcohol abuse, 1989; bd. dirs. Civic Abilene, Inc., 1981-83; treas. Abilene Task Force on Drug and Alcohol Abuse, 1984-86; active March of Dimes. Recipient Polit. Courage award John Ben Shepperd Pub. Leadership Forum, Austin, Tex., 1993, Tex. Urban Leadersip award U. Tex.-Arlington Sch. Urban and Pub. Affairs, 1995. Mem. Nat. League Cities (nat. steering com. on fin., adminstrn. and intergovtl. rels. 1989-90, adv. bd. 1994, bd. dirs. 1992-94), U.S. Conf. Mayors, Internat. Mcpl. Consortium (chmn. 1994-95), Tex. Mcpl. League (legis. policy com. Houston 1986, resolutions com. Dallas 1988, v.p. region 6 1988-89, bd. dirs. 1989-90, pres. 1992), Abilene C. of C. (aviation com. 1981, 94). Republican. Mem. Ch. of Christ. Avocations: art, baseball, jogging. Office: City of Abilene PO Box 60 Abilene TX 79604-0060

MCCALEB, MALCOLM, JR., lawyer; b. Evanston, Ill., June 4, 1945. BA, Colgate U., 1967; JD, Northwestern U., 1971. Bar: Ill. 1971. Ptnr. Foley & Lardner, Chgo. Chmn. Northfield (Ill.) Village Caucus, 1981-82, active, 1977-82, Northfield (Ill.) Zoning Commn., 1985-88, active, 1983-88; pres. bd. dirs. Vols. Am., 1977-79, active 1972-82; active Northfield (Ill.) Sch. and Park Bd. Caucus, 1980-87. Mem. Chgo. Bar Assn., Bar Assn. 7th Fed. Cir., Patent Law Assn. Chgo., Internat. Trademark Assn. Office: Foley & Lardner 330 N Wabash Ave Ste 3300 Chicago IL 60611

MCCALL, BILLY GENE, charitable trust executive; b. Ellerbe, N.C., Mar. 28, 1928; s. Arthur Hall and Letha Belle (Anderson) McC.; m. Betty Sue Berryhill, Aug. 20, 1949; children: Stephen Andrew, Kathryn Elaine McCall Manson. BS magna cum laude, Clemson U., 1950, HHD (hon.), 1991. Adminstrv. resident Charlotte Meml. Hosp., N.C., 1951-53; asst. adminstr. Anderson Meml. Hosp., S.C., 1953-54; field rep. hosp. and child care divs. The Duke Endowment, Charlotte, 1954-62, dir. mgmt. service, 1962-66, asst. exec. dir., 1966-70, assoc. exec. dir., 1970-77, exec. dir., 1977-80, asst. sec., 1966-80, dep. exec. dir., sec., 1980-86, dep. exec. dir., 1987-90, exec. dir., 1990-92; ret., 1992; bd. dirs., mem. exec. com. SunHealth Alliance, Inc., 1992-95; chmn. Commn. on Profl. and Hosp. Activities, Ann Arbor, Mich., 1977-78; mem. N.C. Med. Care Commn., Raleigh, 1977-89; mem. adv. bd. Kate B. Reynolds Health Care Trust, Winston-Salem, N.C., 1977-91, 96—. Past pres. Presbyn. Home at Charlotte; bd. dirs. United Way of Cen. Carolinas, Charlotte; adv. bd. Queens Coll., Charlotte; bd. visitors Davidson Coll., N.C., Lineberger Cancer Ctr., U. N.C., Chapel Hill; past pres., bd. dirs. Charlotte-Mecklenburg Sr. Ctrs., N.C. With U.S. Army, 1946-47, 50-51, PTO. Fellow Am. Coll. Healthcare Execs. (hon.); mem. Am. Hosp. Assn., N.C. Hosp. Assn., S.C. Hosp. Assn., Carmel Country Club. Democrat. Presbyterian. Home: 7724 Cooper Ln Charlotte NC 28217-2387

MC CALL, CHARLES BARNARD, health facility executive, educator; b. Memphis, Nov. 2, 1928; s. John W. and Lizette (Kimbrough) McC.; m. Carolyn Jean Rosselot, June 9, 1951; children: Linda, Kim, Betsy, Cathy. B.A., Vanderbilt U., 1950, M.D., 1953. Diplomate: Am. Bd. Internal Medicine (pulmonary diseases). Intern Vanderbilt U. Hosp., Nashville, 1953-54; clin. assoc., sr. asst. surgeon USPHS, Nat. Cancer Inst., NIH, 1954-56; sr. asst. resident in medicine U. Ala. Hosp., 1956-57, chief resident, 1958-59; fellow chest diseases Nat. Acad. Scis.-NRC, 1957-58; instr. U. Ala. Med. Sch., 1958-59; asst. prof., then assoc. prof. medicine U. Tenn. Med. Sch., 1959-69, chief pulmonary diseases, 1964-69; mem. faculty U. Tex. System, Galveston, 1969-75, prof. medicine med. br., 1971-73; assoc. prof. medicine Health Sci. Center, Southwestern Med. Sch., Dallas, 1973-75, also assoc. dean clin. programs, 1973-75; dir. Office Grants Mgmt. and Devel., 1973-75; dean, prof. medicine U. Tenn. Coll. Medicine, 1975-77, Oral Roberts U. Sch. Medicine, Tulsa, 1977-78; interim assoc. dean U. Okla. Tulsa Med. Coll., 1978-79; clin. prof. medicine U. Colo. Med. Sch., Denver, 1979-80; prof. medicine, assoc. dean U. Okla. Med. Sch., 1980-82; exec. dean and dean U. Okla. Coll. Medicine, 1982-85; v.p. patient affairs, prof. medicine U. Tex. M.D. Anderson Cancer Ctr., 1985-94; chief of staff VA

Med. Center, Oklahoma City, 1980-82; cons. in field; physician cons. Fla. Cancer Network, M.D. Anderson Cancer Ctr., Orlando. Contbr. articles to med. jours. Fellow ACP, Am. Coll. Chest Physicians; mem. AMA, Am. Thoracic Soc., So. Thoracic Soc. (pres. 1968-69), Am. Fedn. Clin. Rsch., Sigma Xi, Alpha Omega Alpha. Baptist. Home: 17056 Crossgate Dr Jupiter FL 33477-5851

MCCALL, CHARLES W., computer company executive; b. Oskaloosa, Iowa, Mar. 11, 1944; s. Charles W. and Esther (Horn) McC.; m. Jacqueline K. Towns, Nov. 26, 1969; 1 child, Chad. B.B.A., U. Iowa, 1966; M.B.A., Roosevelt U., 1972. With sales dept. IBM, Chgo., 1968-73; various mgmt. positions Control Data, Dallas, 1973-77; various mgmt. positions CompuServe, Inc., Columbus, Ohio, 1977-84, pres., chief exec. officer, 1984—, also dir.; bd. dirs. H&R Block, Kansas City, Midland Mut., Columbus. Avocations: running; scuba diving; sports. Home: 1004 Cherbury Ln Alpharetta GA 30202-7146 Office: HBO & Co 301 Perimeter Ctr N Atlanta GA 30346-2402*

MCCALL, DANIEL THOMPSON, JR., retired judge; b. Butler, Ala., Mar. 12, 1909; s. Daniel Thompson and Caroline Winston (Bush) McC.; m. Mary Edna Montgomery, Apr. 3, 1937; children: Mary Winston McCall Laseter, Daniel Thompson III, Nancy McCall Poynor. A.B., U. Ala., 1931, LL.B., 1933, LL.D. (hon.), 1981. Bar: Ala. 1933, U.S. Supreme Ct. 1960. Practice law Mobile, 1933-60; ptnr. Johnston, McCall & Johnston, 1943-60; cir. judge Mobile County, 1960-69; assoc. justice Supreme Ct. Ala., 1969-75; dir. Title Ins. Co., 1959-69; pres. Jr. Bar Ala., 1937. Author McCall Reprot on U. Ala. Hosps. Elected to Mobile County Bd. Sch. commrs., 1950-56, 58-60; co-founder, trustee Julius T. Wright Sch. Girls, 1953-63; dir. U. Ala. Law Sch. Found., Ala. Bar. Commrs., 1957-60; trustee U. Ala., 1965-79, nat. alumni pres., 1963, pres. Mobile chpt., 1961, Disting. Alumnus award, 1995. Lt. USNR, World War II. Named to Ala. Acad. of Hon.; recipient Dean's award, U. Ala. Law Sch., 1974, Julius T. Wright Sch. Disting. Svc. award, 1979, M.O. Beale Scroll Merit, 1979, U.M.S. Preparator Sch. Outstanding Alumnus award, 1980. Mem. ABA, Ala. Bar Assn. (grievance com. 1954-57), Mobile Bar Assn. (pres. 1953), Am. Judicature Soc., Farrah Law Soc. (charter), Cumberland Law Sch. Order Jurisprudence, Inst. Jud. Adminstrn., Nat. Trust Hist. Preservation, Hist. Mobile Preservation Soc., Navy League U.S. (co-founder, pres. Mobile chpt. 1963-65), Am. Legion, Ala. Hist. Soc., Res. Officer's Assn. U.S., 40 and 8, U. Tuscaloosa Club, Omicron Delta Kappa, Phi Delta Phi, Sigma Nu. Democrat. Episcopalian. Home: 2253 Ashland Place Ave Mobile AL 36607-3242

MCCALL, DAVID BRUCE, advertising executive; b. N.Y.C., Mar. 13, 1928; s. Sydney C. and Katharine (Adams) McC.; m. Joan C. Williams, Feb. 10, 1951; children: John Percy, Peter Cortelyou, David Bruce, William Dudley, Robert Dodd, Thomas Clement; m. Susan Alder, Jan. 18, 1975 (dec.); m. Penny Mills McSweeney, Oct. 19, 1979. Student, Hotchkiss Sch., Lakeville Conn., 1942-45, Yale U., 1948-49. Copywriter Young and Rubicam, Inc., 1949-51, Hewitt, Ogilvy, Benson, and Mather, 1951-53; v.p., copy chief David J. Mahoney, Inc., 1953-56; with Ogilvy, Benson, and Mather, 1956-62; copy chief, sr. v.p., dir. Ogilvy, Benson and Mather, 1961-62; vice chmn, bd. C.J. LaRoche, Inc. (named changed to McCaffrey and McCall, Inc.), N.Y.C., 1962-64; pres., chmn. bd. McCaffrey and McCall, Inc., N.Y.C., 1964-87, chmn. bd., creative dir.; chmn. Shepardson, Stern & Kaminsky, 1993—. Served with AUS, 1946-47. Home: 136 E 64th St New York NY 10021-7360 Office: 230 Park Ave New York NY 10169-0005

MCCALL, DAVID WARREN, retired chemistry research director, consultant; b. Omaha, Dec. 1, 1928; s. H. Bryron and Grace (Cox) McC.; m. Charlotte Marion Dunham, July 30, 1955; children—William Christopher, John Dunham. B.S., U. Wichita, 1950; M.S., U. Ill., 1951, Ph.D., 1953. Mem. tech. staff AT&T Bell Labs, Murray Hill, N.J., 1953-62; head dept. phys. chemistry AT&T Bell Labs, Murray Hill, NJ, 1962-69, asst. chem. dir., 1969-73, chem. dir., 1973-91; dir. environ. chemistry rsch. AT&T Bell Labs, Murray Hill, N.J., 1991-92; chmn. bd. trustees Gordon Rsch. Confs.; mem. adv. bd. Chem. Abstract Svcs.; chmn. Nat. Commn. on Super-conductivity; chmn. panels on advanced composites, electronic packaging, and shipboard pollution control NRC, mem. Naval Studies Bd.; bd. dirs., v.p. Randolph (Vt.) Corp. Trustee Matheny Sch. Hosp. Fellow AAAS, Am. Phys. Soc., Royal Soc. Chemistry London; mem. NAE, AICE, Am. Chem. Soc. (Barnes award 1992). Home: 12 Polo Club Rd Far Hills NJ 07931-2467

MCCALL, DOROTHY KAY, social worker, psychotherapist; b. Houston, July 18, 1948; d. Sherwood Pelton Jr. and Kathryn Rose (Gassen) McC. BA, Calif. State U., Fullerton, 1973; MS in Edn., U. Kans., 1978; PhD, U. Pitts., 1989. Lic. social worker. Counselor/intern Ctr. for Behavioral Devel., Overland Park, Kans., 1976-77; rehab. counselor Niagra Frontier Voc. Rehab. Ctr., Buffalo, 1978-79; counselor/instr. dept. motor vehicles Driving While Impaired Program N.Y. State, 1979-80; alcoholism counselor Bry Lin Hosp., Buffalo, 1979-81; instr. sch. social work U. Pitts., 1984, 91; alcohol drug counselor The Whale's Tale, Pitts., 1984-86; sole practice drug and alcohol therapy Pitts., 1986—; faculty Chem. People Inst., Pitts., 1987-89; guest lectr. sch. social work U. Pitts., 1982-87, 89; educator, trainer Community Mental Health Ctr., W.Va., 1986-87, Tenn., 1986; tchr. Tri-Community Sch. System, Western Pa., 1984-87; cons. Battered Women's Shelter, Buffalo, 1980, Buffalo Youth and Alcoholism Abuse program, 1980; lectr. in field. Mem. Spl. Adv. Com. on Addiction, 1981-83; bd. dirs. Chem. People, Task Force Adv. Com., 1984-86; bd. dirs. Drug Connection Hot Line, 1984-86; mem. Coalition of Addictive Diseases, 1984—; co-founder Greater Pitts. Adult Children of Alcoholics Network, 1984; mem. adv. bd. Chem. Awareness Referral and Evaluation System Duquesne U., 1988-93. Recipient Outstanding Achievement award Greater Pitts. Adult Children of Alcoholics Network, 1987, Disting. Svc. award Pa. Assn. for Children of Alcoholics, 1993; Nat. Inst. Alcohol Abuse tng. grantee, 1981; U. Pitts. fellow, 1983. Mem. NASW, Pa. Assn. for Children of Alcoholics (bd. dirs. 1987—, v.p. 1990-94, Disting. Svc. award 1993), Employee Assistance Profls.. Assn. Inc., Am. Soc. for Clin. Hypnosis, Nat. Assn. for Children of Alcoholics, Inst. for Noetic Scis., Internat. Soc. for Study of Subtle Energies and Energy Medicine. Democrat. Avocations: perfumery, film, reading, drawing, playing the synthesizer. Office: 673 Washington Rd Pittsburgh PA 15228-1917

MCCALL, DUKE KIMBROUGH, clergyman; b. Meridian, Miss., Sept. 1, 1914; s. John William and Lizette (Kimbrough) McC.; m. Marguerite Mullinnix, Sept. 1, 1936 (dec. 1983); children: Duke, Douglas H., John Richard, Michael W.; m. Winona Gatton McCandless, Feb. 2, 1984. BA, Furman U., Greenville, S.C., 1936; MDiv, So. Bapt. Sem., Louisville, 1938; PhD, So. Bapt. Sem., 1943; LLD (hon.), Baylor U.; DD (hon.), Furman U., U. Richmond, Stetson U.; LittD, Georgetown Coll. Ordained to ministry, Bapt. Ch., 1937. Pastor Broadway Bapt. Ch., Louisville; pres. New Orleans Bapt. Theol. Sem., 1943-46; exec. sec. So. Bapt. Exec. Com., Nashville, 1946-51; pres. So. Bapt. Theol. Sem., Louisville, 1951-82; chancellor So. Bapt. Theol. Sem., 1982-92; pres. Bapt. World Alliance, Washington, 1980-85; chmn. bd. dirs. Covenant Life Ins. Co., 1989-90. Author: God's Hurry, 1948, Passport to the World, 1951, Broadman Comments, 1957, 2nd edit., 1958, A Story of Stewardship, 1996; editor: What is the Church. Recipient E.Y. Mullins Denominational Svc. award. Avocations: golf; boating. Home: 3534 Lantern Bay Dr Jupiter FL 33477

MC CALL, JERRY CHALMERS, government official; b. Oxford, Miss., June 30, 1927; s. E. Forrest and Mariada (Huffaker) McC.; m. Margaret Denton, Nov. 28, 1952; children: Betsy, Lynn, Kim. B.A., U. Miss., 1951, M.A., 1951; M.S., U. Ill., 1956, Ph.D., 1959. Teaching asst. dept. math. U. Miss., 1950-51, instr. math., 1952-53, prof. math., 1973-76, exec. vice chancellor, 1973-76; rsch. assoc. U. Ill., 1953-57; applied sci. rep. IBM, Springfield, Ill., 1957-58; mgr. IBM, Bethesda, Md., 1966-68, Huntsville, Ala., 1968-71, Owego, N.Y., 1971-72; exec. v.p. Midwest Computer Service, Inc., Decatur, Ill., 1958-59; mem. sci. staff computation lab. Army Ballistic Missile Agy., Huntsville, 1959-60; asst. to dir. Marshall Space Flight Ctr., NASA, Huntsville, 1960-63, dep. dir. rsch. and devel. ops., 1963-66; dir. info. rsch. Miss. Test Facility NASA, Bay St. Louis, 1972-73; pres. 1st State Bank and Trust Co., Gulfport, Miss., 1976-77; dir. Nat. Data Buoy Ctr., Miss., 1977—; pres. McKool, Inc., Gulfport, Miss., 1982-94, Am. Mini Storage, Gulfport, 1985—, Am Crane Rentals, Inc., 1985-89, Cool-Power, Inc., 1988-93; head math. dept. St. Bernard Coll., Cullman, Ala., part-time, 1960-65; asso. prof. math. U. Ala., Huntsville, 1960-62; pub. speaker, 1960-63; chmn. incorporators First State Bank & Trust Co., Gulfport, Miss., 1973-76; tech. cons. Gen. Electric Co., 1974-75. Editor: (with Ernst Stuhlinger) Astronautical Engineering and Science, 1963, From Peenemunde to Outer Space, 1963. Mem. Miss. Criminal Justice Standards Commn., 1974-75; mem. Miss. Marine Resources Council, 1974-76; bd. dirs. U. Miss. Found.; bd. advisers Sch. Engring., U. Miss., 1965-73; mem. indsl. advisors U. New Orleans; chmn. founders U. Ala. Research Inst., Huntsville, 1960-62. Mem. Am. Judicature Soc. (lay mem.), U. Miss. Alumni Assn. (dir. 1966-73). Home: PO Box 7092 Gulfport MS 39506-7092 Office: Nat Data Buoy Ctr Bldg 1100 Stennis Space Center MS 39529

MCCALL, JOHN ANTHONY, banker; b. N.Y.C., Oct. 8, 1940; s. John Agustine and Helen Patricia (Sullivan) McC.; m. Mary Irene Burke, July 11, 1964; children: Kathleen, Stacey, Jennifer, John, Christopher, Matthew. BA, Fairfield U., Conn., 1962; postgrad., Stonier Grad. Sch. Bus., Rutgers U., 1968-70; postgrad. program of mgmt. devel., Harvard Grad. Sch. Bus., 1970. Vice pres. Irving Trust Co., N.Y.C., 1963-77; sr. v.p. E.F. Hutton & Co., Inc., N.Y.C., 1977-89; dir. Swiss Bank Corp., N.Y.C., 1989—. Mem. Pine Valley Golf Club (N.J.), Plainfield Country Club (N.J.).

MCCALL, JOHN PATRICK, college president, educator; b. Yonkers, N.Y., July 17, 1927; s. Ambrose V. and Vera E. (Rush) McC.; m. Mary-Berenice Morris, June 15, 1957; children: Claire, Anne, Ambrose, Peter. AB, Holy Cross Coll., 1949; MA, Princeton U., 1952, PhD, 1955. Instr. Georgetown U., 1955-57, asst. prof. English, 1957-62, asso. prof., 1962-66; prof. U. Cin., 1966-82, head dept. English, 1970-76, sr. v.p., provost, 1976-82; pres. Knox Coll., 1982-93, pres. emeritus and prof. emeritus English, 1993—; vol. Peace Corps, Turkmenistan, 1993—; vis. prof. Turkmen State U., 1994—; vice chmn. Gov.'s Task Force on Rural Ill., 1986; pres. Associated Colls. Ill., 1986-88; chmn. Associated Colls. of M.W., 1991-92; mem. edn. com. Ill. Bd. Higher Edn., 1985, 90; mem. rural libr. panel, State of Ill., 1992; vis. prof. Turkmen State U., 1994—. Author: Chaucer Among the Gods: the Poetics of Classical Myth, 1979; contbr. articles to profl. jours.; research in medieval lit. and Chaucer's poetry. With Signal Corps, U.S. Army, 1952-54. Am. Coun. Learned Socs. fellow, 1962; John Simon Guggenheim Meml. Found. fellow, 1975; Fulbright grantee, 1962. Mem. Medieval Acad. Am. MLA, AAUP. Democrat. Roman Catholic. Home: 6328 Magnolia St New Orleans LA 70118

MC CALL, JULIEN LACHICOTTE, banker; b. Florence, S.C., Apr. 1, 1921; s. Arthur M. and Julia (Lachicotte) McC.; m. Janet Jones, Sept. 30, 1950; children: Melissa, Alison Gregg, Julien Lachicotte Jr. BS, Davidson Coll., 1942, LLD (hon.), 1983; MBA, Harvard U., 1947. With First Nat. City Bank, N.Y.C., 1948-71, asst. mgr. bond dept., 1952-53, asst. cashier, 1953-55, asst. v.p., 1955-57, v.p., 1957-71; 1st v.p. Nat. City Bank, Cleve., 1971-72, pres., 1972-79, chmn., 1979-85, chief exec. officer, from 1979, also bd. dirs.; pres. Nat. City Corp., 1973-80, chmn., chief exec. officer, 1980-86, also bd. dirs., cons.; bd. dirs. Acme Steel Co.; mem. fed. adv. coun. Fed. Res. Bd., 1984-87. Trustee St. Luke's Hosp., United Way Services, Boy Scouts Am., Playhouse Sq. Found., Cleve. Mus. Natural History. Served with AUS, 1942-46, Africa, ETO. Mem. Pepper Pike Club, Chagrin Valley Hunt Club, Kirtland Country Club (Ligonier, Pa.), Mountain Lake Club (Lake Wales, Fla.). Home: Arrowhead Country Line Rd Chagrin Falls OH 44022 Office: 30195 Chagrin Blvd Ste 104W Pepper Pike OH 44124-5703

MC CALL, ROBERT R., retired oil company executive; b. Norman, Okla., June 21, 1926; s. Robert R. and Ida (Smith) McC.; m. Byrdine Grimm, June 12, 1987; children: Claudia, Michael, Melinda, Danial. B.S., U. Okla., 1951, M.S., 1952. With Texaco, Inc., 1952-88, gen. mgr. producing Eastern hemisphere, 1972-78; v.p. producing Texaco, Inc., Harrison, N.Y., 1978-80; sr. v.p. Texaco U.S.A., Houston, 1980-83, exec. v.p., 1983-88. Bd. dirs. Near East Found. Served with USNR, 1944-46. Mem. Am. Inst. Mech. Engrs., Am. Petroleum Inst., Okla. Profl. Engrs., Pi Epsilon Tau. Republican. Home: 27 Grogans Point Ct Spring TX 77380-2648 Office: Texaco USA PO Box 1404 Houston TX 77251-1404

MCCALL, THOMAS DONALD, communications company executive; b. Syracuse, N.Y., Jan. 4, 1958; s. Donald Andrew and Ann Catherine (Lamb) McC.; m. Vicki Lynne Russ; children: Pamella Jean Lanty, Jamie Lynne Lanty, Kathleen Marchand, Matthew Thomas Owen. BS, SUNY, Brockport, 1980. Dir. comm. and pub. rels. Cazenovia (N.Y.) Coll., 1984-86; mgr. corp. pub. rels. Oneida (N.Y.) Silversmiths Ltd., 1986-90; account supr. Eric Mower and Assocs., Syracuse, 1990-91, sr. account supr., 1991-92, mgmt. supr., 1992-94; ptnr. Eric Mower and Assocs., Rochester, N.Y., 1994—; bd. mem. Pub. Rels. Soc. Am.-Ctrl. N.Y. Chpt., Syracuse, 1991-93. Bd. mem. Boys and Girls Club Syracuse, 1994-95; bd. deacons First Presbyn. Ch., Liverpool, N.Y., 1995—. Recipient Prism award Pub. Rels. Soc. Am., Rochester, N.Y., 1992, 93, 94. Democrat. Home: 5473 Saltbox Ln Clay NY 13041 Office: Eric Mower & Assocs 350 Linden Oaks Rochester NY 14625

MCCALL, TINA, critical care nurse; b. Searcy, Ark., Sept. 15, 1960; d. Junior Lee and Doris (Weaver) Barger; m. Todd McCall, Sept. 4, 1981; children: Morgan, Christian. BSN, U. Cen. Ark., Conway, 1982; student, Webster U., Little Rock. Cert. critical care nurse. Cardiac ICU staff nurse St. Vincent Infirmary, Little Rock; asst. head nurse in oncology St. Bernards Hosp., Jonesboro, Ark.; staff devel. instr. Doctors Hosp., Little Rock, nursing dir. intensive care; head nurse intermediate care unit St. paul Med. Ctr., Dallas; asst. divisional dir. med. surg. critical care Arlington (Tex.) Meml. Hosp., staff nurse critical care, adminstrv. coord., 1993—. Mem. AACCN, Am. Heart Assn., Sigma Theta Tau. Home: 934 Rio Vista Ln Arlington TX 76017-1753

MCCALL, WILLIAM CALDER, oil and chemical company executive; b. Hoquiam, Wash., Feb. 1, 1906; s. Dougall Hugh and Hughena (Calder) McC.; m. Marian Hall, Mar. 22, 1946; children—Ernest, Robert. Student U. Oreg., 1924-28; LHD Lewis & Clark Coll., 1992. Asst. sales mgr. Anaconda Sales Co., Chgo., 1932-39; chmn. McCall Oil & Chem. Corp., Portland, Oreg., 1939—, Gt. Western Chem. Co., Portland, 1975—; dir. Oreg. Bank, Portland, King Broadcasting Co., Seattle. Pres. Oreg. Art Mus., Portland; trustee Lewis and Clark Coll., Portland; exec. v.p. Oreg. Symphony Soc.; dir. Oreg. Health Scis. Found., Good Samaritan Hosp. Found., Portland. Republican. Episcopalian. Clubs: Eldorado Country (Indian Wells, Calif.) (pres. 1978-79); Arlington (Portland); Pacific-Union (San Francisco); Los Angeles Country, Vintage (Palm Desert, Calif.), Waverley Country, Rainier (Seattle). Office: McCall Oil and Chem Corp 808 SW 15th Ave Portland OR 97205-1907

MCCALLA, JON P., federal judge; b. 1947; m. Mary R. McCalla; children: Marjorie Katherine, Elizabeth Clair. BS, U. Tenn., 1969; JD, Vanderbilt U., 1974. Law clk. to Hon. Bailey Brown U.S. Dist. Ct. (we. dist.) Tenn., 1974-75; assoc. Armstrong, Allen, Braden, Goodman, McBride & Prewitt, 1975-80; ptnr. Armstrong, Allen, Prewitt, Gentry, Johnson & Holmes, 1980-87, Heiskell, Donelson, Bearman, Adams, Williams & Kirsch, 1987-92; fed. judge U.S. Dist. Ct. (we. dist.) Tenn., Memphis, 1992—. Mem. Fed. Bar Assn., Tenn. Bar Assn., Memphis Bar Assn. Office: US Dist Ct 167 N Main St Ste 907 Memphis TN 38103-1828

MCCALLUM, BENNETT TARLTON, economics educator; b. Poteet, Tex., July 27, 1935; s. Henry DeRosset and Frances (Tarlton) McC.; m. Sally Jo Hart, June 3, 1961. B.A., Rice U., 1957, B.S. in Chem. Engring., 1958, Ph.D., 1969; M.B.A., Harvard U., 1963. Chem. engr. Petro-Tex Chem. Corp., Houston, 1958-61; lectr. U. Sussex, Eng., 1965-66; asst. prof. to prof. U. Va., Charlottesville, 1967-80; prof. econs. Carnegie-Mellon U., Pitts., 1981-86, H.J. Heinz prof. econs., 1986—; cons. Fed. Res Bd., Washington, 1974-75; rsch. assoc. Nat. Bur. Econ. Rsch., Cambridge, Mass., 1979—; adviser Fed. Res. Bank Richmond, Va., 1981—. Author: Monetary Economics, 1989, International Monetary Economics, 1996; co-editor Am. Econ. Rev., 1988-91; contbr. more than 100 articles to profl. publs. NSF grantee, 1977-86; vis. scholar Internat. Monetary Fund, Washington, 1989-90, Bank of Japan, 1993, Victoria U. Wellington and Res. Bank of New Zealand, 1995. Fellow Econometric Soc.; mem. Am. Econ. Assn. Home: 219 Gladstone Rd Pittsburgh PA 15217-1111 Office: Carnegie-Mellon U Grad Sch Indsl Adminstrn 206 Pittsburgh PA 15213

MC CALLUM, CHARLES ALEXANDER, university official; b. North Adams, Mass., Nov. 1, 1925; s. Charles Alexander and Mabel Helen (Cassidy) McC.; m. Alice Rebecca Lasseter, Dec. 17, 1955; children: Scott Alan, Charles Alexander III, Philip Warren, Christopher Jay. Student, Dartmouth Coll., 1943-44, Wesleyan U., Middletown, Conn., 1946-47; D.M.D., Tufts U., 1951; M.D., Med. Coll. Ala., 1957; D.Sc. (hon.), U. Ala., 1975, Georgetown U., 1982, Tufts U., 1988, Chulalongkorn U., Thailand, 1993, U. Medicine & Dentistry, N.J., 1993. Diplomate Am. Bd. Oral Surgery (pres. 1970). Intern oral surgery Univ. Hosp., Birmingham, Ala., 1951-52, resident oral surgery, 1952-54, intern medicine, 1957-58; mem. faculty U. Ala. Sch. Dentistry, 1956-96, prof., chmn. dept. oral surgery, 1959-65, dean sch., 1962-77; prof., dept. surgery U. Ala. Sch. of Medicine, 1965-96; v.p. for health affairs, dir. U. Ala. Med. Center, Birmingham, 1977-87; pres. U. Ala., Birmingham, 1987-93, chief sect. oral surgery Sch. Dentistry, 1958-65, 68-69; prof., 1959-93, disting. prof., 1993—; mem. nat. adv. dental rsch. coun. NIH, 1968-72; mem. Joint Commn. on Accreditation of Hosps., 1980-91, vice chmn., 1985, chmn., 1987-88. Fellow Am. Coll. Dentists, Internat. Coll. Dentists; mem. ADA (council on dental edn. 1970-76), Am. Assn. Dental Schs. (pres. 1969), Ala. Acad. of Honor, AMA, Am. Soc. Oral Surgeons (trustee 1972-73, pres. 1975-76), Southeastern Soc. Oral Surgeons (pres. 1970), Inst. of Medicine of Nat. Acad. of Scis., Assn. Acad. Health Ctrs. (chmn. bd. dirs. 1984-85), Omicron Kappa Upsilon, Phi Beta Pi. Home: 2328 Garland Dr Birmingham AL 35216-3002 Office: Univ Ala at Birmingham 107 MJH Birmingham AL 35294-2010

MC CALLUM, CHARLES EDWARD, lawyer; b. Memphis, Mar. 13, 1939; s. Edward Payson and India Raimelle (Musick) McC.; m. Lois Ann Gowell Temple, Nov. 30, 1985; children: Florence Andrea, Printha Kyle, Chandler Ward, Sabra Nicole Temple. B.S., MIT, 1960; J.D., Vanderbilt U., 1964. Bar: Mich., Tenn. 1964. Assoc. Warner Norcross & Judd LLP, Grand Rapids, Mich., 1964-69; ptnr. Warner, Norcross & Judd, Grand Rapids, Mich., 1969—, mng. ptnr., 1992—; rep. assemblyman State Bar Mich., 1973-78; dir. Rsch. and Tech. Inst. West Mich., 1986—, chmn., 1989-91; lectr. continuing legal edn. programs; chmn., bd. dirs. Butterworth Ventures, 1987—; mem. West Mich. World Trade Week Com., 1988—, chmn., 1990-91; mem. Mich. Dist. Export Coun., 1990—, chmn., 1992—. Chmn. Grand Rapids Area Transit Authority, 1976-79, mem., 1972-79; regional v.p. Nat. Mcpl. League, 1978-86, mem. coun., 1971-78; pres. Grand Rapids Art Mus., 1979-81, trustee, 1976-83, 94—; chmn. Butterworth Hosp., 1979-87, trustee, 1977-87; chmn. Butterworth Health Corp., 1982-89, dir., 1982—, vice chmn., 1989-91, sec., 1991—; vice chmn. Citizens Com. for Consolidation of Govt. Svcs., 1981-82; chmn. Kent County Cultural Svcs. Woodrow Wilson fellow, 1960-61; Fulbright scholar U. Manchester, Eng., 1960-61. Mem. ABA (com. on law firms bus. law sect. 1982-94, chmn. com. on law firms bus. law sect. 1994—, chmn. subcom. on firm mgmt. 1988-95, mem. fed. regulation of securities com. 1982—, mem. internat. bus. law com.), Am. Law Inst., Tenn. Bar Assn., Mich. Bar Assn. (mem. coun. bus. law sect. 1983-89, sect. chmn. 1988-89, ex-officio coun. bus. law sect. 1989—, chmn. takeover laws subcom. 1986-88, co-chmn. internat. bus. law com., internat. law sect. 1988-89), Grand Rapids Bar Assn., Interant. Bar Assn., Grand Rapids c. of C. (pres. 1975, bd. dirs. 1970-76), Univ. Club, Peninsular Club, Order of Coif, Sigma Xi. Home: 110 Bittersweet Ln NE Ada MI 49301-9552 Office: 111 Lyon St NW Grand Rapids MI 49503-2404

MC CALLUM, DAVID, actor; b. Scotland, Sept. 19, 1933; m. Katherine Carpenter; children: Peter, Sophie; children by previous marriage, Paul Jason (dec.), Valentine.

MCCALLUM, JAMES SCOTT, lieutenant governor, former state senator; b. Fond du Lac, Wis., May 2, 1950; s. George Duncan and Marilyn Joy (Libke) McC.; m. Laurie Ann Riach, June 19, 1979; children: Zachary Scott, Rory Duncan, Cara. BA, Macalester Coll., 1972; MA, Johns Hopkins U., 1974. Mem. Wis. State Senate, Madison, 1977-87; lt. gov. State of Wis., Madison, 1987—. Chmn. Fond du Lac County Reps., 1974-76, Wis. Safe Kids Project; mem. resolutions com. Wis. State Rep. Conv., 1977; presdl. appointee to Internat. Trade Adv. Group, 1988-89, U.S. EPA Nat. Adv. Coun. for Environ. Policy and Tech., 1991—; chmn. Gov.'s Conf. on Small Bus. and Gov.'s Com. on Econ. Issues and Safe Kids Project; chair Nat. Conf. of Lt. Govs., 1991—. Named one of Outstanding Young Men Am., Jaycees, 1976; recipient Presdl. award Honor, Jaycees, 1976; Toll Fellow, 1987. Office: State of Wis Office of Lt. Gov. 22 State Capitol Madison WI 53702-0001*

MCCALLUM, KENNETH JAMES, retired university dean, chemistry and chemical engineering educator; b. Scott, Sask., Can., Apr. 25, 1918; s. James Alexander and Alice (Fines) McC.; m. Christine Chorneyko, Sept. 20, 1950 (dec. 1971); children: Patricia Jean, Douglas James; m. Erika Connell, Aug. 16, 1974. B.Sc., U. Sask., 1936, M.Sc., 1939; Ph.D., Columbia U., 1942. Jr. research officer NRC Can., 1942-43; mem. faculty U. Sask., from 1943, prof. chemistry and chem. engring., from 1953, head dept. chemistry and chem. engring., from 1959, dean grad. studies, from 1970. Assoc. editor: Jour. Chem. Physics, 1947-50; research, publs. (in cement chemistry, electron affinities, radioisotope exchange reactions, chem. effects transformations, radiation chemistry). Fellow Royal Soc. Can., AAAS, Chem. Inst. Can. (dir. sci. affairs 1961-64, pres. 1968-69). Home: 1622 Park Ave, Saskatoon, SK Canada

MCCALLUM, RICHARD WARWICK, medical researcher, clinician, educator; b. Brisbane, Australia, Jan. 21, 1945; came to U.S., 1969; MD, BS, Queensland U., Australia, 1968. Rotating intern Charity Hosp. La., New Orleans, 1969-70; resident in internal medicine Barnes Hosp., Washington, 1970-72; fellow in gastroenterology Wadsworth VA Hosp., L.A., 1972-74, chief endoscopic unit, dept gastroenterology, 1974-76; dir. gastrointestinal diagnostic svcs. Yale-New Haven Med. Ctr., New Haven, 1979-85; asst. prof. medicine UCLA, 1974-76; asst. prof. medicine Yale U., New Haven, 1977-82, assoc. prof., 1982-85; prof., chief div. gastroenterology, hepatology and nutrition U. Va., Charlottesville, 1985—, Paul Janssen prof. medicine, 1987—; dir. GI Motility Ctr., U. Va. Health Sci. Ctr., 1990—. Fellow ACP, Am. Coll. Gastroenterology, Royal Australasian Coll. Physicians, Royal Australian Coll. Surgeons; mem. Australian Gastroenterology Soc., Am. Fedn. Clin. Rsch., Am. Assn. Study Liver Diseases, Am. Soc. Gastrointestinal Endoscopy, Am. Soc. for Clin. Investigation, Am. Gastroenterology Assn., Am. Coll. Gastroenterology. Office: U Va Health Scis Ctr Dept Internal Medicine Box 145 Med Ctr Charlottesville VA 22908-0001

MCCALLUM, SCOTT, state official; b. Fond du Lac, Wis.; m. Laurie McCallum; children: Zachary, Rory, Cara. BA, Macalester Coll.; MA in Internat. Studies, Johns Hopkins U. Property developer Fond du Lac; mem. Wis. State Senate; lt. gov. State of Wis.; dir. Workplace Child Care Clearinghouse; chair Repeat Offenders Task Force State of Wis., Trauma and Injury Prevention Task Force; coord. Gov.'s Conf. on Small Bus.; presdl. appointee to Internat. Trade Policy Adv. Com.; past chair Nat. Conf. of Lt. Govs.; gov.'s appointee to Nat. Aerospace States Assn. Office: Lieutenant Governor Rm 22 East State Capitol Madison WI 53702*

MCCALLY, CHARLES RICHARD, construction company executive; b. Dallas, Oct. 5, 1958; s. Richard Holt and Elizabeth Ann (Webster) McC.; m. Shirley Elizabeth Avant, Aug. 18, 1979 (div.); children: Charles Richard Jr., Meredith Holt; m. Judy Lynn Tackett, June 24, 1993. BSME, So. Meth. U., 1981. Engr. McCally Co., Dallas, 1977-83; owner, v.p. DRT Mech. Corp., Dallas, 1983-95; owner McCally Svc. Co., Inc., Dallas, 1995—. Active Young Reps., Dallas, 1980—. Mem. NSPE, ASME, ASHRAE, Am. Soc. Plumbing Engrs. (membership com. 1983-89), Tex. Soc. Profl. Engrs., So. Meth. U. Alumni Assn., SMU Mustang Club, Bent Tree Country Club (Dallas), Oaktree Country Club (Garland, Tex.) (bd. dirs. 1986-89), Sigma Chi. Avocations: tennis, boating, traveling, camping. Home: 4832 Sandestin Dr Dallas TX 75287 Office: McCally Svc Co Inc 2850 Congressman Ln Dallas TX 75220-1408

MCCAMBRIDGE, JOHN JAMES, civil engineer; b. Bklyn., Oct. 27, 1933; s. John Joseph and Florence Josita (McDonnell) McC.; m. Dorothy Antoinette Cook, Mar. 17, 1962; children: Sharon J., John S., Patrick J., Kathleen C. BCE, Manhattan Coll., 1955; MS, Vanderbilt U., 1958; postgrad., UCLA, 1963-66. Civil engr. Raymond Concrete Pile Co., N.Y.C., 1955; commd. 2d lt. USAF, 1955, advanced through grades to col., 1972; exec. sec. Defense Com. On Rsch., Washington, 1971-73, DOD-NASA Supportive Rsch. Tech. Panel, Washington, 1972-74; asst. dir. Def. Rsch. and Engring. (for Life Scis.) Office Sec. Def., Washington, 1974-75; dir. Air Force Life Support Systems Program Office, Wright Patterson AFB, Ohio, 1975-79; retired USAF, 1979; prin. Booz, Allen & Hamilton, Inc., Bethesda, Md., 1979-86; v.p. Espey, Huston & Assoc., Inc., Falls Church, Va., 1986-90; mng. prin. JMC Cons. Group, McLean, Va., 1990—; chmn. air panel on NBC Def., NATO, Evere, Belgium, 1970-71; exec. sec. Def. Com. on Rsch., Washington, 1971-73; def. dept. rep. to physics survey com., Nat. Acad. Scis., Washington, 1971. Contbr. articles to profl. jours. Decorated Legion of Merit with oak leaf cluster. Fellow Aerospace Med. Assn. (exec. coun. 1972-73), Inst. Hazardous Materials Mgmt. (chmn. 1988-94); mem. Coun. Engring. and Sci. Splty. Bds. (exec. com. 1995—), Acad. Cert. Hazardous Materials Mgrs. (pres. 1984-86), Survival and Flight Equipment Assn. (nat. sec. 1977-78), River Bend Golf and Country Club, Fairfax Hunt Club, Black Tie Club, Tower Club, KC, Sigma Xi, Chi Epsilon. Republican. Roman Catholic. Office: JMC Cons Group 9200 Falls Run Rd Mc Lean VA 22102-1028

MC CAMERON, FRITZ ALLEN, retired university administrator; b. Nacogdoches, Tex., Oct. 8, 1929; s. Leland Allen and Gladys (Turner) Mc C.; m. Jeannine Young, June 11, 1957; 1 child, Mary Hartley. B.B.A., Stephen F. Austin State Coll., 1950, M.A., 1951; Ph.D., U. Ala., 1954. C.P.A., La. Asso. prof. La. State U., 1959-62, prof., 1962-67, chmn. dept. accounting, 1967-71, asst. vice chancellor, 1971-73, dean continuing edn., 1973-95; ret., 1995; cons. in field. Author: FORTRAN Logic and Programming, 1968, Cobol Logic and Programming, rev. edit, 1970, 5th edit., 1985, FORTRAN IV, 1970, rev. edit., 1974, 3d edit., 1977. Mem. Am. Inst. C.P.A.'s, La. Soc. C.P.A.'s, Am. Accounting Assn. Home: 930 Rodney Dr Baton Rouge LA 70808-5867

MC CAMMON, DAVID NOEL, automobile company executive; b. Topeka, Nov. 6, 1934; s. Noel F. and Freda E. McC.; m. Valerie L. Palliaer, May 18, 1968; children: Jeff, Mark, Scott. B.S. in Bus. Adminstrn, U. Nebr., 1957; M.B.A. (Baker scholar), Harvard U., 1962. With Ford Motor Co., Dearborn, Mich., 1957—; contr. Ford div. Ford Motor Co., 1970-71, asst. corp. contr., 1971-77, exec. dir. bus. strategy, 1977-78, v.p. corp. strategy analysis, 1979-84, v.p., contr., 1984-87, v.p. fin., treas., 1987-94, v.p. fin., 1995—. Served with U.S. Army, 1957-58. Club: Harvard Bus. Sch. (Detroit). Office: Ford Motor Co The American Rd Dearborn MI 48126-2798

MCCAMMON, JAMES ANDREW, chemistry educator; b. Lafayette, Ind., Feb. 8, 1947; s. Lewis Brown and Jean Ann (McClintock) McC.; m. Anne Elizabeth Woltmann, June 6, 1969. BA magna cum laude, Pomona Coll., 1969; MA, Harvard U., 1970, PhD, 1976. Research fellow Harvard U., Cambridge, Mass., 1976-78; asst. prof. U. Houston, 1978-81, M.D. Anderson prof. chemistry, 1981-94, dir. Inst. for Molecular Design, 1987-94, prof. biochemistry, 1989-94, adj. prof. chemistry, 1995—; adj. prof. molecular physiology and biophysics Baylor Coll. Medicine, Houston, 1986-94, adj. prof. biochemistry, 1992-94; Joseph E. Mayer chair theoretical chemistry U. Calif., San Diego, 1995—, prof. pharmacology, 1995—. Author: Dynamics of Proteins and Nucleic Acids, 1987. Recipient Tchr.-scholar award Camille and Henry Dreyfus Found., 1982, George H. Hitchings award Burroughs-Wellcome Fund, 1987, Computerworld Smithsonian Info. Tech. Leadership award for Breakthrough Computational Sci., 1995; Alfred P. Fellow Am. Phys. Soc.; mem. AAAS, Am. Chem. Soc., Biophys. Soc., Protein Soc., Phi Beta Kappa. Achievements include development of the molecular dynamics simulation method for proteins and nucleic acids, of the thermodynamic cycle perturbation method for studying molecular recognition, and of the Brownian dynamics method for simulating diffusion-controlled reactions. Office: U Calif San Diego Dept Chemistry La Jolla CA 92093-0365

MCCAN, JAMES LAWTON, education educator; b. Plymouth, Ind., Aug. 10, 1952; s.Jean F. and Mildred P. (Hayn) McC.; m. Carolyn G. Splain, Jan. 16, 1971; children: Kendra, Brittany. B of Phys. Edn., Purdue U., 1974; MS in Edn., 1981, PhD, 1983. Tchr. reading and English Waynetown (Ind.) Mid. Sch., 1974-75, Yorkville (Ill.) H.S., 1979-80; reading specialist Purdue U., West Lafayette, Ind., 1983-89; program chair Basic Skills Advancement Ind. Voc-Tech. Coll., Lafayette, 1989-91; asst. prof., coord. student teaching Hillsdale (Mich.) Coll., 1991-95; dir. Student Achievement Zone, South Bend, Ind., 96—. Contbr. articles and poetry to jours. Mem. DARTEP, Internat. Reading Assn., Mich. Reading Assn. Avocations: reading, music. Home: 4205 St Andrews Cir Mishawaka IN 46545 Office: Student Achievement Zone 1202 S Twyckenham South Bend IN 46615

MCCANDLESS, BARBARA J., auditor; b. Cottonwood Falls, Kans., Oct. 25, 1931; d. Arch G. and Grace (Kittle) McCandless; m. Allyn O. Lockner, 1969. BS, Kans. State U., 1953; MS, Cornell U., 1959; postgrad. U. Minn., 1962-66, U. Calif., Berkeley, 1971-72. Cert. family and consumer scientist; enrolled agt. IRS. Home demonstration agt. Kans. State U., 1953-57; teaching asst. Cornell U., 1957-58, asst. extension home economist in marketing, 1958-59; consumer mktg. specialist, asst. prof. Oreg. State U., 1959-62; instr. home econs. U. Minn., 1962-63, research asst. agrl. econs., 1963-66; asst. prof. U. R.I., 1966-67; assoc. prof. family econs., mgmt., housing, equipment dept. head S.D. State U., 1967-73; asst. to sec. Dept. Commerce and Consumer Affairs, S.D., 1973-79, tax cons., 1980-91, revenue auditor, 1991—. Mem. Nat. Council Occupational Licensing, dir., 1973-75, v.p., 1975-79. Mem. Am. Agrl. Econs. Assn., Am. Assn. Family and Consumer Scis., Am. Coun. Consumer Interests, Assn. Govt. Accts., Inst. Internal Auditors, Nat. Coun. on Family Rels., LWV, Kans. State U. Alumni Assn., Pi Gamma Mu. Research on profl. and occupational licensing bds. Address: 2114 SW Potomac Dr Topeka KS 66611-1445

MCCANDLESS, BRUCE, II, aerospace engineer, former astronaut; b. Boston, June 8, 1937; s. Bruce and Sue McCandless; m. Alfreda Bernice Doyle, Aug. 6, 1960; children: Bruce III, Tracy. BS, U.S. Naval Acad., 1958; MSEE, Stanford U., 1965; MBA, U. Houston, Clear Lake, 1987. Commd. ensign USN, 1958, advanced through grades to capt., 1979, naval aviator, 1960, with Fighter Squadron 102, 1960-64; astronaut Johnson Space Ctr., NASA, Houston, 1966-90; mem. Skylab 1 backup crew Johnson Space Center, NASA, Houston, mem. STS-11 shuttle crew, mem. STS-31 Hubble Space Telescope deployment crew; ret. USN, 1990; prin. staff engr. Lockheed Martin Astronautics, Denver, 1990—. Decorated Legion of Merit; recipient Def. Superior Service medal, NASA Exceptional Service medal, NASA Spaceflight medal, NASA Exceptional Engring. Achievement medal, Collier Trophy, 1985, Haley Space Flight award AIAA, 1991. Fellow Am. Astron. Soc.; mem. IEEE, U.S. Naval Inst., Nat. Audubon Soc., Houston Audubon Soc. (past pres.). Episcopalian. Achievements include executing 1st untethered free flight in space using Manned Maneuvering Unit. Office: Lockheed Martin Astronautics MS S8000 PO Box 179 Denver CO 80201-0179

MCCANDLESS, CAROLYN KELLER, entertainment, media company executive; b. Patuxent River, Md., June 6, 1945; d. Stevens Henry and Betty Jane (Bethune) Keller; m. Stephen Porter McCandless, Apr. 22, 1972; children: Peter Keller, Deborah Marion. BA, Stanford U., 1967; MBA, Harvard U., 1969. Fin. analyst Time Inc., N.Y.C., 1969-72, mgr. budgets and fin. analysis, 1972-78, asst. sec., dir. internal adminstrn., 1978-85, v.p., dir. employee benefits, 1985-90; v.p human resources and adminstrn. Time Warner, Inc., N.Y.C., 1990—; bd. dirs. LifeRe Corp. Republican. Mem. Unitarian Ch. Office: Time Warner Inc 1271 Avenue Of The Americas New York NY 10020

MCCANDLESS, J(ANE) BARDARAH, retired religion educator; b. Dayton, Ohio, Apr. 16, 1925; d. J(ohn) Bard and Sarah Catharine (Shuey) McC. BA, Oberlin Coll., 1951; MRE, Bibl. Sem., N.Y.C., 1953; PhD, U. Pitts., 1968. Dir. Christian edn. Wallace Meml. United Presbyn. Ch., Pitts., 1953-54, Beverly Heights United Presbyn. Ch., Mt. Lebanon, Pa., 1956-61; instr. religion Westminster Coll., New Wilmington, Pa., 1961-65, asst. prof., 1965-71, assoc. prof., 1971-83, prof. religion, 1983-94, prof. emeritus, 1994—, chair dept. religion and philosophy, 1988-92; leader Christian edn. workshops Presbytery of Shenango, Presbyn. Ch. (U.S.A.), 1961—, Synod of Trinity, 1972, 76. Author: An Untainted Saint...Ain't, 1978; contbr. articles to profl. jours., Harper's Ency. Religious Edn. Mem. session New Wilmington Presbyn. Ch., 1977-79. Mack grantee Westminster Coll., 1962-63, Faculty rsch. grantee, 1972, 78, 90. Mem. Religious Edn. Assn., Assn. Profs. and Researchers in Religious Edn. (mem. exec. com. 1978-80), Soc. for Sci. Study Religion, Phi Beta Kappa, Pi Lambda Theta.

MCCANDLESS, SANDRA RAVICH, lawyer; b. Revere, Mass., Sept. 5, 1948; d. Merrill Earl and Goldie (Clayman) Ravich; m. Ross Erwin McCandless; 1 child, Phyra. BA, Radcliffe Coll., 1970; JD, Georgetown U., Washington, 1973. Bar: Calif. 1973, U.S. Ct. Appeals (1st and 7th cirs.) 1974, U.S. Ct. Appeals (6th and 9th cirs.) 1975, U.S. Dist. Ct. (no. dist.) Calif. 1976, U.S. Dist. Ct. (ea. dist.) Calif. 1978. Law clk. NLRB, Washington, 1971-73, atty. appellate ct. br., 1973-75; assoc. Pillsbury, Madison & Sutro, San Francisco, 1975-79; from assoc. to ptnr. Graham & James, San Francisco, 1979-93; atty. Sonnenschein, Nath & Rosenthal, San Francisco, 1993—; mem. faculty Nat. Inst. Appellate Advocacy, San Francisco. Mem. ABA, Bar Assn. San Francisco, San Francisco Barrister Club (co-chair com. on labor law 1979-82). Avocations: writing, cruises, theatre. Office: Sonnenschein Nath & Rosenthal 685 Market St Fl 10 San Francisco CA 94105-4200

MCCANDLESS, STEPHEN PORTER, financial executive; b. Denver, Mar. 17, 1941; s. Robert B. and Mary (Porter) McC.; m. Carolyn Keller, Apr. 22, 1972; children: Peter, Deborah. Geol. Engr., Colo. Sch. Mines, 1963; M.B.A., Harvard U., 1969. Geologist Shell Oil Co., Casper, Wyo., 1963-65; securities analyst Kidder Peabody & Co., N.Y.C., 1969-70; fin. analyst Asarco Inc., N.Y.C., 1971-72, asst. to treas., 1972-73, asst. treas., 1973-79, treas., 1979-89, v.p., 1983-89; sr. v.p. fin. The Personalized Mass Media Corp., N.Y.C., 1989—, also bd. dirs.; sr. v.p. fin., mem. adv. bd. Personalized Media Comm., L.L.C., N.Y.C., 1995—. Trustee The Town Sch., 1984-94. Served with C.E., U.S. Army, 1963-65. Recipient Voice for Justice award Support Com. for Battered Women, 1994. Mem. Tau Beta Pi. Office: Personalized Mass Media Corp 110 E 42nd St New York NY 10017-5611

MCCANLES, MICHAEL FREDERICK, English language educator; b. Kansas City, Mo., Mar. 8, 1936; s. Martin and Dorothy (Kaysing) McC.; m. Penelope A. Mitchell, May 27, 1967; children—Christopher, Stephanie, Jocelyn. B.S., Rockhurst Coll., 1957; M.A., U. Kans., 1959, Ph.D., 1964. Instr. dept. English U. Cin., 1962-64; asst. prof. Marquette U., 1964-68, assoc. prof., 1968-76, prof., 1976—. Author: Dialectical Criticism and Renaissance Literature, 1975, The Discourse of Il Principe, 1983, The Text of Sidney's Arcadian World, 1989, Jonsonian Discriminations: The Humanist Poet and the Praise of True Nobility, 1992; contbr. articles to profl. jours. Guggenheim fellow, 1978-79. Home: 2640 N 89th St Milwaukee WI 53226-1808 Office: Dept English Marquette U Milwaukee WI 53233 *As educator, scholar, and citizen I try to encourage in the public domain the same qualities of open-mindedness, secular tolerance of multiple viewpoints, and critical judgement of these viewpoints that I encourage among my students and colleagues.*

MCCANN, CLARENCE DAVID, JR., special events coordinator, museum curator and director, artist; b. Mobile, Ala., Apr. 30, 1948; s. Clarence David and Theresa (Pope) McC.; m. Brenda Clemens (div. 1979); 1 child, Nathan; m. Robin Chiavaroli, 1980; children: Angela, John. BFA, U. South Ala., 1970; MFA, U. Cin., 1972; grad. cert., Mus. Mgmt. Inst., Berkeley, Calif., 1982. Art instr. Spring Hill Coll., Mobile, 1972-75, U. South Ala., Mobile, 1975-76; mem. staff, asst. registrar Fine Arts Mus. of South, Mobile, 1977-78, registrar, 1978-81, curator collection, 1981-84, asst. dir., 1985-86, 88-91, acting dir., 1986-88, mus. curator, 1988-91; asst. mgr. spl. events coord. City of Mobile, 1991—; adj. lectr. U.S. Ala., 1990-91, adj. lectr. Bishop State Community Coll., 1991—. Author: (catalogues) The Ripening of American Art: Duveneck and Chase, 1979, The Artists of Barbizon: The Boone Collection, 1983, Enisled Visions: The Southern Nontraditional Folk Artist, 1987, The Acquisitive Eye: Selections From The Collection of James M. Younger, 1990. Pres. Contemporary Artists Consortium of Mobile, 1979-81. Recipient various painting awards Allied Arts Coun., Mobile, 1974; U. Cin. fellow, 1972. Mem. Am. Assn. Mus., Ala. Mus. Assn., Southeastern Mus. Assn. Democrat. Home: 9080 Rawhide Ct Semmes AL 36575-7275 Office: Office of Spl Events 2900 Dauphin St Mobile AL 36606-2420

MCCANN, DENNIS JOHN, columnist; b. Janesville, Wis., July 25, 1950; s. Thomas G. and Jean E. (Skelly) McC.; m. Barbara Jo Bunker, Sept. 11, 1971. BA, U. Wis., 1974. Reporter WMIR Radio, Lake Geneva, Wis., 1974, Janesville (Wis.) Gazette, 1975-78, 79-83; reporter, columnist Milw. Jour. Sentinel, 1983—; reporter Daily Herald, Arlington Heights, Ill., 1978. Contbg. author: Best of the Rest, 1993. Recipient Writing awards Milw. Press Club, Wis. Newspaper Assn., Newspaper Farm Editors. Avocations: golf, running. Office: The Milw Jour Sentinel 333 W State St Milwaukee WI 53203-1305

MCCANN, EDWARD, investment banker; b. San Diego, June 22, 1943; s. Edward F. and Anna Marie (McKay) McC.; m. Sara Sheffield Hall, Nov. 15, 1980; children: Sheffield Hall, Henry Howland, Edward Brewster. BS, U.S. Naval Acad., 1965, MSEE, 1965; postgrad., MIT, 1970. Staff mem. Rsch. Lab. Electronics MIT, Cambridge, Mass., 1968-70; program mgmt. exec. Westinghouse Corp. Rsch. Lab., Churchill, Pa., 1971-73; chief planner Chevron Shipping Co., San Francisco, 1973-77, div. mgr., 1977-79; corp. planning and acquisition staff exec. Standard Oil Co. Calif., San Francisco, 1979-83; dir. strategic planning, def. sector Sperry Corp., N.Y.C., 1983-85, with merger team, 1986; v.p. corp. fin. Eberstadt Fleming Inc., N.Y.C., 1986-88; sr. v.p. investment banking, dir. aerospace and tech. group Robert Fleming Inc., London and N.Y.C., 1988-90; prin. investment banking Hambrecht & Quist, Inc., N.Y.C., 1990—; bd. dirs. Am. Def. Preparedness Assn., 1986-92, L.I. Biol./Cold Spring Harbor Lab., 1988—. Mem. long-range planning coun. United Way, L.I., 1983-86; treas. Oyster Bay Youth and Family Counseling Agy., 1984-86; trustee Oyster Bay Community Found., 1984—. Recipient class prize systems engring. and naval weaponry, S.R. and Daus. of Am. Colonists awards, 1965. Mem. Coun. Fgn. Rels., Soc. Naval Architects and Marine Engrs., Am. Soc. Naval Engrs., Assn. Old Crows, Navy League, Assn. Naval Aviators, Naval Acad. Alumni Assn., Am. Def. Preparedness Assn. (bd. dirs. 1988-92), Bohemian Club, Seawanhaka Corinthian Yacht Club, Cold Spring Harbor Beach Club. Episcopalian. Home: 398 West Neck Rd Lloyd Harbor NY 11743-1620 Office: Hambrecht & Quist Inc 230 Park 21st Ave New York NY 10169-0005

MCCANN, ELIZABETH IRELAND, theater, television and motion picture producer, lawyer; b. N.Y.C., Mar. 31, 1931; d. Patrick and Rebecca (Henry) McC. BA, Manhattanville Coll., 1952, PhD hon., 1983; MA, Columbia U., 1954; LLD, Fordham U., 1966; ArtsD (hon.), Manhattanville Coll., 1987; LitD (hon.), Marymount Coll., 1993. Bar: N.Y. 1966. Assoc. firm Paul, Weiss, Rifkind, Wharton & Garrison, N.Y.C., 1965-66; assoc. numerous theater mgmts. Robert Joffrey, Hal Prince, Saint Suber, Maurice Evans, 1956-68; mng. dir. Nederlander Orgn., N.Y.C., 1968-76; pres. McCann & Nugent Prodns., Inc., N.Y.C., 1976-86; bd. dirs. City Ctr. Music and Dance, Marymount Coll. Prodr.: (play) My Fat Friend, 1975, Dracula (Tony award 1977), The Elephant Man, 1978 (Tony award, Drama Critics award 1978, Drama Desk award 1978, Outer Critics Circle award 1978, Obie award 1978), Night and Day, 1979, Home, 1980 (Adelco award 1980), Amadeus, 1980 (Tony award 1980, Drama Desk award 1980), Morning's At Seven, 1980 (Tony award 1980), Piaf, 1981, Rose, 1981, The Dresser, 1981, Mass Appeal, 1981, The Life and Adventures of Nicholas Nickleby, 1981 (Tony award 1981, Drama Critics Circle award 1981), Good, 1982, All's Well That Ends Well, 1983, The Glass Menagerie, 1983, Total Abandon, 1983, Painting Churches, 1983, The Lady and the Clarinet, 1983, Cyrano de Bergerac/Much Ado About Nothing, 1984, Pacific Overtures, 1984, Leader of the Pack, 1985, Les Liaisons Dangereuses, 1987 (Drama Critics Circle award 1987), Stepping Out, 1987, Orpheus Descending, 1989, Nick & Nora, 1991, Three Tall Woman, 1995, A Midsummer Nights Dream, 1995; TV show Piaf, 1981, Morning's At Seven, 1982, Philobolus Dance Theatre, 1982; assoc. prodr. Orpheus Descending, 1990. Recipient Entrepreneurial Woman award Women Bus. Owners of N.Y., 1981, 82; recipient James J. and Jame Hoey award for Interracial Justice, 1981, Spl Drama League award for coproducing the Life and Adventures of Nicholas Nickleby on Broadway, 1982, Dr Louis M. Spadero award Fordham Grad. Sch. Bus., 1982.

MC CANN, FRANCES VERONICA, physiologist, educator; b. Manchester, Conn., Jan. 15, 1927; d. John Joseph and Grace E. (Tuttle) Mc C.; m. Elden J. Murray, Sept. 20, 1962 (dec. Nov. 1975). AB with distinction and honors, U. Conn., 1952, PhD, 1959; MS, U. Ill., 1954; MA (hon.), Dartmouth Coll., 1973. Investigator Marine Biol. Lab., Woods Hole, Mass., 1952-62; instr. physiology Dartmouth Med. Sch., Hanover, N.H., 1959-61, asst. prof., 1961-67, assoc. prof., 1967-73, prof., 1973—; adj. prof. biol. scis. Dartmouth Coll., 1974—; mem., cons. physiology study sect. NIH, 1973-77, mem. biomed. rsch. devel. com., 1978-82, chmn, 1979; cons. Hayer Inst., 1979—; cons. staff Hitchcock Hosp., Hanover, 1980—, sr. staff rsch. Norris Catton Cancer Ctr., 1980—; mem. NRC, 1982-86; chmn. Symposium on Comparative Physiology of the Heart, 1968. Editor: Comparative Physiology of the Heart: Current Trends, 1965; contbr. numerous articles to profl. jours. Trustee Lebanon Coll., 1970-73, Montshire Mus. Sic., Hanover, 1975—, Hanover Health Coun., 1976, Lebanon Coll., 1978—; incorporator Howe Libr., 1975—; active LWV, 1980—, Conservation Coun., 1983—, Hist. Soc., 1975—, N.H. Lakes Assn., 1992—; pres. Armington Lake Assn., 1991—. Nat. Heart Inst. fellow, 1959; NIH rsch. grantee, 1959—, Nat. Heart Inst., 1960, N.H. Heart Assn., 1964-65, Vt. Heart Assn., 1966—. Mem. AAAS, Am. Assn. Advancement of Lab. Animal Care, Am. Physiol. Soc., Soc. Gen. Physiologists, Biophys. Soc., Am. Heart Assn. (coun. basic sci., exec. coun. Dallas chpt. 1982-86), Soc. Neurosci. Marine Biol. Lab., LWV, Sigma Xi, Phi Kappa Phi. Avocations: sailing, hiking, reading, keyaking, skiing. Office: Dartmouth Med Sch Lebanon NH 03756

MCCANN, GAIL ELIZABETH, lawyer; b. Boston, Aug. 25, 1953; d. Joseph and Ruth E. (Lagerquist) McC.; m. Stanley J. Lukasiewicz. AB, Brown U., 1975; JD, U. Pa., Phila., 1978. Bar: R.I. 1978, Mass. 1984, U.S. Dist. Ct. R.I. 1978, U.S. Dist. Ct. Mass. 1990. Ptnr. Edwards & Angell, Providence, 1978—. Bd. dirs. Pembroke Ct. Assocs. Coun., Providence, AAA South Ctrl. New Eng., Warwick, R.I., Caritas House, Inc.; mem. R.I. adv. coun. New Eng. Legal Found. Mem. R.I. Bar Assn., Assoc. Alumni of Brown U. (past pres.). Avocations: hiking, travel, aerobics. Office: Edwards & Angell 2700 Hospital Trust Tower Providence RI 02903

MCCANN, JACK ARLAND, former construction and mining equipment company executive, consultant; b. Chestnut, Ill., Apr. 16, 1926; s. Keith Ogden and Miriam Imogene McC.; m. Marian Adele Gordon, Mar. 31, 1956; 1 son, Christopher John. A.B., Bradley U., 1950. Mgr. Washington Office, R.G. LeTourneau Inc., 1950-58; mgr. def. and spl. products Westinghouse Air Brake Co., 1958-64, mgr. nat. accounts, 1964-67, mng. dir. Belgian plant and European mktg., 1967-70; gen. sales mgr. WABCO div. Am. Standard Inc., Peoria, Ill., 1970-73, v.p. mktg., 1973-80, v.p. staff, 1980-82; ret., 1982; now cons. With USNR, 1944-46. Decorated chevalier Ordre de la Couronne (Belgium). Mem. Nat. Def. Transp. Assn. (life), U.S. C. of C., Am. Legion, Bradley Chiefs Club, Country Club Green Valley (pres., dir.), Green Valley Rep. Club (bd. dirs.), Shriners, Masons.

MCCANN, JEAN FRIEDRICHS, artist, educator; b. N.Y.C., Dec. 6, 1937; d. Herbert Joseph and Catherine Brady (Ward) Friedrichs; m. William Joseph McCann, May 14, 1960; children: Kevin, Brian, Maureen McCann Breslin, William, James, Denis Gerard, Kathleen. Student, Caton-Rose Inst. Fine Arts, 1955-57; AAS, SUNY, Farmingdale, 1959; BS, SUNY-Empire State Coll., Binghamton, 1986; MA summa cum laude, Marywood Coll., 1987, MFA in Art summa cum laude, 1989; completed Kellogg Leadership Progam, Sch. Mgmt., SUNY, Binghamton, 1992; PhD, Nova Coll., 1995. Dir. ArtSpace Gallery, Owego, N.Y., 1992-94; completed Kellog Leadership Program-Sch. Mgmt. SUNY; substitute art tchr. Owego-Apalachin Sch. Dist., Owego, 1986-88; tutor, evaluator SUNY-Empire State Coll., 1987—; v.p. bd. dirs. Tioga County Coun. on Arts, 1990-91, pres., 1992-95; demonstrator for various schs., ednl. TV and county museums. One woman shows include IBM, Owego, 1972, Tioga County Hist. Soc. Mus., Owego, 1975, Nat. Hist. Ct. House, 1982, Visual Arts Ctr., Scranton, Pa., 1989-90, Art-Space Gallery, 1991, MacDonald Art Gallery of Coll. Misericordia, Dallas, Pa., 1992, Plaza Gallery, Binghamton, 1992, Artist Guild Gallery, Binghamton, 1993, Wilson Gallery, Johnson City, N.Y., 1994; exhibited in numerous group shows, including IBM, Owego, 1970, Roberson Ctr., Binghamton, 1972, Arnot Art Mus., Elmira, 1974, 89, 92, Nat. Exhibits at Arena, Binghamton, 1974-76, Riise Gallery, St. Thomas, 1975-78, Pennino's Gallery, Burlington Vt., 1975-77, Visual Arts Ctr., Scranton, Pa., 1987, Grand Concourse Gallery, Albany, N.Y., 1987, Tioga County Hist. Soc. Mus., 1990, ArtSpace Gallery, 1990, Contemporary Gallery, Scranton, 1992, 96; art represented in numerous pvt. and pub. collections. Bd. dirs. Birthright of Owego, 1993—. Recipient N.Y. State Artisans award, 1982, Nat. Strathmore Silver award, 1989, 1st pl. in Graphic Arts award Jericho Arts Coun., 1994. Mem. Nat. mus. Women in Arts (charter), Kappa Pi (pres. Zeta Omicron chpt. 1987-89, life). Avocations: traveling, reading, visiting museums. Home: 23 Paige St Owego NY 13827-1617

MCCANN, JOHN FRANCIS, financial services company executive; b. South Orange, N.J., Nov. 30, 1937; s. Frank Charles and Dorothy Marie (Devaney) McC.; m. Mary Ellen Howland, Aug. 4, 1962; children: Sean Francis, Maureen Ellen, Darragh Siobain, Kevin Patrick. Student, LaSalle Mil. Acad., 1951-55, U. Notre Dame, 1955-57, Niagara U., 1959-61, U. Pa., 1984-86. V.p., sales mgr. Imco Container Co., N.Y.C., 1962-68; vice-pres., sales mgr. Eastman Dillon, Union Securities Co., N.Y.C., 1968-72; sr. v.p., sales mgr. Faulkner, Dawkins & Sullivan, N.Y.C., 1972-75; sr. v.p., br. mgr. Faulkner, Dawkins & Sullivan, Chatham, N.J., 1975-77; sr. v.p. Shearson Loeb Rhoades, Chatham, N.J., 1977-83; exec. v.p. Shearson Am. Express, N.Y.C., 1983-84; exec. v.p., dir. Shearson Lehman Bros., N.Y.C., 1984-92, divisional dir. Philanthropic Found., 1989-92; pres. Smith Barney Shearson, N.Y.C., 1993—; bd. dirs. The Robinson-Humphrey Co., Inc., South Atlantic Group, Smith Barney; pres. Great Atlantic Group, 1994—. Fund raiser Riverview Hosp. Found., Red Bank, N.J., 1983; regional dir. Am. Express Found., N.Y.C., 1985—, Shearson Lehman Bros. Philanthropic Found. Mem. N.Y. Stock Exch. (arbitrator 1982—), Securities Industry Assn., Nat. Assn. Securities Dealers (dist. com. 1988-91), Navesink Country Club, Monmouth Beach Bath and Tennis Club, Beacon Hill Club (Summit, N.J.). Republican. Roman Catholic. Avocations: golf; tennis; travel; reading. Home: 135 Bingham Ave Rumson NJ 07760-1852 Office: Smith Barney 151 Bodman Pl Red Bank NJ 07701-1070

MC CANN, JOHN JOSEPH, lawyer; b. N.Y.C., Feb. 4, 1937; s. John and Katherine (McKeon) Mc C.; m. June M. Evangelist, Oct. 16, 1965; children: Catherine Anne, John Bernard, Robert Joseph, James Patrick. AB, Fordham U., 1958; LLB, Columbia U., 1961. Bar: N.Y. 1962, N.J. 1974, Fla. 1994. Ptnr. Donovan Leisure Netwon & Irvine, N.Y.C.; mem. legal adv. com. N.Y. Stock Exch., 1989-92. Mem. ABA (chair bus. law sect. 1992-93), Am. Law Inst., Am. Coll. Investment Counsel (pres. 1984-85), Am. Arbitration Assn. (bd. govs. 1985-96), Tiro A Segno Club, Canoe Brook Golf and Country Club. Roman Catholic. Office: Donovan Leisure Newton & Irvine 30 Rockefeller Plz New York NY 10112

MCCANN, RAYMOND J., utility company executive; b. N.Y.C., Sept. 28, 1934. B.S., Fordham U., 1956; M.B.A., CUNY, 1962. Gen. auditor Consol. Edison Co. N.Y., N.Y.C., 1972-74, controller, 1974-76, v.p. acctg., treas., 1976-77, v.p. Manhattan div., 1977-80, exec. v.p. ops., 1980-87, exec. v.p. fin. and law, 1987-89, exec. v.p., CFO, trustee, 1989—. Served to capt. USAR. Office: Consol Edison Co NY Inc 4 Irving Pl New York NY 10003-3502

MCCANN, RICHARD EUGENE, lawyer; b. Billings, Mont., Aug. 14, 1939; s. Oakey O. and Edith May (Miller) McC.; m. Mona N. Miyagishima, Apr. 27, 1964; children: Tami, Todd (dec.), Jennifer. BA magna cum laude, Rocky Mountain Coll., 1965; JD with highest honors, U. Mont., 1972. Bar: Mont. 1972, Washington 1977, Ala. 1982. Law clk. to Judge W. Jameson U.S. Dist. Ct., Billings, 1972-73; assoc. Crowley, Haughey, Hansen, Toole & Dietrich, Billings, 1973-77; assoc. Perkins Coie, Seattle, 1977-80, ptnr., 1981—. Contbr. articles to profl. jours. Trustee Rocky Mountain Coll., Billings., 1973-77. Served with USMC, 1957-61. Mem. ABA, Mont. Bar Assn., Wash. Bar Assn., Alaska Bar Assn. Office: Perkins Coie 1201 3rd Ave Fl 40 Seattle WA 98101-3000

MCCANN, RICHARD STEPHEN, lawyer; b. Wilmington, Del., Dec. 26, 1938; s. Francis E.B. and Naomi H. (Riley) McC.; m. Gloria M. Baum (div. 1973); 1 child, Heather Marie; m. Sharon R. Cannon. BA, Georgetown U., 1960, JD, 1963; M in City Planning, U. Pa., 1965. Bar: Del. 1964. Pvt. practice law Newark, 1964-66, 70—; alderman City of Newark, 1964-66; city planner Dover, Del., 1966-70; atty. Del. Police Chief's Coun., Dover, 1971—, Del. Police Chief's Found., Dover, 1983—. Atty. Aetna Hose, Hook &

Ladder Co., Newark, 1975—. Mem. ABA, Del. Bar Assn. Avocations: Skiing, gardening, cannons. Home: 19 Carriage Ln Newark DE 19711-2023 Office: 94 E Main St Newark DE 19711-4622

MC CANN, SAMUEL MCDONALD, physiologist, educator; b. Houston, Sept. 8, 1925; s. Samuel Glenn and Margaret (Brokaw) McC.; m. Barbara Lorraine Richardson; children: Samuel Donald, Margaret, Karen Elizabeth. Student, Rice U., Houston, 1942-44; M.D., U. Pa., 1948. Intern in internal medicine Mass. Gen. Hosp., Boston, 1948-49; resident Mass. Gen. Hosp., 1949-50; mem. faculty U. Pa. Sch. Medicine, 1952-65, prof. physiology, 1964-65, acting chmn. dept., 1963-64; prof., chmn. physiology U. Tex. Southwestern Med. Sch., Dallas, 1965-85, dir. neuropeptide div., 1985-95, prof. internal medicine, 1995; prof. Pennington Biomed. Rsch. Ctr. La. State U., Baton Rouge, 1995—; cons. Schering Corp., Bloomfield, N.J., 1958; mem. gen. medicine B study sect. NIH, 1965-67, endocrinology study sect., 1967-69, population research com., 1974-76, reproductive biology study sect., 1978-82, chmn. reproductive biology study sect., 1980-82, neurology study sect., 1985-86. Editorial bd.: Endocrinology, 1963-68, 72-77; editorial bd. Neuroendocrinology, 1967-76, editor, 1985-92; editorial bd. Ann. Rev. Physiology, 1974-79, Soc. Exptl. Biology and Medicine, 1976-85, 91—, Am. Jour. Physiology, 1980-85; editor: Endocrine Physiology, Pioneers in Neuroendocrinology; contbr. articles to profl. jours., chpts. to books. Recipient Spencer Morris prize U. Pa. Med. Sch., 1948, Lindback award for distinguished teaching, 1965, Oppenheimer award for research in endocrinology, 1966, Hartman award Soc. Study of Reproduction, 1986. Mem. Endocrine Soc. (exec. council 1985-88, Fred Conrad Koch award 1979), Am. Physiol. Soc. (council 1979-81), Soc. for Exptl. Biology and Medicine (coun. 1979-83, pres. 1995—), Soc. Clin. Investigation, N.Y. Acad. Scis., Nat. Acad. Scis., Am. Acad. Arts and Scis., Neuroendocrine Discussion Group (chmn. 1965), Internat. Neuroendocrine Soc. (council 1972-79, pres. 1984-88), Internat. Soc. Neuroimmunomodulation (sec. gen. 1990—). Office: La State U Pennington Biomed Rsch Ctr 6400 Perkins Rd Baton Rouge LA 70808-4124

MCCANN, SUSAN LYNN, elementary education educator; b. Forest Hills, N.Y., Feb. 11, 1947; d. Henry August and Frances Susan (Kleist) Kupsch; m. Kevin Daniel McCann, June 28, 1970; children: Christopher, Megan. BS in Edn., St. John's U., 1968, MS in Edn., 1971. Elem. tchr. Bellmore (N.Y.) Schs., 1968-76, Massapequa (N.Y.) Schs., 1987—; pvt. tutor, Massapequa, 1968—; mem., chairperson Unqua Sch. Com., Massapequa, 1990—; chairperson Shared-Decision-Making, Massapequa, 1994—, Ptnrs. in Reading, Massapequa, 1992-93. Chairperson cultural arts Birch Lane PTA, Massapequa, 1986-90; chairperson Earthday com. Unqua Sch., Massapequa, 1991—; vol. Am. Heart Assn., Bohemia, N.Y., 1991—, Nancy Waters Meml. Run, Seaford, N.Y., 1982-92; cmty. outreach chair Massapequa Fedn. Tchrs., 1995—. Recipient Cmty. Svc. Merit cert. Massapequa Bd. Edn., 1995, Nat. Lifetime award PTA, 1995. Mem. Am. Fedn. Tchrs., N.Y. State United Tchrs. (gifts of the heart award 1994, cmty. svc. award 1995). Avocations: cooking, baking, cross-country skiing, reading. Office: Massapequa Schs Merrick Rd Massapequa NY 11758

MCCANN, VONYA B., federal agency administrator. BA, U. Calif., L.A., 1976; MPP, U. Calif., Berkeley, 1979, JD, 1980. Bar: D.C. Law clk. Commr. Tyrone Brown, Fed. Comm. Commn.; policy analyst Nat. Telecom.; ptnr. Arent, Fox, Kintner, Plotkin and Kahn; U.S. coord., dep. asst. sec. internat. comm. & info. policy Dept. State, 1994—, amb., 1994—. Office: Dept of State Internat Comm & Info Policy Bur 2201 C St NW Washington DC 20520-7512*

MCCARD, HAROLD KENNETH, aerospace company executive; b. Corinth, Maine, Dec. 18, 1931; s. Fred Leslie and Ada (Drake) McC.; m. Charlotte Marie Despres, June 29, 1957; children: Robert Fred, Renee Glen. BEE, U. Maine, Orono, 1959; MEE, Northeastern U., 1963; MS in Mgmt., MIT, 1977. Engr. Avco Systems div. Textron, Wilmington, Mass., 1959-60, group leader, 1960-62, section chief, 1962-65, dept. mgr., 1965-72, dir./staff dir., 1972-77, chief engr., 1977-79, v.p. ops., 1979-82, v.p., gen. mgr., 1982-85; pres. Textron Def. Systems (formerly Avco Systems div./Avco Systems Textron), Wilmington, Mass., 1985-95; sr. v.p. ops. Textron, Inc., Providence, 1995—. Mem. AIAA (Leadership in Quality Mgmt. award 1991), Nat. Indsl. Security Assn. (bd. dirs. 1986—), Electronics Industry Assn. (bd. dirs. 1993—, bd. dirs. govt. div. 1989—), Am. Def. Preparedness Assn. (exec. com.). Avocations: golf, tennis, skiing. Home: 6 Lantern Ln Lynnfield MA 01940-1347 Office: Textron Inc 40 Westminster St Providence RI 02903

MCCARDELL, JAMES ELTON, retired naval officer; b. Daytona Beach, Fla., Jan. 22, 1931; s. J. Elton and Margaret Almira (Payne) McC.; m. Nancy Ann Chandler, July 9, 1955; children: Jenise, Patrick. Student, U. Fla., 1948-50; B.A., U.S. Naval Postgrad. Sch., 1965. Commd. ensign U.S. Navy, 1952, advanced through grades to rear adm., 1980; exec. officer USS Forrestal, 1972-73; dep. chief of staff Air Readiness Staff, Chief Naval Res., New Orleans, 1973-76; comdg. officer NAS, Key West, Fla., 1976-78; chief of staff Staff of Chief Naval Res., New Orleans, 1978-80; def. and naval attache U.S. Embassy, Brasilia, Brazil, 1981-83; dir. Inter-Am. Def. Coll., Fort L.J. McNair, Washington, 1983-85; ret., 1985. Decorated Legion of Merit with cluster, Bronze Star medal, Air medal with 12 clusters, Def. Disting. Service medal, Def. Superior Performance medal. Republican. Roman Catholic. Home: PO Box 719 Pass Christian MS 39571-0719 *The absolute measure of successful leadership has always been reflected by performance of subordinates in the achievement of unit goals.*

MCCARDELL, JOHN MALCOLM, JR., college administrator; b. Frederick, Md., June 17, 1949; s. John Malcolm Sr. and Susan (Lane) McC.; m. Bonnie Greenwald, Dec. 30, 1976; children: John Malcolm III, James Benjamin Lee. AB, Washington and Lee U., 1971; postgrad., John Hopkins U., 1972-73; PhD, Harvard U., 1976. Asst. prof. history Middlebury (Vt.) Coll., 1976-80, assoc. prof. history, 1982-87, dean for academic devel., 1985-88, prof. history, 1987—, dean facuty, 1988-89, provost, v.p for academic affairs, 1989-91, acting pres., 1991-92, pres., 1992—; sr. rsch fellow U. S.C., Columbia, 1980-81, 96; bd. dirs. Nat. Bank Middlebury. Author: The Idea of a Southern Nation, 1979 (Allan Nevins award 1977); editor: A Master's Due, 1985. Sgt. USAR, 1971-77. Recipient Algernon Sydney Sullivan prize Washington and Lee U., 1971, Charles Eliot medal Eliot House Harvard U., 1976; Nat. Endowment for Humanities fellow, 1980; Am. Philosophical Soc. fellow, 1979. Mem. Am. Hist. Assn., Orgn. Am. Historians, So. Hist. Assn., Am. Studies Assn., Vt. Hist. Soc., Omicron Delta Kappa, Phi Beta Kappa, Lambda Chi Alpha. Office: Middlebury Coll Old Chapel Bldg Middlebury VT 05753

MC CARDLE, RANDALL RAYMOND, real estate developer; b. Phila., Sept. 2, 1931; s. Russell Henry and Ruth Hertha (Snyder) McC.; m. Yong Suk Yi; 1 child, Mark. AA, Orange Coast Coll., 1956; BA, Chapman Coll., 1958, MA, 1966; PhD, Colo. U., 1974; Real estate broker, Newport Beach, Calif., 1953-95; founder, pres. The Real Estaters, Orange County, Calif., 1961—, Treeco Escrow Co., Inc., Costa Mesa, Calif., 1971—; founder Bank of Costa Mesa, 1972, dir. bus. devel., 1973—; also newspaper columnist, lectr., investment counselor. Fund-raising chmn. Boys' Club of Am., Harbor area, 1979-80; bd. dirs. Boys Club Harbor Area; mem. adv. com. Orange Coast Coll., 1964—, Golden West Coll., 1969—; dir. Harbor Ridge Masters, 1990-95; mem. St. Andrews Presbyn. Ch. With USN, 1950-53. Decorated Nat. Def. Svc. medal, UN Svc. medal, Korean Svc. ribbon with 2 stars; recipient Appreciation award Bd. Realtors, 1967, 68, 70, 76, 80, UN citation; inducted into Orange Coast Coll. Hall of Fame, 1983; named Realtor of Yr., 1989. Mem. Calif. Assn. Realtors (state dir. 1963-67), Calif. Assn. Real Estate Tchrs. (state dir. 1966-80), Orange County Coast Assn. (dir. 1974—), C. of C., Nat. Assn. Real Estate Appraisers, Bd. Realtors (pres. 1966-67 long-range planning com. 1981), U. So. Calif. Faculty Assn., Red Baron Flying Club, Big Canyon Country Club, Mason, Shriner. Contbr. articles to profl. jours. Home: 12 Geneve Newport Beach CA 92660-6813 Office: 1000 Quail St Ste 260 Newport Beach CA 92660-2721

MCCARGAR, JAMES GOODRICH, diplomat, writer; b. San Francisco, Apr. 20, 1920; s. Jesse B. and Addie May (Goodrich) McC.; m. Geraldine Claudia Cooper-Key, Aug. 2, 1948 (div. 1954); m. Emanuela Butculescu, Dec. 22, 1973. BA, Stanford U., 1942. Commd. Fgn. Svc. Officer, 1942; Dept. State, Moscow, 1942, 43; Vladivostok, 1942-43, Santo Domingo, 1943-44; sec. of legation, chief polit. sect. Budapest, Hungary, 1946-47; vice consul Genoa, Italy, 1948; chief div. Southestern European Affairs Office of Policy Coordination, Washington, 1948-50; sec. of embassy, mem. U.S. Del. to Allied Coordinating Com., Paris, 1950-53; asst. to v.p. Free Europe Com., Inc., N.Y.C., 1955; European dir. polit. ops. Free Europe Com., Inc., Paris, 1956-58; cons. to pres. Free Europe Com., Inc., 1959-60, 71-76; spl. asst. to chmn. NEH, Washington, 1978-82; U.S. del. UNESCO confs., 1978, 80, 82; alt. rep. U.S.-Japan Friendship Commn., 1979-82; U.S. del. U.S.-Mexico Commn. on Cultural Cooperation, 1980, Sem. on Funding of Culture, Madrid, 1982, U.S.-Mexico Commn. on Cultural Cooperation, 1980; alt. rep. U.S.-Japan Friendship Commn., 1979-82; cons. BBC-TV, London, 1984, Nat. Dem. Inst. Internat. Affairs, Washington, 1984, African-Am. Labor Ctr., Washington, 1984-85, Am. Inst. Free Labor Devel., Washington, 1985, Dept. Internat. Affairs, AFL-CIO, Washington, 1986-95, Free Trade Union Inst., Washington, 1993-95; editorial adv. Interco Press, Washington, 1988-96; bd. dirs. Ams. for Universality of UNESCO, Washington, 1985—. Author: A Short Course in the Secret War, 1963, rev. edit., 1988, 3d edit., 1992, El Salvador and Nicaragua: The AFL-CIO Views on the Controversy, 1985; co-author: Three-Cornered Cover, 1972, Lost Victory, 1989, Ferenc Nagy: Smallholder or Statesman?, 1995; contbr. articles and book revs., 1940-70; ghostwriter, 1964-96. Co-founder, sec. Ams. Abroad for Kennedy, Paris, 1960. Ensign USNR, 1944-46. Recipient Cert. of Appreciation Internat. Ctr. for Free Trade Unions in Exile, 1958, Fed. Outstanding Performance award NEH, 1979, 81; decorated Knight First Class Royal Norwegian Order St. Olav, 1983, Silver Medallion of the Hungarian Parliament, 1991, Officer's Cross Order of the Hungarian Republic, 1992, Officer's Cross Order of Merit of the Rep. of Poland, 1993. Mem. Polish Inst. Arts and Scis. Am. (elected), Diplomatic and Consular Officers Retired, Chevaliers du Tastevin (France), Vets. of OSS (hon.), Authors' Guild. Democrat. Home and Office: 4201 Cathedral Ave NW Washington DC 20016-4901

MCCARL, HENRY N., economics and geology educator; b. Balt., Jan. 24, 1941; s. Fred Henderson and Mary Bertha (Yaeger) McC.; m. Louise Becker Rys, June 8, 1963 (div. 1986); children: Katherine Lynne, Patricia Louise, Fredrick James; m. Mary Frederica Rhinelander, Jan. 31, 1987; 1 stepchild, Francesca C. Morgan. BS in Earth Sci., MIT, 1962; MS in Geology, Pa. State, 1964, PhD in Mineral Econ., 1969. Cert. profl. geologist. Market rsch. analyst Vulcan Materials Co., 1966-69; asst. prof. econs., asst. prof. geology U. Ala., Birmingham, 1969-72, assoc. prof. econs., 1973-77, assoc. prof. econs. and geology, 1978-91; prof. econs. and geology U. Ala., 1991—; dir. Ctr. for Econ. Edn., Sch. Bus. U. Ala., Birmingham, 1987—; chief econs. div. Ala. Energy Mgmt. Bd., Montgomery, 1973-74; sr. lectr. in energy econs. Fulbright-Hays Program, Bucharest, Romania, 1977-78; mng. dir. McCarl & Assocs., Birmingham, 1969—; vis. fellow Grad. Sch. Arts and Scis., Harvard U., Cambridge, Mass., 1987. Co-author: (book) Energy Conservation Economics, 1986; Introduction to Energy Conservation, 1987; contbr. articles to profl. jours. Mem. Zoning Bd. of Adjustments, Birmingham, 1974-79, Birmingham Planning Commn., 1974-86, chmn. 1980-86; dist. commr. Boy Scouts Am., Birmingham, 1988-94. Mem. SAR (Birmingham chpt. pres. 1994—, Ala. soc. pres. 1995-96), Soc. Mining Engrs. of AIME (bd. dirs. 1978-80), Am. Inst. Profl. Geologists (sect. pres. 1981-83), Mineral Econs. and Mgmt. Soc. (pres. 1992-93), Ala. Geol. Soc., Nat. Assn. Econ. Educators, St. Andrews Soc. Democrat. Episcopal. Avocations: hunting, woodworking, collections, art collections. Home: 1828 Mission Rd Birmingham AL 35216-2229 Summer home: 28 Old Nugent Farm Rd Gloucester MA 01930-3166 Office: U Ala Sch Bus Dept Econs Birmingham AL 35294-4460

MCCARRICK, EDWARD R., magazine publisher. Pub. Life Mag., N.Y.C. Office: Life Time Inc Time & Life Bldg 1271 Ave of the Americas New York NY 10020-1393*

MC CARRICK, THEODORE EDGAR, archbishop; b. N.Y.C., July 7, 1930; s. Theodore Egan and Margaret (McLaughlin) McC. Student, Fordham U., 1950-52; AB, St. Joseph's Sem., 1954, AM, 1958; MA, Cath. U., 1960, PhD, 1963; LLD, Mt. St. Vincent Coll., 1967; STD, Inter-Am. U., 1969; STD (hon.), Niagara U., 1982; LHD (hon.), St. John's U., 1974, St. Peter's Coll., 1987. Ordained priest Roman Cath. Ch., 1958. Asst. chaplain Cath. U. Am., Washington, 1959-61, dean students, 1961-63, asst. to rector, dir. univ. devel., 1963-65, instr. dept. sociology, 1961-65; domestic prelate, 1965; pres. Cath. U. P.R., 1965-69; assoc. dir. edn. Archdiocese of N.Y., 1969-71; sec. to Cardinal-Archbishop N.Y., 1971-77; titular bishop of Rusubisir, aux. bishop N.Y., 1977-81; 1st bishop Diocese of Metuchen, N.J., 1981-86; 4th archbishop Newark, 1986—; mem. policy bd. Washington Consortium, Peace Corps, 1962-63, Pontifical Commn. for Migrants and Refugees, 1987; chmn. U.S. Bishops Com. on Migration, 1986-89, 92-95; mem. Nat. Coun. for Spanish-Speaking People, 1961-65; chmn. Gov.'s Commn. for Higher Edn. in P.R., 1968, P.R. Adv. Coun. on Tech. and Vocat. Edn., 1968-69. Mem. Fed. Commn. for Study of Migration and Econ. Devel., 1989; Episcopal promoter Apostleship of the Sea, 1989-92; chmn. com. aid to ch. in Ctrl. and Ea. Europe, Nat. Conf. Cath. Bishops, 1992—; sec.-treas. Papal Found., 1988—. Named knight grand cross Holy Sepulchre. Clubs: K.C, Am. Assn. Knights Malta (chaplain 1978-82). Office: PO Box 9500 171 Clifton Ave Newark NJ 07104-9500

MCCARROLL, KATHLEEN ANN, radiologist, educator; b. Lincoln, Nebr., July 7, 1948; d. James Richard and Ruth B. (Wagenknecht) McC.; m. Steven Mark Beerbohm, July 10, 1977 (div. 1991); 1 child, Palmer Brooke. BS, Wayne State U., 1974; MD, Mich. State U., 1978. Diplomate Am. Bd. Radiology. Intern/resident in diagnostic radiology William Beaumont Hosp., Royal Oak, Mich., 1978-82, fellow in computed tomography and ultrasound, 1983; radiologist, dir. radiologic edn. Detroit Receiving Hosp., 1984—, vice-chief dept. radiology, 1988-96, chief dept. radiology, 1996—; pres.-elect med. staff Detroit Receiving Hosp., 1992-94, pres., 1994-96; mem. admissions com. Wayne State U. Coll. Medicine, Detroit, 1991—; officer bd. dirs. Dr. L. Reynolds Assoc., P.C., Detroit, 1991-94, 96—; presenter profl. confs.; assoc. prof. radiology Wayne State U. Sch. Medicine, Detroit, 1995—; bd. trustees Detroit Med. Ctr., 1996—. Editor: Critical Care Clinics, 1992; mem. editorial bd. Emergency Radiology; contbr. articles to profl. publs. Trustee Detroit Med. Ctr., 1996—. Mem. AMA, Am. Coll. Radiology (Mich. chpt. sec. 1995—), Radiol. Soc. N.Am., Assn. Univ. Radiologists, Am. Roentgen Ray Soc., Am. Soc. Emergency Radiologists (bd. dirs. 1996—), Mich. State Med. Soc., Wayne/Oakland County Med. Soc., Phi Beta Kappa. Avocations: travelling, skiing, reading. Office: Detroit Receiving Hosp 3L-8 4201 Saint Antoine St Detroit MI 48201-2153

MCCARRON, JOHN FRANCIS, columnist; b. Providence, Jan. 20, 1949; s. Hugh Francis and Katherine Anne (Brooks) McC.; m. Janet Ann Velsor, Sept. 3, 1971; children: Veronica, Catherine. BS in Journalism, Northwestern U., 1970, MS in Journalism, 1973. Gen. assignment reporter Chgo. Tribune, 1973-80, urban affairs writer, 1980-91, fin. editor, 1991-92, editorial bd. columnist, 1992—. Contbr. to Planning mag., World Book Ency., Preservation mag. Lt. USNR, 1970-72. Recipient Editors award AP, 1983, 84, Ann. Journalism award Am. Planning Assn., 1983, Heywood Broun award Am. Newspaper Guild, Washington, 1989, Peter Lisagor award Soc. Profl. Journalists, 1994. Home: 1425 Noyes St Evanston IL 60201-2639 Office: Chicago Tribune Chicago IL 60611

MC CARTAN, PATRICK FRANCIS, lawyer; b. Cleve., Aug. 3, 1934; s. Patrick Francis and Stella Mercedes (Ashton) McC.; m. Lois Ann Buchman, Aug. 30, 1958; children: M. Karen, Patrick Francis, III. AB magna cum laude, U. Notre Dame, 1956, JD, 1959. Bar: Ohio 1960, U.S. Ct. Appeals (6th cir.) 1961, U.S. Ct. Appeals (3rd cir.) 1965, U.S. Ct. Appeals (D.C. cir.) 1980, U.S. Ct. Appeals (5th cir.) 1981, U.S. Ct. Appeals (4th cir.) 1989, U.S. Ct. Appeals (7th cir.) 1992, U.S. Supreme Ct. 1970. Law clk. to Hon. Charles Evans Whittaker, U.S. Supreme Ct., 1959; asso. Jones, Day, Reavis & Pogue, Cleve., 1961-65, ptnr., 1966-93, mng. ptnr., 1993—; bd. trustees Nat. Inst. for Trial Adv., Boulder, Colo., 1987—, U. Notre Dame, Cleve. Clinic Found., Greater Cleve. Roundtable. Fellow Am. Coll. Trial Lawyers, Internat. Acad. Trial Lawyers; mem. ABA, 6th Cir. Jud. Conf. (life), Coun. on Fgn. Rels., U.S.-Japan Bus. Coun., Ohio Bar Assn., Bar Assn. Greater Cleve. (pres. 1977-78), Musical Arts Assn. (trustee). Roman Catholic. Home: 7570 Thistle Ln Novelty OH 44072-9500 Office: Jones Day Reavis & Pogue North Point 901 Lakeside Ave Cleveland OH 44114-1116*

MCCARTER, CHARLES CHASE, lawyer; b. Pleasanton, Kans., Mar. 17, 1926; s. Charles Nelson and Donna (Chase) McC.; m. Clarice Blanchard, June 25, 1950; children—Charles Kevin, Cheryl Ann. BA, Principia Coll., 1950; JD, Washburn U., 1953; LLM, Yale U., 1954. Bar: Kans. 1953, U.S. Supreme Ct. 1962, Mo. 1968. Asst. atty. gen. State of Kans., 1954-57; lectr. law sch. Washburn U., 1956-57; appellate counsel FCC, Washington, 1957-58; assoc. Weigand, Curfman, Brainerd, Harris & Kaufman, Wichita, 1958-61; gen. counsel Kans. Corp. Commn., 1961-63; ptnr. McCarter, Frizzel & Wettig, Wichita, 1963-68, McCarter & Badger, Wichita, 1968-73; pvt. practice law St. Louis, 1968-76; ptnr. McCarter & Greenley, St. Louis, 1976-85; mng. ptnr. Gage & Tucker, St. Louis, 1985-87, Husch and Eppenberger, St. Louis, 1987-89; McCarter & Greenley, 1990—; prof. law, assoc. dir. law sch. Nat. Energy Law and Policy Inst. Tulsa U., 1977-79; prof. law, coach nat. moot ct. coll. of law Stetson U. Coll., St. Petersburg, Fla., 1980-84; mem. govtl. adv. coun. Gulf Oil Corp., 1977-81 ; legal com. Interstate Oil Compact Commn. Co-author: Missouri Lawyers Guide; assoc. editor Washburn U. Law Rev., 1952-53; contbr. articles to profl. jours. Chmn. Wichita Human Rels. Devel. Adv. Bd., 1967-68; bd. dirs. Peace Haven Assn.; active St. Louis estate planning coun., 1987—, bequests and endowment com. Salvation Army, 1995—, YMCA endowment com., 1996—. With USNR, 1944-46. Recipient Excellent Prof. award U. Tulsa , 1979; vis. scholar Yale U., 1980. Mem. ABA (sect. real property, probate and trust law), Kans. Bar Assn., Mo. Bar Assn., Am. Legion, VFW, Native Sons and Daus. Kans (pres. 1957-58), Kappa Sigma, Delta Theta Phi, Principia Dads Club (bd. dirs.). Republican. Office: 1 Metropolitan Sq Ste 2160 Saint Louis MO 63102-2733

MC CARTER, JOHN ALEXANDER, biochemistry educator; b. Wareham, Eng., Jan. 25, 1918; emigrated to Can., 1919; s. Alexander and Helen T. (McKellar) McC.; m. Patricia Jocelyn St. John, Dec. 27, 1941; children: David G., Robert M., Patricia L., William A. B.A., U. B.C., 1939, M.A., 1941; Ph.D., U. Toronto, 1945. Research officer NRC Can. Atomic Energy Project, Chalk River, Ont., 1945-48; asso. prof. Dalhousie U., Halifax, Can., 1948-50; prof. Dalhousie U., 1950-65; prof. biochemistry, dir. Cancer Research Lab., U. Western Ont., London, 1965-83; prof. dept. biochemistry and microbiology U. Victoria, B.C., Can., 1980-83; Mem. Med. Research Council Canada, 1961-67; research adv. group Nat. Cancer Inst. Canada, 1967-72. Contbr. articles to profl. jours. Fellow Brit. Empire Cancer Campaign, 1959-60. Fellow Royal Soc. Can.; mem. Can. Biochem. Soc. (pres. 1966-67), Alpha Omega. Research on tumor virology. Home: 3171 Henderson Rd, Victoria, BC Canada V8P 5A3

MC CARTER, JOHN WILBUR, JR., corporation executive; b. Oak Park, Ill., Mar. 2, 1938; s. John Wilbur and Ruth Rebecca McC.; m. Judith Field West, May 1, 1965; children: James Philip, Jeffrey John, Katherine Field. A.B., Princeton U., 1960; postgrad., London Sch. Econs., 1961; M.B.A., Harvard U., 1963. Cons., assoc., v.p. Booz Allen and Hamilton, Inc., Chgo., 1963-69; White House fellow Washington, 1966-67; dir. Bur. Budget and Dept. Fin., State of Ill., Springfield, 1969-73; v.p. DeKalb AgResearch, Ill., 1973-78, dir., 1975-86, exec. v.p., 1978-80, pres., 1981-82; pres., chief exec. officer DeKalb-Pfizer Genetics, 1982-86, chmn., 1986; pres. DeKalb Corp., 1985-86; sr. v.p. Booz Allen & Hamilton Inc., 1987—; nd. dirs. A.M. Castle & Co., W.W. Grainger, Inc., Harris Insight Funds. Trustee Chgo. Pub. Television, 1973, chmn., 1989—, trustee Princeton U., 1983-87, U. Chgo., 1993—. Office: Booz Allen & Hamilton Inc 225 W Wacker Dr Chicago IL 60606-1224

MCCARTER, P(ETE) KYLE, JR., Near Eastern studies educator; b. Oxford, Mich., July 9, 1945; s. Pete K. and Mary Ann (Hudson) McC.; m. Susan J.F. McCarter; children: Robert, David, Mary. BA, U. Okla., 1967; MDiv, McCormick Theological Seminary, Chgo., 1970; PhD, Harvard U., 1974. Asst. prof. religious studies U. Va., Charlottesville, 1974-79, assoc. prof., 1979-82, prof., 1982-85; William Foxwell Albright prof. of Bibl. and near eastern studies Johns Hopkins U., Balt., 1985—, chmn. dept. near eastern studies, 1991—, assoc. dean sch. arts. and scis., 1987-90; vis. lectr. on bibl. Hebrew Harvard U., Cambridge, Mass., 1978-79; vis. assoc. prof. Dartmouth Coll., Hanover, N.H., 1979; fellow Ctr. for Advanced Studies, U. Va., 1980-82. Author: The Antiquity of the Greek Alphabet and the Early Phoenician Scripts, 1975, I Samuel: A New Translation with Introduction, Notes, and Commentary 1980, II Samuel: A New Translation with Introduction, Notes, and Commentary, 1984, Recovering the Text of the Hebrew Bible: An Introduction fo Textual Criticism, 1986. Mem. Soc. Bibl. Lit., Am. Schs. Oriental Research (pres. 1988-90), Bibl. Colloquium, Colloquium for Bibl. Research. Democrat. Presbyterian. Avocations: squash, fly fishing. Office: Johns Hopkins U 124 Gilman Hall 34th And Charles St Baltimore MD 21218

MC CARTER, THOMAS N., III, investment counseling company executive; b. N.Y.C., Dec. 16, 1929; s. Thomas N., Jr. and Suzanne M. (Pierson) McC.; student Princeton U., 1948-51. Sales exec. Mack Trucks, Inc., N.Y.C., 1952-59; ptnr. Kelly, McCarter, D'Arcy Investment Counsel, N.Y.C., 1959-62; v.p., sec., dir. D'Arcy, McCarter & Chew, N.Y.C., 1962-66; v.p., dir. Trainer, Wortham & Co., Inc., N.Y.C., 1967-71, exec. v.p., 1971-75; chmn. bd., dir. Island Security Bank Ltd., 1976-78; pres. Knottingham Ltd., N.Y.C., 1976-84; gen. ptnr. W.P. Miles Timber Properties, New Orleans, 1974—; exec. v.p., Yorke McCarter Owen & Bartels, Inc., N.Y.C., 1985-89, also bd. dirs.; fins. cons. Laidlaw Holdings, Inc., 1990-92; pres., bd. dirs., Mentor Mgmt. Group, Inc. N.Y.C., 1986-90; chmn. bd. dirs. Ramapo Land Co., Sloatsburg, N.Y., 1990—, Stillrock Mgmt. Inc., N.Y.C., 1992—; bd. dirs. Parock Group Inc., Covenent Fund. Chmn. bd. trustees Christodora Found., Inc., N.Y.C., 1970-93; charter trustee Dalton Sch., N.Y.C., 1968-76, v.p., 1972-76; pres., trustee Civil War Libr. and Mus., Phila., 1985-92; chmn. bd. trustees ASPCA, 1984-95; chmn. Loyal Legion Found., N.Y.C.; trustee Children's Aid Soc. N.Y.C., 1973-94, Joffrey Ballet, Found. for Am. Dance, 1973-77; pres., trustee N.Y.C. Marble Cemetery Assn.; mem. Nat. Com. for Preservation of the U.S. Treasury Bldg., 1988-92; trustee Nat. Symphony Orch., Washington, 1990-94. Chartered investment counselor. Mem. Loyal Legion U.S. (comdr. N.Y. State 1964-66, nat. comdr. in chief 1977-81). Clubs: Racquet and Tennis, Brook, Links, River, St. Nicholas Soc., Pilgrims of U.S. (N.Y.C.), Meadow (Southampton, N.Y.), Ivy (Princeton, N.J.). Republican. Home: 188 E 64th St New York NY 10021-7451 Office: Stillrock Mgmt Inc 18 E 74th St New York NY 10021-2605

MCCARTHY, ABIGAIL QUIGLEY, writer, columnist, educator; b. Wabasha, Minn., Apr. 16, 1915; d. Stephen Michael and Mary Cecelia (O'Leary) Quigley; m. Eugene Joseph McCarthy, June 25, 1945 (separated 1970); children: Ellen Anne, Mary Abigail, Michael Benet, Margaret Alice. BA, Coll. St. Catherine, 1936; MA, U. Minn., 1942; postgrad., U. Chgo., Middlebury Sch. of Eng.; hon. doctorates, Trinity Coll., Cath. U. Am., 9 others. Tchr. Mandan (N.D.) High Sch., 1936-39; asst. prof. Eng. Coll. St. Catherine, St. Paul, 1939-46; columnist Commonweal Mag., N.Y.C., 1974—, RNS, N.Y. Times Syndicate, 1992-94; bd. dirs. Nat. Com. Study of Electorate, Dreyfus Corp., dir. emeritus; pres. Herald Comms., Ltd.; past chmn. bd. Carroll Pub. Co.; Poynter lectr. Ind. U.; Collition lectr. U. Pacific; Audenshaw lectr. Chgo. U.; lectr. Harvard U., Fordham U., Bryn Mawr U., Georgetown U., Hunter U., U. So. Calif., U. Scranton, Boston Coll., Clarke Coll., Stephens U., Trinity U., others. Author: (memoir) Private Faces/Public Places, (novels) Circles, A Washington Story, One Woman Lost; co-author Minnesota Women, At the Edge of Hope, ER: First Lady Without Precedent, Why Catholic?. Founding pres. Clearinghouse Women's Issues; mem. first adv. com. Women's Equity Action League and Women's Polit. Caucus; former mem. Bishops' Com. Edn., Ecumenism; former v.p. Ch. Women United, USA; bd. dirs. Nat. Conf. Interracial Justice. Mem. Wash. Ind. Writers Orgn. (mem. adv. bd.), Phi Beta Kappa. Office: 2126 Connecticut Ave NW Washington DC 20008-1729*

MCCARTHY, BRIAN NELSON, marketing and distribution company executive; b. Detroit, May 24, 1945; s. Andrew Nelson and Ruth Elizabeth (Hill) McC.; married, 1974 (div. 1991); children: Amanda Lang, Kelly Elizabeth, Meghan Virginia; m. Shannon Headley, Sept. 7, 1991; 1 child, Conner Michael. BS in Engring. Sci., Oakland U., Rochester, Mich., 1966; MBA, Harvard U., 1972. Engr. Gen. Motors Corp., Pontiac, Mich., 1965-67; co-owner Sound Wave Systems, Costa Mesa, Calif., 1971-78; chief fin. officer, controller A&W Gershenson Co., Farmington, Mich., 1972-75; chief op. officer Devel. Group, Southfield, Mich., 1975-81; chief exec. officer Brichard & Co., San Francisco, 1982-87; pres., chief exec. officer Watermark Corp., Sausalito, Calif., 1987-89; chief exec. officer Indian Wells Water Co.,

Inc., 1989-95, chief exec. officer Watermark Corp., Ssusalito, Calif., 1995—. Lt. USNR, 1967-70, Rear Adm. supply corps, Res. Decorated Navy Commendation medal with gold star, Meritorious Svc. medal with two gold stars, Def. Meritorious Svc medal with oak leaf cluster. Mem. Navy Supply Corps Assn. (bd. dirs. 1987—), Internat. Bottle Water Assn., Calif. Bottle Water Assn., Harvard Bus. No. Calif. Club, Commonwealth Club. Republican. Office: Watermark Corp 1 Gate 6 Rd Ste 201 Sausalito CA 94965

MCCARTHY, CORMAC (CHARLES MCCARTHY, JR.), writer; b. Providence, R.I., July 20, 1933; s. Charles Joseph and Gladys (McGrail) McC.; m. Lee Holleman, 1961 (div.); 1 child, Cullen; m. Anne deLisle, 1967 (div.). Author: (novels) The Orchard Keeper, 1965 (William Faulkner Found. award 1965), Outer Dark, 1968, Child of God, 1974, Suttree, 1979, Blood Meridian, or The Evening Redness in the West, 1985, All the Pretty Horses, 1992 (Nat. Book award for fiction 1992, Nat. Book Critics Circle award for fiction 1993), The Crossing, 1994; (teleplays) The Gardner's Son, 1977; (plays) The Stonemason: A Play in Five Acts, 1994. Ingram-Merrill Found. creative writing grantee, 1960, Am. Acad. Arts and Letter traveling fellow, 1965-66, Rockefeller Found. grantee, 1966, Guggenheim fellow, 1976, MacArthur Found. grantee, 1981; recipient Jean Stein award Am. Acad. and Inst. Arts and Letters, 1991. Address: 1011 N Mesa El Paso TX 79902

MC CARTHY, D. JUSTIN, emeritus college president; b. Brockton, Mass.; s. Denis Joseph and Jane Vincent (Dempsey) McC.; m. Rose Mary Hoye; children: Daniel Justin, Rosemary, John Emmet, Vincent Joseph. B.S., Bridgewater State Coll., 1938, Ed.M., 1939; Ed.D., Harvard U., 1955; LL.D. (hon.), Framingham State Coll., 1985. Tchr., prin. Hanover (Mass.) Pub. Schs.; tchr., asst. prin. Belmont (Mass.) Elem. Schs.; dean instrn. U. Maine, Farmington, 1947-48; extension lectr. U. Maine, Orono, 1947-48; supr. student teaching U. Mass. at Amherst, 1948-55; supr. edn., asst. dir. div. state colls. Mass. State Colls., 1955-56, dir. div. state colls., 1956-61; pres. Framingham (Mass.) State Coll., 1961-85; assoc. in edn. Harvard Grad. Sch. Edn., 1980-83; past sr. advisor Nat. Commn. on the Role and Future State Colls. and Univs. Contbr.: articles to profl. jours. including Harvard Educational Review. Chmn. evaluation Nat. Coun. Accreditation Tchr. Edn., Mass. Bd. Coll. Authority, New Eng. Assn. Colls.and Secondary Schs.; past pres. New Eng. Tchr. Prep. Assn.; former mem. 1202 Commn. Higher Edn. Mass. Mem. Assn. Supervision and Curriculum Devel. (past pres.), Phi Delta Kappa, Kappa Delta Pi (hon.). Address: 302 Washington St Box 1209 Duxbury MA 02331

MC CARTHY, DANIEL CHRISTOPHER, JR., manufacturing company executive; b. St. Paul, May 10, 1924; s. Daniel Christopher and Isobel Beatrice (Wilmot) McC.; m. Gail Lloyd Allen, Mar. 9, 1951. B.Mech. Engring. with distinction, Cornell U., 1949. Mgr. profit planning Ford div. Ford Motor Co., 1949-56; dir. mfg. staff Chrysler Corp., 1956-58; controller Chrysler Internat., Geneva, Switzerland, 1958-59; exec. v.p. Pratt & Whitney Co., 1959-61, pres., 1961-64; v.p. bus. equipment group Litton Industries, Orange, N.J., 1964-65; pres. Monroe Internat., Inc. div., 1965-67; founder, v.p., dir. Keene Corp., 1967-74; founder, pres. Gale Corp., 1974-80; founder, chmn. Porta-Fab Corp., 1980-88, Norwood Mfg. Corp., 1980-88; pres., sole proprietor Gale Assocs., cons. and investments, Montclair, N.J., 1982—; founder, dir. Am. Mobile Systems, Inc., 1982-90; cons., dir. JJI Lighting Group Inc., 1980—, M.H. Koomey subs. Maritime Group, AS, 1991-93; gen. ptnr. Fiduciary Capital Mgmt., L.P., 1989—; founder, vice chmn. Glenco Holdings Inc., 1992-94. Mem. Cornell U. Council. Served with inf. AUS, 1942-46. Mem. ASME, Tau Beta Pi, Phi Kappa Phi, Pi Tau Sigma, Psi Upsilon. Home and Office: Gale Assocs 78 Lloyd Rd Montclair NJ 07042-1729

MCCARTHY, DAVID JEROME, JR., law educator; b. Hartford, Conn., July 19, 1935; s. David Jerome and Flora Emily (Edmondo) McC.; m. Mary Elizabeth McGlynn, Aug. 13, 1960; children: Emilie Anne, Mary Theresa, Carolyn Elizabeth, Katherine Margaret. AB cum laude, Fairfield (Conn.) U., 1957; LLB, Georgetown U., 1960, LLM, 1962, LLD (hon.), 1983. Bar: Conn. 1960, D.C. 1962. Law clk. U.S. Ct. Appeals D.C. Cir., 1960-61; law clk. to Judge John A. Danaher, 1961-62; atty. Appellate sect. civil div. U.S. Dept. Justice, Washington, 1962-63; dir. D.C. Bail Project, 1963-65; adj. prof. law Georgetown U., 1964-65, assoc. prof., 1965-68, prof., 1968-96, Carmack Waterhouse prof. state and local govt. law, 1996—, asst. dean, 1965-68, assoc. dean, 1968-70, dean, 1975-83, exec. v.p. Law Ctr. Affairs, 1975-83, mem. adv. bd. Health Policy Inst., 1982-88; chmn. exec. com. D.C. Pretrial Services Agy., 1966-87 ; mem. exec. com. Assn. Am. Law Schs., 1981-83, chmn. accreditation com., 1984-86, chmn. accreditation regulations rev. com., 1986-90; mem. Nat. Chamber Found. Task Force on Products Liability, 1978-81; chmn. Nat. Commn. on Taxes and the IRS, 1979-81; mem. Joint Com. on Clin. Legal Edn. Guidelines, Am. Bar Assn.-Am. Assn. Law Schs., 1977-80, Gov.'s Commn. for Modernization of Md. Exec. Br., 1966-67; counsel Md. Gov.'s Fiscal Rev. Com., 1984-86; mem. adv. bd. Nat. Inst. for Citizen Edn. in Law, 1976-86. Author: Local Government Law in a Nutshell, 1975, 4th edit., 1995; co-author: Local Government Law: Cases and Materials, 4th edit., 1992, supplement, 1995; contbr. articles to profl. jours., chpts. to books. Chmn. bd. dirs. Jesuit Internat. Vols., 1986-89. Recipient Profl. Achievement award Fairfield U. Alumni, 1965, 83. Mem. Am. Law Inst. Democrat. Roman Catholic. Home: 12612 Orchard Brook Ter Potomac MD 20854-2326 Office: Georgetown U Law Ctr 600 New Jersey Ave NW Washington DC 20001-2075

MCCARTHY, DENIS, artist, educator; b. N.Y.C., Feb. 21, 1935; s. Patrick and Carmel (Mulvany) McC. Cert. in fine art, The Cooper Union, 1963; B.F.A., Yale U., 1966, M.F.A., 1966. Instr. in drawing Sch. Visual Art, N.Y.C., 1967-72, NYU, 1976-78; prof. fine art Hunter Coll., N.Y.C., 1971—; vis. lectr. Fordham U., Md. Inst., 1979. One-man shows include: Stable Gallery, N.Y.C., 1970, 55 Mercer Gallery, N.Y.C., 1978, N.Y. State Coll., Old Westbury, 1980; exhibited in group shows: Stable Gallery, 1969, Whitney Mus., N.Y.C., 1969, Reese Palley, N.Y.C., 1970, O.K. Harris, N.Y.C., 1972, Warren Benedek Gallery, N.Y.C., 1973, Whitney Mus., N.Y.C., 1973, Aldrich Mus., Ridgefield, Conn., 1973, Paula Cooper Gallery, N.Y.C., 1974, Michael Wyman Gallery, Chgo., 1974, U. Maine, Portland, 1975, Automation House, N.Y.C., 1976, Hundred Acres Gallery, N.Y.C., 1977, NYU, 1977, N.Y. Acad. Scis., 1978. Home: 147 Spring St New York NY 10012-3860

MC CARTHY, DENIS MICHAEL, investment executive; b. Hartford, Conn., Dec. 4, 1942; s. Charles J. and Mary M. (Moynihan) McC.; m. Linda Horn, Aug. 21, 1965; children: Bryan, Kerry, Kevin. B.S., U. Conn., 1964, M.A., 1965. Asst. sec. Mfrs. Hanover Trust Co., N.Y.C., 1965-68; various positions to exec. v.p., chief fin. officer Triangle Industries, Inc., Holmdel, N.J., 1968-81; sr. v.p., chief fin. officer Emery Worldwide, Wilton, Conn., 1981-84; sr. v.p. fin. and adminstrn., chief. fin. officer Emery Worldwide, 1984-85, exec. v.p., chief oper. officer, 1985-87; pres., chief operating officer Emery Air Freight, 1987-89, also bd. dirs.; sr. v.p., CFO Fidelity Investments, Boston, 1989-95; chmn., pres., CEO, Fidelity Mgmt. Trust Co., B, 1995—. Home: 30 Whiting Rd Wellesley MA 02181-6737 Office: A8C 82 Devonshire Ct Boston MA 02109

MC CARTHY, EUGENE JOSEPH, writer, former senator; b. Watkins, Minn., Mar. 29, 1916; s. Michael John and Anna (Baden) McC.; m. Abigail Quigley, June 1945; children—Ellen, Mary, Michael, Margaret. A.B., St. John's U., Collegeville, Minn., 1935; A.M., U. of Minn., 1939. Tchr. pub. schs., 1935-40, 45; prof. econ. edn. St. John's U., 1940-42; civilian tech. work with Mil. Intelligence Div., War Dept., 1944; instr. sociology and econs. St. Thomas Coll., St. Paul, 1946-48; mem. 81st-85th Congresses from 4th Minn. dist., 1949-59, mem. ways and means com.; U.S. senator from Minn., 1959-70; mem. senate finance, fgn. relations and govt. ops. coms.; Adlai Stevenson prof. polit. sci. New Sch. for Social Research, 1973-74; syndicated columnist, 1977—; dir. Harcourt Brace Jovanovich, Inc. Author: Frontiers in American Democracy, 1960, Dictionary of American Politics, 1962, A Liberal Answer to the Conservative Challenge, 1964, The Limits of Power, 1967, The Year of the People, 1969, Other Things and The Aardvark, 1970, Up 'Til Now, 1987; also, The Hard Years, 1975, Mr. Raccoon and His Friends, 1977, America Revisited, 1978, Ground Fog and Night, 1979, The Ultimate Tyrany, 1980, Gene McCarthy's Minnesota, 1982, Complexities and Contraries: Essays of Mild Discontent, 1982, The View from Rappahannock, 1984; co-author: A Political Bestiary, 1978, Up 'Til Now, 1987, Required Reading, 1988, 89, The View from Rappahannock II, 1989, Colony of the World, 1993. Roman Catholic. Office: 271 Hawlin Rd Woodville VA 22749

MC CARTHY, FRANCIS F., construction executive. V.p. Mc Carthy Building Co., St. Louis. Office: Mc Carthy Building Co 1341 N Rock Hill Rd Saint Louis MO 63124-1441*

MC CARTHY, FRANK MARTIN, surgical sciences educator; b. Olean, N.Y., Aug. 27, 1924; s. Frank Michael and Joan (Quinn) McC.; m. Julia Richmond, Nov. 24, 1949; children: Robert Lee, Joan Lee. B.S., U. Pitts., 1943, D.D.S., 1945, M.D., 1949; M.S. in Oral Surgery, Georgetown U., 1954; Sc.D. (hon.), St. Bonaventure U., 1956. Med. intern Mercy Hosp., Pitts., 1949-50; practice oral surgery L.A., 1954-75; teaching fellow Georgetown U., 1952-53; rsch. fellow NIH, 1953-54; prof. oral surgery U. So. Calif. Sch. Dentistry, 1966-75, prof., chmn. sect. anesthesia and medicine, 1975-90, prof. emeritus, 1990—, chmn. dept. surg. scis., 1979-84, assoc. dean adminstrv. affairs, 1977-79, asst. dean hosp. affairs, 1979-84; dir. anesthesiology U.So. Calif. oral surgery sect. L.A. County Hosp., 1958-89; clin. supr., lectr. dental hygiene program Pasadena City Coll., 1992—; v.p. Am. Dental Bd. Anesthesiology, 1984-89; lectr. in field; mem. adv. panel on dentistry sect. anesthesizing agts. Nat. Fire Protection Assn., 1971-79; mem. Am. Nat. Standards Com., 1974-86; cons. in field. Author: Emergencies in Dental Practice, 1967, rev., 1972, 79, Medical Emergencies in Dentistry, 1982, Safe Treatment of the Medically Compromised Patient, 1987, Essentials of Safe Dentistry for the Medically Compromised Patient, 1989; mem. editorial bd.: Calif. Dental Assn. Jour; contbr. articles to profl. publs. Bd. councilors Sch. Dentistry, U. So. Calif., 1972-75. Served as lt., M.C. USNR, 1950-52. Fellow Internat. Assn. Oral Surgeons (founder), Am. Coll. Dentists, Internat. Coll. Dentists; mem. ADA (editorial bd. jour.), Am. Dental Soc. Anesthesiology (Heidbrink award 1977), Am. Assn. Oral-Max Surgeons (chmn. anesthesia com. 1971), So. Calif. Soc. Oral Surgeons (pres. 1974), Calif., Los Angeles County dental assns., Delta Tau Delta, Psi Omega, Phi Rho Sigma, Omicron Kappa Upsilon. Home and Office: 480 S Orange Grove Blvd Apt 11 Pasadena CA 91105-1720

MCCARTHY, G. DANIEL, lawyer; b. Butte, Mont., Mar. 23, 1949; s. George Denis and Mary Agnes (Kiely) McC.; m. Carolyn M. Scully, June 19, 1976; children: Brendan, Katie, Kelly, Sean. BA, U. Dayton, 1971; JD, U. Notre Dame, 1974; AMP, Harvard U., 1994. Bar: Md. 1974, D.C. 1975, U.S. Ct. Appeals (D.C. cir.) 1976, Pa. 1977, N.Y. 1985, U.S. Ct. Appeals (10th cir.) 1985. Assoc. Bilger & Blair, Washington, 1974-77, 79-80; asst. U.S. atty. U.S. Dist. Ct. (ea. dist.) Pa., Phila., 1977-78; assoc. Abourezk, Shack & Mendenhall, Washington, 1980-83; atty. AT&T, N.Y.C., 1983-85; sr. v.p., gen. counsel and sec. AT&T Credit Corp., Morristown, N.J., 1985-89; sr. v.p., gen. counsel, sec., chief risk mgmt. officer. AT&T Capital Corp., Morristown, 1990—; vis. lectr. Marymount Coll., Arlington, Va., 1979-83; bd. dirs. AT&T Credit Corp., AT&T Capital Ltd., NCR Credit Corp., Eaton Fin. Corp., AT&T Comml. Fin. Corp., AT&T Capital Svcs. Corp., AT&T Systems Leasing Corp., AT&T Capital Holdings Internat., Inc. Mem. ABA, D.C. Bar Assn. Avocation: golf, fly fishing. Home: 82 Van Doren Ave Chatham NJ 07928-2253 Office: AT&T Capital Corp 44 Whippany Rd Morristown NJ 07960-4558

MCCARTHY, GERALD MICHAEL, electronics executive; b. Chgo., June 13, 1941; s. John J. and Hannah (Naughton) McC.; m. Margaret-Mary O'Neill, June 20, 1964; children: John, Michael, Gerald Jr., Kevin. BS, Loyola U., Chgo., 1963; MBA, U. Chgo., 1976. Order dept. rep. Zenith Electronics Corp., Chgo., 1965-66, supr. sales plans, 1967-69, asst. mgr. product devel. TV, 1970-71, product mgr. B&W TV, 1971-72, nat. sales tng. mgr., 1972-74, dir. TV product planning, 1974-79, v.p. sales western div., 1979-82, exec. v.p. sales-consumer products, 1982-83; pres. Zenith Sales Co., Chgo., 1983—, Zenith Radio Can., Ltd., 1983—; corp. sr. v.p., mem. office of the pres. Zenith Electronics Corp., Chgo., 1991; corp. exec. v.p. Zenith Electronics Corp., 1993—; chmn. video divsn. Consumer Electronics Mfrs. Assn., Glenview, Ill., 1995—. Trustee Resurrection Health Care Corp., Chgo., 1983—, Jr. Achievement Chgo., 1983—. Served to 1st lt. U.S. Army, 1963-65. Mem. Electronics Industries Assn. (bd. govs. 1983—). Avocations: fishing, golf. Home: 1745 Dartmouth Ln Deerfield IL 60015-3946 Office: Zenith Electronics Corp 1000 Milwaukee Ave Glenview IL 60025-2423

MC CARTHY, HAROLD CHARLES, retired insurance company executive; b. Madelia, Minn., Dec. 5, 1926; s. Charles and Merle (Humphry) McC.; m. Barbara Kaercher, June 24, 1949; children: David, Susan. B.A., Carleton Coll., Northfield, Minn., 1950; postgrad. With Federated Mut. Ins. Co., Owatonna, Minn., 1950-67; with Meridian Mut. Ins. Co., Indpls., 1967-91; exec. v.p., then exec. v.p., gen. mgr. Meridian Mut. Ins. Co., 1972-75, pres., 1975-90, bd. dirs., past chmn. bd., 1990-91; past pres. North Meridian Bus. Group; past pres., chmn. bd. Meridian Ins. Group, Inc.; chmn. bd., dir. Meridian Life Ins. Co.; past chmn., exec. com., bd. dirs. Ind. Ins. Inst. Former mem. Met. Devel. Commn., Corp. Community Council; bd. dirs. Meth. Health Found., Family Services Assn., Boy Scouts Am.; trustee Butler U. With USNR, 1944-46. Named Sagamore of the Wabash. Mem. Nat. Assn. Ind. Insurers (past chmn. bd. govs.) Indpls. C. of C. (bd. dirs.), Ind. C. of C. (bd. dirs.), Skyline Club, Reserve Golf & Tennis Club. Republican. Methodist. Office: 2955 N Meridian St Indianapolis IN 46208-4714

MCCARTHY, J. THOMAS, lawyer, educator; b. Detroit, July 2, 1937; s. John E. and Virginia M. (Hanlon) McC.; m. Nancy Irene Orrell, July 10, 1976. BS, U. Detroit, 1960; JD, U. Mich., 1963. Bar: Calif. 1964. Assoc. Julian Caplan, San Francisco, 1963-66; prof. law U. San Francisco, 1966—; vis. prof. law Univ. Coll., Dublin, summer 1975; vis. prof. law U. Calif., Berkeley, 1976-77, Davis, 1979-80; vis. prof. law Monash U., Melbourne, Australia, 1985; cons. in field; mem. Trademark Rev. Commn., 1986-88. Author: McCarthy on Trademarks and Unfair Competition, 5 vols., 3d edit., 1992; (with Oppenheim and Weston) Federal Antitrust Laws, 1981, McCarthy on Rights of Publicity and Privacy, 1987, McCarthy's Desk Encyclopedia of Intellectual Property, 2d edit., 1995; mem. editl. bd. Trademark Reporter. Recipient Rossman award Patent Office Soc., 1979, Jefferson medal N.J. Intellectual Property Assn., 1994. Mem. Am. Intellectual Property Law Assn. (Watson award 1965), Internat. Assn. for Advancement of Teaching and Rsch. in Intellectual Property, Am. Law Inst. (adv. com. on restatement of law of unfair competition), IEEE.

MCCARTHY, JAMES, sociology researcher, educator. AB in Sociology, Coll. Holy Cross, 1971; MA in Sociology, Ind. U., 1972; PhD in Sociology, Princeton U., 1977. Rsch. assoc. Office Population Rsch. Princeton (N.J.) U., 1977-79; asst. prof. population dynamics and sociology Johns Hopkins U., Balt., 1979-82, assoc. prof., 1982-88, dir. Hopkins Population Ctr., 1984-88; assoc. prof. pub. health Columbia U., N.Y.C., 1988-91, prof. pub. health, 1991—, dir. Ctr. for Population and Family Health, 1988—; cons. UN Fund for Population Activities, 1979, East-West Population Inst., 1979, UN Population Divsn., 1980, World Fertility Survey, 1980, USAID, 1984, 85, NIMH, 1986, NAS, 1987, The World Bank, 1991, U. Mich., 1988-94, Nat. Inst. Child Health and Human Devel., 1991-92, Alan Guttmacher Inst., 1993—, Kuwait U., 1993—, others; grant reviewer NIH, 1983, 84, 85, NSF, 1985, Dept. Health and Human Svcs., 1982, 84, Andrew Mellon Found., 1993, Klingenstein Fund, 1993; presenter papers to numerous confs. Manuscript reviewer for numerous jours.; contbr. articles to profl. jours. Mem. APHA, Population Assn. Am. (chair subcom. fertility stats. 1984-85), Internat. Union for Sci. Study of Population. Office: Columbia U Ctr Population & Family Health 60 Haven Ave # B-3 New York NY 10032-2604

MCCARTHY, JAMES JOSEPH, oceanography educator, museum director; b. Ashland, Oreg., Jan. 25, 1944; m. 1969, 2 children. B.S., Gonzaga U., 1966; Ph.D., Scripps Inst. Oceanography, U. Calif.-San Diego, 1971. Research assoc. biol. oceanography Chesapeake Bay Inst., Johns Hopkins U., 1971-72, assoc. research scientist, 1972-74; asst. prof. Harvard U., 1974-77, assoc. prof., 1977-80, prof. biol. oceanography, 1980—, assoc. dean faculty Arts and Scis., 1986-90; dir. Agassiz Mus. Comparative Zoology, 1982—. Editor: Global Biogeochemical Cycles, 1986-90. Past chmn. Internat. Coun. of Scientific Unions, Scientific Com. Internat. Geosphere-Biosphere Program, 1987—. Fellow AAAS, Am. Acad. Arts and Scis.; mem. Phycol. Soc. Am., Am. Soc. Limnology and Oceanography, Am. Geophys. Union. Office: Mus Comparative Zoology 26 Oxford St Cambridge MA 02138-2902

MC CARTHY, JEAN JEROME, retired physical education educator; b. St. Paul, Sept. 11, 1929; s. Joseph Justin and Florence (Quirin) McC.; m. Norma Louise Shermer, July 30, 1955; children: Patrick J., Anne L., Kevin M. BS, U. Minn., 1956, PhD, 1986; MS, Wash. State U., 1958. Teaching asst. Wash. State U., 1956-57, U. Minn., 1957-59, adminstrv. asst., 1959-60; asst. prof. phys. edn. U. South Fla., 1960-62; asst. prof. phys. edn. Mankato State U., 1962-71, assoc. prof., 1971-86, prof. 1986-91, ret. 1991, baseball coach, 1962-77; cons. AAU. Contbr. articles to profl. jours. Mem. Minn. Gov.'s Phys. Fitness Adv. Com. Served with USAF, 1950-54. Recipient Outsanding Faculty award Mankato State U., 1979; named Region 2 Coach of Yr., NCAA, 1971, Outstanding Educators Am., 1970; named to Mankato State U. Athletic Hall of Fame, 1993; U. Minn. Grad. Sch. fellow, 1959-60; Lilly Found. scholar, 1974—; Rsch. Consortium fellow. Mem. AAHPER, Minn. Assn. Health, Phys. Edn. Recreation and Dance, Phi Delta Kappa, Phi Epsilon Kappa (scholarship award 1972), Phi Kappa Phi. Roman Catholic.

MCCARTHY, JOHN, computer scientist, educator; b. Boston, Sept. 4, 1927; s. Patrick Joseph and Ida McC.; children: Susan Joanne, Sarah Kathleen, Timothy Talcott. B.S., Calif. Inst. Tech., 1948; Ph.D., Princeton U., 1951. Instr. Princeton U., 1951-53; acting asst. prof. math. Stanford U., 1953-55; asst. prof. Dartmouth Coll., 1955-58; asst. and asso. prof. communications scis. M.I.T., Cambridge, 1958-62; prof. computer sci. Stanford U., 1962—, Charles M. Pigott prof. Sch. Engring., 1987-94. Served with AUS, 1945-46. Recipient Kyoto prize, 1988, Nat. medal of Sci. NSF, 1990. Mem. NAS, NAE, Am. Acad. Arts and Scis., Assn. for Computing Machinery (A.M. Turing award 1971), Am. Math. Soc., Am. Assn. Artificial Intelligence (pres. 1983-84). Home: 885 Allardice Way Stanford CA 94305-1050 Office: Stanford U Dept Computer Sci Stanford CA 94305

MC CARTHY, JOHN EDWARD, bishop; b. Houston, June 21, 1930; s. George Gaskell and Grace Veronica (O'Brien) McC. Student, St. Mary's Sem., Houston, 1949-56; M.A., St. Thomas U., Houston, 1979. Ordained priest Roman Catholic Ch., 1956; served various Houston Cath. parishes; exec. dir. Nat. Bishops Com. for Spanish speaking, 1966-68; asst. dir. Social Action Office, U.S. Cath. Conf., 1967-69; exec. dir. Tex. Cath. Conf., Houston, 1973-79; ordained aux. bishop Diocese of Galveston-Houston, 1979-86; installed third bishop of Austin, 1986—; Bd. dirs. Nat. Center for Urban Ethnic Affairs, Mexican-Am. Cultural Center, Sisters of Charity of the Incarnate Word, Houston, from 1981, St. Thomas U., Houston, from 1980. Mem. Cath. Conf. for Urban Ministry. Democrat. Office: Chancery N Congress &16th PO Box 13327 Austin TX 78711-3327*

MCCARTHY, JOSEPH GERALD, plastic surgeon, educator; b. Lowell, Mass., Nov. 28, 1938; s. Joseph H. and Eva (Murphy) McC.; m. Karlan von L. Sloan, June 6, 1964; children: Cara, Stephen. AB, Harvard U., 1960; MD, Columbia U., 1964. Diplomate: Am. Bd. Surgery, Am. Bd. Plastic Surgery. Surg. intern and resident Columbia-Presbyn. Med. Ctr.; resident in plastic surgery NYU Med. Ctr., N.Y.C., 1964-73; Lawrence D. Bell prof. plastic surgery NYU Sch. Medicine, N.Y.C., 1981—; dir. NYU Med. Ctr. Inst. Reconstructive Plastic Surgery; attending physician Univ. Hosp.; vis. plastic surgeon Bellevue Hosp.; attending surgeon Manhattan Eye, Ear and Throat Hosp., N.Y.C. VA Hosp. Editor: Symposium on Diagnosis and Treatment of Craniofacial Anomalies, 1979, Plastic Surgery, 1990; assoc. editor Reconstructive Plastic Surgery, 1977, Jour. Plastic and Reconstructive Surgery, Jour. Craniofacial, Genetics and Developmental Biology. Served to lt. comdr. USPHS, 1965-67. Recipient Joseph Garrison Parker prize Columbia U., 1964, 1st prize Plastic Surgery Edn. found., 1980, James Barret Brown prize, 1991, 1st prize Am. Soc. Maxillofacial Surgeons, 1991, 93, 94; Am. Cancer Soc. fellow Presbyn. Hosp., N.Y.C., 1969-70, prin. investigator NIH, 1974. Fellow ACS; mem. Am. Soc. Plastic and Reconstructive Surgeons, Assn. Acad. Chairmen Plastic Surgery (pres. 1988-89), N.Y. Regional Soc. Plastic and Reconstructive Surgeons (pres. 1984-85), Am. Assn. Plastic Surgeons (historian 1990-93), Internat. Soc. Craniomaxillofacial Surgeons (pres. 1989-91). Office: NYU Med Ctr Univ Hosp 550 1st Ave New York NY 10016-6481 also: 727 Park Ave New York NY 10021

MCCARTHY, JOSEPH HAROLD, consultant, former retail food company executive; b. Derby, Conn., Dec. 21, 1921; s. Joseph Harold and Kathryn (Feeley) McC.; m. Jean Karak, June 7, 1947; children: Timothy J., Maureen, Barbara, Richard, Joseph Harold. B.S. in Econs., Villanova U., 1944. Sr. v.p. First Nat. Stores Inc., Boston, 1947-76, Grand Union Co., Elmwood Park, N.J., 1976-80; exec. v.p., chief oper. officer Great Atlantic and Pacific Tea Co., Inc., Montvale, N.J., 1980-90, ret., 1990; cons. Great Atlantic and Pacific Tea Co., Inc., North Chatham, Mass., 1990-92. Served to capt. USMC, 1943-46, PTO; served to capt. USMC, 1951-52, Korea. Home: 2030 Imperial Golf C Blvd Naples FL 33942 Office: 38 Captains Walk North Chatham MA 02650-1041

MC CARTHY, JOSEPH MICHAEL, historian, educator; b. Lynn, Mass., Oct. 2, 1940; s. Joseph Donald and Johanna (Downing) Mc C.; AB, St. John's Sem., 1961, postgrad., 1961-63; AM, Boston Coll., 1968, PhD, 1972; m. Kathleen Theresa Wright, July 30, 1966; children: Joanna, Kristenmarie, Erika, Joseph Michael. Tchr., Bishop Fenwick H.S., Peabody, Mass., 1964-67; fin. adminstr. Boston Coll., 1967-71; lectr. in edn. Boston Coll., 1971-74, vis. prof., 1990; prof. edn., dir. leadership programs Suffolk U., 1973—; adj. lectr. Merrimack Coll., 1975, Boston U., 1973; prin. Ednl. Mgmt. Svcs., 1976—; gen. editor Garland Pub., 1979-92; bd. dirs. Inst. for Study of Academia, 1992-94. Recipient Hearn scholarship, 1959-61, fellowship, 1961-63. Mem. Am. Hist. Assn., Soc. for Medieval and Renaissance Philosophy, Soc. Romanian Historians, East European Rsch. Inst., Phi Alpha Theta, Phi Delta Kappa. Author: An International List of Articles on the History of Education, 1977; Guinea-Bissau and Cape Verde Islands, 1977; Humanistic Emphases in the Educational Thought of Vincent of Beauvais, 1976; Pierre Teilhard de Chardin, 1981; assoc. editor The Urban and Social Change Rev., 1969-72; asst. editor occasional papers series The Bureaucrat, Inc., 1974-76; contbr. to numerous scholarly jours. Home: 344 West St Duxbury MA 02332-3609 Office: Suffolk U Beacon Hill Boston MA 02114

MCCARTHY, KAREN P., congresswoman, former state representative; b. Mass., Mar. 18, 1947. BS in English, Biology, U. Kans., 1969, MBA, 1985; MEd in English, U. Mo., Kansas City, 1976. Tchr. Shawnee Mission (Kans.) South High Sch., 1969-75, The Sunset Hill (Kans.) Sch., , 1975-76; mem. Mo. House of Reps., Jefferson City, Mo., 1977-94; cons. govt. affairs Marion Labs., Kansas City, Mo., 1986-93; congresswoman, Mo. 5th Dist. U.S. Congress, Washington, D.C., 1995—; rsch. analyst pub. fin. dept. Stearn Bros. & Co., 1984-85, Kansas City, Mo.; rsch. analyst Midwest Rsch. Inst., econs. and mgmt. scis. dept., Kansas City, 1985-86. Del. Dem. Nat. Conv., 1992, Dem. Nat. Party Conf., 1982, Dem. Nat. Policy Com. Policy Commn., 1985-86. Recipient Outstanding Young Woman Am. award, 1977, Outstanding Woman Mo. award Phi Chi Theta, Woman of Achievement award Mid-Continent Coun. Girl Scouts U.S., 1983, 87, Annie Baxter Leadership award, 1993; named Conservation Legislator of Yr., Conservation Fed. Mo., 1987. Fellow Inst. of Politics; mem. Nat. Inst. of Politics; mem. Nat. Conf. on State Legis. (del. on trade and econ. devel. to Fed. Republic of Germany, Bulgaria, Japan, France and Italy, mem. energy com. 1978-84, fed. taxation, trade and econ. devel. com. 1986, chmn. fed. budget and taxation com. 1987, vice chmn. state fed. assembly 1988, pres.-elect 1993, pres. 1994), Nat. Dem. Inst. for Internat. Affairs (instr. No. Ireland 1988, Baltic Republics 1992, Hungary 1993). Office: US House Reps House Office Bldg 1232 Longworth Washington DC 20515-2505

MC CARTHY, KATHRYN A., physicist; b. Lawrence, Mass., Aug. 7, 1924; d. Joseph Augustine and Catherine (Barrett) McCarthy. A.B., Tufts U., 1945, M.S., 1946; Ph.D., Radcliffe Coll., 1957; D.Sc. (hon.), Coll. Holy Cross, 1978; D.H.L. (hon.), Merrimack Coll., 1981. Instr. physics Tufts U., 1946-53, asst. prof., 1953-59, assoc. prof., 1959-62, prof., 1962-95, emerita, 1995—, dean Grad. Sch., 1969-74, provost, sr. v.p., 1973-79; research fellow in metallurgy Harvard, 1957-59, vis. scholar, 1979-80; research assoc. Baird Assocs., 1947-49, 51, Boston U. Optical Research Lab., summer 1952; assoc. research engr. U. Mich., summer 1957-58; dir. Mass. Electric Co., State Mut. Assurance Co. Trustee Southeastern Mass. U., 1972-74, Merrimack Coll., 1974-83, Coll. Holy Cross, 1980—; corporator Lawrence Meml. Hosp., 1975—, dir., 1978—, chmn., 1991. Fellow Optical Soc. Am., Am. Phys. Soc.; mem. Soc. Women Engrs. (sr.), Phi Beta Kappa, Sigma Xi. Roman Catholic. Home: 1580 Massachusetts Ave Apt 5D Cambridge MA 02138-2926 Office: Tufts U Dept Physics 4 Colby St Medford MA 02155-6013

MCCARTHY, MARIE GERALDINE, program director, coordinator, educator; b. San Francisco, Nov. 7, 1940; d. Emmett Francis and Marie Delores (Costello) McC.; children: Peter, Robert, Todd Brockman. BA, Lone Mountain Coll., 1962; MA, Dominican Coll., San Rafael, Calif., 1972. Gen. secondary credential; cert. cmty. coll. chief adminstrv. officer, supr., history, basic edn., spl. edn., profl. edn. educator, counselor. Coord., counselor Work Incentive Program, Employment Devel. Dept., Marin County, Calif., 1970-72; coord., instr. Neighborhood Youth Corps Program, Marin County, Calif., 1972-74; coord. Marin City Project Area Com., Marin County, Calif., 1978-79; coord. basic skills program Coll. of Marin, Kentfield, Calif., 1973-79, edn. cons., 1980-83, pres. acad. senate, 1993—, coord. Disabled Students Program, 1984—; faculty advisor Challenged Students Club, Coll. of Marin, Kentfield, 1983—, exec. coun. United Profs. of Marin, Local 1610, 1984-92, mem. staff devel. com., 1986-88, event coord. ann. student fundraiser for students with disabilities, 1985—, dist. psychol. disabilities task force, 1994—, dist. councilmem. Faculty Assn. Calif. C.C.s, 1994—, dist. budget com., 1994—, dist. master planning com., 1994—, mem. crisis intervention team, 1990—, editor DSPS Forum, 1995—; exec. com. Statewide Acad. Senate, 1995-96. Author: How To Learn To Study: Bridging the Study Skills Gap, 1982, The Faculty Handbook on Disabilities, 1993. Bd. dirs., v.p. CENTERFORCE, 1992—; bd. dirs. Marin Coalition, Marin Athletic Found., 1992—, Marin Ctr. for Ind. Living, 1994—, EXODUS, 1992—, sec.; past v.p. Bay Faculty Assn.; founder Youth Helping Homeless, 1990—; mem. Alliance for the Mentally Ill., 1994—, JERICHO, 1994—; founding bd. dirs. INSPIRIT, 1984—. Recipient Spl. Achievement award Calif. Youth Soccer Assn., 1980, Marin County Mother of Yr. award, 1984, Spl. Recognition awards The Indoor Sports Club for Physically Handicapped, 1984, 88-90, 92-93, Mom Makes the Difference honoree Carter Hawley Hale Stores, Inc., 1994, Cert. of Recognition, Marin Human Rights Commn., 1994, Hayward award, 1995, Buckelew Partnership award, 1995, Disting. Faculty award Com. Alumni Assn., 1995. Mem. AAUW, Calif. Assn. Postsecondary Educators for the Disabled, Faculty Assn. Calif. C.C.'s, Amnesty Internat. Platform Assoc., AHEAD, Commonwealth Club Calif., U.S. Soccer Fedn. Avocations: piano, singing, hiking, aerobics, meditation. Home: 6004 Shelter Bay Ave Mill Valley CA 94941-3040 Office: Coll of Marin College Ave Kentfield CA 94904

MCCARTHY, MARK FRANCIS, lawyer; b. Boston, July 8, 1951; s. William Alfred and Martha Louise (Blodgett) McC.; m. Karen Marie Umerley; children: Kevin Francis, Daniel Henry. AB in Theology, Georgetown U., 1973, JD, 1976. Bar: Ohio 1976. Assoc. Sweeney, Mahon, & Vlad, Cleve., 1976-80; ptnr. Arter & Hadden, Cleve., 1980—; atty. asst. to bd. pres. Bd. Cuyahoga County Commrs., Cleve., 1976-80; adj. prof. Case Western Reserve Law Ctr., Cleve., 1986—. Active Greater Cleve. Growth Assn. Leadership Cleve., 1979-80; pres. bd. trustees Parmadale, Parma, Ohio. Mem. Ohio Assn. Civil Trial Attys. (chmn. product liability sect. 1989—), Fedn. Ins. & Corp. Counsel, Ct. of Nisi Prius, Rowfant Club. Democrat. Roman Catholic. Avocations: book collecting, fly fishing, upland shooting. Home: 404 Regatta Dr Avon Lake OH 44012-2910 Office: Arter & Hadden 1100 Huntington Bldg 925 Euclid Ave Cleveland OH 44115

MCCARTHY, MARY FRANCES, hospital foundation administrator; b. Washington, Apr. 16, 1937; d. Joseph Francis and Frances (Oddi) McGowan; m. Charles M. Sappenfield, Dec. 14, 1963 (div. June 1990); children: Charles Ross, Sarah Kathleen; m. Daniel Fendrick McCarthy, Jr., Aug. 25, 1990. BA, Trinity Coll., Washington, 1958; cert. in bus. adminstrn., Harvard U.-Radcliffe Coll., 1959; MA, Ball State U., Muncie, Ind., 1984. Systems engr. IBM, Cambridge, Mass., 1959-61; editorial asst. Kiplinger Washington Editors, 1961-63; feature writer pub. info. dept. Ball State U., 1984-85, coll. editor Coll. Bus., 1985-86, coord. alumni and devel., 1986-88, dir. major gift clubs and donor rels., 1988-90; dir. devel. Sweet Briar (Va.) Coll., 1990-91; adminstr. St. Mary's Hosp. and Med. Ctr. Found., Grand Junction, Colo., 1991—. Editor: A History of Maxon Corporation, 1986, Managing Change, 1986, Indiana's Investment Banker, 1987; assoc. editor Mid-Am. Jour. Bus., 1985-86. Participant Leadership Lynchburg, 1990, Jr. League; mem. Sr. Companions Bd., Grand Junction, 1992—; mem. Mesa County Healthy Communities Steering Com., 1992—; mem. Mesa County Health Assessment, 1994—; mem. bd. Sta. KRMJ TV Channel 18, 1995—; interim regional dir. region 9 AHP, 1996—. Recipient Golden Broom award Muncie Clean City, 1989; svc. of distinction award Ball State U. Coll. Bus., 1990. Mem. Coun. for Advancement and Support of Edn., Assn. of Healthcare Philanthropy (regional 9 cabinet 1992—), Nat. Soc. Fundraising Execs. (cert., Colo. chpt. bd. dirs. 1994—). Republican. Avocations: biking, walking, cross-country skiing, gardening.

MCCARTHY, MARY LYNN, social work educator; b. Buffalo, Sept. 26, 1950; d. Joseph Timothy and Jean Marie (Weber) McC.; m. David R. Gardam; children: Rachel Lamb, Ethan Gardam. BA, SUNY, Oswego, 1973; MSW, SUNY, Albany, 1982. Cert. social worker. Asst. program dir. Huntington Family Ctr., Syracuse, N.Y., 1973-75; caseworker child protection Onondaga County Dept. Social Svcs., Syracuse, 1975; coord. Community Svc. Alliance, Syracuse, 1976-79; asst. and assoc. human svcs. Profl. Devel. Program - SUNY, Albany, N.Y., 1979-84; intake coord., dir. parent aides St. Catherines Ctr. for Children, Albany, 1983-84; edn. asst. N.Y. State Edn. Dept., Albany, 1984-87; field edn. asst. coord., instr. SUNY Sch. of Social Welfare, Albany, 1987-93, asst. dean student svcs., 1990—, undergrad. field coord., 1993—; chmn. Child Welfare Issues Com., Albany, 1983-88; com. mem. N.Y. State Welfare Adv. Coun., Albany, 1983-84. Recipient Disabled Student Svcs. Achievement award U. Albany, 1993. Mem. NASW (sec. 1983-85, v.p. 1985-88, pres. N.E. divsn. 1988-90, nat. trustee Polit. Action for Candidate Election 1989—, chair 1994-96, N.Y. state trustee 1993—, treas. 1990-92, mem. nat. strategic planning com. 1990-91, Social Worker of Yr. N.E. divsn. N.Y. state chpt. 1992), N.Y. State Social Work Edn. Assn. (bd. dirs. 1989), Coun. on Social Work Edn. Avocations: canoeing, camping, gardening. Office: Rockefeller Coll Sch Social Welfare 114 Richardson Hall Albany NY 12222

MCCARTHY, MICHAEL JOSEPH, communications company executive; b. Davenport, Iowa, Oct. 21, 1944; s. Thomas Patrick and Mary Elizabeth (McCabe) McC.; m. Monica Catherine Martin; children: Michael, Maureen. BA, U. Notre Dame, 1966; MSc, London Sch. Econs., 1968; JD, George Washington U., 1973. Speech writer Office of Telecommunications Policy, Office of Pres. of U.S., Washington, 1972-73; assoc., ptnr. Dow, Lohnes & Albertson, Washington, 1973-85; sr. v.p., sec., gen. counsel A.H. Belo Corp., Dallas, 1985—. Author fiction books. Trustee Dallas Bar Found., 1987; bd. dir. N. Tex. Commn. Home: 6138 Aberdeen Ave Dallas TX 75230-4208 Office: A H Belo Corp 400 S Record St Dallas TX 75202-4841

MCCARTHY, MICHAEL M., construction executive. CEO McCarthy, St. Louis. Office: McCarthy Bldg Cos 1341 N Rock Hill Rd Saint Louis MO 63124-1441*

MCCARTHY, MICHAEL SHAWN, health care company executive, lawyer; b. Evergreen Park, Ill., May 16, 1953; s. Martin J. and Margaret Anne (McNeill) McC.; m. Jane F. Alberding, Oct. 28, 1988; children: Caroline Margaret, Nicholas Michael. BA, Georgetown U., 1975; MS, U. Ill., 1976; JD, Loyola U., 1980. Bar: Ill. 1980, U.S. Dist. Ct. (no. dist.) Ill. 1980. V.p., sec., gen. counsel Luth. Gen. Health Care System, Park Ridge, Ill., 1980-85, sr. v.p., sec., gen. counsel, 1985-91, sr. v.p. corp. svcs., sec., gen. counsel, 1990-93; chmn., CEO Parkside Sr. Svcs., L.L.C., Park Ridge, Ill., 1993—; bd. dirs. Cath. Lawyers Guild, Hosps. Organized for Polit. Edn., Juv. Protection Assn. Mem. ABA, Am. Assn. for Preferred Providers Orgn., Ill. Hosp. Assn., Ill. Pub. Health Assn., Ill. State Bar Assn., Chgo. Bar Assn. Roman Catholic. Avocations: golf, travel. Office: Parkside Sr Svcs LLC 205 W Touhy Ave Park Ridge IL 60068

MCCARTHY, PATRICK, magazine publishing executive. Joined Women's Wear Daily, 1977; reporter Women's Wear Daily, D.C.; bur. chief Women's Wear Daily, London, Paris; editor Women's Wear Daily, N.Y.C., 1985-88, exec. editor, 1988-92; editor W, N.Y.C., 1985-88, exec. editor, 1988-92; exec. v.p. Fairchild Publs., N.Y.C., 1992—. Recipient Eugenia Sheppard award for fashion journalism CFDA, 1994. Office: Fairchild Publs Seven West 34th St New York NY 10001 also: care Susan Magrino Susan Magrino Agency 40 W 57th St New York NY 10019-4071

MCCARTHY, PATRICK A., English educator; b. Charlottesville, Va., July 12, 1945; s. Thomas Blair and Virginia Rose (Feuerstein) McC.; children: Keely, Cailin, Brendan. BA, U. Va., 1967, MA, 1968; PhD, U. Wis., Milw., 1973. Asst. prof., English U. Miami, Coral Gables, Fla., 1976-81, assoc. prof., 1981-84, prof., 1984—; dir. grad. studies English Dept., U. Miami, 1986-95; manuscript cons. various univ. presses. Author: The Riddles of Finnegans Wake, 1980, Olaf Stapledon, 1982, Ulysses: Portals of Discovery, 1990, Forests of Symbols: World, Text, and Self in Malcolm Lowry's Fiction, 1994; editor: Critical Essays on Samuel Beckett, 1986, Critical Essays on James Joyce's Finnegans Wake, 1992, Malcolm Lowry's La Mordida: A Scholarly Edition, 1996; co-editor: The Legacy of Olaf Stapledon, 1989. Travel grantee Am. Coun. Learned Socs., 1977; recipient Max Orovitz summer stipend U. Miami, 1980, 82, 85, 90, 92, gen. rsch. support grant, 1990, 92, 93. Mem. MLA, Assn. Lit. Scholars and Critics, South Atlantic MLA, Internat. James Joyce Found., Am. Coun. Irish Studies. Office: U Miami Dept English Coral Gables FL 33124

MCCARTHY, PAUL, lawyer; b. N.Y.C., Jan. 3, 1940. AB, Cornell U., 1961; JD, U. Mich, 1964; MCL, U. Chgo., 1966. Bar: Ill. 1972. Ptnr. Baker & McKenzie, Chgo. Office: Baker & McKenzie 1 Prudential Pla 130 E Randolph St Chicago IL 60601*

MCCARTHY, PAUL FENTON, aerospace executive, former naval officer; b. Boston, Mar. 3, 1934; s. Paul Fenton and Jane Gertrude (O'Connor) McC.; m. Sandra Williams, June 20, 1959; children: Paul Fenton III, Susan Stacy. B.S. in Marine and Elec. Engring., Mass. Maritime Acad., 1954; M.S. in Mgmt., U.S. Naval Postgrad. Sch., 1964; D of Pub. Adminstrn. (hon.), Mass. Maritime Acad., 1987. Commd. ensign U.S. Navy, 1954, advanced through grades to vice adm., 1985; 7 command tours have included Aircraft Carrier USS Constellation, Carrier Group One, Task Force Seventy; commdr. U.S. 7th Fleet, 1980-82; dir. R & D USN, Washington, 1980-83; negotiator Naval Air, Incidents at Sea Agreement, Moscow, 1980; ret., 1990; cons. in field Alexandria, Va., 1990-92; pres. McCarthy and McCarthy, Ltd.; v.p., chief engr., dep. gen.mgr. McDonnell Douglas Aerospace, St. Louis, 1992-95, v.p. processes and sys. integration, 1995—; Mem. engring adv. coun. Fla. State U. Trustee Naval Mus., 1990; bd. visitors Mass. Maritime Acad., 1993. Decorated D.S.M., Legion of Merit, D.F.C., also by govts. of South Vietnam, Korea, Japan. Mem. Mass. Maritime Acad. Alumni Assn., Soc. Exptl. Test Pilots, Naval Inst., Nat. Soc. Profl. Engrs. (mem. industry adv. group). Episcopalian. Avocations: research, development and acquisition, aircraft and missile systems, financial management. Home: 16475 Saddle Creek Rd Chesterfield MO 63005

MCCARTHY, PAUL LOUIS, pediatrics educator; b. Springfield, Mass., Aug. 9, 1941; s. Alfred Lawrence and Minnie Josephine (Vivian) McC.; m. Barbara Jean Burns, Nov. 30, 1963; children: Paul, Scott, Brian. BA, Dartmouth Coll., 1963; MD, Georgetown U., 1969; MA (in privatum), Yale U., 1982. Diplomate Am. Bd. Pediatrics, Am. Bd. Pediatric Rheumatology. Pediat. intern Children's Hosp., Buffalo, 1969-70, pediat. resident, 1970-72; fellow in ambulatory pediatrics Children's Hosp. Med. Ctr., Boston, 1972-74; asst. prof. pediat. Yale U. Sch. Medicine, New Haven, 1974-78, assoc. prof., 1978-82, prof., 1982—, head gen. pediat., 1985—; Morrison lectr. Geisinger Clinic, Danville, Pa., 1990. Author: Evaluation and Management of Febrile Children, 1985; author 4 monographs; contbr. numerous articles to med. jours., chpts. to books. Fellow Am. Acad. Pediatrics; mem. Ambulatory Pediatric Assn. (pres. 1989-90, Armstrong award 1991), Soc. for Pediatric Rsch., Am. Pediatric Soc. Achievements include research in clinical judgment in acute illnesses in children. Avocations: reading, walking. Office: Yale U Sch of Medicine 333 Cedar St New Haven CT 06510-3206

MCCARTHY, ROBERT EMMETT, lawyer; b. Bklyn., May 26, 1951; s. John Joseph and Leona Mary (Hart) McC.; m. Elizabeth Anne Naumoff, May 20, 1978; children: John Philip, Emily Jane. BS in Fgn. Studies, Georgetown U., 1973, MS in Fgn. Studies, JD, 1978. Bar: N.J. 1978, U.S. Dist. Ct. (ea. and so. dists.) N.Y. 1979. Assoc. Patterson, Belknap et al, N.Y.C., 1978-84; sr. counsel MTV Networks Inc., N.Y.C., 1984-86; v.p., counsel/communications Viacom Internat., N.Y.C., 1986-87; exec. v.p. Nelson Vending Tech., Ltd., N.Y.C., 1987-89; exec. v.p., gen. counsel Cateret Savs. Bank FA, Morristown, N.J., 1989—; cons. UN Ctr. on Transnat. Corps., N.Y.C., 1979; exec. dir. Spl. Master Reapportionment of N.Y., 1982; term mem. Council Fgn. Relations, N.Y.C., 1980-84. Founder, pres. Elizabeth (N.J.) Dem. Assn., 1980; coordinator Florio for Gov., Union County, N.J., 1981. Mem. ABA, N.Y. Bar Assn., N.J. State Bar Assn., N.Y. County Lawyers Assn., Assn. Bar City N.Y. Democrat. Roman Catholic. Home: 1050 Harding Rd Elizabeth NJ 07208-1010 Office: Cateret Savs Bank FA 200 South St Morristown NJ 07960-5390

MCCARTHY, ROGER LEE, mechanical engineer. AB in Philosophy with high distinction, U. Mich., 1972, BSME summa cum laude, 1972; MS in Mech. Engring., MIT, 1973, MechE, 1975, PhD in Mech. Engring., 1977. Registered profl. engr., Calif., Ariz. Project engr. machine design and devel. engring. div. Proctor & Gamble, Inc., Cin., 1973-74; program mgr. Spl. Machinery Group Foster-Miller Assocs., Inc., Waltham, Mass., 1976-78; prin. design engr. Failure Analysis Assocs., Inc., Menlo Park, Calif., 1978—; CEO The Failure Group, Inc., Menlo Park, 1988—. Co-contbr. numerous articles to profl. jours. Mem. Pres.' Commn. on Nat. Medal od Sci., 1992-94. NSF fellow, 1972-75. Mem. Am. Soc. Metals, ASME, Soc. Automotive Engrs., Am. Welding Soc., Am. Soc. for Testing and Materials, Human Factors Soc., ASHRAE, Nat. Fire Protection Assn., Phi Beta Kappa, Sigma Xi (James B. Angell scholar). Office: Failure Group Inc PO Box 3015 149 Commonwealth Dr Menlo Park CA 94025

MCCARTHY, SEAN MICHAEL, air force pilot; b. Tacoma, Feb. 8, 1971; s. Lawrence Joseph and Mary Ann (Kramer) McC. BS with distinction, USAF Acad., Colorado Springs, 1993. Cadet USAF Acad., Colorado Springs, 1989-93; commd. 2d lt. USAF, 1993; student pilot Undergrad. Pilot Tng., Del Rio, Tex., 1993-94; A-10 pilot USAF, Osan Air Base, Korea, 1995—; summer intern Def. Mapping Agy., Alexandria, Va., 1992. Mem. Nat. Geographic Soc. (Dr. John Oliver LaGorce award 1993). Avocations: weight lifting, cycling, swimming, model building. Home: 1717 Devon Ave Linwood NJ 08221-2210 Office: PSC 3 Box 4321 APO AP 96266

MC CARTHY, THOMAS PATRICK, magazine publisher; b. Elizabeth, N.J., Mar. 17, 1928; s. Thomas Joseph and Genevieve Elizabeth (Duffy) McC.; m. Joan Ellen Bodet, Jan. 16, 1954; children: Kathleen E., Patricia E., Thomas Patrick. BA, Seton Hall U., East Orange, N.J., 1955. Salesman, Joseph Davis Plastics Co., Kearney, N.J., 1955-57; nat. accounts mgr. ESB Corp., N.Y.C., 1957-65, Bekins Van & Storage Co., N.Y.C., 1965-67; nat. sales mgr. Traffic Mgmt. mag., N.Y.C., 1967-74; pub. Traffic Mgmt. mag., Boston, 1974—; v.p. Traffic Mgmt. mag., 1980-83; pres. Am. Resource Devel. Group, 1983-86, Land-Air-Sea-Transp. Pub. Co., N.Y.C., 1983-95; ptnr. PROMATE Energy Systems, Inc., Marshfield, Mass., 1994—; pres. Transp. Mktg. Cons., Marshfield, Mass. Served with AUS, 1950-53. Mem. Bus. Publ. Advt. Assn., Assn. R.R. Advt. Mgrs., Sales & Mktg. Council Am. Trucking Assn. Roman Catholic. Clubs: Lions, K.C. Home: 57 Salt Meadow Waye Marshfield MA 02050-2427 Office: 741 Plain St Marshfield MA 02050-1105

MCCARTHY, TIMOTHY MICHAEL, career non-commissioned officer; b. Mpls., July 18, 1944; s. Howard Allen and Elonora H. (Joa) McC.; m. Kang Suk Yi, Jan. 7, 1969; 1 child, Sony Srithai. AAS in Gen. Mgmt., El Paso C.C., 1995. With U.S. Army, 1965-95; platoon sgt. B Co., 143rd Signal BN, Frankfurt, Germany, 1979-81; discom platoon sgt., 1st sgt. 143d Signal Bat., Frankfurt, 1981-82; 1st sgt. 501st Signal Bat., Clarksville, Tenn., 1983-84; divsn. chief signal NCO 101st Airborne Divsn., Clarksville, 1984-85; bat. ops. sgt. 102nd Signal Bat., Frankfurt, 1986-87; sgt. maj. 7th Signal Brigade, Mannheim, Germany, 1987-88; command sgt. maj. 72d Signal Bat., Karlsruhe, Germany, 1988-90, 7th Signal Bridgade, Karlsruhe, 1990-93, Comm.-Electronics Command, Ft. Monmouth, N.J., 1993-95; ret. U.S. Army, 1995; asst. instr. Jr. ROTC Allendale-Fairfax (S.C.) H.S. Jr. ROTC, 1995. Mem. Noncommissioned Officers Assn. (life, chpt. chmn.), Knights of the Square Table, Assn. of the U.S. Army (life), Armed Forces Comm. Electronics Assn., Signal Corps Regimental Assn. Democrat. Roman Catholic. Avocations: golf, running, skiing. Home: 3534 Biltmore Pl Augusta GA 30906-4577 Office: Allendale-Fairfax HS Jr ROTC Rte 2, Box 222 Fairfax SC 29827-0222

MCCARTHY, VINCENT PAUL, lawyer; b. Boston, Sept. 25, 1940; s. John Patrick and Marion (Buckley) McC.; children: Vincent, Sybil, Hope. AB, Boston Coll., 1962; JD, Harvard U., 1965. Bar: Mass. 1965. Ptnr. Hale and Dorr, Boston, 1965—, sr. ptnr., 1976—. Bd. dirs., sec. Robert F. Kennedy Action Corps, Inc.; bd. dirs. Boston Alcohol Detoxification Project, Inc.; mem. Mass. Gov.'s Adv. Coun. on Alcoholism, Boston, 1984—, Gov.'s Jud. Nominating Com., 1991—; chmn. Mass. Housing Partnership Fund; past chmn. Boston Ctr. for Arts; mem. adv. coun. Harvard Internat. AIDS Inst.; trustee, sec. Franklin Square House; past pres. Mass. Assn. for Mental Health; bd. dirs., past sec.-treas. Human Rights Campaign Found. Recipient Vols. of Am. Outstanding Svc. award, 1989. Mem. ABA (Pro Bono Publico award 1987), Mass. Bar Assn., Boston Bar Assn. (Pub. Svc. award 1995).

MC CARTHY, WALTER JOHN, JR., retired utility executive; b. N.Y.C., Apr. 20, 1925; s. Walter John and Irene (Trumbl) McC.; m. Linda Lyon, May 6, 1988; children by previous marriage: Walter, David, Sharon, James, William. B.M.E., Cornell U., 1949; grad., Oak Ridge Sch. Reactor Tech., 1952; D.Eng. (hon.), Lawrence Inst. Tech., 1981; D.Sc. (hon.), Eastern Mich. U., 1983; LHD, Wayne State U., 1984; LLD, Alma (Mich.) Coll., 1985. Engr. Public Service Electric & Gas Co., Newark, 1949-56; sect. head Atomic Power Devel. Assos., Detroit, 1956-61; gen. mgr. Power Reactor Devel. Co., Detroit, 1961-68; with Detroit Edison Co., 1968-90, exec. v.p. ops., 1975-77, exec. v.p. divs., 1977-79, pres., chief operating officer, 1979-81, chmn., chief exec. officer, 1981-90; bd. dirs. Comerica Bank Calif., Energy Conversion Devices Inc. Author papers in field. Past chmn., bd. dirs. Inst. Nuclear Power Ops. Fellow Am. Nuclear Soc., Engring. Soc. Detroit; mem. ASME, NAE. Methodist.

MCCARTHY, WILBERT ALAN, mechanical engineer; b. Wadesboro, N.C., Mar. 22, 1945; s. Wilbert Albert and Myrtle (Greene) McC. Student, Va. Poly. Inst., 1963-66, U. Va. Extension, Falls Church, 1967-70, SUNY, Albany, 1990-91; BS in Mech. Engring., Pacific Western U., 1991, MS in Engring. and Constrn. Mgmt., 1993. Registered profl. engr., Wis., Vt., D.C., N.H., Maine, W.Va., Md. Mech. engring. designer Edward L. Middleton and Assocs., Marlow Heights, Md., 1967-72; mech. engr., project mgr. H.D. Nottingham & Assocs., McLean, Va., 1972-79, sr. mech. engr., project mgr., profl. engr., 1982-83; mech. engr., project mgr., profl. engr. E/A Design Group, Washington, 1979-82; firm assoc., mech. dept. head, sr. mech. engr., profl. engr. Engring. Applications Cons., Burke, Va., 1983-87; firm assoc., dep. ops. mgr., mktg. coord., dir. engring. SAIC Architects, Inc., McLean, 1987-90; pvt. practice Dumfries, Va., 1990-91; project dir., project mgr., mktg. coord., sr. mech. engr. Advanced Cons. Engring., Arlington, Va., 1991-92; program dir., project mgr., mktg. field rep., sr. mech. engr. Engring. Design Group, Washington, 1992-95; pvt. practice mech. cons. Locust Grove, Va., 1995—; mechanical sect. head, sr. mechanical engr 1995—; mem. panel arbitrators Am. Arbitration Assn. for disputes in govt., commercial and private constrn. industry. lectr., speaker Inst. for Internat. Rsch., N.Y.C., 1988—, Nat. Energy Mgmt. Inst., N.Y.C., 1988—. Sgt. USAFR, 1966-72. Recipient Award of Excellence for Design of Hynson Bldg. Rehab. Va. Downtown Devel. Assn., 1988, Commendation for Engring. and Mgmt. Proficiency U.S. Dept. Navy, 1987, 88. Mem. ABA (assoc.), Assn. Energy Engrs. (sr.), NSPE, ASHRAE, Am. Soc. Plumbing Engrs., Nat. Coun. Examiners for Engring. and Surveying (cert. profl. engr.). Methodist. Achievements include development of HVAC design projects for American embassies and consulates throughout the world, complete redesign of boiler plant facilities bldg., steam distbn. sys. for Ft. Belvior Va., chilled water distbtn. sys., Goddard space Flight Ctr., Beltsville Md. Home: HC75 Box 40 LOW Locust Grove VA 22508 Office: Engring Design Group Inc 218 Cornwallace Ave Locust Grove VA 22508

MCCARTHY, WILLIAM DANIEL, retired banking educator; b. Telmore, Ga., Mar. 11, 1935; s. William Allen and Lillian Virue (Fales) McC.; m. Patricia Ann McQuaig, Mar. 17, 1961; children: Lillian Lea, Mary Rosann, Martha Joi, Tricia Hope. BBA in Acctg., U. Ga., 1960, MBA in Acctg., 1961, PhD in Fin., Banking, 1969. Instr. U. Ga., Athens, 1963-65, Valdosta (Ga.) State Coll., 1965-66; prof., div. chmn. South Ga. Coll., Douglas, 1967-75; assoc. prof. Armstrong State Coll., Savannah, Ga., 1976-79; prof. fin. and banking, MBA coord. Savannah State Coll., 1979-90, prof. emeritus fin., 1991—; pres., CEO McCarthy Farms. Contbr. articles to fin. publs. Pres., Ware County Property Owners Assn., Waycross, Ga., 1986—; economist Nat. Wildlife Assn., Washington; mem. budget rev. com. United Way Savannah; mem. com. on grad. studies Bd. Regents, U. System of Ga., 1980-87, chmn., 1987. Sgt. USMC, 1954-57. Mem. NRA, So. Fin. Assn., Midwest Fin. Assn., Southwest Fin. Assn., Ea. Fin. Assn., Sons of Confederacy, Southside Kiwanis Club (pres. 1989-90), Ga. Forestry Assn., Forest Farmers Assn., Southeast Ga. Forest Owners Assn., Phi Kappa Phi, Beta Gamma Sigma, Omicron Delta Epsilon, Beta Alpha Psi. Methodist. Home: 6043 Telmore & Dix Union Rd Millwood GA 31552-9727

MCCARTNEY, CHARLES PRICE, retired obstetrician-gynecologist; b. Barnesville, Ohio, Aug. 18, 1912; s. Jesse Thomas and Carrie (Price) McC.; m. Phyllis Helen Graybill, Sept. 27, 1940; children—Marilyn B., Ann E. B.S., U. Chgo., 1942, M.D., 1943. Diplomate: Am. Bd. Obstetricians and Gynecologists. Intern U. Chgo. Clinics, 1943-44, resident, 1947-50; mem. faculty U. Chgo. Med. Sch., 1950-71, prof. obstetrics and gynecology, 1960-71, Mary Campeau Ryerson prof., 1967-71; clin. prof. obstetrics and gynecology U. Ill., 1971-80, prof. emeritus, 1980—; attending gynecologist and obstetrician Chgo. Lying-In Hosp., 1950—. Mem. Cook County Com. Maternal Welfare, 1965—. Served to maj., M.C. AUS, 1944-46. Fellow Am. Gynecol. Soc.; mem. Am. Gynecol. and Obstetrical Soc., Chgo. Gynecol. Soc. (pres. 1967), Chgo. Med. Soc. (councillor 1960—, pres. 1973, chmn. bd. trustees 1973), Am. Coll. Obstetricians and Gynecologists (chmn. Ill. sect. 1965—), Cen. Assn. Obstetricians and Gynecologists. Home: 916 Thornwood Dr Saint Charles IL 60174

MCCARTNEY, JAMES HAROLD, newspaper columnist; b. St. Paul, July 25, 1925; s. Floyd Allen and Cora Jeanette (Heilig) McC.; m. Jule Ann Graham, Jan. 19, 1952 (div. 1983); children: Robert, Sharon; m. Molly Kathleen Bowers, Sept. 8, 1984. BA, Mich. State U., 1949; MSJ, Northwestern U., 1951. Reporter South Bend (Ind.) Tribune, 1949-50; reporter Chgo. Daily News, 1952-60, Washington corr., 1960-66, city editor, 1966-68; Washington corr. Knight-Ridder Newspapers, Miami, Fla., 1968-85, columnist, 1985—. With U.S. Army, 1943-45, ETO. Mem. Nat. Press Club, Gridiron Club (pres. 1987). Avocation: golf. Home: 4456 Springdale St NW Washington DC 20016-2716

MCCARTNEY, JAMES ROBERT, psychiatrist; b. Elmira, N.Y., Jan. 6, 1932; s. James L. and Edith T. (Tufs) McC; m. Lois McCartney; 4 children. BA, Ohio Wesleyan U., 1952; MD, Columbia U., 1955; MA (Ad Eundem)(hon.), Brown U., 1989. Diplomate Nat. Bd. Med. Examiners, Am. Bd. Pscyhiatry and Neurology, Am. Bd. Geriatric Psychiatry. Intern Boston City Hosp. for Medicine, 1955-56; resdient in psychiatry Elizabeth's Hosp., Washington, 1958-59; assoc. attending psychiatrist then attending psychiatrist North Shore U. Hosp., 1964-80, dir. tng. and edn. dept. psychiatry, 1972-79, chief of liaison svcs., 1973-80, assoc. dir., 1978-80; attending psychiatrist Meadowbrook Hosp., 1961-64; assoc. attending psychiatrist Nassau Hosp., 1964-71; on staff Butler Hosp., 1980—; psychiatrist-in-chief The Miriam Hosp., Providence, 1980—; adv. bd. Mental Health Assn. of Nassau County, 1972-80; cons. impaired physician com. R.I. Med. Soc., 1981—; asst. prof. psychiatry Brown U., Providence, 1980-88, assoc. prof., 1988—. Contbr. articles to profl. jours. Capt. U.S. Army, 1956-58. Fellow ACP, Am. Psychiat. Assn., Acad. of Psychosomatic Medicine; mem. AMA, R.I. Med. Soc., Am. Psychosomatic Soc., Assn. for Acad. Psychiatry, Providence Med. Assn., Am. Assn. Gen. Hosp. Psychiatrists, Gerontol. Soc. of Am., Am. Geriatrics Soc. Office: Miriam Hosp 164 Summit Ave Providence RI 02906-2800

MCCARTNEY, N.L., investment banker; b. Jameson, Mo., Oct. 12, 1923; m. Helen M. Walsh, Feb. 11, 1950; children: Patricia, Deborah, Patrick. BS, U. Md., 1956; MBA, Syracuse U., 1959; MPA, George Washington U., 1963. Enlisted U.S. Army, 1944, advanced through grades to col., ret., 1972; dir. S.W. Mo. Health Care Foun., Springfield, 1974-88; pres. Resource Mgmt. Co., Springfield, 1988-96; exec. v.p. Spencer and Assocs., Springfield, 1990-94; instr. Southwest Mo. State U., Springfield, 1972-82. Pres. S.W. Mo. Adv. Coun. Govts., Ozarks Crime Prevention Coun., 1983-93, Vis. Nurse Assn.; mayor of Springfield, 1993-95. Mem. Rotary. Methodist. Home:

1233 E Loren St Springfield MO 65804-0041 Office: PO Box 389 Springfield MO 65801

MCCARTNEY, PATRICK KEVIN, newspaper editor, writer; b. L.A., Sept. 9, 1948; s. Warren Phil and Mildred Pauline (Weiler) McC. BA, U. San Diego, 1970; MA, U. So. Calif., 1983. Statis. analyst L.A. County Probation Dept., Downey, Calif., 1973-79; writer Free Venice (Calif.) Beachhead, 1984-88; editor Westchester (Calif.) Jour., 1987-88; reporter Blade-Citizen newspaper, Solana Beach, Calif., 1988-89; staff writer Press-Courier, Oxnard, Calif., 1990-91; corr. L.A. Times, Ventura, Calif., 1991-94; mng. editor North Lake Tahoe Bonanza, Incline Village, Nev., 1994-96; sr. writer Tahoe Daily Tribune, South Lake Tahoe, Calif., 1996—. Pres. Venice Town Coun., 1984-86; candidate for L.A. City Coun., 1987. Mem. Venice Hist. Soc. (co-founder, bd. dirs. 1986-88), Encinitas Hist. Soc. (bd. dirs. 1989). Avocations: hiking, outdoor sports, natural science, Calif. history. Home: PO Box 5228 Incline Village NV 89450

MCCARTNEY, (JAMES) PAUL, musician; b. Liverpool, Eng., June 18, 1942; s. James and Mary Patricia (Mohin) McC.; m. Linda Eastman, Mar. 12, 1969; 4 children. Hon., Univ. Sussex, Brighton, 1988. With John Lennon and George Harrison in groups Quarrymen, Moondogs, Silver Beatles, 1956-62, also with Ringo Starr in group The Beatles, 1962-70, solo performer and with group, Wings, 1970-80, The Paul McCartney World Tour, 1989; film appearances include: A Hard Day's Night, 1964, Help!, 1965, Let It Be, 1970, Give My Regards to Broad Street, 1984, Get Back, 1991; TV appearances include Magical Mystery Tour, 1967, James Paul McCartney, 1973, Wings Over the World, 1979; producer animated film The Oriental Nightfish, 1978; composer numerous songs including (with John Lennon) Please Please Me, I Want To Hold Your Hand, All My Loving, Can't Buy Me Love, I Saw Her Standing There, Love Me Do, Yesterday, Michelle, She's a Woman, Here, There and Everywhere, Good Day Sunshine, Penny Lane, She's Leaving Home, Fool on the Hill, Back in the USSR, Martha My Dear, Blackbird, Helter Skelter, Hey Jude, Let It Be, The Long and Winding Road, Get Back, (solo) Maybe I'm Amazed, My Love, Live and Let Die, Band on the Run, Silly Love Songs, Another Day, No More Lonely Nights, With a Little Luck; rec. artist: (albums with The Beatles) Meet the Beatles, Introducing the Beatles, Hard Day's Night, Help!, Rubber Soul, Revolver, Sgt. Pepper's Lonely Hearts Club Band, Magical Mystery Tour, The Beatles, Yellow Submarine, Abbey Road, Hey Jude, Let It Be; solo albums include McCartney, 1970, Ram, 1971, Red Rose Speedway, 1973, Band on the Run, 1973, Venus and Mars, 1975, Wings Over America, 1975, Wings at the Speed of Sound, 1976, London Town, 1978, Wings Greatest, 1978, Back to the Egg, 1979, McCartney II, 1980, Tug of War, 1982, Press to Play, 1986, All The Best, 1987, Flowers in the Dirt, 1989, Jet, 1989, Tripping the Live Fantastic,1990, Unplugged/The Official Bootleg, 1991, Off the Ground, 1993, Paul is Live, 1993; composer The Liverpool Oratorio, 1991. Decorated Order of Brit. Empire, 1965; recipient Acad. award (with Beatles) for Best Original Song Score, Let It Be, 1970, 5 Grammy awards with Beatles, 2 solo, 1 with Wings, Ivor Novello award for outstanding services to Brit. music, 1989; named to Rock and Roll Hall of Fame, 1988, Lifetime Achievement award, 1990.

MC CARTNEY, RALPH FARNHAM, lawyer; b. Charles City, Iowa, Dec. 11, 1924; s. Ralph C. and Helen (Farnham) McC.; J.D., U. Mich., 1950; B. Sci., Iowa State U., 1972; m. Rhoda Mae Huxsol, June 30, 1950; children: Ralph, Julia, David. Bar: Iowa 1950. Mem. firm Miller, Heuber & Miller, Des Moines, 1950-52, Frye & McCartney, Charles City, 1952-73, McCartney & Erb, Charles City, 1973-78; judge Dist. Ct. Iowa, Charles City, 1978-87; chief judge 2d. Judicial Dist., 1987-92; sr. judge Ct. Appeals, 1992—; mem. jud. coordinating com. Iowa Supreme Ct. Chmn. Supreme Ct. Adv. Com. on Adminstrn. of Clks. Offices; mem. Iowa Ho. of Reps., 1967-70, majority floor leader, 1969-70; mem. Iowa Senate, 1973-74. Bd. regents U. Iowa, Iowa State U., U. No. Iowa, Iowa Sch. for Deaf, Iowa Braille and Sight Saving Sch. Served with AUS, 1942-45. Mem. Iowa Bar Assn., Iowa Judges Assn. Home: 1828 Cedar View Dr Charles City IA 50616-9129 Office: Cty Chambers Courthouse Charles City IA 50616

MCCARTNEY, RHODA HUXSOL, farm manager; b. Floyd County, Iowa, June 30, 1928; d. Julius Franklin and Ruth Ada (Carney) Huxsol; m. Ralph Farnham McCartney, June 25, 1950; children: Ralph, Julia, David. AA, Frances Shimer, 1948; BA, U. Iowa, 1950. Mng. dir. McCartney-Huxsol Farms, Charles City, Iowa, 1969—; prin. trustee J.F. Huxsol Trusts, Charles City, Iowa, 1984—. Pres. Nat. 19th Amendment Soc., Charles City, 1991—; mem. Terace Hill Commn., Des Moines, 1988-94; bd. dirs. Iowa Children and Family Svcs., Des Moines, 1963-68; mem. Iowa. Arts Coun., Des Moines, 1974-78. Mem. AAUW, Iowa LWV, PEO. Congregationalist. Avocations: church work, gardening, travel. Home: 1828 Cedar View Dr Charles City IA 50616-9129 Office: McCartney-Huxsol Farms 117 N Jackson St Charles City IA 50616-2002

MC CARTNEY, ROBERT CHARLES, lawyer; b. Pitts., May 3, 1934; s. Nathaniel Hugh and Esther Mary (Smith) McC.; m. Janet Carolyn Moore, June 16, 1956; children: Ronald K., Sharon S., Carole J. AB, Princeton U., 1956; JD, Harvard U., 1959. Bar: D.C. 1959, Pa. 1960, U.S. Dist. Ct. (we. dist.) Pa. 1960, U.S. Ct. Appeals (3d dist.) 1960, U.S. Supreme Ct. 1966. Assoc. Eckert, Seamans, Cherin & Mellott, Pitts., 1959-64, ptnr., 1965-93, mem. exec. com., 1991-93, of counsel, 1993—; sec., gen. counsel Ryan Homes, Inc., 1969-93; bd. dirs. United Meth. Found. of Western Pa., 1971—, v.p., 1981-85, chmn., 1985-86; gen. coun. Rimoldi of Am., Inc., 1989—. Solicitor North Pitts. Cmty. Devel. Corp., 1968-76, alt. dir., 1968-80; mem. McCandless Twp. Govt. Study Commn., 1973-74; solicitor, asst. sec. McCandless Indsl. Devel. Authority, 1972—; mem. exec. com. Princeton U. Alumni coun., 1966-70, 76=85, vice chmn., 1981-83, chmn., 1983-85, co-chair Spl. Com. for 250th Anniversary of Princeton U.; trustee Otterbein Coll., 1975-83, Pa. S.W. Assn., 1992—, Pitts. Cultural Trust, 1992—; copr. bd. North Hills Passavant Hosp., 1976—; chmn. conf.-wide endowment program Untied Meth. Conf. Western Pa., 1985-87; bd. dirs. Pitts. Civic Light Opera Assn., 1986—, v.p., 1987-92, pres., 1992—; gen. counsel, dir. The Ireland Inst. Pitts., 1991—; mem. No. Ireland Partnership, 1991—. Princeton fellow Harvard U., 1956-59. Mem. ABA, Pa. Bar Assn., Internat. Bar Assn., Allegheny County Bar Assn., Princeton U. Alumni Assn. West Pa. (pres. 1976-78), Duquesne Club, Princeton Club, Nassau Club. Republican. Home: 9843 Woodland Rd Pittsburgh PA 15237-4362 Office: Eckert Seamans Cherin & Mellott 600 Grant St Ste 42 Pittsburgh PA 15219-2703

MC CARTY, BRUCE, architect; b. South Bend, Ind., Dec. 28, 1920; s. Earl Hauser and Hazel (Beagle) McC.; m. Julia Elizabeth Hayes, Apr. 5, 1945; children: Bruce Hayes, Douglas Hayes, Sarah Elizabeth. B.A., Princeton U., 1944; B.Arch., U. Mich., 1949. Ptnr. Painter, Weeks & McCarty, 1955-65, Bruce McCarty & Assocs., 1965-70; pres. McCarty Bullock Holsaple (Architects, Planners, Engrs., Inc.), Knoxville, Tenn., 1970-84; pres., chmn. McCarty Holsaple McCarty (Architects), Knoxville, Tenn., 1984—; Mem. Knox County Met. Planning Commn., 1967-72; master architect planner 1982 World's Fair, 1976-82; prin. architect Knoxville Waterfront Master Plan, 1989. Works include residential, pub. and instnl. architecture. Trustee Dulin Gallery of Art, 1969-74; bd. dirs., co-founder East Tenn. Cmty. Design Ctr., 1970-80; bd. dirs. Knoxville Beautification Bd., 1984-87, 89-91, Knoxville Arts Coun., 1984-87; exec. com. Mayor's Waterfront Task Force, 1989; chair Design Tenn., 1992—. 2d lt. USAAF, 1942-45. Recipient AIA EFL 1st honor for Humanities Bldg. U. Tenn.; Prestressed Concrete Inst. award for Mountain View Parking Garages; AIA regional awards for Humanities Bldg., Clarence Brown Theatre, Townview Terrace Housing, U. Tenn., Pedestrian Bridge, Art and Architecture Bldg., St. Johns Luth. Ch.; State of Tenn. Competition winner for U. Tenn. Art and Architecture Bldg., 1975; Mayor's award for Arts, 1975, 82; U. Tenn. Chancellor's assoc.; E. Tenn. chpt. AIA award, 1982; named to Leadership Knoxville, 1994—. Fellow AIA; mem. Tenn. Soc. Architects (pres. 1972), Knoxville C. of C. (dir. 1965-69). Presbyterian (elder). Office: Mc Carty Holsaple Mc Carty Inc Nations Bank Ctr 550 W Main Ave Knoxville TN 37902-2567

MCCARTY, DENNIS L., insurance executive; b. Des Moines, Aug. 27, 1937; s. Francis L. McCarty and Edna V. (Olson) Hall; m. S. Jane Umsted, Sept. 5, 1970; children: Cindy, Adam. BS, Drake U., 1966. CLU, ChFC. Patrolman Des Moines Sheriff's Dept., 1966-69; capt. Johnston (Iowa) Police Dept., 1970-73; sales rep. Travelers Ins. Co., Des Moines, 1973-75, agy. supr., 1975-76; regional mktg. dir. Old Am. Ins. Co., Kansas City, Mo., 1976-79, regional v.p., 1979-87, v.p., 1987—. Sgt. U.S. Army, 1954-62. Mem. Amvets (pub. rels. officer State of Iowa 1964-65), Shriners, Masons, Scottish Rite, Am. Soc. CLU & ChFC. Avocations: golf, boating.

MCCARTY, DONALD JAMES, retired education educator; b. Ulster, Pa., July 17, 1921; s. James Leonard and Louise (Golden) McC.; m. Mary Elizabeth Donahue, Aug. 23, 1951; children: Mary Louise, Donald James, Kevin, Maureen. B.S. cum laude, Columbia U., 1949; M.A., Tchrs. Coll., Columbia U., 1950; Ph.D., U. Chgo., 1959. Jr. high sch. tchr. Brookings, S.D., 1950-51; sr. high sch. tchr. Toms River, N.J., 1951- 52, Brookings, 1952-53; supt. schs. Colman, S.D., 1953-56; staff assoc. U. Chgo., 1956-59; prof. ednl. adminstrn. Cornell U., Ithaca, N.Y., 1959-66; dean U. Wis. Sch. Edn., Madison, 1966-75; prof. ednl. adminstrn. U. Wis. Sch. Edn., 1975-95. Author: (with Charles E. Ramsey) The School Managers: Power and Conflict in American Public Education, 1971, The Dilemma of the Deanship, 1980; also articles. Served to maj. USAAF, 1939-46. Mem. Nat. Coun. Profs. Ednl. Adminstrn. Home: 2926 Harvard Dr Madison WI 53705-2206

MCCARTY, FREDERICK BRIGGS, electrical engineer; b. Dilley, Tex., Aug. 11, 1926; s. John Frederick Briggs and Olive Ruth (Snell) Briggs McCarty; m. Doris Mary Cox, May 3, 1950 (div. 1970); children: Mark Frederick, David Lambuth, Jackson Clare; m. Nina Lucile Butman, Aug. 17, 1973. B.S.E.E., U. Tex., 1949. Registered profl. engr., Calif. Design engr. Gen. Electric Co., Schenectady, N.Y., 1949-51; sr. design engr. Convair, Ft. Worth, Tex., 1951-55; sr. engr. Aerojet Gen., Azusa, Calif., 1955-61; sr. engrng. specialist Garrett Corp., Torrance, Calif., 1961-91; v.p., founder Patio Pacific, Inc., Torrance, 1973-84; owner, operator Textiger Co., Torrance, 1980-91; cons., 1991—. Author computer software, Textiger word processor, Tiger Tools, Big Mag and Roundrot generator synthesizers. Designer superconducting acyclic motor for U.S. Navy and various high speed elec. machines for aerospace and transp. Patentee in field. Served with USNR, 1944-46, PTO. Mem. IEEE (sr. life), Tau Beta Pi, Eta Kappa Nu. Democrat. Home and Office: 1366 Stonewood Ct San Pedro CA 90732-1550

MCCARTY, HARRY DOWNMAN, tool manufacturing company executive; b. Balt., Aug. 30, 1946; s. H. Downman and Melissa (Dunham) McC.; m. Helen Hilliard, May 13, 1948; children: Cormac Downman, Henning Hilliard. BA, Johns Hopkins U., 1968. Math. instr. Gilman Sch., Balt., 1970-71; sales mgr. Balt. Tool Works Inc., Balt., 1971-79, pres., 1979—; bd. dirs. Tool Ins. Co., Ltd., Hamilton, Bermuda. Co-chmn. Robert Nicolls scholarship fund Friends Sch., Balt., 1986-89. 1st lt. U.S. Army, 1968-70. Recipient Barton Cup winner for campus leadership, Johns Hopkins U., 1968, 1st Team All-Am.-Lacrosse, 1968. Mem. Hand Tools Inst. (bd. dirs. 1985-86, 1990-92)), Am. Hardware Mfg. Assn., Am. Supply and Machinery Mfg. Assn., Specialty Tools and Fastener Distbn. Assn., Am. Soc. Metals, Md. Club, L'Hirondelle Club (bd. dirs. 1989-92)), ODK Hon. Soc. Republican. Episcopalian. Avocations: tennis, squash, platform tennis, flyfishing. Office: Balt Tool Works Inc 110 W West St Baltimore MD 21230-3725

MCCARTY, MACLYN, medical scientist; b. South Bend, Ind., June 9, 1911; s. Earl Hauser and Hazel Dell (Beagle) McC.; m. Anita Alleyne Davies, June 20, 1934 (div. 1966); children: Maclyn, Richard E., Dale, Colin; m. Marjorie Steiner, Sept. 3, 1966. AB, Stanford U., 1933; MD, Johns Hopkins U., 1937; ScD (hon.), Columbia U., 1976, U. Fla., 1977, Rockefeller U., 1982, Med. Coll. Ohio, 1985, Emory U., 1987, Wittenberg U., 1989; MD (hon.), U. Cologne, Fed. Republic Germany, 1988; LHD (hon.), Mount Sinai Sch. of Medicine, 1995. House officer, asst. resident physician Johns Hopkins Hosp., 1937-40; assoc. Rockefeller Inst., 1946-48, assoc. mem., 1948-50, mem., 1950—, prof., 1957—, v.p., 1965-78, physician in chief to hosp., 1961-74; research in streptococcal disease and rheumatic fever; Cons. USPHS, NIH. Author: The Transforming Principle: Discovering That Genes are Made of DNA, 1985. Mem. distbn. com. N.Y. Community Trust, 1966-74; chmn. Health Research Council City N.Y., 1972-75; Mem. bd. trustees Helen Hay Whitney Found; chmn. bd. dirs. Pub. Health Research Inst. of N.Y., 1985-92. Served with Naval Med. Research Unit, Rockefeller Hosp. USNR, 1942-46. Fellow medicine N.Y. U. Coll. Medicine, 1940-41; NRC fellow med. scis. Rockefeller Inst., 1941-42; Recipient Eli Lilly award in bacteriology and immunology, 1946, 1st Waterford Biomed. Rsch. award, 1977, Wolf Found. prize in medicine, Israel, 1990, Lasker Spl. Pub. Health award, 1994. Mem. Am. Soc. for Clin. Investigation, Am. Assn. Immunologists, Soc. Am. Bacteriologists, Soc. for Exptl. Biology and Medicine (pres. 1973-75), Harvey Soc. (sec. 1947-50, pres. 1971-72), N.Y. Acad. Medicine, Assn. Am. Physicians (Kober medal 1989), Nat. Acad. Scis. (Kovalenko medal 1988), Am. Acad. Arts and Scis., N.Y. Heart Assn. (1st v.p. 1967, pres. 1969-71), Am. Philos. Soc. Home: 400 E 56th St New York NY 10022-4147 Office: Rockefeller U 66th St and York Ave New York NY 10021

MCCARTY, RICHARD CHARLES, psychology educator; b. Portsmouth, Va., July 12, 1947; s. Constantine Ambrose and Helen Marie (Householder) McC.; m. Sheila Adair Miltier, July 12, 1965; children: Christopher Charles, Lorraine Marie, Ryan Lester, Patrick James. BS in Biology, Old Dominion U., 1970, MS in Zoology, 1972; PhD in Pathobiology, Johns Hopkins U., 1976. Rsch. assoc. NIMH, Bethesda, Md., 1976-78; asst. prof. U. Va., Charlottesville, 1978-84, assoc. prof., 1984-88, prof., 1988—, chair psychology, 1990—, chair Coun. of Grad. Depts. Psychology, 1996—. Co-editor: Stress: Neuroendocrine and molecular Approaches, 1992; mem. editl. bd. Behavioral and Neural Biology, 1985-90, Physiology and Behavior, 1989—; editor-in-chief of Stress, 1995—; sec. gen. 6th Symposium on Stress, 1995; contbr. articles to profl. jours. Lt. comdr. USPHS, 1976-78. Recipient Rsch. Scientist Devel. award NIMH, 1985-90; sr. fellow Nat. Heart Lung Blood Inst., NIH, 1984-85. Fellow Soc. Behavioral Medicine, Acad. Behavioral Med. Rsch., Am. Psychol. Soc., Am. Inst. Stress, Coun. for High Blood Pressure Rsch., AHA. Roman Catholic. Avocations: sports, gardening. Office: U Va Dept Psychology 102 Gilmer Hall Charlottesville VA 22903

MCCARTY, RICHARD EARL, biochemist, biochemistry educator; b. Balt., May 3, 1938; s. Maclyn and Anita (Davies) McC.; m. Kathleen Connolly, June 17, 1961; children—Jennifer A., Richard E., Jr., Gregory P. A.B., Johns Hopkins U., 1960, Ph.D., 1964. Postdoctoral assoc. Pub. Health Research Inst., N.Y.C., 1964-66; asst. prof. Cornell U., Ithaca, N.Y., 1966-72, assoc. prof., 1972-77, prof., 1977-90, prof., chmn., 1981-85; dir. biotech. program Cornell U., Ithaca, 1988-90; prof., chmn. Johns Hopkins U., Balt., 1990—; mem. panel NSF, Washington, 1984-86; panel mgr. Photosynthesis and Respiration Program, USDA, Nat. Rsch. Initiative Competitive Grants Program, 1994. Author: (with D. Wharton) Experiments and Methods in Biochemistry, 1972; mem. editl. bd. Jour. Biol. Chemistry, 1978-88, 95—, assoc. editor, 1981-82; mem. editl. bd. Biochemistry, 1996; contbr. articles to profl. jours. Recipient Career Devel. award NIH, 1968-73, Charles F. Kettering award for Excellence in Photosynthesis Am. Soc. Plant Physiologists, 1994. Mem. AAAS, Am. Soc. Biochemistry and Molecular Biology, Am. Soc. Plant Physiologists. Home: 2204 Dalewood Rd Lutherville Timonium MD 21093-2701 Office: Johns Hopkins U Dept Biology 3400 N Charles St Baltimore MD 21218-2608

MC CARTY, ROBERT LEE, lawyer; b. New London, Conn., Mar. 1, 1920; s. Robert Patrick and Lyda (Griser) McC.; m. Eileen Joan Noone, Sept. 1, 1945; children: Michael N., Patrick J., Charles Barry. B.S., Bowdoin Coll., 1941; LL.B., Yale U., 1948; LL.M., Georgetown U., 1953. Bar: D.C. 1948, U.S. Supreme Ct 1953, Va. 1976. Assoc. Northcutt Ely, 1948-54; mem. Ely, McCarty & Duncan, 1955-60; ptnr. McCarty and Wheatley, 1961-67, McCarty & Noone, 1968-80, McCarty, Noone & Williams, 1981-87, Heron, Burchette, Ruckert & Rothwell, Washington, 1987-90, Ritts Brickfield & Kaufman, Washington, 1990-92, Brickfield, Burchette & Ritts, Washington, 1993—; mem. Adminstrv. Conf. U.S., 1972-74; mem. edn. appeals bd. U.S. Dept. Edn., 1978-83. Contbr. chpts. to books. Pres. bd. dirs. Belle Haven Citizens Assn., 1959-60. Served with USAAF, 1942-46; Served with USAF, 1951-53; col. Res. Decorated D.F.C. (2), Air medal with 3 oak leaf clusters, Army Commendation medal. Fellow Am. Bar Found.; mem. ABA (chmn. sect. adminstrv. law 1966-67), (sect. del. to ho. dels. 1968-70), Fed. Bar Assn., D.C.Bar Assn., Va. Bar Assn. Roman Catholic. Clubs: University (Washington), Belle Haven Country (Va.). Home: 2108 Woodmont Rd Alexandria VA 22307-1155 Office: 8th flr West Tower 1025 Thomas Jefferson St NW Washington DC 20007-5201 *If you are to be satisfied with your product, there is no substitute for work.*

MCCARTY, ROGER LELAND, chemical company official; b. Coos Bay, Oreg., Apr. 6, 1953; s. James Cleo and Dorothy Jean (Beach) McC.; m. Marsha Lee Peterson, Dec. 18, 1976; children: Margie, Heather, Aura Lee, Becky, Allison, Katy, Chelsea, Lori. BSChemE, Brigham Young U., 1977; MBA, Keller Grad. Sch. Mgmt., Chgo., 1981. Registered engr.-in-tng., Mich. Missionary LDS Ch., Washington, 1972-74; with mktg. devel. program Dow Chem. Co., Denver, 1977-78; sales rep. organic chems. Dow Chem. Co., Chgo., 1978-82; sr. sales specialist Dow Chem. Co., Houston, 1982-84, sales supr., 1984-85, mgr. product mktg., 1985-88; mgr. product mktg. Dow Chem. Co., Midland, Mich., 1988-89, mgr. bus. rsch. chems. and performance products dept., 1989-92, group mktg. mgr. new ventures, strategy facilitator, 1989-92, sr. econ. planning assoc. value-based mgmt., 1992-95; sr. VBM strategy devel. mgr. Dow Chem. Co., Midland, 1995—; sales trainer Dow Chem. Co., Houston, 1987-88; presenter in mktg. strategy field. Author: Value Based Strategy Development Guide Book, 1989-94; contbr. articles to profl. jours. Mem. Coos Bay Mayor's Adv. Coun., 1970-71; pres. men's group LDS Ch., Elgin, Ill., 1979-82; mem. stake high coun., Houston, Ill., 1979-82, 89-94, mem. Midland State Presidency, 1995—; explorer leader Boy Scouts Am., Houston, 1985-87; mem. Music Soc. Chorale, 1993-96, Camarata Singers, 1995, LDS choir dir., 1992-94; music and computer vol. elem. sch., Midland, 1989-90. Mem. AICE (sec.-treas. mktg. divsn. 1989-90, bd. dirs. 1986-89, nat. program dir. 1985-89, mem. nat. program com. 1985-89), Gas Processors Assn. (mem. com. 1987-88). Republican. Avocations: music, drama, sports, dancing, reading. Home: 1200 Wakefield Dr Midland MI 48640-2733 Office: Dow Chem Co Larkin Ctr Midland MI 48674

MCCARTY, THOMAS JOSEPH, publishing company executive; b. Waltham, Mass., June 10, 1938; s. Raymond Anthony and Mary Agatha (Riley) McC; m. Colette Ann Koechley, Aug. 3, 1963; children: Matthew Thomas, Brendan James, Sarah Katherine. BA, Holy Cross Coll., 1960; cert., Harvard U., 1961. Various mgmt. positions Oxford U. Press, N.Y.C., 1960-71, mgr. ops., 1971-79, dir. distbn., 1980-81, v.p. distbn., 1982-84, v.p. distbn. and info. systems, 1985-88, sr. v.p., 1988-90; sr. v.p.,gen. mgr. Oxford U. Press, Cary, N.C. ops., 1990—. Trustee N.C. Symphony Found.; mem. adv. adv. bd. Sch. Info. and Libr. Sci., U. N.C., Chapel Hill;; bd. dirs. Shakti for Children Found., English Speaking Union of Rsch. Triangle; mem. N.C. Mus. Art. Mem. Assn. Am. Pubs., Am. Mgmt. Assn., Capital City Club (Raleigh, N.C.), MacGregor Downs Country Club (Cary), Carolina Club, U. N.C. Faculty Club (Chapel Hill). Office: Oxford U Press Inc 2001 Evans Rd Cary NC 27513-2009

MCCARUS, ERNEST NASSEPH, retired language educator; b. Charleston, W.Va., Sept. 10, 1922; s. Nasseph Mitchell and Della (Saad) McC.; m. Adele Najib Haddad, Sept. 10, 1955; children: Peter Kevin, Carol Ann. Student, Morris Harvey Coll., 1939-40; A.B., U. Mich., 1945, M.A., 1949, Ph.D., 1956. Translation team capt. Allied Translators and Interpreters' Service, Allied Hqrs., Tokyo, Japan, 1946-47; mem. English Lang. Inst. staff U. Mich., 1948-52, mem. univ. expdn. to Near East, 1951, instr. univ., 1952-56, asst. prof. Arabic, 1956-61; dir. Fgn. Service Inst., Field Sch. Arabic Lang. and Area Study, U.S. Dept. State, Beirut, Lebanon, 1958-60; asso. prof. dept. Near Eastern studies U. Mich., 1961-67, prof., 1967-95, chmn. dept., 1969-77, dir. Center for Arabic Study Abroad, 1974-83, dir. U. Mich. Center for Near Eastern and North African Studies, 1983-92, assoc. dir. Ctr for Middle Eastern and North African Studies, 1995—, prof. emeritus, 1995—. Author: Grammar of Kurdish of Sulaimania, Iraq, 1958, (with H. Hoenigswald, R. Noss, J. Yamagiwa) A Survey of Intensive Programs in the Uncommon Languages, 1962, (with A. Yacoub) Elements of Contemporary Arabic, 1962, 3d edn., 1966, (with Raji Rammuny) First Level Arabic: Elementary Literary Arabic for Secondary Schools, 1964, Teacher's Manual to Accompany First Level Arabic, 1964, (with Jamal J. Abdullah) Kurdish Basic Course - Dialect of Sulaimania, Iraq, 1967, Kurdish Readers, Vol. I Newspaper Kurdish, Vol. II. Kurdish Essays, Vol. III Kurdish Short Stories, 1967, A Kurdish-English Dictionary, 1967, (with P. Abboud) Elementary Modern Standard Arabic, 1983, (with R. Rammuny) Word Count of Elementary Modern Literary Arabic Textbooks, 1969, (with P. Abboud, E.T. Abdel-Massih, S. Altoma, W. Erwin, R. Rammuny) Modern Standard Arabic Intermediate Level, 1971, (with R. Rammuny) A Programmed Course in Modern Literary Arabic Phonology and Script, 1974; editor: Language Learning, Vol. VII, 1956-57, Language Learning, Vol. XIII, 1963, An-Nashra, 1967-74, Contemporary Arabic Readers, Vols. I-V, 1962-66, The Development of Arab-American Identity, 1994; contbr. articles to scholastic jours. Served with AUS, 1942-46. Rockefeller fellow, 1951. Mem. Mich. Linguistic Soc. (pres. 1962-63), Am. Assn. Tchrs. Arabic (pres. 1973, exec. coun. 1979-81, 89-92), Middle East Studies Assn. (bd. dirs. 1973-75), Linguistic Soc. Am., Am. Oriental Soc., Linguistic Circle N.Y., Arabic Linguistic Soc. (pres. 1992). Home: 1400 Beechwood Dr Ann Arbor MI 48103-2940

MCCARVER, JAMES TIMOTHY, sportscaster; b. Memphis, Oct. 16, 1941; s. Grover Edward and Alice Levonia (Phelan) McC.; m. Anne McDaniel, Dec. 29, 1964; children: Kathryn Leigh, Kelly Lorraine. Student, Memphis State U., 1963-66. Catcher St. Louis Cardinals, 1959-69, 73, 74, Phila. Phillies, 1970-72, 75-79, Sept.-Oct., 1980, Montreal (Can.) Expos., June to Nov., 1972, Boston Red Sox, 1974-75; sportscaster Phila. Phillies, 1980-82, N.Y. Mets, WWOR-TV, 1983—; former sportscaster ABC Sports, N.Y.C., 1984; sportscaster CBS Sports, 1990—. Author: Oh Baby, I Love It, 1987; contbr. articles to sports mags. Chmn. fund raising McGee Rehab. Hosp., Phila., 1988. With U.S. Army, 1962-69. Recipient Emmy awards for local baseball broadcasting, 1986, 87; profl. baseball park named after him by Memphis Chicks, 1977. Mem. AFTRA. Roman Catholic. Avocations: bridge, reading, traveling. Office: care CBS Sports 51 W 52nd St New York NY 10019-6119

MCCARVILLE, MARK JOHN, food company executive; b. Moorland, Iowa, Sept. 13, 1946; s. Robert A. and Lucille (Hillman) McC.; m. Kathryn Mary Frith, June 3, 1972; children: Megan, Erin, Michael, Patrick. B.A., Loras Coll., 1968; M.B.A., U. Iowa, 1971. Asst. nat. bank examiner U.S. Treasury Dept., Chgo., 1968-72; bus. services officer Am. Nat. Bank, Chgo., 1972-76; sr. v.p. corp. devel. Sara Lee Corp., Chgo., 1976—. Bd. dirs. Chgo. Commons, 1990—, United Charities, 1991—. Office: Sara Lee Corp 3 First National Plz Chicago IL 60602*

MCCARY, STEPHEN C., health facility administrator. Adminstr., COO Stevens Meml. Hosp., Edmonds, Wash., 1989-90; adminstr., CEO Stevens Meml. Hosp., 1990—; dir. HealthSource, divsn. of Stevens Hosp. that focuses on health and wellness by offering ednl. programs, recorded health info. and physician referrals. Recipient Robert S. Hudgens Meml. award for young healthcare exec. of yr. Assn. Chief Healthcare Execs., 1995. Achievements include helping to create Stevens Health Network, a physician-hosp. org. that manages 5,500 lives and Health Washington, an independent network of physicians and hosps. dedicated to providing cmty. mems. with access to quality healthcare. Office: Stevens Meml Hosp 21601 76th Ave West Edmonds WA 98026*

MCCASKEY, EDWARD W., professional football team executive; b. Phila., Apr. 27; m. Virginia Halas; 11 children. Student, U. Pa., 1940. Mgr. merchandising Nat. Retail Tea and Coffee Assn., Chgo.; exec. v.p. Mdse. Services, Inc., Chgo.; account exec. E.F. McDonald Co., Chgo.; v.p., treas. Chgo. Bears, 1967-83, chmn. bd. dirs., 1983—. Served to capt., AUS. Office: Chgo Bears 55 E Jackson Blvd Ste 1200 Chicago IL 60604-4105 also: Chicago Bears Halas Hall 250 Washington Rd Lake Forest IL 60045-2471*

MCCASKEY, MICHAEL B., professional football team executive; b. Lancaster, Pa., Dec. 11, 1943; s. Edward B. and Virginia (Halas) McCaskey; m. Nancy McCaskey; children: John, Kathryn. Grad., Yale U., 1965; PhD, Case Western Res. U. Tchr. UCLA, 1972-75, Harvard U. Sch. Bus., Cambridge, Mass., 1975-82; pres., chief exec. officer Chgo. Bears (NFL), 1983—. Author: The Executive Challenge: Managing Change and Ambiguity. Named Exec. of Yr. Sporting News, 1985. Office: Chgo Bears Halas Hall 250 Washington Rd Lake Forest IL 60045-2471

MC CASKEY, RAYMOND F., insurance company executive; b. 1942. With Continental Assurance Co., Chgo., 1963-73; with Health Care Svc. Corp., Chgo., 1976—, now pres., CEO. Office: Health Care Service Corp 233 N Michigan Ave Chicago IL 60601-5519*

MCCASLIN, BOBBY D., soil scientist, educator; b. Wichita, Kans., July 26, 1943; s. Floyd and Alice (Rosendale) McC.; m. Betty L. Shinn, Dec. 19, 1964; children: Michael D., Nancy L. MS, Colo. State U., 1969; PhD, U. Minn., 1974. Rsch. asst. Colo. State U., Ft. Collins, 1966-69; rsch. fellow in soil sci. U. Minn., St. Paul, 1969-74; asst. prof. agronomy N.Mex. State U., Las Cruces, 1974-80, assoc. prof., 1980-87, prof. agronomy, 1987—, asst. dept. head, 1990—; program bd. adminstr. Great Plains Soil Fertilizer Workshop, Soil, Water, Air Testing Lab. Contbr. numerous articles to profl. jours. Recipient Svc. award, Coll. Agr., Las Cruces, 1990. Mem. Am. Soc. Agronomy, Soil Sci. Soc. Am., Western Soil Sci. Soc., Sigma Xi. Achievements include research on utilization of wastes for plant nutrients and soil amendments; plant mineral nutrition and soil management, genetic selection of plants to better fit problem soils. Home: 2030 Tyre Cir Las Cruces NM 88001-5816 Office: NM State U Agl and Hort Dept 3Q Las Cruces NM 88003

MCCASLIN, RICHARD BRYAN, history educator; b. Atlanta, Feb. 21, 1961; s. Jerry L. and Ann Elizabeth (Sharman) McC.; m. Jana Dawn Maryovich, Apr. 5, 1979; 1 child, Christina Michele. BA, Delta State U., 1982; MA, La. State U., 1983; PhD, U. Tex., 1988. Tchg. asst. La. State U., 1982-83, grad. asst. La. Bus. Rev., 1983; tchg. asst. U. Tex., Austin, 1983-87, rsch. assoc., 1984-87; rsch. asst. prof. U. Tenn., Knoxville, 1988-90; asst. prof. history High Point (N.C.) U., 1990-94, assoc. prof., 1994—; instr. Pellissippi State C.C., 1988-89, Roane State C.C., 1989; adj. prof. Corpus Christi (Tex.) State U., 1989; lectr. East Tenn. Hist. Soc., 1990; rsch. cons. Huston-Tillotson Coll., 1985-86, Tex. Senate, 1986-89, Nat. Pk. Svc., 1989-90; assoc. historian Futurepast: History Co., Spokane, Wash., 1987-89; presenter Southwestern Social Sci. Assn., AAAS. Author: (with Earnest F. Gloyna) Commitment to Excellence: One Hundred Years of Engineering Education at The University of Texas at Austin, 1986, Andrew Johnson: A Bibliography, 1992, Portraits of Conflict: A Photographic History of South Carolina in the Civil War, 1994, Tainted Breeze: The Great Hanging at Gainesville, Texas, October 1862, 1994 (Tullis prize Tex. State Hist. Assn.), Remembered Be Thy Blessings: High Point University—The College Years, 1924-1991, 1995; contbr. chpt. to: 100 Years of Science and Technology in Texas: A Sigma Xi Centennial Volume, 1986; columnist Greensboro News and Record, 1993-94; referee Southwestern Hist. Quar., 1990—; asst. editor, then assoc. editor Papers of Andrew Johnson, U. Tenn., 1988-90; contbr. articles and book revs. to various profl. publs. U. Tex. dissertation fellow, 1987-88, Clara H. Driscoll fellow in Tex. history Daus. of Republic of Tex., 1985-87; James H. and Minnie M. Edmonds Ednl. Found. scholar, 1983-85, Colonial Dames Am. grad. scholar, 1987. Mem. So. Hist. Assn. (presenter), Soc. Civil War Historians, Tex. State Hist. Assn. (presenter). Espiscopalian. Home: 714 Ferndale Blvd High Point NC 27262 Office: High Point Univ Dept History and Polit Sci High Point NC 27260

MCCAUGHEY, ELIZABETH P. (BETSY MCCAUGHEY), state official; b. Oct. 20, 1948; d. Albert Peterkin; m. Thomas McCaughey, 1972 (div. 1994); children: Amanda, Caroline, Diana. BA, Vassar Coll., 1970; MA, Columbia Univ., 1972, PhD, 1976. Public policy expert Manhattan Inst., N.Y.C.; lt. gov. State of N.Y., 1995—; instr. Vassar Coll., 1979, Columbia Univ., 1980-84; chmn. Governor's Medicaid Task Force, 1994. Author: From Loyalist to Founding Father, 1980, Government By Choice, 1987; also articles including an article in The New Republic (Nat. Mag. award for Pub. Policy 1995). Recipient Bancroft Dissertation award, Richard B. Morris prize; Woodrow Wilson fellow, Herbert H. Lehman fellow, Honorary Vassar fellow, John Jay fellow, Post Doctoral Rsch. fellow NEH, 1984, John Molin fellow Manhattan Inst., 1993, sr. fellow Ctr. Study of the Presidency. Republican. Office: Office of Lt Governor Executive Chamber State Capitol Rm 326 Albany NY 12224*

MCCAULEY, BRUCE GORDON, financial consultant; b. St. Louis; s. William Maurice and Evylin Adele (Halbert) McC.; m. Barbara Allen Stevens, Mar. 16, 1945 (dec.); children: David S., Sharon; m. Gwen Crumpton Cummings, Nov. 25, 1967. Student, U. Mo., 1939-41, Yale U., 1944; BS in Engring., U. Calif., Berkeley, 1948, MBA, 1949, MS in Indsl. Engring., 1952. Registered profl. engr., N.Y., Calif., Hawaii. Asst. purchasing agt. Curtis Mfg. Co., St. Louis, 1941-43; teaching asst. U. Calif., Berkeley, 1948-49, asst. prof. mech. engring., 1950-56, chmn. indsl. engring. inst., 1954-55; design engr. Standard Oil Co. of Calif., 1949-50; sr. ptnr. McCauley & Dunmire, San Francisco, 1952-56; v.p. Shand & Jurs Co., Berkeley, 1956-58, dir., 1957-60, exec. v.p., 1958-60; asst. to pres. Honolulu Star-Bulletin, 1960-62; gen. mgr. Christian Sci. Pub. Soc., Boston, 1962-69; gen. mgr., sec. N.Y. Daily News Inc., N.Y.C., 1969-74, v.p., 1971-73, sr. v.p., 1973-75, asst. to pres., 1974-75, dir., 1971-75; v.p. Daseke & Co. Inc., Westport, Conn., 1975-77, sr. v.p., 1977-86, mgr. West Coast office, 1978-86; vis. scholar Principia Coll., Elsah, Ill., 1988-91; pres., dir. Rossmoor Mut. 48 Corp., Walnut Creek, 1994—. Bd. dirs. Better Bus. Bur., N.Y.C., 1973-77, N.Y.C. Conv. and Visitors Bur., 1974-77, Albert Baker Found., 1979-90, Asher Found., 1983-93, Sopac Energy Corp., 1986-92. Capt. USAAF, 1943-46, PTO. Mem. ASME (life), Am. Inst. Indsl. Engrs., Nat. Assn. Accts., Nat. Soc. Profl. Engrs., U. Calif. Alumni Assn., Principia Alumni Assn., Sigma Xi, Tau Beta Pi, Beta Gamma Sigma, Pi Mu Epsilon. Christian Scientist. Club: Rossmoor Golf (Walnut Creek). Lodges: Masons (32 deg.), Kiwanis. Home: 3266 Ptarmigan Dr Apt 3B Walnut Creek CA 94595-3149

MCCAULEY, FLOYCE REID, psychiatrist; b. Braddock, Pa., Dec. 30, 1933; d. John Mitchel and Irene (Garner) Reid; m. James Calvin McCauley, July 15, 1955; children: James Stanley, Lori Ellen. BS in Nursing, U. Pitts., 1956; D.O., Coll. Osteopathic Medicine, Phila., 1972. Bd. eligible in child and adult psychiatry. Intern Suburban Gen. Hosp., Norristown, Pa., 1972-73; resident in adult psychiatry Phila. State Hosp. and Phila. Mental Health Clinic, 1973-75; fellow Med. Coll. of Pa. and Ea. Pa. Psychiat. Inst., Phila., 1975-78; Chief child psychiatry inpatient unit Med. Coll. Pa., Phila., 1978-80; med. dir. Carson ValleySch., Flourtown, Pa., 1980-82; dir. outpatient psychiat. clinic Osteopathic Med. Ctr. Phila., 1980-86; staff psychiatrist Kent Gen. Hosp., Dover, Del., 1986-89; psychiat. cons. Del. Guidance Svcs. for Children, Dover, 1986-91; clin. dir. children's unit HCA Rockford Ctr., Newark, 1991-93; with Kid's Peace Nat. Hosp. for Kids in Crisis, 1993-95, Pa. Found., Sellersville, 1995—; mem. Mental Health Code Rev. Com. for Del., 1991; inducted into the Chapel of Four Chaplains, Phila., 1983; psychiat. cons. Seaford (Del.) Br. of New Eng. Fellowship for Rehab., 1991-93, Cath. Charities Day Treatment Program for 3-6 Yr. Olds, Dover, Del., 1990—; cons. Del. Guidance Day Treatment Program, 1990—; staff psychiatrist Kids Peace Nat. Hosp. for Kids in Crisis, 1993-95, Penn Found., 1995—. Mem. Mayor's Com. for Mental Health, Phila., 1983. Mem. Am. Osteopathic Assn., Am. Coll. Neuropsychiatrists, Am. Psychiat. Assn., Am. Acad. Child Psychiatrists (Del. br.). Democrat. Methodist. Avocations: sewing, decorating, knitting, playing classical guitar, drawing, painting, gardening.

MCCAULEY, LISA FRANCINE, elementary education educator; b. New Haven, Feb. 15, 1966; d. Fred and Elaine Carolyn (Webb) McC. AA, Mt. Sacred Heart Coll., Hamden, Conn., 1988; BA in History, So. Conn. State U., 1989, MS in History, 1992. Cert. secondary edn. grades 7-12, Conn. Tchr. St. Lawrence Sch., West Haven, Conn., 1989—; adj. prof. So. Conn. State U., New Haven, 1993—. Vol. Conn. Spl. Olympics, New Haven, 1989—; dist. coord. Nat. History Day, Conn. Hist. Soc., Hartford, 1993—. Recipient cert. for dedicated svcs. and encouragement of student participation Conn. Hist. Soc., Hartford, 1992, cert. appreciation Jr. Achievement, Wallingford, Conn., 1992. Mem. AAUP, Nat. Cath. Edn. Assn., Conn. Coun. for the Social Studies, Conn. and New Haven Hist. Socs., Conn. Geographic Alliance, Conn. Humanities Coun. Roman Catholic. Avocations: musician, reading. Home: PO Box 4291 590 Benham St Hamden CT 06514

MCCAULEY, MICHAEL STEPHEN, lawyer; b. Dubuque, Iowa, Sept. 2, 1947; s. Francis P. and Alberta (Maiers) McC.; m. Patricia Hanna, July 29, 1972; children: Maura, Michael, Meghan. BA, U. Notre Dame, 1969; MPA, Harvard U., 1974; JD, U. Iowa, 1977. Bar: Wis. 1977, U.S. Dist. Ct. (ea. and we. dists.) Wis. 1977, U.S. Ct. Appeals (7th cir.) 1977. Vol. U.S. Peace Corps, Sri Lanka and South Korea, 1969-71; ptnr. Quarles & Brady, Milw., 1971—; mem. adv. bd. Wis. Environ. Law and Regulation Report; speaker in field. Bd. editors Iowa Law Rev., 1976-77; contbr. articles to profl. jours. Dir. Indo-Chinese Refugee Program; chmn. bd. rev. Village of Shorewood, 1980-90. Mem. ABA (vice chmn. environ. quality com. 1990-92, air quality com. 1993-95), Environ. Law Inst., State Bar Wis. (dir. environ. law sect. 1990-93), Wis. Air and Waste Mgmt. Assn. (bd. dirs.), Wis. Environ. Regulatory Group, Wis. Mfrs. and Commerce Assn., Milw. Bar Assn., Order of Coif. Avocations: golf, running. Office: Quarles & Brady 411 E Wisconsin Ave Milwaukee WI 53202-4409

MC CAULEY, R. PAUL, criminologist, educator; b. Highspire, Pa., Jan. 13, 1943; s. Paul Herbert and Frances Vaden (Harper) McC.; m. Gail Lee Gummo, Jan. 30, 1965; 1 child, Brent Clayton. A.S., Harrisburg Area Community Coll., 1968; B.S., Va. Commonwealth U., 1969; M.S., Eastern Ky. U., 1971; Ph.D. (fellow), Sam Houston U., 1973; certificate Home Office Detective Tng. Course, Eng., 1967. Diplomate Am. Coll. Forensic Examiners. Police officer Highspire Police, 1964-69; adminstr. Burns Internat. Security Services Inc., 1969-71; prof. police sci. and adminstrn., dir. grad. studies in adminstrn. of justice U. Louisville, 1973-82; prof., chmn. dept. criminology Indiana U. of Pa., 1982—; co-founder Sempas Security and Safety Technologies, 1980; advisor Reagan Presdl./Congressional Task Force on Criminal Justice, 1980; mem. staff So. Police Inst., 1973-82, Nat. Crime Prevention Inst., 1973-82; researcher, ptnr. McShan Assocs., 1974-85; cons. U.S. Congress Com. on Emergency Communications, 1967. Co-author: The Criminal Justice System, 1976, 3d edit., 1984; co-founder, editor: Criminal Justice Policy Rev., 1984-86; contbr. chpts. to books, articles to profl. jours.; patents. Active Metro Child Abuse Program, Crime Clinic of Greater Harrisburg, 1965-74; mem. Lower Swatara Twp. Police Civil Service Commn., 1967-69. Served with USMC, 1962-66. Recipient Mayor's Citation, City of Louisville, 1982, Gold medal Educator of the 1980's; honoree Silliman Coll., Yale U., 1984; Fulbright scholar, lectr., Australia, 1987. Mem. Acad. Criminal Justice Scis. (exec. bd. 1980-83, pres. 1985), Navy League (award for disting. community service). Home: 4620 Lucerne Rd Indiana PA 15701-8950 Office: Indiana U of Pa 204 Walsh Hall Indiana PA 15705 *One's philosophy, spirit, and drive contributes more to his relative success than do economic resources, social position, planning, or timing.*

MCCAULEY, ROBERT WILLIAM, biologist, educator; b. Toronto, Ont., Can., July 8, 1926; s. Herbert and Mary (Mahaffy) McC.; m. Erika Augusta Hinz, May 19, 1956; children—Eva-Maria, Heidi, Friedrich. BEd, U. Toronto, 1952, B.A., 1955; student, U. Tuebingen, Federal Republic of Germany, 1955; Ph.D., U. Western Ont., 1962. Cert. fisheries biologist. Asst. scientist Fisheries Research Bd. Can., 1956-62; research scientist Ont. Dept. Lands and Forests, Toronto, 1962-65; prof. Wilfrid Laurier U., Waterloo, Ont., 1965-92, prof. emeritus, 1992—; pres. Robert McCauley & Assocs. Aquatic Ecologists, Inc.; cons. Ont. Hydro;. Contbr. articles to profl. jours. Mem. Am. Fisheries Soc., Am. Inst. Biol. Scis., Am. Lake Mgmt. Soc., Internat. Assn. for Great Lakes Rsch. Lutheran. Home: 118 Forest Hill Dr, Kitchener, ON Canada N2M 4G3 Office: 75 University Ave, Waterloo, ON Canada

MCCAUSLAND, THOMAS JAMES, JR., brokerage house executive; b. Cleve., Nov. 27, 1934; s. Thomas James and Jean Anna (Hanna) McC.; m. Kathryn Margaret Schacht, Feb. 9, 1957; children: Thomas James III, Andrew John, Theodore Scott. BA in Econs., Beloit (Wis.) Coll., 1956. V.p. A.G. Becker & Co., Inc., Chgo., 1959-74; v.p. The Chgo. Corp., 1974-76, sr. v.p., dir., 1976-83, exec. v.p., 1983-90, vice chmn., 1991—; pres. The Chgo. Corp. Internat., 1990—; also bd. dirs. The Chgo. Corp.; bd. dirs. Chicorp, Inc., The Founders Fund, Naples, Fla.; bd. dirs., treas. The LaSalle St. Coun., Chgo. v.p. Hospice the North Shore, Evanston, Ill., 1986-90; bd. dirs. McCormick Theol. Sem., Chgo., 1971-79, Presbyn. Home, Evanston, 1968-74; trustee Beloit Coll., 1987-90. Lt. USN, 1956-59. Mem. Securities Industry Assn. (investment mgmt. com. 1979-82), Union League, United Presbyn. Found. (trustee, vice-chmn. 1980-86), Skokie Country Club (bd. dirs. 1983-85, pres. 1993), Pelican Bay Club (Naples, Fla.), Royal Poinciana Golf Club (Naples). Republican. Avocations: travel, Am. history, golf. Office: The Chgo Corp 208 S La Salle St Chicago IL 60604-1003

MCCAW, BRUCE R., insurance executive, airline and communications executive; b. Washington, June 26, 1946; s. J. Elroy and Marion O. (Oliver) McC. Student Colo. Coll., 1964-66, U. Wash., 1967-68. Lic. ins. broker, comml. pilot. Pres. Jet Air Corp., Everett, Wash., 1968-72, Delta Aviation Ins. Brokers Inc., Bellevue, Wash., 1972-80; v.p. and dir. McCaw Communications Cos. Inc., Bellevue, 1969—, Horizon Air Industries Inc., Seattle, 1981-87; chmn. Westar Ins. Group Inc., Bellevue, 1979—; vice chmn. Forbes Westar Inc., 1986—; barnstormer Mus. of Flight, Seattle, 1983—; exec. dir. Assn. Am. Air Travel Clubs, Bellevue, 1974-79. Bd. trustees Poncho, Seattle, 1983-84; dir. Lynnwood Rotary Air Show, Everett, 1968-77; aviation chmn. Everett C. of C. Recipient Disting. Alumnus Achievement award Lakeside Sch., Seattle, 1984. Mem. Nat. Bus. Aircraft Assn., Aviation Ins. Assn., Regional Airline Assn. Republican. Episcopalian. Lodge: Rotary. Office: Forbes Westar Inc PO Box 1607 Bellevue WA 98009-1607

MCCAW, CRAIG O., communications executive; b. Centralia, Wash., 1949. Grad., Stanford U., 1971. Pilot; chmn., CEO McCaw Cellular Comm., Inc., 1968-88; chmn. bd. dirs., CEO McCaw Cellular Comm., Inc., Kirkland, Wash., 1982—; chmn., CEO Lin Broadcasting Co., 1990—. Office: McCaw Cellular Comm Inc 2300 Carillon Pt Kirkland WA 98033-7356*

MCCAW, JOHN E., JR., professional sports team executive. Co-founder, bd. dirs. McCaw Comm., McCaw Cellular Comm., Inc.; owner, bd. dirs. Seattle Mariners, 1992; co-chmn. Orca Bay Sports and Entertainment, Vancouver, B.C. Office: Vancouver Canucks 800 Griffiths Way Vancouver BC*

MCCAWLEY, AUSTIN, psychiatrist, educator; b. Greenock, Scotland, Jan. 17, 1925; came to U.S., 1954; s. Austin and Anna Theresa (McBride) McC.; m. Gloria Klein, Feb. 15, 1958; children: Joseph, Tessa. MBCHB, U. Glasgow, 1948. Diplomate Am. Bd. Psychiatry and Neurology; DPM Royal Coll. London. Intern Glasgow Royal Infirmary, Scotland, 1948; resident Inst. Living, Harford, Conn., 1954-57, clin. dir., 1960-66; med. dir. Westchester br. St. Vincent's Hosp., N.Y.C., 1966-72; dir. psychiatry St. Francis Hosp., Hartford, 1972-88; prof. psychiatry U. Conn. Med. Sch., Farmington, 1983-93; pvt. practice, West Hartford, Conn., 1988—. Co-author: The Physician, 1983; contbr. articles to profl. jours. Chmn. Bd. Mental Health, State of Conn., 1981-84, Search Com. for Commr. Mental Health, Conn., 1981; mem. Gov.'s Spl. Task Force on Mental health Policy, Conn., 1982. With RAF, 1948-50. Fellow Am. Psychiat. Assn., Am. Coll. Psychiatry (charter fellow, founder); mem. Conn. Psychiat. Soc. (pres. 1978-79), Hartford Golf Club. Democrat. Roman Catholic. Avocations: music, golf. Home: 128 Westmont St West Hartford CT 06117-2926 Office: 18 N Main St West Hartford CT 06107-1919

MCCAY, THURMAN DWAYNE, university administrator; b. Wynne, Ark., Sept. 2, 1946; s. Thurman Ellis and Vetra Marcella (Jones) McC.; m. Mary Helen Johnston, Oct. 3, 1985; children: Audra Lee, Leesa Marie. BS in Physics, Auburn U., 1968, MS in Engring., 1969, PhD in Engring. and Math., 1974; postgrad. mgmt. sci. program, Air Force Inst. Tech., Wright-Petterson AFB, Ohio, 1985. Rsch. engr. gas diagnostics sect. aerospace projects br. ARO, Inc., Arnold Air Force Station, Tenn., 1973-78; sr. rsch. phys. scientist, plume tech. br. Air Force Rocket Propulsion Lab., Edwards AFB, Calif., 1978-81; sr. aerospace engr., br. chief, chief propulsion divsn. NASA, George G. Marshall Center, Ala., 1981-86; prof. engring. sci. and mechanics, adj. prof. engring. U. Tenn. Space Inst., Tullahoma, 1986—, v.p., 1993—; tchr. Auburn U., 1970-72, Calif. State U., Fresno, 1980, U. Ala., Huntsville, 1985, U. Tenn. Space Inst., 1986—; bd. dirs. Tenn. Valley Aerospace Region; mem. rev. bd. NASA Lewis Rocket Thruster Rsch. Program, Dept. of Def. Fellowship Program, Indsl. Laser Handbook; mem. nat. adv. bd. NASA Enring. Rsch. Ctr. for Propulsion, Pa. State U., NASA Ctr. for Advanced Space Propulsion, U. Tenn. Space Inst./Calspan. Reviewer Jour. Spacecraft and Rockets, Jour. Propulsion and Power, Jour. Thermophysics and Heat Transfer, Jour. Heat Transfer; contbr. articles to profl. jours.; patentee in field. Maj. U.S. Army, 1972-73. NRC rsch. fellow, 1980-84. Assoc. fellow AIAA (liquid propulsion tech. com. 1984-88, assoc. editor Jour. Propulsion and Power 1988-91); mem. Am. Soc. Metals, Am. Welding Soc., Laser Inst. Am. (chmn. ICALEO 1994), Am. Soc. Engring. Edn. Roman Catholic. Avocation: tennis. Office: Univ Tenn Vice Pres Office UT Space Inst Tullahoma TN 37388 Office: B H Goethert Pkwy MS01 Tullahoma TN 37388-8897

MCCHESNEY, ROBERT MICHAEL, SR., political science educator; b. Effingham, Ill., Oct. 5, 1942; s. J.D. and Helen Grace (Russell) McC.; m. Laraine Freeman, Aug. 28, 1965; children: Robert M. Jr., Todd Patrick, Jennifer Laraine, Grant Russell, Brent Steven. BA, U. Southwestern La., 1964; MA, U. Va., 1967, PhD, 1969. Asst. instr. U. Va., Charlottesville, 1967-68; chmn. dept. polit. sci. U. Cen. Ark., Conway, 1971-76, dean coll. scis. and humanities, 1976-82, v.p. for acad. affairs, 1982-89, disting. prof., 1989-90; provost U. Montevallo, Ala., 1990-92; pres. U. Montevallo, 1992—; v.p. Survey Rsch., Inc., Conway, 1989-92; spl. cons. U. Ark. System, Little Rock, 1989. Mem. Carmichael Found., Conway, 1975-79; exec. bd. Quapaw coun. Boy Scouts Am., Little Rock, 1982-88; Birmingham Area Coun., 1995—. Capt. Med. Svc. Corps U.S. Army, 1968-71. Grantee State Justice Inst./Adminstrv. Office of Cts., Ark., 1989. Mem. Ark. Polit. Sci. Assn. (pres. 1975), Ala. Coun. Univ. and Coll. Pres. (chmn. 1993-95), Conway C. of C., Montevall C. of C., Rotary (pres. Conway Club 1987-88, Paul Harris fellow 1986), Phi Beta Kappa, Phi Kappa Phi, Alpha Chi, Golden Key, Phi Alpha Theta, Phi Eta Sigma, Blue Key. Mormon. Avocations: hunting, fishing, golfing. Home: Flowerhill UM Montevallo AL 35115 Office: U Montevallo Station 6001 Montevallo AL 35115

MC CHESNEY, ROBERT PEARSON, artist; b. Marshall, Mo., Jan. 16, 1913; s. John and Ruby (Pearson) McC.; m. Mary Ellen Fuller, Dec. 17, 1949. Student, Sch. Fine Arts, Washington U., 1931-34, Otis Art Inst., Los Angeles, 1936-37. Represented by Adrianne Fish, San Francisco, Annex Galleries, Santa Rosa, Calif.; instr. art Calif. Sch. Fine Arts, San Francisco, 1949-51, Santa Rosa Jr. Coll., 1957-58; trustee San Francisco Art Inst., 1965-67. One-man shows include San Francisco Mus. Modern Art, 1949, 53, San Francisco Art Inst., 1957, 20th Century West, 1965, Bolles Gallery, N.Y., 1962, Nev. Mus., 1994, also others; group shows include Art Inst. Chgo., 1947, 3d Biennial Sau Paulo, Brazil, 1955, Whitney Annual, 1955, Corcoran, 1957, Provincetown, 1957, Chgo., 1959, Osaka, Japan, 1970, Whitney, 1980, also others; represented in permanent collections, Fresno Art Mus., Art Inst. Chgo., Worcester (Mass.) Art Mus., Whitney Mus., N.Y., San Francisco Mus. Modern Art, Utah State Mus., Nev. Art Mus., Laguna Beach Art Mus., others; executed mural San Francisco Social Svcs. Bldg., 1978. Address: 2955 Sonoma Mountain Rd Petaluma CA 94954-9559 *The desert wilderness, which I truly love to be in as much as possible, has influenced me a great deal. Of course, the artist is no different from anyone else in that he is influenced by everything around him visually and psychologically, but he has the ability to digest this, you might say, and then transform it into art.*

MCCHESNEY, S. ELAINE, lawyer; b. Bowling Green, Ky., Sept. 14, 1954; d. Kelsey H. McChesney and Lorraine (Carter) Durey; m. Paul Boylan; children: Michael, Jessica, Andrew. AB summa cum laude, Western Ky. U., 1975; JD, Harvard U., 1978. With Bingham Dana & Gould, Boston, 1978—, ptnr., 1985—; chair joint MBA/BBA bar com. on jud. appts., 1988-89, 90-91; trial practice advisor moot ct. exercises Harvard Law Sch.; moot ct. judge Harvard Law Sch., Boston U., Suffolk U. Bd. editors Mass. Lawyer's Weekly, 1987-88; panelist, speaker in field; contbr. articles to profl. jours. Treas., bd. dirs. St. Paul's Nursery Sch., Dedham, Mass., 1990-95; parent rep. Charles River Sch., Dover, Mass., vol. numerous coms.; vol. Am. Heart Found., March of Dimes; vol. street canvassing on zoning issues. Mem. ABA (labor law sect. subcom. individual rights in the workplace 1982—, comml. banking or fin. transactions litigation 1982), Mass. Bar Assn., Boston Bar Assn. (coun. 1994—, law sch. liaison com. 1984-85, IOLTA com., co-chair ann. mtg.), Women's Bar Assn. (editor calendar 1988-92). Office: Bingham Dana & Gould 150 Federal St Boston MA 02110-1745

MCCHRISTIAN, JOSEPH ALEXANDER, international business executive; b. Chgo., Oct. 12, 1914; s. Robert Lee and Lillian (Alexander) McC.; BS in Mil. Sci., U.S. Mil. Acad., 1939; grad. Command and Gen. Staff Coll., 1942, Armed Forces Staff Coll., 1951, Army War Coll., 1955, Army Lang. Sch., 1956; m. Dempsie Catherine Van Fleet, Sept. 26, 1940; children: Joseph Alexander, Anne, Lillian. Enlisted U.S. Army, 1933, commd. 2d lt., 1939, advanced through grades to maj. gen., 1961; various assignments 1933-44; successively armored inf. bn. comdr., asst. chief staff plans and ops., chief staff 10th Armored Div., ETO, 1944-45; asst. chief staff intelligence Hdqrs. 3d U.S. Army, Germany, 1945-47; dep. dir. intelligence U.S. Forces, Austria, 1947-48; comdg. officer 2d Bn., 3d Inf., Ft. McNair, D.C., 1948-49; spl. asst. to chief JUSMAG, Greece, 1949-50; S3 dept. tactics U.S. Mil. Acad., 1951-53, comdg. officer 1st Regt., U.S. Corp Cadets, 1953-54; U.S. Army attache, Greece, 1956-60; comdg. officer 1st Armored Regt. (tng.), also comdg. officer U.S. Army Tng. Ctr., Armor, Ft. Knox, Ky., 1960-61; chief Western div. Office Asst. Chief Staff-Intelligence, Dept. Army, 1962-63; asst. chief staff intelligence Hdqrs. U.S. Army Pacific, 1963-65; chief Army, Navy, Air Force and Marine Corps Intelligence, Hdqrs. U.S. Mil. Assistance Command, Vietnam, 1965-67; comdg. gen. 2d Armored Div., also III Corps, Ft. Hood, Tex., 1967-68; asst. chief of staff for intelligence Dept. Army, 1968-71; v.p. Overseas Basic Industries, Fla., 1972-74; v.p., gen. mgr. Société des Eaux, Athens, Greece, 1972-74; v.p. Ulen Mgmt. Co., Fla., 1972-75, Van Fleet Estates, Inc., Fla., 1970-77. Commr., Town of Jupiter Island (Fla.), 1975-83. Decorated D.S.M. with oak leaf cluster, Silver Star, Legion of Merit, Bronze Star with 3 oak leaf clusters, Air medal, Commendation ribbon, Combat Inf. badge; Croix de Guerre with gold star and bronze star (France); comdr. Royal Order King George 1st, also Disting. Svc. medal (Greece); Nat. Order 5th class and Disting. Svc. Order 1st class (Republic Vietnam); Mil. Merit medal, Chung Mu (Korea). Mem. Mil. Order World Wars, Alumni Assn. U.S. Mil. Acad. Clubs: Army and Navy (Washington); Hobe Sound Yacht, The Island (Hobe Sound, Fla.); Ends of the Earth. Home: 365 South Beach Rd Hobe Sound FL 33455-2428

MCCLAIN, CHARLES JAMES, state educational administrator; b. Ironton, Mo., Sept. 1, 1931; s. John F. and Hazel (Pierce) McC.; children: Anita, Melanie. BEd, S.W. Mo. State U., 1954; MEd, U. Mo., 1957, EdD, 1961; hon. degree, Busan Nat. U., Mo. Western State Coll., Kirksville Coll. Osteo. Medicine, Cen. Meth. Coll. Pres. Jefferson Coll., Hillsboro, Mo., 1963-70, N.E. Mo. State U., Kirksville, 1970-89; commr. higher edn. State of Mo., Jefferson City, 1989—; panelist, presenter nat. and internat. edn. confs. Contbr. articles to profl. jours. Bd. dirs. United Meth. Found., Mo. Higher Edn. Loan Authority. Recipient Disting. Alumnus award S.W. Mo. State U., 1977, Disting. Svc. award U. Mo. Coll. Edn., G. Theodore Mitau award, 1983, Alumni award U. Mo.-Columbia, 1989; named Pub. Adminstr. of Yr. Mo. Inst. Pub. Adminstrn., 1986. Mem. Internat. Assn. Univ. Pres., Am. Assn. State Colls. and Univs., Am. Assn. Higher Edn. (bd. dirs.), Midwestern Higher Edn. Commn., Mo. Coun. Econ. Edn. (exec. com.), Mo. Acad. Sci. Home: PO Box 104503 Jefferson City MO 65110-4503 *One can get a lot done if he/she doesn't care who gets the credit.**

MCCLAIN, GEORGE NELSON, lawyer, economist; b. New Haven, Aug. 10, 1952; s. James and Trina (George) McC.; m. Lisa Crossley, May 5, 1982. BS in Econs., U. Conn., 1975; JD, Yale U., 1978. Pres. McClain Internat., Washington, 1990—. Office: 5325 85th Ave Apt 13 New Carrollton MD 20784

MCCLAIN, LEE BERT, corporate lawyer, insurance executive; b. East Chicago, Ill., Jan. 1, 1943; s. Wilson C. and Ida (Dapra) M.; 1 child, Adam. BS, Purdue U., 1966; MBA, Loyola U., Chgo., 1968, JD, 1975. Bar: Ill. 1975. Div. contr. Armour-Dial, Chgo., 1970-73; mgr. corp. planning Spiegel Inc., Chgo., 1973-76; with Kemper Group, Long Grove, Ill., 1976—, employee rels. officer, 1978-81, gen. counsel, corp. sec., mgr. govt. affairs, 1986-91; of counsel, co-chair ins. practice group Wildman, Harold, Allen & Dixon, Chgo., 1991—; CEO, pres. Arabella Capital, Mass.; mem. Supreme Ct. Ill. Atty. Disciplinary Commn. Inquiry Bd., 1990, 91; bd. dirs. Arbella Ins. Group, Mass.; bd. dirs. Preferred Am. Ins. Co., Iowa. Mem. staff Presdl. Commn. on Drunk Driving, 1982. Sgt. U.S. Army, 1968-70, Vietnam. Decorated Bronze Star. Mem. ABA (nat. commn. on minorities 1990-93), Ill. Bar Assn., Chgo. Bar Assn., Fedn. Ins. & Corp. Counsel. Avocations: tennis, running. Office: Wildman Harold Allen & Dixon 225 W Wacker Dr Chicago IL 60606

MCCLAIN, MARILYN RUSSELL, admission and retention counselor; b. Laurelton, N.Y., Aug. 18, 1956; d. Russell H. and Lillian A. (Yarbrough) McC.; 1 child, Amy Lynne Roberts. BS in Social Work, Harding U., 1977; postgrad., Okla. State U. Career counselor Foothills Vo-Tech Sch., Searcy, Ark., 1977-78; social worker Dept. of Social Svcs., Tulsa, Okla., 1978-79;

owner, operator, instr. Spl. Deliveries Childbirth Preparation Ctr., Tulsa, 1980-85; mgr. One Hour Moto Photo, Tulsa, 1986-89; area mgr. Mervyn's, Tulsa, 1989-92; admission/retention counselor Rogers State Coll., Claremore, Okla., 1992—; primary advisor Adult Students Aspiring to Prosper, Claremore, Okla., 1993—; pres. RSC Staff Assn., 1995—; parent educator Parenting Ptnrs., Claremore, 1994—. Sec. Oologah-Talala Sch. Found., 1994-95, pres. 1995—; mem. statue and hotel coms., Rogers County Hist. Soc., Claremore, 1994—; planning com. Leadership Claremore, 1994—; mem. Oologah PTA, 1990—. Mem. Okla. Acad. Advising Assn. (comm. com. 1994—), Am. Assn. for Adult and Continuing Edn. Republican. Avocations: needlework, reading, piano. Home: 3612 N Oaklawn Dr Claremore OK 74017-1828 Office: Rogers State Coll Will Rogers & College Hill Claremore OK 74017

MCCLAIN, PAULA DENICE, political scientist; b. Louisville, Jan. 3, 1950; d. Robert Landis and Mabel (Molock) McC.; stepdau. of Annette Williams McClain; m. Paul C. Jacobson, Jan. 30, 1988; children: Kristina L., Jessica A. BA, Howard U., Washington, 1972; MA, Howard U., 1974, PhD, 1977; postgrad., U. Pa., 1981-82. Asst. prof. dept. polit. sci. U. Wis., Milw., 1977-82; assoc. prof. and prof. pub. affairs Ariz. State U., Tempe, 1982-91; prof. govt. and fgn. affairs U. Va., Charlottesville, 1991—, chair govt. and fgn. affairs, 1994—. Co-author: Can We All Get Along? Racial and Ethnic Minorities in American Politics, 1995, Race, Place and Risk: Black Homicide in Urban America, 1990; editor: Minority Group Influence, 1993; co-editor: Urban Minority Administrators, 1988. Mem. Nat. Conf. Black Polit. Scientists (pres. 1989-90), Am. Polit. Sci. Assn. (mem. coun. 1985-87, v.p. 1993-94), So. Polit. Sci. Assn. (exec. coun. 1992-95). Office: U Va Dept Govt 232 Cabell Hall Charlottesville VA 22901

MCCLAIN, THOMAS E., communications executive; b. East Liverpool, Ohio, July 26, 1950; s. Thomas E. and Helen Marie (Polinski) McC. BA, Case Western Reserve, Cleve., 1972; MA, Kans. State U., 1973. With intergovtl. rels. Ohio EPA, Columbus, 1974-77; legis. liaison Ohio Consumers Counsel, Columbus, 1977-80; dep. dir. Ohio Consumers Counsel, 1980-81; press sec. Ohio Atty. Gen., Columbus, 1982-83; asst. dir. Pub. Utilities Commn., Columbus, 1983; with instnl. rels. dept. Battelle Project Mgmt. Div., Chgo., 1983-84; mgr. instl. rels. Battelle Project Mgmt. Div., 1984-86; mgr. comms. Battelle, Columbus, 1986-88, dir. corp. comms., 1989-95, v.p. corp. comms., 1995—; sec. devel. bd. Children's Hosp., Columbus, 1990—. Vol. Ohio Youth Commn., Columbus, 1975-76; active ARC-Cen. Ohio chpt., 1986-87. Warren Lahr scholar Case Western Reserve U., 1971-72. Mem. Rotary (chmn. program com. 1991-93, bd. dirs. 1994-95, 2d v.p. 1996—). Presbyterian. Avocations: basketball, golf, travel. Home: 2689 Camden Rd Upper Arlington OH 43221-3221 Office: Battelle 505 King Ave Columbus OH 43201-2696

MCCLAIN, WILLIAM ANDREW, lawyer; b. Sanford, N.C., Jan. 11, 1913; s. Frank and Blanche (Leslie) McC.; m. Roberta White, Nov. 11, 1944. AB, Wittenberg U., 1934; JD, U. Mich., 1937; LLD (hon.), Wilberforce U., 1963, U. Cin., 1971; LHD, Wittenberg U., 1972. Bar: Ohio 1938, U.S. Dist. Ct. (so. dist.) Ohio 1940, U.S. Ct. Appeals (6th cir.) 1946, U.S. Supreme Ct. 1946. Mem. Berry, McClain & White, 1937-58; dep. solicitor, City of Cin., 1957-63, city solicitor, 1963-72; mem. Keating, Muething & Klekamp, Cin., 1972-73; gen. counsel Cin. Br., SBA, 1973-75; judge Hamilton County Common Pleas Ct., 1975-76; judge Mcpl. Ct., 1976-80; of counsel Manley, Burke, Lipton & Cook, Cin., 1980—; adj. prof. U. Cin., 1963-72, Salmon P. Chase Law Sch., 1965-72. Exec. com. ARC, Cin., 1978—; bd. dirs. NCCJ, 1975—. Served to 1st lt. JAGC, U.S. Army, 1943-46. Decorated Army Commendation award; recipient Nat. Layman award, A.M.E. Ch., 1963; Alumni award Wittenberg U., 1966; Nat. Inst. Mcpl. Law Officers award, 1971. Fellow Am. Bar Found.; mem. Am. Judicature Soc., Cin. Bar Assn., Ohio Bar Assn., ABA, Fed. Bar assn., Nat. Bar Assn., Alpha Phi Alpha, Sigma Pi Phi. Republican. Methodist. Clubs: Bankers, Friendly Sons of St. Patrick Lodge: Masons (33 deg.). Home: 2101 Grandin Rd Apt 904 Cincinnati OH 45208-3346

MCCLAIN, WILLIAM THOMAS, lawyer; b. Louisville, June 4, 1926; s. George Lee and Catherine (Spalding) McC.; m. Wanda Barry, Feb. 28, 1949; children: Nina, Catherine, Ann, William, Mary. BS in Metall. Engring., U. Ky., 1948; JD, Loyola U., New Orleans, 1958. Bar: Ill. 1960, D.C. 1988. Engr. Shell Oil Co., Deer Park, Tex., 1948-55; asst. prof. U. Houston, 1951-55; sales engr. Pacific Valves, Inc., New Orleans, 1955-58; assoc. Wier, Greene & Nelson, New Orleans, 1958, Amoco Corp., Chgo., 1959-86, Finnegan, Henderson, Farabow, Garrett & Dunner, Washington, 1987—. With USN, 1944-46. Mem. ABA (chmn. 1987—), Am. Intellectual Property Law Assn. (dir., treas. 1986-90). Republican. Avocations: golf, tennis, reading. Office: Finnegan Henderson Farabow & Dunner LLP 1300 I St NW Washington DC 20005-3315

MCCLAMROCH, N. HARRIS, aerospace engineering educator, consultant, researcher; b. Houston, Oct. 7, 1942; s. Nathaniel Harris and Dorthy Jean (Orand) McC.; m. Margaret Susan Hobart, Aug. 10, 1963; 1 child, Kristin Jean. B.S., U. Tex., 1963, M.S., 1965, Ph.D., 1967. Prof. dept. elec. engring. and computer sci. U. Mich., Ann Arbor, 1967—, chair dept. aerospace engring., 1992-95; research engr. Cambridge U., Eng., 1975, Delft U., Netherlands, 1976, Sandia Labs., Albuquerque, 1977, C.S. Draper Lab., Cambridge, Mass., 1982. Author: State Models of Dynamic Systems, 1980; contbr. numerous articles to profl. jours. Chmn. U. Mich. Faculty Senate, 1987-88, dept. aerospace engring., 1992—. Fellow IEEE (editor Transactions on Automatic Control 1989-92); mem. AAAS. Home: 4056 Thornoaks Dr Ann Arbor MI 48104-4254 Office: U Mich Aerospace Engring Ann Arbor MI 48109

MCCLANAHAN, CONNIE DEA, pastoral minister; b. Detroit, Mar. 1, 1948; d. Manford Bryce and Dorothy Maxine (Keely) McC. BA, Marygrove Coll., 1969; MRE, Seattle U., 1978; D Ministry, St. Mary Sem. and U., Balt., 1988. Cert. in spiritual direction, youth ministry, advanced catechist. Campus minister Flint (Mich.) Newman Ctr., 1970-80; coord. religious edn. Blessed Sacrament Ch., Burton, Mich., 1981-84; pastoral assoc. Good Shepherd Cath. Ch., Montrose, Mich., 1984-90; pastor Sacred Heart Ch., Flint, 1990—; music min. New Light Prayer Cmty., Flint, 1979—; co-chaplain Dukette Cath. Sch., Flint, 1991—; ind. spiritual dir., 1988—; resp. Diocesan Regional Adult Edn., 1993-96; mem. Nat., State and Lansing Diocese Catholic Campus Ministry Assns., 1970-80; mem. campus ministry task force Interfaith Metro. Agy. for Planning, 1974-76; mem. Lansing Diocesan Liturgical Commn., 1977-80; mem. Flint Cath. Urban Ministry, 1977-80, 90—, co-chair, 1992-94; mem. Flint Cath. Healing Prayer Team, 1977-84; coord. nat. study week Cath. Campus Ministry Assn., 1978; mem. steering com. All-Mich. cath. Charismatic Com. on Lay Ministry, 1984-86; convener Diocesan Lay Ministry Com. on Cert./Continuing Edn./Spirituality, 1985-86; mem. Diocesan Com. to Update Catechist Formation Handbook, 1989-91; mem. Diocesan All Family Conf. Steering Com., 1990—; mem. Lansing Diocese svc. com. of Cath. Charismatic Renewal, 1979-85, 95—. Mem. Assn. Cath. Lay Ministers (co-chair Region III 1986-87), Profl. Pastoral Ministers Assn. (co-chair 1988-90). Roman Catholic. Avocations: guitar, singing, leather crafting, reading. Office: Sacred Heart Ch 719 E Moore St Flint MI 48505-3905

MCCLANAHAN, LELAND, academic administrator; b. Hammond, Ind., Mar. 14, 1931; s. Alonzo Leland and Eva (Hermanson) McC.; m. Lavaughn Adell Meyrer, June 5, 1954; children: Lindel, Loren. Diploma, Ctrl. Bible Coll., 1954; PhBB, Nat. Postgrad. Bible Acad., 1969; BA, Southwestern Coll., 1973; MA, Fla. State Christian Coll., 1964, ThD, 1970; PhD, Faith Bible Coll. and Sem., Ft. Lauderdale, Fla. and Marina, Lagos, Nigeria, 1969; MA, Bapt. Christian U., 1988; PhD, Freedom U., 1989; ThD, Bapt. Christian U., 1989, DLitt, 1990, PsyD, 1991; PhD (hon.), Freedom U., 1989, Hawaii U., 1995; DEd, Bapt. Christian U., 1992, D in Bus. Adminstrn., 1993; DD (hon.), Internat. Evangelism Crusades, 1969, Trinity Union Coll., 1991; LLD, La. Bapt. U., 1994; StD, PhD, Trinity Internat. U., 1994; HHD (hon.), La. Bapt. U., 1995; LittD (hon.), Cambridge Theol. Sem., 1995; PhD, LittD, PsyD, DBA, LLD, EdD, U. Hawaii, 1995. Diplomate Nat. Bd. Christian Clin. Therapists; ordained pastor, Christian Ch., 1950. Founder, pastor Evangel Temple, Griffith, Ind., 1954-73, Abundant Life Temple, Cocoa, Fla., 1974-77; mgr. ins. divsn. United Agys., Cocoa, Fla., 1979-81; assoc. pastor Merritt Assembly of God, Merritt Island, Fla., 1982-85, Palm Chapel, Merritt Island, 1987-89, 1990-93; founder Hawaii U., Merritt Island Offices, Merritt Island, Fla., 1990—; chancellor Hawaii U. Merritt Island Offices, 1995—; dir. Fla. Hawaii U. Schs.; founder, dir. Griffith Youth Ctr., 1960-70, Todd Nursery Sch., Griffith, 1971-73; founder, chancellor Ind. Bible Coll., Griffith, 1971-73; dir. Chapel Counseling Ctr., Merritt Island, 1990-94; mem. national accreditation com. Hawaii U. Author: Is Divine Healing For Today?, 1989, Truths From the Gospel of St. John, 1991, An Outline of the Revelation, 1993, Numbers in the Bible, 1994, An Outline of the Acts of the Apostle, 1995; author 142 coll. courses and books. Recipient Disting. Svc. award U.S. Jaycees, 1966; named Hon. Lt. Col., Gov. Guy Hunt, 1988. Fellow Am. Biog. Inst. (life); mem. Internat. Platform Assn., Order of Internat. Fellowship (life), Am. Inst. Clin. Psychotherapists, Am. Assn. christian Counselors, Nat. Christian Counseling Assn. (assoc., lic.), Internat. Assn. Pastoral Psychologists (lic.), Order of St. John, Knight of Malta (comdr. 1990). Republican. Avocations: reading, walking, watching sports, watching television adventures, weight lifting. Office: Hawaii U Merritt Island Offices 670 N Courtenay Pky Ste 15 Merritt Island FL 32953-4676 Office: Hawaii U Merritt Island Ofcs 670 N Courtenay Pky Ste 15 Merritt Island FL 32953-4770

MC CLANAHAN, RUE (EDDI-RUE MC CLANAHAN), actress; b. Healdton, Okla.; d. William Edwin and Dreda Rheua-Nell (Medaris) McC.; m. 1st, Tom Bish, 1958; 1 child, Mark Thomas Bish; m. 2nd, Norman Hartweg; m. 3rd, Peter DeMaio; m. 4th, Gus Fisher, 1976; m. 5th, Tom Keel, 1984 (div. 1985). B.A. cum laude, U. Tulsa, 1956. Appearances include (theatre) Erie (Pa.) Playhouse, 1957-58, Harvey (London); (Broadway) Jimmy Shine, 1968-69, Sticks and Bones, 1972, California Suite, 1977, After-Play, 1995; (TV appearances) L.A., 1959-664, N.Y.C., 1964-73; (TV series) Maude, 1973-78, Apple Pie, 1978, Mama's Family, 1982-84, Golden Girls, 1985-92, Golden Palace, 1992-93; (TV movies) Having Babies III, 1978, Sgt. Matlowch vs. the U.S. Air Force, 1978, Rainbow, 1978, Topper, 1979, The Great American Traffic Jam, 1980, Word of Honor, 1981, The Day the Bubble Burst, 1982, The Little Match Girl, 1987, Liberace, 1988, Take My Daughters Please, 1988, Let Me Hear You Whisper, 1988, To the Heroes, 1989, After the Shock, 1990, Children of the Bride, 1990, To My Daughter, 1990, The Dreamer of Oz, 1990, Baby of the Bride, 1991, Mother of the Bride, 1993, Danielle Steele's Message from Nam, 1993, Burning Passion: The Margaret Mitchell Story, 1994; (films) The People Next Door, 1970, They Might Be Giants, 1971, The Pursuit of Happiness, 1971, Modern Love, 1990, (mini-series) Innocent Victims, 1995. Recipient Obie award for leading off-Broadway role in Who's Happy Now, 1970; Emmy award Best Actress in a comedy, 1987; named Woman of Yr., Pasadena Playhouse, 1986; Spl. scholar Pasadena (Calif.) Playhouse, 1959, Phi Beta Gamma scholar, 1955. Mem. Actors Studio, Actors Equity Assn., AFTRA, Screen Actors Guild. Office: Agy for Performing Arts 9000 W Sunset Blvd Ste 1200 Los Angeles CA 90069-5812*

MCCLANE, DRAYTON, JR., professional baseball team executive. Owner, chmn. bd. Houston Astros, also chief exec. officer. Office: Houston Astros PO Box 288 Houston TX 77001-0288*

MCCLANE, ROBERT SANFORD, bank holding company executive; b. Kenedy, Tex., May 5, 1939; s. Norris Robert and Ella Addie (Stockton) McC.; m. Sue Nitschke, Mar. 31, 1968; children: Len Stokes McClane Brown, Norris Robert. BS in Bus. Adminstrn., Trinity U., San Antonio, 1961. With Ford Motor Co., Detroit, 1961-62; with Frost Nat. Bank, San Antonio, 1962—, mem. staff, 1962-68, v.p., 1968-78; exec. v.p. Cullen/Frost Bankers, Inc., 1976—, pres., dir., 1985—; bd. dirs. Frost Nat. Bank, San Antonio, C/F Life Ins. Co., San Antonio, Main Plaza Corp., San Antonio, Daltex Gen. Agy., San Antonio. Crusade chmn. Baxar County chpt. Am. Cancer Soc., 1974; bd. dirs. Bexar County ARC, 1969-72; sr. warden St. Luke's Episopal Ch., San Antonio, 1980; trustee Alamo Pub. Telecomms. Coun., San Antonio, 1981-88, Trinity U., 1990—; chmn. San Antonio Econ. Devel. Found., 1987-89, exec. com. 1985-91. Mem. Greater San Antonio C. of C. (chmn. leadership San Antonio 1975-76, bd. dirs. exec. com. 1994—, chmn. 1996), Trinity U. Alumni Assn. (pres. 1968-69, disting. alumnus 1987), San Antonio German Club, Order Alamo, Tex. Cavaliers, Argyle Club, Town Club, Plaza Club (bd. dirs. 1973-92). Episcopalian. Office: Cullen/Frost Bankers Inc 100 W Houston St San Antonio TX 78205-1457

MCCLARD, JACK EDWARD, lawyer; b. Lafayette, La., May 13, 1946; s. Lee Franklin and Mercedes Cecile (Landry) McC.; m. Marilyn Kay O'Gorman, June 3, 1972; 1 child, Lauren Minton. BA in Hist., Rice U., 1968; JD, U. Tex., 1974. Bar: Va. 1974, U.S. Dist. Ct. (ea. and we. dists.) Va. 1974, D.C. 1981, U.S. Dist. Ct. D.C. 1981, N.Y. 1985, U.S. Dist. Ct. (so. and ea. dists.) N.Y. 1985, U.S. Ct. Appeals (4th cir.) 1978, U.S. Ct. Appeals (D.C. cir.) 1980, U.S. Ct. Appeals (5th cir.) 1993. Assoc. Hunton & Williams, Richmond, Va., 1974-81; ptnr. Hunton & Williams, Richmond, 1981—. Contbr. articles to profl. jours. Served to lt. (j.g.) USN, 1968-71. Mem. ABA, Va. Bar Assn., Richmond Bar Assn., Va. Trial Lawyers Assn., 5th Cir. Bar, John Marshall Inns of Ct. Democrat. Episcopalian. Avocations: bridge, gardening. Home: 100 Trowbridge Rd Richmond VA 23233-5724 Office: Hunton & Williams 951 E Byrd St Riverfront Plz E Tower Richmond VA 23219-4074

MCCLARON, LOUISIANNA CLARDY, retired secondary school educator; b. Clarksville, Tenn., Dec. 12, 1929; d. Abe and Chinaster (Simpson) Clardy; m. Joe Thomas McClaron, July 17, 1965. BS, Tenn. State U., 1952; MA, Ohio State U., 1956; EdS, Tenn. State U., 1977; PhD, Vanderbilt U., 1981. Cert. secondary tchr., sch. adminstr., supr., Tenn. Tchr. Madison County Bd. Edn., Normal, Ala., 1952-58, Metro Nashville Bd. Edn., 1958-94; ret., 1994; presenter workshops in field. Mem. ASCD, NEA, Tenn. Edn. Assn., Metro Nashville Edn. Assn. (exec. bd., dist. dir., del.), Tenn. Bus. Edn. Assn., Nat. Bus. Edn. assn., Am. Vocat. Assn., Delta Pi Epsilon (former v.p. Omega chpt., now pres.), Alpha Kappa Alpha, Alpha Delta Omega Chpt. Found. (housing treas.).

MC CLARREN, ROBERT ROYCE, librarian; b. Delta, Ohio, Mar. 15, 1921; s. Dresden William Howard and Norma Leona (Whiteman) McC.; m. Margaret Aileen Weed, May 31, 1947; children: Mark Robert, Todd Adams. Student, Antioch Coll., 1938-40; AB, Muskingum Coll., 1942; MA in English, Ohio State U., 1951; MS in L.S., Columbia, 1954; DLitt (hon.), Rosary Coll., 1989. Registration officer VA, Cin., 1946-47; instr. English Gen. Motors Inst., 1949-50; head circulation dept. Oak Park Public Library, Ill., 1954-55; acting head librarian Oak Park Public Library, 1955; head librarian Crawfordsville Public Library, Ind., 1955-58, Huntington Public Library, also Western Counties (W.Va.) Regional Public Library, W.Va., 1958-62; dir. Ind. State Library, 1962-67; system dir. North Suburban Library System, 1967-89; system dir. emeritus, 1990—; cons. libr. Chgo. Pub. Libr. Found., 1990; del. White House Conf. on Librs., 1979; instr. U. Wis., summer 1964, Rosary Coll., 1968-80, U. Tex., summer 1979, 82, No. Ill. U., 1980; pres. W.Va. Libr. Assn., 1960; mem. Gov. Ind. Commn. Arts, 1964-65, Ill. State Libr. Adv. Com., 1972-79, 87-89, chmn., 1975-79, vice chmn., 1988-89; bd. dirs. Ill. Regional Libr. Coun., 1972-82, pres., 1977; chmn. adv. commn. Nat. Periodical System, Nat. Commn. on Librs. and Info. Sci., 1978-81; treas. Ill. Coalition Libr. Advs., 1982-89. Contbr. articles to profl. jours. Served to 1st lt. AUS, 1942-46, 51-52; maj. Res. Named Ill. Librarian of Yr., 1978. Mem. ALA (councilor 1966-68, 74-78, treas. 1968-72, endowment trustee 1972-78, mem. publ. bd. 1972-75, pres. reference and adv. svc. div. 1975-76, Melville Dewey award 1989), Ill. Libr. Assn. (pres. 1981, Robert R. McClarren Legis. award 1989), Am. Libr. Trustee Assn. (v.p. 1976-77), Assn. Spl. and Coop. Libr. Agys. (pres. 1978-79, Exceptional Achievement award 1982), Ohio Hist. Soc., Am. Philatelic Soc., Sagamore of Wabash (Ind.), Ry. and Locomotive Hist. Soc. Home: 1560 Oakwood Pl Deerfield IL 60015-2014 Office: 200 W Dundee Rd Wheeling IL 60090-4750

MCCLARY, JAMES DALY, retired contractor; b. Boise, Idaho, July 19, 1917; s. Neil Hamaker and Myrtle (Daly) McC.; m. Mary Jane Munger, Feb. 2, 1939; children: Pamela, John. Student, Boise Jr. Coll., 1934-36, AA, 1957; AB, Stanford U., 1938; LLD, Gonzaga U., 1976. Laborer to supt. Morrison-Knudsen Co., Inc., Boise, 1932-42, project mgr., asst. dist. mgr., 1942- 47; gen. mgr. Mexican subs. Morrison-Knudsen Co., Inc., 1947-51, asst. to gen. mgr., 1951-53, asst. gen. mgr., 1953-60, dir., 1955-78, v.p., 1956-60, exec. v.p., 1960-72, chmn. bd., 1972-78; mem., vice chmn. Idaho Permanent Bldg. Fund Adv. Council, 1961-64, chmn., 1964-71. Treas. Idaho Rep. Cen. Com., 1964-70; presdl. elector, 1968; trustee Boise Jr. Coll., 1960-83, vice chmn., 1967-73, chmn., 1973-83; bd. dirs. Boise State U. Found., Inc., 1964-91, pres., 1970-81; bd. dirs. AGC Edn. and Rsch. Found., 1974-91, pres., 1974-90; elector Hall of Fame for Great Ams., 1976—; trustee St. Alphonsus Regional Med. Ctr., 1976-82, vice chmn., 1981-82. Recipient George Washington medal of honor Freedoms Found., Valley Forge, Pa., 1977, Disting. Alumnus award Boise State U., 1988, Silver medallion, 1996; decorated Chevalier and Legion of Honor, Order of DeMolay; named Disting. Alumnus of Yr. Boise State U. Alumni Assn., 1971, Ky. Col. Fellow ASCE, Am. Inst. Constructors; mem. Internat. Rd. Fedn. (bd. dirs. 1972-78, vice chmn. 1977-78), Soc. Am. Mil. Engrs., Assoc. Gen. Contractors Am. (bd. dirs. 1958—, mem. exec. com. 1961-78, pres. 1972), Cons. Constructors Coun. Am., Newcomen Soc., Conf. Bd. (sr.), Idaho Assn. Commerce and Industry (bd. dirs., chmn. 1974-77, Harwood award 1994), Moles (hon., mem. award for Outstanding Achievement in Constrn. 1978), Hillcrest Country Club (bd. dirs. 1965-67, 69, pres. 1967), Arid Club (mem. exec. com. 1966), Ariz. Club (Scottsdale), Ariz. Country Club (Phoenix), Univ. Club (Mexico City), Stanford Club (Washington). Episcopalian. Home: 4903 Roberts Rd Boise ID 83705-2805

MCCLATCHY, J. D., editor, writer, educator; b. Bryn Mawr, Pa., Aug. 12, 1945; s. J. Donald and Mary Jane (Hayden) McC. BA summa cum laude, Georgetown U., 1967; PhD, Yale U., 1974. Instr. English dept. LaSalle Coll., Phila., 1968-71; asst. prof. English dept. Yale U., New Haven, Conn., 1974-81, lectr. English dept., 1983, 86-87; writer-in-residence CCNY, 1982; writer-in-residence Poetry Ctr. 92d St. YMCA, N.Y.C., 1983-84, workshop leader Poetry Ctr., 1982-91; lectr. Creative Writing program, English dept. Princeton U., 1981-87, 89-93; editor The Yale Rev., New Haven, 1991—; poet-in-residence Southampton Writers Conf., 1988; lectr. MFA Parsons/New Sch., 1989, English dept. Rutgers U., 1989, writing divsn. Columbia U., 1989, 92; vis. prof. English dept. UCLA, 1990, 92; selection com. Conn. Poetry Cir. Author: (poetry) Scenes from Another Life, 1981, (London 1983), Lantskip, Platan, Creatures Ramp'd, 1983, Stars Principal, 1986, Kilim, 1987, The Rest of the Way, 1990, The Art of Poetry, 1994; librettist: A Question of Taste, 1989, Mario and the Magician, 1994, Orpheus Decending, 1994; editor: The Yale Review, 1991—, (books) Anne Sexton: The Artist and Her Critics, 1978, For James Merrill: A Birthday Tribute, 1986, Recitative: Prose by James Merrill, 1986, Poets on Painters: Essays on the Art of Painting by Twentieth Century Poets, 1988, The Vintage Book of Contemporary American Poetry, 1990, Woman in White: Selected Poems of Emily Dickinson, 1991; assoc. editor Four Quarters, 1968-71; contbg. editor Am. Poetry Review; poetry editor The Yale Review, 1981-91; trans. articles, contbr. poems, stories, articles, reviews to various jours. Bd. dirs. Ingram Merrill Found., 1986—. Recipient gold medal Vergilian Acad., 1967, O. Henry award, 1972, prize Am. Acad. Poets ,1972, Chase Going Woodhouse Poetry prize, 1976, Michener award, 1982, Gordon Barber Meml. award Poetry Soc. Am., 1984, Eunice Tietjens Meml. prize Poetry Mag., 1985, Witter Bynner Poetry prize Am. Acad. and Inst. Arts and Letters, 1985, award in lit., 1991, Oscar Blumenthal prize Poetry Mag., 1988, Levinson prize, 1990, Melville Cane award Poetry Soc. Am., 1991, Literary Lion N.Y. Pub. Libr., 1992; grantee Ingram Merrill Found., 1979, Conn. Commn. Arts, 1981; fellow NEA, 1987, John Simon Guggenheim Meml. Found., 1988; fellow lit. Acad. Am. Poets, 1991; artist resident Djerassi Found., 1988; Woodrow Wilson fellow 1967-68; Yale U. fellow, 1971-72; Ethel Boise Morgan fellow, 1972-74; artist's fellow N.Y. Found. Arts, 1986; artist resident Yaddo, 1991, MacDowell Colony, 1991. Mem. Phi Beta Kappa, Alpha Sigma Nu. Home: 15 Grand St Stonington CT 06378-1340 Office: The Yale Review Yale Univ PO Box 208243 New Haven CT 06520-8243

MCCLATCHY, JAMES B., editor, newspaper publisher; b. Sacramento; s. Carlos K. and Phebe (Briggs) McC.; m. Susan Brewster; children: Carlos F., William B. B.A., Stanford U.; M.S., Columbia U. Reporter Sacramento Bee; reporter, editor Fresno Bee, Calif.; pub. McClatchy Newspapers, Sacramento.; past pres., dir. InterAm. Press Assn. Pilot USAFR, 1945-47. Mem. Calif. Nature Conservancy (dir.), Am. Press Inst. (dir.). Office: McClatchy Newspapers 21st & Q Sts Sacramento CA 95813

MCCLAUGHERTY, JOHN LEWIS, lawyer; b. Bluefield, W.Va., Feb. 13, 1931; s. William N. and N. Louisa (Shelton) McC.; m. Sallie M. Fredeking, June 27, 1953; children: Martha M. Nepa, John W. BS, Northwestern U., 1953; LLB, W.Va. U., 1956. Bar: W.Va. 1956, U.S. Dist. Ct. (so. dist.) W.Va. 1956, U.S. Ct. Appeals (4th cir.) 1956, U.S. Supreme Ct. 1975, U.S. Ct. Mil. Appeals 1957. Assoc. Jackson & Kelly, Charleston, W.Va., 1959-65, ptnr., 1965—; mem. Nat. Conf. Commrs. on Uniform State Laws, Chgo., 1977—; pres. Ea. Mineral Law Found., Morgantown, W.Va., 1983-84; dir. Wesbanco South Hills, Charleston. Contbr. articles to profl. jours., chpts. to books. Pres. W.Va. Symphony Orch., Charleston, 1982—; trustee Am. Symphony Orch. League, Washington, 1991—, W.Va. Wesleyan Coll., Buckhannon, 1989-94; dir. Charleston Renaissance Corp., 1989—. 1st lt. USAF, 1956-59. Named Coal Lawyer of the Yr. Nat. Coal Lawyers Conf., 1983, Mayor's Award for Arts Vol., Fund for the Arts, Charleston, 1990; listed in The Best Lawyers in America. Fellow Am. Bar Found. (life); mem. ABA, W.Va. Bar Found. (pres. 1992—), Am. Judicature Soc., W.Va. Bar Assn. (pres. 1995—), Kanawha County Bar Assn. (pres. 1980-82), Kiwanis, Masons, Shriners, Order of Coif. Democrat. Methodist. Home: 3 Bendcrest Pl Charleston WV 25314-1510 Office: Jackson & Kelly PO Box 553 1600 Laidley Twr Charleston WV 25322

MCCLAVE, DONALD SILSBEE, professional society administrator; b. Cleve., May 7, 1941; s. Charles Green and Anne Elizabeth (Oakley) McC.; m. Christine Phyllis Mary Tomkins, Feb. 19, 1966; children: Andrew Green, Susan Elizabeth (dec.). BA, Denison U., 1963. Mktg. rsch. officer Bank of Calif., San Francisco, 1968-70; v.p. Cen. Nat. Bank, Chgo., 1970-75; v.p. First Interstate Bank, Portland, Oreg., 1975-77, sr. v.p., 1977-79, exec. v.p., 1979-86; pres., chief exec. officer Portland Met. C. of C., 1987—; instr. Grad. Sch. Mktg. and Strategic Planning, Athens, 1982-84, Pacific Coast Sch. Banking, Seattle, 1976-78. Pres. Oreg. Episc. Sch. Bd., Portland, 1983-84; pres. Assn. Oreg. Industries Found., Salem, 1984-85; pres., co-chmn. Japan-Am. Conf. Mayors and C. of C., Portland, 1985, trustee, 1991—, exec. com., 1992—; trustee YMCA of Columbia-Willamette, 1990-92, Portland Student Svcs. Corp., 1991-93; mem. METRO Urban Growth Mgmt. Adv. Com., 1989-92; mem. adv. com. Downtown Housing Preservation Partnership Adv. Com., 1989-94; mem. City of Portland Mayoral Transition Team, 1992, Mayor's Bus. Roundtable, 1993—; bd. dirs. Oreg. Trail chpt. ARC, 1994-95, Tri-Met, 1994—, chair fin. com., 1995—. Avocations: reading, travel, golf, model building. Office: Portland Met C of C 221 NW 2nd Ave Portland OR 97209-3999

MCCLEAN, GRAHAM J., commercial printing company executive. Formerly pres. Moore Bus. Forms & Systems Div., Inc., Lake Forest, Ill.; now pres., COO Quebecor Printing (USA) Corp., Boston. Office: Quebecor Printing (USA) Corp 125 High St 23 Fl Boston MA 02110-2704*

MCCLEARY, BENJAMIN WARD, investment banker; b. Washington, July 9, 1944; s. George William and Nancy (Grim) McC.; m. Dierdre Marsters, May 6, 1967 (div. 1977); children: Benjamin, Katherine; m. Jean Muchmore, Oct. 15, 1984. AB, Princeton U., 1966. With Chemical Bank, N.Y.C., 1969-81; trainee, asst. sec., asst. v.p., v.p. Chemical Bank; sr. v.p. Lehman Bros. Kuhn Loeb, N.Y.C., 1981-83; mng. dir. Shearson Lehman Bros., 1983-87, Shearson Lehman Hutton Internat., London, 1987-88, Shearson Lehman Hutton, Inc., N.Y.C., 1988-89; ptnr. McFarland Dewey & Co., N.Y.C., 1989—; dir. Detrex Corp., Detroit, Harvel Plastics, Easton. Lt. (j.g.) USN, 1966-69. Office: McFarland Dewey & Co 230 Park Ave Rm 1450 New York NY 10169-1499

MCCLEARY, ELLIOTT HAROLD, magazine editor; b. Dixon, Ill., Sept. 12, 1927; s. Harold Elliott and Ruth C. (LieVan) McC.; m. Ann Roberts Morgan, Aug. 18, 1962 (div. 1976); children: Bryan, Heather; m. Patricia Mary Sherburne McCabe, Feb. 10, 1996. BA in English, Beloit Coll., 1952. Asst. editor Popular Mechs. mag., Chgo., 1952-56, Rotarian Mag., Evanston, Ill., 1956-65; editor-in-chief Today's Health mag., Chgo., 1966-69; free-lance writer, editor Evanston, 1969-78, 81-82; sr. editor Rand McNally, Skokie, Ill., 1978-81; sr. editor Consumers Digest mag., Chgo., 1983-85, exec. editor, 1986—. Author: New Miracles of Childbirth, 1974; co-author: American Medical Association Book of Heartcare, 1982. With U.S. Army, 1946-48. Mem. Am. Soc. Journalists and Authors (pres. Midwest chpt. 1980, 93-95). Avocation: photography. Home: 2747 Meadowlark Ln Evanston IL 60201

MCCLEARY, HENRY GLEN, geophysicist; b. Casper, Wyo., June 4, 1922; s. Raymond and Wyoma N. (Posey) McCleary Grieve; m. Beryl Tenney Nowlin, May 28, 1950; children: Gail, Glenn, Neil, Paul. Geol. Engr., Colo. Sch. Mines, 1948. From geophysicist to party chief seismic Amoco, various locations, 1948-53; exploration mgr. Woodson Oil Co., Fort Worth, 1953-60; resident mgr. NAMCO, Tripoli, Libya, 1961-62; chief geophysicist to staff geophys. assoc. Amoco Internat. Oil Co., 1963-68, Cairo, London and Buenos Aires, 1963-72, Chgo., 1972-82, Denver, 1982-84, Houston, 1984-86; internat. geophys. cons., 1986—. Served with USN, 1943-46. Named Hon. Admiral Tex. Navy, 1968. Mem. Soc. Exploration Geophysicists, Soc. Petroleum Engrs., AAAS, Houston Gem and Mineral Soc., Profl. Oil People, Sigma Alpha Epsilon, Theta Tau. Republican. Episcopalian. Clubs: Adventurers, Meml. Forest (Houston). Home: 232 Warrenton Dr Houston TX 77024-6226

MCCLEARY, LLOYD E(VERALD), education educator; b. Bradley, Ill., May 10, 1924; s. Hal and Pearl McC.; m. Iva Dene Carter, June 13, 1971; children: Joan Kay, Victoria Lea, Karen Ann. Student, Kans. U., 1941-42; B.S., U. Ill., 1948, M.S., 1950, D.Ed., 1956; postgrad., Sorbonne, Paris, 1946. Tchr., asst. prin. Portland (Oreg.) Public Schs., 1949-51; asst. prin. Univ. High Sch., Urbana, Ill., 1951-52; prin. Univ. High Sch., 1953-56; asst. supt. Evanston Twp. (Ill.) High Sch., 1956-60; assoc. Roosevelt U., 1957-69; mem. faculty U. Mich., summers, 1958-59; prof. ednl. adminstrn. U. Utah, 1969—, chmn. dept., 1969-74; assoc. CFK Ltd. Found., 1971-76; dir. projects in Latin Am. for AID, World Bank, Ford Found., Bolivian Govt.; dir. Nat. Sch. Prin. Study, 1976-79, 86-89, res. project Families in Edn., 1992-94; edn. rep. to Utah People to People Program; Keynoter Asian Conf. Edn., 1985; edn. adviser Office of the Queen, Jordan, 1985-86; advisor Nat. Commn. on Standards in the Principalship; U.S. del. Conf. on Status Children, Senegal, 1992, Yr. of the Family, Malta, 1993; J. Lloyd Trump lectr., New Orleans, 1994. Author: Organizational Analysis X-Change, 1975, Politics and Power in Education, 1976, The Senior High School Principalship, 1980, Educational Administration, Today, 1984, High School Leaders and Their Schools, vols. 1 and 2, 1990; editor: Western Hemisphere Edn. Sch. Orgn., 1989—. Served with inf. AUS, 1941-46. Decorated Bronze Star with oak leaf cluster, Army Commendation medal; S.D. Shankland fellow, 1956; Grantee Ford Found., 1968, 72, AID, 1966, 67, 70, 72, 74, 76, CFK Ltd., 1970-74, Rockefeller Family Found., 1979-80, U.S. Dept. State, 1981, 86-87, U.S. Dept. Def., 1986—; recipient Hatch Prize, 1988-89. Mem. Nat. Assn. Secondary Sch. Prins. (cert. of merit 1978, scholar-in-residence fall 1989, grantee 1969, 77, 86—), Assn. Supervision and Curriculum Devel., Nat. Assn. Elem. Sch. Prins., Phi Delta Kappa, Kappa Delta Pi. Methodist. Home: 1470 Wilton Way Salt Lake City UT 84108-2549 Office: 339 MBH University of Utah Salt Lake City UT 84112

MCCLELLAN, BENNETT EARL, producer; b. Sedalia, Mo., Nov. 20, 1952; s. G. Earl and Ruth E. (McQueen) McC.; m. Gail Jones, Sept. 5, 1981; children: Ian Michael, Elizabeth Gayle. MBA, Harvard U., 1981; MFA in Film and TV, UCLA, 1989. Writer, dir. Old Globe Theater, San Diego, 1973-76; artistic dir. Genesis Theater, San Diego, 1977-79; cons. McKinsey & Co., L.A., 1981-87, Arthur D. Little Media & Entertainment Group, Cambridge, Mass., 1987-89; prodn. exec. Hanna-Barbera Prodns., 1990-91; gen. mgr. L.A. Philharmonic Assn., 1992-94, Nicktoons/Games Animation, Studio City, Calif., 1995—. Producer: (TV series) Good News, Bad News, 1988. Paramount fellow Paramount Pictures, 1989; named Outstanding Grad. Student UCLA Alumni Assn., 1990. Mem. Hollywood Radio and TV Soc. (Internat. Broadcasting award 1989), Acad. TV Arts and Scis. Office: Nickelodeon 4040 Vineland Ave Studio City CA 91604-3350

MC CLELLAN, CATHARINE, anthropologist, educator; b. York, Pa., Mar. 1, 1921; d. William Smith and Josephine (Niles) McClellan; m. John Thayer Hitchcock, June 6, 1974. A.B. magna cum laude in Classical Archaeology, Bryn Mawr Coll., 1942; Ph.D. (Anthropology fellow), U. Calif. at Berkeley, 1950. Vis. asst. prof. U. Mo. at Columbia, 1952; asst. prof. anthropology U. Wash., Seattle, 1952-56; anthrop. cons. USPHS, Arctic Health Research Center, Alaska, 1956; asst. prof. anthropology, chmn. dept. anthropology Barnard Coll., Columbia U., 1956-61; asso. prof. anthropology U. Wis. at Madison, 1961-65, prof., 1965-83, prof. emeritus, 1983—, John Bascom prof., 1973; vis. lectr. Bryn Mawr (Pa.) Coll., 1954; vis. prof. U. Alaska, 1973, 87. Assoc. editor: Arctic Anthropology, 1961; editor, 1975-82; assoc. editor: The Western Canadian Jour. of Anthropology, 1970-73. Served to lt. WAVES, 1942-46. Margaret Snell fellow AAUW, 1950-51; Am. Acad. Arts and Scis. grantee, 1963-64; Nat. Mus. Can. grantee, 1948-74. Fellow Am. Anthrop. Assn., Royal Anthrop. Inst. Gt. Britain and Ireland, AAAS, Arctic Inst. N.Am.; mem. Am. Ethnol. Soc. (sec.-treas. 1958-59, v.p. 1964, pres. 1965), Kroeber Anthrop. Soc., Am. Folklore Soc., Am. Soc. Ethnohistory (exec. com. 1968-71), Sigma Xi. Various archaeol. and ethnographic field investigations in Alaska and Yukon Territory in Can.

MCCLELLAN, EDWIN, Japanese literature educator; b. Kobe, Japan, Oct. 24, 1925; came to U.S., 1952; s. Andrew and Teru (Yokobori) McC.; m. Rachel Elizabeth Pott, May 28, 1955; children: Andrew Lockwood, Sarah Rose. M.A., U. St. Andrews, Scotland, 1952; Ph.D., U. Chgo., 1957. Instr. English U. Chgo., 1957-59, asst. prof. Japanese lang. and lit., 1959-63, asso. prof., 1963-65, prof., 1965-70, Carl Darling Buck prof., 1970-72, chmn. dept. Far Eastern langs. and civilizations, 1966-72; prof. Japanese lit. Yale U., 1972-79, Sumitomo prof. Japanese studies, 1979—, chmn. dept. East Asian langs. and lits., 1973-82, 88-91, chmn. council humanities, 1975-77, chmn. council East Asian studies, 1979-82; vis. lectr. Far Eastern langs. Harvard U., spring 1965; mem. adv. coun. dept. Oriental studies Princeton U., 1966-71; mem. Com. to Visit East Asian Studies, Harvard U., 1982-88; mem. Am. adv. com. Japan Found., 1985-95; mem. bd. Coun. for Internat. Exch. Scholars, 1981-84. Translator: Kokoro (Natsume Soseki), 1957, Grass on the Wayside (Soseki), 1969, A Dark Night's Passing (Naoya Shiga), 1976, Fragments of a Past (Eiji Yoshikawa), 1992; author: Two Japanese Novelists: Soseki and Toson, 1969, Woman in the Crested Kimono, 1985; mem. bd. editors Jour. Japanese Studies, 1986—; contbr. articles to profl. jours. Bd. trustees Society Japanese Studies U. Wash., 1992—; mem. Com. on Emerson-Thoreau Medal and Am. Acad. Award for Humanistic Studies Am. Acad. Arts and Scis., 1995—. Recipient Kikuchi Kan prize for contbn. to study of Japanese lit., Tokyo, 1994, Noma Lit. Translation prize, 1995. Mem. Am. Acad. Arts and Scis. Home: 641 Ridge Rd Hamden CT 06517-2516

MCCLELLAN, JAMES HAROLD, electrical engineering educator; b. Guam, Oct. 5, 1947; s. Harold James McClellan and Esther Mary (Rosenbach) Matkin; m. Carolyn Frances Monjure, May 31, 1969; children—Amy, Scott. B.S., La. State U., 1969; M.S., Rice U., 1972, Ph.D., 1973. Research staff Lincoln Lab., Lexington, Mass., 1973-75; asst. prof. MIT, Cambridge, 1975-78, assoc. prof., 1978-82; tech. cons. Schlumberger Well Services, Austin, Tex., 1982-87, Ga. Inst. of Tech., 1987—; cons. Lincoln Lab., 1975-82, Lawrence Livermore Nat. Lab., Calif., 1979-82, Schlumberger, 1988-89, MathWorks, Inc., Natick, Mass., 1990—. Author: Number Theory in Digital Signal Processing, 1979, Computer-Based Exercises for Signal Processing, 1994. NSF fellow, 1971-73. Fellow IEEE; mem. Speech and Signal Processing Soc. of IEEE, Tau Beta Pi, Eta Kappa Nu. Home: 5169 Sandlewood Ct Marietta GA 30068-2875 Office: Ga Inst Tech Sch of Elec Engring Atlanta GA 30332-0250

MCCLELLAN, JOHN R., school system administrator. Supt. Centennial Sch. Dist. 12, Circle Pines, Minn. State finalist Nat. Supt. of Yr., 1992. Office: Centennial Sch Dist 12 4707 North Rd Circle Pines MN 55014-1545

MCCLELLAN, KARI TURNER, minister; b. Wheeling, W.Va., Apr. 17, 1951; d. William John and Flora Bella (McQuiston) Turner; m. Ralph L. McClellan Jr., Apr. 1988; 1 child, Mardi Lyn. BA in Religion and Philosophy, Westminster Coll., 1973; MDiv, Princeton Theol. Sem., 1976; DMin., Evangel. Theol. Sem., 1992. Ordained to ministry Presbyn. Ch. (U.S.A.), 1976. Asst. to pastor Lenape Valley Ch., New Britain, Pa., 1973-74, St. Mark's Luth. Ch., Trenton, N.J., 1974-76; chaplain Yardville (N.J.) Prison, 1974-76; asst. pastor, then assoc. pastor 1st Presbyn. Ch., Levittown, Pa., 1976-79, sr. pastor, 1979—; chaplain Lower Bucks Hosp., 1993—. Pres. Local Ministerium, Levittown/Fairless Hills, 1980-81; trustee Princeton Theol. Sem., 1983—; mem. chaplains bd. Lower Bucks Hosp. Named Citizen of Yr. Levittown/Fairless Hills, 1982. mem. Evangelical Coalition, Network Presbyn. Women in Leadership, Presbyns. for Faith, Family and Ministry (pres.), Princeton Regional Alumni Assn. (v.p. Pa. and Del. chpts. 1979-81). Home: 28 Fruitree Rd Levittown PA 19056-1904 Office: 1st Presbyn Ch 5918 Emilie Rd Levittown PA 19057-2606

MCCLELLAN, LARRY ALLEN, educator, writer; b. Buffalo, Nov. 3, 1944; s. Edward Lurelle McClellan and Helen (Denison) Greenlee; m. Diane Eunice Bonfoey, Aug. 19, 1973; children: Kara E., Seth C. Student, U. Ghana, 1964-65; BA in Psychology, Occidental Coll., 1966; MTh, U. Chgo., 1969, D Ministry, 1970. Ordained to ministry Presbyn. Ch. (U.S.A.), 1970. Prof. of sociology and community studies Govs. State U., University Park, Ill., 1970-86; interim pastor Presbyn. Ch. (U.S.A.), Chgo. area, 1980-86; sr. pastor St. Paul Community Ch., Homewood, Ill., 1986-96; adj. prof. Govs. State U., University Park, Ill., 1987-96; dir. South Met. Regional Leadership Ctr., Govs. State U., University Park, Ill., 1996—; newspaper columnist Star Publs. Chgo., 1993—; trustee Internat. Coun. Community Chs., 1989-91, pres., 1991-93. Author: Local History South of Chicago, 1988; developer social simulation games; contbr. articles to profl. publs. Mayor Village of Park Forest South (name now University Park), Ill., 1975-79; co-organizer S. Region Habitat for Humanity, Chgo. area, 1989; pres. S. Suburban Heritage Assn., Chgo. area, 1988-91. Fellow Layne Found., 1966-70, NEH, 1979. Mem. Urban Affairs Assn., Am. Acad. Religion, Assn. for Sociology of Religion, Am. Assn. State and Local History, Ill. State Hist. Soc. (Spl. Achievement award 1989), Chgo. Hist. Soc., South Suburban Ministerial Assn. (pres. 1989-91). Office: Govs State U So. Met. Regional Leadership Ctr University Park IL 60466

MCCLELLAN, ROBERT EDWARD, civil engineer; b. Atlanta, Feb. 27, 1922; s. Robert Edward and Maria Elizabeth (Ameln) McC.; m. Mary Margaret Billetter, Oct. 21, 1944; children: Kathleen Mary, Mary Elizabeth, Patricia Maura, Eileen Mary, Robert Edward III, Mary Margaret, Thomas Francis. BCE, U. So. Calif., 1947, MSCE, 1956, PhD in Engring., 1970. Registered profl. civil and structural engr., Calif. Gen. supr. design Rocketdyne, Canoga Park, Calif., 1959-62; mem. tech. staff The Aerospace Corp., El Segundo, Calif., 1962-69, mgr. strategic studies, 1980-85; chief tech. staff The Ralph M. Parsons Co., Pasadena, Calif., 1969-80; v.p. research and devel. Apollo Systems Tech., Canyon Country, Calif., 1985-88, also bd. dirs. Served to lt. (j.g.) USN, 1943-46, PTO. Recipient Outstanding Civil Engring. Grad. award U. So. Calif., 1977. Mem. AIAA, Am. Def. Preparedness Assn., Am. Soc. Indsl. Security, AAAS, Internat. Platform Assn., N.Y. Acad. Scis., L.A. Athletic Club, Sigma Xi, Tau Beta Pi, Chi Epsilon. Republican. Roman Catholic.

MCCLELLAN, ROGER ORVILLE, toxicologist; b. Tracy, Minn., Jan. 5, 1937; s. Orville and Gladys (Paulson) McC.; m. Kathleen Mary Dunagan, June 23, 1962; children: Eric John, Elizabeth Christine, Katherine Ruth. DVM with highest honors, Wash. State U., 1960; M of Mgmt, U. N.Mex., 1980. diplomate Am. Bd. Vet. Toxicology, cert. Am. Bd. Toxicology. From biol. scientist to sr. scientist Gen. Electric Co., Richland, Wash., 1957-64; sr. scientist biology dept. Pacific N.W. Labs., Richland, Wash., 1965; scientist med. research br. div. biology and medicine AEC, Washington, 1965-66; asst. dir. research, dir. fission product inhalation program Lovelace Found. Med. Edn. and Research, Albuquerque, 1966-73; v.p., dir. research adminstrn., dir. Lovelace Inhalation Toxicology Research Inst., Albuquerque, 1973-76, pres., dir., 1976-88; chmn. bd. dirs. Lovelace Biomedical and Environ. Research Inst., Albuquerque, 1988—; pres. Chem. Industry Inst. Toxicology Research, Triangle Park, N.C., 1988—; mem. research com. Health Effects Inst., 1981-92; bd. dirs. Toxicology Lab. Accreditation Bd., 1982-90, treas., 1984-90; adj. prof. Wash. State U., 1980—, U. Ark., 1970-88; clin. assoc. U. N.Mex., 1971-85, adj. prof. toxicology, 1985—; adj. prof. toxicology and occupational and environ. medicine Duke U., 1988—; adj. prof. toxicology U. N.C. Chapel Hill, 1989—; adj. prof. toxicology N.C. State Univ., 1991—; mem. dose assessment adv. group U.S. Dept. Energy, 1980-87, mem. health and environ. research adv. com., 1984-85; mem. exec. com. sci. adv. bd. EPA, 1974-95, mem. environ. health com., 1980-83, chmn., 1982-83, chmn. radionuclide emissions rev. com., 1984-85, chmn. Clean Air Sci. Adv. Com., 1987-92, chmn. rsch. strategies adv. com., 1992-94; mem. com. on toxicology NAS-NRC, 1979-87, chmn., 1980-87; bd. dirs. Lovelace Anderson Endowment Found.; mem. com. risk assessment methodology for hazardous air pollution NAS-NRC, 1991-94, com. biol. effects of Radon, 1994—; pres. Am. Bd. Vet. Toxicology, 1970-73; mem. adv. council Ctr. for Risk Mgmt., Resources for the Future, 1987—; council mem. Nat. Council for Radiation Protection, 1970—; bd. dirs. N.C. Assn. Biomedical Rsch., 1989-91, N.C. Vet. Medical Found., 1990-95, pres., 1993-94; bd. govs. Rsch. Triangle Inst., 1994—. Contbr. articles to profl. jours. Editorial bd. Jour. Toxicology and Environ. Health, 1980—, assoc. editor, 1982—; editorial bd. Fundamental and Applied Toxicology, 1984-89, assoc. editor, 1987-89; editorial bd. Toxicology and Indsl. Health, 1984—; editor CRC Critical Revs. in Toxicology, 1987—; assoc. editor Inhalation Toxicology Jour., 1987—; mem. edit. bd. Regulatory Toxicology and Pharmacology, 1993—. Recipient Herbert E. Stokinger award Am. Conf. Govtl. Indsl. Hygienists, 1985, Alumni Achievement award Wash. State U., 1987, Disting. Assoc. award Dept. Energy, 1987, 88, Arnold Lehman award Soc. Toxicology, 1992; co-recipient Frank R. Blood award Soc. Toxicology, 1989. Fellow AAAS, Am. Acad. Vet. and Comparative Toxicology, Soc. Risk Analysis; mem. Am. Chem. Soc., Inst. Medicine (elected), NAS, Radiation Research Soc. (sec.-treas. 1982-84, chmn. fin. com. 1979-82), Health Physics Soc. (chmn. program com. 1972, Elda E. Anderson award 1974), Soc. Toxicology (v.p.-elect to pres. 1987-90; inhalation specialty sect. v.p. to pres. 1983-86; bd. publs. 1983-86, chmn. 1983-85), Am. Assn. Aerosol Research (bd. dirs. 1982-94, treas. 1986-90, v.p. to pres. 1990-93), Am. Vet. Med. Assn., Gesellschaft fur Aerosolforschung, Sigma Xi, Phi Kappa Phi, Phi Zeta. Republican. Lutheran. Home: 1111 Cuatro Cerros Trl SE Albuquerque NM 87123-4149 also: 2903 Bainbridge Dr Apt Q Durham NC 27713-1448 Office: Chem Industry Inst Toxicology PO Box 12137 Research Triangle Park NC 27709

MC CLELLAN, WILLIAM MONSON, library administrator; b. Groton, Mass., Jan. 7, 1934; s. James Lewis and Ruth Caldwell (Monson) McC.; m. Jane Muir, Sept. 3, 1955; children—Jennifer, Anne, Margaret, Amy. B.A., Colo. Coll., 1956, M.A., 1961; A.M. in L.S, U. Mich., Ann Arbor, 1959. Music librarian U. Colo., Boulder, 1959-65; dir. Music Library, U. Ill., Urbana, 1965—; cons. music library resources and services to colls. and univs.; co-dir. Inst. Music Librarianship, Kent State U., 1969. Editor: Music Library Assn. Notes, 1977-82; Contbr. articles to profl. jours. Council on Library Resources fellow, 1976-77. Mem. Internat. Assn. Music Librs., Music. Libr. Assn. (pres. 1971-73, conf. panelist, chmn. stats. subcom. 1990-93). HOme: 1701 Gentry Sq Ln #108 Champaign IL 61821-5956 Office: Music Bldg University of Illinois Urbana IL 61801 *To commit myself daily to giving and opening myself to others in all professional and other contexts.*

MCCLELLAND, EMMA L., state legislator; b. Springfield, Mo., Feb. 26, 1940; m. Alan McClelland; children: Mike, Karen. BA, U. Mo., 1962. Dir. field office, corp. divsn. Mo. Sec. of State, St. Louis; committeewoman Gravis Township; mem. St. Louis County Rep. Cent. Com., Mo. Rep. State Com.; mem. Mo. State Ho. Rep., 1991—, mem. appropriations, edn., budget, and mcpl. corps. coms. Bd. dirs. Epworth Children's Home, Family Support Network; elder Webster Groves Presbyn. Ch. Recipient Silver Svc. award Nat. Soc. Autistic Children, Outstanding Svc. award Am. Assn. Mental Deficiency, Spl. Leadership award for govt. YWCA of St. Louis. Mem. Webster Groves C. of C., Pi Lambda Theta. Republican. Presbyterian. Home: 455 Pasadena Ave Webster Grove MO 63119-3126 Office: Mo Ho of Reps State Capitol Building Jefferson City MO 65101-1556

MC CLELLAND, JAMES CRAIG, lawyer; b. New Alexandria, Pa., Sept. 8, 1901; s. James Craig and Cora Blanche (Barnhart) McC.; m. Eleanor May Hamilton, June 15, 1929 (dec. July 1964); children—Louise (Mrs. Gerhard Urban), James Craig, Jr.; m. Marjorie Brown Hilkert, Mar. 29, 1969. B.A., Coll. Wooster, 1923; LL.B., Western Res. U., 1926. Bar: Ohio bar 1926. Pvt. practice Cleve., 1926—; mem. firm Boer, Mierke, McClelland & Caldwell (and predecessor firms), 1926-82; of counsel Wilson Caldwell, 1982—. Counsel Berea City Sch. Dist., Southwest Gen. Hosp. Mem. ABA, Ohio Bar Assn. (past mem. council of dels.), Cleve. Bar Assn. (past mem. exec. com.), Order of the Coif, Delta Sigma Rho. Home: 38 E Carriage Dr Chagrin Falls OH 44022-2875 Office: Park Bldg 140 Public Sq Cleveland OH 44114-2213

MCCLELLAND, JAMES LLOYD, psychology educator, cognitive scientist; b. Cambridge, Mass., Dec. 1, 1948; s. Walter Moore and Frances (Shaffer) McC.; m. Heidi Marsha Feldman, May 6, 1978; children: Mollie S., Heather Ann. BA in Psychology, Columbia U., 1970; PhD in Cognitive Psychology, U. Pa., 1975. Asst. prof. dept. psychology U. California, San Diego, 1974-80, assoc. prof., 1980-84; assoc. prof. Carnegie-Mellon U., Pitts., 1984-85, prof. psychology, 1985—, prof. computer sci., 1987—, acting head psychology, 1989-90, co-dir. Ctr. for Neural Basis of Cognition, 1994—; adj. prof. neurosci. U. Pitts., 1995—; vis. scientist dept. psychology and Ctr. Cognitive Sci., MIT, 1982-84; vis. scholar dept. psychology Harvard U., 1982-84; mem. com. on basic rsch. in behavioral and social scis. NRC, 1985, rev. panel for cognition, emotion and personality NIMH, 1983-87, behavioral scis. rsch. br. assessment panel, 1987-88, Cognitive Functional Neurosci., 1995—; co-organizer NSF workshop on connectionism and cognitive sci., 1986. Author: (with others) Parallel Distributed Processing: Explorations in the Microstructure of Cognition, Vols. I, II, 1986; co-author: A Handbook of Models, Programs, and Exercises, 1988; contbr. numerous articles, reports, book chpts. to profl. publs.; sr. editor Cognitive Sci., 1988-91; mem. editorial bd. Perception and Psychophysics, 1977-82, Jour. of Verbal Learning and Verbal Behavior, 1980-84, Cognitive Sci., 1983-88, Cognitive Neuropsychology, 1983—, (book series) Computational Approaches in Cognitive Sci., 1983—, Cognitive Psychology, 1984—, Jour. Exptl. Psychology: General, 1984-87, Lang. and Cognitive Processes, 1988—, Neural Computation, 1989—. Recipient William W. Cumming prize Columbia U., 1970, Rsch. Scientist Career Devel. award NIMH, 1981-86, 87—; NSF fellow, 1970-73, grantee, 1976-79, 80-84, 86-87, 88—; grantee Office Naval Rsch., 1982-87. Fellow AAAS; mem. Cognitive Sci. Soc. (governing bd. 1988—, chmn. 1991), Psychonomics Soc., Internat. Assn. for Study Attention and Performance (governing bd. 1986—, lectr. 1986), Soc. Exptl. Psychologists (Warren medal 1993), Phi Beta Kappa. Office: Carnegie Mellon U Dept Psychology Pittsburgh PA 15213-3890

MCCLELLAND, JEFFERY M., advertising and public relations executive, consultant; b. Media, Pa., Apr. 20, 1962; s. John Howard and Elizabeth Mary (Paynter) McC. Student, Goldey Bencom Coll., 1985. Mktg. mgmt. account exec. Shipley Assocs., Wilmington, Del., 1985-86; pres., media dir. Bryan Charles and Assocs., Wilmington, 1986—. Recipient Silver and Merit awards Addes Advt. Club Del., 1987. Mem. Am. Mktg. Assn., Del. Contenders Assn. Avocations: athletics, reading, travel. Office: Bryan Charles & Assocs 1719 Delaware Ave Wilmington DE 19806-2353

MCCLELLAND, MICHAEL, wholesale distribution executive; b. 1947. BS, Ball State U., 1969; MS, St. Francis Coll., 1971. With Hardware Wholesalers Inc., Fort Wayne, Ind., 1974-77, v.p., pres., 1977-81, v.p. sales, 1981-84, v.p. sales mktg., 1984-87, exec. v.p., 1987-92, pres., CEO, 1992—. Office: Hardware Wholesalers Inc PO Box 868 6502 Nelson Rd Fort Wayne IN 46803*

MCCLELLAND, NORMAN P., food products executive. Ceo., chmn. Shamrock Foods Co., Phoenix, Ariz., 1949—. Office: Shamrock Foods Co 2228 N Black Canyon Hwy Phoenix AZ 85009-2707*

MC CLELLAND, ROBERT NELSON, surgeon, educator; b. Gilmer, Tex., Nov. 20, 1929; s. Robert Hilton and Verna Louise (Nelson) McC.; m. Connie Logan, May 5, 1958; children: Robert Christopher, Alison, Julie. B.A., U. Tex., Austin, 1952; M.D., U. Tex., Galveston, 1954. Diplomate Am. Bd. Surgery. Rotating intern U. Kans. Med. center, 1954-55; resident in gen. surgery Parkland Hosp., Dallas, 1957-59, 60-62; instr. surgery Southwestern Med. Sch., U. Tex., Dallas, 1962-63; asst. prof. Southwestern Med. Sch., U. Tex., 1963-67, asso. prof., 1967-71, prof., 1971—, Alvin Baldwin prof. surgery, 1977—; examiner Nat. Bd. Med. Examiners. Editor Audio Jour. Rev. Gen. Surgery, 1971-82, Selected Readings in Gen. Surgery, 1974—; contbr. numerous articles to profl. jours., chpts. to books. Served to capt. M.C. USAF, 1955-57. Fellow ACS (mem. grad. edn. com.); mem. AMA, Am. Surg. Assn., Western Surg. Assn., Soc. Surgery of Alimentary Tract, Am. Gastroent. Assn., Southwestern Surg. Soc., So. Surg. Assn., Dallas Soc. Gen. Surgeons (pres. 1987-88), Tex. Surg. Soc., Tex. Med. Assn., Dallas Country Med. Soc., Soc. Internatale de Chiurgie (bd. dirs. Am. chpt.), Phi Beta Kappa, Alpha Omega Alpha. Republican. Lutheran. Home: 3601 Potomac Ave Dallas TX 75205-2110 Office: 5323 Harry Hines Blvd Dallas TX 75235-7200

MCCLELLAND, TIMOTHY REID, baseball umpire; b. Jackson, Mich., Dec. 12, 1951; s. Reid Nathan and Geraldine Betty (Donaldson) McC.; m. Sandra Ann Seltz; children: Cole, Molly, Maggie. BS, Mich. State U., 1974, MA, 1975. Umpire Fla. State League of Minor League Baseball, Lakeland, 1976-77, So. League of Minor League Baseball, Montgomery, Ala., 1978, P.R. Baseball League, 1979, 80, Am. Assn. Minor League Baseball, Wichita, Kans., 1979-82, Am. League of Profl. Baseball, N.Y.C., 1983—. Mentor Valley H.S., West Des Moines, 1993-94; playing Santa Claus to orgns. Mem. Major League Umpires Assn. Mem. Lutheran Ch. Mo. Synod. Umpire Major League All-Star Game, Houston, 1986, Am. League Championship Series, Boston, Oakland, Calif., 1988, World Series of Profl. Baseball, Toronto, Can., Phila., 1993. Home: 5405 Woodland Ave West Des Moines IA 50266-7259 Office: Am League Profl Baseball 350 Park Ave New York NY 10022-6022

MCCLELLAND, W. CLARK, retail company financial executive; b. Detroit, Feb. 6, 1939; s. Fauvia McClelland; m. Marjorie Mele; children: Michael, Troy, Cory, Deborah. Grad., Elizabethtown Coll., 1965. Acct. Coopers and Lybrand, Phila., 1967-70; treas., chief fin. officer Heilig Meyers Corp., Richmond, Va., 1970-74; dir., chief fin. officer Gas Spring Corp., Montgomeryville, Pa., 1974-75; exec. v.p., CFO Hechinger Co., Landover, Md., 1975—. Mem. AICPA, Nat. Capital Group Fin. Execs. Inst. Office: Hechinger Co 3500 Pennsy Dr Landover MD 20785-1633

MC CLELLAND, W. KENT, food products executive. With Shamrock Foods Co., Phoenix, Ariz., 1975-79, Mercantile Bank, Canada, 1980-84, MB Financial Services Corp., L.A., 1980-84; v.p., dir. Shamrock Foods Co., Phoenix, Ariz., 1984-87, pres., coo, 1987—. Office: Shamrock Foods Co 2228 N Black Canyon Hwy Phoenix AZ 85009-2707*

MCCLELLAND, WILLIAM CRAIG, paper company executive; b. Orange, N.J., Apr. 21, 1934; s. William N. and Pauline (Lee) McC.; m. Alice Garrett, Dec. 28, 1956; children: Suzanne, Alice Elizabeth, Heather. BS in Econs., Princeton U., 1956; MBA, Harvard U., 1965. Salesman, branch mgr. PPG Industries, Cleve. and Erie, Pa., 1960-63; pres. Watervliet Paper Co. div. Hammermill Paper Co., Mich., 1969-73; product, mktg. mgr. Hammermill Paper Co., Erie, Pa., 1965-69, v.p., 1973-80, sr. v.p., 1980-83, exec. v.p., dir., 1983-85, pres., chief exec. officer, 1985-88, also bd. dirs.; sr. v.p. Internat. Paper Co., 1986-87, exec. v.p., 1987-88, also bd. dirs.; exec. v.p. Union Camp Corp., Wayne, N.J., 1988-89, chmn., pres. chief operating officer, 1989—; bd. dirs. Quaker State Corp., PNC Fin. Corp., Allegheny Ludlum Corp. Mem. Coun. Fellows, Behrend Coll. of Pa. State U., 1980-88; dir. Pitts. Theol. Seminary, 1988—. Lt. (j.g.) USN, 1956-59. Home: 7 Ridge Crest Rd Saddle River NJ 07458-3107*

MCCLELLAN-HOLT, JEAN ELIZABETH, physical education educator, administrator; b. Pine Bluff, Ark., June 25, 1960; d. James Fennimore and Lois Jean (DeDeaux) McClellan; m. William Howard Holt, Dec. 15, 1990. BS, James Madison U., 1981; cert., N.C. State U., 1986; MS, Va. Commonwealth U., 1990. Cert. leisure profl., Va., recreational sports specialist. Jr. athletic specialist, then sr. athletic specialist Chesterfield (Va.) Parks and Recreation, 1981-83; athletic supr. Chesapeake (Va.) Parks and Recreation, 1983-88; program supr., then grad. asst. Va. Commonwealth U., Richmond, 1988-90; dir. recreation Mary Washington Coll., Fredericksburg, Va., 1990-92; dir. intramurals Fla. State U., Tallahassee, 1992-93; sr. program dir. student activities U. Ctrl. Fla., Orlando, 1993-94, dir. student activities, 1994—; rsch. cons. Richmond Conv. and Visitors Bur., 1990; bd. regents Sch. Sports Mgmt., Raleigh, N.C., 1992—; bd. dirs. Leadership Tng. Inst., Richmond, 199-92. Recipient Robert F. Kennedy Merit award Fla. Jaycees, 1993; named to Outstanding Young Women of Am., 1991. Mem. Nat. Assn. Campus Activities, Va. Recreation and Park Soc., Va. Recreational Sports Assn. (exec. bd. 1990-92), Nat. Intramural-Recreational Sports Assn., Nat. Recreation and Parks Assn., Jaycees Am., Delta Sigma Theta. Democrat. Roman Catholic. Avocations: power walking, photography, sewing. Home: 700 Macglenross Dr Oviedo FL 32765-8772 Office: U Cen Fla SC Rm 203 PO Box 163240 Orlando FL 32816-3240

MCCLENDON, EDWIN JAMES, health science educator; b. Troy, Okla., Dec. 3, 1921; s. Charles Wesley and Mattie (Reed) McC.; m. Ruby Wynona Scott, May 5, 1950; children—Edwin James, Melody Jan, Joy Renee. B.S., Okla. East Central State U., 1946; M.Ed., U. Okla., 1954; Ed.D., Wayne State U., Detroit, 1964. Instr. U. Okla., Norman, 1946-47; head speech dept., tchr. Wewoka High Sch., Okla., 1947-49; assoc. dir. Tb Control, Oklahoma City, 1949-51; dir. sch health project Okla. Dept. Health and Edn., Oklahoma City, 1951-54; assoc. dir. Tb Control, Wayne County, Mich., 1954-56; dir. sch. health Wayne County, Mich., 1956-63; dir. secondary edn. Wayne County Intermediate Sch., Detroit, 1963-67; supt. schs. Highland Park, Mich., 1967-68; v.p. Highland Park Coll., Mich., 1968-69; asst. supt. health Mich. Dept. Edn., Lansing, 1969-71; prof., chmn. health edn. U. Mich., Ann Arbor, 1971-88, prof. health behavior and pub. health, 1971-88, prof. emeritus, 1988—; cons. pub. health care, 1985—; cons. WHO, 1978-89, dir. field study for Western Pacific, 1981; health field study of Arabic states, 1979-80; cons., Papua, New Guinea, Japan, Korea, Philippines, 1983-84, Fiji and Malaysia, 1987-88. Author Drug Education-A Teacher's Guide, 1969, Maxi Minds in Mini Cages, The Gifted, 1972, HEalthful Living for Today and Tomorrow, 1981, Health and Wellness, 1987, Evaluation Study of Growing Healthy, 1993; contbr. 60 articles to profl. publs. Chmn. bd. dirs. Am. Cancer Soc., Detroit, 1977-78, mem. nat. pub. edn. com., 1969-83, hon. life mem., 1980—; mem. adv. coun. alcohol abuse NIH, 1976-80; pres. Plymouth-Canton Sch. Bd., 1974-78, 82-91; Tax Rev. Bd., Plymouth, Mich., 1980-85; chmn. Jr. Red Cross S.E. Mich., 1969-73; chmn., cons. Polio Plus immunization campaign, WHO, Rotary Internat; bd. dirs. ARC S.E. Mich., 1992—, exec. com., 1993—, mem. health, safety, youth and internat. coms. Served with USN, 1942-46. Decorated Bronze Star; recipient Disting. Health Edn. award Cen. Mich. U., 1978; adminstrn. bldg. Plymouth-Canton (Mich.) schs. dedicated E. J. McClendon Edn. Ctr., 1992. Fellow Am. Pub. Health Assn., Am. Sch. Health Assn. (pres. 1970-71, Disting. Service award 1962, William A. Howe award 1976), Am. Cancer Soc. (hon. life mem., bd. dirs.), Royal Soc. Health; mem. NEA, AAUP, Mich. Sch. Health Assn. (hon. life mem., Disting. service award 1967, Golden Anniversary award 1985), Am. Social Health Assn. (dir.), Nat. Assn. Curriculum and Devel., Am. Venereal Disease Assn., Alliance Advancement Health Edn., Soc. Pub. Health Edn., Soc. Sex Educators and Counselors, Nat. Council for Internat. Health, Am. Assn. for WHO, Soc. Native Am. Indians, Rotary (pres. 1989-91), Phi Delta Kappa. Democrat. Methodist. Home and Office: 40742 Crabtree Ln Plymouth MI 48170-2742

MCCLENDON, FRED VERNON, real estate professional, business consultant, equine and realty appraiser, financial consultant; b. Vernon, Tex.; s. Guy C. and Lexie M. (Johnson) Mc C.; m. Dorothy J. Seibert, June 1943 (div. 1953); children: Cathy, Kent, Tracy; m. Ethel R. Cherry, Sept. 15, 1959; children: Tess, Rob, J.T. Assoc. degree, Hannibal La Grange Coll., 1947; BBA, Baylor U., 1949; MBA, Harvard U., postgrad. law, 1951; postgrad. in banking, Colo. U., 1951-52; postgrad., Denver U., 1951-52. Lic. ins. agt., Tenn.; cert. real estate broker, Tenn.; sr. cert. valuer. Asst. cashier U.S. Nat. Bank, Denver, 1951; gen. mgr. Nat. Paper Band Co., Denver, 1952-53; personnel mgr. Houston Fire & Casualty Co., Ft. Worth, 1954-56; gen. sales mgr. City Lincoln/Mercury, Dallas, 1957-58; owner INS-Bank Personnel Agy., Dallas, 1959-61; mng. ptnr. Allen & Mc Clendon Ins., Dallas, 1959-63; owner, broker Mc Clendon Real Estate, Dallas, 1959-63; pres. Mc Clendon Realty Co., Hampton, Tenn., 1961—; gen. mgr. Eagle Nest Ranch, Roan Mountain, Tenn., 1963-88, Mile High Ranch, Roan Mountain, 1988—; pres. FMV Appraisal Co., Hampton, 1988—; cons. Gen. Adjustments Bur., 1981—, Debourdieux Corp., 1985—, Wachesaw Corp., 1985—, Hidden Lakes Devel. Corp., various ins. cos. and law firms in U.S. and Can., IRS, U.S. Marshals Svc., U.S. Customs, 1993—; exec. cons. El Dorado Ranch, 1991—; cons. IRS; lectr. to lodges and assns; gen. ptnr. Flexnet Investments, Ltd., Dallas, 1988—; pres. Bus. Realty Internat. Cons., Roan Mountain, Tenn., 1990—; exec. v.p. OmniVue, Inc., S.C., 1992—; chmn. AmeriFund Ventures, Inc., Tenn., 1995—; pres. U.S. Med-Am. Fin. Svcs., 1995—. Contbr. articles to profl. jours. Recipient W.T. Grant fellow Harvard U., 1950-51. Mem. Am. Quarter Horse Assn. (life), Australian Appaloosa Assn., Appaloosa Horse Club U.S., Tenn. Walking Horse Breeders Assn., Am. Paint Horse Assn., Am. Soc. Equine Appraisers, Am. Horse Coun., Am. Soc. Appraisers (Accredited sr. appraiser, bd. examiners 1990—), Internat. Real Estate Inst., Nat. Assn. Real Estate Appraisers, Environ. Assessment Assoc. (cert. onspector 1991—), Appraisers Assn. Am. (cert. sr. appraiser). Republican. Mem. Seventh Day Adventists. Avocations: boating, travel, fishing, swimming. Home: PO Box 190 Roan Mountain TN 37687-0190 Office: FMV Appraisal Co PO Box 330 Hampton TN 37658-0330

MCCLENDON, SARAH NEWCOMB, news service executive, writer; b. Tyler, Tex., July 8, 1910; d. Sidney Smith and Annie Rebecca (Bonner) McClendon; 1 child, Sally Newcomb Mac Donald. Grad., Tyler Jr. Coll., U. Mo. Mem. staff Tyler Courier-Times and Tyler Morning Telegraph, 1931-39; reporter Beaumont (Tex.) Enterprise; Washington corr. Phila. Daily News, 1944; founder McClendon News Svc., Washington, 1946—; talk show host Ind. Broadcasters Network; lectr. Faneuil Hall, Boston, Poor Richard's Club, Phila., Cobo Hall, Detroit, Chautauqua Instn., N.Y., Comstock Club, Sacremento; adv. to Senior Beacon; v.p. Nat. Press Club. Author: My Eight Presidents, 1978 (1st prize); contbr. articles to mags. including Esquire, Penthouse, Diplomat; TV appearances include Merv Griffin Show, Tomorrow, Inside the White House, PBS, NBC Meet the Press, KUP Show, NBC Today Show, C-Span, CNN, Fox Morning News, Late Night with David Letterman, Michael Jackson Show (L.A. radio). Mem. VA Adv. Bd. on Women Vets, def. adv. com. Women in the Svcs.; army advisor, mem. task force Women in the Army Policy Rev.; bd. dir. Sam Rayburn Libr., In Our Own Way, So. Poverty Relief Orgn. Served with WAC. Recipient Woman of Achievement award Tex. Press Women, 1978, 2d prize Nat. Fedn. Press Women, 1979, Headliner award Women in Comm., 1st Pres. award for Journalism in Washington, Nat. Fedn. Press Women, Pub. Rels. award Am. Legion, Bob Considine award, 1990, Am. Woman award Women's Rsch. Edn. Inst., 1991. Mem. DAR (Nat. Constn. award 1990), U. Mo. Alumni Assn. (chpt. pres.), Women in Comm. (Margaret Caskey award), Am. Legion (post comdr.), Nat. Woman's Party (v.p.), Nat. Coun., Soc. Profl. Journalists (Hall of Fame Washington chpt.), Nat. Press Club (v.p.), Am. Newspaper Women's Club (pres.), Capitol Hill First Friday Club (pres.). Club: Capitol Hill First Friday (pres.). *After covering eleven presidents, I still feel that I am my own self, honest and owned by no one. I believe that journalism is a public trust and that I must uphold that public trust.*

MC CLENDON, WILLIAM HUTCHINSON, III, lawyer; b. New Orleans, Feb. 19, 1933; s. William H. and Eleanor (Eaton) McC.; m. Eugenia Mills Slaughter, Feb. 6, 1960; children: William Hutchinson, IV, Virginia Morris, Eleanor Eaton, Bryan Slaughter. B.A., Tulane U., 1956, LL.B., 1958. Bar: La. 1958, U.S. Supreme Ct. 1964. Atty. Humble Oil & Refining Co., 1958-60; with firm Taylor, Porter, Brooks & Phillips, Baton Rouge, 1960—; ptnr. Taylor, Porter, Brooks & Phillips, 1966—; instr. comml. law and negotiable instruments Am. Inst. Banking, 1963-74; lectr. movable Property La. Bar Assn. Bridging the Gap Inst., 1965; lectr. La. State U. LAw Sch. and Real Estate Seminar chmn., 1972, 74, 76, 80, 82, 85, 87, 95, La. Soc. of Profl. Surveying, 1989, La. Soc. CPA's, 1991, Banking Seminar, 1995; adj. prof. La. State U. Legal Negotiation, 1983—. Contbr. articles to legal jours. Bd. dirs. Cancer Soc. Baton Rouge, 1968-71; trustee Episcopal High Sch., 1976-78; mem. Dean's council Tulane U. Law Sch., 1984-88. Served to capt. AUS. Mem. ABA, Am. Judicature Soc., La. Bar Assn. (chmn. sect. trust estates, probate and immovable property law 1969-70, Meml. award article 1987), Baton Rouge Bar Assn. (chmn. title standards com. 1968-69), Tulane Alumni Assn. Greater Baton Rouge (pres. 1968-69), Baton Rouge Green (bd. dirs. 1991-93), Hilltop Aboretum (bd. dirs. 1993-95), La. Civil Svc. League (pres. 1992-94), La. Tulane Law Alumni (treas., 2d v.p. 1964-65), Kappa Alpha. Republican. Episcopalian (vestry, sr. warden 1975, 81, 84, diocesan standing com. 1985-89). Clubs: Baton Rouge Assembly (treas. 1983); Toastmasters (Baton Rouge) (pres. 1970), Baton Rouge Country (Baton Rouge), Camelot (Baton Rouge); Pickwick (New Orleans). Lodge: Rotary (bd. dirs. Baton Rouge club 1972). Home: Oakland at Gurley 6165 Highway 963 Ethel LA 70730-3615 Office: 451 Florida St Baton Rouge LA 70801-1700

MC CLENNEN, LOUIS, lawyer, educator; b. Cambridge, Mass., May 29, 1912; s. Edward F. and Mary (Crane) Mc C.; m. Miriam Jacobs, Apr. 25, 1969; children by previous marriage: Adams, James, Helen, Persis, Crane, Emery. AB cum laude, Harvard U., 1934, JD, 1937. Bar: Mass. 1937, Ind. 1940, Ariz. 1946. Practice in Boston, 1937-39, Indpls., 1940-42, Phoenix, 1946—; now pres. McClennen & Fels, P.C.; adj. prof. law (fed. taxation) Ariz. State U., 1974-80, pres. Law Soc., 1981-83. Author: (with others) Arizona Estate Tax, 1953, (with J.T. Melczer Jr.) Arizona Income Tax Regulations, 1954; contbr. articles to profl. mags. Pres. Ariz. Bd. Edn., 1965-69; trustee No. Ariz. Mus.; past pres., bd. dirs. Maricopa County Legal Aid Soc., Phoenix Symphony Assn.; v.p., bd. dirs. Phoenix United Fund; sec., bd. dirs. Phoenix Country Day Sch.; bd. dirs. Ariz. Acad.; regional dir. Harvard Alumni Assn. Maj. USAAF, 1942-46. Mem. ABA, Ariz. Bar Assn., Maricopa County Bar Assn. (dir., past v.p.), Harvard Law Sch. Assn. (v.p.) Lawyers Club Phoenix (pres.), Phoenix Country Club, Eastward Ho Country Club (Chatham, Mass.). Unitarian. Home and Office: 5311 N La Plaza Cir Phoenix AZ 85012-1415

MC CLENNEY, BYRON NELSON, community college administrator; b. San Antonio, Dec. 14, 1939; s. Thomas B. and Lorene Holley McC.; children: Mark Nelson, Don Alan; m. Kay McCullough, May 17, 1986. BS, U. Tex., 1961, MEd, 1963, EdD, 1969. Asst. dean evening divsn. San Antonio Coll., 1966-68; dean instrn. McLennan C.C., Waco, Tex., 1968-70; dean instrn. Eastfield Coll., Dallas County, Tex., 1970-71, pres., 1971-78; pres. Parkersburg (W.Va.) C.C., 1978-81, San Antonio C.C. Dist., 1981; chancellor Alamo C.C. Dist., 1982-86; pres. C.C. Denver, 1986—; cons. Ctr. for Higher Edn. Mgmt. Sys. Author: Management for Productivity, 1980. NDEA fellow, 1965-66; recipient Disting. Alumni award U. Tex. Coll. Edn., 1982-83, Thomas J. Peters Nat. Leadership award League for Innovation, 1989. Mem. Am. Assn. Cmty. and Jr. Colls. (chmn. pres.'s acad. 1983-84, mem. urban commn. 1987-90), Commn. on Instns. of Higher Edn., Rotary (past dist. gov.). Presbyterian. Club: Rotary (past dist. gov.). Office: Community Coll Denver PO Box 173363 Denver CO 80217-3363

MCCLENON, JOHN RAYMOND, chemistry educator; b. Grinnell, Iowa, May 1, 1937; s. Raymond Benedict and Erika (Weber) McC.; m. Mary Alice Thornton, June 7, 1959; children: Anne Jeanette, Marca Kay, Maureen. B.A., Grinnell Coll., 1959; Ph.D., UCLA, 1964. Asst. prof. Milton Coll., Wis., 1963-65; asst. prof. chemistry Sweet Briar (Va.) Coll., 1965-72, assoc. prof., 1972-76, prof., 1976-82, Charles A. Dana prof., 1982—; head FBN Microcomputing, Lynchburg, Va., 1980—, Johnny McClenon Big Band, Lynchburg, Va., 1978—. Editor: (newsletter) Macintosh User's Group, Sweet Briar Coll. Chmn. ACLU local chpt., 1966-75; prin. clarinettist Lynchburg Symphony, Va., 1976—. Mem. Am. Chem. Soc., AAUP (chmn. Sweet Briar chpt. 1982-83). Democrat. Unitarian. Home: 712 Riverside Dr Lynchburg VA 24503-1327 Office: Sweet Briar Coll PO Box 73 Sweet Briar VA 24595-0073

MCCLIMON, TIMOTHY JOHN, lawyer; b. Clinton, Iowa, July 17, 1953; s. Leonard James and Celeste Margaret (Borman) McC.; m. Suzanne Berman, Jan. 30, 1994. BA magna cum laude, Luther Coll., 1975; MS, St. Cloud State U., 1976; JD, Georgetown U., 1986. Bar: N.Y. 1987. Asst. dir. student activities St. Cloud (Minn.) State U., 1975-76; performing arts coordinator Western Ill. U., Macomb, 1976-79; program specialist Nat. Endowment for the Arts, Washington, 1979-82, program adminstr., 1982-86, law clk., 1985-86; assoc. Webster and Sheffield, N.Y.C., 1986-88; v.p. AT&T Found., N.Y.C., 1988-96, exec. dir., 1996—; adj. prof. NYU, 1990—; bd. dirs. Am. Coun. for Arts, N.Y.C., Second Stage Theatre, N.Y.C., Theatre Comms. Group, N.Y.C., Field Papers, Inc., N.Y.C., Performance Space 122, N.Y.C.; speaker Confs. on Arts Mgmt., 1979—; cons. NEA, Washington, 1986—; mem. mayor's cultural affairs adv. commn. City of N.Y.C., 1992-94. Author: (textbook chpt.) Audiences and the Arts, 1981; contbr. articles to Jour. of Law and the Arts, 1986, other publs., 1989—. Recipient Eagle Scout award Boy Scouts Am., 1967, Faculty award Blue Key Nat. Honor Frat., 1979. Mem. N.Y.C. Bar Assn. (com. mem. 1987-92), ABA (com. mem. 1986-88), N.Y. State Bar Assn., Vol. Lawyers for the Arts. Avocations: photography, tennis, bicycling, traveling, reading. Home: Penthouse 2-C 222 Riverside Dr New York NY 10025-6809 Office: AT&T Found Ste 3100 1301 Avenue Of The Americas New York NY 10019-6022

MCCLINTIC, FRED FRAZIER, simulation engineer; b. Chester, Pa., Aug. 15, 1948; s. Fred F. and Maxene Mary (Felter) McC.; m. Janet Mary DeVitis, May 23, 1970; children: Shannon Janet, Sharon Marie. BS in Engring., Widener U., Chester, Pa., 1970; MS in Indsl. Engring., Tex. A&M U., 1972. Ops. rsch. analyst U.S. Army Civil Svc., Ft. Knox, Ky., 1970-78; prof. wargaming U.S. Army War Coll., Carlisle, Pa., 1978-83, tech. dir. dept. wargaming, 1978-83; pres. McClintic Wargaming Inc., Media, Pa., 1983-85; sr. assoc. CACI, Mechanicsburg, Pa., 1985-86; lead scientist Computer Scis. Corp., Moorestown, N.J., 1986-89; mgr. rsch. and devel. Lockheed Martin, Orlando, Fla., 1989—. Author: The Armor Development Plan, 1976-78; (wargames) McClintic Theater Model, 1979, VII Corps Model, 1981, Warrior Preparation Model, 1983, TACAIR, 1975. Mem. TAu Beta Pi, Sigma Pi Sigma, Alpha Pi Mu, Phi Kappa Phi, Alpha Chi. Roman Catholic. Achievements include tech. leadership in Army, Navy and Air Force interactive simulations, models and wargames; designing and setup of USAF Warrior Preparations Ctr. Models derived from work include JTLS, JESS, CBS, JOINTWARS, and others; lead scientist for Enhanced Naval Wargaming System. Home: 1700 Woodbury Rd #2302 Orlando FL 32828

MCCLINTIC, HOWARD GRESSON, foundation executive; b. Pitts., Feb. 27, 1951; s. Stewart and Pamela Mary (Gresson) McC.; m. Katherine Davis Foss, Sept. 14, 1948; children: Margaret Gresson, Katherine Davis, Henry Stewart. BA in Polit. Sci./Econs., George Washington U., 1973. Legis. asst. U.S. Sen. Howard H. Baker, Washington, 1973-75; assoc. cons. Energy Decisions, Inc., Washington, 1975-78; energy policy analyst Chem. Sys., Inc., N.Y.C., 1978-80; sr. cons. Coal Use Group, Inc., Washington, 1980-83; staff officer NAS, Washington, 1983-87; exec. dir. The Jefferson Energy Found., Washington, 1987—; spl. cons. NAS, 1973-74, Law Offices of Dudley & Warner, N.Y.C., 1979, Internat. Bus. Counsellors, Washington, 1982, Japan Nat. Oil Co., Washington, 1983. Co-editor: NAS Com. Rpt., Oceans in Year 2000, 1974, staff coord. rpts., 1984, 86; exec. producer energy films: Everything Starts With Energy, Energy Policy On Trial, Future Energy Sources, Double Jeopardy, Access to Public Lands and Waters, Nuclear Waste and the West, What Price Cheap Oil?, The Emerging National Energy Strategy. Co-founder Decade Soc., Washington, 1979-83; coord. Washingtonians for Bush, 1983; chmn. subcom. U.S. Dept. Energy, 1988; assoc. mem. Naval War Coll. Found. Mem. Am. Energy Assurance Coun. (advisor 1988—), Internat. Assn. Energy Economists, Atlantic Coun. U.S. (participant energy study 1989), Rolling Rock Club, Mid-Ocean Club (Bermuda), Gibson Island Club, Chevy Chase Club, Potomac Boat Club. Republican. Episcopalian. Avocations: skiing, golf, tennis, sailing. Home: 5115 Palisade Ln NW Washington DC 20016-5337 Office: The Jefferson Energy Found Connecticut Ave NW 12th Fl Washington DC 20036-9999

MC CLINTOCK, ARCHIE GLENN, lawyer; b. Sheridan, Wyo., Mar. 26, 1911; s. James Porter and Martie E. (Glenn) McC.; m. Ina Jean Robinson, May 27, 1939 (dec. 1974); children: Ellery, Jeffry, Kathleen. B.A., U. Wyo., 1933, LLB with honor, 1935. Bar: Wyo. 1935, Calif. 1982. Pvt. practice law Cheyenne, Wyo., 1935-73, 81-83, 87—; justice Wyo. Supreme Ct., Cheyenne, 1973-81; atty. gen. State of Wyo., 1982-87; semi-ret.; adj. prof. law U. Wyo., 1988, 90-92. Mem. Wyo. Fair Employment Practices Commn., 1965-71. Served with USNR, 1944-45. Mem. Wyo. State Bar (pres. 1950-51), Am. Judicature Soc., Order of Coif (hon. mem.) Sigma Nu. Democrat. Club: Elks. Home: 1211 Richardson Ct Cheyenne WY 82001-2424

MCCLINTOCK, EUGENE JEROME, minister; b. San Diego, Calif., Jan. 25, 1924; s. Alberta Jerome and Gladys Elizabeth (Wilsie) McC.;m. Lena LaVerne Brown, Feb. 16, 1947; children: Nathan-Calvin, Joseph, Mark. Student, Caldwell Seminary, 1942-45; BTh, Pentecostal Bible Inst., 1951. Ordained to ministry United Pentecostal Ch. Pastor United Pentacostal Ch., Twin Falls, Idaho, 1945-47, 1st Pentecostal Ch., Aberdeen, Miss., 1949-60, Dupo (Ill.) Pentecostal Ch., 1960-64, Calvary Apostolic Ch., Mt. Vernon, Ill., 1964-79; gen. sec. Sunday sch. United Pentecostal Ch., St. Louis, 1979-82, gen. dir. Sunday sch., 1982—; part time instr. Pentecostal Bible Inst., Tupelo, Miss., 1950-60. Author: Achieving Excellence in the Sunday School, Vols. I, II, III, IV, 1992; editor Christian Educator, 1982-94. Active ministerial fellowship, Aberdeen, Miss., 1950-60, Dupo, 1960-64, Mt. Vernon, 1964-79. Avocations: golf, photography, travel, writing. Office: United Pentecostal Ch Internat 8855 Dunn Rd Hazelwood MO 63042-2212

MCCLINTOCK, GEORGE DUNLAP, lawyer; b. Pocatello, Idaho, Nov. 30, 1920; s. George Dunlap and Jessie (McCabe) McC.; m. Aileen McHugh, Sept. 19, 1945; children—Jessie Kelly, Catharine, George, Jane Wyatt, Michael, Anne. A.B. cum laude, Dartmouth Coll., 1942; LL.B., Harvard U., 1948. Bar: Minn. 1948. Ptnr. Faegre & Benson, Mpls., 1948-90; dir. Merchants Bank, Rugby, N.D.; trustee Douglas Rees Trust, 1966—, Paul R. Held Testamentary Trusts, 1980—. Trustee, mayor City of Woodland, Minn., 1970-79; exec. bd., Viking council Boy Scouts Am., Mpls., 1959-74, pres., 1966-67; gen. campaign chmn. United Way of Mpls., 1972, bd. dirs., 1973-81, pres., 1976; trustee Convent of Visitation Sch., St. Paul, 1975-81; trustee North Meml. Med. Ctr., Robbinsdale, Minn., 1959-75; trustee, sec. Minn. Med. Found., Mpls., 1982-90. Served to lt. USNR, 1942-46. Recipient Disting. Eagle Scout award Boy Scouts Am., 1982. Mem. Mpls. Club (governing com. 1983-89, pres. 1987), Woodhill Country Club (trustee 1985-94). Republican. Presbyterian. Avocations: golf; waterfowl hunting. Office: care Faegre & Benson 2200 Norwest Ctr 90 S 7th St Minneapolis MN 55402-3903

MCCLINTOCK, JESSICA, fashion designer; b. Frenchville, Maine, June 19, 1930; d. Rene Gagnon and Verna Hedrich; m. Frank Staples (dec. 1964); 1 child Scott. BA, San Jose State U., 1963. Elem. sch. tchr. Marblehead, Mass., 1966-68, Long Island, N.Y., 1968, Sunnyvale, Calif., 1964-65, 68-69; fashion designer Jessica McClintock, Inc., San Francisco, 1969—. Active donor, AIDS and Homeless programs; scholarship sponsor Fashion Inst. Design and Merchandising. Recipient Merit award Design, 1989, Dallas Fashion award, 1988, Tommy award, 1986, Pres. Appreciation award, 1986, Best Interior Store Design, 1986, Calif. Designer award, 1985, Earnie award, 1981, numerous others. Mem. Coun. Fashion Designers of Am., Fashion Inst. Design & Merchandising (adv. bd. 1979—), San Francisco Fashion Industry (pres. 1976-78, bd. dirs. 1989). Office: Jessica McClintock Inc 1400 16th St San Francisco CA 94103-5110*

MCCLINTOCK, WILLIAM THOMAS, health care administrator; b. Pittsfield, Mass., Oct. 23, 1934; s. Ernest William and Helen Elizabeth (Clum) M.; m. Wendolyn Hope Eckerman, June 22, 1963; children: Anne Elizabeth, Carol Jean, Thomas Daniel. BA, St. Lawrence U., Canton, N.Y., 1956; MBA, U. Chgo., 1959, MHA, 1962. Prodn. planner Corning Glass Works, Corning, N.Y., 1959-60; adminstrv. resident Highland Hosp., Oakland, Calif., 1961-62; adminstrv. asst. Univ. Hosps. of Cleve., 1962-65; asst. adminstr. Presbyn. Hosp., Whittier, Calif., 1965-68; regional asst. Kaiser Found. Hosps., Oakland, Calif., 1968-70; assoc. dir., exec. dir. Conn. Hosp. Planning Commn., New Haven, 1970-75; project dir., lectr. sch. health studies U. N.H., Durham, 1975-77; regional mgr. Tex. Med. Found., Austin, 1977-81; adminstr. Schick Shadel Hosp., Fort Worth, 1981-87; mgmt. cons. George S. May Internat. Co., Park Ridge, Ill., 1987-88; mgr. Nat. Ctr. Rsch. Programs Am. Heart Assn., Dallas, 1988-89; adminstr. Ambulatory Svcs. Health Care of Tex., Ft. Worth, 1990-92; CEO Boundary Community Hosp. & Nursing Home, Bonners Ferry, Idaho, 1992—. 1st lt. U.S. Army, 1957. Fellow Am. Coll. Health Care Execs., Am. Coll. Addiction Treatment Adminstrs.; mem. Am. Hosp. Assn. (life), Am. Heart Assn. (mem. bd. dirs. Idaho/Mont. affiliate 1993—), Idaho Hosp. Assn. (bd. dirs. 1995—), Unity Lodge No. 9, F&AM, N.Y. Republican. Presbyterian. Avocations: book collections, gardening, photography. Home: County Rd 62C PO Box 1226 Bonners Ferry ID 83805-1226 Office: 6640 Kaniksu St Bonners Ferry ID 83805

MC CLINTON, DONALD G., diversified holding company executive; b. Pitts., June 30, 1933; s. Donald K. and Ethel M. McC.; m. Jane Ann Knoebel, Apr. 12, 1958; children: Catherine, D. Scott. B.S., Miami U., Oxford, Ohio, 1955. Audit mgr. Arthur Andersen & Co., Cleve., 1955-62; mgr. accounting E. Ohio Gas Co., Cleve., 1962-66; exec. v.p. Nat. Industries, Inc., Louisville, 1966-79; pres. Yellow Cab Co., Louisville, 1979-94; owner, chmn. bd. Interlock Industries, Inc., 1994—; pres. Skylight Thoroughbred Tng. Ctr., Inc., 1994—; bd. dirs. Bank of Louisville, Cartenders Heathcorp; trustee Jewish Hosp. Health Care Systems, Inc., 1983—. Mem. Louisville-Jefferson County Bicentennial Commn., 1976-77; mem. coun. treas. Old Kentucky Home. coun. Boy Scouts Am., 1976-94; mem. Citizens at Large Jefferson County Budget Com., 1978-84; bd. overseers Bellarmine Coll., 1978-84; bd. dirs. Ky. Derby Festival, 1978—, Jewish Hosp., Louisville, 1980-86; trustee Spalding U., 1985-91. Mem. Fin. Execs. Inst. Home: 6205 Deep Creek Dr Prospect KY 40059-8606 Office: Skylight Thoroughbred Tng Ctr Inc PO Box 4 Goshen KY 40026

MCCLINTON, WENDELL C., religious organization administrator; b. Waco, Tex., Jan. 10, 1933; s. Clyde E. and Gertrude (Cotton) McC.; m. Beverly A. Harrison, Oct. 19, 1954; children: Kent, Jana, Lori, Meg. BBA, Baylor U., 1960.

MCCLOSKEY, GUY CORBETT, Buddhist religious leader; b. Akron, Ohio, Aug. 15, 1943; s. Burr Clark McCloskey and Rose (Brody) Marlin; m. Doris Jean Dye, Aug. 1, 1971; children: Brian, Vincent, Mary. Dir. adminstrn. Nichiren Shoshu of Am., Santa Monica, Calif., 1967-78; regional dir. Nichiren Shoshu Soka Gakkai of Am., Washington, 1978-91; corp. v.p. Soka Gakkai Internat.-USA, Santa Monica, 1991—; sr. vice gen. dir. Soka Gakkai Internat.-USA, Chgo., 1991—, also bd. dirs. With U.S. Army, 1965-67. Office: Sokai Gakkai Internat-USA 1455 S Wabash Ave Chicago IL 60605-2806

MCCLOSKEY, J(OHN) MICHAEL, trade association administrator; b. Eugene, Oreg., Apr. 26, 1934; s. John Clement and Agnes Margaret (Studer) McC.; m. Maxine Mugg Johnson, June 17, 1965; stepchildren: Claire, Laura, James, Rosemary Johnson. BA, Harvard U., 1956; JD, U. Oreg., 1961. N.W. rep. Sierra Club, Eugene, 1961-65; asst. to pres. Sierra Club, San Francisco, 1965-66, conservation dir., 1966-69, exec. dir., 1969-85; chmn. Sierra Club, Washington, 1985—, acting exec. dir., 1986-87; vice-chmn. Commn. on Environ. Law and Policy (Internat. Union for Conservation of Nature), Gland, Switzerland, 1978-88; mem. Pres.'s Commn. on Agenda for 1980's, Washington, 1979-80; co-chmn. OSHA-Environ. Conf., Washington, 1983-87; vice chmn. Am. Com. on Internat. Conservation, 1988-90; mem. Internat. Union for Conservaton of Nature Commn. Nat. Parks and Protected Areas, 1988—; mem. adj. faculty Sch. Natural Resources, U. Mich., 1988—. Contbr. articles to profl. jours. Bd. dirs. Nat. Resources Coun. Am., 1988-94, vice chmn., 1989-91, chmn., 1992-93, chmn. advocacy forum, 1989-91; bd. dirs. Ind. Sector, 1990—, Mineral Policy Ctr., 1988—, Coalition for Environmentally Responsible Economies, 1989—; mem. steering com. Blueprint for Environ., 1987-88; nominated candidate Oreg. Ho. of Reps., 1962. Recipient award Calif. Conservation Coun., 1969, John Muir award Sierra Club, 1979, UN Environ. Program Global 500 award, 1992. Mem. Harvard Club, Explorers Club (N.Y.C.). Democrat. Office: Sierra Club 408 C St NE Washington DC 20002-5818

MC CLOSKEY, PAUL N., JR., lawyer, former congressman; b. San Bernardino, Calif., Sept. 29, 1927; m. Helen Hooper McCloskey (div.); children—Nancy, Peter, John, Kathleen. A.B., Stanford, 1950, LL.B., 1953; J.D., Santa Clara Law Sch., 1974. Bar: Calif. bar 1953. Deputy dist. atty. Alameda County, Calif., 1953-54; mem. firm McCloskey, Wilson, Mosher & Martin, Palo Alto, 1956-67; mem. 90th-94th Congresses from 17th Calif. dist., 95th-97th Congresses from 12th Calif. dist., 1967-83; ptnr. Brobeck Phleger & Harrison, 1983-89; now counsel McClung & Davis, Laguna Hills, Calif.; founder, ptnr. Law Office of Paul Mc Closkey; del. UN Law of Sea Conf.; lectr. in law Stanford Law Sch., 1964-67, Santa Clara Law Sch., 1964-67. Author: Truth and Untruth, 1972. Served with USN, 1945-47, to col. USMC, 1950-52. Decorated Navy Cross, Silver Star, Purple Heart. Mem. ABA, Palo Alto Bar Assn. (pres. 1960-61), Santa Clara County Bar Assn. (trustee 1965-67), State Bar Calif. (pres. conf. barristers 1961-62), Phi Delta Phi. Republican. Office: Law Office of Paul Mc Closkey 2925 Woodside Rd Woodside CA 94062*

MC CLOSKEY, ROBERT, artist; b. Hamilton, Ohio, Sept. 15, 1914; s. Howard Hill and Mabel (Wismer) McC.; m. Margaret Durand, Nov. 23, 1940; children: Sarah, Jane. Student, Vesper George Sch., N.Y.C., NAD; Litt.D. (hon.), Miami U., Oxford, Ohio, 1962, Mt. Holyoke Coll., South

Hadley, Mass., 1967, U. Maine, 1990; hon. degree, Bowdoin Coll., 1991. Artist, illustrator, host, Am. Songfest, Weston Woods bicentennial film.; Executed bas-reliefs, Hamilton Municipal Bldg., Ohio, 1935; author: Lentil, 1940, Make Way for Ducklings, 1941 (bronze ducklings sculpted by Nancy Schön installed Boston Pub. Garden, 1987, replicas placed in Moscow Park, 1991), Homer Price, 1943, Blueberries for Sal, 1948, Centerburg Tales, 1951, One Morning in Maine, 1952, Time of Wonder, 1957, Bert Dow, Deep Water Man, 1963. Recipient numerous awards including President's award for creative work NAD, 1936; recipient numerous awards including Prix de Rome Am. Acad. in Rome, 1939, Caldecott medal for most disting. picture book for children published in 1941, 1942, Caldecott medal for Time of Wonder, 1958, Regina medal Cath. Library Assn., 1974; hon. by. ALA, 1991. Fellow Am. Acad. Rome; mem. P.E.N., Authors League Am. Home: Little Deer Isle ME 04650

MC CLOSKEY, ROBERT JAMES, former diplomat; b. Phila., Nov. 25, 1922; s. Thomas and Anna (Wallace) McC.; m. Anne Taylor Phelan, July 8, 1961; children: Lisa Siobhan, André Taylor McCloskey. B.S. in Journalism, Temple U., 1953; postgrad., George Washington U., 1958-59. Engaged in hotel work, 1945-50, newspaper reporter, 1952-55; joined U.S. Fgn. Svc., 1955; assigned Hong Kong, 1955-57; publs. officer State Dept., 1957-58; press officer Office of News, 1958-60; assigned U.S. Mission to UN 15th Gen. Assembly, 1960-62; spl. asst. Bur. Pub. Affairs, State Dept., 1962-63; dep. dir. Office News, 1963-64, dir., 1964-66, dep. asst. sec. of state, 1966-69; dep. asst. sec., spl. asst. to sec. for press rels. Office Press Rels., 1969-73; amb. to Republic of Cyprus, 1973-74; amb.-at-large U.S. State Dept., 1974-75, amb.-at-large, asst. sec. state for congl. rels., 1975-76; amb. to The Netherlands, 1976-78, amb. to Greece, 1978-81; ombudsman Washington Post, 1981-83; sr. v.p. Cath. Relief Svcs., Washington, 1984-89; editor Mediterranean Quar., Washington, 1988-90; bd. dirs. Anatoia Coll., Boston, 1981—. Bd. dirs. Am. Acad. Diplomacy. Staff sgt. USMC, 1942-45. Home: 111 Hesketh St Chevy Chase MD 20815-4222

MCCLUNG, A(LEXANDER) KEITH, JR., lawyer; b. Gallipolis, Ohio, Sept. 13, 1934; s. Alexander Keith and Florence (Juhling) McC.; m. Sandra B. Foley, Aug. 17, 1957; children: Alexander Keith III, Martha E. AB, W.Va. U., 1956; JD, Harvard U., 1959. Bar: W.Va. 1959, Md. 1970, Mich. 1972. Assoc. Jackson, Kelly, Holt & O'Farrell, Charleston, W.Va., 1959-69; assoc. counsel Comml. Credit Corp., Balt., 1969-70, v.p., counsel, 1973-82, gen. atty., 1982-85; sr. gen. atty. Comml. Credit Co., Balt., 1985-89, sr. v.p., gen. counsel, 1989—; v.p., counsel McCullagh Leasing, Inc., Roseville, Mich., 1970-73; bd. dirs. Travelers Bank; trustee Roland Park Found.; mem. adv. coun. Coll. Arts and Sci., W.Va. U. Lt. U.S. Army, 1961-62. Mem. ABA (subcom. uniform comml. code, com. equipment leasing). Democrat. Home: 214 Ridgewood Rd Baltimore MD 21210-2539 Office: Comml Credit Co 300 St Paul Pl Baltimore MD 21202-2120

MC CLUNG, JIM HILL, light manufacturing company executive; b. Buena Vista, Ga., Nov. 8, 1936; s. Jim Hill and Marjorie (Oxford) McC.; m. Jo Patrick, July 5, 1958; children—Jim Hill, Karen Mareese. B.A., Emory U., 1958; M.B.A., Harvard U., 1964. With Lithonia Lighting div. Nat. Svc. Industries, Inc., Conyers, Ga., 1964—; now pres., assoc. dir. Lithonia Lighting div. Nat. Svc. Industries, Inc. Served with USAF, 1958-62. Mem. Illuminating Engring. Soc. N.Am. (vice chmn. lighting rsch. and edn. fund), Nat. Elec. Distbrs. Assn. (mfrs. bd.), Nat. Elec. Mfrs. Assn. (nat. lighting bur., bd. dirs.), Intelligent Bldgs. Inst. (bd. dirs.), Lighting Rsch. Inst. (bd. dirs.), Elec. Mfrs. Club, World Pres.'s Orgn. Methodist. Office: Lithonia Lighting Div PO Box A Conyers GA 30207-0067

MCCLUNG, KENNETH AUSTIN, JR., training executive, performance consultant; b. Decatur, Ga., Apr. 11, 1947; s. Kenneth Austin Sr. and Marianne (Conklin) McC.; m. Christina June Palensar, Mar. 21, 1975. BA, North Ga. Coll., 1969; MS, EdD, U. So. Calif., 1976. Commd. 2d lt. U.S. Army, 1969, advanced through grades to maj., 1980; lt. col. USAR; cons. in field Suffern, N.Y., 1980-81; sr. ptnr. Instrl. Design Group, Inc., Morristown, N.J., 1981—; bd. dirs. Nat. Productivity Ctr., Boulder, Colo., LTI, Inc., Washington; author/mgr. more than 100 mgmt., sales, and tech. tng. programs for major corps.; performance cons. to sr. corp. mgmt. Author: Microcomputers for Medical Professionals, 1984, Microcomputers for Legal Professionals, 1984, Microcomputers for Investment Professionals, 1984, Microcomputers for Insurance Professionals, 1984, Personal Computers for Executives, 1984, French edit. 1985; co-author: Sales Training Handbook, 1989. Mem. ASTD, Nat. Soc. Performance Instruction (pres. N.J. chpt. 1986-88, N.E. regional cons. 1989-90, nat. nomination chmn. 1990-91, nat. emerging tech. chmn. 1991-92). Avocations: sailing, tennis, bicycling, rock climbing, skiing. Office: Instrnl Design Group Inc 144 Speedwell Ave Morristown NJ 07960-3850

MC CLUNG, LELAND SWINT, microbiologist, educator; b. Atlanta, Tex., Aug. 4, 1910; s. Joe Baker and Roxie Buelah (Swint) McC.; m. Ruth Wilhelmien Exner, Dec. 25, 1944. A.B., U. Tex., 1931, A.M., 1932; Ph.D., U. Wis., 1934. Research bacteriologist Am. Can Co., Maywood, Ill., 1934-36; instr. in fruit products and jr. bacteriologist Coll. Agr., U. Calif., 1936-37; instr. research medicine George Williams Hooper Found. for Med. Research, U. Calif., 1937-39; asst. prof. Ind. U., Bloomington, 1940-44; assoc. prof. Ind. U., 1944-48, prof., chmn. dept. bacteriology, 1946-66, prof. microbiology, 1966-81, prof. emeritus, 1981—, asst. dir. div. biol. scis., 1965-68; sec. pub. health and nutrition sect. 5th Pacific Sci. Congress. Author: (with Elizabeth McCoy), 2 vols.) The Anaerobic Bacteria and Their Activities in Nature and Disease: A Subject Bibliography, 1939, supplement, 1941; The Anaerobic Bacteria: Their Activities in Nature and Disease: The Literature for 1940-75 (7 vols.), 1982; contbr. articles to sci. jours. John Simon Guggenheim Meml. Found. fellow, 1939-40; rsch. fellow in bacteriology Harvard Med. Sch., 1939-40. Fellow AAAS, Am. Acad. Microbiology (gov. 1961-67, 76-77), Ind. Acad. Sci.; mem. Am. Soc. Microbiology (hon., archivist 1960-82), Soc. Am. Bacteriologists (editl. bd. Jour. Bacteriology 1953-57, archivist 1953-60, chmn. com on edn. 1958-61, Chas. A. Behrens award Ind. br. 1981, Barnett Cohen award Md. br. 1984), Am. Inst. Biol. Scis. (gov. bd. 1968-74), Inst. Food Tech., Nat. Assn. Biology Tchrs. (pres. 1965), Soc. Indsl. Microbiology, Sigma Xi, Phi Sigma, Gamma Alpha, Alpha Epsilon Delta. Office: Ind U Dept Biology Jordan Hall # 138 Bloomington IN 47405-6801

MCCLUNG, RICHARD GOEHRING, lawyer; b. Butler, Pa., June 26, 1913; s. Frank A. and Mary A. (Goehring) McC.; m. Jean Barrett Coffin, Dec. 1, 1951 (dec.); children: Jean C., Mary G., Priscilla B. A.B., Princeton U., 1935; LL.B., Yale U., 1939; cert., Harvard U. Bus. Sch., 1937. Bar: N.Y. 1940. Pvt. practice N.Y.C., 1940—; with Carter, Ledyard & Milburn, 1946—, ptnr., 1948, of counsel, 1983—. Served to comdr. USNR, 1942-46. Home: 101D Lewis St Greenwich CT 06830-6606 Office: 2 Wall St New York NY 10005-2001

MCCLURE, ANN CRAWFORD, lawyer; b. Cin., Sept. 5, 1953; d. William Edward and Patricia Ann (Jewett) Crawford; m. David R. McClure, Nov. 12, 1983; children: Kinsey Tristen, Scott Crawford. BS magna cum laude, Tex. Christian U., 1974; JD, U. Houston, 1979. Bd. cert. in family law and civil appellate law Tex. Bd. Legal Specialization. Assoc. Piro and Lilly, Houston, 1979-83; pvt. practice El Paso, Tex., 1983-92; ptnr. McClure and McClure, El Paso, 1992-94; justice Eighth Ct. of Appeals, El Paso, 1995—; past mem. Tex. Bd. Law Examiners; past dir. Appellate and Advocacy Sect. Coun.; past mem. Bd. Disciplinary Appeals; mem. Family Law Specialization Exam Comm., 1989-93; dir. Family Law Coun., 1987-91. Contbr. numerous articles to profl. jours.; past editor The Family Law Forum; contbg. editor: Texas Family Law Service; mem. Tex. Family Law Practice Manual editl. com., 1982-93. Mem. State Bar Tex. (treas. 1993-94, sec. family law sect. 1994-95, vice chair family law sect. 1995-96), Tex. Acad. Family Law Specialists. Democrat. Presbyterian.

MCCLURE, BROOKS, management consultant; b. N.Y.C., Mar. 8, 1919; s. Walter Harsha and Angelica (Mendoza) McC.; m. Olga Beatrice Gallik, Oct. 15, 1949; 1 child, Karen. AB summa cum laude, U. Md.; disting. grad., U.S. Naval War Coll. N.Y. corr. Western Press Ltd., Australia, 1939-42; copy editor Washington Eve. Star, 1946-51; joined U.S. Fgn. Service, 1951; information officer, attache embassy Copenhagen, 1951-53; press attache embassy Vienna, 1953-55; information officer, attache embassy Cairo, 1956-57, Seoul, 1957-60, Bonn, 1960-63; policy officer Europe USIA, 1963-66; pub. affairs officer 1st sec. embassy, Copenhagen, 1967-72; spl. asst. policy plans and nat. security council affairs, internat. security affairs Dept. Def., 1972-76; internat. security adviser USIA, 1976-77; program coordinator Crisis Assessment Staff, Dept. Commerce, 1977-78; dir. ops. Internat. Mgmt. Analysis and Resources Corp., 1978-81, v.p., 1982—; sec. Cross-Continent Assocs. Ltd., 1994—; various spl. assignments, Europe, Middle East, Asia, Africa; lectr. FBI Acad., Fgn. Svc. Inst., Inter-Am. Def. Coll., Army War Coll., Navy War Coll. Contbg. author: Modern Guerrilla Warfare, 1962, Dynamics of Terrorism, 1977, International Terrorism in Contemporary World, 1978, Corporate Vulnerability and How to Assess it: Political Terrorism and Business, 1979, Business and the Middle East, 1981, Political Terrorism and Energy, 1981; Contbr. articles profl. jours.; author report to Senate Judiciary Com. on internat. terroism and hostage def. measures; testifier on internat. security, hostage behavior, def. of Alaskan pipeline, FBI charter U.S. Senate, 1975-79. With AUS, 1942-46, ETO. Mem. Am. Fgn. Svc. Assn., Assn. for Diplomatic Studies, Nat. Press Club, DACOR, Phi Kappa Phi, Alpha Sigma Lambda. Home: 6204 Rockhurst Rd Bethesda MD 20817-1756 Office: IMAR Corp PO Box 34528 Bethesda MD 20827-0528

MCCLURE, DANIEL M., lawyer; b. Enid, Okla., Feb. 5, 1952; s. Larry M. and Marie Dolores (Sarver) McC.; m. Judy Lynn Pinson, Jan. 3, 1976; children: Andrew Mead, Mark William, Kathleen Claire. BA with highest hons., U. Okla., 1974; JD cum laude, Harvard U., 1978. Bar: Tex. 1978, U.S. Dist. Ct. (so. dist., ea. dist.) Tex. 1979, U.S. Ct. Appeals (5th cir., 11th cir.) 1981. Assoc. Fulbright & Jaworski, Houston, 1978-86, ptnr., 1986—. Fellow Tex. Bar Found.; mem. ABA, Nat. Health Lawyers Assn., Nat. Assn. R.R. Trial Counsel, Tex. Bar Assn., Houston Bar Assn. (cert. civil trial law), Harvard Law Sch. Assn. Avocation: tennis. Home: 2 Long Timbers Ln Houston TX 77024-5445 Office: Fulbright & Jaworski 1301 Mckinney St Houston TX 77010

MCCLURE, DONALD EDWIN, electrical construction executive, consultant; b. Pasadena, Calif., Mar. 13, 1934; s. Robert Wirt and Edna Buela (Williamson) McC.; m. Diana Lee Myrick, Feb. 9, 1958; children: Scott Patrick, Christopher Daniel. BS in Bus. Adminstrn., San Diego State U., 1957. Lic. gen. engring., bldg., elec. Elec. estimator Calif. Electric Works, San Diego, 1953-57; v.p. JCS Elec., San Diego, 1958-61; owner, proprietor McClure Electric, San Diego, 1961-63; chief estimator Am. Electric Contracting Corp., La Mesa, Calif., 1963-65; pres. Cal Pacific Electric Inc., San Diego, 1965-69; v.p., sec., dir. Am. Elec. Contracting, La Mesa, 1969-79; v.p. Steiny and Co., Inc., San Diego, 1979—; cons. constrn., expert witness Don E. McClure, San Diego, 1987—. Active Nat. Rep. Com., Washington, 1984—. Mem. Am. Subcontractors Assn., Singing Hills Tennis Club, Big Bear Tennis Ranch, Friendly Sons' of St. Patrick, Kappa Sigma Alumni Assn. Presbyterian. Avocations: skiing, tennis, fly fishing, deep sea fishing, boating, golf. Office: 1083 N Cuyamaca St El Cajon CA 92020-1803

MC CLURE, DONALD STUART, physical chemist, educator; b. Yonkers, N.Y., Aug. 27, 1920; s. Robert Hirt and Helen (Campbell) McC.; m. Laura Lee Thompson, July 9, 1949; children: Edward, Katherine, Kevin. B.Chemistry, U. Minn., 1942; Ph.D., U. Calif., Berkeley, 1948. With war research div. Columbia U., 1942-46; mem. faculty U. Calif., Berkeley, 1948-55; group leader, mem. profl. staff RCA Labs., 1955-62; prof. chemistry U. Chgo., 1962-67; prof. chemistry Princeton (N.J.) U., 1967-91, prof. emeritus, 1991—; vis. lectr. various univs.; cons. to govt. and industry. Author: Electronic Spectra of Molecules and Ions in Crystals, 1959, Some Aspects of Crystal Field Theory, 1964; also articles. Guggenheim fellow Oxford (Eng.) U., 1972-73; Humboldt fellow, 1980; recipient Irving Langmuir prize, 1979. Fellow Am. Acad. Arts and Scis., Nat. Acad. Scis.; mem. Am. Chem. Soc., Am. Phys. Soc. Home: 23 Hemlock Cir Princeton NJ 08540-5405

MCCLURE, GEORGE MORRIS, III, lawyer; b. Danville, Ky., Nov. 12, 1934; s. George Morris Jr. and Helen Louise (McCormack) McC.; m. Judith DeGolier Selee, July 6, 1957 (div. Jan. 1969); 1 child, George Morris IV; m. Patricia Moberly, Dec. 11, 1971; children: Joseph Scott Kirk, Patrick Spencer McClure. AB, Princeton U., 1956; JD, Denver U., 1963. Bar: Colo. 1963, Ky. 1970, U.S. Dist. Ct. (ea. dist.) Ky. 1970. Assoc. Yegge, Hall, Schulenberg, Denver, 1963-65; sole practitioner Denver, 1965-67; assoc. Zarlengo, Mott & Carlin, Denver, 1967-69, James G. Sheehan, Danville, Ky., 1970-71; sole practitioner Danville, 1971-72, 72—; county atty. Boyle County, Danville, 1972—. Adv. div. Comty. Theatre, Danville, 1984—. 1st lt. USMC, 1956-59. Mem. ABA, Ky. Bar Assn. Democrat. Avocations: golf, fishing, amateur radio, flying, gardening. Office: Boyle County Court House 321 W Main St Danville KY 40422-1848

MCCLURE, GROVER BENJAMIN, management consultant; b. Houstonia, Mo., Oct. 15, 1918; s. Grover B. and Sue F. (Cook) McC. B.A., U. Richmond, 1939. Pres. internat. div. Richardson-Merrell, N.Y.C., 1954-62; pres. Europe and Africa divs. Paris, 1960-81; exec. v.p. Richardson-Vicks, Inc., Wilton, Conn., 1981-85; cons. New Canaan, Conn., 1985—; bd. dirs. Northrup & Johnson Cannes, France. Served to lt. comdr. USNR, 1941-46. Republican. Presbyterian. Clubs: Silver Springs (Ridgefield, Conn.). Avocations: tennis, golf, travel, yachting. Home and Office: 12 St John Place New Canaan CT 06840-4005

MCCLURE, JAMES FOCHT, JR., federal judge; b. Danville, Pa., Apr. 6, 1931; s. James Focht and Florence Kathryn (Fowler) McC.; m. Elizabeth Louise Barber, June 14, 1952; children: Holly McClure Kerwin, Kimberly Ann Pacala, Jamee McClure Sealy, Mary Elizabeth Hudec, Margaret McClure Persing. AB, Amherst Coll., 1952; JD, U. Pa., 1957. Bar: D.C. 1957, Pa. 1958, U.S. Dist. Ct. D.C. 1957, U.S. Dist. Ct. (ea. and mid. dist.) Pa. 1958, U.S. Ct. Appeals (3d cir.) 1959. Atty., advisor Dept. State, Washington, 1957-58; assoc. Morgan, Lewis & Bockius, Phila., 1958-61; atty. Merck & Co., Inc., N.Y.C., 1961-65; ptnr. McClure & McClure, Lewisburg, Pa., 1965-77, McClure & Light, Lewisburg, 1978-84; pres., judge Ct. Common Pleas, 17th Jud. Dist. Pa., Lewisburg, 1984-90; dist. judge U.S. Dist. Ct. (mid. dist.) Pa., Williamsport, Pa., 1990—; dist. atty. Union County, Lewisburg, 1974-75. Pres. bd. sch. dirs. Lewisburg Area Sch. Dist., 1969-74. Cpl. U.S. Army, 1952-54. Mem. Pa. Bar Assn., Union County Bar Assn., Bucknell U. Golf Club, Susquehanna Valley Chorale, Order of Coif, Phi Beta Kappa. Republican. Presbyterian. Office: US Dist Ct Federal Bldg 240 W 3rd St # 1448 Williamsport PA 17701-6412

MC CLURE, JAMES J., JR., lawyer, former municipal executive; b. Oak Park, Ill., Sept. 23, 1920; s. James J. and Ada Leslie (Baker) McC.; m. Margaret Carolyn Phelps, Apr. 9, 1949; children: John Phelps, Julia Jean, Donald Stewart. BA, U. Chgo., 1942, JD, 1949. Bar: Ill. 1950. Ptnr. Gardner, Carton & Douglas, Chgo., 1962-91, of counsel, 1991—; mem. Oak Park Plan Commn., 1966-73; mem. Northeastern Ill. Planning Commn., 1973-77, pres., 1975-77; pres. Village of Oak Park, 1973-81, Oak Park Exch. Congress Inc., 1981—. Pres. United Christian Community Svcs., 1967-69, 71-73, Erie Neighborhood House, 1953-55, Oak Park-River Forest Community Chest, 1967; moderator Presbytery Chgo., 1969; mem. Gov.'s Spl. Com. on MPO, 1978-79; bd. dirs. Leadership Council of Met. Open Communities, 1981—, sec., 1990—; bd. dirs. Met. Planning Coun., 1982-93, honorary dir., 1993—; bd. dirs. Community Renewal Soc., 1982-91, v.p., 1984-88, treas. 1988-91; chmn. Christian Century Found., 1981—; bd. trustees McCormick Theol. Sem., 1981—, chmn. bd. 1987-90. hon. trustee, 1990—; mem. ch. vocations unit, 1987-92, vice chair 1990; mem. gen. assembly coun. Presbyn. Ch. U.S.A., 1987-90; bd. dirs. Oak Park Edn. Found., 1991-96, Oak Park River Forest Community Found., 1991—; mem. Vision 2000 (Oak Park) Coordinating Com., 1995. With USNR, 1942-46. Recipient Disting. Citizen award Oak Park, 1976; Silver Beaver award; Disting. Eagle Scout award Boy Scouts Am. Mem. ABA, Am. Coll. Trust and Estate Counsel, Ill. Bar Assn., Chgo. Bar Assn., Am. Law Inst., Lambda Alpha. Clubs: Univ. (Chgo.). Home: 200 S Maple Ave Oak Park IL 60302-3026 Office: Gardner Carton & Douglas 321 N Clark St Chicago IL 60610-4714 *Love of God, love of family, awareness of both the uniqueness and the contribution of every other human being, a sense of the wholeness of life with my religious faith, my profession of law, my family and my community service each playing an important part and complimenting each other.*

MCCLURE, LUCRETIA WALKER, medical librarian; b. Denver, Jan. 2, 1925; d. Oscar W. and Rachel E. (Stander) Low; m. Arnold L. McClure, May 26, 1946 (dec. Oct. 1992); children: John N., Paul W. BJ, U. Mo., 1945; MA in Librarianship, U. Denver, 1964. Cataloging/serials libr. Edward G. Miner Libr., U. Rochester, N.Y., 1964-68, readers svcs. libr., 1968-72, assoc. libr., 1972-78, med. libr., assoc. prof. med. bibliography, 1979-93, med. libr. emerita, 1993—; bd. dirs. Friends of Nat. Libr. of Medicine, Bethesda, Md., 1991—. Editor Bull., Edward G. Miner Libr., 1979-93; editor IFLA sect. Biol. and Med. Scis. Librs., 1993—; contbr. articles to profl. jours. Recipient Disting. Svc. award U. Rochester, 1992. Fellow Med. Libr. Assn. (chair Upstate N.Y. and Ont. chpt. 1969, parliamentarian 1993—, pres. 1990-91, bd. dirs., fin. chair 1981-83, Marcia C. Noyes award 1996, Pres.'s award 1995), Assn. Acad. Health Scis. Libr. Dirs. (pres. 1985-86), Internat. Fedn. Libr. Assns., Acad. Health Info. Profls. (Disting. mem.). Home: 164 Elmore Rd Rochester NY 14618-3651

MCCLURE, MICHAL CLYDE, corporate executive; b. Cin., Nov. 8, 1940; s. Harold L. and Harriet E. (Hissong) McC.; m. Ilse Eleanor Brall, July 26, 1976; children: Brian H., Christopher M. BS in Physics, Purdue U., 1962, M in Indsl. Adminstrn., 1966; MS in Physics, U. Toledo, 1965. Physicist Goodyear Atomic Corp., 1962, Toledo Scale Corp., 1963-64; mgmt. cons. Booz-Allen & Hamilton, Chgo., 1966-69; investment banker Lehman Bros., N.Y.C., 1969-71; pres. McRand Internat. Ltd., Lake Forest, Ill., 1971—; mem. Ind. U. Slavic Lang. Study in the Soviet Union, 1963. Bd. dirs. Lake Fores Symphony, 1992-95. Mem. Internat. Sporthouse Registry (founder, advisor 1980-84), Collectible and Platemakers Guild (bd. dirs. 1992-94), Cliff Dwellers Club Chgo., Winter Club of Lake Forest. Avocations: golf, horseback riding. Office: McRand Internat Ltd 1 Westminster Pl Lake Forest IL 60045-1885

MCCLURE, ROGER JOHN, lawyer; b. Cleve., Nov. 22, 1943; s. Theron R. and Colene (Irwin) McC. BA, Ohio State U., 1965, JD cum laude, 1972; MA, Northwestern U., 1966. Bar: U.S. Ct. Appeals (D.C. cir.) 1974, U.S. Supreme Ct. 1978, Va. 1983, Md. 1983, Ohio, U.S. Ct. Appeals (4th, 5th & 10th cirs.). Asst. atty. gen. State of Ohio, Columbus, 1972; trial atty. FTC, Washington, 1972-76; sr. assoc. Law Offices of A.D. Berkeley, Washington, 1976-81; pvt. practice, Alexandria, Va., 1981-86; pres. Roger J. McClure, P.C., Alexandria, 1987—; del. Va. Gen. Assembly, 1992—; adj. prof. Antioch Sch. Law, Washington, 1982-84; mem. adv. bd. Va. Commerce Bank; host talk show Sta. WRC Radio, 1987-93, Sta. WPGC, 1993-94. Co-author: Winning the Syndication Game, 1988; bd. editors Ohio State U. Law Rev., 1970-72; contbr. numerous articles to profl. jours. Bd. dirs. No. Va. Cmty. Found., 1995—. Served with U.S. Army, 1967-69. Decorated Bronze Star. Mem. D.C. Bar Assn. (real estate steering com. 1982-84, chmn. antitrust divsn. 1975-76), No. Va. Apt. Assn. (bd. dirs. 1988—, 1st v.p. 1987-88, pres. 1988-89), Nat. Network Estate Planning Attys. Avocation: sailing. Office: 500 N Washington St Alexandria VA 22314-2314

MCCLURE, WILLIAM OWEN, biologist; b. Yakima, Wash., Sept. 29, 1937; s. Rexford Delmont and Ruth Josephine (Owen) McC.; m. Pamela Preston Harris, Mar. 9, 1968 (div. 1979); children: Heather Harris, Rexford Owen; m. Sara Joan Rorke, July 27, 1980. BSc, Calif. Inst. Tech., 1959; PhD, U. Wash., 1964. Postdoctoral fellow Rockefeller U., N.Y.C., 1964-65; rsch. assoc. Rockefeller U., 1965-68; asst. prof. U. Ill., Urbana, 1968-75; assoc. prof. U. So. Calif., L.A., 1975-79; prof. biology, prof. neurology U. So. Calif., 1979—; v.p. sci. affairs Nelson Rsch. & Devel. Co., Irvine, Calif., 1981-82; acting v.p. rsch. & devel. Nelson Rsch. & Devel. Co., 1985-86; dir. program. neurol. info. sci. U. So. Calif., 1982-92, dir. program in psychobiology, 1991—; dir. cellular biology U. So. Calif., 1979-81, dir. neurobiology, 1982-88, dir. prog. psychobiology, 1991—; cons. in field; dir. Marine & Freshwater Biomed. Ctr., U. So. Calif., 1982-83; co-dir. Baja Calif. Expedition of the R/V Alpha Helix, 1974, others; chmn. Winter Conf. on Brain Rsch., 1979, 80, others; lectr. in field; sci. adv. bd. Nelson R & D, 1972-91; mem. bd. commentators Brain and Behavioral Scis., 1978—. Editor or author 3 books; co-editor: Wednesday Night at the Lab; patentee in field; mem. editorial bd. Neurochem. Rsch., 1975-81, Jour. Neurochemistry, 1977-84, Jour. Neurosci. Rsch., 1980-86; contbr. over 100 articles to profl. jours. Bd. dirs. San Pedro and Peninsula Hosp. Found., 1989—, Faculty Ctr., U. So. Calif., 1991-95, San Pedro Health Svcs., 1992—. Scripps Inst. fellow, 1958, NIH fellow, 1959-64, 64-65, Alfred P. Sloan fellow, 1972-76, others; recipient rsch. grants, various sources, 1968—; Intersci. Rsch. Inst. fellow, 1989. Mem. AAAS, Am. Soc. Neurochemistry, Soc. for Neurosci., Am. Soc. Biol. Chemistry and Molecular Biology, Interant. Soc. Neurochemistry, Assn. Neurosci. Depts. and Programs, Univ. Park Investment Group, Bay Surgical Soc., N.Y. Acad. Scis. Republican. Presbyterian. Avocations: computing, travel. Home: 30533 Rhone Dr Palos Verdes Peninsula CA 90275-5742 Office: U So Calif Dept Biol Scis Los Angeles CA 90089

MCCLURE, WILLIAM PENDLETON, lawyer; b. Washington, May 25, 1925; s. John Elmer and Helen Newsome (Pendleton) McC.; children: Marilyn Alexander, Helen Pendleton, Elizabeth Ruffin, Melinda Geoghegan. B.S., U. Pa., 1949; J.D., George Washington U., 1951, LL.M., 1954; postgrad., The Hague (Netherlands) Acad. Internat. Law, 1952. Bar: D.C. 1951. Sr. ptnr. McClure & Trotter, Washington, 1952-91, McClure, Trotter & Mentz, Washington, 1991-93, McClure, Trotter & Mentz, chartered, Washington, 1993-95; ptnr. White & Case, Washington, 1995—. Chmn. D.C. div. Crusade Against Cancer, Am. Cancer Soc., 1966, 67. Served from pvt. to 1st lt., inf. U.S. Army, 1943-46, PTO. Mem. Am. Bar Assn., Bar Assn. D.C., Am. Judicature Soc., Order of Coif, Phi Delta Phi, Phi Delta Theta. Clubs: Metropolitan (Washington), Columbia Country (Washington), Nat. Press (Washington). Home: 9505 Brooke Dr Bethesda MD 20817-2207 Office: 1747 Pennsylvania Ave NW Washington DC 20006-4604

MCCLURE-BIBBY, MARY ANNE, former state legislator; b. Milbank, S.D., Apr. 21, 1939; d. Charles Cornelius and Mary Lucille (Whittom) Burges; m. D.J. McClure, Nov. 17, 1963 (dec. Apr. 1990); 1 child, Kelly Joanne Kyro; m. John E. Bibby, May 1, 1993. BA magna cum laude, U. S.D., 1961; postgrad., U. Manchester, Eng., 1961-62; M of Pub. Adminstrn., Syracuse (N.Y.) U., 1980. Staff asst. U.S. Senator Francis Case, Washington, 1959-61; sec. to lt. gov. State of S.D., Pierre, 1963, with budget office, 1964; exec. sec. to pres. Frontier Airlines, Denver, 1963-64; tchr. Pub. High Schs., Pierre and Redfield, S.D., 1965-66, 68-70; mem. S.D. State Senate, Pierre, 1975-89, pres. pro tem, 1979-89, vice chmn. coun. of state govts., 1987, chmn. coun. of state govts., 1988; spl. asst. to Pres. Bush for intergovernmental affairs, 1989-92; exec. dir. S.D. Bush-Quayle Campaign, 1992. Vice chmn. sch. bd. Redfield Ind. Sch. Dist., 1970-74. Fulbright scholar, 1961-62, Bush Leadership fellow, 1977-80. Mem. Phi Beta Kappa. Republican. Congregationalist. Home: 817 8th Ave Brookings SD 57006-1315

MCCLURG, DOUGLAS P., lawyer; b. Cleve., Feb. 17, 1949; s. Donald Wayne and Helen Mildred (Tulin) McC.; m. Christie Jene Cobourn, Aug., 1976; children: Kelly Cobourn, Douglas Paul, Jr., Lauren Christie. BA, U. Fla., 1973, JD, 1976. Bar: Fla. 1976, U.S. Ct. Appeals (11th cir.) 1981, U.S. Dist. Ct. (mid. dist.) Fla. 1976. Assoc., shareholder Mahoney, Hadlow & Adams, Jacksonville, Fla., 1976-81; shareholder Smith & Hulsey, Jacksonville, Fla., 1981-84; ptnr. Holland & Knight, Tampa, 1984-92; shareholder Hill, Ward & Henderson, Tampa, 1992—; chmn. Bankruptcy/UCC com. of Bus. Law Section of The Fla. Bar, 1984-85, chmn. Legislation Comm. Bus. Law Sect., 1986-87, pres., chmn. Tampa Bay Bankruptcy Bar Assoc., 1989-91. Trustee The Tampa Mus. of Art, 1991-92, pres. The Tampa Club, 1992, Exec. Com. mem. Young Life of Tampa, 1994—. U.S. Army, 1968-70. Decorated Bronze Star (with Vdevice), Purple Heart (with Oak Leaf Cluster). Mem. Ye Mystic Krewe of Gasparilla, The Tampa Yacht and Country Club. Republican. Episcopalian. Avocation: competitive shooting, gun collecting, hunting, camping. Office: Hill Ward & Henderson 101 E Kennedy Blvd Ste 3700 Tampa FL 33602 Home: 2721 Terrace Dr Tampa FL 33609

MCCLURG, JAMES EDWARD, research laboratory executive; b. Bassett, Nebr., Mar. 23, 1945; s. Warren James and Delia Emma (Allyn) McC. B.S., N.E. Wesleyan U., 1967; Ph.D., U. Nebr., 1973. Instr., U. Nebr. Coll. Medicine, Omaha, 1973-76, research instr., 1973-76, clin. asst. prof. Med. Ctr., 1984—; v.p., tech, dir. Harris Labs., Inc., Lincoln, Nebr., 1976-82, exec. v.p., 1982-84, pres., chief exec. officer, 1984—; bd. dirs. Lincoln Mut. Life Ins. Co., Lincoln Gen. Hosp. (chmn.), Unemed Corp., Lincoln, Harris Labs. Ltd, Belfast No. Ireland. Mem. editorial bd. Clin. Rsch. Practices and Drug Regulatory Affairs, 1984. Contbr. articles to profl. jours. Trustee Univ. Nebr. Found.; mem. Commn. on Human Rights, Lincoln, 1982-85; com. mem. Nebr. Citizens for Study Higher Edn., Lincoln, 1984; chmn. U. Nebr.

Found. Recipient ann. research award Central Assn. Obstetricians and Gynecologists, 1982. Mem. Am. Assn. Lab. Accreditation (bd. dirs.). Republican. Clubs: Century (pres. Nebr. Wesleyan U. 1983-84), Nebraska (Lincoln). Lodge: Rotary. Avocation: boating. Office: Harris Labs Inc PO Box 80837 Lincoln NE 68501-0837

MCCLUSKEY, EDWARD JOSEPH, engineering educator; b. N.Y.C., Oct. 16, 1929; s. Edward Joseph and Rose (Slavin) McC.; m. Lois Thornhill, Feb. 14, 1981; children by previous marriage: Edward Robert, Rosemary, Therese, Joseph, Kevin, David. AB in Math. and Physics, Bowdoin Coll., Brunswick, Maine, 1953, BS, MS in Elec. Engring., 1953; ScD, MIT, 1956; doctor honoris causa Inst. Nat. Polytech. de Grenoble, 1994. With Bell Telephone Labs., Whippany, N.J., 1955-59; assoc. prof. elec. engring. Princeton, 1959-63, prof., 1963-66, dir. Computer Center, 1961-66; prof. elec. engring. and computer sci. Stanford (Calif.) U., 1967—, dir. Digital Systems Lab., 1969-78; dir. Center for Reliable Computing, 1976—; tech. advisor High Performance Systems, 1987-90. Author: A Survey of Switching Circuit Theory, 1962; Introduction to the Theory of Switching Circuits, 1965; Design of Digital Computers, 1975; Logic Design Principles with Emphasis on Testable Semicustom Circuits, 1986. Editor: Prentice-Hall Computer Engineering Series, 1988-90; assoc. editor: IRE Transactions on Computers, 1959-65; editorial bd. IEEE Design and Test, 1984-86; assoc. editor, IEEE Trans. Computer Aided Design, 1986-87. Patentee in field. Recipient Emanuel R. Piore award, 1996. Fellow AAAS, IEEE (pres. computer soc. 1970-71, Centennial medal 1984), Assn. Computing Machinery (assoc. editor jour. 1963-69); mem. IEEE Computer Soc. (Tech. Achievement award 1984, Taylor L. Booth Edn. award 1991), Am. Fedn. Info. Processing Socs. (dir., exec. com.), Internat. Fedn. Info. Processing (charter), Japan Soc. Promotion of Sci. Office: Stanford U Ctr for Reliable Computing ERL-460 Stanford CA 94305-4055

MCCLUSKEY, JEAN LOUISE, civil and consulting engineer; b. Pitts., Jan. 8, 1947; d. Matthew Ralph McCluskey Sr. and Violet (Banas) Fontaine. BS in Civil Engring., Northeastern U., 1969; MA in Urban Affairs, Boston U., 1974; postgrad., MIT, 1984. Registered profl. engr., N.Y., Maine, Mass. Staff engr. Metcalf & Eddy, Inc., Boston, 1969-74, project planner/engr., 1974-75, 76-79; sr. environ. engr. Exxon Co. USA, Pelham, N.Y., 1975-76; environ. engr. Stone and Webster Engring. Corp., Boston, 1979-84, project mgr., 1984-89, v.p., 1989-94, dir. project mgmt., 1991-93; also bd. dirs. Stone & Webster Engring. Corp., Boston; pres. Stone & Webster Civil & Transp. Svcs., Inc., 1993-94, Parsons, Brinckerhoff, Quade & Douglas, Inc., Boston, 1995—. Mem. Hull (Mass.) Fin. Com., 1985-88; mem. adv. com. Hull H.S., 1989-95; trustee New Eng. Aquarium, 1993—, South Shore Charter Sch., 1994—; mem. govt. affairs com., chair Am. Cons. Engrs. Coun. New Eng. Mem. Hull (Mass.) Fin. Com., 1985-88; mem. adv. com. Hull H.S., 1989—; trustee New Eng. Aquarium, 1993—, South Shore Charter Sch., 1994—; chmn. govt. affairs com. am. Cons. Engrs. Coun. New England, 1995-96, bd. dirs. 1996—. Recipient Outstanding Woman award Cambridge (Mass.) YWCA, 1986; fellow MIT, 1984. Mem. Water Environ. Fedn., Greater Boston C. of C. (bd. dirs. 1992-94), Chi Epsilon. Roman Catholic. Office: 120 Boylston St Boston MA 02116

MC CLYMONT, HAMILTON, entertainment industry executive; b. Montreal, Que., Can., Mar. 20, 1944; s. Hamilton, Jr. and Zoe Annis (Cook) McC.; children from previous marriage: Alexander H., Laura C.; m. Torill Samuelsen, Aug. 25, 1990. BA, Dalhousie U., 1969. Adminstrv. dir. Toronto Arts Prodns., 1971-74; adminstr. Neptune Theatre, Halifax, N.S., 1974-76; music officer, fin. Can. Council, Ottawa, Ont., 1976-78; dir., gen. mgr. Vancouver (B.C.) Opera, 1978-82; producer spl. events Expo 86, 1983-85, v.p. entertainment, 1986; prin. Lamont Mgmt. Inc., 1986—; pres. Alpha Projects Internat. Ltd., 1989-90; gen. mgr. Can. Stage Co., Toronto, Ont., 1990—; chmn. Can. Com. of Opera America, 1980-83; pres. Profl. Opera Cos. of Can., 1980-81. Mem. Can. Owners and Pilots Assn.

MCCOBB, JOHN BRADFORD, JR., lawyer; b. Orange, N.J., Oct. 14, 1939; s. John Bradford and Dorothea Joyce (Hoffman) M.; m. Maureen Kelly, Oct. 6, 1973; 1 dau., Carrie Elizabeth. A.B., Princeton U. cum laude, 1961; J.D., Stanford U., 1966; LL.M., NYU, 1973. Bar: Calif. 1967. Assoc., IBM, Armonk, N.Y., 1966-1974, gen. counsel, Tokyo, 1974-77, lab. counsel, Endicott, N.Y., 1977-79, sr. atty., White Plains, N.Y., 1979-81, regional counsel, Dallas, 1981-83; counsel, sec. IBM Instruments, Inc., Danbury, Conn., 1983-87; area counsel European Labs, Hursley, England, 1987-90; counsel govtl. programs IBM, Washington, 1990—. Trustee Princeton-in-Asia, Inc., 1970-86 . Princeton-in-Asia-teaching fellow at Chinese Univ. of Hong Kong, 1963-65. Mem. ABA, State Bar of Calif., Phi Beta Kappa. Contbr. articles to profl. jours. Office: IBM 1301 K St NW Washington DC 20005-3317

MCCOID, DONALD JAMES, bishop; b. Wheeling, W.Va., Dec. 31, 1943; s. Roy Conrad and Alberta Virginia (Sturm) McC.; m. Saundra Ernette Piisila, Oct. 20, 1973; children: Kimberly, Elizabeth. AB, West Liberty (W.Va.) State Coll., 1965; MDiv, Luth. Theol. Sem., Phila., 1968; DD (hon.), Thiel Coll., 1983. Ordained to ministry Evang. Luth. Ch. in Am., 1968. Pastor St. Luke's Luth. Ch., Monessen, Pa., 1968-72; assoc. pastor St. John's Luth. Ch. Highland, Pitts., 1972-74; area luth. coord. Western Pa.—W.Va. synod, Luth. Ch. Am., Clarksburg, W.Va., 1974-77; sr. pastor Trinity Luth. Ch., Latrobe, Pa., 1977-87; bishop Southwestern Pa. synod, Evang. Luth. Ch. in Am., Pitts., 1987—; bd. dirs. Pa. Coun. Chs., Harrisburg. Bd. dirs. Religious Leadership Forum, Pitts., 1988—; mem. exec. com. Christian Assocs. S.W. Pa., Pitts., 1988—; chair Coun. Christian Assocs. SW Pa., 1994—. Office: Evang Luth Ch in Am SW Pa Synod 9625 Perry Hwy Pittsburgh PA 15237-5555

MCCOLL, HUGH LEON, JR., banking executive; b. Bennettsville, S.C., June 18, 1935; s. Hugh Leon and Frances Pratt (Carroll) McC.; m. Jane Bratton Spratt, Oct. 3, 1959; children: Hugh Leon III, John Spratt, Jane Bratton. B.S. in Bus. Adminstrn, U. N.C., 1957. Trainee NCNB Nat. Bank, Charlotte, 1959-61, officer, 1961-65, v.p., 1965-68, sr. v.p., 1968, div. exec., 1969, exec. v.p., 1970-73, vice chmn. bd., 1973-74, pres., 1974-83, also dir.; chmn., CEO NationsBank Corp., Charlotte, 1983—; bd. dirs. Sonoco Products Inc., Hartsville, S.C., CSX Corp., Richmond, Va., Jefferson-Pilot Corp., Greensboro, N.C. Trustee Heineman Found., Charlotte, 1976—, Queens Coll., Charlotte; bd. visitors Grad. Sch. Bus. U. N.C. at Chapel Hill; chmn. Charlotte Uptown Devel. Corp., 1978-81, 85. 1st lt. USMCR, 1957-59. Mem. Bankers Roundtable (mem. trialateral commn.), Am. Bankers Assn., N.C. Bankers Assn. (pres. 1974). Democrat. Presbyterian. Office: NationsBank Corp 1 Nationsbank Plz Charlotte NC 28255*

MCCOLL, JOHN GRAHAM, plant and soil biology educator; b. Sydney, New South Wales, Australia. B.S., Sydney U., Australia, 1963; M.S., Australian Nat. U., 1965; Ph.D., U. Wash., 1969. Postdoctoral research assoc. Yale U., New Haven, 1970; asst. prof. U. Minn., Mpls., 1970-74; prof. Environ. Sci. U. Calif., Berkeley, 1974—. Contbr. articles to profl. jours. Mem. Soil Sci. Soc. Am. Office: U Cal Dept Environ Sci Policy & Mgmt 151 Hilgard Hall Berkeley CA 94720

MCCOLLAM, WILLIAM, JR., utility company executive; b. New Orleans, Mar. 15, 1925; s. William and Marie (Mason) McC.; m. Hope Flower Joffrion, Apr. 20, 1947; children: Ellendale McCollam Hoffman, William Cage, Stephen Mason. B.S., La. State U., 1943; B.S. in Engring., U.S. Mil. Acad., 1946; M.S. in Civil Engring., MIT, 1954. Registered profl. engr., N.Y. Commd. 2d lt. U.S. Army, 1946; advanced through grades to lt. col. U.S Army; resigned U.S. Army, 1961; with Ark. Power and Light Co., Little Rock, 1961-70, exec. asst., 1961-64; v.p. Ark Power and Light Co., Little Rock, 1964-68; sr. v.p. Ark. Power and Light Co., Little Rock, 1968-70; exec. v.p. New Orleans Pub. Service, 1970-71, pres., 1971-78; pres. Edison Electric Inst., Washington, 1978-90, pres. emeritus, 1990—; cons. energy mgmt. Washington, 1990—; bd. dirs. McDermott Internat., Inc., New Orleans, Burns and Roe Enterprises, Inc., Oradell, N.J.; trustee Thomas Alva Edison Found., Detroit, 1978-89; past chmn. S.W. Power Pool, Little Rock, 1973-74, Nat. Elec. Reliability Coun., Princeton, N.J., 1975-78; bd. dirs., exec. com. U.S. Mem. Com., World Energy Coun., Washington, 1978-94. Past pres. Greater New Orleans area C. of C., 1974-75; former dir. Loyola U., New Orleans, 1975-78; pres.'s council Tulane U., 1982-86. Named to La. State U. Alumni Hall of Distinction, 1985; recipient U.S. Energy award in recognition of outstanding contbn. to world energy coun., 1991. Mem. La. Soc. Profl. Engrs. (A.B. Paterson award 1975). Republican. Episcopalian. Clubs: Chevy Chase, Metropolitan (Washington); Boston, New Orleans Country. Home: 2411 Tracy Pl NW Washington DC 20008-1628 Office: Edison Electric Inst 701 Pennsylvania Ave NW Washington DC 20004-2696

MCCOLLEY, ROBERT MCNAIR, history educator; b. Salina, Kans., Feb. 2, 1933; s. Grant and Alice Elizabeth (McNair) McC.; m. Diane Laurene Kelsey, Aug. 30, 1958; children: Rebecca, Susanna, Teresa, Margaret, Carolyn, Robert Lauren. B.A., Harvard U., 1954, M.A., 1955; Ph.D., U Calif.-Berkeley, 1960. Instr. to prof. history U. Ill., Urbana, 1960—; mem. Com. for Advanced Placement Test in Am. History, 1987-90, chmn. 1988-90. Author: Slavery and Jeffersonian Virginia, 1964 (Dickerson award 1964); editor: Federalists, Republicans and Foreign Entanglements, 1969; editor: Henry Adams, John Randolph, 1995; co-editor: Refracting America, 1993; mem. editorial bd. Jour. Early Republic, 1981-85, Va. Mag. of History and Biography, 1994—; mem. editorial bd. Ill. Hist. Jour., 1984-93, chair, 1991-94; classical recs. reviewer Fanfare mag., 1989—. Mem. Am. Hist. Assn., Soc. Historians of Early Republic (pres. 1982), Orgn. Am. Historians, Va. Hist. Soc., Ill. Hist. Soc. (bd. dirs. 1978-81, 92-95, pres. elect 1996), Chgo. Hist. Soc., Cliff Dwellers. Episcopalian. Home: 503 W Illinois St Urbana IL 61801-3927 Office: U Ill Dept History 810 S Wright St Urbana IL 61801-3611

MC COLLISTER, JOHN CHARLES, writer, clergyman, educator; b. Pitts., June 1, 1935; s. John Charles and Caroline Jesse (Hall) Mc C.; m. Beverly Ann Chase, Aug. 6, 1960; children: Beth Ann, Amy Susan, Michael John. BA, Capital U., 1957; MDiv, Luth. Theol. Sem., Columbus, Ohio, 1961; PhD, Mich. State U., 1969. Ordained to ministry Luth. Ch., 1961. Pastor Zion Luth. Ch., Freeland, Mich., 1961-65, Bethlehem Luth. Ch., Lansing, Mich., 1965-71; prof. religion and Greek Olivet (Mich.) Coll., 1970-74; prof. religion and philosophy Bethune-Cookman Coll., Daytona Beach, Fla., 1974-76; prof. religion and philosophy Embry-Riddle Aero. U., 1976-82, dir. profl. programs, 1979-80, cons. to pres., 1980-82; pres. Wright Advt. Co., Daytona Beach, 1975-76; CEO New Arran Prodns., Inc., Daytona Beach, 1993—, Yongestreet Prodns., Ormond Beach, Fla., 1986; pres., CEO McCollister/Grofe Prodns., Daytona Beach, 1992—; arbitrator Fed. Mediation and Conciliation Svc., 1978; spl. master Fla. Pub. Employees Rels. Commn., 1975—; mgmt. cons. Hoover Ball and Bearing, Charlotte, Mich.; bd. dirs. Am. Writers Inst. Host: Open Phone Forum, radio sta. WROD, Daytona Beach, 1974-76; author: A Philosophy of Flight, 1981, So Help Me, God, 1981, The Christian Book of Why, 1983, Problem Solving for Executives, 1984, The Sky is Home, 1986; co-author: The Sunshine Book, 1979, Day by Day, 1990; editor and compiler: A Child is Born, 1972, Portraits of the Christ, 1974, Writing for Dollars, 1995; ; contbr. articles to various mags. Vol. probation officer, Mich., 1961-71, hearing officer, 1970-74; commr. Mich. Dept. Commerce, 1969-72; speaker Nat. Lincoln Day Observance, Washington, 1982; internat. adviser Han Nam U., Taejon, Republic of Korea, 1989. Recipient Outstanding Am. award Daytona Beach Jaycees, 1974. Mem. Am. Arbitration Assn. Home and Office: 26 Lazy Eight Dr Daytona Beach FL 32124-6775

MC COLLOM, KENNETH ALLEN, retired university dean; b. Sentinel, Okla., June 17, 1922; s. Walter William and Irene Pearl (Allen) McC.; m. Katherine Tompkins, Jan. 4, 1944; children: Alan Tompkins, Neal Norman. B.S., Okla. State U., 1948; M.S., U. Ill., 1949; Ph.D., Iowa State U., 1964. Engr. Phillips Petroleum Co., Bartlesville, Okla., 1949-51, 54-57; sect. chief, br. mgr. Phillips Petroleum Co. (Atomic Energy div.), Idaho Falls, Idaho, 1951-54, 57-62; project leader Ames (Iowa) Lab. Research Reactor, 1962-64; prof. elec. engring. Okla. State U., Stillwater, 1964-68; asst. dean engring. Okla. State U., 1968-73, assoc. dean engring., 1973-77, dean engring., architecture and tech., 1977-86; adminstrv. judge, mem. atomic safety and licensing bd. panel Nuclear Regulatory Commn., 1976—; cons. AEC; mem. Okla. State Bd. Registration for Profl. Engrs. and Land Surveyors, 1986-92, chmn. 1991-92; mem. Nat. Council for Examiners of Engring. and Surveying, 1986-92. Patentee in field. Asst. condr. Idaho Falls Civic Symphony Orch., 1958-60; bd. mem., Cub Pack leader, asst. scoutmaster Boy Scouts Am., 1960-72; campaign chmn. Stillwater United Fund, 1971-72. Served with AUS, 1942-46, ETO. Recipient Disting. Alumnus award elec. engring. dept. U. Ill., Profl. Devel. citation in engring. Iowa State U., Disting. Svc. award Nat. Coun. for Examiners of Engring. and Surveying, 1992. Fellow Am. Soc. Engring. Edn. (Chester F. Carlson award 1973, Outstanding Engr. in Okla. 1990); mem. IEEE (life, Centennial Medallion award 1993), Am. Nuclear Soc. (chmn. Okla. sect. 1974-75), Nat. Profl. Engrs. Soc. (nat. dir. 1975-78), Okla. Profl. Engrs. Soc. (adminstrv. v.p. 1974-75, exec. v.p. 1975-76, pres. 1976-77). Pres.'s Disting Scholarship established in his name Okla. State U. Home: 1107 W Knapp Ave Stillwater OK 74075-2712

MCCOLLOUGH, MICHAEL LEON, astronomer; b. Sylva, N.C., Nov. 3, 1953; s. Stribling Mancell and Vivian Hazel (Bradley) McC. B.S., Auburn U., 1975, M.S., 1981; PhD, Ind. U., 1989. Lab. instr. Auburn (Ala.) U., 1974-75, grad. asst., 1975-77, lab. technician, 1977-78; assoc. instr. Ind. U., Bloomington, 1978-86; ops. astronomer Computer Scis. Corp., Balt., 1988-90, sci. planning and scheduling system dep. br. chief, 1990-92; data processing and distbn. mgr. U.S. ROSAT Sci. Data Ctr., 1992-93; asst. system mgr. BATSE Data Analysis System, 1993—; vis. lectr. Okla. State U., 1986-87; vis. asst. prof. U. Okla., 1987-88. Recipient Achievement award Space Telescope Sci. Inst., 1990, 91, Pub. Svc. Group Achievement award NASA, 1991, Cert. Recognition, 1991, 93. Mem. Am. Astron. Soc., Royal Astron. Soc., Astron. Soc. Pacific, Am. Phys. Soc., Soc. Physics Students, Sigma Xi (assoc.), Sigma Pi Sigma. Baptist. Home: 201 Water Hill Rd Apt G13 Madison AL 35758-2919 Office: NASA/MSFC Code ES84 Huntsville AL 35812

MCCOLLUM, ALLAN LLOYD, artist; b. L.A., Aug. 4, 1944; s. Warren Whiting and Elizabeth Ann (Hinton) McC. One-man shows include Jack Glenn Gallery, Corona Del Mar, Calif., 1971, 72, Nicholas Wilder Gallery, L.A., 1973, 74, Cusack Gallery, Houston, 1973, Douglas Drake Gallery, Kansas City, 1975, 79, 83, Claire S. Copley Gallery, L.A., 1977, Julian Pretto & Co., N.Y.C., 1979, 87, 88, 89, 90, Galerie Yvon Lambert, Paris, 1980, 88, 90, Artists Space, N.Y.C., 1980, 112 Workshop, N.Y.C., 1980, Dioptre, Geneva, 1981, Hal Bromm Gallery, N.Y.C., 1981, Galerie Nicole Gonet, Lausanne, France, 1982, Health Gallery, Atlanta, 1982, Ben Shahn Galleries William Patterson Coll., Wayne, N.J., 1982, Marian Goodman Gallery, N.Y.C., 1983, Rhona Hoffman Gallery, Chgo., 1984, 85, 86-87, Richard Kuhlenschmidt Gallery, L.A., 1984, 89, 90, Diane Brown Gallery, N.Y.C., 1984, 86, 87, 89, Lisson Gallery, London, 1985, 87, 91, Cash/Newhouse Gallery, N.Y.C., 1985, 86, Gallery Nature Morte, N.Y.C., 1985, Heath Gallery, Atlanta, 1985, Tex. Gallery, Houston, 1985, Kuhlenschmidt Simon Gallery, L.A., 1985, 86, Guttenbergstrasse 62, Stuttgart, 1986, Inst. Contemporary Art U. Pa., Phila., 1986, Portikus, Frankfurt, Germany, 1988, John Weber Gallery, N.Y.C., 1988, 89, 90, 92, Centre d'Art Contemporain, Geneva, Switzerland, 1993, Castello Di Rivara, Turin, Italy, 1993, Modulo Centro Difusor De Arte, Lisbon, Portugal, 1993, Kohji Ogura Gallery, Nagoya, Japan, 1993, Galerie Franck & Schulte, Berlin, 1993, Studio Trisorio, Naples, Italy, Shiraishi Contemporary Art Inc., Tokyo, 1993, Mus. Haus Esters, Krefeld, Germany, 1994, S.L. Simpson Gallery, Toronto, Can., 1994, others; exhibited in group shows at Los Angeles County Mus. Art, L.A., 1971, 87, Seattle Art Mus., 1972, Detroit Inst. Arts, 1973, Whitney Mus. Am. Art, N.Y.C., 1975, 85, 89, 89-90, L.A. Inst. Contemporary Art, 1977, Pratt Inst. Gallery, N.Y.C., 1982, Mus. Fine Arts, Mus. N.Mex., Santa Fe, 1983, Nexus Contemporary Art Ctr., Atlanta, 1985, New Mus. Contemporary Art, N.Y.C., 1986, Padigolione d'Arte Contemporanea, Milan, Italy, 1986-87, Moderna Museet, Stockholm, 1987, Israel Mus., Jerusalem, 1987, 90, Sidney Janis Gallery, N.Y.C., 1987, 88, Milw. Art Mus., 1987-88, Internat. Ctr. Photography, N.Y.C., 1988, 89, 90, Mus. Contemporary Art, L.A., 1989, Nat. Mus. Am. Art, Washington, 1989, Galeria 57, Madrid, 1990, Mus. Contemporary Art, Chgo., 1990, La Gerenne Lemot Getigne, Paris, 1991, Carnegie Mus. Art, Pitts., 1991-92, Mus. Modern Art, N.Y.C., 1992, Museo Nacional de Arte Reina Sofia, Madrid, 1992, Lillehammer Art Mus., Norway, 1993, Lieu D'Art Contemporain, France, 1993, numerous others; represented in permanent collections Met. Mus. Art, N.Y.C., Mus. Modern Art, N.Y.C., Mus. Fine Arts, Boston, Mus. Modern Art, San Francisco, Los Angeles County Mus. Art, Mus. Contemporary Art, L.A., Denver Art Mus., Art Inst. Chgo., Detroit Inst. Arts, Mus. Fine Arts, Houston, Hirshhorn Mus., Washington, Seattle Art Mus., Newark (N.J.) Mus., Long Beach (Calif.) Mus. Art, Springfield (Mo.) Mus. Fine Art, John & Mable Ringling Mus. Art, Sarasota, Fla., Nelson Gallery Art, Kansas City, Santa Fe Mus. Art, Grey Art Gallery NYU, N.Y.C., Weatherspoon Art Gallery, Greensboro, N.C., Washington U., St. Louis, Cin. Art Mus., Van Abbe Mus., Eindhoven, The Netherlands, Louisiana Mus. Modern Art, Humlebaek, Denmark, Inst. Valenciano de Arte Moderno, Valencia, Spain, Mus. Boymans van Beunigen, Rotterdam, The Netherlands, New Tokyo Met. Mus., Ctr. Georges Pompidou, Paris, Musee National d'Art Moderne, Paris, Sprengel-Mus., Hannover, Germany, Rooseum, Malmo, Sweden, Le Consortium, Dijon, France, Fonds Regional d'Art Contemporain Bourgogne, KunstMuseum Wolfsburg, Germany, Ctr. d'art Contemporain, Geneva, Musée d'art Contemporain et Moderne, Geneva. Short Term Activities Fellowships grantee NEA, 1973; Individual Visual Artist fellow NEA, 1988. Democrat. Studio: 17 White St Apt 2B New York NY 10013-2485

MCCOLLUM, BETTY, state legislator; b. July 12, 1954; m. Douglas McCollum; 2 children. BS in Edn., Coll. St. Catherine. Retail store mgr. Minn.; mem. Minn. Ho. Reps., 1992—, mem. edn. com., environ. and natural resources com., mem. gen. legis. com., vet. affairs and elections com., mem. transportation and transit com., asst. majority leader, chair Legis. Commn. on Econ. Status of Women. Mem. St. Croix Valley Coun. Girl Scouts, Greater East Side Boy Scouts. Democrat. Home: 2668 4th Ave E North Saint Paul MN 55109-3116 Office: Minn Ho of Reps State Office Bldg 100 Constitution Ave Rm 501 Saint Paul MN 55155-1606

MCCOLLUM, CLIFFORD GLENN, college dean emeritus; b. South Gifford, Mo., May 12, 1919; s. William Henry and Aultie V. (Westfall) McC.; m. Alice Elizabeth Erickson, Aug. 18, 1940; children: Eric Edward, Lisa Buren. Student, Central Coll., 1935-37; B.S., U. Mo., 1939, M.A., 1947, Ed.D., 1949. Tchr. pub. schs. Monett, Mo., 1938-39, Poplar Bluff, Mo., 1939-41, Boonville, Mo., 1941-42; asst. prof. sci. U. No. Iowa, 1949-55, assoc. prof., 1956-59, prof., 1959-84, prof. emeritus, 1984—, head dept. sci., 1957-68; dean U. No. Iowa (Coll. Natural Scis.), 1968-84, dean emeritus, 1984—; prof. State U. N.Y. at Oneonta, 1955-56; Dir., instl. rep. Central States Univs., Inc.; cons. Coronet Instrnl. Films; cons. on sci. curricula to pub. schs. and colls.; speaker in field. Contbr. articles to profl. jours. Served with USAAF, 1943-46. Fellow AAAS (nat. committeeman 1964-67), Iowa Acad. Sci. (pres. 1979-80); mem. Am. Inst. Biol. Scis., Nat. Assn. Biology Tchrs. (regional dir. 1963-65), Nat. Assn. Research in Sci. Teaching, Nat. Sci. Tchrs. Assn., Sigma Xi, Phi Delta Kappa. Home: 2002 Chapel Hill Rd Columbia MO 65203-1916 *My personal response to the philosophical conditions in which we live today is one of preparing to live rather consistently with crises. It is my conviction that the mood of our time is toward a growing pessimism, and much of this is associated with the concomitants of a galloping technology. Yet we are not willing at this point to give up our human condition to the natural evolution that would result from basic environmental mechanisms. We will still try to condition that destiny.*

MCCOLLUM, GARY WAYNE, government official; b. Mineral Wells, Tex., Apr. 14, 1939; s. Buster Len and Edna Sue (Fowler) McC.; m. Sonja Dru Woodham, May 27, 1960 (div. 1973); children: Scott, Greg, Cynthia; m. Barbara Jean Millican, Sept. 16, 1978. BS in Biology, East Tex. State U., 1962, MS in Biology, 1963. Quarantine control officer Lunar Receiving Lab., Apollo Program to Moon, NASA Johnson Space Ctr., Houston, 1969-71; mgr. med. surveillance office Apollo Flight Crew Health Stabilization Program, Houston, 1971-72, Skylab Flight Crew Health Stabilization Program, Houston, 1972-74; life scis. ground ops. mgr. NASA Life Sci. Project Div., Houston, 1974-78, discipline mgr., 1978-83; payload integration mgr. NASA Space Shuttle Program Office, Houston, 1983-88; program mgr. NASA Hdqs. Office Sci. & Applications, Washington, 1988-93, NASA Hdqs. Office Life & Microgravity Scis. & Applications, Washington, 1993-95; space sta. program officer NASA Johnson Space Ctr., Houston, 1995—; successful completion of STS-40/Spacelab Life Scis.-1 mission, 1991, STS-47/Spacelab-J, coop. mission with Japan, 1992, STS-58/Spacelab Life Scis.-2 mission, 1993, STS-65/Internat. Microgravity Lab.-2 mission, 1994. 1st lt. USAF, 1963-66. Mem. AIAA (sr.), Sr. Exec. Assn., Delta Tau Delta. Avocations: all sports, travel. Office: NASA Johnson Space Ctr Mail Code SC Houston TX 77058

MC COLLUM, IRA WILLIAM, JR. (BILL MC COLLUM), congressman; b. Brooksville, Fla., July 12, 1944; s. Ira William and Arline Gray (Lockhart) McC.; m. Ingrid Mary Seebohm, Sept. 25, 1971; children: Douglas Michael, Justin Randolph, Andrew Lockhart. BA, U. Fla., 1965, JD, 1968. Bar: Fla. 1968. Ptnr. Pitts, Eubanks & Ross (P.A.), Orlando, Fla., 1973-80; mem. 97th-102nd Congresses from 5th Dist. Fla., 1981-92, 103d-104th Congresses from 8th Dist. Fla., 1993—; ranking minority mem., mem. banking and fin. svcs. subcom. on fin. instns. supervision, mem. regulation and deposit ins. com., chmn. judiciary subcom. on crime, mem. select com. on intelligence; vice chair House Rep. Conf. 101st-103d Congresses. Chmn. Rep. Exec. Com. Seminole County, Fla., 1976-80; county chmn.'s rep. 5th Dist. Fla. State Rep. Exec. Com., 1977-80; co-chmn. rep. platform com., 1992. With USN, 1969-72. Mem. Fla. Bar, Naval Res. Assn., Res. Officers Assn., Orange County Bar Assn. (exec. coun. 1975-79), Am. Legion, Mil. Order World Wars, Fla. Blue Key, Phi Delta Phi, Omicron Delta Kappa, Kiwanis. Episcopalian. Office: 2266 Rayburn HOB Washington DC 20515*

MCCOLLUM, JAMES FOUNTAIN, lawyer; b. Reidsville, N.C., Mar. 24, 1946; s. James F. and Dell (Frazier) McC.; m. Susan Shasek, Apr. 26, 1969; children: Audra Lynne, Amy Elizabeth. BS, Fla. Atlantic U., 1968; JD, Fla. State U., 1972. Bar: U.S. Ct. Appeals (5th cir.) 1973, Fla. 1972, U.S. Ct. Appeals (11th cir.) 1982. Assoc. Kennedy & McCollum, 1972-73; prin. James F. McCollum, P.A., 1973-77, McCollum & Oberhausen, P.A., 1977-80, McCollum & Rhoades, Sebring, Fla., 1980-86; pres. Highlands Devel. Concepts, Inc., Sebring, 1982—; sec. Focus Broadcast Communications, Inc., Sebring, 1982-87; mng. ptnr. Highlands Investment Service. Treas. Highlands County chpt. ARC, 1973-76; vestryman St. Agnes Episcopal Ch., 1973—, chancellor, 1978—; mem. Fla. Sch. Bd. Atty.'s Assn., 1974—, bd. dirs., 1989—, pres., 1995-96; mem. Com. 100 of Highlands County, 1975-83, bd. dirs., 1985-87, chmn., 1991-92; chmn. Highlands County High Speed Rail Task Force; chmn. bd., treas. Ctrl. Fla. Racing Assn., 1976-78; chmn. Leadership Sebring: life mem., past pres. Highlands Little Theatre, Inc.; bd. dirs. Palms of Sebring Nursing Home, 1988-90, Palms Estate Mobile Home Park, Sebring Airport Authority, 1988-90, treas., 1988, chmn. indsl. com., 1988, vice-chmn., 1989-90, chmn., 1990-91, Highlands County High Speed Rail Task Force, 1986-89; bd. dirs. Highlands County Family YMCA, 1985-93, pres. Sebring br., 1992-93, chmn. bldg. com., 1992-94. Recipient ARC citation, 1974, Presdl. award of appreciation Fla. Jaycees, 1980-81, 82, 85, Outstanding Svc. award Highlands Coun. of 100, 1988, Most Valuable Player award Highlands Little Theatre, Inc., 1986, Zenon Significant Achievement award, 1991; named Jaycee of Year, Sebring Jaycees, 1981, Outstanding Local Chpt. Pres., U.S. Jaycees, 1977. Outstanding Service award Highlands Council of 100, 1988. Mem. ABA, ATLA, Comml. Law League Am., Am. Arbitration Assn. (comml. arbitration panel), Nat. Assn. Retail Credit Attys., Fla. Bar (jour. com.), Highlands County Bar Assn. (past chmn. legal aid com.), Fla. Sch. Bd. Attys. Assn. (dir. 1989—, v.p. 1993-94, pres. 1994-95), Greater Sebring C. of C. (dir. 1982-89, pres. 1986-87, chmn. transp. com. 1986—, Most Valuable Dir. award 1986, 87), Fla. Jaycees (life mem. internat. senate 1977—), Lions (bd. dirs. 1972-73, v.p. 1994—, Disting. award 1984). Republican. Episcopalian. Office: 129 S Commerce Ave Sebring FL 33870-3602

MCCOLLUM, JEAN HUBBLE, medical assistant; b. Peoria, Ill., Oct. 21, 1934; d. Claude Ambrose and Josephine Mildred (Beiter) Hubble; m. Everett Monroe Patton, Sept. 4, 1960 (div. Jan. 1969); 1 child, Linda Joanne; m. James Ward McCollum, Jan. 2, 1971; 1 child, Steven Ward. Student, Bradley U., Ill. Cen. Coll. Stenographer Caterpillar Tractor Co., Peoria, 1952-53, supr. stenographer pool, 1953-55, adminstrv. sec., treas., 1955-60, sec., asst. dept. mgr., 1969-71; med. staff sec. Proctor Cmty. Hosp., Peoria, 1978-82; med. asst. Drs. Taylor, Fox and Morgan, Peoria, 1982-84; freelance med. asst. Meth. Hosp. and numerous physicians, Peoria, 1984-89; office mgr. Dr. Danehower, McLelland and Stone, Peoria, 1989—. Vol. tutor Northmoor Sch., Peoria, 1974-78; bd. dirs., mem. exec. com., com. chmn. Planned Parenthood, Peoria, 1990-92. Recipient Outstanding Performance award Proctor Hosp., 1981, also various awards for svc. to schs., ch. and hosps. for mentally ill. Mem. Nat. Wildlife Fedn., Mensa Internat. (publs.

officer, editor 1987-89), Mothers League (treas. 1977), Willow Knolls Country Club (social com. 1989-90), Nature Conservancy, World Wildlife Fund, Forest Park Found., Jacques Cousteau Soc., Wilderness Soc. Methodist. Avocations: socializing, reading, travel, theatre, yoga. Home: 2822 W Pine Hill Ln Peoria IL 61614-3256

MCCOLLUM, JOHN MORRIS, tenor; b. Coalinga, Calif., Feb. 21, 1922; s. Fay James and Ingabord Telette (Mason) McC.; m. Mary Margaret Wilson, Jan. 23, 1944; children: Kristi Elizabeth, Timothy James. Student, Coalinga Coll., 1939-40; B.A. in Journalism, U. Calif. at Berkeley, 1947; student voice and acting, Am. Theatre Wing, 1951-53. Reporter, city editor Coalinga Record, 1947-50; editor agrl. news U. Calif. Coll. Agr., 1950-51; prof. music and chmn. voice faculty U. Mich.; dir. U. Mich. div. Nat. Music Camp; faculty Aspen Music Festival and School, 1963-76. Concert and opera singer, 1951—, soloist, Fifth Ave. Presbyn. Ch., N.Y.C., 1953-56, debut, Town Hall, N.Y.C., 1952, with, Boston Symphony Orchestra, Tanglewood, Mass., summer 1952, engagements with Symphony Orchestras in, N.Y.C., Chgo., Phila., San Francisco, Cleve., Washington, St. Louis, Detroit, New Orleans, Toronto, London, Mexico; with opera companies of, Boston, Washington, Toronto, Ft. Worth, Central City, Colo., also, NBC-TV, music festivals and oratorio societies, European debut, Festival of Two Worlds, Spoleto, Italy, summer 1958, Santa Fe Opera Co., leading tenor, N.Y.C. Opera Co., performing mem., Music Assos. of Aspen. (Recipient award Atwater Kent Auditions 1950, Am. Theatre Wing award 1952). Mem. Rep. Ctrl. Com., Fresno County, Calif., 1950; pres. Ann Arbor Civic Theatre, 1987-88; mem. Sarasota County Rep. exec. com.; mem., bd. dirs. Sarasota Concert Assn.,; bd. dirs. Univ. Mich. Alumni Club. Mem. U. Calif. Alumni Assn., Nat. Assn. Tchrs. Singing, Am. Acad. Tchrs. Singing, Alpha Tau Omega, Sigma Delta Chi, Pi Kappa Lambda. Episcopalian (lay reader). Clubs: Rotary (pres. 1977, Paul Harris fellow), Ann Arbor Golf and Outing (pres. 1979), The Meadows Country Club (Sarasota, Fla.). Home: 3380 W Chelmsford Ct Sarasota FL 34235-0947

MCCOLLUM, ROBERT WAYNE, physician, educator; b. Waco, Tex., Jan. 29, 1925; s. Robert Wayne and Minnie (Brown) McC.; m. Audrey Talmage, Oct. 16, 1954; children: Cynthia, Douglas Scott. A.B., Baylor U., 1945; M.D., Johns Hopkins, 1948; D.P.H., London Sch. Hygiene and Tropical Medicine, 1958; MA (hon.), Yale U., 1965, Dartmouth Coll., 1985. Intern pathology Columbia-Presbyn. Med. Center, N.Y.C., 1948-49; intern internal medicine Vanderbilt Hosp., Nashville, 1949-50; asst. resident internal medicine Yale-New Haven Med. Center, 1950-51; mem. faculty Yale Sch. Medicine, 1951-81, prof. epidemiology 1965-81, chmn. dept. epidemiology and public health, 1969-81; dean Sch. Medicine Dartmouth Coll., Hanover, N.H., 1982-90, prof. epidemiology, 1982-95, dean emeritus, 1990—; prof. emeritus, 1995—; assoc. physician Yale-New Haven Hosp., from 1954; v.p. Dartmouth-Hitchcock Med. Ctr., 1983-90; cons. WHO, 1962-79; surgeon gen. U.S. Army, from 1960. Contbr. articles on epidemiology and control infectious diseases to profl. jours. Bd. sci. advisers Merck Inst., 1981-85; trustee Mary Hitchcock Meml. Hosp., Hanover, 1982-90. Capt. M.C., AUS, 1952-54. Mem. Assn. Tchrs. Preventive Medicine, Am. Epidemiological Soc., Internat. Epidemiological Assn., Infectious Diseases Soc. Am., Conn. Acad. Sci. and Engring., Am. Coll. Epidemiology. Office: Dartmouth Coll Med Sch Hanover NH 03755-3861

MCCOMAS, DAVID JOHN, science administrator, space physicist; b. Milw., May 22, 1958; s. Harrold James and Hazelyn (Melconian) McC.; m. Richelle Wolff, May 30, 1981; children: Random A., Koan I., Orion G. BS in Physics, MIT, 1980; MS in Geophysics and Space Physics, UCLA, 1985, PhD in Geophysics and Space Physics, 1986. Mem. staff Los Alamos (N.Mex.) Nat. Lab., 1980-91, sect. leader space plasma and planetary physics, 1991-92, group leader space and atmospheric scis., 1992—; mem. strategic planning com. earth and space scis. divsn. Los Alamos Nat. Lab, 1986; mem. advanced composition explorer phase A study team NASA, 1988-89, mem. space physics data system steering com., 1990-91, mem. inner magnetosphere imaging study team, 1991-94; mem. com. solar-terrestrial rsch. Nat. Rsch. Coun., 1991-94, mem. com. space sci. tech. planning Aeronautics and Space Engring. Bd./space studies bd., 1992, mem. task group rsch. prioritization future space sci. space studies bd., 1994—. Assoc. editor Jour. Geophys. Rsch.-Space Physics, 1993-94; contbr. over 170 sci. papers to profl. jours. Grad. fellow Inst. Geophysics and Planetary Physics, 1983-84. Fellow Am. Geophysical Union (Macelwane medal 1993). Office: Los Alamos Nat Lab MS-D466 Los Alamos NM 87545

MCCOMBS, HUGH R., JR., lawyer; b. Flint, Mich., July 30, 1946. BA, Yale U., 1968; JD cum laude, Boston U., 1973. Bar: Ill. 1975, U.S. Dist. Ct. (no. dist. trial bar) Ill. 1975, U.S. Ct. Appeals (7th cir.) 1979, U.S. Supreme Ct. 1980. Law clk. to Hon. Herbert F. Murray U.S. Dist. Ct. (Md. dist.), 1973-74; ptnr. Mayer, Brown & Platt, Chgo. With U.S. Army, 1968-70, Vietnam. Mem. ABA (mem. litigation sect.), Chgo. Bar Assn. Office: Mayer Brown & Platt 190 S La Salle St Chicago IL 60603-3410*

MC COMIC, ROBERT BARRY, real estate development company executive, lawyer; b. Selmer, Tenn., Nov. 6, 1939; s. Richard Donald and Ila Marie (Prather) McC.; children: Thomas Christopher, Robert Geoffrey. BS, Union U., 1961; LLB, Tulane U., 1964; postgrad. in law, U. Freiburg, W. Ger., 1964-65, Hague (Netherlands) Internat. Acad. Law, 1965. Bar: Tenn. 1964, N.Y. 1966, Calif. 1971. Assoc. Donovan Leisure Newton & Irvine, N.Y.C., 1965-68; assoc. gen. counsel Avco Corp., Greenwich, Conn., 1968-70; exec. v.p., pres., CEO Avco Community Developers, Inc., 1973-82; chmn., CEO R.B. McComic, Inc., 1982-92, McComic Consolidated, Inc., 1992—; bd. dirs. CDC Small Bus. Fin. Corp. Pres. emeritus U. Calif. San Diego Found. Honoree Human Relations Inst. Am. Jewish Com., 1981, Kellog's Celebrity Tribute, 1988. Mem. ABA, Calif. Bar Assn., San Diego County Bar Assn., Assn. of Bar of City of N.Y., San Diego Bldg. Industry Assn., San Diego Yacht Club, Order of Coif, Sigma Alpha Epsilon, Omicron Delta Kappa, Lambda Alpha. Home: 2032 Via Casa Alta La Jolla CA 92037-5732 Office: McComic Consolidated Inc 4920 Carroll Canyon Rd San Diego CA 92121-1725

MCCONAHEY, STEPHEN GEORGE, securities company executive; b. Fond du Lac, Wis., Nov. 8, 1943; s. George and Charlotte McC.; m. Kathleen Louise Litten, Aug. 19, 1967; children: Heather, Benjamin. BS, U. Wis., 1966; MBA, Harvard U., 1968. Assoc. McKinsey & Co., Washington, 1968-72; White House fellow Washington, 1972-73; program adminstr. Dept. Transp., Washington, 1973-75; spl. asst. to Pres. Gerald Ford The White House, 1975-77; underwriter, ptnr. Boettcher & Co., Inc., Denver, 1977-80, mgr. pub. fin., 1980-82, mgr. corp. fin., 1982-84, pres., chief exec. officer, 1984-86, chmn. bd., 1986-87; chmn. bd. Boettcher Investment Corp., Denver, 1987-90; sr. v.p. for corp. and internat. devel. Kemper Corp., Chgo., 1991—; exec. v.p. Kemper Fin. Svcs., Inc., Chgo., 1991—; pres., COO EVEREN Capital Corp., Chgo., 1994—; chmn. oper. com. EVEREN Securities, Chgo., 1994—. Trustee Denver Symphony Assn., 1986; chmn. Greater Denver Corp., 1987; bd. dirs. The Denver Partnership; bd. fellows U. Denver. Served with USAR, 1968-74. Mem. Young Presidents Orgn., Greater Denver C. of C. (bd. dirs.), Denver Club, Colo. Harvard Bus. Sch. Club (Denver), Cherry Hills Country Club (Englewood, Colo.), Castle Pines Country Club (Castle Rock, Colo.), Chgo. Club. Home: 1050 E Green Oaks Dr Littleton CO 80121-1325 Office: EVEREN Securities Inc 77 W Wacker Dr Chicago IL 60601-1629

MC CONAHEY, WILLIAM MCCONNELL, JR., physician, educator; b. Pitts., May 7, 1916; s. William McConnell and Charlotte Maude (Hixson) McC.; m. Adrienne Parsons Magness, June 15, 1940; children: William McConnell III, Meredith McConahey Pollak, Peter Magness. A.B., Washington and Jefferson Coll., 1938; M.D., Harvard U., 1942; M.S., U. Minn., 1948. Resident internal medicine Mayo Clinic, 1946-48, asst. to staff, 1949, mem. staff internal medicine and endocrinology, 1949-85, emeritus staff, 1986—; cons. internal medicine St. Mary's, Rochester Methodist hosps., 1949-85; chmn. dept. endocrinology Mayo Clinic, 1967-74; prof. medicine Mayo Grad. Sch. Medicine U. Minn., 1966-73, prof. medicine Mayo Med. Sch., 1973—. Author articles in field. Served with M.C. AUS, 1943-45; now col. Res. (ret.). Decorated Silver Star, Bronze Star; recipient Disting. Alumni Service award Washington and Jefferson Coll., 1978. Fellow ACP; mem. Am. Thyroid Assn. (Disting. Service award 1973, pres. 1976), Endocrine Soc., Am. Diabetes Assn., Am. Fedn. Clin. Investigation, AMA, Central Soc. Clin. Research, Zumbro Valley Med. Soc., Phi Beta Kappa, Sigma Xi. Home: 1122 6th St SW Rochester MN 55902-1950

MCCONKEY, JAMES RODNEY, English educator, writer; b. Lakewood, Ohio, Sept. 2, 1921; s. Clayton Delano and Grace (Baird) McC.; m. Gladys Jean Voorhees, May 6, 1944; children: Lawrence Clark, John Crispin, James Clayton. BA, Cleve. Coll., 1943; MA, Western Res. U., 1946; PhD, U. Iowa, 1953. Teaching fellow, instr. Cleve. Coll., 1945-46; teaching asst. U. Iowa, Iowa City, 1949-50; asst. prof. Morehead State Coll., Ky., 1950-54, assoc. prof., 1954-56; asst. prof. Cornell U., Ithaca, N.Y., 1956-62, assoc. prof., 1962-67, prof., 1967-87, Goldwin Smith prof. English lit., 1987-92; Goldwin Smith prof. emeritus, 1992—; dir. Morehead Writers Workshop, 1951-56, Antioch Seminar in Writing and Pub., Yellow Springs, Ohio, 1957-59. Author: The Novels of E.M. Forster, 1957, Night Stnad, 1965, Crossroads, 1968, Journey to Sahalin, 1971, The Tree House Confessions, 1979, Court of Memory, 1983, To a Distant Island, 1984; editor: The Structure of Prose, 1963, Chekhov and Our Age, 1985, Kayo: The Authentic and Annotated Autobiographical Novel From Outer Space, 1987, Rowan's Progress, 1992, Stories From My Life With the Other Animals, 1993, The Anatomy of Memory, 1996. Served with U.S. Army, 1943-45. Guggenheim fellow, 1970; Eugene Saxton Meml. Trust Fund fellow, 1962; recipient Nat. Endowment of Arts essay award, 1968, Am. Acad. and Inst. Arts and Letters award in lit., 1979. Democrat. Home: 402 Aiken Rd Trumansburg NY 14886-9733 Office: Cornell Univ Goldwin Smith Hall Dept English Ithaca NY 14853

MC CONKIE, GEORGE WILSON, education educator; b. Holden, Utah, July 15, 1937; s. G. Wilson and Mabel (Stephenson) McC.; m. Orlene Carol Johnson, Sept. 6, 1962; children: Lynnette Mooth, Heather Usevitch, April Rhiner, Faline Coffelt, George Wilson, Bryce Johnson, Camille, Elissa, Esther, Bryna, Ruth, Anna May, Cynthia, Thomas Oscar. A.A., Dixie Jr. Coll., 1957; B.S., Brigham Young U., 1960, M.S., 1961; Ph.D., Stanford U., 1966. Asst. prof. edn. Cornell U., 1964-70, asso. prof., 1970-75, prof., 1975-78, chmn. dept. edn., 1977-78; prof. U. Ill., Champaign, 1978—, chmn. dept. ednl. psychology, 1993-94, 95—; sr. scientist Ctr. for Study of Reading, 1978—, Beckman Inst., 1989—; rsch. fellow Cath. U. Leuven, Belgium, 1991-92. Contbr. articles to profl. publs. Recipient Outstanding Sci. Contbn. award Soc. for Sci. Study of Reading, 1995; NIMH spl. fellow, 1991-92; grantee U.S. Office Edn., 1970-73, Nat. Inst. Edn., 1974-77, NIMH, 1974-84, NICHHD, 1983-89, 91-95, AT&T, 1986-89, NSF, 1989-91, CIA, 1991—, Army Rsch. Lab., 1996—. Fellow Am. Psychol. Assn.; mem. Am. Ednl. Research Assn., Psychonomic Soc., Cognitive Sci. Soc. Mem. Ch. of Jesus Christ of Latter-day Saints. Home: 2605 Berniece Dr Champaign IL 61821-7225 Office: Beckman Inst for Advanced Sci and Tech 405 N Mathews Ave Urbana IL 61801-2325

MCCONNAUGHEY, GEORGE CARLTON, JR., lawyer; b. Hillsboro, Ohio, Aug. 9, 1925; s. George Carlton and Nelle (Morse) McC.; m. Carolyn Schlieper, June 16, 1951; children: Elizabeth, Susan, Nancy. B.A., Denison U., 1949; LL.B., Ohio State U., 1951, J.D., 1967. Bar: Ohio 1951. Sole practice Columbus; ptnr. McConnaughey & McConnaughey, 1954-57, McConnaughey & Stradley, 1957-62, Laylin, McConnaughey & Stradley, 1962-67, George, Greek, King, McMahon & McConnaughey, 1967-79, McConnaughey, Stradley, Mone & Moul, 1979-81, Thompson, Hine & Flory (merger McConnaughey, Stradley, Mone & Moul with Thompson, Hine & Flory), Cleve., Columbus, Cin., Dayton and Washington, 1981-93; ret. ptnr. Thompson, Hine & Flory, Columbus, 1993—; bd. dirs. N.Am. Broadcasting Co. (Sta. WMNI and WBZX Radio); asst. atty. gen. State of Ohio, 1951-54. Pres. Upper Arlington (Ohio) Bd. Edn., 1967-69, Columbus Town Meeting Assn., 1974-76; chmn. Ohio Young Reps., 1956; U.S. presdl. elector, 1956; trustee Buckeye Boys Ranch, Columbus, 1967-73, 75-81, Upper Arlington Edn. Found., 1987-93; elder Covenant Presbyn. Ch., Columbus. With U.S. Army, 1943-45, ETO. Fellow Am. Bar Found., Ohio Bar Found., Columbus Bar Found.; mem. ABA, Ohio Bar Assn., Columbus Bar Assn., Am. Judicature Soc., Scioto Country Club, Athletic Club, Rotary, Masons. Home: 1993 Collingswood Rd Columbus OH 43221-3741 Office: Thompson Hine & Flory One Columbus 10 W Broad St Columbus OH 43215

MCCONNAUGHY, THOMAS BOWEN, JR., advertising executive; b. Massillon, Ohio, June 21, 1942; s. Thomas Bowen and Emma Jean (Heskett) M.; m. Gwen Jones; children: Molly Bowen, Thomas Bowen III. BFA, Ohio U., 1964. TV art dir. Ketchum, MacLeod & Grove, Pitts., 1965, TV producer, 1969-71, v.p., assoc. creative dir., 1971-73; sr. art dir. Leo Burnett, Chgo., 1973-75; with Ogilvy & Mather, Chgo., 1976-84, sr. v.p., 1980-84, group creative dir., 1981-84; sr. v.p. exec. creative dir. Bozell, Jacobs, Kenyon & Eckhardt, Chgo., 1984-86; pres. McConnaughy, Stein, Schmidt & Brown, Chgo., 1986—. Sgt. USAF, 1968-69, Korea. Recipient 12 Clio awards, 18 Addy merit, gold and silver awards, 3 gold Effie awards, 1983, 7 Addy gold awards, 2 One Show awards, 2 merit award Art Dirs. Club N.Y., 1984, cert. of distinction Art Dirs. mag., 1984, 6 excellence award Comm. Arts, 1984, President's award Lipton Co., 1985, Lio de bronze award, Cannes, 1995. Mem. Indian Hill Country Club, Masons. Republican. Avocations: curling, golf. Home: 160 Old Farm Rd Winnetka IL 60093-1039 Office: McConnaughy Stein Schmidt Brown 401 E Illinois St Ste 500 Chicago IL 60611-4363

MCCONNELL, ADDISON MITCHELL, JR. (MITCH MCCONNELL, JR.), senator, lawyer; b. Tuscumbia, AL, Feb. 20, 1942; s. Addison Mitchell and Julia (Shockley) McC.; children: Eleanor Hayes, Claire Redmon, Marion Porter; m. Elaine Chao, Feb. 6, 1993. B.A. with honors, U. Louisville, 1964; J.D., U. Ky., 1967. Bar: Ky. 1967. Chief legis. asst. to Senator Marlow Cook, Washington, 1968-70; sole practice Louisville, 1970-74; dep. asst. U.S. atty. gen. Washington, 1974-75; judge Jefferson County, Louisville, 1978-85; U.S. Senator from Ky., 1985—, chmn. select com. on ethics 104th Congress. Chmn. Jefferson County Republican Com., 1973-74; co-chmn. Nat. Child Tragedies Coalition, 1981; chmn., founder Ky. Task Force on Exploited and Missing Children, 1982; mem. Pres.'s Partnership on Child Safety. Recipient commendation Nat. Trust on Hist. Preservation in U.S., 1982, Conservationist of Yr. award League Ky. Sportsmen, 1983, cert. of appreciation Am. Correctional Assn., 1985. Mem. Ky. Assn. County Judge Execs. (pres. 1982), Nat. Inst. Justice (adv. bd. 1982-84). Republican. Baptist. Avocations: fishing; cooking. Office: SR-120 Russell Office Bldg Washington DC 20510-1702*

MCCONNELL, CALVIN DALE, clergyman; b. Monte Vista, Colo., Dec. 3, 1928; s. Roy and Leota Fern (Taylor) McC.; m. Mary Caroline Bamberg, Sept. 2, 1952 (dec. Apr. 1986); children: David William, Mark Andrew; m. Velma Duell, Dec. 17, 1988. B.A., U. Denver, 1951; M.Div., Iliff Sch. Theology, 1954; S.T.M., Andover Newton Theol. Sem., 1967. Ordained to ministry United Meth. Ch.; pastor Meth. Ch., Williams, Calif., 1955-58, 1st United Meth. Ch., Palo Alto, Calif. and Stanford U. Wesley Found., 1958-61; chaplain and asst. prof. religion Willamette U., Salem, Oreg., 1961-67; pastor Christ United Meth. Ch., Denver, 1968-72; pastor 1st United Meth. Ch., Boulder, Colo., 1972-79, Colorado Springs, Colo., 1979-80; bishop United Meth. Ch., Portland Area, 1980-88, Seattle Area, 1988—. Trustee U. Puget Sound, Iliff Sch. Theology; pres. United Meth. Ch. Bd. Higher Edn. and Ministry. Office: 2112 3rd Ave Ste 301 Seattle WA 98121-2310

MCCONNELL, CHARLES WARREN, marketing management executive; b. Los Angeles, Sept. 24, 1939; s. Lemuel John and Madeline B. (Bumcrot) McC.; m. Nancy Hackler, Aug. 19, 1961; 1 dau., Melanie Gwen. Student, U. Exeter, Eng., 1959-60; B.A., DePauw U., 1961; M.B.A., Northwestern U., 1963. Product mgr. Gen. Foods Corp., White Plains, N.Y., 1967-71; mktg. dir. Ideal Toy Corp., N.Y.C., 1971-72; area dir. internat. mktg. Playtex, N.Y.C., 1972-74; v.p. mktg. Hanes Corp., Winston-Salem, 1974-77; sr. v.p., mgmt. dir. D'Arcy Masius Benton & Bowles Advt., N.Y.C., 1977-86; exec. v.p., gen. mgr. Bozell/Poppe Tyson, 1986-87; exec. v.p. bus. devel. WPP (subs. Harvard Group), N.Y.C., 1988-89; corp. v.p. mktg. communications McGraw-Hill, Inc., N.Y.C., 1989-90; sr. v.p. mktg. Warner's Intimate Apparel, Bridgeport, Conn., 1990-91; pres. B.D. Baggies div. Apparel Group, Ltd., N.Y.C., 1992-94; exec. v.p. Apparel Group, Ltd., 1992-94; ptnr. The Watson Group, N.Y.C., 1994—. Served to capt. USAF, 1963-67. Mem. Advt. Club N.Y., Am. Mktg. Assn., Innis Arden Golf Club, Delta Chi. Republican. Congregationalist. Office: 37 W 20th St New York NY 10011-3706

MCCONNELL, DAVID GRAHAM, research biochemist, educator; b. Bronxville, N.Y., Dec. 3, 1926; s. Luther Graham and Helen (Slagle) McC.; m. Patricia Barnes, Sept. 5, 1970; children: Ross, Paul D., Teresa Barnes, Alex, Debora Barnes, Margaret H.K. A.B., Columbia U., 1949, A.M., 1949; Ph.D., Ind. U., 1957. Research assoc. Ohio State U., Columbus, 1956-61; assoc. prof. Ohio State U., 1962-71, prof., 1971-72; prof. biochemistry Mich. State U., East Lansing, 1973—. Author: novel The Destruction of Crown City, 1974. Labor ofcl. NAACP, 1966-72. Served with USNR, 1944-46; Served with USMCR, 1950-52. Mem. Am. Soc. Biochemistry and Molecular Biology, Am. Soc. for Cell Biology, Biophys. Soc., Am. Soc. Neurochemistry. Home: East Lansing MI Office: Mich State U Dept Biochemistry East Lansing MI 48824

MCCONNELL, DAVID M., secondary school principal. Prin. Kennebunk (Maine) High Sch. Recipient Blue Ribbon Sch. award U.S. Dept. Edn., 1990-91. Office: Kennebunk H S 89 Fletcher St Kennebunk ME 04043-1904

MCCONNELL, DAVID MOFFATT, lawyer; b. Chester, S.C., June 12, 1912; s. Harvey Elzaphon and Elizabeth (Simpson) McC.; m. Ona Altman, Dec. 31, 1952; children: David Moffatt, Lynn Torbit, Joseph Moore. B.S. summa cum laude, Davidson Coll., 1933; student, Harvard. Grad. Bus. Sch., 1933-34, Law Sch., 1934-35; J.D., Georgetown U., 1939, LL.M., 1940; LLD (hon.), Mex. Acad. Internat. Law, 1987. Bar: S.C. 1936, D.C. 1945, N.C. 1946, U.S. Supreme Ct 1946. With firm Henry & Henry, Chester, 1936; counsel com. govt. reorgn. U.S. Senate, 1937-38; spl. atty. to chief counsel Internal Revenue Service, 1938-41; practice in Charlotte, N.C., 1946—; v.p., gen. counsel Belk Stores, Charlotte, 1946-76; gen. counsel Leggett Stores, 1946-76; dir. So. Nat. Bank, Lumberton, N.C., also chmn. Charlotte bd., 1970-76; U.S. ambassador to UN, 1968-69; Spl. adviser UN Econ. and Social Council; mem. U.S. delegation Fed. Republic Germany Marshall Plan, 1967. Chmn., sec. N.C. Bd. Elections, 1952-62; chmn. exec. com. Mecklenburg County (N.C.) Democratic Party, 1952-57; mem. nat. platform com. Dem. Party, 1964-72; elector U.S. Electoral Coll., 1948, 52; Donor McConnell Collection Tibetan Art to Baton Rouge Arts Mus., 1965; bd. dirs. emeritus Billy Graham Evangelistic Assn.; bd. visitors Davidson Coll., 1972-76; trustee Erskine Coll., Due West, S.C., 1954-58, bd. advisers, 1968-72; trustee Robert Lee Stowe, Jr. Found., Henderson Belk Found. Served to col. U.S. Army, 1940-46, CBI; brig. gen. N.C. State Militia. Decorated Legion of Merit with oak leaf cluster; Order Cloud with banner (Republic China); knight comdr. Order of the Knights of Malta. Fellow Mexican Acad. Internat. Law; mem. Am., N.C., 26th Jud. Dist. bar assns., St. Andrews Soc., Newcomen Soc., Phi Beta Kappa, Kappa Alpha. Presbyterian. Clubs: Mason (Charlotte) (Shriner), Charlotte Country (Charlotte), City (Charlotte), University (Washington). Home: 920 Granville Rd Charlotte NC 28207-1832

MCCONNELL, DAVID STUART, insurance agent, retired federal executive; b. Charlotte, Mich., Dec. 5, 1935; s. Russell and Beatrice (Martin) McC.; m. Marchelle Elizabeth Wiltshire, June 10, 1960; children: Marchelle Kern, Martin. BA, Olivet Coll., 1957; grad., Union Theol. Sem., Union Sch. Sacred Music, N.Y.C., 1958, 62. Position classifier U.S. Dept. State, Washington, 1961-62; rsch. specialist U.S. Nat. Interdepartmental Seminar, Washington, 1962-66; head East Asia sect. Am. Specialist Program, 1966-68; asst. to acad. advisor U.S. Bd. Fgn. Scholarships, Washington, 1968-69; desk officer Near East br. Bur. Ednl. and Cultural Affairs, Washington, 1969-72; coord. for multi-regional seminars U.S. Office Internat. Visitors, Washington, 1972-87; head internat. visitor programs for Andean nations U.S. Info. Agy., Washington, 1978-87; agt. Liberty Nat. Life Ins., 1994-95. Compiler: Problems of Development and Internal Defense, 1966. Mem. 3 cabinet subcoms. on narcotics, Washington, 1973-78; coord. narcotics U.s. Bur. Ednl. and Cultural Affairs, 1973-78, U.S. Info. Agy., Washington, 1978; mem. Montgomery County Econ. Coun. With U.S. Army, 1958-61. Grantee (9) White House Spl. Action Office for Drug Abuse Prevention, Ford Found., 1973. Home and Office: RR 3 Box 152 Carrollton MS 38917

MCCONNELL, DONALD JOSEPH, ambassador; b. Massillon, Ohio, Sept. 28, 1939; m. Frances C. Ruegsegger. BA, John Carroll U.; MA, Stanford U., Harvard U. Joined Fgn. Svc., 1967; staff asst. to asst. sec. for Near East and South Asian Affairs Dept. State, Washington, 1967-68; officer Dept. State, Asmara, 1969-71; with Office of Pres. Dept. State, Washington, 1972; internat. rels. officer Dept. State, Mbabane, Swaziland, 1972-75; polit. counselor Dept. State, Abidjan, Ivory Coast, 1975-77; politico-mil. officer Office European Security and Polit. Affairs Dept. State, 1977-79; with NATO Dept. State, Brussels, 1980-83; dep. polit. counselor Dept. State, Cairo, 1983-85; exec. sec. U.S. Intermedia-Range Nuc. Forces Del. to Arms Control and Disarmament Agy. Dept. State, 1985-87, exec. asst. to counselor, 1987-88, dep. dir. Office European Security and Polit. Affairs, 1988-89; dep. chief of mission Dept. State, Brussels, 1989-92, charge d'affaires, 1993; amb. to Burkina Faso Dept. State, Ouagadougou, 1993—. Fulbright scholar U. Freiburg, Germany;. Office: OUAGADOUGOU Dept State Washington DC 20521-2440

MCCONNELL, E. HOY, II, advertising executive; b. Syracuse, N.Y., May 14, 1941; s. E. Hoy and Dorothy R. (Schmitt) McC.; m. Patricia Irwin, June 26, 1965; children: E. Hoy, III, Courtney. B.A. in Am. Studies magna cum laude with high honors, Yale U., 1963; M.B.A. in Mktg, Harvard Bus. Sch., 1965. With Foote, Cone & Belding, 1965-76; v.p. account supr. Foote, Cone & Belding, Chgo., 1971-72, 74-76, Phoenix, 1972-74; with D'Arcy-MacManus & Masius, Chgo., 1976-85, sr. v.p., dir. client services, then vice chmn., 1978-80, pres., 1980-84, chmn., 1984-85; mng. dir. D'Arcy Masius Benton & Bowles, Chgo., 1986-96; sr. v.p., acct. dir. Leo Burnett Co., 1996—; also bd. dirs. D'Arcy Masius Benton & Bowles, Chgo.; sr. v.p., account dir. Leo Burnett Co., Chgo., 1996—. Bd. dirs. Evanston (Ill.) United Way, 1980-83, Evanston Youth Hockey Assn., 1980-89, pres. 1981-83; bd. dirs. Off-the-Street Club, 1980-90, Bus. Profl. People for Pub. Interest, 1981-83, 96—, v.p. 1984-89, pres. 1990-95; bd. dirs. Harvard Bus. Sch. Club, 1990-92; mem. Chgo. Coun. on Fgn. Rels., 1989—. Mem. Am. Assn. Advt. Agys. (gov.-at-large Chgo. coun. 1984, sec. 1986, vice chmn. 1987, chmn. 1988-89), BBB Chgo. (advt. rev. bd.), Tavern Club, Glen View Country Club (bd. dirs. 1992—), Dairymen's Country Club, Chgo. Club (membership comm. 1994—), Yale Club Chgo. (bd. dirs. 1996—). Democrat. Unitarian. Home: 2703 Colfax St Evanston IL 60201-2035 Office: Leo Burnett Co 35 W Wacker Dr Chicago IL 60601

MCCONNELL, EDWARD BOSWORTH, legal organization administrator, lawyer; b. Greenwich, Conn., Apr. 3, 1920; s. Raymond Arnott and Anna Bell (Lee) McC.; m. Jeanne M. Rotton (dec. 1984); children: Annalee, Marilyn, Edward, Barbara, William; m. Florence M. Leonard, (dec. 1991); stepchildren: Susan L. Little, William R. Leonard, Molly M. Leonard. A.B., U. Nebr., 1941, LL.B., 1947; M.B.A. with distinction, Harvard U., 1943. Bar: Nebr. 1947, N.J. 1950. Mem. faculty Rutgers U. Sch. Bus. Adminstrn., Newark, 1947-53; assoc. firm Toner, Speakman and Crowley, Newark, N.J., 1949-50; adminstrv. asst. and law sec. to Chief Justice of N.J., 1950-53; adminstrv. dir. Cts. of N.J., Trenton, 1953-73; also standing master Supreme Ct., 1953-73; pres. Nat. Center for State Cts., Williamsburg, 1973-90, bd. dirs., 1980-90, pres. emeritus, 1990—, cons. on ct. mgmt., 1990—; mem. U.S. Dept. Justice Coun. on Role of Cts. in Am. Soc., 1978-83; mem. adv. com. Dispute Resolution Policy Study, Social Sci. Rsch. Inst., U. So. Calif., 1975-79, Civil Litigation Rsch. Project, U. Wis. and U. So. Calif., 1979-83, nat. judg. edn. program to promote equality for men and women in the cts., 1980—; mem. Nat. Inst. Criminal Justice Task Force, Urban Consortium, 1979-83; participant Access To Justice Colloquium, European Univ. Inst., Florence, Italy, 1979; nat. adv. coun. Ctr. Adminstrn. Justice, Wayne Stae U., 1973-77; nat. project com. State Jud. Info. Sys. Project SEARCH Group, 1973-76; lectr. Inst. of Local and State Govt. Wharton Sch. U. Pa., 1955-65, Appellate Judges Seminar, Inst. Jud. Adminstrn., NYU, 1962-75; vis. expert UN Asia and Far East Inst., Tokyo, 1971; mem. Cts. Task Force Nat. Adv. Commn. Criminal Justice Standards and Goals, 1971-73; nat. adv. com. D.C. Ct. Mgmt. Project, 1966-70; trustee Inst. Ct. Mgmt., 1969-73, 84-86; chmn. Nat. Conf. Ct. Adminstrv. Officers, 1956; mem. nat. task force on gender bias in cts. Nat. Assn. Women Judge's 1985-90; mem. adv. bd. Nat. Ctr. for Citizen Participation in Adminstrn. of Justice, 1984-90; mem. Nat. Commn. Trial Ct. Performance Standards, 1991-95. Mem. adv. com. on article III Commn. on the Bicentennial of the Constitution, 1989-91; adv. com. Judicary Leadership Coun., 1990-95. Maj. C.E., AUS, 1943-46. Decorated Bronze Star medal; recipient Warren E. Burger award for greatest contbn. to improvement of ct. adminstrn. Inst. for Ct. Mgmt., 1975, Herbert Lincoln Harley award for efficient adminstrn. justice Am. Judicature Soc., 1973, Glenn R. Winters award for outstanding service in jud. adminstrn. Am. Judges Assn., 1974, Tom C. Clark award for outstanding contbns. to field of ct. adminstrn. Nat. Conf. Met. Cts., 1983, Award of Merit Nat. Assn. Ct. Mgmt., 1987, Spl. award, Nat. Assn. Women Judges, 1989, Paul C. Reardon award for disting. svc. Nat. Ctr. for State Cts., 1991, Alumni Achievement award U. Nebr., 1991. Fellow Nat. Acad. Pub. Adminstrn. (mem. panel on evaluation budget decentralization project of fed. cts. 1989-91, chmn. panel long range planning in fed. cts. 1991-92, mem. panel for study of fed. trial ct. adminstrv. structure 1995-96—); mem. ABA (fellow-at-large, coun. mem. 1960-66, 71-80, house of dels., 1977-80, chmn. com. on oversight and goals 1975-76, chmn. com. on jud. compensation jud. adminstrn. div. 1984-89, chmn. jud. adminstrn. div. 1976-77, sect. of litigation task force on excess litigiousness in Am. 1986-88, task force on reduction of litigation cost and delay, jud. adminstrn. dir. 1984-94, chmn. 1991-94, mem. long range planning com. 1989-94), N.J. Bar Assn., Nebr. Bar Assn., Kingsmill (Va.) Golf, Tennis and Yacht Clubs, Order of Coif (hon.), Delta Upsilon, Sigma Delta Phi, Phi Delta Phi.

MCCONNELL, ELLIOTT BONNELL, JR., oil company executive; b. Elizabeth, N.J., June 2, 1928; s. Elliott Bonnell and Mildred A. (Snibbe) McC.; m. Sara Gerber, Aug. 16, 1952; children: Marilyn McConnell Huston, James D. A.B., Duke U., 1951; M.S., Pa. State U., 1953; postgrad. Advanced Mgmt. Program, Harvard U., 1973. Exploration mgr. Mobil Oil Corp., U.S. and Can., 1953-69; v.p. land and exploration Gen. Crude Oil Co., Houston, 1969-79; pres. Pennzoil Internat., Houston, 1979-81; exec. v.p. exploration and prodn. Santa Fe Energy Co. subs. Santa Fe S.P. Corp., Houston, 1981-86, petroleum cons. Chmn. Appraisal Rev. Bd., Aransas County, 1989-92; pres. Key Allegro Property Owners Assn., 1989-92; chmn. Rockport Redistricting Commn., 1991, Rockport Charter Rev. Commn., 1991; elected county commr. Aransas County, 1992. Republican. Clubs: Rockport Country. Avocation: tennis.

MCCONNELL, HARDEN MARSDEN, biophysical chemistry researcher, chemistry educator; b. Richmond, Va., July 18, 1927; s. Harry Raymond and Frances (Coffee) McC.; m. Sophia Milo Glogovac, Oct. 6, 1956; children: Hunter, Trevor, Jane. BS, George Washington U., 1947; PhD, Calif. Inst. Tech., 1951; DSc (hon.), U. Chgo., 1991, George Washington U., 1993. NRC fellow dept. physics U. Chgo., 1950-52; research chemist Shell Devel. Co., Emeryville, Calif., 1952-56; asst. prof. chemistry Calif. Inst. Tech., 1956-58, prof. chemistry and physics, 1963-64; prof. chemistry Stanford U., Calif., 1964-79, Robert Eckles prof. chemistry, 1979—, chmn. dept., 1989—; founder Molecular Devices Corp., 1983—; cons. in field. Contbr. numerous articles to profl. publs.; patentee (in field). Pres. Found. for Basic Rsch. in Chemistry, 1990—; hon. assoc. Neurosci. Rsch. Program. Recipient Calif. sect. award Am. Chem. Soc., 1961, award in pure chemistry Am. Chem. Soc., 1962, Harrison Howe award, 1968, Irving Langmuir award in chem. physics, 1971, Pauling medal Puget Sound and Oreg. sects., 1987, Peter Debye award in phys. chemistry, 1990; Am. Achievement award George Washington U., 1971; Disting. Alumni award Calif. Inst. Tech., 1982, Sherman Fairchild Disting. scholar, 1988; Dickson prize for sci. Carnegie-Mellon U., 1982, Wolf prize in chemistry, 1984, ISCO award, 1984; Wheland medal U. Chgo., 1988; Nat. Medal Sci., 1989, Brucker prize, 1995. Fellow AAAS, Am. Phys. Soc.; mem. Nat. Acad. Scis. (award in chem. scis. 1988), Am. Acad. Arts and Scis., Am. Soc. Biol. Chemists, Internat. Acad. Quantum Molecular Scis., Am. Chem. Soc., Biophysical Soc., Internat. Coun. on Magnetic Resource in Biol. Systems, Brit. Biophysical Soc. Office: Stanford U Dept Chemistry Stanford CA 94305

MCCONNELL, J. DANIEL, sports marketing professional; b. Noblesville, Ind., Oct. 5, 1944; s. John Worley and Nadine Lillian (McFarlin) McC.; m. Jane Brant Linger, June 29, 1968. AB in English/Journalism, Ind. U., 1966, MS in Bus., 1968. Asst. to pres. Ind. U. Found., Bloomington, 1966-67; legis. liaison Dept. Housing, Employment and Welfare, Washington, 1968; dir. pub. rels. Commins Engine Co., Columbus, Ind., 1970-72, dir. investor comm., 1972-75, dir. exec. recruiting, 1975-77; prin., CEO The McConnell Co. Pub. Rels., Seattle, 1977-93; sr. v.p., group dir. Elgin Syferd/DDB Needham, Seattle, 1993—; founder The Mountain Summit Internat. Symposium, 1987—; co-founder College Baseball Classic Found., 1990—; bd. dirs. Great Adventures Ltd., N.J. Bd. dirs. Child Haven, Seattle, 1985-91, Internat. Snow Leopard Trust, Seattle, 1991-95, Pacific Crest Outward Bound Sch., Portland, Oreg., 1992—; trustee Seattle Ctrl. C.C., 1992—. Capt. U.S. Army, 1968-70. Mem. Pub. Rels. Soc. (Hoosier chpt. bd. dirs. 1975-77, Puget Sound bd. dirs. 1995—). Avocations: snow skiing, mountaineering, racquetball, sailing. Office: Elgin/DDB Needham 1008 Western Ave Ste 601 Seattle WA 98104-1032

MC CONNELL, JOHN DOUGLAS, retail corporation executive, owner; b. Dimboola, Victoria, Australia, May 13, 1932; s. William Thomas and Ada Maud (Gardner) McC.; came to U.S., 1964; BA, Melbourne U., 1954; PhD, Stanford U., 1967; m. Gloria Ann Revak, Oct. 12, 1968; children: Joanne Patricia, Meredith Lorraine. Asst. to mng. dir. Automotive & Gen. Industries Ltd., Melbourne, 1954-59; mgr. Eagle M.R. Svc. Pty. Ltd., Melbourne, 1959-64; dir. mgmt. systems SRI Internat., Washington, 1975-77, dir. mgmt. econs. Europe and Middle East, 1977-78, dir. mgmt. svcs. group, Menlo Park, Calif., 1978-80, dir. Food and Forest Products Ctr., 1980-83; v.p. Sungene Techs. Corp., Palo Alto, 1983-85; dir. fin. svcs. ctr. SRI Internat., 1986-87, prin., 1987-91, Menlo Park; pres., CEO, owner Remnant World Inc., San Jose, 1991—; vis. lectr. U. Bradford (Eng.); lectr. San Francisco State U. Contbr. articles to profl. mags. Life gov. Royal Victorian Inst. Blind, 1957—; mem. exec. bd. Stanford Area Council Boy Scouts Am., 1974-94. Decorated comdr. The Most Venerable Order of St. John of Jerusalem; recipient Silver Beaver award, 1986; Alfred P. Sloan Fellow, 1964-65; GE fellow, 1966. Fellow Australian Inst. Mgmt., Advt. Inst. Australia; mem. Royal Scottish Country Dance Soc. Presbyterian. Clubs: St. Andrews Soc. San Francisco, The Queen's, Army and Navy. Lodge: Masons. Home: 4174 Oak Hill Ave Palo Alto CA 94306-3720 Office: Remnant World Inc 5158 Stevens Creek Blvd San Jose CA 95129-1019

MCCONNELL, JOHN EDWARD, electrical engineering company executive; b. Minot, N.D., July 28, 1931; s. Lloyd Waldorf and Sarah Gladys (Mathis) McC.; m. Carol Claire Myers, July 4, 1952 (dec. Feb. 1989); children: Kathleen Anne, James Mathis, Amy Lynn; m. Heidi Banziger, Sept. 29, 1990. Registered profl. engr., Pa. B.S. in Mech. Engring., U. Pitts., 1952; M.S., Drexel Inst. Tech., 1958. With mktg. and design depts. for turbomachinery Westinghouse Electric Corp., Lester, Pa., 1954-60, 63-67, Pitts., 1960-63; mgr. power generation equipment activities in U.S., ASEA Inc., White Plains, N.Y., 1967-79; regional mgr. power equipment activities Middle Atlantic and Southeastern U.S. regions, 1967-79, mgr. turbine generator dept., 1980-83, mgr. internat. ops. Power Systems div., 1983-84, mgr. transmission substas. dept., 1984-85; mgr. Eastern U.S. ops. ASEA Power Systems Inc., 1985-86, mgr. eastern ops. measurements div. GEC, 1986-91; mgr. eastern region Protection and Control div. GEC Alsthom T&D Inc., 1991—; adviser on energy matters to U.S. congressman 1968-74; speaker and author on energy and electric power topics. Served to 1st lt., C.E., U.S. Army, 1952-54. Mem. IEEE (sr.; energy com., past chmn. sub-com. cogeneration, chmn. membership com., power sys. relay com.), IEEE Power Engring. Soc. (sr.; past chmn. chpts. public affairs subcom.), ASME. Republican. Contbr. numerous articles on energy and electric power to industry publs.; developer analytical techniques for power systems performance characteristics and econs. of cogeneration systems. Home: 173 Remington Rd Ridgefield CT 06877-4324 Office: GEC Alsthom T&D Inc 4 Skyline Dr Hawthorne NY 10532 *1) If it doesn't produce revenue, is it worthwhile? 2) Problem solving begins with careful listening. 3) Keep people informed. If the don't know, they'll assume the worst. 4) The truth is the most credible explanation you'll find.*

MCCONNELL, JOHN HENDERSON, metal and plastic products manufacturing executive, professional sports team executive; b. New Manchester, W.Va., May 10, 1923; s. Paul Alexander and Mary Louise (Mayhew) McC.; m. Margaret Jane Rardin, Feb. 8, 1946; children—Margaret Louise, John Porter. B.A. in Bus., Mich. State U., 1949; Dr. Law (hon.), Ohio U., 1981. Sales trainee Weirton Steel Co., W.Va., 1950-52; sales mgmt. Shenango-Steel Co., Farrell, Pa., 1952-54; founder, chmn. bd. Worthington Industries, Inc., Columbus, Ohio, 1955—, also past CEO; bd. dirs. Pitts. Pirates; dir. Alltel Corp., Hudson, Ohio, Anchor Hocking, Lancaster, Ohio, Nat. City Corp., Cleve. Bd. dirs. Children's Hosp., Columbus; trustee Ashland Coll., Ohio. Served with USN, 1943-46. Recipient Ohio Gov.'s award Gov. State of Ohio, 1980; Horatio Alger award Horatio Alger Assn., 1983; named Outstanding Chief Exec. Officer, Fin. World Mag., 1981. Mem. Columbus Area C. of C. (chmn. 1978). Republican. Presbyterian. Clubs: Golf (New Albany, Ohio) (pres. 1983—); Brookside Country (Columbus) (pres. 1964-65). Lodge: Masons. Avocations: flying; golf. Office: Worthington Industries Inc 1205 Dearborn Dr Columbus OH 43085-4769*

MCCONNELL, JOHN MICHAEL, former federal agency administrator; b. Greenville, S.C., July 26, 1943; s. Harold Eddie and Dorothy Beatrice (Cassell) Mc.; children from previous marriage: Susan Erin McConnell, Jennifer Michelle McConnell; m. Mary Theresa Wagner, Jan. 29, 1988; children: Mark Richard Sentner, Christine Marie Sentner. BA in Econs., Furman U., 1966; MPA in Govt./Pub. Adminstrn., George Washington U., 1986; grad., Nat. Def. U., 1986; PhD in Strategic Intelligence (hon.), Defense Intelligence Coll., 1992. Asst. engr., damage control officer USS Colleton, Mekong Delta, Vietnam, 1967-68; counterintelligence analyst Naval Investigative Svc., Yokosuka, Japan, 1968-70; analyst and supr. CNO Undersea Warfare Intelligence Watch, Washington, 1971-74; force intelligence officer Commdr. Middle East Force Persian Gulf, Indian Ocean, 1974-76; ops. officer Fleet Ocean Surveillance Info. Facility, Rota, Spain, 1976-79; intelligence analyst CNO Intelligence Staff, Washington, 1979-81; intelligence officer Commdr. in Chief Pacific Fleet, Honolulu, 1981-83; fleet intelligence officer Commdr. Seventh Fleet Western Pacific, 1983-85; exec. asst. Dir. Naval Intelligence, Washington, 1985-86; chief naval forces divsn. Nat. Security Agy., Ft. Meade, Md., 1987-88; asst. chief staff/intelligence Commdr. in Chief Pacific Fleet, Honolulu, 1988-90; dir. joint staff intelligence Joint Staff, Washington, 1990-92; dir. Nat. Security Agy., Ft. Meade, 1992—. Vice admiral U.S. Navy, 1992—. Recipient Navy Unit Commendation Sec. Navy, 1968, Presdl. Unit Citation Combat Action ribbon CINCPACFLT, Navy Achievement medal Sec. Navy, 1974, Navy Commendation medalw/Combat V, 1968, Navy E ribbon Sec. of the Navy, 1984, Nat. Defense Svc. medal with 1 Bronze star, Vietnam Svc. medal with 2 Bronze Stars, Humanitarian Svc. medal, Sea Svc. Deployment ribbon, Navy & Marine Corps Overseas Svc. ribbon, Rep. Vietnam Meritorious Unit Citation Civil Actions Color, Campaign medal Rep. Vietnam, Meritorious Svc. medal with 2 Gold Stars Sec. Navy, 1981, 85, Legion of Merit with 2 Gold Stars, 1985, 87, 90, Defense Superior Svc. medal, 1988, Defense Dist. Svc. medal, 1992. Avocations: world affairs, foreign policy, reading. Office: Dept of Defense National Security Agy Fort George G Meade MD 20755*

MCCONNELL, JOHN THOMAS, newspaper executive, publisher; b. Peoria, Ill., May 1, 1945; s. Golden A. and Margaret (Lyon) McC.; 1 child, Justin. B.A., U. Ariz., 1967. Mgr. Fast Printing Co., Peoria, 1970-71; mgmt. trainee Quad-Cities Times, Davenport, Iowa, 1972-73; asst. gen. mgr., then v.p., gen. mgr. Peoria Jour. Star, 1973-81, pub., 1981—, pres., 1987—. Bd. dirs. Peoria Downtown Devel. Council, Peoria Devel. Corp.; past trustee Methodist Hosp., Peoria. Served with USAR, 1967-69. Named Young Man of Year Peoria Jaycees, 1979. Mem. Peoria Advt. and Selling Club, Peoria C. of C. Congregationalist. Club: Peoria Country. Office: Peoria Jour Star Inc 1 News Plz Peoria IL 61643-0001

MCCONNELL, JOHN WESLEY, real estate-resort developer, corporate executive; b. Steubenville, Ohio, Dec. 3, 1941; m. Clare Yenchochic; 5 children. BS, U. Steubenville, 1967. Various corp. fin. positions Diamond Shamrock Corp., 1967-76, asst. treas., 1976-81, v.p. fin. and adminstrn. coal co., 1981-83, v.p. fin. and adminstrn., 1983-85, exec. v.p., COO, 1985-86; sr. v.p., CFO, treas. Fairfield Communities, Inc., Little Rock, 1986-90, pres., COO, 1990-91, pres., CEO, 1990—, also bd. dirs. With U.S. Army, 1962-64. Avocations: golf, tennis. Office: Fairfield Communities Inc 2800 Cantrell Rd Little Rock AR 72202-2040

MC CONNELL, JOHN WILKINSON, labor relations educator, labor arbitrator, former socio-economics educator; b. Phila, Oct. 18, 1907; s. John and Lucy (Wilkinson) McC.; m. Harriet Hawley Barlow, July 29, 1933; children: Janet (Mrs. John Alexander), Kathleen (Mrs. David Mervin), Grace (Mrs. Alfred Clark), Judith Ann (Mrs. Henry Sondheimer), John C. B.A., Dickinson Coll., 1929, D.Sc., 1959; Ph.D., Yale U., 1937; LL.D., U. R.I., 1967, Ricker Coll., 1968, U. N.H., 1971. Instr. Am. U. at Cairo, 1929- 32; instr. Yale U., 1935; research asso. Inst. Human Relations, 1934-37; asst. prof. econs. and sociology Am. U., Washington, 1937-39; prof. sociology N.Y. U., 1939-46; prof. indsl. and labor relations Cornell U., 1946-63, dean grad. sch., 1955-59, dean sch. indsl. and labor relations, 1959-63; dir. research in indsl. retirement, 1959—; pres. U. N.H., 1963-71; counselor to coll. Ithaca (N.Y.) Coll., 1971-75, lectr., 1975; adj. prof. labor econs. Cornell U., 1971—; dir. research Twentieth Century Fund, 1951-54; Fulbright lectr. in, India, 1953-54; Pub. mem. region II Nat. War Labor Bd., 1943-46, Nat. WSB, 1950-52; mem. Fgn. Service Grievance Bd., Dept. State, 1974-82; cons. pension and retirement systems, mem. human resources research adv. bd. USAF, 1948-53, Social Security Adminstrn.; mem. adv. council Nat. Inst. Child Health and Human Devel., NIH, 1965-69; mem. labor arbitration panel N.Y. State Mediation Service; mem. Fed. Mediation and Conciliation Service; pub. mem. minimum wage bd., P.R., 1956—, chmn., 1960, 1968; chmn. study group on edn. of fgn. students Land-Grant Coll. Assn., 1961. Author: Evolution of Social Classes, 1942, Basic Teachings of Great Economists, 1943, (with Robert Risley) Economic Security, 1951, (with others) America's Needs and Resources, 1955, (with John Corson) Economic Needs of Older People, 1955, Ideas of the Great Economists, 1980; Contbr. articles to profl. jours. Pres. bd. dirs. Tompkins Community Hosp., 1984-86, v.p., 1986-94. Recipient Outstanding Svc. medal Army Dept., 1967, with oak leaf cluster, 1971, Alumni award of Petee medal U. N.H., 1995; named to Hall of Fame, U. N.H., 1989. Mem. Nat. Acad. Arbitrators, Am. Arbitration Assn., Indsl. Relations Research Assn. (dir. 1951-54), Phi Beta Kappa, Phi Kappa Phi, Omicron Delta Kappa, Pi Gamma Mu. Methodist. Home: 21 Cayuga St # 636 Trumansburg NY 14886-9184

MCCONNELL, JOHN WILLIAM, JR., lawyer; b. Bessemer, Ala., Apr. 17, 1921; s. John W. and Elizabeth (Sheridan) McC.; m. Margaret B. Snider, Jan. 7, 1944; children—Margaret E. (Mrs. John Evans), Rebecca L. (Mrs. A.D. Braden), Catherine L., John W. III. A.B., U. Ala., 1942, M.A., 1946; LL.B., Yale, 1948. Bar: Ala. 1948, D.C. 1977. Atty. Inge, Twitty, Armbrecht & Jackson, Mobile, Ala., 1948-56, Armbrecht, Jackson, McConnell & DeMouy, 1956-65; dir. U.S. Peace Corps, Nigeria, 1965-68; v.p. legal Sea-Land Service, Inc., Menlo Park, N.J., 1968-76; also dir., of counsel Haight, Gardner, Poor & Havens, Washington, 1977-94; Atty. for Reynolds v. Sims on legislative reapportionment, U.S. Supreme Ct., 1963-64. Mem. Ala. Dem. Exec. Com., 1963-65. Served to capt. AUS, 1943-46, 50-52. Mem. ABA, Ala. Bar Assn., D.C. Bar Assn., Maritime Law Assn. Methodist. Home: 926 Seagull Dr Mount Pleasant SC 29464-4145

MCCONNELL, LORELEI CATHERINE, library director; b. Port Jefferson, N.Y., Dec. 5, 1938; d. Alvin and Mary (McConnell) Philibert; m. Thomas McConnell, Jan. 20, 1962; children: Catherine, Michael. BA, Drew U., 1960; MLS, Rutgers U., 1963. Reference libr. Irvington (N.J.) Pub. Libr., 1963-90, dir., 1990—; founder Irvington Literacy Program, 1986, dir., 1986-90. Mem. ALA, N.J. Libr. Assn. (mem. exec. bd. 1990-93, N.J. Libr. of Yr. 1993-94), Irvington (N.J.) C. of C. (exec. bd. 1992—, Civic award 1996), Internat. Primal Assn., Beta Phi Mu. Home: 563 Park St Montclair NJ 07043-2027 Office: Irvington Pub Libr Civic Sq Irvington NJ 07111 *The world would be a better place if we could find ways to reward and honor evelry single perosn who works hard and does the right thing.*

MCCONNELL, MICHAEL, opera company director; b. Charlotte, N.C., Dec. 25, 1954; s. Jackson McConnell and Patsy Anne (King) White. MusB, Coll. Conservatory of Music, U. Cin., 1976, postgrad., 1979. Adj. lectr. Cin. Coll. Conservatory, 1980-81; resident stage dir. Opera Memphis, 1982-84; exec. dir. Lyric Opera Cleve., 1984-94; dir. opera Cleve. Inst. Music, 1991-95; stage dir. Fla. State Opera, Tallahassee, 1995—; dir. opera workshop Baldwin-Wallace Conservatory, Berea, Ohio, 1987-91; frequent panelist opera-music theater NEA. With prodn. staff Santa Fe Opera, Opera Theatre St. Louis, Edinburgh Festival, Opera Memphis, others; stage dir. Opera Theatre St. Louis, Opera Memphis, Opera Theatre Rochester, Memphis Playhouse on Sq., Cin. Opera, Skylight Opera Theatre, Cleve. Inst. Music, Cin. Coll. Conservatory Music, Cleve. Orch., others; contbr. articles to profl. jours. Mem. OPERA Am. (bd. dirs. 1993—), Actor's Equity Assn. Office: Fla State U School of Music Tallahassee FL 32306-2098

MCCONNELL, MICHAEL ARTHUR, lawyer; b. Ft. Worth, Jan. 15, 1947. BA, Loyola U., New Orleans, 1969; JD, U. Tex., 1975. Bar: Tex. 1976, U.S. Dist. Ct. (no. dist.) Tex. 1976, U.S. Dist. Ct. (ea. dist.) Tex. 1981, U.S. Dist. Ct. (we. dist.) Tex. 1982, U.S. Dist. Ct. (so. dist.) Tex. 1989, U.S. Ct. Appeals (5th cir.) Tex. 1980, U.S. Ct. Appeals (10th cir.) 1987. Briefing atty. U.S. Dist. Ct. Hon. Eldon B. Mahon, Ft. Worth, 1976-77; assoc. atty. Cantey, Hanger, Gooch, Munn and Collins, Ft. Worth, 1977-81, ptnr., 1981-83; judge no. dist. U.S. Bankruptcy Ct., Ft. Worth, 1983-86; ptnr. Kelly, Hart & Hallman, Ft. Worth, 1986-88, Jackson & Walker, Ft. Worth, 1988-95. Sgt. USAF, 1969-73. Mem. Nat. Conf. Bankruptcy Judges, Assn. Former Bankruptcy Judges. Office: McConnell Goodrich & Lenox 303 Main St Ste 220 Fort Worth TX 76102-4067

MCCONNELL, ROB, jazz musician, composer; b. Ont., Can., 1935. Hon. doctorate, St. Francis Xavier U., Nova Scotia, Can. Mem. The Boss Brass, 1968—; mem. faculty staff, head of the profl. instrumental program Grove Sch. Music, Van Nuys, Calif., 1988—. Recs. include All in Good Time (Grammy award for Best Big Band Album of Yr. 1984), Brassy & Sassy, Overtime, Don't Get Around Much Anymore, Mel Tormeé-Rob McConnell and The Boss Brass, Trio Sketches, Our 25th Year, The Brass is Back, Mutual Street. Recipient 4 Juno awards, 7 Juno nominations, Toronto Musician's award, 1994; named Best Arranger Nat. Assn. Jazz Educators. Office: Concord Jazz Inc PO Box 845 Concord CA 94522

MC CONNELL, ROBERT CHALMERS, former city official; b. Santa Fe, Aug. 7, 1913; s. Chalmers and Mary (Foree) McC.; m. Colleen Alford, Feb. 3, 1948; 1 dau., Julie. B.A., U. N.Mex., 1935; LL.B., George Washington U., 1939. Bar: N.Mex. bar 1941, U.S. Supreme Ct. bar 1947. Law clk. to U.S. circuit judge, 1939-40; asst. dist. atty. N.Mex., 1940-41, 45-47, adminstrv. asst. to congressman from, 1947-57, 57-61; spl. asst. to asst. sec. interior, 1961-62; asst. to sec. for congl. liaison Dept. Interior, Washington, 1962-67; asst. sec. for adminstrn. Dept. Interior, 1967-69; mayor City of Redington Beach, Fla., 1971-72; partner McConnell-Wilroy Cons., St. Petersburg, Fla., 1976-77. Mgr. Madeira Beach (Fla.) Little League Baseball; pres. Gulf Beaches Little League; chmn. bd. govs. Redington Beach Assn., 1977-79; chmn. Chaves County Dem. Com., 1946-48, The Biog. History of N.Mex. Recipient Distinguished Service award U.S. Dept. Interior, 1967. Mem. Sigma Chi. Club: Rotary. Home: 15849 Redington Dr Redington Beach FL 33708-1743

MC CONNELL, ROBERT EASTWOOD, architect, educator; b. Spokane, Wash., July 15, 1930; s. Robert Ervie and Alma (Eastwood) Mc C.; m. Beverly Ann Vincent, Sept. 12, 1953; children: Kathleen Ann, Karen Eileen, Terri Lynn. B in Archtl. Engring., Wash. State U., 1952; MArch, Mass. Inst. Tech., 1954. Project architect John W. Maloney (Architect), Seattle, 1956-62; asst. prof. architecture Ariz. State U., Tempe, 1962-66; asso. prof. Ariz. State U., 1966-67; prof. U. Kans., Lawrence, 1967-69; prof., head dept. art and architecture U. Idaho, Moscow, 1969-71; prof. U. Ariz., Tucson, 1971-92; dean Coll. Architecture U. Ariz., 1971-77; prof. emeritus, dean emeritus U. Ariz., Tucson, 1992—, acting assoc. dean, 1994; partner McConnell & Peterson, Architects, Tempe, 1963-66; pvt. practice architecture, 1962-96. Author, project dir.: Land Use Planning for Ariz., Ariz. Acad, 1974; Contbr. articles to profl. jours. Chmn. Idaho Gov.'s Awards Program in Arts and Humanities, 1970; project dir. Rio Salado Conceptual Study, Phoenix, 1966; bd. dirs. Tucson Regional Plan, 1972-79. Served with USAF, 1954-56. Fellow AIA (awards 1969, 76, pres. So. Ariz. chpt. 1975-76, bd. dirs. 1971-77); mem. AAUP, Ariz. Town Hall, Ariz. Soc. Architects (mem. coun. of dels. 1971-77, chmn. honor awards jury 1975), Phi Kappa Phi, Scarab, Tau Beta Pi, Sigma Tau. Home: 7001 N Edgewood Pl Tucson AZ 85704-6924 Office: U Ariz Coll Architecture Tucson AZ 85721

MCCONNELL, WILLIAM THOMPSON, commercial banker; b. Zanesville, Ohio, Aug. 8, 1933; s. William Gerald and Mary Gladys McC.; m. Jane Charlotte Cook, Aug. 25, 1956; children: Jennifer Wynne, William Gerald. BA, Denison U., 1955; MBA, Northwestern U., 1959. Pres. Park Nat. Bank, Newark, Ohio, 1979-83, pres., chief exec. officer, 1983-93; chmn., chief exec. officer Park Nat. Bank, Newark, 1993—; also bd. dirs. Park Nat. Bank, Newark, Ohio; pres., chief exec. officer Park Nat. Corp., Newark, 1987-94, chmn., CEO, 1994—; bd. dirs. Freight Svcs., Inc., Newark, Consol. Computer Ctr., Newark. Mem. Newark Area C. of C. (past pres., dir. 1977-83), Ohio Bankers Assn. (pres., chmn. 1981-83). Office: Park Nat Bank PO Box 3500 Newark OH 43058-3500

MCCONOMY, JAMES HERBERT, lawyer; b. Pitts., Mar. 24, 1937; s. Murray Michael and Catherine Elizabeth (Herbert) McC.; m. Jeanne Margaret Cronin, Sept. 3, 1960 (div. Apr. 1989); children: Margaret Jeanne, Michael Murray; m. Roberta L. Cavanaugh, June 30, 1989. AB cum laude, Harvard U., 1959, LLB, 1962. Bar: Pa. 1963, U.S. Ct. Appeals (3d cir.) 1972, U.S. Supreme Ct. 1977. Ptnr. Reed, Smith, Shaw & McClay, Pitts., 1962-92; mng. ptnr. Titus & McConomy, Pitts., 1992—. Fellow Am. Coll. Trial Lawyers; mem. ABA, Pa. Bar Assn. (chmn. comml. litigation sect. 1986—), Allegheny County Acad. Trial Lawyers. Republican. Roman Catholic. Clubs: Duquesne, Harvard-Yale-Princeton (Pitts.). Avocations: photography, travel. Home: 1117 Harvard Rd Pittsburgh PA 15205-1726 Office: Titus & McConomy Four Gateway Ctr 20th Fl Pittsburgh PA 15222

MCCONVILLE, WILLIAM, academic administrator. Rsch. fellow Divinity Sch. Yale U., until 1989; pres. Siena Coll., Loudonville, N.Y., 1989—. Office: Siena Coll Office of Pres Loudonville NY 12211

MCCOOK, KATHLEEN DE LA PEÑA, university educator; b. Chgo.; d. Frank Eugene and Margaret L. (de la Peña) McEntee; m. Philip G. Heim, Mar. 20, 1972 (div.); 1 child, Margaret Marie; m. William Woodrow Lee McCook, Oct. 12, 1991; stepchildren: Cecilia, Billie Jean, Nicole. B.A., U. Ill.; M.A., Marquette U., U. Chgo.; Ph.D., U. Wis.-Madison. Reference librarian Elmhurst Coll. Library, Ill., 1971-72; dir. pub. services Rosary Coll. Library, River Forest, Ill., 1972-76; lectr. U. Wis., Madison, 1976-78; asst. prof. library sci. U. Ill., Urbana, 1978-83; dean, prof. La. State U. Sch. Library and Info. Sci., Baton Rouge, 1983-90; dean grad. sch. La. State U., 1990-92; dir. Sch. Libr. and Info. Sci. U. South Fla., 1993—. Author: (with L. Estabrook) Career Profiles, 1983, (with William E. Moen) Occupational Entry, 1989, Adult Services, 1990, (with Gary O. Rolstad) Developing Readers' Advisory Services, 1993, Toward a Just and Productive Soc., 1994; contbr. essays to books, articles to profl. jours. Chmn. Equal Rights Amendment Task Force, Ill., 1977-79; mem. Eugene McCarthy campaign, U. Ill., Chgo., 1968; mem. La. Gov.'s Commn. for Women, 1985-88; bd. dirs. La. Endowment for Humanities, 1991-92. Recipient Disting. Alumnus award U. Wis., 1991; Bradshaw scholar Tex. Woman's Univ., 1994. Mem. ALA (com. chmn. 1980—, editor RQ jour. 1982-88, Pub. Librs. Jour. 1989-90, Am. Librs. adv. com. 1994-96, Equality award 1987, Adult Svc. award 1991), Assn. for Libr. and Info. Sci. Edn. (com. chmn. 1981—, pres. 1987-88), Fla. Libr. Assn. (bd. dirs. 1995—, Transformer award 1996), Tampa Bay Libr. Consortium (bd. dirs. 1994—), Women Libr. Workers, Ill. Libr. Assn. (treas. 1981-83), Beta Phi Mu. Democrat. Roman Catholic. Avocation: reading. Office: U South Fla Sch Libr and Info Sci 4202 E Fowler Ave CIS 1040 Tampa FL 33620-9951

MCCOOK, TERRY L., business executive, consultant; b. Jacksonville, Fla., Aug. 17, 1946; s. Vernon L. and Frances H. (Ulrich) McCook; m. Eileen Marie Hutchin, Sept. 22, 1979; children: Clare Marie, Theresa Renee, Mary Catherine. BA, N.C. State U., 1968; MA, Am. U., 1978, postgrad., 1978. Asst. buyer Thalheimer Bros., Richmond, Va., 1969-70; grad. teaching asst. Am. U., Washington, 1971-73, asst. dir. admissions, 1973-77; sys. analyst Solite Corp., Richmond, 1978-81; corp. br. ops. coord. United Va. Bank, Richmond, 1981-83; mktg. rep. Decimus Corp., Pitts., 1984-85; area sales mgr. Systeme Corp., Orlando, Fla., 1985-86; v.p., mktg. dir. The Citizens Banking Co., Salineville, Ohio, 1986-90; v.p., dimension sales Kirchman Corp., Orlando, 1992-94; CEO Profl. Asset Mgmt., Inc., Orlando, 1990—; mng. dir. Rad-Health Internat., Pitts., 1991-92. Author book revs. and article. Past nat. treas., provincial minister of Secular Franciscan Order. With USAR, 1968-74. Named to Outstanding Young Men in Am., 1978. Mem. Bank Mktg. Assn. (pres. tri-state chpt. 1990-91), Kiwanis Internat.

Club (pres. 1988-90), Sigma Phi Epsilon, Omicron Delta Kappa, Phi Alpha Theta. Roman Catholic. Avocations: golf, fishing. Home: 2669 Lazy Meadow Ln Apopka FL 32703-5858

MCCOOMB, LLOYD ALEXANDER, transportation executive; b. Edmonton, Alta., Can., Sept. 22, 1945. BASc, U. Toronto, Ont., Can., 1968, PhD, 1981; SM, MIT, 1970. With mil. engrng. bd. Can. Armed Forces, 1964-74; sr. devel. officer Transport Devel. Agy. Transport Can., 1974-83; dir. stats. and forecasts Air Adminstrn., Ottawa, Ont., Can., 1983-86; from dir. gen. mktg. to dir. gen. safety and tech. svcs. Airports Group, Ottawa, 1986-94; airport gen. mgr. Toronto-Lester B. Pearson Internat. Airport, 1994—. Office: Lester B Pearson Intl Airport, Transport Canada PO Box 6003, Toronto, ON Canada L5P 1B5

MCCOPPIN, PETER, symphony orchestra conductor; b. Toronto, Ont., Can.; m. Roswitha McCoppin, 1975. BMus in Performance Art, U. Toronto; studied conducting with, Erich Leinsdorf, Prof. Hans Swarosky, Lovro von Maticic, Seriu Celibidache. Formed chamber choir Toronto, 1970-75; condr. orchestral program, prof. conducting Cleve. Inst. Music, 1975-78; guest condr. Alta. Ballet Co., Nat. Ballet Can., major orchs. Can.; music. advisor, condr. Vancouver (B.C.) Symphony Orch., 1988-89, now guest condr.; music dir. Victoria (B.C.) Symphony Orch., 1989—, Charlotte (N.C.) Symphony Orch., 1993—. Guest condr. Thunder Bay (Ont.) Symphony, Syracuse (N.Y.) Symphony; condr. Shanghai Symphony, Ctrl. Philharmonic, Beijing, Tokyo Symphony, Osaka Philharmonic, Gunma Symphony, Sapporo Symphony, Nat. Symphony Mex., Rochester Philharmonic, Buffalo Philharmonic, Tucson Symphony, most major orchs. in Can.; concerts with KBS Symphony, Korea; host B.C. TV Knowledge Network Classic Theatre, TV spls., radio programs. Office: Victoria Symphony Orch, 846 Broughton St lower level, Victoria, BC Canada V8W 1E4

MCCORD, ALICE BIRD, trade association administrator; b. Enid, Okla.; d. Glenn and Lottabel (Bird) McC. BS, NYU, 1964; MA, Columbia U., 1974. Tng. dir. Gimbels Dept. Store, N.Y.C., 1965-69; personnel dir. The May Dept. Stores, N.Y.C. and St. Louis, 1972-75; cons. Arthur Young & Co., N.Y.C., 1976-78; v.p. personnel Nat. Retail Mchts. Assn., N.Y.C., 1978-85, sr. v.p., 1986-92; sr. v.p. rsch. and planning Nat. Retail Fedn., Inc., N.Y.C., 1976-92; cons., prin. ABM Assocs. (specializing in svcs. to internat. retailers U.S. and abroad), 1992—; assn. and retail cons.; guest on nat. and local TV programs. Author: Training and Development. Mem. Am. Psychol. Assn., Am. Soc. Tng. and Devel., Gifts In Kind (bd. dirs.).

MCCORD, JEAN ELLEN, secondary art educator, coach; b. Ilion, N.Y., Oct. 20, 1952; d. Harold Shepard and Marian Alice (Bernier) Shepard; m. Colin McCord, May 10, 1977 (div. Sept. 1993). AA, Mohawk Valley C.C., Utica, N.Y., 1972; BA, SUNY, New Paltz, 1975, postgrad., 1976-77. Cert. art educator, N.Y. Jr. kindergarten tchr. Norfolk (Va.) Naval Base, 1978-79; jr. kindergarten and art tchr. Sunnybrook Day Sch., Virginia Beach, Va., 1979-81; tchr. art Fisher Elem. Sch., Mohawk, N.y., 1982-84, Mechanicstown Sch., Middletown, N.Y., 1984-88, Middletown (N.Y.) Start Ctr., 1986-87, tchr. synergetic edn., Middletown Tchr. Ctr., 1986-87; pvt. portfolio tutor Middletown, 1989-91; tchr. art Middletown Elem. Summer Sch., 1989—, Middletown H.S., 1987—; sec. of policy and exec. bds. Middletown Tchr. Ctr., 1988-91, chmn. policy and exec. bds., 1991-92; mem. Bicentennial of Edn. com.; advisor NAt. Art Honor Soc., 1989—; coord. After Sch. Program for Youth at Risk, 1995-96, tchr., 1992-94. Actress, vocalist, designer in regional theatre, 1993-94; artistic designer sch. plays and Creative Theatre Group; writer, dir. for local cabarets. County svc. coord. Orange County Youth-In-Govt. (adv. 1988—), Goshen, N.Y., 1991-93; Odyssey of the Mind Coach, 1984-92;. Named for outstanding set design Times Herald Record, 1994. Named for outstanding set design Times Herald Record, 1994; honored by Bd. Edn. Outstanding Educator, 1992. Episcopalian. Avocations: theatrical design, singing, calligraphy. Home: 638 Route 211 E Middletown NY 10940-1718 Office: Middletown City Schs Wisner Ave Middletown NY 10940

MC CORD, KENNETH ARMSTRONG, consulting engineer; b. Balt., May 4, 1921; s. William Ellermeyer and Bertha (Turnt) McC.; m. Carol Blanton, Oct. 12, 1946; children—Thomas B., Kenneth Armstrong, William C., David M., Jean E. B. Engring., Johns Hopkins U., 1941. Registered profl. engr., Md., Va., N.J., D.C., Del. registered profl. surveyor, Md., Del. registered profl. planner, N.J. Ret. ptnr. Whitman, Requardt and Assos., Balt.; gen. ptnr. B&H Investments, Manassas, Va. Served with C.E. U.S. Army, 1942-46. Decorated Silver Star, Croix de Guerre France. Fellow ASCE; mem. NSPE, Am. Water Works Assn., Am. Cons. Engrs. Coun., Water Pollution Control Fedn., L'Hirondelle Club. Democrat. Presbyterian. Home: 1010 W Wind Ct Baltimore MD 21204-6738

MC CORD, MARSHAL, civil engineer; b. Balt., July 4, 1917; s. William Ellermeyer and Bertha (Turnt) McC.; m. Ruth Helen Schultz, Apr. 20, 1946; 1 dau., Barbara Lynn. B. Engring., Johns Hopkins U., 1937. Draftsman Modjeski & Masters, Harrisburg, Pa., 1937-40; design and project engr. J.E. Greiner Co., Balt., 1946-57; chief engr., v.p. Century Engring., Inc., Towson, Md., 1957-77; dir. engring. and constrn. State of Md., Balt., 1977-86; mem. Md. State Bd. Registration for Profl. Engrs. and Land Surveyors, 1966-76, chmn., 1971-76. Moderator Presbytery of Balt., 1977—. Served with C.E. U.S. Army, 1941-46. Fellow ASCE; mem. Nat. Soc. Profl. Engrs., Md. Soc. Profl. Engrs. (Meritorious Service award 1971). Club: Johns Hopkins. Home: 11630 Glen Arm Rd Glen Arm MD 21057-9403

MCCORD, SCOTT ANTHONY, chemistry educator; b. Orlando, Fla., Sept. 15, 1956; s. Randolph John and Genevieve (Sbordone) M. BA in Limnology and Music Edn., U. Ctrl. Fla., 1980; MME, Ind. U., 1982; EdD in Sci. Edn., U. Ctrl. Fla., 1995. Cert. tchr., Fla. Lab./field chemist U. Ctrl. Fla., Orlando, 1977-79; instr. chemistry Titusville (Fla.) High Sch., 1983—; mem. lab. safety com. Brevard County (Fla.) Schs., 1989, chmn., 1991; cons. Space Port Fla. Authority, Cocoa, 1992, co-prin. investigator, 1992; sci. rsch. supr. Bionetics Corp., Kennedy Space Ctr., Fla., 1992; chemistry specialist Lockheed Space Ops., Kennedy Space Ctr., 1993; chmn. Brevard County Clash of Titans Sci. Acad. Competition, 1994, master of ceremonies, 1995; sci. and music adjudicator Nat. Excellence in Acads. Competition, Orlando, 1994. Co-author, editor: Brevard County Laboratory Safety Manual, 1991. Honorary liaison officer USAF Acad., Colorado Springs, 1986—. Named Outstanding Chemistry Tchr. Am. Chem. Soc., 1986-94; recipient various outstanding sci. rsch. teaching awards from industry and cmty. including NASA, Harris and Lockheed Martin Corps. Achievements include development of computer model program which simulates thermodynamic changes in neurons which undergo plasticity changes during learning. Home: 1720 York Town Ave Titusville FL 32796 Office: Titusville High Sch 150 Terrier Tr Titusville FL 32780

MCCORD, WILLIAM CHARLES, retired diversified energy company executive; b. San Antonio, Apr. 1, 1928; s. Sam Byard and Helen (Schoepfer) McC.; div.; children: Kathleen McCord Burnett, Martha McCord Pennington, Billy, Helen McCord Curry, Elizabeth McCord Baker, Richard, Douglas, James, Quannah, Korrin Li, Minta Ann Tilden; m. Kay Moran; stepchildren: Heather Moran, Caitlin Moran, James Moran Jr. B.S. in Mech. Engring, Tex. A & M U., 1949. With Enserch Corp. (formerly Lone Star Gas Co.), 1949—, dir. bldg. mgmt., 1965-67; v.p. Enserch Corp. (Dallas div.), 1967, sr. v.p. operations, 1968-70, pres., prin. exec. officer, 1970-77, chmn., pres., 1977-91, chmn., chief exec. officer, 1991-93; sr. v.p. Nipak, Inc., chem. subsidiary, Dallas, 1991-93; ret., 1993; bd. dirs. Enserch Corp., Pool Energy Svcs. Co., Lone Star Techs., Inc. Past pres., mem. exec. bd. Circle Ten council Boy Scouts Am.; mem. nat. exec. bd. Boy Scouts Am.; bd. dirs., former chmn. Tex. Research League, Dallas Citizens Council, State Fair Tex. Mem. Tau Beta Pi. Baptist. Office: 4925 Greenville Ave Dallas TX 75206-4026

MCCORISON, MARCUS ALLEN, librarian, cultural organization administrator; b. Lancaster, Wis., July 17, 1926; s. Joseph Lyle and Ruth (Mink) McC.; m. Janet Buckbee Knop, June 10, 1950; children: Marcus Allen II, Judith McC. Gove, Andrew Buckbee, Mary McC. Rosenbloom, James Rice, Peter Gardner. AB, Ripon Coll., 1950; MA, U. Vt., 1951, LittD (hon.), 1992; MS, Columbia U., 1954; LHD (hon.), Assumption Coll., Worcester, Mass., 1987, Coll. of the Holy Cross, 1992; LittD (hon.), Clark U., 1992. Librarian Kellogg-Hubbard Library, Montpelier, Vt., 1954-55; chief of rare books dept. Dartmouth Coll. Library, Hanover, N.H., 1955-59; head spl. collections dept. State U. Iowa Libraries, 1959-60; libr. Am. Antiquarian Soc., Worcester, Mass., 1960-91, editor Procs., 1960-67, dir., 1967-89, pres., 1989-92, pres. emeritus, 1993—; cons. Christie, Manson & Woods, Internat., 1993—, A.W. Mellon Found., 1994-95, Libr. Congress, Hist. Soc. of Pa., 1996; mem. N.Am. steering com. 18th Century Short Title Catalogue, 1977—; mem. Com. for a New Eng. Bibliography, 1968-90, treas., 1970-77; mem. adv. com. Eleutherian Mills-Hagley Found., 1971-74, 87-89; mem. adv. coun. Princeton U. Libr., 1988-92; bd. govs. Rsch. Librs. Group, 1980-91, chmn. preservation com., 1982-85, chmn. governance com., 1989-91, chmn. writings of James Fenimore Cooper, 1991-93. Author: Vermont Imprints 1778-1820, 1963, The 1764 Catalogue of the Redwood Library, 1965; contbr.: The Pursuit of Knowledge in the Early American Republic, 1976, Publishing and Readership in Revolutionary France and America, 1993; editor: History of Printing in America by Isaiah Thomas, 1970; mem. editorial bd.: History of the Book in America, 1993—. Trustee Fruitlands Mus., 1978-89, Old Sturbridge Village, 1981-92, Hist. Deerfield, Inc., 1991—; mem. bd. mgrs. Lewis Walpole Libr., Yale U., 1995—; nat. trustee Newbury Libr., 1995—. With USNR, 1944-46, U.S. Army, 1951-52. Recipient Samuel Pepys medal Ephemera Soc., London, 1980, Disting. Alumni award Ripon Coll., 1989, Columbia U. Sch. Libr. Svc., 1992. Fellow Pilgrim Soc.; mem. Am. Antiquarian Soc., Mass. Hist. Soc., Coll. and Rsch. Librs. Assn. (chmn. rare books sect. 1965-66), Bibliog. Soc. Am. (pres. 1980-84, del. to ACLS 1985—), Vt. Hist. Soc. (trustee 1956-66), Worcester Hist. Mus. (exec. com. 1967-80), Ind. Rsch. Librs. Assn. (chmn. 1972-73, 78-80), Ctr. for Rsch. on Vt. (assoc.), N.E. Am. Soc. 18th Century Studies (pres. 1978-79), Colonial Soc. Mass., Odd Vols. Club, Grolier Club (councillor 1979-82, 83-84), Century Assn. Democrat. Congregationalist. Home and Office: 3601 Knightsbridge Close Worcester MA 01609-1161

MCCORKLE, HORACE JACKSON, physician, educator; b. Center Point, Tex., Feb. 5, 1905; s. Homer Thomas and Helen Hart (Cason) McC.; m. Marion Fisher, June 10, 1939; children—Alan, Donald, Malcolm, Douglas, Jeanette. M.D., U. Calif., 1934. Intern San Francisco City and County Hosp., 1933-34; surgeon U. Calif. Med. Sch., 1938—, prof. surgery, 1953—. Mem. Am., Pan Pacific, Western, Pacific Coast surg. assns., Internat. Surg. Soc., Pan Am. Med. Soc., Soc. Exptl. Biology and Medicine, Soc. Univ. Surgeons, Am. Gastroenterol. Assn., Nu Sigma Nu, Kappa Delta Rho. Home: 35 San Fernando Way San Francisco CA 94127-1503

MCCORKLE, ROBERT ELLSWORTH, agribusiness educator; b. Salinas, Calif., Apr. 3, 1938; s. Stanley Harold and Muriel Eugenia (Vosti) McC.; m. Mary E. McCorkle, June 26, 1965; children: Bonnie Kathleen, Robyn Krystyna. BSc in Farm Mgmt., Calif. Poly. State U., San Luis Obispo, 1960; MSc in Agrl. Econs., U. Calif., Davis, 1962; postgrad., U. Wis., 1969, Oreg. State U., 1966. Rsch. statistician U. Calif., Davis, 1960-62; asst. prof. agrl. bus. Calif. Poly. State U., San Luis Obispo, 1962-66, dir. internat. edn., 1970-74, asst. prof. agrl. mgmt., 1969-76, prof. agribus., 1976—; chief farm mgmt. officer Ministry Agr., Lusaka, Zambia, 1967-69; dir., owner McCorkle Farms, Inc., Willows, Calif., 1970—; vis. prof. Mich. State U., U.S. AID, Washington, 1984-85; dir., owner McCorkle Trucking, Glenn, Calif., 1988—; agrl. economist U.S. AID-Redso ESA, Nairobi, Kenya, 1984-85. Author: Guide for Farming in Zambia, 1968. Pres. Cabrillo Property Owners Assn., Los Osos, Calif., 1976-78; vol. Atty. Gen.'s Adv. Com., Calif., 1972-74. U.S. Peace Corps strategy grantee, Washington, 1976—. Mem. Am. Agrl. Econs. Assn., Western Agrl. Econs. Assn., Calif. Poly. Farm Mgmt. Club, Calif. Poly. Alumni Assn., Blue Key, Alpha Zeta (sr. advisor Delta chpt., nat. high coun. chronicler, treas., bd. dirs., found.). Republican. Episcopalian. Avocations: hunting, fishing. Office: Calif Poly State U San Luis Obispo CA 93407

MCCORKLE, RUTH, oncological nurse, educator. BS, U. Md., 1968; MA, U. Iowa, 1972, PhD, 1975. Staff nurse CCU Vanvouver (Wash.) Med. Hosp., 1968-69; oncological clin. nurse specialist U. Iowa Hosps. and Clinics, Iowa City, 1971-73; instr. psychiat. nursing and oncological nursing Sch. Nursing, U. Iowa, Iowa City, 1974-75; from asst. prof. to prof. dept. cmty. health care sys. U. Wash., Seattle, 1975-85; prof. adult health and illness divsn. Sch. Nursing, U. Pa., Phila., 1986—, chairperson, 1988-89, dir. Ctr. Advancing Care in Serious Illness, 1989—, dir. cancer control Cancer Comprehensive Ctr., 1990—; mem. nursing sci. rev. com. Nat. Ctr. Nursing Rsch., 1988-92. Contbr. articles to profl. jours. Fellow Am. Acad. Nursing; mem. ANA, NAS, Internat. Soc. Nurses Cancer Care (dir.-at-large 1983-89), Am. Assn. Cancer Edn., Oncology Nursing Soc. (charter mem., mem. rsch. com. 1981-82, dir.-at-large 1983-85). Office: U Pa Sch Nursing 420 Guardian Dr Philadelphia PA 19104-6096

MCCORMAC, BILLY MURRAY, physicist, research institution executive, former army officer; b. Zanesville, Ohio, Sept. 8, 1920; s. Samuel Dennis and Phyllis (Murray) M.; m. Dorothy Boros, 1948; children: Norene Leslie, Candace Elizabeth, Lisbeth Phyllis; m. Diana Root, 1968; children: Billy Murray II, Samuel Dennis Root. B.S., Ohio State U., 1943; M.S., U. Va., 1956, Ph.D. in Nuclear Physics, 1957. Commd. 2d lt. U.S. Army, 1943; advanced through grades to lt. col.; physicist U.S. Army (Office Spl. Weapons Devel.), 1957-60; scientist U.S. Army (Office of Chief of Staff), 1960-61; physicist U.S. Army (Def. Atomic Support Agy.), 1961-62, chief electromagnetic br., 1962-63; ret., 1963; sci. advisor rsch. inst. Ill. Inst. Tech., 1963, dir. div. geophysics rsch. inst., 1963-68; sr. cons. scientist Lockheed Rsch. Labs., Palo Alto, Calif., 1968-69, mgr. Radiation Physics Lab., 1969-74, mgr. Electro-optics Lab., 1974-76, mgr. solar and optics physics, 1976-89, staff exec. physical and electronic scis., 1989-92; Chmn. radiation trapped in earth's magnetic field Adv. Study Inst., Norway, 1965, chmn. aurora and airglow, Eng., 1966, Norway, 1968, Can., 1970, chmn. physics and chemistry of atmospheres, France, 1972, Belgium, 1974, chmn. earth's particles and fields, Germany, 1967, Calif., 1969, Italy, 1971, Eng., 1973, Austria, 1975; chmn. Shuttle Environment and Ops.-I, Washington, 1983, -II, Houston, 1985; chmn. Space Station in 21st Century, Reno, 1986, Space Station I, Washington, 1988. Editor Jour. Water, Air and Soil Pollution, Geophysics and Astrophysics Monographs; editor-in-chief Natural Sinks CO2, 1991, Quantification of Sinks and Sources, 1993, Acid Reign Proceedings, 1996. Fellow AIAA (assoc., mem. publ. com. 1981—, v.p. publs. 1987-91); mem. AAAS, Am. Astron. Soc. (sr.), Am. Phys. Soc., Am. Geophys. Union, Marine Tech. Soc. Home: 1312 Cuernavaca Cir Mountain View CA 94040

MC CORMAC, JOHN WAVERLY, judge; b. Zanesville, Ohio, Feb. 8, 1926; s. Samuel D. and Phyllis (Murray) McC.; m. Martha Ann Cunningham, June 22, 1952; children: Michael Paul, John Mark, James Samuel. B.S., Muskingum Coll., 1951; J.D., Capital U., 1961. Bar: Ohio 1961. Fire protection engr. Ohio Insp. Bur., 1951-60; pvt. practice Columbus, 1961-65; prof. law Capital U., Columbus, 1965-66, 71-74; dean Law Sch. Capital U., 1966-71; judge 10th Dist. Ct. Appeals, 1975-92; prof. law Ohio State U., Columbus, 1993—; mem. staff cons. rules adv. com. Supreme Ct. Ohio; chmn. adv. bd. Vols. in Probation, 1972-74; chmn. ohio Jud. Conf., 1982-84; commr. Ohio Dispute Resolution Com., 1989-96, chmn., 1993-95; chief justice Ohio Ct. Appeals Assn., 1989-91. Author: Ohio Civil Rules Practice, 1970, 2nd edit., 1992, Anderson's Ohio Civil Practice, Vol. 1, 1971, Vol. 2, 1976, Vol. 3, 1977, Wrongful Death in Ohio, 1982. Served with USNR, 1943-46. Fellow Ohio Bar Assn. Found.; mem. League Ohio Law Schs. (pres. 1969-70), ABA, Ohio Bar Assn. (council of dels. 1973-77), Columbus Bar Assn. (bd. govs. 1968-72, sec.-treas. 1973-74, pres. 1975-76), Am. Judicature Soc., Phi Alpha Delta. Republican. Club: Masons (33 deg.). Home: 395 Longfellow Ave Columbus OH 43085-3024

MC CORMAC, WESTON ARTHUR, retired educator and army officer; b. Tacoma, Mar. 5, 1911; s. Jesse Carney and Jessie (Myron) McC.; B.A., Golden Gate U., M.B.A., 1968; diploma Nat. War Coll., 1956; M.P.A., U. So. Calif., 1972; M.A., Calif. Poly. State U., 1975. m. Mary Jeanne Rapinac, Sept. 5, 1940. Account exec. Merrill, Lynch, Pierce, Fenner & Beane, Tacoma, Seattle, 1929-40; commd. lt. U.S. Army, 1940, advanced through grades to col., 1946; asst. chief of staff 7th Army G 1, 1952-54; comdg. officer 35th F.A. Group, Germany, 1956-58; dep. chief of staff V Corps, 1958-60, asst. chief of staff G 1, Pacific, 1962-65; ret., 1966; prof. bus., dept. chmn. Calif. Poly. State U., San Luis Obispo, 1968-80, ret., 1980. Decorated Legion of Merit with 2 oak leaf clusters, Silver Star, Bronze Star medal, Commendation medal with oak leaf cluster. Fellow Fin. Analysts Fedn.; mem. Los Angeles Soc. Fin. Analysts. Home: 16732 Lew Allen Cir Riverside CA 92518-2909

MCCORMACK, DENNIS K., clinical psychologist; m. Nancy K. McCormack; children: Kelly, Karen. BA in Math., Calif. Western U., 1969; MA, U.S. Internat. U., 1971, PhD in Leadership and Human Behavior, PhD in Psychology, 1974, 78. Diplomate Internat. Council Profl. Counseling and Psychotherapy, Am. Inst. Counseling and Psychotherapy, Internat. Acad. Health Care Profls. Pvt. practice family therapist Coronado, Calif.; chief family therapy Winn Army Cmty. Hosp.; guest spkr. at numerous clubs, lodges and local orgns. Contbr. articles to profl. jours. Mem. Sr. Citizen Adv. Com., 1982—, Land Use Adv. Com., Coronado, 1979-80; chmn. Coronado Planning Commn., 1978-83, St. Paul's United Meth. Ch., 1978-81, personnel com., 1978-81, mem. adminstrv. bd., 1983—; pres. Coronado Coordinating Council, 1983—; mem. adv. bd. Mil. Affairs Com., 1984—; bd. dirs. Vietnam Vets. Leadership Program, 1984—, Coronado Hosp. Found., 1988—; mem. Southbay Chember Exec. Com., 1986—, Coronado Visitor Promotion Bd., 1986—. Fellow Internat. Council of Sex Edn. and Parenthood of Am. U., Am. Bd. Med. Psychotherapists (clin. assoc.), S.D. Acad. Psychologists (chmn. membership com. 1988—), Coronado C. of C. (pres. 1986—). Office: PO Box 577 Richmond Hill GA 31324-0577

MCCORMACK, DONALD PAUL, newspaper consultant; b. Brockton, Mass., Jan. 15, 1926; s. Everett G. and Esther (Lufkin) McC.; m. Petronella Ruth Seger, Apr. 28, 1951; 1 son, Christopher Paul. B.A., U. Pitts., 1949. Corr. U.P.I., 1949-52; asst. city editor Pitts. Sun-Telegraph, 1952-56; pub. relations exec., 1956-64; copy reader N.Y. News, 1964-67, editorial writer, 1967-72, chief editorial writer, 1972-82; cons., 1982—. With USAAF, 1944-46, Pa. N.G., 1954-57. Home and Office: PO Box 3539 Westport CT 06880-8539

MCCORMACK, ELIZABETH J., foundation administrator; b. Mar. 7, 1922; m. Jerome I. Aron, Dec. 23, 1976. BA, Manhattanville Coll., 1944; PhD, Fordham U., 1966. Headmistress Acad. Sacred Heart, Greenwich, Conn., 1954-58; asst. to pres. Manhattanville Coll., Purchase, N.Y., 1958-62, acad. dean, 1962-66, pres., 1966-74; asst. to pres. Rockefeller Bros. Fund, N.Y.C., 1974-76; philanthropic advisor Rockefeller Family & Assocs., N.Y.C., 1976—. Trustee Alliance Capital, N.Y., 1984—, Am. Acad. in Rome, N.Y.C., 1990—, Asian Cultural Coun., N.Y.C., 1980; supervisory dir. Arrow Ventures, N.V., N.Y.C., 1983—; bd. dirs. United HealthCare Corp., 1991—; overseer Meml. Sloan-Kettering Cancer Ctr., Inc., N.Y.C., 1979—, mgr., 1980—; trustee emeritus Swarthmore (Pa.) Coll., 1980—. Mem. Am. Acad. Arts and Scis., Century Assn., Coun. on Fgn. Rels. Office: Rockefeller Found 30 Rockefeller Plz Rm 5600 New York NY 10112

MC CORMACK, FRANCIS XAVIER, lawyer, former oil company executive; b. Bklyn., July 9, 1929; s. Joseph and Blanche V. (Dengel) Mc C.; m. Margaret V. Hynes, Apr. 24, 1954; children: Marguerite, Francis Xavier, Sean Michael, Keith John, Cecelia Blanche, Christopher Thomas. AB cum laude, St. Francis Coll., Bklyn., 1951; LLB, Columbia U., 1954. Bar: N.Y. 1955, Mich. 1963, Calif. 1974, Pa. 1975. Assoc. Cravath, Swaine & Moore, N.Y.C., 1956-62; sr. atty. Ford Motor Co., 1962-64, asst. gen. counsel, 1970-72; v.p., gen. counsel, sec. Philco-Ford Corp., 1964-72; v.p., gen. counsel Atlantic Richfield Co., 1972-73, sr. v.p., gen. counsel, 1973-94; arbitrator, mediator JAMS-Endispute. Editor Columbia U. Law Rev., 1954. Decorated commendatore Ordine al Merito (Italy); Stone scholar Columbia U., 1954. Mem. Calif. Club, Chancery Club, Annandale Golf Club. Home and Office: 975 Singingwood Dr Arcadia CA 91006-1924

MC CORMACK, FRED ALLEN, state social services administrator; b. Bklyn., June 10, 1930; s. Frank J. and Rhea (Del Castro) Mc C.; m. Ellen Anne Lockwood, June 19, 1954 (div.); children: Mary Lee, Lynn Anne, Rosemarie, Fred A., Julie Ellen, Rhea Michelle, Claire Eileen; m. Elin Howe, Jan. 1994. BS, Seton Hall U., 1953; MSW, U. Conn., 1955. Social worker Montrose (N.Y.) VA Hosp., 1955-61; adminstr., dir. Tappan Zee Mental Health Ctr., North Tarrytown, N.Y., 1957-62; supr. social worker Orange County Mental Health Clinic, Goshen, N.Y., 1961-62; dir. Sweetwater Counseling Svc., Rock Springs, Wyo., 1962-65; asst. supt., dir. geriatric program Manteno (Ill.) State Hosp., 1965-68; dir. Tacoma Comprehensive Mental Health Ctr., 1968-69; cons. Dept. Instns. Wash., 1968-69, Laurel Haven Sch., Ballwin, Mo., 1977-78; supt. W.G. Murray Children's Ctr., Centralia, Ill., 1969-71, Elisabeth Ludeman Ctr., Park Forest, Ill., 1971-76; dir. San Luis Valley Mental Health Ctr., Alamosa, Colo., 1976-77, Monroe Devel. Ctr., Rochester, N.Y., 1977-80, Suffolk Devel. Ctr., Melville, N.Y., 1980-85; assoc. commr. N.Y. State Office Mental Retardation and Devel. Disabilities, Albany, 1985-93; ret., 1993; part-time tchr. Western Wyo. Jr. Coll., 1963-65, Prairie State Coll., Chicago Heights, Ill., 1965-68, Green River C.C., 1968-69; instr. Adams State Coll., Alamosa, 1977; cons. Snohomish Community Action Coun., Everett, Wash., 1969. Past mem. citizens adv. bd. Sch. Dist. 162, Matteson, Ill.; chmn. Park Forest Sr. Citizens Commn., State Employees Federated Appeal, United Way Rochester, 1978-80, L.I., 1984-85; past bd. dirs. Gavin Found., Park Forest; bd. Jones Cmty. Ctr., Chicago Heights, Four County Devel. Disabilities Conf.; vol. Prescott Spl. Olympics, 1993, 94, 95, 96; advisor Prescott Oasis. Recipient cert. of merit Nat. Assn. Physically Handicapped, Dir. of Yr. award N.Y. State Family Care Providers Assn., 1984. Fellow Am. Assn. Mental Deficiency (pres. Ill. chpt. 1972); mem. NASW, Acad. Cert. Social Workers. Home: 1408 Myers Holw Prescott AZ 86301-5145

MCCORMACK, JOHN JOSEPH, JR., insurance executive; b. Morristown, N.J., Aug. 22, 1944; s. John Joseph and Marion Loretta (Smith) McC.; m. Judith Gail Harvey, July 20, 1968; children—Brendan, Matthew, Margaret. B.B.A., St. Bonaventure U., 1966. Group underwriter Tchrs. Ins. and Annuity Assn.-Coll. Retirement Equities Fund, N.Y.C., 1966-71, benefit plan counselor, 1971-72, asst. adv. officer, 1972-73, adv. officer, 1973-74, asst. v.p., 1974-75, 2d v.p., 1975-78, v.p., 1978-80, sr. v.p., 1980-83, exec. v.p., 1983—; trustee Am. Psychol. Assn. Ins. Trust, Washington, 1980-90, chmn., 1985-86, trustee investment com., 1990—; trustee Employee Benefit Research Inst., Washington, 1983—, treas., 1986-90. Mem. pres.'s coun. St. Bonaventure U., 1986—, chmn., 1986-89; bd. visitors Ctr. for Study Future Mgmt., 1987-92; trustee Coll. and Univ. Pers. Assn. Found., 1992-94; bd. govs. Investment Co. Inst., 1994—. Roman Catholic. Office: Tchrs Ins & Annuity Assn Am 730 3rd Ave New York NY 10017-3206

MCCORMACK, MARK HUME, lawyer, business management company executive; b. Chgo., Nov. 6, 1930; s. Ned and Grace (Wolfe) McC.; m. Nancy Ann Breckenridge, Oct. 9, 1954 (div.); children: Scott, Todd, Leslie; m. Betsy Nagelsen. BA, William and Mary Coll., 1951; LLB, Yale U., 1954. Assoc. Arter and Hadden, Cleve., 1957-63; ptnr. Arter and Hadden, 1963—; pres., chief exec. officer Internat. Mgmt. Group, Cleve., 1964—. Author: The World of Professional Golf, 1967, Arnie, The Evolution of a Legend, 1967, Arnie, The Man and the Legend, 1967 (British edit.), Arnie, What They Did Not Teach You in Harvard Business School, 1984, Terrible Truth About Lawyers, 1987, What They Still Don't Teach You at Harvard Business School, 1989. Served with U.S. Army, 1955-56. Mem. Cleve. Bar Assn., Author's Guild, Royal and Ancient Club (St. Andrews, Scotland), Union Club, Pepper Pike Club, The Club (Cleve.), Isleworth Club, Deepdale Club, Theta Delta Chi. Office: Internat Mgmt Group One Erieview Plz Ste 1300 Cleveland OH 44114

MCCORMACK, PATRICIA SEGER, independent press service editor, journalist; b. Pitts., June 11, 1927; d. Arthur John and Anne Irene (McCaffrey) Seger; m. Donald P. McCormack, Apr. 28, 1951; 1 son, Christopher Paul. B.A., U. Pitts., 1949; certificate, A.P. Inst. Seminar, 1967. News editor weekly newspapers Mt. Lebanon, Pa., 1950-52; med. editor Pitts. Sun Telegraph, 1952-57; med. sci. editor INS, N.Y.C., 1958-59; columnist, family, health and edn. editor UPI, 1959-84, sr. editor, 1987-90. Mem. Boy of Year selection com. Boys Clubs Am., 1966; mem. Coty Fashion award jury, 1965-72, nat. selection com. Century III Leader Scholarship Competition Nat. Assn. Secondary Sch. Prins., 1986. Recipient Biennial Media award Family Service Assn. Am., 1965, Freedom Found. medal; 1st place Sci. Writing award Am. Dental Assn., 1976; Nat. Media award United Negro Coll. Fund, 1977; John Swett award for disting. educating reporting Calif. Edn. Assn., 1981. Mem. AAAS, Nat. Assn. Sci. Writers (life), Edn. Writers Assn., Women's Forum Inc. (N.Y.C.), Nat. Fedn. Press Women (Comm. Achievement medal 1993), Conn. Press Club (v.p., Communicator of Achievement

1993), Conn. Women's Forum. Home and Office: PO Box 3539 Westport CT 06880-8539

MCCORMACK, RICHARD THOMAS FOX, government official; b. Bradford, Pa., Mar. 6, 1941; s. C.H. and Ruth N. (Fox) McC.; m. Karen L. Hagstrom, Oct. 18, 1980; children: Charlotte Louise, Justin Randall, Elizabeth Caroline. B.A., Georgetown U., 1963; Ph.D., U. Fribourg (Switzerland), 1966. With Peace Corps, 1966-67; sr. staff mem. Pres.' Adv. Council on Exec. Orgn., White House, Washington, 1969-71; with Am. Enterprise Inst., 1975-77; dep. asst. sec. for internat. econ. affairs Dept. Treasury, 1974; mem. staff U.S. Senate, 1979-81; asst. sec. state for econ. and bus. affairs U.S. Dept. State, Washington, 1982-85; ambassador Orgn. Am. States U.S. Dept. State, 1985-89, undersec. of state for econ. affairs, 1989-91; candidate in primary elections for U.S. Congress, 1972, 74; cons. Office Telecommunications Policy, 1971, Coun. on Internat. Econ. Policy, 1972, Office Spl. Trade Rep., 1975, Exec. Office of the Pres., Washington; guest scholar Woodrow Wilson Ctr. Smithsonian Instn., Washington, 1991-92; bus. advisor Am. companies, cons. U.S. Govt. on Internat. Econ. Affairs, 1992—. Author: Asians in Kenya, 1971, The Twilight War, 1979, Economic Reforms for Israel's Economy, 1991, Managing Japan's Financial Crisis, 1992. Recipient Superior Honor award Dept. State, 1987, Sec. of State's Disting. Svc. award, 1991; decorated Legion of Honor (France). Mem. Econ. Club N.Y. Republican. Home: 1601 Walden Dr McLean VA 22101-3160 Office: 818 Connecticut Ave NW Ste 800 Washington DC 20006-2702

MCCORMACK, ROBERT CORNELIUS, investment banker; b. N.Y.C., Nov. 7, 1939; m. Mary Lester, Dec. 14, 1963; children: Robert Cornelius Jr., Walter, Scott. BA, U. N.C., 1962; MBA, U. Chgo., 1968. V.p. Dillon Read & Co. Inc., 1968-81; mng. dir. Morgan Stanley & Co., Inc., Chgo., 1981-87; dep. asst sec. def. prodn. support U.S. Dept. Def., Washington, 1987-88, dep. under sec. def. indsl. and internat. programs, 1988-89; acting dep. under sec. of def. acquisition U.S. Dept. Def., 1989-90; asst. sec. Navy fin. mgmt. U.S. Dept. Def., Washington, 1990-93; founding ptnr. Trident Capital L.P., Chgo., 1993—. Served to lt. USNR, 1963-66. Office: Trident Capital LP 190 S La Salle St Ste 2760 Chicago IL 60603

MCCORMACK, THOMAS JOSEPH, publishing company executive; b. Boston, Jan. 5, 1932; s. Thomas Joseph and Lena Carolyn (Allen) McC.; m. Sandra Harriet Danenberg, Aug. 21, 1964; children: Daniel Aaron, Jed Charles (dec.), Jessie Ann. Student, U. Conn., 1950-51; A.B. summa cum laude (James Manning scholar), Brown U., 1954; postgrad. (G.H. Palmer scholar, Woodrow Wilson fellow), Harvard U., 1956. Writer radio news WSTC, Stamford, Conn., 1957-59; editor Doubleday & Co., Inc., N.Y.C., 1959-64, Harper & Row, N.Y.C., 1964-67; edn. editor New Am. Library, N.Y.C., 1967-69; dir. trade dept. St. Martin's Press, N.Y.C., 1969-70; pres. St. Martin's Press, 1970-87, chmn., chief exec. officer, editorial dir.; pres., chmn. bd. St. James Press, Ltd., London, 1973-79; dir. Macmillan Ltd., London, Prudential-Bache Govt. Securities Trust; dir. Prudential-Bache High Yield Mcpls., Inc., Prudential-Bache Tax Free Money Fund, Inc., Prudential-Bache High Yield Fund, Inc.; dir. Chancellor New Decade Growth Fund, Inc.; v.p., treas. Sandra D. McCormack, Inc. (Interior Designer.), dir. Pan Books, London; chmn., chief exec. officer Tor Books, N.Y.C.;. Author: Afterwords, Novelists on Their Novels, 1969, The Fiction Editor, the Novel and the Novelist, 1988; (play) American Roulette, 1969. Served with AUS, 1954-56. Mem. Assn. Am. Pubs. (dir. 1973-76), Phi Beta Kappa. Clubs: The Players (N.Y.C.), Century Assn. (N.Y.C.). Home: 50 Central Park W New York NY 10023-6028 Office: St Martin's Press Inc 175 5th Ave New York NY 10010-7703*

MCCORMALLY, KEVIN JAY, editor; b. Boston, Mar. 13, 1950; s. John Patrick and Marguerite Louise (Wichert) McC.; m. Anne Louise Long, May 27, 1972; children: Niamh Anna, Patrick Henry. BA with honors, U. Iowa, 1972. Area editor Burlington (Iowa) Hawk Eye, 1969-70; city editor Daily Iowan, Iowa City, 1971-72; press sec. U.S. Rep. Edward Mezvinsky, Washington, 1972-77; assoc. editor Changing Times Mag., Washington, 1977-85, sr. editor, 1985-90; exec. editor Kiplinger's Personal Fin. Mag. (formerly Changing Times), Washington, 1991—; commentator Nightly Bus. Report PBS. Author: Successful Tax Planning, 1988, Sure Ways to Cut Your Taxes, 1989, 90, 91, 92, 93, 94, Cut Your Taxes, 1996; co-author: A Term to Remember, 1977; editor: Get More for Your Money, 1981. Mem. Nat. Press Club (best consumer journalism award 1986, 88), Sigma Delta Chi. Democrat. Roman Catholic. Avocations: photography, camping. Home: 161 D St SE Washington DC 20003-1809 Office: Kiplingers Personal Fin Mag 1729 H St NW Washington DC 20006-3904

MCCORMICK, ALMA HEFLIN, writer, retired educator, psychologist; b. Winona, Mo., Sept. 2, 1910; d. Irvin Elgin and Nora Edith (Kelley) Heflin; m. Archie Thomas Edward McCormick, July 14, 1942 (dec.); children: Thomas James, Kelly Jean. BA, Ea. Wash. Coll., 1936, EdM, 1949; PhD, Clayton U., 1977. Originator dept. severely mentally retarded Tri-City Public Schs., Richland, Wash., 1953, Parkland, Wash., 1955; co-founder, dir. Adastra Sch. for Gifted Children, Seattle, 1957-64; author profl. publs., novels; contbr. articles to various publs., 1937—. Mem. Am. Psychol. Assn., OX 5 Aviation Pioneers, Kappa Delta Pi. Republican. Roman Catholic. Editor: Cub Flyer, Western Story Mag., Wild West Weekly; assoc. editor: Mexico City Daily News (English sect. of Novedades). One of the first Am. woman test pilot's, 1942. Home and Office: 11437 Chimayo Rd Apple Valley CA 92308-7754

MCCORMICK, BARNES WARNOCK, aerospace engineering educator; b. Waycross, Ga., July 15, 1926; s. Barnes Warnock and Edwina (Brogdon) McC.; m. Emily Joan Hess, July 18, 1946; 1 dau., Cynthia Joan. B.S. in Aero. Engring, Pa. State U., 1948, M.S., 1949, Ph.D., 1954. Research assoc. Pa. State U., University Park, 1949-54, assoc. prof., 1954-55, prof. aero. engring., 1959-92, Boeing prof. aero. engring., 1985-92, prof. emeritus, cons., 1992—, head dept. aerospace engring., 1969-85; assoc. prof., chmn. aero. dept. Wichita U., 1958-59; chief aerodynamics Vertol Helicopter Co., 1955-58; mem. Congl. Adv. Com. Aeros., 1984-86; U.S. coord. flight mechanics panel Adv. Group for Aerospace R&D, 1988—; cons. to industry. Author: Aerodynamics of V/Stol Flight, 1967, Aerodynamics, Aeronautics and Flight Mechanics, 1979, 2d edit., 1995; co-author: (with M.P. Papadakis) Aircraft Accident Reconstruction and Litigation, 1996; contbr. articles to profl. jours. Served with USNR, 1944-46. Recipient joint award for achievement in aerospace edn. Am. Soc. Engring. Edn.-Am. Inst. Aeros. and Astronautics, 1976. Fellow Am. Inst. Aeros. and Astronautics (assoc.); mem. ASEE, Am. Helicopter Soc. (tech. council, hon. fellow), Sigma Xi, Sigma Gamma Tau, Tau Beta Pi. Club: Masons. Patentee in field. Home: 611 Glenn Rd State College PA 16803-3475 Office: Pa State U Coll Engring University Park PA 16802

MCCORMICK, CHARLES PERRY, JR., food products company executive; b. Balt., May 29, 1928; s. Charles P. and Marion (Hinds) McM.; m. Marlene Darby Hicks, July 29, 1950 (div. 1980); children: Charles P. III, William C., Linda M., Gail P.; m. Jimi Helen Faulk, July 1, 1980. Student, Johns Hopkins U., 1946-47, Duke U., 1948-49; D Bus. Administration (hon.), Johnson and Wales U., 1991. V.p. new products McCormick Co., Inc., Hunt Valley, Md., 1964-75, v.p. corp. devel., 1975-81, v.p. packaging group, 1985-87, pres., chief exec. officer, 1987-88, chmn., chief exec. officer, 1988-93, chmn. bd., 1994—; chmn., pres. Setco, Inc., Anaheim, Calif., 1981-87, Tubed Products Inc., Easthampton, Mass., 1985-87. Mem. Annapolis Yacht Club, Hunt Valley Golf Club, Sailfish Point Yacht, Sailfish Point Golf Club. Republican. Avocations: sailing, racing, golf, tennis. Office: McCormick & Co Inc 18 Loveton Cir Sparks MD 21152-9202*

MCCORMICK, DAVID ARTHUR, lawyer; b. McKeesport, Pa., Oct. 26, 1946; s. Arthur Paul and Eleanor Irene (Gibson) McC. BA, Westminster Coll., 1967; JD, Duquesne U., 1973; MBA, U. Pa., 1975. Bar: Pa. 1973, D.C. 1978, U.S. Ct. Appeals (3d cir.) 1977, U.S. Ct. Appeals (4th and D.C. cirs.) 1980, U.S. Supreme Ct. 1980. Asst. commerce counsel Penn Cen. R.R., Phila., 1973-76; assoc. labor counsel Consol. Rail Corp., Phila., 1976-78; atty. Dept. Army, Washington, 1978—. Author various general. and hist. works; contbr. articles to profl. jours. Mem. Pa. Bar Assn., Phila. Bar Assn., D.C. Bar Assn., Assn. Transp. Practitioners, Soc. Cin. (Del. chpt.), SAR (Pitts. chpt.), Phi Alpha Delta. Presbyterian. Lodge: Masons.

MCCORMICK, DONALD BRUCE, biochemist, educator; b. Front Royal, Va., July 15, 1932; s. Jesse Allen and Elizabeth (Hord) McC.; m. Norma Jean Dunn, June 6, 1955; children: Susan Lynn, Donald Bruce, Michael Allen. B.A., Vanderbilt U., 1953, Ph.D., 1958; postdoctoral fellow, U. Calif., Berkeley, 1958-60. Asst. prof. Cornell U., 1960-63, assoc. prof., 1963-69, prof. nutrition, biochemistry and molecular biology, biol. scis., 1969-79, Liberty Hyde Bailey prof. nutritional biochemistry, 1978-79; chmn. dept. biochemistry Emory U., Atlanta, 1979-94, Fuller E. Callaway prof. biochemistry, 1979—; exec. assoc. dean sci. Emory U. Sch. Medicine, 1985-89; vis. lectr. U. Ill, 1963; Wellcome vis. prof. U. Fla., 1986, Med. Coll. Pa., 1989; Hurley lectr. U. Calif., Davis, 1992; O'Dell lectr. U. Mo., Columbia, 1993; biochem. cons. Interdeptl. Com. on Nutrition for Nat. Def., Spain, 1958; mem. and chmn. nutrition study sect. NIH, 1977-81; mem. diet and health com., dietary guidelines implementation com., vice chmn. food and nutrition bd. NRC, Inst. Medicine, NAS; exec. com., chmn. dept. med. biochemistry, Council Acad. Soc., Am. Assn. Med. Colls., 1984-87. Author: (with others) Spain: Nutrition Survey of the Armed Forces, 1958, Molecular Associations in Biology, 1968, Flavins and Flavin Enzymes, 1968, Flavins and Flavoproteins, 1980, 82, 84, 88, 89, 91, Comprehensive Biochemistry, Vol. 21, 1971, Riboflavin, 1974, Metal Ions in Biological Systems, Vol. 1, 1974, Present Knowledge in Nutrition, 6th edit., 1990, Natural Sulphur Compounds, 1979, Vitamin B6, Metabolism and Role in Growth, 1980, Ann. Rev. of Nutrition, Vol. 1, 1981, Vol. 9, 1989, Mechanisms of Enzymatic Reactions: Stereochemistry, 1986, Chemical and Biological Aspects of Vitamin B6 Catalysis, Part A, 1984, Biochemistry of Vitamin B6, 1987, Textbook of Clinical Chemistry, 1987, 94, Modern Nutrition in Health and Disease, 1988, 94, New Trends in Biological Chemistry, 1990, Chemistry and Biochemistry of Flavins, 1991, Encyclopedia of Human Biology, 1991, Liver, 1994, Molecular Biology and Biotechnology, 1995; editor: Vitamins and Hormones, Vitamins and Coenzymes, Ann. Rev. of Nutrition. Recipient award Bausch and Lomb, 1950, award Mead Johnson, 1970, award Osborne and Mendel, 1978, award Ga. Nutrition Coun., 1989; Westinghouse Sci. scholar, 1950; fellow NIH, 1957-58, 58-60; Guggenheim fellow, 1966-67. Fellow AAAS; mem. Am. Soc. Biochemistry and Molecular Biology, Am. Inst. Nutrition (pres. 1991), Soc. Exptl. Biology and Medicine, Am. Chem. Soc., Am. Inst. Biol. Sci., Biophysics Soc., Fedn. Am. Socs. Exptl. Biology (bd. dirs., scientific steering group), Microbiol. Soc., Photobiol. Soc., N.Y. Acad. Sci., Protein Soc., Sigma Xi. Home: 2245 Deer Ridge Dr Stone Mountain GA 30087-1129 Office: Emory U Dept Biochemistry Atlanta GA 30322

MCCORMICK, DONALD E., librarian, archivist; b. Hartford, Conn., 1941. BA, Trinity Coll., 1963; MLS, Columbia U., 1967. Drama libr. N.Y. Pub. Libr., N.Y.C., 1965-72, sound recording libr., 1972-73, asst. chief libr., 1973-85, sound archive curator, 1985—. Mem. Assn. Recorded Sound Colls. (past pres. 1988-90), Assoc. Audio Archives (chmn. 1990-94), Music Libr. Assn. Office: NY Pub Libr for Performing Arts 40 Lincoln Center Plz New York NY 10023-7498

MCCORMICK, DOUGLAS WALTER, cable, broadcast executive; b. N.Y.C., Dec. 15, 1949; s. Howard George and Hazel Frances (Sullivan) McC.; m. Karen J. Lane, Dec. 9, 1980; children: Douglas Jr., Luke Patrick. BA, U. Dayton; MBA, Columbia U., 1990. Rsch analyst TeleRep, Inc., L.A., 1970; account exec. Sta. KCOP-TV, L.A., 1970-71, Petry TV, N.Y.C., 1971-80; composer, staff writer The Entertainment Co., N.Y.C., 1980-82; v.p. ea. sales, mgr. Lifetime Cable TV, N.Y.C., 1982-85; v.p. TV sales The Samuel Goldwyn Co., L.A., 1985-86; sr. v.p. sales Lifetime TV Network, L.A., 1986-90, exec. v.p., 1990-95, pres., CEO, 1995—. Composer popular songs for artists including Paul Anka, Gladys Knight, Dusty Springfield, others. Bd. dirs. Parent Action. Mem. Internat. Radio and TV Soc. (bd. dirs.), Nat. Acad. Cable Programming. Office: Lifetime TV Network 36-12 35th Ave Astoria NY 11106-1227

MC CORMICK, EDWARD ALLEN, foreign language educator; b. Fairfax County, Va., July 1, 1925; s. Jesse Allen and Elizabeth (Hord) McC.; m. Diana Festa, Mar. 1, 1952 (div. Aug. 1973); children: Allen Sergio, Marco Kevin, Carlo Brian; m. Marie Parrice, Apr. 2, 1974 (div. Apr. 1980); m. Phyllis van Slyck, June 10, 1980 (div. May 1985); 1 son, Andrew Stuart; m. Ping Tsai, Mar. 19, 1993. A.B., Randolph-Macon Coll., 1948; Ph.D., U. Berne, Switzerland, 1951; M.A. (hon.), Dartmouth, 1965. Instr. German Princeton U., 1952, asst. prof. German, 1954-58; instr. German U. Mich., 1952-53, Harvard U., 1953-54; asst. prof. German Brown U., 1958-59; mem. faculty Dartmouth, 1959—; prof. German, German and comparative lit., dir. comparative lt. Queens Coll., CUNY, 1966-70; prof. German and comparative lit. Queens Coll., CUNY (Grad. Ctr.), 1970—, exec. officer comparative lit., 1970-74, exec. officer German, 1980-92; retired, 1992. Author: Whitman's Leaves of Grass in deutscher Übertragung, 1953, (with F.G. Ryder) Lebendige Literatur, 1960, 2d edit., 1974, 3d edit., 1986, Theodor Storm's Novellen, 1964; editor: Lessing's Laokoon, 1962, (J.E. Schlegel) On Imitation, 1965, Germans in America, 1983; also articles in jours., encys. Served with 82d Airborne Div. AUS, 1943-46, ETO. Recipient Princeton Bicentennial Preceptorship, 1954-58; Dartmouth Faculty fellow, 1963. Mem. MLA, Am. Comparative Lit. Assn., Am. Assn. Tchrs. German. Home: 309 Calzada De Bougainville Marathon FL 33050-2513

MCCORMICK, EDWARD JAMES, JR., lawyer; b. Toledo, May 11, 1921; s. Edward James and Josephine (Beck) McC.; m. Mary Jane Blank, Jan. 27, 1951; children: Mary McCormick Krueger, Edward James III, Patrick William, Michael J. B.S., John Carroll U., 1943; J.D., Western Res. U., 1948. Bar: Ohio 1948, U.S. Supreme Ct. 1980. Mem. teaching staff St. Vincent Hosp. Sch. Nursing, 1951-67. Pvt. practice 1948—; Trustee Toledo Small Bus. Assn., 1950-75, pres., 1954-55, 56-58, 67-68; trustee Goodwill Industries Toledo, 1961-74, chmn. meml. gifts com., mem. exec. com., 1965-70; trustee Lucas County unit Am. Cancer Soc., 1950-61, sec., 1953, v.p., 1954-56, pres., 1957-58; founder, incorporator, sec., trustee Cancer Cytology Research Fund Toledo, Inc., 1956-79; trustee Ohio Cerebral Palsy Assn., 1963-70; incorporator, sec., trustee N.W. Ohio Clin. Engring. Ctr., 1972-74; trustee Friendly Ctr., 1973-83, Ohio Blind Assn., 1970-79; founder-incorporator, trustee, sec. Western Lake Erie Hist. Soc., 1978-85; mem. Toledo Deanery Diocesan Coun. Cath. Men; asst. gen. counsel U.S. Power and Sail Squadrons; life mem. China, Burma and India Vets. Assn., Inc. 1st lt. U.S. Army, 1942-46, USAR, 1946-52. Named Outstanding Young Man of Yr., Toledo Jr. C. of C., 1951; Man of Nation, Woodmen of World, Omaha, 1952. Fellow Ohio State Assn.; mem. ABA, Ohio Bar Assn. (chmn. Am. citizenship com. 1958-67, mem. pub. rels. com. 1967-72, estate planning, probate and trust law com.), Toledo Bar Assn. (chmn. pub. rels. com. 1979, mem. grievance com. 1974-92, chmn. probate, estate planning and trust law com. 1986-90, Disting. Svc. award in memory Robert A. Kelb, Esq. 1993), Lucas County Bar Assn. (chmn. Am. citizenship com.), Assn. Trial Lawyers Am., Am. Judicature Soc., Am. Arbitration Assn., Conf. Pvt. Orgns. (sec.-treas.), Toledo C. of C., Toledo Yacht Club (mem. com. 1970-71), Toledo Torch Club, Blue Gavel, Elks (grand esteemed leading knight 1964-65, mem. grand forum 1965-70), Lions (trustee, legal advisor Ohio Eye Research Found. 1956-70; pres. 1957-58, chmn. permanent membership com. 1961-85, hon. mem. 1984, pres. 1957, A.B. Snyder award 1979), Ky. Col. Office: PO Box 1336 Toledo OH 43603-1336

MCCORMICK, EUGENE F., JR., transportation company executive; b. Chgo., 1942; m. Patricia Landini; children: James, Matthew, Erin. Grad., U.S. Mcht. Marine Acad., 1964; MS, Northwestern U., Evanston, Ill., 1969. From deck officer to chief officer Lykes Bros. Steamship Co., Inc., New Orleans, 1964-68, mgr. mktg. services, 1969-72, dep. dir. traffic and ops. for SEABEE vessel, 1972-74, asst. v.p. div. pricing, 1974-77, asst. v.p. fin., 1977-79, sr. v.p. fin., chief fin. officer, 1979-82, pres., chief operating officer, 1986—, also bd. dirs.; founder Interocean Steamship Corp. parent co., 1982, also bd. dirs.; ptnr. The McCormick Jahnke Group, New Orleans; mem. Transp. Research Forum. Mem. Met. Leadership Forum; bd. dirs. USF&G Golf Classic. Serving as lt. comdr. USNR. Recipient Outstanding Achievement award U.S. Mcht. Marine Acad., 1979. Mem. Fin. Execs. Inst., Council Am.-Flag Ship Operators (chair fin. officers' com.), Navy League, U.S. Mcht. Marine Acad. Alumni Assn. (past pres. New Orleans chpt.). Avocations: golf, coaching baseball. Office: The McCormick Jahnke Group 200 Carondelet St New Orleans LA 70130 also: Dept Transp Fed Hwy Adminstrn 400 7th St SW Washington DC 20590-0001*

MCCORMICK, FLOYD GUY, JR., agricultural educator, college administrator; b. Center, Colo., July 3, 1927; s. Floyd Guy and Gladys (Weir) McC.; m. Constance P. Slane, Sept. 18, 1965; children: Angela Lynn, Craig Alan, Kim Ann, Robert Guy. BS, Colo. State U., 1950, MEd, 1959; PhD, Ohio State U., 1964. Tchr. vocat. agr. State of Colo., 1956-62; asst. prof. agrl. edn. Ohio State U., 1964-67; mem. com. agr. edn. com. edn. in agr. and natural resources Nat. Acad. Scis., 1967-69; prof. agrl. edn., head dept. U. Ariz., 1967-89, prof. emeritus, dept. head emeritus, 1990—; cons. in-svc. edn., div. vocat. edn. Ohio Dept. Edn., 1963-64; vis. prof. Colo. State U., 1973, U. Sierra Leone, Njala Univ. Coll., 1989; external examiner U. Sierra Leone, 1984, 85, 87; adv. trustee Am. Inst. Cooperatives, Washington, 1985-88; mem. Nat. Coun. Vocat. and Tech. Edn. in Agr., Washington, 1985-88. Co-author: Teacher Education in Agriculture, 1982, Supervised Occupational Experience Handbook, 1982; author: The Power of Positive Teaching, 1994, also instrl. units, tech. bulls., articles in profl. jours.; spl. editor: Agrl. Edn. mag., 1970-74. Trustee Nat. FFA Found. Served with USNR, 1945-46. Named hon. state farmer Colo., 1958, Ariz., 1968, Am. farmer, 1972; recipient Centennial award Ohio State U., 1970, E.B. Knight award NACTA Jour., 1980, Regional Outstanding Tchr. award Nat. Assn. Coll. Tchrs. Agr., 1989, also fellow, 1988, VIP citation Nat. FFA Assn., 1990, Diamond Anniversary award Ohio State U., 1992. Mem. Am. Vocat Assn. (mem. policy com. agrl. edn. divsn. 1976-79, v.p. divsn. 1985-88, chmn. membership com. 1980-83, sec. agrl. edn. divsn. 1983-86, pres. 1985-88, outstanding svc. awrd 1989), Nat. Vocat. Agr. Tchrs. Assn. (life, Outstanding Svc. award Region I 1974, 83), Am. Assn. Tchr. Educators in Agr. (disting. lectr. 1984, editor newsletter 1975-76, pres. 1976-77, Disting. Svc. award 1978, 88, Rsch. award western region rsch. 1988), Alpha Zeta, Alpha Tau Alpha (hon.), Gamma Sigma Delta, Phi Delta Kappa, Epsilon Pi Tau. Home: 6933 E Paseo San Andres Tucson AZ 85710-2203

MCCORMICK, HUGH THOMAS, lawyer; b. McAlester, Okla., Nov. 24, 1944; s. Hugh O. and Lois (McGucken) McC.; m. Suzanna G. Weingarten, Dec. 5, 1975; 1 child, John B. BA, U. Mich., 1968; JD, Rutgers U., 1977; LLM in Taxation, Georgetown U., 1980. Bar: N.Y. 1977, D.C. 1979, Maine 1981. Atty. office chief counsel interpretative div. IRS, Washington, 1977-81; assoc. Perkins, Thompson, Hinkley & Keddy, Portland, Maine, 1981-83; assoc. LeBoeuf, Lamb, Leiby & MacRae, N.Y.C., 1983-88, counsel, 1989-91; ptnr. LeBoeuf, Lamb, Greene & MacRae, L.L.P., N.Y.C., 1992—; dir. Ins. Tax Conf., 1993—. Mem. bd. contbrs. and advisors Jour. of Taxation of Investments; contbr. articles to profl. jours. Bd. dirs. Ins. Tax Conf.; trustee U.S. Team Handball Found., N.J., 1985-95. Fellow Am. Bar Found.; mem. ABA (chmn. com. on taxation of ins. cos. 1989, chmn. subcom. sect. of taxation 1989—, mem. torts and ins. practice sect., sect. on taxation), D.C. Bar Assn. Democrat. Home: 555 Pelham Manor Rd Pelham Manor NY 10803-2525 Office: LeBoeuf Lamb Greene MacRae LLP 125 W 55th St New York NY 10019-5369

MC CORMICK, JAMES CHARLES, leasing and financial services company executive; b. Cleve., Jan. 23, 1938; s. Michael Patrick and Agnes Christine (Mortensen) McC.; m. Claire A. Maskaly, Nov. 28, 1963 (div. June 1978); children: Kelly, Shannon.; m. Patricia A. Lelko, May 28, 1982. B.S. in Acctg., Regis Coll., Denver, 1960. C.P.A. Accountant Ernst & Ernst, Allentown, Pa., 1963-73; treas. Fuller Co., Catasauqua, Pa., 1973-82; asst. controller GATX Corp., Chgo., 1982-93, dir. internal audit, 1993—. Vol. Chgo. council Boy Scouts Am. Served with USNR, 1960-63. Mem. AICPA, Fin. Execs. Inst. Home: 835 Arbor Ln Glenview IL 60025-3233

MCCORMICK, JAMES EDWARD, oil company executive; b. Providence, Nov. 5, 1927; s. James Edward and Edna Josephine (Smith) McC.; m. Catherine Sullivan, Aug. 30, 1952. AB in Geology, Boston U., 1952. Engr. trainee Sun Oil Co., Beaumont, Tex., 1953-54; jr. geologist Sun Oil Co., Houston, 1954-67, exploration mgr., 1967-70; regional mgr. geology Sun Oil Co., Dallas, 1970-71, exploration program mgr., 1971-74, div. mgr. strategy planning, 1974-77, v.p. internat. exploration and prodn., 1977-86, pres. exploration and prodn., 1986-88; pres. Oryx Energy, Dallas, 1988-92; bd. dirs. Petrolite Corp., St. Louis, Tex. Commerce Bank, B.J. Svcs. Co., Lone Star Tech., Dallas, Snyder Oil Co., Ft. Worth, Tex. Bd. dirs. United Way Met. Dallas, 1986-92; mem. Dallas Citizens Council, 1986-88. Served as sgt. USAF, 1945-48. Mem. Am. Assn. Petroleum Geologists, N.Y. Acad. Scis., Nat. Ocean Industries Assn. (bd. dirs. 1986-92), Northwood Country Club, Las Colinas Country Club, Energy Club, Dallas Petroleum Club. Roman Catholic. Clubs: Northwood Country, Las Colinas Country. Office: McCormick Enterprises 5949 Sherry Ln # 98 Dallas TX 75225-6532

MCCORMICK, JAMES HAROLD, academic administrator; b. Indiana, Pa., Nov. 11, 1938; s. Harold Clark and Mary Blanche (Truby) McCormick; m. Maryan Kough Garner, June 7, 1963; children: David Harold, Douglas Paul. BS, Indiana U. of Pa., 1959; MEd, U. Pitts., 1961, EdD, 1963, postdoctoral, 1966; postdoctoral, Columbia U., U. Mich., 1966-67, Harvard U., 1982. Tchr. Punxsutawney (Pa.) Area Joint Sch. Dist., 1959-61; adminstr. Baldwin-Whitehall Schs., Pitts., 1961-64; grad. asst. U. Pitts., 1962-63; asst. supt. instrn. Washington (Pa.) City Schs., 1964-65; prof. dept. edn. and psychology, asst. dean acad. affairs, acting dean acad. affairs, acting dean tchr. edn., asst. to pres., v.p. adminstrn. and fin. Shippensburg (Pa.) U., 1965-73; pres. Bloomsburg (Pa.) U., 1973-83, pres. emeritus, 1983—; chancellor Pa. State System Higher Edn., Harrisburg, 1983—; Falk intern in politics, 1959; mem. adv. bd. Pa. Ednl. Policy Seminar, Nat. Ctr. for Study Sport in Soc.; mem. Gov.'s Econ. Devel. Partnership Bd.; mem. higher edn. adv. coun. pa. State Bd. Edn.; past commr. Edn. Commn. of the States. Contbr. articles profl. jours. Named One of 10 Outstanding Young Men of Yr., Pa. Jr. C. of C.; recipient Young Leader in Edn. award Phi Delta Kappa, 1981, Disting. Alumnus award Indiana U. Pa., 1981, Outstanding Alumni award Bloomsburg U., 1984, Outstanding Alumnus award U. Pitts., 1985, Adler award Pa. Edn. assn., 1992; selected CIVITAS Prague mission, 1995, Presdl. Lectures, Kuwait U., 1993. Mem. Am. Assn. State Colls. and Univs. (pa. state rep. 1988-93, former chmn. acad. and student pers. com., mem. com. on state rels. and task force on ednl. equity, vice chmn. policies and purposes com. 1996), Am. Coun. on Edn. (commn. on women in higher edn.), Nat. Assn. Sys. Heads, (exec. com., past pres.), Commn. State Colls. and Univs. (mem. and past chmn. govt. rels. and student rels. coms.), Assn. Governing Bds. (adv. coun.), Am. Assn. for Affirmative Action, Am. Assn. Higher Edn., Am. Assn. Sch. Adminstrs., Am. Assn. Univ. Adminstrs. (Tosney Leadership award 1993), Pa. Assn. Colls. and Univs. (bd. dirs., chair 1982), Pers. Assn., Bloomsburg Area C. of C. (pres. 1983), Rotary (bd. dirs. through 1992), Phi Delta Kappa. Presbyterian. Home: 2991 N Front St Harrisburg PA 17110 Office: Pa State Sys Higher Edn Dixon Univ Ctr 2986 N 2nd St Harrisburg PA 17110-1201

MCCORMICK, JAMES HILLMAN, retired broadcast executive; b. Montgomery, Ala., Sept. 10, 1921; s. James Hillman and Odessa (Garrett) McC.; m. Myra Sage, May 20, 1945; children: James Hillman III, Carol. BA in Cinema, U. So. Calif., 1947; postgrad., So. Meth. U., 1974. Theatre mgr. Malco Theatres, Memphis, 1940-41; prodn. asst. So. Film Svc. U. Ga., Athens, Ga., 1947-48; sales exec. Columbia Pictures, Atlanta, 1948-50, Warner Bros., Atlanta, 1950-54; Memphis mgr., Atlanta mgr., ea. sales mgr. CBS, N.Y., 1954-64; divsn. mgr. CBS, Dallas, 1964-71; v.p. Viacom Internat., Dallas, 1971-86; prin. James H. McCormick Broadcast Counselor, Dallas, 1986-89; bd. dirs. Tex. Enfield, Inc., Victoria, 1989-91; nat. v.p. Colosseum Motion Picture Salesmen, 1953-54; mem. founding group which established Viacom as world leader in comms. and entertainment, 1971-86; bd. mem. Assn. Broadcasting Execs. Tex., 1967. Author: Smart Selling--An Advertising/Media Guide; prodn. mgr. The School That Learned to Eat (U.S. Documentary award Edinbergh Film Festival, 1948). Charter mem. Cowboy Hall of Fame, Western Heritage Ctr., Oklahoma City, 1965—; mem. Dallas Mus. Art, 1967—; mem. Tex. State Hist. Assn. Sgt. U.S. Army, 1942-45. Recipient Lifetime Achievement award TV Program Conf., 1986, Rep. Presdl. Legion of Merit, 1993. Mem. Acad. TV Arts and Scis., Internat. Radio and TV Soc., Nat. Assn. TV Program Execs. (charter), Tex. Assn. Broadcasters, TV Program Conf. (bd. dirs. 1968-69), Cinema Circulus, Broadcast Pioneers, Northwood Club, Kiwanis Internat., Alpha Delta Sigma, Delta Kappa Alpha, Pi Kappa Alpha. Republican. Presbyterian. Avocations: oil painting, tennis, western art. Home: 7318 Kenshire Ln Dallas TX 75230-2432 Office: PO Box 515987 Dallas TX 75251-5987 *A persistence of vision, when strengthened by your own enthusiasm, will provide your days with much happiness. Always remember, however, that nothing ever happens in this old world until the sale is made.*

MCCORMICK, JAMES MICHAEL, management consultant; b. Arlington, Va., Dec. 12, 1947; s. James J. and Emma H. (Fisher) McC.; m. Marsha E. Durham, 1971; 1 child, James M. McCormick Jr. BS with distinction, Cornell U., 1969, M in Engring. and Ops. Research with distinction, 1970. Mem. tech. staff Bell Telephone Labs., Holmdel, N.J., 1968-73; div. head, planning N.Y. Stock Exchange, N.Y.C., 1973-75; engagement mgr. McKinsey & Co., N.Y.C., 1975-77; v.p. ROI Cons., N.Y.C., 1977-80; pres. First Manhattan Cons. Group, N.Y.C., 1980—; cons. various U.S. banks, investment banks and fin. instns., 1975—; speaker various profl. assn. meetings. Club: Larchmont (N.Y.) Yacht. Avocations: boating, auto racing, photography. Office: First Manhattan Cons Group 90 Park Ave New York NY 10016*

MCCORMICK, JOHN OWEN, retired comparative literature educator; b. Thief River Falls, Minn., Sept. 20, 1918; s. Owen Charles and Marie Antoinette Beauchemin (Smith) McC.; m. Helen Manuel, 1942; m. Mairi Clare MacInnes, 1954; children: Jonathan, Peter, Antoinette, Fergus. B.A. magna cum laude, U. Minn., 1941; M.A., Harvard U., 1947, Ph.D., 1951. Dean, lectr. Salzburg Seminar in Am. Studies, 1951-52; lectr., prof. Free U., Berlin, 1952-59; prof. comparative lit. Rutgers U., 1959-87, prof. emeritus, 1987—; vis. prof. Nat. U. Mexico, 1961-62, Hachioji (Tokyo) seminar, 1979; Christian Gauss Seminar lectr. Princeton, 1969; resident fellow Sch. Letters of Ind. U., 1970. Author: The Middle Distance: a Comparative History of American Imaginative Literature, 1919-32, 1971, The Complete Aficionado, 1967, (with Mairi MacInnes McCormick) Versions of Censorship, 1962, Der moderne amerikanische Roman, 1960, Amerikanische Lyrik, 1957, Catastrophe and Imagination, 1957, Fiction as Knowledge, 1975, George Santayana: A Biography, 1987, Wolfe, Malraux, Hesse, 1987. Served with USNR, 1941-46. Recipient prize for non-fiction Longview Found., 1960, Am. Acad. and Inst. Arts and Letters award, 1988; Gugenheim fellow, 1964-65, 79-80, Bruern fellow Leeds (Eng.) U., 1975-76, NEH fellow, 1983-84, hon. fellow U. York, 1992. Mem. Taurino Club, Harvard Club.

MCCORMICK, KATHLEEN ANN KRYM, geriatrics nurse, computer information specialist, federal agency administrator; b. Manchester, N.H., June 27, 1947. BSN, Barry Coll., 1969; MSN, Boston U., 1971; MS, U. Wis., 1975, PhD, 1978. Capt. nurse officer USPHS; COSTEP nurse USPHS, Staten Island, N.Y., 1968; staff nurse, instr. USPHS, Brighton, Mass., 1970; staff nurse Mercy Hosp., Miami, 1969, St. Elizabeth's Hosp., Brighton, 1970-71; clin. nurse specialist Boston U. Hosp., 1970-71; clin. nurse specialist, instr. U. Wis., Madison, 1971-72; asst. rsch. to chief nursing clin. ctr., dept. Nursing NIH, Bethesda, 1978-83; rsch. nurse, co-dir. inpatient geriatric continence project, Lab. Behavioral Scis., Gerontology Rsch. Ctr. Nat. Inst. Aging, Balt., 1983-88, dir. nursing rsch., 1988-91; dir. office forum quality and effectiveness health care Agy. Health Care Policy and Rsch., Rockville, Md., 1991-93; sr. sci. adviser Agy. Health Care Policy and Rsch., 1993—; adj. asst. prof. Cath. U., Washington, 1979, 82; faculty assoc. U. Md., Balt., 1979-81; ad hoc reviewer biomed. rsch. grants NIH, 1979-80, divsn. nursing rsch. and tng. HRA, 1979-82; instr. Found. Advanced Edn. in Scis., 1981-82; exec. com. Bat. Inst. Aging Liaison Ctr. Nursing Rsch., 1986-91; Surgeon Gen.'s rep. Sec. Alzheimer's Task Force, 1989—; Surgeon Gen. alternate to Bd. Regents Nat. Libr. Medicine, 1989—; co-chair panel guidelines for urinary incontinence in adult, 1990-91; speaker. Editor: Nursing Outlook, 1988-90; mem. editorial staff Mil. Medicine, 1985-93; assoc. editor: Internat. Jour. Tech. and Aging, 1985-87. Recipient award Jour. Acad. Sci., 1965, travel award NSF, 1973, J.D. Lane Jr. Investigator award USPHS Profl. Assn., 1979, Excellence in Writing award Nat. League Nursing/Humana, 1983, award Spl. Recognition Rsch., U. Pa. Sch. Nursing, 1986, Federal Svc. Nursing award, 1987, Surgeon Gen.'s medallion, 1989,; grantee U. Wis. Grad. Sch., 1977, Upjohn Co., 1977; Queen's Vis. scholar Royal Adelaide (Austrailia) Hosp., 1990. Fellow Am. Acad. Nursing, Royal Coll. Nursing (Australia), Coll. Am. Med. Informatics, Gerontologic Soc. Am. (clin. med. sect., computer program coord. 1985-87, clin. medicine rep. publs. com., Nurse of Yr. 1992), Nat. Acad. Scis. Inst. Medicine; mem. ANA (sec., editor newsletter coun. nurse rschrs. 1980-85, vice chairperson exec. com. coun. computer applications in nursing 1984-86), AACN (strategic planning com. 1987-89, Disting. Rsch. award 1986), Am. Lung Assn./Am. Thoracic Soc. (cert. appreciation mid.-Md. chpt. 1982, 83, 84, chairperson 1983-84, nominating com. 1989, nat. rsch. rev. com.), Am. Med. Informatics Assn., Inst. Medicine, Acad. Medicine, Am. News Women's Club, Internat. Med. Informatics Assn. (working group 8, program com. 1984—), Assn. Mil. Surgeons (sustaining mem. award 1982), Commd. Officers Assn., Met. Area Nursing Rsch. Consortium, Md. Lung Assn. (awards and grants subcom. 1978, 92, v.p. exec. bd. dirs. 1980-87), Capital Spkrs. Club (10 M), Lambda Sigma, Sigma Delta Epsilon (Eloise Gerry grant-in-aid fellow 1979-80), Sigma Theta Tau (grantee 1976). Office: US Agy Health Care Policy Rsch 2101 E Jefferson St Rockville MD 20852-4908

MC CORMICK, KENNETH DALE, retired editor; b. Madison, N.J., Feb. 25, 1906; s. John Dale and Ida Pearl (Wenger) McC.; children: Dale, Kevin; m. Anne Hutchens, 1968; 1 son, John Bradley. A.B., Willamette U., 1928. With Doubleday and Co., Inc., 1930-92, successively clk., mgr., bookshop, promotion mgr. pub. house, reader in editorial dept., chief asso. editor, 1938, editor in chief, 1942-71, v.p., 1948-71, sr. cons. editor, 1971-92; lectr. on books. Contbr. to Publishers' Weekly. Democrat. Conglist. Clubs: Century Assn, Coffee House, Dutch Treat. Home: 670 W End Ave New York NY 10025-7313

MCCORMICK, LINDA YANCEY, elementary education educator; b. Harrisonburg, Va., Sept. 7, 1965; d. Edward Custer and Margaret Joan (Caldwell) Yancey; m. James Coelman McCormick, Jr., Mar. 2, 1991; 1 child, Sarah Grace. BA in Polit. Sci., Hollins Coll., 1987; MEd, James Madison Univ., 1992. Tchr. Rockingham County Schs., Harrisonburg, 1987-88; tchr., instrnl. team leader Harrisonburg City Pub. Schs., 1988—, mem. early childhood adv. com., 1994; adv. com. early childhood adv. com. Harrisonburg City Pub. Schs., 1994. Exec. bd. dirs. Big Bros./Big Sisters, Harrisonburg, 1991—; mem. Harrisonburg Rockingham Hist. Soc., 1994; exec. bd. dirs. Spotswood Elem. PTA, 1994-95, tchr. liason. Mem. DAR. Baptist. Avocations: geneological research. Home: 37 Paul St Harrisonburg VA 22801-4032

MCCORMICK, LOYD WELDON, lawyer; b. Wilson, Tex., Dec. 4, 1928; s. Loyd Franklin and Clara Edith (Monroe) M.; m. Jeanne Alyce Welch, Jan. 29, 1956; children: David W., Janet W. McCormick Riley, Kenneth W. BA, U. Calif., Berkeley, 1950, JD, 1956. Bar: Calif. 1956, U.S. Dist. Ct. (no. dist.) Calif. 1956, U.S. Ct. Appeals (9th cir.) 1956, U.S. Supreme Ct. 1971. Assoc. McCutchen, Doyle, Brown & Enersen, San Francisco, 1956-65, ptnr., 1965—; chmn. legal and tax coms. Nat. Coun. Farmer Coops., Washington, 1980-81; mem. adv. bd. Ojai (Calif.) Ranch and Investment Co., 1987-89; lawyer del. 9th Cir. Jud. Conf., San Francisco, 1988-92, chair, 1990; mem. Commn. Calif. Agriculture and Higher Edn., 1993-95. Pres. Young Reps. of Lafayette, Calif., 1964; mem. Calif. State Rep. Cen. Com., 1968. Lt. (j.g.) USN, 1950-53, Korea. Fellow Am. Coll. Trial Lawyers; mem. ABA, Calif. State Bar, Bar Assn. San Francisco, Am. Judicature Soc., Conf. Bd., Phi Delta Phi, Boalt Hall Alumni Assn. (bd. dirs. 1983-86), Pacific Union Club, Orinda Country Club, Commonwealth Club. Episcopalian. Avocations: tennis, golf, gardening, reading, politics. Home: 21 Via Callados Orinda CA 94563-1123

MCCORMICK, LYLE BERNARD, JR., management consultant; b. Charleston, W.Va., May 31, 1944; s. Lyle Bernard Sr. and Beatrice Lee (Haynes) McC.; m. Linda Marie Brandt, Dec. 27, 1968; 1 child, Stephen Lyle. Degree in bus. adminstrn., U. Ctrl. Fla., 1972. Cert. mgmt. cons. With GE Co., Daytona Beach, Fla., 1967-76; cons. Ingersoll Mfg. Consts., Rockford, Ill., 1976-78; project ind. engr. Daniel Constrn. Co., Warm Springs, Va., 1978-79; v.p. Emerson Cons., Inc., N.Y.C., 1979-86; pres. Omega Cons., Inc., DeLand, Fla., 1986—. With U.S. Army, 1965-67. Mem. Inst. Mgmt. Cons. Democrat. Baptist. Avocations: fishing, tennis, golf, bicycling. Office: Omega Cons Inc 980 Cedar Ridge Ln Deland FL 32720-2329

MCCORMICK, MARIE CLARE, pediatrician, educator; b. Haverhill, Mass., Jan. 7, 1946; d. Richard John and Clare Bernadine (Keleher) McC.; m. Robert Jay Blendon, Dec. 30, 1977. BA magna cum laude, Emmanuel Coll., 1967; MD, Johns Hopkins Medical Sch., 1971; ScD, Johns Hopkins, 1978; MA, Harvard, 1991. Diplomate Am. Bd. Pediatrics. Pediatric resident, fellow Johns Hopkins Hosp., Balt., 1971-75; rsch. fellow Johns Hopkins Hosp., 1972-75; asst. prof. U. Ill. Schs. Medicine & Pub. Health, Chgo., 1975-76; pediatrics instr. Johns Hopkins Medical Sch., Balt., 1976-78; asst. prof. healthcare orgn. Johns Hopkins Sch. Hygiene & Pub. Health, 1978-81; asst. prof. pediatrics U. Pa., Phila., 1981-86, assoc. prof. pediatrics, 1986-87; assoc. prof. pediatrics Harvard Medical Sch., Boston, 1987-91; prof., chair. maternal & child health Harvard Sch. Pub. Health, 1992—; prof. pediatrics . Harvard Medical Sch., 1992—; adj. assoc. prof. pediatrics U. Pa., 1987-92; active attending physician, Johns Hopkins Hosp., 1976-81, asst. physician Children's Hosp. Phila., 1981-84, assoc. physician, 1984-86, sr. physician, 1986-87, assoc. pediatrician Brigham & Women's Hosp., 1987, 88—; vis. prof. Wash. U., St. Louis, 1993; editorial bds. Health Svcs. Rsch., 1985-94, Pediatrics in Review, 1986-91, Pediatrics, 1993—; adv. coun. Ctr. Perinatal & Family Health Brigham & Women;s Hosp., 1991—; cons. to numerous coms., orgns. and bds. Contbr. articles to profl. jours. Adv. The David and Lucile Packard Found., 1993-95; bd. dirs. Family Planning Coun. S.E. Pa., 1984-87; chair com. child health Mayor's Commn. Phila., 1982-83. Named Henry Strong Denison scholar Johns Hopkins Sch. Medicine, 1971, Leonard Davis inst. Health Econs. fellow U. Pa. 1984; recipient Johns Hopkins U. Soc. Scholars award, 1995, Ambulatory Pediat. Assn. Rsch. award, 1996. Fellow Am. Acad. Pediatrics; mem. AAAS, Ambulatory Pediatrics Assn. (Rsch. award 1996), Soc. Pediatric Rsch. (sr.), Am. Pediatric soc., Am. Pub. Health Assn., Internat. Epidemiological Assn., Assn. Health Svcs. Rsch., Eastern Soc. Pediatric Rsch., Soc. Pediatric Epidemiologic Rsch., Assn. Tchrs. Maternal and Child Health, Mass. Med. Soc., Norfolk Dist. Med. Soc., Mass. Pub. Health Assn., Johns Hopkins U. Soc. Scholars. Office: Harvard Sch Pub Health 677 Huntington Ave Boston MA 02115-6028

MCCORMICK, MICHAEL D., lawyer; b. Vincennes, Ind., Mar. 18, 1948; m. Margaret A. McCormick; children: Claire E., Brooks R. AB, Duke U., 1970; JD, Ind. U., 1980. V.p. I & S McDaniel Inc., Vincennes, 1970-77; ptnr. Scopelitis & Garvin, Indpls., 1980-83; pres. Wales Transp. Co., Dallas, 1983-85; v.p., gen. counsel Overland Express Inc., Indpls., 1985-87, Bindley Western Industries Inc., Indpls., 1987—. Mem. ABA, Ind. Bar Assn., Indpls. Bar Assn. *

MCCORMICK, MICHAEL JERRY, judge; b. Fort Lewis, Wash., Oct. 17, 1945; s. Thaddeus Charles and Geraldine (Fogle) McC.; m. Kathleen Karen Kelley, Sept. 2, 1967; children: Patrick Kelley, Karen Michelle. BA, U. Tex.-Austin, 1967; JD, St. Mary's U., 1970. Bar: Tex. 1970. Briefing atty. Tex. Ct. Criminal Appeals, 1970-71; asst. dist. atty., Travis County, Tex., 1971-72; exec. dir. Tex. Dist. and County Attys. Assn., Austin, 1972-80; judge Tex. Ct. Criminal Appeals, Austin, 1981—, presiding judge 1988—; dir. Tex. Ctr. for Judiciary, 1983; vice-chmn. Tex. Commn. on Sentencing, 1984; mem. Tex. Jud. Budget Bd., 1983. Pres. Joslin P.T.A., 1981-82. Served with U.S. Army, 1966-72. Named Rosewood Gavel Outstanding Jurist, St. Mary's U. Sch. Law, 1984, Disting. Law Grad., 1992. Mem. State Bar Tex., Tex. Dist. and County Attys. Assn. Episcopalian. Author: Branch's Annotated Penal Code, 3d edit., Criminal Forms and Trial Manual, 10th edit., Texas Justice Court Deskbook, Texas Constables' Civil Process Handbook. Office: Tex Ct Criminal Appeals PO Box 12308 Austin TX 78711-2308

MCCORMICK, RICHARD, telecommunications company executive; b. Fort Dodge, Iowa, July 4, 1940; s. Elmo Eugene and Virgilla (Lawler) McC.; m. Mary Patricia Smola, June 29, 1963; children: John Richard, Matthew David, Megan Ann, Katherine Maura. B.S. in Elec. Engring., Iowa State U., 1961. With Bell Telephone Co., 1961-85; N.D. v.p., CEO Northwestern Bell Telephone Co., Fargo, 1974-77; asst. v.p. human resources AT&T, Basking Ridge, N.J., 1977-78; sr. v.p. Northwestern Bell, Omaha, 1978-82, pres., CEO, 1982-85; exec. v.p. U S West Inc., Englewood, Colo., 1985-86, pres., COO, 1986-90, pres., CEO, 1990-91, chmn., pres., CEO, 1992—; bd. dirs. Norwest Corp., United Airlines Corp. Mem. Phi Gamma Delta. Office: U S West Inc 7800 E Orchard Rd Ste 200 Englewood CO 80111-2533

MCCORMICK, RICHARD ARTHUR, priest, religion educator, writer; b. Toledo, Oct. 3, 1922; s. Edward J. McCormick. BA, Loyola U., Chgo., 1945, MA, 1950, hon. degree, 1989; STD, Gregorian U., Rome, 1957; hon. degree, U. Scranton, 1975, Wheeling Coll., W.Va., 1976, Jesuit Sch. Theology, Berkeley, Calif., 1982, Siena Coll., 1985, U. Louvain, 1986, Coll. Holy Cross, 1986, Seattle U., 1987, Fordham U., 1988, Xavier U., 1988, U. San Francisco, 1989, Georgetown U., 1990, Cath. Theol. Union, 1991. Joined S.J., Roman Cath. Ch., 1940, ordained priest, 1953. Prof. moral theology Jesuit Sch. Theology, Chgo., 1957-73; Rose F. Kennedy prof. Christian ethics Georgetown U., Washington, 1974-86; John A. O'Brien prof. U. Notre Dame, Ind., 1986—; rsch. assoc. Woodstock Theol. Ctr., Washington, 1974-86; past mem. Ethics Adv. Bd., HEW; mem. Cath. Commn. on Intellectual and Cultural Affairs; lectr. in field. Author: Ambiguity in Moral Choice, 1973, Notes on Moral Theology, 1965 through 1980, 1980, Notes on Moral Theology 1981-1984, 1984, Health and Medicine in the Catholic Tradition, 1984, The Critical Calling: Moral Dilemmas Since Vatican II, 1989, Corrective Vision: Explorations in Moral Theology, 1994; co-author: (with Paul Ramsey) Doing Evil to Achieve Good, 1978; contbr. to numerous books, articles to Christianity and Crisis, New Cath. World, other religious jours.; co-editor: (with Charles E. Curran) Readings in Moral Theology I: Moral Norms and Catholic Tradition, 1979, Readings in Moral Theology II: The Distinctiveness of Christian Ethics, 1980, Readings in Moral Theology III: Morality and Authority, 1981, Readings in Moral Theology IV: The Use of Scripture in Moral Theology, 1982, Readings in Moral Theology V: Official Catholic Social Teaching, 1986, Readings in Moral Theology VI: Dissent in the Church, 1988, Readings in Moral Theology VII: The Natural Law, 1990, Readings in Moral Theology VIII: Dialogue about Catholic Sexual Teaching, 1993; former assoc. editor Am. mag.; editorial advisor Theology Digest, Hosp. Progress jours.; mem. editorial bd. Jour. Religious Ethics, Jour. Contemporary Health Law and Policy. Former trustee U. Detroit, Fairfield U. Recipient Henry Knowles Beecher award Hastings Ctr., 1988; Inst. Soc., Ethics and Life Scis. fellow. Mem. Am. Acad. Arts and Scis., Cath. Theol. Soc. Am. (past pres., Cardinal Spellman award 1969), Am. Soc. Christian Ethics (past bd. dirs.), Am. Hosp. Am. (spl. bioethics com.), Nat. Hospice Orgn. (bioethcis com.), Cath. Health Assn. (bioethics com.), Am. Fertility Soc. (ethics com.). Office: U Notre Dame Dept Theology Notre Dame IN 46556

MC CORMICK, RICHARD PATRICK, history educator; b. N.Y.C., Dec. 24, 1916; s. Patrick Austin and Anna (Smith) McC.; m. Katheryne Crook Levis, Aug. 25, 1945; children: Richard Levis, Dorothy Irene. BA, Rutgers U., 1938, MA, 1940, LittD (hon.), 1982; PhD, U. Pa., 1948. Historian, Phila. Q.M. Depot, 1942-44; instr. U. Del., 1944-45; mem. faculty Rutgers U., 1945—, univ. historian, 1948—; dean Rutgers Coll., 1974-77, Univ. prof. history, 1977-82, Univ. prof. emeritus, 1982—; research adviser Colonial Williamsburg, 1953-61; Fulbright lectr. Cambridge (Eng.) U., 1961-62; Commonwealth lectr. U. London, 1971; chmn. N.J. Hist. Commn., 1967-70. Author: Experiment in Independence, 1950, History of Voting in N.J, 1953, N.J. From Colony to State, 1964, Second American Party System, 1966, Rutgers: a Bicentennial History, 1966, The Presidential Game, 1982, The Black Student Protest Movement at Rutgers, 1990; co-author: The Case of the Nazi Professor, 1989. Mem. N.J. Tercentenary Commn., 1958-60, Am. Revolution Bicentennial Commn., 1971-74. Social Sci. Research Council fellow, 1956-57. Mem. Am. Hist. Assn., Soc. Historians of Early American Republic (pres. 1988-89), N.J. Hist. Soc. (pres. 1950-57), Phi Beta Kappa. Home: 938 River Rd Piscataway NJ 08854-5504 Office: Summer 42 Julien Rd Harwich Port MA 02646

MCCORMICK, ROBERT JUNIOR, government official; b. Boone, Iowa, Aug. 1, 1929; s. Ivyl Robert and Darlene Adel (Bowes) McC.; m. Shirley May Zerbe, Dec. 24, 1950; children: Elaine, Kathleen, Michael, Tara McCormick Wieting, Tammy McCormick Kirby. Grad., Flying Sch., Williams Field, Ariz., 1951, Parachute Jump Sch., 1964, Armed Forces Staff Coll., Norfolk, Va., 1966, Def. Systems Mgmt. Coll., Ft. Belvoir, Va., 1975; B.S., Tex. Tech. U., 1963. Served as enlisted man USAF, 1948-51, commd. 2d lt., 1951, advanced through grades to col., 1971; pilot USAF, U.S., Japan, Korea, Europe, Vietnam; exec. officer to Gen. George Brown 7th Air Force, Saigon, Vietnam, 1969-70; mil. asst. to asst. sec. of Air Force for research and devel. USAF, Washington, 1970-74; ret. USAF, 1975; exec. officer NASA, Washington, 1976-80; adminstrv. asst. to sec. of Air Force USAF, Washington, 1980—; mem. U.S. Sr. Exec. Service, 1979—. Decorated Air Force Legion of Merit, Bronze star, Air medal, Meritorious Svc. medal, Air Force Exceptional Civilian Svc. medal, 1985, 88, others; recipient Exceptional Svc. medal NASA, 1980, Presdl. Meritorious Rank, 1989, Dept. Def. Disting. Civilian Svc. award, 1994. Mem. ASME, DAV, Air Force Assn., Am. Def. Preparedness Assn., Order of Daedalians, St. Andrews Soc. Washington, Mil. Order of Carabao, Chevaliers du Testevin. Club: Army-Navy Country (Fairfax, Va.). Office: Office of Sec Air Force 1720 Air Force The Pentagon Washington DC 20330-1720

MCCORMICK, ROBERT WILLIAM, court reporting educator; b. Hornell, N.Y., Sept. 7, 1949; s. Charles F. and Catherine M. (Bulock) McC.; m. Rose A. Belden, Dec. 29, 1970; children: Tara R., Erin R., Nicole L. AAS in Court Reporting, SUNY, Alfred, 1969; BS in Bus. Edn., SUNY, Albany, 1971, MS in Bus. Edn., 1974; MA in Theology, Colgate Rochester Divinity Sch, 1988. Cert. reporting instr. Prof. ct. reporting SUNY, Alfred; deacon St. Ann's Roman Catholic Ch., Hornell, N.Y.; chaplain-on-call St. James Mercy Hosp., Hornell. Series editor for ct. and realtime reporting theory textbooks.

MCCORMICK, ROD, sculptor, art educator; b. Battle Creek, Mich., Sept. 2, 1952; s. Rodney Lawrence and Joan (Kaminski) McC.; m. Barbara Mail, Dec. 29, 1985; children: Anna, Sonya. BFA, Tyler Sch. Art, 1974; MFA, RISD, 1978. Sculptor Phila., 1974—; vis. prof. Kent State U., Ohio, 1978-79; assoc. prof. U. Arts, Phila., 1981—, chair crafts dept., 1993-94, 95—. One-man shows include Owen Patrick Gallery, Phila., 1990, U. Arts, 1993; exhibited in group shows at Phila. Mus. Art, 1990, Pa. State U., 1991, Meredith Gallery, Balt., 1991, Leo Kaplan Modern Gallery, N.Y.C., 1992, Paley Design Ctr., Phila., 1993, Peter Joseph Gallery, N.Y.C., 1994. Recipient Young Americans Metal exhbn. award Am. Craft Mus., 1980; grantee Nat. Endowment Arts, 1990, Pa. Coun. Arts, 1991. Mem. Soc. N.Am. Goldsmiths, Internat. Sculpture Ctr. Home: PO Box 29578 Philadelphia PA 19144 Office: University of the Arts 320 S Broad St Philadelphia PA 19102

MCCORMICK, STEVEN D., lawyer; b. Waterloo, Iowa, Apr. 24, 1946. AB, U. Notre Dame, 1968; JD, Northwestern U., 1971. Bar: Ill. 1972. Ptnr. Kirkland & Ellis, Chgo. Office: Kirkland & Ellis 200 E Randolph St Chicago IL 60601-6436*

MCCORMICK, STEVEN THOMAS, insurance company executive; b. Phila., Dec. 18, 1955; s. Howard C. and Ruth Marion (Stahl) McC.; m. Helene Mary Trommler, Nov. 21, 1981; children: Matthew Thomas, Bria Helene. BBA, U. Ky., 1978; gen. ins cert., Ins. Inst. Am., 1980. Cert. adminstrv. mgr., purchasing mgr., ins. agt., Ky., 1980. Supr. trainee Ky. Farm Bur. Ins. Cos., Louisville, 1978-79, supr. micrographics dept., 1979-83, supr. adminstrv. services, 1983-85, mgr. adminstrv. services, 1985-89; asst. v.p. operation, 1989—. Named to Hon. Order Ky. Cols., Outstanding Employee of Yr., Nat. Assn. of Mutual Ins. Cos., 1986; recipient Cert. of Excellence Jefferson County Bd. End., 1988. Mem. Adminstrv. Mgmt. Soc. (internat. top recruiter 1985, chpt. pres. 1988, internat. dir. area 7 1990-91, internat. v.p. profl. devel. 1992-93), Acad. Adminstrv. Mgmt. (bd. regents 1991-92, internat. v.p. 1992-93, internat. pres. 1993-94), U. Ky. Alumni Assn., Sigma Nu. Republican. Home: 706 Elsmere Cir Louisville KY 40223-2764 Office: Ky Farm Bur Ins Cos PO Box 20700 Louisville KY 40250-0700

MC CORMICK, THOMAS JULIAN, art history educator; b. Syracuse, N.Y., Nov. 14, 1925; s. Thomas Julian and Doris (Rafferty) McC.; m. Margaret Emily Dorkey, Mar. 23, 1957; children: Sarah Elizabeth, Martha Dorcas. AB, Syracuse U., 1948, AM, 1949; MFA, Princeton U., 1953, PhD, 1971. Research asst. Va. Mus. Fine Arts, Richmond, 1953-54; instr. Smith Coll., Northampton, Mass., 1954-56; dir., asst. prof. Robert Hull Fleming Mus., U. Vt., 1956-58; assoc. prof., chmn. art dept. Wells Coll., Aurora, N.Y., 1958-60; assoc. prof., dir. Art Gallery, Vassar Coll., Poughkeepsie, N.Y., 1960-70; Wright-Shippee prof. Wheaton Coll., Norton, Mass., 1970-79; A. Howard Meneely prof. Wheaton Coll., 1981-82, prof., 1979-91, prof. emeritus, 1991—, chmn. art dept., 1970-79, 90-91; Frederic Lindley Morgan prof. archtl. design U. Louisville, 1991; vis. assoc. prof. Williams Coll., 1969; lectr. Worcester (Mass.) Art Mus., 1978; vis. prof. Sch. Architecture, Canterbury, Eng., 1985-86. Author: Charles-Louis Clérisseau and the Genesis of Neo-Classicism, 1990; contbr. articles to profl. jours., exhbn. catalogs. Bd. dirs. Dutchess County (N.Y.) Landmarks Assn., 1968-70, Olana State Historic Site, 1968-70. With AUS, 1944-46, ETO. Corning Mus. Glass fellow, 1954; Fulbright sr. research fellow Gt. Britain, 1966-67, Yugoslavia, 1976-77. Fellow Soc. Antiquaries (London); mem. Coll. Art Assn., Archeol. Inst. Am., Soc. Archtl. Historians (book rev. editor Jour. 1958-65, dir. 1960-63), Am. Soc. for Eighteenth Century Studies, Delta Kappa Epsilon. Episcopalian. Clubs: Princeton (N.Y.C.); Club of Odd Vols. (Boston). Home: 18 Still St Brookline MA 02146-3444

MCCORMICK, WILLIAM EDWARD, environmental consultant; b. Potters Mills, Pa., Feb. 9, 1912; s. George H. and Nellie (Mingle) McC.; m. Goldie Stover, June 6, 1935; children: John F. (dec.), Kirk W. B.S., Pa. State U., 1933, M.S., 1934. Tchr., Centre Hall (Pa.) High Sch., 1934-37; chemist Willson Products, Inc., Reading, Pa., 1937-43; indsl. hygienist Ga. Dept. Pub. Health, Atlanta, 1946; mgr. indsl. hygiene and toxicology B.F. Goodrich Co., Akron, Ohio, 1946-70; mgr. environ. control B.F. Goodrich Co., 1970-73; mng. dir. Am. Indsl. Hygiene Assn., Akron, 1973-83; exec. sec. Soc. Toxicology, 1976-83; chmn., treas. Envirotox Mgmt., Inc., 1983-93; pres. WRC Environmental, 1996—; mem. exec. com. rubber sect. Nat. Safety Coun., 1955-73, gen. chmn., 1971-72; mem. environ. health com. Chlorine Inst., 1968-73; mem. food, drug and cosmetic chems. com. Mfg. Chemists Assn., 1960-73, chmn., 1967-69, also mem. occupational health com., 1965-73; mem. adv. com. on heat stress U.S. Dept. Labor, 1973; mem. Nat. Adv. Com. Occupational Safety and Health, 1983-85; pres. Am. Indsl. Hygiene Found., 1984, trustee, 1982-89. Contbr. articles to profl. jours. Served to capt. USPHS, 1943-46. Recipient Borden award Am. Indsl. Hygiene Assn., 1993. Mem. AAAS, Am. Chem. Soc., Soc. Toxicology, Am. Indsl. Hygiene Assn. (pres. 1964, charter), Indsl. Hygiene Roundtable (charter), Am. Acad. Indsl. Hygiene (charter), Mason (33 degree), Shriner. Republican. Episcopalian. Home and Office: 419 Dorchester Rd Akron OH 44320-1315

MCCORMICK, WILLIAM THOMAS, JR., electric and gas company executive; b. Washington, Sept. 12, 1944; s. William Thomas and Lucy Valentine (Offutt) McC.; m. Ann Loretta du Mais, June 13, 1969; children: Christopher, Patrick. B.S., Cornell U., 1966; Ph.D., M.I.T., 1969. Mem. staff Inst. for Def. Analysis, Arlington, Va., 1969-72; mem. staff Office of Sci. and Tech., Exec. office of the Pres., Washington, 1972-73; sr. staff mem. Energy Policy Office, The White House, 1973-74; chief sci. and energy tech. br. Office Mgmt. and Budget, Exec. Office of the Pres., 1974-75; dir. commercialization U.S. Energy Research and Devel. Adminstrn., 1975-76; v.p. policy and govt. relations Am. Gas Assn., 1976-78; v.p., asst. to chmn. Am. Natural Resources Co., Detroit, 1978-80; exec. v.p. Mich. Wis. Pipeline Co., Am. Natural Resources System, Detroit, 1980-82; pres. Am. Natural Resources Co., Detroit, 1982-85; chmn., chief exec. officer Consumers Power Co., Jackson, Mich., 1985-92, chmn., 1992—; chmn., CEO CMS Energy Corp.; bd. dirs. Bancorp. Prin. author, editor: Commercialization of Synthetic Fuels in the U.S, 1975. Bd. dirs. Detroit Symphony, St. John Hosp. Alfred P. Sloan scholar, 1962-66. Mem. Econ. Club Detroit (bd. dirs.), Greater Detroit C. of C. (bd. dirs.), Econ. Alliance Mich. (bd. dirs.). Roman Catholic. Clubs: Cosmos (Washington); Detroit Athletic, Country of Detroit, Detroit. Office: Consumers Power Co 212 W Michigan Ave Jackson MI 49201-2236 also: CMS Energy Corp 1100-330 Town Center Dr Dearborn MI 48126*

MCCOTTER, CHARLES KENNEDY, JR., lawyer; b. New Bern, N.C., Oct. 29, 1946; s. Charles Kennedy and Lucy (Dunn) McC.; m. Patricia Byrum, Aug. 3, 1968; children—Virginia Byrum, Patricia Dunn. B.S. in Bus., U. N.C.-Chapel Hill, 1968, J.D., 1971. Bar: N.C. 1971, U.S. Dist. Ct. (ea. dist.) N.C. 1971, U.S. Ct. Appeals (4th cir.) 1973. Law clk. to judge U.S. Dist. Ct. (ea. dist.) N.C. 1971-72; sole practice, New Bern, 1973; ptnr. McCotter and Mayo, New Bern, 1974-79; U.S. magistrate judge U.S. Dist. Ct. (ea. dist.) N.C., 1979-95; lectr. in field; permanent del. to 4th Cir. Jud. Conf.; mem. Ea. Dist. N.C. Com. on Arraignment Procedures, 1986, chmn. local rules com. for Revision of Local Admiralty Rules, 1985; jud. rep. to local adv. com. Implementation of Civil Justice Reform Act, 1991-94. Bd.

visitors U. N.C. Marine Scis. Inst., mem. law alumni bd.; lic. mcht. marine master. Mem. ABA, N.C. Bar Assn., Craven County Bar Assn., N.C. Trial Lawyers Assn., Maritime Law Assn. U.S., Nat. Council U.S., Ea. N.C. Inn of Ct., New Bern. C. of C. Episcopalian. Lodges: Rotary. Office: 3010 Trent Rd New Bern NC 28562

MCCOTTER, JAMES RAWSON, lawyer; b. Denver, May 19, 1943; s. Charles R. and Jane M. (Ballantine) McC.; m. Carole Lee Hand, Sept. 5, 1965; children: Heidi M., Sage B. BA, Stanford U., 1965; JD, U. Colo., 1969. Bar: Colo. 1969, D.C. 1970, U.S. Dist. Ct. Colo. 1969, U.S. Ct. Appeals (10th and D.C. cirs.) 1970, U.S. Ct. Appeals (5th cir.) 1972, U.S. Supreme Ct. 1974. Law clk. U.S. Ct. Appeals (10th cir.), Denver, 1969-70; assoc. Covington & Burling, Washington, 1970-75; assoc. Kelly, Stansfield & O'Donnell, Denver, 1975-76, ptnr., 1977-86; assoc. gen. counsel Pub. Svc. Co. Colo., 1986-88; sr. v.p., gen. counsel, corp. sec., 1988-93; of counsel LeBoeuf, Lamb, Greene & MacRae, Denver, 1993-94, v.p. dep. gen. counsel, El Paso Natural Gas Co., Tex., 1994—. Editor in chief U. Colo. Law Rev., 1968-69 (Outstanding Achievement award 1969). Dem. precinct committeeman, Denver, 1983-84; bd. dirs. Sewall Rehab. Ctr., Denver, 1979-84, Opera Colo., 1987-95; dir., vice chmn. Denver Civic Ventures, Inc., 1988-94; mem. law alumni bd. U. Colo., 1988-91; bd. dirs. Colo. Coun. on Econ. Edn., Found. for Denver Ctr. for Performing Arts Complex, 1991-94. Recipient Disting. Achievement award U. Colo. Law Sch., 1989; named to Outstanding Young Men Am., U.S. Jaycees, 1971; Storke scholar U. Colo., Boulder, 1967. Mem. ABA, Colo. Bar Assn. (adminstrv. law com. 1979-84), Fed. Energy Bar Assn. (chmn. com. on environment 1982-83), Tex. Bar Assn., Coronado Country Club (El Paso), Univ. Club, Denver Country Club, Order of Coif. Episcopalian. Home: 1036 Broadmoor Dr El Paso TX 79912-2004 Office: El Paso Natural Gas Co PO Box 1492 El Paso TX 79978-0001

MCCOUBREY, R. JAMES, advertising executive; b. Grand Mere, Que., Can., Sept. 1, 1944; s. James Addison and Margaret G. F. (Scarratt) McC.; m. Annette L. Hebert, Sept. 16, 1972; children: James Andrew, Matthew Alexander. B. of Commerce, McGill U., 1966, MA, 1967. With brand mgmt. Procter and Gamble, Toronto, Ont., Can., 1967-69; asst. mgr. Young and Rubicam, Montreal, Que., 1969-72; dir. client svcs. Young and Rubicam, Toronto, 1972-74, mgr., 1974-77, pres., 1977-80; area dir. Americas Young and Rubicam, N.Y.C., Toronto, 1980-82; gen. mgr. Europe Young and Rubicam, London, 1982-83; group and area dir. Young and Rubicam, N.Y.C., 1983-85; chmn. Young and Rubicam, Toronto, 1985-90; exec. v.p. Young and Rubicam, N.Y.C., 1984; area dir. Young and Rubicam, Africa, Australia, New Zealand and Can., 1984-90; pres., chief exec. officer Telemedia Inc., North York, Ont., Can., 1990—, Telemedia Communications USA Inc, Charlotte, Vt., 1991—; chmn. Inst. Can. Advt., Toronto, 1981-82; bd. dirs. Greyhound Lines of Can. Dir. Coun. for Bus. and the Arts in Can.; chmn. regional divsn. McGill Univ. Twenty-First Century Fund. Mem. Can. Assn. Broadcasters (bd. dirs., vice chmn.), Young Pres. Orgn. (past chmn.), Mag. Assn. Can. (chmn. 1992-94), Royal Can. Yacht Club, Mt. Royal Club. Anglican. Home: 54 Bernard Ave, Toronto, ON Canada M5R 1R5 Office: Telemedia Communications USA Inc Ferry Rd Charlotte VT 05445

MCCOUBREY, SARAH, artist and art educator; b. New Haven, Conn., Sept. 5, 1956; d. John Walker and Betty (Morse) McC.; m. Michael Crockett Olmsted, Sept. 12, 1987; 1 child, Emily Crockett Olmsted. BA, U. Pa., 1979, BFA in Painting, 1979, MFA in Painting, 1981. Instr. Phila. C.C., 1984-87, Drexel U. Sch. of Art, Phila., 1983-87, No. Va. C.C., Annandale, Va., 1988-89, Geo. Washington U., Washington, 1989-90, Corcoran Sch. of Art, Washington, 1990-91; asst. prof. Syracuse (N.Y.) U. Coll. of Visual and Performing Arts, 1991—. Artist: solo exhibitions: The More Gallery, Phila., 1985, Leslie Cecil Gallery, N.Y.C., 1989, Recent Paintings, Comfort Gallery, Haverford, Pa., 1990, Recent Paintings Robert Brown Contemporay Art, Washington, 1990, Recent Paintings, Robert Brown Gallery, Washington, 1994, Robert Brown Contemporary Art, Washington, 1996; selected group exhibits New Talent Show, Marion Locks Gallery, Phila., 1981, New Figurative Painting, Univ. City Arts League, Phila., 1982, Forty first Award Exhibition of the Cheltenham Art Ctr., Phila., 1982, The More Gallery, Phila., 1985, 86, 88, Art in City Hall, Phila. Urbanscape, Phila. City Hall, Twentieth Juried Exhibition, Allentown (Pa.) Art Mus., 1986, Four Contemporary Artists, 1987, Landscape Transformed, The Dimock Gallery, George Washington U., Washington, 1988, Collectors Exhibition, Ark. Art Ctr., Little Rock, 1989, 90, Bauhaus, Charles St., Balt., 1990, Evidence of Man, Gallery 10, Washington, Back to Basics, Washington, 1991, Cheekwood Nat. Contemporary Painting Competition, Fine Arts Ctr., Nashville (Merit award), 1991, Perspective VI, Am. Soc. Architectural Perspectivists, Security Pacific Gallery, Seattle, AIA Nat. Conv., Boston, Gwenda Jay Gallery, Chgo., 1992, Matrilineage: Women, Art and Change, Altered Space, Syracuse, 1993, Patricia Shea Gallery, Santa Monica, Calif., 1993, Women's Art Works 4: Work on Paper, Shoestring Gallery, Rochester, N.Y., Nat. Women's Hall of Fame, Seneca Falls, N.Y., 1994 (Hon. Mention), Everson Mus., Syracuse, 1994, Erector Square Gallery, New Haven, Conn., 1995, Wright State U. Galleries, Dayton, Ohio, 1996. Recipient Elizabeth Greenshields Found. Grant award, 1981, McDowell Colony fellowship, 1990, Md. State Arts Coun. Individual Artist award, 1990; grantee NEA, 1989. Hon. Mention Vietnam Women's Meml. Competition, 1990. Home: 7027 Woodchuck Hill Rd Fayetteville NY 13066 Office: Syracuse Univ Dept Found Sch Art and Design Syracuse NY 13200

MC COVEY, WILLIE LEE, former professional baseball player; b. Mobile, Ala., Jan. 10, 1938; s. Frank and Ester (Jones) McC. Baseball player, minor league, 1955-59; baseball player, minor league San Francisco Giants, 1959-73, 77-80, active in pub. rels., 1981-86, spl. asst. to the pres., 1986—; baseball player San Diego Padres, 1974-76; coach Oakland Athletics, 1976-81. Named Nat. League Rookie of Year, 1959, Most Valuable Player, 1969; Home Run Champion, 1963, 68, 69; Runs Batted In Leader, 1968, 69; Comeback Player of Year, 1977; 8th on All-Time Major League List of Career Home Runs; All-Time Nat. League leader in grand slam home runs; mem. Nat. League All-Star Team, 1963, 66, 68-71; inducted into Baseball Hall of Fame, 1986. Office: care San Francisco Giants Candlestick Park San Francisco CA 94124-3998

MCCOWAN, RODNEY A., federal agency administrator; b. Jan. 15, 1959; married; two children. BA in Ethics and Religion, U. Okla., 1984; MA in Religion, Yale U., 1985; M in Pub. Policy, Harvard U., 1990; postgrad., Stanford U., 1995. From asst. to dir. govtl. programs to account mktg. rep. IBM Corp., Washington, 1984-91; White House fellow U.S. Agy. for Internat. Devel., Washington, 1991-92; assoc. pub. finance investment banking group Merrill Lynch Capital Markets, N.Y.C., 1992-93; asst. sec. for mgmt. U.S. Dept. Edn., Washington, 1993—. Trustee, vice chmn. bd. Episc. Divinity Sch., Cambridge, Mass.; bd. visitors, vis. lectr. Terry Sanford Inst. Pub. Policy Duke U.; regional panelist Pres.' Commn. on White House Fellowships; active fundraising campaign United Way. Office: US Dept Edn Office Management Ste 2164 600 Independence Ave SW Washington DC 20202-4500*

MCCOWN, GEORGE E., venture banking company executive; b. Portland, Oreg., July 1, 1935; s. Floyd Conly and Ada Elizabeth (Stephens) McC.; m. Karen Stone, Mar. 22, 1986; children: Taryn, Daniel, David; stepchildren: Bryan, Norman, Mark, Amy. BSME, Stanford U., 1957; MBA, Harvard U., 1962. Assoc. Am. Rsch. and Devel. Corp, 1962-63; from asst. to the pres. to sr. v.p. Boise (Idaho) Cascade, 1963-80; pres. Boise Cascade Home & Land Corp., 1974-80; chmn. Sequoia Corp., Boise, 1981-83; co-founder, mng. gen. ptnr. McCown De Leeuw & Co., Menlo Park, Calif., 1984—; chmn. bd. BMC West Corp., VANS, Internat. Data Response Corp., Pelican Cos. Inc. Thrifty Foods, Inc., vice chmn. Specialty Paperboard, Inc.; bd. dirs. Tiara Motorcoach, Nimbus CD Internat. Inc., Fitness Holding Inc., Trustee Stanford U., chmn. fin. com. and investment policy subcom., 1980-85; dir. Packard Childrens Hosp., Stanford; trustee Nueva Learning Ctr., Pacific Crest Outward Bound Sch.; chmn. bd. govs. Wyo. Centennial Everest Expdn.; mem. and past chmn. policy adv. bd. Harvard Joint Ctr. for Housing Studies; Ctr. for Real Estate and Urban Econs, U. Calif.or Real Estate and Urban Econs, U. Calif. at Berkeley, chmn. World Bus. Acad.; overseer Hoover Inst. War, Revolution and Peace. Capt. USAF, 1957-60. Mem. Harvard Bus. Assn. No. Calif. (chmn.), Chief Execs. Orgn., World Pres. Orgn., Explorers Club., Bus. Execs. for Nat. Security. Republican. Avocations: classical piano, mountaineering, adventure travel, aviation, tennis, skiing. Home: 250 Greer Rd Woodside CA 94062-4206 Office: McCown De Leeuw & Co 3000 Sand Hill Rd # 3-290 Menlo Park CA 94025-7116

MCCOWN, GLORIA BOOHER, school system administrator; b. Dallas, Apr. 5, 1945; d. George T. and Lillian (Martine) Booher; m. James R. McCown, July 22, 1962 (dec. May 1994); children: Kelley Lynn, William Scott. BS, Houston Bapt. U., 1976; MEd, U. North Tex., 1983, EdD, 1992. Tchr. Fort Bend Ind. Sch. Dist., Stafford, Tex., 1976-78; tchr. Lancaster (Tex.) Ind. Sch. Dist., 1978-83, prin., 1983-87, dir. curriculum, 1987-88, asst. supt. instrn., 1988-91; dir. elem. edn. Keller (Tex.) Ind. Sch. Dist., 1992—. Author: Site Based Management The Role of The Central Office, 1992. Life mem. Lancaster Coun. PTA, 1987—. Named Prin. of Yr., U. North Tex., 1987. Mem. ASCD, Tex. ASCD, Tex. Elem. Sch. Prins., Tex. Assn. Sch. Adminstrs., Internat. Reading Assn., Phi Delta Kappa. Office: Keller Ind Sch Dist 304 Lorine St Keller TX 76248-3435

MCCOWN, HALE, retired judge; b. Kansas, Ill., Jan. 19, 1914; s. Ross S. and Pauline (Collins) McC.; m. Helen Lanier, July 15, 1938; children: Robert B., William L., Mary Lynn. AB, Hastings Coll., 1935; LLB, Duke U., 1937. Bar: Oreg. 1937, Nebr. 1942. With firm Carey, Hart, Spencer & McCulloch, Portland, 1937-42; pvt. practice Beatrice, Nebr., 1942-65; ptnr. McCown, Baumfalk & Dalke; justice Supreme Court Nebr., 1965-83. Author articles in legal jours. Served to lt. USNR, 1943-45. Fellow Am. Coll. Trial Lawyers, Am. Coll. Trust and Estate Counsel; mem. ABA (legal ethics com. 1957-62), Nebr. Bar Assn. (chmn. ho. dels. 1955-56, pres. 1960-61), Am. Law Inst. (mem. council 1969—), Am. Judicature Soc. Presbyterian.

MCCOY, BERNARD ROGERS, television anchor; b. Cortland, N.Y., Dec. 24, 1955; s. Donald Richard and Vivian Alicia (Rogers) McC.; m. Joanne Louise Lohr, Apr. 29, 1989; children: Emily Louise, Marian Alicia. BS in Journalism, U. Kans., 1979; postgrad., Mich. State U. Mgmt. trainee Garney Constrn. Co., Kansas City, Mo., 1979-80; reporter, anchor Sta. WIBW-AM-FM-TV, Topeka, 1979-80, Sta. KCTV-TV, Kansas City, 1980-89; anchor Sta. WKBD-TV, Detroit, 1989-93, WILX-TV, NBC, Lansing, Mich., 1993—; chmn. Earthwork Environ. Adv. Bd., Southfield, Mich., 1989—. Bd. dirs. Judson Ctr.; celebrity fundraiser Salvation Army, Detroit, 1989, March of Dimes, Detroit, 1989, hon. co-chair Mid-Mich. WalkAmerica, 1996; celebrity fundraiser Cancer Soc., Detroit, 1989, The Sanctuary, Royal Oak, Mich., 1989; mem. YMCA, 1991—; mem. Sparrow Hosp. Children's Miracle Network Com., 1996, Mid-Mich. Environ. Action Coun., 1996; project coord. News-10 Computer Edn., 1996. Recipient Spot News awards Mo. Broadcasters Assn., 1987, Kansas City Press Club, 1987, Kans. Broadcasters Assn., 1987, Disting. Environ. Reporting awards Detroit Audubon Soc., 1991, Mich. Audubon Soc., 1992, Ben East award Mich. United Conservation Clubs, 1991, 93, Mich. Outstanding Individual Reporting award UPI, 1991, Emmy award for Outstanding Reporting in Mich., 1994. Mem. Nat. Acad. of TV Arts and Scis. (bd. dirs. Mich. chpt.), Nat. Geo. Soc., Soc. Environ. Journalists (charter, planner nat. conf.). Avocations: back-packing, golf, fishing, tennis, running. Office: WILX-TV PO Box 30380 Lansing MI 48909-7880

MC COY, DONALD RICHARD, historian; b. Chgo., Jan. 18, 1928; s. Patrick Emmett and Rose Roma (Hewitt) O'Day; m. Sondra Jo Van Meter, June 29, 1980; children: Patricia, Bernard, William. B.A., U. Denver, 1949; M.A., U. Chgo., 1949; Ph.D., Am. U., 1954. Archivist interior sect. Nat. Archives, 1951-52; faculty dept. social studies State U. Coll., Cortland, N.Y., 1952-57; faculty dept. history U. Kans., Lawrence, 1957—; Univ. distinguished prof. U. Kans., 1974—; Fulbright prof. history U. Bonn, Germany, 1962; Mary Ball Washington profl. history Univ. Coll., Dublin, Ireland, 1976-77; dir. spl. rsch. project Harry S. Truman Libr. Inst., 1967-72; prin. investigator Ctrl. Am. Oral History Project, univs. Costa Rica and Kans., 1970-72; mem. adv. com. for protection archives and record ctrs. U.S. GSA, 1974-76; mem. nat. Archives Adv. Coun., 1976-79, Joint com. Historians and Archivists, 1977-80, chmn., 1979-80, adv. com. on the records of Congress, 1991-94. Author: Angry Voices, Left-of-Center Politics in the New Deal Era, 1958, Landon of Kansas, 1966, Calvin Coolidge, The Quiet President, 1967, (with R.T. Ruetten) Quest and Response: Minority Rights during the Truman Administration, 1973, Coming of Age: The United States during the 1920s and 1930s, 1973, The National Archives: America's Ministry of Documents, 1978, The Presidency of Harry S. Truman, 1984. Editor: (with M.L. Fausold) Student Guide to the American Story, II, 1957, (with R.G. O'Connor) Readings in Twentieth Century American History, 1963, (with R.T. Ruetten and J.R. Fuchs) Conference of Scholars on the Truman Administration and Civil Rights, 1968, (with B.K. Zobrist) Conference of Scholars on the Administration of Occupied Areas, 1943-1955, 1970; Contbr. articles to profl. jours. Alderman, Cortland, 1955-57. Served with Signal Corps U.S. Army, 1945-47. Recipient Byron Caldwell Smith award for distinguished writing, 1970; Waldo Gifford Leland prize Soc. Am. Archivists, 1979; Nat. Endowment for Humanities research grantee, 1968-70, 73-74, 81-82. Fellow Soc. Am. Archivists; mem. Am. Hist. Assn., Orgn. Am. Historians, Kans. Hist. Soc. (pres. 1981-82), Phi Beta Kappa. Home: U Kans Dept History 3213 Saddlehorn Dr Lawrence KS 66049

MCCOY, EDWARD FITZGERALD, social services facility administrator; b. Enid, Okla., July 11, 1938; s. Leonard Edward and Florence Wortman (Fitzgerald) McC.; m. Patricia Jean Semon, Sept. 11, 1970 (div. July 1986); children: Mary Clare, Leonard Edward II, Edward Fitzgerald Jr. BA in Polit. Sci., Park Coll., 1961; MA in Rehab. of Blind, Western Mich. U., 1969; postgrad., U. Md., 1971-74. Sales mgr. St. Joseph (Mo.) Surg. Supply, 1961-63; house master Nebr. Sch. for Blind, Nebraska City, 1963-65; dir. recreation Mo. Sch. for Blind, St. Louis, 1965-68; orientation and mobility specialist Montgomery County Pub. Schs., Rockville, Md., 1969-76; child find specialist Montgomery County Pub. Schs., Rockville, Mo., 1976-77, diagnostic prescriptive resource tchr., 1977-78; exec. dir. Fla. Lions Conklin Ctr. for Multihandicapped Blind, Daytona Beach, Fla., 1978—. Charter mem. Planned Giving Coun. Ctrl. Fla.; mem. East Ctrl. Fla. Radio Reading Svc.; mem. bd. counselors Bethune-Cookman Coll.; chmn. Fla. divsn. Blind Svcs. Statewide Rehab. Adv. Coun., 1993—, chmn., 1996-97. Named to Ky. Cols., 1991; Western Mich. U. fellow, 1968-69; acad. leave grantee Montgomery County Pub. Sch., 1973-74. Mem. Fla. Assn. for Edn. and Rehab. of the Blind and Visually Impaired (pres. 1992-94), Nat. Soc. Fund Raising Execs. (cert.), Nat. Coun. Pvt. Agys. for the Blind and Visually Impaired, Nat. Accreditation Coun. for Agys. Serving Blind (team chmn.), Fla. Assn. Agys. Serving Blind (pres. 1985-87, treas. 1994—), Nat. Rehab. Assn., Am. Assn. Workers for Blind (pres. Washington chpt. 1977-78), Daytona Beach C. of C. (leadership coun.), Lions (pres. Daytona Beach Club 1982-83, chmn. sight conservation com. 1985—). Democrat. Roman Catholic. Avocations: camping, cooking, water sports. Home: 640 N Nova Rd Apt 115 Ormond Beach FL 32174-4408 Office: Conklin Ctr Multihandicapped Blind 405 White St Daytona Beach FL 32114-2925

MCCOY, EILEEN CAREY, academic dean; b. Jersey City; d. James Bernard and Nan (Dalton) Carey; m. Thomas James McCoy; children: Thomas James III, Mary Eileen McCoy Whang. BA, Coll. St. Elizabeth, Convent Station, N.J., 1954; MA, Fairleigh Dickinson U., 1969, EdD, 1983; postgrad., Harvard U., 1985. Mem. faculty County Coll. Morris, Dover, N.J., 1970-75; dir. community relations Raritan Valley Community Coll., Somerville, N.J., 1977-79, dean continuing, community edn. and svcs., 1979-95; dean Evening Coll. and Extension Site, 1995—. Author: The Community Education Component of the Community College: New Jersey in Comparative Perspective, 1983. Mem. Morris County Bd. Freeholders, 1975-77; founding chmn. Somerset County Commn. on Women, 1985-88; mem. adv. coun. Somerset County Office on Aging, 1987—; bd. dirs. Rolling Hills Girl Scout Coun., 1991-93, Irish Am. Pub. Action Com., 1993, pres., 1994—; bd. advisors Somerset County United Way; mem. mcpl. com. Montgomery Twp., 1993-95; bd. dirs. Edn. Found. Bridgewater-Raritan, 1993—. Recipient Righteous Gentile award Jewish Fedn. Somerset, Hunterdon and Warren Counties, 1989, Somerset County Tercentennial award, 1989. Mem. Nat. Coun. Continuing Edn. and Community Svc. (bd. dirs. and region rep. 1987—, Person of Yr. region 2 1989), Greater Somerset County C. of C. (v.p. and bd. dirs. 1988-92, Outstanding Woman in Business and Industry 1982), Rotary (pres. Branchburg, N.J., club 1989-90). Republican. Roman Catholic. Office: Raritan C C Box 3000 Somerville NJ 08876-1262

MC COY, FRANK MILTON, concert pianist, educator, lecturer; b. El Centro, Calif., s. Henderson C. and Annie (Lee) McC.; A.B. (Rotary scholar), San Francisco State Coll., 1949, MA, 1960; postgrad. U. Wash., 1952-53, U. Calif. at Santa Barbara, 1957-58, U. So. Calif., 1961-65, U. Valencia (Spain), summer 1967; PhD Walden U., 1980; studied piano under Jean Le Duc, 1947-49, Madame Berthe Poncy-Jacobsen, 1952-53, Amparo Iturbi, 1960-62, Oria Kenah, Gladys Fawcette. Grad. asst. Sch. Music, U. Wash., Seattle, 1952-53; tchr. music edn. San Diego City Schs., 1953-54, El Centro Pub. Schs., 1954-57; counselor Social Service Center, Calexico, Calif., 1955-59; prof. piano and English Compton Coll., 1971-73; chmn. dept. music Portola Jr. H.S., L.A., 1985; personal rep. Odyssey Internat. Attractions. Piano, soloist All Am. Chorus tour 1956; 1st Am. to concertize on islands of St. Pierre and Miguelon, 1960; made concert tours Europe, Can., Latin Am., U.S., North Africa, Carribean, Middle East, USSR, China, Hong Kong; TV appearance CBC, 1965; appeared in Ebony mag., Sepia mag.; music critic Gilmore Piano Festival, Kalamazoo, Mich., 1994; adjudicator piano div. Southwestern Youth Music Festival, 1964; mem. bd. adjudicators Nat. Piano Playing Auditions, 1965; music-drama critic Post-Press Newspapers; founder, chmn. Annie Lee McCoy-Chopin Meml. Piano Award, 1975—; Mem. Founders Ch. of Religious Sci.; master tchr. in music L.A. City Schs., 1983-84. Bd. dirs. El Centro Cmty. Concert Assn. Recipient Leona M. Hickman award U. Wash., 1953, Mayor Tom Bradley commendation, 1991. Mem. Music Educators Nat. Conf., Nat. Guild Piano Tchrs., Am. Guild Mus. Artists, Music Critics Assn. North Am., Southeast Symphony Assn. (bd. dirs.), Internat. Platform Assn., Greater L.A. Press Club. Author: Black Tomorrow: A Portrait of Afro-American Culture, 1976 (children's book) Fruits and Vegetables A.B.C. Book; Playlet: Music Masters, Old and New, 1966, We, Too, Are Americans, 1977; music critic L.A. Sentinel, 1988—. Home: 234 S Figueroa St Apt 431 Los Angeles CA 90012-2509

MC COY, FREDERICK JOHN, retired plastic surgeon; b. McPherson, Kans., Jan. 17, 1916; s. Merle D. and Mae (Tennis) McC.; m. Mary Bock, May 17, 1972; children: Judith, Frederick John, Patricia, Melissa, Steven. B.S., U. Kans., 1938, M.D., 1942. Diplomate: Am. Bd. Plastic Surgery (dir. 1973-79, chmn. 1979). Intern Lucas County Hosp., Toledo, 1942-43; resident in plastic surgery U. Tex. Med. Sch., Galveston, 1946; preceptorship in surgery Grand Rapids, Mich., 1947-50; practice medicine specializing in plastic and reconstructive surgery Kansas City, Mo., 1950-93; staff St. Mary's Hosp., 1950-83, St. Joseph's Hosp., 1950—, N. Kansas City Meml. Hosp., 1955—; mem. staff, chief plastic surgery Kansas City Gen. Hosp. and Med. Center, 1952-72, Children's Mercy Hosp., 1954-93, Research Hosp., 1950—, St. Luke's Hosp., 1951—, Baptist Hosp., 1958—, Menorah Hosp., 1950—; chief div. plastic surgery Truman Med. Ctr., 1972-91; chmn. maxillo-facial surgery U. Kansas City Sch. Dentistry, 1950-57; assoc. prof. surgery U. Mo. Med. Sch., Kansas City, 1964-69; clin. prof. surgery U. Mo. Med. Sch., 1969—; pres. McCoy Enterprises, Kansas City, Mo. Contbr. articles to, profl. jours.; editor: Year Book of Plastic and Reconstructive Surgery, 1971-88. Bd. govs. Kansas City Mus., 1959-93, pres., 1973-74. Served to maj. M.C. U.S. Army, 1943-46. Mem. ACS (pres. Mo. chpt. 1973), AMA, Am. Acad. Pediatrics, Am. Soc. Plastic and Reconstructive Surgeons (sec. 1969-73, dir. 1973-76, pres. 1976, chmn. bd. 1977, Spl. Achievement award 1988), Am. Soc. Pediatric Plastic Surgeons, Pan Pacific Surg. Soc., Singleton Surg. Soc. (v.p. 1965), Am. Assn. Plastic Surgeons (founding mem. plastic surgery rsch. coun.), Internat. Soc. Aesthetic Plastic Surgery, Am. Soc. Aesthetic Plastic Surgery, Jackson County Med. Soc. (pres. 1964-65), Kansas City Southwest Clin. Soc. (pres. 1971), Mo. Med. Assn. (v.p. 1975), Internat. Coll. Surgeons (v.p. 1969), Royal Soc. Medicine (London), Kansas City C. of C., Conservation Fedn. Mo., Natural Sci. Soc. (founder, chmn. 1973), Citizens Assn. Kansas City, Explorer's Club, Mission Hills Country Club, Boone and Crocket Club, Phi Delta Theta, Nu Sigma Nu. Republican. Mem. Christian Ch. Home: 5814 Mission Dr Shawnee Mission KS 66208-1139 Office: 500 Nichols Rd Ste 401 Kansas City MO 64112-2013

MCCOY, JERRY JACK, lawyer; b. Pitts., Aug. 4, 1941; s. Norris and Martha (Jack) McC.; m. Alexandra Armstrong; children: MadeleineRena, Allison Norah, Jonathan Howard. BS, W.Va. U., 1963; LLB, Duke U., 1966; LLM in Taxation, N.Y.U., 1967. Bar: D.C. 1968, N.Y. 1967. Assoc. Silverstein & Mullens, Washington, 1968-72, ptnr., 1973-92; of counsel Reid and Priest, N.Y.C., Washington, 1992-94; sole practitioner Washington, 1994—; adj. law faculty George Washington U., Washington, 1977-87, U. Miami, Fla., 1983—, Law Ctr. Georgetown U., 1996—. Exec. editor Tax Mgmt., Estates Gifts and Trusts series, Washington, 1972-92; co-editor Charitable Gift Planning News, Dallas, 1983—; contbr. articles to profl. jours. Mem. Am. Law Inst., Am. Coll. Trust and Estate Counsel, Am. Coll. Tax Counsel, ABA. Democrat. Jewish. Home: 3560 Winfield Ln NW Washington DC 20007 Office: PO Box 66491 1050 Connecticut Ave NW Washington DC 20035-6491

MC COY, JOHN BONNET, banker; b. Columbus, Ohio, June 11, 1943; s. John Gardner and Jeanne Newlove (Bonnet) McC.; m. Jane Deborah Taylor, Apr. 21, 1968; children: Tracy Bonnet, Paige Taylor, John Taylor. B.A., Williams Coll., 1965; M.B.A., Stanford U., 1967; LLD (hon.), Williams Coll., 1991; D of Bus. Adminstrn. (hon.), Ohio State U., 1993; LLD (hon.), Kenyon Coll., 1994. With Banc One Corp., Columbus NA, Columbus, Ohio, 1970—, banking officer, 1970-73, v.p., 1973-77, pres., 1977-83; pres., chief operating officer Banc One Corp., Columbus, Ohio, 1983-84, pres., chief exec. officer, 1984-87, chmn., chief exec. officer, 1987—, also bd. dirs.; pres., COO Banc One Corp., Columbus, Ohio, 1983-84, pres., CEO, 1984-87, chmn. CEO, 1987—, also bd. dirs.; pres. Bank One Trust Co., 1979-81; bd. dirs. Cardinal Health, Inc., Fed. Nat. Mortgage Assn., Ameritech Corp., Tenneco Inc.; fed. adv. coun. Fed. Res. Sys., 1991-93. Active Boy Scouts Am.; trustee, chmn. bd. dirs. Kenyon Coll.; trustee Stanford U., Battelle Meml. Inst.; bd. dirs. Sr. PGA Tour; pres. Columbus Area Growth Found.; chmn. Capitol South Urban Redevel. Corp. Capt. USAF, 1967-70. Recipient Ernest C. Arbuckle award Stanford U., 1994. Mem. Columbus C. of C. (past chmn., trustee), Am. Bankers Assn., Bankers Roundtable (bd. dirs. 1989-94), Assn. Bank Holding Cos., Young Pres. Orgn. (chmn. Columbus chpt. 1982-83), Cypress Point Club, Seminole Golf Club, Links Club N.Y.C. Episcopalian. Office: Banc One Corp 100 E Broad St Columbus OH 43215-3607

MCCOY, JOHN GARDNER, banker; b. Marietta, Ohio, Jan. 30, 1913; s. John Hall and Florence (Buchanan) McC.; m. Jeanne N. Bonnet, Jan. 4, 1941; children: John Bonnet, Virginia B. Fickle. A.B., Marietta Coll., 1935; M.B.A., Stanford, 1937; LL.D. (hon.), Kenyon Coll., 1970, Marietta Coll., 1981. With City Nat. Bank & Trust Co. (now Bank One of Columbus), Columbus, 1937-84; v.p. City Nat. Bank & Trust Co. (now Bank One of Columbus), 1946-58, pres., chmn., chief exec. officer, 1959-77, dir., 1949—; pres., vice chmn., chief exec. officer Banc One Corp., 1966-84, dir., chmn. exec. com. Trustee Marietta Coll., 1966—. Recipient Ernest C. Arbuckle award Stanford Bus. Sch., 1986. Mem. Assn. Bank Holding Cos. (past pres.). Episcopalian. Clubs: Columbus, Columbus Country, Muirfield Golf, Golf, Wequetonsing (Mich.) Golf, Little Harbor (Harbor Springs, Mich.), Royal Poinciana Golf (Naples, Fla.), Hole In-the-Wall Golf (Naples, Fla.), Naples Yacht (Naples, Fla.). Home: 8 Edge Of Woods New Albany OH 43054 Office: Banc One Corp 100 E Broad St Columbus OH 43215-3607

MCCOY, JOHN JOSEPH, lawyer; b. Cin., Mar. 15, 1952; s. Raymond F. and Margaret T. (Hohmann) McC. BS in Math. summa cum laude, Xavier U., 1974; JD, U. Chgo., 1977. Bar: Ohio 1977, D.C. 1980. Ptnr. Taft, Stettinius & Hollister, Cin., 1977—; lectr. Greater Cin. C. of C., 1984. Pro bono rep. Jr. Achievement Greater Cin., 1978; fund raiser Dan Beard coun. Boy Scouts Am., 1983; fund raising team leader Cin. Regatta, Cin. Ctr. Devel. Disorders, 1983; account mgr. United Appeal, Cin., 1984; mem. green areas trust adv. com. Village of Indian Hill, 1994—. Mem. ABA, Ohio State Bar Assn. (banking, comml. and bankruptcy law com., corp. law com., fed. ct. practice com.), Cin. Bar Assn. (fed. cts., common pleas cts. and negligence law coms., trustee Vol. Lawyers for the Poor Found. 1994—, chmn. 1996), Cin. Inn. of Ct. (barrister 1984-86), Cin. Athletic Club (pres. bd. trustees 1986-89). Home: 6700 Wyman Ln Cincinnati OH 45243-2730

MCCOY, LARRY, journalist; b. Frankfort, Ind., Sept. 30, 1937; s. Lavon James and Ethel Marie (Smith) McC.; m. Irene Theresa Kristoff, July 2, 1960; children: Julie, Jack. AB, Ind. U., 1959, HB, 1962. Writer UPI, Chgo., 1960-64; editor, sr. editor ABC News, N.Y.C., 1964-69; editor Radio

Free Europe, Munich, 1969-71, sr. editor, asst. news dir., 1973-80; writer CBS News Radio, N.Y.C., 1971-73, editor, asst. bur. mgr., news dir., 1980—. Contbr. articles to opinion/editorial pages in newspaper. Office: CBS News Radio 524 W 57th St New York NY 10019

MC COY, LEE BERARD, paint company executive; b. Ipswich, Mass., July 27, 1925; d. Damase Joseph and Robena Myrtle (Bruce) B.; student U. Ala., Mobile, 1958-60; m. Walter Vincent de Paul McCoy, Sept. 27, 1943; children: Bernadette, Raymond, Joan, Richard. Owner, Lee's Letter Shop, Hicksville, L.I., N.Y., 1950-56; mgr. sales adminstrn. Basila Mfg. Co., Mobile, Ala., 1957-61; promotion mgr., buyer Mobile Paint Co., Inc., Theodore, Ala., 1961—. Curator, Shepard Meml. Libr., 1972—; bd. dirs. Monterey Tour House, Mobile, 1972-78, Old Dauphin Way Assn., 1977-79, Friends of Mus., Mobile, 1978—, Miss Wheelchair Ala., 1980—; del. Civic Roundtable, 1977-78, bd. dirs., 1980-81, 1st v.p., 1980-81, pres., 1981-82; pres.'s Com. Employment of Handicapped, 1981—; chmn. Mobile, Nat. Yr. Disabled Persons, 1982; chmn. Mobile, Internat. Decade Disabled Persons, 1983—; mem. Nat. Project Adv. Bd., 1983—, Nat. Community Adv. Bd., 1983—, World Com. for Decade of Disabled Persons, 1983—; v.p. Bristol Sister City Soc.; active Mobile Area Retarded Citizens, Am. Heart Assn.; mem. City of Mobile Cultural Enrichment Task Force, 1985—, Mobile United Recreation and Culture Com.; dir. Culture Mobile, 1986—; v.p., bd. dirs. Joe Jefferson Players, 1986; co-chmn. Brit. Faire, 1983; chmn. Mobile Expo, 1990, Culture & Recreation Com. Mobile United, 1989, steering com., 1990. Recipient Honor award Civic Roundtable, 1979, 80; Service award Women's Com. of Spain Rehab. Center, State of Ala., 1980; award Nat. Orgn. on Disability, 1983, Gayfer's Outstanding Career Woman award, 1988; Golden Rule award, 1991. Mem. Spectromatic Assos., Nat. Paint Distbrs., Hist. Preservation Soc., Color Mktg. Group, English Speaking Union (v.p., pres. 1992, 94, 95, 96), U.S. C. of C. (chmn. local cultural enrichment task force 1986), Toastmasters (pres. 1995-96), The Nat. Mus. of Women of the Arts, Washington, Internat. Platform Assn. Methodist. Republican. Clubs: Quota (charter mem. Mobile chpt., dir. 1977—, pres. 1978-80, chmn. numerous coms., recipient Service award Dist. 8, 1979, Internat. award for serving club objectives, 1980, editor Care-Gram, Weekly newsletter for nursing homes 1980—), Bienville; writer 10 books; lectr., worldwide traveler. Home: 1553 Monterey Pl Mobile AL 36604-1227 Office: 4775 Hamilton Blvd Theodore AL 36582-8523

MC COY, LOIS CLARK, emergency services professional, retired county official, magazine editor; b. New Haven, Oct. 1, 1920; d. William Patrick and Lois Rosilla (Dailey) Clark; m. Herbert Irving McCoy, Oct. 17, 1943; children: Whitney, Kevin, Marianne, Tori, Debra, Sally, Daniel. BS, Skidmore Coll., 1942; student Nat. Search and Rescue Sch., 1974. Asst. buyer R.H. Macy & Co., N.Y.C., 1942-44, assoc. buyer, 1944-48; instr. Mountain Medicine & Survival, U. Calif. at San Diego, 1973-74; cons. editor Search & Rescue Mag., 1975; cons. editor, Rescue Mag., 1988—; editor Press On Newsletter, 1992—. coord. San Diego Mountain Rescue Team, La Jolla, Calif., 1973-75; exec. sec. Nat. Assn. for Search and Rescue, Inc., Nashville and La Jolla, 1975-80, comptr., 1980-82; disaster officer San Diego County, 1980-86, Santa Barbara County, 1986-91, ret. Contbr. editor Rescue Mag., 1989—, editor-in-chief Response! mag., 1982-86; editor Press On! Electronic mag., 1994—; mem. adv. bd. Hazard Montly, 1991—; cons. law enforcement div.; Calif. Office Emergency Svcs., 1976-77; pres. San Diego Com. for Los Angeles Philharmonic Orch., 1957-58. Bd. dirs. Search and Rescue of the Californias, 1976-77, Nat. Assn. for Search and Rescue, Inc., 1980-87, pres., 1985-87, trustee, 1987-90, mem. Calif. OES strategic com., 1992—; pres., CEO Nat. Inst. For Urban Search & Rescue, 1989—; mem. Gov.'s Task Force on Earthquakes, 1981-82, Earthquake Preparedness Task Force, Seismic Safety Commn., 1982-85. Recipient Hal Foss award for outstanding service to search and rescue, 1982. Mem. IEEE, Armed Forces Comm. and Electronics Assoc., Nat. Assn. for Search & Rescue (life, Svc. award 1985), San Diego Mountain Rescue Team (hon. life), Santa Barbara Amateur Radio Club. Episcopalian. Author: Search and Rescue Glossary, 1974; contbr. to profl. jours. Office: PO Box 91648 Santa Barbara CA 93190-1648

MCCOY, MARILYN, university official; b. Providence, Mar. 18, 1948; d. James Francis and Eleanor (Regan) McC.; m. Charles R. Thomas, Jan. 28, 1983. BA in Econs., Smith Coll., 1970; M in Pub. Policy, U. Mich., 1972. Dir. Nat. Ctr. for Higher Edn. Mgmt. Systems, Boulder, Colo., 1972-80; dir. planning and policy devel. U. Colo., Boulder, 1981-85; v.p. adminstrn. and planning Northwestern U., Evanston, Ill., 1985—; bd. dirs. First Prairie Mutual Funds; mem. nat. adv. panel Nat. Ctr. for Postsecondary Governance and Fin. Co-author: Financing Higher Education in the Fifty States, 1976, 3d edit., 1982. Bd. dirs. Evanston Hosp., 1988—, United Charities, Chgo., 1988—, Mather Found., 1995—. Mem. Am. Assn. for Higher Edn., Soc. for Coll. and Univ. Planning (pres., v.p., sec., bd. dirs. 1980—), Assn. for Instnl. Rsch. (pres., v.p., exec. com., publs. bd. 1978-87), Chgo. Network (chmn. 1992-93), Chgo. Econ. Club. Home: 1100 N Lake Shore Dr Chicago IL 60611-1053 Office: Northwestern U 633 Clark St Evanston IL 60208-0001

MCCOY, MARY ANN, state official; b. Duluth, Minn., Oct. 13, 1924; d. Homer Burke and Avis (Woodworth) Hursh; B.A., Grinnell Coll., 1946; postgrad. Laval U., 1946, Mankato State U., 1964-65, U. Minn., 1970-73; m. Charles Ramon McCoy, June 11, 1949; children—Jeffrey, Mary, Jeremy. Exec. trainee Younkers, Inc., Des Moines, 1946; advt. copywriter Des Moines Register & Tribune, 1947; field dir. Duluth (Minn.) Girl Scout Council, 1947-49; with merchandising dept. Dayton's, Inc., Mpls., 1966-75; dir. election and legis. manual div. Office of Sec. of State of Minn., St. Paul, 1975-81; exec. dir. Minn. State Ethical Practices Bd., St. Paul, 1981-95. Mem. Minn. Hist. Soc. (life, hon. council), Council on Govt. Ethics Laws (steering com. 1986-89, treas. 1987-88, hon. life), exec. council Minn. Hist. Soc., 1972-81, 82-90 ; mem. Minn. Supreme Ct. Bd. for Continuing Legal Edn., 1981-87; sec. State Rev. Bd. for Nominations to Nat. Register, 1976-89 . Mem. Minn. Assn. Pub. Adminstrs., Am. Judicature Soc., Women Historians of Midwest, Am. Assn. State and Local History. Editor, Minn. Legis. Manual, 1975-81.

MCCOY, MILLINGTON F., management recruitment company executive; b. Cape Girardeau, Mo., Jan. 22, 1941; d. Howard Hanscom and Mary Helen (Kinder) Flentge; m. W. David McCoy; 1 child, Daniel Phipps. BA, U. Mo., 1962; Cert. in Bus. Adminstrn. program, Harvard-Radcliffe U., 1963. Field market researcher Procter & Gamble Co., N.Y.C., 1964-65; advt. and market rsch. analyst Gardner Advt. Agy., N.Y.C., 1965-66; v.p. Handy Assocs., N.Y.C., 1966-77; mng. dir. Gould, McCoy & Chadick, Inc., N.Y.C., 1977—; founding mem. Com. of 200; panel of experts Boardroom Reports. Mem. Phi Beta Kappa. Avocations: dressange, Enneagram. Office: Gould McCoy & Chadick Inc 300 Park Ave New York NY 10022-7402

MCCOY, NEAL S., lawyer; b. Winfield, Kans., Nov. 22, 1940; s. R. Stewart and Alma Elnora (Fry) McC.; m. Catherine Collins, June 6, 1980. A.B. in Polit. Sci., U. Kans., Lawrence; LL.B., Harvard U., 1965; postgrad., Cambridge U., Eng., 1965-66. Bar: Calif. 1965, D.C. 1978. Mem. br. adminstrv. procs. and investigations, div. corp. fin. SEC, Washington, 1966-69; legal asst. to chmn. SEC, 1969-70, chief counsel div. corp. fin., 1970-74, assoc. dir. (compliance) div. corp. fin., 1974-77; ptnr. firm Skadden, Arps, Slate, Meagher & Flom, Washington, 1977—; mem. adv. coun. George Washington U. Med. Ctr., 1990—, Nat. Commn. on Fin. Instn. Reform, Recovery and Enforcement, 1991-93, ad hoc com. ALT Corp. Governance Project. Mem. ad hoc com. ALI Corp. Governance Project; mem. Nat. Commn. on Fin. Instn. Reform, Recovery and Enforcement, 1991—. Mem. ABA, Fed. Bar Assn. (exec. coun. securities law com. 1988—), Nat. Assn. Securities Dealers (legal adv. bd. 1988-93). Office: Skadden Arps Slate Meagher Flom 1440 New York Ave NW Washington DC 20005-2111

MCCOY, PATRICIA A., counseling administrator, art critic,; b. Seattle, Wash., Dec. 20, 1951; d. Robert Wilson and Barbara (Foss) McC. BS, U. Nev., 1974; MA, NYU, 1983; postgrad. in psychoanalysis, Ctr. for Modern Psychoanalytic, Studies, N.Y. Lectr. in English CUNY, N.Y.C., 1984-88, John Jay Coll. of Criminal Justice, N.Y.C., 1988-91; clin. educator August Aichhorn Resdl. Treatment Ctr., N.Y.C., 1991-93, St. Vincent's Hosp. Psychiatry Inpatient, N.Y.C., 1993-95; residence Louise Wise maternity for teenage girls NYC Bd. of Edn., 1995—; lectr. contemporary art New Arts Program and others, east coast, 1991—; ind. curator, 1987—. Editor: N.A.P. Text jour., 1993—; contbr. articles to profl. jours., art criticism; curated shows include Lang and O'Hara Gallery, N.Y.C., Sandra Gering Gallery, N.Y.C., 1989, Northampton Gallery, Pa., 1994, La Mama Gallery, N.Y., 1994. Grantee N.Y. State Found. for the Arts, 1987, Pa. Coun. for the Arts, 1991, Mid-Atlantic, 1991, Nat. Endowment for the Arts, 1992, Pew Charitable Trust, 1993. Mem. Nat. Soc. Modern Psychoanalysts, Assn. Internat. des Critiques D'Art, Am. Orthopsychiatric Assn., N.Y. Coun. for Humanities.

MCCOY, RHONDA LUANN, daycare administrator; b. Muncy, Pa., Apr. 22, 1968; d. Gary Edward Sr. and Twila Marie (Koch) McC. BS in Edn., Millersville (Pa.) U., 1990. Cert. in elem./early childhood edn., Pa. Substitute pre-sch. tchr. Magic Years, Williamsport, Pa., 1991-92, pre-kindergarten tchr., 1991-92; asst. dir. Angel Sta., Hughesville, Pa., 1992-93; dir., adminstr. Westfield (Pa.) Child Devel. Ctr., 1993—; adminstr. R.B. Walter Sch. Age, Lawrenceville, Pa., 1994—, Westfield Sch. Age, 1993—, Millerton (Pa.) Sch. Age, 1994-95. Home: PO Box 156 Westfield PA 16950-0156

MC COY, ROBERT BAKER, publisher; b. Arrowsmith, Ill., Mar. 26, 1916; s. Robert Benton and Charlotte (Miller) McC. B.S., Northwestern U., 1950; M.S., 1951; postgrad., U. Ill. extension. Various positions with branches U.S. Govt., 1939-51; mng. editor book dept. Popular Mechanics Mag. Co., Chgo., 1951-60; mng. editor high sch. textbook div. J.B. Lippincott Co., Chgo., 1960-62; owner, pres., chmn. bd. Rio Grande Press Inc. (pubs. nonfiction Western Americana books), Chgo., 1962—; chmn. bd., pres. Rio Grande Press of N.Mex., Inc. Lectr., author articles on Am. Indian, ornithology, travel. Served with AUS, 1941-45. Office: The Rio Grande Press Inc La Casa Escuela PO Box 33 Glorieta NM 87535

MCCOY, RONALD WAYNE, physician; b. Memphis, Sept. 25, 1940; s. Loren Alonzo and Esther Maxine (Terry) McC.; m. Marjorie Louise Gray, Aug. 3, 1963; children: Loren Edward, Molly Kay. AB, Wabash Coll., 1962; MD, U. Ill., 1966. Diplomate Am. Bd. Internal Medicine. Intern Cook County Hosp., Chgo., 1966-67, resident in internal medicine, 1967-70; co-owner Med. Ctr. Pa., Sheffield, 1972-85; owner, pres. Ronald W. McCoy, P.C., Muscle Shoals, Ala., 1985-92; pres., co-owner Avalon Med. Ctr., Muscle Shoals, 1992—; mem. at large exec. bd. Humana Hosp., Muscle Shoals, 1989—, bd. dirs. ICU. Mem. Sheffield Bd. Edn., 1989—, pres., 1990-91, 95—. Maj. USAF, 1970-72. Fellow ACP; mem. AMA, Med. Assn. State Ala., Colbert County Med. Assn. (pres. 1978), Sportsmans Club, Presidents Club Wabash Coll. Republican. Avocations: riding, boating, water skiing, farming, horseback riding. Home: 103 Highland Pl Sheffield AL 35660-7221 Office: 203 W Avalon Ave Sheffield AL 35661-2855

MCCOY, SANDRA JO, pharmacist; b. Burkesville, Ky., July 30, 1953; d. Jesse Martin and Wanda Lee (Biggerstaff) McC. BS in Pharmacy, Samford U., 1977; D Pharmacy, 1983. Lic. pharmacist Ala., Ky., Tenn. Staff pharmacist St. Vincent's Hosp., Birmingham, Ala., 1977-83; staff pharmacist St. Thomas Hosp., Nashville, 1983—, ptnrs. in excellence quality leadership process trainer, pharmacy dept. coord., 1992—, drug interaction specialist pharmacy, 1992—, profl. achievement system participant, 1994-95; pres. S.J. McCoy Timber, S.J. McCoy Properties; mem. Consumer Mail Panel, Chgo., 1989—; cons. Clin. Mgmt. Cons., Nashville, 1991—; adv. bd. Town and Country Mag. Mem. Opera Guild, Nashville, 1989, mem. com., standing bd. mem., com. event chair, 1994-95, 95-96; mem. Symphony Guild, Nashville, 1992—, Ballet Guild, 1992—, founding mem. Ballet Friends '92, com. chair, 1993-94, 94-95; mem. Friends of Checkwod, Nashville, 1994—, Tenn. Performing Arts Ctr. Friends, 1994—; founding mem. The Abbey Leix Soc. of the O'more Coll. of Design, 1995; stewarship Ky. Dept. Forestry, Ky. Dept. Fish & Wildlife, 1994. Mem. Am. Soc. Hosp. Pharmacists (midyear presentation 1993, 94, alt. del. state of Tenn. 1994), Mid. Tenn. Soc. Hosp. Pharmacists (bd. dirs. 1987-91, sec. 1987-88, pres. elect 1988-89, pres. 1989-90, scholarship com. 1992, poster presentation 1995), Tenn. Soc. Hosp. Pharmacists (membership com. 1989-90), Nashville Area Pharmacists Assn., Lambda Kappa Sigma (Women in Pharm. Leadership in Am. award 1993). Republican. Avocations: travel, stock market, arts, fashion, current events. Home: 3415 W End Ave Apt 608 Nashville TN 37203-1025 Office: St Thomas Hosp Dept Pharmacy 4220 Harding Rd Nashville TN 37205-2005

MCCOY, THOMAS RAYMOND, lawyer, educator; b. Cin., Apr. 14, 1943; s. Raymond F. and Margaret T. (Hohmann) McC.; m. Judith A. Huth, July 27, 1968; children—Jennifer A., Ellen M. B.S., Xavier U., Cin., 1964; J.D., U. Cin., 1967; LL.M., Harvard U., 1968. Bar: Ohio 1967. Asst. prof. law Vanderbilt U., Nashville, 1968-71, assoc. prof., assoc. dean for acad. affairs, 1971-75, prof., 1975—; mem. Tenn. Supreme Ct. Commn. on Dispute Resolution, 1992-94. Mem. editorial bd. Soundings jour., 1972-85. Bd. dirs. Opportunity House, Inc., Nashville, 1969-81, pres. bd., 1978-80. Mem. ABA, Am. Assn. Law Schs., Nat. Gov.'s Assn. (adv. com. on federalism 1988). Home: 1502 Lynnhurst Ct Brentwood TN 37027-7218 Office: Vanderbilt U Sch Law 21st Ave S Nashville TN 37240

MC COY, TIDAL WINDHAM, former government official; b. Gainesville, Fla., Apr. 25, 1945. Grad., U.S. Mil. Acad., 1967; M.A. in Bus. Fin, George Washington U., 1975. Officer U.S. Army, 1967-72; mem. long-range planning and net assessment group Office of Sec. Def., Washington, 1972-73; mem. staff Nat. Security Council, 1973; staff asst. and then dep. asst. to Sec. Def., 1973-77; sci. asst. to asst. sec. for research, engring. and systems Dept. Navy, 1977-78; dir. policy research, office of under sec. for policy Dept. Def., 1978-79; asst. for nat. security affairs to Sen. Jake Garn, 1979-81; asst. sec. for manpower, res. affairs and installations Dept. Air Force, Washington, 1981-87; asst. sec. for readiness support USAF, Washington, 1987-88; acting sec. and undersec. USAF, 1981-88; sr. assoc. Hecht, Spencer & Assocs., 1988-89; v.p. govt. rels. Thiokol Corp., 1989—. Recipient DOD Outstanding Civil Svc. medal Sec. Defense. Mem. Space Transp. Assn. U.S.A. (chmn. 1996—).

MCCOY, WESLEY LAWRENCE, musician, conductor, educator; b. Memphis, Jan. 27, 1935; s. Harlan Eftin and Gladys (Coggin) McC.; m. Carolyn June Noble, Aug. 26, 1960; children: Jill Laurene McCoy Kurtz, Scott Edward. B.Music Edn., La. State U., 1957, Ph.D., 1970; M of Music Edn, U. Louisville, 1958; M Sacred Music, So. Bapt. Theol. Sem., 1960. Minister of music Beechmont Bapt. Ch., Louisville, 1959-62; also instr. music So. Bapt. Theol. Sem., Louisville; asst. prof. music, dir. bands Carson Newman Coll., Jefferson City, Tenn., 1962-67; asst. prof. music U. S.C., Columbia, 1969-72; asso. prof. music U. Ark., Little Rock, 1972-77; prof. U. Ark., 1977-80, asst. dean for public service Coll. Fine Arts,, 1978-79; condr. Wind Ensemble, River City Community Band, 1972-80, Oklahoma City Youth Symphony, 1985-89; chmn. dept. music Phillips U., Enid, Okla., 1980-82, chmn. fine arts div., 1982-84; minister music 1st United Meth. Ch., Edmond, Okla., 1983—; owner Centre Office, Travel Agts. Internat. French horn player, Knoxville (Tenn.) Symphony Orch., 1962-67, Columbia Philharm. Orch., 1969-72, Ark. Symphony Orch., 1972-80, Enid-Phillips Symphony, 1980-84; contbr. to Ch. Musician, 1974-76, 85-86. Co-chmn. Jefferson County (Tenn.) Com. for Goldwater for Pres., 1962; mem. Pulaski County Republican Com., 1977-81; mem. Oklahoma County Exec. Com., 1995—. Mem. S.C. Music Educators Assn. (pres. coll. div. 1971-73), Ark. Music Edn. Assn. (chmn. rsch. 1975-80), Phi Mu Alpha, Pi Kappa Lambda, Phi Delta Kappa, Alpha Tau Omega. Republican. Baptist. Home: 1904 Blue Jay Ct Edmond OK 73034-6105 Office: 1331 W Memorial Rd Oklahoma City OK 73114-1423

MCCOY, WILLIAM O., retired telecommunications executive; b. Snow Hill, N.C., Oct. 26, 1933; s. Marcus Cicero and Anna Kathleen (Shirley) McC.; m. Sara Jane Hart, Dec. 18, 1955; children—Laura Jo McCoy Foster, Kathleen Sue. BS, U. N.C., 1955; MS, MIT, 1968. Gen. mgr. South Central Bell, New Orleans, 1973-76; v.p. South Central Bell, Nashville, 1978; exec. v.p. South Central Bell, Birmingham, Ala., 1978-82, vice chmn., 1982-83; asst. v.p. Am. Tel & Tel, Basking Ridge, N.J., 1976-78; vice chmn. BellSouth Corp., Atlanta, 1993—; dir. First Am. Corp., Nashville, Liberty Corp., Greenville. Chmn. Middle Tenn. Heart Assn., Nashville, 1971; div. chmn. Greater New Orleans Fedn. of Chs., 1974; gen. vice chmn. New Orleans Symphony Campaign, 1975; co-chmn. Ala. United Way Campaign, Birmingham, 1982; adv. council Coll. Bus. Adminstrn., Ga. State U., 1983—. Served to capt. USMC, 1955-59. Republican. Methodist. Office: BellSouth 675 Peachtree St NE Atlanta GA 30308-1928 also: BellSouth Corp 1155 Peachtree St NE Atlanta GA 30309-3600

MCCRABB, DONALD RAYMOND, religious ministry director; m. Catherine Olds; 1 child, Andrew Thomas. BA in Religion, BA in Polit. Sci., Wright State U., 1975; MA in Theology, U. Dayton, 1978; grad. program, Jesuit Renewal Ctr., Milford, Ohio, 1984. Cert. catechetical leader, Roman Cath. Ch. Campus min. Newman Ctr., Wright State U., Dayton, Ohio, 1975-76; grad. asst. U. Dayton, 1976-78; pastoral assoc. St. Raphael Cath. Ch., Springfield, Ohio, 1978-82; Cath. campus min. Cen. State U., Wilberforce U., 1982-85; exec. dir. Cath. Campus Ministry Assn., 1985—; mem. planning com. Cath. Edn. Futures Project, 1985-88; bd. dirs., site visitor Commn. on Cert. and Accreditation, U.S. Cath. Conf., 1986—. Home: 1433 Constance Ave Dayton OH 45409-1807 Office: Cath Campus Ministry Assn 3000 College Park Ave Dayton OH 45469-2515

MCCRACKEN, CARON FRANCIS, computer company executive, consultant; b. Detroit, Jan. 12, 1951; d. WIlliam Joseph and Constance Irene (Kramer) McC. AS, Mott C.C., 1971; BS, Ctrl. Mich. U., 1973; MA, U. Mich., 1978; postgrad., Wayne State U., 1979-81, 93—. Tchr. Elkton, Pigeon, Bayport (Mich.) High Sch., 1973-74, Davison (Mich.) Jr. High Sch., 1974-75; instr. Mott C.C., Flint, Mich., 1974-78; planning and rsch. specialist Flint Police Dept., 1977-79; campus coord., programmer Systems & Computer Tech. Corp., Detroit, 1981-82, acad. specialist, 1982-83, mgr. acad. computing systems, 1983-84, mgr. adminstrv. computing systems, 1984-85; communications analyst Fruehauf Corp., Detroit, 1985-86, sr. comms. analyst, 1986-87; account cons. US Sprint Communications Co., Detroit, 1987-89; account mgr. US Sprint Communications Corp., Detroit, 1989-90; sr. mgr. Technology Specialists, Inc., Phila., 1990-91; sr. tech. cons. Digital Mgmt. Group, Detroit, 1991-92; sr. assoc. info. tech. practice, tech. delivery svcs. Coopers & Lybrand, Detroit, 1992—; adv. bd. CONTEL Bus. Networks, Atlanta, 1987. Contbr. articles to profl. jours. Vol. charitable and homeless orgns., including COTS - Coalition on Temporary Shelter, Core Cities, Paint the Town; vol. computer project Wayne State U., 1993-95; vol. tech. advisor on 1992 elections project City of Detroit; vol. St. Joseph's Mercy Hosp., Pontiac, Mich., 1995; bd. dirs. Bloomfield Hills Condominium Assn., 1996—. Mem. Data Processing Mgmt. Assn., Assn. Computing Machinery, Detroit Inst. Arts, Alumni Assn. U. Mich., Alumni Assn. Wayne State U., Smithsonian Instn. (assoc.), Adventure Cycling Assn. (Missoula, Mont.). Avocations: distance bicycling and running, golf, personal research, travel. Home: 100 W Hickory Grove H4 Bloomfield Hills MI 48304-2169 Office: Coopers & Lybrand 400 Renaissance Ctr Detroit MI 48243-1507

MC CRACKEN, DANIEL DELBERT, computer science educator, author; b. Hughsville, Mont., July 23, 1930; s. Albert Ray and Blanche (Spear) McC.; m. Evelyn Edwards, 1952; children: Charles, Judith, Cynthia, Virginia, Rachel, Aliza, Thomas.; m. Helen Blumenthal, 1980; 1 stepson, Michael Cohen. B.A. in Math., Central Wash. U., 1950, B.A. in Chemistry, 1951; student, NYU, 1958-59; M.Div., Union Theol. Sem., N.Y.C., 1970. With Gen. Electric Co., 1951-58, dir. tng., computer dept., 1956-57; with AEC Computing Center, N.Y.U., 1958-59; cons. computer programming, writing and tng., 1958—; prof. computer sci. CCNY, 1981—, dept. chair, 1989-91. Author: Digital Computer Programming, 1957, (with H. Weiss and T.H. Lee) Programming Business Computers, 1959, A Guide to FORTRAN Programming, 1961, A Guide to IBM 1401 Programming, 1962, A Guide to ALGOL Programming, 1962, A Guide to COBOL Programming, 1963, (with U. Garbassi) 2d edit., 1970, (with F.J. Gruenberger) Introduction to Electronic Computers, 1963, (with W.S. Dorn) Numerical Methods and FORTRAN Programming, 1964, A Guide to FORTRAN IV Programming, 1965, 2d edit., 1972, FORTRAN with Engineering Applications, 1967, Public Policy and the Expert, 1971, Numerical Methods with FORTRAN IV Case Studies, 1972, A Simplified Guide to FORTRAN Programming, 1974, A Simplified Guide to Structured Cobol Programming, 1976, (with Donald G. Golden) 2d edit., 1988, A Guide to PL/M Programming for Microcomputer Applications, 1978, A Guide to NOMAD for Applications Development, 1981, Computing for Engineers and Scientists with Fortran 77, 1984, (with William I. Salmon) 2d edit., 1988, A Second Course in Computer Science with Pascal, 1987; (with William I. Salmon) A Second Course in Computer Science with Modula-2, 1987, (with Donald G. Golden) Simplified Structured Cobol with Microsoft/Microfocus Cobol, 1990; editor: (with M. Mead, R.L. Shinn and J.E. Carothers) To Love or To Perish: The Technological Crisis and the Churches, 1972. Pres. bd. edn., Ossining, N.Y., 1965-66. Recipient Norbert Wiener award Computer Profls. for Social Responsibility, 1989. Fellow Assn. Computing Machinery (chmn. com. on computers and pub. policy 1972-76, mem. council 1974-82, v.p. 1976-78, pres. 1978-80, Outstanding Contbns. Computer Sci. Edn. award 1992). Democrat. Address: 160 Cabrini Blvd New York NY 10033-1137

MCCRACKEN, JOE C., school system administrator. Supt. Lockwood Schs., Billings, Mont. State finalist Nat. Supt. of Yr., 1993. Office: Lockwood Schs 1932 Us Highway 87 E Billings MT 59101-6651

MCCRACKEN, JOHN HARVEY, painter, sculptor; b. Berkeley, Calif., Dec. 9, 1934; s. John H. and Marjorie (Strain) McC.; m. Gail Barringer, May 4, 1991; children: David Gordon, Patrick Daniel. BFA, Calif. Coll. Arts & Crafts, 1962, postgrad., 1962-65. Tchr., U. Calif., Irvine, 1965-66, L.A., 1966-68, Santa Barbara, 1974-85, Sch. Visual Arts, N.Y.C., 1968-69, Hunter Coll., N.Y.C., 1970-71, U. Nev., Reno, 1971-72, Las Vegas, 1972-75. One man shows include: Robert Elkon Gallery, N.Y.C., 1966, 67, 68, 72, 73, Galerie Ileana Sonnabend, Paris, 1969, Sonnabend Gallery, N.Y.C., 1970, Ace Gallery, L.A., 1985, PS 1, Long Island City, N.Y., 1986, Newport Harbor Art Mus., Calif., 1987, Contemporary Arts Mus., Houston, 1989, Hoffman Borman Gallery, Santa Monica, Calif., 1988, Konrad Fischer Gallery, Düsseldorf, Germany, 1989, Lisson Gallery, London, 1990, Galerie Nordenhake, Stockholm, 1990, Fred Hoffman Gallery, L.A., 1990, Galerie Froment & Putman, Paris, 1991, 96, Sonnabend Gallery, N.Y.C., 1992, Louver Gallery, L.A., 1993-95, Galerie Xavier Hufkens, Brussels, 1993, Galerie Art & Public, Geneva, 1994, Galerie Tanit, Munich, 1995, Hochshule Fur Angwandte Kunst, Vienna, 1995, Kunsthalle Basel, Switzerland, 1995; exhibited in group shows at Solomon R. Guggenheim Mus., N.Y.C., 1967, Saatchi Gallery, London, 1985, Venice (Italy) Biennale, 1986, Centro de Arte Reina Sofia, Madrid, 1987, Musee St. Pierre Art Contemporain, Lyon, France, 1988, Solomon R. Guggenheim Mus., N.Y.C., 1989-90, Carnegie Internat., Carnegie Mus. Art, Pitts., 1991, Corcoran Biennal, Washington, 1995; represented in permanent collections at Art Inst. Chgo., Solomon R. Guggenheim Mus., N.Y.C., Mus. Modern Art, N.Y.C., San Francisco Mus. Art, Whitney Mus. Art, N.Y.C., Mus. Contemporary Art, L.A., L.A. County Mus. Art. Grantee, NEA, 1968.

MC CRACKEN, PAUL WINSTON, economist, business educator; b. Richland, Iowa, Dec. 29, 1915; s. Sumner and Mary (Coffin) McC.; m. Emily Ruth Siler, May 27, 1942; children—Linda Jo, Paula Jeanne. Student, William Penn Coll., 1937; MA, Harvard U., 1942, PhD, 1948. Faculty Found. Sch., Berea Coll., Ky., 1937-40; economist Dept. Commerce, Washington, 1942-43; fin. economist, dir. research Fed. Res. Bank of Mpls., 1943-48; assoc. prof. Sch. Bus. Adminstrn., U. Mich., 1948-50, prof., 1950-66, Edmund Ezra Day Univ. prof. bus. adminstrn., 1966-86, prof. emeritus, 1986—; chmn. Nat. Bur. Econ. Rsch.; trustee Earhart Found.; mem. pub. oversight bd. AICPA. Author: monographs Can Capitalism Survive?; articles on financial, econ. subjects. Fellow Am. Statis. Assn.; mem. Am. Econ. Assn., Am. Finance Assn., Royal Econ. Soc., Harvard Grad. Soc. (coun.). Presbyn. Clubs: Cosmos (Washington); Harvard (N.Y.C.). Home: 2564 Hawthorne Rd Ann Arbor MI 48104-4032

MC CRACKEN, PHILIP TRAFTON, sculptor; b. Bellingham, Wash., Nov. 14, 1928; s. William Franklin and Maude (Trafton) McC.; m. Anne MacFetridge, Aug. 14, 1954; children—Timothy, Robert, Daniel. B.A. in Sculpture, U. Wash., 1954. Asst. to Henry Moore Eng., 1954. One-man shows: Willard Gallery, N.Y.C., 1960, 65, 68, 70, Seattle Art Mus., 1961, Wash. State Capitol Mus., Olympia, 1964, Art Gallery of Greater Victoria, B.C., 1964, LaJolla (Calif.) Mus. Art, 1970, Anchorage Hist. and Fine Arts Mus., 1970, Tacoma Art Mus., 1980, Kennedy Galleries, N.Y.C., 1985, Lynn McAllister Gallery, Seattle, 1986, 89, Valley Mus. N.W. Art, La Conner, Wash., 1993, Whatcom Mus., Bellingham, Wash., 1994, others; group shows include: Mus. Art, Ogunquit, Maine, 1957, Chgo. Art Inst., 1958, Detroit Inst. Arts, 1958, Pa. Acad. Fine Arts, 1958, Contemporary Art Gallery, Houston, 1958, DeYoung Meml. Mus., San Francisco, 1960, Los Angeles Mcpl. Art Mus., 1960, Galerie Claude Bernard, Paris, 1960, Phillips Gallery, Washington, 1966, Corcoran Gallery, 1966, Mus. Art, Akron, 1967, Finch

Coll., N.Y.C., 1968, Rutgers U., 1968, Whitney Mus. Art, 1978, Portland Art Mus., 1976, Mont. State U., Bozeman, 1979, Brigham Young U., 1980, Bellvue (Wash.) Art Mus., 1986, Lynn McAllister Gallery, 1986, Am. Acad. Arts and Letters, N.Y.C., 1986, Schmidt Bingham Gallery, N.Y.C., 1987, Wash. State Capital Mus., 1987, 89, Cheney-Cowles Mus., Spokane, Wash., 1988, Smithsonian Instn., 1991—, Nat. Mus., Ottawa, Can., 1991-92, Gallery Three-Zero, N.Y.C., 1993, Seattle Art Mus., 1994, others; sculptures represented: Norton Bldg., Seattle, Kankakee (Ill.) State Hosp., Swinomish Indian Tribal Center, LaConner, UN Assn., N.Y.C., King County King Dome, Seattle, City Hall, Everett, Wash., others. (Recipient numerous prizes, awards). Address: 401 Guemes Island Rd # B Anacortes WA 98221-9534

MCCRACKEN, ROBERT DALE, anthropologist, writer; b. Fairplay, Colo., Aug. 8, 1937; s. Robert Gerald McCracken and Martha Lucile (Grice) Foster; m. Susan Shihadeh Cline, June 24, 1967 (div. Oct. 1974); 1 child, Bambi Michelle McCracken Metscher. BA in Psychology, U. Colo., 1962, MA in Anthropology, 1965, PhD in Anthropology, 1968; postgrad., Washington U., St. Louis, 1972. Instr. extension ctr. U. Colo., Grand Junction, 1965; instr. dept. anthropology Met. State Coll., Denver, 1966; instr. Colo. Women's Coll., Denver, 1966-67; asst. prof. anthropology Calif. State U., Long Beach, 1968-69; asst. prof. Memphis State U., 1976-79; asst. prof. Sch. Pub. Health UCLA, 1969-71; postdoctoral fellow dept. psychology Washington U., St. Louis, 1971-72; freelance writer, 1972-74; dir. rsch. Colo. Migrant Coun., Denver, 1974-76; asst. prof. U. Tenn., Knoxville, 1979-80; ind. social sci. cons. RDM Assocs., Las Vegas, 1980—; rsch. and field experience at Navajo Urban Relocation Project, U. Colo., Boulder, 1964-67, Navajo Reservation, summers, 1966-71; cons., researcher, presenter in field; dir. rsch. and new programs Colo. Migrant Coun., 1974-75. Contbr. articles to profl. publs. Mem. Nev. Town History Project, Nye County, 1987—; active with Sioux, Ute, Hopi, Shoshoni, Navajo Native Ams., 1965—, with migrant farmworkers, Colo., 1974-76; educator on sch. nutrition and learning performance West L.A., 1970-71. Mem. Anthropolical Assn. Avocations: hiking, film research. Home: PO Box 1232 Tonopah NV 89049-1232 Office: 3930 Swenson St Apt 810 Las Vegas NV 89119-7271

MCCRACKEN, STEVEN CARL, lawyer; b. Artesia, Calif., Oct. 29, 1950; s. Glenn A. and Helen V. (Fears) McCracken; m. Susan Lee Waggener, July 29, 1979; children: Casey James, Scott Kevin. BA magna cum laude, U. Calif., Irvine, 1972; JD, U. Va., 1975. Bar: Calif. 1975, U.S. Dist. Ct. (cen. dist.) Calif. 1975, U.S. Ct. Appeals (9th cir.) 1976, U.S. Dist. Ct. (no. dist.) Calif. 1977, D.C. 1979, U.S. Supreme Ct. 1985, U.S. Dist. Ct. (so. dist.) Calif. 1990. Assoc. Gibson, Dunn & Crutcher, L.A., 1975-82; ptnr. Gibson, Dunn & Crutcher, Irvine, Calif., 1983-94; v.p., sec. and gen. counsel Callaway Golf Co., Carlsbad, Calif., 1994-96; exec. v.p., gen. counsel, sec., 1996—; lawyer rep. Ninth Cir. Jud. Conf., 1989-91. Editor Va. Law Rev., 1973-75, mng. bd. 1974-75, bd. editors The Computer Lawyer, 1984—. Mem. ABA (antitrust sect.), Orange County Bar Assn. (bd. dirs. 1988-90, chmn. fed. ct. com. 1988-89, chmn. bus. litigation sect. 1990, sec. 1991, treas. 1992, pres.-elect 1993, pres. 1994). Democrat. Office: Callaway Golf Co 2285 Rutherford Rd Carlsbad CA 92008-8815

MCCRACKEN, THOMAS JAMES, JR., lawyer; b. Chgo., Oct. 27, 1952; s. Thomas J. Sr. and Eileen (Brophy) McC.; m. Peggy A. Jamrok; children: Catherine, Michael, Amanda, Quinn. BA, Marquette U., 1974; JD, Loyola U., 1977. Bar: Ill. 1977, U.S. Dist. Ct. (no. dist.) Ill., U.S. Ct. Appeals (7th cir.) 1984. Asst. state's atty. DuPage County State's Atty.'s Office, Wheaton, Ill., 1977-81; assoc. atty. McCracken & Walsh, Chgo., 1981-84; ptnr. McCracken, Walsh deLaVan & Hetler, Chgo., 1984—; commr. Nat. Conf. of Commns. on Uniform State Laws, 1989—; bd. dirs. Oak Trust and Savs. Bank, Chgo. Contbr. articles to profl. jours. State rep. Ill. Gen. Assembly, Springfield, Ill., 1983-93, state senator, 1993; chmn. Regional Trans. Authority, Chgo., 1993—. Named Top Ten Legislators Chgo. Mag., 1990. Mem. Chgo. Bar Assn., Ill. State Bar Assn. Avocations: skiing, fishing, hunting, coaching children's sports. Office: McCracken Walsh deLaVan & Hetler 134 N La Salle St Ste 600 Chicago IL 60602-1004

MCCRADY, JAMES DAVID, veterinarian, educator; b. Beaumont, Tex., June 26, 1930; s. James Homer and Lucyle (Ward) McC.; m. Mary Elizabeth McDougald, Sept. 8, 1951; children—David, Diane, Darla. B.S., Tex. A. and M. Coll., 1952, D.V.M., 1958; Ph.D., Baylor U., 1965. Instr., then asst. prof. Tex. A. and M. Coll., 1958- 62; dir. animal rsch., instr. Baylor U. Coll. Medicine, 1962-64; mem. faculty Tex A&M U., 1964—; prof., head dept. vet. physiology and pharmacology Tex. A. and M. Coll., 1966-90, prof., dir. spl. programs, 1990—; dir. Russian-Am. Tng. Partnership, 1995—; adj. prof. Baylor Coll., Medicine, M.D. Anderson Hosp. and Tumor Inst. Served with USAF, 1952-54. Mem. AVMA, Tex. Acad. Sci., Am. Physiol. Soc., Sigma Xi, Phi Kappa Phi, Phi Zeta. Research on comparative cardiovascular and respiratory physiology. Home: 511 Olive St Bryan TX 77801-3506 Office: Tex A&M U College Station TX 77843

MCCRAIN, MICHAEL WILLIAM, accountant, consultant; b. Bklyn., Apr. 25, 1952; s. William Joseph Sr. and Penelope (Malarios) McC.; m. Kathleen Jean O'Donnell, June 9, 1974; children: Michael Walter, Kevin O'Donnell, Christopher William. AS in Computer Sci. with honors, Suffolk County C.C., Selden, N.Y., 1973; BBA in Pub. Acctg. cum laude, Hofstra U., 1975; MS in Bus., Columbia U., 1988. CPA, N.Y. Supervising sr. acct. Peat, Marwick, Mitchell Co., Jericho, N.Y., 1974-79; corp. acctg. mgr. Pall Corp., Glen Gove, N.Y., 1979-81; v.p. CFO North Atlantic Industries, Inc., Hauppauge, N.Y., 1981-88; v.p. fin. Loral Fairchild Sys., Syosset, N.Y., 1988-89; prin. owner, pres. McCrain & Co., Ltd., Smithtown, N.Y., 1989—. Trustee Sachem Schs. Dist., Lake Ronkonkuma, N.Y., 1992-93; v.p. Sachem Athletic Booster Club, Lake Ronkonkuma, 1993-94, pres., 1994-95; vice chairperson Sachem Cmty. Adv. Coun., Lake Ronkonkuma, 1994-95. Mem. AICPA, N.Y. Soc. CPAs, Monarch Bus. Group, Beta Gamma Sigma. Avocations: racquetball, skiing, golfing, computers, coaching lacrosse. Office: McCrain & Co Ltd 22 Lawrence Ave Ste 109A Smithtown NY 11787-3619

MCCRARY, EUGENIA LESTER (MRS. DENNIS DAUGHTRY MCCRARY), civic worker, writer; b. Annapolis, Md., Mar. 23, 1929; d. John Campbell and Eugenia (Potts) Lester; m. John Campbell Howard, July 15, 1955 (dec. Sept. 1965); m. Dennis Daughtry McCrary, June 28, 1969; 1 child, Dennis Campbell. AB cum laude, Radcliffe Coll.-Harvard U., 1950; MA, Johns Hopkins U., 1952; postgrad., Harvard U., 1953, Pa. State U., 1953-54, Drew U., 1957-58, Inst. Study of USSR, Munich, 1964. Grad. asst. dept. Romance langs. Pa. State U., 1953-54; tchr. dept. math. The Brearley Sch., N.Y.C., 1954-57; dir. Sch. Langs., Inc., Summit, N.J., 1958-69; trustee Sch. Langs., Inc., Summit, 1960-69. Co-author: Nom de Plume: Eugenia Campbell Lester, (with Allegra Branson) Frontiers Aflame, 1987. Dist. dir. Eastern Pa. and N.J. auditions Met. Opera Nat. Coun., N.Y.C., 1960-66, dist. dir. publicity, 1966-67, nat. vice chmn. publicity, 1967-71, nat. chmn. public rels., 1972-75, hon. nat. chmn. pub. rels., 1976—; bd. govs., chmn. Van Cortlandt House Mus., 1985-90. Mem. Nat. Soc. Colonial Dames Am. (bd. mgrs. N.Y. 1985-90), Met. Opera Nat. Coun., Soc. Mayflower Desc. (former bd. dirs. N.Y. soc., chmn. house com. 1986-89), Soc. Daus. Holland Dames (bd. dirs. 1982-87, 3d directress gen. 1987-92, directress gen. 1992-96), L'Eglise du St.-Esprit (vestry 1985-88, sr. warden 1988-90), Huguenot Soc. Am. (governing coun. 1984-90, asst. treas. 1990-91, sec. 1991-95, 2d v.p. 1995—), Colonial Dames Am., Daus. of Cin., Colony Club (bd. govs. 1988-96). Republican. Episcopalian. Home: 24 Central Park S New York NY 10019-1632

MCCRAVEN, EVA STEWART MAPES, health service administrator; b. L.A., Sept. 26, 1936; d. Paul Melvin and Wilma Zech (Ziegler) Stewart; m. Carl Clarke McCraven, Mar. 18, 1978; children: David Anthony, Lawrence James, Maria Lynn Mapes. ABS magna cum laude, Calif. State U., Northridge, 1974, MS, Cambridge Grad. Sch. Psychology, 1987; PhD, 1991. Dir. spl. projects Pacoima Meml. Hosp., 1969-71, dir. health edn., 1971-74; asst. exec. dir. Hillview Community Mental Health Center, Lakeview Terrace, Calif., 1974—; past dir. dept. consultation and edn. Hillview Ctr., developer, mgr. long-term residential program, 1986-90; former program mgr. Crisis Residential Program, Transitional Residential Program and Day Treatment Program for mentally ill offenders, dir. mentally ill offenders svcs.; former program dir. Valley Homeless Shelter Mental Health Counseling Program; dir. Integrated Services Agy., Hillview Mental Health Ctr., Inc., 1993—; Former pres. San Fernando Valley Coordinating Coun. Area Assn., Sunland-Tujunga Coordinating Coun.; bd. dirs. N.E. Valley Health Corp., 1970-73, Golden State Community Mental Health Ctr., 1970-73. Recipient Resolution of Commendation award State of Calif., 1988, Commendation award, 1988, Spl. Mayor's plaque, 1988, Commendation awards for community svcs. City of L.A., 1989, County of L.A., 1989, Calif. State Assembly, 1989, Calif. State Senate, 1989, award Sunland-Tujunga Police Support Coun., 1989, Woman of Achievement award Sunland-Tujunga BPW, 1990. Mem. Assn. Mental Health Adminstrs., Am. Pub. Health Assn., Valley Univ. Women, Health Services Adminstrs. Alumni Assn. (former v.p.), Sunland-Tujunga Bus. and Profl. Women, LWV. Office: Hillview Community Mental Health Ctr 11500 Eldridge Ave San Fernando CA 91342-6523

MCCRAW, JOAN, magazine publisher. Pub. L.A. mag., 1994—. Office: LA Mag 11100 Santa Monica Blvd Los Angeles CA 90025

MCCRAW, JOHN RANDOLPH, JR., assistant principal; b. Lynchburg, Va., Nov. 23, 1942; s. John Randolph and Mabel L. (Bethel) McC.; m. Carolyn Lynn Mason, Aug. 3, 1968. BA, Emory and Henry Coll., 1965; MEd, U. Va., 1971; LLB, LaSalle Extension U., 1977; EdD, Va. Poly. Inst. and State U., 1987; cert., Oxford U., 1992. Cert. tchr., adminstr., Va. Tchr. govt. Martinsville (Va.) City Schs., 1965-89; asst. prin. Martinsville Jr. High Sch., 1989-90, Albert Harris Elem. Sch., Martinsville, 1990-93, Martinsville High Sch., 1993—; dir. Martinsville City Schs. Self Studies, Va. Dept. Edn./So. Assn. Colls. and Schs., 1988-90. Author: The Legal History of Teacher Certification in the Commonwealth of Virginia, 1987, Hands-On-Learning, 1993. Chmn. Martinsville Henry County Rep. party, state senate Rep. dist.; candidate for Martinsville City Coun. Mem. ASCD, Nat. Assn. Elem. Sch. Prins., Va. Assn. Elem. Sch. Prins., Va. Coaches Assn., Mid-Atlantic Notary Assn., Phi Delta Kappa. Baptist. Avocations: politics, law, current events, reading. Home: 1724 Meadowview Ln Martinsville VA 24112-5708 Office: Martinsville City Schs 710 Smith Rd Martinsville VA 24112-2531

MCCRAW, LESLIE G., engineering and construction company executive; b. Sandy Springs, S.C., Nov. 3, 1934; s. Leslie Gladstone and Cornelia (Milam) McC.; m. Mary Earle Brown; children: Leslie Gladstone III, James B., John. BSCE, Clemson U., 1956. Registered profl. engr., Del. Design engr. Gulf Oil Corp., Phila., 1956-57; various engrng. and constrn. positions E.I. DuPont Co., Wilmington, Del., 1960-75; v.p., mgr. div. Daniel Constrn. Co., Greenville, S.C., 1975-82, pres., 1982-84; pres., chief exec. officer Daniel Internat., Greenville, 1984-86, Fluor Daniel, Greenville and Irvine, Calif., 1986-88; pres. Fluor Corp., Irvine, 1988-90, vice chmn., chief exec. officer, 1990-91, chief exec. officer, chmn. bd. dirs., 1991. Bd. dirs. Allergan, N.Y. Life Ins. Co., U.S.-China Bus. Coun.; trustee Hampden-Sydney Coll., Va.; adv. bd. rsch. found., pres.'s adv. coun. Clemson U.; bd. visitors U. Calif. Grad. Sch. Mgmt.; internat. adv. bd. Br.-Am. Bus. Coun. Mem. NAM (bd. dirs.), Bus. Roundtable, Constrn. Industy's Presidents' Forum, Calif. Bus. Roundtable, Palmetto Bus. Forum, Pres.'s Export Coun. Republican. Presbyterian. Office: Fluor Corp Inc 3333 Michelson Dr Irvine CA 92715

MCCRAW, THOMAS KINCAID, business history educator, editor, author; b. Corinth, Miss., Sept. 11, 1940; s. John Carey and Eugenia Olive (Kincaid) McC.; m. Susan Morehead, Sept. 22, 1962; children: Elizabeth Morehead, Thomas Kincaid Jr. BA, U. Miss., 1962; MA, U. Wis., 1968, Ph.D., 1970; MA (hon.), Harvard U., 1978. Tchg. asst. U. Wis., Madison, 1968-69; asst. prof. U. Tex., Austin, 1970-74, assoc. prof., 1974-78; vis. assoc. prof. Bus. Sch., Harvard U., Boston, 1976-78, prof., 1978-89, Straus prof. bus. history, 1989—; dir. research Bus. Sch., Harvard U., 1985-87, co-chmn. bus. govt. and competition area, 1986—; ednl. cons. to cos., U.S., Japan, 1977—. Author: Morgan versus Lilienthal, 1970, TVA and the Power Fight, 1971, Prophets of Regulation, 1984; co-author: Management Past and Present, 1996; editor: Regulation in Perspective, 1981, America Versus Japan, 1986, The Essential Alfred Chandler, 1988; editor: Bus. History Rev., 1994—; contbr. numerous articles to various publs., chpts. to books. Trustee Bus. History Conf., 1986—, pres., 1989; mem. coun. Mass. Hist. Soc., 1987-92. Lt. USN, 1962-66. Recipient Lyons Master's Essay award Loyola U., Chgo., 1969, Younger Humanist award NEH, 1975, Pulitzer prize in history Columbia U., 1985, Thomas Newcomen Book award, 1986; Woodrow Wilson fellow, 1966-67; named to Alumni Hall of Fame, U. Miss., 1986; Newcomen fellowship Harvard U., 1973-74. Mem. Orgn. Am. Historians, Econ. Hist. Assn., Am. Econ. Assn. Democrat. Roman Catholic. Office: Harvard U Bus Sch Soldiers Field Boston MA 02163

MCCRAY, CURTIS LEE, university president; b. Wheatland, Ind., Jan. 29, 1938; s. Bert and Susan McCray; m. Mary Joyce Macdonald, Sept. 10, 1960; children: Leslie, Jennifer, Meredith. B.A., Knox Coll., Galesburg, Ill., 1960; postgrad. U. Pa., 1960-61; Ph.D., U. Nebr., 1968. Chmn. dept. English, Saginaw Valley Coll., University Center, Mich., 1972-73, dean arts and scis., 1973-75, v.p. acad. affairs, 1975-77; provost, v.p. acad. affairs Govs. State U., Chgo., 1977-82; pres. U. North Fla., Jacksonville, 1982-88, Calif. State U., Long Beach, 1988-93, Millikin U., Decatur, Ill., 1993—. Bd. dirs., 1982-88, campaign chmn. Jacksonville United Way, 1987; bd. dirs. Sta. WJCT Channel 7 and Stereo 90, Jacksonville, 1982-88, Jacksonville Art Mus., 1983-88, Meml. Med. Ctr., Jacksonville, 1983-88, Jacksonville Community Council, Inc., 1982-88, Arts Assembly Jacksonville, 1984-88, Jacksonville Urban League, 1985-88; hon. dir. Jacksonville Symphony Assn., 1983; mem. Dame Point Bridge Commn., Jacksonville, 1982; mem. Jacksonville High Tech Task Force, 1982; chmn. SUS High Tech. and Industry Council, 1986-88; mem. state relations and undergrad. edn. com. Am. Assn. State Colls. and Univs., 1985-88. Woodrow Wilson fellow, 1960; Johnson fellow, 1966; George F. Baker scholar, 1956; Ford Found. grantee, 1969; recipient Landee award for excellence in teaching Saginaw State Coll., 1972. Mem. AAUP. Club: Torch. Office: Millikin U 1184 W Main St Decatur IL 62522-2039

MCCRAY, RICHARD ALAN, astrophysicist, educator; b. Los Angeles, Nov. 24, 1937; s. Alan Archer and Ruth Elizabeth (Woodworth) McC.; m. Sandra Broomfield; children—Julia, Carla. B.S., Stanford U., 1959; Ph.D., UCLA, 1967. Research fellow Calif. Inst. Tech, Pasadena, 1967-68; asst. prof. astronomy Harvard U., Cambridge, Mass., 1968-71; assoc. prof. astrophysics U. Colo., Boulder, 1971-75, prof., 1975—, chmn. Joint Inst. Lab. Astrophysics, 1981-82, chmn. Ctr. for Astrophysics and Space Astronomy, 1985-86. Contbr. articles to profl. jours. Guggenheim fellow, 1975-76. Mem. NAS, Am. Astron. Soc. (councilor 1980-83, chmn. high energy astrophysics div. 1986-87, Heineman Prize for Astrophysics, 1990), Internat. Astron. Union. Office: U Colo Joint Inst Lab Astrophysics Boulder CO 80309-0440

MCCREADY, KENNETH FRANK, past electric utility executive; b. Edmonton, Alta., Can., Oct. 9, 1939; s. Ralph and Lilian McCready; m. Margaret E. Randall, Sept. 2, 1961; children: John, Janet, Brian. BSc, U. Alta., 1963. Supr. data processing and systems Calgary (Alta.) Power Ltd., 1965-67, supr. rates and contracts, 1967-68, adminstrv. asst. to exec. v.p., 1968-72, asst. mgr. mgmt. cons. div., 1972-75; mgr. mgmt. systems dept., gen. mgr. Montreal Engrng. Co., Calgary, 1975-76; v.p. adminstrn. Calgary (Alta.) Power Ltd., 1976-80; sr. v.p. ops. TransAlta Utilities, Calgary, 1980-85, pres., COO, 1985-89, also bd. dirs., 1988-96; pres., CEO TransAlta Utilities, TransAlta Energy, 1989-94, K. F. McCready & Assocs. Ltd., Calgary; bd. dirs. PanCan. Petroleum Ltd., Hewlett Packard (Can.) Ltd., Marigold Found. Ltd., The Van Horne Inst.; chmn. Conf. Bd. Can.; mem. environ. adv. coun. Dow Chem. Co.; past chmn. bd. Advanced Computing Techs., Inc. Past dep. chmn. bd. govs. So. Alta. Inst. Tech.; past chair Alta. Round Table on Environment and Econ.; past mem. com. on trade and environment Govt. Can. Internat. Trade Adv.; past pres. Western Electric Power and Light Assn. Mem. Assn. Profl. Engrs., Geologists and Geophysicists of Alta., Asea Brown Boveri, World Bus. Coun. for Sustainable Dvel., Can. Exec. Svc. Orgn. (adv. coun.), Constrn. Owners Assn. Alta. (past pres.), Calgary C. of C., Men's Can. Club Calgary (past pres.), Ranchmen's Club. Avocations: computers, cycling, photography.

MC CREARY, JAMES FRANKLIN, banker, lawyer; b. Farmington, Mo., June 15, 1942; s. Frank J. and Bernice E. (Dugal) McCreary; m. Martha Jean Tucker, June 30, 1962; children: James Franklin, III, Jason Tucker, Josh Adam. BSBA, U. Evansville, 1964; JD, Nashville Law Sch., 1969; MBA, Vanderbilt U., 1980. Bar: Tenn. 1969. With Old Nat. Bank, Evansville, Ind., 1960-64; with First Am. Corp., Nashville, 1972-80, exec. v.p., corp. sec., gen. counsel, 1974-80; with First Am. Nat. Bank Nashville (N.A.), 1964-72, 80-86, exec. v.p., 1980-86; ptnr. Borod & Huggins Attys., Memphis, 1986-87; ptnr. Gerrish & Mc Creary, Memphis, 1988, of counsel, 1988-92, dir., 1993—; pres. Met. Fed. Bank, 1988-91; vis. prof. bus. law David Lipscomb U., 1975-77; instr. law and banking Am. Inst. Banking, 1969-75. Mem. Beta Gamma Sigma. Mem. Ch. of Christ. Office: Gerrish & Mc Creary PC 222 2nd Ave N Nashville TN 37201-1649

MCCREDIE, JAMES ROBERT, fine arts educator; b. Chgo., Dec. 31, 1935; s. William and Mareta (Black) McC.; m. Marian Lucille Miles, Sept. 3, 1960; children: Miles William, Meredeth Black. AB in History and Literature summa cum laude, Harvard U., 1958, AM, 1961, PhD, 1963; student, Am. Sch. Classical Studies, Athens, Greece, 1958-59, 61-62. Instr. NYU, 1963-64, asst. prof., 1965-66, assoc. prof., 1967-70, prof., 1970, 78-88, Sherman Fairchild Prof. Fine Arts, 1988—, dep. dir. Inst. Fine Arts, 1967-69, acting dir., 1982-83, dir., 1983—, asst. field dir. Excavations in Samothrace, 1962, field dir., 1963-65, dir. excavations, 1966—; dir. Am. Sch. Classical Studies at Athens, Greece, 1969-77, chmn. mng. com., 1980-90, trustee, 1980—; vis. mem. Inst. Advanced Study, Princeton, N.J., 1977-78; mem. vis. com. dept. classical and near eastern Archeology Bryn Mayr Coll., 1982, dept. european paintings Met. Mus. Art, 1983—, Ctr. Old World Archaeology and Art Brown U., Providence, 1985; mem. adv. bd. Alexander S. Onassis Ctr. for Hellenic Studies NYU, 1990—; cons. in field. Author: Fortified Military Camps in Attica, Hesperia, 1966, Samothrace, 7, The Rotunda of Arsinoe, 1992; mem. adv. bd. Am. Jour. Archaeology, 1969-81; contbr. articles to prof. jours.. Bd. dirs. Hellenic-Am. Union, Athens, 1973-77, vice chmn., 1974-77, U.S. Ednl. Found., Greece, 1969-75; active Pres. Adv. Com. on Cultural Property, 1992-95. Charles Norton fellow, 1961-62; named hon. citizen Community of Samothrace, 1976. Mem. Am. Philos. Soc., Archaeol. Inst. Am. (life, trustee 1972-75, mem. exec. com. 1978-81), Archaeol. Soc. Athens (hon.), Deutsches archaeologisches Inst. (corr.). Home: 30 Battle Rd Princeton NJ 08540-4902 also summer: Palaiopolis GR-680 02, Samothrace Greece Office: NYU Inst Fine Arts 1 E 78th St New York NY 10021-0102

MCCREE, DONALD HANNA, JR., banker; b. Orange, N.J., Sept. 17, 1936; s. Donald Hanna and Elna (Van Houten) McC.; m. Patricia H. Jones, June 13, 1959; children: Donald, Douglas, David. A.B., Dartmouth Coll., 1958. With Mfrs. Hanover Trust Co., N.Y.C., 1960-90; sr. v.p., mgr. Mfrs. Hanover Trust Co. (London br.), 1976-78; sr. v.p., dep. gen. mgr. Mfrs. Hanover Trust Co., N.Y.C., 1978-79, sector exec. v.p. corp. banking, mem. gen. adminstrv. bd., 1980-90,91—; pres., CEO IBJ Schroder Bank and Trust Co., N.Y.C., 1995—. Served with USNR, 1958-60. Mem. Bankers Roundtable, Am. Bankers Assn. (exec. com. comml. lending div.), United Way of N.Y.C. (bd.of dirs.). Club: Whippoorwill, Loblolly. Office: IBJ Schroder Bank & Trust Co 1 State Ste New York NY 10004

MCCREERY, WILLIAM See RAMSEY, BILL

MCCREIGHT, JOHN A., management consultant; b. Phila., Jan. 29, 1938; s. John A. and Marion R. (Vetter) McC.; m. Kim Amet Healey; children: Laura, Cindy, Brian, Kimberly. BS in Mgmt. Scis., Northeastern U., 1968. Cert. mgmt. cons. Chief systems devel. AVCO Apollo Systems, Boston, 1964-68; sr. mgmt. cons. Touche, Ross & Co., Detroit, 1968-72, ptnr., Detroit and N.Y.C., 1972-80, nat. dir., mem. exec. com., N.Y.C., 1980-83 mng. dir. Hayes Hill, N.Y.C., 1983; pres. McCreight & Co., Inc. New Canaan, Conn. and Phila., 1983-86; mng. dir. Hay Group, Inc., N.Y.C., 1986-91; pres. McCreight & Co., Inc., New Canaan and Wilton, Conn., 1991—; mem. Presdl. Task Force to Reduce Cost and Improve Effectiveness of USN; dir., officer Inst. Mgmt. Cons. Adv. Carnegie Hall Bd. Trustees, NIH, N.Y. Mayor's Office, Salvation Army; past chmn. N.Y. Corp. Fund Raising, NIMH; mem. N.Y. Ireland U.S. Coun.; Served with USNR, 1955-63. Mem. Univ. Club (N.Y.C.). Office: McCreight & Co Inc 487 Danbury Rd Wilton CT 06897-2126

MCCRENSKY, EDWARD, international consultant, former organization executive; b. Boston, June 19, 1912; s. Benjamin and Anna (Miller) McC.; m. Louise C. Marshall, Apr. 16, 1942; children: Myron Wilson, Richard Marshall. B.A., Boston Coll., 1933; M.Ed., Boston Tchrs. Coll., 1935; student, Harvard Grad. Sch. Edn., 1940-41. High sch. tchr. Boston, 1936-41; govt. ofcl. U.S. Civil Service Commn., 1941-46; dir. civilian personnel and service Office Naval Research, Washington, 1946-66; chief personnel adminstrn. dept. social and econ. affairs UN, N.Y.C., 1966-68; inter-regional adviser UN, 1968-77; team leader UN, Bangkok, Thailand, 1977-81; internat. cons., 1981—; prof. George Washington U., 1950-68; guest prof. Royal Coll. Sci. and Tech., Strathclyde U., Glasgow, Scotland, 1961; cons. U.S. and internat. orgns.; lectr. human relations and internat. sci. manpower. Author: Wartime Practices in Recruitment, 1946, Scientific Manpower in Europe, 1959, Strategy and Tactics, Professional Recruitment, 1963; Contbr. articles U.S. fgn. jours. Recipient Rockefeller Pub. Service award and fellowship, 1957; Merit citation Nat. Civil Service League, 1955; Distinguished Civilian Service award Navy Dept., 1966. Mem. Soc. Pers. Adminstrn. (pres. 1955-56), Rotary (bd. dirs. Surfside club 1986-89, Paul Harris fellow). Home: 614 7th Ave N Surfside Beach SC 29575-4104 *I have always sought to broaden my experience in work, geographical location and cultural differences by accepting available opportunities for personal growth. I have constantly tried to prepare myself through research, planning, and authorship for improved professional capability.*

MCCRERY, DAVID NEIL, III, lawyer; b. Ames, Iowa, Mar. 7, 1957; s. David Neil Jr. and Judith Ann (Purlee) McC.; m. Katherine Marie Meridith, June 9, 1979; children: Evelyn Judith, David Neil IV. BS in Agr., U. Ill., 1979; JD, So. Ill. U., Carbondale, 1993. Bar: Ill. 1993, U.S. Dist. Ct. (ctrl. dist.) Ill. 1993. Dist. mgr. Ralston Purina Co., St. Louis, 1979-83; farmer, businessman McCrery Farms, Monmouth, Ill., 1984-90; grad. rsch. asst. So. Ill. U. Sch. Law, 1991-93; pvt. practice Law Offices David N. McCrery, III, Galesburg, Ill., 1993—. Assoc. del. U.S.-Can. Gt. Lakes Conf., 1984; assoc. bd. dirs. Warren County Soil and Water Dist., Monmouth, 1986; mem. Ill. Agr. Leadership Program, 1986, 87. Recipient Outstanding State Dir. award Monmouth Jaycees, 1988. Mem. Knox County Bar Assn. Methodist. Avocations: hunting, fishing, collecting antiques. Home: 105 N Carlysle Ave Abingdon IL 61410-1403 Office: 311 E Main St Ste 511 Galesburg IL 61401-4834

MCCRERY, JAMES (JIM MCCRERY), congressman; b. Shreveport, LA, Sept. 18, 1949; m. Johnette Hawkins, Aug. 3, 1991; 1 child, Claiborne Scott. BA, La. Tech. U., 1971; JD, La. State U., 1975. Bar: La. 1975. Pvt. practice Leesville, La., 1975-78; asst. city atty. City of Shreveport, 1979-80; mem. staff U.S. Rep. Buddy Roemer, 1981-84; regional mgr. Ga.-Pacific Corp., 1984-88; mem. 100th-103rd Congresses from 4th (now 5th) La. dist., 1988—; mem. ways and means com. Office: US Ho of Reps 225 Cannon Ho Ofc Bldg Washington DC 20515*

MC CRIE, ROBERT DELBERT, editor, publisher, educator; b. Sarnia, Ont., Can., Oct. 8, 1938; s. Robert Newton and Evelyn May (Johnston) McC.; m. Fulvia Madia, Dec. 22, 1965; children: Carla Alexandra, Mara Elizabeth. B.A., Ohio Wesleyan U., 1960; M.S., U. Toledo, 1964; postgrad., U. Chgo., 1962-63; MA, Hunter Coll., 1994; MPhil, CUNY, 1994, PhD, 1995. Cert. protection profl. Researcher Connective Tissues Research Lab., Copenhagen, 1963; copywriter numerous advt. agys., 1965-70; owner, editor Security Letter, N.Y.C., 1970—; editor, pub. HBJ Publs., N.Y.C., 1973-76; pres. Mags. for Medicine, Inc., N.Y.C., 1972-81; faculty John Jay Coll. Criminal Justice, 1985—, asst. prof., 1986-91, assoc. prof., 1992—; bd. dirs. numerous cos.; cons. in field; speaker at numerous meetings. Editor: Behavioral Medicine, 1978-81, Security Letter Source Book, 1983—, Security Jour., 1989—; contbr. books and articles on security and urban crime and policing. Mem. AAUP, Am. Hist. Assn., Am. Correctional Assn., Am. Soc. Indsl. Security (pres.'s cert. of merit 1990), Nat. Coun. Investigation and Security Svcs. (Duffy Meml. Achievement award 1992), Internat. Security Mmgt. Assn. (Brennan award 1993), Urban History Assn., Union League Club, Alpha Tau Omega, Delta Sigma Rho, Pi Delta Epsilon. Presbyterian (deacon). Home: 49 E 96th St New York NY 10128-0782 Office: 166 E 96th St New York NY 10128-2565 also: John Jay Coll Criminal Justice 899 10th Ave New York NY 10019-1029

MCCRIMMON, JAMES MCNAB, language educator; b. Renton, Scotland, June 16, 1908; came to U.S., 1929, naturalized, 1939; s. John and Margaret (Patterson) McCrimmon; m. Barbara Smith, June 10, 1939; children: Kevin M., John M. B.A., Northwestern U., 1932, M.A., 1933, Ph.D.,

1937. Asst. instr. English, Northwestern U., 1935; instr. English, U. Toledo, 1936-38, asst. prof., 1938-43, asso. prof., 1943-47; faculty U. Ill., 1947—, chmn. humanities div. Galesburg extension, 1947-49; asso. prof. humanities U. Ill., Urbana, 1949-55, prof., 1955-65; prof. emeritus U. Ill., 1965—, head div. gen. studies, 1954-62, dir. U. High Sch. English project, 1962—; vis. prof. English Fla. State U., 1967-70, lectr., 1970-78. Author: (with MacMinn and Hainds) Bibliography of the Writings of John Stuart Mill, 1945, Writing with a Purpose, 1950, Open Door to Education, (with Louttit and Habberton), 1951, From Source to Statement, 1968. Mem. Nat. Council Tchrs. English, College Conf. Composition and Communication, Phi Kappa Phi. Home: 1330 W Indianhead Dr Tallahassee FL 32301-4763

MCCRONE, ALISTAIR WILLIAM, university president; b. Regina, Can., Oct. 7, 1931. BA, U. Sask., 1953; MSc, U. Nebr., 1955; PhD, U. Kans., 1961. Instr. geology NYU, 1959-61, asst. prof., 1961-64, assoc. prof., 1964-69, prof., 1969-70, supr. Rsch. Ship Sea Owl on L.I. Sound, 1959-64; asst. dir. univ. program NYU, Sterling Forest, 1965-66; resident master Rubin Internat. Residence Hall NYU, 1966-69, chmn. dept. geology, 1966-69, assoc. dean Grad. Sch. Arts and Scis., 1969-70; prof. geology, acad. v.p. U. Pacific, 1970-74, acting pres., 1971; prof. geology, pres. Calif. State U. Sys. Humboldt State U., Arcata, 1974—; mem. sys. exec. coun. Calif. State U. Sys., 1974—, acad. senate Humboldt State U., 1974—, mem. chancellor's com. on innovative programs, 1974-76, trustees' task force on off-campus instrn., 1975-76, presdl. search com. Sonoma State U., 1976-77, exec. com. Chancellor's Coun. of Pres., 1976-79, Presdl. search com. Calif. State U., Chico, 1979-80, adv. group. exec. coun., 1980-81; Calif. state del. Am. Assn. State Colls. and Univs., 1977-80; mem. Commn. on Ednl. Telecomm., 1983-86; chair Statewide Task Force on Earthquake and Emergency preparedness, 1985-88; chair Statewide Com. on Emergency Preparedness, 1994-95; chmn., mem. accreditation teams Western Assn. Schs. and Colls.; mem. western sect. Am. Coun. Edn. Adminstrv. Intern Selection Panel, 1973; chair com. on energy and environ. Am. Assn. State Colls. and Univs., 1980-84; chair program com. Western Coll.Assn., 1983-84, panelist, 1983; mem. bd. dirs. Assn. Am. Colls., 1989-93, chair, 1992-93. Contbr. articles to profl. jours.; lectr. on geology Sunrise Semester program CBS Nat. Network, 1969-70; various appearances on local TV stas.; editl. cons. sci. series Harcourt, Brace, Jovanovich, pubs. Bd. trustees Presbyn. Hosp.-Pacific Med. Ctr., San Francisco, 1971-74; mem. Calif. Coun. for Humanities, 1977-82; mem. local campaign bd. United Way, 1977-83; mem. Am. Friends Wilton Park, 1980—; bd. dirs. Humboldt Convention and Visitors Bur., 1980-87, Redwood Empire Assn., 1983-87; bd. dirs. Calif. State Automobile Assn., 1988—, Am. Automobile Assn., 1990-93; bd. trustees Calif. State Parks Found., 1994—. Shell fellow in geology U. Nebr., 1954-55; Danforth assoc. NYU, 1964. Fellow Calif. Acad. Scis.; mem. AAAS, Geol. Soc. Am., Am. Assn. U. Adminstrs. (nat. bd. 1986-89, 96—), Rotary, St. Andrews Soc. N.Y. (life), Sigma Xi (pres. NYU chpt. 1967-69), Phi Kappa Phi. Avocation: golf. Home: 3493 Buttermilk Ln Arcata CA 95521-6946 Office: Humboldt State U Univ Campus Dept Geology Arcata CA 95521-8299

MCCRONE, WALTER COX, research institute executive; b. Wilmington, Del., June 9, 1916; s. Walter Cox and Bessie Lillian (Cook) McC.; m. Lucy Morris Beman, July 13, 1957. B Chemistry, Cornell U., 1938, PhD, 1942. Microscopist, sr. scientist Armour Research Found., Ill. Inst. Tech., Chgo., 1944-56; chmn. bd. Walter C. McCrone Assos. Inc., Chgo., 1956-81; sr. research advisor Walter C. McCrone Assos. Inc., 1956-78; pres. McCrone Research Inst., Inc., 1961-94, chmn. bd., 1961—; vis. prof. chem. microscopy Cornell U., 1984—; adj. prof. IIT, 1950—, NYU, 1974—, U. Ill., 1989—. Author: Fusion Methods in Chemical Microscopy, 1957, The Particle Atlas, 1967, Particle Atlas Two 6 vols., 1973-78, Particle Atlas Three Electronic CD-ROM edit., 1992, Polarized Light Microscopy, 1978, Asbestos Particle Atlas, 1980, Asbestos Identification, 1987; editor Microscope Jour., 1962-95; contbr. articles to profl. jours. Pres. bd. dirs. Ada S. McKinley Cmty. Svcs., 1962-95, emeritus pres., 1995—; chmn. bd. trustees Vandercook Coll. Music, 1986-95, emeritus pres. 1995—; trustee Campbell Ctr., 1990—. Recipient Benedetti-Pichler award Am. Microchem. Soc., 1970, Anachem award Assn. Analytical Chemists, 1981, cert. of merit Franklin Inst., 1982, Forensic Sci. Found., 1983, Madden Disting. Svc. award Vandercook Coll. Music, 1988, Fortissimo award, 1991, Irving Selikoff award Nat. Asbestos Coun., 1990, Founder's Day award Calif. Assn. Criminalists, 1990, Roger Green award, 1991, Pub. Affairs award Chgo. Pub. Schs., 1993, Disting. Svc. award USAF AFTAC program. Mem. Am. Chem. Soc. (Pub. Affairs award 1993, Disting. Svc. award USAF AFTAC Program 1994), Am. Phys. Soc., Am. Acad. Forensic Sci. (Disting. Svc. award criminalistics sect. 1984), Am. Inst. Conservators Art (hon.), Internat. Inst. Conservators, Australian Micros. Soc., N.Y. Micros. Soc. (Ernst Abbe award 1977), La. Micros. Soc., Can. Micros Soc., Midwest Micros. Soc., Royal Micros Soc. (hon.), Ill. Micros. Soc., Quekett Micros. Club, Sigma Xi, Phi Kappa Phi, Phi Lambda Upsilon, Alpha Chi Sigma. Achievements include discovery of highly sensitive polymorphs of HMX, development of a safe prodn. method, prodn. method for casting of artillery rounds with TNT; proved the Vinland map to be a modern forgery, the Turin Shroud to be a medieval painting; developed the analytical methods for detection and identification of asbestos; first zoning ordinance based on performance stds. instituted in Chgo. Home: 501 E 32nd St Chicago IL 60616-4053 Office: McCrone Rsch Inst 2820 S Michigan Ave Chicago IL 60616-3292

MCCRORY, COLLEEN, environmental group administrator; b. New Denver, Can., Jan. 5, 1950; d. Patrick Joseph and Mabel Clifford (Lundy) McC.; children: Sean, Rory, Shea. Leg. asst. to Jim. Fulton Parliament Ottawa, Ottawa, Ont., Can., 1990-91. Organizer Meals on Wheels, New Denver; sch. trustee Arrowlakes # 10 Sch. Bd., New Denver. Recipient Goldman Environ. prize Goldman Found., 1992, UN Global 500 Roll of Honor, 1992, Fred M. Packard Internat. Pks. Merit award Internat. Union for the Conservation of Nature, 1988, Equinox Citation for environ. achievement Equinox Mag., 1990, Conservation award Can. Gov. Gens., 1983. Mem. Valhalla Wilderness Soc. (chairperson). Avocation: hiking. Office: Valhalla Wilderness Society, 307 Sixth Ave Box 329, New Denver, BC Canada V0G 1S0

MCCRORY, JOHN BROOKS, retired lawyer; b. St. Cloud, Minn., Oct. 23, 1925; s. John Raymond and Mary Lee (Rutter) McC.; m. Margaret Joan Dickson, Sept. 4, 1954 (dec. Apr. 1957); 1 child, William B.; m. Elizabeth Ann Quick, June 27, 1959; children—John B., Ann Elizabeth. B.A., Swarthmore Coll., 1948; J.D., U. Pa., 1951. Bar: N.Y. 1952, D.C. 1985. Assoc. Donovan, Leisure, Newton, Lumbard & Irvine, N.Y.C., 1951-52; assoc. Nixon, Hargrave, Devans & Doyle, Rochester, N.Y., 1952-62, ptnr., 1963-92; retired, 1992. Author: Constitutional Privilege in Libel Law, 1977-90. Served to lt. comdr. USNR, 1943-47, PTO. Fellow Am. Coll. Trial Lawyers; mem. ABA, Monroe County Bar Assn., N.Y. State Bar Assn., D.C. Bar Assn. Republican. Presbyterian. Home: 210 Whitewood Ln Rochester NY 14618-3226 Office: Nixon Hargrave Devans & Doyle LLP Clinton Sq PO Box 1051 Rochester NY 14603-1051

MCCRORY, PATRICK, mayor; b. Columbus, Oct. 17, 1956; m. Ann Gordon. BA in Polit. Sci. and Edn., Catawba Coll., 1978. With Duke Power Co., N.C., 1978—, now mgr. bus. rels.; mem. Charlotte City Coun., N.C., 1989—, mayor protem, 1993-95, mayor, 1995—. Co-chmn. Charlotte's Fighting Back Commn.; mem. Children Svcs. Network; hon. chmn. Cystic Fibrosis Found., Arthritis Found.; former chmn. United Way Corp. Campaign; former mem. U. N.C.-Charlotte Bus. Adv. Com., Charlotte Bond Campaign, ARC Pers. Recruitment Com.; H.S. basketball ofcl.; former bd. dirs. Drug Free Workplace Alliance Com.; founder Uptown Crime Prevention Coun. Office: Office of the Mayor 600 E 4th St Charlotte NC 28202

MCCRORY, ROBERT LEE, physicist, mechanical engineering educator; b. Lawton, Okla., Apr. 30, 1946; s. Robert Lee Sr. and Marjorie Marie (Garrett) McC.; m. Betsey Christine Wahl, June 14, 1969; children: Katherine Anne, John Damon, George Garrett. BSc, MIT, 1968, PhD, 1973. Physicist Los Alamos Nat. Lab., Albuquerque, 1973-76; scientist, coleader Lab. for Laser Energetics, U. Rochester, N.Y., 1976-77, sr. scientist, 1977—, dir. theoretical dir., 1979-90; dir. Lab. for Laser Energetics, U. Rochester, 1983—; assoc. prof. of physics and astronomy U. Rochester, 1980, prof. of mech. engring., 1983—. Author: Laser Plasma Interactions, 1989, Computer Applications in Plasma Science and Engineering, 1991; contbr. articles to profl. publs. Alfred P. Simon scholar, 1964-67; AEC fellow, 1985; recipient Edward Teller medal, 1994. Fellow Am. Phys. Soc. (mem. fellowship com., mem. exec. com. div. plasma physics, Excellence in Plasma Physics award). Office: U Rochester Lab Laser Energetics 250 E River Rd Rochester NY 14623-1212

MC CRORY, WALLACE WILLARD, pediatrician, educator; b. Racine, Wis., Jan. 19, 1920; s. Willard L. and Beulah (St. Clair) McC.; m. Sylvia E. Hogben, Feb. 6, 1943; children—Pamela, Michael, Christine. B.S., U. Wis., 1941, M.D., 1944. Diplomate: Am. Bd. Pediatrics. Rotating intern Phila. Gen. Hosp., 1944-45; resident pediatrics Children's Hosp., Phila., 1945-46; chief resident physician Children's Hosp., 1948-49, asso. pediatrician, 1953-55, sr. pediatrician, 1955-58; provisional asst. pediatrician to out-patients, Lewis Cass Ledyard, Jr. fellow pediatrics N.Y. Hosp., 1949-50, pediatrician-in-chief, 1961-80, sr. pediatrician, chief pediatric nephrology, 1980—; chief pediatric service Univ. Hosp., Iowa City, 1958-61; instr. pathology U. Wis. Med. Sch., 1942-43; instr. pediatrics U. Pa. Sch. Medicine, 1948-49, instr., research fellow pediatrics, 1950-53, asst. prof., 1953-55, asso. prof., 1955-58; prof. pediatrics, chmn. dept. State U. Iowa Coll. Medicine, 1958-61; prof. pediatrics Cornell U. Med. Coll., 1961—. Pres. Nat. Kidney Found., 1964-66. Served to capt., M.C. AUS, 1946-48. Fellow N.Y. Acad. Medicine, Royal Soc. Medicine; mem. Am. Pediatric Soc., Am. Acad. Pediatrics, Soc. Pediatric Research, Am. Soc. Nephrology, Am. Soc. Pediatric Nephrology, AAAS, Sigma Xi, Alpha Omega Alpha. Home: 171 Salem Rd Pound Ridge NY 10576-1324 Office: NY Hosp Cornell Med Ctr 525 E 68th St New York NY 10021-4873

MCCROSKEY, WILLIAM JAMES, aeronautical engineer; b. San Angelo, Tex., Mar. 9, 1937; s. J. M. and W. Elizabeth (Adams) McC.; m. Elizabeth W. Wear, Jan. 31, 1960; children: Nancy E., Susan C. BS, U. Tex., 1960; MS, Princeton U., 1962, PhD, 1966. Rsch. assoc. Princeton U., 1966; rsch. engr. U.S. Army Aeromechanics Lab., Moffett Field, Calif., 1966-80; sr. rsch. scientist U.S. Army and NASA Aerophysics Directorate, 1980—; exch. scientist Office Nat. Etudes et Recherches Aérosspatiale, Châtillon, France, 1972-73; mem. fluid dynamics panel NATO Adv. Group for Aerospace R & D, 1976-94, chmn., 1989-91. With U.S. Army, 1966-68. Recipient French Medaille l'Aeronautique, 1994, AGARD von Kármán medal, 1995, Nat. Acad. Engring., 1996. Fellow AIAA (Outstanding Engr. San Francisco sect. 1975, fluid dynamics tech com. 1984-88, internat. activities com. 1990—); mem. ASME (Freeman scholar award 1976), Am. Helicopter Soc. (Howard Hughes award 1991). Office: Ames Rsch Ctr N258-1 Moffett Field CA 94035

MCCUAN, WILLIAM PATRICK, real estate company executive; b. Muskogee, Okla., Oct. 28, 1941; s. Lee L. and LaRee A. (Beverage) McC.; m. Jill Pamela Thomas, May 5, 1982; children: LaRee, Megan. Student, U. Tulsa, 1961-62; BA in Psychology, Baylor U., 1965; MRE, So. Sem., Louisville, 1967; MS, U. Louisville, 1969; postgrad., U. Md., 1971-73. Prof., asst. dean grad. sch. U. Md., Balt., 1969-73; lobbyist, cons. Washington, 1973-76; chmn. bd. KMS Group, Inc., Columbia, Md., 1976-84; CEO MGD Cos. of Naples, Fla., 1994—, MDG Cos. of Md.; chmn. bd. Tuscasrora Real Estate Corp., Berkeley Springs, W.Va., 1991—; adj. prof. Cmty. Coll., Balt., 1969-72, U. Md. College Park, 1969-71; lectr. Univ. Coll.-Univ. Md., Balt., 1970-71, Howard C.C., Columbia, 1987-88; chmn. Pet Holiday, Inc., Toledo, 1973-94; CEO Uniglobe Columbia Travel Ctr., 1986-94; non-lawyer mem. Atty. Grievance Commn., Md., 1990-96. Contbr. to numerous publs. Chmn., bd. dirs. Concert Soc. Md., 1988—; chmn. United Way, Howard County, Md., 1984, Am. Presdl. Inaugural Com., Md., 1988, Howard County Cmty. Partnerships; fin. chmn. Rep. Ctrl. Com., Howard County, 1988-92; trustee Columbia Found., Howard County; mem. Pres.'s Commn. on Food, Nutrition and Health, Washington, 1970, Howard County Environ. Affairs Bd., Columbia Archives Com.; mem. bus. adv. coun. Howard C.C.; bd. dirs. Congl. Commn. on Mental Health of Children, Washington, 1973-75, Human Svcs. Inst. for Children & Families. Mem. Nat. Assn. Home Builders (bd. dirs. 1979-87, fed. govt. affairs com.), Md. Builders Assn. (pres. 1981-82), Home Builders Assn. Md. (bd. dirs. 1977-82, Award of Honor 1979, Award of Excellence 1980, Presdl. award 1982), Howard County Home Builders Assn. (pres. 1978-80), Howard County C. of C. (pres. bd. dirs. 1984-86). Home: 11838 Farside Rd Ellicott City MD 21042-1526 Office: MDG Bldg 5550 Sterrett Pl Columbia MD 21044-2611

MCCUBBIN, SHARON ANGLIN, elementary school educator; b. Fullerton, Calif., Nov. 20, 1948; d. Floyd Calvin and Grace Ann Anglin; m. David Paul White (div. 1990); children: Julie, Adrian, Matthew; m. Robert Patrick McCubbin, July 13, 1991. BA, U. Calif., 1973; MEd, Cleveland State U., 1993. Cert. clear multiple subject profl. pre-K, Calif., elem. Montessori tchr., early childhood edn. Tchr. Primanti Montessori, Orange, Calif., 1977-81; tchr., adminstr. Montessori of Orange, 1981-83, Tustin Hills Montessori, Santa Ana, Calif., 1983-89; tchr., cons. for Montessori programs Irvine (Calif.) Unified Sch. Dist., 1990—; Montessori elem. mentor tchr., 1990—; cons. title VII programs Irvine Unified Sch. Dist., 1990—, GATE adv. bd. mem.; cons. for early childhood programs to local corps. Asst. Jr. Disabled Programs, Orange, 1988—. Mem. ASCD, AAUW, Assn. Montessori Internat., Assn. Montessori Internat./U.S.A., Assn. Montessori Internat. Elem. Alumni Assn. (regional rep. 1984), Am. Montessori Soc., N.Am. Montessori Tchrs. Assn., Pvt. Sch. Adminstrs., U. Calif.-Irvine Alumni Assn., Calif. Tchrs. Assn., Irvine Tchrs. Assn. Home: 19082 Ervin Ln Santa Ana CA 92705-2828 Office: Irvine Unified Sch Dist 5050 Barranca Pky Irvine CA 92714-4652 also: Santiago Hills Elem 29 Christamon W Irvine CA 92720-1836

MCCUBBIN, SUSAN BRUBECK, real estate executive, lawyer; b. Decatur, Ill., Mar. 16, 1948; d. Rodney Earl Brubeck and Marilyn Jean (McMahon) Hopkins; 1 child, Martin Charles Jr.; m. William James McCubbin, May 30, 1987. LLB, Western State U., Fullerton, Calif., 1977. Bar: CAlif. 1977; lic. real estate broker, Calif. Ptnr. Blue Chip Constrn. Co., Santa Ana, Calif., 1969-73; pres. Brubeck Co., San Francisco and Newport Beach, Calif., 1973-78; sole practice San Francisco, 1978-79; sr. mktg. cons., broker Grubb & Ellis Co., San Francisco, 1979-87; pres. Greenwich Corp., San Rafael, Calif., 1987—; broker assoc. Fox & Carskadon, Mill Valley, Calif. Columnist Automotive Age Mag., 1974-75. Chmn. U.S. Senate Primary Campaign, Orange County, Calif., 1976. Republican. Avocations: computers/videography, tennis, historical study, travel, music.

MC CUE, CAROLYN MOORE, retired pediatric cardiologist; b. Richmond, Va., June 26, 1916; d. Thomas Justin and Caroline (Willingham) Moore; m. Howard M. McCue, Jr., Apr. 5, 1941; children—Carolyn McCue Osteen, Howard McDowell. Student, Wellesley Coll., 1933-35; A.B., Leland Stanford U., 1937; M.D., Med. Coll. Va., 1941. Intern Wis. Gen. Hosp., Madison, 1941-42; resident in pediatrics Children's Hosp., Phila., 1942-43, Med. Coll. Va., 1946-47; dir. pediatric cardiology Med. Coll. Va., Richmond, 1947-81; prof. pediatrics Med. Coll. Va., 1963-91; clin. dir. pediatric cardiology clinics State of Va., 1958-81. Contbr. articles to profl. jours. Named Va. Laureate, 1982. Fellow Am. Acad. Pediatrics, Am. Coll. Physicians, Am. Coll. Cardiology, A.C.P.; mem. Richmond Acad. Medicine (pres. 1975), Richmond Area Heart Assn. (pres. 1959-60), Phi Beta Kappa, Alpha Omega Alpha. Club: Country of Va. Home: 12 Huntley Rd Richmond VA 23226-3306

MCCUE, GERALD MALLON, architect; b. Woodland, Calif., Dec. 5, 1928; s. Floyd F. and Lenore (Mallon) McC.; m. Barbara Walrond, Sept. 1, 1951; children: Scott, Mark, Kent. BA, U. Calif. at Berkeley, 1951, MA, 1952; MA (hon.), Harvard U., 1977. Ptnr. archtl. firm Milano-McCue, Berkeley, Calif., 1953-54; pres. Gerald M. McCue & Assocs., Berkeley, 1954-70, McCue, Boone, Tomsick, San Francisco, 1970-76; prin. MBT Assocs., San Francisco, 1976-80; faculty U. Calif. at Berkeley, 1954-76; prof. architecture and urban design U. Calif. at Berkeley, 1966-76; chmn. dept. U. Calif. at Berkeley, 1966-71; prof. architecture/urban design, chmn. dept. and assoc. dean Grad. Sch. Design Harvard U., 1976-80, dean, 1980-92; John T. Dunlop prof. housing studies Sch. Design and Kennedy Sch. Govt., Harvard U., 1992-96. Planning and designn commns. executed for variety pub. and pvt. clients with over 30 nat., regional and local design awards. Fellow AIA, Urban Land Inst. Office: Harvard U Grad Sch Design 48 Quincy St Cambridge MA 02138-3000

MCCUE, HOWARD MCDOWELL, III, lawyer, educator; b. Sumter, S.C., Jan. 4, 1946; s. Howard McDowell and Carolyn Hartwell (Moore) McC.; m. Judith Weiss, Apr. 3, 1972; children—Howard McDowell IV, Leigh. A.B., Princeton U., 1968; J.D., Harvard U., 1971. Bar: Mass. 1971, Ill. 1975, U.S. Tax Ct. 1977. Assoc. Hale and Dorr, Boston, 1971-72; assoc. Mayer, Brown & Platt, Chgo., 1975-77, ptnr., 1977—; adj. prof. law master in tax program Chgo. Kent Coll. Law, 1981—. Author: (with others) Drafting Wills and Trust Agreements, 1979, 82, 85, 87, 90; mem. editorial adv. bd. Trusts and Estates mag., 1981—; contbr. articles to profl. jours. Bd. dirs. Art Inst. Chgo., Lawrence Hall Youth Svcs., Northwestern U. Libr. Coun.; bd. dirs., vice chmn. Ravinia Festival Assn. Lt. USN, 1972-75. Princeton U. scholar, 1965. Mem. ABA, Ill. Bar Assn., Chgo. Bar Assn. (fed. tax com., past chmn., exec. coun.), Chgo. Bar Found. (bd. dirs., past pres.), Am. Coll. Tax Counsel, Am. Coll. Trust and Estate Counsel, Harvard Law Soc. Ill., Internat. Acad. Estate and Trust Law, Chgo. Club, Kenilworth Club, Phi Beta Kappa. Office: Mayer Brown & Platt 190 S La Salle St Chicago IL 60603-3410

MCCUE, JUDITH W., lawyer; b. Phila., Apr. 7, 1948; d. Emanuel Leo and Rebecca (Raffel) Weiss; m. Howard M. McCue III, Apr. 3, 1971; children: Howard, Leigh. BA cum laude, U. Pa., 1969; JD, Harvard U., 1972. Bar: Ill. 1972, U.S. Tax Ct. 1984. Ptnr. McDermott, Will & Emery, Chgo., 1995—; dir. Schawk, Inc., Des Plaines, Ill.; sec., dir. Chgo. Estate Planning Coun. Trustee The Orchestral Assn., 1995—. Fellow Am. Coll. Trust and Estate Counsel (com. chair 1991-94, regent 1993—); mem. Chgo. Bar Assn. (chmn. probate practice com. 1984-85, chmn. fed. estate and gift tax divsn. fed. tax com. 1988-89). Office: McDermott Will & Emery 227 W Monroe St Chicago IL 60606-5096

MCCUEN, JOHN FRANCIS, JR., lawyer; b. N.Y.C., Mar. 11, 1944; s. John Francis Sr. and Elizabeth Agnes (Corbett) McC.; children: Sarah, Mary, John. AB, U. Notre Dame, 1966; JD, U. Detroit, 1969. Bar: Mich. 1970, Fla. 1970, Ohio 1978. Legal counsel Kelsey-Hayes Co., Romulus, Mich., 1970-77; corp. counsel Sheller-Globe Corp., Toledo, 1977-79; v.p., gen. counsel Sheller-Globe Corp., 1979-86, sec., 1982-87, sr. v.p. gen. counsel, 1986-89; ptnr. Marshall & Melhorn, Toledo, 1989-92; pvt. practice Law Offices John F. McCuen, Toledo, 1992-93; counsel Butzel Long, Ann Arbor, Mich., 1994; v.p. legal Kelsey Hayes Co., Livonia, Mich., 1994—; bd. dirs. Preferred Rubber Compounding Corp. Trustee Kidney Found. N.W. Ohio, 1979-88, pres., 1984-86. Mem. ABA, Fla. Bar, Mich. Bar, Inverness Club. Home: 2734 Winter Garden Ct Ann Arbor MI 48105-2952 Office: Kelsey Hayes Co 11878 Hubbard St Livonia MI 48150-1733

MCCUEN, JOHN JOACHIM, financial company executive; b. Washington, Mar. 30, 1926; s. Joseph Raymond and Josephine (Joachim) McC.; m. Gloria Joyce Seidel, June 16, 1949; children: John Joachim Jr., Les Seidel. BS, U.S. Mil. Acad., 1948; M of Internatl. Affairs, Columbia U., 1961; grad., U.S. Army War Coll., 1968. Commd. 2d. lt. U.S. Army, 1948, advanced through grades to col.; dir. internal def. and devel. U.S. Army War Coll., Carlisle Barracks, Pa., 1969-72; chief U.S. Def. Liaison Group, Jakarta, Indonesia, 1972-74; chief field survey office U.S. Army Tng. and Doctrine Command, Ft. Monroe, Va., 1974-76; ret. U.S. Army, 1976; mgr. tng. Chrysler Def., Center Line, Mich., 1977-82; mgr. modification ctr. Land Systems div. Gen. Dynamics, Sterling Heights, Mich., 1982-83; mgr. field ops. Land Systems div. Gen. Dynamics, Warren, Mich., 1983-94; pres. Mich. Econ. Devel. Corp., Birmingham, 1994—, The Magic Christmas Tree, Inc., Birmingham, 1994—; owner Adventure and Exotic Travel Outfitters, Inc., Birmingham, 1995—; pres. First Internat. Corp., Birmingham, 1995—; ptnr. East West Connection, Birmingham, Mich.; past pres. Energy Resource Mgmt. Sys., Inc., Birmingham; armor advisor 3d Royal Thai Army, Utaradit, 1957-58; U.S. rep. users' com. NATO Missile Firing Installation Crete, Paris, 1964-66; advisor Vietnamese Nat. Def. Coll., Saigon, 1968-69; spkr. on terrorism and counter insurgency. Author: The Art of Counter Revolutionary War-The Strategy of Counter Insurgency, Faber 1966, Stackpole, 1967, Circulo Militar, 1967. Pres. Troy (Mich.) Cmty. Concert Assn., 1985—, bd. dirs., 1992; past pres. Mich. Oriental Art Soc., Birmingham; pres. Grander View Found. Sr. Housing and Nursing, Milford, Mich., 1984—; past 1st reader First Ch. of Christ Scientist, Birmingham, 1989-92; past chmn. region VI N.E. unit Detroit United Way Campaign. Mem. Soc. Logistics Engrs., Nat. Mgmt. Assn., Assn. U.S. Army, Oriental Art Soc. Republican. Avocation: collecting and selling Oriental antiques, lecturing on terrorism and national security. Home: 32863 Balmoral St Beverly Hills MI 48025-3008 Office: Mich Econ Devel Corp 700 E Maple Rd Ste 203 Birmingham MI 48009

MCCUISTION, PEG OREM, hospice administrator; b. Houston, July 28, 1930; d. William Darby and Dorothy Mildred (Beckett) Orem; m. Palmer Day McCuistion, Sept. 4, 1949 (div. 1960); 1 child, Leeanne E. BBA, Southwest Tex. State, 1963; MBA, George Washington U., 1968; EdD, Wayne State U., 1989. Patient care adminstr. Holy Cross Hosp., Silver Spring, Md., 1968-79; exec. dir. Hospice of S.E. Mich., Southfield, 1979-86, Hospice Austin, Tex., 1987-94; CEO EMBI, Inc., Arlington, Tex., 1994—. Bd. dirs. Cmty. Home for the Elderly, Austin, 1989-92. Fellow Am. Coll. Health Care Execs. (membership com.); mem. Internat. Hospice Inst. (assoc.), Nat. Hospice Orgn. (chair standards and accreditation com.), Tex. Hospice Orgn. (pres. 1993-94), exec. com., standards and ethics com., edn. com., chair legis. com.), Mich. Hospice Orgn. (chair edn. com., bd. dirs.). Office: Embi Inc 511 Chaffee Dr Arlington TX 76006-2009

MCCUISTION, ROBERT WILEY, lawyer, hospital administrator, management consultant; b. Wilson, Ark., June 15, 1927; s. Ed Talmadge and Ruth Wiley (Bassett) McC.; m. Martha Virginia Golden, June 11, 1949 (dec. Nov. 1991); children: Beth, Dan, Jed.; m. Sudola M. Getz, Feb. 12, 1994. A.B. in History and Polit. Sci, Hendrix Coll., Conway, Ark., 1949; J.D., U. Ark., 1952. Bar: Ark. 1952. Practice in Dermott, Ark., 1952-57; dep. pros. atty. 10th Jud. Dist. Ark., 1953-57; bus. mgr. St. Mary's Hosp., Dermott, 1953-56, asst. adminstr., 1956-57; adminstr. Stuttgart (Ark.) Meml. Hosp., 1957-60, Forrest Meml. Hosp., Forrest City, Ark., 1960-68; assoc. adminstr. St. Edward Mercy Hosp., Ft. Smith, Ark., 1968-70; pres. Meml. Med Center, Corpus Christi, Tex., 1970-79; adminstr. Methodist Hosp., Mitchell, S.D., 1979-85, cons., 1985-86; mgmt. cons., owner Creative Leadership Concepts, Arlington, Tex., 1985—; adminstr. Cen. United Meth. Ch., Fayetteville, 1986-91; sec. Ark. Hosp. Adminstrs. Forum, 1958-59, pres., 1959-60; pres. Ark. Hosp. Assn., 1964-65, Areawide Health Planning, 1970; pres. Ark. Conf. Cath. Hosps., 1970; chmn. Twin City Hosp. Council, 1968; v.p. Ark. Assn. Mental Health, 1966-70. Div. chmn. Forrest City United Community Svcs., 1961, Corpus Christi United Way Community Svcs., 1972, DeSoto coun. Boy Scouts Am., Explorer adviser, 1954-57. With USAAF, World War II. Recipient Eminent Leadership award DeSoto Area council Boy Scouts Am., 1956. Mem. Am. Assn. Hosp. Accountants (pres. Ark. chpt. 1957), S.D. Hosp. Assn. (dist. chmn. 1980-81), Mid-West Hosp. Assn. (trustee 1963-65), Am. Coll. Health Execs. (life). Methodist (vice chmn., sec. ofcl. bd. 1957, lay del. S.D. ann. conf. 1980-85). Lodge: Rotary (pres. Forrest City 1964-65). Home and Office: 1912 S Saint Andrews Ct Arlington TX 76011-3251

MCCULLAGH, GRANT GIBSON, architect; b. Cleve., Apr. 18, 1951; s. Robert Ernest and Barbara Louise (Grant) McC.; m. Suzanne Dewar Folds, Sept. 13, 1975; children: Charles Weston Folds, Grant Gibson Jr. BArch, U. Ill., 1973; MArch, U. Pa., 1975; MBA, U. Chgo., 1979. Registered architect, Ill. Project designer Perkins & Will, Chgo., 1975-77; dir. mktg. The Austin Co., Chgo., 1977-83, asst. dist. mgr., 1983-84, dist. mgr., 1984-88, v.p., 1987-88; chmn., chief exec. officer McClier Corp., Chgo., 1988—. Contbr. articles to various indsl. publs. Bd. dirs. Friends of Prentice Hosp. Mem. FAIA, Chgo. Architecture Found. (pres. 1988-91, adv. bd. trustee 1994—, dir. Design/Build Inst. Am. 1994—, treas. 1995-96), Econ. Club, Chgo. Club, Comml. Club, Casino Club, Univ. Club, Indian Hill Country Club. Republican. Episcopalian. Home: 43 Locust Rd Winnetka IL 60093-3725 Office: McClier Corp 401 E Illinois St Chicago IL 60611-4363

MCCULLAGH, JAMES CHARLES, publishing company executive; b. London, Oct. 22, 1941; s. James Christopher and Violet Anne (Smith) McC.; children: Declan, Deirdre. BS, Ind. U. Pa., 1968; MA, Lehigh U., 1970, PhD, 1974. Tchr. Holidaysburg (Pa.) Area High Sch., 1968; teaching asst. Lehigh U., Bethlehem, Pa., 1968-71, doctoral fellow, 1971-73; vis. poet Pa. Council on Arts Inc., Harrisburg, 1974-78; editor Rodale Press Inc., Emaus, Pa., 1979-83, pub., editor dir., group v.p., 1984—; pub. Novii Fermer, USSR, 1991—; pub. dir. Scuba Diving, 1992; sr. v.p. Internat. Mag. Devel.; mng. dir. Rodale Press, Inc., Russia, 1996—. Author: Bicycle Fitness Book, 1984,

Bicycling for Health and Fitness, 1995, Cycling for Health, Fitness and Well-Being, 1995, (poetry) That Kingdom Coming Business, 1984; pub.: Mountain Bike, 1994. Served with USN, 1960-64. Recipient Man of Yr. award Bicycle Mfrs. Assn. Am., Washington, 1983. Mem. Am. Assn. Mag. Editors, Mag. Pubs. Assn., Bicycle Fedn. (bd. dirs. 1980—), Bicycle Inst. Am. (pres. 1993—). Democrat. Roman Catholic. Avocations: cycling, running. Home: PO Box 265A PO Box 265A 4040 Lower Saucon Rd RD #1 Hellertown PA 18055

MC CULLOCH, ERNEST ARMSTRONG, physician, educator; b. Toronto, Ont., Can., Apr. 27, 1926; s. Albert E. and Letitia (Riddell) McC.; m. Ona Mary Morganty, 1953; children: James A., Michael E., Robert E., Cecelia E., Paul A. M.D. with honors, U. Toronto, 1948. Intern Toronto Gen. Hosp., 1949-50, sr. intern, 1951-52; NRC fellow dept. pathology U. Toronto, 1950-51; asst. resident Sunnybrook Hosp., Toronto, 1952-53; pvt. practice specializing in internal medicine Toronto, 1954-67; clin. tchr. dept. medicine U. Toronto, 1954-60, asst. prof. dept. med. biophysics, 1959-64, assoc. prof., 1964-66, prof., 1966, asst. prof. dept. medicine, 1967-68, assoc. prof., 1968-70, prof., 1970—, univ. prof., 1982-91, univ. prof. emeritus, 1991—; mem. grad. faculty U. Toronto (Inst. Med. Sci.), 1968—; dir. Inst. Med. Sci. U. Toronto, 1975-79, asst. dean Sch. Grad. Studies, 1979-82; physician Toronto Gen. Hosp., 1960-67; sr. scientist, sr. physician Ont. Cancer Inst., 1957-91, head divsn. biol. rsch., 1982-89, head divsn. cell and molecular biology, 1989-91, sr. scientist emeritus, 1991-93; vis. prof. U. Tex. Med. Ctr. Anderson Cancer Ctr., Houston, 1992-93, adj. prof., 1993—; cons. Nat. Cancer Plan, 1972—; mem. standing com. on health rsch. and devel. Ont. Coun. Health, 1974-82. Author numerous articles on research in hematology; editorial bd.: Blood, 1969-80, Biomedicine, 1973, Clin. Immunology and Immunopathology, 1972-76; assoc. editor: Jour. Cellular Physiology, 1966-68; editor, 1968-91. Trustee Banting Rsch. Found., 1975-84, hon. sec.-treas., 1958-74, v.p., 1977-79. Decorated officer Order of Can., 1988; recipient William Goldie prize U. Toronto, 1964, Ann. Gairdner award Internat. Gairdner Found., 1969, Starr Medallist award Dept. Anatomy U. Toronto, 1957; Thomas W. Eadie Medal, 1991, Royal Soc. Canada, Nat. Cancer Inst. Can. fellow, 1954-57. Fellow Royal Soc. Can. (pres. Acad. Sci. 1987-90, Thomas W. Eadie Medal 1991), Royal Coll. Physicians and Surgeons Can.; mem. Can. Acad. Sci., Am. Soc. Exptl. Pathology, Am. Assn. Cancer Rsch., Can. Soc. Cell Biology, Can. Soc. Clin. Investigation, Am., Internat. socs. hematology, Internat. Soc. Exptl. Hematology, Inst. Acad. Medicine (charter mem.). Clubs: Badminton, Racquet. Home: 480 Summerhill Ave, Toronto, ON Canada M4W 2E4 Office: 610 University Ave, Toronto, ON Canada M5G 2M9 *Research success depends on associating with agreeable and talented people.*

MCCULLOCH, JAMES CALLAHAN, manufacturing company executive; b. Pittsfield, Mass., Aug. 20, 1947; s. G. Robert and Marion Elizabeth (Callahan) McC.; m. Patricia A. Greene, Dec. 28, 1970; children: William Brennan, Patrick Callahan, Daniel Daly, Peter Brennan, James Callahan II. BS in Commerce, St. Louis U., 1969, MS in Commerce, 1970. With Ford Motor Co., 1970-72; group contr. Chemetron Corp., 1972-80; corp. contr. Six Flags Corp., L.A., 1980-82; v.p. fin. and planning Indsl. Controls Group Allen-Bradley Co., Milw., 1982-86; v.p., chief fin. officer and treas. Sybron Corp., Saddle Brook, N.J., 1986-87, also bd. dirs.; pres. McCulloch Investments, Madison, N.J., 1987—; bd. dirs. Summit Industries, Chgo. Mem. Fin. Exec. Inst., Morris County Golf Club. Republican. Office: McCulloch Investments 14 Main St Ste 200 Madison NJ 07940-1818

MCCULLOCH, RACHEL, economics researcher, educator; b. Bklyn., June 26, 1942; d. Henry and Rose (Offen) Preiss; m. Gary Edward Chamberlain; children: Laura Meressa, Neil Dudley. BA, U. Pa., 1962; MA in Teaching, U. Chgo., 1965, MA, 1971, PhD, 1973; student, MIT, 1966-67. Economist Cabinet Task Force on Oil Import Control, Washington, 1969; instr., then asst. prof. Grad. Sch. Bus. U. Chgo., 1971-73; asst. prof., then assoc. prof. econs. Harvard U., Cambridge, Mass., 1973-79; assoc. prof., then prof. econs. U. Wis., Madison, 1979-87; prof. Brandeis U., Waltham, Mass., 1987—, Rosen Family prof., 1989—, dir. Lemberg Program in Internat. Econs. and Fin., 1990-91, dir. PhD program Grad. Sch. Internat. Econs. and Fin., 1994—; mem. Pres.'s Commn. on Indsl. Competitiveness, 1983-84; mem. adv. coun. Office Tech. Assessment U.S. Congress, 1979-88; cons. World Bank, Washington, 1984-86; mem. com. on internat. rels. studies with People's Republic of China, 1984-91; rsch. assoc. Nat. Bur. Econ. Rsch., Cambridge, 1985-93; mem. adv. com. Inst. for Internat. Econs., Washington, 1987—; faculty Advanced Mgmt. Network, La Jolla, Calif., 1985-92; mem. com. examiners econs. test Grad. Record Exam. Ednl. Testing Svc., 1990-96, chair, 1992-96; mem. discipline adv. com. for Fulbright scholar awards in econs. Coun. Internat. Exch. Scholars, 1991-93, chair, 1992-93; cons. Global Economy Project, Edn. Film Ctr., 1993-94; mem. study group on pvt. capital flows to developing and transitional economies Coun. Fgn. Rels., 1995—. Author: Research and Development as a Determinant of U.S. International Competitiveness, 1978; contbr. articles to profl. jours. and books. Grantee NSF, 1975-79, Hoover Inst., 1984-85, German Marshall Fund of U.S., 1985, Ford Found., 1985-88, U.S. Dept. Edn., 1990-91. Mem. Am. Econ. Assn. (dir. summer program for minority students 1983-84), Internat. Trade and Fin. Assn. (bd. dirs. 1993-95), New England Women Economists Assn. Home: 10 Frost Rd Lexington MA 02173-1904 Office: Brandeis U Dept Econs Waltham MA 02254

MC CULLOCH, SAMUEL CLYDE, history educator; b. Ararat, Australia, Sept. 3, 1916; came to U.S., 1936, naturalized, 1944; s. Samuel and Agnes Almond (Clyde) McC.; m. Sara Ellen Rand, Feb. 19, 1944; children: Ellen (Mrs. William Henry Meyer III), David Rand, Malcolm Clyde. A.B. with highest honors in History, UCLA, 1940, M.A. (grad. fellow history), 1942; Ph.D., U. Calif. at Los Angeles, 1944. Asst. U. Calif. at Los Angeles, 1943-44; instr. Oberlin Coll., 1944-45; asst. prof. Amherst Coll., 1945-46; vis. asst. prof. U. Mich., 1946-47; mem. faculty Rutgers U., 1947-60, prof. history, assoc. dean arts and scis., 1958-60; dean coll., prof. history San Francisco State Coll., 1960-63; dean humanities, prof. history U. Calif. at Irvine, 1963-70, prof., 1970-87, prof. emeritus, 1987—, coordinator Edn. Abroad Program, 1975-85, dir. Australian Study Ctr., 1986, 87; vis. summer prof. Oberlin Coll., 1945, 46, U. Calif. at Los Angeles, 1947, U. Del., 1949; Fulbright Research prof. Monash U., Melbourne (Australia) U., 1970; Am. Philos. Soc. grantee, 1970. Author: British Humanitarianism, 1950, George Gipps, 1966, River King: The Mc Culloch Carrying Company and Echura, 1865-1898, 1986, Instant University: A History of U.C.I., 1957-1993, 1995, numerous articles, revs.; assoc. editor Jour. Brit. Studies, 1960-68, bd. advisors, 1968-70; bd. corrs. Hist. Studies: Australia and New Zealand, 1949-83. Mem. Calif. Curriculum Commn., 1961-67, Highland Park (N.J.) Bd. Edn., 1959-60. Grantee Am. Philos. Soc., Social Sci. Research Council and Rutgers U. Research Council to Australia, 1951; Fulbright research fellow U. Sydney, Australia, 1954-55; grantee Social Sci. Research Council to Eng., summer 1955. Fellow Royal Hist. Soc.; mem. Am. Hist. Assn., Church, Royal Australian hist. socs., A.A.U.P., Conf. Brit. Studies (exec. sec. 1968-73, pres. 1975-77), English Speaking Union (pres. New Brunswick 1957-59), Phi Beta Kappa, Pi Gamma Mu. Episcopalian (vestry). Home: 2121 Windward Ln Newport Beach CA 92660-3820 Office: Dept of History Univ of California Irvine CA 92717

MCCULLOCH, WILLIAM LEONARD, trade association administrator; b. Providence, Mar. 11, 1921; s. William Fraser and Elsie Cornelia (Westeberg) McC.; m. Dolores Ione Collier, July 26, 1952; children—William Fraser, II, Bruce Collier. B.S., U.S. Naval Acad., 1945; M.A. in Internat. Relations, Georgetown U., 1958. Commd. 2d lt. USMC, 1944, advanced through grades to brig. gen., 1971; service in Okinawa, China, Korea and Vietnam; comdg. gen. (1st Marine Div.), 1974-75; congl. aide, 1975-76; exec. dir. Am. Assn. Orthotists and Prosthetists, Washington, 1976-86; pres. nat. office Orthotics and Prosthetics, 1986-88; pres. Assn. Communications and Mktg. Svcs., Washington, 1988—; bd. dirs. Hanger Orthopedic Group. Decorated Legion of Merit with 2 stars, Bronze Star. Mem. Am. Soc. Assn. Execs., U.S. Naval Acad. Class of 1945 Assn. (pres. 1979-80), U.S. Naval Acad. Athletic Assn., Ret. Officers Assn., Capitol Hill Club (Washington), Army-Navy Country Club (Arlington, Va.), Marine Meml. Club (San Francisco), Army and Navy Club (pres.). Republican. Presbyterian. Home and Office: 528 Ft Williams Pky Alexandria VA 22304-1849

MCCULLOH, JUDITH MARIE, editor; b. Spring Valley, Ill., Aug. 16, 1935; d. Henry A. and Edna Mae (Traub) Binkele; m. Leon Royce McCulloh, Aug. 26, 1961. BA, Ohio Wesleyan U., 1956; MA, Ohio State U., 1957; PhD, Ind. U., 1970. Asst. to dir. Archives of Traditional Music, Bloomington, Ind., 1964-65; asst. editor U. Ill. Press, Champaign, 1972-77, assoc. editor, 1977-82, sr. editor, 1982-85, exec. editor, 1985—, dir. devel., 1992—; advisor John Edwards Meml. Forum, Los Angeles, 1973—. Mem. Editorial Bd. Jour. Am. Folklore, Washington, 1986-90; co-editor Stars of Country Music, 1975; editor (LP) Green Fields of Ill., 1963, (LP) Hell-Bound Train, 1964, Ethnic Recordings in America, 1982; gen. editor Music in America Life series. Trustee Am. Folklife Ctr., Libr. of Congress, Washington, 1986—, chair, 1996—. Fulbright grantee, 1958-59; NDEA grantee, 1961, 62-63; grantee Nat. Endowment for the Humanities, 1978; Disting. Achievement citation Ohio Wesleyan U. Alumni Assn. Fellow Am. Folklore Soc. (pres. 1986-87), Soc. for Ethnomusicology (treas. 1982-86), Sonneck Soc. (1st v.p. 1989-93), Women in Scholarly Pub., Am. Anthropological Assn. Democrat. Office: U Ill Press 1325 S Oak St Champaign IL 61820-6903

MCCULLOUGH, BENJAMIN FRANKLIN, transportation researcher, educator; b. Austin, Mar. 25, 1934; s. Benjamin Franklin and Mabel Comelia (Kitteridge) McC.; m. Norma Jean Walsh, Sept. 1, 1956; children: Michael Wayne, Bryan Scott, Steven Todd, Franklin Norman, Melanie Jean. MSCE, U. Tex., 1962; PhD of Civil Engring., U. Calif., Berkeley, 1969. Registered profl. engr., Tex. Testing engr. Covair Aircraft Co., Ft. Worth, 1957; design and rsch. engr. Tex. Hwy. Dept., Austin, 1957-66; rsch. engr. Materials R&D, Inc., Oakland, Calif., 1966-68; from asst. to prof. U. Tex., Austin, 1969—, dir. transp. rsch., 1980—. Contbr. articles to profl. jours. Mem. ASCE (Outstanding Paper award 1987), Transp. Rsch. Bd., Coun. Univ. Transp. Ctrs., Univ. Transp. Ctrs. Program, Am. Concrete Inst. Mem. LDS Ch. Avocations: coaching, sports, golfing, U.S. and Tex. history. Office: U Tex Transp Rsch Ctr 3208 Red River St Ste 200 Austin TX 78705-2650

MCCULLOUGH, COLLEEN, author; b. Wellington, N.S.W., Australia, June 1, 1937; m. Ric Robinson, Apr. 13, 1984. Student, U. Sydney, Australia; student Inst. Child Health, London U.; LittD (hon.), Macquarie U., Sydney, 1993. Neurophysiologist Sydney, London, Yale U. Sch. Medicine, 1967-77. Author: Tim, 1974, The Thorn Birds, 1977, An Indecent Obsession, 1981, Cooking with Colleen McCullough and Jean Easthope, 1982, A Creed for the Third Millennium, 1985, The Ladies of Missalonghi, 1987, The First Man in Rome, 1990, The Grass Crown, 1991, Fortune's Favorites, 1993, Caesar's Women, 1996.

MCCULLOUGH, DAVID, author; b. Pitts., July 7, 1933; s. Christian Hax and Ruth (Rankin) McC.; m. Rosalee Ingram Barnes, Dec. 18, 1954; children: Melissa (Mrs. John E. McDonald, Jr.), David, William Barnes, Geoffrey Barnes, Doreen Kane. BA, Yale U., 1955; HLD, Skidmore Coll., 1983, Rensselaer Poly. Inst., 1983; D of Engring. (hon.), Villanova U., 1984; hon. doctorate, Worcester Poly. Inst., 1984; LittD (hon.), Allegheny Coll., 1984; LHD (hon.), Wesleyan U., Middletown, Conn., 1984, Colo. Coll., 1985; LittD (hon.), Middlebury Coll., 1986, U. Indiana at Pa., 1991, U. S.C., 1993; HLD (hon.), U. N.H., 1991; LittD (hon.), U. Pitts., 1994, Union Coll., 1994, Washington Coll., 1994; LHD (hon.), Chatham Coll., 1994. Writer, editor Time, Inc., N.Y.C., 1956-61, USIA, Washington, 1961-64, Am. Heritage Pub. Co., N.Y.C., 1964-70; sr. contbg. editor Am. Heritage mag.; free-lance author, 1970—; Newman vis. prof. American civilization, Cornell U., fall 1989; mem. Bennington (Vt.) Coll. Writers Workshop, 1978-79; scholar-in-residence U. N. Mex., 1979, Wesleyan U. Writers Conf., 1982, 83; mem. adv. bd. Ctr. for the Book, Libr. of Congress. Author: The Great Bridge, 1972, The Path Between the Seas, 1977, The Johnstown Flood, 1978, Mornings on Horseback, 1981, Brave Companions, 1991, Truman, 1992 (Pulitzer Prize for biography 1993), host TV series: Smithsonian World, 1984-88, The American Experience, 1988—. Mem. Harry S. Truman Centennial Commn.; trustee Nat. Trust Hist. Preservation, Harry S. Truman Libr. Inst., Hist. Soc. Western Pa., Jefferson Legacy Found.; hon. trustee Carnegie Inst. Recipient N.Y. Diamond Jubilee award, 1973, cert. of merit Mcpl. Art Soc. N.Y., 1973, Nat. Book award for history, 1978, Francis Parkman prize, 1978, 93, Samuel Eliot Morison award, 1978, Cornelius Ryan award, 1978, Civil Engring. History and Heritage award, 1978, L.A. Times prize for biography, 1981, Am. Book award for biography, 1982, Harry S. Truman Pub. Svc. award, 1993, St. Louis Lit. award, 1993, Pa. Gov.'s award for excellence, 1993, Pa. Soc. Gold Medal award, 1994. Fellow Soc. Am. Historians (v.p.); mem. ASCE (hon.), Soc. Am. Historians (pres. 1991—). Office: Janklow & Nesbit Associates 598 Madison Ave New York NY 10022-1614*

MCCULLOUGH, DAVID L., urologist; b. Chattanooga, 1938. MD, Bowman Gray, 1964. Intern U. Hosps. Case Western Reserve U., Cleve., 1964-65, resident in surgery, 1965-66; fellow urology Baylor U. Coll. Medicine, Houston, 1968-69; resident in urology Mass. Gen. Hosp., Boston, 1969-72; chief urologist N.C. Bapt. Hosp., Winston-Salem, 1983—; prof., chmn. urology Bowman Gray, Winston-Salem; pres. Am. Bd. Urology. Mem. ACS, AMA, Am. Urological Assn. (sec. southeastern sect.), Clin. Soc. Urol. Surgeons.

MCCULLOUGH, EDWARD EUGENE, patent agent, inventor; b. Baldwin, N.D., June 4, 1923; s. Elmer Ellsworth and Emma Izelda, (Nixon) McC. BA, U. Minn., 1957; postgrad., Utah State U., 1965. Machine designer Sperry Rand Corp., Mpls., 1952-58; patent adminstr. Thiokol Corp., Brigham City, Utah, 1958-86; patent cons. Thiokol Corp., Brigham City, 1986; pvt. practice, 1986—. Inventor instruments for making perspective drawings, apparatus for forming ignition surfaces in solid propellant motors, passive communications satellite or similar article, flexible bearings and process for their manufacture, rocket nozzel support and pivoting system, cavity-shaping machine, among others; patents in field. Pianist Meth. Ch., Brigham City, 1959—. Staff Sgt. U.S. Army, 1949-52. Decorated two battle stars. Avocations: helping people, inventing, philosophy, music composition, hiking in the mountains. Home: PO Box 46 784 Highland Blvd Brigham City UT 84302

MCCULLOUGH, GAYLE JEAN, graphic artist, publisher; b. Mare Island, Calif., Feb. 7, 1943; d. Earl Martin and Dorothy Clare (Vincent) Hoos; m. Norris Henry Hill; m. James Arthur McCullough, Feb. 19, 1979; children: Kareena Jean, Michael Earl, Michelle Lin. AA in Graphic Arts, Sacramento City Coll., 1970. Composing operator Cal-West Life Ins., Sacramento, 1972-75; sr. graphic artist Dept. Social Svcs. State of Calif., Sacramento, 1975—; mem. AOA implementation team State COSS, Sacramento, 1993—, mem. equal employment opportunity disabled adv. bd., 1986-87. Author, illustrator: Feud for Thought, 1993; author: Everything Hearing People Know About Deafness, 1994, What's Next?, 1994; author, illustrator, pub. (mag.) Life After Deafness, 1993-94. V.p. cmty. coun. NorCal Ctr. on Deafness, Sacramento, 1993-94. Recipient Swimming and Diving Champion award Sacramento City and County, 1957-59, Gold Keys for Art award Brueners & Hallmark Cards, 1959, 60; grantee Bank of Am., 1970. Mem. Calif. Assn. Late Deafened Adults (bd. dirs. 1993-94), Assn. Late Deafened Adults Sacramento (pres., founder 1990—). Avocations: oil painting, art, swimming, tennis. Home: 6773 Starboard Way Sacramento CA 95831-2413 Office: COSS MS 7-182 744 P St Sacramento CA 95814-6413

MCCULLOUGH, GEORGE BIERCE, oil company executive; b. Chgo., Jan. 24, 1925; s. George Bierce McCullough and Willie Pauline (Lynch) Oden; m. Alice Colleen Beacham, Jan. 20, 1951; children: Glen, Greg, Pat, Mike. B.B.A., Tulane U., 1948, M.B.A., 1952. Employee relations mgr. Humble Oil & Refining Co., Houston, 1966-69, Esso Europe, Inc., London, 1969-71; employee relations mgr. Exxon Corp., N.Y.C., 1971-80, v.p. employee relations, 1980-86; sr. fellow Orgn. Resources Counselors Inc., N.Y.C., 1986-88; chmn., bd. dirs. Nat. Energy Group, Inc., Dallas, 1988—. Mem. nat. adv. bd. Salvation Army, 1986-95; mem. overseas schs. adv. coun. U.S. Dept. State, chmn., 1982-86. Lt. (j.g.) USN, 1943-46. Mem. Personnel Round Table (chmn. 1982-83). Home: 6510 Pauma Dr Houston TX 77069-1741 Office: Nat Energy Group Inc 1350 One Energy Sq 4925 Greenville Ave Dallas TX 75206-4026

MC CULLOUGH, HELEN CRAIG, Oriental languages educator; b. Hollywood, Calif., Feb. 17, 1918; d. Everett Emerson and Mabel (Bishop) Craig; m. William Hoyt McCullough, July 19, 1952; 1 son, Dundas Craig. A.B., U. Calif., Berkeley, 1939, M.A., 1952, Ph.D., 1955. Lectr. in history, Asian langs. Stanford (Calif.) U., 1964-69; lectr. Oriental langs. U. Calif., Berkeley, 1969-75, prof., 1975-88, emerita, 1988—; vis. prof. Harvard U., 1978-79. Author: Yoshitsune, 1966, Tales of Ise, 1968, Okagami, The Great Mirror, 1980; (with William H. McCullough) A Tale of Flowering Fortunes, 1980; Brocade by Night, 1985, Kokin Wakashu, 1985, The Tale of the Heike, 1988, Classical Japanese Prose: An Anthology, 1990, Genji and Heike, 1994; translator, author research articles in field of classical Japanese lit. Served with WAVES, 1943-46. Recipient Order of the Precious Clown, Japan, 1996. Mem. Sierra Club. Democrat. Home: 40 Alta Rd Berkeley CA 94708-1204 Office: U Calif Dept East Asian Langs Berkeley CA 94720

MC CULLOUGH, JOHN PRICE, retired oil company executive; b. Dallas, May 10, 1925; s. John A. and Alta (McGee) McC.; m. Mary Ann Calvert, Aug. 5, 1946; children: Sherri, Cathryn, Patricia. Student, U. Denver, 1942-43; B.S. in Chem. Engring, U. Okla., 1945; M.S., Oreg. State U., 1948, Ph.D. in Chemistry, 1949. With U.S. Bur. Mines, Bartlesville, Okla., 1949-63, phys. chemist, 1949-57, chief thermodynamics br., 1958-63; mgr. central research div. Mobil Oil Corp., Princeton, N.J., 1963-69, mgr. applied research and devel., 1969-71; gen. mgr. research and devel. Mobil Chem. Co., 1971-78; v.p. environ. health and safety Mobil Research & Devel. Corp., Princeton, N.J., 1978-89; adj. prof. chemistry Okla. State U., Stillwater, 1961-63; vis. fellow Woodrow Wilson Found., 1991-95; dir. Internat. petroleum Industry Environ. Conservation Assn., 1981-89, chmn., 1985-88; dir. Mobil Found., Inc., 1987-89. Co-author: (with Donald Scott) Experimental Thermodynamics, Volume I: Calorimetry of Non-reacting Systems, 1968; contbr. 90 articles on thermodynamics, molecular structure and energetics, environ. and health policy to profl. jours. mem. adv. com. Mercer County (N.J.) C.C., 1968-69; bd. dirs. Chem. Industry Inst. Toxicology, 1977-89, chmn., 1986-88; bd. dirs. United Cmty. Fund, Princeton, 1963-69, Middlesex-Somerset-Mercer Regional Study Coun., 1968-69, 86-89, World Environ. Ctr., 1986-89; mem. adv. bd. Georgetown U. Inst. Health Policy Analysis, 1986-89; trustee Stony Brook-Millstone Watershed Assn., 1989-95, vice chmn., 1991-93; trustee Art Mus. Princeton U., 1994—; elder, pres. corp. Nassau Presbyn. Ch., 1995—. Lt. (j.g.) USNR, 1943-54. DuPont fellow, 1947-48; recipient Meritorious Service award U.S. Dept. Interior, 1959, Distinguished Service award, 1962; Am. Chem. Soc. award petroleum chemistry, 1963; Chemtech award, 1977; Huffman award Internat. Calorimetry Conf., 1963. Mem. AAAS, Gordon Rsch. Conf. (trustee, chmn. bd. trustees, mem. coun.), Am. Chem. Soc. (editorial bd. Jour. Chem. and Engring. Data, Jour. Phys. Chemistry, mem. coun. com. on chemistry and pub. affairs 1984-92, chmn. 1987-89), Internat. Calorimetry Conf. (chmn. 1960), Am. Inst. Chemists, Sigma Xi. Home: 30 Boudinot St Princeton NJ 08540-3008

MCCULLOUGH, JOSEPH, college president emeritus; b. Pitts., July 6, 1922; s. Joseph Phillip and Margaret (List) McC.; m. Elizabeth Cramer, Mar. 31, 1945; children—Marjorie Ann, Warren. BFA, Yale U., 1949-50, MFA, 1951; Diploma, Cleve. Sch. Art, 1948; DFA (hon.), U. Evansville, Ind., 1980. Instr. San Jose State Coll., Calif., 1948-49; asst. instr. Yale U., New Haven, 1949-51; asst. dir. Cleve. Inst. Art, 1952-54, dir., 1954-74, pres., 1974-88. Artist paintings, nat. regional and local exhbns., 1948—. Chmn. Fine Arts Adv. Com., Cleve. Planning Commn., 1963-91; trustee Mpls. Coll. of Art and Design, 1988—, Sculpture Ctr. Cleve., 1990—; trustee, sec. Access to the Arts, Cleve., 1991-95. Capt. USAAF, 1943-46, ETO. Recipient Cleve. Arts prize Women's City Club, 1971. Mem. Coll. Art Assn. (past dir.), Union Club, Rowfant Club. Home: 20101 North Park Blvd Cleveland OH 44118-5006

MCCULLOUGH, KATHRYN T. BAKER, social worker, utility commissioner; b. Trenton, Tenn., Jan. 5, 1925; d. John Andrew and Alma Lou (Wharey) Taylor; m. John R. Baker, Sept. 30, 1972 (dec. Oct. 1981); m. T.C. McCullough, May 14, 1988. BS, U. Tenn., 1945, MSW, 1954; postgrad., U. Chgo., 1950, Vanderbilt U., 1950-51. Lic. social worker, Tenn.; emeritus diplomate in clin. social work Am. Bd. Examiners. Home demonstration agt., agrl. extension svc. U. Tenn., Hardeman County, 1946-49; Dyer County, 1949-50; dir. med. social work dept. Le Bonheur Children's Hosp., Memphis, 1954-57; chief clin. social worker clinic mentally retarded children U. Tenn. Dept. Pediatrics, Memphis, 1957-59; clin. social worker Children's Med. Ctr., Tulsa, 1959-60; dir. med. social work dept. Coll. of Medicine U. Tenn., Memphis, 1960-69; dir. community svcs. regional med. program Coll. of Medicine, 1969-76; dir. regional clinic program Child Devel. Ctr. Coll. of Medicine, 1976-85; mem. faculty Coll. of Medicine, Coll. of Social Work U. Tenn., Memphis, 1960-85; social worker admissions rev. bd. Arlington Devel. Ctr., Memphis, 1976—. Author 14 books. Active Gibson County Fedn. Dem. Women, 1987—; commr. Dist. I, Gibson Utility Dist., 1990—. Fellow Am. Assn. Mental Retardation (life); mem. NASW, AAUP, Acad. Cert. Social Workers, Tenn. Conf. on Social Welfare, Trenton Music Club, Sigma Kappa Alumni. Mem. Ch. of Christ. Avocations: piano, organ, symphony. Home: 627 Riverside Yorkville Rd Trenton TN 38382-9513

MCCULLOUGH, KEVIN, CNBC anchorperson. CNBC anchor The Money Wheel, Fort Lee, N.J. Office: CNBC The Money Wheel 2200 Fletcher Ave Fort Lee NJ 07024-5005

MCCULLOUGH, M. BRUCE, judge; b. Princeton, N.J., July 26, 1944; s. Malcolm S. and Ruth S. (Strandness) McC.; m. Kathleen M. Ryan, Apr. 12, 1985. BA in Polit. Sci. and Econs., Whitworth Coll., 1966; JD, U. Mich., 1969. Bar: Pa., Fla., D.C. Ptnr. Buchanan Ingersoll P.C., Pitts., 1969-95; judge U.S. Bankruptcy Ct., Pitts., 1995—. Chmn. ARC (southwest Pa., 1994—). With USAR, 1969-75. Mem. Am. Land Title Assn. (lenders counsel), Chartiers Country Club, Duquesne Club, Rivers Club. Avocations: golf, boating, hunting. Office: US Bankruptcy Ct 1000 Liberty Ave Pittsburgh PA 15222

MCCULLOUGH, R. MICHAEL, management consultant; b. Springfield, Ohio, Dec. 31, 1938; s. Jerome Edward and Sara Amelia (Fitzsimmons) McC.; m. Frances P. Kelly, Nov. 24, 1962; children: Jeanne M., Michael F., Colleen T., Brian A., Kathleen H., Christopher E., Brendan P. B.S. in Elec. Engring., U. Detroit, 1962. Engr. Gen. Electric Co., Washington, 1962-65; engr., rsch. dir. Booz Allen & Hamilton, Bethesda, Md., 1965-71, ptnr., 1971-73, mng. ptnr., 1973-84; chmn., chief exec. officer Booz Allen & Hamilton, New York, N.Y., 1984-91; sr. chmn. Booz Allen & Hamilton, McLean, Va., 1991—; bd. dirs. Profl. Svcs. Coun., Washington, pres., 1983-84; bd. dirs. Interstate Hotels, Caterair Internat., O'Sullivan Corp. Mem. adv. coun. Stanford U., 1985-91; bd. dirs. Wolf Trap Found., 1989—; trustee U. Detroit Mercy, 1990, U.S. - Panama Bus. Coun., U.S. - Russia Bus. Coun. Club: Columbia Country (Chevy Chase, Md.); Burning Tree Country (Bethesda, Md.); Country of Fla. (West Palm Beach); Robert Trent James Golf Club (Manassas, Va.); Pine Valley (N.J.) Golf Club. *

MC CULLOUGH, RALPH CLAYTON, II, lawyer, educator; b. Daytona Beach, Fla., Mar. 28, 1941; s. Ralph C. and Doris (Johnson) McC.; m. Elizabeth Grier Henderson, Apr. 5, 1986; children from previous marriage: Melissa Wells, Clayton Baldwin. B.A., Erskine Coll., 1962; J.D., Tulane U., 1965. Bar: La. 1965, S.C. 1974. Assoc. Baldwin, Haspel, Maloney, Rainold and Meyer, New Orleans, 1965-68; asst. prof. law U. S.C., 1968-71, asso. prof., 1971-75; prof. U. S.C., 2, 1975—; chair prof. of advocacy U. S.C., 1982—, asst. dean Sch. Law, 1970-75, instr. Med. Sch., 1970-79, adj. prof. law and medicine Med. Sch., 1979—; adj. prof. medicine Med. U. of S.C., 1984—; of counsel Finkel, Goldberg, Sheftman & Altman, 1978—; adj. prof. pathology Med. U. S.C., 1985—; asst. dean U. S.C. Sch. Law 1970-75. Author: (with J.L. Underwood) The Civil Trial Manual, 1974, 7th supplement, 1987, The Civil Trial Manual II, 1984, 87, (with Myers and Felix) New Directions in Legal Education, 1970, (with Finkel) S.C. Torts II, 1986, III, 1990; co-reporter S.C. Criminal Code, 1977, S.C. Study Sentencing, 1977. Trustee S.C. dist. U.S. Bankruptcy Ct., 1979—; exec. dir. S.C. Continuing Legal Edn. Program.; bd. visitors Erskine Coll.; reporter S.C. Jury Charge Commn., 1991—. Mem. ABA, La. Bar Assn., S.C. Bar (sec. 1975-76, exec. dir. 1972-76, award of service 1978), New Orleans Bar Assn., Am. Trial Lawyers Assn., Am. Law Inst., Southeastern Assn. Am. Law Schs. (pres.), S.C. Trial Lawyers Assn. (bd. govs. 1984-88), Phi Alpha Delta. Republican. Episcopalian. Club: Forest Lake. Home: PO Box 1799 Columbia SC 29202-1799 Office: U SC Sch Law Columbia SC 29208

MCCULLOUGH, RAY DANIEL, JR., insurance company executive; b. Daytona Beach, Fla., Feb. 28, 1938; s. Ray Daniel and Clarice (Malphurs) McC.; m. Barbara Jean Winchester, Aug. 16, 1963; children—Courtney Ann, Justin Ray. BSBA with honors, U. Fla., 1960. C.P.A., Fla. Accountant Deloitte Haskins & Sells (C.P.A.'s), Jacksonville, Fla., 1960-63; with Gulf

Life Ins. Co., Jacksonville, 1963-85; v.p., controller Gulf Life Ins. Co., 1971-85; sr. v.p. fin. Dependable Ins. Group, 1985-88; pvt. practice acctg. Jacksonville, 1988—; Mem. bus. adv. council U. Fla., Gainesville, 1979-85. Mem. Am., Fla. insts. C.P.A.'s, Jacksonville Toastmasters Club (pres. 1966), Beta Alpha Psi, Beta Gamma Sigma. Home: 10312 Sylvan Ln W Jacksonville FL 32257-6240 Office: 2700 University Blvd W Ste 1A Jacksonville FL 32217-2147

MCCULLOUGH, RICHARD LAWRENCE, advertising agency executive; b. Chgo., Dec. 1, 1937; s. Francis John and Sadie Beatrice McCullough; m. Julia Louise Kreimer, May 6, 1961; children: Stephen, Jeffery, Julie. BS, Marquette U., 1959. Commd. U.S. Army, 1959, advance through grades to sgt., 1966; account exec. Edward H. Weiss Advt., Chgo., 1960-66; account supr. Doyle Dane Bernbach, N.Y.C., 1966-68; sr. v.p. J. Walter Thompson Co., Chgo., 1969-86; pres. E.H. Brown Advt., Chgo., 1986—. Author: Building Country Radio, 1986, A New Look at Country Music Audiences, 1988, (video) Country Music Marketing, 1989. Bd. dirs. Gateway Found., Chgo., 1976—, chmn., 1988-91; bd. dirs. Catholic Charities, Chgo. Mem. Country Music Assn. (Nashville dir. 1979—, pres. 1983-85, Pres.'s award 1987), Nat. Assn. Rec. Artists and Scis. (Nashville chpt.), North Shore Country Club (Glenview, Ill.), Tower Club, Dairymen's Country Club (Boulder Junction, Wis.), Quail Creek Country Club (Naples, Fla.). Roman Catholic. Home (summer): 2720 Lincoln St Evanston IL 60201-2043 also (winter): St Simone 5633 Turtle Bay Dr Naples FL 33963-2749 Office: EH Brown Advt 20 N Wacker Dr Chicago IL 60606-2806

MCCULLOUGH, ROBERT WILLIS, former textile executive; b. Monclair, N.J., Sept. 19, 1920; s. Willis G. and Viola (Mock) McC.; m. Margaret Elizabeth Hammons, Aug. 12, 1942; children—Constance Joan, Sandra Margaret, D. Scott, Linda Anne. Student, Phila. Textile Sch.; grad., Brown U., 1943. With Collins & Aikman Corp., N.Y.C., 1946-84; exec. v.p. Collins & Aikman Corp., 1955—, chmn. exec. com., 1961-84; ret.; bd. dirs. parent org. Collins & Aikman; adviser to supt. U.S. Naval Acad. Trustee, past chmn. South Street Seaport Mus.; trustee Brown U., Am. Scottish Found., Textile Research Inst. at Princeton. Served from ensign to lt. comdr. USCGR, 1942-46. Named to Brown U. Hall of Fame. Mem. Am. Arbitration Assn. Clubs: Riverside Yacht, N.Y. Yacht (past commodore; chmn. Am.'s Cup Com.), Storm Trysail, Cruising of Am. Home and Office: 93 Club Rd Riverside CT 06878-2003

MCCULLOUGH, ROY LYNN, chemical engineering educator; b. Hilsboro, Tex., Mar. 20, 1934; s. Roy Lee and Rubye Maye (Ingram) McC.; m. Jamis Carol Petersen, Sept. 5, 1958; children: Catherine Lynne, Amanda Kaye, Roy Lawrence. BS, Baylor U., 1955; PhD, U. N.Mex., 1960. Mem. staff Los Alamos (N.Mex.) Sci. Lab., 1955-60; group leader, sect. head Monsanto Co., Durham, N.C., 1960-69; sr. scientist Boeing Co., Seattle, 1969-71; prof. chem. engrng. U. Del., Newark, 1971—, dir.Ctr. for Composite Material, 1990-94. Author: Concepts of Fiber-Resin Composites, 1971; mem. editorial bd. Jour. Composite Sci. and Tech., 1984—; contbr. articles to profl. jours. Mem. Am. Inst. Chem. Engrs., Am. Chem. Soc., Am. Phys. Soc., Am. Soc. Composites. Home: 107 Reynard Dr Landenberg PA 19350-1145 Office: U Del Ctr for Composite Material Newark DE 19716

MCCULLOUGH, SAMUEL ALEXANDER, banker; b. Pitts., Nov. 10, 1938; s. Alexander and Mary Ruth (Brady) McC.; m. Katharine Graham, Sept. 23, 1967; children: Bonnie McCullough Wideman, Elizabeth McCullough White, Rebecca D., Anne D., Mary D. BBA, U. Pitts., 1960; LLD (hon.), Albright Coll., Reading, Pa., 1990. With Mellon Bank, N.A., Pitts., 1956-75, asst. cashier, 1964-68, asst. v.p., 1968-71, v.p., 1971-75; sr. v.p. corp. banking group Am. Bank and Trust Co. of Pa., Reading, 1975, exec. v.p., 1977, pres., chief exec. officer, 1978-82, chmn., chief exec. officer, 1982—; pres., chief exec. officer Meridian Bancorp., Inc., Reading, 1983-88, chmn., chief exec. officer, 1988—, also bd. dirs.; and bd. dirs. to all prin. subs. cos.; pres. CoreStates Financial Corp.; former rep. 3d Fed. Res. Dist., bd. mem.; chmn. nominating com., past chmn., bd. dirs., exec. com. Greater Phila. 1st Corp.; exec. com. Pa. Chamber Bus. and Industry; former bd. dirs. Fed. Res. Bank Phila. Bd. dirs. Phila. Orch. Assn., exec. com., chmn. facilities com., chmn. audit com., Commonwealth Found., U. Pitts. Joseph M. Katz Grad Sch. Bus.; bd. dirs., mem. planning com. Reading Hosp. and Med. Ctr.; mem. coun. Pa. Soc.; trustee Albright Coll., exec. com., chmn. nominating com.; mem. exec. bd. Valley Forge coun. Boy Scouts Am.; bd. govs. former chmn. Pennsylvanians for Effective Govt.; mem. steering com. Bus. Leaders Organized for Cath. Schs. Recipient Disting. Pennsylvanian award, 1982, Pagoda award for outstanding contbns. to community Berks County Jr. Achievement, 1985, William H. Doran Meml. award, 1987, Bicentennial medal U. Pitts., 1988, Disting. Citizen award Valley Forge coun. Boy Scouts Am., 1988, Ann. Enterprise award Pa. Coun. on Econ. Edn., 1989, Outstanding Vol. Fund Raiser award Greater Northeastern Pa. chpt. Nat. Soc. Fund Raising Execs., 1989; Good Scout award Phila. coun. Boy Scouts Am., 1990, Silver Antelope award, 1991, Torch of Liberty award Ea. Pa.-Del. Region Anti-Defamation League, 1992; named Bus. Person of Yr. Berks County C. of C., 1985, Disting. Alumnus U. Pitts., 1993. Mem. Am. Inst. Banking, Am. Bankers Assn., Pa. Bankers Assn., Berks County Bankers Assn., Bankers Roundtable (govt. rels. com.), Internat. Fin. Conf. (past chmn.), Pa. Bus. Roundtable (bd. dirs.), Allegheny Country Club, Berkshire Country Club. Republican. Presbyterian. Office: CoreStates Fin. Group 35 N 6th St PO Box 1102 Reading PA 19603*

MC CUNE, BARRON PATTERSON, federal judge; b. West Newton, Pa., Feb. 19, 1915; s. James Patterson and Lyda Barron (Hammond) McC.; m. Edna Flannery Markey, Dec. 23, 1943; children: Edward M., James H., Barron Patterson. AB, Washington and Jefferson Coll., 1935; LLB, U. Pa., 1938. Bar: Pa. bar 1939. Practiced in Washington, Pa., 1939-64; judge 27th Jud. Dist. Ct. Common Pleas, Washington, Pa., 1964-71; judge U.S. Dist. Ct., Western Dist. Pa., Pitts., 1971-95, sr. fed. judge; ret., 1995. Trustee emeritus Washington and Jefferson Coll.; bd. dirs. emeritus Washington (Pa.) Hosp. Served with USNR, 1942-45. Home: 144 Le Moyne Ave Washington PA 15301

MCCUNE, DAVID FRANKLIN, publisher; b. Trenton, N.J., Jan. 15, 1954; s. George David and Mary Jane McCune; m. Susan Ruth Watt, Apr. 11, 1981; 1 child, Douglas David. BA summa cum laude, Williams Coll., 1975. Free-lance journalist Malmö, Sweden, 1975-80; editor Time Inc., N.Y.C., 1981-83; pres. The Proteus Group Inc., N.Y.C., 1983-87; mktg. dir. Sage Publs. Inc., Newbury Park, Calif., 1988, pres., 1989—. Mem. Soc. for Scholarly Pub., Assn. for Computing Machinery, Young Pres.'s Orgn. Avocations: sailing, skiing. Office: Sage Publications Inc 2455 Teller Rd Thousand Oaks CA 91320-2218

MCCUNE, ELLIS E., retired university system chief administrator, higher education consultant; b. Houston, July 17, 1921; s. Ellis E. and Ruth (Mason) McC.; m. Hilda May Whiteman, Feb. 8, 1946; 1 son, James Donald. Student, Sam Houston State U., 1940-42; B.A., UCLA, 1948, Ph.D., 1957; LHD, Golden Gate U., 1994. Teaching asst. UCLA, 1949-51; from instr. to assoc. prof. polit. sci. Occidental Coll., Los Angeles, 1951-59; chmn. applied politics and econs. curriculum Occidental Coll., 1951-56; asst. prof. Calif. State U., Northridge, 1959-61, assoc. prof., chmn. dept. polit. sci., 1961-63, prof., 1963, dean letters and sci., 1963; dean acad. planning Calif. State Univs. and Colls., 1963-67; pres. Calif. State U., Hayward, 1967-90, pres. emeritus, 1991—; acting chancellor The Calif. State U. System, 1990-91, ret., 1991; cons. govtl. units and agys.; lectr., panelist; mem. Calif. State Scholarship and Loan Commn., 1964-68, chmn., 1967-68; pres. Govtl. Adminstrn. Group Los Angeles, 1959; chair planning com., mem. exec. com., bd. dirs. Eden Med. Ctr. Found., 1994—, pres.-elect, 1995—. Chmn. univs. and colls. div. United Bay Area Crusade, 1969-70, 73-74; bd. dirs. Oakland (Calif.) Museum Assn., 1974-77, 86-88; vice chmn. higher edn. div., East Bay United Way, 1989-90; mem. arts adv. council, 1986-87, devel. com., 1988-89, Bay Area Urban League, bd. trust Calif. Coun. Econ. Edn. No. sect., Emergency Shelter Program Adv. Coun., Hayward Area Hist. Assn., NAACP Hayward chpt.; trustee Calif. Council Econ. Edn.; sec. bd. dirs. Eden Community Found., 1978-79; rsch. fellow Haynes Found., 1957. With USAAF, 1942-46. Mem. Am. Coun. Edn. (adv. com. 1970-72, inst. coll. & univ. adminstrs. 1973-74, bd. dirs. 1985-86), Western Assn. Schs. and Colls. (accrediting commn. sr. colls. and univs. 1974-78, chmn., 1978-82, pres. 1979-81), N.W. Assn. Schs. and Colls. (commn. colls. 1974-80), Assn. Am. Colls. (bd. dirs. 1972-75, vice chmn. 1975-76), Assn. Western Univs. (bd. dirs.), Coun. Postsecondary Accreditation (bd. dirs. 1977-88, exec. com. 1979-88, chmn. 1985-87, immediate past chmn., 1988-89, chmn. com. recognition 1982-84), Am. Assn. State Colls. and Univs. (chmn. accreditation com. 1983-86, com. acad. pers. and acad. freedom 1987-88, com. on acad. affairs 1988-91), Calif. Coun. Edn. (trustee), Western Polit. Sci. Assn. (exec. coun. 1958-61), Hayward C. of C. (dir. 1968-71, 73-76, 77-80, 82-85, 86-90), Regional Assn. East Bay Colls. and Univs. (exec. com. 1974-90, sec. 1975-76, 87-88, vice chmn. 1976-77, 84-85, chmn. 1977-79, 85-86), Rotary, Phi Beta Kappa, Pi Gamma Mu, Pi Sigma Alpha. Club: Bohemian (San Francisco). Home: 17577 Parker Rd Castro Valley CA 94546-1227 Office: Calif State U Pres Emeritus LI 3167 Hayward CA 94542-3053

MC CUNE, JOHN FRANCIS, III, retired architect; b. New Castle, Pa., Oct. 23, 1921; s. John Francis and Alice (Miles) McC.; m. Jeanne Ramsay, Sept. 28, 1946; children—Morgan R., Martha (Mrs. Dennis L. Maddox), David M., William S. Student, Vanderbilt U., 1938-40; B.S. in Architecture, U. Mich., 1943. Draftsman firm Walter E. Bort (Architect), Clinton, Iowa, 1946-47; firm Pope & Kruse (Architects), Wilmington, Del., 1947-54; asso. Pope & Kruse (Architects), 1955-60; partner firm Pope, Kruse & McCune (Architects), Wilmington, 1961-72; owner McCune Assos. (Architects), Wilmington, 1972-81; v.p., prin. architect Diamond/McCune (Architects & Engrs.), Wilmington, 1981-88. Projects include Gander Hill Correctional Facility; renovation of Wilmington Public Bldg, all Wilmington; historic preservation projects include Presbyn. Ch, New Castle, Old Court House, New Castle, Barrett's Chapel, Frederica, Del., Old State House, Dover, Del., Loockerman Hall, Dover. Mem. Hist. Area Commn., New Castle, Del., 1974-88. Mem. AIA (pres. Del. chpt. 1970-71, mem. nat. com. historic resources 1975-88, state preservation coordinator Del. 1975-88), Soc. Archtl. Historians, Assn. for Preservation Tech., ASTM (com.), Nat. Trust Hist. Preservation, Del. C. of C., Nat. Fire Protection Assn. (com. libraries, museums and hist. bldgs. 1975-88), Kappa Sigma. Home: 14011 Antelope CT Sun City West AZ 85375

MCCUNE, MARY JOAN HUXLEY, microbiology educator; b. Lewistown, Mont., Jan. 14, 1932; d. Thomas Leonard and Anna Dorothy (Hardie) Huxley; m. Ronald William McCune, June 7, 1965; children: Anna Orpha, Heather Jean. BS, Mont. State Coll., 1953; MS, Wash. State U., 1955; PhD, Purdue U., 1965. Rsch. technician VA Hosp., Oakland, Calif., 1956-59; bacteriologist U.S. Naval Radiol. Def. Lab., San Francisco, 1959-61; teaching assoc. Purdue U., West Lafayette, Ind., 1961-65, vis. asst. prof., 1965-66; asst. prof. Occidental Coll., L.A., 1966-69; asst. rsch. bacteriologist II U. Calif., L.A., 1969-70; affiliate asst. prof. Idaho State U., Pocatello, Idaho, 1970-80, from asst. prof. to prof. microbiology, 1980—; instr. U. Calif., Davis, 1964. Contbr. articles to profl. jours. Pres. AK chpt. PEO, Pocatello, 1988-89; chair faculty senate Idaho State U., 1994-95. David Ross fellow Purdue U., 1964. Mem. AAAS, N.Y. Acad. Sci., Idaho Acad. Sci. (trustee 1989-95, v.p. 1992-93, pres. 1993-94), Am. Soc. for Microbiology (v.p. Intermountain br. 1988-89, pres. 1989-90), Idaho Edn. Alliance for Sci. (bd. dirs.), Sigma Xi, Sigma Delta Epsilon. Presbyterian. Home: 30 Colgate St Pocatello ID 83201-3459 Office: Idaho State U Dept Biol Scis Pocatello ID 83209

MCCUNE, SARA MILLER, foundation executive, publisher; b. N.Y.C., Feb. 4, 1941; d. Nathan M. and Rose (Glass) M.; m. George D. McCune, Oct. 16, 1966 (dec. May 1990). BA, Queens Coll., 1961. Asst. to v.p. sales Macmillan Pub. Co., N.Y.C., 1961-63; sales mgr. Pergamon Press Ltd., Oxford, England, 1963-64; pres., pub. Sage Publs. Inc., N.Y.C., 1965-66, Beverly Hills, Calif., 1966-83; pub., chmn. Sage Publs. Inc., Newbury Park, Calif., 1984—; bd. dirs. Sage Publs. Ltd., London, chmn., 1990—; bd. dirs. Sage Publs. India, New Delhi; pres. McCune Found., Newbury Park, Calif., 1990—; mem. bd. dirs. UCSB Comm. Dept. Adv. Bd., Santa Barbara, Calif., 1994—, USCB Bd. Trustees, 1994—, The Fielding Inst., 1994—, Am. Acad. Pol. Scis., Phila., 1994—. Mem. Am. Evaluation Assn. (spl. award for disting. contbns. 1988). Office: Sage Publications Inc 2455 Teller Rd Newbury Park CA 91320-2218

MCCUNE, THOMAS, construction executive contractor. CEO M. A. Mortenson, Mpls. Office: M A Mortenson PO Box 710 Minneapolis MN 55440

MCCUNE, WILLIAM MINTON, retired construction company executive; b. L.A., Oct. 13, 1922; s. William Wade and Lola Jewel (Minton) McC.; m. Lorraine R. Juelson, Dec. 4, 1943; 1 child, Carol McCune Mann. Chief estimator Diversified Builders, Paramount, Calif., 1948-56; v.p. Diversified Builders, Paramount, 1956-63, pres., 1963-69; exec. v.p. Zapata Constructors, Paramount, 1969-71, pres., 1971-78; exec. v.p. Zapata Corp., Houston, 1978-81; pres., chief exec. officer Macco Constructors, Inc., Paramount, 1981-90, chief exec. officer, 1990-92, chmn. bd. Pilot U.S. Army Air Corps, 1942-46. Mem. Nat. Assn. Corp. Dirs., L.A. World Affairs Coun., Navy League U.S., Huntington Harbour Anglers, Huntington Harbour Yacht Club, Jonathan Club, Tuna Club Avalon. Republican. Avocation: yachting. Office: Macco Constructors Inc 14409 Paramount Blvd Paramount CA 90723-3418

MCCURDY, GILBERT GEIER, retired retailer; b. Rochester, N.Y., May 25, 1922; s. Gilbert J.C. and Virginia (Geier) McC.; m. Katherine W. Babcock, Nov. 9, 1946; children—Gilbert Kennedy, Lynda Babcock (Mrs. Hotra). B.A., Williams Coll., 1944. With McCurdy & Co., Inc., Rochester, 1946—; controller, asst. treas. McCurdy & Co., Inc., 1953-55, v.p., 1956-59, exec. v.p., 1959-62, pres., gen. mgr., 1962-80, chief exec. officer, 1969-80, chmn. bd., chief exec. officer, 1980-92, chmn. exec. com. of bd., 1993—; chmn. bd. Frederick Atkins, 1968-70; dir. Chase Lincoln First Bank of Rochester. Bd. dirs. Pathway Houses of Rochester; former mem. bd. dirs. United Way Rochester and Monroe County; sr. trustee U. Rochester. 1st lt. Signal Corps, AUS, 1943-46. Mem. Rochester C. of C. (pres. 1975). Baptist. Home: 1 Whitney Ln Rochester NY 14610-3551 Office: Midtown Plaza Rochester NY 14645

MC CURDY, HAROLD GRIER, psychologist; b. Salisbury, N.C., May 30, 1909; s. McKinnon Grier and Nellie (Curd) McC.; m. Mary Burton Derrickson, Sept. 15, 1937; children: John Derrickson, Ann Lewis. A.B., Duke U., 1930, Ph.D., 1938. Asst. prof. biology High Point Coll., 1931-32; caseworker Fed. Transient Bur., Salisbury, N.C., 1934; prof. psychology Milligan Coll., 1938-41; assoc. prof. to prof. psychology and philosophy Meredith Coll., 1941-48; assoc. prof. to Kenan prof. psychology U. N.C., Chapel Hill, 1948-71; Kenan prof. psychology emeritus U. N.C., 1971—. Author: The Personality of Shakespeare, 1953, reprint, 1973, The Personal World, 1961, Personality and Science, 1965, Barbara, 1966, About Mary, 1989, (poetry) Oblation, 1990, 50 Metaphysical Sonnets for a Rock Age, 1993; contbg. author: Historical Roots of Contemporary Psychology, 1968, Humanistic Psychology, 1981, Foundations of Psychology, 1984; poetry The Chastening of Narcissus, 1970, Novus Ordo Seclorum, 1981, And Then the Sky Turned Blue, 1982, Twenty Four Bagatelles in an Antique Mode, 1989, others. Mem. AAAS, Am. Psychol. Assn., Sigma Xi. Democrat. Methodist. Home: 6 Gooseneck Rd Chapel Hill NC 27514-4600

MCCURDY, HARRY WARD, otolaryngologist; b. Branchton, Pa., Aug. 15, 1918; s. Adam Oscar and Sarah Fern (Hindman) McC.; m. Joan Jacqueline Talty, Dec. 10, 1955; children: Bridget Elizabeth, Peter Adam. A.B., Allegheny Coll., 1940; M.D., U. Pa., 1943. Diplomate: Am. Bd. Otolaryngology. Intern Geisinger Meml. Hosp., Danville, Pa., 1944; resident in otolaryngology Geisinger Meml. Hosp., 1944-45, 48-49; resident in pathology Hamot Hosp., Erie, Pa., 1945-48; mem. staff Geisinger Med. Center, Danville, 1948-50; commd. 2d lt. U.S. Army, 1945, advanced through grades to col., 1962-74; mil. cons. Surgeon Gen., U.S. Army, 1964-74; ret., 1974; exec. v.p. Am. Acad. Otolaryngology-Head and Neck Surgery, Washington, 1974-84; mem. staff Walter Reed Army Hosp.; Mem. resources council Gallaudet Coll., 1975-80; mem. nat. adv. council Sertoma Found., 1976-84; chmn. FDA Panel on Otolaryngologic Med. Devices, 1974-78, cons., 1978-84. Mem. ACS, AMA, Royal Soc. Medicine (U.K.), Am. Acad. Otolaryngology, Mil. Surgeons Assn., Am. Soc. Assn. Execs., Soc. Med. Consultants to Armed Forces, AAAS, Am. Soc. Facial Plastic Surgery, Soc. Mil. Otolaryngologists, Am. Acad. Facial Plastic and Reconstructive Surgery, Am. Laryngol., Rhinol. and Otol. Soc., Anglo-Am. Med. Soc., Am. Audiology Soc., Royal Soc. Health, Osler Med. Soc., Acad. Medicine, Soc. Univ. Otolaryngologists, Am. Council Otolaryngology, Pan-Am. Soc. Bronchoesophagology., Internat. Fedn. Otolaryngol. Socs. (sec. gen. 1981—), Soc. Mil. Cons. to Armed Forces (sec. 1993—). Republican. Methodist. Clubs: Army Navy, Press, Mil. Attaches of London, Les Chevaliers du Tastevin. Home and Office: 6006 Dellwood Pl Bethesda MD 20817-3812

MCCURDY, LARRY WAYNE, automotive parts company executive; b. Commerce, Tex., July 1, 1935; s. Weldon Lee and Eula Bell (Quinn) McC.; m. Anna Jean Ogle, June 2, 1956; children: Michael, Kimberly, Laurie. BBA, Tex. A&M U., 1957. Jr. acct. Tenneco Inc., Houston, 1958-60; sr. acct. Tenneco Oil Co., Houston, 1960-64; acctg. supr. Tenneco Chems., Houston, 1964-69; div. controller Tenneco Chems., Saddle Brook, N.J., 1970-72, corp. controller, 1972-74, v.p., fin., 1974-78; sr. v.p. fin. Tenneco Automotive, Deerfield, Ill., 1978-80; pres. Walker Mfg. Co., Racine, Wis., 1980-81; exec. v.p. N.Am. ops. Tenneco Automotive, Deerfield, 1981-82; v.p. fin. Echlin Inc., Branford, Conn., 1983, pres. chief operating officer, 1983-85; pres., chief exec. officer Moog Automotive Inc., St. Louis, 1985-94; exec. v.p. ops. Cooper Industries, Houston, 1994—; bd. dirs. Lear Seating Corp., Mohawk Industries, Inc., Breed Tech., Inc. Trustee Somerset County Coll., Somerville, N.J., 1974-78, Millikin U., Decatur, Ill., 1991—; former mem. bd. dirs. Jr. Achievement, Chgo.; bd. dirs. Sam Houston coun. Boy Scouts Am., 1995—; mem. adv. coun. Tex. A&M U. Engrng. Sch., 1995—. Mem. Fin. Execs. Inst., Nat. Assn. Accts., Motor Equipment Mfrs. Assn. (chmn. bd. dirs. 1989). Office: Cooper Industries 1001 Fannin St Ste 4000 Houston TX 77002-6711

MCCURDY, MICHAEL CHARLES, illustrator, author; b. N.Y.C., Feb. 17, 1942; s. Charles Errett and Beatrice (Beatson) McC.; m. Deborah Lamb, Sept. 7, 1968; children: Heather, Mark. BFA, Tufts U., 1964, MFA, 1971. Dir. Penmaen Press, Lincoln, Mass., 1968-85; instr. Concord (Mass.) Acad., 1972-75, Wellesley (Mass.) Coll., 1976. Illustrator: The Man Who Planted Trees, 1985, American Tall Tales, 1991, American Buffalo, 1992, The Winged Life: The Poetry of Henry David Thoreau, 1992, The Beasts of Bethlehem, 1992, McCurdy's World, 1992, The Way West: Journal of a Pioneer Woman, 1993, Giants in the Land, 1993, The Gettysburg Address, 1995; author, illustrator: Hannah's Farm, 1988, The Old Man and the Fiddle, 1992; editor, illustrator: Escape From Slavery: The Boyhood of Frederick Douglass in His Own Words, 1994. Mem. Great Barrington (Mass.) Housing Authority, 1990-93. Small press grantee Nat. Endowment Arts, 1978, Mass. Arts and Humanities, 1978. Mem. Soc. Printers, St. Botolph Club. Democrat. Episcopalian.

MC CURDY, PATRICK PIERRE, editor, consultant; b. Angers, France, Sept. 14, 1928; s. Joseph Alexander and Constance Yolande (Hillairet de Boisferon) McC.; m. Eiko Yamada, May 30, 1953; children: Alan J., Wendy C., Alec J., Jeffrey R. B.S. in Chem. Engrng., Carnegie Inst. Tech., 1949. Chem. engr. tech. service dept. Humble Oil & Refining Co., Baytown, Tex., 1949-50; chem. engr. Callery Chem. Co., Pa., 1954-56; sr. chem. engr. U.S. Army Engr. R & D Labs., Ft. Belvoir, Va., 1956-60; asst. editor Chem. & Engrng. News, Washington, 1960-61, N.Y.C., 1961-62; bur. head Chem. & Engrng. News, Frankfurt, Germany, 1962-64, Tokyo, 1964-67; mng. editor Chem. & Engrng. News, Washington, 1967-69; editor Chem. & Engrng. News, 1969-73; editor in chief Chemical Week, 1973-80, 84-87, editor-in-chief, assoc. pub., 1987-88; dir. communications Am. Chem. Soc., 1988-91, dir. industry rels., 1991-93, editor Today's Chemist at Work, 1989—; cons. American Chemical Soc., 1993—; pub. issues mgr. Dow Chem. Co., Midland, Mich., 1980-82, dir. tech. communications, 1982-84; bd. dirs. Centcom, Ltd. Served to 1st lt. C.E. AUS, 1950-54. Recipient Jesse H. Neal award, 1979, finalist 1985; recipient Carnegie Mellon Univ. Alumni Merit award, 1988. Mem. AIChE, Am. Chem. Soc., Fgn. Corrs. Club Japan, Chemists Club (suburban v.p.), Societe de Chimie Industrielle (bd. dirs. Am. sect., past pres.), Soc. Chem. Industry (Am. sect.), Comml. Devel. Assn., Tokyo Am. Club, Tau Beta Pi, Phi Kappa Phi, Theta Tau, Phi Kappa. Home: 11717 Chauncey Ln Mason Neck VA 22079-4140 Office: 1155 16th St NW Washington DC 20036-4800

MCCURDY, RICHARD CLARK, engineering consultant; b. Newton, Iowa, Jan. 2, 1909; s. Ralph Bruce and Florence (Clark) McC.; m. Harriet Edith Sutton, Sept. 11, 1933; children: Gregor, Richard, Carolyn, Robert. A.B., Stanford U., 1931, E.M., 1933. With engrng. and prodn. div. Shell Oil Co., 1933-47; with prodn. mgmt. Shell Caribbean Petroleum Co., 1947-50; gen. mgr. Shell Group Companies, Venezuela, 1950-53; pres. Shell Chem. Co., N.Y.C., 1953-65; dir. Shell Oil Co., mem. exec. com., 1959-69, pres., chief exec. officer, 1965-69; assoc. adminstr. orgn. and mgmt. NASA, Washington, 1970-73; cons. NASA, 1974-82. Trustee United Seamans Service, 1954-70, Stanford U., 1965-70; trustee Hood Coll., 1968-86, trustee emeritus, 1986—, hon. trustee, 1987—; trustee Rensselaer Poly. Inst., 1974-86, hon. trustee, 1986—. Recipient Disting. Service medal NASA, 1972. Mem. Mfg. Chemists Assn. (dir. 1955-65, chmn. bd. 1961-62, chmn. exec. com. 1964-65), Am. Inst. Mining, Metall. and Petroleum Engrs., Am. Phys. Soc., Am. Petroleum Inst., N.Y. Yacht Club, Noroton (Conn.) Yacht Club (commodore), Cruising of Am. (commodore 1980-82), Beta Theta Pi. Home: Contentment Island Darien CT 06820

MCCURLEY, MARY JOHANNA, lawyer; b. Baton Rouge, La., Oct. 3, 1953; d. William Edward and Leora Elizabeth (Block) Trice; m. Carl Michael McCurley, June 6, 1983; 1 stepchild, Melissa Reneé McCurley. BA, Centenary Coll., 1975; JD, St. Mary's U., 1979. Bar: Tex. 1979; cert. family law 1984. Assoc. Martin, Withers & Box, Dallas, 1979-82, Raggio & Raggio, Inc., Dallas, 1982-83; ptnr. Bruner, McColl, McColloch & McCurley, Dallas, 1983-87; assoc., ptnr. Dallas, 1987-90; jr. ptnr. Koons, Fuller, McCurley & VanderEykel, Dallas, 1990-92; ptnr. McCurley, Webb, Kinsar, McCurley & Nelson, Dallas, 1992—; Contbr. numerous articles to profl. jours. Adv. Women's Service League, Dallas, 1993—. Mem. Am. Acad. Matrimonial Lawyers (treas. Tex. chpt. 1995, sec. 1996), Dallas Bar Assn. (chairperson family law sect. 1985), Tex. State Bar Assn. (mem. family law coun.), Tex. Acad. Family Law Specialist, Dallas Bar Assn. Methodist. Avocations: golf, travel, jogging, horseback riding. Home: 4076 Hanover Dallas TX 75225 Office: McCurley Webb Kinser McCurley & Nelson 1201 Elm 4242 Renaissance Tower Dallas TX 75270

MC CURLEY, ROBERT LEE, JR., lawyer; b. Gadsden, Ala., Sept. 7, 1941; s. Robert Lee and Nellie Ruth McC.; 1 child, Allison Leah. BS, U. Ala., 1963, JD, 1966. Bar: Ala. 1966, D.C. 1973, U.S. Ct. Mil. Appeals 1966, U.S. Supreme Ct. 1970, U.S. Ct. Appeals (5th cir.) 1972, U.S. Ct. Appeals (11th cir.) 1973, U.S. Ct. Appeals (fed. cir.) 1981. Am. Law Inst. asst. to dir. Fed. Savs. & Loan Ins. Corp., Washington, 1966-67; partner firm Rains, Rains, McCurley & Wilson, Gadsden, Ala., 1967-75; city judge Southside, Ala., 1970-75; dir. Ala. Law Inst.; assoc. dir. U. Ala. Center Public Law and Service, 1981-82; asst. dean Sch. Law U. Ala., 1978-81; panelist White House Conf. on Volunteerism; pres. Gadsden Jaycees, 1972; mem. White House Fifty States Project; Henry Toll fellow Coun. State Govt., 1992. Editor: Divorce, Alimony and Child Support Custody, 3d edit., 1993, Land Laws of Alabama, 5th edit., 1990, The Legislative Process, 6th edit., 1995, Alabama Law Office Practice Deskbook, 7th edit., 1995, Federally Mandated State Legislation, 1990, Alabama Legislation, Cases and Statutes, 3d edit., 1992, Alabama Election Handbook, 7th edit., 1996. Pres. Gadsden Boys Club, 1971; mem. Nat. Dem. Charter Commn., 1974. Mem. ABA, Am. Law Inst. Order of Coif, Scribes, Farrah Law Soc., Commn. Uniform State Laws, Nat. Conf. State Legislatures (exec. com. legal staff sect.), Kiwanis (pres. Tuscaloosa club 1976, gov. Ala. dist. 1984, internat. v.p. 1991-92, trustee Internat. Found. 1994-97, treas. 1996-97), Indian Hills County Club, Univ. Club. Baptist.

MCCURN, NEAL PETERS, federal judge; b. Syracuse, N.Y., Apr. 6, 1926. LL.B., Syracuse U., 1952, J.D., 1960. Bar: N.Y. 1952. Ptnr. Mackenzie Smith Lewis Mitchell & Hughes, Syracuse, 1957-79; judge U.S. Dist. Ct. (no. dist.) N.Y., 1979-88; chief judge U.S. Dist. Ct. (no. dist.), N.Y., 1988-93; sr. judge, 1993—; del. N.Y. State Constl. Conv., 1976; mem. 2d Cir. Jud. Council. Pres. Syracuse Common Coun., 1970-78. Mem. ABA, N.Y. State Bar Assn. (chmn. state constn. com.), Onondaga County Bar Assn. (past pres.), Am. Coll. Trial Lawyers, Am. Judicature Soc. (bd. dirs. 1980-84). Office: US Dist Ct 100 S Clinton St Rm 33 Syracuse NY 13261-9211

MCCURRY, MARGARET IRENE, architect, educator; b. Chgo., Sept. 26, 1942; d. Paul D. and Irene B. McC.; m. Stanley Tigerman, Mar. 17, 1979. BA, Vassar Coll., 1964. Registered architect, Ill., Mass., Mich.; registered interior designer, Ill. Design coord. Quaker Oats Co., Chgo., 1964-66; sr. interior designer Skidmore, Owings & Merrill, Chgo., 1966-77; pvt. practice architect Margaret I, Chgo., 1977-82; ptnr. Tigerman, McCurry, Chgo., 1982—; vis. studio critic Art Inst. Chgo., 1985-86, 88, lectr., 1988, bd. dirs. Archtl. Soc., 1988—, adv. bd. textile dept., 1992—; vis. studio critic U. Ill., Chgo., Miami U., Oxford, Ohio, 1990; juror Internat. furniture awards Progressive Architecture mag., N.Y.C., 1986, advt. awards, 1988; juror design grants Nat. Endowment for Arts, Washington, 1983; NEA Challenge Design Rev., 1992; peer reviewer design excellence program Gen. Svcs. Administrn., 1992—; juror, Wis., Minn., Calif., Va., Washington, Pitts., Ky., Conn. Soc. Architects, Detroit, N.Y.C., Memphis, Austin, L.A. chpts. AIA, Am. Wood Coun., Am. Inst. Architecture Students Design Competition, 1993. Contbr. Chgo. Archtl. Club Jour.; designer, contbr. archtl. exhibit Art Inst. Chgo., 1983-85, 93, Chgo. Hist. Soc., 1984, Gulbenkian Found., Lisbon Portugal, 1989, Chgo. Athenaeum, 1990, Gwenda Jay Gallery, 1992, Women of Design Traveling Exhbn., 1992-96; archtl. drawings and models in permanent collection Art Inst. Chgo. and Deutsches Architektur Mus., Frankfurt. Chmn. furniture sect. fundraising auction Sta. WTTW-TV, PBS, Chgo., 1975-76; mem. Chgo. Beautiful Com., 1968-70; mem. alumni coun. Grad. Sch. Design, Harvard U.; bd. mem. Architecture and Design Soc. Art Inst. Chgo., mem. textile adv. bd. textile dept. Loeb fellow Harvard U., 1986-87; recipient Builders Choice Grand award Builders Mag., 1985, Interior Design award Interiors Mag., 1983, Dean of Architecture award Chgo. Design Source and the Merchandise Mart, 1989; inducted into Interior Design Hall of Fame, Interior Design Mag., 1990. Fellow AIA (v.p. bd. dirs. Chgo. chpt. 1984-89, chairperson 1993, nat. design com., lectr. Colo. chpt. 1985, nat. conv. 1988, Monterey Design Conf. 1989, Washington Design Ctr. 1989, Nat. Honor award 1984, Nat. Interior Architecture award 1992, Disting. Bldg. award Chgo. chpt. 1984, 86, 91, 94, Disting. Interior Architecture award 1981, 83, 88, 91, product display Neocon award 1985, 88), Coll. of Fellows AIA, Internat. Interior Design Assn., Chgo. Network, Am. Soc. Interior Designers (Nat. Design award 1992, 94, Ill. chpt. Design award 1994, Ill. chpt. Merit award 1994, v.p. bd. dirs. Chgo. chpt.), Chgo. Archtl. Club, Arts Club Chgo., Womens Athletic Club. Episcopalian. Avocations: drawing, travel, tennis, skiing, folk art. Office: Tigerman McCurry Archs 444 N Wells Chicago IL 60610-4522

MCCURRY, MICHAEL DEMAREE, government spokesman, press secretary; b. Charleston, S.C., Oct. 27, 1954; s. William Joseph and Rosemary (Demaree) McC.; Debra Lyn Jones, June 16, 1984; children: William Harry, Marjorie Vera, Christopher Michael. BA, Princeton U., 1976; MA, Georgetown U., 1985. Press sec. Sen. Harrison Williams, Washington, 1976-81, Sen. Daniel P. Moynihan, Washington, 1981-83, Sen. John Glenn, Washington, 1984; pub. affairs dir. ERISA Industry Com., Washington, 1985; press sec. Gov. Bruce Babbitt, Phoenix, 1986-88; dir. comms. Dem. Nat. Com., Washington, 1988-90; sr. v.p. Robinson, Lake, Lerer & Montgomery, Washington, 1990-93; spokesman U.S. Dept. State, Washington, 1993-95; press sec. White House, Washington, 1995—. Mem. coun. St. Paul's United Meth. Ch., Kensington, Md., 1992—. Office: The White House Office Office of the Press Secretary 1600 Pennsylvania Ave NW Washington DC 20500

MCCUSKER, JOHN, financial executive; b. Bklyn., May 28, 1939; s. John Michael and Helen Frances (Sweeney) McC.; BBA, St. John's U., 1961; m. Brenda Ann Caprio, June 27, 1964; children: John Christian, Joseph Andrew, David Douglas. Sr. acct. Haskins & Sells, N.Y.C., 1961-67; asst. dir. fin. planning Colt Industries, Inc., N.Y.C., 1967-69; dir. fin. planning Shearson Hammill & Co., N.Y.C., 1969-70; dir. fin. analysis The Allen Group, Inc., Melville, N.Y., 1971-73; asst. corporate contr., Geraghty & Miller, Inc., Plainview, N.Y., 1974-76, v.p., contr., 1976-82, v.p. fin., 1983-87, sr. v.p. fin., 1989—. Bd. dirs. Nassau-Sufffolk Hosp. Coun., 1983-88, chmn., 1986-89; bd. dirs. Huntington (N.Y.) Hosp., 1979—, chmn., 1989-92, Family Svc. League Suffolk County, Huntington, N.Y. Served with U.S. Army, 1963. CPA, N.Y. Mem. AICPAs, N.Y. State Soc. CPAs, Fin. Execs. Inst., Nassau-Suffolk Hosp. Assn. (chmn. bd. dirs.). Republican. Roman Catholic. Home: 4 Harbor View Dr Huntington NY 11743-6710 Office: 125 E Bethpage Rd Plainview NY 11803-4228

MCCUSKER, MARY LAURETTA, library science educator; b. Sillery, Que., Can., Jan. 18, 1919; came to U.S., 1938, naturalized, 1942; d. Albert James and Laura (Cleary) McC. B.A., Western Md. Coll., 1942; M.S.L.S., Columbia U., 1952, D.L.S., 1963. Joined Order of Preachers, Roman Catholic Ch., 1961; librarian Annapolis (Md.) High Sch., 1942-44, McDonogh Mil. Sch., 1944-47; asst. prof. Iowa State Tchrs. Coll. (now No. Iowa U.), Cedar Falls, 1948-59; vis. prof. library sci. U. Minn., Mpls., summers, 1958-59; assoc. prof. Sch. Library Sci. Rosary Coll., 1963-67, dir., prof. Grad. Sch., 1967-81, prof. emeritus, rsch. assoc., 1981-94, dean grad. sch., 1969-81, prof. emeritus, 1994—. Contbr. articles to profl. jours. Continuing Edn. grantee World Book Ency., 1994. Mem. ALA, Assn. Libr. and Info. Sci. Edn., Nat. Cath. Libr. Assn. (pres. No. Ill. chpt. 1987-89, chair acad. sect. No. Ill. chpt. 1992—, v.p. pres.-elect 1995—), Ill. Libr. Assn., Ill. Sch. Libr. Media Assn. (chair awards com. 1990-91, 94-95, co-chair cert. and stds. com. 1995—), Chgo. Libr. Club, Sch. Libr. Assn. Office: Rosary Coll Grad Sch Library and Info Sci 7900 Division St River Forest IL 60305-1066

MCCUSKEY, ROBERT SCOTT, anatomy educator, researcher; b. Cleve., Sept. 8, 1938; s. Sidney Wilcox and Jeannette M. (Scott) M.; m. Rebecca Woodworth, July 19, 1958 (div.); children: Geofrey, Gregory, Michael; m. Margaret A. Krasovich, Apr. 17, 1993. A.B., Western Res. U., 1960, Ph.D., 1965. Instr. anatomy U. Cin., 1965-67, asst. prof., 1967-71, assoc. prof., 1971-75, prof., 1975-78; prof., chmn. anatomy W.Va. U., Morgantown, 1978-86; prof., head dept. cell biology and anatomy U. Ariz., Tucson, 1986—, prof. physiology, 1987—; vis. prof. U. Heidelberg, Fed. Republic Germany, 1981-83, 87-88, 93-95; cons. Hoffmann-La Rouche, N.J., 1972-75, Procter & Gamble Co., Cin. 1966-86. Recipient NIH Rsch. Career Devel. award, 1969-74; Humboldt Sr. U.S. Scientist prize, Fed. Republic Germany, 1982, Nishimaru award Japan Microcirculatory Soc., 1987; grantee NIH, NSF, 1966—. Mem. AAAS, Microcirculatory Soc., Am. Assn. Anatomists, Am. Assn. Study Liver Diseases, Rsch. Soc. on Alcoholism, Internat. Soc. Exptl. Hematology, Microscopy Soc. Am. Mem. editorial bd. Microvascular Rsch., 1974-84, Shock, 1993—, Am. Jour. Physiology, 1995—; contbr. numerous articles to profl. jours. Office: Ariz Health Scis Ctr Dept Cell Biology and Anatomy P O Box 245044 Tucson AZ 85724-5044

MCCUTCHAN, GORDON EUGENE, lawyer, insurance company executive; b. Buffalo, Sept. 30, 1935; s. George Lawrence and Mary Esther (De Puy) McC.; m. Linda Brown; children: Lindsey, Elizabeth. B.A., Cornell U., 1956, M.B.A., 1958, LL.B., 1959. Bar: N.Y. 1959, Ohio 1964. Pvt. practice Rome, N.Y., 1959-61; atty., advisor SEC, Washington, 1961-64; ptnr. McCutchan, Druen, Maynard, Rath & Dietrich, 1964-94; mem. office of gen. counsel Nationwide Mut. Ins. Co., Columbus, Ohio, 1964-94, sr. v.p., gen. counsel, 1982-89; exec. v.p., gen. counsel Nationwide Mut. Ins. Co., 1989-94; exec. v.p. Law and Corp. Svcs., Nationwide Ins. Enterprise, 1994—. Trustee, bd. govs. Franklin U.; trustee Ohio Tuition Trust Authority. Mem. Columbus Bar Assn., Ohio Bar Assn., Am. Corp. Counsel Assn., Assn. Life Inst. Counsel (bd. govs. 1990-94), Fedn. Ins. and Corp. Counsel, Am. Coun. Life Ins. (chair legal sect. 1992-93). Home: 2376 Oxford Rd Columbus OH 43221-4011 Office: Nationwide Mut Ins Co 1 Nationwide Plz Columbus OH 43215-2423 also: Employers Ins Wausau 2000 Westwood Dr Wausau WI 54401-7802

MCCUTCHEN, CHARLES WILLIAM, chemical engineer; b. Wichita Falls, Tex., Nov. 20, 1928; s. William Urlin and Karis (Jameson) McC.; m. Joyce Forse, June 10, 1956; children: David William, Karis Ann. BSChE, MIT, 1949. Engrng. trainee Dow Chem. Co., Midland, Mich., 1949; R&D engr. Dow Chem. Co., Freeport, Tex., 1949-68; sr. process engr. Dow Chem. Co., —, —, 1968-79, internal process cons., 1979-86; ret., 1986. Mem. AIChE. Achievements include 4 U.S. patents. Home: 109 Blossom St Lake Jackson TX 77566

MCCUTCHEON, HOLLY MARIE, accountant; b. Pitts., Aug. 14, 1950; d. George and Ruth (Bradburn) Rudawski. Student, Ohio Dominican Coll., 1968-69, Wittenburg U., 1979-81; BS in Acctg. and Fin. magna cum laude, Wright State U., 1983. Cert. mgmt. acct. Acct. Morris Bean & Co., Yellow Springs, Ohio, 1983-86; contr. Speco Aerospace Corp., Springfield, Ohio, 1986-96, AIDA-Dayton (Ohio) Techs. Corp., Dayton, Ohio, 1996—; cons. Glenwood Tng. Ctr., Yellow Springs, 1983-86. Coach City Recreation Youth Soccer, Springfield, 1982-85; mem. st. Raphael Adult Choir, Springfield, 1986-89. Mem. Inst. Mgmt. Accts. (pres. Dayton chpt. 1994-95). Avocations: fishing, golf, tennis, cross country skiing. Office: AIDA-Dayton Techs Corp 3131 S Dixie Dr Ste 401 Dayton OH 45439

MCDADE, JAMES RUSSELL, management consultant; b. Dallas, Jan. 15, 1925; s. Marion W. and Jeannette (Reneau) McD.; m. Elaine Bushey, Sep. 10, 1955. BSEE, So. Meth. U., Dallas, 1947; MBA, Northwestern U., Evanston, Ill., 1950. Asst. to pres. Davidson Corp., Chgo., 1951-52; asst. to pres. Mergenthaler Linotype Co., Bklyn., 1952-53, comml. works mgr., 1953-56; chief indsl. engr. Tex. Instruments, Inc., Dallas, 1956-57, product gen. mgr., 1958-60, v.p., 1961-64; chmn. bd. McDade Properties Co., Aspen (Colo.), Denver, Dallas, 1964—; bd. dirs. Pitkin County Bank, Aspen; chmn. bd. dirs. Harley-Davidson Tex., Westec Security of Aspen, Aspen Security, Inc. Founding mem. Aspen Art Mus., 1980; mem. Ballet Aspen, 1980—; pres. club Aspen Valley Hosp., 1984—. Served to 1st lt. USAF, 1943-46. Mem. Rep. Senatorial Inner Circle, Am. Mgmt. Assn., Presidents Assn. Avocations: skiing, horseback riding, camping, swimming. Home and Office: 1000 Red Mountain Rd PO Box 9090 Aspen CO 81612-9090

MCDADE, JOE BILLY, federal judge; b. 1937. BS, Bradley U., 1959, MA, 1960; JD, U. Mich., 1963. Staff atty. antitrust divsn. U.S. Dept. Justice, 1963-65; exec. trainee First Fed. Savs. and Loan Assn., 1965; exec. dir. Greater Peoria (Ill.) Legal Aid Soc., 1965-69; ptnr. Hafele & McDade, Peoria, Ill., 1968-77; pvt. practice Peoria, 1977-82; assoc. cir. judge State of Ill., 1982-88; cir. judge Cir. Ct. Ill., 1988-91; fed. judge U.S. Dist. Ct. (ctrl. dist.) Ill., 1991—. Bd. dirs. Peoria (Ill.) Pub. Libr., 1965-77, Peoria YMCA, ARC, Peoria Tri-Centennial; fin. chmn. St. Peters Cath. Ch.; active Peoria Civic Ctr. Authority, 1976-82; pres. Ill. Health Systems Agy., 1978-80, bd. dirs., 1975-82. Mem. Ill. State Bar Assn., Peoria County Bar Assn. (bd. dirs. 1980-82). Office: US Dist Ct 100 NE Monroe St Peoria IL 61602-1003

MCDADE, JOSEPH MICHAEL, congressman; b. Scranton, Pa., Sept. 29, 1931; s. John B. and Genevieve (Hayes) McD.; children: Joseph, Aileen, Deborah, Mark; m. Sarah Scripture, May 1988; 1 child, Jared. B.A. in Polit. Sci. with honors, U. Notre Dame, 1953; LL.B., U. Pa., 1956; LL.D. (hon.), St. Thomas Aquinas Coll., 1968, U. Scranton, 1969, Misericordia Coll. and Kings Coll., 1981, Mansfield State Coll., 1982; H.H.D., Kings Coll. Bar: Pa. bar 1957. Clk. to fed. judge, 1956-57; pvt. practice law Scranton, 1957—, city solicitor, 1962; mem. 88th-103rd Congresses from 10th Pa. dist., Washington, D.C., 1963—; mem. appropriations com. Mem. Am., Pa., Lackawanna County bar assns., Scranton C. of C. Republican. Roman Catholic. Clubs: K.C; James Wilson Law (Phila.). Office: US Ho of Reps 2107 Rayburn Ho Office Bldg Washington DC 20515-3810*

MCDADE, LINNA SPRINGER, retired academic program administrator; b. Lincoln, Ill., May 18, 1932; d. Clifford Harry and Lois Mae (Lovett) S.; m. Wesley Dale McDade, June 13, 1951; children: Kimberly Rachel, Chance Linnea, Wesley Dale Jr., Bryan Anthony, Darby Erin. Student, Northwestern U., 1950; AB with honors, U. Ill., 1971. Cert. tchr., Ill. Substitute tchr. Sch. Dist. 116, Urbana, Ill., 1972-74; mng. editor Am. Sociol. Rev., Am. Sociol. Assn., Urbana, 1977-80; asst. to head dept. sociology U. Ill., Urbana, 1980-90; ret., 1990; grants coord. The Reading Group, Urbana, Ill., 1995-96. Chorus mem. Ill. Opera Theatre, 1979-82; pres. Evening Etude Music Club, 1958-60; dir. children's choir 1st Presbyn. Ch., Urbana, 1977, deacon, 1985—, elder, 1989—; co-pres. Washington Sch. PTA, Urbana, 1963-64; bd. dirs. Frances Nelson Health Ctr., Champaign, Ill., 1989-93; vol. fundraising coord. New Hope Jobs, Champaign, 1994—; bd. dirs. Adoption Studies Inst., Washington, 1995-96. Recipient " So Proudly We Hail" Community Svc. award The Exch. Club Urbana, 1990. Mem. Phi Alpha Theta. Avocations: singing, swimming, horseback riding. Home: 2433 County Road 1225 N Saint Joseph IL 61873-9727

MCDANIEL, BOYCE DAWKINS, physicist, educator; b. Brevard, N.C., June 11, 1917; s. Allen Webster and Grace (Dawkins) McD.; m. Jane Chapman Grennell, Aug. 3, 1941; children: Gail P., James G. B.S., Ohio Wesleyan U., 1938; M.S., Case Inst. Tech., 1940; Ph.D., Cornell U., 1943. Staff mem. radiation lab. Mass. Inst. Tech., 1943; physicist Los Alamos Sci. Lab., 1943-46; mem. faculty Cornell U., Ithaca, N.Y., 1945—, prof., 1956-87, assoc. dir. lab. nuclear studies, 1960-67, dir. lab. nuclear studies, 1967-85, Floyd R. Newman prof. nuclear studies, 1977-87, prof. emeritus, 1987—; head accelerator sect. Nat. Accelerator Lab., Batavia, Ill., 1972; mem. high energy physics adv. panel ERDA, 1975-78. Contbr. articles to profl. jours. Trustee Associated Univs., Inc., 1962-75. Vis. fellow Brookhaven Nat. Lab., 1966; Fulbright Research grantee Australian Nat. U., 1953; Guggenheim and Fulbright grantee U. Rome and Synchrotron Lab., Frascati, Italy, 1959-60. Fellow Am. Phys. Soc.; mem. NAS, Univs. Rsch. Assn. (trustee 1971-77, 83-84, chmn. superconducting super-collider bd. overseers 1984-91, mem. 1991-93). Spl. research neutron spectroscopy, gamma ray spectroscopy, high energy photoprodn. K mesons and hyperons, instrumentation for high energy physics, accelerator design and constrn. Home: 318 Savage Farm Dr Ithaca NY 14850

MCDANIEL, CHARLES-GENE, journalism educator, writer; b. Luxora, Ark., Jan. 11, 1931; s. Charles Waite and Edith Estelle (Kelly) McD. B.S., Northwestern U., 1954, M.S. in Journalism, 1955. Reporter Gazette and Daily, York, Pa., 1955-58; sci. writer Chgo. bur. A.P., 1958-79; assoc. prof. journalism dept. Roosevelt U., Chgo., 1979-83, prof., 1984-96, chmn. dept., 1979-93, head faculty of journalism and communication studies, 1993-95, prof. emeritus, 1996—. Contbg. editor Libido; contbr. to anthologies, poems, Ency. Britannica, World Book Ency.; contbr. articles to profl. jours.; Chgo. corr. The Med. Post, Toronto, 1979—. Trustee Roosevelt U., 1985-94; bd. dirs. Internat. Press Ctr. Chgo., 1993—; mem. Ill. Gay and Lesbian Task Force. Recipient writing awards Erikson Inst. for Early Edn., 1972, writing award AMA, 1974, writing awards Chgo. Inst. for Psychoanalysis, 1971, 73, writing awards Ill. Med Soc., 1972, 73, writing awards ADA, 1975, Am. Psychol. Assn., 1982. Mem. ACLU, Fellowship of Reconciliation, War Registers League, Art Inst. Chgo. (life), Mus. Contemporary Art (charter), Nat. Lesbian and Gay Journalists Assn., Ill. Arts Alliance, Handgun Control Inc. Home and Office: 5109 S Cornell Ave Chicago IL 60615-4215 *That which we achieve for ourselves is for naught unless we have at the same time contributed to a world in which peace and justice prevail.*

MCDANIEL, DOLAN KENNETH, oil exploration service company executive; b. Clarksville, Ark., June 9, 1935; s. Lowell William and Dana Estelle (Kinney) McD.; m. Letha Patricia Craven, Jan. 2, 1957; children: Laurie McDaniel Holgate, David. BS, Kans. State U., 1957. Field ops. Geophys. Service Inc., various locations, 1957-66; mgr. Rocky Mountains region Geophys. Service Inc., Denver, 1966-70; mgr. N. Latin Am. Geophys. Service Inc., Bogota, Colombia, 1970-72; mgr. land data collection Geophys. Service Inc., Dallas, 1973-77, mgr. marine exploration, 1977, pres., 1977-88; cons. geophys. industry, 1989—; v.p. Tex. Instruments, Dallas, 1978-88. Mem. Soc. Exploration Geophysicists, Dallas Geophys. Soc., Internat. Assn. Geophys. Contractors (bd. dirs. 1982-89). Home and Office: 213 Crooked Creek Dr Richardson TX 75080-2024

MCDANIEL, DONALD HAMILTON, lawyer; b. Washington, Apr. 26, 1948; s. Roy Hamilton and Mildred Dean (Borden) McD.; m. Eva Styron, Dec. 29, 1973; children: Sharon, Michelle. BS, La. State U., 1970; JD, U. Miss., 1973. Bar: Miss. 1973; bd. cert. tax atty., 1987—. Atty. IRS, Washington, 1974-77; tax law specialist Bourgeois Bennett Thokey, New Orleans, 1977-81; ptnr. McCloskey Dennery Page, New Orleans, 1981-85, Lemle & Kelleher, New Orleans, 1985—. Author: Estate Planning in Louisiana, 1991. Trustee St. Martins Episcopal Sch., New Orleans, 1993, East Jefferson Hosp. Found., New Orleans, 1995, United Meth. Found., New Orleans, 1995. Mem. ABA, La. State Bar Assn., Miss. State Bar Assn., New Orleans Estate Planning Council. Avocations: golf, fishing. Office: Lemle & Kelleher LLP 601 Poydras St Ste 2100 New Orleans LA 70130

MCDANIEL, GERALDINE HOWELL, geriatrics rehabilitation nursing consultant; b. Como, N.C., Feb. 21, 1943; d. Jarvis Littleton and Nell Carson (Daughtley) Howell; m. Paul G. McDaniel; children: Christopher Louis Winstead, Kimberley Ann Winstead. Student, Old Dominion U., 1961-62; diploma, RN, Norfolk (Va.) Gen. Hosp. Sch., 1964. RN, Va.; cert. nurse adminstr. ANA; cert. rehab. RN Am. Rehab. Assn. Office nurse obgyn. Dr. A.R. Garnett, Norfolk, Va., 1964; staff nurse Radford (Va.) Cmty. Hosp., 1965-66, Med. Coll. Va., Richmond, 1965; student health nurse Union Coll., Schenectady, N.Y., 1966-69; DON Confederate Home for Women, Richmond, 1975-80; clin. coord. Catawba (Va.) Hosp. Mental/ Geriatric, 1981-86; DON Friendship Manor, Roanoke, Va., 1986-89, Avanté of Roanoke, Va., 1989-92, Va. Vets. Care Ctr., Roanoke, 1992-94; rehab. nurse cons. Mariner Rehab., Chapel Hill, N.C., 1994—; mem. Task Force to Study How Regulations Affect Patient Outcomes in Long Term Care, Roanoke, 1994; state coord. for parish nursing Va. Bapt. Women's Missionary Union. Sunday sch. tchr., com. chairperson, mission trips to Argentina, Mexico, Peru First Bapt. Ch., Roanoke, 1987—. Mem. ANA (cert. nurse adminstr.), Am. Rehab. Assn. (cert. rehab. RN), Assn. Rehab. Nurses, Va. Bapt. Nurses Fellowship (sec., treas., area rep. 1993—), Noble Dirs. Nurses S.W. Va., Va. Nurses Assn., Va. Dirs. Nurses Long Term Care (past dist. rep.). Baptist. Avocations: parish nurse, volunteering for med. mission trips.

MC DANIEL, JAMES EDWIN, lawyer; b. Dexter, Mo., Nov. 22, 1931; s. William H. and Gertie M. (Woods) McD.; m. Mary Jane Crawford, Jan. 22, 1955; children: John William, Barbara Anne. AB, Washington U., St. Louis, 1957, JD, 1959. Bar: Mo. 1959. Assoc. firm Walther, Barnard, Cloyd & Timm, 1959-60; assoc. firm McDonald, Barnard, Wright & Timm, 1960-63, ptnr., 1963-65; ptnr. firm Barnard, Timm & McDaniel St. Louis, 1965-73; ptnr. firm Barnard & Baer, St. Louis, 1973-82; ptnr. Lashly & Baer, St. Louis, 1982—, prosecuting atty., 1968—; city atty. City of Glendale, Mo., 1996—; bd. dirs. Eden. Theol. Sem., Airtherm Mfg. Co.; lectr. Latvian U., Riga, Inst. Fgn. Rels., Banking in Am., 1992-93. Leader legal del. Chinese-Am. Comparative Law Study, People's Republic China, 1988, Russian-Am. Comparative Law Study, USSR, 1990; trustee, past chmn., past treas. 1st Congl. Ch. St. Louis. With USAF, 1951-55. Fellow Am. Bar Found. (life), St. Louis Bar Found. (life); mem. ABA (ho. of dels. 1976-80, 84-92, state del. 1986-92, chmn. lawyers conf., jud. adminstrn. divsn. 1985-86, 8th cir. rep. standing com. on fed. judiciary 1992-95), The Mo. Bar (pres. 1981-82, bd. govs. 1974-83, mem. standing com. on jud. qualification, tenure and compensation 1996—), Mo. Assn. Def. Counsel, Bar Assn. Met. St. Louis (pres. 1972), Internat. Assn. Ins. Counsel, Assn. Def. Counsel St. Louis (past pres.), Phi Delta Phi. Home: 767 Elmwood Ave Saint Louis MO 63122-3216 Office: Lashly & Baer 714 Locust St Saint Louis MO 63101-1603

MCDANIEL, JARREL DAVE, lawyer; b. Clovis, N. Mex., Oct. 17, 1930; s. Raymond Lee and Blanch (Booth) McD.; m. Anne Louise McAllister; children: Jarrel Dave Jr., Julia Anne. A.A., Riverside Coll., 1951; B.A., U. Tex., 1956, LL.B., 1957. Bar: Tex. 1957. Assoc. Vinson & Elkins, Houston, 1957-69, ptnr., 1969—; author, lectr. in field. Served with USAF, 1950-54. Mem. ABA, Am. Coll. Bankruptcy, State Bar Tex., Am. Bankruptcy Inst., Tex. Bd. Legal Specialization in Bankruptcy (mem. adv. com. 1976—). Roman Catholic. Clubs: Houston, Houston Ctr. Home: 649 Bunker Hill Rd Houston TX 77024-5118 Office: Vinson & Elkins LLP 2500 First City Tower 1001 Fannin St Houston TX 77002

MCDANIEL, JOHN PERRY, health care company executive; b. Findlay, Ohio, Sept. 4, 1942; s. Oliver Perry and Lorraine (Schraeding) McD.; m. Ellen Rachel Garb, June 18, 1966; children—Celia Lorraine, Michael Perry. BS, Wittenberg U.; MHA, U. Mich.; LHD (hon.), Wittenberg U., 1990. Adminstrv. resident Wilmington Med. Ctr., Del. Hosp., 1965-66, asst. adminstrs., 1966-67; asst. adminstr. Community Hosp., Springfield, Ohio, 1967-68; assoc. adminstr. Md. Gen. Hosp., Balt., 1968-72; pres., chief exec. officer Lutheran Hosp. Md., Inc., Balt., 1972-81, Md. Health Care Systems, Inc., Balt., 1977-81; pres. Washington Hosp. Ctr. and Medlantic Healthcare Group, 1981—; pres. Medlantic Mgmt. Corp., 1983—, now CEO; cons. Westchester Med. Ctr. Found. Inc., White Plains, N.Y., 1980-81; mem. adv. coun. Nat. Ctr. for Therapeutic Riding, Washington, 1983—. Contbr. articles to profl. jours. Mem., bd. dirs. Vol. Hosps. of Am.-Mid. Atlantic, Greater Washington Bd. Trade ; mem. Washington Trustees of Fed. City Coun. Fellow Am. Coll. Hosp. Adminstrs.; mem. Royal Soc. Health, U. Mich. Program in Hosp. Adminstrn. Alumni Assn. (bd. dirs.), Howard County Hist. Soc., Univ. Club (Washington), Econ. Club of Washington. Republican. Avocations: horseback riding and other related sports. Office: Medlantic Healthcare Group 100 Irving St NW Washington DC 20010-2911*

MCDANIEL, JOSEPH CHANDLER, lawyer; b. Covington, Va., Mar. 24, 1950; s. Everts Hardin and Betty (Chandler) McD.; m. Sandra Lee Bonds, Dec. 27, 1976; children: Sean Kenneth, Caitlin Bonds. BA in Philosophy, Ariz. State U., 1974, JD, 1980. Bar: Ariz. 1980, U.S. Dist. Ct. Ariz. 1981; cert. specialist bankruptcy law Ariz. Bd. Legal Specialization, cert. specialist consumer bankruptcy law Am. Bankruptcy Bd. Specialization, cert. specialist bus. bankruptcy law. Law clk. U.S. Bankruptcy Ct., Phoenix, 1980-82; pvt. practice Phoenix, 1982-84; ptnr. McDaniel and Jaburg, P.C., Phoenix, 1984-89, McDaniel and Lee, Phoenix, 1989-91, McDaniel & Gan, P.C., 1991-93, McDaniel & Kaup, P.C., 1993-94, Lerch, McDaniel & Kaup, P.L.C., 1994—; lectr. in field; mem. Scriveners Com. Local Rules of Ct. for Dist. of Ariz. Bankruptcy Cts., Phoenix, 1980. Author: A Guide to Researching Bankruptcy Law, 1980; editor: (with others) Arizona Civil Remedies, 1982; lectr. in field. Bd. dirs. St. Patrick's Day Parade, 1988-89, Irish Cultural Assn. Phoenix, 1988-89. Mem. ABA (gen. practice sect. bankruptcy com., chmn., dep. chmn. membership com. pubs. bd.), Ariz. Bar Assn. (lectr., co-chmn. continuing legal edn. com., bankruptcy sect. 1987-88, chmn. 1988-89, co-chmn. jud. rels. com. 1990-92), Maricopa County Bankruptcy Practitioners (chmn.), Ariz. Bankruptcy Coalition (bd. dirs. 1986—, chair speakers com. 1994-96), Maricopa County Bar Assn., Am. Bankruptcy Inst. Democrat. Roman Catholic. Avocations: computer tech., chess, hiking. Office: Lerch McDaniel & Kaup PLC 3636 N Central Ave Ste 990 Phoenix AZ 85012-1939

MCDANIEL, MICHAEL CONWAY DIXON, bishop, theology educator; b. Mt. Pleasant, N.C., Apr. 8, 1929; s. John Henry and Mildred Juanita (Barrier) McD.; m. Marjorie Ruth Schneiter, Nov. 26, 1953; 1 son, John Robert Michael. B.A., U. N.C., 1951; B.D., Wittenberg U., 1954; M.A., U. Chgo., 1969, Ph.D., 1978; D.D. (hon.), Lenoir-Rhyne Coll., 1983; LL.D., Belmont Abbey Coll., 1984. Ordained to ministry United Lutheran Ch. in America, 1954. Pastor Faith (N.C.) Luth. Ch., 1954-58, Ch. of the Ascension, Savannah, Ga., 1958-60; assoc. dir. evangelism United Luth. Ch. in Am., N.Y.C., 1960-62; sr. pastor Edgebrook Luth. Ch., Chgo., 1962-67; pastor, guest lectr. Wittenberg U., Springfield, Ohio, 1970-71; prof. Lenoir-Rhyne Coll., Hickory, N.C., 1971-82, Raymond Morris Bost disting. prof., 1982, dir., prof. Ctr. for Theology, 1991—; bishop N.C. Luth. Ch. in Am., Salisbury, 1982-87, Evang. Luth. Ch. Am., Salisbury, 1988-91; chmn. humanities div. Lenoir-Rhyne Coll., 1973-82; cons., grant coord. NEH, 1977-79; master tchr. Hickory Humanities Forum, 1981—; chmn. task force on ecumenical and interfaith relationships Commn. Forming a New Luth. Ch., 1983-87; rep. Luth. Orthodox Dialogue In U.S.A., 1983-89;; chmn., cons. bishops governing coun. Evang. Luth. Ch. Am., 1987-89. Author: Welcome to the Lord's Table, 1972. Mem. Englewood Human Relations Council, N.J., 1959-60; pres., bd. trustees Edgebrook Symphony, Chgo., 1965-67; sec. Chgo. Astron. Soc., 1966-67; pres. Community Concerts Assn., Hickory, N.C., 1977-80. Served to sgt. U.S. Army, 1946-48, Korea. Luth. World Fedn. fellow, 1967-69, Mansfield Coll. fellow U. Oxford, 1989; recipient Disting. Alumnus award Trinity Luth. Sem., 1990. Home: 125 42nd Avenue Cir NE Hickory NC 28601-9012 Office: Lenoir-Rhyne Coll Hickory NC 28603 *Since Christian faith is a joyous relationship with God, Christian hope is courageously counting on God's promises, and Christian love a daily adventure. The Christian approaches each aspect of life as An Adventure in Courageous Joy.*

MCDANIEL, MYRA ATWELL, lawyer, former state official; b. Phila., Dec. 13, 1932; d. Eva Lucinda (Yores) Atwell; m. Reuben Roosevelt McDaniel Jr., Feb. 20, 1955; children: Diane Lorraine, Reuben Roosevelt III. BA, U. Pa., 1954; JD, U. Tex., 1975; LLD, Huston-Tillotson Coll., 1984, Jarvis Christian Coll., 1986. Bar: Tex. 1975, U.S. Dist. Ct. (we. dist.) Tex. 1977, U.S. Dist. Ct. (so. and no. dists.) Tex. 1978, U.S. Ct. Appeals (5th cir.) 1978, U.S. Supreme Ct. 1978, U.S. Dist. Ct. (ea. dist.) Tex. 1979. Asst atty. gen. State of Tex., Austin, 1975-81, chief taxation div., 1979-81, gen. counsel to gov., 1983-84, sec. of state, 1984-87; asst. gen. counsel Tex. R.R. Commn., Austin, 1981-82; gen. counsel Wilson Cos., San Antonio and Midland, Tex., 1982; assoc. Bickerstaff, Heath & Smiley, Austin, 1984, ptnr., 1987-96; mng. ptnr. Bickerstaff, Heath, Smiley, Pollan, Kener & McDaniel, Austin, 1996—; mem. asset. mgmt. adv. com. State Treasury, Austin, 1984-86; mem. legal affairs com. Criminal Justice Policy Coun., Austin, 1984-8, Inter-State Oil Compact, Oklahoma City, 1984-86; bd. dirs. Austin Cons. Group, 1983-86; mem. Jud. Efficiency Coun., Austin, 1995-96; lectr. in field. Contbr. articles to profl. jours., chpts. to books. Del. Tex. Conf. on Librs. and Info. Sci., Austin, 1978, White House Conf. on Librs. and Info. Scis., Washington, 1979; mem. Libr. Svcs. and Constrn. Act Adv. Coun., 1980-84, chmn., 1983-84; mem. long range plan task force Brackenridge Hosp., Austin, 1981; clk. vestry bd. St. James Episcopal Ch., Austin, 1981-83, 89-90; bd. visitors U. Tex. Law Sch., 1983-87, cice chmn., 1983-85; bd. dirs. Friends of Ronald McDonald House Ctrl. Tex., Women's Advocacy, Inc., Capital Area Rehab. Ctr.; trustee Episcopal Found. Tex., 1986-89, St. Edward's U., Austin, 1986—, chmn. acad. com., 1988—; chmn. divsn. capital area campaign United Way, 1986; active nat. adv. bd. Leadership Am.; trustee Episcopal Sem. S.W., 1990-96, Assn. Governing Bds. Univs. and Colls., Leadership Edn. Arts Program, 1995—. Recipient Tribute to 28 Black Women award Concepts Unltd., 1983; Focus on women honoree Serwa Yetu chpt. Mt. Olive grand chpt. Order of Eastern Star, 1979, Woman of Yr. Longview Metro C. of C., 1985, Woman of Yr. Austin chpt. Internat. Tng. in Communication, 1985, Citizen of Yr. Epsilon Iona chpt. Omega Psi Phi. Master Inns of Ct.; mem. ABA, Am. Bar Found., Tex. Bar Found. (trustee 1986-89), Travis County Bar Assn., Travis County Women Lawyers' Assn., Austin Black Lawyers Assn., State Bar Tex. (chmn. Profl. Efficiency & Econ. Rsch. subcom. 1976-84), Golden Key Nat. Honor Soc., Longhorn Assocs. for Excellence in Women's Athletes (adv. coun. 1988—), Order of Coif (hon. mem.), Omicron Delta Kappa, Delta Phi Alpha. Democrat. Home: 3910 Knollwood Dr Austin TX 78731-2915 Office: Bickerstaff Heath Et Al 1700 Forst Bank Plz 816 N Congress Ave Austin TX 78701-2443

MCDANIEL, RANDALL CORNELL, professional football player; b. Phoenix, Dec. 19, 1964. BPE, Ariz. State U., 1988. Offensive guard Minn. Vikings, 1988—. Named NFL All-Pro Team Guard by Sporting News, 1991-93. Played in Pro Bowl, 1988-93. Office: Minn Vikings 9520 Viking Dr Eden Prairie MN 55344-3825

MCDANIEL, RICKEY DAVID, senior living executive; b. Rochester, Minn., Apr. 10, 1946; s. Malcolm David and Elaine (Lee) McD.; m. Shelley Ann Sorenson, May 10, 1980; children: Michael, Mathew, Joseph. AA, Rochester Jr. Coll., 1966; BA, Winona State U., 1969. Clin. mgr. St. Mary's Hosp., Rochester, Minn., 1971-74; long term care adminstr. Roderick Enterprises, Inc., Portland, Oreg., 1974-78; regional dir. Roderick Enterprises, Inc., Portland, 1978-80, v.p. ops., 1980-84; pres. Health Sys. Mgmt. and Devel., L.A., 1984-86; ops. dir. Brim Enterprises, Inc., Portland, 1987-88, v.p., 1988-92, sr. v.p., 1992-93; pres. Brim Sr. Living, Inc., Portland, 1993—; bd. dirs. Brim Homestead, Inc., Portland, Dominican Life Care Svcs., Portland, Belmar, Inc., Portland, also v.p. 1989—; pres. Care Mgmt., Inc., A Fla. Employee Leasing Corp., 1991—; developer alzheimer patients care and housing program, 1993. Cpl. USMC, 1969-71. Republican. Lutheran. Avocations: ice hockey, coaching basketball, baseballand hockey. Home: 16492 S Arrowhead Dr Oregon City OR 97045-9287 Office: Brim Inc 305 NE 102nd Ave Portland OR 97220-4170

MCDANIEL, ROBERT STEPHEN, chemist; b. Nashville, Sept. 26, 1946; s. Robert Stephen and Dorothy (Leahy) McD.; m. Katherine Wood Johnson, May 26, 1972; 1 child, Benjamin C. BS in Chemistry, U. Notre Dame, Ind., 1968; PhD in Organic Chemistry, U. Mo., Rolla, 1974. Sr. rsch. chemist Armak Co., McCook, Ill., 1975-79, sect. head process devel., 1979-80; mgr. new products R&D A.E. Staley Mfg. Co., Decatur, Ill., 1980-88; sr. scientist Henkel Corp., Ambler, Pa., 1988-91; mgr. R&D Endura Products, Quakertown, Pa., 1992—. Contbr. articles to profl. jours. Mem. Tree Bd., Decatur, 1986-88. U. Chgo. Ben May Lab. for Cancer Rsch. fellow, 1974-75. Fellow Sigma Xi; mem. TAPPI (specialty coated papers com. 1994—), Am. Chem. Soc. Roman Catholic. Achievements include 12 patents. Avocations: golf, fencing, soap making. Office: Endura Products Divsn Specialty Paperboard Inc 45 N 4th St Quakertown PA 18951-1239

MCDANIEL, RODERICK ROGERS, petroleum engineer; b. High River, Alta., Can., 1926; s. Dorsey Patton and Daisy (Rogers) McD.; m. Marilyn Bouck, Oct. 16, 1948; children: Nancy, Leslie. BS, U. Okla., 1947. Petroleum reservoir engr. Creole Petroleum Corp., 1947; petroleum reservoir engr. Imperial Oil Ltd., 1948-52, chief reservoir engr., 1952-55; chmn. McDaniel Cons., Calgary, 1955—, PWA Corp, Calgary, 1974-91, Can. Regional Airlines, Calgary, 1991-92; bd. dirs. Honeywell Can. Ltd., Prudential Steel Ltd. Bd. dirs. Calgary Exhbn. and Stampede, 1979-88, hon. bd. dirs., 1988—; dir. Calgary Stampeder Football Team, 1988, Corp. Commissionaires S.A.B. Mem. Assn. Profl. Engrs. Alta and Sask., Can. C. of C. (bd. dirs. 1973), Calgary C. of C. (past pres.), Calgary Petroleum Club (past pres.), Calgary Highlanders (hon. col.), Ranchmen's Club, Calgary Golf and Country Club, Outrigger Club (Honolulu), Mission Hills Country Club. Mem. Progressive Conservative Party. Home: 11 3231 Rideau Ridge Pl SW, Calgary, AB Canada T2S 2T1 Office: McDaniel & Assoc, 2200-255 5th Ave SW, Calgary, AB Canada T2P 3G6

MCDANIEL, SARA SHERWOOD (SALLY MCDANIEL), trainer, consultant; b. St. Louis, Apr. 24, 1943; d. Edward Leighton and Dolores Edic (Pitts) Sherwood; m. Allen Polk McDaniel, Dec. 29, 1967; children: James Polk, Fontaine Maury. AA, Mt. Vernon Coll., 1963; BS, Vanderbilt U., 1965. Tchr. Kanawha Valley Schools, Charleston, W.Va., 1965-66, Fulton County Schools, Atlanta, 1966-68; tournament dir. Atlanta Classic, 1972-77; dir. alumni affairs Leadership Atlanta, 1988-89; pvt. practice cons., trainer Atlanta, 1988—. Bd. dirs. Girl Scouts U.S., Ga., High Mus. Art, Atlanta Opera, UNICEF Atlanta, Aid Atlanta, Fine Art Collectors; active Com. on Women and Minorities for 1996 Olympics; mem. exec. com. Leadership Atlanta, Jr. League; mem. Friends of Spelman; trustee Mt. Vernon Coll.; bd. chair Atlanta Women's Fund. Mem. Am. Soc. Trainers and Dirs., Atlanta Women's Network (bd. dirs., pres.), Vanderbilt U. Alumni Assn., Alumni Assn. Peabody Coll. Presbyterian. Home and Office: 3777 Paces Ferry Rd NW Atlanta GA 30327-3003

MCDANIEL, TERENCE LEE, professional football player; b. Saginaw, Mich., Feb. 8, 1965. Student, U. Tenn. With L.A. Raiders (name changed to Oakland Raiders), 1988-94; cornerback Oakland Raiders, 1995—. Named to Sporting News Coll. All-Am. 2d team, 1987, selected to Pro Bowl, 1992-94. Office: Oakland Raiders 332 Center St El Segundo CA 90245*

MCDANIELS, B. T., bishop. Bishop Northeastern Nebr. region Ch. of God in Christ, Omaha. Office: Ch of God in Christ 1106 N 31st Ave Omaha NE 68131-1433

MCDANIELS, PEGGY ELLEN, special education educator; b. Pulaski, Va., Jan. 4, 1945; d. James H. and Gladys M. (Hurd) Fisher; m. Robert A. McDaniels, Feb. 17, 1973; children: Dawn Marie, Robert C. A Gen. Studies, Schoolcraft Coll., 1976; BA, Ea. Mich. U., 1980, MA, 1985. Cert. adminstr. Woodcock Johnson Psychoednl. Battery (Orton-Gillingham Tng). Payroll sec. Otto's Painting and Drywall, West Bloomfield, Mich., 1964-75; office mgr., closing sec. Bing Constrn. Co., West Bloomfield, 1964-75; substitute tchr. Wayne-Westland Schs., Westland, Mich., 1980-83, Farmington (Mich.) Schs., 1980-83; tchr. spl. edn. Romulus (Mich.) Community Schs., 1983-85, Cros-Lex Schs., Croswell, Mich., 1985-87, Pointe Tremble Elem. Sch., Algonac, Mich., 1987—; organizer, recorder Tchr. Assistance Team, Algonac, 1991—. Mem. Coun. Exceptional Children, Learning Disability Assn. (treas. 1988-90), Mich. Assn. Learning Disability Edn., ASCD. Avocations: camping, bicycling, reading. Home: 2406 Military St # 1 Port Huron MI 48060-6665

MC DANNALD, CLYDE ELLIOTT, JR., management consultation company executive; b. N.Y.C., June 29, 1923; s. Clyde E. and Evelyn (Tunison-Morgan) McD.; BA, Columbia Coll., 1948, MBA, 1950; m. Virginia Washington, Apr. 25, 1953; children: Leslie Ann, Clyde Elliott III, Bruce Robert, Bonnie Washington, Brian Christopher (dec.), Laura Leigh. Market rsch. analyst J. Walter Thompson Co., N.Y.C., 1948-50; asst. dir. market rsch. Nat. Lead Co., N.Y.C., 1950-51; product rsch. supr., account exec. Foote, Cone & Belding, Inc., N.Y.C., 1951-52; product mgr., asst. advt. mgr. Am. Safety Razor Corp., N.Y.C., 1953-54; account exec., account supr. Meldrum & Fewsmith, Inc., Cleve., 1954-56; sr. account exec. Young & Rubicam, N.Y.C., 1956-58; exec. asst. to v.p., advt. mgr. Brown & Williamson Tobacco Corp. subs. Brit.-Am. Tobacco Co., Ltd., Louisville, 1959-63; dir. advt. and mktg. svcs., dir. mktg. Miller Brewing Co., Milw., 1963-65; div. gen. mgr., v.p. consumer products, corp. v.p. Revere Copper & Brass Inc., N.Y.C., 1966-71; pres., COO H.H. Pott Distillers Ltd. U.S. subs. H.H. Pott NFGR, N.Y.C., 1972-80, also bd. dirs.; pres., CEO Oxbridge Cons., Inc., N.Y.C., 1981—; ptnr. Hilbert, Peers and Young, Inc., N.Y.C., 1984—; bd. dirs. West Indies Distillers, Ltd., Distilled Spirits Inst., Washington, McFrank & Williams Inc. and Cooperating Cons. Corp., N.Y.C.; vis. prof. mktg. Fairfield U. Sch. Bus., 1975-77. Apptd. to staff Col. Ky. Govs., 1959-63, 92—; mem. Ky. Hwy. Commn. 1960-63, N.Y. Gov.'s Indsl. Com., 1967-72; bd. govs. N.Y. Mil. Acad., 1970-76, trustee, 1975-92. Served from pvt. to capt. Inf. USAAF, 1942-45, ETO. Decorated D.F.C., Air medal with 4 oak leaf clusters; recipient Conspicuous Service Cross State of N.Y. with 5 oak leaf clusters, Valor medal UDC, Knickerbocker Greys City of N.Y., War Cross, Sons of Confederate Vets., Medaille de la France Liberee, Croix de Guerre (Belgium), Roi Leopold III, Battle of Britain, Knight Mil. Order of Malta, Knight Sovereign Mil. Order Temple Jerusalem. Mem. SAR, SR (bd. mgrs. 1988—), Alumni Fedn. Columbia U., Am. Mgmt. Assn., NAM (mktg. com.), Audit Bur. Circulation, Navy League, St. Andrews Soc. State of N.Y., Am. Revolution Round Table, Am. Legion, VFW, N.Y. Soc. Mil. and Naval Officers World Wars, Sons of Confederate Vets., Soc. Colonial Wars, Sigma Chi (life), Alpha Chi Sigma. Clubs: Columbia U., Explorers, University. Presbyterian. Democrat. Home: 57 Canterbury Ln Wilton CT 06897-4103

MCDARRAH, FRED WILLIAM, photographer, editor, writer, photography reviewer; b. Bklyn., Nov. 5, 1926; s. Howard Arthur and Elizabeth (Swahn) McD.; m. Gloria Schoffel, Nov. 5, 1960; children: Timothy Swann, Patrick James. BA, NYU, 1954. Mem. staff Village Voice Newspaper, N.Y.C., 1959—, picture editor, 1971—; book reviewer ASMP Infinity Mag., 1972-73, Photo Dist. News, 1985-88, The Picture Profl., 1990—. Exhibited in Soho Photo Gallery, 1973, Whitney Mus., 1974, 76-77, Dallas Mus. Art, 1974, San Francisco Mus. Art, 1975, Wadsworth Atheneum, 1975, Sidney Janis Gallery, 1976, Basel (Switzerland) Art Fair, 1976, Alfred Stieglitz Gallery, 1976, Empire State Mus., Albany, N.Y., 1978, Lightworks Gallery, Syracuse, N.Y., 1981, Cape Cod Gallery, Provincetown Mass., 1982, Galleria di Franca Mancini, Pesaro, Italy, 1983, Musée du Quebec, 1987, Anita Shapolsky Gallery, N.Y.C., 1988, Hartnett Gallery U. Rochester, N.Y., 1989, G. Ray Hawkins Gallery, L.A., 1989, Read Gallery Antioch (Ohio) Coll., 1989, Mus. Art/Sci./Industry, Bridgeport, Conn., 1989, N.Y.C. Gallery Queens Mus., 1989, Ctr. Photography, Woodstock, 1989, Frumkin/Adams Gallery, 1990, Musée d'Art Moderne De La Ville de Paris, 1990, Musée d'Art Contemporain, Montreal, 1990, Pollack-Krasner Mus., East Hampton, N.Y., 1990, Found. Cartier, Paris, 1990, Marty Carey Pictures Gallery, Woodstock, N.Y., 1992, Galerie Gilles Ringuet, Belfort, France, 1992, Galerie Contre Jour, Belfort, France, 1992, Galleria La Pescheria, Cesena, Italy, 1994, Whitney Mus. Am. Art, 1995—, Nat. Portrait Gallery, 1996; exhbns. include Jack Kerouac Visions of the Road, Les Rencontres D'Arles, Arles, France, 1991, Jack Kerouac Travelling Writers, Saint-Malo (France) Internat. Festival, 1991, Images of Greenwich Village N.Y. Camera Club, 1992; author: The Beat Scene, 1960, The Artist's World in Pictures, 1961, rev. edit. 1988, Greenwich Village, 1963, New York, New York, 1964, Sculpture in Environment, 1967, Museums in New York, 1973, French edit., 1979, 5th edit., 1990, Photography Marketplace, 2d edit., 1977, Stock Photo and Assignment Source Book, 1977, 2d edit., 1984, Kerouac and Friends: A Beat Generation Album, 1984, Japanese edit, 1990, Frommer's Atlantic City and Cape May, 4th edit., 1991, 5th edit., 1993 ; co-author: The New Bohemia, 1967, 2d edit., 1990 Guide for Ecumenical Discussion, 1970, Greenwich Village Guide, 1992, Frommer's Virginia, 1992, 2d edit. 1994, Gay Pride: Photographs from Stonewall to Today, 1994; editor: Saturday Rev. Executive Desk Diary, 1962-64; photographer: Personality Posters, Fotofolio (post cards) (polit. and social figures); contbr. articles, picture features to various publs. including N.Y. Mag., Vanity Fair, Entertainment Weekly, Vogue. With U.S. Army, 1944-47. Recipient numerous photography awards including 1st place spot news photo award N.Y. Press Assn., 1964, 68; recipient 1st place feature photo award N.Y. Press Assn., 1967, 1st place picture story award N.Y. Press Assn., 1969, 2nd place spot news photo award N.Y. Press Assn., 1967, 70, 3d place spot news photo award N.Y. Press Assn., 1965, 3d place feature photo award N.Y. Press Assn., 1965, 3d place picture story award N.Y. Press Assn., 1970, 1st place Best Pictorial Series Nat. Newspaper Assn., 1966, Page One award Newspaper Guild N.Y., 1971, 80; Guggenheim fellow in photography, 1972. Mem. Nat. Press Photographers Assn., N.Y. Press Photographers Assn., Am. Soc. Mag. Photographers, Soc. Photog. Edn., Photog. Hist. Soc. N.Y., Authors Guild, N.Y. Press Club, Am. Soc. Picture Profls., Photog. Soc. Am. Office: 36 Cooper Sq New York NY 10003-7118

MCDARRAH, GLORIA SCHOFFEL, editor, author; b. Bronx, N.Y., June 22, 1932; d. Louis and Rose Schoffel; m. Fred W. McDarrah, Nov. 5, 1960; children: Timothy, Patrick. BA in French, Pa. State U., 1953; MA in French, NYU, 1966. Editorial asst. Crowell-Collier, N.Y.C., 1957-59; exec. asst. to pub. Time Inc., N.Y.C., 1959-61; libr., tchr. N.Y.C. Pub. Schs. and St. Luke's Sch., 1972-76; exec. asst. to pres. Capital Cities Communications Inc., N.Y.C., 1972-76; analyst N.Y.C. Landmarks Preservation Commn., 1976-79; project editor Grosset & Dunlap Inc., N.Y.C., 1979-80; sr. editor Prentice Hall trade div. Simon & Schuster Inc., N.Y.C., 1980-88; pres. McDarrah Media Assocs., N.Y.C., 1988—. Author: Frommer's Guide to Virginia, 1992, 2d edit., 1994-95, Frommer's Atlantic City and Cape May, 1984, 4th edit., 1991, 5th edit., 1993-95, The Artist's World, 2d edit., 1988; co-author: Museums in New York, 5th edit., 1990, Photography Marketplace, 1975 (book rev. sect.), The Beat Generation: Glory Days in Greenwich Village, 1996; co-editor Exec. Desk Diary Saturday Rev., 1962-64; contbg. editor quar. Dollarwise Traveler, Fodor's Cancun, Cozumel, Yucatan Peninsula, Fodor's Arizona; editor book rev. The Picture Profl., 1990—; book columnist Manhattan Spirit, 1989—; book reviewer Pub.'s Weekly, 1994—.

MC DAVID, GEORGE EUGENE (GENE MC DAVID), newspaper executive; b. McComb, Miss., June 30, 1930; s. O.C. and Inez S. McDavid; m. Betty Ernestine Tinsley, Sept. 24, 1949; children: Carol McDavid, Martha Gene Newman. B.B.A. cum laude, U. Houston, 1965. Owner, publisher Wilk Amite Record, Gloster, Miss., 1949-58; with Houston Chronicle, 1958—, prodn. mgr., 1967-74, v.p. ops., 1974-85, v.p., gen. mgr., 1985-90, pres., 1990—; adv. bd. Am. Press Inst.; past pres. bd. dirs. S.W. Sch. Printing Mgmt. Chmn. Greater Houston chpt. ARC, nat. bd. govs.; mem. pres.'s counsel Houston Bapt. U.; vice-chmn. Sam Houston Boy Scouts Am., United Negro Coll. Fund, Asia Soc. Goodwill Industries, YMCA; bd. dirs., Greater Houston Partnership, Nat. Conf. Christians and Jews, Houston region Am. Cancer Soc.; bd. dirs., pres. Houston Symphony; bd. dirs., v.p. Books of the World; mem. devel. bd. U. Houston; spl. deacon Second Bapt. Ch., Houston. Recipient Franklin award U. Houston, 1961, Disting. Alumnus award, 1990, Taggart award Tex. Newspaper, 1992, Man of Yr. award NCCJ, 1993; named Outstanding Ex-Citizen Gloster, 1973, Hon. Father of Yr., 1996. Mem. Am. Newspaper Pubs. Assn. (chmn. newsprint com.), So. Newspaper Pubs. Assn. (pres.) Tex. Daily Newspaper Assn. (pres.), Houston C. of C. (Houston Citizen's Community Svc. award 1993), Phi Kappa Phi, Beta Gamma Sigma. Clubs: Houston, Houstonian, Texas, Pine Forest Country. Home: 403 Hunters Park Ln Houston TX 77024-5438 Office: Houston Chronicle 801 Texas St Houston TX 77002-2906

MCDAVID, J. GARY, lawyer; b. Colorado Springs, Colo., May 13, 1947; s. John Arthur and Dorothy Jean (Collins) McD.; m. Janet Louise Kurzeka, June 9, 1973; 1 child, Matthew Collins. Student, U. Bonn., 1968-69; BA, Ohio State U., 1970; JD, Georgetown U., 1973. U.S. Dist. Ct. (D.C. dist.), D.C. Ct. Appeals 1973, U.S. Ct. Appeals (Fed. and D.C. cirs.), U.S. Tax Ct., U.S. Supreme Ct. Law clk. to chief judge U.S. Ct. Claims, Washington, 1973-75; with Hamel & Park, Washington, 1975-86; ptnr. McDermott, Will & Emery, Washington, 1986—; adj. prof. Georgetown U., Washington, 1982-85; speaker tax and corp. issues, 1982—. Served with USAR, 1970-78. Mem. ABA, U.S. Claims Ct. Bar Assn., Fed. Cir. Bar Assn. (bd. dirs. 1987-90), Bar Assn. D.C. (Cert. of Appreciation 1978). Avocations: golf, tennis, jogging. Office: McDermott Will & Emery 1850 K St NW Ste 500 Washington DC 20006-2213

MCDAVID, JANET LOUISE, lawyer; b. Mpls., Jan. 24, 1950; d. Robert Matthew and Lois May (Bratt) Kurzeka; m. John Gary McDavid, June 9, 1973; 1 child, Matthew Collins McDavid. BA, Northwestern U., 1971; JD, Georgetown U., 1974. Bar: D.C. 1975, U.S. Supreme Ct., 1980, U.S. Ct. Appeals (fed. cir.) 1975, (D.C. cir.) 1976, (5th cir.) 1983, (9th cir.) 1986. Assoc. Hogan & Hartson, Washington, 1974-83, ptnr., 1984—; gen. counsel ERAmerica, 1977-83; mem. antitrust task force Dept. Defense, 1993-94; mem. antitrust coun. U.S. C. of C., 1994—. Contbr. articles to profl. jours. Participant Clinton Administrn. Transition Team FTC. Mem. ABA (antitrust sect., vice chmn. civil practice com. 1986-89, sect. 2 com. 1989-90, chmn. franchising com. 1990-91, coun. mem. 1991-94, program officer 1994—, governing com. of forum on franchising 1991—), ACLU, U.S. C. of C. (antitrust coun. 1995—), Washington Coun. Lawyers, D.C. Bar Assn., Fed. Bar Assn., Womens Legal Def. Fund, Antitrust Coun. C. of C. Democrat. Office: Hogan & Hartson 555 13th St NW Washington DC 20004-1109

MCDAVID, SARA JUNE, librarian; b. Atlanta, Dec. 21, 1945; d. William Harvey and June (Threadgill) McRae; m. Michael Wright McDavid, Mar. 23, 1971. BA, Mercer U., 1967; MLS, Emory U., 1969. Head librarian Fernbank Sci. Ctr., Atlanta, 1969-77; dir. rsch. libr. Fed. Res. Bank of Atlanta, 1977-81; mgr. mem. services SOLINET, Atlanta, 1981-82; media specialist Parkview High Sch., Atlanta, 1982-84; ptnr. Interncontinental Travel, Atlanta, 1984-85; librarian Wesleyan Day Sch., Atlanta, 1985-86; mgr. info. svcs. Internat. Assn. Fin. Planning, Atlanta, 1986-90; dir. rsch. Korn Ferry Internat., Atlanta, 1990-95; rschr. Lamalie Amrop Internat., Atlanta, 1995—; bd. dirs. Southeastern Library Network, Atlanta, 1977-80, vice chmn. bd., 1979-80. Contbr. articles to profl. jours. Pres., mem. exec. com. Atlanta Humane Soc., 1985-86, bd. dirs. aux., 1978-90. Mem. Ga. Library Assn. (v.p. 1981-83), Spl. Libraries Assn. Home: 1535 Knob Hill Dr NE Atlanta GA 30329-3206 Office: Lamalie Amrop Internat 191 Peachtree St Ste 800 Atlanta GA 30303-1747

MCDAVID, WILLIAM HENRY, lawyer; b. N.Y.C., May 10, 1946; s. William H. and Margaret B. (Carmody) McD.; m. Sylvia Noin, Dec. 21, 1984; children: Andrew, Madeline, William, Flora. AB, Columbia Coll., N.Y.C., 1968; JD, Yale U., 1972. Assoc. Debevoise & Plimpton, N.Y.C., 1972-81; asst. gen. counsel Bankers Trust Co., N.Y.C., 1981-83, assoc. gen. counsel, 1983-84, v.p., 1984-85, v.p., counsel, 1986-88; gen. counsel Chem. Banking Corp., N.Y.C., 1988—; spl. counsel Adminstrv. Conf. of U.S., Washington, 1988-91. Mem. Bank Capital Markets Assn. (vice chmn. 1988-89, chmn. lawyers com. 1989-90). Office: Chemical Bank Office Gen Coun 270 Park Ave 8th Fl New York NY 10017

MCDERMOTT, AGNES CHARLENE SENAPE, philosophy educator; b. Hazelton, Pa., Mar. 11, 1937; d. Charles G. and Conjetta (Ranieri) Senape; children: Robert C., Lisa G., Jamie C. B.A., U. Pa., 1956, Ph.D., 1964; postgrad., U. Calif.-Berkeley, 1960-61, U. Amsterdam, Netherlands, 1965, U. Wis., 1967-69. Instr. math. Drexel Inst. Tech., Phila., 1962-63; asst. prof. philosophy SUNY-Buffalo, 1964-65, Hampton Inst., Va., 1966-67; asst. prof. U. Wis.-Milw., 1967-70; assoc. prof. philosophy U. N.Mex., Albuquerque, 1970-80, prof., dean grad. studies, 1981-86; dean in residence Council of Grad. Schs., Washington, 1985-86; provost, v.p. acad. affairs CUNY, CUNY, 1986-89; prof. philosophy CUNY, 1986-91; dean for acad. and student affairs, cons. Albuquerque Acad., 1991-93; ind. cons. Corrales, N.Mex., 1993—; vis. assoc. prof. U. Wash., Seattle, 1974, U. Calif.-Berkeley, 1973-74, U. Hawaii, Honolulu, 1975; vis. prof. U. Calif.-Berkeley, 1980; lectr., panelist. Author: An Eleventh Century Buddhist Logic of 'Exists', 1969, Boethius' Treatise on the Modes of Signifying, 1980; compiler, editor anthology: Comparative Philosophy: Selected Essays, 1983; rev. editor Phil. East West, 1986—; contbr. articles to profl. jours. Vol. Albuquerque Care Alliance, 1988—. AAUW postdoctoral fellow, 1965-66; NEH Younger Humanist fellow, 1971-72; faculty rsch. fellow U. N.Mex., 1978, 79, 80; U. Pa. grad. fellow, 1961-62; S. Fels Found. fellow, 1963-64;U. Pa. tuition scholar; Pa. Hist. Soc. scholar. Mem. N.Y. Acad. Scis., Am. Philos. Soc., Am. Philos. Assn. (exec. com. 1977-80), Assn. Asian Studies (exec. com. 1977-80), Am. Oriental Soc., Western Assn. Grad. Schs. (pres. 1986-87), Phi Beta Kappa, Pi Mu Epsilon. Democrat. Avocations: skiing, fly-fishing.

MC DERMOTT, ALBERT LEO, lawyer; b. Lowell, Mass., Jan. 21, 1923; s. John Thomas and Josephine (Rohan) McD. AB, Boston Coll., 1944; LLB, Georgetown U., 1949. Bar: Mass. 1950, D.C. 1950, U.S. Supreme Ct. 1972. Practice of law Washington, 1950-54; asso. Ingoldsby & Coles, 1950-52, partner, 1952-54; spl. asst. to Sec. Labor, 1954-61; ptnr. law firm McDermott & Russell (and predecessor), 1961-92; Washington rep. Am. Hotel and Motel Assn., 1963-88; adv. bd. Maritime Cargo Transp. conf., Fed. Svc. Impasses Panel, 1972-78; alt. rep. Pres. Nixon's Pay Bd., 1971-73; staff dir. Senate Rules Com., 1994-95, Senate Com. on Govtl. Affairs, 1995—. Served as lt. USNR, World War II. Mem. Nat. Acad. Sci. (mem. research council 1957-60), ABA, Bar Assn. D.C. Clubs: Congl. Country, Capitol Hill (Washington); Tavern (N.Y.C.); Rehoboth Country (Del.). Home: 4813 Van Ness St NW Washington DC 20016-2353 Office: US Senate Washington DC 20510

MCDERMOTT, CECIL WADE, mathematics educator, educational program director; b. Parkin, Ark., Aug. 19, 1935; s. Joe E. and Myrtle L. (Davis) McD.; m. Nelda Grace Lyons, June 4, 1961; children: Kevin Scott, Stephen Kyle. BS in Math., U. Ark., 1957; MS in Stats., Purdue U., 1962; EdD in Math. Edn., Auburn (Ala.) U., 1967. Cert. tchr. math., gen. sci., phys. sci., curriculum specialist supr., designated ind. fee appraiser, rsch. analyst. Instr. math. Sikeston (Mo.) H.S., 1957-59; state math. supr. Ark. Dept. Edn., Little Rock, 1959-65; ednl. cons. Auburn U., 1965-67; chmn., prof. math. Hendrix Coll., Conway, Ark., 1967-83; program dir. IMPAC Learning Sys., Inc., Little Rock, 1983—; co-dir. NSF Inst. Tulane U., New Orleans, summers 1967-71; residential appraiser Morrilton (Ark.) Savs. & Loan, summers 1977-82; cons. Okla. Legis. Coun., Oklahoma City, 1987, America 2000 Project, Dallas, 1991; mem. tchr. tng. panel Office Tech. Assessment, 1994; pres. Ark. Intercoll. Conf. Faculty Rep., 1974-84. Author: (audio-tutorial film) Primary School Mathematics, 1975; co-author: Modern Elementary Mathematics, 1978, Landmarks, Rudders and Crossroads, 1993; designer: (computer courseware) Mathematics/Basic Skills, 1989, 93. Plan coord. Gov.'s Task Force on Telecomm. Planning, 1991-95. Rsch. grantee U.S. Office Edn., Washington, 1972-73, Rockefeller Found., Little Rock, 1983-85; recipient Cert. of Merit award Electronic Learning, 1987, Endowment Scholarship Hendrix Coll., Conway, Ark., 1987. Mem. Ark. Amateur Union (chmn. state long distance running program 1969-72), Ark. Coun. Tchrs. Math. (chmn. regional conf. 1970), Am. Math. Soc., Math. Assn. Am. (pres. Okla./Ark. 1976-77), Phi Delta Kappa, Phi Kappa Phi, Pi Mu Epsilon. Episcopalian. Avocations: long distance running, creative writing, farming. Home: 1204 Hunter St Conway AR 72032-2716 Office: IMPAC Learning Sys Inc 501 Woodlane Dr Ste 122 Little Rock AR 72201-1024

MCDERMOTT, DREW VINCENT, computer science educator; b. Madison, Wis., Dec. 27, 1949; s. James Kenneth and Lucy Lea (Hurt) McD.; m. Judith Claire Rosenbaum, July 22, 1974; children: Noel Timothy, Katherine Anne. SB, SM, MIT, 1972, PhD, 1976. Asst. prof. computer sci. Yale U., New Haven, 1976-83, prof., 1983—, chmn. dept., 1991-96. Co-author: Introduction to Artificial Intelligence, 1985, Artificial Intelligence Programming, 1987. Fellow Am. Assn. for Artificial Intelligence; mem. Assn. for Computing Machinery. Roman Catholic. Avocations: philosophy of mind, chess. Office: Yale Univ Dept of Computer Sci PO Box 2158 New Haven CT 06520

MCDERMOTT, EDWARD ALOYSIOUS, lawyer; b. Dubuque, Iowa, June 28, 1920; s. Edward L. and Sarah (Larkin) McD.; m. Naola Spellman, Sept. 1, 1945; children: Maureen, Edward Aloysious, Charles Joseph, Daniel John. B.A., Loras Coll., Dubuque, 1939; J.D., State U., Iowa, 1942; J.D. (hon.), Xavier U., 1962, Loras Coll., 1973. Bar: Iowa 1942, D.C. 1942, Nebr. 1942. Mem. legal dept. Travelers Ins. Co., Omaha, 1942-43, Montgomery Ward & Co., Chgo., 1943-46; atty. firm O'Connor, Thomas & O'Connor, Dubuque, 1946-50; chief counsel sub-com. privileges and elections U.S. Senate, 1950-51; partner firm O'Connor, Thomas, McDermott & Wright, Dubuque, 1951-61; prof. bus. law and econs. Loras Coll., also Clarke Coll., Dubuque; dep. dir. U.S. Office Civil and Def. Moblzn., 1961-62, U.S. Office Emergency Planning, 1961-62; dir. Office Emergency Planning, 1962-65; ptnr. firm Hogan & Hartson, Washington, 1965-88; ret., 1989; U.S. rep. to sr. com. and other coms. NATO, 1962-65; chmn. Pres.'s Exec. Stockpile Com., 1962-65; mem. bd. advisers Indsl. Coll. Armed Forces, 1962-65; mem. Nat. Conf. Uniform Commrs. State Laws, 1959-64; chmn. Nat. CD Adv. Coun., 1962-65; mem. Pres.'s Com. Employment Handicapped, 1962-65, Pres.'s Com. Manpower, 1963-65, Pres.'s Com. Econ. Impact Def. and Rearmament, 1963-65, Pres.'s Sr. Adv. Com. on Govt. Reorgn., 1978-79; chmn. Com. on Assumptions for Nonmil. and Devel. Commn., Alaska, 1964-65; bd. dirs. Mercedes-Benz N.A., 1985—, mem. ops. com., 1986—; mem. adv. com. Office Comptr. Gen. of U.S., 1990—. Del. Democratic Nat. Conv., 1952, 56, 60, 64; trustee, sec. Ford's Theatre, Christ Child Soc., Religious Educators Found., Loras Coll.; mem. fin. council Archdiocese of Washington, 1985-89; chmn. emeritus Lombardi Cancer Inst.; regent emeritus Coll. Notre Dame; trustee emeritus Colgate U.; mem. council Hosp. St. John and St. Elizabeth, London, Maynooth Coll., Ireland; regent emeritus U. Santa Clara, Calif; bd. advisers Lynchburg (Va.) Coll., Iowa Law Sch. Found., Up With People; v.p. Flax Trust, No. Ireland. Decorated knight Holy Sepulchre; recipient Amvets Spl. Silver Helmet award, 1963. Fellow ABA; mem. Fed. Bar Assn., Iowa Bar Assn. (bd. govs. 1956-60), D.C. Bar Assn., Am. Judicature Soc., John Carroll Soc. (pres. 1972), Am. Ireland Fund (bd. dirs.), Friendly Sons St. Patrick (pres. 1978-79), Ireland Club Fla., The City Club (bd. dirs.), 1925 F Street Club, Met. Club (Washington), Delray Beach Club (Fla.), Knights of Malta Fed. Assn. (pres. 1979-82). Democrat. Home: Lake House South 875 E Camino Real Boca Raton FL 33432-6356 Office: Columbia Sq 555 13th St NW Washington DC 20004-1109

MCDERMOTT, FRANCIS OWEN, lawyer; b. Denver, Feb. 25, 1933; s. Paul Harkins and Agnes (Clarke) McD.; divorced; children: Diana, Daniel, Christopher, Anthony, Justine; m. Estella Marina Idiaquez, June 6, 1986. JD, Am. U., 1960. Bar: D.C. 1960, U.S. Dist. Ct. D.C., 1960, U.S. Ct. Appeals (D.C. cir.) 1960, u.S. Tax Ct. 1961, U.S. Supreme Ct. 1964. Trial atty. office regional counsel IRS, Washington, 1961-65; mem. profl. staff com. on fin. U.S. Senate, Washington, 1965-68; tax counsel Assn. Am. R.R.s, Washington, 1968-73; assoc. Hopkins & Sutter, Washington, 1973-76, ptnr., 1976—; gen. counsel Inst. Ill., Washington, 1987—. Mem. ABA, Fed. Bar Assn., Nat. Def. Transp. Assn. (v.p., gen. counsel 1974—). Roman Catholic. Avocation: tennis.

MCDERMOTT, JAMES A., congressman, psychiatrist; b. Chicago, Ill., Dec. 28, 1936; children: Katherine, James. BS, Wheaton Coll., 1958; MD, U. Ill., 1963. Intern Buffalo Gen. Hosp., 1963-64; resident in adult psychiatry U. Ill. Hosps., Chgo., 1964-66; resident in child psychiatry U. Wash. Hosps., Seattle, 1966-68; asst. clin. prof. dept. psychiatry U. Wash., Seattle, 1970-83; mem. Wash. Ho. of Reps., 1971-72, Wash. Senate, 1975-87; regional med. officer U.S. Fgn. Svc., 1987-88; mem. 101st-104th Congresses from 7th Wash. dist., 1989—; former chmn. stds. of ofcl. conduct com., mem. ways and means com., ranking minority mem., mem. stds. of ofcl. conduct com.; mem. exec. and edn. com. Nat. Conf. State Legislatures, chair ethics com. Mem. Wash. State Arts Commn., Wash. Coun. for Prevention Child Abuse and Neglect; Dem. nominee for gov., 1980. Lt. comdr. M.C., USN, 1968-70. Mem. Am. Psychiat. Assn., Wash. State Med. Assn., King County Med. Soc. Democrat. Episcopalian. Office: US Ho of Reps 2349 Rayburn HOB Washington DC 20515

MCDERMOTT, JOHN H(ENRY), lawyer; b. Evanston, Ill., June 23, 1931; s. Edward Henry and Goldie Lucile (Boso) McD.; m. Ann Elizabeth Pickard, Feb. 19, 1966; children: Elizabeth A., Mary L., Edward H. BA, Williams Coll., 1953; JD, U. Mich., 1956. Bar: Mich. 1955, Ill. 1956. Assoc. McDermott, Will & Emery, Chgo., 1958-64, ptnr., 1964—; bd. dirs. Patrick Industries Inc. 1st lt. USAF, 1956-58. Mem. ABA, Ill. Bar Assn., Chgo. Bar Assn. Clubs: Commerical of Chgo., Econ. of Chgo., Legal Chgo. (pres. 1981-82), Law Chgo. (pres. 1986-87). Home: 330 Willow Rd Winnetka IL 60093-4130 Office: McDermott Will & Emery 227 W Monroe St Chicago IL 60606-5096

MC DERMOTT, JOHN JOSEPH, philosophy educator; b. N.Y.C., Jan. 5, 1932; s. John J. and Helen (Kelly) McD.; m. Virginia Picarelli, June 14, 1952 (div. Aug., 1990); children: Marise, Michele, David, Brian, Tara; m. Patricia Anne Garner, Dec. 29, 1990. B.A. cum laude, St. Francis Coll., 1953; M.A., Fordham U., 1954, Ph.D., 1959; LL.D., U. Hartford, 1970. Tchr. Latin Loughlin High Sch., Bklyn., 1953-54; instr. philosophy St. Francis Coll., Bklyn., 1954-57; mem. faculty Queens Coll., Flushing, N.Y., 1956-77; assoc. prof. philosophy Queens Coll., 1965-67, prof., 1968-77; prof., head dept. philosophy and humanities Tex. A. and M. U., 1977-81; disting. prof. philosophy Tex. A&M U., 1981—, prof., head dept. med. humanities Coll. Medicine, 1981-90, Abell Prof. liberal arts, 1986—; vis. prof. Am. lit. SUNY-Stony Brook, 1970. Author: The Culture of Experience, 1976, Streams of Experience, 1986; editor: Writings of William James, 1967, Basic Writings of Josiah Royce, 2 vols., 1969, The Philosophy of John Dewey, 2 vols., 1973, Cultural Introduction to Philosophy, 1985; adv. editor: Collected Works of William James; gen. editor: Correspondence of William James; mem. editorial bd. Cross Currents, 1968—, Transactions, Jour. Speculative Philosophy; contbr. articles to profl. jours. Trustee Nat. Faculty for Humanities, Arts, Scis. Postdoctoral fellow Union Theol. Sem., 1964-65; recipient E. Harris Harbison award for gifted teaching, 1969-70. Mem. Am. Philos. Assn. (exec. com., 1979-82, Nat. Bd. Officers, 1989-92), Am. Studies Assn., History of Sci. Soc., Peirce Soc. (editorial bd. Trans.), Soc. for Advancement Am. Philosophy (exec. com. 1973, pres. 1977-80, Herbert W. Schneider award 1993). Home: 701 Dexter Dr S College Station TX 77840-6171

MCDERMOTT, KEVIN J., engineering educator, consultant; b. Teaneck, N.J., Nov. 21, 1935; s. Francis X. and Elizabeth (Casey) McD.; m. Ann McDermott, Aug. 3, 1959; children: Kathleen, Kevin, Donna, Michael. BSEE, N.J. Inst. Tech., 1965; MS Indsl. Engring., Columbia U., 1970; EdD, Fairleigh Dickinson U., 1975. Registered profl. engr., N.J. With Bell Telephone Labs., Murray Hill, N.J., 1960-65, Westinghouse Electic, Newark, 1965-67, Columbia U., NASA, N.Y.C., 1967-70, RCA Corp., N.Y.C., 1970-76, Ramapo (N.J.) Coll., 1976-80; prof. N.J. Inst. Tech., Newark, 1980—; chmn. engring. dept. N.J. Inst. Tech., 1983—; dir. Computer Aided Design/Computer Aided Manufacture Robotics Consortium. Contbr. more than 50 articles to tech. jours. IBM fellow, 1987. Fellow IEEE, Soc. Mech. Engrs.; mem. Inst. Indsl. Engrs. Achievements include research in industrial robot work cells, manufacturing systems, expert systems, analysis of industrial robotics, flexible manufacturing systems, expert and vision systems in compuer aided design and manufacturing.

MCDERMOTT, KEVIN R., lawyer; b. Youngstown, Ohio, Jan. 26, 1952; s. Robert J. and Marion D. (McKeown) McD.; m. Cindy J. Darling, Dec. 11, 1976; children: Ciara, Kelly. AB, Miami U., Oxford, Ohio, 1974; JD, Ohio State U., 1977. Bar: Ohio 1977, U.S. Dist. Ct. (so. dist.) Ohio 1978, U.S. Dist. Ct. (no. dist.) Ohio 1988, U.S. Dist. Ct. (we. dist.) Mich. 1993, U.S. Supreme Ct. 1990. Assoc. ptnr. Murphey Young & Smith, Columbus, Ohio, 1977-88; ptnr. Squire Sanders & Dempsey, Columbus, Ohio, 1988-90, Schottenstein Zox & Dunn, Columbus, Ohio, 1990—; adv. bd. mem. Capital U. Legal Asst. Program, Columbus, Ohio, 1988—. Bd. pres. Easter Seal Soc. Ctrl. Ohio, Columbus, 1992-94, bd. mem. 1988-92; pres. Upper Arlington Civic Svc. Commn., Columbus, Ohio, 1988-93. Office: Schottenstein Zox & Dunn 41 S High St Columbus OH 43215-6101

MCDERMOTT, LARRY ARNOLD, newspaper publisher, newspaper editor; b. Parkin, Ark., Apr. 27, 1948; s. John Allen and Ila Mae (Harris) McD.; m. Linda Louis Lancaster, Mar. 20, 1969; children: Marshall, Kelly, Amanda. BS, Ark. State U., 1970. Reporter Jonesboro (Ark.) Sun, 1968-70; reporter AP, Richmond, Va., 1970-71, 72-75, Norfolk, Va., 1975-76; polit. correspondent AP, Lansing, Mich., 1976-78; bur. chief AP, Little Rock, 1978-80, Mpls., 1980-84, Detroit, 1984-87; asst. to the pres. AP, N.Y.C., 1987-88; info. specialist UN Command, Seoul, Republic of Korea, 1971-72; copy editor Korea Times, Seoul, 1971-72; editor, bur. chief Booth Newspapers, Lansing, 1988-90; pub. Bay City (Mich.) Times, 1990-92; exec. editor Springfield Union News, Mass., 1993—; v.p., bd. dirs. Mich. State News, East Lansing, 1990-91. Bd. dirs. Bay Area Econ. Growth Alliance, Bay City, 1990-91. With U.S. Army, 1970-72. Presbyterian. Avocations: fly fishing, golf, camping. Home: 26 Tennyson Dr East Longmeadow MA 01106-2334 Office: Bay City Times 311 5th St Bay City MI 48708-5806 also: Union-News 1860 Main St Springfield MA 01103-1000

MCDERMOTT, LUCINDA MARY, minister, teacher, philosopher, poet, author; b. Lynwood, Calif., June 3, 1947; d. R. Harry and Cathrine Jaynne (Redmond) Boand. BA, U. So. Calif., L.A., 1969; MS, Calif. State U., Long Beach, 1975; PhD, Saybrook Inst., 1978. Pres. Environ. Health Systems, Newport Beach, Calif., 1976-90, Forerunner Publs., Newport Beach, 1985—; founder, pres. Life-Skills Learning Ctr., Newport Beach, 1985—; founder, dir. Newport Beach Ecumenical Ctr., 1993—; pres. Tri Delta Mgmt.; bd. dirs. The Boand Family Found.; founder, dir. Truthsayers Minstrels, 1996—. Author: Bridges to Another Place, 1972, Honor Thy Self, Vol. I and II, 1973, Hello-My-Love-Good Bye, 1973, Life-Skills for Adults, 1982, Au Courants, 1983, Life-Skills for Children, 1984, Myrika-An Autobiographical Novel, 1989, White Knights and Shining Halos: Beyond Pair Bonding, 1996. Mem. APA, Truthsayer Minstrels (founder, dir. 1996—), Alpha Kappa Delta, Kappa Kappa Gamma.

MCDERMOTT, RENÉE R(ASSLER), lawyer; b. Danville, Pa., Sept. 26, 1950; d. Carl A. and Rose (Gaupp) Rassler; m. James A. McDermott, Jan. 1, 1986. BA, U. So. Fla., 1970, MA, 1972; JD, Ind. U., 1978. Bar: Ind. 1978, U.S. Dist. Ct. (so. and no. dists.) Ind. 1978, U.S. Dist. Ct. Ariz. 1984, U.S. Ct. Appeals (7th cir.) 1979, U.S. Ct. Appeals (9th cir.) 1985. Law clk. to presiding judge U.S. Dist. Ct. (no. dist.) Ind., Ft. Wayne, 1978-80; assoc. Barnes & Thornburg, Indpls., 1980-84, ptnr., 1985-93; pvt. practice Nashville, Ind., 1994—; county atty. County of Brown, Ind., 1994—. Editor in chief Ind. U. Law Jour., 1977-78. Bd. visitors Ind. U. Law Sch., Bloomington, 1979—; bd. dirs. Environ. Quality Control Inc., Indpls. Named one of Outstanding Young Women Am., 1986. Fellow Ind. Bar Found., Am. Bar Found. (life); mem. ABA (bus. sect. coun. 1995—, chmn. environ. controls com. 1991-95, liaison to standing com. on environ. law bus. law sect.), Ind. State Bar Assn. (chmn. young lawyers sect. 1985-86, chmn. environ. law sect. 1989-91), Bar Assn. 7th Fed. Cir., Ind. Mfrs. Assn. (environ. affairs com.), Order of Coif. Avocations: scuba diving, horseback riding, music, reading, hiking. Home and Office: 1008 W McLary Rd Nashville IN 47448-9176

MCDERMOTT, RICHARD T., lawyer, educator; b. Milw., Jan. 30, 1940; s. Richard A. and Sylvia Carmen (Portuondo) McD.; m. Mary Patricia Scanlon, Aug. 24, 1963; children: Richard B., Christina M. BA, Marquette U., 1962; LLB, Fordham U., 1966. Bar: N.Y. 1967. Assoc. Alexander & Green, N.Y.C., 1966-73, ptnr., 1973-86; ptnr. Walter, Conston, Alexander & Green, N.Y.C., 1987-90, Rogers & Wells, N.Y.C., 1990—; adj. prof. law NYU Sch. Law, N.Y.C., 1980—. Author: Legal Aspects of Corporate Finance, 1985, 2d edit., 1995. Fellow Am. Bar Found.; mem. ABA, N.Y. State Bar Assn., Bar Assn. City N.Y., Univ. Club, Woodstock Golf Club (N.Y.). Avocations: foreign relations, golf. Office: Rogers & Wells 200 Park Ave New York NY 10166-0005

MCDERMOTT, ROBERT B., lawyer; b. Washington, June 16, 1927; s. Edward H. and Goldie Lucile (Boso) McD.; m. Julia Wood, Nov. 16, 1950; children: John, Jeanne, Charles; m. Jane S. Whitman, July 31, 1973; m. Sarah Jaicks, Jan. 6, 1996. A.B., Princeton U., 1948; LL.B., Harvard U., 1951. Bar: D.C. 1951, Ill. 1955. Atty. Office Gen. Counsel, Navy Dept., Washington, 1951-52; assoc McDermott, Will & Emery, Chgo., 1954-60, ptnr., 1961-92, chmn., 1986-91, of counsel, 1992—; bd. dirs. The Cherry Corp., Waukegan, Ill., Furst-McNess Co., Freeport, Ill., Maynard Oil Co., Dallas. Trustee Ill. Inst. Tech., Chgo., 1985—, The Mather Found., Evanston, Ill., 1988—; bd. dirs. Ct. Theatre, Alliance Francaise de Chgo. Lt. USNR, 1945-46, 52-54. Mem. Chgo. Bar Assn. Clubs: Chicago, Economic, University (Chgo.). Home: 990 N Lake Shore Dr Chicago IL 60611-1353 Office: 227 W Monroe St Chicago IL 60606-5016

MCDERMOTT, ROBERT FRANCIS, JR., lawyer; b. Cambridge, Mass., Nov. 3, 1945; s. Robert F. and Alice McD.; children: Robert F. III, Peter M. BA, Harvard U., 1967; LLB, Yale U., 1970. Bar: Ga. 1973, Va. 1976, U.S. Dist. Ct. D.C. 1980, U.S. Ct. Appeals 1980, U.S. Dist. Ct. (ea. dist.) Va. 1976, U.S. Supreme Ct. 1982. Staff asst. to the pres. White House, Washington, 1970-72; staff asst. to dep. atty. gen. and assoc. dep. atty. gen. Dept. of Justice, Washington, 1974-75; asst. U.S. atty. U.S. Dist. Ct. (ea. dist.) Va., 1975-79; atty. Jones, Day, Reavis & Pogue, Washington, 1979—. Office: Jones Day Reavis & Pogue 1450 G St NW Washington DC 20005-2001*

MCDERMOTT, THOMAS JOHN, JR., lawyer; b. Santa Monica, Calif., Mar. 23, 1931; s. Thomas J. Sr. and Etha Irene (Cook) McD.; m. Yolanda; children: Jodi Friedman, Kimberly E., Kish S. BA, UCLA, 1953, JD, 1958. Bar: Calif. 1959. Ptnr., Gray, Binkley and Pfaelzer, Los Angeles, 1964-67, Kadison, Pfaelzer, Woodward, Quinn and Rossi, Los Angeles, 1967-87, Rogers & Wells, 1987-93, Bryan Cave, 1993-95, Manatt, Phelps & Phillips, 1995—. Served with U.S. Army, 1953-56, Korea. Fellow Am. Coll. Trial Lawyers; mem. ABA, UCLA Law Alumni Assn. (pres. 1961-62), Assn. of Bus. Trial Lawyers (pres. 1980-81, mem. exec. com. 9th cir. jud. conf. 1993—), State Bar Calif. (chair litigation sect. 1993-94), Order of Coif. Office: Manatt Phelps & Phillips 11355 W Olympic Blvd Los Angeles CA 90064-1614

MC DERMOTT, WILLIAM VINCENT, JR., physician, educator; b. Salem, Mass., Mar. 7, 1917; s. William Vincent and Mary A. (Feenan) McD.; m. Blanche O'Riorden, May 15, 1943 (dec. July 1969); children: Blanche Anne, William Shaw, Jane Travers Hoch; m. Mary Boit Bingham, June 1, 1976 (dec. 1984); m. Frances Weld Gardiner, June 16, 1989 (dec. 1993). A.B., Harvard U., 1938, M.D., 1942. Diplomate: Nat. Bd. Med. Examiners (chmn. surgery test com.), Am. Bd. Surgery. Intern Mass. Gen. Hosp., Boston, 1942; asst. resident surgeon Mass. Gen. Hosp., 1946-49, chief resident surgeon, 1950; practice medicine specializing in surgery Boston, 1951—; mem. staff Mass. Gen. Hosp., 1951—, New Eng. Deaconess Hosp., 1963—; dir. Fifth (Harvard) Surg. Svc. and Sears Surg. Lab. Boston City Hosp., 1963-73; mem. corp. vis. com., 1968—; USPHS fellow dept. biochemistry Sch. Medicine, Yale U., 1949-50; from instr. to prof. surgery Med. Sch. Harvard U., 1951-69, Cheever prof. surgery, 1969-87, prof. surgery emeritus, 1987—, sec. Faculty of Medicine, 1985-87; tutor premed. adv. Cabot House, Harvard Coll., 1989—; vis. prof. pro tem Kings Coll. Hosp. Med. Sch., London, 1960; dir. Harvard Surg. Svc. and Cancer Rsch. Inst., 1973-80; chmn. dept. surgery New Eng. Deaconess Hosp., 1980-85, mem. vis. com., 1987—, bd. dirs. Author four books, over 200 sci. papers; contbr. 12 chapters to books; mem. editorial bd. Jour. Surg. Rsch., 1960-73, Jour. Surg. Oncology, 1970—. Pres. Med. Found., Boston, 1968-70, trustee, 1970-87, hon. trustee, 1987—; bd. trustees Nat. Youth Leadership Forum, 1995—. Maj. M.C. AUS, 1943-46, ETO. Decorated Bronze Star, oak leaf cluster, 5 battle stars; recipient Disting. Alumnus award Harvard U., 1992. Mem. ACS (bd. govs. 1984-90, pres. Mass. chpt. 1980), Soc. Univ. Surgeons, Am. Surg. Assn., Am. Acad. Arts and Scis., New Eng. Surg. Soc. (pres. 1985-86), Boston Surg. Soc. (pres. 1971), Harvard Med. Alumni Assn. (treas. 1965-68, pres. 1975-76, dir. alumni rels. 1987-93, bd. dirs. 1993-95), Harvard Coll. Alumni Assn., Soc. de Chirurgie Internat., Assn. Acad. Surgery, Soc. Surgery Alimentary Tract, Aesculapian Club (pres. 1971), Harvard Club of Boston (bd. govs. 1971-77), Nat. Youth Leadership Forum, Tavern Club, Country Club. Home: 570 Bridge St Dedham MA 02026-4131 Office: New Eng Deaconess Hosp Boston MA 02215

MCDEVITT, BRIAN PETER, history educator, educational consultant; b. Jersey City, Dec. 29, 1944; s. Bernard Aloysius and Veronica Sabina (Decker) McD.; m. Dorothy Helen Gilligan, Oct. 19, 1968; children: Peter David, Timothy Bernard. BS, Seton Hall U., 1966; MA, Columbia U., 1971. Tchr. history St. Patrick's High Sch., Elizabeth, N.J., 1966-68, Vail Deane High Sch., Elizabeth, N.J., 1968-70; fed. grant writer Alexian Bros. Hosp., Elizabeth, N.J., 1970-72, Union County Coll., Cranford, N.J., 1972-76; prin., owner Ednl. Svcs., Westfield, N.J., 1976—; adj. prof. history Union County Coll., Cranford, N.J., 1976—; adj. prof. classics Montclair (N.J.) State U., 1990—. Author: The Irish Librists, 1988, The Irish Librists and the Scrolls of Aristotle, 1993, A Historian's Thematic Study of Western Civilization, 1994, Evidence of an Ancient Greek Navigation System, 1995, The Irish Librists and The Vatican Library Mystery, 1996, (video) The Minoans According to Sir Arthur Evans; contbr. articles to profl. jours. N.J. Dept. Higher Edn. grantee. Mem. Trireme Trust U.S.A. (internat. rowing team 1990), Friends of Trireme (London), Soc. Naval Architects and Marine Engrs., Assn. Ancient Historians, Soc. Ancient Greek Philosophy, Assn. Muslim Social Scientists, Westfield United Fund, Westfield P.A.L., Westfield Basketball Assn., Westfield Baseball Assn., Boy Scouts Am. Roman Catholic. Avocations: golfing, rowing, basketball, playing piano, stamp collecting. Home: 607 S Chestnut St Westfield NJ 07090-1369

MCDEVITT, CHARLES FRANCIS, state supreme court justice; b. Pocatello, Idaho, Jan. 5, 1932; s. Bernard A. and Margaret (Hermann) McD.; m. Virginia L. Heller, Aug. 14, 1954; children: Eileen A., Kathryn A., Brian A., Sheila A., Terrence A., Neil A., Kendal A. LLB, U. Idaho, 1956. Bar: 1956. Ptnr. Richards, Haga & Eberle, Boise, 1956-62; gen. counsel, asst. sec. Boise Cascade Corp., 1962-65; mem. Idaho State Legislature, 1963-66; sec., gen. counsel Boise Cascade Corp., 1965-67, v.p., sec., 1967-68; pres. Beck Industries, 1968-70; group v.p. Singer Co., N.Y.C., 1970-72, exec. v.p., 1973-76; pub. defender Ada County, Boise, 1976-78; co-founder Givens, McDevitt, Pursley & Webb, Boise, 1978-89; justice Idaho Supreme Ct., Boise, 1989—, chief justice, 1993—; served on Gov.'s Select Com. on Taxation, Boise, 1988-89. Home: 4940 Boise River Ln Boise ID 83706-5706 Office: Idaho Supreme Ct 451 W State St Boise ID 83702-6006

MCDEVITT, HUGH O'NEILL, immunology educator, physician; b. Cin., 1930. M.D., Harvard U., 1955. Diplomate: Am. Bd. Internal Medicine. Intern Peter Bent Brigham Hosp., Boston, 1955-56, sr. asst. resident in medicine, 1961-62; asst. resident Bell Hosp., 1956-57; research fellow dept. bacteriology and immunology Harvard U., 1959-61; USPHS spl. fellow Nat. Inst. Med. Research, Mill Hill, London, 1962-64; physician Stanford U. Hosp., Calif., 1966—; assoc. prof. Stanford U. Sch. Medicine, Calif., 1969-72, prof. med. immunology, 1972—, prof. med. microbiology, 1980—, Burt and Marian Avery Prof. Immunology, 1990—; cons. physician VA Hosp., Palo Alto, Calif., 1968—. Served as capt. M.C., AUS, 1957-59. Mem. NAS, AAAS, Am. Fedn. Clin. Rsch., Am. Soc. Clin. Investigation, Am. Assn. Immunologists, Transplantation Soc., Inst. Medicine, Royal Soc. (fgn.). Office: Stanford U Dept Microbiology Stanford CA 94305

MC DEVITT, JOSEPH BRYAN, retired university administrator, retired naval officer; b. McGehee, Ark., Dec. 22, 1918; s. John and Mary Ann (Zimmer) McD.; m. Kathleen Rita Vaughan, 1943 (dec. 1961), m. Catherine Irene Beatty, Jan. 30, 1965 (dec. 1980); m. Ernestine Moody Minshew, Oct. 9, 1982; children: Jeffrey Bryan, Paul Killian, Rodney Peter, Rita Elizabeth, John Stephen, David Andrew, Joseph Bryan, Richard Vincent, Eugena Rose, Edward Francis, Gerald Christopher, Lisa Ernestine. Student, So. Ill. U., 1936-38; B.A., U. Ill., 1940, J.D., 1942. Bar: Ill. 1952. Commd. ensign U.S. Navy, 1943, advanced through grades to rear adm., 1968; boat group comdr. U.S.S. Leon, 1944-46; with legal office 8th Naval Dist. New Orleans, 1950; legal officer to comdr. Amphibious Force, Atlantic Fleet, 1952, mem. mil. justice div. Office Judge Adv. Gen., 1954, naval liaison officer to U.S. Senate, 1956; staff legal officer Marine Corps. Schs. Quantico, Va., 1958; student Naval War Coll., 1958-59, assigned Joint Chiefs Staff, 1959-61, dir. internat. law div. Office Judge Adv. Gen., 1962-65, legal affairs officer to comdr. in chief Pacific, 1965-68, judge adv. gen. of navy, 1968-72, ret., 1972; chief exec. officer People to People Programs Inc., Washington, 1972-73; v.p. exec. affairs, univ. counsel, sec. bd. trustees Clemson U., S.C., 1973-85, ret., 1985. Decorated Purple Heart, Legion of Merit, D.S.M. Mem. Am., Ill., Fed., Inter-Am. bar assns., Judge Advs. Assn., Am. Soc. Internat. Law. Catholic.

MCDEVITT, SHEILA MARIE, lawyer, energy company executive; b. St. Petersburg, Fla., Jan. 15, 1947; d. Frank Davis and Marie (Barfield) McD. AA, St. Petersburg Jr. Coll., 1966; BA in Govt., Fla. State U., 1968, JD, 1978. Bar: Fla. 1978. Research asst. Fla. Legis. Reference Bur., Tallahassee, 1968-69; adminstr., research assoc. Constitution Revision Commn. Ga. Gen. Assembly, Atlanta, 1969-70; adminstrv. asst., analyst Fla. State Sen., Tallahassee, Tampa, 1970-79; assoc. McClain, Walkley & Stuart, P.A., Tampa, Seminole, Fla., 1979-81; govtl. affairs counsel Tampa Electric Co., 1981-82, corp. counsel, 1982-86; sr. corp. counsel Teco Energy, Inc., Tampa, 1986-89, asst. v.p., 1989-92; v.p., asst. gen. counsel, 1992—; mem. Worker's Compensation Adv. Council Fla. Dept. Labor, Tallahassee, 1984-86. Bd. dirs. Vol. Ctr. Hillsborough County, Tampa, 1984-85; chmn., trustee Tampa Lowry Park Zoo Soc., 1968-94, also legal advisor; bd. dirs. Hillsborough County Easter Seal Soc., 1994-95; mem. Fla. Rep. Exec. Com., Tallahassee, 1974-75, Hillsborough County Rep. Exec. Com., 1974-75; mem. transition team for Fla. Gov. Bob Martinez, 1986-87; mem. Fed. Jud. Adv. Commn., 1989—. Mem ABA, Fla. Energy Bar Assn., Fla. Bar (vice chmn., then chmn. energy law com. 1984-87, jud. nominating procedures com. 1986-91, jud. adminstrn. selection and tenure com. 1991-93), Hillsborough County Bar Assn. (chmn. law week com. 1990, corp. counsel com. 1986-87, internat. law com. 1994-95), Am. Corp. Counsel Assn. (bd. dirs. Ctrl. Fla. chpt. 1986-87), Tampa Club, Tiger Bay Club, Tampa Yacht and Country Club. Roman Catholic. Avocations: photography, bicycling, reading, boating. Office: TECO Energy Inc PO Box 111 702 N Franklin St Tampa FL 33602

MCDIARMID, LUCY, English educator, author; b. Louisville, Mar. 29, 1947; m. Harris B. Savin, Oct. 13, 1984; children: Emily Clare, Katharine Eliza. BA, Swarthmore (Pa.) Coll., 1968; MA, Harvard U., 1969, PhD, 1972. Asst. prof. Boston U., 1972-74; from asst. prof. to assoc. prof. Swarthmore Coll., 1974-81; asst. prof. U. Md. Balt. County, Catonsville, 1982-84; prof. Villanova (Pa.) U., 1984—; vis. prof. English Princeton U., 1995; mem. exec. com. Am. Conf. for Irish Studies, 1987-91, v.p., 1995—. Author: Saving Civilization: Yeats, Eliot and Auden Between the Wars, 1984, Auden's Apologies for Poetry, 1990; co-editor: Selected Writings of Lady Gregory, 1995, High and Low Moderns: Literature and Culture, 1889-1939, 1996; contbr. articles to profl. jours. NEH fellow, 1981-82; ACLS grantee, 1976, Bunting Inst. fellow, 1981-82, Guggenheim fellow, 1993-94; vis. fellow N.Y. Inst. Humanities, 1993-95. Mem. MLA (exec. com. Twentieth Century Lit. divsn.), Internat. Assn. for Study Anglo-Irish Lit. (Am. sec.-treas. 1994—), Phi Beta Kappa. Home: 1931 Panama St Philadelphia PA 19103-6609 Office: Villanova U Dept Of English Villanova PA 19085

MCDILL, THOMAS ALLISON, minister; b. Cicero, Ill., June 4, 1926; s. Samuel and Agnes (Lindsay) McD.; m. Ruth Catherine Starr, June 4, 1949; children: Karen Joyce, Jane Alison, Steven Thomas. Th.B., No. Baptist Sem., Oakbrook, Ill., 1951; B.A., Trinity Coll., 1954; M.Div., Trinity Evang. Div. Sch., 1955, DD, 1989; D.Ministries, Bethel Theol. Sem., 1975. Ordained to ministry Evang. Free Ch. Am., 1949. Pastor Community Bible Ch., Berwyn, Ill., 1947-51, Grace Evang. Free Ch., Chgo., 1951-58, Liberty Bible Ch., Valparaiso, Ind., 1959-67, Crystal Evang. Free Ch., Mpls., 1967-76; v.p., moderator Evang. Free Ch. of Am., 1973-74, chmn. home missions bd., 1968-72, chmn. exec. bd., 1973-90, pres., 1976-90, ret., 1990; min. at large Evang. Free Ch. Am., 1991—. Contbr. articles to publs. Chmn. bd. Trinity Coll., Deerfield, Ill., 1974-76; bd. govs. Trinity Western Coll.; bd. dirs. Trinity Evang. Divinity Sch. Mem. Evang. Free Ch. Ministerial Assn., Evang. Ministers Assn., Nat. Assn. Evangelicals (bd. adminstrn. 1976—, mem. exec. com. 1981-88), Greater Mpls. Assn. Evangelicals (bd. dirs., sec. bd. 1969-73). Home: 4246 Goldenrod Ln N Minneapolis MN 55441-1241 Office: 901 E 78th St Bloomington MN 55420-1334

MC DONAGH, EDWARD CHARLES, sociologist, university administrator; b. Edmonton, Alta., Can., Jan. 23, 1915; came to U.S., 1922, naturalized, 1936; s. Henry Fry and Aletta (Bowles) McD.; m. Louise Lucille Lorenzi, Aug. 14, 1940 (dec.); children: Eileen, Patricia. A.B., U. So. Calif., 1937, A.M., 1938, Ph.D., 1942. Asst. prof. So. Ill. U., Carbondale, 1940-46, asst. to pres., 1942-44; asst. prof. U. Okla., Norman, 1946-47; asst. prof. U. So. Calif., L.A., 1947-49, assoc. prof., 1949-56, prof., 1956-69, head dept., 1958-62; chmn., acad. univ. affairs com., 1961; assoc. dean divsn. social scis. and comms. U. So. Calif., L.A., 1960-63, chmn. univ. acad. affairs com., 1963; head dept. sociology U. Ala., 1969-71; chmn. dept. sociology Ohio State U., Columbus, 1971-74, acting dean Coll. Social and Behavioral Scis., 1974-75, dean Coll. Social and Behavioral Scis., 1975-78, chmn. coordinating coun. deans Colls. Arts and Scis., 1977-78, prof. emeritus Colls. Arts and Scis., 1981—; Smith-Mundt prof., Sweden, 1956-57; vis. prof. U. Hawaii, 1965; cons. Los Angeles and related sch. dists.; mem. Region XV Woodrow Wilson Selection Com., 1961-62. Author: (with E.S. Richards) Ethnic Relations in the U.S, 1953, (with J.E. Nordskog, M.J. Vincent) Analyzing Social Problems, 1956, (with Jon Simpson) Social Problems: Persistent Challenges, 1965, rev., 1969; Assoc. editor: Sociology and Social Research, 1947-69; editorial cons.: Sociometry, 1962-65; Contbr. articles to profl. publs. Served with AUS, 1944-46. Fellow Am. Sociol. Assn. (co-chmn. nat. conf. com. 1963, budget and exec. office com. 1975-78); mem. AAUP, AAAS, Am. Assn. Pub. Opinion Rsch., Alpha Kappa Delta (pres. united chtps. 1965-66), Phi Beta Kappa (chpt. pres. 1959-60), Blue Key, Skull and Dagger. Democrat. Home: 201 Spencer Dr Amherst MA 01002-3364

MCDONAGH, THOMAS JOSEPH, physician; b. N.Y.C., Feb. 29, 1932; s. John and Delia (Lee) McD.; m. Helen Marie Drury, May 18, 1957; children: Kevin T., Eileen D., Thomas J., Brian P., Patricia M. B.S., CCNY; M.D.,

Columbia U. Diplomate Am. Bd. Internal Medicine, Am. Bd. Preventive Medicine-Occupational Medicine. Intern Bronx Mcpl. Hosp., N.Y., 1957-58, resident, 1958-60; fellow in medicine, trainee in gastroenterology Albert Einstein Coll. Medicine, Bronx, 1960-62; pvt. practice internal medicine Coatesville, Pa., 1962-64; sr. physician Exxon Corp., N.Y.C., 1964-69, asst. med. dir., 1969-79; dir. medicine and environ. health Exxon Chem. Co., Darien, Conn., 1979-80, dir. medicine and environ. affairs, 1980-81; v.p. medicine and occupational health Exxon Corp., Dallas, 1981—; dir. medicine and environ. health Exxon Co. Internat., Florham Park, N.J., 1986—; bd. dirs. Nat. Assn. Drug Abuse Problems, N.Y.C., 1981-92; bd. dirs. Nat. Found. Med. Edn., San Francisco, 1983-95. Contbr. articles to med. jours. Chmn. bd. appeals Inc. Village of Bellerose, N.Y., 1977-84, trustee, 1965-77, dep. mayor, 1975-77. Fellow ACP, Am. Coll. Occupational and Environ. Medicine (bd. dirs. 1989-92), Am. Coll. Preventive Medicine; mem. AMA, N.Y. Acad. Scis., N.Y. Acad Medicine. Roman Catholic. Office: Exxon Co Internat 200 Park Ave Florham Park NJ 07932-1002

MCDONALD, AGNES GRANTHAM, home health care; b. Terry, Miss., Nov. 15, 1941; d. John T. and Carrie L. (McDonald) Grantham; m. John A. McDonald, Sr., Mar. 10, 1962; children: John A. Jr., D. James, Angela M. Diploma, Gilfoy Sch. of Nursing, 1962; BSN, Miss. Coll., 1975; MSN, U. So. Miss., 1993. RN, Miss.; Cert. in nursing adminstrn. Staff nurse labor and delivery Miss. Bapt. Hosp., Jackson, Miss., 1962-63; office nurse Dr. John Murphy, Jackson, Miss., 1964-66; staff nurse Hinds Gen. Hosp., Jackson, 1966-75; nurse evaluator UMC, Jackson, 1975-76; instr. St. Dominic Sch. of Nursing, Jackson, 1976; staff nurse/supr. Capitol Home Health, Clinton, Miss., 1976-77; state surveyor nurse Miss. State Bd. of Health, Jackson, 1977-81; DON Van Winkle Home Health, Jackson, 1981-85; govt. regulations nurse Ctrl. Miss. Home Health, Jackson, 1985-88; patient care coord MMRC Home, Jackson, 1988-92; dir. continuous quality improvement Sta. Home Health Agy., Jackson, 1992-95; v.p. of clin. svcs. Mid-Delta Home Health, Inc., Belzoni, Miss., 1995—. Mem. Woodville Bapt. Heights Bapt. Ch., Jackson, 1960-95, Calvary Bapt. Ch., 1995—. Mem. ANA, Miss. Nurse Assn., Sigma Theta Tau. Avocations: sewing, reading, crafts. Home: 406 E Jackson St Belzoni MS 39038 Office: Mid Delta Home Health Inc PO Box 373 Belzoni MS 39038

MCDONALD, ALAN ANGUS, federal judge; b. Harrah, Wash., Dec. 13, 1927; s. Angus and Nell (Britt) McD.; m. Ruby K., Aug. 22, 1949; children: Janelle Jo, Saralee Sue, Stacy. BS, U. Wash., 1950, LLB, 1952. Dep. pros. atty. Yakima County, Wash., 1952-54; assoc. Halverson & Applegate, Yakima, 1954-56; ptnr. Halverson, Applegate & McDonald, Yakima, 1956-85; judge U.S. Dist. Ct. (ea. dist.) Wash., Yakima, 1985—. Fellow Am. Coll. Trial Lawyers; Yakima C. of C. (bd. dirs.). Clubs: Yakima Country, Royal Duck (Yakima). Office: US Dist Ct PO Box 2706 Yakima WA 98907-2706

MCDONALD, ALICE COIG, state education official; b. Chalmette, La., Sept. 26, 1940; d. Olas Casimere and Genevieve Louise (Heck) Coig; m. Glenn McDonald, July 16, 1967; 1 child, Michel. B.S., Loyola U., New Orleans, 1962; M.Ed., Loyola U., 1966; cert. rank I sch. adminstrn., Spalding Coll., 1975. Tchr. St. Bernard Pub. Schs., Chalmette, La., 1962-67; counselor, instructional coordinator Jefferson County Schs., Louisville, 1967-77; ednl. adviser Jefferson County Govt., Louisville, 1977-78; chief exec. asst. Office of Mayor, Louisville, 1978-80; dep. supt. pub. instrn. Ky. Dept. Edn., Frankfort, 1980-83, supt. pub. instrn., 1984-88; bd. dirs., com. mem. Ky. Coun. on Higher Edn., 1984-88, Ky. Juvenile Justice com., 1984-88, Ky. Ednl. TV Authority, 1984-88, So. Regional Coun. Ednl. Improvement, 1984-88. Mem. Pres.'s Adv. Com. on Women, 1978-80; active Dem. Nat. Conv., 1972, 76, 80, 84; pres. Dem. Woman's Club Ky., 1974-76, mem. exec. com., 1977-88; bd. dirs. Ky. Found. for Blind; exec. dir. Ky. Govtl. Svcs. Ctr., 1996—. Mem. NEA, Coun. Chief State Sch. Officers, Women in Sch. Adminstrn., Ky. Edn. Assn., River City Bus. and Profl. Women. Home: 6501 Gunpowder Ln Prospect KY 40059-9334 Office: 4th Fl W Acad Bldg Ky State Univ Frankfort KY 40601

MCDONALD, ALONZO LOWRY, JR., business and financial executive; b. Atlanta, Aug. 5, 1928; s. Alonzo Lowry Sr. and Lois (Burrell) McD.; m. Suzanne Moffitt, May 9, 1959; four children. AB in Journalism, Emory U., 1948; MBA with distinction, Harvard U., 1956. Asst. to sales mgr. air conditioning div. Westinghouse Electric Corp., Staunton, Va., 1956-57; Western zone mgr. Westinghouse Electric Corp., St. Louis, 1957-60; assoc. N.Y. office McKinsey & Co., Inc., 1960-64, prin. London office, 1964-66, mng. prin. Zurich Office, 1966-68, mng. dir. Paris Office, 1968-73; mng. dir., chief exec. officer of firm worldwide, 1973-76; dir. N.Y. Office, 1976-77; dep. spl. trade rep., also ambassador in charge U.S. del. Tokyo round of Multilateral Trade Negotiations, 1977-79; acting spl. trade rep. Washington, 1979; asst. to Pres. U.S., White House staff dir., 1979-81; mem. faculty Harvard U. Grad. Sch. Bus. Adminstrn., Boston, 1981; pres. The Bendix Corp., Southfield, Mich., 1981-83; chmn., chief exec. officer Avenir Group, Inc., Bloomfield Hills, Mich., 1983—. Mem. Coun. Fgn. Rels.; vestry Am. Cathedral in Paris, 1970-73; vestry, warden St. Joseph of Arimathea Episcopal Ch., Elmsford, N.Y., 1974-77; trustee CED, 1975—; chmn. Williamsburg Charter Found., Washington, 1986-90; chmn. bd. trustees Trinity Forum, Washington, 1991—; mem. dean's adv. coun. Harvard U. Div. Sch., Boston, 1989—; trustee Emory U., 1992—, Carter Ctr., Atlanta, 1994—. With USMCR, 1950-52. Office: 5505 Corporate Dr Suite 400 Troy MI 48098

MC DONALD, ANDREW J., bishop; b. Savannah, Ga., Oct. 24, 1923; s. James Bernard and Theresa (McGrael) McD. AB, St. Mary's Sem., Balt., 1945, STL, 1948; JCB, Cath. U. Am., 1949; JCD, Lateran U., Rome, 1951. Ordained priest Roman Cath. Ch., 1948. Consecrated bishop, 1972; curate Port Wentworth, Ga., 1952-57; chancellor Diocese of Savannah, 1952-68; vicar gen., from 1968, vice officialis, 1952-57, officialis, 1957; pastor Blessed Sacrament Ch., 1963; named papal chamberlain, 1956, domestic prelate, 1959; bishop Diocese of Little Rock, 1972—. Office: Diocese of Little Rock PO Box 7239 2415 N Tyler St Little Rock AR 77217*

MC DONALD, ANDREW JEWETT, securities firm executive; b. Cin., Sept. 7, 1929; s. Matthew Arnold and Jane (Jewett) Mc D. Grad., Hotchkiss Sch., 1947, Yale U., 1951. With Paine, Webber, Jackson & Curtis Inc., Boston, 1955—; dir. Paine, Webber, Jackson & Curtis Inc. (New Eng. region), 1972-73; sr. v.p., dir. Paine, Webber, Jackson & Curtis Inc. (Eastern div.), 1973—; dir. F. W. Paine Found., 1973—; pvt. trustee and investor, 1985—; allied mem. N.Y. Stock Exch., 1971—. Mem. Flight Safety Found., 1971—. Served with USAF, 1951-55. Mem. Am. Farmland Trust (life), Am. Aviation Hist. Soc. (life). Clubs: Aero of New Eng. (Boston), Fed. (Boston), Down Town (Boston), Yale (Boston). Home: 5 Stonehill Dr Stoneham MA 02180-3927

MCDONALD, ARTHUR BRUCE, physics educator; b. Sydney, N.S., Canada, Aug. 29, 1943; s. A. Bruce and Valerie M. (DeRoche) McD.; m. Janet Catherine MacDonald, July 16, 1966; children: Bruce, Heather, Ross, Fraser. BSc in Physics, Dalhousie U., 1964, MSc in Physics, 1965; PhD, Calif. Inst. Tech., 1969. Post doctoral fellow Chalk River (Ont., Can.) Nuclear Labs., 1969-70, research scientist, 1970-82; prof. physics Princeton (N.J.) U., 1982-89; prof. physics Queen's U., Kingston, Ont., Can., 1989—, dir. Sudbury Neutrino Obs. Inst., 1989—; mem. nuclear sci. adv. com. Dept. Energy, NSF, 1987-89; adv. com. Triumf Experiment, 1987-89; mem. subatomic physics rev. com. Natural Sci. and Engring. Rsch. Coun. Can., 1987-89; mem. adv. com. nuclear sci. divsn. Lawrence Berkeley Lab., 1992-95. Fellow Am. Physical Soc.; mem. Can. Assn. Physicists (bd. dirs. 1978-80). Avocations: skiing, swimming. Office: Queens U Stirling Hall, Dept Physics, Kingston, ON Canada K7L 3N6

MCDONALD, AUDRA ANN, actress. BFA, Juilliard Sch., 1993. Stage appearances include (regional) Man of La Mancha, Evita, The Wiz, A Chorus Line, Grease, Anything Goes (Broadway) The Secret Garden, Carousel (Antoinette Perry award for featured actress in a musical 1994), Master Class. Office: c/o Linda Jacobs - Writers & Artists Agency 924 Westwood Blvd Ste 900 Los Angeles CA 90024*

MCDONALD, BERNARD ROBERT, federal agency administrator; b. Kansas City, Kans., Nov. 17, 1940; s. Bernard Luther and Mabel McD.; m. Jean Graves, June 7, 1963; children: Aaron Michael, Elizabeth Kathleen. BA, Park Coll., Parkville, Mo., 1962; MA, Kans. State U., 1964; PhD, Mich. State U., 1968. Prof. math. U. Okla., Norman, 1968-83, chmn. math. dept., 1981-83; program dir. div. math. scis. NSF, Washington, 1983-86, program dir. spl. projects, 1986-88, dep. dir. div. math. scis., 1988—. Author: R-linear Endomorphism, 1983, Geometric Algebra, 1976, Finite Rings, 1974, Ring Theory III, 1980. Mem. Am. Math. Soc., Math. Assn. Am., Soc. Ind. and Applied Math., Assn. Women Math., Sigma Xi. Home: 4001 9th St N Apt 721 Arlington VA 22203-1961 Office: NSF Div Math Scis Rm 1025 4201 Wilson Blvd Arlington VA 22230

MCDONALD, BRONCE WILLIAM, community activist, advocate; b. Dayton, Ohio, Mar. 21, 1949; s. Lawrence and Pauline Elizabeth (Macknight) McD. Student, Wright State U., 1968-71, U. Dayton, 1971, Dayton Art Inst., 1967-68. Trainer, cons. Nat. Assn. Youth Orgns. United, Washington, 1971-73; program assoc. Dayton (Ohio) Model Cities, 1973-74; child care worker II Montgomery County Children's Svcs. Bd., Dayton, 1974-78; inventory control Mark Morris Tires, San Francisco, 1979-82; office mgr. Bio-Feedback Internat., San Francisco, 1978-84; speaker, bd. dirs. Dayton Area AIDS Task Force, 1987—, AIDS Found. Dayton, 1988-92; community activist People With AIDS, Dayton, 1987—; co-chair Dayton HIV Prevention Cmty. Planning Group Montgomery County Combined Health Dist.; com. mem. Direct Svcs. Dayton Area AIDS Task Force, 1987-92, speaker bur., 1987-92, edn. com., 1987-92, AIDS Found. Miami Valley, 1992—, speaker bur., 1992—, edn. com., 1992—, Pub. Policy and Conflict Mgmt., Ohio Statewide HIV Prevention Cmty. Planning Group, Ohio Dept. Health, The Prevention Summit: HIV Prevention Cmty. Planning Co-chairs meeting, Ctr. for Disease Control and Prevention, Nat. Alliance of State & Territorial AIDS Dirs., Nat. Minority AIDS Coun., Atlanta, 1995—; hotline vol. Dayton Lesbian & Gay Ctr., 1988—; mem. minority AIDS coalition Montgomery County Health Dept., Dayton, 1987—, minority health and social issues coalition, 1988—; bd. dirs. The African Am. Forum on AIDS, Dayton, 1990—, nat. AIDS awareness program So. Christian Leadership Conf., Dayton, 1993—; speaker numerous orgns. on AIDS; bd. dirs. Miami Valley AIDS Partnership, mem. membership, outreach, and needs assessment coms., 1995—. Founding mem., treas. Dayton Area People with AIDS Coalition, 1987-92, Men of All Colors Together, Dayton, 1988-90; co-chair Regional Cmty. Prevention Coord. Com., 1996—. Recipient Pres.'s Citation, 1989, Ohio AIDS Svc. award Ohio Dept. Health, 1990, Cert. of Merit Ohio Dept. Health, Columbus, 1994, Plaque of Vol. Outstanding Merit Montgomery County Combined Health Dist., Dayton, 1995, Outstanding Vol. Svc. Plaque Ohio Dept. Health, 1995, Man of Yr. award Met. Cmty. Ch., Cmty. Unity Health and Wholeness Project, Dayton, 1995. Mem. Nat. Assn. Black and White Men Together. Avocations: drawing, painting, writing, col. work. Home: 39 Central Ave Apt 323 Dayton OH 45406-5514

MCDONALD, BRYANT EDWARD, physicist, oceanographer; b. Louisville, Nov. 12, 1944; s. Blythe Orman and Mildred Eloise (Poythress) McD.; m. Kathleen Lucille Maiorana, July 28, 1968; children: Leah, Esther. BA, Utah State U., 1966; MA, Princeton U., 1968, PhD, 1971. Computational physicist U.S. Naval Rsch. Lab., Washington, 1971-80, physicist, 1990—; oceanographer Naval Ocean Rsch. & Devel., Bay St. Louis, Miss., 1980-90; cons. Sandia Nat. Lab., Albuquerque, 1985-89, Lawrence Livermore (Calif.) Nat. Lab., 1993—; site review panelist Office of Naval Rsch., Arlington, Va., 1990—. Contbr. articles to profl. jours. PhD thesis com. mem. Pa. State U., State College, 1994, U. Calif., San Diego, 1996; rehab. vol. ARC, Princeton, 1966-68. NSF fellow, 1968. Fellow Acoustical Soc. Am. (mem. tech. com. on underwater acoustics 1993-94, tech. com. acoustic oceanography 1994-95); mem. Am. Geophys. Union. Achievements include first successful computer simulation of ionospheric electrojet turbulence, of sonic boom focusing; theory/computer model for global scale ocean acoustic tomography. Avocations: boating, biking, skiing, hiking. Home: 4708 Randolph Ct Annandale VA 22003-6216 Office: US Naval Rsch Lab 4555 Overlook Ave SW Washington DC 20375-0001

MCDONALD, C. W., mining executive; b. 1940. BA in Mining Engring., U. Ala., 1965. With Consolidated Coal Co., Pitts., 1966—, now exec. v.p. Office: Consolidation Coal Co Consol Plz Pittsburgh PA 15241*

MCDONALD, CAPERS WALTER, biomedical engineer, corporate executive; b. Georgetown, S.C., Nov. 29, 1951; s. WalBern and Cecilia (Lockwood) McD.; m. Marion E. Kiper, Aug. 23, 1975; child, Adam Capers. BS in Engring. magna cum laude, Duke U., 1974; MS in Mech. Engring., MIT, 1976; MBA, Harvard U., 1983. Registered profl. engr., N.C. Dir. mktg. dept. Becton Dickinson Co., Sunnyvale, Calif., 1978-81; cons. Booz, Allen & Hamilton, San Francisco, 1982-84; v.p. HP Genenchem, S. San Francisco, Calif., 1984-87; bio-analytic systems mgr. Hewlett-Packard Corp., Palo Alto, Calif., 1987; v.p. Orion Instruments, Inc., Redwood City, Calif., 1987-88; v.p. Spectroscopy Imaging Systems, Fremont, Calif., 1988-90, pres., 1990-92; pres., ceo Microbiological Assoc., Inc., Rockville, Md., 1992—; pres., CEO MAGENTA Corp., Rockville, 1993—; chmn., dir. MAGENTA Svcs., Ltd., Stirling, Scotland, 1994—; guest lectr. Weizmann Inst., Rehovot, Israel, 1977, All-Union Cardiology Ctr., Moscow, 1978, Inst. Hematology Munich, 1978, Christ Church (New Zealand) Clin. Sch., 1980, U. Edinburgh, Scotland, 1981; co-founder, chmn. Md. Biosci. Alliance, 1995; bd. dirs. Md. State C. of C., 1996; bd. visitors U. Md. Biotech. Inst., 1996. Author: chpt. Flow Cytometry and Sorting, 1979; patentee flow microfluorometer; contbr. articles to profl. jours. Asst. scout master Boy Scouts Am., Georgetown, 1965-66. Duke U. scholar, 1970-74, MIT scholar, 1974-76; NSF fellow, 1974; recipient High Tech. Firm of Yr. award Md. High Tech. Coun., 1995. Mem. N.C. Acad. Scis., Harvard U. Alumni Assn., Duke U. Alumni Assn., MIT Alumni Assn., Rotary, Sigma Xi, Tau Beta Pi, Phi Eta Sigma, Pi Mus Epsilon. Republican. Methodist. Avocations: fresh and salt water fishing, travel. Home: 12221 Lake Potomac Ter Potomac MD 20854-1222 Office: 9900 Blackwell Rd Rockville MD 20850-3301

MCDONALD, CAROLYN ANN, dance educator, choreographer; b. Blytheville, Ark., Aug. 27, 1963; d. Travis Eugene and Barbara Jean (Myers) McD. BA in Dance, U. Calif., Irvine, 1987; postgrad., U. Iowa, 1995—. Instr. dance Kirkwood C.C., Cedar Rapids, Iowa, 1987-90; choreographer Kirkwood C.C., Cedar Rapids, 1987—, coord. performing arts camp, 1990-96, artistic dir., 1996—; Choreographer Colorguard dance ensemble Wash. H.S., Cedar Rapids, 1996—; instr. dance Coe Coll., Cedar Rapids, 1989—; owner, pres. McDonald Arts Ctr., Marion, Iowa, 1988—; cons. Jane Boyd Cmty. House, Cedar Rapids, 1993-94; choreographer, color guard dance ensemble Washington H.S., Cedar Rapids, 1996—. Avocations: wine tasting, gourmet cooking, flying, gardening. Office: 105 Southview Dr Marion IA 52302-3055

MCDONALD, CHARLES EDWARD, lawyer; b. El Paso, Tex., Nov. 13, 1957; s. Carlos and Armida (Adauto) McD.; children: Miranda Lee, Ashley Lee Ann. BA in Philosophy, U. St. Thomas, Houston, 1980; JD, South Tex. Coll. Law, 1985. Bar: Tex. 1985, U.S. Ct. Appeals. (5th cir.) 1991, U.S. Supreme Ct. 1992. Prin. Law Office Charles E. McDonald, El Paso, 1985—. Comms. liaison Coleman Re-election Congl. Campaign, El Paso, 1984, 86. Mem. ATLA, Tex. Trial Lawyers Assn., State Bar Tex., El Paso County Bar Assn. Roman Catholic. Avocations: cave diving, chess, traveling. Office: Law Office Charles E McDonald 4100 Rio Bravo #117 El Paso TX 79902

MC DONALD, CHARLES J., physician, educator; b. Tampa, Fla., Dec. 6, 1931; s. George B. and Bertha C. (Harbin) Mc D.; m. Maureen McDonald; children—Marc S., Norman D., Eric S. B.S. magna cum laude, A&T Coll. N.C., 1951; M.S., U. Mich., 1952; M.D. with highest honors, Howard U., 1960. Diplomate: Am. Bd. Dermatology. Rotating intern Hosp. St. Raphael, New Haven, 1960-61; asst. resident in medicine Hosp. St. Raphael, 1961-63; asst. resident in dermatology Yale U., 1963-65, spl. USPHS research fellow, chief resident in dermatology, 1965-66, instr. in medicine and pharmacology, 1966-67, asst. prof. medicine and pharmacology, 1967-68; asst. prof. med. sci. Brown U., 1968-69, assoc. prof., 1969-74, prof., 1974—, dir. dermatology program, 1970-74, head subsect. dermatology, 1974-82, dir. dermatology, 1982—, chair dept. dermatology, 1996—; dir. dermatology Roger Williams Gen. Hosp., 1968—; physician-in-charge dermatology R.I. Hosp., 1989—; mem. com. and task force, chmn. task force on minority affairs Am. Acad. Dermatology, 1975-80; mem. dermatology adv. panel FDA, until 1978, cons., 1978—; mem. pharm. scis. rev. commn. NIH, 1979-83, mem. adv. com. Arthritis, Muscular/Skeletal and Skin Disease Inst., 1993-95; chmn. com. pub. edn., dir., v.p. R.I. divsn. Am. Cancer Soc., 1978-80, pres., 1980-83, bd. dir. nat. soc., 1983—, nat. dir. at large, 1990—, mem. nat. exec. com., 19916; mem. residency rev. com. dermatology ACGME, 1992—. Dermatology editor Postgrad. Medicine; contbr. numerous articles to med. publs. Trustee Howard U., 1993—, chair health affairs com., 1994—, mem. exec. com., 1994—; bd. dirs. Providence Health Care Found., chmn. mem. adv. com., 1976-87; bd. dirs. Providence Fund for Edn.; bd. dirs. Providence Pub. Libr., 1987—, sec., 1991; mem. R.I. State Bd. Edn., 1970-72. Served to maj. USAF, 1952-56. Recipient Disting. Svc. award Hosp. Assn. R.I., 1971, Disting. Alumni award Howard U. Coll. Medicine, 1983, St. George medal nat. divsn. Am. Cancer Soc., 1992. Mem. AAAS, Am. Dermatol. Assn. (bd. dirs. 1995—), New Eng. Dermatol. Assn. (v.p. 1983-84, pres. 1984-85), R.I. Dermatol. Assn., Noah Worcester Dermatol. Assn. (bd. dirs. 1983-86), Soc. Investigative Dermatology, Am. Fedn. Clin. Rsch., Am. Acad. Dermatology (bd. dirs. 1987-91, Nat. Med. Assn. (chmn. sect. dermatology 1973-75), Am. Soc. Clin. Oncology, Dermatology Found. (chmn. sci. com. 1972-76), Assn. Profs. Dermatology (bd. dirs. 1991-94), Sigma Xi, Alpha Omega Alpha, Alpha Kappa Mu, Beta Kappa Chi. Democrat. Office: 825 Chalkstone Ave Providence RI 02908-4728

MCDONALD, DANNY LEE, federal agency administratorr; b. Sand Springs, Okla.; m. Gail McDonald. BA, Okla. State U.; postgrad., Harvard U. Sec. Tulsa County Election Bd., Tulsa, chief clk.; gen. adminstr. Okla. Corp. Commn.; mem. Fed. Election Commn., Washington, 1981—, vice chmn., 1982, 88, 94, chmn., 1983, 89, 95—; former mem. adv. bd. for state and local govt. Harvard U. John F. Kennedy Sch. Govt. Pres. Am. Coun. Young Polit. Leaders. Democrat. Office: Fed Election Commn Office of Chairman 999 E St NW Washington DC 20463*

MCDONALD, DARYL PATRICK, lawyer; b. Detroit, Aug. 27, 1950; s. Donald Angus and Rita Martha (Tymoszek) McD.; m. Deborah Ann Wenzinger, Dec. 29, 1972; children: Andrea, Laura. BA, U. Toledo, 1972; JD, Tulane U., 1975. Bar: Mich. 1975, U.S. Dist. Ct. (we. dist.) Mich. 1975, U.S. Dist. Ct. (ea. dist.) Mich. 1982. Magistrate 93d Dist. Ct., Munising, Mich., 1976-78; sole practice Munising, 1977-82; assoc. Patterson & Patterson, Whitfield, Manikoff, Ternan & White, Bloomfield Hills, Mich., 1982-85, ptnr., 1986; asst. corp. counsel Tecumseh (Mich.) Products Co., 1986-92, corp. counsel, sec., 1993—; city atty., City of Munising, 1978-82. Asst. editor Tulane U. Law Rev., 1973-75. Trustee Munising Meml. Hosp., 1980-82. Recipient Oustanding Service award Alger County Hist. Soc., Munising, 1982. Mem. ABA, ATLA, Mich. Bar Assn., Lenawee County Bar Assn., Rotary (sec. Munising 1975-76, sec. Tecumseh 1989-91, pres. 1992-93), Order of Coif. Roman Catholic. Avocations: jogging, reading, family activities. Home: 707 W Chicago Blvd Tecumseh MI 49286-1203 Office: Tecumseh Products Co Legal Dept Tecumseh MI 49286

MC DONALD, DAVID WILLIAM, retired chemist, educator; b. Shreveport, La., Aug. 4, 1923; s. Maxwell Wood and Mary Estelle (Weber) McD.; m. Nell Cullen Welch, July 31, 1948; children: Mason, Thomas, Daniel, David. BS, U. Southwestern La., 1943; PhD, U. Tex., 1951. Chemist Humble Oil & Refining Co., Baytown, Tex., 1943-44, 46-47; rsch. chemist, group leader Monsanto Co., Texas City, Tex., 1951-59; rsch. sect. leader, mgr. Monsanto Co., 1959-67; product adminstr. Monsanto Co., St. Louis, 1967-69, dir. research plastics div., 1969-74; dir. tech. plastics div. Monsanto Co., 1974-80, dir. tech. plans, corp. rsch. and devel. staff, 1980-82; sr. assoc. Pugh-Roberts Assocs., Inc., Cambridge, Mass., 1983-93; mng. cons. PA Consulting Group, Santa Rosa, Calif., 1993—; affiliate prof. tech. mgmt. Washington U., St. Louis, 1983-88; cons. in field, 1982—; vis. lectr., scholar Stanford U., 1989. Served with USNR, 1944-46. Mem. Am. Chem. Soc., Soc. Plastics Engrs., AAAS, Sigma Xi. Episcopalian. Patentee in field. Home and Office: 423 Pythian Rd Santa Rosa CA 95409-6324

MCDONALD, FORREST, historian, educator; b. Orange, Tex., Jan. 7, 1927; s. John Forrest and Myra (McGill) McD.; m. Ellen Shapiro, Aug. 1, 1963; children from previous marriage: Kathy, Forrest Howard, Marcy Ann, Stephen, Kevin. BA, MA, U. Tex., 1949, PhD, 1955; MA (hon.), Brown U., 1962; LHD (hon.), SUNY, Geneseo, 1989. Exec. sec. Am. History Research Ctr., Madison, Wis., 1953-58; assoc. prof. history Brown U., Providence, 1959-63, prof., 1963-67; prof. Wayne State U., Detroit, 1967-76; prof. U. Ala., Tuscaloosa, 1976-87, disting. univ. research prof., 1987—; James Pinckney Harrison prof. Coll. of William and Mary, Williamsburg, Va., 1986-87; presdl. appointee Bd. Fgn. Scholarships, Washington, 1985-87; mem. fellowship selection com. Richard M. Weaver Fellowships, Bryn Mawr, Pa., 1980—. Author: We The People, 1958, Insull, 1962, E Pluribus Unum, 1965, Alexander Hamilton, 1979 (Frances Tavern Book award 1980), Novus Ordo Seclorum, 1985, Requiem, 1988, The American Presidency: An Intellectual History, 1994. Trustee Phila. Soc., North Adams, Mich., 1983-86, 87-90, pres. 1988-90; co-chmn. New Eng. for Goldwater, 1964. Served with USN, 1945-46. Recipient George Washington medal Freedom's Found., Valley Forge, Pa., 1980, Best Book award Am. Revolution Round Table, N.Y., 1986, Richard M. Weaver award Ingersoll Found., 1990, First Salvatori award Heritage Found., 1992, Salavatori Book award Intercollegiate Studio Inst., 1994; Guggenheim fellow, N.Y., 1962-63; Jefferson lectr. NEH, 1987. Republican. Avocations: horticulture, tennis. Office: U Alabama PO Box 870212 Tuscaloosa AL 35487-0212

MC DONALD, FRANK BETHUNE, physicist; b. Columbus, Ga., May 28, 1925; s. Frank B. and Lucy (Kyle) McD.; m. Virginia Ballew, June 15, 1951 (dec. 1977); children: Kyle Louise McDonald Jossi, Robert Kyle, Douglas Frank; m. Irene Negosh Kelejian, Nov. 7, 1987. BS, Duke U., 1948; MS, U. Minn., 1951, PhD (AEC fellow), 1955. Rsch. assoc. State U. Iowa, Iowa City, 1953-56, asst. prof. physics, 1956-59; chief lab. for high energy astrophysics Goddard Space Flight Ctr. NASA, Greenbelt, Md., 1959-82; mem. phys. scis. com. space program adv. coun. NASA, 1974-76; the NASA chief scientist, 1982-87; assoc. dir., chief scientist Goddard Space Flight Ctr. NASA, 1987-89; sr. policy analyst Office Sci. and Tech. Policy, Exec. Office of Pres., Washington, 1982; sr. rsch. scientist Inst. for Phys. Sci. and Tech. U. Md., College Park, 1989—; part-time prof. U. Md., College Park, 1963-82; mem. Geophysics Rsch. Forum, 1985-88; Internat. Union Pure and Applied Physics mem. Internat. Commn. on Cosmic Rays, 1981-84, sec. to commn., 1984-87, chmn., 1987-90; NASA rep. to NASA Adv. Coun., 1984-89. Editor: High Energy Particles and Quanta in Astrophysics, 1974; assoc. editor: Jour. Geophys. Research, 1964-67; mem. editorial bd.: Space Sci. Revs.; Research in cosmic ray physics. With USNR, 1942-45. Recipient Exceptional Sci. Achievement award NASA, 1964, 78, 86, Outstanding Leadership medal, 1981; Presdl. Mgmt. Improvement cert., 1971; Presdl. rank of meritorious exec. Sr. Exec. Service, 1980, 89, W. Randolph Lovelace II award Am. Astronautical Soc., 1986. Fellow Am. Phys. Soc. (chmn. div. cosmic physics 1973-74, mem. council 1982—, mem. exec. com. 1983); mem. Am. Inst. Physics (council, governing bd. 1983-86), Am. Geophys. Union, Washington Philos. Soc., Am. Astronom. Soc., Nat. Acad. Sci., Sigma Xi, Phi Beta Kappa. Office: U Md IPST Rm 3245 Computer Sci Space Bui College Park MD 20742

MCDONALD, GAIL CLEMENTS, government official; b. Ft. Worth, Tex., Mar. 9, 1944; d. Eugene and Cornelia (Nagle) Clements; m. William C. Scott, Aug. 26, 1967 (div. 1976); 1 child, Jill Miriah Scott; m. Danny Lee McDonald, Aug. 6, 1982. BA, Tex. Christian U., Ft. Worth, 1966, MA, 1967. Instr. social sci. Cooke County Jr. Coll., Gainesville, Tex., 1967-69, Langston (Okla.) U., 1969, Tulsa Jr. Coll., 1977-79; instr. humanities Okla. State U., Stillwater, 1971-74; adminstrv. asst. edn. and cultural affairs Gov. David L. Boren, Oklahoma City, 1975-78; legis. aide Sen. David L. Boren, Tulsa, 1979; state assoc. Inst. for Ednl. Leadership, George Washington U., Washington, 1979-81; exec. asst. Commr. Norma H. Eagleton, Okla. Corp. Commr., Oklahoma City, 1990-95; commr. ICC, Washington, 1990—, vice chmn., 1993, chmn., 1993-95; adminstr. St. Lawrence Seaway Devel. Corp. U.S. Dept. Transp., Wahsington, 1995—. Bd. dirs. Okla. Sci. & Arts Found., 1975-83; exec. com. Frontiers of Sci. Found., 1976-80; fundraiser Washington chpt. Spl. Olympics. Named Woman of Yr., Women's Transp. Seminar, 1991. Mem. Nat. Assn. Regulatory Commrs. (transp. com.), Exec. Women in Govt., Conservation Round Table (chmn. 1990), Transp. Table Washington, Toastmasters (pres. 1988), Phi Alpha Theta. Democrat. Episcopalian. Avocations: gardening, bird watching. Office: US Dept Transp St Lawrence Seaway Devel Co 400 7th St SW Ste 5424 Washington DC 20590

MCDONALD, GAIL JACOLEV, lawyer; b. Port Arthur, Tex., Nov. 18, 1945; d. Leon and Ruth Jacolev. BA cum laude, Mount Holyoke Coll., 1967; MA, Columbia U., 1968; JD with high honors, U. Tex., 1974. Bar:

Tex. 1974. Mgmt. intern U.S. Office of Edn., Washington, 1968-70; planning cons. Tex. Edn. Agy., Austin, 1970-71; student devel. specialist U. Tex., Austin, 1971-72; assoc. Butler & Binion, L.L.P., Houston, 1974-81; ptnr. Butler & Binion, Houston, 1981—. Mem. ABA, Tex. State Bar Assn., Order Coif, Chancellors. Home: 3715 Darcus St Houston TX 77005-3703 Office: Butler & Binion LLP Ste 1600 1000 Louisiana Houston TX 77002

MCDONALD, GARY HAYWOOD, mechanical engineering educator; b. Nashville, June 27, 1955; s. Haywood and Hallie Bea (Black) McD.; stepmother Virginia Nell (Hart) McD.; m. Shirley Ann Cantrell; 1 child, Emily Ann. BSME, Tenn. Technol. U., 1977, MSME, 1979, PhD in Engring., 1984. Registered profl. engr., Tenn. Grad. tchg. asst. Tenn. Technol. U., Cookeville, 1977-79, grad. instr., 1979-84; asst. prof. mech. engring. U. Tenn., Chattanooga, 1985-92, assoc. prof., 1992—, U. Chattanooga Found. prof., 1992. Contbr. articles to profl. jours. Recipient Young Engr. of Yr. award Chattanooga Engrs. Week, 1989, Outstanding Prof. award Student Govt. Assn., U. Tenn., Chattanooga, 1991-92. Mem. ASME, NSPE, Am. Soc. Engring. Edn. (soc./NASA summer faculty fellow 1987, 88, 90, 91), Chattanooga Engrs. Club. Republican. Methodist. Home: 6508-B Still Meadows Ln Harrison TN 37341 Office: Univ Tenn Grote Hall 615 McCallie Ave Chattanooga TN 37403

MCDONALD, GREGORY ANTHONY, microbiologist, researcher; b. N.Y.C., July 21, 1956; s. William Patrick McDonald and Carolyn Martin; m. Annette Jama Howard, Dec. 4, 1982; children: Jason Derrick, Marjorie Veronica. BS in Biology, Guilford Coll., 1978; PhD in Microbiology, U. Va., 1984. Staff fellow NIAID, NIH, Hamilton, Mont., 1984-87, sr. staff fellow, 1987-89; asst. prof. dept. molecular microbiology and immunology U. Mo., Columbia, 1989-1995, assoc. prof. molecular biology and immunology, 1995—. Contbr. articles to profl. jours. and books. Den leader Webelos, 1992-93. Recipient Pub. Health Svc. Spl. Recognition award Pub. Health Svc., 1989. Mem. Am. Soc. Microbiology, Am. Soc. Rickettsiology and Rickettsial Diseases. Democrat. Methodist. Avocations: camping, fishing, reading, softball, martial arts instruction. Office: Univ Mo NW609 Medical School Columbia MO 65212

MCDONALD, GREGORY CHRISTOPHER, author; b. Shrewsbury, Mass., Feb. 15, 1937; s. Irving Thomas and Mae (Haggerty) M.; m. Susan Aiken, Jan. 12, 1963 (div. Oct. 1990); children: Christopher Gregory, Douglas Gregory. BA, Harvard U., 1958. bd. dirs. Camaldon Corp. Novelist, critic Boston Globe, 1966-73; author: (novels) Running Scared, 1964, Fletch, 1974, Confess, Fletch, 1976, Flynn, 1977, Love Among the Mashed Potatoes, 1978, Fletch's Fortune, 1978, Fletch Forever, 1978, Who Took Toby Rinaldi?, 1980, Fletch and the Widow Bradley, 1981, The Buck Passes Flynn, 1981, Fletch's Moxie, 1982, Fletch and the Man Who, 1983, Carioca Fletch, Flynn's In, 1984, Fletch Won, Safekeeping, 1985, Fletch, Too, 1986; (non-fiction) The Education of Gregory Mcdonald, 1985, Fletch Chronicle, Vol. 1, Bull's Eye (drama), 1986, A World Too Wide, 1987, Fletch Chronicle, Vol. 2, 1987, Exits and Entrances, 1988, Fletch Chronicle, Vol. 3, 1988, Merely Players, 1988, The Brave, 1991, Son of Fletch, 1993, Fletch Reflected, 1994, Skylar, 1995; editor: Last Laughs, 1986; dir. Bach Cantata Singers, 1973-80. Mem. vis. com. Boston Mus. Fine Arts, 1970-73, 85—; mem. Lincoln Recreation Com., 1977, 78; mem. Winthrop House Sr. Commons Harvard Coll. 1982—. Recipient Humanitarian of Yr. award Tenn. Assn. Fed. Execs., 1989, Citizen of Yr. award Nat. Assn. Social Workers, 1990, Roger William Straus award NCCJ, 1990, Alex Haley award, 1992. Mem. Authors Guild, Dramatists Guild, Mystery Writers Am. (dir. 1977—, pres. 1985-86, Poe award 1975, 77), Crime Writers Eng., Writers Guild Am., Mass. Chiefs Police Assn., Giles Countians United. Clubs: Harvard (Boston); Overseas Press (N.Y.C.); Hillcrest Country (Pulaski, Tenn.). Office: care Arthur Greene Esq 101 Park Ave New York NY 10178

MC DONALD, HENRY STANTON, electrical engineer; b. Carlisle, Pa., Oct. 28, 1927; s. Robert Clarence and Olive Elizabeth (Berry) McD.; children: H. Stanton, Pattie Elizabeth. B.E.E., Catholic U. Am., 1950; D.Eng., Johns Hopkins U., 1955. Instr. elec. engring. Johns Hopkins U., 1952-55; head gov. systems research dept. AT&T Bell Labs., Whippany, N.J., 1955-91; cons. Dept. Def., 1976—. Contbr. chpts. to books, articles to profl. jours. Served with U.S. Navy, 1945-46. Fellow IEEE, AT&T Bell Labs.; mem. Assn. Computing Machinery, AAAS, Sigma Xi. Republican. Unitarian. Patentee in field. Home: 810 Skyline Dr San Luis Obispo CA 93405-1054

MCDONALD, JACQUELYN MILLIGAN, parent and family studies educator; b. New Brunswick, N.J., July 28, 1935; d. John P. and Emma (Mark) Milligan; m. Neil Vanden Dorpel; five children. BA, Cornell U., 1957; MA, NYU, 1971; MEd, Columbia U., 1992, EdD, 1993. Cert. behavior modification, N.J.; cert. tchr. grades K-8, N.J.; cert. family life educator Nat. Coun. on Family Rels. Instr. Montclair (N.J.) State Coll., 1982-93, Edison C.C., Naples, Fla., 1994—; mem. steering com. Fla. Gulf Coast U. Family Ctr.; parent vol. tng. project coord. Montclair (N.J.) Pub. Schs., 1984-86; coord. Collier County IDEAS, Inc. for Parenting, Naples, 1993—, Parenting Coalition, Naples Alliance for Children. Chairperson Interfaith Neighbors Juvenile Delinquency Prevention, N.Y.C., 1960-68; support family Healing the Children, 1970-90; founder The Parent Ctr., Montclair, 1983, Essex County N.J. Fair Housing Coun., 1990. Mem. Pre-Sch. Interagy. Couns., Family Svc. Planning Team, Raven and Serpent Hon. Soc. (pres. 1956), Psi Chi, Kappa Delta Pi. Avocations: swimming, tennis, golf, boating. Home: 27075 Kindlewood Ln Bonita Springs FL 33923-4370

MCDONALD, JAMES L., accounting firm executive; b. 1943. Mng. ptnr. in charge internat. tax svcs. West Coast region Price Waterhouse. Office: Price Waterhouse 1177 Avenue Of The Americas New York NY 10036*

MC DONALD, JAMES MICHAEL, JR., research institute consultant; b. Chgo., Jan. 19, 1924; s. James Michael and Gertrude Isabel (Dame) McD.; m. Helen Elizabeth Sharp, Feb. 3, 1948; children: Megan, Melissa, Rebecca. AB cum laude, Syracuse U., 1949; MA, Sch. Advanced Internat. Studies, 1950; postgrad., Bologna Ctr, 1956-57; grad., Nat. War Coll., 1969. Joined U.S. Fgn. Service, 1950; assigned Germany, 1951-56, Italy, 1956-57, France, 1957-58, Washington, 1958-61, Nicaragua, 1961-65, Dominican Republic, 1969-71; dep. pub affairs officer Rome, 1971-74; chief resource and ops. analysis USIA, Washington, 1974-75; dir. seminar and studies program Battelle Meml. Inst., 1975-83, internat. programs mgr., corp. edn. and tng. advisor, 1983-85, cons., 1985—. Trustee, v.p., past pres. Seattle Opera. With USAAF, 1943-47. Recipient Superior Honor award USIA, 1975. Mem. Rainier Club. Address: 1278 NW Blakely Ct Seattle WA 98177-4340

MCDONALD, JOHN CECIL, lawyer; b. Lorimor, Iowa, Feb. 19, 1924; s. Cecil F. and Mary Elsie (Fletcher) McD.; m. Barbara Joan Berry, May 8, 1943; children: Mary Elisabeth (Mrs. Dell Richard), Joan Frances (Mrs. Andrew Ackerman), Jean Maurine. Student, Simpson Coll., 1942, So. Ill. U., 1943; J.D., Drake U., 1948. Bar: Iowa 1948, U.S. Ct. Mil. Appeals 1956, U.S. Supreme Ct. 1956. Practiced in Dallas Center, Iowa, 1948—; sr. ptnr. McDonald, Brown & Fagen and predecessor firms, 1971—; county atty. Dallas County, 1958-62; asst. county atty., 1963-69; city atty. Dallas Center, 1956-80. Mem. Simpson Coll. Alumni Council, pres., 1977-80; legal adviser Dallas Community Bd. Edn., 1953-69, pres., mem., 1968-76; nat. adv. com. Cen. Coll.; alt. del. Iowa Coordinating Council for Post-High Sch. Edn.; finance chmn. Dallas County Rep.Cen. Com., 1954-63, chmn., 1963-68; chmn. Iowa 7th Congl. Dist. Rep. Cen. Com., 1968-69, Iowa Rep. Cen. Com., 1969-75; mem. Rep. Nat. Com., 1969-88, mem. exec. com., 1973—; mem. Rule 29 com., com. on reform; mem. Gov. Iowa's inaugural com., 1969, 71, 73, 75, 79; del. Rep. Nat. Conv., 1964, 72, 76, 80, 84, chmn. com. on contests, 1976, 80, 84, 88, chmn. com. on credentials, 1976, 80, 88, mem. com. on arrangements and exec. com. of com. on arrangements, 1976, 80, 84, mem. rules rev. com., 1977-84; chmn. Midwest Rep. State Chairmen's Assn., 1973-75, Nat. Rep. State Chairmen's Adv. Com., 1973-75; hon. co-chmn. Vice Pres.'s Inaugural, 1981; trustee Dallas County Hosp., Perry, Iowa; bd. visitors U.S. Air Force Acad., 1975-78, chmn., 1977-78; trustee Simpson Coll., 1978—; bd. dirs. Iowa Student Loan Liquidity Corp., 1987—; mem. Iowa Coll. Aid Commn., 1989—; mem. Iowa Bd. Regents, 1981-87, pres., 1985-87; bd. dirs. Iowa Public Broadcasting Network, 1981-85; U.S. commr. Am. Battle Monuments Commn., 1982—. Served with USAAF, 1942-46; Col. USAF, 1951-52, ret. Recipient Alumni Achievement award Simpson Coll., 1974; Disting. Service award Drake U., 1978. Mem. ABA, Iowa Bar Assn. (past chmn. spl. com. on mil. affairs, mem. mil. affairs com.), Dallas County Bar Assn. (past pres.), Am. Legion, Farm Bur., Blackfriars, Drake U. Law Sch. Alumni Assn. (class officer), Comml. Club (past pres.) (Dallas Ctr.), Hillcrest Country Club (past pres.) (Adel, Iowa), Des Moines Club, Masons (32 degree), Shriners, Rotary (past pres. Dallas Ctr.), Alpha Tau Omega, Delta Theta Phi, Alpha Psi Omega. Presbyterian. Club: Des Moines. Lodges: Masons (32 deg.), Shriners, Rotary (pas pres. Dallas Ctr.). Home: PO Box 250 Dallas Center IA 50063-0250 Office: McDonald Brown & Fagen PO Box 250 Dallas Center IA 50063-0250

MCDONALD, JOHN CLIFTON, surgeon; b. Baldwyn, Miss., July 25, 1930; s. Edgar Hone and Ethel (Knight) McD.; m. Martha Dennis, Sept. 9, 1956; children: Melissa Lee, Karen Ann, Martha Knight. B.S., Miss. Coll., 1951; M.D., Tulane U., 1955. Diplomate: Am. Bd. Surgery. Intern Confederate Meml. Med. Ctr., Shreveport, La., 1955-56; asst. resident Meyer Meml. Hosp., Buffalo, 1958-62, resident, 1962-63, from asst. attending surgeon to attending surgeon, 1963-68, assoc. dir. surg. research lab., 1965-68; from asst. attending surgeon to attending surgeon Deaconess Hosp., Buffalo, 1965-69, head sect. transplantation, 1966-68; dir. transplantation Charity Hosp. of La., New Orleans, 1969-77, vis. surgeon, 1969-77; clin. asst. surgeon Touro Infirmary, New Orleans, 1969-77; mem. med. staff So. Bapt. Hosp., New Orleans, 1969-77; assoc. mem. dept. surgery Hotel Dieu Hosp., 1969-77; surgeon in chief La. State U. Med. Ctr., Shreveport, 1977—, prof., chmn. dept. surgery, 1977—; asst. prof. surgery SUNY-Buffalo, 1965-68; cons. surgeon various La. Hosps., 1969-77; dir. La. Organ Procurement Program, 1971-77; cons. N.W. La. Emergency Med. Services, 1977—; Buswell research fellow in immunology SUNY-Buffalo, 1963-65, instr. surgery, 1963-65, assoc. prof., 1965-68; assoc. prof. surgery Tulane U. Sch. Medicine, 1969-72, prof., 1972-77, assoc. prof. microbiology and immunology, 1969-77, dir. surg. research labs., 1969-77, dir. transplantation labs., 1969-77, dir. Med. Ctr. Histocampatability Testing Lab., 1969-77. Contbr. articles to med. jours. Served to capt. USAF, 1956-58. Recipient Owl Club award for outstanding teaching Tulane U., 1977; grantee Kidney Found., 1966-67, NIH, 1969—, Schlieder Found., 1970-73, Cancer Assn. Greater New Orleans, 1971-72, La. Regional Med. Program, 1971-73. Mem. AMA, ACS, Am. Assn. Clin. Histocompatability Testing (founding), Am. Assn. Immunologists, Am. Soc. for Artificial Internal Organs, Am. Soc. Transplant Surgeons (founding, pres. 1987), Buffalo Surg. Soc. (sec. 1968), So. Surg. Assn. (Arthur H. Shipley award 1972, treas. 1988-91, sec. 1991-3, pres. 1993-94), Surg. Assn. La. (dir. 1977—, pres. 1983), Am. Assn. for Surgery of Trauma, Transplantation Soc., Southeastern Surg. Congress, Am. Surg. Assn., Halsted Soc. (pres. 1991), Soc. U. Surgeons, La. Med. Soc., Shreveport Med. Soc., United Network for Organ Sharing (pres. 1986-88). Office: Dept Surgery Sch of Medicine La State U Shreveport LA 71130

MCDONALD, JOHN FRANCIS PATRICK, electrical engineering educator; b. Narberth, Pa., Jan. 14, 1942; s. Frank Patrick and Lulu Ann (Hegedus) McD.; m. Karen Marie Knapp, May 26, 1979. BSEE, MIT, 1963; MS in Engring., Yale U., 1965, PhD, 1969. Instr. Yale U., New Haven, 1968-69, asst. prof., 1969-74; assoc. prof. Rensselaer Poly. Inst., Troy, N.Y., 1974-86, prof., 1986—; founder Rensselaer Ctr. for Integrated Electronics, 1980—. Contbr. articles to 185 profl. publs. Patentee in field. Recipient numerous grants, 1974—. Mem. ACM, IEEE (assoc. editor Transactions on VSLI Design 1995—), Optical Soc., Acoustical Soc., Vacuum Soc., Materials Rsch. Soc. Office: Rensselaer Poly Inst Ctr for Integrated Electronics Troy NY 12181

MCDONALD, JOHN GREGORY, financial investment educator; b. Stockton, Calif., 1937; m. Melody McDonald. BS, Stanford U., 1960, MBA, 1962, PhD, 1967. Mem. faculty Grad. Sch. Bus. Stanford U., Calif., 1968—; now The IBJ prof. fin. Grad. Sch. Bus. Stanford U.; vis. prof. U. Paris, 1972, Columbia Bus. Sch., 1975, Harvard Bus. Sch. 1986; vice chmn., bd. govs. NASD/NASDAQ Stock Market, 1989-90; mem. adv. bd. InterWest Venture Capital; dir. Investment Co. of Am., New Perspective Fund, Inc., Scholastic Corp., Varian, EuroPacific Growth Fund. Contbr. articles to profl. jours. Bd. overseers vis. com. Harvard U. Bus. Sch., Cambridge, Mass., 1994—. Fulbright scholar, Paris, 1967-68. Office: Stanford U Grad Sch Bus Stanford CA 94305

MC DONALD, JOHN JOSEPH, electronics executive; b. N.Y.C., Apr. 18, 1930; s. John J. and Margaret (Shanley) McD.; m. Tessa de R. Greenfield, Aug. 22, 1956; children: Kathryn, Elizabeth, Andrew. B.A., Bklyn. Coll., 1951. With Sperry Rand Corp., Blue Bell, Pa., 1954-75; v.p. Sperry Rand Corp., 1972-75; mng. dir. Casio Electronics Ltd., London, 1975-78; pres. Casio Europe Casio Electronics Ltd., 1975-78; pres., CEO Casio, Inc., Dover, N.J., 1978—; also bd. dirs. Casio, Inc., Fairfield, N.J.; chmn. Casio Can. Ltd., 1988-90, pres., chief exec. officer, 1990—; bd. dirs. Casio Mfg. Corp., Casio de Mex. S.A. Served with U.S. Army, 1952-54. Mem. Brit. Inst. Mktg., Am. Mgmt. Assn., Electronic Industries Assn. (bd. govs.), Electronic Industries Found. (trustee 1987—), Consumer Electronics Group (bd. dirs.). Home: PO Box 322 Hope NJ 07844-0322 Office: 570 Mount Pleasant Ave Dover NJ 07801-1620

MC DONALD, JOHN RICHARD, lawyer; b. Connersville, Ind., Aug. 8, 1933; s. Vernon Louis and Thelma (Venham) McD.; m. Mary Alice Boyd, Aug. 17, 1957; children: Anne Elizabeth, John Richard, Colleen Lynn. B.A., U. Ariz., 1957, LL.B., 1960. Bar: Ariz. 1960. Since practiced in Tucson; assoc. Richard N. Roylston, 1961-62; pvt. practice, 1963-65; ptnr. McDonald & Rykken, 1965-68, DeConcini & McDonald (now DeConcini, McDonald, Brammer, Yetwin, Lacy, P.C.), 1968—; mem. adv. bd. Dependable Nurses, Inc., 1994—. Mem. Ariz. Law Rev. Pres., bd. dirs. Comstock Children's Hosp. Found.; v.p. Ariz. Sch. Bds. Assn., 1979, pres., 1981; v.p. All Ariz. Sch. Bd., 1981; v.p., bd. dirs. Tucson Assn. for Blind; trustee Catalina Foothills Sch. Dist., 1976-82; mem. Tucson Com. on Fgn. Rels., 1989—;bd. dirs. Tucson Unified Sch. Dist. Ednl. Enrichment Found., Ariz. Acad., 1981—. Mem. Ariz. Bar Assn., Ariz. Law Rev. Assn. (pres. 1994), Pima County Bar Assn. (dir. 1978-86, pres. 1984-85), Nat. Coun. Sch. Attys. (dir. 1992-96), Delta Chi. Republican. Presbyterian. Home: 6151 N Camino Almonte Tucson AZ 85718-3729 Office: 2525 E Broadway Blvd Tucson AZ 85716-5398

MC DONALD, JOHN WARLICK, diplomat, global strategist; b. Coblenz, Germany, Feb. 18, 1922; s. John Warlick and Ethel Mae (Raynor) McD.; m. Barbara Jane Stewart, Oct. 23, 1943 (div.); children: Marilyn Ruth, James Stewart, Kathleen Ethel, Laura Ellen; m. Christel Meyer, Oct. 24, 1970. AB, U. Ill., 1943, JD, 1946; D (hon.), Mt. Mercy Coll., 1989, Teikyo Marycrest U., 1991, Salisbury State U., 1993. Bar: Ill. 1946, U.S. Supreme Ct. 1951. With legal div. Office Mil Govt., Berlin, 1947; asst. dist. atty. U.S. Mil. Govt. Cts., Frankfort, Germany, 1947-50; with Allied High Commn., Bonn, Germany, 1950-52; U.S. mission to NATO and OEEC, Paris, 1952-54; fgn. affairs officer Dept. State, Washington, 1954-55; exec. sec. to dir. ICA, Washington, 1955-59; U.S. econ. coord. for CENTO affairs Ankara, Turkey, 1959-63; chief econ. and comml. sect. Am. Embassy, Cairo, 1963-66; student Nat. War Coll., Washington, 1966-67; dep. dir. office econ. and social affairs Bur. Internat. Orgn. Affairs, Dept. State, 1967-68, dir., 1968-71; coord. UN Multilateral Devel. Programs, Dept. State, 1971-74, acting dep. asst. sec. econ. and social affairs, 1971, 73; dep. dir. gen. ILO, Geneva, 1974-78; pres. INTELSAT Conf. Privileges and Immunities, 1978; U.S. coord. Tech. Coop. among Developing Countries, 1978; rep. with rank of amb. to UN Conf., 1978—; sec. gen. 27th Colombo Plan Ministerial Meeting, 1978; U.S. coord. UN Decade on Drinking Water and Sanitation, 1979; U.S. coord., ambassador Third World Conf. on Indsl. Devel., 1979, World Assembly on Aging, 1980-82; chmn. fed. inter-agy. com. Internat. Yr. of Disabled Persons, 1980-81; U.S. rep. Internat. Youth Yr., 1981-83; coord. multilateral affairs Ctr. Study of Fgn. Affairs, 1983-87; profl. lectr. in law George Washington U. Nat. Law Ctr., 1987-88, lectr. in conflict resolution, multilateral diplomacy and art of negotiation; pres. Iowa Peace Inst., Grinnell, 1988-92; prof. polit. sci. Grinnell Coll., 1989-92; Disting. vis. prof. George Mason U., Fairfax, Va., 1992-93; chmn. Inst. for Multi-Track Diplomacy, Washington, 1992—; mem. Fgn. Affairs Res. Corps., 1993—. Author: The North-Shore Dialogue and the UN, 1982, How to Be a Delegate, 1984, 2nd edit., 1994; co-editor: International Negotiation, 1985, Perspectives on Negotiation, 1986, Conflict Resolution: Track Two Diplomacy, 1987, 2nd edit., 1995, U.S. Soviet Summitry, 1987, US Bases Overseas: Negotiations with Spain, Greece and The Philippines, 1990, Multi-Track Diplomacy, 1991, revised, 1993, 3rd edit., 1996, Defining A U.S. Negotiating Sytle, 1996; contbr. articles on aging, terrorism, water conflict resolution. Bd. dirs. Global Water, 1982—, Touchstone Theatre, 1982-88, World Com.-UN Decade of Disabled Persons, 1987—, Countdown 2001, 1987-93, People-to-People Com. on Disability, 1987, Am. Impact Found., 1987-89, chmn. bd., 1988-89; dir. Am. Assn. Internat. Aging, 1983—, chmn., 1983—; v.p. nat. capital area UN Assn., 1993—, mem., 1978—. Recipient Superior Honor award, 1972, Presdl. Meritorious Service award, 1984; named Patriot of Yr., Kansas City, 1987. Mem. ABA, Am. Fgn. Svc. Assn., U.S. Assn. for Club of Rome, Soc. Profls. in Dispute Resolution, Consortium of Peace Rsch., Edn. and Devel., Cosmos Club, Delta Kappa Upsilon, Phi Delta Phi. Office: IMTD 1819 H St NW Ste 1200 Washington DC 20006-3603

MC DONALD, JOSEPH VALENTINE, neurosurgeon; b. N.Y.C., June 7, 1925; m. Carolyn Alice Patricia Peterson, Apr. 30, 1955; children: Judith Katherine McDonald Aquadro, Elizabeth Ann McDonald Iwanicki, Catherine Eleanor McDonald Schneider, Joseph Bede, David Randolph. A.B., Coll. Holy Cross, 1945; M.D., U. Pitts., 1949. Intern St. Vincent's Hosp., N.Y.C., 1949-50; rsch. fellow neuroanatomy Vanderbilt U., 1950-51; gen. surgery asst. resident Cushing VA Hosp., Boston, 1951-52; neurology extern Lenox Hill Hosp., 1952; asst. resident neurosurgery Johns Hopkins Hosp., 1953-55, resident neurosurgeon, 1955-56; practice medicine specializing in neurol. surgery Rochester, N.Y., 1956—; emeritus prof. neurosurgery and neurology U. Rochester Med. Sch. Mem. Soc. Neurol. Surgeons, A.C.S., Am. Assn. Neurol. Surgeons, Congress Neurosurgeons. Home: 800 Allens Creek Rd Rochester NY 14618-3412 Office: Strong Meml Hosp Div Neurosurgery Rochester NY 14642

MCDONALD, LESLEY SCOTT, clinical nurse specialist; b. Toronto, Jan. 29, 1946; d. Louis Johnstone and Frances Elizabeth (Pruder) McD.; m. Richard Eldon Jacobson, May 26, 1984. Grad. in nursing, Health Scis. Ctr., Winnipeg, Man., Can., 1969; BA, U. Winnipeg, 1974; MS, Johns Hopkins U., 1984. RN, Md., Wis., Ill., Tenn.; cert. neurosci. RN, ANCC. Neuro nurse clinician, staff nurse Johns Hopkins Hosp., Balt., 1974-83; neuro clin. nurse specialist Madison (Wis.) Gen., 1983-84, St. Anthony Med. Ctr., Rockford, Ill., 1984-90, Nashville Meml., 1990-94; charge nurse, neuro Vanderbilt-Stallworth, Nashville, 1994—; lectr. No. Ill. U. Sch. Nursing, Rockford, 1989-90, Austin Peay State U. Sch. Nursing, Clarksville, Tenn., 1991-94. Mem. AACN, Am. Assn. Neurosci. Nurses (Madison chpt. pres. 1983-84, Rockford chpt. pres. 1986-90). Avocations: breeding, raising and showing Great Pyrenees. Home: 147 Flat Rock Rd Lebanon TN 37090-9217

MCDONALD, LESLIE, art director, production designer. Prodn. designer: (films) The Grifters, 1990, (with Dennis Gassner) Hero, 1992; art dir.: (films) Bugsy, 1991 (Academy award nomination best art direction 1991), (with Jim Teergarden) Forrest Gump, 1994 (Academy award nomination best art direction 1994). Office: care Art Directors Guild 11365 Ventura Blvd Ste 315 Studio City CA 91604-3148

MCDONALD, MALCOLM GIDEON, education educator; b. Boise, Idaho, Mar. 22, 1932; s. Gideon L. and Annette (Connell) McD.; m. Glenda S. Yarbrough, Nov. 23, 1962; children: Ronald, Steven, Michael. AA, Boise Jr. Coll., 1951; BA, Wash. State U., 1954, MA, 1972; EdD, U. Idaho, 1991. Prof. North Idaho Coll., Coeur d'Alene, Idaho, 1977-78; exec. dir. Spokane Higher Edn. Office, 1978-84; dir. CAREERS, Eastern Wash. U., 1984-86; dir. continuing edn. Eastern Wash. U., Cheney, Wash., 1986-89, asst. prof. dept. comm. studies, 1989-94. Ret. lt. col. U.S. Army. Recipient Legion of Merit award, Bronze stars (2), Air medals (11), Meritorious Svc. medal, Commendation medal (5), Vietnam medal of Gallantry, 1954-76. Presbyterian. Avocation: sports. Home: 2841 Spalding Dr Las Vegas NV 89134-7555

MCDONALD, MARIANNE, classicist; b. Chgo., Jan. 2, 1937; d. Eugene Francis and Inez (Riddle) McD.; children: Eugene, Conrad, Bryan, Bridget, Kirstie (dec.), Hiroshi. BA magna cum laude, Bryn Mawr Coll., 1958; MA, U. Chgo., 1960; PhD, U. Calif., Irvine, 1975, doctorate (hon.) Am. Coll. Greece, 1988, hon. diploma Am. Archaeological Assn. Teaching asst. classics U. Calif., Irvine, 1974, D Litt (hon.) U. Athens, Greece, 1994, U. Dublin, 1994. instr. Greek, Latin and English, mythology, modern cinema, 1975-79, founder, rsch. fellow Thesaurus Linguae Graecae Project, 1975—; bd. dir. Centrum. Bd. dirs. Am. Coll. of Greece, 1981-90, Scripps Hosp., 1981; Am. Sch. Classical Studies, 1986—; mem. bd. overseers U. Calif. San Diego, 1985—; nat. bd. advisors Am. Biog. Inst., 1982—; pres. Soc. for the Preservation of the Greek Heritage, 1990—; founder Hajime Mori Chair for Japanese Studies, U. Calif., San Diego, 1985, McDonald Ctr. for Alcohol and Substance Abuse, 1984, Thesaurus Linguarum Hiberniae, 1991—; vis. prof. U. Dublin, 1990—; adj. prof. theatre U. Calif., San Diego, 1990, prof. theatre and classics, 1994. Recipient Ellen Browning Scripps Humanitarian award, 1975; Disting. Svc. award U. Calif.-Irvine, 1982, Irvine medal, 1987, 3rd Prize Midwest Poetry Ctr. Contest, 1987; named one of the Community Leaders Am., 1979-80, Philanthropist of Yr., 1985, Headliner San Diego Press Club, 1985, Philanthropist of Yr. Honorary Nat. Conf. Christians and Jews, 1986, Woman of Distinction Salvation Army, 1986, Eleventh Woman Living Legacy, 1986, Woman of Yr. AHEPA, 1988, San Diego Woman of Distinction, 1990, Woman of Yr. AXIOS, 1991; recipient Bravissimo gold medal San Diego Opera, 1990, Gold Medal Soc. Internationalization of Greek Lang., 1990, Athens medal, 1991, Piraeus medal, 1991, award Desmoi, 1992, award Hellenic Assn of Univ. Women, 1992, Academy of Achievement award AHEPA, 1992, Woman of Delphi award European Cultural Ctr. Delphi, 1992, Civis Universitatis award U. Calif. San Diego, 1993, Hypatia award Hellenic U. Women, 1993, Am.-Ireland Fund Heritage award, 1994, Contribution to Greek Letters award Aristotle U. Thessaloniki, 1994, Order of the Phoenix, Greece, 1994, citations from U.S. Congress and Calif. Senate, Alezander the Gt. award Hellenic Cultural Soc., 1995, made hon. citizen of Delphi and gold medal of the Amphiktuonon, Delphi, Greece, 1995, award European Cultural Ctr. of Delphi, 1995, Women Who Mean Bus. award for Fine Arts San Diego Bus. Jour., 1995. Vol. Decade Women's International Ctr., 1994. Mem. MLA, AAUP, Am. Philol. Assn., Soc. for the Preservation of the Greek Heritage (pres.), Libr. of Am., Am. Classical League, Philol. Assn. Pacific Coast, Am. Comparative Lit. Assn., Modern and Classical Lang. Assn. So. Calif., Hellenic Soc., Calif. Fgn. Lang. Tchrs. Assn., Internat. Platform Assn., Greek Language Found., Royal Irish Acad., Greece's Order of the Phoenix (commdr. 1994), KPBS Producers Club, Hellenic Univ. Club (bd. dir.). Author: Terms for Happiness in Euripides, 1978, Semilemmatized Concordances to Euripides' Alcestis, 1977, Cyclops, Andromache, Medea, 1978, Heraclidae, Hippolytus, 1979, Hecuba, 1984, Hercules Furens, 1984, Electra, 1984, Ion, 1985, Trojan Women, 1988, Iphigenia in Taurus, 1988, Euripides in Cinema: The Heart Made Visible, 1983; translator: The Cost of Kindness and Other Fabulous Tales (Shinichi Hoshi), 1986, (chpt.) Views of Clytemnestra, Ancient and Modern, 1990, Classics and Cinema, 1990, Modern Critical Theory and Classical Literature, 1994, A Challenge to Democracy, 1994, Ancient Sun/Modern Light: Greek Drama on the Modern Stage, 1990; contbr. numerous articles to profl. jours. Avocations: karate, harp (medieval), skiing, diving. Home: PO Box 929 Rancho Santa Fe CA 92067-0929 Office: U Calif at San Diego Dept Theatre La Jolla CA 92093

MCDONALD, MARK DOUGLAS, electrical engineer; b. Princeton, N.J., Aug. 3, 1958; s. James Douglas and Jacquelyn (Milligan) McD.; m. Patricia Joann Watson, Sept. 12, 1980. BSE, Duke U.; MS, N.C. State U. Product engr. Exide Electronics, Raleigh, N.C., 1981-84; rsch. asst. N.C. State U., Raleigh, 1985-86; mem. tech. staff Avantek (Hewlett Packard), Newark, Calif., 1987-90; prin. engr. Nat. Semiconductor, Santa Clara, Calif., 1990-92, engring. project mgr., 1992-95; design engring. mgr. Linear Tech. corp., Milpitas, Calif., 1995—; session chmn. Wireless Symposium, Santa Clara, 1993-96, RF and Microwave Applications Conf., Santa Clara, 1992; mem. com. Sumposium on VLSI Circuits Program, 1995-96. Contbr. articles to profl. jours. Precinct capt. various polit. campaigns, Fremont, Calif., 1988. Mem. IEEE (sr.), Cairn Terrier Club of No. Calif. (asst. chairperson 1995, specialty show chairperson 1996—, bd. govs. 1996—). Achievements include U.S. and foreign patents in area of high-speed analog circuits; designed front-end integrated circuits in first wireless digital European cordless telecomm. transceiver (DECT) for voice comm.; design of first selective frequency trip circuit for parallel uninterruptible power supplies. Office: Linear Tech Corp 1630 McCarthy Blvd Milpitas CA 95035-7487

MCDONALD, MARY M., lawyer; b. 1944. BA, D'Youville Coll., 1966; JD, Fordham U., 1969. Bar: N.Y. 1969. Counsel corp. staff Merck & Co., v.p., gen. counsel, 1991—, now sr. v.p., gen counsel. Office: Merck & Co P.O. Box 100 Whitehouse Station NJ 08889-0100*

MCDONALD, MICHAEL BRIAN, economist, consultant; b. Tulsa, Jan. 1, 1948; s. William Gerald and Agnes Gertrude (Sellman) McD.; m. Jane Anne Fahey, Aug. 25, 1969; children: Kelly, Anne. BA in Econs. cum laude, Georgetown U., 1969; PhD in Econs., U. Pa., 1978. Teaching fellow U. Pa., Phila., 1976-77; rsch. fellow Logistics Mgmt. Inst., Washington, 1977-78; assoc. dir. Bur. Bus. and Econ. Rsch. U. N.Mex., Albuquerque, 1978-82, dir. Bur. Bus. and Econ. Rsch., 1982—; dir. Kirtland Fed. Credit Union, Albuquerque, 1982—. Contbr. articles to profl. jours. Lt-Col. USAFR, 1978—. Capt. USAF, 1972-76. NDEA Title IV fellow U. Pa., 1969-72. Mem. Phi Beta Kappa. Avocations: tennis, golf, fishing. Office: U NMex Bur Bus and Econ Rsch 1920 Lomas NE Albuquerque NM 87131

MCDONALD, MICHAEL LEE, health care consultant, retired naval officer; b. Salt Lake City, Oct. 23, 1949; s. Jack Alex and Dorothy Elsie (Mantle) McD.; m. Celia McKean Smoot, June 23, 1975; children: Sarah Lynn, Michelle Elise, AnnMarie, Jeffrey Michael, Matthew David, Emily Jane. BA, U. Utah, 1973; MA, U. Iowa, 1977. Commd. ensign USN, 1975; advanced through grades to comdr., 1991; patient adminstr. Naval Hosp., Great Lakes, Ill., 1977-80, Oakland, Calif., 1980-82; med. recruiter Navy Recruiting Dist., San Francisco, 1982-84; adminstr. Navy Environ. and Preventative Medicine Unit # 7, Naples, Italy, 1984-87; staff officer Navy Med. Commd. Europe, London, 1987-89; healthcare advisor U.S. Naval Forces Europe, London, 1989-91; exec. officer Naval Med. Clinic, Seattle, 1991-93, commdg. officer, 1993-94; officer in charge Branch Med. Clinic, Everett, Wash., 1994-96; ret., 1996, health care cons., 1996—. Coach Northshore Little League, Bothell, Wash., 1992, 93; scoutmaster Boy Scouts Am., Dublin, Calif., 1981-85, instl. sponsor, Naples, Italy, 1985-87. Fellow Am. Coll. Healthcare Execs. Mem. LDS Ch. Avocations: golf, basketball, English literature, cycling. Home and Office: 19225 4th Dr SE Bothell WA 98012-7013

MCDONALD, MICHAEL SCOTT, lawyer; b. Ft. Stockton, Tex., Feb. 6, 1962; s. Roland R. and Harriett L. McD.; m. Sara; children: Matthew, Michael. BA, U. Tex., El Paso, 1984; JD, U. Tex., Austin, 1987. Bar: Tex. 1987, U.S. Ct. Appeals (5th cir.), U.S. Dist. Ct. (all dists.) Tex. Assoc. Johnson, Bromberg & Leeds, Dallas, 1987-92; assoc. Littler, Mendelson, Fastiff, Tichy & Mathiason, Dallas, 1992-94, ptnr., shareholder, 1994—; presenter in field. Co-author, editor: The 1994 Texas Employer, 1994; contbg. editor: Model Jury Instructions-Employment Litigation, 1994, Covenents Not to Compete-A State by State Survey, 1995; contbr. articles to profl. jours. Mem. ABA (litigation sect., labor and employment law sect.), Tex. Bar Assn. (labor and employment law sect.), Tex. Assn. Bus., Dallas Bar Assn. (employment law sect.), mem. exec.com. 1994—), Dallas Young Lawyers Assn., Indsl. Rels. Rsch. Assn. Office: Littler Mendelson Fastiff Tichy & Mathiason 300 Crescent Ct Dallas TX 75201

MCDONALD, MILLER BAIRD, management consultant, columnist, historian; b. Huntsville, Tenn., Feb. 16, 1920; s. Melva Lawson and Bertha Clarence (Baird) McD.; m. Lois Fox, Nov. 30, 1941; 4 children. Ed., Lincoln Meml. U., 1939-40, U. Tenn., 1948-49; cert., Cornell U., 1958, U. Wis., 1967, U. Mich., 1971; B.S., Pacific Western U., 1984, Ph.D., 1985. Adminstrv. asst. Home Owners Loan Corp., Washington, 1940-41; personnel officer AEC, Oak Ridge, 1946-51; pers., tng. and intelligence officer AEC, Albuquerque, 1953-59; policy devel. officer FAA, Washington, 1959-60; chief out-service tng. IRS, Washington, 1960-66; dir. mgmt. tng. Sec. Commerce, Washington, 1966-72; pres., cons. to mgmt. Miller McDonald and Assocs., La Follette, Tenn., 1973—, Arlington, Va., 1972—; syndicated columnist County Line, Tenn., 1980—; owner, mgr. County Services Syndicate, 1981—; commr. for human devel. State of Tenn., 1979—; instr. internat. program in taxation Harvard U. Law Sch., 1964-66; instr. U. Ga., 1970, La. State U., 1971; bd. dirs. Wesleyan Found., 1978—; mem. nat. adv. bd. Am. Security Council, 1979—; del. White House Conf. on Aging, 1981—; mem. Gov.'s Conf. on Aging, 1982—. Author: Campbell County Tennessee, 3 vols., 1993, (news series) Our Government, What's Wrong, 1982, also profl. papers. Mem. Presdl. Task Force on Career Advancement, 1965; charter mem. Statue of Liberty Found., 1983; chmn. Pres. Ford Com. East Tenn., 1976; mem. Senator Baker for Pres. Com., 1979; chmn. Campbell County Republican Exec. Com., Tenn., 1976-80, 2d Congl. dist. Reagan for Pres. Com., 1980, Upper 4th Dist. Reagan-Bush Com., 1984; dir. Tenn. Citizen's Against Govt. Waste (Grace Commn.), 1986—; mem. U.S. Capitol Hist. Soc., 1987—; historian Campbell County, Tenn., 1988—; incorporator, dir. Campbell County Hist. Soc., 1989—, pres. bd., 1991—. Served to col. U.S. Army, 1942-46, 50-53. Decorated Presdl. award for Outstanding Meritorious Svc.; decorated numerous other medals; recipient Superior Performance award AEC, 1960, cert. recognition IRS, 1966, medal Sec. Army, 1971, Cert. svc. Dept. Commerce, 1972, Presdl. Achievement award Rep. Nat. Com., 1982, Tenn. Gov.'s Outstanding Achievement award, 1992, Merit award Tenn. Hist. Commn., 1993, Proclamation Tenn. Ho. of Reps., 1993, Tenn. Libr. Assn. award of Merit, 1994. Mem Inst. Applied Behavioral Sci., NEA, Am. Soc. Tng. and Devel., Adult Edn. Assn., Libr. of Congress Assocs. (charter), Am. Legion, Clan Donald U.S.A., Rotary, Masons. Methodist. Home and Office: 109 Crestview Dr La Follette TN 37766-4822 *Society has lost much because of failure to persist. To be sure you are right and go ahead is the thing. Many of life's goals have been lost simply because one has given up too soon. To have the steadfastness to persist in the face of great odds has largely accounted for what measure of success I have achieved.*

MCDONALD, PATRICIA LESLIE, education educator; b. Detroit, Apr. 5, 1945; d. Joseph Aloysious and Ethel Irene (Reynolds) McD. BA, Siena Heights Coll., 1969, MA, 1976; EdD, Western Mich. U., 1983. Elem. tchr. St. Anthony, St. Patrick, Ft. Lauderdale, Fla., 1969-75; coll. counselor Siena Hts. Coll., Adrian, Mich., 1975-76; faculty Siena Heights Coll., 1992—; therapist Macomb County Com. Mental Health, Mt. Clemens, Mich., 1976-83; adminstr. Human Devel. Program, Detroit, 1983-85; v.p., therapist Macomb Family Svcs., Mt. Clemens, 1985-92; assoc. dir. Archdiocese of Detroit, 1992-95; faculty Assumption Univ., Windsor, Ont., Can., 1995—, Univ. Detroit, 1994—; asst. dean met. Detroit program Siena Heights Coll., 1995—; cons. IBM, various colls. and univs., Mich., Calif., 1980—. Adv. bd. Dominican Consultation Ctr., Detroit, 1983-91; bd. dirs. Macomb County Child Abuse and Neglect Coun., Mt. Clemens, 1985-92, bd. dirs. ARC, Detroit, 1994. Mem. Mich. Counselors Personal Assn. Roman Catholic. Home: 22727 Corteville St Saint Clair Shores MI 48081-2563

MCDONALD, PATRICK ALLEN, lawyer, arbitrator, educator; b. Detroit, May 11, 1936; s. Lawrence John and Estelle (Maks) Mc D.; m. Margaret Mercier, Aug. 10, 1963; children: Michael Lawrence, Colleen Marie, Patrick Joseph, Timothy, Margaret, Thomas, Maureen. PhB cum laude, U. Detroit, 1958, JD magna cum laude, 1961; LLM (E. Barrett Prettyman Trial scholar, Hugh J. Fegan fellow), Georgetown U., 1962. Bar: D.C. 1961, Mich. 1961, Colo. 1993. Case worker Dept. Pub. Welfare, Detroit, 1958; field examiner NLRB, Detroit, 1961; practiced in Washington, 1961-62; trial cons. NIH, Bethesda, Md., 1962; staff judge adv. USAF, France, 1962-65; ptnr. Monagham, LoPrete, Mc Donald, Yakima & Grenke, Detroit, 1965—; bd. dirs., chmn. Delta Dental Plan of Mich.; chmn. Delta Dental Plan of Ohio; bd. dirs., v.p. Guest House, Lake Orion, Mich., Rochester, Minn., Detroit Athletic Club, Brighton Hosp.; instr. polit. sci. and law U. Md., 1963-65, U. Detroit Law Sch., adj. prof., 1965—. Co-author: Law and Tactics in Federal Criminal Cases, 1963. Mem. Detroit Bd. Edn., 1966-76, pres.; sec., trustee Mt. Elliott Cemetary Assn.; mem. U. Detroit Sports Hall of Fame; mem. adv. bd. Providence Hosp., Southfield, Mich.; exec. bd. U. Detroit Pres.'s Cabinet. Named one of Five Outstanding Young Men of Mich., Outstanding Young Man of Detroit. Mem. ABA, Detroit Bar Assn., State Bar Mich. (commr.), U. Detroit Alumni Assn. (bd. dirs.), Mensa, Blue Key, Alpha Phi Omega (pres. Eta Pi chpt. 1955), Alpha Sigma Nu (v.p. 1960). Home: 13066 Lashbrook Ln Brighton MI 48116-9002 Office: 1700 N Woodward Ave Bloomfield Hills MI 48304-2249 *In the field of law, as an attorney, professor and arbitrator, I have prayed and attempted to be able in argument, accurate in analysis, correct in conclusion, candid with clients, honest with adversaries, and responsible for obligations assigned to me. I have advocated moderation in all things with the exception of my love for Him who created me.*

MCDONALD, ROBERT BOND, chemical company executive; b. Seattle, Oct. 31, 1936; s. Theodore Day and Elizabeth Wood (Robbins) McD.; m. Eleanore Mary Beca, June 27, 1959; children: James Arthur, Kylie Robbins. BE, Yale U., 1958; MS, U. Wash., 1960. Mng. dir. Gt. Lakes Chem. Corp., Lancaster, Eng., 1976-79; asst. to pres. Great Lakes Chem. Corp., West Lafayette, Ind., 1979-81, v.p., 1981-87, sr. v.p., 1987-94, exec. v.p., COO, pres., CEO, 1994—; also bd. dirs. Gt. Lakes Chem. Corp., West Lafayette, Ind.; v.p. COB Octel Am., Inc.; adv. bd. Inst. for Applied Neurology, Purdue U., deans adv. coun. Krannert Sch. Mgmt.; bd. dirs. Kao-Quaker, Japan, Tetrabrom Tech., Ltd., Israel, QO Chems., Assoc. Octel, U.K., The Lafayette Life Ins. Co. Mem. Tippecanoe County Hist. Assn., Greater Lafayette Mus. Art. Mem. Ind. Soc. Chgo., Greater Lafayette C. of C. (bd. dirs. 1987-90), Lafayette Country Club (bd. dirs.). Republican. Episcopalian. Office: Gt Lakes Chem Corp 1 Great Lakes Blvd PO Box 2200 West Lafayette IN 47906

MCDONALD, ROBERT DELOS, manufacturing company executive; b. Dubuque, Iowa, Jan. 30, 1931; s. Delos Lyon and Virginia (Kolck) McD.; m. Jane M. Locher, Jan. 16, 1960 (div. Jan. 1970); children: Jean, Patricia, Maria, Sharon, Rob; m. Marilyn I. Miller, July 4, 1978. BA in Econs., U. Iowa, 1953. With A.Y. McDonald Mfg. Co., Dubuque, 1956—, salesman, 1956-60, sales mgr., 1961-64, mgr. Dubuque wholesale br., 1965-72, v.p., 1971-72, v.p., corp. sec., 1972-83, sr. v.p., corp. sec., 1983-85, pres., 1985-95, chmn. bd., chief exec. officer, 1987—, also bd. dirs., 1964—; bd. dirs. Brock-McVey Co., Lexington, Ky., A.Y. McDonald Supply Co., Inc., Dubuque, Dubuque Bank & Trust Co.; sr. v.p., bd. dirs. A.Y. McDonald Industries, Inc., Dubuque, 1983—; chmn. bd., pres., CEO, bd. dirs. A.Y.M. Inc., Albia, Iowa. Trustee, bd. dirs. A.Y. McDonald Mfg. Co. Charitable Found., 1978—, pres., 1982—; bd. dirs. Stonehill Care Ctr., Dubuque, 1984-92, chmn. bd., 1991-92; mem. Stonehill Renovation and Financing Task Force, 1994—; bd. dirs. Dubuque Boys Club, 1989—, Save Iowa's Civil War Monument Restoration Fund, 1995—, Dubuque County Hist. Soc., 1996—; trustee United Way Svcs., Inc., Dubuque, 1989—; vice chmn. Stonehill Benevolent Found., Dubuque, 1988-92; mem. adv. coun. region VII SBA, Cedar Rapids, 1984—; mem. adv. bd. Jr. Achievement Tri-States, Inc., 1991—, Iowa State Fair Blue Ribbon Found., 1993—. Lt. USNR, 1953-56, Korea. Mem. Am. Mgmt. Assn., Am. Supply Assn., Am. Water Works Assn., Nat. Assn. Mfrs., Dubuque Area C. of C., Am. Legion, Dubuque Shooting Soc., Dubuque Golf and Country Club, Sigma Alpha Epsilon. Republican. Roman Catholic. Home: Fountain Hill 3399 Eagle Point Dr Dubuque IA 52001 Office: AY McDonald Mfg Co PO Box 508 Dubuque IA 52004-0508

MC DONALD, ROBERT EMMETT, company executive; b. Red Wing, Minn., Apr. 29, 1915; s. Mitchell W. and Olivia (Carlson) McD.; m. Marion L. Wigley, Sept. 14, 1946; children: Patricia L., Barbara C. B.B.A., B.E.E., U. Minn., 1940; postgrad., U. Chgo., 1942. Employment interviewer Commonwealth Edison Co., Chgo., 1940-43; supr. accessory maintenance Northwest Airlines, St. Paul, 1946-51; dir. maintenance No. region Braniff Airways, Mpls., 1951-53; mgr. ops., then v.p., mgr. def. div. Univac, St. Paul, 1953-64; pres. Univac div. Sperry Rand Corp., Blue Bell, Pa., 1966-71; exec. v.p. parent co. Univac div. Sperry Rand Corp., 1966-72; pres., COO Sperry Rand Corp., N.Y.C., 1972-79; vice chmn. bd. Sperry Rand Corp., 1979-80; dir. CertainTeed Corp., Valley Forge, Pa., SKF Industries, Phila., 1979-85, Glenmede Corp., Phila.; mgmt. cons. Trustee U. Minn. Found., 1975-85. Served to lt. USNR, 1943-46. Mem. Tau Beta Pi, Eta Kappa Nu, Acacia. Clubs: Phila. Country, Union League (Phila.). Home: 1125 Robin Rd Gladwyne PA 19035-1007

MCDONALD, STANFORD LAUREL, clinical psychologist; b. Lincoln, Nebr., Mar. 14, 1929; s. Laurel C. and Irene Virginia (Frey) McD.; m. Shirley P. Peterson, Apr. 26, 1964; children: Stacia E. V., Jeffrey J.S., Kathleen S., Patricia M. AB, Nebr. Wesleyan U., 1956; MA, U. Nebr., 1959, postgrad., 1958-60; PhD, Fielding Inst., 1974. Licensed clin. psychologist, Ill. Intern Nebr. Psychiat. Inst., Omaha, 1957-58; staff psychologist Presbyn. St. Lukes Hosp., Chgo., 1960-61; sch. psychologist Chgo. Bd. Edn., 1961-65; chief psychologist SPEED Devel. Ctr., Chicago Heights, Ill., 1965-79; pvt. practice psychology Park Forest, Ill., 1980—; cmty. prof. Gov.'s State U., University Park, Ill., 1974—; clin. dir. Dr. Stanford L. McDonald and Assocs., Park Forest, 1980; vis. prof. U. Witwatersrand, Johannesburg, S.A., spring 1996. Contbr. papers for profl. convs. With USMC, 1950-52, Korea. Fellow Am. Orthopsychiat. Assn.; mem. Am. Psychol. Assn., Biofeedback Soc. Ill. (past. pres.), N.Y. Acad. Scis., Midwestern Psychological Assn., 1st Marine Divsn. Assn., Zeta Psi, Psi Chi. Avocations: personal computers, automotive design. Home: 255 Rich Rd Park Forest IL 60466-1629 Office: 24 Centre Ste 4 Park Forest IL 60466-2032

MC DONALD, STEPHEN LEE, economics educator; b. Arkadelphia, Ark., Aug. 8, 1924; s. Claud Bethel and Ruth Jane (Gresham) McD.; m. Elizabeth Gene Brewer, Aug. 14, 1945; children: Martha Elizabeth Mc Donald Worchel, Kathryn Ann Mc Donald McGlothlin. B.A., La. Poly. Inst., 1947; M.A., U. Tex., 1948, Ph.D., 1951. Asst. prof. U. Tex., Austin, 1950-56, prof. econs., 1961—, Josey prof. in energy studies, 1983-85, Duncan prof. econs., 1985—; chmn. dept. U. Tex., 1972-76, 78-79, 88-89; sr. fellow Bur. Bus. Rsch., 1990—; economist Humble Oil & Refining Co., 1956-57; assoc. prof., prof., chmn. dept. La. State U., 1957-61; mem. faculty Stonier Grad. Sch. Banking; staff assoc., Brookings Instn., 1961-63; mem. econs. adv. panel NSF, 1962-64; cons. to govt. and industry, 1957—. Author: Federal Tax Treatment of Income from Oil and Gas, 1963, Petroleum Conservation in the United States, 1971, The Leasing of Federal Lands for Fossil Fuels Production, 1979; mem. editorial bds.: So. Econ. Journal, 1961-64, Energy Jour., 1979-86; contbr. articles to profl. jours. Served with USNR, 1943-46. Recipient Citation for Excellence Am. Bankers Assn.; Ford Found. grantee, 1964; Resources for Future grantee, 1967, 76; Pres. Assocs. award teaching excellence, 1982. Mem. Am. Econ. Assn., So. Econ. Assn. (v.p. 1969-70), Southwestern Econ. Assn. (pres. 1964-65), Internat. Assn. Energy Econs., Gamma Epsilon, Phi Kappa Phi. Democrat. Methodist. Home: 4002 Sierra Dr Austin TX 78731-3914

MCDONALD, SUSAN F., business executive, county official; b. Rockford, Ill., Jan. 18, 1961; d. John Augustus and Jeanne (Reitsch) Floberg; m. Robert Arthur McDonald, June 19, 1981; children: Molly Jeanne, Amanda Elizabeth. AAS in Bus. Mgmt., Colo. Mountain Coll., Glenwood Springs, 1981. Teller, bookkeeper Alpine Bank, Glenwood Springs, 1981-82; teller Macktown State Bank, Rockford, 1982-83; treas., mgr., owner Roscoe (Ill.) Movie House, 1984-94; sales cons. Lou Bachroot, Inc., Rockford, 1992-93; mem. bd. suprs. Winnebago County Bd., Rockford, 1992—; exec. v.p., owner Corp. Svc. Alliance, Machesney Park, Ill., 1993-95; leasing and fleet mgr. Budweiser Motors, Inc., Beloit, Wis., 1994-95; bus. mgr. Finley Oldsmobile GMC, South Beloit, Ill., 1995—. Pres. Roscoe Bus. Assn., 1990, 91, v.p., 189; chair, founder Roscoe Beautification Assn., 1991; mem. county bd. dirs. Winnebago County, 1992—, vice chmn. econ. devel. com., 1993—; chmn. econ. devel. environ. com. Winnebago County Bd., 1994—; commr. Winnebago County Forest Preserve, Rockford, 1992—; co-founder, bd. dirs. Very Important Pregnancy, Rockford Meml. Hosp.; bd. dirs. Family Advocate Aux., Rockford, 1987-88; bd. dirs. U. Ill. Extension Svc./Winnebago County, 1994—. Nominated Video Retailer of Yr., Am. Video Assn., 1989, Leadership award, Stateline YWCA, 1989. Republican. Methodist. Avocations: horseback riding, hunting and jumping equestrian activities, golfing, skiing. Office: Finley Oldsmobile GMC 1790 Gardner St South Beloit IL 61080

MCDONALD, THERESA BEATRICE (PIERCE) (MRS. OLLIE MCDONALD), church official; b. Vicksburg, Miss., Apr. 11, 1929; d. Leonard C. Pierce and Ernestine Morris Templeton; m. Ollie McDonald, Apr. 23, 1966. Student, Tougaloo Coll., 1946-47, Roosevelt U., 1954-56, 59-62, U. Chgo. Indsl. Rels. Ctr., 1963-64. Vol. rep. Liberty Bapt. Ch., Am. Legion Aux., VA West Side Hosp., Chgo., 1971-73; nat. instr. ushers dept. Prog. Nat. Bapt. Conv. Inc., Washington, 1973-75, nat. sec. ushers dept., 1975-76, v.p. at large, 1980-82, chmn. pers. com., 1982-84; mem. faculty Congress of Christian Edn., 1978-85; mem. pub. rels. staff Liberty Bapt. Ch., Chgo., 1973-79, trustee, 1987-91; asst. Christian edn. dir. Maryland Ave. Bapt. Ch., Chgo., 1995—; cons., lectr. in field; guest speaker TV and radio programs. Participant White House Regional Confs., 1961. Recipient Christian Svc. award Prog. Nat. Bapt. Conv. Inc., 1986, 92, 94, Disting. Svc. award, 1990-94. Mem. Bethlehem Bapt. Dist. Assn. Chgo. (asst. sec. 1982-84), Ch. Women United in Greater Chgo. (Ecumenical Actions com. 1981-83), Am. Legion (Outstanding Svc. award 1972, 73), Order Ea. Star. Address: 9810 S Calumet Ave Chicago IL 60628-1432

MCDONALD, THOMAS ALEXANDER, lawyer; b. Chgo., Aug. 20, 1942; s. Owen Gerard and Lois (Gray) McD.; m. Sharon Diane Hirk, Nov. 25, 1967; children: Cristin, Katie, Courtney, Thomas Jr. AB, Georgetown U., 1965; JD, Loyola U., Chgo., 1968. Bar: Ill. 1969, U.S. Dist. Ct. (no. dist.) Ill. 1969. Ptnr. Clausen Miller, PC, Chgo., 1969—. Mem. ABA, Ill. Bar Assn., Chgo. Bar Assn. Office: Clausen Miller PC 10 S La Salle St Chicago IL 60603-1098

MCDONALD, THOMAS PAUL, controller; b. Williamsport, Pa., Aug. 13, 1949; s. Paul Tripp and Ethel Mary (Cowden) McD.; m. Debra Ann Rosamilia, July 17, 1976; children: Kevin, Gail. BS in Acctg., U. Scranton, 1971. CPA, N.Y. Auditor Coopers & Lybrand, N.Y.C., 1971-79; internal audit dir. Ward Foods, N.Y.C., 1979-81; contr. Mallory Randall Corp., N.Y.C., 1981-83; asst. contr. Sullivan & Cromwell, N.Y.C., 1983—. Mem. AICPA, N.Y. State Soc. CPAs. Avocations: golf, coaching recreational sports. Home: 34 Dawson Dr West Caldwell NJ 07006-8128 Office: Sullivan & Cromwell 125 Broad St New York NY 10004-2400

MCDONALD, THOMAS ROBERT, materials technologist, consultant, business owner; b. Denver, Dec. 2, 1945; s. Phillip John and Anne Winslow (Jewell) McD.; m. Mary Kathleen Pfannenstiel, Mar. 6, 1970; children: Michael T., Patrick R. BS in Bus. Fin., U. Colo., 1974. Project material technician Colo. Dept. Hwys., Denver, 1964-71; pub. works inspector, project mgr. City of Lakewood, Colo., 1971-76; quality control supr., lab. mgr. Brannan Sand & Gravel Co., Denver, 1976-82; area mgr. Soiltest, Inc., Evanston, Ill., 1982-84; pavement maintenance specialist Western Technologies, Phoenix, 1984-87, Brewer Cote of Ariz., Glendale, 1987-88; sales mgr., estimator Driveway Maintenance of Ariz., Phoenix, 1988-92; owner Pavement Maintenance Info. Source, Mesa, Ariz., 1992—; materials quality control cons. Colo. Dept. Hwys., Denver, 1964-71, Brannan Sand & Gravel, Denver, 1976-82; pavement maintenance cons. Western Technologies, Phoenix, 1984-87, Brewer Cote of Ariz., Glendale, 1987-88, Pavement Maintenance Inf. Source, Mesa, 1992—. Author: (software) Ecopave, 1986, (book) Property Managers Guide to Pavement Maintenance, 1992, Asphalt Estimating, 1995; contbr. articles to property mgmt. and pavement maintenance mags. on pavement maintenance applications, distress inventories and devel. budgets. Mem. Leadership Mesa, 1986. With USN, 1965-68. Recipient Most Innovative Pavement Maintenance Program award FAA, 1986. Mem. Bldg. Owners and Mgrs. Assn. (bd. dirs. 1984-93), Multihousing Assn. Ariz. (instr. 1987, 89, 91), Nat. Assn. Aviation Ofcls., Calif. Assn. Aero. Execs. Achievements include development of a property management training course on pavement maintenance and budgeting; developed effective specification manual for pavement maintenance applications for property managers. Office: Pavement Maintenance Info Source PO Box 30567 Mesa AZ 85275-0567

MCDONALD, TIM, professional football player; b. Fresno, Calif., Jan. 6, 1965. Student, U. So. Calif. With St. Louis Cardinals, 1987; safety Phoenix Cardinals (formerly St. Louis Cardinals), 1988-92; with S.F. 49ers, 1993—. Named defense back The Sporting News All-America team, 1985. Played in Pro Bowl, 1989, 1991, 92, 93. Office: San Francisco 49ers 4949 Centennial Blvd Santa Clara CA 95054-1229

MCDONALD, WARREN GEORGE, accountant, former savings and loan executive; b. Oakland, Calif., Feb. 14, 1939; s. George Daniel and Barbara (Sainsot) McD.; m. Roberta Anne Peterson, Apr. 27, 1968; children: Edward Bruce, Deborah Lynn. B.A., San Francisco State Coll., 1962. CPA, Calif. Ptnr. Main Lafrentz & Co., CPAs, San Francisco, 1969-74; v.p., treas. Imperial Corp. Am., San Diego, 1975-80; v.p. fin. No. Calif. Savs. & Loan, Palo Alto, 1980-82; sr. v.p. fin. Unified Mortgage Co., Santa Clara, Calif., 1982-85; pres. Saratoga Savs., 1985-89; pvt. practice cons. San Francisco, 1989—. Co-author: Power Above The Law, 1990. Served to capt. USCGR. Mem. AICPA, Calif. Soc. CPAs, Inst. Mgmt. Accts., Res. Officers Assn. Home: 1430 Wendy Way Menlo Park CA 94025-6022

MCDONALD, WILLIAM ANDREW, classics educator; b. Warkworth, Ont., Can., Apr. 26, 1913; came to U.S., 1936, naturalized, 1943; s. William Douglas and Jean (Lane) McD.; m. Elizabeth Jackson Anderson, June 28, 1941; children: Susan, Elizabeth. B.A., U. Toronto, 1935, M.A., 1936; Ph.D., Johns Hopkins, 1940. Asst. prof. classics Lehigh U., 1939-43; tech. writer Consol. Vultee Aircraft Co., 1943-45; asso. prof. classics U. Tex., Austin, 1945-46; prof. classics, chmn. dept. Moravian Coll., Bethlehem, Pa., 1946-48; prof. classics U. Minn., 1948-80, Regents' prof. classical studies, 1973-80; dir. honors div. U. Minn. (Coll. Liberal Arts), 1964-67; dir. Minn. Messenia expdn. in S.W. Greece, 1961-92, dir. grad. center for ancient studies, 1973-78, 85-86; Research prof. Am. Sch. Classical Studies, Athens, 1978-79; excavation staff Johns Hopkins U. at Olynthus, 1938, U. Cin. at Pylos, 1939, 53; dir. Nichoria excavation, 1969-75. Author: Political Meeting Places of Greeks, 1943, Progress into the Past, 1967, (with C.C. Thomas) 2d edit., 1990, (with D. J. Georgacas) Place Names of Southwest Peloponnesus, 1969, (with G. Rapp Jr.) Minnesota Messenia Expedition: Reconstructing A Bronze Age Regional Environment, 1972, (with W.D.E. Coulson and John Rosser) Excavations at Nichoria in Southwest Greece: Dark Age and Byzantine Occupation, 1983, (with N.C. Wilkie) Bronze Age Occupation, 1992. Vogeler Meml. fellow Johns Hopkins, 1936-38; Royal Soc. Can. fellow Am. Sch. Classical Studies, Athens, 1938-39; Guggenheim fellow, 1958-59, 67-68. Mem. Archaeol. Inst. Am. (exec. com. Gold medal for Disting. Archaeol. Achievement 1981), Am. Philol. Assn., Assn. for Field Archaeology (v.p.), Soc. Prof. Archaeologists (dir.). Home: 1666 Coffman St Apt 333 Saint Paul MN 55108-1340 Office: Univ Minn 331 Folwell Hall Minneapolis MN 55455

MCDONALD, WILLIAM HENRY, lawyer; b. Niangua, Mo., Feb. 27, 1946; s. Milburn and Fannie M. McDonald; m. Janice E. Robinson, July 13, 1968; children: Melissa L., Meghan M. BS in Pub. Adminstrn., Southwest Mo. State U., 1968; JD, U. Mo., 1971. Bar: Mo. 1971, U.S. Dist. Ct. (we. dist.) Mo. 1973, U.S. Supreme Ct. 1978, U.S. Ct. Appeals (8th cir.) 1982. Pres. William H. McDonald & Assocs., P.C., Springfield, Mo., 1973-95, Springfield, 1995; ptnr. Woolsey, Fisher, Whiteaker & McDonald, P.C., 1973-95; pres. William H. McDonald & Assocs., 1995—. Chmn. blue ribbon task force on Delivery of Mental Health Services to Southwest Mo., Mo. Commn. Continuing Legal Edn.; pres. Tan Oaks Homeowners Assn.; mem. fin. com. Child Adv. Council, Rep. Nat. Com., Mo. Rep. Com., Greene County Nat. Com.; active various Southwest Mo. State U. Clubs; bd. dirs. Greene County div. Am. Heart Assn., Ozarks regional Am. Athletic Union Jr. Olympics; pres., bd. dirs. Springfield Little Theatre; bd. dirs., v.p. pub. affairs Springfield Area C. of C. Served to capt. U.S. Army, 1971-73. Named one of Outstanding Young Men Am., 1978, 81, Outstanding Young Men Springfield, 1980. Fellow ABA (litigation and torts and ins. sects.); mem. ATLA, Mo. Bar Assn. (chmn. spol. com. on mandatory continuing edn., various coms., Pres.'s award 1986), Greene County Bar Assn. (bd. dirs., chmn. pub. edn. speakers bur.), Met. Bar Assn. St. Louis, Def. Rsch. Inst., Am. Judicature Soc., Am. Bd. Trial Advs., Nat. Bd. Trial Advs., 31st Jud. Cir. Bar Com. (chmn.), Supreme Ct. Hist. Soc., U. Mo.-Kansas City Sch. Law Found., Springfield Area C. of C. (bd. dirs., v.p. pub. affairs), Beta Omega Tau, Kappa Epsilon. Presbyterian. Home: 4857 E Royal Dr Springfield MO 65809-2425

MCDONALD, WILLIAM HENRY, financial executive; b. Ottawa, Ont., Can., Sept. 8, 1924; s. Joseph and Constance Mary (Gordon) McD.; m. D. Gwen Selkirk, July 8, 1950; 1 child, Barbara Elaine. Grad. high sch. Credit and operating mgr. B.F. Goodrich Co., Winnipeg, Man., Can., 1945-49; fin. adminstrn. officer Govt. Can., Ottawa, 1949-55; asst. gen. mgr. mortgages Bank of N.S., 1955-66; mng. dir. Boyd Stott & McDonald Ltd., Toronto, Ont., 1966-79; exec. v.p., dir. Morguard Trust Co., 1966-74; chmn. bd. Can. Comml. Bank, Toronto, 1976-81, chmn. exec. com., 1981-84; chmn. bd. Can. Comml. Bank Mortgage Investment Corp., 1983-84; pres., CEO, dir. Boyd Stott and McDonald Techs., Ltd., 1984—; pres. Thornton McDonald Assocs., Inc. Chmn. bd. govs. J. Douglas Ferguson Hist. Research Found.,

1971—. Served with RCNVR, 1943-45. Mem. Can. Paper Money Soc. (hon. pres.), Internat. Bank Note Soc. (life), Can. Credit Inst., Classical & Medieval Numismatic Soc. (exec. sec.). Conservative. Anglican. Office: PO Box 956 Sta B, Willowdale, ON Canada M2K 2T6

MCDONALD, WILLIS, IV, lawyer; b. N.Y.C., Aug. 25, 1926; s. Willis McDonald III and Elizabeth Beaumont (Pfaff) McD.; m. Mary Lou H. Bellows, May 12, 1967; stepchildren: Randall F. Bellows Jr., Lisa L. Acker. B.S., Yale U., 1949; LL.B., U. Va., 1953. Bar: Va. 1952, N.Y. 1955. Assoc. White & Case, N.Y.C., 1953-63, ptnr., 1963—. Pres. Mesa Ranch Inc., Cody, Wyo.; trustee Buffalo Bill Hist. Ctr., Cody. Fellow Am. Bar Found., Am. Coll. Investment Counsel (pres. 1981-82, trustee); mem. ABA, Va. Bar Assn., N.Y. State Bar Assn., Assn. of Bar of City of N.Y. Republican. Episcopalian. Clubs: N.Y. Yacht, Yale, Indian Harbor Yacht, Wigwam Country (Litchfield Park, Ariz.). Office: White & Case 1155 Ave Of The Americas New York NY 10036-2711

MCDONALD-WEST, SANDI M., headmaster, consultant; b. Lowell, Mass., May 8, 1930; d. Walter Allan and Celina Louise (Lalime) MacLean; m. Thomas D. McDonald, Sept. 8, 1951 (div.); children: Todd F. McDonald, Brooke McDonald Killian, Ned M. McDonald, Reid A. McDonald, Heather McDonald Acker. BA, DePauw U., 1951; MA, Fairleigh Dickinson U., 1966; MEd, North Tex. State U., 1980. Cert. in Montessori teaching. Tchr., adminstr. Hudson (Ohio) Montessori Sch., 1966-68, Berea (Ohio) Montessori Sch., 1968-70, Creative Learning Ctr., Dallas, 1970-71; tchr., head of lower sch. The Selwyn Sch., Denton, Tex., 1971-83; tchr., headmaster Cimarron Sch., Enid, Okla., 1983-87; cons. Corpus Christi (Tex.) Montessori Sch., 1987-89, Azlann-Eren Horn Montessori Sch., Denton, 1989-95, Highland Meadow Montessori Acad., Southlake, Tex., 1994—; ednl. dir., pres. Southwestern Montessori Tchg. Ctr., Inc., Denton, 1974—; adj. prof. North Tex. State U., Denton, 1979-80; cons., lectr. Am. Montessori Soc., N.Y.C., 1970—, Japanese Montessori Soc., 1978—, also pub. and pvt. schs., 1972—; chair commn. for accreditation Montessori Accreditation Coun. Tchr. Edn., Denton, 1991—. Developer various Montessori materials; contbr. articles to profl. jours. Mem. Am. Montessori Soc., No. Ohio Montessori Assn. (pres. 1968-70), Assn. Montessori Internat., N.Am. Montessori Tchrs. Assn., Wheat Capital Assn. for Children Under Six (pres. 1986-87), LWV. Mem. Am. Montessori Soc., No. Ohio Montessori Assn. (pres. 1968-70), Assn. Montessori Internat., N.Am. Montessori Tchrs. Assn., Wheat Capital Assn. for Children Under Six (pres. 1986-87), LWV, Concerned Scientists. Avocations: ecology, golf, reading, travel. Home: 2005 Marshall Rd Denton TX 76207-3316

MCDONELL, HORACE GEORGE, JR., instrument company executive; b. N.Y.C., Sept. 23, 1928; s. Horace Gustave and Anabel (Armstrong) McD.; m. Eileen Romar, Sept. 6, 1952; children: Victoria (dec.), Diane, Horace. A.B., Adelphi Coll., 1952; postgrad., Harvard U., 1962. Engr. Sperry Gyroscope Co., N.Y.C., 1952; with Perkin-Elmer Corp., Norwalk, Conn., 1963—; mgr. instrument group Perkin-Elmer Corp., 1967-77, v.p., 1966-69, sr. v.p., 1969-77, exec. v.p., 1977-80, pres., 1980-85, chmn., 1985-90, ret., 1990; bd. dirs. Perkin Elmer, Ltd., U.K. UniRoyal, Inc., Perkin Elmer Internat., Inc., Harvey Hubbell, Inc., Ethan Allen Inc.; Mem. adv. task force on export controls U.S. Def. Sci. Bd., 1975—, chmn. instrumentation subcom., 1975—. Mem. Bd. Edn., Ridgefield, Conn., 1969; Bd. dirs. Conn. Sci. Fair.; Trustee, bd. dirs. Danbury (Conn.) Hosp.; trustee Adelphi U.; bd. dirs. Danbury Health Svcs. With AUS, 1946-48. Mem. Sci. Apparatus Maker Assn. (dir., chmn. analytical instrument sect.), Am. Inst. Physics, AAAS, Instrument Soc. Am., Am. Electronics Assn. (bd. dirs. 1984-89, chmn. 1987). Home: 740 Bald Eagle Dr Naples FL 33942 Office: Perkin-Elmer Corp 761 Main Ave Norwalk CT 06859-0002

MCDONELL, KATHERINE MANDUSIC, professional society administrator; b. Mansfield, Ohio, Nov. 8, 1954; d. Sam and Ann Julia (Konves) Mandusic; m. Edwin D. McDonell, Aug. 18, 1979 (div. Dec. 1994). BA, Ohio Wesleyan U.; MA in History and Mus. Studies, Case Western Res.; MBA, Ind. U. Rschr. Conner Prairie Mus., Fishers, Ind., 1978-82; exec. dir./rsch. historian Ind. Med. History Mus./Ind. Hist. Soc., Indpls., 1982-91; asst. dir. for comm. and mktg. Ind. U. Ctr. on Philanthropy, 1991-93; exec. dir. Roller Skating Assn., Indpls., 1993—. Author: The Journals of William A. Lindsay, 1989; contbg. editor The Encyclopedia of Indianapolis, 1994; contbr. articles to profl. jours. Pres. Altrusa Internat. of Indpls., 1995—; bd. dirs. Nat. Mus. of Roller Skating, Lincoln, 1994—; rec. sec. Crown Hill Soc., Indpls., 1993-95. Mem. Am. Soc. of Assn. Execs., Nat. Soc. of Fund Raising Execs. (cert.), Am. Mktg. Assn., Beta Gamma Sigma, Sigma Iota Epsilon, Phi Beta Kappa. Avocations: reading, walking, gourmet cooking, traveling. Office: Roller Skating Assn Ste 123 7301 Georgetown Rd Indianapolis IN 46268

MCDONELL, ROBERT TERRY, magazine editor, novelist; b. Norfolk, Va., Aug. 1, 1944; s. Robert Meinard and Irma Sophronia (Nelson) McD.; m. Joan Raffeld Hitzig, June 15, 1981; Robert Nicholas Campbell, Thomas Hunter Campbell. Student, U. Calif., Berkeley, 1962-63, San Jose State U., 1963-64; BA in Art, U. Calif., Irvine, 1967. With AP, N.Y.C., 1970-72; reporter Los Angeles Weekly, 1972-73; asso. editor San Francisco mag., 1974-76, City mag., San Francisco, 1976-77; sr. editor San Francisco mag., 1977, Outside mag., San Francisco, 1978-79; founding editor Rocky Mountain mag., Denver, 1979-80; mng. editor Rolling Stone mag., N.Y.C., 1980-83; asst. mng. editor Newsweek Mag., N.Y.C., 1983-86; founder Smart mag., N.Y.C., 1986-90; editor-in-chief Esquire mag., N.Y.C., 1990-93; editor-in-chief, pub. Sports Afield Mag., N.Y.C., 1994—. Author: California Bloodstock, 1980, paperback edit., 1989; screenwriter: Miami Vice, China Beach. Office: Sports Afield 250 W 55th St New York NY 10019-5201

MCDONNELL, ARCHIE JOSEPH, environmental engineer; b. N.Y.C., June 3, 1936; s. Patrick and Margaret (O'Reilly) McD.; m. Nancy Carol Schaeffer, June 18, 1966; children: Patrick, Sean. BS in Civil Engring., Manhattan Coll., 1958; MS in Civil Engring., Pa. State U., 1960, PhD in Civil Engring., 1963. Prof. Pa. State U., University Park, 1963-96; asst. dir. Water Resources Rsch. Ctr., Pa. State U., 1969-82; dir. Inst. for Rsch. on Land and Water Resources, Pa. State U., 1982-86, Environ. Resources Rsch. Inst., Pa. State U., 1986—; bd. dirs. Pa. Environ. Coun., 1989-92, Nat. Assn. State Univs. & Land Grant Colls., 1990-92, chmn. water resources com., 1985-91; mem. rsch. & modeling subcom. EPA Chesapeake Bay Program, 1984-86, sci. & tech. adv. com., 1984—, exec. com., 1988-92; U.S. rep. Internat. Joint Commn., 1976-79, 87-89; mem. Pa. State Conservation Com., 1988-89, water resources policy adv. com. Pa. Dept. Environ. Resources, 1979-82, air & water quality tech. adv. com., 1983—, chmn. water quality subcom., 1986-88; chmn. Northeast Assn. Water Inst. Dirs., 1973-74; mem. exec. com. Nat. Assn. Water Inst. Dirs., 1975-78. Contbr. articles to profl. jours. Fellow U.S. Pub. Health Svc., 1961-62; recipient Commendation cert. Internat. Joint Commn., Conservationist of Yr. award Chesapeake Bay Found., Washington, 1986, Outstanding Rsch. award Pa. State U. Engring. Soc., 1988, Outstanding Profl. Rsch. award Water Pollution Control Assn. Pa., 1990, Karl M. Mason medal Pa. Assn. Environ. Profls., 1991, Gabriel Narutowicz medal Ministry Environ. Protection and Natural Resources, Poland, 1991. Mem. ASCE (chmn. 1972-73, exec. com. 1976-80, J. James R. Croes Rsch. medal 1976, Outstanding Svc. award 1981), Water Environ. Fedn. (co-chmn. 1991—), Fed. Water Pollution Control Fedn., Internat. Assn. Water Pollution Rsch., Am. Soc. Limnology and Oceanography, Chi Epsilon, Sigma Xi, Phi Kappa Phi. Achievements include demonstration of low cost treatment method for renovation of acidmine waters. Office: Pa State U 100 Land Water Research Bldg University Park PA 16802

MCDONNELL, BARBARA, health facility administrator. B., Univ. Ill.; M, Univ. Iowa; JD magna cum laude, Univ. Pa. Law Sch. With Sherman & Howard, 1982-87; staff atty. Colo. Ct. Appeals, 1988-89; law clerk Phila.; legal adv. Gov. Romer, dep. dir. policy and rsch., 1989-90; exec. dir. Colo. Dept. Human Svcs., 1991—. Rep. Nursing Adv. bd., team leader Policy Acad. Team on Families & Children At Risk. Home: 1575 Sherman St Denver CO 80203-1714

MCDONNELL, DENNIS J., securities industry executive; b. Chgo., May 20, 1942; s. Lawrence J. and Eleanor (Lama) McD.; m. Kate A. McDonnell, Sept. 13, 1986. B.S. in Econs., Loyola U., Chgo., 1965; M.A. in Econs., UCLA, 1969. Vice pres. Continental Bank, Chgo., 1969-83; pres., dir. Van Kampen Am. Capital Investment Adv. Corp., Lisle, Ill., 1983—; dir. Van Kampen Am. Capital Investment Adv. Corp., Naperville, Ill., 1983—; dir. McCarthy, Crisanti & Maffei, Inc., N.Y.C. Lt. USN, 1965-68. Mem. Soc. Mcpl. Analysts (pres. 1978-79), Nat. Fedn. Mcpl. Analysts, Mcpl. Bond Club Chgo., Columbia Yacht Club. Roman Catholic. Avocation: yacht racing. Office: Van Kampen American Capital Investment Adv Corp 1 Parkview Plz Villa Park IL 60181-4400

MCDONNELL, JAMES, English educator; b. London, Eng., May 2, 1937; came to U.S., 1965; s. Patrick and Mary (Brennan) McD.; m. Jane Rutherford Taylor, Aug., 1968; children: Paul A., Katherine R. BA in English, Cambridge (Eng.) U., 1965, MA in English, 1967; PhD, Washington U., 1974. Instr. Carleton Coll., Northfield, Minn., 1969-74, asst. prof., 1974-77, assoc. prof., 1977-84, prof., 1984—; vis. lectr. in English, Trinity Coll., Dublin, Ireland, 1986; advanced placement cons. Concord Coll., Athens, W.Va., 1986; chair dept. English, Carleton Coll., 1989-92; external evaluator English dept. Furman U., Greenville, S.C., 1992; external reviewer English dept. Samford U., Birmingham, Ala., 1992. Contbr. articles to profl. jours. Cons., panelist and lectr. Guthrie Theatre, Minn., 1985, 88, 90. Mem. MLA, AAUP, Nat. Coun. Tchrs. of English, English Inst., Assn. Depts. English, Cambridge Union. Avocation: acting. Home: 309 Washington St Northfield MN 55057-2026 Office: Carleton Coll 100 S College St Northfield MN 55057-4002

MCDONNELL, JOHN FINNEY, aerospace and aircraft manufacturing executive; b. Mar. 18, 1938; s. James Smith and Mary Elizabeth (Finney) McD.; m. Anne Marbury, June 16, 1961. BS in Aero. Engring., Princeton U., 1960, MS in Aero. Engring., 1962; postgrad. in bus. adminstrn., Washington U., St. Louis, 1962-66. Strength engr. McDonnell Aircraft Co. (subs. McDonnell Douglas Corp.), St. Louis, 1962, corp. analyst, 1963-65, contract coord., adminstr., 1965-68; asst. to v.p. fin. Douglas Aircraft Co. (subs. McDonnell Douglas Corp.), 1968; v.p. McDonnell Douglas Fin. Corp. (subs. McDonnell Douglas Corp.), 1968-71; staff v.p. fiscal McDonnell Douglas Corp., 1971-75, corp. v.p. fin. and devel., 1975-77, corp. exec. v.p., 1977-80, pres., 1980—, mem. exec. com., 1975—, chmn., 1988—, past CEO, also bd. dirs.; bd. dirs. Ralston Purina Co. Bd. commrs. St. Louis Sci. Ctr.; trustee KETC, Washington U., also chmn. nat. coun. faculty arts and scis. com. Office: McDonnell Douglas Corp PO Box 516 Saint Louis MO 63166-0516*

MCDONNELL, MARY, actress; b. Wilkes-Barre, Pa., 1952; m. Randle Mell; 1 child, Olivia. Appearences include (theatre) Buried Child, 1978-79, Letters Home, 1979, Still Life, 1981 (Obie award 1981), The Death of a Miner, 1981-82, A Weekend Near Madison, 1982-83, Red River, 1982-83, Black Angel, 1982-83, All Night Long, 1984, The Three Sisters, 1984-85, Savage in Limbo, 1985, Stitchers and Starlight Talkers, 1985-86, Execution of Justice, 1986, A Doll's House, 1986-87, Three Ways Home, 1988, The Heidi Chronicles, 1990, (TV series) E/R, 1984-85, (TV movies) Money on the Side, 1982, Courage, 1986, O, Pioneers!, 1991, The American Clock, 1993, Blue Chips, 1993, (films) Garbo Talks, 1984, Matewan, 1987, Tiger Warsaw, 1988, Dances with Wolves, 1990 (Golden Globe award nomination 1990, Acad. Award nomination 1990), Grand Canyon, 1991, Sneakers, 1992, Passion Fish, 1992 (Acad. Award nomination 1993), Blue Chips, 1994. Office: William Morris Agy 151 S El Camino Dr Beverly Hills CA 90212-2704*

MCDONNELL, ROSEMARY CYNTHIA, special populations programmer; b. Washington, July 31, 1969; d. Joseph Patrick and Judith Ann (Bruscino) McD. BS, Bradley U., Peoria, Ill., 1991; postgrad., Ill. Ctrl. Coll., 1993. Qualified mental retardation profl. Team leader Community Workshop and Tng. Ctr., Peoria, 1989-92; polit. sci. intern City of Peoria, 1991; undergrad. teaching asst. Bradley U., Peoria, 1991; family support coord. Tazewell County Resource Ctr., Pekin, Ill., 1992-93, early intervention asst., 1993-94; spl. populations programmer Pekin Pk. Dist. Recreation Office, 1994—. Asst. coach Spl. Olympics, Peoria, 1992. Olive B. White scholar Bradley U., 1990. Mem. NOW, Pi Gamma Mu, Phi Alpha Theta. Roman Catholic. Avocations: reading, weight lifting, basketball, history, travel. Home: PO Box 363 Pekin IL 61555-0363

MCDONNELL, SANFORD NOYES, aircraft company executive; b. Little Rock, Oct. 12, 1922; s. William Archie and Carolyn (Cherry) McD.; m. Priscilla Robb, Sept. 3, 1946; children: Robbin McDonnell MacVittie, William Randall. BA in Econs., Princeton U., 1945; BS in Mech. Engring., U. Colo., 1948; MS in Applied Mechanics, Washington U., St. Louis, 1954. With McDonnell Douglas Corp. (formerly McDonnell Aircraft Corp.), St. Louis, 1948—, v.p., 1959-66, pres. McDonnell Aircraft div., 1966-71, corp. exec. v.p., 1971, corp. pres., from 1971, chief exec. officer, from 1972, chmn., 1980-88, chmn. emeritus, 1988—. Active St. Louis United Way; mem. exec. bd. St. Louis and nat. councils Boy Scouts Am.; trustee, elder Presbyn. Ch. Fellow AIAA; mem. Navy League U.S. (life), Tau Beta Pi. Office: McDonnell Douglas Corp PO Box 516 Saint Louis MO 63166-0516

MCDONOUGH, JOHN MICHAEL, lawyer; b. Evanston, Ill., Dec. 30, 1944; s. John Justin and Anne Elizabeth (O'Brien) McD.; m. Susan J. Moran, Sept. 19, 1982; children: John E., Catherine Anne. AB, Princeton U., 1966; LLB, Yale U., 1969. Bar: Ill. 1969, Fla. 1991. Assoc. Sidley & Austin, Chgo., 1969-75, ptnr., 1975—. Bd. dirs. Met. Planning Coun., 1978—, pres., 1982-84; bd. dirs. Ctr. Am. Archeology, 1980-85, chmn., 1982-84; bd. dirs. Leadership Greater Chgo., 1984-90, sec.-treas., 1987-90; bd. dis. Brian Rsch. Found., 1985—, pres., 1989-94. With JAGC, USAR, 1969-75. Mem. ABA, Ill. Bar Assn., Chgo. Bar Assn., Chgo. Club, Racquet Club, Commonwealth Club, Econ. Club, Phi Beta Kappa. Democrat. Episcopalian. Home: 1209 N Astor St Chicago IL 60610-2300 Office: Sidley & Austin 1 First Nat Plz Ste 4400 Chicago IL 60603

MC DONOUGH, JOHN RICHARD, lawyer; b. St. Paul, May 16, 1919; s. John Richard and Gena (Olson) McD.; m. Margaret Poot, Sept. 10, 1944; children—Jana Margaret, John Jacobus. Student, U. Wash., 1937-40; LL.B., Columbia U., 1946. Bar: Calif. 1949. Asst. prof. law Stanford U., 1946-49, prof., 1952-69; assoc. firm Brobeck, Phleger & Harrison, San Francisco, 1949-52; asst. dep. atty. gen. U.S. Dept. Justice, Washington, 1967-68; asso. dep. atty. gen. U.S. Dept. Justice, 1968-69; of counsel and ptnr. firm Keatinge & Sterling, L.A., 1969-70; ptnr. Ball, Hunt, Hart, Brown and Baerwitz, 1970-90, Calsmith Ball Wichman Case & Ichiki, L.A., L.A., 1990—; exec. sec. Calif. Law Revision Commn., 1954-59, mem. commn., 1959-67, vice chmn., 1960-64, chmn., 1964-65; participant various continuing edn. programs. Served with U.S. Army, 1942-46. Mem. ABA, State Bar Calif., Los Angeles County Bar Assn., Am. Coll. Trial Lawyers. Democrat. Office: Carlsmith Ball Wichman Case & Ichiki 555 S Flower St Fl 25 Los Angeles CA 90071-2326

MCDONOUGH, JOSEPH CORBETT, former army officer, aviation consultant; b. N.Y.C., Sept. 30, 1924; s. Joseph Walter and Catherine Loretta (Corbett) McD.; m. Mary Patricia Aaron, June 10, 1945; children—Joseph Corbett, Thomas Michael, Robert Timothy. B.S., U.S. Mil. Acad., West Point, N.Y., 1945; M.A., Georgetown U., Washington, 1957; grad., U.S. Command and Gen. Staff Coll., 1954, Brit. Staff Coll., Camberly, 1958, U.S. Army War Coll., 1965. Commd. 2d lt. U.S. Army, 1945, advanced through grades to maj. gen., 1973, served in Philippine Scouts, 1945-47, served with 82d Airborne Div., 1948-51; served with 40th Inf. Div. U.S. Army, Korea, 1952-53; instr. U.S. Naval Acad., 1954-57; staff and command U.S. Army, Europe, 1958-61; with Office Personnel Mgmt., Dept. Army, Washington, 1961-64; mem. staff Office Under Sec. Army, Washington, 1965-67; bn. and brigade comdr. 1st Calvary Div. U.S. Army, Vietnam, 1967-68; with Joint Chiefs of Staff, Washington, 1968-71; brigade and asst. div. comdr. Vietnam, 1971-72; chief of staff CENTO, Turkey, 1972-73; comdg. gen. 8th Inf. Div. U.S. Army, Germany, 1973-75; U.S. Comdr. Berlin, 1975-78; ret. U.S. Army, 1978; cons. numerous govt. agys., 1978-79; v.p., gen. mgr. Butler Aviation, BWI Airport, Md., 1980-83; v.p. ops. Butler Aviation Internat., 1983-86; cons., 1986-88; exec v.p. Butler Aviation Internat., 1988-90; cons., 1990—. Decorated D.S.M. with oak leaf cluster, Silver Star, Legion of Merit with oak leaf cluster, D.F.C., Bronze Star, Air medal with 32 oak leaf clusters, Army Commendation medal with 2 oak leaf clusters. Mem. Assn. U.S. Army, Army Aviation Assn. Address: 219 Greenbury Ct Annapolis MD 21401-6302

MCDONOUGH, PATRICK DENNIS, academic administrator; b. Virginia, Minn., Jan. 30, 1942; s. James Morris and Vivian S. (Knudtson) McD.; children: Jeffrey, Anne; m. Karen Howe, June 27, 1981. BA cum laude, Moorhead State U., 1964; MA, U. Kans., 1969; PhD, U. Minn., 1972. Asst. prof. theatre Emporia (Kans.) State U., 1966-70; dir. sales, mktg. Guthrie Theater, Mpls., 1971, 72; asst. prof. speech, dir. of forensics Moorhead (Minn.) State U., 1972-73; assoc. prof., mng. dir., chair Marshall Performing Arts Ctr. U. Minn., Duluth, 1973-76; dean fine arts, prof. U. Evansville (Ind.), 1976-81; vice chancellor, prof. U. Wis., Stevens Point, 1981-84; program dir. (edn. and leadership) W.K. Kellogg Found., Battle Creek, Mich., 1984-89; 15th pres., prof. theatre and mgmt. Marietta (Ohio) Coll., 1989-95, exec. dir. McDonough Ctr. for Leadership and Bus.; assoc. vice chancellor planning and analysis Calif. State U. Sys., Long Beach, 1995—; pres. Emporia chpt. AAUP, 1969; cons. Lexington (Ky.) Children's Theatre, 1979; festival evaluator Am. Coll. Theatre Festival, 4 states, 1975, 76; mem. theatre panel Ind. Arts Commn., Indpls., 1977-79; mem. arts orgn. panel Mich. Arts Bd., Detroit, 1985-89; presenter workshops, conv. programs. Producer, dir. 100 plays and musicals, 1964-84; contbr. articles to profl. publs. Bd. visitors U. Wis., Stevens Point, 1988-90; dist. organizer Eugene McCarthy Presdl. Campaign, Emporia, 1968; mem. leadership commn. Am. Coun. Edn., 1989-94; mem. exec. com. Campus Compact, 1990-95; bd. dirs. numerous civic and arts orgns., 1973-90; chmn. govs. adv. com. on vol. svc., Ohio, 1990-93; mem. leadership studies project U. Md., 1994—. Recipient Disting. Alumnus award Moorhead State U., 1989; grantee Minn. Arts Bd., 1974-76, Ind. Arts Commn., 1976-79. Mem. Am. Assn. Higher Edn., Univ. and Coll. Theatre Assn. (v.p. 1982-83), Marietta Country Club, Stevens Point Country Club, Athletic Club of Columbus. Democrat. Episcopalian. Avocations: travel, international relations, arts. Office: Calif State U Sys 400 Golden Shore Long Beach CA 90802-4275

MCDONOUGH, PATRICK JOSEPH, lawyer; b. Los Angeles, Oct. 11, 1943; s. Thomas John and Cecilia Veronica (Roach) McD.; m. Susan Ann Singletary, Dec. 30, 1967; 1 child, Colleen Marie. BA, Calif. State U., Northridge, 1967; JD, Loyola U., Los Angeles, 1971. Bar: Calif. 1971, U.S. Dist. Ct. (cen. dist.) Calif. 1971. Assoc. counsel. Auto Club So. Calif., Los Angeles, 1971-77, sec., assoc. counsel, 1977-86; sr. v.p., gen. counsel Johnson & Higgens Calif., Los Angeles, 1986—. Active United Way Koko Challenge, 1993—; bd. visitors Loyola Law Sch., 1994—. Mem. ABA, Calif. State Bar Assn. (ins. law com. 1993-95), L.A. Bar Assn. (chmn. corp. law sect. 1987-88, Outstanding Corp. Coun. 1992), Univ. of Calif. Law Ctr., Inst. of Corp Counsel (chmn. 1986-87, bd. govs. 1982—), Am. Corp. Counsel Assn. So. Calif. (bd. dirs. 1985-87), Assn. Calif. Tort Reform (bd. dirs. 1986—), L.A. Bar Found. (bd. dirs. 1993-94), Town Hall Calif. Roman Catholic. Avocations: boating, sailing, fishing. Office: Johnson & Higgins Calif 2029 Century Park E Fl 24 Los Angeles CA 90067-2901

MCDONOUGH, PATRICK JOSEPH, JR., lawyer; b. Paterson, N.J., Sept. 13, 1941; s. Patrick Joseph and Margaret Mary (Bohan) McD.; m. Joanne Catherine Hansen, Dec. 26, 1966; children: Patrick Joseph III, Katherine Ann. BS, St. Joseph's U., Phila., 1964; AM, NYU, 1969; JD, Seton Hall Law Sch., Newark, 1976. Bar: N.J. 1978. Tchr. N.J. high schs., Elizabeth, N.J., 1964-69; dist. mgr. AT&T Hdqrs., N.Y.C., 1969-79; spl. asst. and mgr. external affairs, exec. dept., law dept. AT&T Hdqrs., Basking Ridge, N.J., 1981-90; mng. dir. internat. div. AT&T Hdqrs., Morristown, N.J., 1991-96; legis. asst. U.S. Senate, Washington, 1980-81; pvt. practice, 1996—; speaker in field. Author: Are Your Electronic Files Secure?, 1989; co-author: Guide to Prosecution of Telecommunication Fraud, 1989. Mem. exec. bd. Watchung (N.J.) Area Boy Scouts Am., 1985—; chair Utility Adv. Bd., Cranford, N.J., 1976-79; mem. Zoning Bd. Adjustment, Cranford, 1978-79; mem. Union County (N.J.) Com., 1977-79; pres. Cranford (N.J.) Rep. Club, 1977-78. NSF grantee, 1968. Mem. ABA (chmn. computer crime com. 1986—, coun. mem. sci. and tech. sect. 1992-95), N.J. Bar Assn., Summit (N.J.) Bar Assn., Comm. Fraud Control Assn. Home and Office: 93 Pine Grove Ave Summit NJ 07901-2436

MCDONOUGH, REGINALD MILTON, religious organization executive; b. Mt. Vernon, Tex., Aug. 16, 1936; s. J.C. McDonough and Gladys (White) Branch; m. Joan Bird, Aug. 28, 1956; children: Michael Keith, Teri Royce. BS, East Tex. Bapt. U., 1957; MRE, New Orleans Bapt. Theol. Sem., 1960, DEd, 1967; DD, U. Richmond, 1988. Ordained to ministry Bapt. Ch. Minister Bapt. Ch., Arcadia, La., 1959-60; instr. East Tex. Bapt. U., Marshall, 1960-61; minister edn. North End Bapt. Ch., Beaumont, Tex., 1961-64; cons. ch. adminstrn. Bapt. Sun. Sch. Bd., Nashville, 1964-65, supr. ch. adminstrn., 1965-78, dept. dir., 1978-80; exec. v.p. exec. com. So. Bapt. Conv., Nashville, 1981-86; exec. dir. Bapt. Gen. Assn. Va., Richmond, 1987—. Author: Working with Volunteer Leaders in the Church, 1976, Keys to Effective Motivation, 1979, A Church on Mission, 1980; editor monthly mag. Bapt. Program, 1981-86. Recipient Eagle Scout award Boy Scouts Am., 1951, Disting. Alumnus award, New Orleans Bapt. Theol. Sem., 1979, Disting. Achievement award East Tex. Bapt. U. Alumni Assn., 1984. Mem. Soc. Religious Orgns. Mgrs. Avocations: flying, skiing, golfing. Home: 12800 Knightcross Rd Midlothian VA 23113-9608 Office: Va Bapt Gen Bd PO Box 8568 Richmond VA 23226-0568

MC DONOUGH, RICHARD DOYLE, retired paper company executive; b. St. Stephen, N.B., Can., May 8, 1931; s. Kenneth Paul and Mary (Doyle) McD.; m. Caroline Wilkins, July 7, 1956; children: Elizabeth Wilkins, Richard David, Philip Bradford. AB, Dartmouth Coll., 1952. Mgmt. trainee Gen. Electric Co., Lynn, Mass., 1953-56; various fin. positions lamp div. Gen. Electric Co., Monterrey, Mex., 1956-59; controller Mexican subs. Gen. Electric Co., Mexico City, 1959-63; cost supr. Singer Co., N.Y.C., 1964; fin. dir. Singer Co., Clydebank, Scotland, 1965-66; controller Eur. div. Singer Co., London, 1967-69; v.p. ops. Home Furnishings Group, 1969; v.p., corp. contr. Singer Co., N.Y.C., 1970-73; corp. v.p., pres. mail order div. Singer Co., Hanau, Fed. Republic of Germany, 1973-76; v.p. Singer Co., London, 1976-79; sr. v.p., CFO, dir. Bowater Inc., Darien, Conn., 1979-92, vice chmn., CFO, 1992-93, vice chmn., 1993-94, ret., 1994; dir. Xylem Investments, Compensation Resources Group. Mem. Am. Forest and Paper Assn. (fin. com. 1980-94, steering com. 1987-94, vice chmn. 1989-91, chmn. 1991-93), Fin. Execs. Inst., Greenwich Country Club. Republican. Episcopalian. Avocations: scuba, opera. Home: Barons Mead E Point Ln Old Greenwich CT 06870-2403 Office: 25 East Point Ln Old Greenwich CT 06870-2403

MCDONOUGH, RUSSELL CHARLES, retired state supreme court justice; b. Glendive, Mont., Dec. 7, 1924; s. Roy James and Elsie Marie (Johnson) McD.; m. Dora Jean Bidwell, Mar. 17, 1946; children: Ann Remmich, Michael, Kay Jensen, Kevin, Daniel, Mary Garfield. JD, George Washington U., 1949. Bar: Mont. 1950. Pvt. practice Glendive, Mont., 1950-83; judge Gen. Jurisdiction State of Montana, Glendive, 1983-87; justice Mont. Supreme Ct., Helena, 1987-93, ret., 1993. City atty. City of Glendive, 1953-57; county atty. Dawson County, Mon., 1957-63; del. Mont. Constl. Conv., Helena, 1972. 1st lt. AC, U.S. Army, 1943-45, ETO. Decorated DFC. Mem. Mont. Bar Assn. Roman Catholic. Home: 1805 Joslyn St Trlr 131 Helena MT 59601-0113

MC DONOUGH, WILLIAM, corporate lawyer; b. 1943. Executive v.p., gen. counsel Federal Reserve Bank of Boston, Mass. Office: Federal Reserve Bnk of Boston 600 Atlantic Ave Boston MA 02106*

MCDONOUGH, WILLIAM ANDREW, dean. Dean sch. architecture U. Va., Charlottesville. Office: U Va Dept Architecture 206 Campbell Hall Charlottesville VA 22903*

MCDONOUGH, WILLIAM J., banker; b. Chgo., 1934; married. B.S., Coll. of Holy Cross, 1956; M.A., Georgetown U., 1962. Spl. asst. to amb. Am. Embassy, Uruguay, 1961-67, sr. economist Inter-Am. affairs to amb., 1961-67; with 1st Nat. Bank of Chgo., 1967-89, asst. v.p. internat. banking dept., 1967-70; v.p., gen. mgr. 1st Nat. Bank of Chgo., Paris, 1970-72; area head, Europe, Middle East and Africa 1st Nat. Bank of Chgo., 1972-73, sr. v.p., head internat. banking dept., 1973-75, exec. v.p., 1975-89; CFO 1st Nat. Bank of Chgo., Chgo., 1982-89; chmn. asset and liability mgmt. com. 1st Nat. Bank of Chgo., until 1989; vice chmn. 1st Chgo. Corp. and 1st Nat. Bank Chgo., 1986-89; exec. v.p., head bank fin. markets group Fed. Res. Bank of N.Y., N.Y.C., 1992-93, pres., CEO, 1993—; vice chmn. fed. open market com. Fed. Res. Sys.; bd dirs. Bank for Internat. Settlements, N.Y. Philharmonic Orch. Office: Fed Res Bank of NY 33 Liberty St New York NY 10045-0001

MCDORMAND, FRANCES, actress; b. Ill., 1957. Student, Yale U. Sch. Drama. Stage appearances include Awake and Sing!, N.Y.C., 1984, Painting Churches, N.Y.C., 1984, The Three Sisters, Mpls., 1985, N.J., 1991, All My Sons, New Haven, 1986, A Streetcar Named Desire, N.Y.C., 1988, Moon for the Misbegotten, 1992, Sisters Rosensweig, N.Y.C., 1993, The Swan, N.Y.C., 1993; TV appearances include The Twilight Zone, The Equalizer, Spencer: For Hire, Hill Street Blues, (series) Legwork, 1986-87, (TV movies) Scandal Sheet, 1985, Vengeance: The Story of Tony Cimo, 1986, Crazy In Love, 1992; film appearances include Blood Simple, 1984, Crime Wave, 1986, Raising Arizona, 1987, Mississippi Burning, 1988, Chattahoochee, 1990, Darkman, 1990, Miller's Crossing, 1990, Hidden Agenda, 1990, The Butcher's Wife, 1991, Passed Away, 1992, Short Cuts, 1993, Beyond Rangoon, 1995. Office: William Morris Agy 1325 Avenue Of The Americas New York NY 10019-4702*

MCDOUGAL, ALFRED LEROY, publishing executive; b. Evanston, Ill., Feb. 12, 1931; s. Alfred L. and Mary (Gillett) McD.; m. Gudrun Fenger, May 7, 1960 (div. 1982); children: Thomas, Stephen; m. Nancy A. Lauter, Mar. 1, 1986. BA, Yale U., 1953; MBA, Harvard U., 1957. Asst. to pres. Rand McNally & Co., Skokie, Ill., 1962-65, mgr. sch. dept., 1965-69; pres. McDougal, Littell & Co., Evanston, Ill., 1969-91, chmn., CEO, 1991-94; dir. Houghton Mifflin Co., Boston, 1994—; CEO Alth Corp., 1994—; chmn. McDougal Family Found. Trustee Hadley Sch. for Blind, Winnetka, Ill., 1980-83; chmn. budget com. Evanston United Fund, 1974-76, bd. dirs.; bd. dirs. Evanston YMCA, 1988-94, Youth Job Ctr., 1987—, chmn., 1989-91, Opportunity Internat., 1994—, Literacy Chgo., 1992—, treas., 1994—. With U.S. Army, 1953-55. Mem. Assn. Am. Pubs. (exec. com. sch. divsn. 1981—, chmn. 1988-89, 92-94, dir. 1987-89), No. Ill. Assn. (1st v.p. 1984, chmn. 1985). Office: ALM Corp 401 N Michigan Ave 27th Fl Chicago IL 60611

MCDOUGAL, LUTHER LOVE, III, law educator; b. Paris, Tex., Oct. 19, 1938; s. Luther Love and Dorothy Harriet (Atkinson) McD.; m. Mary Anne McDougal, Apr. 12, 1959; children—Luther IV, Katherine, Kim, Mark, Myres. Student, Vanderbilt U., 1956-58; B.A., U. Miss., 1959, LL.B., 1962; LL.M., Yale U., 1966. Assoc. Blair & Anderson, Tupelo, Miss., 1962; ptnr. Riley & McDougal, Tupelo, 1963-64; prof. law U. Miss., Oxford, 1964-70, U. Ariz., Tucson, 1970-74; W. R. Irby prof. law Tulane U., New Orleans, 1974—; chmn. bd. N. Miss. Rural Legal Services, Oxford, 1967-70, Ctr. for Legal Studies of Intergovtl. Relations, New Orleans, 1982-86. Author: Property, Wealth, Land: Allocation, Planning and Development, 1981, Cases on American Conflicts Law, 1982, 2d edit., 1989, American Conflicts Law, 1986, Louisiana Oil and Gas Law, 1988; contbr. articles to profl. jours. Mem. Am. Law Inst. Democrat. Office: Tulane U Law Sch 6329 Freret St New Orleans LA 70118-5670*

MCDOUGAL, STUART YEATMAN, comparative literature educator, author; b. L.A., Apr. 10, 1942; s. Murray and Marian (Yeatman) McD.; m. Menakka Weerasinghe, Apr. 29, 1967 (div. 1977); children—Dyanthe Rose, Gavin Rohan; m. Nora Gunneng, Aug. 4, 1979; children—Angus Gunneng, Tobias Yeatman. B.A., Haverford Coll., 1964; M.A., U. Pa., 1965, Ph.D., 1970. Lectr. U. Lausanne, Switzerland, 1965-66; asst. prof. Mich. State U., East Lansing, 1970-72; from asst. prof. to prof. English, comparative lit. and film /video U. Mich., Ann Arbor, 1972-85; dir. program in comparative lit. U. Mich., Ann Arbor, 1981—. Author: Ezra Pound and the Troubadour Tradition, 1972 (Bredvold prize 1973), 2d edit. 1993; Made into Movies: From Literature to Film, 1985, 5th edit. 1994. Editor: Dante Among the Moderns, 1985. Contbr. articles to profl. jours. Am. Council of Learned Socs. fellow, 1974-75; U. Mich. Rackham Research grantee, 1975-76; Fulbright Assn. sr. lectr., Italy, 1978; recipient Faculty Recognition award, U. Mich., 1987; Vis. scholar Senapulli, Brazil, 1996. Fellow Dirs. Guild Am. (summr workshop, 1993), Aegean Inst. (vis. prof. film, 1994); mem. MLA, Am. Comparative Lit. Assn. (sec.-treas. 1983-89, v.p. 1989-91, pres. 1991-93), Internat. Comparative Lit. Assn., Soc. Cinema Studies. Democrat. Office: U Mich Program in Comparative Lit 411 Mason Hall Ann Arbor MI 48109

MCDOUGAL, WILLIAM SCOTT, urology educator; b. Grand Rapids, Mich., 1942; s. William Julian and Verna Wilma (Pasma) McD.; m. Mary Stuart Logan, Sept. 19, 1992; 1 child, Molly Katherine. AB, Dartmouth Coll., 1964; MD, Cornell U., 1968. Intern in surgery U. Hosps., Cleve., 1968-69, resident in surgery, 1969-75, attending urologist, 1977-80; postdoctoral fellow in physiology Yale U., New Haven, 1971-72; postdoctoral fellow in surgery Case-Western Res. U., Cleve., 1972-75; chief, burn study div. Inst. Surg. Rsch. Brook Army Med. Ctr., Ft. Sam Houston, 1975-77; instr. surgery U. Tex., San Antonio, 1975-77; asst. prof. urology Case Western Res. U., Cleve., 1977-78, assoc. prof., 1978-80; assoc. prof. Dartmouth Coll., Hanover, N.H., 1980-84, chmn. dept. urology, 1982-84; prof., chmn. dept. urology Vanderbilt U., Nashville, 1984-90; prof. surgery Harvard Med. Sch., 1991—; chief urology Mass. Gen. Hosp., Boston, 1991—. Office: Mass Gen Hosp Dept Urology Fruit St Boston MA 02114

MCDOUGALL, DONALD BLAKE, retired government official, librarian; b. Moose Jaw, Sask., Can., Mar. 6, 1938; s. Daniel Albert and Donela (McRae) McD.; m. Norma Rose Peacock, May 19, 1962. BA, U. Sask., 1966, BEd, 1966; BLS, U. Toronto, 1969, MLS, U. Alta., 1983, cert. pub. adminstrn. U. Alta., 1990. Classroom tchr., Regina Bd. Edn., Sask., 1960-63, vice prin., 1963-68; asst. chief libr. Stratford Pub. Libr., Ont., Can., 1969, chief. libr., 1970-72; supr. info. svcs. Edmonton Pub. Libr., Alta., Can., 1972, head pub. svcs., 1973-74; legislature libr. Province of Alta., Edmonton, 1974-87; asst. dep. min., legis. libr. Legis. Assembly Alta., 1987-93, ret., 1993. Editor microfilm: Alberta Scrapbook Hansard, 1906-1964, 1976, editor Book: A History of the Legislature Library, 1979, Princess Louise Carline Alberta, 1988, Canada's Parliamentary Libraries, 1989, Lieutenant-Governors of the Northwest Territories and Alberta, 1876-1991, 1991, Premiers of the Northwest Territories and Alberta, 1897-1991, 1991. Govt. Sask. scholar, 1965; recipient Queen's Silver Jubilee medal Govt. Can., 1977; named Hon. Clk.-At-The-Table, Legis. Assembly Alta., 1987-93. Mem. Alta. Govt. Libraries Coun. (chmn. 1975), Assn. Parliamentary Librarians in Can. (pres. 1980-82), Edmonton Libr. Assn., Hist. Soc. Alta. (v.p. Edmonton chpt. 1987), Libr. Assn. Alta., Can. Libr. Assn., Beta Phi Mu. Presbyterian. Clubs: Edmonton Jaguar Drivers, Edmonton Scottish Soc. Home: 209 Rhatigan Rd W, Edmonton, AB Canada T6R 1A2

MC DOUGALL, DUGALD STEWART, retired lawyer; b. Indpls., May 15, 1916; s. George and Effie (Barclay) McD.; m. Carol Brueggeman, Aug. 1938; children: George, Duncan, Walter, Robert; m. Judith Stephen, Dec. 1967. A.B., U. Chgo., 1935, J.D., 1937. Bar: Ill. 1937. Since practiced in Chgo.; sr. ptnr. McDougall, Hersh & Scott, 1961-87; sec., dir. Aladdin Industries, Inc. Served with USNR, 1942-46. Fellow Am. Coll. Trial Lawyers; mem. ABA, Am. Patent Law Assn., Patent Law Assn. Chgo., Law Club Chgo. Clubs: Union League (Chgo.); Olympia Fields (Ill.) Country. Office: Theodore R Scott 77 W Wacker Dr Chicago IL 60601-1629

MCDOUGALL, GERALD DUANE, lawyer; b. Hammond, Ind., Sept. 18, 1931; s. John and Carol Maxine (Lind) McD.; m. Ingrid Rosina Kempf, Jan. 26, 1960; children: Manfred, James. JD, Mercer U., 1971. Bar: U.S.V.I. 1972, Colo. 1973, Germany 1973, Tex. 1985. Atty. USVI Dept. Labor, St. Thomas, 1971-72; pvt. practice Denver, 1972-74, 76-84, Heilbronn, Neckar, Germany, 1974-76, Amarillo, Tex., 1985—. Precinct committeeman Rep. Ctrl. Com., Denver, 1978-84. Sgt. U.S. Army, 1951-54, ETO, 61-67, Vietnam. Mem. Tex. Bar Assn., Amarillo Bar Assn. Home: 7910 Merchant Dr Amarillo TX 79121 Office: PO Box 50898 Amarillo TX 79159

MCDOUGALL, IAIN ROSS, nuclear medicine educator; b. Glasgow, Scotland, Dec. 18, 1943; came to U.S., 1976; s. Archibald McDougall and Jean Cairns; m. Elizabeth Wilson, Sept. 6, 1968; children: Shona, Stewart. MB, ChB, U. Glasgow, 1967, PhD, 1973. Diplomate Am. Bd. Nuclear Medicine (chmn. 1985-87), Am. Bd. Internal Medicine (gov. 1984-86). Lectr. in medicine U. Glasgow, 1969-76; fellow Harkness-Stanford Med. Ctr., 1972-74; assoc. prof. radiology and medicine Stanford (Calif.) U., 1976-84, prof. radiology and medicine, 1985—. Contbr. numerous articles to sci. jours. Fellow Royal Coll. Physicians (Glasgow), Am. Coll. Physicians; mem. Am. Thyroid Assn., Soc. Nuclear Medicine, Western Assn. for Clin. Research. Office: Stanford U Med Ctr Divsn Nuclear Medicine Stanford CA 94305

MCDOUGALL, JACQUELYN MARIE HORAN, therapist; b. Wenatchee, Wash., Sept. 24, 1924; d. John Rankin and Helen Frampton (Vandivort) Horan; m. Robert Duncan McDougall, Jan. 24, 1947 (div. July 1976); children: Douglas, Stuart, Scott. BA, Wash. State U., 1946. Lic. therapist, Wash.; cert. nat. addiction counselor II. Pres. oper. bd. Ctr. for Alcohol/Drug Treatment, Wenatchee, 1983-85; sec. Wash. State Coun. on Alcoholism, 1988-89, supr. out-patient svcs., 1989-90; case mgmt. counselor Lakeside Treatment Ctr., East Wenatchee, Wash., 1991-92; ret., 1994. Treas. Allied Arts, Wenatchee, 1984; pres. Rep. Women, Wash., 1969-70.

MCDOUGALL, JOHN ROLAND, civil engineer; b. Edmonton, Alta., Can., Apr. 4, 1945; s. John Frederick and Phyllis Eirene (Sladden) McD.; m. Susan Carley, July 2, 1971 (div. 1995); children: John Christopher, Jordan Page, Michael Tait. BSCE, U. Alta., Edmonton, 1967. Registered profl. engr., Alta. Engr. Imperial Oil Ltd., Calgary, Alta., 1967-69; sr. engr. Imperial Oil Ltd., Edmonton, Alta., 1969-75; treas. McDougall & Secord, Edmonton, 1969-85; v.p. McDougall & Secord, Ltd., 1975-90, pres., 1990—; pres., chief exec. officer Dalcor Cos., Edmonton, 1975-91; chmn. Trade Innoventures, Inc., 1992—; chair engring. mgmt. U. Alta., Edmonton, 1991—; chmn. D.B. Robinson & Assocs., Edmonton; bd. dirs. Edmonton Northlands; chmn. World Trade Centre, Edmonton, 1994—; mem. adv. bd. Royal Trust Corp., 1984-94. Chmn. Edmonton Civic Govt. Assn., 1975-77; mem. Premiers Coun. on Sci. and Tech., 1990. Fellow Can. Acad. Engrs. (bd. dirs. 1992—); mem. Can. Coun. Profl. Engrs. (pres. 1990-91), Assn. Profl. Engrs. Alta. (hon. life, pres. 1980-81), Can. Engring. Manpower Bd. (chmn. 1985-88), Edmonton C. of C. (pres. 1989), Loyal Edmonton Regiment (hon.), Edmonton Club (pres. 1983-84). Anglican. Avocations: skiing, travel, cycling, philately, railroad modeling. Office: U Alta Faculty Engring, Edmonton, AB Canada T6G 2G8

MCDOUGALL, RONALD ALEXANDER, restaurant executive; b. Chgo., Aug. 12, 1942; s. John A. and Doris E. (Sengstock) McD.; m. Dale O. Ryser, Feb. 1, 1964 (div. July 1969); children: Timothy, Jonathan; m. Carolyn Kay Conley, Aug. 9, 1979; 1 child, Matthew. BBA, U. Wis., 1964, MBA, 1965. With Procter & Gamble, Cin., 1967-68, Sara Lee, Deerfield, Ill., 1969-72, The Pillsbury Co., Mpls., 1972-74, S&A Restaurant Corp., Dallas, 1974-82, Burger King, Miami, Fla., 1982-83; pres., CEO Brinker Internat., Dallas, 1983—. Bd. dirs. Susan G. Komen Found., U. Wis. 1st lt. U.S. Army, 1965-67. Mem. Nat. Restaurant Assn., Am. Mgmt. Assn., Bent Tree Country Club, Aerobics Activity Ctr., Employment Policies Inst. Republican. Presbyterian. Avocations: tennis, running, baseball, cycling, golf. Office: Brinker Internat 6820 Lyndon B Johnson Fwy Dallas TX 75240-6515

MC DOW, JOHN JETT, agricultural engineering educator; b. Covington, Tenn., Jan. 6, 1925; s. Robert Simpson and Lucy Ann (Cocke) McD.; m. Dorothy Virginia Glass, Dec. 22, 1946; children: Ronald Allan, Jane Virginia. Student, Franklin and Marshall Coll., 1944-45; B.S., U. Tenn., 1948; M.S., Mich. State U., 1949, Ph.D., 1957. Registered profl. engr., Tenn., La. Instr. Mich. State U., 1949; instr. Okla. State U., 1949-51, asst. prof. agrl. engring., 1951; assoc. prof. La. Poly. U., 1951-57, prof., 1957-62, head agrl. engring. dept., 1953-62; prof., head dept. agrl. engring. U. Tenn., Knoxville, 1962-73; dean admissions and records U. Tenn., 1973-83, prof. agrl. engring., 1983-92, prof. emeritus, 1992—; cons./collaborator Agrl. Research Service, U.S. Dept. Agr., 1970-76; leader Rotary Internat. Found. Group Study Exchange Team to Philippines, 1984; mem. scholarship selection com. N.Am. Philips Corp., 1976-88. Contbr. articles to profl. jours. Mem. La. Engring. Council, 1955-56; Bd. dirs. Tenn.-Venezuela-Amazonas Partners, 1977-80. Comdr. USNR, World War II, ret. So. Fellowship grantee, 1957. Mem. Am. Soc. Agrl. Engring. (dir. 1973-75), Am. Soc. Engring. Edn. (sec. agrl. engring. div. 1971-72, vice chmn. 1972-73, chmn. 1973-74), Sigma Xi, Tau Beta Pi, Pi Mu Epsilon, Omicron Delta Kappa, Gamma Sigma Delta, Phi Kappa Phi (v.p. 1971-77, nat. pres. elect 1977-80, pres. 1980-83, pres. found. 1974-78). Lodge: Rotary (pres. 1989-90, chmn. dist. scholarship selection com., 1982-87, 88-91). Home: 2008 Walnut Hills Dr Knoxville TN 37920-2946

MC DOWALL, RODDY, actor; b. London, Sept. 28, 1928; s. Thomas Andrew and Winifred Mc D. Educated, St. Joseph's Sch., London. Actor, films include: Scavenger Hunt, Man Hunt, 1941, How Green Was My Valley, 1941, Confirm or Deny, 1941, Son of Fury, 1942, On the Sunny Side, 1942, The Pied Piper, 1942, My Friend Flicka, 1943, Lassie Come Home, 1943, White Cliffs of Dover, 1944, Macbeth, 1948, Kidnapped, 1948, Tuna Clipper, 1949, Black Midnight, 1949, Killer Shark, 1950, Steel Fist, 1952, The Subterraneans, 1960, Midnight Lace, 1960, The Longest Day, 1962, Cleopatra, 1963, The Greatest Story Ever Told, 1965, That Darn Cat, 1965, The Loved One, 1965, The Third Day, 1965, Inside Daisy Clover, 1965, It, 1966, Lord Love a Duck, 1966, The Defector, 1966, Bullwhip Griffin, 1967, The Cool Ones, 1967, Planet of the Apes, 1968, The Poseidon Adventure, 1972, Funny Lady, 1975, Charlie Chan and the Curse of the Dragon Queen, 1981, Evil Under the Sun, 1982, Class of 84, 1984, Fright Night, 1985, Dead of Winter, 1986, Overboard, 1987, The Big Picture, 1989, Destroyer, 1989, Fright Night Part 2, 1988, Cutting Class, 1989, Shakma, 1990; debut as dir. in The Devil's Widow, 1971; Broadway appearances include: Misalliance, Mean Johnny Barrows, Escapade, Doctor's Dilemma, No Time for Sergeants, Good as Gold, Compulsion, Handful of Fire, Look after Lulu, The Fighting Cock, 1959-60, Camelot, 1960-61, The Astrakhan Coat, 1966; numerous TV appearances on Macmillan & Wife; regular on TV series Planet of the Apes, 1974, Bridges to Cross, 1986; TV films include: Miracle on 34th Street, The Elevator, 1974, Hart to Hart, 1979, The Martian Chronicles, 1980, The Memory of Eva Ryker, 1980, Mae West, 1982, This Girl for Hire, 1983, The Zany Adventures of Robin Hood, 1984; author: Double Exposure: Take Two, 1989. Recipient Emmy award for Best Supporting Actor, 1960; Tony award for Best Supporting Actor. Office: Innovative Artists Talent & Lit Agy 1999 Avenue Of The Stars Ste 2850 Los Angeles CA 90067-6022*

MCDOWELL, ANGUS, accountant; b. Redhill, Eng., Mar. 28, 1946; came to U.S., 1974; s. Horace John and Una (Ferguson) McD.; A.C.A., Inst. Chartered Accts. in Eng. and Wales, 1969; M.S. in Bus. Policy, Columbia U., 1978. From articled clk. to sr. acct. Ernst & Whinney, London, 1964-70; mgmt. acct. P&O Steam Nav., London, 1971; chief acct. travel and transp. div. Grindlays Internat. Banking Group, London, 1972-74; treas., gen. mgr., dir. M&J Comml., Inc., N.Y.C., 1974-79; partner AECC (Am. European Cons. Co.), N.Y.C., 1980-81; man. part. Pavie Et Associes C.P.A.s, 1984-88; propr. Angus Mc Dowell, C.P.A., 1981—. C.P.A., N.Y. State. Fellow Inst. Chartered Accts. Eng. and Wales; mem. Assn. Chartered Accts. in U.S. (founder, past pres.), Am. C. of C., Am. Inst. CPAs, N.Y. State Soc. CPAs (internat. ops. com.), Danish Am. C. of C. (dir.), Danish Bus. Club. also: Vysehradska 51, 128 00 Praha Czech Republic

MCDOWELL, CHARLES EAGER, lawyer, retired military officer; b. Manchester, N.H., Sept. 9, 1923; s. Joseph Curry and Mildred (Eager) McD.; m. Carolyn A. Gibbons, June 21, 1947; children—Robin, Patricia. A.B., Dartmouth Coll., 1947; J.D., U. Va., 1950. Bar: Tex. 1950, Va. 1981, D.C. 1981. With land div. Shell Oil Co., Houston, 1950; commd. lt. (j.g.) USN, 1951, advanced through grades to rear adm., 1976; staff legal officer Comdr. Service Force, U.S. Pacific Fleet; staff judge adv., head internat. law div. Naval War Coll., 1963-66; staff legal officer, comdr. 7th Fleet, 1966-68; sr. Navy mem. ad hoc com., dep. asst. judge adv. gen. Office Judge Adv. Gen. Dept. Def., Washington, 1968-72; staff judge adv. on staff comdr. in chief U.S. Naval Forces, Europe, London, 1972-75; comdg. officer Naval Justice Sch., Newport, R.I., 1975-76; dep. judge adv. gen. Navy Dept., Washington, 1976-78, judge adv. gen., 1978-80; pvt. practice Dumfries, Va., 1981—. Served to 2d lt. AUS, 1943-46. Decorated D.S.M., Bronze Star, Joint Service Commendation medal, Navy Commendation medal with Combat V, Purple Heart, Combat Inf. badge. Mem. FBA, Tex. Bar Assn., Va. Bar Assn., Judge Advs. Assn., Order of Coif, Chi Phi, Square Dancer Club. Methodist. Home: 1106 Croton Dr Alexandria VA 22308-2008 Office: The Law Bldg 201 Waters Ln Dumfries VA 22026-2209

MCDOWELL, CHARLES R., columnist, news analyst, lecturer; b. Danville, Ky., June 24, 1926; m. Ann Webb, Apr. 26, 1952. BA, Washington & Lee U., 1948; MS in Journalism, Columbia U., 1949; LHD (hon.), Washington & Lee U., 1975; hon. degree, Centre Coll. With Richmond (Va.) Times-Dispatch, 1949-65, Washington corr., columnist, 1965—; panelist PBS Washington Week in Review, 1977—. Author: One Thing After Another, 1960, What Did You Have in Mind?, 1963, Campaign Fever, 1965; author: (with others) Beyond Reagan, 1986; writer, narrator (documentary) Summer of Judgment, 1983, 84; voices (TV series) The Civil War, 1990, Baseball, 1994; commentator weekly TV series The Lawmakers; contbr. articles to profl. jours. Past chmn. Standing Com. Corrs. Recipient Burkett Miller Presdl. award White-Burkett Miller Ctr. Pub. Affairs at U. Va., 1984; named to Soc. Profl. Journalists' Washington Hall of Fame, 1992. Mem. Gridiron Club (past pres.). Office: 1214 National Press Building Washington DC 20045-2200

MCDOWELL, DAVID E., pharmaceutical executive; b. 1942. AA, Orange Coast Jr. Coll., 1962; MS, Stanford U., 1978. V.p., gen. mgr. quality control Internat. Bus. Machines, Armonk, N.Y., 1962-91; pres., COO, bd. dirs. McKesson Corp., 1991—. Office: McKesson Corp 1 Post St San Francisco CA 94104-5203*

MCDOWELL, DONALD L., hospital administrator; b. Indpls., June 9, 1934; married; 5 children. BS Acctg., Ohio State U., 1956; grad. Edn. Adminstrn., U. Fla. Acctg. tng. program Chevrolet divsn. Gen. Motors Corp., Toledo, Ohio, 1956-58, acctg. asst. supr. Chevrolet divsn., 1958-59; acctg. supr. Chevrolet divsn. Gen. Motors Corp., Atlanta, 1959-61; controller U. Fla., Gainesville, 1961-67; dir. mgmt. info. systems Fla. Bd. Regents, Tallahassee, 1967-68; v.p. adminstrv. affairs Fla. Internat. U., Miami, 1969-74; exec. dir. ops. Vanderbilt U., 1974-76, v.p. bus. affairs, 1976-80; exec. v.p., treas. Maine Med. Ctr., 1980-91, interim pres., 1990-91, pres., 1991—; bd. dirs. Maine Bank and Trust; com. mem. So. Assn. Colls. and Schs., program classification com. Nat. Ctr. Higher Edn. Mgmt. Systems; educator Fla. Internat. U.; city mgrs. adv. com. Portland. Mem. Bldg. com. YWCA Portland; chmn. Hosp. adv. com. Maine Health Care Fin. Commn.; at-large mem. House Dels. Am. Hosp. Assn.; Pres'. coun. visitors U. So. Maine; bd. dirs. ARC, Greater Portland United Way, Park Danforth Home for the Aged, Portland C. of C. (pres. 1990-91), Community Health Svcs., Portland Stage Co., Maine Hosp. Assn., Portland Symphony Orchestras, Voluntary Hosps. Am., New England (treas.), Regional C. of C. (chmn.), Maine Devel. Found., Ptnrs. for Progress, New England Healthcare Assembly. Office: Maine Med Ctr 22 Bramhall St Portland ME 04102-3134*

MCDOWELL, DONNA SCHULTZ, lawyer; b. Cin., Apr. 23, 1946; d. Robert Joseph and Harriet (Parronchi) Schultz; m. Dennis Lon McDowell, June 20, 1970; children: Dawn Megan, Donnelly Lon. BA in English with honors, Brandeis U., 1968; MEd, Am. U., 1972; CASE with honors, Johns Hopkins U., 1979; JD with honors, U. Md., 1982, MS, Hood Coll., 1995. Bar: Md. 1982. Instr., Anne Arundel & Prince George's C.C., Severna Park and Largo, Md., 1977-78; coll. adminstr. Bowie State Coll. (Md.), 1978-79; assoc. Miller & Bortner, Lanham, Md., 1982-83; sole practice, Lanham, 1983-87; Gaithersburg, Md. 1987—; ednl. cons. Chmn. Housing Hearing Com., Bowie, 1981-83; trustee Unitarian-Universalitst Ch., Silver Spring, Md., 1979-83; bd. dirs. New Ventures, Bowie, 1983, Second Mile (Runaway House), Hyattsville, Md., 1983; officer Greater Laytonsville Civic Assn., 1989—; founding mem. People to Preserve, Laytonsville; mem. Solid Waste Adv. Com., Montgomery County, Md.; election judge. Recipient Am. Jurisprudence award U. Md., 1981. Mem. Montgomery County Bar Assn., Prince George's Bar Assn., Phi Kappa Phi. Democrat. Avocations: gardening, reading, bluebirds. Home: 24308 Hipsley Mill Rd Gaithersburg MD 20882-3132 Office: 965 C Russell Ave Gaithersburg MD 20879

MCDOWELL, EDWARD R. H., chemical engineer; b. Cleve., Aug. 13, 1932; s. Blake and Lois (Held) McD.; m. Joyce Patricia Dudley, June 18, 1955; children: Edward R. H. Jr., James D. BSChemE, Cornell U., 1955; MS, Calif. Inst. Tech., 1960, PhD, 1964. Registered prof. chem. engr., Calif. Instr. Cornell U., Ithaca, N.Y., 1955; assoc. rsch. engr. Calif. Rsch. Corp., El Segundo, 1955-59; instr. Calif. Inst. Tech., Pasadena, 1959-63; rsch. engr. Chevron Rsch. Corp., La Habra, Calif., 1963-66, sr. rsch. engr., 1966-68; sr. engring. assoc. Chevron Oil Field Rsch. Co., La Habra, 1968-74, mgr., 1974-86; gen. ptnr. C. Blake McDowell Ltd. Partnership, Akron, Ohio, 1986—. NSF fellow Calif. Inst. Tech., 1961-63; recipient Engring. Merit award Orange County Engring. Coun., 1985. Fellow Am. Inst. Chem. Engrs. (pres. 1989, v.p. 1988, dir. 1982-84, Civic Achievement award 1983, F.J. & Dorothy Van Anwepen award 1992), Inst. for Advancement of Engring.; mem. Soc. Petroleum Engrs., Am. Assn. Engring. Socs. (bd. govs.), King Harbor Yacht Club (commodore 1990, vice commodore 1989, rear commodore 1988), St. Francis Yacht Club (San Francisco), Transpacific Yacht Club (Long Beach, Calif.), Assn. Santa Monica Bay Yacht Clubs (commodore 1989, vice commodore 1988, rear commodore 1987), Nawiliwili Yacht Club (Lihue, Hawaii), Magic Castle Club, Manhattan Country Club, The Cornell Club (N.Y.C.). Avocations: offshore sailboat racing (winner ULDB70 Season Sailing Championship 1990, 92), magic. Home: 2510 The Strand Hermosa Beach CA 90254-2553

MCDOWELL, ELIZABETH MARY, retired pathology educator; b. Kew Gardens, Surrey, Eng., Mar. 30, 1940; came to U.S., 1971; d. Arthur and Peggy (Bryant) McD. B Vet. Medicine, Royal Vet. Coll., London, 1963; BA, Cambridge U., 1968, PhD, 1971. Gen. practice vet. medicine, 1964-66; Nuffield Found. tng. scholar Cambridge (Eng.) U., 1966-71; instr. dept. pathology U. Md., Balt., 1971-73, asst. prof., 1973-76, assoc. prof., 1976-80, prof., 1980-96, ret., 1996. Co-author: Biopsy Pathology of the Bronchi, 1987; editor: Lung Carcinomas, 1987; contbr. over 120 articles to sci. jours., chpts. to books. Rsch. grantee NIH, 1979-92. Fellow Royal Coll. Vet. Surgeons Gt. Britain and Ireland. Avocations: conservation education, gardening, swimming. Home: 606 W 37th St Baltimore MD 21211

MCDOWELL, FLETCHER HUGHES, physician, educator; b. Denver, Aug. 5, 1923; married. BA, Dartmouth Coll., 1943; MD, Cornell U., 1947. From instr. to assoc. prof. medicine Cornell U. Med. Coll., N.Y.C., 1968—, assoc. dean Med. Coll., 1970-95, Winifred Masterson Burke prof. rehab. medicine; med. dir. Burke Rehab. Hosp., White Plains, N.Y., 1973-95; pres. Winifred Masterson Burke Rsch. Inst., White Plains, 1992—. Mem. Am. Acad. Neurology, Am. Neurol. Assn., Am. Fedn. Clin. Research. Office: Burke Rehab Ctr 785 Mamaroneck Ave White Plains NY 10605-2523

MCDOWELL, JACK BURNS, professional baseball player; b. Van Nuys, Calif., Jan. 16, 1966. Grad., Stanford U. Baseball player Chgo. White Sox, 1987-88, 90-95, N.Y. Yankees, 1995, Cleve. Indians, 1996—. mem. Am. League All-Star Team, 1991-93; Sporting News All-Star Team, 1992, 93; Am. League Complete Games Leader, 1991-92; recipient Cy Young award Baseball Writers Assn. Am., 1993; named Sporting News Pitcher of Yr., 1993. Office: Cleveland Indians 2401 Ontario St Cleveland OH 44115*

MC DOWELL, JACK SHERMAN, political consultant; b. Alameda, Calif., Feb. 23, 1914; s. John Sherman and Myra Lorraine (Frierson) McD.; m. Jeanette California Ofelth, June 18, 1938; children: Nancy Lynn (Mrs. Henry A. Swanson, Jr.), Peggy Joanne (Mrs. G.P. Cramer), Judy Carolina. Student, San Jose State Coll., 1931-32. With Alameda Times-Star, 1926-31, San Jose Evening News, 1932; owner, operator with brother Turlock Daily Jour., 1933-40, Eugene (Oreg.) Daily News, 1941-42; staff writer San Francisco Call-Bull. (now Examiner), 1942-50, war corr. Pacific, 1944, daily columnist, 1946-50, city editor, 1950-56, polit. editor, columnist, 1956-69; specialist in ballot measures Woodward & McDowell (polit. campaign mgmt. advt. and pub. relations), 1969—; News dir. Gov. Ronald Reagan campaign, 1970, Senator S.I. Hayakawa campaign, 1976. Co-author: (with Chaplain Howell M. Forgy) And Pass the Ammunition, 1944; Contbr. articles to mags. Recipient best news photo award Calif. Newspaper Pub. Assn., 1939, Pulitzer prize for distinguished reporting, 1944. Mem. Am. Assn. Polit. Cons. Club: Press (San Francisco). Home: 97 Normandy Ln Atherton CA 94027-3816 Office: 111 Anza Blvd Burlingame CA 94010-1932

MCDOWELL, JAY HORTENSTINE, lawyer; b. New Orleans, July 10, 1936; s. Jacob Leonidas Hortenstine and Martha (Grace) Babcock; m. Kari Keyser, Oct. 24, 1959; children: Paul H., Sean C., Kari K. Student, Eastbourne Coll., Sussex, Eng., 1954-55; BA, Yale U., 1959; LLB, U. Va., 1963. Bar: N.Y. 1964. Assoc. Cadwalader, Wickersham & Taft, N.Y.C., 1963-71, ptnr., 1972—; mem. bd. dirs. Bacardi Ltd., Hamilton, Bermuda, 1996—. V.p., bd. dirs. St. Mary's Hosp. for Children, Bayside, N.Y., 1972—. Mem. ABA, Assn. Bar of City of N.Y. Clubs: Union (N.Y.), Shelter Island Yacht (N.Y.). Office: Cadwalader Wickersham & Taft 100 Maiden Ln New York NY 10038-4818

MCDOWELL, JENNIFER, sociologist, composer, playwright, publisher; b. Albuquerque; d. Willard A. and Margaret Frances (Garrison) McD.; m. Milton Loventhal, July 2, 1973. BA, U. Calif., 1957; MA, San Diego State U., 1958; postgrad., Sorbonne, Paris, 1959; MLS, U. Calif., 1963; PhD, U. Oreg., 1973. Tchr. English Abraham Lincoln High Sch., San Jose, Calif., 1960-61; free-lance editor Soviet field, Berkeley, Calif., 1961-63; rsch. asst. sociology U. Oreg., Eugene, 1964-66; editor, pub. Merlin Papers, San Jose, 1969—, Merlin Press, San Jose, 1973—; rsch. cons. sociology San Jose, 1973—; music pub. Lipstick and Toy Balloons Pub. Co., San Jose, 1978—; composer Paramount Pictures, 1982-88; tchr. writing workshops; poetry readings, 1969-73; co-producer radio show lit. and culture Sta. KALX, Berkeley, 1971-72. Author: (with Milton Loventhal) Black Politics: A Study and Annotated Bibliography of the Mississippi Freedom Democratic Party, 1971 (featured at Smithsonian Inst. Spl. Event 1992), Contemporary Women Poets, 1977, Ronnie Goose Rhymes for Grown-Ups, 1984; co-author: (plays off-off Broadway) Betsy and Phyllis, 1986, Mack the Knife Your Friendly Dentist, 1986, The Estrogen Party To End War, 1986, The Oatmeal Party Comes To Order, 1986, (plays) Betsy Meets the Wacky Iraqui, 1991, Bella and Phyllis, 1994; contbr. poems, plays, essays, articles, short stories, and book revs. to lit. mags., news mags. and anthologies; rschr. women's autobiog. writings, contemporary writing in poetry, Soviet studies, civil rights movement, and George Orwell, 1962—; writer: (songs) Money Makes a Woman Free, 1976, 3 songs featured in Parade of Am. Music; co-creator mus. comedy Russia's Secret Plot To Take Back Alaska, 1988. Recipient 8 awards Am. Song Festival, 1976-79, Bill Casey Award in Letters, 1980; doctoral fellow AAUW, 1971-73; grantee Calif. Arts Coun., 1976-77. Mem. Am. Sociol. Assn., Soc. Sci. Study of Religion, Poetry Orgn. for Women, Dramatists Guild, Phi Beta Kappa, Sigma Alpha Iota, Beta Phi Mu, Kappa Kappa Gamma. Democrat. Office: care Merlin Press PO Box 5602 San Jose CA 95150-5602

MC DOWELL, JOHN B., bishop; b. New Castle, Pa., July 17, 1921; s. Bernard A. and Louise M. (Hannon) McD. B.A., St. Vincent Coll., 1942, M.A., 1944; M.A., Catholic U. Am., 1950, Ph.D., 1952; Litt.D. (hon.), Duquesne U., 1962; grad., St. Vincent Sem., Latrobe, Pa. Ordained priest Roman Catholic Ch., 1945, consecrated as titular bishop of Tamazuca and aux. bishop of Pitts., 1966—; asst. pastor St. Irenaeus Ch., Oakmont, 1945-49; asst. supt. schs. Diocese of Pitts., 1952-55, supt. schs., 1955-70, vicar for edn., from 1970; now vicar gen.; pastor Epiphany Parish, Pitts., 1969—; papal chamberlain to Pope Pius XII, 1956, to Pope John XXIII, 1958; domestic prelate to Pope Paul VI, 1964; chmn. ad hoc com. on moral values in our soc. Nat. Conf. Cath. Bishops, from 1973, Bishops Com. for Pastoral on Moral Values, from 1976; mem. Internat. Council for Catechesis, from 1975. Co-author elem. sch. religions series, jr. high sch. lit. series, elem. sci. series and elem. reading series; contbr. ednl. articles to various publs.; former editor: Cath. Educator Mag. Bd. dirs. Allegheny County Community Coll.; bd. dirs. Western Pa. Safety Council, Duquesne U. Named Man of Yr. in Religion Pitts., 1970, 93, Educator of Yr., United Pvt. Acad. Schs. Assn., 1978, Man of Yr., Pitts. chpt. KC, 1989. Mem. Nat. Cath. Ednl. Assn., Cath. Ednl. Assn. Pa., Omicron Delta Kappa Gamma Circle (hon.). Office: Epiphany Ch 1018 Centre Ave Pittsburgh PA 15219-3502 also: Chancery Office 111 Blvd Of The Allies Pittsburgh PA 15222-1618*

MCDOWELL, JOHN EUGENE, lawyer; b. Toledo, Nov. 22, 1927; s. Glenn Hugh and Evelyn (Millspaugh) McD.; m. Jean Ann Hepler, June 18, 1950; children: Jane Lynn McDowell Thummel, Sheila Lorraine McDowell Laing. BS, Miami U., Oxford, Ohio, 1949; JD, U. Mich., 1952. Bar: Ohio 1952. Assoc. Dinsmore & Shohl, Cin., 1952-59, ptnr., 1959—; bd. dirs. Structural Dynamics Rsch. Corp., Milford, Ohio. Mem. solicitation coms. United Appeal, Cin., NCCJ, Cin., Boy Scouts Am., Cin. Mem. ABA, Ohio Bar Assn., Cin. Bar Assn., Cin. Country Club, Queen City Club, Order of Coif. Democrat. Episcopalian. Office: Dinsmore & Shohl 1900 Chemed Ctr 255 E 5th St Cincinnati OH 45202-4700

MCDOWELL, MALCOLM, actor; b. Leeds, Eng., June 13, 1943; m. Mary Steenburgen, 1980 (div.); 2 children. Began career with: Royal Shakespeare Co., Stratford, Eng., 1965-66; early TV appearances include: role of Dixon of Dock Green in Z Cars, British TV; other TV appearances: Little Red Riding Hood, Faerie Tale Theatre, Showtime TV, 1983, Gulag, HBO, 1985; stage appearance: In Celebration, N.Y.C., 1984; films include: Poor Cow, 1967, If..., 1969, Figures in a Landscape, 1970, The Raging Moon, 1971, A Clockwork Orange, 1971, O Lucky Man, 1973, Royal Flash, 1975, Aces High, 1976, Voyage of the Damned, 1977, Caligula, 1977, The Passage, 1978, Time After Time, 1979, Cat People, 1981, Britannia Hospital, 1984, Blue Thunder, 1983, Get Crazy, 1983, Cross Creek, 1983, Sunset, 1987, Buy and Cell, 1989, Class of 1999, 1989, Bopha!, 1993, Milk Money, 1994, The Caller, Star Trek: Generations, 1994, Tank Girl, 1995. *

MCDOWELL, MARION, state agency director. BA in Sociology, U. Ariz.; MA in Pub. Personnel Adminstrn., George Washington U. Mem. grad. faculty for pub. personnel mgmt. Coll. Notre Dame, Belmont, Calif.; dep. supt. personnel svcs. Sequoia Union High Sch. Dist., 1988-95; pres. Calif. State Bd. of Edn., 1995—. Mem. Civil Svc. Commn. for San Mateo County, 1987—. Mem. Am. Soc. Personnel Adminstrn., Am. Assn. for Sch. Personnel Adminstrn., Calif. Ednl. Placement Assn., Assn. Calif. Sch. Adminstrs., No. Calif. Human Resources Coun. Office: State Bd of Edn Rm 532 721 Capitol Mall Sacramento CA 95814

MCDOWELL, MICHAEL DAVID, lawyer, utility executive; b. Lewisburg, Pa., May 10, 1948; s. David Leonard and Mary Ellen (Scallan) McD.; m. Martha LaMantia, Aug. 4, 1973; 1 child, Daniel Joseph. B.S. in Bus. Mgmt., U. Dayton, 1970; J.D., U. Pitts., 1973. Bar: Pa. 1973, U.S. Dist. Ct. (mid. dist.) Pa. 1973, U.S. Tax Ct. 1974, U.S. Ct. Appeals (3d cir.) 1974, U.S. Dist. Ct. (we. dist.) Pa. 1975, U.S. Supreme Ct. 1977, U.S. Ct. Internat. Trade 1981, U.S. Ct. Appeals (fed. cir.) 1982. Asst. U.S. atty. Dept. Justice, Lewisburg, Pa., 1973-75; assoc. Hirsch, Weise & Tillman, Pitts., 1975-76, Plowman & Spiegel, Pitts., 1976-80; counsel Dravo Corp., Pitts., 1980-86, sr. counsel, 1987; atty. West Penn Power Co., Greensburg, Pa., 1987-95, counsel, 1995—; mem. panel of arbitrators Am. Arbitration Assn., 1978-94, Pa. Bur. Mediation, 1983—, Pa. Labor Relations Bd., 1985—. Contbr. articles to profl. jours. Mem. Union County Child Welfare adv. com., 1974-75; account exec. Southwestern Pa. United Way, Pitts., 1983; bd. govs. Pine Run Homeowners Assn., 1986-87; mem. nat. panel consumer arbitrators Better Bus. Bur., 1986—; sr. arbitrator, 1989—; mem. supervisory com. ALCOBAR Credit Union, 1986-87. Recipient Dravo Corp. Editorial Achievement awards, 1982, 83, 85, 86; nominated as one of Outstanding Young Men. Am., 1983,84. Fellow Am. Bar Found., Pa. Bar Found.; mem. ABA (Ho. of Dels. 1985-91, exec. coun. sect. labor and employment law 1983-85, exec. council young lawyers div. 1982-84, chmn. YLD Labor Law Com. 1981-83, fellow, 1985—), Pa. Bar Assn. (Ho. of Dels. 1980-94, chmn. special rules subcom. Disciplinary Bd. Study Com. 1983-93, com. on legal ethics and profl. responsibility, 1983—, arbitrator lawyer dispute resolution program 1987—, house com. on rules and calendar 1991-94, Outstanding Young Lawyer award 1984, Spl. Achievement award 1986,), Allegheny County Bar Assn. (profl. ethics com. 1980-94, bd. govs. 1979, 85-91, asst. sec.-treas. 1979, chmn. young lawyers sect. 1978, council professionalism 1988-90, bylaws com. 1990—, award for outstanding leadership and valuable contbns. to bar 1979), Nat. Contractors Assn. (gen. counsels com. 1983-87), Am. Corp. Counsel Assn., McCandless Swimming Club (Pitts., bd. govs. 1982-85), Phi Alpha Delta (justice 1972-73, cert. Outstanding Service 1973). Republican. Roman Catholic. Office: West Penn Power Co 800 Cabin Hill Dr Greensburg PA 15601-1650

MCDOWELL, NAN HAZEL, occupational therapist, rehabilitation services professional; b. Quincy, Mass., June 23, 1940; d. Arthur Pierce and Hazel Florence (Foley) Thomas; m. Billy M.L. McDowell, Dec. 16, 1966; 1 child, Tara Brooke. BS in Occupational Therapy, Edn., Tufts U., 1964; Cert. in Rehab. Facilities Adminstrn., U. Mo., 1991. Registered occupational therapist, Mo. Spl. edn. tchr. Anchorage Borough Sch. Dist., 1965-70; dir. occupational therapy Mid Maine Med. Ctr., Waterville, 1978-80, Hillcrest Med. Ctr., Tulsa, 1980-84; dir. adjuctive therapy St. Vincent Hosp., Santa Fe, 1985-86; rehab. coord., analyst Muskogee (Okla.) Regional Med. Ctr., 1986-87; mgr. rehab. svcs. and in-patient clinics U. Mo. Hosps. and Clinics, Columbia, 1988-89; mgr. rehab. svcs. Still Regional Med. Ctr., Jefferson City, Mo., 1990-91, Claremore (Okla.) Regional Hosp., 1992-93; mgr. outpatient rehab. Sisters of St. Mary's Rehab. Inst., Jefferson City, 1994; dir. rehab. therapies Rehab Visions at Lake of the Ozarks Gen. Hosp., Osage Beach, Mo., 1994—; cons. occupational therapy svcs. EPIC-Cornerstone Geriatic Psychology, Miami, Okla., 1989-90; cons. program devel. Coffyville (Kans.) Meml. Hosp., 1984; chmn. hosp. safety com. Claremore Regional Hosp., 1992; mem. mgmt. coun. U. Mo. Hosp. and Clinics, Columbia, 1987-88. Active Spl. Olympics, Alamosa, Colo., 1977. Mem. Am. Occupational Therapy Assn. Democrat. Methodist. Avocations: oil painting, pottery, dryweed arrangements, decorating. Home: HC 3 Box 1137 Rocky Mount MO 65072-9038

MCDOWELL, THEODORE NOYES, public relations consultant; b. Washington, Oct. 20, 1925; s. Ralph Walker McDowell and Ruth Noyes Sheldon; m. Mildred Bowen, Mar. 5, 1945; children: Patricia B., Janet Ruth Curtis, Theodora McDowell Herskovitz, Theodore Noyes Jr. BA, Duke U., 1947. Reporter Washington Star Newspaper, 1947-51, asst. promotion mgr., 1951-53; account exec. Evening Star Broadcasting Co., Washington, 1953-55, TV program mgr., 1955-62, gen. mgr. news and pub. affairs and sec., 1962-70; dir. office of pub. affairs U.S. Dept. Transp., Washington, 1970-71; regional rep. of the sec. U.S. Dept. Transp., Atlanta, 1971-76; self-employed media cons. Hilton Head Island, S.C., 1976—. Former mem. and vice chmn. governing bd. Nat. Cathedral Sch., Washington; former bd. dirs. Children's Hosp., Washington, chmn. Pres.'s Cup Regatta, 1960-61; elder Presbyn. Ch. With USN, 1943-46. Recipient Meritorious Achievement award Sec. Transp., 1971, Sec.'s award, 1973, Nat. Def. Transp. Assn. award, 1972-73. Mem. Radio TV News Dirs. Assn. (former bd. dirs.), AP Radio/TV Assn. (bd. dirs., past pres.), Soc. Profl. Journalists, Broadcast Pioneers, Toastmasters. Presbyterian (elder). Home and Office: 29 Ruddy Turnstone Rd Hilton Head Island SC 29928-5704

MCDOWELL, WILLIAM S., lawyer; b. Chgo., Mar. 16, 1941. BBA, U. Mich., 1963, JD with distinction, 1966. Bar: Ill. 1966. Ptnr. Baker & McKenzie, Chgo. Office: Baker & McKenzie 1 Prudential Plz 130 E Randolph St Chicago IL 60601*

MCDUFFIE, FREDERIC CLEMENT, physician; b. Lawrence, Mass., Apr. 27, 1924; m. Isabel Simpson Wiggin, May 31, 1952; children: Elisabeth Wiggin, Joan Selden, Deborah Howard, Charles Dennett. Grad., Harvard U., M.D. cum laude, 1951. Diplomate Am. Bd. Internal Medicine and Subbd. Rheumatology. Intern Peter Bent Brigham Hosp., Boston, 1951-52; resident Peter Bent Brigham Hosp., 1952-53, 56-57; tng. in phys. chemistry Harvard U., 1953-54; in immunology Columbia Coll. Physicians and Surgeons, 1954-56; asst. prof. internal medicine U. Miss., Jackson, 1957-62; asst. prof. microbiology U. Miss., 1957-64, assoc. prof., 1964-65; cons. medicine and microbiology Mayo Clinic and Mayo Found., Rochester, Minn., 1965; asst. prof. internal medicine and microbiology Mayo Grad. Sch. Medicine, 1965-69, asso. prof., 1969-73; asso. prof. Mayo Med. Sch., 1973, prof. internal medicine and immunology, 1974-79; prof. medicine Emory U., Atlanta, 1979—; vis. investigator Center for Disease Control, Atlanta, 1979-88; sr. v.p. med. affairs Arthritis Found., Atlanta, 1979-87; dir. Piedmont Hosp. Arthritis Ctr., 1988—; pres. Minn. chpt. Arthritis Found., 1962-63; bd. dirs., mem. exec. com. Miss. chpt. Arthritis Found. (Minn. chpt.), 1974-79, chmn. med. and sci. com., 1975-79, nat. trustee, 1978-79, chmn. nat. research com., 1978-79; trustee Nat. Health Coun., 1984—. Editorial bd. Arthritis and Rheumatism, 1976-81, Jour. Rheumatology, 1974—; editor Jour. Lab. and Clin. Medicine, 1977-79; contbr. articles to profl. jours. Served with U.S. Army, 1943-45. Mem. Am. Assn. Immunologists, Am. Rheumatism Assn., Central Rheumatism Assn. (pres. 1973-74), Central Soc. Clin. Research (council 1977-79), Soc. Exptl. Biology and Medicine, Am. Fedn. Clin. Research, A.C.P., Alpha Omega Alpha. Home: 3201-H Post Woods Dr NW Atlanta GA 30339 Office: Ste 205 2001 Peachtree Rd NE Atlanta GA 30309-1476

MCDUFFIE, KEITH A., literature educator, magazine director; b. Spokane, Wash., Feb. 12, 1932; s. Clair L. and Helen Marie (Yaeger) McD.; m. Helen E. Ferry, June 5, 1965 (div. Aug. 1995); children: Anne Leslie, Andrew Keith; m. Pamela Philips Bacarisse, Aug. 14, 1995. BA in English, Gonzaga U., Spokane, 1954; MA in Spanish, Middlebury (Vt.) Coll., 1960, Univ. Complutense, Madrid, Spain, 1960; PhD in Hispanic Lit., U. Pitts., 1969. Prof. U. Mont., 1969-74; Mellon postdoctoral fellow U. Pitts., 1974, prof., chair dept. Hispanic Lit., 1975-92, prof. Hispanic Lit., 1992—; editor Revista Iberoamericana, Pitts., 1991-96. Co-author: Co-Textes: Cesar Vallejo, 1987; co-editor: Texto y Contexto-Actas 19 Congreso del IILI, 1980, En Este Aire de America: Homenaje a Alfredo Roggiano, 1990. With U.S. Army Security Agy., 1954-56. Mellon Predoctoral fellow U. Pitts., 1965, Title VI fellow U.S. Govt., 1966; Spanish Govt. scholar Spanish Govt., 1959-60. Mem. Instituto Internacional de Literatura Iberoamericana (contbg., bd. dirs. 1991-96, exec. dir. 1991-96). Democrat. Home: 220 N Dithridge St Apt 1001 Pittsburgh PA 15213-1425

MC DUFFIE, MALCOLM, oil company executive; b. San Francisco, Nov. 14, 1915; s. William Chester and Mary (Skaife) McD.; m. Mary Sutherland de Surville, Dec. 8, 1951; children: Cynthia de Surville, Duncan de Surville. A.B. in Econs, Stanford U., 1940. With O.C. Field Gasoline Corp., 1940-41, Wilmington Gasoline Corp., 1941-42; with Mohawk Petroleum Corp., 1945-80, pres., dir., 1969-80; dir. Res. Oil & Gas Co., 1973-80, sr. v.p., 1977-80; sp. asst. to pres. Getty Oil Co., Los Angeles, 1980-82. Bd. overseers Huntington Library, Art Gallery and Bot. Gardens, 1972—; bd. dirs. Calif. Inst. Tech. Assos., 1976-82. Mem. Nat. Petroleum Refiners Assn. (Dir. 1970-80), Ind. Refiners Assn. Calif. (pres. 1967-69, 77-78, dir. 1950-80), Rancheros Visitadores. Republican. Episcopalian. Clubs: California (Los Angeles); Bohemian (San Francisco); Valley Hunt (Pasadena, Calif.), Annandale Golf (Pasadena, Calif.); Birnam Wood (Santa Barbara, Calif.), Valley (Montecito, Calif.). Office: 180 S Lake Ave Ste 315 Pasadena CA 91101-2619

MCEACHEN, RICHARD EDWARD, banker, lawyer; b. Omaha, Sept. 24, 1933; s. Howard D. and Ada Carolyn Helen (Baumann) McE.; m. Judith Ann Gray, June 28, 1969; children: Mark E., Neil H. BS, U. Kans., Lawrence, 1955; JD, U. Mich., 1961. Bar: Mo. 1961, Kans. 1982. Assoc. Hillix, Hall, Hasburgh, Brown & Hoffhaus, Kansas City, Mo., 1961-62; sr. v.p. First Nat. Bank, Kansas City, Mo., 1962-75; exec. v.p. Commerce Bank Kansas City, Mo., 1975-85, Centerre Bank of Kansas City N.A., 1985-87, Security Bank Kansas City, Kans., 1987-88; exec. v.p., trust officer UMB Overland Park Bank, 1988-93; atty. Ferree, Bunn & O'Grady, Chartered, Overland Park, 1994—. Gov. Am. Royal Assn., Kansas City, Mo., 1970—, amb., 1980—; bd. dirs. Harry S. Truman Med. Ctr., Kansas City, 1974-86, mem. fin. com., 1975-86, treas., 1979-84, bd. govs., 1986—, mem. bldg. and grounds com., 1993—; trustee Clearinghouse for Midcontinent Founds., 1980-87; bd. dirs. Greater Kansas City Mental Health Found., 1963-69, treas., 1964-69, v.p., 1967-69; adv. bd. urban svcs. YMCA, Kansas City, 1976-83; cubmaster Kanza dist. Boy Scouts Am., 1982-83, dist. vice chmn., 1982-83, troop com., 1983-90, treas., 1986-88; bd. dirs. Scout Booster Club, Inc., 1989-94; mem. planned gift com. William Rickhill Nelson Gallery Art, Children's Mercy Hosp. Planned Gift Coun., 1991; mem. adv. com. Legal Assistance Program Avila Coll., 1978-80, adv. coun. Future Farmers Am., 1972-82; mgr. Oppenstein Bros. Found., 1979-85; trustee Village Presbyn. Ch., 1987-90, chmn., 1989-90, elder, 1994—; bd. dirs. Village Presbyn. Ch. Found., 1987-89, 94—, chmn., 1996—; bd. dirs. Estate Planning Coun., 1984-86; bd. dirs. Shawnee Mission Med. Ctr. Found., 1988—, fin. com., 1989-92. Mem. Nat. Assn. Securities Dealers Inc. (bd. arbitrators), Am. Arbitration Assn. (panel arbitrators), Estate Planning Soc. Kansas City, Mo. Bar Assn., Kans. Bar Assn., Johnson County Bar Assn., Kansas City Met. Bar Assn., Estate Planning Assn. (pres. 1974-75), Kansas City Jr. C. of C. (v.p. 1964-66), Lawyers Assn. Kansas City, Ea. Kans. Estate Planning Coun., Indian Hills Club, Delta Tau Delta Alumni (v.p. Kansas City chpt. 1978-80). Republican. Home: 9100 El Monte St Shawnee Mission KS 66207-2627 Office: One Glenwood Pl PO Box 12570 Shawnee Mission KS 66212-2570

MCEACHERN, ALEXANDER, electronics company executive; b. Boston, Feb. 18, 1955; s. Alexander William and Elisabeth Helena McEachern; m. Barbara Ruth Pereira, Dec. 18, 1975; children: Alexander Wallis, Ian Wallis. V.p. Mac Systems, 1975-79; dir. R&D Lomac Corp., Santa Clara, Calif., 1979-80; chmn., founder Basic Measuring Instruments, Santa Clara, 1981—; pres. Electrotek Concepts, Inc., 1996—. Author: Handbook of Power Signatures; contbr. articles to profl. jours. Mem. IEEE (sr.). Office: Electrotek Concepts 3250 Jay St Santa Clara CA 95054

MCEACHERN, ALLAN, Canadian justice; b. Vancouver, B.C., Can., May 20, 1926; s. John A. and Blanche L. (Roadhouse) McE.; m. Gloria, July 17, 1953; children: Jean Williams, Joanne Evans. BA, U. B.C., Vancouver, 1949; LLB, U. B.C., 1950. Assoc., sr. ptnr., barrister, solicitor Messrs. Russell & DuMoulin, Vancouver, B.C., 1950-78; chief justice Supreme Ct. B.C., Vancouver, 1979-88, Ct. Appeals B.C., Vancouver, 1988—. Pres. Kats Rugby Club, Vancouver, 1953-64, B.C. Lions Football Club, Vancouver, 1967, 68, 69, We. Football Conf., 1964, Can. Football League, 1967-68, commr. 1967-68. Mem. Can. Bar Assn. (bd. dirs.), Vancouver Bar Assn. (bd. dirs.), Legal Aid Soc. (pres. 1977-78), Law Soc. B.C. (bencher 1971-79). Avocations: sailing, gardening, walking, summer cottage. Home: 1414 W King Edward Ave, Vancouver, BC Canada V6H 2A2 Office: Law Cts, 800 Smithe St, Vancouver, BC Canada V6Z 2E1*

MCEACHERN, SUSAN MARY, database analyst; b. Royal Oak, Mich., May 3, 1960; d. Donald Keith and Lois Jean (Robison) McE.; m. James Paul Corbett, Jan. 8, 1983 (div. 1995). BS, Mich. State U., 1982; MBA, New Mex. State U., 1985. From acct. adminstr. trainee to acct. adminstr. IBM, El Paso, Tex., 1985-89; customer support rep. IBM, Southfield, Mich., 1989-90; sr. adminstrv. specialist IBM, Southfield, 1991-92, adv. customer support rep., 1992-93; fin. analyst IBM, Boulder, Colo., 1993-95, database adminstr., analyst, 1995—; cons. Integrated Sys. Solutions Co., Dallas, 1990-93. Author: Treasury of Poetry, 1992. Vol. supr. Easter Seals, Southfield Mich., El Paso, Tex., 1978-88, Crisis Pregnancy, Las Cruces, New Mex., 1982-86, Multiple Sclerosis, Mich., 1983, Longmont (Colo.) Vol. Assn., 1994. Recipient Photography award Mich. State Fair, 1991, 92. Mem. IBM PC Club, Creative Designs (pres. 1994—, Nat. Sci. and Engring. vol. rep. 1994). Avocations: computers, swimming, white-water rafting, photography. Home: PO Box 6043 Longmont CO 80501-2008

MCEACHRAN, ANGUS, newspaper editor; b. Memphis, Aug. 24, 1939; s. Angus G. and Maxine (Taylor) McE.; m. Ann Blackwell; children: Angus G. III, Amanda Simmons. Student, George Washington U., 1958-59, Memphis State U., 1959-61. Reporter The Comml. Appeal, Memphis, 1960-63, asst. city editor, 1963-65, metro editor, 1965-69, asst. mng. editor, 1969-77; exec. editor Birmingham (Ala.) Post-Herald, 1977-78, editor, 1978-82; exec. editor The Pitts. Press., 1982-83, editor, 1983-92; editor The Commercial Appeal, Memphis, Tenn., 1993-94, editor, pres., 1994—; corr. N.Y. Times, Wall St. Jour., Newsweek, The Nat. Observer. Mem. Am. Soc. Newspaper Editors, Pa. Soc. Newspaper Editors (bd. dirs.), Sigma Delta. Roman Catholic. Avocations: fishing, hiking, reading, racquetball. Home: 872 River Park Dr Memphis TN 38103 Office: Commercial Appeal 495 Union Ave Memphis TN 38103-3242

MCEACHRON, DONALD LYNN, biology educator, researcher; b. Erie, Pa., Nov. 8, 1953; s. Karl Boyer and Marjorie (Blalock) McE.; m. Barbara Anne O'Donnell, Aug. 14, 1987. BA with highest honors, U. Calif., 1977, PhD, 1984. Lab. technician psychiatry VA Med. Ctr., La Jolla, Calif., 1978-82; rsch. technician cell biology U. Tex. Health Sci. Ctr., Dallas, 1983-84; sci. dir. Imaging and Computer Vision Ctr. Drexel U., Phila., 1984-88, vis. asst. prof. dept. biosci., 1986-88, rsch. asst. prof. Biomed. Engring. and Sci. Inst., 1989-92, rsch. assoc. prof., 1992—, acting assoc. dir. Biomed. Engring. and Sci. Inst., 1995—, assoc. dir. Biomed. Engring. and Sci. Inst., 1996—; cons. Hoffman-LaRoche, Nutley, N.J., 1984-86; mem. adv. bd. BioAutomation, Inc., Bridgeport, Pa., 1988—; project dir. NSF Young Scholar's Project/Drexel U., Phila., 1994—; lectr. U. Pa., Phila., 1986-93, adj. asst. prof. dept. psychiatry, 1993—; vis. asst. prof. dept. psychology Haverford (Pa.) Coll., 1987; adj. asst. prof. Thomas Jefferson U., Phila., 1989—. Editor: Functional Mapping in Biology and Medicine, 1986; contbg. editor Diversity in Biomed. Imaging, 1989, Progress in Imaging in the Neurosciences using Microcomputers and Workstations, 1990; mem. editl. bd. Computerized Med. Imaging and Graphics, 1988—, NeuroImage, 1990. 1st lt. USAR, 1993, capt., 1993—. Regent's fellow U. Calif., 1979. Mem. AAAS, Internat. Soc. Chronobiology, N.Y. Acad. Sci., Animal Behavior Soc., Soc. Rsch. on Biol. Rhythms, Internat. Behavioral Neurosci. Soc. (editor newsletter). Republican. Avocations: Am. history, photography. Office: Drexel U Imaging And Computer V Ct Rm. 128 Philadelphia PA 19104

MCELDREW, JAMES JOSEPH, III, lawyer; b. Phila., Sept. 14, 1957; s. James J. and Helen (Haberle) McE.; m. Deborah Anne McCullough, Mar. 23, 1985; children: Caitlin, Theresa Kelly, James, Michael. BS, Georgetown U., 1979; JD, Del. Law Sch., 1982. Bar: Pa., N.Y., U.S. Dist. Ct. (ea. dist.) Pa., U.S. Ct. of Appeals (3rd cir.), U.S. Supreme Ct., U.S. Dist. Ct. (so. dist.) N.Y., U.S. Ct. of Appeals (2d cir.). Assoc. McEldrew, Hanamirian et al, Phila., 1982-88; ptnr. Smith, McEldrew & Levenberg, Phila., 1988-95, McEldrew & Fullam, P.C., N.Y.C., 1996—; legal counsel Transport Worker's Union, Phila., 1983-85, Local 2013, 2001, Phila., 1993—; settlement master Common Ct. of Pleas, Phila., 1994—; dir. Fed. Employers' Liability Act program Transport Workers Union RR Divsn., N.Y.C., 1994—; mem. hearing com. Pa. disciplinary Bd., 1995. Mem. ATLA, Phila. Trial Lawyers (bd. govs. 1995—), Pa. Trial Lawyers, Phila. Bar Assn. (Fee dispute com. 1987—, ecn. com. 1993—, VIP 1988—), Acad. RR and Labor Attys. Roman Catholic. Avocations: tennis, golf, martial arts. Office: McEldrew & Fullam PC 1 Liberty Pl Ste 3170 1650 Market St Philadelphia PA 19103

MCELGUNN, JAMES DOUGLAS, agriculturist, researcher; b. Vancouver, B.C., Can., Mar. 22, 1939; s. Douglas McElgunn and Margret (Gogan) Lastuka; m. Doris Roseann Johnson; children: Kim, Greg, Colleen. BS, Mont. State U., 1962, MS, 1964; PhD, Mich. State U., 1967. Rsch. scientist Rsch. Sta. Agr. Can., Swift Current, Sask., 1967-80; dir. Rsch. Sta. Agr. Can., Kamloops, B.C., 1980-85, Beaverlodge, Alta., 1985—. Chmn. Saskatoon Mountain Econ. Devel. Authority, Beaverlodge, 1987-89, Amisk Ct., Beaverlodge, 1989—. Home: Box 1204, Beaverlodge, AB Canada T0H 0C0 Office: Agr Can Rsch Sta, Box 29, Beaverlodge, AB Canada T0H 0C0

MC ELHANEY, JAMES WILSON, lawyer, educator; b. N.Y.C., Dec. 10, 1937; s. Lewis Keck and Sara Jane (Hess) McE.; m. Maxine Dennis Jones, Aug. 17, 1961; children: David, Benjamin. AB, Duke U., 1960; LLB, 1962. Bar: Wis. 1962. Assoc. Wickham, Borgelt, Skogstad & Powell, 1966; asst. prof. U. Md. Law Sch., 1966-69, assoc. prof., 1969-72; vis. prof. So. Meth. U. Sch. of Law, Dallas, 1973-74; prof. So. Meth. U. Sch. of Law, 1974-76; Joseph C. Hostetler prof. trial practice and advocacy Case Western Res. U. Sch. of Law, Cleve., 1976—; mem. faculty Nat. Inst. Trial Advocacy, Boulder, Colo., 1975—; vis. prof. U. Tulsa Coll. Law, summer 1977, 79, Ind. U. Law Sch., summer 1980; cons. to U.S. Atty. Gen. on Justice Dept. Advocacy Tng. Programs, 1979—; lectr. in field. Author: Effective Litigation: Trials, Problems and Materials, 1974, Trial Notebook, 1981, 3rd edit., 1994, Trial Notebook on Tape: The Basics, 1989, Mc Elhaney's Trial Notebook on Tape: Advanced Techniques, 1991, Mc Elhaney's Trial Notebook on Tape: Evidence, Foundations and Objections, 1992, Mc Elhaney's Trial Notebook on Tape: Winning Tactics, 1994, Mc Elhaney's Litigation, 1995; editor-in-chief Litigation mag., 1984-86, sr. editor, 1986—; contbr. columns to Trial Notebook, Litigation, articles to profl. jours. Mem. ABA (mem. coun. on litigation 1987—, author jour. column Litigation), Assn. Am. Law Schs. (chmn. sect. on trial advocacy 1974-76, chmn. sect. on evidence 1978). Office: Case Western Res U 11075 East Blvd Cleveland OH 44106-5409 *The lamp of doctrine is a flickering and unsteady guide; we are led more by facts than obtuse theory.*

MC ELHANEY, JOHN HESS, lawyer; b. Milw., Apr. 16, 1934; s. Lewis Keck and Sara Jane (Hess) McE.; m. Jacquelyn Masur, Aug. 4, 1962; children—Scott, Victoria. B.B.A., So. Meth. U., 1956, J.D., 1958. Bar: Tex. bar 1958. Pvt. practice law Dallas, 1958—; shareholder Locke Purnell Rain Harrell, 1976—; lectr. law So. Meth. U., 1967-76. Contbr. articles to legal jours. Trustee St. Mark's Sch. Tex., 1980-86. Fellow Am. Coll. Trial Lawyers; mem. Am. Bd. Trial Advs., ABA, Tex. Bar Assn., So. Meth. U. Law Alumni Assn. (pres. 1972-73, dir. 1970-73), Town and Gown Club (pres. 1981-82). Presbyterian. Home: 5340 Tanbark Dr Dallas TX 75229-5555 Office: Locke Purnell Rain Harrell 2200 Ross Ave Ste 2200 Dallas TX 75201-6766

MCELHINNEY, JAMES LANCEL, artist, educator; b. Abington, Pa., Feb. 3, 1952; s. James and Joan Howland (Carpenter) McE.; m. Victoria Maria Dávila, Sept. 12, 1981 (div.). Scholarship student, Skowhegan (Maine) Sch. of Art, 1973; BFA, Temple U., 1974; MFA, Yale U., 1976. Asst. prof. Moore Coll. of Art, Phila., 1977-78, Skidmore Coll., Saratoga Springs, N.Y., 1979-87; adj. instr. UCLA, L.A., 1983, Moore Coll. of Art, Phila., 1983, Tyler Sch. of Art, Phila., 1983-86, Univ. of the Arts, Phila., 1985-89; instr. Milw. Inst. of Art and Design, 1991-93; vis. artist E. Carolina U., Greenville, N.C., 1994—. Artist: (paintings) solo exhbns. include: Peninsula Ctr. for the Fine Arts, Newport News, Va., 1993, Danville (Va.) Mus., 1993, Second Street Gallery, Charlottesville, Va., 1995, F.A.N. Gallery, Phila., 1995, Greenville (N.C.) Mus. Art, 1996. Vol. Richmond (Va.) Nat. Battlefield Park, 1991—. Grantee: (painting) NEA, Washington, 1987-88, Ptnrs. in the Arts, Richmond Arts Coun., 1995. Mem. Coll. Art Assn. Home: 109 A N West Ave Ayden NC 28513

MCELHINNEY, SUSAN KAY (KATE MCELHINNEY), legal assistant; b. Greeley, Colo., May 20, 1947; d. Glenn Eugene and Maxine (Filkins) McE. Student, U. N.C., 1965-67, U. Kans., 1969, U. Colo., 1971-72, 80. Adminstrv. sec. Colo. Pub. Defender, Denver, 1970-74; clk. Colo. Dist. Ct., Boulder, 1974-80; legal asst., office mgr. Law Office Ben Echeverria, San Marcos, Calif., 1986—. Mem. black tie fund raising com. Palomar Community Coll., 1991-92. Democrat. Avocations: reading, golf, travel, classic autos, raising Min Pins. Office: Law Offices Ben Echeverria 1350 Grand Ave Ste 200 San Marcos CA 92069-2461

MCELHINNY, HAROLD JOHN, lawyer; b. San Francisco, Jan. 5, 1947; s. Harold James and Margaret I. (Mahoney) McE.; m. Mary Ellen McElhinny, June 22, 1968; children: Hannah, Jennifer, William. BA in Polit. Sci., U. Santa Clara, 1970; JD, U. Calif., Berkeley, 1975. Bar: Calif. 1976, U.S. Supreme Ct. 1983. Vol. Peace Corps., Tripoli, Libya, 1968-69; juvenile counselor Santa Clara County (Calif.) Juvenile Hall, 1969-72; law clk. U.S. Dist. Ct., Hartford, Conn., 1975-76; ptnr. Morrison & Foerster, San Francisco, 1976—. Mem. ABA, Calif. State Bar Assn., State Bar Calif. (rev. dept. 1986-89, chair 1988), San Francisco Bar Assn., Am. Intellectual Property Law Assn., Assn. Bus. Trial Lawyers (bd. govs. 1992—). Democrat. Roman Catholic. Office: Morrison & Foerster 345 California St San Francisco CA 94104-2635

MCELHINNY, WILSON DUNBAR, banker; b. Detroit, July 27, 1929; s. William Dunbar and Elizabeth (Wilson) McE.; m. Barbara Cheney Watkins, June 6, 1952 (dec.); children: David Ashton, Ward Cheney, Edward Wilson, William Dunbar; m. Lisa Lesher, Mar., 1993. BA, Yale U., 1953. With Union and New Haven Trust Co., 1952-63; with Reading Trust Co., Pa., 1963-68, pres., 1968-70; pres. Nat. Central Bank (formerly Reading Trust Co.), Pa., 1970-79, chief exec. officer, 1975-79; chmn. bd. dirs., pres., chief exec. officer Hamilton Bank (formerly Nat. Central Bank), Lancaster, Pa., 1979-81, chmn. bd. dirs., chief exec. officer, 1981-83, chmn. bd. dirs., 1981-90; pres. CoreStates Fin. Corp., Phila., 1983-86, vice chmn., 1986-90; pres., chmn. Hamilton Bank, Lancaster, Pa., 1988-90, also dir.; bd. dirs. Hunt Mfg. Co., Phila., Educators Mut. Life Ins. Co., Reading Eagle Co., Wohlsen Constrn. Co.; chmn. bd. Irex Corp. Bd. dirs. Lancaster Gen. Hosp. Found. Mem. Pa. C. of C. (chmn. 1990-92), Hamilton Club (Lancaster), Lancaster Country Club. Home and Office: 198 Pinetown Rd Leola PA 17540-9736

MCELLIGOTT, JAMES PATRICK, JR., lawyer; b. Chgo., Jan. 11, 1948; s. James Patrick and Helen Cecelia (Hogan) McE.; children: Michael Sean, Andrew David; m. Trina Reff, Aug. 25, 1985. BA, U. Ill., Urbana, 1970; JD, Harvard U., 1973. Bar: Va. 1974, U.S. Dist. Ct. (ea. and we. dists.) Va. 1974, U.S. Ct. Appeals (4th cir.) 1974, U.S. Supreme Ct. 1979. Research asst. U. Ill., 1970; assoc. McGuire, Woods & Battle, Richmond, 1973-79; ptnr. McGuire, Woods, Battle & Boothe, Richmond, 1979—. Mem. exec. com. Va. Home for Boys, Richmond, 1976—, pres. bd. govs., 1981-83; mem. Leadership Metro Richmond-Met. C. of C., 1984-85; bd. dirs. ARC Greater Richmond Chpt., 1990—, chmn., 1994—. Mem. ABA, Va. Bar Assn. (exec. com., chmn. pub. rels. com. 1978-82, producer pub. svc. message 1973, Hot Spot award 1973), Richmond Bar Assn., Fed. Bar Assn. (pres. Richmond chpt. 1986), Nat. Sch. Bds. Assn., Coun. of Sch. Attys., Phi Beta Kappa, Phi Kappa Phi, Omicron Delta Epsilon. Home: 203 Cyril Ln Richmond VA 23229-7740 Office: McGuire Woods Battle & Boothe One James Ctr Richmond VA 23219-3229

MC ELRATH, RICHARD ELSWORTH, retired insurance company executive; b. Thompsontown, Pa., Oct. 11, 1932; s. Clayton Ellsworth and Jane Elizabeth (Shoop) McE.; m. Donna Gail Booher, Aug. 18, 1952; children—Leslie Jo, Jennifer Jo, Josie Arlene Elizabeth, Rebekah Clare. B.S. cum laude, Elizabethtown (Pa.) Coll., 1955; M.B.A. cum laude, Harvard U., 1961. Research asst. Harvard U., 1961-62; asst. to pres. Callaway Mills Co., LaGrange, Ga., 1963-65; with Irving Trust Co., N.Y.C., 1965-73; v.p. Irving Trust Co., 1969-73; treas. Tchrs. Ins. Annuity Assn. and Coll. Retirement Equities Fund, 1973-81; v.p. Met. Life Ins. Co., 1982-95; pres., dir. MetLife Funding, Inc., MetLife Credit, Inc., 1984-95. Author articles, case studies. Trustee Elizabethtown Coll.; mem. Society Valley Hosp., Ridgewood, N.J.; mem. Boston Rep. Com., 1961-63, Troup County (Ga.) Rep. Com., 1964-65; bd. dirs. Family Counseling Svc., Ridgewood, 1986-92. Lt. comdr. USNR, 1956-59. Mem. Assn. Gov. Bds. Univs. and Colls. Methodist. Club: Harvard (N.Y.C.). Home: 17 Cedar St Glen Rock NJ 07452-1608

MCELROY, CHARLOTTE ANN, principal; b. Dimmitt, Tex., Oct. 24, 1939; d. William Robert and Mary Ilene (Cooper) McE. BA, West Tex. State U., 1962, MEd, 1964; postgrad., Calif. State U., Santa Barbara, 1966-68. Tchr. Amarillo (Tex.) Schs., 1962-65; 1st and 2d grade tchr. Ventura (Calif.) Schs., 1965-66, 4th, 5th and 6th grade tchr., 1966-74, elem. counselor, 1974-76, spl. edn. tchr., 1976-77, counselor, phys. edn. tchr., 1977-78; asst. prin. Cabrillo Jr. High Sch., Ventura Unified Schs., 1978-80; prin. E. P. Foster Elem. Sch., Ventura Unified Schs., 1980-84, Anacapa Middle Sch., Ventura Unified Schs., 1984—; presenter in field. Recipient Nat. Blue Ribbon Sch. award Nat. Edn. Dept., 1990-91, Calif. Disting. Sch. award, 1989-90; named one of Outstanding Principals, State Calif., 1992-93. Mem. Ventura Adminstrs. Assn., Calif. League Middle Schs., Assn. Calif. Sch. Adminstrs., Kappa Kappa Gamma. Democrat. Avocations: skiing, reading, music, gardening. Home: 2250 Los Encinos Rd Ojai CA 93023-9709 Office: Anacapa Middle Sch 100 S Mills Rd Ventura CA 93003-3434

MCELROY, EDMUND G., JR., financial executive; b. N.Y.C., June 26, 1941; s. Edmund G. and Elizabeth (Arnold) McE; m. Marcy Leanne Ham, June 13, 1964; children: Scott E., Elizabeth M., Todd C., Peter J. BA in Econs., Lafayette Coll., 1964; MBA, NYU, 1971. Asst. v.p. Irving Trust Co., N.Y., 1964-71; dir. cash and banking Avon Products, Inc., N.Y.C., 1971-81; asst. treas. Nabisco Brands, East Hanover, N.J., 1981-85; treas. Dyson-Kissner-Moran Corp., N.Y.C., 1985-93; asst. treas. and dir. of corp. treasury Gateway 2000, Inc., North Sioux City, S.D., 1994—. Councilman Borough of Ho-ho-kus, N.J., 1984-94; active Bergen County United Way, Paramus, N.J., 1983-86. Mem. Internat. Fin. Group, N.Y. Treas. Group, Nat. Assn. Corp. Treas., Midwest Treasury Mgmt. Assn. Republican. Episcopalian. Avocations: skiing, running, tennis, hiking. Office: Gateway 2000 Inc 610 Gateway Dr North Sioux City SD 57049

MCELROY, EDWARD J., union officer; b. Providence, Mar. 17, 1941; s. Edward J. Sr. and Clara (Angelone) McE.; m. Edwina Barbara Ricci, Apr. 20, 1963; children: Kathleen, Mary, Stephen, Elizabeth. AB, Providence Coll., 1962. Cert. tchr. Tchr. Lockwood Jr. High Sch., Warwick, R.I., 1962-72; pres. Warwick Tchrs. Union, Warwick, R.I., 1967-69, R.I. Fed. Tchrs., Am. Fed. Tchrs., Providence, 1971-92; v.p. Am. Fed. Tchrs., AFLCIO, Providence, 1974-92; sec. treas. Am. Fed. Tchrs., AFLCIO, Washington, 1992—; pres. R.I. AFLCIO, Providence, 1977-92. Exec. com. mem. R.I. Democratic State Com., Providence, 1976-92; sec. exec. com. United Way So. New England, Providence, 1978-92; devel. commn. R.I. State, 1984-85, mem. Workforce 2000, 1987-92. Recipient Quirk Inst. award Providence Coll., 1980. Mem. Aurora Civic Assn. Democrat. Roman Catholic. Avocations: golf, photography, reading. Office: Am. Fed Tchrs AFL CIO 555 New Jersey Ave NW Washington DC 20001-2029

MCELROY, FRANCES MARION (ZELENT), occupational health nurse practitioner; b. Ashuelot, N.H., Nov. 8, 1926; d. Gotfread and Helen (Sucharzewska) Zelent; m. David L. McElroy, Nov. 25, 1950. RN, St. Michael's (Hosp.) Med. Ctr., 1948; cert. occupational health, 1973; occupational nurse pratitioner, Boston U., 1977. Oper. rm. supr., 1948-57; founder, adminstr. occupl. health program Dept. Army Military & Civilians, Ft. Devens, Mass., 1974; researcher diabetes testing devel. ASA Rule Inc., Waltham, Mass., 1990—. Dir. Rep. City Com., Newton, Mass.; bd. dirs. Am. Cancer Soc., vol. Shrine Burn Ctr., Boston; Women of Old North Ch., Boston. Avocations: golfing, crafts, gardening, mushroom foreys, skiing, horseback riding. Home: 124 Rowe St Auburndale MA 02166-1528

MCELROY, FREDERICK WILLIAM, economics educator, consultant; b. Dublin, Ireland, May 18, 1939; came to U.S., 1963; s. Herbert John and Annie Maureen (McDowell) McE.; m. Kathleen Child, Sept. 8, 1964; children: Dominique, Hugh. BA, Nat. U. of Ireland, Dublin, 1960; MA, U. Coll. Dublin, 1961; PhD, Georgetown U., 1967. Asst. prof. econs. SUNY, Buffalo, 1967-68; asst. prof. econs. Georgetown U., Washington, 1968-71, assoc. prof. econs., 1971-77, prof. econs., 1977—, chair econs. dept., 1994—; cons. in antitrust cases. Contbr. articles to profl. jours. Trustee, treas. Help the Aged, Washington, 1982-86; bd. dirs. Oxfam-Am., Boston, 1976-79. Mem. Am. Econs. Assn., Phi Beta Kappa, Alpha Sigma Nu. Democrat. Roman Catholic. Avocations: tennis, golf. Home: 5013 Brookdale Rd Bethesda MD 20816-1709 Office: Georgetown U Dept Econs Washington DC 20057

MC ELROY, JOHN HARLEY, electrical engineering educator; b. Marion, Ohio, June 27, 1936; s. Francis and Alice Marie McElroy; m. Eleonore Hildegard Schmidt, Mar. 18, 1957. B.S. in Elec. Engring, U. Tex., Austin, 1966; M.E.E., Cath. U. Am., 1973, Ph.D., 1978. Instr. guided missles Air Defense Sch. U.S. Army, 1957-63; rsch. asst. Quantum Electronics rsch. Lab U. Texas, Austin, 1963-66; staff Goddard Flight Center, Greenbelt, Md., 1966-79, 80-82; chief communications tech. div. Goddard Flight Center, 1978-79, dep. dir. center, 1980-82; dir. communications programs NASA Hdqrs., Washington, 1979-80; asst. adminstr. NOAA, Washington, 1982-85; dir. spl. projects Hughes Aircraft Co., Los Angeles, 1985-86; v.p. tech. Hughes Communications, Inc., 1986-87; dean Coll. Engring., prof. elec. engring. U. Tex., Arlington, 1987-96, vice provost for rsch. and grad. studies, 1996—; cons. satellite communications and earth observations. Contbr. articles to profl. jours. Served with AUS, 1954-63. Recipient Apollo Achievement award NASA, 1969, Applications Tech. Satellite award, 1975, Earth Resources Satellite award, 1973; named Wernher von Braun Meml. Lectr. Smithsonian Instn. Fellow AIAA, Washington Acad. Scis., IEEE. Home: PO Box 1122 Arlington TX 76004-1122 Office: U Tex Arlington PO Box 19019 Arlington TX 76019

MCELROY, JOHN LEE, JR., brokerage house executive; b. Richmond, Va., Feb. 28, 1931; s. John Lee and Margaret (Williams) McE.; m. Aminta Sorrel Mackall, Oct. 12, 1957; children: John Lee III, Mary Earle McElroy Robertson, Sorrel M., Margaret W. B, U. Va., 1953, postgrad., 1964. Securities analyst State Planters Bank, Richmond, 1955-58; stockbroker Wheat, 1st Securities, Inc., Richmond, 1958-63, mgr., ptnr., 1963-86, chmn., chief exec. officer, 1986—, also bd. dirs.; vice chmn., chief exec. officer WFS Fin. Corp., 1986—, also bd. dirs.; bd. dirs. Piper, Jaffray & Hopwood, Mpls. Pres. Va. Hist. Soc., Richmond, Children's Home Soc., Richmond; bd. dirs. Cen. Richmond Assn., Ch. Schs. of Diocese Va., St. Catherine's Sch., St. Timothy's Sch., Vestry St. Paul's Ch.; trustee St. Paul's Episcopal Ch. Home. Lt. (j.g.) USCG, 1953-55. Republican. Episcopalian. Avocations: golf, sailing, hunting. Home: 13 River Rd Richmond VA 23226-3310 Office: Wheat First Securities Inc 707 E Main St Richmond VA 23219-2814*

MCELROY, LEO FRANCIS, communications consultant, journalist; b. Los Angeles, Oct. 12, 1932; s. Leo Francis and Helen Evelyn (Silliman) McE.; m. Dorothy Frances Montgomery, Nov. 3, 1956 (div. 1981); children: James, Maureen, Michael, Kathleen; m. Judith Marie Lewis, May 30, 1992. BS in English, Loyola U., L.A. 1953. News dir. KFI, KRLA, KABC Radio, L.A., 1964-72; pub. affairs host Sta. KCET, Pub. TV, L.A., 1967-74; v.p. Sta. KROQ AM/FM, L.A., 1972-74; polit. editor Sta. KABC-TV, L.A., 1974-81; pres. McElroy Communications, L.A. and Sacramento, 1981—; pres. sec. Lt. Gov.'s Office, Sacramento, 1983-84; chmn. Calif. AP Broadcasters, 1972-74; cons. State Office Migrant Edn., Sacramento, 1974, Californians for Water, L.A. , 1982, Calif. Water Protection Coun., Sacramento, 1982, Planning and Conservation League, Sacramento, 1984—, Common Cause, Sacramento, 1988—. Author: Uneasy Partners, 1984; author plays: Mermaid Tavern, 1956, To Bury Caesar (Christopher award 1952), 1952, Rocket to Olympus, 1960, The Code of Whiskey King, 1995. State del. Western Am. Assembly on Prison Reform, Berkeley, Calif., 1973; chmn. State Disaster Info. Task Force; Calif., 1973-74; campaign media cons. statewide issues, various candidates, Sacramento, L.A., 1981—; bd. dirs. Vols. in Victim Assistance, Sacramento, 1984, Rescue Alliance, Sacramento, 1987—, Mental Health Assn., Sacramento, 1985-89, Leukemia Soc., 1992—. Recipient Gabriel award Cath. Archdiocese, L.A., 1972, Golden Mike award Radio-TV News Assn., L.A., 1973; Hon. Resolution, Calif. State Assembly, Sacramento, 1981. Mem. ASCAP, AFTRA, Screen Actors Guild, Am. Assn. Polit. Cons. Mem. Reform Party. Roman Catholic. Home: 8217 Oakenshaw Way Orangevale CA 95662-2953 Office: McElroy Comm 2410 K St Ste C Sacramento CA 95816-5002 *No gift is greater than the gift of oneself - honestly given, honestly received.*

MCELROY, SISTER MAUREEN, secondary school principal. Prin. St. Mary Acad.-Bay View, Riverside, R.I. Recipient Blue Ribbon Sch. award U.S. Dept. Edn., 1990-91. Office: St Mary Acad-Bay View 3070 Pawtucket Ave Riverside RI 02915-5105

MCELROY, MICHAEL, physicist, researcher, educator; b. Shercock, County Cavan, Ireland, May 18, 1939; married, 1963. B.A., Queen's U., Belfast, Ireland, 1960; Ph.D. in Math., Belfast, Ireland, 1962. Project assoc. Theoretical Chemistry Inst., U. Wis., 1962-63; from asst. physicist to physicist Kitt Peak Nat. Obs., 1963-71; physicist Ctr. Earth and Planetary Physics Harvard U., Cambridge, Mass., 1971—, now Abbott Lawrence Rotch prof. atmospheric sci.; chmn. Dept. Earth and Planetary Scis. Harvard U., 1986—; mem. Mars panel Lunar and Planetary Missions Bd., NASA, 1968-69, Stratospheric Research Adv. Com., Space and Terrestrial Applied Adv. Com., Com. Atmospheric Sci., Nat. Acad. Sci. Space Sci. Bd.; chmn. Com. Planetary and Lunar Exploration. Recipient James B. Macelwane award Am. Geophys. Union, 1968; recipient Newcomb Cleve. prize AAAS, 1977, Pub. Service medal NASA, 1978. Fellow AAAS, Am. Geophys. Union, Internat. Acad. Aeronautics and Astronautics, Am. Acad. Arts and Scis. Office: Harvard U Dept Earth and Planetary scis 20 Oxford St Cambridge MA 02138-2902

MC ELROY, WILLIAM DAVID, biochemist, educator; b. Rogers, Tex., Jan. 22, 1917; s. William D. and Ora (Shipley) McE.; m. Nella Winch, Dec. 23, 1940 (div.); children—Mary Elizabeth, Ann Reed, Thomas Shipley, William David; m. Marlene A. DeLuca, Aug. 28, 1967; 1 son, Eric Gene. B.A., Stanford, 1939; M.A., Reed Coll., 1941; Ph.D., Princeton U., 1943; D.Sc., U. Buffalo, 1962, Mich. State U., 1970, Loyola U., Chgo., 1970, U. Notre Dame, 1975, Calif. Sch. Profl. Psychology, 1978; D.Pub. Service, Providence Coll., 1970; LL.D., U. Pitts., 1971, Johns Hopkins U., 1977. War research, cons. med. research OSRD, Princeton, 1942-45; NRC fellow Stanford, 1945-46; instr. biology dept. Johns Hopkins, 1946, successively asst. and asso. prof., prof. biology, 1951-69, chmn. biology dept., 1956-69; also dir. McCollum-Pratt Inst., 1949-64; dir. NSF, Washington, 1969-71; chancellor U. Calif., San Diego, 1972-80, prof., from 1980, now prof. emeritus. Author textbook.; Editor: (with Bentley Glass) Copper Metabolism, 1950, Phosphorus Metabolism, 2 vols, 1951, 52, Mechanism of Enzyme Action, 1954, Amino Acid Metabolism, 1955, The Chemical Basis of Heredity, 1957, The Chemical Basis of Development, 1959, Light and Life, 1961, Cellular Physiology and Biochemistry, 1961, (with C.P. Swanson) Foundations of Modern Biology series, 1961-64. Mem. Sch. Bd. Baltimore City, 1958-68. Recipient Barnett Cohen award in bacteriology, 1958; Rumford prize Am. Acad. Arts and Scis., 1964. Mem. AAAS (pres. 1976, chmn. 1977), Am. Inst. Biol. Scis. (pres. 1968), Am. Chem. Soc., Nat. Acad. Sci., Am. Soc. Biol. Chemists (pres. 1963-64), Soc. Gen. Physiology (pres. 1960-61), Soc. Naturalists, Soc. Zoologists, Am. Acad. Arts and Scis., Am. Soc. Bacteriologists, Am. Philos. Soc.,Sigma Xi, Kappa Sigma. Office: Univ Calif San Diego Dept Biology La Jolla CA 92093

MC ELROY, WILLIAM THEODORE, lawyer; b. Newark, Jan. 20, 1925; s. William J. and Matilda (Hamilton) McE.; m. Emilie Hoinowski, Jan. 18, 1947; children: Karen L., William J., Ruth P. LL.B. cum laude, Rutgers U., 1950. Bar: N.J. 1949, U.S. Dist. Ct. (fed. dist.) N.J. 1950, U.S. Dist. Ct. (ea. and so. dists.) N.Y. 1986. Assoc. Duggan, Shaw & Hughes, Newark, 1949-50; with McElroy, Connell, Foley & Geiser (and predecessor firms), Newark, 1950-78; ptnr. McElroy, Connell, Foley & Geiser (and predecessor firms), 1956-78; judge Superior Ct. N.J., Morristown, 1978-80; Appellate Div. Superior Ct. N.J., 1980-85; presiding judge part H, 1984-85; ptnr. McElroy, Deutsch & Mulvaney, Morristown, N.J., 1985—. Served with USNR, 1942-45. Fellow Am. Coll. Trial Lawyers; mem. ABA, N.J. Bar Assn. (chmn. civil procedure sect. 1973-74), Essex County Bar Assn., Morris County Bar Assn., Trial Attys. N.J. (Disting. Svc. in cause of justice award 1986).d. Home: 80 Old Farm Rd Basking Ridge NJ 07920-3309 Office: 1300 Mt Kemble Ave PO Box 2075 Morristown NJ 07960

MCELVAIN, DAVID PLOWMAN, retired manufacturing company financial executive; b. Chgo., Oct. 16, 1937; s. Carl R. and Ruth P. (Plowman) McE.; B.B.A., U. Ariz., 1961, M.B.A., 1962; m. Mary Rosalind Hysong, Dec. 20, 1961; children—Jana, Jodi. Consolidation accountant, exec. div. Dresser Industries, Inc., Dallas, 1962-67, corporate fin. controller, 1973-76, dir. fin. services, 1976-78, staff v.p. fin. service and risk mgmt., 1978-82, exec. v.p. fin. services group, 1982-83, pres. fin. services group, 1984-86, v.p. fin., chief fin. officer, 1987-1993; controller crane, hoist & tower div., Muskegon, Mich., 1967-73. Cert. mgmt. acct. Mem. Nat. Assn. Accts., Beta Gamma Sigma, Phi Delta Theta. Episcopalian. Home: 3806 Beverly Dr Dallas TX 75205-2808

MCELVEEN, JOSEPH JAMES, JR., author, journalist, public broadcasting executive; b. Sanford, Fla., Feb. 23, 1939; s. Joseph James Sr. and Genevieve (Stoll) McE.; m. Mary Louise Young, Aug. 18, 1979; 1 child, Ryan Leighton. BA, Furman U., 1961; MA, U. S.C., 1968. Editor, pub. West Ashley News, Charleston, S.C., 1951-57; reporter, photographer Charleston Post, 1955-57; tchr. English and journalism St. Andrew's Parish High Sch., Charleston, 1961-65; dir. info., prof. journalism Columbia Coll., S.C., 1965-68; prof. journalism U. S.C., Columbia, 1968-79; staff pub. affairs FCC, Washington, 1979-81; dir. pub. affairs adminstrn. Nat. Cable TV Assn., Washington, 1981-87; dir. internal communications Corp. for Pub. Broadcasting, Washington, 1987-92, dir. program adminstrn., 1992—; ombudsman, columnist Alexandria (Va.) Gazette, 1981-88. Author: Introduction to Creative Writing, 1963, Modern Communications, 1964; contbr. chpt. to International Biography (Mencken), 1986. Mem. Orgn. of News Ombudsmen, Soc. Profl. Journalists, Mencken Soc. Democrat. Episcopalian. Avocations: photography, reading, desktop pub. Office: Corp for Pub Broadcasting 901 E St NW Washington DC 20004-2037

MCELVEEN, JUNIUS CARLISLE, JR., lawyer; b. Rogersville, Tenn., Feb. 17, 1947; s. Junius Carlisle and Martha Kathleen (Harrison) McE.; m. Mary Wallace Pyles, Sept. 22, 1973; children: Kathryn Carlisle, Sarah Elizabeth. BA cum laude, U. Va., 1969, JD, 1972. Bar: Va. 1972, Calif. 1975, U.S. Dist. Ct. (ea. dist.) Va. 1976, D.C. 1978, U.S. Ct. Appeals (4th cir.) 1978, U.S. Ct. Appeals (Fed. cir.) 1986, U.S. Ct. Appeals (11th cir.) 1990. Rsch. assoc. Atlantic Richfield, Washington, 1972; assoc. Pender & Coward, Norfolk, Va., 1976-77; assoc. Seyfarth, Shaw, Washington, 1977-80, ptnr., 1981-83, Jones, Day, Reavis & Pogue, Washington, 1983—; mem. adv. com., reproductive hazards in the workplace Office of Tech. Assessment, Washington, 1984-86; mem. adv. council Ctr. Environ. Health, U. Conn., 1986—; mem. editorial bd. The Occupational and Environ. Medicine Report, 1986—; contbr. articles to legal jours. Elder Kirkwood Presbyn. Ch., Springfield, Va., 1984-86. Served as lt. USN, 1972-75. Mem. ABA, Va. State Bar, State Bar Calif., Phi Beta Kappa, Phi Delta Phi (sec. local chpt. 1971-72, Outstanding Grad. award 1972). Home: 10113 Homar Pond Dr Fairfax VA 22039-1650 Office: Jones Day Reavis & Pogue 1450 G St NW Ste 600 Washington DC 20005-2001

MCELVEEN, WILLIAM HENRY, minister; b. Winston-Salem, N.C., June 7, 1932; s. Adam Ezra and Selma Anita (Adams) McE.; m. Carol Lee Sloan, Aug. 28, 1955; children: Miriam Lee Story, Gregory William, David William. BA, Davidson Coll., 1954; MDiv, Moravian Theol. Sem., 1958, DD (hon.), 1994; MA, Wake Forest U., 1971. Assoc. pastor Home Moravian Ch., Winston-Salem, N.C., 1958-61; pastor Messiah Moravian Ch., Winston-Salem, 1961-70; exec. dir. Bd. Christian Edn. So. Province Moravian Ch. in Am., Winston-Salem, 1970-80, v.p., asst. to pres., 1993—; founding pastor Unity Moravian Ch., Lewisville, N.C., 1980-93. Contbr. articles to profl. jours. Chair Model Cities Com., Winston-Salem, 1970s. Democrat. Avocations: carpentry, electrical wiring, gardening, walking, bicycling. Office: Moravian Church in Am Drawer O, Salem Sta Winston Salem NC 27108

MCELVEEN, WILLIAM LINDSAY, broadcasting executive, lecturer; b. Columbia, S.C., Sept. 20, 1950; s. Henry Moody and Dorothy Butler (Sligh) McE.; m. Laurie Wells Boyle, Sept. 8, 1969 (div. 1976); 1 child, Earle Sligh; m. Catharine Elizabeth McCaslin, Aug. 13, 1992; 1 child, Kerry Elizabeth McCaslin. BA in English, Univ. of South, 1972. Acct. exec. Sta. WNOK-FM, Columbia, S.C., 1972-73; mng. dir. Sta. WNOK-FM, Columbia, 1973-79; v.p., gen. mgr. Stas. WNOK-AM-FM, Columbia, 1979-84; pres. Audubon Broadcasting Co., Columbia, 1984-89, Radio South Carolina, Columbia, 1989—; lectr. Internat. Media Fund, Washington, 1993—. Chmn. bd. dirs. Columbia Urban League, 1983-85; bd. dirs. Crimestoppers of Midlands, 1984-88, S.C. Law Inst., Columbia, 1985-88, Helpline of Midlands, 1986-90; gen. campaign chair United Negro Coll. Fund, Columbia, 1985-86; mem. exec. com. United Way of Midlands, Columbia, 1987-88. Mem. Nat. Assn. Broadcasters (bd. dirs. 1988-92, 96—), S.C. Broadcasters Assn. (exec. com., bd. dirs. 1980-87, pres. 1988-92, Hall of Fame inductee 1996), Columbia Advt. Fedn. (pres. 1980-81), Media Club of Columbia (bd. dirs., pres. 1983-84). Presbyterian. Avocations: golf, tennis, travelling. Home: 263 Tombee Ln Columbia SC 29209-0804 Office: Radio SC 1801 Charleston Hwy Cayce SC 29033-2019

MCELVEIN, THOMAS I., JR., lawyer; b. Buffalo, Apr. 19, 1936; s. Thomas I. and Edith Marian (Bowen) McE.; m. Ernesta F. McElvein, June 26, 1965; children—Christopher, Andrew, Kathryn. B.A., Antioch Coll., 1959; J.D., Yale U., 1962. Bar: N.Y. 1962, U.S. Dist. Ct. (we. dist.) N.Y. 1969. atty. Village Akron (N.Y.); dir. Pollack Printing Corp.; trustee, mgr., Yager Found. Mem. N.Y. State Bar Assn., Erie County Bar Assn. Home: 295 Nottingham Ter Buffalo NY 14216-3125 Office: 1500 Liberty Building Bldg Buffalo NY 14202-3612

MCELWAIN, FRANKLIN ROY, educational administrator; b. Caribou, Maine, Oct. 22, 1954; s. Ralph Bearce and Adrina (Roy) McE.; m. Joan Aucoin, June 17, 1978; children: Diana, Lauren, Spencer. BS in Agrl. Mechanization, U. Maine, 1977, MPA, 1988. Farmer Red Wagon Farms, Caribou, 1973-75; tchr. Cen. Aroostook High Sch., Mars Hill, Maine, 1977-85; rsch. asst. U. Maine Agrl. Experiment Sta., Presque Isle, summers 1982-85; tchr. Limestone (Maine) Jr./Sr. High Sch., 1985-93; asst. prin. Caribou (Maine) High Sch., 1993—; advisor Future Farmers Am., Limestone High Sch., 1985—; assoc. supr. Cen. Aroostook Soil and Water, Presque Isle, 1990—; text reviewer Delmar Pubs., Albany, N.Y., 1990-92; academic team leader Limestone High Sch., 1991-92. Sec. Caribou PTA, 1982; mem. Caribou Bd. of Edn. review com., 1991-92; mem. Parish Coun., Caribou, 1988-90; advisor Cath. Youth Orgn., Caribou, 1979-81. Named Maine Tchr. Yr., 1992, Agriscience Tchr. Yr., 1986; recipient Excellence in Edn. award U. Maine, 1992. Mem. Nat. Tchrs. Assn., Nat. Vocat. Agr. Tchrs. Assn., Maine Assn. Agr. Tchrs., Maine Resource Bank, Maine Edn. Talent Pool, Limestone Future Farmers Am. Alumni Assn. (sec. 1986—), Maine Dirigo Found., Maine Plant Food Ednl. Soc. Republican. Roman Catholic. Avocations: running, basketball, cross-country skiing, woodworking. Home: Sweden Rd Box 551 Caribou ME 04736

MC ELWAIN, JOSEPH ARTHUR, retired power company executive; b. Deer Lodge, Mont., Nov. 13, 1919; s. Lee Chaffee and Johanna (Petersen) McE.; m. Mary Cleaver Witt, Mar. 8, 1945 (dec. June 1992); children—Lee William and Lori Louise (twins). B.A., U. Mont., 1943, LL.B., 1947. Bar: Mont. 1947. Individual practice law Deer Lodge, 1947-63; Washington legis. counsel Mont. Power Co., Butte, 1954-63, counsel, 1963-65, asst. to pres., 1965-67, v.p., 1967-70, exec. v.p., dir., 1970, then chmn., chief exec. officer, now ret.; dir. Mont. Power Co., First Bank System 1975-84, Devel. Credit

Corp. Mont.; MHD Devel. Corp. 1986—; mem. U.S. nat. com. World Energy Conf.; Mont. dir. for U.S. Savs. Bonds, 1980-81; cons. in field. Mem. Mont. Pub. Land Law Rev. Adv. Com. City atty. Deer Lodge, 1950-57, 60-63; mem. Mont. Ho. of Reps., 1949-55, majority floor leader, 1951; mem. Mont. State Senate, 1962-64; state chmn. Republican Central Com., Mont., 1952-54; mem. adv. com. Edison Electric Inst., U. Mont. Found., Missoula, Rocky Mountain Coll., Billings; bd. dirs. Mont. Internat. Trade Commn. Served with AUS, World War II and Korea. Recipient Judstin Miller award, 1947. Mem. Mont., Am. bar assns. Episcopalian. Clubs: Masons, Shriners, Kiwanis. Home: 205 Aspen Ln Butte MT 59701-5550 Office: 40 W Broadway St Butte MT 59701-9222

MCELWEE, ANDREW ALLISON, finance executive, lawyer; b. Dover, N.J., Apr. 10, 1955; s. Andrew Allison and Grace Lloyd (Lloyd) M.; m. Connie Chapman, May 24, 1980; children: Alexandra Chapman, Andrew Allison III. BA, Davidson Coll., 1977; JD, U. Va., 1980. Bar: N.Y. 1981, N.J. 1981, U.S. Dist. Ct. (ea. and so. dists.) N.Y. Assoc. Dewey, Ballantine, Bushby, Palmer & Wood, N.Y.C., 1980-83, Morgan Stanky & Co. Inc., N.Y.C., 1984-85; v.p. fin. Bellemead Devel. Corp., Roseland, N.J., 1985—, exec v.p., 1995; bd. dirs. Lamont Fin. Services, Inc., Essex Falls, N.J. Bd. dirs. World Impact, Inc., Newark, 1986—; elder First Presbyn. Ch., Caldwell, N.J., 1983-87. Mem. ABA, N.J. Bar Assn., N.Y. Bar Assn. Home: 4 Stone House Rd Mendham NJ 07945-3125 Office: Bellemead Devel Corp 4 Becker Farm Rd Roseland NJ 07068-1734*

MCELWEE, DENNIS JOHN, lawyer, pharmaceutical company executive; b. New Orleans, July 30, 1947; s. John Joseph and Audrey (Nunez) McE.; m. Nancy Lu Travis, Sept. 3, 1976. BS, Tulane U., 1970; JD, U. Denver, 1992, Hague Acad. Internat. Law, 1990-91. Clean room and quality control analyst Sci. Enterprises Inc., Broomfield, Colo., 1975-76; analytical chemist in toxicology Poisonlab. Inc., Denver, 1977; analytical chemist, then dir. analytical quality control program Colo. Sch. Mines Rsch. Inst., 1977-79; dir. quality control, then dir. compliance Benedict Nuclear Pharms. Co., Golden, Colo., 1979-84; pres. MC Projections, Inc., Morrison, Colo., 1985-86, dir. regulatory affairs, Electromedics Inc., Englewood, Colo., 1986-89; pvt. practice 1992—. Author: Mineral Research Chemicals, Toxic Properties and Proper Handling, 2d edit., 1979; contbr. articles to profl. jours. Bd. dirs. Denver Chpt. Cystic Fibrosis Found., 1996. Mem. Colo. Bar Assn., Colo. Criminal Def. Bar, Denver Bar Assn., 1st Judicial Dist. Bar Assn. Recipient Sutton prize in internat. law U. Denver Sch. Law, 1991. Home: PO Box 56 Morrison CO 80465-0056 Office: 2009 Wadsworth Blvd Ste 200 Lakewood CO 80215-2031

MC ELWEE, JOHN GERARD, retired life insurance company executive; b. Port Bannatyne, Scotland, Dec. 19, 1921; came to U.S., 1925; s. James and Margaret (Fitzgerald) McE.; m. Barbara Sullivan, Mar. 31, 1951; children: Neal, Janet, Sheila, Brian. Attended, Boston Coll., 1939-42, LLB, 1950, LLD (hon.), 1987; grad. advanced mgmt. program, Harvard U., 1960; LLD (hon.), Bentley Coll., 1986. With John Hancock Mut. Life Ins. Co., Boston, 1945-93, asst. sec., 1957-61, 2d v.p., 1961-65, v.p., 1965-71, sr. v.p., sec., 1972-74, exec. v.p., sec., 1974-79, pres., 1979-81, chmn., 1982-86, also bd. dirs., 1976-93; bd. dirs. Data Gen. Corp. Trustee, assoc. Boston Coll.; life trustee Boston Mus. Sci. With USN, 1941-45. Mem. Weston Golf Club, Comml. Club, Knights of Malta. Roman Catholic. Home: 139 Buckskin Dr Weston MA 02193-1131

MCELYEA, ULYSSES, JR., veterinarian; b. Ft. Collins, Colo., Oct. 29, 1941; s. Ulysses and Hazel (Hall) McE.; m. Rexanna Bell, Dec. 29, 1975 (div. 1980). BS in Pharmacy, U. N.Mex., 1963; DVM, Colorado State U., 1967, MS, 1968. Diplomate Am. Bd. Vet. Practicioners; cert. in companion animals. Owner Alta Vista Animal Clinic, Las Cruces, N.Mex., 1970—; bd. dirs. N.Mex. Acad. Vet. Practice, Albuquerque, bd. dirs. state of N.Mex. Bd. Vet. Examiners, v.p., 1989-92, vice chair, 1992, chair, 1992—, Bank of the Rio Grande. Pres. Las Cruces Community Theater, 1974; founder, bd. dirs. Dona Ann Arts Coun., Las Cruces, 1976-80. Capt. U.S. Army, 1968-70. Mem. AVMA, Am. Pharm. Assn., Am. Assn. Feline Practitioners, Am. Soc. Vet. Ophthalmologists, N.Mex. Vet. Med. Assn. (bd. dirs. 1976-82), So. N.Mex. Vet. Assn. (pres. 1974, 84), N.Mex. State U. Athletic Assn. 9bd. dirs. 1976—, pres.-elect 1992-93, pres. 1993-94), N.Mex. State U. Pres.'s Assn. 9bd. dirs. 1988-91), U. N.Mex. Alumni Assn. (bd. dirs. 1976-80). Democrat. Home: 2635 Fairway Dr Las Cruces NM 88011-5044 Office: Alta Vista Animal Clinic 725 S Solano Dr Las Cruces NM 88001-3244

MC EMBER, ROBERT ROLAND, association executive, musician; b. Ludington, Mich., Feb. 26, 1919; s. Francis Roland and Lillian Laurentine (Hansen) McE.; B.A., John B. Stetson U., 1946, B.M., 1946, M.A., 1951; m. Elizabeth Anderson Futch, Dec. 15, 1942; children—Sharon Leigh, Elizabeth Anne. Critic tchr. Western Mich. U., 1950-55; asst. prof. Purdue U., 1955-63; asso. prof. U. Wis., 1964-67; mgr. flight tng. aids and tech. writing Am. Airlines, 1967-69; mgr. flight tng. program devel. Eastern Airlines, Miami, Fla., 1970—; guest lectr.; leader workshops and seminars on instrnl. tech.; mus. dir., condr. Ludington Civic Symphony Orch., 1948-50; condr. Central Wis. Symphony Orch., 1964-67. Served with USAAF, 1942-45; col. Res., 1945-72. Recipient cert. of appreciation U.S. Air Force, 1972. Mem. Nat. Acad. Rec. Arts and Scis., Nat. Soc. Scabbard and Blade, Mil. Order World Wars, Daedalian Soc., Am. Soc. Tng. and Devel., Internat. TV Assn. (pres. 1974-75, dir., chmn. bd. 1976-77), Res. Officers Assn. U.S., Audio Visual Mgmt. Assn., Am. Fedn. Musicians, Phi Delta Kappa. Republican Lutheran. Author: C-124 Aircraft Homestudy, 1970; (with others) Communication Security for AF Personnel, 1972, Principles and Practices of Occupational Safety and Health, 1975; editorial adv. bd. Am. Soc. Tng. and Devel. Jour., 1979-82; editor Flight Line (Flight Safety Found. Publs. award 1980), 1957-81; contbr. articles to ednl. jours.; composer: All-American Bands, 1958; several works for symphony orch. Home: PO Box 490115 Leesburg FL 34749-0115 Office: Audio Visual Mgmt Assn 7907 NW 53d St Suite 346 Miami FL 33166

MCENERY, TOM, professional sports team executive; married; three children. BA, MA degress, Santa Clara U. Mayor of City of San Jose, Calif., 1983-90; vice-chmn. San Jose Sharks. Contbr. editl. to L.A. Times, 1995; author: The New City-State: Change and Renewal in America's Cities. Office: San Jose Sharks 525 West Santa Clara St San Jose CA 95113

MCENIRY, ROBERT FRANCIS, education educator; b. Milw., Feb. 22, 1918; s. Frank Michael and Mary (Brown) McE. BA, St. Louis U., 1941, Philosophiae Licentiatus cum laude, 1944, Theologiae Licentiatus cum laude, 1953, PhL, ThL cum laude, 1953; PhD, Ohio State U., 1972. Instr. classics St. Louis U. High Sch., 1944-47, Creighton Prep. Sch., Omaha, 1947-48; asst. prof., chmn. classics Rockhurst Coll., Kansas City, Mo., 1953-58; retreat dir. White House Retreat, St. Louis, 1958-68; assoc. research prof. Creighton U., Omaha, 1972-89; dir., facilitator Growth for Couples, 1975-89; lectr. Creighton Natural Family Planning Ctr.; facilitator groups Adult Children of Alcoholism and Dysfunctional Families, 1989-93; vis. lectr. San Francisco Sch. Theology, San Anselmo, Calif., 1985; presenter over 700 lectrs., seminars and workshops in 43 states and 12 fgn. countries on value decisions during high anxiety and stress; exec. dir. Studies Adult Survivors of Abuse, 1993—; tchr., counselor in marriage and family issues. Editor and pub. Interaction Review, 1982-89; editor Scholar and Educator, 1974-76; mem. editorial bd. Counseling and Values, 1976-82; editor (book) Pastoral Counseling, 1977, Premarriage Counseling, 1978; contbr. over 180 articles to profl. jours.; literary agent, 1992—. Mem. Bd. of Pastoral Ministry, Omaha, 1972-78. Research grantee Council for Theol. Reflection, 1975-77; recipient Research award Creighton U., 1977. Fellow Nat. Acad. Counselors and Family Therapists (editor book rev. 1979-91); mem. APA, Am. Assn. for Religious Values in Counseling (editor newsletter 1982-89, Outstanding Svc. award 1985, Meritorious Svc. award 1989), Phi Delta Kappa (exec. com. 1977-83, del. 1981-83). Avocations: barbershop quartets, photography, Civil War sites, yoga. Home: 3016 Paddock Rd Apt 12B Omaha NE 68124-2942 Office: Creighton U Dept of Education 2500 California St Omaha NE 68178

MCENROE, JOHN PATRICK, lawyer; b. N.Y.C., Mar. 25, 1935; s. John Joseph and Kathleen C. (Kellaghan) McE.; m. Katherine Callender Tresham, Dec. 7, 1957; children: John, Mark T., Patrick W. BA, Cath. U. Am., 1955; JD, Fordham U., 1964. Bar: N.Y. 1965, U.S. Dist. Ct. (so. dist.) 1966, D.C. 1982. Assoc. Kelley, Drye, Newhall, Maginess & Warren, N.Y.C., 1964-67; assoc. Paul, Weiss, Rifkind, Wharton & Garrison, N.Y.C., 1967-74, ptnr., 1974—. Served to 1st lt. USAF, 1955-59. Mem. ABA, Assn. of Bar of City of N.Y. Office: Paul Weiss Rifkind Wharton & Garrison 1285 Ave Of The Americas New York NY 10019-6028*

MCENROE, JOHN PATRICK, JR., retired professional tennis player, commentator; b. Wiesbaden, Fed. Republic of Germany, Feb. 16, 1959; s. John Patrick and Katy McEnroe; m. Tatum O'Neal, Aug. 1, 1986; children: Kevin Jack, Sean. Grad., Trinity Sch., N.Y.C., 1977; student, Stanford U. Winner numerous U.S. jr. singles and doubles titles; winner jr. titles French Mixed Doubles, 1977, French Jr. Singles, 1977, Italian Indoor Doubles, 1978; winner Nat. Coll. Athletic Assn. Intercollegiate U.S. Men's Singles title, 1978; professional tennis player, 1978-93; played on victorious U.S. Davis Cup Team, 1978, 79, 81, 82, 92; winner Stockholm Open, 1978, Benson and Hedges Tournament, 1978, Grand Prix Masters singles and doubles, Wembley, 1978, Grand Prix Masters Tournament, N.Y.C., 1979, New Orleans Grand Prix, 1979, WCT Milan Internat., Italy, 1979, Stella Artois Tournament, London, 1979, U.S. Open Men's Singles Championship, 1979, 80, 81, 84, World Championship Tennis Championship, 1979, 83, Australian Indoor Singles Championship, 1980-83, U.S. Indoor Singles Championship, 1980-83, Wimbledon Singles, 1981, 83, 84, Tournament of Champions, 1981, 83, AT & T Challenge, 1987, Japan Open, 1988, U.S. Hard Court Singles, 1989, Wimbledon Doubles, 1992; tennis sportscaster USA Network, 1993; mem. Men's Seniors' Tour Circuit, 1994. Office: care John P McEnroe Sr Paul Weiss Rifkind Wharton & Garrison 1285 Ave the Americas New York NY 10019-6028*

MCENROE, PATRICK, professional tennis player; b. Manhasset, N.Y., July 1, 1966; s. John Patrick Sr. and Katy McEnroe. Student, U. Stanford. Ranked 12th U.S. Tennis Assn., 1991. Mem. U.S. Davis Cup Team, 1993, 94.

MCENROE, PAUL, reporter. Gen. assignment reporter, National writer Mpls. Star Tribune, Mpls. Office: Star Tribune 425 Portland Ave Minneapolis MN 55488-0001

MCENTEE, GERALD W., labor union official; b. Phila., Jan. 11, 1935; four children. B in Econs., LaSalle Coll., 1956; postgrad., Temple U., Harvard U. With Am. Fedn. State County and Mcpl. Employees, 1973—; former leader Dist Coun. 13, Harrisburg, Penn.; union internat. v.p., mem. exec. bd., since 1974; internat. pres. Washington, 1981—. Office: AFSCME 1625 L St NW Washington DC 20036-5601*

MCENTEE, ROBERT EDWARD, management consultant; b. Franklin, N.J., Mar. 22, 1932; s. William J. and Marie C. (Gorman) McE.; m. Ruth M. Kathalynas, Sept. 29, 1956; children—Kathleen, Susan, Jane, Robert, Christopher. B.S., Villanova U., 1953. C.P.A., N.J. With Price Waterhouse, 1955-63; sr. fin., adminstrv. exec. Beecham Inc., West Paterson, N.J., 1963-88; pres. fin. div. Beecham Inc., 1974-88; pres., chief oper. officer Russ Berrie & Co., Inc., Oakland, N.J., 1988-90; pvt. practice cons., 1990—; bd. dirs. Valley Nat. Bancorp, Wayne, N.J. Trustee Archdiocese of Newark, pension bd. Served with U.S. Army, 1953-55. Mem. Am. Inst. C.P.A.s, N.J. Soc. C.P.A.s, Fin. Exec. Inst. Roman Catholic. Home: 398 Autumn Chase Dr Venice FL 34292

MCENTEGART, PATRICK JOSEPH, cost consultant, program designer; b. Crossmaglen, Newry, Ireland, Jan. 20, 1946; s. Michael G. and Catherine Ann (Lennon); separated; children: Michael, Roisin, Catherine, Adrian, Patrick Jr. Student surveying & levelling, St. McCartans, Dublin, 1968; quantity surveying, St. Philbin's, Dublin, 1970. Cost cons. M.J. Fitzgerald Corp., N.Y.C., 1986-90, Kafki Corp., N.Y.C., 1990-94; project mgr. to castle abatement N.J., 1991-94; pres. Fortview Internat., Long Island City, N.Y., 1986—; pres. Fortview Constrn. Co., N.Y.C., Fortview Drywall, Inc., N.Y.C., Fortview Assoc. Ltd., Ireland, Fortview Devel. Ltd., UK. Mem. Celts Who Care; founder mem. Civil Rights Assn. in No. Ireland. Mem. Am. Inst. Physics, Internat. Acoustics Assn., County Armagh Gaelic Athletic Assn. of N.Y., Inc. (pres.), Nat. Athletic and Cycling Assn. of Ireland, Constrn. Specification Inst. Am. Avocations: composer, poet. Office: Fortview Internat 24-16 Steinway St Ste 636 Long Island City NY 11103

MCENTIRE, REBA N., country singer; b. McAlester, Okla., Mar. 28, 1955; d. Clark Vincent and Jacqueline (Smith) McE.; m. Narvel Blackstock, 1989; 1 child, Shelby Steven McEntire Blackstock. Student elem. edn., music, Southeastern State U., Durant, Okla., 1976. Rec. artist Mercury Records, 1978-83, MCA Records, 1984—. Albums include Whoever's in New England (Gold award), 1986, What Am I Gonna Do About You (Gold award), 1987, Greatest Hits (Gold award, Platinum award, U.S., Can.), 1987, Merry Christmas To You, 1987, The Last One To Know (Gold award), 1988, Reba (Gold award 1988), Sweet 16 (Gold award 1989, U.S.), Rumor Has It (Gold award 1991, Platinum award 1992, Double Platinum 1992), Reba Live (Gold award 1990, Gold award 1991, Platinum award 1991), For My Broken Heart, 1991, Forever in Your Eyes, 1992, It's Your Call, 1992, Read My Mind, 1994, Reba compilation video (Gold award, Platinum award 1992); author: (with Tom Carter) Reba: My Story, 1994; actress: (miniseries) Buffalo Girls, 1995. Spokesperson Middle Tenn. United Way, 1988, Nat. and State 4-H Alumni, Bob Hope's Hope for a Drug Free Am.; Nat. spokesperson Am. Lung Assn., 1990-91. Recipient numerous awards in Country music including Disting. Alumni award Southeastern State U., Female vocalist award Country Music Assn., 1984, 85, 86, 87, Grammy award for Best Country Vocal Performance, 1987, 2 Grammy nominations, 1994, Grammy award, Best Country Vocal Collaboration for "Does He Love You" with Linda Davis, 1994, Entertainer of Yr. award Country Radio Awards, 1994, Female Vocalist award, 1994; named Entertainer of Yr., Country Music Assn., 1986, Female Vocalist of Yr. Acad. Country Music, 1984, 85, 86, 87, 92, Top Female Vocalist, 1991, Am. Music award favorite female country singer, 1988, 90, 91, 92, 93, Am. Music award, 1989, 90, 91, 92, Best Album, 1991, Favorite Female Vocalist, 1994, Favorite Female Vocalist, Peoples Choice Award, 1992, Favorite Female Country Vocalist, 1992, 93, Favorite Female Vocalist, TNN Viewer's Choice Awards, 1993, Favorite Female Country Artist, Billboard, 1994. Mem. Country Music Assn., Acad. County Music, Nat. Acad. Rec. Arts and Scis., Grand Ol' Opry, AFTRA, Nashville Songwriters Assn. Inc. Avocations: golf, shopping, being with Narvel and Shelby, horse racing, raising horses.

MCERLANE, JOSEPH JAMES, insurance company executive; b. Phila., Mar. 5, 1948; s. Joseph Leo and Theophila Mary (Szymanski) McE.; m. Florence Mary Myhasuk; children: Joan Reardon, Rebecca Ann, Megan Diane, Erin Moira, Joseph James Jr. BA, Villanova U., 1970. CLU; cert. employee benefit specialist. Group sales asst. Metro. Life Ins. Co., Phila., 1970-72; mgr. group bus. svcs. Investors Diversified Svcs., Valley Forge, Pa., 1972-74; from mgr. to dir. to v.p. and divisional mgr. group ins. sales Investors Diversified Svcs., Mpls., 1974-84; pres. Nat. Benefit Resources Group Svcs., Inc., Mpls., 1984—. Mem. sch. bd. Annunciation Sch., Mpls., 1984-87, chmn., 1986-87. Mem. Mass. Mktg. Inst., Self-Insured Inst. Am. (bd. dirs. 1993—), Sertoma (Mpls. Sertoman of Yr. 1982). Office: Nat Benefit Resources Group Svcs Inc 5353 Gamble Dr Minneapolis MN 55416-1509 also: 5402 Parkdale Dr Minneapolis MN 55416

MCEVILLY, MICHAEL JAMES, civil engineer; b. Newburgh, N.Y., Sept. 29, 1958; s. William George and Mary Elizabeth (Waye) McE.; m. Mary Ellen Hilton, May 23, 1980; children: Melissa Renee, Michael Patrick. BS in Civil Engring., U. Mo., Rolla, 1980, MS in Engring. Mgmt., 1981. Registered profl. engr., Tex. Prodn. engr. Cities Svc. Co., Houston, 1981-84, sr. prodn. engr., 1984-85; sr. constrn. engr. Anadarko Petroleum Corp., Houston, 1985-92, staff constrn. engr., 1992-94, divsn. constrn. supr., 1994—; offshore platform staff Cities Svc. Co., Houston, 1981-85; facilities, pipeline design, fabrication, installation and commissioning Gulf of Mex., onshore Gulf Coast, Alaska and internat. Anadarko Petroleum Corp., Houston, 1985—. Mem. Little League Umpires, Spring, Tex., 1988—. Named Young Engr. of Yr., Tex. Soc. Profl. Engrs., Houston, 1992. Mem. ASCE, Am. Welding Soc., Masters, Warden and Secs. Assn. (sec. 1993—), Order Ea. Star (patron, v.p.), Masons (pres. 1992-93, master, dist. instr.), Lions Club, Shriners, Elks. Republican. Presbyterian. Achievements include multiple derrick barge (2) lift of a 1700 ton offshore drilling/production platform. Avocations: baseball umpiring, sporting events, coaching youth sports. Home: 5210 Nodaway Ln Spring TX 77379-8048 Office: Anadarko Petroleum Corp 17001 Northchase Dr Houston TX 77060-2139

MC EVILLY, THOMAS VINCENT, seismologist; b. East Saint Louis, Ill., Sept. 2, 1934; s. Robert John and Frances Nathalie (Earnshaw) Mc E.; m. Dorothy K. Hopfinger, Oct. 23, 1970; children: Mary, Susan, Ann, Steven, Joseph, Adrian. BS, St. Louis U., 1956, PhD, 1964. Geophysicist California Co., New Orleans, 1957-60; engring. v.p. Sprengnether Instrument Co., St. Louis, 1962-67; asst. prof. seismology U. Calif., Berkeley, 1964-68, assoc. prof., 1968-74, prof., 1974—, chmn. dept. geology and geophysics, 1976-80, asst. dir. seismographic sta., 1968-90; dir. earth sci. div. Lawrence Berkeley Lab., 1982-93; chmn. bd. dirs. Inc. Research Instns. for Seismology, 1984-86; cons. numerous govt. agys., geotech. cos. Contbr. numerous articles to profl. jours. Mem. Am. Geophys. Union, Royal Astron. Soc., Seismol. Soc. Am. (editor bull. 1976-85), Soc. Exploration Geophysicists, AAAS, Phi Beta Kappa. Office: Univ Calif Dept Geology and Geophysics Berkeley CA 94720

MCEVOY, NAN TUCKER, publishing company executive; b. San Mateo, Calif., July 15, 1919; s. Nion R. and Phyllis (de Young) Tucker; m. Dennis McEvoy, 1948 (div.); 1 child, Nion Tucker McEvoy. Student, Georgetown U., 1975. Newspaper reporter San Francisco Chronicle, 1944-46, N.Y. Herald Tribune, N.Y.C., 1946-47, Washington Post, 1947-48; rep. in pub. rels. John Homes, Inc., Washington, 1959-60; spl. asst. to dir. U.S. Peace Corps, Washington, 1961-64; mem. U.S. delegation UNESCO, Washington, 1964-65; dir. Population Coun., Washington, 1965-70; co-founder, dep. dir. Preterm, Inc., Washington, 1970-74; former chmn. bd. Chronicle Pub. Co., San Francisco, 1975-95, dir. emeritus, 1995—. Mem. nat. bd. dirs. Smithsonian Instn., Washington, 1994—; mem. Brookings coun. Brookings Instn., Washington, 1994—; commr. Nat. Mus. Art, Washington; mem. U. Calif. San Francisco Found., 1993—; formerly arbitrator Am. Arbitration Assn., Washington. Named Woman of Yr., Washingtonian Mag., 1973. Mem. Am. Art Forum, Burlingame Country Club, The River Club, Commonwealth Club of Calif., World Affairs Coun., Villa Taverna. Avocation: overseeing California olive grove ranch in anticipation of producing fine olive oil. Office: 655 Montgomery St Ste 1430 San Francisco CA 94111

MCEVOY, SHARLENE ANN, business law educator; b. Derby, Conn., July 6, 1950; d. Peter Henry Jr. and Madaline Elizabeth (McCabe) McE. BA magna cum laude, Albertus Magnus Coll., 1972; JD, U. Conn., West Hartford, 1975; MA, Trinity Coll., Hartford, 1980, UCLA, 1982; PhD, UCLA, 1985. Bar: Conn., 1975. Pvt. practice Derby, 1984—; asst. prof. bus. law Fairfield (Conn.) U. Sch. Bus., 1986—; adj. prof. bus. law, polit. sci. Albertus Magnus Coll., New Haven, Conn., 1978-80, U. Conn., Stamford, 1984-86; acting chmn. polit. sci. dept. Albertus Magnus Coll., 1980; assoc. prof. law Fairfield U., 1992—; Chmn. Women's Resource Ctr., Fairfield U., 1989-91. Staff editor Jour. Legal Studies Edn., 1989-94; reviewer Am. Bus. Law Assn. jour., 1988—, staff editor, 1995—; sr. articles editor N.E. Jour. of Legal Studies in Bus., 1995-96. Mem. Darby Tercentennial Commn., Derby, 1973-74; bd. dirs. Valley Transit Dist., Derby, 1975-77, Justice of Peace, City of Derby, 1975-83; alt. mem. Parks and Recreation Commn., Woodbury, 1995—; mem., treas. Woodbury Dem. Town Com., 1995-96, corr. sec. 1996—. Recipient Best Paper award N.E. Regional Bus. Law Assn., 1990, Best Paper award Tri-State Regional Bus. Law Assn., 1991; Fairfield U. Sch. Bus. rsch. grantee 1989, 91, 92, Fairfield U. rsch. grantee, 1994. Mem. ABA, ATLA, Conn. Bar Assn., Acad. Legal Studies in Bus. (coord. SINISTRAL spl. interest group 1977—). Democrat. Roman Catholic. Avocations: running, chess, tennis, swimming. Office: 198 Emmett Ave Derby CT 06418-1258

MC EWAN, LEONARD, former judge; b. Great Falls, Mont., Feb. 17, 1925; s. Leonard Wellington and Olga (Trinastich) McE.; m. Cameon Wolfe, Sept. 2, 1953 (dec. 1977); m. Mary Hurst Amschel, Feb. 20, 1988. B.S., U. Wyo., 1955, J.D., 1957. Bar: Wyo. bar 1957. Practice in Sheridan, 1957-69; municipal judge City Sheridan, 1958-69; justice Wyo. Supreme Ct., Cheyenne, 1969-75; chief justice Wyo. Supreme Ct., 1975; dist. judge Sheridan, Wyo., 1975-85. Trustee Sheridan Coll., 1963-69, Sheridan County YMCA, 1963-68, All-American Indian Days, 1959-63, N. Am. Indian Found., 1960-67. Served with USAAF, 1943-46. Recipient Distinguished Service award Jr. C. of C., 1960. Mem. Wyo. State Bar, Am. Bar Assn., Am. Legion, U. Wyo. Alumni Assn. (bd. dirs. 1962-66), Sigma Alpha Epsilon. Episcopalian. Lodges: Elks, Eagles, Masons, Rotary, Quarterback. Address: PO Box 460 Story WY 82842-0460

MCEWEN, ALEXANDER CAMPBELL, cadastral studies educator, former Canadian government official, surveying consultant; b. Ryde, Isle of Wight, Eng., Aug. 22, 1926; emigrated to Can., 1949; s. Walter Scott and Florence Lilian (Goodall) McE.; m. Patricia Stuart Richards, July 27, 1956 (div. 1988); m. Sherry Lee Wilson, June 13, 1993; children: Ann Florence, Sheila Jean, Laura Susan. LL.B., U. London, 1966, Ph.D., 1979; LL.M., U. East Africa, 1970. Sr. surveyor H. Wheeler Assocs., Toronto, Ont., Can., 1961-62; sec. treas. Assn. Ont. Land Surveyors, Toronto, 1963-64; prin. Survey Tng. Centre, Dar es Salaam, Tanzania, 1964-70; survey cons. Ottawa, Ont., Can., 1970-72; dir. lands and surveys Govt. Nfld., St. John's, 1972-76; commr. Internat. Boundary Commn., Ottawa, Ont., 1976-90; survey adviser Govt. Can., Jesselton, North Borneo, 1954-56, Lagos, Nigeria, 1989-90; tech. expert UN, Victoria, Seychelles, 1958-61; survey cons. Can. Exec. Service Orgn., Kingston, Jamaica, 1981, Quito, Ecuador, 1986; prof. cadastral studies, dept. geomatics engring. U. Calgary, Alta., Can., 1991—. Author: International Boundaries of East Africa, 1971 In Search of the Highlands, 1988; contbr. articles to profl. jours. Served with Royal Armoured Corp. Mem. Can. Inst. Geomatics (mem. coun. 1977-81, Jim Jones award 1967, 83, 90, Presdl. citation 1981), Western Can. Bd. Examiners for Land Surveyors (registrar, bd. dirs. 1991—), Assn. Ont. Land Surveyors (sec.-treas. 1963-64), Assn. Nfld. Land Surveyors (bd. examiners 1975-76), PEN, Writer's Union Can. Home: 2129 2d Ave NW, Calgary, AB Canada T2N OG8 Office: U Calgary, Dept Geomatics Engring, 2500 University Dr NW, Calgary, AB Canada T2N 1N4

MCEWEN, ALFRED SHERMAN, planetary geologist; b. Lawrence, Kans., July 22, 1954; s. William Edwin and Miriam (Sherman) McE.; m. Eileen Haney; 1 child, Ian. B.S., SUNY-Syracuse, 1975; B.S. No. Ariz. U., 1981, M.S., 1983; PhD Ariz. State U., 1988. Vol. Peace Corps, Guatemala, Central Am., 1975-77; soil conservationist Soil Conservation Service, USDA, 1978-80; geologist U.S. Geol. Survey, Flagstaff, Ariz., 1981—. Mem. Galileo, Cassini, Mars Global Surveyor, and Clementine Spacecraft Sci. Teams. Contbr. articles, image processing-color images to profl. jours. Mem. Am. Geophys. Union, Am. Astron. Soc. Home: 3890 N Paradise Rd Flagstaff AZ 86004-1613 Office: US Geol Survey 2255 N Gemini Dr Flagstaff AZ 86001-1637

MCEWEN, JAMES, publishing executive. Pub. Family Cir., N.Y.C. Office: Gruner & Jahr USA Pub Family Cir 110 Fifth Ave New York NY 10011*

MCEWEN, JEAN, painter; b. Montreal, Que., Can., Dec. 14, 1923; s. William and Elaine (Renaud) McE.; m. Indra Kagis, Sept. 18, 1976; children: Jean Sabin, Marianne Jérémie; children by previous marriage: Isabelle, Domenique. Grad., U. Montreal, 1947. Tchr. U. Concordia, Montreal. One-man exhbns. include, Gallery Godart-Lefort, Montreal, 1962-69, Gallery Montreal, 1963, Gallery Moos, Toronto, 1963-69, Gallery Martha Jackson, N.Y.C., 1963, Mayer Gallery, Paris, 1964, group exhbns. include, Dunn Internat. Exhbn., Tate Gallery, London, 1963; rep. permanent collections, Mus. Modern Art, N.Y.C., Walker Art Center, Mpls., Albright-Knox Art Gallery, Buffalo, Hirshhorn Mus., Smithsonian Instn., Ottawa Mus., Toronto Mus.; commd. for stained glass window, Sir George Williams U., 1966, murals for, Toronto Airport, Plase Arts, Montreal. (Winner Quebec Art competition 1962, recipient Jessie Dow award Montreal Spring Exhbn. 1964), large mural Bank Scotia, Montreal, head office, 1991; major retrospect Mont. Mus. Fine Arts, 1987—. grantee Can. Council, 1977-78. Academician Royal Can. Acad. Arts. Roman Catholic. Address: 3908 Parc Lafontaine Rue, Montreal, PQ Canada H2L 3M6

MCEWEN, JOSEPH, JR., distributing company executive; b. Rahway, N.J., June 20, 1921; s. Joseph and Thora (Thompson) McE.; m. Aila; children: Joseph, Jacqueline, Anne, Susan. Student in engring., Temple U. Test engr. Wright Aero. Co., 1941, Lawrence Engring. Co., 1941-43; sales engr. Rapistan of Pa., 1946-55; v.p. Modern Handling Equipment Co., Bristol, Pa., 1955-79, pres., 1960-79, pres. modern group, 1979—. Bd. dirs. Distbn., Research and Edn. Found., World Affairs Council, Phila. Served to 2d lt. U.S. Army 1943-45. Mem. Internat. Material Handling Soc., Nat. Assn. Wholesalers and Distbrs. (presl 1976), Material Handling Distbrs. Assn. (pres. 1966), Pa. C. of C. (bd. dirs.). Clubs: Mfrs. Golf and Country, St. Petersburg Yacht. Office: Modern Group Ltd 2501 Durham Rd Bristol PA 19007-6923 Address: 1904 Kansas Ave NE Saint Petersburg FL 33703-3430

MCEWEN, LARRY BURDETTE, retired English and theater arts educator, author; b. Clay Center, Nebr., Aug. 4, 1934; s. Gerald E. and Marie L. (Pennington) McE.; m. Charlotte E. Alloway, Feb. 14, 1978; children: Diana J., Sheila J. AB, Augustana Coll., Rock Island, Ill., 1962; MS, Ill. State U., 1968. Cert. tchr., Nebr. Prof. theatre arts Blackburn Coll., Carlinville, Ill., 1969-75; counselor div. vocat. rehab. Nebr. Dept. Edn., Lincoln, 1976-82; tchr. English Hastings (Nebr.) Sr. High Sch., 1983-92; vis. lectr. Mt. Senario Coll., Ladysmith, Wis., 1971, Knox Coll., Galesburg, Ill., 1974, Hastings (Nebr.) Coll., 1976. Author: Much Ado About Shakespeare, 1992, Goose and Fables, 1994, To Honor Our Fathers and Mothers, 1996; author Apple Software; dir. 63 theatrical prodns.; contbr. numerous articles to profl. publs. With USAF, 1951-52. Grad. fellow Ind. U., 1968-69; Quad-City Music Guild scholar, 1961-62. Mem. NEA, Neb. State Edn. Assn., Acad. Computers in Eng., Apple Programmers and Developers Assn., Nat. Apple Users Group, Nat. Coun. Tchrs. English, Alpha Psi Omega, Alpha Phi Omega. Home and Office: 603 E 5th St Hastings NE 68901-5336

MCEWEN, WILLARD WINFIELD, JR., lawyer, judge; b. Evanston, Ill., Dec. 26, 1934; s. Willard Winfield Sr. and Esther (Sprenger) McE.; children: Michael, Elizabeth, Allison. BS, Claremont Men's Coll., 1956; LLB, U. Calif., San Francisco, 1959. Bar: Calif. 1960, U.S. Dist. Ct. (no. and so. dists.) Calif. 1960, U.S. Supreme Ct. 1974. Commd. U.S. Army, 1956, advanced through grades to capt., 1965, resigned, 1968; dep. legis. counsel. City of Sacramento, Calif., 1960-61; asst. city atty. City of Santa Barbara, Calif., 1961-62; sole practice Santa Barbara, 1962—; judge U.S. Magistrate Ct., Santa Barbara County, 1973—; atty. Goleta Water Dist., 1986-87; lectr. Santa Barbara Adult Edn. Program. Founder, bd. dirs., officer, gen. legal coun. Santa Barbara Coun. for Retarded, 1962-72; active WORK Workshop for Handicapped, Assn. Retarded Citizens, Santa Barbara City Landmarks Adv. Com., 1967-73; v.p. Santa Barbara Harbor Pageants and Exhibits Com., 1964; chmn. Citizens Save our Shoreline Com., 1964, Citizens Cmty. Master Plan Com., 1964, YMCA Membership Drive, 1964, Citizens Adv. Com. on Sch. Dist. Tax Needs, 1965; commr. Santa Barbara City Water Commn., 1965, City of Santa Barbara Recreation Commn., 1970-73; elected to founding bd. dirs. City Commerce Bank. Recipient Disting Svc. award Santa Barbara Jaycees, 1965; named Santa Barbara's Young Man of Yr. Sanata Barbara C. of C. 1983. Mem. Am. Heart Assn. (pres. Santa Barbara County chpt. 1981-82), Santa Barbara Heart Assn. (bd. dirs., pres. bd. dirs. 1981-82, chmn. Heart Sunday 1973, 75), Santa Barbara Malacological Soc., Santa Barbara Kiwanis (pres. 1967), C. of C. (com. on local govt., state legisaltion com., bd. dirs., past v.p. bd. dirs., pres. bd. dirs. 1981-82, chmn. several coms.). Republican. Roman Catholic. Avocations: golf, skiing. Office: US Courthouse 8 E Figueroa St Ste 210 Santa Barbara CA 93101-2720

MCFADDEN, DAVID REVERE, museum director; b. Devils Lake, N.D., Aug. 28, 1947; BA, U. Minn., 1972, MA, 1978. Assoc. curator Mpls. Inst. Arts, 1976-78, curator, 1978; asst. dir. collections and rsch., curator decorative arts Cooper-Hewitt, Nat. Mus. of Design, N.Y.C., 1978-95; exec. dir. Millicent Rogers Mus., Taos, N.Mex., 1995—; adj. prof. art Cooper-Hewitt-Parsons M.A. program, N.Y.C., 1983—; gov. Decorative Arts Trust; pres. applied arts com. Internat. Coun. Mus., 1993-95; mem. exhbn. com. Am. Fedn. Arts. Author: Scandinavian Modern Design (Wittenborn award 1984), 1983, L'Art de Vivre: Decorative Arts and Design in France 1789-1989, 1989. Decorated knight 1st class Order of the Lion (Finland), 1984; knight commdr. Order of No. Star (Sweden); chevalier des l'Ordre des Arts et des Letrres (France). Recipient Awards of Merit Smithsonian Instn., 1981, 88, 89, Presdl. Design award, 1994; fellow Kress Found., 1973-74. Mem. Worshipful Co. Goldsmiths London. Office: Millicent Rogers Mus PO Box A Taos NM 87571

MCFADDEN, DENNIS, experimental psychology educator; b. Oct. 2, 1940; s. Samuel John and Evelyn (Dinnerson) McF.; m. Nancy L. Wilson, Dec. 28, 1960; children: Tracie Ann, Devin James. BA, Sacramento State Coll., Calif., 1962; PhD, Ind U., 1967. Asst. prof. U. Tex., Austin, 1967-72, assoc. prof., 1972-77, prof., 1977—. Contbr. articles to profl. jours. Recipient Jacob K. Javits Neurosci. Investigator award, 1984-89, Claude D. Pepper award, 1989-91; named Piper Prof., Minnie Stevens Piper Found., 1987. Fellow AAAS, Acoustical Soc. Am.; mem. Assn. for Rsch. Otolaryngology, CHABA (NAS-NRC com. on hearing, bioacoustics, and biomechanics). Office: U Tex Dept Psychology Mezes Hall # 330 Austin TX 78712

MCFADDEN, EDWARD REGIS, JR., pulmonary educator; b. Pitts., Aug. 2, 1936. BA, St. Vincent Coll., 1958; MD, U. Pitts., 1963. Assoc. prof. medicine U. Tex. Med. Br., Galveston, 1972-73; asst. prof. Harvard U., Boston, 1973-77, assoc. prof., 1977-81, 81-84; assoc. prof. MIT div. health sci., Boston, 1979-84; prof. medicine Case Western Res. U., Cleve., 1984—; dir. Airway Disease Ctr. Univ. Hosp., Cleve., 1984—, respiratory therapy, 1985—, Clin. Research Ctr., 1986—. Editor-in-chief Airway Diseases, N.Y.C., 1985—; contbr. articles to profl. jours. Recipient George W. Thorn Teaching award Peter Bent Brigham Hosp., Boston, 1980. Fellow ACP; mem. Am. Fedn. Clin. Research, Am. Thoracic Soc., So. Soc. Clin. Investigation, Am. Physiol. Soc., Am. Acad. Allergy and Immunology, Am. Soc. Clin. Investigation, Assn. Am. Physicians. Home: 2706 Landon Rd Cleveland OH 44122-2008 Office: Univ Hosps Cleve 2074 Abington Rd Cleveland OH 44106-5067

MCFADDEN, FRANK HAMPTON, lawyer, business executive, former judge; b. Oxford, Miss., Nov. 20, 1925; s. John Angus and Ruby (Roy) McF.; m. Jane Porter Nabers, Sept. 30, 1960; children—Frank Hampton, Angus Nabers, Jane Porter. B.A., U. Miss., 1950; LL.B., Yale U., 1955. Bar: N.Y. 1956, Ala. 1959. Assoc. firm Lord, Day & Lord, N.Y.C., 1955-58; assoc. firm Bradley, Arant, Rose & White, Birmingham, Ala., 1958-63, partner, 1963-69; judge U.S. Dist. Ct. No. Dist. Ala., Birmingham, 1969-73; chief judge U.S. Dist. Ct. No. Dist. Ala., 1973-81; sr. v.p., gen. counsel Blount, Inc., Montgomery, Ala., 1982-91, exec. v.p. adminstrn. and govt. affairs, 1991, exec. v.p. legal affairs, 1991-93, exec. v.p., gen. counsel, 1993-95; mem. Capell, Howard, Knabe & Cobbs, P.A., Montgomery, 1995—; chmn. Blount Energy Resource Corp., Montgomery, 1983-88. Mem. jud. panel Ctr. for Pub. Resources, 1985—. Served from ensign to lt. USNR, 1944-49, 51-53. Fellow Am. Coll. Constrn. Lawyers; mem. Am. Corp. Counsel Assn. (bd. dirs. 1984-93, chmn. 1989). Office: Capell Howard Knabe 57 Adams Ave Montgomery AL 36104

MC FADDEN, G. BRUCE, hospital administrator; b. Winchester, Va., Feb. 19, 1934; s. S. Donald and Ruth D. McF.; m. Lois F. Richardson, Aug. 22, 1964; children—Christopher, Amy. BS, Va. Poly. Inst., 1953; MHA, Med. Coll. Va. (Va. Commonwealth U.), 1961. Asst. adminstr. Meml. Hosp. at Easton, Md., Inc., 1963-70; v.p. Pa. Hosp., Phila., 1970-75; dir. U. Md. Hosp., Balt., 1975-82; pres. Robert Wood Johnson, University Hosp., 1982-88; exec. dir. N.Y. Health Career Ctr., N.Y.C., 1989-91, N.Y. Regional Transplant Program, N.Y.C., 1991-95; v.p. One Call Med., 1995—; cons. Hosp. Joint Practice Demonstration Project, Nat. Joint Practice Commn. of AMA, ANA; preceptor for programs in health care adminstrn. Med. Coll. Va., Columbia U., N.Y. U., U. Pa., Temple U.; bd. dirs., mem. recognition com. Am. Blood Commn.; bd. dirs., mem. exec. com. Central Md. Health Systems Agy.; chmn. Accreditation Council on Grad. Med. Edn.; chmn. Cen. Jersey Health Care Corp., New Brunswick; bd. dirs. New Brunswick Savs. Bank;. Bd. dirs. Vis. Nurse Soc., Phila., George St. Playhouse, New Brunswick, N.J., Westfield YMCA, N.J.; bd. dirs., vice chmn. Community Nursing Svcs. of Phila.; pres. Robert Wood; mem. Bd. of Edn., Westfield, N.J. Fellow Am. Coll. Hosp. Adminstrs.; mem. Am. Hosp. Assn. (chmn. coun. on human resources, chmn. spl. coms. on mandatory continuing edn., gen. coun.). Home: 585 Trinity Pl Westfield NJ 07090

MC FADDEN, GEORGE LINUS, retired army officer; b. Sharon, Pa., Oct. 16, 1927; s. George Linus and Frances Jane (Byrne) McF.; m. Floretta Theresa McFadden, Nov. 20, 1948; children: Kenneth William, Mark Edward, Mary Kathleen, Robert Bernard, George Linus, William. B.E., U. Omaha, 1961; M.S., George Washington U., 1967; grad., Advanced Mgmt. Program, Harvard U., 1971. Pvt. U.S. Army, 1946, advanced through grades to maj. gen., 1976; comdg. officer (7th inf. div. arty.), Korea, 1969-70; dep. comdg. gen. U.S. Army Security Agy., Arlington, Va., 1972-74; dep. dir. for field mgmt. and evaluation, dep. chief central security service Fort George G. Meade, Md., 1975-78; dep. dir. ops. Nat. Security Agy., 1978-79; comdg. gen. U.S. Army So. European Task Force, Vicenza, Italy, 1979-82; corp. v.p. CompuDyne Corp., 1986-89; sr. v.p. The Abbott Group, Inc., Annapolis, Md., 1989—; dir. Washington Studies and Analysis Group McDonnell Douglas Corp., 1985-86; dir. security affairs Dept. Energy, 1991—. Pres., chmn. bd. Met. Washington chpt. Arthritis Found., 1986-95. Decorated D.F.C., D.S.M., Silver Star, Bronze Star, Purple Heart, others. Roman Catholic.

MCFADDEN, JAMES FREDERICK, JR., surgeon; b. St. Louis, Dec. 5, 1920; s. James Frederick and Olivia Genevieve (Imbs) McF.; m. Mary Cella Switzer, Sept. 15, 1956 (div. Sept. 1969); children: James Frederick, Kenneth Michael, John Switzer, Mary Cella, Joseph Robert; m. Deanne Nemec Puls, Apr. 29, 1989. AB, St. Louis U., 1941, MD, 1944. Intern Boston City Hosp., 1944-45; ward surgeon neorsurg. and orthopedics McGuire Gen. Hosp., Richmond, Va., 1945; ward surgeon in internal medicine Regional Hosp., Fort Knox, Ky., 1946; ward surgeon plastic surgery Valley Forge Gen. Hosp., Phoenixville, Pa., 1946-47; intern St. Louis City Hosp., 1947-48; resident in surgery VA Hosp., St. Louis, 1948-52; clin. instr. surgery St. Louis U., 1952-62; gen. practice medicine specializing in surgery St. Louis, 1952—; mem. staff St. Mary's Hosp., 1952-77, St. John's Mercy Hosp., 1952-74, Desloge Hosp., 1952-62, Frisco RR Hosp., 1953-64, DePaul Hosp., 1954—, Christian Hosp., 1955-66, 83—. Mem. St. Louis Ambassadors, 1979-81; officer St. Louis County Aux. Police, 1973-75. Served to capt. AUS, 1945-47. Recipient Eagle Scout award, Order of the Arrow Honor award Boy Scouts Am. Fellow ACS, Royal Soc. Medicine, Internat. Coll. Surgeons; mem. St. Louis Med. Soc., Am. Coll. Occupl. and Environ. Medicine, Am. Soc. Clin. Hypnosis, Internat. Soc. Hypnosis, Am. Assn. RR Surgeons, St. Louis U. Student Conclave, Alpha Sigma Nu, Phi Beta Pi. Roman Catholic. Avocations: hypnosis, photography. Home: PO Box 411933 Saint Louis MO 63141-1933 Office: 11500 Olive Blvd Saint Louis MO 63141-7143

MCFADDEN, JOHN VOLNEY, retired manufacturing company executive; b. N.Y.C., Oct. 3, 1931; s. Volney and Mary Lucile (McConkie) McF.; m. Marie Linstead, June 27, 1953; children—Deborah, John Scott, David. B.S. in Commerce and Fin, Bucknell U., 1953; J.D., Detroit Coll. Law, 1960. Pres., vice-chmn. MTD Products, Inc., Cleve., 1960-92; pres. MTD Products Inc., Cleve., 1980-91, vice chmn., 1990-92; gen. ptnr. Camelot Ptnrs., Cleve., 1992—; chmn. AC Products Co., Inc.; bd. dirs. Nat. Machinery Inc., Fusion Inc., Star Bank, Flambeau Corp.; chmn. bd. dirs. Guarantee Spltys. Inc.; chmn. financing adv. bd. State of Ohio Devel.; past pres. Cleve. World Trade Assn. Trustee, chmn. Fairview Health Svcs. Lt. Supply Corps, USN. Mem. Cleve. Yachting Club. Office: Camelot Ptnrs 20160 Parkside Dr Cleveland OH 44116-1347

MC FADDEN, JOSEPH MICHAEL, academic administrator; b. Joliet, Ill., Feb. 12, 1932; s. Francis Joseph and Lucille (Adler) McF.; m. Norma Cardwell, Oct. 10, 1958; children: Timothy Joseph, Mary Colleen, Jonathan Andrew. B.A., Lewis Coll., 1954; M.A., U. Chgo., 1961; Ph.D., No. Ill. U., 1968. Tchr. history Joliet Cath. High Sch., 1957-60; mem. faculty history dept. Lewis Coll., Lockport, Ill., 1960-70, assoc. prof., 1967-70, v.p. acad. affairs, 1968-70; prof. history, dean sch. Nat. and Social Sci., Kearney (Nebr.) State Coll., 1970-74; prof. history, dean Sch. Social and Behavioral Scis., Slippery Rock (Pa.) State Coll., 1974-77; pres. No. State Coll., Aberdeen, S.D., 1977-82, U. S.D., Vermillion, 1982-88, U. St. Thomas, Houston, 1988—. Served with USNR, 1954-56. Roman Catholic. Office: U St Thomas Office of Pres 3812 Montrose Blvd Houston TX 77006-4626

MCFADDEN, JOSEPH PATRICK, insurance company executive; b. Norristown, Pa., Jan. 1, 1939; s. Joseph Patrick and Anna (Brennan) McF.; m. Patricia Ann Burke, Jan. 28, 1961; children: Mary Ann, Linda, Patricia, Joseph, Nancy, Meghan. BA, LaSalle U., 1961. Claim adjuster Allstate Ins. Co., Valley Forge, Pa., 1963-66; various mgmt. positions Valley Forge and Harrison, N.Y., 1966-74; regional claim mgr. Rochester, N.Y., 1974-76, Murray Hill, N.J., 1976-79; zone claim mgr. Bannockburn, Ill., 1979-81; asst. regional mgr. Skokie, Ill., 1981-83; asst. v.p. Northbrook, Ill., 1983-84; regional v.p. Santa Ana, Calif., 1984-86; claim v.p. Northbrook, 1986-91, territorial v.p., 1991—. Served to 1st lt. U.S. Army, 1961-63. Mem. Nat. Auto Theft Bur. (bd. govs. 1986), Nat. Assn. Ind. Insurers (claims com. 1986), Ins. Crime Prevention Inst., Ins. Info. Inst. (adv. panel on legal issues). Roman Catholic. Home: 1005 Ashley Ln Libertyville IL 60048-3813 Office: Allstate Ins Co 2775 Sanders Rd Ste F6B Northbrook IL 60062-6110

MCFADDEN, LEON LAMBERT, artist, inventor; b. St. Paul, Apr. 19, 1920; s. Frank Grover and Irene Manilla Lambert McF.; m. Karyn Flannery, Nov. 6, 1986. Student, several colls., univs., art insts. Prin. McFadden Commercial Studios, 1946-50; with McFadden-Kaump Art Service, 1952-54; pres. McFadden Advt. (merger with Sundial Services, Inc.), 1954-70; mktg. dir. Kinelogic Corp., Mountain View, Calif., 1965-70; dir. rsch. and devel. proprietary patents Sundial Svcs., Inc., 1968-70; art instr. various Calif. community colls., 1972-74; minority bus. cons. VISTA/ACTION, 1974-75; pres., CEO Prometheus Project, Inc., Yreka, Calif., 1975—. Inventor, patentee 18 mechanical tools and devices; prin. artistic works include large assemblage painting of liberty, found image works (represented in White House spl. collection). Served with USN, 1942-46, PTO. Mem. AAAS, Mensa, Artists Equity Assn. Inc., Artists Equity Assn. N.Y., Siskiyou Artists Assn., Sierra Club. Home: 551 N Main St Yreka CA 96097-2524 Office: Liberty Painting Corp 6725 Old Highway 99 S Yreka CA 96097-9760

MCFADDEN, MARY JOSEPHINE, fashion industry executive; b. N.Y.C., Oct. 1, 1938; d. Alexander Bloomfield and Mary Josephine (Cutting) McF.; m. Philip Harari; 1 child, Justine. Ed., Sorbonne, Paris, France, Traphagen Sch. Design, 1957, Columbia, 1959-62; DFA, Internat. Fine Arts Coll., 1984. Pub. relations dir. Christian Dior, N.Y.C., 1962-64; merchandising editor Vogue South Africa, 1964-65, editor, 1965-69; polit. and travel columnist Rand (South Africa) Daily Mail, 1965-68; founder sculptural workshop Vukutu, Rhodesia, 1968-70; spl. projects editor Vogue U.S.A., 1973; pres. Mary McFadden, Inc., N.Y.C., 1976—; ptnr. MMcF Collection by Mary McFadden, 1991—; bd. dirs., advisor Sch. Design and Merchandising Kent State U., Eugene O'Neill Meml. Theatre Ctr.; mem. profl. com. Cooper-Hewitt Mus., Smithsonian Inst., Nat. Mus. of Design. Fashion and jewelry designer, 1973—. Advisor Nat. Endowment for Arts. Recipient Am. Fashion Critics award-Coty award, 1976, 78, 79, Audemars Piguet Fashion award, 1976, Rex award, 1977, award More Coll. Art, 1977, Pa. Gov.'s award, 1977, Roscoe award, 1978, Pres.'s Fellows award RISD, 1979, Neiman-Marcus award of excellence, 1979, Design Excellence award Pratt Inst., 1993, award N.Y. Landmarks Conservancy, 1994, NU Breed Fashion award, 1996, Marymount Coll. Fashion award, 1996; named to Fashion Hall of Fame, 1979; fellow RISD. Mem. Fashion Group, Coun. Fashion Designers Am. (pres., past bd. dirs.). Office: Mary McFadden Inc 240 W 35th St Fl 17 New York NY 10001-2506

MCFADDEN, NANCY ELIZABETH, lawyer; b. Wilmington, Del., Oct. 20, 1958; d. William P. and Mary Elizabeth (Adams) McF. BA, San Jose State U., 1984; JD, U. Va., 1987. Judicial clk. Hon. John P. Wiese U.S. Claims Ct., Washington, 1987-88; atty. O'Melveny & Myers, Washington, 1988-91; deputy communications dir. Office of Pres.-Elect, Washington, 1992-93; asst. ti atty. gen. U.S. Dept. Justice, Washington, 1993, prin. deputy assoc. atty. gen., 1993—; gen. counsel Dept. Transp., Washington, 1996—. Nat. deputy polit. dir. Clinton for Pres. Campaign, 1992, nat. surrogate dir. Clinton-Gore for Pres. Campaign, 1992.

MCFADDEN, PETER WILLIAM, mechanical engineering educator; b. Stamford, Conn., Aug. 2, 1932; s. Kenneth E. and Marie (Gleason) McF.; children: Peter, Kathleen, Mary. B.S. in Mech. Engring, U. Conn., 1954, M.S., 1956; Ph.D., Purdue U., 1959. Registered profl. engr., Ind. Asst. instr. U. Conn., 1954-56, prof. mech. engring., 1971—, dean Sch. Engring., 1971-85, dir. devel., 1985-88, provost, v.p., 1988, exec. asst. to pres., exec. sec. to bd. trustees, 1989—; mem. faculty Purdue U., 1956-71; prof. mech. engring., head Purdue U. (Sch. Mech. Engring.), 1965-71; postdoctoral research Swiss Fed. Inst., Zurich, 1960-61; cons. to industry, 1959—. Mem. ASME, Am. Soc. Engring. Edn. Research in cryogenics, heat transfer, mass transfer. Office: U Conn Gulley Hall U-48 352 Mansfield Rd Storrs Mansfield CT 06268

MC FADDEN, ROBERT DENNIS, reporter; b. Milw., Feb. 11, 1937; s. Francis Joseph and Violet (Charleston) McF.; student U. Wis., Eau Claire, 1955-57; B.S. cum laude, U. Wis., Madison, 1960; m. Judith Marian Silverman, June 20, 1971; 1 son, Nolan Seth. Reporter, Wisconsin Rapids (Wis.) Daily Tribune, 1957-58, Wis. State Jour., Madison, 1958-59, Cin. Enquirer, 1960-61; sr. writer, reporter N.Y. Times, 1961—; mem. adv. coun. St. John's U. dept journalism, 1996—. Co-author: No Hiding Place, 1981; Outrage: The Story Behind the Tawana Brawley Hoax, 1990. Served with U.S. Army, 1960-61, Res., 1961-68. Recipient Byline award N.Y. Press Club, 1973, 74, 80, 87, 89, 92, Page One award Newspaper Guild N.Y., 1978, Spot News award Uniformed Firemen's Assn., 1967, Spot News award L.I. Press Club, 1984, 95, Chancellor's award for Disting. Svc. U. Wis., 1987, Excellence in Local Reporting award N.Y. Newspaper Publ. Assn., 1988, Spot News award N.Y. State Associated Press, 1989, 91, Continuing Coverage award, 1995, In Depth Reporting award, 1989, 91, Ochs Prize in Journalism, 1989, Best News/Feature Story award Internat. Assn. Fire Fighters, 1991, Pulitzer Prize for Spot News Reporting (N.Y. Times team), 1994, 96, Nat. Spot News award Asian-Am. Journalists Assn., 1994, Comprehensive Reporting award, N.Y. Uniformed Fire Officers Assn., 1995. Mem. N.Y. Soc. Silurians (Spot News Story award 1977, Peter Kihss award 1987, Investigative reporting award 1989, Excellence in Journalism award 1994, gov. 1988—). Office: NY Times 229 W 43rd St New York NY 10036-3913

MCFADDEN, THOMAS, academic administrator; b. N.Y.C., Nov. 12, 1935; m. Monica A. Dowdall; children—Monica, David. B.A., Cathedral Coll., 1957; S.T.L., Gregorian U., 1961; S.T.D., Cath. U., 1963. Asst. prof. St. Joseph's Coll., Bklyn., 1963-66; chmn. theology dept. Cathedral Coll., Douglaston, N.Y., 1966-68; asst. prof. Loyola Coll., Balt., 1968-69; prof. St. Joseph's U., Phila., 1970-82, dean Coll. Arts and Scis., 1982-87; acad. v.p. St. John Fisher Coll., Rochester, N.Y., 1987-92; pres. Marymount Coll., Calif., 1992—; vis. prof. Cath. U., Washington, 1967-68, LaSalle U., Phila., summer 1974-79. Author, editor: New Cath. Ency., 1974, 79. Editor, Dictionary of Religion, 3 vols., 1979; editor: Liberation, Revolution and Freedom, 1975, America in Theological Perspective, 1976. Recipient Disting. Teaching award Lindback, 1978, N.Y. State Excelsior award Bd. Examiners, 1991; HEW grantee, 1972; CAPHE grantee, 1985. Mem. AAUP, Coll. Theology Soc. (chmn. pubs. com. 1973-77). Democrat. Roman Catholic. Office: Marymount Coll 30800 Palos Verdes Dr E Rancho Palos Verdes CA 90275-6299

MCFADIN, HELEN LOZETTA, retired elementary education educator; b. Tucumcari, N.Mex., Sept. 7, 1923; d. Henry J. and LaRue Altha (Ford) Stockton; m. John Reece McFadin, July 3, 1946; 1 child, Janice Lynn McFadin Koenig. AB in Edn./Psychology, Highlands U., Las Vegas, N.Mex., 1956; MA in Teaching, N.Mex. State U., 1968; postgrad., U. N.D., 1965, St. Leo's Coll., St. Leo, Fla., 1970. Cert. tchr., K-12 reading/psychology specialist, N.Mex. Tchr. 1st and 2d grades Grant County Schs., Bayard, N.Mex., 1943-44; tchr. 4th grade Durango (Colo.) Pub. Schs., 1946-48; tchr. 2d grade Artesia Pub. Schs., Loco Hills, N.Mex., 1955; tchr. 3d grade Alamogordo (N.Mex.) Pub. Schs., 1957-66, h.s. reading specialist, 1966-72, elem. reading specialist, 1972-77, tchr. 4th grade, 1977-82, reading tchr. 7th grade, dept. chair, 1982-87; ret. N.Mex. State U., Alamogordo, 1987, instr. edn., 1987-90; organizer reading labs. h.s., elem. schs., Alamogordo, 1966-77, designer programs and curriculum, 1957-89; presenter/cons. in field; cons. Mary Kay Cosmetics. Contbr. articles to profl. jours. Local and dist. judge spelling bees and sci. fairs Alamogordo Pub. Schs., 1987—. Recipient Literacy award Otero County Reading Coun., 1986; inducted in Women's Hall of Fame, Alamogordo Women's Clubs, 1989. Mem. Am. Bus. Women's Assn. (pres. 1986-87, Woman of the Yr. 1988), C. of C., NEA (del. 1957-87, Dedicated Svc. award 1987), N.Mex. Edn. Assn., Internat. Reading Assn. (mem. Spl. League of the Honored 1985, pres. 1975-76), N.Mex. Reading Assn. (bd. dirs. 1988-94, del. to 1st Russian reading conf. 1992, Dedicated Svc. award 1994), Beta Sigma Phi, Kappa Kappa Iota (Disting. Educator Emeritus Cert. of Merit 1988). Republican. Baptist. Avocations: reading, fashion modeling. Home: 2364 Union Ave Alamogordo NM 88310-3848

MCFALL, CATHERINE GARDNER, poet, critic, educator; b. Jacksonville, Fla., July 10, 1952; d. Albert Dodge and Joan (Livingston) McF.; m. Peter Forbes Olberg, Oct. 21, 1978; 1 child, Amanda Olberg. Baccalaureat, U. Paris, 1973; AB magna cum laude, Wheaton Coll., Norton, Mass., 1974; MA, Johns Hopkins U., 1975; PhD, NYU, 1990. Editorial asst., short story editor Ladies' Home Jour., N.Y.C., 1975-77; adminstrv. dir. Poetry Soc. Am., N.Y.C., 1981-83; instr. writing NYU, N.Y.C., 1983-87, asst. dir. Poetics Inst., 1984-86; asst. prof. humanities Cooper Union, N.Y.C., 1990—. Author: Jonathan's Cloud, 1986, Discovery, 1989 (Nation award), Naming the Animals, 1994, The Pilot's Daughter, 1996; contbr. poetry and revs. to mags. including Paris Rev., New Yorker, N.Y. Times, others. MacDowell Colony fellow, 1980, 86, Yaddo fellow, 1981, 84, 91, 93, Nat. Arts Club Poetry scholar Bread Loaf Writers Conf., 1983. Mem. MLA, Poets and Writers, Poetry Soc. Am., Nat. Book Critics Circle.

MCFARLAN, FRANKLIN WARREN, business administration educator; b. Boston, Oct. 18, 1937; s. Ronald Lyman and Ethel Warren (White) McF.; m. Margaret Karen Nelson, Dec. 17, 1971; children: Andrew, Clarissa, Elizabeth. A.B., Harvard Coll., 1959, M.B.A., 1961, D.B.A., 1965. Asst. prof. Harvard Bus. Sch., Boston, 1964-68, assoc. prof., 1968-73, prof. bus. adminstrn., 1973—, sr. assoc. dean, dir. rsch., 1991-95, sr. assoc. dean external rels., 1995—; dir. Providian Corp., Louisville, Pioneer Hy-Bred Corp., Des Moines, Computer Sci. Corp., L.A. Author: (with Richard Nolan) Information Systems Administration, 1973; (with Linda Applegate and James L. McKenney) Corporate Information Management, 1987, 4th edit., 1996; editor: (with Richard Nolan) Information Systems Handbook, 1973, Information Systems Research Challenge, 1984; sr. editor MIS Quar., 1986-88. Bd. dirs., pres. Belmont (Mass.) Day Sch., 1982-86; bd. dirs. Dana Hall Sch., Wellesley, Mass., 1982-94, chmn. bd., 1990-93; trustee Mt. Auburn Hosp., 1991—, chmn. bd., 1995—; trustee Winsor Sch., 1994—. 1st lt. U.S. Army, 1962-67. Republican. Episcopalian. Club: The Country (Brookline, Mass.). Home: 37 Beatrice Cir Belmont MA 02178-2657 Office: Harvard Bus Sch Soldiers Field Rd Boston MA 02163

MCFARLAND, DAVID E., university official; b. Enid, Okla., Sept. 25, 1938; s. Eugene James McF. and Lydia May (Catlin) Lawson; m. Marcia Ruth Lake, Nov. 27, 1958 (div. 1978); children: Jennifer, Jeffrey, Jon, Julie; m., Susan Kaye Siler, Mar. 3, 1979 (div. 1994); 1 child, Matthew Chapple; m. Barbara Ambrogro, Oct. 1994. BS, Wichita State U., 1961, MS, 1964; PhD, U. Kans., 1967. Stress analysis engr. Boeing Co., Wichita, Kans., 1957-64; instr. U. Kans., Lawrence, 1964-67; asst. v.p., dean Wichita State U., 1967-81; dean. sch. tech., Pittsburgh State U., Kans., 1981-85; provost, v.p. acad. affairs Cen. Mo. State U., 1985-88; pres. Kutztown U. of Pa., 1988—. Author: Mechanics of Materials, 1977; Analysis of Plates, 1972. Contbr. articles to tech. jours. Office: Kutztown U of Pa Office of Pres Kutztown PA 19530

MCFARLAND, DONALD JOE, hardware engineer; b. Oak Creek, Colo., Dec. 8, 1932; s. Donald Coleman McFarland and Barbara (Yirsa) Schwabe; m. Betty Irene Johnson, Nov. 17, 1951; children: Donald J. Jr., Diana D., Cheryl R. BSEE, Okla. State U., 1958. Elec. engr. Rockedyne divsn. N.Am. Aviation, Canoga Park, Calif., 1958-60; elec. engr. space and info. divsn. N.Am. Aviation, Lakewood, Calif., 1964-66; elec. engr. Lockheed Missile & Space, Van Nuys, Calif., 1960-64; sys. engr. Northrip Space Lab., Hawthorn, Calif., 1964-66; sr. elec. engr. MTS Jet Propulsion Lab., Pasadena, 1966—. Cpl. USMC, 1952-54. Achievements include design and testing of rocket engine test bed controls; prodn. of various items of surveillance satellite and polaris missile operational support equipment, mariner and voyager attitude control subsy. operational support equipment, drop dynamics module for Spacelab Three, drop physics module for U.S. Microgravity Lab. One, tempus incandescence measuring instrument for Internat. Microgravity Lab. One; design of a Martian surface seismometer prototype design, production and testing of Apollo and Lunar Exploration Module factory and launch Automatic Checkout Equipment. Home: 4945 Boston Ave La Crescenta CA 91214-1012 Office: Jet Propulsion Lab 4800 Oak Grove Dr Pasadena CA 91109-8001

MC FARLAND, FRANK EUGENE, university official; b. Ft. Towson, Okla., Sept. 8, 1918; s. Thomas Edward and Sadie Margaret (Gayer) McF.; m. Trudy Hudson Lively, Dec. 20, 1947 (dec.); children—Marsha Lane, Martha Lynne McFarland Cox. B.A. cum laude, Baylor U., 1950; M.A., Columbia U., 1953, Ed.D., 1959; postgrad., U. Tex., 1956, Tex. A. and M. U., 1956. Lic. psychologist, Okla. Counselor Tex. A&M U., College Station, 1950-51; acting dir. counseling Tex. A&M U., 1951, personal and vocat. counselor, 1951-55, instr., 1951-53, asst. prof. psychology, 1953-55, acting dir. testing and research basic div., asst. prof. psychology, 1955-56, dir. testing and research, basic div., assoc. prof., 1956-69; dir. student personnel Coll. Arts and Scis., assoc. prof. Okla. State U., Stillwater, 1959-61; dean student affairs, prof. psychology Okla. State U., 1961-68, prof. edn. Coll. Edn., 1968-73, dir. student services, prof. applied behavioral studies, 1973-84, dir. student svcs., prof. applied behavioral studies emeritus, 1984—; treas., adminstrv. sec. Okla. State U. Emeriti Assn., 1990—. Author: Compilation of Research Studies from 1953-59, 1959, Student Attitudes Toward the Basic Division, 1958; contbr. articles to profl. jours. First v.p. United Fund Stillwater, Inc., 1963-64, pres., 1964-65; cabinet adviser Will Rogers council Boy Scouts Am., 1961-63; mem. Mayor's Com. on Hosp. Adv. Bd., 1963-66; mem. devel. council Baylor U., 1983—; treas., bd. dirs. YMCA Found.; treas. Stillwater YMCA Found., Inc., 1986—. Served with AUS, 1941-45. Decorated Purple Heart with oak leaf cluster, Bronze Star; recipient Okla. State U. Student Senate award of recognition, 1968; Columbia U. faculty fellow, 1952-53. Mem. Am. Psychol. Assn., Okla. Psychol. Assn. (assoc.), Am. Personnel and Guidance Assn., Southwestern Assn. Student Personnel Adminstrs., Okla. Personnel, Guidance and Counseling Assn., Okla. Deans and Counselors Assn., Okla. Edn. Assn. (pres. 1972-73), Omicron Delta Kappa (achievement award for outstanding contbn. to Okla. State U. 1968), Phi Delta Kappa, Kappa Delta Pi, Alpha Chi, Psi, Chi, Sigma Epsilon Sigma, Phi Kappa Phi, Omicron Delta Kappa (coll. rep.). Lodge: Rotary. Home: 1224 N Lincoln St Stillwater OK 74075-2749

MC FARLAND, H. RICHARD, food company executive; b. Hoopeston, Ill., Aug. 19, 1930; s. Arthur Bryan and Jennie (Wilkey) McF.; m. Sarah Forney, Dec. 30, 1967. BS, U. Ill., 1952. With Campbell Soup Co., Camden, N.J., 1957-67; mgr. purchasing Campbell Soup Co., 1961-67; dir. procurement Keebler Co., Elmhurst, Ill., 1967-69; v.p. purchasing and distbn. Ky. Fried Chicken Corp., Louisville, 1969-74; v.p. food svcs., sales and distbn. Ky. Fried Chicken Corp., 1974-75; pres., dir. Mid-Continent Carton Co., Louisville, 1974-75, Ky. Fried Chicken Mfg. Corp., Nashville, 1974-75; owner, pres., dir. McFarland Foods Corp., Indpls., 1975—; bd. dirs. Fountain Trust Co., Ind., Covington Svc. Corp., Ind.; pres., bd. dirs. Ky. Fried Chicken Advt., Inc., Ind., 1975-87, exec. coun., 1988-91; mem. exec. coun., nat. franchise coun. Ky. Fried Chicken, 1979-85; bd. dirs. Ky. fried Chicken Nat. Purchasing Coop., 1981-85, chmn. ins. com., 1982-84; chmn. processed foods com. World's Poultry Congress, 1974; dir. nat. advt. coun. Ky. Fried Chicken, 1985-91, exec. com., 1988-90, chmn., 1989-90; mem. devel. com. U. Ill., 1989—. Mem. U. Ill. Found., 1992—, bd. dirs., 1993—; chmn. U. Ill. Nat. Advocates, 1994—; life pres. U. Ill. Sr. Class of '52; bd. dirs. Ind. Fedn. Children and Youth, 1983-84; chmn. campaign Ind. Ky. Fried Chicken March of Dimes, 1978-87; nat. trustee McCormick Theol. Sem., 1993—. 1st lt. USAF, 1952-54, Korea. Recipient Award of Merit U. Ill. Coll. Agr., 1988, Achievement award U. Ill. Alumni Assn., 1996. Mem. Ky. Restaurant Asns. (bd. dirs. 1970-75), Nat. Broiler Coun. (bd. dirs. 1971-74), Ind. Restaurant Assn., Am. Shorthorn Breeders Assn., Great Lakes Ky. Fried Chicken Franchise Assn. (bd. dirs. 1975-91, 1st v.p. 1978-79, pres. 1979-80), Delta Upsilon. Presbyterian. Clubs: Main Line Ski (Phila.) (pres. 1964); Hillcrest Country. Home: 6361 Avalon Ln Indianapolis IN 46220-5009 Office: 6284 Rucker Rd Ste M Indianapolis IN 46220-4851

MCFARLAND, JAMES W., academic administrator. Dean bus. adminstrn. U. Houston, University Park, until 1988; dean Freeman Sch. Bus. Tulane U., New Orleans, 1988—. Office: Dean School of Business Tulane University New Orleans LA 70118

MCFARLAND, JAMES WILLIAM, real estate development company executive; b. Montgomery, Ala., Sept. 7, 1948; s. Ward Wharton and Frances Adelia (Morrow) McF.; B.S., U. Ala., 1970; m. Miriam Melinda Webster, Feb. 20, 1971; children—James William, Mimi Morrow. Dir. real estate for Ky., Ind. and Tenn., Winn-Dixie Stores, Inc., Louisville, 1970-72; v.p. Ward McFarland, Inc., Tuscaloosa, Ala., 1972—, also dir. Mem. Coun. for Devel. of French in La., 1976—, Friends of Libr., 1975—; commr. Dept. Mental Health, 1987-89; ; Rep. nominee U.S. Congress Ala. 7th Dist., 1986; young churchmen adviser Episcopal Diocese Ala., 1976—, conv. del.; charter investor, chair of real estate U. Ala.; chmn. Ala. Rapid Rail Transit Commn.; vice chmn. La.-Miss.-Ala. Rapid Rail Transit Commn., 1983-84, chmn., 1984—; state advisor Congl. Adv. Com., Am. Security Coun.; sr. warden Christ Episc. Ch., 1984; bd. dirs. Tuscaloosa Kidney Found.; mem. Rep. State Exec. Com., 1991—; commr. Dept. Mental Health State of Ala.; chmn. Tuscaloosa County Reps., 1991—; flotilla staff officer USCG Aux., 1994—. Named hon. citizen of Mobile and New Orleans, hon. mem. mayor's staff, Mobile. Mem. Nat. Assn. Realtors, Tuscaloosa Bd. Realtors, Nat. Small Bus. Assn., U. Ala. Commerce Execs. Soc., U. Ala. Alumni Assn., Nat. Assn. R.R. Passengers, Ala. Assn. R.R. Passengers (pres. 1982, 90, 91), North River Yacht, Kiwanis of Greater Tuscaloosa, Delta Sigma Pi. Home: 4714 7th Ct E Tuscaloosa AL 35405-4104 Office: 325 Skyland Blvd E Tuscaloosa AL 35405-4030

MCFARLAND, JANE ELIZABETH, librarian; b. Athens, Tenn., June 22, 1937; d. John Homer and Martha Virginia (Large) McFarland. AB, Smith Coll., 1959; M in Divinity, Yale U., 1963; MS in LS, U. N.C., 1971. Tchr. hist. and religion Northfield Schs., Mass., 1961-62; head librarian reference and circulation Yale Divinity Library, New Haven, Conn., 1963-71; head librarian Bradford (Mass.) Coll., 1972-77; reference librarian U. Tenn., Chattanooga, Tenn., 1977-80; head librarian reference dept Chattanooga-Hamilton County Bicentennial Library, Tenn., 1980-86, acting dir., 1986, dir., 1986—. Mem. Chattanooga Library Assn., Tenn. Library Assn., Southeastern Library Assn., Am. Library Assn., Phi Beta Kappa (treas. 1987, 88). Democrat. Roman Catholic. Avocations: reading, travel, needlework. Home: 1701 Estrellita Cir Chattanooga TN 37421-5754 Office: Chattanooga-Hamilton County Libr 1001 Broad St Chattanooga TN 37402-2620

MCFARLAND, JANET CHAPIN, consulting company executive; b. New Castle, Pa., Jan. 5, 1962; d. Robert Chapin McFarland and Dorothy Jean (Heade) Jost; m. Steven Mitchell Walter, July 30, 1994. BS in Imaging Sci. and Engring., Rochester Inst. Tech., 1985; MBA in Innovation Mgmt. and Mktg., Syracuse U., 1990. Rsch. engr. Shipley Co., Inc., Newton, Mass., 1985-88; mktg. cons. Syracuse (N.Y.) U. Sch. Mgmt., 1988-90; market rsch. coop. AT&T Consumer Comms. Svcs., Basking Ridge, N.J., summer 1989; tech. analyst DynCorp Meridian, Alexandria, Va., 1991-93; dir. studies and analysis Tech. Strategies & Alliances, Burke, Va., 1993-94; pres. ArBar, Inc., Alexandria, Va., 1994—; presenter in field. Mem. Internat. Soc. Optical Engrs., Soc. Mfg. Engrs. (chpt. chair 1995), Beta Gamma Sigma, Alpha Mu Alpha. Office: ArBar Inc 312 S Washington St Ste 5B Alexandria VA 22314

MCFARLAND, JON WELDON, county commissioner; b. Wenatchee, Wash., Aug. 23, 1938; s. Charles Edward and Maud Elizabeth (Brennan) McF.; m. Kay Annette Erbes, Apr. 5, 1956; children: Colleen, Michael, Heather. BS in Edn., Eastern Wash. State U., 1961; MS in Personnel Adminstrn., George Washington U., 1966; Grad., Command and Gen. Staff Coll., Fort Leavenworth, Kans., 1970, U.S. Army War Coll., Carlisle Barracks, Pa., 1980. Commd. U.S. Army, 1961, advanced through grades to col., 1981, retired, 1988; ops. officer European Hdqtrs. U.S. Army, Heidelberg, Fed. Republic Germany, 1980-83; commdr. 16th mil. police brigade U.S. Army, Fort Bragg, N.C., 1983-85, provost marshal 18th Airborne Corps, 1983-85; asst. commandant, commdr. of troops U.S. Army Mil. Police Sch., Fort McClellan, Ala., 1985-88; county commr. Columbia County, Wash., 1989-96; dir., owner Mr. Mc's Direct Mktg. Svcs., 1992—; owner, dir. Spectro-Optics of Ea. Wash., Dayton, 1994—; Wash. staff for courthouse security, 1995—9; vice chmn. Southeastern Emergency Med. and Trauma Coun., Wash., 1990-94, chmn., 1995-96; chmn. Columbia County Bd. Commrs., 1990, 93; bd. dirs. Emergency Mgmt. Svcs., Columbia County. Author: History of Civil Disturbance 1960-68, 1969. Bd. dirs. Columbia County Pub. Health Dist., Dayton, 1989-96, chmn., 1995-96; bd. dirs. Project Timothy Pub. Svcs., Columbia County Health Found., 1989—; vice chmn. Palouse Econ. Devel. Corp., 1990-92, chmn., 1993-95. Decorated Legion of Merit, Bronze Star, numerous others. Mem. Assn. U.S. Army, Wash. State Assn. Counties, U.S. Army War Coll. Found., Kiwanis (bd. dirs. Dayton 1990—). Democrat. Roman Catholic. Avocations: woodworking, pottery, fishing, hunting, travel. Home: RR 3 Box 248 Dayton WA 99328-9792 Office: Columbia County 341 E Main St Dayton WA 99328-1361

MCFARLAND, KAY ELEANOR, state supreme court chief justice; b. Coffeyville, Kans., July 20, 1935; d. Kenneth W. and Margaret E. (Thrall) McF. BA magna cum laude, Washburn U., Topeka, 1957, JD, 1964. Bar: Kans. 1964. Sole practice Topeka, 1964-71; probate and juvenile judge Shawnee County, Topeka, 1971-73; dist. judge Topeka, 1973-77; assoc. justice Kans. Supreme Ct., 1977-95, chief justice, 1995—. Mem. Kans. Bar Assn. Office: Kans Supreme Ct Kans Jud Ctr 301 W 10th St Topeka KS 66612

MCFARLAND, KAY FLOWERS, medical educator; b. Daytona Beach, Fla., Jan. 27, 1942; d. Ernest Clyde and Sarah Elizabeth (Holder) Flowers; m. Dee Edward McFarland, Aug. 18, 1963; children: Grace, Joy, Eric, Sarah. BS, Wake Forest Coll., 1963; MD, Bowman Gray Sch. Medicine, 1966. Diplomate Am. Bd. Internal Medicine, Endocrinology, Geriatrics. Intern N.C. Bapt. Hosp., Winston-Salem; resident medicine Cleve. Clinic; fellow endocrinology Med. Coll. Ga., Augusta, from instr. to asst. prof. medicine, 1971-77; assoc. prof. to prof. ob-gyn. Sch. Medicine U. S.C., Columbia, 1977-86, prof. medicine Sch. Medicine, 1986—, assoc. dean continuing edn. Sch. Medicine, 1986-91. Contbr. chpts. to books and articles to profl. jours. Fellow ACP, ACE; mem. Am. Diabetes Assn. (past pres. Augusta chpt., Profl. award 1975, Woman of Valor award 1996). Avocations: music, writing. Office: USC Sch Medicine Ste 506 Two Medical Park Columbia SC 29203

MCFARLAND, LESLIE KING, special education educator; b. Canton, Ohio, July 13, 1954; d. John Edward and Nadine Mae (Phillips) King; m. James David McFarland, July 16, 1977. BS in Edn., Bowling Green State U., 1976. Cert. specific learning disabilities, spl. edn. tchr. K-12, developmentally handicapped spl. edn. tchr. K-12, elem. tchr. 1-8, Ohio. Tchr. developmentally handicapped Warren (Ohio) City Schs., 1976—; bd. dirs. McFarland and Son Funeral Svcs., Inc., v.p., 1992—. Mem. Fine Arts Coun. Trumbull County, 1988—; bd. dirs. Warren Dance Ctr., sec., 1988-90; bd. dirs. Warren Chamber Orch., 1986-92; mem. Trumbull County Women's History Com., 1993—; deacon 1st Presbyn. Ch., 1994. Mem. NEA, Ohio Edn. Assn., Warren Edn. Assn., AAUW (past sec.), Embroiderers' Guild Am. (Western Res. chpt., rep. to Fine Arts Coun. Trumbull County). Avocations: embroidery, needlepoint, camping, travel. Home: 197 Washington St NW Warren OH 44483-4732

MCFARLAND, MARY A., elementary and secondary school educator, administrator; b. St. Louis, Nov. 12, 1937; d. Allen and Maryann (Crawford) Mabry; m. Gerald McFarland, May 30, 1959. BS in Elem. Edn., S.E. Mo. State U., 1959; MA in Secondary Edn., Washington U., St. Louis, 1965; PhD in Curriculum and Instrn., St. Louis U., 1977. Cert. tchr. elem., secondary, supt., Mo. Elem. tchr. Berkeley Sch. Dist., St. Louis, 1959-64; secondary tchr. Parkway Sch. Dist., St. Louis, 1965-75, social studies coord. K-12, 1975—, dir. staff devel., 1984—; adj. prof. Maryville U., St. Louis, 1990—; cons. pvt. practice, Chesterfield, Mo. Co-author: (text series) The World Around Us, 1990, 3d rev. edit., 1995; contbr. articles to profl. jours. Nat. faculty Nat. Issues Forum, Dayton, Ohio. Mem. ASCD, Social Sci. Edn. Consortium, Nat. Coun. for Social Studies (pres. 1989-90), Mo. Coun. for Social Studies (pres. 1980-81). Democrat. Methodist. Avocations: music, sailing. Office: Parkway Schs Dist Instrnl Svcs 12657 Fee Fee Rd Saint Louis MO 63146-3855

MC FARLAND, NORMAN FRANCIS, bishop; b. Martinez, Calif., Feb. 21, 1922; student St. Patrick's Sem., Menlo Park, Calif.; J.C.D., Cath. U. Am. Ordained priest Roman Catholic Ch., 1946, consecrated bishop, 1970; titular bishop of Bida and aux. bishop of San Francisco, 1970-74; apostolic adminstr. Diocese of Reno, 1974-76; bishop Diocese of Reno-Las Vegas, 1976-87, Diocese of Orange, Calif., 1987—. Office: Marywood Ctr 2811 E Villa Real Dr Orange CA 92667-1999

MCFARLAND, RICHARD M., executive recruiting consultant; b. Portland, Maine, Sept. 10, 1923; s. George Fiske and Phillys C. (Macomber) McF.; BChemE, Rensselaer Poly. Inst., 1944; postgrad. U. Mich., 1946-47; m. Virginia Fitz-Randolph Ripley, Dec. 6, 1947; children: Richard Macomber, Kirk, Jane. Prodn. supr. E. I. duPont, 1947-51; mgr. agrl. chem. market research Brea Chem. (Calif.) subs. Union Oil Co., 1953-55; product mgr. chem. div. FMC Corp., N.Y.C., 1955-59; mgr. mktg. devel. Tex. Butadiene & Chem., N.Y.C., 1959-60; pres. Cumberland Chem. Corp., N.Y.C., 1960-67; gen. mgr. inorganic div. Wyandotte Chem. Co. (Mich.), 1967-69; asso. Heidrick & Struggles, Inc., N.Y.C., 1969-72, v.p., 1972-81; founder, pres. Brissenden, McFarland, Wagoner & Fuccella, Inc. and predecessors, Stamford, Conn., 1981-94 . Ensign USNR, 1943-46, lt. comdr., 1951-53. Mem. Am. Chem. Soc., Lambda Chi Alpha. Clubs: Landmark, Cedar Point Yacht, Nutmeg Curling. Patentee in field. Home: 16 Clover Ln Westport CT 06880-2626

MCFARLAND, RICHARD MACKLIN, retired journalist; b. Blockton, Iowa, Mar. 27, 1922; s. William Harold McFarland and Elsie (Sisson) McFarland Chavannes; m. Jacquelyn Jean Folske, Mar. 22, 1955; children: Marcy Ann, Scott Macklin, Elizabeth Ann McFarland Heyda, Kathryn Belle. BA, U. Iowa, 1944. Newsman UPI, Des Moines, 1944, Chgo., 1945, 46-47; bur. mgr. UPI, Bismarck, N.D., 1944-45, Herrin, Ill., 1945, Sioux Falls, S.D., 1947-49, Milw., 1949-51; legis. reporter UPI, Des Moines, 1947, Pierre, S.D., 1949; Iowa mgr. UPI, Des Moines, 1951-54; NW mgr. UPI, Mpls., 1954-55; Wis. mgr. UPI, Milw., 1956-57, regional exec. sales, 1958-59; bur. mgr. UPI, Chgo., 1960-61; Minn. mgr. UPI, Mpls., 1961-69; Mich. editor UPI, Detroit, 1969-71; Minn. editor UPI, Mpls., 1971-84; bur. mgr.-capitol reporter UPI, St. Paul, 1985-89; bd. dirs. Minn. Press Club, 1981-84. Former deacon, Advent Luth. Ch., Roseville, Minn., 8 yrs. Served with USN, 1943-44. Avocations: reading, music, fishing, backpacking, golf. Home: 7312 5th Ave Bradenton FL 34209-1522

MCFARLAND, ROBERT EDWIN, lawyer; b. St. Louis, July 25, 1946; s. Francis Taylor and Kathryne (Stevens) M.; m. Jeannine M. Ghekiere, Feb. 26, 1982. B.A., U. Mich. 1968, J.D., 1971. Bar: Mich. 1971, U.S. Dist. Ct. (ea. dist.) Mich. 1971, U.S. Ct. Appeals (6th cir.) 1974, U.S. Supreme Ct. 1975, U.S. Ct. Appeals (D.C.) 1978. Law clk. to chief judge Mich. Ct. Appeals, 1971-72; assoc. William B. Elmer, St. Clair Shores, Mich., 1972-74, James Elsman, Birmingham, Mich., 1974-75; ptnr. McFarland, Schmier, Stoneman & Singer, Troy, Mich. 1975-77; sr. ptnr. McFarland & Bullard, Bloomfield Hills, Mich., 1977-90; sr. ptnr. McFarland & Niemer, Farmington Hills, Mich., 1990-91; shareholder, Foster, Swift, Collins & Smith, P.C., Farmington Hills, Mich., 1992—. Chmn. bd. of govs. Transp. Law Jour., U. Denver Coll. of Law, 1981-83; mem. rulemaking study com. Mich. Pub. Svc. Commn., 1983-84, Motor Carrier adv. bd., 1984-88; mem. bd. of control Intercollegiate Athletics, U. Mich., 1966-68. Served to capt. USAR, 1971-80. Mem. Transp. Lawyers Assn., Assn. Interstate Commn. Practioners, ABA, State Bar Mich. (vice-chmn. transp. law com. adminstrn. law sect. 1990—, sect. coun. aol law sect. 1994—), Am. Judicature Soc.

MC FARLAND, ROBERT HAROLD, physicist, educator; b. Severy, Kans., Jan. 10, 1918; s. Robert Eugene and Georgia (Simpson) McF.; m. Twilah Mae Seefeld, Aug. 28, 1940; children: Robert Alan, Rodney Jon. B.S. and B.A., Kans. State Tchrs. Coll., Emporia, 1940; Ph.M. (Mendenhall fellow), U. Wis., 1943, Ph.D., 1947. Sci. instr., coach high sch. Chase, Kans., 1940-41; instr. navy radio sch. U. Wis., Madison, 1943-44; sr. engr. Sylvania Elec. Corp., 1944-46; faculty Kans. State U., 1947-60, prof. physics, 1954-60, dir. nuclear lab., 1958-60; physicist U. Calif. Lawrence Radiation Lab., 1960-69; dean Grad. Sch., U. Mo., Rolla, 1969-79, dir. instnl. analysis and planning, 1979-82; prof. physics U. Mo., Rolla, 1969-84, prof. emeritus physics dept., 1985—; v.p. acad. affairs U. Mo. System, 1974-75; Intergovtl. Personnel Act appointee Dept. Energy, Washington, 1982-84; vis. prof. U. Calif., Berkeley, 1980-81; mem. Grad. Record Exams. Bd., 1971-75, chmn. steering com., 1972-73; cons. Well Surveys, Inc., Tulsa, 1953-54, Argonne Nat. Lab., Chgo., 1955-59, Kans. Dept. Pub. Health, 1956-57, cons. in residence Lawrence Radiation Lab., U. Calif., 1957, 58, 59, med. physics U. Okla. Med. Sch., 1971, grad. schs., PhD physics program, Utah State U., 1972; physicist, regional counselor Office Ordnance Research, Durham, N.C., 1955. Contbr. articles to profl. jours. Active Boy Scouts Am., 1952—, mem. exec. bd. San Francisco Bay Area council, 1964-68, Ozark Council, 1986—; chmn. Livermore (Calif.) Library Bond drive, 1964. Mem. Kans. N.G., 1936-40. Recipient Silver Beaver award Boy Scouts Am., 1968, Community Service award C. of C., 1965, Disting. Alumnus award Kans. State Tchrs. Coll., 1969; named Disting. Lt. Gov., Kiwanis, 1985. Fellow Kiwanis Internat., 1992, fellow AAAS, Am. Phys. Soc.; mem. AAUP (chpt. pres. 1956-57), Am. Assn. Physics Tchrs., Mo. Acad. Sci., Mo. Assn. Phys. Sci. Tchrs., Am. Soc. Engring. Edn., Kiwanis (lt. gov. Mo.-Ark. dist. 1984-85, internat. accredited rep. 1985-92), Sigma Xi, Lambda Delta Lambda, Xi Phi, Kappa Mu Epsilon, Kappa Delta Pi, Pi Mu Epsilon, Gamma Sigma Delta, Phi Kappa Phi. Patentee in field of light prodn., vacuum prodn., controlled thermonuclear reactions. Home: 309 Christy Dr Rolla MO 65401-4073 Office: U Mo Physics Dept Rolla MO 65401 *Continuation of the last hundred years of major progress in the quality of life for the human race will not only require the best of our educational systems and technological talents but a sincere interest in all of us to contribute positively toward our collective well-being.*

MCFARLAND, SHIRLEY ANN, women's health nurse; b. Greensburg, Pa., Sept. 25, 1935; d. Charles Thomas and Hettie Jane (Kunkle) Brown; m. Marion Luther McFarland, July 5, 1958; children: Shirley Marie McKinney, David Eugene, Kevin Paul. Diploma in Nursing, Johnstown (Pa.) Meml. Hosp., 1956; BS, U. Kans., 1976; MSN, Wayne State U., 1985. Cert. nurse practitioner; RN, Pa., Mich. Operating rm. staff nurse Conemaugh Valley Meml. Hosp., Johnstown, 1956, chg. nurse, 1957-58; staff nurse, clin. instr. Torrence State Hosp., Blairsville, Pa., 1956-57; instr. classroom and clinic Clarinda (Iowa) C.C., 1960-62; head nurse Standish (Mich.) Cmty. Hosp., 1971-82; insvc. dir. Geriatric Village, West Branch, Mich., 1982-83; instr. classroom and clinic Kirtland C.C., Roscommon, Mich., 1982-83; nurse practitioner Dist. Health Dept. #2, West Branch, 1988-94, Primary Care Practice, West Branch, 1985—. Contbg. author: Protocols for Cervical Cancer, 1995. Precinct del. Rep. Party, Rose City, 1984; singer Ogeman Players. Named Woman of the Yr., Bus. and Profl. Women, 1987. Mem. Mich. Nurses Assn. (Outstanding Nurse in Advanced Practice 1992), Sigma Theta Tau. Reformed Presbyterian. Avocations: knitting, camping, exploring historical sites. Home: 1832 N Ogemaw Trail West Branch MI 48661 Office: Primary Care Practice 2331 Progress St West Branch MI 48661-9384

MC FARLAND, THOMAS L., book publishing executive; m. Dianne L. McFarland; 2 children. BA in English and Journalism, Westminster Coll.; MA in History of Ideas, Johns Hopkins U. Reporter Intelligencer Jour., Lancaster, Pa., 1957; editor-in-chief Stanwix House, Inc., Pitts., 1958-63; mktg. mgr. Johns Hopkins U. Press, Balt., 1963-67, asst. dir. ops. and mktg., 1967-73; part-time jours. mgr. & acquisitions editor, asst. dir. ops. and mktg. U. Calif. Press, Berkeley, 1973-79; dir., editor Univ. Press New Eng., Hanover, N.H., 1979—; dep. chmn., dir. European mktg. office several Am. univ. presses, Trevor Brown Assocs., Ltd., London, 1970—; invited speaker Translation Ctr. Columbia U., Buenos Aires, 1989; met with scholarly pubs. univs. sponsored USIA, China, 1985; mem. adv. bd. NAS Press, 1980-89; cons. U. Calgary Press, U. Alta. Press, 1991, U. Tenn. Press, 1989, U. Minn. Press, 1988, U. Colo. Office of Pres., 1987, Duke U. Press Office of Provost, 1978, others; judge New Eng. Book Show, 1990, Sara Josepha Hale Award, 1989—; student, lectr. Graphic Arts Ctr., Dartmouth Coll., Hanover; faculty mem. pub. seminar. Bd. dirs. Opera North, 1992—; pres. Congregl. Ch. Dartmouth Coll., 1985-88, bd. elders, 1985-88; mem. book and author event com. Friends of Hopkins Ctr./Hood Mus. Art, Dartmouth Coll., 1984—, bd. dirs., 1987-89. Mem. AAUP (del. univ. press pub. meeting Soviet Union 1989, pres. 1989-90, bd. dirs. 1975-78, 88-91, chair govt. and found. rels. com. 1989—, chair exec. dir. search com. 1990, chair membership and standards com. 1985, chair annual meeting program com. 1984, numerous panels, workshops). Avocations: community chorus, piano, house and garden projects. Home: 23 Valley Rd Hanover NH 03755-2230 Office: Univ Press Of NE 23 S Main St Hanover NH 03755-2048

MCFARLANE, BETH LUCETTA TROESTER, former mayor; b. Osterdock, Iowa, Mar. 9, 1918; d. Francis Charles and Ella Carrie (Moser) Troester; M. George Evert McFarlane, June 20, 1943 (dec. May 1972); children: Douglas, Steven (dec.), Susan, George. BA in Edn., U. No. Iowa, 1962, MA in Edn., 1971. Cert. tchr. Tchr. rural and elem. schs., Iowa, 1936-50, 55-56; elem. tchr. Oelwein Cmty. Schs., Iowa, 1956-64, jr. high reading tchr., 1964-71, reading specialist, 1971-83; mayor of Oelwein, 1982-89; evaluator North Cen. Accreditation Assn. for Ednl. Programs; mem. planning team for confs. for Iowa Cities, N.E. Iowa, 1985; v.p. N.E. Iowa Regional Council for Econ. Devel., 1986-89; mem. Area Econ. Devel. Com. N.E. Iowa, 1985, Legis. Interim Study Com. on Rural Econ. Devel., 1987-88; mem. policy com. Iowa League Municipalities, 1987-88; bd. dirs. Oelwein Indsl. Devel. Corp., 1982-91, Oelwein Betterment Corp., 1982-94. V.p. Fayette County Tourism Council, 1987-88; Iowa State Steering Com. on Road Use Tax Financing, 1988-89; chmn. bd. govs. Oelwein Community Ctr, 1990-94; chmn. Reorganized LDS Ch. Bldg. and Fin. Com., 1980—, Dist. Ch. Fin. Com., 1992—, Dist. Ch. Revolving Loan Com., 1982—. Named Iowa Reading Tchr. of Yr., Internat. Reading Assn. Iowa, 1978; recipient Outstanding Contbrn. to Reading Council Activities award Internat. Reading Assn. N.E. Iowa, 1978, State of Iowa's Gov.s' Leadership award, 1988. Mem. N.E. Iowa Reading Council (pres. 1975-77), MacDowell Music and Arts Orgn. (pres. 1978-80), Oelwein Bus. and Profl. Women (Woman of Yr. 1983), Oelwein Area Ret. Sch. Pers. (pres. 1994-96), Oelwein Area C. of C. (bd. dirs. 1986-89, Humanitarian award 1987), Delta Kappa Gamma (pres. 1980-82). Republican. Mem. Reorganized Ch. of Jesus Christ of Latter Day Saints. Avocations: hiking, refinishing antiques, gardening, jogging, creative sewing. Home: 512 7th Ave NE Oelwein IA 50662-1326

MC FARLANE, KAREN ELIZABETH, concert artists manager; b. St. Louis, Jan. 2, 1942; d. Nicholas and Bonita Margaret (Fults) Walz; m. Ralph Leo McFarlane, Nov. 30, 1968 (div.); children: Sarah Louise.; m. Walter Holtkamp, June 19, 1982. B.Mus.Ed. (Presser Music Found. scholar), Lindenwood Coll., 1964. Public sch. music tchr. St. Louis County, 1964-66; music asst. Riverside Ch., N.Y.C., 1966-70; dir. music St. Mark's Episc. Ch., San Marcos, Tex., 1971-73, Park Ave. Christian Ch., N.Y.C., 1974-81; also pres. Murtagh/McFarlane Artists, Inc., Cleve., 1976-88; pres. Karen McFarlane Artists, Cleve., 1989—. Mem. Am. Guild Organists, Nat. Assn. Performing Arts Mgrs. and Agts., Inc., Internat. Soc. Performing Arts Adminstrn. Republican. Presbyterian. Office: 12429 Cedar Rd Ste 29 Cleveland OH 44106-3172

MCFARLANE, NEIL, church administrator. Children's dir. The Missionary Church, Fort Wayne, Ind. Office: The Missionary Ch PO Box 9127 3811 Vanguard Dr Fort Wayne IN 46809-3304

MCFARLANE, WALTER ALEXANDER, lawyer, educator; b. Richlands, Va., May 4, 1940; s. James Albert and Frances Mae (Padbury) McF.; m. Judith Louise Copenhaver, Aug. 31, 1962; children: Brennan Alexander, Heather Copenhaver. BA, Emory and Henry Coll., 1962; JD, T.C. Williams Sch. Law, U. Richmond, 1966. Bar: Va. 1966, U.S. Supreme Ct. 1970, U.S. Ct. Appeals (4th cir.) 1973, U.S. Ct. Appeals (D.C. cir.) 1977, U.S. Dist. Ct. (ea. dist.) Va. 1973. Asst. atty. gen. Office Va. Atty. Gen., Richmond, 1969-73, dep. atty. gen., 1973-90; exec. asst. chief counsel, dir. policy Gov.'s office, Commonwealth Va., 1990-94; supt. Dept. Correctional Edn. Commonwealth of Va., 1994—. prof. adj. staff U. Richmond, 1978—. Contbr. articles to profl. jours. Chmn. transp. law com. Transp. Research Bd., Nat. Research Bd. Nat. Acads. Scis. and Engring., Washington, 1977-85, 88-94, chmn. legal affairs com., 1978-85, chmn. environ., archeological and hist. com., 1985-90; mem. State Water Commn., 1994—; mem. exec. com., bd. govs. Emory and

Henry Coll., 1985—; pres. Windsor Forest Civic Assn., Midlothian, Va., 1975-76; bd. dirs. Greater Midlothian Civic League, 1981-86, v.p., 1980; instr. water safety ARC, 1962-87; chmn. bldg. com. Mt. Pisgah United Meth. Ch., 1980-85, pres. men's club, 1980-81; bd. dirs. cen. Va. chpt. Epilepsy Assn. Va., 1988-91, Woodland Pond Civic Assn., 1988-89; mem. State Criminal Justice Svcs. Bd., 1994—. Capt. JAGC, USAF, 1966-69. Recipient J.D. Buscher Disting. Atty. award Am. Assn. State Hwy. and Transp. Ofcls., 1983, John C. Vance legal writing award Nat. Acads. Sci. and Engring., 4th ann. outstanding evening lectr. award Student Body U. Richmond, 1980. Mem. Chesterfield Bar Assn., Richmond Bar Assn. (bd. dirs. 1989-93), Richmond Scottish Soc. (bd. dirs. 1980-82), Emory and Henry Coll. Alumni Assn. (chpt. pres. 1971-73, regional v.p. 1974-77, pres. 1981-83), Meadowbrook Country Club. Home: 9001 Widgeon Way Chesterfield VA 23838-5274 Office: 101 N 14th St Richmond VA 23219

MCFARLEN, GERALD DALE, lawyer; b. Corpus Christi, Tex., Aug. 15, 1951; s. Julian Detroy and Dorothy (Fuller) McF.; ;m. Jane Ann Wrede, July 4, 1976; children: Christopher Joel, Sarah Catherine. BA in Govt., U. Tex., 1975; JD, U. Houston, 1981. Bar: Tex. 1981, U.S. Dist Ct. (so. dist.) Tex. 1982, U.S. Dist. Ct. (we. dist.) Tex. 1990, U.S. Dist. Ct. (no. dist.) Tex. 1992, U.S. Ct. Appeals (5th cir.) 1993. Briefing atty. 13th Ct. Appeals, Corpus Christi, Tex., 1981-83; assoc. Porter, Rogers, Dahlman & Gordon, Corpus Christi, 1983-84, Law Offices Robert Patterson, Corpus Christi, 1984=86, Brin & Brin P.C., San Antonio, Tex., 1986-90; shareholder Brin & Brin P.C., San Antonio, 1990—. Episcopalian. Avocations: sailing, golf. Office: Brin & Brin 8200 IH 10 W Ste 610 San Antonio TX 78230

MCFARLIN, DIANE H., newspaper editor; b. Lake Wales, Fla., July 10, 1954; d. Ruffie Denton Hooten and Anna Loraine (Peeples) Huff; m. Henry Briggs McFarlin, Aug. 28, 1976 (div. 1993). BS, U. Fla., 1976. Reporter Sarasota (Fla.) Jour., 1976-77, asst. news editor, 1977-78, city editor, 1978-82; asst. mng. editor Sarasota (Fla.) Herald Tribune, 1983-84, mng. editor, 1985-87; exec. editor Gainesville (Fla.) Sun, 1987-90, Sarasota Herald-Tribune, 1990—; mem. adv. bd. U. Fla. Coll. Journalism and Comm., 1987—. Mem. accrediting coun. Edn. in Journalism and Mass Comms., 1994—. Mem. Am. Soc. Newspaper Editors (com. chair 1992, 94, bd. dirs. 1994—), Fla. Soc. Newspaper Editors (sec.-treas. 1993, v.p. 1994, pres. 1995). Office: Sarasota Herald-Tribune PO Box 1719 Sarasota FL 34230

MCFARLIN, RICHARD FRANCIS, industrial chemist, researcher; b. Oklahoma City, Oct. 12, 1929; s. Loy Lester and Julie Mae (Collins) McF.; m. Clare Jane Burroughs, Apr. 4, 1953; children: Robin Sue McFarlin Godwin, Richard Prescott, Rebecca Lynn McFarlin Bray, Roger Whitsitt. BS, Va. Mil. Inst., 1951; MS, Purdue U., 1953, PhD, 1956. Rsch. chemist Monsanto Chem. Co., St. Louis, 1956-60; supr. inorganic rsch. Internat. Minerals and Chems., Mulberry, Fla., 1961; mgr. Agr. Rsch. Ctr. Armour Agrl. Chem. Co., Atlanta, 1962; v.p. rsch., ops., devel. & adminstrn. div. agri-chems. U.S. Steel, Atlanta, 1986; tech. dir. Lester Labs. Inc., Atlanta, 1986-88; exec. dir. Fla. Inst. Phosphate Rsch., Bartow, 1988-96; ret., 1996; mem. bd. advisors engring. coun. U. South Fla., Lakeland, 1990—, U. Fla., Gainesville, 1991—; mem. bd. advisors Inst. Recyclable Materials La. State U., Baton Rouge, 1990—. Capt. USAR, 1951-61. M. M. Cohn Found. scholar, 1947, L. D. Wall scholar, 1949, O. M. Baldinger scholar, 1950. Presbyterian. Achievements include eight U.S. and foreign patents for selective organic reducing agents, fertilizer processes and selective biocides. Home: 6611 Sweetbriar Ln Lakeland FL 33813-3598

MCFARLIN, ROBERT PAUL, former army officer, consultant; b. L.A., Dec. 6, 1942; s. Paul Combs and Marion Esther (Fair) McF.; m. Barbara Jean Hinson, Sept. 6, 1962; children: Douglas Paul, Erin Elizabeth McFarlin Wheeler. BA, Trinity U., 1964; MS, Fla. Inst. Tech., 1978. Commd. 2d lt. U.S. Army, 1964, advanced through grades to brig. gen., 1989; student U.S. Army Command and Gen. Staff Coll., Ft. Leavenworth, Kans., 1975-76; logistics staff officer Hdqrs. Dept. Army, Arlington, Va., 1978-80; bn. comdr. 705th Maintenance Bn., Ft. Polk, La., 1980-82; student U.S. Army War Coll., Carlisle, Pa., 1982-83; dir. materiel mgmt. U.S. Army Armament, Munitions and Chem. Command, Rock Island, Ill., 1983-84, chief of staff, 1984; comdr. support command 5th Inf. Div., Ft. Polk, 1984-87; asst. comdt. U.S. Army Ordnance Ctr. and Sch., Aberdeen Proving Ground, Md., 1987-89; comdg. gen. 2d Corps Support Command, Nellingen, Germany and Saudi Arabia, 1989-91, 200th Theater Army Materiel Mgmt. Ctr., Zweibruecken, Germany, 1991-92; exec. dir. distbn. Def. Logistics Agy., Washington, 1992—. Decorated D.S.M., Legion of Merit; recipient Keys to City award Mayor of Natchitoches, La., 1986, Ehrenkreuz der Bundeswehr award German Govt., 1991, Ehrenurkunde award Flak Rgt. 25, 1991. Mem. Assn. U.S. Army, U.S. Army Ordnance Assn., Coun. of Logistics Mgmt., Warehouse Edn. and Rsch. Presbyterian (elder). Avocations: golf, skiing, history, languages. Address: 1522 NW 44th Ave Carrolls WA 98609

MCFARLING, DAVID, physician, neurologist; b. L.A., Sept. 21, 1945; s. Joe A. and Kate I. (Gossett) McF.; m. Sandra D. Holman, Aug. 26, 1967; children: Laura, Sean. BS, Tulane U., 1967, MD, 1972. Commd. officer U.S. Army, 1973, advanced through grades to col., 1986; intern Gorgas Hosp.; resident Walter Reed Army Med. Ctr., Washington; fellow U. Fla., Gainesville; chief neurology Brooke Army Med. Ctr., Ft. Sam Houston, Tex., 1980-87, comdr. U.S. Army Health Care Studies Activity, 1987-92, dep. comdr., 1992-93, comdr., 1993-94; dir. clin. ops. U.S. Army Med. Command, Ft. Sam Houston, 1994—; cons. staff San Antonio State Chest Hosp., San Antonio, 1981-84; mem. staff South Tex. Epilepsy Ctr., San Antonio, 1983-94; pres. Epilepsy Found. South Tex., San Antonio, 1985-88. Fellow Am. Acad. Neurology; mem. Assn. Mil. Surgeons U.S., Soc. Clin. Neurologists (pres. 1991-92). Home: 157 Trillium Ln San Antonio TX 78213-2514

MCFATE, KENNETH LEVERNE, trade association administrator; b. LeClaire, Iowa, Feb. 5, 1924; s. Samuel Albert and Margaret (Spear) McF.; m. Imogene Grace Kness, Jan. 27, 1951; children: Daniel Elliott, Kathryn Margaret, Sharon Ann. BS in Agrl. Engring., Iowa State U., 1950; MS in Agrl. Engring., U. Mo., 1959. Registered profl. engr., Mo. Agrl. sales engr. Ill. No. Utility Co., Aledo, 1950-51; extension agrl. engr. Iowa State U., Ames, 1951-53, rsch. agrl. engr., 1953-56; prof. agrl. engr. U. Mo., Columbia, 1956-86, prof. emeritus, 1986; dir. Mo. Farm Electric Coun., Columbia, 1956-75; exec. mgr. Nat. Farm Electric Coun., Columbia, 1975-86; pres., exec. mgr. Nat. Food and Energy Coun., Columbia, 1986-91, pres. emeritus, 1991; mgr. Electrotechnology Rsch., 1991-93; bd. dirs. Internat. Congress Agrl. Engrs., Brussels, 1989-94. Editor, author: (with others) Handbook for Elsevier Science, Electrical Energy in World Agriculture, 1989; mem. editl. bd. Energy in Agriculture for Elsevier Sci., Amsterdam, The Netherlands, 1981-88. 2d lt. USAAF, 1943-45. Recipient Outstanding Svc. awards Nat. Safety Coun., 1975, MOFEC, 1976, Nat. 4-H Coun., 1982, Nat. Hon. Extension Frat., 1984, Hon. award Future Farmers Assn., 1991. Fellow Am. Soc. Agrl. Engrs. (George Kable elec. award 1974); mem. Alpha Epsilon, Gamma Sigma Delta. Republican. Presbyterian. Avocations: technical writing, gardening, old car restoration, woodworking. Home: 9450 E Highway HH Hallsville MO 65255-9724

MC FATE, PATRICIA ANN, scientist, education, foundation executive; b. Detroit, Mar. 19, 1936; d. John Earle and Mary Louise (Bliss) McF.; m. Sidney Norman Graybeal, Sept. 10, 1988. B.A. (Alumni scholar), Mich. State U., 1954; M.A., Northwestern U., 1956, Ph.D., 1965; M.A. (hon.), U. Pa., 1977. Assoc. prof. English, asst. dean liberal arts and scis. U. Ill., Chgo., 1967-74; assoc. prof. English, assoc. vice chancellor acad. affairs U. Ill., 1974-75; assoc. prof. folklore Faculty Arts and Scis., U. Pa., Phila., 1975-81; prof. tech. and soc. Coll. Engring. and Applied Sci., 1975-81, vice provost, 1975-78; dep. chmn. Nat. Endowment for Humanities, Washington, 1978-81; exec. v.p. Am.-Scandinavian Found., N.Y.C., 1981-82, pres., 1982-88; sr. scientist Sci. Applications Internat. Corp., Mc Lean, Va., 1988—, program dir. Ctr. for Nat. Security Negotiations, 1988—; cons. UN, 1994—; vis. assoc. prof. dept. medicine Rush U., Chgo., 1970-85; bd. dir. CoreStates Bank, N.A., CoreStates Fin. Corp., Raoul Wallenberg Com. of U.S. Author: The Writings of James Stephens, 1979, Uncollected Prose of James Stephens, 1983; exec. producer Northern Stars, 1985, Diego Rivera: I Paint What I See, 1989; contbr. articles in fields of sci. policy and lit. to various jours. Mem. sci. and policy adv. com. Arms Control and Disarmament Agy., 1995—; bd. dirs. Raoul Wallenberg Com. of U.S., Swedish Coun. Am., Santa Fe Stages. Decorated officer Order of Leopold II Belgium, comdr. Order Icelandic Falcon, comdr. Royal Order of Polar Star (Sweden), comdr. Order of Lion (Finland), comdr. Royal Norwegian Order Merit, Knight 1st class Royal Order Dannebrog (Denmark); U. Ill. Grad. Coll. faculty fellow, 1968; Swedish Bicentennial Fund grantee, 1981. Fellow N.Y. Acad. Scis.; mem. AAAS (chmn. com. on sci., engring. and pub. policy 1984-87, com. on sci. and internat. security 1976-79, 88-93), Coun. on Fgn. Rels., Acad. Scis. Phila. (founding mem., corr. sec. 1977-79), N.Y. Sci. Policy Assn., Am. Women for Internat. Understanding, Cosmopolitan Club (Phila.), Theta Alpha Phi, Omega Beta Pi, Delta Delta Delta.

MC FEATTERS, DALE STITT, retired electric company executive; b. Avella, Pa., Aug. 20, 1911; s. James Dale and Alice Mabel (Stitt) McF.; m. Tirzah McHenry Bigham, Sept. 29, 1938; children: Dale Bigham, Ann Carol McFeatters Koepke, Susan Love. Student, Art Inst. Pitts., U. Pitts. Reporter, feature writer, news commentator, fin. editor Pitts. Press., 1931-45; with Westinghouse Electric Corp., Pitts., 1945-73; dir. employee info., dir. info. services, v.p. Westinghouse Electric Corp., 1945-73. Creator: nationally syndicated cartoon Strictly Business. Mem. Nat. Cartoonists Soc. Republican. Episcopalian. Clubs: Duquesne (Pitts.), Chartiers Country (Pitts.); Rolling Rock (Ligonier, Pa.); Nat. Press (Washington). Lodge: Masons. Home: 1461 Navahoe Dr Pittsburgh PA 15228-1617

MC FEE, ARTHUR STORER, physician; b. Portland, Maine, May 1, 1932; s. Arthur Stewart and Helen Knight (Dresser) McF.; m. Iris Goeschel, May 13, 1967. B.A. cum laude, Harvard U., 1953, M.D., 1957; M.S., U. Minn., 1966, Ph.D., 1967. Diplomate: Am. Bd. Surgery. Intern U. Minn. Hosp., 1957-58, resident in surgery, 1958-65; asst. prof. surgery U. Tex. Med. Sch., San Antonio, 1967-70; asso. prof. U. Tex. Med. Sch., 1970-74, prof., 1974—; co-dir. surg. ICU Med. Ctr. Hosp., San Antonio, 1968—; spl. cons. on emergency med. care text to AAOS. Contbr. articles to profl. jours. Served with USNR, 1965-67. Fellow ACS; mem. AMA, Am. Assn. History of Medicine, Assn. Acad. Surgery, Tex. Med. Assn., Bexar County Med. Soc., Tex. Surg. Soc., Western Surg. Assn., San Antonio Surg. Soc., Soc. Surgery Alimentary Tract, So. Med. Assn., N.Y. Acad. Scis., Royal Soc. Medicine, So. Surg. Assn., Internat. Surg. Soc., Halsted Soc., J. Bradley Aust Surg. Soc. Home: 131 Brittany Dr San Antonio TX 78212-1721 Office: 7703 Floyd Curl Dr San Antonio TX 78284-6200 *Most of my life has been spent in training surgeons. It has been an informative experience.*

MCFEE, RICHARD, electrical engineer, physicist; b. Pitts., Jan. 24, 1925; s. William and Beatrice (Allender) McF.; m. Anne Stauffer, June 26, 1947 (div. 1960); m. 2d., Joanellen Lewis, Dec. 31, 1974. BEE, Yale U., 1947; MS in Physics, Syracuse U., 1949; PhDEE, U. Mich., 1955. Rsch. asst. Syracuse U. Med. Sch., 1947-48; instr. Syracuse U. elec. engring. dept., 1948-49; rsch. assoc. U. Mich. Med. Sch., 1949-51; engr. Electro-Mech. Rsch. Inc., Ridgefield, Conn., 1951-52; mem. tech. staff Bell Telephone Labs., Whippany, N.J., 1952-57; prof. elec. engring. Syracuse U., 1957-82; ind. researcher Union Springs, N.Y., 1982-86, Hawi, Hawaii, 1986—; cons. Arthur D. Little Inc., Cambridge, Mass., 1960-61, cardiovascular study sect. NIH, GE Inc., Crouse Hinds Inc., Syracuse, N.Y., 1970, Stanford U. physics dept., 1974-75. Author numerous articles on electronics, electrocardiography, magnetocardiography, superconductivity, circuit theory, thermodynamics, inertial navigation, elec. measurements, energy conservation, rehab. equipment; patentee in field. Sgt. U.S. Army, 1943-46. Sci. Faculty fellowship NSF, Stanford U., 1970. Fellow IEEE; mem. AAAS, Sigma Xi. Home and Office: PO Box 989 Kapaau HI 96755-0989

MC FEE, THOMAS STUART, retired government agency administrator; b. Delafield, Wis., Nov. 19, 1930; s. Leon Worrick and Margurette Ella (Morris) McFee; m. Mary Virginia Butler, June 7, 1952; children: Richard Stuart, John Worrick, Charles Paxton. BS, U. Md., 1953, postgrad., 1956-60. Mathematician math. computation divsn. David Taylor Model Basin, Navy Dept., Washington, 1956-58; dir. sys. analysis br. ops. rsch. divsn. David Taylor Model Basin, Navy Dept., 1958-62; project leader weapons sys. evaluation group U.S. Dept. Def., 1962-65; tech. asst. to dir. Sci. and Tech. Office, Exec. Office of Pres., White House, 1965-66; dir. sys. devel. HEW, 1967-69, dep. asst. sec. for program sys., planning and evaluation, 1969-71, dep. asst. sec. for mgmt. planning and tech., 1971-77, dep. asst. sec. for mgmt., 1977-78; asst. sec. for pers. adminstrn. HHS, 1978-95. With USAF, 1954-56. Mem. Am. Soc. Pub. Adminstrn., Am. Consortium for Internat. Pub. Adminstrn., Nat. Acad. Pub. Adminstrn. (elected).

MCFEE, WILLIAM WARREN, soil scientist; b. Concord, Tenn., Jan. 8, 1935; s. Fred Thomas and Ellen Belle (Russell) McF.; m. Barbara Anella Steelman, June 23, 1957; children—Sabra Anne, Patricia Lynn, Thomas Hallie. B.S., U. Tenn., 1957; M.S., Cornell U., 1963, Ph.D., 1966. Mem. faculty Purdue U., 1965—, prof. soil sci., 1973—, dir. natural resources and environ. sci. program, 1975-91, head dept. agronomy, 1991—; vis. prof. U. Fla., 1986-87; cons. U.S. Forest Svc., Desert Rsch. Inst. Author articles in field, chpts. in books. Served with USAR, 1958-61. Alpha Zeta scholar, 1957; named Outstanding Agr. Tchr. Purdue U., 1972; recipient Am. Educator award Soil Sci. Soc., 1987. Fellow Am. Soc. Agronomy (pres.-elect 1995-96, resident edn. award 1989), Soil Sci. Soc. Am. (pres. 1991-92); mem. Internat. Soil Sci. Soc., Sigma Xi. Presbyterian. Home: 708 Mccormick Rd West Lafayette IN 47906-4915 Office: Purdue U Agronomy Dept LILY West Lafayette IN 47907

MC FEELEY, JOHN JAY, chemical engineer; b. Bklyn., Aug. 15, 1945; s. John Joseph and Maude May (Irvine) McF.; m. Jacquelyn Anne Ratzin, Oct. 30, 1971; children: Christine, John Jay. BS, Poly. Inst. Bklyn., 1966, MS, 1967, Phd, 1972. Engr. Polaroid Corp., Cambridge, Mass., 1971-72, sr. engr., 1972-74, sr. scientist, 1974-77, prin. engr. research and devel., 1977-79, tech. mgr. chem. engring. devel., 1979-83, sr. mgr. chem. engring., 1983—. Mem. water supply study com. Town of Norfolk (Mass.), 1976-77, mem. adv. bd., 1979-81, mem. bicentennial com., 1975-76, chmn. adv. bd., 1980-81, selectman, 1981-84, chmn., 1983-84; registrar of voters, 1991—, chmn., 1993—; mem. Dem. Town Com., 1981—, vice-chmn., 1988—; mem. Norfolk Community TV, 1989—, pres., 1992-94, 95—. NDEA fellow, 1969-71; NSF fellow, 1968-69, teaching fellow, 1967-68, rsch. fellow, 1966-67. Mem. AAAS, Am. Chem. Soc., Am. Inst. Chem. Engrs., N.Y. Acad. Scis., Lions (pres. 1977-78, 89-90), Tau Beta Pi, Sigma Xi, Omega Chi Epsilon, Phi Lambda Upsilon. Democrat. Roman Catholic. Contbr. articles in field to profl. jours. Home: 10 Chicatabut Ave Norfolk MA 02056-1164 Office: 103 Fourth Ave Waltham MA 02154

MCFEELY, WILLIAM DRAKE, publishing company executive; b. Port Chester, N.Y., July 15, 1954; s. William Shield and Mary (Drake) McF.; m. Karen Gail Eliason, Aug. 12, 1978; children: Matthew Bensen, Eric Daniel, Laura Mae. BA cum laude, Amherst Coll., 1976. Coll. traveler W.W. Norton & Co., Inc., N.Y.C., 1976-80, asst. sales mgr., 1980-82, editor, 1982—, v.p., 1990-94, bd. dirs., 1990—, pres., 1994—; dir. W.W. Norton & Co., Ltd., 1994—, Liveright Pub. Corp., N.Y.C., 1994—, Nat. Book Co., Scranton, Pa., 1994—. Mem. Pubs. Lunch Club, Seven Bridges Field Club (pres. 1989). Home: 106 Seven Bridges Rd Chappaqua NY 10514 Office: W.W. Norton & Co 500 Fifth Ave New York NY 10514

MC FEELY, WILLIAM SHIELD, historian, writer; b. N.Y.C., Sept. 25, 1930; s. William C. and Marguerite (Shield) Mc F.; m. Mary Drake, Sept. 13, 1952; children: William Drake, Eliza, Jennifer. B.A., Amherst Coll., 1952, L.H.D., 1982; M.A., Yale U., 1962, Ph.D., 1966; LD, Washington Coll., 1986. Asst. prof. history and Am. studies Yale U., 1966-69, assoc. prof., 1969-70; dean faculty Mount Holyoke Coll., 1970-73, prof. history, 1970-80, Rodman prof. history, 1980-82, Andrew W. Mellon prof. in the humanities, 1982-86; Richard B. Russell prof. Am. history U. Ga., Athens, 1986-94, Abraham Baldwin prof. of Humanities, 1994—; tchr. Yale-Harvard-Columbia intensive summer studies program, 1967-69; vis. prof. history Univ. Coll. London, 1978-79, Amherst Coll., 1980-81, U. Mass., 1984-85, John J. McCloy prof., 1988-89 ; cons. to com. on judiciary U.S. Ho. of Reps., 1974. Author: Yankee Stepfather: Gen. O.O. Howard and the Freedmen, 1968, Grant: A Biography, 1981, Frederick Douglass, 1991, Sapelo's People, 1994. Recipient Pulitzer Prize in biography, 1982, Francis Parkman prize, 1982, Lincoln prize, 1992, Avery O. Craven award, 1992; Morse fellow, 1968-69, fellow Am. Coun. Learned Socs., 1974-75, Huntington Library, 1976, 83, Guggenheim fellow, 1982-83, assoc. fellow Charles Warren Ctr., 1991-91, vis. scholar W.E.B. Du Bois Inst., Harvard U., 1992—; NEH grantee, 1986-87. Mem. Am. Hist. Assn., So. Hist. Assn., Assn. Study Afro-Am. Life and History, Orgn. Am. Historians, PEN Ctr., Century Assn., Authors Guild. Home: 445 Franklin St Apt 25 Athens GA 30606-3086 Office: U Ga 301 LeConte Hall 210 Joseph Brown Hall Athens GA 30602

MC FERON, DEAN EARL, mechanical engineer; b. Portland, Oreg., Dec. 24, 1923; s. Wallace Suitor and Ruth Carolyn (Fessler) McF.; m. Phyllis Grace Ehlers, Nov. 10, 1945; children: David Alan, Phyllis Ann, Douglas Dean, Donald Brooks. Student, Oreg. State Coll., 1942-43; BSME with spl. honors, U. Colo., 1945, MSME, 1948; PhD, U. Ill., 1956. Instr. U. Colo., Boulder, 1946-48; assoc. prof. U. Ill., 1948-58; rsch. assoc. Argonne (Ill.) Nat. Lab., 1957-58; prof. mech. engring., assoc. dean U. Wash., Seattle, 1958-82; prof. emeritus U. Wash., 1983—; cons. to industry, 1959-80. Served with USNR, 1942-46, to comdr. Res., 1946-72. Co-recipient Outstanding Tech. Applications Paper award ASHRAE, 1974; Ednl. Achievement award Soc. Mfg. Engrs., 1970; NSF faculty fellow, 1967-68. Mem. ASME, Am. Soc. Engring. Edn., U.S. Naval Inst. (life), Sigma Xi (nat. dir. 1972-80, nat. pres. 1978), Tau Beta Pi, Sigma Tau, Pi Tau Sigma. Home: 4008 NE 40th St Seattle WA 98105-5422 Office: U Wash Dept Mech Engring Seattle WA 98195 *What matters most in life is what you can do for others.*

MCFERRIN, BOBBY, singer, musician, composer and conductor. Creative chair St. Paul Chamber Orch. Albums: Bobby McFerrin, 1982, The Voice, 1984, Spontaneous Inventions, 1986, Simple Pleasure, 1988, Medicine Music, 1990, (with Chick Corea) Play, 1992, (with Yo Yo Ma) Hush, 1992, (with St. Paul Chamber Orch.) Paper Music, 1995. Recipient 10 Grammy awards, Emmy award, ACE award. Office: c/o Original Artists 853 Broadway Ste 1901 New York NY 10003-4703

MCFERSON, D. RICHARD, insurance company executive; b. 1937; m. Darlene Moss; 7 children. BA, UCLA, 1959; MA, U. So. Calif., 1972. CPA, CLU. With Ernst & Young; sr. v.p. finance Surety Life Ins. Co., Salt Lake City, New Eng. Life, until 1979; sr. v.p. fin., then exec. v.p. Nationwide Mut. Ins. Co., 1978-88, pres., dir., 1988—; also pres. Nationwide Mut. Fire Ins., Nationwide Gen. Ins. Co.; sr. v.p. fin., dir. Nationwide Fin. Svcs. Inc.; sr. v.p. Nationwide Devel. Co. Office: Nationwide Mut Ins Co 1 Nationwide Plz Columbus OH 43215-2220

MCGAFFEY, JERE D., lawyer; b. Lincoln, Nebr., Oct. 6, 1935; s. Don Larsen and Doris (Lanning) McG.; m. Ruth S. Michelsen, Aug. 19, 1956; children: Beth, Karen. B.A., B.Sc. with high distinction, U. Nebr., 1957; LL.B. magna cum laude, Harvard U., 1961. Bar: Wis. 1961. Mem. firm Foley & Lardner, Milw., 1961—, ptnr., 1968—; dir. Wis. Gas Co., Smith Investment Co., WICOR. Author works in field. Chmn. bd. dirs. Helen Bader Found.; former chmn. bd. dirs. Aurora Health Care; vice chmn. legis. Milw. Met. Assn. Commerce; former chmn. Wis. Taxpayers Alliance, sec., treas., 1994—; chmn. bd. visitors U. Wis. Med. Sch., Madison; chmn. bd. advisors U. Wis. Nursing Sch., Milw. Mem. ABA (chmn. tax sect. 1990-91), AICPA, House of Del., 1995—, Wis. Bar Assn., Wis. Inst. CPA's, Am. Coll. Tax Counsel (chmn., regent), Am. Coll. Trust and Estate Counsel (chmn. bus. planning com.), Am. Law Inst., Univ. Club, Milw. Club, Milw. Country Club, Harvard Club N.Y.C., Univ. Club Washington, Phi Beta Kappa, Beta Gamma Sigma, Delta Sigma Rho. Home: 12852 NW Shoreland Dr Thiensville WI 53097-2304 Office: Foley & Lardner 777 E Wisconsin Ave Ste 3600 Milwaukee WI 53202-5302

MCGAGH, WILLIAM GILBERT, financial consultant; b. Boston, May 29, 1929; s. Thomas A. and Mary M. (McDonough) McG.; m. Sarah Ann McQuigg, Sept. 23, 1961; children: Margaret Ellen, Sarah Elizabeth. BSBA, Boston Coll., 1950; MBA, Harvard U., 1952; MS, MIT, 1965. Fin. analyst Ford Motor Co., Dearborn, Mich., 1953-55; mem. staff treas. office Chrysler Corp., Detroit, 1955-64; compt., treas. Canadian div. Chrysler Corp., Windsor, 1965-67; staff exec.-fin. Latin Am. ops. Chrysler Corp., Detroit, 1967-68, asst. treas., 1968-75, treas., 1975-76, v.p., treas., 1976-80; sr. v.p. fin., dir. Northrop Corp., Los Angeles, 1980-88; owner McGagh Assocs., Beverly Hills, Calif., 1988—; bd. dirs. Pacific Am. Income Shares, Inc., Western Asset Trust, Inc. Board dirs. Greater L.A. Zoo Assn., John Tracy Clinic (pres. 1994—), Mt. St. Mary's Coll. With USAF, 1952-53. Sloan fellow MIT, 1965. Mem. Fin. Execs. Inst. (pres. Detroit chpt. 1979-80). Clubs: Orchard Lake Country; Harvard (N.Y.C. and Boston); Beach (Santa Monica, Calif.); Los Angeles Country, California (Los Angeles), Eastward Ho Country. (Chatham, Mass.). Home: 2189 Century Hl Los Angeles CA 90067-3516 Office: McGagh Assocs 9601 Wilshire Blvd Ste 623 Beverly Hills CA 90210-5208

MCGAHREN, RICHARD GEORGE, lawyer; b. Bayonne, N.J., June 18, 1928; s. Eugene Dewey and Cecelia (Paulsen) McG.; m. Marjorie J. Waterhouse, Jan. 29, 1994; stepchildren: Lawrence Waterhouse III, Kevin Waterhouse, Patrick Waterhouse, Christine Waterhouse Krizman, Jennifer Waterhouse Pacchiana. AB, Columbia U., 1952, LLB, 1959. Bar: N.Y. 1960, U.S. Dist. Ct. (so. and ea. dists.) N.Y. 1961, U.S. Ct. Appeals (2nd cir.) 1962. Assoc. LeBoeuf Lamb Leiby & MacRae, N.Y.C., 1960-71; ptnr. D'Amato Costello & Shea, N.Y.C., 1971-78; founding ptnr. D'Amato & Lynch, N.Y.C., 1978-94, counsel, 1994—. With U.S. Army, 1946-47. Mem. ABA. Avocations: skiing, sailing. Office: D'Amato & Lynch 70 Pine St New York NY 10270-0002

MCGANN, JEROME JOHN, English language educator; b. N.Y.C., July 22, 1937; s. John Joseph and Marie Violet (Lecouffe) McG.; m. Anne Patricia Lanni, July 26, 1938; children: Geoffrey, Christopher, Jennifer. BS, Le Moyne Coll., 1959; MA, Syracuse U., 1962; PhD, Yale U., 1966. From asst. prof. to prof. U. Chgo., 1966-75; prof. Johns Hopkins U., Balt., 1975-80; Dreyfuss prof. humanities Calif. Inst. Tech., Pasadena, 1980-86; John Stewart Bryan prof. English U. Va., Charlottesville, 1987—. Author: Swinburne: An Experiment in Criticism, 1972 (Melville Cane award 1972), The Romantic Ideology, 1983, The Beauty of Inflections, 1985, Social Values and Poetic Acts, 1987, Towards a Literature of Knowledge, 1989, The Textual Condition, 1991, Black Riders: The Visible Language of Modernism, 1993; editor: The New Oxford Book of Verse of the Romantic Period, 1993, Poetics of Sensibility: A Revolution in Literary Style, 1996, Byron: Complete Poetical Works, 7 vols., 1980-93; author, editor 22 scholarly books and 3 poetry books. Fulbright fellow, Fels Found. fellow, Eng., 1965-66; Guggenheim fellow, Eng., 1970-71, 74-75; NEH fellow, Eng. and Europe, 1975-76, 87-88. Fellow Am. Acad. Arts and Scis.; mem. MLA. Office: U Va Dept English Charlottesville VA 22903

MCGANN, JOHN RAYMOND, bishop; b. Bklyn., Dec. 2, 1924; s. Thomas Joseph and Mary (Ryan) McG. Student, Cathedral Coll. Immaculate Conception, 1944, Sem. Immaculate Conception, Huntington, 1950; LL.D., St. Johns U., 1971; L.H.D., Molloy Coll., 1977, Niagara U., 1983, St. Joseph's Coll., 1983, Adelphi U., 1985. Ordained priest Roman Cath. Ch., 1950, ordained bishop, 1971. Asst. priest St. Anne's, Brentwood, 1950-57; asst. chaplain St. Joseph Convent, Brentwood, 1950-54; tchr. religion St. Joseph Acad., 1950-54; assoc. Cath. chaplain Pilgrim State Hosp., 1950-57; asst. chancellor Diocese of Rockville Centre, 1957-67, vice chancellor, 1967-71; sec. to Bishop Kellenberg, 1957-59; elevated to papal chamberlain, 1959; sec. to Bishop Kellenberg, 1959-70; apptd. titular bishop of Morosbisdus and aux. bishop Diocese of Rockville Centre, 1970-76, bishop, 1976—; Del. Sacred Congregation for Religious to Marianists, 1973-76; theol. cons. Nat. Conf. Cath. Bishops, Rome, 1974, treas. 1984-87; mem. adminstrv. com., 1977-79; Anglican/Roman Cath. task force on pastoral ministry of bishops, 1978-81, nat. adv. coun. U.S. Cath. Conf., 1969-70, 81-83, treas. 1984-87; mem. health affairs com., 1972-75, adminstrv. bd., 1976-79, sem. admissions bd. Diocese Rockville Centre, 1971-76, diocesan boundary commn., 1971-76, Tri-Conf. Religious Retirement Project, 1985-88; mem. Papal visit, 1986-87. Bd. Diocesan Svcs., Inc., 1971-76; com. that established Consultation Svcs. for Religious, 1972-74; vicar gen. Diocese Rockville Centre, 1971-76, Episc. vicar, Suffolk County, 1971-76; mem. N.Y. State Cath. Conf. Com. on Prison Apostolate, 1971-74, U.S. Bishops' Com. for Apostolate to Laity, 1972-76, Rockville Centre Diocesan Bd. Consultors, 1969-76; Episc. mem. N.Y. State Cath. Com., 1974-78; chmn. N.Y. State Bishops' Com. on Elective Process, 1974—, Com. Religious Studies in Pub. Edn., 1975-79; mem. com. on ednl. concerns, com. on priests senates and couns. N.Y. State Cath. Conf.; bd. dirs. Good Samaritan Hosp., West Islip, N.Y., 1972-76, chmn., 1976—; trustee Cath. Charities Diocese of Rockville Centre, 1971-76; trustee St. Charles Hosp., Port Jefferson, N.Y., 1972-76, chmn., 1976—; pres. Mercy

Hosp., St. Francis Hosp., 1976—; chmn. Consolation Residence, 1976—; bd. advisers Sem. Immaculate Conception, 1975—; treas. Nat. Conf. Cath. Bishops U.S. Cath. Conf., 1984-87, ad hoc com. on stewardship, 1988—, tri-conf. commn. on religious life and ministry, 1988-91; mem. Papal Visit, 1986-87, Tri-conf. Religious Retirement Project., 1985-88; chmn. Nat. Conf. Cath. Bishops/U.S. Cath. Conf. Telecommunications Network Am., 1990-93; mem. adminstrv. bd. Nat. Conf. Cath. Bishops, 1991-93. Office: 50 N Park Ave Rockville Centre NY 11570-4129*

MCGANNEY, THOMAS, lawyer; b. San Mateo, Calif., Mar. 12, 1938; s. Daniel James and Mary Irene (West) McG.; m. Mildred Kalik; children—Jennifer, Abigail, Melanie, Juliana. B.A., Stanford U., 1959; LL.B., Harvard U., 1962. Bar: N.Y. 1963, U.S. Dist. Ct. (so. and ea. dists.) N.Y. 1965, U.S. Ct. Appeals (2d cir.) 1966, (3d cir.) 1969, (10th cir.) 1970, U.S. Supreme Ct. 1971, U.S. Ct. Appeals (9th cir.) 1990. Law clk. U.S. Dist. Ct., So. Dist. N.Y., 1962-64; assoc. White & Case, N.Y.C., 1964-72, ptnr., 1973—; adj. prof. NYU Law Sch., 1984-86. Mem. Am. Coll. Trial Lawyers, N.Y. State Bar Assn., ABA, Fed. Bar Council, Assn. Bar City N.Y. Office: White & Case 1155 Ave Of The Americas New York NY 10036-2711

MCGARR, FRANK JAMES, retired federal judge, dispute resolution consultant; b. 1921. A.B., Loyola U., Chgo., 1942; J.D., Loyola U., 1950. Bar: Ill. 1950. Assoc. firm Dallstream Schiff Stern & Hardin, Chgo., 1952-54; asst. U.S. atty. No. dist. of Ill., 1954-55, first asst. U.S. atty., 1955-58; ptnr. firm McKay Solum & McGarr, Chgo., 1958-69; first asst. atty. gen. State of Ill., 1969-70; judge U.S. Dist. Ct. for No. Ill., 1970-88, chief judge, 1980-86, sr. judge, 1986-88; of counsel Phelan Cahill & Quinlan, Chgo., 1988-96, Foley & Lardner, Chgo., 1996—. Served with USN, 1942-45. Mem. Am. Coll. Trial Lawyers, 7th Cir. Bar Assn., Chgo. Bar Assn. Home: 4146 Venard Rd Downers Grove IL 60515-1908 Office: Foley & Lardner One IBM Plz Ste 3300 330 N Wabash Ave Chicago IL 60611-3608

MCGARRELL, JAMES, artist, educator; b. Indpls., Feb. 22, 1930; s. James and Gretchen (Heermann) McG.; m. Anna Harris, June 24, 1955; children: Andrew Rider, Flora Raven. B.A., Ind. U., 1953; M.A., UCLA, 1955. Artist-in-residence Reed Coll., Portland, Oreg., 1956-59; prof. fine arts, dir. grad. painting Ind. U., Bloomington, 1959-80; prof. fine arts Washington U., St. Louis, 1981-93, prof. emeritus, 1993—; artist in residence Dartmouth Coll., 1992. One man exhbns. include Frumkin/Adams Gallery, N.Y.C., 1961, 64, 66, 68, 71, 73, 77, 80, 84, 86, 88, 89, 90, 91, 93, Galerie Claude Bernard, Paris, 1967, 70, 74, Galleria Il Fante de Spade, Rome and Milan, 1967, 71, 72, 74, 76, 79, Galeria Gian Ferrari, Milan, 1981, 83, Galerie Simonne Stern, New Orleans, 1989, 91, 94, 95, Struve Gallery, Chgo., 1988, 90, More Gallery, Phila., 1987, 89, Utah Mus. Art, Salt Lake City, 1972, Art Mus. U. N.Mex., Albuquerque, 1982, St. Louis Art Mus., 1985, Art Mus. U. Ariz., Tucson; represented in permanent collections at Mus. Modern Art, Met. Mus. Art, Whitney Mus. Am. Art, Pa. Acad., Phila., Santa Barbara Mus. Art, San Francisco Art Mus., Art Inst. Chgo., Joseph Hirshhorn Mus., Washington, St. Louis Art Mus., Hamburg (Germany) Mus. Art, Centre Georges Pompidou, Paris. Bd. govs. Skowhegan Sch. Painting and Sculpture. Recipient Am. Acad. Arts and Letters Lifetime Achievement award, 1995; Fulbright fellow, 1955-56; Guggenheim Found. fellow, 1965; Nat. Endowment for Arts grantee, 1967, 85. Mem. Coll. Art Assn. (bd. dirs. 1969-73), Academie des Beaux Arts de L'Institut de France, Nat. Acad. Design. Home: PO Box 39 Newbury VT 05051-0039

MCGARRY, EUGENE L., university official; b. West Chicago, Ill., June 9, 1930; s. Joseph C. and Rose (Gorgal) McG.; m. Jetta F. Grubbs, June 11, 1955; 1 son, Michael. B.A., Cornell Coll., 1952; M.A., Northwestern U., 1956; Ph.D., U. Iowa, 1961. Asst. prof. social scis. U. Minn., Mpls., 1960-62; asst. prof., advisement coordinator, assoc. prof. and assoc. dean edn., prof. and dean edn. Calif. State U., Fullerton, 1962-71; asso. v.p. acad. adminstrn. Calif. State U., 1971-77, dir. Univ. Learning Ctr., 1977-92, chmn. tchr. edn., 1983-84; ret., 1992. Served with AUS, 1952-54. Home: 403 S Paseo Serena Anaheim CA 92807-4214

MCGARRY, FREDERICK JEROME, civil engineering educator; b. Rutland, Vt., Aug. 22, 1927; s. William John and Ellen (Dunn) McG.; m. Alice M. Reilly, Oct. 7, 1950 (dec. Jan. 1971); children: Martha Ellen, Alice Catherine, Joan Louise, Carol Elizabeth, Susan Elizabeth, Janet Marian. A.B., Middlebury (Vt.) Coll., 1950; S.B., Mass. Inst. Tech., 1950, S.M., 1953. Faculty MIT, 1950—, prof. civil engring., 1965—, prof. materials sci. and engring., 1974—, head materials div., 1964—, dir. materials research lab., 1964—, assoc. dir. inter-Am. program civil engring., 1961—, dir. summer session, 1983—. Contbr. numerous articles to profl. jours. Recipient Best Paper award Soc. Plastics Industry, 1968, 91. Mem. AAAS, ASTM, Soc. Rheology, Soc. Plastics Engrs., Am. Soc. Metals, Sigma Xi. Home: 90 Bakers Hill Rd Weston MA 02193-1774 Office: Mass Inst Tech 77 Massachusetts Ave Cambridge MA 02139-4301

MCGARRY, J. MICHAEL, III, lawyer; b. Sacramento, Calif., July 30, 1943. BS, U. Pa., 1965; LLB, U. Va., 1969. Bar: D.C. 1969, Md. 1972. Law clk. to Hon. Matthew F. McGuire U.S. Dist. Ct. (D.C. dist.), 1969-70; asst. U.S. atty. U.S. Attys. Office, 1970-73; ptnr. Winston & Strawn, Washington. Office: Winston & Strawn 1400 L St NW Washington DC 20005-3509*

MCGARRY, JOHN EVERETT, lawyer; b. Madison, Wis., May 11, 1939; s. Daniel E. and Margaret A. (Haas) McG.; m. Kate Wilkinson, Aug. 26, 1961; children: John Eric, Andrew Lawrence. BA, Lehigh U., 1961, BS in Metall. Engring., 1962; LLB, Georgetown U., 1966. Bar: Okla. 1966, Mich. 1968. Atty. Phillips Petroleum Co., Bartlesville, Okla., 1966-67, Price, Heneveld, Huizenga & Cooper, Grand Rapids, Mich., 1967-70; pvt. practice, Grand Rapids, 1970-72; ptnr. McGarry & Waters, Grand Rapids, 1973-78, Varnum Riddering Wierengo & Christenson, Grand Rapids, 1979-84, Varnum Riddering Schmidt & Howlett, Grand Rapids, 1984—. Mem. Opera Grand Rapids, 1984-92, pres., 1991. Mem. Am. Intellectual Property Law Assn. (chair harmonization com. 1993-95). Office: Varnum Riddering Schmidt & Howlett PO Box 352 Bridgewater Pl Grand Rapids MI 49501-0352

MCGARRY, JOHN PATRICK, JR., advertising agency executive; b. Elizabeth, N.J., Nov. 22, 1939; s. John Patrick and Elizabeth (Weber) McG.; m. Gilda R. Spurio, Oct. 24, 1964; children: Victoria Elizabeth, John Patrick, III. BS in Mktg. Econs, Villanova U., 1961. Salesman Exxon Corp., Elizabeth, 1961-64; advt. exec. Young and Rubicam Inc., N.Y.C., 1965-69, sr. v.p., mgmt. supr., 1969-87, pres., mem. ops. com., advt. exec. com., 1987—; vice chmn. Young and Rubicam Advt. Worldwide, N.Y.C., 1990—; chmn. Client Svcs. Worldwide, N.Y.C., 1987—; pres., CEO Young and Rubicam N.Am., N.Y.C., 1992-94; pres. Young & Rubicam Inc., N.Y.C., 1996—; bd. dirs. Caramoor; mem. corp. exec.'s com. Young and Rubicam, 1992. Bd. dirs. New Youth Performing Theatre, Bedford, N.Y., Regional Rev. League, Westchester, 4 A's, Louisville Opera Assn., 1981-83, Dominican Coll., Drop-out Prevention Fund, United Negro Coll. Fund, 1994—; bd. dirs. N.Y. coun. Boy Scouts Am., 1992; head parents fund St. Lawrence U. Mem. Internat. Advt. Assn. (pres. U.S. and Can.), Proprietary Assn. (bd. dirs.), Bedford Club, Golf and Tennis Club, N.Y. Athletic Club, The Roundabout Theater (adv. bd. 1994—). Democrat. Roman Catholic. Home: 465 Cantitoe St Bedford NY 10506-1103 Office: Young & Rubicam Inc 285 Madison Ave New York NY 10017-6401

MCGARRY, JOHN WARREN, government official. Grad. cum laude, Holy Cross Coll, Georgetown U. Law Ctr. Asst. atty gen. State of Mass.; practicing atty.; chief counsel House Spl. Com to Investigate Campaign Expenditures; mem. spl. counsel on Elections Com. on House Adminstrn., 1973-78; appointed to Fed. Election Commn., 1978—, chmn., 1981, 85, 91. Office: Fed Election Commn 999 E St NW Washington DC 20463-0001

MCGARRY, ROBERT GEORGE, safety engineer; b. Mpls., Jan. 4, 1917; s. Emmett Frank and Ethel Florence (Bryant) McG.; m. Janalee Judy, Sept. 22, 1986; children from previous marriage: Mary Kathleen, Nancy Margaret, Susan Elaine, Kevin Robert. BS in Indsl. Engring., U. Minn., 1939; MS in Safety Engring., Ga. Inst. Tech., 1947. Registered profl. engr., Calif.; cert. safety profl. Sr. safety engr. U.S. Fidelity & Guaranty Co., Atlanta, Mpls., 1950-63; Bechtel Corp., San Francisco, 1963-77; corp. safety engr. Burns & McDonnell Engrs., Cons., Kansas City, Mo., 1977-82; con. safety engr., Lee's Summit, Mo., 1982—. With USN, 1942-46. Recipient Minn. Gov.'s Outstanding Safety Achievement award, 1969; scholar Advanced Inst. Nuclear Studies. Mem. NSPE, Am. Soc. Safety Engrs. (chmn. engring. com.), Vets. of Safety Internat. (dir.-at-large), NSPE, Mo. Soc. Profl. Engrs., Profl. Engrs. in Pvt. Practice, Am. Arbitration Assn. (arbitrator), Masons, Shriners. Home and Office: PO Box 9914 Kansas City MO 64134-0914

MCGARY, BETTY WINSTEAD, minister, counselor, individual, marriage, and family therapist; b. Louisville, June 21, 1936; d. Philip Miller and Mary Jo (Winstead) McG.; married, 1960 (div. 1979); children: Thomas Edward, Mary Alyson, Andrew Philip Pearce. BS, Samford U., 1958; MA, So. Bapt. Theol. Sem., 1961; EdD, U. Louisville, 1988. Ordained to ministry Bapt. Ch., 1986; cert. secondary tchr., Ky., Ga.; lic. profl. counselor, marriage and family therapist, Tex. Min. to youth Broadway Bapt. Ch., Louisville, 1958-60; learning disability and behavior disorders specialist Jefferson County Schs., Muscogee Schs., Cobb County Schs., Louisville, Columbus, Ga., Atlanta, 1964-88; min. to adults South Main Bapt. Ch., Houston, 1986-90; assoc. pastor Calder Bapt. Ch., Beaumont, Tex., 1991—; marriage enrichment cons. Pastoral Inst., Columbus, 1973-76; co-founder and coord. Ctr. for Women in Ministry, Louisville, 1983-86, exec. bd. dirs., 1983-90; cons. Tex. Christian Life Commn., Ft. Worth, 1989-93; co-therapist pvt. practice, Houston, 1989—. Author: (with others) The New Has Come, 1988, A Costly Obedience: Sermons by Women of Steadfast Spirit, 1994; co-editor nat. newsletter Folio: A Newsletter for Southern Bapt. Women in Ministry, 1983-86. Vice-chairperson exec. bd. dirs. handicapped Boy Scouts Am., Houston, 1986-90; mem. leadership coun. Triangle Interfaith Project, Beaumont, 1995—. Recipient citation for Disting. Svc. So. Bapt. Theol. Sem., 1984, Dean's citation Outstanding Achievement U. Louisville, 1988. Mem. The Alliance of Baptists (exec. bd. dirs. 1988-90, v.p. 1990-91), So. Bapt. Women in Ministry (pres. 1988-90, treas. 1995-96), Bapt. Gen. Conv. of Tex. (exec. bd. dirs.), Leadership Beaumont. Avocations: gardening, interior design, travel. Home: 2107 Bartlett St Houston TX 77098-5305 Office: Calder Bapt Ch 1005 N 11th St Beaumont TX 77702-1204 *All around us there are new opportunities for creating, ordering, liberating and healing our world. It is our calling and our challenge to be God's partners in this holy purpose.*

MC GAUGHAN, ALEXANDER STANLEY, architect; b. Phila., May 18, 1912; s. Henry T. and Mable (Colgan) McG.; m. Virginia Storm, July 11, 1936 (dec. Sept. 1989); 1 son, Alexander Stanley; m. Maria R. Drayer, Oct. 27, 1990.. BArch, U. Mich., 1934. Draftsman, designer Pontiac, Mich., 1934-36; architect Resettlement Adminstrn. and Farm Security Adminstrn., 1936-44; labor economist, planner WPB, Washington, 1944-45; housing economist, prodn. engr. Nat. Housing Agy., Washington, 1945-47; indsl. designer Cairns Corp., N.Y.C., also Hugh Johnson Assos., Washington, 1947-50; partner McGaughan & Johnson, Washington, 1950-80; asst. dir. design and constrn. Gallaudet U., Environ. Design Center for the Deaf, 1980-84; univ. architect Am. U., Washington, 1984-87; archtl. cons., 1988—; spl. cons. Nat. Security Resources Bd., Def. Prodn. Adminstrn., HHFA, HUD, Dept. Def.; mem. D.C. Bd. Examiners and Registrars Architects, 1966-73, pres., 1969-72; dir. Mid. Atlantic region Nat. Coun. Archtl. Registration Bds., 1966-73, chmn., 1970-71, chmn. exam. com. on design and site planning, 1972-73. Prin. works include Charred Oak Estates, Md., doctor's residence D.C. Gen. Hosp., housing, Carlisle Barracks, Pa., housing for USAF and U.S. Army C.E., ea. U.S., shopping ctrs., McLean, Va., Greenbelt, Md., Fairfax County, Va., Prince Georges County, Md., Washington pub. schs., Andrew Radar Clinic, Ft. Myer, Va., D.C. Police Acad., 2d, 4th and 5th dist. police hdqrs., Washington; patentee aluminum bldg. systems. Bd. govs. Washington Bldg. Congress, 1968-71, bd. dirs., 1973-76; mem. President's Com. on Employment People with Disabilities, 1974-93; bd. dirs. Nat. Ctr. for Barrier Free Environ., 1974-79. Recipient 1st award for contemporary architecture and land planning Md. Homebuilders, 1962; disting. urban landscape award U.S. Army C.E., 1968; disting. archtl. award, 1969; nat. archtl. award of excellence Am. Inst. Steel Constrn., 1973. Fellow AIA (pres. Washington met. chpt. 1963, chmn. nat. com. archtl. competitions 1966-67, mem. barrier free task force 1974-77, rep. to Am. Nat. Stds. Inst. A 117.1 com. 1977-88); mem. Am. Arbitration Assn. (nat. panel arbitrators), Cosmos Club (bd. mgmt. 1978-80). Home and Office: 2028 Hillyer Pl NW Washington DC 20009-1006

MCGAUGHEY, EMMETT CONNELL, advertising agency executive; b. St. Paul, May 20, 1911; s. Emmett Walter and Frances (Connell) McG.; m. Mary Etta Freese, Oct. 27, 1939; children: Terrence, Dennis, Mark, Mary Frances. B.S., U. Wash., 1934. Sales promotion Gen. Motors Corp., 1934-41; spl. agt. FBI, 1941-49; So. Calif. mgr. Cappel, MacDonald & Co., 1950-51; exec. v.p. Erwin Wasey, Ruthrauff & Ryan, Inc., Los Angeles and N.Y.C., 1951-63; sr. v.p. Hixson & Jorgenson, Inc., Los Angeles, 1964-65; exec. v.p. Hixson & Jorgenson, Inc., 1965-68; chmn. Dailey & Assos., Los Angeles, 1968—, Dailey Internat. Group, 1981—; mem. adv. bd. Calif. Pacific Nat. Bank. Past officer-or-dir. Los Angeles chpt. ARC, So. Calif. chpt. Arthritis and Rheumatism Found. (Nat. Distinguished Service award 1963), Calif. chpt. Multiple Sclerosis Soc., Los Angeles County Heart Assn., Am. Cancer Soc.; chmn. Los Angeles-Auckland Sister City Com., Com. to Secure a Mayors Residence; mem. Los Angeles Police Commn., 1952-61, 66-73, v.p., 1954-55, 57-58, 69-70, pres., 1955-56, 58-59, 70-71, sr. mem., 1959-61; mem. assos. Calif. Inst. Tech.; mem. commerce assos. U. So. Calif.; bd. dirs. So. Calif. Symphony, Hollywood Bowl Assn.; mem. bd. airport commrs. City of Los Angeles, 1979-85, v.p., 1981-82, pres., 1982-83; chmn. bd. trustees Orthopedic Hosp.; envoy to New Zealand and Tonga Summer Olympics, 1984; trustee Ireland's Children, Inc., mem. com. on internat. trade, City of Los Angeles; pres. Southern Calif. chpt. Am. Irish Found., 1985; 1st v.p. Greater Los Angeles Vis. & Conv. Bur., 1985-87, pres., 1988. Recipient award merit Blind Children's Center, 1971. Mem. Nat. Outdoor Advt. Bur., Soc. Former Spl. Agts. FBI (nat. pres. 1964), Los Angeles C. of C. (dir.), Air Force Assn., Aerospace Council, U. Wash. Alumni Assn. (trustee), Chi Psi (Distinguished Service award 1966), Alpha Delta Sigma. Clubs: Masons, Shriners, Rotary (pres. Los Angeles 1978, dir.); Capitol Hill (Washington); California (Los Angeles), 100 (Los Angeles); Lake Arrowhead Country, Los Angeles Athletic. Office: 3055 Wilshire Blvd Los Angeles CA 90010-1108

MC GAUGHY, JOHN BELL, civil engineer; b. Norfolk, Va., Nov. 5, 1914; s. John Bell and Frances Vivian (Coleman) McG.; m. Charlotte Edna Schwartz, Jan. 20, 1940 (dec. Dec. 1978); 1 child, John Bell; m. Page Cook Axson, Sept. 26, 1981. Student, U. Va., 1933-35; B.S. in Civil Engring. Duke U., 1938. Asst. to project engr. U.S. Dept. Agr., Farmville, Va., 1936-37; tech. asst. civil engring. sect. U.S. Coast Guard, Norfolk, Va., 1938-39; civil engr. constrn. q.m. U.S. Army, Albrook Field, C.Z., 1939-41; chief mil. design sect. U.S. Engrs. Office, Norfolk, 1941-44; sr. partner McGaughy, Marshall & McMillan (architects and cons. engrs.)(formerly Lublin, McGaughy & Assocs), Norfolk, 1945-65; pres. MMM Design Group (formerly McGaughy, Marshall & McMillan), Norfolk, Washington, Dublin, Ireland, Frankfurt, Fed. Republic Germany, 1965-81, chmn. bd., chief exec. officer, 1981—; spl. cons. Office Coal Research U.S. Dept. Interior; mem. Va. Gov.'s Met. Areas Study Commn.; chmn. faculty Norfolk extension U. Va., 1943-46. Named Va. Engr. of Yr., 1970. Fellow ASCE; mem. Am. Concrete Inst., ASTM, Am. Road Bldg. Assn. (bd. dirs. engring. div. 1966-68), Nat. Soc. Profl. Engrs. (v.p. 1957-59), Va. C. of C., Norfolk C. of C. (bd. dirs. 1960-63), Va. Soc. Profl. Engrs. (past pres.), Engrs. Club Hampton Roads (past pres.), Soc. Am. Mil. Engrs., Va. Engring. Found. (bd. dirs. 1970-72, 90—), Phi Delta Theta, Thelta Tau. Clubs: Cedar Point Golf (Suffolk); Harbor, Norfolk Yacht and Country (Norfolk); Princess Anne Country (Virginia Beach, Va.). Home: 5905 Studeley Ave Norfolk VA 23508-1030 Office: 229 W Bute St PO Box 269 Norfolk VA 23501

MCGAVIC, JUDY L., coal company official; b. Evansville, Ind., June 29, 1944; d. M. Galen and Helen L. (Sims) Barclay; m. Ronald R. McGavic, Aug. 22, 1962; 1 child, Michael D. Student, Ky. Wesleyan Coll., 1965-66, Murray (Ky.) State U., 1968, U. Ky., 1969; B of Liberal Arts, U. Evansville, 1994. Mine clk. Peabody Coal Co., Centertown, Ky., 1973-78, chief mine clk., 1978-81, sr. mine clk., 1981-86, panel technician, 1986, sr. coord. employee rels., 1987-88, employee rels. rep., 1988-92; sr. employee rels. rep. Peabody Coal Co., Lynnville, Ind., 1993-95. Peabody Coal Co. campaign chmn. United Way, 1992, 93, also chmn. blood drive. Mem. NAFE. Avocations: golf, boating, walking, bowling. Home: 7600 Edgedale Dr Newburgh IN 47630-3062

MCGAVIN, DARREN, actor, director, producer; b. Spokane, Wash., May 7, 1922; s. Reid Delano Richardson and Grace (Bogart) McG.; m. Kathie Browne, Dec. 31, 1969; children: York, Megan, Bridget, Bogart. Student, U. of Pacific, 1 year, Neighborhood Playhouse, 6 months, Actors Studio. pres., chief exec. Taurean Films (S.A.), Tympanum Corp. Films include Fear, 1946, Queen for a Day, 1951, Summer Madness, 1955, The Court Martial of Billy Mitchell, 1955, The Man with the Golden Arm, 1956, The Delicate Delinquent, 1957, Beau James, 1957, The Case Against Brooklyn, 1958, Bullet for a Badman, 1964, The Great Sioux Massacre, 1963, Mrs. Pollifax, Spy, 1970, The Petty Story, 1972, B Must Die, 1973, The Poetry Story, 1974, No Deposit, No Return, 1975, Mission Mars, Airport '77, 1977, Hot Lead and Cold Feet, 1978, Repo, 1980, Zero to Sixty, 1980, Hangar 18, 1980, Firebird, 1981, A Christmas Story, 1984, The Natural, 1984, Raw Deal, 1985, From the Hip, 1986, Captain America, 1988, Blood and Concrete, 1990, Billy Madison, 1994; plays include Captain Brassbound's Conversion, The Rainmaker, Tunnel of Love, My Three Angels, Dinner at Eight, The Innkeepers, The King and I (revival, Lincoln Ctr., N.Y.C.); TV series Mike Hammer, 1958-59, Riverboat, 1960-61, The Outsider, 1968-69, The Night Stalker, 1974-75; TV films The Challenge, 1970, Tribes, 1970, Something Evil, 1972, Law and Order, 1976, Brink's, 1976, The Night Stalker, 1977, The Night Strangler, 1978, Child of the Night, 1990, Perfect Harmony, 1990, Greetings, 1993-94; TV series Kolchak: The Night Stalker, 1978-79, Murphy Brown, 1990 (Emmy award); directorial debut with film Happy Mother's Day . . . Love, George, 1973. Mem. Screen Actors Guild, Actors Equity Assn., Dirs. Guild Am., Writers Guild Am., AFTRA. Office: Gersh Agency 232 N Canon Dr Beverly Hills CA 90210 *Do nothing you will be ashamed of, honor all commitments, and hope for the best.**

MCGAVRAN, FREDERICK JAEGER, lawyer; b. Columbus, Ohio, Apr. 24, 1943; s. James Holt and Marion (Jaeger) McG.; m. Elizabeth Dowlig, Jan. 5, 1980; children: Sarah Ann, Marian Katherine. BA, Kenyon Coll., 1965; JD, Harvard U., 1972. Bar: Ohio 1972, U.S. Supreme Ct. 1984, Ky. 1992. Assoc. Kyte, Conlan, Wulsin & Vogeler, Cin., 1972-78, Frost & Jacobs, Cin., 1978—. Editor: Sixth Circuit Federal Practice Manual, 1993. Lt. USN, 1965-69. Mem. Fed. Bar Assn. (pres. Cin. chpt. 1984-85, mem. exec. com. Cin. chpt. 1985—), Ohio State Bar Assn. (chmn. com. on fed. cts. 1982-85), Univ. Club of Cin., The Literary Club. Home: 2560 Perkins Ln Cincinnati OH 45208-2723 Office: Frost & Jacobs 2500 PNC Ctr Cincinnati OH 45202

MCGAW, KENNETH ROY, wholesale distribution executive; b. Parry Sound, Ont., Can., Aug. 25, 1926; s. Dalton Earnest and Grace (Crockford) McG. Student, Denison U., 1946-48; B.A., Western Res. U., 1949. With Bigelow Carpets, N.Y. and Ohio, 1949-53; representing Frederick Cooper Lamps, Inc., Chgo., 1953—; home furnishing salesman Gates Mills, Ohio, 1958-74, Fort Lauderdale, 1974-77, Dallas, 1978-79; pres. Ken McGaw, Inc., Dallas, 1979—; factory rep. for maj. furniture and furniture accessory mfrs. Bd. dirs. Big Bros. Cleve., 1963-65, Dallas Opera Co., 1981-92; v.p. Nat. Council on Alcoholism, Cleve., 1972-74; chmn. fundraising drive Wholesale div. Dallas Industry for Dallas Opera, 1982-83; ruling elder 1st Presbyterian Ch., Dallas., 1981—. Served to 2d lt. U.S. Army, 1944-46. Mem. Greater Dallas Home Furnishings Assn. (bd. dirs. 1985-86), S.W. Homefurnishings Assn., S.W. Roadrunners Assn., Internat. Homefurnishings Reps. Assn. Lodge: Rotary. Home: 8360 E San Bernardo Dr Scottsdale AZ 85258-2430

MCGEADY, SISTER MARY ROSE, religious organization administrator, psychologist; b. Hazelton, Pa., June 28, 1928; d. Joseph James and Catherine Cecilia (Mundie) McG. BA in Sociology, Emmanuel Coll., 1955; MA in Clin. Psychology, Fordham U., 1961; DHL (hon.), St. John's U., Queens, N.Y., 1982, Coll. New Rochelle, N.Y., 1991, Fordham U., 1991, Niagara U., 1991, Coll. St. Rose, Albany, N.Y., 1991, DePaul U., 1991. Joined Daus. of Charity St. Vincent De Paul, Roman Cath. Ch., 1946. Dir. Astor Home Clinics, Rhinebeck, N.Y., 1961-66; exec. dir. Nazareth Child Care Ctr., Boston, 1966-71; dir. mental health Cath. Charities Bklyn., 1971-79, assoc. exec. dir., 1987-90; dir. Kennedy Child Study Ctr., N.Y.C., 1979-81; provincial supr. Daus. of Charity St. Vincent DePaul, Albany, 1981-87; pres., chief exec. officer Covenant House, N.Y.C., 1990—; bd. dirs. Cardinal Cooke Health Care Ctr., N.Y.C., Meninger Found., Kans., St. Michael's Coll., Vt., Ctr. for Human Devel., Washington. Author: Catholic Special Education, 1979. Mem. N.Y. State Mental Health Svcs. Coun., Albany, 1983-90, N.Y. State Mental Health Planning Coun., Albany, 1986-91, Cath. Charities USA, 1966—. Recipient svc. award N.Y.C. Dept. Mental Health, 1988, Encouragement award Cath. U. Am., 1991. Home: 75 Lewis Ave Brooklyn NY 11206-7015 Office: Covenant House 346 W 17th St New York NY 10011-5002

MCGEE, DOROTHY HORTON, writer, historian; b. West Point, N.Y., Nov. 30, 1913; d. Hugh Henry and Dorothy (Brown) McG.; ed. Sch. of St. Mary, 1920-21, Green Vale Sch., 1921-28, Brearley Sch., 1928-29, Fermata Sch., 1929-31. Asst. historian Inc. Village of Roslyn (N.Y.), 1950-58; historian Inc. Village of Matinecock, 1966—. Author: Skipper Sandra, 1950; Sally Townsend, Patriot, 1952; The Boarding School Mystery, 1953; Famous Signers of the Declaration, 1955; Alexander Hamilton-New Yorker, 1957; Herbert Hoover: Engineer, Humanitarian, Statesman, 1959, rev. edit., 1965; The Pearl Pendant Mystery, 1960; Framers of the Constitution, 1968; author booklets, articles hist. and sailing subjects. Chmn., Oyster Bay Am. Bicentennial Revolution Commn., 1971—; historian Town of Oyster Bay, 1982—; mem. Nassau County Am. Revolution Bicentennial Commn.; hon. dir. The Friends of Raynham Hall, Inc.; treas. Family Welfare Assn. Nassau County, Inc., 1956-58; dir. Family Service Assn. Nassau County, 1958-69. Recipient Cert. of award for outstanding contbn. children's lit. N.Y. State Assn. Elem. Sch. Prins., 1959; award Nat. Soc. Children of Am. Revolution, 1960; award N.Y. Assn. Supervision and Curriculum Devel., 1961; hist. award Town of Oyster Bay, 1963; Cert. Theodore Roosevelt Assn., 1976. Fellow Soc. Am. Historians; mem. Soc. Preservation L.I. Antiquities (hon. dir.), Nat. Trust Hist. Preservation, N.Y. Geneal. and Biol. Soc. (dir., trustee), Oyster Bay Hist. Soc. (hon., pres. 1971-75, chmn. 1975-79, trustee), Theodore Roosevelt Assn. (trustee), Townsend Soc. Am. (trustee). Republican. Address: PO Box 142 Locust Valley NY 11560-0142

MCGEE, HALL THOMAS, JR., newspaper, radio and television executive; b. Charleston, S.C., Aug. 7, 1913; s. Hall Thomas and Gertrude Wyman (Frampton) McG.; m. Margaret Anne Pringle, June 29, 1939; children—Margaret Anne McGee McManes, Hall Thomas, III. B.S., Coll. Charleston, 1935; postgrad., Harvard U. Bus. Sch., 1936. With Eve. Post Pub. Co. and News and Courier Co., Charleston, 1936-87; treas. Eve. Post Pub. Co. and News and Courier Co., 1945-81, v.p., gen. mgr., 1969-84, pres., 1984-87, also dir., 1945—; trustee retirement plan, 1955—; treas., dir. Rochelle Corp., Beaufort, S.C., 1962-75, Aiken Cablevision, Inc., S.C., 1965-83, Banner Corp., Cambridge, Md., 1965-86, Aiken Communications, Inc., 1968-87 , Georgetown Communications, Inc., S.C., 1973-87 , Waynesboro Pub. Co., Va., 1974-82; treas., dir. Portal Communications, Inc., El Paso, Tex., 1974-86, Sangre de Cristo Communications, Inc., Pueblo, Colo., Editors Press Service Inc., N.Y.C., Buenos Aires (Argentina) Herald, Mardel Communications, Inc., Salisbury, Md., 1980-86. Bd. dirs. Charleston YMCA; treas. Charleston Indsl. Assn., 1964-80; pres., trustee Grant Home, Charleston, 1975-86; trustee Coll. Charleston, 1952-68, Magnolia Cemetery, Charleston, 1970-86, Roper Found., 1988—; elder Second Presbyn. Ch., 1958—. Mem. Am. Newspaper Pubs. Assn. (chmn. taxation com.), So. Newspaper Pubs. Assn. (dir.), S.C. Press Assn. (past pres.), St. Cecilia Soc., S.C. Soc., St. Andrews Soc., Agrl. Soc. S.C., Huguenot Soc. S.C., Rotary (dir. Charleston chpt.), Carolina Yacht Club, Supper Club. Home: 200 Wentworth St Charleston SC 29401-1233 Office: Executive Suites 171 Church St Ste 300 Charleston SC 29401-3165

MCGEE, HAROLD JOHNSTON, academic administrator; b. Portsmouth, Va., Apr. 13, 1937; s. Harold Valentine McGee and Clara Mae (Johnston) Webber; m. Mary Frances Eure, Mar. 22, 1959; children: Harold Johnston, Mary Margaret, Matthew Hayden; m. Linda Gayle Stevens, Apr. 3, 1976; 1 child, Andrew Meade. BS, Old Dominion U., 1959; MEd, U. Va., 1962, EdD, 1968. Tchr. Falls Church (Va.) City Schs., 1959-62; asst. dean, then dean of admissions Old Dominion U., Norfolk, Va., 1962-65; field rep., program officer, sr. program officer U.S. Office Edn. Bur. Higher Edn., Charlottesville, 1965-70; provost Tidewater Community Coll., Portsmouth, 1970-71; founding pres. Piedmont Va. Community Coll., Charlottesville, 1971-75; various offices including dean grad. sch., asst. to pres., v.p. student affairs, v.p. adminstrv. affairs, sec. bd. visitors James Madison U., Harrisonburg, Va., 1975-86; pres. Jacksonville (Ala.) State U., 1986—; bd. dirs. Marine Environ. Scis. Consortium, Dauphin Island, Ala., Gulf South Conf. Conf., chmn. 1990-92; bd. dirs. Birmingham Calhoun County C. of C., vice chmn. 1988-90; chmn. Ala. Coun. Univ. Pres., 1991-93; mem. Gov.'s Tax Reform Task Force, 1991-92; bd. dirs. Trans America Athletic Conf., 1995—, Southland Farm League, 1995—. Author: Impact of Federal Support, 1968, The Virginia Project, 1976. Mem. United Way of Calhoun County Ala. 1986-92, Knox Concert Series Adv. Bd., Anniston, Ala., Leadership Ala., Anniston Mus. Natural History Found. Mem. NCAA (coun. 1991-95), ACA, Soc. Coll. and Univ. Planning Am. Assn. Higher Edn., Capital City Club (Montgomery, Ala.), Rotary, Phi Delta Kappa. Episcopalian. Office: Jacksonville State U Office of Pres Jacksonville AL 36265

MCGEE, HENRY ALEXANDER, JR., university official; b. Atlanta, Sept. 12, 1929; s. Henry Alexander and Arrie Mae (Mallory) McG.; m. Betty Rose Herndon, July 29, 1951; children: Henry Alexander, Charles Nelson, Kathy Nan. BChemE, Ga. Inst. Tech., 1951, PhD, 1955; postgrad., U. Wis., 1955-56. Rsch. scientist Army Rocket and Guided Missile Agy. and NASA, Huntsville, Ala., 1956-59; from assoc. prof. to prof. chem. engring. Ga. Inst. Tech., Atlanta, 1959-71; prof. Va. Poly. Inst. and State U., Blacksburg, 1971-94, head dept. chem. engring., 1971-82; assoc. provost for engring. Va. Commonwealth U., Richmond, 1994-95, founding dean engring., 1995—; vis. prof. Calif. Inst. Tech., 1964; dir. chem. and thermal sys. div. NSF, Washington, 1990-93; cons. in field. Author: Molecular Engineering, 1991; editorial adv. bd.: Chemical Abstracts; contbr. numerous articles to profl. publs. Danforth Assoc.; recipient various rsch. grants NSF, NASA, Air Force Office Sci. Rsch.; named one of five Outstanding Young Men of Yr. Atlanta, 1964, Acad. Disting. Engring. Alumni, Ga. Tech., 1994. Fellow AIChE (chmn. nat. program com., mem. editl. bd. jour), AAAS (chmn. sect. on engring. 1985-86), Am. Chem. Soc.; mem. Sigma Xi. Republican. Home: 6 River Court Ln Richmond VA 23233 Office: Va Commonwealth U Richmond VA 23284

MCGEE, HUMPHREY GLENN, architect; b. Hartsville, S.C., June 26, 1937; s. James Gladney and Elizabeth Adams (Williams) McG.; BArch, Clemson U., 1960. Designer, Clark, McCall & Leach, Hartsville-Kingstree, S.C., 1961; Designer prodn. A. G. Odell & Assocs., Charlotte, N.C., 1962; chief designer Clark, McCall & Leach, Hartsville-Kingstree, S.C., 1963; sr. designer LBC & W, Inc., Columbia, S.C., 1965-69, pres., 1969-76, sr. v.p. client services and design, 1976; pres. CEDA, Inc., Columbia, S.C., 1976-86; pres., treas. McGee-Howle & Assocs., Vero Beach, Fla, 1986—. With USAR, 1961-67. Mem. Am. Inst. Architects, Nat. Soc. Interior Designers (award 1972), Am. Soc. Interior Designers (chmn. S.C. chpt. com. on Found. Interior Design Edn. and Rsch. 1976). Published: Who's Who in Interior Design, 1993-95; cited in 100 Designer's Favorite Rooms, 1993-95. Home: 251 Johns Island Dr Indian River Shores FL 32963-3238 Office: 2801 Ocean Dr Ste 302 Vero Beach FL 32963-2025

MCGEE, JAMES SEARS, historian; b. Houston, July 12, 1942; s. William Sears and Mary Elizabeth (Peterson) McG.; m. Mary Arnall Broach, Aug. 20, 1966; children: Elizabeth, Claude. BA, Rice U., 1964; MA, Yale U., 1966, M in Philosophy, 1968, PhD, 1971. Asst. prof. Ga. So. Coll., Statesboro, 1969-71; asst. prof. history U. Calif., Santa Barbara, 1971-78, assoc. prof., 1978-84, prof., 1984—, chmn. dept., 1990-95. Author: The Godly Man in Stuart England, 1976; editor: The Miscellaneous Works of John Bunyan, Vol. 3, 1987. Named Disting. Tchr. in Soc. Scis., U. Calif., Santa Barbara, 1989; fellow Abraham Found., 1962-63; Woodrow Wilson fellow, 1964-65; recipient summer stipend NEH, 1975. Mem. Royal Hist. Soc., Am. Soc. Ch. History, Am. Hist. Assn., N.Am. Conf. on Brit. Studies. Democrat. Episcopalian. Avocation: gardening. Office: U Calif Dept History Santa Barbara CA 93106

MCGEE, JERRY EDWARD, academic administrator; b. Rockingham, N.C., Nov. 4, 1942; s. Sam McGee and Mary (McKinnon) Caddell; m. Hannah Covington, Aug. 15, 1965; children: Jeremy Ryan, Marcus Samuel. BS, East Carolina U., 1965; MA, Appalachian State U., 1974; EdD, Nova U., 1979; AA (hon.), Richmond C.C., 1993. Insdl. engr. Burlington Inc., Rockingham, 1965-68; program dir. Tri-County Cmty. Action, Laurinburg, N.C., 1968-71; counselor, program dir. Richmond C.C., Hamlet, N.C., 1971-75; exec. asst. to pres. Gardner Webb U., Boiling Springs, N.C., 1975-80; v.p. for devel. Meredith Coll., Raleigh, N.C., 1980-87, Furman U., Greenville, S.C., 1987-92; pres. Wingate (N.C.) U., 1992—; bd. dirs. Bank of Union, Monroe, N.C., First Charter Corp., Concord, N.C.; bd. visitors Johnson C. Smith U., Charlotte, N.C., 1995—. Dist. gov. Civitan Internat., Western N.C., 1974-75; football referee divsn. I NCAA. With USNG, 1967-73. Democrat. Baptist. Home: 1204 Irongate Dr Monroe NC 28110 Office: Wingate Univ Office of Pres Wingate NC 28174

MC GEE, JOHN FRAMPTON, communications company executive; b. Charleston, S.C., Jan. 9, 1923; s. Hall Thomas and Gertrude (Frampton) McG.; m. Ruth Bouknight Smedley, June 19, 1971; children: Beverly C. McGee Kinder, Catharine F. McGee Mebane, Charles V. Smedley. BS in Bus. and Polit. Sci., Davidson Coll., 1943. With Charleston (S.C.) Post-News and Courier, 1946-62; asst. gen. mgr. State-Record Newspapers, Columbia, S.C., 1962-64, gen. mgr., pres., co-pub., 1964-69; gen. exec. Knight Newspaper, Inc., Miami, Fla., 1969-70; pres., associated pub. Charleston (W.Va.) Daily Mail, 1970-87, pub., 1987-90; pres. Clay Communications, Inc. Charleston parent co. Charleston Daily Mail, Raleigh Register, Post-Herald, Beckley (W.Va.), Enquirer-Jour., Monroe, N.C., Shelby (N.C.) Daily Star, Sta. WWAY-TV, N.C., Sta. KFDX-TV, Tex., Sta. KJAC-TV, Tex., Sta. WAPT-TV, Miss., 1970-87; gen. ptnr. McGee Enterprises, Charleston, 1987—; bd. dirs., mem. exec. com. AP, N.Y.C.; bd. dirs. Thomson Newspapers, Inc., N.Y.C. and Toronto, Can., United Nat. Bank, Charleston, W.Va.; mem. adv. bd. Sch. Journalism, W.Va. U.; vis. prof. Grad Sch. Journalism, U. Nairobi, Kenya, 1992, 93, Harare Zimbabwe, 1993, 94; vis. lectr. media matters USIS Wind Hook Namibia, 1994; print media counselor, Namibia, Botswana, 1995. Vice chmn. Charleston Area Med. Ctr., U. Charleston; chmn. bd. visitors Davidson (N.C.) Coll., trustee; mem. gen. exec. bd. Presbyn. Ch., U.S.A., 1974-76; mem. S.C. Commn. for Higher Edn., 1966-69. Capt. inf. U.S. Army, 1943-45. Decorated Purple Heart with one oak leaf cluster, Bronze Star with three oak leaf clusters, Combat Infantry badge, Croix de Guerre with palm (France and Belgium), Presdl. Merit citation, Knight Fellow Knight Found., 1995. Mem. So. Newspaper Pubs. Assn. (bd. dirs. 1967-69), Internat. Press Inst. (bd. dirs. Am. com., mem. Internat. Press Inst.-UNESCO commn. for free press during South African elections 1994), W.Va. Press Assn. (pres. 1977-78), New Eng. Soc. S.C. Clubs: Cosmos (Charleston, W.Va.); Edgewood Country of W.Va. Office: McGee Enterprises Bank One Ctr Ste 812 Charleston WV 25301

MC GEE, JOSEPH JOHN, JR., former insurance company executive; b. Kansas City, Mo., Dec. 2, 1919; s. Joseph J. and Margaret (Cronin) McG.; m. Anne Cunningham, Apr. 30, 1949; children: Sally, Peter, Mary, John, David, Julie, Simon. Attended, Rockhurst Coll., Kansas City, Georgetown U. Asst. sec. Old Am. Ins. Co., Kansas City, Mo., 1939-45; v.p. Old Am. Ins. Co., 1946-51, exec. v.p., 1952-55, pres., 1956-87; ins. cons. Kansas City, Mo., 1987-91. Bd. dirs. Truman Med. Ctr., Truman Libr. Inst. for Nat. and Internat. Affairs; trustee emeritus Rockhurst Coll.; pres. McGee Found. Office: 4800 Main St Ste 458 Kansas City MO 64112-2510

MCGEE, MARY ALICE, health science research administrator; b. Winston-Salem, N.C., Oct. 14, 1950; d. C.L. Jr. and Mary Hilda (Shelton) McG. AB, Meredith Coll., 1972. Tchr. Augusta (Ga.) Schs., 1972-73; specialist grants Med. Sch. Brown U., Providence, R.I., 1974-76; profl. basketball player, 1975-76; dir. research adminstn. Med. Sch. Brown U., Providence, 1976-94; tchr., coach Providence Country Day Sch., East Providence, R.I., 1995—. Bd. dirs. Sojourner House, Providence, 1983—, v.p., 1986, 91, treas. 1987-89. Mem. Soc. Rsch. Adminstrs., Nat. Coun. U. Rsch. Adminstrs., R.I. Assn. Women in Edn. Avocations: sports, travel, dogs. Home: 121 Plain St Rehoboth MA 02769-2540 Office: Providence Country Day Sch 2117 Pawtucket Ave East Providence RI 02914-1724

MCGEE, REECE JEROME, sociology educator, researcher; b. St. Paul, Oct. 19, 1929; s. Reece John and Vivian Jeanette (McFarland) McG.; m. Betty Ann Enns, June 10, 1950 (div. 1978); children: Kaelin Christine, Reece Jon, Shanna Beth; m. Sharron Ann Onken, Dec. 2, 1978. BA, U. Minn., 1952, MA, 1953, PhD, 1956. Asst. prof. Humboldt State Coll., Arcata, Calif., 1956; rsch. assoc. U. Minn., Mpls., 1957; asst. prof. U. Tex., Austin, 1957-61, assoc. prof., 1961-64; vis. assoc. prof. Macalester Coll., St. Paul, 1964-65, prof., 1965-67; prof., master tchr. Purdue U., West Lafayette, Ind., 1967-94, prof. emeritus, 1994—, head. dept. sociology and anthropology, 1987-92. Co-author: The Academic Marketplace, 1958; author: Academic Janus, 1971; co-editor: Teaching Sociology: The Quest for Excellence, 1984; editor: Teaching the Mass Class, 1986, 2nd edit., 1991. Sgt. U.S. Army, 1950-51. Mem. Am. Sociol. Assn. (Teaching award sect. on undergrad. edn. 1982, Teaching award 1994), North Cen. Sociol. Assn. (Teaching award 1987), AAUP, Phi Beta Kappa. Democrat. Episcopalian. Avocations: sailing, motorcycles. Office: Purdue U Stone Hall 1365 Dept Sociology & Anthropol West Lafayette IN 47907-1365

MCGEE, ROBERT MERRILL, oil company executive; b. Laramie, Wyo., Dec. 15, 1946; s. Gale William and Loraine (Baker) McG.; m. Mary Louise Lehman, July 26, 1969; children: Kirk Lehman, Scott Baker. BA in Polit. Sci., Allegheny Coll., 1969. Bus. assoc. B.F. Goodrich Co., Akron, Ohio, 1969-70; dir. of info. Nat. Petroleum Coun., Washington, 1970-73; asst. dir. pub. rels. Occidental Internat. Corp., Washington, 1973-74, exec. asst. to pres., 1974-76, v.p., 1976-78, exec. v.p., 1978-82, sr. exec. v.p., 1982-91, pres., 1991—; v.p. Occidental Petroleum Corp., 1994—. Trustee Pan Am. Devel. Found., Washington, 1985, pres., 1991-93; bd. govs. Ford's Theatre, Washington, 1991—; trustee Bus. Coun. for Internat. Understanding, N.Y.C., 1991—, Karl Landegger program in internat. bus. diplomacy, Sch. Fgn. Svc., Georgetown U., Washington, 1991—; mem. The Pres.'s Commn. on White House Fellowships, 1993—; bd. dirs. Inst. for Environment and Nat. Resources Rsch. and Policy, U. Wyo., 1994—, Meridian Internat. Ctr., 1994—, Ctr. Democracy, 1995, U.S.-Can. Pvt. Sector Adv. Coun. IDB, 1995. Mem. The Econ. Club of Washington, Met. Club Washington, Nat. Press Club, Robert Trent Jones Golf Club. Office: Occidental Internat Corp Ste 375 1747 Pennsylvania Ave NW Washington DC 20006-4604

MCGEE, WILLIAM HOWARD JOHN, library system coordinator; b. Rochester, N.Y., May 15, 1942; s. William Peter and Cecilia Matilda (Kuhn) McG.; m. Sheila Anne Drumm, Sept. 4, 1965; children: Kathleen Moira, Margaret Frances. BA with honors, U. Toronto, Ont., Can., 1965; MEd, U. Toronto, 1973; MLS, U. Western Ont., London, 1980. Tchr. Mimico (Ont.) High Sch., 1966-67; tchr., libr. Applewood Secondary Sch., Mississauga, Ont., 1967-71; libr. Crestwood Secondary Sch., Peterborough, Ont., 1971-74; libr. cons. Cayman Islands Edn. Dept., Grand Cayman, B.W.I., 1975-79; adminstrv. asst. Lake Erie Regional Libr., London, Ont., 1980-83; chief libr. Ft. Erie (Ont.) Pub. Libr., 1983-86; asst. dir. McAllen (Tex.) Pub. Libr., 1986-89; coord. Hidalgo County Libr. System, McAllen, 1989—; cons. Grand Ct. Libr., Grand Cayman, 1974-79; mem. Tex. State Libr. Task Force, Austin, Tex., 1991-93; adv. coun. Libr. Svcs. Consultation Act, Austin, 1993—. Editor InTraLogue jour., 1980-83; assoc. editor Can. Jour. Info. Sci., 1980. Mem. ALA, Ont. Libr. Assn., Tex. Libr. Assn. (chmn. dist. #4 1994—, chmn. intellectual freedom com. 1995-96), Bibliothecaires Francophones Internat. Roman Catholic. Avocations: gourmet cooking, music, travel, reading. Office: Hidalgo County Libr Sys 4305 N 10th St Ste E Mcallen TX 78504-3009

MCGEE, WILLIAM TOBIN, intensivist; b. Port Chester, N.Y., May 23, 1957; s. James R. and Mary (Delzotto) McG.; m. Sarah McGrath; children: Erin, Kelly, Mary. BA in Physics, Dartmouth Coll., 1979; MD, N.Y. Med. Coll., 1983. Diplomate Am. Bd. Internal Medicine with spl. qualifications in Critical Care. Resident in internal medicine Baystate Med. Ctr., Springfield, Mass., 1983-86, intensivist, acting dir. surg. ICU, 1990-95; fellow in critical care St. Louis U./St. John's Mercy Med. Ctr., St. Louis, 1986-88. DeWitt Wallace fellow rehab. medicine Rusk Inst. NYU Med. Ctr. Fellow Coll. Chest Physicians; mem. AMA, Soc. Critical Care Medicine, Am. Soc. Parenteral and Enteral Nutrition. Roman Catholic. Avocations: skiing, biking, hiking, sailing, windsurfing. Office: Baystate Med Ctr 759 Chestnut St Springfield MA 01199-1001

MCGEEN, DANIEL SAMUEL, dentist, ornithology and ecology educator; b. Waukesha, Wis., Mar. 30, 1918; s. Norman John and Rhoda Lillian (Eales) McG.; m. Jean Jordan; children: Daniel Thomas, Susan Jean, Donald John, David Norman, Mary Elizabeth. BA summa cum laude, Carroll Coll., Waukesha, Wis., 1942; DDS, U. Detroit, 1947. Grad. tchg. asst. in biology U. Oreg., Eugene, 1942-43; pvt. practice dentistry Pontiac, Mich., 1975-88; pvt. practice dentist Waterford, Mich., 1953-88; base dental officer USCG, Boston, 1951-53; pres. pvt. corp. Waterford, 1976-88; tchr. ornithology and ecology Cranbrook Inst. Sci., Bloomfield Hills, Mich., 1968-74; tchr. ornithology and ecology divsn. continuing edn. Oakland U., Rochester Hills, Mich., 1968-74; pvt. rschr. Auburn Hills, Mich., 1988—; head oral protection for athletes Pontiac Pub. Schs., 1962-64; ednl. cons. natural history, bird banding Pontiac Sch. Dist., 3 County Sch. Dist., Oakland, Waimo, and Macomb County Sch. Dists., 1953-92. Contbr. articles to profl. publs. Scouter, resource person Boy Scouts Am., 1953-67; founder, past pres. Pontiac, Oakland, Macomb Audubon Soc.; past pres. Eugene (Oreg.) Nat. History Soc.; sr. warden, lay min., cup bearer St. Mary's-in-the Hills Episcopal Ch., Lake Orion, Mich., 1953—. Lt. USPHS, 1951-53. Fellow Royal Soc. Health; mem. AAAS (2 stripes, life mem.), AOU, ADA, Mich. Dental Assn., Oakland County Dental Assn., Wilson Ornithol. Assn., Assn. Field Ornithologists, Sigma Xi, Delta Sigma Nu, Phi Sigma, Beta Beta Beta. Achievements include research in two types of host-cowbird interaction patterns, delineation of habitat--Kirtland's Warbler-Brown-Headed Cowbird cycles; originator of hypothesis that sodium limits the Kirtland's cycle and probably that of other species of animals; that sodium is the deeper invariant of the basic allometric invariant 0.25. Home: 552 Lake Angelus Rd Auburn Hills MI 48326

MCGEENEY, JOHN STEPHEN, lawyer; b. Manhasset, N.Y., Dec. 22, 1934; s. John Joseph and Marion Alice (Morse) McG.; m. Diane Tyler; children: Michael Morse, Luke Stephen. AB, Amherst Coll., 1956; LLB, Harvard U., 1959. Bar: Conn., U.S. Dist. Ct. Conn. 1961, U.S. Supreme Ct. 1965, U.S. Dist Ct. (ea. dist.) Va. 1967, U.S. Ct. Appeals (2d cir.) 1969, U.S. Ct. Appeals (4th cir.) 1971, U.S. Dist. Ct. (so. dist.) N.Y. 1980, U.S. Dist. Ct. Mont. 1987. Assoc. Cummings & Lockwood, Stamford, Conn., 1959-68, ptnr., 1968-89; ptnr. Paul, Hastings, Janofsky & Walker, Stamford, 1989—, chmn.; bd. dirs. Dorr-Oliver Inc., Milford, 1989—. Fellow Am. Coll. Trial Lawyers; mem. ABA, Fed. Bar Coun., Conn. Bar Assn. (Fed. Practice com.). Office: Paul Hastings Janofsky & Walker 1055 Washington Blvd Stamford CT 06901-2216

MCGEER, EDITH GRAEF, neurological science educator emerita; b. N.Y.C., Nov. 18, 1923; d. Charles and Charlotte Annie (Ruhl) Graef; m. Patrick L. McGeer, Apr. 15, 1954; children: Patrick Charles, Brian Theodore, Victoria Lynn. BA, Swarthmore Coll., 1944; PhD, U. Va., 1946; DSc (hon.), U. Victoria, 1987. Research chemist E.I. DuPont de Nemours & Co., Wilmington, Va., 1946-54; research assoc. div. neurological sci. U. B.C., Vancouver, Can., 1954-74; assoc. prof. U. B.C., Vancouver, 1974-76, prof., acting head, 1976-83, prof., head., 1983-89, prof. emerita, 1989—. Author: (with others) Molecular Neurobiology of the Mammalian Brain, 1978, 2d. edit., 1987; editor: (with others) Kainic Acid as a Tool in Neurobiology, 1978, Glutamine, Glutamate, and GABA, 1983; contbr. articles to profl. jours. Decorated officer Order of Can.; recipient Citation Am. Chem. Soc., 1958, Rsch. Prize in Psychiatry Clarke Inst., 1992, Lifetime Achievement spl. award Sci. Coun. B.C., 1995. Fellow Can. Coll. Neuropsychopharmacology; mem. Can. Biochemical Soc., Internat. Brain Research Orgn., Internat. Soc. Neurochemistry, Soc. Neuroscience, Am. Neurochemical Soc. (councilor 1979-83), North Pacific Soc. Neurology and Psychiatry (hon. fellow), Lychnos Soc., Sigma Xi, Phi Beta Kappa. Office: U BC Div Neurol Scis, 2255 Wesbrook Mall, Vancouver, BC Canada V6T 1Z3

MCGEER, JAMES PETER, research executive, consultant; b. Vancouver, B.C., Can., May 14, 1922; s. James Arthur and Ada Alice (Schwenger) McG.; m. Catherine Pearson Deas, June 22, 1948; children: Mary, Allison, James, Thomas. BA, U. B.C., 1944, MA, 1946; MA, Princeton U., 1948, PhD, 1949. Researcher Alcan R & D, Arvida, Que., Can., 1949-52, group leader, 1952-59, pilot plant dir., 1960-67; dept. head Alcan Smelters, Arvida, Que., Can., 1968-71, asst. div. head, 1972-73; mgr. tech. transfer Alcan Smelter Svcs., Montreal, Que., 1973-77; dir. rsch. Alcan Internat. Ltd., Kingston, Ont., Can., 1978-82, dir. lab., 1983-87; mng. dir. Ont. Ctr. Materials, Kingston, 1988—; chmn. bd. Can. Rsch. Mgmt. Assn., Toronto, Ont., 1990-91, Welding Inst. Can., Mississauga, Ont., 1988-90, Can. U. Ind. Coun. Advanced Ceramics, Ottawa, Ont., 1986-88; dir. Metall. Soc., Pitts., 1987-89; Can. Coun. lectr. Am. Soc. Metals, 1985-86; disting. lectr. Can. Inst. Mining Metallurgy, 1987. Contbr. articles to profl. jours. Chmn. bd. Que. Assn. Protestant Sch. Bds., Montreal, 1968-70. Recipient Airey award Can. Inst. for Mining and Metallurgy, 1993, Forum award Xerox Can., 1994. Mem. Anglican Ch. Office: Ontario Ctr Materials Rsch, PO Box 1146, Kingston, ON Canada K7L 4Y5*

MCGEHEE, FRANK SUTTON, paper company executive; b. Aug. 15, 1928; s. Clifford G. and Ray (Sutton) McGehee; m. Ann Whitehurst, Mar. 18, 1949; children: Frank Sutton, David Searcy, Ann Lynwood Riley. BA in Econs., U. Ala., 1950. Co-founder, co-chmn. bd. Jacksonville Paper Co. (now UNIJAX), 1950-64; dir. Flagship Banks of Jacksonville; co-founder, co-chmn. bd. Mac Paper Converters, Inc., now chmn. bd., CEO. Trustee, mem. exec. com. Bolles Sch.; past pres., dir. Wolfson Childrens Hosp.; past pres., pres. bd. Ga. Christian Sch. and Home, North Fla. Coun. Boy Scouts Am.; past chmn. Weyerhaeuser Mcht. Coun., Kimberly Clark Mcht. Coun.; active San Jose Ch. of Christ. Mem. Nat. Paper Trade Assn. (dir.), Jacksonville Businessmen Club (sec., dir.), Tournament Players Club (founder), River Club, San Jose Country Club, Sawgrass Country Club, Plantation Country Club. Home: 6750 Epping Forest Way N Jacksonville FL 32217-2688 Office: MAC Papers Inc 3300 Phillipps Hwy PO Box 5369 Jacksonville FL 32247

MC GEHEE, H(ARRY) COLEMAN, JR., bishop; b. Richmond, Va., July 7, 1923; s. Harry Coleman and Ann Lee (Cheatwood) McG.; m. June Stewart, Feb. 1, 1946; children: Lesley, Alexander, Harry III, Donald, Cary. BS, Va. Poly. Inst., 1947; JD, U. Richmond, 1949; MDiv, Va. Theol. Sem., 1957, DD, 1973. Bar: Va. 1949, U.S. Supreme Ct. 1954; ordained to ministry Episcopal Ch., 1957. Spl. counsel dept. hwys. State of Va., 1949-51, gen. counsel employment svc., 1951, asst. atty. gen., 1951-54; rector Immanuel Ch.-on-the-Hill, Va. Sem., 1960-71; bishop Diocese of Mich., Detroit, 1971-90; adv. bd. Nicaraguan Network, Ctr. for Peace and Conflict Studies, Wayne State U.; bd. dirs. Mich. Religious Coalition for Abortion Rights, 1976-84; trustee Va. Theol. Sem., 1978-93; pres. Episc. Ch. Pub. Co., 1978-85. Columnist: Detroit News, 1979-85; weekly commentator pub. radio sta. WDET-AM, Detroit, 1984-90. Mem. Gov.'s Commn. on Status of Women, 1965-66, Mayor's Civic Com., Alexandria, 1967-68; sponsor Nat. Assn. for ERA, 1977-85; pres. Alexandria Legal Aid Soc., 1969-71; bd. dirs. No. Va. Fairhousing Corp., 1963-67; pres. Mich. Coalition for Human Rights, 1980-89; chmn. Citizens' Com. for Justice in Mich., 1983-84; sponsor Farm Labor Orgn. for Children, 1983-85; bd. dirs. Pub. Benefit Corp., Detroit, 1988-90, Mich. Citizens for Personal Freedom, 1989-92, Poverty and Social Reform Inst., Detroit, 1989—, Bread for the World, 1990-94, Ams. United for Separation of Ch. and State, 1990, ACLU Oakland County, Mich., 1991-94; co-chair Lesbian-Gay Found. Mich., 1991—. 1st lt. C.E., U.S. Army, 1943-46. Named Feminist of Yr., Detroit NOW, 1978; recipient Humanitarian award Detroit ACLU, 1984, Phillip Hart medal Mich. Women's Studies Assn., 1984, Sayre award for justice and peace Episc. Peace Fellowship, 1988, Spirit of Detroit award, 1989, Archbishop Romero award Mich. Labor Com., 1990, Brotherhood award AME Ch., Detroit, 1993, Ira Jayne award Detroit br. NAACP, 1993, Martin Luther King, Jr. award United Ch. of Christ, 1995. Mem. Detroit Econ. Club (bd. dirs.). Home: 1496 Ashover Dr Bloomfield Hills MI 48304-1215 Office: Diocese of Mich 4800 Woodward Ave Detroit MI 48201-1310

MC GEHEE, LARRY THOMAS, university administrator; b. Paris, Tenn., May 18, 1936; s. George Eugene and Margaret Elizabeth (Thomas) McG.; m. Elizabeth Hathhorn Boden, Aug. 26, 1961; children: Elizabeth Hathhorn, Margaret Thomas. BA, Transylvania Coll., 1958; BD, Yale U., 1963, MA, 1964, PhD, 1969. Dir., asst. v.p. for univ. relations U. Ala., 1966-68, exec. asst. to pres., 1968-69, exec. v.p., 1969-71; lectr., assoc. prof. dept. Am. studies, 1969-71, acad. v.p., 1971; chancellor U. Tenn., Martin, 1971-79; spl. asst. to pres. U. Tenn., Knoxville, 1979-82; v.p. coll., prof. religion Wofford Coll., Spartanburg, S.C., 1982—. Danforth fellow Yale U., 1960-66. Home: 1047 Woodburn Rd Spartanburg SC 29302-2867 Office: Wofford Coll 429 N Church St Spartanburg SC 29303-3663

MCGEHEE, THOMAS RIVES, paper company executive; b. Jacksonville, Fla., July 12, 1924; s. Clifford Graham and Ray (Sutton) McG. Student Davidson Coll., 1942-43, BS in Chemistry, U. Ala. 1948; m. Delia Houser, Nov. 3, 1950; children: Delia McGehee II, Thomas R. Jr. V.p. Jacksonville Paper Co., 1948-56, pres., 1956-64, Mac Papers, Inc., Jacksonville, 1964-79, co-founder, chief exec. officer, chmn. bd., 1979—; co-chmn., chief exec. officer Mac Papers Converters, Inc., 1965—, pres., North Fla. TV-47, Inc., 1979-90; pres. Higley Pub. Co., 1968-90; bd. dirs. Barnett Bank of Jacksonville, 1961-89; chmn. exec. com. Sta. WTLV-TV 12, 1972-78; numerous real estate interests. Chmn. and founder Greater Jacksonville Community Found., 1964-84, trustee, 1964-89; trustee Jacksonville U., 1959—, vice chmn., 1962-65, chmn., 1991-92; trustee Regent U., 1996—; mem. U. Fla. Pres.' Coun., U. Fla. Health & Sci. Ctr.; mem. post secondary edn. planning commn. State of Fla., 1987-90; bd. dirs. Dreams Come True, pres. and founder 1984-90, chmn. emeritus, 1990—; bd. dirs. Bapt. Hosp. Found., 1986-90; vice chmn. Every Home For Christ, 1987—; past mem., officer numerous other community orgs. Served with U.S. Army, 1943-46, ETO. Recipient 3 Battle Stars, Fla. Gov.'s award, 1962. Mem. NAM (dir. 1964-66), Asso. Industries Fla. (dir. 1961-63), Nat. Paper Trade Assn., So. Paper Trade Assn., Nat. Assn. Broadcasters, Fla. State C. of C., Phi Gamma Delta (pres. 1948). Republican. Episcopalian. Clubs: River (dir. 1980-83), Fla. Yacht, Timuquana Country, Ponte Vedra, Plantation Country, Blowing Rock Country (bd. dirs. 1991-94). Home: Park Plz Condominiums 505 Lancaster St 6B Jacksonville FL 32204-4136 Office: MAC Papers Inc 3300 Phillips Hwy PO Box 5369 Jacksonville FL 32247

MCGEORGE, RONALD KENNETH, hospital executive; b. Fredericton, N.B., Can., June 7, 1944; s. Hubert Oswald and Ruth Johanna (Kolding) McG.; m. Gail F. Mitchell, July 17, 1970; children: Ronald Millard, Scott, Dacia Gail. B.S., Houghton Coll., 1966; diploma in hosp. adminstrn., U. Toronto, 1969. Adminstrv. counsellor N.S. Hosp. Ins. Commn., Halifax, 1969-70; asst. exec. dir. Izaak Walton Killam Hosp. for Children, Halifax, 1970-72; v.p. Greater Niagara Gen. Hosp., Niagara Falls, Ont., 1972-74; chmn. Council Teaching Hosps.; exec. dir. Halifax Infirmary, 1974-79, Kingston Gen. Hosp., Ont., 1980-90; CEO Dr. Everett Chalmers Hosp., 1990-92; pres., chief exec. officer Region 3 Hosp. Corp., Fredericton, N.B., Can., 1992-95; dir. outreach and discipleship Moncton Wesleyan Ch., 1995—; Atlantic Provinces dir. Promise Keepers, 1995; preceptor hosp. adminstrn. U. Ottawa, U. Toronto; chmn. Ont. Council Adminstrn. Teaching Hosps.; cons. in field. Contbr. articles to profl. jours. Chmn., pres. Wesleyan Men, 1st Wesleyan Ch. Named Bus. Alumnus of Yr., Houghton Coll., 1987. Mem. Can. Coll. Health Services Execs. (pres. 1979-80), Assn. Hosp. Adminstrs. N.S. (pres.-elect 1972), N.S. Assn. Health Orgns. (dir.), Ont. Council Adminstrs. of Teaching Hosps. (pres.), Ont. Hosp. Assn. (mem. exec. com., chmn. exec. com. 1989-90), Alumni Assn. of Bethany Bible Coll. (pres.). Home: Steeves Mountain RR # 1, Moncton, NB Canada E1C 8J5 Office: 945 St George Blvd, Moncton, NB Canada E1E 2C9

MCGERVEY, JOHN DONALD, physics educator, researcher; b. Pitts., Aug. 9, 1931; s. Daniel Donald and Eleanor (Rogerson) McG.; m. Nancy Ruth Maher, July 6, 1957; children: Anne, Donald, Joan. BS in Math., U. Pitts., 1952; postgrad., U. Chgo., 1952-53; MS in Physics, Carnegie Inst. Tech., 1955, PhD in Physics, 1960. Instr. math. Carnegie Inst. Tech., Pitts., 1957-60; asst. prof. physics Case Western Res. U., Cleve., 1960-65, assoc. prof., 1965-78, prof. physics, 1978—; vis. scientist Kernforschungsanlage, Julich, Fed. Republic Germany, 1972-73, U. der Bundeswehr München, Fed. Republic Germany, 1988, U. Göttingen, Germany, 1994, U. Bristol, Eng., 1996; Sci. Rsch. Coun. vis. fellow U. East Anglia, Norwich, Eng., 1978-79; resident rsch. assoc. Argonne (Ill.) Nat. Lab., 1963; faculty participant Oak Ridge Assoc. Univs., 1974-90; cons. WQED-TV, Pitts., 1994, Glencoe-Merrill Pub., 1992—. Author: Introduction to Modern Physics, 1971, Spanish lang. edit., 1975, 2d edit., 1983, Probabilities in Everyday Life, 1986, paperback edit., 1989, Quantum Mechanics: Concepts and Applications, 1995; newspaper columnist Numbers, 1994—. Pres. Cath. Interracial Coun. of Cleve., 1969-72; bd. dirs. Commn. on Cath. Cmty. Action, Cleve., 1969-

78; pres. Project Equality of Ohio, Columbus, 1970-72; mem. Physicians for Social Responsibility, Cleve., 1982—; mem. speakers bur. Union Concerned Scientists, 1992—. NSF fellow, 1952; grantee AEC, 1963-66, NSF, 1969-72, 74-81, 85, 87, 90-96, NASA, 1981-85, Army Rsch. Office, 1986—. Mem. AAAS, AAUP (pres. chpt. 1983-84), Am. Phys. Soc., Am. Assn. Physics Tchrs., Cleve. Astron. Soc., Sierra Club, Cleve. Philosophical Club, S. Shore Skeptics, Cleveland Heights Tennis Club, Sigma Xi. Democrat. Roman Catholic. Home: 1819 Wilton Rd Cleveland OH 44118-1628 Office: Case Western Reserve U Dept Physics Cleveland OH 44106

MCGERVEY, TERESA ANN, technology information specialist; b. Pitts., Sept. 27, 1964; d. Walter James and Janet Sarah (Donehue) McG. BS in Geology, Calif. U. Pa., 1986, MS in Earth Sci., 1988. Phys. sci. technician U.S. Geol. Survey, Reston, Va., 1989-90; editor, indexer Am. Geol. Inst., Alexandria, Va., 1990-91; cartographer Def. Mapping Agy., Reston, 1991-93; tech. info. specialist Nat. Tech. Info. Svc., Springfield, Va., 1993—; intern Dept. Mineral Scis., Smithsonian Instn., summers 1985, 1986.

MCGETTIGAN, CHARLES CARROLL, JR., investment banker; b. San Francisco, Mar. 28, 1945; s. Charles Carroll McGettigan and Molly (Fay) McGettigan Pedley; m. Katharine Havard King, Nov. 1, 1975 (div. 1981); m. Meriwether Lewis Stovall, Aug. 6, 1983; 1 child, Meriwether Lewis Fay. AB in Govt., Georgetown U., 1966; MBA in Fin., U. Pa., 1969. Assoc., asst. v.p., v.p. Blyth Eastman Dillon, N.Y.C., 1970-75, 1st v.p., 1975-78, sr. v.p., San Francisco, 1978-80; sr. v.p. Dillon, Read & Co., San Francisco, 1980-83; gen. ptnr. Woodman Kirkpatrick & Gilbreath, San Francisco, 1983-84; prin. corp. fin. Hambrecht & Quist, Inc., San Francisco, 1984-88, mng. dir, founder McGettigan, Wick & Co., Inc., San Francisco, 1988—; gen. ptnr., founder Proactive Ptnrs. L.P., San Francisco, 1990—, Proactive Investment Mgrs., L.P., 1991—; gen. ptnr. Fremont Proactive Ptnrs., L.P., 1991—; bd. dirs. Digital Dictation, Inc., Vienna, Va., NDE Environ. Corp., Austin, Tex., PMR Corp., San Diego, I.-Flow Corp., Irvine, Calif., Sonex Rsch., Inc., Annapolis, Md., Modtech, Inc., Perris, Calif., Wray-Tech Instruments, Inc., Stratford, Conn.; chmn. Onsite Energy Corp., Carlsbad, Calif.; adv. dir. Chesapeake Ventures, Balt., 1984-94. Trustee St. Francis Meml. Hosp., San Francisco, 1980-86; mem. United San Francisco Rep. fin. com., 1983—, steering com., 1986—; adv. bd. dirs. Leavey Sch. Bus. Adminstrn., Santa Clara U., Calif., 1984-1990. With USN, 1966. Named Confrerie des Chevaliers du Tastevin, 1991. Mem. Soc. Calif. Pioneers, The Brook, Racquet and Tennis Club (N.Y.), The Pacific Union Club, Bohemian Club (San Francisco), San Francisco Golf Club, Burlingame Country Club (Hillsborough, Calif.), Calif. Club (L.A.), Boston Club (New Orleans), Piping Rock Club (Locust Valley, N.Y.). Republican. Roman Catholic. Home: 3375 Clay St San Francisco CA 94118-2006 Office: McGettigan Wick & Co Inc 50 Osgood Pl San Francisco CA 94133-4617

MCGHEE, GEORGE CREWS, petroleum producer, former government official; b. Waco, Tex., Mar. 10, 1912; s. George Summers and Magnolia (Spruce) McG.; m. Cecilia Jeanne De Golyer, Nov. 24, 1938; children: Marcia Spruce, George DeGolyer, Dorothy Hart, Michael Anthony, Cecilia Goodrich, Valerie Foster. Student, So. Meth. U., 1928, DCL, 1953; BS, U. Okla., 1933; DPhil (Oxon), (Rhodes scholar), Oxford U., 1937; postgrad., U. London, 1937; LL.D., Tulane U., 1957, U. Md., 1965; D.Sc., U. Tampa, 1969. Registered profl. engr., Tex. Geologist Atlantic Refining Co., 1930-31; geophysicist Continental Oil Co., 1933-34, Compagnie Generale de Geophysique, Morocco, 1935; v.p. Nat. Geophys. Co., 1937-40; partner DeGolyer, MacNaughton & McGhee, Dallas, 1940-41; ind. explorer, producer oil, 1940—; sole owner McGhee Prodn. Co.; chmn. bd. Saturday Rev., 1973-77; Coordinator for aid to Greece and Turkey Dept. State, 1947-49, spl. asst. to sec. state, 1949; asst. sec. for Dept. State (Near Eastern, South Asian, African affairs), 1949-51; mem. various adv. groups to pvt., govtl. orgns., 1940—; U.S. ambassador, chief Am. Mission for Aid to Turkey, 1951-53; sr. adviser N. Atlantic Treaty Council, Ottawa, Can., 1951; mem. bd. Middle East Inst., 1953-58; cons. Nat. Security Council, 1958-59; mem. Pres.'s Com. to study U.S. Mil. Assistance program, 1958-59; chmn. policy planning council, counselor Dept. State, 1961; under-sec. state for polit. affairs, 1961-63; ambassador Fed. Republic of Germany, 1963-68; ambassador-at-large, 1968-69; spl. rep. to chmn. Urban Coalition, 1969-70; chmn. bd. Bus. Council for Internat. Understanding, 1969-73; mem. bd. Fed. City Council, Washington, 1958-61, 70—; pres. Fed. City Council, 1970-74; vice chmn. Japan-U.S. Internat. Adv. Council, 1970-74; chmn. adv. com. on housing and urban devel. Nat. Acad. Scis., 1970-74; bd. dirs. Procter & Gamble Co., Am. Security Bank, Washington, TransWorld Corp., Transworld Airlines.; mem. Am. Council on Germany, 1969—, Fed. City Housing Corp., 1972—; hon. fellow Queen's Coll., Oxford, 1968—; guest lectr. Nat., Air, Naval War Colls., Salzburg Seminar, Austria, 1960. Author: Envoy to the Middle World, 1983, At the Creation of a New Germany, 1989, The U.S.-Turkish-NATO Middle East Connection, 1990, Dance of the Billions, 1990, International Community: A Goal for a New World Order, 1992, Life in Alanya: Turkish Delight, 1992; editor: Diplomacy for the Future, 1987, National Interest and Global Goals, 1989; contbr. to profl. publs.; patentee in field. Trustee Thessalonica (Greece) Agrl. and Indsl. Inst. (Am. Farm Sch.), 1949-61; mem. bd. devel. So. Meth. U., 1949-61; bd. dirs. Near East Found., 1956-61, Aspen Inst. Humanistic Studies, 1958—, Atlantic Council, Atlantic Inst. for Internat. Affairs, Resources for Future; vice chmn. bd. dirs. Inst. for Study of Diplomacy, Georgetown U., Washington; trustee or bd. dirs. Com. for Econ. Devel., 1957—, Fgn. Service Edn. Found. and Sch. Advanced Internat. Studies, Johns Hopkins, 1947—, Nat. Civil Service League, 1969-73, Population Crisis Com., 1969—, Population Crisis Found. Tex., 1969-70, Nat. Trust for Historic Preservation, 1971-75, Duke U., 1962—, Vassar Coll., 1959-61, Am. U., 1980—, Asia Found., 1973—, Va. Outdoors Found.; adv. council Renewable Natural Resources Found., 1973-74; bd. dirs., treas. Piedmont Environmental Council; internat. com. YMCA, 1949-61; adv. council dept. Oriental langs. and lits. Princeton, 1949-61; vis. com. Middle Eastern Studies and Summer Sch., Harvard, 1954-61; sponsor Atlantic Inst., 1954-60; chmn. nat. adv. com. Ctr. for Book, Library of Congress, 1980-82; mem. Folger Library Council, 1983-85, Inst. Turkish Studies, 1983-85, Carnegie Coun.; mem. vis. com. Arthur M. Sackler Gallery, Smithsonian Instn.; trustee Am. U., 1981—; mem. German Am. Cultural Fund, 1992—, Circle Nat. Gallery Art, 1991, Carnegie Coun., 1990—, CED subcom. Global Econ. Strategy for U.S., 1991—; bd. dirs. adv. bd. Am.-Turkish Friendship Coun., Nat. Tree Trust, 1992—. Served with USNR, 1943-45; lt. col. USAF Res., 1945-72. Decorated Legion of Merit with 3 battle stars; Order of Cherifien Empire Morocco; recipient Distinguished Service award U.S. Jr. C. of C., 1949, Distinguished Service citation U. Okla., 1952, So. Meth. U. Distinguished Alumnus award, 1955; Andrew Wellington Cordier fellow Columbia U.; named Hon. citizen Ankara, Turkey, 1954. Mem. NAS (pres.'s circle), Am. Assn. Petroleum Geologists, Soc. Exploration Geophysicists (Spl. Commendation award 1992), m. Inst. Mining, Metall. and Petroleum Engrs., English SPeaking Union (chmn. bd. 1970-74), Am. Philos. Soc., Coun. Am. Mbs., Smithsonian Nat. Assocs. (chmn. 1975-78), Sigma Si. Phi Beta Kappa, Cosmos Club, Metro. Club, Washington. Episcopalian. Home and Office: Farmers Delight 36276 Mountville Rd Middleburg VA 22117 also: Turkish Delight, Alanya Turkey

MCGIBBON, WILLIAM ALEXANDER, rancher, photographer, state legislator; b. Evanston, Ill.; s. Edmund L. and Catherine (Klink) M.; m. Nancy Hornaday, Aug. 27, 1966; children: Heather M., Andrew W. BA, U. Pa., 1966; postgrad., U. Ariz., 1970-71. Pres., chief exec. officer Santa Rita Ranch, Inc., Green Valley, Ariz., 1970--; mem. Ariz. Ho. of Reps.; chmn. econ. devel. com., mem. ways and means, agr. and natural resources, edn. coms.; adv. com. Coll. Agr., U. Ariz., Tucson. Photographer: photographs pub. in numerous agrl. and livestock publs., 1980--. Mem. Continental Sch. Bd. Green Valley, 1976-84, pres., 1978-84; mem. Ariz. Bd. Pesticide Control, Phoenix, 1983-86; bd. dirs. Green Valley Community Fund, 1988--. Mem. Ariz. Cattlemen's Assn. (bd. dirs.), Nat. Cattlemen's Assn., Green Valley Rotary Club (pres. 1986, v.p. Green Valley Rotary Club Found. 1988—), So. Ariz. Cattlemen's Assn. (past pres.), Cattle Growers Assn. (past pres.), Ariz. Town Hall. Republican. Avocations: cattle ranching, photography, politics. Home and Office: Santa Rita Ranch Inc 8200 E Box Canyon Rd PO Box 647 Green Valley AZ 85622-0647

MCGIFF, JOHN C(HARLES), pharmacologist; b. N.Y.C., Aug. 6, 1927; s. John Francis and Rose (Rieger) McG.; m. Sara Leighton Babb, Feb. 8, 1958 (dec.); children: John, Katharine, Sara, Jeremiah, Elizabeth. B.S., Georgetown U., 1947; M.D., Columbia U., 1951; Doctorate Honoris Causa, Copernicus Acad. Medicine, Cracow, Poland, 1987. Diplomate: Am. Bd. Internal Medicine. Intern U. Cin., 1951-52; resident in medicine U. Va. Med. Center, 1952-53; tng. in physiology and pharmacology Columbia Presbyn. Hosp., N.Y.C., 1957-58; mem. faculty U. Pa. Med. Sch., 1961-66; dir. cardiovascular sect. St. Louis U. Med. Sch., 1966-71; dir. clin. pharmacology Med. Coll. Wis., Milw., 1971-75; prof., chmn. dept. pharmacology U. Tenn. Center Health Scis., 1975-79, N.Y. Med. Coll., Valhalla, 1979—; vis. scientist Wellcome Rsch. Labs., Beckenham, Eng., 1975-76; adv. bd. Am. Heart Assn., Kidney Found.; mem. nat. vis. coun. for health sci. faculties Columbia U. Coll. Physicians and Surgeons, 1987; mam. arteriosclerosis hypertension and lipid adv. com. NIH, 1987; cons. in field; chmn. cardiovascular renal study sect. Nat. Heart, Lung and Blood Inst. NIH, 1994. Author articles in books; contbr. articles to profl. jours. Pres. sch. bd. St. Louis Cathedral Sch., 1970. Served as flight surgeon M.C. USMCR, 1955-57, Korea. Recipient Medal of Achievement Copernicus Acad. Medicine, Cracow, Poland, 1984; Terence Cardinal Cooke medal for Disting. Service in Health Care, 1985; CIBA award Am. Heart Assn., 1986, Merit award Nat. Heart, Lung, and Blood Inst. of NIH, 1990; burroughs Wellcome Fund scholar, 1971-74. Mem. Am. Physiol. Soc., Am. Soc. Pharmacology and Exptl. Therapeutics, Council High Blood Pressure Research (med. adv. bd. 1968), Am. Soc. Clin. Investigation, Brit. Pharmacology Soc. Roman Catholic. Home: 5 Bay Rd East Patchogue NY 11772-6201 Office: NY Med Coll Dept Pharmacology Valhalla NY 10595

MC GIFFERT, DAVID ELIOT, lawyer, former government official; b. Boston, June 27, 1926; s. Arthur Cushman and Elizabeth (Eliot) McG.; m. Enud De Kibedi-Varga, Jan. 21, 1966; children: Laura, Carola.; m. Nelse Greenway, Apr. 9, 1983. Student, U. Calif.-Berkeley, 1944; B.A., Harvard U., 1949, LL.B., 1953; postgrad., Cambridge (Eng.) U., 1950. Bar: D.C. 1954. With firm Covington & Burling, Washington, 1953-55, 57-61; ptnr. Covington & Burling, 1969-77, 81—; lectr. law U. Wis., 1956; asst. to sec. def. for legis. affairs Dept. Def., 1962-65, undersec. army, 1965-69, asst. sec. for internat. security affairs, 1977-81. Served with USNR, 1944-46. Mem. Am. Bar Assn., Council Fgn. Relations, Alpha Delta Phi. Club: Metropolitan (Washington). Home: 3819 Veazey St NW Washington DC 20016-2230 Office: Covington & Burling 1201 Pennsylvania Ave NW PO Box 7566 Washington DC 20044

MCGIFFERT, MICHAEL, history educator, editor; b. Chgo., Oct. 5, 1928; s. Arthur Cushman and Elisabeth (Eliot) McG.; m. Genevieve White Mischel, Aug. 13, 1960; m. Elizabeth Eastman, June 19, 1949 (div. 1960). B.A., Harvard Coll., 1949; B.D., Yale U., 1952, Ph.D., 1958; postgrad., Union Theol. Sem., N.Y.C., 1949-50. Instr. history Colgate U., Hamilton, N.Y., 1954-55, 56-60, U. Md., College Park, 1955-56; asst. prof. history U. Denver, 1960-64, assoc. prof., 1964-69, prof. history, 1969-74; editor William and Mary Quar., Inst. Early Am. History and Culture, prof. history, Coll. William and Mary, Williamsburg, Va., 1972—. Author: The Higher learning in Colorado, 1964; editor: The Character of Americans, 1964 (rev. edit.), 1969, Puritanism and the American Experience, 1969, (with Robert A. Skotheim) American Social Thought, 1972, God's Plot: The Paradoxes of Puritan Piety, 1972, God's Plot: Puritan Spirituality in Thomas Shepard's Cambridge, 1994. Faculty rsch. grantee U. Denver, 1970, Coll. William and Mary, 1981-82, 89; rsch. fellow NEH, 1977-78. Mem. Am. Hist. Assn., Orgn. Am. Historians, Confr. of Hist. Jours. (pres.1987-89). Home: 102 Old Glory Ct Williamsburg VA 23185-4914 Office: Inst Early Am History & Culture PO Box 8781 Williamsburg VA 23187-8781

MCGILBERRY, JOE HERMAN, university administrator; b. Mobile, Ala., Aug. 6, 1943; s. Thomas Henry and Yvonne (Jorden) McG.; m. Betty Sue Reynolds, Dec. 20, 1964; children: Joe H. Jr., Michele, Brent. BS, Auburn U., 1965; MS, U. Tenn., 1972; PhD, TEx. A&M U., 1978. Gen. plant asst. Gen. Telephone Fla., Tampa, 1966; systems analyst E.I. DuPont de Nemours & Co., Old Hickory, Tenn., 1966-68; research asst. U. Tenn., Knoxville, 1968-69; advanced materials engr. Union Carbide Corp., Texas City, TX, 1969-70; asst. prof. Tenn. Tech. U., Cookeville, 1970-72, 73-75, 76-77; mgr. prodn. support Fleetguard div. Cummins Engine, Cookeville, 1972-73; assoc. research engr. Tex. A&M U., College Station, 1975-76; mgr. food and fiber ctr. Miss. State Coop. Extension Program, 1978-94, state program leader in cmty. resource devel. coop. ext. svc., 1994—; cons. Dunlap Industries, U. Tenn. at Nashville, Norwalk Furniture Corp., Teledyne-Stillman, Genco Stamping, Inc., Riley Enterprises; lectr. various seminars and presentations, 1978—. Author numerous articles in field. Mem. Inst. Indsl. Engrs. (sr.), Miss. Indsl. Devel. Coun., Order Engrs., Nat. Assn. County Agrl. Agts., Alpha Phi Mu. Office: Miss State U Coop Ext Svc 201 Bost Ext Bldg Box 9601 Mississippi State MS 39763-9600

MC GILL, ARCHIE JOSEPH, venture capitalist; b. Winona, Minn., May 29, 1931; s. Archibald Joseph and Anne (Lettner) McG.; m. Jeanne Sullivan, Mar. 17, 1974; children: Archibald Joseph, III, Mark E., Gregory P., Debora, Karen, Susan, Brian. BA in Econs., St. Mary's Coll., Winona, 1956. With IBM Corp., 1956-69; v.p. market ops. IBM Corp., White Plains, N.Y., 1956-69; founder, pres. McGill Assocs., White Plains, 1970-73; dir. market mgmt. AT&T Co., 1973-78, v.p. bus. mktg., 1978-83; pres. Advanced Info. Systems Am. Bell, Inc., 1983; pres., chief exec. officer Rothschild Ventures, Inc., 1983; now pres. Chardonnay, Inc.; dir. various cos. Bd. dirs. Steadman/Hawkins Found. With USAF, 1951-54. Named Mktg. Statesman of Year Sales Execs. Club, 1978.

MCGILL, CATHY BROOME, gifted and talented education educator; b. Gastonia, N.C., Sept. 26, 1945; d. Harold Beeler and Christine (Hicks) Broome; m. Paul Furman McGill, July 5, 1969; children: Paul Bryan, Harold Marcus. BA, Mars Hill Coll., 1967; MA, Appalachian State U., 1968. Tchr. 6th grade Victory Elem., Gastonia, N.C., 1968-69; lang. arts, social studies & music tchr. Northside Mid. Sch., West Columbia, S.C., 1969-71, Fulmer Mid. Sch., West Columbia, 1972-76; tchr. Pine View Elem. Sch., West Columbia, 1978-81; sci. & lang. arts tchr. Heiskell Sch., Atlanta, 1981-82; lang. arts & gifted tchr. Fulmer Mid. Sch., 1982-85; itinerant gifted educator Lex II, West Columbia, 1985—; in-svc. presenter Lex II, 1992-95. Pianist Holland Ave. Baptist Ch., Cayce, S.C., 1970—, vacation Bible sch. dir., 1982-93, youth choir dir., 1982-85; neighborhood solicitor Arthritis Found., Columbia, S.C., 1993-95. Mem. Nat. Assn. for Gifted Children, Palmetto State Tchrs. Assn., Alpha Delta Kappa (chaplain 1993—). Republican. Avocations: music, reading. Home: 100 Sweetgum Dr Cayce SC 29033-1930

MCGILL, DAN MAYS, insurance business educator; b. Greenback, Tenn., Sept. 27, 1919; s. John Burton and Jane (Mays) McG.; m. Elaine Kem, June 22, 1952; children: Douglas Russell, Melanie Mays. BA, Maryville Coll., 1940, LLD (hon.), 1982; MA, Vanderbilt U., 1941; PhD, U. Pa., 1947. Assoc. prof. fin. U. Tenn., Knoxville, 1947-48; Julian Price assoc. prof. ins. U. N.C., Chapel Hill, 1948-51; assoc. prof. ins. U. Pa., Phila., 1952-56, Frederick H. Ecker prof. life ins., 1959-90; trustee N.W. Mut. Life Ins. Co., Milw., 1978-90; bd. dirs. NRG Life Reassurance Corp., Phila., 1984-94, Phila. Reins. Corp., 1990—, Independence Blue Cross, 1990—; exec. dir. S.S. Huebner Found., 1954-75, 78-86, chmn., 1965-94; dir. rsch. Pension Rsch. Coun., 1952-90; chmn., mem. governing bd. Leonard Davis Inst. Health Econs., 1967-90; 1st chmn. adv. commn. Pension Benefit Guaranty Corp., 1975-78, mem. 1978-81. Author: An Analysis of Government Life Insurance, 1949, The Fundamentals of Private Pensions, 7th edit., 1996, Legal Aspects of Life Insurance, 1959, Fulfilling Pension Expectations, 1962, Life Insurance, 1967, Preservation of Pension Benefit Rights, 1972, others; editor: (with others) World Insurance Trends, 1959, others. Chmn. bd. pensions Presbyn. Ch. U.S., 1977-78; trustee Presbyn. Found. for Phila., 1996—, Presbyn. Med. Ctr. Phila., 1987-96; chmn. Boettner Inst. Fin. Gerontology, 1993—; mem. retirement bd. Mass. Bay Transp. Authority, 1980-96. Maj. USAAF, 1942-46, 51-52. Recipient Disting. Alumni award Maryville Coll., 1962, Huebner Gold medal award Am. Coll., 1977, Gold medal Internat. Ins. Soc., 1987. Mem. Am. Risk and Ins. Assn. (pres. 1959, Eluzur Wright award 1955, 81), Union League. Republican. Presbyterian. Avocations: music, travel, sports. Home: 50 Belmont Ave Bala Cynwyd PA 19004-2437 Office: 2 Bala Plaza Ste 300 Bala Cynwyd PA 19004

MCGILL, ESBY CLIFTON, former college official; b. Omaha, Ark., Jan. 12, 1914; s. James Preston and Celia (Stafford) McG.; m. Ruth Evelyn Jones, Oct. 22, 1932 (dec.); children: Barbara (Mrs. Forrest E. Nelson), Marilyn (Mrs. Joel Pahk); m. Mary Elizabeth Beardsley, July 5, 1978. BS, S.W. Mo. State U., 1940; MS, Okla. State U., 1941; EdD, NYU, 1955. Tchr. public schs. Mo., 1932-33, 35-39; head bus. dept. High Sch. Stillwater, Okla., 1941-42; assoc. prof. in charge of U.S. Naval Radio Sch., Tex. A&M U., College Station, 1942-44; chmn. div. bus. Emporia State U., Kans., 1945-59; chmn. bus. edn. dept. Utah State U., Logan, 1959-60; dean faculties, dir. acad. planning, dir. summer sessions So. Oreg. State Coll., Ashland, 1960-77; dir. summer sessions So. Oreg. State Coll., 1976-79, dir. continuing edn., 1976-78, dir. non-traditional programs, 1978-79; comml. loan officer for Jackson-Josephine Counties Coos, Curry, Douglas Bus. Devel. Corp., Medford, Oreg., 1990-91; cons. curriculum for schs. in cen. states, 1950-69; mem. regional adv. bd. So. Oreg. State Coll., 1st term, 1987-89, 2d term, 1989-91, 3d term, 1991-93, 4th term, 1994—. Author: Communications Typing, 1944, Production Typing, 1955, Business Principles, Organization and Management, 1958, rev., 1963, Briefhand, 1957, manuals in field; also contbr. over 100 articles to profl. jours.; spl. editor: Nat. Bus. Edn. Quar, 1951-55; mem. editorial bd.: Bus. Edn. Forum, 1956-59, Nat. Assn. Bus. Tchr. Tng. Instns. Bull, 1951-55. Chmn. Downtown Redevel. Com., Ashland, Oreg., 1967-71; bd. dirs. Peter Britt Music and Arts Festival Assn., Jacksonville, Oreg., 1966-69, Ashland Rotary Found., Jackson-Josephine Counties, Oreg. Comprehensive Health Planning Unit. Recipient Founder's Day award NYU, 1956, Man of Yr. award Ashland C. of C., 1965. Mem. NEA, Oreg. Edn. Assn., Nat. Assn. Bus. Tchr. Edn. Instns. (past pres., bd. dirs.), United Bus. Edn. Assn. (past pres., bd. dirs.), Mountain Plains Bus. Edn. Assn. (past pres., bd. dirs.), North Ctrl. Assn. Conf. Summer Schs. and Future Bus. Leaders Am. (past bd. dirs. both), Nat. Office Mgmt. Assn. (hon.), Ashland C. of C. (pres., bd. dirs.), Am. Assn. Colls. Tchrs. Edn. (liaison officer for Oreg. 1970-73), Svc. Corp. Ret. Execs. (chmn. chpt. 269 1985-86, 86-87, 87-88, 88-89), SCORE (alternate dist. rep. Portland dist. 1988-89, dist. rep. Portland dist. 1990-91, asst. regional dir. region 10 1991-92, dir. region 10 States of Alaska, Idaho, Oreg. and Wash., 1993-95, 95—, nat. treas. 1994—), Masons, Rotary (past sec., pres. bd. Ashland, gov. internat. dist. 5110, 1983-84, materials chmn. pres. elect tng. program 9 dists. U.S. N.W., Can. S.W. 1990-94, ext. chmn. 1991—, rep. Rotary Internat. Coun. Legislation dist. 5110 1995, Paul Harris fellow), Phi Delta Kappa, Kappa Delta Pi, Delta Pi Epsilon, Pi Omega Pi, Pi Gamma Mu, Sigma Tau Gamma. Home: 1785 Zemke Rd Talent OR 97540-9718

MCGILL, HENRY COLEMAN, JR., physician, educator, researcher; b. Nashville, Oct. 1, 1921; s. Henry Coleman and Thursa (Lowry) McG.; m. Cloace Laurite Ferguson, Sept. 12, 1945; children: Margaret Ann, Laurilynn, Elizabeth Gail. BA, Vanderbilt U., 1943, MD, 1946. Intern Vanderbilt Hosp., Nashville, 1946-47; asst. prof. La. State U. Med. Ctr., New Orleans, 1950-55, assoc. prof., 1955-61, prof., chmn. pathology, 1961-66, U. Tex. Health Sci. Ctr., San Antonio, 1966-72, prof., 1972-91; sci. dir. S.W. Found. for Biomed. Rsch., San Antonio, 1979-92, sr. scientist, 1992—. Served to capt. U.S. Army, 1948-50. Mem. Phi Beta Kappa, Sigma Xi, Alpha Omega Alpha. Contbr. numerous articles to profl. jours. Home: 4102 Fawnridge Dr San Antonio TX 78229-4212 Office: PO Box 760549 San Antonio TX 78245-0549

MCGILL, JAY, magazine publisher. Pub. Country Living, N.Y.C. Office: Country Living Hearst Mags 224 West 57th St New York NY 10019-5201*

MCGILL, JENNIFER HOUSER, non-profit association administrator; b. Abingdon, Va., Mar. 3, 1957; d. Mason L. and Margaret Jane (Powers) H.; m. James B. McGill, July 15, 1978; children: Melissa Diane, Mark James. AA, Va. Highlands C.C., Abingdon, 1978; BA, U. S.C., 1980. Reporter, editor Sumter (S.C.) Daily ITEM, 1980-81; assoc. editor Sandlapper Mag., Columbia, S.C., 1981-82; membership editor Assn. for Edn. in Journalism/Mass Comm., Columbia, 1982-83, adminstrv. asst., 1984-85, exec. dir., 1985—; mem. nat. steering com. Journalist-in-Space Project, Columbia, 1985-86. Mem. Lioness Club (3d v.p. 1990-91, 2d v.p. 1991-92). Avocations: reading, cooking, biking. Office: Assn Schs Journalism & Mass Comm Univ SC Columbia SC 29208-0251

MCGILL, MAURICE LEON, financial executive; b. Malden, Mo., Aug. 22, 1936; s. William Howard and Iris (Phillips) McG.; m. Wanda Coral Wirt, Feb. 2, 1957; children—Melany, Melinda, William Shannon. B.S., U. Mo., 1958, M.A., 1959. C.P.A., Mo., Iowa, Ariz. Mgr. Touche, Ross, Bailey & Smart, Kansas City, Mo., 1959-64; fin. v.p., treas. Iowa Beef Packers, Inc., Dakota City, Nebr., 1964-69; exec. v.p., treas. Spencer Foods, Inc., Iowa, 1969-71, also dir.; sr. v.p. Diamond Reo Trucks, Inc., Lansing, Mich., 1971-72; fin. v.p. Ariz. Colo. Land & Cattle Co., Phoenix, 1972-75; ptnr. Touche Ross & Co., Phoenix, 1975-81; exec. v.p. fin. and adminstrn., treas., bd. dirs. IBP, Inc., Dakota City, Nebr., 1981-89; pres., bd. dirs. Wirmac Corp., Garland, Tex., 1989—; bd. dirs. Bluebonnet Savs. Bank, Dallas. Mem. AICPA, Iowa Soc. CPAs, Ea. Hills Country Club. Home: 1414 Seminary Rdg Garland TX 75043-1241

MCGILL, ROBERT ERNEST, III, retired manufacturing company executive; b. San Francisco, Apr. 30, 1931; s. Robert Ernest and Madeleine Melanie (Ignace) McG.; m. Daphne Urquhart Driver, Apr. 26, 1958; children: Robert Ernest, Meredith Louise, Christina Elizabeth, James Alexander. B.A., Williams Coll., 1954; M.B.A., Harvard U., 1956. With Morgan Stanley & Co. (investment bankers), N.Y.C., 1956-63; mem. fin. staff Air Products & Chems., Inc., Allentown, Pa., 1963-64; dir. corp. planning and devel. Air Products & Chems., Inc., 1964-68; v.p. Gen. Interiors Corp., N.Y.C., 1968-70; exec. v.p. Gen. Interiors Corp., 1970-73; v.p. fin. Ethan Allen, Inc., Danbury, Conn., 1973-75; v.p. fin., sec. Dexter Corp., Windsor Locks, Conn., 1975-83, sr. v.p. fin. and adminstrn., dir., 1983-89, exec. v.p., 1989-94; dir. Dexter Corp., Windsor Locks, 1989-95; pres. Kettlebrook Ins. Co. Ltd., 1983-93, chmn., 1993-94; pres. Dexter Credit Corp., 1982-88; bd. dirs. The Conn. Surety Corp., Chemfab Corp., Calbiochem; bd. mgrs. Travelers Funds for Variable Annuities; trustee Travelers Mut. Fund. Trustee Colt Bequest, Inc., Assn. des Amis L'Abbaye Valmont, Arts Coun., 1989-94; bd. overseers U. Conn. Sch. Bus., 1991-95; bd. dirs. Conn. Pub. Expenditures Coun., 1980-95. Home: 295 Hancock Rd Williamstown MA 01267-3005

MCGILL, THOMAS CONLEY, physics educator; b. Port Arthur, Tex., Mar. 20, 1942; s. Thomas Conley and Susie Elizabeth (Collins) McG.; m. Toby Elizabeth Cone, Dec. 27, 1966; children: Angela Elizabeth, Sara Elizabeth. BS in Math., Lamar State Coll., 1963, BEE, 1964; MEE, Calif. Inst. Tech., 1965, PHD, 1969. NATO postdoctoral fellow U. Bristol, Eng., 1969-70; NRC postdoctoral fellow Princeton (N.J.) U., 1970-71; from asst. to assoc. prof. applied physics Calif. Inst. Tech., Pasadena, 1971-77, prof., 1977-85, Fletcher Jones prof. applied physics, 1985—; cons. United Techs. Corp., 1988—, Advance Projcets Agy./Def. Sci. Rsch. Coun., Arlington, Va., 1979—; chief Naval Ops. Exec. Panel, 1995—; mem. Semiconductor Tech. Coun., 1995—; adv. bd. Sematech U., 1992—. Alfred P. Sloan Found. fellow, 1974. Fellow Am. Physical Soc.; mem. AAAS, IEEE, Am. Vacuum Soc., Sigma Xi. Office: Calif Inst of Tech Mail Code 128 # 95 Pasadena CA 91125

MCGILL, THOMAS EMERSON, psychology educator; b. Sharon, Pa., Sept. 26, 1930; s. Emerson Dickson and Margaret Hughes (McCallen) McG.; m. Nancy C. Welch, June 14, 1955; children: Michael Howard, Steven Emerson. BA, Youngstown State U., 1954; MA, Princeton U., 1957, PhD, 1958. Instr. psychology Williams Coll., Williamstown, Mass., 1958-59, asst. prof., 1960-64, asso. prof., 1965-69, prof., 1969-91, chmn. dept. psychology, 1976-82, 85-86, Hales prof., 1970-91, prof. emeritus, 1991—; postdoctoral fellow U. Calif., Berkeley, 1959-60; sr. postdoctoral fellow U. Edinburgh, 1964-65, vis. research fellow, 1969-70. Editor: Readings in Animal Behavior, 3d edit, 1977, (with Dewsbury and Sachs) Sex and Behavior, 1977. USPHS grantee, 1960-82; sr. postdoctoral fellow Nat. Acad. Sci., 1964-65. Fellow AAAS; mem. Newfoundland Club N.Am. (dir. 1980-94, pres. 1990-92), Newfoundland Club New Eng. (pres. 1980-82), Sigma Xi. Home: 137 Laura Ln Tiverton RI 02878-4711 Office: Williams Coll Dept Of Psychology Williamstown MA 01267

MCGILL, WARREN EVERETT, lawyer, consultant; b. Brazil, Ind., Sept. 10, 1923; s. Ira and Joyce S. (Wenning) McG.; m. Irene Marie Kish, Aug. 31, 1946; children: Cecelia, Daniel, Nancy, Mary Beth, Mark. BS, Ind. U., 1944, JD with honors, 1945. Bar: Ind. 1945. Assoc. Oare, Thornburg, McGill & Deahl, South Bend, Ind., 1945-60; ptnr. Thornburg, McGill, Deahl, Harman, Carey & Murray, South Bend, 1960-83; ptnr. Barnes & Thornburg, South Bend, 1983-89, of counsel, 1989—; chmn. Probate Code

Study Commn., Ind., 1972-90. Editor, co-author: Indiana Land Trust Practice, 1980, Trust Litigation, 1981; asst. editor, co-author: Probate Code 1975 Reform, 1975; author: Special Comment on Indiana Probate Code, 1982. Sec., dir. Michiana Arts and Scis. coun., Inc., South Bend, 1965—; pres. Com. of 100, South Bend, Mishawaka, Ind., 1960-64; community adv. bd. Channel 34 Pub. TV, No. Ind., So. Mich., 1982-86. Recipient Cmty. Achievement citation City of South Bend, 1985, 50 Yr. award Ind. Bar Found., 1996. Fellow Ind. Acad. Law Alumni; mem. ABA, St. Joseph County Bar Assn., Am. Coll. Trust and Estate Counsel (chmn. membership com. 1972-90), Ind. State Bar Assn. (chmn. ho. dels. 1982-83, Presdl. citation 1985), Ind. Bar Found. (pres. 1984-86, bd. dirs. 1984-89), Ind. Continuing Legal Edn. Forum (bd. dirs. 1984-90), Morris Park Country Club (pres. 1978), Summit Club. Avocations: golf, history, travel. Home: 2831 Caroline St South Bend IN 46614-1543 Office: Barnes & Thornburg 600 1st Source Bank Ctr 100 N Michigan St South Bend IN 46601-1630

MCGILL, WILLIAM JAMES, JR., academic administrator; b. St. Louis, Mo., Mar. 25, 1936; s. William James Sr. and Ethel (Williams) McG.; m. Ellen Buck, June 18, 1960; children: Sara Louise, Susan Elizabeth, Alison Marcia. BA, Trinity Coll., 1957; MA, Harvard U., 1958, PhD, 1961, grad. Inst. Ednl. Mgmt., 1989. Instr. history Western Md. Coll., Westminster, 1960-62; asst. prof. history Alma (Mich.) Coll., 1962-68, assoc. prof., 1968-72; dean of coll. Washington & Jefferson Coll., Washington, Pa., 1972-75, prof. history, 1972-84; asst. dir., div. edn. programs NEH, Washington, 1984-86; v.p., dean faculty Lebanon Valley Coll., Annville, Pa., 1986—, acting pres., 1987-88. Author: Maria Theresa, 1972; contbr. 53 articles to profl. jours., 43 book revs., numerous poems; poetry editor Spitball Mag., 1993—. Assoc. to rector St. Luke's Episc. Ch., Lebanon, Pa., 1986—; priest-in-charge St. George's Episc. Ch., Waynesburg, Pa., 1974-83; actor Washington Theater Wing, 1984-86, Gretna Playhouse, Mt. Gretna, Pa., 1987-90; bd. dirs. Lebanon County United Way, 1987-95, Gretna Prodns., Mt. Gretna, 1986-90, 91-92; trustee Penn Sch. Art and Design, 1992—. Mem. Am. Assn. Higher Edn., Phi Beta Kappa. Avocations: sailing, writing, acting. Home: PO Box 682 Cornwall PA 17016-0682 Office: Lebanon Valley Coll Office Academic Affairs Annville PA 17003

MC GILLEM, CLARE DUANE, electrical engineering educator; b. Clinton, Mich., Oct. 9, 1923; s. Virgil and Starlie (Weaver) McG.; m. Frances Ann Wilson, Nov. 29, 1947; 1 child, Mary Ann. BSEE, U. Mich., 1947; MSE, Purdue U., 1949, PhD, 1955. Rsch. engr. Diamond Chain Co. Inc., Indpls., 1947-51; head functional design U.S. Naval Avionics Ctr., Indpls., 1951-56; head mil. and elec. engring. AC Spark Plug, GM, Flint, Mich., 1956-58; dir. elec. and applied rsch. AC Spark Plug, GM, Milw., 1958-59; program mgr. def. rsch. div. GM, Santa Barbara, Calif., 1959-62; prof. elec. engring. Purdue U., West Lafayette, Ind., 1963-92, assoc. dean engring., 1968-72, prof. emeritus of elec. engring., 1992—; dir. engring. expt. sta. Purdue U., West Lafayette, Ind., 1968-72; bd. dirs. VETRONICS Inc., West Lafayette, 1984—, pres., 1984-87; pres. Tech. Assocs. Inc., West Lafayette, 1977—. Co-author: Probabilistic Methods of Signal and System Analysis, 1971, Continuous and Discrete Signal and System Analysis, 1974, Modern Communications and Spread Spectrum, 1986. Lt. (j.g.) USN, 1943-46, PTO. Recipient Meritorious Civilian Svc. award USN, 1955. Fellow IEEE (Centennial award 1984, J. Fred Peoples award 1988). Avocation: duplicate bridge, amateur radio. Office: Sch Elec Engring Purdue U West Lafayette IN 47907

MCGILLEY, SISTER MARY JANET, nun, educator, writer, academic administrator; b. Kansas City, Mo., Dec. 4, 1924; d. James P. and Peg (Ryan) McG. B.A., St. Mary Coll., 1945; M.A., Boston Coll., 1951; Ph.D., Fordham U., 1956; postgrad., U. Notre Dame, 1960, Columbia U., 1964. Social worker Kansas City, 1945-46; joined Sisters of Charity of Leavenworth, 1946; tchr. English Hayden High Sch., Topeka, 1948-50, Billings (Mont.) Central High Sch., 1951-53; faculty dept. English St. Mary Coll., Leavenworth, Kans., 1956-64; pres. St. Mary Coll., 1964-89, Disting. prof. English and Liberal Studies, 1990—. Contbr. articles, fiction and poetry to various jours. Bd. dirs. United Way of Leavenworth, 1966-85; mem. Mayor's Adv. Coun., 1967-72; bd. dirs. Kans. Ind. Coll. Fund, 1964-89, exec. com., 1985-86, vice chmn., 1984-85, chmn., 1985-86. Recipient Alumnae award St. Mary Coll., 1969; Disting. Service award Baker U., 1981, Leavenworth Bus. Woman of Yr. Athena award, 1986. Mem. Nat. Coun. Tchrs. of English, Nat. Assn. Ind. Colls. and Univs. (bd. dirs. 1982-85), Kans. Ind. Coll. Assn. (bd. dirs. 1964-89, treas. 1982-84, v.p. 1984-85, chmn. exec. com. 1985-86), Am. Coun. Edn. (com. on women in higher edn. 1980-85), Am. Assn. Higher Edn., Kansas City Regional Coun. for Higher Edn. (bd. dirs. 1965-89, treas. 1984-85, v.p. 1986-88), Ind. Coll. Funds Am. (exec. com. 1974-77, trustee-at-large 1975-76), North Cen. Assn. Colls. and Schs. (exec. commr. Com. on Insts. Higher Edn. 1980-88, vice chair 1985-86, chair 1987-88), Leavenworth C. of C. (bd. dirs. 1964-89), Assn. Am. Colls. (commn. liberal learning 1970-73, com. on curriculum and faculty devel. 1979-82) St. Mary Alumni Assn. (hon. pres. 1964-89), Delta Epsilon Sigma. Democrat. Office: St Mary Coll 4100 S 4th St Leavenworth KS 66048-5082

MC GILLICUDDY, JOHN FRANCIS, retired banker; b. Harrison, N.Y., Dec. 30, 1930; s. Michael J. and Anna (Munro) McG.; m. Constance Burtis, Sept. 9, 1954; children: Michael Sean, Faith Burtis Benoit, Constance Erin Mc Gillicuddy Mills, Brian Munro, John Walsh. A.B., Princeton, 1952; LL.B., Harvard, 1955. With Mfrs. Hanover Trust Co. subs. Mfrs. Hanover Corp., N.Y.C., 1958-91, v.p., 1962-66, sr. v.p., 1966-69, exec. v.p., asst. to chmn., 1969-70, vice chmn., dir., 1970, pres., 1971-91, chmn., chief exec. officer, 1979-91; chmn. bd., chief exec. officer Chem. Banking Corp., N.Y.C., 1992-93, ret., 1994; bd. dirs. USX Corp., Chem. Banking Corp., Continental Copr., Empire Blue Cross and Blue Shield, UAL Corp. Bd. dirs. Nat. Multiple Sclerosis Soc.; trustee, chmn. N.Y. Hosp., N.Y. Pub. Libr.; trustee emeritus Princeton U.; pres. Boy Scouts Am., Greater N.Y. Couns. Lt. (j.g.) USNR, 1955-58. Mem. Bus. Coun., Westchester Country Club (Rye, N.Y.), Blind Brook Club (Port Chester, N.Y.), Princeton Club (N.Y.C.), Augusta Nat. Golf Club (Ga.), Pine Valley Golf Club (N.J.), Laurel Valley Golf Club (Ligonier, Pa.), Seminole Golf Club (north Palm Beach, Fla.), Links Club (N.Y.C.), Sky Club (N.Y.C.). Roman Catholic. Office: Chem Banking Corp 270 Park Ave New York NY 10017-2014*

MCGILLIS, KELLY, actress; b. Newport, Calif., July 9, 1957; m. Fred Tillman, Dec. 31, 1988; 3 children. Student, Pacific Conservatory of Performing Arts, Juilliard Sch. Music. Actress: (feature films) Reuben, Reuben, 1983, Witness, 1985, Top Gun, 1986, Made in Heaven, 1987, Promised Land, 1988, The House on Carroll Street, 1988, The Accused, 1988, Winter People, 1989, The Babe, 1992, North, 1994; (TV films) Sweet Revenge, 1984, Private Sessions, 1985, Grand Isle (also prod.), 1991, Bonds of Love, 1993, In the Best of Families: Marriage, Pride and Madness, 1994; (stage) Hedda Gabler, Roundabout Theatre Company, 1994. *

MCGILLIVRAY, DONALD DEAN, seed company executive, agronomist; b. Muscatine, Iowa, Aug. 28, 1928; s. Walter C. and Pearl E. (Potter) M.; m. Betty J. Anderson, June 24, 1951; children—Ann E., Jean M. B.S. in Agronomy, Iowa State U., 1950. Asst. mgr. Iowa, Minn., Wis. sect. Funk Seeds Internat., Belle Plaine, Iowa, 1965-69, mgr., 1969-70, mgr. hybrid corn ops., Bloomington, Ill., 1970-75, v.p. ops., 1976-82, pres., 1982-88; assoc. Smart Seeds, Inc., 1989—; dir. U.S. Feed Grains Coun., Washington, D.C., 1984-87. Bd. dirs. Ill. Agrl. Leadership Found., Macomb, Ill., 1985—, chmn. bd. 1990—. Ill. Wesleyan Assocs., 1986-89; adv. bd. Bro-Menn Hosp., pres., 1989-90. Sgt. U.S. Army, 1951-53. Mem. Am. Seed Trade Assn. (bd. dirs. 1978—, div. chmn. 1978-79, 2d v.p. 1986-87, 1st v.p. 1987-88, pres. 1988-89), Am. Seed Rsch. Found. (bd. dirs. 1982-95, pres. 1984-87), Masons.

MCGILLIVRAY, KAREN, elementary school educator; b. Richland, Oreg., Aug. 24, 1936; d. Kenneth Melton and Catharina (Sass) McG. BS in Edn. cum laude, Ea. Oreg. State Coll., 1958; MRE, Pacific Sch. Religion, 1963. Cert. tchr., Oreg. 4th grade tchr. Salem (Oreg.)-Keizer Pub. Schs.; ret., 1995. Contbr. articles, stories to ednl. mags. U.S. Govt. grantee. Mem. NEA (rep. assembly, former state exec. bd.), Oreg. Edn. Assn. (rep. assembly), Oreg. Ret. Educators Assn., Salem Edn. Assn. (officer), Phi Kappa Gamma (officer). Methodist. Home: 325 SW Cedarwood Ave McMinnville OR 97128

MC GIMPSEY, RONALD ALAN, oil company executive; b. Cleve., June 7, 1944; s. John E. and Muriel N. McGimpsey; m. Linda V. Tiffany, Apr. 20, 1974. BS, Case Inst. Tech., 1966; MS, Case Western Res. U., 1974; grad. exec. program, Stanford U., 1987. With BP Am. Inc. (formerly Standard Oil Co.), Ohio, 1966—; treas. BP Am. Inc. (formerly Standard Oil Co.), 1977-81, v.p. fin., 1981-82, sr. v.p. crude trading and transp., 1982-86; sr. v.p. petroleum products and refining BP Am. Inc. (formerly Standard Oil Co.), Cleve., 1986-89; group contr. BP-London, 1989-91; regional sr. v.p., CFO BP America, Cleve., 1991-92, sr. v.p., fin. officer, 1992-93; CEO BP Australia, Melbourne, 1994—. Chmn. bd. trustees Marymount Hosp., Cleve., 1986-88; adv. bd. Case Inst. Tech. Mem. Bus. Coun. Australia, Australia Inst. of Petroleum (chmn. 1995—). Office: BP Australia, 360 Elizabeth St, Melbourne 3000, Australia

MC GIMSEY, CHARLES ROBERT, III, anthropologist; b. Dallas, June 18, 1925; s. Charles Robert, Jr. and Ellen Randolph (Parks) McG.; m. Mary Elizabeth Conger, Dec. 20, 1949; children—Charles Robert, Brian Keith, Mark Douglass. Student, Vanderbilt U., 1942-43, U. of South, 1943-44; B.A., U. N.Mex., 1949; M.A., Harvard U., 1954, Ph.D., 1958. Instr. U. Ark., Fayetteville, 1957; asst. prof. U. Ark., 1958-62, assoc. prof., 1962-67, prof. anthropology, 1967-90, prof. emeritus, 1990—, chmn. dept., 1969-72; asst. curator U. Ark. Mus., 1957-59, dir., 1959-83; dir. Ark. Archeol. Survey, 1967-90, dir. emeritus, 1990—; cons. archeology U.S. GAO, 1979-87, U.S.-Internat. Com. on Monuments and Sites; Rep. to Internat. Com. on Archeol. Heritage Mgmt., 1988-95. Author: (with G.R. Willey) Monagrillo Culture of Panama, 1954, Mariana Mesa, 1980, Indians of Arkansas, 1969, Public Archeology, 1972, Archeology and Archeological Resources, 1973, (with H.A. Davis) The Management of Archeological Resources, 1977; assoc. editor Am. Antiquity, 1972-80; Co-editor (with H. A. Davis) Southeastern Museums Conf., 1964-73; Contbr. articles to profl. jours. Mem. Ark. Rev. Com., Historic Preservation Program, 1968-76; collaborator Nat. Park Service, 1971-74, adviser, 1974-77; mem. Com. on Recovery Archeol. Remains, 1971-78; mem. adv. bd. dirs. Red River Mus., 1975-76; mem. adv. bd. Am. Indian Archeol. Inst., 1975-80, Ark. Natural and Cultural Heritage Dept., 1976-90. Served to lt. (j.g.) USNR, 1943-47. Recipient Cert. Recognition State of Ark., 1990; rsch. grantee Am. Philos. Soc., Am. Acad. Arts and Scis., Andean Rsch. Inst., Nat. Park Service, NSF, Smithsonian Instn., Wenner-Gren Found.; rsch. fellow dept. archaeology U. Cambridge, 1985-86, assoc. mem. Darwin Coll., 1985—. Fellow Am. Anthrop. Assn.; mem. Soc. for Am. Archeology (pres. 1974-75, Disting. Svc. award 1975, award for excellence in cultural resource mgmt. 1995), Ark. Archeol. Soc. (editor 1960-83, Preservationist award 1989), Southeastern Mus. Conf. (coun. 1962-71, editor 1964-71), Am. Soc. for Conservation Archeology (founding, award for outstanding contbn. 1980), Soc. Profl. Archeologists (founder, bd. dirs. 1976-79, pres. 1983-84, Seiberling award 1989), Am. Assn. Mus., Am. Assn. for State and Local History (award of merit 1985). Home: 435 Hawthorne St Fayetteville AR 72701-1935 Office: Ark Archeol Survey PO Box 1249 Fayetteville AR 72702-1249

MCGINLEY, EDWARD STILLMAN, II, naval officer; b. Allentown, Pa., June 9, 1939; s. Edward Stillman and Dorothy Mae (Kandle) McG.; m. Connie Lee Mayo, July 1, 1962; children: Amanda Lee, Edward Stillman III. BS, U.S. Naval Acad., 1961; advanced degree in naval architecture, MIT, 1970; MSA, George Washington U., 1972; cert. exec. program, U. Va., 1981. Commd. ensign USN, 1961, advanced through grades to rear adm., 1990, various positions in submarine engring., 1962-76; repair officer USN, Rota (Spain) and Charleston, S.C., 1976-83; ops. mgr. Mare Island Naval Shipyard, Vallejo, Calif., 1983-87; comdr. Norfolk Naval Shipyard, Portsmouth, Va., 1987-90; maintenance officer U.S. Pacific Fleet, Honolulu, 1990-93; comdr. Naval Surface Warfare Ctr., Washington, 1993-94; vice-comdr. Naval Sea Sys. Command, Washington, 1994—. Contbr. articles to profl. jours. Recipient Environ. award Sec. of Navy, 1987, Productivity Improvement award Inst. Indsl. Engrs., 1988, Quality Improvement award Office Mgmt. and Budget, 1989, Productivity award U.S. Senate, 1990. Mem. Am. Soc. Naval Engrs. (nat. counselor), Soc. Naval Arch. and Marine Engrs., U.S. Naval Inst., Am. Soc. for Quality Control, Rotary, Sigma Xi, Tau Beta Pi. Republican. mem. United Church of Christ. Avocations: art, running. Home: Washington Navy Yard Qtrs M-1 Washington DC 20374 Office: Naval Sea Sys Command SEA 09 2531 Jefferson Davis Hwy Arlington VA 22242-0001

MCGINLEY, JOSEPH PATRICK, brokerage house executive; b. Phila., Mar. 17, 1947; s. Joseph Robert and Kathaleen (Brennan) McG.; m. Linda L. Irvin, May 15, 1970 (div. 1981); children: Lisa C., Andrew S.; m. Sharon A. Malloy, Sept. 7, 1984; 1 child, Christopher J. BSBA, Villanova U., 1965-69. Sr. v.p. Dean Witter, Phila., 1974—; bd. dirs. Tara Investments Ltd., Phila., Orion Assoc., Phila., Florence Ave. Corp., Phila. Co-founder A Better Chance of Lower Merion. Mem. Union League Yacht Club (commodore), Union League of Phila., Cynwyd Club, Corinthian Yacht Club (Phila.). Republican. Roman Catholic. Avocation: yachting. Office: Dean Witter Reynolds 2 Logan Sq Philadelphia PA 19103-2707

MCGINLEY, MORGAN, newspaper editor; b. New London, Conn., Mar. 1, 1942; s. Morgan Sr. and Elizabeth (Zuccardy) McG.; m. Mary Elizabeth Dowd, Sept. 11, 1971; children: John, Carolyn, Brendan. BA, Colby Coll., 1964. Reporter Providence Jour., 1965; reporter The Day, New London, 1965-75, asst. city editor, 1975-78, night city editor, 1978-81, asst. editorial page editor, 1981-82, editorial page editor, 1982—; writer in residence Emerson Coll., Boston, 1992. Bd. dirs. Salvation Army, New London, 1976—. Found. Open Govt., Conn., 1993—; chmn. Conn. Coun. on Freedom of Info.; mem. Task Force on Minorities in the Newspaper Bus.; panelist Conn. Pub. TV Fourth Estate Show, 1987—. With U.S. Army, 1965, cpl. Army NG, 1965-70. Fellow Washington Journalism Ctr., 1969, Knight Ctr. Specialized Journalism U. Md., 1991, 94, 95; recipient 1st place edit. writing award new Eng. AP New Execs. Assn., new Eng. Press Assn., 1st place award Soc. Profl. Journalists. Mem. Nat. Conf. Editl. Writers (chmn. minorities com. 1988—, bd. dirs. 1989-90, 92-93, chair mem. 1993-94, mem. editl. mgmt. and ops. com., sec. 1995, treas. 1996), New Eng. Soc. Newspaper Editors (bd. govs. 1987—, minority affairs com., pres. 1992, past v.p., treas. and sec.), New Eng. Newspaper Assn. (mem. minority affairs com.), Trout Unltd. (bd. dirs. Thames Valley chpt. 1972—). Episcopalian. Avocations: fly fishing, fly tying. Home: 119 Glenwood Ave New London CT 06320-4302 Office: The Day Pub Co 47 Eugene Oneill Dr New London CT 06320-6306

MCGINLEY, NANCY ELIZABETH, lawyer; b. Columbia, Mo., Feb. 29, 1952; d. Robert Joseph and Ruth Evangeline (Garnett) McG. BA with high honors, U. Tex., 1974, JD, 1977. Bar: Tex. 1977, U.S. Dist. Ct. (no. dist.) Tex. 1979. Law clk. U.S. Dist. Ct. (no. dist.) Tex., Fort Worth, 1977-79; assoc. Crumley, Murphy and Shrull, Fort Worth, 1979-81; staff atty. SEC, Fort Worth, 1981-87, br. chief, Houston, 1990-92, sr. counsel, Washington, 1992—. Mem. editorial staff Urban Law Rev. Mem. Mortar Bd., Phi Beta Kappa, Phi Kappa Phi, Alpha Lambda Delta. Methodist. Home: 1505 Crystal Dr Apt 1008 Arlington VA 22202-4120

MCGINLEY, SUZANNE, enrivonmental and civil engineer; b. Jamaica Queens, N.Y., Aug. 24, 1964; d. John Joseph and Bobbie Sue (Herron) McG. BSCE, SUNY, Buffalo, 1986; postgrad., U. Tenn. Registered profl. engr., N.Y., Ala., Ky., Tenn. Civil engr. Nelson & Pope Engrs., Melville, N.Y., 1986-91; environ. engr. Advanced Scis. Inc., Oak Ridge, Tenn., 1992-94; project mgr., engr., lead engr. Geraghty & Miller, Inc., Oak Ridge, 1994-95. Sponsor contact Habitat for Humanity, Oak Ridge, 1994-95. Mem. ASCE (tech. rep. WATTec com. 1996—), Nat. Soc. Profl. Engrs. Home: 507 Cross Creek Rd Apt A Knoxville TN 37923-6419

MCGINN, BERNARD JOHN, religious educator; b. Yonkers, N.Y., Aug. 19, 1937; s. Bernard John and Catherine Ann (Faulds) McG.; m. Patricia Ann Ferris, July 10, 1971; children: Daniel, John. BA, St. Joseph's Sem., Yonkers, N.Y., 1959; Licentiate in Sacred Theology, Gregorian U., Rome, 1963; PhD, Brandeis U., 1970. Diocesan priest Archdiocese N.Y., N.Y.C., 1963-71; prof. U. Chgo., 1969—, Naomi Shenstone Donnelly Prof., 1992—; program coord. Inst. for Advanced Study of Religion, Divinity Sch., U. Chgo., 1980-92. Author: The Calabrian Abbott, 1985, Meister Eckhart, 1986, Foundations of Mysticism, 1991, Growth of Mysticism, 1994, Antichrist, 1994; editor: (series) Classics of Western Spirituality, 1978, (book) God and Creation, 1990. Fellow Medieval Acad. Am. Home: 5701 S Kenwood Ave Chicago IL 60637-1718 Office: U Chgo Divinity Sch 1025 E 58th St Chicago IL 60637-1509

MCGINN, CHERIE M., secondary education educator; b. Oil City, Pa., Feb. 5, 1949; d. Rendall Baxter and Helen Joyce (Kunselman) Agnew; 1 child from previous marriage, Joshua Edward; m. Stephen James McGinn, Jan. 1, 1983; 1 child, Kathleen Erin. BS Clarion State Coll., 1971. Cert. secondary tchr., Md. Grad. asst. Clarion State Coll., Pa., 1971-72; tchr. Montgomery County Pub. Schs., 1972—; chairperson Montgomery Blair H.S., Silver Spring, Md., 1994—; cons. curriculum, Upper Marlboro, Md., 19; panelist Odyssey 1984, Excellence in Edn., Md. Humanities Coun., Balt., 1984. Vol. reader grant proposal Coun. for Basic Edn., fellow, 1983.91. NEH, Washington, 1984—. NEH fellow, 1989, 92, 95. Mem. Nat. Coun. for Social Studies, U.S. Capitol Hist. Soc., Assn. Supervision and Curriculum Devel., Md. Social Studies Assn., Montgomery County Social Studies Coun., NEA, Md. State Tchrs. Assn., Montgomery County Educators Assn. Democrat. Mem. Unitarian Ch. Home: 14228 Rutherford Rd Upper Marlboro MD 20774-8564 Office: Montgomery Blair HS 313 Wayne Ave Silver Spring MD 20910

MCGINN, DONALD JOSEPH, English language educator; b. Indian Lake, N.Y., Apr. 1, 1905; s. James and Mary Elizabeth (McCarthy) McG.; m. Margaret Mary Howley, June 27, 1940 (dec. 1979); children: Kathleen McGinn Spring, Donald J. Jr. AB, Cornell U., 1926, MA, 1929, PhD, 1930. Tchr. Rutgers Prep., New Brunswick, N.J., 1930-36, Rutgers U., 1936-73; prof. English Georgian Court Coll., Lakewood, N.J., 1945-93, ret., 1993. Author: Shakespeare's Influence on the Drama of His Age, 1938, The Admonition Controversy, 1949, (with George Howerton) Literature as a Fine Art, 1959, John Penry and the Marprelate Controversy, 1966, Thomas Nashe, 1981. Home: PO Box 387 Saint Petersburg FL 33731-0387

MCGINN, MAX DANIEL, lawyer; b. Lexington, N.C., July 30, 1942; s. Max Terry and Ethel Mae (Peck) McG.; m. Judith Eaton McBee, June3, 1965; children: Brian, Tracie. BA magna cum laude, Wake Forest U., 1964, JD cum laude, 1967. Bar: U.S. Dist. Ct. (mid. dist.) N.C. 1971, U.S. Supreme Ct. 1977, U.S. Ct. Appeals (4th cir.) 1976, U.S. Dist. Ct. (we. and ea dists.) N.C. 1979. Atty. NLRB, Winston-Salem, N.C., 1967, 1970; ptnr. Brooks, Pierce, McLendon, Humphrey & Leonard, Greensboro, N.C., 1971—. Lt., atty. Judge Adv. Gen.'s Corps, USN, 1967-70. Fellow Am. Coll. of Trial Lawyers; mem. ABA, N.C. Bar Assn. (chmn. Labor and Employment Law sect. 1989). Presbyterian. Avocations: tennis, sports, reading. Home: 3008 Redford Dr Greensboro NC 27408-3116 Office: Brooks Pierce McLendon Humphrey & Leonard 230 N Elm St Greensboro NC 27401-2436

MC GINNES, EDGAR ALLEN, JR., forestry educator; b. Chestown, Md., Feb. 15, 1926; s. Edgar Allen and Emily Frances (Howard) McG.; m. Jean Marie Heidemann, June 23, 1951; children—Jeffrey, Christine, Karen. B.S., Pa. State U., 1950, M.F., 1951; Ph.D., N.Y. State Coll. Forestry, 1955. Research chemist Am. Viscose Corp., 1951-52, research scientist, 1955-60; prof. forestry U. Mo., Columbia, 1960-88; cons. abnormal wood formation. Contbr. articles to profl. jours. Served with AUS, 1944-46. Fellow AAAS (coun. 1970-74), Am. Inst. Chemists, Soc. Am. Foresters, Mo. Acad. Scis. (pres. 1981-82); mem. Am. Chem. Soc., TAPPI, Forest Products Rsch. Soc. chmn. midwest sect. 1986-87), Internat. Assn. Wood Anatomists, Soc. Wood Sci. and Tech. (pres. 1986-87), Kappa Sigma. Club: Cosmopolitan Internat. (Columbia) (pres. 1971-72). Home: 900 Bourn Ave Columbia MO 65203-1457

MCGINNIES, ELLIOTT MORSE, psychologist, educator; b. Buffalo, Sept. 19, 1921; s. Elliott Morse and Mabel Christina (Hussong) McG.; m. Bessie Yeh, Jan. 27, 1967; children: Michelle, Lisa, Amy. BA, SUNY-Buffalo, 1943; MA, Brown U., 1944; PhD, Harvard U., 1948. Teaching fellow Harvard U., 1944-47; asst. prof. U. Ala., 1947-52; assoc. prof., then prof. U. Md., 1952-70; prof., chmn. dept. psychology Am. U., 1970-86, prof. emeritus, 1987— ; vis. scholar U. Calif., Berkeley, 1987-88; Fulbright prof. Nat. Taiwan U. With AUS, 1943. Fellow Am. Psychol. Assn.; mem. Eastern Psychol. Assn., Psychonomic Soc., Sigma Xi. Author: Social Behavior: A Functional Analysis, 1970, The Reinforcement of Social Behavior, 1971, Attitudes, Conflict and Social Change, 1972, Perspectives on Social Behavior, 1994. Office: The Am Univ Dept of Psychology 4400 Massachusetts Ave NW Washington DC 20016-8001

MC GINNIS, ARTHUR JOSEPH, publisher; b. Paterson, N.J., Apr. 5, 1911; s. Arthur J. and Rose (Seyer) McG.; m. Roselind P. Diskon, May 17, 1939; children: Roselind P. (Mrs. Joseph W. Mullen, Jr.), Carolyn M., Kathleen M. (Mrs. A.A. Stein III), Patricia A., Arthur J. B.A., Fordham U., 1932; M.B.A., Harvard, 1934. Traveling auditor, 1934-35; staff statistician Western Union Telegraph Co., 1935-40; assoc. editor Ry. Age, 1940-44, fin. editor, 1944-46; asst. treas. Simmons-Boardman Pub. Corp., 1946-50; mem. White House press corps, Washington, 1950-58; treas., dir. Simmons-Boardman Pub. Corp., 1950-54, exec. v.p., treas., 1954-58, pres., treas., 1958-72, chmn. exec. com., treas., chief exec. officer, 1972—; pub. Am. Builder mag., 1955-61. Trustee Monmouth Med. Center, Long Branch, N.J., 1956—, chmn. devel. com. Roman Catholic. Clubs: N.Y. Athletic (N.Y.C.), Harvard Business (N.Y.C.), Nat. Arts (N.Y.C.); Deal (N.J.) Golf and Country (pres.), Allenhurst (N.J.) Bathing. Home & Office: 345 Hudson St New York NY 10014-4502

MCGINNIS, CHARLES IRVING, civil engineer; b. Kansas City, Mo., Jan. 31, 1928; s. Paul Sherman and Sidney (Bacon) McG.; m. Shirley Ann Meyer, Nov. 5, 1955; children: Gail B., Ann K., James P. B.S., Tex. A&M., 1949; M.Engring., Tex. A & M Coll., 1950; grad., Army Engring. Sch., 1955, Command and Gen. Staff Coll., 1959, Armed Forces Staff Coll., 1962, Army War Coll., 1969. Registered profl. engr., Tex., Mo. Enlisted as pvt. U.S. Army, 1945, advanced through grades to maj. gen., 1976; area engr. Ethiopia and Somali Republic, 1962-65; dist. engr. St. Paul, 1969-71; dir. engring. and constrn. bur. Panama Canal Co., 1971-72, v.p., 1972-74; lt. gov. C.Z., 1972-74; div. engr. southwestern div. C.E., Dallas, 1974-77; dir. civil works Office Chief of Engrs. U.S. Army, Washington, 1977-79; civil engr., 1979—; exec. v.p. Fru-con Corp.; pres. Fruco Engrs., Inc., 1983-87; assoc. dir. Constrn. Industry Inst. U. Tex., 1987-93; sr. lectr. civil engring. dept. U. Tex., Austin, 1992—; mem. vis. com., dept. civil engring. M.I.T., 1978-81; mem. Mississippi River Commn., 1975-77, Bd. Engrs. for Rivers and Harbors, 1975-77. Chmn. Combined Fedn. Campaign coordinating com., C.Z., 1972-74; pres. C.Z. coun. Boy Scouts Am., 1973-74; mem. exec. bd. St. Louis area coun., 1983-87, Capitol area coun., 1987-90; mem. com. mgmt. Balboa YMCA, 1973-74; trustee C.Z. United Way, 1972-74. Decorated D.S.M., Legion of Merit with oak leaf cluster, Joint Svcs. Commendation medal, U.S. Army Commendation with oak leaf cluster, Chuong My medal 1st class Vietnam. Fellow ASCE, Soc. Am. Mil. Engrs. (past pres. Twin Cities post and Panama post); mem. NSPE (chmn. water policy task force 1979-81), Assn. U.S. Army, Mil. Order of the World Wars, Tau Beta Pi, Chi Epsilon. Episcopalian. Address: 10006 Sausalito Dr Austin TX 78759-6106 *The simple four-part philosophy which has well served three generations of my family requires an uncompromising commitment to honesty in all things, industry, concentration on the job and on personal objectives, and economy of all resources, both natural and man-made.*

MCGINNIS, GARY DAVID, science educator; b. Everett, Wash., Oct. 1, 1940. BS, Pacific Lutheran U., 1962; MS, U. Wash., 1968; PhD in Organic Chem., U. Mont., 1970. Prodn. chemist Am. Cyanamid Co., 1964-67; fell. U. Mont., 1970-71; from asst. prof. wood chemistry to assoc. prof. wood sci. Forest Products Utilization Lab. Mich. State U. Mem. Am. Chem. Soc., Forest Products Rsch. Soc., Sigma Xi. Office: Michigan Technology University Institute of Wood Research Houghton MI 49931*

MC GINNIS, JAMES MICHAEL, physician; b. Columbia, Mo., July 12, 1944; s. Leland Glenn and Lillian Ruth (Mackler) McG.; m. Patricia Anne Gwaltney, Aug. 4, 1978; children—Brian, Katherine. A.B., U. Calif., Berkeley, 1966; M.A., M.D., UCLA, 1971; M.P.P., Harvard U., 1977. House officer in internal medicine Boston City Hosp., 1971-72; internat. med. officer HEW, 1972-74; dir. Office for Asia and Western Pacific, 1974-75; state coordinator smallpox eradication program WHO, India, 1974-75; fellow Harvard Center for Community Health and Med. Care, Boston, 1976-77; cons. to sec. HEW, Washington, 1977; dep. asst. sec. for health, dir. office disease prevention HEW, 1977-95, asst. surgeon gen., 1980-95, acting dir. office of rsch. integrity, 1992-93; scholar-in-residence Nat. Acad. Scis., Washington, 1995—; instr. medicine George Washington U. Med. Sch.,

1973-75; adj. prof. pub. policy Duke U., 1979-81; chair, sec. task force on smoking and health; chair exec. com. HHS Environ. Health Policy Com.; mem. U.S. Japan Leadership program; chair World Bank/European Commn. Task Force on Reconstrn. of Health Sector, Bosnia, 1996—. Mem. editl. bd. Jour. Med. Edn., 1975-78, Jour. Preventive Medicine, 1987—, Jour. Health Promotion, 1992—; editor-in-chief: Healthy People 2000, Surgeon General's Report on Nutrition and Health, Determining Risks to Health. Served with USPHS, 1972-75, 77—. Recipient Arthur S. Flemming Pub. Svc. award, 1979, USPHS Disting. Svc. medal, 1989, Surgeon Gen.'s medallion, 1995, Fed. Profile in Leadership award, 1989, Wilbur Cohen award, 1995. Fellow Am. Coll. Epidemiology, Am. Coll. Preventive Medicine. Office: 330 C St SW Washington DC 20201-0001

MCGINNIS, JOÁN ADELL, secondary school educator; b. Erie, Pa., Jan. 20, 1932; d. Roy Hamilton and Sara Zelma (Gorman) Sjöberg; m. Richard H. Edwards, Aug. 6, 1954 (div. 1965); m. George William McGinnis, Dec. 29, 1966 (dec. Apr. 1994). BA, St. Lawrence U., Canton, N.Y., 1953. Cert. tchr., Calif. Spl. proxies Sun Life Assurance Co., Montreal, 1952-53; pvt. sec. Detroit Trust, 1953-54; sec. Meth. Ch., Lancaster, Calif., 1964—; tchr. Sunny Hills H.S., Fullerton, Calif., 1966—; contr. Mission Viejo (Calif.) Sheet Metal, 1980-81; dept. sec. Fgn. Lang. Dept. Sunny Hills H.S., 1966-80, dept. chair, 1987-89; internat. baccalaureate examiner in Spanish, 1991—, French, 1992—; advanced placement examiner in Spanish, 1990—. Mem. Am. Assn. Tchrs. Spanish and Portuguese, Modern Classical Lang. Assn. Calif., Fgn. Lang. Assn. Orange County (Exptl. Tchr. of Orange County award 1994), Am. Women's Orgn. Republican. Avocations: languages, music, drama. Home: 26382 Estanciero Dr Mission Viejo CA 92691-5401 Office: Sunny Hills HS 1801 W Warburton Way Fullerton CA 92633-2235

MCGINNIS, JOHN OLDHAM, lawyer, educator; b. N.Y.C., Mar. 21, 1957; s. John Patrick and Pauline Ruth (Oldham) McG. BA magna cum laude, Harvard U., 1978, JD magna cum laude, 1983; MA, Oxford U., Eng., 1980. Bar: N.Y. 1984. Law clk. to judge U.S. Ct. Appeals (D.C. cir.), Washington, 1983-84; assoc. Sullivan & Cromwell, N.Y.C., 1984-85; atty./advisor Office Legal Counsel, Dept. Justice, Washington, 1985-87, dep. asst. atty. gen., 1987-91; prof. Benjamin N. Cardozo Sch. Law, N.Y.C., 1991—. Contbr. articles to profl. jours.; editor Harvard Law Rev., 1982-83. Home: 21 E 22nd St New York NY 10010-5332 Office: Cardozo Law Sch 55 5th Ave New York NY 10003-4301

MCGINNIS, ROBERT CAMPBELL, lawyer; b. Dallas, Jan. 1, 1918; s. Edward Karl and Helen Louise (Campbell) McG.; m. Ethel Clift, May 14, 1945; children: Mary, Campbell, John, Robert, Michael. AB, U. Tex., 1938; LLB, Yale U., 1941. Bar: Tex. 1941, Ohio 1942, U.S. Dist. Ct. (no. dist.) Tex. 1948, U.S. Dist. Ct. (we. dist.) Tex. 1950. Assoc. Squires, Sanders & Dempsey, Cleve., 1941-42, Carrington, Gowan, Dallas, 1946-49; ptnr. McGinnis, Lochridge & Kilgore and predecessor firm Powell, Wirtz & Rauhut, Austin, Tex., 1950-95; chmn. Tex. Com. Jud. Ethics, 1972-78; bd. dirs. Republic Bank, Austin. Served to lt. USNR, 1942-46, PTO. Fellow Am. Bar Found.; mem. ABA, Tex. Bar Assn., U.S. Lawn Tennis Assn. (hon. life). Presbyterian. *Died Feb. 22, 1995.*

MCGINNIS, ROBERT E., lawyer; b. Caldwell, Ohio, May 1, 1931; s. Earl Peregoy and Mary Ethel (Richner) McG.; m. Jane Ann Lindenmeyer, Sept. 12, 1953; children: Sharon Ann, David E. BA, Ohio Weslayan U., 1952; JD, Ohio State U., 1954. Bar: Ohio 1954, Calif. 1956. Asst. judge advocate USAF, 1954-56; sr. ptnr. Luce, Forward, Hamilton, & Scripps, San Diego, 1956—; counsel to pub. utilities, pub. agys., savs. and loan instns., ins. cos. and contractors. Trustee Wesley Meth. Ch., San Diego, Fine Arts Soc., First Meth. Ch., La Mesa, Calif.; counsel Kensington Community Ch.; dir. San Diego Opera Assn., corp. sec., v.p. Mem. Order of Coif. Republican. Mem. United Ch. Christ. Office: Luce Forward Hamilton & Scripps 600 W Broadway Ste 2600 San Diego CA 92101-3311

MCGINNIS, THOMAS MICHAEL, lawyer; b. Royal Oak, Mich., July 13, 1954; s. Donalo Edward Sr. and Maryane Carney (Jex) McG.; m. Tracy Chris, Mar. 4, 1993. BA, Regis U., 1976; JD, Thomas Cooley Coll., 1980. Bar: Mich. 1981, U.S. Dist. Ct. (ea. dist.) Mich. 1981, U.S. Ct. Appeals 1984. Wilson, Portnoy & Leader, 1980-83; Pvt. practice law Troy, Mich.; chairperson Lawyer Referral Svc., Pontiac, Mich., 1985-86. Mem. Soc. Irish/Am. Lawyers. Avocations: water skiing, snow skiing, guitar. Office: 802 E Big Beaver Rd Troy MI 48083

MCGINNIS, TINA MARIE, art educator; b. Flint, Mich., July 26, 1954; d. Keith Raymond and Katherine Ann (Luce) McG.; children: Katrina Marie, Robert Raymon. A of Liberal ARts, Mott. C.C., 1990, A in Gen. Studies, 1992; BS, U. Mich., 1993. Tchr. art Valley Sch., Flint, Mich., 1991-92; substitute tchr. Swartz Creek (Mich.) Schs., 1993-94, Flint Cmty. Schs., 1993-94; tchr. Mott Adult High Sch., Flint, 1986-94; tchr. art Flint Inst. Art, 1991-94, Grand Blanc (Mich.) Parks & Recreation, FLint, 1993—, Lapeer (Mich.) Cmty. Schs., 1994—. Author of poems. Mem. ASCD, NEA, Nat. Art Edn. Assn., Mich. Edn. Assn., Mich. Art Edn. Assn. (conf. demonstrator 1993), Greater Flint Arts Coun., U. Mich. Alumni Assn., Kappa Delta Pi. Avocations: making jewelry, painting, metal smithing, reading, floral design.

MCGINNITY, MAUREEN ANNELL, lawyer; b. Monroe, Wis., Apr. 6, 1956; d. James Arthur and Marie Beatrice (Novak) McG.; m. Richard W. Ziervogel, July 17, 1982; 1 child, Brigitte Kathleen. BS, U. Wis., Milw., 1977; JD, U. Wis., 1982. Bar: Wis. 1982, U.S. Dist. Ct. (ea. and we. dists.) Wis. 1982, U.S. Ct. Appeals (7th cir.) 1989, U.S. Supreme Ct. 1991, U.S. Ct. Appeals (1st cir.) 1991. Assoc. Foley & Lardner, Milw., 1982-91, ptnr., 1991—; mem. Wis. Supreme Ct. Planning and Policy Adv. Com., Madison, 1991-94; adv. bd. Domestic Violence Legal Clinic, Milw., 1991—. Treas. Waukesha (Wis.) Food Pantry, 1988-94; trustee Boys & Girls Club Greater Milw., 1991—; bd. dirs. Task Force on Battered Women & Children, Inc., 1994—. Recipient Outstanding Svc. award Legal Action Wis., Milw., 1984, 93 Outstanding Fundraising awards Boys & Girls Club Greater Milw., 1987-92, Cert. Recognition, Common Coun. Task Force on Sexual Assault & Domestic Violence, Milw., 1991, Cert. Appreciation, Wis. Equal Justice Task Force, Madison, 1991, Cmty. Svc. award Wis. Law Found., 1995. Mem. ABA, State Bar Wis. (bd. govs. 1992—, Pro Bono award 1990, chair 1993-94), Assn. for Women Lawyers (various offices, pres. 1992-93), Milw. Young Lawyers Assn. (bd. dirs. 1987-92, pres. 1990-91, Pres.' award 1991), Profl. Dimensions. Office: Foley & Lardner 777 E Wisconsin Ave Milwaukee WI 53202-5302

MCGINTY, JOHN, marketing consultant; b. Neosho, Mo., Dec. 5, 1911; s. Abner Crawford and Blanche (Hale) McG.; m. Glenella Florence Davison, July 15, 1934; children: Marilyn McGinty Stewart, Marjorie McGinty Kilpatrick, Maureen, John Edward, Melanie McGinty Tate, Melinda. BCS, Drake U., 1932; LLB, City Coll. Law, St. Louis, 1936; DHL (hon.), Drury Coll., 1988. Bar: Mo. bar 1936. Mgr. closing div. Fed. Land Bank of St. Louis, 1933-44; with Ralston Purina Co., St. Louis, 1944-73; editor sales publs., mgr. publs., sales promotion mgr. Ralston Purina Co., 1944-59, v.p. and dir. sales promotion, 1959-63, v.p., dir. advt. and sales promotion, 1963-69, v.p., dir. mktg. services, 1969-73; meeting cons. for firms including Ralston Purina, DeLaval Separator Co., Monsanto Co., Babcock Industries Inc., Mktg. Intercontinental, Hudson Foods, Inc., 1973—; chmn. bd. Christian Bd. Publs., St. Louis, 1955-84. Author: How to Raise the Level of Giving in Your Church, 1978. Trustee Disciples Div. House, U. Chgo., Drake U., 1966-74; chmn. bd. trustees Drury Coll., 1970-73, life trustee. Home: 12 Country Club Ter Saint Louis MO 63122-4673

MC GINTY, JOHN MILTON, architect; b. Houston, Apr. 24, 1935; s. Milton Bowles and Ruth Louise (Dreaper) McG.; m. Juanita Jones, May 4, 1957; children: Christopher Harold, Jacqueline Ruth McGinty Carlson. B.S., Rice U., 1957; M.F.A., Princeton U., 1961. With archtl. firm Barnes, Landes & Goodman, Austin, Tex., 1957-58, Ingram & Harris, Beaumont, Tex., 1958-59; prin. McGinty Partnership, Architects, Inc., Houston, 1961-89, City Assos., Inc., 1979-91, Bovay-McGinty, Inc., engrs. & architects, Houston, 1989-91; co-owner, pres. Am. Constrn. Investigations Inc., Houston, 1991—; instr. archtl. design U. Houston, 1965-67; White House fellow, asst. to Sec. of Interior, 1967-68; vis. prof. architecture Rice U., 1969-70. Named Disting. Alumnus Rice U., 1986. Fellow AIA (mem. U.S. delegation to USSR 1972, pres. Houston chpt. 1973, nat. pres. 1977). Home: HC-02 Box 308 Palacios TX 77465 Office: Am Constrn Investigations Ste 200 602 Sawyer St Houston TX 77007-7510

MCGINTY, KATHLEEN, federal official. Dep. asst. to pres., dir. environ. policy Exec. Office of Pres. of U.S., Washington, 1993-95, chairperson coun. on environ. quality, 1995—. Office: Council on Environ Quality 722 Jackson Place NW Washington DC 20503*

MCGINTY, MICHAEL DENNIS, air force officer; b. Waukegan, Ill., Sept. 20, 1942; s. Roy Leonard and Betty Jane (Anderson) McG.; m. Karen Lee Dibble, July 2, 1965; children: Shannon, Timothy. BA in Math., U. Minn., 1964; MA in Pub. Adminstrn., Shippensburg U., 1983. Commd. 2d lt. USAF, 1965, advanced through grades to maj. gen., 1992; chief of standarization and evaluation 3d Tactical Fighter Wing, Clark Air Base, The Philippines, 1975-76; ops. officer 9th Tactical Fighter Squadron, Holloman AFB, N.Mex., 1976-78; grad. student Air Command and Staff Coll., Maxwell AFB, Ala., 1979; chief of officer assignments Hdqrs. Tactical Air Command, Langley AFB, Va., 1979-82; grad. student U.S. Army War Coll., Carlisle, Pa., 1983; dep. comdr. for ops. 355th Tactical Tng. Wing, Davis-Monthan AFB, Ariz., 1983-85; chief cols. group Air Force Mil. Pers. Ctr., Randolph AFB, Tex., 1985-87; vice comdr. 10th Tactical Fighter Wing, RAF Alconbury, U.K., 1987-88, comdr., 1988-90; dep. chief of staff for plans and requirements Hdqrs. Air Tng. Command, Randolph AFB, 1990; vice comdr. Air Force Mil. Pers. Ctr., Randolph AFB, 1990-92, comdr., 1992-94; dir. pers. programs, edn. and tng. USAF The Pentagon, Washington, 1994—, dep. chief of staff, personnel. Author: Low Altitude Training for F-4 Aircrews, 1979, Theory Z Management: Can It Be Used Effectively in the Air Force, 1983. Decorated Disting. Svc. medal, Legion of Merit (2), DFC (2), Meritorious Svc. medal (4), Air medal (10). Mem. Air Force Assn., Ret. Officers Assn., Order of Daedalians (flight capt. Tucson club 1984-85), Pi Sigma Alpha. Republican. Roman Catholic. Avocations: running, hiking, camping, outdoor activities. Home: 75 Westover Ave SW Washington DC 20336-5409 Office: Hq USAF/DPP 1040 Air Force Pentagon Washington DC 20330-1040*

MCGINTY, THOMAS EDWARD, management consultant; b. Holyoke, Mass., Aug. 20, 1929; s. Patrick John and Alice May (Hill) McG.; m. June Theresa Coutu, Jan. 27, 1951; children: Thomas, Michael, Matthew. B.S. in Econs. and Commerce, U. Vt., 1951; M.B.A., NYU, 1957. Chartered fin. analyst. Sr. fin. analyst Moody's Investor Service, 1955-59, Model, Roland and Stone, N.Y.C., 1959-62; with Cleve.-Cliffs Iron Co., 1962-83, v.p. fin., 1971-75, sr. v.p., 1975-83; pres. Belvoir Cons., Inc., 1983—; chmn. bd. Ormet Corp., 1986-89; bd. dirs. Horsburgh & Scott Co., Park Ohio Industries. Author: Project Organization and Finance, 1981. Bd. advisers Notre Dame Coll. Served with U.S. Army, 1951-55, Korea. Decorated Bronze Star. Mem. Assn. Investment Mgmt. and Rsch., Cleve. Skating Club, Wilderness Country Club (Naples, Fla.). Roman Catholic. Home: 2705 Belvoir Blvd Cleveland OH 44122-1925 Office: Belvoir Cons 23200 Chagrin Blvd Ste 325 Cleveland OH 44122-5403

MCGIRR, DAVID WILLIAM JOHN, investment banker; b. Glasgow, Scotland, May 19, 1954; came to U.S., 1991; s. Edward McCombie and Diane Curzon (Woods) McG.; m. Margaret Joslin Richardson, May 9, 1981; children: William David, Katherine Joslin, Lucy Ann, Elizabeth Margaret. BSc with honors, U. Glasgow, 1976; MBA, U. Pa., 1978. Assoc. S.G. Warburg & Co. Ltd., London, 1978-80, exec. dir., 1981-86; mng. dir. S.G. Warburg & Co. Inc., N.Y.C., 1991-95, CFO, 1992-95; assoc. Warburg Paribas Becker Inc., N.Y.C., 1980-81; exec. dir. S.G. Warburg Securities, London, 1986-87; CEO S.G. Warburg Securities (Can.) Ltd., Toronto, Ont., Can., 1987-89; COO, CFO Bunting Warburg Inc., Toronto, 1989-91; pres. GAB Robins North Am. Inc., Parsippany, N.J., 1996—; mem. selection com. Thouron Scholarship. Thouron scholar, 1976-78. Mem. Apawamis Club (Rye, N.Y.), Nat. Club (Can.). Avocations: collecting cars, motor racing, family, golf. Office: GAB Robins N Am Inc 9 Campus Dr Parsippany NJ 07054-4476

MCGIVERIN, ARTHUR A., state supreme court justice; b. Iowa City, Iowa, Nov. 10, 1928; s. Joseph J. and Mary B. McG.; m. Mary Joan McGiverin, Apr. 20, 1951; children: Teresa, Thomas, Bruce, Nancy. BSC with high honors, U. Iowa, 1951, JD, 1956. Bar: Iowa 1956. Pvt. practice law Ottumwa, Iowa, 1956; alt. mcpl. judge Ottumwa, 1960-65; judge Iowa Dist. Ct. 8th Jud. Dist., 1965-78; assoc. justice Iowa Supreme Ct., Des Moines, 1978-87, chief justice, 1987—. Mem. Iowa Supreme Ct. Commn. on Continuing Legal Edn., 1975. Served to 1st lt. U.S. Army, 1946-48, 51-53. Mem. Iowa State Bar Assn., Am. Law Inst. Roman Catholic. Avocation: golf. Office: Iowa Supreme Ct State Capital Bldg Des Moines IA 50319*

MC GLAMERY, MARSHAL DEAN, agronomy, weed science educator; b. Mooreland, Okla., July 29, 1932; s. Walter Gaiford and Bernice (Gardner) McG.; m. Marilyn Hudson, June 2, 1957; children—Paul, Steve. B.S., Okla. State U., 1956, M.S., 1958; Ph.D., U. Ill., 1965. Instr. Panhandle A. and M. Coll., 1958-60; agronomist Agribus. Co., Lawrence, Kans., 1960-61; teaching asst. U. Ill., 1961-63, research fellow, 1963-65, asst. prof. weed sci., 1965-70, asso. prof., 1970-76, prof., 1976—, extension agronomist, 1965—. Served with U.S. Army, 1953-55. NSF fellow, 1963. Mem. Am. Soc. Agronomy, Weed Sci. Soc. Am., Council Agr. and Tech. Baptist. Home: 35 Lange Ave Savoy IL 61874-9705 Office: 1102 S Goodwin Ave Urbana IL 61801-4730

MCGLAMRY, MAX REGINALD, lawyer; b. Wilcox County, Ga., Sept. 12, 1928; s. Edgar Lee and Allie Bea (Faircloth) McG.; m. Jean Louise Hilyer, Dec. 28, 1950; children: Sharon Kay McGlamry Hendrix, Michael Lee. BS, Auburn U., 1948; LLB cum laude, Mercer U., 1952, JD cum laude, 1970. Bar: Ga. 1953, U.S. Dist. Ct. (mid. dist.) Ga. 1954, U.S. Dist. Ct. (no. dist.) Calif. 1988, U.S. Dist. Ct. (no. dist.) Ga. 1989, U.S. Ct. Appeals (5th cir.) 1964, U.S. Ct. Appeals (11th cir.) 1981, U.S. Ct. Appeals (4th cir.) 1985, U.S. Supreme Ct. 1972. Pvt. practice Columbus, Ga., 1953-64; from ptnr. to officer Swift, Pease, Davidson & Chapman (name changed to Page, Scrantom, Harris, McGlamry, & Chapman, P.C.), Columbus, 1964-85; ptnr. Pope, Kellogg, McGlamry, Kilpatrick & Morrison, Columbus, 1985-90, Pope, McGlamry, Kilpatrick & Morrison, Columbus, 1990—. Mem. exec. com. Muscogee County Dem. Orgn., Columbus, 1956-60; bd. dirs. Columbus Jr. C. of C. With USN, 1948-49. Am. Coll. Trust & Estate Counsel fellow, 1973, Ga. Bar Found., Inc. fellow, 1983. Mem. ABA, ATLA, State Bar Ga., Ga. Trial Lawyers Assn., Assn. U.S. Army, Metro Columbus Urban League, Inc., Columbus Lawyers Club (pres. 1964-65), Lions (Columbus chpt. pres. 1967-68), Chattahoochee River Club, Green Island Country Club, Phi Kappa Phi, Alpha Epsilon Delta, Phi Alpha Delta, Pi Kappa Alpha. Democrat. Methodist. Avocations: golf, fishing. Home: 2937 Lynda Ln Columbus GA 31906-1337 Office: Pope McGlamry Kilpatrick & Morrison PO Box 2128 318 11th St 2nd Fl Columbus GA 31902

MCGLATHERY, JAMES MELVILLE, foreign language educator; b. New Orleans, Nov. 22, 1936; s. Samuel Lyon and Mary Jackson (Garrott) McG.; m. Nancy Judith Beyer, June 1, 1939; children: Samuel Lyon, Daniel Beyer, Andrew James, Benjamin Kim. AB, Princeton U., 1958; AM, Yale U., 1959, PhD, 1964. Instr. German Phillips Andover (Mass.) Acad., 1959-60; lectr. German Harvard U., 1963-64, instr. German, 1964-65; from asst. prof. to assoc. prof. U. Ill. at Urbana-Champaign, 1965-84, prof. German, 1984—, acting dept. head, spring 1985, dept. head, 1985-95; instr. Colby Coll. Summer Lang. Sch., 1964, Harvard U. Summer Lang. Sch., 1965, 66, 70, U. Ill. at Urbanan-Champaign summer session, 1972, 74, 76, 78, 80, 82, 87, 90; lectr. and presenter conf. papers numerous orgns. Author: Mysticism and Sexuality: E. T. A. Hoffmann, Part One: Hoffmann and His Sources, 1981, Desire's Sway: The Plays and Stories of Heinrich von Kleist, 1983, Mysticism and Sexuality: E. T. A. Hoffmann, Part Two: Interpretations of the Tales, 1985, Fairy Tale Romance: The Grimms, Basile, Perrault, 1991, Grimms' Fairy Tales: A History of Criticism on a Popular Classic, 1993; editor: German Source Readings in the Arts and Sciences, 1974, Journal of English and Germanic Philology, 1976, The Brothers Grimm and Folktale, 1988, 91, Music and German Literature: Their Relationship since the Middle Ages, 1992; contbg. author: Reader in German Literature, 1969, Molière and the Commonwealth of Letters: Patrimony and Posterity, 1975, Fairy Tales as Ways of Knowing: Essays on Märchen in Psychology, Society, and Literature, 1981, Reflection and Action: Essays on the Bildungsroman, 1991; mng. editor: Jour. English and Germanic Philology, 1972—; contbr. articles and book revs. to profl. jours. Full undergrad. tuition scholar Princeton U., 1954-58; undergrad. rsch. assistantship Princeton U., 1956-58; Woodrow Wilson Nat. fellow Yale U., 1958-59, Jr. Sterling fellow Yale U., 1960-61, Nat. Def. Edn. Act fellow in Russian, Yale U., 1961-63; grad. rsch. bd. grantee U. Ill. Urbana-Champaign, 1975, 79, 80, 86, 89, 92. Mem. MLA (exec. com. divsn. comparative studies in 18th century lit. 1984-89), Am. Assn. Tchrs. of German, E. T. A. Hoffmann-Gesellschaft, Heinrich von Kleist-Gesellschaft, N.Am. Heine Soc. Home: 1204 Thomas Dr Champaign IL 61821 Office: U Ill Urbana-Champaign Dept Germanic Langs & Lits 707 S Mathews Ave Urbana IL 61801

MCGLAUCHLIN, TOM, artist; b. Turtle, Wis., Sept. 14, 1934; s. Charles Orion and Frances Lenore (Cadman) McG.; m. Patricia Ann Smith, Aug. 5, 1961; children: Christopher, Jennifer (dec.), Patrick (dec.). BS in Art, U. Wis., 1959, MS in Art, 1960; studied pottery with James McKinnell, 1962. Instr. dept. art and art edn. U. Wis., Madison, 1960-61; instr. art dept. Cornell Coll., Mt. Vernon, Iowa, 1961-64, asst. prof. art dept., 1964-68; assoc. prof., chmn. art dept. Cornell Coll., Mt. Vernon, N.Y., 1968-71; instr. Toledo Mus. Art, 1971-82, prof., dir. glass program, 1982-84. One-man exhbns. include Habatat Gallery, Dearborn, Mich., 1979, Glass Art Gallery, Toronto, 1981, 85, Glass Gallery, Bethesda, Md., 1981, 85, 87, 91, Heller Gallery, N.Y.C., 1983, B.Z. Wagman Gallery, St. Louis, 1983, Running Ridge Gallery, Santa Fe, 1990; selected group exhbns. include Toledo Mus. Art, 1972, 88, Glasmuseum Frauenau, Franenau, Germany, 1977, Habatat Gallery, 1980, 84, The Hand and the Spirit Gallery, Scottsdale, Ariz., 1980, Gallery of Contemporary Crafts, Detroit, 1980, The Naples (Fla.) Art Gallery, 1981, The Craftsman's Gallery, Scarsdale, N.Y., 1981, 84, The Nat. Mus. Modern Art, Kyoto and Tokyo, 1981, Perception Gallery, Houston, 1985, The AirLoft Gallery, Honolulu, 1986, The Corning (N.Y.) Mus. Glass, 1987; selected competitive exhbns. include Everson Mus. Art, Syracuse, N.Y., 1961, 62, Mus. Contemporary Crafts, N.Y.C., 1962, Corning Glass Mus., Met. Mus. Art, N.Y.C., Victoria and Albert Mus., London, Musee Ars Decoratif, Paris; public collections include Toledo Mus. Art, The Smithsonian Collection, Washington, Portland (Oreg.) Art Mus., New Orleans Mus. Art, Mus. Contemporary Crafts, Musee des arts decoratifs de la Ville de Lausanne, Switzerland, Minn. Mus. Art, St. Paul, Kunstmuseum, Dusseldorf, Germany, Corning Glass Mus. Grantee Associated Colls. Midwest, 1966-67; recipient First Jury award Toledo Glass Nat. II, 1968. Mem. Am. Crafts Coun., Internat. Sculpture Soc., Ohio Designer-Craftsmen, Glass Art Soc. Office: The Glass Studio 1940 W Central Ave Toledo OH 43606-3944

MCGLINCHEY, JOSEPH DENNIS, retail corporation executive; b. Lowell, Mass., Mar. 14, 1938; s. Patrick Joseph and Grace E. (Curley) McG.; m. Joan Fitzgerald, Sept. 12, 1964; children: Joseph II, Mark, Christopher, David. BA in Acctg., Bentley Coll., 1965; MBA, Babson Coll., 1971. Internal auditor The Stop and Shop Cos., Inc., Boston, 1962-65, dir. fin. planning and control, 1973-74, corp. controller, 1974-77, v.p., corp. controller, 1977-83, v.p. fin., chief acctg. officer, 1983-86, sr. v.p., chief fin. officer, 1986—; controller Gilchrist Co., Boston, 1969-72; mem. adv. bd. New Eng. region Arkwright Mus. Ins. Co., Norwalk, Conn., 1988-92. Bd. overseers, mem. fin. com. Harvard Cmty. Health Plan, Brookline, Mass., 1985-91; treas. St. Mary's Parish, Randolph, Mass.; mem. gen. bd. Greater Boston YMCA, 1993—, treas., 1995—. Roman Catholic. Home: 360 Beacon St Boston MA 02116 Office: Stop & Shop Cos Inc 1 Quincy Center Plz Quincy MA 02169

MCGLINN, FRANK CRESSON POTTS, lawyer; b. Phila., Nov. 19, 1914; s. John Alexander and Emma Frances (Potts) McG.; m. Louise Cabeen Lea, Sept. 9, 1942; children: Marion McGlinn Lockwood, Louise McGlinn Preston, Alice McGlinn Fetter, Ann. AB, U. N.C., 1937; JD, U. Pa., 1940; LLD (hon.), Villanova U., 1970. Assoc. Pepper, Hamilton & Scheetz, Phila., 1945-53; dir. Rep. Fin. Com. of Pa., Phila., 1945-53; v.p., asst. to pres. Al Paul Lefton Co. Advt., Phila., 1953-57; exec. v.p. Fidelity Bank, Phila., 1957-78; sr. v.p. Western Savs. Bank, Phila., 1978-82; exec. v.p. Barra Found., Wyndmoor, Pa., 1982-83; pres. McGlinn Assocs., Haverford, Pa., 1983—; dir. Rittenhouse Trust Co., Phila., 1984—; cons. William Penn Found., 1978-82, Barra Found., 1983-85. Trustee, bd. dirs. Free Libr. Phila., 1955-73, Hist. Soc. Pa., 1978-85; mem. Pa. Coun. on the Arts, 1964-71, 79-87; mem. coun. mgrs. Archdiocese of Phila., 1970-89; dir. chmn. ARC, 1949; chmn. cancer Crusade, 1954, Cath. Charities Appeal, 1966; chmn. Young Rep. Nat. Com., 1949-51; chmn. Pa. Young Reps., 1949-51; chmn. Rep. Fin. com., Pa., 1963-65, vice chmn. 1972-76, chmn. rep. Exec. Co., 1965-77; chmn. NCCJ, Phila., 1961-66, Hon. chmn., 1966-95;. Decorated Purple Heart; knight comdr. Equestrian Order of St. Gregory the Great; recipient Humanitarian award NCCJ, 1967. Mem. Phila. Bar Assn., Merion Cricket Club, Knights of Malta. Republican. Roman Catholic. Avocations: theater, fishing. Home: 729 Millbrook Ln Haverford PA 19041-1210 *Peace-understanding-tolerance in the world can only be achieved through complete freedom of expression and the opportunity to freely question all such expressions. To work toward such a goal is the first step toward one's own success and a better world.*

MCGLOCKTON, CHESTER, professional football player; b. Whiteville, N.C., Sept. 16, 1969. Student, Clemson U. Defensive tackle Oakland Raiders, 1992—. Named to Sporting News NFL All-Pro Team, 1994, to NFL Pro Bowl Team, 1994. Office: Oakland Raiders 332 Center St El Segundo CA 90245

MC GLOTHLIN, JAMES HARRISON, lawyer; b. Louisville, May 31, 1910; s. William Joseph and May Belle (Williams) McG.; m. Patricia Charlotte Dowd, Dec. 31, 1944; children: Susan Louise Detchon, Patricia Anne Stewart, Kathryn Holly. B.A. summa cum laude, Furman U., 1929; M.A., U. Va., 1930; J.D. magna cum laude, Harvard, 1936. Bar: D.C. 1937, N.Y. 1939, U.S. Supreme Ct. 1946. Tchr. Tech. High Sch., Atlanta, 1930-33; law clk. Judge H.M. Stephens, 1936-37; practice in Washington, 1940—; asso. Cravath, Swaine & Moore, N.Y.C., 1937-40; asso. Covington & Burling, 1940-50, partner, 1950-78, sr. ptnr., 1979—; prof. Cath. U. Law Sch., 1947-49; v.p. law So. Ry. Co., 1967-70, exec. v.p. law and fin., 1970-75, cons. to CEO, 1975-79; mem. financial adv. panel Nat. Rail Passenger Transp. Corp., 1971-76. Contbr. articles to legal jours. Mem. adv. council Furman U. Served with AUS, 1941-42; to lt. comdr. USNR, 1942-46. Mem. ABA (anti-trust com., P.U. sect.), D.C. Bar Assn., Am. Arbitration Assn., Met. Club, Chevy Chase (Md.) Club, Sea Island Golf Club (Ga.), Madison Beach Club (Conn.), Phi Gamma Delta. Democrat. Baptist. Home: 247 W 27th St Sea Island GA 31561 also: 14 Cambridge Dr Madison CT 06443-3016 Office: 1201 Pennsylvania Ave PO Box 7566 NW Washington DC 20044

MCGLOTHLIN, JAMES W., wholesale distribution executive; b. 1940. Grad., William & Mary Coll. Bar: Va. 1964. CEO United Ctrl. Indsl. Supply Co., Big Rock, Va. Office: United Co Inc PO Box 1280 Bristol VA 24203*

MCGLYNN, BETTY HOAG, art historian; b. Deer Lodge, Mont., Apr. 28, 1914; d. Arthur James and Elizabeth Tangye (Davey) Lochrie; m. Paul Sterling Hoag, Dec. 28, 1936 (div. 1967); children: Peter Lochrie Hoag, Jane Hoag Brown, Robert Doane Hoag; m. Thomas Arnold McGlynn, July 28, 1973. BA, Stanford U., 1936; MA, U. So. Calif., 1967. Cert. secondary tchr., Calif. Rsch. dir. So. Calif. Archives of Am. Art, L.A., 1964-67, Carmel (Calif.) Mus. Art, 1967-69; dir. Triton Mus. Art, Santa Clara, Calif., 1970; archivist, libr. San Mateo County (Calif.) Hist. Soc. Mus., 1972-74; cons. Monterey Peninsula Mus. Art, Calif., 1964—; tchr. art extension Monterey Peninsula Coll., Calif., 1970, San Jose City Coll., 1971; lectr. in field. Author: The World of Mary DeNeale Morgan, 1970, Carmel Art Association: A History, 1987; contbg. author: Plein Air Painters of California, The North, 1986, Orchid Art and The Orchid Isle, 1982, Hawaiian Island Artists and Friends of the Arts, 1989; editor, author of jours. La Peninsula, 1971-75, Noticias, 1983-88, 95; author of booklets; contbr. articles to profl. jours. Appraiser art work City of Carmel, 1967, City of Monterey, 1981; mem. Friends of Harrison Meml. Libr., Carmel, Friends of Sunset Found., Carmel, Pacific Grove Art Ctr., Monterey Bay Aquarium. Mem. Butte (Mont.) Arts Chateau, Carmel Art Assn. (hon.), Carmel Heritage Soc., Carmel Found., Carmel Residents Assn., Chinese Hist. Soc., Monterey History and Art Assn. (art cons.), Monterey Peninsula Mus. Art (acquisitions bd.), Monterey County Geneal. Soc., Gallatin County Hist. Soc. (Mont.), Stanford Alumni Assn., Robinson Jeffers Tor House Found. (art cons.), Hawaiian Hist. Soc., Mont. Hist. Soc., Nat. Mus. of

Women in Arts, The Westerners, P.E.O., Book Club of Calif. Republican. Avocations: research archives and library. Home and Office: PO Box 7189 Carmel CA 93921-7189

MCGLYNN, JOSEPH LEO, JR., federal judge; b. Phila., Feb. 13, 1925; s. Joseph Leo and Margaret Loretta (Ryan) McG.; m. Jocelyn M. Gates, Aug. 26, 1950; children: Jocelyn, Leo, Timothy, Suzanne, Alisa, Deirdre, Caroline, Elizabeth, Meghan, Brendan. B.S., Mt. St. Mary's Coll., 1948; LL.B., U. Pa., 1951. Bar: Pa. 1952. Asst. U.S. atty. Phila., 1953-60; assoc., then ptnr. Blank Rudenko Klaus & Rome, Phila., 1960-65; judge County Ct. of Phila., 1965-68, Ct. of Common Pleas, 1st Jud. Dist. of Pa., 1968-74, U.S. Dist. Ct. (ea. dist.) Pa., Phila., 1974—. Served with USN, 1943-46, PTO. Mem. Phila. Bar Assn. Office: US Dist Ct 16614 Us Courthouse Philadelphia PA 19106*

MCGLYNN, MICHAEL JAMES, bakery company executive; b. Mpls., June 10, 1950; s. Burton James and Patricia (Jones) M.; m. Elizabeth Cravens, July 8, 1972 (div. 1983); children: Elizabeth Ann, Emily Katherine; m. Julie Bean, Sept. 23, 1983; stepchildren: Jennifer Leslie, Elissa Hill. BS, U. Colo., 1972. V.p. McGlynn Bakeries Co., Mpls., 1972-80, pres., 1981—. Dir. Minn. Family Bus. Council, Mpls., 1979; contact exec. United Way, 1981-87. Mem. Minn. Bakers Assn., Retail Bakers Am., Am. Bakers Assn. Republican. Roman Catholic. Clubs: Interlachen, Country (Edina, Minn.), Mpls. Home: 5025 Schaefer Rd Edina MN 55436-1142 Office: McGlynn Bakeries Inc 7350 Commerce Ln Minneapolis MN 55432

MCGLYNN, RICHARD BRUCE, lawyer; b. Kearny, N.J., Dec. 16, 1938; s. William Edward and Irene Louise (Mohr) M.; m. Victoria Sargent Bell, June 15, 1963; children: Margaret, Mary Elizabeth, Melissa. AB, Princeton U., 1960; LLB, Rutgers U., 1963. Bar: N.J. 1963, U.S. Dist. Ct. N.J. 1963, U.S. Supreme Ct. 1976, U.S. Ct. Appeals (3d cir.) 1984. Asst. prosecutor Essex County, Newark, N.J., 1965-67; dep. atty. gen. State of N.J., Trenton, 1970-73; judge Essex County Dist. Ct., Newark, 1974-76; commr. Bd. Pub. Utilities, State of N.J., Newark, 1976-80; ptnr. Stryker Tams & Dill, Newark, 1980-92, LeBoeuf, Lamb, Greene & MacRae, Newark, 1992-94; v.p., gen. counsel United Water Resources, Harrington Park, N.J., 1994—; bd. dirs. Atlantic Energy Inc., Pleasantville, N.J. Candidate Rep. Gubernatorial primary, N.Y., 1981; chmn. N.J. Shakespeare Festival, N.J., 1989-92, dir., 1994—; dir. Ctr. for the Analysis of Pub. Issues, N.J., 1983—. Mem. ABA, N.J. Bar Assn. (Young Lawyer of Yr. young lawyers sect. 1975), Am. Law Inst., Am. Judicature Soc., Nassau Club, Short Hills Club, Univ. Glee Club N.Y.C., Princeton Club of N.Y. Episcopalian. Avocations: small group singing, tennis, paddle tennis. Home: 30 Hurlingham Club Rd Far Hills NJ 07931 Office: United Water Resources 200 Old Hook Rd Harrington Park NJ 07640-1716

MC GLYNN, SEAN PATRICK, physical chemist, educator; b. Dungloe, Ireland, Mar. 8, 1931; came to U.S., 1952, naturalized, 1957; s. Daniel and Catherine (Brennan) McG.; m. Helen Magdalena Salacz-von Dohnanyi, 4Apr. 11, 1955; children: Sean Ernst, Daniel Julian, Brian Charles, Sheila Ann, Alan Patrick. B.S., Nat. U. Ireland, 1951, M.S., 1952; Ph.D., Fla. State U., 1956. Fellow Fla. State U., 1956, U. Wash., 1956-57; mem. faculty La. State U., 1957—, prof. chemistry, 1964—, Boyd prof. chemistry, 1967—, dean Grad. Sch., 1981-82, vice chancellor for research, 1981-91; asso. prof. biophysics Yale U., 1961; Humboldt prof. physics U. Bonn, W.Ger., 1979-80; cons. to pvt. cos. Author: (with others) Molecular Spectroscopy of the Triplet State, 1969, Introduction to Applied Quantum Chemistry, 1971, Photophysics and Photochemistry in the Vacuum Ultraviolet, 1985, The Geometry of Genetics, 1988; editor Wiley-Interscience Monographs in Chem. Physics; contbr. over 400 articles and chpts. to profl. pubs. Fellow Research Corp., 1960-63; Sloan fellow, 1964-68; recipient award Baton Rouge Council Engring. and Sci. Socs., 1962-63; Sr. Scientist award Alexander von Humboldt Found., 1979; Disting. Research medal U. Bologna, Italy, 1979. Mem. Am. Chem. Soc. (S.W. regional award 1967, Fla. sect. award 1970, Coates award 1977), AAAS, Am. Phys. Soc. Research molecular electronic spectroscopy, electronic structure, energy transfer, molecular genetics, bioenergetics, mathematical biology, optoacoustics, optogalvanics. Home: 1056 E Lakeview Dr Baton Rouge LA 70810-4621

MCGOFF, EDYTHE ANNA, nursing administrator; b. Phila., Mar. 13, 1946; d. Edward and Ida Julianna (Damerau) Hintz; m. James Charles McGoff, May 6, 1972; children: Jennifer Leigh, James Charles II. Diploma in nursing, Albert Einstein Med. Ctr., 1969; BSN, George Mason U., 1993, postgrad., 1993—. RN, Va., W.Va., Pa.; cert. ACLS, emergency nurse, TNCC. Charge nurse emergency dept. Lower Bucks County Hosp., Bristol, Pa., 1969-72; charge nurse orthopedic dept. Winchester (Va.) Med. Ctr., 1969-72, charge nurse, asst. head nurse emergency dept., 1974-85, head nurse emergency dept., 1989-94, staff nurse emergency dept., 1989-94; dir. patient svcs. War Meml. Hosp., Berkeley Spring, W.Va., 1994—. Peer counselor Critical Incident Stress Debriefing, Winchester, 1989—; parent-to-parent facilitator Kids Are Our Concern, Winchester, 1992—; dir. vols. Emergency Nurses C.A.R.E., Winchester, 1994—; dir. disaster svcs. ARC, Winchester, 1986-92. Maj. W.Va. Air NG, 1989—. Mem. Emergency Nurses Assn. (pres. 1992-94), Air Force Assn. (v.p. mil. affairs 1994), Air NG Nurses Assn., Albert Einstein Med. Ctr. Alumni Assn. Lutheran. Avocations: sewing, reading, travel. Home: 260 Little Mountain Church Rd Winchester VA 22603-3053 Office: War Meml Hosp 1127 Fairfax St Berkeley Springs WV 25411-1717

MC GOLDRICK, JOHN GARDINER, lawyer; b. Grand View-on-Hudson, N.Y., July 25, 1932; s. Francis Michael and Elizabeth Theresa (Leitner) McG.; m. Cathleen Elinor Cloney, June 5, 1965; children: John Francis, Ann Cathleen. Student, Coll. of Holy Cross, Worcester, Mass., 1950-51; seminarian, S.J., 1951-58; AB, Fordham U., 1957; JD, Georgetown U., 1961. Bar: N.Y. 1962, U.S. Dist. Ct (so. and ea. dists.) N.Y. 1975, U.S. Ct. Appeals (2d cir.) 1975, U.S. Supreme Ct. 1975. Assoc. Lowenstein, Pitcher, Hotchkiss, Amann & Parr, N.Y.C., 1961-66, Kaye, Scholer, Fierman, Hays & Handler, N.Y.C., 1966-69; ptnr. Schulte & McGoldrick, N.Y.C., 1969-81; counsel to Gov. Hugh L. Carey, N.Y., 1981-82; ptnr. Schulte Roth & Zabel, 1983—; commr. Port Authority N.Y. and N.J., 1982-93, chair audit com., 1985-93; bd. dirs. Com. on Modern Cts., Inc., 1983-94; mem. N.Y.C. Mayor's Com. on Judiciary, 1990-93. Bd. dirs., mem. exec. com. Georgetown U., 1973-79, vice chmn. bd., 1975-79. Fellow Am. Bar Found., Am. Law Inst., N.Y. State Bar Assn. (com. on state constitution 1985-93, chmn. 1987-90, mem. ho. of dels. 1985-91, spl. com. lawyers in pub. svc. 1986-88, com. on fin. 1990-96), Assn. of Bar of City of N.Y. (com. on profl. responsibilities 1974-76, com. on grievances 1976-79, com. profl. discipline 1980, com. 2d century 1982-88, treas., mem. exec. com. 1984-87, com. on govt. ethics 1988-93), Univ. Club. Home: 111 E 80th St New York NY 10021-0334 Office: Schulte Roth & Zabel 900 3rd Ave New York NY 10022-4728

MCGOLDRICK, MARGARET MARY, hospital administrator; b. Phila., Dec. 17, 1952; d. Owen Francis McGoldrick and Helen Merrick (Welsh) Pancoast; m. Richard William Owens, Aug. 10, 1984; 1 child, Sarah Katelin. BA, Temple U., 1973, MBA, 1976. Lic. nursing home adminstr., Pa. Vice pres. Am. Med. Ctrs., Spring House, Pa., 1976-80; asst. exec. dir. Hahnemann U. Hosp., Spring House, 1980-81, assoc. exec. dir., 1982—; exec dir., ceo Medical College Pa Hosp., Philadelphia. Contbr. articles to profl. jours. Vice pres. Phoenixville (Pa.) YMCA, 1982, Delaware Valley Hosp. Laundry, Phila., 1985—; bd. dirs. Keystone Kidney Ctr., Willow Grove, Pa., 1987—. Mem. Am. Coll. Health Care Execs., Hosp. Assn. Pa., Delaware Valley Hosp. Coun., Temple U. Health Adminstrn. Alumni Assn. (pres. 1979-80). Avocations: jogging, cross country skiing, golf, bicycling, orienteering. Home: 1030 W King Rd Malvern PA 19355-3120 Office: Medical College Pa Hospital 3300 Henry Ave Philadelphia PA 19129*

MCGONIGAL, PEARL, former lieutenant governor; b. Melville, Sask., Can., June 10, 1929; d. Fred and Kathryne Kuhlman; m. Marvin A. McGonigal, Nov. 3, 1948; 1 child, Kimberly Jane. Ed., Melville, Sask.; LLD (hon.), U. Man. Formerly engaged in banking, mdse. rep., mem. St. James-Assiniboia (Man.) City Council, 1969-71; mem. Greater Winnipeg (Man.) City Council, 1971-81, chmn. com. on recreation and social services, 1977-79, dep. mayor and chmn. exec. policy com., 1979-81; lt. gov. Man., 1981-86; mem. adv. bd. Royal Trust Co., 1987—; trustee First Can. Mortgage Fund; bd. dirs. Mediacom. Inc., Can. Imperial Bank of Commerce; commr. Man. Law Reform Commn. Author: Frankly Feminine Cookbook, 1975, Bringing It All Together. Cookbook, 1990; weekly columnist: Reliance Press Ltd. Newspapers, 1970-81. Bd. dirs. Winnipeg Conv. Centre, 1975-77, Red River Exhbn., 1975-81, Rainbow Stage, 1976-81, Man. Blue Cross; ex-officio mem. Man. Theatre Centre, 1977-81; mem. Winnipeg Conv. and Visitors Bur., 1973-75, Man. Environ. Concil, 1974-76, Man. Aviation Council, 1974-77; mem. selection com. Faculty Dental Hygiene, U. Man., 197-80; bd. mgmt. Winnipeg Home Improvement Program, 1979-81; chmn. adv. com. Sch. Nursing, Grace Gen. Hosp., 1972-93; past chmn. St. James-Assiniboia Inter-faith Immigration Council; former mem. vestry St. Andrew's Anglican Ch.; former vol. Lions Manor, Sherbrook Day Centre; chmn. bd. mgmt. Grace Gen. Hosp., 1987-93; chmn. bd. reference Catherine Booth Bible Coll., 1987; commr. Man. Law Reform Commn.; campaign chmn. United Way of Winnipeg, 1990; vice chair Grey Cup Festival, '91; hon. col. 402 City of Winnipeg Squadron, 1992. Decorated dame Order of St. John; recipient award dist. 64 Toastmasters, 1974, award Elks, Winnipeg, 1975, Nat. B'nai B'rith Humanitarian award, 1984, Citizen of Yr. award KC, 1987, Order of Disting. Aux. Svc., Salvation Army, 1991, Hadassah-Wizo Woman of Yr. award, 1994; named hon. col. 735th Comm. Regt., Citizen of Yr., Chinese Cultural Ctr., 1995. Mem. Order of Can., Beta Sigma Phi (1st Lady of Yr. 1986). Liberal. Club: Winnipeg Winter. Lodge: KC (Citizen of Yr. 1987). Home: 51-361 Westwood Dr, Winnipeg, MB Canada R3K 1G4

MCGONIGLE, JAMES GREGORY, financial consultant; b. Bklyn., Nov. 17, 1945; s. William John and Helen Bernadette (Dennin) McG.; m. Francine Anne Falango, May 27, 1972; children: MarieElena, Lauren Anne. AAS in Acctg., CUNY, 1972; BS in Fin. summa cum laude, L.I. U., 1980. Cert. fin. planner Internat. Bd. Cert. Fin. Planners. Account exec. Coburn Credit Corp., Rockville Centre, N.Y., 1965-66; asst. credit mgr. UNI-CARD, Greatneck, N.Y., 1966-68; accounts receivable mgr. Granite Leasing Corp., Garden City, N.Y., 1968-73; v.p. Citicorp., N.Y.C., 1973-88; cons. O/E Learning, Inc., Detroit, 1988-90; regional dir. Ednl. Techs., Inc., Troy, Mich., 1989—; adj. faculty Coll. for Fin. Planning, Denver. Vol. Family Svc. Assn., Nassau, N.Y., 1981-84, Better Bus. Bur., Farmingdale, N.Y., 1987—; vol., career advisor L.I. U., Brookville, N.Y., 1990—; treas. W. Tresper Clarke Friends of Arts, 1988-89. Mem. ABA (assoc.), Fin. Mgmt. Assn., Internat. Assn. Fin. Planning, Adelphi Soc. Cert. Fin. Planners, Internat. Assn. Registered Fin. Planners (speaker's bur.), Nat. Assn. Life Underwriters, Nat. Panel Consumer Arbitrators, Nat. Ctr. for Fin. Edn., Inst. Cert. Fin. Planners (bd. dirs. L.I. 1989-92), N.Y. State Assn. Cert. Fin. Planners, Delta Mu Delta. Republican. Roman Catholic. Avocations: bicycling, public speaking, traveling, writing, gardening. Home: 2167 Plum Tree Rd N Westbury NY 11590-6029 Office: 33 Willis Ave Mineola NY 11501-4411

MCGONIGLE, JOHN LEO, JR., civil engineer; b. Pitts., May 2, 1921; s. John L. and Marie (Cannon) McG.; m. Mary Frances McInerney, Oct. 10, 1953; children: Loretta, John III, Maureen, Charles, Thomas, Robert. BS in Civil Engring., Lehigh U., 1942. Registered profl. engr. N.Y., Pa., Conn. Field engr. Bethlehem Steel Corp., N.Y., Boston, 1947-50, resident engr., 1950-57; constrn. mgr. Bethlehem Steel Corp., San Francisco, 1957-67; mgr. estimates Bethlehem Steel Corp., Bethlehem, Pa., 1967-78; project mgr. C. F. Braun, Berkeley Heights, N.J., 1978-83; prin. resident engr. Berger-Lehman Assocs., Rye, N.Y., 1983-93; self-employed project mgmt. cons., 1993—; com. mem. Am. Inst. Steel Constrn., Pitts., 1970-73. Mem. Hanover Twp. (Pa.) Planning Commn. Mem. Am. Soc. Engrs., Lehigh U. Alumni Assn. (pres. San Francisco 1960). Republican. Roman Catholic. Achievements include resident engineer for high level bridges over Passaic River, N.J., Rappahonnock, Va., Missouri River, Annisquam River, Mass., Raritan River, N.J., and Newark Bay; also high rise buildings in Detroit, N.Y., S.I. Ferry Terminal, John Hancock, Boston.

MCGONIGLE, RICHARD THOMAS, lawyer; b. Columbus, Ohio, Jan. 29, 1951; s. Francis Phillip and Mary Lou (Daughtery) McG.; m. Janet Christine Bowser, Aug. 17, 1974; children: Richard K., Michael P., Robin C. BA, St. Leo Coll., 1978; JD, Duquesne U., 1981. Bar: Pa. 1981, Okla. 1986, U.S. Supreme Ct. 1994, U.S. Dist. Ct. (we. dist.) Pa. 1981, U.S. Dist. Cts. (ea., we., and no. dists.) Okla. 1985, U.S. Ct. Appeals (5th and 10th cirs.) 1985. Police officer City of Hilliard, Ohio, 1973-74, City of Virginia Beach, Va., 1974-78; atty. Eckert Seamans Cherin & Mellot, Pitts., 1981-85, Hall, Estill, Tulsa, Okla., 1985-95; of counsel Ronald D. Wood & Assocs., Tulsa, 1995—; faculty mem., co-author seminar materials Nat. Bus. Inst., 1992. Author: (case notes) Duquesne Law Review, 1979. Pres. Eastwood Lake Homeowners Assn., Owasso, Okla., 1993—; mem. Associated Builders & Contractors, Inc., Tulsa, 1994—. Recipient Acad. Achievement award Franklin County Sheriff's Acad., Columbus, 1973, Honor Grad. award Fraternal Order of Police Assn., Norfolk, Va., 1975, Best Oralist award Mugel Nat. Tax Moot Ct., Buffalo, N.Y., 1980. Mem. ABA, Okla. Bar Assn., Pa. Bar Assn., Tulsa County Bar Assn., Muscogee (Creek) Nation Bar Assn. Republican. Roman Catholic. Avocations: motorcycling, hunting, fishing, camping, reading. Home: 18432 E 90th St N Owasso OK 74055-8019 Office: Ronald D. Wood & Assocs 2727 E 21st St Ste 500 Tulsa OK 74114

MCGOOHAN, PATRICK JOSEPH, actor; b. Astoria L.I., N.Y., Mar. 19, 1928; s. Thomas and Rose McG.; m. Joan Drummond, 1951; children: Ann, Frances, Catherine. Worked with Sheffield (Eng.) Repertory Co., Bristol (Eng.) Old Vic. Co. Stage debut in London in The Brontes, St. James Theatre, 1948; appeared: stage prodns. Serious Charge, London, 1955, Moby Dick, London, 1955, Pack of Lies, 1985; acted in films including: Passage Home, 1955, High Tide at Noon, 1956, Hell Drivers, 1957, The Quare Fellow, 1962, Life for Ruth, 1962, Ice Station Zebra, 1968, Mary Queen of Scots, 1972, The Genius, 1975, Silver Streak, 1976, Brass Target, 1978, Scanners, 1981, Baby...Secret of the Lost Legend, 1985, Braveheart, 1995; TV series includes: Danger Man, 1961 (in U.S. as "Secret Agent" 1965-66), The Prisoner, 1968-69, Rafferty, 1977; TV movies include: The Man in the Iron Mask, 1978, Koroshi, 1978, 3 Sovereigns for Sarah, 1985, Jamaica Inn, 1985; wrote, directed and appeared in various episodes in Columbo series. Recipient Brit. award for best TV actor of yr. 1963, Brit. award for best stage actor of yr. in play Brand, 1959, Emmy award Nat. Acad. TV Arts and Scis., 1975. Office: care Jack Fields and Assocs 9255 W Sunset Blvd Ste 1105 Los Angeles CA 90069-3308 also: Directors Guild of America 7920 W Sunset Blvd Los Angeles CA 90046-3300*

MC GOON, DWIGHT CHARLES, retired surgeon, educator; b. Marengo, Iowa, Mar. 24, 1925; s. Charles Douglas and Ada Belle (Buhlman) McG.; m. Betty Lou Hall, Apr. 2, 1948; children: Michael, Susan, Betsy, Sarah. Student, Iowa State U., 1942-43, St. Ambrose Coll., Davenport, Iowa, 1943-44; M.D., Johns Hopkins U., 1948. Intern Johns Hopkins Hosp., 1948-49, resident in surgery, 1949-54; cons. in surgery Mayo Clinic, Rochester, Minn., 1957—; Stuart W. Harrington prof. surgery Mayo Med. Sch., 1975-79. Editor-in-chief: Jour. Thoracic and Cardiovascular Surgery, 1977-87; editorial bd.: Circulation, 1970-76, Surgery, 1971-77, Am. Jour. Cardiology, 1969-77, Am. Heart Jour, 1969-76; contbr. numerous articles to profl. jours. Served with USN, 1943-45; with M.C. USAF, 1954-56. Fellow ACS; mem. Am. Assn. Thoracic Surgery (pres. 1983-84), Am. Coll. Cardiology (trustee 1979-83), Am. Surg. Assn., Soc. Clin. Surgery, Soc. Univ. Surgeons, Johns Hopkins Soc. Scholars, Phi Beta Kappa, Alpha Omega Alpha. Presbyterian. Home: 706 12th Ave SW Rochester MN 55902-2028 Office: Mayo Clinic 200 1st St SW Rochester MN 55905-0001

MCGOUGH, DUANE THEODORE, economist, government official; b. Rice Lake, Wis., Aug. 3, 1932; s. James Patrick and Josephine Margaret (Huerth) McG.; m. Donna Mae Jones, June 13, 1959. Student, Wis. State Coll., Eau Claire, 1950-52, U. Wis., 1952-54, 56-60; B.S. in Light Constrn. Industry, U. Wis., 1959, M.B.A. in Urban Land Econs., 1962; postgrad., U. So. Calif., 1968-69. Housing mgmt. officer Pub. Housing Adminstrn. Atlanta, 1960-62; program planning analyst Pub. Housing Adminstrn. Phila., 1962-67; program analyst HUD, Washington, 1967-68, 69-70; industry economist HUD, 1970-73, supervisory economist, 1973-77, dir. housing and demographic analysis, 1977—, govt. tech. rep. ann. housing survey, 1977-83; govt. tech. rep. Am. Housing Survey, 1984—; acting dep. asst. sec. for econ. affairs (chief economist) HUD, Washington, 1977, 82, 84-85; U.S. rep housing subcom. UN Econ. Commn. for Europe, Geneva, 1976, 79, 82; HUD rep. Interagy. Com. on Population Rsch., 1978—, Interagy. Forum on Aging-Related Stats., 1986—; mem. Fed. Task Force on Household Survey Redesign, 1988—; mem. policy com. Year 2000Census. Editor: President's Report on Housing Goals, 1974-78, Nat. Housing Prodn. Report, 1980, 82; sec. Quarterly U.S. Housing Market Conditions Report, 1994—. With U.S. Army, 1954-56; saxophonist 7th Army Band. Fellow NAt. Inst. Pub. Affairs, 1969; recipient Outstanding Performance award Pub. Housing Adminstrn., Phila., 1966, HUD, 1984, 92, Career Edn. award Nat. Inst. Pub. Affairs, 1968-69, Cert. Spl. Achievement, HUD, 1978, 83, 84, Cert. Superior Svc., HUD, 1988, Cert. Appreciation, Bur. Census, 1990. Mem. Am. Econ. Assn., Am. Real Estate and Urban Econ. Assn., Nat. Economists Club, Lambda Alpha Internat. (v.p. programs 1987-89, chmn. real estate and fin. com. George Washington chpt. 1990-92, dir.-at-large 1992-93). Avocations: music, gardening, rockhounding. Office: HUD Office Econ Affairs 7th and D Sts SW Washington DC 20410

MCGOUGH, JOHN PAUL, conveyor and power transmission company executive; b. Pitts., June 14, 1935; s. Patrick J. and Adelean R. (Skillen) McG.; m. Alice M. Gase, Feb. 15, 1958 (div. Dec. 1974); children: Mary G., Paul, Daniel J., Timothy F.X. Student, St. Vincent Coll., Latrobe, Pa., 1953-57; BA, DePaul U., Chgo., 1966; MA, Montclair State Coll., 1973. Sales rep. Shields Rubber Corp., Pitts., 1957-62; dist. mgr. Fabreeka Products Co., Skokie, Ill., 1962-67; regional mgr. Fabreeka Products Co., Wayne, N.J., 1967-75, Continental Rubber Works, Erie, Pa., 1975-76; dir. mktg. Daneline Inc., Kenilworth, N.J., 1976-80; exec. v.p., chief exec. officer Volta Internat., Livingston, N.J., 1980-83; pres., chief exec. officer J. E. Rhoads & Sons Inc., Newark, Del., 1983-90, vice chmn., 1990—. Mem. county com. Wayne Dem. Orgn., 1968-72; vice chmn. Wayne Dem. Club, 1969-70 . With U.S. Army, 1957-62. Mem. Pitts. Athletic Club. Unitarian.

MCGOUGH, WALTER THOMAS, JR., lawyer; b. Pitts., Nov. 7, 1953; s. Walter Thomas and Jane (Fitzpatrick) McG.; m. Rebecca Gai Frazier, June 24, 1978; children: Emily Ann, Walter Thomas III. BA, Princeton U., 1975; JD, U. Va., 1978. Bar: Pa., D.C., U.S. Dist. Ct. (we. dist.) Pa. 1980, U.S. Ct. Appeals (3d cir.) 1983, U.S. Ct. Appeals (6th cir.) 1984, Pa. Supreme Ct. 1978, U.S. Supreme Ct. 1983. Law clk. to judge U.S. Ct. Appeals 3d Cir., Wilmington, Del., 1978-79; law clk. to Hon. William H. Rehnquist U.S. Supreme Ct., Washington, 1979-80; asst. U.S. atty. We. Dist. Pa., 1980-82; assoc. Reed, Smith, Shaw & McClay, Pitts., 1982-86, ptnr., 1987—; assoc. counsel Sen. Select Com. on Secret Mil. Asst. to Iran and the Nicaraguan Opposition, Washington, 1987; mem. lawyers adv. com. U.S. Ct. Appeals (3d cir.), 1987-89, chmn., 1989; atty. Fed. Criminal Justice Def. Panel West Dist. Pa., 1983—. Contbr. articles to profl. jours. Mem. Allegheny County (Pa.) Bd. Assistance, 1986-90, chmn., 1989-90; bd. visitors H. John Heinz III Pub. Policy and Mgmt., Carnegie-Mellon U., Pitts., 1987—; mem. 3d Cir. Task Force on Rule 11, 1987-89. Mem. Allegheny County Bar Assn. (ethics com. 1983-86, bd. gov.'s 1994—), Allegheny County Acad. Trial Lawyers, Duquesne Club, Ross Mountain Club, World Affairs Coun. Office: Reed Smith Shaw & McClay 435 6th Ave Pittsburgh PA 15219-1809

MCGOVERN, BARBARA ELIZABETH ANN, elementary education educator; b. Newton, Mass., July 24, 1936; d. Joseph and Katherine Frances (Broderick) McG. BS in Edn., Lowell State Tchrs. Coll., 1957; postgrad., Salem State Coll., 1959-64, Andover-Newton Theol. Sem., 1965-68. Cert. tchr., Mass. 2d grade tchr. Thomson Sch., North Andover, Mass., 1957-58; 1st, 4th and 5th grade tchr. Franklin Sch., North Andover, 1958-95, coord. various intergenerational programs, 1970-95, ret., 1995; owner B.E.A.M.S Dreams, North Andover, 1994-95; cons. City of Lawrence Youth Commn., 1993—; panelist Holy Cross Coll., 1993. Camp counselor, 1952-70; tchr. arts and crafts Lawrence Jewish Comty. Ctr., 1954-55; asst. coach 6th-8th grade Girl's Basketball and Softball and Jr. Varsity Softball, 1958-67; sec. Kings Daus., 1958-65; leader Girl Scouts Am., 1960-63; vol. Civil Def., 1965-68; coord. holiday programs Franklin Sch., 1970-93, 95-96, Spl. Friends Program, 1989-95, 96, Hobby Show, 1982-95, 96, Audio Visual com., Pen Pals with City of Lawrence Sch., 1989-95; sec. North Andover PTO, 1970-74, v.p., 1974-79, rep., 1979-84, chair social com., 1972-90; day capt. Ground Observer Corp., Methuen, Mass., 1958-65; softball umpire ASA, 1974-76; supt. Sunday sch. Lawrence St. Congl. Ch., 1958-67, tchr., 1951-57, asst. ch. flower com., 1957-67; leader jr. and sr. pilgrim fellowships, 1957-67, also mem. choir; coach bantam group Pro Bowl, North Reading, Mass., 1990—; coun. mem. Sch. Improvement, 1985-90; active Matching Families with Shut Ins in Chs., 1994—; mem. Trinitarian Congl. Ch., 1995—; mem. Interfaith Choir, Derry, N.H., 1995—; vol. cons. North Andover Sch. Sys., 1995; mem. 350th Anniversary North Andover commn., 1995-96; coord. Carvell chpt. Blind in Merrimack Valley, 1995-96. Recipient citation of recognition Mass. Ho. of Reps., 1988, Congressman Chet Akins, 1988, award Nevins Home, 1988, Point of Light award Eagle Tribine, 1990, Those Who Care award Elder Svcs. of Merrimack Valley, 1990, Living Tribute award Acad. Manor Nursing Home, 1990, plaque Prescott Nursing Home, 1992, Sportsmanship award Lawrence Recreation Women's Softball League, 1989, 90. Mem. AARP, Mass. Intergenerational Network (sec. 1991—), North Andover Tchrs. Assn., Lawrence Sports Club (life, bd. dirs. 1972-73, v.p. 1973-75, pres. 1975-84). Republican. Avocations: softball, ten pin bowling, Mickey Mouse, drawing, painting. Home: 42 York St Andover MA 01810-2601 Office: Franklin Sch Cypress Ter North Andover MA 01845

MCGOVERN, DOUGLAS EDWARD, mechanical engineer; b. Schenectady, N.Y., Apr. 15, 1946; s. Arthur Douglas and Virginia Seibert McGovern; divorced; children: Thomas A., Robert D., Joanna M. BS with distinction, Northwestern U., 1968; MS in Elec. Engring., U. N.Mex., 1972; MS in Mech. Engring., Stanford U., 1969, PhD, 1975. Design engr., project leader Sandia Nat. Labs., Albuquerque, 1969-82; mgr. Dallas Devel. Lab. Gearhart Industries, Inc., Ft. Worth, 1982-83; unit mgr., staff engr. Govt. Comm. Systems, RCA, Camden, N.J., 1983-85; project leader Sandia Nat. Labs., Albuquerque, 1985-89, dep. mgr., 1989—. Contbr. articles to profl. jours.; patentee in field. Mem. Sigma Xi, Tau Beta Pi, Sigma Tau, Pi Tau Sigma, Phi Eta Sigma. Avocation: refereeing soccer games. Home: 6621 Orphelia Ave NE Albuquerque NM 87109-3752

MC GOVERN, GEORGE STANLEY, former senator; b. Avon, S.D., July 19, 1922; s. Joseph C. and Frances (McLean) McG.; m. Eleanor Stegeberg, Oct. 31, 1943; children: Ann, Susan, Teresa, Steven, Mary. BA, Dakota Wesleyan U., 1945; MA, Northwestern U., 1949, PhD, 1953. Prof. history and polit. sci. Dakota Wesleyan U., 1949-53; exec. sec. S.D. Dem. Party, 1953-55; mem. 85th-86th Congresses, 1st Dist. S.D.; spl. asst. to Pres., dir. Food for Peace, 1961-62; U.S. senator from S.D., 1963-81, chmn. senate select com. on nutrition and human needs; pres. Middle East Policy Coun.; chmn. Ams. for Common Sense, Washington, 1981-82; guest lectr. Northwestern U., Evanston, Ill., Duke U., Columbia U., Cornell U., Munich, Berlin, and numerous others in U.S. and Europe, from 1981. Author: The Colorado Coal Strike, 1913-14, 1953, War Against Want, 1964, Agricultural Thought in the Twentieth Century, 1967, A Time of War, A Time of Peace, 1968, (with Leonard Guttridge) The Great Coalfield War, 1972, An American Journey, 1974, Grassroots, 1978. Democratic candidate for Pres. U.S., 1972; candidate for presdl. nomination Dem. Party, 1984. Served as pilot USAAF, World War II. Decorated D.F.C. Mem. Am. Hist. Assn. Methodist. Clubs: Mason (33 deg., Shriner), Elk, Kiwanian. *

MCGOVERN, JOHN HUGH, urologist, educator; b. Bayonne, N.J., Dec. 18, 1924; s. Patrick and Mary (McGovern) McG.; m. Mary Alice Cavazos, Aug. 2, 1980; children by previous marriage: John Hugh, Robert, Ward, Raymond. BS, Columbia U., 1947; MD, SUNY, Bklyn., 1952. Diplomate Am. Bd. Urology. Rotating intern Bklyn. Hosp., 1952-53; asst. resident in surgery Bklyn. VA Hosp., 1953-54; with urology N.Y. Hosp., 1954-56; exchange surg. registrar West London Hosp., Eng., 1956-57; resident in urol. surgery N.Y. Hosp., 1957-58, rsch. asst. pediatric urology, 1958-59, asst. attending surgeon James Buchanan Brady Found., 1959-61, assoc. attending surgeon, 1961-66, attending surgeon, 1966—; asst. in surgery Med. Coll. Cornell U., 1957-59, asst. prof. clin. surgery, 1959-64, assoc. prof., 1964-72, prof., 1972—; attending staff in urology Lenox Hill Hosp., 1969—, in-charge urology, 1969-83; cons. urology Rockefeller Inst., St. Vincent's Hosp., Mercy Hosp., Phelps Meml. Hosp.; chmn. coun. on urology Nat. Kidney Found., 1982. Contbr. articles to profl. jours., chpts. to books. Lt. M.C., U.S. Army, 1942-45. Recipient Conatvoy mos medal Chile, 1975, Tree of Life award Nat. Kidney Found., 1990; named Huesped de Honor, Mimunicipalidad de Guayaquil (Ecuador), 1976; award in urology Kidney Found. N.Y., 1977, Sir Peter Freyer medal, Galway, Ireland, 1980. Fellow N.Y. Acad. Medicine (exec. com. urol. sect. 1968-72, chmn. 1972), ACS (credentials com. 1991—), Am. Acad. Pediatrics (urological); mem. AMA (diagnostic and therapeutic tech. assessment bd. 1991—, diagnostic and therapeutic tech. assessment program panel 1991, DATTA panel 1991—), Am. Assn. G.U. Surgeons, N.Y. State Med. Soc. (chmn. urol. sect. 1975), Med. Soc. County N.Y., Am. Urol. Assn. (hon. mem. 1994—, pres.-elect 1988-89, pres. 1989-90, pres. N.Y. sect. 1979-80, N.Y. rep. exec. com. 1982-87, socioecons. com. 1987, chmn. fiscal affairs rev. com. 1987, chmn. awards com. 1990, time and place com. 1989-90), N.Y. State Urol. Soc. (exec. com. 1982—), Pan Pacific Surg. Assn., Am. Assn. Clin. Urologists (pres.-elect 1987-88, pres. 1988-89, bd. dirs. 1984—, mem. interpersonal rels. com. 1975—, govt. rels. com. 1989-90, program com. 1989-90, nominating com. 1979—90), Assn. Am. Physicians and Surgeons, Pan Am. Med. Assn. (diplomate 1981—), Urol. Investigators Forum, Soc. Pediatric Urology (pres.-elect 1979-80, pres. 1980-81), Am. Trauma Soc., Kidney Found. (med. adv. bd. N.Y. sect., trustee, 1979) Société Internationale d'Urologie (exec. com. U.S. sect.); hon. mem. Sociedad Peruana de Urología, Sociedad Guatemale de Urología, Sociedad Ecuadorians de Urología, Royal Coll. Surgeons (London). Home and Office: 53 E 70th St New York NY 10021-4941

MCGOVERN, JOHN JOSEPH, retired air pollution control executive; b. Pitts., June 21, 1920; s. John J. and Philomene (Henigin) McG.; m. Doris I. Judy, Sept. 25, 1947 (dec. 1986); children: John Joseph, Joseph Edgar, Daniel Paul, Michael James, William Patrick, Edward Vernon; m. Patricia E. Carothers, Apr. 1987. B.S., Carnegie Inst. Tech., 1942, M.S., 1944, Sc.D., 1946. Fellow, then sr. fellow Mellon Inst., Pitts., 1945-50; head research services Mellon Inst., 1958-71; dir. edn1. and research services Carnegie-Mellon U., 1971-73, asst. dir. div. sponsored research, 1973; asst. dir. Carnegie-Mellon Inst. Research, 1974-76; info. scientist U. Pitts., 1976—; edn. services mgr. Air Pollution Control Assn., 1979-83, mem. services mgr., 1983-87; now ret.; asst. chief chemist, then chief chemist Koppers Co., Inc., 1950-58. Editor: The Crucible, 1970-76. Mem. Spectroscopy Soc. Pitts. (chmn. 1951), Am. Chem. Soc. (sec. Pitts. 1960, chmn. sect. 1964, dir.), PITTCON (pres. 1951). Club: Chemists (pres. Pitts. 1968-69). Home: 1606 Parkline Dr # 4 Pittsburgh PA 15227-1645

MCGOVERN, MICHAEL BARBOT, lawyer; b. N.Y.C., Mar. 6, 1947; s. Michael Malachy and Annette (Barbot) McG.; m. Christine Anne Beaudet, Sept. 2, 1972; children: Kathleen, Ellen, Maura. AB, Georgetown U., 1969, JD, 1972; LLM (Taxation), George Washington U., 1987. From assoc. to ptnr. Wilkes & Artis, Washington, 1973-79; sole practice Washington, 1980, 84-87; ptnr. Lambert, Griffin & McGovern, Washington, 1981-84, Venable, Baetjer, Howard & Civiletti, Washington, 1987-93; counsel Montedoninco, Hamilton & Altman, D.C., 1994—. Bd. dirs. Hist. Soc. Washington, 1984-93; co-founder, vice-chair, bd. dirs. Greater Bethesda-Chevy Chase Coalition Inc., 1986—; pres. Westmoreland Citizens Assn. Inc., 1988-90; mem. Leadership Washington, 1987—. Capt. USAFR, 1969-82. Recipient Distinguished Service award Fed. Bar Assn., 1978. Mem. ABA, Fed. Bar Assn., D.C. Bar Assn., Md. State Bar Assn., Columbia Country Club (Chevy Chase), Met. Club (Washington), Barristers, John Carroll Soc. Republican. Catholic. Home: 5414 Albemarle St Bethesda MD 20816-1825 Office: Montedonico Hamilton & Altman 5301 Wisconsin Ave NW Ste 400 Washington DC 20015-2015

MCGOVERN, PATRICK J., communications executive. BA in Physics, M.I.T. With Internat. Data Corp., Framingham, Mass., 1964—, chmn., 1976—; with IDG Comm. Inc., Framingham, 1987—. Office: Internat Data Group One Exeter Plaza Boston MA 02116*

MCGOVERN, R(ICHARD) GORDON, food company executive; b. Norristown, Pa., Oct. 22, 1926; s. James Joseph and Marion (Stritzinger) McG.; m. Julia Merrow, June 4, 1955; children: Lucinda, Jennifer, Martha, Douglas. Student, Williams Coll., 1944-45, Coll. Holy Cross, 1945-46; AB, Brown U., 1948; MBA, Harvard U., 1950. With Pepperidge Farm, Inc., 1956-80, pres., 1968-80; dir., v.p. Campbell Soup Co., 1976-80, exec. v.p., 1980, pres., 1980-89, ret., 1989; bd. dirs. Merrow Machine Co., Newington, Conn., George Weston Ltd., Toronto. Lt. USNR, 1944-46, 52-54. Mem. Am. Mktg. Assn., Am. Soc. Bakery Engrs., Grocery Mfrs. Assn. (past. bd. dirs.), Phi Beta Kappa, Sigma Xi, Delta Upsilon. Home: 182 Lounsbury Rd Ridgefield CT 06877-4725

MCGOVERN, THOMAS AQUINAS, retired utility executive; b. N.Y.C., Mar. 2, 1933; s. Thomas Aquinas and Helen Frances (Carroll) McG.; m. Miriam Anne Howley, July 16, 1955; children: Cecilia, Louise, Pamela. BS in History, Coll. of the Holy Cross, 1954; MA in Econs., L.I. U., 1965. Dep. asst. Consol. Edison Co. of N.Y., N.Y.C., 1958-61, supts. asst., 1961-66, asst. supt., 1967-68, supt., 1968-69, staff dir., 1969-70, asst. to exec. v.p., 1970-72, exec. dir., 1972-82, asst. v.p., 1982-89, v.p., 1989-95; sr. assoc. John Hall Co., Danbury, Conn., 1995—; mem. Edison Elec. Inst. Sec. Commn., Washington, 1976-90, Mailers' Tech. Adv. Com., Washington, 1990-91; vice-chmn. Nat. Postal Coun., Washington, 1982—; pres. D.C.K. Mgmt. Corp., N.Y.C., 1982—; mem. Real Estate Bd. N.Y., N.Y.C., 1988—. Mem. N.Y.C. (N.Y.) Health and Hosps. Security Adv. Com., 1985; pres. Westchester County Police Meml., White Plains, N.Y., 1987—. With U.S. Army, 1954-56. Recipient Svcs. to Nation and FBI award FBI, N.Y.C., 1984, Svc. to Law Enforcement Community award N.Y. State Chiefs of Police, Albany, N.Y., 1989, Appreciation for Svc. award N.Y. State Fedn. of Police, Briarcliff Manor, N.Y., 1989, Svc. to Orgns. award FBI Marine Corps Assn., Cresskill, N.J., 1989, Svc. to Orgns. award N.Y.C. Honor Legion, Richmond Hill, N.Y. Mem. KC, Am. Legion, Assn. of U.S. Army, U.S. Naval Inst., FBI Marine Corps Assn., Friendly Sons of St. Patrick, Pi Gamma Mu. Roman Catholic. Avocations: U.S. mil. history, post card collecting, toy soldier collecting, Royal Doulton china collecting.

MCGOVERN, THOMAS JOHN, environmental engineer; b. Rockville Ctr., N.Y., May 31, 1968; s. Thomas Edward and Barbara Ann (Bukoski) McG. BSCE, U. Hartford, 1990; JD, St. Johns Sch. Law, 1995. Engr. Suffolk County Dept. Health Svcs., Farmingville, N.Y., 1988, N.Y.C. Dept. Environ. Protection, 1989; environ. engr. Camp Dresser and McKee, Woodbury, N.Y., 1990—. Contbr. articles to profl. jours.; speaker in field. Mem. ABA, Water Environ. Fedn., Tau Beta Pi, Sigma Xi, Alpha Chi. Home: 24 Sycora Ln Central Islip NY 11722 Office: Camp Dresser & McKee 100 Crossways Park W Woodbury NY 11797

MC GOVERN, WALTER T., federal judge; b. Seattle, May 24, 1922; s. C. Arthur and Anne Marie (Thies) McG.; m. Rita Marie Olsen, June 29, 1946; children: Katrina M., Shawn E., A. Renee. B.A., U. Wash., 1949, LL.B., 1950. Bar: Wash. 1950. Practiced law in Seattle, 1950-59; mem. firm Kerr, McCord, Greenleaf & Moen; judge Municipal Ct., Seattle, 1959-65, Superior Ct., Wash., 1965-68, Wash. Supreme Ct., 1968-71, U.S. Dist. Ct. (we. dist.) Wash., 1971—; chief judge, 1975-87; mem. subcom. on supporting personnel Jud. Conf. U.S., 1981-87, chmn. subcom., 1983, mem. adminstrn. com., 1983-87, chmn. jud. resources com., 1987-91. Mem. Am. Judicature Soc., Wash. State Superior Ct. Judges Assn., Seattle King County Bar Assn. (treas.), Phi Delta Phi. Club: Seattle Tennis (pres. 1968). Office: US Dist Ct US Courthouse 5th Fl 1010 5th Ave Seattle WA 98104-1130

MCGOWAN, DAVID, broadcast executive. BA in History cum laude, Yale U., 1982. Mem. MIS profl. staff Morgan Stanley & Co., N.Y.C., 1982-84; editor-in-chief, publisher Prism Mag., N.Y.C., 1983-85; tchr. history Collegiate Sch., N.Y.C., 1984-86; dir. media development and exec. prodr. TIME Mag., N.Y.C., 1986-91; sr. v.p. news, pub. affairs and program prodn. WETA, Washington, D.C., 1992—. Exec.-in-charge: (TV) Washington Week in Review, 1992—, Convention Night in Review, 1992, For the Living, 1993, Challenge to America, 1994, Coming and Going, 1994, Off Limits, 1994, Inside the FBI, 1995, Mystery of the Senses, 1995, Here and Now, 1995; exec. prodr. or co-prodr.: (TV) TIME Man of the Yr., 1987-91, Images of the 80's, 1988, 1968, 1988, Man in Space, 1989, You've Come the Wrong Way, Maybe, 1990, Vision of Freedom, 1990; co-prodr.: (TV) The Defense of Europe, 1988, The Choice, 1988, Forum on Cambodia, 1989, Forum on Guns, 1989; writer: (TV) TIME Man of the Yr., 1986; exec. prodr.: (interactvie multimedia) NewsQuest, 1985-88, Desert Storm, 1991, Seven Days in August, 1993, Washington Week in Review Online, 1994. Avocations: music (Whiffenpoofs of 1982), skiing, bicycling, squash. Office: WETA PO Box 2626 Washington DC 20013

MCGOWAN, GEORGE VINCENT, public utility executive; b. Balt., Jan. 30, 1928; s. Joseph H. and Ethna M. (Prahl) McG.; m. Carol Murray, Aug. 6, 1977; children by a previous marriage: Gregg Blair, Bradford Kirby. BS in M.E., U. Md., 1951; LHD (hon.), Villa Julie Coll., 1991, Loyola Coll., Md., 1992. Registered profl. engr., Md. Project engr. nuclear power plant Balt. Gas & Electric Co., 1967-72, chief nuclear engr., 1972-74, pres., chief operating officer, 1980-87, chmn. bd. dirs., CEO, 1988-92, chmn. exec. com., 1993—, mgr. corp. staff services, 1974-78, v.p. mgmt. and staff services, 1978-79; bd. dirs. Balt. Life Ins. Co., McCormick & Co., Life of Md., Inc., UNC Inc., Orgn. Resources Counselors, Inc., NationsBank, N.A. Bd. dirs. U. Md. Med. Sys., United Way Ctrl. Md., Coll. Bound Found., Md. Pride of Balt.; chmn. Balt. Symphony Orch. Recipient Disting. Alumnus award U. Md. Coll. Engring., 1980, U. Md., 1987, Disting. Marylander award Advt. and Profl. Club Balt., 1992, Disting. Citizen award U. Md., 1991, Disting. Citizen of Yr. award Balt. Coun. Boy Scouts Am., 1991, Disting. Alumnus award Balt. Poly. Inst., 1992, Nat. Multiple Sclerosis Soc. Corp. Honoree, Md. chpt., 1993, Outstanding Vol. Fund Raiser award Nat. Soc. Fund Raising Execs., 1993, Pub. Affairs award Md. Bus. Coun., 1994, United States Energy award, 1995. Mem. ASME (James N. Landis medal 1992), Am. Nuclear Soc., U.S. Energy Assn. of the World Energy Conf., Engring. Soc. Balt. (Founders Day award 1988), Caves Valley Golf Club, The Ctr. Club (pres. bd. govs.), U. Md. M. Club, Talbot Country Club, Annapolis Yacht Club, Md. Club. Presbyterian. Office: Balt Gas & Electric Co PO Box 1475 Baltimore MD 21203-1475

MCGOWAN, HAROLD, real estate developer, investor, scientist, author, philanthropist; b. Weehawken, N.J., June 23, 1909; s. Sylvester and Grace (Kalbfleish) McG.; m. Anne Cecelia McTiernan, Jan. 15, 1938; children—Linda Anne, Harold Charles, Janice Marie. Ed., Bklyn. Poly. U., Pratt Inst., N.Y. U.; student, N.Y. Tech.; ed., Hubbard U. (Eng.); D.Sc., Coll. Fla. Chmn. bd. Atomic Rsch. Inc.; pres. Harold McGowan Builders; owner, developer Central Islip Shopping Center, Central Islip Indsl. Center; developer, builder Brinsley Gardens, Rolling Green, Slater Park, Clover Green, Maple Acres, Wheeler Acres; owner-donor Little League Baseball Pks. Sculptures include: Bless Them; Victory, Eternity, Love and Hate, Triumph; author: Green Flight, (originator) The Thoughtron Theory of Life and Matter, Race with Death across the Sahara, The Incorrigibles, The Frigid Trap, The Shah's Swiss Secret, Another World for Christmas, The Spirit of Christmas in Words and Sculpture, The Making of a Universalist, The Journeyman, $800,000 for Love, Beyond the Visible, Shock after Shock, Christmas Stories, Short Stories, Born Again, You Are Forever, Black Shroud Over Bagdad, The Gold Mine; mural Back to Creation; holder U.S. patent to form one-piece plywood corner units, U.S. patent apparatus for forming one-piece plywood corner units. Hwy. commr., Suffolk County; chmn. Recreation & Parks-Islip; past dir. Suffolk County Girl Scouts; land donor St. John of God R.C. Ch., The Episcopal Ch. of the Messiah, Ctrl. Islip Sch. Dist. Recipient Winston Churchill Medal of Wisdom, 1986, Wisdom Hall of Fame, Beverly Hills, Calif., 1970; Churchill fellow, 1989. Mem. AAAS, IEEE, Explorers Club, Mensa Internat. Avocations: sculpture, art, philanthropy. Address: 28 2nd Ave Central Islip NY 11722-3012 *To become a really whole and successful person, one should recognize the efforts and good will of those living and dead who developed the culture, the fruits of which he enjoys, and repay his benefactors by contributing more to that society than he takes and also by doing good deeds to make the society better than he found it. He must also strive to understand the world and his relationship to it and know that the universe is neither capricious nor mysterious, that miracles do not happen. Everything and every action can only occur within the bounds of the laws of physics, chemistry, biology and communication. He must further realize that he is eternal and the basic purpose of human life is to become aware of and to live by these universal laws. The acme of a person's accomplishments would be his comprehension of the structure of the physical universe, the processes of life, the nature of his mind and his own being and intelligence. Our intellect, like eternity, is unbounded. It is inde*

MC GOWAN, JAMES ATKINSON, business executive, financial consultant; b. De Soto, Mo., Nov. 10, 1914; s. James Electra and Dora Mercer (Atkinson) McG.; m. Barbara Louise Bevan, Apr. 5, 1941; m. Margaret Mercier Johns, Dec. 21, 1974; children: James Michael, John Barrie, Susan Alexandra, Jean Christine. AA, Little Rock Jr. Coll., 1934; BSChemE, Iowa State U., 1936. With Aluminum Co. Am., 1936-79; dist. sales mgr. Aluminum Co. Am., Cleve., 1959-60; gen. mgr. indsl. sales Aluminum Co. Am., Pitts., 1962-67, v.p., 1967-75; exec. v.p. Aluminum Co. Am., 1975-79; v.p. Amcan Trading Co. subs. Am. Can Corp., Pitts., 1980-81; fin. cons.; arbitrator Better Bus. Bus. Mem. AICE, Chem. Mfg. Assn. (dir.), Aluminum Assn., Nat. Assn. Corrosion Engrs., Sigma Chi. Republican. Episcopalian. Clubs: Duquesne, Fox Chapel Golf, Rolling Rock.

MCGOWAN, JOHN EDWARD, JR., clinical microbiology educator, epidemiologist, infectious diseases specialist; b. Poughkeepsie, N.Y., June 30, 1942; s. John Edward and Doris Robinson (Wearne) McG.; m. Linda Kay Hudson, May 28, 1967; 1 child, Angela Kay. B.M.S., Dartmouth Coll., 1965; M.D., Harvard U., 1967. Diplomate Am. Bd. Internal Medicine, Am. Bd. Infectious Diseases, Am. Bd. Pathology in Med. Microbiology. Intern, resident Harvard Service, Boston City Hosp., 1967-69; research fellowship Thorndike Lab. Harvard Med. Sch., 1971-72; instr. Harvard Med. Sch., Boston, 1972-73; asst. prof. Emory Med. Sch., Atlanta, 1973-76, assoc. prof., 1977-81, prof. pathology and medicine, 1982—; prof. epidemiology Emory Sch. Pub. Health, 1992—; dir. microbiology Grady Meml. Hosp., Atlanta, 1982—, asst. dir. clin. labs., 1985—. Assoc. editor, Infection Control and Hosp. Epidemiology jour., 1980-92; contbr. 200 sci. articles to profl. jours. Governing bd. Young Singers of Callanwolde, Decatur, Ga., 1981-86; treas. Leafmore Creek-Park Club, Decatur, 1982-84; mem. panel on microbial devices FDA, 1985-89, cons., 1989-91, chmn., 1992-94. Served to sr. surgeon with USPHS, 1969-71. Fellow Infectious Diseases Soc. Am. (antimicrobial agts. com. 1980-93, tuberculosis com. 1993—, governing bd. 1995—). So. Soc. for Clin. Investigation, Coll. of Am. Pathologists, Am. Coll. of Epidemiology; mem. Am. Soc. for Microbiology (div. chmn. 1982-84, governing bd. 1984-87), Soc. Hosp. Epidemiologists of Am. (pres. 1981), Am. Hosp. Assn. (panel on infections in hosps. 1989-95). Office: Emory U Sch Medicine 69 Butler St SE Atlanta GA 30303-3033

MCGOWAN, JOSEPH ANTHONY, JR., news executive; b. Sheridan, Wyo., May 16, 1931; s. Joseph Anthony and Eda B. (Harris) McG.; m. Patricia Donnette Mitchell, June 7, 1958 (div. 1980); children: Joseph Howard, Colleen Diane; m. Catherine Doris Netick, June 12, 1982; stepchildren: Nancy Malick, Diane Malick, Laura Malick. B.S., U. Wyo. Newsman AP, Miami, Fla., 1960-64; bur. chief AP, New Delhi, India, 1965-68, Lima, Peru, 1968-70, Indpls., 1970-75, Boston, 1975-78, Denver, 1978—; lectr. U. Denver, 1978—, Colo. U., Boulder, 1978—, Northeastern U., Boston, 1975-78. Scoutmaster Boy Scouts Am., Sudbury, Mass., 1977-78. Served with USNR, 1953-55. Named Disting. Alumnus, U. Wyo., 1992; Knight Internat. Press fellow to Pakistan, 1995. Mem. Denver Press Club (bd. dirs. 1989-92), Press Club Boston, Colo. Assn. Commerce and Industry (communications council 1986-89), Sigma Delta Chi (Big Hat award 1983). Republican. Avocations: bird hunting; cross country skiing; fishing, cross country bicycling. Office: AP 1444 Wazee St Ste 130 Denver CO 80202-1326

MCGOWAN, MICHAEL BENEDICT, investment banker; b. Wilkes-Barre, Pa., Jan. 21, 1950; s. John W. and Catherine (Hore) McG.; m. Nancy King, May 24, 1980; children: Nicholas King, Grace Caroline. BArch, U. Ark., 1977; MBA, U. Va., 1981. Architect Cromwell Firm, Little Rock, 1976-79; v.p. Oliver Carr Co., Washington, 1981-85; sr. v.p. Stephens Inc., Little Rock, 1985—. Mem. econ. cluster team Clinton-Gore Transition Team, Washington, 1992. Home: PO Box 542 Turner Mountain Rd Ivy VA 22945 Office: Stephens Inc 111 Center St PO Box 3507 Little Rock AR 72201

MCGOWAN, PATRICK FRANCIS, lawyer; b. N.Y.C., July 23, 1940; s. Francis Patrick and Sonia Veronica (Koslow) M.; m. Patricia Neil, June 6, 1964; children: Susan Claire, Kathleen Anne. BA, Rice U., 1962; JD, U. Tex.-Austin, 1965. Bar: Tex. 1965, U.S. Tax Ct., 1972, U.S. Ct. Appeals (5th cir.) 1969, U.S. Ct. Appeals (fed. cir.) 1993, U.S. Supreme Ct. 1970. Briefing atty. Tex. Supreme Ct., Austin, Tex., 1965-66; ptnr. Strasburger & Price, Dallas, 1966—; pres., chmn. bd. Tex Lex, Inc. Contbr. numerous articles on trademark, copyright and franchise law. Bd. advisors Dallas Ft. Worth Sch. Law. Mem. ABA (forum com. on franchising, trademark and unfair competition com., patent, trademark and copyright law sect.), State Bar Tex. (intellectual property sect., com. continuing legal edn.), Coll. State Bar Tex. (faculty Franchising inst., 1987—, Intellectual Property Inst., 1992—, S.W. Legal Found. Patent Law Inst., 1992—, Practising Law Inst. 1996), Dallas Bar Assn. (dir. intellectual property law section, 1994—), Internat. Anti Counterfeiting Assn., Tex. Law Review Editors Assn., Phi Delta Phi. Office: Strasburger & Price 4300 NationsBank Plz 901 Main St Dallas TX 75202-3714

MCGOWAN, THOMAS RANDOLPH, religious organization executive; b. Balt., Apr. 19, 1926; s. Robert and Mary (Miller) McG.; m. Bernice A. Bernard, May 20, 1967 (dec. Nov. 1981); children: Howard, James, Terry; m. Roedean Olivia Oden, Feb. 9, 1985; children: Karen White, Kevin, Kurt. AA, Oakland Jr. Coll., 1964; postgrad., San Francisco State Coll., 1964-68; BS, U. Md., 1978. Lt. security police Oakland (Calif.) Army Base, 1955-60; chief motor pool San Francisco Procurement Agy., Oakland, 1960-64, contract specialist, 1964-68; contract specialist Harry Diamond Labs., Washington, 1968-79, br. chief procurement divsn., 1972-79; chief procurement directorate Yuma (Ariz.) Proving Ground, 1979-82; dir. ecumenism Roman Cath. Diocese of Oakland, 1983—; dir. African Am. Cath. Pastoral Ctr., Diocese of Oakland, 1991—. Convenor Interreligious Coun. of Oakland, 1988—; trustee Greater Oakland Interfaith Network, 1989-92; mem. East Oakland Renewal Task Force, 1990—; bd. dir. Columbia (Md.) Found., 1972-74, chmn., 1975-79; div. Bd. Cons., Graymoor, N.Y., 1990—; bd. dirs. Thea Bowman Manor, Oakland, 1989—. With U.S. Army, 1944-46. Mem. Knights of Peter Claver, Rotary. Democrat. Avocations: tennis, woodworking. Home: 139 Pinto Dr Vallejo CA 94591-8451

MC GOWIN, WILLIAM EDWARD, artist; b. Hattiesburg, Miss., June 2, 1938; s. William Edward and Emily (Ratliff) Mc G.; m. Claudia DeMonte, May 28, 1977; children: Leah, Jill. BS, U. So. Miss., 1961; MA, U. Ala., 1964. prof. art SUNY, Old Westbury, 1978—, Coll. Old Westbury; mem. faculty Corcoran Gallery Art, 1966-77, head sculpture dept., 1967-74; lectr. in field. One-man shows include Corcoran Gallery Art, Washington, 1962, 71, 75, Martha Jackson Gallery, N.Y.C., 1968, Am. Cultural Ctr., Paris, 1974, Mus. Modern Art, Paris, 1978, Brooks Jackson Gallery, Iolas, N.Y.C., 1978-80, Fendrick Gallery, Washington, 1977-80, U. Colo., New Orleans Contemporary Art Ctr., 1982, Project Studios 1, L.I., N.Y., Cranbrook Acad., Bloomfield Hills, Mich., 1983, Art Park, Lewiston, N.Y., 1984, Gracie Mansion Gallery, N.Y.C., 1985, 86, 89, Mus. Fine Arts, Miami, Jones, Troyer Gallery, Washington, 1987, 89, 91, Boca Raton (Fla.) Mus., 1991, Margulis-Taplin Gallery, Miami, 1993, Paris-New York-Bangkok Gallery, Bangkok, Thailand, 1994, Grey Art Gallery, NYU, 1995; group shows include Contemporary Mus., Houston, Miss. Mus. Art, Whitney Mus., N.Y.C., Detroit Inst. Art, Guggenheim Mus., Speed Mus., Ky., Cologne (Germany) Art Fair, Zurich (Switzerland) Art Fair; represented in permanent collections Phillips Collection, Washington, Indpls. Mus. Art, Addison Mus. Art, Andover, Mass, Corcoran Gallery Art, Nat. Collection Fine Arts, Washington, New Orleans Mus. Art, Whitney Mus. Am. Art, N.Y.C., Guggenheim Mus., N.Y.C., Hirshorn Gallery and Sculpture Garden; commd. State of Va., 1985, Percent for Art, N.Y.C., 1992, City of Jubai, Saudi Arabia, 1993, Dallas Rapid Transit Authority, 1994, VA (sculpture, Ind.), GSA (sculpture, Miss.). Recipient Oscar for painting, 1977, Painting prize 9th Internat. Painting Festival, Cagnes-sur-Mer, France, 1977, Miss. Arts and Letters award for visual arts, 1980; Nat. Endowment for Arts grantee, 1967-68, 79-80; pub. outdoor sculpture grantee, 1977, 79; GSA grantee, 1978-79; Cassandra Found. grantee. Home and Office: 96 Grand St New York NY 10013-2660

MCGRADY, CLYDE A., secondary school principal. Prin. A. S. Staley Mid. Sch., Americus, Ga. Recipient Elem. Sch. Recognition award U.S. Dept. Edn., 1989-90. Office: A S Staley Middle Sch 915 N Lee St Americus GA 31709-3047

MCGRADY, DONALD LEE, retired Spanish language educator; b. Greenhurst, Md., Jan. 17, 1935; s. Francis Guy and Lida Amelia (Ewing) McG.; m. Marina Ignacia Pedroza, Sept. 6, 1958; children: Martha, Sandra, Daniel, Arthur. BA, Swarthmore Coll., 1957; AM, Harvard, 1958; PhD, Indiana Univ., 1961. Instr. U. Tex., Austin, 1961-63, asst. prof., 1963-64; asst. prof. U. Calif., Santa Barbara, 1964-67, assoc. prof., 1967-69; assoc. prof. U. Va., Charlottesville, 1969-71, prof., 1971-94; prof. emeritus, 1994—; vis. assoc. prof. U. Calif., Berkeley, 1969. Author: La Novela Histórica en Colombia, 1877-1959, 1962, Mateo Alemán, 1968, Critical edition of Jorge Isaacs María, 1970, Bibliografía sobre Jorge Isaacs, 1971, Jorge Isaacs, 1972, Critical edition of Cristóbal de Tamariz Novelas en verso, 1974, Critical edition of Lope de Vega's La francesilla, 1981, Edition of Lope de Vega's La bella malmaridada, 1986, Critical edition of Lope de Vega, Fuente Ovejuna, 1993. Guggenheim fellow Guggenheim Found., N.Y., 1972-73, NEH fellow NEH, Washington, 1976-77. Mem. Asociación Internacional de Hispanistas, Asociación Internacional Siglo de Oro., Comediantes. Home: 530 N 1st St Charlottesville VA 22902-4613

MCGRATH, ANNA FIELDS, librarian; b. Westfield, Maine, July 4, 1932; d. Fred Elber and Nancy Phyllis (Tarbell) Fields; m. Bernard McGrath (div.); children: Timothy, Maureen, Patricia, Colleen, Rebecca. BA, U. Maine, Presque Isle, 1976; MEd, U. So. Maine, 1979; MLS, U. R.I., 1982. Libr. U. Maine, Presque Isle, 1976-86, assoc. libr. dir., 1986-89, interim libr. dir., 1989-92, dir., 1992-94, spl. coll. libr., 1994—. Editor: County: Land of Promise, 1989. Mem. Friends of Aroostook County Hist. Ctr. at Libr., U. Maine-Presque Isle. Mem. ALA, Maine Libr. Assn., Friends of Arrostook County Hist. Ctr. at Libr. U. Maine-Presque Isle, Inst. Noetic Scis., Am. Mensa. Office: U Maine Libr 181 Main St Presque Isle ME 04769-2888

MCGRATH, CHERYL JULIA, elementary education educator; b. Milw., Feb. 17, 1947; d. Elmer William and Marjorie (Bleiler) Scherkenbach; m. Robert Edward McGrath, July 25, 1970; children: Edward, Erin, Molly. BA in Edn., Alverno Coll., Milw., 1969. Cert. tchr., Wis. Tchr. grade 1 Greenfield (Wis.) Pub. Schs., 1969-72, St. Lawrence Sch., Wisconsin Rapids, Wis., 1972-80; tchr. grades 7-8 Our Lady Queen of Heaven, Wisconsin Rapids, Wis., 1980-85; substitute work Wisconsin Rapids (Wis.) Pub. Schs., 1987-88, tchr. grade 2, 1988—; bd. mem. Girl Scouts Samoset Coun., Stevens Point, Wis., 1979-84; com. Math Their Way, 1992-94, Report Card, 1990-93, Able Learner, 1990-92, Peer Tutoring, 1989-91, Wisconsin Rapids Pub. Schs. Recipient Advance Religious Cert. award Diocese of Lacrosse, Wis., 1978. Mem. NEA, Wis. Rapids Edn. Assn., Wis. Edn. Assn., Alverno Coll. Alumnae Assn. Republican. Roman Catholic. Avocations: reading, boating, early childhood development, travel, computer programming. Home: 4711 Townline Rd Wisconsin Rapids WI 54494-8988 Office: Wisconsin Rapids Pub Schs 510 Peach St Wisconsin Rapids WI 54494-4663

MCGRATH, DANIEL BERNARD, newspaper editor; b. Chgo., Apr. 9, 1950; s. James Joseph and Margaret Mary (Mackey) McG.; m. Jo-Anna Marie Grannon, Nov. 27, 1971; children—Megan, Matthew. Grad., Marquette U., 1972. Sports editor Freeport Jour. Standard, Ill., 1972-75; sports writer, columnist Nev. State Jour., Reno, 1975-77; sports editor Sacramento Union, 1977-79, San Francisco Chronicle, 1979—. Editor: "Super Season" San Francisco 49ers, 1984, 1984. Recipient Nev. Sportswriter of Yr. award Nat. Assn. Sportswriters, Sportscasters, 1976-77; Best Sports Sect. award Calif. Newspaper Pubs. Assn., 1978; Best sports Story award San Francisco Press Club, 1983. Mem. AP Sports Editors. Democrat. Roman Catholic. Avocations: golf; reading; movies. Home: 194 Ashland Dr Daly City CA 94015-3406 Office: The Sacramento Bee 21st & Q Sts PO Box 15779 Sacramento CA 95852

MCGRATH, DENNIS BRITTON, public relations executive; b. Mpls., Mar. 11, 1937; s. James William and Rosalia Clara (Britton) McG.; m. Susan J. Smith, Apr. 15, 1961 (div. 1972); children: Daniel Scott, Amy Susan; m. Elizabeth Ann Buckley, Sept. 15, 1983; 1 stepson, Felix Buckley Jones. BA in Journalism, U. Minn., 1963. Publs. editor Mut. Service Ins. Co., St. Paul, 1963-65; pub. relations account exec. Kerker, Peterson Advt., Mpls., 1965-69; dir. advt. and pub. relations Dain, Kalman & Quail, Mpls., 1969-70; v.p., dir. pub. relations Carmichael Lynch Advt., Mpls., 1970-75; editor Corp. Report Goldletter Dorn Communications, Mpls., 1975; sr. account supr. Kerker & Assocs., Mpls., 1975-77; v.p. Padilla & Speer Inc., Mpls., 1977-79; v.p. communications Gelco Corp., Mpls., 1979-81; v.p., regional mgr. Doremus & Co., Mpls., 1981-83; pres. Mona Meyer McGrath & Gavin,

Mpls., 1983-93, CEO, 1993-95; mng. dir. Shandwick USA (formerly Mona Meyer McGrath & Gavin), Bloomington, Minn., 1995—. Bi-monthly columnist corp. report mag. Communications, 1974-88. Bd. dirs. Cricket Theatre, Mpls., 1985-89, Women's Econ. Devel. Corp., St. Paul, 1986-88, Project Pride in Living, Mpls., 1970—, Minn. Hearing Soc., 1990, The Mpls. Youth Trust, 1991-94, De LaSalle H.S., 1991-94, Mpls. Aquatennial, 1992—, pres., 1993, Greater Mpls. Visitor and Conv. Assn., 1991—. Mem. Pub. Rels. Soc. Am. (accredited, bd. dirs. 1988-90), Nat. Investor Rels. Inst. (pres. Twin Cities chpt. 1984), Pub. Rels. Soc. Counselors Acad. (exec. com. 1994—), Minn. Press Club (chmn., pres. 1980, 81, bd. dirs. 1979-80), Mpls. Club, Mpls. Athletic Club. Democrat. Roman Catholic. Avocations: squash, biking, fishing, reading. Home: 284 Pelham Blvd Saint Paul MN 55104-4935 Office: Shandwick USA Ste 500 8400 Normandale Lake Blvd Bloomington MN 55437-1080

MCGRATH, DON JOHN, banker; b. Springfield, Ill., June 15, 1948; s. Donald John and Wilma P. (Beck) McG.; m. Patricia Ratti, May 7, 1983. B.S. in Mktg., U. Ill., 1970; M.B.A., Boston U., 1973. Investment officer Banque Nationale de Paris, San Francisco, 1975-76, treas., San Francisco and Los Angeles, 1976-78, v.p. and treas., 1978-80; v.p., treas. Bank of the West, San Francisco, 1980, v.p., CFO, 1980-81, sr. v.p., CFO, 1981-84, sr. exec. v.p., CFO, 1984-87, sr. exec. v.p., COO, 1987-91, pres., COO, 1991-95, pres., CEO, 1996—. Bd. dirs. Commonwealth Club Calif., Nature Conservancy Calif. Mem. Calif. Bankers Assn. (bd. dirs.), Univ. Club, St. Francis Yacht Club (San Francisco), Silicon Valley Capital Club (San Jose, Calif.), Diablo (Calif.) Country Club. Office: Bank of the West 1450 Treat Blvd Walnut Creek CA 94596-2168

MCGRATH, ERIKA WEIS, economics educator, management consultant; b. Laufenselden, Hessen, Federal Republic of Germany, Nov. 17, 1937; d. Wilhelm A. and Auguste Louise (Vogt) Weis; m. Thomas J. McGrath, Oct. 1, 1963 (dec. Sept. 1984). BA, U. Calif., Santa Cruz, 1982; MA, Calif. State U., San Jose, 1984; PhD, U. Calif., Santa Barbara, 1989. Adj. asst. prof. Golden Gate U., Monterey, Calif., 1990—, Monterey Inst. Internat. Studies, 1992—; mgmt. cons. Weis Consulting, Monterey, 1992—. Mem., 1st chair Monterey County Commn. on Status of Women, Monterey, 1990-93; mem. LWV, Monterey, 1994—, Dem. Women's Club, Monterey, 1994—, Profl. Women's Network, Monterey, 1991—. Mem. ASTD, Profl. Orgn. Women in Edn., Kappa Delta Pi. Democrat. Avocations: travel, classical music, hiking, reading, political discussions. Home: 625 Filmore St Monterey CA 93940-1614

MCGRATH, EUGENE R., utility company executive; b. New York City, 1942. BSME, Manhattan Coll., 1963; MBA, Iona Coll., 1980. With Consol. Edison Co. N.Y., N.Y.C., 1963—, from v.p. to pres. and chief oper. officer, 1978-89, now chmn., pres., chief exec. officer, 1989—, also bd. dirs., 1989—. Office: Consol Edison Co NY Inc 4 Irving Pl Rm 1610 New York NY 10003-3502

MCGRATH, J. NICHOLAS, lawyer; b. Hollywood, Calif., Feb. 12, 1940; m. Margaret Crowley, Oct. 4, 1980; children: Nicholas Gerald, Molly Inez. BA with honors, Lehigh U., 1962; LLB magna cum laude, Columbia U., 1965. Bar: D.C. 1966, Calif. 1969, U.S. Supreme Ct. 1970, Colo. 1971. Law clk. to presiding justice U.S. Ct. Appeals (D.C. cir.), 1965-66; law clk. to assoc. justice Thurgood Marshall U.S. Supreme Ct., Washington, 1967-68; assoc. Pillsbury, Madison & Sutro, San Francisco, 1968-70; from assoc. to ptnr. Oates, Austin, McGrath, Aspen, Colo., 1970-80; ptnr. Austin, McGrath & Jordan, Aspen, 1980-82; sole practice Aspen, 1982—; chmn. grievance com. Colo. Supreme Ct., 1989, mem. 1984-89. Mem. bd. editors Columbia Law Review, 1964-65. Mem. Planning Commn., Town of Basalt, Colo., 1992-93, town trustee, 1993-94; bd. dirs. CLE in Colo., Inc., 1995-96, lectr.; pres. Basalt Children's Recreation Fund, Inc., 1994—. Mem. Colo. Bar Assn., Assn. Trial Lawyers Am., Pitkin County Bar Assn. (pres. 1977). Democrat. Avocations: skiing, tennis, computers. Office: 600 E Hopkins Ave Ste 203 Aspen CO 81611-2933

MCGRATH, JAMES CHARLES, III, financial services company executive, lawyer, consultant; b. Davenport, Iowa, May 25, 1942; s. James Charles and Genevieve (Clarke) McG.; m. Sherbourne Everett, Apr. 11, 1970. BA, U. Notre Dame, 1964; JD, U. Iowa, 1967. Bar: Iowa 1967, D.C. 1971, U.S. Ct. Mil. Appeals 1974, U.S. Ct. Appeals (D.C. cir.) 1971, U.S. Supreme Ct. 1970. Spl. agt. FBI, Balt., N.Y.C., 1967-71; trial atty. Dept. Justice, Washinton, 1971-75; dir. investigations Am. Express Co., N.Y.C., 1975-77, v.p. corp. security, 1978-82, sr. v.p. security, 1982-89; pres. McGrath Internat., Inc., 1989—; mem. overseas security adv. coun. U.S. State Dept., 1985-88; bd. dirs. Barringer Techs. Inc., New Providence, N.J. Mem. Soc. Former Spl. Agts. FBI, Am. Soc. Indsl. Security (chmn. white collar crime com. 1985-88), Internat. Assn. Credit Card Investigators (exec. adv. bd. 1985-88), Iowa State Bar Assn., D.C. Bar Assn., U.S. C. of C. (white collar crime adv. panel 1979—), Debordieu Club (Georgetown, S.C.), Phi Delta Phi. Office: McGrath Internat Inc PO Box 1384 Georgetown SC 29442-1384

MCGRATH, JAMES EDWARD, chemistry educator; b. Easton, N.Y., July 11, 1934; s. Thomas Augustine and Marguerite Monica (Hiland) McG.; m. Marlene Mary Potter, May 9, 1959; children: Colleen McGrath Kraft, Patricia McGrath Hoover, Matthew, Barbara, Elizabeth McGrath Throckmorton, Joseph. BS in Chemistry, St. Bernadine of Siena Coll., 1956; MS in Chemistry, U. Akron, 1964, PhD in Polymer Sci., 1967. Rsch. chemist rsch. divsn. Rayonier, Inc., Whippany, N.J., 1956-59, Goodyear Tire & Rubber Co., Akron, Ohio, 1959-65; mem. staff Inst. Polymer Sci., U. Akron, 1965-67; sr. rsch. chemist Union Carbide Corp., Bound Brook, N.J., 1967-69, project scientist, 1969-72, rsch. scientist, 1972-74, rsch. scientist, group leader, 1974-75; asst. prof. chemistry Va. Poly. Inst. and State U., Blacksburg, 1975-76, assoc. prof. chemistry, 1976-79, prof. chemistry, 1980-87; dir. Materials Inst. Va. Poly. Inst. and State U., 1987-89, prof. dept. chem., co-dir. polymer materials and interface lab., 1979—, Ethyl prof. polymer chemistry, 1986—, dir. Ctr. for Polymer Adhesives and Composites, 1989—; bd. dirs. ChemFab Inc., N.H.; mem. fire safety report com. NAS/NRC; mem. external adv. com. High Performance Polymers and Ceramics Ctr., Clark Atlanta U. Author, editor: Polyimides: Materials, Chemistry and Characterization, 1989; co-author (with Noshay): Block Copolymers: Overview and Critical Survey, 1977; mem. editl. bd. Jour. Polymer Sci., 1987—, Polymer, 1990—, High Performance Polymeric Polymers, 1990—; adv. bd. Jour. Polymer Sci., 1989—, Advances in Polymeric Sci. Capt. U.S. Army, 1957. Mem. NAS (mem. nat. materials bd. 1992—), NAE, Soc. Plastics Engrs. (Internat. Rsch. award 1987, Outstanding Achievement award 1992). Republican. Roman Catholic. Avocations: music, tennis, travel. Office: Va Poly Inst Ctr Polymeric Adhesives and Composites 2108 Hahn Hall Blacksburg VA 24061-0344

MCGRATH, JAMES THOMAS, real estate investment company executive; b. N.Y.C., Nov. 10, 1942; s. Thomas James and Mary Ita (Finnegan) McG.; m. Paulette L. Franck, Aug. 16, 1980; 1 child, Tara (dec.). BS in Acctg., Providence Coll., 1964. CPA, N.Y. Sr. auditor Coopers & Lybrand, N.Y.C., 1968-72, mgmt. cons., 1972-74; group controller IU Internat. Corp., Phila., 1974-77; v.p. fin. Taylor Engring. Corp. subs. IU Internat., Detroit, 1977-78; controller Pool Co. subs. Enserch Corp., Houston, 1978-85; sr. v.p. fin., treas. Lone Star Gas Co. subs. Enserch Corp., Dallas, 1985-91; pres. McGrath & Assocs., Inc., Dallas, 1991—. Bd. dirs. ARC, Dallas chpt., 1990-93. Lt. USN, 1964-68. Mem. AICPA, Dallas Athletic Club, St. Vincent de Paul Soc. Republican. Roman Catholic. Avocations: golf, cooking, skiing, scuba diving, sailing. Home and Office: 2838 Colleen Dr Garland TX 75043-1215

MCGRATH, JOHN FRANCIS, utility executive; b. Freeport, N.Y., May 4, 1925; s. John Francis and Catherine Frances (Maune) McG.; m. Catherine Elizabeth Zainor, June 22, 1946; children—Joseph R., Susan M., Martha J., Thomas J. B.S., U.S. Mcht. Marine Acad., 1944; A.B., Muhlenberg Coll., Allentown, Pa., 1948; J.D., St. John's U., Bklyn., 1952; grad. bus. exec. program, U. Minn. Grad. Sch., 1973. Bar: N.Y. bar 1952, Minn. bar 1958. Atty. firm Casey, Lane & Mittendorf, N.Y.C., 1953-58; jud. inquiry asst. counsel N.Y. State Supreme Ct., 1957-58; atty. U.S. Steel Corp., Duluth, Minn., 1958-64; with Minn. Power & Light Co., Duluth, 1964-83; sr. v.p. Minn. Power & Light Co., 1978-83, gen. counsel, 1975-83, sec., 1979-88; adj. prof., gen. counsel Coll. St. Scholastica, Duluth; vol. atty. Bay Area Legal Svcs., Tampa, Fla. Bd. dirs. emeritus Duluth Cathedral H.S., 1972, St. Anne's Residence, Duluth, 1963-83; commr. Seaway Port Authority, Duluth, 1966-76, pres., 1970, 75; bd. dirs., sec. Good Samaritan Fund Greater Sun City Center, Fla.; mem. Hillsborough County Bd. Zoning Adjustment, 1992-94. With U.S. Mcht. Marine, 1943-46. Mem. Minn. Bar Assn., St. Louis County Bar Assn., Golf Club of Cypress Creek, K.C. (4th degree). Democrat. Roman Catholic. Home: 2036 Hampstead Cir Sun City Center FL 33573-7350

MCGRATH, JUDITH, broadcast executive; b. Scranton, PA, 1952. Former fashion copywriter Mademoiselle; now pres. MTV, New York, NY. Office: MTV 1515 Broadway New York NY 10036*

MCGRATH, KATHRYN BRADLEY, lawyer; b. Norfolk, Va., Sept. 2, 1944; d. James Pierce and Kathryn (Hoyle) Bradley; m. John J. McGrath Jr., June 8, 1968; children: Ian M., James D. AB, Mt. Holyoke Coll., 1966; JD, Georgetown U., 1969. Ptnr. Gardner, Carton & Douglas, Washington, 1979-83; dir. div. investment mgmt. SEC, Washington, 1983-90; ptnr. Morgan, Lewis & Bockius, LLP, Washington, 1990—. Named Disting. Exec. Pres. Reagan, 1987. Mem. Fed. Bar Assn. (exec. council securities law com.). Office: Morgan Lewis & Bockius LLP 1800 M St NW Washington DC 20036-5802

MC GRATH, LEE PARR, author, public relations executive; b. Robstown, Tex.; d. James Carl and Margaret Marden (Russ) Parr; m. Richard J. McGrath, Nov. 5, 1955 (div. 1975); children: John Parr, Margaret Lee, Maureen Alison; m. Robert Lansing Phipps, Jan. 1, 1989. B.A., So. Methodist U., 1955. Book reviewer Dallas Morning News, 1953, New Orleans Times-Picayune, 1956; guest editor Mademoiselle mag., 1952; chmn. bd. McGrath/Power Assocs., N.Y.C., 1973-93; chmn. bd. dirs. McGrath/Crossen Assocs., Richmond, Va., chmn., 1993—; pub. rels. cons. Waldenbooks, Campbell Soup Co., Reebok, N.Y. Times Mag. Group, Citibank. Author: Creative Careers For Women, 1968, Do-It-All-Yourself Needlepoint, 1971, What is a Father?, 1969, What Is a Mother?, 1969, What Is a Grandmother?, 1970, What Is a Grandfather?, 1970, What is a Brother?, 1971, What Is a Sister?, 1971, What Is a Friend?, 1971, What Is a Pet?, 1971, Celebrity Needlepoint, 1972, Housekeeping With Antiques, 1971. Recipient Prix de Paris Vogue, 1954. Mem. Pub. Rels. Soc. Am., Am. Soc. Journalists and Authors, Cousteau Soc. (bd. dirs.), Cosmopolitan Club, Phi Beta Kappa. Home: Bolan Hall Plantation Ridgeland SC 29936 Office: McGrath/Crossen Assocs 5805 River Rd Richmond VA 23226-3313

MCGRATH, MARY HELENA, plastic surgeon, educator; b. N.Y.C., Apr. 12, 1945; d. Vincent J. and Mary M. (Manning) McG.; m. Richard H. Simon, Apr. 11, 1970; children: Margaret E. Simon, Richard M. Simon. BA, Coll. New Rochelle, 1966; MD, St. Louis U., 1970; MPH, George Washington U., 1994. Lic. surgeon, D.C. Resident in surg. pathology U. Colo. Med. Ctr., Denver, 1970-71, intern in gen. surgery, 1971-72, resident in gen. surgery, 1971-75, chief resident in gen. surgery, 1975-76; resident in plastic and reconstructive surgery Yale U. Sch. Medicine, New Haven, Conn., 1976-77; chief resident plastic and reconstructive surgery Yale U. Sch. Medicine, New Haven, 1977-78; fellow in hand surgery U. Conn.-Yale U., New Haven, 1978; instr. in surgery divsn. plastic and reconstructive surgery Yale U. Sch. Medicine, New Haven, 1977-78, asst. prof. plastic surgery, 1978-80; attending in plastic and reconstructive surgery Yale-New Haven Hosp., 1978-80, Columbia-Presbyn. Hosp., N.Y.C., 1980-84, George Washington U. Med. Ctr., Washington, 1984—, Children's Nat. Med. Ctr., Washington, 1985—; asst. prof. plastic surgery Columbia U., N.Y.C., 1980-84; assoc. prof. plastic surgery Sch. Medicine, George Washington U., Washington, 1984-87, prof. plastic surgery, 1987—; attending physician VA Hosp., West Haven, Conn., 1978-80; attending in surgery Hosp. Albert Schweitzer, Deschapelles, Haiti, 1980; co-investigator Charles W. Ohse Fund, Yale U. Sch. Medicine, 1979; prin. investigator various rsch. grants, 1979-89; historian, bd. dirs. Am. Bd. Plastic Surgery, 1991-95; guest examiner certifying exam., 1986-88, 95-96; specialist site visitor Residency Rev. Com. for Plastic Surgery, 1985, 87, 91, 94; presenter in field; cons. in field; senator med. faculty senate George Washington U., bd. govs. Med. Faculty Assocs. Co-editor: (with M.L. Turner) Dermatology for Plastic Surgeons, 1993; assoc. editor: The Jour. of Hand Surgery, 1984-89, Plastic and Reconstructive Surgery, 1989-95, chmn. nominating com., 1994—; contbr. book chpts.: Problems in General Surgery, 1985, Human and Ethical Issues in the Surgical Care of Patients with Life-Threatening Disease, 1986, Problems in Aesthetic Surgery, Biological Causes and Clinical Solutions, 1986; guest reviewer numerous jours.; contbr. articles, abstracts to profl. jours. Fellow ACS (bd. govs. 1995—, chmn. adv. coun. for plastic surgery 1995—); mem. AAAS, AMA, Am. Assn. Hand Surgery (exec. sec. 1988-90, rsch. grants com. 1983-86, chmn. edn. com. 1983-88, 1st prize ann. resident contest 1978, numerous other coms., D.C. chpt. program ann. meeting chmn. 1992, v.p. 1993-94, pres. 1994—), Am. Assn. Plastic Surgeons (pub. info. com. 1988-89, James Barrett Brown com. 1990-92, rsch. and edn. com. 1992-95), Am. Burn Assn., Am. Soc. for Aesthetic Plastic Surgery (FDA implant task force 1990—, pub. edn. com. 1991-92, sci. rsch. com. 1990—), Am. Soc. Maxillofacial Surgeons, Am. Soc. Plastic and Reconstructive Surgery (chmn. ethics com. 1985-87, chmn. device/tech. evaluation com. 1993-94, bd. dirs. 1994—, mem. ednl. found. bd. dirs. 1985-96, treas. 1989-92, v.p. 1992-93, pres.-elect 1993-94, pres. 1994-95), Am. Soc. Reconstructive Microsurgery (mem. edn. com. 1992-94), Am. Soc. Surgery of Hand (chmn. 1987 ann. residents' and fellows conf. 1986-87, mem. rsch. com. 1988-90), Assn. Acad. Chmn. Plastic Surgery (mem. prerequesite tng. com. 1990-92, mem. com. aesthetic surgery tng. 1992—), Assn. Acad. Surgery, D.C. Met. Area Soc. Plastic and Reconstructive Surgeons, Internat. Soc. Reconstructive Surgery, Met. D.C. Soc. Surgery Hand, N.Y. Surg. Soc., Northeastern Soc. Plastic Surgeons (chmn. sci. program com. 1991, chmn. fin. com. 1992-93, treas. 1993—), Plastic Surgery Rsch. Coun. (chmn. 1990), Surg. Biology Club III, The Wound Healing Soc., Washington Acad. Surgery, Washington Med. and Surg. Soc. Office: George Washington U # 6B-422 2150 Pennsylvania Ave NW Washington DC 20037-2396

MCGRATH, MICHAEL ALAN, state government officer; b. Trenton, N.J., Oct. 27, 1942; s. Lyman Levitt and Ada Frances (Hofreiter) McG.; m. Marsha Louise Palmer, Aug. 6, 1966; children: David Patrick, Stephen Gregory, Christopher Andrew. AA, Daytona Beach Jr. Coll., 1967; BA, Stetson U., 1969. Supr. 1st Trust Co., St. Paul, 1969-72; v.p. Internat. Dairy Queen, Inc., Bloomington, Minn., 1972-84; dir. ops. WISCECO, Inc., Bloomington, 1984; bus. mgr. McGraw-Hill, Inc., Edina, Minn., 1985; pres. Policy Advisors, Inc., Bloomington, 1986; treas. State of Minn., St. Paul, 1987—; mem. State Bd. Investment, State Exec. Coun., 1987—; bd. dirs. Minn. State Retirement Systems, St. Paul; Minn. rep. Pub. Fin. Network, 1989—. Mem. editorial bd. Pension Fund News, 1988-90. Chmn. bd. dirs. Urban Concerns Workshop, Inc., St. Paul, 1984-86; sec. League Minn. Human Rights Commn., Mpls., 1985-86; chmn. sen. dist. 41 Dem. Farm Labor Party, 1984-86, treas. 3d congl. dist., New Hope, Minn., 1986, pres. Dem. Farm Labor Club, Bloomington, 1982-84. Served with USAF, 1962-66. Mem. Nat. Assn. State Treas. (midwest v.p. 1988-89, sec.-treas. 1990-94, sr. v.p. 1994-95, pres. 1995-96, coun. of state govts., fin. com. 1993-94, long-range planning com. 1995, exec. com. 1995-96), Coun. of Instnl. Investors, Govt. Fin. Officers Assn., Nat. Assn. State Auditors, Comptrs. and Treas. (exec. com. 1995-96, nat. electronic benefits transfer coun., 1995—). Office: Office of Treasury State Minn 50 Sherburne Ave Ste 303 Saint Paul MN 55155-1402

MCGRATH, PETER, editor; b. Macclesfield, Eng., Aug. 19, 1944; came to U.S., 1947; s. Hugh P. and Barbara W. (Collins) McG.; m. Susan Seliger, June 17, 1972; children: Alexander S., Evan S. BA, Amherst Coll., 1966; MA, U. Chgo., 1971, PhD, 1974. Press, legis. asst. Congressman Timothy E. Wirth, Washington, 1975-77; founding editor Washington Journalism Rev., 1977; sr. editor Washingtonian mag., Washington, 1977-81; spl. corr. The Economist, Washington, 1979-81; gen. editor Newsweek, N.Y.C., 1981-83, sr. editor, 1983-86, fgn. editor, 1986-92; mng. editor Newsweek Internat., N.Y.C., 1992-95; editor new media Newsweek, N.Y.C., 1995—. Contbr. articles to profl. jours. Office: Newsweek 251 W 57th St New York NY 10019

MCGRATH, RICHARD PAUL, lawyer; b. Chgo., Aug. 10, 1929; s. John Francis and Helen Leone (Hoyer) M.; m. Luisa Sacco y Artze, Aug. 12, 1956; children: Lisa, Deborah, Holly. BA magna cum laude, Georgetown U., 1951; JD cum laude, Harvard U., 1954. Bar: D.C. 1954, N.Y. 1955, Mass. 1957, Conn. 1960, U.S. Supreme Ct. 1965. Assoc. Hughes, Hubbard, Blair and Reed, 1954-57; corp. counsel Raytheon Co., 1957-60; assoc. Cummings & Lockwood, Stamford, Conn., 1960-63, ptnr., 1963—; bd. dirs. Stamford Partnership, Landmark Club; gen. counsel, corp. sec. Internat. Exec. Svc. Corps, 1990—, mem. coun., 1990—. Editorial bd. Harvard Law Rev., 1952-54; contbr. articles to profl. jours.; panelist law seminars. Past pres. Fairfield County Coun. Boy Scouts Am. Mem. ABA, Conn. Bar Assn. (chmn. corp. law com. 1984-86, fee disputes arbitration com. 1980-84), Pi Gamma Mu, Eta Sigma Phi, Gold Key Soc., Stamford Rotary Club (past pres.), Woodway Country Club (Darien, Conn., bd. govs., sec. 1983-91). Avocations: golf, trap, chess. Office: Cummings & Lockwood 4 Stamford Plz Stamford CT 06901-3215

MCGRATH, THOMAS J., lawyer, writer, film producer; b. N.Y.C., Oct. 8, 1932; m. Mary Lee McGrath, Aug. 4, 1956 (dec.); children: Maura Lee, J. Connell; m. Diahn Williams, Sept. 28, 1974; 1 child, Courtney C. B.A., NYU, 1956, J.D., 1960. Bar: N.Y. 1960. Assoc. Milbank, Tweed, Hadley & McCloy, N.Y.C., 1960-69; ptnr. Simpson, Thacher & Bartlett, N.Y.C., 1970-95; retired, 1995; lectr., writer Practicing Law Inst., 1976—, Am. Law Inst. ABA, 1976-81. Author: Carryover Basis Under Tax Reform Act, 1977; contbg. author: Estate and Gift Tax After ERTA, 1982; producer: feature film Deadly Hero, 1977. Bd. dirs. N.Y. Philharm.; trustee Am. Austrian Found., Tanzania Wildlife Fund; dir. Olofsson Corp., Fast Food Devel. Corp. With U.S. Army, 1953-54. Fellow Am. Coll. Trust and Estate Coun.; mem. ABA, N.Y. State Bar Assn., Assn. Bar City N.Y. Home: 988 5th Ave New York NY 10021-0143 Office: Simpson Thacher & Bartlett 425 Lexington Ave New York NY 10017-3903

MCGRATH, WILLIAM JOSEPH, lawyer; b. Cleve., July 6, 1943; s. William Peter and Marie Agnes (Wolf) McG.; m. Mary Ann Ostrenga; children: William Peter, Geoffrey Walton, Megan Joy. AB, John Carroll U., 1965; MA, Loyola U., 1967; JD, Harvard U., 1970. Bar: Ill. 1970. Assoc. McDermott, Will & Emery, Chgo., 1970-75, ptnr., 1976—, mem. mgmt. com., 1993—, mem. exec. com., 1994—; bd. dirs. Tomy Am., Inc., Brea, Calif. Trustee Boys and Girls Club Found., 1983. Mem. ABA. Democrat. Roman Catholic. Clubs: Evanston Golf; Union League (Chgo.). Home: 943 Edgemere Ct Evanston IL 60202-1428 Office: McDermott Will & Emery 227 W Monroe St Chicago IL 60606-5016

MC GRATH, WILLIAM RESTORE, transportation planner, traffic engineer; b. Stratford, Conn., Oct. 4, 1922; s. Thomas Christopher and Alpha Retta (Perry) McG.; m. Lillian Joyce DeAngelis, Mar. 9, 1945; children: Brian, David, Raymond, Harold, Vincent, Mary, Kevin, Rita, Beverly, Nora, Margaret. B.C.E., Rensselaer Poly. Inst., 1950; diploma, Yale Bur. Hwy. Traffic, 1951. Registered profl. engr. Calif., Conn., Mass., N.J., N.Y., Fla., Maine, N.H. Mem. faculty Yale Bur. Hwy. Traffic, New Haven, 1951-55; dir. traffic and parking City of New Haven, 1955-63; transp. coordinator Boston Redevel. Authority, 1963-68; commr. dept. traffic and parking City of Boston, 1968-70; v.p. Raymond Parish Pine & Weiner, Tarrytown, N.Y., 1970-79; mgr. traffic and parking Daniel, Mann, Johnson & Mendenhall, 1980-83; ptnr. McGrath, O'Rourke & Assocs., 1983-85; owner/mgr. McGrath Engring., Cape Coral, Fla., 1985-87; transp. planner Lee County Dept. Transp. & Engring., 1987-94; cons. AID, Madras, India, 1963, Dublin, Ireland, 1965; Cons. World Trade Center, Moscow, USSR, 1974. Mem. exec. com. Met. Area Planning Council, Boston, 1965-70, Gov.'s Council on Transp., 1968-70; mem. urban ecology adv. council Inst. Ecology, 1973—. Served with USNR, 1943-45. Mem. NSPE, Inst. Transp. Engrs. (hon., nat. pres. 1973, chmn. equal opportunity com., chmn. U.S. legis. com.), Transp. Rsch. Bd., Fla. Engring. Soc., Sigma Xi, Tau Beta Pi, Chi Epsilon. Roman Catholic. Home: 215 SE 14th Ct Cape Coral FL 33990-1799 Office: 4906 Victoria Dr Unit 104 Cape Coral FL 33904

MC GRAW, DARRELL VIVIAN, JR., attorney general; b. Mullens, W.Va., Nov. 8, 1936; s. Darrell Vivian and Julia (ZeKany) McG.; m. Jorea Marple; children: Elizabeth, Sarah, Darrell, Elliott. AB, W.Va. U., 1961, JD, 1964, MA, 1977. Bar: W.Va. 1964. Gen. atty. Fgn. Claims Settlement Commn., U.S. Dept. State, 1964; counsel to gov. State of W.Va., 1965-68; pvt. practice Charleston, Shepherdstown and Morgantown, 1968-76; judge W.Va. Supreme Ct. Appeals, Charleston, 1977-88, chief justice, 1982-93; atty. gen. State of W.Va., Charleston, 1993—. Served with U.S. Army, 1954-57. Fellow W.Va. U., Nat. Ctr. Edn. in Politics/Ford Found. Fellow Am. Polit. Sci. Assn. Democrat. Office: Office of Atty Gen 1900 Kanawha Blvd E Bldg 1 Rm E-26 Charleston WV 25305-0220

MCGRAW, DELOSS HOLLAND, illustrator, painter; b. Okemah, Okla., Feb. 1, 1945. Student, Ea. Ctrl. State Coll., 1963-65, Otis Art Inst., L.A., 1965-67; BA, Calif. State Coll., Long Beach, 1969; MFA, Cranbrook Acad. Art, 1972. Commissioned mural Whittier Inst., La Jolla, Calif., 1989, bronze sculptor Homart Corp., L.A., 1990, sculpture and painting Carlsbad Libr. Ctr., Calif., 1991-94, mural Luce, Forward & Assocs., San Diego, 1992, set design Shakespeare Festival, L.A., 1994; exhibited at The Book in Art, U. Art Mus., Calif. State U., Laguna Beach, 1986, Book as Art, Victoria and Albert Mus., London, 1987; one-man shows include La Maison Visinand, Montreux, Switzerland, 1988, The Death of Cock Robin, DeSaisset Mus., Santa Clara (Calif.) U., 1991, A Mus. in the Making, Scottsdale (Ariz.) Ctr. for Arts, 1991, Calif. Gothic, Mary Ryan Gallery, N.Y., 1994. Office: c/o Harcourts Modern Cont 460 Bush St San Francisco CA 94108

MCGRAW, DONALD JESSE, biologist, historian of science, writer; b. Altadena, Calif., Oct. 27, 1943; s. Jesse E. and Mary L. (Hajostek) McG.; m. Laura Lee Hansen, July 13, 1968; children: Adrienne, Holly, Rachel. BS in Biol. Scis., Calif. State Poly. Coll., 1965; MS, Utah State U., 1967; PhD, Oreg. State U., 1976. Registered microbiologist Am. Acad. Microbiology. Research asst. microbiology Utah State U., 1965-66, teaching asst. food and aquatic microbiology, 1966-67; grad. teaching asst. gen. biology Oreg. State U., 1970-72, instr., 1972-73; tchr. phys. and biol. scis. U.S. Bur. Indian Affairs Boarding Sch., Shonto, Ariz., 1974-75; asst. prof. biology Franklin Coll., Ind., 1975-78; adj. asst. prof. biology Ind. Central U., Indpls., 1977-78; adj. asst. prof. Ind. U.-Purdue U., Columbus, 1978; mem. faculty Yavapai Community Coll., Prescott, Ariz., 1978-79; assoc. dir. Ute Research Lab., Ft. Duchesne, Utah, 1980-81, dir., 1981-82; vis. prof. biology Bard Coll., N.Y., Spring 1984, Coll. St. Thomas, Minn., 1985-87; adj. asst. prof. biology, assoc. provost U. San Diego, 1988—; ranger-naturalist U.S. Nat. Park Svc., summers, 1970-79, 83-86, vol., 1989—; writer, 1968—; adj. faculty Southwestern Coll., 1989-92. Contbr. numerous articles on history of microbiology and history of antibiotics to sci. publs. Commr. San Diego County Columbian Quincentenary Commn., 1990-93, chmn. edn. com., 1990-93; mem. pres.'s adv. com. San Diego Zool. Soc., 1995—; trustee Quail Bot. Gardens Found., 1995—. Recipient Disting. Alumnus award, Calif. State Poly. U., 1991, Monrovia High Sch., 1991; Eli Lilly doctoral grantee Oreg. State U., 1973-74. Mem. AAAS, History of Sci. Soc., Soc. for Econ. Botany, Cabrillo Hist. Assn. (bd. dirs. 1989-94, vice chair 1992, chair 1993, 94), Alpha Scholastic Honor Soc. of Franklin Coll. (pres. 1976-78), Sigma Xi, Beta Beta Beta. Office: U San Diego Office of Provost 5998 Alcala Park San Diego CA 92110-2429

MCGRAW, FRANK WILLIAM, JR., lawyer; b. Newport News, Va., Aug. 21, 1944; s. Frank William and Mary Jean (Head) McG.; 1 child, Virginia LaVaughan. AA, U. Fla., 1965, BS in Journalism, 1967; BA in Polit. Sci., U. N.C., 1974; MS in Criminal Justice, Nova U., 1980; MPA in Justice Adminstrn., Golden Gate U., 1981; JD, U. Houston, 1973. Bar: Va. 1975, U.S. Dist. Ct. (ea. dist.) Va. 1978, U.S. Claims Ct., U.S. Mil. Appeals, U.S. Dist. Ct. (we. dist.) Va. 1979, D.C. 1979, U.S. Supreme Ct. 1979, U.S. Ct. Appeals (D.C. cir.) 1980. Asst. commonwealth atty. City of Va. Beach, Virginia Beach, 1976-79, 85-87, dep. commonwealth atty., 1987-89; pvt. practice Virginia Beach, 1975-76, 79-85, 89—; bd. dirs. Ea. Va. Health Sys. Agy., Inc., 1982-86; faculty advisor Nat. Coll. Dist. Attys., Houston, 1978; faculty advisor Nat. Coll. Dist. Attys., 1978; adj. prof. Nova U., 1982; adj. faculty mem. Tidewater C.C., 1980-85. 1st lt. U.S. Army, 1967-70, Vietnam. Recipient bronze star with oak leaf cluster U.S. Army, 1969. Mem. ATLA (mem. criminal and family law sects.), ABA (criminal justice and family law sects.), Nat. Assn. Criminal Def. Lawyers, Va. State Bar (criminal and family law sects.), Va. Bar Assn. (criminal law sect. coun., domestic rels. sect.), D.C. Bar Assn. (criminal law and individual rights divsn.), Virginia Beach Bar Assn., Va. Trial Lawyers Assn. (mem. criminal and family law sects.).

Home: 1024 Collection Creek Way Virginia Beach VA 23454 Office: 1200 1st Colonial Rd #204G Virginia Beach VA 23454

MCGRAW, HAROLD WHITTLESEY, JR., publisher; b. Bklyn., Jan. 10, 1918; s. Harold Whittlesey and Louise (Higgins) McG.; m. Anne PerLee, Nov. 30, 1940; children: Suzanne, Harold Whittlesey III, Thomas Per-Lee, Robert Pearse. Grad., Lawrenceville (N.J.) Sch., 1936; A.B., Princeton U., 1940. With G.M. Basford (advt. agy.), N.Y.C., 1940-41, Brentano's Bookstores, Inc., 1946; with McGraw-Hill Book Co., Inc., N.Y.C., 1947—, successively promotion mgr., dir. co. advt. and trade sales, 1947-55, dir., v.p. charge trade book, indsl. and bus. book depts., co. advt., 1955-61, sr. v.p., 1961-68, pres., chief exec. officer, 1968-74; pres., chief exec. officer McGraw-Hill, Inc., 1974-83, chairman, 1976-88; chairman emeritus, 1988—; bd. dirs. McGraw Hill, Inc., 1954-88. Founder, pres., bd. dirs. Bus. Council Effective Literacy and Bus. Press Ednl. Found. Served as capt. USAAF, 1941-45. Clubs: Bent Pine (Vero Beach); Blind Brook (Purchase, N.Y.); Wee Burn (Darien, Conn.). Home: Watch Tower Rd Darien CT 06820 Office: McGraw-Hill Inc 1221 Ave Of The Americas New York NY 10020-1001

MCGRAW, JACK WILSON, government official; b. Balt., May 19, 1943; s. P.W. and Nina (Gwinn) McG.; m. Nancy F. Foster, Aug. 31, 1974; children—David, Mark. B.A., Morris Harvey Coll., 1964; B.Div., Tex. Christian U., 1967. Ordained minister Christian Ch. (Disciples of Christ). Dir. temporary housing HUD, Washington, 1979-82; asst. assoc. dir. Fed. Emergency Mgmt. Agy., Washington, 1982, dep. asst. dir., 1982-83; dep. asst. adminstr. EPA Office Solid Waste and Emergency Response, Washington, 1983-88, acting asst. adminstr.; dep. regional adminstr. EPA Regional Office, Denver, 1988—. Nominee William H. Jump award HUD, 1972, Presdl. Rank award for sr. exec. service. Presbyterian. Avocation: skiing. Home: 8074 S Oneida Ct Englewood CO 80112-3128 Office: EPA Regional Office 999 18th St Denver CO 80202-2440

MCGRAW, JAMES L., retired ophthalmologist, educator; b. Syracuse, N.Y., Sept. 7, 1917; s. John J. and Elizabeth B. (Hemmer) M. A.B., Syracuse U., 1938, M.D., 1941; D.M.S., Columbia U., 1946. Diplomate Am. Bd. Ophthalmology. Intern, Grad. Hosp. U. Pa., 1941-42; resident Inst. Ophthalmology of Presbyn. Hosp., N.Y.C., 1942-46; teaching and research fellow Inst. Ophthalmology, Columbia U. Coll. Physicians and Surgeons, N.Y.C., 1945-46, instr. ophthalmology, 1945-46; clin. instr. ophthalmology SUNYHealth Sci. Ctr. Hosp., Syracuse, N.Y., 1947-54, clin. asst. prof., 1954-57, prof., dept. chmn., 1957-84, prof. emeritus, 1984—; attending ophthalmologist Crouse-Irving Meml. Hosp.; Univ. Hosp. SUNY; cons. VA Hosp. Contbr. articles to profl. jours, papers to profl. orgns. Served to maj. M.C., U.S. Army, 1950-52. Mem. Onondaga County Med. Soc., N.Y. State Med. Soc., AMA, Am. Acad. Ophthalmology (Honor award 1963), Nat. Soc. for Prevention Blindness, Nat. Med. Found. for Eye Care, Am. Bd. Ophthalmology, N.Y. Ophthal. Soc., Inst. Ophthalmology Alumni Assn., N.Y. Eye Bank, Alpha Omega Alpha. Roman Catholic. Club: Skaneateles Country. Home: 3069 E Lake Rd Skaneateles NY 13152-9002 Office: Eye Cons of Syracuse 224 Harrison St Syracuse NY 13202-3052

MCGRAW, LAVINIA MORGAN, former retail company executive; b. Detroit, Feb. 26, 1924; d. Will Curtis and Margaret Coulter (Oliphant) McG. AB, Radcliffe Coll., 1945. Mem. Phi Beta Kappa. Home: 2501 Calvert St NW Washington DC 20008-2620

MCGRAW, ROBERT PIERCE, publishing executive; b. Bronxville, N.Y., June 13, 1954; s. Harold W. Jr. and Anne (Per-Lee) McG.; m. Dawn A. Watson, Sept. 15, 1979; children: Avery Christine, Dale Per-Lee. AB, Princeton U., 1976. Sales rep. McGraw Hill Book Co., Chgo., 1976-79; editor McGraw-Hill Inc., N.Y.C., 1979-82, editorial dir., 1982-83, gen. mgr., 1983-85, group v.p., 1985-87, exec. v.p., 1987—; bd. dirs. McGraw-Hill Cos.; dep. dir. Med. China Ltd., Hong Kong, 1986—. Republican. Presbyterian. Office: McGraw-Hill Inc 1221 Ave Of The Americas New York NY 10020-1001

MCGREAL, JOSEPH A., JR., publishing company executive; b. Bklyn., Mar. 6, 1935; s. Joseph A. and Aresta (Noon) McG.; m. Margaret A. Molloy, June 6, 1959; children—Patrick, Pegeen, Joseph. BBA, St. Francis Coll., 1962. Pres. Med./Pharm. Pub. Co., Inc., Manhasset, N.Y., 1996—. Served with U.S. Army, 1955-57. Home: 52 Rockywood Rd Manhasset NY 11030-2513 Office: Med/Pharm Pub Co Inc 29 Park Ave Manhasset NY 11030

MC GREGOR, DONALD THORNTON, newspaper editor, journalist; b. McLennan County, Tex., Mar. 20, 1924; s. Marshall Thornton and Flora Elvira (Welch) McG.; m. Alice Carlene Barnhill, Dec. 21, 1946; children: Alice Diane McGregor Tyrone, Robert Thornton, Donald Wayne. B.A., Baylor U., Waco, Tex., 1947; postgrad., Southwestern Baptist Theol. Sem., Ft. Worth, 1951-52. Agr. reporter Midland (Tex.) Reporter-Telegram, 1948-49; continuity dir. Sta. KCRS, Midland, 1949-50; editorial asso. Bapt. Standard, Dallas, 1952-55; real estate editor Dallas Times Herald, 1959; pub. relations exec. Union Bankers Ins. Co., Dallas, 1955-58; assoc. editor Bapt. Standard, 1959-71; editor Calif. So. Bapt., Fresno, 1971-73; publisher Kemp (Tex.) News, Ferris (Tex.) Wheel, also Dawson (Tex.) Herald, 1973-74; assoc. editor Bapt. Record, Jackson, Miss., 1974-76, editor, 1976-90; ret., 1990. Chmn. public rels. adv. com. So. Bapt. Conv., 1979-80. Served with AUS, 1943-45; prisoner of war, Germany, 1944-45. Decorated Purple Heart; recipient Distinguished Service award So. Bapt. Conv., 1973. Mem. So. Bapt. Press Assn. (sec.-treas. 1964-68, pres. 1981, chmn. Bapt. press liaison com. 1988-90), Associated Bapt. Press (co-founder and bd. dirs., exec. dir. 1994—). Home: PO Box 850547 Mesquite TX 75185-0547

MCGREGOR, F. DANIEL, education educator; b. Indiana, Pa., Aug. 8, 1946; s. Ralph Murray and Elaine (Kennedy) McG. BS in Edn., Ind. U., 1972, MEd, 1977; cert. prin., U. Pitts., 1979, cert. supt., 1988. Prin. Blairsville (Pa.) Saltsburg Sch. Dist., Kiski Area Sch. Dist., Vandergrift, Pa.; regional coord. Dept. of Edn., Harrisburg, Pa.; prof. Elem. Edn. Indiana (Pa.) U.; prin. Duquesne Sch. Dist.; dir. edn. Pa. Dept. Corrections; prof. Westmoreland C.C. Mem. Pa. Congress of Parents and Tchrs. (life).

MCGREGOR, JACK EDWIN, natural resource company executive; b. Kittanning, Pa., Sept. 22, 1934; s. Russell Alexander and Leah Rachel (Hampton) McG.; m. Carol Dangerfield, Nov. 23, 1955 (div. Mar. 1992); children: Nancy, Douglas, Elisabeth, Heather; m. Mary-Jane Foster, Jan. 2, 1993. BS, Yale U., 1956; LLB, U. Pitts., 1962. Bar: Pa. 1963, D.C. 1971, U.S. Supreme Ct. 1971. Pres. Pitts. Penguins Hockey Club, 1966-70; assoc. Reed Smith Shaw & McClay, Pitts., 1962-68, 70; gen. counsel U.S. Pay Bd., Washington, 1971-72; asst. legal adviser econ. affairs Dept. State, Washington, 1971; v.p., gen. counsel Potomac Electric Power Corp., Washington, 1972-74; exec. v.p., COO Carey Energy Corp., N.Y.C., 1974-79; pres., CEO Hampton-Douglas Corp., Bedford, N.Y., and Washington, 1979-85; exec. v.p. Aquarion Co., Bridgeport, 1985-88, pres., dir., 1988—, CEO, 1990-95, chmn., 1995—; bus. and econ. devel. advisor Cohen & Wolf, P.C., Bridgeport, 1995—; prin. Bridgeport Waterfront Investor, 1995—; dir. People's Bank, Bay State Gas Co. Mem. Pa. Senate, 1962-70; del., asst. floor mgr. Republican Nat. Conv., 1964; co-chair Conn. Gov.-elect John Roland's Transition Team, 1994-95; bd. dirs. Barnum Mus. Found., Mystic Marinelife Aquarium, Conn. Gov.'s. Greenways Com., Conn. Com. Regional Plan Assn. Capt. USMC, 1956-59. Mem. ABA, D.C. Bar Assn., Pa. Bar Assn., Nat. Assn. Water Cos. (immediate past pres.), Country Club of Fairfield, Chevy Chase (Md.) Club, Conn. Golf Club. Presbyterian. Home: 74 Freeborn Rd Easton CT 06612-1141 Office: Aquarion Co 835 Main St Bridgeport CT 06604-4914

MCGREGOR, JANET EILEEN, elementary school educator; b. Pittsfield, Mass., Jan. 6, 1949; d. Joseph Patrick and Edith Cecilia (Wendell) Feeley; m. Ronald Lee McGregor, Jan. 21, 1972; children: Joshua, Jason. BS in Elem./Early Childhood Edn., Fla. State U., 1971; MS in Elem. Edn., U. South Fla., 1996. Tchr. 4th grade South Lake Elem. Sch., Titusville, Fla., 1971-74; tchr. 1st and 2d grades Peace River Elem. Sch., Port Charlotte, Fla., 1974-90; tchr. 1st grade Deep Creek Elem. Sch., Punta Gorda, Fla., 1990—; workshop presenter Charlotte County Schs., Port Charlotte, 1989—; cons. Lee County Schs., Ft. Myers, Fla., 1993; seminar presenter (level 3 interns) U. South Fla., Ft. Myers, 1992-94; presenter in field. Co-author: Charlotte's Arithmetic Basic Skills, 1980. Religious edn. tchr. Sacred Heart Ch., Punta Gorda, 1988—, lector, 1994—; Brownie leader Girl Scouts U.S., Port Charlotte, 1976; bd. dirs. Swim Team, Lane 4, Punta Gorda, 1991-93, cert. stroke and turn official, 1995—. Recipient Nat. Presdl. award for excellence in teaching math. NSF/Nat. Coun. Tchrs. Math., 1994, State Presdl. award for excellence in teaching math., 1993; named Charlotte County Tchr. of the Yr., Charlotte County Schs., 1993; profiled on Disney Presents the Am. Teacher, 1994; Disney/Am. Tchr. Honoree in Maths., Disney Corp. along with Campbells Soup Co., 1994. Mem. Nat. Coun. Tchrs. Math., Fla. Coun. Tchrs. Math., Coun. of Presdl. Awardees in Math., Fla. League Tchrs., Phi Delta Kappa, Alpha Delta Kappa. Democrat. Roman Catholic. Avocations: reading, sailing, camping, cross-stitch. Home: 3114 Newbury St Pt Charlotte FL 33952-7100 Office: Deep Creek Elem Sch 26900 Harbor View Rd Punta Gorda FL 33983-3601

MCGREGOR, RALPH, textile chemistry educator, consultant, researcher, author; b. Leeds, Eng., Feb. 11, 1932; s. Robert and Evelyn (Hutchison) McG.; m. Maureen Mabel McGaul, Aug. 8, 1959; children—Alasdair, Ralph, Francine. B.Sc with 1st class honors, Leeds U. (Eng.), 1953, Ph.D. in Applied Chemistry, 1957, D.Sc., 1979. Chemistry tchr. Roundhay Sch., Leeds, 1956-58; Courtauld research fellow U. Manchester, 1958-59, lectr. in polymer and fiber sci., 1959-68; vis. sr. researcher Ciba A.G., Basel, Switzerland, 1965-66; sr. scientist Fibers div. Allied Corp., Petersburg, Va., 1968-70; from assoc. prof. to prof., Cone Mills Disting. prof. textile chemistry N.C. State U., Raleigh, 1970—; spl. invited prof. Tokyo Inst. Tech., 1986. Recipient LeBlanc medal Leeds U., 1953; research medal Dyers Co., 1976; Perkin travel fellow, 1962; U.S.-Japan NSF Coop. Sci. Program grantee, 1981; N.C. Japan Ctr. fellow. Mem. Am. Chem. Soc., Am. Assn. Textile Chemists and Colorists (Olney medal 1984), Soc. Dyers and Colorists, Fiber Soc., AAUP, Sigma Xi, Phi Kappa Phi, Phi Sigma Iota. Author: Diffusion and Sorption in Fibres and Films, 1974. Contbr. articles to profl. jours. Home: 8276 Hillside Dr Raleigh NC 27612 Office: NC State Univ Box 8301 Raleigh NC 27695

MCGREGOR, WALTER, medical products company designer, inventor, consultant, educator; b. Kyiv, Ukraine, Nov. 2, 1937; came to U.S., 1957; s. William and Lydia (Aplass) McG.; m. Helen McGregor, July 18, 1965; children: Roxanne, Walter Jr. BS, Fairleigh Dickinson U., 1973, MBA in Pharm. Mktg., 1975. Sect. leader Ethicon Inc., Somerville, N.J., 1965-68, supr., 1968-76, mgr., 1976-83, dir. surg. products devel. and materials engring., 1983-92, dir. of tech., 1992-94; pres., CEO Biomark Tech. Inc., Flemington, N.J., 1994—; sr. v.p. Global Med. Countertrade Corp., 1994—; pres. Global Med. Countertrade Svcs., Inc., 1994—; guest cons. Wilmer Inst., Johns Hopkins Hosp. Rsch. Lab., Balt., 1965-70; guest lectr. dept. plastic surgery U. Va. Med. Sch., Charlottesville, 1986—. Contbr. articles to profl. jours. Patentee surg. instruments. Life mem. Rep. Presdl. Task Force, Washington, 1984—; mem. Rep. Nat. Com., 1991. Fellow Soc. for Advancement of Med. Instrumentation; mem. Am. Med. Informatics Assn. (founding), Am. Mktg. Assn. (profl.), Med. Mktg. Assn. Avocations: stamp collecting, fishing, reading in surgical developments. Home: 104 Hoffman Rd Flemington NJ 08822-7023 Office: Biomark Tech Inc 104 Hoffman Rd Flemington NJ 08822-7023

MCGREW, JEAN B., superintendent. Supt. Northfield Twp. High Sch. Dist. 225, Glenview, Ill. Recipient State Finalist for Nat. Supt. of Yr. award, 1992. Office: Northfield Twp HS Dist 225 1835 Landwehr Rd Glenview IL 60025-1241

MCGRIFF, DEBORAH, school system administrator. Supt. Detroit public schs.

MCGRIFF, FRED (FREDERICK STANLEY MCGRIFF), baseball player; b. Tampa, Oct. 31, 1963. Grad. high sch., Tampa. Baseball player N.Y. Yankees, 1981-82, Toronto Blue Jays, 1982-90, San Diego Padres, 1990-93, Atlanta Braves, 1993—. Named to Sporting News All-Star team, 1989, 92, 93; recipient Silver Slugger award, 1989, 92, 93; mem. Nat. League All-Star Team, 1992, 94; Am. League Home Run Leader, 1989; Nat. League Home Run Leader, 1992. Mem. World Series championship team, 1995. Office: Atlanta Braves PO Box 4064 Atlanta GA 30302*

MCGROARTY, BRUCE JAMES, building products manufacturing executive; b. Montreal, Que., Can., Sept. 1, 1942; came to U.S., 1980; s. Herbert Thomas and Margaret Ann (Langon) McG.; m. Bernice Dianne MacArthur, May 15, 1965; children: Shannon, Tracey, Brent, Leigh, Ryan. BBA, Ryerson U., Toronto, Ont., Can., 1968, BBM, 1975; MBA, McMaster U., Hamilton, Ont., Can., 1977. Rep. maj. accts. Abitibi-Price, Inc., Toronto, 1972-75, corp. planner, 1975-80; mgr. mktg. services Abitibi-Price Corp., Troy, Mich., 1980-83; plant mgr. Abitibi-Price Corp., Toledo, 1983-84; exec. v.p. Abitibi-Price Corp., Troy, 1984-85; pres. Abitibi-Price Corp. subs. Abitibi-Price, Inc., Troy, 1985—; chmn. bd., chief exec. officer, dir. Azerty, Inc., Orchard Park, N.Y., now pres. Avocations: skiing, squash, hockey, boating, education. Home: 20435 Ronsdale Dr Franklin MI 48025-3865 Office: Azerty Inc 13 Centre Dr Orchard Park NY 14127-4103*

MC GRODDY, JAMES CLEARY, computer company executive; b. N.Y.C., Apr. 6, 1937; s. Charles B. and Helen F. (Cleary) McG.; children: Kathleen, Sheila, Christine, James. B.S., St. Joseph's U., 1958; Ph.D., U. Md., 1964. With IBM, 1965—; dir. rsch., sr. v.p. rsch. IBM, White Plains, N.Y., 1989-96; prof. Tech. U. Denmark, 1970-71. Contbr. articles to profl. jours.; patentee in field. Recipient Frederik Philips award Inst. of Elec. and Electronics Engrs., 1995. Fellow IEEE, Am. Phys. Soc. (George E. Pake prize 1995). Office: IBM Corp Hdqrs Old Orchard Rd Armonk NY 10504-1709

MC GRORY, MARY, columnist; b. Boston, 1918; d. Edward Patrick and Mary (Jacobs) McGrory. A.B., Emmanuel Coll. Reporter Boston Herald Traveler, 1942-47; book reviewer Washington Star, 1947-54, feature writer for nat. staff, 1954-81; now syndicated columnist The Washington Post, Universal Press Syndicate. Recipient George Polk Meml. award; Pulitzer prize for commentary, 1975. Office: Washington Post 1150 15th St NW Washington DC 20071-0001

MCGRORY, MARY KATHLEEN, non-profit organization executive; b. N.Y.C., Mar. 22, 1933; d. Patrick Joseph and Mary Kate (Gilvary) McG. BA, Pace U., 1957; MA, U. Notre Dame, 1962; PhD, Columbia U., 1969; DHL, Albertus Magnus Coll., 1984; LLD, Briarwood Coll., 1990; DHL, Trinity Coll., 1991. Prof. English Western Conn. State U., Danbury, 1969-78; dean of arts and scis. Eastern Conn. State U., Willimantic, 1978-80, v.p. for acad. affairs, 1981-85; pres. Hartford Coll. for Women, Conn., 1985-91; sr. fellow U. Va. Commonwealth Ctr., Charlottesville, 1991-92; exec. dir. Soc. Values in Higher Edn./Georgetown U., Washington, 1992—; pres. MKM Assocs., Holland, Ma., 1983—. Author: Yeats, Joyce & Beckett, 1975. Bd. dirs. Hartford Hosp., 1985-93; chmn. bd. govs. Greater Hartford Consortium Higher Edn., 1989-90. Fels Found. fellow, 1966-67, NEH summer fellow, 1975; Ludwig Vogelstein Found. travel grantee, 1973. Mem. New Eng. Jr. Community and Tech. Coll. Coun. (v.p. 1988-91), Am. Assn. Higher Edn., Med. Acad. of Am., Greater Hartford C. of C. (bd. dirs. 1989-91), Hartford Club (bd. dirs. 1988-91). Avocations: writing, swimming, piano. Home: Apt 809 1727 Massachusetts Ave NW Washington DC 20036-2153 Office: Georgetown U Soc for Values Higher Edn Washington DC 20057

MCGRUDER, ROBERT, newspaper publishing executive. Exec. editor Detroit Free Press. Office: 321 W Lafayette Blvd Detroit MI 48226-2705

MC GRUDER, STEPHEN JONES, portfolio manager; b. Louisville, Nov. 14, 1943; s. Clement W. and Elizabeth Boyer (Short) McG.; m. Angeline W. Goreau, Mar. 19, 1983; 1 child, Keaton A. BS in Chemistry, Stanford U., 1966; BA in Econs, Claremont Men's Coll., 1966. Chartered fin. analyst. V.p. Surveyor Fund, N.Y.C., 1978-86, The Portfolio Group, N.Y.C., 1986-88, Wafra Investment Adv. Group, N.Y.C., 1988-95, Lord Abbett, N.Y.C., 1995—. Mem. Fin. Analysts Fedn., Univ. Club. Republican. Presbyterian. Office: Lord Abbett & Co 767 5th Ave New York NY 10153

MCGUANE, THOMAS FRANCIS, III, author, screenwriter; b. Wyandotte, Mich., Dec. 11, 1939; s. Thomas Francis and Alice Rita (Torphy) McG.; m. Portia Crockett, Sept. 8, 1962 (div. 1975); 1 child, Thomas Francis; m. Margot Kidder, 1976 (div. 1977); 1 child, Maggie; m. Laurie Buffett, Sept. 19, 1977; 1 child, Anne Buffett; 1 stepchild, Heather. BA, Mich. State U., 1962; MFA, Yale U., 1965; Wallace Stegner fellow, Stanford U., 1966; PhD (hon.), Mont. State U., 1993. Author: The Sporting Club, 1969, The Bushwacked Piano, 1971 (Richard and Hinda Rosenthal Found. award for fiction 1971), Ninety-Two in the Shade, 1973 (Nat. Book award nomination 1974), Panama, 1977, An Outside Chance: Essays on Sport, 1980, Nobody's Angel, 1982, Something to be Desired, 1984, In the Crazies: Book and Portfolio, 1984, To Skin a Cat, 1986, Keep the Change, 1989, An Outside Chance: Classic and New Essays on Sport, 1990, Nothing But Blue Skies, 1992, Sons, 1993; screenwriter: (films) Rancho Deluxe, 1975, Missouri Breaks, 1976, Tom Horn, 1980, Cold Feet, 1989; screenwriter, dir.: (films) Ninety-Two in the Shade, 1975; editor: Best American Sports Writing, 1992; contbr. to Sports Illustrated mag., 1969-73. Wallace Stegner fellow Stanford Univ., 1966-67; recipient Mont. Gov.'s award 1988, N.W. Bookseller's award 1992, Golden Plate award Am. Acad. Achievement, 1993. Mem. Tale Club of N.Y. Address: PO Box 25 Mc Leod MT 59052-0025*

MCGUCKIN, WENDY MICHELLE BLASSINGAME, accounting specialist; b. Guymon, Okla., June 11, 1966; d. Ronald Clifford Blassingame and Evelyn Marie (Maddox) Martin; m. Randall Mack McGuckin, Sept. 11, 1993. BS, U. Okla., 1989. Tchr. Norman (Okla.) Pub. Schs., 1989-90; pub. rels. coord. Hatfield and Bell, Inc., Norman, 1990-91; fin. cons. Sun Fin. Group, Oklahoma City, 1991; acctg. specialist U. Okla., Norman, 1991—; co-owner Wildfire Horse Ranch, EnviroPin; chair awards com. U. Okla. Staff Senate. Environ. activist, Oklahoma City, 1990; vol. Okla. Equine Hosp., 1994. Mem. NAFE, Okla. Equestrian Trail Riders Assn. Avocations: golf, scuba diving, gourmet cooking, skiing, western riding. Office: Univ Okla 620 Elm Ave Norman OK 73069-8801

MCGUE, CHRISTIE, federal official; b. Columbus, Ohio, Feb. 1, 1949; m. Robert Calt, Nov. 13, 1992. Sr. mgmt. analyst Nuclear Regulatory Comm., Washington, 1973-76; asst. sec., asst. dir. Office of Elec. Power Regulations, asst. dir. Office of Hydropower Licensing Fed. Energy Regulatory Comm., Washington, 1977-85; with Dept. Interior, Washington, 1986-88; dep. exec. dir. Fed. Energy Regulatory Commn., Washington, 1990-93, exec. dir., CFO, 1994—. Office: Fed Energy Regulatory Commn 888 1st St NE Rm 11-J Washington DC 20002-4232

MC GUIGAN, FRANK JOSEPH, psychologist, educator; b. Oklahoma City, Dec. 7, 1924. BA, UCLA, 1945, MA, 1949; PhD, U. So. Calif., 1950. Instr. Pepperdine Coll., 1949-50; asst. prof. U. Nev., 1950-51; rsch. assoc. Psychol. Corp., 1950-51; rsch. scientist, sr. rsch. scientist, acting dir. rsch. Human Resources Rsch. Office, George Washington U., 1951-55; prof. psychology (Hollins Coll.), Roanoke, Va., 1955-76; chmn. dept. (Hollins Coll.), 1955-76; rsch. prof. (Grad. Sch.); prof. dept. psychology, dep. psychiatry and behavioral scis. (Sch. Medicine); dir. Performance Rsch. Lab., Inst. Advanced Study, U. Louisville, 1976-83; prof. psychology, dir. Inst. Stress Mgmt. U.S. Internat. U., San Diego, 1983—; adj. prof. psychiatry and behavioral scis. U. Louisville Sch. Medicine, 1986—; adj. rsch. prof. N.C. State U., 1970-72; vis. prof. U. Hawaii, summer 1965, U. Calif., Santa Barbara, 1966, Hiroshima Shudo U., 1984; Nat. Acad. Scis. vis. scientist, Hungary, 1975, Bulgaria, 1987; sr. rsch. fellow Naval Health Rsch. Ctr., summer 1991. Author: numerous books in field including The Biological Basis of Behavior, 1963, Contemporary Studies in Psychology, 1972, Cognitive Psychophysiology - Principles of Covert Behavior, 1978, Experimental Psychology: Methods of Research, 6th edit., 1993, Psychophysiological Measurement of Covert Behavior—A Guide for the Laboratory, 1979, Calm Down—A Guide for Stress and Tension Control, 2d edit., 1992, Stress and Tension Control: Procs. of Internat., Interdisciplinary Conf. on Stress and Tension Control, 1980, vol. 2, 1984, vol. 3, 1989; (with Edmund Jacobson) cassettes Self-Directed Progressive Relaxation Training Instructions, 1981, Critical Issues in Psychology, Psychiatry and Physiology, 1986, Biological Psychology--A Cybernetic Science, 1994; editor numerous works in field.; editor, Internat. Jour. Stress Mgmt.; contbr. articles to profl. jours.; mem. editorial bd. Archiv fur Arzneitherapie, Biofeedback and Self-regulation, Activitas Nervosae Superioris. Served with USNR, 1942-46. Recipient award for outstanding contbns. to edn. in psychology Am. Psychol. Found., 1973, Blue medal of honor Union Scientists Bulgaria, 1980, medal of Sechenov USSR Acad. Med. Scis., 1983, medal of Anohkin, 1984, Pres.'s medal U. Hiroshima-Shudo, 1982, medal Okayama U., 1987, medal Tbilisi (USSR) Inst. Physiology, 1989, Edmund Jacobson award for stress mgmt., 1995, Gold medal award for lifetime achievement in application of psychology Am. Psychol. Found., 1995. Fellow APA, Internat. Soc. Rsch. on Aggression; mem. Am. Assn. Advancement of Tension Control (now Internat. Stress Mgmt. Assn.) (exec. dir. 1973-82, pres. 1985-89, exec. dir. 1992—, chmn. bd. dirs.), Pavlovian Soc. (mem. exec. bd. 1973—, pres. 1975-86, editor, chmn. publ. bd. Pavlovian Jour. Biol. Sci.), Am. Physiol. Soc., Biofeedback Soc. Am., Internam. Soc. Psychology, Internat. Congress of Applied Psychology, Psychonomic Soc., Soc. Psychophysiol. Rsch., Bulgarian Soc. for Psychiatry (hon.), Sigma Xi. Office: US Internat U Inst for Stress Mgmt 10455 Pomerado Rd San Diego CA 92131-1717

MC GUIGAN, JAMES EDWARD, physician, scientist, educator; b. Paterson, N.J., Aug. 20, 1931; s. Harold Taylor and Marie (Lloyd) McG.; m. Nancy Baron; children: Sheila, Maura, John. Student, Coll. Holy Cross, 1949-50; BS, Seattle U., 1952; MD, St. Louis U., 1956; PhD (hon.), Uppsala U., Sweden, 1989. Diplomate Am. Bd. Internal Medicine, Am. Bd. Gastroenterology. Intern Pa. Hosp., 1956-57; asst. resident in medicine U. Wash. Sch. Medicine, Seattle, 1960-62; fellow in gastroenterology U. Wash. Sch. Medicine, 1962-64; spl. fellow in immunology Washington U. Sch. Medicine, St. Louis, 1964-66; asst. prof. medicine Washington U. Sch. Medicine, 1966-69; chief div. gastroenterology U. Fla. Coll. Medicine, Gainesville, 1969-78; prof. U. Fla. Coll. Medicine, 1969—, chmn. dept. medicine, 1976—; Mem. program projects com. Nat. Inst. Arthritis, Metabolic and Digestive Diseases, NIH, 1971-73, mem. gen. medicine A study sect., 1974-76, chmn., 1976-78. Served to capt. USAF, 1957-60. Research fellow in gastroenterology; Spl. fellow in immunology; Career Devel. award; research grantee NIH; research grantee Am. Heart Assn.; research grantee Am. Cancer Soc. Mem. Am. Assn. Immunologists, Am. Gastroent. Assn. (Disting. Achievement award 1974), Am. Soc. Clin. Investigation, Assn. Am. Physicians, Assn. Profs. of Medicine, Fla. Clin. Practice Assn. (pres. 1985-91), Alachua County Med. Soc. (pres. 1985-86), Sigma Xi. Research and publs. in gastroenterology and immunology.

MCGUIGAN, THOMAS J., engineering company executive; b. Toronto, Ont., Can., Jan. 3, 1942; s. Thomas F. and Priscilla M (Robitaille) McG.; m. Ileana Petrie, Aug. 3, 1968; children: Andrea, Mark. BSc., U. Toronto, Can., 1963. Project engr. Litton Systems Can. Ltd., Etobicoke, Ont., 1963-71, dir. advance programs, 1971-81, v.p. mktg., 1981-86, pres., 1986—; v.p. Litton Industries, L.A., 1988—. Office: Litton Systems Can Ltd, 25 City View Dr, Etobicoke, ON Canada M9W 5A7

MCGUINN, MARTIN GREGORY, banker, lawyer; b. Phila., Sept. 9, 1942; s. Martin G. and Rita (Horgan) McG.; m. Ann M. Muldoon, Sept. 17, 1977; children: Patrick J., Christopher M. A.B., Villanova U., 1964, J.D., 1967. Bar: Pa. bar 1967, N.Y. bar 1970. Assoc. Sullivan & Cromwell, N.Y.C., 1970-77; mng. counsel The Singer Co., Stamford, Conn., 1977-80; vice chmn. Mellon Bank, Pitts., 1981—; bd. consultors Villanova Law Sch., 1972—, chmn. 1985-87. Editor in chief Villanova Law Rev., Vol. 12, 1966-67. Bd. dirs. U. Pitts. Med. Ctr., Carnegie Inst., Carnegie Mus. Art; mem. Carnegie 100, World Affairs Coun. Pitts. Mem. ABA, N.Y. State Bar Assn., Pa. Bar Assn., Allegheny County Bar Assn., Am. Law Inst., The Bankers Roundtable, Am. Soc. Corp. Secs. (chmn. 1990-91), Pa. Chamber of Bus. and Industry (bd. dirs.). Home: 714 Amberson Ave Pittsburgh PA 15232-1446 Office: Mellon Bank Corp 1 Mellon Bank Ctr Pittsburgh PA 15258-0001

MCGUINN, MICHAEL EDWARD, III, retired army officer; b. Spartanburg, S.C., Feb. 22, 1925; s. Michael Edward Jr. and Margaret Cordelia (Shackleford) McG.; m. Betty Gay Corn, 1948 (div. 1951); m. Phyllis Fryer, Oct. 7, 1952; childen: Michael Edward IV, Carol Ann McGuinn Branch. Student, Clemson U., 1941-43, 46, Coll. William and Mary, 1962-63. Served with U.S. Navy, PTO, 1943-46; commd. 2d lt. U.S.

Army, 1949, advanced through grades to col., 1971; asst. mil. attache Am. Embassy, Copenhagen, 1958-61; posted to svc. British Army, Longmoor, Eng., Eng., 1964-66; served on U.S. Dept. Army Gen. Staff, Washington, 1966-68; comdr. 10th Transp. Bn. U.S. Army, Vietnam, 1968-69; chief transp. div. U.S. Readiness Command, MacDill AFB, Fla., 1969-72; ret. U.S. Army, 1972; state govt. svc. various locations, 1972-82; chief of staff Ga. State Def. Force, an Agy. of the State of Ga., Atlanta, 1987-95. Decorated Legion of Merit (2), Army Commendation medal (2), Naval Commendation medal. Mem. U.S. Army Transp. Mus., The Old Guard of the Gate City Guard. Avocations: military history, photography, home workshop. Home: 6420 Tanacrest Ct NW Atlanta GA 30328-2837 Office: Ga State Def Force PO Box 17965 Atlanta GA 30316-0965 *Since boyhood when a young cadet,I have lived by one code "Duty, Honor and Country". In good times and bad, it has kept me faithful to principles of personal responsibility, personal integrity, and the importance of service to something greater than oneself. The code has never failed our nation nor has it ever failed me.*

MCGUINNESS, CATHERINE SUZANNE, graphic designer, illustrator; b. Providence, R.I., 1956; d. William Eugene and Dawn Elizabeth McG.; m. Irwin Frederick Kraus, June 12, 1993. Student, Art Inst. of Boston, 1974-75, San Francisco Art Inst., 1976-78; BFA in Graphic Design, Swain Sch. of Design, New Bedford, Mass., 1981; postgrad. in Illustration, R.I. Sch. of Design, Providence, 1987. Asst. to art dir. Harvey Probber, Inc., Fall River, Mass., 1981-82; sr. designer Delaney Design Group, Providence, R.I., 1982-88; graphic designer, project mgr. The MITRE Corp., Bedford, Mass., 1989-90; graphic designer The Laux Co., Maynard, Mass., 1991-94. Mem. Save the Bay, R.I. Recipient 1st and 2nd pl. in Corp. Identity Super Show, Art Dirs. Club of Boston, Merit award, 1983, 84, 85, 86, Design Excellence award, Am. Inst. Graphic Arts, 1985, award of excellence DESI 9 Exhbn., 1986, Merit award Art Dirs. Club of N.Y., 1987, Ozzie award, hon. mention, 1991. Avocations: sailing, skiing, guitar, drums.

MCGUINNESS-MUKERJEE, JOANNE HELENE, nursing administrator, consultant; b. Providence, Aug. 22, 1942; d. John William and Helen Louise (McCormack) McGuinness; m. Dilip K. Mukerjee, Feb. 6, 1975 (div. 1979). BS in Nursing, Simmons Coll., 1979; MEd, Cambridge Coll., 1982. Clin. specialist Lawrence (Mass.) Gen. Hosp., 1980-81; asst. dir. nursing Essex Hall, Beverly, Mass., 1981-82, Greenery Rehab. Ctr., Brighton, Mass., 1982-83; dir. nursing Elder Care Services, Tewksbury, Mass., 1983-84; asst. adminstr. Webster Manor, Mass., 1984-85, adminstr., exec. dir., 1985-89; adminstr. ADS Mgmt., Boston, 1989-93; CEO Univ. Commons Nursing Care Ctr., Worcester, Mass., 1993—; lectr. Regis Coll., Weston, Mass., 1990—, Assn. Mass. Homes for the Aging, 1993; presenter in field. Author: An Understanding of Policy Analysis, 1982. Mem. ANA (cert. adminstr., mem. gerontol. council), Am. Coll. Health Care Execs., Mass. Nurses Assn. (mem. nominating com. dist. IV 1987-88, mem. long term care task force, conveyor for nurse practice act legis.), Mass. Fedn. Nursing Homes (program chair 1984-85), Am. Nurses Found. Roman Catholic. Avocations: private and comml. pilot multiengine rating, golf, collecting 17th and 18th century French antiques. Home: 378 Plantation St Worcester MA 01605-2324 Office: 120 Fisher Ave Boston MA 02120-3320

MC GUIRE, ALFRED JAMES, former basketball coach, sports equipment company executive, basketball commentator; b. N.Y.C., Sept. 7, 1931; s. John and Winifred (Sullivan) McG.; m. Patricia Sharkey, Aug. 22, 1953; children: Alfred J., Noreen, Robert. B.A., St. John's Coll., Bklyn., 1952. Coach Dartmouth Coll., Hanover, N.H., 1955-57, Belmont Abbey Coll., Belmont, N.C., 1957-64; athletic dir., head basketball coach Marquette U., Milw., 1964-77; v.p., dir. sports edn. publs. Medalist Industries, Milw., 1970-78, also bd. dirs.; basketball commentator NBC, 1978-95; profl. basketball player, N.Y., 1951-52, Balt., 1954; pres. Hall of Fame Basketball Camps, 1967—. Trustee Milw. County Stadium Recreation Commn., 1972—. Named Sports Figure of Year Wis. C. of C., 1974; Coach of Year AP, UPI, Sporting News, U.S. Basketball Writers Assn., 1971, 74. Mem. Nat. Assn. Basketball Coaches. Club: Westmoor Country. Office: care NBC Sports 30 Rockefeller Plz New York NY 10112

MCGUIRE, CAMILLE HALL, elementary education educator; b. Wayne County, Miss., Mar. 2, 1949; d. Howard Edward Sr. and Margaret Louise (Cochran) Hall; m. Richard Jay McGuire Sr., Mar. 17, 1972; 1 child, Richard Jay Jr. BS, U. Mobile, 1971; MEd, U. South Ala., 1978. Cert. early childhood edn. 1st grade tchr. Holloway Elem. Sch., Mobile, Ala., 1971-75, Orchard Elem. Sch., Mobile, 1976-87; v.p., buyer Pestop Exterminator Inc., Mobile, 1987-91; 2nd grade tchr. O'Rourke Elem. Sch., Mobile, 1991—; pvt. tutor, Mobile, 1978—; 1st and 2nd grade chairperson Orchard and O'Rourke Schs., mobile, 1978—; supr. tchr.-trainer coll. students, 1973-86; chairperson So. Accreditation for Pub. Schs., 1979, 94; leader constant profl. growth through workshops, 1971-94. Mem. Mobile Opera Guild, 1986-91; mem. adult choir Hilcrest Bapt.Ch., 1971—, dir. children's choir, 1983—. Named Outstanding Reading Tchr. Metro Mobile Reading Coun., 1985-86. Mem. ASCD, Ashley Estates Garden Club (achievement task force 1995), Assn. Univ. Women. Avocations: reading, water sports, snow skiing in Montana and New Mexico. Office: Pauline ORourke Elem 1975 LeRoy Stevens Rd Mobile AL 36695

MC GUIRE, DOROTHY HACKETT, actress; b. Omaha, June 14, 1916; d. Thomas Johnston and Isabel (Flaherty) McG.; m. John Swope, July 18, 1943 (dec.); children: Topo Swope, Mark Swope. Student, Pine Manor Jr. Coll., 1936-38. Stage debut in A Kiss for Cinderella, Omaha, 1933; played stock in Deertrees, Maine; N.Y.C. debut as understudy in Stop-Over, 1938; played role of Emily in Our town, on Broadway, 1938; toured with My Dear Children, 1939; starred in Claudia, 1941; toured in USO prodn. Dear Ruth, Europe, 1945, USO prodn. Tonight at 8:30, 1947, Summer and Smoke, 1950; appeared in Broadway prodn. Legend of Lovers, 1951, Joan at the Stake, 1954, Winesburg, Ohio, 1958, The Night of the Iguana, 1976, Cause Celebre, 1979; film appearances include: Claudia, 1943, A Tree Grows in Brooklyn, 1945, The Enchanted Cottage, 1945, Claudia and David, 1946, The Spiral Staircase, 1946, Gentlemen's Agreement, 1947, Mr. 880, Invitation, 1952, Make Haste to Live, 1954, Three Coins in the Fountain, 1954, Trial, 1955, Friendly Persuasion, 1956, Old Yeller, 1957, This Earth is Mine, 1959, A Summer Place, 1959, The Remarkable Mr. Penny Pincher, The Swiss Family Robinson, 1960, The Dark at the Top of the Stairs, 1960, Susan Slade, 1961, Summer Magic, 1962, The Greatest Story Ever Told, 1965, Flight of the Doves, 1971; film appearances include (voice only) Jonathan Livingston Seagull, 1973; appeared in: TV movie She Waits, 1971, TV prodn Am. Playhouse: I Never Sang For My Father, 1988; radio serial Big Sister, 1937; Juliette in: Romeo and Juliette; Ophelia in Hamlet, 1951; TV appearances include U.S. Steel Hour, 1954, Lux Video Theatre, 1954, Climax, 1954, 56, Play House 90, Another Part of the Forest, 1972, The Runaways, 1975, The Philadelphia Story, 1954, Rich Man Poor Man, 1970, Little Women, 1978, The Incredible Journey of Doctor Meg Laurel, Ghost Dancing, 1983, Love Boat, 1984. Recipient N.Y. Drama Critics Circle award, 1941; named Best Actress by Nat. Bd. Rev., 1955. Mem. Screen Actors Guild, Actors Equity Assn., AFTRA. Office: Raymond J Gertz Acctg Corp 10351 Santa Monica Blvd Los Angeles CA 90025-6908

MCGUIRE, E. JAMES, lawyer; b. Kansas City, Mo., Feb. 10, 1914; m. Jean McGregor McGuire; children: Andrew, Kathleen Carroidas, Wendy, Thomas, William C. McGuire, Morton Willie, John K. McGuire. AB, U. Calif., 1936, JD, 1948. Bar: Calif. 1948. Jr. acct. exec. McCann-Erickson Inc., San Francisco, 1938-39; mgr. advt. and sales promotion Calif. Almond Growers Exchange, Sacramento, 1939-41; asst. advt. mgr. Pacific Rural Press, San Francisco, 1941-42; officer Dist. Legal Office 12th Naval Dist., San Francisco, 1946-49; ptnr. McGuire, Prom & La Lanne (formerly O'Gara and McGuire), San Francisco, 1949—; lectr. Calif. Continuing Edn. of Bar, 1964. Served to lt. comdr. USNR, 1942-46, Philippines. Mem. Calif. State Bar Assn., Phi Delta Phi, Sequoyah Country Club (Oakland, dir. 1970-74, v.p. 1973-74). Home: 889 Longridge Rd Oakland CA 94610-2451 Office: 160 Sansome St Fl 11 San Francisco CA 94104-3717

MCGUIRE, EDWARD DAVID, JR., lawyer; b. Waynesboro, Va., Apr. 11, 1948; s. Edward David and Mary Estelle (Angus) McG.; m. Georgia Ann Charuhas, Aug. 15, 1971; children: Matthew Edward, Kathryn Ann. BS in Commerce, U. Va., 1970; JD, Coll. William and Mary, 1973. Bar: Va. 1973, D.C. 1974, Md. 1990, U.S. Dist. Ct. (ea. dist.) Va. 1974, U.S. Dist. Ct. D.C. 1974, U.S. Dist. Ct. Md. 1990, Pa. 1995, U.S. Ct. Appeals (4th cir.) 1974, U.S. Ct. Appeals (D.C. cir.) 1974, U.S. Supreme Ct. 1993. Assoc. Wilkes and Artis, Washington, 1973-78; gen. corp counsel Mark Winkler Mgmt., Alexandria, Va., 1978-80; sr. contracts officer Amtrak, Washington, 1980-81; sr. real estate atty., asst. corp. sec. Peoples Drug Stores, Inc., Alexandria, 1981-88; of counsel Cowles, Rinaldi & Arnold, Ltd., Fairfax, Va., 1989-91; sr. assoc. Radigan, Rosenberg & Holmes, Arlington, Va., 1991; pvt. practice, Annandale, Va., 1992—. Bd. dirs. Dist. XVI Va. Student Aid Found., 1978-85, George Washington dist. Boy Scouts Am., 1986; active William and Mary Law Sch. Assn., bd. dirs., pres., 1987-88, treas., 1990-91. Capt. JAGC, USANG, 1973-79. Mem. ABA, Va. Bar Assn., Va. State Bar, D.C. Bar, Md. State Bar Assn., Fairfax Bar Assn., Arlington County Bar Assn., Va. Trial Lawyers Assn., Nat. Network Estate Planning Attys., William and Mary Alumni Soc. (bd. dirs. D.C. chpt. treas. 1992-94), U. Va. Club of Washington (schs. com. chmn. 1995—), Rotary (treas. Springfield chpt. 1985-86, sec. 1986-87, pres.-elect 1987, chmn. World Affairs Conf. 1985-88, 93-94, Dist. 7610 youth leadership awards chmn. 1994—, Outstanding Rotarian award 1985). Greek Orthodox. Avocations: racquetball, coaching youth sports. Home: 31 W Myrtle St Alexandria VA 22301-2422 Office: 4306 Evergreen Ln Ste 103 Annandale VA 22003-3217

MCGUIRE, JAMES CHARLES, aircraft company executive; b. St. Louis, Aug. 8, 1917; s. John Patrick and Anna Beulah (Erbar) McG.; AB, Washington U., St. Louis, 1949, MA (Univ. fellow), 1953, PhD, 1954; m. Eunice Leota Sloop, Mar. 21, 1942 (div. June 1948); 1 child: Judith Lynn; m. Ingrid Elisabeth Getreu, Sept. 16, 1954. Research assoc. Ohio State U., 1953-56; rsch. psychologist Aeromed. Lab., Wright-Patterson AFB, Ohio, 1956-59; group supr. Boeing Airplane Co., Seattle, 1959-61; dept. mgr. Internat. Electric Corp., Paramus, N.J., 1961-62; sr. human factors scientist System Devel. Corp., Santa Monica, Calif., 1962-67; v.p. Booz-Allen Applied Rsch., Saigon, Vietnam, 1967-72; v.p. Assoc. Cons. Internat., Saigon, 1972-75, Bethesda, Md., 1975-78; br. chief Human Factors, System Tech. Devel., 1978-82; prin. staff engr. tech. modernization methodology Douglas Aircraft Co., Long Beach, Calif., 1982-85; program mgr. cockpit automation tech. program, Northrop Aircraft div., Hawthorne, Calif., 1985-87; sect. mgr. aircraft programs human factors engring. dept. Douglas Aircraft Co., Long Beach, 1987—, sr. staff engr. Crew Systems Tech., 1990-93; prin. engr. tech. McDonnell Douglas Aerospace Transport Aircraft, 1993-94; prin. engr.-scientist, crew sys. tech., advanced transport aircraft devel., McDonnell Douglas Aerospace, 1995—; lectr. Nat. Def. Coll., Vietnamese Armed Forces, Saigon, 1971. Served with AUS, 1940-46. Decorated Bronze Star medal with oak leaf cluster; recipient Tech. Svc. First Class medal Republic South Vietnam Armed Forces, 1968. Mem. Am. Psychol. Assn., IEEE, Computer Soc. of IEEE, Human Factors Soc., Am. Assn. Artificial Intelligence, Phi Beta Kappa, Sigma Xi. Republican. Home: 23201 Mindanao Cir Dana Point CA 92629 Office: McDonnell Douglas Aerospace Advanced Transport Aircraft Devel 1510 Hughes Way Mail Code 71-11 Long Beach CA 90810-1870

MCGUIRE, JOHN MURRAY, chemist, researcher; b. New Bedford, Mass., May 15, 1929; s. Thomas C., Jr. and Mary W. (Murray) McG.; m. Harriet S. Drake, Aug. 5, 1954; children: Joseph P., John M. Jr., Thomas C., David Vincent, James E., M. Catherine. BS in Chemistry, U. Miami, Coral Gables, Fla., 1948, MS in Phys. Chemistry, 1951; PhD in Phys. Chemistry, U. Fla., Gainesville, 1955. Product chemist GE, Waterford, N.Y., 1955-57; sr. rsch. chemist W. R. Grace R & D, Clarksville, Md., 1957-60; sr. chemist, supr. GE, Syracuse, N.Y., 1960-70; engr. advanced materials GE, Decatur, Ill., 1970-71; rsch. chemist EPA, Athens, Ga., 1971-73, supervisory rsch. chemist, 1973-95; ret., 1995; rec. for blind, 1995—; ham radio operator, 1995—. Editorial advisor Biomedical Mass Spectrometry jour., 1974-83; contbr. articles to tech. publs. Decorated knight and knight comdr. of Holy Sepulchre of Jerusalem. Mem. Am. Chem. Soc. (sect. chmn. 1986), Am. Soc. Mass Spectrometry (chmn. environ. com. 1973-75), KC (grand knight Athens 1973-79, state dep. Ga. 1986-87, Ga. master 4th degree 1988-92). Republican. Roman Catholic. Avocations: reading, church work.

MC GUIRE, JOSEPH WILLIAM, business educator; b. Milw., Mar. 14, 1925; s. William B. and Marion (Dunn) McG.; m. Margaret Drewek, Aug. 20, 1946; children: Laurence, Karen, Eileen, Kevin. Ph.B., Marquette U., 1948, D.B.A. (hon.), 1981; M.B.A., Columbia U., 1950, Ph.D., 1956; LL.D. (hon.), St. Benedict's Coll., 1968. Asst. prof. U. Wash. Coll. Bus. Adminstrn., Seattle, 1954-56; assoc. prof. U. Wash. Coll. Bus. Adminstrn., 1956-61, prof., 1961-63; prof., dean U. Kans. Sch. Bus., 1963-68; dean Coll. Commerce and Bus. Adminstrn., prof. U. Ill., Urbana, 1968-71; v.p. planning U. Calif., Berkeley, 1971-74; prof. adminstrn. U. Calif., Irvine, 1973-95—, assoc. dean exec. degree programs, 1990-94, prof. emeritus, 1995—; vis. prof. Netherlands Coll. Econs., Rotterdam, 1957-58, dept. econs. U. Hawaii, 1962-63, Michael Smrfit Grad. Sch. of Bus. Univ. Coll., Dublin, Ireland, 1993, Am. U. of Armenia, 1993; Ford. vi. rsch. prof. Carnegie-Mellon U. Grad. Sch. Indsl. adminstrn., 1987-88; cons. editor Wadsworth Pub. Co., 1964-70, Goodyear Pub. Co., 1973-81, Scott Foresman & Co., 1981-90. Author: Business and Society, 1963, Theories of Business Behavior, 1964, Factors Affecting the Growth of Manufacturing Firms, 1963, Inequality; The Poor and the Rich in America, 1968; Editor, contbr.: Interdisciplinary Studies in Business Behavior, 1962, Contemporary Management: Issues and Viewpoints, 1973. Served with USAAF, 1943-45. Recipient McKenzie awards, 1963, 65. Fellow Am. Acad. Mgmt. (bd. govs. 1967-70), Internat. Acad. Mgmt.; mem. Am. Assn. Collegiate Schs. Bus. (dir. 1970-71), Am. Econ. Assn., AAUP, Am. Inst. Decision Scis., Western Econs. Assn., Western Tax Assn. (dir. 1977-80), Assn. Social Econs. (exec. council 1970-75, pres. 1973-74), Western Acad. Mgmt. (dir. 1975-81, pres. 1980-81), Phi Beta Kappa, Beta Gamma Sigma. Home: 54 Lessay Newport Beach CA 92657

MCGUIRE, MAVIS LOUISE, professional society administrator; b. Sioux Falls, S.D., Oct. 6, 1948; d. Francis and Beverly Beatrice McG.; m. Kenneth Chatzinoff, May 22, 1983. BSN, U. Iowa, 1974, MA in Nursing, 1976. Cert. pediatric nurse practitioner. Pediatric nurse practitioner Children & Youth Project, Davenport, Iowa, 1976-77; dir. pediatric nurse practitioner program Gwynedd Mercy Coll., Gwynedd Valley, Pa., 1977-84; exec. dir. Nat. Assn. Pediatric Nurse Assocs. & Pracitioners, Cherry Hill, N.J., 1981—; bd. dirs. Pa. Nurses Assn. Dist. Level, 1978-80; cons. in field. Mem. edit. bd. Jour Pediatric Health Care, 1986—. Fellow Nat. Assn. Pediatric Assocs. and Practitioners; mem. NAFE, Nat. Assn. Assn. Execs., Sigma Theta Tau. Avocation: music. Home: 2 Greenbriar Ln Riverton NJ 08077-3876 Office: Nat Assn Pediatric Nurse Assocs and Practitioners 1101 Kings Hwy N # 206 Cherry Hill NJ 08034-1912

MCGUIRE, MICHAEL FRANCIS, plastic and reconstructive surgeon; b. St. Louis, Oct. 4, 1946; s. Arthur Patrick and Virginia Claribel (Gannon) McG. BA, Columbia U., 1968, MD, 1972. Diplomate Am. Bd. Surgery, Am. Bd. Plastic Surgery. Intern UCLA, 1972-73, resident in gen. surgery, 1973-77, resident in plastic surgery, 1978-80; fellow in plastic surgery rsch. Stanford (Calif.) U., 1977-78; traveling fellow in plastic surgery Gt. Britain, 1980; chief plastic surgery L.A. County-Olive View Med. Ctr., Sylmar, Calif., 1980-85; pvt. practice Santa Monica, Calif., 1980—; bd. dirs. Calif. Med. Rev., Inc.; pres. Pacific Coast Plastic Surgery Ctr., Inc., Santa Monica, 1987—; asst. clin. prof. surgery UCLA, 1980—, mem. exec. com., 1993—; vice chmn. plastic surgery St. John's Hosp., Santa Monica, 1987-91. chmn. plastic surgery, 1992—, chmn. surg. svc. rev. com., 1995—; dir. cleft palate team Los Angeles County-Olive View Med. Ctr., 1986—; mem. ops. com. Med. Profl. Group, 1995. Charter patron L.A. Music Ctr. Opera, 1983—; sponsoring patron Los Angeles County Art Mus., 1986—; patron Colleague Helpers in Philanthropic Svc., Bel Air, Calif., 1987, 93, 95; pres. Found. for Surg. Reconstrn., 1996—. Fellow ACS, Royal Soc. Medicine; mem. Am. Soc. Plastic and Reconstructive Surgeons, Am. Soc. Aesthetic Plastic Surgery, Los Angeles County Med. Assn. (v.p. 1995), Calif. Soc. Plastic Surgery (exec. com., auditor 1988-89, program chmn. 1990, exec. coun. 1991-94, treas. 1994—), Am. Assn. Accreditation of Ambulatory Surgery (facilities ops. com. 1995-96, bd. dirs. 1996—), Alpha Omega Alpha. Democrat. Episcopalian. Avocations: golf, travel, collecting antique Irish glass, opera, modern art. Office: 1301 20th St Ste 460 Santa Monica CA 90404-2050

MC GUIRE, MICHAEL JOHN, environmental engineer; b. San Antonio, June 29, 1947; s. James Brendan and Opal Mary (Brady) McG.; BS in Civil Engring., U. Pa., 1969; MS in Environ Engring., Drexel U., 1972, PhD in Environ. Engring., 1977; diplomate Am. Acad. Environ. Engring.; m. Deborah Marrow, June 19, 1971; children: David, Anna. San. engr. Phila. Water Dept., 1969-73; rsch. assoc. Drexel U., Phila., 1976-77; prin. engr. Brown & Caldwell Cons. Engrs., Pasadena, Calif., 1977-79; water quality engr. Met. Water Dist. of So. Calif., L.A., 1979-84, water quality mgr., 1984-86, dir. water quality, 1986-90, asst. gen. mgr., 1990-92; pres. McGuire Environ. Cons., Inc., Santa Monica, Calif., 1992—; cons. to subcom. on adsorbents, safe drinking water com. Nat. Acad. Scis., 1978-79; cons. mem. Techs. Workgroup USEPA, DBP Reg Neg, 1992-93. Registered profl. engr., Pa., N.J., Calif. Mem. Am. Water Works Assn. (Acad. Achievement award 1978, edn. div. chmn. 1982-83, chair taste and odor com. 1993—, Calif.-Nev. sect., chmn. water quality and resources div. 1982-83, governing bd. 1984-87, 89-96, exec. com. 1989-96, chmn. 1991-92, nat. dir. 1993-96, trustee Research Found. 1983-86, nat. v.p. 1994-96, nat. exec. com. 1994-96, Fuller award 1994), Am. Chem. Soc., ASCE, Internat. Water Supply Assn., Internat. Assn. on Water Quality (specialist group on taste and odor control 1982—, chmn. organizing com. 1991, off-flavor symposium 1987-91), Internat. Ozone Assn. (internat. bd. dirs. 1992-95), Sigma Xi, Sigma Nu, Sigma Tau. Editor: (with I.H. Suffet) Activated Carbon Adsorption of Organics From the Aqueous Phase, 2 vols., 1980; Treatment of Water by Granular Activated Carbon, 1983; contbr. articles to profl. jours. Office: McGuire Environ Cons Inc 469 25th St Santa Monica CA 90402-3103

MCGUIRE, PATRICIA A., lawyer, academic administrator; b. Phila., Nov. 13, 1952; d. Edward J. and Mary R. McGuire. BA cum laude, Trinity Coll., 1974; JD, Georgetown U., 1977. Bar: Pa. 1977, D.C. Ct. Appeals 1979. Program dir. Georgetown U. St. Law Clinic, Washington, 1977-82; asst. dean for devel. and external affairs Georgetown U. Law Ctr., Washington, 1982-89; pres. Trinity Coll., Washington, 1989—; adj. prof. law Georgetown U., 1977-82, Georgetown Law Ctr., 1987—; commr. Mid. States Commn. on Higher Edn., 1991—; bd. dirs. Acacia Group. Editor: Street Law Mock Trial Manual, 1984; contbr. articles to profl. jours. Trustee Trinity Coll., 1986—; bd. dirs. Assn. Cath. Colls. and Univs., 1991—, Eugene and Agnes Meyer Found.; mem. adv. bd. Merion Mercy Acad. and Sisters of Mercy, 1990—; bd. dirs. Nat. Assn. Ind. Colls. and Univs.; mem. commn. govt. rels. Am. Coun. Edn. Recipient Daytime Emmy, TV Acad., N.Y.C., 1979-80. Mem. ABA, Assn. Am. Law Schs. (instl. advancement 1985—), Coun. for the Advancement and Support of Edn., Trinity Coll. Alumnae Assn. (pres. 1986-89). Democrat. Roman Catholic. Office: Trinity Coll Office of the President 125 Michigan Ave NE Washington DC 20017-1094

MCGUIRE, ROGER ALAN, foreign service officer; b. Troy, Ohio, July 1, 1943; s. Charles M. and Mary L. (Coppock) McG.; m. Harriet H. Cooke, July 12, 1969; children: Sara, Casey. BA, Beloit Coll., 1965; MA, U. Wis., 1967. Country desk officer Dept. State, Washington, 1974-78; dep. chief of mission Am. Embassy, Maputo, Mozambique, 1978-80; congl. fellow Am. Polit. Sci. Assn., Washington, 1980-81; polit. officer Am. Embassy, Asuncion, Paraguay, 1981-83, Lusaka, Zambia, 1983-86; dep. dir. Office of West African Affairs Dept. of State, Washington, 1986-88; chief of mission Am. Embassy, Windhoek, Namibia, 1988-90; consul Am. Consulate, Porto Alegre, Brazil, 1990-92; U.S. amb. to Guinea-Bissau, 1992-95; counselor for polit. affairs Am. Embassy, Canberra, Australia, 1995—. Recipient Superior Honor award U.S. Agy. for Internat. Devel., 1969. Mem. Rotary Internat., Phi Beta Kappa. Home and Office: Am Embassy-Canberra Box 18 PSC 277 APO AP 96549

MCGUIRE, TIMOTHY JAMES, lawyer, county and state official; b. Mount Pleasant, Mich., Mar. 24, 1949; s. James Edward and Anita Matilda (Starr) McG.; m. T. Jean Fannin, May 10, 1975; children: Tracy, Jason, Jeffrey. BA, Aquinas Coll., Grand Rapids, Mich., 1971; JD cum laude, William Mitchell Coll. Law, St. Paul, 1987. Bar: Minn. 1987. Mng. editor Ypsilanti Press, Mich., 1973-75, Corpus Christi Caller, Tex., 1975-77, Lakeland Ledger, Fla., 1977-79, Mpls. Star, 1979-82; mng. editor features and sports Mpls. Star and Tribune, 1982-84, mng. editor, 1984-91, exec. editor, 1991-93; editor, gen. mgr. reader customer unit, 1993—; Pulitzer Prize juror, 1988-89, 95-96. Mem. Oakland County Bd. Commrs., 1985—, pers. com., 1985-94, vice chmn. pub. svcs. com., 1988-89, vice chmn. planning and bldg. com., 1989-91, majority party caucus, 1987-89; chmn. Oakland County Zoning Coordinating Bd., 1991, 93, vice chmn., 1992; mem. exec. coun. Southeast Mich. Coun. Govts., 1993-95; pub. hearing officer Oakland County Road Commn., 1983-85; adminstr. emeritus David L. Moffit Scholarships for Outstanding Legal Editl. Achievement and Outstanding Achievement in Legal Journalism, U. Detroit Sch. Law; apptd. to Mich. State Hazardous Waste Site Rev. Bd., 1995—. Mem. Am. Soc. Newspaper Editors (bd. dirs. 1992—, chmn. change com. 1994-95, chmn. program com. 1996—), Minn. State Bar Assn. Roman Catholic. Home: 3645 Rosewood Ln N Minneapolis MN 55441-1127 Office: Star Tribune 425 Portland Ave Minneapolis MN 55488-0001

MCGUIRE, TIMOTHY WILLIAM, economics and management educator, dean; b. Englewood, N.J., Nov. 30, 1938; s. Charles James and Marie (McCarthy) McG.; children: Timothy William Jr., Gretchen Elizabeth, Michael Joseph; m. Nancy Paule Melone, 1991. BS in Indsl. Mgmt., Carnegie Inst. Tech., 1960, MS in Econs., 1961; PhD in Econs., Stanford U., 1968. Staff mem. Coun. Econ. Advisors, 1963-64; rsch. assoc. in econs. Grad. Sch. Indsl. Adminstrn., Carnegie Mellon U., Pitts., 1964-66, asst. prof. econs., 1966-69, assoc. prof., 1969-75, prof., 1975-79, prof. mgmt. and econs., 1982—, dep. dean, 1983-90; prof. social scis. and econs. Dept. Social Scis. Carnegie Mellon U., Pitts., 1981-82; prof. econs., chmn. dept. U. Iowa, Iowa City, 1979-80; dean, Harry B. Miller prof. bus. Charles H. Lundquist Coll. Bus., U. Oreg., Eugene, 1994—; sr. visitor U. Cambridge, Eng., summer, 1970; vice chmn. bd. dirs. Mgmt. Sci. Assocs., Inc., Pitts. Contbr. articles to profl. jours. Woodrow Wilson Nat. Hon. fellow Carnegie Inst. Tech., 1960-61; Stanford U. fellow, 1961-62; fellow Ford Found., 1962-63, 70-71. Mem. Internat. Soc. Bayesian Analysis, Am. Econ. Assn., Am. Mktg. Assn., Inst. Mgmt. Scis., Ops. Rsch. Soc. Am., Soc. Judgment and Decision Making, Am. Statis. Assn., Tau Beta Pi, Omicron Delta Kappa. Home: 3302 Stoney Ridge Rd Eugene OR 97405-7009 Office: Charles Lundquist Coll Bus 1208 U Oreg Eugene OR 97403-1208

MC GUIRE, WILLIAM, civil engineer, educator; b. S.I., N.Y., Dec. 17, 1920; s. Edward Joseph and Phoebe (Sellman) McG.; m. Barbara Weld, Feb. 5, 1944; children—Robert Weld, Thomas Rhodes. B.S. in Civil Engring, Bucknell U., 1942; M.Civil Engring., Cornell U., 1947. Structural designer Jackson & Moreland (engrs.), Boston, 1947-49; faculty Cornell U., Ithaca, 1949—; prof. civil engring. Cornell U., 1960-90, prof. emeritus of civil engring., 1990—; dir. Cornell U. (Sch. Civil Engring.), 1966-68; vis. prof. civil engring. Asian Inst. Tech., Bangkok, Thailand, 1968-70; vis. research engr. Nat. Bur. Standards, 1972; Gledden vis. sr. fellow U. Western Australia, 1973; cons. structural engr., 1951—; vis. prof. U. Tokyo, 1979, U. Strathclyde, 1986. Author: Steel Structures, 1967, (with R.H. Gallagher) Matrix Structural Analysis, 1979. Served to lt. USNR, 1942-45. Recipient Naval Letter of Commendation, award for Outstanding Achievement, Bucknell U., 1987, T.R. Higgins Lectureship award Am. Inst. Steel Constrn., 1992. Fellow ASCE (pres. Ithaca 1964, Norman medal 1962, 94, Hardesty award 1992, honorary mem. 1994); mem. Internat. Assn. Bridge and Structural Engring., Nat. Acad. Engring., Sigma Xi, Chi Epsilon, Kappa Delta Rho. Congregationalist. Home: 121 Simsbury Dr Ithaca NY 14850-1728

MCGUIRE, WILLIAM B(ENEDICT), lawyer; b. Newark, Feb. 14, 1929; m. Joan Glinane, June 3, 1968; children: Joan Ellen, Ralph R., James C., Keith P., Grant W. BS, Fordham U., 1950; JD, Seton Hall U., 1958; LLM in Taxation, NYU, 1963. Bar: N.J. 1958, U.S. Dist. Ct. N.J. 1958, U.S. Supreme Ct. 1971, U.S. Ct. Appeals (3rd cir.) 1980, N.Y. 1982. Chief acct. Hanover Fire Ins. Co., N.Y.C., 1950-58; sr. ptnr. Lum, Biunno & Tompkins, Newark, 1958-83, Tompkins, Mc Guire & Wachenfeld, 1984—; asst. prosecutor Essex County, N.J., 1964-65; bd. dirs. Ind. Coll. Fund of N.J., St. Peter's Coll., Delbarton Sch.; trustee St. Barnabas Hosp.; mem. Essex County Ethics Com., 1974-77; mem. com. to review State Commn. of Investigation, 1982. Fellow Am. Coll. Trial Lawyers, Am. Bar Found., Am. Bd. Trial Advocates, Internat. Acad. Trial Lawyers, Internat. Soc. Barristers; mem. ABA, N.J. State Bar Assn. (trustee 1982-89, sec. 1989-90, treas. 1990-91, 2nd v.p. 1991-92, 1st v.p. 1992-93, pres. elect 1993-94, pres. 1994-95), N.J. State Bar Found. (pres. 1988-89), Essex County Bar Assn. (pres. 1975-76), Internat. Assn. Ins. Counsel, Fedn. Ins. Counsel, Def. Research Inst., Maritime Law Assn. U.S., Am. Arbitration Assn., Trial Attys. N.J., Assn. Fed. Bar N.J. (pres. 1985-88). Roman Catholic. Club: Essex County Country (pres. 1983), Newark. Office: 4 Gateway Ctr 100 Mulberry St Newark NJ 07102-4004

MCGUIRE, WILLIAM DENNIS, health care system executive; b. Glen Ridge, N.J., Sept. 24, 1943; s. John William and Kathleen Mary (Sexton) McG.; B.A., U. Notre Dame, 1965; M.H.A., U. Mich., 1968; m. Nancy Katherine Hoyne, Aug. 13, 1966; children: Kathleen Anne, Colleen Dempsey. Asst. adminstr. U. Wis. Hosps., Madison, 1971-74; adminstr. Children's Med. Ctr., Dayton, Ohio, 1974-79; sr. v.p. Mercy Cath. Med. Ctr., Phila., 1979-80; chief exec. officer Wills Eye Hosp., Phila., 1980-85; pres., chief exec. officer Mercy Health Care System, Scranton, Pa., 1985-89; pres., chief exec. officer Mt. Carmel Health, Columbus, Ohio, 1989-92; pres., chief exec. officer Incarnate Word Health Services, San Antonio, 1992-95; pres., CEO Catholic Med. Ctr. Bklyn. & Queens, 1996—; adj. faculty dept. health care Trinity U., 1992-95; asst. prof. Ohio State U., 1990-92; asst. clin. prof. Wright State U. Sch. Medicine, Dayton, Ohio, 1978-79; instr. U. Wis., Madison, 1972-73; mem. Wilkes Coll. Health Adminstrn. Adv. Com., 1988-89, Coll. Misericordia Health Care Task Force, 1988-89. Trustee Community Blood Ctr., 1977-79, Cath. Social Svcs., 1976-79, pres., 1978-79; bd. dirs. Coop. Purchasing Corp., 1974-79; mem. Dayton Pub. Schs. Lay Adv. Com. on Vocat. Edn., 1974-79; pres. Dayton Area Young Adminstrs. Group, 1977; pres. elect Greater Dayton Area Hosp. Assn., 1979; mem. allied health technologies adv. com. Sinclair Community Coll., 1974-79; bd. dirs. Covenant Health System, 1992—, Consolidated Cath. Casualty Risk Retention Group, 1992-95; active United Way, ARC. Mem. Am. Coll. Healthcare Execs., Acad. for Cath. Health Care Leadership, Mercy Leadership Group, Nat. Commn. Cath. Health Care Ministry-Resource Devel. Com., 1988-89, Maj. Cath. Hosp. Alliance, 1989—, chmn.- elect, 1995—, sec. 1990-95, Health Care Fin. Mgmt. Assn., Am. Assn. Univ. Profs. Ophthalmology, Am. Soc. Law and Medicine, Am. Hosp. Assn., Am. Assn. Eye and Ear Hosps. (pres.-elect 1984-85), Health Mgmt. Edn. Assn. (pres. 1987-88), Hosp. Assn. N.Y. State, Greater N.Y. Hosp. Assn., Tex. Hosp. Assn., Ohio Hosp. Assn., Hosp. Assn. Pa., Cath. Health Assn., Am. Pub. Health Assn., Pa. Pub. Health Assn., Del. Valley Hosp. Council, Pa. Emergency Health Svcs. Coun., Del. County Emergency Health Svcs. Coun., Nat. Union Hosp. and Health Care Employees (plan trustee), Pa. Hosps. Ins. Co. Adv. Coun., 1988-89, C. of C., U. Notre Dame Alumni Assn., U. Mich. Alumni Assn., U. Wis. Med. Sch. Alumni Assn., Wills Eye Soc., Sorin Soc., Notre Dame Club (pres. 1971, v.p. 1983-84), Plaza Club, Dominion Country Club. Republican. Roman Catholic. Office: Catholic Med Ctr Bklyn & Queens 88-25 153 St Jamaica NY 11432

MC GUIRE, WILLIAM JAMES, social psychology educator; b. N.Y.C., Feb. 17, 1925; s. James William and Anne M. (Mitchell) McG.; m. Claire Vernick, Dec. 29, 1954; children—James William, Anne Maureen, Steven Thomas. BA, Fordham U., 1949, MA, 1950; PhD, Yale U., 1954; PhD (hon.), Eötvös U., Budapest, Hungary, 1990. Postdoctoral fellow U. Minn., 1954-55; assoc. prof. psychology U. Ill., 1958-61; prof. Columbia U., 1961-67, U. Calif., San Diego, 1967-70; vis. prof. London Sch. Econs., 1970-71; asst. prof. Yale U., New Haven, 1955-58, prof., 1971—, chmn. dept. psychology, 1971-73; Mem. adv. panel for sociology and social psychology NSF, 1963-65; mem. review panel for social scis. NIMH, 1968-72, cons., 1974-85. Author: Content and Processes in the Experience of Self, 1988, A Perspectivist Approach to Strategic Planning, 1989, Structure of Attitudes and Attitude Systems, 1989, The Content, Structure, and Operation of Thought Systems, 1991; contbr. to Ency. Brit.; editor Jour. Personality and Social Psychology, 1967-70; cons. editor European Jour. Social Psychology, 1978—, Jour. Applied Social Psychology, 1983—, Jour. Exptl. Social Psychology, 1994—. With AUS, 1943-46. Recipient Ann. Social Psychology award AAAS, 1964, Gen. Electric Found. awards, 1963, 64, 66, Disting. Scientist award Soc. Exptl. Social Psychology, 1992; grantee NSF, 1960-79, NIH, 1979—; Fulbright fellow Louvain (Belgium) U., 1950-51, Ctr. for Advanced Study in Behavioral Scis. fellow, 1965-66, Guggenheim fellow, 1970-71, William James fellow Am. Psychol. Soc., 1989—. Fellow APA (pres. divsn. personality and social psychology 1973-74, Disting. Sci. Contbn. award 1988); mem. Am. Sociol. Assn., Am. Assn. Pub. Opinion Rsch., Sigma Xi. Home: 225 Saint Ronan St New Haven CT 06511-2313 Office: Yale U Dept Psychology Box 208205 New Haven CT 06520-8205

MC GUIRE, WILLIAM W., health maintenance organization executive; b. Troy, N.Y., 1948. Grad., U. Tex., 1970, U. Tex., 1974. Chmn., CEO, pres., dir. United Healthcare Corp.; dir. SciMed Life Ins. Co., Systems, Inc., Mpls. Office: United Healthcare Corp 300 Opus Ctr 9900 Bren Rd E Minnetonka MN 55343-9664*

MCGUIRK, RONALD CHARLES, banker; b. Balt., Dec. 9, 1938; s. Charles F. and Grace E. (Delcher) McG.; m. Katherine Sauer, Oct. 1, 1960; children: Frank D., Ann E. Student St. John's Coll., Annapolis, Md., 1956-59. Sr. data processing officer 1st Nat. Bank, Balt., 1966-72, v.p. data processing, 1972-76, v.p. mktg., 1976-80, sr. v.p. mktg., 1980-90, sr. v.p. corp. plan, chief of staff to CEO, 1990-94; sr. v.p., corporate sec. First Md. Bancorp, Balt., 1995—. Bd. dirs. North Arundel Hosp., Glen Burnie, Md., 1974—, Internet, Inc., 1990-95, Glen Burnie Urban Renewal Com., 1995—, Annapolis Symphony, 1991-92; mem. adv. bd. Hist. Annapolis Found., 1982-85, dir., 1985-90; chmn. Annapolis Boundary Commn., 1983-84; mem. Anne Arundel County Coun., 1974-82, Anne Arundel County Libr. Bd., 1974-84; pres. Anne Arundel County Scholarship for Scholars/Bd. Edn., 1983-85, treas., 1985-88; mem. Anne Arundel County Charter Rev. Commn., 1986, Anne Arundel County Govt. Salary Commn., 1985, 89; chmn. Anne Arundel County Impact Fee Study Task Force, 1987; pres. Anne Arundel County YMCA, 1987-89, bd. dirs. 1982-87, 89-90; mem. Commn. for Ednl. Excellence, 1988-90; vice chmn. Ft. Meade Coordinating Coun., 1989-91; mem. Exec. Com. Md. Bus.-Industry PAC 1991—, Anne Arundel County Charter and Orgn. Transition Group, 1991; corp. ptnr. Sch. bus. and Mgmt. Morgan State U., 1991-92; bd. trustees Md. Hist. Soc., 1995—. Mem. Ctr. Club. Democrat. Roman Catholic. Office: 1st Nat Bank Md 25 S Charles St Baltimore MD 21201

MCGUIRK, TERRENCE, former broadcasting company executive; b. Bklyn., Apr. 2, 1925; s. William Edward and Loretta Beatrice (Lanigan) McG.; m. Gloria Helen Geoghan, June 17, 1950; children: Terence F., Sara McGuirk Duncan, Susan McGuirk Blank, Elizabeth McGuirk Magee, Melissa McGuirk Bowman, Bryan, Michelle McGuirk O'Connor. B.S., Fordham U., 1950. Nat. sales mgr. St. WAGA-TV, Atlanta, 1966-68; mgr. Sta. WAGA-TV, Atlanta, 1970-75; eastern sales mgr. Storer TV Sales, N.Y.C., 1968-70; pres., gen. mgr. Sta. WTEN-TV, Albany, N.Y., 1976-82; pres. Knight-Ridder Broadcasting, Inc., 1982-85; ret. Assoc. trustee Siena Coll., Loudonville, N.Y., 1979-83; trustee Meml. Hosp. Found., 1980-83; dir. Albany chpt. ARC, 1987-91. Served with U.S. Army, 1943-46. Mem. Mariner Sands Country Club, Schuyler Meadows Club (dir. 1979-84), Babylon Yacht Club (hon.).

MCGUIRL, MARLENE DANA CALLIS, law librarian, educator; b. Hammond, Ind., Mar. 22, 1938; d. Daniel David and Helen Elizabeth (Baludis) Callis; m. James Franklin McGuirl, Apr. 24, 1965. AB, Ind. U., 1959; JD, DePaul U., 1963; MALS, Rosary Coll., 1965; LL.M., George Washington U., 1978, postgrad. Harvard U., 1985. Bar: Ill. 1963, Ind. 1964, D.C. 1972. Asst., DePaul Coll. of Law Libr., 1961-62, asst. law libr., 1962-65; ref. law librarian Boston Coll. Sch. Law, 1965-66; libr. dir. D.C. Bar Library, 1966-70; asst. chief Am.-Brit. Law Div. Libr. of Congress, Washington, 1970, chief, 1970-90, environ. cons., 1990—; counsel Cooter & Gell, 1992-93; adminstr. Washington Met. Transit Authority, 1994—; libr. cons. s. Nat. Clearinghouse on Poverty Law, OEO, Washington, 1967-69, Northwestern U. Nat. Inst. Edn. in Law and Poverty, 1969, D.C. Office of Corp. Counsel, 1969-70; instr. law librarianship Grad. Sch. of U.S. Dept. of Agr., 1968-72; lectr. legal lit. Cath. U., 1972; adj. asst. prof., 1973-91; lectr. environ. law George Washington U., 1979—; judge Nat. and Internat. Law Moot Ct. Competition, 1976-78, 90—; pres. Hamburger Heaven, Inc., Palm Beach, Fla., 1981-91, L'Image de Marlene Ltd., 1986-92, Clinique de Beauté Inc., 1987-92, Heads & Hands Inc., 1987-92, Horizon Design & Mfg. Co., Inc., 1987—; dir. Stoneridge Farm Inc., Gt. Falls, Va., 1984—. Contbr. articles to profl. jours. Mem. Georgetown Citizens Assn.; trustee D.C. Law Students in Ct.; del. Ind. Democratic Conv., 1964. Recipient Meritorious Svc. award Libr. of Congress, 1974, letter of commendation Dir. of Pers., 1976, cert. of appreciation, 1981-84. Mem. ABA (facilities law libr. Congress com. 1976-89), Fed. Bar Assn. (chpt. council 1972-76), Ill. Bar Assn., Women's Bar Assn. (pres. 1972-73, exec. bd. 1973-77, Outstanding Contbn. to Human Rights award 1975), D.C. Bar Assn., Am. Bar Found., Nat. Assn. Women Lawyers, Am. Assn. Law Libraries, (exec. bd. 1973-77), Law Librarians Soc. of Washington (pres. 1971-73), Exec. Women in Govt. Home: 3416 P St NW Washington DC 20007-2705

MC GUIRT, WAYNE ROBERT, publishing company executive; b. Englewood, N.J., May 19, 1943; s. Wayne Paul and Helen Elaine (Rinaldi) McG.; B.A., Fordham U., 1965; M.B.A. in Fin., Columbia U., 1972; M.B.A. in Mktg., N.Y. U., 1981; m. Lisa Berger, Sept. 12, 1975. Computer ops. mgr. CIT Fin. Co., N.Y.C., 1966-68; fin. leasing specialist Efficient Leasing Corp., Ft. Lee, N.J., 1968-71; comptrollers asst. Time Inc., N.Y.C., 1972-73 ; asst. bus. mgr. Sports Illustrated, N.Y.C., 1973-75; bus. mgr. U.S. edit. Time Mag., N.Y.C., 1975-77; dir. planning Dow Jones & Co., Inc., N.Y.C., 1978-81; v.p. devel. Richard D. Irwin, Subs. Dow Jones, Homewood, Ill., 1981-84; chmn., CEO Probus Pub. Co., Chgo., 1984—. Mem. unit bd. Boys & Girls Clubs, Chgo. Bank of N.Y. fellow, 1971-72. Mem. Beta Gamma Sigma. Republican. Roman Catholic. Clubs: Tower, East Bank. Office: Probus Pub Co 1925 N Clybourn Ave Chicago IL 60614-4946

MCGUNIGLE, BRIAN EDWARD, lawyer; b. Boston, Nov. 2, 1947; s. Daniel H. and Mona (Tyldesley) McG.; m. Mary Ann Caven, Aug. 9, 1974. BA, Harvard U., 1968; MA, Nat. Univ. of Ireland, 1969; JD, Harvard U., 1973; LLM, U. London, 1974. Bar: N.Y. 1975. Assoc. Coudert Bros., N.Y.C., 1974-80, ptnr., 1981—. Fulbright scholar, Ireland, 1968-69; Knox fellow, Eng., 1973-74. Office: Coudert Bros 1114 Avenue Of The Americas New York NY 10036-7794*

MCGURHILL, GERALD, chemical engineer, lawyer; b. Montreal, Que., Can., Mar. 28, 1934; s. James Owen and Mary (Quig) McGurhill; m. Lyanne Margaret Fielding, June 20, 1992. BEng in Chem., McGill U., 1957, MBA, 1961; BCL, McGill U., Montreal, 1980, LLB in Common Law, 1980. Cert. engr., Que.; Bar: Que. Plant mgr. Coty, Pfizer Canada, Inc., Montreal, 1962-65; mgr. prodn. planning and inventory control Pfizer Canada, Inc., Montreal, 1964-65, mgr. materials and distbn., 1965-70, fin. projects coord., 1970-71; project coord.-materials Pfizer Canada, Inc., Cornwall, Ont., Can., 1971-72; mgr. corp. projects Pfizer Canada, Inc., Kirkland, Que., 1972-80, mgr. legal affairs, 1980-82, dir. legal affairs, 1982-90, sec. and corp. counsel, 1990—. Co-author: Canadian Trademark Law and Practice, 1993. Ch. warden St. Malachy's Ch., Montreal, 1983-89, 90-92; treas. Can. Assn. for Prodn. and Inventory Control, Montreal, 1967-68. Mem. AIChE, Can. Bar Assn., Can. Soc. Mech. Engrs., Barreau du Que., Patent and Trademark Assn. Can., Internat. Trademark Assn. (mem. edn. com. 1994—, mem. publs. com. 1990-94). Roman Catholic. Avocations: railroading, travel, classical, military and western music, reading. Office: Pfizer Can Inc, 17300 Trans-Can Hwy, Kirkland, PQ Canada H9J 2M5

MC GURN, BARRETT, communications executive, writer; b. N.Y.C., Aug. 6, 1914; s. William Barrett and Alice (Schneider) McG.; m. Mary Elizabeth Johnson, May 30, 1942 (dec. Feb. 1960); children: William Barrett III, Elizabeth (Mrs. John J. Hehn), Andrew; m. Janice Ann McLaughlin, June 19, 1962; children: Summers, Martin Barrett, Mark Barrett. AB, Fordham U., 1935, LittD, 1958. Editor Fordham Ram, 1934-35; with N.Y. Herald Tribune, 1935-66; asst. corr. N.Y. Herald Tribune, Rome, 1939, bur. chief, 1946-52, 55-62; reporting staff N.Y. Herald Tribune, 1935-42, 62-66; bur. chief N.Y. Herald Tribune, Paris, 1952-55; acting chief bur. N.Y. Herald Tribune, Moscow, 1958; with, assignments in Morocco, Algeria, Tunisia, Hungary (1956 revolution), Egypt, Greece, Yugoslavia, Poland, Cen. Africa, Gaza Strip. N.Y. Herald Tribune, 1946-62; press attache Am. Embassy, Rome, 1966-68; counselor for press affairs Am. Embassy, Vietnam, 1968-69; U.S. consular officer, sec. appointed by Pres., 1969; dir. U.S. Govt. Press Ctr., Vietnam, 1968-69; White House and Pentagon liaison for State Dept. spokesman Washington, 1969-72; World Affairs commentator USIA, 1972-73; dir. pub. info. U.S. Supreme Ct., Washington, 1973-82; dir. communications Cath. Archdiocese of Washington, 1984-87; pres. Carroll Pub. Co. pub. Cath. Standard and El Pregonero, 1987-91; dir. Our Sunday Vistor Pub. Co., 1988—; mem. Italian-Am. com. to select Italian fellowship winners for study in U.S., 1950-52; mem. U.S. Nat. Cath. Com. on Comm. Policy, 1970-74, White House Com. on Drug Control Info., 1970-72; mem. interdept. com. on U.S. govt. press info. policy, 1970, interdept. U.S. govt. task force to rescue 100 Ams. kidnapped in Jordan, 1970, one-man U.S. Presdl. mission to Cambodia on media news problems, 1970; archivist John Carroll Soc., Washington, 1990—. Author: Decade in Europe, 1959, A Reporter Looks at the Vatican, 1962, A Reporter Looks at American Catholicism, 1967; contbg. author: The Best from Yank, 1945, Yank, the GI Story of the War, 1946, Combat, 1950, Highlights from Yank, 1953, Overseas Press Club Cook Book, 1962, I Can Tell it Now, 1964, U.S. Book of Facts, Statistics and Information, 1966, New Catholic Treasury of Wit and Humor, 1967, How I Got that Story, 1967, Heroes for Our Times, 1968, Newsbreak, 1975, Saints for all Seasons, 1978, Informing the People, 1981, The Courage to Grow Old, 1989, Am. Peoples Encyclopedia Yearbook, Close To Glory: Yank Correspondents Untold Stories of World War II, 1992; contbr. articles to profl. jours. Trustee Corrs. Fund, 1965-68; mem. bd. Anglo-Am. Charity Fund in Italy, 1967-68; v.p. Citizens Assn., Westmoreland Hills, Md., 1984-86. Sgt. AUS, 1942-45. Decorated Purple Heart; grand knight Italian Order of Merit; Vietnam Psychol. Warfare medal 1st class; recipient Polk award for outstanding fgn. reporting L.I. U., 1956; named best press corr. abroad Overseas Press Club, 1957; recipient N.Y.C. Fire Dept. Essay Silver Medal, 1924, N.Y. Times Oratorical Contest Bronze Medal, 1930; Christopher award for one of ten most inspiring books of year, 1959; named Man of Year Cath. Inst. Press, 1962, Fordham U. Alumnus of Year in communications, 1963; co-winner ann. Golden Typewriter award N.Y. Newspaper Reporters Assn., 1965, nominated by N.Y. Herald Tribune for Journalism Pulitzer Prize, 1965; outstanding pub. service award N.Y. chpt. Sigma Delta Chi, 1965; recipient Page One award N.Y. Newspaper Guild, 1966, Silurians award, 1966, award N.Y. Newspaper Reporters Assn., 1966, Citation for pub. service N.Y.C. Citizens Budget Commn., 1966, Meritorious Honor award Dept. State, 1972; Ann. Achievement award Fordham U. Club, Washington, 1986. Mem. Fgn. Press Assn. Italy (v.p. 1951-52, pres. 1961-62), SHAPE Corrs. Assn. Paris (treas. 1955), Authors Guild, Am. Fgn. Svc. Assn., Pax Romana Soc. for Cath. Intellectuals (Washington chmn. 1986—, dir. 1994—), Overseas Press Club (pres. 1963-65), Nat. Press Club, Kenwood Club, Cosmos Club, Fordham U. Club Washington (bd.s. 1990—). Roman Catholic. Home: 5229 Duvall Dr Bethesda MD 20816-1875 *Providing information to our democratic public has been the work of my life both as a foreign correspondent, as a government spokesman, and as a lecturer. The newsman and the person who speaks for government share the same objective of explaining government policy. The spokesman has an added responsibility—to help government policy succeed. The reporter and the spokesman sometimes are at war with one another, but it is a war in behalf of the same beneficiary: the people.*

MCGURN, GEORGE WILLIAM, lawyer; b. Chgo., May 10, 1914; s. George William and Margaret Anna (Gavin) McG.; m. Margaret Mary Daley (dec. Oct. 1967); children: Margaret Mary (dec.), George, Anne, Jane, Mary, Michael, Susan; m. Antoinette Margaret Feuce, Nov. 28, 1970. Student, Clemson U., 1932-34; JD, Ill. Inst. Tech., 1938; LLM, U. Chgo., 1946. Bar: Ill. 1938, U.S. Dist. Ct. (no. dist.) Ill. 1951, U.S. Supreme Ct. 1955, U.S. Ct. Appeals (7th cir.) 1974. Assoc. LaRochelle, Brooks & Beardsley, Chgo., 1938-40; asst. gen. counsel Pabst Brewing Co., Chgo., 1946-48; ptnr. Reum, Casello and McGurn, Chgo., 1948-51; asst. counsel Chgo. Dist. Engr. Office U.S. Army, Chgo., 1951-53; asst. atty. gen. Office of Ill. Atty. Gen., Springfield, Ill., 1953-54; chief counsel and sec. Ill. State Toll Highway Commn., Chgo. and Oak Brook, Ill., 1954-63; ptnr. Healy and McGurn, Chgo. and Oakbrook, 1963-82; ret. Healy and McGurn, 1982-88; counsel Law Offices of Michael McGurn, Warrenville, Ill., 1988—. Editor Chgo.-Kent Law Rev., 1936-38. Rep. committeeman, Elmhurst, Ill., 1960-63. Served to maj. U.S. Army, 1941-46; col. res. ret. Postgrad scholar Chgo.-Kent Coll. Law Ill. Inst. Tech., 1938; recipient Citizenship award Ill. Inst. Tech., 1988. Mem. ABA, Ill. State Bar Assn. (sr. counselor 1988), DuPage County Bar Assn., Rotry (sec. Oak Brook club 1962-63, v.p 1963-64), K.C., Delta Theta Phi (scholarship key). Roman Catholic. Home: 1572 S Prospect St Wheaton IL 60187-7750 Office: McGurn & Assocs Ltd Unit 101 29W140 Butterfield Rd Warrenville IL 60555

MCGURN, WILLIAM BARRETT, III, lawyer; b. N.Y.C., Apr. 3, 1943; s. Barrett and Mary Elizabeth (Johnson) McG.; m. Catherine Roche, June 17, 1972; children Mary Anne, Edward Johnson. BA, Yale U., 1965; JD, Harvard U., 1972. Bar: D.C. 1973, Paris 1992. Assoc.t Cleary, Gottlieb, Steen & Hamilton, Paris and Washington, 1972-80, ptnr., 1981—. Chmn. Dem. Abroad, France, 1987-89, mem. exec. com., 1989—; gov. Am. Hosp. Paris, 1991—, sec., 1992—. Lt. USNR, 1967-69. Mem. ABA, Am. Club Paris. Democrat. Home: 29 Ave Bosquet, 75007 Paris France Office: Cleary Gottlieb Steen & Hamilton, 41 Ave Friedland, 75008 Paris France

MCGWIRE, MARK DAVID, professional baseball player; b. Pomona, Calif., Oct. 1, 1963; s. John and Ginger McGwire; m. Kathy McGwire; 1 child, Matthew. Student, U. So. Calif. With Oakland Athletics, 1984—; player World Series, 1988, 89, 90. Named Am. League Rookie of Yr. Baseball Writers' Assn. Am., 1987, Sporting News, 1987; recipient Gold Glove award, 1990; named to All-Star team, 1987-92, 95-96; recipient Silver Slugger Award, 1992; Am. League Home Run Leader, 1987; mem. U.S. Olympic Baseball Team, 1984. Office: Oakland Athletics Oakland-Alameda County Coliseum 7000 Coliseum Way Oakland CA 94621-1945*

MCHALE, EDWARD ROBERTSON, retired lawyer; b. Chgo., Jan. 24, 1921; s. Edward F. and Martha (Robertson) McH.; m. Helen Louise Lindgren, Aug. 28, 1953; children: Nancy Ellen McHale Kaufman, Sally Jane McHale Cutler, John Robertson. B.S.S., Northwestern U., 1942; LL.B., Harvard U., 1948. Bar: Calif. 1949. Asst. U.S. atty. U.S. atty. So. Dist. Calif., 1949-61, chief tax div., 1954-61; assoc. Mitchell, Silberberg & Knupp, Los Angeles, 1961-64; partner Mitchell, Silberberg & Knupp, 1965-86, mgr. litigation dept, 1978-82; pres. Edward R. McHale, P.C., 1979—; lectr. U. So. Calif. Law Center, 1958-61. Co-author: Handling Federal Tax Litigation, 1961. Served to lt. USNR, 1943-46. Mem. Fed. Bar Assn. (past pres. Los Angeles chpt., past nat. v.p. for 9th Circuit), Assn. Bus. Trial Lawyers (bd. govs. 1981-83), State Bar Calif., Delta Sigma Rho. Lutheran. Clubs: South Hills Country (West Covina); Clan Donnachaidh Soc. Home: 1116 S Serena Dr West Covina CA 91791-3754

MCHALE, KEVIN EDWARD, former professional basketball player; b. Hibbing, Minn., Dec. 19, 1957; m. Lynn McHale; children: Kristyn, Michael. Student, U. Minn., 1976-80. Basketball player Boston Celtics, 1980-93; v.p. Minn. Timberwolves. Named to NBA All Rookie Team, 1981, NBA All-Defensive First Team, 1986-88, All-NBA First Team, 1987, NBA All-Star Game, 1984, 86-91; recipient NBA Sixth Man award, 1984, 85. Played on NBA Championship Team, 1981, 84, 86. Office: Minn Timberwolves Target Ctr 600 First Ave N Minneapolis MN 55403*

MCHALE, MICHAEL JOHN, lawyer; b. N.Y.C., Apr. 14, 1960; s. Michael Joseph and Mary Beatrice (Graddy) McH. BA, U. of the South, 1982; JD, Samford U., 1985. Bar: Ala. 1986, U.S. Dist. Ct. (no., mid. and so. dists.) Ala. 1986, U.S. Ct. Appeals (11th cir.) 1986, Fla. 1991, U.S. Dist. Ct. (mid. and so. dists.) 1991, U.S. Supreme Ct. 1991. Assoc. Wagner, Nugent, Johnson, Roth, Romano, Eriksen & Kupfer, West Palm Beach, Fla., 1989-92; ptnr. Whalen & McHale, West Palm Beach, Fla., 1992-95, Daves, Whalen. McHale & Considine, West Palm Beach, Fla., 1995—. Author: Strategic Use of Circumstantial Evidence, 2d edit., 1991, Evaluating and Settling Personal Injury Claims, 1992, supplement through present, Making Trial Objections, 1993, supplement through present, Expert Witnesses: Direct and Cross Examination, 1993, supplement through present; editor, author: Litigating TMJ Cases, 1993 and yearly supplements. Named one of Outstanding Young Men of Am., 1988. Mem. ABA (mem. admiralty com.), ATLA, Am. Acad. Fla. Trial Lawyers, Maritime Law Assn. U.S., Southeastern Admiralty Law Inst., Fla. Bar (admiralty law com. editl. bd.), Palm. Beach Bar Assn., Sigma Nu Phi. Avocation: fishing. Home: 23018-D Oxford Pl Boca Raton FL 33433 Office: Daves Whalen McHale & Considine 301 Clematis St Ste 200 West Palm Beach FL 33401

MCHALE, PAUL, congressman, lawyer; b. Bethlehem, Pa., July 26, 1950; m. Katherine McHale; children: Matthew, Mary, Luke. BA in Govt. sigma cum laude, Lehigh U., 1972; JD, Georgetown U. Law Sch., 1977. Atty. Bethlehem, 1977-82; mem. Pa. Ho. of Reps., 1983-92, 103rd-104th Congresses from 15th Pa. dist., 1993—; mem. nat. security com., mem. sci. com. Infantry officer USMC, Okinawa, Philippines, 1972-74; Maj. USMCR Persian Gulf, 1990-92. Decorated Navy Commendation medal. Mem. Phi Beta Kappa. Democrat. *

MCHALE, ROBERT MICHAEL, lawyer; b. Youngstown, Ohio, Oct. 14, 1932; s. John F. and Elizabeth (Prendergast) M.; children: John F. II, Rachel Anne, Robert M. Jr. Student, St. Mary's Coll., Moraga, Calif., 1950-53; JD, Tulane U., 1956. Bar: La. 1956, U.S. Dist. Ct. (we. dist.) La. 1958, U.S. Ct. Mil. Appeals 1959, U.S. Supreme Ct. 1959, U.S. Ct. Appeals (5th cir.) 1960, U.S. Dist. Ct. (ea. dist.) La. 1963. Ptnr. Rogers, McHale & St. Romain, Lake Charles, La., 1960-70; prin. McHale, Bufkin & Dees, Lake Charles, 1970-94, McHale Schwartzberg, Lake Charles, 1995—; bd. dirs. Cameron (La.) State Bank; chair mineral bd. State of La., 1992-94, chair legal and title controversy commn., 1994—. Democrat. Roman Catholic. Avocations: horse racing, railroads. Office: 1901 Oak Park Blvd Lake Charles LA 70601-8915

MCHALE, VINCENT EDWARD, political science educator; b. Jenkins Twp., Pa., Apr. 17, 1939; m. Ann Barbara Cotner, Nov. 8, 1963; 1 child, Patrick James. A.B., Wilkes Coll., 1964; M.A., Pa. State U., 1966, Ph.D. in Polit. Sci., 1969. Asst. prof. polit. sci. U. Pa., Phila., 1969-75, dir. grad. studies, 1971-73; assoc. prof. Case Western Res. U., Cleve., 1975-84, prof., 1984—, chmn. dept. polit. sci., 1978—; vis. lectr. John Carroll U., summer 1980, Beaver Coll., spring 1975. Author: (with A.P. Frognier and D. Paranzino) Vote, Clivages Socio-politiques et Developpement Regional en Belgique, 1974. Co-editor; contbr.: Evaluating Transnational Programs in Government and Business, 1980; Political Parties of Europe, 1983; edtl. adv. bd. Worldmark Ency. of Nations, 1994—. Contbr. chpts. to books, articles to profl. jours. Project cons. Council Econ Opportunity in Greater Cleve., 1978-81; mem. Morris Abrams Award Com., 1977—. Recipient Outstanding Prof. award Lux chpt. Mortar Bd., 1989, 90; named one of Most Interesting People of 1988, Cleve. Mag.; NSF grantee, 1971-72; HEW grantee, 1976-78; Woodrow Wilson fellow, 1968, Ruth Young Boucke fellow, 1967-68; All-Univ. fellow, 1967-68. Mem. Phi Kappa Phi. Home: 3070 Coleridge Rd Cleveland OH 44118-3556 Office: Case Western Res U Cleveland OH 44106

MCHARG, IAN LENNOX, landscape architect, regional planner, educator; b. Clydebank, Scotland, Nov. 20, 1920; came to U.S., 1946, naturalized, 1960; s. John Lennox and Harriet (Bain) McH.; m. Pauline Crena de Iongh, Aug. 30, 1947 (dec. 1974); children: Alistair Craig, Malcolm Lennox, Ian William, Andrew Maxwell; m. Carol Ann Smyser, May 28, 1977. B.Landscape Architecture, Harvard U., 1949, M.Landscape Architecture, 1950, M.City Planning, 1951; L.H.D. (hon.), Amherst Coll., 1970, Bates Coll., 1978; H.H.D. (hon.), Lewis and Clark Coll., 1970; D.L. (hon.), Heriot-Watt U., Edinburgh, Scotland. Planner Dept. Health, Scotland, 1950-54; prof. dept. landscape architecture and regional planning U. Pa., Phila., 1954-86; disting. sci. lectr. Brookhaven Nat. Lab., 1968; Horace Albright Meml. lectr. U. Calif., Berkeley, 1969, sr. vis. prof., 1986-87; Danz lectr. U. Wash., Seattle, 1971; Brown and Haley lectr. U. Puget Sound, 1971; Found. prof. U. Auckland, 1986; vis. prof. Pa. State U., Harvard U., 1994; Bruce Gott prof. architecture Okla. U., 1994. Prin. works include Ecol. Study for Mpls.-St. Paul Met. Area, San Francisco Met. Area, plan for New Town, Pontchartrain, New Orleans, plan for New Town, Woodlands, Tex., Environ. Park for Tehran, Iran, Amelia Island, Medford, Sanibel, EMAP, Nat. Ecol. Inventory; author: Design With Nature, 196, Quest for Life, 1996. Prin. works include Ecol. Study for Mpls.-St. Paul Met. Area, San Francisco Met. Area, plan for New Town, Pontchartrain, New Orleans, plan for New Town, Woodlands, Tex., Environ. Park for Tehran, Iran, Amelia Island, Medford, Sanibel, EMAP, Nat. Ecol. Inventory; author: Design With Nature, 1969, Quest for Life, 1996. Recipient B.Y. Morrison medal N.Am. Wildlife Mgmt. Assn., 1971, Creative Arts award Brandeis U., 1972, Phila. Art Alliance award, 1975, Rene du Bos award, 1986, Alfred La Gasse award, 1987, Nat. Medal of Art, 1990, Richard Neutra medal, 1992, CELA Outstanding Educator award, 1992, Outstanding Achievement award Harvard U., 1992, Thomas Jefferson medal U. Va., 1995. Fellow Royal Soc. Art, Am. Soc. Landscape Architects (Bradford Williams medal 1968, 76, ASLA medal 1984), Inst. Landscape Architects, Royal Inst. Brit. Architects; mem. NAS (com. on sci. in nat. pks. 1991-92), AIA (hon., Allied Professions medal 1972). Office: U Pa Dept Landscape Architecture & Regional Planning Philadelphia PA 19104

MC HARGUE, CARL JACK, research laboratory administrator; b. Corbin, Ky., Jan. 30, 1926; s. John David and Virginia (Thomas) McH. B.S. in Metall. Engring., U. Ky., 1949, M.S., 1951, Ph.D., 1953; m. Edith Troville, Aug. 28, 1948; children: Anne Odell McHargue Diegel, Carol Virginia, Margaret Katherine McHargue Behrendt; m. Betty Ford, Sept. 30, 1960. Instr. U. Ky., Lexington, 1949-53; with Oak Ridge Nat. Lab., 1953-90, sect. head, 1960-80, program mgr. for materials scis., 1961-88, sr. rsch. staff 1980-90; prof. metall. engring. U. Tenn., Knoxville, 1963—, dir. ctr. materials processing, 1991—; vis. prof. U. Newcastle upon Tyne, Eng., 1987; adj. prof. Vanderfilt U., 1988—. With AUS, 1944-46. Fellow Metall. Soc. AIME, Am. Soc. for Metals; mem. Am. Nuclear Soc., Materials Rsch. Soc., Sigma Xi, Tau Beta Pi. Republican. Presbyterian. Contbr. numerous articles in field to profl. jours. Home: 7201 Sheffield Dr Knoxville TN 37909-2414 Office: U Tenn 102 Estabrook Hall Knoxville TN 37996-2350

MCHENRY, BARNABAS, lawyer; b. Harrisburg, Pa., Oct. 30, 1929; s. William Cecil and Louise (Perkins) McH.; m. Marie Bannon Jones, Dec. 13, 1952; children: Thomas J.P., W.H. Davis, John W.H. A.B., Princeton U., 1952; LL.B., Columbia U., 1957. Bar: N.Y. 1957. Assoc. Lord, Day, & Lord, N.Y.C., 1957-62; gen. counsel The Reader's Digest Assn., Inc., N.Y.C., 1962-85; exec. dir. Wallace Funds, N.Y.C., 1985-86; now chmn. N.Y. state orgns. Trustee Boscobel Restoration, Inc., 1964, Am. Conservation Assn., 1977, Supreme Ct. Hist. Soc., 1980, Hudson River Found. for Sci. and Environ. Rsch., Inc., Saratoga Performing Arts Ctr., 1984, Aperture Found., 1986; trustee emeritus Met. Mus. Art, 1980; mem. N.Y. State Commn. on Restoration of Capitol, 1979; coun. mem. Villa I Tatti, Harvard Sch. Renaissance Studies, 1982; regent emeritus Smithsonian Instn., 1985; commr. Palisades Interstate Park Commn., 1987; chmn. Hudson River Valley Greenway Coun., 1989, adv. coun. hist. preservation, 1992. Home: 164 E 72nd St New York NY 10021-4363

MC HENRY, DEAN EUGENE, academic administrator emeritus; b. nr. Lompoc, Calif., Oct. 18, 1910; s. William Thomas and Virgie (Hilton) McH.; m. Jane Snyder, Feb. 23, 1935; children—Sally (Mrs. Kenneth Mackenzie), Dean Eugene, Nancy (Mrs. L.S. Fletcher), Henry. A.B., U. Calif. at Los Angeles, 1932; M.A., Stanford U., 1933; Ph.D., U. Calif. at Berkeley, 1936; Litt.D., U. Western Australia, 1963; LL.D., U. Nev., 1966, Grinnell Coll., 1967. Instr. govt. Williams Coll., 1936-37; asst. prof. polit. sci. Pa. State Coll., 1937-39; asst. prof. polit. sci. U. Calif. at Los Angeles, 1939-45, assoc. prof., 1945-50, prof. polit. sci., 1950-63, coordinator Navy tng. program, 1943-46, dean div. social scis., 1947-50, chmn. dept. polit. sci., 1950-52; Fulbright vis. prof. U. Western Australia, 1954; acad. asst. to pres. U. Calif. (statewide), 1958-60, dean of acad. planning, 1960-61; prof. comparative govt., chancellor U. Calif., Santa Cruz, 1961-74; chancellor emeritus U. Calif., 1974—; ptnr. McHenry Vineyard, 1979—; cons. S.Am. univs. Ford Found., 1961; mem. Coll. Entrance Exam. Bd., 1964-67; dir. State Nev. U. Survey, 1955-57, Survey of Higher Edn. in Kansas City Area, 1957; mem. Master Plan Survey of Higher Edn. in Cal., 1959- 60; mem. adv. bd. U.S. Naval Postgrad. Sch., 1970-74. Author: The Labor Party in Transition, 1931-38, 1938, California Government: Politics and Administration, (with W.W. Crouch), 1945, The American Federal Government, (with J.H. Ferguson), 1947, 14th edit., 1981, The American System of Government, (with J.H. Ferguson), 1947, 14th edit., 1981, The Third Force in Canada, 1950, Elements of American Government, (with J.H. Ferguson), 1950, 9th edit., 1970, American Government Today, (with E.B. Fincher and J.H. Ferguson), 1951, State and Local Government in California, (with W.W. Crouch and others), 1952, California Government and Politics, 1956, 4th edit., 1967, Academic Departments: Problems, Variations and Alternatives, 1977. Candidate for mayor, City Los Angeles, 1950; for rep. in Congress 22d Dist., 1952. Carnegie fellow in New Zealand, 1946-47; Fullbright lectr. in Australia, 1954. Office: McHenry Libr U Calif Santa Cruz CA 95064

MCHENRY, HENRY MALCOLM, anthropologist, educator; b. Los Angeles, May 19, 1944; s. Dean Eugene and Emma Jane (Snyder) McH.; m. Linda Jean Conway, June 25, 1966; children: Lindsay Jean, Annalisa Jane. BA, U. Calif., Davis, 1966, MA, 1967; PhD, Harvard U., 1972. Asst. prof. anthropology U. Calif., Davis, 1971-76, assoc. prof. anthropology, 1976-81, prof. anthropology, 1981—, chmn. dept. anthropology, 1984-88. Fellow Am. Anthrop. Assn., Calif. Acad. Sci.; mem. Am. Assn. Phys. Anthropologists (exec. com. 1981-85), Soc. Study Evolution, Soc. Vertebrate Paleontology, Phi Beta Kappa, Phi Kappa Phi. Democrat. Buddhist. Avocation: winemaker. Home: 330 11th St Davis CA 95616-2010 Office: U of Calif Davis Dept Of Anthropology Davis CA 95616

MC HENRY, MARTIN CHRISTOPHER, physician, educator; b. San Francisco, Feb. 9, 1932; s. Merl and Marcella (Bricca) McH.; m. Patricia Grace Hughes, Apr. 27, 1957; children: Michael, Christopher, Timothy, Mary Ann, Jeffrey, Paul, Kevin, William, Monica, Martin Christopher. Student, U. Santa Clara, 1950-53; MD, U. Cin., 1957; MS in Medicine, U. Minn., 1966. Intern, Highland Alameda County (Calif.) Hosp., Oakland, 1957-58; resident, internal medicine fellow Mayo Clinic, Rochester, Minn., 1958-61, spl. appointee in infectious diseases, 1963-64; staff physician infectious diseases Henry Ford Hosp., Detroit, 1964-67; staff physician Cleve. Clinic, 1967-72, chmn. dept. infectious diseases, 1972-92, sr. physician infectious diseases, 1992—. Asst. clin. prof. Case Western Res. U., 1970-77, assoc. clin. prof. medicine, 1977-91, clin. prof. medicine, 1991—; assoc. vis. physician Cleve. Met. Gen. Hosp., 1970—; cons. VA Hosp., Cleve., 1973—. Chmn. manpower com. Swine Influenza Program, Cleve., 1976. Served with USNR, 1961-63. Named Disting. Tchr. in Medicine Cleve. Clinic, 1972, 90; recipient 1st ann. Bruce Hubbard Stewart award Cleve. Clinic Found. for Humanities in Medicine, 1985, Nightingale Physician Collaboration award Cleve. Clinic Found. Divsn. Nursing, 1995. Diplomate Am. Bd. Internal Medicine. Fellow ACP, Infectious Diseases Soc. Am., Am. Coll. Chest Physicians (chmn. com. cardiopulmonary infections 1975-77, 81-83), Royal Soc. Medicine of Great Britain; mem. Am. Soc. Clin. Pharmacology and Therapeutics (chmn. sect. infectious diseases and antimicrobial agts., 1970-77, 80-85, dir.), Am. Thoracic Soc., Am. Soc. Clin. Pathologists, Am. Fedn. Clin. Rsch., Am. Soc. Tropical Medicine and Hygiene, Am. Soc. Microbiology, N.Y. Acad. Scis. Contbr. numerous articles to profl. jours., also chpts. to books. Home: 2779 Belgrave Rd Pepper Pike OH 44124-4601 Office: 9500 Euclid Ave Cleveland OH 44195-0001

MC HENRY, POWELL, lawyer; b. Cinn., May 14, 1926; s. L. Lee McHenry and Marguerite L. (Powell) Heinz; m. Venna Mae Guerrea, Aug. 27, 1948; children: Scott, Marshall, Jody Lee, Gale Lynn. AB, U. Cinn., 1949; LLB, Harvard U., 1951, JD, 1969. Bar: Ohio 1951, U.S. Ct. Appeals (6th cir.) 1964, U.S. Supreme Ct. 1966. Assoc. Dinsmore, Shohl, Sawyer & Dinsmore, Cinn., 1951-58; ptnr. Dinsmore, Shohl, Coates & Deupree (and predecessors), Cinn., 1958-75; gen. counsel Federated Dept. Stores, Inc., 1971-75; assoc. gen. counsel Procter & Gamble Co., 1975-76, v.p., gen. counsel, 1976-83, sr. v.p., gen. counsel, 1983-91; counsel Dinsmore & Shohl, Cin., 1991—; bd. dirs. Eagle Picher Industries, Inc., 1991—. Mem. com. Hamilton County Pub. Defender, Cinn. With USNR, 1944-46. Recipient award of merit Ohio Legal Center Inst., 1969. Mem. ABA, Ohio Bar Assn., Cin. Bar Assn. (pres. 1979-80, exec. com. 1975-81), Harvard U. Law Sch. Assn. Cin. (pres. 1960-61), Am. Law Inst., Assn. Gen. Counsel (pres. 1986-88), Harvard Club, Western Hill Country Club (bd. dirs. 1964-70, sec. 1966-69, 87-89, treas. 1969-70, 89-90), Queen City Club, Commonwealth Club. Republican. Methodist. Office: Dinsmore & Shohl 1900 Chemed Ctr 255 E 5th St Cincinnati OH 45202-4700

MCHENRY, ROBERT (DALE), editor; b. St. Louis, Apr. 30, 1945; s. Robert Dale and Pearl Lenna (Nalley) McH.; m. Carolyn F. Amundson, Oct. 2, 1971; children: Curran, Zachary. BA in English Lit., Northwestern U., 1966; MA in English Lit., U. Mich., 1967; MBA in Mgmt., Northwestern U., 1987. Proofreader, prodn. editor Ency. Britannica, Inc., Chgo., 1967-69, editor, 1974-75, dir. yearbooks, 1985-86, mng. editor, 1986-90, gen. editor, v.p., 1990-92, editor-in-chief, 1992—. Editor: Documentary History of Conservation in America, 1972, Webster's American Military Biographies, 1978, Liberty's Women, 1980, Webster's New Biographical Dictionary, 1983. Mem. United Ch. of Christ.

MCHUGH, EARL STEPHEN, dentist; b. Colorado Springs, Colo., Feb. 27, 1936; s. Earl Clifton and Margaret Mary (Higgins) M.; m. Joan Bleckwell, Aug. 24, 1957; children: Kevin, Stacey, Julie. BA, Cornell U., 1958; DDS, U. Mo., 1962. Pvt. practice, Kansas City, Mo., 1964—; lectr. U. Mo. Dental Sch., Kansas City, 1988, clin. staff, 1989, 90, 91, 92, 93, 94, 95, ethics seminar faculty staff, addiction in dentistry faculty, 1995; cons. Hallmark, Inc., Kansas City, 1988; adv. dir. Rsch. Hosp., Kansas City. Contbr. articles to profl. jours. Deacon Presbyn. Ch. Prairie Village, Kans., 1982-84; vol. Shawnee Mission Hosp. Kans., 1985-88; lectr. Drug Recovery Program, Kansas City, Kans., 1988-89, 92, 93, 94. Capt. Dental Corp, U.S. Army, 1962-64. Mem. Valley Hope Assn. (rsch. hos. adv. bd. 1995-96), Audubon Soc. (Ortnithologist of Yr. award Kansas City chpt. 1990), Kans. Ornithol. Soc. (v.p. 1989-90, pres. 1990-91), Internat. Coun. Bird Preservation (Kans. del. 1990, coord. Kans. Breeding Bird Atlas 1992, 93, 94, 95, chmn. Kans. bird records com.), Omicron Kappa Upsilon, Chi Psi.

MCHUGH, EDWARD FRANCIS, JR., lawyer; b. Cambridge, Mass., Sept. 6, 1932; s. Edward Francis and Eleanor (Whelton) McH.; m. Mary Judith Murchison, Sept. 15, 1962; children: Mary, Alexandra, Edward III, Michael. AB, Georgetown U., 1953, LLB, 1958. Bar: Mass., 1958, U.S. Dist. Ct. Mass. 1958, D.C. 1958, U.S. Ct. Appeals (D.C. cir.) 1958. Law clk. U.S. Ct. Appeals (D.C. cir.), Washington, 1958-59; assoc., jr. ptnr, then ptnr. Nutter, McClennen & Fish, Boston, 1959—; gen. counsel Two/Ten Found., Watertown, Mass., 1975-95; counsel, sec. New Eng. Aquarium Corp., Boston, 1987—; gen. counsel and clk. South Shore Health and Ednl. Corp. and South Shore Hosp., 1991—. Editor in chief Georgetown Law Journal, 1958; contbr. to profl. publs. Trustee Notre Dame Acad., Hingham, Mass., 1975-85, Harold Brooks Found., Quincy, Mass., 1987-88; chmn. bd. trustees South Shore Hosp. and South Shore Health and Ednl. Corp., Weymouth, Mass., 1986-88. 1st lt. USAF, 1953-55. Mem. Boston Bar Assn. (coun. 1984-87), Knights of Malta, Hatherly Country Club (pres. 1978-79), Clover Club. Roman Catholic. Office: Nutter McClennen & Fish 1 International Pl Boston MA 02110-2699

MCHUGH, HEATHER, poet; b. Calif., Aug. 20, 1948. BA, Radcliffe Coll., 1970; MA, U. Denver, 1972. Assoc. prof. English SUNY, Binghamton, 1976-82; prof. English, Milliman writer-in-residence U. Wash., Seattle, 1983—; vis. prof. Columbia U., 1987; Holloway lectr. U. Calif., Berkeley, 1987; judge Nat. Poetry Series book award, 1986, 95. Author: (poetry) Dangers, 1977, A World of Difference, 1981, To the Quick, 1987, Shades, 1988, (essays) Broken English: Poetry and Partiality, 1993, Hinge & Sign: Poems, 1968-93, 1994 (Nat. Book award nomination 1994); translator: D'Apres Tout: Poems by Jean Follain, 1981; (with Nikolai Popov) Because the Sea Is Black: Poems by Blaga Dimitrova, 1989. Recipient Harvard U./Pollock prize, 1995, Lila Wallce/Reader's Digest Writer's award, 1996. Office: Univ of Washington Box 354330 Dept of English Seattle WA 98195-4330

MCHUGH, HELEN FRANCES, research administrator, consumption economist; b. Tucson, Aug. 19, 1931; d. James Patrick and Mary Catherine (Hochstatter) McH.; m. Herbert J. Brauer, Mar. 26, 1982. B.S. with distinction, U. Mo.-Columbia, 1958, M.S., 1959; Ph.D., Iowa State U., 1965. Instr. U. Tex., Austin, 1961-63; asst. prof. U. Tex., 1963-66, asso. prof., 1966-67; asso. prof. Ind. State U., Terre Haute, 1967-69; asso. prof., dept. head Oreg. State U., Corvallis, 1969-73; prof., dean Coll. Home Econs., U. Del., Newark, 1973-75; prof. consumer econs. Colo. Experiment Sta., Colo. State U., Ft. Collins, 1976—; dean Coll. Human Resource Scis. Colo. State U., Ft. Collins, 1976-86, assoc. dir. Colo. Experiment Sta., 1976-86, dep. dir. Colo. Experiment Sta., 1986—; cons. in field. Chmn. policy bd.: Jour. Consumer Research, 1978-80. Recipient Disting. Service award U. Mo. Alumni Assn., 1975. Mem. Am. Econ. Assn., Am. Agrl. Econs. Assn., Am. Assn. of Family and Consumer Scis. (bd. dirs. 1973-75), Assn. Adminstrs. Home Econs. (pres. 1978-79), Western Assn. Agrl. Experiment Sta. Dirs., Great Plains Agrl. Coun. (bd. dirs. 1994-96, chair 1995-96), Sigma Xi, Gamma Sigma Delta, Phi Kappa Phi. Roman Catholic. Office: Colorado State U Agricultural Experimen Fort Collins CO 80523

MCHUGH, JAMES JOSEPH, retired naval officer, retired associate dean; b. Phila., Aug. 12, 1930; s. James Joseph and Patience Mary (McGowan) McH.; m. Rita Marie Huber, May 21, 1960; children: Margaret Marie, James Joseph IV. B.A. (with honors), U. Pa., 1951, LL.B., 1954; M.S. in Internat. Relations, George Washington U., 1972. Bar: Pa. 1955. Commd. ensign U.S. Navy, 1955, advanced through grades to rear adm., 1980; legal officer Naval Air Station, Point Mugu, Calif., 1955-58; staff officer Office Judge Adv. Gen., Washington, 1959-63; staff instr. U.S. Naval Justice Sch., Newport, R.I., 1963-65; counsel Bur. Naval Personnel, Washington, 1965-68; asst. fleet judge adv. to comdr. in chief U.S. Pacific Fleet, 1968-71; spl. counsel to chief naval ops. Washington, 1972-76; officer in charge Naval Legal Service Office, San Francisco, 1976-78; asst. judge adv. gen. Washington, 1978-80; dep. judge adv. gen. Alexandria, Va., 1980-82, judge adv. gen., 1982-84; asst. dean McGeorge Sch. Law, Sacramento, 1984-86, assoc. dean, 1987-93. Decorated D.S.M., Legion of Merit (2), Meritorious Svc. medal (2), Navy Commendation medal. Mem. ABA, Order of Coif (hon.), Phi Beta Kappa. Republican. Roman Catholic. Home: 4704 Olive Oak Way Carmichael CA 95608-5663

MCHUGH, JAMES LENAHAN, JR., lawyer; b. Pitts., June 28, 1937; s. James Lenahan and Annette (Dalton) McH.; m. Mary-Ann Curto, Feb. 16, 1963 (div. 1988); children: Angela Dalton Sherrill, Hillary Lenahan Clagett; m. Rosa Lamoreaux, Sept. 8, 1991. BA, Duquesne U., 1959; LLB, Villanova U., 1962. Bar: D.C. 1963. Law clk. U.S. Dist. Ct. (ea. dist.) Pa., Phila., 1962-63; law clk. to Assoc. Justice Tom C. Clark, U.S. Supreme Ct., Washington, 1963-64; assoc. Steptoe & Johnson, Washington, 1967-70, ptnr., 1970-94; gen. counsel APA, Washington, 1994—; mem. bd. consultors Law Sch., Villanova (Pa.) U., 1973—; dir. Higher Achievement Program, Washington, 1984-87; coord. Washington Lawyers' Project, Robert F. Kennedy Meml. Found., Washington, 1972-75. Editor-in-chief Villanova Law Rev., Vol. VII, 1961-62; chmn. editorial adv. bd. Fed. Comm. Law Jour., 1981-84. Bd. dirs. Columbia Hosp. for Women's Found., Washington, 1985—, Children's Radio Theatre, Washington, 1983-86; chmn. exec. giving Archbishop's Appeal, Archdiocese of Washington, 1982-84; mem. bd. visitors Ctr. for Study of Orgns. and Mgmt., U. Md. Univ. Coll., 1987-92; bd. dirs. Human Resources Rsch. Orgn., Inc., 1978—; chmn. bd. dirs., 1991—; mem. advisors Inst. for Conflict Analysis and Resolution, George Mason U., 1990-94. Capt. U.S. Army, 1964-67. Mem. ABA (forum com. health law, sect. on tax, antitrust and intellectual property), Nat. Health Lawyers Assn., D.C. Bar Assn., Choral Arts Soc., Order of Coif. Home: 4112 Fessenden St NW Washington DC 20016-4227 Office: APA 750 1st St NE Washington DC 20002-4241

MCHUGH, JAMES T., bishop; b. Orange, N.J., Jan. 3, 1932. Educated at Seton Hall Univ., Immaculate Conception Sem. (Darlington, N.J.), Fordham Univ., Catholic Univ., Angelicum (Rome). Ordained priest, 1957; consecrated bishop, 1988. Asst. dir. Family Life Div., U.S. Cath. Conf., 1965-67, dir., 1967-75; dir. Office for Pro-Life Activities, Nat. Conf. Cath. Bishops, 1972-78; aux. bishop Newark, 1987-89; bishop Diocese of Camden, N.J., 1989—. Home: Marywood PO Box 577 Blackwood NJ 08012 Office: The Chancery PO Box 709 1845 Haddon Ave Camden NJ 08101*

MC HUGH, JOHN LAURENCE, marine biologist, educator; b. Vancouver, B.C., Can., Nov. 24, 1911; came to U.S., 1946, naturalized, 1958; s. John and Annie Margaret (Woodward) McH.; m. Sophie Kleban, Mar. 30, 1979; children by previous marriage—Peter Chadwick, Heather, Jan Margaret. B.A., U. B.C., 1936, M.A., 1938; Ph.D., U. Calif. at Los Angeles, 1950. Summer sci. asst. Fisheries Research Bd. Can., 1929-37, fishery biologist, 1938-41; research asso. Scripps Instn. Oceanography, 1948-51; dir. Va. Fisheries Lab., Gloucester Point, 1951-59; prof. marine biology Coll. William and Mary, 1951-59; chmn. sci. com. Atlantic States Marine Fisheries Commn., 1956-58; chief div. biol. research Bur. Comml. Fisheries, Dept. Interior, 1959-63, asst. dir. for biol. research, 1963-66, dep. dir. bur., 1966-70; acting dir. Office Marine Resources, 1968-70; head NSF Office for Internat. Decade Ocean Exploration, 1970; prof. marine resources SUNY-Stony Brook, 1970-82, prof. emeritus, 1982—; U.S. commr. Inter-Am. Tropical Tuna Commn., 1960-70, sec. commn., 1960-61, 67-68, sec. U.S. sect., 1961-67, head U.S. del., 1967-70; dep. U.S. commr. Internat. Whaling Commn., 1961-67, commr., 1967-73, vice chmn., 1968-71, chmn., 1971-72; mem. U.S. nat. com. Internat. Biol. Program, 1968-70; adv. com. marine resources research to dir.-gen. FAO, 1967-71; mem. U.S. dels. to internat. sci., fishery meetings, 1959-72, NRC, 1963-69; mem. com. on internat. marine sci. affairs policy, ocean affairs bd. Nat. Acad. Scis.-Nat. Acad. Engring., 1971-74, com. on aquatic food resources, food and nutrition bd., 1973-74, vice chmn., 1973; mem. blue ribbon panel to rev. fed. programs on continental shelf. Office Sci. and Tech., Exec. Office Pres., 1971; chmn. select com. to rev. Eastern Pacific Oceanic Conf., Scripps Instn. Oceanography, 1972; mem. steering com., chmn. panel on fisheries, chmn. working group on information needs for effective mgmt. Coastal Zone workshop Woods Hole Oceanographic Instn., 1971-72; hon. mem. Whaling Mus. Soc., Cold Spring Harbor, N.Y., 1972-76; sec. Internat. Marine Archives, Nantucket, Mass., 1973-78; cons. to Nat. Council Marine Resources and Engring. Devel., 1970-71, Smithsonian Instn., 1970-72, Nat. Oceanic and Atmospheric Adminstrn., 1971-73, Riverside Research Inst., N.Y.C., 1971-72, Town of Islip, N.Y., 1974-78; mem. Mid-Atlantic Regional Fishery Mgmt. Council, 1976-79, mem. sci. and statis. com., 1980-84; mem. steering com. Nat. Acad. Sci.-NRC Panel to Review Fishery Research, 1975-76. Author: Fishery Management; contbr. numerous sci. papers, book chpts., articles to profl. lit. Served to capt. Canadian Army, 1941-45. Recipient Disting. Teaching award Marine Scis. Rsch. Ctr. Assocs., 1977, cert. for meritorious svc. Marine Scis. Rsch. Ctr./U. Stony Brook, 1994; fellow Internat. Oceanographic Found., 1955-74; trustee emeritus, 1974—; fellow Woodrow Wilson Internat. Ctr. for Scholars Smithsonian Instn., summer 1971. Mem. AAAS (selection com., Rosensteil award 1976), Am. Fisheries Soc. (Bronze medal, award of excellence 1984), Nat. Shellfisheries Assn. (citation 1984, hon. mem.), Va. Acad. Scis. (past chmn. biology sect.), Atlantic Estuarine Research Soc. (hon., past pres.), Am. Inst. Fishery Research Biologists, Nat. Shellfisheries Assn. (hon. mem.), Estuarine Research Fedn. (hon. mem.), Sigma Xi, Beta Theta Pi. Home: Vinson Hall Apt 170 6251 Old Dominion Dr Mc Lean VA 22101

MCHUGH, JOHN MICHAEL, congressman, former state senator; b. Watertown, N.Y., Sept. 29, 1948; s. Donald and Jane (O'Neill) McH. BA in Polit. Sci., Syracuse U., 1970; MPA, Nelson A. Rockefeller Grad. Sch. Pub. Affairs, 1977. Asst. city mngr. Watertown, 1968-73; confidential asst. Watertown City Mgrs. Office, 1971-76; chief of research, liaison with local govts. Office of N.Y. State Senator H.D. Barclay, 1976-84; U.S. senator from 46th N.Y. dist., 1984-93, chmn. joint legis. commn. on dairy industry devel., 1987-92; mem. 103rd-104th Congresses from 24th N.Y. dist., 1993—; chmn. govt. reform and oversight subcom. on postal svc., mem. nat. sucurity com. Mem. Legis. Commn. on Modernization of the Tax Code, Nat. Conf. State Legis., Commerce & Econ. Devel. Com., Commerce, Labor and Regulation Com. of the State Fed. Assembly, Coun. State Govt. Eastern Regional Conf. Com. on Fiscal Affairs. Recipient 40 Outstanding Alumni awards Syracuse U., Individual Achievement award N.Y. State Dept. Econ. Devel.; named to Hon. First Citizen, City of Watertown, 1976. Mem. Legis. on State Legislators (nat. conf. state legislators), Nat. Conf. State Legislators (vice chmn. agrl. and internat. trade com. State-Fed. Assembly), Am. Soc. Young Polit. Leaders. Republican. Roman Catholic. Avocations: boating, snow skiing, music. Office: US Ho of Reps 416 Cannon HOB Washington DC 20515-3224*

MC HUGH, PAUL R., psychiatrist, neurologist, educator; b. Lawrence, Mass., May 21, 1931; s. Francis Paul and Mary Dorothea (Herlihy) McH.; m. Jean Barlow, Dec. 27, 1959; children: Clare Mary, Patrick Daniel, Denis Timothy. AB, Harvard U., 1952, MD, 1956. Diplomate: Am. Bd. Psychiatry and Neurology. Intern Peter Bent Brigham Hosp., Boston, 1956-57; resident in neurology Mass. Gen. Hosp., 1957-60, fellow in neuropathology, 1958-59; teaching fellow in neurology and neuropathology Harvard, 1957-60; clin. asst. psychiatry Maudsley Hosp., London, Eng., 1960-61; mem. neuropsychiatry div. Walter Reed Army Inst. Research, Washington, 1961-64; asst. prof. psychiatry and neurology Cornell U., N.Y.C., 1964-68; assoc. prof. Cornell U., 1968-71, prof., 1971; dir. electroencephalography N.Y. Hosp., 1964-68; founder, dir. N.Y. Hosp. Bourne Behavioral Rsch. Lab., 1967-68, clin. dir., supr. psychiat. edn., founder, dir. Weschester divsn. dept. psychiatry, 1968-73; prof., chmn. dept. psychiatry U. Oreg. Health Sci. Center, Portland, 1973-75; Henry Phipps prof. psychiatry Johns Hopkins, Balt., 1975—; chmn. dept. psychiatry Johns Hopkins, 1975—, prof. dept. mental hygiene, 1976—; psychiatrist-in-chief Johns Hopkins Hosp., 1975—; dir. Blades Ctr. for Clin. Practice and Rsch. in Alcoholism Johns Hopkins Med. Inst., 1992—; chmn. med. staff Johns Hopkins Hosp., 1983-89, trustee, 1983—; vis. prof. Guys Hosp., London, Eng., 1976; chmn. bio-psychology Study sect. NIH, 1986-89. Author: The Perspectives of Psychiatry, 1983; (with Phillip R. Slavney) Psychiatric Polarities, 1987, Genes, Brain and Behavior, 1990; contbg. author: Cecil-Loeb Textbook of Medicine; mem. editorial bd. Am. Jour. Physiology, Jour. Nervous and Mental Disease, Comprehensive Psychiatry, Medicine, Psychol. Medicine, 1976—, Am. Scholar; contbr. articles to profl. jours. Mem. Md. Gov.'s Adv. Com., 1977-80. Grantee NIH, 1964-68, 67-70, 70-74, 75—; recipient William C. Menninger award ACP, 1987. Fellow Royal Coll. Psychiatry, Am. Psychiat. Assn.; mem. Inst. Medicine-NAS, Am. Neurol. Assn., Am. Physiol. Soc., Harvey Soc., Am. Coll. Neuropsychopharmacology, Am. Psychopath. Assn., Pavlovian Soc., W Hamilton St. Club. Home: 3707 St Paul St Baltimore MD 21218-2403 Office: Johns Hopkins Med Insts 600 N Wolfe St Baltimore MD 21205-2110*

MCHUGH, RICHARD WALKER, lawyer; b. Sullivan, Ind., Dec. 9, 1952; s. Richard Harrison and Virginia Ann (Robinson) McH.; m. Marsha J. Marshall, May 24, 1975; children: Walker, Cora. BA, Wabash Coll., 1975; JD, U. Mich., 1978. Bar: Mich. 1984, Ky. 1979, U.S. Supreme Ct. 1987. Assoc. Youngdahl Law Firm, Little Rock, 1978-79; staff atty. Legal Aid Soc., Louisville, 1979-84; assoc. gen. counsel Internat. Union UAW, Detroit, 1984-95; pvt. practice, Ann Arbor, Mich., 1995—; dir. Mich. Legal Svcs., Detroit, 1986-91. Mem. ABA (com. on unemployment ins. law 1985—), Nat. Acad. Social Ins. Democrat. Avocations: fishing, backpacking. Office: 255 E Liberty St Ste 277 Ann Arbor MI 48104-2019

MCILVAINE, JOSEPH PETER, professional baseball team executive; b. Bryn Mawr, Pa., Jan. 18, 1948; s. Joseph Francis and Mary Margaret (Wack) McI.; m. Martha Anne Marmer, Nov. 24, 1973; children: Timothy, Susan, Patrick. BA, St. Charles Borromeo Sem., Phila., 1969. Tchr. Our Mother of Good Counsel, Bryn Mawr, Pa., 1969-72; deliveryman United Parcel Svc., West Chester, Pa., 1972-73; profl. baseball player Detroit Tigers, 1969-73; major league baseball scout Balt. Orioles, 1974-76, Calif. Angels, Anaheim, 1977-78, Milw. Brewers, 1979-80; dir. scouting N.Y. Mets, Flushing, 1980-85, v.p., dir. baseball ops., 1986-90; exec. v.p., gen. mgr. San Diego Padres, 1990-93; former gen. mgr. N.Y. Mets, now exec. v.p. baseball ops.; cons. Athletes for Life, Washington, 1988—; bd. dirs. Major League Scouting Bur., Newport Beach, Calif., Returning Baseball to Inner Cities, L.A. Recipient World Series ring Major League Baseball, Flushing, 1986. Mem. Fla. Diamond Club (pres. 1980-81, Exec. of Yr. award 1984). Avocation: golf. *

MC ILVEEN, WALTER, mechanical engineer; b. Belfast, Ireland, Aug. 12, 1927; s. Walter and Amelia (Thompson) McI.; came to U.S., 1958, naturalized, 1963; M.E., Queens U., Belfast, 1948; H.V.A.C., Borough Polytechnic, London, 1951; m. Margaret Teresa Ruane, Apr. 17, 1949; children: Walter, Adrian, Peter, Anita, Alan. Mech. engr. Davidson & Co., Belfast, 1943-48; sr. contract engr. Keith Blackman Ltd., London, 1948-58; mech. engr. Fred S. Dubin Assos., Hartford, Conn., 1959-64; chief mech. engr. Koton & Donovan, West Hartfor, Conn., 1964-66; prin., engr. Walter McIlveen Assos., Avon, Conn., 1966—. Mem. IEEE, ASME, ASHRAE, Illuminating Engring. Soc., Hartford Engring. Club, Conn. Engrs. in Pvt. Practice. Mem. Ch. of Ireland. Home: 3 Valley View Dr Weatogue CT 06089-9714 Office: 195 W Main St Avon CT 06001-3685

MCILVEEN, WALTER RONALD, architectural engineer; b. London, Sept. 9, 1950; came to U.S., 1959; s. Walter and Margaret Theresa (Ruane) McI.; m. Barbara Lee O'Neill, June 8, 1974 (div. June 1993); 1 child, Daniel Walter. BS in Mech. Engring., Worcester (Mass.) Poly. Inst., 1972; MS in Mech. Engring., Rensselaer Poly. Inst., Hartford, Conn., 1975; MBA, Wayne State U., 1979. Registered profl. engr., Conn., Fla., Tenn., Ga., Mich., Ala. Design engr. Walter McIlveen Assocs., Avon, Conn., 1972-77, project engr., 1977; project engr. Smith Hinchman & Grylls Assocs., Detroit, 1977-78, divsn. discipline head, 1978-81; divsn. mgr. Diaz Seckinger Assocs., Tampa,

1981-84; chief mech. and elec. engr. Archtl. Engring. Inc., Palm Harbor, Fla., 1984—; pres. Archtl. Engrs., Inc., Palm Harbor, 1993—. Mem. ASHRAE, NSPE, Nat. Fire Protection Assn., Nat. Coun. Engring. Examiners, Inc., So. Bldg. Code Congress Internat. Inc., Greater Tampa C. of C. Leadership Tampa. Republican. Roman Catholic. Avocations: tennis, water skiing, stone sculpting, snorkeling. Home: 3526 Shoreline Cir Palm Harbor FL 34684-1743 Office: Archtl Engring Inc 3442 E Lake Rd Palm Harbor FL 34685-2406

MCILWAIN, CARL EDWIN, physicist; b. Houston, Mar. 26, 1931; s. Glenn William and Alma Ora (Miller) McI.; m. Mary Louise Hocker, Dec. 30, 1952; children—Janet Louise, Craig Ian. B.A., N. Tex. State Coll., Denton, 1953; M.S., State U. Iowa, 1956, Ph.D., 1960. Asst. prof. State U. Iowa, 1960-62; assoc. prof. physics U. Calif.-, San Diego, 1962-66; prof. U. Calif., 1966—; mem. space scis. steering com., fields and particles subcom. NASA, 1962-66; mem. anti-submarine warfare panel President's Sci. Adv. Com., 1964-67; mem. com. potential contamination and interference from space expts. Space Sci. Bd., Nat. Acad. Scis.-NRC, 1964-71; mem. advisory com. for radiation hazards in supersonic transports FAA, 1967-71; mem. Fachbeirat Inst. Extraterrestrial Physics, Max Planck Inst., Garching, Fed. Republic Germany, 1977-83, Space Sci. Bd., NRC, 1983-86. Author. Guggenheim fellow, 1968, 72; recipient Space Sci. award Am. Inst. Aeros. and Astronautics, 1970; Computer Art award U.S. Users Automatic Info. Display Equipment, 1971; Sr. U.S. Scientist award Alexander von Humboldt Found., Ger., 1976. Fellow Am. Geophys. Union (John A. Fleming award 1975); mem. Am. Phys. Soc., Am. Astron. Soc. Patentee in field. Home: 6662 Avenida Manana La Jolla CA 92037-6228 Office: Cass, 0111 Univ Calif San Diego La Jolla CA 92093-0111

MCILWAIN, THOMAS DAVID, fishery administrator, marine biologist, educator; b. Pascagoula, Miss., Nov. 15, 1940; s. Julius Coleman and Kathleen (Folsom) McI.; m. Janet Ellen Chapman, Dec. 29, 1962; 1 child, Stacey Lee. BS in Biology and Psychology, U. So. Miss., 1964, MS in Biology, 1966, PhD in Zoology, 1978. Lab. aid U.S. Bur. Comml. Fisheries, Pascagoula, summer 1958; instr. biology U. So. Miss., Hattiesburg, 1964-66; tchr. sci. St. Martin (Miss.) High Sch., 1965-66; rsch. biologist Gulf Coast Rsch. Lab., Ocean Springs, Miss., 1966-67, sect. leader, 1967-78, asst. dir. fisheries, 1978-83, dir., 1989-94; legis. asst. U.S. Congressman Trent Lott, Washington, 1983-84; fishery adminstr. Nat. Marine Fisheries Svc., Pascagoula, Miss., 1994—; fishery cons. Gulf and South Atlantic Fishery Devel. Found., Tampa, Fla., 1984-86, Republic of Honduras, 1990; pres. bd. dirs. Miss.-Ala. Sea Grant Consortium, Ocean Springs, 1991-94. Contbr. numerous articles to profl. jours. Chmn. Harbor Commn., Ocean Springs, 1980—; bd. dirs. Jackson County United Way, Pascagoula, 1991-95, Walter Anderseum Art Mus. Fellow Am. Inst. Fish Rsch. Scientists (regional bd. dirs. 1980); mem. Am. Fisheries Soc. (cert. fishery scientist), World Mariculture Soc., Miss. Acad. Scis. (bd. dirs. 1981), U.S. C. of C. (chmn. environ. com. 1990-95), So. Assn. Marine Labs. (pres. 1991-94). Presbyterian. Avocations: sailing, scuba diving, fishing. Office: Nat Marine Fisheries Svc Pascagoula Lab PO Drawer 1207 Pascagoula MS 39568-1207

MC ILWAIN, WILLIAM FRANKLIN, newspaper editor, writer; b. Lancaster, S.C., Dec. 15, 1925; s. William Franklin and Docia (Higgins) McI.; m. Anne Dalton, Nov. 28, 1952 (div. 1973); children: Dalton, Nancy, William Franklin III; m. K. L. Brelsford, June 5, 1978 (div. 1983). B.A., Wake Forest Coll., 1949; postgrad., Harvard, 1957-58. Various positions with Wilmington (N.C.) Star, 1943, Charlotte (N.C.) Observer, 1945, Jacksonville (Fla.) Jour., 1945, Winston-Salem (N.C.) Jour.-Sentinel, 1949-52, Richmond (Va.) Times-Dispatch, 1952-54; chief copy editor Newsday, Garden City, N.Y., 1954-57; day news editor Newsday, 1957-60, city editor, 1960-64, mng. editor, 1964-66, editor, 1967-70; writer-in-residence Wake Forest U., 1970-71; dorm leader Alcoholic Rehab. Ctr., Butner, N.C., 1971; dep. mng. editor Toronto Star, 1971-73; mng. editor The Record, Hackensack, N.J., 1973-77; editor Boston Herald Am., 1977-79; dep. editor Washington Star, 1979-81, exec. mng. editor, 1981; editor Ark. Gazette, 1981-82; founding editor N.Y. Newsday, 1982-84; exec. editor Sarasota (Fla.) Herald-Tribune, 1984-90; sr. editor N.Y. Times Regional Newspaper Group, 1991-92; chmn. Bill Mc Ilwain, Inc., 1993—; Stone Ridge lectr., 1978. Author: The Glass Rooster, 1960, (with Walter Friedenberg) Legends of Baptist Hollow, 1949; collaborator: (with Newsday staff) Naked Came The Stranger, 1969, A Farewell to Alcohol, 1973; contbr. to: Reader's Digest, Harper's, Esquire, Atlantic Monthly. Mem. Pres. Johnson's Commn. on Civil Rights. With USMC, 1944. Mem. Am. Soc. Newspaper Editors, Soc. Nieman Fellows. Home and Office: 305 N Channel Dr Wrightsville Beach NC 28480 *As Fats Waller said, "One never knows, do one?".*

MC INDOE, DARRELL WINFRED, nuclear medicine physician, former air force officer; b. Wilkinsburg, Pa., Sept. 28, 1930; s. Clarence Wilbert and Dorothy Josephine (Morrow) McI.; m. Carole Jean McClain, Aug. 23, 1952; children: Sherri L., Wendy L., Darrell B., Ronald S., Holly B. BS, Allegheny Coll., 1952; MD, Temple U., 1956, MS, 1960. Commd. 2d lt. M.C. U.S. Air Force, 1956, advanced through grades to col., 1971; intern Brooke Army Med. Ctr., San Antonio, 1956-57; resident in medicine Temple U. Med. Ctr., Phila., 1957-60; chief internal medicine and hosp. svcs. Norton AFB, 1960-64; chief internal medicine and hosp. services 7520 U.S. Air Force Hosp., U.K., 1964-68; vis. rsch. fellow Royal Post Grad. Med. Sch., London, 1968-69; chief endocrinology svcs., chmn. dept. nuclear medicine USAF Med. Center, Keesler AFB, Miss., 1969-75; dep. dir. Armed Forces Radiobiology Rsch. Inst., Def. Nuclear Agy., Bethesda, Md., 1975-77; dir. Armed Forces Radiobiology Rsch. Inst., Def. Nuclear Agy., 1977-79; staff physician nuclear medicine br., dept. radiology Nat. Naval Med. Center, Bethesda, 1979-82; sr. lectr. mil. medicine Uniformed U. of Health Scis., Bethesda, 1975-80; asst. prof. radiology/nuclear medicine and rsch. program coord. Uniformed U. of Health Scis., 1980-82; assoc. div. nuclear medicine St. Joseph Hosp., Towson, Md., 1982-91, dir. div. nuclear medicine, 1992—; med. advisor Nev. ops. office Dept. Energy, Las Vegas; cons. in field. Fellow Royal Soc. Medicine, Am. Coll. Nuclear Physicians (regent Ea. USA); mem. Am. Coll. Nuclear Physicians, Air Force Soc. Physicians (bd. govs. 1973-77), Uniformed Services Nuclear Medicine Assn. (pres. 1975), Soc. Nuclear Medicine (pres. Mideastern chpt.), Md. Soc. Nuclear Medicine (pres.-elect), AMA, Health Physics Soc. (dir. Balt., Washington chpt.), Assn. Mil. Surgeons U.S., Soc. Med. Cons.'s to Armed Forces, Alexander Graham Bell Soc. Home: 15510 Foxpaw Tr Woodbine MD 21797 Office: St Joseph Hosp Towson MD 21204

MC INERNEY, DENIS, lawyer; b. N.Y.C., May 31, 1925; s. Denis and Anne (Keane) McI.; m. Mary Irene Murphy, Nov. 14, 1953; children: Kathleen Mc Inerney O'Hare, Denis J., Maura Mc Inerney Romano. BSS, Fordham U., 1948, JD cum laude, 1951, LLD (hon.), 1996. Bar: N.Y. 1951, D.C. 1961. Instr. philosophy Fordham U., 1948-51; assoc. Cahill Gordon & Reindel, N.Y.C., 1951-61, prtnr., 1961-90, sr. counsel, 1991—; vice chmn. Com. Character and Fitness Admission State Bar N.Y., 1st Jud. Dept., 1979—; lectr. in field. Co-author: Practitioners Handbook for Appeals to the Appellate Divisions of the State of New York, 1979, Practitioners Handbook for Appeals to the Court of Appeals of the State of New York, 1981. Bd. dirs. Vols. of Legal Svc., Inc., 1985—, Cath. Youth Orgn., 1975—; mem. adv. bd. St. Vincent's Hosp., Westchester, N.Y., 1988—; chmn. bd. visitors Fordham Law Sch., 1989—; trustee Fordham U., 1988-94. Sgt. 82d Airborne Divsn. U.S. Army, 1943-46, ETO. Decorated Knight of Malta, Knight of the Holy Sepulcher; recipient Achievement in Law award Fordham U., 1977. Fellow Am. Coll. Trial Lawyers (state chmn. 1980-82); mem. ABA, N.Y. State Bar Assn., New York County Lawyers Assn. (pres. 1982-84), Fordham U. Law Alumni Assn. (pres. 1968-72, medal of achievement 1975). Roman Catholic. Clubs: Westchester Country, Univ. Office: Cahill Gordon & Reindel 80 Pine St New York NY 10005-1702

MCINERNEY, JAMES EUGENE, JR., trade association administrator; b. Springfield, Mass., Aug. 3, 1930; s. James Eugene and Rose Elizabeth (Adikes) McI.; m. Mary Catherine Hill, July 17, 1963; children: Anne Elizabeth, James Eugene, III. B.S., U.S. Mil. Acad., 1952; M.S. in Engring., Princeton U., 1960; postgrad., Royal Air Force Staff Coll., 1964; M.S. in Internat. Affairs, George Washington U., 1970. Commd. 2d lt. USAF, 1952, advanced through grades to maj. gen., 1976; fighter pilot Korea, Japan and Ger.; comdr. tactical fighter squadron Thailand, 1967; tactical fighter wing Ger., 1971; sr. U.S. adviser Turkish Air Force, 1973; dir. mil. assistance and sales Hdqrs. USAF, 1975-78; comdt. Indsl. Coll. Armed Forces, 1978-79; dir. programs Hdqrs. USAF, 1979-80, asst. dep. chief of staff for programs and evaluation, 1980; dir. legis. liaison McDonnell Douglas Corp., Washington, 1980-83, dir. internat. affairs, 1983-86; v.p. Am. League for Exports and Security Assistance, 1986-89, exec. v.p., 1989-92; v.p. Am. Def. Preparedness Assn., 1992—. Decorated Air Force Cross, D.S.M. (2), Silver Star (3), D.F.C. (7), Bronze Star, Meritorious Service medal (2), Air medal (18), Air Force Commendation medal; Vietnamese Crosses of Gallantry with palm and star; Republic of Korea Cheongsu medal. Mem. Air Force Assn. (citation of honor 1968), Brit.-Am. Bus. Assn.-Washington (pres. 1982-94, chmn. 1994—), Brit.-Am. Bus. Coun. (US-UK) (chmn. 1996—), Am.-Air Mus. in Britain (exec. dir. 1994—). Roman Catholic. Home: 1031 Delf Dr Mc Lean VA 22101-2009

MCINERNEY, JAY, author; b. Hartford, Conn., Jan. 13, 1955; s. John Barrett and Marilyn Jean (Murphy) McI.; m. Merry Reymond, June 2, 1984 (dec.); m. Helen Bransford, Dec. 27, 1991. BA, Williams Coll., 1976; postgrad., Syracuse U. Reporter Hunterdon County Democrat, Flemington, N.J., 1977; textbook editor Time Life Pubs., Osaka, Japan, 1978-79; fact checker New Yorker, N.Y.C., 1980; reader Random House Pubs., N.Y.C., 1980-81; instr. English Syracuse U., 1983; writer, 1983—. Author: (novels) Bright Lights, Big City, 1984, Ransom, 1985, Story of My Life, 1988, Brightness Falls, 1992, The Last of the Savages, 1996; screenwriter: (films) Bright Lights, Big City, 1988; contbr. articles to profl. jours. Princeton in Asia fellow, 1977. Mem. Authors Guild, PEN, Writers Guild. Address: 1572 Old Hillsboro Rd Franklin TN 37064-9135 Office: care Amanda Urban Intl Creative Mgt 40 W 57th St New York NY 10019-4001 Office: 50 E 77th St New York NY 10021

MCINERNEY, JOSEPH ALOYSIUS, hotel executive; b. Oak Park, Ill., Sept. 2, 1939; s. Joseph Aloysius and Helene (Mustari) McI.; m. Ruth McClelland, Aug. 29, 1969; children—Joseph A., Susan B. Student, Loyola U., Chgo., 1959-61; B.A. cum laude, Boston Coll., 1974. With Sheraton-Chgo. Hotel, 1961-65, regional dir. franchise ops., 1966-67, dir. franchise devel., 1968-69; gen. mgr. Sheraton-Winston, Salem, 1969-70; v.p., asst. to pres. Sheraton Corp., 1970-73, sr. v.p., dir. franchise ops., 1973-79; sr. v.p. Sheraton Corp., pres. Sheraton Corp. (Franchise div.), 1979-86; pres. Hawthorn Suites, 1986-91; pres., chief exec. officer Travelodge Internat., 1991-92; pres., CEO Forte Hotels, Inc., 1992—; guest lectr. Cornell Hotel Sch., Boston U. Hotel Sch., U. N.H. Hotel Sch., Mich. State U., San Diego State U. Former mem. industry sect. adv. com. U.S. Dept. Commerce, also U.S. trade rep.; mem. adv. bd. Master Sci. degree program in hospitality industry studies at NYU; mem. hospitality adv. bd. N.Mex. State, Calif. Poly. Hosp.; former trustee Boston U. Med. Ctr., Bethune-Cookman Coll.; bd. trustees St. Vincent de Paul Village; exec. com. CEO San Diego Roundtable. Mem. Am. Hotel & Motel Assn. (govtl. affairs com.), Am. Hotel & Motel Ednl. Inst. (chmn.). Office: Forte Hotels Inc 1973 Friendship Dr El Cajon CA 92020-1140

MCINERNEY, JOSEPH JOHN, biomedical engineer, educator; b. Boston, Aug. 13, 1932; s. John Joseph and Anne (Berry) McI.; m. Suzanne Finke, Oct. 20, 1970; children by previous marriage: Joseph, Lynn, Maureen; children by present marriage: Kathleen, John. B.S. in Mech. Engring., Northeastern U., 1960; M.S. in Nuclear Engring., Pa. State U., 1962, Ph.D. in Theoretical Physics, 1964, M.S. in Human Physiology, 1980. Nuclear physicist Knolls Atomic Lab., Schenectady, 1964-76; postdoctoral fellow Sch. Medicine, Pa. State U., Hershey, 1976-79, staff rsch. scientist, 1979—; asst. prof. depts. biomed. engring. and medicine, Pa. State U., State College, 1984-90, assoc. prof., 1990—; referee Am. Nuclear Soc., Hinsdale, Ill., 1966—, Med. Biol. Engring., 1986—; cons. Whitaker Found., Harrisburg, Pa., 1981—, NIH; mem. standard com. Am. Nuclear Soc., Hinsdale, 1966—. Patentee in field. Contbr. articles to profl. jours. Served with USN, 1951-55. NIH fellow, 1976-79; Whitaker Found. grantee, 1979-81; Am. Heart Assn. grantee, 1979-80; NIH grantee, 1976-84, 84—, Pa. Rsch. Corp. grantee, 1983-84, Applied Rsch. Labs. grantee, 1985—. Mem. Am. Nuclear Soc., Am. Heart Assn., AAAS, Am. Physiol. Soc., Am. Fedn. Clin. Rsch., Am. Assn. Physicists in Medicine, IEEE (referee 1986—), Sigma Xi, Pi Tau Sigma. Democrat. Home: 260 Quarry Rd Hummelstown PA 17036-8902 Office: Pa State U Milton S Hershey Med Ctr PO Box 850 Hershey PA 17033-0850

MCINERNY, RALPH MATTHEW, philosophy educator, author; b. Mpls., Feb. 24, 1929; s. Austin Clifford and Vivian Gertrude (Rush) McI.; m. Constance Terrill Kunert, Jan. 3, 2953; children: Cathleen, Mary, Anne, David, Elizabeth, Daniel. BA, St. Paul Sem., 1951; MA, U. Minn., 1952; PhD summa cum laude, Lval U., 1954; DHL, St. John Fisher Coll., 1993, St. Anselm Coll., 1995. Instr. Creighton U., 1954-55; prof. U. Notre Dame, Ind., 1955—, Michael P. Grace prof. medieval studies, 1988—, dir. dept., 1978-85; vis. prof. Cornell U., 1988, Cath. U., 1971, Louvain, 1983, 95; founder Internat. Catholic Univ. Author: (philos. works) The Logic of Analogy, 1961, History of Western Philosophy, vol. 1, 1963, vol. 2, 1968, Thomism in an Age of Renewal, 1966, Studies in Analogy, 1967, New Themes in Christian Philosophy, 1967, St. Thomas Aquinas, 1976, Ethica Thomistica, 1982, History of the Ambrosiana, 1983, Being and Predication, 1986, Miracles, 1986, Art and Prudence, 1988, A First Glance at St. Thomas: Handbook for Peeping Thomists, 1989, Boethius and Aquinas, 1989, Aquinas on Human Action, 1991, The Question of Christian Ethics, 1993, Aquinas Against the Averroists, 1993; (novels) Jolly Rogerson, 1967, A Narrow Time, 1969, The Priest, 1973, Gate of Heaven, 1975, Rogerson at Bay, 1976, Her Death of Cold, 1977, The Seventh Station, 1977, Romanesque, 1977, Spinnaker, 1977, Quick as a Dodo, 1978, Bishop as Pawn, 1978, La Cavalcade Romaine, 1979, Lying Three, 1979, Abecedary, 1979, Second Vespers, 1980, Rhyme and Reason, 1981, Thicker than Water, 1981, A Loss of Patients, 1982, The Grass Widow, 1983, Connolly's Life, 1983, Getting Away with Murder, 1984, And Then There Were Nun, 1984, The Noonday Devil, 1985, Sine Qua Nun, 1986, Leave of Absence, 1986, Rest in Pieces, 1985, Cause and Effect, 1987, The Basket Case, 1987, Veil of Ignorance, 1988, Abracadaver, 1989, Body and Soil, 1989, Four on the Floor, 1989, Frigor Mortis, 1989, Savings and Loan, 1990, The Search Committee, 1991, The Nominative Case, 1991, Sister Hood, 1991, Judas Priest, 1991, Easeful Death, 1991, Infra Dig, 1992, Desert Sinner, 1992, Seed of Doubt, 1993, The Basket Case, 1993, Nun Plussed, 1993, Mom and Dead, 1994, The Cardinal Offense, Law and Ardor, 1995; editor The New Scholasticism, 1967-89; editor, pub. Crisis, 1982-96; pub. Catholic Dossier, 1995—. Exec. dir. Wethersfield Inst., 1989-92; bd. govs. Thomas Aquinas Coll., Santa Paula, Calif., 1992—. With USMCR, 1946-47. Fulbright rsch. fellow, Belgium, 1959-60, NEH fellow, 1977-78, NEA fellow, 1983, Fulbright scholar, Argentina, 1986, 87. Fellow Pontifical Roman Acad. St. Thomas Aquinas; mem. Am. Philos. Assn., Am. Cath. Philos. Assn. (past pres., recipient medals), Am. Metaphys. Soc. (pres. 1992), Internat. Soc. for Study Medieval Philosophy, Medieval Acad., Mystery Writers Am., Authors Guild, Fellowship Cath. Scholars (pres. 1992-95). Home: 2158 Portage Ave South Bend IN 46616-2035 Office: U of Notre Dame Dept of Philosophy 336 O Shaugnessy Hall Notre Dame IN 46556-5639

MCINNES, DONALD GORDON, railroad executive; b. Buffalo, Nov. 6, 1940; s. Milton Gordon and Blanche Mae (Clunk) McI.; m. Betsy Campbell, Mar. 18, 1967; children: Campbell Gordon, Cody Milton. B.A., Denison U., 1963; M.S., Northwestern U., 1965; cert. in transp. Yale U., 1965. Budget mgr. operating AT&SF R.R. Co., Chgo., 1969-71, asst. trainmaster, San Bernardino, Calif., 1971-73, trainmaster, Temple, Tex., 1973-76, asst. supt., Carlsbad, N.M., 1976-77, supt. eastern divsn., Emporia, Kans., 1977-79, supt. Los Angeles divsn., San Bernardino, Calif., 1979-81, asst. to exec. v.p., Chgo., 1981-82, gen. supt. transp., 1983-87, gen. mgr. transp., 1987, gen. mgr. ea. region, 1988, v.p. adminstrn., 1989, v.p. intermodal, 1989-91, sr. v.p. intermodal, 1991-93, sr. v.p., COO, 1994-95; sr. v.p., COO Burlington No. Santa Fe Corp., 1995—; bd. dirs. AT & SF Railway Co., TTX Corp., leader of group Intermodal Assn. N.Am., 1st chmn., 1991-93. Bd. dirs. Jr. Achievement Chgo. Served to 2d lt., USAF, 1965-67; capt. U.S. Army, 1967-69. Decorated Bronze Star. Rivercrest C. of C. (Ft. Worth). Republican. Episcopalian. Clubs: Union League (Chgo.), Meadow (Rolling Meadow), Pass (Boca Grande), Boca Grande Pass Yacht, Lemon Bay Golf (Englewood, Fla.). Home: 429 Rivercrest Dr Fort Worth TX 76107 also: 148 Carrick Bend Ct Boca Grande FL 33921 Office: Burlington No Santa Fe Corp PO Box 961034 Fort Worth TX 76161-0034

MCINNES, HAROLD A., manufacturing company executive; b. Groton, Conn., 1927. B.S.M.E., MIT, 1949. With Delco Appliance div. Gen. Motors Corp., 1949-55, Tracerlab, Inc., 1955-60, Reed Rolled Thread Die Co., 1960-62, Dresser Industries, Inc., 1962-65, AMP, Inc., Harrisburg, Pa., 1965—; mfg. mgr. packaging components AMP, Inc., 1966-70, mgr. automach div., 1970-73, group dir. gen. products, 1973-78, v.p. mfg. resources planning, 1978-79, corp. v.p. engring. and tech. resources, 1979-81, pres., 1981-86, vice chmn., bd. dirs., 1986-90, chmn., chief exec. officer, 1990-93, chmn. exec. com., 1993—; bd. dirs. PPG Industries, Pitts. Mem. Elec. Mfrs. Club. Office: AMP Inc 470 Friendship Rd MS 176-40 Harrisburg PA 17111-1203*

MC INNES, ROBERT MALCOLM, lawyer, business consultant; b. Pictou, N.S., Can., July 17, 1930; naturalized U.S. citizen, 1964; s. John Logan and Jenny MacKay (Malcolm) McI.; m. June Hughena O'Brien, Apr. 19, 1952; children: Donald, Elizabeth, Susan. B.A., Dalhousie U., Halifax, N.S., 1951, LL.B., 1953; postgrad., Harvard U. Bus. Sch., 1968. Assoc. firm Duquet, MacKay, Weldon & Tetreault, Montreal, Que., Can., 1953-57; with Pickands Mather & Co., Cleve., 1957-69, 71-87; v.p. Pickands Mather & Co., 1971-73, exec. v.p., 1973-83, pres., chief exec. officer, 1983-87; gen. counsel, treas. Diamond Shamrock Corp., 1969-71; group exec. v.p. Cleve. Cliffs Inc., 1987-88; of counsel Arter and Hadden, Cleve., 1988-94; bd. dirs. Brush Wellman Inc., Cliffs Drilling Co., Seaforth Mineral and Ore Co. Mem. Mayfield Country Club, Union Club. Republican. Methodist. Home: 32300 Meadow Lark Way Pepper Pike OH 44124-5510

MC INNES, WILLIAM CHARLES, priest, campus ministry director; b. Boston, Jan. 20, 1923; s. William Charles and Mary (Byrne) McI. B.S., Boston Coll., 1946, A.B., 1950, M.A., 1951; S.T.L., Weston Coll., 1958; Ph.D., N.Y. U., 1955. Joined Soc. of Jesus, 1946; ordained priest Roman Cath. Ch., 1957; prof. mktg. and bus. ethics Boston Coll. Sch. Bus. Adminstrn., 1959-63, assoc. dean, 1961-63, dir. honors program, 1963-64, mem. citizens seminar planning com., 1959-63; pres. Fairfield (Conn.) U., 1964-73, prof. urban problems, 1969-72; pres. U. San Francisco, 1972-77, Assn. Jesuit Colls. and Univs., 1977-89; campus min. U. Conn., Storrs, 1990—; vis. fellow Woodstock Theol. Ctr., 1990-91. Past chmn. bd. ABCD (cmty. action agys.); pres. Conn. Assn. for Cmty. Action Programs; founder Fairfield County Cmty. forum, Conn. Charter Oak Coll.; life mem. United Cerebral Palsy Assn. Fairfield County; bd. dirs., vice chmn. Nat. Better Bus. Bur. Found.; mem. adv. com. Conn. Dept. Social Svcs., 1993—. Served to capt. USAAF, 1942-46, CBI. Mem. Beta Gamma Sigma, Alpha Sigma Nu, Delta Sigma Pi, Phi Kappa Theta, Alpha Epsilon Delta. Home: 46 N Eagleville Rd Storrs Mansfield CT 06268-1710

MCINNIS, HELEN LOUISE, publishing company executive; b. Fall River, Mass.; d. Hugh Michael and Louise Patricia (Waldron) McI. B.A., Merrimack Coll., 1967; M.A., Duquesne U., 1969. Asst. editor Holt, Rinehart & Winston, N.Y.C., 1971-73; editor D. Van Nostrand Co., N.Y.C., 1972-75; sr. v.p., dir. coll. dept. Scribner Book Cos., Inc., N.Y.C., 1976-91; asst. v.p., exec. editor Macmillan Pub. Co., 1985-91; v.p., editl. dir. acad./trade Oxford U. Press, N.Y.C., 1991—. Editor, author: Viewpoints: American Cities, 1972. Mem. Assn. Am. Pubs. (chmn. com. higher edn. div. 1980-82, exec. bd. 1982-84). Democrat. Roman Catholic. Home: 253 W 72nd St Apt 1505 New York NY 10023-2708 Office: Oxford U Press 200 Madison Ave New York NY 10016-3903

MCINNIS, SCOTT STEVE, congressman, lawyer; b. Glenwood Springs, Colo., May 9, 1953; s. Kohler McInnis and Carol Kreir; m. Lori McInnis; children: Daxon, Tessa, Andrea. BA, Ft. Lewis Coll., 1975; JD, St. Mary's Law Sch., 1980. Atty. Delaney & Balcomb P.C., Glenwood Springs, Colo., 1981—; mem. Colo. Ho. of Reps., 1984-93; majority leader, 1990-93; mem. 103d-104th Congresses from 3d Colo. Dist., 1993—; chmn. agrl. livestock and natural resources com., 1986-90, mem. rules com. Recipient Florence Sabin award, 1984, Guardian of Small Bus. award Nat. Fed. Ind. Bus., 1990, Lee Atwater Leadership award, 1991, and various awards from United Vets. Commn.; named Legislator of Decade and Legislator of Yr by Colo. Ski Country and Colo. Wildlife Found. Mem. Elks, Rotary, Phi Delta Phi. Republican. Roman Catholic. Office: US Ho of Reps 215 Cannon HOB Washington DC 20515-0603*

MCINTIRE, JERALD GENE, investment executive, former municipal official; b. Abilene, Tex., Mar. 16, 1938; s. Andrew Noble and Viola (Richey) McI.; m. Linda Carole Sanders, Aug. 28, 1964 (div. Mar. 1976); children: Chrisitan Tilghman, Ross Andrew, John Patrick Morgan. AA, N.Mex. Mil. Inst., 1958; BA, Ea. N.Mex. U., 1964. Ptnr., officer Ruffino Prodns., Dallas, 1960-64; tchr., drama dir. Roswell (N.Mex.) Pub. Schs., 1966-70; tchr. curriculum Thiokol Chem., Roswell, 1970-74; pvt. bus. mgr. Dallas, 1974-77; career coordinator Soc. Ednl. Reconstrn./Jobs for Progress, Dallas, 1977-82; council asst. City of Dallas, 1982-83, asst. to mayor pro tem, 1983-87, asst. to mayor, 1987-89; pres., chief exec. officer Multinational Investments, Multinational Offshore Venture, M'N'M Antiquities, Grand Caymen, Bahamas, 1990—; ptnr., officer Multi-Nat. Investments, Inc., Dallas, 1980. Con., v.p. Chrysalis Home & Health Care, Dallas, 1985-87; devel. dir., mem. sch. bd. Immaculate Conception Sch, Grand Prairie, Tex., 1983-85; bd. dirs. Hist. Soc. Southeast N.Mex., 1996. Mem. Nat. Assn. Council Assts. Democrat. Jewish. Avocations: gardening, travel, writing, music, riding. Office: Multinational Investments, M'N'M Brokers Internat, Grand Cayman Bahamas

MCINTIRE, LARRY VERN, chemical engineering educator; b. St. Paul, June 28, 1943; s. James Lawrence and Lenore Vineal (Converse) McI.; m. Mary Beth McEnery, July 5, 1969. BChemE, MS, Cornell U., 1966; MA, Princeton U., 1968, PhD, 1970. Registered profl. engr., Tex. Asst. prof. Rice U., Houston, 1970-74, assoc. prof., 1974-78, prof. chem. engring., 1978—, E.D. Butcher prof., 1983—, chmn. dept., 1981-91, chmn. Bioscis. and Bioengring. Inst., 1991—, chmn. rsch. coun., 1988-91, dir. Biomed. Engring. Lab., 1980—; speaker faculty coun., 1994-95; adj. prof. medicine Baylor Coll. Medicine, Houston, 1982—, U. Tex. Med. Sch., Houston, 1982—; chmn. blood/materials working group NIH, Bethesda, Md., 1982-85; mem. surgery and bioengring. study sect. NIH, 1984-88; mem. com. on bioprocessing NRC, 1991—; chmn. rheology subcom. Internat. Coun. on Thrombosis and Hemostasis, 1985-89. Contbr. over 160 articles to profl. jours. Recipient Merit award NIH, 1989; NSF fellow Cornell U., Princeton U., 1965-69, NATO-NSF postdoctoral fellow Imperial Coll., London, 1976-77. Fellow Am. Inst. Med. Biol. Engring. (sec., treas. 1993—), AICHE (officer lical sect. 1980-81, 86, Food Pharm. and Bioengring. divsn. award 1992); mem. AAAS, Biomed. Engring. Soc. (bd. dirs. 1992—, pres. 1995—, Disting. lectr. 1992), N.Am. Soc. Biorheology (v.p. 1992-94, pres. 1994—), N.Y. Acad. Scis., Am. Heart Assn. (coun. on thromposis, exec. com. 1994—), Faculty Club Rice U. (bd. dirs., chmn. 1982-84), Sigma Xi (nat. lectr. 1993—). Presbyterian. Avocations: tennis, squash, classical music, hiking. Office: Rice U Inst Bioscis and Bioengring John W Cox Lab Biomed Engring Houston TX 77251-1892

MCINTOSH, CAROLYN MEADE, retired educational administrator; b. Waynesburg, Ky., Oct. 21, 1928; d. Clarence Hobert and Sarah Letitia (Bentley) Meade; m. Edgar G. McIntosh, Aug. 21, 1948; children: Wayne, Jeanne, Penny, Jimmi, Carol. BS, Miami U., Oxford, Ohio, 1962; MEd, Xavier U., Cin., 1966. Elem. tchr. Ohio, 1961-79; prin. New Richmond (Ohio) Sch. Dist., 1980-91; ret., 1991; tchr. Clermont County Adult Edn. Program, 1970-95, Clermont County dir.of Headstrart 1971-72, Clearmont County Rep. to Ohio elem. adminstr., 1985-87, Pres. Clermont and Brown County adminstr., 1988-89. Editor Ret. Tchrs. Newsletter. Pres. New Richmond Bd. Edn.; v.p. U.S. Grant Vocat. Sch. Bd. Edn.; mem. Clermont County Excellence in Edn. Com.; mem. edn. adv. com. Clermont Coll.; mem. adv. bd. Bethany Children's Home; mem. Clermont 2001 Com.; mem. Rep. Ctrl. Com. of Clermont County. Recipient New Richmond Adminstr. of the Yr. award City of New Richmond, 1989. Mem. AAUW, ASCD, NAESP, Nat. Sch. Bd. Assn., Ohio Sch. Bd. Assn., Ohio Assn. Elem. Sch. Adminstrs. (all county legis. liaison), Ohio County Ret. Tchrs. Assn., Clermont County Ret. Tchrs. Assn. (pres.), Order Eastern Star, Phi Delta Kappa, Delta Kappa Gamma (pres. chpt.). Baptist.

MCINTOSH, CECILIA ANN, biochemist, educator; b. Dayton, Ohio, Apr. 30, 1956; d. Russell Edward McIntosh and Geraldine Rita (Cochran) Slemp; m. Kevin Smith Schweiker, May 28, 1978 (div. Mar. 1989); children: Katrina Lynn McIntosh Schweiker, Rebecca Sue McIntosh Schweiker. BA in Biology cum laude, U. South Fla., 1977, MA in Botany, 1981, PhD in Biology, 1990. Rsch. assoc. U. South Fla., Tampa, 1981-86, teaching/rsch. asst. dept. biology, 1986-90; postdoctoral fellow dept. biochemistry U. Idaho, Moscow, 1990-93; asst. prof. dept. biol. scis. East Tenn. State U., Johnson City, 1993—; adj. asst. prof. dept. biochemistry Quillen Coll. Medicine, East Tenn. State U., Johnson City, 1995—; sci. mentor U. So. Fla. Ctr. for Excellence, Tampa, 1984-90; rsch. forum judge Coll. Medicine Rsch. Forum, East Tenn. State U., Johnson City, 1994—. Author: (rev. articles) The Molecular Biology of Mitrochondria, 1995, Biotechnology of Medicinal and Aromatic Plants, 1991; contbr. rsch. articles to profl. jours. including Plant Physiology, Archives of Biochemistry & Biophysics. Sci. fair judge East Tenn. Regional Sci. Fair, Johnson City, 1994—. Strenghthening program grantee USDA, 1994-95, Seed grantee, 1995-97; rsch. devel. grantee East Tenn. State U. Rsch. Devel. Coun., 1994-96. Mem. Am. Assn. Women in Sci., Am. Soc. Plant Physiologists, Phytochem. Soc. N.Am., Sigma Xi (sci. fair workshop coord. Appalachian chpt. 1995—, dissertation award 1991). Achievements include characterization of new enzyme in plant flavonoid biosynthesis; biochemical characterization of plant mitrochondrial membrane tricarboxylate and phosphate transporters. Avocations: outdoor activities, sports, mysteries. Office: East Tenn State U Dept Biol Scis Box 70 703 Johnson City TN 37614-0703

MCINTOSH, DAVID M., congressman; b. June 8, 1958; m. Ruthie McIntosh. Grad., Yale Coll., 1980, U. Chgo., 1983. Bar: Ind., U.S. Supreme Ct. Spl. asst. domestic affairs to Pres. Reagan; spl. asst. to Atty. Gen. Meese; liaison Pres.'s Commn. on Privatization; spl. asst. to V.P. Quayle, dep. legal counsel to; exec. dir. Pres.'s Coun. on Competitiveness; sr. fellow Citizens for a Sound Economy; founder Federalist Soc. for Law & Pub. Policy, now co-chmn.; mem. U.S. Ho. of Reps., 104 Congress, Washington, 1995—, mem. Govt. Reform & Oversight Com., chmn. panel's Econ. Growth, Natural Resources and Regulatory Affairs Subcom. Mem. State Bar of Ind. Republican. Office: US House Reps 1208 Longworth House Office Bldg Washington DC 20515-1402*

MCINTOSH, DECOURCY EYRE, museum director; b. Balt., Dec. 1, 1942; s. David Gregg and Grace (Wright) McI.; m. Susan Reed Bell, Nov. 11, 1967; children: Madeline Eyre, David Gregg. AB, Harvard U., 1965. Program officer Richard King Mellon Found., Pitts., 1969-74; exec. dir. Hist. Savannah (Ga.) Found., 1974-77; mng. dir. Minn. Landmarks, St. Paul, 1977-79; v.p. Mpls. Soc. Fine Arts, 1979-84; exec. dir. Helen Clay Frick Found., Pitts., 1984—, Frick Art & Hist. Ctr., Pitts., 1990—. Editor: (exhbn. catalogues) 19th Century French Drawings from Lyon, 1992, Renaissance & Baroque Bronzes in The Frick Art Museum, 1993, Florentine Drawings of the 17th & 18th Centuries from Lille, 1994. Trustee Pitts. History & Landmarks, 1984—, Art Svcs. Internat., Alexandria, 1990—; bd. dirs. Pitts. Parks & Playgrounds Fund, 1986—, Preservation Pa., 1991—. Mem. Am. Assn. Mus., Century Assn., Pitts. Golf Club, Walpole Soc. Office: The Frick Art & Hist Ctr 7227 Reynolds St Pittsburgh PA 15208-2919

MCINTOSH, DENNIS KEITH, veterinary practitioner, consultant; b. Newark, June 12, 1941; s. Sheldon Weeks and Enid Nicholson (Casey) McI.; m. Rachel McIntosh; children: Rebecca, Kevin, Jamie. BS in Animal Sci., Tex. A&M U., 1963, BS in Vet. Sci., 1967, DVM, 1968. Asst. county agrl. agt., Cleburne, Tex., 1963-65; owner, operator Park North Animal Hosp., San Antonio, 1970-75, El Dorado Animal Hosp., San Antonio, 1973—; co-chmn. vet. tech. adv. coun. Palo Alto Coll. tchr. Animal Health Tech., San Antonio Coll., 1985-95; pres., mgr. Bexar County Emergency Animal Clinic, Inc., 1978-81; cons. vet. practice mgmt., mktg., client relations; speaker for vet. meetings, assns.; vet. mem. Tex. Bd. Health, 1984-89, chmn. disease control com., personnel com.; mem. environ. health, hosps. com. Team capt. Alamo Roundup Club and Pres.' Club of San Antonio C. of C., 1970-75; mem. Guadalupe County Youth Fair Bd., 1978-80; 1st v.p. No. Hills Lions Club, 1972-73. Served with Vet. Corps, USAF, 1968-70. Recipient Alumnus award Guadalupe County 4-H Club, 1979, Outstanding Service award San Antonio Coll., 1986-87. Mem. Tex. Vet. Med. Assn. (pres., chmn. bd.), Tex. Acad. Vet. Practice (pres.), Am. Assn. Human-Animal Bond Vets., AVMA, Vet. Hosp. Mgrs. Assn., San Antonio C. of C. (Life), Tex. County Agrl. Agts. Assn. (4th v.p. 1964), Delta Soc. (pres. San Antonio chpt. 1989-90), Conservative. Contbr. articles to profl. jours. Office: 13039 Nacogdoches Rd San Antonio TX 78217-1960

MC INTOSH, DOUGLAS J., insurance company executive. With Blue Cross Blue Shield of R.I., Providence, 1966-77, pres., 1977—. Office: Blue Cross Blue Shield of RI 444 Westminster St Providence RI 02903-3254*

MCINTOSH, ELAINE VIRGINIA, nutrition educator; b. Webster, S.D., Jan. 30, 1924; d. Louis James and Cora Boletta (Bakke) Nelson; m. Thomas Henry McIntosh, Aug. 28, 1955; children: James George, Ronald Thomas, Charles Nelson. BA magna cum laude, Augustana Coll., Sioux Falls, S.D., 1945; MA, U. S.D., 1949; PhD, Iowa State U., 1954. Registered dietitian. Instr., asst. prof. Sioux Falls Coll., 1945-48; instr. Iowa State U., Ames, 1949-53, rsch. assoc., 1955-62; postdoctoral rsch. assoc. U. Ill., Urbana, 1954-55; asst. prof. human biology U. Wis., Green Bay, 1968-72, assoc. prof., 1972-85, prof., 1985-90, emeritus prof., 1990—, writer, cons., 1990—, chmn. human biology dept., 1975-80, asst. to vice chancellor, asst. to chancellor, 1974-76. Author 2 books including American Food Habits in Historical Perspective, 1995; contbr. numerous articles on bacterial metabolism, meat biochemistry and nutrition edn. to profl. jours. Fellow USPHS, 1948-49. Mem. Am. Dietetic Assn., Inst. Food Technologists, Wis. Dietetics Assn., Wis. Nutrition Coun. (pres. 1974-75), Sigma Xi. Avocation, travel. Office: U Wis - Green Bay ES 301 Human Biology 2420 Nicolet Dr Green Bay WI 54311-7001

MCINTOSH, HENRY DEANE, cardiologist; b. Gainesville, Fla., July 19, 1921; s. Thomas Irvin and Nelle Deane (Calwell) McI.; m. Harriet Owens, Nov. 6, 1945; children: Thomas Irvin, James Owens, Willa Elizabeth. BS, Davidson Coll., 1943; MD, U. Pa., 1950; DSc (hon.), U. Francisco Martinique, Guatemala de la Asuncion, 1987; hon. prof., Kunming Med. Coll., Yunnan, People's Republic of China, 1996. Diplomate Am. Bd. Internal Medicine, subspecialty bd. cardiovascular disease. Intern medicine Duke U., Durham, N.C., 1950-51, fellow cardiology, 1952-54, instr. medicine Sch. Medicine, 1954-55, assoc., 1955-57, from asst. prof. to assoc. prof., 1957-62, prof., 1962-70, chief cardiology divsn., 1966-70; asst. resident medicine Lawson VA Hosp., Atlanta, 1951-52; chief resident medicine VA Hosp., Durham, N.C., 1954-55, asst. chief cardiovascular-renal sect., 1955-56; prof., chmn. dept. medicine Baylor Coll. Medicine, Houston, 1970-77, chief sect. cardiology, 1977, adj. prof. medicine, 1977—; chief med. svc. The Meth. Hosp., Houston, 1970-77; clin. prof. medicine U. Fla. Sch. Medicine, Gainesville, 1977—, U. South Fla. Sch. Medicine, Tampa, 1993—; cons. VA Hosp., Durham, 1956-70, Watts Hosp., Durham, 1956-79, Womack U.S. Army Hosp., Ft. Bragg, N.C., 1957-70, Portsmouth (Va.) Naval Hosp., 1957-70, VA Hosp., Hosuton, 1970-77, Harris County Dist. Hosps., Houston, 1970-77, St. Luke's Episc. Hosp., Houston, 1970-77, Hermann Hosp., Houston, 1970-77, Lakeland (Fla.) Regional Med. Ctr., 1977-92, St. Joseph's Hosp., Tampa, 1992—; med. dir. prevention and rehab. ctr. St. Joseph's Heart Inst., Tampa, 1992—. Editl. bd. Circulation, Heart and Lung, Am. Jour. Cardiology, Am. Jour. Geriatric Cardiology; asst. editor Modern Concepts in Cardiovascular Disease, 1967; editor Baylor Cardiology Series, 1975-77; contbr. 240 articles to profl. jours. Founder, bd. dirs. Heartbeat Internat., Lakeland, Fla., 1983-92, Tampa, Fla., 1992—, pres., 1993-95, chmn. bd. dirs., 1995—. Capt. U.S. Army, 1943-45. Decorated Silver Star; decorated Croix de Guerre with two bronze and one silver star; recipient Disting. Alumni award Duke U. Med. Ctr., 1972, Rotary Internat. Hon. Fellowship, 1985, Paul Harris Fellow, 1986, U.S. Presdl. Citation from Ronald Reagan, Heartbeat Internat., 1986, Disting. Kennedy Lectureship, Univ. Assn. Emergency Medicine, 1986, Disting. Alumni award Davidson Coll., 1988. Fellow Am. Coll. Cardiology (disting., pres. 1974-75, govt. rels. com. 1986-93, prevention com. 1986-90, chair 1987-90, rep. to pub. health svc. objectives for the yr. 2000, 1988—, Spl. Achievement award Fla. chpt. 1994, Disting. Svc. award 1996); mem. AMA, ACP (Laureate award Fla. chpt. 1994), NASPE (continuing med. edn. coun. 1988-91, bldg. com. 1992-94, Disting. Svc. award 1991), Am. Fedn. Clin. Rsch., Soc. Clin. Investigation (Founders award 1984), Assn. Univ. Cardiologists, Am. Clin. and Climatological Soc., Am. Soc. Internal Medicine, Assn. Am. Physicians, Assn. Profs. medicine, Am. Heart Assn. (v.p. 1977-78, rsch. com. 1986-90, chair sci. sessions com. 1971-73, coun. clin. cardiology 1975-76, Disting. Achievement award coun. clin. cardiology 1986), Coun. Geriatric Cardiology (membership com. 1986—, pres. 1991-92, Disting. Svc. award 1995). Presbyterian. Avocations: jogging, fostering international good will, public education. Home: PO Box 1788 Lakeland FL 33802-1788 Office: St. Joseph's Heart Inst PO Box 4227 3003 Dr Martin Luther King Blvd Tampa FL 33677-4227

MC INTOSH, JAMES EUGENE, JR., interior designer; b. Dadeville, Ala., Nov. 13, 1938; s. James Eugene and Jessie (Latimer) McI. B.Interior Design, Auburn (Ala.) U., 1961. Designer contract div. Rich's Dept. Store, Atlanta, 1961-64; assoc. William Trapnell & Assocs., Atlanta, 1964-70; dir. Interior Concepts, Inc., Atlanta, 1970-72; dir. design comml. design div. Rich's Dept. Store, 1972-80; v.p. Comml. Interior Designs, Inc., 1980-82; exec. staff Rollins Inc., 1982-85; owner Gene Mc Intosh & Assocs., 1985—. Fellow Am. Soc. Interior Designers (Presdl. citation 1974); mem. Nat. Trust Hist. Preservation, Ala. Hist. Soc., High Mus. Art, Soc. Archtl. Historians. Office: Gene McIntosh & Assocs 1000 Iris Dr Conyers GA 30208

MC INTOSH, J(OHN) RICHARD, biologist, educator; b. N.Y.C., Sept. 25, 1939; s. Rustin and Millicent Margaret (Carey) McI.; m. Marjorie Rogers Keniston, Aug. 30, 1961; children—Robert K., Elspeth R., Craig T. B.A. in Physics, Harvard U., 1961, Ph.D. in Biophysics, 1968. Instr. in math. and physics Cambridge Sch., Weston, Mass., 1961-63; asst. prof. biology Harvard U., 1968-70; asst. prof. U. Colo., Boulder, 1970-72; assoc. prof. U. Colo., 1972-76, prof., 1977—, chmn. dept. molecular, cellular and devel. biology, 1977-78, dir. Lab for High Voltage Electron Microscopy, 1986—. Mem. editl. bd. Jour. Cell Biology, 1978-82, 86-90, Cell Motility, 1986-87, Jour. Structural Biology, 1990—, Molecular Biology Cell, 1995—; contbr. articles to profl. jours. Recipient Teaching Recognition award U. Colo., 1974, Scholar award Am. Cancer Soc., 1976, 90; Am. Cancer Soc. grantee, 1971-90, NSF grantee, 1970-82, NIH grantee, 1973-78, 80—; Eleanor Roosevelt Internat. Cancer fellow, 1984; Guggenheim fellow, 1990-91. Mem. Am. Soc. Cell Biology (coun. 1977-80, 86-89, pres. 1994), Am. Cancer Soc. (cell biology panel 1983-87, rsch. prof. 1994—), NIH (molecular cytology study sect. 1988-92). Home: 870 Willowbrook Rd Boulder CO 80302-7439 Office: Dept Molecular Devel and Devel Biology U Colo Boulder CO 80309-0347

MCINTOSH, L(ORNE) WILLIAM, marketing executive; b. Kingston, Ont., Can., May 1, 1945; s. Jack Lorne and Lillian (Oaks) McI.; m. Delthyn Lee Johnson, Mar. 11, 1965. BSBA, Lehigh U., 1967, MBA, 1968. Asst. prof. Union Coll., Cranford, N.J., 1968-72; sr. market rsch. analyst Merck, Sharp & Dohme, West Point, Pa., 1972-75, advt. copywriter, 1975-77, product mgr., 1977-80, assoc. dir. advt., 1980-82, dir. licensing and acquisitions, 1982, sr. dir. mktg., 1983-86; exec. v.p. mktg. Medco Containment Svcs., Inc., Fair Lawn, N.J., 1987-88; v.p. mktg. and bus. devel. Boehringer Mannheim Pharms., Rockville, Md., 1988-92; chmn. bd., chief exec. officer Target Mktg. Systems, Inc., Blue Bell, Pa., 1992-93; sr. v.p. bus. devel. and com. ops. Zynaxis, Inc., Malvern, Pa., 1993-95; sr. cons. SmithKline Beecham, Phila., 1995—. Mem. Am. Econ. Assn., Am. Mktg. Assn., Lic. Execs. Soc., Antique Automobile Club Am., Model A Ford Club Am., Vintage Chevrolet Club Am., Beta Gamma Sigma. Avocations: antique automobiles, woodworking, antique furniture restoration, boating, music. Home: 161 Polo Dr North Wales PA 19454-4273 Office: SmithKline Beecham 206 Welsh Rd Horsham PA 19044

MCINTOSH, ROBERT EDWARD, JR., electrical engineering educator, consultant, electronics executive; b. Hartford, Conn., Jan. 19, 1940; s. Robert Edward and Natalie Rose (Glynn) McI.; m. Anne Marie Potvin, July 7, 1962; children—Robert Edward III, Edgar J., Michael T., William P., Matthew P. B.S.E.E., Worcester Poly. Inst., 1962; S.M. in Applied Physics, Harvard U., 1964; Ph.D. in Elec. Engring., U. Iowa, 1967. Mem. tech. staff Bell Telephone Labs, North Andover, Mass., 1962-65; asst. prof. elec. engring. U. Mass., Amherst, 1967-70, assoc. prof., 1970-73, prof., 1973—, coord. microwave electronics group, 1980-87, dir. microwave remote sensing lab., 1981—, acting head dept. elec. and computer engring., 1983-84; treas. Quadrant Engring., Inc., Amherst, 1982-84, 88-91, pres. 1984-87, 91—; mem. adv. bd. ECE Dept. Worcester Poly. Inst., 1992—. Assoc. editor Radio Sci., 1987-89; contbr. articles to profl. jours. Recipient sr. faculty scholarship award Alumni Coll. Engring., U. Mass., 1984, dept. of ECE Faculty award, 1987, 90, 92, GE Tchg. award, 1988, Univ. Disting. Lectr. award, 1992, Hobart Newell award WPI, 1993; Univ. Faculty Rsch. fellow, 1995; rsch. grantee NSF, NASA, Dept. Energy, Air Force Office Sci. Rsch., Army Rsch. Office, Office Naval Rsch., numerous electronics cos., 1967—. Fellow IEEE (Centennial medal 1984, tech. activities bd. 1984-85, fellows com. 1986-89); mem. Antennas Propagation Soc. (sec.-treas. 1980-83, v.p. 1984, pres. 1985, editor newsletter 1979-81, assoc. editor Trans. 1984-87, editor 1989-92), Geosci. Remote Sensing Soc. (sec.-treas. 1980-83, pres. 1984), Internat. Radio Sci. Union (U.S. nat. com. 1984-92), Am. Phys. Soc. Democrat. Roman Catholic. Avocations: athletics, music, theatre. Office: U Mass Dept Elec Computer Eng Amherst MA 01003

MCINTOSH, SUSAN KEECH, anthropology educator; b. Dunkirk, N.Y., Feb. 2, 1951; d. S. Elwin and Lucille M. (Stone) Keech; m. Roderick J. McIntosh, June 28, 1976; children: David Alexander, Annick Michelle. Student, Wellesley Coll., 1969-71; BA in Anthropology summa cum laude, U. Pa., 1973; MA in Archaeology, Cambridge U., Eng., 1975; MA in Anthropology, U. Calif., Santa Barbara, 1976, PhD in Anthropology, 1979. Vis. asst. prof. Washington U., St. Louis, 1978-80; from adj. asst. prof. to assoc. prof. anthropology Rice U., Houston, 1980-88, prof., 1988—; master Baker Coll., Rice U., 1984-89, treas. com. masters, 1986-89, chair com. campus climate women, pres.'s commn. women, 1988-89; mem. archaeology panel NSF, 1988-90; co-dir. various excavations and surveys. Author: Excavations at Jenne-jeno, Hambarketolo and Kaniana, 1995, (with R.J. McIntosh) Prehistoric Investigations in the Region of Jenne, Mali, 1980; contbr. articles to profl. jours.; assoc. editor for archaeology Current Anthropology, 1985-87; mem. editl. bd. Jour. World Prehistory, 1987—, Jour. African History, 1989-94, Antiquity, 1993—; contbg. editor Jour. Archaeol. Rsch., 1992—, African Archaeol. Rev., 1995—. Fulbright-Hays grantee, 1973; grantee NSF, 1977—, Nat. Geog. Soc., 1983-92; Thouron Brit.-Am. Exch. fellow, 1973-75; fellow Ctr. for Advanced Study in the Behavioral Scis., Stanford U., 1989-90. Mem. Am. Anthrop. Assn., Soc. Am. Archaeology, Am. Assn. Phys. Anthropologists, Soc. Africanist Archaeologists Am., Prehistoric Soc., West African Archeol. Assn., Société des Africanistes, Panafrican Congress Prehistory, Mande Studies Assn., Phi Beta Kappa. Avocations: classical music, tennis, skiing. Office: Rice University Anthropology Dept PO Box 1892 Dept Houston TX 77251-1892

MCINTOSH, TERRIE TUCKETT, lawyer; b. Ft. Lewis, Wash., July 20, 1944; d. Robert LeRoy and Elda (Perry) Tuckett; m. Clifton Dennis McIntosh, Oct. 13, 1969; children: Alison, John. BA, U. Utah, 1967; MA, U. Ill., 1970; JD, Harvard U., 1978. Bar: N.Y. 1979, Utah 1980. Assoc. Hughes, Hubbard & Reed, N.Y.C., 1978-79; assoc. Fabian & Clendenin, Salt Lake City, 1979-84, shareholder, 1984-86; staff atty. Questar Corp., Salt Lake City, 1986-88, sr. atty., 1988-92, sr. corp. counsel, 1992—; instr. philosophy Douglass Coll. Rutgers U., New Brunswick, N.J., 1971-72; mem. adv. com. civil procedure Utah Supreme Ct., Salt Lake City, 1987—; mem. jud. nominating com. 5th Cir. Ct., Salt Lake City, 1986-88. Mem. Utah State Bar (ethics and discipline screening panel 1989—, co-chair law related edn. com. 1985-86), Women Lawyers of Utah (chair exec. com. 1986-87), Harvard Alumni Assn. Utah (bd. dirs. 1987—), Phi Beta Kappa, Phi Kappa Phi. Office: Questar Corp PO Box 45433 180 E 1st South St Salt Lake City UT 84147

MCINTYRE, ANITA GRACE JORDAN, lawyer; b. Louisville, Ky., Jan. 29, 1947; d. Blakely Gordon and Shirley Evans (Grubbs) Jordan; m. Kenneth James McIntyre, Oct. 11, 1969; children: Abigail, Jordan Kenneth. BA, Smith Coll., 1969; JD, U. Detroit, 1975. Bar: Mich. 1975, U.S. Dist. Ct. (ea. dist.) Mich. 1975, U.S. Dist. Ct. (we. dist.) Mich. 1979, U.S. Ct. Appeals (6th cir.) 1979. Ptnr. Rollins White & Rollins, Detroit, 1975-79; vis. assoc. prof. Detroit Coll. Law, 1979-81; assoc. Tyler & Canham, Detroit, 1981-82; prin. Anita G. McIntyre, P.C., Grosse Pointe, Mich., 1982-87, 91—; of counsel Nederlander Dodge & Rollins, Detroit, 1987-90; assoc. Damm & Smith, P.C., Detroit, 1990-91. Editor, author (case notes) U. Detroit Jour. Urban Law, 1975; contbr. articles to profl. jours. Sec. Berry Subdivsn. Assn., Detroit, 1975-77; pres. Smith Coll. Club Detroit, 1982-86; mem. parents bd. U. Liggett Sch., Grosse Pointe, Mich., 1991-95. Mem. State Bar Mich., Detroit Bar Assn. (family law, debtor-creditor sect. 1980-95), Wayne County (Mich.) Probate Bar Assn., Wayne County Juvenile Trial Lawyers Assn. Episcopalian. Avocations: skiing, swimming, needle point. Office: 15324 Mack Ave Grosse Pointe Park MI 48224

MCINTYRE, BRUCE HERBERT, publishing company executive; b. Takoma Park, Md., Jan. 24, 1930; s. Orrin Raymond and Leila Hazel (Olmsted) McI.; m. Natalie Ann Wolff, Oct. 10, 1953; children: Douglas A., Elizabeth W., Emily O., Catherine N., Jane A. Student, Gannon Coll., 1954-57, U. Akron, 1958-61. Reporter, city editor Erie (Pa.) Times and News, 1949-57; reporter, city editor, asst. to exec. editor Akron (Ohio) Beacon Jour., 1958-67; with Battle Creek (Mich.) Enquirer & News, 1967-71, asst. mng. editor, 1967-68, mng. editor, 1968-71; exec. v.p., editor Oakland Press, Pontiac, Mich., 1971-77; pub. Oakland Press, 1977-95; v.p., pub. div. Capital Cities/ABC Inc., 1987—; chmn. Great Lakes Media Inc., Birmingham, Mich., 1995—; lectr. Am. Press Inst., 1968—; journalism juror Pulitzer Prizes, 1972—. Served with AUS, 1951-53; lt. col. Res. ret. Mem. Soc. Profl. Journalists. Episcopalian. Club: Pine Lake Country (Bloomfield, Mich.). Office: Great Lakes Media Inc 700 E Maple Rd Ste 303 Birmingham MI 48009-6360

MCINTYRE, CHARLES EARL, insurance executive; b. L.A., Mar. 28, 1944; s. Donald Earl and Helen (Walker) McI.; m. Linda W. McIntyre, Oct. 17, 1969; children: Amanda, Margaret. BA, U. Redlands, Calif., 1966. CLU, ChFC. With Ray C. Watson Co., L.A., 1966-70; dir. human resources Leadership Housing, Newport Beach, Calif., 1970-75; agt. Northwestern Mut. Life, Ft. Lauderdale, Fla., 1975-80, dist. agt., 1980-85, gen. agt., 1985—. Bd. dirs. Bonnet House, Ft. Lauderdale, 1993—; bd. advisors Fla. Atlantic U., Ft. Lauderdale, 1994. Mem. Gen. Agts. and Mgrs. Assn. (pres. 1989-90, Master Agy. award 1987—), Gen. Agts. Assn. (bd. dirs. 1988—), Broward County Life Underwriters, Chartered Life Underwriters Assn. Republican. Episcopalian. Avocations: reading, cards, jogging, travel. Office: Northwestern Mutual Life 2101 W Commercial Blvd Ste 5100 Fort Lauderdale FL 33309-3071

MCINTYRE, COLLEEN ALISON, special education educator; b. Seattle, Sept. 20, 1963; d. David Joseph and Lois Ann McIntyre. BA in Spl. Edn., Seattle Pacific U., 1985, MA in Curriculum and Instrn., 1993. Tchr. spl. edn. Seattle Pub. Schs., 1985-86, substitute tchr. spl. edn., 1986-87; tchr. spl. edn. Sumner (Wash.) Sch. Dist., 1987-89, Lower Yukon Sch. Dist., Alakanuk, Alaska, 1989—. Recipient Exemplary Tchr. of Yr. award Edmark Corp., 1994. Mem. NEA, Nat. Assn. Edn. Young Children, Coun. for Exceptional Children (v.p. 1985, sec. 1990-91, pres. 1991-93). Avocations: photography, writing, watercolor, braille. Home: PO Box 69 Alakanuk AK 99554-0069

MCINTYRE, DEBORAH, psychotherapist, author; b. Pensacola, Fla., Sept. 11, 1955; d. John Joseph and Mary Cecelia (Campbell) McI.; m. Denis Miller Donovan, Sept. 6, 1985. BA in Psychology, George Mason U., 1976; MA Counseling Psychology, U. West Fla., 1980; AA in Nursing, Pensacola Jr. Coll., 1981. Diplomate Am. Bd. Med. Psychotherapists (fellow); RN, Va., Fla. Child psychotherapist Holly Hall Sch. for Exceptional Children, Vienna, Va., 1975-77; area rep. Youth For Understanding, Vienna, 1976-78; vol. child psychotherapist Children's Resource Ctr. of N.W. Fla., Pensacola, Fla., 1979-80; staff/charge nurse med. surgery Va. Beach Gen. Hosp., 1981-83; intake coord., child and family psychotherapist Psychiatric Inst., Norfolk, Va., 1982-83; head nurse, program coord., child and family therapist Children's Service, Horizon Hosp., Clearwater, Fla., 1983; child and adolescent psychotherapist The Children's Ctr. for Devel. Psychiatry, St. Petersburg, Fla., 1983—; cons., trainer Project Playpen, Juvenile Welfare Bd., St. Petersburg, 1985-87; cons. Early Childhood Coun. of Pinellas County; mem. adv. bd. New Traumatology Ann. Conf.; participant in workshops and seminars for mental health care. Author: (with Denis M. Donovan) Healing the Hurt Child: A Developmental-Contextual Approach, 1990; editl. adv. bd. The New Child Psychiatry; contbr. articles to profl. jours., chpts. to books. Fellow Am. Psychol. Soc.; mem. Am. Orthopsychiat. Assn. Roman Catholic. Office: Childrens Ctr Devel Psychiatry 6675 13th Ave N Ste 2-A Saint Petersburg FL 33710-5483

MCINTYRE, DONALD CONROY, opera singer, baritone; b. Auckland, New Zealand, Oct. 22, 1934; s. George D. and Hermyn McI.; m. Jill Redington, 1961; 3 children. Student, Auckland Tchrs. Tng. Coll., Guildhall Sch. Music, London; MusD, Auckland U., 1992. Prin. bass Sadler's Wells Opera, London, 1960-67, Royal Opera House-Covent Garden, London, from 1967. Appeared at Bayreuth Festival, 1967-81, 87, 88; frequent internat. guest appearances maj. opera houses including Metropolitan, N.Y.C., La Scala, Milan, Vienna, Paris, Munich, Berlin, Hamburg, Zurich, Chgo., Savonlinna Festival, Sydney, Buenos Aires; roles include: Wotan and Wanderer, Der Ring, Dutchman, Der Fliegende Hollander, Telramund, Lohengrin, Barak, Die Frau ohne Schatten, Pizzaro, Fidelio, Golaud, Pelleas et Melisande, Kurwenal, Tristan and Isold, Gurnemanz, Klingsor and Amfortas, Parsifal, Heyst, Victory, Jochanaan, Salome, Macbeth, Scarpia, Tosca, The Count, Marriage of Figaro, Nick Shadow, The Rake's Progress, Hans Sachs, Die Meistersinger, The Doctor, Woyzeck, Cardillac, Cardillac Hindemith, Kasper, Der Freischütz, Rocco, Fidelio, Prospero, Un Re In Ascolto (Brit. premier), Balstrode, Peter Grimes, Shakloviti, Khovanshchina, Sarastro Zauberflöte; recs. include Pelleas et Melisande, Oedipus Rex, Il Trovatore, Parsifal, The Ring, Damnation of Faust, Messiah Beethoven's 9th, Boris, Lady Macbeth of Mtsensk. Decorated comdr. Order of Brit. Empire; created knight, 1992; recipient Worldwide Fidelio medal Assn. Internat. Dirs. of Opera, 1989, New Zealand Commemoration award, 1990. Home: Foxhill Farm, Jackass Ln, Keston, Bromley, Kent BR2 6AN, England Office: care Ingpen & Williams, 14 Kensignton Ct, London W8 5DN, England also: Org Interntional Opera et Concert, 19, rue Vignon, F-7 rue Vignon Paris France

MCINTYRE, DOUGLAS ALEXANDER, magazine publisher; b. Erie, Pa., Mar. 16, 1955; s. Bruce Herbert and Natalie Ann (Wolff) McI.; divorced; children: Garrett Wolff, Hunter Garrahan; m. Patricia Yarberry Allen, Apr. 20, 1995. B.A. magna cum laude, Harvard U., 1977. Strategic planner Time Inc., N.Y.C., 1977-81; asst. to pres. Penthouse Internat., N.Y.C., 1981-82; assoc. Veronis, Suhler and Assocs., N.Y.C., 1982-83; gen. mgr. Fin. World, N.Y.C., 1983-84, pres., pub., 1984-95; pres., CEO McIntyre Media Properties, 1996—; pres. Harvard Advocate Trustees Inc., 1983—; bd. dirs. Oster Comms., Inc.; corps. and founds. subcom. NYU Hosp./Cornell Med. Ctr. Mem. Harvard Club. Episcopalian.

MCINTYRE, ELIZABETH GEARY, Olympic athlete; b. Hanover, N.H., 1965. AB, Dartmouth Coll., 1988. Silver medalist, women's moguls final freestyle skiing Olympic Games, Lillehammer, Norway, 1994. Office: US Olympic Com 1750 E Boulder St Colorado Springs CO 80909-5724*

MCINTYRE, GUY MAURICE, professional football player; b. Thomasville, Ga., Feb. 17, 1961. Student, U. Ga. Offensive guard San Francisco 49ers, 1984-94; played in Super Bowl XIX, 1984, XXIII, 1988, XXIV, 1989. Played in Pro Bowl, 1989-93.

MC INTYRE, JAMES A., diversified financial services executive; b. 1932. BS, U. So. Calif., 1954. With Ernst & Ernst, L.A., 1958-63; pres. Fremont Indemnity Co., 1963-80; pres., CEO, chmn. Fremont Gen. Corp., Santa Monica, Calif., 1980—. Office: Fremont Gen Corp 2020 Santa Monica Blvd, Ste 600 Santa Monica CA 90404-2023*

MCINTYRE, JOEL FRANKLYN, lawyer; b. Fairbury, Nebr., Sept. 19, 1938; s. Frank Otto and Maxine Olive (Ward) McI.; m. Suzanne Jane Sahl, June 22, 1958; children: Joel Franklyn, Jr., David William, Jeffrey Bayne, Erin Suzanne, Matthew Kay, Karyn Suzanne, Kathleen Suzanne, Michael Joel. B.A., Stanford U., 1960; J.D., UCLA, 1963. Bar: Calif. 1963. Assoc., Paul, Hastings, Janofsky & Walker, Los Angeles, 1963-70, ptnr., 1970-93; sr. ptnr. McIntyre & Lubeck, Costa Mesa, Calif., 1993—; dir. Internat. Aluminum Corp., Crown City Plating Co. Mem. Phi Delta Phi. Republican. Club: San Gabriel Country. Home: 60 W Arthur Ave Arcadia CA 91007-8201 Office: McIntyre & Lubeck 3070 Bristol St Ste 450 Costa Mesa CA 92626-3070*

MCINTYRE, JOHN ARMIN, physics educator; b. Seattle, June 2, 1920; s. Harry John and Florence (Armin) McI.; m. Madeleine Forsman, June 15, 1947; 1 son, John Forsman. B.S., U. Wash., 1943; M.A., Princeton U., 1948, Ph.D., 1950. Mem. faculty elec. engring. Carnegie Inst. Tech., Pitts., 1943; radio engr. Westinghouse Elec. Co., Balt., 1944; research asso. Stanford, 1950-57; mem. faculty Yale, 1957-63, asso. prof., 1960-63; prof. physics Tex. A&M U., College Station, 1963-95, emeritus prof., 1995—; asso. dir. Cyclotron Inst., 1965-70; Mem. council Oak Ridge Asso. Univs., 1964-71. Fellow Am. Phys. Soc., Am. Sci. Affiliation (exec. council 1968-73); mem. AAAS. Presbyn. Research and publs. on scintillation counters for gamma ray spectroscopy; determination of nuclear charge distbns. by electron scattering; study of nuclear structure by neutron transfer reactions; devel. variable energy gamma ray cameras. Home: 2316 Bristol St Bryan TX 77802-2405 Office: Tex A&M U Dept Physics College Station TX 77843

MCINTYRE, JOHN GEORGE WALLACE, real estate development and management consultant; b. Toronto, Ont., Can., July 26, 1920; s. George Crerar and Gwendolyn Alberta (Wallace) McI.; m. Ruth Elizabeth Wilson, July 26, 1945 (dec.); children: Angus, Heather, Robert, Anne. B of Commerce, U. Toronto, 1941; MBA, Harvard U., 1947. Budget acct. Abitibi Paper Co., Toronto, 1947-51; budget mgr., asst. gen. mgr. Ford of Can., Windsor, Ont., 1951-58, gen. mgr. mfg. ops., 1963-65; asst. mng. dir., mng. dir. Ford of Australia, Melbourne, 1958-63; exec. v.p., pres. Columbia Cellulose Ltd., Vancouver, B.C., Can., 1965-67; v.p. retail devel. and distbn. Hudson's Bay Co., Toronto, 1967-84; pres. Rupert's Land Tng. Co., Hudson's Bay Co. Devels. Ltd.; trustee Internat. Council of Shopping Ctrs., 1970-84; v.p., gen. mgr. Broadcast Ctr. Devel. Project Can. Broadcasting Corp., 1984-88; cons., 1988—. Served to capt. Royal Can. Ordnance Corps., 1942-45, ETO. Address: 53 Widdicombe Hill Blvd Ste 401E, Weston, ON Canada M9R 1Y3

MCINTYRE, KENNETH J., lawyer; b. Port Huron, Mich., Oct. 20, 1944; s. Kenneth E. and Loretta A. (Parker) McI.; m. Anita Grace Jordan, Nov. 11, 1969; children: Abigail Evans, Jordan Kenneth. AB with honors, U. Mich., 1967, JD with honors, 1970. Bar: Mich. 1970, U.S. Dist. Ct. (ea. dist.) Mich. 1970, U.S. Ct. Appeals (6th cir.) 1970, U.S. Ct. Claims 1972, U.S. Dist Ct. (we. dist.) Mich. 1972, U.S. Supreme Ct. 1978, U.S. Ct. Appeals (fed. cir.) 1987. Ptnr. Dickinson, Wright, Moon, Van Dusen & Freeman, Detroit, 1970—; Chmn. Antitrust Law Sect. State Bar of Mich., 1980-81. Mem. Am. Law Inst., Phi Beta Kappa. Home: 834 Edgemont Park Grosse Pointe MI 48230-1855 Office: Dickinson Wright Moon Van Dusen & Freeman 500 Woodward Ave Ste 4000 Detroit MI 48226-3423

MCINTYRE, LOUISE S., income tax consultant; b. Cin., Jan. 29, 1924; d. George Washington and Bertha (McDaniels) Sullivan; m. Harry McIntyre Jr., Jan. 18, 1947; children: Carol L., Patricia A., Harriet L., Harry J., Brenda R. AA, Mira Costa Coll., Oceanside, Calif., 1972; grad. in auditing, Nat. Tax Practice Inst., 1989. Hydraulic testor Paterson Field, Fairfield, Ohio, 1942-45; control clk. Hickam Field, Honolulu, 1945-47; clk.-typist Patterson Field, Fairfield, 1947-49, Camp LeJeune, Jacksonville, N.C., 1951-56; sec., bookkeeper Mission Bowl, Oceanside, 1973-79; income tax cons. Oceanside, 1974—. Mem. Oceanside Human Rels. Commn., 1970; bd. dirs. Armed Forces YMCA, Oceanside, 1969-71, Oceanside Christian Women's Club, 1988-91. Mem. Inland Soc. Tax Cons. (bd. dirs. 1988—), Am. Soc. Women Accts. (v.p. 1989-90), Enrolled Agts. Palomar, Nat. Assn. Enrolled Agts., Nat. Soc. Pub. Accts., Calif. Assn. Ind. Accts., Palmquist PTA (hon. life). Avocations: bowling, dancing, crafts, interior decorating, cake decorating. Home: 328 Camelot Dr Oceanside CA 92054-4515

MCINTYRE, MILDRED JEAN, clinical psychologist, writer, neuroscientist; b. Boston; d. William James and Theodora Grace (Jackson-McCullough) McI. BA, Swarthmore Coll., 1965; MA, Clark U., 1972, PhD, 1975. Lic. psychologist, Mass., Alaska, Hawaii. Ford Found. fellow, 1972, 73. Mem. APA, Internat. Neuropsychol. Soc., Cognitive Neurosci. Soc. Avocations: art, music, travel. Office: PO Box 990124 Boston MA 02199-0124

MCINTYRE, NORMAN F., petroleum industry executive; b. Pangman, Sask., Can., Oct. 21, 1945; s. Donald and Jean (Cruickshank) McI.; m. Lana Jean, June 10, 1967; children: Jason Lee, Spencer James. BSc in Petroleum Engring., U. Wyo., 1971; MS in Mgmt., MIT, 1991. Various positions with Mobil Oil, U.S., Can., to 1982; group mgr. engring. offshore divsn. Petro-Can., 1982-83, gen. mgr. frontier devel. offshore divsn., 1983, v.p. frontier devel., 1983-86, v.p. prodn. devel., 1986-89; sr. v.p. western region Petro-Can. Products, 1989-90; pres. Petro-Can. Resources, Calgary, Alta., Can., 1990-95, exec. v.p., 1995—; chmn., dir. Panarctic Oils Ltd.; dir. Petroleum Transmission Co.. Office: Petro-Canada, 150-6th Ave SW PO Box 2844, Calgary, AB Canada T2P 3E3

MCINTYRE, OSWALD ROSS, physician; b. Chgo., Feb. 13, 1932; m. Jean Geary, June 5, 1957; children—Margaret Jean, Archibald Ross, Elizabeth Geary. A.B. cum laude, Dartmouth Coll., 1953, postgrad, 1953-55; M.D., Harvard U., 1957. Intern U. Pa. Hosp., 1957-58; resident in medicine Dartmouth Med. Sch. Affiliated Hosps., 1958-60; instr. medicine Dartmouth Coll., 1964-66, asst. prof. medicine, 1966-69, assoc. prof., 1969-75, prof., 1976—, James J. Carroll prof. oncology, 1980-95, dir. Norris Cotton Cancer Center, 1975-92, prof. emeritus, 1995—; attending physician VA Hosp., White River Junction, Vt., 1964; cons. in hematology and oncology; acting chmn. dept. medicine Dartmouth-Hitchcock Med. Ctr., 1987-89; chmn. Cancer and Leukemia Group B.; 1990-95. Fellow AAAS; mem. Am. Fedn. Clin. Rsch., Am. Soc. Hematology, Internat. Assn. Study Lung Cancer, Am. Assn. Cancer Rsch., Am. Soc. Clin. Oncology, Assn. Cancer Inst. (pres. 1988-89), New Eng. Cancer Soc. (pres. 1989-90). Home: 34 Lamphere Hill Ln Lyme NH 03768-5003

MCINTYRE, PETER MASTIN, physicist, educator; b. Clewiston, Fla., Sept. 26, 1947; s. Peter Mastin and Ruby Eugenia (Richaud) McI.; m. Rebecca Biek, June 29, 1968; children: Peter B., Colin H., Jana M., Robert J. BS, U. Chgo., 1967, MS, 1968, PhD, 1973. Asst. prof. Harvard U., Cambridge, Mass., 1975-80; group leader Fermilab, Batavia, Ill., 1978-80; assoc. prof. Tex. A&M U., College Station, 1980-84, prof. physics, 1985—, assoc. dean Coll. of Sci., 1990-92; pres. Accelerator Tech. Corp., College Station, 1988—; dir. Tex. Accelerator Ctr., The Woodlands, 1991-93. Prin. author Tex. SSC Site Proposal, 1988. Sloan Found. fellow, 1976-78; recipient IR-100 award Indsl. Rsch. Mag., 1980. Mem. AAAS, Am. Phys. Soc. (pres. Tex. sect. 1990-91). Achievements include Proton-Antiproton Colliding Beams; patents for Continuous Unitized Tunneling System, Gigatron High Power Microwave Amplifier, Gas Microstrip Chamber for X-ray Disinfestation of Foods; development of 16 Tesla Superconducting magnets for future hadron colliders; micro-fabricated silicon array for DNA sequencing by hybridization. Home: 611 Montclair Ave College Station TX 77840-2868 Office: Tex A&M U Dept Physics College Station TX 77843

MCINTYRE, ROBERT WALTER, church official; b. Bethlehem, Pa., June 20, 1922; s. Simon Jesse and Ruth (Young) McI.; m. Edith Jones, Sept. 1, 1944 (dec. Jan. 1953); m. Elizabeth Norman, Nov. 6, 1953; children: Judith McIntyre Keilholtz, Joy McIntyre McCallum, John, James, June McIntyre Brannon. Student, Miltonvale Wesleyan Coll., 1939-43; B.Religion, Marion Coll., 1944, LittD (hon.), 1980, B.A., 1959; postgrad., Ball State U., 1960-61; D.D. (hon.), Ea. Pilgrim Coll., 1969; LLD (hon.), Houghton Coll., 1976; DHL (hon.), Ctrl. Wesleyan Coll., 1988. Ordained to ministry The Wesleyan Ch., 1945. Pastor Marengo, Ohio, 1944-47, Columbus, Ohio, 1947-52, Coshocton, Ohio, 1952-55; exec. sec. youth The Wesleyan Ch., Marion, Ind., 1955-68; editor The Wesleyan Youth, Marion, 1955-68; gen. editor The Wesleyan Ch., editor The Wesleyan Adv., Marion, 1968-73; assoc. editor The Preacher's Mag., Marion, 1973-88; gen. supt. The Wesleyan Ch., Marion, 1973-88; mem. gen. bd. adminstrn. The Wesleyan Ch., 1955-88, mem. Commn. Christian Edn., 1959-73, 76-80, chmn. Commn. Christian Edn., 1976-80, mem. exec. bd., 1968-88; chmn. Commn. on World Missions, 1973-76, Commn. on Publs., 1980-84, Commn. on Extension and Evangelism, 1984-88; spl. asst. to the pres. Ind. Wesleyan U., Marion, 1988-93; denominational rep., bd. adminstrn. Nat. Assn. Evangelicals, 1973-83, exec. com., 1978-80, 81-87, 2d v.p., 1981-82, 1st v.p., 1982-84, pres., 1984-86, mem., 1973—; denominational rep. The Lord's Day Alliance, 1973-76; trustee Marion Coll., Asbury Theol. Sem., 1976—. Author: Ten Commandments for Teen-Agers, 1965; editor: Program Pathways for Young Adults, 1964, Mandate for Mission, 1970; contbr. articles to religious jours. Mem. Christian Holiness Assn. (chmn. social action commn. 1971-73, sec. 1973-76), Wesleyan Theol. Soc., Best Yrs. Fellowship (gen. dir. 1992—). Home: 4613 S Star Dr Marion IN 46953-7303

MCINTYRE, RONALD LLEWELLYN, electric utility executive; b. Detroit, May 12, 1934; s. Nathaniel Francis McIntyre and Cheaber (Hudson) Farmer; m. Amalia Rosario Leon, June 17, 1961; children: Carmen Maria, Norman Lawrence, Maritza Cheaber, Yvonne Amalia, Carlos Leonel. BSEE, Wayne State U., 1962, MSEE, 1968. Registered profl. engr., Mich. Rsch. engr. Detroit Edison Co., 1963-68, instr., control systems engr., 1968-71, reactor systems engr., 1971-72, assoc. project engr., 1972-74, supr. power supply planning, 1974-80, corp. strategic planning, 1980-81, bus. mgr. dist. heating, 1981-86, dir. engring. rsch., 1986-90, gen. dir. tech. and engring. svcs., 1990-91; supt. River Rouge Power Plant, 1991-94, dir. environ. initiatives, 1994—; v.p. Utility Tech. Svcs., Detroit, 1984—; adv. bd. Wayne State U., 1987—; bd. vis. Oakland U., Rochester, Mich., 1988—; exec. com. and bd. dirs. Metro Ctr. High Tech., Detroit, 1988—. Contbr. articles to profl. jours. Bd. dirs. Detroit Sci. Ctr., 1988—; active Mich. Emergency Preparedness Adv. Coun., Lansing, 1985—; deacon Archdiocese Detroit, 1986—. Mem. IEEE, Engring. Soc. Detroit, Edison Boat Club, Etta Kappa Nu. Roman Catholic. Avocations: golfing, sailing, photography, reading, biking. Office: Detroit Edison Co 2000 2nd Ave Detroit MI 48226-1203

MCINTYRE, THOMAS, recording industry executive; b. 1948. Treas. BMG Entertainment, N.Y.C., 1985—. Office: BMG Entertainment 1540 Broadway New York NY 10036-4039

MC ISAAC, GEORGE SCOTT, business policy educator, past business executive; b. Auburn, N.Y., July 25, 1930; s. Robert Scott and Agnes Congalton (Aitchison) McI.; m. Betsy Clark, Sept. 11, 1954; children: Ian Scott, Christopher Clark. BS, Yale U., 1952; MS, U. Rochester, 1961. In mfg. mgmt. Eastman Kodak Co., Rochester, N.Y., 1954-62; prin., dir. McKinsey & Co. (Mgmt. Consultants), N.Y.C., Dusseldorf, Ger., Washington, 1962-78; asst. sec. of energy for resource applications U.S. Dept. Energy, Washington, 1978-80; sr. v.p. Schlegel Corp., Rochester, 1980-85; AT&T resident mgmt. fellow; exec. prof. bus. and pub. policy William E. Simon Grad. Sch. Bus. Adminstrn., U. Rochester, 1985—; cons. Dept. Def., U.S. Postal Service, HUD, German Agrl. Ministry, Govt. of Tanzania, various pvt. clients. Contbr. articles to bus. jours. Bd. dirs. Rochester Hosp. Corp.; trustee Internat. Mus. Photography, George Eastman House. Lt. USMC, 1952-54. Clubs: Met. (Washington), Genesee Valley (Rochester). Office: Grad Sch Mgmt U Rochester Carol G Simon Hall Rochester NY 14627

MCISAAC, PAUL ROWLEY, electrical engineer, educator; b. Port Washington, N.Y., Apr. 20, 1926; s. Robert Milton and June Zatella (Barrus) McI.; m. Mary Lou Heldenbrand, Sept. 10, 1949; children—Wendy Lee, Karen Jo, Hugh Paul, Kathleen Anne. B.E.E., Cornell U., 1949; M.S.E., U. Mich., 1950, Ph.D., 1954. Research engr. Microwave Tube div. Sperry Gyroscope Co., Great Neck, N.Y., 1954-59; assoc. prof. elec. engring. Cornell U., 1959-65, prof., 1965—, assoc. dean engring., 1975-80. Served with USN, 1944-46. Rotary Found. fellow, 1951-52. Mem. IEEE, AAAS, Sigma Xi. Office: Cornell University 306 Phillips Hall Ithaca NY 14853-5401

MCIVOR, DONALD KENNETH, retired petroleum company executive; b. Winnipeg, Man., Can., Apr. 12, 1928; s. Kenneth MacIver and Nellie Beatrice (Rutherford) McI.; m. Avonia Isabel Forbes, 1953; children: Gordon, Deborah, Duncan, Donald, Daniel. B.S. with honors in Geology, U. Man., 1950; postgrad., Nat. Def. Coll., 1973. Geophysical trainee seismic crew Imperial Oil Ltd., Alta., 1950, various operational and rsch. positions in exploration, 1950-58; held various positions including asst. to exploration mgr., suprv. exploration planning, mgr. exploration rsch. Imperial Oil Ltd., Calgary, 1958-68; with Jersey Prodn. Rsch. Co. Imperial Oil Ltd., Angola, France and Tulsa, Okla.; asst. mgr., mgr. corp. planning Toronto HO, 1968-69, mgr. exploration, 1970-72, sr. v.p., dir., 1973, exec. v.p., 1975; v.p. oil and gas exploration and prodn. Exxon Corp., 1977-81; dep. chmn., dir. Imperial Oil Ltd., 1981, chmn., chief exec. officer, 1982-85; dir., sr. v.p. Exxon Corp., Dallas, 1985-92; bd. dirs. Nat. Coun. on Econ. Edn.; exec. v.p. Internat. Exec. Svc. Corps. Mem. Can. Soc. Petroleum Geologists, Am. Petroleum Inst. Home: 111 Hemlock Hill Rd New Canaan CT 06840-3004

MCKAGAN, DUFF (MICHAEL MCKAGAN), bassist; b. Feb. 5, 1964. Bassist Guns n' Roses, 1985—. Albums with Guns n' Roses include Live Like a Suicide, 1986, Appetite for Destruction, 1987, Guns n' Roses Lies, 1988, Use Your Illusion I, 1991, Use Your Illusion II, 1991, The Spaghetti Incident?, 1993; solo album: Believe in Me, 1993. Office: care Geffen Records 9130 W Sunset Blvd West Hollywood CA 90069-3110

MCKANE, DAVID BENNETT, business executive; b. Salem, Mass., July 10, 1945; s. Vernon Wilson and Barbara Inez (Bennett) McK.; m. Wilson Lineburgh Baldwin, Apr. 16, 1977; adopted daughters, Taylor A., Lee and Paige Baldwin. BA, Dartmouth Coll., 1967; MBA, Amos Tuck Sch., 1969. Product mgr. Church & Dwight Co. Inc. (Arm and Hammer Products), N.Y.C., 1969-72; v.p. NTA Inc. N.Y.C., Nanuet, N.Y., 1972-75; v.p., exec. asst. to chmn. Schick Inc., Westport, Conn., 1975-77, sr. v.p., 1977-79, COO, exec. v.p., 1979-84, treas., 1980-84, also bd. dirs.; chmn., CEO A.I. Friedman, Inc., N.Y.C., 1985-87; chmn. McKane Robbins & Co. Inc., N.Y.C. and Westport, 1986—; bd. dirs. Oakhurst Dairy, Portland, Maine. Mem. bd. trustees Greens Farms (Conn.) Acad., 1991—; vice chmn. Associated Schs., Dartmouth Coll. Capital Campaign, 1991—. Mem. New Eng. Soc. in City N.Y., Mass. Mayflower Soc., Union Club (N.Y.C.), Country Club Fairfield, John's Island Club. Episcopalian. Home: 48 Owenoke Park Westport CT 06880-6833

MC KAUGHAN, HOWARD PAUL, linguistics educator; b. Canoga Park, Calif., July 5, 1922; s. Paul and Edith (Barton) McK.; m. Barbara Jean Budroe, Dec. 25, 1943; children: Edith (Mrs. Daniel Skene Santoro), Charlotte (Ms. Charlotte Barnhart), Patricia (Mrs. Stephen B. Pike), Barbara (Mrs. Ronald Chester Bell), Judith (Mrs. Frank L. Achilles III). AB, UCLA, 1945, MTh, Dallas Theol. Sem., 1946; MA, Cornell U., 1952, PhD, 1957. Mem. linguistic rsch. team Summer Inst. Linguistics, Mexico, 1946-52; asso. dir. Summer Inst. Linguistics, Philippines, also assoc. dir. summer sessions U. N.D., 1952-57, dir. Philippine br., 1957-61; rsch. asst. prof. anthropology U. Wash., 1961-62; rsch. assoc. prof., 1962-63; assoc. prof. linguistics U. Hawaii, 1963-64, prof. linguistics, 1964-88, prof. emeritus, 1988—, chmn. dept., 1963-66, dir. Pacific and Asian Linguistics Inst., 1964, 1966-69, assoc. dean grad. div., 1965-72, dean grad. div., dir. rsch., 1972-79, acting chancellor, 1979, interim vice chancellor acad. affairs, 1981-82, acting dir rsch., 1982-84, acting dean grad. div., 1982-83, dean, 1984-87, dir. rsch. rels., 1987-88; lectr. linguistics U. Philippines, summers, 1954, 60; Fulbright vis. prof. Philippine Normal Coll.-Ateneo De La Salle Consortium, Philippines, 1977, De La Salle U., Philippines, 1992; vis. prof. linguistics Bukidnon State Coll., Malaybalay, Philippines, 1993, 94; prin. Wycliffe Sch. Linguistics, summers 1953, 61; vis. prof. Australian Nat. U., Canberra, 1970; adj. prof. linguistics U. Okla., summers 1984, 85, 86; vis. prof., head dept. linguistics Payap U., Chiang Mai, Thailand, 1989-90. Sr. scholar East-West Ctr., Honolulu, 1964; NDEA Maranao-Philippines research grantee, 1963-65; Office of Edn. Hawaii English grantee, 1965-66; NSF Jeh Language of South Vietnam grantee, 1969-70, Maranao Linguistic Studies, 1971-72, numerous other research grants. Mem. linguistic socs. Am., Philippines, Western Assn. Grad. Schs. (pres. 1978), Hawaii, Linguistic Circle N.Y., Philippine Assn. Lang. Tchrs., Hawaii Govt. Employees Assn., Phi Beta Kappa, Phi Kappa Phi. Author (with B. McKaughan): Chatino Dictionary, 1951; (with J. Forster) Ilocano: An Intensive Language Course, 1952; The Inflection and Syntax of Maranao Verbs, 1959; (with B. Macaraya): A Maranao Dictionary, 1967. Editor: Pali Language Texts: Philippines, 21 vols., 1971; The Languages of the Eastern Family of the East New Guinea Highlands Stock, 1973, Maranao Stories, 1996, Stories from the Darangen, 1996; contbr. articles, chpts. to books, sci. jours. Home: 420 S Hill Rd McMinnville OR 97128

MC KAY, ALEXANDER GORDON, classics educator; b. Toronto, Dec. 24, 1924; s. Alexander Lynn and Marjory Maude Redfern (Nicoll) McKay; m. Helen Jean Zulauf, Dec. 24, 1964; stepchildren: Julie Anne Stephanie Brott, Danae Helen Fraser. BA, U. Toronto, 1946; MA, Yale U., 1947, Princeton U., 1948; PhD, Princeton U., 1950; LLD (hon.), U. Man., 1986, Brock U., 1990, Queen's U., 1991; DLitt (hon.), McMaster U., 1992, U. Waterloo, 1993. Mem. faculty classics Wells Coll., 1949-50, U. Pa., 1950-51, U. Man., 1951-52, 55-57, Mt. Allison U., 1952-53, Waterloo Coll., 1953-55; mem. faculty McMaster U., 1957-90, prof., chmn. dept. classics, 1962-68, 76-79, dean humanities, 1968-73, mem. faculty senate, 1968-73, 85-87, prof. emeritus, 1990—; Disting. vis. prof. classics U. Colo., 1978; prof. in charge Intercollegiate Center for Classical Studies, Rome, 1975; vis. mem. Inst. Advanced Study, Princeton, 1979, 81; vis. scholar U. Tex., Austin, 1987, Hardt, Vandoeuvres, Geneva, 1988; vis. fellow Trinity Coll., Cambridge, 1988; adj. prof. Miami U., Oxford, Ohio, 1989, 92-95; adj. prof. humanities York U., 1990-96; Disting. vis. lectr. Concordia U., Montreal, 1992-93, Rockefeller Study and Conf. Ctr., Bellagio (Como) Italy, 1993. Author: Naples and Campania: Texts and Illustrations, 1962, Roman Lyric Poetry: Catullus and Horace, 2d edit., 1974, Vergil's Italy, 1970, Cumae and the Phlegraean Fields, 1972, Naples and Coastal Campania, 1972, Houses, Villas and Palaces in the Roman World, 1975, Roman Satire, 1976, Vitruvius, Architect and Engineer, 1978, 2d edit., 1985, Römische Häuser, Villen und Paläste, 1980, Roma Antiqua: Latium and Etruria, 1986; co-author: Selections from Vergil, Aeneid I, IV and VI (Dido and Aeneas), 1988, Festschrift, The Two Worlds of the Poet: New Perspectives on Vergil, 1992, Tragedy, Love, and Change: Roman Poetic Themes and Variations, 1994. Pres., bd. govs. Hamilton Philharm. Orch., 1967-96, Hamilton Chamber Music Soc., 1965-67, Hamilton br. Archtl. Conservancy Ont., 1965-67, Hamilton and Region Arts coun., 1971-72; bd. dirs. Can. Fedn. Humanities, 1980-82; v.p., dir. Internat. Acad. Union, 1978-90; trustee Hamilton Found., 1972-75; bd. govs. Art Gallery Hamilton; bd. govs., dir. Boris Brott Summer Music Festival, 1989—; presdl. bd. trustees McMaster U. Art Gallery, 1985-91; pres. Sir Ernest MacMillan String Ensemble, 1988-90; mem. adv. bd. Inst. for Classical Tradition, Boston U., 1987-88; v.p., dir. Bach-Elgar Choral Soc., Hamilton, 1992-95. Decorated knight comdr. Order St. John of Jerusalem; officer Order of Can.; recipient Silver Jubilee medal Queen Elizabeth II, 1977, 125th Anniversary medal Can. Confedn.; Woodrow Wilson fellow, 1947-48, Can. Coun. fellow, 1973-74, Killam rsch. fellow, 1979-80, fellow Vanier Coll., York U., 1991-95. Fellow Royal Soc. Can. (hon. editor 1970-83, pres. 1984-87, past pres. 1987-89, Centennial medal 1982); mem. Vergilian Soc. (pres. 1972-74, Hon. Pres. for Life 1988—, chmn. Villa Vergiliana mgmt. com. 1993—), Classical Assn. Mid. West and South award of merit com. 1989-91), Classical Assn. Can. (v.p. 1970-72, 76-78, pres. 1978-80), Ont. Classical Assn. (hon. pres. 1994—), Societas Cumana (trustee 1993—), The Campanian Soc., Inc. (dir. 1994—), Yale Club (N.Y.C.), Univ. Club (Pitts.), Tamahaac Club (Ancaster), Arts and Letters Club (Toronto), X Club (Toronto), Faculty Club (McMaster). Home: 1 Turner Ave, Hamilton, ON Canada L8P 3K4 Office: McMaster U, Dept of Classics, Hamilton, ON Canada L8S 4M2

MCKAY, CRAIG, film editor. Editor: (films) Scarecrow, 1973, Thieves, 1977, Melvin and Howard, 1980, (with Dede Allen) Reds, 1981 (Academy award nomination best film editing 1981), Swing Shift, 1984, Something Wild, 1986, (with Alan Miller) Crack in the Mirror, 1987, Married to the Mob, 1988, She-Devil, 1989, Miami Blues, 1990, The Silence of the Lambs, 1991 (Academy award nomination best film editing 1991), Shining Through, 1992, (with Elena Maganini) Mad Dog and Glory, 1993, Philadelphia, 1993, (TV movies) Private Sessions, 1985. Address: 345 W 58th St New York NY 10019-1145

MC KAY, DEAN RAYMOND, computer company executive; b. Seattle, Nov. 13, 1921; s. Joseph and Nora (MacDermitt) McK.; m. Jean Davis, Dec. 26, 1942; children: Dean Brian, Bruce Thompson, Robert Joseph. BA, U. Wash., 1944; postgrad., Harvard U., 1955. With IBM Corp., Armonk, N.Y., 1946-82, from br. mgr. to dir. pers. div. data processing, 1957-61, v.p. communications, 1961-69, v.p. corp. ops. and services staff, 1969, mem. mgmt. com., 1970, sr. v.p., 1971, sr. v.p., group exec. data processing mktg., 1972—, sr. v.p. corp. ops. and services staffs, mem. corp. mgmt. com., bd. dir., 1978-82, mem. adv. bd., 1982—; bd. dirs. Marsh & McLennan Cos., Inc., N.Y.C., MCI Communications Corp., Washington, MARCAM, Newton, Mass., Du Pont, Wilmington, Del. Served to lt. (s.g.) Intelligence Corps USNR, 1942-46. Mem. Phi Beta Kappa. Clubs: Ekwanok (Manchester, Vt.); Gulf Stream (Delray Beach, Fla.), Blind Brook (Purchase, N.Y.).

MCKAY, DIANE ADELE MILLS, humanities educator; b. New Brunswick, N.J., Mar. 23, 1947; d. George M. and Dorothy Allen Mills; m. Thomas McKay III; children: Robert Allen, Heather Anne. BA in Am. Studies, Douglass Coll., 1969; MA, U. Pa., 1970, postgrad. Cert. substitute tchr., N.J. Mgr., trainer Fidelity Mut. Life Ins. Co., 1977-80; instr. humanities U. So. Colo., 1991—, Burlington County Coll., 1990—. Trustee New Covenant Presbyn. Ch., 1988—; mem. Hainesport Twp. Bd. Edn., 1983-90, 92—, v.p., 1985-90; mem. Hainesport Twp. Zoning Bd. Adjustment, 1983—, chair, 1985-89; bd. dirs. Burlington County Girl Scout Coun., 1993—, Burlington County Red Cross, 1994—; Burlington County Com. on Women, 1993-96, chair, 1994; adv. com. mem. N.J. Coalition for Battered Women, 1993-95; gender equity task force N.J. State Employment and Tng. Commn., 1993-95; equity adv. com. N.J. Dept. Edn., 1993-94. Mem. AAUW (pres. 1994—, bd. dirs., exec. com, v.p. N.J. membership 1989—, br. pres. 1985-87), Assn. Alumnae of Douglass Coll. (bd. dirs. 1989—, alumnae class pres. 1985-89, 94—), N.J. Women's Political Caucus, LWV. Home: 12 Whittier Dr Mount Holly NJ 08060-4812

MC KAY, EMILY GANTZ, civil rights professional; b. Columbus, Ohio, Mar. 13, 1945; d. Harry S. and Edwina (Bookwalter) Gantz; BA, Stanford U., 1966, MA, 1967; m. Jack Alexander McKay, July 3, 1965. Pub. info. specialist Community Action Pitts., 1967-68, exec. asst. to manpower dir., 1968-69, rsch. assoc., 1969-70; free-lance cons., 1969-70; pub. rels. and materials specialist Metropolitan Cleve. JOBS Coun., 1971-72; rsch. and mgmt. cons. BLK Group, Inc., Washington, 1970-73; dir. tech. products Am. Tech. Assistance Corp., McLean, Va., 1973-74; rsch. and mgmt. cons. CONSAD Rsch. Corp., Pitts., 1974-76, v.p., 1976-78; spl. asst. to Pres. for planning and eval. Nat. Coun. La Raza, Washington, 1978-82, v.p. rsch., advocacy and legislation, 1981-88, exec. v.p., 1983-88, cons. to the pres., 1988-90, v.p. for instl. devel., 1991-93, sr. v.p. instl. devel., 1993-94; pres. MOSAICA Ctr. for Nonprofit Devel. and Pluralism, 1994—; mem. adv. merit selection panel Superior Ct. D.C., 1987-90; cons. resource devel. New Israel Fund, 1989-91; cons. City of Cleve., Nat. Assn. Cmty. Devel., Nat. Coun. La Raza, 1975-78, Ford Found., 1989, Nat. AIDS Network, 1988-89, Am. Cultural Ctr., Israel, 1990, Nat. Hispana Leadership Inst., 1993; vol. orgnl. cons. SHATIL, Jerusalem and community based groups in Israel, 1987—; guest faculty Union Grad. Sch.; adj. faculty Am. U., Washington, 1995—. Author: numerous tng. nonprofit orgn. devel. materials. Co-chmn. Citizens Adv. Com. to D.C. Bar, 1986-87; mem. Mayor's Commn. Coop. Econ. Devel., 1981-83; non-lawyer mem. bd. govs. D.C. Bar, 1982-85; exec. com., bd. dirs. Indochina Resource Action Ctr., 1982-92; bd. dirs. exec. com. Southeast Asia Resource Action Ctr., 1993—; co-chmn. Citizens Commn. Adminstrn. Justice, 1982-84; mem. exec. com. Coalition on Human Needs, 1981-88; mem. Washington area steering com. New Israel Fund, 1989-91; co-chmn. adv. com. to Washington dist. office dir. Immigration and Naturalization Svc., 1984-88; chair Refugee Women in Devel., 1987-90, vice chair, 1990-94; mem. nat. adv. bd. Project Blueprint United Way Am., 1992-94, mem. diversity com., 1994—; vice chair Fund for the Future of Our Children, 1994—; sec. bd. dirs. New Bosnia Fund, 1995—; bd. advisors Internat. Ctr. for Residential Edn., 1994—; treas. bd. dir. Mary's Ctr. for Maternal and Child Care, 1995—. Ford Found. nat. honors fellow, 1966-67; recipient I. Pat Rios award Guadalupe Ctr., 1988; mem. working group Memorandum of Understanding between HHS and Israeli Ministry of Labour and Social Welfare, 1990-94, chairperson subcom. Youth at Risk, 1992-94. Mem. NAACP, Phi Beta Kappa. Democrat. Home: 3200 19th St NW Washington DC 20010-1006 Office: 1000 16th St NW Ste 604 Washington DC 20036

MCKAY, EUGENE HENRY, JR., food company executive; b. Battle Creek, Mich., June 25, 1929; s. Eugene Henry and Ella Florence (Everest) McK.; m. Beverly June Blakeman, Nov. 6, 1951 (div. 1981); children: Eugene Henry III, John Blakeman, Heather Melinda; m. Janice Lee Rook, 1989. BA, Mich. State U., 1951. Prodn. mgr. Battle Creek Food Co., 1955-60; franchise mgr. Archway Cookies, Inc., 1960-65, v.p., 1965-75, exec. v.p., 1975-85, pres., ptnr., 1985-96, ptnr., co-chmn., CEO, 1996—. Maj. U.S. Army, 1951-54. Republican. Presbyterian. Office: Archway Cookies Inc 5451 W Dickman Rd Battle Creek MI 49015-1034

MCKAY, JACK ALEXANDER, electronics engineer, physicist; b. Alhambra, Calif., Apr. 3, 1942; s. Gordon Alexander and Helen Leona (Lappin) McK.; m. Emily Gantz, July 3, 1965. BS in Physics, Stanford U., 1964, MSEE, 1967; MS in Physics, Carnegie-Mellon U., 1969, PhD in Physics, 1974. Rsch. physicist Naval Rsch. Lab., Washington, 1974-84; rsch. scientist Phys. Scis. Inc., Alexandria, Va., 1984-91; scientist Rsch. Support Instruments, Hunt Valley, Md., 1991-96; cons. Remote Sensor Concepts, Washington, 1996—. Home: 3200 19th St NW Washington DC 20010-1006 Office: Remote Sensor Concepts 3200 19th St NW Washington DC 20010

MC KAY, JIM, television sports commentator; b. Phila., Sept. 24, 1921; s. Joseph F. and Florence (Gallagher) McManus; m. Margaret Dempsey, Oct. 2, 1948; children: Mary Edwina, Sean Joseph. A.B., Loyola Coll., Balt., 1943, HLD (hon.), 1981. Reporter Balt. Evening Sun, 1946-47; news and sports commentator sta. WMAR- TV, Balt., 1947-50; sports commentator CBS Network, 1950-61; host This is New York, 1958-59; sports commentator for Winter and Summer Olympics, 1960-88; host ABC Wide World of Sports, from 1961; now commentator ABC Sports; chmn. "Maryland Million" Horse Racing Program, 1986—. Author: My Wide World, 1973. Served to lt. USNR, 1943-46. Decorated Officer's Cross Order of Merit (Fed. Republic Germany), 1974; recipient 12 Emmy awards, George Polk Meml. award, 1973, Olympic medal Austria, 1977, Engelhard award Thoroughbred Breeders of Ky., 1978, 90, Humphrey S. Finney award Md. Racing Writers, 1985, Nat. Turf Writers award, 1987, Peabody Award, 1989; named to Sportscasters Hall of Fame, 1987, U.S. Olympic Hall of Fame, 1989. Clubs: Jockey, Balt. Country, Md. Club, Hamilton St., Pinetree (Fla.) Golf Club. Avocations: raising and breeding race horses. Office: ABC Sports 47 W 66th St New York NY 10023-6201

MCKAY, JOHN, lawyer; b. Seattle, June 19, 1956; s. John Larkin and Kathleen (Tierney) M. BA, U. Wash., 1978; JD, Creighton U., 1982. Bar: Wash. 1982, U.S. Dist. Ct. (we. dist.) Wash. 1982, U.S. Supreme Ct. 1990, U.S. Ct. Appeals (9th cir.) 1990. Ptnr. Lane Powell Spears Lubersky, Seattle, 1982-92, Cairncross & Hempelmann, Seattle, 1992—. White House fellow, Washington, 1989-90. Mem. ABA (bd. govs. 1991-94), Wash. State Bar Assn. (pres. young lawyers divsn. 1988-89). Republican. Roman Catholic. Avocations: soccer, golf. Office: Cairncross & Hempelmann 701 5th Ave Ste 7000 Seattle WA 98104-7016

MCKAY, JOHN JUDSON, JR., lawyer; b. Anderson, S.C., Aug. 13, 1939; s. John Judson and Polly (Plowden) McK.; m. Jill Hall Ryon, Aug. 3, 1961 (div. Dec. 1980); children: Julia Plowden, Katherine Henry, William Ryon, Elizabeth Hall; m. Jane Leahey, Feb. 18, 1982; children: Andrew Leahey, Jennifer McFaddin. AB in History, U. S.C., 1960, JD cum laude, 1966. Bar: S.C. 1966, U.S. Dist. Ct. S.C. 1966, U.S. Ct. Appeals (4th cir.) 1974, U.S. Supreme Ct. 1981, U.S. Dist. Ct. (so. dist.) Ga. 1988, U.S. Ct. Appeals (11th cir.), 1990. Assoc. Haynsworth, Perry, Bryant, Marion & Johnstone, Greenville, S.C., 1966-70; ptnr. Rainey, McKay, Britton, Gibbes & Clarkson, P.A., and predecessor, Greenville, 1970-78; sole practice, Hilton Head Island, S.C., 1978-80; ptnr. McKay & Gertz, P.A., Hilton Head Island, 1980-81, McKay & Mullen, P.A., Hilton Head Island, 1981-88, McKay & Taylor, Hilton Head, 1988-91; pvt. practice, 1991—. Served to lt. (j.g.) USNR, 1961-64; lt. comdr. Res. (ret.). Mem. ABA, S.C. Bar Assn. (pres. young lawyers sect. 1970, exec. com. 1971-72, assoc. mem. grievance and disciplinary com. 1983-87), S.C. Bar, Beaufort County Bar Assn., Hilton Head Bar Assn., Assn. Trial Lawyers Am., S.C. Trial Lawyers Assn., S.C. Bar Found. (pres. 1977), Blue Key, Wig and Robe, Phi Delta Phi. Episcopalian. Clubs: Poinsett (Greenville). Editor-in-chief U. S.C. Law Rev., 1966; contbr. articles to legal jours. Home: 17 Foxbriar Ln Hilton Head Island SC 29926 Office: 203 Watersedge Hilton Head Island SC 29928-3541

MCKAY, KENNETH GARDINER, physicist, electronics company executive; b. Montreal, Que., Can., Apr. 8, 1917; came to U.S., 1946, naturalized, 1954; s. James Gardiner and Margaret (Nicholas) McK.; m. Irene C. Smith, July 25, 1942; children—Margaret Craig, Kenneth Gardiner. B.Sc., McGill U., 1938, M.Sc., 1939; Sc.D, MIT, 1941; D.Eng. (hon.), Stevens Inst. Tech., 1980. Research engr. Nat. Research Council Can., 1941-46; with Bell Telephone Labs., 1946-66, 73-80, dir. solid state device devel., 1957-59, v.p. systems engring., 1959-62, exec. v.p. systems engring., 1962-66, exec. v.p., 1973-80; v.p. engring AT&T, 1966-73; chmn. bd. Bellcomm Inc., 1966-73, Charles Stark Draper Lab., 1982-87; advisor Min. of Transp. and Comms., Republic of China, 1992-95. Trustee Stevens Inst. Tech., 1974-87; bd. govs. McGill U., 1972-77, N.Y. Coll. Osteo. Medicine, 1980-89; mem. vis. com. for engring. Stanford U., 1974-87; mem. sci. and acad. adv. com. U. Calif., 1980-88; mem. Sci. and Tech. Adv. Group, Republic of China, 1982—. Fellow IEEE, Am. Phys. Soc., N.Y. Acad. Scis.; mem. NAS, NAE (councillor 1970-73), Century Assn. Home and Office: 5 Carolina Meadows # 206 Chapel Hill NC 27514-8522

MCKAY, MICHAEL DENNIS, lawyer; b. Omaha, May 12, 1951; s. John Larkin and Kathleen (Tierney) McK.; m. Christy Ann Cordwin, Apr. 22, 1978; children: Kevin Tierney, Kathleen Lindsay, John Larkin. BA in Polit. Sci. with distinction, U. Wash., 1973; JD, Creighton U., 1976. Bar: Wash. 1976, U.S. Dist. Ct. (we. dist.) Wash. 1978, U.S. Dist. Ct. (ea. dist.) Wash. 1982, U.S. Ct. Appeals (9th cir.) 1982, U.S. Supreme Ct. 1993. Sr. dep. pros. atty. King County, Seattle, 1976-81; ptnr. McKay & Gaitan, Seattle, 1981-89; U.S. atty. we. dist. Wash. Seattle, 1989-93; ptnr. Lane Powell Spears Lubersky, Seattle, 1993-95, McKay, Chadwell & Matthews PLLC, Seattle, 1995—. Bd. dirs. Mental Health North, Seattle, 1982-85, St. Joseph Sch. Bd., 1984-87, Our Lady of Fatima Sch. Commn., 1994—, Creighton U., 1988-90; mem. stadium adv. bd. Seattle Kingdome, 1987-89; state vice chmn. George Bush for Pres., 1988; mem. U.S. Atty. Gen. Adv. Com., 1991-93, vice chmn., 1992. Mem. Creighton U. Alumni Assn. (pres. 1988-90, nat. alumni bd. 1988-92), Wash. Athletic Club, Columbia Tower Club. Republican. Roman Catholic. Avocations: tennis, running, swimming. Office: McKay Chadwell & Matthews 7201 Columbia Ctr 701 5th Ave Seattle WA 98104

MCKAY, MIMI, pediatric nurse, psychiatric nurse; b. Louisville, June 7, 1954; d. Charles Henry and Helen Dorothy (Palla) McK. BSN, Ind. U., New Albany, 1986; MSN, IUPUI, Indpls., 1992. RN, Ky.; cert. RNC-mental health, psychiat. nursing. Charge nurse Kosair Children's Hosp., Louisville, 1988-94; clin. nurse specialist child/adolescent psychiat. Alliant Health System/Kosair Children's Hosp., Louisville, 1994—; adolescent group psychotherapist Bingham Child Guidance Ctr., Louisville, 1994—; lectr. Ind. U. Southeast; course leader psychiat. mental health nursing; pvt. practive cons., psychotherapy.

MCKAY, MONROE GUNN, federal judge; b. Huntsville, Utah, May 30, 1928; s. James Gunn and Elizabeth (Peterson) McK.; m. Lucile A. Kinnison, Aug. 6, 1954; children: Michele, Valanne, Margaret, James, Melanie, Nathan, Bruce, Lisa, Monroe. B.S., Brigham Young U., 1957; J.D., U. Chgo., 1960. Bar: Ariz. 1961. Law clk. Ariz. Supreme Ct., 1960-61; assoc. firm Lewis & Roca, Phoenix, 1961-66; ptnr. Lewis & Roca, 1968-74; assoc. prof. Brigham Young U., 1974-76, prof., 1976-77; judge U.S. Ct. Appeals for 10th Cir., Denver, 1977-91, chief judge, 1991-94, sr. judge, 1994—. Mem. Phoenix Community Council Juvenile Problems, 1968-74; pres. Ariz. Assn. for Health and Welfare, 1970-72; dir. Peace Corps, Malawi, Africa, 1966-68; bd. dirs., pres. Maricopa county Legal Aid Soc., 1972-74. Served with USMCR, 1946-48. Mem. ABA, Ariz. Bar Assn., Maricopa County Bar Assn., Am. Law Inst., Am. Judicature Soc., Order of Coif, Blue Key, Phi Kappa Phi. Mem. LDS Ch. Office: US Ct Appeals for 10th Cir Rm 6404 Fed Bldg 125 S State St Salt Lake City UT 84138-1102

MCKAY, NEIL, banker; b. East Tawas, Mich., Aug. 9, 1917; s. Lloyd G. and Rose (McDonald) McK.; m. Olive D. Baird, Nov. 11, 1950; children: Julia B., Lynn B., Hunter L. A.B., U. Mich., 1939, J.D. with distinction, 1946. Bar: Mich. 1946, Ill. 1947. With firm Winston & Strawn, Chgo., 1946-63; partner Winston & Strawn, 1954-63, mem. mgmt. com., 1958-63; with First Nat. Bank of Chgo., 1963-83, from v.p. charge heavy industry lending div., gen. mgr. London br., to exec. v.p., cashier, 1970-75, vice chmn. bd., 1976-83, also dir.; exec. v.p., sec. First Chgo. Corp., 1970-75, vice chmn. bd., 1976-83; also bd. dirs.; bd. dirs. Baird & Warner, Inc., Chgo.; founding dir. Student Loan Mktg. Assn. Mem.: U. Mich. Law Rev; assoc. editor-in-chief: U. Mich. Law Rev., 1942, sr. editor, 1946. Trustee Morton Arboretum; former trustee Kalamazoo Coll. and Ill. Inst. Tech. Served with USNR, 1942-46. Mem. ABA, Ill. Bar Assn., Chgo. Bar Assn., Order of Coif, Dunham Woods Riding Club, CHgo. Hort. Soc. (sec., bd. dirs.). Clubs: Chicago (Chgo.), Mid-Day (Chgo.); Geneva Golf. Office: One First Nat Plz First National Plz Rm 2538 Chicago IL 60603

MC KAY, ROBERT JAMES, JR., pediatrician, educator; b. N.Y.C., Oct. 8, 1917; s. Robert James and Mary (Montgomery) McK.; m. Elizabeth Stewardson Foote, May 30, 1943; children: Robert James III, David Montgomery, Daniel Graham, Timothy Foote. Grad., Lawrenceville (N.J.) Sch., 1934; A.B., Princeton U., 1939; M.D., Harvard U., 1943. Intern Columbia-Presbyn. Med. Center, N.Y.C., 1943; asst. resident Columbia-Presbyn. Med. Center, 1947; chief resident Childrens Hosp. Med. Center, Boston, 1948; Milton fellow pharmacology Harvard Med. Sch., 1949; asst. prof. dept. pediatrics U. Vt. Coll. of Medicine, 1950-52, asso. prof., 1952-55, prof., 1955-87, prof. emeritus, 1987—, chmn. dept., 1950-83; Fulbright lectr. U. Groningen, Netherlands, 1960. Contbr. articles to profl. jours. Served from 1st lt. to capt. M.C. AUS, 1944-46. Decorated Bronze Star medal; recipient Jaycee Distinguished Service award, 1953; John and Mary Markle Found. scholar in med. sci., 1950-55. Mem. AMA, Am. Acad. Pediatrics (pres. 1971), Soc. for Pediatric Research, Am. Soc. Human Genetics, Am. Pediatric Soc., New Eng. Pediatric Soc. (pres. 1966), Can. Pediatric Soc., Ambulatory Pediatric Assn., Soc. Behavioral Pediatrics, Sigma Xi, Alpha Omega Alpha. Home: 99 Sunset Hill Rd Williston VT 05495-9614

MC KAY, SAMUEL LEROY, clergyman; b. Charlotte, N.C., Oct. 15, 1913; s. Elmer Ranson and Arlena (Benfield) McK.; AB cum laude, Erskine Coll., 1937; BD cum laude, Erskine Theol. Sem., 1939; postgrad. U. Ga., 1941-42, Union Theol. Sem., 1957; m. Martha Elizabeth Caldwell, Apr. 29, 1939; children: Samuel LeRoy, Mary Louise, William Ranson. Ordained to ministry of Presbyn. Ch., 1940; pastor Prosperity Assoc. Ref. Ch., Fayetteville, Tenn., 1942-46, Bethel Assoc. Ref. Ch., Oak Hill, Ala., 1946-50, 1st Asso. Ref. Ch., Salisbury, N.C., 1950-53, 1st Ch. U.S., Dallas, N.C., 1953-60, First Ch., Kernersville, N.C., 1960-66, Cooleemee (N.C.) Presbyn. Ch., 1966-69, Broadway (N.C.) Presbyn. Ch., 1969-80, Cape Fear Presbyn. Ch., 1983-91, Sardis Presbyn. Ch., 1984-86; stated clk. Gen. Synod Assoc. Ref. Presbyn. Ch., 1950-53; commr. Gen. Assembly Presbyn. Ch. U.S., 1960, 69; permanent clk. Winston-Salem Presbytery, 1961-69, chmn. leadership edn. com., 1962-66, chmn. Christian edn. com., 1967-68; chmn. nominations com. Fayetteville Presbytery, 1977-79; mem. hunger task force Fayetteville Presbytery, 1984-88, chmn. com. on Bangladesh, 1985-87; supr. chaplaincy program Davie County Hosp., 1968-69. Pres. Dallas PTA, 1955-56; bd. mgrs. Kernersville YMCA, 1962-66, chmn. membership com., 1963, treas., 1964, pres., 1965-66; bd. dirs. Winston-Salem-Forsyth County YMCA, 1965-66. Mem. Kernersville Area Ministers Assn. (pres. 1963-64), N.C. Poetry Soc. (dir. 1971—, chmn. poetry contests 1970-72, 83-88, editor ann. book Award-Winning Poems 1970-90; pres. 1971-74), Clan MacKay Soc. N.Am. (pres. 1971-75, chaplain 1976-90—, coun. 1983-90, honored guest, prin. speaker 1985 internat. gathering Glasgow, Scotland 1985, speaker at Clan Mackay Soc. Centenary Celebration, Edinburgh, Scotland, 1988, elected hon. mem. 1988, keynote speaker at meeting, Atlanta 1994). Lodge: Lions. Author: (poems) Harbinger, 1992; contbr. articles and sermons to periodicals and publs. *Perhaps the first thing to mark one's breeding is respect for the person of others and courtesy in matters of disagreement.*

MC KAY, THOMAS, JR., lawyer; b. Kearny, N.J., Sept. 26, 1920; s. Thomas and Mary (Paterson) McK.; m. Rosemary T. LaMarra, Oct. 5, 1946; children—Thomas III, Barbara Anne, Robert Michael. AB, Rutgers U., 1941; LLB, NYU, 1944. Bar: N.J. 1945, Ill. 1967. Assoc. to Arthur T. Vanderbilt, 1944-47; assoc. firm Toner, Speakman & Crowley, Newark, 1947-50; with McGraw-Edison Co. (and predecessor), 1950-80, sec., gen. counsel, 1967-80, v.p., 1973-80; v.p., gen. counsel, sec. Swift Ind. Corp., Chgo., 1980-84; of counsel Boodell Sears Giambalvo & Crowley, Chgo., 1984-87; securities industry arbitrator pub., 1988-95. Vol. legal aid atty. Prairie State Legal Svcs., Inc., St. Charles, Ill., 1987—. Mem. Am. Arbitration Assn. (comml. and securities law arbitrator). Home: 1435 Hampton Crse Saint Charles IL 60174-1319

MC KAYLE, DONALD COHEN, choreographer, director, writer, dance educator; b. N.Y.C., July 6, 1930; s. Philip Augustus and Eva Wilhelmina (Cohen) McK.; m. Esta Beck, 1954; m. Leah Levin, 1965; children—Gabrielle, Liane, Guy Eylon. Student, CCNY. mem. faculty Bennington Coll., Sarah Lawrence Coll., Conn. Coll., Bard Coll., Neighborhood Playhouse, Juilliard Sch., Martha Graham Sch., Am. Dance Festival; artistic dir., dean Calif. Inst. Arts Sch. of Dance; prof. dance, artistic dir. U. Calif., Irvine. Dancing debut, 1948; dir., 1964—; choreographer, 1950—, for cos. including, Alvin Ailey Am. Dance Theater, Batsheva Dance Co. Israel, Repertory Dance Theater, San Francisco Ballet, Cleve. San Jose Ballet, Dayton Comtemporary Dance Co., Cleo Parker Robinson Dance Ensemble; dir., choreographer stage prodns.: Free and Easy, 1961, Trumpets of the Lord, 1963 (Tony award nominee for best dir. and best choreographer 1975), Raisin, 1974 (Tony award nominee for best choreographer 1974), Dr. Jazz, 1975 (Tony award nominee for best choreographer 1975), The Last Minstrel Show, 1978, Evolution of the Blues, 1978-79, My Heart Belongs to Daddy, 1979, Sophisticated Ladies, 1981 (Best Choreographer award Outer Critics Cir. 1981, Tony award nominee for best choreographer 1981); choreographer stage prodns.: The Tempest, 1963-64, Anthony and Cleopatra, 1963-64, As You Like It, 1963-64, Golden Boy, 1964 (Tony award nominee for Best Choreographer, 1965), A Time for Singing, 1966, The Four Musketeers, 1967, I'm Solomon, 1968, Mass., 1972; choreographer films: The Great White Hope, 1968, Bed Knobs and Broomsticks, 1970, Charlie and the Angel, 1972, The Jazz Singer, 1980; T.V. works include: Baseball Ballet, 1963, Amahl and the Night Visitors, 1963, Fan Fare, 1965, Jazz Dance, U.S.A., 1965, The Strolling Twenties, 1965, Ten Blocks of the Camino Real, 1966, The Ed Sullivan Show, 1966-67, The Bill Cosby Special, 1967, Soul, 1968, Soul, 1968, TCB, 1968, The Second Bill Cosby Special, 1968, The Sounds of Summer, 1969, The Leslie Uggams Show, 1969, Dick Van Dyke and the Other, 1969, And Beautiful, 1969, Yesterday, Today and Tomorrow, 1970, The Super Comedy Bowl, 1971, A Funny Thing Happened on the Way to a Special, 1972, The New Bill Cosby Show, 1972-73, Angelitos Negros, 1973, Free to Be You and Me, 1974, Good Times, 1974-78, The Minstrel Man, 1977 (Emmy nominee 1977), The Richard Pryor Special, 1977, Cindy, 1978; choreographer concert works: Games, 1951, Nocturne, 1952, Rainbow Round My Shoulder, 1959, Dist. Storyville, 1962, They Called Her Moses, Incantation, 1968, Migrations, 1972, Album Leaves, 1976, Blood Memories, 1976, and numerous others, (staged club acts and TV specials for Diana Ross, Ann-Margret, Harry Belafonte, Mary Tyler Moore and others. Recipient Drama League Critics award Evolution of the Blues, Samuel H. Scripps Am. Dance Festival award, 1992, Capezio award, 1963, Lauds and Laurels profl. achievement award U. Calif. Irvine Alumni Assn., 1992, Lifetime Achievement award Am. Dance Guild, 1994, Living Legend award Nat. Black Arts Festival, 1994.

MCKEACHIE, WILBERT JAMES, psychologist, educator; b. Clarkston, Mich., Aug. 24, 1921; s. Bert A. and Edith E. (Welberry) McK.; m. Virginia Mae Mack, Oct. 30, 1942; children: Linda, Karen. BA, Mich. State Normal Coll., 1942; MA, U. Mich., 1946, PhD, 1949; LLD, Ea. Mich. U., 1957, U. Cin.; ScD, Northwestern U., 1973, Denison U., 1975, Nat. Acad. Edn., 1977, Alma Coll., 1995; DLitt (hon.), Hope Coll., 1985; LHD (hon.), Shawnee State U., 1994. Faculty U. Mich., 1946—, prof. psychology, 1961—, chmn. dept., 1961-71, dir. Center for Research in Learning and Teaching, 1975-83; mem. nat. adv. mental health council NIMH, 1976-80; mem. spl. med. adv. group VA, 1967-72. Author: (with J.E. Milhollaand) Undergraduate Curricula in Psychology, 1961, (with Charlotte Doyle and Mary Margaret Moffett) Psychology, 1966, 3d edit., 1977 (also Spanish edit. and instr.'s manual), Teaching Tips, 9th edit., 1994. Trustee Kalamazoo Coll., 1964-77; trustee-at-large Am. Psychol. Found., 1974-84, 92-96, pres., 1979-82. Officer USNR, 1943-45. Recipient Outstanding Tchr. award U. Mich. Alumni Assn., Am. Coll. Testing-Am. Ednl. Rsch. Assn. award for outstanding rsch. on coll. students, 1973, career contbns. award, 1990, award for disting. teaching in psychology Am. Psychol. Found., 1985. Mem. Am. Psychol. Assn. (sec., dir., pres. 1976-77, Disting. Career Contbn. to Edn. and Tng. in Psychology award 1987, E.L. Thorndike award for outstanding rsch., 1988), Internat. Assn. Applied Psychology (pres. div. ednl. instrn. and sch. psychology 1982-86), Am. Assn. Higher Edn. (dir. 1974-80, pres. 1978), AAUP (pres. U. Mich. chpt. 1970-71), AAAS (chmn. sect. on psychology 1976-77), Sigma Xi. Baptist. Home: 4660 Joy Rd Dexter MI 48130-9706 Office: U Mich Dept Psychology 525 E University Ann Arbor MI 48109-1346

MCKEAGUE, DAVID WILLIAM, district judge; b. Pitts., Nov. 5, 1946; s. Herbert William and Phyllis (Forsyth) McK.; m. Nancy L. Palmer, May 20, 1989; children: Mike, Melissa, Sarah, Laura, Elizabeth, Adam. BBA, U. Mich., 1968, JD, 1971. Bar: Mich. 1971, U.S. Dist. Ct. (we. dist.) Mich. 1972, U.S. Dist. Ct. (ea. dist.) 1978, U.S. Ct. Appeals (6th cir.) 1988. Assoc. Foster, Swift, Collins & Smith, Lansing, Mich., 1971-76, ptnr., 1976-92; sec.-treas. Foster, Swift, Collins & Smith, 1990-92; judge U.S. Dist. Ct., Western Dist. Mich., Lansing, 1992—. Mem. nat. com. U. Mich. Law Sch. Fund, 1980-92; gen. counsel Mich. Rep. Com., 1989-92; mem. adv. coun. Wharton Ctr., Mich. State U., 1996—. Mem. FBA (bd. dirs. Western Mich. chpt. 1991—), Mich. Bar Assn., Ingham County Bar Assn., Country Club Lansing (bd. govs. 1988-92, 96—). Roman Catholic. Office: US Dist Ct 315 W Allegan St Lansing MI 48933-1514

MC KEAN, JOHN ROSSEEL OVERTON, university dean; b. Cortland, N.Y., July 31, 1928; s. Norman Dodge and Janet (Passage) McK.; m. Ruth MacDonald, July 2, 1955; children: Janet, Annalise. B.A., Coll. William and Mary, 1951; M.Ed., Cornell U., 1956, Ed.D., 1961. Tchr. Landon Sch. for Boys, Washington, 1952-53; tchr. Central Sch., Homer, N.Y., 1953-55; asst. prof. history, dean students Allegheny Coll., 1957-67; headmaster Kingswood Sch. for Girls, Cranbrook, Bloomfield Hills, Mich., 1967-68; dean Hobart Coll., 1968-73; v.p. Coll. Kenyon Coll., Gambier, Ohio, 1973-77; dean arts and scis. State U. N.Y. at Canton, 1977-92. Mem. SUNY Coun. Deans Arts and Scis., Nat. Assn. Student Personnnel Adminstrs. (pres. Pa. 1958-59), SUNY Coun. Two-Yr. Bus. Adminstrs., Nat. Assn. Student Personnel Adminstrs. (dir. 1959-61), Am. Assn. Higher Edn., Community Coll. Gen. Edn. Assn., Middle States Assn. Colls. and Secondary Schs., Direct Descs. Signers Declaration Independence (pres. gen. Va.), St. Lawrence County Hist. Soc., Geneva Concerts Assn., (dir. 1969-72), Am. Hist. Assn., Round Table, English-Speaking Union, Phi Delta Kappa, Kappa Sigma. Club: Rotarian. Home: 1184 Jamestown Rd Apt 46 Williamsburg VA 23185-3357

MC KEAN, KEITH FERGUSON, former education educator; b. Beaver Falls, Pa., Aug. 18, 1915; s. Arthur and Eleanor (Ferguson) McK.; m. Catherine Stevenson, Oct. 31, 1942 (div. 1965); children—Kevin, Bruce; m. Joan Sanford Canter, Sept. 26, 1969. AB, Williams Coll., 1938; MA, U. Chgo., 1940; Ph.D. (Rackham fellow), U. Mich., 1950. Instr. U. Toledo, 1940-42; prof. N.C. State U., 1949-62, Elmira Coll., 1962-68; prof. U. No. Iowa, Cedar Falls, 1968-80, prof. emeritus, 1980—; lectr. Morse Mus. Am. Art, 1981—. Author: Cross Currents in the South, 1960, The Moral Measure of Literature, 1961, Critical Approaches to Fiction, 1968, Informative and Persuasive Prose, 1971. Bd. dirs. Winter Park Libr., 1982-86, Friends of Orlando Libr., 1987-90, Winter Park Hist. Assn., 1993-95; mem. evaluation com. Orlando Human Svcs. Coun., 1989-91; pres. Morse Mus. Am. Art Assocs., 1991—. 1st lt. USAAF, 1942-46. Ford Faculty fellow for postdoctoral study, 1954-55. Mem. AAUP, Univ. Club of Winter Park, Delta Kappa Epsilon. Home: 1272 Sara Ct Winter Park FL 32789-5922 *I am deeply impressed with the part that plain chance plays in one's success or failure. Everything I have achieved that is really desirable was, in large measure, an accident of such things as time or place. Indeed, I might have accomplished far less than I actually have or far more—depending on factors over which I had no control. We are all created equal, in one sense, because all men are created equally dependent on blind chance, and a full realization of this fact can temper foolish pride and guard against excessive self-abasement.*

MC KEAN, MICHAEL, actor; b. N.Y.C., Oct. 17, 1947; s. Gilbert and Ruth McKean; m. Susan McKean; children: Colin Russell, Fletcher. Student, Carnegie Inst. Tech., NYU. Toured with satirical comedy group The Credibility Gap; TV appearances include The Goodtime Girls, More Than Friends, American Bandstand, The TV Show ; regular on ABC-TV series Laverne and Shirley, 1976-83, Grand, 1989, Dream On, 1990—, Sessions, 1991, Spinal Tap Anniversary Spl., 1992, Saturday Night Live, 1994—; actor: (films) 1941, 1979, Used Cars, 1980, Young Doctors in Love, 1982, This is Spinal Tap, 1984, Clue, 1985, D.A.R.Y.L., 1985, Jumpin Jack Flash, 1986, Light of Day, 1987, Planes, Trains, & Automobiles, 1987, Short Circuit II, 1988, Earth Girls Are Easy, 1989, Flashback, 1989, The Big Picture, 1989, Book of Love, 1991, True Identity, 1991, Memoirs of an Invisible Man, 1992, Man Trouble, 1992, Mojo Flats, 1993, Coneheads, 1993, Airheads, 1994, Radioland Murders, 1994, The Brady Bunch Movie, 1995; (Broadway) Accomplice, 1989, (TV movies) More Than Friends, 1978, Classified Love, 1986, Murder in High Places, 1991; rec. artist: (with David Lander) Lenny and the Squiggtones, This is Spinal Tap. Office: care William Morris Agy 151 El Camino Beverly Hills CA 90212*

MCKEAN, ROBERT JACKSON, JR., retired lawyer; b. N.Y.C., Dec. 21, 1925; s. Robert Jackson and Isabel (Murphy) McK.; m. Sally H. Ament; children from previous marriage: Katherine, Douglas, Lauren, Andrew. B.A., Amherst Coll., 1950; LL.B., Harvard U., 1953. Bar: N.Y. 1954. Assoc. Simpson Thacher & Bartlett, N.Y.C., 1953-62, ptnr., 1962-85; pres. Nat. Bldg. Mus., Washington, 1986. Trustee Amherst Coll., Mass., Folger Shakespeare Library, Washington. Served with U.S. Army, 1944-46, ETO. Recipient medal for eminent service Amherst Coll., 1968. Mem. Phi Beta Kappa. Democrat.

MCKEAN, THOMAS WAYNE, dentist, retired naval officer; b. Adams County, Ind., May 18, 1928; s. Gorman F. and Elmira B. (Staley) McK.; m. Marilyn Kimberlin, Aug. 9, 1952; children: Thomas Wayne, Randall K., Dana K. D.D.S., Ind. U., 1953; grad., Naval Dental Sch., 1963. Diplomate: Am. Bd. Oral Surgery. Commd. ensign Dental Corps USN, 1949, advanced through grades to rear adm., 1980; stationed at Naval Tng. Ctr., Great Lakes, Ill., 1953; dental officer U.S.S. Randall, 1953-56; head dental svc., asst. dental officer U.S. Naval Acad./Naval Hosp., Annapolis, Md., 1956-59; dental officer FASRON III; asst. dental officer U.S. Naval Sta., Bermuda, 1959-63; postgrad. student Naval Dental Sch., Bethesda, Md., 1963-64; resident oral and maxillofacial surgery Naval Hosp., Great Lakes, Ill., 1964-66; dental officer U.S.S. America, 1966-68; chief oral surgery Naval Hosp., Orlando, Fla., 1968-70; dir. oral surgery and gen. practice residency tng. programs Naval Regional Med. Ctr., Great Lakes, 1970-74, chmn. dept. dentistry, 1970-74; cons., lectr. U.S. Army, Fort Sheridan, Ill., 1970-74; dir. oral surgery and gen. practice residency tng. programs Naval Regional Med. Ctr., Oakland, Calif., 1974-78; chmn., dept. dentistry Naval Regional Med. Ctr., 1974-78; lectr. oral surgery Letterman Army Med. Ctr., San Francisco, 1974-78; clin. lectr. dept. oral surgery U. of Pacific Sch. Dentistry, San Francisco, 1974-78; comdg. officer Naval Regional Dental Ctr., Pensacola, Fla., 1978-80; lectr. oral surgery Pensacola (Fla.) Jr. Coll., 1978-80; cons., lectr. Dwight D. Eisenhower Army Regional Med. Ctr., Augusta, Ga., 1978-80; insp. gen. dental Bur. Medicine and Surgery, Dept. of Navy, Washington, 1980-81; comdg. officer Naval Regional Dental Ctr., San Diego, 1981-82; insp. gen. Naval Med. Command, Washington, 1983-85; ret. USN, 1985. Contbr. articles to profl. jours. Chmn. bd. trustees UMC, Winter Park, 1992, mem. bd. adminstrs. 1995-96; bd. dirs. Circle of Friends Fla. Hosp. Found., 1989-91, Fla. Hosp. Found., 1991—, chmn. bd., 19953-96. Decorated Humanitarian Service medal, Legion of Merit with Gold Star, Meritorious Service medal, Nat. Def. Service medal with star, Vietnam Service medal, Republic of Vietnam Campaign medal with device, others; recipient Alumnus of Yr. award Ind. U. Sch.of Dentistry Alumnus Assn., 1988. Fellow Am. Dental Soc. of Anesthesiology, Internat. Coll. Dentists, Am. Coll. Dentists, Internat. Assn. Oral Surgeons; mem. Am. Assn. Oral and Maxillofacial Surgeons, ADA, Western Soc. Oral Surgeons, Assn. Mil. Surgeons U.S. (medal), Fla. Soc. Oral Surgeons, Delta Sigma Delta, Sigma Chi (Significant Sig award 1983). Home: 1309 Temple Grove Ct Winter Park FL 32789-2716

MCKEE, ALAN REEL, foreign service officer; b. Des Moines, May 23, 1943; s. T. Bonar and Lois Ellen (Reel) McK.; m. Martha Berry, July 16, 1966; children: Alexander, Amanda. BA, Dartmouth Coll., 1964; MA, Tufts U., 1968, MA in Law and Diplomacy, 1969. Country officer for Nigeria Dept. of State, 1972-73, mem. secretariat staff, 1974-75, country officer Norway & Denmark Office No. European Affairs, 1983-85, dep. dir. Office So. African Affairs, 1989-91, dir. Office West African Anglophone & Lusophone Affairs, 1991-93; chief polit.-econ. sect. Am. Embassy, Dakar, Senegal, 1975-78; polit. officer Am. Embassy, Ottawa, Can., 1978-82; congl. fellow Office of Senator Edward M. Kennedy, 1982-83; polit. counselor U.S. Embassy, The Hague, The Netherlands, 1985-89; U.S. consul gen. Johannesburg, South Africa, 1993—; rsch. intern U.S. AID, Accra, Ghana, 1968. Participant Operation Crossroads Africa, Zimbabwe, 1962. Capt. U.S. Army, 1964-67, Vietnam. Decorated Bronze Star. Mem. Am. Fgn. Svc. Assn., Johannesburg South Rotary (hon.). Home: 6611 River Rd, Bethesda. South Africa Office: US Consulate Gen, PO Box 2155, Johannesburg 2000, South Africa

MCKEE, CHRISTOPHER FULTON, astrophysics and astronomy educator; b. Washington, Sept. 6, 1942; m. Suzanne P. McKee; 3 children. AB in Physics summa cum laude, Harvard U., 1963; PhD in Physics, U. Calif., Berkeley, 1970. Physicist Lawrence Livermore (Calif.) Labs., 1969-70, cons., 1970—; rsch. fellow in astrophysics Calif. Inst. Tech., Pasadena, 1970-71; asst. prof. astronomy Harvard U., Cambridge, 1971-74; asst. prof. physics and astronomy U. Calif., Berkeley, 1974-77, assoc. prof., 1977-78, prof., 1978—, Miller Rsch. prof., 1984-85; assoc. dir. Space Scis. Lab., Berkeley, 1978-83, acting dir., 1983-84, dir., 1985—; dir. Theoretical Astrophysics Ctr., Berkeley, 1985. Fannie and John Hertz Found. fellow, 1963-69; Sherman Fairchild Disting. scholar, 1981, Nat. Acad. Scis., 1992. Fellow Am. Phys. Soc. (exec. com. astrophysics div. 1986-88); mem. Am. Astron. Soc. (councillor 1981-84), Internat. Astron. Union, Phi Beta Kappa. Office: U Calif Dept Physics Berkeley CA 94720

MCKEE, CHRISTOPHER FULTON, librarian, naval historian, educator; b. Bklyn., June 14, 1935; s. William Ralph and Frances (Manning) M.; m. Ann Adamczyk, 1993; children: Sharon, David B. AB, U. St. Thomas, Houston, 1957; AMLS, U. Mich., 1960. Catalogue libr. Washington and Lee U., Lexington, Va., 1958-62; social sci. libr. So. Ill. U., Edwardsville, 1962-66; book selection officer So. Ill. U., 1967-69, asst. dir., 1969-72; libr. of coll. Grinnell Coll., Iowa, 1972—, Samuel R. and Marie-Louise Rosenthal prof.; Sec. of Navy rsch. chair in naval history Naval Hist. Ctr., Washington, 1990-91; trustee Bibliog. Ctr. Rsch., Denver, 1984-88. Author: Edward Preble, 1972, A Gentlemanly and Honorable Profession: The Creation of the U.S. Naval Officer Corps, 1794-1815, 1991. NEH-Newberry Libr. fellow, 1978-79, Newberry Libr.-Brit. Acad. fellow, 1995-96; recipient U.S. Naval History prize for best pub. article, 1985, John Lyman book award N.Am. Soc. Oceanic History, 1994, Samuel Eliot Morison Disting. Svc. award USS Constitution Mus., Boston, 1992. Mem. Am. Hist. Assn., Navy Records Soc., Soc. for Mil. History, Orgn. Am. Historians, Soc. Historians of Early Republic, U.S. Naval Inst. Home: PO Box 272 Grinnell IA 50112-0272 Office: Grinnell Coll Burling Libr PO Box 805 Grinnell IA 50112-0811

MCKEE, ELLSWORTH, food products executive. CEO McKee Foods. Office: McKee Foods PO Box 750 10260 Mc Kee Rd Collegedale TN 37315 Office: PO Box 750 Collegedale TN 37315

MC KEE, FRAN, retired naval officer; b. Florence, Ala., Sept. 13, 1926; d. Thomas W. and Geneva (Lumpkins) McK. BS, U. Ala., 1950; postgrad., Gen. Line Sch., Postgrad. Sch. USN, Monterey, Calif., 1957; MS in Internat. Affairs, George Washington U., 1970, Naval War Coll., 1970; D. in Pub.Adminstrn. (hon.), Mass. Maritime Acad., 1978. Commd. ensign USN, 1950, advanced through grades to rear adm., 1976; svc. in various U.S. locations and in Morocco and Spain; dep. asst. chief for human goals (Bur. Naval Personnel), 1972-73; comdg. officer Naval Security Group Activity Ft. Meade, Md., 1973-76; dir. naval ednl. devel. Staff of Chief Naval Edn. and Tng. Naval Air Sta., Pensacola, Fla., 1976-78; dir. human resource mgmt. div. Office Chief of Naval Ops., Navy Dept. Washington, 1978-81; ret., 1981. Mem. Nat. Com. Armed Svcs. YMCA of U.S.A., 1981-83; VA Women's Adv. Com. for Vets.' Affairs, 1988-91; mem. Nat. Adv. Com. for Women in Mil. Svc. Meml. Found., 1988—. Decorated Legion of Merit with gold star, Meritorious Svc. medal; recipient DAR Medal of Honor, 1982, Nat. Vets. award, 1993; elected to Ala. Acad. Honor, 1979; first woman line officer in USN promoted to rear adm. Episcopalian. Home: 7420 Adams Park Ct Annandale VA 22003-5722

MC KEE, GEORGE MOFFITT, JR., civil engineer, consultant; b. Valparaiso, Nebr., Mar. 27, 1924; s. George Moffitt and Iva (Santrock) McK.; student Kans. State Coll. Agr. and Applied Sci., 1942-43, Bowling Green State U., 1943; B.S. in Civil Engring., U. Mich., 1947; m. Mary Lee Taylor, Aug. 11, 1945; children—Michael Craig, Thomas Lee, Mary Kathleen, Marsha Coleen, Charlotte Anne. Draftsman, Jackson Constrn. Co., Colby, Kans., 1945-46; asst. engr. Thomas County, Colby, 1946; engr. Sherman County, Goodland, Kans., 1947-51; salesman Oehlert Tractor & Equipment Co., Colby, 1951-52; owner, operator George M. McKee, Jr., cons. engrs., Colby, 1952-72; sr. v.p. engring. Contract Surety Consultants, Wichita, Kans., 1974—. Adv. rep. Kans. State U., Manhattan, 1957-62; mem. adv. com. N.W. Kans. Area Vocat. Tech. Sch., Goodland, 1967-71. Served with USMCR, 1942-45. Registered profl. civil engr., Kans., Okla., registered land Surveyor, Kans. Mem. Kans. Engring. Soc. (pres. N.W. profl. engrs. chpt. 1962-63, treas. cons. engrs. sect. 1961-63), Kansas County Engr's. Assn. (dist. v.p. 1950-51), N.W. Kans. Hwy. Ofcls. Assn. (sec. 1948-49), Nat. Soc. Profl. Engrs., Kans. State U. Alumni Assn. (pres. Thomas County 1956-57), Am. Legion (Goodland 1st vice comdr. 1948-49), The Alumni Assn. U. Mich. (life), Colby C. of C. (v.p. 1963-64), Goodland Jr. C. of C. (pres. 1951-52). Methodist (chmn. ofcl. bd. 1966-67). Mason (32 deg., Shriner); Order Eastern Star. Home: 8930 Suncrest St # 502 Wichita KS 67212-4069 Office: 6500 W Kellogg Dr Wichita KS 67209-2212

MC KEE, JAMES, JR., retired bank executive; b. Utica, N.Y., Aug. 29, 1918; s. James and Marie Roze (Tuller) McK.; m. Doris Elsie Nafis, June 28, 1947; children: James III, Nancy C. (dec.), Peter C., David R., John S. BS, Syracuse U., 1940. Exec. v.p., cashier First Nat. Bank, Richfield Springs, N.Y., 1940-56; with State Bank of Albany, 1956-83, v.p., cashier, 1969-83, sr. v.p., cashier, 1982-83. Co-chmn. United Fund, Clinton County, 1969; treas. Ea. Adirondack Econ. Devel. Commn., 1967-69; treas., mem. bd. mgrs. Parsons Child and Family Ctr., 1971-78, assoc. mem. bd., 1978; mem. Plattsburgh Coll. Found., bd. dirs., 1995—, mem. planned giving commn.; bd. dirs. Champlain Devel. Corp., 1969, New Industries for Clinton County, 1969; trustee Albany Rotary Found., Inc., 1980-85, v.p., 1986-88; trustee Champlain Valley Physicians Hosp., 1969. Maj. C.E., AUS, 1942-46, ETO. Decorated Bronze star. Mem. Norstar Bank Quarter Century Club (pres. 1974-75), Elks, Rotary (treas. dist. 7190 1983-89, mem. Plattsburgh N.Y. 1989—, asst. treas. dist. 7040 1989-91, Paul Harris fellow 1980, Rotarian of Yr. 1988, bd. dirs.), Ft. Orange Club, Alpha Kappa Psi, Delta Kappa Epsilon, Phi Kappa Phi, Beta Gamma Sigma, Beta Alpha Psi. Home: 30 Tanglewood Dr Port Kent NY 12975

MCKEE, KATHRYN DIAN GRANT, human resources consultant; b. L.A., Sept. 12, 1937; d. Clifford William and Amelia Rosalia (Shacher) G.; m. Paul Eugene McKee, June 17, 1961; children: Scott Alexander, Grant Christopher. BA, U. Calif., Santa Barbara, 1959; grad. Sch. Mgmt. Exec. Program, UCLA, 1979. Cert. compensation and benefits. Mgr. Mattel, Inc., Hawthorne, Calif., 1963-74; dir. Twentieth Century Fox Film Corp., L.A., 1975-80; sr. v.p. 1st Interstate Bank, Ltd., L.A., 1980-93; sr. v.p. and human resources dir. Am.'s Standard Chartered Bank, 1993-95; pres. Human Resources Consortia, Santa Ana, Calif., 1995—; dir. Accordia benefits of Southern Calif., 1991—, mem. exec. com. H.R. div. of Am. Bankers Assn., 1991-93; bd. dirs. Bank Certification Inst. Am. Bankers Assn., 1992-94; treas. Pers. Accreditation Inst., 1983-86, pres., 1986. Contbr. articles to profl. jours. Pres. GEM Theatre Guild, Garden Grove, Calif., 1984-86; bd. dirs. Vis. Nurses Assn., L.A., 1984-88; bd. dirs. SHRM, 1986-92, treas., 1989, vice-chmn., 1990, chmn., 1991, pres. SHRM Found., 1994, 95. Recipient Sr. Honor Key award U. Calif., Santa Barbara, 1959, named Outstanding Sr. Woman, 1959; recipient William Winter award Am. Compensation Assn., 1986, Excellence award L.A. Pers. Indsl. Rels. Assn., 1990, Profl. Excellence award SHRM, 1994. Mem. Internat. Assn. Pers. Women (various offices, past nat. pres., Mem. of Yr. 1986), Orgn. Women Execs. Office: Human Resources Consortia 2700 N Main St Ste 800 Santa Ana CA 92705-6636

MCKEE, KEITH EARL, manufacturing technology executive; b. Chgo., Sept. 9, 1928; s. Charles Richard and Maude Alice (Hamlin) McK.; m. Lorraine Marie Celichowski, Oct. 26, 1951; children: Pamela Ann Houser, Paul Earl. BS, Ill. Inst. Tech., 1950, MS, 1956, PhD, 1962. Engr. Swift & Co., Chgo., 1953-54; rsch. engr. Armour Rsch. Found., Chgo., 1954-62; dir. design and product assurance Andrew Corp., Orland Park, Ill., 1962-67; dir. engring. Rsch. Ctr. Ill. Inst. Tech., Chgo., 1967-80, dir. mfg. prodn. ctr., 1977—; adj. prof. Ill. Inst. Tech., Chgo., 1979—; coord. Nat. Conf. on Fluid Power, Chgo., 1983-88; mem. com. on materials and processing Dept. Def., Washington, 1986—. Author: Productivity and Technology, 1988; editor: Automated Inspection and Process Control, 1987; co-editor: Manufacturing High Technology Handbook, 1987; mng. editor: Manufacturing Competitiveness Frontier, 1977—. Capt. USMC, 1950-54. Recipient oustanding presentation award Am. Soc. of Quality Control, Milw., 1983. Fellow World Acad. Productivity Scis.; mem. ASCE, Am. Def. Preparedness Assn. (pres. Chgo. chpt. 1972—), Am. Assn. Engring. Soc. (Washington) (coor. com. on productivity 1978-88), Inst. of Indsl. Engrs., Soc. Mfg. Engrs. (Gold medal 1991), Am. Assn. for Artificial Intelligence, Robotic Industry Assn. (bd. dir. 1978-81), Assn. for Mfg. Excellence, Soc. for Computer Simulation. Democrat. Roman Catholic. Home: 18519 Clyde Rd Homewood IL 60430-3015 Office: Illinois Inst Tech Mfg Productivity Ctr 3350 S Federal St Chicago IL 60616-3732

MC KEE, KINNAIRD ROWE, retired naval officer; b. Louisville, Ky., Aug. 14, 1929; s. James H. and Kathleen (Sutton) McK.; m. Betty Ann Harris, June 23, 1953; children: James Henry III, Anne Arnold. BS, U.S. Naval Acad., 1951; grad., Nuclear Power Tng., 1958. Commd. ensign U.S. Navy, 1951, advanced through grades to adm., 1982; served in (Pacific fleet destroyer Marshall), Korean War; served in div. naval reactors (AEC), 1964-66; comdg. officer nuclear attack submarine (DACE), 1966-69; asst. to dir. program planning (Office Chief of Naval Ops.), Washington, 1969-70; exec. dir. (Chief Naval Ops. Exec. Panel), 1970-73; comdr. (U.S. and NATO submarine forces), 1973-75; supt. (U.S. Naval Acad.), Annapolis, 1975-78; comdr. U.S. Third Fleet, 1978-79; dir. naval warfare (Chief of Naval Ops.), Washington, 1979-82; dir. naval nuclear propulsion Washington, 1982-88, ret.; bd. dirs. Peco Energy Corp., Energy Corp., Entergy Ops., Inc. Mem. U.S. Naval Inst. Home: 214 S Morris St Oxford MD 21654-1309

MCKEE, MARGARET JEAN, federal agency executive; b. New Haven, June 20, 1929; d. Waldo McCutcheon and Elizabeth (Thayer) McKee; A.B., Vassar Coll., 1951. Staff asst. United Rep. Fin. Com., N.Y.C., 1952; staff asst. N.Y. Rep. State Com., N.Y.C., 1953-55; staff asst. Crusade for Freedom (name later changed to Radio Free Europe Fund), N.Y.C., 1955-57; researcher Stricker & Henning Research Assocs., Inc., N.Y.C., 1957-59; exec. sec. New Yorkers for Nixon (name later changed to N.Y. State Ind. Citizens for Nixon Lodge), N.Y.C., 1959-60; asst. to Raymond Moley, polit. columnist, N.Y.C., 1961; asst. campaign com. Louis J. Lefkowitz for Mayor, N.Y.C., 1961; research programmer, treas. Consensus, Inc., N.Y.C., 1962-67; spl. asst. to U.S. Senator Jacob K. Javits, N.Y., 1967-73, adminstrv. asst., 1973-75; dep. adminstr. Am. Revolution Bicentennial Adminstrn., 1976, acting adminstr., 1976-77; chief of staff Perry B. Duryea (minority leader) N.Y. State Assembly, 1978; public affairs cons., 1979-80; dir. govt. relations Gen. Mills Restaurant Group, Inc., 1980-83; exec. dir. Fed. Mediation and Conciliation Service, 1983-86; mem. Fed. Labor Rels. Authority, 1986-89, chmn., 1989-94; mem. Nat. Partnership Coun., 1993-94; bd. dirs. Interam. Life Ins. Co., 1979-86. Mem. N.Y. State Bingo Control Commn., 1965-72, U.S. Adv. Commn. on Public Diplomacy, 1979-82; mem. Nat. Partnership Coun., 1993—; pres. Bklyn. Heights Slope Young Rep. Club, 1955-56; co-chmn. Bklyn. Citizens for Eisenhower-Nixon, 1956; chmn. 2d Jud. Dist. Assn. N.Y. State Young Rep. Clubs, Inc., 1957-58, vice-chmn., mem. bd. govs., 1958-60, v.p., 1960-62; pres., 1962-64; mem. exec. com. Fedn. Women's Rep. Clubs N.Y. State, Inc., 1960-64, mem. council, 1964-70; mem. exec. com. N.Y. Rep. State Com. 1962-64; co-chmn. spl. assts. Rockefeller for Pres. Nat. Campaign com., N.Y.C., 1964; co-dir. N.Y. Rep. State Campaign Com., 1964; asst. campaign mgr. Kenneth B. Keating for Judge Ct. Appeals, N.Y., 1965; dir. scheduling Gov. Rockefeller campaign, 1966, Sen. Charles E. Goodell campaign, 1970; dir. scheduling and speakers' bur. N.Y. Com. to Re-elect the Pres., 1972; dir. planning and strategy, Conn. Reagan-Bush campaign, Hartford, 1980; mem. annual fund adv. com. Vassar Coll., 1992—. Mem. bd. govs. Women's Nat. Rep. Club, N.Y.C., 1963-66. Mem. Jr. League of Bklyn. (past (dir.), Exec. Women in Govt. (chmn. 1986), Nat. Women's Edn. Fund (mem. bd.), Am. Newspaper Women's Club, Nat. Soc. Colonial Dames Am. Episcopalian. Club: Vassar (past dir., Bklyn.). Home: 532 S Brooksvale Rd Cheshire CT 06410

MCKEE, MARY ELIZABETH, producer; b. Syracuse, N.Y., Feb. 14, 1949; d. Anthony Henry and Mary (Robards) Krystosik; m. Peter S. Fama, June 27, 1970 (div. Mar. 1973); 1 child, Kiralie Fama; m. Michael R. McKee, Feb. 15, 1975 (Oct. 1978); 1 child, Quinn. BFA, Fla. Internat. U., Miami, 1974; MFA, Memphis State U., 1977. Copywriter announcer Sta. WREC/WZXR Radio, Memphis, 1978-79; creative dir. Cit Neifert & Assoc. Advt., Memphis, 1979-82; promotion dir. Sta. WGNX-TV, Atlanta, 1982-86; program mgr. Sta. WVEU-TV, Atlanta, 1986-90; v.p., sta. mgr. Sta. WHSP-TV, Vineland, N.J., 1990-95; v.p. V Boxes Worldwide, Phila., 1995—, V Box Prodns., Atlantic City, 1995—; adj. prof. Glassboro State U., 1990—. Actor in field (Top 10 Memphis Mag. 1979). Vol. Com. to Feed the Hungry, Atlanta, 1988, Tenn. Talking Libr., Memphis, 1982; mem. Greenpeace, 1987—; mem. adv. coun. SES, Easter Seal Soc. N.J. Recipient Merit award Tenn. Talking Libr., 1982; named Best TV Comml. Memphis Advt. Club, 1982; Hair scholar Fla. Internat. U., 1973. Mem. AFTRA, Nat. Assn. Broadcasters, Am. Women in Radio and TV (publicity chmn. 1985-86), Nat. Assn. TV Program Execs., N.J. Broadcasters Assn. (TV chair 1995—), Broadcast Cable Fin. Mgmt. Assn., Chelsea Neighborhood Assn. (exec. bd.), Rotary. Democrat. Roman Catholic. Avocations: writing journals, published poet, running and video production bus., bicycling. Home: 55 S Dover Ave Atlantic City NJ 08401-5912 Office: 5918 Hammond Ave Philadelphia PA 19120

MCKEE, PENELOPE MELNA, library director; b. New Liskeard, Ont., Can., Dec. 31, 1938; d. Melvin Hugh and Violet Mary (Hooton) Olimer; m. Arthur Donald McKee, Mar. 5, 1960 (div. 1985); children: Suzanne, Carolyn, Stephen. BA with honors, U. Toronto, Can., 1960, BLS, 1961, MLS, 1980; diploma, Coll. Applied Arts and Tech., 1976. Cert. mcpl. mgr., Ont. Mcpl. Mgmt. Devel. Bd. Fine arts libr. North York Pub. Libr., Ont., Can., 1961-63, reference libr., 1969-74; reference libr. Toronto Montessori Schs., Thornhill, Ont., 1974-76; cons. Grolier Pub., Toronto, 1976; libr. supr. Toronto Pub. Libr., 1977-80; dir. Aurora Pub. Libr., Ont., Can., 1980-86, Peterborough Pub. Libr., Ont., Can., 1986-90, Edmonton Pub. Libr., Alta., Can., 1990—; adj. assoc. prof. U. Alta., Edmonton, 1992—; cons. Edmonton Cath. Sch. Bd., 1992. Contbr. articles to profl. jours. Vice chmn. Project Hostel, Aurora, 1986-89; bd. dirs. Friends of Trent Severn Waterway, Peterborough, 1990; active Edmonton Centennial Celebrations Com., 1992. Russell scholar U. Toronto, 1956. Mem. Canadian Libr. Assn., Ontario Libr. Assn. (pres.), Libr. Assn. Alta., Alta. Pub. Libr. Dirs. Coun. (chair), Rotary Club of Downtown Edmonton (pub. rels. chmn. IVT Woman of Vision 1995, ABI Woman of Yr. 1995). Avocations: reading, music, curling, canoeing. Office: Edmonton Pub Libr, 7 Sir Winston Churchill Sq, Edmonton, AB Canada T5J 2V4

MCKEE, RICHARD MILES, animal studies educator; b. Cottonwood Falls, Kans., Oct. 8, 1929; m. Marjorie Fisk, June 22, 1952; children: Dave, Richard, Annell, John. BS in Agriculture, Kans. State Coll. Agriculture and Applied Sci., 1951; MS in Animal Husbandry, Kans. State U., 1963; PhD in Animal Science, U. Ky., 1968. Herdsman Moxley Hall Hereford Ranch, Coun. Grove, Kans., 1951-52, 54-55, Luckhardt Farms, Tarkio, Mo., 1955-58; asst. mgr. L&J Crusoe Ranch, Cheboygan, Mich., 1958-59; asst. instr., cattle herdsman Kans. State U., Manhattan, 1959-65, from asst. prof. to assoc. prof., 1959-65, prof., departmental teaching coord., 1976—; program participant and/or official judge numerous shows, field days including Kans. Jr. Hereford Field Day, Kans. Jr. Shorthorn Field Day, Better Livestock Day, Kans. Jr. Livestock Assn., Am. Jr. Hereford Assn. Field Day, Cheyenne, Wyo., 1973, Kans. Jr. Polled Hereford Field Day, Am. Jr. Shorthorn Assn., Kans. City, Mo., 1965, Am. Internat. Jr. Charolais Assn. Show, Lincoln, Nebr., 1976, Am. Royal 4-H Livestock Judging Contest, Kans. City, 1975, Jr. Livestock Activities various cattle breed assns. nationwide, 1977-81; served on many breed assn. coms.; judge County Fairs; official judge 14 different Nat. Beef Breed Shows U.S. and Can.; conducted 60 livestock judging and showmanship schs. at county level. Contbr. articles to profl. jours. Deacon 1st Presbyn. Ch., Manhattan, 1969-75, Sunday Sch. tchr., Chancel choir, elder; project leader com. mem. 4-H; foster parent Kans. State U. Football Program. Lt. USMC, 1952-54, Korea. Named Hon. State Farmer of Kans.; Hall of Merit Honoree for Edn. by Am. Polled Hereford Assn., 1985; NDEA scholar U. Ky., 1966-67; Miles McKee Student Enrichment Fund established at Kans. State U. Mem. Am. Soc. Animal Sci., Kans. Livestock Assn. (beef cattle improvement com. 1970-78, cow-calf clinic com. 1973, 74, 75, 76, 77, 78), Nat. Assn. Colls. and Tchrs. Agriculture, Block and Bridle Club, Am. Jr. Hereford Assn. (hon.), FarmHouse, Sigma Xi, Phi Kappa Phi, Alpha Zeta, Gamma Sigma Delta, Alpha Tau Alpha (hon.). Home: 901 Juniper Dr Manhattan KS 66502-3148 Office: Dept of Animal Scis & Industry Kansas State U Manhattan KS 66506

MCKEE, ROGER CURTIS, federal magistrate judge; b. Waterloo, Iowa, Feb. 11, 1931; s. James A. and Leonace (Burrell) McK.; m. Roberta Jeanne Orvis, Sept. 3, 1954; children: Andrea Jane, Brian Curtis, Paul Robert. BA, State Coll. of Iowa, 1955; MA, U. Ill., 1960; JD, U. San Diego, 1968. Bar: Calif. 1970, U.S. Dist. Ct. (so. dist.) Calif. 1969, U.S. Ct. Appeals (9th cir.) 1971. Telegrapher, agt. Ill. Cen. R.R., 1950-55; tng. asst. No. Ill. Gas Co., Aurora, 1959-60; with indsl. rels. dept. Convair div. Gen. Dynamics Corp., San Diego, 1960-68; contract adminstr. and supr. Datagraphix div. Gen. Dynamics Corp., San Diego, 1968-69, asst. counsel, 1969-70; ptnr. Powell & McKee, San Diego, 1970-75, Millsberg, Dickstein & McKee, San Diego, 1975-83; magistrate judge U.S. Dist. Ct. for So. Dist. Calif., San Diego, 1983—; presiding magistrate judge, 1993—. Bd. trustees So. Calif. Presbyn. Homes, L.A., 1979-81; moderator Presbytery of San Diego, 1980. Capt. USNR, 1949-85. Mem. Calif. Bar Assn., Fed. Magistrate Judges Assn., Navy League U.S., Naval Res. Officers Assn., Res. Officers Assn., Dixieland Jazz Soc. (bd. dirs. San Diego chpt. 1984—). Republican. Office: US Cts Bldg 940 Front St San Diego CA 92101-8994

MCKEE, THEODORE A., federal judge; b. 1947. B.A., SUNY, Cortland, 1969; J.D. magna cum laude, Syracuse U. Coll. of Law, 1975. Dir. of minority recruitment & admissions SUNY, Binghamton, 1969-72; atty. Wolf, Block, Schorr & Solis-Cohen, Phila., 1975-77; asst. U.S. atty., Eastern Dist. PA, 1977-80, asst. U.S. atty., Eastern Dist. Gen. Crimes Unit, Narcotics and Firearms Unit, then Polit. Corruption Unit; lecturer Rutgers U. Coll. of Law, 1980-91; dep. city solicitor Law Dept., Phila., 1980-83; gen. counsel Phila. Parking Auth., 1983; judge Ct. of Common Pleas, 1st Jud. Dist. PA, 1984-94, judge major felony program, 1986, judge orphans' ct. divsn., 1992; circuit judge Third Circuit, Phila., 1994—; bd. dirs. Diagnostic and Rehab. Ctr. of Phila. Mem. World Affairs Coun., New Directions for Women, Inc.; trustee Edna McConnell Clark Found. Mem. ABA, Nat. Bar Assn., Am. Law Inst., Barristers' Assn. Phila., Temple Inn of Ct., Crime Prevention Assn. (bd. dirs.). Office: 601 Market St Rm 20614 Philadelphia PA 19106-1510

MCKEE, THOMAS FREDERICK, lawyer; b. Cleve., Oct. 27, 1948; s. Harry Wilbert and Virginia (Light) McK. BA with high distinction, U. Mich., 1970; JD, Case Western Rs. U., 1975. Bar: Ohio 1975, U.S. Dist. Ct. (no. dist.) Ohio 1975, U.S. Supreme Ct. 1979. Assoc. firm Calfee, Halter & Griswold, Cleve., 1975-81, ptnr., 1982—, also mem. exec. com., chmn. operating com.; sec. McDonald & Co. Investments, Inc., Chart Industries, Inc.; bd. dirs. Mr. Coffee, Inc. Contbg. editor Going Public, 1985. Mem. ABA (com. fed. regulation securities law sect.), Bar Assn. Greater Cleve., Order of Coif., Union Club, Tavern Club, Country Club, Hillbrook Club. Home: 210 Pheasant Run Dr Chagrin Falls OH 44022-2968 Office: Calfee Halter & Griswold Ste 1400 McDonald Investment Ctr 800 Superior Ave E Cleveland OH 44114

MCKEE, TIMOTHY CARLTON, taxation educator; b. South Bend, Ind., Mar. 9, 1944; s. Glenn Richard and Laura Louise (Niven) McK.; m. Linda Sykes Mizelle, Oct. 13, 1984; children: Brandon Richard. BS in Bus. Econs., Ind. U., 1970, MBA in Fin., 1973, JD, 1979; LLM in Taxation, DePaul U., 1980. Bar: Ill. 1980, U.S. Dist. Ct. (no. dist.) Ill. 1980; CPA, Ill., Va.; cert. govt. fin. mgr. Procedures analyst Assocs. Corp., South Bend, Ind., 1969-71; asst. dir. fin. Ind. U., Bloomington, Ind., 1971-79; sr. tax mgr. Peat Marwick Mitchell & Co., Chgo., Norfolk, Va., 1979-84; corp. counsel K & K Toys, Norfolk, 1984; assoc. prof. acctg. Old Dominion U., Norfolk, 1985—, chmn. dept., 1994-95, chmn. acctg., fin. and law dept., 1995; computer coord. Peat, Marwick, Mitchell & Co., 1982-84; micro computer cons. Old Dominion U., 1985-91. Contbr. articles to profl. jours. Mem. Friends of Music, Bloomington, 1978, Art Inst., Chgo., 1981; loaned exec. United Way, Chgo., 1981; telethon chmn. Va. Orch. Group, Norfolk, 1983. Mem. Assn. Govt. Accts., Am. Acctg. Assn., Am. Assn. Atty. CPAs, Inc., Am. Tax Assn., Fin. Execs. Inst. (pres. 1995-96), Hampton Rds. Tax Forum, Inst. Internal Auditors, Beta Alpha Psi. Home: 412 Rio Dr Chesapeake VA 23320-7144 Office: Old Dominion U Hughes Hall # 2065 Norfolk VA 23529-0229

MCKEE, WILLIAM DAVID, lawyer; b. N.Y.C., Aug. 11, 1926; s. H. Harper and Mabel (Hughes) McK.; m. Eleanor Lyn Messenkopf, Sept. 13, 1947; children: Rebecca Inez, Harper Charles, Joshua Monte. BSME, Duke U., 1946; LLB, Columbia U., 1949. Bar: Calif. 1950. Rsch. assoc. Am. Law Inst., Berkeley, Calif., 1949-50; assoc. Orrick, Herrington & Sutcliffe, San Francisco, 1950-57, ptnr., 1958-88, chmn., chief exec. officer, 1983-86; bd. dirs. Golden West Fin. Corp., Oakland, Calif., World Savs. & Loan Assn. Served as ensign USNR, 1943-46. Mem. Calif. Bar Assn. Democrat. Home: 1271 Redwood Ln Lafayette CA 94549-2429 Office: Orrick Herrington & Sutcliffe Old Federal Reserve Bank Bldg 400 Sansome St San Francisco CA 94111-3308

MCKEEL, LILLIAN PHILLIPS, education educator; b. Rocky Mount, N.C., Aug. 23, 1932; d. Ellis Elma and Lillian Bonner (Archbell) Phillips; m. James Thomas McKeel Jr., July 23, 1955; children: Sarah Lillian McKeel Youngblood, Mary Kathleen McKeel Welch. BA, U. N.C., 1954; MEd, Pa. State U., 1977, DEd, 1993. Tchr. State Coll. (Pa.) Area Schs., 1964-90; instr. Pa. State U., University Park, 1990-93; asst. prof. Shippensburg (Pa.) U., 1993-94; mem. of panel NSTA Book Rev. Panel/Outstanding Sci. Tradebooks for Children, Washington, 1992; faculty sponsor Shippensburg U. Sch. Study Coun., 1993-95. Contbr. articles to profl. jours. Recipient Presdl. award for Excellence in Sci. and Math. Tchng., NSF, Washington, 1990; finalist Tchr. of Yr. program Pa. Dept. Edn., Harrisburg, 1992, cert. Recognition, Hon. Robert Casey/Gov., Harrisburg, Pa., 1991; named Achieving Women of Penn State, Pa. State U., 1993. Mem. Nat. Sci. Tchrs. Assn., Soc. Presdl. Awardees, Assn. Edn. Tchrs. in Sci., Coun. Elem. Sci. Internat., Phi Delta Kappa (Disting. Svc. award 1992), Pi Lambda Theta, Pi Kappa Pi. Avocations: photography, collecting antique toys. Office: Shippensburg U 1871 Old Main Dr Shippensburg PA 17257-2200

MCKEEN, ALEXANDER C., engineering consulting company owner; b. Albion, Mich., Oct. 10, 1927; s. John Nisbet and Janet (Callander) McK.; m. Evelyn Mae Feldkamp, Aug. 18, 1951; Jeffrey, Brian, Andrew. BSME, U. Mich., 1950; MBA, Mich. State U., 1968. Registered profl. engr., Mich. Asst. supt. maintenance Cadillac Motor Car div. GM, Detroit, 1961-65, plant engr., 1965-67, supt. final assembly, 1967-69, asst. dir. reliability, 1969-72; exec. engr. Product Assurance GM, Warren, Mich., 1972-75, asst. dir. Engring. Analysis, 1975-77, dir. Engring Analysis, 1977-87; pres., owner Engring. Analysis Assocs., Inc., Bingham Farms, Mich., 1987—. Pres. Dells of Bloomfield Home Owners Assn., Bloomfield Hills, Mich., 1987-88; trustee Kirk in Hills, Bloomfield Hills, 1990-93, elder, 1995—. Mem. Soc. Auto. Engrs., Am. Soc. Quality Control, Engring. Soc. Detroit, Detroit Athletic Club, Stonycroft Hills Golf Club, Pelican Nest Golf Club, Beta Gamma Sigma. Avocations: tennis, golf, photography, travel, gardening. Home: 5286 Kellen Ln Bloomfield Hills MI 48302-2738 Office: Engring Analysis Assocs Inc 30700 Telegraph Rd Ste 4566 Bingham Farms MI 48025-4532

MC KEEN, CHESTER M., JR., business executive; b. Shelby, Ohio, Mar. 18, 1923; s. Chester Mancil and Nettie Augusta (Fox) McK.; m. Alma Virginia Pierce, Mar. 1946; children: David Richard, Karin, Thomas Kevin. BS in Mil. Sci., U. Md., 1962; MBA, Babson Coll., Wellesley, Mass., 1962. Advanced through grades to maj. gen. U.S. Army, 1942-77; dir. logistics Bell Helicopter Internat., Tehran, Iran, 1977-79; v.p. procurement Bell Helicopter Textron, Ft. Worth, 1979-82; v.p. materiel Bell Helicopter Textron, 1982-89; pres. Logistics Svcs. Internat., Arlington, Tex.; chmn. bd. dirs. ISES Inc.; bd. dirs. Exec. Svc. Corps Tarrant County, chmn. Decorated D.S.M., Legion of Merit (3), Commendation medal (3). Mem. Am. Mgmt. Assn., Am. Def. Preparedness Assn. (v.p. S.W. region), Assn. U.S. Army, Ridglea Country Club, Rotary, Masons (33 degree), Shriners, Sigma Pi. Home: 2310 Woodsong Trl Arlington TX 76016-1037 Office: ISES Inc 328 Pipeline Rd Hurst TX 76053 *To live for oneself is to pursue emptiness. To live for others is to insure fulfillment.*

MCKEEVER, JEFFREY D., computer company executive; b. Marion, Ind., 1942. Grad., U. Ariz., Tucson, 1965; MBA, U. Ariz., 1973. Chmn., CEO, dir. MicroAge Inc., Tempe. Office: MicroAge Inc 2400 S MicroAge Way Tempe AZ 85282-1896*

MCKEEVER, JOHN EUGENE, lawyer; b. Phila., Oct. 24, 1947; s. John James and Marie Julia (Supper) McK.; m. Kathleen Marie Wynne, Dec. 9, 1995; children: John Joseph, Jeannine Marie. BA magna cum laude with distinction, U. Pa., 1969, JD magna cum laude, 1972. Bar: Pa. 1972, U.S. Dist. Ct. (ea. dist.) Pa. 1972, U.S. Dist. Ct. (mid. dist.) Pa. 1977, U.S. Ct. Appeals (3rd cir.) 1979, U.S. Ct. Appeals (D.C. cir.) 1981, U.S. Supreme Ct. 1981. Assoc. Schnader, Harrison, Segal & Lewis, Phila., 1972-80, ptnr., 1980—. Mem. Pres. Coun. Allentown Coll. St. Francis De Sales, Center Valley, Pa., 1980—, Bus. Leadership Organized for Cath. Schs., Phila., 1984—, adv. com. De Sales Sch. Theology, Washington, trustee, 1988-91; capt. spl. gifts com. Cath. Charities Appeal, Phila., 1986-91; bd. dirs. Jr. Achievement, Phila., 1986—. Mem. Pa. Bar Assn., Phila. Bar Assn., Pro-Life Lawyers' Guild (bd. dirs. 1983-84, chancellor 1984-86), St. Thomas More Soc. (gov. 1979-91, pres. 1981-82), Order of Coif, Phi Beta Kappa, Pi Gamma Mu. Republican. Roman Catholic. Office: Schnader Harrison Segal & Lewis 1600 Market St Ste 3600 Philadelphia PA 19103-7240

MCKEITHEN, WALTER FOX, secretary of state; b. Columbia, La., Sept. 8, 1946; s. John Jesse and Marjorie (Funderburk) McK.; m. Yvonne May; children: Marjorie, Marianne, Rebecca, John Jesse. B in History and Social Studies, La. Tech. U., 1972. Owner, operator Apparel Mart Dept. Store, Columbia, 1974-83, McKeithen Chem. & Cementing, Columbia, 1979-88; mem. appropriation, natural resources and joint budget coms. La. Ho. of Reps., Baton Rouge, 1983-87; sec. of state State of La., Baton Rouge, 1987—; tchr., coach Caldwell Parish High Sch., Grayson, La., 1975-78; past mem. La. Assn. Educators. Past v.p. Caldwell Parish Jaycees; trustee La. Sch. Employees' Retirement System; mem. La. Tourist Devel. Commn.; second injury bd. La. Workmen's Compensation; mem. State Bd. Election Supervisors and State Bond Commn., La. Farm Bur., Am. Petroleum Inst.; administrv. bd. Broadmoor Meth. Ch. Recipient Outstanding Legislator award La. Assn. Educators, 1985, Golden Apple award La. Fedn. Tchrs., 1986. Republican. Methodist. Office: Dept of State State Capitol 20th Fl PO Box 94125 Baton Rouge LA 70804-9125*

MCKELDIN, WILLIAM EVANS, management consultant; b. Richmond, Va., Aug. 14, 1927; s. Robert A.W. and Mary E. (Burke) McK.; BS in Bus. Adminstrn., Temple U., 1951, postgrad., 1951-53; postgrad. U. Pitts., 1953-54; m. Phyllis Shellhase, Jan. 23, 1982; children by previous marriage: William Evans, Roberts E. Various employee relations and mgmt. positions with Westinghouse Corp., Pitts., 1950-62, Farrel Corp., Rochester, N.Y., 1963-66, Gen. Signal Corp., Norwalk, Conn. and Watertown, N.Y., 1966-71, Copperweld Steel Co., Warren, Ohio, 1971-75, Tenn. Forging Steel, Knoxville, 1975-77, Val Bradley Assocs., West Chester, Pa., 1977-79; pres. and owner McKeldin Assocs., West Chester, 1979—. Bd. dirs. United Fund, YMCA, ARC, Rochester Inst. Tech., Jefferson Community Coll., Kent State U. Served with USAAF, 1945-47. Mem. Inst. Mgmt. Cons., Am. Soc. Safety Engrs., Am. Soc. Personnel Adminstrn., C. of C. (dir.). Republican. Presbyterian. Clubs: Masons, Rotary. Contbr. articles to trade jours. Office: McKeldin Assocs 125 Willowbrook Ln West Chester PA 19382-5571

MCKELL, CYRUS M., college dean, plant physiologist, consultant; b. Payson, Utah, Mar. 19, 1926; s. Robert D. and Mary C. (Ellsworth) McK.; m. Betty Johsnon; children: Meredith Sue, Brian Marcus, John Cyrus. BS, U. Utah, 1949, MS, 1950; PhD, Oreg. State U., 1956; postgrad., U. Calif., Davis, 1957. Instr. botany Oreg. State U., Corvallis, 1955-56; range rsch. plant physiologist U. Calif. USDA-Agrl. Research Service, Davis, 1956-60; prof., dept. chmn. U. Calif., Riverside, 1960-69; prof. dept. head., dir. Utah State U., Logan, 1969-80; v.p. research NPI, Salt Lake City, 1980-88; dean Coll. of Sci. Weber State U., Ogden, Utah, 1988-94; pres. Applied Ecol. Svcs. Inc., Salt Lake City, 1995—; cons. Ford Found. 1968-72, Rockefeller Found., 1964-70, 89, UN, 1978, 90, NAS, 1980, 89, 91, 92, 93, USAID, 1972, UN Devel. Program, 1989. Editor: Grass Biology and Utilization, 1971, Useful Wildland Shrubs, 1972, Rehabilitation of Western Wildlife Habitat, 1978, Paradoxes of Western Energy Development, 1984, Resource Inventory and Baseline Study Methods for Developing Countries, 1983, Shrub Biology and Utilization, 1989, Wilderness Issues, Arid Lands of the Western United States, 1992; contbr. over 230 articles to profl. jours. Chmn. Cache County Planning Commn., Logan, 1974-79; mem. Utah Energy Conservation and Devel. Coun., 1976-79, Gov.'s Sci. Adv. Coun., 1988—, chmn., 1990-91; mem. Commn. of the Californians, Riverside, 1965-68. Recipient Utah Gov.'s Sci. and Tech. medal, 1990; Fulbright scholar Spain, 1967-68; World Travel grantee Rockefeller Found., 1964. Fellow AAAS (com. chmn. 1979-89, sci. exchange to China grantee 1984-85, 89, sci. panel U.S.-Chile 1987); mem. Am. Soc. Agronomy, Soc. Range Mgmt. (pres. Calif. sect. 1965, pres. Utah sect. 1982). Mem. LDS Ch. Avocations: travel, photography. Home: 2248 E 4000 S Salt Lake City UT 84124-1864

MCKELLAR, C. H., grocery chain executive; b. 1937. With Winn-Dixie Stores, Inc., 1957—; supt. retail ops. Jacksonville (Fla.) div., 1978-80, corp. v.p., mgr., 1980-81; v.p., mgr. Montgomery div., 1981-83; sr. v.p., regional dir. Jacksonville, from 1986, now exec. v.p., dir. Office: Winn-Dixie Stores Inc PO Box B Jacksonville FL 32203-0297*

MCKELLEN, IAN, actor; b. Burnley, Eng., May 25, 1939; s. Denis Murray and Margery (Sutcliffe) McK.; ed. St. Catharine's Coll., Cambridge, Eng. Prof. Oxford U., 1990-91. First stage appearance as Roper in A Man for All Seasons, Belgrade Theatre, Coventry, Eng., 1961; numerous other parts include title roles in Henry V, Luther, Ipswich, 1962-63, Aufidius in Coriolanus, Arthur Seaton in Saturday Night and Sunday Morning, title role in Sir Thomas More, Nottingham Playhouse, 1963-64; London debut as Godfrey in A Scent of Flowers, 1964, Claudio in Much Ado About Nothing, Andrew Cobham in Their Very Own and Golden City, 1966; title part in O'Flaherty, V.C. and Bonapart in The Man of Destiny, 1966, (Broadway debut) Leonidik in The Promise, London, 1966-67, Richard II, Edward II, Hamlet, Prospect Theatre Co., 1968-71; Capt. Plume in The Recruiting Officer; founder-mem. Actors' Co., Edinburgh Festival, 1972 and touring as Giovanni in Tis Pity She's A Whore, Page-Boy in Ruling the Roost, title role Wood Demon; debut with R.S.C. as Dr. Faustus, Edinburgh Festival, 1974; title role in The Marquis of Keith, Philip the Bastard in King John, 1974-75, Young Vic Colin in Ashes, 1975; Royal Shakespeare Co.: Burglar in Too True to be Good, Romeo, Macbeth, Leontes in The Winter's Tale, Face in The Alchemist, Bernick in Pillars of the Community, Langevin in Days of the Commune, 1976-78, Ivanov in Every Good Boy Deserves Favour, Toby Belch in Twelfth Night, Andrei in The Three Sisters, Max in Bent, 1979, Amadeus, N.Y.C., 1980, Iago in Othello, The Other Place, Stratford, 1989; European tour of one-man show Acting Shakespeare, 1983, also Los Angeles, N.Y.C., 1984, one-man show A Knight Out at the Lyceum (devised especially for Gay Games IV U.K. and South African tour), 1994; assoc. dir. Nat. Theatre, London, 1984-86, plays include: Venice Preserved, Wild Honey, Coriolanus, Duchess of Malfi, The Cherry Orchard, King Lear, Richard m. Napoli Milionaria, Uncle Vanya, others; dir. first prodn. The Prime of Miss Jean Brodie, Liverpool Playhouse, 1969, A Private Matter, 1973, The Clandestine Marriage, 1975; films include: Alfred the Great, 1969, The Promise, 1969, A Touch of Love, 1969, The Keep, 1982, Plenty, Zina, 1985, Scandal, 1988, The Ballad of Little Jo, 1992, I'll Do Anything, 1992, Last Action Hero, 1993, Six Degrees of Separation, 1993, The Shadow, 1994, Jack and Sarah, 1994, Restoration, 1994, Richard III, 1995, Apt Pupil, 1996; TV appearances include: David Copperfield, 1965, Ross, 1969, Richard II, Edward II and Hamlet, 1970, Hedda Gabler, 1974, Macbeth, Every Good Boy Deserves Favour, Dying Day, 1979, Acting Shakespeare, 1981, The Scarlet Pimpernel, 1982, And the Band Played On, 1993 (Emmy nomination, Supporting Actor - Special, 1994), Cold Comfort Farm, 1995, Rasputin, 1995. Recipient Clarence Derwent award, 1964; Variety and Plays and Players awards, 1966; Actor of Year, Plays and Players, 1976; award Soc. of West End Theatres for Best Actor in Revival, 1977, for Best Comedy Performance, 1978, for Best Actor in a New Play, 1979, Tony Award for Best Actor, Drama Desk Award, Outer Critics' Circle Award, N.Y. Drama League Award, 1981; Performer of Yr. award Royal TV soc., 1983. Decorated comdr. Order Brit. Empire, knight Bachelor. Mem. Brit. Actors' Equity (coun. 1970-71). Office: ICM, Oxford House, 76 Oxford St, London W1N 0AX, England

MCKELVEY, JACK M., bishop; b. Wilmington, Del., Dec. 8, 1941; m. Linda Boardman; children: Heather, Glen, Drew, Marissa. B in Psychology, U. del.; MDiv, Va. Theol. Seminary. ordained to deaconate Episc. Ch., 1966, to priesthood, 1967. Vicar St. John the Baptist Ch., Milton, Del., 1965-70, Holy Trinity Ch., Wilmington, 1970-79; rector St. Paul's Ch., Englewood, N.J., 1979—; elected Suffragan Bishop Diocese of Newark, 1990—; mem. faculty Inter-Met Seminary, Washington, 1976; former mem. diocesan coun. Del., commns. on ministry and standing coms.; pres. standing com. diocese of Newark; co-founder Van Ost Family Inst. Co-author: Inter-Met Seminary: Bold Experiment in Theological Education. Office: 24 Rector St Newark NJ 07102-4512

MCKELVEY, JAMES MORGAN, chemical engineering educator; b. St. Louis, Aug. 22, 1925; s. James Grey and Muriel (Morgan) McK.; m. Edith Rothbauer, Dec. 28, 1957; children: James, Robert; m. Judith Hood Forgotson, Sept. 4, 1992. B.S., U. Mo.-Rolla, 1945; M.S., Washington U., St. Louis, 1947, Ph.D., 1950. Research engr. E.I. DuPont de Nemours & Co., Inc., 1950-54; asst. prof. chem. engring. Johns Hopkins U., Balt., 1954-57; mem. faculty Washington U., St. Louis, 1957—, dean Sch. Engring. and Applied Sci., 1964-91, prof. chem. engring., 1991—. Recipient Disting. Educator award Soc. Plastics Engrs., 1979. Home: 9861 Copper Hill Rd Saint Louis MO 63124

MC KELVEY, JEAN TREPP, industrial relations educator; b. St. Louis, Feb. 9, 1908; d. Samuel and Blanche (Goodman) Trepp; m. Blake McKelvey, June 29, 1934. AB, Wellesley Coll., 1929; MA, Radcliffe Coll., 1931, PhD, 1933. Mem. faculty Sarah Lawrence Coll., 1932-45, N.Y. State Sch. Indsl. and Labor Rels., Cornell U., Ithaca, N.Y., 1946—; from asst. prof. to assoc. prof. indsl. rels. N.Y. State Sch. Indsl. and Labor Rels., Cornell U., 1946-49, prof., 1949—; vis. prof. Sch. Law Cornell U., 1977-78; mem. pub. panel, hearing officer, arbitrator Nat. War Labor Bd., 1944-45; mem. inquiry into Rochester Transit dispute N.Y. State Bd., 1952; mem. pub. adv. com. to sec. of labor, 1953; mem. N.Y. State Bd. Mediation, 1956-66; mem. presdl. emergency bd. on ry. shopcrafts dispute, 1964, ry. signalmen dispute, 1971; mem. Fed. Svc. Impasses Panel, 1970-90. Author: The Uses of Field Work in Teaching Economics, 1939, AFL Attitudes Toward Production, 1952, Dock Labor Disputes in Great Britain, 1953, Fact Finding in Public Employment Disputes, 1969, Sex and the Single Arbitrator, 1971. Editor: The Duty of Fair Representation, 1977; The Changing Law of Fair Representation, 1985, Cleared For Takeoff: Airline Labor Relations Under Deregulation, 1988; also several vols. on arbitration. Alumnae trustee Wellesley Coll., 1946-53. Mem. Nat. Acad. Arbitrators (past pres.), Am. Fedn. Tchrs. (mem. pub. rev. bd. 1969-73), Am. Arbitration Assn. (mem. nat. panel, mem. UAW pub. rev. bd. 1957—), Indsl. Rels. Rsch. Assn., Phi Beta Kappa. Home: 1570 East Ave Apt 501 Rochester NY 14610-1638 Office: Cornell U NYS-SILR 16 Main St W Rochester NY 14614-1601

MC KELVEY, JOHN CLIFFORD, research institute executive; b. Decatur, Ill., Jan. 25, 1934; s. Clifford Venice and Pauline Lytton (Runkel) McK.; m. Carolyn Tenney, May 23, 1980; children: Sean, Kerry, Tara, Evelyn, Aaron. B.A., Stanford U., 1956, M.B.A., 1958. Research analyst Stanford Research Inst., Palo Alto, Calif., 1959-60; indsl. economist Stanford Research Inst., 1960-64; with Midwest Research Inst., Kansas City, Mo., 1964—; v.p. econs. and mgmt. sci. Midwest Research Inst., 1970-73, exec. v.p., 1973-75, pres., chief exec. officer, 1975—; chmn. Menninger Found. Bd., 1994. Trustee Rockhurst Coll., 1993; mem. Civic Coun. of Greater Kansas City; bd. regents Rockhurst Coll., Kansas City, Mo., 1977; bd. dirs. Yellow Corp., North Star Found., 1981, Mid-Am. Mfg. Tech. Ctr., 1991; trustee The Menninger Found., 1975. Clubs: Carriage, Mission Hills, Hallbrook Country. Home: 1156 W 103rd St # 232 Kansas City MO 64114-4511 Office: Midwest Rsch Inst 425 Volker Blvd Kansas City MO 64110-2241

MC KELVEY, JOHN JAY, JR., retired foundation executive; b. Albany, N.Y., July 16, 1917; s. John Jay and Louise E. (Brunning) McK.; m. Josephine G. Faulkner, June 28, 1941; children: John Jay III, Richard Drummond, Edward Faulkner, Laurence Brunning. A.B., Oberlin Coll., 1939; M.S., Va. Poly. Inst., 1941; Ph.D., Cornell U., 1945. Investigator N.Y. State Agrl. Expt. Sta., 1942-45; with Rockefeller Found., 1945-83, dep. dir. agrl. sci., 1966-68, assoc. dir. agrl. scis., 1968-83; cons. in field, 1959—; Mem. survey team natural resources No. Region Nigeria FAO-ICA, 1960; cons. UN spl. fund project agrl. research, Thailand, 1964; study com. manpower needs and ednl. capabilities in Africa Edn. and World Affairs, 1964-65; rev. commn. higher edn. Botswana, Lesotho and Swaziland Overseas Devel. Ministry U.K., 1966; overseas liaison com. study team higher edn., Sierra Leone, 1968; mem. agrl. edn. mission to U.S. Pacific, Overseas Devel. Ministry of U.K., 1970; mem. Africa sci. bd. Nat. Acad. Scis., 1961-68, vice chmn., 1964-68, mem. sci. orgn. devel. bd., 1966-68, mem. bd. sci. and tech. internat. devel., also chmn. Africa sci. panel, 1968—, chmn. adv. panel on arid lands of, sub-Saharan Africa, 1974; chmn. com. African agrl. research capabilities Nat. Acad. Scis./Agrl. Bd., 1971-74; mem. vis. com. for biology and related research facilities Harvard Coll., 1975-81; mem. area adv. com. for Africa Council for Internat. Exchange of Scholars, 1976-80; mem. Chappaqua Internat. Exchange, 1976-78; chmn. USAID/IBAR Task Force, 1978-79. Author: Man Against Tse-tse, 1973; editor: (with R.L. Metcalf) The Future for Insecticides, 1976, (with H.H. Shorey) Chemical Control of Insect Behavior, 1977, (with Louis H. Miller and John A. Pino), Immunity to Blood Parasites of Animals and Man, 1977, (with Bruce F. Eldridge and Karl Maramorosch) Vectors of Disease Agents, 1980, (with K. Maramorosch) Subviral Pathogens of Plants and Animals, 1985; contbr. articles to profl. jours., chpts. to books. Trustee Internat. Inst. Tropical Agr., Ibadan, Nigeria, 1971-87, chmn., 1983-87; vice chmn. governing coun. Internat. Trypanotolerance Ctr., The Gambia, 1981-89, chmn., 1988-89; pres. Internat. Fund for Agrl. Rsch., 1985-87, bd. dirs. 1988, chmn., 1989-93; bd. govs. Inst. for Agrl. Rsch., Ahmadu Bello U., Zaria, Nigeria, 1971-74; moderator Federated Ch. West Winfield, 1995—. Mem. AAAS, Entomol. Soc. Am., Assn. for Advancement Agrl. Sci. in Africa (founding). Home: Richfield Springs NY 13439

MCKELVEY, JUDITH GRANT, lawyer, educator, university dean; b. Milw., July 19, 1935; d. Lionel Alexander and Bernadine R. (Verdun) Grant. B.S. in Philosophy, U. Wis., 1957, J.D., 1959. Bar: Wis. 1959, Calif. 1968. Atty. FCC, Washington, 1959-62; adj. prof. U. Md., Europe, 1965; prof. law Golden Gate U. Sch. Law, San Francisco, 1968—; dean Golden Gate U. Sch. Law (Sch. Law), 1974-81; mem. State Jud. Nominees Evaluation Commn., 1981-82. Contbr. to: Damages Book, 1975, 76. Bd. dirs. San Francisco Neighborhood Legal Assistance Found. Fellow Am. Bar Found.; mem. ABA, Wis. Bar Assn., Calif. Bar Assn., San Francisco Bar Assn. (dir. 1975-77, chmn. legis. com., sec.-treas., pres.-elect 1980-83, pres. 1984), Calif. Women Lawyers (1st pres.), Law in a Free Soc. (exec. com.), Continuing Edn. of Bar (chmn. real estate subcom., mem. joint adv. com.), Legal Svcs. to Children Inc. (pres. 1987-89), San Francisco Neighborhood Legal Assistance Found. (dir. and exec. com. 1985-87), Lawyers Com. for Urban Affairs (dir. and exec. com. 1985-87, co-chairperson 1988-90). Office: Golden Gate U Sch Law 536 Mission St San Francisco CA 94105-2921

MCKELVIE, RODERICK R., federal judge; b. 1946. BA, Harvard U., 1968; ME, Roosevelt U., 1970; JD, U. Pa., 1973. Law clk. to Hon. Caleb Layton U.S. Dist. Ct., Wilmington, Del., 1973-74; assoc. Richards, Layton & Finger, Wilmington, 1974-79; ptnr. Ashby, McKelvie & Geddes, Wilmington, 1979-92; fed. judge U.S. Dist. Ct. (Del. dist.), Wilmington, 1992—. Active World Affairs Coun., 1988—, United Way Govt. Rels. Commn. Mem. ABA, Del. State Bar, Richard S. Rodney Inn of Ct. (mem. exec. com., pres. 1992-93). Office: US Dist Ct 844 N King St Ste Box 10 Wilmington DE 19801-3519*

MCKELWAY, ALEXANDER JEFFREY, religion studies educator; b. Durham, N.C., Dec. 8, 1932; s. Alexander Jeffrey and Alice (Gibbon) McK.; m. Adelaide Bullard, Sept. 17, 1960; children: Alexander J., Daniel, Matthew Phillip. AB, Davidson Coll., 1954; BD, Princeton Theol. Sem., 1954-57; ThD, U. Basil, 1963. Minister Vienna (Austria) Community Ch., 1958-60; asst. prof. Dartmouth Coll., Hanover, N.H., 1963-65; Paul B. Freeland prof. religion Davidson (N.C.) Coll., 1965—, faculty chair, 1991-94; vis. prof. Princeton (N.J.) Theol. Sem., 1973, 86, 87; active The Fulbright Commn., Vienna, Austria, 1958-60. Author: The Systematic Theology of Paul Tillich, 1964, The Freedom of God and Human Liberation, 1991; editor: The Context of Contemporary Theology, 1974. Chair jud. com. Synod of N.C., 1975; moderator Charlotte (N.C.) Presbytery, 1985, active, 1972—; active Kincaid for Congress Com., Charlotte, N.C., 1980, Ex. Com. Dem. Party, Davidson, 1975-77. Grad. fellow in theology Princeton Sem., 1957, Younger Scholars fellow NEH, 1969. Mem. Am. Acad. Religion, Calvin Studies Soc., Duodecim Theol. Soc. (sec.), Am. Theol. Soc. Office: Davidson Coll Dept Religion Davidson NC 28036

MCKENNA, ALVIN JAMES, lawyer; b. New Orleans, Aug. 17, 1943; s. Dixon N. Sr. and Mabel (Duplantier) McK.; m. Carol Jean Windheim, 1963; children: Sara, Alvin James Jr., Martha, Andrea, Erin, Rebecca. AB, Canisius Coll., 1963; JD, Notre Dame U., 1966. Bar: N.Y. 1966, Ohio 1967, U.S. Dist. Ct. (so. dist.) Ohio 1968, U.S. Dist. Ct. (no. dist.) Ohio 1978, U.S. Ct. Appeals (6th cir.) 1969, U.S. Supreme Ct. 1977. Law clk. to presiding justice U.S. Dist. Ct. (so. dist.), Columbus, Ohio, 1966-68; asst. U.S. atty., 1968-70; ptnr. Porter, Wright, Morris & Arthur, 1970—. Mem. Gahanna (Ohio) City Council, 1972-80, 82-84; chmn. Gahanna Charter Rev. Commn., 1981; v.p. Community Urban Redevel. Corp., Gahanna, 1984—. Named one of Ten Outstanding Young Persons in Columbus, Jaycees, 1974. Mem. ABA, Ohio Bar Assn., Fed. Bar Assn. (pres. Columbus chpt. 1973-74), Columbus Bar Assn. (chair fed. cts. com. 1972-74). Home: 202 Academy Ct Columbus OH 43230-2104 Office: Porter Wright Morris & Arthur 41 S High St Columbus OH 43215-6101

MCKENNA, ANDREW JAMES, paper distribution and printing company executive, baseball club executive; b. Chgo., Sept. 17, 1929; s. Andrew James and Anita (Fruin) McK.; m. Mary Joan Pickett, June 20, 1953; children: Suzanne, Karen, Andrew, William, Joan, Kathleen, Margaret. B.S., U. Notre Dame, 1951; J.D., DePaul U., 1954. Bar: Ill. Chmn., CEO Schwarz Paper Co. (name now Schwarz), Morton Grove, Ill., 1964—; dir. Chgo. Nat. League Ball Club Inc., Chgo. Bears.; bd. dirs. Dean Foods Co., 1st Nat. Bank Chgo., Skyline Corp., Tribune Co., AON Corp., McDonald's Corp.; bd. govs. Chgo. Stock Exch. Chmn. bd. trustees U. Notre Dame, Mus. Sci. & Industry, Chgo.; bd. dirs. Cath. Charities of Chgo., Children's Meml. Med. Ctr. Chgo. Mem. Chgo. Athletic Assn., Econ. Club, Lyric Opera (bd. dirs.), Chgo. Club, Comml. Club, Econs. Club., Execs. Club Chgo. (chmn.), Glenview Golf Club, Old Elm Club, Merit Club, Casino Club, The Island Club. Home: 60 Locust Rd Winnetka IL 60093-3751 Office: Schwarz 8338 Austin Ave Morton Grove IL 60053-3209

MCKENNA, DAVID LOREN, academic administrator, clergyman, consultant, author; b. Detroit, May 5, 1929; s. William Loren and Ilmi E. (Matson) McK.; m. Janet Voorheis, June 9, 1950; children: David Douglas, Debra Lynn, Suzanne Marie, Robert Bruce. AA, Spring Arbor Jr. Coll., 1949; BA magna cum laude in History, Western Mich. U., 1951; MDiv, Asbury Theol. Sem., 1953; MA, U. Mich., 1955, PhD (Clifford Woody scholar), 1958; LLD, Houghton Coll., 1974, Spring Arbor Coll., 1976, Lewis and Clark Coll., 1978, Seattle U., 1982, Marion Coll., 1983; LHD, Roberts Wesleyan Coll., 1986; DD, Asbury Coll., 1994. Ordained to ministry Free Methodist Ch. N.Am., 1950; dean of men Spring Arbor Jr. Coll., 1953-55, instr. psychology, 1955-60, acad. dean, 1955-57, v.p., 1958-60, pres., 1961-68; lectr. higher edn. U. Mich., 1958-60; asst. prof., coord. Ctr. for the Study of Higher Edn., Ohio State U., Columbus, 1960-61; pres. Seattle Pacific U., 1968-82, Asbury Theol. Sem., 1982-94, pres. emeritus, 1994—; del. World Meth. Coun., London, 1966, Nairobi, Kenya, 1987, Singapore, 1991, v.p. N.Am. sect., 1987—; chmn. Mich. Commn. Coll. Accrediting, 1966-68; bd. dirs. Council Advancement Small Colls., 1964-67; pres. Assn. Free Meth. Colls., 1968-70; chmn. Christian Coll. Consortium, 1970-74; participant Internat. Congress World Evangelization, 1974, Consultation on World Evangelization, Pattaya, Thailand, 1980, Lausanne II, Manila, 1989; mem. bd. adminstrn., exec. com. Nat. Assn. Evangelicals, 2d v.p., 1975-81; bd. reference Black Evangelistic Enterprise, Evangelicals for Social Action, Ugandan Relief, Youth for Christ Internat. Author: The Jesus Model, 1976, Awake, My Conscience!, 1977, The Communicator's Commentary: Mark, 1982, The Communicator's Commentary: Job, 1986, Renewing Our Ministry, 1986, Mega Truth, 1986, The Whisper of His Grace, 1987, Discovering Job, 1988, Power to Follow, Grace to Lead, 1989, Love Your Work, 1990, The Coming Great Awakening, 1990, Communicator's Commentary on Isaiah, vol. I, 1993, vol. II, 1994, When Our Parents Need Us Most, 1994, A Future With A History: The Wesleyan Witness of the Free Methodist Church, vols. I and II, 1995; exec. editor: The Urban Crisis, 1969, Minister's Personal Library, 1987-89, Religious Book Club, 1989—; nat. radio commentator: This Is Our World, 1983—; contbr. articles to profl. jours. Pres. United Community Services, Jackson, Mich., 1968, Wash. Coll. Assn., 1970, 76; trustee United Way, Pacific Sci. Ctr., Seattle Found., Spring Arbor Coll., 1983—; bd. dirs. Bread for the World, 1980-86, Jr. Achievement, 1966-68, Land O'Lakes council Boy Scouts Am., 1965-68; mem. Wash. State Council Postsecondary Edn., 1969-74, Pacific Sci. Ctr., 1969-82, Seattle Found., 1975-82; v.p. Bluegrass Tomorrow, 1989-93; chmn. R & D com. United Way Bluegrass, 1984-89, bd. dirs., 1987-93; sec. Nat. Religious Partnership Environment, 1993-95. Named One of Outstanding Young Men of Yr., Jr. C. of C., Seattle and Puget Sound, 1965, Outstanding Citizen of Yr., 1976, Outstanding Educator, Religious Heritage of Am., 1993; recipient Others award Salvation Army, 1994; Named in his honor McKenna Hall, Seattle Pacific U., 1983, David L. and Janet McKenna Chapel, Ashbury Theol. Sem., 1994. Mem. Assn. Am. Colls. (dir. 1974-77), Ind. Colls. Wash. (pres. 1969-71, co-chmn. 1968-70, 79-80), Wash. State Council Econ. Edn. (dir. 1980), Am. Council Edn. (interassn. pres.'s com. on accreditation 1979-80), N.W. Assn. Schs. and Colls. (commr. 1975-79), N. Central Assn. Colls. and Schs. (chmn., dir. 1966-68), Nat. Assn. Ind. Colls. and Univs. (dir. 1976-80, sec. 1978), Council Postsecondary Accreditation (dir. 1979—), Seattle C. of C., Wash. Friends of Higher Edn., Wash. Athletic Club (bd. govs.), Rainier Club (Seattle), The Diet Club, Lafayette (Ky.) Club, Lexington Tennis Club, Rotary (pres. Jackson chpt. 1966-67, Paul Harris fellow 1982), Phi Kappa Phi.

MCKENNA, FRANK JOSEPH, Canadian politician, lawyer; b. Apohaqui, N.B., Can., Jan. 19, 1948; s. Durward and Olive (Moody) McK.; m. Julie Friel; children: Tobias John, Christine Alice, James Durward. BA with honors, St. Francis Xavier U., 1970; postgrad., Queen's U., 1970-71; LLB, U. N.B., 1974; DSc (hon.), Université de Moncton, Can., 1988; LLD (hon.), University of N.B., Can., 1988, Mt. Allison U., Can., 1991. Spl. asst. to pres. Privy Council, 1971; rsch. asst. Constl. Law Unit, 1973-74; v.p. U. N.B. Faculty of Law Liberal Assn., Fredericton, 1974; ptnr. Martin, Lordon, McKenna & Bowes, Chatham, 1974-87; mem. N.B. Liberal Party, 1982, leader, 1985; premier Province of N.B., Fredericton, 1987—. Recipient Vanier award, 1988, Distinction award Can. Advanced Tech. Assn., 1994; named Econ. Developer of Yr., Econ. Developers' Assn. Can., 1993, Chair, Can. Quality Month, 1994. Mem. Can. Bar Assn., N.B. Bar Assn. Liberal. Avocations: jogging, baseball, hockey. Office: PO Box 6000, Fredericton, NB Canada E3B 5H1

MCKENNA, GEORGE LAVERNE, art museum curator; b. Detroit, Dec. 7, 1924; s. John LaVerne and Carolyn Georgia (Schwab) McK.; m. Janice Ballinger, July 22, 1966. Student, U. Oreg., 1943-44, U. Calif., Berkeley, 1948-49, U. Chgo., 1950; AB, Wayne State U., 1948, MA, 1951. Curator prints, drawings and photographs Nelson-Atkins Mus. Art, Kansas City, Mo., 1952—; cons. Hallmark Cards, Inc., Kansas City, 1974-76. Curator, author exhbn. and coll. catalogues. With U.S. Army, 1943-46. Mem. Am. Assn. Mus., Print Coun. Am. Office: Nelson-Atkins Mus Art 4525 Oak St Kansas City MO 64111-1818

MCKENNA, J. FRANK, III, lawyer; b. Pitts., Nov. 9, 1948; s. J. Frank Jr. and Antoinette (Schlafly) McK.; m. Colleen Shaughnessy, Mar. 25, 1972; children: Collette M., J. Frank IV, Laura J., Stephen J. BA, Williams Coll., 1970; JD, U. Pitts., 1973. Bar: Pa. 1973. Assoc. Thorp, Reed & Armstrong, Pitts., 1973-82, ptnr., 1982-88; ptnr. Babst, Calland, Clements & Zomnir, Pitts., 1988—. Served to lt. USAFR, 1973-74. Named one of Outstanding Young Men In Am., 1982. Mem. ABA, Pa. Bar Assn., Allegheny County Bar Assn. (chmn. young lawyers sect. 1980, v.p. 1987, bd. govs. 1988-90, pres.-elect 1991, pres. 1992), Am. Law Inst., Acad. Trial Lawyers Allegheny County, Am. Judicature Soc., Pitts. Field Club, Pitts. Athletic Assn. Home: 101 Fox Ridge Farms Dr Pittsburgh PA 15215-1142 Office: Babst Calland Clements & Zomnir 2 Gateway Ctr Pittsburgh PA 15222-1402

MCKENNA, JOHN DENNIS, environmental testing engineer; b. N.Y.C., Apr. 1, 1940; s. Hubert Guy and Elizabeth Ann (Record) McK.; BSChemE,

Manhattan Coll., 1961; MSChemE, Newark Coll. Engring., 1968; MBA, Rider Coll., 1974, PhD, Walden U., 1991; m. Christel Klages, Dec. 26, 1964; children: Marc, Michelle. Tech. asst. to pres. Eldib Engring. & Rsch. Co., Newark, 1964-67; project mgr. Princeton Chem. Rsch., Inc. (N.J.), 1967-68; projects dir. Rsch. Cottrell Environ. Systems, Bound Brook, N.J., 1968-72; v.p., then pres. Enviro-Systems & Rsch., Inc., Roanoke, Va., 1973-79; pres. ETS, Inc., Roanoke, 1979-91; chmn. bd., pres. ETS Internat. Inc., 1991—; chmn. air pollution adv. bd. State of Va., 1993; workshop lectr. and sci reviewer publs. EPA, 1978-79. Author chpts. to books; contbr. articles to profl. jours. Recipient Outstanding Engring. Grad. Manhattan Coll. Centennial award, 1992. Mem. AIChE (treas. Ctrl. Va. chpt.), Air Pollution Control Assn., Air and Waste Mgmt. Assn. (divsn. chmn. tech. coun., Pitts.), Tau Beta Pi (N.Y. Xi chpt., Eminent engr.). Roman Catholic. Home: RR 1 Box 1925 Rocky Mount VA 24151-9607 Office: ETS Inc 1401 Municipal Rd NW Roanoke VA 24012-1309

MCKENNA, KATHLEEN KWASNIK, artist; b. Detroit, Nov. 6, 1946; d. John J. and Eleanor H. (Ciosek) K.; m. Frank J. McKenna, Jr., Mar. 16, 1968. Cert., Cooper Sch. Art, Cleve., 1973; student, Art Students' League, N.Y.C., 1972, 74. Instr. portrait painting Baycrafters, Bay Village, Ohio, 1976-79; self-employed painter, 1972—. One-person shows include Ctrl. Nat. Bank, Cleve., 1975, Women's City Club Gallery, Cleve., 1979, Kennedy Ctr. Art Gallery, Hiram, Ohio, 1980, Chime Art Gallery, Summit, N.J., 1985, Bolton Art Gallery, Cleve., 1986, 91, Lakeland C.C. Gallery, Kirtland, Ohio, 1996; group shows include Butler Inst. Am. Art, 1981, 89, 91, 93, Mansfield (Ohio) Art Ctr., 1990, Circle Gallery, N.Y.C., 1978, Canton (Ohio) Art Inst., 1990, others. Recipient Pres.'s award Am. Artists Profl. League, 1993, other awards. Mem. New Orgn. for the Visual Arts, Catharine Lorillard Wolfe Art Club (Pastel Soc. plaque 1989, Mae Berlind Bach award 1983, Cert. of Merit 1981), Allied Artists Am. (assoc.; Gold medal of Honor 1989). Roman Catholic. Avocations: art-related travel, tennis, skiing. Studio: 15914 Chadbourne Rd Shaker Heights OH 44120

MCKENNA, LAWRENCE M., federal judge; b. 1933. AB, Fordham Coll., 1956; LLB, Columbia U., 1959. With Simpson Thacher & Bartlett, N.Y.C., 1959-69, Wormser, Kiely, Alessandroni, Hyde & McCann, N.Y.C., 1969-90; judge U.S. Dist. Ct. (so. dist.), N.Y., 1990—. Mem. N.Y. State Bar Assn., Copyright Soc. USA. Office: US Dist Ct US Courthouse 500 Pearl St New York NY 10007*

MC KENNA, MALCOLM CARNEGIE, vertebrate paleontologist, curator, educator; b. Pomona, Calif., July 21, 1930; s. Donald Carnegie and Bernice Caroline (Waller) McK.; m. Priscilla Coffey, June 17, 1952; children: Douglas M., Katharine L., Andrew M., Bruce C. B.A., U. Calif., Berkeley, 1954, Ph.D., 1958. Instr. dept. paleontology U. Calif., Berkeley, 1958-59; asst. curator dept. vertebrate paleontology Am. Mus. Natural History, N.Y.C., 1960-64; assoc. curator Am. Mus. Natural History, 1964-65; Frick assoc. curator, chmn. Frick Lab., 1965-68, Frick curator, 1968—; asst. prof. geology Columbia U., N.Y.C., 1960-64, assoc. prof., 1964-72, prof. geol. scis., 1972—; research assoc. U. Colo. Mus., Boulder, 1962—. Contbr. articles on fossil mammals and their evolution, the dating of Mesozoic and Tertiary sedimentary rocks, and paleogeography and plate tectonics to profl. jours. Bd. dirs. Bergen Community (N.J.) Mus., 1964-67, pres., 1965-66; trustee Flat Rock Brook Nature Assn., N.J., 1979-93, Raymond Alf Mus., Webb Sch. of Calif., 1980—, Dwight-Englewood Sch., Englewood, N.J., 1968-80; bd. dirs. Flat Rock Brook Nature Assn., N.J., 1979-84; trustee Claremont McKenna Coll., Calif., 1983-91; Planned Parenthood Bergen County, N.J., 1979-88, Mus. No. Ariz., 1978-85, 87-93. Nat. Acad. Scis. exchange fellow USSR, 1965. Fellow AAAS, Explorers Club, Geol. Soc. Am.; mem. Grand Canyon Natural History Assn. (bd. dirs. 1972-76), Soc. Systematic Zoology (coun. 1974-77), Soc. Vertebrate Paleontology (v.p. 1975, pres. 1976), Am. Geophys. Union, Am. Soc. Mammalogists, Paleontol. Soc. (award 1992), Soc. for Study Evolution, Polish Acad. Scis. (fgn.), Sigma Xi. Office: Am Mus Nat History Vertebrate Paleontology Central Park St W New York NY 10026-4355

MCKENNA, MARGARET ANNE, college president; b. R.I., June 3, 1945; d. Joseph John and Mary (Burns) McK.; children: Michael Aaron McKenna Miller, David Christopher McKenna Miller. BA in Sociology, Emmanuel Coll., 1967; postgrad., Boston Coll. Law Sch., 1968; JD, So. Meth. U., 1971; LLD (hon.), U. Upsala, N.J., 1978, Fitchburg (Mass.) State Coll., 1979, Regis Coll., 1982; D Community Affairs, U. R.I., 1979. Bar: Tex. 1971, D.C. 1973. Atty. Dept. Justice, Washington, 1971-73; exec. dir. Internat. Assn. Ofcl. Human Rights Agys., Washington, 1973-74; mgmt. cons. Dept. Treasury, Washington, 1975-76; dep. council to Pres. White House, Washington, 1976-79; dep. undersec. Dept. Edn., Washington, 1979-81; dir. Mary Ingraham Bunting Inst., Radcliffe Coll., Cambridge, Mass., 1981-85; v.p. program planning Radcliffe Coll., Cambridge, 1982-85; pres. Lesley Coll., Cambridge, 1985—; bd. dirs. Stride Rite Corp., Cambridge, Best Products Co., Inc., Richmond, Va., Consolidated Natural Gas Co., Pitts., Coun. of Ind. Colls., Washington. Chair higher edn. task force Clinton Transition, 1992-93; chair edn. task force Mayor Thomas Menino Transition Com., 1994. Recipient Outstanding Contribution award Civil Rights Leadership Conf., 1978; named Woman of Yr. Women's Equity Action League, 1979, Outstanding Woman of Yr. Big Sister Assn., 1986. Democrat. Office: Lesley Coll Office of the President 29 Everett St Cambridge MA 02138-2790

MCKENNA, MARIANNE, architect; b. Montreal, Que., Can., Sept. 25, 1950; d. Richard D. and Anna M. (Lohr) McK.; m. Ian C.; children: Cameron Lohr, Portia McKinley. Attended, The Study Montreal, 1969; BA, Swarthmore Coll., 1972; MArch, Yale U., 1976. Asst. architect Bobrow & Fieldman, Montreal, Can., 1976-78; architect Denys Lasdun, Redhouse & Softley, London, 1978-79; architect Barton Myers Assocs., 1980-87, assoc., 1981—; founding ptnr. Kuwabara Payne McKenna Blumberg Archs., Toronto, 1987—; assoc. prof. architecture U. Toronto, 1994—; guest critic, U. Toronto, U. Waterloo, McGill U., Yale U., 1975-87; exec. dir. Ont. Coll. of Art. Selected projects include Union Libr., Toronto, Hasbro Toy Co., N.Y.C.; selected projects present firm York U. Ctr. Fine Arts 3, Tudhope Assocs. Design Studios Toronto, 35 E. Wacker Addition Corp., Kitchener City Hall, Royal Conservatory of Music Master Plan, Facility for Federally Sentenced Women, Kitchener, Home for the Aged Providence Ctr. Recipient Gov. Gen.'s award for Architecture, Royal Archtl. Inst. Can., 1994. Mem. Ont. Assn. Architects, Ordre des architectes de Québec, Royal Architecture Inst. Can. Office: Kuwabara Payne McKenna Blumberg Archs, 322 King St W 3rd Fl, Toronto, ON Canada M5V 1J2

MCKENNA, MATTHEW MORGAN, lawyer; b. Washington, Apr. 29, 1950; s. James Aloysius and Rebecca (Rial) McK.; m. Nancy Fitzpatrick, Sept. 11, 1976; children: Matthew, James, Christine, Connor. BA, Hamilton Coll., 1972; JD, Georgetown U., 1975, LLM, 1978. Bar: N.Y. 1977. Clk. to Hon. Fred B. Ugast, Superior Ct., Washington, 1975-76; assoc. Olwine, Connelly, N.Y.C., 1976-79; assoc. Winthrop, Stimson, Putnam & Roberts, N.Y.C., 1979-83, ptnr., 1984-93; v.p. taxes PepsiCo, Purchase, N.Y., 1993—; adj. prof. Sch. Law, Fordham U., N.Y.C., 1983-94. Trustee Merrill Lynch Found., 1986-95, Mt. St. Mary's Coll., Emmitsburg, Md., 1994—. Mem. ABA (tax sect.), N.Y. State Bar Assn. (chmn. com. on fgn. activities of U.S. taxpayers), Assn. Bar City N.Y. (com. internat. taxation). Home: 35 Valley Rd Bronxville NY 10708-2226 Office: PepsiCo 700 Anderson Hill Rd Purchase NY 10577-1403

MCKENNA, MICHAEL JOSEPH, manufacturing company executive; b. Phila., Feb. 18, 1935; s. Michael J. and Stella Marie (Gramigna) McK.; B.S., LaSalle Coll., 1962; m. Letitia Ward, Feb. 9, 1957; children—Letitia, Carol, Suzanne, Kathleen Jane, Margaret. With Crown Cork & Seal Co., Phila., 1957—, sales rep., 1969, dist. sales mgr., Phila., 1970, regional sales mgr., 1974, v.p. sales and mktg., 1979-86, former sr. v.p., also bd. dirs., exec. v.p., pres. N.Am. Divsn., Crown Cork & Seal Co., Inc., now pres. and COO. Founding bd. dirs. Northampton Twp. Library, 1967-71; pres. Churchville PTA, 1969-70. Served with U.S. Army, 1955-57. Mem. Can. Mfrs. Inst. (standing com. 1980—). Republican. Roman Catholic. Club: Old Guard Soc. Home: 247 Magnolia Dr Southampton PA 18966-1456 Office: Crown Cork & Seal Co Inc 9300 Ashton Rd Philadelphia PA 19136

MCKENNA, RICHARD HENRY, hospital consultant; b. Covington, Ky., Dec. 19, 1927; s. Charles Joseph and Mary Florence (Wieck) McK.; m. Patricia M. Macdonald, Jan. 6, 1979; children: Linda Ann, Theresa K., Joan Marie; stepchildren: Stuart J Goodman, Ann Elizabeth Goodman. BS in Commerce, U. Cin., 1959; MBA, Xavier U., 1963. CPA. Acct., Andrew Jergens Co., Cin., 1947-55; treas., dir. Ramsey Bus. Equipment, Inc., Cin., 1955-59; asst. to pres. Oakley Die and Mfg. Co., Cin.,1959-60, Electro-Jet Tool Co., Inc., Cin., 1959-60; pvt. practice acctg., No. Ky. and Cin., 1960-62; bus. mgr. St. Joseph Hosp., Lexington, Ky., 1962-66; asst. adminstr. fin. U. Ky. Hosp., Lexington, 1966-70; v.p., CFO St. Lawrence Hosp., Lansing, Mich., 1970-87; adj. faculty Aquinas Coll., Grand Rapids, Mich., 1980-89, asst. prof.; chmn. bd. McKenna & McKenna Assocs., Inc., 1983—; chmn. bd. North Grand River Coop. Laundry, 1986-87; v.p., CFO, asst. sec. and treas. St. Joseph's Hosp., Inc., Savannah, Ga., 1987-95, St. Joseph's Health Ctr., Inc., 1987-90, v.p. Midland Enterprises, Richmond Hill, Ga. Former mem. adv. com. to commr. of fin. State of Ky.; chmn. cath. divsn. Oak Hills Bus. Com.; mem. speakers com. Oak Hill Sch. Dist.; bd. dirs. Savannah YMCA, 1992-94, exec. com., 1994-96, YMCA Habersham Branch, 1992-96, chmn. bd. 1994-96. Served with U.S. Mcht. Marine, 1945-47, U.S. Army, 1948-51. Mem. Healthcare Fin. Mgmt. Assn. (Follmer award, past dir. Ky. chpt.), Am. Mgmt. Assn., Am. Inst. CPAs, Ky. Soc. CPAs, Mich. Hosp. Assn. (former mem. com. on reimbursement), Ga. Hosp. Assn. (com. on fin. and mgmt.), Delta Mu Delta, Alpha Sigma Lambda.

MCKENNA, SIDNEY F., technical company executive; b. Detroit, Nov. 27, 1922; s. Michael James and Elizabeth Josephine McK.; m. Helen Mary Spiroff, Sept. 20, 1944; children—Lynne Marie McKenna Hoss, Dennis Michael, Patrick Conlon, Mary Elizabeth McKenna Raimondi, Maureen T. McKenna Anderson, Christopher John. A.B., U. Mich., Ann Arbor, 1947; M.A., Wayne State U., 1948. With Ward Baking Co., Detroit, 1939-41; prodn. worker Cadillac Motor Co. (div. Gen. Motors Corp.), Detroit, 1941-42; mem. indsl. relations staff Ford Motor Co., Dearborn, Mich., 1942-79, v.p., 1974-79; sr. v.p. human resources United Techs. Corp., Hartford, Conn., 1980-86, sr. v.p. employee and external relations, 1986-87, sr. v.p. pub. affairs, 1987-90; ret., 1990; bd. dirs. Schwartz Value Fund. Chmn. adv. bd. Providence Hosp., Detroit, 1972-80; bd. dirs. Brighton (Mich.) Hosp., 1976-80, Mercy Coll., Detroit, 1976-80, United Found., 1976-80, St. Francis Hosp., Hartford, Conn., 1983-89, St. Joseph's Coll., 1988-89. Served with USN, 1942-46. Decorated knight St. Gregory. Mem. Labor Policy Assn. (chmn.), Bus. Roundtable, Orgn. Resources Counselors, Nat. Assn. Mfrs. (bd. dirs. 1988-89), Bloomfield Hills Country Club, Birmingham Athletic Club, Mariner Sands Golf Club, K.C. Roman Catholic. Home: 5680 SE Winged Foot Dr Stuart FL 34997-8642

MCKENNA, STEPHEN JAMES, lawyer, corporate executive; b. Islip, N.Y., Sept. 4, 1940; s. John Paul and Margaret (Foley) McK.; m. Lolita Andrea deLeon, Aug. 24, 1963; children: Stephen Jr., Christopher, Matthew, Andrew. BA magna cum laude, Boston Coll., Chestnut Hill, Mass., 1962; JD, Fordham U., 1965. Bar: N.Y. 1966. D.C. 1970, U.S. Supreme Ct. 1990. Atty. Pan Am. World Airlines, N.Y.C., 1965-67, Ea. Airlines, Washington, 1967-69, Lockheed Aircraft Corp., Washington, 1969-72; pvt. practice law Washington, 1972-73; v.p., assoc. gen. counsel Marriott Corp., Bethesda, Md., 1973-93; v.p., gen. counsel Host Marriott Corp., Bethesda, Md., 1993-95, exec. v.p., gen. counsel, 1995—; continuing legal edn. panelist Georgetown U. Law Ctr. Founder, pres. Civic Assn. River Falls, Potomac, Md., 1976; committeeman troop 1427 Boy Scouts Am., Potomac, 1977-93; mem. fin. com. St. Bartholomew's Ch., Bethesda, 1979—, chmn. sch. bd., 1979; bd. trustees Marymount U., Arlington, Va., 1992—. Mem. ABA (panelist), Am. Coll. Real Estate Lawyers (panelist), D.C. Bar Assn., Assn. Bar City N.Y., N.Y. State Bar Assn. Democrat. Office: Host Marriott Corp 10400 Fernwood Rd Bethesda MD 20817-1109

MCKENNA, TERENCE PATRICK, insurance company executive; b. Oldham, Lancashire, Eng., Sept. 3, 1928; came to U.S., 1929, naturalized, 1939; s. Patrick A. and Mary F. McK.; m. Patricia Buckley, Sept. 22, 1973. Student, St. Thomas Coll., Bloomfield, Conn., 1946-48. With John Hancock Mut. Life Ins. Co., 1951-87; gen. agt. John Hancock Mut. Life Ins. Co., Cherry Hill, N.J., 1963-67; field v.p. gen. agy. dept. John Hancock Mut. Life Ins. Co., Atlanta, 1967-69; field v.p. dist. agy. dept. John Hancock Mut. Life Ins. Co., Boston, 1969-73, 2d v.p. mktg. ops. dept., 1973-74, v.p. dept., 1974-76, sr. v.p. dept., 1976-83, sr. v.p. gen. agy. sales dept., 1983-87; ret. 1987; v.p., also bd. dirs. John Hancock Variable Life Ins. Co.; chmn. bd. mgrs. I.V.A.; bd. dirs. John Hancock Distbrs. Inc., John Hancock Property and Casualty Ins. Co. Served with USMC, 1952-54. Mem. Am. Coll. Life Underwriters, Am. Soc. CLU's, Palm Beach Gardens, Ballen Isles C. C., Univ. Club (Boston), Woods Hole Golf Club (Falmouth, Mass.). Clubs: Univ. (Boston).

MCKENNA, THOMAS MORRISON, JR., social services organization executive; b. Chgo., July 19, 1937; s. Thomas Morrison and Martha (Stanley) McK.; m. Kay Mary O'Connor, Sept. 10, 1960; children: Mark, Lisa. BA, De Pauw U., 1959; MSW, Columbia U., 1961. Group worker Hamilton-Madison House, N.Y.C., 1961-63, exec. dir., 1967-71; assoc. exec. dir. Bronx (N.Y.) River Neighborhood House, 1963-67; exec. dir. United Neighborhood Houses, N.Y.C., 1971-76, State Communities Aid Assn., N.Y.C. and Albany, N.Y., 1976-85; nat. exec. dir. Big Bros./Big Sisters Am., Phila., 1985—; asst. prof. NYU Sch. Social Work, 1974-82; mem. bd. overseers U. Pa. Sch. Social Work, 1991—. Mem. bd. local sch. dist. 8, Bronx, 1964-67; coun. against poverty N.Y.C. Antipoverty Bd., 1971-76; adv. bd. Columbia U. Sch. Social Work, 1980-84; chmn. adv. bd. N.Y.C. Dept. Social Svcs., 1977-85. Mem. NASW (pres. N.Y.C. chpt. 1983-85), One to One Found. Avocations: sailing, tennis. Home: 1307 E Susquehanna Ave Philadelphia PA 19125-2823 Office: Big Bros/Big Sisters Am 230 N 13th St Philadelphia PA 19107-1538

MC KENNA, WILLIAM EDWARD, business executive; b. Boston, Aug. 9, 1919; s. Alfred W. and Mary E.C. (Quigley) McK.; children: William P., Kathleen M., Daniel J., Eileen F., Paul V., Mary Ellen; m. Mary N. Smith, Oct. 3, 1968. A.B., Holy Cross Coll., 1947; M.B.A., Harvard, 1949. Diplomate: C.P.A., N.Y., Calif. Staff accountant Touche, Niven, Bailey & Smart, N.Y.C., 1949-52; v.p., controller Monroe Calculating Machine Co., Orange, N.J., 1952-60; also dir.; v.p., treas., controller Litton Industries, Beverly Hills, Calif., 1960-63; sr. v.p. Litton Industries Bus. Equipment Group, Beverly Hills, 1964-67; also dir.; chmn., chief exec., dir. Hunt Foods & Industries, Inc., Fullerton, Calif., 1967-68; chmn., chief exec., dir. Norton Simon, Inc., Fullerton, 1968-69; bus. cons., 1969-70; chmn., dir. Technicolor, Inc., Hollywood, Calif., 1970-76; chmn. bd. Sambo's Restaurants, Inc., Santa Barbara, Calif., 1979-81, Vencap, Inc., Irvine, Calif., 1977-79; now gen. ptnr. MCK Investment Co., Beverly Hills, Calif.; bd. dirs. Calif. Amplifier, Inc., Safeguard Health Enterprises, Inc., Calprop Corp., WMS Industries, Inc., Williams Hospitality Group, Drexler Tech., Inc.. Mem. pres.'s council, regent, assoc. trustee Coll. Holy Cross; trustee St. John's Hosp. Found.; regent St. Mary's Coll., Calif. Mem. Am. Inst. C.P.A.s, Nat. Assn. Accts., Fin. Execs. Inst., Calif. Soc. C.P.A.s, N.Y. Soc. C.P.A.s, N.J. Soc. C.P.A.s, Tailhook Assn., Delta Epsilon, Alpha Sigma Nu. Home and Office: 912 Oxford Way Beverly Hills CA 90210-2841

MCKENNA, WILLIAM JOHN, textile products executive; b. N.Y.C., Oct. 11, 1926; s. William T. and Florence (Valis) McK.; m. Jean T. McNulty, Aug. 27, 1949 (dec. Nov. 1984); children: Kevin, Marybeth, Peter, Dawn; m. Karen Lynne Hilgert, Aug. 6, 1988; children: Katherine Lynne, William John IV. BBA, Iona Coll., 1949; M.S. (Univ. Store Service scholar), NYU, 1950. V.p. Hat Corp. Am., N.Y.C., 1961-63, v.p. mktg., 1961-63, exec. v.p., 1963-67; pres. Manhattan Shirt Co., N.Y.C., 1967-74, Lee Co., Inc., Shawnee Mission, Kans., 1974-82, also dir.; pres., dir. Kellwood Co., St. Louis, 1982—, chief exec. officer, 1984—, also bd. dirs., chmn., CEO, 1991—; dir. Genovese Drug Stores, Melville, N.Y., United Mo. Bancshares, Kansas City, Mo., United Mo. Bank of St. Louis, Cardinal Ritter Inst. Trustee St. Louis U., Boys Hope; permanent deacon Archdiocese St. Louis. With USN, 1944-46, PTO. Mem. Sovereign Mil. Order Malta, St. Louis Club, Bellerive Country Club. Roman Catholic. Office: Kellwood Co PO Box 14374 Saint Louis MO 63178-4374

MCKENNA, WILLIAM MICHAEL, advertising executive; b. Washington, Apr. 4, 1951; s. William H. and Betty Ann (Cashin) McK.; m. Lynn Stevenson, Dec. 18, 1976; children: James Langdon, Lee Stevenson. BA, Wesleyan U., 1973; MS in Journalism, Boston U., 1978. V.p., creative dir. Ingalls Quinn & Johnson, Boston, 1981-88; sr. v.p., creative dir. Young & Rubicam, N.Y.C., 1988-94; chief creative officer, exec. v.p. AF GL Internat., N.Y.C., 1994-95; mng. dir., chief creative officer Citigate Albert Frank, N.Y.C., 1996—. Recipient Clio, Hatch, N.Y. Film Soc. creative advt. awards, 1982-95. Home: 16 Salt Box Ln Darien CT 06820 Office: Citigate Albert Frank 850 3d Ave New York NY 10022

MCKENNEE, ARDEN NORMA, art educator, retired, consultant; b. N.Y.C.; d. Archibald McKennee and Norma (Bischof) Kirkley. BA, U. Minn., 1953. Exec. sec. John & Mable Ringling Mus. of Art, Sarasota, Fla., 1964-79, mus. edn. programmer, 1980-94; ret., 1994. Mem. Very Spl. Arts Adv. Bd. for Sarasota County, 1988-94. Mem. Nat. Art Edn. Assn., Delta Gamma Alumni Assn.

MC KENNEY, WALTER GIBBS, JR., lawyer, publishing company executive; b. Jacobsville, Md., Apr. 22, 1913; s. Walter Gibbs and Mary (Starkey) McK.; m. Florence Roberta Rea, July 17, 1939. Student, Dickinson Sem., 1935-37; Ph.B. Dickinson Coll., 1939; J.D., U. Va., 1942; LL.D., Dickinson Sch. Law, 1964; LHD, Lycoming Coll., 1984. Bar: Md. 1942. Practiced in Balt., 1942—; partner McKenney, Thomsen & Burke; partner, gen. mgr., editor Taxes & Estates Pub. Co., Balt., 1946—; chmn. trust com. Equitable Bank, N.A., Balt., 1970-84; dir. Equitable Bancorp., 1960-84; lectr. Southwestern Grad. Sch. Banking, 1966-76. Editor Taxes and Estates, 1946—, Minimizing Taxes, 1946-84, The Educator, 1965—, The Patron, 1968-84. Pres. Kelso Home for Girls; mem. bd. child care Balt. Conf. Meth. Ch., pres., 1961-64; pres. Balt. Estate Planning Council, 1963-64; trustee Goucher Coll., 1968-84, Dickinson Coll., Lycoming Coll., Wesley Theol. Sem., Loyola Coll. at Balt., 1975-83, Franklin Sq. Hosp., Franklin Square Found., Franklin Square Health System, Helix Health System. Served to lt. USNR, 1942-45. Mem. ABA, Md., Balt. bar assns. Republican. Methodist. Home: 105 Brightwood Club Dr Lutherville MD 21093-3628 Office: One N Charles St Ste 400 Baltimore MD 21201

MCKENNON, KEITH ROBERT, chemical company executive; b. Condon, Oreg., Dec. 25, 1933; s. Russel M. and Lois E. (Edgerton) McK.; m. Patricia Dragon, Sept. 30, 1961; children: Brian, Marc, Kevin. B.S., Oreg. State U., 1955. Rsch. chemist Dow Chem. Co., Pittsburg, Calif., 1955-67; sales mgr. Dow Chem. Co., Houston, 1967; research mgr. Dow Chem. Co., Midland, Mich., 1968-69, bus. mgr., 1969-80, v.p., 1980-83, group v.p., 1983-87, exec. v.p., 1987-92, also bd. dirs.; pres. Dow USA, 1987-90; chmn., chief exec. officer Dow Corning Corp., 1992-94, also bd. dirs.; chmn. PacifiCorp, Portland, Oreg., 1994—; bd. dirs. PacifiCorp, Tektronix. Patentee. Recipient Chemical Industry medal Soc. of Chemical Industry, 1994. Republican. Presbyterian. Home: PO Box 5542 Stateline NV 89449-5542 Office: PacifiCorp Ste 1600 700 NE Multnomah St Portland OR 97232-4116

MCKENNY, COLLIN GRAD, banker; b. Seattle, July 29, 1944; d. Edward Paul and Betty B. (Collins) Grad; m. Jon W. McKenny, June 15, 1975 (div. June 1982); m. Spencer Frank Lson, Dec. 31, 1985. BA, U. Wash., Seattle, 1966; MBA, Seattle U., 1969; grad., Pacific Coast Banking Sch., 1979. From mgmt. trainee to v.p. Peoples Nat. Bank, Seattle, 1966-85; sr. v.p. Barclays Bank of Calif., San Francisco, 1985-88, Star Banc Corp., Cin., 1988—. Treas. Salvation Army, Federal Way, Wash., 1981-83; bd. dirs. Boys and Girls Clubs, Seattle, 1982-85; mem. risk adv. bds. Visa USA and Visa Internat. Mem. Am. Bankers Assn. (bd. dirs. bancard exec. com., chmn. ann. conf. 1989—, chmn. bankcard schools 1990-94), Cin. Bus. Incubator (chmn.), Bankers Club, Chi Omega. Office: Star Banc Corp 311 Elm St PO Box 956 Cincinnati OH 45201-0956

MCKENNY, LAWRENCE, religious organization administrator; m. Debbie McKenny; 2 children. BS in Bible, Phila. Coll. Bible, Langhorne, Pa., 1972; MA in Ednl. Ministries, Wheaton (Ill.) Coll., 1974; EdD in Ednl. Adminstrn., Temple U., 1986. Ordained to ministry Evang. Free Ch., 1974. Former pastor local chs., N.J., Pa.; exec. dir. Fay-West Youth for Christ, Uniontown, Pa., 1972-73, 74-80; dean students, v.p. for student devel. Phila. Coll. Bible, 1980-93; pres. Providence Coll. and Sem., 1993—, Assn. Can. Bible Colls., Three Hills, Alta.; former instr. numerous grad. and postgrad. ednl.-related fields; frequent spkr. for chs., confs., seminars; former mem. or chmn. 6 evaluation teams Accrediting Assn. Bible Colls.; mem. coun. Evang. Fellowship Can. Contbr. numerous articles to mags. and ednl. jours. Avocations: reading, history, running, weightlifting, watching sports. Office: Assn Can Bible Colls, PO Box 173, Three Hills, AB Canada T0M 2A0

MC KENZIE, HAROLD CANTRELL, JR., retired manufacturing executive; b. Carrollton, Ga., Dec. 25, 1931; s. Harold Cantrell and Sue (Tanner) McK.; m. Katherine Branch, Apr. 11, 1958; children—Ansley, Katherine, Harold Cantrell, III. B.Indsl. Engring., Ga. Inst. Tech., 1953; J.D., Emory U., 1955; A.M.P., Harvard Bus. Sch. Bar: Ga. 1955. Law clk. to judge U.S. Dist. Ct., Atlanta, 1956; ptnr. firm Troutman, Sams, Schroder & Lockerman, Atlanta, 1957-67; with Ga. Power Co., 1967-81; dir. Intermet Corp., 1971—; pres. So. Electric Internat., Inc., 1981-85; chmn., chief exec. officer Machine Techs., Inc. (doing bus. as MacTech Inc.), Martinsville, Va., 1986-89; sr. adv. facilities Atlanta Project of Carter Presdl. Ctr., 1992—. Mem. State Bar Ga., Capital City (Atlanta), Piedmont Driving Club. Episcopalian. Office: 172 Huntington Rd NE Atlanta GA 30309-1504

MCKENZIE, HERBERT A(LONZA), pharmaceutical company executive; b. Savannah, Ga., Dec. 23, 1934; s. Herbert A. and Marie L. (Lytjen) McK.; m. Joan B. Baggs, Dec. 17, 1959; children: Catherine B. McKenzie Bowman, Gregory M., Susan M. McKenzie Carson. BS, Clemson U., 1956; grad. exec. program, Stanford U., 1986. Sales mgmt. positions Am. Cyanamid, Wayne, N.J., 1956-71, mktg. mgr., 1971-73, gen. mgr., 1973-80; pres. Hilton Davis Chem. Co. div. Sterling Drug, Inc.; corp. v.p. Sterling Drug, Inc., 1980-81; pres. Sterling Chem. Group, 1982-85, Sterling Japan, Can., Australasia and Pacific Rim Group, Sterling Chem. Group, 1985-88, Sterling Internat.; corp. v.p. Sterling Drug, Inc. subs. Eastman Kodak, 1988-90, corp. exec. v.p.; pres. Sterling Consumer Health Group, N.Y.C., 1991-92; advisor Synthetic Organic Chem. Mfrs. Assn., 1976-78, Industry Sector. Adv. Com., 1977-80, Office Spl. Trade Negotiations, Dept. Commerce, 1977-80, Romanoff Internat., Inc., Charlotte, N.C., 1990-91. Patentee in field. Bd. dirs. Coop. Ireland, 1988-92, Coun. Better Bus. Bur., 1991-92. With USN, 1959. Mem. Dry Colors Mfg. (pres. 1976-78).

MC KENZIE, JOHN MAXWELL, physician; b. Glasgow, Scotland, Nov. 13, 1927; came to U.S., 1980; s. Thomas Wilson and Isabell Connor (Spencer) McK.; m. Vieno Laine Kangas, June 29, 1957; children—Ann, Ian, Lesley, Gordon. M.B., Ch.B., U. St. Andrews, Scotland, 1950, M.D., 1958. Intern U. St. Andrews, 1950-51, resident, 1953-55, fellow, 1955-56, 57-58; research trainee, fellow Tufts U., 1956-57, 58-59; clin. asst. medicine McGill U., Montreal, Que., Can., 1959-61; asst., then assoc. prof. McGill U., 1961-68, prof., 1968-80; prof. U. Miami, 1980—, chmn. dept. medicine, 1980-94. Contbr. numerous articles to profl. jours. Served with Royal Army Med. Corps, 1951-53. Recipient Killam award Can. Coun., 1980. Mem. Am. Thyroid Assn. (Parke-Davis disting. lectr. 1981, pres. 1983-84), Am. Soc. Clin. Investigation, Endocrine Soc. (Ayerst award 1961, Rorer Pharm. Clin. Investigator award 1990), Am. Physiol. Soc., Assn. Am. Physicians, Am. Fedn. Clin. Rsch., AAAS, Internat. Soc. Neuroendocrinology, European Thyroid Assn. (corr.). Home: 12505 SW 63rd Ave Miami FL 33156-5531 Office: U Miami Jackson Meml Med Ctr 1611 NW 12th Ave Miami FL 33136-1005

MCKENZIE, KAY BRANCH, public relations executive; b. Atlanta, Feb. 12, 1936; d. William Harllee and Katherine (Hunter) Branch; m. Harold Cantrell McKenzie, Jr., Apr. 11, 1958; children: Ansley, Katherine, Harold Cantrell III. Student, Sweet Briar Coll., 1955, Emory U., 1956-57. Account exec. Hill and Knowlton Inc., Atlanta, 1979-80, account supr./dir. S.E. govt. rels., 1981-83; ptnr. McKenzie, Gordon & Potter, Atlanta, 1983-85; pres. McKenzie & Assocs. Inc., Atlanta, 1986-89; sr. v.p. Manning Selvage & Lee, Atlanta, 1989-93; v.p. comm. and creative svcs. 1996 Atlanta Paralympic Games, 1993-96. Mem. Commn. on Future of South, 1974; co-chmn. John Lewis for Congress, Atlanta, 1986; bd. dirs. Bedford Pines Day Care Ctrs., Atlanta, 1987-92, Ga. Clean and Beautiful, 1987-88, Ga. Fund for Edn., 1987-92; regional bd. dirs. Inst. Internat. Edn., 1987-93. Fellow Internat. Bus. Fellows (bd. dirs. 1983-85, 92-93, v.p. 1986-88); mem. Pub. Rels. Soc. Am., Ga. C. of C. (bd. dirs. 1983—), Leadership Atlanta. Democrat. Episcopalian. Home: 172 Huntington Rd NE Atlanta GA 30309-1504 Office: 1201 W Peachtree St NW Ste 2500 Atlanta GA 30309-3400

MCKENZIE, KENNETH, retail grocery executive. Chmn. Grocery Supply Cos., Inc., Sulphur Springs, Tex., also bd. dirs. Office: Grocery Supply Cos Inc PO Box 638 130 Hillcrest Dr Sulphur Springs TX 75483-0638*

MCKENZIE, KEVIN PATRICK, artistic director; b. Burlington, Vt., Apr. 29, 1954; s. Raymond James and Ruth (Davison) McK. Grad. high sch., Washington. Mem. corps de ballet Nat. Ballet of Washington, 1972-74; prin. Joffrey Ballet, N.Y.C., 1974-78, Am. Ballet Theatre, N.Y.C., 1979-91; artistic assoc. Washington Ballet, 1991-92; artistic dir. Am. Ballet Theatre, N.Y.C., 1992—; pres. bd. dirs. Am. Ballet Theatre Dancers Fund, Inc., 1982-89; assoc. dir. New Amsterdam Ballet, N.Y.C., 1984—. Appeared in film Unicorn, Gorgon and Monticore, Sta. WETA-TV, Washington, 1971; guest dancer Houston Ballet, 1978, Spoleto Festival, 1980, 84, Theatre des Champs Elysees, Paris, 1981, Sadler's Wells Theatre, London, 1981, Asami Maki Ballet Co., Tokyo, 1983, Aspen Festival, 1982; producer, dir. The Party of the Year, 1982; choreographer Groupo Zambaria Ballet, 1984, Liszt Etudes, 1991, Lucy and the Count, 1992, The Nutcracker, 1993; created roles in Adrienne Dellos' The Blind Man's Daughter, Seoul, Korea, 1986, Amnon V'Tamar, S.P.E.B.S.Q.S.A.; appeared with Martine Van Hamel in Swan Lake, Nat. Ballet of Cuba, Havanna, 1986, Merrill Ashley in Tchaikowsky Pas de Deux, Bolshoi Theater, Moscow, 1986; repertoire as dancer includes La Bayadere, Carmen, Cinderella, Coppelia, Dim Lustre, Don Quixote, Giselle, The Garden of Villandry, Jardin aux lilas, The Leaves Are Fading, Pillar of Fire, Raymonda, Requiem, Rodeo, Romeo and Juliet, The Sleeping Beauty, Swan Lake, La Sylphide; other dances include Paquita, Sylvia Pas de Deux, Theme and Variations. Recipient Silver medal Varna (Bulgaria) Internat. Ballet Competitions, 1972, Artistic Achievement medal Dept. State, U.S. Govt., 1972, Artistic Achievement medal Mayor of Burlington, Vt., 1984, Performing Arts award, Am. Ireland Fund, 1994; Kevin McKenzie Day proclaimed by City of Burlington, 1985. Office: Am Ballet Theatre 890 Broadway New York NY 10003-1211

MC KENZIE, LIONEL WILFRED, economist, educator; b. Montezuma, Ga., Jan. 26, 1919; s. Lionel Wilfred and Lida (Rushin) McK.; m. Blanche Veron, Jan. 2, 1943; children—Lionel Wilfred, Gwendolyn Veron, David Rushin. AB, Duke U., 1939; MA, Princeton U., 1946, PhD, 1956; BLitt, Oxford (Eng.) U., 1949; postgrad., U. Chgo., 1950-51, LLD (hon.), 1991. Asst. economist WPB, 1942; instr. Mass. Inst. Tech., 1946; asst. prof., then asso. prof. Duke, 1948-57; prof. econs. U. Rochester, 1957-64, John Munro prof. econs., 1964-67, Wilson prof. econs., 1967-89, Wilson prof. emeritus, 1989—, chmn. dept., 1957-66; Taussig research prof. Harvard U., 1980-81; Mem. math. div. NRC, 1960-63, mem. behavioral scis. div., 1964-70; mem. math., social scis. bd. Center Advanced Study in Behavioral Scis., Palo Alto, Calif., 1964-70, chmn., 1969-70. Assoc. editor Internat. Econs. Rev., 1964—, Jour. Econ. Theory, 1970-73, Jour. Internat. Econs., 1970-84, Econ. theory, 1991-95; contbr. articles to profl. jours. Served to lt. (s.g.) USNR, 1943-45. Recipient Rising Sun award Japan, 1995; Rhodes scholar Oriel Coll. Oxford U., 1939; Guggenheim fellow, 1973-74; fellow Center for Advanced Study in Behavioral Scis., 1973-74. Fellow Econometric Soc. (coun. 1973-78, pres. 1977), Am. Acad. Arts and Scis., Am. Econ. Assn.; mem. NAS, Royal Econ. Soc., Am. Math. Soc., Am. Econ. Assn. (Disting. Fellow 1993), Phi Beta Kappa (chpt. v.p. 1968-70, chpt. pres. 1972-73). Home: 225 Dorchester Rd Rochester NY 14610-1322

MCKENZIE, LORENE LANDS, marriage and family counselor, educator; b. Arab, Ala., Mar. 3, 1932; d. Alver Lee and Maggie Jane (Nixon) Lands; m. Jesse E. McKenzie, Nov. 22, 1947; children: Barbara Hemrick, Dennis, Rayford J., Debbie Argo, Dianne Morgan. BA in Psychology, West Ga. Coll., 1977, MEd, 1980, postgrad., 1982. Clergy counselor Mt. Pleasant Bapt. Ch., Carrollton, Ga., 1964-84; tchr. Bremen (Ga.) High Sch., 1980-81, Spemedial-Bowdon H.S., 1981-82, Heritage Pvt. Sch., Newman, Ga., 1982-83; pvt. practice counselor in field; indsl. supr. Sewell Mfg. Co., Bremen, Ga., 1970-72, mental health counselor, Carrrollton, 1978. Chaperoned tour group pen-pals to Eng.; mem. Rep. campaign, Carrollton, 1980; speaker, Bible lectr. to women's groups. Avocations: travel, research, reading, flower gardening, music. Home and Office: 218 Perry St Carrollton GA 30117-2423

MCKENZIE, MARY BETH, artist; b. Cleve.; d. William Jennings and Mary Elizabeth (McCray) McK.; m. Tony Mysak, May 8, 1974; children: Zsuzsa McKenzie Mysak, Maria McKenzie Mysak. Student, Mus. Fine Arts, Boston, 1964-65, Cooper Sch. Art, Cleve., 1965-67; diploma, Nat. Acad. Design, N.Y.C., 1974. Painting instr. Nat. Acad. Design, N.Y.C., 1981—. Author: A Painterly Approach, 1987; contbr. articles to profl. jours.; one-woman shows include Nat. Arts Club, N.Y.C., 1976, FAR Gallery, N.Y.C., 1980, Perin and Sharpe Gallery, New Canaan, Conn., 1981, Frank Caro Gallery, N.Y.C., 1988-89, Joseph Keiffer Gallery, N.Y.C., 1991; exhibited in group shows at Sindin Gallery, N.Y.C., 1985-86; permanent collections include Met. Mus. Art, N.Y.C., The Butler Mus. Am. Art, Mus. City of N.Y., NAD, Art Student's League of N.Y. Recipient Nat. Scholastic award Mus. Fine Arts, Boston, numerous awards including Thomas B. Clark prize and the Isaac N. Maynard prize Nat. Acad. Design, Greenshields Found. grantee, Stacey Found. grantee. Mem. Nat. Acad. Design, Pastel Soc. Am. (Best In Show, Award of Exceptional Merit, Exhbn. Com. award), Allied Artists Am. (Gold medal, The Jane Peterson award, Grumbacher Cash award, Silver medal), Audubon Artists (Pastel Soc. Am. award). Home: 525 W 45th St New York NY 10036-3405

MCKENZIE, MICHAEL K., wholesale executive. Past pres., CEO G.S.C. Enterprises, Inc., Sulphur Springs, Tex., now chmn. bd., CEO, also bd. dirs. Office: GSC Enterprises Inc 130 Hillcrest Dr Sulphur Springs TX 75482*

MC KENZIE, RAY, anesthesiologist, educator; b. Turua, N.Z., July 9, 1927; s. Robert Keith and Edith Harfield (Collingwood) McK.; m. Barbara Mavis Snelling, Dec. 11, 1954; children: Robyn Kay, William Brett, Melvern Craig, Glenn Carrick. Student, Hauraki Plains Coll., 1939-45; M.B. Ch.B., U. Otago, 1952. Intern Auckland (N.Z.) Hosp., 1953, resident, 1954-56, cons. anesthetist, 1961-66; dir. anesthesia Mowasat Hosp., Kuwait, 1967-69; asst. prof. U. Pitts., 1969-71, assoc. prof., 1971-77, prof., 1977—; dir. surg. anesthesia Magee-Women's Hosp., Pitts., 1971-73, chief anesthesia, 1973-92, prof. rsch., 1992—. Mem. Bro.'s Bro. Found., 1971—. Served with Royal N.Z. Air Force, 1957-59. Fellow Faculty Anesthetists Royal Coll. Surgeons (Eng.); mem. Internat. Rsch. Soc. Am., Pa., Western Pa. socs. anesthesiologists. Home: 325 Richland Ln Pittsburgh PA 15208-2730 Office: Magee Womens Hosp Halket And Forbes St Pittsburgh PA 15213 *There is no electric elevator to success. Step up the stairs. Don't stare up the steps.*

MCKENZIE, THOMAS JAMES, lawyer, insurance consultant; b. Hastings, Nebr., May 7, 1930; s. Martin O. and Mary Ella (Graves) McK.; m. Harriet J. Beck, Nov. 10, 1951; children: Bruce, Craig, Scot, Mark. BA, State U. Iowa, 1955, JD, 1958. Bar: Iowa 1958, Ind. 1967, Pa. 1972, U.S. Dist. Ct. (we. dist.) Pa. 1993; CPCU. Atty. Benke & McKenzie, Parkersburg, Iowa, 1958; adjuster State Farm Ins., Dubuque, Iowa, 1958-64; claim and litig. mgr. State Auto Ins., Indpls., 1964-71; ins., claim and litig. mgr. Motor Freight Express, York, Pa., 1971-83; v.p. claims-litig. Mut. Benefit Ins., Huntingdon, Pa., 1983-92; ins. litigator Murphy, Taylor & Trout, P.C., Pitts., 1992—; seminar speaker in field. Served to staff sgt. USAF, 1951-53. Mem. ABA, Pa. Bar Assn., Masons, Shriners, Phi Alpha Delta. Home: 2802 Glenmore Ave Pittsburgh PA 15216-2124 Office: Murphy Taylor and Trout 326 3rd Ave Pittsburgh PA 15222-1911

MCKEON, HOWARD P. (BUCK MCKEON), congressman, former mayor; b. Los Angeles; m. Patricia; 6 children. BS, Brigham Young U. Mem. Coun. City of Santa Clarita, Calif., 1987-92, mayor, 1987-88; mem. 103rd Congress from 25th Calif. dist., 1993—; founding dir., chmn. Valencia Nat. Bank; co-owner Howard & Phil's Western Wear, Inc. Hon. chmn. Leukemia Soc. Celebrity program, 1990, Red Cross Community Support Campaign, 1992; active Dist. Com. Boy Scouts Am.; chmn., trustee William S. Hart Sch. dist., 1979-87; chmn., dir. Henry Mayo Newhall Meml. Hosp., 1983-88; mem. Calif. Rep. State Ctrl. Com., 1988-92; bd. dirs. Santa Clarita Valley Sml. Bus. Devel. Ctr., 1990-92, Canyon Country C. of C., 1988-92. Office: US Ho of Reps 307 Cannon Ho Ofc Bldg Washington DC 20515*

MCKEOUGH, WILLIAM DARCY, investment company executive; b. Chatham, Ont., Can., Jan. 31, 1933; s. George Grant and Florence Sewell (Woodward) McK.; m. Margaret Joyce Walker, June 18, 1965; children: Walker Stewart, James Grant. BA, U. Western Ont., 1954; LLD (hon.), Wilfred Laurier U., 1980, LL.D. (hon.), 1980. Chmn. McKeough Sons Co., Ltd.; bd. dirs. Can. Imperial Bank Commerce, Can. Gen. Tower Ltd., Global Stone Corp., Intertan Inc., Medicom Inc., Numac Energy Ltd., Noranda Mines Ltds., St. Mary's Cement Ltd., Varity Corp. Inc. Former mem. exec. com. Anglican Diocese of Huron; former mem. Gen. Synod, Anglican Ch., Can.; mem. Chatham City Council, 1960-63; also mem. Planning Bd. and Lower Thames Valley Conservation Authority; former mem. Chatham-Kent adv. bd. Can. Nat. Inst. of the Blind; former bd. dirs. Chatham YMCA, Chatham Little Theatre; former chmn. and pres. bd. govs. pres. Ridley Coll.; former bd. govs. Stratford Shakespearian Festival, Wilfrid Laurier U.; former mem. Can. group Trilateral Commn.; mem. Ont. Legislature, 1963-78, minister without portfolio, 1966, minister mcpl. affairs, 1967; treas. and minister of econs., also chmn. Treasury Bd., 1971-72, minister mcpl. affairs, 1972, treas. and minister of econs. and intergovtl. affairs, 1972, parliamentary asst. to premier Ont., 1973, minister of energy, 1973-75, treas. and minister econs. and intergovtl. affairs, 1975-78. Decorated officer of Order of Can. Home and Office: PO Box 940, Chatham, ON Canada N7M 5L3

MCKEOWN, JAMES CHARLES, accounting educator, consultant; b. Cleve., Nov. 3, 1945; s. Charles Joseph and Dara Ferrol (Prew) McK.; m. Mary Alinda Park, Jan. 2, 1965 (div. May 1980); children—Jeffrey Charles, Pamela Lynn; m. 2d, Nancy Ann Stratton, Jan. 3, 1981. B.S. in Math. with high honors, Mich. State U., 1966, Ph.D. in Bus. Adminstrn., 1969. Asst. prof. accountancy U. Ill., Urbana-Champaign, 1968-73, assoc. prof., 1973-76, prof., 1976-80, Weldon Powell prof. accountancy, 1980-83, A.C. Littleton prof. accountancy, 1983-89; disting. prof. acctg. Pa. State U., University Park, 1989-92, Ernst & Young prof. acctg., 1992—; cons. research, computers; expert witness. Editor: Inflation and Current Value Accounting, 1979; author computer-delivered acctg. course PLATO for Elementary Accounting, 1978; contbr. numerous articles to acad. jours. Recipient Instructional award U. Ill., Urbana-Champaign, 1970, Weldon Powell award, 1973; Fred Roedgers Research award U. Ill., 1978; Ford Found. fellow, 1967-68. Mem. Am. Acctg. Assn. (Manuscript award 1970), Am. Statis. Assn., Decision Scis. Inst., Inst. Mgmt. Accts. Republican. Office: Pa State U 210 Beam Bus Adminstrn Bldg University Park PA 16802

MC KEOWN, WILLIAM TAYLOR, magazine editor, author; b. Ft. Collins, Colo., July 4, 1921; s. Stuart Ellison and Eunice Harris (Akin) Mc K.; m. Lorraine Laredo; children: Elizabeth Ellison, Katherine, Suzanne. AB, Bowdoin Coll., 1942; student, Columbia U. Grad. Sch., 1948. Editor Fawcett Library Series, 1953-56; founding editor True's Boating Yearbook, 1955-56; founding editor Popular Boating mag., 1956, editor-in-chief, 1956-62; CEO The Mc Keown Co., N.Y.C., 1993—; editl. dir. Computer Travel Info., 1994—; travel editor Davis Publs.; outdoor/boating/travel editor Popular Mechanics, 1971-82; sr. editor Outdoor Life, 1983-93. Author weekly NEA syndicated newspaper column American Afloat, 1959-65; contbr. fiction, non-fiction to nat. mags., 1947—; author: Boating Handbook, 1956, Boating in America, 1960. Pilot USAAF, WW II, ETO. Mem. Am. Power Boat Assn., U.S. Power Squadrons, 357 FIghter Group Assn., N.Y. Yacht Club, Overseas Press Club, Royal Danish Yacht Club (Copenhagen), Turtles Internat. Avocation: international competitor in power and sail racing events. Office: The Mc Keown Co 420 Lexington Ave New York NY 10170-0002

MCKERNAN, LEO JOSEPH, manufacturing company executive; b. Phila., Feb. 17, 1938; s. Leo Joseph and Mary (Dever) McK. Student, Iona Coll., 1956-59, NYU, 1961-62, U. Bridgeport, 1962-64. With Eaton Corp., Carol Stream, Ill., 1959-74, mgr. mfg. Controls div., 1974; v.p., gen. mgr. Axle div. Clark Equipment Co., Buchanan, Mich., 1974-77, group v.p., 1977-83, sr. v.p., then exec. v.p., then chief oper. officer, 1983-86; pres., chief exec. officer Clark Equipment Co., South Bend, Ind., 1986—, chmn., 1988—, also bd. dirs.; mem. supervisory bd. VME Group N.V.; bd. dirs. 1st Source Corp., Lincoln Nat. Corp., Nat. Assn. Mfrs. Bd. dirs. St. Joseph Community Found., Ind.; mem. U. Notre Dame Engring. Adv. Coun., 1985—, corp. grants com., 1988—.

MCKERNS, CHARLES JOSEPH, lawyer; b. Shenandoah, Pa., July 17, 1935; s. Charles Francis and Bridgett Ann (Barrett) McK.; m. Helen Patricia Nott, Feb. 13, 1960; children: Charles J. Jr., Michael H., Patricia B. BS, Georgetown U., 1957, JD, 1960. Bar: D.C. 1960, U.S. Ct. Appeals (D.C. cir.) 1961, U.S. Supreme Ct. 1971, Va. 1992. Law clk. to assoc. judge U.S. Ct. Appeals (D.C. cir), Washington, 1960-61; assoc. Dow, Lohnes & Albertson, Washington, 1961-65, ptnr., 1965-91, of counsel, 1991-95; ptnr. McKerns and McKerns, Heathsville, Va., 1991—; bd. dirs. Palmer Communications Inc. 1st lt. U.S. Army, 1957-59. Mem. ABA, University Club, Belle Haven Country Club (Alexandria, Va.), Indian Creek Yacht and Country Club (Kilmarnock, Va.). Republican. Roman Catholic. Avocations: reading, swimming. Home: Windy Blue Ophelia VA 22530 Office: McKerns & McKerns PO Box 188 McKerns Bldg Heathsville VA 22473-0188 also: Dow Lohnes & Albertson 1255 23rd St NW Washington DC 20037-1125

MCKERROW, AMANDA, ballet dancer; b. Albuquerque; d. Alan and Constance McKerrow; m. John Gardner. Student, Met. Acad. Ballet, Bethesda, Md., Washington Sch. Ballet. With Washington Ballet Co., 1980-82; with Am. Ballet Theatre, N.Y.C., 1982—, soloist, from 1983, prin. dancer, 1987—. Toured Europe with Washington Ballet; danced in Margot Fonteyn Gala at Metropolitan Opera House; featured in Pavlova Tribute film, also many guest appearances; leading roles in Ballet Imperial, La Bayadere, Manon, Birthday Offering, Dim Lustre, Donizetti Variations, Giselle, Graduation Ball, The Leaves Are Fading, Nine Sinatra Songs, The Nutcracker, Pillar of Fire, Requiem, Romeo and Juliet, The Sleeping Beauty, Les Sylphides, Push Comes to Shove, Symphony Concertante, Symphonic Variations, Theme and Variations, Stravinsky Violin Concerto, Swan Lake, Triad, Duets, Etudes, Coppelia, Voluntaries and Rodeo; created leading role in Bruch Violin Concerto No. 1, Some Assembly Required and Agnus De Mille's The Other. Recipient N.Y. Woman award for dance, 1991; co-winner gold prize for women Moscow Internat. Ballet Competition, 1981. Office: Am Ballet Theatre 890 Broadway New York NY 10003-1211

MCKESSON, JOHN ALEXANDER, III, international relations educator; b. N.Y.C., Mar. 29, 1922; s. John Alexander and Mildred Fleming (Warner) McK.; m. Erna Jensson, Jan. 4, 1950 (dec. May 1971); 1 child, John A. IV. AB, Columbia U., 1941, MA in Internat. Rels., 1942, MA in Art History, 1982; LLD (hon.), Ea. Mich. U., 1972. Fgn. svc. officer Dept. of State, Washington and abroad, 1947-75; Am. amb. Libreville, Gabon, 1971-75; v.p. Etudes Travaux et Gestion, Paris, 1975-78; editor-in-chief UN Plaza Mag., N.Y.C., 1980-81; prof. NYU, N.Y.C., 1983—. Contbr. articles to profl. jours. Lt. USN, 1942-46. Decorated Commdr. Order of Equatorial Star of Gabon, 1975, Nat. Order of Senegal, 1967. Mem. Fgn. Svc. Assn., Regency Club. Episcopalian. Avocation: bridge. Home: 880 5th Ave New York NY 10021-4951

MCKESSY, STEPHEN W., accounting firm executive; b. 1937. Vice chmn. Coopers & Lybrand, N.Y.C. Office: Coopers & Lybrand 1251 Avenue Of The Americas New York NY 10020-1104*

MC KETTA, JOHN J., JR., chemical engineering educator; b. Wyano, Pa., Oct. 17, 1915; s. John J. and Mary (Gelet) McK.; m. Helen Elisabeth Smith, Oct. 17, 1943; children: Charles William, John J. III, Robert Andrew, Mary Anne. B.S., Tri-State Coll., Angola, Ind., 1937; B.S.E., U. Mich., 1943, M.S., 1944, Ph.D., 1946; D.Eng. (hon.), Tri-State Coll., 1965, Drexel U., 1977; Sc.D., U. Toledo, 1973. Diplomate: registered profl. engr., Tex., Mich. Group leader tech. dept. Wyandotte Chem. Corp., Mich., 1937-40; asst. supt. caustic soda div. Wyandotte Chem. Corp., 1940-41; teaching fellow U. Mich., 1942-44, instr. chem. engring., 1944-45; faculty U. Tex., Austin, 1946—; successively asst. prof. chem. engring., assoc. prof., then prof. chem. engring. U. Tex., 1951-52, 54—, E.P. Schoch prof. chem. engring., 1970-81, Joe C. Walter chair, 1981—; asst. dir. Tex. petroleum research com., 1951-52, 54-56, chmn. chem. engring. dept., 1950-52, 55-63, dean Coll. Engring., 1963-69; exec. vice chancellor acad. affairs U. Tex. System, 1969-70; J.C. Walter in Chem. Engring. U. Tex., 1970—; editorial dir. Petroleum Refiner, 1952-54; pres. Chemoil Cons., Inc., 1957-73; dir. Gulf Pub. Co., Howell Corp., Houston, Tesoro Petroleum Co., San Antonio; Chmn. Tex. AEC, So. Interstate Nuclear Bd., 1963-70; mem. Tex. Radiation Adv. Bd., 1978-84; chmn. Nat. Energy Policy Com., 1970-72, Nat. Air Quality Control Com., 1972-85; mem. adv. bd. Carnegie-Mellon Inst. Research, 1978-84; pres. Reagans's rep. on U.S. Acid Precipitation Task Force, 1982-88; apptd. mem. Nuclear Waste Tech. Rev. Bd., 1992—. Author: series Advances in Petroleum Chemistry and Refining; Chmn. editorial com.: series Petroleum Refiner; mem. adv. bd.: series Internat. Chem. Engring. mag; editorial bd.: series Ency. of Chem. Tech; exec. editor: series Ency. of Chem. Processing and Design (65 vols.). Bd. regents Tri-State U., 1957—. Recipient Bronze plaque Am. Inst. Chem. Engrs., 1952, Charles Schwab award Am. Steel Inst., 1973, Lamme award as outstanding U.S. educator, 1976, Joe J. King Profl. Engring. Achievement award U. Tex., 1976, Gen. Dynamics Teaching Excellence award, 1979, Triple E award for contbns. to nat. issues on energy, environment and econs. Nat. Environ. Devel. Assn., 1976, Boris Pregal Sci. and Tech. award NAS, 1978, Internat. Chem. Engring. award, Italy, 1984, Pres. Herbert Hoover award for advancing well-being of humanity and developing richer and more enduring civilization Joint Engring. Socs., 1989, Centennial award exceptional contbn. Am. Soc. Engring. Edn., 1993; named Disting. Alumnus U. Mich Coll. Engring., 1953, Tri-State Coll., 1956; fellow Allied Chem. & Dye, 1945-46; named Disting. fellow Carnegie-Mellon U., 1978. Mem. Am. Chem. Soc. (chmn. Central Tex. sect. 1950), Am. Inst. Chem. Engrs. (chmn. nat. membership com. 1955, regional exec. com., nat. dir., nat. v.p. 1961, pres. 1962, service to soc. award 1975), Am. Soc. Engring. Edn., Chem. Markets Research Assn., Am. Gas Assn. (adv. bd. chems. from gas 1954), Houston C. of C. (chmn. refining div. 1954, vice chmn. research and statistics com. 1954), Engrs. Joint Council (dir.), Engrs. Joint Countil Profl. Devel. (dir. 1963-85), Nat. Acad. Engring., Sigma Xi, Chi Epsilon, Alpha Psi Omega, Tau Omega, Phi Lambda Upsilon, Phi Kappa Phi, Iota Alpha, Omega Chi Epsilon, Tau Beta Pi, Omicron Delta Kappa. Home: 5227 Tortuga Trl Austin TX 78731-4501

MCKEWEN, JACK LEARD, insurance sales executive; b. Tuscumbia, Ala., May 21, 1919; s. Harry Stoddard and Addie Mae (Simpson) McK.; m. Ruth Peeples, Apr. 14, 1945; children: JAck L., Debra Mae and Peggy (twins). BS of Commerce and Bus., U. Ala., 1942. Chartered life underwriter. With sales dept. Prudential Ins. Co., Birmingham, Ala., 1948-50, 52-54, Fidelity Mutual Ins. Co., Birmingham, Ala., 1954—. Past pres. Jefferson County Alumni Assn., U. Ala., Homewood YMCA, Shades Valley Athletic Assn.; past chmn. heart fund dr. Brimingham Life Underwriters Assn., 1969. 2nd lt. WWII, 1943, capt., 1946; capt., Korea, 1950, maj., 1952; col. USNG, 1952-63. Mem. Advanced Assn. Life Underwriters, Million Dollar Round Table (pres. 1978). Baptist. Avocation: sailing. Home: 29 Cross Creek Park Birmingham AL 35213-2302

MCKHANN, GUY MEAD, physician, educator; b. Boston, Mar. 20, 1932; s. Charles Fremont and Emily (Priest) McK.; m. Katherine E. Henderson, Nov. 30, 1957 (div. 1983); children: Ian, James, Emily, Guy, Charles. Student, Harvard U., 1948-51; M.D., Yale U., 1955. Intern New York Hosp., 1955-56; asst. resident pediatrics Johns Hopkins Hosp., Balt., 1956-57; clin. asso. NIH, Bethesda, Md., 1957-60; resident neurology Mass. Gen. Hosp., Boston, 1960-63; asst. and asso. prof. pediatrics and neurology Stanford (Calif.) U., 1963-69; prof. neurology Johns Hopkins, Balt., 1969—, Kennedy prof. neurology, head neurology dept., 1969-88, prof. neurology, dir. Zanuyl Krieger Mind Brain Inst., 1988—. Served with USPHS, 1957-60. Markle scholar, 1964-69; Joseph P. Kennedy Jr. scholar, 1963-69. Fellow AAAS; mem. Am. Acad. Neurology, Am. Neurol. Assn., Am. Neurochem. Soc., Soc. Neuroscis., Inst. Medicine, Alpha Omega Alpha. Research on normal and abnormal human nervous system. Home: 6526 Montrose Ave Baltimore MD 21212-1023 Office: Zanvyl Krieger Mind Inst Johns Hopkins U 338 Krieger Hall Baltimore MD 21218

MCKIBBEN, HOWARD D., federal judge; b. Apr. 1, 1940; s. James D. and Bernice McKibben; m. Mary Ann McKibben, July 2, 1966; children: Mark, Susan. B.S., Bradley U., 1962; M.P.A., U. Pitts., 1964; J.D., U. Mich., 1967. Assoc. George W. Abbott Law Office, 1967-71; dep. dist. atty. Douglas County, Nev., 1969-71, dist. atty., 1971-77; dist. ct. judge State of Nev., 1977-84; judge U.S. Dist. Ct. Nev., Reno, 1984—. Mem. ABA, Nev. Bar Assn., Am. Inns of Ct. (pres. Nev. chpt. 1986-88). Methodist. Avocations: tennis, golf, racquetball. Home: PO Box 588 Verdi NV 89439-0588 Office: US Dist Ct 300 Booth St Rm 5137 Reno NV 89509-1356

MCKIBBEN, RYAN TIMOTHY, newspaper executive; b. Watertown, S.D., June 25, 1958; s. Bernard Dean and Patricia Martha (Loehr) McK.; m. Mary Elizabeth O'Donnell, Oct. 3, 1981; children: Sean Robert, Michael Patrick. Grad. high sch., Janesville, Wis. Classified advt. exec. Green Bay (Wis.) Press Gazette, 1977-79; display advt. exec. Racine (Wis.) Jour. Times, 1979-80; advt. dir. Oshkosh (Wis.) Northwestern, 1980-82, dir. sales/mktg., 1982-84; advt. dir. Reno Gazette-Jour., 1984-85, Madison (Wis.) Newspapers Inc., 1985-88; v.p., advt. dir., sr. v.p. advt. and mktg. Denver Post, 1988-90, exec. v.p., gen. mgr., 1990-93, pub., 1993—; bd. dirs. Newspapers First, N.Y.C. Mem. mktg. com. Metro Area Boys Clubs, Denver, 1988—; bd. dirs. Nat. Jewish Ctr. for Immunology and Respiratory Medicine, Denver, Denver Metro Conv. Bur., Denver Ctr. for Performing Arts, Colo. Symphony, Colo. Forum, Colo. Concer, Castle Pines Golf Club. Mem. Am. Press Inst., Newspaper Advt. Coop. Network (bd. dirs. 1989—), Internat. Newspaper Advt./Mktg. Execs., (com. mem. 1989—), Denver Advt. Fedn., Boys and Girls Club, Columbine Country Club. Republican. Roman Catholic. Home: 5350 S Race Ct Littleton CO 80121-1430 Office: Denver Post 1560 Broadway Denver CO 80202-5133

MCKIE, FRANCIS PAUL, journalist; b. Jarrow-upon-Tyne, England, Dec. 18, 1958; arrived in Can., 1963; s. Francis David and Sonia (Marley) McK.; m. Ellen Frances Robinson, May 26, 1984; 1 child, Sean David. BA, U. Toronto, 1982. Free-lance film critic Winnipeg (Man., Can.) Free Press, 1985-87, staff film critic, 1988-92, features writer, 1992-94; news reporter, features writer, columnist Winnipeg (Man., Can.) Free Press, $, 1994-95; bus. reporter Winnipeg (Man., Can.) Free Press, 1996—. Mem. Winnipeg Press Club (pres. 1990, house chair/treas. 1989), Media Union Manitoba (bd. dirs. 1994—). Avocations: movies, Trekkies, Blue Jays. Office: Winnipeg Free Press, 1355 Mountain Ave, Winnipeg, MB Canada R2X 3B6

MC KIE, TODD STODDARD, artist; b. Boston, Apr. 25, 1944; s. Roy Albert and Lois E. (Barwood) McK.; m. Judy Anne Kensley, Apr. 10, 1967; 1 son, Jesse Simon. BFA, RISD, 1966. Vis. artist RISD, 1977, Mass. Coll. Art, 1977-78, Sch. Mus. Fine Arts, Boston, 1979; lectr. schs. and museums. Exhibited in one-man shows Harcus Krakow Gallery, Boston, 1977, 79, 83, Aquavella Gallery, N.Y.C., 1978, 79, 81, Hokin-Kaufman Gallery, Chgo., 1983, Helander Gallery, N.Y.C., 1990, 92, Toale Gallery, Boston, 1994; exhibited in group shows including, Whitney Museum Am. Art, N.Y.C., 1975, Harcus Krakow Gallery, 1975, 78, Mus. Fine Arts, Boston, 1975, 77, 81, Acquavella Gallery, 1976, 78, 79, 81, Inst. Contemporary Art, Boston, 1979, Addison Gallery Am. Art, 1981; represented in permanent collections including Fogg Art Mus., Cambridge, Mass., M.I.T., Cambridge, Brockton (Mass.) Mus., Mus. Fine Arts, Boston, DeCordova Mus., Lincoln, Mass., Rose Art Mus. Brandeis U.; also numerous pvt. collections. Recipient Blanch E. Colman award Colman Found., 1974; Artists fellowship Villa Montalvo, 1995; Artists Found. fellow Boston, 1975, 89. Home and Office: 117R Magazine St Cambridge MA 02139-3955

MCKIE, W. GILMORE, human resources executive; b. Marquette, Mich., Aug. 25, 1927; s. Walter G. and Amy Gertrude (Larson) McK.; m. Elenore R. MacNally, Sept. 9, 1950 (div. Nov. 1962); 1 child, Janet; m. Mary Simmons, Mar. 21, 1964 (dec. Aug. 1970) 1 child, Gwen DeBuck; m. Eunice Winifred Curtis, July 10, 1971; children: Ellen Sheive, Norine Halvorsen. BS in Econs., U. Rochester, 1951. Employment interviewer Taylor Instruments Cos', Rochester, N.Y., 1951-60; employment mgr. Graflex, Inc., Rochester, 1960-62, Gen. Railway Signal Co., Rochester, 1962-67; dir. human resources The Singer Co., Rochester, Binghamton,, N.Y.C., 1967-77, Norwich-Eaton Pharms., Norwich, N.Y., 1977-80; personnel mgr. Ness Automatic Machine Products, Rochester, 1980-84; v.p. human resources Marine Midland Bank, N.A., Rochester, 1984-89; pres. HRM Cons., Inc., Rochester, 1989-93; founder, pres. adr Support Svcs., Rochester, N.Y., 1993—; mgmt. adv. bd. Cornell U. Extension div., Rochester, 1984-90; mem. job svc. employer com. N.Y. State Dept. Labor, 1993—. Co-author: The Contingent Worker - A Human Resource Perspective, 1995. Adv. bd. Salvation Army, Rochester, 1986—; vice chair N.Y. State divsn. Human Rights, Rochester, 1987—; bd. dirs. Ralph Bunche Scholarship Fund,

Rochester, 1990-93, Youth at Risk, Rochester, 1988-92; bd. govs. N.Y. State Fingerlakes Regional Edn. Ctr. for Econ. Devel., Rochester, 1984—; exec. com. United Negro Coll. Fund, Rochester, 1986—; adv. bd. chair Coll. Continuing Edn. Rochester Inst. Tech., 1985-90; chair Loftus C. Carson Human Rights Awards Luncheon, Rochester, 1991. Mem. Soc. for Human Resource Mgmt. (dist. dir. N.Y. state 1985-89, pers. rsch. com. 1989—, pres. Genesee Valley chpt. 1982-84, chmn. bd. 1984-87, founder 1982), Industrial Mgmt. Coun. Rochester (mem. human resource adv. com. 1988-90, chmn. industrial pers. group 1983-84, vice chmn. bank pers. group 1985-90), Rochester Assn. Automatic Machining (pres. 1982-83), Rochester Profl. Cons. Network, Pers. Testing Coun. Upstate N.Y., Broome County C. of C. (pres. Industrial Rels. Com. 1977), Chenango C. of C. (dir. 1978), Chenango-Deleware Bus. Edn. Ctr. (past v.p. 1977-78). Republican. Lutheran. Avocations: golf, trap and skeet shooting, woodworking. Office: HRM Support Svcs 2854 St Paul Blvd Rochester NY 14617-3740 *I have always endeavored to enhance the growth and achievements of my staff and co-workers. In that same vein guide the youth in our society, so that they might make use of their potential.*

MCKIERNAN, HELEN, airport executive. Gen. mgr. Ottawa (Ont., Can.) MacDonald-Cartier Internat. Airport. Office: Ottawa International Airport, 50 Airport Rd Ste 3120, Gloucester, ON Canada K1V 9B4*

MCKIERNAN, JOHN WILLIAM, mechanical engineer; b. Hannibal, Mo., Jan. 12, 1923; s. Charles and Anna Laura (Turner) McK.; m. Jeannette Dorothy Hagen, Aug. 26, 1945; children—Kathleen J., Linda J., John E. B.S., U. Mo., 1947; M.S., Iowa State Coll., 1950. With E.I. duPont de Nemours & Co., Inc., Richmond, Va., 1947-48; faculty Iowa State Coll., 1948-51; mech. engr. Sandia Nat. Lab., Albuquerque, 1951-85. Served with USAAF, 1943-45. Decorated D.F.C., Air medal. Fellow ASME (v.p., bd. govs.). Mem. Christian Ch. Home: 1709 Cardenas Dr NE Albuquerque NM 87110-6629

MCKILLOP, DANIEL JAMES, insurance company real estate executive; b. N.Y.C., June 18, 1948; s. Daniel James and Martha (Laux) McK.; m. Irene M. Flood, June 22, 1974. BA in History, Siena Coll., 1969; MBA in Fin., St. John's U., 1975. Cert. property mgr. V.p. real estate N.Y. Life Ins. Co., 1969—. Roman Catholic. Avocations: hunting, fishing. Home: PO Box 332 Port Monmouth NJ 07758-0332 Office: New York Life Insurance CO 51 Madison Ave Rm 904 New York NY 10010-1603

MCKIM, PAUL ARTHUR, management consultant, retired petroleum executive; b. Milford, Conn., Feb. 1, 1923; s. Arthur Wheatley and Helen Agnes (Brennan) McK.; m. Daisy Flora Brown, June 18, 1945; 1 dau., Meredith Ann. Student, Lamar Inst. Tech., 1940-42; BS in Chem. Engring., La. State U., 1943, MS, 1947, PhD, 1949; grad. Advanced Mgmt. Program, Harvard, 1959; grad. Aspen Inst. Humanistic Studies Exec. Program, 1970. With Ethyl Corp., 1949-62, asst. gen. mgr. research and devel. operations, 1958-62; v.p., gen. mgr. rsch. and devel. Atlantic Refining Co., Phila., 1962-66; v.p. Atlantic Richfield Co., 1966-78; v.p. comml. devel. Arco Chem. Co., 1966-69, v.p. nuclear operations and comml. devel., 1969-73; exec. v.p. Sinclair Koppers Co., 1973; pres. Arco Polymers, Inc., 1974-78; asst. to pres. Tex. Eastern Corp., 1978-80, v.p., 1980-84, sr. v.p., 1985-88; Chmn. US Organizing com. for 12th World Petroleum Congress, Houston, 1987. Past bd. mgrs. Franklin Inst. Research Labs; past vice chmn. bd. mgrs. Spring Garden Coll., Phila. Coll. Art.; past vice chmn. World Affairs Council of Phila. Served to lt. (j.g.) USNR, 1944-46. Mem. AIChE, Am. Petroleum Inst., Union League, Merion (Pa.) Cricket Club, Merion Golf Club, Houston Club, Shreveport (La.) Country Club, Alpha Chi Sigma, Omicron Delta Kappa, Tau Beta Pi, Phi Lambda Upsilon, Phi Kappa Phi, Delta Kappa Epsilon. Home: 5405 Holly Springs Dr Houston TX 77056-2021

MCKIM, SAMUEL JOHN, III, lawyer; b. Pitts., Dec. 31, 1938; s. Samuel John and Harriet Frieda (Roehl) McK.; children: David Hunt, Andrew John; m. Eugenia A. Leverich. AA cum laude, Port Huron Jr. Coll., 1959; BA cum laude, U. Mich., 1961, JD cum laude, U. Mich., 1964. Bar: Mich. 1965, U.S. Dist. Ct. (so. dist.) Mich. 1965, U.S. Ct. Appeals (6th cir.) 1969, U.S. Supreme Ct., 1994. Assoc. Miller, Canfield, Paddock and Stone, P.L.C., Detroit, Bloomfield Hills, Howell, Kalamazoo, Lansing, Monroe, Traverse City and Grand Rapids, Mich., Washington, N.Y.C., Pensacola, St. Petersburg, Fla., Gdansk, Warsaw, Poland, 1964-71, sr. mem., 1971—, head state and local tax sect., 1985—, chmn. tax dept., 1989-94, mng. ptnr., 1979-85, chmn., mng. ptnr., 1984-85; mem. tax coun. State Bar Mich., 1981-84, chmn. state and local tax com. real property sect., 1982-90; adj. prof. law sch. Wayne State U., 1993—. Bd. dirs., past chmn. Goodwill Industries of Greater Detroit, 1970—; dir. Goodwill Industries Found., 1982-95; elder Presbyn. ch., Stevens min.; coun. mem. at large Detroit area coun. Boy Scouts Am., 1987—. Fellow Am. Coll. Tax Counselors; mem. ABA, Mich. Bar Assn., Detroit Bar Assn., Detroit Club, Barrister's Soc., Ostego Ski Club, Port Huron Golf Club, Order of Coif, Phi Delta Phi. Assoc. editor Mich. Law Rev. Home: 32778 Friar Tuck Ln Beverly Hills MI 48025 Office: Miller Canfield Paddock & Stone 150 W Jefferson Ave Ste 2500 Detroit MI 48226-4415

MCKIMMEY, MARTHA ANNE, elementary education educator; b. Uvalde, Tex., Apr. 9, 1943; d. Aubrey Allan and Nellie Grey (Roberts) Stovall; m. Vernon Hobart McKimmey Jr., July 3, 1965; children: Annette Gay, Patrick Allan. BS, Howard Payne Coll., Brownwood, Tex., 1964; MEd, Tex. Christian U., 1969; PhD, Tex. Women's U., 1995. Cert. elem. tchr., Tex. Tchr. Ft. Worth Ind. Sch. Dist., 1964-66, White Lake Sch., Ft. Worth, 1979-80, Meadowbrook Christian Sch., Ft. Worth, 1982-87. Contbr. articles to mags. Mem. ASCD, Internat. Reading Assn. Home: 7104 Jewell Ave Fort Worth TX 76112-5712

MCKINLESS, KATHY JEAN, accountant; b. Augusta, Ga., June 15, 1954; d. Jack M. and Jean K. (Norby) VanderWood; m. Darryl P. Calderon, Mar. 17, 1979 (dec. June 1988); children: Christopher, Jackie; m. Richard T. McKinless, July 1, 1989; children: Ashley, Thomas. BS in Acctg., U. S.C., 1975, MBA, 1978. CPA, D.C. Acct. Clarkson, Harden & Gantt, Columbia, 1975-79; sr. acct. KPMG Peat Marwick, Washington, 1979-80, mgr., 1980-86, ptnr., 1986—; spkr. Mortgage Bankers Assn., Fin. Mgrs. Soc., Nat. Assn. Coll. and Univ. Bus. Officers, Fed. Fin. Insts. Exam. Coun., Diocesan Fiscal Mgrs. Mem. governance com., treas., pres. bd. dirs. Nations Capital coun. Girl Scouts U.S., 1985—; mem. fin. com. Cath. Charities, U.S.A. Mem. AICPAs, D.C. Inst. CPAs. Office: KPMG Peat Marwick 2001 M St NW Washington DC 20036-3310

MCKINLEY, BRUNSON, diplomat; b. Miami, Fla., Feb. 8, 1943; s. Kenneth William and Lois Rebecca (Hiestand) McK.; m. Nancy Padlon, Sept. 11, 1971; children: Harley Joseph, Sarah Elizabeth. BA, U. Chgo., 1962; MA, Harvard U., 1964. Third sec. U.S. Embassy, Rome, 1971-72; spl. asst. U.S. Liaison Office, Peking, China, 1973-74; dep. prin. officer U.S. Consulate Gen., Danang, Republic of Vietnam, 1975; staff officer Dept. State, Washington, 1975-76, officer-in-charge Italian affairs, 1976-78; first sec. Am. Embassy, London, 1978-81; dep. polit. advisor U.S. Mission, Berlin, 1981-83; dep. exec. sec. Dept. State, Washington, 1983-86; U.S. ambassador Am. Embassy, Port-Au-Prince, Haiti, 1986-89; deputy for policy bur. european affairs U.S. Dept. State, Washington, 1990-91, dep. asst. sec. state for refugee programs, 1991-93, sr. dep. asst. sec. state for population, refugees and migration, 1993-95; Bosnia humanitarian coord. U.S. Dept. of State, Washington, 1995—. Contbr. various publs. in field of migration. Served to capt. U.S. Army, 1965-71, Vietnam. Decorated Air medal, Bronze star, Award for Valor, Superior Hon. award. Mem. Army and Navy Club, Bath Club (London), Washington Figure Skating Club, Phi Beta Kappa. Avocations: walking, running, riding, ice skating, languages. Home: 7064 31st St NW Washington DC 20015-1402 Office: Dept of State Washington DC 20520-6317

MCKINLEY, DONALD ROBERT, former school system administrator, education advisor; b. Cottonwood, Idaho, Nov. 17, 1924; s. Howard R. and Elsie May (Wortman) McK.; m. Margaret Faye Burson, March 27, 1948; children: Constance, Kathryn, Philip. BS, U. Idaho, 1948, MS, 1953; EdD, Wash. State U., 1958. Tchr. music and govt. Grangeville (Idaho) Sch. Dist., Idaho, 1948-50; tchr. music and math. Cajon Valley Sch. Dist., El Cajon, Calif., 1952-56; supt.-prin. Ferndale (Calif.) H.S. Dist., 1957-59; prin. Davis (Calif.) Sr. H.S., 1959-67; asst. supt. Davis Unified Sch. Dist., 1967-70; supt. Placer Union H.S. Dist., Auburn, Calif., 1970-72, San Ramon Valley Sch. Dist., Danville, Calif., 1972-73; chief dep. state supt. Calif. State Dept. Edn., Sacramento, 1973-83; sales and regional mgr. WICAT Edn. Sys., Provo, Utah, 1983-86; mktg. advisor Edn. Sys. Corp., San Diego, 1986-89; edn. advisor Photo & Sound Co., San Francisco, 1989-92, Edunetics Corp., Arlington, Va., 1992-94; search cons. Wilson Riles & Assocs., Sacramento, Calif., 1990—; chmn. Coun. of Chief State Sch. Officers-Study Commn., Washington, 1975-76; mem. Sec. of Edn. Adv. Com., Washington, 1981-86; cons. Optical Data Corp., 1995—, Ameri Data Corp., 1995—. Lt. USN, 1943-46, World War II, 1950-52, Korea. Mem. Am. Assn. Sch. Adminstrs., Calif. Assn. Secondary Sch. Adminstrs. (pres. 1969-70), Assn. Calif. Sch. Adminstrs. (pres. 1971-72). Avocations: golf, fishing, travel. Home: 5332 Adelaide Way Sacramento CA 95841-4304

MCKINLEY, ELLEN BACON, priest; b. Milw., June 9, 1929; d. Edward Alsted and Lorraine Goodrich (Graham) Bacon; m. Richard Smallbrook McKinley, III, June 16, 1951 (div. Oct. 1977); children: Richard IV, Ellen Graham, David Todd, Edward Bacon. BA cum laude, Bryn Mawr Coll., 1951; MDiv Yale U., 1976; STM, Gen. Theol. Sem., N.Y.C., 1979; PhD, Union Theol. Sem., N.Y.C., 1988. Ordained to ministry Episcopal Ch. as deacon, 1980, as priest, 1981. Intern St. Francis Ch., Stamford, Conn., 1976-77; pastoral asst. St. Paul's Ch., Riverside, Conn., 1979-80, curate, 1980-81; priest assoc. St. Saviour's Ch., Old Greenwich, Conn., 1982-90; asst. St. Christopher's Ch., Chatham, Mass., 1987-88, interim asst., Trinity Ch., Princeton, N.J., 1990-91; priest assoc. All Saints Ch., Princeton, 1992—, interim rector, 1993; mem. major chpt. Trinity Cathedral, Trenton, 1992-96. Mem. Episcopal Election Com., Diocese of Conn., 1986-87, Com. on Human Sexuality, 1987-90; Com. on Donations and Bequests Diocese of Conn., 1987-90; sec., Greenwich Com. on Drugs, 1970-71; bd. dirs. Greenwich YWCA, 1971-72. Mem. Episcopal Women's Caucus, Colonial Dames Am., Jr. League. Clubs: Sulgrave. *God has a sense of humor and is unwilling for me to take myself too seriously or think I am in charge of my life. Whenver I have had my life organized, something unexpected rearranged it. I have come to chuckle at myself with God while following unexpected paths.*

MC KINLEY, JOHN KEY, retired oil company executive; b. Tuscaloosa, Ala., Mar. 24, 1920; s. Virgil Parks and Mary Emma (Key) McK.; m. Helen Grace Heare, July 19, 1946; children: John Key Jr., Mark Charles. B.S. in Chem. Engring, U. Ala., 1940, M.S. in Organic Chemistry, 1941, LL.D. (hon.), 1972; grad., Advanced Mgmt. Program, Harvard U., 1962; LL.D. (hon.), Troy State U., 1974. Registered profl. engr., Tex. With Texaco Inc., 1941-86; asst. dir. research Texaco Inc., Beacon, N.Y., 1957-59; asst. to v.p. Texaco Inc., 1959-60, mgr. comml. devel., 1960; gen. mgr. petrochem. dept. Texaco Inc., N.Y.C., 1960-67; v.p. petrochem. dept., v.p. in charge supply and distbn. Texaco Inc., 1967-71, sr. v.p. worldwide refining, petrochems., also supply and distbn., 1971, pres., dir., 1971-80, pres., chief operating officer, chmn. exec. com., 1980, chmn. bd., pres., chief exec. officer, 1980-83, chmn. bd., chief exec. officer, 1983-86, ret., 1986; bd. dirs. emeritus Federated Dept. Stores, Inc. Patentee for chem. processing. Hon. bd. dirs. Met. Opera Assocs.; nat. chmn. Met. Opera Centennial Fund, 1980; bd. dirs. The Ams. Soc.; mem. Bus. Coun. Maj. AUS, 1941-45, ETO. Decorated Bronze Star; recipient George Washington Honor medal Freedoms Found., 1972; Andrew Wellington Cordier fellow Columbia U.; named to Ala. Bus. Hall of Fame, 1982, Ala. Acad. Honor, 1983, State of Ala. Engring. Hall of Fame, 1992. Fellow Am. Inst. Chem. Engrs.; mem. Am. Petroleum Inst. (hon. dir.), Wee Burn Country Club, Links Club, Brook Club, Augusta Nat. Golf Club, Blind Brook County Club, North River Yacht, Sigma Xi, Tau Beta Pi, Gamma Sigma Epsilon, Kappa Sigma. Office: One Canterbury Green Stamford CT 06901

MCKINLEY, LOREN DHUE, museum director; b. Tillamook, Oreg., Feb. 1, 1920; s. Henry Raymond and Flora (Phillips) McK.; m. Mary Eileen Sessions, May 22, 1942; children: Candace Eileen, Scott Dhu, Kevin Loren, Laurie Lee, Maris Colleen. Student, Oreg. State U., U. Oreg.; D.Sc., U. Portland, 1973. Advt. mgr. Headlight Herald, Tillamook, 1946; partner Kenwood Press, Tillamook, 1949; dir. Oreg. Mus. Sci. and Industry, Portland, 1960-78; chief exec. officer Oreg. Mus. Sci. and Industry, 1978—; bd. dirs. Fred Hutchinson Cancer Rsch. Ctr. Found.; Portland ops. mgr. Office of Devel. Oreg. State U. Mayor of Tillamook, 1954-60; pres. Leukemia Assn. Oreg. Inc., 1983—; bd. dirs. St. Mary's Acad., 1993—; mem. Oreg. State U Found. Served with AUS, World War II, ETO, MTO. Decorated Bronze Star with oak leaf cluster; named 1st Citizen of Oreg., 1951; recipient award Oreg. Mus. Sci. and Industry, 1965, Elsie M.B. Naumberg award as outstanding sci. mus. dir., 1968, citation for outstanding svc. Oreg. Acad. Sci., 1971, Aubrey Watzek award Lewis and Clark Coll., 1973. Mem. Assn. Sci. and Tech. Ctrs. Am. (pres. 1973—), League Oreg. Cities (past pres.), Kappa Sigma. Republican. Home and Office: 11925 SW Belvidere Pl Portland OR 97225-5805

MCKINLEY, (JENNIFER CAROLYN) ROBIN, writer; b. Warren, Ohio, Nov. 16, 1952; d. William and Jeanne Carolyn (Turrell) McK; m. Peter Dickinson, Jan. 3, 1992. Student, Dickinson Coll., 1970-72; BA, Bowdoin Coll., 1975, PhD (hon.), 1986. Editor, transcriber Ward and Paul, Washington, 1972-73; rsch. asst. Rsch. Assocs., Brunswick, Maine, 1976-77; tchr., counselor pvt. secondary sch., Natick, Maine, 1978-79; edit. asst. Little, Brown & Co., Boston, 1979-81; barn mgr. horse farm Holliston, Mass., 1981-82; clerk Books of Wonder, N.Y.C., 1983—; freelance reader, copy and line editor, 1983—. Author: Beauty: A Retelling of the Story of Beauty and the Beast, 1978 (Horn book Honor list citation 1978), The Door in the Hedge, 1981, The Blue Sword, 1982 (Best Young adult books citation ALA 1982, Newbery Honor citation 1983), The Hero and the Crown, 1984 (Horn book honor list citation 1985, John Newbery medal 1985), The Outlaws of Sherwood, 1988, Rowan, 1992, My Father is in the Navy, 1992, Deerskin, 1993 (Best Young Adult Books citation ALA 1993, Best Adult Books for Young Adults citation ALA 1993), A Knot in the Grain and Other Stories, 1994, The Sea King's Son, 1994; contbr.: Elsewhere Vol. II, 1982, Vol. III, 1984, Faery, 1985, Writers for Children, 1988; editor, contbr.: Imaginary Lands, 1985 (World Fantasy award Best Anthology 1986); adapter: Jungle Book Tales, 1985, Black Beauty, 1986, The Light Princess, 1988. Office: c/o Merrilee Heifetz Writers House 21 W 26th St New York NY 10010-1003*

MCKINLEY, WILLIAM THOMAS, composer, performer, educator; b. New Kensington, Pa., Dec. 9, 1938; s. Daniel Edward and Ellen Lee (Henson) M.; m. Marlene Marie Mildner, Apr. 11, 1956; children: Thomas Jr., Derrick, Jory, Sean, Elliott. BFA, Carnegie-Mellon U., 1960; MM, Yale U., 1966, DMA, 1969. Mem. music faculty SUNY-Albany, 1968-69; prof. music U. Chgo., 1969-73; prof. composition and jazz studies New Eng. Conservatory Music, Boston, 1973—. Composer numerous works for orch., chamber ensembles, choral works, oratorio, also solo works; commns. include works for Koussevitsky Music Found., 1982, Lincoln Ctr. Chamber Music Soc., 1985, Boston Symphony Pops, 1986, Concert Artist Guild, 1988, Stan Getz, 1988, Am. Symphony, 1988, (2) Fromm Found., John Williams, 1989, NEA Consortium, Rheinische Philharmonie, Fed. Republic Germany, 1990, Queensland Youth Orch., Australia, 1990, Bolshoi Ballet Theatre Orch. USSR, 1990, Pitts. New Music Ensemble, 1991, Quintet Ams., 1992, Md. Bach Aria Group, 1992, Berlin Saxophone Quartet, 1992, 93, Richard Stolzman, 1993, Seattle Symphony, 1993, Absolut Vodka, 1994; performance recs. with Berlin Radio Symphony and Richard Stolzman, Rheinische Philharm., Warsaw Philharm., St. Petersburg Philharm., Slovak Radio Symphony, Seattle Symphony, Krakow Philharm., Silesian Philharm., Prague Radio Symphony, Solati Trio, Manhattan Sinfonia, Cleve. Quartet. Recipient Naumberg prize Naumberg Found., 1975; Nat. Endowment Arts composer fellow, 1975-83; Am. Acad. Music award, Am. Acad. and Inst. Arts and Letters, 1983; Guggenheim fellow, 1985; 3 Mass Council fellowships. Mem. Am. Composers Alliance, Am. Music Ctr. Home: 240 West St Reading MA 01867-2847

MCKINLEY BALFOUR, STEPHANIE ANN, learning resources director, librarian; b. Galesburg, Ill., Mar. 27, 1948; d. William Chester and Virginia Ann (Clugsten) McKinley; m. James Robert Miller, Mar. 2, 1968 (div. Mar. 1978); 1 child, Christopher Antonin Miller; m. David Alan Balfour, Nov. 23, 1991. BA in Speech, Drama, Western Ill. U., 1970; MLS, Drexel U., 1974. Cert. tchr., Ill., media specialist, Ill. Libr. William McKinley Elem. Sch., Phila., 1971-76, Regional Jr. H.S., Amherst, Mass., 1976-77, Garfield Elem. Sch., Monmouth, Ill., 1977-79; dir. learning resources Spoon River Valley Sch. Dist., London Mills, Ill., 1979-95; dir. librs. Spoon River Valley Sch. Dist./Avon Sch. Dist., Ill., 1995—; dir. summer reading program Avon (Ill.) Pub. Libr., 1980-95. Leader 4-H, Avon, 1983-92; vol. EMT Galesburg Hosp. Ambulance Svc., Galesburg/Avon, 1978—; dir. religious edn. Avon Federated Ch., 1984—. Named Outstanding Young Educator by Monmouth Jaycees, 1979. Mem. Am. Found. Vision Awareness Ill. Affiliate (pres.), Nat. Edn. Assn., Ill. Edn. Assn., Ill. Sch. Libr. Media Assn., Phi Delta Kappa, Gamma Lambda-Delta Kappa Gamma Soc. Internat. (pres. 1992-94, 1st v.p. 1990-92, recording sec. 1988-92). Republican. Mem. United Ch. of Christ. Avocations: reading, knitting, crocheting, gardening. Home: RR2 274 Funcheon Ct Avon IL 61415 Office: Spoon River Valley Sch Dist RR 1 London Mills IL 61544-9801

MCKINNELL, ROBERT GILMORE, zoology, genetics and cell biology educator; b. Springfield, Mo., Aug. 9, 1926; s. William Parks and Mary Catherine (Gilmore) McK.; m. Beverly Walton Kerr, Jan. 24, 1964; children: Nancy Elizabeth, Robert Gilmore, Susan Kerr. AB, U. Mo., 1948; BS, Drury Coll., 1949, DSc (hon.), 1993; PhD, U. Minn., 1959. Research assoc. Inst. Cancer Research, Phila., 1958-61; asst. prof. biology Tulane U., New Orleans, 1961-65; asso. prof. Tulane U., 1965-69, prof., 1969-70; prof. zoology U. Minn., Mpls., 1970—; prof. genetics and cell biology U. Minn., St. Paul, 1976—; vis. scientist Dow Chem. Co., Freeport, Tex., 1976; guest dept. zoology U. Calif., Berkeley, 1979; Royal Soc. guest rsch. fellow Nuffield dept. pathology John Radcliffe Hosp., Oxford U., 1981-82; NATO vis. scientist Akademisch Ziekenhuis, Ghent, Belgium, 1984; faculty rsch. assoc. Naval Med. Rsch. Inst., Bethesda, Md., 1988; secretariat Third Internat. Conf. Differentiation, 1978; mem. amphibian com. Inst. Lab. Animal Resources, NRC, 1970-73, mem. adv. coun., 1974; mem. panel genetic and cellular resources program NIH, 1981-82, spl. study sect., Bethesda, 1990. Author: Cloning: Amphibian Nuclear Transplantation, 1978, Cloning, A Biologist Reports, 1979; sr. editor: Differentiation and Neoplasia, 1980, Cloning: Leben aus der Retorte, 1981, Cloning of Frogs, Mice, and other Animals, 1985; mem. editorial bd. Differentiation, 1973—; assoc. editor: Gamete Research, 1980-86; contbr. articles to profl. jours. Served to lt. USNR, 1944-47, 51-53. Recipient Outstanding Teaching award Newcomb Coll., Tulane U., 1970; Disting. Alumni award Drury Coll., 1979, Morse Alumni Teaching award U. Minn., 1992; Research fellow Nat. Cancer Inst., 1957-58; Sr. Sci. fellow NATO, 1974. Fellow AAAS, Linnean Soc. (London); mem. Am. Assn. Cancer Rsch., Am. Assn. Cancer Edn., Metastasis Soc., Am. Inst. Biol. Scis., Soc. for Devel. Biology, Indian Soc. Devel. Biology (lifetime emeritus mem.), Internat. Soc. Study of Comparative Oncology, Inc., Internat. Soc. Differentiation (exec. com., sec.-treas. 1975-92, pres. elect 1992-94, pres. 1994—), Gown-in-Town Club, Sigma Xi. Home: 2124 Hoyt Ave W Saint Paul MN 55108-1315 Office: U Minn Dept Genetics Cell Bio Saint Paul MN 55108-1095

MC KINNEY, ALEXIS, public relations consultant; b. Cin., Mar. 13, 1907; s. John Austin and Gertrude (Kofler) McK.; m. Esther Ryker Simmons, Aug. 27, 1930 (dec. 1985); 1 dau., Eunice Christine; m. Margaret Jane Miles, Sept. 14, 1986 (dec. 1990); m. Irene Vogel Stevenson, Apr. 6, 1991. Ed. pub. schs., Colo., and Tex. Enlisted in U.S. Navy, 1923, served aboard U.S.S. New Mexico, 1923-27; circulation agt. Pueblo (Colo.) Star-Jour., 1928; reporter Pueblo Chieftain, 1929, state editor, 1930, city editor, 1931-32; co-pub. and editor Rocky Ford Tribune, 1933-34; news editor Alamosa (Colo.) Daily Courier, 1934-42; statehouse reporter Denver Post, 1942-45; information officer U.S. Bur. Reclamation, Denver, 1945-46; asst. city editor Denver Post, 1946, city editor, 1946-47, mng. editor, 1947-49, asst. pub., 1949-63; project dir. Rio Grande-land, Durango, Colo., 1963-65; dir. pub. relations Denver & Rio Grande Western R.R. Co., 1965-73; pub. relations cons. Rio Grande Industries, Inc., 1973—. Trustee Colo. R.R. Hist. Found. and Mus. Mem. all-Navy championship rifle team, 1927. Mem. Pub. Relations Soc. Am., R.R. Pub. Relations Assn., Sigma Delta Chi. Conglist. Address: 3131 E Alameda Ave #505 Denver CO 80209-3411

MCKINNEY, CHARLES CECIL, investment company executive; b. Newdale, N.C., Nov. 30, 1931; s. Sherbert Day and Florence Van (Hall) McK.; children—Emry Lynn, Robin Ashley, Marc Jason; m. Suzanne Reeves, Apr. 3, 1988. B.S.B.A., U. N.C.-Chapel Hill, 1957; student, U. Tenn., 1950-52. V.p., creative dir. J.T. Howard Advt., 1957-68; chmn. bd., chief exec. officer McKinney & Silver, Raleigh, N.C., 1968-90; chmn., pres., chief exec. officer Onyx Corp., 1991—. Trustee N.C. Symphony, Raleigh, 1983-87; bd. visitors U. N.C., Chapel Hill, 1989-91; bd. vis. Kenan Flagler Sch. Bus., 1985-94. Recipient profl. awards. Mem. N.C. Mus. Art, Sphinx Club, Carolina Country Club, Figure Eight Yacht Club. Republican. Home: 1021 Cowper Dr Raleigh NC 27608-2228

MCKINNEY, CYNTHIA ANN, congresswoman; b. Mar. 17, 1955; d. Billy and Leola McKinney; 1 child, Coy Grandison, Jr. B, U. So. Calif.; post-grad., Ga. State U., U. Wis.; Tufts U. Former instr. Clark Atlanta U., Atlanta Met. Coll.; former mem. Ga. Ho. of Reps.; mem. 103rd Congress from 11th Ga. dist., 1993—; instr. Agnes Scott Coll. Diplomatic fellow Spellman Coll. Home: 765 Shorter Ter NW Atlanta GA 30318-7140 Office: US Ho of Reps 124 Cannon Washington DC 20515*

MCKINNEY, DENNIS KEITH, lawyer; b. Ottawa, Ill., May 12, 1952; s. Robert Keith and Delroy Louise (Clayton) McK.; m. Patricia Jean Boyle, Oct. 4, 1986; 1 child, Geoffrey Edward. BS, Ball State U., 1973; JD, Ill. Inst. Tech., 1976. Bar: Ind. 1977, U.S. Dist. Ct. (so. dist.) Ind. 1977, U.S. Supreme Ct. 1993. Appellate dep. Ind. Atty. Gen, Indpls., 1977-78, trial dep., 1978-79, sr. trial dep., 1979-81, chief real estate litigation sect., 1981-94; clk. to Hon. James S. Kirsch Ind. Ct. Appeals, Indpls., 1994-95; staff atty. Ind. Supreme Ct. Disciplinary Commn., Indpls., 1995—. Author: Eminent Domain, Practice and Procedure in Indiana, 1991, A Guide to Indiana Easement Law, 1995; contbg. author: Indiana Real Estate Transactions, 1996; contbr. articles to profl. jours. Active Indpls.-Scarborough Peace Games, 1983-84. Avocations: reading, volleyball, wargaming. Office: Ind Supreme Ct Disciplinary Commn Ste 1060 South Tower 115 W Washington St Indianapolis IN 46204

MCKINNEY, DONALD, art gallery director, art dealer; b. N.Y.C., May 2, 1931. Student, Columbia U., 1954-57, London U., 1960-62. Pres. Marlborough Gallery, N.Y.C., 1974-78; dir. Hirschl & Adler Modern Galleries, N.Y.C., 1981-93; pres. Andre Emmerich Gallery, N.Y.C., 1993—. Co-author: Mark Rothko, 1971; contbr. Jackson Pollack Catalogue Raisonne, 1978. Mem. The Century Club.

MCKINNEY, DONALD LEE, magazine editor; b. Evanston, Ill., July 12, 1923; s. Guy Doane and Cora Redfield (Brenton) McK.; m. Mary Frances Joyce, Dec. 14, 1958; children—Jennifer Joyce, Douglas Guy. A.B., U. N.C., 1948. Salesman textbooks John Wiley & Sons, N.Y.C., 1949-52; freelance writer mostly comic books with some short articles and fiction, 1952-54; asst. mng. editor True mag., N.Y.C., 1955-62; editor articles Saturday Evening Post, 1962-69; spl. features editor N.Y. Daily News, 1969-70; mng. editor McCalls mag., N.Y.C., 1969-86; Gonzales prof. journalism U. S.C., Beaufort, 1986-90, prof. emeritus, 1990—. Author: Writing Magazine Articles That Sell, 1994; reporter, book reviewer. Served with USNR, 1943-46. Democrat. Home: 9 Spanish Moss Rd Hilton Head Island SC 29928-4412 *I learned early that it is important to speak up if you think you are being treated unfairly; sometimes it's true, and nobody else will complain if you don't. I also learned that in my business, and probably in most others, it is best to always say what you think. Truth is usually more helpful than any assortment of euphemisms, and it also saves a lot of worry over who you have lied to and just what you've said. Truth is not only the best policy—by all odds it's the easiest to keep track of.*

MCKINNEY, E. KIRK, JR., retired insurance company executive; b. Indpls., Mar. 27, 1923; s. E. Kirk and Irene M. (Hurley) McK.; m. Alice Hollenbeck Greene, June 18, 1949; children: Kirk Ashley, Alan Brooks, Nora Claire McKinney Hiatt, Margot Knight. A.B., U. Mich., 1948. Asst. treas. Jefferson Nat. Life Ins. Co., Indpls., 1949-52, asst. to pres., asst. treas., 1952-53, treas., asst. to pres., 1953-55, v.p., treas., 1955-59, pres., 1959-90, chmn. bd., 1970-90, ret., 1990; vice chmn. bd. Somerset Group Inc., 1986-89, ret., 1990; bd. dirs. Zimmer Paper Products, Inc. Corp. relations com. U. Mich.; former pres., former chief exec. officer, bd. govs. Indpls. Mus. Art, now treas.; bd. dirs., mem. exec. com., past bd. dirs. (hon.) Greater Indpls. Progress Com.; former vice chmn. Indpls.-Marion County Bd. Ethics; former dir. Park Tudor Sch., Community Svc. Coun. Indpls., Hosp. Devel. Corp.,

Ind. Repertory Theater; past adv. com. Indpls. Retirement Home; former bd. dirs., and pres. Episcopal Community Services, Inc.; former vice chmn., life trustee Nature Conservancy; mem. adv. bd. Ind. U., Purdue U.; active Indpls. Symphony Orch.; former bd. dirs. Ind. Pub. Broadcasting Soc. Capt. Q.M.C., AUS, 1942-46. Mem. Life Office Mgmt. Assn. (bd. dirs. 1981-83), Am. Council Life Ins. (state v.p. 1973-75, dir., exec. com. 1976-79), Assn. Ind. Life Ins. Cos. (pres. 1969-71), Indpls. C. of C., Sigma Chi. Democrat. Club: Economic of Indpls. (bd. dirs.). Home: 250 W 77th St Indianapolis IN 46260-3608 Office: 1330 W 38th St Indianapolis IN 46208-4103

MC KINNEY, GEORGE WESLEY, JR., banking educator; b. Amigo, W.Va., May 27, 1922; s. George W. and Charlotte (Ashworth) McK.; m. Lucille Christian, Sept. 5, 1941; children: George Wesley III, Mary, Ruth. A.B., Berea Coll., 1942; M.A., U. Va., 1947, Ph.D., 1949; postgrad., Stonier Grad. Sch. Banking, 1958. With Fed. Res. Bank Richmond, Va., 1948-60; asst. v.p. Fed. Res. Bank Richmond, 1958-60; with Irving Trust Co., N.Y.C., 1960-82; sr. v.p. Irving Trust Co., 1968-82, head econ. research and planning div., 1968-78, chmn. econ. adv. com., 1978-82; Va. Bankers prof. bank mgmt. McIntire Sch. Commerce U. Va., 1982-88, prof. emeritus, 1988—. Author: Federal Taxing and Spending in Virginia, 1949, Federal Reserve Discount Window, 1960, Management of Commercial Bank Funds, 1974, rev. edit., 1980; Contbr. to books. Bd. visitors Nat. Def. U., 1979-82. Served to capt. AUS, 1942-45. Fellow Nat. Assn. Bus. Economists (pres. 1965-66); mem. Phi Kappa Phi. Office: University of Virginia McIntire School of Commerce Charlottesville VA 22903

MCKINNEY, JAMES CARROLL, baritone, educator; b. Minden, La., Jan. 11, 1921; s. William C. and Carolyn (Hilman) McK.; m. Elizabeth Richmond, Aug. 28, 1949; children: James Carroll, Timothy Richmond, John Kevin. Student, La. Poly. Inst., 1938-41; student, Stanford U., 1943-44; MusB, La. State U., 1949, MusM, 1950; D.Mus. Arts, U. So. Calif., 1969; student in, London, 1979-80, 86. Grad. asst. La. State U., 1949-50; asst. prof. music theory Southwestern Baptist Theol. Sem., Ft. Worth, 1950-54; chmn. dept. music theory, composition Southwestern Baptist Theol. Sem., 1954-56, dean Sch. Ch. Music, disting. prof. of voice, 1956-94, emeritus dean and disting. prof., 1994—; baritone soloist First Presbyn. Ch., Hollywood, Calif., 1957-58, First Methodist Ch., Ft. Worth, 1963-67; guest tchr. U. So. Calif., 1958; vis. evaluator Nat. Assn. Schs. Music; vis. lectr. Hong Kong Bapt. Coll., Hong Kong Bapt. Theol. Sem., 1971-72; participant Internat. Congress Voice Tchrs., Strasbourg, France, 1987; faculty mem. Symposium on Care of the Profl. Voice, N.Y.C., 1988, Phila., 1989-96; master tchr. in NATS intern program, in Singapore, Hong Kong, Indonesia, The Philippines, and Romania, 1995, 96; spkr. in field. Presented solo recitals; appeared TV and choral prodns., Bangkok, Thailand, Hong Kong, Israel, Jordan, 1971-72; Author: The Beginning Music Reader, 1958, The Progressing Music Reader, 1959, You Can Read Music, 1960, The Advanced Music Reader, 1961, Mastering Music Reading, 1964, Study Guide for Fundamentals of Music, 1964, Vocal Fundamentals Kit, 1976, Vocal Development Kit, 1977, The Diagnosis and Correction of Vocal Faults, 1982, 2nd edit., 1994, Five Practical Lessons in Singing, 1982 (trans. into Indonesian, Korean, Portuguese, and Spanish). Bd. dirs. Ft. Worth Symphony Orch. Assn., Ft. Worth Civic Music Assn., Van Cliburn Internat., Piano Competition, Ft. Worth Opera, 1987-94. Mem. Music Tchrs. Nat. Assn. (pres. Ft. Worth chpt.), Music Educators Nat. Conf., Nat. Assn. Tchrs. Singing (lt. gov., editor jour. 1987—, pres. elect 1996—), Am. Acad. Tchrs. Singing, Am. Choral Dirs. Assn., Tex. Assn. Music Schs. (pres.), Ft. Worth Voice Tchrs. Forum (pres.), Phi Mu Alpha Sinfonia, Omicron Delta Kappa, Phi Kappa Phi, Pi Kappa Lambda. Baptist. Office: Southwestern Bapt Theol Sem PO Box 22000 1809 W Broadus Ave Fort Worth TX 76115-2137 *The longer I live, the more certain I become that the basic value systems passed on to me by my parents are valid. Inherent in all their systems were personal integrity and abiding respect for the rights of others. My chief hope is that I may be as effective as they in transmitting these values to my own children and to the students with whom I come in contact.*

MCKINNEY, JAMES CLAYTON, electronics executive, electrical engineer; b. Charleston, W.Va., June 3, 1940; s. George Clayton and Leona (Adams) McK. B.S.E.E., W.Va. Inst. Tech., 1963. Mem. staff Sta. WMON, Montgomery, W.Va., 1961-63; stringer AP, Charleston, W.Va., 1961-63; with FCC, Washington, 1963-87, chief ops. br., 1969-73, chief monitoring div., 1973, chief enforcement div., 1974, dep. chief Field Ops. Bur., 1974-80, chief Field Ops. Bur., 1980-81, chief Pvt. Radio Bur., 1981-83; chief Mass Media Bur. FCC, 1983-87; dep. asst. to Pres., dir. White House Mil. Office Washington, 1987-89; chmn. Advanced TV Systems Com., Washington, 1989-96; CEO Model HDTV Sta. Project, Inc., 1996—; chmn. U.S. del. UN Conf. on Radio, Geneva, 1986.; mem. U.S. Dels., Geneva, 1978-79, Can., 1984, Italy, 1985, Mexico, 1986, S.Am., 1986, Fed. Republic Germany, 1990; mem. presdl. dels., NATO, UN, Mexico, USSR, Can., Eng., Finland, Econ. Summit, 1987-88; U.S. Spokesman High Definition TV Conf., Geneva, 1989. Author: (with Eliot Maxwell) Future of Electronic Information Handling at the FCC—Blue Print for the 80's, 1980; (with G.A. Fehlner) Direct Broadcast Satellites in the United States, 1985; New Look at AM Radio, 1986, HDTV Approaches the End Game, 1991. Vice chmn. Montreux Medal Award Com., 1990-95; chmn. High Definition TV World Conf., 1990-93; chmn. strategic planning roup for Internat. Consultative Com. for Radio, Dept. State, 1990-91; bd. dirs. Bowler Found., 1990-95, PICA Found., Inc., 1996—. Recipient Outstanding Fed. Exec. award FCC, 1979, 80, 82, 83, 85, 86; Presdl. Rank award for disting. exec. svc., 1985, Gold medal for disting. fed. svc., 1987, TV Engring. Achievement award, 1992, NAB award of honor, 1996. Fellow Radio Club Am., Soc. Broadcast Engrs. (sr.), Broadcast Pioneers, Soc. Motion Picture and TV Engrs. (presdl. proclamation 1991); mem. Fed. Exec. Assn., Cosmos Club of Washington. Episcopalian. Home: 6514 Gretna Green Way Alexandria VA 22312-3114

MCKINNEY, JANE-ALLEN, artist and educator; b. Owensboro, Ky., Jan. 8, 1952; d. William Holland and Jane Wilhoit (Moore) McK. BA, Scarritt Coll., Nashville, 1974; MA, Vanderbilt U., 1977; MFA, Memphis Coll. of Art, 1993. Grad. asst. dept. art Peabody Coll. for Tchrs., Vanderbilt U., Nashville, 1975-76; tchr. Smyrna (Tenn.) Comprehensive Vocat. Ctr., 1977-78; pres., bd. dirs. Jane Allen Flighton Artworks Inc., Nashville, 1978—; jeweler Wright's Jewelry Store, Clarksville, Tenn., 1982; tchr. art Belmont U., Nashville, 1984-88, Met. Centennial Park Art Ctr., Nashville, 1988-91, Cheekwood Mus. of Art, Nashville, 1990-94, Nossi Coll. of Art, Nashville, 1991-94, Western Ky. U., Bowling Green, 1991-94; ednl. cons. fine art Nossi Coll. Art, Nashville, 1993—; artist for Women of Achievement awards, sculptures and jewelry YWCA, Nashville, 1992—; artist for Bus. Award Sculpture, C. of C., Nashville, 1990. One and two person shows include Cheekwood Mus. Art, 1981, 93, Owensboro Mus. Fine Art, 1992, Western Ky. U., 1992-94, Belmont U., 1984, others; exhbns. include Watkins Art Inst., Nashville, 1991, Western Ky. U., 1992, Parthenon, Nashville, 1992, Owensboro Mus. Art, 1993, Tenn. Performing Arts Ctr., 1995; invitational and juried exhibits include Sculptors of Mid. Tenn. Arts in the Airport, Nashville, 1996, Nat. Coun. on the Edn. of Ceramics Arts, Rochester, N.Y., 1996, Ceramic Exhibn. Tenn. State U., 1996, and numerous others; represented in permanent collections including City of Chattanooga's Visitors Ctr., IBM, Bapt. Hosp., Nations Bank of Tenn., Mass. Pub. Libr., First Am. Bank Corp., and numerous others. Adv. bd. Belmont U., Nashville, 1984—, Nossi Coll. Art, 1993—; mem edn. com. Nat. Mus. of Women in the Arts, Tenn., 1992—; artist for fundraising sculpture Arthritis Found., Nashville, 1989-90; vol. singer VA Hosp., Nashville, 1989—; bd. dirs. Visual Arts Alliance Nashville, 1996; vol. soloist Vet.'s Hosp., 1991-96; artist for ann. fundraiser YWCA, 1993-96. Recipient Best Tchr. award Nossi Coll. Art, 1992-93; grantee City of Chattanooga Welcome Ctr., 1993, Memphis Arts Festival Spl. Projects, 1994. Mem. AAUW, Assn. of Visual Artists, Soc. of N.Am. Goldsmiths, Visual Artists Alliance of Nashville, Nat. Art Edn. Assn., Internat. Sculpture Ctr., Nat. Coun. on Edn. of the Ceramic Arts, Tenn. Assn. of Craft Artists, Coll. Art Assn. Avocations: boating, running, singing, dancing, hiking. Home: PO Box 120454 Nashville TN 37212-0454

MCKINNEY, JOHN ADAMS, JR., lawyer; b. Washington, Mar. 10, 1948; s. John A. and Cleo G. (Turner) McK., m. Carol A. Cowen, Dec. 22, 1970; children: John III, Thomas. BA, Principia Coll., 1970; JD, Coll. William and Mary, 1973. Bar: N.J. 1973. Assoc. Mason, Griffin & Pierson, Princeton, N.J., 1973-77; gen. atty. Nabisco, Inc., East Hanover, N.J., 1977-79; asst. counsel Republic Steel Corp., Cleve., 1979-84; sr. atty. AT&T, Berkeley Heights, N.J., 1984-90; mem. McCarter & English, 1990—. Mem. ABA (vice-chair sect. natural resources energy and environ. law solid and hazardous waste com. 1990—, chair, teleconf. programs 1994-96), N.J. Bar Assn. (dir. environ. law sect. 1992—). Office: McCarter & English 4 Gateway Ctr 100 Mulberry St Newark NJ 07102-4004

MCKINNEY, JOSEPH F., diversified manufacturing holding company executive; b. Phila., 1931. BS, St. Joseph's Coll., 1952; MBA, Harvard U., 1957. Dir. rsch. Warner, Jennings, Mandel & Longstreth, 1957-60; founder, pres. Electro-Sci. Investors, Inc., Richardson, Tex., 1960-63; v.p. Brown, Allen & Co., 1963-64; dir. corp. fin. Ling & Co., 1964-65, Goodbody & Co., 1965-66; pres. Tyler Corp., Dallas, Tex., 1966-83, 1987-94, chmn., chief exec. officer, 1972—, also bd. dirs. Office: Tyler Corp 2121 San Jacinto St Dallas TX 75201-7901*

MCKINNEY, JUDSON THAD, broadcast executive; b. Sacramento, Aug. 21, 1941; s. Judson Bartlet and Mildred Eoline (Taylor) McK. Student, Sacramento State U., 1959-61, Western Bapt. Bible Coll., 1961-62, Am. River Coll., 1962-63. Prodn. dir. Sta. KEBR, Sacramento, 1962-65; sta. mgr. Sta. KAMB, Merced, Calif., 1965-68, Sta. KEAR, San Francisco, 1975-78, 79-88, WFME, Newark, 1978; western regional mgr. Family Stas. Inc., 1988—. Chmn. bd. 1st Bapt. Ch. of San Francisco, 1985-91. Mem. Nat. Religious Broadcasters., Nat. Assn. Evangelicals. Republican. Lodge: Gideons. Office: Family Stations inc 290 Hegenberger Rd Oakland CA 94621-1436

MCKINNEY, LARRY J., federal judge; b. South Bend, Ind., July 4, 1944; s. Lawrence E. and Helen (Byers) McK.; m. Carole Jean Marie Lyon, Aug. 19, 1966; children: Joshua E., Andrew G. BA, MacMurray Coll., Jacksonville, Ill., 1966; JD, Ind. U., 1969. Bar: Ind. 1970, U.S. Dist. Ct. (so. dist.) Ind. 1970. Law clk. to atty. gen. State of Ind., Indpls., 1969-70, dep. atty. gen., 1970-71; ptnr. Rodgers and McKinney, Edinburgh, Ind., 1971-75, James F.T. Sargent, Greenwood, Ind., 1975-79; judge Johnson County Cir. Ct., Franklin, Ind., 1979-87, U.S. Dist. Ct. (so. dist.) Ind., Indpls., 1987—. Presbyterian. Avocations: reading, jogging. Office: US Dist Ct 330 US Courthouse 46 E Ohio St Indianapolis IN 46204-1903

MCKINNEY, OWEN MICHAEL, special education educator, consultant; b. Jeffersonville, Ind., Mar. 9, 1950; s. Owen Howard and Frances Marie (Hall) McK.; m. Janice Elaine Wilson, Sept. 2, 1972; 1 child, Sean Michael. BS in Police Adminstrn., U. Louisville, 1976, postgrad., 1988—; AA, SUNY, Albany, 1978; MS in Adminstrn. of Justice, U. Louisville, 1978; diploma in pastoral ministries, So. Bapt. Conv., 1980; MAT in Secondary Edn., U. Louisville, 1987. Cert. 5-12 tchr., learning disabilities, behavior disorders, physically handicapped, community-based edn., learning strategies, social skills, history, geography, polit. sci., sociology, Ky. Probation and parole officer Commonwealth of Ky., Louisville, 1978; security mgr. First Nat. Tower John W. Galbreath & Co., Louisville, 1981-82; v.p. Safety Arms Security & Police Equipment Co., Portsmouth, Va., 1980; area mgr. CPP Security Svc., Norfolk, Va., 1979-80, Louisville, 1982-83; tchr. Jefferson County Pub. Schs., Louisville, 1985-88, spl. edn. tchr., 1988—; pres. Cambridge Cons Inc, Louisville, 1995—; owner Owen McKinney Security Cons., Louisville, 1973—; commr. City of Richlawn, Ky., 1990-92; presenter in field. Editor, writer, publisher The Renaissance Magazine, 1979-81; editor, publisher: Security Gazette, 1982, The Private Investigator, 1983-84, Private Security Report, 1983; editor, writer: (newspaper) Richlawn Gazette, 1990, 91; contbr. articles to profl. jours. Mem. George Bush for Pres., Jefferson County, 1988, Rebecca Jackson for Jefferson County Clerk, 1989, Owen M. McKinney for City Comsnr., Richlawn, 1989, Al Brown for U.S. Congress, 3d congl. dist., Louisville, 1990, Vote for the Library Tax campaign, Jefferson County, 1992; Rep. del. 3d congl. dist. meeting 32d Legis. Dist., 1990, del. Rep. State Conv. 32nd legis. dist. chmn. 1993-94. Staff sgt. U.S. Army, 1969-73, Vietnam, mem. USAR, 1977-85. Recipient Commendation medal U.S. Army, 1971, cert. of appreciation Pres. of U.S., 1973, Outstanding Staff award JCPS, 1919, 92, 93, 94, 95, Minerva award U. Louisville, 1993; named to Hon. Order Ky. Cols., sr. fellow U. Louisville Soc., numerous others. Mem. ASCD, Am. Soc. Indsl. Security (cert. protection profl., chmn. seminar com. Louisville chpt. 1983-84, cert. appreciation Louisville chpt. 1984), Coun. Exceptional Children (chpt. gen. bd. 1988-89, v.p. 1989-90, pres. elect 1990-91, chpt. pres. 1991-92, state gen. bd. 1991-92, chpt. past pres. 1992-93, state v.p. 1993-94, state pres.-elect 1994-95, state pres. 1995-96, Svc. award 1990, cert. merit Ky. Fedn. 1990, cert. Outstanding Svc. 1991-92, outstanding mem. of yr. award 1993), Nat. Crime Prevention Alumni Assn., Ky. Ctr. Pub. Issues (charter), Commonwealth Atty.'s Citizen Adv. Coun., DeMolay Alumni Assn. (life, Rep. DeMolay award 1976, 25 Yr. mem.award 1991), U. Louisville Alumni Assn. (program vol. 1990—), Am. Mensa Soc., Am. Legion, Ky. Mid. Sch. Assn., Jesse Stuart Found., York Rite, Scottish Rite, USCG Aux., The Wild Geese (hon.), Masons (past master, grand lodge com.), Order of Eastern Star, Grotto, KP (chancellor comdr. 1994, Internat. Svc. award 1993), Rosicrucian Order, Philalethes Soc., Royal Order Scotland (life), Societas Rosicruciana in Civitatibus Foederatis (life), Shrine, Golden Key Hon. Soc. (life), Internat. High 12 (Internat. Svc. award 1994), Alpha Phi Sigma (nat. criminal justice hon. soc. 19750, Phi Delta Kappa (chpt. sec. 1992-93, v.p. 1993-94. Republican. Baptist. Avocations: reading, tennis, weight lifting, photography, master scuba diver. Home: 212 N Hubbards Ln Louisville KY 40207-2251 Office: Eastern HS 12400 Old Shelbyville Rd Louisville KY 40222 also: Cambridge Cons Inc PO Box 6602 Louisville KY 40206

MCKINNEY, PATRICIA CAROL, mental health nurse; b. Kittanning, Pa., June 7, 1938; d. William Lamont and Grace Garnet (France) Mohney; m. Frank Carl McKinney, Sept. 9, 1961; children: Amy Beth, Kelly Sue. Diploma, St. John's Gen. Hosp., 1959. Civilian staff nurse Ireland Army Hosp., Ft. Knox, Ky.; staff nurse Armstrong County Meml. Hosp., Kittanning, Sugarcreek Rest Home, Kittanning; day supr. Armstrong County Health Ctr., Kittanning; supr. and quality control nurse Wesley Manor Health Care, 1991-92; office nurse, quality control Cowansville Area Health Ctr., 1992-93; dir. health svc. Sugarcreek Home Inc., Kittanning, 1993-96, ret., 1996. Home: RR 8 Box 204 Kittanning PA 16201-7901

MCKINNEY, RICHARD ISHMAEL, philosophy educator; b. Live Oak, Fla., Aug. 20, 1906; s. George Patterson and Sallie Richard (Ellis) McK.; m. Phyllis Vivian Kimbrough, June 27, 1933 (dec. May 1965); children: George Kimbrough, Phyllis Zanaida McKinney Bynum; m. Lena Roberta Martin, Aug. 5, 1967. BA, Morehouse Coll., 1931; BD, Andover Newton Theol. Sch., 1934, STM, 1937; PhD, Yale U., 1942; DD, St. Paul's Coll., Lawrenceville, Va., 1978. Pastor Pond St. Bapt. Ch., Providence, 1933-35; asst. prof. philosophy and religion Va. Union U., Richmond, Va., 1935-42, dean Sch. of Religion, 1942-44, acting v.p., 1978-79; pres. Storer Coll., Harpers Ferry, W.Va., 1944-50; chmn. dept. philosophy Morgan State U., Balt., 1951-76, acting dean Coll. Arts and Scis., 1977-78; disting. scholar in philos. theology Coppin State Coll., Balt., 1983; vis. prof. U. Pa., Phila., spring 1972, U. Ife, Ife-Ife, Nigeria, spring 1974. Author: Religion in Higher Education Among Negroes, 1945, History of First Baptist Church of Charlottesville, Va., 1863-1980, 1981, History of the Black Baptists of Florida, 1850-1985, 1987; contbr. articles to profl. jours. Bd. dirs. Balt. Urban League, 1958-59, Luth. Hosp., Balt., 1963-65, Am. Cancer Soc., Balt., 1965-70, Enoch Pratt Libr., Balt., 1991—. Mem. AAUP, NEA, Am. Philos. Assn., Soc. for Values in Higher Edn., Soc. for Existential Philosophy and Phenomenology, Phi Beta Kappa, Omega Psi Phi, Sigma Pi Phi (nat. pres. 1986-88), Phi Sigma Tau (nat. pres. 1959-62). Democrat. Avocation: cabinet maker. Home: 2408 Overland Ave Baltimore MD 21214-2440

MC KINNEY, ROBERT MOODY, newspaper editor and publisher; b. Shattuck, Okla., Aug. 28, 1910; s. Edwin S. and Eva (Moody) McK.; married, 1943; 1 child, Mrs. Meade Martin; m. Marie-Louise de Montmollin, May 7, 1970. AB, U. Okla., 1932; LLD, U. N.Mex., 1964. Investment analyst Standard Stats. Co., Inc. (now Standard and Poor's Co.), 1932-34; ptnr. Young-Kolbe & Co., 1934-38, Robert R. Young & Co., 1938-42; exec. v.p., treas. Pathe Film Co., 1934-39, Allegheny Corp., 1936-42, Pittston Corp. and subs., 1936-42; v.p. Fremkir Corp., 1937-50, Allan Corp., 1937-50; exec. v.p., treas. Mo. Pacific R.R., 1938-42; ptnr. Scheffmeyer, McKinney & Co., 1945-50; editor, pub. Santa Fe New Mexican, 1949—; chmn. bd. The New Mexican, Inc., 1949—; profl. corp. dir. 10 N.Y.S.E. cos., 1934-86; chmn. Robert Moody Found.; chmn. N.Mex. Econ. Devel. Commn. and Water Resources Devel. Bd., 1949-51; asst. sec. U.S. Dept. Interior, 1951-52; chmn. panel to report to Congress on impact of Peaceful Uses of Atomic Energy, 1955-56; permanent U.S. rep. to Internat. Atomic Energy Agy., Vienna, 1957-58; U.S. rep. Internat. Conf. Peaceful Uses Atomic Energy, Geneva, 1958; U.S. ambassador to, Switzerland, 1961-63; exec. officer Presdl. Task Force on Internat. Investments, 1963-64; chmn. Presdl. Commn. on Travel, 1968; chmn. bd. visitors U. Okla., 1968-72; U.S. rep. Internat. Centre Settlement Investment Disputes, Washington, 1967-74. Author: Hymn to Wreckage: A Picaresque Interpretation of History, 1947, The Scientific Foundation for European Integration, 1959, On Increasing Effectiveness of Western Science and Technology, 1959, The Red Challenge to Technological Renewal, 1960, Review of the International Atomic Policies and Programs of the United States, 1960, The Toad and the Water Witch, 1985, Variations on a Marxist Interpretation of Culture, 1986. Served from lt. (j.g.) to lt. USNR, 1942-45. Recipient Disting. Service medal U.S. Dept. Treasury, 1968, Disting. Service medal U. Okla., 1972. Mem. Am. Soc. Newspaper Editors, Coun. Fgn. Rels., Coun. of Am. Ambs., Newspaper Assn. of Am., Phi Beta Kappa, Phi Gamma Delta. Democrat. Episcopalian. Clubs: Chevy Chase (Md.); F Street, Metropolitan (Washington); University, Brook, Century, Links, Knickerbocker, River (N.Y.C.). Home: Wind Fields 39850 Snickersville Tpke Middleburg VA 22117-3002 Office: PO Box 1705 Santa Fe NM 87504-1705

MC KINNEY, ROSS ERWIN, civil engineering educator; b. San Antonio, Aug. 2, 1926; s. Roy Earl and Beatrice (Saylor) McK.; m. Margaret McKinney Curtis, June 21, 1952; children: Ross Erwin, Margaret E., William S., Susanne C. B.A., So. Meth. U., 1948, B.S. in Civil Enging, 1948; S.M., MIT, 1949, Sc.D., 1951. Sen. scientist S.W. Found. for Research and Edn., San Antonio, 1951-53; asst. prof. MIT, 1953-58, assoc. prof., 1958-60; prof. U. Kans., 1960-63, chmn. dept. civil engring., 1963-66, Parker prof. civil engring., 1966-76, N.T. Veatch prof. environ. engring., 1976-93, prof. emeritus, 1993—; adv. prof. Tongji U., Shanghai, Peoples Rep. China, 1985; v.p. Rolf Eliassen Assocs., Winchester, Mass., 1954-60; pres. Environ. Pollution Control Services, Lawrence, Kans., 1969-73. Author: Microbiology for Sanitary Engineers, 1962; Editor: Nat. Conf. on Solid Waste Research, 1964, 2d Internat. Symposium for Waste Treatment Lagoons, 1970. Mem. Cambridge (Mass.) Water Bd., 1953-59, Lawrence-Douglas County Health Bd., 1969-76, Kans. Water Quality Adv. Council, 1965-76, Kans. Solid Waste Adv. Council, 1970-76, Kans. Environ. Adv. Bd., 1976-85. Served with USNR, 1943-46. Recipient Harrison P. Eddy award, 1962, Water Pollution Control Fedn. Rudolph Hering award, 1964, U.S. Presdl. Commendation, 1971, Environ. Quality award EPA Region VII, 1979, Chancellors Teaching award, U. Kans., 1986. Mem. ASCE (hon.), Am. Water Works Assn., Water Pollution Control Fedn. (Thomas R. Camp medal 1982), Am. Pub. Works Assn., Am. Chem. Soc., Am. Soc. Microbiologists, AAAS, Internat. Assn. Water Pollution Rsch., Am. Acad. Environ. Engrs., Kans. Water Pollution Control Assn. (hon., Gordon M. Fair medal 1991), NAE, Sigma Xi, Sigma Tau, Kappa Mu Epsilon, Chi Epsilon, Tau Beta Pi. Achievements include patent for water treatment process. Home: 2617 Oxford Rd Lawrence KS 66049-2822

MCKINNEY, SALLY VITKUS, realty company executive, business owner; b. Muncie, Ind., Aug. 6, 1944; d. Robert Brookins and Mary (Mann) Gooden; m. Alan George Vitkus (div. Jan. 1979); m. James Larry McKinney, Feb. 1, 1986. AA, William Woods Coll., 1964; BSBA, U. Ariz., 1966; postgrad., U. Nev., Las Vegas, 1966-68. Tchr. Las Vegas Day Sch., 1972-76; salesperson Globe Realty, Las Vegas, 1976-79; owner, pres. Realty West, Las Vegas, 1979—. Rec. sec. Clark County Rep. Cen. Com., Las Vegas, 1982, 1st vice chmn., 1985; vice chmn. Nev. Rep. com., 1986, chmn., 1987-88; mem. Assistance League Las Vegas. Recipient award Nat. Assn. Home Builders, 1981, 82, 83. Mem. Nat. Assn. Realtors, Las Vegas Bd. Realtors, Greater Las Vegas C. of C., Gen. Fedn. Womens Clubs (Outstanding Young Woman Am. 1979, exec. bd. 1980-82), Jr. League Las Vegas, Mesquite Club (chmn. pub. affairs com. 1986-87, past pres., secret witness exec. bd. 1994—). Presbyterian. Avocations: tennis, bridge. Home: 132 Ultra Dr Henderson NV 89014-8306

MCKINNEY, VENORA WARE, librarian; b. Meridian, Okla., June 16, 1937. BA, Langston U., 1959; MLS, U. Ill., 1965. Librarian Milw. Pub. Library, 1962-68, br. librarian, 1979-83, dep. city librarian, 1983—; librarian Peoria Pub. Schs., Ill., 1969, Milw. Pub. Schs., 1972-79; adj. faculty U. Wis., Milw.; mem. Wis. Govs. Coun. on Libr. Devel., 1983-92; bd. dirs. V.E. Carter Child Devel. Group. Bd. dirs. Milw. Repertory Theatre; coun. adv. Sch. Libr. and Info. Sci., U. Wis., Madison, 1992-96. Nat. Forum for Black Pub. Adminstrs. fellow Exec. Leadership Inst., George Mason U. Mem. ALA Black Caucus, Wis. Libr. Assn. (v.p. 1994, pres. 1995—, bd. dirs. 1996), Wis. Libr. Assn. Found., Wis. Black Librs. Network, ALA Pub. Libr. Assn., Links, Delta Sigma Theta. Baptist. Office: Milw Pub Libr 814 W Wisconsin Ave Milwaukee WI 53233-2309

MCKINNEY, WILLIAM T., psychiatrist, educator; b. Rome, Ga., Sept. 20, 1937. BA cum laude, Baylor U., 1959; MD, Vanderbilt U., 1963. Diplomate Nat. Bd. Med. Examiners (mem. psychiatry test com. 1982-87, chmn. 1984-87); cert. Am. Bd. Psychiatry and Neurology (sr. examiner 1979-90, bd. dirs. 1991—, mem. rsch. com., co-chair part I test com., chair added qualifications in geriatric psychiatry test com., mem. part II audio visual com., mem. disability accomodations com., rep. to residency rev. com.). Intern in medicine Bowman Gray Sch. Medicine, Wake Forest U., Winston-Salem, N.C., 1963-64; resident dept. psychiatry Sch. Medicine, U. N.C., Chapel Hill., 1964-66, Sch. Medicine, Stanford (Calif.) U., 1966-67; clin. assoc. psychosomatic sect. adult psychiatry br., tng. specialist, asst. br. chief NIMH, Bethesda, Md., 1967-69; asst. prof. psychiatry dept. psychiatry Sch. Medicine, U. Wis., Madison, 1969-72, assoc. prof. psychiatry, 1972-74, prof. psychiatry, 1974-93; Asher prof. of psychiatry dept. psychiatry and behavioral scis., dir. Asher Ctr. for Study and Treatment of Depressive Disorders Med. Sch., Northwestern U., Chgo., 1993—; part-time clin. pvt. practice, Bethesda, 1967-69; NIMH rsch. career investigator Sch. Medicine, U. Wis., Madison, 1970-75, rsch. psychiatrist Primate Lab., 1974-93, affiliate sci. Wis. Regional Primate Rsch. Ctr., 1974-93, affiliate prof. psychology dept. psychology, 1974-93, chmn. dept. psychiatry, 1975-80, dir. Wis. Psychiat. Rsch. Inst. Ctr. Health Scis., 1975-80; sr. staff psychiatrist William S. Middleton Meml. VA Hosp., Madison, Wis., 1974-93; rschr. sub dept. animal behaviour U. Cambridge, Eng., 1974; mem. rsch. rev. com. VA Behavioral Scis., 1976-79; Abbott Sigma XI Club lectr., 1976; Milw. Psychiat. Hosp. lectr., 1977; mem. program adv. com. and workshop chmn. Dahlem Found. Internat. Conf. on Depression, Berlin, 1982; U. Minn. lectr. at Festshrift, 1982; cons. grad. sch. U. Minn., 1982; fellow Ctr. Advanced Study in Behavioral Scis., Stanford, Calif., 1983-84; mem. external adv. bd. Clin. Rsch. Ctr. Dept. Psychiatry U. N.C., Chapel Hill, 1984—, cons., bd. advisors clin. rsch. fellow tng. program dept. psychology, 1988—; William F. Orr lectr. Vanderbilt U., 1985; vis. prof. dept. psychiatry U. Tex. Health Scis. Ctr., Dallas, 1986, U. Utah Sch. Medicine, Salt Lake City, 1987, U. Minn. Sch. Medicine, Mpls., 1988; cons. biol. scis. tng. br. divsn. manpower and tng. programs NIMH, 1975-76, mem. psychiatry spl. tng. com. 1983, plenary lectr., Clearwater, Fla., 1987, co-chairperson Workshop on Non-Human Primate Models of Psychopathology, 1987, mem. biol. psychopathology spl. rev. com., 1992—; mem. sci. core group MacArthur Found. Mental Health Rsch. Network I: The Psychobiology of Depression and Other Affective Disorders, 1988-93; vis. spkr. So. Calif. Psychiat. Soc., L.A., 1988; plenary lectr. Soc. Biol. Psychiatry ann. meeting, Montreal, 1988; vis. prof. Dalhousie U. Sch. Medicine, N.S., 1989, HCA Riveredge Hosp., Chgo., 1989, U. Pa., Phila., 1991, U. N.Mex., Albuquerque, 1992, Northwestern U., Chgo., 1992; invited spkr. Animal Models in Psychopharmacology Symposium, Duphar, Amsterdam, 1990; vis. spkr., cons. CIBA-GEIGY, Basel, Switzerland, 1990; mem. minority instns. rsch. devel. rev. com. Alcohol, Drug Abuse and Mental Health Adminstrn., 1990; guest spkr. Inst. Pa. Hosp., Phila., 1991; reviewer Human Frontier Sci. Program, 1992—; external cons. dept. psychiatry Mental Health Clin. Rsch. Ctr. U. Tex. Southwestern Med. Ctr., Dallas, 1992—; presenter in field. Author: Animal Models of Mental Disorders: A New Comparative Psychiatry, 1988; co-author: Mood Disorders: Towards a New Psychobiology, 1984; mem. editl. bd. Archives of Psychiatry and Neurol. Scis., Contemporary Psychiatry, 1981-82, Ethology and Sociobiology, Experientia, 1982-89, Trends in Neurosciences, 1982-86, Neuropsychopharmacology, 1987-90; manuscript and book reviewer numerous sci. jours.; contbr. articles to profl. jours. USHPS fellow in biostats.bilt U., 1962; recipient Beauchamp award Vanderbilt U. Med. Sch., 1963, Rsch. Career Devel. award NIMH, 1975, Rsch. Leave award U. Wis., 1983-84, Am. Acad. Pediats. award, 1991. Fellow Am. Psychiat. Assn. (cons. psychiat. edn. consultation svc. 1983—), Am. Coll. Psychiatrists, Am. Coll. Neuropsychopharmacology (mem. constn.

and rules com. 1985-87, mem. ethics com. 1987-89, mem. fin. com. 1990-92, panel chair San Juan, P.R. 1992, panel presenter 1992); mem. Am. Soc. Primatologists, Am. Psychosomatic Soc. (mem. program com. 1975-76), Internat. Primatology Soc., Internat. Coll. Neurobiology, Biol. Psychiatry and Psychopharmacology (lectr. Zurich 1985), Internat. Soc. Devel. Psychobiology, Internat. Soc. Ethological and Behavioral Pharmacology (bd. advisors 1983—), Collegium Internat. Neuro-Psychopharmacologicum, Psychiat. Rsch. Soc., Soc. Neuroscience, Wis. Psychiat. Assn. (chmn. program com. 1972, co-chairperson task force on sexual misconduct and membership edn. 1986-88, pres.-elect 1989-91, pres. 1991-93). Office: Northwestern U Med Sch Dept Psychiatry and Behavioral Scis 303 E Chicago Ave Bldg 9-176 Chicago IL 60611-3008

MCKINNEY-KELLER, MARGARET FRANCES, retired special education educator; b. Houston, Mo., Nov. 25, 1929; d. George Weimer and Thelma May (Davis) Van Pelt; m. Roy Calvin McKinney Sr., Nov. 11, 1947 (dec. Feb. 1990); children: Deanna Kay Little, Roy Calvin Jr.; m. Clarence Elmore Keller, June 8, 1991; 1 child, Dennis Lee Keller. BS with honors, Bradley U., 1963, MA in Counselor Edn., 1968, postgrad., 1992; postgrad., U. Ill., 1993—, Aurora Coll., Ill. Ctrl. Coll. In real estate Peoria, Ill., 1951-57; tchr. Oak Ridge Sch., Willow Springs, Mo., 1947-48, pvt. kindergarten, Washington, Ill., 1957-59, Dist. 50 Schs., Washington, Ill., 1959-67; tchr. socially maladjusted Washington Twp. Spl. Edn. Coop., 1967-70; tchr. behavior disordered Tazewell-Mason Counties Spl. Edn., Washington, Ill., 1970-78; resource tchr. Dist. 50 Schs., Washington, 1978-94; ret., 1994; cons. moderator Active Parenting Group, Washington, 1972—. Vol. Proctor Hosp., 1994—; com. mem. to establish Tazewell County Health Dept., 1960s; pres. gov. bd. Faith Luth. Day Care Ctr., Washington, 1970—, Washington Sr. Citizens, 1982-91; coach Spl. Olympics, Washington, 1979—; pres. Faith Luth. Ch. Coun., Washington, 1985-86; laity v.p. No. Conf. Evang. Luth. Ch. Am., Ctrl. Ill., 1986-92. Mem. AAUW, Washington Bus. and Profl. Women (pres. 1979-80, 88-89, dist. 9 dir. 1995-96), Am. Legion Aux., German-Am. Soc., Alpha Delta Kappa (state office, ctrl. region). Avocations: travel, cooking, oil painting, crocheting. Home: 603 Sherwood Park Rd Washington IL 61571-1828

MCKINNIS, MICHAEL B., lawyer; b. St. Louis, May 31, 1945; s. Bayard O. and Doris (Lammert) McK.; m. Patricia Butow, Aug. 24, 1968; children: Scott, Christopher, Elizabeth. BS, Drake U., 1967; JD, U. Mo., 1970. Bar: Mo. 1970, U.S. Dist. Ct. (ea. dist.) Mo. Ptnr., exec. com. Bryan Cave, St. Louis. Editor U. Mo. Law Rev., 1969-70. Mem. ABA, Mo. Bar Assn., Order of Coif, Phi Delta Phi. Office: Bryan Cave 1 Met Sq 211 N Broadway Saint Louis MO 63102-2733

MCKINNON, ARNOLD BORDEN, transportation company executive; b. Goldsboro, N.C., Aug. 13, 1927; s. Henry Alexander and Margaret (Borden) McK.; m. Oriana McArthur, July 19, 1950; children: Arnold Borden Jr., Colin McArthur, Henry Alexander. AB, Duke U., 1950, LLB, 1951; grad. Advanced Mgmt. Program, Harvard U., 1972. Bar: D.C. 1951, N.C. 1966. With Norfolk So. Corp. (formerly So. Ry. System), Norfolk, Va., 1951—, v.p. law, 1971-75, sr. v.p. law and acctg., 1975-77, exec. v.p. law and acctg., 1977-81, exec. v.p. law and fin., 1981-82, exec. v.p. mktg., 1982-86, vice chmn., 1986-87, chmn., pres., CEO, 1987-91; chmn., 1991-92, chmn. exec. com., 1992—, also bd. dirs.; bd. dirs. Norfolk Works, Inc. Mem. Va. Port Authority Nat. Maritime Ctr. Found., Global Transpark Found., Norfolk Forum, Inc., CADRE Found.; active Mil. Civilian Liaison Group; mem. bus. adv. com. Northwestern U. Transp. Ctr.; trustee Med. Coll. Hampton Roads Found., Va. Union Theol. Sem.; vice chmn. Va. Gov.'s Econ. Adv. Coun.; commr. Norfolk Redevel. and Housing Authority. With U.S. Army, 1946-47. Mem. ABA, N.C. Bar Assn., D.C. Bar Assn., Am. Soc. Corp. Execs., Norfolk Yacht and Country Club, Harbor Club, Chevy Chase Club, Met. Club (Washington), Laurel Valley Golf Club, India House (N.Y.C.), Cedar Point Club (Suffolk, Va.), Rotary (bd. dirs. Norfolk). Presbyterian. Home: 552 Mowbray Arch Norfolk VA 23507-2130 Office: Norfolk So Corp 3 Commercial Pl Norfolk VA 23510-2191

MC KINNON, CLINTON DAN, aerospace transportation executive; b. San Bernardino, Calif., Jan. 27, 1934; s. Clinton Dotson and Lucille V. (McVey) McK.; m. Janice Bernard; children: Holly Jean, Sherri Lynn, Clinton Scott, Lisa Caroline. B.A., U. Mo., 1956; honorary doctorate, Nat. U., 1987. Page U.S. Ho. of Reps., 1950-52; reporter, photographer, advt. salesman Sentinel Newspaper, San Diego, 1960-62; owner, pres. KSON Radio, San Diego, 1962-85, KSON-FM, San Diego, 1964-85; pub. La Jolla (Calif.) Light Jour., 1969-73; owner House of Hits (book and music pub.), San Diego, 1972—; co-owner KIII-TV, Corpus Christi, Tex., 1964—, KBMT-TV, Beaumont, Tex., 1976—, KUSI-TV, San Diego, 1992—; chmn. CAB, Washington, 1981-84; with spl. projects CIA, 1985-86; chmn., pres. North Am. Airlines, Jamaica, N.Y., 1989—. Author: The Good Life, 1974, Bullseye--One Reactor (aka Bullseye Iraq), 1986, Everything You Need to Know Before You're Hijacked, 1986, The Ten Second Message, 1994, Rescue Pilot, 1994, Words of Honor, 1995. Chmn. exec. com. Greater San Diego Billy Graham Crusade. Served as aviator USNR, 1956-60. Recipient Advt. Man of Year award San Diego Advt. and Sales Club, 1971; Radio Sta. Mgr. of Year award Billboard Mag., 1973; Internat. Pres.'s award Youth for Christ, 1975; Man of Distinction award Mexican-Am. Found., 1976; George Washington Honor medal Freedoms Found., 1976; Headliner of Yr. (govt.), San Diego Press Club, 1985. Mem. Country Music Assn. (pres. 1977, recipient pres. award 1980), C. of C. (dir.), Nat. Assn. Broadcasters (bd. dirs. 1970-74), Calif. Broadcasters Assn. (dir.), Navy League (Media Man of Yr. 1980). Club: Rotary (San Diego). Set Navy helicopter peacetime rescue record of 62 air/sea rescues, 1958; 1st person to close down fed. govt. regulatory agy., CAB, 1984. Office: N Am Airlines JFK International Ste 250 Jamaica NY 11430

MCKINNON, DANIEL WAYNE, JR., naval officer; b. St. Joseph, Mo., Apr. 26, 1934; s. Daniel Wayne and Amber Ruth (McClanahan) McK.; m. Rae Lynne Hopper, Apr. 21, 1957; 1 child, Daniel W. III. BSBA, U. Mo., 1956; MBA with distinction, U. Mich., 1966; grad. (disting.), Indsl. Coll. Armed Forces, Washington, 1975. Commd. ensign USN, 1956, advanced through grades to rear adm., 1983; exec. asst. to comdr. Naval Supply Systems Command, Washington, 1970-74, dir. supply corps pers., 1982-83, dep. comdr. for inventory and systems integrity, 1983-84, vice comdr., 1984-86, comdr., 1988-91; ship supply readiness officer, supply systems ops. officer Naval Logistic Command, Pacific Fleet, Pearl Harbor, Hawaii, 1975-78; dir. shipbuilding contracts div. Naval Sea Systems Command, Washington, 1978-80; comdg. officer Naval Supply Depot, Subic Bay, The Philippines, 1980-82; dep. dir. for acquisition mgmt. Def. Logistics Agy., Cameron Station, Va., 1986-88; chief Navy supply corps, comdr. Naval Supply Systems, 1988-91; ret. USN, 1991—; pres., CEO NISH (formerly Nat. Industries for Severely Handicapped), Vienna, Va., 1992—. Chmn. Annandale (Va.) Ctrl. Bus. Dist. Planning Com., 1986-91, Pres.'s Com. for Purchase from the Blind and Other Severely Handicapped, Washington, 1986-91; mem. strategic devel. bd. U. Mo.; bd. dirs. Va. Industries for Blind, 1991—, Project Handclasp, 1994—. Decorated D.S.M., Legion of Merit. Recipient Disting. Svc. award Nat. Industries for Severely Handicapped, 1991; Capstone fellow Nat. Def. U., 1986. Mem. Navy Supply Corps Assn. (pres. 1988-91), Nat. Contract Mgmt. Assn. (bd. advisors 1986—), Navy Fed. Credit Union (vice chmn. 1986-92), Navy Mut. Aid Assn. (bd. dirs. 1982-91), Comprehensive Tech. Internat. (bd. dirs. 1992—), Army and Navy Club, Beta Theta Pi, Beta Gamma Sigma, Phi Kappa Phi.

MCKINNON, FLOYD WINGFIELD, textile executive; b. Columbus, Ga., Dec. 1, 1942; s. Malcolm Angus and Sarah C. (Bullock) McK.; m. Barbara Evans Roles, June 18, 1966; children: James Wingfield, Sarah Elizabeth, Robert Kent. AB, Washington and Lee U., 1964. Lic. airplane pilot. V.p. Cotswold Industries, Inc., N.Y.C., 1966—, also bd. dirs.; v.p., corp. sec. Cen. Textiles, Inc., S.C., 1984—, also bd. dirs.; arbitrator Am. Arbitration Assn., 1983—. Pres. Berkley-in-Scarsdale Assn., 1980, Scarsdale Leasing Corp., 1996; admissions rep. Washington and Lee U., 1979-89, 93—. Mem. Aircraft Owner's and Pilot's Assn., St. Andrews Soc. N.Y., Ch. Club N.Y. Republican. Episcopalian. Clubs: Union League (bd. govs. 1974-77, 88-91, sec. 1981-83, chmn. admissions com. 1996) (N.Y.C.); Scarsdale Golf (bd. govs. 1983—, pres. 1990-91) (Hartsdale, N.Y.); Bras Coupe (exec. com. 1980—) (Maniwaki, Can.). Home: 26 Taunton Rd Scarsdale NY 10583-5610 Office: Cotswold Industries 10 E 40th St New York NY 10016-0200

MC KINNON, F(RANCIS) A(RTHUR) RICHARD, utility executive; b. Delburne, Alta., Can., Mar. 5, 1933; s. John Donald and Ruth Rebecca (Sundberg) McK.; m. Elma Lorraine Lebsack, June 1, 1957; children: Kenneth Richard, Stephen David, Karen Diane. B. Commerce, U. Alta., 1954; postgrad., Stanford Exec. Program, Stanford U., 1982. With Alta. Gas Trunk Line Co. Ltd., Calgary, 1960-75, treas., 1971-75; dir. fin. TransAlta Utilities Corp. (formerly Calgary Power Ltd.), 1975—, treas., 1976-81, v.p. fin., 1981—; v.p. fin. Trans Alta Energy Corp., Trans Alta Corp.; bd. dirs. AEC Power Ltd. Past bd. dirs. Foothills Gen. Hosp., Calgary. Fellow Inst. Chartered Accts. of Alta.; mem. Can. Inst. Chartered Accts., Fin. Execs. Inst. Can. (past chmn., past pres., bd. dirs. Calgary chpt., v.p.), Fin. Execs. Inst. (bd. dirs.). Clubs: Calgary Petroleum, Canyon Meadows Golf and Country. Home: 1412 Windsor St NW, Calgary, AB Canada T2N 3X3 Office: TransAlta Utilities Corp, 110 12th Ave SW, Calgary, AB Canada T2P 2M1

MCKINNON, ISAIAH, police chief; b. Montgomery, Ala., June 21, 1943; s. Cota and Lula (Jones) McK.; m. Patrice Anne McKinnon; children: Jeffrey Christopher, Jason Patrick. BA in History/Law Enforcement, Mercy Coll. of Detroit, 1975; MA in Criminal Justice, U. Detroit, 1978; PhD in Administrn. and Higher Edn., Mich. State U., 1981; grad., FBI Nat. Acad., 1977. Police officer Detroit Police Dept., 1965-71, sgt., 1971-74, lt., 1974-77, inspector, 1977-84, chief of police, 1994—; dir. pub. safety U. Detroit, 1984-89; dir. security Renaissance Ctr., Detroit, 1989-93; lectr. Detroit Met. Police Acad., Mich. State Police Acad., Mich. Assn. Police; trainer in field; presenter Nat. Bapt. Ministers Conv., Ala. State U.; mem. Leadership and Mgmt. Adv. Bd.; adj. prof. criminal justice U. Detroit, 1984, Wayne State U., 1985-86, Wayne County C.C., 1988—; asst. prof. criminal justice Mercy Coll. of Detroit, 1978-86; security cons. Limbach Co., Detroit, Marathon Petroleum Co., Detroit, State of Mich. Workers Disability Compensation Bldg., Detroit, Rubloff Mgmt. Co., Chgo. Author: Police and the Nurse, 1984, Police and Child Abuse, 1992; contbr. articles to newspapers; guest columnist Mich. Chronicle. Trustee Grosse Point Acad.; past mem., bd. dirs. Ronald McDonald House, Children's Ctr. Wayne County; past mem. youth devel. com. Detroit Urban League; mem. Dad's Club U. Detroit Jesuit H.S.; bd. dirs. U. Detroit, 1974—, Wayne County C.C., Detroit, 1975—. With USAF, 1961-65. Recipient Spirit of Detroit award, numerous citations, commendations. Mem. F.B.I. Nat. Acad. Grads. Office: Police Dept 1300 Beaubien St Detroit MI 48226-2308

MCKINNON, JAMES BUCKNER, real estate sales executive, writer, researcher; b. Tacoma, Dec. 5, 1916; s. James Mitchell and Rochelle Lenore (Buckner) McK.; m. Mary C. Corbitt, Dec. 1961 (div. June 1963); 1 child, James H.C.; m. Marylyn Adelle Coote, Mar. 12, 1967 (div. May 1977); 1 child, Michelyn; m. Martha Sackmann, June 12, 1977. BA in Internat. Studies, U. Wash., 1983, H.M. Jackson Sch. Police detective Los Angeles Police Dept., 1946-50; bn. security officer 1st med. bn. 1st Marine div. Fleet Marine Force, 1950-53; owner, operator, mgr., dir. promotional sales The Saucy Dog Drive-In, Venice, Calif., 1953-63; salesman new car sales and leasing Burien Mercury, Seattle, 1963-66; real estate salesman and appraiser various firms Seattle, 1966—; instr., lectr. U.S. Naval Support Activity, Sandpoint, Wash., 1964-74; mem., lectr. NRC 11-8, Naval Postgrad. Sch., Monterey, Calif., 1975-76; Burien Mercury announcer KOMO TV. Author: (poetry) On the Threshold of a Dream, Vol. III, 1992, Best Poems of the 90's, 1992; contbr. to anthologies: Where Words Haven't Spoken, 1993, Fire From Within, 1994; contbr. articles to various newspapers and mil. jours. Mem. br. adv. com. Wash. State YMCA, Seattle, 1994—, treas., 1986-94, 95, mem. so. dist. fin. bd., 1989-93, 94, 95-96. With USN, 1939-53, PTO, Korea. Recipient Wilmer Culver Meml. award Culver Alumni Fictioneers, Seattle, 1979, Silver Poet award World of Poetry Press, 1986, Golden Poet award, 1987-92, Best Poet of the 90's Nat. Libr. of Poetry, 1992; Occidental Coll. scholar, 1935; named to Honorable Order Ky. Cols., 1976; named One of Best New Poets, Am. Poetry Assn. Anthology, 1988. Mem. Internat. Soc. Authors and Artists, Internat. Platform Assn., U.S. Naval Inst. (life), Internat. Soc. Poets (life), N.W. Writers Conf., Ret. Officers Assn. (life), Mensa, Acad. Am. Poets, KP, Masons. Republican. Home: 2312 41st Ave SW Seattle WA 98116-2060 *Personal philosophy: To realize one's greatest potential pursue goals that hold the greatest potential meaning in life.*

MCKINNON, ROBERT HAROLD, insurance company executive; b. Holtville, Calif., Apr. 4, 1927; s. Harold Arthur and Gladys Irene (Blanchar) McK.; m. Marian Lois Hayes, Dec. 18, 1948; children: Steven Robert, Laurie Ellen, David Martin. BS, Armstrong Coll., 1950, MBA, 1952. Regional sales mgr. Farmers Ins. Group, Austin, Tex., 1961-66, Aurora, Ill., 1966-68; dir. life sales Farmers New World Life, L.A., 1968-75; v.p. mktg. Warner Ins. Group, Chgo., 1975-82; mem. Canners Exchange Dairy Adv. Com., 1977-82; sr. v.p. mktg. The Rural Ins. Cos., Madison, Wis., 1982-89; mktg. cons. ins. and fin. svcs. Nat. Guardian Life Fin. Svcs., Madison, 1989-90, exec. recruiter Sales Cons. Madison, 1990—. Scoutmaster Boy Scouts Am., 1971-72; vestry mem. St. Dunstan's Episcopal Ch., chair redevel. of Ch. With U.S. Army, 1944-45. Fellow Life Underwriters Tng. Coun.; mem. Madison Life Underwriters Assn., Soc. CPCUs, Rotary (bd. dirs., pres., Paul Harris fellow 1994), Elks. Home: 5 Connecticut Ct Madison WI 53719-2202

MCKINZIE, CARL WAYNE, lawyer; b. Lubbock, Tex., Dec. 3, 1939; s. J. Clyde and Flora (Cates) McK.; m. Rowena Ann Williams; children: Wayne, Clinton, Morgan (dec.). BBA, Tex. Tech U., 1962, MBA, 1963; JD, So. Meth. U., 1966. From assoc. to ptnr. Nossaman, Guthner & Knox, L.A., 1966-80; prin. Riordan & McKinzie, L.A., 1980—; bd. dirs. IXC Comm., Inc. Contbr. articles to law jours. Mem. bd. visitors Sch. Law So. Meth. U., Dallas, 1979-82, 90—, bd. dirs., 1970-73, 84-89; mem. bd. visitors Coll. Law Ariz. State U., 1990—; bd. dirs. Riordan Found., Rx for Reading, Calif. Cmty. Found.; mem. bd. govs. Nat. Assn. Real Estate Investment Trusts, 1986-89. Capt. USAF, 1967-70. Mem. ABA (chmn. current devel. subcom., com. tax problems 1978-80), Calif. Bar Assn., Los Angeles County Bar Assn., Jonathan Club, City Club on Bunker Hill. Republican. Home: 527 1st Pl Santa Monica CA 90402 Office: Riordan & McKinzie 29th Fl 300 S Grand Ave Fl 29 Los Angeles CA 90071-3109

MCKIRAHAN, RICHARD DUNCAN, JR., classics and philosophy educator; b. Berkeley, Calif., July 27, 1945; s. Richard Duncan and Helen Marion (Hixson) McK.; m. Voula Tsouna, June 3, 1961; 1 child, Helen Hamilton. AB, U. Calif., Berkeley, 1966; BA, U. Oxford, Eng., 1969; MA, Oxford U., Eng., 1979; PhD, Harvard U., 1973. Teaching fellow, tutor Harvard U., Cambridge, Mass., 1971-73; asst. prof. classics and philosophy Pomona Coll., Claremont, Calif., 1973-79, assoc. prof., 1979-87, E.C. Norton prof. classics and philosophy, 1987—, chair dept. classics, 1992—. Author: Socrates and Plato, A Comprehensive Bibliography, 1958-73, 78, Plato's Meno, 1986, Principles and Proofs: Aristotle's Theory of Demonstrative Science, 1992, Philosophy Before Socrates, 1994, A Presocratics Reader, 1996; also articles on Greek philosophy, math. and scis. Marshall Aid Commemoration Commn. scholar, U. Oxford, 1966-69; Woodrow Wilson Found. fellow, 1966-67; NEH grantee, 1975, 85, 90. Mem. Am. Philol. Assn., Soc. Ancient Greek Philosophy, Phi Beta Kappa. Office: Pomona Coll Dept Classics 140 W 6th St Claremont CA 91711

MCKISSOCK, PAUL KENDRICK, plastic surgeon; b. Lakeland, Fla., Oct. 27, 1925; s. Percival Kendrick and Helen Williams (Morse) McK.; m. Joan McShane, 1951; children—Ellen, John, Scott. B.A. in Zoology, UCLA, 1950; M.D. (James A. Gibson Anat. award 1953), U. Buffalo, 1956. Diplomate: Am. Bd. Plastic Surgery. Intern Los Angeles County Gen. Hosp., 1956-57; resident VA Hosp., Los Angeles, UCLA, 1957-63; fellow in plastic surgery Queen Victoria Hosp., East Grinstead, Eng., 1963; practice medicine specializing in plastic and reconstructive surgery Torrance, Calif., 1963—; pres. Paul K. McKissock M.D. Inc., 1968—; mem. staff Torrance Meml. Hosp., Little Company of Mary Hosp.; clin. prof. UCLA Med. Sch. Contbr. articles med. publs. Served with USNR, 1943-46. Mem. Am. Soc. Plastic and Reconstructive Surgeons, Am. Soc. Aesthetic Plastic Surgeons, Am. Assn. Plastic Surgeons, Calif. Soc. Plastic Surgeons. Republican. Presbyterian. Home: 75-280 Inverness Dr Indian Wells CA 92210-7636 Office: D-513 44489 Town Center Way Palm Desert CA 92260-2729

MC KITRICK, ERIC LOUIS, historian, educator; b. Battle Creek, Mich., July 5, 1919; s. Fred Louis and Colleen (Hodges) McK.; m. Edyth Carol Stevenson, Dec. 26, 1946; children—Frederick Louis II, Enid Lael, Charles Keith, Mary Caroline. B.S., Columbia U., 1949, M.A., 1951, Ph.D., 1959. Asst. prof. history U. Chgo., 1955-59; asst. prof. history Douglass Coll., Rutgers U., 1955-60; asso. prof. history Columbia, 1960-65; prof. Columbia U., N.Y.C., 1965-89, prof. emeritus, 1989—; Pitt prof. Am. history and instns. Cambridge (Eng.) U., 1973-74; Harmsworth prof. Am. history Oxford (Eng.) U., 1979-80. Author: Andrew Johnson and Reconstruction, 1960, Slavery Defended: Views of the Old South, 1963, Andrew Johnson: A Profile, 1969, The Hofstadter Aegis: A Memorial, 1974, (with Stanley Elkins) The Age of Federalism, 1993. Served with AUS, 1941-45. Recipient Dunning prize Am. Hist. Assn., 1960, Bancroft prize, 1994, prize Soc. of the Cincinnati, 1995; fellow Ford Found., 1957-58, Rockefeller Found., 1962-63, Nat. Endowment for Humanities, 1967-68, Guggenheim Found., 1970-71, 76-77. Fellow Am. Philos. Soc., Am. Council Learned Socs. Club: Century (N.Y.C.). Office: Dept of History Columbia University New York NY 10027

MCKITRICK, JAMES THOMAS, retail executive; b. Cin., Sept. 14, 1945; s. Harry J. and L. May (Buck) McK.; m. Margaret J. Haynes, Sept. 6, 1975; children: Angela, Greg, Randal, Paul, Sheri, Richard, Mike. Student, Salem Coll., 1963-64. Dir. mdse. K Mart Corp., Troy, Mich., 1965-84; exec. v.p., gen. mgr. T.G. & Y. Stores, Oklahoma City, 1984-86, exec. v.p. merchandising and mktg., 1986; pres., chief exec. officer Warehouse Club, Skokie, Ill., 1986-87; pres., chief operating officer G.C. Murphy Co. subs. Ames, Rocky Hill, Conn., 1987—; chmn. Zayre Discount, Rocky Hill, 1988—. Republican. Methodist. Home: 13769 Bay Hill Dr Des Moines IA 50325-8566 Office: Central Tractor Farm Family Ctr 3915 Delaware Ave Des Moines IA 50313-2541*

MCKITTRICK, WILLIAM DAVID PARRISH, lawyer; b. Phila., June 10, 1942; s. Robert William and Marianna Virginia (Jones) McK.; m. Maureen Elaine Kerr, Jan. 20, 1964 (div. June 1980); children: Terrance, Allison; m. Teresa Jane Hopkins, Mar. 20, 1982; children: Parrish, Tyler. BA, Marshall U., Huntington, W.Va., 1965; JD, W.Va. U., 1968. Bar: W.Va. 1968, U.S. Dist. Ct. (so. dist.) W.Va. 1968. Asst. prosecutor Kanawha County, Charleston, W.Va., 1968-70; ptnr. McKittrick & Vaughn, St. Albans, W.Va., 1970-85, McKittrick & Murray, St. Albans, 1968-89, McKittrick & Assocs., St. Albans, 1990-93, McKittrick & Tantlinger, St. Albans, 1993—; lectr. numerous seminars. Mem. Am. Trial Lawyers Assn., W.Va. Trial Lawyers Assn. Office: McKittrick & Tantlinger 450 2nd St Saint Albans WV 25177-2832

MCKITTRICK, WILLIAM WOOD, lawyer; b. Mt. Carmel, Ill., July 11, 1915; s. Lafe E. and Mary Lynn (Wood) McK.; m. Carolyn Lenne Davis, Dec. 19, 1942; children—Lynn McKittrick Pond, Bruce W. A.B., DePauw U., 1936; J.D., Northwestern U., 1939. Bar: Ill. Assoc. Pope & Ballard, Chgo., 1939-48, ptnr., 1948-52; atty. Office Gen. Counsel, Panama C.Z., 1942; ptnr. Vedder, Price, Kaufman & Kammholz, Chgo., 1952-95; lectr. on labor law Northwestern U. Sch. Law, Chgo., 1961-62. Case note editor, mem. editorial bd. Ill. Law Rev., 1938-39. Life trustee Orchestral Assn. of Chgo. Symphony Orch., 1980—, Chgo. Symphony Musicians Pension Trust, 1987—; bd. dirs. Am. Symphony Orch. League, 1986-93, mem. exec. com., 1988-91; trustee Newberry Libr., Chgo., 1984—, mem. exec. com., 1989—; vice chmn. exec. bd. Libr. Coun., Northwestern U., 1984—; chmn. Friends of Ryerson & Burnham Librs., Art Inst. Chgo., 1988-90, mem. com. on librs., 1982—. Served to lt. USNR, 1943-45, PTO. Recipient Service award Northwestern U., 1968. Mem. ABA, Ill. Bar Assn., Chgo. Bar Assn. (lectr. various programs 1940-70, bd. mgrs. 1961-63), Legal Club of Chgo., Univ. Club (Chgo.), Michigan Shores Club, Skokie Country Club, Caxton Club of Chgo. (v.p. 1982-83, pres. 1983-85). Home: 232 Essex Rd Kenilworth IL 60043-1122

MCKNIGHT, FREDERICK L., lawyer; b. Kansas City, Mo., Nov. 28, 1947; s. Harry A. and Donna Ruth (Breining) McK.; m. Linda Jean McKnight, June 20, 1970; children: Justin Teague, Cristin Ruth. AB honors, Princeton U., 1969; JD, U. Calif., Berkeley, 1972. Bar: Calif. 1973, N.Y. 1973. adv. com. Jones, Day, Reavis & Pogue, Cleve., 1991—. Bd. dirs. Econ. Devel. Corp., L.A., 1992—. Mem. ABA (health care sect.), Assn. Bus. Trial Lawyers. Office: Jones Day Reavis & Pogue 555 W 5th St Ste 4600 Los Angeles CA 90013-3002*

MC KNIGHT, JOHN LACY, physics educator; b. Monroe, Mich., Sept. 13, 1931; s. Joseph Daniel and Esther (Lacy) McK.; m. Joyce Nunn, May 30, 1964; 1 son, Andrew. A.B., U. Mich., 1953; M.S., Yale, 1954, Ph.D., 1957. Mem. Faculty Coll. William and Mary, 1957—, prof. physics, 1968—; cons. to Colonial Williamsburg Found. on 17th and 18th century sci. instruments. Mem. editorial bd. Eighteenth Century Life. Pres. Va. Wilderness Com., 1969-70; bd. dirs. Conservation Coun. Va., 1969-71; trustee Va. chpt. Nature Conservancy, 1971-78, chmn. bd., 1975-77. Mem. AAAS, Am. Phys. Soc., Philosophy of Sci. Assn., History of Sci. Soc., Soc. History of Tech., Sci. Instrument Soc., Internat. Sci. Instruments Commn., Phi Beta Kappa, Sigma Xi, Phi Kappa Phi. Home: 701 College Ter Williamsburg VA 23185-3532

MCKNIGHT, JOSEPH WEBB, law educator, historian; b. San Angelo, Tex., Feb. 17, 1925; s. John Banning and Helen Katherine (Webb) McK.; m. Julia Ann Dyer, July 19, 1957; children—John Banton, Joseph Adair; m. Mildred Katherine Virginia Payne, Aug. 9, 1975. B.A., U. Tex., 1947, Oxford U., Eng., 1949; B.C.L., Oxford U., Eng., 1950, M.A., 1954; LL.M., Columbia U., 1959. Bar: Tex. 1951, U.S. Ct. Appeals (5th cir.) 1982. Assoc. Cravath, Swaine & Moore, N.Y.C., 1951-55; asst. prof. So. Meth. U., Dallas, 1955-57, assoc. prof., 1957-63, prof. law, 1963—, acad. dean, 1977-80, Larry and Jane Harlan faculty fellow, 1991—; vis. prof. various univs. Gen. editor Creditors' Rights in Texas, 1963; author: (with William A. Reppy, Jr.) Texas Matrimonial Property Law, 1983; contbr. articles to profl. jours. Pres., Tex. Old Missions and Forts Restoration Assn., 1977-79; bd. dirs. San Jacinto Mus. History Assn., 1976—; mem. exec. com. Tex. State Hist. Assn., 1988-91. Served to lt. USNR, 1942-47. Rhodes scholar, 1947-50; James Kent fellow, 1958-59; Academico, Acad. Mexicana de Derecho Internat., 1988. Mem. ABA, State Bar Tex., Dallas Bar Assn., Tex. Bar Found. (v.p. 1959), Nat. Legal Aid and Defenders Assn. (bd. dirs. 1963-66), Selden Soc., Am. Soc. Legal History (v.p. 1967-68, bd. dirs. 1967-75), Inst. Texan Cultures (exec. bd. 1990—), Sigma Chi. Democrat. Episcopalian. Office: So Meth U Law School Dallas TX 75275-0116

MCKNIGHT, STEVEN LANIER, molecular biologist; b. El Paso, Tex., Aug. 27, 1949; s. Frank Gillespie and Sara Elise (Stevens) McK.; m. Jacquelynn Ann Zimmer, Sept. 16, 1978; children: Nell, Grace, Frances, John Stevens. BA, U. Tex., 1974; PhD, U.Va., 1977. Postdoctoral fellow Carnegie Instn. Washington, Balt., 1977-79, staff assoc., 1979-81, mem. staff, 1984-92; co-founder, dir., dir. rsch. Tularik Inc., 1991—; prof. U. Tex. Southwestern Med. Ctr., 1995—; hon. prof. Johns Hopkins U. Contbr. articles to jours. in field. With U.S. Army, 1969-71, Vietnam. Decorated ARCOM medal; recipient Eli Lilly prize Am. Soc. Microbiology, 1987, Newcomb-Cleveland prize Sci. mag., 1989, NAS Molecular Biology award Nat. Acad. Sci., 1991. Fellow Carnegie Inst. Washington (hon.); mem. NAS, Am. Acad. Arts and Scis., Am. Soc. for Biochemistry and Molecular Biology, Am. Soc. for Cell Biology, Japanese Biochem. Soc. (hon.). Democrat. Home: 3717 Euclid Ave Dallas TX 75205 Office: U Tex Southwestern Med Ctr 5323 Harry Hines Blvd Dallas TX 75235 Office: Tularik Inc 270 Grand Ave San Francisco CA 94080

MCKNIGHT, THOMAS FREDERICK, artist; b. Lawrence, Kans., Jan. 13, 1941. BA in Art, Wesleyan U., Middletown, Conn.; postgrad., Columbia U. One-man shows Basel (Switzerland) Art Fair, 1975-77, Tomic Galerie, Dusseldorf, Germany, 1976, Hartmann Gallery, Munich, 1977, Newport (R.I.) Art Assn., 1981; exhibited in group shows Llubljana, Yugoslavia, 1981, Tokyo, 1989, Davison Art Ctr., Wesleyan U., 1988, numerous others; represented in permanent collections Davison Art Ctr., N.Y. State Mus., Albany, Smithsonian Instn., Washington, Met. Mus. Art, N.Y.C.; commns. include poster and print U.S. Constn. Bicentennial, 1989, prints Am.'s Cup, 1992, paintings and prints Urban Fair, Kobe, Japan, 1991, White House Christmas card, 1994.

MCKNIGHT, WILLIAM BALDWIN, physics educator; b. Macon, Ga., July 4, 1923; s. Gilbert Franklin and Exie (Baldwin) McK.; m. Helen Mabel Bowling, Oct. 1, 1955; children: Tandy Ringoringo, Linda McKnight Way. BS, Purdue U., 1950; PhD, Oxford U., 1968. Physicist Underwater Sound Reference Lab., Orlando, Fla., 1952-53, U.S. Army Missile Command, Redstone Arsenal, Ala., 1953-61; supervisory research physicist Army Missile Command, Redstone Arsenal, 1961-74; cons. Ballistic Missile Def. Advanced Tech. Ctr., 1975; research prof. physics U. Ala., Huntsville, 1974—; pres. Tech. Research Assocs. Inc., 1984—. Contbr. articles to profl. jours. Vice pres. Cotaco Communities League, Somerville, Ala., 1964-65; mem. Madison County Rep. Exec. Com.; mgr. Gordo Area C. of C., 1993—; chmn. Pickens County Health Coun., 1994—. With USAAF, 1943-45. Decorated D.F.C., Air medal with three oak leaf clusters; recipient Research and Devel. award U.S. Army, 1961, 64; Sec. of Army fellow, 1966-67. Fellow Optical Soc. Am.; mem. IEEE (sr.), Am. Phys. Soc., Sigma Xi, Sigma Pi Sigma. Mem. Ch. of Christ. Clubs: United Oxford, Cambridge Univ. Home: RR 1 Box 141A Gordo AL 35466-9728 Office: PO Box 1247 Huntsville AL 35807-0247

MCKNIGHT, WILLIAM EDWIN, minister; b. Grenada, Miss., Mar. 21, 1938; s. Leslie Spurgeon and Lucy Jennings (Sistrunk) McK.; m Sue Belle Roberts, Aug. 5, 1960; children: Susan Michele, William Roberts. BA, Millsaps Coll., 1960; BD, Lexington (Ky.) Theol. Sem., 1963. Ordained to ministry, 1964. Chaplain intern Grady Hosp., Atlanta, 1963-64; pastor First Christian Ch., Cleveland, Miss., 1964-67, Inverness, Miss., 1964-67; assoc. pastor First Christian Ch., Jackson, Miss., 1967-70; regional minister Christian Ch. (Disciples of Christ) in Miss., Jackson, 1971—; bd. dirs. Nat. City Christian Ch., Washington, Christian Brotherhood Homes, Jackson, So. Christian Svcs., Macon, Ga.; mem. Gen. Bd. the Christian Ch., Indpls., 1969—, bd. dirs. fin. coun., 1979-82; mem. bd. higher edn., St. Louis, 1979-80. Named one of Outstanding Young Men Am. U.S. Jaycees, 1976. Mem. Miss. Religious Leadership Conf. (pres. 1984-85), Conf. Regional Ministers and Moderators (pres. 1985-86). Office: Christian Ch in Miss 1619 N West St Jackson MS 39202-1418

MC KNIGHT, WILLIAM WARREN, JR., publisher; b. Normal, Ill., June 9, 1913; s. William Warren and Isabel Alida (Travis) McK.; m. Alice McGuire, Oct. 30, 1937; children: William Warren, III, Michael Joe, John James. B.S. in Bus. Adminstrn., Northwestern U., 1938. With McKnight Pub. Co., Bloomington, Ill., 1938-83; sec.-treas. McKnight Pub. Co., 1949-56, pres., 1956-67, chmn. bd., 1968-79; bd. dirs. Gen. Telephone Co. Ill., Champion Fed. Savs. & Loan Assn., chmn. bd. Pres. Bloomington Rotary Club, 1952, Bloomington C. of C., 1954; mem. Ill. Commn. Higher Edn., 1956-60; chmn. Bloomington-Normal Airport Authority, 1965-70, CETA Pvt. Industry Council Ill. Balance of State, 1979-81. Served with USNR, 1942-46. Recipient Disting. Service award Bloomington Kiwanis Club, 1963, Disting. Service award Normal C. of C., 1973; Good Govt. award Bloomington Jaycees, 1970; Edn. Constrn. award Edn. Council Graphic Arts Industry, 1974; Disting. Alumni award Ill. State U., 1978; Disting. Service award Spirit of McLean County, 1982; Disting. Service citation Epsilon Pi Tau, 1983; award of Merit Am. Vocat. Assn., 1990; disting. assoc. award Coun. on Tech. Tchr. Edn., 1995. Mem. Graphic Arts Edn. Assn., Internat. Tech. Edn. Assn., Nat. Assn. Indsl. and Tech. Tchrs. Educators, Ill. C. of C. (dir. 1964-69), Ill. Mfrs. Assn. (dir. 1954-62). Republican. Presbyterian. Clubs: Coll. Alumni, Bloomington Country. Home: 401 W Vernon Ave Normal IL 61761-3542 Home (winter): 7788 E Stallion Rd Scottsdale AZ 85258-3485

MCKOWN, CHARLES H., dean. Dean Marshall U. Sch. Medicine, Huntington, W.Va. Office: Marshall U Sch Medicine 1801 6th Ave Huntington WV 25755

MC KOY, BASIL VINCENT CHARLES, theoretical chemist, educator; b. Trinidad, W.I., Mar. 25, 1938; came to U.S., 1960, naturalized, 1973; s. Allan Cecil and Doris Augusta McK.; m. Anne Ellen Shannon, Mar. 18, 1967; 1 son, Christopher Allan. B.Chem. Eng., N.S. Tech. U., 1960; Ph.D. in Chemistry (Univ. fellow), Yale U., 1964. Instr. chemistry Calif. Inst. Tech., 1964-66, asst. prof. chemistry, 1966-69, asso. prof., 1969-75, prof. theoretical chemistry, 1975—, chmn. of faculty, 1985-87; cons. Lawrence Livermore Lab., U. Calif., Livermore, 1974—, Inst. Def. Analysis, 1984—; vis. prof. Max Planck Inst., Munich, Ger., 1976—, U. Paris, 1968—, U. Campinas, Brazil, 1976—; lectr. Nobel Symposium, Goteborg, Sweden, 1979. Contbr. articles to Jour. Physics, London, chem. Physics Letters, Phys. Rev., Jour. Chem. Physics; bd. editors; Chem. Physics Jour., 1977-79, mem. adv. editoral bd., 1992—; co-editor: Electron-Molecule and Photon-Molecule Collisions, 1979, 83, Swarm Studies and Inelastic Electron-Molecule Collisions, 1986; co-author: Electron-Molecule Collisions and Photoionization Processes, 1982. Recipient medal Gov.-Gen. Can., 1960; Alfred P. Sloan Found. fellow, 1969-73; Guggenheim fellow, 1973-74. Fellow Am. Phys. Soc. Home: 3855 Keswick Rd La Canada Flintridge CA 91011-3945 Office: Calif Inst Tech Div Chemistry Pasadena CA 91125

MCKUSICK, MARSHALL KIRK, computer scientist; b. Wilmington, Del., Jan. 19, 1954; s. Blaine Chase and Marjorie Jane (Kirk) McK.; domestic ptnr. Eric P. Allman. BSEE with distinction, Cornell U., 1976; MS in Bus. Adminstrn., U. Calif., Berkeley, 1979, MS in Computer Sci., 1980, PhD in Computer Sci., 1984. System designer Hughes Aircraft Co., 1977-79; software cons., 1982—; rsch. computer scientist U. Calif., Berkeley, 1984-93. Author: The Design and Implementation of the 4.3BSD UNIX Operating System, 1989, (trans. into German, 1990, Japanese, 1991), The Design and Implementation of the 4.3BSD UNIX Operating System Answer Book, 1991, (trans. into Japanese, 1992), The Design and Implementation of the 4.4BSD Operating System, 1996; contbr. articles to profl. publs. Mem. IEEE, Usenix Assn. (Lifetime Achievement award 1992, pres. 1990-92, bd. dirs. 1986-92), Assn. Computing Machinery. Democrat. Avocations: swimming, scuba diving, hiking. Office: 1614 Oxford St Berkeley CA 94709-1608

MCKUSICK, VICTOR ALMON, geneticist, educator, physician; b. Parkman, Maine, Oct. 21, 1921; s. Carroll L. and Ethel M. (Buzzell) Mc K.; m. Anne Bishop, June 11, 1949; children: Carol Anne, Kenneth Andrew, Victor Wayne. Student, Tufts Coll., 1940-43; MD, Johns Hopkins U., 1946; DSc (hon.), N.Y. Med. Coll., 1974; MD (hon.), Liverpool U., 1976; DSc (hon.), U. Maine, 1978, Tufts U., 1978, U. Rochester, 1979, Meml. U., Nfld., 1979; DMCh (hon.), U. Helsinki, 1981; D Med. Sci. (hon.), Med. U. S.C., 1979; MD (hon.), Edinburgh U., 1984; DSc (hon.), Aberdeen U., 1988, Med. Coll. Ohio, 1988, Bates Coll., 1989; PhD (hon.), Tel Aviv U., 1989; MD (hon.), Zurich (Switzerland) U., 1990; DSc (hon.), Colby Coll., 1991, U. Chgo., 1991, Mt. Sinai Sch. Medicine, 1992. Diplomate Am. Bd. Internal Medicine. Tng. in clin. medicine, lab. rsch. Johns Hopkins U./USPHS, 1946-52; instr. medicine Johns Hopkins Sch. Medicine, 1952-54, asst. prof., 1954-57, assoc. prof., 1957-60, chief divsn. med. genetics, dept. medicine, 1957-73, prof. medicine, 1960-85, prof. epidemiology, biology, 1969-78, William Osler prof. medicine, 1978-85, chmn. dept. medicine, 1973-85; physician-in-chief Johns Hopkins Hosp., 1973-85, Univ. prof. medical genetics, 1985—, chief div. med. genetics, 1957-73, 85-89; mem. rsch. adv. com. Nat. Found., 1959-78, med. adv. bd. Howard Hughes Med. Inst., 1967-83, com. mapping and sequencing of human genome Nat. Acad. Sci., 1986-88; pres. Internat. Med. Congress, Ltd., 1972-78; mem. Nat. Adv. Rsch. Resources Coun., 1970-74; mem. bd. sci. advisers Roche Inst. Molecular Biology, 1967-71; trustee Jackson Lab., 1979—; founding mem. Am. Bd. Med. Genetics, 1979-82; pres. 8th Internat. Congress of Human Genetics, 1991; mem. human genome adv. com. NIH, 1988-92, NIH/DOE work group on ethical, legal and societal implications of human genome project, 1990-95; co-chmn. Centennial of Johns Hopkins Hosp., 1989-90; co-founder, co-dir. ann. short course in med. and exptl. mammalian genetics, Bar Harbor, Maine, 1960—; co-founder, co-dir. European Sch. Med. Genetics Sestri Levante, 1988—; chmn. com. on DNA tech. in forensic sci. NRC/NAS, 1989-92, adv. update com., 1993-96. Author: Heritable Disorders of Connective Tissue, 1956, 60, 66, 72, 93, Cardiovascular Sound in Health and Disease, 1958, Medical Genetics 1958-60, 1961, Human Genetics, 1964, 69, On the X Chromosome of Man, 1964, Mendelian Inheritance in Man, 1966, 68, 71, 75, 78, 83, 86, 88, 90, 92, 94, (with others) Osler's Textbook Revisited, 1967, Genetics of Hand Malformations, 1978, Medical Genetic Studies of the Amish, 1978, A Model of its Kind, 1989, Osler's Legacy, 1990, A Century of Biomedical Science at Johns Hopkins, 1993; author, editor: Online Mendelian Inheritance in Man, 1985—; editor-in-chief Medicine jour., 1985—; founding co-editor-in-chief Genomics jour. 1987—; editor med. textbook. Recipient Disting. Achievement award Modern Medicine, 1965, John Phillips award ACP, 1972, Silver medal U. Helsinki, 1974, Gairdner Internat. award, 1977, Premio Internazionale Sanremo per le Ricerche Genetiche, 1983, Col. Saunders award March of Dimes, 1988, Disting. Alumnus award Johns Hopkins U., 1983, Alumnus Svc. award Johns Hopkins Med. Sch., 1989, Passano award, 1989, Disting. Svc. award Miami Biotech. Winter Symposium, 1991, Frank Bradway Rogers Info. Advancement award Med. Libr. Assn., 1991, Silver Columbus medal Comune di Genova, 1992, Maine prize (with twin), 1993, Mendel medal Villanova U., 1995, Big "M" award Maine State Soc. Washington, D.C., 1995; named to Internat. Pediatrics Hall of Fame, 1987. Fellow AAAS (chair med. scis. sect. 1991), Am. Acad. Orthopedic Surgeons (hon.), Royal Coll. Physicians (London), Hastings Ctr., Am. Coll. Med. Genetics (hon.); mem. Nat. Acad. Sci. (James Murray Luck award 19820, Am. Philos. Soc. (v.p. 1996—, Benjamin Franklin medal for disting. achievement in scis. 1996), Am. Soc. Human Genetics (pres. 1975, Wm. A. Allan award 1977), Assn. Am. Physicians (Kober medal 1990), Am. So Investigation (v.p. 1967), The Human Genome Orgn. (founder, pres. 1988-89), Am. Acad. Arts and Sci., Little People of Am. (hon. life), Acad. Nat. Medicine (France; corr.), Am. Bd. Med. Genetics (founding), Inst. Medicine, Phi Beta Kappa, Alpha Omega Alpha, Johns Hopkins Club, West Hamilton St. Club, St. Andrew's Soc. Balt. Presbyterian (elder). Home: 221 Northway Baltimore MD 21218-1141 Office: Johns Hopkins Hosp Ctr Med Geneetics-Blalock 1007 600 N Wolfe St Baltimore MD 21287-4922

MCKUSICK, VINCENT LEE, former state supreme court chief justice, lawyer; b. Parkman, Maine, Oct. 21, 1921; s. Carroll Lee and Ethel (Buzzell) McK.; m. Nancy Elizabeth Green, June 23, 1951; children: Barbara Jane McKusick Liscord, James Emory, Katherine McKusick Ralston, Anne Elizabeth. A.B., Bates Coll., 1943; S.B., S.M., MIT, 1947; LL.B., Harvard U., 1950; LL.D., Colby Coll., 1976, Nasson Coll., 1978, Bates Coll., 1979, Bowdoin Coll., 1979, Suffolk U., 1983; L.H.D., U. So. Maine, 1978, Thomas Coll., 1981. Bar: Maine 1952. Law clk. to Chief Judge Learned Hand, 1950-51; to Justice Felix Frankfurter, 1951-52; partner Pierce, Atwood, Scribner, Allen & McKusick and predecessors, Portland, Maine, 1953-77; chief justice Maine Supreme Jud. Ct., 1977-92; of counsel to Pierce Atwood (formerly Pierce, Atwood, Scribner, Allen, Smith, & Lancaster), Portland, Maine, 1992—; mem. adv. com. rules civil procedure Maine Supreme Jud. Ct., 1957-59, chmn., 1966-75, commr. uniform state laws, 1968-76, sec. nat. conf., 1975-77; mem. Conf. Chief Justices, 1977-92, bd. dirs., 1980-82, 91-92, pres.-elect, 1989-90, pres., 1990-91; dir. Nat. Ctr. for State Ctrs., 1988-89, chmn.-elect, 1989-90, chmn., 1990-91; spl. master U.S. Supreme Ct. Conn. v. N.H., 1992-93, La. v. Miss., 1994-96; master Mass. S.V.C. Liquidation Am. Liberty Mutual Liability Ins. Co., 1995-96; leader Am. Judges Del. to China, 1983, USSR, 1988, U.S. State Dept. Rule of Law Del. to Republic of Ga., 1992; mem. permanent com. Oliver Wendell Holmes Devise, 1993—. Author: Patent Policy of Educational Institutions, 1947, (with Richard H. Field) Maine Civil Practice, 1959, supplements, 1962, 67, (with Richard H. Field and L. Kinvin Wroth) 2d edit., 1970, supplements, 1972, 74, 77; also articles in legal publs. Trustee emeritus Bates Coll.; mem. adv. com. on pvt. internat. law U.S. State Dept., 1980-85, Fed.-State Jurisdiction com., Jud. Conf. of U.S., 1987-89. With AUS, 1943-46. Recipient The Maine prize U. Maine Sys., 1993, Benjamin E. Mays award Bates Coll., 1994, Big M award Maine State Soc. Washington, 1995. Fellow Am. Bar Found. (bd. dirs. 1977-87), Am. Philos. Soc. (coun. 1990-96); me,. ABA (chmn. fed. rules com. 1966-71, bd. editors jour. 1971-80, chmn. 1976-77, mem. study group to China 1978, ho. dels. 1983-87), Maine Bar Assn., Cumberland County Bar Assn., Am. Arbitration Assn. (bd. dirs. 1994—), Am. Judicature Soc. (dir. 1976-78, 92—), Am. Law Inst. (coun. 1968—), Maine Jud. Coun. (chmn. 1977-92), Inst. Jud. Adminstrn., Supreme Ct. Hist. Soc. (trustee 1994—), Rotary Club (hon., past pres.), Portland Yacht Club, Downeast Yacht Club, Phi Beta Kappa, Sigma Xi, Tau Beta Pi. Republican. Unitarian. Home: 1152 Shore Rd Cape Eliz ME 04107-2115 Office: 1 Monument Sq Portland ME 04101-4033

MCLACHLIN, BEVERLEY, supreme court judge; b. Pincher Creek, Alta., Can., Sept. 7, 1943; m. Roderick McLachlin (dec. 1988); 1 child, Angus; m. Frank E. McArdle, 1992. B.A., U. Alta., MA in Philosophy, LLB, LLD (hon.), 1990; LLD (hon.), U. B.C., 1990, U. Toronto, 1995. Bar: Alta. 1969, B.C. 1971. Assoc. Wood, Moir, Hyde and Ross, Edmonton, Alta., Can., 1969-71, Thomas, Herdy, Mitchell & Co., Fort St. John, B.C., Can., 1971-72, Bull, Housser and Tupper, Vancouver, B.C., 1972-75; lectr., assoc. prof., prof. with tenure U. B.C., 1974-81; appointed to County Ct., Vancouver, 1981; justice Supreme Ct. of B.C., 1981-85, B.C. Ct. of Appeal, 1985-88; chief justice Supreme Ct. of B.C., 1988; justice Supreme Ct. Can., Ottawa, Ont., 1989—. Co-author: B.C. Supreme Court Practice, B.C. Court Forums, Canadian Law of Arch. and Engring.; mem. editorial adv. bd. Family Law Restatement Project, 1987-88, Civil Jury Instruction, 1988; contbr. numerous articles to profl. jours. Office: Supreme Ct Bldg, Wellington St, Ottawa, ON Canada K1A 0J1

MCLAFFERTY, FRED WARREN, chemist, educator; b. Evanston, Ill., May 11, 1923; s. Joel E. and Margaret E. (Keifer) McL.; m. Elizabeth E. Curley, Feb. 5, 1948; children: Sara L., Joel E., Martha A., Samuel A., Ann E. B.S., U. Nebr., 1943, D.Sc. (hon.), 1983, M.S., 1947; Ph.D., Cornell U., 1950; D.Sc. (hon.), U. Liege, Belgium, 1987; DSc (hon.), Purdue U., 1995. Postdoctoral fellow U. Iowa, 1949-50; research chemist, div. leader Dow Chem. Co., 1950-56; dir. Eastern Research Lab., 1956-64; prof. chemistry Purdue U., 1964-68, Cornell U., 1968—; mem. chem. sci. and tech. bd., numerical data adv. bd., bd. Army sci. tech., bd. radioactive waste mgmt. NRC; chem. co-chmn. World Bank's Chinese Univ. Devel. Project. Author: Mass Spectrometry of Organic Ions, 1963, Mass Spectral Correlations, 2d edit., 1981, Interpretation of Mass Spectra, 4th edit., 1993, Tandem Mass Spectrometry, 1983, Advances in Analytical Chemistry and Instrumentation, (with C.N. Reilley), Vols. 4-7, 1967-70, Index and Bibliography of Mass Spectrometry, (with J. Pinzelik), 1967, Atlas of Mass Spectral Data; (with E. Stenhagen and S. Abrahamsson), 1969, Registry of Mass Spectral Data, 1974; (with D.B. Stauffer) Wiley/NBS Registry of Mass Spectral Data, 1989, Important Peak Index of Mass Spectral Data, 1991; editor: Accounts of Chemical Research, 1986-94; co-editor: (with E. Stenhagen and S. Abrahamsson) Archives of Mass Spectral Data, 1969-72. Served with AUS, 1942-45, ETO. Decorated Purple Heart, Combat Inf. badge, Bronze Star with 4 oak leaf clusters; recipient Pitts. Spectroscopy award Spectroscopy Soc. Pitts., 1975, Gold medal U. Naples, 1989, W. L. Evans award Ohio State U., 1987; John Simon Guggenheim fellow, 1972, Overseas fellow Churchill Coll., Cambridge (Eng.) U., 1979. Fellow NAS, AAAS, N.Y. Acad. Scis., Am. Acad. Arts and Scis.; mem. Soc. Analytical Chemists (Pitts. Analytical Chemist award 1987, Pioneer Analytical Instrumentation award 1994), Am. Chem. Soc. (chmn. analytical chem. divsn. 1969, chmn. Midland sect. 1956, Northeastern sect. 1964, award chem. instrumentation 1971, award analytical chemistry 1981, Nichols medal N.Y. sect. 1984, Oesper award Cin. sect. 1986, award mass spectrometry 1989), Internat. Spectrometry Orgn. (Sir J. J. Thomson medal 1985), Assn. Analytical Chemists (Anachem award 1985), Am. Soc. Mass Spectrometry (founder, sec. 1957-58), Am. Inst. Chemists (Chem. Pioneer award 1996), Sigma Xi, Phi Lambda Upsilon, Alpha Chi Sigma. Home: 103 Needham Pl Ithaca NY 14850-2120

MCLAIN, DAVID ANDREW, internist; b. Chgo., Aug. 16, 1948; s. William Rex and Wilma Lucille (Raschka) McL.; m. Pamela Rose Fullmer, June 15, 1974; children: Edward, Richard. BA, Northwestern U., 1970; MD with Honors, Tulane U., 1974. Diplomate Am. Bd. Internal Medicine, Am. Bd. Rheumatology. Intern Oschner Clinic, New Orleans, 1974-75; resident Barnes Hosp., St. Louis, 1975-77; fellow in rheumatology Washington U., St. Louis, 1977-79, instr. dept. medicine, 1979-81; with VA Hosp., St. Louis, 1979-81; pvt. practice Birmingham, Ala., 1981—; chief rheumatology sect. dept. internal medicine Brookwood Med. Ctr., Birmingham, 1983-87, 89-90, 91-94, med. dir. phys. therapy, 1986—; mem. staff St. Vincent's Hosp., Birmingham, 1981—, Shelby Med. Ctr., Alabaster, Ala., 1982—, Lakeshore Rehab. Hosp., Birmingham, 1983—, HealthSouth Hosp., 1989—; dir. courses continuing med. edn., 1983—. Editor: (jour. series) Internal Medicine; contbr. articles, abstracts to profl. jours. Mem. med. adv. com. Birmingham chpt. Lupus Found. Am., 1982—, co-originator Lupus Day, Brookwood Med. Ctr., 1983—; bd. dirs. north ctrl. br. Arthritis Found., 1982—, organizer, originator Benefit Horse Show and Art Fair, Birmingham, 1985, del. nat. coun., 1987, chmn. med. and sci. com. Ala. chpt., 1988-89; active Nat. Arthritis Found.; med. advisor Sjogren's Syndrome Found., 1988—. Recipient award of Appreciation Ala. Podiatry Assn., 1984, Ala. Chpt. Arthritis Found., 1986, award for Decade of Leadership in Rheumatology, 1992, Excellence in Tchg. award Med. Assn. State of Ala., 1995. Fellow ACP, Am. Coll. Rheumatology (founding); mem. AMA (Physicians Recognition award 1979, 82, 85, 88, 91, 94), Am. Soc. Internal Medicine, Ala. Soc. Rheumatic Diseases (founding, sec.-treas. 1996—), Am. Med. Equestrian Assn. (bd. dirs. 1995—), Ala. Soc. Internal Medicine, Med. Assn. State Ala. (Excellence in Tchg. award 1995), Jefferson County Med. Soc., Brookwood Splty. Physicians Assn. (founding incorporator, bd. dirs., pres. 1990—), U.S. Combined Tng. Assn. (area coun. 1992-94, editor newsletter 1992-94, bd. govs. 1992-94, chmn. safety com. 1992—, adult riders com. 1992-94, chmn. ad hoc coalition to promote equestrian helmet safety 1993—), U.S. Dressage Fedn. (founder aux. U.S. Tes Callers Assn.), Alpha Omega Alpha. Avocation: equestrian combined training or eventing. Office: Birmingham Rheumatology McLain Med Assocs 2022 Brookwood Med Ctr Dr Ste 509 Birmingham AL 35209-6807

MCLAIN, WILLIAM ALLEN, lawyer; b. Chgo., Oct. 19, 1942; s. William Rex and Wilma L. (Raschka) McL.; divorced; children: William A., David M., Heather A.; m. Kristine R. Zierk. BS, So. Ill. U., 1966; JD, Loyola U., Chgo., 1971. Bar: Ill. 1971, U.S. Dist. Ct. (no. dist.) Ill. 1971, U.S. Ct. Appeals (7th cir.) 1971, Colo. 1975, U.S. Dist. Ct. Colo. 1975, U.S. Ct. Appeals (10th cir.) 1975. Law clk. U.S. Dist. Ct. (no. dist.) Ill., Chgo., 1971-72; assoc. Sidley & Austin, Chgo., 1972-75; ptnr. Welborn, Dufford, Brown & Tooley, Denver, 1975-86; pres. William A. McLain PC, 1986—; ptnr. McLain & Singer, 1990—. Mem. Dist. 10 Legis. Vacancy Commn., Denver, 1984-86. Served with U.S. Army, 1966-68. Recipient Leadership and Scholastic Achievement award Loyola U. Alumni Assn., 1971. Mem. ABA, Colo. Bar Assn. (lobbyist 1983-85), Denver Bar Assn., Colo. Assn. Commerce and Industry (legis. policy coun. 1983-88), Colo. Mining Assn. (state and local affairs com. 1978-88), Inst. Property Taxation. Republican. Clubs: Mount Vernon Country Club, Roundup Riders of the Rockies. Lodges: Masons, Shriners, Scottish Rite, York Rite. Home and Office: 3962 S Olive St Denver CO 80237-2038

MCLAIN, WILLIAM TOME, principal; b. Washington, July 10, 1935; s. Ronald Alpha and Dorothy Smithson (Tome) McL.; m. Meurial Claire Webb, Nov. 20, 1977; 1 child, Laura Louisa McLain. BA, U. Del., 1957, MEd, 1966. Secondary Prin. Cert., Del. Math. tchr. Newark Sch. Dist., 1957-69, high sch. adminstrv. asst., 1969-78; high sch. assoc. prin. New Castle County Sch. Dist., Newark, 1978-81; high sch. asst. prin. Christina Sch. Dist., Newark, 1981-84, middle sch. asst. prin., 1984-87, prin. adult edn. program, 1987—. chmn. Del. Coalition for Literacy. Recipient Tchrs. medal Freedom's Found., 1968, Silver Beaver award Boy Scouts Am., 1967, Walace Johnson Community Svc. award New Castle County C. of C., 1979, Adult, dFamily Lit. Outstanding Svc. award State of Del., 1992. Mem. Del Assn. for Adult and Community Edn., Interagency Coun. on Adult Lit. United Methodist. Avocations: travel, history. Home: 95 Dallas Ave Newark DE 19711-5123 Office: Christina School District 83 E Main St Newark DE 19711-4645

MC LANATHAN, RICHARD (BARTON KENNEDY), author, consultant; b. Methuen, Mass., Mar. 12, 1916; s. Frank Watson and Helen (Kennedy) McL.; m. Jane Fuller, Jan. 2, 1942. Grad., Choate Sch., 1934; A.B., Harvard U., 1938, Ph.D., 1951. Instr. English and history Allen-Stevenson Sch., N.Y.C., 1938-43; asst. curator paintings Mus. Fine Arts, Boston, 1946-48; asst. curator decorative arts Mus. Fine Arts, 1949-54, sec. of museum, 1949-56, editor museum publs., 1952-57, asso. curator decorative arts, 1954, curator decorative arts, 1954-57; dir. Mus. Art, Munson-Williams-Proctor Inst., Utica, N.Y., 1957-61; exec. dir. Am. Assn. Museums, Washington, 1976-78; trustee, mem. exec. com. Boston Arts Festival, 1954-59; curator Am. nat. art exhbn., Moscow, 1959, Am. specialist to, W. Ger., Poland and Denmark, 1959, Yugoslavia, 1961; mem. U.S. Nat. Commn. for UNESCO, 1976-79, Corcoran Biennial Jury, 1960, N.Y. State Council Arts, 1960-64; bd. advisers Albany (N.Y.) Inst. History and Art, 1958-70; cons. in field, 1961-75, 79—. Author: Images of the Universe: Leonardo da Vinci, The Artist as Scientist, 1966, The Pageant of Medieval Art, 1966, The American Tradition in the Arts, 1968, A Guide to Civilisation: The Kenneth Clark Films on the Cultural Life of Western Man, 1970, The Brandywine Heritage, 1971, Art in America, 1973, The Art of Marguerite Stix, 1977, National Gallery of Art, East Building: A Profile, 1978, Romantic America; catalogue of the inaugural exhbn. of Tampa Museum, 1979, World Art in American Museums, A Personal Guide, 1983, Gilbert Stuart, 1986, Leonardo da Vinci, 1990, fgn. lang. edits., 1991, Michelangelo, 1993, Rubens, 1995; co-author: M. and M. Karolik Collection of American Paintings, 1815-1855, 1949; editor: Catalogue of Classical Coins, 1955; cons. editor: Art and Man, Nat. Gallery Art, 1969-76; adv. editor: The Great Contemporary Issues: The Arts, 1978; decorative arts editor: Webster's Unabridged Dictionary, 1955; contbr.: Am. Foundation Philanthropy, 1967. Bd. advisers Boys Club Boston, 1950-57; trustee Boys' Club Utica, 1959-61, Brandywine River Mus., 1970-75, Maine Maritime Mus., 1984-89; bd. dirs. St. Luke's Meml. Hosp. Center, Utica, 1957-61. Sr. fellow Am. Acad. Rome, 1948-49; recipient Distinguished Service award USIA, 1959; Prix de Rome, 1948; Rockefeller sr. fellow Met. Mus., 1975-76. Mem. Am. Assn. Museums, Harvard Soc. Fellows. Home: The Stone School House Phippsburg ME 04562

MCLANE, DAVID GLENN, lawyer; b. Dallas, Jan. 17, 1943; s. Alfred Ervin and Dixie Marie (Martin) McL.; m. Sally Ruth Payne, Apr. 5, 1963; children: Cynthia Lynn, Kathleen Michelle, Michael Scott; m. Beverly Anne Bledsoe, Feb. 5, 1983; children: Morgan Elizabeth, Nicholas Martin, Elizabeth Clark. BA, So. Meth. U., 1963, LLB, 1966. Bar: Tex. 1966, U.S. Supreme Ct. 1971. Briefing atty. Supreme Ct. Tex., 1966-67; assoc., then ptnr. Gardere & Wynne and predecessors, Dallas, 1967—; mem. faculty So. Meth. U.; lectr. in field. Bd. dirs. Urban Services br. Dallas YMCA, 1977-84, Dallas Symphony Assn., 1980-93; mem. Dallas County AIDS Planning Commn. Task Force, 1988; pres. coun. Dallas Theol. Sem., 1994—. Mem. ABA, Tex. Bar Assn., Dallas Bar Assn., S.W. Benefits Assn. (bd. dirs. 1975-80, pres. 1978-79), So. Meth. U. Law Alumni Assn. (sec., bd. dirs. 1981-85, Vol. of Yr. award 1984), So. Meth. U. Alumni Assn. (bd. dirs. 1972-77). Presbyterian. Contbg. author: Texas Corporations—Law and Practice, 1984; editor: Incorporation Planning in Texas, 1977. Office: 3000 Thanksgiving Tower Dallas TX 75201

MCLANE, FREDERICK BERG, lawyer; b. Long Beach, Calif., July 24, 1941; s. Adrian B. and Arlie K. (Burrell) McL.; m. Lois C. Roberts, Jan. 28, 1967; children: Willard, Anita. BA, Stanford U., 1963; LLB, Yale U., 1966. Bar: Calif. 1967, U.S. Dist. Ct. (cen. dist.) Calif. 1967. Assoc. prof. law U. Miss., Oxford, 1966-68; assoc. O'Melveny & Myers, L.A., 1968-74, ptnr., 1975—; com. of counsel HUD, Los Angeles, 1979-84; lectr. in field. Pres., bd. dirs. Legal Aid Found., L.A., 1974-83; deacon Congl. Ch., Sherman Oaks, Calif., 1979-83; vice-chair L.A. Music Ctr., Unified Fund, 1992-94; bd. dirs. Calif. Mus. Found., 1991—. Mem. ABA (banking com.), Calif. Bar Assn. (fin. insts. com., uniform comml. codes), L.A. Bar Assn., Order of Coif, Calif. Club (L.A.), L.A. Country Club, Lakeside Golf Club (L.A.), Lake Arrowhead Country Club (Calif.). Democrat. Avocations: golf, skiing, walking, reading. Office: O'Melveny & Myers 400 S Hope St Los Angeles CA 90071-2801

MCLANE, HENRY EARL, JR., philosophy educator; b. Statesboro, Ga., Aug. 18, 1932; s. Henry Earl and Lillie Ora (Beasley) McL.; m. Barbara Helen Gardner, Nov. 7, 1934; children—Debra Lynn, Shawn Creg. B.A., George Washington U., 1955; postgrad., Johns Hopkins U., 1955-56; M.A., Yale U., 1958, Ph.D., 1961. Instr. philosophy Washburn U. of Topeka, Kans., 1960-61; asst. prof. Washburn U. of Topeka, 1961-64, assoc. prof., 1964-65; vis. assoc. prof. Coll. of William and Mary, Williamsburg, Va., 1965-66; assoc. prof. Coll. of William and Mary, 1966-77, prof. philosophy, 1978—; diving coach Coll. of William and Mary, 1976-87. Contbr. articles to profl. publs. Danforth Found. fellow, 1955-60. Mem. Am. Philos. Assn. Democrat. Baptist. Avocations: playing violin; music. Home: 116 Dogwood Dr Williamsburg VA 23185-3743 Office: Coll of William and Mary Dept Philosophy PO Box 8795 Williamsburg VA 23187-8795

MCLANE, JAMES WOODS, insurance executive; b. New Canaan, Conn., Jan. 27, 1939; s. William Lawrence and Elizabeth Fish (Benjamin) McL.; m. Fay Sargent, Apr. 27, 1963 (div. 1980); children—James Woods, Benjamin Sargent; m. Nancy Coe, May 5, 1984; 1 child, Joshua Coe. B.A., Yale U., 1961; M.B.A., Harvard U., 1967. Cons. Booz, Allen & Hamilton, N.Y.C., 1967-69; exec. asst. to sec. HEW, Washington, 1969-70; staff asst. to Pres. U.S., White House, 1971-72; dep. dir. Cost of Living Council, Washington, 1972-74; v.p. mcht. banking group Citibank N.A., N.Y.C., 1974-79; sr. v.p. and head corp. fin. div. Citibank N.A., 1980-83; sr. v.p., mng. dir. Citicorp Internat. Bank Ltd., 1983-84; head Europe, Middle East, Africa div (Global Investment Bank), London, 1983-84; pres., chief exec. officer Citicorp Ins.

Group Inc., 1985-91; div. exec. Citibank Global Ins. Div., 1985-91, Capital Investments Div., 1988-90; chief exec. officer Aetna Health Plans, Hartford, Conn., 1991—; group exec. Aetna Life & Casualty, 1992-93, exec. v.p., 1993—; chmn. AMBAC, Inc., AMBAC Indemnity, Capital Markets Assurance Corp., Citicorp Ins. (U.S.A.) Inc., Citicorp Ins. (Bermuda) Ltd.; bd. dirs. Citicorp Ins. Brokers Ltd. Chmn. Outward Bound U.S.A., 1993-96; trustee Old State House Assn., Jackson Hole Group, 1992-96, St. George's Sch., 1981-85; mem. exec. com. Health Leadership Coun., 1996—; campaign mgr. Mass. Gov. Sargent's Reelection Campaign, 1970; mem. hon. degrees com. Yale U., 1973-74; bd. dirs., 1st v.p., campaign chmn. Greenwich (Conn.) Health Assn., 1981-83; elder Brick Ch., N.Y.C., 1988-91. With USN, 1961-65, Vietnam. Mem. Yale Club of N.Y., Twin Lakes Beach Club, Hartford Golf Club. Republican. Office: Aetna Health Plans 151 Farmington Ave # B66 Hartford CT 06156-0001

MC LANE, JOHN ROY, JR., lawyer; b. Manchester, N.H., Feb. 19, 1916; s. John R. and Elisabeth (Bancroft) Mc L.; m. Blanche Marshall, Feb. 15, 1935; children: John Roy III, Andrew M. (dec.), Lyn, Blanche M., Angus; m. 2d, Elisabeth Deane, Dec. 30, 1960; children: Towner D., Virginia W., Kathryn E., Duncan C. Bar: N.H. 1941. Practiced in Manchester, since 1941; dir. firm McLane, Graf, Raulerson & Middleton, P.A., 1941-42, 45—. Alderman, Manchester, 1952-53; trustee Spaulding-Potter Charitable Trusts, 1958-72, N.H. State Hosp., 1949-62, Hurricane Island Outward Bound Sch., 1972-79; chmn. N.H. Adv. Commn. on Health and Welfare, 1965-68; trustee, sec. Norwin S. and Elizabeth N. Bean Found., 1967-94; trustee, clk. St. Paul's Sch., 1952-83; distbg. dir. N.H. Charitable Fund, 1962-69; bd. dirs. Coun. on Founds, 1968-74, chmn., 1970-72; bd. dirs. Child and Family Svcs. N.H., 1946-71, pres., 1963-71; bd. dirs. Palace Theatre Trust, 1974—. Lt. USNR, 1942-45. Mem. ABA, N.H. Bar Assn., Manchester Bar Assn. Republican. Episcopalian (vestry 1963, 68). Home: 106 McLane Ln Manchester NH 03104-1641 Office: 900 Elm St Manchester NH 03101-2007

MCLANE, ROBERT DRAYTON, JR., food products company executive; b. Cameron, Tex., July 22, 1936; s. Robert Drayton and Gladys (Blaylock) McL.; m. Mary Elizabeth Cockrell, Feb. 2, 1972; children: Robert Drayton III, Denton. BBA, Baylor U., 1958; MS, Mich. State U., 1959. With McLane Co., Inc., Temple, Tex., 1957—, v.p., 1964-74, exec. v.p., sec.-treas., 1974-78, chief exec. officer, pres., 1978—, also bd. dirs.; bd. dirs. First Nat. Bank, Temple, Tex. Pres. United Way Campaign, Temple, 1985—; mem. Tex. State Bd. Mental Health and Mental Retardation, 1985—, exec. bd. Heart O'Tex. Council Boy Scouts Am., 1968—; bd. dirs. Scott and White Meml. Hosp., Temple, 1985—. Recipient Mgmt. Excellence and Achievement award Coll. Bus. Mgmt. U. Ga., 1986; named Entrepreneur of Yr. Arthur Young/Venture, Dallas, 1987. Mem. Nat. Am. Wholesale Grocers Assn. (chmn. 1986-88), Nat. Assn. Convenience Stores, Grocery Mfrs. Am., Tex. Food Industry Assn. Baptist. Avocation: tennis. Office: McLane Group PO Box 549 Temple TX 76503*

MCLANE, WILLIAM DELANO, mechanical engineer; b. Ralls, Tex., Aug. 22, 1936; s. Clyde and Lillian Helen (Earp) McL.; m. Mary Ann Clark, Feb. 17, 1962; children: William Devin, Keri, Kristi, Mandy. BSME, Tex. Tech. U., 1961. Profl. engr. Tex. Engr. Texaco Inc., Tulsa, 1961-63; plant engring. mgr. Owens-Corning Fiberglas Corp., Toledo, 1963-72; pres., CEO Tucker-McLane Tire Corp., Waxahachie, Tex., 1972-89; commr. County of Ellis, Waxahachie, 1989-93; engr. Morrison Knudsen Corp., Dallas, 1993-94; MK-Ferguson, Albuquerque, 1994-95, Parsons Brinckerhoff, Dallas, 1995-96; quality control mgr. Sedalco, Inc., Fort Worth, Tex., 1996—; mem. adv. bd. Guaranty Fed. Bank, Waxahachie, 1993—, Citizens Nat. Bank, Waxahachie, 1991-92, City of Waxahachie, 1990-91. Sec. bd. Waxahachie Sch. Dist., 1979-86; vice chmn. Ctrl. Tex. Econ. Devel. Dist., Waco, Tex., 1989-93. Mem. ASME, ASCE, NSPE, Tex. Soc. Profl. Engrs., Waxahachie C. of C. (pres. 1977), Internat. Conf. Bldg. Officials. Republican. Presbyterian. Avocations: civic and political volunteer work, varmint hunting, photography, cooking. Home: 1612 Alexander Dr Waxahachie TX 75165 Office: 2554 E Long Ave Fort Worth TX 76137

MCLAREN, DIGBY JOHNS, geologist, educator; b. Carrickfergus, Northern Ireland, Dec. 11, 1919; m. Phyllis Mary Matkin, Mar. 25, 1942; children: Ian, Patrick, Alison. Student, Queen's Coll., Cambridge U., 1938-40; BA, Cambridge U., 1941, MA (Harkness scholar), 1948; PhD, Mich. U., 1951; DSc (hon.), U. Ottawa, 1980, Carleton U., 1993, U. Waterloo, 1996. Geologist Geol. Survey Can., Ottawa, Ont., 1948-80; dir. gen. Geol. Survey Can., 1973-80; sr. sci. advisor Can. Dept. Energy, Mines and Resources, Ottawa, 1981-84; vis. prof. U. Ottawa, 1981-90; 1st dir. Inst. Sedimentary and Petroleum Geology, Calgary, Alta., Can., 1967-73; pres. Commn. on Stratigraphy, Internat. Union Geol. Scis., 1972-76; apptd. 14th dir. Geol. Survey Can., 1973; chmn. bd. Internat. Geol. Correlation Program, UNESCO, 1976-80. Contbr. memoirs, bulls., papers, geol. maps, sci. articles in field of Devonian geology and paleontology of Western and Arctic Canada, internat. correlation and boundary definition, global extinctions and asteroid impacts, and global change. Served to capt. Royal Arty. Brit. Army, 1940-46. Decorated officer Order of Can.; recipient Gold medal (sci.) Profl. Inst. Pub. Service of Can., 1979, Hollis D. Hedberg Energy award So. Meth. U., 1994. Fellow Royal Soc. Can. (pres. 1987-90), Royal Soc. London, European Union of Geoscis. (hon.), U.S. Nat. Acad. Scis. (fgn. assoc.), Geol. Soc. France (hon.), Geol. Soc. London (hon., Coke medal 1986), Am. Philos. Soc. (fgn. mem.); mem. Geol. Soc. Germany (hon., Leopold von Buch medal 1983), Geol. Soc. Am. (pres. 1982), Paleontol. Soc. (pres. 1969), Geol. Assn. Can. (Logan medal 1987), Can. Soc. Petroleum Geologists (pres. 1971, hon.). Home: 248 Marilyn Ave, Ottawa, ON Canada K1V 7E5

MCLAREN, FRED B., supermarket chain executive; b. 1934. With Hughes Mkts. Inc., L.A., 1959—, formerly dir. ops., pres., 1974—, also bd. dirs. Office: Hughes Markets Inc 14005 Live Oak Ave Irwindale CA 91706*

MCLAREN, JAMES CLARK, French educator; b. Halifax, N.S., Can., June 19, 1925; came to U.S., 1947, naturalized, 1960; s. Philip Doane and Margaret (MacGregor/Clark) McL.; m. Helen Elizabeth Oestreich, Jan. 25, 1957; children: Susan Atwell, James Philip. B.A., Dalhousie U., 1945, M.A., 1946; diplôme d'études, Sorbonne, Paris, 1947; Ph.D., Columbia U., 1951. Lectr. French Columbia U., N.Y.C., 1947-48; instr. Johns Hopkins U., Balt., 1948-52, asst. prof., 1952-56; assoc. prof., then prof. Chatham Coll., Pitts., 1956-65, chmn. dept. modern langs., 1957-65; prof. French U. Del., Newark, 1965-85, prof. emeritus, 1985—, chmn. grad. program French, 1966-81; vis. lectr. French lit. U. Pitts., 1957-63. Author: The Theatre of André Gide, 1953; essayist in field, reviewer; writer poetry. Recipient Buhl Humanities award Chatham Coll., 1964; French Govt. scholar, Sorbonne, 1946-47; Grad. residence scholar Columbia U., 1948-49; Todd scholar Columbia U., 1948-49. Mem. MLA, Am. Assn. Tchrs. of French. Home: 802 S Chapel St Newark DE 19713-3718 Office: U Del Dept French Newark DE 19716 *My goal as a teacher and writer has been to try to view the relativity and interrelationship of ideas and themes: to attempt a critical synthesis out of any specific analysis of a text or author. However specialized the topic, it loses its relevance if isolated from the broader contexts within which it evolves or contrasts. This, I think, is the real meaning of the Humanities.*

MC LAREN, JOHN ALEXANDER, retired physician; b. Vancouver, B.C., Can., Mar. 21, 1919; came to U.S., 1948, naturalized, 1952; s. Henry Moncrieff and Elizabeth Jean (Dingwall) McL.; m. Valerie Jean Adams, June 24, 1944; children: John Alexander, Jeannie McLaren Martz, Duncan R., Laurie McLaren Gates. B.A., U. B.C., 1939; M.D., C.M., McGill U., Montreal, 1943. Diplomate: Am. Bd. Internal Medicine. Intern and resident Montreal Gen. Hosp.; resident Toronto Gen. Hosp., 1946-48; gen. practice internal medicine Wilmette and Evanston, Ill., 1948-68; v.p. patient care services Evanston (Ill.) Hosp., 1968-74, v.p. mktg., 1976-80; v.p. orgn., planning and staffing Glenbrook Hosp., Glenview, Ill., 1974-76; physician Northcare Med. Group, 1980-84; asst. prof. medicine Northwestern U. Med. Sch.; mem. Nat. Bd. Med. Examiners, 1975-78; long-term care council Joint Commn. Accreditation Hosps., 1971-78. Served with M.C. Can. Army, 1943-46. Mem. Chgo. Med. Soc., AMA. Club: Mission Hills Country (Northbrook). Home: 3741 Mission Hills Rd #201 Northbrook IL 60062-5747

MC LAREN, MALCOLM GRANT, IV, ceramic engineering educator; b. Denver, July 22, 1928; s. George W. and Evelyn (Hodgson) McL.; m. Barbara Stephen, Sept. 23, 1950; children: Malcolm Grant, George, Thomas, Michael. B.S., Rutgers U., 1950, M.S., 1951, Ph.D., 1962. Research asst. Rutgers U., New Brunswick, N.J., 1950-54, mem. faculty, 1962—, prof. ceramics, chmn. dept. ceramics, 1969-94, dir. Inst. for Engineered Materials, 1987—; chief ceramist Paper Makers Importing Co., Easton, Pa., 1954-55; v.p., dir. Paper Makers Importing Co., 1957-62; hon. life prof. Tsing Hua U., Beijing, China, 1992. Author articles in field. Served to 1st lt. USAF, 1955-57. Recipient Gardner award Rutgers U., 1970; Man of Yr. award Associacão Brasiliera de Cerâmica, 1978; Dr. Harvey Wiley medal FDA, 1984; Ann. award Ceramic Assn. N.J.; Outstanding Engr. award Rutgers U., 1989. Fellow Am. Ceramic Soc. (Disting. life, v.p. 1974, pres. 1979-80, Albert Victor Bleininger award 1979, Founders award Phila. sect. 1983), Brit. Inst. Ceramics; mem. Am. Soc. Engring. Edn., Ceramic Ednl. Coun. (pres.), Internat. Ceramic Fedn. (pres. 1989-90), The Acad. Ceramics (pres., bd. trustees 1993-96), Associacão Brasiliera de Cerâmica (hon. life), Cap and Skull Rutgers U., Sigma Xi, Phi Lambda Upsilon, Phi Gamma Delta, Tau Beta Pi, Keramos. Home: 297 Spring Mills Rd Milford NJ 08848-1945 Office: Rutgers U Ceramics Dept New Brunswick NJ 08903

MCLARNAN, DONALD EDWARD, banker, corporation executive; b. Nashua, Iowa, Dec. 19, 1906; s. Samuel and Grace (Prudhon) McL.; m. Virginia Rickard, May 5, 1939; children: Marilyn, Marcia, Roxane. A.B., U. So. Calif., 1930; grad., Southwestern U. Law Sch., 1933; postgrad., Cambridge U. Trust appraiser, property mgr. Security-Pacific Nat. Bank, Los Angeles, 1935-54; regional dir. SBA for, So. Calif., Ariz., Nev., 1954-61; area adminstr. SBA for, Alaska, Western U.S., Hawaii, Guam, Samoa, U.S. Trust Terr., 1969-73; pres. Am. MARC, Inc. (offshore oil drillers and mfr. diesel engines), 1961-63, Terminal Drilling & Prodn. Co., Haney & Williams Drilling Co., Western Offshore, 1961-63; v.p., dir. Edgemar Dairy, Santa Monica Dairy Co., 1954-70; founder, pres., chmn. bd. Mission Nat. Bank, 1963-67; pres. Demco Trading Co., Mut. Trading Co.; dir. Coast Fed. Savs. & Loan; cons. numerous corps.; guest lectr. various univs. Contbr. articles on mgmt. and fin. to profl. jours. Chmn. fed. agys. div. Community Chest, 1956; nat. pres. Teachers Day, 1956; bd. councillors U. So. Calif.; founder, chmn., pres. Soc. Care and Protection Injured Innocent; adv. bd. Los Angeles City Coll.; bd. dirs. Calif. Easter Seal Soc.; nat. chmn. U. So. Calif. Drug Abuse Program. Recipient Los Angeles City and County Civic Leadership award, 1959. Mem. Nat. Assn. People with Disabilities (pres.); Mem. Skull and Dagger, Delta Chi. Clubs: Mason (Los Angeles) (K.T., Shriner), Los Angeles (Los Angeles), Jonathan (Los Angeles). Home: 135 S Norton Ave Los Angeles CA 90004-3916 Office: 1111 Crenshaw Blvd Los Angeles CA 90019-3112

MCLARNON, MARY FRANCES, neurologist; b. Montreal, Que., Canada, May 13, 1944; came to U.S., 1969; d. John Francis and Patricia Jessica (Dore) McL.; m. Malcolm Weiner, Dec. 21, 1975; m. Lawrence Zingesser, Oct. 12, 1982; children: Andrea, Eliza. BS, McGill U., 1965, MD, 1969. Intern St. Vincent's Hosp., N.Y.C., 1969-70; fellow seizure unit Boston Children's Hosp., 1970-71; resident in neurology Albert Einstein Coll. Medicine, Bronx, N.Y., 1971-73; resident in radiology N.Y. Hosp.-Cornell Med. Ctr., N.Y.C., 1973-76; pvt. practice.

MCLARTY, THOMAS F., III (MACK MCLARTY), federal official; b. Hope, Ark., June 14, 1946; s. Thomas Franklin and Helen (Hesterly) McL.; m. Donna Kay Cochran, June 14, 1969; children: Mark Cochran, Franklin Hesterly. BA, U. Arkansas, Fayetteville, 1968. Founder, pres. McLarty Leasing System Inc., Little Rock, 1969-79; pres. McLarty Cos., 1979-83; with Arkla Inc., Shreveport, from 1983, pres., CEO Arkla Gas divsn., 1983; pres., COO Arkla Gas divsn. Arkla, Inc., Shreveport, 1984, chmn. bd., pres., CEO, from 1985; chief of staff The White House, Washington, 1993-94, sr. adviser to President Clinton, 1994—; chmn. Arkla Energy Mktg. Co., Shreveport, La., Arkla Chem. Corp., Shreveport, AER-Ark. Gas Transit Co., Shreveport; chmn., chief exec. officer, Miss. River Transmission Corp., St. Louis, MRT Energy Mktg. Co., St. Louis, Ark. La. Fin. Corp., Shreveport. Mem. Ark. Ho. of Reps., 1970-72; chmn. Ark. Dem. Com.; mem. Dem. Nat. Com., 1974-76; treas. David Pryor Gubernatorial Campaign, 1974, Gov. Bill Clinton campaign, 1978; bd. dirs. Hendrix Coll., Conway, Ark.; bd. visitors U. Ark., Little Rock; former chmn. United Negro Coll. Fund Campaign, fund-raising campaign Ark. Symphony. Mem. Greater Little Rock C. of C. (pres. 1983). Office: The White House 1600 Pennsylvania Ave NW Washington DC 20500*

MCLAUGHLIN, ANN, public policy, communications executive; b. Newark, Nov. 16, 1941; d. Edward Joseph and Marie (Koellhoffer) Lauenstein; m. John McLaughlin, 1975 (div. 1992). Student, U. London, 1961-62; B.A., Marymount Coll., 1963; postgrad., Wharton Sch., 1987. Supr. network comml. schedule ABC, N.Y.C., 1963-66; dir. alumnae relations Marymount Coll., Tarrytown, N.Y., 1966-69; account exec. Myers-Infoplan Internat. Inc., N.Y.C., 1969-71; dir. communications Presdl. Election Com., Washington, 1971-72; asst. to chmn. and press sec. Presdl. Inaugural Com., Washington, 1972-73; dir. Office of Pub. Affairs, EPA, Washington, 1973-74; govt. relations and communications exec. Union Carbide Corp., N.Y.C. and Washington, 1974-77; pub. affairs, issues mgmt. counseling McLaughlin & Co., 1977-81; asst. sec. for pub. affairs Dept. Treasury, Washington, 1981-84; under sec. Dept. of Interior, Washington, 1984-87; cons. Ctr. Strategic and Internat. Studies, Washington, 1987; sec. of labor Dept. of Labor, Washington, 1987-89; vis. fellow The Urban Inst., 1989-92; pres., CEO New Am. Schs. Devel. Corp., 1992-93; chmn. Pres.'s Commn. Aviation Security and Terrorism, 1989-90; mem. Am. Coun. on Capital Formation, 1976-78; mem. environ. edn. task force HEW, 1976-77; mem. Def. Adv. Com. of Women in the Svcs., 1973-74; bd. dirs. GM, Union Camp Corp., Kellogg Co., Nordstrom Co., Host Marriott Corp., Vulcan Materials Co., AMR Corp., Fannie Mae, Potomac Electric Power Co., Pub. Agenda Found.; vice-chmn., trustee Aspen Inst.; pres. Fed. City Coun., 1990-95. Mem. bd. overseers Wharton Sch. U. Pa.; bd. dirs. Charles A. Dana Found., The Conservation Fund; trustee Urban Inst., 1989—. Mem. Cosmos Club, Met. Club, Econ. Club, F St. Club. Republican. Roman Catholic.

MCLAUGHLIN, AUDREY, Canadian government official; b. Dutton, Ont., Can., Nov. 7, 1936; d. William and Margaret Brown; children: David, Tracy. BA, U. Western Ont.; MSW, U. Toronto, Ont. M.P. from Yukon Ter. Ho. of Commons, 1987—; leader New Dem. Party, 1989-94; apptd. Privy Coun., 1991; social scientist, cons. Office: House of Commons, 649-D Ctr Block 11 Wellington St, Ottawa, ON Canada K1A 0A6

MCLAUGHLIN, CALVIN STURGIS, biochemistry educator; b. St. Joseph, Mo., May 29, 1936; s. Calvin Sturgis and Agnes Jane McLaughlin; m. Chin Helen Moy, Sept. 7, 1960; children—Heather Chin Chu, Christine Leng Oy, Andrew Calvin Moy. BS, King Coll., 1958; postgrad., Yale U., 1958-59; PhD, MIT, 1964. Postdoctoral fellow Institut de Biologie Physico-Chimique, Paris, 1964-66; prof. biochemistry U. Calif., Irvine, 1966—, dir. Cancer Research Inst., 1981-83; vis. prof. Sch. Botany Oxford U., Eng., 1976, 80; mem. peer rev. panels Am. Cancer Soc., NSF, NIH, VA. Contbr. numerous articles to profl. jours.; mem. editorial bds. Jour. Bacteriology, 1975-80, Exptl. Mycology, 1980-86; reviewer profl. jours. Bd. dirs. Am. Cancer Soc., Orange County, 1980-89; mem. Traffic Affairs Com., Newport Beach, Calif., 1972-78. Named Outstanding Tchr. U. Calif.-Irvine, 1978, Gabriel Lester Meml. Lectr. Reed Coll., 1979; fellow Rockefeller Found., 1958-59, Upjohn Found., 1959-60, Nutrition Found., 1960-61, NIH, 1961-64, Am. Cancer Soc., 1964-66. Mem. Genetics Soc. Am., Am. Soc. Biochemistry and Molecular Biology, Am. Soc. Microbiology, Am. Soc. Mycology, Am. Soc. for Cell Biology, Yeast Genetics and Molecular Biology Soc. Am. (co-chair 1986-88), Electrophoresis Soc. Presbyterian. Office: U Calif-Irvine Dept Biol Chemistry Irvine CA 92717

MCLAUGHLIN, CAROLYN LUCILE, elementary school educator; b. Pensacola, Fla., June 16, 1947; d. John Franklin and Mamie Lou (Rayburn) Wells; m. Richard Allen McLaughlin, Sept. 5, 1969; children: Allen Wayne, Kristen Lynn. BA, U. West Fla., 1970. Cert. early childhood, elem. edn. tchr., ESOL. Elem. tchr. Santa Rosa Sch. Bd., Milton, Fla., 1970-95. Youth ch. tng tchr., music and youth dir., Sunday sch. youth tchr. Billory Bapt. Ch., East Bay Bapt. Ch., Midway Bapt. Ch., 1970-95; mem. County Tchr. Edn. Coun., Santa Rosa, County Ins. Com. Grantee Jr. League 1986, 91-94, Chpt. II Fed. grantee Elem. and Secondary Edn. Act, 1992. Mem. Santa Rosa Profl. Educators (dist. VII rep., negotiations team com., county calendar com., sec. county restructuring steering com., county curriculum com., tchr. of yr. com.). Home: 3586 Ginger Ln Navarre FL 32566-9616

MCLAUGHLIN, DAVID JORDAN, botanist; b. Providence, Oct. 19, 1940; s. Walter Joseph and Abby Christina (Kilmartin) McL.; m. Esther Tuckerman Gaw, Feb. 1, 1964; children: Abigail Gaw, Elise Manning. AB, Brown U., 1962; postgrad., McGill U., Montreal, 1962-63; PhD, U. Calif., Berkeley, 1968. Postdoctoral fellow U. Copenhagen, Denmark, 1968-69; asst. prof. U. Minn., Mpls., 1969-73, assoc. prof., 1973-80, prof., 1980—, curator of fungi Herbarium, 1989—; vis. assoc. prof. U. Colo., Boulder, 1975-76; vis. scientist U. Bristol, Eng., 1983-84. Author: (with others) An Atlas of Fungal Ultrastructure, 1974; contbr. articles to profl. jours. NSF grantee. Fellow Linnean Soc. London' mem. AAAS, Mycol. Soc. Am. (editl. bd. 1982-90, editor in chief Mycologia 1990-95). Office: U Minn Dept Of Plant Biology Saint Paul MN 55108

MC LAUGHLIN, DAVID THOMAS, academic administrator, business executive; b. Grand Rapids, Mich., Mar. 16, 1932; s. Wilfred P. and Arlene (Sunderlin) McL.; m. Judith Ann Landauer, Mar. 26, 1955; children: William, Wendy, Susan, C. Jay. B.A., Dartmouth Coll., 1954, M.B.A., 1955. With Champion Internat. Co., 1957-70; v.p., gen. mgr. Champion Internat. Co. (Champion packages div.), 1957-70; pres., chief exec. officer Toro Co., Bloomington, Minn., 1970-77; chmn., chief exec. officer Toro Co., Mpls., 1977-81; pres. Dartmouth Coll., Hanover, N.H., 1981-87; chmn. The Aspen Inst., Aspen, Colo., 1987-88, Queenstown, Md., 1987—; pres., CEO The Aspen Inst., Aspen, Colo., Queenstown, Md.; bd. dirs. Westinghouse Elec. Corp., Pitts., Atlas Air, Denver, Arco, L.A.; chmn. bd. dirs. PartnerRe, Bermuda, Arco, Std. Fusee Corp., Easton, Md. Served with USAF, 1955-57. Office: The Aspen Inst PO Box 222 Carmichael Rd Queenstown MD 21658-0222

MCLAUGHLIN, EDWARD DAVID, surgeon, medical educator; b. Ridley Park, Pa., Jan. 8, 1931; s. Edward D. and Catherine J. (Hilbert) McL.; m. Mary Louise Hanlon, June 20, 1959; children: Catherine, Louise, Edward, Patricia. BS magna cum laude Georgetown U., 1952; MD, Jefferson Med. Coll., 1956. Intern, Jefferson Med. Coll., Phila., 1956-57, resident in surgery, 1957-59; resident in surgery Jefferson Med. Coll. Hosp., Phila., 1962-64; practice medicine specializing in surgery; surg. asso. Nat. Cancer Inst., NIH, 1959-61, surgeon, 1961-62; teaching fellow Harvard Med. Sch., Boston and clin. research fellow Mass. Gen. Hosp., Boston, 1964-66; sr. surg. registrar Hawkmoor Chest Hosp., Devon, Eng., 1966-67; sr. surgeon Chestnut Hill Hosp., 1967-71; asst. prof. surgery Jefferson Med. Coll., 1968-72, assoc. prof., 1972—, lectr. Jefferson continuing med. edn. program, 1976-77; assoc. chmn. of surgery Mercy Cath. Med. Center, Phila., 1972-88; pres., treas. Cedar Mgmt. Corp., 1981-86; pres., treas. Garnet Moor Ltd., 1981-91, Garnetmoor Pub. Svc. Ltd., 1986-91, Garnet Valley Acad. Alliance, 1991—, Garnet Valley Academic Assn., 1995—; treas. Physicians and Surgeons Ltd., 1983-86. Chmn., Bethel Twp. Planning Study Group, 1971-72, Bethel Twp. Sewer Authority, 1972-78, Bethel Twp. Planning Commn., 1989-91; mem. bd. of sch. dirs. Garnet Vally Sch. Dist., 1990—; mem. resources com., Garnet Valley Sch. Bd., 1991-95, chmn. curriculum com., 1992-95, chmn. edn. com., 1995-96, alt. mem. fin. com., 1995-96, mem. policy com., 1995—, mem. bldg. com., 1995—, mem. facility com., 1995—. With USPHS, 1959-62. Recipient Mead Johnson award for research, 1962, Americus award KC, 1963, Lindback award Jefferson Med. Coll., 1974; named Outstanding Prof. of 1976-77, Phi Alpha Sigma Jefferson Med. Coll. Diplomate Am. Bd. Surgery. Fellow ACS; mem. Phila. Acad. Surgery, N.Y. Acad. Scis., Med. Soc. State Pa., AAAS, Am. Soc. Artificial Internal Organs, AMA, Pa. Thoracic Soc., Georgetown U. Alumni (dir. 1970-72, senator 1972—), Nu Sigma Nu, Alpha Kappa Kappa. Contbr. articles on research in cancer to med. jours. and articles on edn. to ednl. jours. Home and Office: 3112 Garnet Mine Rd Boothwyn PA 19061-1718

MC LAUGHLIN, HARRY ROLL, architect; b. Indpls., Nov. 29, 1922; s. William T. and Ruth E. (Roll) McL.; m. Linda Hamilton, Oct. 23, 1954; 1 child Harry Roll Jr. Grad., Wabash Coll., 1983. Registered architect, Ind., Ohio Ill., Nat. Coun. Archtl. Registration Bds.; lic. real estate broker, Ind. Past pres. James Assocs. Inc., Indpls.; specializing in restoration of historic bldgs. and domestic architecture. Restorations include Old State Bank State Meml, Vincennes, Andrew Wylie House, Bloomington, Old Opera House State Meml, New Harmony, Old Morris-Butler House, Indpls. (Merit award 1972), Market St. Restoration and Maria Creek Baptist Ch., Vincennes, Ind., Benjamin Harrison House, Old James Ball Residence, Lafayette, Ind. (1st Design award 1972), Lockerbie Sq. Master Plan Park Sch., Indpls., Knox County Ct. House, Vincennes, 1972, J.K. Lilly House, Indpls., 1972, Waiting Station and Chapel, Crown Hill Cemetery, Indpls., 1972, Blackford-Condit House Ind. State U., Terre Haute, Ind. several Indian houses Angel Mounds Archaeol. Site and Interpretive Center, nr. Evansville, Ind.; architect: Glenn A. Black Mus. Archaeology, Ind. U., Bloomington; Restoration Morgan County Ct. House, Indpls. City Market, Hist. Schofield House, Madison, Ind., Ernie Pyle Birthplace, Dana, Ind., Phi Kappa Psi Nat. Hdqrs, Indpls., 1980 (Design award), East Coll. Bldg, DePauw U., Greencastle, Ind., Pres.'s House Restoration, DePauw U., 1992; contbr. articles to profl. jours.; Illustrator: Harmonist Construction. Past chmn. bd., past pres., now chmn. emeritus Historic Landmarks Found., Ind.; bd. dirs., archtl. adviser, bd. advisers Historic Madison, Inc.; mem. adv. coun. Historic Am. Bldgs. Survey, Nat. Park Svc., 1967-73; past mem. Ind. profl. rev. com. for Nat. Register nominations, 1967-81; past adv. bd. Conner Prarie Mus., Patrick Henry Sullivan Found.; past adviser Indpls. Historic Preservation Commn.; past mem. preservation com. Ind. U.; architect mem. Meridian St. Preservation Commn., Indpls.; hon. mem. Ind. Bicentennial Commn.; bd. dirs. Park-Tudor Sch., 1972-85; past nat. bd. dirs. Preservation Action; bd. dirs. Historic New Harmony; trustee Masonic Heritage Found.; bd. dirs. Masonic Home, 1984-91, Inpls. Pub. Libr. Found., 1986—, treas. 1988, 95—, v.p., 1989, pres. 1990; trustee Eiteljorg Mus. Western Art; past mem. Hamilton County Tourism Commn., 1989-91. Recipient numerous award including gov.'s citation State of Ind., 1967, Sagamore of Wabash award, 1967, 80, 82; Mayor's citation for svcs. in preservation archtl. heritage City of Indpls., sec.'s citation U.S. Dept. Interior, design and environ. citation for work in preservation, 1975. Fellow AIA (mem. nat. com. historic bldgs., chmn. historic resources com. 1970); mem. Ind. Soc. Architects (state preservation coord. 1960—, Biennial award 1972, Design award 1978), Nat. Trust Historic Preservation (past trustee, bd. advisers), Soc. Archtl. Historians (Wilbur D. Peat award Ctrl. Ind. chpt. outstanding contbns. to understanding and appreciation of archtl. heritage 1993, past bd. dirs.), Ind. Com. for Preservation of Archtl. Records, Indpls. Mus. Art. (trustee, chmn. bldgs. com., bd. govs. 1986-95), Assn. Preservation Tech., Zionsville C. of C. (hon. bd. dirs.), U.S. Capitol (hon. trustee), Ind. Hist. Soc. (trustee, bldg. com.), Marion County Hist. Soc. (past v.p., bd. dirs.), Zionsville Hist. Soc. (hon. life), Navy League U.S. (life), Ind. State Mus. Soc. (charter), English Speaking Union (bd. dirs. Indpls.), Newcomen Soc. of U.S., Hamilton County Hist. Soc. (life), Woodstock Club (bd. dirs. 1982-86, pres. 1985, ex-officio 1986), Literary Club Found. (trustee), Amateur Movie Club, Skyline Club (life), Packard Club, Masons (33 deg.). Home and Office: 950 W 116th St Carmel IN 46032-8864

MCLAUGHLIN, JAMES DANIEL, architect; b. Spokane, Wash., Oct. 2, 1947; s. Robert Francis and Patricia (O'Connel) McL.; B.Arch., U. Idaho, 1971; m. Willa Kay Pace, Aug. 19, 1972; children: Jamie Marie, Robert James. Project architect Neil M. Wright, Architect, AIA, Sun Valley, Idaho, 1971-74, McMillan & Hayes, Architects, Sun Valley, 1974-75; now pres., prin. McLaughlin Architects Chartered, Sun Valley. Prin. works include Oakridge Apts., Moscow, Idaho (Excellence in Design award AIA), Walnut Ave. Mall, Ketchum, Idaho (Excellence in Design award AIA, 1987), McMahan Residence, Sun Valley (Excellence in Design award AIA, 1987). Chmn., Ketchum Planning and Zoning Commn., Ketchum Planning Commn., Ketchum Zoning Commn.; chmn. Sun Valley Planning and Zoning Commn.; vice-chmn. Idaho Archtl. Licensing Bd. Served to 1st lt. U.S. Army. Registered architect, 10 states including Idaho. Mem. AIA, Nat. Coun. Archtl. Registration Bds., Nat. Home Builders Assn., Ketchum-Sun Valley C. of C. (dir.). Roman Catholic. Club: Rotary. Prin. archtl. works include James West Residence, First Fed. Savs., Fox Bldg. Rehab., Walnut Ave. Mall, First St. Office Bldg. Home: PO Box 6 Lot # 5 Red Cliffs Subdivsn Ketchum ID 83340-0006 Office: McLaughlin Architects Chartered PO Box 479 Sun Valley ID 83353-0479

MCLAUGHLIN, JEAN WALLACE, art director, artist; b. Charlotte, N.C., Dec. 19, 1950; d. John Mason and Caroline (Garner) McL.; m. Thomas Hudson Spleth, Jan. 1991. BA, U. N.C., 1972; postgrad., Calif. Coll. Arts & Crafts, 1983-85; MA, N.C. State U., 1994. Spl. projects coord. Divsn. of the Arts, Dept. Cultural Resources, Raleigh, N.C., 1975-77; arts program coord. Gov.'s Adv. Coun. for Persons with Disabilities, Raleigh, 1978-79; visual and literary arts coord. N.C. Arts Coun., Raleigh, 1979-82; pvt. practice arts cons. San Francisco, 1982-85; visual arts sect. dir. N.C. Arts Coun., Raleigh, 1985—; art educator Charlotte (N.C.) Latin Sch., 1973-75; panelist and spkr. in field. Author: The Arts in the Churches and Synagogues of North Carolina, 1976; prodr. (book) Public Art Dialogue: SE, 1988. Bd. mem. New Langton Arts, San Francisco, 1983-85, N.C. World Ctr., Raleigh, 1988-91; program com. mem. Fiberworks, Berkeley, 1984-85. Mem. Nat. Campaign for Freedom of Expression, Nat. Assn. Artists Orgns., N.C. Arts Advs., Am. Assn. Mus., Am. Crafts Coun., N.C. Mus. Coun., City Gallery of Contemporary Art, New Langton Arts, Internat. Sculpture Ctr. Avocations: gardening, traveling, reading, writing, making art. Office: NC Arts Coun Dept Cultural Resources Raleigh NC 27601

MC LAUGHLIN, JEROME MICHAEL, lawyer, shipping company executive; b. St. Louis, Jan. 11, 1929; s. John Thomas and Mary Adelaide (White) McL.; m. Delphine M. McClellan, June 15, 1957; children—Margaret D., Mary Martha, Elizabeth O., Jerome Michael, John T. A.B., St. Louis U., 1950, J.D., 1954. Bar: Mo. 1954, U.S. Supreme Ct. 1972. V.p. Internat. Indemnity, St. Louis, 1955-56; asst. circuit atty. City of St. Louis, 1957-58; partner firm Wilson, Cunningham & McClellan, St. Louis, 1958-78; v.p., gen. counsel Alexander & Baldwin, Inc., Honolulu, 1978-79; sr. v.p. Philippines, Micronesia & Orient Navigation Co., San Francisco, 1979-87, exec. v.p., 1987—; instr. philosophy St. Louis U., 1955-60. Served to capt. USMC, 1951-53, Korea. Mem. Mo. Bar Assn., Maritime Law Assn. U.S., Soc. Maritime Arbitrators San Francisco (past pres.). Republican. Roman Catholic. Home: 1225 Hillview Dr Menlo Park CA 94025-5510 Office: 353 Sacramento St San Francisco CA 94111-3620

MC LAUGHLIN, JOHN FRANCIS, civil engineer, educator; b. N.Y.C., Sept. 21, 1927; s. William Francis and Anna (Goodwin) McL.; m. Eleanor Thomas Trethewey, Nov. 22, 1950; children: Susan, Donald, Cynthia, Kevin. B.C.E., Syracuse U., 1950; M.S. in Civil Engring., Purdue U., 1953, Ph.D., 1957. Mem. faculty Purdue U., 1950—, prof. civil engring., 1963—, head Sch. Civil Engring., 1968-78, asst. dean engring. Sch. Civil Engring., 1977-80, assoc. dean engring., 1980-94, interim dean engring., 1994-95; ret. Sch. Civil Engring., 1995; cons. in field. Served with USAAF, 1945-47. Fellow ASCE, Hwy. Rsch. Bd.; mem. ASTM (bd. dirs. 1984-86), Am. Concrete Inst. (hon. mem., bd. dirs., v.p. 1977-79, pres. 1979), Am. Nat. Studies Inst. (bd. dirs. 1992-94), Sigma Xi, Tau Beta Pi, Chi Epsilon, Theta Tau. Home: 112 Sumac Dr West Lafayette IN 47906-2157

MCLAUGHLIN, JOHN JOSEPH, broadcast executive, television producer, political commentator, journalist; b. Providence, Mar. 29, 1927; s. Augustus Hugh and Eva Philomena (Turcotte) McL.; m. Ann Lauenstein, Aug. 23, 1975 (div. 1992). AB, Boston Coll., 1951, MA in Philosophy, 1952, BDiv, 1959, MA in English, 1961; PhD, Columbia U., 1967. Ordained priest Roman Catholic Ch., 1960. Mem. Jesuit Order, N.E., N.Y. and Washington; resigned order and priesthood, 1975; tchr., dir. communications Fairfield (Conn.) Univ. and Preparatory Sch., 1960-64; assoc. editor America Mag., N.Y.C., 1967-70; dep. spl. asst. to Pres. Richard Nixon and Gerald Ford, Washington, 1971-74; pres. McLaughlin and Co. Pub. Policy Cons., Washington, 1975-79; radio talk-show host Sta. WRC-AM, Washington, 1979-82; pres., chmn. bd. dirs. Oliver Prodns., Inc., Washington, 1983—; lectr. numerous univs., corps. and orgns. nationwide, 1963—; host various TV series, Sta. WJAR-TV, Providence, 1962-63, Sta. WNHC-TV, New Haven, 1963, Sta. WTIC-TV, Hartford, 1963, Sta. WOR-TV, N.Y.C., 1964; host, exec. producer Biafra Today report ABC-TV Network, 1969; radio commentator Sta. WSTC, Stamford, Conn., 1964, CBS Network Radio, N.Y.C., 1964, Nat. Pub. Radio All Things Considered, Washington, 1981-85; dir. film insts. Yale U., Holy Cross Coll., Manhattanville Coll.; juror Am. Film Festival, 1969; congressional testimony pub. broadcasting and TV license renewal, Washington, 1967, 69. Author: Love Before Marriage, 1970; editor National Review, Washington, 1981-89, columnist From Washington Straight, 1982-89; TV host and exec. producer The McLaughlin Group NBC and PBS TV stas., 1982—, John McLaughlin's One on One, 1984—, McLaughlin CNBC cable system, 1989-94; host spl. episode (TV show) Cheers, 1990. Rep. candidate U.S. Senate, R.I., 1970. Recipient Excellence in Journalism award Cath. Press Assn., 1969, News Media award VFW, 1984; nominee Nat. Acad. Cable Programming ACE award, 1989, 90, 91, 94; The McLaughlin Group named Best Polit. Talk Show, Washingtonian mag., 1987-93. Mem. NATAS (Emmy award 1984), Am. Fedn. TV and Radio Artists, Screen Actors Guild. Office: Oliver Prodns Inc 1211 Connecticut Ave NW Ste 810 Washington DC 20036-2701*

MCLAUGHLIN, JOHN SHERMAN, lawyer; b. Pitts., Apr. 1, 1932; s. John H. and Dorothy I. (Schrecongost) McL.; m. Suzanne Shaver, June 5, 1971; children—Dorothy, Sarah, Martha. A.B., Harvard U., 1954, LL.B., 1957. Bar: Pa. 1958, U.S. Supreme Ct. 1967. Assoc. Reed, Smith, Shaw & McClay, Pitts., 1957-71; ptnr. Reed, Smith, Shaw & McClay, 1971—. Trustee Harmarville Rehab. Ctr., Inc., 1980-87, Western Pa. Sch. for the Deaf, 1985—; pres. Pa. NG Assn., 1976-78; justice of peace Borough of Edgewood, 1963-73; dir. Pitts. Symphony soc., 1987-94, Winchester Thurston Sch., 1985—; life trustee Carnegie Libr. of Pitts. and Carnegie Inst., 1994—. Lt. col. Air NG, 1957-79. Mem. Am. Law Inst., Am. Coll. Trust and Estate Counsel, Allegheny County Bar Assn., Duquesne Club, Rolling Rock Club (Ligonier, Pa.). Office: Reed Smith Shaw & McClay 435 6th Ave Pittsburgh PA 15219-1809

MCLAUGHLIN, JOSEPH, lawyer; b. Newark, Aug. 1, 1941; s. Joseph Nicholas and Genevieve Veronica (Lardiere) McL.; m. Elisabeth Lippold, July 31, 1965; children: Elisabeth, Jessica, Emilie. AB, Columbia U., 1962, LLB, 1965. With Sullivan & Cromwell, N.Y.C., 1968-76; v.p., gen. counsel Goldman, Sachs & Co., 1976-88, cons., 1988-90; ptnr. Brown & Wood, N.Y.C., 1993—; adj. prof. law NYU Sch. Law, 1988-92; spkr., presenter in field. Contbr. articles to profl. jours. Trustee Greenwich (Conn.) Acad., 1988—; treas. Presbyn. Ch. Old Greenwich, 1988-91; bd. dirs. United Way, Greenwich, 1993—; mem. Rep. Town com., Greenwich, 1993-96. Jervey fellow Parker Sch. Fgn. Comparative Law, Columbia Law Sch., U. Munich, 1966-68. Mem. ABA (sect. bus. law, fed. regulation securities com., subcom. broker-dealer matters 1985—, subcom. civil litigation and SEC enforcement matters 1989—, chair task force rule 10b-6 1995—, co-chair task force sellers' due diligence and similar defenses under fed. securities laws 1989-92), Am. Law Inst., Assn. of Bar of City of N.Y. (internat. law com. 1979-84, chair 1981-84, civil rights com. 1984-87, internat. arms control and security affairs com. 1988-90), N.Y. Stock Exch. (legal adv. com. to bd. govs. 1985-88, subcom. corp. governance, subcom. internat. issues 1988—), Securities Industry Assn. (fed. regulations com. 1978-88, chair 1982-84), Nat. Assn. Securities Dealers, Inc. (corp. financing com. 1983-86), Am. Arbitration Assn. (dir. 1986-90). Republican. Congregationalist. Office: Brown & Wood 1 World Trade Ctr New York NY 10048-0202

MC LAUGHLIN, JOSEPH MAILEY, lawyer; b. Los Angeles, July 10, 1928; s. James Aloysius and Cecilia Ann (Mailey) McL.; m. Beverly Jane Walker, July 24, 1949; children: Stephen Joseph, Lawrence James, Suzanne Carol, Eileen Louise. J.D., Loyola U., Los Angeles, 1955. Bar: Calif. 1955, U.S. Supreme Ct. 1959. Mem. firm McLaughlin and Irvin, L.A., 1955—, San Francisco, 1969—; lectr. labor relations Loyola U., Los Angeles, 1958-60, mem. bd. visitors law sch., 1987—; pres. Food Employers Council, Inc., 1984-89. Contbg. author: Labor Law for General Practitioners, 1960. Served to 1st lt. USAF, 1951-53. Mem. San Francisco, Long Beach, Los Angeles County, Fed., Am., Internat., Inter-Am. bar assns., State Bar Calif., Am. Judicature Soc., Assn. Bus. Trial Lawyers, Am. Soc. Internat. Law. Clubs: California, Los Angeles Stock Exchange (pres. 1972). Office: 333 S Grand Ave Fl 33 Los Angeles CA 90071-1504

MCLAUGHLIN, JOSEPH MICHAEL, federal judge, law educator; b. Brooklyn, N.Y., Mar. 20, 1933; s. Joseph Michael and Mary Catherine (Flanagan) McL.; m. Frances Elizabeth Lynch, Oct. 10, 1959; children: Joseph, Mary Jo, Matthew, Andrew. A.B., Fordham Coll., 1954, LL.B., 1959; LL.M., NYU, 1964; LL.D., Mercy Coll., White Plains, N.Y., 1981. Bar: N.Y. 1959. Assoc. Cahill, Gordon, N.Y.C., 1959-61; prof. law Fordham U., N.Y.C., 1961-71, dean Sch. of Law, 1971-81, adj. prof., 1981—; judge U.S. Dist. Ct. Eastern Dist. N.Y., Bklyn., 1981-90, U.S. Ct. Appeals (2nd Cir.), N.Y.C., 1990—; adj. prof. St. John's Law Sch., N.Y.C., 1982—; chmn. N.Y. Law Revision Commn., Albany, 1975-82. Author: (with Peterfreund) New York Practice, 1964, Evidence, 1979; also articles. Served to capt. U.S. Army, 1955-57, Korea. Mem. ABA, Assn. of Bar of City of N.Y., N.Y. State Bar Assn. Roman Catholic. Club: Lotos. Office: US Courthouse US Ct Appeals 40 Foley Sq/Rm 2402 New York NY 10007-1502*

MCLAUGHLIN, JOSEPH THOMAS, lawyer; b. Boston, Mar. 30, 1944; s. James Francis and Madeline Louise (Hickman) McL.; m. Christine E. Mullen, Sept. 2, 1967; children: Amy Melissa, Caitlin Christine, Ian Michael. BA magna cum laude, Boston Coll., 1965; JD, Cornell U., 1968. Bar: Mass. 1969, N.Y. State 1968, U.S. Supreme Ct. 1974. Research asst. Brit. Council of Archaeology, Winchester, Eng., 1964; site supr. Brit. Council of Archaeology, 1966; legis. asst. Rep. Thomas P. O'Neill, Washington, 1967; research asst. Cornell U., 1967-68; law clk. to chief justice Mass. Superior Ct., 1968-69; assoc. Shearman & Sterling, N.Y.C., 1969-76, ptnr., 1976—; adj. prof. Fordham Law Sch., 1981—; vis. prof. Cornell Law Sch., 1995—. Author: Federal Class Action Digests, 1974, 1976; contbr. articles to profl. jours. Exec. dir. Brooklyn Heights Draft Counseling Svc., 1970-74, Presbyn. Task Force for Justice Counseling Svc., 1973-75; v.p., bd. dirs. Brooklyn Heights Assn., 1973-77; bd. dirs. Willoughby Settlement House, Inc., Ingersoll-Willoughby Cmty. Ctr., Inc., 1970-75, United Neighborhood Houses, 1976-78, Good Shepherd Svcs., Resources for Children with Spl. Needs, Inc., Internat. House. Mem. ABA, Assn. of Bar of City of N.Y. (mem. com. on profl. discord 1986—), N.Y. State Bar Assn. (chmn. com. on marijuana and drug abuse 1972-75), Am. Law Inst., Am. Arbitration Assn., N.Y. Lawyers for Pub. Interest (chmn. bd. dirs.) ABAC (com. on promoting settlements), Heights Casino Club. Home: 174 State St Brooklyn NY 11201-5610 Office: 153 E 53rd St New York NY 10022-4602

MC LAUGHLIN, LEIGHTON BATES, II, journalism educator, former newspaperman; b. Evanston, Ill., Apr. 10, 1930; s. Leighton Bates and Gwendolyn I. (Markle) McL.; m. Beverly Jean Jeske, May 5, 1962; children: Leighton Bates III, Jeffrey, Steven, Patrick. Student English lit., Kenyon Coll., Gambier, Ohio, 1948-50, Northwestern U., 1951; BA in English lit., UCLA, 1983; MA in communications, Calif. State U., Fullerton, 1990. Copyboy, reporter, rewriteman City News Bur., Chgo., 1957-58; reporter, rewriteman Chgo. Sun-Times, 1958-62; rewriteman, asst. city editor Ariz. Jour., Phoenix, 1962; reporter Miami (Fla.) Herald, 1962-64; successively rewriteman, night city editor, 1st asst. city editor, telegraph editor Chgo. Sun-Times, 1964-74; dir. Chgo. Daily News/Sun-Times News Service, 1974-79; editorial coord. electronics newspaper div. Field Enterprises, 1975-79; adminstr. reference libr. and communications ctr. Field Newspapers, 1976-79; editor News Am. Syndicate, Irvine, Calif., 1979-85; mng. editor San Gabriel Valley Daily Tribune, 1986; assoc. prof. journalism Riverside (Calif.) Community Coll., 1987—, chmn. performing arts and media dept., 1993—; lectr. in journalism Calif. State U.-Fullerton, 1984—; fill-in editor The Press-Enterprise, Riverside, Calif., 1988—; lectr., condr. seminars in field. Author articles in field. Served to 1st lt. USMC, 1951-54. Recipient Stick-o-Type award for best feature story Chgo. Newspaper Guild, 1961, Best News story award Ill. AP and UPI, 1967. Mem. Soc. Profl. Journalists, Verban Soc., Psi Upsilon. Office: Riverside Community Coll 4800 Magnolia Ave Riverside CA 92506-1242 *Reporting the news is like any other intellectual activity in that it involves research, verification, organization, and clarity of presentation. But news reporting is unique in that all this is done on a dead run, in time for the day's editions.*

MCLAUGHLIN, LINDA LEE HODGE, federal judge; b. 1942. BA, Stanford U., 1963; LLB, U. Calif., Berkeley, 1966. With Keatinge & Sterling, L.A., 1966-70, Richards, Martin & McLaughlin, Beverly Hills and Newport Beach, Calif., 1970-73, Bergland, Martin & McLaughlin, Newport Beach, 1973-76, Bergland & McLaughlin, Costa Mesa, Calif., 1976-80; judge North Orange County Mcpl. Ct., Fullerton, Calif., 1980-82, Orange County Superior Ct., Santa Ana, Calif., 1982-92, U.S. Dist. Ct. (ctrl. dist.) Calif., Santa Ana, 1992—; mem. adv. com. jud. forms Jud. Coun., 1978—, mem. adv. com. gender bias in cts., 1987-90. Active Edgewood Sch. Parents Assn., Cate Sch. Parents Aux.; mem. governing bd. Victim-Witness Assistance Program Orange County. Mem. Nat. Assn. Women Judges, Calif. State Bar Assn. (mem. com. profl. ethics 1976-80, disciplinary referee dist. 8 1978-80), Calif. Women Lawyers (gov. dist. 8 1978-80), Calif. Judges Assn. (chair civil law and procedure com. 1985-86), Orange County Bar Assn. (mem. com. adminstrn. justice 1975-78, client rels. com. 1978-80, com. jud. appointments 1979-80), Orange County Women Lawyers, Boalt Hall Alumni Assn., Stanford U. Alumni Assn., Cap and Gown Hon. Soc.

MCLAUGHLIN, MARY RITTLING, magazine editor; b. Buffalo; d. Joseph and Irene (Meyer) Rittling; m. Charles Edward McLaughlin, June 21, 1962 (div. June 1981) children—Daniel (dec.), Maud Rosie. BA, Manhattanville Coll., 1956. Reporter Buffalo Evening News, 1956-58; copywriter Harper's Bazaar, N.Y.C., 1959-61; editor McCall's Mag., N.Y.C., 1973-79; mng. editor Working Mother Mag., N.Y.C., 1979-85; exec. editor Working Mother Mag., 1985—. Mem. Am. Soc. Mag. Editors, Women's Media Group. Office: Working Mother Mag 230 Park Ave New York NY 10169-0005

MCLAUGHLIN, MICHAEL JOHN, insurance company executive; b. Cambridge, Mass., Feb. 14, 1944; s. Michael John and Evelyn Katherine (Quinn) McL. A.B., Boston Coll., 1965; J.D., N.Y. U., 1968. Bar: N.Y., Mass. With N.Y. Life Ins. Co., 1968—, sr. v.p. info. systems and services dept., 1982-88, sr. v.p., 1988-91, sr. v.p., dep. gen. counsel, 1991-95, sr. v.p., gen. counsel, 1995—. Mem. ABA, N.Y. State Bar Assn. Office: NY Life Ins Co 51 Madison Ave New York NY 10010-1603

MCLAUGHLIN, MICHAEL JOHN, financial executive; b. Bklyn., Apr. 13, 1951; s. Michael John and Dorothy May (Reposky) McL.; m. Patricia Ann Concannon, June 24, 1978; children: Michael, Matthew, Brian. BS, Manhattan Coll., 1972; MBA, St. John's U., Queens, N.Y., 1978; JD, Pace U., 1984. Bar: N.Y. 1985; CPA, N.Y. Auditor Arthur Young & Co., N.Y.C., 1972-75; asst. controller Montrex Corp., N.Y.C., 1975-78; mgr. corp. acctg. Gen. Housewares Corp., Stamford, Conn., 1977-79, asst. controller, 1979-81, controller, 1981-86; v.p.-controller Preway Inc., Stamford and Wisconsin Rapids, Wis., 1986-87, v.p.-controller, sec., treas., 1987-88, v.p. fin., treas., sec., 1988-89; v.p. fin. and adminstrn. Hayden Roofing Co., Inc., West Nyack, N.Y., 1989-91; v.p. fin., chief fin. officer Celadon Group, Inc., 1991-93; v.p. fin. and adminstrn. A.T. Clayton & Co. Inc., Greenwich, Conn., 1993—. Mem. ABA, N.Y. State Bar Assn., Am. Inst. CPA's, N.Y. State Soc. CPA's. Republican. Roman Catholic. Office: A T Clayton & Co Inc 600 Steamboat Rd Greenwich CT 06830-7149

MCLAUGHLIN, PATRICK MICHAEL, lawyer; b. Monahans, Tex., July 23, 1946; s. Patrick John and Ann (Donnelly) McL.; m. Christine Manos, Aug. 21, 1970; children—Brian Patrick, Christopher Michael, Conor Andrew. B.Gen. Studies, Ohio U., 1972; J.D., Case Western Res. U., 1976. Bar: Ohio 1976, U.S. Dist. Ct. (no. dist.) Ohio 1978, U.S. Ct. Appeals (6th cir.) 1979, U.S. Supreme Ct. 1980; U.S. Dist. Ct. (so. dist.) Ohio 1989, U.S. Ct. Appeals (5th cir.). Dir. vets. edn. project. Am. Assn. Community and Jr. Colls., Washington, 1972-73; law clk. Common Pleas Ct., Cleve., 1976-77; law clk. to judge 8th Jud. Dist. Ct. of Appeals, Cleve., 1977-78; asst. U.S. atty. No. Dist. Ohio, Cleve., 1978-82; chief civil div. No. Dist. Ohio, 1982-84; U.S. atty. No. Dist. Ohio, Cleve., 1984-88; ptnr. Janik & McLaughlin, Cleve., 1988-89, Mansour, Gavin, Gerlack & Manos Co., L.P.A., Cleve., 1989—; appt. and ind. spl. prosecutor Ohio Attorneys General, 1993-96; cons. Nat. League of Cities, U.S. Conf. Mayors, 1971-72; co-creator Opportunity Fair for Veterans Concept, 1971. Editor-in-chief Case Western Res. Jour. Internat. Law, 1975-76. Chmn. North Ohio Drug Abuse Task Force, 1986-88; chmn. Law Enforcement Coordinating Commn., North Ohio, 1985-88; chmn. civil issues subcom. Atty. Gen.'s Adv. Com., 1986-88; exec. v.p. Greater Cleve. Vets. Meml., Inc., 1993, pres., 1994-96. Decorated Silver Star, Bronze Star, Purple Heart, Army Commendation medal, Vietnamese Cross of Gallantry with Silver and Bronze Stars. Mem. ABA, FBA, Ohio Bar Assn., Cleve. Bar Assn., Nat. Assn. Former U.S. Attys., Soc. 1st Divsn., Order of Ahepa, Vietnam Vets. Am., Nat. Vietnam Vets. Network (Disting. Vietnam Vet. award 1985), Nat. Assn. Concerned Vets. (nat. v.p. external affairs 1971-72, exec. dir. 1972-73), Cuyahoga County Vets. (award 1985), Nat. Soc. SAR (law enforcement commendation medal 1989). Republican. Roman Catholic. Office: Mansour Gavin Gerlack & Manos 2150 Illuminating Bldg 55 Public Sq Cleveland OH 44113-1913

MCLAUGHLIN, PHILIP VANDOREN, JR., mechanical engineering educator, researcher, consultant; b. Elizabeth, N.J., Nov. 10, 1939; s. Philip VanDoren and Ruth Evans (Landis) McL.; m. Phoebe Ann Feeney, Aug. 19, 1961; children: Philip VanDoren III, Patrick Evans, Christi Duff. BSCE, U. Pa., 1961, MS in Engring. Mechanics, 1964, PhD in Engring. Mechanics, 1969. Assoc. engr. Boeing-Vertol, Morton, Pa., 1962-63, engr. II, 1963; rsch. engr. Scott Paper Co., Phila., 1963-65, rsch. project engr., 1965-69, sr. rsch. project engr., 1969; asst. prof. theoretical and applied mechanics U. Ill., Urbana, 1969-73, asst. dean engring., 1971-72; project mgr. Materials Scis. Corp., Blue Bell, Pa., 1973-76; assoc. prof. mech. engring. Villanova (Pa.) U., 1976-81, prof., 1981—; judge Cons. Engrs. Coun. Ill. 1st Ann. Engring. Excellence Awards Competition, 1972; cons. Naval Air Engring. Ctr., Lakehurst, N.J., 1977-79, U.S. Steel Crop., Trenton, 1980-82, RCA Corp., Moorestown, N.J., 1986, Coal Tech Crop, Merion Station, Pa., Air Products and Chems., Inc., Allentown, Pa., 1986, Aircraft divsn. Naval Air Warfare Ctr., Patuxent River, Md., 1995—; vis. prof. dept. engring. U. Cambridge, Eng., 1990-91. Reviewer Prentice Hall, 1980—, Jour. Engring. Mechanics, 1973-83, AIAA Jour., 1970-87, Materials Evaluation, 1988, Jour. Composite Materials, 1988—, Composites Sci. and Tech., 1990—, others; contbr. articles to Jour. Applied Mechanics, Internat. Jour. Solids and Structures, Jour. Engring. Materials and Tech., NDT Internat., others. Rsch. grantee NSF, 1970-72, Naval Air Engring. Ctr., 1978-84, Lawrence Livermore Nat. Lab., 1979-81, Naval Air Warfare Ctr., 1985-86, RCA Corp., 1986-87; sr. rsch. assoc. NRC, Washington, 1983-84; USN-Am. Soc. for Engring. Edn. sr. faculty fellow, 1995. Mem. ASCE (chmn. engring. mechanics divsn. com. on inelastic behavior 1977-79, assoc. editor Jour. Engring. Mechanics Divsn. 1977-79, mem. aerospace divsn. com. on structures and materials 1986—), ASME (chmn. applied mechanics divsn. Phila. sect. 1981-83, mem. materials divsn. com. on composites 1992—), Am. Acad. Mechanics, Am. Soc. for Engring. Edn., Am. Soc. Composites, Sigma Xi. Achievements include research and consulting on composite materials and structures, structural analysis and design and inelastic behavior. Office: Villanova U Dept Mech Engring 800 Lancaster Ave Villanova PA 19085-1681

MCLAUGHLIN, RICHARD WARREN, retired insurance company executive; b. Boston, Nov. 25, 1930; m. Marilyn Slye, 1956; children: Kathleen, Richard Warren Jr., Thomas, Judy. B.S., Boston Coll., 1952; grad. Advanced Mgmt. Program, Harvard U., 1979. Trainee Travelers Ins. Co., Hartford, Conn., 1956, asst. sec., 1966-69, sec., 1969-70, 2d. v.p., 1970-73, v.p., 1973-81, sr. v.p., 1981-85; exec. v.p. Travelers Corp., Hartford, Conn., 1985-91; pres. Travelers Ins. Co., Hartford, Conn., 1991—; chmn. Travelers Indemnity Co., Hartford, 1991—. Corporator St. Francis Hosp. Capt. USAF, 1952-56, Korea. Mem. Eastward Ho Club (Chatham, Mass.), Hawks Nest Club (Vero Beach, Fla.). Home: PO Box 947 Eastham MA 02642-0947

MCLAUGHLIN, RONALD PAUL, labor union administrator; b. Kansas City, Mo., Nov. 13, 1929; s. Joseph Henry and Gladys Merl (Thomas) McL.; m. Barbara Joyce Runyon, Nov. 11, 1954; children: Gregory, Brian, Mark, Kevin. Grad. high sch., Kansas City. Local chmn. Brotherhood of Locomotive Engrs., Ottumwa, Iowa, 1959-81, gen. chmn., 1981-86; v.p. Brotherhood of Locomotive Engrs., Cleve., 1986-87, 1st v.p., 1987-91, pres., 1991—. Councilman City of Pleasant Valley, Mo., 1964. Cpl. USMC, 1946-48. Mem. Rail Labor Exec. Assn. (vice chmn. 1991—), Masons. Home: 225 Westwind Dr Apt 2 Avon Lake OH 44012-2417

MCLAUGHLIN, STEPHEN, sound recording engineer. Recipient Grammy award for Best Engineered Album, Non Classical ("Wildflowers" by Tom Petty), 1996. Office: c/o Robert Urband 860 Lexington Ave New York NY 10122*

MCLAUGHLIN, T. MARK, lawyer; b. Salem, Mass., Apr. 20, 1953; s. Terrence E. and Mary E. (Donlon) McL.; m. Sandra L. Roman, Oct. 16, 1982; children: Daniel, Kathleen, Eileen. BA in Econs., U. Notre Dame, 1975, JD, 1978. Bar: Ill. 1978, U.S. Dist. Ct. (no. dist.) Ill. 1978, U.S. Dist. Ct. (cen. dist.) Ill. 1992, U.S. Dist. Ct. (ea. dist.) Wis. 1992, U.S. Ct. Appeals (7th cir.) 1982, U.S. Ct. Appeals (11th cir.) 1982. Assoc. Mayer, Brown & Platt, Chgo., 1978-84, ptnr., 1985—; adj. faculty law Loyola U., Chgo., 1983, 86-90. Bd. dirs. no. Ill. affiliate Am. Diabetes Assn., Chgo., 1985-94. Mem. ABA (franchising forum com. antitrust law sect.), Phi Beta Kappa. Office: Mayer Brown & Platt 190 S La Salle St Chicago IL 60603-3410

MCLAUGHLIN, WILLIAM F., paper company executive; b. 1948. Student, West Point Acad.; MBA, Syracuse Univ. Pres. L.J. Minor Co.; exec. v.p. Nestle Brands Foodservice Co.; CEO Sweetheart Holdings, Chgo. Office: 7575 South Kostner Ave Chicago IL 60652

MC LAUGHLIN, WILLIAM GAYLORD, health care services company executive; b. Marietta, Ohio, Sept. 28, 1936; s. William Russell and Edna Martha (Hiatt) McL.; children: Debora, Cynthia, Leslie, Teresa, Kristin, Jennifer (dec.). BS in Mech. Engring., U. Cin., 1959; MBA, Ball State U., 1967. Plant engr. Kroger Co., Marion, Ind., 1959-62; with Honeywell, Inc., Wabash, Ind., 1962-75, mgr. metal products ops., 1971-72, gen. mgr. ops., 1972-75; pres. MarkHon Industries Inc., Wabash, 1975-90, pres. Healthy Industries Inc., 1991—; mem. N. Cen. Ind. Pvt. Industry Coun., 1983-84; mem. bus. adv. bd. Manchester Coll. Patentee design electronic relay rack cabinet. Pres. Wabash Assn. for Retarded Children, 1974-75; gen. chmn. United Fund Drive, 1971; mem. Wabash County Arts Coun.; pres. Wabash Valley Dance Theater; treas., Young Reps., Wabash, 1968-70; bd. dirs. Youth Svc. Bur., Sr. Citizens, Jr. Achievement; mem. ofcl. bd. Meth. ch., 1966-71; pres. Meth. men, 1975-77; area comm. chmn. Am. Heart Assn. Recipient Ind. Jefferson award for public service, 1981, Disting. Citizen award Wabash, 1981; named Outstanding Young Man of Year, Wabash Jr. C. of C., 1972. Mem. Indsl. C. of C. (pres. 1973-74), Wabash Area C. of C. (pres. 1976), Precision Metal Forming Assn. (chmn. Ind. dist. 1978, chmn. metal fabrication div.), Ind. Mfg. Assn. (bd. dirs.), Young Pres.'s Orgn. Club: Wabash Country (v.p. 1972-76). Lodges: Rotary (pres. 1970-71, dist. youth exchange officer 1974-77, dist. gov. 1979-80), Masons. Home: 141 W Maple St Wabash IN 46992 Office: PO Box 218 Wabash IN 46992-0218

MCLAUGHLIN, WILLIAM IRVING, space technical manager; b. Oak Park, Ill., Mar. 6, 1935; s. William Lahey and Eileen (Irving) McL.; student Calif. Inst. Tech., 1953-57; BS, U. Calif.-Berkeley, 1963, MA, 1966, PhD, 1968; m. Karen Bjorneby, Aug. 20, 1960; children: William, Margot, Walter, Eileen. Mem. tech. staff Bellcomm, Inc., 1968-71; mem. tech. staff Jet Propulsion Lab., Pasadena, Calif., 1971—; supr. terrestrial planets mission design group, 1981-83, mission design mgr. for Infrared Astron. Satellite, 1977-83, mgr. flight engring. office for Voyager/Uranus project, 1983-86; mgr. mission profile and sequencing sect., 1986-92; dep. mgr. astrophysics and fundamental physics program office, 1992-96, mgr. mission and syss. architecture sect., 1996—. Served with USMC, 1957-60. Recipient Apollo Achievement award, 1969, Exceptional Svc. medal NASA, 1984, Outstanding Leadership medal NASA, 1986. Fellow Brit. Interplanetary Soc. (Space Achievement Bronze medal 1993); mem. Internat. Acad. Astros., Phi Beta Kappa, Sigma Xi. Columnist Spaceflight mag., 1982—. Office: Jet Propulsion Lab 4800 Oak Grove Dr Pasadena CA 91109-8001

MCLAUGLIN, ROBERT BRUCE, software designer; b. Camden, N.J., Aug. 30, 1959; s. Robert Bruce and Patricia Ann (Renner) McL. Programmer/analyst Computron, N.Y.C., 1979-81; systems analyst Wincester Computer, N.Y.C., 1982-83, Geometric Solutions, N.Y.C., 1983-85; instrument maker Fusion Energy Found., N.Y.C., 1985-87; rsch. engr. Community Computer, Arlington, Va., 1987-89; prin. engr. Pilot Rsch., Vienna, Va., 1989-91; systems architect Unitel Comm., Toronto, Ont., Can., 1991-93; chief scientist Image Telecom, Reston, Va., 1993—; design authority Energis Comm., London, 1993-94; chief scientist Winstar Comm., Vienna, Va. Author: Fix Your LAN, 1994, Troubleshooting Your Own LAN, 1992, Fix Your PC, 1989-93; contbr. numerous articles to profl. jours. Mem. IEEE, Assn. Computing Machinery, Soc. of Old Crows, Am. Soc. for Quality Control. Achievements include 5 patents in the areas of video on-demand interactive and multimedia services.

MCLAURIN, HUGH MCFADDIN, III, military officer, historian consultant; b. Sumter, S.C., Jan. 30, 1936; s. Hugh McFaddin and Louise Mellette (Nettles) McL.; m. Virginia Anne Harvin, Aug. 22, 1958; children: Mary Louise, Virginia Harvin, Hugh IV. BS, Clemson U., 1959; hon. grad., Command & Gen. Staff Coll., Ft. Leavenworth, Kans., 1978. Ptnr. McLaurin Farms, Wedgefield, S.C., 1959—; commd. 2d lt. U.S. Army, 1958, advanced through grades to col., 1985; exec. officer 151st Field Artillery Brigade, Sumter, 1975-85; dir. pers. S.C. NG, Columbia, 1986-91, dir. logistics, 1991-95; cons. S.C. Ednl. TV, Columbia, 1992-93; moderator Nat. Def. Seminar, Washington, 1978. Author: History of South Carolina National Guard and Militia, 1989. Elder, Presbyn. Ch., Wedgefield, 1961; v.p. Com. for Progress, Sumter, 1963; chmn. bd. dirs. S.C. NG Mus., Columbia, 1982—. Fellow Co. Mil. Historians; mem. Field Artillery Soc. S.C. (pres. 1987), SAR (historian), The Sumter Assembly (pres. 1991), Hon. Order St. Barbara, Fortnightly Club. Avocation: American Revolution research. Home: 6380 McLaurin Rd Wedgefield SC 29168

MC LEAN, DON, singer, instrumentalist, composer; b. New Rochelle, N.Y., Oct. 2, 1945; s. Donald and Elizabeth (Bucci) McL.; m. Patrisha Shnier, Mar., 1987. Student, Villanova U., 1964; BBA, Iona Coll., 1968. Pres., owner The Benny Bird Co., Inc., Fairfield, Conn.; recorded for United Artists, Artista Records, EMI Records; star BBC-TV spls., 1973, 78. Albums include Tapestry, 1972, American Pie, 1972, Don McLean, 1972, Playin' Favourites, 1973, Homeless Brother, 1974, Solo, 1976, Prime Time, 1987, Chain Lightning, 1979, Very Best of, 1980, Believers, 1982, Dominion, 1983, The Best of Don McLean, 1987, Don McLean's Greatest Hits Then & Now, 1987, Love Tracks, 1988, For the Memories, 1989, Don McLean's Greatest Hits Live, 1990, Headroom, 1991, Classics, 1992; singles include American Pie, 1971, Vincent, 1971, Crying, 1980; wrote Perry Como hit And I Love You So, 1973. Mem. bd. Hudson River Sloop Restoration, World Hunger Yr., Advs. for Arts; fund raiser Scenic Hudson, Hudson River Fisherman's Assn. Recipient more than 30 gold and platinum records worldwide, 5 grammy award nominations and others; Israel Cultural award, 1981. Mem. Coffee House Club. Office: Benny Bird Co 1838 Black Rock Tpke Fairfield CT 06432-3500

MC LEAN, DONALD MILLIS, microbiology, pathology educator, physician; b. Melbourne, Australia, July 26, 1926; s. Donald and Nellie (Millis) McL.; married. B.Sc., U. Melbourne, 1947, M.B., 1950, M.D., 1954. Fellow Rockefeller Found., N.Y.C. and Hamilton, Mont., 1955; vis. instr. bacteriology U. Minn., Mpls., 1957; med. officer Commonwealth Serum Labs., Melbourne, 1957; virologist Research Inst., Hosp. for Sick Children, Toronto, Ont., Can., 1958-67; assoc. prof. microbiology, assoc. in pediatrics U. Toronto Med. Sch., 1962-67; prof. med. microbiology U. B.C. Med. Sch., Vancouver, Can., 1967-91, prof. emeritus Pathology, 1991—. Author: Virology in Health Care, 1980, Immunological Investigation of Human Virus Disease, 1982, Same-Day Virus Diagnosis, 1984, Virological Infections, 1988, Medical Microbiology Synopsis, 1991, Acute Viral Infections, 1991; contbr. articles to profl. jours. Fellow Royal Coll. Physicians (Can.), Royal Coll. Pathologists; mem. Am. Epidemiological Soc., Am. Soc. Tropical Medicine, Can. Med. Assn., Am. Soc. Microbiology, Am. Soc. Virology. Home: 6-5885 Yew Street, Vancouver, BC Canada V6M 3Y5

MCLEAN, EDGAR ALEXANDER, physicist; b. Gastonia, N.C., July 25, 1927; s. Alexander Milton and Nell Blythe (Miller) McL.; m. Anna Jane Hess, Dec. 29, 1951; children: Susan, Sandra, William, Frederick, Mary Anne. BS Physics, U.N.C., 1949; MS Physics, U. Del., 1951. Rsch. physicist Naval Rsch. Lab., Washington, 1951—; rsch. cons. Rep. Aviation Corp., Farmingdale, N.Y., 1963-65, Vitro Labs., West Orange, N.J., 1964-69, Cath. U. of Am., Washington, 1964-69, U. Western Ont., London, 1972-76. Contbr. articles to profl. jours., books. Troop com. mem. Boy Scouts of Am., Oxon Hill, Md., 1970-80; sci. fair judge Prince George's County Schs., Md., 1952—. With USN, 1945-46. Mem. Am. Phys. Soc., Optical Soc. Am., IEEE (exec. com. 1976-82), Sigma Xi (local exec. com. 1989-94). Achievements include optical diagnostics in the field of plasma physics, including spectroscopic, laser scattering, interferometric and ultra high-speed photographic measurements on shock waves, laser-matter interactions, and various controlled fusion devices. Discovered high-order harmonic generation produced in 1-micron laser-plasma interactions; discovered x-ray lasing in Cu, Zn, Ga, Ge, and As; demonstrated a new technique for optical imaging in turbid water using range gating. Home: 19 Mel Mara Dr Oxon Hill MD 20745

MCLEAN, EPHRAIM RANKIN, information systems educator; b. Jan. 7, 1936; married; 3 children. BME, Cornell U., 1958; SM in Mgmt., MIT, 1967, PhD in Mgmt., 1970. Mfg. mgmt., then sys. analyst positions Procter & Gamble Co., 1958-65; instr. tracked vehicle sect. automotive br. U.S. Army Ordnance Sch., Aberdeen Proving Ground, Md., 1959; sys. analyst Cambridge (Mass.) Thermionic Corp., 1966-67; rsch. asst. Sloan Sch. Mgmt. MIT, Cambridge, 1966-69, instr. info. sys., 1969; asst. prof. Grad. Sch. Mgmt. UCLA, 1969-75, assoc. prof., 1975-87; prof., George E. Smith eminent scholar's chair Ga. State U., Atlanta, 1987—; dir. computing svcs. Grad. Sch. Mgmt., UCLA, 1970-74, chmn. computers and info. systems, 1972-73, 77-80, 83-84, 86-87, founder/dir. computers and info. systems rsch. program, 1978-87; mem. adv. bd. Info. Inst., Internat. Acad. Santa Barbara, Calif., 1983-87; mem. adv. com. Info. Systems Faculty Devel. Inst., Am. Assembly Collegiate Sch. Bus. and U. Minn., Mpls., 1982, 84; cons. numerous bus. and ednl. orgns., 1967—; vis. prof. U. South Australia, Adelaide, 1993. Author: (with J.V. Soden) Strategic Planning for MIS, 1977; (with E. Turban and J. Wetherbe) Information Technology for Management, 1996; co-editor: Management Applications in APL, 1981, Decision Support Systems: A Decade in Perspective, 1986, The Management of Information Systems, 1989, 2nd edit., 1994, prof. conf. procs.; assoc. editor Data Base, 1990-94, co-editor, 1994—; mem. editl. bd./adv. bd., referee many profl. publs. and pub. cos.; contbr. numerous articles and revs. to profl. jours., mags., other publs. 2nd lt. ordnance corps USAR, 1958-59; 1st lt. ordnance corps N.J. Army N.G., 1959-65; capt. ordnance corps Mass. Army N.G., 1965-68. NDEA doctoral fellow MIT, 1967-69; recipient 1st prize nat. engring. design contest Lincoln Arc Welding Found., 1958; rsch. grantee IBM Corp., 1985, McCormick & Co., Hunt Valley, Md., 1989, InformationWEEK mag., Manhasset, N.Y., 1989, Sellinger Sch. Bus. and Mgmt. Loyola Coll. Md., Balt., 1992. Mem. Internat. Acad. Info. Mgmt. (bd. dirs. 1992—), EDUCOM (affiliate) Decision Scis. Inst., Internat. Fedn. Info. Processing (founding mem. working group on decision support sys. 1981—), Internat. Conf. on Info. Sys. (founding mem. adv. bd. 1980—, chmn. exec. com. 1986-87), Soc. for Info. Mgmt. (Atlanta chpt., mem. nat. pres.'s coun. 1985—, mem. nat. exec. com. 1976-79, 85-87, 3d pl. juried paper award competition 1987), Inst. Mgmt. Scis., ACM, Assn. for Info. Sys. (founding mem., v.p. affiliated orgns.), Mensa, Sigma Xi. Home: 2257 Old Brooke Point Dunwoody GA 30338 Office: Ga State U Computer Info Sys Dept Box 4015 Atlanta GA 30302-4015

MC LEAN, GEORGE FRANCIS, philosophy of religion educator, clergyman; b. Lowell, Mass., June 29, 1929; s. Arthur and Agnes (McHugh) McL. Ph.L., Gregorian U., Rome, 1952, S.T.L., 1956; Ph.D., Cath. U. Am., 1958. Joined Order Oblates of Mary Immaculate, 1949; ordained priest Roman Catholic Ch., 1955; prof. metaphysics, philosophy of religion Cath U. Am., Washington, 1958-94, prof. emeritus, 1994—; rsch. scholar U. Madras, 1969, 77-78, 85, U. Paris, 1970, Ctr. for Oriental Rsch., Cairo, 1991-94; adv. prof. Fudan U., Shanghai, 1994—. Author: Man's Knowledge of God According to Paul Tillich, 1958, Perspectives on Reality, 1966, An Annotated Bibliography of Philosophy in Catholic Thought, 1966, A Bibliography of Christian Philosophy and Contemporary Issues, 1966, Readings in Ancient Western Philosophy, 1970, Ancient Western Philosophy, 1971, Plenitude and Participation, 1978, Tradition and Contemporary Life: Hermeneutics of Perennial Wisdom and Social Change, 1986; editor: numerous books including Philosophy and the Integration of Contemporary Catholic Education, 1962, Philosophy in a Technological Culture, 1964, Christian Philosophy and Religions Renewal, 1966, Philosophy and Contemporary Man, 1968, Religion in Contemporary Thought, 1973, Traces of God in a Secular Culture, 1973, The Impact of Belief, 1974, The Role of Reason in Belief, 1974, New Dynamics in Ethical Thinking, 1974, Philosophy and Civil Law, 1975, Freedom, 1976, Ethical Wisdom East and/or West, 1977, Act and Agent: Philosophical Foundations of Moral Education and Character Development, 1986, 92, Psychological Foundations of Moral Education and Character Development, 1986, 92, Character Development in Schools and Beyond, 1987, 92, Person and Nature, 1988, Person and Society, 1988, Person and God, 1988, The Nature of Metaphysical Knowledge, 1988, The Social Context and Values: Perspectives of the Americas, 1989, Culture Human Rights and Peace in Central America, 1989, On Reading the Philosophers for the 21st Century, 1989, Research on Culture and Values, 1989, Man and Nature: The Chinese Tradition and The Future, 1989, Relations Between Cultures, 1991, Urbanization and Values, 1991, Place of the Person in Social Life, 1991, Chinese Foundations for Moral Education and Character Development, 1991, Morality, Metaphysics and Chinese Culture, 1992, The Foundations of Social Life, 1992, Person and Community, 1992, Tradition, Harmony and Trancendence, 1993, Islam and the Political Order, 1993, Psychology, Phenomenology and Chinese Philosophy, 1994, Values in Philippine Culture and Education, 1994, The Filipino Mind, 1994, The Philosophy of Person: Solidarity and Cultural Creativity, 1994, Private and Public Social Inventions in Modern Societies, 1994, Traditions and Present Problems of Czech Political Culture, 1994, Czech Philosophy in the XXth Century, 1994, Language, Values and the Slovak Nation, 1994, Morality and Public Life in a Time of Change, 1994, National Identity as an Issue of Knowledge and Morality, 1994, Personal Freedom and National Resurgence, 1994, Philosophy of Science and Education, 1995, Civil Society in Chinese Context, 1996, Civil Society and Social Reconstruction, 1996; area editor: New Cath. Ency. Mem. Am. Cath. Philos. Assn. (nat. sec. 1965-80), World Union Cath. Philos. Socs. (sec. gen. 1973—), InterUniv. Com. Research and Policy Studies (sec. 1975-77), Internat. Soc. Metaphysics (gen. sec. 1974—), Council Research in Values and Philosophy (sec. 1980—), Internat. Fedn. Philos. Socs. (dir. 1978-88), Cath. Learned Socs. and Scholars (sec. 1975-77). Home: 391 Michigan Ave NE Washington DC 20017-1586 Office: Cath U Am Dept Metaphysics Washington DC 20064

MCLEAN, IAN SMALL, astronomer, physics educator; b. Johnstone, Scotland, U.K., Aug. 21, 1949; s. Ian and Mary (Small) McL.; (div.); 1 child, Jennifer Ann; m. Janet Wheelans Yourston, Mar. 4, 1983; children: Joanna, David Richard, Graham Robert. BS with hons., U. Glasgow, 1971, PhD, 1974. Rsch. fellow Dept. Astronomy U. Glasgow, Scotland, 1974-78; rsch. assoc. Steward Observatory U. Ariz., Tucson, 1978-80; sr. rsch. fellow Royal Observatory U. Edinburgh, Scotland, 1980-81, sr. scientific officer Royal Observatory, 1981-86; prin. scientific officer Joint Astronomy Ctr., Hilo, Hawaii, 1986-89; prof. Dept. Physics and Astronomy UCLA, 1989—. Author: Electronic and Computer-Aided Astronomy: From Eyes To Electronic Sensors, 1989; contbr. articles to profl. jours. Recipient Exceptional Merit award U.K. Serc, Edinburgh, 1989; NSF grantee, 1991. Fellow Royal Astron. Soc.; mem. Internat. Astron. Union (pres. com. Paris chpt. 1988-91, v.p. 1985-88), Inst. Physics, Am. Astron. Soc. Achievements include discovery of relationship between polarization of light and orbital inclination of close binary stars; development of first CCD spectropolarimeter, first fully automated infrared camera for astronomy used to achieve images of faintest high redshift galaxies; research in polarization measurements of radiation from astronomical sources, use of CCDs and infrared array detectors. Office: UCLA Dept Astronomy 405 Hilgard Ave Los Angeles CA 90095-1362

MC LEAN, JACKIE, jazz saxophonist, educator, composer, community activist; b. N.Y.C., May 17, 1932. Bandmaster, counselor N.Y. State Correction Dept.; chmn., prof. Hartt Sch. Music, Hartford, Conn., from 1968; founder Artist Collective, Inc., Hartford, 1970; founder African Am. music program (jazz degree) Hartt sch. music U. Hartford. With Art Blakey's Jazz Messengers, performed with, Charles Mingus; actor: film The Connection; albums include Monuments, New York Calling, Antiquity, Live at Montmarte, Ode To Super, A Ghetto Lullaby, Lights Out, Dr. Jackle, The Meeting, Jack Knife, New and Old Gospel, Let Freedom Ring, Destination Out, One Step Beyond, Grachan Moncur III, (with Jackie McLean Quintet) Dynasty, 1990, Rites of Passage, 1991, Triloka: Rhythm of the Earth, 1992, Jackie MacAttack, 1993, Rhythm of the Earth, 1993; guest artist album by Jazz Messengers Midnight Session, 1993; led McLean Jazz Dynasty tour with son Rene in 6 countries in Southern Africa, 1993. Decorated officer of the Arts (France); recipient Bent award U. Hartford; named # 1 in Downbeat Mag. Critics Poll, 1993, 94, 95, # 1 in Jazz Times Mag. Readers' Poll, 1993, 94, 95. Office: care Artists Collective Inc 35 Clark St Hartford CT 06120-2010

MCLEAN, JAMES ALBERT, artist, educator; b. Gibsland, La., Nov. 25, 1928; s. Charles Edward and Lucille (Bowdon) McL.; m. Ocelia Jo Perkins, Nov. 27, 1954; 1 child: Gregory Scott. BA, Southwestern La. Inst., 1950; BD, So. Meth. U., 1953; MFA, Tulane U., 1961. Meth. student dir. Centenary Coll., Shreveport, La., 1957-59; head art dept. LaGrange (Ga.) Coll., 1964-66; assoc. prof. art Ga. State U., Atlanta, 1967-68, prof. art, 1968-95; ret., 1995. Exhibited in numerous group shows including Brooklyn Mus., 1976-77, Positive/Negative Exhbn., 1988, Siggraph Exhbn. 1988, 89, Clemson U. Nat. Print and Drawing Exhbn., 1989, Purdue U. Small Print Exhbn., 1990. Mem. Siggraph. Avocations: animation, puppetry. Home: 1256 Dunwoody Knolls Dr Atlanta GA 30338-3219

MCLEAN, KIRK, professional hockey player; b. Willowdale, Ont., Can., June 26, 1966. Goalie Vancouver (Can.) Canucks. Named to NHL All-Star 2nd Team, 1991-92. Office: Vancouver Canucks, 100 N Renfrew St, Vancouver, BC Canada V5K 3N7*

MCLEAN, ROBERT DAVID, lawyer; b. Mar. 1, 1945; s. Edward D. McLean; children by previous marriage: Ann P., Robert P.; m. Leslie Taft Breed; children: Edward B., Katherine T. BA, Northwestern U.; JD, Yale U. Law clk. to Justice Thurgood Marshall U.S. Supreme Ct.; ptnr. Sidley & Austin, Chgo., 1975—, also exec. com. chrmn., 1993—. Note and comment editor Yale U. Law Rev. Office: Sidley & Austin 1 First Nat Plz Chicago IL 60603

MCLEAN, (ANDREW) STUART, educator, journalist; b. Montreal, Que., Can., Apr. 19, 1948; s. Andrew Thompson and Margret Patricia (Godkin) McL.; m. Linda Read, July 10, 1982; children: Andrew, Robert, Christopher Trowbridge. Adminstr. Dawson Coll., Montreal, 1971-74; exec. prodr. Sunday Morning CBC Radio, 1981-83; dir. broadcast journalism Ryerson Poly U., Toronto, Ont., Can., 1984—; prof. Ryerson Poly. Inst., Toronto, Ont., Can., 1987—. Co-writer (film) Looking for Miracles; author: The Morningside World of Stuart McLean, 1989, Welcome Home: Travels in Small Town Canada, 1992 (Best Non-fiction award Can. Authors Assn. 1993), Stories from the Vinyl Cafe, 1995; contbr.: The New Morningside Papers, 1987, The Latest Morningside Papers, 1989. Recipient Best Documentary award ACTRA, 1979, Human Rights Broadcast Journalism award B'nai Brith, 1985; Rooke fellow for tchg. and writing Trent U., 1994. Office: care Ryerson Polytechnic U, 350 Victoria St, Toronto, ON Canada M5B 2K3

MCLEAN, SUSAN RALSTON, lawyer, federal government; b. Fayetteville, Tenn., Feb. 28, 1948; d. Joseph Frederick and Clara (Robertson) Ralston; m. Arthur Edward McLean, Apr. 16, 1983. AB, Randolph-Macon Woman's Coll., 1970; MAT in English, Vanderbilt U., 1971; JD, U. Tenn., 1979; LLM in Taxation, So. Meth. U., 1984. Bar: Tenn. 1979, Tex. 1981, Ark. 1984. Assoc. Rose Law Firm, Little Rock, 1984-85, Brice & Mankoff, Dallas, 1986-87; counsel tax divsn. Dept. Justice, Dallas, 1987—. Mem. ABA (tax litigation, bus. law sects., exempt orgn. com. tax sect.), Tex. Bar Assn. (tax and litigation sects.), Dallas Bar Assn., Randolph-Macon Woman's Coll. Alumnae (pres. 1992-94). Republican. Presbyterian. Avocations: swimming, golf, art, music, hiking. Home: 4025 McFarlin Blvd Dallas TX 75205-1723

MC LEAN, THOMAS EDWIN, retired manufacturing company executive; b. St. Petersburg, Fla., Feb. 14, 1925; s. Annis and Grace (Bell) McL.; m. Virginia Starr, Feb. 20, 1948; children—Brent Starr, Thomas Edwin, Lynn Elizabeth. B.S. in Bus. Adminstrn, U. Fla., 1950; grad., Ind. U. Sch. Savs. and Loan, 1967, also Am. Savs. and Loan Inst. Partner firm Gassner and McLean (C.P.A.'s), St. Petersburg, 1953-65; sr. v.p., sec. First Fed. Savs. & Loan Assn., St. Petersburg, 1965-69; exec. v.p. St. Petersburg Fed. Savs. & Loan Assn., 1969-71, pres., 1971-75; also dir.; pres. Manufactured Housing Products Co., 1978-86; pres. Abilities, Inc. of Fla., 1968-70; dir. Southwestern Suppliers Inc. Pres. Jr. Achievement Pinellas County, 1968-71, St. Petersburg Relocation Assistance Corp., 1971-75; mem. bishop's finance com. Episcopal Diocese S.W. Fla.; chmn. Bishop's Com. on State of Ch., 1973-75; mem. Com. of 100, chmn., 1970; mem. Pinellas County Budget Commn., 1954-56, Pinellas County Tourist Devel. Commn., 1978—; Chmn. bd. dirs. Anclote Psychiat. Center, 1973—; bd. dirs. St. Petersburg Speech and Hearing Clinic, pres., 1968-69, Pinellas Assn. Retarded Children, 1969-72, Police Athletic League, 1971-74, Community Alliance, 1972-74, Sunny Shores Villas, 1964-68, Suncoast Manor, 1969-75, Pinellas Horizon Mental Health Center and Hosp., 1977-79. Served with AUS, 1943-45. Decorated Purple Heart; named Sertoman of Yr., 1957-58; Liberty Bell award St. Petersburg Bar Assn., 1975. Mem. Nat. League Insured Savs. Assns. (chmn. finance com. 1973, mem. exec. com. 1972-74), U.S. Savs. and Loan Leagues, Fla. Savs. and Loan Leagues (chmn. advt. and pub. relations com. 1970-72), Sales and Mktg. Club (pres. 1968-69), St. Petersburg Area C. of C. (dir., pres. 1975-76), Suncoast C. of C. (dir.). Republican. Episcopalian (treas., sr. warden). Clubs: Rotary, Yacht (St. Petersburg), Dragon (dir.), Tiger Bay (pres.), Suncoasters, Golden Triangle. Home: 1339 43rd Ave N Saint Petersburg FL 33703-4437

MCLEAN, VINCENT RONALD, former manufacturing company financial executive; b. Detroit, June 1, 1931; s. Frederick Ronald and Bernice Mary (Vincent) McL.; m. Joyce Adrienne Koch, July 23, 1960; children—Judith Adrienne, Bruce Ronald. B.B.A., U. Mich., 1954, M.B.A., 1955. Fin. analyst Ford Motor Co., Detroit, 1954-55, Mobil Oil Corp., N.Y.C., 1958-69; treas. Mobil Chem. Co., N.Y.C., 1966-69; v.p. fin., treas. NL Industries, N.Y.C., 1969-76, exec. v.p. fin. and planning, dir., 1976-82; exec. v.p., chief fin. officer, dir. Sperry Corp., N.Y.C., 1982-86; sr. advisor Wertheim Schroder & Co., N.Y.C., 1988-89; bd. dirs. Alexander and Alexander Svcs., Inc., Legal and Gen. Am., Inc., William Penn Life Ins. Co. N.Y., Banner Life Ins. Co., Md., MAS Funds. Served with U.S. Army, 1955-57. Mem. N.Y. Soc. Security Analysts, Econ. Club N.Y. Home: 702 Shackamaxon Dr Westfield NJ 07090-3408

MCLEAN, WALTER FRANKLIN, international consultant, pastor, former Canadian government official; b. Leamington, Ont., Can., Apr. 26, 1936; s. J.L.W. McL.; m. Barbara Muriel Scott, Aug. 19, 1961; children: Scott, Chima, Ian, Duncan. BA, Victoria Coll., U. B.C., 1957; M.Div., Knox Coll., U. Toronto, 1960; LLD (hon.), Wilfrid Laurier U., 1995. Ordained to ministry, Presbyterian Ch. Minister Knox Presby. Ch., Waterloo, 1971-79; mem. House of Commons, Ottawa, Ont., Can., 1979-93, Sec. of State of Can., 1984-85, min. of immigration, 1985-86; min. resp. for status of women Govt. of Can., 1984-86; pres. Franklin Consulting, Ltd., Waterloo, Ontario, Canada, 1994; CUSO, Nigeria coord., 1962-67; chaplain U. Nigeria, 1962-67; dep. dir. Internat. Program Can. Centennial, 1967; exec. dir. Man. Assn. for World Devel., 1970; past chmn. World Concerns Commn. Canadian Coun. Chs.; Can. del. Gen. Assemblies UN, 1986-93; apptd. spl. rep. Commonwealth and South African affairs, 1989-93; Can. rep. So. Africa Devel. Coordination Conf., 1987-93; del. Commonwealth Fgn. Mins. Against Apartheid, 1987-93, African Devel. Bank, 1990-91, Assn. West European Parliamentarians Against Apartheid, 1988-89; leader fact finding mission to Mozambique, 1987, Can. delegation UN Conf. on Women, Nairobi, 1985; led Parliamentary del. to observe the pre-election process and attended Namibian Indpedence, Mar. 21, 1990; chmn. paliamentary Com. on Devel. and Human Rights; Commonwealth observer South African and Sri Lanka elections 1994; pres. Franklin Cons. Assoc. KPMG-Can. Alderman City of Waterloo, Ont., 1976-79; co-founder UN based Parliamentarians Global Action; hon. consul of the Rep. of Namibia. Chaplain 404 wing RCAF. Recipient award Can. U. Svcs. Overseas, 1990. Mem. Can. Bur. Internat. Edn., Waterloo Rotary, UN Assn. (chair human rights com.). Progressive Conservative.

MC LEAN, WILLIAM L., III, publisher; b. Phila., Oct. 4, 1927; s. William L., Jr. and Eleanor Ray (Bushnell) McL.; m. Elizabeth D. Peterson, Sept. 4, 1954; children: Elizabeth, William L. IV, Helen Brooke Katzenbach, Sandra, Warden. BA, Princeton U., 1949. With The Bull., Phila., 1949-80; v.p. The Bull., 1969-74, sr. v.p., 1974-75, editor, pub., 1975-80; pres. Ind. Publs., Inc., Bryn Mawr, Pa., 1976—; chmn. bd. Ind. Publs., Inc., 1980—. Trustee Acad. Natural Scis.; trustee, treas. Pa. chpt. Nature Conservancy. Mem. Pa. Newspapers Pubs. Assn. (pres. 1964, trustee Pa. Newspaper Pubs. Found.), Blooming Grove Hunting and Fishing Club, Franklin Inn Club. Episcopalian. Home: 139 Cherry Ln Wynnewood PA 19096-1208 Office: Ind Publs Inc 945 E Haverford Rd Bryn Mawr PA 19010-3819

MCLEAN, WILLIAM RONALD, electrical engineer, consultant; b. Bklyn., Mar. 26, 1921; s. Harold W. and Helena Winifred (Farrell) McL.; m. Cecile L. Mills, Aug. 17, 1946 (div.); m. 2d, Evelyn Hupfer, Nov. 29, 1968. BA, Bklyn. Coll., 1980, BS, 1981. Chief electrician U.S. Mcht. Marine, 1942-64; elect. designer, engr., 65-76; sr. elect. engr. M. Rosenblatt & Son, Inc., N.Y.C., 1976-86; cons., 1986—. Mem. Soc. Naval Architects and Marine Engineers, IEEE, Am. Soc. Naval Engrs. Home and Office: 57 Montague St Brooklyn NY 11201-3374

MCLELLAN, A. ANNE, Canadian government official; b. Hants County, N.S., Can., Aug. 31, 1950; d. Howard Gilmore and Joan Mary (Pullan) McL. BA, Dalhousie U., LLB, 1974; LLM, King's Coll., U. London, 1975. Bar: N.S., 1976. Asst. prof. law U. N.B., Can., 1976-80; assoc. prof. law U. Alta., Edmonton, Can., 1980-89, assoc. dean faculty of law, 1985-87, prof. law, 1989-93, acting dean, 1991-92; M.P. for Edmonton Northwest Ho. of Commons, Can., 1993—; min. Natural Resources Can., Ottawa, Ont., Can., 1993—; commentator on Can. Charter of Rights and Freedoms and on human rights issues. Contbr. articles to profl. publs. Past bd. dirs. Can. Civil Liberties Assn., Alta. Legal Aid; past v.p. U. Alta. Faculty Assn. Office: House of Commons, Rm 323 West Block, Ottawa, ON Canada K1A 0A6 Office: House of Commons, Rm 323 West Block, Ottawa, Canada K1A 0A6

MCLELLAN, JOSEPH DUNCAN, critic, journalist; b. Quincy, Mass., Mar. 27, 1929; s. Malcolm and Elsie May (Turner) McL.; m. Estelle Marie Cajolet, Feb. 3, 1951; children—Joseph, Laura, Andree, Sandra. B.A., Boston Coll., 1951, M.A., 1953. Reporter, columnist The Pilot, Boston, 1953-67; editor fgn. news Religious News Service, N.Y.C., 1967-70; editor mag. AD 1970, S. Bend, Ind., 1970; dir. spl. projects N.C. News Service, D.C., 1970-72; writer, editor The Washington Post, D.C., 1972-82, music critic, 1982-95; music critic emeritus, 1995—. Mem. Music Critics Assn., Book Critics Circle, Assn. U.S. Chess Journalists. Club: Mensa (D.C.). Avocations: chess; computers; video equipment and software; poetry translation. Home: 1224 Fairmont St NW Washington DC 20009-5322

MCLELLAN, KATHARINE ESTHER, health physicist, consultant; b. Boston, Apr. 14, 1963; d. Paul Edward and Esther Charlotte (Smith) McL. BA in Chemistry and Biology, Regis Coll., 1985; MS in Health Physics, Ga. Inst. Tech., 1986. Rsch. asst. dept. nuclear engring. Ga. Inst. Tech., Atlanta, 1985-86; asst. analyst NUS Corp., Gaithersburg, Md., 1986-88; health physicist NIH, Bethesda, Md., 1988—; lectr. Radiation Safety Tng. Program, 1988—; ex officio mem. Animal Care and Use com. Nat. Inst. Child Health and Devel./NIMH, Bethesda, 1990-95. Activities dir. Chase Knoll Apts., Germantown, Md., 1988-90; coord. St. Rose of Lima Young Adults, Gaithersburg, 1990—; mem. St. Rose Coun. Ministries, Gaithersburg, 1990-94, chair youth ministry com., 1992-94, co-chair fiesta, 1992-94; coord. neighborhood watch program Churchill View Condominium Assn., 1994—, pres., 1995—. Mem. Nat. Health Physics Soc. (Balt., Washington chpt.), Appalachian Compact Users of Radioactive Isotopes. Roman Catholic. Office: NIH Bldg 21 Radiation Safety Br 21 Wilson Dr Bethesda MD 20892-6780

MCLELLAN, SHIRLEY ANN, nursing administrator, educator; b. Franklin, N.C., July 2, 1935; d. Clifford B. and Callie L. (Stewart) Lawrence; m. Hebert C. White, June 10, 1957 (div. June 1976); children: Herbert, Linda D., Tina M.; m. Lee McLellan, Sept. 1, 1979. BS, SUNY-Plattsburg, 1957, MS in Edn., 1966; MSN, Russell Sage Coll., 1975; MS in Ednl. Adminstrn., SUNY-Albany, 1976; EdD, U. S.D., 1991. RN; cert. specialist. Head nurse Physicians Hosp., Plattsburgh, 1959; tchr. New Lebanon (N.Y.) Cen. Sch., 1963-70; ESEA Title I dir. Pittsfield (Mass.) Pub. Schs., 1970-72; staff nurse Berkshire Med. Ctr., Pittsfield, 1966-73; clin. nurse specialist VA Med. Ctr., Albany, 1974-85; assoc. chief nurse svc./edn. VA Med. Ctr., Sioux Falls, S.D., 1986-90, VA Med. Ctr., East Orange, N.J., 1990—. Mem. Am. Nurses Assn. (cert.), Nat. League for Nursing, Nat. Nursing Staff Devel. Orgn., Kripalu Yoga Club. Home: 433 Lincoln Ave Apt 8C Orange NJ 07050-2267

MCLENDON, GEORGE LELAND, chemistry educator, researcher; b. Ft. Worth, June 6, 1952; s. George and Beata (Shaw) McL.; m. Donna Turner, Aug. 20, 1973; children: Heather, Audrey. BS, U. Tex., El Paso, 1972; PhD, Tex. A&M U., 1976. Asst. prof. chemistry U. Rochester (N.Y.), 1976-80, assoc. prof., 1980-84, prof., 1984—, Tracy Harris prof., 1990-94; R.W. Moore prof. Princeton (N.J.) U., 1994—; cons., mem. vis. bd. Solar Energy Rsch. Inst., 1986-89; adv. com. NSF, 1988-91. Contbr. 150 articles and revs. to profl. jours. Recipient Dreyfus Tchr. Scholar award, 1979-84; A.P. Sloan fellow, 1980-85; Guggenheim Found. and Worcester Coll. fellow, Oxford, Eng., 1989. Mem. Am. Chem. Soc. (Pure Chemistry award 1987, Eli Lilly award 1990, Akron sect. award 1992), Am. Phys. Soc., Materials Rsch. Soc. Episcopalian.

MC LENDON, HEATH BRIAN, securities investment company executive; b. San Francisco, May 24, 1933; s. Jesse Heath and Clara Martha (Nelson) McL.; m. Judith Nelson Locke, May 30, 1959; children: Laurie, Eric, Brian and Michael (twins). BA, Stanford U., 1955; MBA, Harvard U., 1959. With Shearson Lehman Brothers, N.Y.C., 1960-93; mng. dir. Smith Barney, 1993—; chmn. Strategy Advisors, N.Y.C., 1971—; bd. dirs. East N.Y. Savs. Bank; chmn. The Italy Fund, Inc., 1986—, Zenix Income Fund; adv. dir. First Empire State Corp. Pres. bd. trustees N.J. Shakespeare Festival, 1975-76; trustee Drew U., 1975—, chmn. bd., 1992. Served to 1st lt. AUS, 1955-57. Mem. N.Y. Soc. Security Analysts, N.Y. Assn. Bus. Economists, Money Marketeers. Presbyterian. Clubs: Baltusrol, Bay Head Yacht. Home: 70 Hillcrest Ave Summit NJ 07901-2023 Office: Smith Barney 388 Greenwich St New York NY 10013

MCLENNAN, BARBARA NANCY, consultant; b. N.Y.C., Mar. 25, 1940; d. Sol and Gertrude (Rochkind) Miller; m. Kenneth McLennan, Aug. 14, 1962; children: Gordon, Laura. BA magna cum laude, CCNY, 1961; MS, U. Wis., 1962, PhD, 1965; JD, Georgetown U., 1983. Bar: D.C. 1983, Va. 1991, U.S. Ct. Internat. Trade 1988, U.S. Ct. Appeals (D.C. cir.) 1988, U.S. Supreme Ct. 1988. From asst. prof. to assoc. prof. Temple U., Phila., 1965-78; budget analyst Com. on Budget, U.S. Ho. of Reps., Washington, 1978-81; legis. asst. fin. and budget Sen. Dan Quayle, Washington, 1981-84; internat. tax specialist IRS, U.S. Dept. Treasury, Washington, 1984-89; dep. asst. sec. trade, info. and analysis U.S. Dept. Commerce, Washington, 1989-91; prin., atty.-at-law Bitonti and Wilhelm, PC, McLean, Va., 1991-93; staff v.p. govt.-legal affairs consumer electronics group Electronic Industries Assn., Washington, 1993-94, staff v.p. tech. policy, consumer electronics group, 1994-95; v.p. Van Scoyoc Assocs., Washington, 1995—; sr. polit. scientist SRI-Internat., Arlington, Va., 1971-74; vis. prof. Am. Coll., Paris, 1975-76; cons. UNESCO, Paris, 1977-78. Author: Comparative Political Systems, 1975; contbr. numerous articles to profl. jours. Mem. parents adv. coun. Randolph-Macon Coll., Ashland, Va., 1989-92. NDEA fellow, 1962-65. Mem. ABA, Am. Soc. Assn. Execs., D.C. Bar Assn., Fed. Bar Assn., Phi Beta Kappa. Home: 6950 Duncraig Ct Mc Lean VA 22101-1568 Office: Van Scoyoc Assocs Ste 1050 1420 New York Ave NW Washington DC 20005

MCLENNAN, BERNICE CLAIRE, human resources professional; b. Malden, Mass., Dec. 26, 1936; d. Ralph Cyril Worth and Alice Seaman (Hunter) Worth Barrett; m. Hubert Earle McLennan, Oct. 28, 1961; 1 child, Cynthia Alice. Student, Moody Bible Inst., 1958, Salem State Coll., 1988, Bentley Coll., 1989. Youth dir. Faith Evangelical Ch., Melrose, Mass., 1971-77; adminstrv. asst. Boston Redevel. Authority, 1977-85, adminstr. coord., 1985-87, asst. sec. to the authority, 1981—, dir. human resources, 1988-95, asst. dir., 1995—; moderator Faith Evangelical Ch., Melrose, 1985-88, Christian edn. chair, 1973-76. Sec. Melrose (Mass.) Sch. Com., 1983-85; vol. Boston (Mass.) Youth Campaign, 1989, 90. Mem. Internat. Pers. Mgmt. Assn., Assn. Affirmative Action Profls. Avocations: Christian edn., women's issues, drug/alcohol edn. Home: 31 Botolph St Melrose MA 02176-1126 Office: Boston Redevel Authority City Hall One City Hall Sq Boston MA 02201

MCLENNAN, MYRA ANN, technical information specialist; b. Albany, Ky., Sept. 17, 1936; d. Logan Cyrus Frost and Mabel Delane (Bertram) Williams; m. Lawrence William McLennan, Aug. 25, 1962 (div. Sept. 1972); children: Mary Jana Sagastegui, William Lane, Laura Michelle. BA, Union Coll., 1960; BSCE, U. Louisville, 1989. Civil engring. tech. U.S. Army Corps of Engrs., Louisville, 1989-90; tech. info. specialist Def. Tech. Info. Ctr., Alexandria, Va., 1990—. Publicity chmn. Christian County Reps., Hopkinsville, Ky., 1983; coord. Christian County Rep. Com., Hopkinsville, 1980; del. Dist. Rep. Conv., Hopkinsville, 1980, 83. Mem. ASCE, Chi Epsilon (sec. 1988—). LDS Ch. Avocations: painting, grandchildren, watching/listening to Rush Limbaugh, reading, patio gardening. Office: Def Tech Info Ctr DTIC-OCS Ste 0944 8725 John J Kingman Rd Fort Belvoir VA 22060-6218

MCLEOD, E. DOUGLAS, real estate developer, lawyer; b. Galveston, Tex., Aug. 6, 1941; s. Vaughn Watkins McL. and Dorothy (Milroy) Burton; m. Sarah Jackson Helms, Mar. 20, 1965 (div. 1979); children: Chanse, Alexandra, Lindsey; m. Joan Margaret Williams, Dec. 26, 1979; 1 child, Joanie; stepchildren: Meg, Libbie. BBA, U. North Tex., 1965; postgrad., So. Meth. U., 1965-66; JD, South Tex. Coll. Law, 1990; LLM, U. Houston, 1993. Lic. real estate broker. Pres., owner McLeod Properties & co., Galveston, Tex., 1967—; tchr. Galveston Ind. Sch. Dist., 1967-69; banker W.L. Moody & Co., Galveston, 1969-72; developer, broker McLeod Properties/Builders, Galveston, 1972-82; developer Moody Found., Galveston, 1982—; bd. dirs. Am. Nat. Ins. Co., Galveston, Nat. Western Life Ins. Co., Austin, Anrem Corp., Galveston, Moody Gardens Inc., Galveston, , chmn., 1984—; bd. dirs. Colonel Inc., Galveston, v.p., 1985—; bd. dirs. Ctr. Transp. & Commerce, Glaveston. Pres., trustee Galveston Ind. Sch. Dist., 1969-73; mayor pro-tem, mem. city coun. City of Galveston, 1973-76; state legislator Tex. Ho. of Reps., Austin, 1976-83; bd. visitors So. Tex. Coll. Law, 1990—; mem. adv. bd. U. Houston, 1986—; bd. dirs. Ronald McDonald House, 1986-93, Trinity Episcopal Sch., 1990—. With USMC, 1961-67. South Tex. Coll. Law fellow, 1990-95. Mem. Tex. Trial Lawyers Assn. (mem. legis. com. 1991—), Granaderos De Galvez, Marine Corps League. Episcopalian. Avocations: physical fitness advocate, legal history collector, family archivist. Home: 53 Cedar Lawn Cir Galveston TX 77551-4631 Office: The Moody Found 2302 Post Office St Ste 704 Galveston TX 77550-1936

MCLEOD, JOHN WISHART, architect; b. Edinburgh, Scotland, Mar. 24, 1908; s. Thomas and Catherine (Wishart) McL.; m. Helen G. Rath, July 11, 1936; children: Ian Wishart, Cathie Ann. Student, Columbia U., NYU, Beaux-Arts Inst. Design, Columbia Tchrs. Coll. Archtl. tng. in N.Y., N.J. area, 1930-36; ptnr. McLeod, Ferrara & Ensign and predecessor firms, Elizabeth, N.J., 1936-41, Washington, 1946-80; with WPB, 1941-46; mem. Bd. Examiners and Registrars Architects of D.C., 1959-66; mem. U.S. del. UNESCO-IBE Conf. Sch. Bldg., Geneva, 1957; mem., vice chmn. U.S. del. UNESCO-U.K. Conf. Sch. Bldg., London, 1962; mem., co-chmn. constrn. adv. com. fallout shelters Dept. Def., 1962-76; planning cons. Found. Barre De La Maja, La Corunna, Spain, 1976. Prin. works include ednl. facilities; author: Urban Schools in Europe, 1968; co-author: Planning America's School Buildings, 1960. Fellow AIA (chmn. nat. com. ednl. facilities 1950-63, pres. Washington-Met. chpt. 1961); mem. Coun. Ednl. Facility Planners Internat. (Planner of Yr. award 1975), Palm Beach Watercolor Soc. (spl. award 8th ann. exhbn. 1991). Home: 404 NW 72nd St Boca Raton FL 33487-2361

MCLEOD, NORMAN CARL, librarian; b. Sackville, New Brunswick, Can., Nov. 11, 1943; s. Carl Victor and Marjorie Pauline (Hicks) McL.; m. Marie-Reine Marguerite Yolande Dubois, July 8, 1972; 1 child, Isabelle. BA, Mt. Allison U., Sackville, 1965; BLS, U. Toronto, Ont., Can., 1967; MLS, McGill U., Montreal, Que., Can., 1975; diploma in pub. adminstrn., U. Western Ont., 1987. Librarian Kitchener (Ont.) Pub. Library, 1967-69, Bishop's U., Lennoxville, Quebec, Can., 1969-75; chief librarian Sources Pub./Bibliotheque Municipaledes Sources, Roxboro, Quebec, Can., 1975-77, Guelph (Ont.) Pub. Library, 1977—. Mem. Rotary. Avocations: reading, music. Office: Guelph Pub Library, 100 Norfolk St, Guelph, ON Canada N1H 4J6

MCLEOD, PHILIP ROBERT, publishing executive; b. Winnipeg, Man., Can., May 4, 1943; s. Donald G. and Phyllis (Brown) McL.; m. Cheryl Amy Stewart, Sept. 25, 1965 (div. 1992); children: Shawn Robert, Erin Dawn; m. Virginia Mary Corner, Nov. 6, 1992. Journalist Bowes Pub., Grande Prairie, Alta Truro, N.S., 1962-76; journalist, dep. mng. editor Toronto (Ont., Can.) Star, 1976-87; editor-in-chief London (Ont.) Free Press, 1987—. Southam fellow Southam Newspapers, 1970. Mem. The London Club. Avocations: canoeing, skiing. Office: The London Free Press, 369 York St, London, ON Canada N6A 4G1

MCLEOD, ROBERT MACFARLAN, lawyer, arbitrator; b. Toronto, Ont., Can., Oct. 13, 1925; s. William Green and Eliza Vest (Macfarlan) McL.; m. Siddney Anne Mercer, June 21, 1950; children—Ann Payne, William Mercer, Elizabeth Macfarlan. B.S., U. Wis.-Madison, 1950; J.D., U. Va., 1952. Bar: Calif. 1953, Va. 1952. Assoc. faculty U. Calif. Law Sch., Berkeley, 1952-53; assoc., then ptnr. Thelen Marrin Johnson & Bridges, San Francisco, 1953-86, of counsel, 1986—; real estate broker Hill & Co., San Francisco, 1986-92; vis. lectr. U. Calif. Law Sch., Berkeley, 1965-86; arbitrator Calif. State Constrn. Arbitration Panel, 1978-90; arbitrator constrn. industry panel Am. Arbitration Assn., 1982—; judge pro tem San Francisco Mcpl. Ct., 1980-81; mem. Calif. Pub. Contract Code Com., 1980-85. Contbr. chpts. to books, articles to profl. jours.; bd. editors Va. Law Rev., 1951-52. Sustaining mem. Mus. Soc., San Francisco, 1974—; mem. Nat. Trust, London, 1982—, Forum for Architecture, N.Y.C., 1984-86, Found. for San Francisco's Archtl. Heritage, 1987-93, Nat. Trust for Hist. Preservation, 1987—. With inf. U.S. Army, 1943-46, ETO. Decorated Bronze Star medal. Mem. Bar Assn. San Francisco, State Bar Calif., The Guardsmen, San Francisco Golf Club, Order of Coif, Phi Alpha Delta, Delta Kappa Epsilon. Republican. Avocations: travel; golf. Office: Thelen MarrinJohnson & Bridges 2 Embarcadero Ctr San Francisco CA 94111-3823

MCLEOD, WILLIAM LASATER, JR., judge, former state legislator; b. Marks, Miss., Feb. 27, 1931; s. William Lasater and Sara Louise (Macaulay) McL.; m. Marilyn Qualls, June 16, 1962; children: Sara Nelson Judson, Martha Ellen, Ruth Elizabeth. AB, Princeton U., 1953; JD, La. State U., 1958. Bar: La. 1958, U.S. Supreme Ct. 1980. Sole practice, Lake Charles, La., 1958-62; ptnr. McLeod & Little, Lake Charles, 1976-90; dist. judge Calcasieu Parish, 1991—; mem. La. Ho. of Reps., 1968-76; mem. La. Senate, 1976-90. Chmn. Lake Charles Salvation Army Adv. Bd., 1965-66; pres. Calcasieu Area Coun. Boy Scouts Am., 1978; elder Presbyn. Ch. Served with U.S. Army, 1953-55. Recipient Disting. Service award Lake Charles Jaycees, 1963, Civic Service award S.W. La. C. of C., 1986. Mem. ABA, La. Bar Assn., S.W. La. Bar Assn. (pres. 1980). Democrat. Lodge: Masons. Office: Calcasieu Parish Courthouse 1000 Ryan St Lake Charles LA 70601-5250

MCLEOD, WILSON CHURCHILL, lawyer; b. Hamilton, Ont., Can., Aug. 25, 1938; s. Wilson Churchill and Christine Carol (Ard) McL.; m. Lynn Ann Winston, Nov. 6, 1962 (div. 1977); children: Wilson Churchill, Alexandra Lynn; m. Mary Alwina Van Ogtrop, Aug. 15, 1978 (separated). BA, McMaster U., Can., 1960; LLB cum laude, Harvard U., 1963. Bar: Mass. 1969; solicitor Eng., 1975. Asst. trust officer The Nat. Shawmut Bank Boston, 1963-67; cons. Crane & Hawkins, London, 1967-82; ptnr. Bryan Cave, London, 1982-92, Brown & Wood, London, 1992—; mem. internat. adv. bd. Boston Private Bank & Trust Co. Home: Longholt, Hall Ln, Ingatestone, Essex CM4 9NN, England Office: Brown & Wood, Blackwell House Guildhall Yard, London EC2V 5AB, England

MC LERAN, JAMES HERBERT, university dean emeritus, oral surgeon; b. Audubon, Iowa, Apr. 9, 1931; s. Louis D. and Alma K. (Christensen) McL.; m. Hermine Weinert Hayden, July 15, 1979; 1 children, Stephen Andrew; step children: John Wilson Hayden, Charles Matthew Hayden. BS, Simpson Coll., 1953; DDS, U. Iowa, 1957, MS, 1962. Diplomate: Am. Bd. Oral and Maxillofacial Surgeons. Instr. U. Iowa, 1959-60, asst. prof., 1963-67, assoc. prof., 1967-69, prof. oral surgery, 1972—, assoc. dean Coll. Dentistry, 1972-74, dean, 1974—; prof. and chmn. dept. oral surgery U. N.C., Chapel Hill, 1969-72. Served with Dental Corps USN, 1957-59. Recipient Finkbine Leadership award U. Iowa, 1957; named Instr. of Yr. Jr. ADA, 1964, Outstanding Instr. award, 1965. Mem. ADA, Am. Assn. Oral and Maxillofacial Surgeons, Iowa Assn. Oral and Maxillofacial Surgeons, Internat. Assn. Dental Rsch., Midwestern Assn. Oral and Maxillofacial Surgeons, N.C. Soc. Dental Surgeons, N.C. Dental Soc., Iowa Dental Assn. (Disting. Svc. award 1992), Univ. Dist. Dental Soc., Johnson County Dental Soc., Am. Coll. Dentists, Internat. Coll. Dentists, Fedn. Dentaire Internat., Am. Assn. Dental Schs. (pres. 1978-79), Psi Omega. Lodge: Rotary. Office: U Iowa Coll Dentistry Iowa City IA 52242

MCLESKEY, CHARLES HAMILTON, anesthesiology educator; b. Phila., Nov. 8, 1946; s. W. Hamilton and Marion A. (Butts) McL.; m. Nanci S. Simmons, June 3, 1972; children: Travis, Heather. BA, Susquehanna U., 1968; MD, Wake Forest U., 1972. Diplomate Am. Bd. Anesthesiology. Intern Maine Med. Ctr., Portland, 1972-73; resident in anesthesiology U. Wash. Sch. Medicine, Seattle, 1973-76, NIH rsch. trainee, 1974-75; clin. teaching assoc. dept. anesthesiology U. Calif., San Francisco, 1976-78; asst. prof. anesthesiology Wake Forest U. Bowman Gray Sch. Medicine, Winston-Salem, N.C., 1978-83, assoc. prof., 1983-84; assoc. prof. U. Tex. Med. Br., Galveston, 1985-87; assoc. prof. anesthesiology U. Colo. Health Sci. Ctr., Denver, 1987-91, prof., 1991-93, dir. acad. affairs, 1987-93; prof., chmn. dept. anesthesiology Tex. A&M U., 1993—; chmn. dept. anesthesiology, med. dir. perioperative svcs. Scott and White Clin. and Meml. Hosp., Temple, Tex., 1993—; assoc. med. dir. Scott and White Health Plan, 1995—; cons., lectr. Janssen Pharmaceutica, Piscataway, N.J., 1980—, Alza Corp., Palo Alto, Calif., 1986—; cons. Glaxo-Wellcome Co., Research Triangle Park, N.C., Abbott Labs., Chgo., Marion Merrill Dow, Kansas City, Kans., Aspect Med., Natick, Mass.; lectr. to over 500 nat. and state med. orgns., 1982—; examiner Am. Bd. Anesthesiology. Assoc. editor Anesthesiology Rev.; editor Geriatric Anesthesiology, 1996; contbr. numerous articles to med. jours. Mem. choir Friendswood (Tex.) Meth. Ch., 1985-87; mem. Friendswood Fine Arts Commn., 1985-87. Lt. comdr. M.C., USN, 1976-78. Woodruff-Fisher scholar, 1964-68. Mem. Internat. Platform Assn., Nat. Spkrs. Assn., Assn. U. Anesthetists, Am. Soc. Anesthesiologists (del. 1983-85, 88—), Soc. for Edn. in Anesthesio (past v.p., now pres.), Colo. Soc. Anesthesiologists (pres.), Internat. Anesthesia Rsch. Soc., Evergreen Newcomers, Alpha Omega Alpha. Republican. Presbyterian. Avocations: running, fishing, racquetball, squash.

MCLIN, RHINE LANA, state legislator, funeral service executive, educator; b. Dayton, Ohio, Oct. 3, 1948; d. C. Josef, Jr., and Bernice (Cottman) McL. B.A. in Sociology, Parsons Coll., 1969; M.Ed., Xavier U., Cin., 1972; postgrad. in law U. Dayton, 1974-76, AA in Mortuary Sci., Cin. Coll., 1988. Lic. funeral dir.; cert. tchr., Ohio. Tchr. Dayton Bd. Edn., 1970-72; divorce counselor Domestic Relations Ct., Dayton, 1972-73; law clk. Montgomery Common Pleas Ct., Dayton, 1973-74; v.p., dir., embalmer McLin Funeral Homes, Dayton, 1972—; instr. Central State U., Wilberforce, Ohio, 1982—; mem. Ohio Ho. of Reps., 1988-94; state senator Ohio State Senate, 1994—. com. mem. Human Svcs. and Aging Com., Agrl. Com., Hwys. and Transp. Com., Energy, Natural Resources and Environ. Com. Mem. Democratic Voters League, Dayton, Dem. Nat. Com.; mem. inspection com. V.C. Correctional Instn. Mem. Nat. Funeral Dirs. Assn., Ohio Funeral Dirs. Assn., Montgomery County Hist. Soc., NAACP (life), Nat. Council Negro Women (life), Delta Sigma Theta. Home: 1130 Germantown St Dayton OH 45408-1465 Office: Ohio State Senate State House Columbus OH 43215

MCLOONE, EUGENE P., education educator; b. Phila., Nov. 11, 1929; married. BA, LaSalle Coll., 1951; MS, U. Denver, 1952; PhD, U. Ill., 1961. Rsch. dir. Nat. Ctr. for Edn. Stats./U.S. Dept. Edn., Washington, 1979-81; prof. edn. dept. edn. policy, planning and adminstrn. U. Md. Coll. Edn., College Park, 1975—, assoc. prof., 1967-75, assoc. prof. dept. econs., 1967—; assoc. dir. Rsch. Divsn. NEA, Washington, 1968-69, staff contact, 1968-70; atty. gen. State of N.J., 1981-83, State of W.Va., 1981; cons. Addison-Wesleyan Pubs., 1992-93, Bur. of Spl. Edn., Dept. Edn., 1992, Jour. Econs. and Edn., 1989-90, Jour. Edn. Fin., 1989-95, Nat. Tax Assn., 1989, Office Edn. Rsch. and Improvement, 1989, others; lectr. in field; mem. various rsch. couns.; panel mem. Statis. for Supply and Demand of Pre-Collegiate Sci. and Math. Tchrs., Nat. Rsch. Coun., NAS, 1986-90, others. Author: Pre-College Science and Mathematics Teachers: Monitoring Supply, Demand, and Quality, 1990, Report of Panel, Toward Understanding Teacher Supply and Demand: Priorities for Research and Development Interim Report, Profiles in School Support, 1969-70; others; co-author: Public School Finance: Profiles of the State, 1979, Documentation and Analysis of Maryland Special Services Information System, 1977, others; contbr. articles to profl. jours.; editor books in field. Grantee Bur. of the Handicapped, U.S.O.E., 1977, Nat. Ctr. for Edn. Stats., 1971, 73, others; recipient numerous awards in field. Mem. NEA, Am. Econ. Assn., Am. Assn. Sch. Adminstrs., Am. Edn. Fin. Assn. (pres.-elect 1996-97), Phi Delta Kappa.

MCLOUGHLIN, MERRILL, publishing executive. Co-editor U.S. News & World Report, Washington. Office: US News & World Report 2400 N St NW Washington DC 20037

MC LUCAS, JOHN LUTHER, aerospace company executive; b. Fayetteville, N.C., Aug. 22, 1920; s. John Luther and Viola (Conley) McL.; m. Patricia Knapp, July 27, 1946 (div. 1981); children: Pamela McLucas Byers, Susan, John C., Roderick K.; m. Harriet D. Black, Sept. 25, 1981. B.S., Davidson Coll., 1941; M.S., Tulane U., 1943; Ph.D., Pa. State U., 1950, D.Sc., 1974. V.p., tech. dir. Haller, Raymond & Brown, Inc., State College, Pa., 1950-57; pres. HRB-Singer, Inc., State College, 1958-62; dep. dir. rsch. and engring. Dept. Def., 1962-64; asst. sec.-gen. for sci. affairs NATO, Paris, France, 1964-66; pres., chief exec. officer Mitre Corp., Bedford, Mass., 1966-69; undersec. of Air Force, 1969-73, sec. of Air Force, 1973-75; adminstr. FAA, 1975-77; pres. Comsat Gen. Corp., Washington, 1977-79; exec. v.p. COMSAT, 1979-80, pres. world systems div., 1980-83, exec. v.p., chief strategic officer, 1983-85; chmn. bd. dirs. External Tanks Inc.; bd. dirs. Dulles Access Rapid Transit, Inc., Orbital Scis. Corp.; mem. USAF Sci. Adv. Bd., 1967-69, 77-84, Def. Sci. Bd., 1968-69; chmn. USAF SDAG, 1979-83; chmn. bd. dirs. Internat. Space U., 1987-93, active, 1987—. Author: Space Commerce, 1991; contbr. articles to tech. lit. Chmn. bd. Wolf Trap Found., 1986-88; chmn. bd. Arthur C. Clarke Found. of U.S.; chmn. bd. dirs. ISY Internat. Space Yr. Assn. U.S., 1987-93; chmn. NASA adv. council, 1988-91. Served with USNR, 1943-46. Recipient Disting. Service award Dept. Def., 1964, 1st bronze palm, 1973, silver palm, 1975. Fellow IEEE, AAAS, AIAA (hon., pres.); mem. NAE (coun. 1988-93), Nat. Rsch. Coun. (chmn. Air Force studies bd. 1987-91), Tower Club, Belle Haven Club, Sigma Xi, Sigma Pi Sigma. Patentee and author in field. Home and Office: 1213 Villamay Blvd Alexandria VA 22307-2051

MC LURE, CHARLES E., JR., economist; b. Sierra Blanca, Tex., Apr. 14, 1940; s. Charles E. and Dessie (Evans) McL.; m. Patsy Nell Carroll, Sept. 17, 1962. B.A., U. Kans., 1962; M.A., Princeton U., 1964, Ph.D., 1966. Asst. prof. econs. Rice U., Houston, 1965-69, assoc. prof., 1969-72, prof., 1972-79, Allyn R. and Gladys M. Cline prof. econs., 1973-79; exec. dir. for research Nat. Bur. Econ. Research, Cambridge, Mass., 1977-78, v.p., 1978-81; sr. fellow Hoover Instn., Stanford U., 1981—; dep. asst. sec. Dept. Treasury, 1983-85; sec. Dept. Treasury, 1983-85; sr. staff economist Coun. Econ. Advisers, Washington, 1969-70; vis. lectr. U. Wyo., 1972; vis. prof. Stanford U., 1973; cons. U.S. Treasury Dept., Labor Dept., World Bank, UN, OAS, Interam. Devel. Bank, Tax Found., Com. Econ. Devel., IMF, govts. Can., Colombia, Malaysia, Panama, Jamaica, Bolivia, Indonesia, New Zealand, Trinidad and Tobago, Venezuela, Guatemala, Peoples Republic China, Egypt, Malawi, Mex., Bulgaria, Brazil, Russia, Ukraine, Kazakhstan, South Africa, Vietnam. Author: Fiscal Failure: Lessons of the Sixties, 1972, (with N. Ture) Value Added Tax: Two Views, 1972, (with M. Gillis) La Reforma Tributaria Colombiana de 1974, 1977, Must Corporate Income Be Taxed Twice?, 1979, Economic Perperspectives on State Taxation of Multijurisdictional Corporations, 1986, The Value Added Tax: Key to Deficit Reduction, 1987; co-author: Taxation of Income from Business and Capital in Colombia, 1989; also numerous articles on econs. and public finance. Ford Found. faculty research fellow, 1967-68. Mem. Am. Econ. Assn., Nat. Tax Assn., Beta Theta Pi. Home: 250 Yerba Santa Ave Los Altos CA 94022-1609 Office: Stanford U Hoover Instn Stanford CA 94305-6010

MCLURKIN, THOMAS CORNELIUS, JR., lawyer; b. L.A., July 28, 1954; s. Thomas Cornelius and Willie Mae (O'Connor) McL.; m. Charmaine Bobo. BA, U. So. Calif., 1976, MPA, 1980, PhD in Pub. Adminstrn., 1996; JD, U. LaVerne, 1982. Bar: Calif. 1984, U.S. Dist. Ct. (ctrl. dist.) Calif. 1984, U.S. Dist. Ct. Hawaii 1984, U.S. Ct. Appeals (9th cir.) 1984, U.S. Dist. Ct. (ea., no. and so. dists.) Calif. 1985, U.S. Tax Ct. 1988, U.S. Ct. Mil. Appeals 1989, U.S. Army Ct. Mil. Rev. 1993, U.S. Supreme Ct., 1995. Law clk. Dept. Water and Power City of L.A., 1979-82; jud. clk. U.S. Dist. Ct. (cen. dist.) Calif., L.A., 1982-83; law clk. Office City Atty., L.A., 1983-84, Dep. City Atty., 1984—. Author (with others): Facts in American History, 1968, 2nd edit. 1989, Eagle Scout, 1970. Mem. L.A. World Affairs Coun., 1980—, Smithsonian Assocs.; bd. dirs. L.A. Area coun. Boy Scouts Am., Hillsides Homes for Children; provisional patron Tournament of Roses Assn., Pasadena, 1994—; mem. Verdugo Hills Area coun. Boy Scouts Am. Mem. ABA, ALA, L.A. County Bar Assn., Assn. Trial Lawyers Am., Langston Law Assn. L.A., Am. Soc. Pub. Adminstrs., U. So. Calif. Gen. Alumni Assn. (bd. govs. exec. bd. 1986-90), U. So. Calif. Black Alumni Assn.-Ebonics (pres. 1988-89), U. So. Calif. Pres.'s Cir., Elks, Am. Legion, Phi Alpha Delta, Kappa Alpha Psi. Republican. United Methodist. Avocations: sailing, tennis, volunteer work, American and world history. Office: LA City Atty Office Ste 340 111 N Hope St Los Angeles CA 90012-5701

MCLURKIN-HARRIS, KIMBERLY ELANA, secondary education educator; b. Washington, Mar. 9; d. Samuel Louis and Wheatley McLurkin; m. David Harris, Oct. 11, 1986; 1 child, David Jr. BA, Clark Atlanta U., 1982; MA, U. Ky., 1985. Tchr. U.S. history Montgomery County Pub. Schs., Rockville, Md., 1985—; mem. editorial bd. Montgomery Times, Silver Spring, Md., 1992-93. Bd. dirs. Friends of Olney Theatre. Mem. Theta Omega Omega (v.p. 1990-92, pres. 1993-95), Alpha Kappa Alpha (Pres. of Yr. 1994 for Atlantic Region). Office: 1901 Randolph Rd Silver Spring MD 20902

MCMAHON, ANITA SUE, women's health nurse; b. Elgin, Ill., Dec. 11, 1940; d. Herman Henry and Neva Imogene (Lusted) Mass; m. Daniel D. McMahon, Aug. 20, 1960; children: Daniel, Patrick, Christine, Joseph, Susanne. AAS with high honors, Elgin C.C., 1983; BS, St. Francis Coll., Joliet, Ill., 1992; student, Alverno Coll., Milw. Cert. inpatient obstet. nurse; cert. childbirth educator. Nurse preceptor, staff nurse med.-surg. Sherman Hosp., Elgin, 1983-90, ob-gyn. nurse, 1990—, childbirth instr., 1991—, charge nurse, 1992—, obstet. leadership coun., 1995—. Creator, editor quar. Nurse's Notes. Home: 617 Hawthorne Ct Carpentersville IL 60110-1970

MCMAHON, CATHERINE DRISCOLL, lawyer; b. Mineola, N.Y., Apr. 28, 1950; d. Matthew Joseph and Elizabeth (Driscoll) McM.; m. Gregory Arthur McGrath, Sept. 10, 1977 (div. 1991); children: Elizabeth Driscoll, Kerry Margaret, Michael Riley. BA, Simmons Coll., 1972; JD, Boston Coll., 1975; postgrad., Suffolk U., 1972-73; LL.M., NYU, 1980. Bar: N.Y. 1976, D.C. 1979, U.S. Supreme Ct. 1980, U.S. Tax Ct., 1991. Tax atty. asst. Exxon Corp., N.Y.C., 1975-76, asst. tax atty., 1976-77, sr. tax atty., 1979-81; tax atty. Exxon Internat. Co., N.Y.C., 1977-79, sr. tax counsel, Florham Park, N.J., 1990-92; sr. tax counsel Exxon Co., U.S.A., Houston, 1992—; tax mgr. Exxon Rsch. & Engring. Co., Florham Park, 1981-90. Bd. dirs. S.E. Morris chpt. ARC, Madison, N.J., 1983. Recipient TWIN award YMCA, Plainfield/Westfield, N.J., 1983. Mem. ABA, N.Y. State Bar Assn., D.C. Bar Assn. Roman Catholic. Office: Exxon Co USA 800 Bell St Houston TX 77002-7426

MC MAHON, CHARLES JOSEPH, JR., materials science educator; b. Phila., July 10, 1933; s. Charles Joseph and Alice (Schu) McM.; m. Helen June O'Brien, Jan. 31, 1959; children: Christine, Charles, Elise, Robert, David. B.S., U. Pa., 1955; Sc.D., MIT, 1963. Instr. metallurgy MIT, 1958-62, research asst., 1962-63; postdoctoral fellow U. Pa., 1963-64; asst. prof. dept. materials sci. and engring., 1964-68, assoc. prof., 1968-74, prof., 1974—; cons. in field. Editor: Microplasticity, 1968; contbr. articles to profl. jours. Served with USN, 1955-58. Churchill Overseas fellow Churchill Coll., Cambridge U., Eng., 1973-74; recipient Alexander von Humboldt Sr. U.S. Scientist award, U. Göttingen, 1983-84. Fellow AIME, Am. Soc. Metals, Nat. Acad. Engring., Inst. Metals U.K.; mem. AAAS, U.S. Rowing Assn., Vesper Boat Club (Phila.). Democrat. Roman Catholic. Home: 7103 Sherman St Philadelphia PA 19119-3306 Office: U Pa Dept Materials Sci & Engring Philadelphia PA 19104

MCMAHON, COLLEEN, judge; b. Columbus, Ohio, July 18, 1951; d. John Patrick and Patricia Paterson (McDanel) McM.; m. Frank V. Sica, May 16,

1981; children: Moira Catherine, Patrick McMahon, Brian Vincent. BA summa cum laude, Ohio State U., 1973; JD cum laude, Harvard U., 1976. Bar: N.Y. 1977, U.S. Dist. Ct. (so. and ea. dists.) N.Y. 1977, U.S. Ct. Appeals (2d cir.) 1978, U.S. Supreme Ct. 1980, U.S. Ct. Appeals (5th cir.) 1985, D.C. 1985. Spl. asst. U.S. mission to the UN, N.Y.C., 1979-80; assoc. Paul, Weiss, Rifkind, Wharton & Garrison, N.Y.C., 1976-79, 80-84, ptnr., 1984-95; judge N.Y. Ct. Claims, N.Y.C., 1995—; acting justice N.Y. Supreme Ct., 1995—; bd. dirs., gen. counsel Danceworks, Inc., N.Y.C., 1977-81; mem. Coun. N.Y. Law Assocs., 1977-81; chair The Jury Project, N.Y. Office Ct. Adminstrn., 1993-94. Bd. dirs. Vol. Lawyers for the Arts, N.Y.C., 1979-83, Dance Theater Workshop, 1978-83; vice chancellor Episcopal Diocese of N.Y., 1992-95. Mem. ABA, Assn. of Bar of City of N.Y. (mem. coun. on jud. adminstrn. 1983-89, chmn. com. on state cts. of superior jurisdiction 1983-86, com. on women profession 1989-95, chmn. 1992-95), Am. Law Inst., Am. Judicature Soc., Westchester County Bar Assn., N.Y. State Bar Assn. (mem. ho. of dels. 1986-89), Fed. Bar Coun. Republican. Episcopalian. Office: Chamber 1146 111 Center St New York NY 10013

MCMAHON, DONALD AYLWARD, investor, corporate director; b. N.Y.C., Feb. 20, 1931; s. William F. and Anne (Aylward) McM.; m. Nancy Lantz, Apr. 12, 1953; children: Gail, Brian, Lisa, Glenn, Ann, Carol, William, Douglas. M.B.A., Emory U., 1982. With Dime Savs. Bank, Bklyn., 1952; salesman Monroe Calculating Machine Co., Bklyn., 1952-55; asst. br. mgr. Monroe Calculating Machine Co., Pitts., 1955-56; br. mgr. Monroe Calculating Machine Co., Phila., 1956-63; asst. gen. sales mgr. Monroe Calculating Machine Co., Orange, N.J., 1963-64; Eastern regional gen. sales mgr. Monroe Calculating Machine Co., 1964-65, v.p. mktg., 1965-66; pres. Monroe Calculator Co. div. Litton Industries, Inc., Orange, 1966-70; v.p. Litton Industries, 1967-70; pres., chief operating officer, dir. Baker Industries, Inc., Parsippany, N.J., 1970-74; pres., chief exec. officer, dir. Royal Crown Cos., Inc., Atlanta, 1975-85; bd. dirs. Intelligent Systems Corp., Atlanta, Norrell Corp., Atlanta. Bd. dirs. Boys Clubs Metro Atlanta. Mem. Sovereign Order of Knights of Malta. Home: 1665 Winterthur Close NW Atlanta GA 30328-4688

MC MAHON, ED, television personality; b. Detroit, Mar. 6, 1923; children: Claudia, Michael, Linda, Jeffrey, Katherine Mary, Alexis. Ed., Boston Coll.; B.A., Cath. U. Am. TV announcer: Tonight Show, 1962-92; appeared in films The Incident, 1967, Fun with Dick and Jane, 1975, Butterfly; host TV series The Kraft Music Hall, 1968, Whodunnit?, 1979, TV's Bloopers and Practical Jokes, Ed McMahon's Star Search; host TV specials: Thanksgiving Day Parade, (co-host) Jerry Lewis Labor Day Telethon; numerous other TV appearances; appeared on Broadway in The Impossible Years. Active Muscular Dystrophy Assn. With USMC, PTO; col. res., ret. Address: McMahon Communications 12000 Crest Court Beverly Hills CA 90210

MCMAHON, EDWARD PETER, systems engineer, consultant; b. Jersey City, May 30, 1940; s. Edward Patrick and Blanche Elizabeth (Verbout) McM.; m. Barbara Ann Reedy, May 7, 1966; children: Joseph, James. AB, BEE, Cath. U. Am., 1963; SMEE, MIT, 1964; PhD, Poly. Inst. Bklyn., 1969. Engr. GE, King of Prussia, Pa., 1964-70; systems engr. GE, Washington, 1970-71; dir. optics system dept. Gen. Rsch. Corp., Arlington, Va., 1971-74; mem. staff CIA, Washington, 1974-81; mem. tech. staff MRJ, Inc., Oakton, Va., 1981-86, v.p., 1986-87, pres., 1987—. Dir. Perkin-Elmer Advanced Devel. Ctr., 1986; cubmaster, asst. scoutmaster Nat. Capitol Area coun. Boy Scouts Am., 1977-86; chmn. edn. com N.Va.Tech. Coun., 1992—; mem. supts. bus. and industry adv. com. Fairfax Pub. Schs., 1992—. Mem. IEEE, Ops. Rsch. Soc. Am., Phi Beta Kappa, Sigma Xi (assoc.), Tau Beta Pi. Republican. Roman Catholic. Avocations: fine art photography, woodworking, hiking, cross-country skiing, model making. Home: 8224 Inverness Hollow Ter Rockville MD 20854-2726

MCMAHON, EDWARD RICHARD, lawyer; b. Jersey City, June 7, 1949; s. Edward Barnawall and Jean (Sullivan) McM.; m. Ellen Mary Bosek; children: Meghan Jean, Kerry Eileen, Ryan Edward. AB, Colgate U., 1972; JD, Seton Hall U., 1975. Bar: N.J. 1975, U.S. Dist. Ct. N.J. 1975, U.S. Ct. of Appeals (3rd circ.) 1980. Law clk. to judge U.S. Dist. Ct., Newark, 1975-77; assoc. Lum, Biunno & Tompkins, Newark, 1977-83; ptnr. Lum, Danzis, Drasco, Positan & Kleinberg, Roseland, 1983—. Mem. Morris County Rep. Com., N.J., 1982-94; mem. Chatham (N.J.) Boro Rep. com., 1982-94, chmn., 1986-94; bd. dirs. Madison area YMCA, 1989-95; mem. N.J. State Rep. Com., 1994—. Mem. ABA (litigation and banking sects.), N.J. Bar Assn., Assn. Fed. Bar N.J., Am. Judicature Soc., Morris County Bar Assn., Essex County Bar Assn., Delbarton Sch. Alumni Assn. (class rep. 1984—), 200 Club Morris County, Delta Upsilon, Phi Alpha Delta. Republican. Roman Catholic. Club: Colgate (No. N.J.). Home: 150 Van Houton Ave Chatham NJ 07928-1239 Office: Lum Hoens Conant Danzis & Kleinberg 103 Eisenhower Pky Roseland NJ 07068-1029

MC MAHON, GEORGE JOSEPH, academic administrator; b. N.Y.C., June 20, 1923; s. Martin Joseph and Mary (O'Connor) McM. A.B., Woodstock Coll., 1946, Ph.L., 1947, M.A., 1948, S.T.L., 1954; M.A., Fordham U., 1951; Ph.D., Laval U., 1959. Joined Soc. of Jesus, 1940; ordained priest Roman Catholic Ch., 1953; instr. physics and Latin Regis High Sch., N.Y.C., 1947-49; instr. philosophy St. Peter's Coll., Jersey City, 1958-60; asst. dean, dir. St. Peter's Coll. (Sch. Bus. Adminstrn.), 1961-62; instr. philosophy Loyola Sem., Shrub Oak, N.Y., 1960-61; dean Fordham Coll., Fordham U., Bronx, N.Y., 1962-74; v.p. adminstrn. Fordham U., 1974-87, v.p. Lincoln Ctr. campus, 1987-94, chaplain, 1994—. Author: The Order of Procedure in the Philosophy of Nature, 1958, The Proemium to the Physics of Aristotle, 1957. Vice pres. Friends of U. Laval, Que., Can.; trustee Marymount Sch. N.Y., Wheeling (W.Va.) Coll., Xavier High Sch., N.Y.C.

MCMAHON, GERRI LYN, illustrator, educator; b. Bklyn., Jan. 31, 1952; d. Roger and Josephine M.; m. Mel Giptson, Oct. 17, 1975; children: Rupert, Sanford, Delavan. BFA, Pratt Inst., 1973; MFA, Parsons Sch. Design, 1975; attended, Rutgers, 1978-80. Art instr. New Sch., N.Y.C., 1975-94; instr. illustration Raleigh C.C., 1994—. Works exhibited at Freer Gallery, N.Y.C., 1980, 84, 88, 90, Reed Gallery, N.J., 1992, 94, 96, Bklyn. Mus., 1982, 85, Soc. Illustrators, N.Y.C, 1987, 89, 93, Franklin Lakes Gallery, N.J., 1995, 96, numerous others; illustrator (children's books) Susie Sunshine and the Grump, 1986, Happiness in Hackensack, 1988, I Have a Dinosaur in My Pocket, 1990, The Day the Popcorn Exploded, 1992, Do Ducks See In Color?, 1994 (Caldecott medal), Do Bugs Sleep At Night?, 1996; freelance illustrator Highlights mag., Humpty Dumpty, Cricket, Ladybug, Grasshopper, Stone Soup, New Yorker, Natural Hist. mag. Art for Art's Sake Found. (pres. Raleigh chpt. 1991-92), Friends of the Libr. Raleigh, Assoc. for Freedom From Censorship. Recipient Design award Graphic Soc., 1980, award Brownstone Gallery, 1976, 85, 92. Mem. Soc. Illustrators (award 1983, 96),ICP, ALA, NJLA, NCLA., Ducks Unlimited. Avocations: creating handmade books, holiday plays and performances.

MCMAHON, JOHN ALEXANDER, lawyer, educator; b. Monongahela, Pa., July 31, 1921; s. John Hamilton and Jean (Alexander) McM.; m. Betty Wagner, Sept. 14, 1947 (div. Mar. 1977); children: Alexander Talpey, Sarah Francis, Elizabeth Wagner, Ann Wallace; m. Anne Fountain Willets, May 1, 1977. A.B. magna cum laude, Duke U., 1942; student, Harvard U. Bus. Sch., 1942-43; J.D., Law Sch., 1948; LL.D., Wake Forest U., 1978; D.Sc. (hon.), Georgetown U. Sch. Medicine, 1985. Bar: N.C. 1950. Prof. pub. law and govt., asst. dir. Inst. Govt. U. N.C., 1948-59; gen. counsel, sec.-treas. N.C. Assn. County Commrs., Chapel Hill, 1959-65; v.p. spl. devel. Hosp. Saving Assn., Chapel Hill, N.C., 1965-67; pres. N.C. Blue Cross and Blue Shield, Inc., Chapel Hill, 1968-72, Am. Hosp. Assn., Chgo., 1972-86; chmn. dept. health adminstrn. Duke U., Durham, N.C., 1986-92, exec.-in-residence Fuqua Sch. Bus., 1992—; mem. Chapel Hill bd. N.C. Nat. Bank, 1967-72; bd. govs. Blue Cross Assn., 1969-72; mem. Orange County Welfare Bd., 1956-63; chmn. N.C. Comprehensive Health Planning Coun., 1968-72, Health Planning Coun. of Ctrl. N.C., 1963-69; mem. Pres.' Com. on Health Edn., 1971-72; mem. com. health svcs. industry and health industry adv. com. Econ. Stablzn. Program, 1971-74; mem. adv. coun. Kate Bitting Reynolds Health Care Trust, 1971-95; mem. adv. coun. Northwestern U., 1973-86; mem. med. adv. com. VA, 1975-85; bd. dirs. Eason, Earl and Assocs., Greenville, S.C., The Forest at Duke, Durham, N.C. Author: North Carolina County Government, 1959, The North Carolina Local Government Commission, 1960; editor: N.C. County Yearbook, 1959-64, Proceedings of the Annual National Forum on Hospital and Health Affairs, 1993—. Mem. Orange County Dem. Exec. Com., also chmn. Kings Mill Precinct, 1964-68; chmn. bd. trustees Duke U., 1971-83, chmn. emeritus, 1983—; bd. dirs. Rsch. Triangle Found., 1971-83, 92—, Nat. Ctr. for Health Edn., 1974-86; bd. mgrs., mem. exec. com. Internat. Hosp. Fedn., London, 1975-85, pres., 1981-83. With USAAF, 1942-46, col. Res., ret. Mem. N.C. State Bar, Inst. Medicine of NAS, Duke Alumni Assn. (pres. 1968-70), Hope Valley Country Club (Durham), Dunes Golf and Beach Club (Myrtle Beach). Presbyterian. Home: 181 Montrose Dr Durham NC 27707-3929 Office: Duke U Fuqua Sch Bus Durham NC 27708-0120

MCMAHON, JOHN J., JR., metal processing company executive. Pres., sec., treas. McWane, Inc., Birmingham, Ala.; now also chief exec. officer Clow Corp., Birmingham. Office: McWane Inc PO Box 43327 Birmingham AL 35243*

MCMAHON, JOHN PATRICK, lawyer; b. Monroeville, Ohio, Feb. 8, 1919; s. George James and Eleanor Helene (Ruffing) McM.; m. Patricia Patterson McDanel, May 6, 1950 (dec. July 1983); children: Colleen, Kevin, Patricia, Brian, Barry, Michael; m. Mary Echard, Mar. 7, 1987. B.A. cum laude, Ohio State U., 1940, J.D. summa cum laude, 1942. Bar: Ohio 1942, U.S. Supreme Ct. 1949, U.S. Dist. Ct. Ohio 1949, U.S. Ct. Appeals (6th cir.) 1959, U.S. Ct. Appeals (D.C. cir.) 1975. Ptnr. George, Greek, King, McMahon, Columbus, Ohio, 1954-79, Baker & Hostetler, Columbus, 1979-85; with nat. coun. Ohio State U. Coll. Law, 1980—. Capt. USAAF, 1943-46, PTO. Mem. ABA, Ohio Bar Assn., Columbus Bar Assn., Transp. Lawyers Assn., Univ. Club (Columbus), Maennerchor (Columbus), Pres.' Club of Ohio State U. (Columbus). Clubs: University (Columbus), Faculty (Columbus), Pres.' of Ohio State U. (Columbus). Home: 2880 Halstead Rd Columbus OH 43221-2916 Office: Baker & Hostetler 65 E State St Columbus OH 43215-4213

MCMAHON, JOSEPH EINAR, lawyer, consultant; b. Chgo., Aug. 26, 1940; s. Reynold Bernard and Dorothy Marie (Oftedahl) McM. B.A. cum laude, Denison U., 1962; J.D., U. Mich., 1965. Bar: Mass. 1968, D.C. 1980. Asst. to Atty. Gen. and Senator Edward Brooke, Boston and Washington, 1965-67; exec. asst. Lt. Gov. Sargent of Mass., Boston, 1967-69; v.p. BedStuy D&S Corp. Restoration, Bklyn., 1969-74; dir. govt. regulations Westinghouse Electric Corp., Washington, 1974-78; v.p. corp. affairs Federated Dept. Stores, Cin., 1978-80; atty., cons. McMahon and Assocs., Washington, 1980—; exec. dir. (part time), bd. dirs. The Get Ahead Found./USA, 1991—. Trustee Denison U.; visitor U. Mich. Law Sch.; 1st v.p. Boston Rep. Com., 1968-69; presdl. appointee Nat. Coun. Econ. Opportunity, 1975-76; exec. dir. Nat. Bus. for Reagan-Bush Com., 1980; dir. Luther Inst., Washington, Fgn. Students Svc. Coun., Rodale Inst., Emmaus, Pa.; trustee Gettysburg Luth. Sem.; dir. Luth. Lesbian and Gay Min., San Francisco; mem. outreach bd. Evang. Luth. Ch. in Am., 1995—. Mem. Phi Delta Phi, Pi Sigma Alpha, Omicron Delta Kappa. Lutheran. Clubs: Nat. Press, University, Capitol Hill (Washington). Office: McMahon & Assocs 1924 N St NW Washington DC 20036-1604

MCMAHON, LILLIAN ELIZABETH, hematologist; b. Bklyn., Sept. 17, 1937; d. Manuel Dos Santos and Eufemia (Diaz) Caldeira; m. Leonard George McMahon, June 25, 1966; 1 child, David Leonard Caldeira McMahon. MD, U. Pará, Belém, Brazil, 1963. Intern Carney Hosp., Dorchester, Mass., 1964-65, med. resident, 1965-66; pediatric resident Boston City Hosp., 1966-68, hematology/oncology fellow, 1968-69, dir. Boston Sickle Cell Ctr., 1978—, chief clin. pediatric hematology, 1989—; ped. hematology/oncology fellow N.Y. Hosp.-Cornell Med. Ctr., N.Y.C., 1969-70; assoc. clin. prof. pediatrics Boston U. Sch. Medicine, 1989—. Author, presenter abstracts in field. Comprehensive sickle cell ctr. grantee Nat. Heart, Blood & Lung Insts., NIH, 1978—. Avocations: gardening, travel, music. Home: 35 Ridgecrest Ter West Roxbury MA 02132-5253 Office: Boston City Hosp Boston Sickle Cell Ctr 818 Harrison Ave # 2 Boston MA 02118-2905

MCMAHON, MAEVE, principal. Prin. St. Leo the Great Elem. Sch., New Orleans. Recipient DOE Elem. Sch. Recognition Program award, 1989-90. Office: St Leo the Great Elem Sch 1501 Abundance St New Orleans LA 70119-2052

MCMAHON, MARIBETH LOVETTE, physicist; b. Bradford, Pa., June 8, 1949; d. James Harry and Josephine Rose (Sylvester) Lovette; m. Frank Joseph MaMahon, Nov. 19, 1976. B.S. in Math., Pa. State U., 1971, B.S. in Physics, 1971, M.S. in Physics, 1974; Ph.D. in Physics, 1976. Research asst. Pa. State U., 1971-76; advanced research and devel. engr. GTE Sylvania, Danvers, Mass., 1976-78; sr. physicist 3M Co., St. Paul, 1978-79, market devel. supr., 1979-83; market devel. mgr. Galileo Electro-Optics Corp., Sturbridge, Mass., 1983-84; product mgr. Varian Assocs., Lexington, Mass., 1984-85; mktg. dir. Bowmar, Acton, Mass., 1985-86; pres. Kilduff Inc., Sturbridge, Mass., 1986—. Recipient Cert. in Appreciation of Service Pa. State U., 1971. Mem. Optical Soc. Am., Assn. Women in Sci., Assn. Physicists in Medicine, Sigma Pi Sigma, Sigma Chi. Home: 140 Brookfield Rd Fiskdale MA 01518-1136 Office: Kilduff Inc Sturbridge MA 01566

MCMAHON, PAUL FRANCIS, international management consultant; b. Malone, N.Y., Apr. 28, 1945; s. Philip Francis and Shirley (Roy) M.; m. Sheila Ann Lester, Nov. 30, 1963; children—Michael, Marsha. B.S., Syracuse U., 1968. CPA, N.Y.; cert. mgmt. acct., cert. mgmt. cons. Various staff positions Ernst & Young, Syracuse, N.Y., 1968-73, mgr., 1975-79; ptnr. in charge of mgmt. cons. in Europe Ernst & Young, Brussels, 1979-84; vice chmn. Ernst & Young, Cleve., 1984-87; exec. ptnr. Ernst & Young Internat., N.Y., 1987-93; chmn. Ernst & Young Ea. Europe, 1990-93; regional dir. Asia/Pacific Ernst & Young Internat., Singapore, 1994—; controller Coop. Mktg. Agy., Syracuse, 1973-75. Treas. Bus. Coun. for Internat. Understanding. Mem. AICPA, N.Y. Soc. CPA's, Inst. Mgmt. Acctg., Assn. Mgmt. Cons. Firms (bd. dirs.), Coun. Cons. Orgns. (past chmn.). Republican. Roman Catholic. Avocations: photography, natural history, travel, gardening, biographies. Home: PO Box 4070 Wilsonville OR 97070 Office: Ernst & Young Internat, PO Box 384, Singapore 9007, Singapore

MCMAHON, ROBERT LEE, JR. (BOB MCMAHON), information systems executive; b. Weatherford, Tex., Feb. 19, 1944; s. Robert Lee Sr. and Gusta Rosann (Collins) McM. AA, Weatherford Coll., 1964; BA, U. Tex., Arlington, 1970; postgrad. in mgmt., Tex. Christian U., 1970-73. Announcer Sta. KZEE, Weatherford, Tex., 1963-65; asst. gen. mgr. Sta. KZEE, Weatherford, 1972-75; programmer Gen. Dynamics, Ft. Worth, 1967-68, sr. programmer, 1968-72, sr. engr., 1975-78, project engr., 1978-79, group supr., 1979-80, sect. chief, 1980-83, dept. mgr., 1983-93; staff specialist Lockheed Ft. Worth Co., 1994-95, retired, 1995; mem. adv. bd. Mfg. Tech. Directorate, USAF, Dayton, Ohio, 1981-91, Automation and Robotics Rsch. Inst., Ft. Worth, 1986-91. Editor: Manufacturing Engineer's Handbook, 1988; mem. editorial bd. Mfg. Engrng. mag., 1989-91. Dir. adult edn. program Parker County, Tex., 1972-75; chmn. Weatherford City Charter Revision Commn., 1974-75; mem. Weatherford Planning and Zoning Bd., 1984-88; chmn. 4th precinct Parker County Dem. Com., 1982-92, 27th precinct, 1992—; foreman Grand Jury, 1993. Mem. Soc. Mfg. Engrs., (cert., sr.), Robotic Industries Assn. (sr., bd. dirs. 1984-88), Computer and Automated Sys. Assn. (sr.), Robotics Inst. (sr.), Am. Inst. Indsl. Engrs., Nat. Mgmt. Assn., Masons (33d degree, past master), Phi Theta Kappa (v.p. Weatherford chpt.). Mem. Ch. of Christ. Avocations: photography, pocket billiards, reading, model railroading. Home: 1418 E Bankhead Dr Weatherford TX 76086-4607

MCMAHON, TERRENCE JOHN, retired foriegn service officer; b. Rockford, Ill., Aug. 7, 1936; s. Hugh Raymond McMahon and Lucile Isabelle (Hayes) Driscoll; m. Phyllis Ruth Anderson, Dec. 2, 1967; children: Kevin, Michael, Kathleen, Marianne. BS in Accountancy, U. Ill., 1958; M Internat. Pub. Policy, Johns Hopkins U., 1983. CPA, Ill. Audit supr. Coopers and Lybrand, Rockford, Ill., 1958-68; fin. analyst U.S. AID, Washington, 1968-70; dep. contr. U.S. AID, Rio de Janeiro, 1970-73; contr. U.S. AID, Kabul, Afghanistan, 1973-77, Amman, Jordan, 1977-79; dep. contr. U.S. AID, Washington, 1979-83; contr. U.S. AID, Cairo, 1983-86; dir. Office of Procurement U.S. AID, Washington, 1986-92; dir. U.S. AID, Kiev, Ukraine, 1993-95. Recipient Presdl. Meritorious Svc. award for fgn. svc. Pres. of U.S., 1985, 92. Mem. AICPA. Roman Catholic. Avocations: fishing, boating, travel. Home: 430 Marine Dr Sequim WA 98382

MCMAHON, THOMAS ARTHUR, biology and applied mechanics educator; b. Dayton, Ohio, Apr. 21, 1943; s. Howard Oldford and Lucille (Nelson) McM.; m. Carol Ehlers, June 20, 1965; children: James Robert, Elizabeth Kirsten. B.S., Cornell U., 1965; S.M., MIT, 1967, Ph.D., 1970. Postdoctoral fellow Harvard U., Cambridge, Mass., 1969-70, lectr. bioengrg., 1970-71, asst. prof., 1971-74, assoc. prof., 1974-77, prof. applied mechanics and biology, 1977—; cons. numerous industries, legal firms. Author: (novels), Principles of American Nuclear Chemistry, 1970, McKay's Bees, 1979, Loving Little Egypt, 1987; (non-Fiction) Muscles, Reflexes and Locomotion, 1984; (with others) On Size and Life, 1983. Grantee NIH; System Devel. Found., Sloan Found.; recipient Richard and Hinde Rosenthal award Am. Acad. and Inst. Arts and Letters, 1988. Mem. Biomed. Engrng. Soc., Am. Physiol. Soc., N.Y. Acad. Scis., PEN. Home: 65 Crest Rd Wellesley MA 02181-4620 Office: Harvard U Dept Applied Scis Pierce Hall Cambridge MA 02138

MCMAHON, THOMAS MICHAEL, lawyer; b. Evanston, Ill., May 11, 1941; s. Robert C. and Kathryn D. (Dwyer) McM.; m. M. Ann Kaufman, July 11, 1964; children—Michael, Patrick. Student, U. Notre Dame, 1959-61; B.A., Marquette U., 1963; J.D. magna cum laude, Northwestern U., 1970. Bar: Ill. 1970. Mgr. legal adv. sect. Ill. EPA, Springfield, 1970-72; assoc. firm Sidley & Austin, Chgo., 1972-75, ptnr., founder nat. environ. group, 1975—; lectr. environ. law Euromoney, Centaur and Inst. for Internat. Rsch. confs., London, Japanese EPA Conf., Tokyo; mem. City of Evanston Environ. Control Bd., 1981-83. Author: The Superfund Handbook, 1989, International Environmental Law and Regulation, 1992, Legal Guide to Working with Environmental Consultants, 1992, The Environmental Manual, 1992. Served to lt. USN, 1963-67. Decorated Republic of Vietnam Campaign medal. Mem. ABA (vice chmn. environ. quality com. and environ. aspects of bus. trans. com., vice chmn. internat. environ. law com., lectr. confs., teleconfs. and satellite seminars), Order of Coif. Office: Sidley & Austin 1 First Nat Plz Chicago IL 60603*

MCMAINS, MELVIN L(EE), controller; b. Oskaloosa, Iowa, Aug. 1, 1941; m. Kathryn Elaine Murphy; children: Kimberly, Lindsay. BA, U. Northern Iowa, 1966, MA, 1968. CPA, Iowa; CMA. Corp. contr., chief acctg. officer HON Industries, Inc., Muscatine, Iowa, 1979—. Mem. AICPA, Fin. Execs. Inst., Iowa Soc. CPA's, Inst. Mgmt. Accts., Geneva Golf and Country Club. Office: HON Industries PO Box 1109 Muscatine IA 52761-7109

MCMANAMAN, KENNETH CHARLES, lawyer; b. Fairfield, Calif., Jan. 25, 1950; s. Charles James and Frances J. (Holys) McM.; m. Carol Ann Wilson, Apr. 15, 1972; children: Evan John, Kinsey Bridget, Kierin Rose. BA cum laude, S.E. Mo. State U., 1972; JD, U. Mo., Kansas City, 1974; grad. Naval Justice Sch., Newport, RI., 1975; MS in Bus. Mgmt. summa cum laude, Troy State U., Montgomery, Ala., 1978. Bar: Mo. 1975, Fla. 1976, U.S. Dist. Ct. (we. dist.) Mo. 1975, U.S. Dist. Ct. (ea. Dist.) Mo. 1978, Fla. 1976, U.S. Dist. Ct. (no., mid. dists.) Fla. 1976, U.S. Ct. Mil. Appeals 1977, U.S. Ct. Appeals (5th, 8th cirs.) 1977, U.S. Supreme Ct. 1978, D.C. 1991; cert. mil. judge. Ptnr. firm O'Loughlin, O'Loughlin & McManaman, Cape Girardeau, Mo., 1978—; prof. bus. law Troy State U., Ala., 1976-78; prof. bus. law S.E. Mo. State U., Cape Girardeau, 1978-84; instr. Mo. Dept. Pub. Safety, S.E. Mo. Regional Law Enforcement Tng. Acad., 1979—, Cape Girardeau Police Res., 1983-93; mcpl. judge City of Jackson, Mo., 1980-89, 94—; spl. mcpl. judge City of Cape Girardeau, 1981-89; atty. Ct. Apptd. Spl. Advs./Guardians in Ct. for Children, 1994—; spl. mcpl. judge City of Fredricktown, Mo., 1995. Mem. Cape Girardeau County Coun. on Child Abuse, 1980-89; membership dir. S.E. Mo. Scouting coun. Boy Scouts Am., 1980-82; mem. Cape Girardeau County Mental Health Assn., 1982-92; active local and state Dem. Party, del. Nat. Dem. Conv., San Francisco, 1984, chmn. County Dem. Com., 1984-86; mem. 8th Congl. Dist. Dem. Com., 1984-86, 27th State Dem. Senatorial Com., 1984-86, ward committeeman, 1984-94; bd. dirs. Area wide Task Force on Drug and Alcohol Abuse, 1984-87; sponsor drug edn./prevention program in schs.; bd. dirs. Cape County chpt. Nat. Kidney Found, 1988-93; pres. Jackson Area Soccer Assn., 1987-93. Capt. JAGC, USNR, 1994—. Recipient Robert Chilton award City of Jackson for leadership, integrity, and responsibility, 1995—; named One of Outstanding Young Men of Am. 1981, 82, 84, 85. Mem. ABA (Mo. del. for young lawyers div. 1982-83)., Mo. Bar Assn. (chmn. trial advocacy task force 1982, psychology and the law task force 1983), Mo. Bar (young lawyers sect. council, rep. dist. 13, 1980-85), Fla. Bar Assn., Kansas City Bar Assn., Assn. Trial Lawyers Am., Fed. Bar Assn., Nat. Coll. Dist. Attys., Cape Girardeau County Bar Assn. (founder, pres. young lawyers sect. 1981-82), Naval Res. Assn. (v.p. Southeast Mo.-So. Ill. chpt. 1980-85), S.E. Mo. State U. Alumni Coun., Sigma Chi (numerous awards), Sigma Tau Delta, Pi Delta Epsilon. Roman Catholic. Home: 400 Oak Forest Dr Jackson MO 63755-3504 Office: O'Loughlin O'Loughlin McManaman 1736 N Kingshighway St Cape Girardeau MO 63701-2122

MCMANIGAL, SHIRLEY ANN, university dean; b. Deering, Mo., May 4, 1938; d. Jadie C. and Willie B. (Groves) Naile. BS, Ark. State U., 1971; MS, U. Okla., 1976, PhD, 1979. Lic. med. technologist, clin. lab. dir. Med. technologist, 1958-75; chair dept. med. tech. U. So. Miss., Hattiesburg, 1979-83; chair dept. med. tech. Tex. Tech U. Health Scis. Ctr., Lubbock, 1983-87, dean Sch. Allied Health, 1987—; gov.'s appointee to statewide health coord. coun., 1994—. Leadership Tex., 1992; Lt. Alumnae Regl. dir., 1994—. Recipient Citation, State of Tex., 1988; named Woman of Yr., AAUW, Tex. div., 1990, Woman of Excellence in Edn. YWCA, Lubbock, 1990. Mem. AAUW (bd. dirs. Tex. 1990-94), Am. Coun. on Edn./Nat. Identification Program (steering com. for Tex.), Clin. Lab. Mgmt. Assn. (chair edn. com. 1989, 91), Am. Soc. Med. Tech., Nat. Assn. Women in Edn., So. Assn. Allied Health Deans at Acad. Health Ctrs., S.W. Assn. Clin. Microbiology, Tex. Soc. Allied Health Professions (pres. 1990-91), Tex. Soc. Med. Tech. (Educator of Yr. 1990), Alpha Eta, Phi Beta Delta. Home: 5003 94th St Lubbock TX 79424-4839 Office: Tex Tech U Health Scis Ctr Sch Allied Health Lubbock TX 79430

MCMANMON, THOMAS ARTHUR, JR., oil industry executive; b. Boston, Sept. 10, 1943; s. T. Arthur and Maura (Sullivan) M.; m. Suzanne Cole, Nov. 17, 1973; children: Katherine, Suzanne, Thomas III. BA in History, U. Notre Dame, 1966; MBA, Dartmouth Coll., 1968. V.p. N.E. Merchants Bank, Boston, 1968-77; sr. v.p. Entwistle Corp., Hudson, Mass., 1977-78, Global Petroleum Corp., Waltham, Mass., 1978—; dir. Griffith Consumers Corp., Cheverly, Md., 1985—, Atlantic Petroleum Corp., Chelsea, Mass., 1989, Montello Oil Corp., Waltham, Mass., 1980, Carl King, Dover,Del., 1985, Nimrod Nat. Gas, Tulsa. Dir. New England Fuel Inst., Watertown, Mass., 1980—. Mem. Marion-Beverly Yacht Club, Sippican Tennis Club, Boston Algonquin Club, Brookline Country Club. Office: Global Petroleum Corp 800 South St Waltham MA 02154-1439*

MCMANUS, CLARENCE ELBURN, judge; b. New Orleans, June 3, 1934; s. Otis Clarence and Odell (Hawsey) McM.; m. Barbara Isabella Edmundson, Apr. 3, 1976; children—Elizabeth Ann, Bryan Stephen. B.B.A., Tulane U., 1958; J.D., 1961. Bar: La. 1961, U.S. Ct. Appeals (5th cir.) 1961, U.S. Dist. Ct. (ea. dist.) La. 1961, U.S. Supreme Ct. 1987. Sole practice, Metairie, La., 1961-69; asst. dist. atty. Jefferson Parish, La., 1969-82; state dist. judge 24th Jud. Dist. Ct., Gretna, La., 1982—. Republican. Home: 824 Bonnabel Blvd Metairie LA 70005-2059 Office: Gretna Courthouse Annex Gretna LA 70053

MCMANUS, DECLAN PATRICK See COSTELLO, ELVIS

MCMANUS, EDWARD HUBBARD, government official; b. Roxbury, Mass., Jan. 11, 1939; s. Paul Carter and Dorothy (Shaw) McM.; m. Sharon Pickett, Feb. 10, 1968; children: Kevin, Keith, Michael. B.A., U. Mass., 1960; M.A., U. Wis., 1970. Mgmt. analyst Bur. Internat. Commerce, Dept. Commerce, Washington, 1965-66; asst. to adminstrv. officer NIMH, NIH, Bethesda, Md., 1966-68; adminstrv. officer div. research resources NIH, Bethesda, 1968-69; asst. exec. officer div. research resources NIH, Bethesda, Md., 1970-71; fin. mgmt. officer Nat. Library Medicine, NIH, Bethesda, 1971-73; exec. officer Nat. Eye Inst., Bethesda, 1973-81, dep. dir., 1981—. Served to lt. (j.g.) USN, 1961-64. Mem. Am. Mgmt. Assn., Am. Soc. Pub. Adminstrn., Internat. Agy. for Prevention of Blindness (exec. bd.). Office: Nat Eye Inst 31/6A05 31 Center Dr MSC 2510 Bethesda MD 20892-2510

MC MANUS, EDWARD JOSEPH, federal judge; b. Keokuk, Iowa, Feb. 9, 1920; s. Edward W. and Kathleen (O'Connor) McM.; m. Sally A. Hassett, June 30, 1948 (dec.); children: David P., Edward W., John N., Thomas J., Dennis Q.; m. Esther Y. Kanealy, Sept. 15, 1987. Student, St. Ambrose Coll., 1936-38; B.A., U. Iowa, 1940, J.D., 1942. Bar: Iowa 1942. Gen. practice of law Keokuk, 1946-62, city atty., 1946-55; mem. Iowa Senate, 1955-59; lt. gov. Iowa, 1959-61; chief U.S. judge No. Dist. Iowa, 1962-85, sr. U.S. judge, 1985—. Del Democratic Nat. Conv., 1956, 60. Served as lt. AC USNR, 1942-46. Office: US Dist Ct 329 US Courthouse 101 1st St SE Cedar Rapids IA 52401-1202

MCMANUS, HUGH F., principal. Prin. John T. Hoggard High Sch., Wilmington, N.C. Recipient Blue Ribbon Sch. award, 1990-91. Office: John T Hoggard High Sch 4305 Shipyard Blvd Wilmington NC 28403-6160

MCMANUS, JAMES WILLIAM, chemist, researcher; b. Atlanta, Oct. 7, 1944; s. Claude William and Sara Louise (Cook) McM.; m. Ruth Krieger, Apr. 10, 1971; children: Angela Ruth, Meagan Joy. BS in Chemistry, Auburn U., 1971. Mgr. Cook's Grocery Co., Atlanta, 1970-73; analytical chemist North Chem. Co., Atlanta, 1973-74; analytical chemist Merck & Co., Inc., Albany, Ga., 1974-75, staff chemist, 1975-76, sr. staff chemist, 1976-78, sr. chemist, 1978-89, rsch. fellow, 1989-94; bd. dirs. M. Taylor, Inc., Albany, 1988—, chmn. chemistry sect., 1994—. Mem. editorial bd. Process Control and Quality, 1990-95; inventor, patentee in field. Mem. Am. Chem. Soc. (cert.). Republican. Baptist. Office: Merck and Co Inc 3517 Radium Springs Rd Albany GA 31705-9596

MCMANUS, JAMES WILLIAM, lawyer; b. Kansas City, Mo., Aug. 1, 1945; s. Gerald B. and Mary M. (Hagan) McM.; m. Julie C. Waters, Feb. 17, 1973. BA, Rockhurst Coll., 1967; JD, St. Louis U., 1971. Bar: Mo. 1971, U.S. Dist. Ct. (we. dist.) Mo. 1972, U.S. Ct. Appeals (8th cir.) 1974, U.S. Supreme Ct. 1979, U.S. Ct. Appeals (10th cir.) 1984. Law clk. to presiding justice U.S. Dist. Ct. (we. dist.) Mo., 1971-73; assoc. Shughart, Thomson & Kilroy, P.C., Kansas City, 1973-76, dir., 1977-94; counsel Dysart, Taylor, Penner, Lay & Lewandowski, Kansas City, 1994—; course lectr. med. jurisprudence U. Health Scis., Coll. Osteo. Medicine, Kansas City, 1994. Mem. adv. coun. St. Joseph Health Ctr., 1989—. Mem. ABA, Mo. Bar Assn., Kansas City Lawyers Assn., Kansas City Met. Bar Assn. (chmn. alternate dispute resolution com. 1996—, vice chmn. 1994-95, chmn. med. malpractice com. 1989), Mo. Orgn. Def. Lawyers, St. Louis Alumni Assn. (pres. 1984-92), St. Louis U. Law Sch. Alumni Assn. Home: 6824 Valley Rd Kansas City MO 64113-1929 Office: Dysart Taylor Penner Lay & Lewandowski PC 4420 Madison Ave Kansas City MO 64111-3407

MCMANUS, JASON DONALD, editor; b. Mission, Kans., Mar. 3, 1934; s. John Alan and Stella Frances (Gosney) McM.; m. Patricia Ann Paulson, Oct. 18, 1958 (div. Feb. 1966); 1 child, John Alan; m. Deborah Hall Murphy, Dec. 2, 1973; children: Sophie Eleanor, Mage Caroline. B.A., Davidson Coll., 1956, Litt.D. (hon.), 1979; M.P.A., Princeton U., 1958; postgrad., Oxford U., 1958-59; LittD (hon.), Monmouth Coll., 1988, U. N.C., 1991, Loyola U., Balt., 1992. Common Market bur. chief Time Mag., Paris, 1962-64; assoc. editor Time Mag., N.Y.C., 1964-68, sr. editor, 1968-75, asst. mng. editor, 1975-78, exec. editor, 1978-83, mng. editor, 1985-87; corp. editor Time Inc., N.Y.C., 1983-85; editor-in-chief Time Warner Inc., N.Y.C., 1987-95; ret. Author: short stories Introduction, 1960. Mem. presdl. adv. commn. Internat. Edn. Exchange, 1982-83. Rhodes scholar, 1958-59. Club: Century Assn. (N.Y.C.). Office: Time & Life Bldg New York NY 10020

MCMANUS, JOHN FRANCIS, association executive, writer; b. Bklyn., Jan. 24, 1935; s. V. Paul and Dorothy F. (Devenport) McM.; m. Mary Helen O'Reilly, Oct. 19, 1957; children: John G., Margaret A. Strauss, Paul J., Mary Anne Power. BS in Physics, Holy Cross Coll., 1957. Elec. engr. Transitron Corp., Wakefield, Mass., 1960-66; field coord. The John Birch Soc., Belmont, Mass., 1966-68, projects mgr., 1968-73, dir. pub. rels., 1973-91; pres. The John Birch Soc., Appleton, Wis., 1991—. Author: An Overview of Our World, 1971, The Insiders: Architects of the New World Order, 1992, 4th edit., 1995, Financial Terrorism: Hijacking America Under the Threat of Bankruptcy, 1993, Changing Commands: The Betrayal of America's Military, 1995; author weekly column, 1973—. Lt. USMC, 1957-60, capt., USMCR, 1960-68. Avocations: reading, golf, family. Home: PO Box 3076 Wakefield MA 01880-0772 Office: John Birch Society PO Box 8040 Appleton WI 54913-8040

MCMANUS, JOHN FRANCIS, III, advertising executive; b. Bklyn., Mar. 8, 1919; s. John Francis and Helen Jane (Cleary) McM.; m. Regina Delores Smith, Feb. 12, 1942 (div. June 1950); m. Sara Grace Scerra, Mar. 8, 1951 (dec. Aug. 1970); children: John Francis IV, Jane Frances, Stephan George, Kathleen Elizabeth; m. Jane Caroline Lewis, Apr. 25, 1974. BFA, Cooper Union Inst. Art, N.Y.C., 1941; student, Silvermine Guild Art Ctr., Norwalk, Conn., 1987, 88, 89; BA, NYU, 1947. Advt. dir. Thayer, Inc., Gardner, Mass., 1948-52; account supr. and copy chief Zimmer, Keller, Calvert, Detroit, 1952-57; account mgmt. McCann-Erickson, Inc., N.Y.C., 1957-58; v.p., mgmt. supr. Doyle, Dane, Bernbach, Inc., N.Y.C., 1958-69; sr. v.p., mgmt. Super-Smith/Greenland, Inc., N.Y.C., 1969-70; pres., creative dir. The McManusCo., Westport, Conn., 1970—; bd. dirs. Stamford Art Assn., Homes Conn., Holiday Cruise Lines; official artist USCG, 1988—. Writer series on Am. Way of Life, mag., 1949 (Freedom Found. gold medals 1949, 50); mgmt. supr. Avis, We Try Harder campaign, 1964, Mobil Detergent Campaign, 1968, Rheingold Would You Have the Guts? campaign, 1971 (Clio, Effie awards 1971). Capt. USAAF, 1942-46. Recipient Le Premier Prix Festival Internat., DU Film Publicitaire, Venice, France, 1960, Freedoms Found. Gold medals, Freedoms Found. Inc., Valley Forge, Pa., 1969-70, Effie, Am. Mktg. Assn., N.Y.C., 1972, Archie award, Nat. Assn. Indsl. Advts., N.Y.C., 1984. Mem. Am. Watercolor Soc., Am. Soc. Marine Artists, Westport Arts Council, Fairfield County Bus. Execs. Republican. Roman Catholic. Avocations: painting marine and seascapes, writing, photography, travel. Office: The McManus Co PO Box 446 Greens Farms CT 06436-0446

MCMANUS, LANA RAE, court reporter; b. New Orleans, Mar. 8, 1965; d. Calvin Claiborne and Betty Jane (Reed) McM. AAS, Alvin (Tex.) C.C., 1992. Court reporter A. William Roberts Jr. & Assocs., Charleston, S.C., 1992—. Glassell Sch. Art scholar, 1982-83. Mem. Nat. Ct. Reporters Assn., Tex. Ct. Reporters Assn., S.C. Shorthand Reporters Assn. Roman Catholic. Avocations: art, guitar, church-related activities. Office: A. William Roberts Jr & Assocs 46 State St # A Charleston SC 29401-2810

MCMANUS, MARY HAIRSTON, English language educator; b. Danville, Va., Nov. 23; d. Benjamin and Essie (Walton) Hairston; m. Booker Taliaferro McManus, June 27; children: Philip, Kenneth. BA, Va. State U., Petersburg, MA; PhD, U. Md. Cert. in English lang. and lit. edn. Instr. English Va. State U., Petersburg, 1965-70; lectr. English European div. U. Md., Berlin, 1972-73; instr. English Fayetteville (N.C.) State U., 1975-78; instr. ESOL Venice (Ill.)-Lincoln Tech. Ctr., 1978-83; lectr. English Anne Arundel C.C., Arnold, Md., 1983-84; asst. prof. English Bowie (Md.) State U., 1984—, dir. honors program, 1993—; cons. Anne Arundel County Govt., Glen Burnie, Md., 1983-84, Prince George's County Govt., Upper Marlboro, Md., 1985-86; mem. adv. bd. Collegiate Press, Alta Loma, Calif., 1992—. Recipient Outstanding Educator award Prince George's County Fire Dept., 1988; NEH fellow, 1991. Mem. MLA, Nat. Coun. Tchrs. English, Coll. Lang. Assn., CHUMS Inc. (pres. 1995—), Alpha Kappa Alpha, Sigma Tau Delta. Democrat. Avocations: reading, travel. Home: 432 Lakeland Rd N Severna Park MD 21146-2420 Office: Bowie State U 14000 Jericho Park Rd Bowie MD 20715-3318

MCMANUS, PATRICK FRANCIS, educator, writer; b. Sandpoint, Idaho, Aug. 25, 1933; s. Francis Edward McManus and Mabel Delana (Klaus) DeMers; m. Darlene Madge Keough, Feb. 3, 1954; children: Kelly C., Shannon M., Peggy F., Erin B. BA in English, Wash. State U., 1956, MA in English, 1962, postgrad., 1965-67. News reporter Daily Olympian, Olympia, Wash., 1956; editor Wash. State U., Pullman, 1956-59; with Ea. Wash. U., Cheney, 1959—; ret., 1983; news reporter Sta. KREM-TV, 1960-62; assoc. prof. Ea. Wash. U., Cheney, 1971-74, prof., 1974-83, prof. emeritus, 1983—. Author: A Fine and Pleasant Misery, 1978, Kid Camping form Aaaaiii! to Zip, 1979, They Shoot Canoes, Don't They?, 1981, Never Sniff a Gift Fish, 1983, The Grasshopper Trap, 1985, Rubber Legs & White Tail-Hairs, 1987, The Night The Bear Ate Gommbaw, 1989, Whatchagot Stew, 1989, Real Ponies Don't Go Oink!, 1991, The Good Samaritan Strikes Again, 1992, How I Got This Way, 1994, (stage play) A Fine and Pleasant: The Humor of Patrick F. McManus, 1994, Misery II: McManus In Love, 1995; assoc. editor Field & Stream mag., 1977-81; editor-at-large Outdoor Life, 1981—. Recipient Booksellers award P.N.W. Booksellers, 1983, Trustees medal EWU, 1984, Gov.'s award Wash. State Libr., 1985, Excellence in Craft award OWAA, 1986, Disting. Achievement award WSU, 1994, Founder's Day award EWU, 1994; named to Idaho's Hall of Fame, 1995. Mem. Authors Guild, Outdoor Writers Am. (bd. dirs. 1981-84, Excellence award 1986). Roman Catholic. Avocations: outdoor sports, woodworking, traveling. Office: PO Box 28216 Spokane WA 99228-8216

MCMANUS, PATRICK J., mayor, lawyer, accountant; b. Lynn, Mass., July 20, 1954; s. Robert A. and Kathryn M. (Gainey) McM. BA in Govt., Bowdoin Coll., 1976; MBA, Suffolk U., 1981; JD, Boston Coll., 1985. CPA, Mass.; cert. managerial acct., Mass. Tchr. Lynn Pub. H.S.; assoc. prof. bus. and fin. Salem (Mass.) State Coll.; lawyer pvt. practice Lynn; councillor at large City of Lynn, 1986-91, mayor, 1992—; mem. adv. bd. U.S. Conf. of Mayors, Washington, Brownsfield Task Force, Washington, Urban and Econ. Policy, Washington, Arts, Culture and Recreation, Washington. Mem. KC, Ancient Order of Hibernians. Democrat. Roman Catholic. Office: Mayor's Office 3 City Hall Sq Lynn MA 01905

MCMANUS, RICHARD PHILIP, lawyer, agricultural products company executive; b. Keokuk, Iowa, Oct. 20, 1929; s. Edward William and Kathleen (O'Connor) M.; m. Marjorie Theresa Mullaney, Nov. 5, 1955; children: Michael L., Mark J., Matthew A. BA, St. Ambrose U., Davenport, Iowa, 1949; JD, U. Mich., 1952; MBA, Roosevelt U., Chgo., 1965. Bar: Calif. 1982, Ill. 1958, Iowa 1952. Ptnr. McManus & McManus, Keokuk, 1953-63; div. counsel USN Facility Engring. Command, Great Lakes, Ill., 1963-66; v.p., dir. law Household Fin. Corp., Chgo., 1966-81; exec. v.p., sec. Security Pacific Fin. Svcs., Inc., San Diego, 1981-92; pres., bd. dirs. Mosamac Co., Inc., 1992—; mem. gen. com. Conf. Consumer Fin. Law, Chgo., 1975-92. Contbr. articles to profl. jours. Bd. dirs., treas., atty. Tijuana/San Diego Habitat for Humanity, Inc., 1992-95; trustee Village of Lake Bluff, Ill., 1974-78. Mem. ABA, Calif. Bar Assn., Ill. Bar Assn., San Diego Bar Assn., Calif. Fin. Svcs. Assn. (chmn. law com. 1981-92), Am. Fin. Svcs. Assn. (chmn. law forum 1980-81, Disting. Svc. award 1990), Lions, Elks, KC, Beta Gamma Sigma. Democrat. Roman Catholic. Avocations: golf, flying, sailing, woodworking. Home: 17305 Campillo Dr San Diego CA 92128-2149

MC MANUS, SAMUEL PLYLER, chemist, academic administrator; b. Edgemoor, S.C., Oct. 29, 1938; s. Henry Plyler and Louise (Sanders) McM.; m. Nancy Fincher, Mar. 26, 1959; children: Samuel Plyler, Robert Adair. B.S. in Chemistry, The Citadel, 1960; M.S., Clemson U., 1962, Ph.D. in Chemistry, 1964. Research chemist Du Pont, Phila., 1964; asst. prof. chemistry U. Ala., Huntsville, 1966-68; assoc. prof. U. Ala., 1968-73, prof., 1973—, chmn. dept. chemistry, 1970-72, 77-78, dir. materials sci. program, 1988-89, grad. dean, 1989-94, assoc. v.p. acad. affairs, 1990-91, assoc. provost, 1991-93, interim provost, 1993-94, provost, v.p. acad. affairs, 1994—; vis. faculty mem. U. S.C., 1974-75; mem. Ala. Coun. Grad. Deans, 1989-94, (chmn. 1992-93), Conf. So. Grad. Schs. (com. Issues and Planning, 1993-94), Cons. to govt. and industry. Author: Neighboring Group Participation; Editor: Organic Reactive Intermediates, Nucleophilicity; Contbr. articles on chemistry to sci. jours. Committeeman Tenn Valley council Boy Scouts Am., 1973-75. Served to capt. U.S. Army, 1964-66. Named Outstanding Educator U. Ala., Huntsville, 1971, 74; Sigma Xi Researcher of Yr., 1978; Alumni fellow Clemson U., 1961; Petroleum Research Fund grantee, 1968-87 ; NASA-Am. Soc. Engring. Edn. fellow, 1981, 82. Mem. Am. Chem. Soc. (councillor 1970-74, 78-80, 83-93, bd. dirs. 1966-74, 78-80, 83-93, nat. awards com. 1987-89), Ala. Acad. Sci. (v.p. 1973-74, exec. com. 1967, 73-74), AAAS, Am. Assn. State Colls. and Univs. (com. sci. and tech. 1978), Ala. Coun. Chief Acad. Officers (chmn. 1994—), Sigma Xi (chpt. sect. 1967-69, pres. 1970-71, exec. com. 1967-72), Phi Kappa Phi (chpt. v.p. 1988-89, pres. 1989-90). Clubs: Rotary Internat., Lake Guntersville Yacht (treas. 1975, gov. 1974-83, 88-90, 93—, commodore 1977, chmn. bd. govs. 1978, chmn. exec. com. 1978-79, 93-94), Yacht Club Assn. Ala. (pres., chmn. bd. commodores 1977). Office: Office of the Provost U Ala Huntsville AL 35899 *At the beginning of my academic career I was fortunate to have realized that opportunity always exists. Success requires that one seize even the fleeting opportunity and to be creative with the available resources.*

MCMANUS, WALTER LEONARD, investment executive; b. N.Y.C., Apr. 27, 1918; s. Charles E. and Eva M. (Olt) McM.; m. Lillian Ziegler, June 6, 1941; children: Walter Leonard, Peter David, Susan. Student, Harvard Bus. Sch.; BS in Fin. Sci., Georgetown U., 1940. With Crown Cork & Seal Co., Inc., Balt., 1940-60; became sec. Crown Cork & Seal Co., Inc., 1945, v.p., 1949, sec.-treas., 1958-60; pres., dir. Cem Securities Corp.; assoc. Castlewood Realty Co.; dir. Hospice of Martin County, Fla. Mem. Halifax River Yacht Club, Lighthouse Point Yacht Club, Cocoanut Point Yacht Club, Internat. Order of Blue Gavel. Home: 1766 NW Harbor Pl North River Shores Stuart FL 34994 Office: E Joppa Rd Ste 204 Baltimore MD 21286

MCMARTIN, JOHN, actor; b. Warsaw, Ind.; children: Kathleen Alice, Susan Helen. Actor Broadway prodns. including Artist Descending a Staircase, 1989, The Conquering Hero, Blood, Sweat and Stanley Poole, Children From Their Games, A Rainy Day in Newark, Sweet Charity, Follies, The Great God, Brown, Don Juan, The Visit, Chemin de Fer, Love For Love, Rules of the Game, Happy New Year, A Little Family Business, Show Boat, 1994-95 (Tony nominee - Lead Actor in a Musical, 1995); Off-Broadway prodns. Little Mary Sunshine, The Misanthrope, Too Much Johnson, Henry IV, Julius Caesar; films: Sweet Charity, All The President's Men, Pennies From Heaven, Brubaker, Legal Eagles. Recipient Theatre World award, 1959; nominee 2 Tony awards, 1967, 74; recipient 2 Drama Desk awards, 1974. Club: The Players (N.Y.C.). Office: The Artists Agy 1000 Santa Monica Blvd North Hollywood CA 91601

MCMASTER, BELLE MILLER, religious organization administrator; b. Atlanta, May 24, 1932; d. Patrick Dwight and Lila (Bonner) Miller; m. George R. McMaster, June 19, 1953; children: Lisa McMaster Stork, George Neel, Patrick Miller. BA, Agnes Scott Coll., 1953; MA, U. Louisville, 1970, PhD, 1974. Assoc. corp. witness Presbyn. Ch. USA, Atlanta, 1974-77, dir. corp. witness, 1977-81, dir. div. corp. and social mission, 1981-87; dir. social justice and peacemaking unit Presbyn. Ch. USA, Louisville, Ky., 1987-93; acting dir. program women in theology and ministry Candler Sch. Theology Emory U., 1993-96; dir. advanced studies Candler Sch. Theology Emory U., 1995—; 1993-96; vice moderator chs. commn. internat. affairs World Coun. Chs., 1984-91; chair commn. internat. affairs Nat. Coun. Chs., N.Y.C., 1986-89, v.p., 1990-95, chair ch. world svc. and witness unit com., 1990-95; bd. dirs. Ecumenical Devel. Corp. U.S.A., 1992—, Orison Ministries with Women, 1995—. Author: Witnessing to the Kingdom, 1982, book columnist "What I Have Been Reading" in Church and Society Magazine, 1993—; contbr. articles to profl. jours. Pres. League of Women Voters, Greenville, S.C., 1963-64; bd. dirs. Interfaith Housing, Atlanta, 1975-81. Danforth fellow, 1969-74. Mem. MLA, Acad. Am. Religion, Soc. for Values in Higher Edn., Phi Beta Kappa. Office: Emory U Candler Sch Theology Atlanta GA 30322

MCMASTER, BRIAN JOHN, artistic director; With internat. artists dept. EMI, 1968-73; controller opera planning English Nat. Opera, 1973-76; mng. dir. Welsh Nat. Opera, Cardiff, 1976-91; dir. Edinburgh (Scotland) Internat. Festival, 1991—; artistic dir. Vancouver Opera (B.C., Can.), 1983-89. Office: Edinburgh Festival, 21 Market St, Edinburgh EH1 1BW, Scotland

MCMASTER, JAMES HENRY, orthopedic surgeon; b. Pitts., Feb. 14, 1939; s. James J. and Clara (Ketter) McM.; m. Judith L. Ryan, June 30; children: Laurie R. McMaster Southern, Amy L., Kristin R. (dec.). BA, Washington and Jefferson U., 1960; MD, Temple U., 1964. Diplomate Am. Bd. Orthopaedic Surgeons; lic. physician, Pa. Rotating intern Harrisburg (Pa.) Polyclinic Hosp., 1964-65, gen. surgery resident, 1965-66; orthopaedic surgery resident U. Pitts. Sch. Medicine, 1966-69, asst. prof. dept. orthopaedic surgery, 1971-75, dir. Orthopaedic Rsch. Lab., 1971-76, assoc. prof. dept. orthopaedic surgery, 1975-79, assoc. clin. prof., 1979-82, clin. prof., 1982—; prof. surgery orthopaedics dept. surgery Med. Coll. Pa., Phila., 1988—; mem. attending staff Children's Orthopaedic Clinic, Jackson Meml. Hosp., Miami, 1969-71; chmn. dept. orthopaedic surgery Allegheny Gen. Hosp., Pitts., 1976; exec. v.p. clin. affairs Allegheny Health Svcs., Inc., Pitts., 1988—; pres., COO Allegheny-Singer Rsch. Inst., Pitts., 1988-89, pres., CEO, 1990—; orthopaedic cons. Princess Margaret Hosp., Nassau, Bahamas, 1972—; bd. dirs. Allegheny Health Svcs., Inc., Allegheny Gen. Hosp., Allegheny Health Found., Allegheny Health Svcs. Providers Ins. Co. Contbr. articles to profl. jours., chpts. to books. Mem. Pres. Circle, Pitts. Symphony Soc. Maj. USAF, 1969-71. Kappa Scholar award Washington and Jefferson Coll., Disting. Am. award Pitts. chpt. Nat. Football Found., 1984; grantee The Robert and Mary Weisbrod Found., 1986-90. Mem. AMA, Am. Acad. Orthopaedic Surgeons, Am. Fedn. Clin. Rsch., Ea. Orthopaedic Assn., Orthopaedic Rsch. Soc., Am. Coll. Sports Medicine, Pa. Med. Soc., Allegheny County Med. Soc., Pa. Med. Soc., Am. Orthopaedic Soc. Sports Medicine, Am. Orthopaedic Assn., Pa. Orthopaedic Soc., Musculoskeletal Tumor Soc., Assn. Arthritic Hip and Knee Surgery, Alexis deTocqueville Soc. Republican. Avocations: golf, jogging, reading. Office: Allegheny-Singer Rsch Inst 320 E North Ave Pittsburgh PA 15212*

MCMASTER, JULIET SYLVIA, English language educator; b. Kisumu, Kenya, Aug. 2, 1937; emigrated to Can., 1961, naturalized, 1976; d. Sydney Herbert and Sylvia (Hook) Fazan; m. Rowland McMaster, May 10, 1968; children: Rawdon, Lindsey. B.A. with honors, Oxford U., 1959; M.A., U. Alta., 1963, Ph.D., 1965. Asst. prof. English U. Alta., Edmonton, Can., 1965-70; assoc. prof. U. Alta., 1970-76, prof. English, 1976-86, Univ. prof., 1986—. Author: Thackeray: The Major Novels, 1971; editor: Jane Austen's Achievement, 1976, Jane Austen on Love, 1978, Trollope's Palliser Novels, 1978, (with R.D. McMaster), The Novel from Sterne to James, 1981, Dickens the Designer, 1987, Jane Austen the Novelist, 1995; gen. editor Juvenilia Press, 1993—; illustrator/editor children's picture book: (by Jane Austen) The Beautifull Cassandra, 1993; contbr. articles to profl. jours. Fellow Can. Coun., 1969-70, Guggenheim Found., 1976-77, Killam Found., 1987-89; recipient Molson prize in Humanities for Outstanding Contbn. to Canadian Culture, 1994. Fellow Royal Soc. Can.; mem. Victorian Studies Assn. Western Can. (founding pres. 1972), Assn. Can. Univ. Tchrs. English (pres. 1976-78), MLA, Jane Austen Soc. N.Am. (dir. 1980-91). Office: U Alta, Dept English, Edmonton, AB Canada T6G 2E5

MCMASTER, ROBERT RAYMOND, accountant; b. Cleve., June 14, 1948; s. William G. and Elizabeth (Smith) McM.; m. Jane M. Pepple, June 27, 1970; children: William R., Sarah J. BS in Acctg., Miami U., Oxford, Ohio, 1970. CPA, Ohio, N.Y. Mem. audit staff Sta. KPMG, Columbus, Ohio, 1970-75; mgr. Sta. KPMG, N.Y.C., 1975-76; sr. mgr. Peat Marwick Main & Co., Columbus, 1977-81, ptnr., 1981, mng. ptnr., 1988—, area mng. ptnr., 1992. Pres. Planned Parenthood Ctrl. Ohio, Columbus, 1988, 89; bd. dirs. Riverside Meth. Hosp. Found., Columbus, 1988-91, Unverferth House, 1990-92, Children's Hosp. Found., 1990—, Children's Hosp., chmn., 1993—; mem. fin. com. Columbus Found.; chmn. Blue Ribbon Commn. on Columbus Pub. Sch. Fins., 1995. Mem. AICPA, Ohio Soc. CPAs (pres. Columbus chpt. 1983-84), Columbus Bar Assn. (ethics com. 1989-91), Scioto Country Club, Muirfield Village Golf Club, Columbus Club. Avocations: golf, tennis, skiing, basketball. Office: KPMG Peat Marwick 2 Nationwide Plz Columbus OH 43215-2422

MCMASTERS, PAUL KENNETH, foundation executive; b. Dade County, Mo., Jan. 18, 1942; s. James Harvey and Evelyn Gail (Carmack) McM.; m. Priscilla Jean Thomas, Feb. 19, 1967; 1 child, Amy Elaine. BA, SW Mo. State U., 1965, MA, 1973. From gen. assignment reporter to asst. mng. editor The Daily News, Springfield, Mo., 1970-79; mng. editor Coffeyville (Kans.) Jour., 1979-82; state editor USA Today, Arlington, Va., 1982-83, editorial editor, then ops. dir. editorial dept., 1983-87, dep. editorial dir., 1987-91, assoc. editor editorial page, 1991-92; v.p. The Freedom Forum, Arlington, 1992-95; exec. dir. The Freedom Forum 1st Amendment Ctr., Nashville, 1992-95; 1st amendment ombudsman The Freedom Forum, Arlington, Va., 1995—; speaker in field. Mem. editorial bd.: Newspaper Rsch. Jour.; contbr. articles to profl. jours. Bd. dirs. Student Law Press Ctr., The Media Inst., Sox Found. Recipient Inglehart First Amendment award Coll. Media Advisors, 1992, Human Rights Leadership award Freedom Mag., 1993. Mem. Soc. Profl. Journalists (pres. 1993-94, past chmn. freedom of info., past sec.-treas., Wells Meml. Kay award 1990), Am. Soc. Newspaper Editors (freedom of info. com.), Assn. Educators in Journalism and Mass Comm. (newspaper divsn. exec. com.). Home: 11871 Troika Ct Woodbridge VA 22192 Office: The Freedom Forum 1st Amendment Ctr 1101 Wilson Blvd Arlington VA 22209-9999

MCMATH, CARROLL BARTON, JR., past college administrator, retired army officer; b. Godfrey, Wash., Sept. 18, 1910; s. Carroll Barton and Grace Jenness (Matthews) McM.; BS, Oreg. State U., 1932; MS (A. Olson Research scholar), N.Y. U., 1936; m. Betty Ruth Thompson, Nov. 26, 1937; children: Robert Thompson, Carol. With Sacramento Bee Newspaper, 1932-35; jr. exec. Lord & Taylor, N.Y.C., 1936-39; head dept. bus. Boise (Ida.) Jr. Coll., 1939-40; Res. officer on active duty U.S. Army, 1940-46, assigned gen. staff War Dept., 1943-45; commd. capt. regular U.S. Army 1947, advanced through grades to lt. col., assigned Joint Chiefs of Staff, 1951-53, Office Sec. of Army, 1953-55, ret., 1963; campaigns include Okinawa, Korea, Vietnam; mem. faculty U. Hawaii, Honolulu, 1964-77, asst. to dir. research, profl. adviser to faculty on rsch., 1964-77; faculty Indsl. Coll. of Armed Forces, Washington, 1945-46; asst. prof. retailing N.Y. U., N.Y.C., 1946-47. Mem. Assn. U.S. Army, AAAS, AAUP, Ret. Officers Assn., Honolulu Acad. Arts, Hawaiian Hist. Soc., Am. Theatre Organ Soc., Hawaii Found. History and Humanities, Scabbard and Blade, Alpha Delta Sigma, Alpha Kappa Psi, Eta Mu Pi, Elk, Koa Anuenue. Democrat. Home: 1624 Kanunu St Honolulu HI 96814-2747

MCMEEKIN, DOROTHY, botany, plant pathology educator; b. Boston, Feb. 24, 1932; d. Thomas LeRoy and Vera (Crockatt) McM. BA, Wilson Coll., 1953; MA, Wellesley Coll., 1955; PhD, Cornell U., 1959. Asst. prof. Upsala Coll., East Orange, N.J., 1959-64, Bowling Green State U., Ohio, 1964-66; prof. natural sci. Mich. State U., East Lansing, 1966-89, prof. botany, plant pathology, 1989—. Author: Diego Rivera: Science and Creativity, 1985; contbr. articles to profl. jours. Mem. Am. Phytopath. Soc., Mycol. Soc. Am., Soc. Econ. Bot., Mich. Bot. Soc. (bd. dirs. 1985—), Mich. Women's Studies Assn., Sigma Xi, Phi Kappa Phi. Avocations: gardening, sewing, travel, drawing. Home: 1055 Marigold Ave East Lansing MI 48823-5128 Office: Mich State U Dept Botany-Plant Pathology 335 N Kedzie Hall East Lansing MI 48824-1031

MC MEEL, JOHN PAUL, newspaper syndicate and publishing executive; b. South Bend, Ind., Jan. 26, 1936; s. James E. and Naomi R. (Reilly) McM.; m. Susan S. Sykes, Apr. 16, 1966; children: Maureen, Suzanne, Bridget. BS, U. Notre Dame, 1957. Sales dir. Hall Syndicate, 1960-67; asst. gen. mgr., sales dir. Publishers-Hall Syndicate, 1968-70; co-founder Universal Press Syndicate, Kansas City, Mo., 1970; pres. Universal Press Syndicate, 1970—; bd. dirs. Newspaper Features Coun., Universal/Belo Prodns.; chmn. bd. Andrews & McMeel Inc., 1973—; chmn. bd. dirs. Nat. Cath. Reporter; mem. adv. coun. Inst. for Ch. Life, U. Notre Dame; bd. dirs. Christmas in April U.S.A. Co-founder Christmas in October, Kansas City, 1984—, James F. Andrews fellowship program U. Notre Dame, 1981. Mem. Fed. Assn. USA, Sovereign Mil. Order Malta, Internat. Press Inst. (bd. dirs. Am. com.). Home: Three Sunset Pl 5300 Sunset Dr Kansas City MO 64112-2358 Office: Universal Press Syndicate 4900 Main St Fl 9 Kansas City MO 64112-2630

MCMEEN, ALBERT RALPH, III, writer, lecturer; b. Lewistown, Pa., Oct. 4, 1942; s. Albert Ralph and Margaret McDowell (Parker) McM.; BA in Econs., Williams Coll., 1964; MBA in Fin. (Columbia Internat. Fellows scholar 1964), Columbia U., 1966; m. A. Mary Kelley, June 6, 1965 (div.); children: Albert Ralph, Christopher Benjamin; life ptnr., Hamza Yaldiz. Asst. v.p. Chem. Bank, N.Y.C., 1966-75; v.p. mktg. Irving Leasing Co. subs. Irving Trust Co., N.Y.C., 1975-80; v.p. regional ops. USI Capital and Leasing affiliate U.S. Industries, Inc., N.Y.C., 1980-83; pres. Tng. Assocs., Inc., 1983—; assoc. adj. prof. NYU, 1979-93; asst. prof. L.I. U., 1986-93; tng. cons. Citibank, 1986-87, Barclay's Bank, 1986-89; lectr. Am. Mgmt. Assn., 1986—, cons. N.Y. Life Ins., 1989-91, Am. Bankers Assn., 1992-94, Kocbank, Istanbul, 1993, Fund Democracy and Devel., Moscow, 1995—. Mem. legis. com. Citizens' Union, 1968-75; bd. dirs. Columbia U. Alumni Assn., 1970-75; sec. Gay Fathers Inc. Recipient Columbia Bus. Sch. service award, 1966. Mem. ASTD, Fin. Ind. Tng. Assn. (exec. dir. 1994—).

Democrat. Author: Treasurers and Controllers New Equipment Leasing Guide, 1984, Equipment Leasing Guide for Lessees, 1990, Debt Repayment Capacity, 1992, Financial Statement Analysis, 1993, Statement Analysis Series, 1994, Guide to Consumer Lending Computer Based Training, 1995. Home: 333 W 88th St New York NY 10024-2219

MCMEEN, ELMER ELLSWORTH, III, lawyer, guitarist; b. Lewistown, Pa., June 3, 1947; s. Elmer Ellsworth II and Frances Josephine McM.; m. Sheila Ann Taenzler, July 31, 1971; children—Jonathan Ellsworth, Daniel Biddle, James Cunningham and Mary Josephine (twins). A.B. cum laude, Harvard U., 1969; J.D. cum laude, U. Pa., 1972. Bar: 1973, U.S. Ct. Appeals (2d cir.) 1973, U.S. Dist. Ct. (so. and ea. dists.) N.Y. 1975. Assoc. Cravath, Swaine & Moore, N.Y.C., 1972-75; assoc. LeBoeuf, Lamb, Greene & MacRae L.L.P., N.Y.C., 1975-78, ptnr., 1979—; lectr. Editor U. Pa. Law Rev., 1970-72. Author numerous guitar books; contbr. articles to profl. jours; solo guitar recs. Of Soul and Spirit, Irish Guitar Encores by Shanachie Records, Solo Guitar Serenade and Playing Favorites by Piney Ridge Music, solo guitar instructional audio and video lessons Stefan Grossman's Guitar Workshop. Chmn. N.Y.C. regional com. for U. Pa. Law Sch., 1984-86; class sec. Mt. Hermon Sch. Class of 1965, Mass., 1984-91. Fellow Am. Coll. Investment Counsel; mem. ABA, N.Y. State Bar Assn. (mem. corp. law com.), Rockaway River Country Club, Harvard Club (N.Y.C.). Office: LeBoeuf Lamb Greene & MacRae LLP 125 W 55th St New York NY 10019-5369

MCMENAMIN, HELEN MARIE FORAN, home health care, pediatric, maternal nurse; b. Buffalo, May 21, 1943; d. John Michael and Helen Marie (McCarty) Foran; m. John Patrick McMenamin, Aug. 21, 1965; children: Maureen Regina, Kathleen Noelle, Terence Michael, Amy Colleen, Shannon Rosemary, Barry Patrick. BSN, Niagara U., 1965; cert. instr. natural family planning, St. Margaret's Hosp., Boston, 1983. RN N.Y., N.H., Maine, D.C., Va., Md., Pa. Instr. perinatal, neonatal nursing Mercy Hosp. Sch. of Nursing, Portland, Maine, 1981-83; staff nurse neonatal intensive care unit Georgetown Univ. Hosp., Washington, D.C., 1984-93; staff nurse neonatal ICU, renal unit, home care case mgr. Children's Hosp. Nat. Med. Ctr., Washington, 1986-93; educator infant APNEA/CPR, Fairfax Hosp. Infant APNEA Program, Fairfax, Va., 1988-89; pediatric and maternal-child case mgr. Vis. Nurse Assn. No. Va., Arlington, 1992; staff nurse pediatric emergency room Mercy Hosp., Balt., 1992-93; case mgr. maternal-child pediatrics, high-risk neonatal home care Bay Area Health Care, Balt., 1993-95; mgr. maternal-child/neonatal and pediatric program 1st Am. Home Care, Hanover, Pa., 1994-95; pvt. duty pediatric home care Mount Washington Pediatric Hosp., Balt., 1995; coord. high risk maternal-child pediatric program Future Health Corp., Timonium, Md., 1995—; organizer, co-dir. health clinics Cathedral Elem. Sch., Portland, Maine, 1981-83. Block capt. Am. Cancer Assn., Springfield, Va., 1986-90, Healthy Mothers/Healthy Babies and Teen Pregnancy Coalition York County. Mem. Nat. Assn. Neonatal Nurses, Nat. Assn. Pro-Life Nurses (bd. dirs. of Pa.), Nat. Assn. Pediatric Nurses. Roman Catholic. Avocations: art, gardening, knitting, piano, baking. Home: RR 1 Box 1456 Brodbecks PA 17329-9603

MCMENAMIN, JOAN STITT, headmistress; b. N.Y.C., May 7, 1925; d. William Britton and Josephene Lloyd (White) Stitt; m. Edward B. McMenamin, Jan. 24, 1953. BA in Econs., Smith Coll., 1946. With Econ. Cooperation Adminstrn., Paris, 1949-50; office mgr. Ford Found., N.Y.C., 1951-52; history tchr. Nightingale-Bamford Sch., N.Y.C., 1962-63, asst. to headmistress, 1963-65, asst. headmistress, 1965-71, headmistress, 1971-92, headmistress emerite, 1992; mem. adv. council for nonpub. schs. N.Y. State Commr. of Edn., 1985-87; pres. Guild Ind. Schs. N.Y., 1983-85; mem. admissions com. Nat. Assn. Ind. Schs., 1977-79. Former vice chmn. English-Speaking Union Exchange Scholarship Program; former spl. advisor Parents League N.Y.; bd. dirs. Council for Religion in Ind. Schs., 1976-79, Ind. Sch. Orchs., Inc., 1980-84; trustee A Better Chance, Inc., 1977-83, The Town Sch., 1975-77, Ind. Ednl. Svcs., 1985-89, The Laurenceville School, 1989—, Buckley Sch., 1977-92, Coun. for Basic Edn., Washington, 1978—, Clark Found., 1979—, Robert Coll. of Istanbul, Turkey, 1979—, WICAT Founds., 1976—, Axe-Hought Found., 1985—. Mem. Nat. Assn. Prins. of Girls' Schs. (pres. 1983-85), N.Y. State Assn. Ind. Schs. (chmn. 1985-87), Headmasters Assn., Country Day Sch. Headmasters Assn. (vice pres. 1987-90, exec. com. 1987-90), Headmistresses Assn. of East. Democrat. Episcopalian. Club: Cosmopolitan (N.Y.C.); Bridehampton (N.Y.). Avocation: reading. Home: PO Box 768 172 Church Ln Bridgehampton NY 11932

MCMENAMIN, JOHN ROBERT, lawyer; b. Evanston, Ill., Sept. 30, 1946. BA, U. Notre Dame, 1968, JD, 1971. Bar: Ill. 1971. Law clk. to presiding judge U.S. Ct. Appeals (7th cir.), 1971-72; ptnr. Mayer, Brown & Platt, Chgo., 1978-89, McDermott, Will & Emery, Chgo., 1989—. Chmn. adv. bd. Holy Trinity High Sch., Chgo., 1986-88. Mem. ABA, Mid-Am. Com. Roman Catholic. Clubs: Law, Legal, University (Chgo.), Econ. (Chgo.). Office: McDermott Will & Emery 227 W Monroe St Chicago IL 60606-5016

MCMENAMIN, RICHARD F., lawyer; b. Nov. 23, 1946. BA, St. Joseph's Coll., 1968; MA, Boston U., 1971; JD, Temple U., 1977. Bar: Pa. 1977. Ptnr. Morgan, Lewis & Bockius, Phila. Office: Morgan Lewis & Bockius 2000 One Logan Sq Philadelphia PA 19103*

MCMENAMY, KRISTEN, model; b. Easton, Pa.; d. Charles and Eileen McM. Modelling contracts with Gianni Versace, Calvin Klein, Karl Lagerfeld. Named Harper's Bazaar Model of Yr., 1993. Office: Elite Model Mgmt Corp 111 E 22nd St Fl 2 New York NY 10010-5400

MC MENNAMIN, GEORGE BARRY, advertising agency executive; b. N.Y.C., May 23, 1922; s. Harold G. and Hazel F. (Stanbridge) McM.; m. Marilynn L. Simon, Sept. 9, 1946; children: Marilynn Breeze, Karen Foster. BS, Harvard U., 1945. With Doremus & Co., N.Y.C., 1946-88, exec. v.p., 1967-73, pres., 1973-84, vice chmn., 1984-88, also mem. exec. com.; pub. Worldpaper, Boston, 1988. Served to lt. (j.g.) USNR, 1944-46. Mem. Fin. Advt. and Mktg. Assn. Met. N.Y. (pres. 1967), Down Town Assn., Hasty Pudding Inst. 1770, Harvard Coll. Speakers Club, Harvard Club, New Canaan Country Club, Pilgrims Club of U.S. Republican. Episcopalian. Home: 28 Cross Ridge Rd New Canaan CT 06840-2311

MCMENNAMY, ROGER NEAL, community development company executive; b. Amarillo, Tex., Oct. 9, 1942; s. Wilson Foch and Mildred Evelyn (Freudiger) McM.; m. Marilyn Kay Gibbons, Jan. 1, 1967; children: Timothy Neal, Traci Nicole. Student, Abilene Christian U., 1961-62; BBA in Mgmt. cum laude, U. Tex., Arlington, 1970; MBA in Fin., U. Tex., Austin, 1971. CPA, Tex. Contr., treas. E.N. Wolcott Corp., Houston, 1971-73; mem. corp. staff ELPAC, Inc., Houston, 1973-74; gen. mgr. BS&B Mfg., Houston, 1974-75; gen. mgr. adminstrn. Gulf Interstate Co., Houston, 1975-77; exec. v.p., chief fin. officer NWS Supply Group, Houston, 1977-83; v.p., chief fin. officer Newpark Resources, Inc., Metairie, La., 1983-86; sr. v.p., chief fin. officer Gemcraft, Inc., 1986-88; exec. v.p., chief fin. officer Cooper Communities, Inc., Bella Vista, Ark., 1988-90, pres., chief exec. officer, 1990—, also bd. dirs.; bd. dirs. Boatmen's Bank of N.W. Ark., Fayetteville. Mem. N.W. Ark. Coun., Fayetteville; bd. dirs. Walton Arts Ctr., Fayetteville, 1994—. With USMC, 1962-66, Viet Nam. Mem. AICPA, Am. Resort Devel. Assn. (bd. dirs. 1991—), Ark. State C. of C. (bd. dirs.). Avocations: skiing, travel, golf, waterfowl hunting. Office: Cooper Communities Inc 1801 Forest Hills Blvd Bella Vista AR 72714-2395

MCMICHAEL, FRANCIS CLAY, civil engineering educator, environmental engineering consultant; b. Phila., Aug. 8, 1937; s. Francis and Estella Marie (Walker) McM.; m. Catherine Patricia Barati, Aug. 16, 1969; children: Jessica Elizabeth, Laureen Marie. B.S., Lehigh U., 1958; M.S., Calif. Inst. Tech., 1959, Ph.D., 1963. Asst. prof. Princeton U., 1965-67; sr. fellow Mellon Inst., Pitts., 1967-72; assoc. prof. Carnegie-Mellon U., Pitts., 1972-75, prof., 1975—; The Walter J. Blenko Sr. prof. environ. engring. Carnegie-Mellon U., 1981—, dept. head civil engring., 1975-80; sr. tech. advisor ERT Inc., Pitts., 1979-81. Mem. editorial bd. Waste Mgmt. and Rsch. Jour. Served with USPHS, 1962-65. AT&T Found. Indsl. Ecology faculty fellow, 1994-95, 95-96. Mem. ASCE, Water Pollution Control Fedn., Am. Inst. Chem. Engrs., Am. Geophys. Union, Soc. for Risk Analysis, Internat. Solid Wastes Assn. Presbyterian. Home: 7001 Penn Ave Pittsburgh PA 15208-2407 Office: Carnegie-Mellon U Pittsburgh PA 15213

MCMICHAEL, GUY H., III, federal official; b. South Bend, Ind., Dec. 26, 1939; m. Nancy Moore. AB, Harvard U., 1962; JD, U. Mich., 1967. Pvt. practice, 1967-71; dept. prosecuting atty. State of Ind., 1967-71; gen. counsel com. vet. affairs U.S. Senate, Washington, 1971-77; gen. coun. Dept. Vet. Affairs (formerly VA), Washington, 1977-81; adminstrv. judge bd. contract appeals Dept. Vet. Affairs, Washington, 1981-90, chmn., chief adminstrv. judge, 1990—. With U.S. Army, 1962-64. Mem. ABA, Bds. Contract Appeals Judges Assn. (pres. 1989-90), Ind. Bar Assn., D.C. Bar Assn. Office: Dept Vet Affairs Bd Contract Appeals 1800 G St NW Rm 545 Washington DC 20006-4407

MCMICHAEL, JEANE CASEY, real estate corporation executive; b. Clarksville, Ind., May 7, 1938; d. Emmett Ward and Carrie Evelyn (Leonard) Casey; m. Norman Kenneth Wenzler, Sept. 12, 1956 (div. 1968); m. Wilburn Arnold McMichael, June 20, 1978. Student Ind. U. Extension Ctr., Bellermine Coll., 1972-73, Ind. U. S.E., 1973—, Kentuckiana Metroversity, 1981—; Grad. Realtors Inst., Ind. U., 1982; grad. Leadership Tng., Clark County, Ind.; lic. real estate broker, Ind., Ky.; master Grad. Realtors Inst., Cert. Residential Specialist, Cert. Real Estate Broker, Leadership Tng. Grad. Owner, pres. McMichael Real Estate, Inc., Jeffersonville, 1979-88, 90-95; mgr., owner Buzz Bauer Realtors, Clark County, 1989-91; mng. broker Parks & Weisberg Realtors, Jeffersonville, Ind., 1989-91; instr. pre-license real estate Ivy Tech. State Coll., 1995-96, real estate Tng. Concepts, Inc. Pres. of congregation St. Mark's United Ch. of Christ, 1996, pres., Mr. and Mrs. Class, chmn., fin. trustee and bus. adv., chmn. devel. com., 1993, 94; chmn. bd. trustees, Brooklawn Youth Svcs., 1988-94, chmn. 1994-95; chmn. social com. Rep. party Clark County (Ind.); v.p. Floyd County Habitat for Humanity, 1991, 94/95. Recipient cert. of appreciation Nat. Ctr. Citizen Involvement, 1983; award Contact Kentuckiana Teleministries, 1978. Mem. Nat. Assn. Realtors (nat. dir. 1989—), Ind. Assn. Realtors (state dir. 1987—, quick start speaker 1989-91), Nat. Women's Council Realtors (state pres., chmn. coms., state rec. sec., 1984, state pres. 1985-86, Nat. Achievement award 1982, 83, 84, 85, 86, 87, 88, 89, 90, nat. gov. Ind. 1987, v.p. region III 1988, Ind. Honor Realtor award 1982—), Women's Council of Realtors (speaker 1990-94, Mem. of Yr. 1988), Ky. Real Estate Exchange, So. Ind. Bd. Realtors (program chmn. 1986-87, bd. dirs., pres., 1988—, Realtor of Yr. 1985, instr. success series, 1989-92, Snyder Svc. award 1987, Omega Tau Rho award 1988, Excellence in Edn. award 1989), Ind. Assn. Realtors (state dir. 1985—, bd. govs., instr./trainer, speaker 1989-94, chair bd. govs. 1991), Toastmasters (pres. Steamboat chpt.), Psi Iota Xi. Office: McMichael Real Estate Inc 1402 Blackiston Mill Rd Jeffersonville IN 47129-1227 Address: 23 Arctic Springs Rd Jeffersonville IN 47130 *Personal philosophy: The constant pursuit of excellence brings quality service and respect for every individual.*

MCMICHAEL, RONALD L., superintendent. Supt. Longview (Tex.) ISD. Named state finalist Nat. Supt. of Yr. award, 1992. Office: Longview ISD PO Box 3268 Longview TX 75606-3268

MC MILLAN, BROCKWAY, former communications executive; b. Mpls., Mar. 30, 1915; s. Franklin and Luvena (Brockway) McM.; m. Audrey Wishard, Sept. 2, 1942; children—Sarah Linn McMillan Taylor, Douglas Wishard, Gordon Brockway. Student, Armour Inst. Tech., 1932-34; B.S., Mass. Inst. Tech., 1936, Ph.D., 1939. Procter fellow Princeton, 1939-40, H.B. Fine instr., 1940-41; with Bell Telephone Labs., 1946-61, dir. mil. research, 1959-61; asst. sec. research and devel. U.S. Air Force, 1961-63, under-sec., 1963-65; exec. dir. mil. research Bell Telephone Labs., Whippany, N.J., 1965-69; v.p. mil. devel. Bell Telephone Labs., 1969-79. Mem. Bd. Edn. Summit, N.J., 1958-61. Served with USNR, 1942-45. Fellow IEEE; mem. Soc. Indsl. and Applied Math. (pres. 1959-60), Am. Math. Soc., Math. Assn. Am., Inst. Math. Stats., AAAS, Nat. Acad. Engring. Home: Carter Point Rd Sedgwick ME 04676

MCMILLAN, CAMPBELL WHITE, pediatric hematologist; b. Soochow, China, Jan. 10, 1927; s. Henry Hudson and Leila McNeill (Memory) McM.; m. Florence Jean MacKenzie, June 11, 1955; children: Ian Johnson, Sally Hudson, Donna Jean, Andrew Duncan, Bridget White, Wendy McNeill. B.S. summa cum laude, Wake Forest Coll., 1948; M.D., Bowman Gray Sch. Medicine, 1952. Diplomate Am. Bd. Pediatrics, Pediatric Hematology-Oncology. Intern Harvard Med. Service, Boston City Hosp., 1952-53; resident in pediatrics Children's Hosp. Med. Center, Boston, 1953-55; registrar in pediatrics St. Mary's Hosp., London, 1955; pediatrician Nemazee Hosp., Shiraz, Iran, 1956-58; fellow in pediatric hematology Harvard U., 1958-60; instr. pediatrics, 1960-61; gen. practice pediatrics Laurinburg, N.C., 1961-63; asst. prof. pediatrics U. N.C., Chapel Hill, 1963-68; asso. prof. U. N.C., 1968-72, prof., 1972-92, chief div. pediatric hematology, 1963-83, prof. emeritus, 1992—; Asso. dir. Clin. Research Center, U. N.C., 1966-78. Assoc. editor: Blood Diseases of Infancy and Childhood, 1978, 84; contbr. articles profl. jours., chpts. in books. Served with USNR, 1945-46. Recipient Lederle Med. Faculty award, 1964, Disting. Alumnus award Bowman Gray Sch. Medicine, 1972. Fellow Am. Acad. Pediatrics; mem. Soc. Pediatric Rsch., Am. Pediatric Soc., Phi Beta Kappa, Alpha Omega Alpha. Democrat. Episcopalian. Home: 408 Ridgecrest Dr Chapel Hill NC 27514-2103 *It was my extremely good fortune to live and to work in a time of the most explosive growth medical knowledge had ever undergone.*

MCMILLAN, CHARLES WILLIAM, consulting company executive; b. Ft. Collins, Colo., Feb. 9, 1926; s. Charles and Margaret (Jennings) McM.; m. Jardell Hollier, Feb. 12, 1951; children: Brett W., Kurt C., Scott P. B.S., Colo. State U., 1948. Asst. 4-H agt. Denver, 1948; county agrl. agt. LaJara, Colo., 1949-50, Julesburg, 1950-53; faculty Colo. State U., 1954; div. head, agrl. research dept. Swift & Co., Chgo., 1954-59; exec. v.p. Am. Nat. Cattlemen's Assn., 1959-77; v.p. Nat. Cattlemen's Assn., 1977-81; asst. sec. for mktg. and inspection services USDA, Washington, 1981-85; pres. McMillan and Farrell Assocs., Inc., Washington, 1985-94, C.W. McMillan Co., Alexandria, Va., 1994—; bd. dirs. RTI Inc.; vice chmn. Western Assocs. Inc. Served to lt. (j.g.) USNR, World War II. Mem. Inst. for Sci. in Soc. (bd. dirs.), Newcomen Soc. N.Am., Sigma Alpha Epsilon. Club: Capitol Hill. Home: 4003 Pine Brook Rd Alexandria VA 22310-2144 Office: PO Box 10009 Alexandria VA 22310-0009

MCMILLAN, DONALD EDGAR, pharmacologist; b. Butler, Pa., Sept. 23, 1937; s. Chandler Burdell and Ruth Elizabeth (Beach) McM.; m. Marjorie Ann Leavitt, Feb. 4, 1963; children: David Craig, Pamela Jean. B.S., Grove City Coll., 1959; M.S., U. Pitts., 1962, Ph.D., 1965. Postdoctoral fellow Harvard U. Med. Sch., 1965-66; instr. in pharmacology SUNY Downstate Med. Ctr., N.Y.C., 1967-68, asst. prof., 1968-69; asst. prof. pharmacology U. N.C., 1969-72, asso. prof., 1972-76, prof., 1976-78; prof., chmn. dept. pharmacology U. Ark. for Med. Scis., 1978-80, prof., chmn. dept. pharmacology and toxicology, 1980—, prof. psychiatry, 1985—, Wilbur D. Mills prof. alcoholism and drug abuse prevention, 1991—; dir. Substance Abuse Treatment Ctr.; vis. lectr. U. Ctrl. Caracas, Venezuela, 1974; IRG mem. neurobiology rev. panel NSF, 1979-80; IRG mem. Nat. Inst. Drug Abuse, 1982-88, 92-95, chair 1994-95, SRC mem., 1988-95; bd. dirs. Chapel Hill (N.C.) Drug Action Com., 1971-78; cons. Health Effects Inst., 1985-87; cons. sci. adv. bd. EPA, 1985-89; spl. merit rev. bd. Armed Forces Radiobiology Rsch. Inst., 1982; mem. com. toxicity data elements NRC, 1980-83. Author: Central Nervous System Pharmacology— A Self Instruction Text, 1974, 2d, rev. edit., 1979; research, numerous publs. in behavioral pharmacology and drug abuse; bd. editors Jour. Pharmacology and Exptl. Therapeutics, 1972—, Psychopharmacology, 1973-81, Neurotoxicology, 1979-82, Toxicology and Applied Pharmacology, 1982-89, Neurobehavioral/Toxicology and Teratology, 1982-90, Behavioral Pharmacology, 1989—. Grantee NIMH, 1971-74, Nat. Inst. Environ. Health Scis., 1976-80, N.C. Alcoholism Rsch. Authority, 1975-77, EPA, 1982-85, Kellogg Found., 1987-92, U.S. Dept. Edn., 1989-91, Nat. Inst. Drug Abuse, 1976—. Mem. AAAS, Behavioral Pharmacology Soc. (pres. 1982-84), Behavioral Toxicology Soc. (pres. 1988-90), Am. Soc. Pharmacology and Exptl. Therapeutics, Am. Psychol. Soc., European Behavioral Pharmacology Soc., Soc. Toxicologists (pres. So. Cen. chpt. 1985-86), Com. on Problems of Drug Dependence. Home: 100 Longway Dr Little Rock AR 72211-9531 Office: U Ark Med Scis Sch Medicine Dept Pharmacology & Toxicol 4301 W Markham St Little Rock AR 72205-7101

MCMILLAN, DONALD ERNEST, small business owner, educator; b. San Francisco, Dec. 13, 1931; s. George Ernest and Agnes Josephine (McGaffigan) McM.; m. Marilyn Marshal, June 23, 1956; children: David, Mark, Kathleen, Robert, Bruce, Rhannon. AB with distinction, Stanford U., 1953, MD, 1957. Diplomate Am. Bd. of Internal Medicine, Am. Bd. of Endocrinology and Metabolism. Intern USPHS Hosp., San Francisco, 1957-58; resident USPHS Hosp., New Orleans, San Francisco, 1959-63, dir. metabolic service, 1965-68, assoc. chief of medicine, endocrinology, 1968-82; chief endocrine and diabetes clinics Santa Barbara (Calif.) Gen. Hosp., 1968-82; lab. dir. Sansum Med. Rsch. Found., Santa Barbara, 1972-82; dir. research Hal B. Wallis Research Facility, Rancho Mirage, Calif., 1982-87; prof. internal medicine U. So. Fla., 1987-94; co-dir. diabetes ctr. State Fla. Sch. Medicine, 1987-94; staff physician James A. Haley Vets. Hosp., 1987-94, rsch. prof. engring., 1989—, clin. prof. physiology and biophysics, 1992—; spl. reviewer NIH Spl. Study Sect., 1980-81; clin. prof. of medicine, U. So. Calif., 1980-94; cons. numerous agys. and founds. including NIH, 1995—. Reviewer numerous sci. jours.; contbr. articles to profl. jours. Recipient USPHS Clin. Soc. Research Prize, 1963, Mary Jane Kugel award Juvenile Diabetes Found., 1982; fellow U. Calif. Med. Ctr., San Francisco, 1963-65. mem. AAAS, Am. Diabetes Assn. (pres. So. Calif. affiliate 1982-83, bd. dirs. 1984-87, pres. Fla. affiliate 1995-96), Am. Fedn. for Clinical Research, AMA, Am. Physiological Soc., Biorheology Soc., Endocrine Soc., Glycoconjugate Soc., Microcirculatory Soc., Sigma Xi, Phi Beta Kappa. Republican. Roman Catholic. Avocations: grandparenting, computer games, camping. Home: 2409 W Watrous Ave Tampa FL 33629-5342 Office: U South Fla 12901 Bruce B Downs Blvd Tampa FL 33612-4742

MC MILLAN, GEORGE DUNCAN HASTIE, JR., lawyer, former state official; b. Greenville, Ala., Oct. 11, 1943; s. George Duncan Hastie and Jean (Autrey) McM.; m. Ann Louise Dial, Nov. 20, 1971; children: George Duncan Hastie, III, Ann Dial. B.A. magna cum laude, Auburn U., 1966; LL.B. (Southeastern Regional scholar), U. Va., 1969. Bar: Ala. bar 1969. Research asst. dept. agronomy Auburn U., summers 1963-65; law clk. firm Lange, Simpson, Robinson & Somerville, Birmingham, Ala., summers 1967-68; law clk. to judge U.S. Dist. Ct. No. Dist. Ala., 1969-70; instr. U. Ala. Law Sch., 1969-70; individual practice law Birmingham, 1970-71; ptnr. firm McMillan & Spratling, Birmingham, 1971-86; of counsel Haskell, Slaughter, Young and Lewis, 1986; ptnr. McMillan, Jones and Assocs., 1987-90; pres. McMillan & Assocs., 1990—; mem. Ala. Ho. of Reps., 1973, Ala. Senate, 1974-78; lt. gov. Ala., 1979-83; vice-chmn. Nat. Conf. Lt. Govs., 1980-82; mem. Permanent Study Commn. on Ala.'s Jud. System, 1975-79. Chmn. Ala. Film Commn., 1976-83; mem. Arts Task Force, Nat. Conf. State Legislatures, 1978-80, Multi-State Transp. Adv. Bd., 1974-79; mem. exec. com. So. Growth Policies Bd., 1974-83, vice chmn., 1981-83; bd. dirs. Campfire, Inc., 1975-82, Met. YMCA, Birmingham, Boys and Girls Ranches, Ala., Positive Maturity, 1987—; chmn. bd., pres. Birmingham Cultural and Heritage Found., 1988—; pres., bd. dirs. Birmingham Repertory Theatre, 1989—; exec. producer City Stages; Served to lt. USAR, 1969. Recipient award Ala. Nurses Assn., 1975; named Legislator of Yr. Ala. Forestry Assn., 1978; Hardest Working Senator Capitol Press Corps, 1976; 1 of 4 Outstanding Young Men Ala. Jaycees, 1977; 1 of 10 Most Outstanding State Legislators Assn. Govtl. Employees, 1978; award Birmingham Emancipation Assn., 1977; award Ala. Hist. Commn., 1978; James Tingle award, 1979, Citizen of Yr. award City of Birmingham, 1990. Mem. Birmingham Bar Assn., Ala. Bar Assn., Am. Bar Assn., Birmingham Jaycees, Ala. Jaycees (dir. 1970-72), Birmingham Urban League, United Negro Coll. Fund. Democrat. Mem. Ch. of Christ. Club: Rotary (Birmingham). Office: PO Box 11311 Birmingham AL 35202-1311

MCMILLAN, HOWARD LAMAR, JR., banker; b. Jackson, Miss., Aug. 29, 1939; s. Howard Lamar and Mary Frances (Byars) McM.; m. Mary Eliza Love, July 5, 1964; children: Eliza Love McMillan Garraway, Howard Lamar III. BA in Banking & Finance, U. Miss., Oxford, 1960; postgrad., La. State U., 1966, Harvard U., 1979. With Deposit Guaranty Nat. Bank, Jackson, 1960, v.p., 1972-73, sr. v.p., 1973-77, exec. v.p. corp. div., 1977-81, exec. v.p. state bank div., 1981-84, pres., dir., 1987—; pres., dir. Deposit Guaranty Corp., Jackson, 1984—. Gen. chmn. United Way, Jackson, 1989—. Mem. Am. Bankers Assn. (bd. dirs. 1988—), Miss. Bankers Assn. (chmn. fed. legis. com.), Jackson C. of C. (bd. dirs. 1989—), Univ. Miss. Alumni Assn. (pres. 1988), 100 Club (Jackson). Avocations: golfing, snow skiing, reading. Office: Deposit Guaranty Nat Bank PO Box 1200 Jackson MS 39215-1200*

MC MILLAN, JAMES, manufacturing executive; b. Grosse Pointe Farms, Mich.; s. James Thayer and Anne Davenport (Russel) McM.; m. Virginia Cutting, Jan. 4, 1935; children: Francis Wetmore (Sandy), Virginia. A.B., Yale, 1934. With Detroit & Cleve. Nav. Co., supt., asst. gen. mgr., gen. mgr., pres., chmn. bd., 1934-48; pres. McMillan Packard, Inc.; pres., dir. Great Lakes-Oceanic Line, Inc.; security-ins. broker Multivest Financial Corp., Inc.; dir. Detroit Bank & Trust Co., Packard Motor Car Co., Studebaker Corp., Detroit Bank, Detroit Trust Co., Ferry-Morse Seed Co., Detroit & Cleve. Nav. Co., Am. Presidents Life Ins. Co., Grand Rapids, Mich.; v.p., dir., treas. Boyer-Campbell Co.; adminstrv. exec. asst. Am. Nat. Gas Service Co.; cons. Glover Assos., Inc., N.Y.C., Ordnance Tank Automotive Center, U.S. Army; mgmt. cons. Glover Assos. (Can.) Ltd. Exec. asst. United Found., 1964—; Bd. dirs. ARC; trustee Grosse Pointe War Meml. Assn., Detroit Hist. Assn., Mich. State Appellate Defender Commn., Grace Hosp., Grosse Pointe Country Day Sch., Detroit U., Sch. Corp., Estate James T. McMillan, Katherine K. Brookfield Trust.; Village commr., police commr. Grosse Pointe Park. Mem. Nat. Assn. Security Dealers, Detroit Bd. Commerce (dir. 1938-43), Mich. Hort. Soc. (trustee, treas.), Newcomen Soc. N.Am., Mason Club, St. Clair Flats Shooting Club, Yondotega Club, Detroit Country Club, Grosse Pointe Club (pres. 1953), Detroit Club (pres. 1962), Sakonnet Golf Club (Little Compton, R.I.). Republican. Presbyn. (elder, trustee). Home: 46 Sunningdale Dr Grosse Pointe MI 48236-1664 Office: Free Press Bldg Detroit MI 48226

MCMILLAN, JOANETTE HART, elementary educator; b. Mayo, Fla., Apr. 28, 1932; m. William R. McMillan, June 19, 1959; 1 child, Leenette. BS, Fla. State U., 1954; MS, Valdosta State U., 1973. Cert. elem. tchr., early childhood tchr., reading tchr., Fla. Tchr. various sch. dists. Gadsden, Brevard Counties, Fla., 1955-68, Suwannee County, Fla., 1968-78; tchr., chpt. 1 coord. Lafayette County, Fla., 1978-94. Active Dem. Ctrl. Com., Mayo, 1982—; chairperson Mayo Family Med. Svcs., 1986-94; mem. Seminole Boosters, 1987—, Builders Guild Advent Christian Village, 1974—, United Meth. Ch., 1942—, PTA. Mem. Fla. Edn. Assn., Order Eastern Star (assoc. matron, sec. 1989—), Fla. State U. Alumni Assn., Alpha Delta Kappa (pres., v.p., sec., historian, altruistic chmn. 1967—). Office: Lafayette Elem Sch RR 2 Box 260 Mayo FL 32066-9642

MCMILLAN, JOHN A., retail executive; b. 1931. BA, U. Wash., 1957. With Nordstrom Inc., Seattle, 1957—, exec. v.p., 1975—, pres., 1989—, co-chmn., 1991—. Office: Nordstrom Inc 1501 5th Ave Seattle WA 98101-1603*

MCMILLAN, JULIA A., pediatrician; b. Pinehurst, N.C., July 10, 1946. MD, SUNY, Syracuse, 1976. Intern SUNY Upstate Med. Ctr., Syracuse, 1976-77, resident in pediatrics, 1977-78, 79-80, fellow in infectious diseases, 1979-81; mem. staff Johns Hopkins U. Hosp., Balt.; assoc. prof. Johns Hopkins U., Balt. Mem. Am. Acad. Pediatrics, ASM, IDSA. Office: Johns Hopkins Hosp Dept Pediatrics 600 N Wolfe St Baltimore MD 21287-3224

MCMILLAN, LEE RICHARDS, II, lawyer; b. New Orleans, Aug. 26, 1947; s. John H. and Phoebe (Skillman) McM.; m. Lynne Clark Pottharst, June 27, 1970; children: Leslie Clark, Hillary Anne, Lee Richards III. BS in Commerce, Washington and Lee U., 1969; JD, Tulane U., 1972; LLM in Taxation, NYU, 1976. Bar: La. 1972. Assoc. Jones, Walker, Waechter, Poitevent, Carrere & Denegre, New Orleans, 1976-79, ptnr., 1979—, sect. head, corp. and securities sect., 1987-90, 94—, exec. com., 1990-94, 96—, chmn. exec. com., 1991-94, 96—; vice-chmn. Mech. Equipment Co., Inc., New Orleans, 1980-86, chmn. bd., 1986—, pres. 1989—, bd. dirs.; bd. trustees Alton Ochsner Med. Found., 1995—. Bd. trustees New Orleans Mus. Art., 1989-95; bd. dirs. bur. Govt. Rsch. New Orleans, 1987-93, Louise S. McGehee Sch., New Orleans, 1982-88, co-chmn. capital fund dr., 1984-86, pres. bd. dirs., 1986-88; bd. govs. Isidore Newman Sch., New Orleans, 1991-

95. Lt. JACG USNR, 1972-75. Mem. ABA (com. on negotiated acquisitions 1986-94), La. State Bar Assn. (chmn. corp. and bus. law sect. 1985-86, mem. com. on bar admissions 1986-87), Young Pres. Orgn., Washington and Lee U. Alumni Assn. (bd. dirs. 1995—). Republican. Episcopalian. Avocation: sailing. Office: Jones Walker Waechter Poitevent Carrere & Denegre 201 Saint Charles Ave New Orleans LA 70170-5100

MCMILLAN, M. SEAN, lawyer. Diploma U. Munich, 1963; cert. Internat. Sch., Copenhagen, Denmark, 1962; SB, U. So. Calif., 1967; JD, Harvard U., 1970. Bar: Calif. 1971. Spl. projects dir. Mass. Gen. Hosp., Boston, 1967-70; ptnr. Keatinge, Libbott, Bates & Loo, Los Angeles, 1970-74, Loo, Merideth & McMillan, Los Angeles, 1974-85, Bryan Cave LLP, Los Angeles/Santa Monica, 1986—. Mem. Assn. Computing Machinery, ABA, Am. Soc. Internat. Law, Phi Beta Kappa, Phi Kappa Phi. Editor: Harvard Internat. Law Jour., 1968-70. Office: Bryan Cave LLP 120 Broadway Ste 500 Santa Monica CA 90401-2386

MCMILLAN, MARY BIGELOW, retired minister, volunteer; b. St. Paul, July 30, 1919; d. Charles Henry and Allison (McKibbin) Bigelow; m. Richard McMillan, June 26, 1943; children: Richard Jr., Charles B., Douglas D., M. Allison, Anne E. BA, Vassar Coll., 1941; MDiv, United Theol. Sem. Twin Cities, 1978, DDiv (hon.), 1989. Ordained to ministry Presbyn. Ch., 1978. Asst. min. House of Hope Presbyn. Ch., St. Paul, 1978-82; interim pres. United Theol. Sem. Twin Cities, New Brighton, Minn., 1982-83, ret., 1987. Contb. author: The Good Steward, 1983. Trustee Minn. Ch. Found., Mpls., 1984—, United Theol. Sem. Twin Cities, 1977-89, also chmn. bd. trustees; bd. dirs. Inst. for Ecumenical and Cultural Rsch., Collegeville, Minn., 1982—; regional dir. Assn. Jr. Leagues, N.Y.C., 1959-61, pres. St. Paul chpt., 1957-59; vice chair Ramsey County Welfare Bd., St. Paul, 1962-66, St. Paul Health and Welfare Planning Coun., 1964-70, F.R. Bigelow Found., St. Paul, 1988-95, also 1st vice chair; trustee Wilder Found., 1973-89, also 1st vice chair. Recipient award for community planning United Way, 1965, also for yr. round leadership, 1973, Leadership in Community Svc. award YWCA, 1980, Sisterhood award NCCJ, Mpls., 1989; named Disting Alumna award St. Paul Acad. and Summit Sch., 1988. Mem. New Century Club. Avocations: golf, knitting, reading. Home: 2532 Manitou Is Saint Paul MN 55110-3901

MCMILLAN, NATHANIEL, professional basketball player; b. Raleigh, N.C., Aug. 3, 1964; m. Michelle McMillan; children: Jamelle, Brittany Michelle. Student, Chowan Coll., 1982-84, N.C. State U., 1984-86. Guard Seattle SuperSonics, 1986—. Dir. summer basketball camp. Holder NBA single-game rookie record assists; Seattle SuperSonics all-time leader steals, assists, single-game record assists, single-game playoff record assists; named Jr. Coll. All-Am., top 10 N.C. State list assists, 2d team All-NBA def., 1993-94, 94-95. Avocation: football. Office: Seattle SuperSonics Ste 200 190 Queen Anne Ave N Seattle WA 98109-9711*

MCMILLAN, ROBERT ALLAN, chemical company executive; b. Santa Barbara, Calif., Dec. 18, 1942; s. Edward and Thelma (Zuercher) McM.; m. Peggy Sue Damron, Oct. 17, 1964; children: Donald James, Jeffrey Scott; m. Christine Collins, June 17, 1983; children: Michelle Diane Ball, Suzanne Mary Ball. BS in Econs., U. Calif., Santa Barbara, 1968; PhD in Econs., U. Calif., Berkeley, 1972. Cons., economist Bank of Am., San Francisco, 1968-71; economist FRS, Cleve., 1971-74; economist BF Goodrich Co., Akron, Ohio, 1974-75, dir. econ. research, 1975-77, dir. analysis and control, 1977-78, dir. investor relations, 1978-82, exec. dir. planning and devel., 1982-86, v.p., treas., 1986—. Chmn. Akron Area Joint Econ. Council, 1985. Named Seer of Yr., Harvard U., 1977, 84. Mem. Fin. Execs. Inst., Conf. Bus. Econmists, Nat. Assn. Corp. Treas. Office: B F Goodrich Co 3925 Embassy Pky Akron OH 44333-1763*

MC MILLAN, R(OBERT) BRUCE, museum executive, anthropologist; b. Springfield, Mo., Dec. 3, 1937; s. George Glassey and Winnie Mae (Booth) McM.; m. Virginia Kay Moore, Sept. 30, 1961; children: Robert Gregory, Michael David, Lynn Kathryn. B.S. in Edn, S.W. Mo. State U., 1960; M.A. in Anthropology, U. Mo., Columbia, 1963; Ph.D. in Anthropology (NSF fellow), U. Colo., Boulder, 1971. Rsch. assoc. in archaeology U. Mo., 1963-65, 68-69; assoc. curator anthropology Ill. State Mus., Springfield, 1969-72; curator anthropology Ill. State Mus., 1972-73, asst. mus. dir., 1973-76, mus. dir., 1977—; exec. sec. Ill. State Mus. Soc., 1977—; lectr. in anthropology Northwestern U., 1973; bd. dirs. Found. Ill. Archaeology, 1978-83. Editor: (with W. Raymond Wood) Prehistoric Man and His Environments, 1976. Mem. Ill. Spl. Events Commn., 1977-79, program chmn., 1977-78; commr. Ill. and Mich. Canal Nat. Heritage Corridor Commn., 1988—. NSF grantee, 1971, 72, 80; Nat. Endowment for Humanities grantee, 1978. Fellow AAAS, Am. Anthrop. Assn.; mem. Am. Assn. Mus. (council 1982-86), Midwest Mus. Conf. (pres.), Soc. Am. Archaeology, Current Anthropology (asso.), Am. Quaternary Assn., Sigma Xi. Office: Ill State Mus Spring and Edwards Sts Springfield IL 62706 also: Dickson Mounds Museum Lewistown IL 61542

MCMILLAN, ROBERT RALPH, lawyer; b. N.Y.C., May 21, 1932; s. Harry and Vivian (Beatty) McM.; m. Jane Gail Arbo, June 7, 1958; children: Robin, Karen, Kenneth. Student, Adelphi U., 1951-52, 55-56; JD, Bklyn. Law Sch., 1960. Bar: N.Y. 1960. Spl. asst. staff of Richard M. Nixon, N.Y., Washington, 1960, 64-65; counsel Senator Kenneth B. Keating, Washington, 1960-62; govt. rels. advisor Mobil Oil Co., N.Y.C., 1962-63, 65-68; v.p. Avon Products, N.Y.C., 1973-78, 79-85; sr. v.p. A&S Dept. Stores, N.Y.C., 1978-79; counsel Rivkin, Radler, Bayh, Hart & Kremer, Uniondale, N.Y., 1986-91; ptnr. McMillan, Rather, Bennett & Rigano, P.C., Melville, N.Y., 1991—; bd. dirs. Lumex, Inc., Bayshore, N.Y., Key Bank N.Y., Empire Blue Cross Blue Shield, Panama Canal Commn., 1989-94, chmn., 1993-94. News commentator Sta. WLIW-TV, 1993—. Trustee Adelphi U., 1984-89; bd. dirs. L.I. (N.Y.) Assn.; chmn. L.I. Housing Parntership, 1988—. 1st lt. U.S. Army, 1952-54. Decorated Bronze Star. Mem. Nassau County Bar Assn., Suffolk County Bar Assn. Republican. Avocations: golf, fishing. Office: McMillan Rather Bennett & Rigano 395 N Service Rd Melville NY 11747-3139

MCMILLAN, TERRY L., writer, educator; b. Port Huron, Mich., Oct. 18, 1951; d. Edward McMillan and Madeline Washington Tillman; 1 child, Solomon Welch. BA in Journalism, U. Calif., Berkeley, 1979; MFA, Columbia Univ., N.Y.C., 1979. Instr. U. Wyoming, Laramie, 1987-90; prof. U. Ariz., Tucson, 1990-92. Author: Mama, 1987, Disappearing Acts, 1989, Waiting to Exhale, 1992, How StellaGot Her Groove Back, 1996, (with Nawal El Saadawi) Ergo! the Bumbershoot Literary Magazine (vol. 8 no. 1), 1993; editor: Breaking Ice: An Anthropology of Contemporary African-American Fiction, 1990; screenwriter (with Ron Bass) (movie) Waiting to Exhale, 1995. Recipient National Endowment for the Arts fellowship, 1988. Office: care Free at Last PO Box 2408 Danville CA 94526-7408 also: care Molly Friedrich Aaron Priest Literary Agency 708 Third Ave 23rd Fl New York NY 10017

MCMILLAN, WENDELL MARLIN, agricultural economist; b. Dallastown, Pa., June 14, 1923; s. John Walter and Alice Mary (McCormick) McM.; m. Eleanor Unser, July 14, 1946; children: Susan, Barbara, Douglas. Grad., York (Pa.) Jr. Coll., 1943; BS, Juniata Coll., 1948; MS, Pa. State U., 1950, PhD, 1954. Agrl. economist, asst. dir. U.S. Dept. Agriculture, Washington, 1955-64; project mgr., mktg. advisor Food and Agriculture Orgn. of UN, Jordan, Saudi Arabia and Afghanistan, 1964-72; agrl. economist The World Bank, Caribbean, Sudan, 1972-76; agrl. and policy economist U.S. Dept. Agr./USAID, Syria, Indonesia, Lesotho, Liberia, 1977-80; agrl. economist Africa Bur. USAID, Washington, 1980-89; mem. mktg. subcom. Nat. Commn. on Cooperative Devel., Washington, 1964; adj. prof. York (Pa.) Coll., 1990. Author tech./policy publs. on agr. Past dist. chmn. Campfire Girls, No. Va., 1959-61; bd. dirs. Hist. York, Inc., 1987—, pres., 1995—; mem. Hist. Soc. York County, 1987—, mem. libr. com., 1990—; mem. Hist. Soc. York County, 1987—; bd. trustees York County Acad., 1991—. Recipient Fulbright award U.S. Dept. State, Denmark, 1954-55, Merit certificates USDA, 1960, 84. Mem. Am. Agrl. Econs. Assn., Soc. for Internat. Devel., Alumni Assn. York Coll. (bd. dirs. 1986-91, Svc. award 1991, Disting. Alumnus 1982), Alumni Assn. Juniata Coll. (Nat. Alumni Achievement award 1984), Pi Gamma Mu. Democrat. Avocations: stamp collecting, nature study, opera. Home and Office: 101 E Springettsbury Ave York PA 17403-3126

MCMILLEN, ELIZABETH CASHIN, artist; b. Chgo.; d. James Blaine and Hortense (Fears) Cashin; m. John Stephen Jerabek; 1 child, Michael N. Student, Western Coll. for Women, 1961-63; BA, Bard Coll., 1965. coord. com. and juror Spectra I, sponsor state exhbn. women artists Westbrook Coll., Portland, Maine, 1979; dir. Hancock County Auditorium Art Gallery, Ellsworth, Maine, 1984, 85. Prin. works include sculpture Ahimsa Gallery, Maine, 1976; exhibited at Frick Gallery, Belfast, Maine, 1993, 94, Maine Coast Artists Juried Show, Rockport, 1994, Portland Children's Mus., 1995, Lakes Gallery, Sebago, Maine, 1995; one-person shows include Frick Area Gallery, Belfast, Maine, 1995; two persons show Maine Coast Artists, Rockport, 1996. Dem. chair Town of Lamoine, Maine, 1984-85, 86-87, 88-89; legislation coord. Amnesty Internat., Ellsworth, 1991—. Democrat. Episcopalian. Avocations: writing, politics, teaching, African-Am. history.

MCMILLEN, LOUIS ALBERT, architect; b. St. Louis, Oct. 24, 1916; s. Drury A. and Eleanor (Stockstrom) McM.; m. Persis White, Aug. 26, 1949; children: Michael Albert, Louis Stockstrom, Leander A.C. Grad., St. George's Sch., Newport, R.I., 1935; B.F.A., Yale U., 1940; M.Arch., Harvard U., 1947. Vice pres., dir. Architects Collaborative Inc., Cambridge, Mass., 1947-70; pres. Architects Collaborative Inc., 1970-80; pres. Architects Collaborative Internat. Ltd., Vaduz, 1959—; Architect in residence Am. Acad. Rome, 1968, 69; Mem. planning bd., Concord, Mass., 1958-60. Prin. works include master planning air bases in U.S., ednl. facilities in, New Eng.; commd. to do: U. Bagdad, Iraq, 1959, U. Mosul, Iraq, 1965, W.Va. State Parks, Hawks Nest, Canaan Valley, Pipestem/Bluestone and Twin Falls; office bldg., Kuwait Fund for Arab Econ. Devel., 1968, total tourist facilities, Porto Carras, Sithonia, Greece, 1969. Served to lt. USNR, 1942-46. Fellow AIA; mem. Boston Soc. Architects, Soc. Fellows Am. Acad. in Rome, Zeta Psi. Clubs: Naval and Military (London); Old North Bridge Hounds (joint master); Somerset (Boston). Home: PO Box 490 Essex MA 01929-0009

MCMILLEN, PATRICIA B., television producer; b. Dayton, Ohio, Feb. 7, 1938; d. Herman K. and Helen (Foureman) Baker; m. William A. McMillen, Sept. 7, 1957 (div. June 1969). Cert., Humbolt Inst.; student, Miami U., Oxford, Ohio. Comms. staff Capital/United Airlines, Washington; stenographer, billing clk. NCR, Dayton; from assoc. prodr., to exec. prodr. Donahue Syndicated TV Talk Show, Dayton, Chgo. and N.Y.C.; exec. prodr. Pozner & Donahue, N.Y.C., 1991-92; mem. ad hoc com., developer women's study class Wright State U., Dayton, 1971. Host pub. svc. TV program Home on Saturday, 1969-74; author: Working Woman's Cookbook and Entertainment Guide, 1983; co-author: Donahue: My Story, 1979. Mem. NATAS (4 Nat. Emmy awards, 1 local Emmy award). Avocations: snow and water skiing, in-line skating, decorating, sewing, reading.

MCMILLEN, ROBERT STEWART, lawyer; b. Yonkers, N.Y., Feb. 25, 1943; s. David Harry and Blodwyn Elizabeth (Evans) McM; m. Dorothea Anne Murray, July 2, 1966; children: Elissa London, Tara Evans. BS, U. Rochester, 1964; JD cum laude, Albany Law Sch. Union U., 1969. Bar: N.Y. 1969, U.S. Dist. Ct. (no. dist.) N.Y. 1969. Assoc. Clark, Bartlett & Caffry, Glens Falls, N.Y., 1969-73; ptnr. Caffry, Pontiff, Stewart, Rhodes & Judge, Glens Falls, 1974-80; prin. Bartlett, Pontiff, Stewart & Rhodes, P.C., Glens Falls, 1981—; sr. law examiner N.Y. State Bd. Law Examiners, Albany, 1986—; pres., bd. dirs. Community Title Agy., Inc., Glens Falls, 1984—. Editor-in-chief Albany Law Rev., 1968-69. Bd. dirs., officer Voluntary Action Ctr. of Glens Falls Area, Inc., 1970—; bd. dirs., treas. Arts and Crafts Ctr. of Warren County, Inc., Glens Falls, 1984-94; mem. Warren County Rep. Com., Queensbury, N.Y., 1979—; alt. or del. Rep. Jud. Nominating Com. 4th Jud. Dist. N.Y., 1977—. Recipient Disting. Svc. award Voluntary Action Ctr. of Glens Falls Area, Inc., 1990. Mem. ABA, N.Y. State Bar Assn. (mem. com. profl. ethics 1990—), Warren County Bar Assn. (bd. dirs. 1979-82). Avocations: family activities, downhill skiing, boating, hockey. Home: 27 Moorwood Dr Queensbury NY 12804-1040 Office: 1 Washington St Glens Falls NY 12801-2963

MC MILLEN, THOMAS ROBERTS, lawyer, arbitrator, mediator, retired judge; b. Decatur, Ill., June 8, 1916; s. Rolla C. and Ruth (Roberts) Mc M.; m. Anne Ford, Aug. 16, 1946; children: Margot F., Patricia R., Anne C. Scheyer. AB, Princeton U., 1938; LLB, Harvard U., 1941. Bar: Ill. 1941, U.S. Supreme Ct. 1948. Mem. firm Bell, Boyd, Lloyd, Haddad & Burns, Chgo., 1946-66; judge Cook County Cir. Ct., Cook County, Ill., 1966-71, U.S. Dist. Ct. (no. dist.) Ill., Chgo., 1971-85, ret.; pvt. practice Chgo., 1985—. Mem. arbitration panels Fed. Med. and Conciliation Svc., Chgo. Bd. Options Exch., Ill. State Bd. Edn., Judicate. Maj. CIC, AUS, 1941-45. Decorated Bronze Star medal, European Battle Stars (4), Croix de Guerre. Mem. Chgo. Bar Assn. (mem. bd. mgrs. 1964-66), 7th Cir. Bar Assn., Counter Intelligence Corps Assn., Chgo. Farmers (bd. dirs. 1989), Assn. Am. Rhodes Scholars, Indian Hill Country Club, Univ. Club Chgo., Phi Beta Kappa. Home and Office: 231 Forest St Winnetka IL 60093-3856

MCMILLER, ANITA WILLIAMS, army officer, transportation professional, educator; b. Chgo., Dec. 23, 1946; d. Chester Leon and Marion Claudette (Martin) Williams; m. Robert Melvin McMiller, July 29, 1967 (div. 1980). BS in Edn., No. Ill. U., 1968; MBA, Fla. Inst. Tech., 1979; M of Mil. Arts and Sci., U.S. Army Command & Gen. Staff Coll., 1990; postgrad., U.S. Army War Coll., Carlisle, Pa., 1993-94. Social worker Cook County, Chgo., 1968-69; recruiter analyst, dir. pers. State of Ill., Chgo., 1969-75; commd. 1st lt. U.S. Army, 1975, advanced through grades to lt. col., 1991; platoon leader, motor officer, exec. officer 155th Transp. Co., Ft. Eustis, Va. and Okinawa, Japan, 1976-78; S-1 pers. and adminstrn. officer 38th Transp. Bn., Ft. Eustis, 1978-79; installation transp. officer, fin. mgr. 3d Armor Div., Hanau, Germany, 1979-82, transp. co. comdr., 1982-83; transp. plans officer Mil. Traffic Mgmt. Command, Falls Church, Va., 1983-85; tour with Sea Land Corp., Menlo Park, N.J., 1985-86; dep. comdr., ops. officer Bremerhaven (Germany) Terminal, 1986-89; logistics staff officer The Pentagon, Washington, 1990-91; comdr. 1320th Port Battalion Mil. Traffic Mgmt. Command, U.K. Terminal, Felixstowe, Great Britain, 1991-93; dep. legis. asst. to chmn. Office Joint Chiefs of Staff, The Pentagon, Washington, 1994—; instr. Ctrl. Tex. Coll., Hanau, Germany, 1981-83, Phillips Bus. Coll., Alexandria, Va., 1983-84, City Colls. Chgo., 1987-89. Editor: Rocks, Inc. Pictoral Album, 1996; contbr. articles to profl. jours. Child adv., foster mother Army Cmty. Svc., Hanau, 1980-83; tutor Parent-Tchr. Club Hanau Schs., 1981-83; vol. Vis. Nurses Assn. No. Va., 1983-85; coord., English tutor Adopt-a-Sch. Project, Washington, 1983-85; treas. Bremerhaven Girl Scouts Coun., 1987-89, mem. ARC. Mem. Nat. Def. Transp. Assn. (world affairs coun.), Assn. U.S. Army, Fedn. Bus. Profl. Women, Club: Rocks, Inc., Am. Legion, British Legion, Alpha Kappa Alpha. Avocations: skiing, golf, running, hist. rsch. Home: PO Box 46344 Washington DC 20050-6344 Office: Office of Chmn Joint Chiefs of Staff The Pentagon Washington DC 20318-9999

MCMILLIAN, THEODORE, federal judge; b. St. Louis, Jan. 28, 1919; m. Minnie E. Foster, Dec. 8, 1941. BS, Lincoln U., 1941, HHD (hon.), 1981; LLD, St. Louis U., 1949; HHD (hon.), U. Mo., St. Louis, 1978. Mem. firm Lynch & McMillian, St. Louis, 1949-53; asst. circuit atty. City of St. Louis, 1953-56; judge U.S. Ct. Appeals (8th cir.), 1978—; judge Circuit Ct. for City St. Louis, 1956-72, Mo. Ct. Appeals eastern div., 1972-78; asso. prof. adminstrn. justice U. Mo., St. Louis, 1970—; asso. prof. Webster Coll. Grad. Program, 1977; mem. faculty Nat. Coll. Juvenile Justice, U. Nev., 1972—. Served to 1st lt. Signal Corps U.S. Army, 1942-46. Recipient Alumni Merit award St. Louis U., 1965, ACLU Civil Liberties award, 1995, Disting. Lawyer award Bar Assn. Met. St. Louis, 1996. Mem. Am. Judicature Soc., Am. Bd. Trial Advs. (hon. diplomate), Lawyers Assn. Mo., Mound City Bar Assn., Phi Beta Kappa, Alpha Sigma Nu. Office: US Ct Appeals 8th Circuit 526 US Ct & Custom House 1114 Market St Saint Louis MO 63101-2043

MCMILLIN, DAVID ROBERT, chemistry educator; b. E. St. Louis, Jan. 1, 1948; s. Robert Cecil and Clara Rose (Thereon) McM.; m. Nicole Wilson, Nov. 3, 1974; children: Robert Stephen, Andrew Wilson. BA, Knox Coll., 1969; PhD, U. Ill., 1973. Postdoctoral fellow Calif. Inst. Tech., Pasadena, 1974; asst. prof. chemistry Purdue U., West Lafayette, Ind., 1975-80, assoc. prof., 1980-85, prof., 1985—. Contbr. articles to profl. jours. Recipient F.D. Martin Teaching award Purdue U., 1975. Mem. Am. Chem. Soc., Inter-Am. Photochem. Soc. (sec. 1986-90, v.p. 1994—), Phi Beta Kappa, Sigma Xi. Presbyterian. Avocations: sports, reading. Office: Purdue U Dept Chemistry West Lafayette IN 47907-1393

MC MILLION, JOHN MACON, retired newspaper publisher; b. Coffeyville, Kans., Dec. 25, 1929; s. John Dibrell and Mattie Anna (Macon) McM.; m. Melanie Ann McMillion; children: John Thomas, Johanna, Jennifer, Amanda. Student, Vanderbilt U., 1947-49; B.S. in Journalism, U. Kans., 1956. Police reporter Amarillo (Tex.) Globe-News, 1956; sports editor, telegraph editor Grand Junction (Colo.) Daily Sentinel, 1956-58; mng. editor Alliance (Nebr.) Times-Herald, 1958-59, Clovis (N.Mex.) Jour., 1959-62; gen. mgr. Pasadena (Tex.) Citizen, 1962; bur. mgr. UPI, 1962-66; exec. editor Albuquerque Jour., 1966-69; bus. mgr. Albuquerque Pub. Co., 1971-75; pub. Herald and News-Tribune, Duluth, Minn., 1975-86, Akron (Ohio) Beacon Jour., 1986-90, ret.; campaign mgr. gubernatorial campaign, 1969-71. Served with USN, 1950-54. Address: 12404 Royal Oak Ct NE Albuquerque NM 87111-6237

MCMINDES, ROY JAMES, aggregate company executive; b. Essex, Md., July 12, 1923; s. Roy Preston and Edith S. (Sh) McM.; m. Prudence Atsinger, June 8, 1946; children: Gail Karen, Joan Susan, James Lee. B.S., U. Md., 1948. Pres., Sheridan Corp., Lebanon, Pa., 1951—, Grays Ferry Brick Co., Lebanon, 1971—; pres., Waylite Co., Lebanon, 1976-88; pres. Sheridan Co., Lebanon, PA; chmn. bd. Peoples Nat. Bank, Lebanon, 1984-92, dir., 1965-92. Bd. dirs. Lebanon YMCA, 1968-86, Good Samaritan Hosp., Lebanon, 1970-93. With A.C., USN, 1943-46, mem. USNR, 1946-52. Recipient Founders Day award Lebanon Valley Coll., 1987. Mem. Lebanon Valley C. of C. (pres. 1973), Lebanon Country Club, Shriners, Jesters. Republican. Presbyterian. Office: 1212 W Maple St Lebanon PA 17046-2701

MCMINN, VIRGINIA ANN, human resources consulting company executive; b. Champaign, Ill., Apr. 7, 1948; d. Richard Henry and Esther Lucille (Ellis) Taylor; m. Michael Lee McMinn, Dec. 29, 1973. BA in Teaching of English, U. Ill., 1969; MS in Indsl. Rels., Loyola U., Chgo., 1985. Pers. sec. Solo Cup Co., Urbana, Ill., 1972-74; pers. asst. Rust-Oleum Corp., Evanston, Ill., 1974-75, asst. pers. mgr., 1974-80; mgr. employee rels. Rust-Oleum Corp., Vernon Hills, Ill., 1980-81, mgr. human resources, 1981-84; dir. human resources Field Container Corp., Elk Grove Village, Ill., 1984-87; regional mgr. human resources Hartford Ins. Corp., Chgo., 1987-90; owner, pres. McMinn & Assocs., Ltd., Palatine, Ill., 1988—; founder S.W. Human Resources Group, Chandler, Ariz., 1995; instr. bus. and mgmt. divsn. Trinity Coll., Deerfield, Ill., 1984-85; instr. bus. and social scis. Harper Coll., Palatine, Ill., 1990-93; bd. dirs. Nierman's Hard-To-Find Sizes Shoes, Chgo.; spkr. on legal issues, terminations, employment at will, career planning, job search, and human resources function to area colls., industry and profl. and women's groups. Bd. dirs. Ill. Crossroads coun. Girls Scouts USA, Elk Grove, 1988-92; mem. Ill. Com. to Implement Clean Indoor Air Act, Chgo., 1990-91; past mem. adv. bd. Coll. of Lake County, 1982-84. Mem. Soc. for Human Resource Mgmt., Nat. Network Sales Profls. (program chmn. 1990-93), Women in Mgmt. (chpt. Leadership award corp. category, past pres.), Palatine C. of C., Rotary Club Palatine. Avocations: reading, golf, crafts. Office: 1423 Michele Dr Palatine IL 60067-5656

MCMINN, WILLIAM A., chemicals company executive; b. 1931. With FMC Corp., Chgo., 1967-85, Cain Chemical Co., Kearney, N.J., 1987-88; chmn., dir. Arcadian Corp., Memphis, 1989—; dir. Sterling Chems., Houston. Office: Arcadian Corp 6750 Poplar Ave Ste 600 Memphis TN 38138-7424*

MCMORRIS, JERRY, transportation company executive. CEO NW Transport Svc, Denver. Office: NW Transport Svc 717 17th St Ste 500 Denver CO 80202

MCMORROW, RICHARD MARK, holding company executive; b. Boston, Aug. 8, 1941; s. J. Edward and Marie L. (Martine) McM.; m. Ursula M. Rodgers, Apr. 24, 1965; children: Ethan Rodgers, Juliet Marie. Student, Northeastern U., 1959-61, Bentley Coll., Waltham, Mass., 1962-65; J.D., New Eng. Sch. Law, Boston, 1968. Bar: Mass. 1971. With Commonwealth Energy Co., Cambridge, Mass., 1969-76; sec. Commonwealth Energy Co., 1973-76, Columbus So. Power Co., Columbus, 1976-79; v.p. law and risk mgmt. Columbus So. Power Co., 1979—; asst. v.p. Am. Electric Power, 1983-94; pres. CoconaRsch. Corp., Columbus, 1994-96; pres., CEO, Camac Co., Nantucket, Mass., 1996—; bd. dirs. Elford Inc., System Sports Inc. Trustee Columbus Zoo, Ctr. Sci. and Industry,, Columbus, Ballet Met., Columbus, Columbus Assn. for Performing Arts; chmn. bd. trustees Grant Med. Ctr. Found., Nat. Safety Coun., Columbus. With USCGR, 1963-68. Mem. ABA, Ohio Bar Assn., Mass. Bar Assn., Columbus C. of C., Rotary. Office: Camac Co 32 Main St Nantucket MA 02554

MCMULKIN, FRANCIS JOHN, steel company executive; b. Sault Ste. Marie, Ont., Can., Dec. 7, 1915; s. George Alexander and Leanor Augusta (Zryd) McM.; m. Margaret Lilian Winch, Sept. 21, 1946; children: John Bruce, Mary Diane. B.S. in Metallurgy, Mich. Coll. Mining and Tech., 1937; M.E., Mich. Tech. U., 1945, D.Engring. (hon.), 1972. Formerly metallurgist Algoma Steel Corp., Sault Ste. Marie; then research fellow Ont. Research Found., Mississauga, 1942-47; research and devel. engr. Dominion Foundries & Steel Ltd., Hamilton, Ont., Can., from 1947; then dir. research Dominion Foundries & Steel Ltd., until 1964, v.p. research, 1964-85. Contbr. articles to profl. publs. Recipient Disting. Alumnus award Mich. Tech. U., 1976. Fellow Am. Soc. Metals (life mem., William Hunt Eisenman award 1968), Engring. Inst. Can. (life mem., John Galbraith prize 1945); mem. Can. Inst. Mining and Metallurgy (H.T. Airey Meml. Ann. Conf. lectr. award), AIME (Basic Oxygen Steel award 1963; charter disting. mem. Iron and Steel Soc. 1976, Metall. Soc. Howe meml. lectr. 1973), Iron and Steel Inst., U.K., Royal Over-Seas League (London), Hamilton Club, Hamilton Golf and Country Club, Mid Ocean Club (Bermuda). Mem. United Ch. of Canada. Home: 270 Roseland Crescent, Burlington, ON Canada L7N 1S3 Office: PO Box 2460, Hamilton, ON Canada L8N 3J5

MC MULLAN, DOROTHY, nurse educator; b. Bloomfield, N.J., June 19, 1911; d. Samuel H. and Anne (Gardiner) McM.; m. Bernard J. Pisani, July 10, 1982. Diploma, Cornell U.-N.Y. Hosp. Sch. Nursing, 1935; B.S., N.Y. U., 1948, M.A., 1950, Ed.D., 1962. Pub. health nurse Henry St. Vis. Nurse Service, N.Y.C., 1935-39; pvt. duty nurse N.Y.C., 1939-41; instr. N.Y. Hosp.-Cornell U. Sch. Nursing, 1947-55; supr. N.Y. Hosp.-Cornell Med. Center, 1947-50, asst. dept. head, 1950-53, adminstrv. asst. nursing services for methods improvements, 1953-55; instr. N.Y. Hosp.-Cornell Med. Center (Sch. Nursing); dir., prof. nursing Russell Sage Coll., 1955-61; dean, prof. Ind. State U. Sch. Nursing, Terre Haute, 1962-71; dir. div. nursing Nat. League for Nursing, N.Y.C., 1971-77; chmn. dept. baccalaureate and higher edn. N.Y. League, 1960-62; mem. Nat. Commn. on Allied Health Edn., 1977-80; cons. on nurse edn., 1977-80; cons. Council on Postsecondary Accreditation, 1977-78; v.p. N.Y. Nurses Assn., 1960-61; pres. Vigo County Coordinating Council, 1966-69; mem. adv. bd. Ind. Regional Med. Planning, 1966-71; sec. exec. com. Ind. Comprehensive Health Council, 1967-71; mem. adv. com. on women in services U.S. Dept. Def., 1971-73; mem. nursing adv. com. Am. Cancer Soc., 1975-77; mem. com. on health manpower Nat. Health Council, 1975-79. Author: (with Hayt, Groeschel) Law of Hospital and Nurse, 1958, The Role of the Nurse as Employee: A Case of Mutual Responsibilities, 1976, Preparation of the Nurse Specialist, 1977. Bd. dirs. Vigo County cancer Soc., Vigo County cerebral Palsy Assn., Goodwill Industries Terre Haute, Cmty. Found. Wabash Valley, 1964-71; mem. Heritage Found.; mem. coun. Citizens Against Govt. Waste. Recipient Ann. award of Vigo County Ind. Bus. and Profl. Women's Orgn., 1967, Army Nurse Corps Spl. award, 1973, Dept. of Def. cert., NYU Founders Day cert., 1963, Pres.'s award Ind. State U., 1988, Disting. Alumnus award Cornell U./N.Y. Hosp. Sch. Nursing Alumni Assn., 1990; recognized for disting. and devoted svc. as pres. Ind. League for Nursing, 1966-71; named in People of Progress in Terre Haute, 1967. Mem. APHA, Cornell U.-N.Y. Hosp. Sch. Nursing Alumnae Assn. (pres. 1950-52), Ind. League for Nursing (pres. 1966-71), So. N.Y. League for Nursing (pres. 1980-82, exec. sec. 1982-88, award 1987, Dorothy McMullan Pisani ann. award 1987), League Nursing (mem. exec. com., chmn. Gt. Lakes Regional Assembly 1969-71), Nat. League Nursing (bd. dirs. 1981-83), Assn. Higher Edn., Inst. Biomed. Edn. (bd. dirs. 1984-89), Am. Assn. for World Health (exec. com. 1980-90, exec. 1984-89), N.Y. County Med. Soc. Auxiliary (v.p. 1984-90), Kappa Delta Pi. Republican. Episcopalian. Home: 209 Sunset Ave Englewood NJ 07631-4413 *The important ingredients to success include self reliance, identifying goals and how* *to reach them through perseverance, willingness t work hard and to enjoy every step of the way.*

MCMULLAN, WILLIAM PATRICK, III, investment banker; b. Newton, Miss., Dec. 29, 1952; s. William Patrick Jr. and Rosemary (Lyons) McM.; m. Rachel Smiley McPherson, Oct. 16, 1982. BA, Vanderbilt U., 1974; MBA, U. Pa., 1976. V.p. Lehman Bros. Kuhn Loeb, N.Y.C., 1976-82; assoc. dir. Prudential-Bache Securities, N.Y.C., 1982-85; mng. dir. Donaldson, Lufkin & Jenrette Securities Corp., N.Y.C., 1985—. Mem. Metropolitan Club, Mashomack Fish and Game Club, Lawrence Beach Club. Home: 607 6th St Brooklyn NY 11215-3701 Office: Donaldson Lufkin & Jenrette Securities Corp 140 Broadway New York NY 10005-1101

MC MULLEN, EDWIN WALLACE, JR., English language educator; b. Quincy, Fla., Dec. 8, 1915; s. Edwin Wallace and Sara Della (Moore) McM.; m. Marian Elizabeth Hoper, June 9, 1946; children: William Wallace, Charles Edwin. B.A., U. Fla., 1936; M.A., Columbia U., 1939, Ph.D., 1950. Instr. English Pa. State U., 1946-48, State U. Iowa, 1950-52; spl. instr. in report writing U.S. Dept. Def., Washington, 1953; sr. reporter U.S. Dept. Def., 1952-57; asst. editor Merriam Webster Dictionary Co., 1957; asst. prof. English Lehigh U., 1957-61, Fairleigh Dickinson U., Madison, N.J., 1961-62; assoc. prof. Fairleigh Dickinson U., 1962-72, prof., 1973-82, chmn. dept. lang. and lit., 1962-65, emeritus, 1982; founder, dir. Names Inst., 1962-86; chmn. publs. subcom. Morris County Tercentenary Com., N.J., 1962-63. Author: English Topographic Terms in Florida, 1563-1874, 1953; contbr. articles to profl. publs.; editor: Names, 1962-65; editor, contbr.: Pubs, Place-Names and Patronymics: Selected Papers of the Names Institute, 1980; editor, contbr. Names New and Old: Papers of the Names Inst., 1993. Served with Signal Corps, U.S. Army, 1942-46. Mem. MLA, Am. Name Soc. (pres. 1976), Internat. Congress on Onomastic Scis., Internat. Linguistic Assn., Am. Dialect Soc., English Place-Name Soc., Morris County Hist. Soc., Old Guard of Summit (N.J.), Nat. Coun. Tchrs. English, Meth. Friendship Club (past co-pres.). Democrat. Methodist. Home: 15 Rosewood Dr Madison NJ 07940-1120 Office: Fairleigh Dickinson U English Dept Madison NJ 07940 *Chaucer sums up my philosophy in his description of the Clerk: "And gladly wolde he lerne and gladly teche."*.

MCMULLEN, JOHN J., professional hockey team executive; m. Jacqueline McMullen; children: Peter, Catharine, John Jr. BSEE, U.S. Naval Acad., 1940; DMechE, Swiss Fed. Tech. Inst.; M in Naval Architecture and Marine Engring., MIT. Commd. ensign USN, 1940, advanced through grades to comdr., resigned, 1954; chief ship constrn. and repair U.S. Maritime Adminstrn. Office, Washington, 1954-57; chmn. John J. McMullen Assocs., Inc., 1957—; ltd. ptnr. N.Y. Yankees Baseball Team, 1974; chmn. Houston Astros Baseball Team, 1979-92, N.J. Devils Hockey Team, East Rutherford, N.J., 1981—. Office: NJ Devils PO Box 504 East Rutherford NJ 07073-0504*

MC MULLEN, THOMAS HENRY, retired air force officer; b. Dayton, Ohio, July 4, 1929; s. Clements and Adelaide Palmer (Lewis) McM.; m. Clara Faye Kirkwood, Mar. 28, 1956; children—Susan Marie, Thomas Clements, John Kirkwood. Student, St. Mary's U. Tex., 1945-47; B.S. in Mil. Engring, U.S. Mil. Acad., 1951; M.S. in Astronautics, Air Force Inst. Tech., 1964; M.S. in Adminstrn, George Washington U., 1971; student, Indsl. Coll. Armed Forces, Ft. McNair, Washington, 1970-71. Commd. 2d lt. U.S. Air Force, 1951, advanced through grades to lt. gen., 1980; flight trainee Hondo AB, Tex., Bryan AFB, Tex. and Nellis AFB, Nev., 1951-52; fighter pilot/flight comdr. (K-13 AB), Suwon, Korea, 1952-53; flight test maintenance officer Kelly AFB, Tex., 1953-59; Air Force flight acceptance test pilot at (Gen. Dynamics Inc.), Ft. Worth, 1959-62; project officer, Gemini Launch Vehicle Program, officer (Space Systems Div.), Los Angeles, 1964-66; air liaison officer 25th Inf. Div. Cu Chi, South Vietnam, 1967-68; asst. mission dir. Apollo Program Hdqrs. NASA Washington, 1968-70; B-1 dep. system program dir. Wright Patterson AFB, Ohio, 1971-73; A-10 System program dir., 1973-74; vice comdr. Tactical Air Warfare Center Eglin AFB, Fla., 1974-75; comdr. (Tactical Air Warfare Center), 1975-76; dep. chief of staff/requirements Hdqrs. Tactical Air Command Langley AFB, Va., 1976-79; dep. chief of staff/systems Hdqrs. Air Force Systems Command Andrews AFB, Md., 1979-80; vice comdr. Tactical Air Command, 1980-82; comdr. Aero. Systems Div. Wright-Patterson AFB, Ohio, 1982-86; ret. USAF, 1986; cons. in aerospace Washington, 1986—. Decorated D.S.M. with two oak leaf clusters, Silver Star, Legion of Merit, D.F.C. with oak leaf cluster, Bronze Star, Meritorious Service medal with oak leaf cluster, Air Force Commendation medal with oak leaf cluster, Air medal with 18 oak leaf clusters, Purple Heart; Cross of Gallantry with palm Vietnam; recipient Exceptional Service medal NASA, 1969, Group Achievement award, 1969, 71. Fellow AIAA (asso.); mem. Air Force Assn., Order Daedalians, Tau Beta Pi. Presbyterian. Home and Office: 6301 Chaucer View Cir Alexandria VA 22304-3548 *The key to success is a combination of fortunate circumstance, hard work, and a willingness to accept responsibility. Few people get ahead without some combination of all three.*

MC MULLIAN, AMOS RYALS, food company executive; b. Jackson County, Fla., Aug. 28, 1937; s. Andrew Jackson and Willie Ross (Ryals) McM.; m. Jackie Williams, Aug. 27, 1960; children: Amos Ryals, Britton Jackelyn. BS, Fla. State U., 1962. Successively asst. controller, data processing coordinator, adminstrv. asst. to gen. mgr., asst. plant mgr., plant mgr. Flowers Baking Co., Thomasville, Ga., 1963-70, pres. Atlanta Baking Co. div., 1970-72, regional v.p. parent co., 1972-74, pres., chief operating officer bakery div., 1974-76, chief operating officer industry, 1976-81, pres., 1976-83, dir., 1981—, chief exec. officer, 1983—, co-chmn. exec. com., 1983—, vice chmn. industry and chmn. exec. com., 1984-85, chmn. bd., CEO, 1985—; bd. dirs. Ga. Rsch. Reliance. Mem. adv. bd. President's Club, Fla. State U.; trustee Southeastern Legal Found.; vestryman, sr. warden Episcopal Ch.; bd. govs. Ga. Pub. Policy Found. With USMC, 1958-61. Named Outstanding Bus. Alumnus, Fla. State U. Mem. NAM (bd. dirs.), Thomasville Landmarks Soc., Atlanta Bakers Club (past pres.), Atlanta Commerce Club, Gridiron Soc. (U. Ga.). Office: Flowers Industries Inc PO Box 1338 Thomasville GA 31799

MCMULLIN, CARLETON EUGENE, automotive business executive; b. Hutchinson, Kans., Feb. 17, 1932; s. Cloys E. and Beatrice (Jennings) McM.; m. Beth Becker; children: Lucinda Lou, Charis Ann. B.A., U. Okla., 1954; M.P.A., U. Kans., 1958. Asst. city mgr. City of Corpus Christi, Tex., 1957-58; city mgr. City of McAlester, Okla., 1958-62, City of Oak Ridge, Tenn., 1962-73, City of Little Rock, 1973-80; pres. NPT, Inc., 1994; pres. Keystone Enterprises Inc., Cemac Corp., Exceltune Corp.; v.p., treas. Devonian Corp.; sec. Precision Tune Franchise Adv. Coun., 1979-80; chmn. Assn. Precision Tune Area Sub-Franchisors, 1979-80, sec., 1991; mem. intergovtl. sci. engring. tech. adv. panel U.S. Office Sci. and Tech. Policy, 1977-79; mem. NSF Adv. Coun., 1977-79; chmn. Urban Tech. Sys. Adv. Bd., 1979; cons. in field. Commr. Little Rock Housing Authority, 1987-92. Served with Signal Corps U.S. Army, 1954-56. Mem. Internat. City Mgmt. Assn., Rotary. Episcopalian. Home: 12821 Ridgehaven Rd Little Rock AR 72211-2207

MC MULLIN, ERNAN VINCENT, philosophy educator; b. Donegal, Ireland, Oct. 13, 1924; came to U.S., 1954; s. Vincent Paul and Carmel (Farrell) McM. BSc, Maynooth (Ireland) Coll., 1945, BD, 1948; postgrad. theoretical physics, Dublin Inst. Advanced Studies, 1949-50; BPh, U. Louvain, Belgium, 1951, LPh, 1953, PhD, 1954; DLitt (hon.), Loyola U., Chgo., 1969, Nat. U. Ireland, 1990; PhD (hon.), Maynooth Coll., Ireland, 1995. Ordained priest Roman Catholic Ch., 1949; faculty U. Notre Dame, 1954-57, 59—, assoc. prof. philosophy, 1964, prof. philosophy, 1966-94, prof. emeritus, 1994—, chmn. dept., 1965-72, O'Hara prof. philosophy, 1984-94; postdoctoral fellow Yale U., 1957-59; vis. prof. U. Minn., 1964-65, U. Cape Town, summers 1972-73, UCLA, 1977, Princeton U., 1991, Yale U., 1992; Cardinal Mercier lectr. U. Louvain, Belgium, 1995; mem. exec. bd. Coun. Philos. Studies, 1970-75; chmn. philosophy of sci. div. Internat. Congress Philosophy, 1968, 73; chmn. U.S. Nat. Com. for History and Philosophy of Sci., 1982-84, 86-87. Author: Newton on Matter and Activity, 1978, The Inference That Makes Science, 1992; editor: The Concept of Matter, 1963, Galileo, Man of Science, 1967, The Concept of Matter in Modern Philosophy, 1978, Death and Decision, 1978, Issues in Computer Diagnosis, 1983, Evolution and Creation, 1985, Construction and Constraint: The Shaping of Scientific Rationality; co-editor: (with J.T. Cushing) The Philosophical Consequences of Quantum Theory, 1989, The Social Dimensions of Science, 1992; cons. editor Jour. Medicine and Philosophy, 1977-93 , Studies History and Philosophy of Science, 1970-75, 1983—, Brit. Jour. Philos. Sci., 1988—, Perspectives on Science, 1992—. Romanell-Phi Beta Kappa Prof. of Philosophy, 1993-94; NSF rsch. grantee Yale U., 1957-59, Cambridge U., 1968-69; vis. rsch. fellow Cambridge U., 1973-74, 83, 87, U. Pitts., 1979. Fellow AAAS (chmn. sect. L 1977-78), Am. Acad. Arts and Scis., Internat. Acad. History Sci.; mem. Am. Cath. Philos. Assn. (pres. 1966-67, Aquinas medal 1981), Philosophy of Sci. Assn. (governing bd. 1969-73, pres. 1980-82), Metaphys. Assn. Am. (exec. coun. 1968-72, pres. 1973-74), Am. Philos. Assn. (exec. coun. 1977-81, pres. western divsn. 1983-84), History of Sci. Soc. (exec. coun. 1988-92), Sigma Xi. Address: PO Box 1066 Notre Dame IN 46556-1066

MCMULLIN, RUTH RONEY, publishing company executive, management fellow; b. N.Y.C., Feb. 9, 1942; d. Richard Thomas and Virginia (Goodwin) Roney; m. Thomas Ryan McMullin, Apr. 27, 1968; 1 child, David Patrick. BA, Conn. Coll., 1963; M Pub. and Pvt. Mgmt., Yale U., 1979. Market rschr. Aviation Week Mag., McGraw-Hill Co., N.Y.C., 1962-64; assoc. editor, bus. mgr. Doubleday & Co., N.Y.C., 1964-66; mgr. Natural History Press, 1967-70; v.p., treas. Weston (Conn.) Woods, Inc., 1970-71; staff assoc. GE, Fairfield, Conn., 1979-82; mng. fin. analyst GECC Transp., Stamford, Conn., 1982-84; credit analyst corp. fin. dept. GECC, Stamford, Conn., 1984-85; sr. v.p. GECC Capital Markets Group, Inc., N.Y.C., 1985-87; exec. v.p., COO John Wiley & Sons, N.Y.C., 1987-89, pres., CEO, 1989-90; pres., CEO Harvard Bus. Sch. Pub. Corp., Boston, 1991-94; mem. chmn.'s com., acting CEO UNR Industries Inc., Chgo., 1991-92, also bd. dirs.; mgmt. fellow, vis. prof. Sch. Mgmt. Yale U., New Haven, 1994-95; now bus. cons.; bd. dirs. Bausch & Lomb, Rochester, N.Y., UNR Industries Inc., Chgo., Middlesex (Conn.) Mut. Assurance, Fleet Financial, 1992-94; vis. prof. Sch. Mgmt., Yale U., New Haven, 1994-95. Mem. dean's adv. bd. Sch. Mgmt. Yale U.; bd. dirs. Yale U. Alumni fund, 1986-92, Yale U. Press, Math. Scis. Edn. Bd., 1990-93. Mem. N.Y. Yacht Club, Stamford Yacht Club. Avocations: sailing, skiing. Home: 274 Beacon St Boston MA 02116-1230

MCMURPHY, MICHAEL ALLEN, energy company executive, lawyer; b. Dothan, Ala., Oct. 1, 1947; s. Allen L. and Mary Emily (Jacobs) McM.; m. Maureen Daly, Aug. 8, 1970; children: Matthew, Kevin, Patrick. BS, USAF Acad., 1969; MA, St. Mary's U., San Antonio, 1972; JD, U. Tex., 1975. Bar: Tex. 1975, U.S. Supreme Ct. 1977, U.S. Ct. Appeals (fed. cir.), D.C. 1978. Commd. 2d lt. USAF, 1969, advanced through grades to capt.; instr. Air U., Ala., 1975-79; resigned USAF, 1979; atty., advisor Oak Ridge (Tenn.) ops. U.S. Dept. Energy, 1979-83; gen. counsel COGEMA, Inc., Washington, 1983-87, v.p., 1987-88; pres., chief exec. officer COGEMA, Inc., Bethesda, Md., 1988—; pres., CEO Va. Fuels, Inc., Lynchburg, 1987-92; bd. dirs. Nuc. Energy Inst., Washington, B&W Fuel Co., Lynchburg, U.G./USA, Atlanta, Transnuclear, Inc., Hawthorne, N.Y., Cogema Resources, Inc., Casper, Wyo.; chmn. Numatec Inc., Bethesda, 1989—; pres. Uranium Producers Am., 1991-92. Mem. editorial bd. Air Force Law Rev., 1977-79. Decorated chevalier Nat. Order of Merit (France). Mem. ABA, Fed. Bar Assn. (pres. E. Tenn. chpt. 1982-83). Avocation: skiing. Office: COGEMA Inc 7401 Wisconsin Ave Bethesda MD 20814

MCMURRAY, WILLIAM, consultant, retired electrical engineer; b. Los Angeles, Aug. 15, 1929; s. William Arthur and Genevieve Leona (Arnold) McM.; m. Marion Elizabeth Schnipp, Oct. 22, 1955; children: William B., Shirley A., Robert C., Barbara C. BSc in Engring. with first class honors, Battersea Poly., London, 1950; MS, Union Coll., 1956; LLD (hon.), Concordia U., Montreal, Que., Can., 1986. Test engr. Gen. Electric, Pittsfield, Mass., 1950-51; elec. engr. corp. rsch. and devel. Gen. Electric, Schenectady, N.Y., 1953-88; cons., 1989—. Author: Theory and Design of Cycloconverters, 1972; contbg. author: Principles of Inverter Circuits, 1964; patentee in field; contbr. 28 articles to profl. jours. Chmn. troop 31 Boy Scouts Am., Schenectady, 1973. Served as pvt. U.S. Army, 1951-53. Recipient William Newell award Power Electronics Specialists Conf., 1978. Fellow IEEE (Magnetics Soc., chmn. static power converter com. Industry Applications Soc. 1982-83, Centennial medal 1984, Lamme medal 1984), Instn. Elec. Engrs. (assoc.). Republican. Avocations: canoeing, archaeology. Office: Cons Engr PO Box 741 Schenectady NY 12301-0741

MCMURRY, IDANELLE SAM, educational consultant; b. Morganfield, Ky., Dec. 6, 1924; d. Sam Anderson and Aurelia Marie (Robertson) McM. B.A., Vanderbilt U., 1945, M.A., 1946. Tchr. English Abbot Acad., Andover, Mass., 1946-50, Hockaday Sch., Dallas, 1951-54, San Jacinto High Sch., Houston, 1954-55; dean of girls Kinkaid Sch., Houston, 1955-63; headmistress Harpeth Hall Sch., Nashville, 1963-79, Hockaday Sch., Dallas, 1979-89, ret.; now pvt. sch. cons. The Edn. Group, Dallas; Bd. dirs. Ednl. Records Bur., 1979-85, trustee, 1980-85. Bd. dirs. Tex. council Girl Scouts U.S., 1980-82, Town North YMCA; trustee Winston Sch., 1979-85, Spl. Care Sch., 1979-81, Asheville Sch., Manzano Day Sch. Mem. Nat. Study Sch. Evaluation (bd. dirs. 1979-83), Headmasters Assn., Nat. Assn. Ind. Schs. (bd. dirs. 1974-84, acad. com. 1974-79, sec. 1978-80, chmn. 1980-84), So. Assn. Ind. Schs. (pres. 1974-75), Tenn. Assn. Ind. Schs. (pres. 1967-68), Mid-South Assn. Ind. Schs. (pres. 1972-73), Ind. Schs. Assn. S.W. (v.p. 1967—), Nat. Assn. Prins. Schs. for Girls (sec. 1970-72, pres. 1975-77, coun. 1970-79), Nat. Assn. Secondary Sch. Prins., Country Day Sch. Headmasters Assn. (exe. com. 1984-87, v.p. 1988-89), So. Assn. Colls. and Schs. (adminstrv. coun. 1974-77, ctrl. reviewing com. 1972-77, vice chmn. secondary commn. 1975-76, chmn. 1976-77, bd. dirs. 1976-81), Ladies Hermitage Assn., Vanderilt Aid Soc. (sec. 1971-73, pres. 1994-96), Ind. Edn. Svcs. (trustee 1980-88, chmn. 1986-88), Susan Komen Found. (adv. bd.), Belle Meade Club, Centennial Club, Phi Beta Kappa, Pi Beta Phi. Republican. Presbyterian. Office: 5 Strawberry Hl Nashville TN 37215-4118

MCMURRY, JOHN EDWARD, chemistry educator; b. N.Y.C., July 27, 1942; s. Edward and Marguerite Ann (Hotchkiss) McM.; m. Susan Elizabeth Sobuta, Sept. 4, 1964; children—Peter Michael, David Andrew, Paul Matthew. B.A., Harvard U., 1964; M.A., Columbia U., 1965, Ph.D., 1967. Prof. chemistry U. Calif., Santa Cruz, 1967-80, Cornell U., Ithaca, N.Y., 1980—. Author: Organic Chemistry, 1984, Chemistry, 1995 and other textbooks. Assoc. editor Accounts of Chem. Research, 1975-95. Recipient Humboldt Sr. Sci. award, 1987; Sloan Found. fellow, 1969-71; Career awardee NIH, 1975-80. Fellow AAAS; mem. Am. Chem. Soc. Home: 625 Highland Rd Ithaca NY 14850-1411 Office: Cornell Univ Dept Chemistry Baker Lab Ithaca NY 14853

MCMURTRY, BURTON JOHN, venture capital investor, electrical engineer; b. Houston, Mar. 26, 1935; s. James G. and Alberta Elizabeth (Matteson) McM.; m. Ann Kathryn Meck, June 9, 1956; children—Cathryn Ann, John Eric. BA, Rice U., 1956, BSEE, 1957; MSEE, Stanford U., 1959, Ph.D. in Elec. Engring. (Raytheon fellow), 1962. Engr. Microwave Tube div. Sylvania, Mountain View, Calif., 1957-62; rsch. asst. Stanford U., 1960-62; head lab. rsch. and devel. in electro-optics GTE, Sylvania, Mountain View, 1962-66; mgr. Equipment Engring. Labs., 1967-68; dir., gen. mgr. electro-optics orgn. Sylvania Electronic Systems, 1968-69; asso. Jack L. Melchor (personal venture capital investment bus.), Los Altos, Calif., 1969-70; pres. Palo Alto Investment Co., Calif., 1970-73; gen. partner Dennis, Jamieson & McMurtry, Menlo Park, Calif., 1973—, TVI Mgmt., TVI Mgmt.-2, TVI Mgmt.-3, TVI IV, Menlo Park, 1980—; bd. dirs. Aradigm, Edify, E.O Networks, Intuit, Spectralink. Contbr. articles, chpts. to electronics publs., mainly on microwave tubes, lasers, optical detectors. Bd. dirs. El Camino Hosp. Found.; elder Menlo Park Presbyn. Ch.; mem. major gifts com. Stanford U.; trustee Rice U. Recipient Alfred Noble prize, 1964. Fellow IEEE; mem. Nat. Venture Capital Assn. (pres. 1986-87, chmn. 1987-88), Western Assn. Venture Capitalists (pres. 1972-73), Am. Phys. Soc., Optical Soc. Am., Sigma Xi (sr. award 1957), Sigma Tau, Tau Beta Pi. Home: 7 Coal Mine Vw Menlo Park CA 94028-8016 Office: Tech Venture Investors 2480 Sand Hill Rd # 101 Menlo Park CA 94025-7116

MC MURTRY, JAMES GILMER, III, neurosurgeon; b. Houston, June 11, 1932; s. James Gilmer and Alberta Elizabeth (Matteson) McM.; student Rice U., Houston, 1950-53; M.D. cum laude, Baylor U., Houston, 1957. Intern, Hosp. U. Pa., Phila., 1957-58; resident gen. surgery Baylor U. Affiliated Hosps., Houston, 1958-59; asst. neurol. surgery Coll. Physicians and Surgeons, Columbia U., N.Y.C., 1959-60; asst. resident neurol. surgery and neurology Neurol. Inst. N.Y., Columbia Presbyn. Med. Center, N.Y.C., 1960-62, chief resident neurol. surgery, 1962-63; Nat. Inst. Neurol. Disease and Blindness spl. fellow neurol. surgery Coll. Physicians and Surgeons, Columbia U., N.Y.C., 1963-64, instr. neurol. surgery, 1963-65, assoc., 1965-68, asst. prof. clin. neurol. surgery, 1968-73, assoc. prof., 1973-89, prof., 1989—; asst. attending neurol. surgeon Neurol. Inst. N.Y., N.Y.C., 1964-73, assoc. attending neurol. surgeon, 1973-89, attending neurol. surgeon, 1989—; chief neurol. surgery clinic Vanderbilt Clinic, Columbia Presbyn. Med. Center, N.Y.C., 1964-68; attending-in-charge neurosurgery Lenox Hill Hosp., N.Y.C., 1970-91; assoc. cons. neurol. surgery Englewood (N.J.) Hosp., 1964—; asst. cons. neurol. surgery Harlem Hosp., N.Y.C., 1964—; cons. neurol. surgery Bronx (N.Y.) VA Hosp., 1964-65; mem. NIH Parkinson Research Group, Columbia U., 1965—; mem. med. adv. bd. N.Y. State Athletic Commn. Jesse H. Jones scholar Baylor U. Coll. Medicine, 1953-57, Allen fellow dept. neurol. surgery Columbia U., 1964-65. Diplomate Am. Bd. Neurol. Surgery. Fellow ACS, Linnean Soc. (London); trustee Glimmerglass Opera, Morris-Jumel, Opera Manhattan. Mem. AAUP, AAAS, AMA, Am. Assn. Neurol. Surgeons, European Congress Pediatric Neurosurgery, Am. Soc. Stereotaxic Surgeons, Pan Am. Med. Assn., N.Y. State Soc. Surgeons, N.Y. State Neurosurgery Soc., N.Y. Acad. Sci., N.Y. Neurosurg. Soc., Med. Soc. State N.Y., N.Y. County Med. Soc., Osler Soc., Baylor U. Coll. Medicine Alumni Assn., Med. Strollers, The Med. Soc. of London, The Harveian Soc., Alpha Omega Alpha. Presbyn. Clubs: The Union (N.Y.C.), The Garrick (London), The Atheneum (London), The Met. Opera (N.Y.C.), The Norfolk Yacht and Country. Author: Medical Examination Review Book-Neurological Surgery, 1970, rev. edit., 1975; Neurological Surgery Case Histories, 1975; contbr. articles to profl. jours. Home: 1 Cobb Ln Tarrytown NY 10591-3003 Office: 710 W 168th St New York NY 10032-2603

MCMURTRY, LARRY JEFF, author; b. Wichita Falls, Tex., June 3, 1936; s. William Jefferson and Hazel Ruth (McIver) McM.; m. Josephine Ballard, July 15, 1959 (div. 1966); 1 child, James. BA, N.Tex. State Coll., 1958; MA, Rice U., 1960. Instr. Tex. Christian U., Ft. Worth, 1961-62; lectr. in English and creative writing Rice U., Houston, 1963-69; co-owner Booked Up Book Store, Washington, from 1970; vis. prof. George Mason Coll., 1970, Am. Univ., 1970-71. Author: (novels) Horseman, Pass By, 1961 (Jesse H. Jones award Texas Inst. of Letters 1962), Leaving Cheyenne, 1963, The Last Picture Show, 1966, Moving On, 1970, All My Friends Are Going to be Strangers, 1972, Terms of Endearment, 1975, Somebody's Darling, 1978, Cadillac Jack, 1982, The Desert Rose, 1983, Lonesome Dove, 1985 (Pulitzer prize for fiction 1986), Texasville, 1987, Anything for Billy, 1988, Some Can Whistle, 1989, Buffalo Girls, 1990, The Evening Star, 1992, Streets of Laredo, 1993, (with Diana Ossana) Pretty Boy Floyd, 1994, The Late Child, 1995, Dead Man's Walk, 1995; (essays) In a Narrow Grave: Essays on Texas, 1968, It's Always We Rambled: An Essay on Rodeo, 1974, Film Flam: Essays on Hollywood, 1987; screenwriter: (with Peter Bogdonovich) The Last Picture Show, 1971 (Academy award nomination best adapted screenplay 1971), Texasville, 1990, Montana, 1990, Falling From Grace, 1992, (with Cybill Shepard) Memphis, 1992; also articles, essays, book revs. in N.Y. Times, Saturday Rev., Washington Post, Am. Film, others. Wallace Stegner fellow, 1960, Guggenheim fellow, 1964; recipient Barbara McCombs/Lon Tinkle award Texas Inst. of Letters, 1986. Mem. Tex. Inst. Letters (Jesse H. Jones award 1962). Office: Simon & Schuster 1230 6th Ave New York NY 10020-1513 also: c/o Jerry Katzman Pres William Morris Agy 151 S El Camino Dr Beverly Hills CA 90212-2704*

MCMURTRY, R. ROY, chief justice; b. Toronto, Ont., Can., May 31, 1932; s. Roland Roy and Doris Elizabeth (Belcher) McM.; m. Ria Jean Macrae, Apr. 18, 1957; children: Janet, James, Harry, Jeannie, Erin, Michael. BA with honors, U. Toronto, 1954; LLB, Osgoode Hall Law Sch., 1958; LLD (hon.), U. Ottawa, 1983, Leeds U., U.K., 1988, York U., 1991. Bar: Called to bar 1958, created Queen's counsel 1970. Partner firm Benson, McMurtry, Percival and Brown; mem. Provincial Parliament for Eglinton, 1975-85; atty. gen. for Ont., 1975-85, solicitor gen. for Ont., 1978-82, high commnr. for Can. to Gt. Brit. and No. Ireland, 1985-88; ptnr. Blaney, McMurtry Stapells, Toronto, 1988-91; chmn. Can. Football League, 1989-91; assoc. chief justice Ont. Ct. Justice, Toronto, 1991-94, chief justice, 1994-96, chief justice on Ont., 1996—; freeman of City of London, 1986. Mem. United Ch. of Can. Office: Ont Ct Gen Div, 130 Queen St W, Toronto, ON Canada M5H 2N5

MCMURTY, ROBERT Y., academic dean. Dean U. Western Ont. Faculty Medicine, Can. Office: U Western Ont, Health Sci Ctr Rm H112, London, ON Canada N6A 5CI

MCNABB, DARCY LAFOUNTAIN, medical management company executive; b. Middletown, N.J., Aug. 27, 1955; d. Donald Mark LaFountain and Suzanne (Gilman) LaFountain Westergard; m. Leland Monte McNabb, July 4, 1981 (div. Feb. 1989); 1 child, Leland Monte Jr. BBA in Internat. Fin. cum laude, U. Miami, 1977. Real estate agent, Grad. Realtor's Inst. Market rsch. asst. Burger King Corp., Miami, Fla., 1975-77; regional mktg. supr. Burger King Corp., Huntington Beach, Calif., 1977-78; mgr., restaurant planning Holiday Inns, Inc., Memphis, 1978-79, mgr., nat. promotions, 1979-83; dir., lodging and travel planning Holiday Corp., Memphis, 1983-86; affiliate broker The Hobson Co., Realtors, Memphis, 1986-88, Crye Leike, Memphis, 1988-92; v.p. comm. and planning Medshares Mgmt. Group, Inc., Memphis, 1991—. Active Friends Pink Palace Mus., Memphis, 1987-91, Family Link/Runaway, Memphis, 1980-88; chmn. Foster Care Rev. Bd., Memphis, 1988—; bd. dirs. Bethany House, Memphis, 1989-95; pres., bd. dirs. Am. Cancer Soc., 1994—; mktg. com. Health Industry Coun., 1994-95. Named Profl. Vol. of Yr., Friends of Pink Palace Mus., Memphis, 1989, 93, U.S. Masters Swimming All-Am., 1993, 94; grad. Leadership Memphis, 1995; named Cmty. Hero for Olympic Torch Relay, 1996. Mem. Le Bonheur Club, Memphis Runners Track Club. Republican. Episcopalian. Avocations: competitive long distance running, tennis, swimming. Home: 1948 Harbert Ave Memphis TN 38104-5216 Office: Medshares Mgmt Group Inc 2714 Union Avenue Ext Memphis TN 38112-4415

MCNAIR, CARL HERBERT, JR., army officer, aeronautical engineer; b. Pensacola, Fla., Sept. 22, 1933; s. Carl Herbert and Hallie Rebecca (Edwards) McN.; m. Jo Ann Wilson, Oct. 26, 1957; children: Cynthia Leigh, Carl Herbert III, Courtney Ann. B.S., U.S. Mil. Acad., 1955; B.Aero. Engring., Ga. Inst. Tech., 1963, M.S. in Aero. Engring., 1963; M.S. in Pub. Adminstrn., Shippinsburg State Coll., 1971. Commd. 2d lt. U.S. Army, 1955, advanced through grades to maj. gen., 1987; comdr. troop brigade U.S. Army Aviation Ctr., Fort Rucker, Ala., 1974-75; dep. for aviation to asst. sec. of Army Office Sec. of Army, U.S. Army, Washington, 1975-77, exec. to dep. chief of staff for research, devel. and acquisition, 1977-78; dep. dir. requirements and aviation officer Office of Dep. Chief of Staff for Ops. and Plans, 1978-79; dep. comdg. gen. U.S. Army Aviation Ctr., Fort Rucker, Ala., 1979-80, comdg. gen., 1980-83; dep. chief staff combat devels. U.S. Army Tng. and Doctrine Command, Fort Monroe, Va., 1983-84, chief of staff, 1985-87; ret. U.S. Army, 1987; v.p. Burdeshaw Assocs., Ltd., Bethesda, Md., 1988-90; pres. Dyncorp Support Svcs. Div., Reston, Va., 1990-94, Dyncorp Enterprise Mgmt., Reston, 1994—; corp. v.p. Dyncorp, Reston, 1994—. Contbr. articles to profl. jours. Pres. Uniformed Svcs. Benefit Assn., Kansas City, Mo., 1980-82, Assn. of U.S. Army, Washington, 1988-92 (Washington chpt., exec. v.p. 2 region 1992—); v.p. Army Aviation Assn. Am., Westport, Conn., 1990-93, sec.-treas., 1993—; v.p. Ala.-Fla. coun. Boy Scouts Am., Dothan, Ala., 1979-83; mem. nat. bd. dirs. Mil. Cmty. Youth Ministries, 1988-93; pres. West Point Soc., Washington, 1992-95; mem. bd. dirs. Army Aviation Mus. Found.; mem. West Poinst Fund Com.; trustee U.S. Mil. Acad., 1992—. Decorated D.S.M. with oak leaf cluster, Legion of Merit with two leaf clusters, D.F.C. with three oak leaf clusters, Bronze Star medal with V devices with oak leaf cluster, Air medal with V devices and 51 oak leaf clusters, Disting. Service medal State of Ala.; named Disting. Grad. Sch. Aerospace Engring. Ga. Inst. Tech., Sigma Gamma Tau, 1963; recipient Silver Beaver Achievement Boy Scouts Am., 1981; recipient Crosses of Military Svc., Korean Conflict, Vietnam, Jeff Davis award United Daus. of the Confederacy, 1987, 88; numerous fgn. awards Korea, Vietnam, France, Republic of China. Mem. Assn. U.S. Army (mil. adviser 1979-87), Army Aviation Assn. Am. (v.p. 1979-83, 85-87, 90-93, sec.-treas. 1993—), Am. Def. Preparedness Assn. (bd. dirs. Washington chpt. 1993—, sec. 1994-95, v.p. 1995-96), Order of Daedalians (life), Am. Helicopter Soc., Air Force Assn., Navy League, Ret. Officers Assn. (life), Masons. Methodist. Home: 7821 Friars Ct Alexandria VA 22306-2717 *The military service, perhaps more than any other profession, provides us with a unique opportunity to* *serve both our fellow man and our God -in preserving the Peace and the Freedom cherished by mankind. It is within such a framework that I have charted the course of my life, remembering always Duty-Honor-Country.*

MCNAIR, JOHN FRANKLIN, III, banker; b. Laurinburg, N.C., Apr. 12, 1927; s. John Franklin and Martha (Fairley) McN.; m. Martha Fowler, June 16, 1951; children: John Franklin IV, Elizabeth Fowler. BS, Davidson Coll., 1949; postgrad., U. N.C., 1954-56. Pres. McNair Automotive Co., Inc., Laurinburg, 1949-66, The State Bank, Laurinburg, 1966-68; sr. v.p. Wachovia Bank & Trust, Laurinburg, 1968-70, Raleigh, N.C., 1970-72; exec. v.p. Wachovia Bank & Trust, Winston-Salem, N.C., 1972-77, vice chmn., 1977-85; vice chmn. The Wachovia Corp., Winston-Salem, N.C., 1977-87, pres., chief exec. officer, 1987-90; pres., chief exec. officer Wachovia Bank & Trust Co, 1987-90, also dir.; exec. v.p. First Wachovia Corp., 1986-90; bd. dirs. Piedmont Natural Gas Co.; bd. dirs., pres. N.C. R.R. Co., 1993—. Mem. N.C. State Hwy. Commn., Raleigh, 1965-69, Commn. on future N.C., raleigh, 1981-83; chmn. N.C. Bd. Econ. Devel., 1979-85, N.C. Coun. Econ. Edn., Greensboro, 1980-82, Ind. Coll. Fund N.C., 1989-91, N.C. Citizens for Bus. and Industry, 1988-89; trustee Peace Coll., Raleigh, 1980-89, Davidson Coll., 1985-93; trustee Old Salem, Inc., 1985—, treas., 1990—; trustee Winston-Salem Found., 1983-91, chmn., 1989-91; co-chmn. gov.'s adv. com. Superconducting Supercollider Project, 1988; trustee, mem. exec. com. rsch. triangle Found., 1986—, vice chmn., 1990-93, chmn., 1992—; trustee exec. com. Winston-Salem Bus., Inc., 1986—, chmn., 1990-95; mem. govt. performance com. State of N.C., 1991-93; bd. dirs. N.C. Enterprise Corp., 1988-93; chmn. Qual Choice of N.C., Inc., 1994—. With USN, 1945-46. Recipient Young Man of Yr. award Laurinburg Jaycees, 1962; recipient Silver Beaver award Boy Scouts Am., 1967. Mem. Am. Bankers Assn. (state v.p. 1980-81), Res. City Bankers Assn., N.C. Bankers Assn. (pres. 1976-77), Cape Fear County Club (Wilmington, N.C.), Old Town Club, Piedmont Club, St. Andrews Soc., Rotary. Democrat. Presbyterian. Home: 234 NW Pine Valley Rd Winston Salem NC 27104-1808 Office: Wachovia Bank NC PO Box 3099 Winston Salem NC 27150

MCNAIR, JOHN WILLIAM, JR., civil engineer; b. Asheville, N.C., June 17, 1926; s. John William and Annie (Woody) McN.; m. June Clemens Kratz; children—Jeffry, Marsha, Cathy. B.S. in Forestry, Pa. State U., 1950; B.S.C.E., Va. Poly. Inst. State U., 1955; postgrad. in engring. U. Va., 1957-58. Registered profl. engr., Va. and other states. Forester U.S. Forest Service, Flagstaff, Ariz., 1950, U.S. Gypsum Co., Buena Vista, VA., 1951; mem. engring. faculty U. Va., Charlottesville, 1955-58; prin. John McNair & Assocs., Waynesboro, VA., 1958—; owner Brucheum Group, Waynesboro, 1983—; with Va. Bd. Architects, Profl. Engrs. and Land Surveyors, 1969-79, v.p., 1977-78, pres., 1978-79. Author numerous engring. and land mgmt. study reports. Mem. Waynesboro City Council, 1968-72, vice mayor, 1970-72; chmn. Waynesboro INdsl. devel. Authority, 1984—. Served to capt. AUS, 1944-46, 51-53; France, Okinawa. Recipient Disting. Service cert. Va. Soc. Profl. Engrs., 1971. Fellow ASCE; mem. Acad. Environ. Engrs. (diplomate). Republican. Presbyterian. Lodge: Rotary. Office: John McNair and Assocs Wayne Ave LB & B Bldg Waynesboro VA 22980

MCNAIR, RUSSELL ARTHUR, JR., lawyer; b. Detroit, Dec. 2, 1934; s. Russell Arthur and Virla (Standish) McN.; m. Rosemary M. Chesbrough, Apr. 6, 1957; children: Julie McNair Schwerin, Russell Arthur III, Douglas S. AB in Econs. cum laude, Princeton U., 1956; JD with distinction, U. Mich., 1960. Bar: Mich. 1960. Assoc. Dickinson, Wright, Moon, Van Dusen & Freeman, Detroit, 1960-67, ptnr., 1968—, chmn., 1994—; adj. prof. U. Detroit Sch. Law, 1968-72; mem. adv. bd. Fin. Transactions Inst., 1984—; adj. prof. Wayne State U. Law Sch., 1994—; spkr. in field. Trustee Children's Home, Detroit, 1975-95, pres. 1986-87, hon. trustee 1995—; mem. adv. bd. United Way, 1994—; dir. Mich. Jobs Commn., 1995—. Mem. ABA, Mich. Bar Assn., Detroit Bar Assn., Am. Law Inst., Am. Coll. Real Estate Lawyers. Republican. Presbyterian. Avocations: golf, tennis, platform tennis. Home: 308 Touraine Rd Grosse Pointe MI 48236-3311 Office: Dickinson Wright Moon et al 1 Detroit Ctr 500 Woodward Ave Ste 4000 Detroit MI 48226-3423

MCNAIRN, PEGGI JEAN, speech pathologist, educator; b. Dallas, Sept. 22, 1954; d. Glenn Alton Harmon and Anna Eugenia (McVay) Hicks; m. Kerry Glen McNairn, Jan. 27, 1979; children: Micah Jay, Nathan Corey. BS in Speech Pathology, Tex. Christian U., 1977, MS in Communications Pathology, 1978; PhD in Ednl. Adminstrn., Kennedy Western U., 1991. Cert. speech pathologist, mid mgmt. Staff speech pathologist, asst. dir. infant program Easter Seal Soc. for Crippled Children and Adults Tarrant County, Ft. Worth, 1978-80; staff speech pathologist, spl. edn. lead tchr. Sherrod Elem. Sch. Arlington (Tex.) Ind. Sch. Dist., 1981-84, secondary speech/lang. specialist, early childhood assessment staff Spl. Services dept., 1984-89; owner, dir. Speech Assocs., 1989-92; mem. state forms com. Arlington (Tex.) Ind. Sch. Dist., 1985-86, chairperson assessment com., 1986-87; cons. augmentative communication Prentke Romich Co., 1992—; adj. prof., clin. supr. Tex. Christian U., Ft. Worth, 1978-79; clin. speech pathologist North Tex. Home Health Assn., Ft. Worth, 1980-92. Author: Quick Tech Activities for Literacy, 1993, Readable, Repeatable Stories and Activities, 1994, Quick Tech Music Magic, 1996. Chairperson United Cerebral Palsy Toy Lending Libr., 1989-90; sunday sch. tchr. 1st United Meth. Ch., Arlington, 1982-87; mem. South Arlington Homeowners Assn., Arlington, 1985-87; 3rd v.p. Bebensee Elem. PTA. Recipient Outstanding Svc. to Handicapped Am. Biog. Inst., 1989; Cert. of Achievement John Hopkins U. for computing to assist persons with disabilities, 1991. Mem. Internat. U.S. Tex. Socs. for Augmentative and Alternate Comm. (sec. Tex. branch), Neurodevelopmental Assn., Assn. for Curriculum and Supervision, Am. Speech and Hearing Assn., Tex. Speech-Lang.-Hearing Assn., Tex. Speech and Hearing Assn. (task force mem for augmentative comm.) Teaching Tex. Tots Consortium, Tex. Christian U. Speech and Hearing Alumni Assn., Kappa Delta Pi, Alpha Lambda Delta. Democrat. Avocations: doll making, sewing. Home and Office: 215 Spanish Moss Dr Arlington TX 76018-1540

MCNALL, BRUCE, professional sports executive, numismatist; m. Jane Cody; children: Katie, Bruce. Student, UCLA. Founder, chmn. bd. Numismatic Fine Arts, Inc., L.A.; owner, chmn. bd. Summa Stable, Inc.; chmn. bd. Gladden Entertainment Corp.; former ptnr. Dallas Mavericks NBA; co-owner L.A. Kings, 1986-87, sole owner, 1988-94, co-owner, 1994—; owner Toronto Argonauts, 1991—. Office: LA Kings 3900 W Manchester Blvd Inglewood CA 90305-2200

MC NALLEN, JAMES BERL, marketing executive; b. Heber Springs, Ark., Feb. 17, 1930; s. George Berl and Sally Lou (Brown) McN.; AB, Columbia, 1951; MBA, N.Y.U., 1960, PhD, 1975; m. Marianne Patricia Kakos, Mar. 4, 1952 (dec. Sept. 1990); children: James Lawrence, Marianne Victoria, Thomas Berl (dec.), John Kennedy. Mktg. asst. Am. Petroleum Inst., N.Y.C., 1954-67, coor. products mktg. 1967-69, asst. dir., div. fin. and acctg., 1969-70; corp. mgr. mktg. research Atlantic Richfield Co., N.Y.C., 1970-71; lectr. bus. adminstrn. Sch. Bus. Adminstrn. U. Conn., Storrs, 1972-75, asst. prof., 1975-76; mktg. research specialist, market research and mktg. div. Office Customer Service Support, Fed. Supply Service, GSA, Washington, 1976-78, mgr. mktg. research Office of Requirements, 1978-82, mgr. forecasting and bus. analysis Office of Mgmt., 1982-84; Mem. U.S. del. U.S.-Saudi Arabian Joint Econ. Commn., Riyadh, 1984-88, mktg. specialist, tng. officer Cen. Supply Mgmt. Devel. Project, 1984-88; spl. asst. commr. Office of Customer Service and Mktg., 1991; chief Program Devel. and Support, Office Transp. Audits, 1992-93, dep. dir. regulations & program developing, 1993—; GSA Fed. Supply Svc., Washingon, 1988—; pres. McNallen Investment Co., Arlington, Va.; ptnr. McNallen Enterprise, Big Spring, Tex.; lectr. mktg. Va. Poly. Inst., Reston, 1976-77, George Mason U., 1977-84, Georgetown U., 1978-80; adj. prof. mgmt. Univ. District Columbia, 1980-84. Mem. planning bd. Twp. of South Brunswick (N.J.), 1966-67; bd. dirs., sec., vice chmn. South Brunswick Mcpl. Utilities Authority, 1966-68; pres. South Brunswick Library Assn., 1965-69; comdg. officer Naval Air Intelligence Res. Unit, Lakehurst, N.J., 1970-71, commdg. officer Naval Investigative Svc. HQ Res. Unit, Washington, 1978-79, inspector gen. Naval Res. Intelligence Area 19, Washington, 1981, dep. area comdr. Co. IVTU, Dist. 19, Washington, 1982. Lt. (jr. gr.) USN, 1951-54, capt. USNR, 1976-87; ret. 1987. Mem. Naval Res. Assn., (pres. Washington chpt. 1978-79, pres. 5th dist. 1979-81, mem. nat. exec. com. 1979-81), Ret. Officers Assn., Naval Order U.S., Mil. Order World Wars, Res. Officers Assn. (exec. v.p. Washington D.C. Nat. Navy chpt. 1982-84), U.S. Naval Inst., Smithsonian Assocs., S. Brunswick Jaycees (pres. 1964-65, state v.p. N.J. State Jaycees 1965-66, named Jr. Chamber Internat. Senator), Ancient Order Hibernians (Chevy Chase, Md.), KC, Wolf Trap Friends, Kennedy Ctr. Friends. Recipient Gold medal Am. Mktg. Assn., 1960. Roman Catholic. Contbr. articles in field to profl. jours. Home: 2 Park Place Apt 21W Hartford CT 06106-5017 Office: GSA - FSS Office Trans Audits 18th & F St NW Rm G35ffwpa Washington DC 20405-0002

MCNALLY, ANDREW, III, printer, publisher; b. Chgo., Aug. 17, 1909; s. Andrew and Eleanor (Vilas) McN.; m. Margaret Clark MacMillin, Nov. 20, 1936 (dec.); children: Betty Jane, Andrew, Edward Clark. AB, Yale U., 1931; LHD (hon.), St. Lawrence U., 1986. With Rand McNally, Chgo., 1931; N.Y. sales office v.p., dir. Rand McNally & Co., Chgo., 1933, pres., 1948-74; chmn. bd. Rand McNally, 1974-93; chmn. emeritus Rand McNally & Co., 1993—. Life trustee Art Inst. Chgo.; trustee Washington Crossing Found., Antique Boat Mus.; past pres., bd. dirs. Girl's Latin Sch., Infant Welfare Soc., Graphic Arts Tech. Found.; internat. adv. bd. Frederic Remington Art Mus.; mem. Northwestern U. Libr. Coun.; governing mem. Orchestral Assn.; past pres., trustee Chgo. Hist. Soc. Capt. C.E., U.S. Army Map Svc., 1942-45. Fellow Royal Geog. Soc.; mem. Geog. Soc. Chgo. (past pres.), Newberry Library (hon. trustee). Office: Rand McNally 8255 Central Park Ave Skokie IL 60076-2908 Office: PO Box 7600 Chicago IL 60680-7600

MCNALLY, ANDREW, IV, publishing executive; b. Chgo., Nov. 11, 1939; s. Andrew and Margaret C. (MacMillin) McN.; m. Jeanine Sanchez, July 3, 1966; children: Andrew, Carrie, Ward. BA, U. N.C., 1963; MBA, U. Chgo., 1969. Bus. mgr. edn. divsn. Rand McNally & Co., Chgo., 1967-70, exec. v.p., sec., 1970-74, pres., 1974—, CEO, 1978—, also chmn. bd. dirs., 1993—; bd. dirs. Mercury Fin. Inc., Hubbell Inc., Morgan Stanley Funds, Zenith Electronics Corp., Allendale Ins., Borg Warner Securities Corp. Trustee Newberry Libr.; bd. dirs. Children's Meml. Hosp.; active vis. com. of libr. U. Chgo. With Air Force N.G., 1963-69. Mem. Chgo. Club, Saddle and Cycle Club, Commonwealth Club, Glen View Golf Club, Links (N.Y.C.). Office: Rand McNally & Co 8255 Central Park Ave Skokie IL 60076-2908

MCNALLY, JAMES HENRY, physicist, defense consultant; b. Orange, N.J., Dec. 18, 1936; s. James Osborne and Edith Maude (Jones) McN.; m. Nancy Lee Eudaley, July 4, 1976. B. in Engring. Physics, Cornell U., 1959; PhD in Physics, Calif. Inst. Tech., 1966. Staff mem. program mgr. Los Alamos (N.Mex.) Nat. Lab., 1965-74; asst. dir for laser and isotope separation tech. AEC/ERDA, Washington, 1974-75; assoc. div. leader, dep. for inertial fusion, asst. for nat. sec. issues Los Alamos Nat. Lab., 1975-86; dep. asst. dir. Arms Control and Disarmament Agy., Washington, 1986-88; dir. office staff Los Alamos Nat. Lab., 1988-90, Washington Inst., 1990-94; cons., 1990—; U.S. del. Geneva Conf. on Disarmament, 1969, 73, 74, Threshold Test Ban Treaty, Moscow, 1974, Nuclear Testing Talks, Geneva, 1986-88. Bd. dirs. Wilson Mesa Met. Water Dist., 1976-88; v.p., pres. Mountain Canine Corps, 1994—. Recipient Meritorious Honor award Arms Control and Disarmament Agy., 1988. Mem. AAAS, Am. Phys. Soc., Internat. Inst. Strategic Studies. Home and Office: 550 Rim Rd Los Alamos NM 87544-2931

MCNALLY, JOHN JOSEPH, lawyer; b. N.Y.C., July 1, 1927; s. Edward E. and Virginia L. (O'Brien) McN.; m. Sally Vose Greeley, Jan. 25, 1958; children: Martha, Sarah, Elizabeth, Julie, Thomas. A.B., Coll. Holy Cross, 1950; LL.B., Harvard U., 1953. Bar: N.Y. 1953. Assoc. White & Case, N.Y.C., 1953-63, ptnr., 1964—; bd. dirs. Mohawk Paper Mills, Inc., Cohoes, N.Y.; panelist in field. Trustee Caedmon Sch., N.Y.C., 1968—; bd. dirs. Community Fund of Bronxville-Eastchester-Tuckahoe, Inc., 1986—, All Hallows High Sch., N.Y.C., 1991—; mem. bd. gov's. Lawrence Hosp., Bronxville, N.Y., 1990—. Fellow Am. Bar Found.; mem. N.Y. State Bar Assn., N.Y. County Lawyers Assn., Bar Assn. City N.Y. Home: 58 Avon Rd Bronxville NY 10708-1723 Office: White & Case 1155 Ave Of The Americas New York NY 10036-2711*

MCNALLY, TERRENCE, playwright; b. St. Petersburg, Fla., Nov. 3, 1939; s. Hubert Arthur and Dorothy Katharine (Rapp) McN. B.A., Columbia U., 1960. Stage mgr. Actors Studio, N.Y.C., 1961, tutor, 1961-62; film critic The Seventh Art,, 1963-65; asst. editor Columbia Coll. Today, N.Y.C., 1965-66. Author: (plays) The Lady of the Camellias, 1963, And Things That Go Bump in the Night, 1964, Apple Pie and Last Gasps, 1966, Sweet Eros, 1968, Witness, 1968, Tour, 1968, Cuba Si!, 1968, Noon, 1968, Next, 1969, Where Has Tommy Flowers Gone?, 1971, Bad Habits, 1971 (Obie award 1971), Botticelli, 1971, Bringing It All Back Home, 1971, Whiskey, 1973, The Tubs, 1974, The Ritz, 1975 (Obie award best play 1974), The Golden Age, 1975, Broadway, Broadway, 1979, The Five Forty-Eight, 1974, The Lisbon Traviata, 1979, It's Only a Play, 1982, The Rink, 1984, Frankie and Johnny in the Clair de Lune, 1988, The Lisbon Traviata, 1989, Up in Saratoga, 1990, Kiss of the Spider Woman, 1990 (Tony award best book of a musical 1993), Andre's Mother, 1990 (Emmy award), Preludes, Fuges & Rifts, 1991, Lips Together, Teeth Apart, 1991, (screenplay) Frankie and Johnny, 1991, A Perfect Ganesh, 1993 (Pulitzer prize for drama nomination 1994), Love! Valour! Compassion!, 1994 (Outer Critics' Circle award best Broadway play 1995), Master Class, 1994. Recipient Dramatists Guild Hull-Warriner award, 1973, 88, 90; Guggenheim fellow, 1966, 69. Mem. Am. Acad. Arts and Letters, Dramatists Guild (v.p. 1981—). Office: care Gilbert Parker William Morris Agy 1350 Avenue Of The Americas New York NY 10019-4702

MCNALLY, THOMAS CHARLES, III, lawyer; b. San Francisco, Dec. 5, 1938; s. Thomas Charles and Claire Marie (Egan) McN.; m. Paula Ann Berger, Sept. 3, 1960; children: Megan, Martin, J. Tevis. B.S., U. San Francisco, 1960; J.D., Hastings Coll. Law, U. Cal. at San Francisco, 1963. Bar: Calif. bar 1964. Dep. atty. gen. State Calif., 1964; assoc. firm Bohnert, Flowers & McCarthy, San Francisco, 1965-68; asst. sec., counsel DiGiorgio Corp., San Francisco, 1968-73; sec., counsel DiGiorgio Corp., 1974-75; sec., gen. counsel Consol. Fibres, Inc., San Francisco, 1975-88, v.p., 1981-88; also dir. Consol. Fibres, Inc.; of counsel McInerney & Dillon, P.C., Oakland, Calif., 1989-91; pvt. practice San Francisco, 1991—; lectr. McGeorge Bar Rev., 1964-65, Continuing Edn. of Bar, U. Calif., 1975-76; judge moot ct. U. San Francisco, 1974-84; arbitrator Am. Arbitration Assn., NASD, 1988—. Co-chmn. Mill Valley Citizens Adv. Com., 1974-76; mem. pub. affairs com. San Francisco Assn. Mental Health, 1965-69; commr. Mill Valley Park and Recreation Commn., 1988-93, chmn., 1990. Mem. ABA, State Bar Calif., San Francisco Bar Assn. Republican. Roman Catholic (lector). Clubs: Olympic, Scott Valley Tennis (founder, dir. 1971-76, pres., dir. 1980-82), World Trade. Home: 3 Midhill Dr Mill Valley CA 94941-1490 Office: 455 Market St Fl 19 San Francisco CA 94105-2420

MC NAMAR, RICHARD TIMOTHY, merchant banker; b. Olney, Ill., Apr. 21, 1939; s. Charles A. and Mary Louise (Diver) McN.; m. Mary Ann Lyons, Aug. 10, 1963 (div.); children: Brendan, Lindsay; m. Karen K. Kwiatt, Dec. 14, 1985. A.B., Villanova U., 1961; J.D., U. Mich., 1963; M.B.A., Dartmouth Coll., 1965. Legal and fin. counselor Standard Oil Co. of Calif., 1965-66; mgmt. cons. McKinsey & Co., Inc., San Francisco, N.Y.C. and Amsterdam, 1966-71; dir. Case Mgmt. and Analysis Bd., 1972; mgmt. cons. Cost of Living Council, Washington, 1973; exec. dir. FTC, Washington, 1973-77; exec. v.p. Beneficial Standard Corp., Los Angeles, 1977-81; dep. sec. Treasury Dept. Treasury, Washington, 1981-85; mem. pvt. investment partnership, 1985-87; mng. dir. Conover & McNamar Inc., Los Angeles, 1987-90; vice chmn. Bank of New Eng. Corp., Boston, 1990-91; mng. dir. Oppenheimer & Co., Inc., L.A., 1991-94; chmn. Finance, Inc., 1994—; dir. NACRE, Inc. Trustee Boston Ballet Co. Mem. ABA, Calif. State Bar Assn., Fin. Execs. Inst., Bretton Woods Comte (bd. dirs.). Republican. Office: Ste 2300 10880 Wilshire Blvd Los Angeles CA 90024-3913

MCNAMARA, A. J., federal judge; b. 1936. BS, La. State U., 1959; JD, Loyola U., New Orleans, 1968. Bailiff, law clk. U.S. Dist. Ct., New Orleans, 1966-68, sole practice, 1968-72; ptnr. Monton, Roy, Carmouche, Hailey, Bivens & McNamara, New Orleans, 1972-78, Hailey, McNamara, McNamara & Hall, 1978-82; judge U.S. Dist. Ct. (ea. dist.) La., New Orleans, 1982—. Mem. La. Ho. of Reps., 1976-80. Office: US Dist Ct C-316 US Courthouse 500 Camp St New Orleans LA 70130-3313*

MCNAMARA, ANN DOWD, medical technologist; b. Detroit, Oct. 17, 1924; d. Frank Raymond and Frances Mae (Ayling) Sullivan; m. Thomas Stephen Dowd, Apr. 23, 1949 (dec. 1980); children: Cynthia Dowd Restuccia, Kevin Thomas Dowd; m. Robert Abbott McNamara, June 15, 1985. BS Wayne State U., 1947. Med. technologist Woman's Hosp. (now Hutzel Hosp.), Detroit, 1946-52, St. James Clin. Lab., Detroit, 1960-62; supr. histo-pathology lab. Hutzel Hosp., Detroit, 1962-72, Mt. Carmel Mercy Hosp., 1972-87, ret., 1987; docent Domino's Ctr. for Architecture & Design, Ann Arbor, Mich., 1988. Mem. Am. Soc. Clin. Pathologists, Am. Soc. Med. Technology, Mich. Soc. Med. Tech., Nat. Soc. Histotechnology, Mich. Soc. Histotechnologists, Wayne State U. Alumni Assn., Smithsonian Assocs., Detroit Inst. Arts Founders Soc. Home: 29231 Oak Point Dr Farmington Hills MI 48331-2774

MCNAMARA, ANNE H., lawyer, corporate executive; b. Shanghai, Republic of China, Oct. 18, 1947; came to U.S. 1949; d. John M. and Marion P. (Murphy) H.; m. Martin B. McNamara, Jan. 15, 1977. AB, Vassar Coll., 1969; JD, Cornell U., 1973. Bar: N.Y. 1973, Tex. 1981. Assoc. Shea, Gould, Climenko & Casey, N.Y.C., 1972-76; from asst. corp. sec. to corp. sec. Am. Airlines, Inc., Dallas, 1976-88, v.p. pers. resources, 1988; sr. v.p., gen. counsel Am. Airlines (AMR Corp.), Dallas, 1988—; bd. dirs. Louisville Gas & Electric Co., LG&E Energy Corp. Office: Am Airlines Inc Mail Drop 5618 PO Box 619616 Dallas TX 75261

MCNAMARA, BRENDA NORMA, secondary education educator; b. Blackpool, Lancashire, Eng., Aug. 8, 1945; came to U.S., 1946; d. Milford Hampson and Nola (Welsby) Jones; m. Michael James McNamara, July 19, 1969. BA in History, Calif. State U., Long Beach, 1967; postgrad., Calif. State U., various campuses, 1967—. Cert. secondary tchr. and lang. devel. specialist, Calif. Tchr. history West High Sch., Torrance, Calif., 1968—, dept. chair, 1989—; cons. in field. Co-author: World History, 1988. Western Internat. Studies Consortium grantee, 1988. Mem. Calif. Tchrs. Assn., Calif. Coun. for Social Studies, Torrance Tchrs. Assn. (bd. dirs. 1992—), South Bay Coun. for Social Studies, Nat. Tchrs. Assn., Nat. Coun. for Social Studies. Avocations: travel, theater, myster reading, gourmet cooking. Office: West High Sch 20401 Victor St Torrance CA 90503-2255

MCNAMARA, EDWARD HOWARD, county official, former mayor; b. Detroit, Sept. 21, 1926; s. Andrew Kursina and Ellen Gertrude (Bennett) McN.; m. Lucille Yvonne Martin, June 26, 1948; children—Colleen, Michael, Nancy, Kevin, Terence. Ph.B., U. Detroit, 1959; Ph.D. (hon.), Madonna Coll., 1982. Mgr. Mich. Bell Telephone Co., Detroit, 1948-70; mayor City of Livonia, Mich., 1970-86; county exec. Wayne County, Detroit, 1987—. Served with USN, 1944-46. Democrat. Roman Catholic. Home: 16501 Park St Livonia MI 48154-2203 Office: Office of the County Exec 350 Wayne County Bldg 600 Randolph St Detroit MI 48226-2831*

MCNAMARA, FRANCIS JOHN, writer; b. Bklyn., Nov. 19, 1915; s. Sylvester John and Adelia Ferris (French) McN.; m. Katherine Elizabeth Foley, Nov. 20, 1945; children: Jane Marie, Ellen Elizabeth. BA, St. John's U., 1938; MA, Niagara U., 1939. Assoc. reg. sales mgr. UN Relief & Rehab. Adminstrn., Jehol & Hupeh Provinces, China, 1946-47; editor Counterattack, N.Y.C., 1950-54; dir. nat. security program VFW, Washington, 1954-58; research analyst and cons. House Com. on Un-Am. Activities, Washington, 1958-61; dir research House Com. on Un-Am. Activities, 1961-62, staff dir., 1962-69; exec. sec. Subversive Activities Control Bd., Washington, 1970-73; exec. dir. The Hale Found., Washington, 1981; vice chmn. Security and Intelligence Found., Arlington, Va., 1987-90; sr. fellow Ctr. for Intelligence Studies, Arlington, 1990-93; bd. dirs. Coun. for Def. of Freedom, Washington, 1952-94; bd. advisors Nathan Hale Inst., Washington, 1983—. Author: U.S. Counterintelligence Today, 1985, Patterns of Communist Espionage, 1959; contbr. articles to profl. jours. Served to maj. U.S. Army, 1941-46. Mem. Assn. Former Intelligence Officers. Republican. Roman Catholic. Avocations: gardening, photography. Address: Apt 1417 8100 Connecticut Ave Chevy Chase MD 20815

MC NAMARA, FRANCIS JOSEPH, JR., foundation executive, lawyer; b. Boston, Nov. 30, 1927; s. Francis Joseph and Louise (English) McN.; m. Noreen E. O'Connor, June 18, 1953 (dec. Feb. 1984); children: Francis Joseph III, Moira Patricia (Mrs. Lance F. James), John Allen, Kathleen Louise (Mrs. Robert J. Hugin), Martha Jeanne (Mrs. James R. Bordewick), Mark Jeffrey; m. Louis L. Magner, Jan. 17, 1986. A.B., Georgetown U., 1949, LL.B., 1951; LL.D. (hon.), Fairfield U., 1983. Bar: Conn. 1952. Assoc. firm Pullman, Comley, Bradley & Reeves, 1953; asst. U.S. Atty., dist. Conn., 1953-57; assoc. firm Cummings & Lockwood, Stamford, Conn., 1957-59; ptnr. Cummings & Lockwood, 1959-91; guest lectr. Salzburg (Austria) Seminar, 1981; chmn. grievance com. U.S. Dist. Ct. Conn., 1983-89. Trustee Fairfield (Conn.) U., 1968-80, trustee emeritus, 1980—; trustee Charles E. Culpeper Trust; chmn. bd. Charles E. Culpeper Found., 1968-91, pres., 1991—. Served with USNR, 1946, 51-53. Fellow Am. Bar Found., Am. Coll. Trial Lawyers (state com. 1985-91, state chmn. 1989-90); mem. U.S. Supreme Ct. Hist. Soc. (Conn. state chmn. 1989-91, trustee 1992—), Navy League U.S., Knight of Holy Sepulchre, Knight of Malta, Knight of St. Gregory the Great, Wee Burn Country Club (Darien, Conn.), Bent Pine Golf Club (Vero Beach, Fla.), Turf and Field Club (N.Y.). Republican. Roman Catholic. Home: 75 Bank St New Canaan CT 06840-6203 also: 10 Lost Beach Ln Vero Beach FL 32963 Office: Charles E Culpeper Found 695 E Main St Stamford CT 06901-2155

MCNAMARA, FRANCIS T., ambassador; b. Troy, N.Y., Nov. 2, 1927; married; 7 children. BA, Russell Sage Coll., 1953; MS, George Washington U., 1972; grad., Armed Forces Staff Coll., 1967, Naval War Coll., 1971-72. Vice-consul, econ. officer Am. Consulate Gen., Salisbury, Rhodesia, 1957-59; consul-polit. officer Am. Consulate Gen., Lubumbashi, Zaire, 1961-63; polit. and econ. officer Am. Consulate Gen., Dar-Es Salaam, Tanzania, 1964-66; dep. chief mission Am. Embassy, Lusaka, Zambia, 1967; provincial advisor Vinh Long and Quang Tri provinces Viet Nam, 1967-69; consul gen. Am. Consulate Gen., Danang, Vietnam, 1969-71; chargé d'affaires, dep. chief mission Am. Embassy, Cotonou, Benin, 1972-74; consul gen. Am. Consulate Gen., Can Tho, Vietnam, 1974-75, Quebec City, Que., Can., 1975-79; dep. asst. sec. of state for pub. affairs Dept. of State, Washington, 1979-81; amb. to Republic of Gabon and Republic of Sao Tome and Principe Am. Embassy, 1981-84; chargé d'affaires, dep. chief of mission Am. Embassy, Beirut, 1985-87; amb. to Republic of Cape Verde Am. Embassy, 1989—; fgn. affairs fellow Hoover Instn. Stanford (Calif.) U., 1984-85; sr. rsch. fellow Nat. Def. U., 1987-89. Author: France in Black Africa, 1989. With USN, 1944-46, 50-51. Home: 102 Gresham Pl Falls Church VA 22046-3440 Office: Am Embassy, Rua Hojl Ya Yenna 81, Praia Cape Verde

MC NAMARA, J(OHN) DONALD, retired lawyer, business executive; b. Bridgeport, Conn., Feb. 28, 1924; s. John T. and Agnes (Keating) McN.; m. Shirley Addison Holdridge, Nov. 5, 1960. BA, Dartmouth Coll., 1945; MA in Govt., Harvard U., 1947, LLB, 1950. Bar: N.Y. 1951, Conn. 1951. Assoc. Hall, Haywood, Patterson & Taylor, N.Y.C., 1951-53, 55-56; asst. U.S. Atty. U.S. Dist. Ct. (so. dist.) N.Y., 1953-55; assoc. Wickes, Riddell, Bloomer, Jacobi & McGuire, N.Y.C., 1956-57; assoc., then ptnr. Nottingham & McEniry (and successor), N.Y.C., 1957-59; sec., gen. counsel Interpub. Group of Cos., Inc., N.Y.C., 1960-79, dir., 1965-85, sr. v.p., 1966-73, exec. v.p., 1973-79, pres., 1980-85, mem. exec. com., 1967-85, mem. fin. com., 1980-85. Chmn. U.S. Nat. Tennis Championships, 1965. Served to lt. (j.g.) USNR, 1943-46. Mem. River Club, Univ. Club, Met. Opera Club, Ekwanok Country Club (mem. bd. govs. Manchester, Vt. 1991-95), Dorset (Vt.) Field Club, West Side Tennis club (pres. Forest Hills, N.Y. 1964-66, 79-80). Home: 350 E 57th St New York NY 10022-2953 also: River Rd Manchester VT 05254

MCNAMARA, JOHN F., health services company executive; b. 1935. V.p., gen. mgr. McKesson Drug Co., L.A., 1974-78, pres. Value Rite div., 1978-81; with Alco Health Svcs. Corp. Inc., Valley Forge, Pa., 1981—, pres. Kauffman-Lettimer div., 1981-83, v.p., 1983-84, exec. v.p., 1984-85, chief operating officer, exec. v.p., 1985-87, pres., chief operating officer, 1987-88, chmn., pres., chief exec. officer, 1988—, also bd. dirs. Office: Ameri Source Corp PO Box 959 Valley Forge PA 19482-0959*

MCNAMARA, JOHN JEFFREY, advertising executive; b. N.Y., Jan. 31, 1937; s. John Joseph and Alexandra (Salem) M. BA, N.Y. Law Sch., 1963.

Asst. v.p. Albert Frank Guenther Law Inc., N.Y., 1959-66; acct. supr., v.p. Doremus and Co., N.Y., 1966-74; v.p., exec. v.p. Wiley Kiernan Inc Charles Barker Ayer, N.Y., 1974-76; v.p. acct. supr. Tinker Campbell Ewald, N.Y., 1976-78; pres., chmn. John McNamara Advt. Inc., N.Y., 1978—; corr. cons. Hamilton College Alumni, Clinton, N.Y., 1978-88. Republican. Presbyterian. Avocations: boating, golf, restoring old cars, houses. Home: 420 Majors Path Southampton NY 11968-2423 Office: 27 Whitehall St New York NY 10004-2117

MC NAMARA, JOHN J(OSEPH), advertising executive, writer; b. Yonkers, N.Y., Mar. 7, 1934; m. Patricia A. Widmann, Sept. 14, 1963; children: Mary, John. B.S., Yale U., 1956; M.B.A., NYU, 1963. Exec. v.p., eastern regional dir. Young & Rubicam, N.Y.C., 1979; pres. Young & Rubicam U.S.A., from 1982; later pres. McCann Erickson Worldwide, ret., 1988; writer, cons., bd. dirs. in field. Author: Advertising Agency Management, 1989. Pres. Pelham United Way, N.Y.; mem. Pelham Manor Zoning Bd.; chmn. Pelham Manor Planning Bd.; trustee City of Pelham Manor, mayor, 1989-90. Served to 1st lt. USMC, 1956-58. Clubs: Pelham Country (pres.), Winged Foot. Office: PO Box 8092 Vero Beach FL 32963-8092

MCNAMARA, JOHN STEPHEN, artist, educator; b. Cambridge, Mass., Feb. 16, 1950; s. John Stephen and Mary (Adams) McN. BFA in Painting, Mass. Coll. Art, Boston, 1971, MFA in Painting, 1977. Tchr. Mus. Fine Arts Sch., Boston, 1983; undergrad. and grad. painting tchr. Mass. Coll. Art, Boston, 1988; undergrad. painting tchr. Boston Archtl. Ctr., Boston, 1977; color fundamentals tchr. Mass. Coll. Art, Boston, 1987, undergrad. drawing, 1975-88; vis. lectr. San Francisco Art Inst., 1992, 93, U. Calif., Berkeley, 1993, 94, 95, 96. One-man shows include Starvaridis Gallery, Boston, 1985, Bess Cutler Gallery, 1986, Mass. Coll. Art, 1986, Honolulu Acad. Fine Art, 1987, Nielson Gallery, 1990, 92, Miller Block Gallery, Boston, 1995; exhibited in group shows at Boston Collects, Mus. Fine Arts, Stavaridis Gallery, 1986, Bess Cutler Gallery, N.Y.C., 1987, Am. Painters and Sculptors, Met. Mus. Art, N.Y.C., 1988, Resonant Abstraciton, Fuller Mus. Art, Brockton, Mass., 1989-90. Mass. Art and Humanities grantee, 1980, 83, 86, 89, Award in the Visual Arts grantee, 1982, Nat. Endowment Arts grantee, 1981. Home: 1150 Sanchez St San Francisco CA 94114-3857

MC NAMARA, JOSEPH DONALD, researcher, retired police chief, novelist; b. N.Y.C., Dec. 16, 1934; s. Michael and Eleanor (Shepherd) McN.; divorced; children: Donald, Laura, Karen. BS, John Jay Coll., 1968; fellow, Harvard Law Sch., 1970; DPA (Littauer fellow), Harvard U., 1973. Served to dep. insp. Police Dept., N.Y.C., 1956-73; police chief Kansas City, Mo., 1973-76, San Jose, Calif., 1976-91; rsch. fellow Hoover Instn., Stanford U., 1991—; adj. instr. Northeastern U., 1972, John Jay Coll., 1973, Rockhurst Coll., 1975-76, San Jose State U., 1980; cons. U.S. Civil Rights Commn., 1978; lectr., appearances on nat. TV; apptd. nat. adv. bd. U.S. Bur. Justice Stats., 1980, U.S. Drug Control Policy Office, 1993; commentator Pub. Broadcasting Radio. Author: (non-fiction) Safe and Sane, 1984, (novel) The First Directive Crown, 1985, Fatal Command, 1987, The Blue Mirage, 1990, Code 211 Blue, 1996; contbr. articles to profl. publs. Bd. dirs. Drug Policy Found., Washington; active NCCJ. Served with U.S. Army, 1958-60. Named one of 200 Young Am. Leaders Time mag., 1975; recipient disting. alumni award John Jay Coll., 1979, Pres.'s award Western Soc. Criminology1979, Morrison Gitchoff award Western Soc. Criminology, 1992, H.B. Spear award Drug Policy Found., 1992; Kansas City police named Best in Country by Nat. Newspaper Enterprises, 1974, San Jose Police Dept. named Nat. Model U.S. Civil Rights Commn., 1980; named Law Enforcement Officer of Yr., Calif. Trial Lawyers Assn., 1991. Mem. Internat. Assn. Chiefs of Police, Calif. Police Chiefs Assn., Calif. Peace Officers Assn., Major Cities Police Chiefs Assn., Police Exec. Research Forum (dir.). Office: Hoover Instn Stanford CA 94305 *In our country, social mobility is possible for people from even the most humble backgrounds. Despite problems, our nation has provided more liberty and dignity for the common individual than any other civilization in history. Continuation of our free society depends upon how successful we are in teaching each new generation an appreciation of our precious freedoms and the patience to achieve progress within our democratic process.*

MC NAMARA, LAWRENCE J., bishop; b. Chgo., Aug. 5, 1928; s. Lawrence and Margaret (Knusman) McN. B.A., St. Paul Sem., 1949; S.T.L., Catholic U. Am., 1953. Ordained priest Roman Catholic Ch., 1953; parish priest, tchr. Kansas City-St. Joseph Diocese, 1953-57; dir. diocesan Refugee Resettlement, 1957-60; chaplain Jackson County Jail, 1957-64; exec. dir. Campaign for Human Devel., 1973-77; bishop of Grand Island Nebr., 1978—. Recipient award Cath. Relief Services. Office: Chancery Office 311 W 17th St PO Box 996 Grand Island NE 68801-3521*

MCNAMARA, MARTIN BURR, lawyer, oil and gas company executive; b. Danbury, Conn., Sept. 10, 1947; s. William Joseph and Geraldine Margaret (Young) McN.; m. Anne Rose Hogan, Jan. 15, 1977. BA in English, Providence Coll., 1969; JD, Yale U., 1972. Bar: N.Y. 1973, U.S. Dist. Ct. (so. and ea. dists.) N.Y. 1973, (no. dist.) Tex. 1993, U.S. Ct. Appeals (2d cir.) 1973, Tex. 1980, U.S. Ct. Appeals (5th and 11th cirs.) 1980. Assoc. Shea & Gould, N.Y.C., 1972-76; asst. U.S. atty. (so. dist.) N.Y., N.Y.C., 1976-79; v.p., gen. counsel, sec. Tex. Oil & Gas Corp., Dallas, 1979-91; gen. counsel, sr. v.p. adminstrn. Delhi Gas Pipeline Corp., Dallas, 1979-91; mng. ptnr. Gibson, Dunn & Crutcher, Dallas, 1991—; lectr. State Bar of Tex., Dallas Bar Assn., U. Tex. Corp. Coun. Inst., Okla. Bar Assn. bd. dirs. Sonat Offshore Drilling, Inc.; lectr. State Bar of Tex., Dallas Bar ASsn., U. Tex. Corp. Counsel Inst., Okla. Bar Assn. Mem. exec. com. Yale Law Sch. Assn., 1983-86. Mem. State Bar of Tex. (vice chmn. corp. counsel sect. 1984-86, chmn.-elect 1987-88, chmn. 1988-89), Bar Assn. Fifth Fed. Cir., Assn. Bar. City of N.Y., N.Y. State Bar Assn., Fed. Energy Bar Assn. Republican. Roman Catholic. Club: Petroleum. Office: Gibson Dunn & Crutcher 5500 Bank One Ctr 1717 Main St Dallas TX 75201-4605

MCNAMARA, MARY E., asset manager, minister; b. Mpls., Dec. 18, 1943; d. Edward Emmanuel and Gladys Theresa (Mattson) Bjorklund; m. Peter Alexander McNamara II; children: Peter Alexander III, Nathaniel Paul. BA, Carleton Coll., 1965; MDiv, Harvard U., 1968. Program dir. St. Peter's Ch., N.Y.C., 1968-72, program dir., dep. exec., 1977-80; program dir. Ctr. Ch. on-the-Green, N.Y.C., 1972-74; program developer Westminster Presbyn. Ch., Springfield, Ill., 1974-77; assoc. Gen. Assembly Coun. Presbyn. Ch., N.Y.C., 1980-87; dir. not-for-profit sector City of N.Y., 1987-90; pres., exec. dir. Interchurch Ctr., N.Y.C., 1990—; v.p. Pathways for Youth, Bronx, N.Y., 1987—; pres. Morningside Area Alliance, N.Y.C., 1991—. Moderator Presbyn. N.Y.C., 1995-96, chair com. on ministry, 1992-95; bd. dirs., exec. com. mem. Polish Conf. Ctr., 1996—. Home: 5411 Palisade Ave Riverdale NY 10471 Office: The Interchurch Ctr 475 Riverside Dr Rm 253 New York NY 10115

MCNAMARA, MICHAEL JOHN, lawyer; b. Hutchinson, Minn., July 1, 1948; s. John Oliver and Lucille Violet (Wedell) M.; m. Kathleen Elizabeth Dahl; children: Jennifer, Kelly. BA, U. Utah, 1976; JD, U. Minn., 1980. Bar: Minn. 1981, U.S. Dist. Ct. Minn. 1981, U.S. Ct. Appeals (8th cir.) 1982, U.S. Supreme Ct. 1988, Wis. 1992. Pvt. practice Mpls., 1981—; panel arbitrator Am. Arbitration Assn., Hennepin County Dist. Ct.; panelist No-Fault Arbitrators Minn. Supreme Ct. Contbr. articles to profl. jours. Sgt. U.S. Army, 1968-71, Vietnam. Nat. merit scholar. Mem. FBA, ATLA, The Federalist Soc., Internat. Platform Assn., Minn. State Bar Assn., Wis. State Bar Assn., Minn. Trial Lawyers Assn., Hennepin County Bar Assn. (mem. spkrs. bur.). Avocations: jogging, biking, hiking. Office: Henderson Howard Pawluk & McNamara PA 6200 Shingle Creek Pky Ste 385 Minneapolis MN 55430-2168

MCNAMARA, PAULA RUTH WAGNER, therapeutic recreation programs director; b. St. Louis, Feb. 23, 1925; d. Paul Brooks and Leah Ruth (Dick) Wagner; m. Raymond Edmund McNamara, May 28, 1949; children: Carol Rae, Marla Ann, Cynthia Ruth, Erin Marie, Brian Francis. BFA, Sch. of Art Inst., 1948; MA, W. Va. Grad. Coll., 1988. Cert. therapeutic recreation specialist. Supr. leisure edn. W. Va. Rehabilitaion Ctr., Institute, 1970-91; exec. dir. W. Va. Therapeutic Recreation Assn., Institute, 1992—; rep. Nat. Therapeutic Recreation Assn., Arlington, Va., 1984—. Amb. Friendship Force, 1993—; conf. del. Partners of the Americas, Washington, 1991. Mem. Nat. Therapeutic Recreation Assn., Am. Therapeutic Recreation Assn., W.Va. Therapeutic Recreation Assn. (sec. 1991). Avocations: graphic arts, drawing, crafts. Office: WVa Therapeutic Recreation Assn PO Box 554 Institute WV 25112-0554

MC NAMARA, ROBERT STRANGE, former banking executive, cabinet member; b. San Francisco, June 9, 1916; s. Robert James and Clara Nell (Strange) McN.; m. Margaret Craig, Aug. 13, 1940 (dec.); children: Margaret Elizabeth, Kathleen, Robert Craig. AB, U. Calif., 1937; MBA, Harvard U., 1939; LLD (hon.), U. Calif., U. Mich., Columbia U., Harvard U., George Washington U., Princeton U., Amherst Coll., Williams Coll., U. Ala., Ohio State U., NYU, U. Notre Dame, U. Pa., U. St. Andrews, U. Philippines, Aberdeen U., Oxford U., U. S.C. Asst. prof. bus. adminstrn. Harvard U., 1940-43; exec. Ford Motor Co., 1946-61, pres. co., 1960-61, co. dir., 1957-61; sec. U.S. Dept. Def., 1961-68; pres. World Bank, 1968-81; mem. , trustee pub. and pvt. instns. including Overseas Devel. Coun., Urban Inst., Enterprise Found., Brookings Inst.; spl. cons. War Dept., 1942. Author: The Essence of Security, 1968, One Hundred Countries-Two Billion People, 1973, The McNamara Years at the World Bank, 1981, Blundering Into Disaster, 1986, Out of the Cold, 1989, In Retrospect, 1995. Served as lt. col. USAAF, 1943-46. Decorated Legion of Merit, D.S.M.; recipient Presdl. Medal of Freedom with distinction, Christian A. Herter Meml. award, Albert Pick Jr. award U. Chgo., 1979, Franklin D. Roosevelt Freedom from Want medal, 1983, Onassis Athinai prize, 1988. Mem. Phi Beta Kappa. Office: 1455 Pennsylvania Ave NW Washington DC 20004-1008

MCNAMARA, STEPHEN, newspaper executive; b. Chgo., July 9, 1934; s. Robert Charles McNamara Jr. and Susan (Deuel) Shattuck; m. Hanne Morgensen Petterson, Feb. 21, 1960 (div. Aug. 1968); children: Lise, Natalie, Kevin; m. Kay Copeland, June 10, 1978; children: Christopher, Morgan. AB in Am. History, Princeton U., 1955. Reporter Winston-Salem (N.C.) Jour., 1955-57; sports writer Miami Herald, 1957-59; contbg. European editor Car & Driver, N.Y.C., 1960; asst. news editor, exec. sports editor, Sunday editor San Francisco Examiner, 1961-67; CEO, editor, pub. Pacific Sun, Mill Valley, Calif., 1967—; co-pub. The Ark, Tiburon, Calif., 1987—; pres. Marin Sun Printing Co., Mill Valley, 1967-93; mng. gen. ptnr. Sunrise Investment Co., Mill Valley, 1980—; vis. lectr. San Francisco State U., 1967; mem. innovation and planning comm. Calif. Dept. Edn., Sacramento, 1980; co-founder, pres. Marin Solar Village Corp., Mill Valley, 1976—, Marin Cmty. Video, Mill Valley, 1973-78. Mem. Soc. Profl. Journalists, Nat. Assn. Alternative Newsweeklies (pres. 1978-81), Calif. Assn. Alternative Newsweeklies (pres. 1990-92), Calif. Soc. Newspaper Editors (pres. 1985-86, bd. dirs. 1983-93), Calif. Newspaper Pubs. Assn. (bd. dirs. 1989-93), San Francisco Press Club (1st place newspaper writing award 1967, 3-2d place awards), Cap and Gown Club (Princeton U.), Scott Valley Swimming and Tennis Club. Democrat. Home: 2 Bradford Ave Mill Valley CA 94941 Office: Pacific Sun Publ Co 21 Corte Madera Ave Mill Valley CA 94941-1800

MCNAMARA, THOMAS NEAL, lawyer; b. Washington, Dec. 1, 1930; s. Philip Joseph and Louise Loretta (Ryan) McN.; children: John Michael, George Denison, Mary Louise Higgins; m. Deana Hollingsworth, Dec. 21, 1986; stepchildren: John W. Hollingsworth, Christopher M. Hollingsworth, Kim R. Hollingsworth. B.A., Duke U., 1952; J.D. with honors, George Washington U., 1959. Bar: Va. 1959, Calif. 1960. Assoc. Pillsbury, Madison & Sutro, San Francisco, 1959-66, ptnr., 1967-86; mng. ptnr. L.A., 1986-89, chmn., 1990-95; adv. ptnr. Pillsbury, Madison & Sutro, San Francisco, 1996—. Contbr. articles to profl. jours. Trustee Dixie Sch. Dist., San Rafael, Calif., 1964-76; dir. San Francisco Home Health Svc., 1975-82, Hospice of Marin (Calif.), 1988-91, Bay Area Coun., 1990-95; mem. bd. advisors Nat. Law Ctr., George Washington U. Law Sch., 1991—. Served to Lt. comdr. USNR, 1952-56, Korea. Fellow Am. Bar Found. (life), Am. Coll. Tax Counsel; mem. ABA, Calif. Bar Assn., San Francisco Bar Assn., Va. Bar Assn., Internat. Game Fish Assn. (Calif. rep. 1983—), Order of Coif, Pacific-Union Club, The Family Club, Presidio Golf Club. Republican. Roman Catholic. Office: Pillsbury Madison & Sutro PO Box 7880 San Francisco CA 94120-7880

MCNAMARA, TIMOTHY JAMES, secondary education educator; b. Buffalo, June 24, 1952; s. Vincent Michael and Peggy Jo (Matthews) McN.; m. Julie Ann McCready, Aug. 25, 1979; children: James Vincent, Lucille Ann. BA in Math., Niagara U., 1975; EdM, SUNY, Buffalo, 1979; MBA, SUNY, 1984, postgrad., 1995—. Tchr. Williamsville East High Sch., East Amherst, N.Y., 1975-84, Maryvale Sr. High Sch., Cheektowaga, N.Y., 1984-86; tchr. gifted math. program SUNY, 1987-90; coord. math. The Nichols Sch , Buffalo, 1991-93; K-12 math. supr. West Irondequoit Schs., Rochester, 1993—; lectr. in field. Faculty editor student math. jour. The Nth Degree; contbr. articles to profl. jours. Recipient N.Y. State Presdl. award for Excellence in Secondary Math. Teaching, 1993, finalist, 1990, 91. Mem. Nat. Coun. Tchrs. Math., Assn. Math. Tchrs. N.Y. State (exec. bd. dirs. 1992-94), N.Y. State Assn. Math. Suprs., Ontario Assn. Math. Educators, Phi Delta Kappa. Avocations: gardening, travel, bicycling. Home: 1093 Marigold Dr Webster NY 14580-8765 Office: Irondequiot High Sch 260 Cooper Rd Rochester NY 14617-3049

MCNAMARA, TOM, newspaper editor. Managing editor-news USA Today, Arlington, Va. Office: USA Today 1000 Wilson Blvd Arlington VA 22209-3901

MCNAMARA, WILLIAM, priest; b. Providence, Feb. 14, 1926; s. John and Margaret (Gannon) McN. BA in Theology and Philosophy, Cath. U. Am.; MA in Edn. and Psychology, Boston Coll. Became a Discalced Carmelite monk, 1944, ordained Roman Cath. priest, 1951. Founder Spiritual Life Mag., 1955, editor, 1955-62; author: The Art of Being Human, 1962, The Human Adventure: Contemplation for Everyman, 1974, Mystical Passion, 1977, Christian Mysticism, 1981, Earthy Mysticism, 1987. Home: Box 219 Crestone CO 81131

MCNAMEE, SISTER CATHERINE, educational association executive; b. Troy, N.Y., Nov. 13, 1931; d. Thomas Ignatius McNamee and Kathryn McNamee Marois. B.A., Coll. of St. Rose, 1953, D.H.L. (hon.), 1975; M.Ed., Boston Coll., 1955, M.A., 1958; Ph.D., U. Madrid, 1967. Grad. asst. Boston Coll., 1954-55; asst. registrar Boston Coll. (Grad. Sch.), 1955-57; acad. v.p. Coll. St. Rose, Albany, N.Y., 1968-75; dir. liberal arts Thomas Edison Coll., Trenton, 1975-76; pres. Trinity Coll., Burlington, Vt., 1976-79, Coll. St. Catherine, St. Paul, 1979-84; dean Dexter Hanley Coll., U. Scranton, Pa., 1984-86; pres. Nat. Cath. Ednl. Assn., Washington, 1986—. Bd. dirs. Am. Forum, Boston Coll., Internat. Cath. Child Bur. Spanish Govt. grantee, 1965-67; OAS grantee, 1967-68; Fulbright grantee, 1972-73. Mem. Inter-Am. Confedn. Cath. Edn., Internat. Orgn. Cath. Edn., Coun. for Am. Pvt. Edn., Internat. Fedn. Cath. Univs., Delta Epsilon Sigma. Roman Catholic. Office: Nat Cath Ednl Assn 1077 30th St NW Ste 100 Washington DC 20007-3829

MCNAMEE, DANIEL VINCENT, III, management consultant; b. N.Y.C., Sept. 21, 1944; s. Daniel Vincent McNamee Jr. and Barbara Burroughs (Cooley) Dudley; m. Susan Anderson Thompson, Oct. 21, 1978; 1 child, Simon Cooley. BA, Yale U., 1967; post grad., Balliol Coll., Oxford, England. Assoc. pub. MORE mag., N.Y.C., 1973-74; v.p. circulation Downe Communications, Inc., N.Y.C., 1974-77; dir. planning Chartcom, Inc., N.Y.C., 1977-78; v.p. consumer mktg. Charter Pub., N.Y.C., 1978-79; pres. The McNamee Cons. Co., N.Y.C., 1979—; ptnr. The Electronic Pub. Consulting Group; bd. dirs. First Albany (N.Y.) Corp., Silver Eagle Pubs., N.Y.C., Opus Publ., SRDS, Inc. Trustee Assocs. Coun. Oxford Centre for Mgmt. Studies, 1984—, Ocean Liner Mus., N.Y.C., 1985—, E.N. Huyck Preserve Inc. With U.S. Army, 1969-71. Mem. Yale Club (N.Y.C.), Manursing Island Club (Rye, N.Y.). Democrat. Presbyterian. Avocations: reading, skiing, tennis, theater, sailing. Home: 42 Orchard Ln Rye NY 10580-3638 Office: The McNamee Cons Group 355 Lexington Ave New York NY 10017

MCNAMEE, LOUISE, advertising agency executive; m. Tom M. Attended, Mary Baldwin Coll., Va. With rsch. dept. Kelly Nason; exec. v.p., dir. mktg. and rsch. Della Femina, Travisano & Ptnrs., Inc. (now Della Famina McNamee, Inc.), N.Y.C., 1979-84, ptnr., 1982—, acting pres., from 1984, past pres., chief operating officer, chief exec. officer, 1992-93; now ptnr., pres. Messner, Vetere, Berger, McNamee, Schmetterer, Euro RSCG, N.Y.C., 1993—. Named Advt. Woman of Yr., Advt. Women of N.Y., 1988. Office: Messner, Vetere, Berger, McNamee, Schmetterer, Euro RSCG 350 Hudson St New York NY 10014-4504*

MCNAMEE, STEPHEN M., federal judge; b. 1942. B.A., U. Cinn., 1964; M.A., J.D., U. Ariz., 1969. U.S. atty. Dist. of Ariz., Phoenix, 1985-90; judge U.S. Dist. Ct. Ariz., Phoenix, 1990—. Office: City of Phoenix 400 N 7th St Phoenix AZ 85025*

MCNANEY, ROBERT TRAINOR, lawyer; b. Chgo., Nov. 16, 1934; s. Leo F. and Lauretta M. (Scully) McN.; m. Janice M. Haertel, June 21, 1958; children: Susan, Mary, Robert, James. Student, John Carroll U., 1952-54; BS in Humanities, Loyola U., 1956, JD, 1958; postdoctoral, Harvard U., 1984. Bar: Ill. 1959. Jr. atty. Brunswick Corp., Skokie, Ill., 1960-63, atty., 1963-68, sr. atty., 1968-85, gen. counsel, 1985-96; v.p., gen. counsel, 1996—. Served with U.S. Army, 1958-60. Mem. Am. Corp. Counsel Assn., North Shore Gen. Counsels Assn., Chgo. Bar Assn. Avocation: golf. Home: 912 N East Ave Oak Park IL 60302-1330 Office: Brunswick Corp 1 N Field Ct Lake Forest IL 60045-4811

MCNAUGHTON, ALEXANDER BRYANT, lawyer; b. Atlanta, Apr. 2, 1948; s. William James and June Florence (Gibson) McN.; m. Susan Mary Knox, Mar. 7, 1981; children: Alexis Loren, Elizabeth Adelyn. BS, Ga. State U., 1974; postgrad., Oxford (England) U., 1980; JD, U. Okla., 1981. Bar: Okla. 1981, U.S. Dist. Ct. (we. dist.) Okla. 1981, U.S. Ct. Appeals (10th cir.) 1982, U.S. Ct. Mil. Appeals 1984, U.S. Supreme Ct. 1985. Social worker State of Ga. Dept. Human Svcs., Bainbridge, 1974-75; farmer MC Farms, Cole, Okla., 1975-81; trial lawyer Mattoon Law Offices, Norman, Okla., 1981-82, Jones, Gungoll, Jackson et al, Enid, Okla., 1982-83, Jones, McNaughton & Blakley, Enid, 1983-85, McNaughton & McNaughton, Enid, 1985-94; Norman, Edem, McNaughton & Wallace, Enid, 1994—; expert cons. in field. Contbr. to book chpt. Scoutmaster Boy Scouts Am., Norman. With U.S. Army, 1966-68. Mem. ABA (litigation, med. negligence, tort and ins. sects.), Okla. Trial Lawyers Assn. (bd. dirs.), Assn. Trial Lawyers Am. (sustaining). Avocations: camping, bicycling, piloting, snow skiing, swimming. Home: 2567 Homestead Rd Enid OK 73703-1647 Office: Norman Edem McNaughton Wallace 110 N Independence Enid OK 73701

MCNAUGHTON, JOHN D., director. Films include Henry: Portrait of a Serial Killer, 1989, The Borrower, 1991, Sex, Drugs, Rock & Roll, 1991, Mad Dog and Glory, 1993, Girls in Prison, 1994. Office: ICM 8942 Wilshire Blvd Beverly Hills CA 90211-1934 also: 1370 N Milwaukee Ave Chicago IL 60622-2149

MCNAUGHTON, ROBERT FORBES, JR., computer science educator; b. Bklyn., Mar. 13, 1924; s. Robert Forbes and Helen (Brown) McN.; m. Ann Gerardo, Dec. 20, 1948 (div. 1957); children: Nicholas F., Sarah E. McNaughton Deppa; m. Vivien Leonard, June 23, 1974. Student, Bklyn. Coll., 1942-43, 46; BA, Columbia U., 1948; PhD, Harvard U., 1951. Tchr. philosophy Ohio State U., 1951-52, U. Mich., 1953-54, Stanford U., 1954-57; tchr. computer sci. and elec. engrng. Moore Sch. Elec. Engring., U. Pa., 1957-64, MIT, 1964-66; prof. computer sci., math. Rensselaer Poly. Inst., Troy, N.Y., 1966-89, prof. emeritus, 1989—; vis. prof. dept. computer sci. SUNY at Albany, 1989-90; researcher Office Naval Rsch., 1952-53, RCA, Moorestown, summer 1960, Princeton, summer 1963. Served with AUS, 1943-46. Recipient Levy medal Franklin Inst., 1956. Mem. Assn. Symbolic Logic, Assn. Computing Machinery, Am. Math. Soc., Math. Assn. Am., Phi Beta Kappa. Home: 2511 15th St Troy NY 12180-1704

MCNAUGHTON, WILLIAM FRANK, translator, educator; b. Westboro, Mo., May 21, 1933; s. Frank McNaughton and Ruth Ellen (Flanders) Francis; m. Margaret Orminski, Apr. 4, 1956 (div. 1971); children: John Ferenc, Dorothy Ellen; m. Li Ying, Apr. 8, 1990. Student, U. Mo., 1951-53; studied poetry and translation with, Ezra Pound, 1953-56; student, Georgetown U., 1953-54; BA, Bklyn. Coll., 1961; PhD, Yale U., 1965. Asst. prof. Oberlin (Ohio) Coll., 1965-70; lectr. Exptl. Coll., Oberlin, 1970-71; vis. lectr. Bowling Green (Ohio) State U., 1972-74, Denison U., Granville, Ohio, 1972-78; prof. Program for Afloat Coll. Edn. (PACE) USN, Norfolk, Va., 1978-84; vis. prof. King Saud U., Abha, Saudi Arabia, 1984-85; sr. lectr. English, translation City Poly. Hong Kong, 1986-89, prin. lectr. translation, 1989-94; univ. sr. lectr. City U., Hong Kong, 1994-95, assoc. prof., 1995—; guest lectr., U. degli Studii, Venice, Italy, 1975; coord. Tri-Coll. Chinese program, Gt. Lakes Colls. Assn., Ann Arbor, 1965-68; cons., Asian Lit. program, Asia Soc., N.Y.C., 1967-80, Nat. Translation Ctr., Austin, Tex., 1965-68, Ballantine Books, N.Y.C., 1985, Princeton U. Press, 1965; presenter papers at lit. confs. Author: Reading and Writing Chinese, 1979; co-translator: Poem Without a Hero and Selected Poems of Anna Akhmatova, 1989, As Though Dreaming: The Tz'u...of Li Ch'ing-chao, 1977; editor, translator: Light from the East, 1978, The Confucian Vision, 1974, The Book of Songs, 1971, The Taoist Vision, 1971, Guerilla War, 1971; contbr. articles to profl. publs., translations to various lit. mags.; editor-in-chief: City Univ. Bull., 1995—; mem. editl. bd. City Univ. Press, 1996—. Woodrow Wilson Found. fellow, 1961-62; modern fgn. lang. fellow, NDEA, 1962-65; grantee, Nat. Translation Ctr., Austin, 1967, Gt. Lakes Colls. Assn., Ann Arbor, 1965, 67-68, Asia Soc., N.Y.C., 1971-72, 74; Fulbright fellow, 1968-69. Avocations: sailing, music, Venetian culture and history. Home: Flat 5C Block 12, 88 Tat Chee Ave, Kowloon Hong Kong Office: City Univ Hong Kong, 83 Tat Chee Ave, Kowloon Hong Kong

MCNEAL, DALE WILLIAM, JR., biological sciences educator; b. Kansas City, Kans., Nov. 23, 1939; s. Dale William and Geraldine Estelle (Reed) McN.; m. Arlene Joyce Purvis, Feb. 26, 1966. B.A., Colo. Coll., 1962; M.S., SUNY Coll. Environ. Sci. and Forestry, Syracuse, 1964; Ph.D., Wash. State U., 1969. Asst. prof. dept. biol. scis. U. Pacific, Stockton, Calif., 1969-74, assoc. prof., 1974-79, prof., 1979—, chmn. dept., 1978-84. Contbr. articles to profl. jours. Served with U.S. Army, 1964-66. Mem. Am. Bot. Soc., Calif. Bot. Soc. (pres. 1987-88), Am. Soc. Plant Taxonomists, Internat. Soc. Plant Taxonomy, Calif. Acad. Scis., Sigma Xi. Republican. Episcopalian. Office: U Pacific Dept Biol Scis Stockton CA 95211

MCNEAL, SHAY, advertising executive; b. Sturgis, Ky., Nov. 5, 1946; d. John H'Earl Evans and Mary Ellen Baird; 1 child, Richard McNeal (dec. 1972); 1 child, Hethur; m. Gordon K. Smith, Oct. 24, 1975 (div. 1982); 1 child, Paris. Student, DeKalb Coll. Asst. dir. Savannah St. Mission, Atlanta, 1968-70; spl. project asst. Lovable Co., Atlanta, 1970-71; assoc. buyer Montgomery Ward/Knit Div., N.Y., 1971-73; nat. fashion dir. Dan River Mills, N.Y.; mktg. dir. Macy's SE div., Atlanta, 1974-78; pres. Smith McNeal Advt., 1978-86; sr. v.p., gen. mgr. William Cook Advt., Atlanta, 1986-89; pres. Preemptive Ltd., Beverly Hills, Calif., 1989-91, Georgetown Prodns., Washington, 1991—; key cons. Jack Watson for Gov., Atlanta and Savannah; mem. faculty, jurist Portfolio Ctr., Atlanta, 1988-89; media cons. anti David Duke campaign Dem. Party, Washington. Bd. dirs. Travelers Aid, Atlanta, 1982-84; vol. ARC, Atlanta, 1978—, various advt. clubs nationwide; appointed by the gov. to Ga. Film Commn., 1989; media cons. Anti-David Duke Campaign for Dem. Party, Washington. Named one of the Top Advt. Women in the S.E. AdWeek, Atlanta, 1987. Mem. Am. Assn. Advt. Agys., Exec. Womens Assn., Atlanta Advt. Club, Ansley Golf Club Atlanta. Democrat. Avocation: horseback riding.

MCNEALEY, J. JEFFREY, lawyer, corporate executive; b. Cin., Feb. 8, 1944; s. J. Lawrence and Louise McNealey; m. Sara Wilson, Sept. 24, 1988; children: Anne Elizabeth, John Alexander. BA, Cornell U., 1966; JD, Ohio State U., 1969. Ptnr. Porter, Wright, Morris & Arthur, Columbus, Ohio, 1969—; bd. dirs. TRC Cos., Windsor, Conn., 1985—; sec., bd. dirs. The Smoot Corp., Columbus, 1972—. Trustee Columbus Cancer Clinic, 1972—, past pres.; trustee German Village Soc., Columbus, 1986—, past pres.; bd. dirs. Columbus chpt. ARC, 1983-86, Columbus Urban League, 1984-90; active Union League Chgo., 1982—. Mem. ABA, Ohio State Bar Assn. (past chmn. environ. com. 1978-84), Columbus Bar Assn., Columbus Country Club, Capital Club of Columbus, Cornell Club of Ctrl. Ohio (trustee 1978—, past pres.). Episcopalian. Avocations: flying, racquet sports, wood working, flyfishing. Office: Porter Wright Morris & Arthur 41 S High St Fl 30 Columbus OH 43215-6101

MC NEALY, SCOTT, computer company executive; b. 1954. BA, Harvard U., 1976; MBA, Stanford U., 1980. Chmn., pres., chief exec. officer Sun Microsystems Inc., Mountain View, Calif.; with Rockwell Internat. Corp., Troy, Mich., 1976-78, sales engr.; staff engr. FMC Corp., Chgo., 1980-81; dir. ops. Onyx Systems, San Jose, Calif., 1981-82; with Sun Microsystems Inc., Mountain View, Calif., 1982—, now chmn. bd., pres., chief exec. officer, also dir. Office: Sun Microsystems Inc 2550 Garcia Ave Mountain View CA 94043-1109*

MCNEAR, BARBARA BAXTER, financial communications executive, consultant; b. Chgo., Oct. 9, 1939; d. Carl Henden and Alice Gertrude (Parrish) Baxter; m. Robert Erskine McNear, Apr. 13, 1968 (div. 1981); 1 child, Amanda Baxter; m. Glenn Philip Eisen, June 7, 1987. B.S. in Journalism, Northwestern U., 1961. Editorial asst. Scott Foresman & Co., Chgo., 1961; pub. rels. dir. Market Facts Inc., Chgo., 1961-63; account supr. Philip Lesly Co., Chgo., 1963-68, 69; account exec. Burson-Marsteller, Chgo., 1968; dir. communications CNA Fin. Corp., Chgo., 1969-74; dir. pub. rels. Gould Inc., Chgo., 1974; v.p. Harris Bank, Chgo., 1974-80, Fireman's Fund Ins. Co., San Francisco, 1980-83; sr. v.p. First Chgo. Corp., 1983-86; v.p. communications Xerox Fin. Svcs., Inc., Stamford, Conn., 1987-93; mgr. shareholder comm. Xerox Corp., Stamford, 1993—. Mem. Pub. Rels. Soc. Am., Fairfield County Pub. Rels. Assn., Nat. Investor Rels. Inst. (pres. Chgo. chpt. 1974-75, bd. dirs. Chgo. chpt.), Cliffdwellers, Princeton Club. Episcopalian. Home: 23 Telva Rd Wilton CT 06897-3733 Office: Xerox Corp 800 Long Ridge Rd Stamford CT 06902-1227

MCNEEL, VAN LOUIS, chemical company executive; b. Laurel, Miss., July 4, 1925; s. George Louis and Pauline (Webb) McN.; m. Betty Tarwater, July 6, 1959 (div. 1966); 1 child, Clayton Webb; m. Diane Kidd, Dec. 30, 1971 (div. 1994); 1 child, Ian Edward. Student, Sanford U. (formerly Howard Coll.); LLB, U. Ala., 1949. Project mgr. Reynolds Metals, N.Y.C. and Jacksonville, Fla., 1949-51; div. mgr. Olin Mathieson Chem. Corp., Atlanta, 1951-60, dir. internat. ops., 1960-63; pres. Polymer Internat. Corp., N.Y.C., 1963-64; chmn., chief exec. officer McNeel Internat Corp, Tampa, Fla., 1964—. Bd. dirs. Tampa chpt ARC; mem. Golden Triangle Civic Assn., Tampa Bay Area Trade Coun. Fgn. Rels. Mem. Am. Mgmt. Assn., Soc. Plastic Engrs. Clubs: Palma Ceia Golf and Country, Tampa Yacht and Country, Ctr. Club, University (Tampa). Office: McNeel Internat Corp 5401 W Kennedy Blvd Tampa FL 33609-2433

MCNEELEY, DONALD ROBERT, steel company executive; b. Chgo., July 31, 1954; s. Donald Robert and Alma Theresa (Gray) McN.; m. Elizabeth Dianne Smith, Aug. 23, 1975; children: Kelly Dianne, Meghan Maureen. BA, U. Wis., 1979; MBA summa cum laude, George Williams Coll., 1985; PhD cum laude, Columbia Pacific U., 1986; MS in Mgmt. and Organiztional Behavior, Ill. Benedictine Coll., 1991. With Chgo. Tube and Iron Co., 1972-77, ops. mgr., 1977-79, corp. mgr. employee relations, 1979-82, v.p. ops., 1982-84, exec. v.p., 1984-91, pres., chief oper. officer, 1991—, also bd. dirs.; trustee Plumbing and Heating Wholesalers Retirement Income Plan, Chgo., 1987—, negotiator labor com., 1982—; adj. prof. mgmt. De Paul U., Chgo., 1992, mem. bus. adv. coun., mem. Inst. for Bus. and Profl. Ethics, De Paul U. Editor: Employment in Illinois, 1983; contbr. articles to profl. jours. Dir. Com. for Monetary Rsch. and Edn., Greenwich, Conn., 1988—. Mem. Steel Svc. Ctr. Inst. (trustee, 1st v.p. Found. for Continuing Edn. 1981—, chmn. tubular products coun. 1994—), La Grange Country Club (Ill.). Republican. Roman Catholic. Avocations: golf, reading, investing.

MCNEELY, JOHN J., lawyer; b. Mpls., Oct. 8, 1931; s. John J. Sr. and Mae (Carlin) McN.; children: Mary Ann, John J. Jr., Michael F., Patricia C., David C. BS, Georgetown U., 1955, JD, 1958. Bar: Minn. 1958. Law clk. Minn. Supreme Ct., St. Paul, 1958-59; ptnr. Briggs & Morgan, St. Paul, 1959—. Sgt. USMC, 1950-52. Fellow Am. Coll. Trust and Estate Counsel; mem. ABA, Minn. State Bar Assn., Ramsey County Bar Assn., Prestrwick Country Club. Home: 1183 Ivy Hill Dr Saint Paul MN 55118-1827 Office: Briggs & Morgan 2200 1st Nat Bank Bldg Saint Paul MN 55101

MCNEESE, BRENDA LUNNON, community health nurse, researcher; b. Houston; d. George and Mattie (Prescott) Lunnon; 1 child, Marcel Wade McNeese. BSN, Prairie View A&M U., Prairie, Tex., 1973; MS in Nursing, Tex. Woman's U., Houston, 1978; DrPH, U. Tex., Houston, 1994. Cert. gerontol. nurse. Admissions coord. Vis. Nurse Assn., Houston; coord. post hosp. planning VA, Houston. Contbr. articles to profl. jours. 2d lt. USAF, 1971-76. Recipient Diamond Anniversary award Prairie View A&M U. Coll. Nursing, 1993. Mem. Am. Assn. Spinal Cord Injury, Tex. Nurses Assn. (Dist. 9 Nursing Celebration award 1993), Sigma Theta Tau. Home: 4502 University Oaks Blvd Houston TX 77004-6704

MC NEESE, WILMA WALLACE, social worker; b. Chgo., Apr. 30, 1946; d. Nettie Fletcher Wallace; student Wilson City Coll., 1964-66; B.A., So. Ill. U., 1969; M.S.W., Loyola U., Chgo., 1976; m. Mose D. McNeese, Dec. 27, 1969; children—Derrick, Christina. Program coordinator Intensive Tng. and Employment Program, East St. Louis, Ill., 1970-71; methods and procedures adviser Ill. Dept. Pub. Aid, Chgo., 1972-73; social work intern Robbins (Ill.) Presch. Center, 1974; with U.S. Probation Office, Chgo., 1975; officer U.S. Pretrial Services Agy., Chgo., 1976-87; chief U.S. pretrial services officer for western dist. Pa., 1987—; fieldwork instr. Aurora Coll., 1981, Chgo. State U., 1981-82; grad. fieldwork instr. U. Ill. Sch. of Social Work, 1986; mem. bd. trustees The Wesley Inst. Inc., 1993—. Recipient Community Service award Village of Robbins, 1975; advanced tng. cert. Fed. Jud. Ctr. Mem. Nat. Assn. Social Workers, Acad. Cert. Social Workers, Nat. Assn. Pretrial Svcs. Agencies, Greater Pitts. Commn. for Women. Baptist. Home: 833 Chalmers Pl Pittsburgh PA 15243-1967 Office: 1000 Liberty Ave Ste 822 Pittsburgh PA 15222-4003

MC NEICE, JOHN AMBROSE, JR., investment company executive; b. Quincy, Mass., Sept. 28, 1932; s. John Ambrose and Gladys Lydia (Starratt) McN.; m. Margarete Emma Aust, Apr. 2, 1956; children: Gabriele S., Margarete Anne. B.A. magna cum laude, Boston Coll., 1954; M.B.A., Northeastern U., Boston, 1960. Chartered fin. analyst. With Colonial Mgmt. Assos., Inc. (subsidiary of TCG, Inc.), Boston, 1956—, v.p., 1968-73, dir. investment rsch., 1973, exec. v.p., 1974, pres., chief exec. officer, 1975-83, chmn., 1983—; chmn. The Colonial Group, Inc., Boston, 1985—, CEO, 1985-95; bd. dirs., Am. Ireland Fund. Trustee Assoc. Boston Coll.; Trustee Boston Coll. H.S., St. John's Sem.; Cath. Charities of Archdiocese of Boston; chmn. bd. trustees Nativity Prep. Sch.; mem. Carney Hosp. Found., Corp. Westworth Inst. Tech.; bd. visitors Peter F. Drucker Ctr., Claremont U.; bd. dirs., treas., exec. com. Peter F. Drucker Found.; bd. dirs., exec. com. United Way Mass. Bay; bd. overseers Northeastern U.; trustee, pres. Boston Cath. Found., Archdiocese of Boston, mem. fin. coun.; dir. Pope John XXIII Med.-Moral Rsch. and Edn. Ctr.; bd. overseers Facing Hist. and Ourselves Nat. Found., Inc.; pres., trustee Better Opportunities Scholarship Found., Inc.; mem. exec. com. CEOs for Fundamental Change in Edn. With U.S. Army, 1954-56. Mem. Knights of Malta, Union Club, Wollaston Golf Club. Roman Catholic. Home: 47 Green St Canton MA 02021-1023 Office: The Colonial Group Inc 1 Financial Ctr Boston MA 02111-2621

MCNEIL, BARBARA JOYCE, radiologist, educator; b. Cambridge, Mass., Feb. 11, 1941; d. Archibald Pius and Katherine (Joyce) McN. A.B., Emmanuel Coll., 1962; M.D., Harvard U., 1966, Ph.D., 1972. Diplomate: Am. Bd. Nuclear Medicine. Intern Mass. Gen. Hosp., Boston, 1966-67, resident in nuclear medicine, 1971-73; prof. radiology and clin. epidemiology Harvard Med. Sch. and Brigham & Women's Hosp., Boston, 1983—, dir. ctr. for cost effective care, 1980-93; chmn. dept., Ridley Watts prof. health care policy Harvard Med. Sch., 1988—; chmn. Blue Cross-Mass. Hosp. Assn. Fund for Coop. Innovation, 1981-87; mem. Prospective Payment Assessment Commn., 1983-91; mem. nat. adv. coun. Agy. for Health Care Policy, Rsch. and Evaluation, 1991—. Editor: Critical Issues in Medical Technology, 1982; contbr. articles to profl. jours. Fellow AAAS, Am. Coll. Nuclear Physicians; mem. Am. Acad. Arts and Scis., Inst. Medicine (coun. 1991—), Fleischner Soc., Nat. Coun. on Radiation Protection, Am. Coll. Radiology, Soc. Nuclear Medicine. Office: Harvard Med Sch 25 Shattuck St Boston MA 02115-6027

MC NEIL, DONALD LEWIS, retired multiple association management company executive; b. Milw., Dec. 20, 1926; s. Robert Lewis and Elizabeth Barbara (Bloesius) McN.; m. Mildred M. Hancock, Sept. 2, 1950. PhB, Marquette U., 1950. Editor Pewaukee (Wis.) Post, 1948-50; advt. copywriter Sears Roebuck, Milw., 1952-53; press. dir. United Way of Greater Milw., 1953-57; mgr. adminstrv. services Med. Soc. Milwaukee County, 1957-62; v.p. Exec. Dir., Inc., Milw., 1962-67; pres. Exec. Dir., Inc., 1967-94; ret., 1994; organizer, dir. Hartland Nat. Bank (Wis.). Pub. Am. Christmas Tree Jour., 1966-92. Pres. Hartland United Way, 1949-58; active Republican politics. With USN, 1944-46, 50-52. Mem. Am. Soc. Assn. Execs., VFW, Am. Legion, Urgan League, Lac LaBelle Golf Club, St. Charles Ch. Men's Club. Republican. Roman Catholic. Home: 432 E Capitol Dr Hartland WI 53029-2202

MCNEIL, MARY ELIZABETH, school system administrator; b. Boston, Oct. 15, 1946; d. Joseph C. and Margaret A. (Murray) McN.; 1 child, Ryan McNeil Pierce. BS in Social Scis. and Elem. Edn., U. Vt., 1968, MEd in Spl. Edn., 1972; EdD in Systems Devel. and Adaptation, Boston U., 1979. Tchr. remedial reading Burlington (Vt.) Sch. Dist., 1968, tchr. elem. sch., 1968-70; instr. intensive reading program Chittenden South Supervisory Sch. Dist., Hinesburg, Vt., 1972; cons. tchr. Chittenden South Supervisory Sch. Dist., Shelburne, Vt., 1972-76, co-dir. Title VI G Model Demonstration Ctr., 1974-76; lectr. spl. edn. Coll. Edn. and Social Svcs. U. Vt., 1976-79, lectr., coord. responsive teacher program dept. profl. edn., 1979-81, facilitator workshop on effective schs. Vt. Sch. Improvement Inst., 1981, coord. Woodstock/UVM collaborative project Coll. Edn. and Social Svcs., 1981-84, mem. faculty grad. coll., 1980—, asst. prof. responsive tchr. program dept. profl. edn. and cirriculum devel., 1980-83, assoc. prof., 1983-91, coord. respnsive tchr. program, 1980-85, adminstr. Ednl. Devel. Ctr., 1985-86, interim chair dept. profl. edn. and cirriculum devel. Coll. Edn. and Social Svcs., 1988-89; dir. spl. edn. and evaluation, coord. responsive tchr. program. Merced (Calif.) Union High Sch. Dist., 1992—; mem. steering com. Vt. Outcomes-Based Instrn. Network; vis. prof. U. Moncton, N.B., Can., 1983; mem. Calif. Statewide Spl. Edn. Task Force. Author: Partner Learning, 1984; assoc. editor Edn. and Treatment Children, 1982-89, mem. editorial rev. bd., 1982—; co-editor Jour. Tchr. Edn. and Spl. Edn., 1987-90; guest editor Pro Ed Publ., 1981; reviewer Jour. Applied Behavioral Analysis, 1983-86; contbr. articles to profl. jours. Pres. Vt. Coun. for Exceptional Children. Mem. Ptnrs. of Ams. (pres.). Avocations: reading, skiing, traveling, gardening. Office: Merced Union High Sch Dist Merced CA 95344

MCNEIL, STEVEN ARTHUR, food company executive; b. Ft. Thomas, Ky., May 6, 1942; s. Arthur James and Ruby Marie (Lindell) McN.; m. Kathryn Louise Knapp, Aug. 27, 1966; children: Andrew James, Kathryn Marie. BA, Ohio Wesleyan U., 1964; MBA, Dartmouth U., 1966. Mgr. mktg. and devel. Gen. Foods Corp., 1966-80; mgr. mktg. and devel. Campbell Soup Co., Camden, N.J., 1980-81, mgr. Swanson bus. unit, 1981-83, gen. mgr., 1983-84, group gen. mgr., 1984-85, corp. v.p., 1985—; pres. Mrs. Paul's, 1988-90; sr. v.p., gen. mgr. N.Am., The Haagen-Dazs Co., Inc., Teaneck, N.J., 1990-91; pres., chief oper. officer Bumble Bee SeaFoods, Inc., San Diego, 1992-93; dean Rowan Sch. of Bus. Rowan Coll. N.J., 1994—; bd. dirs. South Jersey Industries Inc., Folsom, N.J.; chmn., mem. exec. com. Frozen Food Inst., McLean, Va. Trustee West Jersey Health and Hosp. Found., Camden, sec., 1989-91; co-founder The Friends of the Nyacks, Nyack, N.Y., 1972; bd. dirs. Gloucester County United Way, 1995—. Mem. South Jersey C. of C. (bd. dirs. 1994—, chmn. Camden Fin. Controls com. 1996—), La Costa Country Club.

MCNEILL, ALFRED THOMAS, JR., construction executive; b. Elizabeth, N.J., Dec. 21, 1936; s. Alfred T. and Mary Ellen (Byrne) McN.; m. Dorothy J. Keidat, Oct. 4, 1981; children: Mary McNeill Ivanoski, Gabrielle McNeill Hensley, Matthew, Christopher, Peter, Bartholomew, Elizabeth McNeill Downes, Catherine, Gwyneth Elizabeth. BSCE, Lehigh U., 1958. Registered profl. engr., Ohio, N.Y. With Turner Constrn. Co., 1958—; field engr. Turner Constrn. Co., N.Y.C., 1958; supt. Turner Constrn. Co., Cin., 1961, gen. supt., 1969; corp. v.p. ops. Turner Constrn. Co., N.Y.C., 1973; v.p., gen. mgr. Turner Constrn. Co., Phila., 1975, regional sr. v.p., 1981; pres., chief exec. officer Turner Constrn. Co., N.Y.C., 1985; pres. The Turner Corp., N.Y.C., 1986-89, chmn. bd., chief exec. officer, 1989—, also dir.; chmn. State of Ohio Apprenticeship Coun., Cin., 1970-73; mem. nat. collective bargaining com. Associated Gen. Contractors, 1970-75; mem. labor policy com. Gen. Bldg. Contractors Assn., 1975-80, bd. dirs., 1978-84; bd. dirs. Tchrs. Properties, Inc., Rouse-Tchrs. Properties; adv. bd. Liberty Mut. Ins. Co.; mem. Constrn. Industry Pres.'s Forum; mem. civil engring. adv. bd. Lehigh U. Co-author: Construction Management for the General Contractor, 1974. Mem. chmn.'s circle USA-ROC Econ. Coun., N.Y.C. Partnership, NYU Real Estate Inst. Adv. Bd. 2d lt. U.S. Army, 1959, capt. Res. Recipient award Nat. Associated Gen. Contrators, 1974, De La Salle medal Manhattan Coll., 1991. Mem. Am. Inst. Constructors (constructor), Regional Plan Assn. (bd. dirs. 1985-87), Econ. Club N.Y., Aronimink Country Club (Newtown Square, Pa.), The Sky Club (N.Y.C. v.p., bd. govs.), Blind Brook Club (Purchase, N.Y.), Ocean Reef Club (Key Largo, Fla.). Roman Catholic. Avocation: golf. Office: The Turner Corp 375 Hudson St New York NY 10014-3658*

MC NEILL, CHARLES JAMES, publishing executive; b. Newton, Kans., Dec. 1, 1912; s. Hugh Andrew and Elizabeth (Sheehan) McN.; m. Mary Elizabeth O'Neill, Nov. 6, 1935; 1 dau., Mary Sharon McGlynn. A.B., St. Benedict's Coll., 1933, L.H.D., 1956; postgrad., U. Denver, 1934-36; B.J., Register Coll. Journalism, Denver, 1935, M.J., 1937, D.Journalism, 1939. Librarian Sacred Heart Jr. Coll., 1933; exec. sec. Cath. Action Com. of Men, Wichita, Kans., 1933-34; staff Cath. Advance, Wichita, 1934; asso. editor Register System of Cath. Newspapers, 1934-43; staff Geo. A. Pflaum, Pub., Inc., Dayton, Ohio, 1946-49, asst. to pres., 1949-51, gen. mgr., 1951-57; asst. European dir. Radio Free Europe, Munich, Germany, 1957-61; treas. Internat. Television Devel. Corp., N.Y.C., 1961-63, Inter Tel N.V., Amsterdam, 1961-63; v.p. Kane, McNeill, Inc., N.Y.C., 1963-72, Cath. Lists, Inc., Mt. Vernon, N.Y., 1965-72; pres. Cath. Lists, Inc., 1972-86; dir. Intertel (Prodns.) S.A., Brussels, 1961-63; Ofcl. del. Internat. Union Cath. Press ECOSOC, 1952-56; nat. council USO, 1956; bd. advisers Nat. Fund Raising Conf., 1968-69; bd. dirs. Our Sunday Visitor, Inc., 1968-86. Author: The Sacramentals, 1938, Prayers, 1939, Catholic Church in Colorado, 1943, (with Gregory Smith) Divine Love Story, 1941. Served with AUS, 1943-46. Recipient Disting. Service award Nat. Cath. Devel. Conf., 1984. Mem. Classroom Periodical Pubs. Assn. (chmn. 1950-57), Cath. Press Assn. (pres. 1954-56, St. Francis de Sales award 1987), Cath. Assn. Internat. Peace (v.p. 1953-59), Nat. Cath. Edn. Assn., C. of C. Democrat. Home: 860 Grand Concourse Bronx NY 10451-2814 Office: 22 W 1st St Ste 511 Mount Vernon NY 10550-3000

MCNEILL, CORBIN ASAHEL, JR., utility executive; b. Santa Fe, July 6, 1939; s. Corbin Asahel and Madeline (Thielen) McN.; m. Dorice Schiller, June 16, 1962; children: Michele, Corbin IV, Kevin, Alicia, Timothy. BS in Marine Engring., U.S. Naval Acad., 1962; postgrad., Naval Nuclear Power Sch., Mare Island, Md., 1962-63, U. Calif., Berkeley, 1975-76, Syracuse U., 1983-84. Commd. ensign USN, 1962, advanced through grades to comdr., 1981, ret., 1981; sr. v.p. nuclear generation N.Y. Power Authority, White Plains, 1981-85, Pub. Service Electric & Gas Co., Hancocks Bridge, N.J., 1985-88; exec. v.p. nuclear div. PECO Energy Co., 1988-90; pres., chief operating officer Phila. Electric Co., 1990—; pres. Adwin Equipment Co., Phila., 1990—. Trustee The Meml. Hosp. of Salem County (N.J.) Inc., 1986; chmn. TeamWalk March of Dimes, Salem, 1986; bd. dirs. Oswego (N.Y.) C. of C., 1982-83. Mem. Am. Nuclear Soc., Nuclear Utility Mgmt. and Resources Com. Avocation: skiing, reading. Office: PECO Energy Co PO Box 8699 Philadelphia PA 19101-8699*

MCNEILL, DANIEL RICHARD, writer; b. San Francisco, June 1, 1947; s. Daniel Harry and Maureen Evangeline (Sherriff) McN.; m. Rosalind Deborah Gold, Dec. 20, 1984. AB, U. Calif., Berkeley, 1975; JD, Harvard U., 1982. Author: Fuzzy Logic, 1993 (L.A. Times Book prize 1993). Mem. Authors Guild. Avocations: hiking, swimming. Home and Office: 9905 Farragut Dr Apt 2 Culver City CA 90232-3244

MCNEILL, FREDERICK WALLACE, lawyer, educator, writer, U.S. government consultant, former military and commercial pilot; b. Chgo., Jan. 4, 1932; s. James Joseph and Irene Gertrude (Stevenson) McN.; m. Judith Carol Austin, Feb. 9, 1957; children: Marjorie, Tamelyn, Kenneth, Patricia, Darcy, Sean, Meghan. BBA, U. Ariz., 1974, JD, 1977. Bar: Ariz. 1977, U.S. Dist. Ct. Ariz., 1977. Served to maj. USAF, 1949-73; ret., 1973; bus. mgr. Engring. & Research Assocs., Inc., Tucson, 1973-74; mng. ptnr. ERA Shopping Ctr., Tucson, 1973-75; chief pilot, spl. agt. Narcotics Strike Force, Ariz., 1975-77; dep. county atty. Pima County, Ariz., 1977-79; atty. Ariz. Drug Control Dist., 1977-79; ptnr. Rees & McNeill, Tucson, 1979-84; writer, 1984—; coord. legal asst. studies program and adj. prof. Nova U.-Panama Ctr., Republic of Panama, 1987-90; adj. prof. Ctrl. Tex. Coll., Germany, 1990-92, Univ. Phoenix and Pima County Coll., Tucson, 1992—; pvt. practice U.S. law, U.S. mil. and PCC installations, 1987-90; of counsel Carreira-Pitti P.C. Abogados, Panama, 1987-90; cons. Booz, Allen & Hamilton, Inc., Panama, 1989-90; pvt. practice Wurzburg, Fed. Republic of Germany, 1990-92; pvt. practice, Tucson, 1992—, adj. prof. Ctrl. Tex. Coll., Germany, 1990-92, U. Phoenix, Pima C.C., Tucson, 1992—; lectr. air smuggling seminars, organized crime seminars, Ariz., 1977-79. V.p. Indian Ridge Homeowners Assn., 1980-82; bd. dirs. Tucson Boys Chorus Bldg. Fund Com., 1972-74; lt. Ariz. Rangers. Decorated DFC, Air medal (5), Air Force Commendation medal (2). Mem. ABA, ATLA, Ariz. Bar Assn., Pima County Bar Assn., Ariz. Trial Lawyers Assn., Lawyer Pilots Bar Assn., Internat. Platform Assn., Ret. Officers Assn., Air Force Assn., DAV, Vietnam Vets. Am., Order of Daedelians, Quiet Birdmen. Home: 9957 E Stella Rd Tucson AZ 85730

MCNEILL, G. DAVID, psychologist, educator; b. Santa Rosa, Calif., Dec. 21, 1931; s. Glenn H. and Ethel G. (Little) McN.; m. Nobuko Baba, Dec. 17, 1957; children: Cheryyl, Randall Baba. A.B., U. Calif. at Berkeley, 1953, Ph.D., 1962. Research fellow Harvard U., 1962-65; asst. prof. psychology U. Mich., 1965-66, assoc. prof., 1966-68; prof. psychology and linguistics U. Chgo., 1969—, chmn. dept. psychology, 1991—; mem. Inst. Advanced Study, Princeton, 1973-75; fellow Netherlands Inst. for Advanced Studies, 1983-84. Author: The Acquisition of Language, 1970, The Conceptual Basis of Language, 1979, Psycholinguistics: A New Approach, 1987, Gengo Shinrigaku, 1991, Hand and Mind: What Gestures Reveal about Thought, 1992. Recipient Faculty Achievement award Burlington No., 1991, Ann. Excellence in Pub. award Assn. Am. Pubs., Gordon G. Laing award U. Chgo. Press, 1995; Guggenheim fellow, 1973-74; grantee NSF, 1983-89, Spencer Found., 1979-82, 89-92, 95—, NIDCD, 1992-96. Fellow AAAS, Am. Psychol. Soc.; mem. Cognitive Sci. Soc., Linguistic Soc. Am., Violoncello Soc., Phi Beta Kappa, Sigma Xi. Office: U Chgo Dept Psychology 5848 S University Ave Chicago IL 60637-1515

MCNEILL, JOHN, museum administrator; b. Edinburgh, Scotland, U.K., Sept. 15, 1933; s. Thomas and Helen Lawrie (Eagle) McN.; m. Bridget Mariel Winterton, July 29, 1961 (div. 1990); children: Andrew Thomas, Douglas Paul; m. Marilyn Lois James, Apr. 6, 1990. BSc with honors, U. Edinburgh, 1955, PhD, 1960. Asst. lectr. dept. agrl. botany U. Reading, Eng., 1957-60, lectr. agrl. botany, 1960-61; lectr. dept. botany U. Liverpool, Eng., 1961-69; rsch. scientist Plant Rsch. Inst. Agriculture, Ottawa, Can., 1969-77; sr. rsch. scientist Biosystematics Rsch. Inst. Agr., Ottawa, Can., 1977-81; prof. dept. biology U. Ottawa, Can., 1981-87; regius keeper Royal Botanic Garden, Edinburgh, Scotland, 1987-89; assoc. dir. Royal Ont. Mus., Toronto, Can., 1989-90, acting dir., 1990-91, dir., 1991—; prof. dept. botany U. Toronto, 1991-95; dir., pres. Royal Ont. Mus., Toronto, Can., 1995—; curator herbarium U. Liverpool, 1964-69, dep. sr. tutor faculty sci., 1967-69; vis. assoc. prof dept botany U. Wash., Seattle, 1969; acting assoc. prof. dept. population and environ. biology U. Calif., Irvine, 1969; chief taxonomy and econ. botany sect. Plant Rsch. Inst. Agriculture, Ottawa, Can., 1969-73; sessional lectr. dept. biology U. Ottawa, 1977, chmn. dept. biology, 1981-87, mem. faculty sci. teaching com., 1987, mem. univ. rsch. com., 1986-87, mem. univ. adv. com. on computing, 1984-87, mem. sch. grad. studies, adj. prof., 1987-91; vis. prof. dept. botany U. Toronto, 1978; adj. prof. dept. biology Carleton U., 1973-79; hon. prof. dept. botany U. Edinburgh, 1989, hon. fellow faculty sci., 1988-89; dir. George R. Gardiner Mus. Ceramic Art, Toronto, 1991—; pres. Royal Ont. Mus. Found., 1992—; contbr. to numerous sci. meetings throughout U.S., Can. Europe. Author: (with others) Grasses of Ontario, 1980, The Genus Atriplex (Chenopodiaceae) in Canada, 1983, Preliminary Inventory of Canadian Weeds, 1988, also book chpts.; editor: (with others) Phenetic and Phylogenetic Classification, 1964, International Code of Botanical Nomenclature, 1983, 88, 94, French edit., 1988, 95, German edit., 1989, 95, Japanese edit., 1992, Flora of North America, Vols. 1 and 2, 1993, International Code of Nomenclature for Cultivated Plants, 1995; mem. editl. com. Flora of N.Am., 1985—, nomenclature advisor, 1987—; contbr. articles to profl. jours.; mem. internat. bd. editors Edinburgh Jour. Botany, 1996—. NSERC Operating grantee, 1982-85, 1985-88, 1989-92. Fellow Linnean Soc. London; mem. Am. Soc. Naturalists, Am. Soc. Plant Taxonomists, Biol. Coun. Can. (v.p. 1984-85, v.p. and pres.-elect 1985-86, pres. 1986-87), Can. Coun. Univ. Biology Chmn. (v.p. 1982-84, pres. 1984-85, past pres. 1985-86), Bot. Soc. Brit. Isles, Bot. Soc. Edinburgh (v.p. 1987-89), Can. Bot. Assn. (chmn. systematics and phytogeography sect. 1981-83), Natural Scis. and Engring. Rsch. Coun. Can. (mem. population biology grant selection com. 1981-84), Classification Soc., Hennig Soc., Hunt Inst. Bot. Documentation, Internat. Union Biol. Scis. (voting mem. exec. 1985-88, alt. mem. exec. 1991-94), Internat. Assn. Bot. and Mycological Socs. (sec. 1986-93, chmn. 1993—), Internat. Union Biol. Scis., Internat. Union Microbiol. Socs. (internat. com. for bionomenclature 1994—), Internat. Assn. Plant Taxonomy (mem. coun. 1981-87, 93—, adminstr. fin. 1987-93), Internat. Congress Systematic and Evolutionary Biology (mem. internat. com. 1980-90), Internat. Orgn. Plant Biosystematists (mem. coun. 1989-92), Annales Botanici Fennici (mem. adv. bd. 1987-92), Acta Botanica Fennica (mem. adv. bd. 1987-92), Internat. Assn. Bot. Gardens, Internat. Weed Sci. Soc., Orgn. for Phyto-Taxonomic Investigation of Mediterranean Area (bd. dirs. 1989—), Royal Caledonian Hort. Soc., Royal Hort. Soc., Soc. Systematic Biology, Systematics Assn. (mem. coun. 1959-62, 64-66, gen. sec. 1966-69), Ottawa Field Naturalists Club, Scottish Rock Garden Club. Office: Royal Ontario Museum, 100 Queen's Park, Toronto, ON Canada M5S 2C6

MCNEILL, JOHN HENDERSON, lawyer, government official; b. Phila., Jan. 31, 1941; s. John Henderson and Cecilia Marie (Murphy) McN.; m. Helen Elizabeth Foley, June 18, 1966; children: John Henderson IV, Bronwyn Jane Foley, Andrew Patrick Joseph. BA, U. Notre Dame, 1962; JD, Villanova U., 1965; LLM, London Sch. Econs., 1971, PhD, 1974; diploma Hague Acad. Internat. Law, 1973. Bar: Pa. 1966, U.S. Supreme Ct. 1970, D.C. 1981. Assoc. Sheer & Mazzocone, Phila., 1966; asst. defender Defender Assn. Phila., 1966-67; law clk. to Hon. Wm. W. Vogel, Judge, Ct. Common Pleas, Montgomery County, Pa., 1969-70; internat. rels. officer ACDA, 1974-75, atty. adv., 1975-78, asst. gen. counsel, 1979-83; asst. gen. counsel internat. affairs and intelligence, U.S. Dept. Def., 1983-92, dep. gen. counsel internat. affairs and intelligence, 1992-93, acting gen. counsel, 1993, sr. dep. gen. counsel internat. affairs and intelligence, 1993—; legal adv. U.S. del. SALT, 1977-79, Intermediate Range Nuclear Forces Negotiations with USSR, 1981-82, Strategic Arms Reduction Talks with USSR, 1983, Dept. Def. rep. Maritime Boundary Talks with USSR, 1984-90; chmn. Dept. Def. Task Force on Law of the Sea Conv., 1994—; mem. U.S. del. Internat. Ct. Justice, 1995, participant adv. opinions cases; cons. Amnesty Internat., London, 1971-73, IAEA, Vienna, 1976, Ford Found., 1990; lectr. U. Notre Dame London Centre Legal Studies, 1973-74; profl. lectr. Paul H. Nitze Sch. Advanced Internat. Studies Johns Hopkins U., Washington, 1994—; adj. prof. law Georgetown U., 1987—; Charles H. Stockton prof. internat. law U.S. Naval War Coll., 1990-91. Mem. editorial adv. bd. Internat. Legal Materials, 1992—; mem. editl. bd. Am. Jour. Internat. Law., 1996—. Bd. dirs. Crusade D.C. div. Am. Cancer Soc., 1976-77; bd. consultors Villanova U. Law Sch., 1978—; mem. internat. adv. com. John D. and Catherine T. MacArthur Found. Project on Governing Rules of Internat. Law, 1990-93. 2d lt. USAF, 1967-68. Career mem. U.S. Sr. Exec. Service, 1983—. Recipient Meritorious Honor award ACDA, 1979, Leadership Honor award Nat. Capital Area Combined Fed. Campaign, 1982; awarded rank of meritorious exec., U.S. Pres., 1987, 92, Intelligence Under Law award Nat. Security Agy., 1995; Centre Studies and Rsch. in Internat. Law and Internat. Rels., Hague Acad. Internat. Law scholar, 1974; London Sch. Econs. Internat. Law scholar, 1973. Mem. Am. Soc. Internat. Law. (exec. coun. 1986-89, exec. com. 1988-89), Coun. Fgn. Rels., Internat. Inst. Strategic Studies, Fed. Bar Assn., Inter-Am. Bar Assn., Internat. Law Assn., Cosmos Club (bd. mgmt. 1994—). Office: Pentagon Rm 3e963 Washington DC 20301-1600

MCNEILL, JOHN HUGH, university dean; b. Chgo., July 5, 1938; s. John and Agnes Margaret (McLean) McN.; m. Sharon Keneffly, July 27, 1963;

children: Sandra, Laurie. BS, U. Alta., Can., 1960, MS, 1962; PhD, U. Mich., 1967. Lectr. pharmacy Dalhousie U., 1962-63, U. Alta., 1963; research assoc. U. Mich., Ann Arbor, 1963-65, teaching fellow, 1965-66; asst. instr. Mich. State U., East Lansing, 1966-67, asst. prof., 1967-71; assoc. prof. U. B.C., 1971-72, assoc. prof., chmn. div. pharmacology and toxicology, 1972-75, dir. research and grad. studies Faculty Pharm. Scis., 1977-78; prof. Faculty Pharm. Scis., 1975—; asst. dean U. B.C., 1978-81, research prof. Med. Research Council, 1981-82, prof., assoc. dean research and grad. studies, 1982-84, dean Faculty Pharm. Scis., 1985-96. Contbr. over 400 tech. articles to profl. jours. Mem. Pharm. Soc. Can. (various coms. 1974-88, coun. 1977-83, v.p. 1979, pres. 1980-81), Am. Soc. for Pharm. and Therapeutics (J.J. Abel award com. 1981, Upjohn award com., 1978-80, chmn. mem. com. 1983-86), Western Pharm. Soc. (coun. 1977-81, pres. 1979-80, past pres. 1980-81), N.Y. Acad. Scis., Internat. Soc. for Heart Rsch. (coun. 1986-95), AAAS, B.C. Coll. Pharms. (coun. 1985-96), Internat. Union Pharmacologists (Can. rep. 1982-88), Am. Pharm. Assn. Office: The Univ of BC, The Faculty of Pharm Scis, 2146 East Mall, Vancouver, BC Canada V6T 1Z3

MCNEILL, K(ENNETH) G(ORDON), medical physicist; b. Cheshire, Eng., Dec. 21, 1926; s. Ferguson and Elizabeth (Stevenson) McN.; m. J. Ruth S. Robertson, Nov. 6, 1959; 1 dau., Diane E.S. B.A., Oxford (Eng.) U., 1947, M.A., 1950, D.Phil. (Harmsworth Sr. scholar), 1950. Sir John Dill Meml. fellow Yale U., 1950-51; Nuffield research fellow Glasgow (Scotland) U., 1951-52, lectr., 1952-57; mem. faculty U. Toronto, Ont., Can., 1957-92; prof. physics U. Toronto, Ont., Can., 1963-92, prof. medicine, 1969-92; spl. staff mem. Toronto Gen. Hosp., 1974-92; fellow Trinity Coll., Toronto, 1963-92, prof. emeritus, 1992—; mem. adv. com. radiation protection to Ministry Nat. Health and Welfare, 1964-68; mem. nuclear accident contingency planning bd. Govt. of Ont., 1974—; hon. prof. Monash U., Melbourne, 1988; pres. Kishmul Resources Inc. Author: (with J. Maclachlan, P.T. Spencer, J. Bell) Matter and Energy, 1963, 3d edit., 1987, French edit., 1981; contbr. numerous articles to profl. jours. Mem. governing coun. U. Toronto, 1980-86, 89-92. Fellow Instn. Nuclear Engrs. (U.K.); mem. Can. Assn. Physicists, Can. Radiation Protection Assn. Research on low energy nuclear physics and med. physics. Home: 70 Rathnelly Ave, Toronto, ON Canada M4V 2M6

MCNEILL, ROBERT PATRICK, investment counselor; b. Chgo., Mar. 17, 1941; s. Donald Thomas and Katherine (Bennett) McN.; m. Martha Stephan, Sept. 12, 1964; children—Jennifer, Donald, Victoria, Stephan, Elizabeth. B.A. summa cum laude (valedictorian), U. Notre Dame, 1963; M.Letters, Oxford U., 1967. Chartered investment counselor. Assoc. Stein Roe & Farnham, Chgo., 1967-72, gen. ptnr., 1972-77, sr. ptnr., 1977-86, exec. v.p., 1986-89; pres., mng. dir. Stein Roe Internat., Chgo., 1989—; underwriting mem. Lloyds of London, 1980—; dir. Comml. Chgo. Corp.; vice chmn. bd. Hill Internat. Prodn. Co., Houston, 1982—; dir., 4 dir. Touche Remnant Investment Counselors, London, 1983—; dir. TR Worldwide Strategy Fund, Luxembourg, Konrad Adenauer Fund for European Policy Studies, Fed. Republic Germany. Voting mem., sec Ill. Rhodes Scholarship Selection Com.; voting mem. Ill. rep. Great Lakes Dist. Rhodes Scholarship Selection Com.; bd. dirs. Kennedy Sch. for Retarded Children, Palos Park, Ill., 1972—, Winnetka United Way, Ill., 1984—, Division St. YMCA, Chgo., 1972—; assoc. Rush-Presbyterian-St. Lukes Med. Ctr., Chgo., 1975—; mem. leadership com. Rush Alzheimer's Disease Ctr. Rhodes scholar, 1963. Fellow Fin. Analysts Fedn.; mem. Chgo. Council on Fgn. Relations (bd. dirs., treas. 1975—), Inst. European Studies (bd. govs., vice-chmn. 1981—), Investment Analysts Soc. Chgo. (chgo. com., com. on fgn. affairs, com. on internat. and domestic issues), Assn. for Investment Mgmt. and Rsch., Chgo. Soc. Clubs, Econ. Club of Chgo, Sunset Ridge Country (bd. dirs. Northfield, Ill., 1983—). Avocations: coin collecting; bridge; golf; skiing; art.

MCNEILL, THOMAS B., lawyer; b. Chgo., Oct. 28, 1934; s. Donald T. and Katherine M. (Bennett) McN.; m. Ingrid Sieder, May 11, 1963; children: Christine, Thomas, Stephanie. B.A., U. Notre Dame, 1956, J.D., 1958. Ptnr. Mayer, Brown & Platt, Chgo., 1962—; dir. Deltona Corp., Miami, Fla. Served to capt. JAGC USAF, 1959-62. Mem. Chgo. Bar Assn., Chgo. Council Lawyers, Law Club Chgo., Legal Club Chgo. Club: Indian Hill (Winnetka, Ill.). Home: 930 Fisher Ln Winnetka IL 60093-1563 Office: Mayer Brown & Platt 190 S La Salle St Chicago IL 60603-3410

MCNEILL, THOMAS RAY, lawyer; b. Pitts., June 2, 1952; s. Thomas William McNeill and Mary (Shiveley) Hiss; m. Patsy Lynch, June 25, 1977; children: Elizabeth, Kathleen, Thomas. BSBA, U. Fla., 1974; JD, Emory U., 1977. Bar: Ga. 1977, U.S. Dist. Ct. (no. dist.) Ga. 1977. Assoc. Powell, Goldstein, Frazer & Murphy, Atlanta, 1977-84, ptnr., 1984—, mgr. corp. dept., 1993-95. Mem. Ga. Bar Assn., Emory U. Alumni Assn. (pres. exec. com. Atlanta chpt. 1988-89, co-chmn. barristers com. Atlanta chpt.), Beta Gamma Sigma. Office: Powell Goldstein Frazer & Murphy Ste 1600 191 Peachtree St Atlanta GA 30303-1741

MCNEILL, WILLIAM, environmental scientist; b. Evanston, Ill., Jan. 1, 1930; s. John and Ebba Katrina (Hansen) McN.; m. Caryl Mook, June 15, 1951 (dec. 1969); children: Elizabeth Marie, Charles Craig, Margaret Ruth; m. Caecilia Cinquanto, Oct. 10, 1970. BA, Colgate U., 1951; MA, Temple U., 1955, PhD, 1961. Chief phys. chemistry br. Frankford Arsenal U.S. Army, Phila., 1955-70, dir. applied sci., 1970-75; chief scientist, environ. mgr. Rocky Mountain Arsenal U.S. Army, Denver, 1975-80, dir. tech. ops., 1980-85; gen. mgr. Battelle Denver Ops., 1985-88; sr. tech. adviser Sci. Applications Internat. Corp., Golden, Colo., 1989-92; dir. tech. devel. Sci. Applications Internat. Corp., Oak Ridge, Tenn., 1992—; mem. materials adv. bd. ceramics Nat. Acad. Sci./Nat. Rsch. Coun., Washington, 1966; mem. Gov.'s Task Group on Rocky Mountain Arsenal, 1976, Colo. Pollution Prevention Adv. Bd., Denver, 1991—. Contbr. articles to Jour. Che. Physics, Applied Physics Letters, other profl. publs. Mem. Am. Chem. Soc.,Hazardous Material Control Rsch. Inst., Air and Waste Mgmt. Assn. Achievements include 10 patents for electrochemical processes, inorganic materials sythesis, electro-optical devices; demonstration and use of narrow-band optical absorbers for laser protection; leader in development of Army environmental programs. Home: 319 Cliffrose Ct Lafayette CO 80026

MC NEILL, WILLIAM HARDY, retired history educator, writer; b. Vancouver, B.C., Can., Oct. 31, 1917; s. John Thomas and Netta (Hardy) McN.; m. Elizabeth Darbishire, Sept. 7, 1946; children: Ruth Netta, Deborah Joan, John Robert, Andrew Duncan. B.A., U. Chgo., 1938, M.A., 1939; Ph.D., Cornell U., 1947; 18 hon. degrees. Faculty U. Chgo., 1947-87, prof. history, 1957-87, Robert A. Millikan Disting. Svc. prof., 1969-87, prof. emeritus, 1987—, chmn. dept., 1961-67; pres. Demos Found., 1968-80, chmn. bd., 1980-86; George Eastman vis. prof. Oxford (Eng.) U., 1980-81. Author: Greek Dilemma, War and Aftermath, 1947, Report on the Greeks, 1948, History Handbook of Western Civilization, 1948, rev. and enlarged 6th edit., 1986, America, Britain and Russia, Their Cooperation and Conflict, 1941-46, 1953, Past and Future, 1954, Greece: American Aid in Action, 1947-56, 1957, Rise of the West: A History of the Human Community, 1963, 9th edit., 1991 (Nat. Book award, Gordon J. Laing prize), Europe's Steppe Frontier, 1500-1800, 1964, A World History, 1967, 3d edit., 1979, The Contemporary World, 1967, 2d edit., 1975, The Ecumene: Story of Humanity, 1973, Venice, the Hinge of Europe, 1081-1797, 1974, The Shape of European History, 1974, Plagues and Peoples, 1976, Metamorphosis of Greece since World War II, 1978, The Human Condition, An Ecological and Historical View, 1980, Pursuit of Power, 1982, The Great Frontier, 1983, Mythistory and other Essays, 1986, A History of the Human Community, 1986, 5th edit., 1996, Polyethnicity and National Unity in World History, 1987, Arnold J. Toynbee: A Life, 1989, Population and Politics Since 1750, 1990, Hutchins' University: A Memoir of the University of Chicago 1929-50, 1991, The Global Tradition: Conquerors, Catastrophies and Community, 1992, Keeping Together in Time: Dance & Drill in Human History, 1995, Colebrook: An Historical Sketch, 1996; editor: Lord Acton, Essays in the Liberal Interpretation of History, 1967, (with others) Readings in World History, Vols. I-X, 1968-73, Human Migration, 1978, Jour. Modern History, 1971-79, Jour. Modern Greek Studies, 1983-85; bd. editors Ency. Brit., 1981—; contbr. numerous articles and reviews to profl. jours., chpts. to books. Trustee Athens Coll., 1970-88; vice chmn. Christopher Columbus Quincentenary Jubilee Commn., 1985-93; co-chair curriculum task force Nat. Commn. on Social Studies, 1987-89; mem. Bradley Commn. on the Teaching of History, 1986-89; vice chmn. Nat. Coun. for History Edn., 1990-94, Nat. Coun. for History Standards, 1992-94. Fulbright Research scholar Royal Inst. Internat. Affairs, Eng., 1950-51; Rockefeller grantee, 1951-52; Ford Faculty fellow, 1954-55; Carnegie grantee, 1957-62, 63-64; Guggenheim fellow, 1971-72, 86-87; Josiah H. Macy grantee, 1973-74; Rockefeller grantee, 1976. Fellow Am. Philos. Soc., Am. Acad. Arts and Scis., Brit. Acad. Arts and Scis. (corr.), Royal Hist. Soc. (corr.); mem. Am. Hist. Assn. (council, del. Am. Council Learned Socs., pres. 1985). Office: PO Box 45 Colebrook CT 06021-0045

MCNELLY, JOHN TAYLOR, journalist, educator; b. Lancaster, Wis., Oct. 2, 1923; s. Stephen Sumner and Caroline Hurd (Taylor) McN.; m. Pamela Edith Thompson, Dec. 20, 1952; children: Barbara, Duncan. B.A., U. Wis., 1946, M.A., 1957; Ph.D., Mich. State U., 1961. Reporter AP, Milw., 1948-52, Reuters, London, 1952-53; news editor U. Wis. News Service, Madison, 1957; instr., then assoc. prof. Mich. State U., East Lansing, 1957-66; assoc. prof., then prof. U. Wis., Madison, 1966-82, Evjue-Bascom prof., 1982-88, prof. emeritus, 1988—; asst. dir. Inter-Am. Mass Communications Program, San Jose, Costa Rica, 1961-62; vis. prof. Berlin Inst. Mass. Communication in Developing Nations, W.Ger., 1965, Agrarian U., Lima, Peru, 1968-69; communication cons. UNESCO, Latin Am., 1970-75; lectr. USIA, Latin Am., 1968, 74, 80. Co-author: Communication and Social Change in Latin America, 1968; assoc. editor: Journalism Quar., 1975-77; contbr. monographs and articles to communication publs. Served with USAF, 1942-43. Fulbright-Hays Faculty fellow Lima, Peru, 1968-69. Home: 134 Larkin St Madison WI 53705-5116

MCNEMAR, DONALD WILLIAM, academic administrator; b. Wilmington, Ohio, June 1, 1943; s. Robert Arthur and Kathryn (Hunt) McN.; m. Britta Schein, Aug. 18, 1968; children—Heather Osborn, Galen Rebecca. B.A., Earlham Coll., Richmond, Ind., 1965; Ph.D., Princeton U., 1971. Asst. prof., then asso. prof. govt. Dartmouth Coll., 1970-81, assoc. dean faculty social scis., 1978-81; headmaster Phillips Acad., Andover, Mass., 1981-94; cons. Conflict Mgmt. Group, Cambridge, Mass., 1994-96; pres. Guilford Coll., Greensboro, N.C., 1996—; regional adv. bd. BayBank, 1981-94. Mem. exec. com. N.H. Coun. World Affairs, 1975-81; com. mem. Quaker office UN, 1978-82; trustee Sch. Yr. Abroad, 1981-94, Prep for Prep, 1988-94, Earlham Coll., 1989-95, Northfield Mount Hermon Sch., 1994—. Danforth fellow, 1965-69. Office: Guilford Coll 5800 W Friendly Ave Greensboro NC 27410

MC NERNEY, WALTER JAMES, health policy educator, consultant; b. New Haven, June 8, 1925; s. Robert Francis and Anna Gertrude (Shanley) McN.; m. Shirley Ann Hamilton, June 26, 1948; children: Walter James, Peter Hamilton, Jennifer Allison, Daniel Martin, Richard Hamilton. B.S., Yale U., 1947; M.H.A., U. Minn., 1950. Research asst. Labor-Mgmt. Center, Yale U., 1947; instr. advanced math. Hopkins Prep. Sch., New Haven, 1947-48; adminstrv. resident R.I. Hosp., Providence, 1949-50; asst. to coordinator Hosp. and Clinics of Med. Center, U. Pitts., 1950-53; also instr., then asst. prof. hosp. adminstrn. at univ. Grad. Sch. Pub. Health, U. Pitts., 1953-55; assoc. prof., dir. program hosp. adminstrn. Sch. Bus. Adminstrn., U. Mich., 1955-58; prof., dir. Bur. Hosp. Adminstrn., 1958-61; pres. Blue Cross Assn., Chgo., 1961-77; pres., chief exec. officer Blue Cross and Blue Shield Assns., Chgo., 1977-81; Herman Smith prof. health policy Grad. Sch. Mgmt., Northwestern U., 1982—; cons. in field, 1982—; mem. Nat. Coun. on Health Planning and Devel., HEW, 1976-82; mem. bd. dirs. Nat. Health Coun., 1963-77, pres., 1972-73; mem. nat. commn. on cost of med. care AMA, 1977, mem. com. on pvt. philanthropy, 1977-78; past pres. Internat. Fedn. Vol. Health Svc. Funds; mem. devel. com. Yale U.; trustee Nat. Exec. Svc. Corps; chmn. task force on Medicaid and related progrsm HEW, 1969-70; charter mem. Inst. Medicine-NAS, chmn. bd. on health care svcs., chmn. bd. on spl. initiatives; mem. physican payment rev. commn. U.S. Congress, Dept. Vets.' Affairs; mem. Commn. on the Future Structure of Vets. Health Care; mem. coal commn. U.S. Dept. Labor; mem. coun. on performance measurement Joint Commn. on Accreditation of Healthcare Orgns.; mem. nat. adv. coun. for health care policy, rsch. and evaluation HHS; bd. dirs. Stanley Works, Medicus, Value Health Inc., Nellcor Inc., Ostel Tech., Ventritex, Inc., Hanger Orthopedics Group Inc.; chmn. bd. McNerney Heintz, Inc., Am. Health Properties Inc.; adv. coun. to dean Yale U. Med. Sci.; vis. com. U. Mich. Med. Ctr., adv. coun. chmn. Agy. for Health Care Policy and Rsch., chmn., bd. trustees Med. Outcomes Trust. Author: Hospital and Medical Economics, 1962, Regionalization and Rural Health Care, 1962; contbr. articles to profl. jours. Mem. Pres.' Com. on Health Edn., 1972-73; trustee Hosp. Research and Ednl. Trust, Inst. for Future; vis. com. Harvard Med. and Dental Schs. Served to lt. (j.g.) USNR, 1943-46. Nuffield Provincial Hosps. Trust-Kings Fund (Eng.) fellow, 1970; recipient Justin Ford Kimball award Am. Hosp. Assn., 1967, Outstanding Achievement award U. Minn., 1970, Sec.'s Unit ciatation HEW, 1970, Yale medal, 1979, Meritorious Svc. award AMA, 1981, Award of Honor, Am. Hosp. Assn., 1982, C. Rufus Rorem award Blue Cross/Blue Shield, 1995; named 1 of 100 most important young men and women in U.S., Life Mag., 1962; inducted into Modern Heathcare Mag. Hall of Fame, 1996. Clubs: Commonwealth, Yale (N.Y.C.). Office: Northwestern U Grad Sch Mgmt 2001 Sheridan Rd Evanston IL 60208-0814

MC NEW, BENNIE BANKS, economics and finance educator; b. Greenbrier, Ark., Nov. 12, 1931; s. Roland H. and Stella (Avery) McN.; m. Bonnie Lou Stone, Mar. 31, 1956; children—Bonnie Banks, Mary Kathleen, William Michael. B.S., Ark. State Tchrs. Coll., 1953; M.B.A., U. Ark., 1954; Ph.D., U. Tex., 1961. Asst. nat. bank examiner, 1954-56; indsl. specialist U. Ark. Indsl. Research and Extension Center, 1956-59; lectr. finance U. Tex., 1959-61; prof. banking U. Miss., University, 1961-65; dean U. Miss. (Sch. Bus. Adminstrn.), 1965-79, Sch. Bus., Middle Tenn. State U., Murfreesboro, 1980-88; prof. econs. and fin. U. Cen. Ark., Conway, 1988—; asst. dir., v.p. Grad. Sch. Banking of South, La. State U., 1966—. Author: (with Charles L. Prather) Fraud Control for Commercial Banks, 1962; contbg. author: Money and Banking Casebook, 1966, The Bankers Handbook, 1966, A History of Mississippi, 1973. Served with AUS, 1950-51. Mem. Southwestern Fin. Assn., So. Fin. Assn., Fin. Execs. Inst., Beta Gamma Sigma, Delta Pi Epsilon, Delta Sigma Pi, Omicron Delta Kappa, Phi Kappa Phi, Lions (pres. Oxford, Miss. 1964-65). Home: 12 Bainbridge Dr Conway AR 72032-7217 Office: Univ Central Arkansas PO Box 5025 Conway AR 72035

MCNICHOLAS, DAVID PAUL, automobile rental company executive; b. Youngstown, Ohio, Mar. 1, 1941; s. Paul James and Mary Frances (Dignan) McN.; m. Patricia Marie McAtee; children: Paula, John, Catherine, Tim, Dan. BBA, Youngstown State U., 1962. With Youngstown Sheet and Tube Co. (now subs. LTV), 1964-78, from trainee to dir. data processing; with Avis Inc., N.Y.C., 1978—, sr. v.p., 1985-90, exec. v.p., 1990—, also bd. dirs.; bd. dirs. Ohio Franchise Operater, Inc., Cilva Holding Ltd. Office: Avis Inc 900 Old Country Rd Garden City NY 11530-2128

MCNICHOLS, GERALD ROBERT, consulting company executive; b. Cleve., Nov. 21, 1943; s. Charles Wellington and June Beatrice (Kalal) McN.; m. Paula Kay Austin, Dec. 26, 1964; children: G. Robert Jr., Kay Lynn, Melissa Sue. BS with honors, Case-Western Res. U., 1965; MS, U. Pa., 1966; ScD, George Washington U., 1976. Cert. cost estimator/analyst. Sr. ops. analyst Office of Sec., Dept. of Def., Washington, 1970-76; v.p. GenTech, Inc., Bethesda, Md., 1976-77, J. Watson Noah, Inc., Falls Church, Va., 1977-78; pres., chief exec. officer Mgmt. Cons. and Rsch., Inc., Falls Church, 1978—. Co-author: Operations Research for Decision Making, 1975; editor Cost Analysis, 1984; contbr. articles to profl. jours. Pres. Rondelay Civic Assn., Fairfax Sta., Va., 1985-87. Capt. USAF, 1966-70. Mem. Inst. Cost Analysis (pres. 1985-88), Internat. Soc. Parametric Analysts (bd. dirs. 1982-84), Ops. Rsch. Soc. Am. (chmn. mil. applications sect.), Mil. Ops. Rsch. Soc. (sec., treas. 1986-87, v.p. adminstrn. 1987-88, bd. dirs. 1985-88, 92—), Soc. Cost Estimating and Analysis (bd. dirs. 1990-93). Home: 8133 Rondelay Ln Fairfax VA 22039-2305 Office: Mgmt Cons & Rsch Inc 5113 Leesburg Pike Ste 509 Falls Church VA 22041-3204*

MCNICOL, DAVID LEON, federal official; b. South Gate, Calif., May 18, 1944; s. Charles D. and Mary W. (Heisel) McN.; m. Lore Anne Long, Mar. 25, 1967; children: Katharine Anne, Elizabeth Mary. BA magna cum laude, Harvard U., 1966; MS, MIT, 1968, PhD, 1973. Asst. prof. econs. U. Pa., Phila., 1971-75; sr. staff economist Pres.'s Coun. of Econ. Advisors, Washington, 1976; vis. assoc. prof. econs. Calif. Inst. Tech., Pasadena, 1976-77; sr. economist Office of the Sec., U.S. Dept. of Treasury, Washington, 1977-79; dir. Office of Econ. Analysis U.S. Dept. Energy, Washington, 1980-81, dep. asst. adminstr. Office of Applied Analysis, 1981-82; dir. Econ. Analysis and Resource Planning Div. Office of Sec. of Def., Office of Program Analysis and Evaluation, Washington, 1982-88, dep. asst. sec., dep. dir., 1988—, chmn. cost analysis improvement group, 1988—. Author over 20 publs. on commodity markets, regulatory econs., energy issues and econ. aspects of the U.S. def. program. Recipient Spl. Svc. award Dept. Energy, 1981, Presdl. Rank award U.S. Govt., 1988, 93, Disting Civilian Svc. medal Dept. Def., 1988, 91, 93. Mem. Am. Econ. Assn. Home: 6901 Pineway Univ Park MD 20782-1163 Office: Dept Def OSD: PA&E The Pentagon Washington DC 20301

MC NICOL, DONALD EDWARD, lawyer; b. Kew Gardens, N.Y., Aug. 11, 1921; s. William J. and Margaret (McGirr) McN.; m. Carmen Gallego, July 10, 1988; children: Elaine McNicol Postley, Janet McNicol Barton, Donald Edward, Paul Mansfield, Andrea Gallego. AB, Harvard U., 1942, LLB, 1948. Bar: N.Y. 1949. Asso. Davis, Polk, Wardwell, Sunderland & Kiendl, N.Y.C., 1948-54; assoc. Hall, Haywood, Patterson & Taylor, N.Y.C., 1954-56; ptnr. Hall, McNicol, Hamilton & Clark, 1956-92; of counsel Keck, Mahin & Cate, N.Y.C., 1992—; bd. dirs. Thomas Pub. Co. Trustee Boys and Girls Club Am. Served with AUS, 1942-46. Mem. Assn. Bar City N.Y., Harvard Club (bd. mgrs. N.Y.C. 1967-69). Home: 461 Berry Hill Rd Syosset NY 11791-1117 Office: Keck Mahin & Cate 220 E 42nd St New York NY 10017-5806

MCNISH, SUSAN KIRK, lawyer; b. San Jose, Calif., Nov. 4, 1940; d. Wallace Garland and Dorothy (Kirk) Shaw; m. Thomas A. McNish, May 12, 1989; children: Jenifer, Michael. BA, U. Calif., 1962; JD, U. Santa Clara, Calif., 1981; postgrad., Stanford U., 1979, U. Mich., 1981. Bar: Mich. 1981, U.S. Dist. Ct. (ea. dist.) Mich. 1981. Various positions Stanford (Calif.) U., 1968-79; law clk. U.S. Dist. Ct. (no. dist.) Calif., San Francisco, 1979; atty. Consumers Power Co., Jackson, Mich., 1981-88; gen. counsel, corp. sec. Mich. Consol. Gas Co., Detroit, 1988—. Trustee Harper Hosp., Detroit. Mem. Am. Arbitration Assn. (arbitrator, Mich. adv. panel), Am. Gas Assn. (chair state regulatory com., legal sect. mng. com.). Home: 9130 Woodberry Rd Plymouth MI 48170-3441 Office: Mich Consol Gas Co 500 Griswold St Detroit MI 48226-3700

MC NITT, WILLARD CHARLES, business executive; b. Chgo., June 6, 1920; s. Willard C. and Louise (Richardson) McN.; m. Charlotte D. Boyd, Sept. 14, 1946; children: Willard Charles, James D., Peter B. McNitt. B.A., Amherst Coll., 1942; A.M., Harvard Grad. Sch. Bus. Adminstrn., 1942; student, Northwestern Grad. Sch. Bus. Adminstrn., U. Chgo. Sch. Bus. Adminstrn., 1947. Asst. market planning and research Foote, Cone & Belding Co., Chgo., 1946-47; asst. sales promotion and advt. Bell & Gosset Co., Morton Grove, Ill., 1947-48; v.p. sales and mktg. Bowes Industries, Inc., Chgo., 1948-54; gen. mgr. sales and mktg. Clayton Mark & Co., Evanston, Ill., 1954-58; pres., dir. Bowey's, Inc., Chgo., 1958-62; pres., dir., mem. exec. com. H.M. Byllesby Co., Chgo., 1962-63; group v.p., dir. Consol. Foods Corp., Chgo., 1963-67; exec. v.p. consumer products group W.R. Grace & Co., N.Y.C., 1967-72; exec. v.p., dir., mem. exec. com. Ward Foods, Inc., Wilmette, Ill., 1972-73; chief operating officer, pres., dir., mem. exec. com. Ward Foods, Inc., 1973-76; pres., chief exec. officer, dir. Westgate-Calif. Corp., and Sun Harbor Industries, San Diego, 1977-80; pres., chief exec. officer Nalley's Fine Foods, Tacoma, 1980-83; chmn., dir. Joseph Magnin Inc., 1982-85; chmn. Blue Moon Cheese Co., Thorpe, Wis., 1983—; operating ptnr. Wallner & Co., La Jolla, Calif.; vice chmn., pres., chief exec. officer, dir., mem. exec. com. Foremost Dairies, Inc., San Francisco, 1983-85; chmn. Epcom; bd. dirs. ATI, NCIC, Blue Moon Cheese, Del. Lightweight. Troop head local Boy Scouts Am., 1957-67. Served to lt. (s.g.) USNR, 1942-46. Mem. Executives Club (Chgo.), Amherst Club, Harvard Bus. Sch. Club (Chgo., N.Y.C.), Indian Hill Country Club (Winnetka), Dairymen's Club (Boulder Junction, Wis.), Rancho Santa Fe Country Club, Fairbanks Ranch Country Club (Rancho Santa Fe), Rio Mar Country Club (Vero Beach, Fla.), Chi Psi. Republican. Congregationalist. Address: 1630 Sheridan Rd Apt 2C Wilmette IL 60091-1888

MCNULLY, LYNNETTE LARKIN, elementary education educator; b. Iowa City, Iowa, Jan. 22, 1966; d. Ernest F. and Karen (Schaeferle) Larkin; m. William S. McNully, May 14, 1988. BA in English, U. Okla., 1987; MEd in Early Childhood Edn., East Tex. State U., 1994. Cert. tchr., Tex. Prekindergarten and kindergarten tchr. Dallas Pub. Schs., 1989—; founding mem. site-based mgmt. coun. Arlington Park Sch., 1994—. Vol. North Texas Irish Festival, Dallas, 1992, On the Wing Again, Ferris, Tex., 1993—. Named Tchr. of Yr., Arlington Park Sch., Dallas, 1992; Write, Right! grantee Dallas Jr. League, 1993. Mem. Nat. Assn. for Edn. of Young Children, Assn. for Childhood Edn. Internat., Dallas Quilters Guild, PTA (exec. bd. 1993—), Phi Beta Kappa. Avocations: quilting, hiking, genealogy.

MCNULTY, CAROL JEANNE, elementary education educator; b. Alton, Ill., July 12, 1936; d. Robert Waldemore and Jessie Adele (Scheldt) Fensterman; m. Thomas Wayne McNulty, June 9, 1957; children: Brian Munro, Timothy Robert, Kevin Wayne. BS in Edn., Ill. State U., 1957, MS in Edn., 1967. Cert. tchr., Ill. 1st grade tchr. Bloomington (Ill.) Pub. Schs., 1957-67, remedial reading tchr., 1968-73; instr. reading practicum Ill. State U., Normal, 1972-73, instr. children's lit., 1973-78; 2d grade tchr. Epiphany Sch., Normal, 1978—; summer sch. tchr. grades 1 and 2 Bloomington Pub. Schs., 1985-88, mem. adv. coun., 1973-76, mem. curriculum coun., 1975-78; part-time assoc. Gingerbread House Ednl. Toystore, Bloomington, 1989—. Leader Cub Scouts, Bloomington, 1972-74; tchr. Wesley Meth. Ch., Bloomington, 1972-77, substitute tchr., 1989-92. Golden Jubilee scholar PTA, 1953-57. Mem. Ill. Reading Coun., Tri County Reading Assn., Delta Kappa Gamma (com. chair, recording sec. 1960—). Avocations: reading, travel, crafts, antiquing. Home: 7 Charles Pl Bloomington IL 61701-1803

MCNULTY, CARRELL STEWART, JR., manufacturing company executive, architect; b. Newark, Dec. 4, 1924; s. Carrell Stewart and Marjorie (Yaegerlehner) McN.; m. Barbara Brokaw, June 21, 1952; children: Peter Carrell, Susan Abigail. Student, Emory U., 1941-43, U. N.C., 1943-44; BArch, Columbia U., 1950, MS in Urban Planning, 1963. Registered architect, Pa. Assoc. SMS Architects, Stamford, Conn., 1950-58, gen. ptnr., 1958-73; pvt. practice architecture Weston, Conn., 1973-76; pres. CMW Co., Weston, 1975-77, NB Products, Inc., Horsham, Pa., 1976-94, NB Instruments, Inc., Horsham, 1979-93, Environ. Svcs. and Products, Inc., Horsham, 1994—; mem. Conn. Soc. Architects, 1963-73, sec., 1964-67, pres., 1969-70. Chair S.W. Regional Planning Agy., Norwalk, Conn., 1967-71; mem. Gov.'s Com. on Environment, New Haven, 1970, chair Gov.'s Task Force on Housing, Norwalk, 1972; bd. dirs., sec. Habitat for Humanity of Greater Bucks, Doylestown, Pa., 1990—; pres. Ctrl. Bucks Crossroads, 1995-96. Lt. (j.g.) USNR, 1943-46; PTO. Recipient citation Am. Assn. Sch. Adminstrs., 1960, 6th Biennial Design award HUD, 1973; grantee HUD, Housing Rsch., 1970. Fellow AIA (mem. urban design com. 1963-73, chmn. 1971); mem. Water Pollution Control Fedn., Bucks County Choral Soc., Sigma Nu. Democrat. Mem. United Ch. of Christ (deacon 1965-71, elder 1989-92). Avocations: computers, model building, choral music. Home: Century House # 234 303 W State St Doylestown PA 18901-3559 Office: Environ Svcs and Products Inc 903 Sheehy Dr Horsham PA 19044-1231

MCNULTY, DERMOT, public relations executive; b. Dublin, Ireland, Mar. 11, 1949; s. William J. and Margaret M. (Reigh) McN.; m. Paula Ann Gaber, 1977. BA in Journalism, Marquette U., 1971. Sr. v.p. Burson Marsteller, Hong Kong, 1985-87, Cohn & Wolfe, N.Y.C., 1987-88; exec. v.p. Burson Marsteller, N.Y.C., 1988-89, Shandwick N.Am., N.Y.C., 1989-90; dir. internat. mktg. Shandwick plc, London, 1990-91, COO, 1991-94, CEO, 1994—, also bd. dirs. Avocations: arts, golf, tennis. Office: 61 Grosvenor St, London W1X 9DA, England

MCNULTY, HENRY BRYANT, journalist; b. Hartford, Conn., May 6, 1947; s. J. Bard and Marjorie (Grant) McN.; m. Anne Margaret Schneider, Sept. 7, 1985; 1 child, Frederick Gardiner Bard McNulty. B.A. in English, Cornell U., 1969. Op-Ed editor Hartford Courant, Conn., 1976-78, features editor, 1978-84, assoc. editor, 1984-95, town editorials editor, 1995—. Contbg. author: The British Invasion, 1982. Mem. Orgn. News Ombudsmen (bd. dirs., v.p., pres.), Soc. Decendents of Founders of Hartford, Cornell Club (N.Y.).

MCNULTY, JOHN KENT, lawyer, educator; b. Buffalo, Oct. 13, 1934; s. Robert William and Margaret Ellen (Duthie) McN.; m. Linda Conner, Aug. 20, 1955 (div. Feb. 1977); children: Martha Jane, Jennifer, John K. Jr.; m. Babette B. Barton, Mar. 23, 1978 (div. May 1988). A.B. with high honors, Swarthmore Coll., 1956; LL.B., Yale U., 1959. Bar: Ohio 1961, U.S. Supreme Ct. 1964. Law clk. Justice Hugo L. Black, U.S. Supreme Ct., Washington, 1959-60; vis. prof. Sch. Law U. Tex., summer 1960, Yale U., fall 1990; assoc. Jones, Day, Cockley & Reavis, Cleve., 1960-64; prof. law U. Calif., Berkeley, 1964-91, Roger J. Traynor prof. law, 1991—; of counsel Baker and McKenzie, San Francisco, 1974-75; acad. visitor London Sch. Econs., 1985, Cambridge U., 1994, U. Edinburgh, 1994; vis. fellow Wolfson Coll., Cambridge, 1994; lectr. univs. Cologne, Hamburg, Kansei, Kyoto, London, Munich, Seoul, Tokyo, Tilburg, Amsterdam, Rotterdam, Vienna, Tohoku, Tübingen, others; mem. adv. bd. Tax Mgmt. Author: Federal Income Taxation of Individuals, 5th edit., 1995, Federal Estate and Gift Taxation, 5th edit., 1994, Federal Income Taxation of S Corporations, 1992; (with Westin & Beck) Federal Income Taxation of Business Enterprises, 1995; mem. bd. overseers Berkeley Jour. Internat. Law. Guggenheim fellow, 1977. Mem. ABA, Am. Law Inst., Internat. Fiscal Assn. (coun. U.S. br.), Order of Coif, Phi Beta Kappa. Home: 1176 Grizzly Peak Blvd Berkeley CA 94708-1741 Office: U Calif Sch Law 389 Boalt Hall Berkeley CA 94720

MCNULTY, JOHN WILLIAM, retired public relations executive, automobile company executive; b. N.Y.C., June 29, 1927; s. Christopher and Margaret (Kennedy) McN.; m. Margaret Rose Cooney, Nov. 11, 1950 (dec. Aug. 1978); children: Suellen McNulty Kinna, Jean McNulty Crocker, John, Peter, Jodi Wyatt Phelan, Russell Wyatt; m. Jean Fayette Winslow, Sept. 6, 1980. BS, Fordham U., 1949. Dir. pub. relations Lincoln Ctr., N.Y.C., 1958-63; assoc. John D. Rockefeller 3rd, N.Y.C., 1963-66; asst. to Pres. Lyndon B. Johnson, Washington, 1966-68; exec. asst. to exec. v.p. fin., pub./industry-govt. rels. GM, Detroit, 1968-74, exec. asst. to vice chmn., 1974-76, pub. affairs coord., 1976-77, dir. corp. comm., 1977-79, v.p. pub. rels., 1979-90, ret., 1990. Trustee Nat. Racing Mus., Saratoga. Served with USN, 1945-46, PTO. Recipient Communications Achievement award Fordham U., 1977. Mem. Kenwood Club. Democrat. Home: 1071 Celestial St Cincinnati OH 45202-1661

MCNULTY, JULIA BRIDGET, nurse; b. Ireland, Jan. 23, 1940; came to U.S., 1968; m. John James McNulty, Oct. 8, 1981; children: Deirdre, Fergus. Diploma, Whittington Sch., London, 1962. RN, N.Y.; state registered nurse, Eng. and Wales. Staff nurse Elmhurst (N.Y.) City Hosp., 1970-72, head nurse, 1972-80, rev. analyst, 1980-81; pvt. duty nurse, 1983-86; home care/cmty. supr. Home Svcs. Systems, N.Y.C., 1986-89; discharge planning nurse Parkway Hosp., Queens, N.Y., 1989—. Home: 41-30 77th St Elmhurst NY 11373-1936 Office: The Parkway Hosp 70-35 113th St Forest Hills NY 11375-4651

MCNULTY, MATTHEW FRANCIS, JR., health sciences and health services administrator, educator, university administrator, consultant, horse and cattle breeder; b. Elizabeth, N.J., Nov. 26, 1914; s. Matthew Francis and Abby Helen (Dwyer) McN.; m. Mary Nell Johnson, May 4, 1946; children: Matthew Francis III, Mary Lauren. BS, St. Peter's Coll., 1938, DHL (hon.), 1978; postgrad., Rutgers U. Law Sch., 1939-41; grad., Officer Candidate Sch., U.S. Army, 1941, U.S. Army Staff and Command Sch., Ft. Leavenworth, 1945; MHA, Northwestern U., 1949; MPH, U. N.C., 1952; ScD (hon.), U. Ala., 1969, Georgetown U., 1986. Contract writer, mgmt. trainee acturial div. Prudential Life Ins. Co., Newark, N.J., 1938-46; dir. med. adminstrn. VA, Chgo. and Washington, 1946-49; project officer to take over and operate new VA Teaching Hosps. VA, Little Rock, Birmingham, Ala. and Chgo., 1949-54; adminstr. U. Ala. Jefferson-Hillman Hosp., Birmingham, 1954-60; founding gen. dir. U. Ala. Hosps. and Clinics, 1960-66; founding prof. hosp. adminstrn. U. Ala. Grad. Sch., 1954-69, vs. prof., 1969—, founding dir. grad. program health adminstrn., 1964-69; prof. epidemiology and preventive medicine Sch. Medicine U. Ala., 1960-69; founding dean Sch. Health Adminstrn. (now Sch. Health Related Profls.), 1965-69; pres. Matthew F. McNulty, Jr. & Assocs., Inc., 1954-91; founding dir. Coun. Teaching Hosps. and assoc. dir. Assn. Am. Med. Colls., 1966-69; prof. community medicine and internat. health Georgetown U., 1969-89, prof. emeritus 1989—, v.p. med. ctr. affairs, 1969-72, exec. v.p., med. ctr. affairs, 1972-74; chancellor, dir. Georgetown U. Med. Ctr., 1974-86; chancellor emeritus Georgetown U., 1986—; chmn. acad. affairs com., trustee Hahnemann U., Phila, 1987—; trustee Fla. Found. for Active Aging, 1989—; cons. VA Adv. Com. on Geriatrics & Gerontology, 1991—; founding chmn. bd. Univ. D.C. Affiliated Health Plan, Inc., 1974-78; founding chmn. bd. trustees Georgetown U. Community Health Plan, Inc., 1972-80; vis. prof. Cen. U., Caracas, Venezuela, 1957-61; hosp. cons., 1953—; bd. dirs. Kaiser-Georgetown Community Health Plan, Inc., Washington, 1980-85, bd. dirs. Kaiser Health Plans and Hosps., Oakland, Calif., 1980-85, emeritus, 1985—; mem. Statuatory VA Spl. Med. Adv. Group, 1978-89, Higher Edn. Com. on Dental Schs. Curriculum, 1978-79; preceptor hosp. adminstrn. Northwestern U., Washington U., U. Iowa, U. Minn., 1953-69; mem. nat. adv. com. health research projects Ga. Inst. Tech., 1959-65, 73-85; nat. adv. com. health rsch. projects U. Pitts., 1956-60; adv. com. W.K. Kellogg Found., 1960-65; vis. cons., lectr. Venezuelan Ministry Health and Social Welfare, 1967-69; dir. Blue Cross-Blue Shield Ala., 1960-61, 65-68; trustee, mem. exec. com. Blue Cross and Blue Shield Nat. Capital Area, 1973-89, Washington Bd. Trade, 1972-86; mem. feasability study P.R. VA Med. Care, 1949, feasability study Ariz. Med. Edn., 1956. Bd. dirs. Greater Birmingham United Appeal, 1960-66; trustee, chmn. Jefferson County (Ala.) Tb Sanatorium, 1958-64; mem. health services research study sect. NIH, 1963-67; cons. USPHS, 1959-63; mem. White House Conf. on Health, 1965, on Medicare Implementation, 1966, NIH, USPHS and DHEW Commns., 1967-86, others; trustee Nat. Council Internat. Health, 1975-86; pres. Nat. League Nursing, 1979-81. Served to maj. USAAF, 1942-46, lt. col. USAFR, 1946-55. Recipient Disting. Alumnus award Northwestern U., 1973, Disting. Alumnus award U. N.C., John Benjamin Nichol award Med. Soc. D.C., Mayor and D.C. Coun., Matthew F. McNulty, Jr. Unanimous Recognition Resolution of 1986, Centennial award Georgetown U. Alumni Assn. award, 1982, Patrick Healy Disting. Svc. award, 1985, Alumni Life Senator Election award, 1986; named to Hon. Order Ky Cols., 1984. Fellow Am. Pub. Health Assn., Am. Coll. Healthcare Execs. (life, bd. regents and council of regents 1961-67, Disting. Health Sci. Exec. award 1976); mem AAAS, Am. Hosp. Assn. (life, Disting. Service award 1984), Ala. Hosp. Assn. (past pres.), Nat. Lr Nursing (past pres.), D.C. League Nursing (past dir.), Nat. Forum Health Planning (past pres., Disting. award, 1987), Council Med. Adminstrn., Internat. Hosp. Fedn., Jefferson County Ala. Vis. Nursing Assn. (past pres., Disting. Service award), Ala. Pub. Health Assn. (past chmn. med. care sect.), Southeastern Hosp. Conf. (past dir.), Birmingham Hosp. Council (past pres.), Hosp. Council Nat. Capital Area (pres. 1985-89, exec. com. 1989—, past pres. 1989-93, treas. 1993—), Assn. Univ. Programs in Hosp. Adminstrn. (Disting. award 1971), Greater Birmingham Area C. of C. (Merit award), Washington Acad. of Medicine, Am. Assn. Med. Colls. (founding chmn. teaching hosp. council 1964-69, Disting. Service Mem.), Royal Soc. Health, Am. Systems Mgmt. Soc. (Disting. award), Orgn. Univ. Health Ctr. Adminstrs., Santa Gertrudis Breeders Internat., Bashkir Curley Horse Breeders Assn., Med. Soc. of D.C. (John Benjamin Nichols award 1982), Univ. Club Ala., Cosmos Club, City Tavern Club, KC (3d degree, coun. 10499 Ocean Springs, 4th degree Francis Deignan Assembly), Knights of Malta, Omicron Kappa Upsilon. Home and Office: Teoc Pentref 3100 Phil Davis Rd Ocean Springs MS 39564-9076

MCNULTY, MICHAEL ROBERT, congressman; b. Troy, N.Y., Sept. 16, 1947; s. John J. and Madelon McN; m. Nancy Ann Lazzaro; children: Michele, Angela, Nancy, Maria. Grad., St. Joseph's Inst., Barrytown, N.Y., 1965, Loyola U. Rome Ctr., 1968, Hill Sch. Ins., N.Y.C., 1970; B.A. in Polit. Sci., Coll. Holy Cross, 1969; LHD honoris causa, Coll. St. Rose, 1991; LLD honoris causa, Siena Coll., 1993. Town supr. Town of Green Island, N.Y., 1969-77, mayor, 1977-82; mem. N.Y. State Assembly, 1982-88, chmn. sub-com. on town and village elections, mem. legis. commn. on rural resources, 1983-88, asst. dir. adminstrv. regulations rev. commn., 1977-82, mem. adminstrv. regulations rev. com., 1983-88; past chmn. planning com. Capital Dist. Transp. Com.; mem. 101st-102nd Congresses from 23rd N.Y. dist., 1989-92, 103d-104th Congresses from 21st N.Y. dist., 1993—; mem. internat. rels. com.; past chmn. task force for constrn. Troy-Green Island Bridge; chmn. United Way campaign, 1982. Mem. staff com. on edn. N.Y. State Constl. Conv., 1967; del. Dem. Nat. Conv., 1972, 92; campaign mgr. John J. McNulty Jr. for Sheriff of Albany County, N.Y., 1973; participant 1974 polit. campaign mgmt. inst. Kent State U., Ohio; past mem. Albany County Dem. Com.; past chmn. Green Island Dem. Com.; past mem. N.Y. State Dem. Com. Office: US Ho of Reps 2442 Rayburn HOB Washington DC 20510-3221*

MCNULTY, ROBERT HOLMES, non-profit association executive; b. Oakland, Calif., June 20, 1940; s. Frederick James and Ruth (Holmes) McN.; m. Penelope Cuff, Dec. 27, 1964; children: Maria, Abigail. BS in Bus. Adminstrn., U. Calif., Berkeley, 1962, JD, 1965. Property acquisition planner Safeway Stores, Internat., Oakland, 1962; archeol. asst. Colonial Williamsburg, Va., 1968; rsch. asst. Nat. Mus. of History and Tech. The Smithsonian Instn., Washington, 1968-69, asst. to the dir., 1969-70; environ. advisor GSA, Washington, 1970-71; asst. dir. architecture and environ. arts program NEA, Washington, 1971-78; acting dir. grad. program in hist. preservation Sch. Architecture Columbia U., N.Y.C., 1978-79; pres. Ptnrs. for Livable Communities, Washington, 1979—; cons. Task Force on Land Use and Urban Growth, 1972, German Marshall Fund, Washington, 1978; bd. visitors U. Ind. Sch. Pub. Adminstrn., 1991—. Author: Neighborhood Conservation: A Handbook of Methods and Techniques, 1976, Economics of Amenity, 1985, Entrepreneurial American City, 1985, Return of the Livable City, 1986; editor: (report) State of the American Community, 1994. Served to capt. U.S. Army, 1966-68. Smithsonian Inst. grantee, 1972, 73, Graham Found. grantee 1978; Loeb fellow Harvard U., 1973-74; Pierson Coll. guest fellow, Yale U., 1985. Mem. Calif. Bar Assn., Nat. Press Club. Home: 4006 62nd St Bethesda MD 20816-2622 Office: Ptnrs for Livable Community 1429 21st St NW Washington DC 20036-5902

MCNULTY, ROBERTA JO, educational administrator; b. Cin., July 17, 1945; d. Edward Norman and Ruth Marcella (Glass) Stuebing; children: Meredith Corinne, Brian Edward, Stephen Barrett. BS in Edn., U. Cin., 1967; MA in Edn., Coll. of Mount St. Joseph, 1989; PhD in Ednl. Adminstrn. and Supervision, Bowling Green State U., 1993. Elem. tchr. St. Mary Sch., Urbana, Ohio, 1968; elem. tchr. Urbana (Ohio) City Schs., 1968-70, middle sch. tchr., 1970-71; off-campus liaison Mt. St. Joseph Coll., 1987-89; adj. faculty Bowling Green State U., 1990—; gen. edn. supr., testing 540 coord. curriculum devel. and implementation Fulton County Ednl. Svc. Ctr., Wauseon, Ohio, 1992—; Lamaza instr. Scioto Meml. Illustrated Lamaze Edn., Portsmouth, Ohio, 1983-84, Tiffin (Ohio) Childbirth Edn. Assn., 1984-87; edn. symposium com. chair Project Discovery, 1995—; proficiency test rev. com. Ohio Dept. Edn., 1993-94. Grad. editor Am. Secondary Edn., 1989-92. Mem. sch. bd. St. Mary Sch., Urbana, 1971-75; mem. parent adv. com. Wheelersburg (Ohio) Local Schs., 1978-84; mem. parents coun. U. Evansville, 1990-93; exec. dir. Am. Cancer Soc., Tiffin, Ohio, 1985; treas. Parents' Boosters Club, Portsmouth YMCA, 1979-84; chmn. Y-wives com. Tiffin-Cmty. YMCA, 1984-87; mem. Archbold (Ohio) Teen Issues Adv. Com., 1995—. Recipient Doctoral fellowship Bowling Green State U., 1989-92, Svc. Appreciation award Cub Scouts, 1990-92. Mem. ASCD, Ednl. Leadership Assn., N.W. Ohio Assn. for Supervision and Curriculum Devel., Ohio Sch. Suprs. Assn., Ohio Coun. Tchrs. English Language Arts, Assn. Tchr. Educators, Ohio Assn. Tchr. Educators (nat. del.), Phi Delta Kappa. Office: Fulton County Ednl Svc Ctr 602 S Shoop Ave Wauseon OH 43567-1712

MCNUTT, CHARLIE FULLER, JR., bishop; b. Charleston, W.Va., Feb. 27, 1931; s. Charlie Fuller and Mary (Ford) McN.; m. Alice Turnbull, Mar. 3, 1962; children: Thomas Ford, Charlie Fuller III, Alison Turnbull. AB, Washington and Lee U., 1953; MDiv, Va. Theol. Sem., 1956, DD (hon.), 1981; MS, Fla. State U., 1970. Ordained to ministry Episcopal Ch., 1956; bishop, 1980. Vicar, Christ Ch., Williamston, W.Va., 1956-60; asst. rector St. John's Episc. Ch., Tallahassee, Fla., 1960-62; rector St. Luke's Episc. Ch., Jacksonville, Fla., 1962-68; planning dir. Diocese of Fla., 1968-74; archdeacon of Jacksonville Diocese of Fla., 1970-74; rector Trinity Episc. Ch., Martinsburg, W.Va., 1974-80; bishop coadjutor Diocese Ctrl. Pa., 1980-82, diocesan bishop, 1982-95; COO, exec. dir. presiding bishop's fund The Episcopal Ch., 1995—; bd. dirs. Pa. Coun. Chs., Harrisburg, chmn. dept. social ministry, 1982-86, pres., 1991-94. Bd. dirs. Appalachian People's Svc. Orgn., pres., 1985-87; bd. dirs. Boy Scouts Am., Harrisburg, 1981-86; mem. exec. coun. Nat. Ch., 1988-94; mem. standing com. on program, budget and fin. Nat. Episcopal Ch., 1983-90; co-chmn. Pa. Conf. Interch. Cooperation. Mem. Phi Beta Kappa. Democrat. Home: 2428 Lincoln St Camp Hill PA 17011-3637 Office: Episcopal Ch Ctr 815 2d Ave New York NY 10017

MCNUTT, JACK WRAY, oil company executive; b. Norphlet, Ark., Sept. 7, 1934; s. Fay D. and Mattie E. (Garner) McN.; m. Jordine Chesshir, Aug. 19, 1955; 1 child, Marsha. BS, Harding Coll., 1956; MS, Columbia U., 1957. Acct. Murphy Oil Corp., El Dorado, Ark., 1957-68, exec. mgmt. asst., 1968-69, exec. v.p., 1981-88, chief operating officer, 1986-88, pres., chief exec. officer, 1988-94; ret., 1994; v.p. planning Murphy Ea. Oil Co., London, 1969-72, pres., 1972-81; bd. dirs. First Nat. Bank El Dorado, Ark. Mem. Am. Petroleum Inst. (dir.), 25 Yr. Club. of Petroleum Industry. Home: 1705 W Cedar St El Dorado AR 71730-5309 Office: 101 W Main St Ste 509 El Dorado AR 71730

MCNUTT, KRISTEN WALLWORK, consumer affairs executive; b. Nashville, Nov. 17, 1941; d. Gerald M. and Lee Wallwork; m. David McNutt, Sept. 13, 1969. BA in Chemistry, Duke U., 1963; MS in Nutrition, Columbia U., 1965; PhD in Biochemistry, Vanderbilt U., 1970; JD, DePaul U., 1984. Bar: N.Y. 1984, D.C. 1984. Exec. dir. Nat. Nutrition Consortium, Washington, 1979-81; asst. prof. pub. health U. Ill., Chgo., 1981-83; assoc. dir. Good Housekeeping Inst., N.Y.C., 1982-85; v.p. consumer affairs Kraft Inc., Glenview, Ill., 1985-87; pres. Consumer Choices Unltd. Inc., Evanston, 1988—. Author: Nutrition and Food Choices, 1979; editor: Sugars in Nutrition, 1975, Consumer Mags. Digest, 1989—. Bd. dirs. Better Bus. Bur., Chgo. and No. Ill., 1986-88; FDA Food Adv. Com., 1992-94. Mem. N.Y. Bar Assn., D.C. Bar Assn., Fedn. Am. Socs. Exptl. Biology (Congl. Sci. fellow), Soc. for Nutrition Edn. (pres. 1983-84), Am. Inst. Nutrition, Am. Dietetics Assn., Am. Coun. on Consumer Interests. Home and Office: Consumer Choices Inc 28W176 Belleau Dr Winfield IL 60190

MCNUTT, MARCIA KEMPER, geophysicist; b. Mpls., Minn., Feb. 19, 1952; widowed, 1988; 3 children. BA, Colorado Coll., 1973; PhD, Scripps Inst. Oceanography, 1978. Geophysicist US Geol. Survey, 1979-82; asst. prof. geophysics MIT, 1982-86, assoc. prof., 1986-89, prof., 1989—, Griswold prof., 1991—; pres. tectonophysics sect. AGU, 1994—; mem. com. on criteria for fed. support of rsch. & devel., 1995—. Mem. Am. Geophys. Union (Macelevane award 1988). Office: MIT Dept of Earth Atmospheric& Planetary Sci 77 Massachusetts Ave Cambridge MA 02139-3594

MCNUTT, WILLIAM JAMES, consulting engineer; b. Phila., Aug. 31, 1927; s. Thomas T. and Mary V. McNutt; m. Eleanor M. McGonigal, Aug. 19, 1950. BSEE, Tufts Coll., 1950; MSEE, Ill. Inst. Tech., 1952. Design and devel. engr. large transformer dept. GE, Pittsfield, Mass., 1952-66, mgr. advance devel. engring., large transformer dept., 1966-86; pres. Berkshire Transformer Cons., Pittsfield, 1987—; U.S. rep. transformers study com. Conf. Internat. des Grands Reseaux Electriques, 1977-88; expert advisor on transformers U.S. Nat. Com. of Internat. Electrotech. Commn., 1987—. Editor: (with others) Standard Handbook for Electrical Engineers, 1987; contbr. articles to IEEE Trans., 1958— (prize papers 1974, 83-84, 90). Treas. South Congl. Ch., Pittsfield, 1988-91. Power Systems Engring. fellow Westinghouse Electric Corp., 1950-52. Fellow IEEE (chmn. transformers com. 1981-82). Avocations: golf, tennis, bridge.

MCPARTLAND, JAMES MICHAEL, university official; b. N.Y.C., Sept. 26, 1939; s. James J. and Helen M. (Leddy) McP. BS, Cornell U., 1961, MS, 1963; PhD, Johns Hopkins U., 1968. Rschr. U.S. Office Edn., Washington, 1965-67, U.S. Commn. Civil Rights, Washington, 1967-68; asst. dir. Ctr. Social Orgn. Schs., Johns Hopkins U., Balt., 1968-75, co-dir., 1976-94; dir., 1994—. Co-author: Equality of Educational Opportunity, 1966; author: (with others) Encyclopedia of Educational Research, 1992, Review of Research in Education, 1993; co-editor: Violence in Schools, 1977. Mem. Am. Ednl. Rsch. Assn., Am. Sociol. Assn., Am. Statis. Assn. Democrat. Roman Catholic. Avocation: music. Home: 1102 S Streeper St Baltimore MD 21224-4873 Office: Johns Hopkins U CSOS 3505 N Charles St Baltimore MD 21218-2404

MCPARTLAND, PATRICIA ANN, health educator; b. Passaic, N.J.; d. Daniel and Josephine McP. BA, U. Mo., 1971; MCRP, Ohio State U., 1975, MS in Preventive Medicine, 1975; EdD in Higher and Adult Edn., Columbia U., 1988. Cert. holistic, aromatherapy and hypnotherapy. Sr. health planner Merrimack Valley HSA, Lawrence, Mass., 1977-79; planning cons./adminstr. Children's Hosp., Boston, 1979-80; exec. dir. Southeastern Mass. Area Health Edn. Ctr., Marion, Mass., 1980—; v.p. New Bedford (Mass.) Cmty. Health Ctr., 1993-94; chmn. edn. and tng. com. Health and Human Svc. Coalition, 1988-89; vis. lectr. Bridgewater State Coll.; lectr. in field. Editorial bd. Jour. Healthcare Edn. and Tng., 1989-93; author: Promoting Health in the Workplace, 1991; contbr. articles to profl. jours. Vol. speaker March of Dimes Found., Wareham, Mass., 1992-93; coll.-wide vocat. Cape Cod C.C., Hyannis, Mass., 1989—; planning adv. 2nd Internat. Symposium, Pasco, Wash., 1992; v.p. New Bedford chpt. Am. Cancer Soc., 1985-90. Recipient award Excellence in Continuing Edn. Nat. AHEC Ctr. Dirs. Assn., 1994, 95, 96, Sec.'s awards for Outstanding Progam in Community Health, Nat. Cancer Inst., Washington, 1990. Mem. Am. Pub. Health Assn., Inst. for Disease Prevention (steering com. 1982—), Southeastern Mass Health Planning (bd. dirs., sec., 1982-87), Nat. Planning Conf. (mem. com. 1984-85, 86-87). Avocations: writing, dance, theatre, travel, hiking. Home: PO Box 491 Marion MA 02738-0491 Office: Southeastern Mass AHEC PO Box 280 2 Spring St Marion MA 02738

MCPEAK, MERRILL ANTHONY, business executive, consultant, retired officer; b. Santa Rosa, Calif., Jan. 9, 1936; s. Merrill Addison McPeak and Winifred Alice (Stewart) McPeak Bendall; m. Elynor Fay Moskowitz, Nov. 10, 1956; children—Mark Allen, Brian David. A.B., San Diego State Coll., Calif., 1957; M.S., George Washington U., Washington, 1974. Commd. 2d lt. USAF, 1957, advanced through grades to gen., 1988; pilot USAF Thunderbirds, Nellis AFB, Nev., 1966-68; comdr. Misty Forward Air Controllers, Phu Cat, Republic of Vietnam, 1969, 20th Tactical Fighter Wing, RAF, Upper Heyford, Eng., 1980-81, 12th Air Force, Bergstrom AFB, Tex., 1987-88; comdr.-in-chief Pacific Air Forces, Hickam AFB, Hawaii, 1988-90; chief of staff USAF, Washington, 1990-94; co. dir., cons., 1994—. Officer USAF, retired. Decorated DSM, Silver Star, Legion of Merit, DFC. Mem. Air Force Assn., Coun. Fgn. Rels., Daedalians, Sigma Chi. Home: Air House 17360 SW Grandview Lake Oswego OR 97034

MC PHAIL, ANDREW TENNENT, chemist, educator; b. Glasgow, Scotland, Sept. 23, 1937; s. Archibald Donaldson and Mary (Tennent) McP.; m. Annette Carson Paton, Aug. 4, 1961; children: Neil Andrew, Donald Robert. B.S. with honors, U. Glasgow, 1959, Ph.D., 1963. Asst. lectr. chemistry U. Glasgow, 1961-64; research assoc. dept. chemistry U. Ill., 1964-66; lectr. chemistry U. Sussex, Eng., 1966-68; assoc. prof. chemistry Duke U., 1968-73, prof., 1973—, dir. X-ray Structure Ctr., 1984—; adj. prof. Sch. Pharmacy U. N.C.-Chapel Hill, 1983—; cons. Schering Research Corp., Burroughs Wellcome Co., Research Triangle Inst. Contbr. articles to profl. jours. Fellow Am. Crystallographic Assn.; mem. Royal Soc. Chemistry (London), Am. Chem. Soc., Sigma Xi, Phi Lambda Upsilon. Co-inventor pharmacologically active amine-carboxyboranes and related compounds. Office: Paul M Gross Chemical Lab Duke U Durham NC 27708-0346

MCPHAIL, JOANN WINSTEAD, writer, producer, publisher, art dealer, owner; b. Trenton, Fla., Feb. 17, 1941; d. William Emerson and Donna Mae (Crawford) Winstead; m. James Michael McPhail, June 15, 1963; children: Angela C. McPhail Morris, Dana Denise, Whitney Gold McPhail Casso. Student, Fla. So. Coll., 1959-60, St. John's River Jr. Coll., Palatka, Fla., 1960-61, Houston (Tex.) C.C. With Jim Walter Corp., Houston, 1961-62; receptionist, land lease sec. Oil and Gas Property Mgmt. Inc., Houston, 1962-63; sec. to mng. atty. State Farm Ins. Co., Houston, 1963-64; saleswoman, decorator Oneil-Anderson, Houston, 1973; sec. Law Offices of Ed Christensen, Houston, 1980-82; advt. mgr. Egalitarian Houston (Tex.) C.C. Systems, 1981; fashion display artist, 1985-86; entrepreneur, writer, art agt., playwright Golden Galleries, Houston, 1990—; owner, property mgr. APT Investments, 1994—; producer, publisher Anna Gold Classics, 1995—. Freelance writer, photographer: Elegance of Needlepoint, 1970, S.W. Art Mag., A Touch of Greatness, 1973, Sweet 70's Anthology, The Budding of Tomorrow, 1974; columnist Egalitarian: The New Game, Design Your Own Wall Covering, Student Profile, 1981, National Library of Poetry, Fireworks, 1995; contbr. poetry to various publs.; playwright, 1993—; writer, pub., prodr. Anna Gold Classics, 1995—; prodr. religious drama The Missing Crown, KYND-AM, World Wide Christian Radio, KTEK-AM, KCBI-FM, San Angelo, Tex., Frederick, Okla., 1995—. Vol. PTO bd. Sharptown Mid. Sch. Mem. NAFE, ASCAP, BMI, Internat. Platform Assn. Republican. Methodist. Home: 2608 Stanford St Houston TX 77006-2928

MCPHAIL, ROBERT J. F., management consultant. Prin. Deloitte TCHE THMTSU LLG group, 1984—. Office: 1001 Pennsylvania Ave NW Washington DC 20004

MCPHEDRAN, NORMAN TAIT, surgeon, educator; b. Saskatoon, Sask., Can., Feb. 12, 1924; s. Norman Neil and Olive Mabel (Tait) McP.; m. Jean Anne Young, June 19, 1950; children—Norman, Peter, Duncan, Bruce, James. M.D., U. Toronto, 1950. Lectr., then asst. prof. U. Toronto, 1958-69; prof. surgery U. Calgary Med. Sch., 1969-81, former head prof. surgery, head dept. developing med. sch., 1981-89; prof. emeritus, 1989—. Author: Canadian Medical Schools - Two Hundred Years of Medical History, 1822-1992; contbr. articles to profl. jours.; chpts. in books. Served with Can. Army, 1942-45. Recipient George Armstrong Peter prize U. Toronto, 1960, McLaughlin fellow, 1957-58. Fellow Royal Coll. Surgeons Can.; mem. Can. Med. Assn., Am. Surg. Assn., Cen. Surg. Assn., ACS (regent 1985-93). Mem. United Ch. Christ. Club: Earl Gray Golf.

MC PHEE, HENRY ROEMER, lawyer; b. Ames, Iowa, Jan. 11, 1925; s. Harry Roemer and Mary (Ziegler) McP.; m. Joanne Lambert, May 19, 1956 (div. Dec. 1991); children: Henry Roemer III, Joanne, Larkin, Charles. AB cum laude, Princeton U., 1947; LLB, Harvard U., 1950. Bar: N.J. 1951, Ill. 1961, D.C. 1966. Exec. asst. to gov. State of N.J., Trenton, 1950-52; assoc. R.E. & A.D. Watson, New Brunswick, N.J., 1952-54; asst. to gen. counsel FTC, Washington, 1954; exec. asst. White House, Washington, 1954-57; asst. spl. counsel Pres. U.S., Washington, 1957-58, assoc. spl. counsel, pres., 1958-61; ptnr. Hamel & Park, Washington, 1961-88; mem. mgmt. com. Hamel & Park, 1975-85, mng. ptnr., 1980-83; ptrnr. Hopkins & Sutter, 1988-93, of counsel, 1994—; sec. N.J. Commn. on Interstate Cooperation, 1952-54; gen. counsel Rep. Nat. Fin. Com., 1968-73, Rep. Nat. Com., Washington, 1968. Chmn. bldg. com. Potomac (Md.) Presbyn. Ch., 1965-67; v.p. Rep. Club, Princeton, 1952-54; bd. dirs. Eisenhower World Affairs Inst., 1983—, treas., 1991-93. Mem. ABA, D.C. Bar Assn., N.J. Bar Assn., Lincoln's Inn Soc. Harvard Law Sch. Republican. Presbyterian. Clubs: Tower (Princeton U.); Princeton (Washington) (pres. 1970-72), Metropolitan (Washington), Capitol Hill (Washington). Avocation: tennis. Home: 11615 Partridge Run Ln Potomac MD 20854-1218 Office: Hopkins & Sutter 888 16th St NW Washington DC 20006-4103

MC PHEE, JOHN ANGUS, writer; b. Princeton, N.J., Mar. 8, 1931; s. Harry Roemer and Mary (Ziegler) McP.; m. Pryde Brown, Mar. 16, 1957; children: Laura, Sarah, Jenny, Martha; m. Yolanda Whitman, Mar. 8, 1972; stepchildren: Cole Harrop, Andrew Harrop, Katherine Ryan, Vanessa Speir. AB, Princeton U., 1953; postgrad., Magdalene Coll., Cambridge (Eng.) U., 1953-54; LittD (hon.), Bates Coll., 1978, Colby Coll., 1978, Williams Coll., 1979, U. Alaska, 1980, Coll. William and Mary, 1988, Rutgers U., 1988; ScD, Maine Maritime Acad., 1992. TV playwright for Robert Montgomery Presents, N.Y.C., 1955-56; contbg. editor, assoc. editor Time mag., 1957-64; staff writer The New Yorker mag., 1965—; Ferris prof. journalism Princeton U., 1975—. Author: A Sense of Where You Are, 1965, The Headmaster, 1966, Oranges, 1967, The Pine Barrens, 1968, A Roomful of Hovings, 1968, Levels of the Game, 1969, The Crofter and the Laird, 1970, Encounters with the Archdruid, 1971, The Deltoid Pumpkin Seed, 1973, The Curve of Binding Energy, 1974, Pieces of the Frame, 1975, The Survival of the Bark Canoe, 1975, Coming into the Country, 1977, Giving Good Weight, 1979, Basin and Range, 1981, In Suspect Terrain, 1983, La Place de la Concorde Suisse, 1984, Table of Contents, 1985, Rising from the Plains, 1986, The Control of Nature, 1989, Looking for a Ship, 1990, Assembling California, 1993, The Ransom of Russian Art, 1994. Recipient award in lit. Am. Acad. and Inst. Arts and Letters, 1977, Woodrow Wilson award Princeton U., 1982, John Wesley Powell award U.S. Geol. Survey,

1988, John Burroughs medal, 1990, Walter Sullivan award Am. Geophys. Union, 1993. Fellow Geol. Soc. Am.; mem. Am. Acad. Arts and Letters.

MCPHEE, JONATHAN, music director, conductor, composer, arranger. LRAM, Royal Acad. Music; BM, MM, Juilliard Sch. Music dir., prin. condr. Boston Ballet, 1988—. Condr. dance cos. including The Joffrey Ballet, The Martha Graham Dance Co., The Dance Theatre of Harlem, Am. Ballet Theatre, N.Y.C. Ballet, The Royal Ballet, Covent Garden, Nat. Ballet of Can., orchs. including Buffalo Philharm., Joffrey Ballet Orch., Rochester Philharm., N.Y.C. Opera Orch., BBC Scottish Symphony, Hague Philharm., Boston Pops, Syracuse Symphony, San Diego Symphony, San Francisco Symphony, Orchestre Colonne, Paris, The Nat. Philharm. Orch., London, Danish Radio Symphony Orch.; recs. for filming of Martha Graham works, Cave of the Heart, Errand Into the Maze, El Penintent, Michael Gandolfi's Caution to the Wind: author rev. version Stravinsky's Rite of Spring; arrangements pub. by Boosey & Hawkes. Office: Boston Ballet 19 Clarendon St Boston MA 02116-6107

MCPHEE, RICHARD S., church administrator. Exec. dir. American Baptist Men of the American Baptist Church, Valley Forge, Pa. Office: Am Baptist Church PO Box 851 Valley Forge PA 19482-0851

MC PHEETERS, EDWIN KEITH, architect, educator; b. Stillwater, Okla., Mar. 26, 1924; s. William Henry and Eva Winona (Mitchell) McP.; m. Patricia Ann Foster, Jan. 29, 1950 (div. 1981); children: Marc Foster, Kevin Mitchell, Michael Hunter; m. Mary Louise Marvin, July 21, 1984. B.Arch., Okla. State U., 1949; M.F.A., Princeton U., 1956. Instr. architecture U. Fla., 1949-51; asst. prof. Ala. Poly. Inst., Auburn U., 1951-54; fellow Princeton U., 1955, 81; from asst. prof. to prof. U. Ark., 1956-66; prof. Rensselaer Poly. Inst., 1966-69, dean, 1966-69; prof. Auburn (Ala.) U., 1969-89, dean Sch. Architecture and Fine Arts,, 1969-88, dean, prof. emeritus, 1989—; adj. prof. Frank Lloyd Wright Sch. of Architecture, 1992—; mem. Ala. Bd. Registration for Architects, 1978-87; profl. adviser South Ctrl. Bell Telephone Co., 1977-79, So. Co., 1979-81, Ala. Power Co., 1979-81, Okla. State U., 1983, Ala. Sch. Fine Arts, 1985-86; cons. Taliesin Architects, 1988-92. Served to 2d lt. USAAC, 1943-45; capt. USAFR 1945-57. Fellow AIA (pres. Ala. coun. 1978, Merit award 1976, East Ala. Design awards 1986, 87, 90, 92); mem. Assn. Collegiate Schs. Arch. (bd. dirs. 1970-77, Disting. Prof. 1989), Blue Key, Kappa Sigma, Omicron Delta Kappa, Kappa Kappa Psi, Tau Sigma Delta, Rotary. Episcopalian.

MC PHERSON, ALICE RUTH, ophthalmologist; b. Regina, Sask., Can., June 30, 1926; came to U.S., 1938, naturalized, 1958; d. Gordon and Viola (Hoover) McP. BS, U. Wis., 1948, MD, 1951. Diplomate Am. Bd. Ophthalmology. Intern Santa Barbara (Calif.) Cottage Hosp., 1951-52; resident anesthesiology Hartford (Conn.) Hosp., 1952; resident ophthalmology Chgo. Eye, Ear, Nose and Throat Hosp., 1953, U. Wis. Hosps., 1953-55; ophthalmologist Davis and Duehr Eye Clinic, Madison, Wis., 1956-57; clin. instr. U. Wis., 1956-57; fellow retina service Mass. Eye and Ear Infirmary, 1957-58; ophthalmologist Scott and White Clinic, Temple, Tex., 1958-60; practice medicine specializing in ophthalmology and retinal diseases Houston, 1960—; mem. staff Meth., St. Luke's, Tex. Children's Hosps., Houston; clin. asst. prof. Baylor Coll. Medicine, Houston, 1959-61, asst. prof. ophthalmology, 1961-69, clin. asst. prof., 1969-75, clin. prof., 1975—, chmn. search com. dept. otorhinolaryngology and communicative scis., 1996; cons. retinal diseases VA Hosp., Houston, 1960—, Ben Taub Hosp., Houston, 1960—; mem. adv. com. for active staff appt. sect. ophthalmology Meth. Hosp., 1986-91, mem equipment com., 1993-95; vol. clin. faculty appts. and promotions com., 1993—. Editor: New and Controversial Aspects of Retinal Detachment, 1968, New and Controversial Aspects of Vitreoretinal Surgery, 1977, Retinopathy of Prematurity: Current Concepts and Controversies, 1986. Ambassador Houston Ballet, mem. Houston Ballet Found.; mem. pres.'s council Houston Grand Opera, mem.; mem. conductors circle Houston Symphony, mem. Houston Symphony Soc.; mem. campaign for 80s Baylor Coll. Medicine; mem. Assn. for Community TV, Better Bus. Bur., Physicians' Benevolent Fund, South Tex. Diabetes Assn. Inc., Jr. League Houston. Recipient Honor award Am. Acad. Ophthalmology, 1956, Award of Appreciation, Knights Templar Eye Found., 1978, Woodlands Medal for Outstanding Contbn. to the Econ. Devel. of Community, 1988; Alice R. Mc Pherson Lab for Retina Rsch. dedicated Baylor Ctr. for Biotech., 1988,; Alice R. Mc Pherson Day proclaimed in her honor Mayor of City of Houston, Mar. 12, 1988. Fellow Am. Acad. Ophthalmology (2d v.p. 1979, com. for pub. and profl. rels., vice chmn. program devel. found. bd. trustees, sr. honor award 1986), ACS (credentials and Tex. credentials com., com. on applications); mem. Vitreous Soc., AMA, Tex. Med. Assn., Pan-Am. Med. Assn., Internat. Coll. Surgeons (vice regent 1991—), Am. Med. Women's Assn., Retina Soc. (v.p. 1976-77, pres. 1978-79, credentials com.), Internat. Coll. Ocular Surgeons (vice regent 1991), Am. Soc. Contemporary Ophthalmology (Charles Schepens Hon. award), Am. Bd. Laser Surgery, Internat. Assn. Ocular Surgeons, Harris County Med. Soc., Houston Acad. Medicine, Houston Ophthalmol. Soc. (credentials com., pres. 1990-91), Internat. Soc. Eye Research (cred. com. 1992—), Macula Soc. (credentialling com. 1992—), 9th Dist. Med. Soc., Pan Am. Assn. Ophthalmology (bd. dirs., membership com., bd. dirs. Pan Am. ednl. fund, v.p. 1991-92, AJO lectr. 1993, pres.-elect 1992-95, pres. 1995—), Research to Prevent Blindness, So. Med. Soc., Tex. Med. Assn., Vitreous Soc., Tex. Ophthal. Assn., Soc. Eye Surgeons, Harris County Med. Soc., Assn. Research Surgeons, U. Wis. Ophthal. Alumni Assn. (founding pres. 1990-93, founded Alice R. McPherson lectureship 1994), French Ophthal. Soc., Internat. Med. Assembly S.W. Tex., Schepens Internat. Soc. (sec. 1986-93, v.p. 1993-95, pres. 1995—), Jules Gonin Club. Research in vision and ophthalmology. Office: Tex Med Ctr 6560 Fannin St Ste 2200 Houston TX 77030-2707

MCPHERSON, DONALD J., metallurgist; married; children: Marjorie, Linda. B.S., M.S., Ph.D., Ohio State U., D.Sc. (hon.), 1975. Assoc. metallurgist Argonne Nat. Lab., to 1950; research metallurgist, asst. div. mgr., div. mgr., v.p. IIT Research Inst., 1950-69; v.p., dir. tech. Kaiser Aluminum and Chem. Corp., Oakland, Calif., 1969-82; Mem. numerous govt. coms. on devel. titanium for def. applications.; chmn. nat. materials adv. bd. NRC, 1982-84. Contbr. numerous articles on titanium and its alloys to profl. jours. Bd. dirs. Research Found. Ohio State U., Jr. Achievement of Bay Area, 1980-82. Recipient Outstanding Young Men award Chgo. Jr. Assn. Commerce and Industry, 1956; Distinguished Alumnus and Centennial Achievement awards Ohio State U. Fellow Am. Soc. Metals (trustee, Campbell Meml. lectr. 1974), hon. mem.; mem. AIME (chmn. titanium com.; chmn. Inst. of Metals div.; bd. dirs. Metall. Soc.), Am. Ceramic Soc. Home: 9369 E Via Montoya Scottsdale AZ 85255-5013

MCPHERSON, DONALD PAXTON, III, lawyer; b. Balt., Aug. 9, 1941; s. Donald Paxton Jr. and Janet Lewis Russell McPherson; children: David Russell, Cynthia Quandt. AB, Princeton U., 1963; LLB, Columbia U., 1966. Bar: Md. 1966, U.S. Dist. Ct. Md. 1967, U.S. Ct. Appeals (4th cir.) 1967. Assoc. Piper & Marbury, Balt., 1966-74, ptnr., 1974—, head real estate dept., 1980-94. Mem. ABA, Md. Bar Assn. Democrat. Presbyterian. Avocations: swimming, bicycling, hiking. Office: Piper & Marbury 36 S Charles St Baltimore MD 21201-3020

MC PHERSON, FRANK ALFRED, manufacturing corporate executive; b. Stilwell, Okla., Apr. 29, 1933; s. Younce B. and Maurine Francis (Strauss) McP.; m. Nadine Wall, Sept. 10, 1955; 4 children. B.S., Okla. State U., 1957. With Kerr-McGeeCorp., 1957—; gen. mgr. Gulf Coast Oil and gas ops., Morgan City, La., 1969-73; pres. Kerr-McGee Coal, 1973-76, Kerr-McGee Nuclear, 1976-77; vice chmn. Kerr-McGee Corp., 1977-80, pres., 1980—, chmn., CEO, 1983—; bd. dirs. Kimberly-Clark Corp. Patentee in field. Bd. dirs. Okla. chpt. Nature Conservancy, U.S. Olympic Com. for Okla., Bapt Med. Ctr. Okla., Okla. Med. Rsch. Found., Okla. State U. Found., Okla. State Fair, Bank of Okla., Boys and Girls Clubs of Am., J.&W., Seligman & Co., Inc.; pres. Okla. Found. Excellence; active Bus. Roundtable; adv. com. U. Okla. Coll. Medicine, Oklahoma City Pub. Schs. Mem. Conf. Bd., Soc. Mining Engrs. Am., Am. Petroleum Inst. (dir.), Nat. Petroleum Council, 25-Yr. Club of Petroleum Industry Oklahoma City C. of C. (dir.), Okla. State C. of C. Republican. Baptist. Office: Kerr-McGee Corp PO Box 25861 Oklahoma City OK 73125-0861

MCPHERSON, GARY LEE, lawyer, state representative; b. Auburn, Wash., Dec. 4, 1962; s. Percy Ivan and Vicki Mae (Voyles) McP.; children: Christina, Elizabeth, Ashley. BS in Bus. Adminstrn., Union Coll., 1985; JD, U. Nebr., 1988. Bar: Colo. 1989, Nebr. 1989, U.S. Dist. Ct. Colo. 1989, U.S. Ct. Appeals (10th cir.) 1989. Legal/legis. aide Knudsen, Berkheimer & Richardson, Lincoln, Nebr., 1981-85; law clk. Crosby, Guenzel & Davis, Lincoln, 1986; law clk. ethics com. Nebr. State Bar Assn., Lincoln, 1987; assoc. Hall & Evans, Denver, 1987-89, Elrod, Katz, Preeo & Look, P.C., Denver, 1989-90, Fortune & Lawritson, P.C., Denver, 1990-93; ptnr. McPherson & Hull, P.C., Aurora, Colo., 1993—; state rep. State of Colo., Denver, 1994—. Author: Handbook on Professional Malpractice, 1987, rev. edit., 1988; contbr. articles to profl. jours. Bd. dirs. Arapahoe Park and Recreation Bd., Aurora, 1991-95; dist. capt. Arapahoe County Rep. Dist. 8, Aurora, 1992-95; vice chmn. Ho. Dist. 40, Aurora, 1993-95, state rep.; chmn. Senate Dist. 28, Aurora, 1993-95. Recipient Internat. Acad. Trial Lawyers award, 1987, 88, Aurora Pub. Schs. Supts. award, 1992. Mem. ABA (bd. dirs., litigations com. 1992-93, chmn. young lawyers divsn. prelaw counseling com. 1992-94), Colo. Bar Assn. (sec., treas. young lawyers divsn. 1991-93, chair-elect 1993-94, chmn. 1994-95), Arapahoe County Bar Assn., Aurora Rep. Forum, Arapahoe County Rep. Mens Club. Avocations: aviation, scuba, politics, backpacking, snow skiing. Office: 14291 E 4th Ave Ste 206 Aurora CO 80011-8724

MC PHERSON, HARRY CUMMINGS, JR., lawyer; b. Tyler, Tex., Aug. 22, 1929; s. Harry Cummings and Nan (Hight) McP.; m. Clayton Read, Aug. 30, 1952 (div.); children: Courtenay, Peter B.; m. Mary Patricia DeGroot, Oct. 17, 1981; 1 child, Sam B. B.A., U. South, 1949, D.C.L. (hon.), 1965; student, Columbia U., 1949-50; LL.B., U. Tex., 1956. Bar: Tex. 1955. Asst. gen. counsel Democratic policy com. U.S. Senate, 1956-59, asso. counsel, 1959-61, gen. counsel, 1961-63; dep. under sec. internat. affairs Dept. Army, 1963-64; asst. sec. ednl. and cultural affairs Dept. State, 1964-65; spl. asst. and counsel to Pres. Johnson, 1965-66, spl. counsel, 1966-69; pvt. practice law Washington, 1969—; chmn. task force on domestic policy Dem. Adv. Coun. Elected Ofcls., 1974-76; mem. Pres.'s Commn. on Accident at Three Mile Island, 1979; vice chmn. John F. Kennedy Ctr. for Performing Arts, 1969-76, gen. counsel, 1977-91; bd. dirs. Woodrow Wilson Internat. Ctr. for Scholars, 1969-74; pres. Fed. City Coun., 1983-88; apptd. vice chmn. U.S. Internat. Cultural and Trade Ctr. Commn., 1988-93. Author: A Political Education, 1972, 88, 95. Mem. U.S. Base Closure and Realignment Commn., 1993. 2d lt. USAF, 1950-53. Recipient Disting. Civilian Svc. award Dept. Army, 1964, Arthur S. Flemming award, 1968, Judge Learned Hand Human Rels. award Am. Jewish Com., 1994. Mem. D.C. Bar Assn., N.Y. Council on Fgn. Relations (dir. 1974-77), Econ. Club. of Washington (pres. 1992—). Democrat. Episcopalian. Home: 10213 Montgomery Ave Kensington MD 20895-3325 Office: 901 15th St NW Washington DC 20005-2327

MCPHERSON, JAMES ALAN, writer, educator; b. Savannah, Ga., Sept. 16, 1943; s. James and Mable (Smalls) McP.; 1 dau., Rachel Alice. BA, Morris Brown Coll., 1965; LLB, Harvard, 1968; MFA, U. Iowa, 1971. Asst. prof. lit. U. Calif., Santa Cruz, 1969-71, Morgan State U., 1975-76; assoc. prof. English U. Va., Charlottesville, 1976-81; prof. English U. Iowa, 1981—; mem. lit. panel Nat. Endowment for Arts, 1977-80; lectr., Japan, 1989-90; vis. scholar Yale Law Sch., 1978-79. Author: Hue and Cry, 1969, Railroad, 1976, Elbow Room, 1977 (Pulitzer prize 1978), A World Unsuspected, 1987, The Prevailing South, 1988, Confronting Racial Differences, 1990, Lure and Loathing, 1993, Crossings, 1993; editor Double Take Mag., 1995—; contbr. editor Atlantic Monthly, Boston, 1969. Recipient award in lit. Nat. Inst. Arts and Letters, 1970, MacArthur Found. award, 1981, Excellence in Tchg. award U. Iowa, 1991, Green Eyeshades award Soc. So. Journalists, 1994; stories selected for O'Henry Collection and Best American Short Stories, 1969, 73, best Am. Essays, 1990, 93, 94; Guggenheim fellow 1972-73; Atlantic grantee, 1968. Mem. ACLU, NAACP, P.E.N., Am. Acad. Arts and Scis. (elected mem. 1995), Authors League.

MC PHERSON, JAMES MUNRO, history educator; b. Valley City, N.D., Oct. 11, 1936; s. James Munro and Miriam (Osborn) McP.; m. Patricia Rasche, Dec. 28, 1957; 1 dau., Joanna Erika. B.A., Gustavus Adolphus Coll., 1958; Ph.D., Johns Hopkins U., 1963. Mem. faculty Princeton U., 1962—, prof. history, 1972—, Edwards prof. Am. history, 1982, George Henry Davis '86 prof. Am. history, 1991. Author: Struggle for Equality, 1964 (Ainsfield-Wolf award race rels. 1965), The Negro's Civil War, 1965, Marching Toward Freedom: The Negro in the Civil War, 1968, Blacks in America: Bibliographical Essays, 1971, The Abolitionist LEgacy: From Reconstruction to the NAACP, 1975, Ordeal by Dire: The Civil War and Reconstruction, 1981, 2d edit., 1992, Battle Cry of Freedom: The Civil War Era, 1988 (Pulitzer prize for history 1989), Abraham Lincoln and the Second American Revulotion, 1991, Images of the Civil War, 1992, Gettysburg, 1993, What They Fought For, 1861-1865, 1994, The Atlas of the Civil War, 1994. Danforth fellow, 1958-62, Guggenheim fellow, 1967-68, Huntington-Nat. Endowment for Humanities fellow, 1977-78, fellow Behavioral Scis. Ctr., Stanford U., 1982-83, Huntington-Seaver Inst. fellow, 1987-88. Mem. Am. Philos. Soc., Am., So. hist. assns., Orgn. Am. Historians, Phi Beta Kappa. Home: 15 Randall Rd Princeton NJ 08540-3609

MCPHERSON, JOHN BARKLEY, aerospace consultant, retired military officer; b. Virginia, Minn., Oct. 4, 1917; s. Barkley John and Anna (Holmgren) McP.; m. Leota Irene Wilson, July 16, 1940; children—Kenneth, Sue McPherson Cain, Shirley McPherson Curs, Robin McPherson Rohrback. B.C.E., U. Ariz., 1940. Commd. 2d lt., cav. U.S. Army, 1940; advanced through grades to lt. gen. USAF, 1968; assigned (B-29s, World War II, PTO); comdr. Walker AFB, Roswell, N.Mex., 1950-52; dir. faculty (Air War Coll.), 1955-56; dep. comdr. (5th Air Div. Morocco), 1956-58; comdr. (379th Bomb Wing), Homestead AFB, Fla., 1958-59, (823d Air Div.), Homestead AFB, 1959-62, (810th Air Div.), Minot AFB, N.D., 1962-64; vice dir. ops., joint staff (Joint Chiefs Staff), 1964-67, vice dir. joint staff, 1967-68, asst. to chmn., 1968-70; comdt. (Nat. War Coll.), 1970-73; ret., 1973; cons. Martin Marietta Aerospace, 1973-85; mem. Sr. Govt. Rev. Panel, 1985-91. Decorated D.S.M. with two oak leaf clusters, Legion of Merit, Bronze Star; recipient Gen. H.S. Vandenberg Aerospace Edn. award, 1984; Centennial medallion award U. Ariz., 1989, Disting. Citizen award, 1995; named Outstanding Young Man of Yr., Roswell, 1951. Mem. Air Force Hist. Found. (pres. 1974-83), Air Force Assn., Nat. Space Club, Order of Daedalians, Theta Tau, Kappa Sigma. Home: 3881 Rust Hill Pl Fairfax VA 22030-3919

MCPHERSON, LARRY E(UGENE), photographer, educator; b. Newark, Ohio, May 1, 1943; s. Eugene Edward and Ethel Grace (Lehman) McP. BA, MA; B.A., Columbia Coll., Chgo., 1976; M.A., No. Ill. U., 1978. Instr. Columbia Coll., 1971-76; assoc. prof. photography U. Memphis, 1978—; instr. Sch. of Art Inst. Chgo., spring 1972; workshop instr. Ohio State U., Columbus, summer 1980, VSW Summer Inst., Rochester, N.Y., summer 1988. One-man shows include Art Inst. Chgo., 1969, 78, 81, Dayton Art Inst., 1992; exhibited in group shows at Mus. Modern Art, N.Y.C., 1978, Corcoran Gallery Art, Washington, 1982, George Eastman House, Rochester, N.Y., 1982, New Orleans Mus. Art, 1992; represented in permanent collections Mus. Modern Art, Art Inst. Chgo., George Eastman House, New Orleans Mus. Art, Mus. Fine Arts, Houston, Memphis Brooks Mus. Art. Faculty Devel. grantee Memphis State U., springs 1983, 92; grantee-fellow Nat. Endowment for Arts, 1975, 79; Guggenheim fellow, 1980. Mem. Soc. Photog. Edn. Home: 3293 Southern Ave Apt 5 Memphis TN 38111-8321 Office: U Memphis Dept Art Memphis TN 38152

MCPHERSON, MARY PATTERSON, academic administrator; b. Abington, Pa., May 14, 1935; d. John B. and Marjorie Hoffman (Higgins) McP. A.B., Smith Coll., 1957, LL.D., 1981; M.A., U. Del., 1960; Ph.D., Bryn Mawr Coll., 1969; LL.D. (hon.), Juniata Coll., 1975, Smith Coll., 1981, Princeton U., 1984, U. Rochester, 1984, U. Pa., 1985; Litt.D. (hon.), Haverford Coll., 1980; L.H.D. (hon.), Lafayette Coll., 1982, U. Pa., 1985; LHD (hon.), Med. Coll. Pa., 1985. Instr. philosophy U. Del., 1959-61; asst., fellow and lectr. dept. philosophy Bryn Mawr Coll., 1961-63, asst. dean, 1964-69, assoc. dean, 1969-70; dean Bryn Mawr Coll. (Undergrad. Coll.), 1970-78, assoc. prof., from 1970; acting pres. Bryn Mawr Coll., 1976-77, pres., 1978—; bd. dirs. Provident Nat. Bank of Phila., Bell Telephone Co. Pa., Dayton Hudson Corp.; mem. commn. on women in higher edn. Am. Council on Edn., bd. dirs., 1979-82. Bd. dirs. Agnes Irwin Sch., 1971—; bd. dirs. Shipley Sch., 1972—, Phillips Exeter Acad., 1973-76, Wilson Coll., 1976-79, Greater Phila. Movement, 1973-77, Internat. House of Phila., 1974-76, Josiah Macy, Jr. Found., 1977—, Carnegie Found. for Advancement Teaching, 1978-86, Univ. Mus., Phila., 1977-79, University City Sci. Center, 1979-85, Brookings Inst., 1984—, Phila. Contributionship, 1985—, Carnegie Corp. N.Y., 1985—, Nat. Humanities Ctr., 1986—, Amherst Coll., 1986—. Mem. Soc. for Ancient Greek Philosophy, Am. Philos. Soc. Clubs: Fullerton, Cosmopolitan. Office: Bryn Mawr Coll Office of the President 101 N Merion Ave Bryn Mawr PA 19010-2899*

MCPHERSON, MELVILLE PETER, academic administrator, former government official; b. Grand Rapids, Mich., Oct. 27, 1940; s. Donald and Ellura E. (Frost) McP.; m. Joanne McPherson; 1 child, Donald B.; 1 stepchild, Michael D. Kircher. JD, Am. U., 1969; MBA, Western Mich. U., 1967; BA, Mich. State U., 1963. Peace Corps vol. Peru, 1965-66; with IRS, Washington, 1969-75; spl. asst. to pres. and dep. dir. Presdl. Pers. White Ho., Washington, 1975-77; mng. ptnr. Washington office Vorys, Sater, Seymour & Pease, 1977-81; adminstr. AID, Washington, 1981-87; dep. sec. Dept. Treasury, Washington, 1987-89; group exec. v.p. Bank of Am., San Francisco, 1989-93; pres. Mich. State U., East Lansing, 1993—. Mem. D.C. Bar Assn., Mich. Bar Assn. Republican. Methodist. Office: Office of the Pres Mich State U 450 Administration Bldg East Lansing MI 48824-1046

MC PHERSON, PAUL FRANCIS, publishing and investment banking executive; b. Boston, Apr. 30, 1931; s. William Andrew and Margaret Frances (Rice) McP.; m. Mary Loretta Sanders, June 10, 1953; children: Paul, Kevin, Gary, Scott. BSBA, Boston Coll., 1952; MBA, Babson Coll., 1955. With McGraw Hill, Inc., N.Y.C., 1955-89; advt. sales mgr. McGraw-Hill Pub. Co., 1963-66, group v.p., 1973-76, exec. v.p., 1976-79; pres. McGraw-Hill Info. Systems Co., 1979-80; pres. McGraw-Hill Pub. Co., 1980-83, exec. v.p., 1983-89; pres., chief exec. officer FM Bus. Publs. Inc., N.Y.C., 1988-92; sr. advisor AdMedia Corp. Advisors, N.Y.C., 1992-93, mng. dir., 1993—. Served with U.S. Army, 1952-54. Mem. Am. Bus. Press (bd. dirs., past chmn.), Mag. Pubs. Am. (bd. dirs., past chmn.), Advt. Coun. (dir., past vice chmn.), Audit Bur. Circulations (dir., past vice chmn.), Woodway Country Club. Home: 10 Drum Hill Ln Stamford CT 06902-1406 Office: AdMedia Corp Advisors Inc 866 3rd Ave New York NY 10022-6221

MC PHERSON, PETER, academic administrator. BA in Polit. Sci., Mich. State U., 1963; MBA, Western Mich. U., 1967; JD, Am. U., 1969; LHD (hon.), Va. State U., 1984, Mt. St. Mary;s Coll., 1986; LLD (hon.), Mich. State U., 1984. Tax law specialist IRS, 1969-75; spl. asst. to Pres. Ford, deputy dir. presdl. personnel The White House, Washington, 1975-77; ptnr. Vorys, Sater, Swymour & Pease, Washington, 1977-80; adminstr. Agy. for Internat. Devel., 1981-87; deputy sec. Treasury Dept., Washington, 1987-89; group exec. v.p. Bank Am., 1989-93; pres. Mich. State U., East Lansing, 1993—; chmn. bd. Overseas Pvt. Investment Corp., 1981-87. Gen. counsel Reagan-Bush Transition, 1980-81; vol. Peace Corps, Peru, 1964-65. Recipient Humanitarian of Yr. award Am. Lebanese League, 1983, UNICEF award.

MC PHERSON, ROBERT DONALD, retired lawyer; b. Madison, Wis., Dec. 21, 1936; s. Clifford James and Alice Irene (Peterson) McP.; m. Nancy Joann Buenzli, Aug. 17, 1957; children—Sean Kelly, Eileen Patricia, Maureen Teresa, Cathleen Marie. B.A., U. Tex., El Paso, 1960; J.D., South Tex. Coll. Law, Houston, 1969. Bar: Tex. 1969. Tchr. English various schs., El Paso, Tex. and Menomonie, Wis., 1960-62; claims rep. Employers Casualty Co. Tex., 1962-66, staff claims rep., 1966-68; ptnr. Bousquet & McPherson, Houston, 1969-76; pvt. practice Houston, 1976-80; ptnr. McPherson & McPherson, Houston, 1980-87, McPherson & Ruman, Houston, 1987-89; pvt. practice Houston, 1989-90; ptnr. Mc Pherson & Mahar, Houston, 1990-91; instr. history and govt. South Tex. Jr. Coll., 1969-71; adj. prof. law South Tex. Coll. Law, 1972-78. Served with AUS, 1953-56. Mem. State Bar Tex., Order of Lytae.

MC PHERSON, ROLF KENNEDY, clergyman, church official; b. Providence, Mar. 23, 1913; s. Harold S. and Aimee (Semple) McP.; m. Lorna De Smith, July 21, 1931 (dec.); children—Marlene (dec.), Kay. Grad., So. Cal. Radio Inst., 1933; D.D. (hon.), L.I.F.E. Bible Coll., 1944; LLD (hon.), L.I.F.E. Bible Coll., Los Angeles, 1988. Ordained to ministry Internat. Ch. Foursquare Gospel, 1940. Pres. Internat. Ch. Foursquare Gospel, L.A., 1944-88, dir., 1944-92; pres. emeritus, 1988—; pres., dir. L.I.F.E. Bible Coll., Inc., L.A., 1944-88. Mem. Echo Park Evangelistic Assn. (pres. 1944—). Office: Internat Ch Foursquare Gospel 1910 W Sunset Blvd Ste 200 Los Angeles CA 90026-3247

MCPHERSON, SAMUEL DACE, III, technical training consultant; b. Durham, N.C., May 22, 1957; s. Samuel Dace Jr. and Margaret Courtauld (Finney) McP.; m. Grace Carroll Gilliam, Oct. 11, 1986; children: Stuart Dace, Katherine Finney, Rebecca Banks. BA in Edn., U. N.C., 1979; MEd, U. S.C., 1981. Data entry operator Olsten svcs. No. Telecom, Durham, 1985; computer operator GTE Data Svcs., Durham, 1985-86, sr. computer operator, 1986-87, svc. technician, 1987-88; systems tng. analyst GTE Data Svcs., Tampa, Fla., 1988-90, sr. systems tng. analyst, 1990-92; sr. sales tng. specialist Ascom Timeplex, 1992-93; tech. tng. specialist Fujitsu Network Switching, Raleigh, N.C., 1994-95; founder, pres. Technology Tng. Solutions, Inc., 1995—; presenter pub. and ednl. workshops Wake Tech.; instr./lectr. Am. Rsch. Group. Vol. U.S. Olympic Festival, Durham, 1987, GTE Suncoast Classic, Tampa, 1989-91; instr. Jr. Achievement Tampa, 1989; active Village Presbyn. Ch., Tampa, 1990. Recipient Personal Best Group award GTE, 1992, Quest for Quality award, 1992, Outstanding Achievement award Ascom Timeplex, 1993; Cameron scholar U. N.C., 1978-79. Mem. ASTD (spl. projects com. Suncoast chpt. 1989-90, appreciation award 1989), Data Processing Mgmt. Assn. (dir. mem. edn. 1989-91, presenter local workshop 1991). Republican. Avocations: racquetball, golf, tennis, music, working with others. Home: 5201 Lovell Ct Raleigh NC 27613-5618 Office: Tech Tng Solutions Inc 5201 Lovell Ct Raleigh NC 27613

MCPHERSON, SANDRA JEAN, poet, educator; b. San Jose, Calif., Aug. 2, 1943; d. John Emmet and Joyce (Turney) Todd; adopted d. Walter James and Frances K. (Gibson) McP.; m. Henry D. Carlile, 1966 (div. 1985); 1 child, Phoebe; m. Walter D. Pavlich, 1995. BA in English, San Jose (Calif.) State U., 1965; postgrad., U. Wash., 1965-66. Vis. lectr. U. Iowa Writers Workshop, 1974-76, 78-80; Holloway lectr. U. Calif., Berkeley, 1981; tchr. poetry workshop Oreg. Writers Workshop, Portland, 1981-85; prof. English U. Calif., Davis, 1985—. Author: (poetry) Elegies for the Hot Season, 1970, Radiation, 1973, The Year of Our Birth, 1978, Patron Happiness, 1983, Streamers, 1988, The God of Indeterminacy, 1993, The Spaces Between Birds: Mother/Daughter Poems, 1996, Edge Effect: Trails and portrayals, 1996. Recipient Nat. Endowment for the Arts awards; award in lit. Am. Acad. and Inst. Arts and Letters, 1987; Ingram Merrill Found. fellow; grantee Guggenheim Found., 1976, Oreg. Arts Commn., 1984-85. Democrat. Avocation: collector and exhibitor of African-American quilts. Office: U Calif Dept English Davis CA 95616

MCPHERSON, VANZETTA PENN, federal judge; b. Montgomery, Ala., May 26, 1947; d. Luther Lincoln and Sadie Lee (Gardner) P.; m. Winston D. Durant, Aug. 17, 1968 (div. Apr. 1979); 1 child, Raegan Winston; m. Thomas McPherson Jr., Nov. 16, 1985. BS in Speech Pathology, Howard U., Washington, 1969; MA in Speech Pathology, Columbia U., 1971, JD, 1974. Bar: N.Y. 1975, Ala. 1976, U.S. Dist. Ct. (so. dist.) N.Y. 1975, U.S. Dist. Ct. (mid. dist.) Ala. 1980, U.S. Ct. Appeals (2d cir.) 1975, U.S. Ct. Appeals (11th cir.) 1981, U.S. Supreme Ct. Assoc. Hughes, Hubbard & Reed, N.Y.C., 1974-75; asst. atty. gen. Ala. Atty. Gen. Office, Montgomery, 1975-78; pvt. practice Montgomery, 1978-92; magistrate judge U.S. Dist. Ct. (mid. dist.) Ala., Montgomery, 1992—; co-owner Roots & Wings, A Cultural Bookplace, Montgomery, 1989—. Dir. Ala. Shakespeare Festival, Montgomery, 1987—; chmn. trustees Dexter Ave. King Meml. Bapt. Ch., Montgomery, 1988; chmn. Leadership Montgomery; bd. mem. Lighthouse Counseling Ctr., Montgomery, 1981-84, Montgomery County Pub. Libr., 1989-90; v.p. Lanier High Sch. Parent Tchr. Student Assn., Montgomery, 1990-91. Recipient cert. Ala. Jud. Coll.; named Woman of Achievement Montgomery Advertiser, 1989, Boss of Yr. Montgomery Assn. Legal Secs., 1992, Woman of Yr. Gamma Phi Delta, Montgomery, 1992, Citizen of Yr. Delta Sigma Theta, Montgomery, 1992. Mem. ABA (law office design award 1985), Nat. Bar Assn., Ala. State Bar Assn. (chmn. family law sect. 1989-90), N.Y. State Bar Assn., Montgomery Inn of Cts. (master bencher

1992—), Ala. Black Lawyers Assn. (pres. 1979-80). Office: US Dist Ct Mid Dist Ala PO Box 1629 15 Lee St Montgomery AL 36102

MC QUADE, HENRY FORD, state justice; b. Pocatello, Idaho, Oct. 11, 1915; s. M. Joseph and Mary E. (Farnan) McQ.; m. Mary E. Downing, Apr. 11, 1942; children—Sharon McQuade Grisham, Michael, Frances McQuade Munning, Robert, Joseph, Peter, William. A.B., U. Idaho, 1940, LL.B., 1943. Bar: Idaho 1946. Practice in Pocatello, 1946-51; pros. atty. Bannock County, Idaho, 1946-50; judge 5th Jud. Dist., Idaho, 1951-56; justice Idaho Supreme Ct., 1957-76, chief justice, 1972-75; dep. adminstr. Law Enforcement Assistance Adminstrn., U.S. Dept. Justice, Washington, 1976; adminstrv. law judge Occupational Safety and Health Rev. Commn., Washington, 1976-81; mem. Nat. Commn. on Criminal Justice Standards and Goals, 1971-73, Nat. Commn. Hwy. Traffic Safety, 1971-74. Chmn. Idaho Gov.'s Com. Traffic Safety, 1958-59, Idaho YMCA Youth Legislature, 1958-69, Boise chpt. ARC, 1970-71. Mem. Am. Bar Assn., Am. Judicature Soc., Idaho State Bar. Home: 1002 Ranch Rd Boise ID 83702-1440

MC QUADE, LAWRENCE CARROLL, lawyer, corporate executive; b. Yonkers, N.Y., Aug. 12, 1927; s. Edward A. and Thelma (Keefe) McQ.; m. de Rosset Parker Morrissey, Aug. 3, 1968 (dec. Oct. 1978); 1 child, Andrew Parker; m. Margaret Osmer, Mar. 15, 1980. BA with distinction, Yale U., 1950; BA, Oxford (Eng.) U., 1952, MA, 1956; LLB cum laude, Harvard U., 1954; MA (hon.), Colby Coll., 1981. Bar: N.Y. 1955, D.C. 1968. Assoc. Sullivan & Cromwell, N.Y.C., 1954-60; spl. asst. to asst. sec. for internat. security affairs U.S. Dept. Def., Washington, 1961-63; dep. asst. sec. U.S. Dept. Commerce, Washington, 1963-64, asst. to sec., 1965-67, asst. sec., 1967-69; pres. Procon Inc., Des Plaines, Ill., 1969-75; CEO, dir. Procon Inc., 1969-75; v.p. Universal Oil Products Co., 1972-75; v.p. W.R. Grace & Co., N.Y.C., 1975-78, sr. v.p., 1978-83, exec. v.p., 1983-87, also bd. dirs.; vice chmn. Prudential Mut. Fund Mgmt., N.Y.C., 1988-95; mng. dir. Prudential Securities Inc., 1988-92; chmn., CEO Universal Money Ctrs., 1987-88; expert advisor commn. on transnat. corps. UN, 1989-93; bd. dirs. Bunzl, Quixote Corp., Oxford Analytica, Applied Biosci. Internat.; dir. Country Baskets Index Fund, Inc. Author: (with others) The Ghana Report, 1959; contbr. (with others) articles to profl. jours. Bd. dirs. Fgn. Bondholders Protective Coun., N.Y.C., 1978—, The Am. Forum, 1985—, Am. Coun. on Germany, 1985-94; trustee Colby Coll., 1981-89, trustee emeritus, 1989—; chmn., dir. Czech and Slovak Am. Enterprise Funds, 1994-96; chmn. Czech and Slovak AE Fund, 1995-96; mem. Bretton Woods Com. Rhodes scholar Oxford U., 1952. Mem. Coun. Fgn. Rels. N.Y., Chgo. Coun. Fgn. Rels. (bd. dirs. 1969-75), Nat. Fgn. Trade Coun. (bd. dirs. 1979-87), Atlantic Coun. U.S. (bd. dirs. 1969—), Mgmt. and Devel. Inst. (bd. dirs. 1970—), Overseas Devel. Coun. (bd. dirs. 1974-87), Pres.'s Cir. of NAS, Harvard Club, Century Club, Pilgrims Club, Met. Club (Washington), Phi Beta Kappa.

MCQUAGE, CLARETTA DIANNE, surgical care administrator; b. Laurinburg, N.C., July 16, 1951; d. Horace Franklin and Clara M. (Walters) McQ. ADN, Florence-Darlington Tech. Coll. Charge nurse Security Forces Hosp., Riyadh, Saudi Arabia; head nurse King Fahad Hosp., Riyadh, charge nurse; same day surg. coord. Chesterfield Gen. Hosp., Cheraw, S.C. Recipient Cert. of Appreciation Am. Internat. Div.

MCQUAID, J. DENNIS, lawyer; b. San Diego, Apr. 19, 1939. AB, St. Patrick's Coll., 1961; JD, U. San Francisco, 1970. Bar: Calif. 1970. Ptnr. Keck, Mahin & Cate, San Francisco. Mem. planning commn. City of Novato, Calif., 1977-78, mayor of city, 1985, mem. city coun., 1983-87. Mem. State Bar Calif. Office: Keck Mahin & Cate 1 Maritime Plz 23rd fl San Francisco CA 94111-2496*

MCQUAID, JOHN GAFFNEY, lawyer; b. N.Y.C., Jan. 4, 1918; s. Paul Augustine and Louise (Gaffney) McQ.; m. Betty Frances Seay, May 27, 1989; children from previous marriage: John G. Jr., Catherine M., Elizabeth L. BA, Yale Coll., 1940, LLB, 1947. Bar: N.Y. 1948, U.S. Supreme Ct. 1954. Assoc. Townley Updike Carter & Rodgers, N.Y.C., 1947-52; with Nat. Prodn. Auth., Washington, 1952-54; pvt. practice White Plains, N.Y., 1954-60; ptnr. Fingar & McQuaid, White Plains, 1960-65, McCarthy, Fingar, Donovan, Drazen & Smith, White Plains, 1965—; dir., asst. sec. Dewey Electronics Corp., Oakland, N.J., 1955—. co-author, editor: New York Wills and Trusts, 2d edit., 1961, 3d edit., 1990; nat., N.Y. co-editor: West's Trust's and Wills Document Assembly, 1993, New York Will Manual. 2d lt. U.S. Army, 1942-46. Fellow Am. Coll. Trusts and Estate Counsel; mem. N.Y. State Bar Assn. (chmn. trusts and estates law sect. 1981), White Plains Bar Assn. (pres. 1961), Ardsley Country Club. Home: Hudson House PO Box 11 Ardsley-On-Hudson NY 10503-7011 Office: McCarthy Fingar Donovan Drazen & Smith 11 Martine Ave White Plains NY 10606-1934

MCQUAID, JOSEPH WOODBURY, newspaper executive; b. Manchester, N.H., Feb. 12, 1949; s. Bernard John and Margaret (Griffin) McQ.; m. Signe Karin Anderson, Nov. 2, 1975; children—Katharine, Brendan. Student, U. N.H., 1967-69. Reporter Union Leader, Manchester, N.H., 1969-71; Sunday editor N.H. Sunday News, Manchester, N.H., 1971-76; mng. editor Union Leader-Sunday News, Manchester, N.H., 1976-82, editor-in-chief, 1982—, v.p., 1986—; gen. mgr., 1992—; dir. Union Leader Corp., Manchester. Sec. Manchester Indsl. Council, 1974-84. Roman Catholic. Home: 256 N Bay St Manchester NH 03104-2324 Office: Union Leader Corp 100 William Loeb Dr Manchester NH 03109-5309

MCQUARRIE, BRUCE CALE, mathematics educator; b. Easton, Pa., Jan. 6, 1929; s. William Caven Hunter and Florence Mabel (Cale) McQ.; m. Betty Ann Palmer, Dec. 25, 1948 (div. 1983) children—Nancy, Laura, Amy. A.B., Lafayette Coll., 1951; M.A., U. N.H., 1956; Ph.D., Boston U., 1971. Instr. Tucson Indian Sch., Ariz., 1951-52; instr. Wasatch Acad., Mt. Pleasant, Utah, 1956-60; instr. math., asst. prof., assoc. prof. Worcester Poly. Inst., Mass., 1960—, prof. math., dept. head math. scis., 1983-86, prof. emeritus, 1990—. Mem. Democratic Town Com., Auburn, Mass., 1970-90. With U.S. Army, 1952-54. Home: 10 Eames Dr Auburn MA 01501-1308 Office: Worcester Poly Inst 100 Institute Rd Worcester MA 01609-2247

MCQUARRIE, DONALD GRAY, surgeon, educator; b. Richfield, Utah, Apr. 17, 1931; s. John Gray and LoRetta (Smith) McQ.; m. Dolores Jean Dietrich, July 16, 1956; children—William Gray, Michelle Dolores Colton. B.S., U. Utah, 1952, M.D., 1956; Ph.D., U. Minn., 1964. Diplomate Am. Bd. Surgery, Am. Bd. Thoracic and Cardiovascular Surgery. Intern U. Minn. Hosps., 1956-57; resident in surgery U. Minn., Mpls., 1957-59, resident, 1961-65, asst. prof. surgery, 1964-68, assoc. prof. surgery, 1968-72, prof. surgery, 1972—, vice chmn. dept. surgery, 1993—; mem. surg. staff Mpls. VA Hosp., 1964—, chief surgical svc., 1993—, resident in thoracic surgery, 1965-66, dir. surg. research lab., 1964-78; vis. prof. U. Tex.-San Antonio, 1974, U. Ind. and Indpls. VA, 1977, affiliated program U. Ariz., Phoenix, 1982, Case Western Res. U., 1986. Editor, contbg. author: Head and Neck Cancer, 1986, Reoperations in General Surgery, 1991; contbr. articles on surg. and basic med. scis. to profl. publs., 1955—. Served to lt. M.C., USN, 1959-61. USPHS postdoctoral fellow, 1962-65. Fellow ACS (commn. on cancer 1980-89, exec. council commn. on operating room environ. 1985-91, pres. Minn. chpt. 1983-84, liaison to Assn. Oper. Rm. Nurses 1985—, gov. 1990—); mem. Minn. Surg. Soc. (pres. 1980-81), Assn. Acad. Surgery, Mpls. Surg. Soc. (pres. 1978-79), Soc. Head and Neck Surgeons, Central Surg. Assn., Soc. Univ. Surgeons, Société Internationale de Chirurgie, Am. Surg. Assn., Assn. VA Surgeons (pres. 1987), Soc. Surg. Oncology, Hennepin County Med. Soc., Minn. Med. Assn., Am. Soc. Clin. Oncology, Phi Beta Kappa, Phi Kappa Phi. Clubs: Minneapolis, Interlachen Country (Mpls.). Avocations: computer applications to medicine; jewelry design; lapidary work. Home: 6625 Mohawk Trl Minneapolis MN 55439-1029 Office: Mpls VA Med Ctr Dept Surgery 1 Veterans Dr Minneapolis MN 55417-2300

MCQUEEN, JEFFERY THOMAS, meteorologist; b. Bklyn., June 1, 1961; s. Roy and Domenica (Sommese) McQ.; m. Jacqueline Theresa Favilla, Feb. 16, 1991. BA, U. Va., 1982; MS, Colo. State U., 1985. Rsch. asst. Colo. State U., Ft. Collins, 1982-85; rsch. meteorologist NASA/Goddard Space Flt. Ctr., Greenbelt, Md., 1985-91, NOAA/Air Resources Lab., Silver Spring, Md., 1991—; mem. WMO Kuwait Oil Fires, Washington, 1991-92, Air Evaluation Team/WMO, Dhahran, Saudi Arabia, 1991; MARRS evaluation com., NASA/NOAA, Cape Kennedy, Fla., 1992; Inter-Am. Inst. Global Change mem., Montevideo, Uraguay, 1993. Contbr. articles to profl. jours. Vol. Georgetown Ministry Ctr., Washington, 1993—; bd. dirs. 16th St. Civic Assn., Washington, 1992—. DuPont scholarship, 1980; recipient State of Colo. scholarship, 1983, Spl. Achievement award NOAA, 1991. Mem. Am. Meteorology Soc., D.C. Local Am. Meterol. Soc. Roman Catholic. Avocations: woodworking, bicycling. Home: 1429 Longfellow St NW Washington DC 20011-6819 Office: NOAA/Air Resources Lab 1315 E West Hwy Silver Spring MD 20910

MCQUEEN, JUSTICE ELLIS (L. Q. JONES), actor, director; b. Beaumont, Tex., Aug. 19, 1927; s. Justice Ellis and Pat (Stephens) McQ.; m. Sue Helen Lewis, Oct. 10, 1950 (dec.); children: Marlin Randolph, Marilyn Helen, Steven Lewis. Student, Lamar Jr. Coll., 1944, Lon Morris Coll., 1949, U. Tex., 1950-51. Actor numerous motion picture films, TV shows; dir.: motion picture films including A Boy and His Dog, 1975 (recipient Hugo award, Sci. Fiction achievement award for dramatic presentation); producer The Big Thickett, Come In, Children, The Witchmaker; author: The Brotherhood of Satan, 1971. Served with USNR, 1945-46. Mem. Screen Actors Guild. Republican. Methodist. Home and Office: 2144 N Cahuenga Blvd Los Angeles CA 90068-2708 *Contribute to a space that no one can or will fill.*

MCQUEEN, ONELLIA JOY, medical, surgical and oncology nurse; b. Big Springs, Ala., Nov. 29, 1937; d. Lula Cornelia Bonner; m. James L. McQueen, Nov. 29, 1986; children: Joe, Marie, Paula, Anthony, Katherine. ADN, Okla. State U. Tech. Inst., 1971; student, Cen. State U. Cert. oncology and med. surg. nurse. Mem. planning com. Am. Cancer Soc., Oklahoma City; speaker on oncology cert. Okla. Meml. Hosp. Vol. Oklahoma City Bomb Recovery Ctr. for ARC. Mem. ANA, Okla. Nurses Assn., Oncology Nurse Assn. Home: 3904 Valley Rd Oklahoma City OK 73135

MC QUEEN, ROBERT CHARLES, retired insurance executive; b. Santiago, Chile, Jan. 23, 1921; s. Charles Alfred and Grace Juanita (Abrecht) McQ.; m. Donna Marie Ikeler, Oct. 6, 1945; children: Scott, Jerry, Monte, Donald. A.B., Dartmouth Coll., 1942. Mathematician, Equitable Life Assurance Soc., N.Y.C., 1945-49; group actuary Union Central Life Ins. Co., Cin., 1949-57; with Mut. Benefit Life Ins. Co., Newark, 1957-85; exec. v.p. Mut. Benefit Life Ins. Co., 1969-71, sr. exec. v.p., chief adminstrv. officer, 1971-85, dir., 1978-85; bd. dirs. St. Barnabas Corp. (formerly Trimark Corp.). Pres. Millburn Twp. (N.J.) Bd. Edn., 1969-71, Naples (Fla.) Bridge Ctr., 1994-96; chmn. BBB Met. N.Y., 1978-80; chmn. bd. trustees St. Barnabas Hosp., Livingston, N.J., 1983-91, trustee, 1991—. With OSS, 1943-45. Fellow Soc. Actuaries; mem. Am. Acad. Actuaries, Internat. Actuarial Assn., Canoe Brook Country Club, Quail Creek Club. Republican. Episcopalian. Home: 12988 Bald Cypress Ln Naples FL 33999-8526

MCQUEEN, SCOTT ROBERT, broadcasting company executive; b. Peekskill, N.Y., June 30, 1946; s. Robert Charles and Donna Marie (Ikeler) McQ.; m. Loretta A. Dybala, May 17, 1980; children: Geoffrey Scott, Mallory Morgan, Brian Daniel; 1 child, by previous marriage, Tasha Lea. B.A., Dartmouth Coll., 1968. Founder Sconnix Radio Ent., Inc., Laconia, N.H., 1968; Founder Sconnix Radio Ent., Inc. (became Sconnix Group Broadcasting, Inc.), 1971, pres., 1971—. Chmn. Magic Childrens Fund, 1991—; bd. advisors Pincrest Sch., Boca Raton, Fla. With N.H.N.G., 1968-69. Mem. Nat. Assn. Broadcasters, Nat. Radio Broadcsters Assn., Lakes Region C. of C. (dir. 1977-81), Rotary, Royal Palm Yacht and Country Club, Ocean Reef Club (Key Largo, Fla.). Home: 431 Coconut Palm Rd Boca Raton FL 33432-7915 Office: 3000 N 28th Ter Hollywood FL 33020-1302 also: Village West Gilford NH 03246

MCQUEEN, SHERMAN JOHN, JR., entertainment company executive; b. Monrovia, Calif., May 29, 1928; s. Sherman John, Sr. and Ethel (Morrison) McQ.; m. Irene Cecelia Anderson, June 21, 1957 (div. 1965); children: Amy Lynn, Susan Marie; m. Margaret Ann Ross, Dec. 31, 1967. BA, Occidental Coll., 1949. Sports dir. Sta. KREM, Spokane, Wash., 1948-50; newscaster Sta. WIND, Chgo., 1950-52; mgr. sta. rels. Mut. Broadcasting, L.A., 1952-54; mgr. bus. affairs CBS, L.A., 1954-57; v.p., account supr. D'Arcy Advt., L.A., 1957-60; sr. v.p. broadcasting Foote, Cone and Belding, L.A., 1960-79; pres. FCB Entertainment, Burbank, Calif., 1979—; chmn. Old Mill. Adv. Bd., San Marino, Calif. 1974-82, Telecom. Group, City San Marino, 1994—; mem. com. Pasadena (Calif.) Tounament Roses, 1974-94. Prodr. (TV program series) Hallmark Hall of Fame, 1960-83 (Emmy award 1982), Sportslook, 1981-90 (Ace award 1987); editor FCB Network News, 1994. Recipient Silver award Am. Advt. Fedn., 1968. Mem. TV Acad. (chair com. 1990-91), Pacific Pioneer Broadcasters (bd. dirs. 1994—), So. Calif. Sportscasters (bd. dirs. 1982-83), Hollywood Ad Club (pres. 1965, Silver award 1966), Hollywood Radio and TV Soc. (pres. 1966-67, Ollie award 1967-68), San Marino Rotary (bd. dirs. 1978). Republican. Presbyterian. Avocations: book and document collecting, travel, golf, gardening. Office: FCB Entertainment 11601 Wilshire Blvd Los Angeles CA 90025*

MC QUEENEY, HENRY MARTIN, SR., publisher; b. N.Y.C., Oct. 29, 1938; s. John Henry and Catherine Mary (Quigg) McQ.; m. Elizabeth Bernino, May 14, 1960; children: Mary E., Henry M. Jr., John P., Matthew S. B.B.A., St. Johns U., 1960; postgrad., U. Rochester, 1965-67. City sales rep. Curtis Circulation div. Curtis Pub. Co., 1960-62; asst. mgr. Curtis Circulation div. Curtis Pub. Co., N.Y.C., 1962-63; field mgr. Curtis Circulation div. Curtis Pub. Co., Rochester, N.Y., 1964-67; dept. mgr., account exec. Curtis Circulation div. Curtis Pub. Co., Phila., 1968-74; v.p. sales, exec. v.p. mktg. Manor Books, Inc., N.Y.C., 1974-76, pres., 1976-79; pres. Wood Hill Press, Inc., 1979-89, Scott Mag. Dist. Corp., N.Y.C., 1989-93, Kearny Pub., Inc., N.Y.C., 1993-96, Princeton Pub., Inc., N.Y.C., 1996—; chmn. bd. Oui mag., 1981-82; pres., CEO, J.Q., Adams Prodns., Inc., 1983-94; rep. Western N.Y. Pubs.; cons. Bipad Ednl. Program. Pres. parish bd. Roman Catholic Ch., 1965, editor newspaper, Spencerport, N.Y., 1965, diocesan leader, mem. lay bd., Rochester, 1964-67; certified as tchr. Confraternity Christian Doctrine, Diocese of Rochester, 1964. Served with USAFR, 1956-64. Mem. Am. Legion. Home: 12 Blenheim Ln Centerport NY 11721-1704 Office: Princeton Pub Inc 28 W 25th St New York NY 10010-2705

MCQUEENEY, THOMAS A., publisher; b. N.Y.C., Aug. 21, 1937; s. Henry J. and Jeannette A. (Beaton) McQ.; m. Ellyn M. Carney, Oct. 11, 1970; children: Kicha Lee, Miya Lyn, Jana Mai. BBA, Northeastern U., 1964. Market analyst Gillette Co., Boston, 1964-65; research analyst Chase Manhattan Bank, N.Y.C., 1965-68; portfolio mgr. Portfolio Planning, Inc., N.Y.C., 1968-71; pub., pres. Money Market Directories, Inc., Charlottesville, Va., 1971—. Editor: Real Estate Investing by Pension Fund Adminstrs., 1975. Mem. Indsl. Devel. Bd. Authority, Albemarle County, 1980—. Served to 1st lt., U.S. Army, 1956-58. Mem. Assn. Investment Mgmt. Sales Execs. Republican. Presbyterian. Lodge: Rotary. Avocations: sailing, skiing. Home: 121 Indian Spring Rd Charlottesville VA 22901-1019 Office: Money Market Directories Inc Charlottesville VA 22901

MCQUERN, MARCIA ALICE, newspaper publishing executive; b. Riverside, Calif., Sept. 3, 1942; d. Arthur Carlyle and Dorothy Louise (Krupke) Knopf; m. Lynn Morris McQuern, June 7, 1969. BA in Polit. Sci., U. Calif., Santa Barbara, 1964; MS in Journalism, Northwestern U., 1966. Reporter The Press-Enterprise, Riverside, 1966-72, city editor, 1972-74, capitol corrs., 1975-78, dep. mng. editor news, 1984-85, mng. editor news, 1985-87, exec. editor, 1988-94, pres., 1992—; editor, publisher, 1994—; asst. metro editor The Sacramento Bee, 1974-75; editor state and polit. news The San Diego Union, 1978-79, city editor, 1979-84; juror Pulitzer Prize in Journalism, 1982, 83, 92, 93. Mem. editorial bd. Calif. Lawyer mag., San Francisco, 1983-88. Bd. advisors U. Calif.-Berkeley Grad. Sch. Journalism, 1991—, U. Calif.-Riverside Grad. Sch. Mgmt., 1994—. Recipient Journalism award Calif. State Bar Assn., 1967, Sweepstakes award Twin Counties Press Club, Riverside and San Bernardino, 1972, Athena award YWCA, 1994. Mem. Am. Soc. Newspaper Editors (bd. dirs. 1992—), Calif. Soc. Newspaper Editors (bd. 1988-95), Calif. Newspaper Pubs. Assn. (bd. dirs. 1992—), Calif. Press Assn. (bd. dirs. 1996—), Soc. Profl. Journalists, U. Calif.-Santa Barbara Alumni Assn. (bd. dirs. 1983-89). Home: 5717 Bedford Dr Riverside CA 92506-3404 Office: Press-Enterprise Co 3512 14th St Riverside CA 92501-3814

MCQUIGG, JOHN DOLPH, lawyer; b. Abilene, Tex., Oct. 19, 1931; s. John Lyman and Dorothy Elinor (King) McQ.; m. Sandra Elainea Duke, Oct. 18, 1969 (div. 1989); 1 son, John Revel. B.A., Denison U., 1953; LL.B., U. Tex., Austin, 1962. Bar: Fla. 1962, U.S. Supreme Ct. 1971. account exec. San Antonio Light, 1957-59; assoc. Shackleford, Farrior, Stallings & Evans, 1962-66, ptnr. Tampa, Fla., 1966-73; pres. John McQuigg, P.A., Tampa, 1973-80; shareholder Fowler, White, Gillen, Boggs, Villareal & Banker, P.A., Tampa, 1980-92; of counsel, Stephen Rosen, P.A., Tampa, Fla., 1993; pvt. practice. Judge Compensation Claims pro hac vice, 1993; bd. dirs. Fla. Gulf Coast R.R. Mus., Inc., Am. Assn. Pvt. Railroad Car Owners; pres. Fla. Coalition R.R. Passengers, 1990—. 1st lt. USAF, 1953-57. Mem. ABA, Fla. Bar. Episcopalian. Club: Tampa. Home: 1000 W Horatio St Apt 125 Tampa FL 33606-2658 Office: PO Box 2480 Tampa FL 33601-2480

MCQUILKIN, JOHN ROBERTSON, religion educator, academic administrator, writer; b. Columbia, S.C., Sept. 7, 1927; s. Robert C. and Marguerite (Lambie) McQ.; m. Muriel Elaine Webendorfer, Aug. 24, 1948; children: Helen Marguerite, Robert Paul (dec.), David John, Virginia Anne, Amy Lambie, Douglas Kent. BA, Columbia Internat. U., 1947; M.Div., Fuller Theol. Sem., 1950; postgrad., No. Bapt. Theol. Sem., 1947-48. Prof. Greek, religious edn. and theology Columbia (S.C.) Internat. U., 1950-52; pres. Internat. U., 1968-90; chancellor Columbia (S.C.) Bible Coll. and Sem., 1990-93; headmaster Ben Lippen Sch., Asheville, N.C., 1952-55; missionary The Evang. Alliance Mission, Japan, 1956-68; acting pres. Tokyo Christian U., 1963-65. Author: Measuring the Church Growth Movement, 1974, Understanding and Applying the Bible, 1992, The Great Omission, 1984, An Introduction to Biblical Ethics, 1995; contbr. articles to religious jours. Mem. Evangel. Missiological Soc. (gen. dir. 1994—).

MCQUILLAN, WILLIAM HUGH, building company executive; b. Newtown, Conn., Apr. 6, 1935; s. Alexander Jerome and Madeleine (McLaughlin) McQ.; m. Eileen Mary Craig, Aug. 29, 1959; children—Madeleine, William, Maureen, Patrick. B.B.A., Fairfield U., 1959. Asst. v.p. Fairfield Homes Inc., Conn., 1959-64; v.p. Conn. Gen. Contrn. Co., Botsford, 1964-68; various mgmt. positions ITT Levitt and Sons, Lake Success, N.Y., 1968-74; sr. v.p. Gen. Devel. Corp., Miami, 1974-91; pres The McQuillan Corp., Cornwall, Vt., 1991-94; v.p. Nat. Guardian Securities, Inc., Greenwich, Conn., 1994—. Served with U.S. Army, 1959-63. Mem. Nat. Assn. Homebuilders.

MCQUILLEN, HARRY A., publishing company executive. Formerly with Prentice-Hall; former dir. mktg. services Coll. div. McGraw-Hill; former editor-in-chief Coll. div. CBS Pub., pres. Ednl. and Profl. Pub. div., 1983-87; group v.p. Gen. Pub. Group Macmillan Inc., N.Y.C., 1987-88, v.p., 1988; pres. Macmillan Pub. Co., 1988-91; pres., CEO K-III Mag Corp., N.Y.C., 1991—; pres. K-III Media Group, N.Y.C., 1994—. Office: K-III Mags 10th Fl 717 5th Ave Fl 10 New York NY 10022-8101

MC QUILLEN, MICHAEL PAUL, physician; b. N.Y.C., Sept. 9, 1932; s. Paul and Dorothy Marian (Moore) McQ.; m. Louise Devlin; children: Daniel, Thomas, Patrick, Kathleen. B.A. cum laude, Georgetown U., 1953, M.D., 1957; MA, U. Va., 1994. Diplomate Am. Bd. Psychiatry and Neurology (bd. dirs. 1991-95, exec. com. 1995). Rotating intern Royal Victoria Hosp., Montreal, Que., Can., 1957-58; resident in neurology Georgetown U. Med. Center, 1958-60; fellow in physiology Johns Hopkins U. Med. Sch. and Hosp., 1960-62, instr. medicine, 1962-65; mem. faculty U. Ky. Med. Center, 1965-74, prof. neurology, 1972-74, prof., chmn. neurology, 1987-93; prof. neurology, chmn. dept. Med. Coll. Wis., Milw., 1974-87; clin. faculty mem. dept. neurology U. Va. Health Sci. Ctr., Charlottesville, 1993-94; prof. neurology U. Rochester St. Mary's Hosp., N.Y., 1995—; vis. sci. Inst. Neurophysiology U. Copenhagen, 1971-72; vis. prof. U. Ky. Med. Ctr., 1978, Royal Coll. Surgeons, Ireland, 1983. Author articles, papers in field. Mem. Cath. Commn. on Intellectual Affairs. Recipient Neurology medal Georgetown U. Med. Sch., 1957; Clin. Teaching award Med. Coll. Wis., 1976; Disting. Service award N.Y. Med. Coll., 1983; named to Johns Hopkins Soc. Scholars, 1981. Fellow Am. Acad. Neurology; mem. Royal Acad. Medicine Ireland, Nat. Myasthenia Gravis Found. (chmn. 1981-83), Am. Neurol. Assn., N.Y. Acad. Scis., Assn. U. Profs. Neurology, Am. Assn. Electromyography and Electrodiagnosis, AMA, Wis. Neurol. Assn. (pres. 81-82), Milw. Acad. Medicine, Alpha Omega Alpha. Home: 4 Bragdon Dr Rochester NY 14618 Office: St Mary's Hosp Dept Neurology Rochester NY 14611

MC QUINN, WILLIAM P., corporation executive; b. Waterbury, Conn., May 2, 1936; s. William and Bridget (Flynn) McQ.; m. Lorese Hucks, Apr. 17, 1964; children: Kathryn, Norah, Linda, Jennifer. B.S., Bryant Coll., 1956. C.P.A., Conn. Mgmt. auditor NASA, Washington, 1962-64; asst. controller Scovill Mfg. Co., Waterbury, 1964-67; controller C F & I Steel Co., Pueblo, Colo., 1967-71; v.p. financial services Loews Corp., N.Y.C., 1971-73; chief exec. officer Williams Hudson Am. subs. Williams Hudson Group Ltd., Eng., 1973-75; pres. Pegasus Design Group (formerly Williams Hudson Am.), 1975-78; v.p. M.W. Houck, Inc., Rye, N.Y., 1979-82; chief operating officer Cusinarts Inc, Greenwich, CT, 1982-88; exec. v.p. CHC of Conn., Inc., 1988-94; chmn., CEO Fin. Svcs. Inc., Old Greenwich, Conn., 1994—. Served with U.S. Army, 1959. Mem. Am. Inst. C.P.A.s, Fin. Execs. Inst. Home: 8 Vista Ave Old Greenwich CT 06870-2135

MCQUISTON, ROBERT EARL, lawyer; b. Pitts., Feb. 4, 1936; s. Theodore O. and Bertha L. (Kegley) McQ.; m. Mary Hope Missimer, June 30, 1962; children: Mary Hope, Elizabeth Ann. BA magna cum laude, Yale U., 1958; JD cum laude, Harvard U., 1961. Bar: Pa. 1962. Assoc. Ballard, Spahr, Andrews & Ingersoll, Phila., Balt., Denver, Washington, Salt Lake City, 1962-69, ptnr., 1969—; mem. nat. adv. group to Commr. IRS, Washington, 1985-87; lectr. in law Temple U., 1968-69, also various tax insts.; bd. dirs. Macromedia Inc., Hackensack, N.J., Gateway Communications, Inc., Binghamton, N.Y. Contbr. articles to profl. jours. Mem. Rep. Fin. Com., Harrisburg, Pa., 1983-86; trustee Am. Soc. Hypertension, 1992—. Mem. ABA (active numerous coms. sect. taxation 1969—, including coun. mem. 1979-85, vice chmn., sec. 1982-85), Phila. Bar Assn. (bd. govs. 1978-80, mem. coun. 1969—, sec. treas sect. on taxation 1973-75, vice chmn. 1976-78, chmn. 1978-80), Am. Coll. Tax Counsel (charter, regent 1990—, vice chmn. 1993-94, chmn. 1994—), Nat. Conf. Lawyers and CPAs, Pyramid Club. Episcopalian. Home: 111 Ridgewood Rd Wayne PA 19087-2810 Office: Ballard Spahr Andrews et al 1735 Market St Ste 51 Philadelphia PA 19103-7501

MCQUOWN, JUDITH HERSHKOWITZ, author, financial advisor; b. N.Y.C., Apr. 8, 1941; d. Frederick Ephraim and Pearl (Rosenberg) H.; m. Michael L. McQuown, Jan. 13, 1969 (div. 1980); m. Harrison Roth, Dec. 8, 1985 (div. 1996). AB, Hunter Coll., 1963; postgrad., N.Y. Inst. Fin., N.Y.C., 1965-67. Chief underwriting div. mcpl. securities City of N.Y., 1972-73; CEO Judith H. McQuown & Co., Inc., N.Y.C., 1973—. Author: Inc. Yourself: How to Profit by Setting Up Your Own Corporation, 8th edit., 1995, Tax Shelters That Work for Everyone, 1979, The Fashion Survival Manual, 1981, Playing the Takeover Market, 1982, How to Profit After You Inc. Yourself, 1985, Keep One Suitcase Empty: The Bargain Shopper's Guide to the Finest Factory Outlets in the British Isles, 1987, Keep One Suitcase Empty: The Bargain Shopper's Guide to the Finest Factory Outlets in Europe, 1988, Use Your Own Corporation to Get Rich, 1991; contbg. editor Boardroom Reports, Physician's Fin. News, Physician's Guide to Money Mgmt.; seminars The Learning Annex, The Discovery Ctr., Boston Ctr. for Adult Edn. Mem. Am. Soc. Journalists and Authors. Home and Office: 315 E 72nd St New York NY 10021-4626

MCRAE, DAVID CARROLL, hospital administrator; b. Winston-Salem, N.C., Apr. 15, 1946; married. B, U. N.C., 1968, MHA, 1975; M, East Carolina U., 1985. Adminstr. Medictr. of Am., Raleigh, N.C., 1971-72, Hillhaven Convalescent Ctr., Raleigh, 1972-76; v.p. Univ. Med. Ctr. Pitt County Meml. Hosp., Greenville, N.C., 1976-84, sr. v.p., 1985-86, sr. v.p., chief oper. officer, 1986-89, pres., chief exec. officer, 1989—. Home: 403 Tatten Ct Greenville NC 27834-7677 Office: Pitt County Meml Hosp-Univ Med Ctr Ea Carolina-Pitt County PO Box 6028 Greenville NC 27835-6028*

MCRAE, HAMILTON EUGENE, III, lawyer; b. Midland, Tex., Oct. 29, 1937; s. Hamilton Eugene and Adrian (Hagaman) McR.; m. Betty Hawkins, Aug. 27, 1960; children: Elizabeth Ann, Stephanie Adrian, Scott Hawkins. BSEE, U. Ariz., 1961; student, USAF Electronics Sch., 1961-62; postgrad., U. Redlands, Calif., 1962-63; JD with honors and distinction, U.

Ariz., 1967; LHD (hon.), Sterling Coll., 1992; vis. fellow, Darwin Coll., Cambridge (Eng.) U. Bar: Ariz. 1967, U.S. Supreme Ct. 1979; cert. real estate specialist, Ariz. Elec. engr. Salt River Project, Phoenix, 1961; assoc. Jennings, Strouss & Salmon, Phoenix, 1967-71, ptnr., 1971-85, chmn. real estate dept., 1980-85, mem. policy com., 1982-85, mem. fin. com., 1981-85, chmn. bus. devel. com., 1982-85; ptnr. and co-founder Stuckey & McRae, Phoenix, 1985—; co-founder, chmn. bd. Republic Cos., Phoenix, 1985—; magistrate Paradise Valley, Ariz., 1983-85; juvenile referee Superior Ct., 1983-85; pres., dir. Phoenix Realty & Trust Co., 1970—; officer Indsl. Devel. Corp. Maricopa County, 1972-86; instr. and lectr. in real estate; officer, bd. dirs. other corps.; adj. prof. Frank Lloyd Wright Sch. Architecture, Scottsdale, Ariz., 1989—; instr. Ariz. State U. Coll. Architecture and Environ. Design; lead instr. ten-state-bar seminar on Advanced Real Estate Transactions, 1992; evaluation com. for cert. real estate specialist Ariz. Bar, 1994—. Exec. prodr. film documentary on relief and devel. in Africa, 1990; contbr. articles to profl. jours. Elder Valley Presbyn. Ch., Scottsdale, Ariz., 1973-75, 82-85, 96—, chair evangelism com. 1973-74, corp. pres., 1974-75, 84-85, trustee, 1973-75, 82-85, chmn. exec. com., 1984, mem. mission com. 1993—; trustee Upward Found., Phoenix, 1977-80, Valley Presbyn. Found., 1982-83, Ariz. Acad., 1971—; trustee, mem. exec. com. Phi Gamma Delta Ednl. Found., Washington, 1974-84; trustee Phi Gamma Delta Internat., 1984-86; bd. dirs. Archon, 1986-87; founder, trustee, pres. McRae Found., 1980—; bd. dirs. Food for Hungry Inc. (Internat. Relief), 1985-95, exec. com., 1986—, chmn. bd. dirs., 1987-92; chmn. bd. dirs. Food for Hungry Internat., 1993-95; pres. adv. coun., 1995—; trustee, mem. exec. com. Ariz. Mus. Sci. and Tech., 1984—, 1st v.p., 1985-86, pres., 1986-88, chmn. bd. dirs., 1988-90; Lambda Alpha Internat. Hon. Land Econs. Soc, 1988—; sec.-treas. Ariz. State U. Coun. for Design Excellence, 1989-90, bd. dirs. 1988—, pres. 1990-91; mem. Crisis Nursery Office of the Chair, 1988-89, Maricopa Community Colls. Found., 1988—, sec. 1990-91, 2d v.p. 1993-94, 1st v.p. and pres. elect 1994-95, pres. 1995—, capital campaign cabinet, 1995-96, Phoenix Cmty. Alliance, 1988-90, Interchurch Ctr. Corp., 1987-90, Western Art Assocs., bd. dirs., 1989-91, Phoenix Com. on Fgn. Rels., 1988—, U. Ariz. Pres.'s Club, 1984—, chmn., 1991-92; bd. dirs. Econ. Club of Phoenix, 1987— , sec.-treas., 1991-92, v.p., 1992-93, pres. 1993-94; bd. dirs. Ctrl. Ariz. Shelter Svcs., 1995—; mem. adv. bd. Help Wanted USA, 1990-92; vol. fund raiser YMCA, Salvation Army, others; bd. dirs. Frank Lloyd Wright Found., 1992—; mem. Taliesin Coun., 1985—; mem. bd. dirs. Taliesin Arch., 1992—, Taliesin Conservation Com. (Wis.); founding mem. Frank Lloyd Wright Soc., 1993—; mem. fin. com. Kyl for Congress, 1985-92, bd. dir. campaign bd. Kyl for U.S. Senate, 1993-94; Senator Kyl Coun., 1995—; campaign com. Symington for Gov. '90, 1989—, mem. gubernatorial adv. bd., 1990-91; mem. Gov.'s Selection Com. for State Revenue Dir., 1993; mem. bond com. City of Phoenix, 1987-88; mem. Ariz. State U. Coun. of 100, 1985-89, investment com., 1985-89; bd. govs. Twelve Who Care Hon Kachina, 1991; mem. adv. coun. Maricopa County Sports Authority, 1989-93; mem. Ariz. Coalition for Tomorrow, 1990-92; founding mem., bd. dirs. Waste Not Inc., 1992-96, pres., 1990-92, chmn., 1992-94, adv. bd. 1996—; selected as bearer for the Olympic Torch Relay Team, 1996. 1st lt. USAF, 1961-64,. Recipient various mil. award. Mem. ABA, AIEE, AIME, Arizy Bar Assn., U. Ariz. Alumni Assn., Nat. Soc. Fund Raising Execs., Clan McRae Soc. N.Am. Phoenix Exec. Club, Jackson Hole Racquet Club, Teton Pines Country Club, Tau Beta Pi. Republican. Home: 8101 N 47th St Paradise Vly AZ 85253-2907 Office: Republic Cos 2425 E Camelback Rd Ste 900 Phoenix AZ 85016-4215

MC RAE, KENNETH DOUGLAS, political scientist, educator; b. Toronto, Ont., Can., Jan. 20, 1925; s. Douglas Archibald and Margaret Constance McR.; m. Dorothea Annette Simon, Aug. 4, 1950; children: Patricia, Sandra, Karen, Susan. BA, U. Toronto, 1946; AM, Harvard U., 1947, PhD, 1954; postgrad., Oxford (Eng.) U., 1948-50, postdoctoral research, 1953-55. lectr. in polit. sci. U. Toronto, 1950-52; asst. prof. polit. sci. Carleton U., Ottawa, Ont., 1955-57, assoc. prof., 1957-64, prof., 1964-95; rsch. supervisor Royal Commn. on Bilingualism and Biculturalism., 1964-69. Author: (with Louis Hartz and others) The Founding of New Societies: Studies in the History of the United States, Latin America, South Africa, Canada and Australia, 1964, Switzerland: Example of Cultural Coexistence, 1964, Conflict and Compromise in Multilingual Societies, Vol. 1, Switzerland, 1983, Vol. 2, Belgium, 1986; editor: The Six Bookes of a Commonweale (Jean Bodin), 1962; editor and project dir.: The Federal Capital: Governmental Institutions, 1969; editor, contbg. author: Consociational Democracy: Political Accommodation in Segmented Societies, 1974; contbg. author: Conflict and Peacemaking in Multiethnic Societies, 1990. Fellow Royal Soc. Can. (hon. sec. 1980-83); mem. Can. Polit. Sci. Assn. (pres. 1978-79), Soc. Scientiarum Fennica (fgn. mem.), Renaissance Soc. Am. Office: Carleton U, Dept Polit Sci, Ottawa, ON Canada K1S 5B6

MCRAE, ROBERT MALCOLM, JR., federal judge; b. Memphis, Dec. 31, 1921; s. Robert Malcolm and Irene (Pontius) McR.; m. Louise Howry, July 31, 1943; children: Susan Campbell, Robert Malcolm III, Duncan Farquhar, Thomas Alexander Todd. BA, Vanderbilt U., 1943; LLB, U. Va., 1948. Bar: Tenn. 1948. Practice in Memphis, 1948-64; judge Tenn. Circuit Ct., 1964-66; judge U.S. Dist. Ct. (we. dist.) Tenn., Memphis, 1966-94, chief judge, 1979-86, sr. judge, 1987-94; mem. Jud. Council 6th Cir., 1982-85, Jud. Conf. Commn. Adminstrn. Criminal Law, 1979-86, Jud. Conf. U.S., 1984-87. Pres. Episcopal Ch. men of Tenn., 1964-65. Mem. Dist. Judges Assn. 6th Circuit (pres.). Home: 220 Baronne Pl Memphis TN 38117-2906

MCRAE, THOMAS KENNETH, retired investment company executive; b. Richmond, Va., July 7, 1906; s. Christopher Duncan and Sarah Alice (Lawrence) McR.; m. Marion Lanier White, Sept. 11, 1937; children: Thomas Kenneth Jr., John Daniel. B.A., U. Richmond, 1927; postgrad. Sch. Banking, Rutgers U., 1936-38. Asst. cashier First Mchts. Nat. Bank, Richmond, 1940-46, asst. v.p., 1946-49, v.p., 1949-63, sr. v.p., 1963-71; v.p. Davenport and Co., Richmond, 1971-85, sr. investment officer, 1985-90. Trustee Va. Supplemental Retirement System, 1964-71; active Va. Mus. Fine Arts. Mem. Richmond Soc. Fin. Analysts. Republican. Baptist. Clubs: Country of Va. Lodges: Masons, Rotary. Avocations: golf; stamp collecting.

MCRAITH, JOHN JEREMIAH, bishop; b. Hutchinson, Minn., Dec. 6, 1934; s. Arthur Luke and Marie (Hanley) McR. B.A., Loras Coll., Dubuque, Iowa, 1956. Ordained priest, Roman Cath. Ch., 1960. Assoc. pastor St. Mary's Ch., Sleepy Eye, Minn., 1960-64, assoc. pastor, 1968-71; pastor St. Michael's Ch., Mickoy, Minn., 1964-67, St. Leo's Ch., St. Leo, Minn., 1967-68; dir. Nat. Cath. Rural Life, Des Moines, 1971-78; vicar gen. Diocese of New Ulm, Minn., 1978-82; bishop Owensboro, Ky., 1982—. Home: 501 W 5th St Owensboro KY 42301-0765 Office: 600 Locust St Owensboro KY 42301-2130

MC REYNOLDS, MARY BARBARA, retired secondary school educator, community volunteer; b. Los Angeles, Feb. 18, 1930; d. Clyde C. and Dorothy (Slaten) McCulloh; m. Zachariah A. McReynolds, Feb. 9, 1952 (dec.); children: Gregg Clyde, Barbara, Zachariah A.; m. John Richard Street, May 7, 1994. BA, U. N.Mex., 1951, MA, 1972, Edn. Specialist, 1975, postgrad., 1981—. Dept. sec. USAF Intelligence, Wiesbaden, W. Ger., 1953-54; tchr. Annandale (Va.) Elem. Sch., 1962-65, supr. adult edn., 1965-66; tchr. Albuquerque High Sch., 1968-77, 79-91, social studies curriculum dir., 1973-75; instr. U. N.Mex., Albuquerque, 1975-76, acad. decathlon coach Albuquerque High Sch., 1986-91; evaluator N. Central Assn., 1970-81, dir. Cultural Awareness Workshop, 1976, 79; coord. Sex Equality, 1979, 80. Bd. dirs. Greater U. N.Mex. Fund, 1978-79, 79-80, fund raiser, 1976-81, pres. club, 1977-80; campaign mgr. state senatorial campaign, 1976; exec. sec. Civic Assn., 1958-60; sponsor Black Student Union, 1978-80; sponsor Boys and Girls State, 1968-75; rep. Am. Fedn. Tchrs., 1982-91; sponsor Close-Up, 1987—; precinct chmn. Democratic Party, Albuquerque, 1985-86; mem. exec. bd. Albuquerque Rehab. Ctr., 1993—; vol. Cancer Soc., KKM; mem. fin. and pub. rels. coms. RCI Bd. Indian research and tuition edn. grantee, 1971; grantee U. N.Mex., 1975-76, others. Mem. Assn. Supervision and Curriculum Devel., Nat. Social Studies Council, N.Mex. Social Studies Council, Phi Kappa Phi, Phi Delta Kappa, Pi Alpha Theta, Kappa Kappa Gamma. Democrat. Episcopalian. Clubs: N.Mex. Democratic Women, Air Force Officers Wives, Kappa Kappa Gamma Alumni (pres. 1991-93, chmn. ways and means com. 1994, Outstanding Alumna award 1994). Condr. research in field. Home: 749 Tramway Ln NE Albuquerque NM 87122-1601

MCREYNOLDS, NEIL LAWRENCE, consultant; b. Seattle, July 27, 1934; s. Dorr E. and Margaret (Gillies) McR.; m. Nancy Joyce Drew, June 21, 1957; children: Christopher, Bonnie. BA in Journalism, U. Wash., 1956, postgrad., 1973-76. Assoc. editor Bellevue (Wash.) Am., 1956-60, editor, 1960-67; press sec. to Gov. Dan Evans State of Wash., Olympia, 1967-73; N.W. regional mgr. for pub. rels. and pub. affairs ITT Corp., Seattle, 1973-80; v.p. corp. rels. Puget Sound Power & Light, Bellevue, 1980-87, sr. v.p., 1987-95; prin. McReynolds & Assocs., Seattle, 1995—; pub. affairs counsel to CEO Group Health Coop. of Puget Sound, 1996—; bd. dirs. Continental Savs. Bank, Seattle; chmn. adv. com., exec. adv. com. Edison Electric Inst., 1984-85; mem. rsch. adv. coun. Electric Power Rsch. Inst., 1989-90. Bd. dirs. Seattle Symphony, 1980-89, Ind. Colls. of Wash., 1984-95, Mus. of History and Industry, 1995—, Corp. Coun. for Arts, 1985-94, Mt. Rainier, North Cascades & Olympic Fund, 1995—, Forum for Regulatory Balance; chmn. bd. dirs. Fred Hutchinson Cancer Rsch. Ctr., 1993-95, Leadership Tomorrow, Seattle, 1987, Seattle-King County Econ. Devel. Coun., 1994; pres. Seattle Ctr. Found., 1979-80; nat. pres. Electric Info. Coun., 1988; chmn. bd. trustees Bellevue C.C., 1976-77; state chmn. Nature Conservancy, 1988-90; mem. Wash. State Commn. on Trial Cts., 1990; chmn. King County 2000, 1988-90. Named Citizen of Yr., Bellevue, One of Wash. State's Three Outstanding Young Men; recipient Pres. medal Pacific Luth. U. Mem. Pub. Rels. Soc. Am. (accredited), N.W. Elec. Light and Power Assn. (pres. 1992-93), Greater Seattle C. of C. (officer 1979-81), Soc. Profl. Journalists, Rainier Club (trustee 1995—), Overlake Golf and Country Club (trustee 1993—), Rotary (pres. Downtown Seattle Club 1991-92). Republican. Episcopalian. Avocations: golf, hiking, skiing, photography. Home: 14315 SE 45th St Bellevue WA 98006 Office: 2000 Two Union Sq 601 Union St Seattle WA 98101-2326

MCRORIE, WILLIAM EDWARD, life insurance company executive; b. Rutherfordton, N.C., Apr. 8, 1940; s. Cyrus Brown and Rosalie (Thompson) McR.; m. Hope Evangeline Foster, Sept. 9, 1962; children: Mark Edward, Jennifer Lynn. LLB, U. N.C., 1964. CLU; Bar: N.C., Va. State mgr. Sturdivant Life Ins. Co., Lynchburg, Va., 1965-68; sr. v.p. First Colony, Lynchburg, 1969—; sec. Jamestown Life Ins. Co., Lynchburg, 1981—. Vice mayor City of Lynchburg. Mem. ABA, N.C. Bar Assn., Va. Bar Assn., Assn. Life Ins. Counsel, Christian Legal Soc., John Lynch Soc. (sec. 1970—). Home: 2600 Link Rd Lynchburg VA 24503-3012 Office: First Colony Life Ins Co PO Box 1280 Lynchburg VA 24505-1280

MC ROSTIE, CLAIR NEIL, economics educator; b. Owatonna, Minn., Dec. 16, 1930; s. Neil Hale and Myrtle Julia (Peterson) McR.; m. Ursula Anne Schwieger, Aug. 29, 1968. BSBA cum laude, Gustavus Adolphus Coll., 1952; MA in Mktg., Mich. State U., 1953; Ph.D. in Fin., U. Wis., 1963; postgrad., U. Minn., 1971-72, Am. Grad. Sch. Internat. Mgmt., 1980-81; cert., Coll. for Fin. Planning, 1990. Cert. fin. planner. Faculty Gustavus Adolphus Coll., St. Peter, Minn., 1958—; chmn. dept. econs. and bus. Gustavus Adolphus Coll., 1967-83, chmn., mem. various coms., 1971—; teaching asst. Sch. Commerce, U. Wis., 1960-62; lectr. European div. U. Md., 1966-67; vis. prof. Am. Grad. Sch. Internat. Mgmt., 1980-81; pres. World Trade Week, Inc., 1987. Editor: Global Resources: Perspectives and Alternatives, 1978, The Future of the Market Ecomomy, 1979. Congregation pres. First Luth. Ch., St. Peter, Minn., 1972-73, 93, chmn. pastoral call com., 1968-69, chmn. staffing com., 1975, mem. ch. council, 1968-74, 89-93; chmn. social ministry com. Minn. Synod, Luth. Ch. Am., 1975; chmn. Rep. council arts professions, scis., Minn., 1968-70, co-chmn. state task force on Vietnam, 1968; mem. adv. commn. Minn. Dept. Manpower Services, 1967-71; mem. North Central Regional Manpower Adv. Com.; Bd. dirs. Midwest China Resource Study Center; del. White House Conf. Aging, 1971. Served with U.S. Army, 1954-56. Recipient Leavey Found. award Freedoms Found., Valley Forge, Pa.; Research fellow Fed. Res. Bank of Chgo., 1962-63. Mem. Fin. Execs. Inst., Inst. Cert. Fin. Planners, Fin. Profls. Assn., Soc. Coll. and Univ. Planning, Minn. Econs. Assn. (bd. dirs. 1974-75, 79-80), Sierra Club (exec. com. North Star chpt., Midwest regional conservation com.; 4th officer nat. coun. 1972-78), Alpha Kappa Psi, Iota Delta Gamma, Sigma Epsilon. Republican. Lutheran. Avocations: bird watching, backpacking, fitness and health. Home: Rural Rt 1 RR 1 Box 198 Saint Peter MN 56082-9745 Office: Gustavus Adolphus Coll Dept Econ Saint Peter MN 56082

MCRUER, DUANE TORRANCE, aerospace engineering executive; b. Bakersfield, Calif., Oct. 25, 1925; s. John Torrance and Ruth Inez (Bartlett) McR.; m. Betty June Mechura, Oct. 5, 1955; 1 child, Lara McRuer; 1 stepson, Stephen Harsey. BS in Engring., Calif. Inst. Tech., 1945, MEE, 1948. Registered profl. engr., Calif. Tech. chief, flight controls Northrop Aircraft Inc., Hawthorne, Calif., 1948-54; pres. Controls Specialists Inc., Inglewood, Calif., 1954-57; pres., tech. dir. Systems Tech. Inc., Hawthorne, Calif., 1957-92; chmn., 1992—; Regents lectr. U. Calif., Santa Barbara, 1976; Humsaker prof. MIT, 1992-93; mem. NRC Aero. and Space Engring. Bd., Washington, 1987-95, NASA Adv. Coun., 1990—, NASA Aero. Adv. Com., Washington, 1978-88, Am. Automatic Control Coun. (pres. 1969-73). Author: Analysis of Nonlinear Control Systems, 1961, Aircraft Dynamics and Automatic Control, 1974; author more than 150 tech. papers, 1948—; patentee in field. Lt. (j.g.) USNR, 1943-53. Recipient Louis Levy medal Franklin Inst., Phila., 1960, Disting. Alumnus award Calif. Inst. Tech., 1983. Fellow AIAA (Mechanics and Control of Flight award 1970), IEEE, AAAS, Nat. Acad. Engring., Soc. Automotive Engrs., Human Factors and Ergonomics Soc. (A.W. Williams award 1976), Caltech Assocs., Am. Alpine Club (N.Y.C.), Sierra Club. Episcopalian. Avocation: mountaineering. Office: Systems Tech Inc 13766 Hawthorne Blvd Hawthorne CA 90250-7010

MCSHAN, CLYDE GRIFFIN, II, financial executive; b. New Orleans, Feb. 8, 1945; s. Clyde G. and Ursula C. (Mumme) McS.; m. Deborah A. Lark, Oct. 16, 1971; children: Madylin, Kristy, Suzanne. BA, Southeastern La. U., 1966. Cert. internal auditor, cert. govt. fin. mgr., cert. office automation profl. Auditor Office of the Inspector Gen., New Orleans, 1965-72; audit br. chief Cen. Voucher Payment Ctr., New Orleans, 1972-73; evaluation staff chief Nat. Fin. Ctr., New Orleans, 1973-74, processing br. chief, 1974, ops. div. chief, 1974-78, acctg. div. chief, 1978-79, ops. div. chief, 1979-80, dep. dir., 1980-81, dir., 1981-93; dep. chief fin. officer, dir. fin. mgmt. U.S. Dept. Commerce, 1993—. Contbr. articles to profl. jours. Chmn. CASU Tenant Bd. Dirs., New Orleans, 1989-93, policy com. Fed. Exec. Bd., New Orleans, 1990-93, chmn., 1989-90, 92-93; chmn. unit I United Way of Greater New Orleans, 1991, vice chmn. community resources divsn. 1991, chair 1992-93, bd. trustees, 1990-94, chmn. unit VII, 1990, chmn. CFC, 1989; mem. Tulane U. pub. adv. com. for computer info. sys., 1987-93; acctg. dept. advt. bd. U. New Orleans, 1991; pres. acctg. bd. U. New Orleans, 1992-93. With U.S. Army, 1965-71. Named Outstanding 1990 Campaign Vol. of Yr. United Way, 1991, Leadership award, 1989; recipient Communication and Leadership award Toastmasters, 1991, award New Orleans chpt. Federally Employed Women, 1990, 91, Presdl. Meritorious Rank award, 1988, 95, New Orleans Fed. Exec. Bd. award for outstanding leadership, 1989, Spl. award Office of the Comptroller Gen., 1989, Disting. Exec. Svc. award Sr. Exec. Assn. USDA, 1989; named as Fed. 100 info. systems mgr. by Fed. Computer Wk., 1990, Elmer Staats Disting. Leadership award, 1993, Donald L. Scantlebury Meml. award for Disting. Leadership in Fin. Mgmt., 1995. Mem. Assn. Govt. Accts. (New Orleans chpt. pres. 1972-73, dir. 1970-71, 73-74, 74-75, 76-77, S.W. region v.p. 1975-76, South Ctrl. region v.p. 1981-82, mem. nat. exec. com. 1983-84, 93—, chmn. fin. mgmt. enhancement bd. 1988-89, chmn. emerging issues 1990-91, chmn. tech. progrm com. 1991—, nat. pres.-elect 1993-94, nat. pres. 1994-95), Inst. Internal Auditors, Sr. Exec. Assn., Fed. Exec. Inst. Alumni Assn. Republican. Roman Catholic. Avocation: gardening. Home: 5624 Camphor St Metairie LA 70003-2210

MCSHANE, JOSEPH MICHAEL, priest, dean, theology educator; b. N.Y.C., June 19, 1949; s. Owen Patrick and Catherine Veronica (Shelley) McS. AB, Boston Coll., 1972, AM, 1972; MDiv, STM, Jesuit Sch. Theology, Berkeley, Calif., 1977; PhD, U. Chgo., 1981. Ordained priest Roman Cath. Ch., 1977. English tchr. Canisius H.S., Buffalo, 1972-74; asst. prof. religious studies LeMoyne Coll., Syracuse, N.Y., 1982-87, assoc. prof. religious studies, 1987-91, prof., 1991-92, chairperson, 1991-92; dean Fordham Coll., Bronx, N.Y., 1992—, prof. theology, 1992—; vis. prof. history Loyola House, Berkley, Mich., 1986-87; bd. dirs. U. Scranton, Pa., Fordham Prep. Sch., Bronx, N.Y., Regis H.S., N.Y.C., Canisius Coll., Buffalo. Author: Sufficiently Radical: Catholicism, Progressivism and the Bishops' Program of 1919, 1986; author chpt. to book; creator video: The Pilgrimage of the People of God: An Introduction to the Study of Church History, 1991; contbr. articles to profl. jours. Recipient First prize Cath. Press Assn., 1992. Mem. Am. Cath. Hist. Assn., Am. Soc. Ch. History, Phi Beta Kappa. Democrat. Home: 441 E Fordham Rd Bronx NY 10458 Office: Fordham U Dept Theology Bronx NY 10458

MCSHANE, WILLIAM R., systems engineer; b. July 30, 1943. BE, Manhattan Coll.; MS, Poly. Inst. Bklyn., PhD in Systems Engring. Prof., dept. head Indsl. & Systems, Mech. Engring. Poly. U., Bklyn.; cons. Fla Dept. Transp. Co-author of three publs. Mem. IEEE, Ind. Indsl. Engrs., Inst. Traffic Engrs. Office: Poly U Transp Tng & Rsch Ctr 333 Jay St Brooklyn NY 11201-2907*

MCSHEFFERTY, JOHN, research company executive; b. Akron, Ohio, Mar. 14, 1929; s. John and Jean (Conway) McS.; m. Glenna Gloria Childs, Apr. 18, 1959; children: John III, Amy Childs. BSc, U. Glasgow, 1953, PhD, 1957. Various rsch. positions Sterling Winthrop Rsch. Inst., Rensselaer, N.Y., 1957-62; dir. pharm. devel. Ortho Pharm. Corp. div. Johnson and Johnson, Raritan, N.J., 1962-75; dir. rsch. Janssen R & D, Inc., Piscataway, N.J., 1975-77; v.p. R & D family products Internat. Playtex, Paramus, N.J., 1977-79; pres. Gillette Rsch. Inst., Gaithersburg, Md., 1979—. Fellow Royal Pharm. Soc. of Gt. Britain; mem. Indsl. Rsch. Inst. (bd. dirs. 1988-92), Am. Acad. Dermatology, Am. Mgmt. Assn. (bd. dirs. 1994—), Am. Chem. Soc., Am. Pharm. Assn., N.Y. Acad. Scis., Soc. Cosmetic Chemists, Dirs. Indsl. Rsch., Assn. Rsch. Dirs., Sigma Xi. Office: Gillette Rsch Inst 401 Professional Dr Gaithersburg MD 20879-3432

MC SHEFFREY, GERALD RAINEY, architect, educator, city planner; b. Belfast, Ireland, Aug. 13, 1931; s. Hugh and Jane (Piggot) McS.; m. Norma Isabella Lowry, June 4, 1956; children: Laurence, Niall, Aidan. Student, Belfast Coll. Tech., 1950-56; Diploma in Architecture, Univ. Coll., U. London, 1959; Diploma in Civic Design, U. Edinburgh, Scotland, 1963. Archtl. asst. various archtl. firms Belfast, 1950-57; design architect Munce and Kennedy, Belfast, 1957-62; architect/planner Liverpool (Eng.) City Planning Dept. and Livingston New Town, 1963-65; asso. partner James Munce Partnership, Belfast, 1965-68; prin. planning officer (design) Belfast City Planning Dept., 1968-71; prof. architecture U. Kans., 1971-73, dir. archtl. studies, 1976-79; Belfast regional architect, dir. devel. No. Ireland Housing, 1973-76; prof. architecture, dean Coll. Architecture, Planning and Design, Ill. Inst. Tech., 1979-82; dean Coll. Architecture and Environ. Design Ariz. State U., Tempe, 1982-86, prof. architecture, 1988—; v.p. Ariz. State U., West Campus, Phoenix, 1985-88; vis. fellow Princeton (N.J.) U., 1989; external examiner in urban design and landscape studies U. Edinburgh, 1973-76. Author: (with James Munce Partnership) Londonderry Area Plan, 1968. Fulbright award, 1965. Fellow Royal Inst. Brit. Architects, Royal Town Planning Inst.; mem. AIA. Episcopalian. Office: Ariz State U Coll Architecture & Environ Design Tempe AZ 85287-1605

MCSHIRLEY, MARJORIE STONE, art director. Art dir.: (films) Pee-Wee's Big Adventure, 1985, Back to School, 1986, Back to the Future II, 1989, Three Fugitives, 1989, Back to the Future III, 1990, The Addams Family, 1991. Office: care Art Directors Guild 11365 Ventura Blvd Ste 315 Studio City CA 91604-3148

MCSORLEY, CISCO, lawyer; b. Albuquerque, July 8, 1950; s. Frank N. and Virginia E. (Norton) McS. BA, U. N.Mex., 1974, JD, 1979; postdoctoral sch. govt., Harvard U., 1986. Bar: N.Mex. 1980, U.S. Dist. Ct. N.Mex. 1980. Tchr. Academia Cotopaxi, Quito, Ecuador, S. Am., 1973-76; sole practice Albuquerque, 1980—. State rep. N.Mex. Ho. Reps., Albuquerque, 1984—. Mem. ABA, N. Mex. Bar. Assn., N. Mex. Trial Lawyers Assn., Assn. Trial Lawyers Am. Democrat. Mem. Soc. of Friends. Avocations: basketball.

MCSPADDEN, PETER FORD, retired advertising agency executive; b. Montclair, N.J., Oct. 2, 1930; s. Chester F. and Janet (Chase) McS.; m. Barbara Dodds, June 30, 1956; children—Douglas Dodds, David Ford, Peter Chase. A.B., Dartmouth, 1952. Account exec. McCann-Erickson, Inc., N.Y.C., 1956-59; with Dancer-Fitzgerald-Sample, Inc., N.Y.C., from 1959, v.p., account supr., 1965-68, sr. v.p., mgmt. supr., 1968-72, exec. v.p., 1972-74, pres., chief operating officer, from 1974; chmn. bd., chief operating officer Saatchi & Saatchi DFS Inc., N.Y.C., 1986-88, also bd. dirs., ret., 1988; pres., bd. dirs. DFS/Dorland Worldwide; bd. dirs. Am. Advt. Fedn., Am. Assn. Advt. Agys., TriState U.; mem. Nat. Advt. Rev. Bd.; bd. trustees Bradford Coll; vice chmn. Broadstreet TV Inc, 1989—. Chmn. bd. visitors Rockefeller Ctr., Dartmouth Coll.; pres. Greenwich (Conn.) Young Republican Club, 1966-67; bd. dirs. United Way of Tri-State, 1995 Spl. Olympic Games; campaign mgr. Congressman Lowell P. Weicker, 1968, Senator Weicker, 1970, 76, 82, 88; mem. Rep. Town Com., Greenwich, 1965-68; trustee Greenwich Hosp. Served to lt. (j.g.) USNR, 1952-55. Mem. Am. Assn. Advt. Agys. (dir.). Clubs: Riverside (Conn.) Yacht, Greenwich Country, Meguntícook Golf. Home: 46 Carriglea Dr Riverside CT 06878-2402

MCSPARRAN, ROBERT B., food products executive. Pres. Inter-State Milk Producers Coop, Southhampton, Pa. Office: Inter-State Milk Producers Coop 1225 Industrial Blvd Southampton PA 18966-4010*

MCSTEEN, MARTHA ABERNATHY, organization executive; b. Iowa Park, Tex., May 25, 1923; d. King Peyton and Iva Mae (Dawson) Abernathy; m. George Steven McSteen, Oct. 13, 1943 (dec. Jan. 1945); m. Marshall Parks, Apr. 6, 1991. BA, Rice U., 1944; MA, U. Okla., 1972; JD (hon.), Austin Coll., 1985. Claims rep., supr. and dist. mgr. Social Security Adminstrn., Dallas, 1947-65, regional commr., 1976-83; acting commr. Social Security Adminstrn., Washington, 1983-86; regional adminstr. Medicare, Denver and Dallas, 1965-76; cons. Nat. Com. To Preserve Social Security and Medicare, Washington, 1987-89, pres., 1989—; U.S. rep. to Internat. Social Security Assn., 1985, 86. Bd. dirs. Buck Found., San Francisco, 1991—, Setting Priorities for Retirement Yrs. Found., Washington, 1991—, Prevention of Blindness Found., Washington, 1993—, Claude and Mildred Pepper Found. Recipient Commr.'s citation Social Security Adminstrn., 1961, 66, 71, Disting. Svc. award HEW, 1979, Presdl. Meritorious Exec. award, 1980, Nat. Pub. Svc. award Am. Soc. for Pub. Adminstrn., 1986, Presdl. Disting. Exec. award, 1987; fellow Social Security Adminstrn., 1968-69. Office: Nat Com Preserve Soc Sec & Medicare 2000 K St NW Ste 800 Washington DC 20006-1809

MCSWAIN, RICHARD HORACE, materials engineer, consultant; b. Greenville, Ala., Sept. 27, 1949; s. Howard Horace and La Belle (Henderson) McS.; m. Wanda Lynn Hare, June 9, 1972; children: Rachel Lynn, John Angus, Daniel Richard. BS in Materials Engring., Auburn U., 1972, MS in Materials Engring., 1974; PhD in Materials Engring., U. Fla., 1985. Teaching and rsch. asst. Auburn (Ala.) U., 1972-73; metallurgist So. Rsch. Inst., Birmingham, Ala., 1973-76; materials engr. Naval Aviation Depot, Pensacola, Fla., 1977-88, head metallic materials engring., 1988-90; pres. McSwain Engring., Inc., 1991—; cons. materials engr., Pensacola, 1982-90; presenter in field. Contbr. articles to tech. jours. Mem. ASTM, SAE Internat., ASM Internat. (chpt. edn. chmn. 1975-76), Am. Welding Soc., Nat. Assn. Corrosion Engrs., Electron Microscopy Soc., Internat. Soc. Air Safety Investigators. Presbyterian. Avocations: boating, fishing, running. Home: 1405 Kings Rd Cantonment FL 32533-8951 Office: McSwain Engring Inc PO Box 10847 Pensacola FL 32524-0847

MCSWEENEY, FRANCES KAYE, psychology educator; b. Rochester, N.Y., Feb. 6, 1948; d. Edward William and Elsie Winifred (Kingston) McS. BA, Smith Coll., 1969; MA, Harvard U., 1972, PhD, 1974. Lectr. McMaster U., Hamilton, Ont., Can., 1973-74; asst. prof. Wash. State U., Pullman, 1974-79, assoc. prof., 1979-83, prof. psychology, 1983—, chmn. dept. psychology, 1986-94; cons. in field. Contbr. articles to profl. jours. Woodrow Wilson fellow, Sloan Fellow, 1968-69; NSF fellow, 1970-72; NIMH fellow, 1973. Fellow Am. Psychol. Assn., Am. Psychol. Soc.; mem. Western Psychol. Assn., Psychonomic Soc., Assn. Behavior Analysis, Phi Kappa Phi, Phi Beta Kappa, Sigma Xi. Home: SW 860 Alcora Pullman WA 99163 Office: Wash State U Dept Psychology Pullman WA 99164-4820

MCSWEENEY, MAURICE J. (MARC), lawyer; b. Chgo., July 3, 1938; s. Thomas J. and Margaret F. (Ahern) McS.; m. Sandra A. Panosh, Sept. 30, 1967; children: Erin, Sean. BS, DePaul U., 1960; JD, U. Chgo., 1963. Ptnr. Foley and Lardner, Milw., 1963—. Bd. dirs. Milw. Pub. Schs., 1973-79,

Milw. chpt. ARC, 1979-85, Alverno Coll., Milw., 1984—, Health Edn. Ctr. of Wis., 1987—. Fellow Am. Coll. Trial Lawyers; mem. ABA, Wis. Bar Assn., Milw. Bar Assn., Am. Judicature Soc. (bd. dirs. 1988-93), Rotary (bd. dirs. Milw. 1986-88). Avocations: skiing, tennis, karate. Office: Foley & Lardner 777 E Wisconsin Ave Milwaukee WI 53202-5302*

MCSWEENEY, MICHAEL TERRENCE, manufacturing executive; b. Rockford, Ill., Jan. 28, 1937; s. John Carpenter and Julia Elizabeth (McCann) McS.; m. Louise Antionette Walters, Aug. 20, 1960; children—David, Mark. B.S.E., No. Ill. U., 1961. Indsl. engr. MicroSwitch div. Honeywell Inc., Freeport, Ill., 1960-63; sr. v.p. Metromail div. Metromedia, Inc., N.Y.C., 1963-80; v.p., gen. mgr. Harlequin Reader Service, Toronto, Ont., Can., 1980-82; exec. v.p. Harlequin Enterprises, Ltd., Toronto, Ont., Can., 1982-85; pres., chief exec. officer Bear Creek Corp., Medford, Oreg., 1985-88; chmn., CEO, dir. DIMAC Corp., St. Louis, 1988—; mem. mktg./direct mktg. adv bd. U. Mo., Kansas City, 1992—; instr. Am. Mgmt. Assn., N.Y.C., 1976-77, Dale Carnegie Mgmt. Instrn., Iowa, Ill., 1968-71; mem., past chmn. mailers tech. adv. com. to postmaster gen., Washington, 1978—; bd. dirs. So. Oreg. State Coll. Regional Adv. Bd., 1986-88; trustee Peter Britt Music & Arts Assn., Medford, 1986-88, Rogue Valley Community Health Ctr., 1987-88. Contbr. articles to profl. jours. County campaign chmn. U.S. senatorial candidate Henry County, Iowa, 1966, 68; trustee St. Elizabeth Hosp., Lincoln, Nebr., 1973-75; bd. dirs. Regional Airport Authority, Burlington, Iowa, 1976-79; trustee Direct Mktg. Edn. Found., 1995—. Served to sgt. USAF, 1954-58. Recipient Leadership award Boy Scouts Am., 1968, Career Counseling commendation Iowa Wesleyan Coll., 1976, Leadership commendation U.S. Post Office, 1982. Mem. Direct Mktg. Assn. (ethics com. 1970-72, bd. dirs. 1987-94, chmn. govt. affairs com. 1987-94, fin. com. 1987-88), Mail Advt. Svc. Assn. (bd. dirs. 1979-80, Commendation award 1980), Can. Direct Mktg. Assn., Direct Mktg. Assn. Toronto, VFW, Phi Kappa Theta (trustee 1979-83, 90—, nat. treas. 1995—). Republican. Roman Catholic. Lodges: Kiwanis, K.C. Avocations: flying; swimming; golf. Home: 12818 Topping Manor Dr Town & Country MO 63131-1815 Office: DIMAC Corp 1 Corporate Woods Dr Bridgeton MO 63044-3807

MCSWEENEY, WILLIAM LINCOLN, JR., publishing executive; b. Boston, Nov. 9, 1930; s. William Lincoln and Ruth Patricia (Desmond) McS.; B.S., Boston Coll., 1953; M.L.A., So. Meth. U., 1980; m. Anne Cornelia Bulman, Aug. 18, 1956; children: Anne C., William L., Siobhan White, Arthur J., Sean B. Tchr. English, Killingly (Conn.) High Sch., 1956-57; with Hallmark Cards, Inc., Kansas City, Mo., 1957-86, area pers. mgr., 1968, sales tng. mgr., 1969-86, dir. corp. tng. and devel., 1970-86; pub. Nat. Catholic Reporter Co., 1986—. Bd. dirs. Cath. Social Svcs., Kansas City Archdiocese, 1975-88, pres., 1980-84; bd. dirs. United Cmty. Svcs. Kansas City, 1978-84, mem. exec. com., 1978-84; bd. dirs. Kansas City Amigos De Las Americas, 1977-80, pres., 1979; bd. dirs. Johnson County YMCA, 1978-79, Jesuit Vol. Corps, Midwest, 1989-95, Mexican Am. Cultural Ctr., San Antonio, 1990—, Minoroty Mus., 1994—; bd. dirs. Pan Ednl. Inst., 1979-83, pres., 1980-81; mem. Boston Coll. Alumni Admissions Council, 1976—; mem. chancellor's adv. bd. Met. Cmty. Colls., 1979-80; mem. Dem. Com., Johnson County, Kans., 1980-86; bd. advisors Sch. Social Welfare, U. Kans., 1983—, chair 1983-91, 93—, Avila Coll., 1991—, Ctrl. City Parochial Sch. Bd., chair 1996—; chair Mayor's UN Day Dinner, Kansas City, Mo., 1990, Mayor's Prayer Breakfast, 1994—; trustee NCCJ, 1991—. Served with U.S. Army, 1953-56. Mem. Internat. Rels. Coun. of Kansas City (bd. dirs. 1989—), Cath. Press Assn., Assoc. Ch. Press, Internat. Press Inst., UN Assn., Inter-Am. Press Inst., Kans. City Press Inst., Boston Coll. Alumni Assn. (past bd. dirs.), Boston Coll. Club (Kansas City), Bus. Execs. Nat. Security. Recipient Kansas City World Citizen of the Yr. award, 1995. Roman Catholic. Office: 115 E Armour Blvd PO Box 419281 Kansas City MO 64141

MCSWEENY, WILLIAM FRANCIS, petroleum company executive, author; b. Haverhill, Mass., Mar. 31, 1929; s. William Francis and Mary Florence (Doyle) McS.; m. Dorothy Pierce, Jan. 20, 1969; children: William Francis III, Cathy Ann, Ethan Madden Maverick, Terrell Pierce. Reporter, columnist, fgn. corr. Hearst Newspapers, 1943-67; dep. chmn., dir. pub. affairs Democratic Nat. Com., 1967-68; spl. asst. to White House Chief of Staff, 1968-69; sr. exec. v.p., bd. dirs. Occidental Internat. Corp., Washington, 1969—, pres., 1976-91; exec. v.p. Occidental Petroleum Corp., 1984-91; cons. to chmn. Occidental Petroleum Corp., 1991—; dir. Fin. Gen. Bankshares Co., Washington, 1978-82, Chevy Chase Savs. and Loan, 1985—; mem. Lloyd's of London; pres.'s rep. to USSR, 1979; mem. Pres.'s Inaugural Com., 1980, 84, 92; Presdl. spl. rep. to Oman, 1980, Bolivia, 1982; Pres.'s com. Korean War Meml., 1987; Pres.'s commr. Exec. Exch., 1976-81; Pres.'s trustee The Kennedy Ctr., 1995—; mem. N.E. White Ho. Fellows Bd.; mem. U.S. Com. UNESCO; spl. counsel speaker of Ho. of Reps., 1971-72. Author: Go Up for Glory, 1965, Violence Every Sunday, 1966, The Impossible Dream, 1967; also articles. Bd. visitors Fletcher Sch. Law and Diplomacy, Tufts U.; bd. advisors Karl F. Landegger Program Internat. Bus. Diplomacy, Sch. Fgn. Svc., Georgetown U.; trustee, pres. Holton Arms; chmn. Washington Episc. Sch.; chmn. Meridian House Internat., life trustee; mem. World Affairs Coun.; bd. dirs. The Atlantic Coun., Overseer Exec. Coun. Fgn. Diplomates, Dept. of State, The Brookings Instn. Coun., 1991—; vice chmn. Sec. of State Fine Arts Commn.; chmn. Ford's Theatre, 1988—; bd. dirs. Very Spl. Arts, Arena State, Corcoran Gallery Art, Africare, Fed. City Coun., Washington Opera, Folger Shakespeare Theater, Cities in Schs. Nat. Learning Ctr., USO, Arms Control Assn., Nat. Assn. So. Poor, Duke Ellington Sch., Washington Ednl. TV, 1989—; v.p. Ct. of Mary Rose, Portsmouth, Eng.; pres. Commn. to Preserve U.S. Cultural Heritage Abroad; co-chair State Dept. diplomatic rooms endowment; chmn. Lombardi Cancer Ctr. Coun., Georgetown U. Med. Ctr.; pres. Ams. Internat. Insts. for Advanced Studies; vice chmn. Kennedy Ctr. Cmty. Bd., 1991-92; trustee V.P. Residence Found.; juror The Heinz Found., 1995—; chmn. Chevy Chase for Cmty. Com. Recipient Outstanding Young Man award Boston Jaycees, 1961, U.S. Disting. Svc. award, 1968, Outstanding Svc. spl. award, 1969, D.C. Disting. Citizen award, 1981, Paul Hill award Kennedy Ctr., 1983, D.C. Cultural award, 1983, Armenian Earthquake Hero medal, 1989, Lincoln medal, 1991, Helen Hayes award, 1991, Washingtonian of Yr. award, 1995, also numerous awards for domestic reports and reporting from Vietnam and Mid. East, including Best U.S. Reporting award, 1964. Mem. Smithsonian Inst. (mem. nat. adv. com. Kellogg Project), Alfalfa Club, Cosmos Club, 1925 F St. Club (trustee, Washington), Internat. Club (trustee).

MCSWINEY, CHARLES RONALD, lawyer; b. Nashville, Apr. 23, 1943; s. James W. and Jewell (Bellar) Mc.; m. Jane Detrick McSwiney, Jan. 2, 1970. BA, Kenyon Coll., Gambier, Ohio, 1965; JD, U. Cin., 1968. Assoc. Smith & Schnacke, Dayton, Ohio, 1968-72, ptnr., 1972-89, pres. and mng. ptnr., 1984-89; sr. v.p., gen. counsel The Danis Cos., Dayton, 1989-92; vice chmn. Carillon Capital, Inc., Dayton, 1992—; chmn., CEO Crysteco, Inc., Wilmington, Ohio, 1995—; pres. interchange exec. Presdl. Commn. on Personnel Interchange, Washington, 1972-73. Chmn., pres. bd. trustees Dayton Ballet Assn., 1985-88; trustee Columbus (Ohio) Symphony Orch., 1981-84; chmn. Dayton Performing Arts Fund, 1989-92, Dayton Devel. Coun., 1987-90, Wright State U. Found., Dayton, 1988-94, Miami Valley Sch., Dayton, 1988-94, Arts Ctr. Found., 1986—; mem. bd. advisors Wright State U. Coll. Bus. Adminstrn., 1988—; bd. vis. U. Cin. Coll. Law, 1987-89. Recipient Bronze Medal for Performance U.S. EPA, 1973. Mem. ABA, Ohio Bar Assn., Dayton Bar Assn., Dayton Area C. of C. (trustee 1987-90). Republican. Presbyterian. Home: 3780 Ridgeleigh Rd Dayton OH 45429-1253 Office: Carillon Capital Inc Kettering Tower Ste 1480 Dayton OH 45423-1480

MC SWINEY, JAMES WILMER, retired pulp and paper manufacturing company executive; b. McEwen, Tenn., Nov. 13, 1915; s. James S. and Delia (Conroy) McS.; m. Jewel Bellar, 1940; children: Charles Ronald, Margaret Ann. Grad., Harvard Advanced Mgmt. Program, 1954. Lab. technician, shipping clk. Nashville div. The Mead Corp., 1934-39; asst. office mgr. Harriman div., 1939; plant mgr. Rockport, Ind., 1940; asst. office mgr. Kingsport (Tenn.) div.), 1941-44; exec. asst. to pres. Dayton, Ohio, 1954-57; v.p. devel., 1957-59; adminstrv v.p. Harriman div. (Kingsport (Tenn.) div.), 1959; group v.p., gen. mgr. Mead Bd. div., 1961-63, exec. v.p. corp., 1963-67, pres., chief exec. officer, 1968-71, chmn. bd., chief exec. officer, 1971-78, chmn. bd., 1978-82, also dir.; acct., office mgr., asst. sec.-treas. Brunswick Pulp & Paper Co., Ga., 1944-45; bd. dirs. Ultra-Met, Crysteco, Inc., Energy Innovations Inc., Gosinger, Inc., Sea Island Co., Miami Valley Rsch.; chmn. bd. Interstate Resources Inc., Riceboro, Ga. Trustee Com. for Econ. Devel.; chmn. bd. dirs. Air Force Found. Inst. of Tech. Aviation cadet USAAF, 1942-44. Home: PO Box 30604 Sea Island GA 31561-0604 Office: Mead World HQs Dayton OH 45463

MCTAGGART, JAMES M., diversified financial services company executive; b. 1947. BS in Engring., U. Wash., 1970, MBA in Fin., 1972. V.p. fin. dept. Wells Fargo Bank, San Francisco, 1972-78; v.p. Marakon Assocs., Stamford, Conn., 1978—. Office: Marakon Assocs 300 Atlantic St Stamford CT 06901*

MCTAGGART, PATRICK WILLIAM, principal; b. East Chicago, Ind., Dec. 3, 1950; s. Frederick M. and Dolores R. (Gourley) McT. BS, Ball State U., 1972; MS, Purdue U., 1977, EdS, 1985. Cert. secondary adminstrn. and supervision. Tchr. Griffith (Ind.) Jr. H.S., 1973-82, asst. prin., 1982-88; prin. Roosevelt Mid. Sch., Monticello, Ind., 1988—. Deacon First Presbyn. Ch. Monticello, Ind., 1994—. Mem. ASCD, Nat. Mid. Sch. Assn., Ind. Prin. Leadership Acad. (grad. 1992-93), Ind. Assn. Sch Prins., Sportsmen Acting for the Environ, Ducks Unltd. Avocations: fishing, hunting, golf, tennis, wildlife art collecting. Home: 3608 E Bailey Rd Monticello IN 47960-7041 Office: Roosevelt Mid Sch 721 W Broadway St Monticello IN 47960-2010

MCTAGGART-COWAN, IAN, retired university chancellor; b. Edinburgh, Scotland, June 25, 1910; s. Garry McTaggart and Laura (Mackenzie) McTaggart-Cowan; m. Joyce Stewart Racey, Apr. 21, 1936; children: Garry Ian McTaggart, Barbara Ann McTaggart (Mrs. Mikkel Schau). B.A., U. B.C., 1932, D.Sc., 1977; Ph.D., U. Calif.-Berkeley, 1935; LL.D., U. Alta., 1971, Simon Fraser U., 1981; D.Environ. Sci., Waterloo U., 1976; D.Sc., U. Victoria, 1985. Head teaching fellow U. Calif.-Berkeley, 1932-35; asst. biologist B.C. Provincial Mus., Victoria, 1935-38; asst. dir. B.C. Provincial Mus., 1938-40; with U. B.C., Vancouver, 1940-76; asst. prof. zoology U. B.C., 1940-45, prof. zoology, 1945-53, prof., head zoology dept., 1953-64, dean faculty grad. studies, 1964-75, dean emeritus, 1975—, mem. senate, 1952-75; mem. acad. bd. Province B.C., 1964-78, chmn., 1969-75, chmn. acad. council, 1978-84; chancellor U. Victoria, 1979-85. Mem. Environ. Coun. Can., 1971-74, chmn., 1974-82; bd. govs. Arctic Inst., 1950-56, 1985-89, Nature Trust, 1978—; mem. select com. nat. parks U.S. Sec. Interior, 1966-67; chmn. Can. Com. on Whales and Whaling, 1976-93, Habitat Enhancement Com., B.C., 1980—. Decorated officer Order of Can., 1981; Order of B.C., 1991; recipient Leopold medal, 1970, Can. Centennial medal, 1964, Fry medal, 1976, Queen Elizabeth Jubilee medal, 1977, 125th Ann. Can. Confederation medal, 1993. Fellow AAAS, Royal Soc. Can., Calif. Acad. Sci., Pacific Sci. Assn. (hon. life), Wildlife Soc. (hon. life), Alta., B.C. soc. profl. biology (hon. life). Home: 3919 Woodhaven Terr, Victoria, BC Canada V8N 1S7

MCTAGUE, JOHN PAUL, automobile manufacturing company executive, chemist; b. Jersey City, Nov. 28, 1938; s. James Aloysius and Teresa Eugenia (Hanley) McT.; m. Carole Frances Reilly, Dec. 30, 1961; children: Kevin W., Catherine E., Margaret A., Maureen E. BS in Chemistry, Georgetown U., 1960; PhD, Brown U., 1965. Mem. tech. staff N.Am. Rockwell Sci. Ctr., Thousand Oaks, Calif., 1964-70; prof. chemistry, mem. Inst. Geophysics and Planetary Physics UCLA, 1970-82; chmn. nat. synchrotron light source dept. Brookhaven Nat. Lab., Upton, N.Y., 1982-83; dep. dir. Office Sci. and Tech. Policy, Exec. Office of Pres., Washington, 1983-86, acting sci. advisor to Pres. Reagan, 1986; v.p. rsch. Ford Motor Co., Dearborn, Mich., 1986-90; v.p. tech. affairs Ford Motor Co., 1990—; bd. dirs. Raychem Corp.; adj. prof. chemistry Columbia, U., 1982-83. Mem. Pres.'s Coun. Advisors on Sci. and Tech., 1990-93; mem. adv. bd. Sec. Energy, 1990—. Alfred P. Sloan Research fellow, 1971-73; NATO sr. fellow, 1973; John Simon Guggenheim Meml. fellow, 1975-76. Fellow AAAS, Am. Phys. Soc.; mem. Am. Chem. Soc. (Calif. sect. award 1975), Soc. Automotive Engrs., Engring. Soc. Detroit, Barton Hills Country Club, Sigma Xi. Office: Ford Motor Co The American Rd Dearborn MI 48121

MCTARNAGHAN, ROY E., acadamic administrator. Vice chancellor acad. programs State U. System Fla., Tallahassee, 1975—, exec. vice chancellor, 1989—; interim pres. U. North Fla., Jacksonville, 1988-89. Office: State U System Fla 325 W Gaines St Tallahassee FL 32399-6557

MCTEER, ROBERT D., JR., bank executive. Pres., ceo Federal Reserve Bank of Dallas, Tex. Office: Fed Res Bank 2200 N Pearl St Dallas TX 75201-2216*

MCTIER, CHARLES HARVEY, foundation administrator; b. Columbus, Ga., Jan. 28, 1939; s. Roy and Julia (Harvey) McT.; m. Margaret Lucy Ruyl, Aug. 23, 1962; children: Margaret Marie, Charles Harvey Jr. BBA, Emory U., 1961. Administrv. asst. hosp. Emory U., Atlanta, 1961-63, bus. mgr. dept. psychiat. Sch. Med., 1963-66, assoc. dir. personnel, 1966-69, asst. to pres., bd. trustees, 1969-71; sec. Robert W. Woodruff Found., Joseph B. Whitehead Found., Lettie Pate Evans Found., Inc., Lettie Pate Whitehead Found., Inc., Atlanta, 1971-77, sec., treas., 1977-87, v.p., sec., treas., 1987-88, pres., 1988—; chmn. Atlanta Founds. Forum, 1985-86; trustee Southeastern Coun. Founds., Atlanta, 1985-92, chmn. membership com., 1986-89, chmn. program com., 1989, chmn. bd. trustees, 1989-90; vice chmn. Coun. on Founds., Washington, program com., 1985-87, mgmt. com., 1987—, nominating com., 1987-88, chmn. audit and fin. com., 1990-95, chmn. mgmt. com., 1996—; chmn. bd. trustees Found. Ctr. N.Y.C., 1994—, fin. and audit com., 1991—, exec. com., 1992—, chmn. nominating com., 1992, chmn. program and fund devel. adv. com., 1993—; pub. mem. Joint Commn. on Accreditation of Health Care Orgns., 1994—; dir. SunTrust Bank of Ga., SunTrust Bank Atlanta. Trustee, North Ga. United Meth. Found., 1985-92; trustee, treas. Meth. Found. Ret. Mins., 1980; chmn. new ch. devel. com. North Ga. United Meth. Conf., 1980-85; trustee North Ga. United Meth. Found., 1985-92; mem. bd. vis. Emory U., 1985-87. Mem. Mgmt. Execs. Soc., Assn. Emory Alumni (bd. govs. 1987-91), Pres.'s Cir. of NAS/Inst. of Medicine, Commerce Club (bd. dirs.), Druid Hills Golf Club. Avocations: golf, travel. Office: Joseph B Whitehead Found 50 Hurt Plz SE Ste 1200 Atlanta GA 30303-2916

MC TIERNAN, JOHN, film director; b. Albany, N.Y., Jan. 8, 1951. Dir., screewriter Nomads, 1985; dir. Predator, 1987, Die Hard, 1988, The Hunt For Red October, 1990, Medicine Man, 1992, The Last Action Hero, 1993, Die Hard With a Vengeance, 1995. Office: CAA 9830 Wilshire Blvd Beverly Hills CA 90212-1804

MCTURNAN, LEE BOWES, lawyer; b. N.Y.C., Sept. 13, 1937; s. Lee M. and Alice (Light) McT.; m. Susan Cassady, Aug. 2, 1969; children: John M., Sarah D. AB magna cum laude, Harvard U., 1959; Diploma in Law, Oxford (Eng.) U., 1961; JD, U. Chgo., 1963. Bar: Ill. 1965, U.S. Dist. Ct. (no. dist.) Ill. 1965, U.S. Ct. Appeals (7th cir.) 1966, U.S. Supreme Ct. 1969, Ind. 1978, U.S. Dist. Ct. (so. dist.) Ind. 1978, U.S. Dist. Ct. (no. dist.) Ind. 1987. Law clk. to hon. justice U.S. Supreme Ct., Washington, 1963-64; assoc. Sidley & Austin, Chgo., 1964-69, ptnr., 1970-78; ptnr. Hackman, McClarnon & McTurnan, Indpls., 1978-88, McTurnan & Turner, Indpls., 1989—; assoc. spl. counsel procs. on chief justice R.I. Commn. Jud. Tenure and Discipline, Providence, 1985; mem. Civil Justice Reform Adv. Com. for So. Dist. Ind. Adminstrv. bd. Meridian St. United Meth. Ch., 1987-90. Mem. ABA, Ind. Bar Assn., Ill. Bar Assn., Indpls. Bar Assn., 7th Cir. Bar Assn., Ind. Trial Lawyers Assn., Assn. Trial Lawyers Am., Law Club of Indpls. (pres. 1988-90), Legal Club of Chgo., Columbia Club, Woodstock Club, Lit. Club, Rotary. Republican. Avocations: running, reading, gardening. Home: 115 Bennington Dr Zionsville IN 46077-1134 Office: McTurnan & Turner 2400 Market Tower 10 W Market St Indianapolis IN 46204-2954

MCVAY, JOHN EDWARD, professional football club executive; b. Bellaire, Ohio, Jan. 5, 1931; s. John A. and Helen (Andrews) McV.; m. Eva Lee; children: John R., James P., Timothy G. B.S. in Edn., Miami U., Oxford, Ohio, 1953; M.A. in Sch. Adminstrn., Kent (Ohio) State U., 1963. Asst. football coach, instr. phys. edn. Mich. State U., 1962-65; head coach, dir. athletics U. Dayton, Ohio, 1965-74; head coach, gen. mgr. Memphis in World Football League, 1974-76; head football coach N.Y. Giants, NFL, 1976-78; dir. player pers. San Francisco 49ers, NFL, 1979-80, dir. football ops., 1980-81, v.p. adminstrn., 1981-83, gen. mgr., v.p., 1983-89, v.p. football ops., 1990-96; prin. McVay Sports Cons. Inc., Sanibel, Fla., 1996—. Exec. dir. Catholic Youth Council, Canton, Ohio, 1959-62. Recipient Disting. Citizen award Massillon H.S., 1996; named to Miami U. Athletic Hall of Fame; named NFL Exec. of Yr., 1989. Mem. Sigma Chi (Significant Sig award), Phi Epsilon Kappa, Phi Delta Kappa. Won five Super Bowl Championships 1981, 1984, 88, 89, 94.

MCVAY, MARY FRANCES, portfolio manager; b. Washington, Sept. 17, 1955; d. Joseph J. and Stella F. (Walejko) McVay; m. Theodore R. Rosenberg, Sept. 21, 1991. BS in Acctg., Va. Tech., 1978, MBA, 1981. CPA; CFA. Auditor CIA, Washington, 1975-83; sr. cons. Booz, Allen & Hamilton, Arlington, Va., 1983-85; portfolio mgr. Burney Mgmt. Co., Falls Church, Va., 1985—. Mem. Inst. Mgmt. Accts. (dir. newsletter 1992—, dir. mem. acquisition 1993—, dir. program roster 1994-96), Assn. Investment, Mgmt. and Rsch. Office: Burney Mgmt Co 123 Rowell Ct Falls Church VA 22046-3126

MCVEIGH-PETTIGREW, SHARON CHRISTINE, communications consultant; b. San Francisco, Feb. 6, 1949; d. Martin Allen and Frances (Roddy) McVeigh; m. John Wallace Pettigrew, Mar. 27, 1971; children: Benjamin Thomas, Margaret Mary. B.A. with honors, U. Calif.-Berkeley, 1971; diploma of edn. Monash U., Australia, 1975; M.B.A., Golden Gate U., 1985. Tchr., adminstr. Victorian Edn. Dept., Victoria, Australia, 1972-79; supr. Network Control Ctr., GTE Sprint Communications, Burlingame, Calif., 1979-81, mgr. customer assistance, 1981-84, mgr. state legis. ops., 1984-85, dir. revenue programs, 1986-87; communications cons. Flores, Pettigrew & Co., San Mateo, Calif., 1987-89; mgr. telemarketing Apple Computer, Inc., Cupertino, Calif., 1989-94; prin. The Call Ctr. Group, San Mateo, Calif., 1995—; telecomm. cons. PPG Svcs., 1994—; telecomm. spkr. Dept. Consumer Affairs, Sacramento, 1984. Panelist Wash. Gov.'s Citizens Council, 1984; founding mem. Maroondah Women's Shelter, Victoria, 1978; organizer nat. conf. Bus. Women and the Polit. Process, New Orleans, 1986; mem. sch. bd. Boronia Tech. Sch., Victoria, 1979. Recipient Tchr. Spl. Responsibilities award Victoria Edn. Dept., 1979. Mem. Women in Telecommunications (panel moderator San Francisco 1984), Am. Mgmt. Assn., Peninsula Profl. Women's Network, Am. Telemktg. Assn. (bd. dirs. 1992), Women's Econ. Action League. Democrat. Roman Catholic.

MCVERRY, THOMAS LEO, manufacturing company executive; b. Pitts., Aug. 2, 1938; m. Jean L. Smith, Apr. 29, 1961; children: Thomas, Michael, Amy. BA, U. Pitts., 1961, MBA, 1962. CPA, N.Y., CFP. Sr. acct. Deloitte & Touche, N.Y.C., 1962-66; contr., treas. Church & Dwight Co., Inc., N.Y.C., 1966-73; v.p. fin., resources Rexham Corp., Charlotte, N.C., 1973-90, also bd. dirs.; pres. McVerry & Assocs., Charlotte, 1990—; trustee 1st Union Funds, Evergreen Funds; vice chmn. bd. Carolina Coop. Fed. Credit Union. Chmn. bd. edn. Charlotte Cath. High Sch., 1977-84, fin. com. St. Gabriel's Parish, Charlotte, 1976-82; v.p. Waldwick (N.J.) Bd. Edn., 1970-73. Mem. Am. Mgmt. Assn. (fin. coun.), Fin. Execs. Inst. (bd. mem. S.C. chpt.). Home and Office: 4419 N Parview Dr Charlotte NC 28226-3433

MCVEY, HENRY HANNA, III, lawyer; b. Richmond, Va., Aug. 12, 1935; s. Henry Hanna Jr. and Eva Lawson (Jennings) McV.; m. Reba Jean Robinson, Dec. 12, 1964; children: Margaret Anne McVey Singleton, Lewis Lawson, Ian Douglas. BS, BA magna cum laude, Hampden-Sydney Coll., 1957; LLB, U. Va., 1960. Bar: Va., 1960, U.S. Dist. Ct. (ea. dist.) Va. 1960, U.S. Ct. Appeals (4th cir.) 1965, U.S. Supreme Ct. 1970. Assoc. Battle, Neal, Harris, Minor & Williams, Richmond, 1960-66; ptnr. McGuire, Woods, Battle & Boothe (and predecessor firm), Richmond, 1966—; mem. adv. group under Civil Justice Reform Act of 1990, U.S. Dist. Ct. (ea. dist.) Va. Bd. dirs. Richmond Symphony, 1977-78, 87—, v.p., 1979-81, exec. v.p., 1981-83, pres., 1983-85, chmn. bd. dirs., 1985-87; bd. dirs. Carpenter Ctr. for Performing Arts, 1982-89; trustee Hampden-Sydney Coll., 1989-94, 95—; mem. Commn. on Archtl. Rev., City of Richmond, 1985-95. Fellow Am. Coll. Trial Lawyers; mem. ABA, Va. Assn. Def. Attys. (v.p. 1981-83, treas. 1983-84, pres.-elect 1984-85, pres. 1985-86), Def. Research and Trial Lawyers Assn. (past state chmn., regional v.p. 1985-87, bd. dirs. 1987-90), Am. Bd. Trial Advocacy (adv.), Fedn. Ins. and Corp. Counsel, Bar Assn. City of Richmond, Va. Bar Assn., Country Club of Va., Bull and Bear Club, Capital Club. Presbyterian. Home: PO Box 43 Schley VA 23154 Office: McGuire Woods Battle & Boothe One James Ctr Richmond VA 23219

MCVICKER, JESSE JAY, artist, educator; b. Vici, Okla., Oct. 18, 1911; s. Jesse Allen and Clara Mae (Hendrick) McV.; m. Laura Beth Paul, Aug. 20, 1938. B.A., Okla. State U., 1940, M.A., 1941. Faculty Okla. State U., Stillwater, 1941—; prof. art Okla. State U., 1959-77, prof. emeritus, 1977—, head dept., 1959-77. Exhbns. include Med. Mus. Art, Mus. Non-Objective Painting, Chgo, Art Inst., N.A.D., Library of Congress, San Francisco Mus. Art, Denver Art Mus., Pa. Acad. Fine Arts, Carnegie Inst., Print Club Phila., Salon Des Realities Nouvelles, Paris, France, Dallas, Mus. Fine Arts, Galleria Origine, Rome, Italy, Whitney Mus. Am. Art; represented in permanent collections Library of Congress, Seattle Art Mus., Dallas Mus. Fine Arts, Met. Mus. Art, Joslyn Meml. Art Mus.; bibliography Graphic Works by J. Jay McVicker, 1986. Served with USNR, 1943-46. Mem. Soc. Am. Graphic Artists, Audubon Artists (John Taylor Arms award 1990), Print Club Phila., Pi Kappa Alpha.

MC VIE, CHRISTINE PERFECT, musician; b. Eng., July 12, 1943; m. John McVie (div.); m. Eddy Quintela. Student art sch., pvt. student sculpture. Singer, keyboardist, Fleetwood Mac, from 1970; albums with Fleetwood Mac include: Fleetwood Mac, 1968, Fleetwood Mac in Chicago, 1969, Then Play On, 1969, English Rose, 1969, Kiln House, 1970, Future Games, 1971, Bare Trees, 1972, Penguin, Mystery To Me, 1973, Heroes Are Hard to Find, 1974, Fleetwood Mac, 1975, Rumours, 1977, Tusk, 1979, Fleetwood Mac Live, 1980, Mirage, 1982, Jumping at Shadows, 1985, Tango in the Night, 1987, Greatest Hits, 1988, Behind the Mask, 1990; solo albums include Christine Perfect, 1969, Christine McVie, 1984; composer: songs including Spare Me a Little of Your Love, Don't Stop, You Make Loving Fun, Over and Over, Hold Me, Songbird, Got a Hold on Me, Heroes Are Hard to Find, Little Lies, As Long as You Follow, Save Me, Skies the Limit. Office: care Warner Bros Records 3300 Warner Blvd Burbank CA 91505-4632

MCVISK, WILLIAM KILBURN, lawyer; b. Chgo., Oct. 8, 1953; s. Felix Kilburn and June (DePear) Visk; m. Marlaine Joyce McDonough, June 20, 1975. BA, U. Ill, 1974; JD, Northwestern U., 1977. Bar: Ill. 1977, U.S. Dist. Ct. (no. dist.) Ill. 1977, U.S. Ct. Appeals (7th cir.) 1978. Assoc. Jerome H. Torshen, Ltd., Chgo., 1977-80, Silets & Martin, Chgo., 1980-81; assoc. Peterson & Ross, Chgo., 1981-85, ptnr., 1985-95; ptnr. Johnson & Bell, Chgo., 1995—. Contbr. articles to profl. jours. Mem. ABA, Chgo. Bar Assn., Def. Research Inst., Am. Assn. Hosp. Attys., Ill. Assn. Hosp. Attys., Ill. Assn. Def. Trial Lawyers. Office: Johnson & Bell 222 N LaSalle St Chicago IL 60601

MCVOY, KIRK WARREN, physicist, educator; b. Mpls., Feb. 22, 1928; s. Kirk Warren and Phyllis (Farmer) McV.; m. Hilda A. Van Der Laan, Aug. 15, 1953; children—Christopher, Lawrence, Annelies. B.A., Carleton Coll., 1950; B.A. (Rhodes scholar), Oxford U., Eng., 1952; Dipl., U. Gottingen, Germany, 1953; Ph.D., Cornell U, 1956. Research asso. Brookhaven Nat. Lab., Upton, N.Y., 1956-58; asst. prof. Brandeis U., 1958-62; assoc. prof. physics U. Wis., Madison, 1963-67, prof., 1967-93, prof. emeritus, 1993—; vis. distinguished prof. physics Bklyn. Coll., 1970-71; vis. prof. Ind. U., 1971-72. Fulbright research grantee U. Utrecht, Netherlands, 1960-61; sr. scientist awardee A. von Humboldt Found., Max-Planck-Institut für Kernphysik, Heidelberg, W. Ger., 1980-81. Fellow Am. Phys. Soc. Achievements include rsch. and publs. on nuclear reaction theory. Office: U Wis Dept Physics 1150 University Ave Madison WI 53706-1302

MCWALTERS, PETER, state agency administrator; b. Oct. 8, 1946; m. Alice Bond McWalters; children: Jennifer, Molly, Katherine. BA in History and Philosophy, Boston Coll., 1968; MS in Pub. Adminstrn., SUNY Brockport, 1979, cert. advanced study ednl. adminstrn., 1981. Permanent N.Y. State Teaching Cert social studies 7-12, Sch. Adminstrn., Sch. Dist. Adminstrn. Tchr.-trainer Eng. for speakers other langs. U.S. Peace Corps., Rep. Philippines; tchr. Eng. for speakers other langs. City Sch. Dist., Rochester, N.Y., 1970-71; tchr. social studies Interim Jr. High Sch., Rochester, 1971-78; Magnet Sch. planning specialist City Sch. Dist.,

Rochester, 1978-81, coord. Mgmt. Inst., 1980-81, supervising dir. planning and budgeting, 1981-85, supt. schs., 1985-91; commr. elem. and secondary edn. State of R.I., 1992—; bd. dirs. Nat. Ctr. Edn. and Economy, mem. new standards project; bd. dirs. Ctr. Ednl. Devel., Rochester; mem. Edn. Commn. of States, Coun. Chief State Schs. Officers, Coun. Great Cities Schs., 21st Century Edn. Commn. Bd. dirs. Urban League, Rochester; mem. United Way Task Force, Rochester; gov. bd., exec. com. Rochester New Futures Initiative, Inc.; mem. Goals for Greater Rochester, Inc. Mem. Am. Assn. Sch. Adminstrs., Assn. Supervision and Curriculum Devel., Phi Delta Kappa. Home: 26 Diman Pl Providence RI 02906-2104 Office: Elem and Sec Office 22 Hayes St Providence RI 02908-5025*

MCWETHY, JOHN FLEETWOOD, journalist; b. Aurora, Ill., Feb. 28, 1947; s. John Adams and Mary Helen (Bell) McW.; m. Laurie Duncan, June 25, 1971; children: Adam Duncan, James Ian. B.A., DePauw U., 1969; M.S., Columbia U., 1970. Def. writer Congl. Quar., Washington, 1970-72; sci. editor U.S. News & World Report, Washington, 1972-77, chief White House corr., 1977-79; chief Pentagon corr. ABC News, Washington, 1979-84; chief corr. ABC News Nat. Security and Sr. State Dept., Washington, 1984—. Contbg. author: Power of the Pentagon, 1972. Recipient DuPont award Columbia U. Sch. Journalism, 1984; 3 Emmy awards, 1984, 91, 92, Overseas Press Club award for Inside the Other Side, 1987. Home: 5028 30th St N Arlington VA 22207-2717

MCWETHY, PATRICIA JOAN, educational association administrator; b. Chgo., Feb. 27, 1946; d. Frank E. and Emma (Kuehne) McW.; m. H. Frank Eden; children: Kristin Beth, Justin Nicholas. BA, Northwestern U., 1968; MA, U. Minn., 1970; MBA, George Washington U., 1981. Geog. analyst CIA, McLean, Va., 1970-71; research asst. NSF, Washington, 1972-74, spl. asst. to dir., 1975; assoc. program dir. human geography and regional sci. program NSF, 1976-79; exec. dir. Assn. Am. Geographers, Washington, 1979-84, Nat. Assn. Biology Tchrs., Reston, Va., 1984-95, Nat. Sci. Edn. Leadership Assn., Arlington, Va., 1995—; prin. investigator NSF grant on biotech. equipment ednl. resource partnership, 1989-93, NSF funded internat. symposium on "Basic Biol. Concepts: What Should the World's Children Know?", 1992-94; co-prin. investigator NSF grant, 1995—; mem. chmn.'s adv. com. Nat. Com. Sci. Stds. & Assessment, 1992—; mem. Commn. for Biology Edn., Internat. Union Biol. Sci., 1988—; mem. exec. com. Alliance for Environ. Edn., 1987-90, chmn. program com., 1990; condr. seminars in field; lectr. in field. Author monograph and papers in field; editor handbook. NSF grantee, 1989-93, 95—; NSF fellow, 1968-69; recipient Outstanding Performance award, NSF, 1973. Mem. Am. Soc. Assn. Execs., Phi Beta Kappa. Office: PO Box 5556 Arlington VA 22205

MCWHAN, DENIS BAYMAN, physicist; b. N.Y.C., Dec. 10, 1935; s. Bayman and Evelyn (Inch) McW.; m. Carolyn Quick, June 20, 1959; children: Susan, Jeanette, David. BS, Yale U., 1957; PhD, U. Calif., Berkeley, 1961. Disting. mem. tech. staff AT&T Bell Labs., Murray Hill, N.J., 1962-1990; chmn. Nat. Synchrotron Light Source, Brookhaven Nat. Lab., Upton, N.Y., 1990-95; assoc. dir. basic energy scis. programs Brookhaven Nat. Lab., Upton, N.Y., 1995—. Fellow AAAS, Am. Phys. Soc. Achievements include rsch. in condensed matter physics. Office: Brookhaven Nat Lab Bldg 460 Upton NY 11973

MCWHINEY, GRADY, history educator; b. Sherveport, La., July 15, 1928; s. Henry Grady and Mayme (Holland) McW.; m. Sue B. Baca, Nov. 20, 1947. B.S., Centenary Coll. of La., 1950; M.A., La. State U., 1951; Ph.D., Columbia U., 1960. Asst. prof. Troy State U., Ala., 1952-54, Millsaps Coll., Jackson, Miss., 1956-59, Northwestern U., Evanston, Ill., 1960-65; assoc. prof. to prof. U.B. C., Vancouver, Can., 1965-70; vis. prof. U. Calif. - Berkeley, 1959-60, 67-68; prof. Wayne State U., Detroit, 1970-75; vis. prof. Tulane U., New Orleans, summer 1970, U. Mich., Ann Arbor, 1972-73; prof. history, dir. and disting. sr. fellow ctr. for study of so. history and culture U. Ala. University, 1975-83; Lyndon Baines Johnson prof. Am. history Tex. Christian U., Ft. Worth, 1983-96, emeritus, 1996—; disting. historian in residence U. So. Miss., Hattiesburg, 1996—; mem. NEH Selection Com., 1973, Jefferson Davis Award Com., 1970-72, 75-77; rsch. fellow Mosher Inst. for Def. Studies, 1988—; James Murfin Meml. lectr., 1990, Marian Alexander Blake lectr., 1991; Conf. Meml. speaker, 1991. Author: Braxton Bragg and Confederate Defeat, Vol. 1, 1969, 2d edit., 1991, Southerners and Other Americans, 1973, (with Perry D. Jamieson) Attack and Die: Civil War Military Tactics of the Southern Heritage, 1982, Cracker Culture: Celtic Ways in the Old South, 1988, (with J.L. Hallock) Braxton Bragg, 2 vols., 1991, An American Civil War Primer, 1992, Battle in the Wilderness: Grant Meets Lee, 1994; editor: (with Sue McWhiney) To Mexico with Taylor and Scott, 1845-1847, 1969, Grant, Lee, Lincoln and the Radicals, 1964, (with Robert Weibe) Historical Vistas, 2 vols., 1963-64, Reconstruction and the Freedmen, 1963, (with Douglas Southall Freeman) Robert E. Lee's Dispatches to Jefferson Davis, 1957, 94. Served with USMC, 1945-47. Recipient Frank E. Vandiver award Houston Civil War Round Table, 1993, Charles L. "Pie" Dufour award New Orleans Civil War Round Table, 1994, Outstanding Scholar award U. Ala., 1980, Gallant Service award Chgo. Civil War Round Table, 1979, Harry S. Truman award, 1970, Pacific Br. award Am. Hist. Assn., 1969; Huntington Library fellow, 1984; recipient Jefferson Davis medal United Daughters of the Confederacy, 1992, Honor award Sons Confederate Vets Tex. Divsn., 1993; rsch. fellow Mosher Inst. Defense Studies, 1988—. Fellow St. George Tucker Soc.; mem. Ala. Hist. Assn. (pres. 1978-79), So. Hist. Assn. (exec. council 1976-79), Phila. Soc., St. Louis Civil War Round Table (hon.), Civil War Round Table U.K. (hon.), Main St. Com., Phi Beta Kappa. Home: 608 S 34th Ave Hattiesburg MS 39402 Office: U So Miss Dept History Hattiesburg MS 39406

MC WHINNEY, EDWARD WATSON, Canadian government legislator; b. Sydney, Australia, May 19, 1924; s. Matthew and Evelyn Annie (Watson) McW.; m. Emily Ingalore Sabatzky, June 27, 1951. LLB, U. Sydney, 1949; LLM, Yale U., 1951, D Juridical Sci., 1953; diploma, Acad. de Droit Internat., The Hague, 1950. Bar: Called to Australian bar 1949, apptd. Queen's counsel, Can 1967. Crown prosecutor Sydney, 1949-50; lectr., then asst. prof. Law Sch. and Grad. Sch., Yale U., 1951-55; prof. law, mem. Centre Russian Studies, U. Toronto, Ont., Can., 1955-66; prof. law, dir. Inst. Air and Space Law, McGill U., Montreal, Que., Can., 1966-71; prof. law, dir. internat. and comparative legal studies U. Ind., Indpls., 1971-74; disting. prof. Simon Fraser U., Burnaby, B.C., 1974-93; mem. Permanent Ct. Arbitration, The Hague, 1985-91; Paul Martin prof. U. Windsor, Can., 1986; prof. emeritus, 1992; M.P. Ho. of Commons, Ottawa, Ont., Can., 1993—; co-chmn. joint standing com. Senate and Ho. of Commons, Ottawa, Ont., Can., 1993-95, parliamentary sec. (fisheries and oceans), 1996—; vis. prof. Ecole Libre des Hautes Etudes, 1952, Heidelberg and Max-Planck-Inst., 1960-61, 90, NYU, 1954, Faculté Internat. de Droit Comparé, Luxembourg, 1959-60, U. San Antonio, 1963, U. Laval, Que., 1967, U. Paris, 1968, U. Madrid, 1968, U. Aix-Marseille, 1969, U. Nacional Autónoma de México, 1965, Inst. Univ. Luxembourg, 1972, 74, 76, Acad. Internat. Law, The Hague, 1973, 90, Aristotelian U., Thessaloniki, Greece, 1974, 78, 85, U. Nice, 1976-77, Jagellonian U., Cracow, Poland, 1976, U. Paris I (Sorbonne), 1982, 85, Coll. de France, Paris, 1983, Meiji U., Tokyo, 1987, Inst. Internat. Relations, Bejing, 1987, 92; legal cons. UN, 1953-54; cons. Japanese Commn. Constn., mem. prime minister Ont. Adv. Com. Confedn., 1964-71; cons. U.S. Naval War Coll., 1961-68; legal cons. Ministère de la Justice, Que., 1969-70; 74-75; constl. adviser to prime minister of Que., 1974-75; royal commr. Commn. Lang. Rights. Que., 1968-72; cons. U.S. Senate select com. presdl. campaign activities, 1973; spl. commr. inquiry Legislature B.C., 1974-75; chief adv. Fed. Govt.'s Task Force on Nat. Unity, 1978; commr. of enquiry, City of Vancouver, 1979; constl. adv. Fedn. Can. Municipalities, 1978-82; spl. advisor Can. del. UN Gen. Assembly, ann. sessions, 1981, 82, 83; constl. adviser Indian Nations (Treaties 6-9), Can., 1980-82; mem. Assoc. de l'Inst. de Droit Internat., 1967, membre titulaire, 1975; mem. Assoc. de l'Acad. Internat. de Droit Comparé, Paris, 1986, mem. Deutsche Gesellschaft für Völkerrecht, 1992. Author: Judicial Review, 4th edit, 1969, Canadian Jurisprudence, 1958, Föderalismus und Bundesverfassungsrecht, 1961, Constitutionalism in Germany, 1962, Comparative Federalism, 2d edit, 1965, Peaceful Coexistence and Soviet-Western International Law, 1964, Law Foreign Policy and the East-West Détente, 1964, Federal Constitution- Making for a Multi-National World, 1966, International Law and World Revolution, 1967, Conflit idéologique et ordre public mondial, 1970, (with M.A. Bradley) The Freedom of the Air, 1968, New Frontiers in Space Law, 1969, The International Law of Communications, 1970, Aerial Piracy and International Law, 1971, (with Pierre Pescatore) Federalism and Supreme Courts and the Integration of Legal Systems, 1973, Parliament and Parliamentary Power Today, 1976, The Executive and Executive Power Today, 1977, (with J-D Gendron and others) La situation de la lanque française au Québec (3 vols.), 1973, The Illegal Diversion of Aircraft and International Law, 1974, Parliamentary Privilege and the Broadcasting of Parliamentary Debates, 1975, The International Law of Detente, 1978, The World Court and the Contemporary International Law-making Process, 1979, Quebec and the Constitution, 1979, Municipal Government in a New Canadian Federal System, 1980, Conflict and Compromise: International Law and World Order in a Revolutionary Age, 1981, Constitution-Making: Principles, Process, Practice, 1981, Canada and the Constitution, 1982, United Nations Law Making, 1984, Supreme Courts and Judicial Law-Making, 1986, Les Nations-Unies et la Formation du Droit, 1986, Aerial Piracy and International Terorism, 1987, The International Court of Justice and the Western Tradition of International Law, 1987, (with Nagendra Singh) Nuclear Weapons and Contemporary International Law, 1988, Judicial Settlement of International Disputes, 1990, (with G.I. Tunkin and V.S. Vereshchetin) From Coexistence to Cooperation: International Law and Organisation in the Post-Cold War Era, 1991, (with J. Zaslove and W. Wolf) Federalism-in-the-Making, Contemporary Canadian and German Constitutionalism, National and Transnational, 1992, Judge Shigeru Oda and the Progressive Development of International Law, 1992, Judge Manfred Lachs and Judicial Law-Making, 1994; bd. editors Australian Quar., 1949-50, Can. Yearbook of Internat. Law, 1963—, Jour. Media Law and Practice, 1980-85, Annuaire International de Justice Constitutionnelle, 1987—; editorial adv. com. Ency. Britannica, 1985—; contbr. to Ency. Brit. Served as officer Australian Air Force, 1943-45. Fellow Carnegie Endowment, 1951; Fulbright fellow, 1950-51; Sterling fellow Yale, 1950-51; Rockefeller fellow, 1960-61, 66-68; Can. Council fellow, 1960-61; fellow Am. Soc. Internat. Law, 1962-63. Mem. Australian Inst. Polit. Sci. (dir.), Internat. Law Assn. (pres. Toronto br. 1964-66, pres. Montreal br. 1970-71, chmn. exec. com. Canadian br. 1972-75), Canadian Bar Assn. (council Ont. 1956-58), Yale Law Sch. Assn. (pres. Can. 1964-69), Canadian Civil Liberties Assn. (v.p. 1965-67), Am. Soc. Internat. Law (council 1965-68), Am. Fgn. Law Assn., Inst. interamericano de Estudios Juridicos Internacionales (dir. 1965—), Inst. Grand-Ducal de Luxembourg, Internat. Commn. Jurists (mem. coun. Can. br. 1988—), Knights of Mark Twain (U.S.) (hon.). Home: 1949 Beach Ave Ste 402, Vancouver, BC Canada V6G 1Z2 Office: House of Commons 555d Ctr Block, Parliament of Can, Ottawa, ON Canada K1A 0A6

MCWHINNEY, IAN RENWICK, physician, medical educator; b. Burnley, Eng., Oct. 11, 1926; emigrated to Can., 1968, naturalized, 1981; s. Archibald Renwick and Mary (Freeland) McW.; m. Betty Heap, Apr. 30; children: Heather, Julie. MB, BCh, Cambridge (Eng.) U., 1949; MD, Cambridge (Eng.) U., Eng.; MD (hon.), U. Oslo, 1991. Intern St. Bartholomews Hosp., London, 1949-50; resident (Warwick), Eng., 1953-54; pvt. practice medicine Stratford-on-Avon, Eng., 1954-68; prof. family medicine U. Western Ont., London, Can., 1968-92; prof. emeritus U. Western Ont., London, 1992—; med. dir. palliative care unit Parkwood Hosp., 1986-91. Author: The Early Signs of Illness, 1964, Introduction to Family Medicine, 1981, A Textbook of Family Medicine, 1989. Capt. Royal Army M.C., 1951-53. Recipient Excellence cert. Soc. Tchrs. Family Medicine, 1979, Curtis G. Hames Rsch. award, 1989. Fellow Coll. Family Physicians (Victor Johnston orator 1980), Royal Coll. Gen. Practitioners, Royal Coll. Physicians; mem. Inst. Medicine-Nat. Acad. Scis. (fgn. assoc.). Office: U Western Ont, Dept Family Medicine, London, ON Canada N6A 5C1

MCWHINNEY, MADELINE H. (MRS. JOHN DENNY DALE), economist; b. Denver, Mar. 11, 1922; d. Leroy and Alice (Houston) McW.; BA, Smith Coll., 1943; MBA, NYU, 1947; m. John D. Dale, June 23, 1961; 1 child, Thomas Denny. Economist, Fed. Res. Bank N.Y., 1943-73, chief fin. and trade statis. div., 1955-59, mgr. market stats. dept., 1960-65, asst. v.p., 1965-73; pres. First Women's Bank, N.Y.C., 1974-76; trustee Retirement System Fed. Res. Bank, 1955-58; vis. lectr. N.Y.U. Grad. Sch. Bus., 1976-77; pres. Dale, Elliott & Co., Inc., Red Bank, N.J., 1977—; mem. N.J. Casino Control Commn., 1980-82, Women's Econ. Round Table, 1978-89, chmn. 1987-88; bd. govs. Am. Stock Exch., 1977-81. Trustee Monmouth Mus., 1995—, Vis. Nurse Assn. Ctrl. Jersey, 1995—, Planned Parenthood Ctrl. Jersey, 1995—; Carnegie Corp. N.Y., 1974-82, Central Savs. Bank of N.Y., 1980-82, Charles F. Kettering Found., 1975-93, chmn. 1987-91, Inst. Internat. Edn., 1975—, Investor Responsibility Rsch. Ctr., Inc., 1974-81; asst. dir. Whitney Mus. Am. Art, 1983-86; dir. Atlantic Energy Co., 1983-93; trustee The Mgrs. Funds, 1983—; mem. adv. com. prof. ethics N.J. Supreme Ct., 1983—. Recipient Smith Coll. medal, 1971, Alumni Achievement award NYU Grad. Sch. Bus. Adminstrn. Alumni Assn., 1971; NYU Crystal award, 1982. Mem. Am. Fin. Assn. (past dir.), Money Marketeers (v.p. 1960, pres. 1961-62), Alumni Assn. Grad. Sch. Bus. Adminstrn. NYU (dir. 1951-63, pres. 1957-59), Soc. Meml. Ctr., N.J. Com. for Humanities, Phi Beta Kappa Assocs. (v.p. 1979-87). Home: 24 Blossom Cove Rd Red Bank NJ 07701-6302 Office: PO Box 458 Red Bank NJ 07701-0458

MCWHIRTER, BRUCE J., lawyer; b. Chgo., Sept. 11, 1931; s. Sydney and Martha McW.; m. Judith Hallett, Apr. 14, 1960; children: Cameron, Andrew. BS, Northwestern U., 1952; LLB, Harvard U., 1955. Bar: D.C. 1955, Ill. 1955, U.S. Ct. Appeals (7th cir.) 1963, U.S. Supreme Ct. Assoc. Lord, Bissell & Brook, Chgo., 1958-62; assoc., then ptnr. Ross & Hardies, Chgo., 1962-95, of counsel, 1996—. Editor: Donnelley SEC Handbook, 1972-87; contbr. articles to profl. publs. Served with U.S. Army, 1955-57, Japan. Mem. ABA, Chgo. Bar Assn., Law Club Chgo., Harvard Law Soc. Ill. (bd. dirs. 1984), Harvard Club (N.Y.C.), Phi Beta Kappa. Democrat. Home: 111 Sheridan Rd Winnetka IL 60093-4223 Office: Ross & Hardies 150 N Michigan Ave Ste 2500 Chicago IL 60601-7567

MCWHIRTER, GLENNA SUZANNE (NICKIE MCWHIRTER), newspaper columnist; b. Peoria, Ill., June 28, 1929; d. Alfred Leon and Garnet Lorene (Short) Sotier; m. Edward Ford McWhirter (div.); children: Suzanne McWhirter Orlicki, Charles Edward, James Richard. BS in English Lang. and Lit., U. Mich., postgrad., 1960-63. Editl. asst. McGraw-Hill Pub. Co., Detroit, 1951-54; staff writer Detroit Free Press, Inc., Detroit, 1963-88; columnist Detroit News Inc., Detroit, 1988—; advt. copy writer Campbell-Ewald Co., Detroit, 1967-68. Author: Pea Soup, 1984. Winner 1st Place Commentary award UPI, Mich., 1979; 1st Place Columns AP, Mich., 1978, 81; 1st Place Columns Detroit Press Club Found., Mich., 1978; Disting. Service award State of Mich., 1985. Mem. Women in Comm. (Headliner award 1978), Alpha Gamma Delta. Avocations: flower gardening; tennis. Home: 88 Meadow Ln Grosse Pointe MI 48236-3803

MCWHIRTER, JAMES HERMAN, consulting engineering business executive, financial planner; b. Mercer, Pa., July 4, 1924; s. John Herman and Blanche Rebecca (Anderson) McW.; m. Suzanne Kibler, July 5, 1952; children: Kathleen, Meg Allyn, John Richard, Thomas Charles, Robert Brian. BS, Columbia U., 1945; MS, Carnegie Inst. Tech., 1947. Registered profl. engr., Pa; cert. fin. planner. Devel. engr. Westinghouse Electric Corp., Sharon, Pa., 1948-65; rsch. engr. Westinghouse Rsch. Labs., Pitts., 1965-89; registered rep. Allegheny Investments, Ltd., Pitts., 1987—; pres. Optimization, Ltd., Murrysville, Pa., 1989—. Contbr. articles on engring. and fin. planning to profl. jours.; spkr. on fin. planning. Lt. (j.g.) USNR, 1945-58. Fellow IEEE. Republican. Presbyterian. Avocation: "Big Band" musician. Home and Office: 3660 Forbes Trail Dr Murrysville PA 15668-1054

MCWHIRTER, JOHN RUBEN, chemical engineering educator; b. East St. Louis, Ill., Dec. 29, 1937; s. Walter and Mildred (Johnson) McW.; m. Gail Balthrope, June 28, 1958 (div. Aug. 1978); children: John Winfield, Andrew James, Mark Steven, Brian Michael; m. Anne Burlingham, Mar. 31, 1979 (div. Dec. 1990); m. Jeanette D. Heiser, Mar. 21, 1992. BS in Chem. Engring., U. Ill., 1959; MS in Chem. Engring., Pa. State U., 1961, PhD in Chem. Engring., 1962; postgrad. exec. program, Stanford U., 1971. Research engr. E.I. Du Pont de Nemours & Co., Wilmington, Del., 1962-63; mgr. research and devel. Mixing Equipment Co., Rochester, N.Y., 1963-66; section engr. engring. devel. lab. Linde div. Union Carbide Corp., Tonawanda, N.Y., 1966-67, div. engr. engring. devel. lab., 1967-68, mgr. chem. engring. div. and special projects, 1968-69, product mgr., 1969-70; mgr. wastewater treatment systems Linde div. Union Carbide Corp., N.Y.C., 1970-72, gen. mgr. environ. systems dept., 1973-76, v.p., gen. mgr. environ. systems dept., 1977-78; v.p., gen. mgr. insecticides and intermediates agrl. products div. Union Carbide, N.Y.C., 1978-83, v.p., gen. mgr. agrl. chems., 1983-86; prof. chem. engring. Pa. State U., State College, Pa., 1986—. Author: The Use of High Purity Oxygen in the Activated Sludge Process, 1978; contbr. articles to profl. jours.; presented numerous papers at profl. confs.; patentee in field. Recipient Best Paper Presentation award Nat. Am. Inst. Chem. Engrs., 1963, Outstanding Personal Achievement award Chem. Engring. Mag., 1970, Kirkpatrick award, 1971, Outstanding Engring. Alumnus award Pa. State U., 1984, Arthur Dehan Little award Am. Inst. Chem. Engrs., 1991. Mem. AICE, AAAS, Am. Mgmt. Assn., Am. Chem. Soc. (Jacob F. Schoellkopf medal 1976), N.Y. Acad. Scis., Water Pollution Control Fedn., Tau Beta Pi, Phi Lambda Upsilon, Sigma Tau, Alpha Chi Sigma, Delta Tau Delta. Republican. Home: 101 Aspen Dr Boalsburg PA 16827 Office: Pa State U 122 Fenske Lab University Park PA 16802-4400

MCWHORTER, ALAN LOUIS, electronics researcher, electrical engineering educator; b. Crowley, La., Aug. 25, 1930; s. Arthur Walton and Andree (Genet) McW. Student, Tulane U., 1947-48; BEE, U. Ill., 1951; ScD, MIT, 1955. Staff mem. Lincoln Lab., MIT, Lexington, 1955-59, asst. head. solid state div., 1962-63, assoc. head, 1963-65, head, 1965-94, fellow, 1994—; from asst. to assoc. prof. elec. engring. MIT, Cambridge, 1959-66, prof. elec. engring., 1966—; mem. elec. engring. adv. coun. U. Pa., 1987-93; cons. mem. adv. group on electron devices Office of the Under Sec. of Def., Acquisition and Tech., 1991—. Contbr. articles to profl. jours. Fellow IEEE (assoc. editor Transaction on Electron Devices 1961-64, editl. bd. Proc. 1966-68, 74-76, David Sarnoff award 1971), Am. Phys. Soc. (exec. com. divsn. solid state physics 1968-70); mem. Nat. Acad. Engring. Office: MIT Lincoln Lab 244 Wood St Lexington MA 02173-9108

MCWHORTER, HOBART AMORY, JR., lawyer; b. Birmingham, Ala., Dec. 24, 1931; s. Hobart Amory and Marjorie (Westgate) McW.; divorced; children: Margaret G., Marjorie W. BA, Yale U., 1953; LLB, U. Va., 1958. Bar: Ala. 1958. Ptnr. Bradley Arant Rose & White, Birmingham, 1958—. 1st lt. U.S. Army, 1953-55. Fellow Am. Coll. Trial Lawyers; mem. Internat. Assn. Ins. Counsel, Nat. Assn. r.R. Counsel. Republican. Presbyterian. Office: Bradley Arant Rose & White 1400 Park Pl Tower 2001 Park Pl Birmingham AL 35203-2735

MCWHORTER, RALPH CLAYTON, health care company executive; b. Chattanooga, Sept. 27, 1933; s. Ralph C. McWhorter and Gladys (Dover) Franks; children: Jodie, Stuart. Student, U. Tenn., 1951-52; BS, Samford U., 1955. Asst. adminstr. Phoebe Putney Meml. Hosp., 1956-65; adminstr. Americus-Sumter Regional Hosp., 1965-67, West Ga. Med. Ctr., 1967-70; adminstr. Palmyra Park Hosp. Hosp. Corp. Am., Nashville, 1970-73, div. v.p., 1973-76, sr. v.p. domestic ops., 1976-80, exec. v.p. ops., 1980-85, pres., chief oper. officer, 1985-87, also bd. dirs.; chmn., chief exec. officer Health-Trust, Inc., Nashville, 1987—. Co-author: Management Dimensions, 1988. Campaign chair United Way Mid. Tenn., 1991. Fellow Am. Coll. Health-care Execs.; mem. Am. Hosp. Assn. (bd. dirs.), Fedn. Am. Health Systems (pres. 1990, chmn. 1991). Methodist. Avocations: water sports, boating. Office: Columbia/HCA Healthcare Inc 4525 Harding Rd Nashville TN 37205-2101*

MCWHORTER, RUTH ALICE, counselor, marriage and family therapist; b. Norfolk, Va., May 14, 1946; d. Lester Arthur and Mabel Winifred (Hopwood) Gorman; m. R. Dale Lawhorn, Jan. 6, 1972 (div. Nov. 1979); m. Brent Wilson McWhorter, Aug. 16, 1986; stepchildren: Daniel Chastin, Kenley Reid, Scott Jason. BA in Edn., Ariz. State U., 1970, M of Counseling Psychology, 1979. Cert. profl. counselor, Ariz., cert. marriage and family therapist, Ariz. Tchr. lang. arts Globe (Ariz.) Mid. Sch., 1969-72; tchr. English Isaac Jr. High Sch., Phoenix, Ariz., 1973-74; real estate salesperson Ben Brooks & Assocs., Phoenix, 1975-76, Century 21 Metro, Phoenix, 1976-77; overnight counselor The New Found., Phoenix, 1978-80; family therapist Youth Svc. Bur., Phoenix, 1980-81; owner, corp. officer, profl. counselor/marriage & family Family Devel. Resources (now Family Psychology Assocs.), Phoenix, 1981—; cons., vol. counselor Deseret Industries, Phoenix, 1992-96. Bd. dirs. Westside Mental Health Svcs., Phoenix, 1982-87; vol. facilitator Ariz. Multiple Sclerosis Soc., Phoenix, 1988. Mem. ACA, Internat. Assn. Marriage and Family Therapists, Am. Assn. Marriage and Family Therapists, Am. Mental Health Counselors Assn., Ariz. Counselors Assn., Ariz. Mental Health Counselors Assn. (sec.-treas. ctrl. chpt. 1982, sec. ctrl. chpt. 1995), Am. Assn. Christian Counselors, Assn. Mormon Counselors and Psychotherapists (sec.-treas. 1990—). Avocations: genealogy, movies, reading, golf, logic puzzles. Office: Family Devel Resources PC PO Box 55291 Phoenix AZ 85078-5291

MCWHORTER, SHARON LOUISE, business executive, inventor, consultant; b. Detroit, Feb. 22, 1951; d. Leroy Byron Harris Jr. and Josiebell (Richards) Harris Aaron; m. Abner McWhorter II, Mar. 15, 1969 (div. Aug. 1974); 1 child, Abner III. BA, Wayne State U., 1988; cert., SBA, Detroit, 1978; cert. in sound engring. Detroit Rec. Inst., Warren, Mich., 1982. Directory asst. Mich. Bell Telephone Co., Detroit, 1969; quality control clk. Chevrolet Gear & Axle, Detroit, 1971-74; circulation clk. Wayne County Community Coll., Detroit, 1977-85, mem. library standing com. and open house com., 1983-84; pres. Galactic Concepts & Designs, Detroit, 1977-88, cons., 1983—; gen. ptnr., mgr. S.M.J. Corridor Devel., Detroit, 1982—, hist. researcher, 1982; del. Small Bus. Conf., 1981; ad-hoc mem. Minority Tech. Council, 1981-82; elected alt. Mich. del. White House Conf. on Small Bus., Washington, 1985-86. Author, editor Creative Dilemma newsletter, 1985—. Co-patentee cup holding apparatus. Vol. counselor Barat House/March of Dimes, Detroit, 1977; active Concerned Citizens Cass Corridor, Detroit, 1982-87, Cass Corridor Citizen's Patrol, Detroit, 1983-84; pres. Wayne County chpt. MADD, Mich., 1987-88; apptd. citizen review com., 1988—; mem. adv. bd. Neighborhood Family Initiative, Southeastern Community Found.; pres. Am. Res. Tng. Sys., Inc., 1990—; lectr., cons. Recipient Hist. Landmark award Dept. Interior, 1983, cert. appreciation Tri-County Substance Abuse Awareness Com., 1984. Mem. Inventors Council Mich. (bd. dirs. 1985-88), Black Women in Bus. (sec. 1984-85), Greater Detroit C. of C., South Cass Bus. Assn. (v.p. 1987-88, pres. 1988-89), Detroit Econ. Club. Democrat. Methodist. Avocations: inventing; writing, readaptive furniture design, photography, video production. Office: SMJ Corridor Devel Co 453 Myrtle St Ste 102 Detroit MI 48201-2311

MCWILLIAM, JOANNE ELIZABETH, religion educator; b. Toronto, Ont., Can., Dec. 10, 1928; d. Cecil Edward and Edna Viola (Archer) McW.; children, Leslie Mary Giroday, Elizabeth McEwen, Sean Dewart, Colin Dewart; m. C. Peter Slater, June 6, 1987. BA, U. Toronto, 1951, MA, 1953; MA, U. St. Michael's, Toronto, 1966, PhD, 1968. Asst. prof. religious studies U. Toronto, 1968-74, assoc. prof., 1974-87, prof., 1987, chairperson dept. religious studies, 1990-92, 93-94; Mary Crooke Hoffman prof. of Dogmatic Theology The Gen. Theol. Sem., N.Y.C, 1994—. Author: The Theology of Grace of Theodore of Mopsuestia, 1971, Death and Resurrection in the Fathers, 1986; editor: Augustine: Rhetor to Theologian, 1991, Toronto Jour. Theology. Mem. Can. Soc. for Patristic Studies (pres. 1987—), Conf. Anglican Theologians (pres. 1990—), Can. Soc. for the Study of Religion, Can. Theol. Soc., Am. Theol. Soc., Am. Acad. Religion. Anglican. Home: 59 Duggan Ave, Toronto, ON Canada M4V 1Y1 Office: The Gen Theol Sem 175 9th Ave New York NY 10011-4977

MCWILLIAMS, BETTY JANE, science administrator, communication disorders educator, researcher; d. Harry J. and Martha (McClure) McW. B.S., Ohio State U., 1949; M.S., U. Pitts., 1950, Ph.D., 1953. Speech pathologist Ohio County Easter Seal Soc., Wheeling, W.Va., 1950-51; instr. U. Pitts., 1951-54, asst. prof., 1954-59, assoc. prof, 1959-67, prof., 1967-91, prof. emeritus, 1991—, dir. cleft palate craniofacial ctr., 1969-91, dir. emeritus, 1993—; vis. prof. U. N.C., Chapel Hill, 1962, Howard U., Washington, 1977-78; cons. Western Pa. Hosp., Pitts., 1972-91, Montefiore Hosp., N.Y.C., 1975-87, Walter Reed Army Hosp., Washington, 1984-87; mem. Pa. Acad. Com. on Tech. Devel., Harrisburg, 1984-87; mem. standards and peer rev. com. Pa. Fedn. of Cleft Palate Clinics, 1985-87. Sr. author: Cleft Palate Speech, 1984, revised edit., 1990; contbr. articles to profl. jours. Recipient Herbert Cooper Meml. award Cooper Clinic, 1979, award of recognition Pa. Acad. Dentistry for Children, 1989, award of recognition Pa. Dental Soc., 1991. Fellow Am. Speech, Lang. and Hearing Assn. (cert. clin. competence, Frank R. Kleffner Career award 1995), Am. Coll. Dentists; mem. APA, Am. Cleft Palate Craniofacial Assn. (pres. 1965, asst. sec. gen. 1st internat. congress 1969, editor 1975-81, pres. Found. 1982-83, svc. award 1975, Honors of Assn. 1987), Pa. Fedn. Cleft Palate Clinics (pres. 1980-82, 89-90, legis. con.

1991-94). Avocations: antiques; needlework; cooking; reading. Home and Office: 512 Bigham Rd Pittsburgh PA 15211-1412

MCWILLIAMS, BRUCE WAYNE, marketing professional; b. Vancouver, B.C., Can., Sept. 23, 1932; came to U.S., 1975; s. Lloyd and Mamie (Bateman) McW.; m. Heather Oxland, Nov. 15, 1957 (div.); children: Sandra, Roderick, Anna; m. Sheila Albin, June 23, 1990. Student, U. B.C., Vancouver, 1950-54. Advt. asst. Brit. Petroleum Co., London, 1957-62; asst. dir. B.C. Govt. Travel Bur., 1962-64; mng. dir. HCF-Ergon Advt., Athens, Greece, 1964-67; dir. HCF-Internat., London, 1967-70; dir. pub. relations Occidental Internat. Oil Inc., Paris and London, 1970-75; dir. pub. affairs Occidental Petroleum Corp., Los Angeles, 1975-80; dir. pub. relations and advt. Comark, Newport Beach, Calif., 1980-81; ptnr. Chester Burger & Co. Inc., N.Y.C., 1981-83; sr. v.p. Ogilvy & Mather PR, Chgo., 1983-85; sr. corp. relations officer Internat. Fin. Corp., 1985-88; pres. The McWilliams Co., 1988-90; mktg. dir. Nixon, Hargrave, Devans & Doyle, Rochester, N.Y., 1990-92, Powell, Goldstein, Frazer & Murphy, Washington, 1993—. Mem. Pub. Relations Soc. Am. Club: Naval and Mil. (London).

MCWILLIAMS, C. PAUL, JR., engineering executive; b. Louisville, June 4, 1931; s. Cleo Paul and Audrey Dora (Hale) McW.; m. Barbara Ann Sparks, Feb. 22, 1950 (div. 1962); children: Bruce Kevin, Craig Tinsley; m. Barbara Ann Heintz, Apr. 25, 1980; 1 stepchild, Kimberly Jean Moorhouse Swigert. B Chem. Engring., U. Louisville, 1954, M Engring., 1972. Lic. profl. engr., N.Y., N.C. Sr. process devel. engr. Olin Mathieson Chem. Corp., Brandenburg, Ky., 1958-66, Rochester, N.Y., 1958-66; sr. chem. engr. GTE Sylvania, Seneca Falls, N.Y., 1966-74, Eastman Kodak Co., Rochester, 1974-81; prin., treas. Flint & Sherburne Assocs., P.C., Rochester, 1981-89; project engr. Roy F. Weston, Inc., Rochester, 1989-92; engring. mgr. ECCO, Inc. (Environ. Cons. Co., Inc.), Buffalo, 1992-94; pres. ECCO Engring., Buffalo, 1993-94; staff engr. Environ. Products & Svcs., Inc., Rochester, N.Y., 1994—; cons. water tech. Water Tech. Corp., Tonawanda, N.Y., 1973-76; product rsch. panel Chem. Engring. Mag., 1982-83. Author: Waste Disposal Manual, 1976. Life mem. Rep. Presdl. Task Force, Webster, N.Y., 1986—; mem. Rep. Nat. Com., Webster, 1991-92. 1st lt. USAF, 1954-58, ret. lt. col. USAF Res., 1982. Decorated Meritorious Svc. medal. Mem. NSPE, AIChE, Soc. Am. Mil. Engrs., Res. Officers Assn. (life), Monroe Profl. Engrs. Soc. (environ. com. 1972-75, chmn. 1973-75, bd. dirs. 1982-84, program chmn. 1984), Cons. Engrs. Coun. N.Y. State (program chmn. Rochester chpt. 1986-87, sec. 1987-88, treas. 1989). Episcopalian. Achievements include replacing boiler feedwater regulators, related instrumentation and control systems and blowdown at a N.Y. State U. facility; system design for dry fabric dust collectors to remove fly ash from coal-fired boilers' flue gas. Home: 1132 Woodbridge Ln Webster NY 14580-8709 Office: Environ Products & Svcs Inc 230 Mckee Rd Rochester NY 14611-2013

MCWILLIAMS, DAVID BRIAN, pastor; b. Macon, Ga., Jan. 14, 1956; m. Merry Vicky Flesher, Dec. 13, 1974; 1 child, Patrick Evans. BA cum laude, Mercer U., 1981; MA in Religion, Westminster Theol. Sem., 1983, MDiv, 1984. Ordained min. Presbyn. Ch., 1984. Min. Trinity Presbyn. Ch., Elberton, Ga., 1984-87; asst. min. Covenant Presbyn. Ch., Lakeland, Fla., 1987-88; assoc. min. Covenant Presbyn. Ch., Lakeland, 1988-91, sr. min., 1989-91, 1991—; adj. prof. practical theology John Knox Theol. Sem., Ft. Lauderdale, Fla., 1993-94, 95-96; mem., chmn. of candidates and credentials com. in two Presbyteries, 1988—; chmn. com. debate Dr. Richard Gaffin and Wayne Grudem, 1990. Home: 5853 Colony Place Dr Lakeland FL 33813

MCWILLIAMS, EDWIN JOSEPH, banker; b. Spokane, Washington, Aug. 11, 1919; s. Frank S. and Alice (Conlan) McW.; m. Betty J. Galbreath, Aug. 15, 1944; children: Lawrence, Barbara Anne, Marijoan, Peter. Student, U. Notre Dame, 1937-38, Marquette U., 1938-40; B.S. in Bus. Adminstrn, Gonzaga U., 1943. With Fidelity Mutual Savings Bank, Spokane, 1940-82; exec. v.p. Fidelity Mutual Savings Bank, 1955-58, pres., 1958-82; pres. Fidelity Service Corp., 1983-87; mem. adv. council Wash. State Dept. Commerce and Econ. Devel., 1977-80; U.S. del. Internat. Savs. Bank Inst., 1975, 76, 79; vice chair, dir. NW Edn. Loan Assn; pres., dir. Heritage Funeral Home. Pres. United Crusade Spokane County, 1966; past pres., mem. exec. bd. Inland Empire coun., region 11 exec. com. Boy Scouts Am.; past pres. Spokane Unltd.; mem. adv. coun. Sch. Bus., Gonzaga U.; bd. dirs., mem. exec. com. Expo '74 World's Fair; past mem. bd. regents Ft. Wright Coll., Spokane; past bd. dirs. Sacred Heart Med. Ctr.; past bd. regents Wash. State U.; bd. dirs. Fairmont Meml. Assn. Served to lt. (j.g.) USNR, 1943-45. Mem. Nat. Assn. Mut. Savs. Banks (chmn. 1976-77), Mut. Savs. Banks Assn. State of Wash. (pres. 1980), Am. Savs. and Loan Inst. (past gov. dist. XI), Spokane C. of C. (pres. 1974-75). Roman Catholic. Clubs: Rotary of Spokane, K.C. Home: 1717 S Upper Terrace Rd Spokane WA 99203-3558

MCWILLIAMS, JOHN LAWRENCE, III, lawyer; b. Phila., Dec. 21, 1943; s. John Lawrence Jr. and Elizabeth Dolores (Chevalier) McW.; m. Paula Ann Root, July 19, 1969 (dec.); children: John Lawrence, IV, Robert Root, Anne Elizabeth, David Stanford, Peter Farrell; m. Kathleen Nolan Pradella, Apr. 3, 1993. BS, St. Joseph's U., 1965; JD, Seton Hall U., 1969. Bar: N.J. 1969, N.Y. 1975, U.S. Supreme Ct. 1975, Fla. 1977. Trial atty. regional office SEC, N.Y.C., 1969-72; assoc. Mudge Rose Guthrie & Alexander, N.Y.C., 1972-77; mem. Freeman, Richardson, Watson & Kelly, P.A., Jacksonville, Fla., 1977-89, chmn., pres., 1984-89, ptnr. Squire, Sanders & Dempsey, 1989—; apptd. spl. asst. to U.S. atty. Dist. of N.J., 1971. Trustee Mcpl. Service Dist. Ponte Vedra Beach, 1981-85, chmn. bd. trustees, 1984-85; treas. Ponte Vedra Cmty. Assn., 1980-82; mem. Leadership Jacksonville, 1981, mem. steering com., 1982; dir. Jacksonville Country Day Sch., 1985-87; pres. Jacksonville Beaches Ponte Vedra Unit Am. Cancer Soc., 1988-90. Mem. ABA, Nat. Assn. Bond Lawyers, Fla. Bar, Jacksonville C. of C. Republican. Roman Catholic. Clubs: Ponte Vedra, Sawgrass, River. Home: 3040 Timberlake Pt Ponte Vedra Beach FL 32082-3726 Office: Squire Sanders & Dempsey One Enterprise Ctr 225 Water St Ste 2100 Jacksonville FL 32202-5154

MCWILLIAMS, JOHN MICHAEL, lawyer; b. Annapolis, Md., Aug. 17, 1939; s. William J. and Helen (Disharon) McW.; m. Frances Edelen McCabe, May 30, 1970; children: M. Edelen, J. Michael, James McC. B.S., Georgetown U., 1964; LL.B., U. Md., 1967; LLD (hon.), U. Balt., 1993. Bar: Md. 1967, U.S. Supreme Ct. 1970, U.S. Ct. Internat. Trade 1991, U.S. Ct. Mil. Appeals 1992. Law clk. Chief Judge Roszel C. Thomsen, U.S. Dist. Ct. Md., 1967-68; assoc. Piper and Marbury, Balt., 1968-69; asst. atty. gen. State of Md., 1969-76; gen. counsel Md. Dept. Transp., 1971-76; sr. ptnr. Tydings and Rosenberg, Balt., 1977—; permanent mem. 4th Cir. Jud. Conf.; mem. panel of disting. neutrals CPR Inst. for Dispute Resolution, 1994—. Asst. editor Law Rev., U. Md., 1967. Chmn. Md. adv. coun. to Nat. Legal Svcs. Corp., 1975-78; mem. Gov.'s Commn. to Revise Annotated Code of Md., 1973-78; transition dir. Md. Gov.-Elect Harry Hughes, 1978-79; mem. Md. Indsl. Devel. Financing Authority, 1980; mem. Greater Balt. Com., 1979-94; mem. exec. com. Econ. Devel. Coun. Greater Balt., 1979-83; vice chmn. bd. Washington/Balt. Regional Assn., 1980-83; mem. Md. Econ. and Cmty. Devel. Adv. Commn., 1983-87; chmn. bd. Md. Econ. Devel. Corp., 1984-89. Served to 1st lt. U.S. Army, 1958-60. Fellow Am. Bar Found. (bd. dirs. 1986-88, 91-93), Md. Bar Found. (dir. 1980-82); mem. ABA (pres. 1992-93, mem. ho. of dels. 1976—, chmn. 1986-88; chmn. bd. dir. 1976-86, bd. editors jour. 1986-88, 91-93), Md. Bar Assn. (pres. 1981-82), Nat. Conf. Bar Pres. (exec. council 1982-85), Bar Assn. Balt. City, Am. Law Inst., Am. Judicature Soc. (dir. 1974-81, exec. com. 1975-77), Am. Acad. Jud. Edn. (dir. 1977), Am. Arbitration Assn. (various panels), Md. Law Rev. (trustee 1980-83), Md. Inst. Continuing Edn. Lawyers (trustee 1980-83), Inst. Internat. Bus. Law and Practice (corr.), Center Club, Md. Club, Rule Day Club. Democrat. Roman Catholic. Home: 3 Merryman Ct Baltimore MD 21210-2815 Office: 26th Fl 100 E Pratt St Fl 26 Baltimore MD 21202-1009

MCWILLIAMS, MARGARET ANN, home economics educator, author; b. Osage, Iowa, May 26, 1929; d. Alvin Randall and Mildred Irene (Lane) Edgar; children: Roger, Kathleen. BS, Iowa State U., 1951, MS, 1953; PhD, Oreg. State U., 1968. Registered dietitian. Asst. prof. home econs. Calif. State U., L.A., 1961-66, assoc. prof., 1966-68, prof., 1968-92, prof. emeritus, 1992—, chmn. dept., 1968-76; pres. Plycon Press, 1978—. Author: Food Fundamentals, 1966, 6th edit., 1995, Nutrition for the Growing Years, 1967, 5th edit., 1993, Experimental Foods Laboratory Manual, 1977, 4th edit., 1994, (with L. Kotschevar) Understanding Food, 1969, Illustrated Guide to Food Preparation, 1970, 7th edit., 1995, (with L. Davis) Food for You, 1971, 2d edit., 1976, The Meatless Cookbook, 1973, (with F. Stare) Living Nutrition, 1973, 4th edit., 1984, Nutrition for Good Health, 1974, 2d edit., 1982, (with H. Paine) Modern Food Preservation, Fundamentals of Meal Management, 1978, 2d edit., 1993, Foods: Experimental Perspectives, 1989, 2d edit., 1993. Chmn. bd. Beach Cities Symphony, 1991-94. Recipient Alumni Centennial award Iowa State U., 1971, Profl. Achievement award, 1977; Phi Upsilon Omicron Nat. Founders fellow, 1964; Home Economist in Bus. Nat. Found. fellow, 1967; Outstanding Prof. award Calif. State U., 1976. Mem. Am. Dietetic Assn., Inst. Food Technologists, Phi Kappa Phi, Phi Upsilon Omicron, Omicron Nu, Iota Sigma Pi, Sigma Delta Epsilon, Sigma Alpha Iota. Home: PO Box 220 Redondo Beach CA 90277-0220

MCWILLIAMS, MARY ANN, school administrator; b. Shreveport, La., July 5, 1944; d. Joseph Vivian and Helen Claire (McKinney) McW. BS, Northwestern State U., 1966; MEd, U. North Tex., 1989. Cert. composite sci., Tex., adminstrn. cert. Tchr. biology Willapa Valley Schs., Menlo, Wash., 1966-67; med. technologist Meth. Hosp., Houston, 1967-68; tchr. biology Caddo Parish Schs., Shreveport, 1968-74, 77-79; advt. account exec. Sta. KCOZ Radio, Shreveport, 1979-80; coord. tng./documentation Tri-State Computer Svcs., Shreveport, 1980-83; tchr. biology, team leader Plano (Tex.) Ind. Sch. Dist., 1983-94, environ. studies coord., coord. for environ. outdoor sch. camp program, 1994—, coord. for environ. outdoor sch. camp program, 1994—; dir. Holifield Sci. Learning Ctr., Plano, 1994—; chmn. ednl. improvement coun. Plano Ind. Sch. Dist., 1990-94; tchr. trainer Jason V Project, Dallas, 1993-94; dir. Environ. Studies Camp, Plano, 1994—. Mem. Dallas Mus. of Art, 1987—; bd. dirs. Camp Classen, Oklahoma City YMCA, 1996. Named Jane Goodall Environ Educator of Yr., Jane Goodall Inst. and Boreal Labs., Dallas, 1993, one of Outstanding Young Women of Am., 1980. Mem. ASCD, NEA, Nat. Sci. Tchrs. Assn., Sci. Tchrs. of Tex., Jane Goodall Inst. Roots and Shoots. Roman Catholic. Avocations: travel, water sports, walking/hiking, birding, reading. Office: Plano Ind Sch Sys 2700 W 15th St Plano TX 75075-7524

MCWILLIAMS, MICHAEL G., writer, television critic; b. Detroit, Aug. 28, 1952; s. Henry and Mary (Toarmina) McW. BA, Wayne State U., 1975; MFA, Columbia U., 1978. Free-lance writer Detroit News, Monthly Detroit mag., 1979-82, Village Voice, Rolling Stone, TV Guide, Advt. Age, N.Y. Daily News, L.A. Herald Examiner, N.Y.C., 1982-87; TV critic The Detroit News, 1988—. Author: TV Sirens, 1987, (with others) The Premiere Guide to Movies on Video, 1991. Recipient Assn. of Sunday and Feature Editors award, 1st pl. Arts Criticism, 1992. Mem. Phi Beta Kappa. Avocations: TV, movies, theater, music. Office: Detroit News 615 W Lafayette Blvd Detroit MI 48226-3124

MCWILLIAMS, MIKE C., lawyer; b. Dallas, Nov. 10, 1948; s. Earl Dewitt and Mary Louise (Campbell) McW.; m. Sally Swatzell, Sept. 1, 1973; children: Michael, Matthew. BBA in Fin., U. Tex., 1969, JD, 1973. Bar: Tex. 1973. Assoc. Elliott, Meer, Vetter, Denton & Bates, Dallas, 1973-78; ptnr. Denton & Generis, Dallas, 1978-80, Moore & Peterson, P.C., Dallas, 1980-89, Winstead, Sechrest & Minick, Dallas, 1989—. Editor: Texas International Law Journal, 1972-73. Mem. ABA, Tex. State Bar Assn., Dallas Bar Assn., Phi Delta Phi, Beta Gamma Sigma. Office: Winstead Sechrest & Minick 5400 Renaissance Tower 1201 Elm St Dallas TX 75270

MCWILLIAMS, PETER, writer; b. Detroit, Aug. 5, 1949; s. henry G. and Mary McW. Student, Ea. Mich. U., Maharishi Internat. U. co-founder Three Rivers Pr.; pub. Versemonger Pr., Lion Pr.; owner Leo Pr. Author: (with Denise Denniston) The TM Book: How to Enjoy the Rest of Your Life, 1975, (with Melba Colgrove and Harold Bloomfield) How to Survive the Loss of a Love: 58 Things to Do When There Is Nothing to Be Done, 1976, revised edit., 1991, You Can't Afford the Luxury of a Negative Thought: A Book for People with Any Life-Threatening Illness-Including Life, 1988, (with Colgrove and Bloomfield) Surviving, Healing, and Growing: The How to Survive the Loss of a Love Workbook, 1991, LIFE 101: Everything We Wish We Had Learned About Life in School - But Didn't, 1991, Focus on the Positive: The You Can't Afford the Luxury of a Negative Thought Workbook, 1991, The Portable LIFE 101: 179 Essential Lessons, 1992, DO IT! Let's Get Off Our Buts, 1992, Portraits: A Book of Photographs by Peter McWilliams, 1992, WEALTH 101: Wealth Is Much More Than Money, 1993, We Give To Love: Giving Is Such a Selfish Thing, 1993, The Portable DO IT!: 172 Essential Excerpts Plus 190 Quotations, 1993, Ain't Nobody's Business If You Do: The Absurdity of Consensual Crimes in a Free Society, 1993, LIFE 102: What to Do When Your Guru Sues You, 1994, (with Bloomfield) How to Heal Depression, 1994, What Jesus and the Bible Really Said about Drugs, Sex, Gays, Gambling, Prostitution, Alternative Healing, Assisted Suicide and Other Consensual "Sins", 1994, That Book About Drugs, 1995, LOVE 101: To Love Oneself Is the Beginning of a Lifelong Romance, 1995; (poetry) Come Love with Me and Be My Life, 1967, I Have Loved, 1968, For Lovers and No Others, 1968, I Love Therefore I Am, 1969, The Hard Stuff: Love, 1969, Evolving at the Speed of Love, 1971, Surviving the Loss of a Love, 1971, Love: An Experience Of, 1972, Love and All the Other Verbs of Life, 1973, Love Is Yes, 1973, This Longing May Shorten My Life, 1974, Catch Me With Your Smile, 1976, I Marry You Because, 1993. Office: Prelude Press 8159 Santa Monica Blvd Los Angeles CA 90046-4912

MCWILLIAMS, ROBERT HUGH, federal judge; b. Salina, Kans., Apr. 27, 1916; s. Robert Hugh and Laura (Nicholson) McW.; m. Catherine Ann Cooper, Nov. 4, 1942 (dec.); 1 son, Edward Cooper; m. Joan Harcourt, Mar. 8, 1986. A.B., U. Denver, 1938, LL.B., 1941. Bar: Colo. bar 1941. Colo. dist. judge Denver, 1952-60; justice Colo. Supreme Ct., 1961-68, chief justice, 1969-70; judge U.S. Ct. Appeals (10th cir.), Denver, 1970—. Served with AUS, World War II. Mem. Phi Beta Kappa, Omicron Delta Kappa, Phi Delta Phi, Kappa Sigma. Republican. Episcopalian. Home: 137 Jersey St Denver CO 00220 Office: Byron White US Courthouse 1823 Stout St Rm 216 Denver CO 80257

MCWILLIAMS, ROGER DEAN, physicist, educator; b. Ames, Iowa, Aug. 18, 1954; s. Donald Arthur and Margaret Ann (Edgar) McW.; m. Carol Lee Carter, Sept. 7, 1985; children: Alice Louise, Corinne Lee. BA, U. Calif., Irvine, 1975; PhD, Princeton U., 1980. Rsch. asst. Princeton (N.J.) U., 1975-80; asst. prof. in physics U. Calif., Irvine, 1980-87, assoc. prof., 1987-91, prof., 1991—, acting dean undergrad. studies, 1994-95, cons., expert witness for physics and law, 1983—, cons., expert witness for physics in sports, 1988—. Mem. Am. Phys. Soc., Am. Geophys. Union, Phi Beta Kappa, Sigma Xi. Office: U Calif Physics Irvine CA 92717

MEACHAM, CHARLES HARDING, government official; b. Newman, Calif., Sept. 21, 1925; s. Vernon A. and Sara (Paulsen) M.; m. June Lorraine Yunker, June 22, 1946; children—Charles Paulsen, Bruce Herbert. B.S., Utah State U., 1950. Biologist Calif. Dept. Fish and Game, 1950-56, Alaska Dept. Fisheries, 1956-59; regional supr. regions II and III Alaska Dept. Fish and Game, 1959-68; dir. internat. fisheries Office Gov. Alaska, 1968-69; commr. U.S. Fish and Wildlife Service, Dept. Interior, 1969-70, dep. asst. sec. for fish and wildlife, pks. and marine resources, commr. Internat. North Pacific Fisheries Commn. and Gt. Lakes Fishery Commn., 1969-70, commr. Internat. Pacific Salmon Fisheries Commn., 1969-70, commr. Great Lakes Fishery Commn., 1969-70; spl. asst. to area dir. U.S. Fish and Wildlife Service, Dept. Interior, Alaska, 1971-74; dir. internat. affairs Office of Gov., Juneau, Alaska, 1975-80; pres. Meacham & Assocs., Anchorage, 1980—; dep. commr. U.S. North Pacific Fur Seal Commn.; mem. Pacific and North Pacific Fisheries Mgmt. Councils, 1976-81; chmn. nat. park system adv. bd. U.S. Dept. Interior. Bd. dir. Resource Devel. Coun. for Alaska. With USMCR, 1943-46. Mem. Am. Fisheries Soc., Wildlife Soc., Pacific Fisheries Biologists, Internat. Assn. Game, Fish and Conservation Commrs., Ducks Unlimited, Alaska Miners Assn., Am. Legion. Club: Elks. Address: PO Box 428 Sequim WA 98382-0428

MEACHAM, CHARLES P., president, capital consulting; b. Susanville, Calif., Apr. 29, 1947; m. Charlene D. Heriot, 1969; 3 children. BS, Humboldt State U., 1969, MS in Fisheries, 1971. Comml. fisherman Bristol Bay, Alaska, 1963-66; with Bumble Bee Seafoods, Bristol Bay, S.E. Alaska, 1967-69; fisheries cons. Winzler & Kelly Engring., Eureka, Calif., 1970; seafood insp. U.S. Army, Ft. Richardson, Alaska, 1971-74; staff biologist Alaska Dept. of Fish and Game, Juneau, Alaska, 1974-75; rsch. biologist Artic Char investigations Alaska Dept. of Fish and Game, Dillingham, Alaska, 1975-77; Bristol Bay rsch. project leader Alaska Dept. of Fish and Game, Anchorage, 1978-81, regional rsch. supr., 1981-89, mgr. fisher program Exxon Valdez oil spill impact assessment, 1990-91; dep. commr. Alaska Dept. of Fish and Game, Juneau, 1991-95; pres. Capital Consulting, 1995—; affiliate faculty U. Alaska, 1983-87; mem. Bering Sea/Aleutians plan team N. Pacific Fisheries Mgmt. Coun., 1989, Alaska Regional Marine Rsch. Bd., 1992—, Pacific Fisheries Mgmt. Coun., 1991-95; commr. Pacific States Marine Fisheries Commn., 1991-95; presdl. appt. as commr. Pacific Salmon Commn., 1991-95. Mem. Mayor's Task Force on Fisheries, Anchorage, 1988-89, Alaska Tourism Coordinating Commn., 1992—; mem. rev. team Alaska Sci. & Tech. Found., 1989; alt. mem. Exxon Valdez Oil Spill Trustee Coun., 1992-95. Mem. NAS, OSB (fisheries com., 1992, 95), Am. Fisheries Soc. (life, v.p. Alaska chpt. 1975, pres. elect 1977, pres. 1978), Am. Inst. of Fishery Rsch. Biologists. Home: 533 Main St Juneau AK 99801-1153

MEACHAM, STANDISH, historian, educator; b. Cin., Mar. 12, 1932; s. Standish and Eleanor (Rapp) M.; m. Sarah Shartle, Aug. 24, 1957 (div. 1993); children: Edith, Louisa, Samuel. B.A., Yale U., 1954; Ph.D., Harvard U., 1961. Asst. prof. history Harvard U., 1962-67; mem. faculty U. Tex., Austin, 1967—; prof. history U. Tex., 1970—, chmn. dept. history, 1969-72, 84-89, dean Coll. Liberal Arts, 1989-92. Author: Henry Thornton of Clapham, 1964, Lord Bishop: The Life of Samuel Wilberforce, 1970, A Life Apart, 1977, (with R. Flukinger and Larry Schaaf) Paul Martin, Victorian Photographer, 1977, (with E. M. Burns and Robert Lerner) Western Civilizations, 12th edit., 1993, Toynbee Hall and Social Reform, 1987; editor: (Edward Bulwer) England and the English, 1970. Trustee Brooks Sch., North Andover, Mass., 1983—; dir. Live Oak Fund for Change, 1992, Planned Parenthood of Austin, 1993—, Tex. Low Income Housing Info. Svc., 1996—. Am. Council Learned Socs. fellow, 1965-66, 79-80; Guggenheim Found. fellow, 1972-73. Office: U Tex Garrison Hall 101 Austin TX 78712-1163

MEACHAM, WILLIAM FELAND, neurological surgeon, educator; b. Washington, Dec. 12, 1913; s. Marion H. and Mamie (Henderson) M.; m. Alice Marie Mathews, June 14, 1944; children: William Feland, Patrick, Barbara, Robert. B.S., Western Ky. State Coll., 1936; M.D., Vanderbilt U., 1940. Diplomate: Am. Bd. Surgery, Am. Bd. Neurol. Surgery. Intern surgery Vanderbilt U. Hosp., Nashville, 1940-41; asst. resident surgery Vanderbilt U. Hosp., 1941-43, resident surgeon, 1943-44, asst. vis. surgeon, 1944; asso. vis. surgeon Out-Patient Service, 1944; asst. in surgery Vanderbilt U. Sch. Medicine, 1941-43, instr. surgery, 1943-44, William Henry Howe fellow in neurol. surgery, 1945-47, asst. clin. prof. surgery, 1947-50, assoc. clin. prof. surgery, 1950-53, assoc. prof. neurol. surgery, 1953-54, prof. neurol. surgery, 1954-59, clin. prof. neurol. surgery, 1959-85, prof. emeritus clin. neurosurgery, 1985—; vol. asst. Montreal Neurol. Inst., 1947; asst. clin. prof. neurol. surgery Meharry Med. Sch., 1947-50, clin. prof., 1950—; attending neurosurgeon Nashville Gen., St. Thomas, Mid-State Bapt. hosps., Riverside and Madison Sanitaria; cons. in neurosurgery Thayer Vets. Hosp., Murfreesboro (Tenn.) Vets. Hosp., Jr. League Home for Crippled Children.; Chmn. Study Commn. on Stroke, Tenn. Mid South Regional Med. Program, 1968. Mem. Am. Acad. Neurol. Surgery, ACS (chmn. adv. council for neurol. surgery 1959-63, bd. govs. 1964- 66, bd. regents 1966-75, 2d v.p. 1982-83), AMA, Nashville Acad. Medicine (past pres., chmn. bd. dirs.), Nashville Surg. Soc. (past pres.), Am. Surg. Assn., Neurosurg. Soc. Am. (past pres., mem. exec. council), Neurosurg. Travel Club, Soc. Neurol. Surgeons (pres. 1971), Soc. Univ. Surgeons, Southeastern Surg. Congress, So. Med. Assn., So. Neurosurg. Soc. (past pres.), Tenn. Med. Assn., Am. Assn. Neurol. Surgeons (dir., past sec., past treas., pres. 1972), Am. Cancer Soc. (dir.), Sigma Xi, Alpha Omega Alpha. Methodist. Home: 3513 Woodmont Blvd Nashville TN 37215-1427 Office: 709 St Thomas Med Pla 4230 Harding Rd Nashville TN 37205-2013

MEACHIN, DAVID JAMES PERCY, investment banker; b. Teignmouth, Devon, Eng., Jan. 1, 1941; came to U.S., 1969; s. James Alfred and Ena Annie Meachin; m. Barbara Marshall Maxwell, Sept. 25, 1971; children: Jonathan J.M., Philip D.M. BS in Physical Sci., U. Natal, Republic South Africa, 1960; BSChemE, U. Cape Town, Republic South Africa, 1963; MS in Petroleum Engring., French Petroleum Inst., Paris, 1965; diploma in Indsl. Mgmt., Cambridge (Eng.) U., 1966; MBA with distinction, Harvard U., 1971. Project engr. Humphreys and Glasgow Ltd., London, 1966-69; 2d v.p. investment banking Smith Barney and Co. Inc., N.Y.C. and Tokyo, 1971-75; v.p., gen. mgr. internat. corp. fin. Salomon Bros., N.Y.C. and London, 1975-81; mng. dir. investment banking Merrill Lynch Capital Markets, N.Y.C., 1981-91; chmn., CEO, Cross Border Enterprises L.L.C., 1991—. Dir. Spartek Emerging Opportunities of India Fund; dir., past chmn. British Am. Ednl. Found.; elder Brick Presbyn. Ch., N.Y.C., 1988—; bd. dirs., vice-chmn. U. Cape Town Found., N.Y.C., 1985—; mem. UN Assn. Coun. of Fellows. Mem. Misquamicut Club (bd. govs.), Watch Hill Yacht Club, Hurlingham Club, United Oxford and Cambridge Club, Harvard Club, Union Club, Sky Club. Avocations: sailing, golf, tennis, squash. Home: 1105 Park Ave New York NY 10128-1200 Office: Cross Border Enterprises LLC 441 Lexington Ave New York NY 10017-3910

MEAD, BEVERLEY TUPPER, physician, educator; b. New Orleans, Jan. 22, 1923; s. Harold Tupper and Helen Edith (Hunt) M.; m. Thelma Ruth Cottingham, June 8, 1947. B.S., U. S.C., 1943; M.D., Med. Coll. S.C., 1947; M.S., U. Utah, 1958. Intern Detroit Receiving Hosp., 1947-48, resident, 1948-51; asst. prof. U. Utah, 1954-61; assoc. prof. U. Ky., 1961-65; prof. psychiatry and behavioral sci. Creighton U. Sch. Medicine, Omaha, 1965—; chmn. dept. Creighton U. Sch. Medicine, 1965-77, assoc. dean for acad. and faculty affairs, 1980-88. *The approval of others does not concern me as much as my approval of myself.*

MEAD, BEVERLY MIRIUM ANDERSON, author, educator; b. St. Paul, May 29, 1925; d. Martin and Anna Mae (Oshanyk) Anderson; m. Jerome Morton Nemiro, Feb. 10, 1951 (div. May 1975); children: Guy Samuel, Lee Anna, Dee Martin; m. William Isaac Mead, Aug. 8, 1992. Student Reed Coll., 1943-44; BA, U. Colo., 1947; postgrad., U. Denver. Tchr., Seattle Pub. Schs., 1945-46; fashion coord., dir. Denver Dry Goods Co., 1948-51; fashion model, Denver, 1951-58, 78—; fashion dir. Denver Market Week Assn., 1952-53; free-lance writer, Denver, 1958—; moderator TV program Your Preschool Child, Denver, 1955-56; instr. writing and communications U. Colo. Denver Ctr., 1970—, U. Calif., San Diego, 1976-78, Met. State Coll., 1985; dir. pub. relations Fairmont Hotel, Denver, 1979-80; free lance fashion and TV model; author, co-author: The Complete Book of High Altitude Baking, 1961, Colorado a la Carte, 1963, Colorado a la Carte, Series II, 1966, (with Donna Hamilton) The High Altitude Cookbook, 1969, The Busy People's Cookbook, 1971 (Better Homes and Gardens Book Club selection 1971), Where to Eat in Colorado, 1967, Lunch Box Cookbook, 1965, Complete Book of High Altitude Baking, 1961, (under name Beverly Anderson) Single After 50, 1978, The New High Altitude Cookbook, 1980. Co-founder, pres. Jr. Symphony Guild, Denver, 1959-60; active Friends of Denver Libr., Opera Colo. Recipient Top Hand award Colo. Authors' League, 1969, 72, 79-82, 100 Best Best Books of Yr. award N.Y. Times, 1969, 71; named one of Colo.'s Women of Yr., Denver Post, 1964. Mem. Am. Soc. Journalists and Authors, Colo. Authors League (dir. 1969-79), Authors Guild, Authors League Am., Friends Denver Library, Rotary, Kappa Alpha Theta. Address: 23 Polo Club Dr Denver CO 80209-3309

MEAD, CARL DAVID, educator; b. Cadiz, Ohio, May 4, 1913; s. Carl David and Neva Eloine (Walker) M.; m. Lillian Martha Felton, Apr. 15, 1938; children: Susan, Nancy Mead Coates. Student, Washington and Jefferson Coll., 1932-34; B.S., Ohio State U., 1936, M.A., 1938, Ph.D., 1947. Instr. English Denison U., 1938-39, Ohio State U., 1946-47; faculty Mich. State U., 1948-81, prof. English, 1957-81, head dept., 1959-66; Fulbright lectr. Philippines, 1964; cons., chief univ. adv. group to U. Ryukyus, Okinawa, 1955-57. Author: Yankee Eloquence in the Middle West, 1951, (with others) Prentice-Hall Handbook for Writers, 1951, The American Scholar Today, 1970; Adv. editor: Dodd, Mead & Co, 1963-75; editor: Centennial Review, 1966-82. Served with AUS, 1943-46. Decorated Legion of Merit. Mem. MLA, Am. Studies Assn. Home: 1229 Glenmeadow Ln East Lansing MI 48823-2223

MEAD, CARVER ANDRESS, computer science educator; b. Bakersfield, Calif., May 1, 1934. B.S., Calif. Inst. Tech., 1956, M.S., 1957, Ph.D., 1960;

hon. doctorate, U. of Lund, 1987, U. So. Calif., 1991. Prof. Calif. Inst. Tech., Pasadena, 1957—, Gordon and Betty Moore prof. engring. and applied sci., 1980—; bd. dirs. Synaptics Inc., San Jose, Aptix Corp., San Jose. Author: Introduction to VLSI Systems, 1979 (Electronic Achievements award 1981, Harold Pender award 1984, John Price Wetherhill award 1985), Analog VLSI and Neural Systems, 1989. Recipient T.D. Callinan award Electrochem. Soc., 1971, Centennial medal IEEE, 1984, Harry Goode Meml. award Am. Fedn. Info. Processing Socs., Inc., 1985, award for Outstanding Rsch., INNS, 1992, Robert Dexter Conrad award USN, 1994. Fellow IEEE (John von Neumann medal 1996), Am. Phys. Soc., Franklin Inst. (life), Am. Acad. Arts and Scis.; mem. NAE, NAS, Royal Swedish Acad. Engring. Sci. (fgn.), Sigma Xi. Office: Calif Inst Tech Physics Computation MS 136-93 1201 E California Blvd Pasadena CA 91125-0001

MEAD, DANA GEORGE, diversified industrial manufacturing company executive; b. Cresco, Iowa, Feb. 22, 1936; s. George Francis and Evelyn Grace (Derr) M.; m. Nancy L. Cooper, Apr. 12, 1958; children: Dana George, Mark Cooper. B.S. (Disting. Cadet), U.S. Mil. Acad., 1957; Ph.D., M.I.T., 1967. Commd. 2d lt. U.S. Army, 1957, advanced through grades to col., 1974; service in W. Ger. and Vietnam; White House fellow, 1970-71; staff asst. to Pres. Nixon, 1970-72; assoc. dir., then dep. dir. Domestic Council, White House, 1972-74; permanent prof. social sci. dept., dep. head U.S. Mil. Acad., 1974-78; ret., 1978; v.p. human resources Internat. Paper Co., N.Y.C., 1978-81, v.p., group exec., 1981-87; sr. v.p. Internat. Paper Co., Purchase, 1987-89, exec. v.p., dir, 1989-92; pres., COO Tenneco, Inc., Houston, 1992-93, chmn., CEO, 1994—, also bd. dirs.; CEO, chmn. J.I. Case, Racine, Wis., 1992-94, chmn., 1994—; bd. dirs. Nat. Westminster Bancorp, Cummins Engine Co., Alco Standard, Baker Hughes Corp., Logistics Mgmt. Inst., Washington. Author articles on nat. security and domestic policy, business and manufacturing planning. Mem. Pres.'s Commn. on White House Fellowships, West Point Soc., N.Y., 1980—, pres., 1981-83; mem. White House Fellows Assn. and Found., 1981-82; bd. dirs. White House Fellows Found., 1978-83, pres. 1978; mem. MIT Vis. Com. Polit. Scis. Decorated Legion of Merit with oak leaf cluster, Bronze Star with oak leaf cluster, Meritorious Service medal, Air medal with 3 oak leaf clusters, Army Commendation medal, Presdl. Service badge, Combat Inf. badge; Vietnam Cross Gallantry with palm, silver and bronze stars. Mem. Nat. Assn. Mfg. (chmn. 1995-96), Coun. Fgn. Rels., Assn. Grads. West Point (trustee), Univ. Club, Met. Club (N.Y.), Houston Racquet Club, Houstonian Club. Republican. Home: 145 Radney Rd Houston TX 77024-7334 Office: Tenneco Inc PO Box 2511 Houston TX 77252-2511

MEAD, EDWARD MATHEWS, newspaper executive; b. Erie, Pa., Oct. 13, 1926; s. John James and Grace (Finerty) M.; m. Allene Steimer, Feb. 16, 1957; children: John James, Edward Mathews, Daniel Patrick. Student, U. N.C., 1945-46; B.A. in History, Princeton U., 1949. Trainee Trenton Times, 1949-50; night editor Erie Times, 1950-54, Sunday editor, 1954-56, asst. to pub., 1956-64, asst. pub., 1964-73, pres., 1973—, also co-pub., also treas., columnist, editor. Mem. Erie Conf. on Community Devel., 1971—, sec., 1980; bd. dirs. St. Vincent Hosp., from 1974, pres., 1980; bd. dirs. Villa Maria Coll., from 1977, pres., 1979. Served with USMC, 1945-46. Mem. Pa. Asso. Press (pres. 1977), Pa. Newspaper Pubs. Assn. (dir. from 1977). Roman Catholic. Office: Time Publishing Co. Times Sq W 12th & Sassafras Sts Erie PA 16534

MEAD, GILBERT D(UNBAR), geophysicist, lawyer; b. Madison, Wis., May 31, 1930; s. Stanton Witter and Dorothy Elizabeth (Williams) M.; m. Jaylee Montague, Nov. 18, 1968; children: Elizabeth, Diana, Stanton, Robert. BS, Yale U., 1952; PhD in Physics, U. Calif., Berkeley, 1962; JD, U. Md., 1991. Physicist theoretical div. NASA Goddard Space Flight Ctr., Greenbelt, Md., 1962-74, head geophysics br., 1974-79; geophysicist crustal dynamics project NASA Goddard Space Flight Ctr., 1979-87; bd. dirs., chmn. audit com., mem. nominating com. Consolidated Papers, Inc., Wisconsin Rapids, Wis., 1974—. Editor: (with W. Hess) Introduction to Space Science, 1968; contbr. numerous articles to profl. jours. Trustee Beloit Coll., 1976-87, ARena Stage, Washington, 1991—, Levine Sch. Music, Washington, 1996—. Recipient Outstanding Svc. award Goddard Space Flight Ctr., 1978, Washington Post award for disting. cmty. svc., 1996. Mem. Md. Bar, D.C. Bar. Home: 2700 Virginia Ave NW Apt 701 Washington DC 20037-1908

MEAD, JAMES MATTHEW, insurance company executive; b. Erie, Pa., June 10, 1945; s. James Leonard and Olga (Richter) M.; m. Rhoda Ginsburg, Sept. 2, 1967 (div. 1971); m. Elaine Margaret Lytle, Mar. 8, 1975. BS, Pa. State U., 1967, MA, 1970. Instr. bus. Pa. State U., Middletown, 1968-71; asst. to ins. commr. Commonwealth of Pa., Harrisburg, 1971-74; asst. to pres. Capital Blue Cross, Harrisburg, 1974-78, sr. v.p., 1978-84, pres., CEO, 1984—; bd. dirs. Blue Cross & Blue Shield Assn., Chgo., BCS Fin., Chgo., Fed. Res. Bank Phila., chmn. 1994-95. Contbr. articles on health care to profl. publs. Mem. bd. advisors Pa. State U., 1985-93; chmn. savs. bond campaign for Ctrl. Pa., U.S. Treasury Dept., Harrisburg, 1986-87; bd. dirs. United Way Capital Region, pres. 1994. Paul Harris fellow Rotary Internat., 1988. Mem. Capital Region C. of C. (bd. dirs., treas. 1987-90), Country Club of Harrisburg, Blue Ridge Country Club. Avocation: tennis. Home: 201 Hearth Rd Camp Hill PA 17011-8455

MEAD, JOHN MILTON, banker; b. Schenectady, Oct. 26, 1924; s. Milton Samuel and Jane (Drake) M.; m. Marguerite Ann Stone, Jan. 3, 1948; children: Ann Elizabeth, Jane Stone, Mary Ames. B.S., U. Mo., 1950; postgrad., U. Wis., 1963-65. Auditor Schenectady Trust Co., 1950-51; v.p., auditor First Trust & Deposit Co., Syracuse, N.Y., 1955-77; v.p., compliance officer Key Corp., Albany, N.Y., 1977-86, ret., 1986. Served with USAAF, 1943-46; Served with USAF, 1951-55. Mem. Inst. Internal Auditors (past pres. Central N.Y. chpt.), Am. Legion (past post comdr.). Republican. Presbyterian. Clubs: Marcellus Optimist (past pres.), Glens Falls Country. Home: 27 Yorkshire Dr Queensbury NY 12804-8620

MEAD, JOHN STANLEY, university administrator; b. Indpls., Dec. 9, 1953; s. Judson and Jane (Stanley) M.; m. Virginia Potter, Aug. 11, 1979; children: Christopher, Carolyn. BA, Ind. U., 1976; JD, U. Ill., 1979. Bar: Ill. Staff atty. Ill. Energy Resources Commn., Springfield, 1979-82, staff dir., 1982-85; mgr. coal rsch. Ill. Dept. Energy Natural Resources, Springfield, 1985-87, dir. office of coal devel. and mktg., 1987-89; dir. coal rsch. ctr. So. Ill. U., Carbondale, 1989—; b. dirs. Mid-West Univ. Energy Consortium Inc., Chgo.; mem., past chair Ill. Clean Coal Inst., 1986—. adv. com. Carbondale Bus. Devel. Corp., 1994. Recipient gold medal Tech. Univ. Ostrava, Czech Republic, 1992. Mem. Am. Radio Relay League, Ill. State Bar Assn., Mil. Vehicle Preservation Assn., Carbondale Rotary. Lutheran. Home: RR 4 Box 340 Carbondale IL 62901-9241 Office: So Ill U Coal Rsch Ctr Mail Code 4623 Carbondale IL 62901

MEAD, LAWRENCE MYERS, JR., retired aerospace executive; b. Plainfield, N.J., May 11, 1918; s. Lawrence Myers and Eleanor Whitman (Machado) M.; m. Janet Chase, Feb. 21, 1942; children—Lawrence Myers, Kirtland Chase, Jonathan Taylor, Bradford Machado. B.S.E., Princeton U., 1940, C.E., 1941; postgrad. mgmt., Harvard Bus. Sch., 1964. With Grumman Corp., Bethpage, N.Y., 1941-93; v.p. tech. ops. Grumman Aerospace Corp., Bethpage, N.Y., 1972-75, sr. v.p. dept. ops., 1975-81, sr. v.p. tech. ops., 1981-83; sr. mgmt. cons., 1983-93. Trustee, police commr., dep. mayor Village of Huntington Bay, N.Y., 1975-80; trustee N.Y.C. Hall of Sci. Fellow Poly. U., 1981. Fellow AIAA; mem. NAE, L.I. Forum on Tech. (bd. dirs., past chmn. bd.), Soc. Logistic Engrs., Soc. Advancement Materials and Process Engring., Princeton U. Alumni Assn., Am. Model Yacht Assn., Huntington Country Club. Democrat. Patentee in field; designer A6A Intruder Navy All Weather Bomber, Gulfstream III Exec. Jet Transport. Home: 88 Notch Hill Rd Apt 253 North Branford CT 06471-1850

MEAD, LOREN BENJAMIN, writer, consultant; b. Florence, S.C., Feb. 17, 1930; s. Walter Russell and Dorothy (Nauss) M.; m. Polly A. Mellette, Aug. 25, 1951; children: Walter Russell, Christopher Allen, Barbara Holladay Mead Wise, Philip Sidney. BA, U. of the South, 1951, DD (hon.), 1982; MA, U. S.C., 1951; MDiv, Va. Sem., Alexandria, 1955, DD (hon.), 1984; DD (hon.), Berkeley Div. Sch., New Haven, 1986. Ordained priest Episcopal Ch., 1956. Rector Trinity Episcopal Ch., Pinopolis, S.C., 1955-57, Ch. of the Holy Family, Chapel Hill, N.C., 1957-69; exec. dir. Project Test Pattern, Washington, 1969-74; founder, pres. Alban Inst., Washington, 1974-94. Author: New Hope for Congregations, 1972, Critical Moment, 1988, The Once and Future Church, 1991, More Than Numbers, 1993, Transforming Congregations For The Future, 1994. Recipient Spl. Achievement award Interim Pastor Network, 1990. Mem. Acad. Parish Clergy (bd. dirs. 1973-75), Soc. for Advancement of Continuing Edn. for Ministry. Democrat.

MEAD, PHILIP BARTLETT, healthcare administrator, physician; b. Poughkeepsie, N.Y., June 23, 1937; s. Ralph Allen and Altina (Gervin) M.; m. Ann Elaine Smith, June 27, 1964; children: Ralph Allen II, David Smith. BA, Hamilton Coll., 1959; MD, Cornell U., 1963. Diplomate Nat. Bd. Med. Examiners, Am. Bd. Ob-Gyn. Intern in medicine Bellevue Hosp., N.Y.C., 1963-64; resident in ob-gyn. N.Y. Hosp./Cornell Med. Ctr., N.Y.C., 1964-69; asst. prof. U. Vt. Coll. Medicine, Burlington, 1971-76, assoc. prof., 1976-81, prof., 1981—; hosp. epidemiologist Med. Ctr. Hosp. of Vt., Burlington, 1984-93; dir. clin. sys. Vt. Acad. Med. Ctr., Burlington, 1993-95; sr. v.p., med. dir. Fletcher Allen Health Care, Burlington, 1995—. Lt. comdr. M.C., USN, 1969-71. Fellow ACOG, Infectious Disease Soc. Am.; mem. Infectious Disease Soc. Ob-Gyn. (pres. 1987-88), Soc. Hosp. Epidemiologists, Phi Beta Kappa, Alpha Omega Alpha. Republican. Methodist. Home: 10 Pinehurst Dr Shelburne VT 05482-7240 Office: Fletcher Allen Health Care 111 Colchester Ave Burlington VT 05401 also: 1 S Prospect St Burlington VT 05401

MEAD, PHILOMENA, mental health nurse; b. Yonkers, N.Y., June 23, 1934; d. Alfonso F. and Jennie (Saltarelli) D'Amato; m. Kenneth Mead, Nov. 10, 1956; children: Scott Kenneth, Jeanne Bette. RN, St. Vincents Hosp., Bridgeport, Conn., 1955; BS in Psychology, Sacred Heart U., 1980; cert. in nursing mgmt., Fairfield U., 1988. Cert. psychiat. mental health nurse, nursing specialist, nat. chem. dependency nurse, CPR. Day supr.-relief, night supr. Hall Brooke Hosp., Westport, Conn., 1956-58, day supr., asst. dir. nurses, 1958-66, evening supr.-relief, 1967-68, team nurse, 1974-83, coord. nursing care, 1983-86, adminstrv. coord., 1986-87, nursing care coord. substance abuse treatment unit, 1987-91; charge evening nurse Carolton Hosp., Fairfield, Conn., 1971-73; nurse psychiat. emergency rm. and brief treatment unit West Haven (Conn.) VA, 1991—, mem. staff psychiat. emergency rm., 1995—. Roman Catholic. Avocation: genealogy. Home: 67 Adams Rd Fairfield CT 06430-3018

MEAD, PRISCILLA, state legislator; m. John L. Mead; children: John, Willian, Neel, Sarah. Student, Ohio State U. Councilwoman Upper Arlington, Ohio, 1982-90, mayor, 1986-90; mem. Ohio Ho. of Reps. Mem. Franklin County Child Abuse and Neglect Found., Coun. for Ethics and Econs. Recipient Svc. award Northwest Kiwanis, Woman of Yr. award Upper Arlington Rotary, Citizen of Yr. award U.S. C. of C. Mem. LWV, Upper Arlington Edn. Found., Jr. League Columbus, Upper Arlington C. of C., Delta Gamma. Republican. Home: 2281 Brixton Rd Columbus OH 43221-3117 Office: Ohio Ho of Reps State House Columbus OH 43215*

MEAD, TERRY EILEEN, clinic administrator, consultant; b. Portland, Oreg., Mar. 14, 1950; d. Everett L. and Jean (Nonken) Richardson; divorced; 1 child, Sean Wade Adcock. AA summa cum laude, Seattle U., 1972; postgrad., U. Wash., 1971. Project mgr. Assoc. Univ. Physician, Seattle, 1971-74; pathology supr. Swedish Hosp., Seattle, 1974-77; svcs. supr. Transamerica, Seattle, 1977-78; various mgmt. positions Providence Hosp., Seattle, 1978-83; adminstr. Evergreen Surg. Ctr., Kirkland, Wash., 1983-86; bus. mgr. Ketchikan (Alaska) Gen. Hosp., 1986—; instr. U. Alaska, Ketchikan, 1990; adminstr. Bethel (Alaska) Family Clinic, 1994—; CFO Southeast Oreg. Rural Health Network, 1996—; sec. S.E. adv. bd. U. Alaska, Ketchikan, 1987-94; CEO Meads Med. Mgmt.; cons. to hosps. and physicians, Wash., Alaska, 1980—; mgr. Practice Mgmt. Cons., Seattle, 1982-83. Mem. City Charter Rev. Com., Ketchikan, 1990-94; High Sch. Facilities Com. Ketchikan, 1990; S.E. dir. search com. U. Alaska, Ketchikan, 1990; treas. Calvary Bible Ch., Ketchikan, 1989-91; bd. dirs. S.E. Alaska Symphony, 1992-94, Jr. Achievement, 1992-93; chmn. fin. com. City of Bethel, 1994-96. Mem. Rotary Internat. Avocations: computers, politics, fishing, music, writing. Home: PO Box 2221 Bethel AK 99559-2221 Office: PO Box 379 Chiloquin OR 97624

MEAD, WAYLAND MCCON, lawyer; b. Roxbury, N.Y., Nov. 25, 1931; s. Irvin John and Dorothy (Seablom) M.; m. Barbara Jean Wales, Aug. 24, 1958; children: Michael John, David Scott, Deborah Ellen. B.S., Cornell U., 1953, J.D., 1958. Bar: N.Y. 1958. Assoc. Sage, Gray, Todd & Sims, N.Y.C., 1958-59; atty. Mut. Ins. Rating Bur., N.Y.C., 1959-62, Continental Ins. Co., N.Y.C., 1962-65; atty., then sec., counsel Am. Home Assurance Co., N.Y.C., 1965-75; sec., counsel Nat. Union Fire Ins. Co., N.Y.C., 1968-75; asst. v.p., counsel Am. Internat. Group, Inc., N.Y.C., 1969-75; v.p., gen. counsel Am. Internat. Group, Inc., 1975-82, sr. v.p., gen. counsel, 1982—, now acting gen. counsel, 1995; spl. counsel Am. Internat. Group, Inc., N.Y.C., 1995—; dir. Transatlantic Reins. Co., N.Y.C., Am. Home Assurance Co., N.Y.C., Commerce and Industry Ins. Co., N.Y.C., AIU Ins. Co., United Guaranty Corp., United Guaranty NC; chmn. ad hoc com. property and casualty ins. industry, N.Y.C., 1976. Bd. dirs. New Alternatives for Children, 1987—. 2nd Lt. U.S. Army, 1953-55. Mem. ABA. Home: 22 Lucille Ct Massapequa NY 11758-6503 Office: Am Internat Group Inc 70 Pine St New York NY 10270-0002*

MEADE, ANGELA KAYE, special education educator; b. Bryon, Ohio, Mar. 14, 1969; d. Douglas MacAuther and Thelma Judy (Williams) Smith; m. Steven Andrew Meade, June 1, 1991; 1 child, Alexander Jefferson. AA in Edn. summa cum laude, S.W. Va. C.C., 1989, AA in Gen. Studies, 1989; BA in English with distinction, U. Va., 1992, M Tchg. in Spl. Edn., 1992. Cert. K-12 tchr. learning disabilities and mental retardation, Va. Tchr. spl. edn. Newport News (Va.) Pub. Schs., 1992—; yearbook sponsor Newport News (Va.) Pub. Schs., 1992-95, implemented collaborative tchg. program, 1994-95; counselor Summer Yough Program, Lebanon and Richmond, Va., 1993-94. Organizer Spl. Olympics Va., Newport News, 1993-94. Mem. ASCD, Internat. Reading Coun., Newport News Reading Coun. (co-chmn. banquet 1993-95).. Avocations: reading, writing. Office: Reservoir Mid Sch 301 Heacox Ln Newport News VA 23608-1809

MEADE, DALE MICHAEL, laboratory director; b. Lodi, Wis., Aug. 7, 1939; s. Merlin Jones and Valborg (Olson) M.; m. Helen Eva Flentje, Oct. 26, 1959 (div. Dec. 1979); children: Loretta, Carla Fleming. BS with high honors in Elec. Engring., U. Wis., 1961, MS in Physics, 1962, PhD in Physics, 1965. Asst. prof. physics U. Wis., Madison, 1967-69, assoc. prof., 1969-72, prof., 1972-74; head FM-1 Princeton (N.J.) Plasma Physics Lab., 1973, head PDX Ops., 1975-80, head exptl. divsn. rsch. dept., head TFTR rsch. program, 1980-82, head exptl. divsn., head TFTR rsch. ops. divsn., 1982-86, head exptl. physics rsch. dept., head TFTR project, 1986-91, dep. dir., 1991—. Recipient Disting. Svc. Citation U. Wis. Coll. Engring., Madison, 1990, Disting. Assoc. award U.S. Dept. Energy, Washington, 1994. Fellow Am. Phys. Soc.; mem. AAAS. Office: Princeton Plasma Physics Lab US Rt #1 N PO Box 451 Princeton NJ 08543

MEADE, EVERARD KIDDER, JR., retired broadcasting and publishing executive; b. Tappahannock, Va., Oct. 3, 1919; s. Everard Kidder and Della (Wright) M.; m. Alice Amory Winslow, Sept. 1944; children: Mary Devereux, Everard Kidder III, Susanna Fitzhugh. B.S., U.S. Mil. Acad., 1943. Mem. Hoover Commn., U.S. Depts. Def. and State, 1946-53; v.p. Colonial Williamsburg, Inc., 1953-55; assoc. Earl Newsom & Co., 1955-57; v.p. CBS Inc., 1957-82. Served from 2d lt. to lt. col. U.S. Army, 1939-46. Mem. SAR, VFW, Fgn. Policy Assn., Century Assn. (N.Y.C.), Army and Navy Club, Sailfish Club of Fla., Soc. Colonial Wars, Bar Harbor (Maine) Yacht Club, Bath and Tennis Club (Fla.), Rockaway (N.Y.) Hunting Club. Episcopalian.

MEADE, KENNETH ALBERT, minister; b. Sweet Valley, Pa., June 14, 1935; s. Delbert H. and Dorothea I. (Myers) M.; m. Jeanette H. Quigley, Dec. 18, 1954 ; children: Jane M. Meade Ulm, Mark K. Ministerial cert., Ea. Christian Inst., East Orange, N.J., 1955; DD (hon.), Milligan Coll., Tenn., 1986, Ea. Christian Coll., Bel Air, Md., 1986. Ordained to ministry Ch. of Christ, 1955. Student min. Ch. of Christ, Bklyn. and Greenpoint, N.Y., 1952-53; mem. Meade-Bennett Evangelistic Team, East Orange, 1953-55; sr. min. Ch. of Christ at Manor Woods, Rockville, Md., 1956—; pres. N.Am. Christian Conv., Cin., 1986, Ea. Christian Conv., Rockville, 1969, 74, 82. Contbr. numerous articles to religion mags. Trustee Milligan Coll. Recipient Award of Honor, Am. Legion, 1952, Highest Comml. award Lehman High Sch. Alumni Assn., 1952. Office: Ch of Christ at Manor Woods 5300 Norbeck Rd Rockville MD 20853-2303

MEADER, JOHN DANIEL, state agency administrator, judge; b. Ballston Spa, N.Y., Oct. 22, 1931; s. Jerome Clement and Doris Luella (Conner) M.; m. Joyce Margaret Cowin, Mar. 2, 1963; children: John Daniel Jr., Julia Rae, Keith Alan. BA, Yale U., 1954; JD, Cornell U., 1962. Bar: N.Y. 1963, U.S. Dist. Ct. (no. dist.) N.Y. 1963, U.S. Ct. Appeals (2d cir.) 1966, U.S. Supreme Ct. 1967, U.S. Ct. Mil. Appeals 1973, Ohio 1978, U.S. Dist. Ct. (no. dist.) Ohio 1979, Fla. 1983, U.S. Ct. Appeals (4th cir.) 1992, U.S. Ct. Appeals (fed. cir.) 1993. Sales engr. Albany (N.Y.) Internat. Corp., 1954-59; asst. track coach Cornell U., 1959-62; asst. sec., asst. to pres. Albany Internat. Corp., 1962-65; asst. atty. gen. State of N.Y., Albany, 1965-68; ops. counsel, atesting sec. GE, Schenectady, 1968-77; gen. counsel, asst. sec. Glidden div. SCM Corp., Cleve., 1977-81; chmn. bd., pres. Applied Power Tech. Co., Fernandina Beach, Fla., 1981-84; pres. Applied Energy, Inc., Ballston Spa, 1984-88; judge N.Y. State Workers Compensation Bd., Albany, 1988—; dir. Saratoga Mut. Fire Ins. Co. Author: Labor Law Manual, 1972, Contract Law Manual, 1974, Patent Law Manual, 1978. Candidate U.S. Ho. of Reps., 29th Dist. N.Y., 1964, N.Y. Supreme Ct., 1975, 87, 93. Col. JAGC, USAR, 1968—, dep. staff judge adv. 3d U.S. Army & Cen. Command, 1984. Nat. AAU High Sch. 1000 Yard Indoor Track Champion, 1949, Nat. AAU Prep. Sch. 440 and 880 Yard Indoor Track Champion, 1950, Nat. AAU Outstanding Performer award, Melrose Games Assn., 1950, Heptagonal Track 880-Yard Champion 1954. Mem. ABA, N.Y. State Bar Assn., Fla. Bar, Amelia Island Plantation Club, Cyprus Temple Club, Yale Club Jacksonville (pres.), Masons. Republican. Presbyterian. Home: 271 Round Lake Rd Ballston Lake NY 12019-1714 Office: NY State Workers Compensation Bd 100 Broadway Albany NY 12241-0001

MEADERS, PAUL LE SOURD, lawyer; b. Amarillo, Tex., Feb. 1, 1930; s. Paul Le Sourd and Lorna Irene (Pumroy) M.; m. Patricia Rockefeller, Mar. 21, 1953 (dec.); m. Jane W. Dickely, Apr. 2, 1966; children: Phyllis P., Paul Le Sourd III. BA, U. Va., 1952; LLB, U. Tex., 1957; LLM, NYU, 1961. Bar: Tex. 1956, N.Y. 1959. Atty. office chief counsel IRS, 1957-59; asst. U.S. atty. So. Dist. N.Y., 1951-61; assoc. Breed Abbott & Morgan, N.Y.C., 1961-63, Reid & Priest, N.Y.C., 1963-67; ptnr. Morris & McVeigh, N.Y.C., 1967-77, McKenzie, Meaders & Ives, N.Y.C., 1977-90, Meaders, Duckworth & Moore, 1990—. 1st lt. U.S. Army, 1952-54. Mem. ABA, (estate tax com. tax sect.) N.Y. State Bar Assn., Tex. Bar Assn., Internat. Bar Assn., Vets. Corps Arty. (life), U. Va. Alumni Assn. (pres. N.Y.C. chpt. 1982-84), Friendly Sons of St. Patrick (life), Ch. Club, Pilgrims of U.S. Club, Bronxville Field Club, Carlton Club (London). Episcopalian. Office: 551 5th Ave Ste 1704 New York NY 10176

MEADLOCK, JAMES W., computer graphics company executive; b. 1933; married. BSEE, N.C. State U., 1956. Dept. mgr. IBM, 1956-69; pres. Intergraph Corp., Huntsville, Ala., 1969—; also chmn. bd. dirs. Intergraph Corp., Huntsville; chief exec. officer Intergraph Corp., 1989—. Office: Intergraph Corp Huntsville AL 35894-0001*

MEADOR, CHARLES LAWRENCE, management and systems consultant, educator; b. Dallas, Oct. 7, 1946; s. Charles Leon and Dorothy Margaret (Brown), m. Diane E. Collins, May 18, 1985. BSME with honors, U. Tex., 1970; MSME, MS in Mgmt., MIT, 1972. Mem. engring. staff Union Carbide Corp., Houston, 1967-68; instr. Alfred P. Sloan Sch. Mgmt. MIT, Cambridge, 1972-75, asst. dir. Ctr. Info. Systems Rsch., 1976-78, lectr. Sch. Engring., co-dir. Macro-Engring. Rsch. Group, 1978—; founder, pres. Decision Support Tech., Inc., 1974-92; co-founder, vice-chmn., dir. Software Productivity Rsch., Inc., 1985-87; pres., dir. The Softbridge Group, 1989-92, Mgmt. Support Tech. Corp., 1992—; bd. dirs. Coordinated Svcs. Network, Inc., 1993-96; sr. v.p., divsn. info. systems officer CIGNA Property and Casualty. Editor: How Big and Still Beautiful? Macro-Engineering Revisited, 1980, Macro-Engineering: The Rich Potential, 1981, Macro-Engineering and the Future: A Management Perspective, 1982, Macro-Engineering: Global Infrastructure Solutions, 1992; mem. editorial adv. bd. Computer Comm., 1979-91; mem. editorial bd. Comunicacion e Informatica, 1980—; author papers in field. NSF trainee, 1970; MIT Wilfred Lewis fellow, 1971; Draper Lab. fellow, 1974. Mem. Computer Soc. IEEE (vice-chmn. Ea. Hemisphere and Latin Am. area com. 1977-83), Am. Soc. for Macro-Engring. (bd. dirs. 1992—), Cosmos Club, St. Botolph's Club, Sigma Xi, Tau Beta Pi, Pi Tau Sigma. Home: 3 Windy Hill Ln Wayland MA 01778-2612 Office: MIT Rm 3-282 Cambridge MA 02139

MEADOR, DANIEL JOHN, lawyer, educator; b. Selma, Ala., Dec. 7, 1926; s. Daniel John and Mabel (Kirkpatrick) M.; m. Janet Caroline Heilmann, Nov. 19, 1955; children: Janet Barrie, Anna Kirkpatrick, Daniel John. B.S., Auburn U., 1949; J.D., U. Ala., 1951; LL.M., Harvard U., 1954. Bar: Ala. 1951, Va. 1961. Law clk. to U.S. Supreme Ct. Justice Hugo L. Black, 1954-55; assoc. firm Lange, Simpson, Robinson & Somerville, Birmingham, 1955-57; faculty U. Va. Law Sch., 1957-66, prof. law, 1961-66; prof., dean U. Ala. Law Sch., 1966-70; James Monroe prof. law U. Va., Charlottesville, 1970-94, prof. emeritus, 1994—; asst. atty. gen. U.S., 1977-79, dir. grad. program for judges, 1979-95; Fulbright lectr., U.K., 1965-66; vis. prof. U.S. Mil. Acad., 1984; Chmn. Southeastern Conf. Assn. Am. Law Schs., 1964-65; chmn. Cts. Task Force Nat. Adv. Commn. on Criminal Justice, 1971-72; dir. appellate justice project Nat. Center for State Cts., 1972-74; mem. Adv. Council on Appellate Justice, 1971-75, Council on Role of Cts., 1978-84; bd. dirs. State Justice Inst., 1986-92. Author: Preludes to Gideon, 1967, Criminal Appeals-English Practices and American Reforms, 1973, Mr. Justice Black and His Books, 1974, Appellate Courts: Staff and Process in the Crisis of Volume, 1974, (with Carrington and Rosenberg) Justice on Appeal, 1976, Impressions of Law in East Germany, 1986, American Courts, 1991, (with J. Bernstein) Appellate Courts in the United States, 1994, His Father's House, 1994, (with Rosenberg and Carrington) Appellate Courts: Structures, Functions, Processes, and Personnel, 1994; editor: Hardy Cross Dillard: Writings and Speeches, 1995; editor Va. Bar News, 1962-65; contbr. articles to profl. jours. Served to 1st lt. AUS, 1951-53. Decorated Bronze Star.; IREX fellow German Dem. Republic, 1983. Mem. ABA (chmn. standing com. on fed. jud. improvements 1987-90), Ala. Bar Assn., Va. Bar Assn. (exec. com. 1983-86), Am. Law Inst., Am. Judicature Soc. (bd. dirs. 1975-77, 80-83), Soc. Pub. Tchrs. Law, Am. Soc. Legal History (bd. dirs. 1968-71), Order of Coif, Raven Soc., Phi Delta Phi, Omicron Delta Kappa, Kappa Alpha. Presbyn. Office: U Va Sch Law Charlottesville VA 22903

MEADOR, JOHN MILWARD, JR., university dean; b. Louisville, Nov. 4, 1946; s. John Milward and Ruth Inez (Miller) M.; m. Judith Ann Hay, Dec. 22, 1969; children: John Milward III, Elise Kathleen. BA, U. Louisville, 1968; MA, U. Tex., 1972, MLS, 1973; cert. in pub. adminstrn., U. Utah, 1982. Cert. tchr., Ky., Tex. Stacks supr. U. Louisville Librs., 1965-68; English bibliographer M.D. Anderson Libr. U. Houston, 1973-74, head reference dept. social scis. and humanities, 1974-77, head gen. reference dept., 1977-80; asst. dir. pub. svcs. Marriott Libr. U. Utah, Salt Lake City, 1980-84; dean libr. svcs. S.W. Mo. State U., Springfield, 1984-93; dean librs. U. Miss., Univeristy, 1993—; bd. dirs. Mo. Libr. Network Corp., 1984-90, St. Louis, S.W. Mo. Libr. Network, Springfield; cons. Dayco Corp., Springfield, 1984-86; chmn. Mo. Northwestern Online Total Integrated Systems (NOTIS) Users Group, 1988-89. Co-author: The Robinson Jeffers Collection at the University of Houston, 1975; contbr. articles to profl. jours. Sponsor Community Alternative Svc. Program, Springfield and St. Louis, 1985-93; mem. governing bd. Mo. Rsch. and Edn. Network, MOREnet, 1991-93; With U.S. Army, 1969-71, Vietnam. Recipient Nat. Essay award Propeller Club of U.S., 1964; named to Honorable Order of Ky. Colonels, Gov. Ky., 1978; summer scholar English-Speaking Union, Edinburgh, Scotland, 1968; Apple Computer's Higher Edn. Acad. Devel. Donation Program grantee, 1990. Mem. ALA, Am. Assn. for Higher Edn., Assn. Coll. Rsch. Librs., Bibliog. Soc. Am., Libr. Adminstrn. and Mgmt. Assn., other profl. orgns., English-Speaking Union Club, Rotary (chmn. students guests com. Springfield chpt. 1986-89, chmn. scholarships com. 1989-90, bd. dirs. 1990-91, bd. dirs. Oxford chpt. 1995—). Avocations: raising pure bred airedale terriers, fishing, book collecting. Home: PO Box 787 University MS 38677-0787 Office: U Miss J D Williams Libr University MS 38677

MEADOR, RON, newspaper editor, writer; b. Buffalo, N.Y., Nov. 24, 1952; s. Meril E. and Evelyn (Lyons) M.; divorced; 1 child, Benjamin Brian. BA, Ind. U., 1975. Copy editor The Courier-Journal, Louisville, 1975-78, The New York Times, 1978-80; reporter, state editor, city editor Star Tribune, Mpls., Minn., 1980—; asst. mng. editor for spl. projects and nat. news Star Tribune, Mpls. Mem. Investigative Reporters and Editors, Inc. Office: Star Tribune 425 Portland Ave Minneapolis MN 55488-0001

MEADORS, ALLEN COATS, health administrator, educator; b. Van Buren, Ark., May 17, 1947; s. Hal Barron and Allene Coats (Means) M. AA, Saddleback Coll., 1981; BBA, U. Cen. Ark., 1969; MBA, U. No. Colo., 1974; M. in Pub. Administrn., U. Kans., 1975; MA in Psychology, Webster U., 1979; MA in Health Svcs. Mgmt., 1980, PhD in Adminstrn, So. Ill. U., 1981. Assoc. adminstr. Forbes Hosp., Topeka, 1971-73; asst. dir. health svcs. devel. Blue Cross Blue Shield of Kans., Topeka, 1973-76; asst. dir. Kansas City Health Dept. (Mo.), 1976-77; program dir., asst. prof. So. Ill. U., Carbondale, and Webster U., St. Louis, 1978-82; assoc. prof., dir. div. health adminstrn. U. Tex., Galveston, 1982-84; exec. dir. N.W. Ark. Radiation Therapy Inst., Springdale, Ark., 1984-87; prof., chmn. dept. health adminstrn. U. Okla., Oklahoma City, dean Coll. Pub. Health, 1989-90; mem. faculty Calif. State U., Long Beach, 1977-81; grad. faculty U. Ark. Sch. Bus. Adminstrn., Fayetteville, 1984-87; prof., chmn. dept. health administrn. U. Okla., 1987-90; dean Coll. Health, Social and Pub. Svcs. Ea. Wash. U., Cheney, 1990-94; CEO Pa. State U., Altoona, 1994—; cons. Surgeon Gen. Office and Air Force System Command. Bd. dirs. Martin Luther King Hosp., Health Care Svcs. Adv. Bd.; bd. dirs., mem. exec. com. Altoona Symphony Orch.; bd. dirs. Altoona Hosp., 1994—, Home Health Agy., 1995—, Altoona Enterprises, Inc., 1994—. Served with Med. Service Corps, USAF, 1969-73. Fellow Am. Coll. Healthcare Execs., Ark. Hosp. Assn.; mem. Am. Hosp. Assn. Contbr. articles to profl. jours. Home: PO Box 9 Altoona PA 16603-0009 Office: Pa State U 3000 Ivyside Park Altoona PA 16601-3760

MEADORS, HOWARD CLARENCE, JR., electrical engineer; b. Chgo., July 31, 1938; s. Howard Clarence and Eileen May (Baker) M.; m. Phyllis Anne Rennebaum, July 18, 1964; children: Henry Charles, William Howard, Laura Phyllis, Pamela Susan. SB, MIT, 1960, SM, 1962, Profl. Degree in Elec. Engring., 1964; PhD, Poly. Inst. NY., 1976. Mem. tech. staff Bell Tel. Labs., Inc., Holmdel, N.J., 1966-82; disting. mem. tech. staff AT&T Info. Systems Labs., Holmdel, 1983-85, supr. product devel., 1985-86; supr. adv. data communications AT&T Bell Labs., Middletown, N.J., 1986-91; Disting. mem. tech. staff AT&T Bus. Communications Systems, Holmdel, N.J., 1991-94; disting. mem. tech. staff AT&T Network Systems, Holmdel, N.J., 1994-96, Lucent Technologies, Holmdel, N.J., 1996—; ednl. counselor MIT, 1973—, regional vice chmn., 1983—. Inventor in field. With Signal Corps, U.S. Army, 1964-66. Mem. IEEE (sr. mem. 1987), Sigma Xi, Eta Kappa Nu. Office: AT&T Bell Labs Crawfords Corner Rd Holmdel NJ 07733

MEADOW, LYNNE (CAROLYN MEADOW), theatrical producer and director; b. New Haven, Nov. 12, 1946; d. Frank and Virginia R. Meadow. BA cum laude, Bryn Mawr Coll., 1968; postgrad., Yale U., 1968-70. Dir. Theatre Communications Group, 1978-80; adj. prof. SUNY, Stony Brook, 1975-76, Yale U., Circle in the Sq., 1977-78, 89-91, NYU, 1977-80; theatre and music/theatre panelist Nat. Endowment for Arts, 1977-88; artistic advisor Fund for New Am. Plays, 1988-90. Artistic dir. Manhattan Theatre Club, N.Y.C., 1972—; guest dir. Nat. Playwrights Conf., Eugene O'Neill Theatre Ctr., 1975-77, Phoenix Theatre, 1976; dir. Ashes for Manhattan Theatre Club and N.Y. Shakespeare Festival, 1977; prodr. off-Broadway shows Ain't Misbehavin', 1978, Crimes of the Heart, 1981, Miss Firecracker Contest, 1984, Frankie and Johnny, 1987, Eastern Standard, 1988, Lisbon Traviata, 1989, Lips Together, Teeth Apart, 1991, Four Dogs and a Bone, 1993, Love! Valour! Compassion!, 1994; dir. Principia Scritoriae, 1986, Woman in Mind, 1988 (Drama Desk award), Eleemosynary, 1989, Absent Friends, 1991; dir. Broadway prodn. A Small Family Business, 1992, The Loman Family Picnic, 1993; co-prodr. off-Broadway and Broadway show Mass Appeal, 1981. Recipient Citation of Merit Nat. Coun. Women, 1976, Outer Circle Critics award 1977, Drama Desk award, 1977, Obie award for Ashes, 1977, Margo Jones award for Continued Encouragement New Playwrights, 1981, Critics Circle award Outstanding Revival on or off Broadway for Loot, 1986, Lucille Lortel award for Outstanding Achievement, 1987, Spl. Drama Desk award, 1989, N.Y. Drama Critics Circle award Best Fgn. Play for Aristocrats, 1989, Torch of Hope award, 1989, Manhattan Mag. award, 1994, Lee Reynolds award League Profl. Theatre Women, 1994; named Northwood Inst. Disting. Woman of Yr., 1990, Person of Yr., Nat. Theatre Conf., 1992. Office: Manhattan Theatre Club 453 W 16th St Fl 2 New York NY 10011-5835

MEADOW, PHYLLIS WHITCOMB, psychoanalyst; b. Boston, Apr. 12, 1924; d. George Raymond and Marjorie (Loring) Whitcomb; m. Cyril Zachary Meadow; 1 dau., Dena. Cert. in psychoanalysis, Theodor Reik Inst., 1962; Ph.D., NYU, 1969. Practice psychoanalysis N.Y.C. and Boston, 1973—; assoc. adj. prof. L.I. U., 1967-72; dean rsch. Center Modern Psychoanalysis, N.Y.C., 1970—, exec. dir., 1970-76, chmn. bd., 1976—; chmn. bd. Boston Center Modern Psychoanalysis, 1978-89, pres., 1989—. Co-author: Treatment of the Narcissistic Neuroses, 1976; Editor: Jour. Modern Psychoanalysis; contbr. articles to profl. jours. Recipient Disting. Service award Nat. Assn. Psychoanalysis, 1980. Mem. Nat. Assn. Advancement Psychoanalysis, Am. Psychol. Assn., Soc. Modern Psychoanalysis. Home and Office: 245 W 13th St New York NY 10011-7701 Office: Ctr for Modern Psychanalytic Std 16 W 10th St New York NY 10011

MEADOW, SUSAN ELLEN, magazine editor and publisher; b. N.Y.C., Dec. 17, 1936; d. Sol and Betty (Greene) Raunheim; m. Alvin Harvey Meadow, Aug. 17, 1958 (dec. 1994); children—Eric, Douglas, Peter. B.A. in English, U. Mich., 1958; M.S. in Edn., Iona Coll., 1967. Asst. editor N.Y. State Pharmacist, N.Y.C., 1958-60; mng. editor Westchester mag., White Plains, N.Y., 1969-70; editor, pub. Spotlight, Mamaroneck, N.Y., 1977-96. Bd. dirs. ARC, Rye, 1981—; Westchester-Putnam div. Diabetes Assn. Am.; mem. adv. council Westchester Community Coll. Found., 1984-85. Recipient plaque Leukemia Soc., 1983, Am. Cancer Soc., 1984. Mem. Westchester Women in Communications (excellence in periodicals award 1982), Advt. Club Westchester. Democrat. Jewish. Office: Meadow Pub 126 Library Ln Mamaroneck NY 10543-3608

MEADOWS, DONALD FREDERICK, librarian; b. Regina, Sask., Can., Jan. 13, 1937; s. Frederick John and Doris Eileen (Willock) M.; m. Ruth Susan Cochran, June 10, 1960; children—Scott Frederick, George Edward. B.A., U. Sask., 1962; B.L.S., U. B.C., 1968. Library cons. Sask. Provincial Library, Regina, 1968-69; asst. provincial librarian Sask. Provincial Library, 1969-70, provincial librarian, province of Sask., 1970-81; dir. Met. Toronto Library, 1981-86; dir. Vancouver Island Regional Library, Nanaimo, B.C., Can., 1986—, also bd. dirs. Mem. Canadian Library Assn., ALA, B.C. Library Assn. Mem. United. Ch. Can. Office: Vancouver Island Regional Library, PO Box 3333, Nanaimo, BC Canada V9R 5N3

MEADOWS, GEORGE LEE, communications company executive; b. Toronto, Ont., Can., Nov. 17, 1938; m. Donna McKay, Sept. 26, 1964; children: Lee Ann, Shelly. BA, U. Toronto, 1963. Chartered acct. Acct. Clarkson Gordon, Toronto, 1963-73; v.p. fin. Project Group Can. Ltd., Toronto, 1973-74; sec.-treas. Southam Communications Ltd., Toronto, 1974-77, v.p., 1976-77; asst. to pres. Southam Inc., Toronto, 1977-78, v.p. corp. devel., 1978-84, sr. v.p. communications group, 1984-87; mng. dir., chief exec. officer Selkirk Communications Ltd., Toronto, 1987-88, pres., chief exec. officer, 1988—; chmn. Niagara TV Ltd., Selkirk Broadcasting Ltd., Selkirk Communications Inc., Selkirk Communications (Hallandale) Inc.; pres. Selkirk Communications Corp., Selkirk Films Ltd., Selkirk Holdings; bd. dirs. B.C. Broadcasting Co. Ltd., Calgary TV Ltd., Can. Satellite Communications Inc., Lethbridge TV Ltd., Okanagan Valley TV Co. Ltd., Branksome Hall, U. Toronto Press. Mem. Can. Inst. Chartered Accountants. Clubs: Royal Can. Yacht. Avocations: sailing, skiing, squash, badminton, tennis. Office: Univ of Toronto Press Inc, 10 St Mary St Ste 700, Toronto, ON Canada M4Y 2W8

MEADOWS, JENNIFER ELIZABETH, retired editor, tattoo artist; b. Texarkana, Tex., Jan. 20, 1947; d. Walter Edward and Martha Elizabeth (McCoy) Willis; m. Joe R. Matthews (div.); 1 child, Chris; m. Rich Meadows. AA, Cottey Coll., 1965; BS, U. Tex., Arlington, 1978. Actuarial asst. S.W. Life Ins. Co., Dallas; proofreader Royal Bus. Forms, Arlington, Tex.; substitute tchr. Arlington (Tex.) Ind. Sch. Dist.; reporter The Dallas Morning News, 1980-83, asst. editor, 1983-86, editor, 1986-94; columnist The Dallas Morning News, 1980-94. Vol. The Dallas Opera; tng. coord. Kairos Found., 1990—. Avocations: calligraphy, massage, svc. to the community. Office: 904 W Pioneer Pky Arlington TX 76013-6330

MEADOWS, JUDITH ADAMS, law librarian, educator; b. Spartanburg, S.C., June 5, 1945; d. Thomas Taylor and Virginia (Dayton) Adams; m. Bruce R. Meadows; children: Beth Ann Blackwood, Ted Adams Meadows. BA, Am. U., 1967; MLS, U. Md., 1979. Law libr. Aspen Sys. Corp., Gaithersburg, Md., 1979-81; dir. Fairfax (Va.) Law Libr., 1981-84, State Law Libr., Helena, Mont., 1984—; vis. prof. U. Wash., Seattle, 1994; adj. prof. U. Great Falls, Mont., 1989-96; presiding ofcl. Gov.'s Conf. on Libr. Info. Svc., Helena, Mont., 1991. Author: (book chpts.) From Yellow Pads to Computers, 1991, Law Librarianship, 1994; contbr. articles to profl. jours. Bd. dirs. Helena Presents, 1986-92, Holter Mus. Art, 1995—. Recipient Disting. Svc. award State Bar of Mont., 1991. Mem. Am. Assn. Law Librs. (treas. 1992-95, v.p., pres.-elect 1996—), N.W. Consortium of Law Librs. (pres.), Mont. Libr. Assn. (sec. 1986-88). Avocations: gourmet cooking, cross-country skiing, reading, gardening. Office: State Law Libr Mont Justice Bldg 215 N Sanders St Helena MT 59620-3004

MEADOWS, LOIS ANNETTE, elementary education educator; b. Harrisville, W.Va., Jan. 12, 1948; d. Orvle Adam and Una Pauline (Slocum) Ingram; m. David Alan Meadows, June 15, 1969; children: Lynecia Ann, Eric Justin. BA, Glenville State Coll., 1969; MA, W.Va. U., 1980. Cert. music, elem. edn., reading, W.Va. Tchr. grade six Acad. Park-Portsmouth (Va.) City Schs., 1969-73; elem. substitute Wood County Schs., Parkersburg, W.Va., 1973-77; real estate agt. Nestor Realty, Parkersburg, 1974-77; tchr. grade five/music Emerson Elem. Wood County Schs., Parkersburg, W.Va., 1977-78, tchr. grade three, 1978—; edn. cons. World Book, Parkersburg, 1986—; mentor tchr.-trainer Wood County Schs., parkersburg, 1990—; W.Va. S.T.E.P. Test com./trainer W.Va. Dept. Edn., Charleston, 1994—, mem. writing assessment com., 1994—; grant writer and speaker in field; mem. W.Va. Dept. Edn. State Writing Manual Com., 1996—. Author: (reading projects) Operation Blackout, 1986-94 (grant 1994), The Reading Room, 1988 (grant 1990), Storytime at the Mall, 1986— (grant 1994, 95). Life mem. Emerson PTA, Parkersburg, 1977—; Sunday Sch. tchr. North Parkersburg Bapt. Ch., 1976—, children's choir dir., 1976-88; fund raiser local charities, Parkersburg. Women of Excellence and Leadership Timely Honored award, W. Va. State Reading Tchr. of Yr., 1988, Finalist W. Va. State Tchr. of Yr., W.VA. Dept. Edn., 1993, Wood County Tchr. of Yr., 1993, Ashland Oil Golden Apple Achiever award, 1995, Wood Co. PTA Outstanding Educator of Yr. award, 1995-96, award for ann. contbrs. and project work Emerson PTA. Mem. W.Va. Reading Assn. (pres. 1993-94, mem. chmn. 1994—), Internat. Reading Assn., Wood County Reading Coun. (past pres. 1986-88, 90-92, Am. Fedn. Tchrs., Delta Kappa Gamma. Republican. Avocations: children's Lit., collecting autographed books, bridge, family times. Home: 102 Jo Mar Dr Parkersburg WV 26101 Office: Wood County Schs Emerson Elem 1605 36th St Parkersburg WV 26104

MEADOWS, PATRICIA BLACHLY, art curator, civic worker; b. Amarillo, Tex., Nov. 12, 1938; d. William Douglas and Irene Bond Blachly; m. Curtis Washington Meadows, Jr., June 10, 1961; children: Michael Lee, John Morgan. BA in English and History, U. Tex., 1960. Program dir. Ex-Students Assn., Austin, Tex., 1960-61; dir. Dallas Visual Art Ctr., 1981-86, curator, 1987—, founder The Collectors, 1988—; exhbn. dir. Tex. bd. Nat. Mus. Women in Arts, Washington, 1986-91; mem. acquisition com. Dallas Mus. Art, 1988-92; chmn. adv. bd. Oaks Bank and Trust, 1993—; juror numerous exhibits, Dallas and Tex.; speaker on arts subjects; cons. city, state and nat. projects concerning arts; bd. dirs., mem. exec. com. Uptown Pub. Improvement Dist., 1993-96; chmn. bd. dirs. Author: (art catalogues) Critic's Choice, 1983—, Texas Women, 1989-90, Texas: reflections, rituals, 1991; organizer exhbns. Presenting Nine, D-Art Visual Art Ctr., 1984, Mosaics, 1991—, Senses Beyond Sight, 1992-93. Bd. dirs. Mid-Am. Arts Alliance, Kansas City, Mo., 1989-93, Tex. Bd. Commerce, Austin, 1991-93, Women's Issues Network, Dallas, 1994—; bd. dirs. Dallas Summit, 1989-95, pres., 1993-94; mem. Charter 100, 1993—, Dallas Assembly, 1993—, Leadership Tex., 1987; co-founder, mem. steering com. Emergency Artists Support League, Dallas, 1992—; mem. originating task force Dallas Coalition for Arts, 1984; also others. Recipient Dedication to Arts award Tex. Fine Arts Assn., 1984, Assn. Artists and Craftsmen, 1984, Southwestern Watercolor Soc., 1985, Flora award Dallas Civic Garden Ctr., 1987, James K. Wilson award TACA, 1988, Maura award Women's Ctr. Dallas, 1991, Disting. Woman award Northwood U., 1993, Excellence in the Arts award Dallas Hist. Soc., 1993. Mem. Tex. Assn. Mus., Tex. Sculpture Assn. (originating task force), Arts Dist. Mgmt. Assn. (bd. dirs., exec. com. 1984-92, Artists Square design com. 1988-90), Artists and Craftsmen Assn. (pres. bd. dirs. 1982-83), Dallas Woman's Club. Presbyterian. Office: 2707 State St Dallas TX 75204-2634

MEADOWS, WILLIAM J., farmer; s. Victor Noel and Donna Maye (Lilly) M.; m. Betty Marie Lewis, Aug. 6, 1953; children: William J. (dec.), Jay Williams, Cinty Lou (dec.), Kate Marie, Rocky Joe. AB, Marshall U.; MEd, Am. U. Tchr. high sch., football coach, 1959-69; pres., owner Meadows Farms, Inc., Va. & Md., 1969—, Meadows Farms Cattle Co., Locust Grove, Va., 1981—, Meadows Farms Championship Golf Course, Locust Grove, Va., 1992—. Chancellor Bapt. Ch.; mem. Orange County Friends of Libr., Locust Grove Elem. PTA. Named State of Va. Tchr. of Yr., 1965, 66, 67, 68, Entrepreneur of Yr., Washington, 1988. Mem. Am. Nurserymen's Assn., Va. Nurserymen's Assn., No. Va. Nurserymen's Assn., Garden Ctrs. of Am., Santa Gertrudis Internat., No. East Santa Gertrudis Assn., Georgian Santa Gertrudis Assn., Profl. Golf Assn., Va. Golf Assn. Home: 32142 Meadows Farm Rd Locust Grove VA 22508-2517

MEADS, DONALD EDWARD, management services company executive; b. Salem, Mass., Sept. 23, 1920; s. Laurence G. and Gertrude F. M.; m. Jane Lightner, June 15, 1943; children: Edward G., Robert C., Laurence G., Judith C. Antrim, Suzanne M. O'Neil, Clifford L., Nancy Chapin. A.B. in Pre-Law, Dartmouth Coll., 1942; M.B.A. in Fin., Harvard U., 1947. Vice-pres., vice-chmn. investment com. N.Y. Life Ins. Co., N.Y.C., 1947-61; v.p. fin., chmn. investment com. Investors Diversified Services Inc., Mpls., 1961-65; pres., chief exec. officer Internat. Basic Economy Corp., N.Y.C., 1965-67, chmn., chief exec. officer, 1967-71; exec. v.p., dir., chief fin. officer, chmn. investment com. INA Corp., Phila., 1971-74; chmn. bd., chief exec. officer CertainTeed Corp., Valley Forge, Pa., 1974-78, dir., 1973-78; chmn. Mateer-Burt Co., Inc., Plymouth Meeting, Pa., 1984-87; chmn. Phila. First Group Inc., 1982-90; chmn. Carver Assocs., Inc., Plymouth Meeting, 1978—; hon. life trustee Valley Forge Mil. Acad. & Coll., Wayne Pa., trustee emeritus Thomas Jefferson U., Phila.; bd. dirs. Independence Hall Assn., Phila.; hon. dir. Marine Corps Scholarship Found., Princeton, N.J.; mem. Phila. Com. on Fgn. Relations; bd. dirs. World Affairs Council Phila. Served to capt. USMC, 1942-45. Decorated D.F.C., Air medals (6). Mem. Harvard Club of N.Y.C., Sunday Breakfast Club, Union League (Phila.), Rockefeller Ctr. Club (N.Y.C.).

MEADS, WALTER FREDERICK, executive recruitment consultant; b. Ft. Wayne, Ind., Mar. 11, 1923; s. Frederick C. and Minnie E. (Stephenson) M.; m. Mary E. Smith, Mar. 21, 1975; children by previous marriage: Kenneth W., Catherine L. B.S., Kent State U., 1948; M.A., Fairfield U. With Norman Malone & Assos., Akron, Ohio, 1946-48, Griswold-Eshleman Co., Cleve., 1949-53, Fuller, Smith & Ross, Cleve., 1953-55; sr. v.p., head of creative svc., mem. mgmt. com., vice chmn. plans and rev. bds. J. Walter Thompson Co., N.Y.C., 1955-72; pres. Meads & Assocs., 1972—. With USAAF, 1943-45. Recipient numerous nat. and local advt. industry awards. Home: 4420 Orangewood Loop E Lakeland FL 33813-1844 Office: 6700 S Florida Ave Ste 4 Lakeland FL 33813-3310 *Creative freedom is probably the core concept at the heart of my life—not only for myself but for others. Life is never static; it either deteriorates or grows. All growth, to me, springs from the creative doers of the world. The rest of humanity goes along for the ride. And creative growth, in any field or endeavor, demands an attitude of freedom to shake off the shackles of habit and find new and better ways of doing things.*

MEAGHER, GEORGE VINCENT, mechanical engineer; b. Halifax, N.S., Can., Apr. 23, 1919; s. John Nicholas and Blanche Margaret (Seals) M.; m. Evelyn Margaret Hamm, June 2, 1945; children: Maureen, Lindsey, Lise, Shelagh. BSc, Dalhousie U., Halifax, 1940; B of Engring., McGill U., 1942. Engring. and mgmt. positions in industry, 1942-56; with Dilworth, Secord, Meagher & Assocs. Ltd., Toronto, 1957-92; chmn. Dilworth, Secord, Meagher & Assocs. Ltd., 1988-92; pres. Tatacan Ltd., 1985—; vice chmn. Tata-DSMA, Bombay, India; dir. State Bank India, Can. Ltd., Toronto, 1984-94; founding dir., past chmn. Can.-India Bus. Coun.; pres. George V. Meagher Inc. Fellow Engring. Inst. Can.; mem. Designated Cons. Engr., Profl. Engrs. Ont., Nat. Club (Toronto). Home: # 1402, 500 Avenue Rd, Toronto, ON Canada M4V 2J6

MEAGHER, JAMES FRANCIS, atmospheric research executive; b. Sydney, Can., Oct. 23, 1946; came to U.S., 1967; s. James Marcellus and Margaret Evelyn (MacDougall) M.; m. Elizabeth Strapp; children: Jeffrey James, Elizabeth Kathleen. BSc, St. Francis Xavier, 1967; PhD, Cath. U. of Am., 1971. Rsch. fellow U. Wash., Seattle, 1971-73, Pa. State U., 1973-76; dir. atmospheric rsch. Tenn. Valley Authority, Muscle Shoals, Ala., 1976—; sci. adv. com. Nat. Acid Precipitation Assessment Program, Washington, 1987-93; mgr. Atmospheric Scis. TVA, Eviron. Rsch Ctr., 1993—. Contbr. chpt. to book, articles to profl. jours. Mem. Am. Chem. Soc., Am. Geophys. Union, Sigma Xi. Avocations: sailing, youth soccer. Home: 204 Seminole Ct Florence AL 35630 Office: USG TVA 212 Ceb Sheffield AL 35660

MEAGHER, JAMES PROCTOR, editor; b. Rock Island, Ill., June 2, 1935; s. Edmund Joseph and Pauline Marie (Proctor) M.; m. Marie Therese Lyman, Sept. 12, 1959; children: Kathleen Ann, Christopher James. BA, U. Notre Dame, 1957. Copy editor Chgo. Tribune Co., 1959-61; staff writer Nat. Observer, Washington, 1961-62; news editor Nat. Observer, Silver Spring, Md., 1962-65, sr. editor, 1965-76, asst. mng. editor, 1976-77; assoc. editor Barron's Bus. and Fin. Weekly, N.Y.C., 1977-78, news editor, 1978-82, asst. mng. editor, 1982-86, dep. editor, 1986-92, mng. editor, 1992-93; exec. editor Dow Jones Mag. Group, N.Y.C., 1995—. Served to 1st lt. U.S. Army, 1957-59. Mem. Soc. Profl. Journalists, Sigma Delta Chi. Roman Catholic. Home: 25 Hedges Ave Chatham NJ 07928-2503 Office: Barron's Fin Weekly 200 Liberty St New York NY 10281-1003

MEAGHER, MARK JOSEPH, publishing company executive; b. Balt., July 9, 1932; s. Harry Royce and Maria Paula (Demarco) M.; m. Gabriela Sierra, Dec. 24, 1983. Student, U. Notre Dame, 1950-51; B.S., U. Md., 1954. C.P.A. Accountant, auditor Price Waterhouse & Co., Balt., 1954-57; systems analyst IBM, Balt., 1957-58; mgmt. cons. McKinsey Co., Washington, 1958-61; exec. v.p. McGraw Hill Book Co., N.Y.C., 1961-70; v.p. fin. and adminstrn. Washington Post Co., N.Y.C., 1970-74; exec. v.p., gen. mgr. Washington Post Co., 1974-76, pres. newspaper div., 1976-77, pres., chief operating officer co., 1977-80, dir., 1970-81; pres., chief operating officer, dir. Penthouse Internat. Ltd., 1981; ptnr. Holding Capital Group, N.Y.C., 1982—; mem., chmn. Fin. World Ptnrs., N.Y.C., 1983-95; dir. Maple Press. V.p. Urban League New Brunswick, N.J., 1967-69; chmn. housing com. Metuchen/Edison (N.J.) unit NAACP, 1968; bd. dirs. World Affairs Coun.; vice chmn., trustee U. Md. Found., 1978-88. Mem. Hon. Accounting Soc., Am. Inst. CPA's (Eisenhower fellow 1980). Republican. Roman Catholic.

MEAGHER, THOMAS, transportation executive. Chmn. Trans World Airlines, St. Louis. Office: Trans World Airlines 1 City Ctr 515 N 6th St Saint Louis MO 63101*

MEAHL, BARBARA, occupational health nurse; b. N.Y.C., Aug. 15, 1938; d. Raymond G. and Alice (Duncan) Reynolds; m. Robert P. Meahl, Oct. 29, 1988; children: Susan, Mark, Ruth. Diploma in Nursing, Presbyn. Hosp., Phila., 1959; BS, St. Joseph's Coll., Windham, Maine, 1986. Cert. occupl. health nurse, CCM. Staff nurse various hosps. N.J./Pa., 1959-74; staff nurse AMP Inc., Harrisburg, Pa., 1974-75; mgr. safety and health Carlisle (Pa.) Corp., 1975-86; chief nurse Naval Shipyard, Phila., 1986-89; DON Concorde Inc., Phila., 1990-95; cons. Barbara Meahl & Assoc., Springfield, Pa., 1995—; dir., vice chmn. Am. Bd. Occupational Health Nurses, Inc., Palos Hills, Ill., 1988-92; lectr. in field. Mem./chair Cumberland County Drug and Alcohol Commn., Carlisle, Pa., 1986-88; instr. ARC, 1976—; ordained elder Presbyn. Ch., Springfield, Pa., 1987. Mem. Am. Assn. Occupl. Health Nurses, Pa. Assn. Occupl. Health Nurses (v.p. 1985-86, Outstanding Occupl. Health Nurse 1984), Delaware Valley Assn. Occupl. Health Nurses (v.p. 1987-88, sec. 1994—). Avocations: sewing, gardening.

MEAKER, MARIJANE AGNES, author; b. Auburn, N.Y., May 27, 1927; d. Ellis R. and Ida T. M. B.A., U. Mo., 1949; PhD (hon.), Southampton Coll., 1996. Author: novels (under own name) Sudden Endings, 1965, Hometown, 1967, Game of Survival, 1969, Don't Rely on Gemini, 1971, Shockproof Sydney Skate, 1972, 2d edit., 1990; (under pseudonym M.E. Kerr), Dinky Hocker Shoots Smack, 1972, Gentlehands, 1978, If I Love You, Am I Trapped Forever, 1973, I'll Love You When You're More Like Me, 1977, Is That You, Miss Blue?, 1975, Love is a Missing Person, 1975, The Son of Someone Famous, 1975, Little Little, 1981 (Soc. Children's Books Writers award 1982), What I Really Think of You, 1982, Me Me Me Me Me: Not a Novel (Best Books for Young Adults ALA), 1983, Him She Loves?, 1984, I Stay Near You (Best Books for Young Adults ALA), 1985, Night Kites, 1986, Fell, 1987, Fell Back, 1989, Fell Down, 1990; (under pseudonym Mary James) Shoebag, 1990, The Shuteyes, 1993, Frankenlouse, 1994, (M.E. Kerr) Linger, 1993, Deliver Us from Evie, 1994. Recipient Notable Children's Book award ALA, 1972, Book of Yr. award Sch. Library Jour., 1972, 77, 78, Christopher award, 1978, Night Kites award ALA, 1986, Margaret A. Edwards award ALA, 1993.

MEAL, LARIE, chemistry educator, researcher, consultant; b. Cin., June 15, 1939; d. George Lawrence Meal and Dorothy Louise (Heileman) Fitzpatrick. BS in Chemistry, U. Cin., 1961, PhD in Chemistry, 1966. Rsch. chemist U.S. Indsl. Chems., Cin., 1966-67; instr. chemistry U. Cin., 1968-69, asst. prof., 1969-75, assoc. prof., 1975-90, prof., 1990—, researcher, 1980—; cons. in field. Contbr. articles to sci. jours. Mem. AAAS, N.Y. Acad. Scis., Am. Chem. Soc., Internat. Assn. Arson Investigators, NOW, Planned Parenthood, Iota Sigma Pi. Democrat. Avocations: gardening, yard work. Home: 2231 Slane Ave Norwood OH 45212-3615 Office: U Cin 2220 Victory Pky Cincinnati OH 45206-2822

MEALER, LYNDA REAM, physical education educator; b. Lima, Ohio, Sept. 19, 1946; d. Don A. and Sue (Pringle) Duncan; m. Ben T. Mealer, Aug. 29, 1970; children: Thomas Lee, Theresa Lynn. AA, LaSalle U., Chgo., 1976; BS, La. State U., 1983, 1992. Office mgr. M. Quick Ins., Glenmora, La., 1975-77; ind. bus. owner Glenmora (La.) Exxon, 1977-82; kindergarten tchr. Glenmora (La.) Elem. Sch., 1986-87; 4th grade tchr., 1983-86, 92-94; 6th grade tchr. Forest Hill (La.) Acad., 1989-90; 4th grade tchr. Glenmora (La.) Elem. Sch., 1992-94; phys. edn. tchr., 1994—; intervention strategist Drug Free Schs., Rapides Parish, La., 1994-95; crisis intervention Team Glenmora (La.) Elem. Sch., 1994-95. Author: (poem) Who's Who in Poetry, 1993, Vengeance is Mine, 1988. Sec., pres. Glenmora (La.) Garden Club, 1974-87; sec., pres., legis. chair Bus. and Profl. Women, Glenmora, La., 1981-91. Recipient Student Svc. award Student Govt. Assn., La. State U. 1983, Lifetime mem. Gamma Beta Phi, La. State U., 1983, Scholarship award Sm. Assn. Women, Alexandria, La., 1992, Lifetime/charter mem. Golden Key Hon. Soc., Baton Rouge, La., 1992. Mem. NEA, La. Assn. Educators, Rapides Fedn. Tchrs. Avocations: reading, sewing, arts and crafts, home decorating, writing. Home: PO Box 72 806 Hwy 165 S Glenmora LA 71433 Office: Glenmora Elementary School PO Box 1188 Glenmora LA 71433-1188

MEALMAN, GLENN, corporate marketing executive; b. Prescott, Kans., June 10, 1934; s. Edgar R. and Mary E. (Holstein) M.; m. Gloria Gail Proch, June 12, 1955; children: Michael Edward, Cathy Gail. BS in Bus., Kans. State Coll., Emporia, 1957; postgrad., Harvard U., 1970. With Fleming Cos., Topeka, 1957—, sr. v.p. mktg., 1981-82, exec. v.p. mktg., 1982-86, exec. v.p. Mid-Am. region, 1986-93, exec. v.p. nat. accts., 1994—; dir. PBI-Gordon Co., KCCI. Pres. bd. Topeka YMCA, 1981; trustee Ottawa U., Kans., 1980. Served with USNR, 1954-56. Mem. Kans. State C. of C. and Industry (bd. dirs. 1991—), Blue Hills Country Club, Rotary. Baptist. Office: Fleming Cos Inc 7101 College Blvd Ste 850 Overland Park KS

66210-1891 also: Fleming Cos Inc 6301 Waterford Blvd Oklahoma City OK 73118-1103

MEALOR, WILLIAM THEODORE, JR., geography educator, university administrator, consultant; b. Atlanta, Apr. 20, 1940; s. William Theodore and Doris (Pittman) M.; m. Jennifer Joyce Hancock, Dec. 28, 1968; children—Stephen Theodore, Augustus Everett, William Griggs. B.A., U. Fla., 1962; M.A., U. Ga., 1964, Ph.D., 1972. Instr. dept. geography U. Ga., Athens, 1970-71; asst. prof. dept. geography and area devel. U. So. Miss., Hattiesburg, 1971-75, assoc. prof., 1975-78; asst. dean Coll. Liberal Arts, 1977-78; prof., chmn. dept. geography U. Memphis, 1978-83, prof., chmn. dept. geography and planning, 1983-86, interim dean Coll. Arts and Scis., 1987-88, assoc. v.p. for acad. affairs, 1988-92, chmn. dept. geography and planning, 1989-90, dir. instnl. self study, 1992-94, interim vice provost Acad. Affairs, 1992-94, prof. geography and planning, 1994—; cons. real estate devel. and land use analysis. Contbr. articles to profl. jours. Active Memphis Job Conf. Served to 1st lt. U.S. Army, 1964-66; Vietnam. Recipient Miss. Marine Resources Coun. award, 1974-75, U.S. Dept. Transp. award, 1974-76, 79-80, Miss. R&D Ctr. award, 1976-77, Carnegie Corp. award, 1988-89, NSF award, 1981, 89-91, 94—, Nat. Ctr. Acad. Achievement and Transfer award, 1991-94; NASA Remote Sensing grantee, 1972-75. Mem. Assn. Am. Geographers, Am. Geog. Soc., Nat. Council Geog. Edn., Tenn. Geog. Soc. (pres. 1984-86), Sigma Xi, Phi Kappa Phi, Pi Gamma Mu, Gamma Theta Upsilon, Pi Tau Chi, Sigma Chi, Omicron Delta Kappa. Presbyterian. Office: U Memphis Dept Geography Memphis TN 38152

MEANS, GEORGE ROBERT, organization executive; b. Bloomington, Ill., July 5, 1907; s. Arthur John and Alice (Johnson) M.; m. Martha Cowart, Aug. 5, 1950. B.Ed., Ill. State U., 1930; A.M., Clark U., 1932; HHD (hon.), Rikkyo U., Tokyo; H.H.D. (hon.), Ill. State U.; HHD (hon.), Ill. Wesleyan U., Ky. Wesleyan Coll. Cartographer, map editor, 1932-35; with Rotary Internat., 1935—; beginning as conv. mgr., successively head Middle Asia office Rotary Internat., Bombay, India; asst. gen. sec. Rotary Internat., 1948-52, gen. sec., 1953-72; sec. Rotary Found., 1953-72; hon. dir. Washington Nat. Corp.; dir. Hertzberg-New Method, Inc., Ind. State Retirement Home Guaranty Fund, 1982-95. Author: Rotary's Return to Japan, also numerous articles. Mem.-at-large nat. council Boy Scouts Am. Served as comdr. USNR, 1942-46. Decorated Legion of Honor France; Chilean Order of Merit; Japanese Order of Rising Sun; Italian Order of Merit; recipient Disting. Service award Geog. Soc. Chgo., 1972; Paul Harris fellow The Rotary Found. Fellow Am. Geog. Soc.; mem. Rotary Club (Evanston, Bloomington, Ill., Sydney, Australia, Kyoto, Osaka and Tokyo, Japan, Seoul, Korea, Cape Town, South Africa, Ituzaingo, Saavedra, Argentina, Greenwood, Ind.), Gamma Theta Upsilon. Home: 1067 Smock Dr Greenwood IN 46143-2426

MEANS, JOHN BARKLEY, foreign language educator, association executive; b. Cin., Jan. 2, 1939; s. Walker Wilson and Rosetta Miller (Barkley) M. BA, U. Ill., 1960, MA, 1963; PhD, U. Ill. at Urbana, 1968. U.S. govt. rsch. analyst on L.Am. CIA, Washington, 1962-64; assoc. prof. Spanish and Portugese Temple U., Phila., 1972-82, prof. critical langs., 1982—, co-chmn. dept. Spanish and Portuguese, 1971-75, dir. Center for Critical Langs., 1975—, dir. Inst. for Langs. and Internat. Studies, 1987—, chmn. dept. Germanic and Slavic Langs. and lit., 1992-94, chair univ. core programs, 1995-97; cons. on Brazilian-Portuguese and second lang. acquisition and self-instrnl. programs for less commonly taught langs., 1968—; cons. to founds., pubs., univs. and govt. agys. Editor: Essays on Brazilian Literature, 1971; author: (with others) Language in Education: Theory and Practice, 1988—; contbr. numerous articles to profl. jours. Trustee Bristol (Pa.) Riverside Theatre, 1990—; mng. trustee Means Charitable Trust, 1993—. 1st lt. U.S. Army, 1960-62. NDEA fellow, 1962, 64; grantee U.S. Dept. Edn., 1979-81, Japan Found., 1980, 82, 89-91, ARCO Chem. Found., 1991, 93. Mem. MLA, S.E., S.R., Nat. Coun. on Langs. and Internat. Studies (bd. dirs.), Joint Nat. Com. for Langs. (bd. dirs.), Nat. Assn. Self-Instrnl. Lang. Programs (exec. dir. 1977—, editor jour. 1978-94), Am. Coun. on Teaching Fgn. Lang., Nat. Coun. Orgns. Less Commonly Taught Langs. (exec. sec.-treas.), Nat. Assn. State Univs. and Land Grant Colls., Pi Kappa Phi, Phi Lambda Beta, Sigma Delta Pi. Home: PO Box 565 Yardley PA 19067-8565 Office: Temple U Anderson Hall 022-38 Ctr for Critical Langs Philadelphia PA 19122

MEANS, MICHAEL DAVID, hospital administrator; b. Lakeland, Fla., Jan. 19, 1950; married. B, U. Fla., 1971, MHA, 1974. Adminstrv. resident Manatee Meml. Hosp., Bradenton, Fla., 1974, adminstrv. asst., 1974-78; asst. dir. Orlando (Fla.) Regional Med. Ctr., 1978-80, assoc. exec. dir., 1980-81, exec. v.p., chief oper. officer, 1981-88; pres., chief exec. officer Holmes Regional Healthcare System, Melbourne, Fla., 1988—, Health First, Melbourne, Fla. Mem. Fla. Hosp. Assn. Home: 1848 River Shore Dr Indialantic FL 32903-4514 Office: Health First 8247 Devereaux DrSte 103 Melbourne FL 32940*

MEANS, NATRONE JERMAINE, professional football player. Student, U. N.C. Running back San Diego Chargers, 1991—. Selected to Pro Bowl, 1994. Mem. San Diego Chargers AFC Champions, 1994. Office: c/o San Diego Chargers PO Box 609609 San Diego CA 92160*

MEANS, TERRY ROBERT, federal judge; b. Roswell, N.Mex., July 3, 1948; s. Lewis Prude and Doris Emaree (Hightower) M.; m. JoAnn Huffman Harris, June 2, 1973; children: Robert, MaryAnn, Emily. BA, So. Meth. U., Dallas, 1971; JD, So. Meth. U., 1974. Bar: Tex. 1974, U.S. Dist. Ct. (no. dist.) Tex. 1976, U.S. Ct. Appeals (5th cir.) 1978, U.S. Dist. Ct. (we. dist., ea. dist.) Tex. 1991. Ptnr. Means & Means, Corsicana, Tex., 1974-88; justice 10th Ct. Appeals, Waco, Tex., 1989-90; judge U.S. Dist. Ct. for Northern Dist. Tex., Ft. Worth, 1991—. Chmn. Navarro County Rep. Party, Corsicana, 1976-88; pres. YMCA, Corsicana, 1984. Mem. State Bar Tex., Tarrant County Bar Assn., McLennan County Bar Assn. Baptist. Avocations: coaching soccer, racquetball. Office: 201 US Courthouse 501 W 10th St Fort Worth TX 76102-3637

MEANS, THOMAS CORNELL, lawyer; b. Charleston, S.C., Oct. 3, 1947; s. Thomas Lucas and Dean (Cornell) M.; m. Judith Faye Perlmutter, Sept. 10, 1977; children: Benjamin Thomas, Samuel Thomas. AB, Dartmouth Coll., 1969; postgrad., Princeton Theol. Sem., 1970-71; M of Pub. Adminstrn., U. Colo., 1975; JD, George Washington U., 1978. Bar: D.C. 1978, U.S. dist. Ct. (D.C. dist.), U.S. Ct. Appeals (4th and D.C. cirs.) 1979, U.S. Ct. Appeals (10th cir.) 1989, U.S. Ct. Appeals (9th cir.) 1992, U.S. Ct. Appeals (8th cir.) 1993, U.S. Ct. Appeals (5th cir.) 1996. Social worker Vinyard Childcare, Ann Arbor, Mich., 1969-70; rsch. analyst, registered lobbyist Colo. Counties, Inc., Denver, 1972-75; assoc. Jones, Day, Reavis and Pogue, Washington, 1978-79; assoc. then ptnr. Crowell & Moring, Washington, 1979—; mem. state adv. coun. on pub. Pers. Mgmt., Colo. State Govt., Denver, 1974-75; lectr. mining law; chmn. coal com. Ea. Mineral Law Found., 1988-89, chmn. spl. insts., ass. sec., 1989-91, sec., 1991-92, v.p., 1992-93, pres., 1993-94, exec. com., 1989-96; bd. advisors Nat. LAw Ctr., 1993-94. Contbr. articles to profl. jours. Trustee Ea. Mineral Law Found., 1989—, mem. adv. bd. editors, 1994—. Mem. George Washington Law Alumni Assn. (bd. dirs. 1986-96, exec. com. 1987-96, treas. 1987-88, sec. 1988-90, pres. 1992-94), Order of Coif, Cosmos Club (Washington), Phi Beta Kappa. Home: 6411 Dahlonega Rd Bethesda MD 20816-2101 Office: Crowell & Moring 1001 Pennsylvania Ave NW Washington DC 20004-2505

MEANY, JOHN JOSEPH, newspaper publisher; b. Port Jervis, N.Y., Nov. 7, 1939; s. John J. Sr. and Dorothy E. (Simmons) M.; m. Kathleen J. Wukich, June 15, 1978; children: Stephen, Patrick, Matthew, Mary Beth. BS, East Stroudsburg (Pa.) U., 1961; MS, SUNY, New Paltz, 1976. Tchr. Port Jervis High Sch., 1961-77; circulation mgr. Gazette-Jour., Reno, Nev., 1978-82; circulation dir. Tribune Star, Terra Haute, Ind., 1982-85, gen. mgr., 1985-89, pub., 1990—; pub. Times, Leavenworth, Kans., 1989-90. Dir. United Way, Terre Haute, 1985—, Boy Scouts, Terre Haute, 1991-92; bd. assocs. Rose Hulman Coll., Terre Haute, 1990—. Mem. Inland Press Assn., Terre Haute C. of C. (dir. 1990—). Roman Catholic. Avocations: reading, travel. Office: Tribune Star 721 Wabash Ave Terre Haute IN 47807-3220

MEARA, ANNE, actress, playwright, writer; b. Bklyn., Sept. 20; d. Edward Joseph and Mary (Dempsey) M.; m. Gerald Stiller, Sept. 14, 1954; children: Amy, Benjamin. Student, Herbert Berghoff Studio, 1953-54. Apprentice in summer stock, Southold, L.I. and Woodstock, N.Y., 1950-53; off-Broadway appearances include A Month in the Country, 1954, Maedchen in Uniform, 1955 (Show Bus. off-Broadway award), Ulysses in Nightown, 1958, The House of Blue Leaves, 1970, Spookhouse, 1983, Bosoms and Neglect, 1986, also with Shakespeare Co., Two Gentlemen of Verona, Cen. Park, N.Y.C., 1957, Romeo and Juliet, 1988, Eastern Standard, 1989, Anna Christie, 1993 (Tony nomination Best Supporting Actress), After-Play, 1995; film appearances include The Out-of-Towners, 1968, Lovers and Other Strangers, 1969, The Boys From Brazil, 1978, Fame, 1979, Nasty Habits (with husband Jerry Stiller), 1976, An Open Window, 1990, Mia, 1990, Awakenings, 1991, Reality Bites, 1994; comedy act, 1963—; appearances Happy Medium and Medium Rare, Chgo., 1960-61, Village Gate, Phase Two and Blue Angel, N.Y.C., 1963, The Establishment, London, 1963; syndicated TV series Take Five With Stiller and Meara, 1977-78; numerous appearances on TV game and talk shows, also spls. and variety shows; rec. numerous commls. for TV and radio (co-recipient Vocie of Imagery award Advt. Bur. N.Y.); star TV series Kate McShane, 1975; other TV appearances Archie Bunker's Place, 1979, The Sunset Gang, The Detective, 1990, Avenue Z Afternoon, 1991, Alf, 1986, Murphy Brown, 1994; writer, actress TV movie The Other Woman, 1983 (co-recipient Writer's Guild Outstanding Achievement award 1983), Alf, To Make Up to Break Up, The Stiller and Meara Pilot; author: (play) After-Play, 1994; video host (with Jerry Stiller) So You Want to Be an Actor?. Recipient Outer Critic's Cir. Playwriting award for "After-Play", 1995.

MEARS, PATRICK EDWARD, lawyer; b. Flint, Mich., Oct. 3, 1951; s. Edward Patrick and Estelle Veronica (Mislik) M.; m. Geraldine O'Connor, July 18, 1981. BA, U. Mich., 1973, JD, 1976. Bar: N.Y. 1977, U.S. Dist. Ct. (so. and ea. dists.) N.Y. 1977, Mich. 1980, U.S. Dist. Ct. (we. and ea. dists.) Mich. 1980, U.S. Ct. Appeals (6th cir.) 1983. Assoc. firm Milbank, Tweed, Hadley & McCloy, N.Y.C., 1976-79, ptnr. Warner, Norcross & Judd, Grand Rapids, Mich., 1980-91; sr. mem. Dykema Gossett PLLC, Grand Rapids, 1991—; adj. prof. Grand Valley State U., Allendale, Mich., 1981-84. Author: Michigan Collection Law, 1981, 2d edit., 1983, Basic Bankruptcy Law, 1986, Bankruptcy Law and Practice in Michigan, 1987; contbr. articles to profl jours. Chairperson legis. com. East Grand Rapids Parent-Tchr. Assn., 1992-94; dir. Children's Law Ctr., 1994, Grand Rapids Ballet, 1994—, East Grand Rapids Pub. Sch. Found., 1994—. Fellow Am. Coll. Bankruptcy; mem. ABA (vice chmn. workouts, enforcement of creditors rights, and bankruptcy com. ABA real property sect. 1995—), Mich. State Bar Assn. (mem., sec. coun. real property sect. 1993—), Am. Bankruptcy Inst., Fed. Bar Assn. (chairperson bankruptcy sect. We. Mich. chpt. 1992-94), Comml. Law League Am., Am. C. of C. in France, Grand Rapids Rotary, World Affairs Coun. of West Mich., West Mich. World Trade Assn., Peninsular Club (Grand Rapids), East Hills Athletic Club. Office: Dykema Gossett 200 Old Town Riverfront Bu Grand Rapids MI 49503

MEARS, WALTER ROBERT, journalist; b. Lynn, Mass., Jan. 11, 1935; s. Edward Lewis and Edythe Emily (Campbell) M.; m. Sally Danton, Dec. 28, 1956 (dec. Dec. 1962); children: Pamela (dec.), Walter Robert Jr. (dec.); m. Joyce Marie Lund, Aug. 4, 1963 (div. 1983); children: Stephanie Joy, Susan Marie; m. Carroll Ann Rambo, Mar. 1, 1986 (div. 1995). B.A., Middlebury Coll., 1956, Litt.D. (hon.), 1977. Newsman AP, Boston, 1956; corr. AP, Montpelier, Vt., 1956-60; state house corr. AP, Boston, 1960-61; newsman AP, Washington, 1961-69; chief polit. writer AP, 1969-72, asst. chief Washington bur., 1973-74, spl. corr., 1975, chief, 1977-83, v.p., 1978—, exec. editor, 1984-88, v.p., columnist, 1989—. Author: (with John Chancellor) The News Business, 1983, The New News Business, 1995. Trustee Middlebury Coll., 1980-84. Recipient ann. award AP Mng. Editors Assn., 1973; Pulitzer prize for Nat. Reporting, 1977. Mem. Phi Beta Kappa, Delta Kappa Epsilon. Clubs: Gridiron, Burning Tree. Home: 1556N 21st Court Arlington VA 22206 Office: Associated Press 2021 K St NW Ste 600 Washington DC 20006-1003

MEASELLE, RICHARD LELAND, accountant; b. Detroit, Sept. 29, 1938; s. Leland Stanford and Jean Therese (Saydak) M; children: Jeffrey, Laura, Susana, Millicent, Stephen; m. Alison Price, Dec. 2, 1995. BS in Bus., Miami U., Oxford, Ohio, 1961. Office mng. ptnr. Arthur Andersen, Barcelona, Spain, 1970-72, Detroit, 1975-87; mng. ptnr. acctg. and audit worldwide Arthur Andersen, 1987-89, worldwide mng. ptnr., 1989—; area mng. ptnr. Arthur Andersen, Mich., Ohio, Ky. and Wis., 1985-87; mem., bd. ptnrs., mem. exec. com. Arthur Andersen Worldwide Orgn. Co-author: Helping Public Schools Succeed, 1989. Chmn. bd. trustees U. Detroit, 1985; trustee Detroit Econ. Growth Corp., 1975-87; chmn. United Negro Coll. Fund, Detroit, 1982; hon. Spanish consul to Mich.; mem. vis. com. U. Mich. Sch. Bus. Adminstrn., Tax Found.'s Policy Coun, 1990; mem. com. Chgo. Coun. Fgn. Rels., 1991; mem. Brit. N.Am. Com.; bd. dirs. Field Mus. Natural History. With USMC, 1958-64, Res. Named Hon. Alumnus of Yr. U. Detroit, 1984, Acct. of Yr. Beta Alpha Psi-Miami U., 1989; recipient Pres.'s Cabinet award U. Detroit, 1989. Mem. AICPA, The Econ. Club of N.Y. Avocations: skiing, tennis. Office: Arthur Andersen 69 W Washington St Ste 3500 Chicago IL 60602-3004 Office: Arthur Andersen 69 W Washington St Ste 3500 Chicago IL 60602-3004

MEAT LOAF (MARVIN LEE ADAY), popular musician, actor; b. Dallas, Sept. 27, 1951; m. Leslie Aday (Edmonds), 1975; children: Pearl, Amanda. Albums include Featuring Stoney and Meat Loaf, 1970, Free For All, 1976, Bat OutOf Hell, 1977, DeadRinger, 1982, Midnight at The Lost and Found, 1983, Bad Attitude, 1984, Hits Out Of Hell, 1985, Blind Before I Stop, 1986, Meat Loaf Live, 1987, Bat Out Of Hell II: Back Into Hell, 1993; appeared in plays Hair, The RockyHorror Show, National Lampoon Show, More Than You Deserve, Rockabye Hamlet, BillyThe Kid & Jean Harlow, As You Like It, Othello; appeared in films The Rocky Horror Picture Show, 1975, Americathon, 1979, Scavenger Hunt, 1979, Roadie, 1980,Dead Ringer, 1981, The Squeeze, 1986, Out of Bounds, 1986, Motorama, 1990, Gun & Betty Lou's Handbag, 1991, Wayne's World, 1992, Leap of Faith, 1992. Received Grammy for Best Rock Vocal Solo Performance, 1993. Office: c/o MCA Records 70 Universal Terrace Pky Universal City CA 91608

MEBANE, GEORGE ALLEN, corporate executive, rancher; b. Greensboro, N.C., Sept. 28, 1929; s. George Allen III and Elizabeth (Armstrong) M.; m. Pat Pannill, Aug. 23, 1950 (dec.); children: George Allen IV, William Michael, Lucy Mebane Webster; m. Marianne Cheek, June 28, 1987. BS, Phila. Coll. Textile and Sci., 1950, D Textiles (hon.), 1986. Supr. Sale Knitting Co., Martinsville, Va., 1950-52; salesman Am. & Efird Mills, Mt. Holly, N.C., 1954-56, Burlington, Ind., Greensboro, 1956-64; pres., chief exec. officer Throwing Corp. Am., Swepsonville, N.C., 1964-67, Universal Textured Yarns, Inc., Mebane, N.C., 1967-71; pres., chief exec. officer Unifi, Inc., Greensboro, 1971-78, chmn., chief exec. officer, 1978-85, chmn., 1985—. Sgt. U.S. Army, 1952-54; Korea. Mem. Am. Synthetic Yarns Assn. (bd. dirs. 1977-80), Am. Textile Mfg. Inst. (bd. dirs. 1986-89), N.C. Textile Assn. (bd. dirs. 1988-90). Democrat. Presbyterian. Office: Unifi Inc PO Box 19109 Greensboro NC 27419-9109*

MEBANE, WILLIAM BLACK, controller, financial consultant; b. Vernon, Tex., Dec. 15, 1927; s. David Mitchell and Ida Virginia (Black) M.; m. Joan Hebbard Dumper, Nov. 24, 1956; children—David Alexander, Virginia Ann. B.B.A., Tex. A&M U., 1952; M.B.A., Harvard U., 1954. Mem. treas.'s office staff Gen. Motors Corp., N.Y.C., 1954-70; sec.-treas. Alfred P. Sloan Found., N.Y.C., 1971-78; dir. fin. and adminstrn. Am. Diabetes Assn., N.Y.C., 1979-80; dir. planning Am. Diabetes Assn., 1981; v.p., comptroller NCCJ, Inc., N.Y.C., 1981-86, v.p. for fiscal affairs, 1987-88; fin. cons. Internat. House, N.Y.C., 1989-90; ind. fin. cons., 1990-91; contr. Better Bus. Bur., N.Y.C., 1991—. Vol. Essex Council Boy Scouts Am., 1967—. Served with USAAF, 1946-49. Recipient Silver Beaver award Boy Scouts Am., 1982. Republican. Episcopalian. Clubs: Harvard Bus. Sch. (N.Y.C.); Short Hills (N.J.). Home: 36 Haddonfield Rd Short Hills NJ 07078-3402

MEBANE, WILLIAM DEBERNIERE, newspaper publisher; b. Durham, N.C., Jan. 14, 1949; s. John Gilmer and Harriet deBerniere (Elmore) M.; m. Catharine Frampton McGee, May 30, 1970; children—William deBerniere, Harriet Bacot, Jane Bacot, Catharine Frampton, John McGee, Beverly Canby. B.A., U. N.C., 1971, cert. in exec. program, 1981. V.p. Greenville News-Piedmont, S.C., 1976-82, bus. mgr., 1976-78, gen. mgr., 1978-81, co-pub., 1981-84, pres., 1982—, pub., 1984-92; v.p. Multimedia Newspaper Co., Greenville, 1984-92, pres., 1989—; v.p. Multimedia Inc., 1989—. Commr. S.C. Mental Retardation Commn., 1983-89, vice chmn., 1988; past pres. Greenville Symphony Assn.; campaign chmn. United Way Greenville County, 1984, v.p. resource devel., 1985, v.p. mktg. and comms., 1986, 1st v.p., 1987, pres., 1988; treas. Goodwill Industries of Upper S.C., 1980-81; past pres. Greenville Assn. Retarded Children; mem. First Amendment Congress Bd., 1987-88, N.C. Soc. of the Cin., Corp. Coalition on Infant Mortality, 1988; bd. dirs. Greenville Hosp. System, 1993—. Mem. AP (com. 1985—, nominating com. 1991—, chmn. 1992—), Am. Newspaper Pubs. Assn. (com. 1982—), So. Newspaper Pubs. Assn. (treas. 1990, chmn. com. 1983-84, pres. 1992, chmn. 1993), So. Govs. Assn., S.C. Press Assn. (treas. 1984-85, v.p. dailies 1986, pres. 1987), Young Pres.'s Orgn., Huguenot Soc., Greenville C. of C. (bd. dirs., v.p. 1981-82, bd. dirs. 1987-88), Poinsett Club, Delta Kappa Epsilon. Avocation: outdoorsman. Home: 119 Crescent Ave Greenville SC 29605-2812 Office: Multimedia Newspaper Co 305 S Main St PO Box 1688 Greenville SC 29602-1688

MEBUS, ROBERT GWYNNE, lawyer; b. Ft. Worth, Aug. 28, 1940; s. Robert Lee and Lucille (Cooke) M.; children: Elizabeth, Mary Ellen. BBA, So. Meth. U., 1962, LLB, 1965. Bar: Tex. 1965, U.S. Dist. Ct. (no. and ea. dists.) 1966, U.S. Ct. Appeals (5th cir.) 1965, U.S. Supreme Ct. 1969. Assoc. Malone, Seay & Gwinn, Dallas, 1965-67; ptnr. Seay, Gwinn, Crawford, Dallas, 1967-69, Seay, Gwinn, Crawford, Mebus, Dallas, 1969-82, Haynes and Boone, Dallas, 1982—; Mem. Tex. State Bar (chmn. labor law sect. 1982-83, chmn. labor law adv. commn. 1982-83), Tex. Bd. Legal Specialization. Contbg. editor: (book) Developing Labor Law, 1967, 2d edit., 1987. Mem. ABA (labor law sect.), Tex. Bar Found. Avocations: tennis, photography, gardening. Office: Haynes and Boone 3100 NationsBank Plz 901 Main St Dallas TX 75202-3714

MEBUST, WINSTON KEITH, surgeon, educator; b. Malta, Mont., July 2, 1933; s. Hans G. and Anna C. (Leiseth) M.; m. Lora June Peterson, Sept. 15, 1955; children—Leanne, Kevin, Kreg, Kari. Student, U. Wash., 1951-54, M.D., 1958. Diplomate: Am. Bd. Urology (trustee 1983-89, pres. 1988-89). Intern King County Hosp., Seattle, 1958-59; resident Virginia Mason Hosp., Seattle, 1959-63, Kans. U. Med. Center, 1963-66; practice medicine, specializing in urology, 1966—; instr. surgery and urology U. Kans. Med. Center, Kansas City, 1966-69; asst. prof. U. Kans. Med. Center, 1969-72, asso. prof., 1972-76, chmn. urology sect., 1974—, prof., 1977—; chief urology service VA Hosp., Kansas City, Mo., 1966-75. Contbr. articles, chpts. to med. jours. and texts. Served with U.S. Army, 1961-63. Mem. ACS, Am. Cancer Soc., Am. Bd. Surgery, Kansas City Urol. Assn., Assn. for Acad. Surgery, Am. Urol. Assn. (pres South Cen. sect. 1983, exec. com. 1992—), Wyandotte Med. Soc., Kans. Med. Assn., Soc. Univ. Urologists, Am. Assn. Genitourinary Surgeons, Sigma Xi, Alpha Omega Alpha. Republican. Home: 292 Seneca Trl W Kansas City KS 66106-9689 Office: 39th and Rainbow Blvd Kansas City MO 66103

MECH, TERRENCE FRANCIS, library director; b. Birdorup Park, Wiltshire, Eng., Feb. 24, 1953; s. Emil Paul and Madelyn (Tremmel) M. BS, U. Wis., Stevens Point, 1975; MS, Ill. State U., 1978; MLS, Clarion U., 1979; EdD, Pa. State U., 1994. Pub. svcs. libr. Tusculum Coll., Greensville, Tenn., 1979-80; libr. dir. Coll. of the Ozarks, Clarksville, Ark., 1980-82; libr. dir. King's Coll., Wilkes-Barre, Pa., 1982-94, v.p. for info. and instrnl. techs., dir. libr., 1994—; bd. dirs. Northeastern Pa. Bibliographic Ctr., 1982—; mem., officer Coun. Pa. Libr. Networks, 1984-89, chair, 1987-89. Contbr. chpts. to books and articles to profl. jours. Mem. ALA, Pa. Libr. Assn. (bd. dirs. 1986-87, various coms. 1985—). Office: Kings Coll 14 W Jackson St Wilkes Barre PA 18701-2010

MECHAM, GLENN JEFFERSON, lawyer, mayor; b. Logan, Utah, Dec. 11, 1935; s. Everett H. and Lillie (Dunford) M.; m. Mae Parson, June 5, 1957; children: Jeff B., Scott R., Marcia, Suzanne. BS, Utah State U., 1957; JD, U. Utah, 1961; grad. Air Command and Staff Coll., Air War Coll., 1984. Bar: Utah 1961, Supreme Ct. U.S., U.S. Ct. Appeals (10th Cir.), U.S. Dist. Ct. Utah, U.S. Ct. Claims. Gen. practice law, 1961-65; atty. Duchesne County, Utah, 1962, City of Duchesne, 1962; city judge Roy City, Utah, 1963-66; judge City of Ogden, Utah, 1966-69, mayor, 1992—; lectr. law and govt. Stevens-Henager Coll., Ogden, 1963-75; asst. U.S. atty., 1969-72; ptnr. Mecham & Richards, Ogden, Utah, 1972-82; pres. Penn Mountain Mining Co., South Pacific Internat. Bank, Ltd.; mem. Bur. Justice Stats. Adv. Bd., U.S. Dept. Justice, U.S. Conf. Mayors. Chmn. Ogden City Housing Authority; chmn. bd. trustees Utah State U., Space Dynamics Lab. Utah State U.; mem. adv. coun. Fed. Home Loan Bank; pres. Utah League Cities and Towns, 1981-82. Col. USAF, 1957. Mem. ABA, Weber County Bar Assn. (pres. 1966-68), Utah Bar Assn., Am. Judicature Soc., Weber County Bar Legal Svcs. (chmn. bd. trustees 1966-69), Utah Assn. Mcpl. Judges (sec.), Sigma Chi, Phi Alpha Delta. Home: 1715 Darling St Ogden UT 84403-0556 Office: City of Ogden 2484 Washington Blvd # 300 Ogden UT 84401

MECHAM, STEVEN RAY, school system administrator; b. Salt Lake City, Oct. 10, 1938; s. Milton Claudius and Marjorie (White) M.; m. Donna Jean Johnson, Jan. 22, 1943; children: Brian Paul, Allan LeRoy. AS, Weber State Coll., 1958; BS, U. Utah, 1963; MA, Tchrs. Coll., Columbia U., 1965; postgrad. McGill U.; PhD U. Santa Barbara, Calif., 1981. Prin., Montreal (Que.) Oral Sch., 1966-70; state dir. hearing impaired Conn. Dept. Edn., 1970-71; dir. guidance Lexington Sch. for the Deaf, N.Y.C., 1971-72; supt. Exton Elem., Ana Frank Jr. & Sr. High Sch., Mexico City, 1972-77; coord. spl. edn. Weber Sch. Dist., Ogden, Utah, 1977-78; prin. Roosevelt Elem. Sch., Ogden, 1978-82; asst. supt. Weber County Schs., Ogden, 1982-87, Utah Schs., 1990—, assoc. supt. 1990-93; supt. Weber Sch. Dist., 1993—; instr. U. Utah, 1965-66, St. Joseph Coll., Hartford, Conn., 1970-71; pres. Finnish Mission-LDS Russia and Baltic States, 1987-90; adj. prof. McGill U.; instr. Tchrs. Coll., Columbia U., 1968-70; acting chmn. dept. edn. U. Americas, Mexico City, 1976-77; cons. Far West Labs., San Francisco. Bd. dirs. Instituto Mexicano Norte Americano de Relaciones Culturales, Mexico City, 1975-76; bishop Ch. Jesus Christ of Latter-day Saints, chmn. Cancer Crusade; pres. Finnish Mission Ch. Jesus Christ of Latter-day Saints; bd. dirs. Am. Cancer Soc. Weber County. Mem. Am. Orgn. Educators of Hearing Impaired (pres.), Can. Hearing Soc. (dir.), Utah Assn. Elem. Sch. Prins., Nat. Assn. Elem. Sch. Prins., Internat. Reading Assn., Am. Assn. Sch. Adminstrs., Alexander Graham Bell Assn. Club: Rotary. Contbr. articles to profl. jours. Home: 2163 Jennifer Dr Ogden UT 84403-4965 Office: 5320 Adams Ave Ogden UT 84405

MECHANIC, DAVID, social sciences educator; b. N.Y.C., Feb. 21, 1936; s. Louis and Tillie (Penn) M.; m. Kathleen Mars Wiltshire; children: Robert Edmund, Michael Alexander. B.A., CCNY, 1956; M.A., Stanford U., 1957, Ph.D., 1959. Faculty U. Wis., Madison, 1960-79; prof. sociology U. Wis., 1965-73, John Bascom prof., 1973-79; dir. U. Wis. (Center for Med. Sociology and Health Services Research), 1971-79, chmn. dept. sociology, 1968-70; prof. social work and sociology Rutgers U., New Brunswick, N.J., 1979—; acting dean faculty arts and scis. Rutgers U., 1980-81, Univ. prof., dean faculty arts and scis., 1981-84, Univ. prof. and Rene Dubos prof. behavioral scis., 1984—, dir. Inst. for Health, Health Care Policy and Aging Research, 1985—; mem. panel on health svcs. rsch. Pres.'s Sci. Adv. Com., 1971-72; mem. treatment com. on reduction of cancer mortality Nat. Cancer Inst., 1984; vice-chmn. com. pain, disability and chronic illness behavior Inst. Medicine-NAS, 1985-86, mem. panel on prevention of disability, 1989-90; mem. Com. on Prevention of Mental Disorder, 1992-94; coord. panel Pres.'s Commn. Mental Health, 1977-78; mem. Nat. Adv. Coun. Aging, NIH, 1982-86; expert adv. panel on mental health WHO, 1984-89; mem. health adv. bd. GAO, 1987-95; mem. panel on tech., ins. and health care sys. Office of Tech. U.S. Congress, 1992-95; mem. nat. com. on vital and health stats. HHS, 1988-92; mem. commn. on behavioral and social scis. and edn. NRC, 1992-95, commn. on med. edn. Robert Wood Johnson Found., 1990-92; mem. adv. com. Picker/Commonwealth Scholar's Program, 1992—; nat. adv. com. Robert Wood Johnson Scholars in Health Policy Rsch. Program, 1992—; mem. panel on Rethinking Disability Policy, Nat. Acad. Social Ins., 1993-96; vis. scholar Kings Fund Inst., london, 1994-95. Author: Students Under Stress, 1962, 2d edit., 1978, Medical Sociology, 1968, rev. edit., 1978, Mental Health and Social Policy, 1969, rev. edit., 1980, 89, Public Expectations and

Health Care, 1972, Politics, Medicine and Social Science, 1974, (with Charles E. Lewis and Rashi Fein) A Right to Health, 1976, Growth of Bureaucratic Medicine, 1976, Future Problems in Health Care, 1979, From Advocacy to Allocation: The Evolving American Health Care System, 1986, Painful Choices: Research and Essays on Health Care, 1989, Inescapable Decisions: The Imperatives of Health Reform, 1994; author, editor: Symptoms, Illness Behavior and Help-Seeking; editor: Handbook of Health, Health Care and the Health Professions, 1983, Improving Mental Health Services: What the Social Sciences Can Tell Us, 1987; Co-editor: (with Robert Houser, Archibald Haller and Tess Hauser) Social Structure and Personality, 1982, (with Linda Aiken) Applications of Social Science to Clinical Medicine and Social Policy, 1986; Paying for Services: Promises and Pitfalls of Capitation, 1989; (with Marian Osterweis and Arthur Kleinman) Pain and Disability: Clinical Behavior and Public Policy Perspectives, 1987, (with Carl Taube and Ann Hohmann) The Future of Mental Health Services Research, 1989. Fellow Ctr. for Advanced Study in Behavioral Scis., 1974-75, NIMH rsch. fellow, 1965-66, Ford Behavioral Sci. fellow, 1956-57, Guggenheim fellow, 1977-78; recipient Ward medal CCNY, 1956, Med. Sociologists award Am. Sociol. Assn., 1983, Carl Taube award APHA, 1990, Disting. Investigator award Assn. for Health Svcs. Rsch., 1991, Disting. Contbn. award mental health sect. Soc. for Study of Social Problems, 1991, Emily Mumford medal Columbia U., 1991, Investigator award in health policy rsch. Robert Wood Johnson Found., 1995—. Fellow AAAS (chmn. sect. social, econ. and polit. scis. 1985); mem. Am. Sociol. Assn. (governing coun. 1977-78, chmn. med. sociol. sect. 1969-70, chmn. publs. com. 1989-91, chmn. mental health sect. 1992-93), Sociol. Rsch. Assn. (pres. 1991-92), Inst. Medicine-Nat. Acad. Scis. (governing coun. 1972-74), Nat. Acad. Scis., Am. Acad. Arts and Scis., Hogg Found. Mental Health (nat. adv. coun. 1987), Phi Beta Kappa. Office: Rutgers U Inst Health Care Policy and Aging Rsch 30 College Ave New Brunswick NJ 08901-1245 Home: 14 Cameron Ct Princeton NJ 08540-3924

MECHANIC, WILLIAM M., television and motion picture industry executive; b. Detroit. BA in English, Mich. State U.; PhD in Film, U. So. Calif. Dir. programming SelecTV, 1978-80, v.p. programming, 1980-82; v.p. pay TV Paramount Pictures Corp., 1982-84; v.p. pay TV sales Walt Disney Pictures and TV, 1984-85, sr. v.p. video, 1985-87, pres. internat. theatrical distbn. and worldwide video, 1987-93; pres., COO 20th Century Fox Film Entertainment, 1993—. Office: 20th Century Fox PO Box 900 Beverly Hills CA 90213-0900*

MECHEM, CHARLES STANLEY, JR., former broadcasting executive, former golf association executive; b. Nelsonville, Ohio, Sept. 12, 1930; s. Charles Stanley and Helen (Hall) M.; m. Marilyn Brown, Aug. 31, 1952; children: Melissa, Daniel, Allison. A.B., Miami U., Oxford, Ohio, 1952; LL.B., Yale U., 1955. Bar: Ohio 1955. Practice in Cin., 1955-67; partner Taft, Stettinius & Hollister, 1965-67; chmn. bd. Taft Broadcasting Co., Cin., 1967-90; commr. LPGA, Daytona Beach, Fla., 1990-95, commr. emeritus, 1995—; chmn. U.S. Shoe, 1993-95; chmn. Cin. Bell, Inc., 1996—; bd. dirs. Star Bank N.A., Cin., AGCO Corp., Myers Y. Cooper Co., Mead Corp., Ohio Nat. Life Ins. Co., Cin. Bell, J.M. Smucker Co. Capt. JAGC, U.S. Army, 1956-59. Mem. Cin. C. of C. (pres. 1977). Club: Commercial (Cin.). Office: Cin Bell Inc 7th fl 120 E 4th St Cincinnati OH 45202

MECHEM, EDWIN LEARD, judge; b. Alamogordo, N.Mex., July 2, 1912; s. Edwin and Eunice (Leard) M.; Dorothy Heller, Dec. 30, 1932 (dec. 1972); children: Martha M. Vigil, John H., Jesse (dec. 1968), Walter M.; m. Josephine Donavan, May 28, 1976. L.L.B., U. Ark., 1939; L.L.D. (hon.), N.Mex. State U., 1975. Bar: N.Mex. 1939, U.S. Dist. Ct. N.Mex. 1939. Lawyer Las Cruces and Albuquerque, 1939-70; now judge U.S. Dist. Ct. N.Mex., Albuquerque; spl. agt. FBI Dept. Justice, various locations, 1942-45; mem. legislature State of N.Mex., 1947-48, gov., 1951-54, 57-58, 61-62; senator U.S. Govt., Washington, 1963-64. Mem. ABA, N.Mex. Bar Assn., Am. Law Inst. Republican. Methodist. Avocation: travel. Office: US Dist Ct PO Box 97 Albuquerque NM 87103-0097*

MECHLEM, DAPHNE JO, vocational school educator; b. Cin., Oct. 20, 1946; d. Louis Edward Griffith and Esther Eileen (Calvert) Griffith-Schultz; m. James T. Mechlem, Nov. 18, 1967 (div. June 1983); 1 chld, Louis Henry. BS summa cum laude, U. Cin., 1982, MS, 1983, MEd, 1984. Cert. vocat. and adult dir., supr., cosmetology instr., real estate agt. Stylist, mgr. Fashion Flair Styling, Cin., 1965-70, Ann Wolfe Coiffures, Cin., 1970-71; salon owner Curls by Daphne, Cin., 1971-77; tchr. Great Oaks Joint Vocat. Sch. Dist., Cin., 1976-83, adminstrv. intern, 1983; probation officer Hamilton County Juvenile Ct., Cin., 1983—; tchr. Great Oaks Joint Vocat. Sch. Dist., Cin., 1983—; spkr., presenter workshops in field. Author: Critical Issues in Campus Policing, 1983; lectr: workshops, seminars and classes. Mem. ASCD, Nat. Cosmetology Assn., Criminal Justice Assn., Am. Vocat. Assn., Ohio Vocat. Assn., Ohio Vocat. Cosmetology Tchrs. Assn. Avocations: flying, travel, counseling. Home: 5776 Pleasant Hill Rd Milford OH 45150-2301

MECHLIN, GEORGE FRANCIS, electrical manufacturing company executive; b. Pitts., July 23, 1923; s. George Francis and Ruth (Butler) M.; m. Mary Louise Megaffin, June 25, 1949; children—Thomas Walker, Ann Louise. B.S. in Physics, U. Pitts., 1944, M.S. in Physics, 1949, Ph.D. in Physics, 1951. With Westinghouse Electric Corp., 1949-87; gen. mgr. astronuclear/oceanic div. Westinghouse Electric Corp., Balt., 1971-72, v.p. astronuclear lab., oceanic and marine divs., 1972-73; v.p. R & D Westinghouse Electric Corp., Pitts., 1973-87; pub. svc. cons., 1990—. Past bd. dirs. Buhl Planatarium. Recipient Meritorious Public Service award U.S. Navy, 1961, John J. Montgomery award Nat. Soc. Aerospace Profls. and San Diego Aerospace Mus., 1961; Order of Merit award Westinghouse Electric Corp., 1961. Mem. Am. Phys. Soc., AIAA, Nat. Acad. Engring., Sigma Xi. Home: 960 Via Malibu Aptos CA 95003-5617

MECIMORE, CHARLES DOUGLAS, accounting educator; b. Belmont, N.C., Aug. 20, 1934; s. John Edgar and Hattie (Bolick) M.; m. Barbara Jean Chiddie, June 7, 1959; children: Laura Jean, Charles D. Jr., John Amos. BS, Pfeiffer Coll., 1958; MS, U. N.C., 1962; PhD, U. Ala., 1966. CPA, N.C.; CMA. Asst. prof. U. Ala., Tuscaloosa, 1966-67; assoc. prof. U. Ga., Athens, 1967-71; prof. U. Cin., 1971-79; prof. acctg. Sch. Bus. and Econs., U. N.C., Greensboro, 1980—; head dept. U. N.C. Sch. Bus. and Econs., 1980-89, 96—. Served with USAF, 1951-55. Univ. scholar, 1963-66; Haskins and Sells fellow, 1962-64; Beyer bronze medal, 1974. Mem. AICPAs, N.C. Assn. CPAs (Outstanding Educator 1985), Am. Acctg. Assn., Inst. Mgmt. Acctg. Home: 1312 Westridge Rd Greensboro NC 27410-2940 Office: Sch Bus and Econs U NC Greensboro NC 27412

MECKE, THEODORE HART MCCALLA, JR., management consultant; b. Phila., Mar. 6, 1923; s. Theodore Hart McCalla and Genevieve (Loughney) M.; m. Mary E. Flaherty, July 14, 1956; children: William Moyn, Theodore Hart III, John Chetwood, Stephen Campbell. Student, LaSalle U., Phila., 1941, LL.D. (hon.), 1964; D Mgmt. (hon.), Lawrence Technol. U., 1983. Mng. editor Germantown (Pa.) Courier, 1942-43, 46-49; with Ford Motor Co., Dearborn, Mich., 1949-80; gen. pub. rels. mgr. Ford Motor Co., 1957-63, v.p. pub. rels., 1963-69, v.p. pub. affairs group, 1969-80; pres. Econ. Club Detroit, 1980-84, Hartwood Assocs., Detroit, 1984-93; trustee Henry Ford Health Sys., Detroit. Served with AUS, 1943-45. Mem. Mil. Order Loyal Legion, Am. Legion. Roman Catholic. Clubs: Country of Detroit, Detroit, Yondotega. Home: 400 Chalfonte Ave Grosse Pointe MI 48236-2943

MECKEL, PETER TIMOTHY, arts administrator, educator; b. Yankton, S.D., Nov. 28, 1941; s. Myron Eugene and Cynthia Ann (Turnblom) M.; m. Louise Gloria Mudge, Sept. 8, 1962; children: Christina Louise, Christopher Mark; m. Adrienne Dawn Maravich, Dec. 30, 1972; children: Moya Anne, Jon-Peter. Ed. Rockford Coll., Occidental Coll. Founder, gen. dir. Hidden Valley Music Seminars, Carmel Valley, Calif., 1963—, dir. Hidden Valley Opera Ensemble, Masters Festival of Chamber Music, Master Class Series; cons. in field. Mem. Music Educators Nat. Conf. Congregationalist. Office: Hidden Valley Opera Ensemble PO Box 116 Carmel Valley CA 93924-0116

MECKLENBURG, GARY ALAN, hospital executive; m. Lynn Kraemer; children: John, Sarah. BA, Northwestern U., 1968; MBA, U. Chgo., 1970. Adminstrv. resident Presbyn.-St. Luke's Hosp., Chgo., 1969-70, adminstrv. asst., 1970-71, asst. supt., 1971-76, assoc. supt., 1976-77; assoc. supt. U. Wis. Hosps., Madison, 1977-80; adminstr. Stanford U. Hosp. Clinics, Calif.; pres., CEO St. Joseph's Hosp., Milw., 1980-85; pres., dir. Franciscan Health Care Inc., Milw., 1985; pres., CEO Northwestern Meml. Hosp., Northwestern Meml. Corp., Chgo., 1985—; preceptor, guest lectr., mem. adv. bd. Kellogg Sch. Mgmt., chgo., 1986—; pres., chief exec. officer, dir. Northwestern Healthcare Network, 1990-92. Recipient Harold M. Coon, M.D. Merit award Wis. Hosp. Assn., 1974. Mem. Am. Hosp. Assn. (sect. met. hosps., mem. bd. trustees 1996—, chmn. sect. 1991, mem. regional policy bd., #5 1984-85, 87-94, 95—, mem. ho. dels. 1984, 87, mem. com. on med. edn. 1987-90), Ill. Hosp. Assn. (bd. dirs. 1988—, chmn. 1994, mem. steering com. coun. tchg. hosps. 1985—), U. Chgo. Hosp. Adminstrn. Alumni Assn. (pres. 1985-86), Econ. Club Chgo., Comml. Club Chgo. Office: Northwestern Meml Hosp Superior St & Fairbanks Ct Chicago IL 60611

MECKLER, ALAN MARSHALL, publisher, author; b. N.Y.C., July 25, 1945; s. Herman Louis and Lillian (Brodsky) M.; m. Ellen Laurie Finkelstein, Sept. 10, 1969; children—Naomi, Kate, Caroline, John. B.A., Columbia Coll., 1967; M.A., Columbia U., 1968, Ph.D., 1980. Pres., chmn., CEO Mecklermedia Corp., Westport, Conn., 1970—. Author: The Draft and Its Enemies, 1973; Micropublishing: A History of Scholarly Micropublishing in America, 1938-80, 1982; Complete Guide to Winning Lotteries by Mail, 1985. Served with USAR, 1969-75. Office: 20 Ketchum St Westport CT 06880-5808

MECREDY, JAMES R., management consultant; b. Roanoke, Va., Sept. 24, 1918; s. James Roderick and Rosalie Digges (Miller) M.; m. Alice Chatfield, April 8, 1944; children: Robert Clark, Thomas Randolph, Russell Edwards. BSME, Purdue U., 1941; attended, Case Inst. Tech., 1946-48, Alexander Hamilton Inst., 1941-43. Student engr. Gen. Motors Corp., Anderson, Ind., 1941-43; foundry foreman Delco-Remy-G.M., Bedford, Ind., 1943-45; foundry engr., trouble shooter Nat. Bronze and Aluminum Foundry Co., Cleve., 1945-46; machine designer Motch & Merryweather Machinery Co., Cleve., 1946-47; engr. Cleve. Range Co., 1947-54, chief engr., 1954-71, v.p. ops., 1971-74; mgmt. cons., 1974-75; tchr. shop, math. Delco-Remy Foundary, Bedford, Ind., 1943-44, blue print reading, 1943-44. Author: (manual) Instrn. and Maintenance Manual, 1973, District Boy Scouts, 1959; patentee. Dir., coach swimming Anderson YMCA, 1941-42; coach Little League Baseball, Lakewood, Ohio, 1950; precinct committeeman Rep. Com., 1945-46; chmn. dist. fund raising Boy Scouts Am., 1975, scoutmaster, 1955-77, chmn. protestant com., 1974-94. Recipient Scouting Wood badge, 1964, Silver Beaver award Boy Scouts Am., 1968, Nat. Hornaday award N.Y. Zool. Body, 1977, St. Georges award Cleve. Cath. Diocese, 1982, God and Svc. award Presbyn. Western Res., 1991, Nat. Eagle Scout Scoutmaster award, 1990. Mem. Nat. Assn. Presbyn. Scouters (trustee, deacon 1957-66, regional v.p. 1992—), Kiwanis (pres. 1982-83). Avocations: photography, travel, camping, canoeing, wood carving. Home: 13425 Cliff Dr Cleveland OH 44107-1401

MEDAK, PETER, film director; b. Budapest, Hungary; arrived in Eng., 1956; came to U.S., 1979; s. Gyula and Elisabeth (Diamonstein) M.; m. Julia Migenes, July 31, 1989; children: Christopher, Karen, Joshua, Cornelia, Martina, Jessica. Dir. (films) Negatives, 1968, A Day in the Death of Joe Egg, 1970, The Ruling Class, 1971, Ghost in a Nonnday's Sun, 1973, The Odd Job, 1977, The Changling, 1979, Zorro the Gay Blade, 1980, The Men's Club, 1986, The Krays, 1989, La Voix Humane, 1990, Let Him Have It, 1991, Romeo is Bleeding, 1992, Pontiac Moon, 1994, (stage) Miss Julie, 1977 (opera) Salome, 1988, La Voix Humane, and others. Mem. Dir.'s Guild of Am., Dir.'s Guild of U.K., Assn. of Cinematographers, Allied Technicians, Dir.'s Guild of Can. Jewish. Office: Fred Actman & Co 9255 W Sunset Blvd Ste 901 Los Angeles CA 90069-3306

MEDALIE, JACK HARVEY, physician; b. Buhl, Minn., Jan. 8, 1922; m.; 3 children. BSc, Witwatersrand U., Johannesburg, 1941; MD, BChir, Witwatersrand U., 1945; MPH (hon.), Harvard U., 1958. Instr. dept. anatomy U. Witwatersrand, Johannesburg, 1942-43; sr. lectr. dept. social medicine Hebrew U., Hadassah, Jerusalem, 1962-66; from assoc. prof. to prof., chmn. dept. family medicine Tel-Aviv U., 1966-74; chmn. dept. family medicine Case Western Res. U., 1975-87, prof. cmty. health, 1976-87, prof. family medicine, 1976—, prof. med. and pediat., 1978—, prof. emeritus, 1992—; co-prin. investigator congenital abnormality study NIH, 1972-74, Dept. Health, Edn. and Welfare, 1976-82, Robert Wood Johnson Found., 1978-88; vis. prof., family medicine and epidemiology U. N.C., Chapel Hill, 1973-74; vis. sr. rsch. scientist, Nat. Heart, Blood and Lung Inst., Bethesda, Md., 1974, 90-91; med. coun. U. Hosps. Cleve., 1975-87, com. impaired physicians, 1980-87; med. edn. com. Case Western Res. U., 1980-85, chmn. ambulatory and primary care clerkship com., 1981-83; task force health consequences bereavement Nat. Acad. Sci., 1982-85, membership com., 1984-88; dir. dept. family practice U. Hosps., Cleve., 1982-87; rsch. cons. Mt. Sinai Med. Ctr., Cleve., 1991—. Contbr. articles to profl. jours. Fellow Am. Acad. Family Physicians, Am. Heart Assn., Royal Soc. Med. Found.; mem. Inst. Med.-Nat. Acad. Sci., Soc. Tchrs. Family Medicine (chmn. at. task force 1985-87, Curtis Hames Career Rsch. award 1988, Cert. Excellence 1988, Maurice Saltzman award 1988), Soc. Behavioral Medicine. Office: Case Western Res Univ Dept of Family Medicine 2119 Abington Rd Cleveland OH 44106-2333*

MEDALIE, RICHARD JAMES, lawyer; b. Duluth, Minn., July 21, 1929; s. William Louis and Mona (Kolad) M.; m. Susan Diane Abrams, June 5, 1960; children: Samuel David, Daniel Alexander. B.A. summa cum laude, U. Minn., 1952; cert., U. London, 1953; A.M., Harvard U., 1955, J.D. cum laude, 1958. Bar: D.C. 1958, N.Y. 1963. Law clk. to Hon. George T. Washington U.S. Ct. Appeals, Washington, 1958-59; asst. solicitor gen. U.S., 1960-62; assoc. Kaye, Scholer, Fierman, Hays & Handler, N.Y.C., 1962-65; dep. dir. Ford Found. Inst. Criminal Law and Procedure, Georgetown U. Law Ctr., 1965-68; ptnr. Friedman & Medalie and predecessors, Washington, 1968—; pres. Pegasus Internat., Washington, 1970—; exec. dir. The Appleseed Found., Washington, 1993-94, chmn. bd., 1993—; adj. prof. adminstrv. and criminal law Georgetown U. Law Center, 1967-70; Mem. D.C. Law Revision Commn., 1975-87, chmn. Criminal Law Task Force, mem. exec. com., 1978-82; panel comml. arbitrators Am. Arbitration Assn., 1964—; vice chmn. Harvard Law Sch. Fund, 1981-84, chmn. nat. maj. gifts, 1984-86, dep. chmn., 1986-87, chmn. 1987-89. Author: From Escobedo to Miranda: The Anatomy of a Supreme Court Decision, 1966; co-author: Federal Consumer Safety Legislation, 1970; co-author, editor: Commercial Arbitration for the 1990s, 1991; co-editor: Crime: A Community Responds, 1967; staff: Harvard Law Rev., 1956-58; case editor, 1957-58; contbr. articles to legal jours. Bd. dirs. alumni assn. Expt. in Internat. Living, Brattleboro, Vt., 1961-64, pres., 1962-63. Fulbright scholar, 1952-53; Ford fellow, 1954-55. Mem. ABA (program chair 1994, 90, chair legis. subcom. 1986-89, ADR/arbitration com., rep. on adv. com. nat. conf. Emerging ADR Issues in State and Fed. Cts. 1991, vice chair 1991-94, arbitration com. litigation sect., co-chair nat. conf. Critical Issues in Arbitration 1993), D.C. Unified Bar, Assn. Bar City of N.Y., Am. Law Inst., Harvard Law Sch. Assn. D.C. (pres. 1976-77, nat. v.p. 1977-78), Harvard Alumni Assn. (law sch. dir. 1991-95), Cosmos Club, Phi Beta Kappa, Phi Alpha Theta. Home: 3113 Macomb St NW Washington DC 20008-3325 Office: 1901 Pennsylvania Ave NW Washington DC 20006-3405

MEDALIE, SUSAN DIANE, management consultant; b. Boston, Oct. 7, 1941; d. Samuel and Matilda (Bortman) Abrams; m. Richard James Medalie, June 5, 1960; children: Samuel David, Daniel Alexander. BA, Sarah Lawrence Coll., 1960; MA, George Washington U., 1962, Cert. Pubs. Spec., 1977; JD, Am. U., 1986. Bar: Pa., 1987, D.C., 1987. Pres. Medalie Cons., Washington, 1980—; dep. dir. U.S. Holocaust Meml. Coun., Washington, 1980-82; assoc. pub. Campaigns & Elections, Washington, 1983-84; legis. analyst Subcom./House Energy and Commerce, Washington, 1985; ea. regional dir. Josephson Found. for Adv. Ethics, L.A., 1986-88; asst. dean for external affairs George Washington U. Nat. Law Ctr., Washington, 1988-90; exec. dir. Internat. Soc. Global Health Policy, Washington and Paris, 1990-93; pvt. practice law Washington, 1993—; cons. Kettering Found., Washington, 1986; corp. liaison First Hosp. Corp., Norfolk, Va., 1986-88; assoc. producer and cons. Prof. Arthur Miller's "Headlines on Trial" (NBC), N.Y.C., 1987-91. Editor/pub.: Getting There mag., 1977-80; sr. editor: Am. Univ. Law Rev., Washington, 1984-86. Nat. dep. fin. dir. Edward M. Kennedy for Pres. Com., Washington, 1979-80; cons. Lt. Gov. Davis for Senate, Va., 1982; co-chair Patricia Roberts Harris for Mayor, Washington, 1982. Mem. Sarah Lawrence Alumnae Assn. (mem. coun. 1980-83), Florence Crittenton Home (bd. dirs. exec. com. 1980-83), ABA, DC Bar. Office: Medalie Cons 1901 Pennsylvania Ave NW Washington DC 20006-3405

MEDAVOY, MIKE, motion picture company executive; b. Shanghai, China, Jan. 21, 1941; came to U.S., 1957, naturalized, 1962; s. Michael and Dora Medavoy; 1 child, Brian. B.A., UCLA, 1963. With Casting dept. Universal Studios, 1963; agt. Bill Robinson Assos., Los Angeles, 1963-64; v.p. motion picture dept. GAC/CMA Co., 1965-71, IFA Co., 1971-74; sr. v.p. United Artists Corp., 1974-78; one of founders, exec. v.p. Orion Pictures Co., Burbank, Calif., 1978-82; exec. v.p. Orion Pictures Corp. (formerly Orion Pictures Co.), Burbank, 1982-90; chmn. Tri-Star Pictures, Inc., Burbank, 1990—, Phoenix Picture Corp., 1995—; bd. dirs. Sony Pictures Corp., co-chmn. Am. Cinematech.; jury chmn. Tokyo Film Festival 1994; hon. co-chair St. Petersburg Film Festival; adv. bd. Swawghai Film Conf. Mem. vis. com. Boston Museum Fine Arts.; chmn. Ctr. Internat. Strategic Affairs, UCLA, Com. to Cure Cancer through Immunization UCLA; co-chmn. Olympic Sports Fedn. Com., Music Ctr. Unified Fund Campaign; co-founder Sundance Film Inst.; bd. govs. Sundance Inst., 1980-86; bd. dirs. Calif. Mus. Sci. and Industry, 1984-87. Recipient Academy award for One Flew Over the Cuckoo's Nest, Rocky, Annie Hall, Amadeus, Platoon, Dances With Wolves, Silence of the Lamb. Mem. Acad. Motion Picture Arts and Scis. (gov. 1977-81), UCLA Found., UCLA Chancellors Assocs.

MEDDING, WALTER SHERMAN, environmental engineer; b. St. Louis, Mar. 4, 1922; s. Walter Lyman and Elizabeth Steele (Sherman) M.; m. Mary Agnes Patty Johnson, Apr. 22, 1944; children: Jean, Walter, Mauri. BSCE, Va. Poly. Inst., 1947, MS in Sanitary Engring., 1970. Registered profl. engr., Va., N.C., Kans. Various positions U.S. Army, 1942-64; student officer advanced course The Engr. Sch., Ft. Belvoir, Va., 1952-53, head fixed bridges sect., 1953-55; asst. engr. Asmara Eritrea, chief design br. Mediterranean Divsn., Gulf Dist., Tehran, Iran, 1955-57; asst. divsn. engr. 9th Infantry Divsn., Ft. Carson, Colo., 1957-59; resident engr. USACAG, chief constrn. ops. U.S. Army Engring. Command Europe, Frankfurt, Germany, 1959-72; chief contract adminstrn. U.S. Army Engring. Divsn. Europe, Frankfurt, Germany, 1972-75; chief environ. engring. Office, Chif of Engrs., U.S. Army, Washington, 1975-86; sr. engr. Romem Aqua Sys. Co., Woodbridge, Va., 1986—. Co-author: (textbook) Non-standard Military Fixed Bridges, 1954; contbr. articles to profl. jours. Mem. ASCE, Am. Waterworks Assn., Water Environment Fedn., Conf. of Fed. Environ. Engrs. Republican. Episcopalian. Achievements include development of mil. bridge classification procedures for load carrying and rapid field design. Home: 204 Brooke Dr Fredericksburg VA 22408 Office: The Romem Aqua Systems Co 1635-2 Woodside Dr Woodbridge VA 22191

MEDDLES, SHARON DIANE, secondary education educator; b. Pasadena, Calif., Feb. 9, 1947; d. Jarrell William and Vivian Irene (Heffner) Gunstream; m. Larry Wayne Meddles, June 16, 1973; children: Brittany Dawn, Brooke Reneé. BA in English, Pasadena Coll., 1968; MEd in Counseling, U. Phoenix, 1995. Cert. tchr., Ariz. Jr. high tchr. Adams County Dist. 12, Northglenn, Colo., 1969-72; jr. high tchr. Washington Elem. Sch. Dist. 6, Phoenix, 1972-76, homebound tchr., 1985-86, 88-90; sr. high tchr. N.W. Christian Acad., Glendale, Ariz., 1986-87; jr. high tchr. Washington Sch. Dist., Phoenix, 1990—. Core group leader Cmty. Bible Study, Phoenix, 1988-90; bd. dirs. Orangewood Ch. of the Nazarene, Phoenix, 1982-84, 93; local pres. Nazarene World Missionary Soc., 1982-84; dist. dir. Point Loma Alumni Bd., San Diego, 1990-93, sec., 1993—. Republican. Avocations: singing, cooking. Home: 1115 W Le Marche Ave Phoenix AZ 85023-4429

MEDDLETON, DANIEL JOSEPH, health facility administrator; b. July 11, 1936. AA in Bus. Adminstrn., Broome Tech. Community Coll., Binghamton, N.Y., 1959; BSBA, Mich. Technol. U., 1964; M in Health Care Adminstrn., Univ. Minn., 1966. Asst. adminstr. Clifton Springs Hosp. and Clinic, 1966-68, Univ. Cin. Med. Ctr., 1968-70; assoc. adminstr. Providence Hosp., Anchorage, Alaska, 1970-76; exec. v.p. Benedictine Hosp., Kingston, N.Y., 1976-82; dir. Div. Planning, Policy and Prog. Evaluation State of Alaska/Dept. Health and Social Svcs., 1983-84; owner Kits Cameras, Juneau, Alaska, 1984-90; adminstr. Juneau Pioneers' Home, 1988-93, Alaska Psychiat. Hosp., 1993-95; dir. Dept. Health and Social Svcs. North Slope Borough, Barrow, Alaska, 1995—. Bd. dirs. Alaska Econ. Devel. Adv. Coun., Benedictine Hosp, Kingston, N.Y., Bartlett Meml. Hosp., Juneau, Barrow Hosp., Big Bros./Big Sisters, others; mem. steering com. S.E. Alaska Regional Econ. Devel. Inst., 1987. Fellow Am. Coll. Health Care Execs. (regent 1995—); mem. No. N.Y. Met. Hosp. Assn. (past bd. dirs.), Mid Hudson Health Systems Agy. (past bd. dirs.), Rotary, others. Avocations: outdoor sports, photography, camping, backpacking, sailing, flying. Home: PO Box 769 Barrow AK 99723

MEDDLETON, FRANCIS CHARLES, elementary and secondary school educator; b. Johnson City, N.Y., Nov. 17, 1942; s. Willett J. and Julia (Curley) M.; m. Linda I. Albright, July 10, 1965; children: Dennis K., Laura D. AA, Cayuga County C.C., Auburn, N.Y., 1964; BS, Old Dominion U., 1969; MEd, U. Va., 1972; MA, U. South Fla., 1978, EdS, 1979; BA, SUNY, Albany, 1986; postgrad., Brigham Young U., 1991, U. Houston, 1991, U. St. Thomas, Houston, 1992-93. Tchr. Pub. Sch. Systems, Va., 1969-72, Fla., 1972-82, Tex., 1982-96; instr. Lee Coll., Baytown, Tex., 1989-94; tchr. specialist Harris County Children Protective Svcs. Houston Ind. Sch. Dist., 1994—; cons. insvc. tng. Galena Park Ind. Sch. Dist., Houston, 1982-83, North Forest Ind. Sch. Dist., Houston, 1983-89, Lee Coll., Baytown, 1989-94, Houston Ind. Sch. Dist., 1994—, San Jacinto Coll., Houston, 1995—. Mem. Rep. Nat. Com., Houston, 1989, Am. Legion, Houston, 1989. With USNR, 1961-67. Decorated Nat. Def. Svc. medal. Mem. NRA, NEA, Tex. Coll. Tchrs. Assn., Tex. Faculty Assn., Tex. State Tchrs. Assn. Roman Catholic. Home: 12811 Woodlite Ln Houston TX 77015-2053 Office: Children Protective Svcs Houston Ind Sch Dist 6425 Chimney Rock Rd Houston TX 77081-4501

MEDEARIS, DONALD NORMAN, JR., physician, educator; b. Kansas City, Kans., Aug. 22, 1927; s. Donald Norman and Gladys (Sandford) M.; m. Mary Ellen Marble, Aug. 25, 1956; children: Donald Harrison, Ellen Sandford, John Norman, Jennifer Marble. AB, U. Kans., 1950; MD, Harvard U., 1953. Diplomate: Am. Bd. Pediatrics. Intern internal medicine Barnes Hosp., St. Louis, 1953-54; resident pediatrics Children's Hosp., Cin., 1954-56; rsch. fellow pediatrics Harvard U. rsch. div. infectious diseases Children's Med. Ctr., Boston, 1956-58; from asst. to assoc. prof. pediatrics and microbiology Johns Hopkins Sch. Medicine, Balt., 1959-65; Joseph P. Kennedy Jr. Meml. Found. Sr. Rsch. Scholar in Mental Retardation, 1960-65; prof. pediatrics U. Pitts. Sch. Medicine, 1965-74, chmn. dept., 1965-69, dean, 1969-74; med. dir. Children's Hosp., Pitts., 1965-69; prof. pediatrics Case Western Res. U., Cleve., 1974-77; dir. pediatrics Cleve. Met. Gen. Hosp., 1974-77; Charles Wilder prof. pediatrics Harvard U. Med. Sch., 1977-95, Charles Wilder disting. prof. pediatrics, 1995—; chief Children's Svc. Mass. Gen. Hosp., Boston, 1977-95; mem. Pres.'s Commn. on Study Ethical Problems in Medicine and Biomed. and Behavioral Rsch., 1979-82. Contbr. articles to profl. jours., texts. Vestry Trinity Ch., Boston, 1983-87. Served with USNR, 1945-46. Mem. Am. Acad. Pediatrics, Am. Pediatric Soc., Infectious Disease Soc. Am., Inst. Medicine/Nat. Acad. Sci., Alpha Omega Alpha. Office: Massachusetts Gen Hosp Fruit St Boston MA 02114

MEDEARIS, KENNETH GORDON, research consultant, educator; b. Peoria, Ill., Aug. 5, 1930; s. Harold Oscar and Ferol Mae (Rowlett) M.; m. Mary Genevieve Barlow, June 28, 1953; children—Mark Allen, Mary Lynne, Terry Gordon. B.S., U. Ill., 1952, M.S., 1953; Ph.D., Stanford U., 1962. Registered profl. engr., Calif., Colo., N.Mex., Pa. Stress analyst Sandia Corp., Albuquerque, 1957-58; asst. prof. civil engring., U. N.Mex., 1958-62; assoc. prof. engring. Ariz. State U., 1962-63; engr., computer cons., Sunnyvale, Calif., 1963-66; dir. Computer Ctr., prof. civil engring. Colo. State U., Ft. Collins, 1966-69, adj. prof. civil and mech. engring., 1969—; lectr. N.Mex. State U., 1982—; cons. Kenneth Medearis Assocs., Ft. Collins, 1969—; research and vibration engring. cons., Ft. Collins., 1969—; evaluation cons. UN. Author: Numerical-Computer Methods for Engineers and Physical Scientists, 1974. Contbr. articles to profl. jours. Mem. Stanford Regional Cabinet. Served to 1st lt. USAF, 1953-56. Recipient Outstanding Engrng. Achievement award No. Colo. Profl. Engrs., 1974, Outstanding Engrng. Achievement award Profl. Engrs. Colo., 1974, Disting. Engring.

Alumnus award U. Ill., 1988. Mem. Colo. Earthquake Research Soc. (v.p.), Univs. Council for Earthquake Engring., Internat. Orgn. for Standardization, UN Tech. Evaluation Team, ASCE, Seismol. Soc. Am., Larimer County Computer Soc. (chmn. 1974—), Aircraft Owners and Pilots Assn., Sigma Xi, Phi Sigma Kappa, Chi Epsilon, Sigma Tau, Tau Beta Pi. Methodist. Lodge: Rotary. Home: 1901 Seminole Dr Fort Collins CO 80525-1537 Office: 1413 S College Ave Fort Collins CO 80524-4115

MEDEARIS, ROGER NORMAN, artist; b. Fayette, Mo., Mar. 6, 1920; s. Thomas Whittier and Mara (Miller) M.; m. Elizabeth Burrall Sterling, Jan. 16, 1976; 1 son, Thomas Whittier, III. Pupil of, Thomas Hart Benton, 1938-41. One-man exhbns. include Kende Galleries, N.Y.C., 1949, 50, Capricorn Galleries, Bethesda, Md., 1971, 78, 81, 84, 94; group exhbns. include AAA Galleries, Met. Mus. Art, NAD, N.Y.C., Carnegie Mellon U., Pitts., Butler Inst. Am. Art, Youngstown, Ohio, Albrecht-Kemper Mus. Art, St. Joseph, Mo., Spencer Mus. Art, Lawrence, Kans., many others; represented in numerous pvt. and public collections, including, D.C. Mcpl. Ct., Nat. Mus. Am. Art, Washington, Nelson-Atkins Mus. Art, Kansas City, Butler Inst. Am. Art., Hunt Inst., Pitts., Albrecht-Kemper Art Mus., St. Joseph, Mo.; commd. by Nat. Recreation & Park Assn., 1982, Print Club Albany, 1994; work reviewed in various articles, monographs; subject of various art books. With USN Dept., 1942-45, AUS, 1945-46. Address: 2270 Melville Dr San Marino CA 91108-2612

MEDENICA, GORDON, corporate planner; b. Darmstadt, Fed. Republic Germany, Oct. 26, 1951; came to U.S., 1952; s. Walter Vojislav and Heidi Hedwig (Knoerzer) M.; m. Ann Margaret Connolly, Jan. 2, 1982; children: Madeline, Candice. AB, Harvard U., 1973, MBA, 1979. Staff acct. Meahl, McNamara & Co., Boston, 1973-74; exec. dir. BMW Car Club Am., Cambridge, Mass., 1974-77; analyst corp. planning Marriott Corp., Washington, 1979-80, sr. analyst hotel planning, 1981-82; sr. analyst strategic planning N.Y. Times Co., N.Y.C., 1982-83, project mgr. strategic planning, 1984, mgr. strategic planning and corp. devel., 1984-86, dir. planning, 1986-90; v.p. corp. planning, 1990-93, v.p. ops. and planning, 1993-96; sr. v.p., group pub. NYT Mag. Group, N.Y.C., 1996—. Office: NY Times Co Mag Group 8th Fl 1120 Ave of the Americas New York NY 10036-3913

MEDEROS, CAROLINA LUISA, transportation policy consultant; b. Rochester, Minn., July 1, 1947; d. Luis O. and Carolina (del Valle) M. BA, Vanderbilt U., 1969; MA, U. Chgo., 1971. Adminstrv. asst. Lt. Gov. of Ill., Chgo., 1972; sr. research assoc. U. Chgo., 1972; project mgr., cons. Urban Dynamics, Inner City Fund and Community Programs Inc., Chgo., 1972-73; legis. asst. to Senate pres. Ill. State Senate, Chgo. and Springfield, 1973-76; program analyst Dept. Transp., Washington, 1976-79, chief, trans. assistance programs div., 1979-81, dir. programs and evaluation, 1981-88, chairwoman, sec.'s safety rev. task force, 1985-88; deputy asst. sec. for safety Dept. Transp., 1988-89; cons. Patton Boggs LLP, Washington, 1990—. Recipient award for Meritorious Achievement, Sec. Transp. 1980, Superior Achievement award U.S. Dept. Transp., 1981, Sec.'s Gold Medal Award for Outstanding Achievement, 1986, Presdl. Rank award, 1987. Mem. Womens Transp. Seminar, Coun. for Excellence in Govt. Home: 2723 O St NW Washington DC 20007-3128 Office: Patton Boggs LLP 2550 M St NW Washington DC 20037-1301

MEDFORD, RUSSELL MARSHALL, physician; b. Bklyn., Jan. 8, 1955; s. Jerome L. and Doris P. (Pinchuk) M.; m. Margaret K. Offermann, May 31, 1986; children: Arielle, Rochelle. BA, Cornell U., 1976; MS, Albert Einstein Coll. Medicine, 1980, PhD in Cell and Molecular Biology, 1982, MD, 1983. Diplomate Am. Bd. Internal Medicine. Instr. dept. medicine Harvard Med. Sch., Boston, 1986-89; assoc. physician cardiology Brigham and Women's Hosp., Boston, 1986-89; asst. prof. medicine Emory U., Atlanta, 1989-94, assoc. prof. medicine, 1994—; dir. molecular cardiology rsch. ctr., 1994—; founding scientist Athero Genics, Inc., Atlanta, 1994—, exec. v.p., 1994—; pres., CEO, 1995—; bd. dirs. Ga. Biomed. Partnership, Atlanta; mem. site vis. rev. com. Nat. Heart, Lung and Blood Inst., 1992—, NIH, 1993—; scientific rev. Am. Jour. Physiology, Jour. Clin. Investigation, Jour. Biol. Chemistry. Contbr. articles to profl. jours. Grantee NIH, 1993, 94, 95, Am. Heart Assn., 1993, 95. Mem. Am. Fedn. Clin. Rsch., Am. Heart Assn., Am. Soc. Microbiology. Achievements include patent for treatment of atherosclerosis and other inflammatory diseases; studies on the molecular biology of cardiovascular disease and gene-directed therapy. Office: Emory U Sch of Medicine Divsn Cardiology 1639 Pierce Dr WMB 319/LL Atlanta GA 30345

MEDH, JHEEM D., medical educator, biochemistry researcher. BS in Chemistry and Biochemistry, U. Bombay, India, 1982; MS in Biochemistry, U. Bombay, 1984; PhD in Biochemistry, U. Tex. Med. Br., Galveston, 1990. Jr. rsch. fellow, dept. physiology L.T.M. Med. Coll., Bombay, 1984-86; rsch. asst., dept. human biol. chemistry and genetics U. Tex. Med. Br., 1986-90; postgrad. rsch. biochemist, dept. medicine U. Calif., San Diego, 1991-93; asst. rsch. scientist, adj. asst. prof., dept. medicine U. Iowa Coll. Medicine, Iowa City, 1993—. Presenter in field of role of LDL receptor-related protein, receptor-associated protein and lipoprotein lipase on the regulation of lipoprotein metabolism. Juvenile Diabetes Internat. Found. fellow 1992-93; recipient nat. grand-in-aid award Am. Heart Assn., 1995-98; recipient Gip Hudson award Nat. Student Rsch. Forum, 1989, Stephen C. Silverthorne award Grad. Sch. Biomed. Scis., U. Tex. Med. Br. Mem. Am. Heart Assn. (coun. for basic science), Am. Soc. Cell Biology, Juvenile Diabetes Found. Internat. Home: 209 Woodside Dr Iowa City IA 52246

MEDICUS, HEINRICH ADOLF, physicist, educator; b. Zurich, Switzerland, Dec. 24, 1918; came to U.S., 1950; naturalized, 1995; s. Friedrich Georg and Clara Anna (Frey) M.; m. Hildegard Julie Schmelz, June 15, 1961. Dipl. Naturwiss., Swiss Fed. Inst. Tech., Zurich, 1943, Dr.sc.nat., 1949. Research assoc. Swiss Fed. Inst. Tech., 1943-50; visitor Lawrence Berkeley Lab., Calif., 1950-51, MIT, Cambridge, 1951-52; instr., then vis. asst. prof. MIT, 1952-55; assoc. prof. Rensselaer Poly. Inst., Troy, N.Y., 1955-72, prof., 1972-86, prof. emeritus, 1987—; vis. scientist Atomic Energy Research Establishment Harwell, Eng., 1967-68, Swiss Inst. Nuclear Research, Villigen, 1974-75. Co-author: Fields and Particles, 1973; contbr. articles on physics, history of physics and enology. Pres. Hudson-Mohawk Swiss Soc., Albany, N.Y., 1974—. Served to lt. arty. Swiss Army, 1937-50. Fellow, Swiss Found., 1950-52. Mem. Am. Phys. Soc., Swiss Phys. Soc., Hist. of Sci. Soc., Swiss Am. Hist.Soc., Soc. Wine Educators, Société des Vignerons, Delta Tau Delta (pres. house corp. of Upsilon chpt. 1984-91, faculty advisor 1991-95). Presbyterian. Club: Swiss Alpine (Zurich). Avocations: wine education, internat. student exchange programs. Home: 1 The Knoll East Acres Troy NY 12180 Office: Rensselaer Poly Inst Dept Physics Troy NY 12180

MEDIN, A. LOUIS, computer company executive; b. Balt., Oct. 2, 1925; s. Nathan and Bessie (Zell) M.; B.E. in Chem. Engring., Johns Hopkins U., 1948; Ph.D. in Chem. Engring., Ohio State U., 1951; m. Julia A. Levin, Dec. 24, 1950; children—Douglas, David, Thomas, Linda. Registered profl. engr., Md. Chem. engr. AEC, Wilmington, Del., 1951-53; research engr. Ford Motor Co., Dearborn, Mich., 1953-55; chief chem. nuclear reactor tech. ALCO Products, Schenectady, 1955-58; head nuclear research engr. U.S. Steel, Monroeville, Pa., 1958-63; project mgr. missile design AVCO Corp., Wilmington, Mass., 1963-65; mgr. sci. applications IBM, Manassas, Va., 1965-72, mgr. advanced applications, 1975-87; exec. dir. Inst. for Simulation and Tng., Orlando, Fla., 1987—; chmn. symposia on def. research and devel.; asst. dir. environment and life scis. Dept. Def., 1972-74; lectr. in field. Contbr. articles to profl. and tech. jours. Mem. Monroeville Parks and Recreation Commn., 1960; chmn. Monroeville Mental Health Assn., 1961; mem. Monroeville Zoning and Planning Commn., 1961; dep. precinct chmn. Montgomery County Rep. Com., 1982. Served with USN, 1944-46, PTO. Recipient award Am. Chem. Soc., 1957. Fellow Am. Inst. Chemists; mem. Nat. Security Indsl. Assn., Am. Inst. Chem. Engrs., Am. Def. Preparedness Assn. (chmn. sci. and engring. tech. div. 1981-90, editorial advisor Def. Jour., Am. Def. award 1984, Gold medal 1990), Am. Metall. Soc., Johns Hopkin's U. Alumni Assn., Ohio State U. Alumni Assn. Home: 714 Bear Creek Cir Casselberry FL 32708-3857

MEDIN, JULIA ADELE, mathematics educator, researcher; b. Dayton, Ohio, Jan. 16, 1929; d. Caroline (Feinberg) Levitt; m. A. Louis Medin, Dec. 24, 1950; children: Douglas, David, Thomas, Linda. BS in Maths. Edn., Ohio State U., 1951; MA in Higher Edn., George Washington U., 1977; PhD in Counseling and Edn., Am. U., 1985. Cert. tchr., Fla., Md. Rsch. engr. Sun Oil Co., Marcus Hook, Pa., 1951-53; tchr. maths. Montgomery County Pub. Schs., Rockville, Md., 1973-88; asst. prof. maths. U. Ctrl. Fla., Orlando, 1988-90, sr. ednl. technologist Inst. for Simulation and Tng., 1990—; mem. adv. steering com. U.S. Dept. Edn. Title II, Washington, 1985-89; sr. math educator, rschr. Inst. for Simulation and Tng., Orlando, 1988—; judge NII Nar. Awards. Author: Loc. of Cont. and Test Anxiety of Mar. Math. Studies, 1985; contbg. author: Math for 14 & 17 Yr. Olds, 1987; editor: Simulation Technology for Education; contbr. articles to profl. jours. Dem. committewoman Town of Monroeville, Pa., 1962; religious sch. dir. Beth Tikva Religious Sch., Rockville, 1971; cons. Monroeville Mental Health, 1960. Mem. Nat. Coun. Tchrs. Math., Math. Assn. Am. (task force on minorities in math.), Women in Math. in Edn., Nat. Coun. for Tech. in Edn. and Tng., Phi Delta Kappa, Kappa Delta Pi. Home: 714 Bear Creek Cir Casselberry FL 32708-3857 Office: U Ctrl Fla Inst for Simulation and Tng 3280 Progress Dr Orlando FL 32826-3229

MEDIN, LOWELL ANSGARD, security company executive; b. Shafer Twp., Minn., Aug. 28, 1932; s. Ansgaard Phillip Magnus and Adelaide Marie Christine (Grandstrand) M.; m. Frances Irene Knutson, Sept. 13, 1958; children: Kimberly June, James Lowell. AS in Liberal Arts, U. Minn., 1957, BBA, 1959. Dairy farmer Medin Farm, Franconia Twp., 1951-53; silo builder Lindstrom Silo, 1956-58; employment mgr. John Wood Co., St. Paul, 1959; salesperson Diversey Co., LaCrosse, Wis., 1959-60; rebuyer, inventory mgr. Montgomery Ward, St. Paul, 1960-67; rebuyer, rebuyer mgr. Montgomery Ward, Chgo., 1967-85; with sales dept. J.T. Gen. Store, Palatine, Ill., 1986; rebuying mgr. Sportsmen's Guide, Golden Valley, Minn., 1987; inventory mgr. Donald Bruce and Co., Chgo., 1988-91; supr. Pinkerton Security Ops., 1992—; pics coord. Hickory Farms, Itasca, Ill., 1995—. Author: (with others) Shafer Swamp to Village, 1978, The Pioneers of Chisago County 1838-1870, 1992, The Knutson/Stavenau Family Roots, 1994. Candidate for polit. office, Mpls., 1967; del. Minn. State Dem.-Farm Labor Conv., 1956, 58; chmn. cancer drive Village of Palatine, 1968, mem. dist. 6 adv. coun., 1989—; mem. Homeowners Coun., Palatine, 1976-77; mem. coun. Christ Luth. Ch., Palatine, 1981-86; officer Chicago County DFL Party, 1956-60; del. Chicago County DFL Conv., 1956, 58; pres. Palonis Park Homeowners Assn., Palatine, 1976-82. Cpl. U.S. Army, 1953-55, ETO. Mem. No. Ill. Civil War Roundtable (chartered officer 1983-86, trustee, sec., 2d v.p.), VFW (life, post 981, Arlington Hts.), Am. Legion (life, post 690, Palatine), Alpha Phi Omega. Republican. Lutheran. Avocations: genealogy, gardening, Am. history, Civil War period. Home: 121 S Linden Ave Palatine IL 60067-6342

MEDIN, MYRON JAMES, JR., city manager; b. Ladysmith, Wis., July 8, 1931; s. Myron James and Mildred Clara (Johnson) M.; m. Alice Louise Moholt, May 14, 1955; children: John, Karen, Anne. BA, St. Olaf Coll., 1954; MPA, U. Mich., 1959. Adminstrv. asst. to city mgr. City of Fond du Lac, Wis., 1959-64, city mgr., 1967-83; city mgr. City of New Ulm, Minn., 1964-67; city adminstr. City of Kansas City, Kans., 1983-85; pres., gen. mgr. Bella Vista Village Property Owners Assn., Ark., 1986-92; mem. com. human devel. Nat. League of Cities, Washington, 1974-80, com. on govtl. relations, 1971-73; chmn. City Plan Commn., Fond du Lac, Wis., 1967-83. Bd. dirs. United Way, Kansas City, Kans., 1984-85, YMCA, 1984-85, Kansas City C.C. Found., 1984-85; mem. Gov.'s Regionalism Task Force Adv. Com., Madison, Wis., 1968-70; trustee Phillips Pro-Celebrity Golf Tennis Charity Classic, 1991-92; vol. historic house mus. and gardens. Lt. USAF, 1955-57. Recipient Community Service award Fond du Lac Assn. of Commerce, 1978. Mem. Internat. City Mgmt. Assn., Wis. City Mgmt. Assn. (pres. 1975-76), Wis. League of Municipalities (bd. dirs. 1978-80), Wis. Alliance of Cities (v.p. 1972-73), Am. Soc. Pub. Adminstrn. (bd. dirs. 1984-85, Pub. Adminstr. of Yr. award 1985), Bella Vista-Bentonville C. of C. (bd. dirs. 1987-91), Nat. Trust for Hist. Preservation, Benton County Hist. Soc., Ret. Officers Assn. Lutheran. Avocations: swimming, reading, tennis, gardening, genealogy. Home: 1 Audley Cir Bella Vista AR 72714-5645

MEDINA, JOSE ENRIQUE, dentist, educator; b. Santurce, P.R., May 1, 1926; s. Jose Wilfredo and Genoveva (de la Baume) M.; m. Betty Lee Mansfield, June 5, 1948 (dec. Feb. 1975); children—Elizabeth Lee, Jose Enrique, Virginia Genoveva; m. Patricia Fay Pachler, Dec. 26, 1975. Student, Johns Hopkins, 1942-44; D.D.S., U. Md., 1948. Instr. Berlitz Sch. Langs., 1944-48; instr. operative dentistry dept. U. Md. Sch. Dentistry, 1948-50, asst. prof., 1950-52, asso. prof., 1952-57, prof., head, 1957-66, asst. dean, 1964-67; prof. clin. dentistry, assoc. dean Coll. Dentistry, U. Fla., Gainesville, 1967-69; prof. clin. dentistry Coll. Dentistry, U. Fla., 1969—, dean, 1969-74, dir. health center planning and utilization, 1974-76; v.p. for facilities planning and ops. J. Hillis Miller Health Center, 1976-86; Cons. USPHS, U.S. Naval Dental Sch., Bethesda, VA Hosp., Gainesville, Miami.; Pres. So. Conf. Dental Deans and Examiners, 1973; mem. nat. adv. dental research council Nat. Inst. Dental Research, NIH, 1973-76; charter mem. Am. Bd. Operative Dentistry, pres., 1980-87; mentor George M. Hollenback Operative Dentistry Sem. Group, 1961—, N.H. Gold Foil Study Group, 1987—. Pres. Sunnybrook (Md.) Community Assn., 1963-65. Served with USNR, 1944-46. Decorated Knight Comdr., Order of Bernardo O'Higgins (Chile), 1991; recipient Disting. Alumnus award R.I. Alumni Assn. U. Md., 1965, U. Md. Sch. Dentistry Alumni Assn., 1985, Disting. Faculty award U. Fla. Blue Key, 1986, Tchr. of Yr. award U. Fla., 1987, Outstanding Clinician of Yr. award, 1987, 92, Andres Cendan Dentist of Yr. award Dade Dental Study Group, 1990; named to Hall of Fame, U. Md. Alumni Assn. , 1990; hon. prof. U. De San Carlos, Guatemala, 1960—. Fellow Internat. Coll. Dentists (trustee found. 1993—, dep. regent Fla. sect. 1988-91, regent dist 5 USA sect. 1992—), AADS, Acad. Gen. Dentistry (hon.), Acad. Dentistry Internat.; mem. ADA, Fla. Dental Assn. (Disting. Svc. award 1978), Am. Acad. Gold Foil Operators (editor 1958-63, pres. 1965, Disting. Mem. award 1986), Am. Coll. Dentists (Disting. Faculty award 1989, chmn. Fla. sect. 1992-93, William J. Gies award 1990), Internat. Assn. Dental Rsch., Acad. Operative Dentistry (charter, George Hollenback meml. prize 1985, trustee Acad. Found., 1986—, v.p. 1989, pres. elect 1990, pres. 1991), Am. Acad. Restorative Dentistry, Health Edn. Media Assn. (dir.), Royal Soc. Health, N.Y. Acad. Sci., Am. Acad. Oral Medicine (hon.), Fla. Acad. Dental Practice Adminstrn. (hon.), Guatemala Dental Soc. (hon.), Chile Dental Assn. (hon.), Optimists Club (Md.), Masons, Kiwanis, Omicron Kappa Upsilon. Home: 5002 NW 18th Pl Gainesville FL 32605-3430

MEDINA, KATHRYN BACH, book editor; b. Plainfield, N.J.; d. F. Earl and Elizabeth E. Bach; m. Standish F. Medina Jr.; 1 child, Nathaniel Forde. B.A., Smith Coll. Various editorial positions Doubleday Pub. Co., Inc., N.Y.C., 1965-85; exec. editor, v.p. Random House, N.Y.C., 1985—; assoc. fellow Jonathan Edwards Coll., Yale U., New Haven, 1982—. Editor books by James Atlas, Peter Benchley, Amy Bloom, Elizabeth Berg, Anita Brookner, Ethan Canin, Robert Coles, Agnes deMille, Henry Louis Gates, Jr., Mary Gordon, David Halberstam, Bobbie Ann Mason, James A. Michener, Anna Quindlen, Nancy Reagan, James Reston, William Safire, Maggie Scarf, Christopher Tilghman, Daniel Yergin, others.

MEDINA, STANDISH FORDE, JR., lawyer; b. Orange, N.J., June 16, 1940; s. Standish F. and Hope Tyler (Kiesewetter) M.; m. Kathryn L. Bach, Apr. 20, 1968; 1 child, Nathaniel Forde. A.B. cum laude, Princeton U., 1962; LL.B. magna cum laude, Columbia U., 1965, LL.M., 1966. Bar: N.Y. 1965, U.S. Supreme Ct. 1970, U.S. Dist. Ct. (so. dist., ea. dist.) N.Y., U.S. Ct. Appeals (2d, 3d, 4th, 5th, 7th, 11th, D.C. cirs.). Assoc. in law Columbia Law Sch., 1965-66; lectr. Columbia Law Sch., N.Y.C., 1992; instr. law orientation program in Am. law Princeton U., summer 1966; assoc. Debevoise & Plimpton, N.Y.C., 1966-72, ptnr., 1973—. Author: Settlement Practices in the Second Circuit, 1988, Reflections Below, 1991. Trustee The Hill Sch., Pottstown, Pa., 1976-91, St. Bernard's Sch., N.Y.C., 1992—, Episc. Sch., N.Y.C., 1988-93. Fellow Am. Coll. of Trial Lawyers; mem. ABA (vice-chmn. com. on fed. cts., litigation sect. 1981-82, co-chmn. com. pleadings motions and pretrial 1986-87), Fed. Bar Coun., N.Y. State Bar Assn., Assn. of Bar of City of N.Y. (mem. exec. com. 1982-86, chmn. membership com. 1986-90, chmn. com. fed. cts. 1978-81, mem. judiciary com. 1978-81, mem. nominating com. 1988-89, mem. com. on ct. requirements 1978-81, mem. fed. legis. com. 1971-75), Am. Law Inst., 2d Cir. Com. on Improvement Civil Litigation (chmn. 1986-90), Legal Aid Soc. (chmn. assoc. and young lawyers com. 1972). Office: Debevoise & Plimpton 875 3rd Ave New York NY 10022-6225

MEDITCH, JAMES STEPHEN, electrical engineering educator; b. Indpls., July 30, 1934; s. Vladimir Stephen and Alexandra (Gogeff) M.; m. Theresa Claire Scott, Apr. 4, 1964; children: James Stephen Jr., Sandra Anne. BSEE, Purdue U., 1956, PhD, 1961; SM, MIT, 1957. Staff engr. Aerospace Corp., Los Angeles, 1961-65; assoc. prof. elec. engring. Northwestern U., 1965-67; mem. tech. staff Boeing Sci. Research Labs., Seattle, 1967-70; prof. U. Calif., Irvine, 1970-77; prof. U. Wash., Seattle, 1977—, chmn. dept. elec. engring., 1977-85, assoc. dean engring., 1987-90. Author: Stochastic Optimal Linear Estimation and Control, 1969; co-editor: Computer Communication Networks, 1984. Fellow IEEE (Disting. mem. control systems soc., 1983, editor Proceedings 1983-85, Centennial medal 1984). Office: Univ Wash Dept Elec Engring FT-10 Seattle WA 98195

MEDITZ, WALTER JOSEPH, engineering consultant; b. Bklyn., June 4, 1917; s. Joseph and Marie (Gaspar) M.; m. Elizabeth M. Cagney, Jan. 9, 1944; children—Jeannette Jordan, Mary Beth Banks. B.C.E., Bklyn Poly. Inst., 1939, M.M.E., 1941; M.Indsl. Engring., Ga. Inst. Tech., 1951. Research engr., lab. instr. Bklyn. Poly. Inst., 1939-40; civil engr., supt. Spencer, White & Prentice, 1940-41; asst. to design and prodn. mgr. Frederick R. Harris, 1941-43; chief indsl. engr. Naval Aircraft, Norfolk, Va., 1943-46; asst. chief engr. Boyle-Midway, N.Y.C., 1946-47; plant mgr. Boyle-Midway, Atlanta, 1947-51; asst. to pres. Boyle-Midway, N.Y.C., 1951-55, Standard Packaging Corp., N.Y.C., 1955-57; v.p. for mfg. Standard Packaging Corp., 1957-67; mgr. facilities to divisional v.p. Doubleday & Co., Inc., Garden City, N.Y., 1967-83; pres. Meditz Engring. Assocs., 1984—. Served from ensign to lt. (s.g.) USNR, 1943-46. J. Waldo Smith fellow ASCE, 1939; Bklyn. Poly. Inst. fellow, 1939. Mem. Soc. for Adcancement Mgmt., Highland Park Club, Lake Wales Country Club, Alpha Pi Mu. Home: 1639 NE 26th St Fort Lauderdale FL 33305

MEDLAND, WILLIAM JAMES, college president; b. Logansport, Ind., Jan. 1, 1944; s. Thomas Gallagher and Mary Elizabeth (Hassett) M.; m. Donna Lee Bahnaman, Mar. 12, 1977; 1 child, Mark David. BA, U. Notre Dame, 1966; student, St. Louis U., 1972-74; MA in History, Ball State U., 1967, MA in Edn., 1979, PhD in History, 1980; postgrad., Inst. for Mgmt. Lifelong Edn., Harvard U., 1985, Ctr. Internat. Cooperation and Security Studies, U. Wis., 1988, Ctr. Internat. Studies, MIT, 1989, Freie Universitat, Berlin, 1991. Instr. history and philosophy Donnelly coll., Kansas City, Kans., 1967-70; curricular advisor Ball State U., Muncie, Ind., 1970-71, teaching fellow, 1977-80; asst. dean St. Louis (Mo.) U., 1971-75; employee supr. Wilson, Inc., Logansport, 1975-76; ops. mgr. Watson-Jenkins, Inc., Indpls., 1976-77; dean of coll., asst. prof. history Springfield (Ill.) Coll., 1980-81; acad. dean, assoc. prof. history and edn. Marymount Coll., Salina, Kans., 1981-86; exec. v.p., provost, prof. history St. Mary's Coll., Winona, Minn., 1986-91; pres., prof. history Viterbo Coll., LaCrosse, Wis., 1991—; edn. cons. Am. Inst. Banking, Springfield, 1980-81; advisor Adv. Com. to Sch. Bd., Salina, 1984, Salina Diocesan Bd. Edn., 1981-83; evaluator North Ctrl. Assn., Chgo., 1987—. Author: Cuban Missile Crisis of 1962-Needless or Necessary?, 1988, reprint, 1990, A Guide to Writing College Research Papers, 1989, The Catholic School: A Bibliographical Resource Guide, 1990; editor: Ind. Acad. Social Scis. jour., 1979, Perspectives: A Liberal Arts Exchange (faculty jour.), 1988. Coll. solicitor United Way, St. Louis, 1973; coord. Coll./Cmty. Artist Series, Salina, 1981-84; bd. dirs. Immaculate Heart of Mary Sem., Winona, 1987-91, Viterbo Coll., La Crosse Med. Health Sci. Consortium, Wis. Found. for Ind. Colls., ; chair La Crosse Diocesan Edn. Commn. Fellow Ctr. Internat. Studies, MIT/Harvard U., 1989. Mem. am. Assn. Higher Edn., Am. Assn. Coll. Pres., Am. Assn. Ind. Coll. Pres., Wis. Assn. Ind. Colls. and Univs. (bd. dirs.), KC, Rotary, Phi Alpha Theta (rsch. award Ball State U. 1979), Phi Delta Kappa. Democrat. Roman Catholic. Avocations: reading, research, hiking, cross-country skiing. Home: 414 29th St S La Crosse WI 54601-6013 Office: Viterbo Coll Office of Pres 815 9th St S La Crosse WI 54601-4777

MEDLEY, ALEX ROY, executive minister; b. Columbus, Ga., Aug. 4, 1948; s. Howard and Clois Mildred (Chumney) M.; m. Patricia Stauffer, May 10, 1975; children: James Ethan, Christopher Jordan. BA magna cum laude, U. Chattanooga, 1970; cert., Grad. Sch. Ecumenical Studies, Celigny, Switzerland, 1973; MDiv, Princeton Sem., 1974. Ordained to ministry Bapt. Ch., 1975. Assoc. pastor First Bapt. Ch. Trenton, N.J., 1974-77; adminstrv. intern Nat. Ministries Am. Bapt. Chs. U.S.A., Valley Forge, Pa., 1977, nat. dir. Christian ctr., 1978-85; min. of world mission support, area min. Am. Bapt. Chs. N.J., East Orange, 1986-92, exec. min., 1992—; intern World Coun. Chs., Geneva, Switzerland, 1973; rep. N.Am. Bapt. Fellowship, Washington, 1975-77; mem. domestic hunger/poverty working group Nat. Coun. Chs. of Christ, 1978-85, mem. gen. assembly; conf. speaker Am. Bapt. Chs., 1979; Am. Bapt. Ch. U.S.A. del. to Nat. Coun. Chs. of Christ. Editor (newsletter) Social Edn. for Action Newsletter, 1978-79. Bd. dirs. Ch. World Svc./CROP, N.J., 1975-77, Occupational Tng. Ctr., Burlington, N.J., 1992; sec. Key Inmate Edn. Project, Trenton, 1986. Mem. Am. Bapt. Regional Exec. Mins. Coun. Avocations: reading, fishing, hiking. Home: 12 Courtland Ln Willingboro NJ 08046-3406 Office: Am Bapt Chs NJ Ste 101 3752 Nottingham Way Trenton NJ 08690

MEDLEY, DONALD MATTHIAS, education educator, consultant; b. Faulkton, S.D., Feb. 18, 1917; s. Thomas Arnot and Cecilia Agnes (Kellen) M.; m. Betty Ann Robertsen, Aug. 23, 1948; 1 child, Timothy Laurence. B.S., Coll. St. Thomas, St. Paul, 1938; M.A., U. Minn., 1950, Ph.D., 1954. Tchr., Am. Sch. Guadalajara, Mex., 1941-42, Floodwood Pub. Schs., Minn., 1946-48; instr. English, Coll. St. Thomas, 1948-50; asst. prof. CUNY, 1954-59, assoc. prof., 1959-64, prof., 1964-65; sr. research psychologist Ednl. Testing Service, Princeton, N.J., 1965-70; disting. prof. U. Va., Charlottesville, 1970-87, prof. emeritus, 1987—; mem. exec. bd. Consortium for the Improvement of Tchr. Evaluation, Atlanta, 1985-87. Author: Measurement-Based Evaluation of Teacher Performance, 1984; author: (with others) Handbook of Research on Teaching, 1963, The Teacher's Handbook, 1971, Research on Teaching: Concepts, Findings, and Implications, 1979, Encyclopedia of Educational Research, 5th edit., 1982, 6th edit., 1992, Developing Skills for Instructional Supervision, 1984, Advances in Teacher Education, 1984, International Encyclopedia of Education: Research and Studies, 1984, 2d edit., 1994, Assessment of Teaching: Purposes, Practices, and Implications for the Profession, 1990; contbr. articles to profl. jours. Served as staff sgt. U.S. Army, 1942-46. Fellow Am. Psychol. Assn.; mem. Am. Ednl. Research Assn. (div. sec. 1962), Nat. Council on Measurement in Edn., Assn. Tchr. Educators. Democrat. Roman Catholic. Avocations: conjuring, travel.

MEDLIN, JOHN GRIMES, JR., banker; b. Benson, N.C., Nov. 23, 1933; s. John Grimes and Mabel (Stephenson) M. BS in Bus. Adminstrn., U. N.C., 1956; grad., The Exec. Program, U. Va., 1965. With Wachovia Bank & Trust Co., Winston-Salem, N.C., 1959—, pres., 1974; pres., CEO Wachovia Bank and Wachovia Corp., Winston-Salem, N.C., 1977-93; chmn. bd. Wachovia Corp., Winston-Salem, N.C., 1987—; bd. dirs. US Air Group, Inc., RJR Nabisco, Inc., Wachovia Corp., BellSouth Corp., Nat. Svc. Industries, Inc., Burlington Industries Inc., Media Gen. Inc., Nabisco Holdings, Inc. Trustee Nat. Humanities Ctr., Wake Forest U., Kenan Inst. Pvt. Enterprise, Kenan Inst. Arts, The Duke Endorsement; active numerous civic and svc. orgns. With USNR, 1956-59. Mem. Phi Delta Theta. Office: Wachovia Corp PO Box 3099 100 N Main St Winston Salem NC 27150

MEDLOCK, ANN, non-profit organization executive, writer, speaker; b. Portsmouth, Va., May 6, 1933; d. Frank Wesley and Olive Edna (Litz) Medlock; m. Thomas Proctor Crawford, Mar. 5, 1955 (div.); 1 child, Philip Courtney; m. John Peasley Miraglia, June 22, 1966 (div.); children: Cynthia Medlock, David Medlock; m. John A. Graham, June 13, 1982. BA magna cum laude, U. Md., 1964. Free-lance writer N.Y.C., Princeton (N.J.) and Saigon, Republic of Vietnam, 1959-85; editor Vietnam Presse, Saigon, 1959-61, Macmillan Pub. Inc., N.Y.C., 1966-69; founder Medlock & Co. Pub. Rels., 1972-82; speechwriter the Aga Khan, N.Y.C., 1979-80; editor-in-chief Children's Express, N.Y.C., 1978-79; founder, pres. The Giraffe Project, N.Y.C. and Whidbey Island, Wash., 1983—; judge Creative Altruism Awards, Sausalito, Calif., 1988-92, Eddie Bauer Heroes for the Earth Award, 1990-93. Editor: The Giraffe Gazette, 1983-92. Mem. planning bd. City of Langley, Wash., 1986-88; co-founder Citizens for Sensible Devel., Whidbey Island, 1988; mem. bd. advisors Cmty. Action Network, 1986-94, Windstar Found., Snowmass, Colo., 1984-92, U.S.-Soviet Ptnrs. Project, Seattle, 1989-92; bd. dirs. Hedgebrook Writers' Colony, 1994—, Context Inst., 1996—.

Recipient Pub. Svc. award Am. Values, 1989, 1st Pl. award Wash. Press Assn., 1991, Temple award for Creative Altruism, 1996. Avocations: painting, poetry, designing. Office: The Giraffe Project 197 Second St PO Box 759 Langley WA 98260

MEDLOCK, DONALD LARSON, lawyer; b. Port Chester, N.Y., Mar. 8, 1927; s. J. Harold and Emma Adelaide (MacLennan) M.; m. Katharine Smedes Nicholson, May 21, 1955; children: Katharine Baird, Margaret MacLennan, William Nicholson. BA with honors, Yale U., 1947, LLB, 1950. Bar: N.Y. 1950, U.S. Dist. Ct. (so. dist.) N.Y. 1951, U.S. Dist. Ct. (ea. dist.) N.Y. 1952, U.S. Tax Ct. 1952, U.S. Ct. Custom and Patent Appeals, U.S. Ct. Appeals (2d cir.) 1951. Assoc. Putnam & Roberts, N.Y.C., 1950-56, ptnr., 1957-94, sr. counsel, 1995—; bd. dirs. Bancard Sys. of N.Y. Inc., Port Washington. Editor Yale Law Jour., New Haven, 1948-50. Sec., bd. dirs. Port Washington Community Chest, 1959-61; bd. dirs. Port Washington Estates Assn., 1958-61; mem. ann. fund parents com. Taft Sch., 1979-81; bd. mgrs., exec. com. William Sloane Ho. YMCA of Greater N.Y., 1979-84; chmn. univ. coun. com. on Law Sch. Yale U., 1979-86; chmn. Yale Alumni Fund, 1984-86, bd. dirs., 1955—, exec. com., 1980-88; chmn. Yale Law Sch. Fund, 1974-76; mem. devel. bd. Yale U., 1984-88, exec. com., 1984-86; exec. com. Yale Law Sch., 1975-79, hon., 1979—; bd. dirs. Assn. Yale Alumni, 1984-86, rep.-at-large, 1979-82, com. on undergrad. admisssions, 1979-82, com. on Yale medal, 1981; exec. com. Assn. Families U. Denver, 1982-84. Recipient citation Yale Law Sch., 1977, Yale Alumni Fund Chmn.'s award, 1979, 87, Yale medal, 1994. Mem. ABA, Fed. Power Bar Assn., Assn. of Bar of City of N.Y. (com. on profl. ethics 1958-61), Corbey Ct. Yale Law Sch., Tuscarora Club (Margaretville, N.Y., bd. dirs. 1963-95, sec. 1970-86, v.p. 1984-86), Landfall Club, Manhasset Bay Yacht Club, Mory's Assn., India House, Scroll and Key Soc., Yale Club N.Y.C., Phi Beta Kappa, Phi Delta Phi. Avocations: trout fishing, tennis, reading, crossword puzzles. Home: Landfall 800 Oyster Landing Wilmington NC 28405-5292

MEDNICK, MURRAY, playwright; b. Bklyn., Aug. 24, 1939; s. Sol Joseph and Betty (Greenstein) M. Student, Bklyn. Coll., 1957-60. Author: The Hawk, 1968, The Hunter, 1969, The Shadow Ripens, 1969, The Deer Kill, 1971, Are You Lookin?, 1973, Black Hole in Space, 1975, Taxes, 1975, The Coyote Cycle, 1978-84, Iowa and Blessings for Public Broadcasting System, 1977, 78, Scar, 1985, Heads, 1987, Shatter 'n Wade, 1990, Fedunn, 1992, Joe & Betty, 1994; also pub. in West Coast Plays; poems in Transatlantic Rev; others.; 1st prodn. at Theatre Genesis, N.Y.C., 1966; v.p., N.Y. Theatre Strategy, 1972, artistic dir., Padua Hills Playwrights' Workshop, 1978-94. Grantee Rockefeller Found., 1968, 72, Guggenheim Found., 1973; recipient Poetry award Nat. Coun. Arts, 1968, Creative Artists Pub. Svc. award, 1973, Obie award for The Deer Kill, 1970, Ovation lifetime achievement award L.A. Theater League, 1992. Mem. Writers Guild, New Dramatists.

MEDNICK, ROBERT, accountant; b. Chgo., Apr. 1, 1940; s. Harry and Nettie (Brenner) M.; m. Susan Lee Levinson, Oct. 28, 1962; children: Michael Jon, Julie Eden, Adam Charles. BSBA, Roosevelt U., Chgo., 1962. CPA, Ill. Staff asst. Arthur Anderson, Chgo., 1962-63, sr. acct., 1963-66, mgr., 1966-71, ptnr., 1971—, mng. dir. SEC policies, 1973-76, mng. dir. auditing procedures, 1976-79, mng. ptnr. profl. and regulatory matters, 1993—; vice chmn. com. on profl. stds. Andersen Worldwide, 1979-82, chmn. com., 1982—. Contbr. articles to profl. jours. Bd. dirs. Roosevelt U., Chgo., 1980—, vice chmn., 1986—, sr. vice chmn., 1994—; bd. dirs. Auditorium Theatre Coun., 1990—, Lake Shore Drive Synagogue, 1992—; co-chmn. adv. coun. Chgo. Action for Soviet Jewry, Highland Park, Ill., 1983-87; bd. dirs., mem. exec. com. Am. Judicature Soc., 1990-95, vice chmn., 1993-95; bd. overseers Rand Corp. Inst. Civil Justice, 1994—. Sgt. USAFR, 1965-69. Recipient Silver medal Ill. CPA Soc., 1962; named One of Ten Outstanding Young Men in Chgo., Chgo. Jr. C. of C., 1973-74; recipient Rolf A. Weil Disting. Service award, Roosevelt U., Chgo., 1983; Max Block award N.Y. State C.P.A. Soc., 1984; Ann. Literary award Jour. Acctg., 1986, 88. Mem. AICPA (bd. dirs. 1986-87, 92-94, 95—, vice chmn. 1995—, numerous coms., Elijah Watt Sells award 1962), Am. Acctg. Assn., Ill. CPA Soc. (acctg. prins. com. 1973, legal liability com. 1986—, mgmt. of acctg. practice com. 1991—), Mid-Day Club, Standard Club. Jewish. Avocations: tennis, collecting art.

MEDOFF, MARK HOWARD, playwright, screenwriter, novelist; b. Mt. Carmel, Ill., Mar. 18, 1940; s. Lawrence Ray and Thelma Irene (Butt) M.; m. Stephanie Thorne, June 24, 1972; children: Debra, Rachel, Jessica. B.A., U. Miami, Fla., 1962; M.A., Stanford U., 1966; D.H.L., Gallaudet Coll., 1981. Instr. English and drama N.Mex. State U., 1966-79, dramatist in residence, 1974—, head dept. drama, 1978-87, prof. drama, 1979-93, artistic dir., 1982-87; artistic dir. Am. S.W. Theatre Co., 1984-87. Author: (plays) When You Comin' Back, Red Ryder?, 1974, The Wager, 1975, The Kramer, 1975, The Halloween Bandit, 1978, The Conversion of Aaron Weiss, 1978, Firekeeper, 1978, The Last Chance Saloon, 1979, Children of a Lesser God, 1980 (Soc. West Theatres best play award 1982), The Majestic Kid, 1981, The Hands of Its Enemy, 1984, Kringle's Window, 1985, The Heart Outright, 1986 (novel) Dreams of Long Lasting: (films) When You Comin' Back, Red Ryder?, 1979, Off Beat, 1986, Apology, 1986, Children of a Lesser God, 1986, Good Guys Wear Black, 1978, Clara's Heart, 1988, The Majestic Kid, 1988, City of Joy, 1992, Homage, 1995; works appear in Best Plays, 1973-74, 75-75, 79-80, Best Short Plays, 1975, The Homage that Follows, 1987; plays Stumps, 1989, Stefanie Hero, 1990. Guggenheim fellow, 1974-75; recipient Obie award, Drama Desk award, Outer Critics Circle award, Media award Pres.'s Com. Employment Handicapped, Tony award; Oscar award nominee for Best Screenplay for Children of A Lesser God, 1987. Mem. Dramatists Guild, Writers Guild Am., Actors Equity Assn., Screen Actors Guild Pen. Office: PO Box 3072 Las Cruces NM 88003-3072

MEDONIS, ROBERT XAVIER, lawyer; b. Pitts., May 31, 1931; s. Vincent X. and Anastasia T. (Puida) M.; m. M. Kathleen Castor, Dec. 29, 1962; children: Meg Toomey, Robert Xavier, Mark D. BEd, Duquesne U., 1953, MA, 1985; JD, U. Pitts., 1958. Bar: Pa. 1959, U.S. Supreme Ct. 1966, U.S. Ct. Appeals (3d cir.) 1976. Trial atty. criminal div. Legal Aid Soc., Pitts., 1960-61; trial atty. Allegheny County Dist. Atty.'s Office, Pitts., 1964-71; assoc. Cleland, Hurt & Bowman, Pitts., 1961-63; pvt. practice, 1958-60, 63-64, 71-93; assoc. Karlowitz and Cromer, Pitts., 1993-95; v.p., gen. counsel Marquee Group, 1995-96, Internat. Investment Group, Pitts., 1996—. Bd. dirs. World Trade Ctr., Pitts. Capt. U.S. Army, 1953-55. Mem. ABA, Pa. Bar Assn., Allegheny County Bar Assn., Internat. Bar Assn., Pa. Trial Lawyers Assn., We. Pa. Trial Lawyers Assn., Lithuanian Am. Bar Assn., Am. Ins. of Ct., China-Am. Trade Soc. (founder, pres.). Home: 737 Shady Ln Pittsburgh PA 15228-2450 Office: 1550 Koppers Bldg Pittsburgh PA 15219

MEDVECKY, ROBERT STEPHEN, lawyer; b. Bridgeport, Conn., Feb. 12, 1931; s. Stephen and Elizabeth (Petro) M.; m. Ellen R. Munt, Nov. 11, 1966; children—Allison L., Beth A., Craig R. A.B., Dartmouth, 1952; J.D., Harvard, 1955. Bar: Ill. bar 1955, Conn. bar 1958, D.C. bar 1972, Fla. bar 1989. Asso. firm Lord, Bissell & Brook, Chgo., 1955-57; gen. atty. So. New Eng. Telephone Co., New Haven, 1957-71; v.p., gen. counsel, sec. Amtrak, Washington, 1971-75; partner firm Lord, Bissell & Brook, Washington, 1975-78, Reid & Priest, N.Y.C., 1978-87. Clubs: Harvard (N.Y.C.), Fiddlesticks Country (Ft. Meyers, Fla.), Saphire Valley Country (Cashlers, N.C.). Home (winter): 15491 Kilbirnie Dr Fort Myers FL 33912 Home (summer): 29 Pine Ridge Trl Sapphire NC 28774-9625

MEDVED, MICHAEL, film critic, author; b. Phila., Oct. 3, 1948; s. David Bernard and Renate Rosa (Hirsch) M.; m. Nancy Harris Herman, Aug. 5, 1972 (div. 1983); m. Diane Elvenstar, Jan. 27, 1985; children: Sarah Julia, Shayna Elana, Daniel Joshua. BA, Yale U., 1969; MFA, Calif. State U., San Francisco, 1974. Speech writer, polit. cons. various campaigns and politicians, Conn., Calif., D.C., 1970-73; advt. creative dir. Anrick Inc., Oakland, Calif., 1973-74; freelance writer Los Angeles, 1974—; on-air film critic People Now, Cable News Network, Los Angeles, 1980-83; on-air film critic, co-host Sneak Previews PBS, 1985—; chief film critic N.Y. Post, 1993—; Hollywood corr. The Sunday Times of London. Author: What Really Happened to the Class of '65?, 1976, The Shadow Presidents, 1979, Hospital, 1983, Hollywood vs. America, 1992; co-author: (with Harry Medved) The 50 Worst Films of All Time, 1978, The Golden Turkey Awards, 1980, The Hollywood Hall of Shame, 1984, Son of Golden Turkey Awards, 1986. Co-founder, pres. Pacific Jewish Ctr., Venice, Calif., 1977-94; pres. Emanuel Streisand Sch., Venice, 1980-85. Mem. Writers Guild Am., AFTRA. Avocation: classical music. Office: Sta WTTW-TV 5400 N St Louis Ave Chicago IL 60625-4623

MEDVED, PAUL STANLEY, lawyer; b. Milw., May 6, 1956; s. Frank F. and Evelyn F. (Poplawski) M.; m. Danita C. Cole, Aug. 27, 1988. BA with Honors, Marquette U., 1978; JD, Columbia U., 1981. Bar: Wis. 1981, U.S. Dist. Ct. (ea. dist.) Wis. 1981, U.S. Dist. Ct. (we. dist.) Wis. 1984, U.S. Ct. Appeals (7th cir.) 1984. Assoc. Michael, Best & Friedrich, Milw., 1981-88, ptnr., 1988—. Office: Michael Best & Friedrich 100 E Wisconsin Ave Milwaukee WI 53202-4107

MEDVIN, HARVEY NORMAN, financial executive, treasurer; b. Chgo., Sept. 6, 1936; s. Benjamin and Clara (Edelstein) M.; m. Sheila S. Spitzner, July 5, 1965; children: Arla Risa, Steven Merrill. BS in Acctg., U. Ill., 1958. CPA, Ill. Mem. audit staff Coopers & Lybrand, 1958-63; treas., v.p. The Martin Brower Co., Des Plaines, Ill., 1963-73, Ryan Ins. Group, Inc., Chgo., 1983—; sr. v.p., chief fin. officer Combined Internat. Corp. Chgo., Chgo., 1983—; exec. v.p., chief fin. officer, treas. Aon Corp., Chgo., 1987—, also bd. dirs. all subs.; bd. dirs. Schwarz Paper Co., Morton Grove, Ill., La Salle Bank Corp., La Salle Nat. Bank Chgo. Bd. dirs. Highland Park (Ill.) Hosp.; bd. govs. Chgo. Lighthouse for Blind; trustee Ravina Festival Highland Park, Ill., La Salla Nat. Bank, La Salle Nat. Corp., Chgo. With U.S. Army, 1958-59. Mem. AICPA. Office: Aon Corp 123 N Wacker Dr Chicago IL 60606-1700*

MEE, HERB, JR., natural resource/environmental services executive; b. Oklahoma City, June 16, 1928; s. Herbert Martin and Margaret Adair (Lackey) M.; m. Marlene W., Sept. 8, 1978; children from previous marriage: Christopher W., Michael M. (twins). BA cum laude, Harvard U., 1950; advanced transp. mgmt. program, Northwestern U., 1965. Ptnr. in fire and casualty ins. agy. Oklahoma City, 1950-53, ind. oil and gas lease broker, 1953-54; with land dept. Woods Corp., Oklahoma City, 1956-72, v.p., then. exec. v.p., pres., chief exec. officer, 1968-72; pres. Beard Co., Oklahoma City, 1974—; bd. dirs. Alladin Plastics Inc., Liberty Bancorp, Inc.; bd. dirs. Liberty Bank and Trust Co. of Oklahoma City, N.A. and Liberty Band and Trust Co. of Tulsa, N.A., E.F. Craven Co. With U.S. Army, 1955-56. Mem. Chief Execs. Orgn., Oklahoma City Golf and Country Club (pres. 1982-84). Republican. Avocations: golf, backgammon. Office: The Beard Co 5600 N May Ave Oklahoma City OK 73112-4275

MEECH, KAREN JEAN, astronomer; b. Denver, July 9, 1959; d. Lloyd Augustus and Patricia Ann (Marshall) M. BA cum laude in Physics, Rice U., 1981; PhD in Planetary Astronomy, MIT, 1987. Rsch. asst. Maria Mitchell Obs., Nantucket, Mass., 1978, Am. Assn. Variable Star Observation, Cambridge, Mass., 1979, 81-82; rsch. asst. archaeoastronomy EARTHWATCH, Cusco, Peru, 1980; univ. lab. asst. molecular physics Rice U., Houston, 1980-81, quantum physics grader, 1980-81; rsch. asst. Am. Assn. Variable Star Observers, 1981-82; rsch. specialist MIT, Cambridge, 1981-82, grad. teaching asst., 1982-86, grad. rsch. asst., 1986-87; asst. astronomer Inst. for Astronomy, Honolulu, 1987-91, assoc. astronomer, 1992—; mem. IFA Computer Adv. Com., 1991-93, IFA Endowment Com., 1991—, U. Rsch. Coun., 1990-93, NASA Planetary Astronomy Com. II, 1993-94, NASA Planetary Sci. Data Steering Group, 1993-95, IFA Admissions Com., 1992-93, NASA Planetary Astronomy Rev. Panel, 1990-91, Cerro Tololo Interamerican Obs. user's Com., 1991-94, USIA Internat. Teleconf., 1991; chair IFA Scholarship Com., 1991; interviewer Rice U. Alumni, 1989—; reviewer. Contbr. articles to Astron. Jour., Astrophys. Jour., Sci., Icarus, Nature, Bull. Am. Astronomy Soc., Info. Bull. Variable Stars, Minor Planet Circular, IAU Circular. Safety diver U. Hawaii Scuba class, 1988-90; vol. Honolulu Zool. Soc. Zoo Fun Run, 1991-92; active dept. edn. H.S. Student Career Program, Honolulu, 1988; organizer H.S. Tchr.-Student Asst. Workshops, 1993-95; local organizing chair divsn. Planetary Astronomy meeting, Kona, Hawaii, 1995; faculty senate U. Hawaii, 1995—; com. Annie Jump Cannon award, 1988; judge Hawaii State Sci. Fair, 1992—; bd. dirs. Kilolokahi, 1995—. Scholar Bd. of Govs., 1980, Grad. Student Rschrs. fellow NASA, 1986-87; recipient Annie Jump Cannon award in Astronomy, 1988, Harold C. Urey prize in Astronomy Am. Astron. Soc., 1994, Heaps prize in Physics, 1981. Mem. Am. Astron. Soc. (divsn. planetary scis., 1995), Internat. Astron. Union-Commn. 15, Am. Assn. Variable Star Observers. Achievements include co-discovery of the outburst of Halley's comet at the longest distance from the sun for a recorded outburst; discovery of cometary activity on object 2060 Chiron; investigator Hubble space telescope. Office: Inst for Astronomy 2680 Woodlawn Dr Honolulu HI 96822-1839

MEECH, RICHARD CAMPBELL, lawyer; b. Portsmouth, Hampshire, Eng., Sept. 16, 1921; s. Richard George and Elizabeth (Campbell) M.; m. Carol Crockett, Oct. 6, 1951; children: Susan Crockett, Richard George, Peter Campbell, Sarah Elizabeth, Nancy Bingham. BA, U. Toronto, Ont., Can., 1946; LLB, York U., Toronto, 1950; LLM, Harvard U., 1951. Bar: Ont. 1950; created Queen's counsel, 1960. Ptnr. Borden & Elliot, Toronto, 1956-65, sr. ptnr., 1965-92, ptnr. emeritus, counsel, 1992—; bd. dirs. Barclays Bank Can. Ltd., Budd Can. Inc., Continental Ins. Co. Can., Dominion Ins. Co.; chmn. bd. dirs. Eskofot Can. Ltd.; pres., bd. dirs. Austin Knight Can.; v.p., sec., bd. dirs. Textron Can. Ltd., Canaham Ltd.; chmn. Howden Group PLC, 1983-87; sec. Can. Investor Protection Fund, 1969-90. Hon. consul gen. of Thailand, Toronto; sec. Can. Securities Inst.; mem. adv. coun. Ridley Coll., 1971-77; pres. Wellesley Coll. Can. Found.; trustee Can. Found., Queen's U., 1980-92; trustee emeritus Sunnybrook Med. Ctr., Toronto; chmn. Havergal Coll. Found., Toronto, 1972-74, bd. govs., 1971-77; nat. chmn. Queen's U. Parents Assn., 1975-85; mem. Met. Toronto adv. bd. Salvation Army. Pilot RCAF, RAF, 1942-46. Decorated comdr. Order of White Elephant, knight comdr. Order of Crown (Thailand); recipient 125th Anniversary Confedn. Can. Commemorative medal, 1993. Mem. Internat. Bar Assn. (chmn. bus. sect. 1982-84), Harvard Law Sch. Assn. Ont. (pres. 1973-75), York Club, Toronto Club, Badminton and Racquet Club, Nat. Club (pres. 1980-81), Toronto Golf Club, Can. Club (pres. 1974-75), Empire Club, St. George's Soc., Harvard Club (N.Y.C.), Garden of Gods Club (Colorado Springs, Colo.), Coral Beach and Tennis Club (Bermuda). Home: 40 Stratheden Rd, Toronto, ON Canada M4N 1E4 Office: Scotia Pla, 40 King St W 44th Fl, Toronto, ON Canada M5H 3Y4

MEECHAM, WILLIAM CORYELL, engineering educator; b. Detroit; s. William Edward and Mabel Catherine (Wilcox) M.; m. Barbara Jane Brown, Sept. 4, 1948 (dec.); children: Janice Lynn, William James; m. Della Fern Carson,. BS, U. Mich., 1948, MS, 1948, PhD in Physics, 1954. Head acoustics lab. Willow Run Labs., Ann Arbor, Mich., 1959-60; asst. prof. U. Mich., Ann Arbor, 1958-60; prof. U. Minn., Mpls., 1960-67; prof. fluid mechanics and acoustics UCLA, 1967—, chmn. dept. mechanics and structures, 1972-73; cons. Aerospace Corp., El Segundo, Calif., 1975-80, Rand Corp., Santa Monica, Calif., 1964-74, Bolt, Beranek and Newman, Cambridge, Mass., 1968-73, Arete Assocs., Encino, Calif., 1976—, CRT Corp., Chatsworth, Calif., 1985—. Author: (with R. Lutomirski) Lasar Systems, 1973; author 140 papers on fluid mechanics and acoustics. Treas. Unitarian Ch., Ann Arbor, Mich., 1958-60; advisor U.S. Congress Com. on Pub. Works, Congl. Record Report N.J., 1972; mem. Calif. Space and Def. Council, U.S. Congress, 1982—. Served with U.S. Army, 1944-46. Mich. Alumni scholar 1942-44, Donovan scholar U. Mich., 1944-45; UCLA senate rsch. grantee, 1968—, NASA rsch. grantee, 1971—, Office Naval Rsch. grantee, 1977-85; recipient Disting. Svc. award U.S. Army. Fellow Acoustical Soc. Am. (gen. chmn. meeting 1973), AIAA (assoc. fellow); mem. com. aeroacoustics 1972-75); mem. Am. Phys. Soc. (fluid dynamics div.), Inst. Noise Control Engring., Sigma Xi, Tau Beta Pi. Home: 927 Glenhaven Dr Pacific Palisades CA 90272-2202 Office: UCLA Sch Engring & Applied Sci Los Angeles CA 90024

MEEGAN, CHARLES ANTHONY, astrophysics researcher; b. Buffalo, Sept. 24, 1944; s. Charles Anthony and Ruth Marie (Rieman) M.; m. Gerry Louise Allen, May 7, 1983; 1 child, Anna Katharine. BS, Rensselaer Poly. Inst., 1966; PhD in Physics, U. Md., 1973. Rsch. assoc. in astrophysics Rice U., Houston, 1974-75, U. Ala., Huntsville, Ala., 1976, Nat. Rsch. Coun., Huntsville, 1976-78; space scientist in astrophysics NASA Marshall Space Flight Ctr., Huntsville, 1978—; mission scientist Astro Shuttle mission NASA, 1992—, co-investigator burst and transient source expt., Huntsville, 1978—. Mem. Am. Physics Soc., Am. Astron. Soc., Sigma Xi. Avocations: aviation, sailing, woodworking. Office: Marshall Space Flt Ctr NASA ES 84 Huntsville AL 35812*

MEEHAN, GERRY, professional hockey team executive; b. Toronto, Ont., Can.; m. Mirella Meehan; children: Danny, Adam, Katie. Grad., Canisius Coll.; JD, U. Buffalo, 1982. Professional hockey player Toronto Maple Leafs, 1968, Phila. Flyers, 1969; professional hockey player Buffalo Sabres, 1970-74, asst. gen. mgr., 1984-86, former gen. mgr.; player Vancouver (Can.) Canucks, 1975, Atlanta Flames (now Calgary Flames), 1975, Washington Capitals, 1976-79; atty. Cohen Swados Wright Hanifin Bradford Brett, Buffalo, 1984; exec. v.p. for sports operations Buffalo Sabres; prin. George Meehan-Attorney, Williamsville, NY. Office: George Meehan Attorney 300 International Williamsville NY 14221*

MEEHAN, JOHN, artistic director; b. Brisbane, Australia. Studied with, Patricia MacDonald; student, Australian Ballet Sch., Melbourne. Mem. Australian Ballet, 1970-72, soloist, 1972-74, prin. dancer, 1974; artistic dir. Royal Winnipeg Ballet, 1990-93; guest artist, prin. dancer Am. Ballet Theatre, 1977. Leading roles include The Sleeping Beauty, Romeo and Juliet, Giselle, Onegin, Fokine's Firebird, Les Sylphides, George Balanchie's Theme and Variations, Teltley's Sphinx, Pierrot Lunaire and Voluntaries, Anthony Tudor's The Leaves are Fading, Lilac Garden, Baryshnikov's Don Quixote; created leading role in Gemini; Can. debut The Merry Widow with the Nat. Ballet of Can., 1986; danced at Kennedy Centre, Washington; co-starred with Karen Kain TV prodn. The Merry Widow, 1987; created two original pas de deux for ABT, Le ReTour, Adagio for Stings; choreographer Echoes for the Washington Ballet; singer, dancer feature role mus. rev. Noel; mus. debut in Song and Dance; dance premiere Dim Lustre, ABT, 1985; dancer Jacob's Pillow Dance Festival, 1985; guest appearances with the N.Y.C. Ballet; with Merrill Ashley in The Nutcracker, Divertimento No. 15, Swan Lake, Gounod Symphony, Piano Concerto No. 2. Scholar Australian Ballet Sch. Address: Box 12 Russell Ave Rhinecliff NY 12574-0019

MEEHAN, JOHN JOSEPH, brokerage house executive; b. Bklyn., Mar. 18, 1945; s. John Joseph and Marie Kathleen (McGuinness) M.; m. Mary Lou Muniz, June 20, 1970 (div. 1976); 1 child, Michael; m. Janice Anne Napoli, Dec. 5, 1980; children: Matthew, Martin. A.A.S., St. John's U., Jamaica, N.Y.,, 1965. Asst. treas. for trading Chase Manhattan Bank, N.Y.C., 1968-72; sr. trader agys. Goldman, Sachs & Co., N.Y.C., 1972-75; sr. v.p. fin., treas. Fed. Nat. Mortgage Assn., N.Y.C., Washington, 1975-85; sr. v.p., mgr. govt. bond dept. Dean Witter Reynolds Inc., N.Y.C., 1985-88; sr. v.p., dir., mng. dir., dep. chief exec. officer Deutsch Bank Govt. Securities, Inc., N.Y.C., 1988-93; mng. dir. Deutsch Bank Securities Corp., N.Y.C., 1993-95, Deutsch Morgan Grenfell, N.Y.C., 1995—. Served to sgt. USMC, 1966-68, Vietnam. Roman Catholic. Avocations: golf; tennis; coaching boys' football; baseball. Home: 55 Crescent Rd Port Washington NY 11050-3220 Office: Deutsch Morgan Grenfell W 52d St New York NY 10019-6118

MEEHAN, JOHN JOSEPH, JR., hospital administrator; b. Boston, Jan. 29, 1946; s. John Joseph and Marjorie Louise (Hill) M.; m. Pamela Marshall, Mar. 25, 1973; children—Seth, Andrew, Sean. B.A., Dartmouth Coll., Hanover, N.H., 1968; M.H.A., U. Minn., Mpls., 1974. Unit mgr. Boston Hosp. Women, 1971-72; adminstrv. resident Hennepin County Gen. Hosp., Mpls., 1973-74; v.p. Putnam Meml. Hosp., Bennington, Vt., 1974-79; asst. dir. Hartford Hosp., Conn., 1979-81, assoc. exec. dir., 1981-85, exec. v.p., 1985-87, pres., chief operating officer, 1987-89; pres., chief exec. officer, 1989—; faculty Hartford Grad. Ctr., 1979-81; preceptor U. Minn., 1981—,. Yale U., New Haven, 1981—; mem. New Eng. Health Care Assembly, 1975—, officer, 1982-92. Active Bennington Lion's Club, 1975-79, Conn. Hosp. Assn., Urban League Greater Hartford, 1979—, Greater Hartford C. of C., 1979—, also bd. dirs., 1994—; chmn. ARC, Bennington, 1978-79; bd. dirs. St. Joseph Coll., ConnectiCare IPA/HMO, Mech. Savs. Bank, 1993—; corporator St. Francis Hosp., 1988—, Inst. Living, 1993—; fellow Am. Leadership Forum, 1993—. Served to lt. (j.g.) USNR, 1968-70. Decorated Naval medals and ribbons, 1968-70; recipient Disting. Naval Grad. award, 1968, Stuart Thompson M.D. award U. Minn., 1974. Mem. Am. Hosp. Assn., Conn. Hosp. Assn. (bd. dirs.), Capital Area Health Consortium.

MEEHAN, MARTIN THOMAS, congressman, lawyer; b. Dec. 30, 1956; s. Martin T. and Alice (Britton) M. BA in Polit. Sci., Edn. cum laude, U. Mass., Lowell, 1978; MPA, Suffolk U., 1981, JD, 1986; student, Harvard U., 1987-88. Adminstrv. asst. to mayor City of Lowell, Mass., 1978-79; press asst. Congressman James M. Shannon, Mass., 1979-81; del. Dem. Nat. Conv., 1980, 84, 88; head rsch. analyst Joint Com. on Elec. Laws Mass. State Senate, 1981-84; dir. pub. affairs Govt. of Mass., 1985-86, dep. sec. state, 1986-90; 1st asst. dist. atty. Middlesex County, Mass., 1991-92; mem. 103rd-104th Congresses from 5th Mass. dist., 1993—; mem. nat. security com., ranking minority mem., mem. small bus. subcom. on tax and fin.; former teacher, adj. instr. U. Lowell, Mass.; lawyer 1986—. Named Student of Yr. Lowell Exchange Club, 1975. Mem. ABA, Mass. Bar Assn., U. Lowell Alumni Assn., The Newspaper Guild, Internat. Fedn. Journalists. Democrat. Roman Catholic. Office: US Ho of Reps 318 Cannon HOB Washington DC 20515-2105*

MEEHAN, PATRICK J., public health officer; b. Tulsa, Dec. 30, 1956; married; 1 child. BA in Chemistry, U. Calif., Santa Cruz, 1978; MD, Washington U., St. Louis, 1982. Diplomate Am. Bd. Family Practice; lic. physician, N.H., Ga. Resident in family practice Navidad Med. Ctr./U. Calif., Salinas, 1982-85; with Epidemic Intelligence Svc. CDC and Prevention, Ctr. Environ. Health and Injury Control, Atlanta, 1988-89, preventive medicine resident, 1989-91; family practice physician Su Clinica Familiar, Harlingen, Tex., 1985-87; med. dir. prenatal and family planning Region 8 Tex. Dept. Pub. Health, Harlingen, 1986-87; acting health officer, cons. in communicable disease Santa Cruz (Calif.) County Health Dept., 1987-88; dir. N.H. divsn. Pub. Health Svc., 1991-94; dir. Ga. divs. pub. health Dept. Human Resources, Atlanta, 1994—; family practice physician Locum Tenens, Raymondville, Tex., 1987, Salud Para La Gente, Watsonville, Calif., 1987-88; adj. asst. prof. Emory U., Atlanta; clin. assoc. prof. Morehouse Sch. Medicine; lectr. in field. Contbr. numerous articles to profl. jours. Mem. APHA, Med. Assn. Ga., Am. Acad. Family Physicians, Ga. Pub. Health Assn., Assn. of State and Territorial Health Ofcls. (chair com. on injury control, com. on tobacco or health). Office: 2 Peachtree St NW Atlanta GA 30303

MEEHAN, THOMAS PATRICK, veternarian, zoological park administrator; b. Mar. 26, 1952; s. Michael P. and Dorothy (Winkler) M.; m. Judy Geiser; children: Lisa, Laura. BS in Agrl. with honors, U. Mo., 1975, D of Veterinary Medicine, 1977. Small animal veterinarian Woodmar Animal Hosp., Hammond, Ind., 1977-78; veterinary intern Westchester Comty. Veterinary Hosp. for Spl. Svcs., Mt. Kisco, N.Y., 1978-79; veterinary resident St. Louis Zoological Gardens, 1979-81; staff veterinarian Lincoln Park Zoo, Chgo., 1981-93; head dept. of animal health Brookfield (Ill.) Zoo, 1993—; adj. asst. prof. veterinary clin. medicine, Univ. of Ill. Coll. of Veterinary Medicine, 1983—; coord. Dr. Scholl Confs. on Nutrition of Captive Wild Animals and edited proceedings of meetings., 1982-91. Contbr. chpt. to book., articles to profl. jours. and presented papers at sci. meetings. Mem. Am. Vet. Med. Assn., Ill. State Vet. Med. Assn., Am. Assn. of Zoo Vets. (mem. infectious disease com.), Am. Assn. Zool. Parks and Aquariums (vet. advisor spectacled bear spl. survival plan, vet. advisor gorilla spl. survival plan), C. L. Davis Found. for Advancement of Vet. and Comparative Pathology (mem. zool. consortium), Phi Zeta. Achievements include design of equipment that facilitates safe collection of semen from zoo species by electroejaculation; initiated research that contributed to the knowlege of the parasite Geopetitia-aspiculata in bird collection at Lincoln Park Zoo; evaluated use of bio-electric impedence analysis for determining body composition in adult gorillas; collaborated in determining the relationship among vitamin D levels, metabolic bone disease and genetic lines in Emperor tamarins (with Dr. Craig Langman); studied incidence of metabolic bone disease in mother-reared infant great apes (with Dr. Craig Langman). Home: 1241 Alima Terr La Grange Park IL 60526 Office: Brookfield Zoo 3300 Golf Rd Brookfield IL 60513-1060

MEEHL, PAUL EVERETT, psychologist, educator; b. Mpls., Jan. 3, 1920; s. Otto John and Blanche Edna (Duncan) Swedal; m. Alyce M. Roworth, Sept. 6, 1941 (dec. 1972); children: Karen, Erik; m. Leslie Jane Yonce, Nov.

17, 1973. A.B., U. Minn., 1941, Ph.D., 1945; Sc.D., Adelphi U., 1984. Diplomate Am. Bd. Profl. Psychology (clin. psychology, bd. dirs.1957-62, Disting. Svc. and Outstanding Contbns. award 1989). Instr., asst., assoc. prof., chmn. dept. psychology U. Minn., 1951-57, prof., 1952—, prof. dept. psychiatry Med. Sch., 1952-90, regents' prof. psychology, 1968-89, Hathaway-Meehl prof. psychology, 1990-93, regent's prof. psychology emeritus, 1993—; prof. Minn. Ctr. for Philosophy of Sci., 1953-56, 69—, prof. philosophy, 1971—; acting chief clin. psychology VA Hosp., Mpls., 1947-49; participant Dartmouth Conf. on Behavior Theory, 1950; mem. panel on criminal deterrence Nat. Acad. Sci., 1975-77; practice psychotherapy, 1951-94; staff Nicollet Clinic, 1970-80. Author: (with S.R. Hathaway) Atlas for Clinical Use of MMPI, 1951, (with others) Modern Learning Theory, 1954, Clinical Versus Statistical Prediction, 1954, What, Then, Is Man?, 1958, Psychodiagnosis, 1973, Selected Philosophical and Methodological Papers, 1991; contbr. articles to profl., legal and philos. jours. Recipient Ednl. Testing Svc. award for contbns. to measurement, 1994, Clin. Psychology Centennial prize for lifetime achievement APA, Bruno Klopfer disting. contbn. award, 1979, Gold medal for life achievement application of psychology Am. Psychol. Found., 1989, Disting. Svc. award Am. Bd. Profl. Psychologists, 1989, Joseph Zubin prize lifetime contbns. to psychopathology, 1993; William James fellow Am. Psychol. Soc., 1989. Felow Inst. for Advanced Study in Rational Psychotherapy; mem. APA (pres. 1961-62, Disting. Contbr. award clin. divsn. 1967, Disting. Sci. Contr. award 1958, Disting. Scientist award 1976, Disting. Contbn. to Knowledge award 1993, award for Outstanding Lifetime Contbn. to Psychology 1996), Am. Acad. Arts and Scis., Nat. Acad. Sci., Philosophy of Sci. Assn., Phi Beta Kappa, Sigma Xi, Psi Chi. Home: 1544 E River Ter Minneapolis MN 55414-3646 Office: U Minn N218 Elliott Hall 75 E River Rd Minneapolis MN 55455-0280

MEEK, CARRIE P., congresswoman; 3 children. BS, Fla. A&M U., 1946, MS, U. Mich., 1948. Mem. Fla. Senate from Dist. 36, 1982-1992. Mem. 103rd-104th Congress from 17th Fla. dist., 1993—. Democrat. Office: US Ho of Reps 404 Cannon House Office Bldg Washington DC 20515*

MEEK, FORREST BURNS, educational administrator, trading company executive; b. Tustin, Mich., June 11, 1928; s. Robert B. and Electa I. (Gallup) M.; m. Jean R. Grimes, June 26, 1953; children: Sally, Thomas, Nancy, Charles. AA, Spring Arbor Coll., 1950; AB, Mich. State U., 1953; postgrad., U. Ga., 1965; MA, Cen. Mich. U., 1967. Asst. supt. Tranter Mfg. Co., Lansing, Mich., 1951-53; pres. Pioneer Mortgage Co., Clare, Mich., 1966-74; exec. sec., chmn. bd. Edgewood Press, Clare, 1971—; gen. mgr. Blue Water Imports, 1985; dir. Hanover Ednl. Ctr., Clare, 1986—, Ctr. for Chinese-Am. Scholarly Exchs., Inc., 1989—; gen. mgr. Blue-Water Internat. Trading Co., Inc.; vis. prof. Wuhan U., People's Republic China, 1986, 87; dist. office mgr. Fed. Decennial Census, 1990; hon. headmaster Xiaohe H.S., Hubei Province, China, 1994—; CFO AM. Petroleum Corp., 1996; pres. MGF Drilling USA, Inc., 1996—. Author: Michigan Timber Battleground, 1976, Michigan Heartland, 1979, One Year in China, 1988, Michigan Logging Railroad Era, 1850-1963, 1989, Railways and Tramways, 1990, Lumbering in Eastern Canada, 1991, Pearl Harbor Remembered, 1991, Heroes of The Twentieth Century, 1996. Coordinator Clare County Bicentennial Com., 1975-76; Rep. fin. chmn., Clare County, 1966-71, asst. treas. 10th dist. Mich, 1967-69; trustee local sch. bd.; chmn. local county jury bd. Served to staff sgt. U.S. Army, 1946-48. Mem. Am. Entrepreneur Assn., Mich. Sci. Tchrs. Assn., Mich. Hist. Soc., Heartland Mich. Geneal. Soc., White Pine Hist. Soc. (exec. sec.), Ctr. for Chinese-Am. Scholarly Exchs. Republican. Avocations: astronomy, silviculture, beekeeping.

MEEK, J. WILLIAM, III, art gallery owner, dealer; b. Aberdeen Proving Ground, Md., Nov. 8, 1950. BA in Econs., Fla. So. Coll., 1972. Asst. dir. Harmon Gallery, Naples, Fla., 1972-77; dir., owner Harmon-Meek Gallery, Naples, Fla., 1978—. Curator over 200 traveling art exhbns., 1978—. Capt. USAR, 1972-80. Fellow Royal Soc. Arts (London); mem. Nat. Arts Club, Chaine des Rotisseurs (charge de mission 1989—), Naples Yacht Club, Rotary (Paul Harris fellow 1989). Republican. Office: Harmon-Meek Gallery 386 Broad Ave S Naples FL 33940-7031

MEEK, PAUL DERALD, oil and chemical company executive; b. McAllen, Tex., Aug. 15, 1930; s. William Van and Martha Mary (Sharp) M.; m. Betty Catherine Robertson, Apr. 18, 1954; children: Paula Marie Meek Burford, Kathy Diane Meek Hasemann, Carol Ann Meek Miller, Linda Rae Meek. B.S. in Chem. Engring, U. Tex., Austin, 1953. Mem. tech. dept. Humble Oil & Refining Co., Baytown, Tex., 1953-55; with Cosden Oil & Chem. Co., 1955-76, pres., 1968-76; dir. Fina, Inc. (formerly Am. Petrofina, Inc.), Dallas, 1968—, v.p. parent co., 1968-76, pres., chief operating officer, 1976-83, pres., chief exec. officer, 1983-86, chmn. bd., pres., chief exec. officer, 1984-86, chmn. bd., 1986—; apptd. by Gov. Wm. P. Clements, Jr. chmn. Pub. Uitilites Commn. of Tex., 1989-92. Contbg. author: Advances in Petroleum Chemistry and Refining, 1957. Chmn. chem. engring. vis. com. U. Tex., 1975-76; mem. adv. coun. Coll. Engring. Found., U. Tex., Austin, 1979—, U. Tex. Longhorn Found., 1989—, Coll. of NaturalScis. Found., 1989—; life mem.-at-large, bd. visitors McDonald Observatory dept. astronomy U. Tex.; co-chmn. indsl. divsn. United Way of Met. Dallas, 1981-82. Named Disting. Engring. Grad. U. Tex., Austin, 1969. Mem. Am. Petroleum Inst. (bd. dirs.), 25 Yr. Club of the Petroleum Industry, Founders Club of the Petrochem. Industry, Dallas Wildcat Com. (chmn. exec. com. 1987-88). Office: Fina Inc 8350 N Central Expwy PO Box 2159 Dallas TX 75221*

MEEK, PHILLIP JOSEPH, communications executive; b. Los Angeles, Nov. 17, 1937; s. Joseph Alcinus and Clara Amy (Phillips) M.; m. Nancy Jean LaPorte, June 25, 1960; children: Katherine Amy, Brian Joseph, Laurie Noel. B.A. cum laude, Ohio Wesleyan U., 1959; M.B.A., Harvard U., 1961. Fin. analyst Ford Motor Co., 1961-63, supr. capacity planning, 1963-66, supr. domestic scheduling, 1966, controller mktg. services, 1966-68; on loan as pres. Econ. Devel. Corp. Greater Detroit, 1968-70; pres., pub. Oakland Press Co., Pontiac, Mich., 1970-77; exec. v.p., gen. mgr. Ft. Worth Star-Telegram, 1977-79, pres., editorial chmn., 1980-82, pres., pub., 1982-86; sr. v.p., pres. pub. group Capital Cities/ABC Inc., N.Y.C., 1986—; dir. Calyx & Corolla, 1995—, Roadway Express, 1996—. Past mem. Pontiac Stadium Bldg. Authority; pres. United Way Pontiac-North Oakland, 1977; dir. United Way of N.Y.C., 1994—; pres. Tarrant County United Way, 1982-83, chmn., 1983-84; chmn. North Tex. Commn., 1983-84; trustee Ohio Wesleyan U. Mem. Newspaper Assn. of Am., Tex. Daily Newspaper Assn. (pres. 1984), Phi Beta Kappa, Omicron Delta Kappa, Sigma Delta Chi, Pi Delta Epsilon, Phi Gamma Delta. Methodist. Clubs: Stanwich (Conn.); Crystal Downs (Mich.). Office: Capital Cities/ABC Inc 77 W 66th St New York NY 10023-6201

MEEK, VIOLET IMHOF, dean; b. Geneva, Ill., June 12, 1939; d. John and Violet (Krepel) Imhof; m. Devon W. Meek, Aug. 21, 1965 (dec. 1988); children: Brian, Karen; m. Don M. Dell, Jan. 4, 1992. BA summa cum laude, St. Olaf Coll., 1960; MS, U. Ill., 1962, PhD in Chemistry, 1964. Instr. chemistry Mount Holyoke Coll., South Hadley, Mass., 1964-65; asst. prof. to prof. Ohio Wesleyan U., Delaware, Ohio, 1965-84, dean for ednl. svcs., 1980-84; dir. annual programs Coun. Ind. Colls., Washington, 1984-86; assoc. dir. sponsored programs devel. Rsch. Found. Ohio State U., Columbus, 1986-91; dean, dir. Ohio State U., Lima, 1992—; vis. dean U. Calif., Berkeley, 1982, Stanford U., Palo Alto, Calif., 1982, reviewer GTE Sci. and Tech. Program, Princeton, N.J., 1986-92, Goldwater Nat. Fellowships, Princeton, 1990-96. Co-author: Experimental General Chemistry, 1984; contbr. articles to profl. jours. Bd. dirs. Luth. Campus Ministries, Columbia, 1988-91, Lutheran Social Svcs., 1988-91, Americom Bank, Lima, 1992—, Lima Symphony Orch., 1993—, Art Space, Lima, 1993—, Allen Lima Leadership, 1993—, Am. House, 1992—, Lima Vets. Meml. Civic Ctr. Found., 1992—; chmn. synodical coms. Evang. Luth. Ch. im Am., Columbus, 1982, Allen County C. of C., 1995—. Recipient Woodrow Wilson Fellowship, 1960. Mem. Nat. Coun. Rsch. Adminstrs. (named Outstanding New Profl. midwest region 1990), Am. Assn. Higher Edn., Phi Beta Kappa. Avocations: music, skiing, woodworking, Civil War history, travel. Home: 209 W Beechwold Blvd Columbus OH 43214-2012 Office: Ohio State U 4240 Campus Dr Lima OH 45804-3576

MEEKER, GUY BENTLEY, banker; b. Calcutta, India, Nov. 4, 1945; (parents Am. citizens); s. Lincoln Voght and Fortune Helen (Bentley) M.; m. Lavenia Yale Nelson, Apr. 27, 1967 (div. 1979); children: G. Bentley Jr., Melissa Anne ; m. Marcia Lee Zink, Nov. 4, 1984. BSBA, Georgetown U., 1967; MBA, George Washington U., 1970. Cons. OAS, Washington, 1971-73; v.p. The Deltec Banking Corp., Nassau, Bahamas & N.Y.C., 1973-78, Comml. Credit Internat. Banking Corp., Balt., 1978-82; sr. v.p., gen. mgr. Union Planters Internat. Bank, N.Y.C., 1982-84; exec. v.p., gen. mgr. Worthen Bank Internat., N.Y.C., 1984-86; exec. v.p. and chief exec. officer N.Am. Bank Cen. Asia, N.Y.C., 1984-95; supervisory dir. BCA Bank Europe N.V., Amsterdam, The Netherlands, 1993-95; pres. G.B. Meeker & Co., N.Y.C., 1996—. Author articles and monographs in field. Mem. BAnkers Assn. Fgn. Trade (internat. adv. coun. 1992-95, vice chmn. IAC 1994-95), Inst. Internat. Bankers (legis. and regulatory com. 1992-94, bd. trustees 1994-95), Asia Soc. (corp. coun. 1987-95), River Club, Coffe House Club, Dutch Treat Club, Doubles Club. Roman Catholic.

MEEKER, ROBERT ELDON, retired manufacturing company executive; b. Moline, Ill., Sept. 6, 1930; s. Paul Edwin and Esther (Carlson) M.; m. Dorothy Elaine Nelson, Dec. 23, 1951; children: Julie Lynn Meeker Gratton, Laurie Allison Meeker Gamel, Bradford Nelson. B.S. in Chemistry, Ill. Wesleyan U., 1952; Ph.D in Phys. Chemistry, Northwestern U., 1955. Chemist, supr. Shell Devel. Co., Emeryville, Calif., 1955-64; mgr.-dir. synthetic rubber tech. ctr. Shell Chem. Co., Torrance, Calif., 1964-66; mgr. new projects Shell Chem. Co., N.Y.C., 1966-69; dir. exploratory sci., exploration and prodn. rsch. ctr. Shell Devel. Co., Houston, 1969-71; gen. mgr., head new enterprises div. Royal Dutch-Shell Co., London, 1971-72; v.p. comml., gen. mgr. Billiton aluminum B.V. Billiton Internat. Metals subs. Shell Co., The Hague, The Netherlands, 1972-74; pres. Roxana Shale Oil Co. subs. Shell Co., Houston, 1974-76; v.p., gen. mgr. energy systems mgmt. div. TRW, Inc., Redondo Beach, Calif., 1976-80; v.p., gen. mgr. maj. programs TRW, Inc., 1980-86; pvt. practice cons., real estate developer Tucson, 1986-94. Patentee in field. Trustee Ill. Wesleyan U., Bloomington, 1982—; v.p., bd. dirs. Cobblestone Homeowners Assn., 1991-92, pres., bd. dirs., 1992-94, sec., security chmn., 1994—. Recipient Disting. Alumnus award Ill. Wesleyan U., 1981. Mem. Mercedes Benz Club Am. (pres. Chaparral sect. 1992-94). Republican. Lutheran. Avocations: photography; swimming; travel. Home and Office: 7240 N Star Fury Pl Tucson AZ 85718-1345

MEEKS, CAROL JEAN, educator; b. Columbus, Ohio, Mar. 9, 1946; d. Clarence Eugene and Clara Johanna (Schwartz) B.; m. Joseph Meeks, Aug. 17, 1968 (div. 1981); 1 child, Catherine Rachael. BS, Ohio State U., Mex., 1968; MS, Ohio State U., 1969, PhD, 1972. Rsch. asst., assoc. Ohio State U., Columbus, 1968-71; internship Columbus Area C. of C., Ohio, 1970; lectr. Ohio State U., Columbus, 1970, 72; asst. prof. U. Mass., Amherst, 1972-74; asst. prof. Cornell U., Ithaca, N.Y., 1974-78, assoc. prof., 1978-80; legis. fellow Senate Com. Banking, 1984; supr. economist, head housing section USDA, Washington, 1980-85; assoc. prof. housing and consumer econs. U. Ga., Athens, 1985-90, prof., 1990—, head housing and consumer econs., 1992—; rsch. fellow Nat. Inst. for Consumer Rsch., Oslo, Norway, 1982; cons. Yale U., 1976-77, HUD, Cambridge, Mass., 1978, MIT Ctr. for Real Estate Devel. Ford Found. Project on Housing Policy; del. N.E. Ctr. for Rural Devel. Housing Policy Conf. Reviewer Home Econ. Rsch. Jour., 1987—, ACCI conf., 1987—; contbr. articles to profl. mags. Mem. panel town of Amherst Landlord Tenant Bd.; bd. dirs. Am. Coun. Consumer Interests; mem. adv. coun. HUD Nat. Mfg. Housing, 1978-80, 91-93; chair Housing Mfg. Inst. Consensus Commn. on Fed. Standards. Recipient Young Profl. award Ohio State U., 1979; named one of Outstanding Young Women of Am., 1979; Columbus Womens Chpt. Nat. Assn. Real Estate Bds. scholar, Gen. Foods fellow, 1971-72, HEW grantee, 1978, travel grantee NSF bldg. rsch. bd., AID grantee, USDA Challenge grant, 1995—. Mem. Soc. Govt. Economists (bd. dirs. 1984-85, co-chmn. 1985), Am. Assn. Housing Educators (newsletter editor 1976-79, pres. 1983-84), Nat. Inst. Bldg. Sci. (bd. sec. 1984, 85, 89—, bd. dirs. 1981-83, 85, 87-93, features commn.), Am. Real Estate and Urban Econs. Assn., Internat. Assn. Housing Sci., Com. on Status of Women in Econs., Nat. Assn. Home Builders (Smart House contract 1989), Epsilon Sigma Phi, Omicron Nu, Kappa Omicron Nu (v.p. of programs 1995-96), others. Office: U Ga 215 Dawson Hall Athens GA 30602-3622

MEEKS, HERBERT LESSIG, III, pastor, former school system administrator; b. National City, Calif., May 12, 1946; s. Herbert Lessig Jr. and Hazel Evelyn (Howard) M.; m. Ardena Lorraine Bice, June 30, 1971; children: Herbert Lessig IV, Laura Dawn, Misty Danae. Grad. in Theology, Bapt. Bible Coll., 1972; BS in Interdisciplinary Studies, Liberty U., Lynchburg, Va., 1989; MS in Edn., Tenn. Temple U., 1989; MA in Religion, Liberty U., 1990. Tchr. Mt. Vernon Christian Sch., Stockbridge, Ga., 1975-82; prin. Mt. Zion Christian Acad., Jonesboro, Ga., 1982-90; elem. prin. Des Moines Christian Sch., 1990-93; prin. N.W. Acad., Houston, 1993-94; sr. pastor 1st Bapt. Ch. Genoa, Houston, 1994—. Instr. ARC, Atlanta; candidate Ga. Ho. of Reps., Atlanta, 1980; bd. dirs. Concerned Christian for Good Govt., Atlanta, 1980-82; notary pub., Clayton County, Ga., 1983-90. Served to sgt. USAF, 1966-69. Mem. Assn. Christian Schs. Internat. (conv. planning com. 1985-90, accreditation/cons. chmn., Behind the Scenes award 1986), Nat. Rifle Assn. (life), Am. Pistol and Rifle Assn. Republican. Avocations: flying, hunting, politics, econs. Home: 12102 Palmcroft St Houston TX 77034-3721 Office: 1st Bapt Ch Genoa 12717 Almeda Genoa Rd Houston TX 77034-4639

MEEKS, KENNETH, magazine editor; b. Louisville, Oct. 26, 1963; m. Feb. 6, 1996. Grad. high sch., Louisville, 1981. Asst. to feature editor Guideposts mag., N.Y.C., 1986-90; reporter, copy editor Amsterdam News, N.Y.C., 1991-94; mng. editor Black Elegance mag., N.Y.C., 1994—. Contbg. author: (anthology) Brotherman, 1995 (award 1995). Rastafarian. Office: Black Elegance 475 Park Ave S New York NY 10016

MEEKS, PATRICIA LOWE, secondary school educator; b. Enid, Okla., Oct. 21, 1928; d. Henry Preston and Veda Gay (Combs) Lowe; m. James Donald Meeks, Feb. 28, 1953 (div. Aug. 1975); children: Mary Gay, Ann Lowe, James Robert David. BA, Phillips U., 1951; MA in English, U. Colo., 1973. Cert. tchr., Colo., Okla. Tchr. English Garber (Okla.) High Sch., 1952-53; tchr. English and journalism Hillcrest High Sch., Dallas, 1955-57; teaching asst. U. Colo., Boulder, 1965-66; tchr. English Cherry Creek High Sch., Englewood, Colo., 1966-91; supr. grades K-12 reading and lang. arts Oklahoma City Pub. Schs., 1991—; cons. Coll. Bd. Rocky Mt. Region, Denver, 1973-91; advanced placement reader, table leader Coll. Bd. and Ednl. Testing Svc., Princeton, N.J., 1970-80, SAT reader, 1989-94, table leader, 1994—. Mem. alumni bd. Phillips U. Fulbright exch. tchr. U.S. Dept. Edn., 1980-81; grantee NEH, 1986, English-Speaking Union, 1987. Mem. ASCD, NEA, AAUW, Nat. Fulbright Assn., Okla. Coun. Tchrs. English, Nat. Coun. Tchrs. English, English-Speaking Union (v.p. Okla. City chpt.), Nature Conservancy, Audubon Soc. Republican. Episcopalian. Avocations: art history, bird watching, jazz, reading. Home: 5806 N Pennsylvania Ave Apt 104 Oklahoma City OK 73112-7381 Office: Oklahoma City Pub Schs 900 N Klein Ave Oklahoma City OK 73106-7036

MEEKS, WAYNE A., religious studies educator; b. Aliceville, Ala., Jan. 8, 1932; s. Benjamin L. and Winnie (Gavin) M.; m. Martha Evelina Fowler, June 10, 1954; children—Suzanne, Edith, Ellen. BS, U. Ala.-Tuscaloosa, 1953; BD, Austin Presbyn. Theol. Sem., 1956; MA, Yale U., 1964, PhD, 1965; Doctor Theologiae honoris causa, U. Uppsala, Sweden, 1990. Instr. religion Dartmouth Coll., Hanover, N.H., 1964-65; asst. prof. religious studies Ind. U., Bloomington, 1966-68, assoc. prof., 1968-69; assoc. prof. religious studies Yale U., New Haven, 1969-73, prof. religious studies, 1973-84, Woolsey prof. Bibl. studies, 1984—; dir. divsn. of Humanities, 1988-91. Author: Go From Your Father's House, 1964; The Prophet-King, 1967; First Urban Christians, 1983; Moral World of the First Christians, 1986, Origins of Christian Morality, 1993. Contbr. articles to profl. jours. Fulbright fellow, 1956-57; Kent fellow, 1962-64; NEH fellow, 1975-76; Guggenheim fellow, 1979-80. Fellow British Acad.; mem. Soc. Bibl. Lit. (pres. 1985), Am. Acad. Religion (bd. dirs. 1974-77), Studiorum Novi Testamenti Societas (editorial bd. 1979-82). Democrat. Presbyterian. Avocations: cabinet-making; hiking. Office: Yale U Dept Religious Studies PO Box 208287 Yale Station New Haven CT 06520-8287

MEELIA, RICHARD J., healthcare products executive. Pres. Kendall Co., Mansfield, Mass. Office: Kendall Company 15 Hampshire St Mansfield MA 02048-1139*

MEEM, JAMES LAWRENCE, JR., nuclear scientist; b. N.Y., Dec. 24, 1915; s. James Lawrence and Phyllis (Deaderick) M.; m. Buena Vista Speake, Sept. 5, 1940; children: James, John. B.S., Va. Mil. Inst., 1939; M.S., Ind. U., 1947, Ph.D., 1949. Aero. research sci. NACA, 1940-46; dir. bulk shielding reactor Oak Ridge Nat. Lab., 1950-53, in charge nuclear operation aircraft reactor expt., 1954-55; chief reactor sci. Alco Products, Inc., 1955-57; in charge startup and initial testing Army Package Power Reactor, 1957; prof. nuclear engring. U. Va., Charlottesville, 1957-81; dept. chmn., dir. reactor facility U. Va., 1957-77, prof. emeritus, 1981—; cons. U.S. Army Fgn. Sci. and Tech. Ctr., 1981-90; vis. cons. nuclear fuel cycle programs Sandia Labs., Albuquerque, 1977-78; vis. staff mem. Los Alamos Sci. Lab., 1967-68; mem. U.S.-Japan Seminar Optimization of Nuclear Engring. Edn., Tokai-mura, 1973. Author: Two Group Reactor Theory, 1964. Fellow Am. Nuclear Soc. (sec. reactor ops. div. 1966-68, vice chmn. 1968-70, chmn. 1970-71, Exceptional Service award 1980); mem. Am. Phys. Soc., Am. Soc. Engring. Edn., SAR. Home: University Village # 1201 2401 Old Ivy Rd Charlottesville VA 22903-4853

MEENAN, JAMES JOSEPH, communications executive; b. Mpls., Nov. 10, 1943; s. Leonard Louis and Mary (Brennan) M.; m. Clare Hunnewinkel, July 16, 1966; children: Daniel, Marcy, Mark. BSBA, St. Mary's Coll., 1965; M in Mgmt. Sci., Stevens Inst. Tech., 1978. Mgmt. trainee AT&T Teletype Corp., 1966, various positions, 1966-80; asst. contr. ops. Western Electric, 1980-82, corporate contr., 1982-84; v.p. fin. AT&T Network Sys., 1984-85; CFO AT&T Info. Sys., 1985-87; corporate v.p. AT&T Fin. Ops. and Sys., 1987-89; v.p., CFO AT&T Comm. Svcs. Group, Basking Ridge, N.J., 1989-95; pres., CEO AT&T Canada Inc., Toronto, 1995—; bd. dirs. Unitel Comm., Inc., Toronto. Past pres. Fathers and Friends Delbarton Sch., Morristown, N.J., 1986-89; bd. trustees Tri-County Scholarship Fund, Paterson, N.J., 1990—, Coll. of St. Elizabeth, Convent Station, N.J., 1990—. Mem. Fin. Execs. Inst. Office: AT&T Canada Inc, 320 Front Street West, Toronto, ON Canada M5V 3C4*

MEENAN, PATRICK HENRY, state legislator; b. Casper, Wyo., Sept. 24, 1927; s. Hugh Martin and Margaret (Kelly) M.; BS cum laude, U. Notre Dame, 1949; m. Shirley Louise Byron, Dec. 30, 1950; children: Maurya Ann, Kevin Patrick, Michael James, Patricia Kelly. CPA Raab, Roush & Gaymon, Casper, 1949-53, ptnr. 1960-68; asst. treas. Williston Oil & Gas Co., 1953-55; ptnr. Meenan & Higgins, Casper, 1955-60; pres. KATI-AM & FM, Casper, 1963-81, KAWY Stero Radio, 1967-81; ptnr. Meenan, Miracle & Sherrill, CPAs, 1975-76; sec. dir. Bank of Casper, 1980-87; pres. PM Enterprises, Inc., 1981—; Erin Corp. Councilman City of Casper, 1956-65, v.p., 1961, mayor, 1962, 65; mem. Wyo. Ho. of Reps., 1969-89, majority floor leader, 1983-85, Speaker Pro Tem, 1985-87, Speaker of the House, 1987-89, chmn. house-rules com., chmn. mgmt. council, 1987-89; mem. exec. com. Western Legis. Conf. Coun. of State Govts., 1983-89; chmn. Nat. Conf. State Legis. Energy and Environ. Com., 1985. Named Young Man of Year, Jr. C. of C., Casper, 1962; Boss of Year, 1965; Distinguished Pub. Servant award City of Casper. Mem. AICPA, Casper Country Club, Notre Dame Alumni (nat. dir. 1972-75), Wyo. So. CPAs, Nat., Wyo. assns. broadcasters. Elk, K.C. Republican. Roman Catholic. Home: 3070 E 4th St Casper WY 82609-2104 Office: PM Enterprises Inc 300 Country Club Rd Ste 211 Hilltop Nat Tower PO Box 9727 Casper WY 82609

MEENAN, ROBERT FRANCIS, academician, rheumatologist, researcher; b. Cambridge, Mass., Apr. 5, 1947; s. Paul Leo and Anna Bernadine (Curtin) M.; m. Lynda Jane Fortman, Apr. 29, 1972; children: Molly, Mark. BA, Harvard U., 1968; MD, Boston U., 1972; MPH, U. Calif., Berkeley, 1977; MBA, Boston U., 1989. Diplomate Am. Bd. Internal Medicine and Rheumatology. Asst. prof. Sch. of Medicine Boston U., 1977-82, assoc. prof. Sch. of Medicine, 1982-88, prof. Sch. of Medicine, 1988—, assoc. dir. Arthritis Ctr., 1977-88, chief arthritis sect. Sch. of Medicine, 1988-92, dir. Arthritis Ctr., 1988-92, dir. and prof. Sch. Pub. Health, 1992—; mem. nat. arthritis adv. bd. NIH, Washington, 1988-92; Svartz Meml. lectr. Swedish Med. Soc., 1989. Contbr. Jour. Arthritis Impact Measurement Scales, Jour. Social Security Disability, Jour. Dictionary of Rheumatic Disease, Outcome Assessmentation Clin. Moles; contbr. over 75 articles to profl. jours. Trustee Arthritis Found., 1989. Internat. League Against Rheumatism fellow, 1981; recipient Nat. Svc. award Arthritis Found., 1989. Fellow ACP, Am. Coll. Rheumatology (pres. 1990-91); mem. Am. Soc. for Clin. Investigation. Achievements include development of arthritis impact measurement scales. Office: Boston U Sch Pub Health 80 E Concord St Roxbury MA 02118-2307

MEENDSEN, FRED CHARLES, food company executive; b. Garden City, N.Y., Oct. 28, 1933; s. Frederick Herman and Charlotte Mabel (Reiss) M.; B.A., Colgate U., 1954; M.B.A., Harvard U., 1956; m. Nancy Lou Gross, Nov. 16, 1957; children: Fred Charles, Martha Anne. Mem. mktg. and sales mgmt. dept. Velsicol Chem. Corp., Chgo., 1957-63; with CPC Internat., Inc., Englewood Cliffs, N.J., 1963—, pres. subs. Peterson/Puritan, Inc., Danville, Ill., 1977-83, pres. subs. Can. Starch Co., 1983-84, v.p. parent co., 1983—, pres. N.Am. region Corn Wet Milling div., 1984-88, v.p. corp. affairs, 1988-93, v.p. govt. affairs, 1994—; dir. Can. Starch Co., 1983-88; chmn. Casco Co.; mem. U.S. C. of C. Can. Rels. Com., 1986—, Food and Agr. Com., 1988—; sec. Agr. Adv. Comm. on Trade, 1987-92; pres., Colgate U. Alumni Corp., 1991-93, bd. dirs. 1988—; trustee Colgate U., 1993—. Served to 1st lt. U.S. Army, 1956-59. Author: Atomic Energy and Business Strategy, 1956. Home: 24472 Trice Field Ct Saint Michaels MD 21663-2618 Office: CPC Internat Inc Internat Plz Englewood Cliffs NJ 07632

MEER, CARY JESSE, lawyer; b. N.Y.C., Mar. 8, 1957; d. George and Gladys (Dallal) Meer; m. Charles Phipps Thomas, Sept. 23, 1984; 1 child, Daniel Phipps Thomas. BS in Econs. summa cum laude, U. Pa., 1979; JD cum laude, Harvard U., 1982. Bar: N.Y. 1983, D.C. 1986. Assoc. Stroock & Stroock & Lavan, N.Y.C., 1982-86; assoc. Kirkpatrick & Lockhart, Washington, 1986-91, ptnr., 1992—; counselor Am. Woman's Econ. Devel. Corp., Washington, 1993—. Contbr. articles to profl. jours.; co-author chpt. in Money Manager's Compliance Guide, 1994. Democrat. Home: 5417 Nevada Ave NW Washington DC 20015 Office: Kirkpatrick & Lockhart 1800 M St NW Washington DC 20036

MEERS, HENRY W., investment banker; b. Joliet, Ill., July 12, 1908; s. Robert and Mary (Cullen) M.; m. Evelyn Huckins; children: Henry Weber, Albert Huckins, Robert. A.B., U. Ill., 1930. With Halsey, Stuart & Co., Chgo., 1930-35, Harriman, Ripley & Co., 1936-42; resident partner White, Weld & Co., 1946-72, vice chmn., 1972-78; mng. dir. Merrill Lynch & Co. Investment Banking Group, Chgo., 1978—; dir. Merrill Lynch Trust Co., Chgo., 1992—; dir. DuKane Corp., 1962—; chmn. bd. govs. Assn. Stock Exchange Firms, 1968-69; bd. govs. Midwest Stock Exchange, 1957-60, N.Y. Stock Exchange, 1970-71. Del. Nat. Rep. Conv., 1984, alt. del., 1988; bd. dirs. Nat. Recreation Park Assn. Found.; mem. Chgo. Crime Commn.; chmn. Modern Cts. Ill., 1970, Met. Cursade Mercy, 1967; life trustee U. Cgho., Ch. Internat. House; life trustee, chair Chgo. Ednl. TV Sta.-WTTW, PBS, 1978-89; life trustee Lake Forest Acad.; trustee Lake Forest Coll., 1968-76; bd. dirs. Children's Meml. Hosp., chmn., 1970-75; chair bd. trustees Latin Sch. Chgo., 195-658; bd. dirs. U. Ill. Found.; mem. citizens bd. Loyola U.; chmn. Chgo. coun. Boy Scouts Am., 1952-56; mem. Ill. Compensation Rev. Bd., 1985-96; chair Internat. House, U. Chgo. Commdr. USNR, 1942-46. Recipient Man of Yr. award NCCJ, 1969, Founders award, 1992. Mem. Investment Analysts Soc., Ducks Unltd. (nat. trustee 1980-90), Chgo. Club, Comml. Club Chgo., Links Club, Onwentsia Club, Old Elm Club, Seminole Golf Club, Shore Acres Club, Bohemian Club, The Island Club, Phi Beta Kappa. Home: 550 N Green Bay Rd Lake Forest IL 60045-2146 Office: Merrill Lynch 5500 Sears Towers Chicago IL 60606

MEEUSE, BASTIAAN JACOB DIRK, biologist, educator, researcher; b. Sukabumi, Indonesia, May 9, 1916; came to U.S., 1947; s. Adrianus Dirkszoon and Jannigje (Kruithof) M.; m. Johanne Roberta ten Have, Aug. 28, 1942; children: Karen Barbara, Peter Nicholas. BSc in Biology, U. Leiden, The Netherlands, 1936, M, 1939; D in Tech. Sci., U. Delft, The Netherlands, 1943. Tchr. Hort. Inst., Boskoop, The Netherlands, 1939-42; asst. lectr. U. Delft, 1942-46, chief asst. lectr., 1946-49, lectr., 1949-52; asst. prof. U. Wash., Seattle, 1952-55, assoc. prof., 1955-60, prof. botany, 1960-86, prof. emeritus, 1986—; corr. Royal Dutch Acad. Scis., Amsterdam, The Netherlands, 1965—; vis. prof. U. Nijmegen, The Netherlands, 1985; cons. Shell Devel. Co., Modesto, Calif., 1986-87. Author: The Story of Pollination, 1961, The Sex Life of Flowers, 1984, Old Wine in New Glasses, 1996;

contbr. articles to profl. jours. Fellow NSF, 1962-63, Rockefeller Found., 1947-49. Mem. Royal Dutch Bot. Soc., Am. Soc. Plant Physiologists, Am. Bot. Soc., Native Plant Soc., Sigma Xi. Club: Holland-America (Seattle). Avocations: photography, hiking, showing films, lecturing. Office: U Wash Botany Dept KB-15 Seattle WA 98195

MEEZAN, ELIAS, pharmacologist, educator; b. N.Y.C., Mar. 5, 1942; s. Maurice and Rachel (Epstein) M.; m. Elisabeth Gascard, May 14, 1967; children: David, Nathan, Joshua. BS in Chemistry, CCNY, 1962; PhD in Biochemistry, Duke U., 1966. Asst. prof. physiology and pharmacology Duke U., Durham, N.C., 1969-70; asst. prof. pharmacology U. Ariz., Tucson, 1970-75; assoc. prof. U. Ariz., 1975-79; prof., chmn. dept. pharmacology U. Ala., Birmingham, 1979-89, prof., dir. Metabolic Diseases Rsch. Lab., 1989-93, prof. dept. pharmacology, 1993—. Asso. editor: Life Sci, 1973-79. Helen Hay Whitney postdoctoral fellow, 1966-69; recipient NIH Research Career Devel. award, 1977-79. Mem. Am. Soc. Pharmacology and Exptl. Therapeutics, Am. Soc. Biol. Chemistry, AAUP, AAAS, N.Y. Acad. Sci., Assn. Med. Sch.Pharmacology. Democrat. Jewish. Isolated retinal microvasculature; developer method for isolating ultrastructurally and chemically intact basement membranes. Home: 1202 Cheval Ln Birmingham AL 35216-2037 Office: U Ala Dept Pharmacology Birmingham AL 35294

MEFFORD, NAOMI DOLBEARE, secondary education and elementary education educator; b. Pittsfield, Ill., Feb. 10, 1944; d. Donald Pryor and Ruth Allyne (Utter) Dolbeare; m. Clark L. Mefford, Feb. 8, 1964; children: Joseph Clark, Christopher Lee. BA, William Penn Coll., 1977; MA, N.E. Mo. State U., 1986, EdS, 1991. Cert. profl. tchr., adminstr., Iowa. Undergrad. instr. Buena Vista, Ottumwa, Iowa, 1984-87; grad. instr. So. Prairie AEA and Marycrest Coll., Ottumwa, 1988-92; tchr. Ottumwa Schs., 1985—; dir. summer sch. Ottumwa, 1991-93. Chmn. Hosp. Major Fund Raiser, Ottumwa, 1995. Mem. AAUW (pres. Iowa chpt. 1996—), Delta Kappa Gamma. Home: 8 Country Club Pl Ottumwa IA 52501-1417 Office: Horace Mann Sch 1523 N Court St Ottumwa IA 52501-1440

MEGAN, THOMAS IGNATIUS, retired judge; b. Chgo., Dec. 24, 1913; s. Charles P. and May M. (Magan) M.; m. Lucyanne Flaherty, Apr. 17, 1948; children: Anne, Thomas, Jane, Sarah, William, Molly. A.B., U. Ill., 1935; J.D., U. Chgo., 1938. Bar: Ill. 1939, N.Y. 1941. Mem. firm Pruitt & Grealis, Chgo., 1939-40, Pruitt, Hale & MacIntyre, N.Y.C., 1941; atty. U.S. Ordnance Dept., Chgo., 1941-42, Chgo., Rock Island and Pacific R.R. Co., Chgo., 1945-70; v.p., gen. counsel Chgo., Rock Island and Pacific R.R. Co., 1970-74, v.p. law, 1974-75; adminstrv. law judge ICC, Washington, 1975-81, HHS, Washington, 1981, FERC, Washington, 1981-96; ret., 1996. Served to maj. AUS, 1942-45. Mem. ABA, Soc. Trial Lawyers Chgo., Chgo. Law Club, Phi Kappa Tau, Phi Delta Phi. Club: Union League (Chgo.). Home: 11108 Waycroft Way Rockville MD 20852-3217

MEGARGEE, KATHLEEN ANNE, state public information officer; b. Somers Point, N.J., Oct. 12, 1954; d. Irwin Ferdinand and Althea Myrtle (Evans) M. BA in English, Montclair State Coll., 1976. News anchor, reporter Sta. WMID Radio, Atlantic City, 1977-78, Sta. WIIN Radio, Atlantic City, 1979-81, Sta. WHAG-TV, Hagerstown, Md., 1982-84, Sta. WHP-TV, Harrisburg, Pa., 1984-86; news writer The Sun newspaper, Atlantic City, 1978; news reporter, anchor Sta. WRBV-TV, Vineland, N.J., 1981; news anchor Sta. WCAU Radio, Phila., 1981-82; news anchor, reporter, prodr. Sta. WQED-TV, Pitts., 1986-89, Sta. WITF-TV, Harrisburg, 1989-91; anchor KYW News Radio, Phila., 1989; press sec. Pa. Dept. Aging, Harrisburg, 1991—. Vol., fund raiser Mothers Against Drunk Driving, 1985, Alzheimer's Assn., Harrisburg, 1994; vol., reader Harrisburg Area Radio Reading Svc. for the Blind, Harrisburg, 1991—. Recipient N.J. AP Broadcasters Assn. award, 1979, N.J. State Bar Assn. award, 1979, Golden Microphone award Atlantic City Press Club, 1980, Reporter/Prodr. award Chesapeake AP Broadcasters Assn., 1982, Nat. Mature Media Market award, 1993, 94, Corp. Pub. Broadcasting award, 1994. Roman Catholic. Avocations: canoeing, reading, hiking, cross country skiing. Home: 1405D Skyview Cir Harrisburg PA 17110 Office: Pa Dept Aging 400 Market St Harrisburg PA 17101

MEGAW, ROBERT NEILL ELLISON, English educator; b. Ottawa, Ont., Can., Oct. 7, 1920; came to U.S., 1925, naturalized, 1936; s. John Wesley and Eileen (Ellison) M.; m. Ann Barber, Dec. 20, 1947; children—Peter Kenneth McNeill, Margaret McNeill, Laura McNeill. Student, Duke U., 1937-40; M.A., U. Chgo., 1947, Ph.D., 1950. Mem. faculty Williams Colls., 1950-69, prof. English, 1965; Carnegie intern Harvard U., 1955-56; prof. English U. Tex., Austin, 1969-85; chmn. dept. U. Tex., 1969-72, prof. emeritus, 1985—; cons. acad. planning, 1962—; mem. nat. bd. cons. NEH, 1974—. Contbr. poetry to Hellas, Sequoia, Negative Capability, The Spectator, The Formalist, Nimrod, The Lyric, others. Served to 1st lt. USAAF, 1942-45. Nat. Humanities Faculty, 1969—. Mem. MLA, Am. Ednl. Theatre Assn., AAUP (chmn. com. coll. and univ. teaching research and publ. 1965-71, pres. Tex. conf. 1976-78, chmn. assembly state confs. 1979-81), Tex. Assn. Coll. Tchrs., Tex. Faculty Assn., Nat., Fed., State poetry socs., Poetry Soc. Am., Acad. Am. Poets, Common Cause, ACLU, NAACP, Phi Beta Kappa (speaker, panelist 1980—). Democrat. Home: 2805 Bowman Ave Austin TX 78703-1608 Office: U Tex Dept English Parlin Hall Austin TX 78712

MEGGERS, BETTY J(ANE), anthropologist; b. Washington, Dec. 5, 1921; d. William Frederick and Edith (Raddant) M.; m. Clifford Evans, Sept. 13, 1946. AB, U. Pa., 1943; MA, U. Mich., 1944; PhD, Columbia U., 1952; D (hon.), U. de Guayaquil, Ecuador, 1987, U. Fed. Rio de Janeiro, Brazil, 1994. Instr. anthropology Am. U., Washington, 1950-51; rsch. assoc. Smithsonian Instn., 1954—, expert, 1981—; founder, pres. Taraxacum Inc., 1977—; hon. prof. U. de Azuay, Ecuador, 1991. Author: Environmental Limitation on the Development of Culture, 1954, Ecuador, 1966, Amazonia, 1971, 2d edit., 1995, Prehistoric America, 1972, (with Clifford Evans) Archeological Investigations at the Mouth of the Amazon, 1957, Archeological Investigations in British Guiana, 1960, (with Clifford Evans and Emilio Estrada) Early Formative Period of Coastal Ecuador, 1965, (with Clifford Evans) Archeological Investigations on the Rio Napo, Eastern Ecuador, 1968; editor: Prehistoria Sudamericana, 1992. Recipient award for sci. achievement Washington Acad. Sci., 1956; gold medal 37th Internat. Congress of Americanists, 1966; Order Al Merito Govt. Ecuador, 1966; Order Bernardo O'Higgins Govt. Chile, 1985; Sec.'s Gold medal for exceptional service Smithsonian Instn., 1986; Order Andres Bello Govt. Venezuela, 1988; Order Al Mérito por Servicios Distinguidos Govt. Peru, 1989. Hon. fellow Assn. Tropical Biology (councilor 1976-78, pres.-elect 1982, pres. 1983); fellow AAAS; mem. Soc. Am. Archeology (exec. bd. 1962-64), Am. Anthrop. Assn. (exec. sec. 1959-61), Am. Ethnol. Soc., Anthrop. Soc. Wash. (treas. 1955-60, v.p. 1965-66, pres. 1966-68), Academia Nacional Historia, Ecuador (corr.), Phi Beta Kappa, Sigma Xi. Home: 1227 30th St NW Washington DC 20007-3410 Office: Smithsonian Instn Washington DC 20560

MEGGETT, LINDA LINETTE, reporter; b. Charleston, S.C.; d. James Lee and Arabell (Cohen) M. BA in Journalism, Marshall U., 1985. Reporter Herald Dispatch, Huntington, W.Va., 1985-88, Desert Sun, Palm Springs, Calif., 1988-90; reporter govt. Santa Barbara (Calif.) News-Press, 1990-92; reporter higher edn. Post and Courier, Charleston, S.C., 1992—. Author: Black Issues in Higher Education, 1994. Planning com. mem. YWCA, Charleston, 1994—. Mem. Nat. Assn. Black Journalists, S.C. Coastal Assn. Black Journalists (treas. 1993-95), Sigma Gamma Rho (rec. sec. Delta Iota Sigma chpt.). Methodist. Avocations: travel, reading, exercise. Home: 7121 Highway 162 Hollywood SC 29449-5603 Office: Post and Courier 134 Columbus St Charleston SC 29403

MEGHREBLIAN, ROBERT VARTAN, manufacturing executive, physicist; b. Cairo, Sept. 6, 1922; came to U.S., 1923, naturalized, 1946; s. Vahan V. and Mary (Kurkjian) M.; m. Margaret M. Gordon, 1987; children: David V., Susan L. B.Engring. (Gotshall-Powell scholar), Rensselaer Poly. Inst., 1943; M.S. (Guggenheim fellow), Calif. Inst. Tech., 1950, Ph.D. (Guggenheim fellow), 1953. Lectr. Oak Ridge Nat. Lab., 1952-55, asso. project mgr., 1955-58; chief sect. Physics Jet Propulsion Lab., Calif. Inst. Tech., 1958-60, mgr. space scis. div., 1960-68, dep. asst. lab dir., 1968-71, assoc. prof. applied mechanics, 1960-61; v.p. research and engring. Cabot Corp., Boston, 1971-79, v.p., 1971-87; pres. Distrigas Corp., 1979-85; gen. mgr. Cabot Crystals Bus. Unit, 1985-86, dir. corp. planning and devel., 1986-87. Author: Reactor Analysis, 1960. Served to lt. (j.g.) USN, 1941-46, PTO, ATO. Fellow AIAA (assoc.), Am. Nuclear Soc.; mem. Tennis Club Santa Barbara, Santa Barbara Club, Montecito Assn. (bd. dirs., v.p. 1994, pres. 1995, 96, chair archtl. rev. com. 1993-95), Sigma Xi. Home: 440 Woodley Rd Montecito CA 93108-2006

MEGILL, ALLAN D., historian, educator; b. Regina, Sask., Can., Apr. 20, 1947; came to U.S., 1980; s. Ralph Peter and Jean Tudhope (Dickson) M.; divorced; children: Jason Robert, Jessica Susan, Jonathan David. BA, U. Sask., 1969; MA, U. Toronto, 1970; PhD, Columbia U., 1975. From instr. to prof. history U. Iowa, Iowa City, 1974-90; prof. history U. Va., Charlottesville, 1990—; rsch. fellow in history of ideas Australian Nat. U., Canberra, ACT, 1977-79, temp. lectr. modern European studies, 1979. Author: Prophets of Extremity, 1985; editor: Rethinking Objectivity, 1994; co-editor: The Rhetoric of the Human Sciences, 1987; cons. editor Jour. of History of Ideas, 1986-89, mem. editl. bd., 1990—; mem. editl. bd. Social Epistemology, 1986—, U. Press of Va., 1991-94; contbr. articles to profl. jours. Chmn. Page-Barbour and Richard Lectures com. U. Va., 1994—. Mem. Am. Hist. Assn. Office: University of Virginia Corcoran Dept of History Randall Hall # 221 Charlottesville VA 22903-3284

MEGILL, ROBERT EDGAR, retired oil company executive, consultant; b. Lawrence, Kans., Nov. 26, 1923; s. David Lucian and Margaret (Caskey) M.; m. Margaret Ann Webb, Feb. 24, 1945; children: Gregory Alan, Jana Lynn Green. B.S. in Geol. Engring., U. Tulsa, 1948. Various positions Exxon Co., U.S.A., Houston, 1941-84, div. planning mgr., Houston and Corpus Christi, Tex., 1965-73, coordinator planning, Houston, 1973-76, coordinator econ. evaluation, 1976-84; cons., advisor to petroleum industry. Author: An Introduction to Exploration Economics, 3d edit., 1988; How to be a More Productive Employee, 2d edit., 1980; May I Touch Your Life (poems), 1979; An Introduction to Risk Analysis, 2d edit., 1984; Life in the Corporate Orbit, 1981; Long Range Exploration Planning, 1985: contbr. articles to profl. jours. Served with USN, 1942-45, PTO. Mem. Am. Assn. Petroleum Geologists (assoc. editor 1983-89, columnist Explorer Mag. 1984—). Republican. Methodist. Lodge: Masons. Avocations: golf; reading; writing. Home: 4314 Valley Branch Dr Humble TX 77339-1867

MEGIVERN, KATHLEEN, association director, lawyer; b. Apalachin, N.Y., Apr. 16, 1950; d. John David and Katherine Augusta (Gibbons) M.; m. James Albert Mecklenburger, Jan. 5, 1986. BA, SUNY, Oneonta, 1972; JD, Cath. U., 1979. Bar: D.C. 1979. Adminstrv. asst. Am. Coun. of the Blind, Washington, 1973-79, staff lawyer, 1979-81; exec. dir. Assn. for Edn. and Rehab. of the Blind, Alexandria, Va., 1981—. Contbg. editor Braille Forum, 1987-90. Bd. dirs. Nat. Accreditation Coun., N.Y.C., 1982-86; treas. Affiliated Leadership League of and for the Blind, L.A., 1986—; mem. Human Rights Commn., Alexandria, 1990-93; vice chair Commn. on Disabled, Alexandria, 1989—. Recipient Outstanding Article of Yr. award Am. Coun. Blind, 1979, spl. award Task Force on Rights and Empowerment Ams. with Disabilities, 1991. Mem. Am. Blind Lawyers Assn. (hon.), D.C. Bar Assn., Womens Bar Assn. Avocations: movies, folk music, good books. Office: Assn for Edn & Rehab of the Blind 206 N Washington St Alexandria VA 22314-2528

MEGNA, JEROME FRANCIS, university dean; b. Bklyn., Mar. 11, 1939; s. James G. and Irene (Bodkin) M.; m. Doreen Ann Filippi, Dec. 23, 1973; 1 child, Donna Marie. BA, St. Francis Coll., 1966; MA, NYU, 1968; PhD, Ball State U., 1972. Tchr. English Franciscan Bros., Bklyn., 1959-69; instr. English Ball State U., Muncie, Ind., 1969-71; prof. edn. CUNY, Bklyn., 1971-88; dean edn. Rider U., Lawrenceville, N.J., 1988—. Author: Study Guide on Italian Americans, 1978; contbr. articles to profl. jours. Democrat. Roman Catholic. Avocations: reading, music, swimming. Office: Rider U 2083 Lawrenceville Rd Lawrenceville NJ 08648-3099

MEHAFFY, THOMAS N., retired tire company executive; b. Rushden, Northamptonshire, Eng., Sept. 23, 1932; came to U.S., 1977; s. James Edward and Sarah (Moloney) M.; m. Catherine Mary Ryle, Mar. 23, 1963; children: Catherine A., Siobhan M., Deirdre E., Brendan R. BSc in Econs., London Sch. Econs., U. London, 1956. Mgr. econ. studies Dunlop Rubber Co., London, 1959-66; mgr. econs. Ford of Britain, Warley, Essex, Eng., 1966-67; mgr. bus. studies Ford of Europe, Warley, 1967-73; dir. profit analysis Brit. Steel Corp., London, 1973-77; dir. corp. planning and market research Dunlop Tire Corp., Buffalo, 1977-91; bus. advisor Dunlop Tire Corp., 1991-93, Trico Products Corp., Buffalo, N.Y., 1993-94. Served with Brit. Arty., 1951-53. Home and Office: 5129 Willowbrook Dr Clarence NY 14031-1476

MEHLE, ROGER W., federal agency administrator; b. Long Beach, Calif., Dec. 28, 1941. BS, U.S. Naval Acad., 1963; MBA, NYU, 1972; JD, Fordham U., 1976. Mng. dir. The First Boston Corp., N.Y.c., 1969-79; sr. v.p., dir. Dean Witter Reynolds, Inc., N.Y.c., 1979-81; asst. sec. for domestic fin. Dept. Treasury, Washignton, 1981-83; exec. v.p., mng. dir. PaineWebber, Inc., N.Y.C., 1983-84; banking and securities atty. Washington, 1985-86; chmn. dir. Fed. Retirement Thrift Investment Bd., Washington, 1986-94, exec. dir., 1994—. Office: Fed Retirement Thrift Investment Office of the Exec Dir 1250 H St NW Washington DC 20005*

MEHLENBACHER, DOHN HARLOW, engineering executive; b. Huntington Park, Calif., Nov. 18, 1931; s. Virgil Claude and Helga (Sigfridson) M.; m. Nancy Mehlenbacher; children: Dohn Scott, Kimberly Ruth, Mark James, Matthew Lincoln. BS in Civil Engring., U. Ill., 1953; MS in City and Regional Planning, Ill. Inst. Tech., 1961; MBA, U. Chgo., 1972. Structural engr., draftsman Swift & Co., Chgo., 1953-54, 56-57, DeLeuw-Cather Co., Chgo., 1957-59; project engr. Quaker Oats Co., Chgo., 1959-61, mgr. constrn., 1964-70, mgr. real property, 1970-71, mgr. engring. and maintenance, Los Angeles, 1961-64; chief facilities engr. Bell & Howell Co., Chgo., 1972-73; v.p. design Globe Engring. Co., Chgo., 1973-76; project mgr. I.C. Harbour Constrn. Co., Oak Brook, Ill., 1976-78; dir. estimating George A. Fuller Co., Chgo., 1978; pres. Food-Tech Co., Willowbrook, Ill., 1979-80; dir. phys. resources, adj. prof. dept. civil engring. Ill. Inst. Tech., Chgo., 1980-92; pvt. practice facility cons., Chgo., 1993—. Served with USAF, 1954-56. Registered profl. engr. and structural engr., Ill. Fellow ASCE; mem. Am. Arbitrators Assn., Exec. Svc. Corps of Chgo. Office: 436 S Leitch La Grange IL 60525-6126

MEHLINGER, HOWARD DEAN, education educator; b. Hillsboro, Kans., Aug. 22, 1931; s. Alex and Alice Hilda (Skibbee) M.; m. Carolee Ann Case, Dec. 28, 1952; children: Bradley Case, Barbara Ann, Susan Kay. BA, McPherson (Kans.) Coll., 1953; MS in Edn, U. Kans., 1959, PhD, 1964. Co-dir. social studies project Pitts. pub. schs., 1963-64; asst. dir. fgn. relations project North Central Assn. Schs. and Colls., Chgo., 1964-65; mem. faculty Ind. U., Bloomington, 1965—, prof. history and edn., 1974—, dean Sch. Edn., 1981-90, dir. Ctr. for Excellence in Edn., 1990—; social studies adviser Houghton Mifflin Pub. Co.; cons. U.S. Office Edn. Co-author: American Political Behavior, 2d edit., 1977, Count Witte and the Tsarist Government in the 1905 Revolution, 1972, Toward Effective Instruction in the Social Studies, 1974, School Reform in the Information Age, 1995; editl. bd. Education and Society, history tchr.; editor: UNESCO Handbook on the Teaching of Social Studies, 1981; co-editor: Yearbook on the Social Studies, 1981. STAG grantee Dept. State, 1975. Mem. NEA, Nat. Council Social Studies, Am. Edn. Research Assn., Am. Hist. Assn., Am. Assn. for Advancement Slavic Studies, Phi Beta Kappa, Phi Alpha Theta, Pi Sigma Alpha, Phi Delta Kappa. Home: 3271 Ramble Rd E Bloomington IN 47408-1094 Office: Ind Univ Ctr Excellence Edn 230 N Rose St Bloomington IN 47405-1004

MEHLMAN, EDWIN STEPHEN, endodontist; b. Hartford, Conn., Nov. 30, 1935; s. Sol Abraham and Rose (Slitt) M.; m. Lesley Judith Lunin, June 13, 1959; children: Jeffrey Cole, Brian Scott, Erik Van. BA, Wesleyan U., 1957; DDS, U. Pa., 1961; cert. endodontics, Boston U., 1965. Diplomate Am. Bd. Endodontists. Instr. oral medicine Sch. Dental Medicine Harvard U., Boston, 1965-67; clin. instr. endodontics Sch. Dental Medicine Tufts U., Boston, 1968-70; lectr. endodontics Sch. Dental Medicine, Harvard U., Boston, 1970-72, asst. clin. prof. endodontics, 1972—; staff assoc. Forsyth Dental Ctr., Boston, 1965—; asst. prof. endodontics Boston U. Sch. Dental Medicine, 1995—; pvt. practice Providence, 1965—; vis. lectr. dental hygiene U. R.I., Kingston, 1965-71, Community Coll. R.I., Lincoln, 1990—; cons. com. on accreditation of Dentists and Dental Aux. Edn. Programs, 1974-78. Contbr. articles to profl. jours. Pres. Temple Habonim, Barrington, R.I., 1968-70, Bur. Jewish Edn. of R.I., 1980-84; area v.p. Jewish Fedn. R.I., 1975-78; mem. R.I. Legis. Commn. to Study Malpractice Crisis, 1985-86; chmn. R.I. Dental Polit. Action Com., 1987-90. Capt. USAF, 1961-63. Recipient Etherington award Six N.E. Dental Assns. for Outstanding Contbns. to Dentistry. Fellow Am. Coll. Dentists, Internat. Coll. Dentists, Pierre Fauchard Acad. (Award of Merit); mem. ADA (coun. on govt. affairs and fed. dental svcs. 1988-92, vice chmn. 1991-92, 1st v.p. 1994-95), Am. Assn. Endodontists (dir. 1988-91), R.I. Dental Assn. (pres. 1986-87), N.E. Dental Assns. (Outstanding N.E. Dentist 1995). Jewish. Avocations: tennis, reading, civic activities. Home: 6 Ridgeland Rd Barrington RI 02806-4028 Office: 130 Waterman St Providence RI 02906-2010 also: 1090 New London Ave Cranston RI 02920-3016

MEHLMAN, LON DOUGLAS, information systems specialist; b. Los Angeles, Apr. 29, 1959; s. Anton and Diane Mehlman. BA, UCLA, 1981; MBA, Pepperdine U., 1983. Systems programmer Ticom Systems Inc., Century City, Calif., 1978-81; systems analyst NCR Corp., Century City, 1981-83; sr. systems analyst Tandem Computers Inc., L.A., 1983-91; sr. computer scientist Computer Scis. Corp., El Segundo, Calif., 1991—. Author: Establishing an Enterprise Information Systems Infrastructure, 1995, Implimenting TQM, 1995. Mem. Am. Mgmt. Assn., Assn. for Info. and Image Mgmt., Armed Forces Communications and Electronics Assn., Sierra Club, Phi Delta Theta. Avocations: sailing, skiing, world travel. Office: Computer Scis Corp 2100 E Grand Ave El Segundo CA 90245-5024

MEHLMAN, MAXWELL JONATHAN, law educator; b. Washington, Nov. 4, 1948; s. Jacob and Betty (Hoffman) M.; m. Cheryl A. Stone, Sept. 15, 1979; children: Aurora, Gabriel. BA, Reed Coll., 1970, Oxford U., England, 1972; JD, Yale U., 1975. Bar: D.C. 1976, Ohio 1988. Assoc. Arnold & Porter, Washington, 1975-84; asst. prof. Case Western Res. U., Cleve., 1984-87, assoc. prof., 1987-90, prof. law, 1990-96, Arthur E. Petersilge prof., 1996—; spl. counsel N.Y. State Bar, N.Y.C., 1988-94, Nat. Kidney Found., 1991; cons. Am. Assn. Ret. Persons, Washington, 1992. Editor: High Tech Home Care, 1991; contbr. articles to profl. jours. Active steering com. AIDS Commn. Greater Cleve., 1986-90. Rhodes scholar, 1970; Rsch. grantee NIH, 1992-94. Mem. Am. Assn. Law Schs. (chmn. sect. on law, medicine and health care 1990), Phi Beta Kappa. Avocations: skiing, choral music. Office: Case Western Reserve U Sch Law-Law Medicine Ctr Gund Hall 11075 E Blvd Cleveland OH 44106

MEHLMAN, MYRON A., environmental and occupational medicine educator, environmental toxicologist; b. Poland, Dec. 21, 1934; m. Sept. 4, 1960; children: Mara Appel, Hope, Alison, Constance Lloyd. BS, CCNY, 1957; PhD, MIT, 1964. Prof. biochemistry Rutgers U., Newark, 1965-69; prof. biochemistry Coll. of Medicine U. Nebr., Omaha, 1967-71; chief biochem. toxicology FDA, Washington, 1972-73; spl. asst. toxicology dept. HEW, Washington, 1973-75; interagy. liaison officer NIH, Bethesda, Md., 1975-77; dir. toxicology Mobil Oil, Princeton, N.J., 1977-89; prof. U. Medicine and Dentistry of N.J., Piscataway, 1990—. Editor Jour. Environ. Pathology & Toxicology, 1977-81, Jour. Toxicology and Indsl. Health, 1975-78, Jour. Clean Tech. and Environ. Sci., 1989—; contbr. over 100 articles to profl. jours.; edited over 60 books. 1st lt. U.S. Army, 1958-60. Fellow Acad. Toxol. Soc., Am. Coll. Toxicology, Collequim Ramazzinic (bd. dirs.). Achievements include research in toxicology, environmental health, and nutritional and biomedical science. Home: 7 Bouvant Dr Princeton NJ 08540-1208 Office: U Medicine and Dentistry NJ 675 Hoes Ln Piscataway NJ 08854-5635

MEHRA, JAGDISH, physicist; b. Meerut, India, Apr. 8, 1937; came to U.S., 1957; s. Bhagwan Das and Shanti Devi (Kakkar) M.; m. Marlis Helene Lehn, Apr. 27, 1959; 1 child Anil. MS, UCLA, 1960; PhD, U. Neuchatel, 1963. Sr. lectr. U. Neuchatel (Switzerland), 1963-64; asst. prof. physics Purdue U., Hammond, Ind., 1964-65; assoc. prof. U. Mass., North Dartmouth, 1965-67; program dir. Sci. Rsch. Assocs. (IBM), Chgo., 1967-69; spl. rsch. assoc. U. Tex., Austin, Tex., 1969-73; inst. prof. Solvay Inst., Brussels, 1973-88; Sir Julian Huxley prof. UNESCO, Paris, 1989-93; disting. prof. physics The Citadel, Charleston, S.C., 1993-96; prof. sci. and humanities U. Houston, 1996—; mem. edit. bd. Founds. of Physics, Denver, 1988—. Author: The Quantum Principle, 1974, Einstein, Hilbert and Theory of Gravitation, 1974, The Solvay Conferences on Physics, 1975, The Historical Development of Quantum Theory, 1982, 87, The Beat of a Different Drum: The Life and Science of Richard Feynman, 1994; editor: The Physicist's Conception of Nature, 1973. Rsch. grantee Krupp Found., 1978-80, J.D. and C.T. MacArthur Found., 1982-85, Minna-James-Heineman Found., 1985-87; recipient Humboldt prize, 1976. Mem. Am. Phys. Soc., Swiss Phys. Soc., History Sci. Soc., Sherlock Holmes Soc. London. Home: 7830 Candle Ln Houston TX 77071-2114

MEHRA, RAJNISH, finance educator; b. New Delhi, Jan. 15, 1950; came to U.S., 1972; s. Mohan Dev and Raj-Mohini (Vadera) M.; m. Neeru Narula, Jan. 4, 1977; 1 child, Chaitanya. BS in Math. honors, St. Stephen's Coll., U. Delhi, 1966-67; BTech in Elec. Engring., Indian Inst. Tech., Kanpur, 1972; MS in Computer Sci., Rice U., 1974; MS in Indsl. Adminstrn., Carnegie-Mellon U., 1975, PhD, 1978. Instr. adminstrn. and mgmt. sci. Carnegie-Mellon U., Pitts., 1974-76; asst. prof. Queens U., Kingston, Ont., Can., 1976-77; asst. prof., then assoc. prof. fin. Columbia U. Grad. Sch. Bus., 1977-85; assoc. prof., then prof. fin. U. Calif., Santa Barbara, 1985—, dir. Masters of Bus. Econs. program, 1992—; dir. joint econ.-engring. program, 1994—; vis. asst. prof. UCLA, 1980; vis. prof. fin. U. Lausanne, Switzerland, 1981, U. Chgo. Sch. Bus., 1995, Sloan Sch. Mgmt. MIT, 1987-89; vis. scholar U. Chgo., 1979, Norwegian Sch. Econs. and Bus. Adminstrn., 1982, Stockholm Sch. Econs., 1988, Wharton Sch. U. Pa., 1980; vis. assoc. Oxford U., 1986; cons. Internat. Monetary Fund, 1989—. Assoc. editor Jour. Econ. Dynamics and Control; contbr. Growth Theory, Vol. 10, Internat. Library of Critical Writings in Economics, 1991, Encyclopedia of Business Cycles, Panics and Depressions, 1995; contbr. articles to profl. jours.; referee maj. jours. in field. William Larimer Mellon fellow, 1974-76; NSF grantee, 1980—. Mem. IEEE (sr.), Am. Econ. Assn., Am. Fin. Assn., Econometric Soc., Tau Beta Pi. Home: 938 W Campus Ln Santa Barbara CA 93117-9999 Office: U Calif Dept Bus Econ Santa Barbara CA 93106

MEHRA, RAMAN KUMAR, data processing executive, automation and control engineering researcher; b. Lahore, Punjab, India, Feb. 10, 1943; came to U.S., 1964; s. Madan Mohan and Vidya Vati (Khanna) M.; m. Anjoo Talwar; children: Archana, Mandira, Kunal. BEE, Punjab Engring. Coll., 1964; MS in Engring., Harvard U., 1965, PhD, 1968. Assoc. prof. Harvard U., Cambridge, Mass., 1972-76; pres., chief exec. officer Sci. Systems, Co., Inc., Woburn, Mass., 1976—. Author: System Identification, 1976; also tech. papers on model algorithmic control (Best Paper award Internat. Fedn. Automatic Control, 1983). Recipient Eckman award Am. Automatic Control Coun., St. Louis, 1971. Fellow IEEE. Avocations: hiking, skiing, tennis. Home: 5 Angier Rd Lexington MA 02173-1608 Office: Sci Systems Co Inc 500 W Cummings Park Woburn MA 01801-6503

MEHRABIAN, ROBERT, academic administrator; b. Tehran, Iran. Former prof. MIT, U. Ill., Urbana; dean Coll. of Engring. U. Calif., Santa Barbara, until 1990; past dir. Ctr. Materials Sci. Nat. Bur. of Standards; pres. Carnegie-Mellon U., Pitts., 1990—. Office: Carnegie-Mellon U Office of the Pres 5000 Forbes Ave Pittsburgh PA 15213-3816

MEHRING, CLINTON WARREN, engineering executive; b. New Haven, Ind., Feb. 14, 1924; s. Fred Emmett and Florence Edith (Hutson) M.; m. Carol Jane Adams, Mar. 9, 1946; children—James Warren, Charles David, John Steven (dec.), Martha Jane. B.S., Case Inst. Tech., 1950; M.S., U. Colo., 1956. Registered profl. engr., Wyo., Colo., Nev. Design engr. U. S. Bur Reclamation, Denver, 1950-56; design engr. Tipton & Kalmbach, Denver, 1956-58; asst. resident engr. Tipton & Kalmbach, Quito, Equador, 1959-61; asst. chief design engr. Tipton & Kalmbach, Lahore, Pakistan, 1962-65; v.p. Tipton & Kalmbach, Denver, 1966-73, exec. v.p., 1973-79, pres., 1979—, also bd. dirs. Served with AUS, 1943-45. Recipient Theta Tau award as outstanding grad. Case Inst. Tech., 1950. Fellow ASCE (life); mem. Am. Cons. Engrs. Coun., U.S. Com. on Large Dams, Am. Concrete

Inst., U.S. Com. Irrigation and Drainage (life), Sigma Xi, Tau Beta Pi, Theta Tau, Sigma Chi, Blue Key. Methodist. Club: Denver Athletic. Home: 1821 Mt Zion Dr Golden CO 80401-1733 Office: 1331 17th St Denver CO 80202-1566

MEHRINGER, CHARLES MARK, medical educator; b. Dickinson, N.D., Nov. 21, 1945; m. Ruth Mehringer; 1 child, Sydney.; BS in Biology, Lamar U., 1966; MD, U. Tex., 1970. Diplomate Am. Bd. Radiology, Am. Bd. Neuroradiology. Intern UCLA Hosp., 1970-71; resident iin diagnostic radiology Harbor-UCLA Med. Ctr., Torrance, Calif., 1971-74, fellow in neuroradiology, 1976-77; asst. prof. dept. radiology UCLA Sch. Medicine, 1977-80, dir. spl. procedures, 1980-94, assoc. prof. dept. radiology, 1986—; vice-chmn. dept. radiological scis. UCLA Sch. Medicine, Torrance, 1992—, acting chmn. dept. radiology, 1992—, chief diagnostic radiology, 1983-92; chief radiological svcs., cons. U.S. Air Force for Japan and Korea, 1974-76; cons. U. Calif./Irvine (Calif.) Med. Ctr., 1988—, St. Marys Med. Ctr., Long Beach, Calif., 1986—, Long Beach VA Hosp., 1979—, L.A. County Dept. Chief Med. Examiner-Coroner, 1977—; bd. dirs. Rsch. and Ednl. Inst.; presenter in field. Co-author: (with others) Neurological Surgery of the Ear and Skull Base, 1982, Vascular Surgery, 1984, 2d edit., 1994, Youman's Neurological Surgery, 1990, Common Problems in Infertility and Impotence, 1990, Intraluminal Imaging of Vascular and Tubular Organs: Diagnostic and Therapeutic Applications, 1993, Neuroradiology, A Study Guide, 1995; contbr. articles to profl. jours. Bd. dirs., exec. com. Med. Found. Harbor-UCLA Med. Ctr., 1992—. Recipient numerous grants for rsch., 1977—. Mem. Am. Coll. Radiology, Am. Soc. Neuroradiology (sr. mem.), Western Neuroradiologic Soc., So. Calif. Interventional Radiology Soc. (bd. dirs.), L.A. Radiologic Soc., L.A. County Med. Assn. Home: 834 Rome Dr Los Angeles CA 90065 Office: UCLA Med Ctr Box 27 1000 W Carson St Torrance CA 90509

MEHTA, A. SONNY, publishing company executive; b. India, 1943. Student, Cambridge U. Worked in paperback publishing U.K.; formerly with Pan and Picador pubs., U.K.; pub., pres. Alfred A. Knopf div. of Random House, N.Y.C., 1987—, now pres., editor-in-chief; pres. Knopf Pub. Group, N.Y.C. Office: Alfred A Knopf Inc 201 E 50th St New York NY 10022-7703

MEHTA, EILEEN ROSE, lawyer; b. Colver, Pa., Apr. 1, 1953; d. Richard Glenn and Helen (Wahna) Ball; m. Abdul Rashid Mehta, Aug. 31, 1973. Student, Miami U., 1971-73; BA with distinction, Fla. Internat. U., 1974; JD cum laude, U. Miami, 1977. Bar: Fla. 1977, U.S. Dist. Ct. (so. dist.) Fla. 1977, U.S. Ct. Appeals (11th cir.) 1981. Law clk. to presiding judge U.S. Dist. Ct. (so. dist.) Fla., Miami, 1977-79; asst. atty. County of Dade, Miami, 1979-89; shareholder Fine Jacobson Schwartz Nash Block & England, Miami, Fla., 1989-94; partner Eckert Seamans Cherin & Mellott, Miami, 1994; lectr. in field; v.p., bd. dirs. Mehtatron Enterprises, Inc., Miami, Shalimar Homes Inc., Anderson, S.C. Miami U. scholar, 1971-73. Mem. ABA, Fla. Bar Assn. Office: Eckert Seamans Cherin & Mellott Ste 1850 701 Bricknell Ave Miami FL 33131

MEHTA, NARINDER KUMAR, marketing executive; b. Lahore, Punjab, India, Feb. 18, 1938; came to U.S., 1959; s. Puran Chand and Raj Rani Mehta; m. Narayanaswamy Sampath; children: Kiren, Ravi. B of Commerce, U. Delhi, India, 1958; MA, U. Minn., 1961. Program dir. All India Mgmt. Assn., New Delhi, India, 1963-67; with Am. Express Co., Chgo., 1968-82; nat. sales dir. Am. Express Co., N.Y.C., 1975-80, v.p. sales, 1980-82; sr. v.p. Shearson Lehman/Am. Express, Boston, 1982-85, Capital Credit Corp., Fairfield, N.J., 1985—; sr. v.p. Temporary Investment Funds, 1982-85, Trust for Short Term Fed. Securities, 1982-85, Mcpl. Fund for Calif. Investors, 1983-85; conducted seminars for profl. assns., colls. and univs. Contbr. articles to profl. jours. Nat. v.p. Muscular Dystrophy Assn., N.Y.C., 1984-86; student body pres. U. Delhi, India, 1958-59. Recipient 1st prize inter-coll. debate, 1958. Mem. Am. Mgmt. Assn., Tau Kappa Epsilon. Avocations: running, swimming, traveling, reading. Office: Capital Credit Corp 492 Route 46 Fairfield NJ 07004-1906

MEHTA, SHAILESH J., banker; b. Bombay, Maharashtra, India, Apr. 22, 1949; came to U.S., 1971; s. Jayantilal B. and Manjula J. Mehta; m. Kalpa S. Doshi, Dec. 19, 1973; children: Sameet, Sheetal. B.S. in Mech. Engring., Indian Inst. Tech., 1971; M.S. in Ops. Research, Case Western Res. U., 1973, Ph.D. in Ops. Research and Computer Sci., 1975. Sr. ops. analyst Cleve. Trust Co., 1973-75, ops. officer, 1975-76, asst. v.p. card ops., 1976-77, v.p. corp. ops. adminstrn., 1979, v.p. advanced systems planning, 1977-78, v.p. info. systems, 1979-82; exec. v.p. banking services AmeriTrust, Cleve., 1974-86; exec. v.p., COO First Deposit Corp., San Francisco, 1986-88, pres., CEO, 1988—; chmn. bd. First Deposit Nat. Bank, Tilton, N.H., 1986—; pres., chief exec. officer, chmn. bd. First Deposit Savs. Bank, Redding, Calif., 1986-90; CEO, chmn. bd. First Deposit Nat. Credit Card Bank, Concord, N.H., 1990—; pres., dir. A.T. Venture Capital Group, Cleve., 1982-86. Mem. community adv. coun. U. Calif., Berkeley, 1991—. Mem. Am. Bankers Assn. (telecommunications group 1984—), Ohio Venture Assn., Calif. Commn. for Econ. Devel's. Adv. Coun. on Asia. Office: First Deposit Corp 88 Kearny St San Francisco CA 94108-5530*

MEHTA, VED (PARKASH), writer, literature and history educator; b. Lahore, Punjab, India, Mar. 21, 1934; came to U.S., 1949; s. Amolak Ram and Shanti Devi (Mehra) M.; m. Linn Fenimore Cooper Cary, Dec. 17, 1983; children: Alexandra Sage, Natasha Cary. BA, Pomona Coll., 1956, DLitt (hon.), 1972; BA, Oxford U., Eng., 1959; MA, Harvard U., 1961, Oxford U., Eng., 1962; DLitt (hon.), Bard Coll., 1982, Williams Coll., 1986, Bowdoin Coll., 1995; DUniv. (hon.), Stirling U., Scotland, 1988. Staff writer New Yorker mag., 1961-94; Rosenkranz chair in writing Yale U., New Haven, 1990-93, fellow, 1988—, residential fellow Berkeley Coll., 1990-93, lectr. in English, 1991-93, lectr. in History, 1990-93; Randolph Vis. Disting. prof. English and history Vassar Coll., N.Y., 1994—; Arnold Bernhard prof. English and History Williams Coll., Mass., 1994-96; vis. fellow lit. Balliol Coll., Oxford U., 1988-89; vis. scholar Case Western Res. U., 1974; vis. prof. lit. Bard Coll., 1985, 86; Noble Found. vis. prof. art and cultural history Sarah Lawrence Coll., 1988; vis. prof. English NYU, 1989-90. Author: Face to Face, 1957 (Secondary Edn. Ann. Book award 1958), Walking the Indian Streets, 1960, rev. edit., 1971, Fly and Fly-Bottle, 1963, 2d edit., 1983, The New Theologian, 1966, Delinquent Chacha, 1967, Portrait of India, 1970, 2d edit., 1993, John is Easy to Please, 1971, Mahatma Gandhi and His Apostles, 1977, 2d edit., 1993, The New India, 1978, The Photographs of Chachaji, 1980, A Family Affair: India Under Three Prime Ministers, 1982, Three Stories of the Raj, 1986, Rajiv Gandhi and Rama's Kingdom, 1995; (autobiography) Continents of Exile: Daddyji, 1972, Mamaji, 1978, Vedi, 1982, The Ledge Between the Streams, 1984, Sound-Shadows of the New World, 1986, The Stolen Light, 1989, Up at Oxford, 1993, also articles; writer, narrator TV film Chachji, My Poor Relation, 1978 (DuPont Columbia award); mem. usage panel Am. Heritage Dictionary, 1982. Recipient award Assn. Indians in Am., 1978, Signet medal, 1983, Disting. Svc. award Asian/Pacific ALA, 1986, Liberty medal Mayor of N.Y.C., 1986, Centenary Barrows award Pomona Coll., 1987, Lion medal N.Y. Pub. Libr., 1990, Asian-Am. Heritage Month award N.Y. State, 1991; Hazen fellow, 1956-59, Harvard Prize fellow, 1959-60, Residential fellow Eliot House, 1959-61, Guggenheim fellow, 1971-72, 77-78, MacArthur Prize fellow, 1982-87, N.Y. Inst. for Humanities fellow, 1988-92; Ford Found. grantee, 1971-76, grantee Pub. Policy, 1979-82. Mem. Coun. on Fgn. Rels., Century Assn. (trustee 1972-75). Avocations: Indian and Western music, cycling. Home: 139 E 79th St New York NY 10021-0324

MEHTA, ZARIN, music festival administrator; b. Bombay, India, Oct. 28, 1938; came to Can., 1962, naturalized, 1969; s. Mehli and Tehmina Mehta; m. Carmen Lasky, July 1, 1966; children—Rohanna, Rustom. Chartered acct., London, 1957. Acct. Frederic B. Smart & Co., London, 1957-62, Coopers & Lybrand, Montreal, Que., Can., 1962-81; mng. dir. Orchestre Symphonique de Montreal, 1981-90, dir., 1973-81; exec. dir., chief oper. officer Ravinia Festival, 1990—. Fellow Inst. Chartered Accts. in Eng. and Wales; mem. Ordre des Comptables Agrees du Que. Office: Ravinia Festival 400 Iris Ln Highland Park IL 60035-5208

MEHTA, ZUBIN, conductor, musician; b. Bombay, India, Apr. 29, 1936; came to U.S., 1961; s. Mehli Nowrowji and Tehmina (Daruvala) M.; m. Nancy Diane Kovack; children: Zarina, Merwan. Student, St. Xavier's Coll., Bombay, 1951-53, State Acad. Music, Vienna, Austria, 1954-60; LL.D., Sir George Williams U., Montreal, 1965; D.Mus. (hon.), Occidental Coll.; hon. doctorate, Colgate U., Brooklyn Coll., Westminster Choir Coll., Juilliard Sch., Weizmann Inst. Sci. (Israel). Music dir., Montreal (Can.) Symphony Orch., 1961-67, Los Angeles Philharmonic Orch., 1962-78; mus. dir.: Israel Philharmonic, from 1969, appointed dir. for life, 1981; music dir., N.Y. Philharmonic, 1978-91, guest condr., Met. Opera, Salzburg (Austria) Festival, Vienna Philharmonic, Berlin Philharmonic, La Scala, Milan, Italy, music dir., Maggio Musicale Florence, Italy, rec. artist for, Decca, CBS, RCA, New World Records, (recipient 1st prize Liverpool (Eng.) Condrs. Competition 1958). Decorated Padma Bhushan India, 1967, commendatore of Italy. Office: Israel Philharm Orch, 1 Huberman St Box 11292, 61112 Tel Aviv Israel also: Orch Maggio Musicale, Teatro, Comunale Via Solferino 15, I-50123 Florence Italy

MEHTABDIN, KHALID RAUF, economist, educator; b. Sialkot, Pakistan, Nov. 6, 1944; s. Haji and Atiiya Mehtabdin; m. Durdana Ansarie, Jan. 26, 1951; children: Mehvish, Khurram. MA, U. Punjab, 1968; MPA, U. Pitts., 1974, M in Pub. and Internat. Affairs, 1977, PhD, 1979. Asst. prof. econs. Niagara U., Niagara Falls, N.Y., 1980-84, assoc. prof., 1985-86; assoc. prof. St. Rose Coll., Albany, N.Y., 1986—; mem. bus. adv. coun. Niagara U., 1980-86; cons. M.H. Bros., Karachi, Pakistan, 1980-82. Author: Comparative Management, 1986, Reagonomics, 1986, Macro Eco, 1987. Recipient Outstanding Cmty. award Pakistani Cmty. Albany, N.Y., 1995. Mem. Am. Econs. Assn., Ea. Econs. Assn. (bd. dirs. 1986-90), Islamic Ctr. of Capital Dist. Home: 312 Torquay Blvd Albany NY 12203-4927

MEHURON, WILLIAM OTTO, electronics company executive; b. Hammond, Ind., Nov. 20, 1937; s. Arthur and Margaret Irene (Soroka) M.; m. Charlotte Anne Nyheim, Aug. 26, 1982; children: Kimberly Anne, Kristine Lynn. BSEE, Purdue U., 1959; MSEE, U. Pa., 1962, PhD, 1966. Tech. staff RCA, Moorestown, N.J., 1959-64, GE, Phila., 1964-68; group leader Mitre Corp., McLean, Va., 1969-74; tech. dir. naval intelligence Dept. Navy, Washington, 1974-81; dir. rsch. and engring. Nat. Security Agy., Ft. Meade, Md., 1981-85; v.p., gen. mgr. data systems div. Ampex Corp. subs. Allied-Signal Co., Redwood City, Calif., 1985-86; sr. v.p. product ops. Daisy Systems Corp., Mountain View, Calif., 1986-88; v.p., gen. mgr. Networks and Info. Security div. Security div. Unisys Def. Systems, McLean, Va., 1988-91; pres. Mehuron Assocs. Inc., 1991-95; dir. sys. acquisition office NOAA, USG, Washington, 1995—. Mem. IEEE, AAAS, Armed Forces Communication and Electronics Assn., Security Affairs Support Assn., Air Force Assn. Avocations: amateur radio (W4XM), running, tennis, cooking, antiques. Home: 8107 Birnam Wood Dr Mc Lean VA 22102-2712

MEIBURG, CHARLES OWEN, business administration educator; b. Seneca, S.C., Dec. 17, 1931; s. Albert and Gladys Katherine (Burley) M.; m. Elizabeth Rhodes Glenn, June 11, 1955; children: Charles O. Jr., Howard Glenn, Elizabeth Rhodes. BS in Arts and Scis., Clemson U., 1953; MA in Econs., U. Va., 1958, PhD in Econs., 1960. Assoc. prof. U. Va., Charlottesville, 1964-69, prof., 1969-82, J. Harvie Wilkinson, Jr. prof. bus. adminstrn., 1982—; dir. Taylor Murphy Inst. U. Va., 1967-83; assoc. dean Darden Sch. U. Va., 1983-89. Co-author: Cases on Financial Institutions, 1979, Cases in Bank Management, 1986; editor (with others) Loan Officers Handbook, 1986. 1st lt. U.S. Army, 1953-55. Mem. Am. Econ. Assn., Fin. Mgmt. Assn., Assn. for U. Bus. and Econ. Rsch. (pres. 1971). Home: 3345 Kirkwood Ct Keswick VA 22947 Office: U Va Darden Sch PO Box 6550 Charlottesville VA 22906-6550

MEIDER, ELMER CHARLES, JR., publishing company executive; b. Buffalo, Feb. 7, 1946; s. Elmer Charles and Marie (Gress) M.; m. Teri René Mertz; children: Lisa Marie, Elmer Charles III, Tacy L., Anna Simms. B.B.A., Cleve. State U., 1971. Advt. research analyst Meldrum & Fewsmith (advt.), Cleve., 1967-69; sales promotion supr. ESB Inc., Cleve., 1969-72; sr. market research analyst, consumer products group Miles Labs., Elkhart, Ind., 1972-74; v.p., dir. mktg. World Book-Childcraft Internat. Inc., Chgo., 1974-83; v.p., gen. mgr. Tandy Home Edn. Systems (div. Radio Shack), 1983-86; pres. Highlights for Children Inc., 1986—; cons. mktg. research and mktg.; bd. dirs. Fifth-Third Bank, Columbus, Ohio. Bd. dirs. Ctrl. Ohio, Vols. Am.; trustee Westminster Coll., New Wilmington, Pa. Mem. Am. Mktg. Assn., Direct Selling Assn. Republican. Episcopalian. Home: 559 Cardinal Hill Ln Powell OH 43065-9358 Office: Highlights for Children 2300 W 5th Ave Columbus OH 43215-1003

MEIER, AUGUST, historian, educator; b. N.Y.C., Apr. 30, 1923; s. Frank A. and Clara (Cohen) M. AB, Oberlin Coll., 1945; AM, Columbia U., 1949, PhD, 1957; LittD, Rutgers U., 1994. Asst. prof. history Tougaloo (Miss.) Coll., 1945-49; rsch. asst. to Charles S. Johnson, 1953; asst. prof. history Fisk U., 1953-56; asst., assoc. prof. history Morgan State Coll., Balt., 1957-64; prof. history Roosevelt U., Chgo., 1964-67; prof. history Kent (Ohio) State U., 1967-69, univ. prof., 1969-93; univ. prof. emeritus, 1993—. Author: Negro Thought in America, 1880-1915, 1963, (with Elliott Rudwick) From Plantation to Ghetto, 1966, 3d edit., 1976, (with Elliott Rudwick) Black Detroit and the Rise of the UAW, 1979, (with Elliott Rudwick) CORE: A Study In The Civil Rights Movement, 1942-68, 1973, (with Elliott Rudwick) Along the Color Line: Explorations in the Black Experience, 1976, (with Elliott Rudwick) Black History and the Historical Profession, 1986, A White Scholar and the Black Community, 1945-1965, 1993; editor: (with Francis Broderick) Negro Protest Thought in the Twentieth Century, 1966, (with Francis Broderick and Elliott Rudwick) rev. edit. renamed Black Protest Thought in The Twentieth Century, 1971, (with Elliott Rudwick) The Making of Black America, 1969, (with Elliott Rudwick and John H. Bracey, Jr.), Black Nationalism in America, 1970, (with John Hope Franklin) Black Leaders of the Twentieth Century, 1982, (with Leon Litwack) Black Leaders of the Nineteenth Century, 1988; gen. editor: Atheneum Negro in Am. Life Series, 1966-74, University of Illinois Press Blacks in the New World Series, 1972—, (with John H. Bragy), 1994—, (with Elliott Rudwick and John Bracey) University Publications of America Black Studies Research Sources on Microfilm, 1980—; mem. editorial adv. bd.: Booker T. Washington Papers, 1967-85, Civil War History, 1970—, Jour. Am. History, 1974-77. Sec. Newark br. NAACP, 1951-52, 56-57; chmn. Balt. chpt. Ams. for Democratic Action, 1960-61, mem. nat. bd., exec. com., 1960-61; active Newark chpt. CORE, 1963-64, Balt. chpt. SNCC, 1960-63. Advanced grad. fellow Am. Council Learned Socs., 1952; Guggenheim fellow, 1971-72; Nat. Endowment for Humanities fellow, 1975-77; Center for Advanced Study in Behavioral Scis. fellow, 1976-77. Mem. Am. Hist. Assn., So. Hist. Assn. (pres. 1992), Assn. Study Negro Life and History, Orgn. Am. Historians (del. to Am. Coun. Learned Socs. 1979-83, chmn. program com. 1990). Unitarian. Home: 305 W End Ave # 701 New York NY 10023-8102

MEIER, GEORGE KARL, III, pastor, lawyer; b. Glen Ridge, N.J., Jan. 13, 1944; s. George Karl and Mary Claire (Myers) M.; children: G.K., Leslie; m. Therese DesCamp, Oct. 10, 1992. BS, Washington and Lee U., 1966; JD, Dickinson Sch. Law, 1969; MDiv, Pacific Sch. of Religion, 1992. Bar: N.J. 1969, Oreg. 1970, U.S. Dist. Ct. N.J. 1969, U.S. Dist. Ct. Oreg. 1970, U.S. Ct. Appeals (9th cir.) 1971, U.S. Ct. Appeals (fed. cir.) 1987, U.S. Supreme Ct. 1973. Law clk. N.J Superior Court Appellate Div., 1969-70; assoc. Stoel, Rives, Boley, Jones & Grey, Portland, Oreg., 1970-75, ptnr., 1976-89; spl. dep. atty. gen. State of Idaho, 1988-89; spl. asst. to pres. Pacific Sch. Religion, Berkeley, Calif., 1992; pastor Pioneer Cong. Ch., Sacramento, Calif., 1992—. Co-founder Ctrl. City Concern, 1978, SW Youth Svc. Ctr., Portland; chmn. ctrl. adv. bd. Dept. Human Resources; pres. consistory Hillside Cmty. Ch., Portland, 1984-85; acad. com. Pacific Sch. Religion, 1989-91; interim dir. youth programs Epwirth Meth. Ch., 1992; bd. dirs. No. Calif. Nev. Conf. the United Ch. Christ, 1993, v.p., 1995-96, pres., 1996—, Francis House, 1992—, chmn., 1995-96, Cathedral Pioneer Ch. Homes, Inc., 1992—. Recipient Outstanding Svc. award Cen. City Concern 1976-89. Mem. Oreg. State Bar Assn. Mem. United Ch. of Christ. Office: Pioneer Congregational Ch 2700 L St Sacramento CA 95816-5614

MEIER, GERALD MARVIN, economics educator; b. Tacoma, Wash., Feb. 9, 1923; s. Max and Bessie (Nagel) M.; m. Gretl Slote, Oct. 23, 1954; children: David, Daniel, Jeremy, Andrew. BA in Econs., Reed Coll., 1947; BLitt in Econs., Oxford (Eng.) U., 1952; PhD, Harvard U., 1953; MA (hon.), Wesleyan U., Middletown, Conn., 1959. Instr. Williams Coll., Williamstown, Pa., 1952-54; asst. prof. Wesleyan U., 1954-59, prof. econs., 1959-63; prof. econs. Stanford (Calif.) U., 1963—; research assoc. Oxford U., 1957-58; vis. lectr. Yale U., New Haven, 1955-56, vis. assoc. prof., 1956-59, vis. prof., 1959-61; vis. prof. Stanford U., 1962; cons. Asia Soc., Bank Am., East-West Ctr., Food and Agrl. Orgn., Goodyear Internat., NSF, others; internat. lectr. in field. Author: International Trade anbd Development, 1963, Leading Issues in Development Economics, 1964, The International Economics of Development, 1968, 2d edit., 1978, Leading Issues in Economic Development: Studies in International Poverty, 6th edit., 1995; (with R.E. Baldwin) Economic Development, 1957; gen. editor: Econ. Devel. Series, Econ. Theory and the Underdevel. Countries, Human Resources as the Wealth of Nations, 1973, Fin. Deepening in Econ. Devel., 1975, Agrl. and Structural Transformation, 1975, Gen. X-Efficiency Theory of Econ. Devel., 1978; editor: International Economic Reform: Collected Papers of Emile Despres, 1973, Problems of Trade Policy, 1973, Problems of a World Monetary Order, 1982, Problemsod Cooperation for Development, 1977, Toward a New International Development, 1982, La Nueva Era de Desarollo, 1978, Internat. Econs. of Development, International Economics: Theory of Policy, 1982, New International Development Policy, 1982, Pricing Policy for Development Management, 1983, Pioneers in Development, 1985, Emerging from Poverty: The Economics that Really Matters, 1984, Financing Asian Development, 1986, Pioneers in Development, 1987, Asian Development: Economic Success and Policy Lessons; author numerous chpts. to books and articles to profl. jours. Rhodes scholar, 1948-52, Rockefeller Found. Study Ctr. resident scholar, 1981; Guggenheim fellow, 1957-58, Brookings Nat. Research fellow, 1961-62, Russel Sage Found. resident fellow, 1976-77; Social Sci. Research Council Faculty research grantee, 1968, Internat. Legal Ctr. research grantee, 1970, Rockefeller Found. research grantee, 1974-75. Mem. Am. Assn. Rhodes Scholars, Am. Econ. Assn., Royal Econ. Soc., Am. Soc. Internat. Law, Phi Beta Kappa. Home: 774 Santa Ynez St Palo Alto CA 94305-8441 Office: Stanford U Grad Sch of Bus Stanford CA 94305-5015

MEIER, GUSTAV, symphony conductor. Conductor Lansing (Mich.) Symphony.

MEIER, HENRY GEORGE, architect; b. Indpls., July 14, 1929; s. Virgil and Elizabeth (Whiteside) M.; m. Peggy Nelson, June 28, 1953; children: Scott J., Bruce W., Paul T., Thomas A. BArch, U. Cin., 1953. Lic. architect Ind., Mich., Ky., Ill., Iowa, Fla., Ohio; lic. landscape architect Ind. Pvt. practice architecture Indpls., 1964-90; sr. architect Ball State U., Muncie, Ind., 1990—. Contbr. Indiana Architect mag. Bd. dirs. Am. Bapt. Chs./U.S.A., Valley Forge, Pa., 1970-77, Bd. Bldg. Appeals, Indpls., 1979-85. Served to 1st lt. USMC, 1953-55. Fellow AIA (bd. dirs. 1981-85); mem. Ind. Soc. Architects (pres. 1975, Edward D. Pierre award 1979), Constrn. Specifications Inst., Interfaith Forum on Religion Art and Architecture (v.p. 1981). Republican. Lodges: Masons, Shriners.

MEIER, KENNETH J., political science journal editor; b. Aberdeen, S.D., Mar. 3, 1950; s. John and Elizabeth (Malsam) M.; m. Diane Jones Meier, Dec. 31, 1972. BA, U. S.D., 1972; PhD, Syracuse U., 1975. Prof. polit. sci. Rice U., Houston, 1975-78, U. Okla., 1978-85; prof. polit. sci. U. Wis., Madison, 1985-89, Milw., 1989—; fellow com. for hispanic pub. policy issues Inter Univ. Program Social Sci. Rsch. Coun., 1991-92. Author: Race, Class and Education, 1989, The Politics of Hispanic Education, 1991, Politics and the Bureaucracy, 1993, The Politics of Sin, 1994, The Case Against School Choice, 1995; editor Am. Jour. Polit. Sci., 1994—. Recipient Clarence A. Kulp award, 1990, Gustavus Myers award, 1991, 93, Hubert Kaufman award, 1992. Mem. APHA, ASPA, Am. Polit. Sci. Assn. Office: Univ Wisconsin-Milw. Dept Political Science PO Box 413 Milwaukee WI 53201

MEIER, LOUIS LEONARD, JR., lawyer; b. Hawthorne, Calif., Oct. 12, 1918; s. Louis Leonard and Celestine Helen (Gabriel) M.; m. Donna Eleonora Tomacelli-Filomarino, June 5, 1954; children: Renée, Sharon Clark, Catherine, Marina. B.S., U.S. Naval Acad., 1942; LL.B., Georgetown U., 1951; grad., U.S. Naval War Coll., 1963. Bar: Va. 1951, U.S. Supreme Ct. 1970, D.C. 1973. Legal and legis. asst. to Chmn. Joint Chiefs of Staff, Washington, 1965-67; comdr. Guided Missile Destroyer Squadron 18, Atlantic Fleet, U.S. Navy, 1967-69; mem policy planning staff Office Sec. State, Washington, 1969-72; Washington counsel ASCE, 1972-82, exec. dir., 1982-83; sole practice Washington, 1983—. Served to capt. USN, 1941-72. Decorated Legion Merit; recipient U.S.S. Gherardi Battle Efficiency award, 1951, U.S.S. John S. McCain Battle Efficiency award, 1954. Mem. ABA, Nat. Inst. Bldg. Scis., Conf. Fedn. Environ. Engrs., Met. Club, Chevy Chase Country Club, N.Y. Yacht Club, Spouting Rock Beach Assn. Republican. Roman Catholic. Home and Office: 5132 Baltan Rd Bethesda MD 20816-2350

MEIER, MARK F., research scientist, glaciologist, educator; b. Iowa City, Dec. 19, 1925; s. Norman C. and Clea (Grimes) M.; m. Barbara McKinley, Sept. 16, 1955; children: Lauren G., Mark S., Gretchen A. BSEE, U. Iowa, 1949, MS in Geology, 1951; PhD in Geology and Applied Mechanics, Calif. Inst. Tech., 1957. Instr. Occidental Coll., L.A., 1952-55; chief glaciology project office U.S. Geol. Survey, Tacoma, 1956-85; dir. Inst. Arctic & Alpine Rsch. U. Colo., Boulder, 1985-94; vis. prof. Dartmouth Coll., Hanover, N.H., 1964; rsch. prof. U. Wash., Seattle, 1964-86; profl. geol. scis. U. Colo., 1985—; pres. Internat. Comn. on Snow and Ice, 1967-71; pres. Internat. Assn. Hydrol. Scis., 1979-83; Mendenhall lectr. U.S. Geol. Survey, 1982, Walter Orr Roberts Disting. lectr. Aspen Global Change Inst., 1992. Contbr. articles to profl. jours. With USN, 1945-46. Recipient 3 medals Acad. Scis., Moscow, USSR, 1970-85, Disting. Svc. award (Gold medal) U.S. Dept. of the Interior, 1968; Meier Valley, Antarctica named in his honor U.S. and U.K. Bd. Geographic Names. Fellow AAAS (John Wesley Powell Meml. lectr. 1994), Am. Geophys. Union (com. chmn.), Geol. Soc. Am., (com. mem.), Internat. Glaciological Soc. (v.p., coun., Seligman Crystal 1985), Arctic Inst. N.Am. (gov. 1987-93). Office: U Colo Inst Inst Arctic and Alpine Rsch 1560 30th St Boulder CO 80303-1012

MEIER, MATTHIAS S(EBASTIAN), historian; b. Covington, Ky., June 4, 1917; s. Matthias J. and Mary (Berberich) M.; married; 5 children. B.A., U. Miami, 1948; M.A., Mexico City Coll., 1949; Ph.D. in Latin Am. History, U. Calif.-Berkeley, 1954. Lectr. U.S. history San Francisco State Coll., summers 1953-55; lectr. U.S. And Latin Am. history Bakersfield Coll., 1955-63; asst. prof. Fresno State Coll., summer 1956, fall 1962; asst. prof. Latin Am. history Santa Clara U., 1963-66, assoc. prof., 1966-72, prof., 1972-89, Patrick A. Donohoe prof. history, 1983-89, emeritus; Fulbright lectr. Nat. U. Tucuman and Inst. Nacional de Profesorado Secundario, Buenos Aires, Argentina, 1958-59; lect. U. Ibero-Am., summer 1965; vis. prof. San Jose State Coll., spring 1968. Author: (with Feliciano Rivera) The Chicanos: A History of Mexican Americans, 1972, A Bibliography for Chicano History, 1972; editor: (with Feliciano Rivera) Readings on La Raza: Twentieth Century, 1973, Dictionary of Mexican American History, 1981, Bibliography of Mexican American History, 1984, Mexican American Biographies, 1988, update of Carey McWilliams's North From Mexico (publ. 1949), 1990, revision, update The Chicanos (new title Mexiacn Americans/American Mexicans), 1993. Served with Signal Corps U.S. Army, 1942-46. Mem. Pacific Coast Council Latin Am. Studies (pres. 1964-65, 76-77), Latin Am. Studies Assn., Conf. Latin Am. Historians, Assn. Borderlands Scholars, Nat. Assn. for Chicano Studies. Office: Dept History Santa Clara U Santa Clara CA 95053

MEIER, RICHARD ALAN, architect; b. Newark, Oct. 12, 1934; s. Jerome and Carolyn (Kalenbacher) M.; m. Katherine Gormley, Jan. 21, 1978; children: Joseph Max, Ana Moss. BArch, Cornell U., 1957; hon. doctorate, U. Naples, Italy, 1991. Registered profl. arch., N.Y., N.J., Conn., Mich., Va., Fla., Ind., Ga., Calif., Ill., Iowa, Tex., Oreg. Architect Frank Grad & Sons, N.J., 1957, Davis, Brody & Wisniewski, N.Y.C., 1958-59, Skidmore, Owings & Merrill, 1959-60, Marcel Breuer & Assocs., 1960-63; architect, prin. Richard Meier & Assocs., N.Y.C., 1963-80, Richard Meier & Ptnrs., 1980—; resident architect Am. Acad. in Rome, 1973-74; vis. critic Pratt Inst., 1960-62, 65, Princeton, 1963, Syracuse U., 1964; William Henry Bishop vis. prof. architecture Yale U., 1975, 77, vis. critic, 1967, 72, 73, 77; vis. prof. Harvard U., 1977, UCLA, 1988, Eliot Noyes vis. critic in architecture, 1980-81; Harvey S. Perloff vis. prof. architecture UCLA, 1987; mem. adv. coun. Cornell U. Coll. Art, Architecture and Planning; mem. Jerusalem Com. Exhbns., XV Triennale, Milan, 1973, Mus. Modern Art, N.Y.C., 1975, 81, Princeton U., Biennale, Venice, Italy, 1976, Cooper-Hewitt Mus., N.Y.C., 1976-77, Leo Castelli Gallery, N.Y.C., 1977, 94, Rosa Esman Gallery,

N.Y.C., 1978, 80, N.J. State Mus., 1978, Modernism Gallery, San Francisco, Wadsworth Atheneum, Hartford, Conn., High Mus. Art, Atlanta Harvard U., Max Protech Gallery, 1980, Syracuse U., Whitney Mus. Art, N.Y.C., 1982, Knoll Internat., Tokyo, Japan, 1988, October Gallery, London, 1990, Royal Palace, Naples, Italy, 1991, Palazzo delle Esposizione, Rome, 1993, Aichi Prefectural Mus. Art, Nagoya, Japan, 1996; adj. prof. architecture Cooper Union, 1963-73. Prin. works include Westbeth Artists Housing, N.Y.C., Bronx (N.Y.) Devel. Ctr., Smith House, Darien, Conn., Douglas House, Harbor Springs, Mich., Shamberg House, Mt. Kisco, N.Y., Hoffman and Saltzman Houses, East Hampton, N.Y.; houses in Old Westbury, N.Y., Pound Ridge, N.Y., Palm Beach, Fla., Pitts.; Twin Parks NE Housing, N.Y.C., Atheneum, New Harmony, Ind., N.Y., Hartford (Conn.) Sem., Mus. für Kunsthandwerk, Frankfurt, Germany, Des Moines Art Ctr., High Mus. Art, Atlanta, Bridgeport (Conn.) Ctr., Daimler-Benz Office and Lab. Complex, Ulm, Germany, Weishaupt Forum, Schwendi, Germany, Nat. Investment Bank, City Hall and Cen. Libr., The Hague, The Netherlands, Corp. Hdqs., Royal Dutch Paper Mills, Hilversum, The Netherlands, Cornell U. Alumni and Admissions Ctr., Ithaca, N.Y., Canal Hdqs., Paris, Espace Pitot, Montpellier, France, Maybury Office Park, Edinburgh, Scotland, Hypolux Bank Bldg., Luxembourg, Mus. Contemporary Art, Barcelona, Spain, Arp Mus., Rolandswerth, Germany, Swiss Volksbank, Basel Office Bldg., Singapore, The Getty Ctr., L.A., SwissAir Hdqs., Melville, N.Y., Fed. Courthouse, Islip, N.Y., Phoenix, Mus. TV & Radio, L.A., Gagosian Gallery, L.A., Rachofsky House, Dallas, Naples, Fla., others; author: Richard Meier Architect: Buildings & Projects 1966-1976, 1976, On Architecture, 1982, Richard Meier Collages, 1990, The Getty Ctr. Design Process, J. Paul Getty Trust, 1991, Richard Meier Sculpture, 1994; contbr. articles to profl. jours. Decorated officer de l'Ordre des Arts et des Lettres (France), 1984; recipient Arnold Brunner Meml. prize Am. Acad. Arts and Letters, 1972, Albert S. Bard Civic award City Club N.Y., 1973, 1st honor award for excellence in architecture and urban design, 1977, R.S. Reynolds Meml. award, 1977, Archtl. Record award of excellence for design, 1964, 68, 69, 70, 77, Am. Inst. Steel Constrn. award, 1978, 79, design award 1st prize Kunsthandwerk Competition, Frankfurt am Main, Fed. Republic Germany, 1980, Pritzker Prize for Architecture, 1984. Fellow AIA (medal of honor N.Y. chpt. 1980, nat. design com. 1972-74, 12 AIA nat. awards 1968-93, 32 chpt. awards N.Y. 1965-94, Chgo. Arch. award, 5 Progressive Architecture awards 1979, 89, 90, 91, 95; mem. NAD, Internat. Inst. Archs., Royal Inst. Brit. Archs. (Royal Gold medal 1988), Belgian Royal Acad. Art (Lifetime Achievement award Guild Hall 1991, commdr. de l'Ordre des Arts et Lettres, France, 1992). Address: 475 10th Ave New York NY 10018-1120

MEIER, RICHARD LOUIS, futurist, planner, behavioral scientist; b. Kendallville, Ind., May 16, 1920; s. Walter A. and Mary (Lottman) M.; m. Gitta Unger, May 20, 1944 (dec.); children: Karen Reeds, Andrea Meier Whitmore, Alan; m. Robin Standish, Apr. 21, 1992. Student, No. Ill. State Tchrs. Coll., 1936-39; BS, U. Ill., 1940; MA, UCLA, 1942, PhD, 1944. With Calif. Research Corp., 1943-47; exec. sec. Fedn. Am. Scis., 1947-48; with Petrocarbon, Ltd., 1949-50; Fulbright scholar Manchester U., Eng., 1949-50; asst. prof. program of edn. and research in planning U. Chgo., 1950-56; research social scientist Mental Health Research Inst., U. Mich., Ann Arbor, 1957—; asso. prof. conservation Mental Health Research Inst., U. Mich., 1960-65, prof., 1965-67; prof. environ. design U. Calif., Berkeley, 1967-90; prof. emeritus U. Calif., 1990—; vis. lectr. Harvard U., 1959-60; vis. prof. Grad. Sch. Ekistics, Athens, 1962, U. Calif., Berkeley, 1966; cons. on social planning and resources planning Joint Ctr. for Urban Studies, MIT and Harvard U., in Venezuela, 1963-65; developer program for using inter-active media for edn. of illiterates for econ. devel. and population planning in Africa and Asia. Author: Science and Economic Development, 1956, Modern Science and the Human Fertility Problem, 1959, A Communications Theory of Urban Growth, 1962, Developmental Planning, 1965, Resource-Conserving Urbanism for South Asia, 1968, Planning for an Urban World, 1974, Urban Futures Observed: In the Asian Third World, 1980; contbr. numerous articles to profl. jours. Mem. AAAS, Am. Planning Assn., Am. Chem. Soc., Am. Sociol. Assn., Soc. for Gen. Sys. Rsch., Fedn. Am. Scis., Holis-Soc. for Sustainable Future, Internat. Solar Energy Soc. Home: 636 Colusa Berkeley CA 94707

MEIER, THOMAS KEITH, college president, English educator; b. Houston, Apr. 12, 1940; s. Herbert H. and Madeleine (Keith) M.; m. Mila Hillard, June 30, 1962; children: John Hillard, Keith Reilly. BA, U. Tex., 1962; AM, Columbia U., 1963; MBA, Harvard U., 1967; PhD, Columbia U., 1969. Fin. mgr., employee rels. mgr. Exxon Co., U.S.A. and Exxon Rsch. Engring. Co., Houston, Florham Park, N.J., 1969-79; pres. Castleton (Vt.) State Coll., 1979-87, Elmira (N.Y.) Coll., 1987—; regent Lee Coll., Baytown, Tex., 1972-73; pres. Vt. Higher Edn. Coun., 1981-82; mem. Johnson Found. (Troutbeck) Leadership Seminar, 1991—; mem. adv. coun. The Pres.'s Found. for Support of Higher Edn.; bd. dirs. Chemung Canal Trust Co., Coll. Consortium Finger Lakes, N.Y., Ind. Coll. Fund of N.Y. Author: Defoe and the Defense of Commerce, 1987; contbr. articles to profl. jours. Bd. dirs. Union County Urban League, Elizabeth, N.J., 1973-76, Rutland Region C. of C., 1982-86, Arnot Art Mus., 1987—, So. Tier Econ. Growth, 1987—, N.E.-Midwest Congl. Leadership Coun., 1988—; bd. dirs. Chemung County United Way, 1990-93, chmn. 1992-93; corp. bd. dirs. Rutland Hosp., 1980-87. Lt. U.S. Army, 1963-65. Recipient Outstanding Periodical Essay award Tex. Books Rev., 1979, medal of merit Elmira Coll. Alumni Assn., 1991; Weaver fellow, 1968. Mem. Pico Ski Club, Elmira Country Club, Elmira City Club, Harvard Club of N.Y.C., Phi Beta Kappa, Phi Eta Sigma, Phi Alpha Theta, Omciron Delta Kappa, Theta Xi. Episcopalian. Home: The President's Home 855 College Ave Elmira NY 14901-2001 Office: Elmira Coll Office of Pres Elmira NY 14901

MEIER, WILBUR LEROY, JR., industrial engineer, educator, former university chancellor; b. Elgin, Tex., Jan. 3, 1939; s. Wilbur Leroy and Ruby (Hall) M.; m. Judy Lee Longbotham, Aug. 30, 1958; children: Melynn, Marla, Melissa. BS, U. Tex., 1962, MS, 1964, PhD, 1967. Planning engr. Tex. Water Devel. Bd., Austin, 1962-66, cons., 1967-72; research engr. U. Tex., Austin, 1966; asst. prof. indsl. engring. Tex. A&M U., College Station, 1967-68; assoc prof. Tex. A&M U., 1968-70, prof., 1970-73, asst. head dept. indsl. engring., 1972-73; prof., chmn. dept. indsl. engring. Iowa State U., Ames, 1973-74; prof., head sch. of indsl. engring. Purdue U., West Lafayette, Ind., 1974-81; dean Coll. Engring., Pa. State U., University Park, 1981-87; chancellor U. Houston System, 1987-89; prof. indsl. engring. Pa. State U., University Park, 1989-91; dir. div. engring. infrastructure devel. NSF, Washington, 1989-91; dean Coll. Engring. N.C. State U., 1991-93, prof. indsl. engring., 1991—; mem. bd. visitors Air Force Inst. Technology; cons. Ohio Bd. Regents, 1990, U. Arizona, 1989, Indsl. Rsch. Inst., St. Louis, 1979, Environments for Tomorrow, Inc., Washington, 1970-81, Water Resources Engrs., Inc., Walnut Creek, Calif., 1969-70, Computer Graphics, Inc., Bryan, Tex., 1969-70, Kaiser Engrs., Oakland, Calif., 1971, Tracor, Inc., Austin, 1966-68, div. planning coordination Tex. Gov.'s Office, 1969, Office of Tech. Assessment, 1982-86, Southeast Ctr. for Elec. Engring. Edn., 1978—; mem. rev. team Naval Rsch. Adv. Com. Editor: Marcel Dekker Pub. Co., 1978—; Contbr. articles to profl. jours. Recipient Bliss medal Soc. Am. Mil. Engrs., 1986, Am. Spirit award USAF, 1984; named Outstanding Young Engr. of Yr. Tex. Soc. Profl. Engrs., 1966, Disting. Grad. Coll. Engring., U. Tex. at Austin, 1987; USPHS fellow, 1966. Fellow AAAS, Am. Soc. Engring. Edn. (chmn. indsl. engring. divsn. 1978-83), Inst. Indsl. Engrs. (dir. ops. rsch. div. 1975, pres. Ind. chpt. 1976, program chmn. 1973-75, editorial bd. Trans., publ. chmn., newsletter editor engring. economy div. 1972-73, v.p. region VIII 1977-79, exec. v.p. chpt. ops. 1981-83, pres. 1985-86); mem. Ops. Rsch. Soc. Am., Inst. Mgmt. Scis. (v.p. S.W. chpt. 1971-72), ASCE (sec.-treas. Austin br. 1965-66, chmn. rsch. com., tech. coun. water resources planning and mgmt. 1972-74), Am. Assn. Engring. Socs. (bd. govs. 1984-86), Nat. Assn. State Univ. and Land Grant Colls. (mem. engring. legis. task force 1983-87), Assn. Engring. Colls. Pa. (pres. 1985-86, treas. 1981-87), Air Force Assn. (advisor sci. and tech. com. 1984-87), Nat. Soc. Profl. Engrs., Profl. Engrs. in Edn. (vice chmn. N.E. region 1985-87, bd. govs. 1983-85), Sigma Xi, Tau Beta Pi, Alpha Pi Mu (asso. editor Cogwheel 1970-75, regional dir. 1976-77, exec. v.p. 1977-80, pres. 1980-82), Phi Kappa Phi, Chi Epsilon. Lodge: Rotary. Home: 7504 Grist Mill Rd Raleigh NC 27615-5411

MEIERING, MARK C., lawyer; b. Roswell, N.Mex., Sept. 28, 1944; m. Gail Marino. BBA, U. Notre Dame, 1966; JD, NYU, 1969. Bar: N.Mex. 1970, U.S. Dist. Ct. N.Mex. 1970, U.S. Ct. Appeals (10th cir.) 1971, U.S. Supreme Ct. 1977; bd. cert. in civil litigation Nat. Bd. Trial Advocacy. Law clk. Hon. D.C. Hill, U.S. Ct. Appeals, Wichita, Kans., 1969-71; asst. U.S. atty. Dist. of N.Mex., Albuquerque, 1971-76; assoc. Rodey Law Firm, Albuquerque, 1976—; asst. staff judge advocate USAR, Albuquerque, 1971-76. Chmn. bd. dirs. Sandia Prep. Sch., Albuquerque, 1991-92. Mem. Am. Bd. Trial Advocates (assoc.). Office: Rodey Law Firm PO Box 1888 Albuquerque NM 87103-1888

MEIGHER, S. CHRISTOPHER, III, communications and media investor; b. N.Y.C., Sept. 23, 1946; s. Stephen Christopher and Denise (Connor) Todd; m. Grace Tebbutt, Aug. 8, 1970; children: Elizabeth, Amanda. A.B., Dartmouth Coll., 1968; P.M.D., Harvard U., 1974. Dir. circulation Fortune mag., N.Y.C., 1972-74, Sports Illustrated mag., N.Y.C., 1974-76, Time mag., N.Y.C., 1976-79; v.p. circulation Time, Inc., N.Y.C., 1981-83; pres. Time Distbn. Services, N.Y.C., 1979-81; pub. People mag., N.Y.C., 1983-85, exec. v.p., group pub., 1985-90; pres. Time Inc. Mags. N.Y., N.Y.C., 1990-92; bd. dirs. Book of the Month Club, N.Y.C., Asiaweek Ltd., Hong Kong, Sunset Pub. Co., Southern Progress (Birmingham), Advt. Council, Inc., Mag. Publishers Assn., America Online, Washington. Trustee Boys Club, N.Y.C., South St. Seaport, N.Y.; bd. dirs. Meml. Sloan Kettering Dream Team, Am. Ballet Theatre, N.Y. Recipient Disting. Service award Brandeis U., 1983. Mem. River Club, Bath & Tennis Club (Palm Beach), Brook Club, Racquet & Tennis Club (N.Y.), N.Y. Yacht Club (trustee), Lake George Club, Clove Valley Rod and Gun Club. Home: 164 E 72nd St New York NY 10021-4363 Office: Meigher Comm. LP 100 Avenue Of The Americas New York NY 10013-1689

MEIGS, JOHN FORSYTH, lawyer; b. Boston, Dec. 4, 1941; s. Charles H. and Florence S. (Truitt) M.; m. Faith C. Watson; children: Amy, Perry, John. BA, Yale U., 1964; LLB, U. Pa., 1969. Bar: Pa. 1969, U.S. Supreme Ct. 1977. Assoc. Saul, Ewing, Remick & Saul, Phila., 1969-76, ptnr., 1976—. Trustee Independence Seaport Mus., 1978—; mem. Com. of 70, 1976—; trustee Woodmere Art Mus., 1987—. Contbr. articles to profl. jours. Mem. ABA, Pa. Bar Assn., Phila. Bar Assn. Episcopalian. Home: 6 Norman Ln Philadelphia PA 19118-3617 Office: Saul Ewing Remick & Saul 3800 Centre Sq W Philadelphia PA 19102

MEIGS, JOSEPH CARL, JR., retired English language educator; b. New London, N.C., Aug. 29, 1930; s. Joseph Carl and Lola Vann (Eddins) M.; m. Elizabeth Eleanor Stevenson, Sept. 12, 1953; children: Geoffrey Montgomery, Jonathan Hervey, Edward Stevenson. BA, Wake Forest U., 1952; MA, Tulane U., 1957. English and French tchr. Aquadale (N.C.) High Sch., 1952-53; tchr. Metairie (La.) Park Country Day Sch., 1954-55; instr. in English Salem Coll., Winston-Salem, N.C., 1957-62, Tulane U., New Orleans, 1962-64, Marquette U., Milw., 1964-67; asst. prof., then assoc. prof. English Ea. Conn. State U., Willimantic, 1967-93, chmn. dept. English, 1972-74, 87-88, 1990-93; ret., 1993; vis. prof. U. Hawaii, Hilo, 1988-89, 94-95. Grantee Carnegie Inst., 1953, Danforth Found., 1960. Mem. Linguistic Soc. Am., Soc. for Pidgin and Creole Studies, Phi Beta Kappa, Omicron Delta Kappa. Democrat. Avocations: photography, gardening, cooking, hiking, ceramic arts. Home: PO Box 852 Brooklyn CT 06234-0852

MEIGS, MONTGOMERY CUNNINGHAM, JR., military officer; b. Annapolis, Md., Jan. 11, 1945; s. Montgomery Cunningham and Elizabeth Shoemaker (Griggs) M.; m. Mary Ann Mellenbruch, July 6, 1968; children: William Bradford, Matthew Montgomery. BS, U.S. Mil. Acad., West Point, N.Y., 1967; MA in History, U. Wis., 1977, PhD in History, 1982. Commd. 2d lt. U.S. Army, 1967, advanced through grades to maj. gen.; internat. affairs fellow Coun. Fgn. Rels., N.Y.C., 1981-82; exec. officer 2d Armored Cavalry Regiment, Nurnberg, Germany, 1982-84; comdr. 1st Squadron, 1st Cavalry, 1st AD, Schwabach, Germany, 1984-86; rsch. fellow Nat. Def. U., Washington, 1986-87; chief strategic applications br. J-5 Joint Staff, Washington, 1987-90; comdr. 2d Bde 2d Bn., 1st Armored Divsn., Erlangen, Germany, 1990-91; comdg. gen. 7th Army Tng. Command, Grafenwoehr, Germany, 1991-93; chief of staff V U.S. Corps, Frankfurt, Germany, 1993-94; dep. chief of staff ops. HQ USAREUR & 7th Army, Heidelberg, Germany, 1994-95; commanding gen. 3d Infantry Divsn., 1995—. Author: Slide Rules and Submarines, 1990; contbr. articles to profl. jours. Decorated Disting. Svc. medal, Def. Superior Svc. medal, Legion of Merit with oak leaf cluster, Bronze Star medal with V device and 1 oak leaf cluster, Purple Heart. Avocations: history, hunting. Home: 140 Marne Ln, Wurzburg Germany Office: HQ 1ID Unit 26222 APO AE 09036

MEIJER, DOUGLAS, retail company executive; b. 1954. With Meijer Inc., 1967—, co-chmn., dir., 1990—. Office: Meijer Inc 2929 Walker Ave NW Grand Rapids MI 49504-9424*

MEIJER, FREDERIK, retail company executive; b. 1919. married. Former pres. Meijer, Inc., then chmn. bd., chief exec. officer, 1975-90, chmn. exec. com., chief exec. officer, 1990—, also bd. dirs. Office: Meijer Inc 2929 Walker Ave NW Grand Rapids MI 49504-9424*

MEIJER, HENDRIK, retail company executive; b. 1952. With Meijer Inc., Grand Rapids, Mich., 1963—, co-chmn., 1990—. Office: Meijer Inc 2929 Walker Ave NW Grand Rapids MI 49504-9424*

MEIJER, MARK, retail executive. With Bud's Ambulance Service, Grand Rapids, Mich., 1977-79; pres. EMS Inc., Grand Rapids, Mich., 1979—, Meijer Companies LTD, Grand Rapids, Mich. Office: Meijer Companies LTD 2929 Walker Ave NW Grand Rapids MI 49504-9424*

MEIJER, PAUL HERMAN ERNST, educator, physicist; b. The Hague, Netherlands, Nov. 14, 1921; came to U.S., 1953, naturalized, 1959; s. Herman Willem and Elisabet (Kossmann) M.; m. Marianne Schwarz, Feb. 17, 1949; children: Onko Frans (dec.), Miriam, Daniel, Mark, Corinne. Ph.D., U. Leiden, Netherlands, 1951. Research assoc. U. Leiden, 1952-53, Duke U., 1954-55; vis. lectr. Case Inst. Tech., 1953-54; asst. prof. U. Del., 1955-56; asso. prof. Cath. U., Washington, 1956-60; prof. physics Cath. U., 1960-92, prof. emeritus, 1992—, chmn. dept., 1980-83; vis. prof. U. Paris, 1964-65, 72, 78, U. Nancy, 1984, 88; part-time appointment Nat. Bur. Standards; short time appointments at Naval Ordnance Lab., Livermore Radiation Lab., Naval Research Lab., Night Vision Lab., Ft. Belvoir. Author: (with E. Bauer) Group Theory, 1962; editor: Group Theory and Solid State Physics, 1964. Fulbright grantee, 1953-55, 77-78; Guggenheim grantee, 1964-65; Fulbright sr. fellow, 1978. Fellow Am. Phys. Socs.; mem. European Phys. Soc., Phys. Soc. Netherlands, Fedn. Am. Scientists, Fulbright Alumni Assn., Sigma Xi. Research, publs. statis. mechanics solids and liquids, group theory and other fields. Home: 1438 Geranium St NW Washington DC 20012-1518 Office: Physics Dept Hannan Hall Cath U Am Washington DC 20064 also: Phys and Chem Properties div Nat Inst Stds and Tech Gaithersburg MD 20899

MEIKLE, PHILIP G., retired government agency executive; b. Glendale, W.Va., Dec. 5, 1937; s. Philip and Caroline Elizabeth (Stephens) M.; m. Linda Kay Price, July 14, 1961 (div. Aug. 1976); children—Philip Kevin, Melissa Kay. B.S. in Mining Engring., W.Va. U., 1961, M.S. in Mining Engring., 1965; M.Engring. Adminstrn., George Washington U., 1980. Registered profl. engr. Mining engr. Duquesne Light Co., Pitts., 1961-63; research engr. W.Va. U., Morgantown, 1963-66; materials engr. Mobay Chem. Co., New Martinsville, W.Va., 1966-68; asst. dir. Nat. Ash Assn., Washington, 1968-72; staff mining engr. U.S. Bur. Mines, Washington, 1972-82, divsn. chief, 1982-95; ret., 1995; mem. U.S. Nat. Com. for Tunneling Tech., Nat. Acad. Scis., Washington, 1985-90, chmn., 1988-89; lectr. in field. Contbr. articles to profl. jours., chpts. to books. Recipient Superior Svc. award Dept. Interior, 1980, Meritorious Svc. award, 1986, Disting. Svc. award, 1991, Presdl. Rank award, 1991. Mem. Fed. Exec. Inst. Alumni Assn., Sr. Execs. Assn., Sigma Xi (life), Tau Beta Pi (life), Masons, Shriners. Republican. Baptist. Avocations: racquetball; tennis; golf. Home: 6819 Brian Michael Ct Springfield VA 22153-1004

MEIKLE, THOMAS HARRY, JR., neuroscientist, foundation administrator, educator; b. Troy, Pa., Mar. 24, 1929; s. Thomas H. and Elizabeth (MacMorran) M.; m. Jane T. Germer, Aug. 26, 1966 (div. 1983); children: David Andrew, Sarah Elizabeth; m. Jacqueline Winterkorn, Sept. 27, 1986. A.B., Cornell U., 1951, M.D., 1954. Intern Jefferson Hosp., Phila., 1954-55; clin. fellow Inst. Neurology, London, Eng., 1957-58; research fellow Inst. Neurol. Scis., U. Pa., Phila., 1958-61; instr., asst. prof., assoc. prof., prof. anatomy Cornell U. Med. Coll., N.Y.C., 1961-87, acting dean medicine, 1976-77, dep. dean, 1977-79, dean, provost, 1980-87; dean Cornell U. Grad. Sch. Med. Scis., 1969-76; v.p. Josiah Macy, Jr. Found., N.Y.C., 1980, pres., 1987—; career scientist Health Research Council, N.Y.C., 1969-71. Served to capt. M.C. AUS, 1955-57, Korea. Markle Found. scholar in acad. medicine, 1963-68. Home and Office: Josiah Macy Jr Found 44 E 64th St New York NY 10021-7306

MEIKLEJOHN, ALVIN J., JR., state senator, lawyer, accountant.; b. Omaha, June 18, 1923; B.S., J.D., U. Denver, 1951; m. Lorraine J. Meiklejohn; children: Pamela Ann, Shelley Lou, Bruce Ian, Scott Alvin. Mem. Colo. Senate from 19th dist., 1976—, chmn. com. edn.; mem. Edn. Commn. of States, 1981—, chmn. Colo. Commn. on Ach. in Edn., 1995; chmn., 1993—. Mem. Jefferson Sch. Dist. No. R-1 Bd. Edn., 1971-77, pres., 1973-77; commr. Commn. on Uniform State Laws, 1988—. Served to capt. U.S. Army, 1940-46; to maj. USAF, 1947-51. Mem. Colo. Soc. CPA's, Arvada C. of C. Republican. Clubs: Masons, Shriners. Home: 7540 Kline Dr Arvada CO 80005-3732 Office: Jones & Keller PC 1625 Broadway Ste 1600 Denver CO 80202-4730

MEIKLEJOHN, DONALD, philosophy educator; b. Providence, June 1, 1909; s. Alexander and Nannine (LaVilla) M.; m. Betty Moore, Aug. 25, 1941; children: Alexander M., Douglas, Elizabeth, Donald Stuart. AB, U. Wis., 1930; PhD, Harvard, 1936. Instr. philosophy Dartmouth, 1936-38; assoc. prof. philosophy Coll. William and Mary, 1938-46; assoc. prof. U. Chgo., 1946-59, prof., 1959-63; chmn. Coll. Social Sci. Group, 1958-61; prof. philosophy and social sci. Syracuse U., 1963—, dir. pub. affairs and citizenship Maxwell Sch., 1963-75, emeritus, 1975—, adj. prof. pub. affairs, 1989-94; vis. prof. Coll. of the Atlantic, Bar Harbor, Maine, 1979-83, faculty, 1983—. Author: Freedom and the Public, 1965; co-author: Participation in Government, 1988; articles in field. Served from pvt. to 1st lt. AUS, 1942-46. Mem. ACLU (dir. Ill.), AAUP, Phi Beta Kappa. Club: Hyde Park Neighborhood (dir.). Home: 822 Maryland Ave Syracuse NY 13210-2501 *A life-long career as a teacher in American colleges has been tremendously rewarding in terms both of intellectual stimulus and personal association. The chance such a career offers to follow, however inadequately, the example of Socrates in questioning the fundamental values and concepts effective in American public life is as much, I believe, as any teacher may fairly expect. For this I am deeply grateful.*

MEIKSIN, ZVI H., electrical engineering educator; b. 1926. BSEE, Israel Inst. Tech., Haifa, 1950, Dipl. Ing., 1951; MSEE, Carnegie Mellon U., 1953; PhDEE, U. Pitts., 1959. Registered profl. engr., Pa. Design engr. McGraw Edison, Cannonsburg, Pa., 1953-54; sr. project engr. Westinghouse Electric Corp., Pitts., 1956-59; prof. dept. elec. engring. U. Pitts., 1959-91; prof. emeritus, 1991—; pres. Transtek, Inc. (formerly Transcom. Co.), Pitts., 1989-95, Transtek, Inc., Pitts., 1995—; cons. entr. 33 orgns. in U.S., Europe, 1959—. Author: Thin & Thick Films, 1976, Active Filter Design, 1990; co-author: Electronic Design, 1980, 84, Microprocessor Based Design, 1986; jour. referee profl. publs., 1970—; contbr. articles to profl. jours.; inventor, holder 6 patents in field. Fellow IEEE (award coms.); mem. Eta Kappa Nu, Sigma Xi. Office: Transtek Inc PO Box 8113 Pittsburgh PA 15217-0113

MEILAN, CELIA, food products executive; b. Bklyn., Jan. 21, 1920; d. Ventura Lorenzo and Susana (Prego) M. Student, CCNY, 1943-46. Codes and ciphers translator security divsn. U.S. Censorship Office, N.Y.C., 1942-46; sec., treas. Albumina Supply Co., N.Y.C., 1946-55; co-founder, co-owner, sec., treas., fin. officer Internat. Proteins Corp., Fairfield, N.J., 1955-86, exec. v.p., 1986-92, pres., 1992-94, chair emeritus, bd. dirs., 1994—; bd. dirs. Pesquera Taboquilla, Panama City, Republic of Panama, 1969—, Inversiones Pesqueras S.A., Brit. V.I.; v.p., bd. dirs. Atlantic Shippers of Tex. Inc., Port Arthur, 1989, Atlantic Shippers Inc., Morehead City, N.C., Empacadora Nacional S.A., Panama City, Republic of Panama; exec. v.p., bd. dirs. Fairfield Fishing Co., Liberia, Internat. Proteins Chile S.A., Santiago. Named One of Top 50 Women Bus. Owners, Working Woman mag. and Nat. Found. Women Bus. Owners, 1994, 95. Mem. Nat. Found. Women Bus. Owners, Spanish Benevolent Soc. (bd. dirs. 1955-62). Avocations: travel, hand crafts, backgammon, puzzles. Office: 204 Passaic Ave Fairfield NJ 07004-3503

MEILGAARD, MORTEN CHRISTIAN, food products executive, international consultant; b. Vigerslev, Denmark, Nov. 11, 1928; s. Anton Christian Meilgaard and Ane Maria Elisa Larsen; m. Manon Meadows, Oct. 29, 1962; children: Stephen Paul, Justin Christian. MSChemE, Tech. U. Denmark, 1952, DS in Food Sci., 1982. Rsch. chemist Carlsberg Breweries, Copenhagen, Denmark, 1947-57; dir. and co-owner Alfred Jorgensen Lab. for Fermentation, Copenhagen, 1957-67; dir. rsch. and devel. Cerveceria Cuauhtemoc, Monterrey, Mex., 1967-73; v.p. rsch. Stroh Brewery Co., Detroit, 1973-89, pres. Strohtech Inc. div., 1986-91; cons., 1991—; vis. prof. Agrl. U. Denmark, 1994—. Author: Sensory Evaluation Techniques, 1987, 2d edit., 1991; contbr. articles to profl. jours. Recipient Schwarz award, 1974. Fellow Inst. Brewing; mem. Internat. Med. Advisory Group, European Chemoreception Rsch. Orgn., Assn. Chemoreception Scis., Inst. Food Technologists, Am. Chem. Soc., Dansk Ingeniorforening, Am. Wine Soc., Air Pollution Control Assn., Master Brewers Assn. Am. (chmn. various coms., award of merit 1990), Am. Soc. Brewing Chemists (chmn. various coms.), ASTM (chmn. various coms., award of merit 1992), U.S. Hop Rsch. Coun. (pres. 1978-80, 1982-84, founder). Avocations: theatre, music, sailing, skiing. Home: 2938 Moon Lake Dr West Bloomfield MI 48323-1841 Office: Stroh Brewery Co 100 River Place Dr Detroit MI 48207-4295

MEILING, GEORGE ROBERT LUCAS, bank holding company executive; b. Columbus, Ohio, Nov. 28, 1942; s. Richard Lewis and Ann Elizabeth (Lucas) M. BA, Yale U., 1964; MBA, Harvard U., 1966. With Chem. Bank, N.Y.C., 1966; contr. Bank One Columbus, Ohio, 1971-73; asst. treas. Banc One Corp., Columbus, 1973-77, treas., 1977—. Mem. alumni bd. Columbus Acad., 1974-78; bd. dirs. Greater Columbus Arts Coun., 1986-87, Pro Musica, 1987-90, AmeriFlora '92, Columbus Light Opera Co., 1990-92; treas., bd. dirs. Am. Rose Soc., 1987-91. Capt. USAF, 1966-69. Mem. Nat. Investor Rels. Inst., Bank Investors Rels. Assn., Yale Alumni (dir. 1978-80), Green Lawn Cemetary Assn. (dir. 1988—), Army and Navy Club, Yale Club, Columbus Club (dir. 1994—), Yale Ctrl. Ohio Club (pres. 1976-78), Columbus Country Club. Anglican. Home: 2654 Henthorn Rd Columbus OH 43221 Office: Banc One Corp 100 E Broad St Columbus OH 43271-0251

MEILING, GERALD STEWART, materials scientist; b. Provo, Utah, Sept. 12, 1936; s. Harry Louis and Iona (Falker) M.; m. Jane Olive Sprunt, July 20, 1962; children—John Scott, William David, Marcine Elizabeth. B.S., U. Utah, 1958; M.S., MIT, 1959, Sc.D., 1966. Sr. scientist Corning, Inc., N.Y., 1966-69, devel. assoc., 1971-76, devel. mgr., 1976-82, dir. devel., 1982-86, dir. rsch., 1986—, v.p., 1988-94, sr. v.p. 1994—; sr. rsch. scientist Signetics, Sunnyvale, Calif., 1969-71; bd. dirs. Samsung Corning, Seoul, Korea; mem. earth scis. adv. bd. Stanford U., 1985—; mem. materials sci. adv. bd. U. Calif. Santa Barbara, Cornell U., Los Alamos (N.Mex.) Nat. Lab. Patentee in photochromics. Fellow Am. Ceramic Soc.; mem. IEEE, N.Y. Acad. Scis., Indsl. Rsch. Inst., Sigma Xi. Republican. Mem. LDS Ch. Office: Corning Inc R&D Labs Sullivan Park Corning NY 14830

MEILMAN, EDWARD, physician; b. Boston, Apr. 6, 1915; s. Harry and Jennie (Sholofsky) M.; m. Rhoeda Berman, Mar. 6, 1946. A.B., Harvard U., 1936, M.D., 1940. Intern Mt. Sinai Hosp., N.Y.C., 1940-42; resident Beth Israel Hosp., Boston, 1946-48; assoc. in med. and med. research Beth Israel Hosp., 1948-53; chmn. dept. medicine L.I. Jewish-Hillside Med. Center, New Hyde Park, N.Y., 1953-82, chmn. emeritus dept. medicine, 1982—; prof. medicine SUNY, Stony Brook, 1971—. Contbr. articles to profl. jours. Served with USAAF, 1942-46. Fellow N.Y. Acad. Medicine, N.Y. Acad. Scis.; mem. Am. Heart Assn. (fellow council clin. cardiology, council arteriosclerosis), Am. Fedn. Clin. Research, Harvey Soc., Am. Rheumatism Assn., Phi Beta Kappa, Alpha Omega Alpha. Democrat. Jewish. Club: Harvard (N.Y.C.); Harvard (L.I.).

MEIMA, RALPH CHESTER, JR., corporate execuitve, former foreign service officer; b. Chgo., Mar. 29, 1927; s. Ralph Chester and Grace Georgine (Larson) M.; children: Ralph Chester III, Stephen H.; m. Elizabeth B. Frazier, 1994. B.A., U. Americas, Mexico City, 1952; M.B.A., Am. U., 1964. With Carborundum Co., Perth Amboy, N.J., 1952-53, Johns-Manville

Corp., N.Y.C., 1953-58, Security Storage Co., Washington, 1958-61, Dept. Commerce, 1961-68; joined U.S. Fgn. Service, 1968; consul gen. Marseille, France, 1977-80; on loan as export devel. cons. State of Md., 1980-82; pres. Atlantic Eastern Corp., 1982-87, Phoenix Internat. Mktg. Corp., 1987-89; pres., chief exec. officer FTI Inc., Annapolis, Md., 1989-95; pres. DERCO, Inc., Balt., 1995—. Served with USN, 1945-46. Office: 200 E Joppa Rd Ste 206 Baltimore MD 21286

MEINDL, MAX J., III, environmental consultant; b. Buffalo, N.Y., June 21, 1951; s. Max John Jr. and Doris Elisabeth (Wessel) M.; m. Rachel Pratt, Apr. 23, 1983; 1 child, Elisabeth Bancroft Wessel Meindl. Student, U. St. Thomas, 1973-75, U. Houston, 1983-84, Tex. A & M U., 1989-91. Lic. profl. inspector. Prin. E. Daughter & Co., Houston, 1976-91, Texan Inspection & Environ. Svcs., Houston, 1980-89; program mgr. real estate svcs. TSP Inc., Houston, 1989-91; prin. MJM Cons., Houston, 1991—; cons. Resolution Trust Corp., Houston, 1991, Bridas Oil Co., Argentina; Compaq Computer Corp. facility engr.; coord. Spartan Internat. Project, 1993-95; project mgr., estimator Evans Am. Corp., Disaster Restoration. Mem. disaster relief ARC, Houston; disaster insp. Fed. Emergency Mgmt. Agy.; tech. specialist Bechtel/Sonatrach Algerian Pipeline Project, Algeria, 1995. With USN, 1969-71. Mem. Nat. Assn. Environ. Profls., Am. Assn. Energy and Environ. Engrs., Nat. Asbestos Coun., Nat. Environ. Health Assn., Mensa. Office: MJM Cons PO Box 1464 Houston TX 77251-1464

MEINDL, ROBERT JAMES, English language educator; b. Wausau, Wis., Sept. 17, 1936; s. George Martin and Adeline Emilie (Goetsch) M.; m. Victoria Lynn Chavez; children: Karin Rose, George Andrew, Damian Kurt, Erika Wittmer, Christopher Smith, Gabrielle Remelia. BS, U. Wis., 1958; MA, U. Conn., 1960; PhD, Tulane U., 1965. Teaching asst. U. Conn., Storrs, 1958-60; teaching fellow Tulane U., 1960-62; lectr. U. Wis., Green Bay, 1963-65; from asst. to full prof. English Calif. State U., Sacramento, 1965—. Translator: Studies in John Gower, 1981; book rev. editor Studia Mystica Jour., 1984-89; contbr. numerous articles to profl. jours. With USNR, 1953-61, 79-96. Mem. MLA, Medieval Acad. Am., Medieval Assn. of Pacific, Early English Text Soc., John Gower Soc., New Chaucer Soc. Home: 2301 Pennland Dr Sacramento CA 95825-0329 Office: Calif State U 6000 J St Sacramento CA 95819-2605

MEINEL, ADEN BAKER, optics scientist; b. Pasadena, Calif., Nov. 25, 1922; s. John G. and Gertrude (Baker) M.; m. Marjorie Steele Pettit, Sept. 5, 1944; children: Carolyn, Walter, Barbara, Elaine, Edward, Mary, David. AB, U. Calif., Berkeley, 1947, PhD, 1949; DSc (hon.), U. Ariz., 1990, U. Ariz., 1990. Assoc. prof. Yerkes Obs., U. Chgo., Williams Bay, Wis., 1950-57; dir. Kitt Peak Nat. Obs., Tucson, 1958-60; prof. U. Ariz., Tucson, 1961-85; dir. Steward Obs., Tucson, 1962-67, Optical Scis. Ctr., Tucson, 1966-73; Disting. scientist Jet Propulsion Lab., Pasadena, 1985-93; ret., 1993; regent Calif. Luth. Coll., 1961-71; cons. USAF Spl. Projects Office, 1965-80. Co-author: Applied Solar Energy, 1976, Sunsets, Twilights and Evening Skies, 1983. Recipient Warner prize Am. Astron. Soc., 1954, Van Blesbroeck award Astron. Soc. Pacific, 1990, NASA Exceptional Scientific Achievement medal, 1993; Aden B. Meinel bldg. U. Ariz., dedicated 1993. Fellow Am. Acad Arts and Scis., Optical Soc. Am. (pres. 1972-73, Adolph Lomb medal 1952, Ives medal 1980), Internat. Optical Engring. Soc. (Goddard award 1984, Kingslake medal and prize, 1993). Home: 1600 Shoreline Dr Santa Barbara CA 93109-2024

MEINERS, LOUIS MELVIN, JR., accountant, lawyer; b. Louisville, Oct. 4, 1950; s. Louis M. and Norma J. (Reasor) M.; children: Kenneth, Suzanne, Laura, Valarie. BS in Commerce and Acctg., U. Louisville, 1971, JD, 1976. CPA, Ky., Ind. Sr. acct. Amick and Helm, Louisville, 1972-73; tax supr. Touche Ross and Co., Louisville, 1974-78; tax mgr. Blue and Co., Indpls., 1978-79, co-owner, dir. tax dept., 1979—. Mem. AICPA, ABA, Ind. CPA Soc. (chmn. taxation com. 1977—), Ind. Bar Assn., Hunting Creek Country Club, Woodland Country Club. Avocations: aviation, tennis, golf. Office: Blue and Co PO Box 80069 Indianapolis IN 46280

MEINERT, JOHN RAYMOND, clothing manufacturing and retailing executive, investment banker; b. White Cloud, Mich., Aug. 11, 1927; m. Joyce Macdonell, Nov. 5, 1955; children: Elizabeth Tinsman, Pamela Martin. Student, U. Mich., 1944-45; B.S., Northwestern U., 1949. C.P.A., Ill., 1952. With Hart Schaffner & Marx/Hartmarx Corp., Chgo., 1950-90, exec. v.p., 1975-80, vice chmn., 1981-85, sr. vice chmn., 1985-86, chmn., 1987-90, chmn. emeritus, 1990—, also bd. dirs.; prin. investment banking, chmn. J.H. Chapman Group, Ltd., Rosemont, Ill., 1995—; bd. dirs. The John Evans Club; trustee Amalgamated Ins. Fund, 1980-92; dir. Evanston Hosp., 1988-94; instr. acctg. Northwestern U., 1949; faculty Lake Forest Grad. Sch. Mgmt., 1994-95; arbitrator Am. Arbitration Assn., 1993—. Bd. dirs. Better Bus. Bur.; chmn. bus. adv. coun. U. Ill., 1989-90; mem. Fin. Acctg. Stds. Adv. Coun., 1989-92, Chgo. Coun. Fgn. Rels., Sisters City Com.; mem. adv. coun. Northwestern U. Kellogg Grad. Sch. Recipient Alumni Merit award Northwestern U. Kellogg Grad. Sch., 1989; named Humanitarian of Yr., Five Hosp. Found., 1995. Mem. AICPA (v.p. 1985-86, bd. dirs. 1975-78, coun. 1971-93, trustee benevolent fund 1992-95, gold medal 1987), Ill. CPA Soc. (pub. svc. award 1996, pres. 1982-83, bd. dirs. 1966-68, 81-84, hon. award), Clothing Mfrs. Assn. (bd. dirs. 1980-90, pres. 1982-87, chmn. 1987-90), Chgo. C. of C. (bd. dirs.), Rotary (pres. Chgo. 1989-90, trustee found. 1991-95), Univ. Club, Execs. Club, Rolling Green Country Club. Presbyterian (elder). Home: 634 N Ironwood Dr Arlington Heights IL 60004-5818 Office: J H Chapman Group Ltd 9700 W Higgins Rd Des Plaines IL 60018-4796

MEINIG, DONALD WILLIAM, geography educator; b. Palouse, Wash., Nov. 1, 1924; s William August and Annie (Malsed) M.; m. Lee McAuliffe, June 29, 1946; children: Laurel, Kristin, Lee. B.S., Georgetown U., 1948; M.A., U. Wash., 1950, Ph.D., 1953; DHL (hon.), Syracuse U., 1994. From asst. prof. to assoc. prof. U. Utah, Salt Lake City, 1950-59; assoc. prof. geography Syracuse U., N.Y., 1959-73, Maxwell prof. geography, 1973-89; Maxwell rsch. prof. Syracuse U., 1990—; lectr. St. Andrews U., Scotland, 1973, Charles Homer Haskins lectr. ACLS, 1992; vis. prof. Hebrew U., Jerusalem, 1974; adv. editor Wadsworth Pub. Co., 1957-61, Harper & Row, N.Y.C., 1965-83; chief editl. cons. Nat. Geog. Soc., Washington, 1982-88, councilor, 1993-96. Author: On the Margins of the Good Earth, 1962, The Great Columbia Plain, 1968, Imperial Texas, 1969, Southwest, 1971, The Shaping of America, Vol. 1: Atlantic America 1492-1800, 1986, Vol. 2: Continental America 1800-1867, 1993; editor: The Interpretation of Ordinary Landscapes, 1979. Mem. N.Y. Council for Humanities, 1979-86. Served to 2d lt. U.S. Army, 1943-46. Recipient Emil and Kathleen Sick award in Western History, 1968, award of Merit Seattle Hist. Soc., 1968, award of Merit Am. Assn. State and Local History, 1969, Summerfield G. Roberts award Sons Republic of Tex., 1969, Faculty Enrichment award Can Embassy, 1980, Master Tchr. award Nat. Coun. for Geog. Edn., 1986, Charles P. Daly medal Am. Geog. Soc., 1986; Fulbright rsch. scholar U. Adelaide, 1958; Guggenheim fellow, 1966-67, NEH fellow, 1987-88. Fellow Brit. Acad. (corr.); mem. Assn. Am. Geographers (councilor 1965-67, Meritorious Contbn. award), Am. Antiquarian Soc. Office: Syracuse U Dept Geography Syracuse NY 13244-1090

MEINKE, PETER, writer, retired educator; b. Bklyn., Dec. 29, 1932; s. Harry Frederick Meinke and Kathleen Dorothy (McDonald) Lewis; m. Jeanne Clark, Dec. 14, 1957; children: Perrie Sue, Peter Thomas, Gretchen, Timothy Clark. AB, Hamilton Coll., 1955; MA, U. Mich., 1961; PhD, U. Minn., 1965. Tchr. Mountain Lakes (N.J.) High Sch., 1958-60; instr. Hamline U., St. Paul, 1961-66; prof. literature, dir. writing Eckerd Coll., St. Petersburg, Fla., 1966-93; writer-in-residence Hamline U., St. Paul, 1974, George Washington U., Washington, 1981-82, Thurber House, Columbus, Ohio, 1987, Davidson (N.C.) Coll., 1989, Austin Peay State U., Clarksville, Tenn., 1995; writer-in-residence, vis. disting. writer U. Hawaii, 1993; vis. disting. writer U. N.C., Greensboro, 1996. Author: Night Watch on the Chesapeake, 1987, The Piano Tuner, 1986 (Flannery O'Connor award for short fiction 1986), Trying to Surprise God, 1981, The Rat Poems, 1978, The Night Train and the Golden Bird, 1977, Underneath the Lantern, 1986, Liquid Paper: New and Selected Poems, 1991, Far From Home, 1987, Scars, 1996, Campocorto, 1996. With U.S. Army, 1955-57. Recipient Gustav Davidson award, 1976, Lucille Medwick award, 1984, Robert A. Staub Outstanding Tchr. award Eckerd Coll., 1990, Emily Dickinson award, 1992, Paumanok Poetry award, 1993; creative writing fellow Nat. Endowment for Arts, 1974, 89; named Fulbright Sr. Lectr., U. Warsaw, 1978-79; Master Artists's fellowship, 1995. Mem. PEN, Poetry Soc. Am., Nat. Book Critics Circle. Avocations: sports, music. Home: 147 Wildwood Ln SE Saint Petersburg FL 33705-3222

MEINKE, ROY WALTER, electrical engineer, consultant; b. Cleve., Aug. 7, 1929; s. George F. and Marie (Reyer) M. BS, Miami U., Oxford, Ohio, 1952; postgrad. Ohio State U., 1952-53, 67-68; postgrad. in engring. Columbia Pacific U., 1985—. Asst. instr. dept. math. Ohio State U., Columbus, 1953; tchr. high sch., Edgerton, Ohio, 1953-54, Kingman, Ariz., 1954-56; aerodynamics engr. N.Am. Aviation, Los Angeles, 1956-57; instr. physics dept. Central State Coll., Edmond, Okla., 1957-58; elec. engr. Boeing Co., Seattle, 1958-62, Huntsville, Ala., 1962-74; mem. staff engring. mgmt. Lockheed Corp., Houston, 1974-88; ind. lectr., cons. on aerospace dynamic system, 1988—. Co-pilot Mercy Flight Systems, 1973-74; treas. Houston United Campus Christian Life Com., 1983; dir. S.E. Conf. Chs., 1969-73; rep. Tex. Conf. Chs., 1989-93; judge Harris County Optimists Club Youth Scholarship Fund, 1983-85. Recipient Apollo Achievement award NASA, 1970, Group Achievement awards, 1979, 82, 83; recipient Phase III Pilot Proficiency Wings Dept. Transp., 1982, Awareness Cert. of Appreciation, NASA, 1987. Mem. IEEE (sr.), AIAA (assoc. fellow 1991), AAAS. Mem. United Ch. of Christ. Home: 10212 Longmont Houston TX 77042

MEINS, JOHN, publishing executive. Pres. Parents Mag., N.Y.C., 1994—. Office: Parents Magazine 685 3rd Ave New York NY 10017

MEIROVITCH, LEONARD, engineering educator; b. Maxut, Romania, Nov. 28, 1928; came to U.S., 1956, naturalized, 1964; s. Carol and Adelle (Schoenfeld) M.; m. Jo Anne Reifer, Oct. 15, 1960. BSc summa cum laude, Technion-Israel Inst. Tech., 1953; MS in Engring., UCLA, 1957, PhD, 1960. Structural engr. Water Planning for Israel, Tel Aviv, 1953-55; asst. sect. head Water Planning for Israel, 1955-56; asst. research engr., asso. in engring. UCLA, 1956-60; staff engr. IBM, Endicott, N.Y., 1960-62; asso. prof. Ariz. State U., 1962-66; prof. U. Cin., 1967-71, Va. Poly. Inst. and State U., Blacksburg, 1971-79; Reynolds Metals prof. Va. Poly. Inst. and State U., 1979-83, Univ. disting. prof., 1983—; cons. Goodyear Aerospace, Phoenix, 1962-63; cons. C.S. Draper Labs., Cambridge, Mass., 1976-78, Naval Research Lab., Washington, 1977-79, Intelsat, Washington, 1980-82. Author: Analytical Methods in Vibrations, 1967, Methods of Analytical Dynamics, 1970, Elements of Vibration Analysis, 1975, 2d edit., 1986, Computational Methods in Structural Dynamics, 1980, Introduction to Dynamics and Control, 1985, Dynamics and Control of Structures, 1990, also articles; assoc. editor Jour. Spacecraft and Rockets, 1971-76, Jour. Optimization Theory and Applications, 1984—; mem. internat. editorial bd. Jour. European Mechanics, 1977-93. Served with Israeli Army, 1948-49. Recipient Alumni award for rsch. excellence Va. Poly. Inst. and State U., 1981, Japan Soc. Mech. Engrs. medal, 1989, Alexander von Humboldt Sr. Rsch. award Germany, 1991; Am. Soc. Engring. Edn.-NASA fellow, 1964; NAS sr. rsch. assoc. Langley Rsch. Ctr., Hampton, Va., 1966-67. Fellow AIAA (Structures, Structural Dynamics and Materials award 1983, Pendray Aerospace Lit. award 1984, Mechanics and Control of Flight award 1987); mem. Sigma Xi, Tau Beta Pi. Home: 303 Neil St Blacksburg VA 24060-2542

MEIROWITZ, CLAIRE CECILE, public relations executive; b. Frankfurt, Fed. Republic Germany, Jan. 14, 1934; came to U.S., 1939; d. Karl and Margot (Herrmann) Bier; m. Richard Meirowitz, Sept. 12, 1954 (div., July, 1969); children: Diane, Laura, Linda; m. Joseph Spiegel, Apr. 20, 1975. AA, Nassau Community Coll., 1971; BA magna cum laude, Hofstra U., 1976; postgrad., N.Y. Inst. Tech., 1987-90. Pres., owner, editor, writer Profl. Editing Svcs., Massapequa Park, N.Y., 1972-76, 92—; editorial asst. United Technical Publs., Garden City, N.Y., 1976-77; publs. assoc. N.Y. Inst. Tech., Old Westbury, N.Y., 1977-79; asst. dir. coll. rels., dir. publs. SUNY, Old Westbury, 1979-87, dir. of community rels. and publs., 1987-92; pres. SUNY Coun. for Univ. Affairs and Devel., 1987-89; cons. Guarino Graphics, Greenville, N.Y., 1985-92, editor, copywriter, 1986-92. Manuscript editor Jour. of Collective Negotiations in Pub. Sector, 1972-91, editr., 1991—, Jour. of Individual Employment Rights, 1992—; editor art catalog South Africa/South Bronx, 1981 (art excellence award 1982); author: New Student Prospectus, The College at Old Westbury, 1979, Labor-Management Relations Among Government Workers, 1983; co-editor: Strategies for Impasse Resolution, 1992; editor Alzheimer's Assn. L.I. chpt. newsletter; contbr. articles to profl. jours. v.p., treas., sec., Taxpayers Edn. Assn., Hicksville, N.Y., 1962-68; mem. The Nature Conservancy, Cold Spring Harbor, N.Y., 1980—. Recipient Excellence in Profl. Svc. award SUNY at Albany, 1987, Disting. Svc. award SUNY Coun. Univ. Affairs, 1989, award for excellence in communications SUNY Westbury Alumni Assn., 1992, award for disting. leadership L.I. Women's Coun. for Equal Edn., Employment and Tng., 1992. Mem. L.I. Communicators Assn., Internat. Assn. of Bus. Communicators. Democrat. Jewish. Avocation: computers. Home: 167 Cadman Ave Babylon NY 11702-1607

MEIS, PAUL JEAN, obstetrics and gynecology educator; b. Sioux City, Iowa, Oct. 29, 1934; s. Lee Francis and Dorothy (Trexlar) M.; m. Marcia Rose Donsker, June 28, 1958; children: Steven James, Douglas John. BS, U. Iowa, 1956, MD, 1959. Diplomate Am. Bd. Ob-Gyn., Am. Bd. Maternal-Fetal Medicine. Intern Martin Army Hosp., Ft. Benning, Ga., 1959-60; resident ob/gyn. SUNY Upstate Med. Ctr., Syracuse, 1962-65; pvt. practice, La Crosse, Wis., 1965-75; fellow Harbor Gen. Hosp., Torrance, Calif., 1975-77; asst. prof. dept. ob-gyn. Bowman Gray Sch. Medicine Wake Forest U., Winston-Salem, N.C., 1977-80, assoc. prof., 1980-85, prof., 1985—. Capt. M.C., U.S. Army, 1959-62. Office: Bowman Gray Sch Medicine Dept Ob-Gyn Medical Center Blvd Winston Salem NC 27157

MEISCH, JANENE KAY, women's health nurse; b. Caledonia, Minn., Aug. 10, 1950; d. Charles Arvid and Alma Leota (Kannenberg) Rollins; m. Arnold Leo Meisch, Nov. 2, 1968; children: Kelly, Abigail. ADN, Western Wis. Tech. Coll., LaCrosse, 1979. Cert. reproductive endocrinology/infertility NAACOG. Staff nurse ob/gyn. Luth. Hosp. LaCrosse, 1979-86; staff nurse ob/gyn. Gundersen Clinic, LaCrosse, 1986-87, staff nurse infertility, 1987-91, nurse clinician, 1991—; cons. Infertility Support Group, 1988—. Mem. Nurses Profl. Group Am. Soc. Reproductive Medicine, Am. Fertility Soc. Avocations: boating, counted cross stitch, reading, quilting. Office: Gundersen Clinic Ltd 1836 South Ave La Crosse WI 54601-5429

MEISEL, ALAN, law educator; b. Newark, Dec. 24, 1946; s. Stanley and Beatrice (Katz) M.; m. Linda S. Serody, Mar. 6, 1982; children: Matthew, Julia. BA, Yale U., 1968, JD, 1972. Bar: Conn. 1972, Pa. 1973, U.S. Dist. Ct. Conn. 1972, U.S. Dist. Ct. (we. dist.) Pa. 1973, U.S. Ct. Appeals (3d cir.) 1985. Assoc. Goldstein & Peck, P.C., Bridgeport, Conn., 1972-73; prof. psychiatry U. Pitts., 1973—, prof. law, 1976—, Dickie, McCamey Chilcote prof. bioethics/law and psychiatry, 1995—, co-dir. Ctr. Med. Ethics, 1986-91, dir., 1991—; asst. dir. for legal studies Pres.'s Commn. for Study of Ethical Problems in Medicine and Biomed. and Behavioral Rsch., Washington, 1982; mem. ethics working group Presdl. Task Force on Healthcare Reform, 1993. Author: The Right to Die, 1989, 2d edit., 1995; co-author: Informed Consent: A Study of Decision Making in Psychiatry, 1984, Informed Consent: Legal Theory and Clinical Practice, 1987; contbr. articles to legal and med. jours. Grantee NIMH, grantee Pres.'s Commn. for Study of Ethical Problems in Medicine and Biomed. and Behavioral Research, 1981-82, Founds. Fund for Research in Psychiatry grantee, 1979-82, Legal Services Corp. grantee, 1985-87; fellow Hastings Ctr.; award for The Right to Die Am. Assn. Publs., 1989. Office: U Pitts Sch Law Pittsburgh PA 15260

MEISEL, GEORGE IRA, lawyer; b. Cleve., May 5, 1920; s. Herman George and Ethel Lynn (Wright) M.; m. Gladys Ulch, 1946; children: Scott, Craig, David, Keith. A.B., Case Western Res. U., 1942; LL.B., Harvard U., 1948. Bar: Ohio 1948. Assoc. Williams, Eversman & Morgan, Toledo, 1948-51; assoc. Squire, Sanders & Dempsey, Cleve., 1951-58, ptnr., 1958—, vice chmn. mgmt. com., 1980-81, chmn. mgmt. com., 1981-86, sr. ptnr., 1986-87, ret., 1987; bd. dirs. Harris Corp., Melbourne, Fla., 1983-92. Pres. Cleve. Hearing & Speech Center, 1960-61; sec.-treas. Greater Cleve. Growth Assn., 1980-81, chmn. 1984-86. Served with USAAF, 1942-46. Mem. ABA (chmn. litigation sect. 1973-74), Ohio Bar Assn., Bar Assn. Greater Cleve. (pres. 1975-76), Am. Coll. Trial Lawyers, Internat. Assn. Def. Counsel (exec. com. 1977-80, sec.-treas. 1987-90) 6th Circuit Jud. Conf. Home: 13411 NW Wax Myrtle Trl Palm City FL 34990-4826 Office: Squire Sanders & Dempsey Society Center Cleveland OH 44115

MEISEL, GEORGE VINCENT, lawyer; b. St. Louis, Sept. 24, 1933; s. Leo Otto and Margaret (Duggan) M.; m. Joy C. Cassin, May 18, 1963. B.S. summa cum laude, St. Louis U., 1956, J.D. cum laude, 1958. Bar: Mo. 1958. Assoc. Grand Peper & Martin, St. Louis, 1961-64; ptnr. Grand Peper & Martin, 1965; jr. ptnr. Bryan Cave McPheeters & McRoberts, St. Louis, 1966-69; ptnr. Bryan Cave, St. Louis, 1970—. Served to 1st lt. USAF, 1958-61. Mem. ABA, Bar Assn. Met. St. Louis, Mo. Bar Assn. Roman Catholic. Clubs: Saint Louis, Mo. Athletic (St. Louis). Home: 2029 S Warson Rd Saint Louis MO 63124-1151

MEISEL, JEROME, electrical engineer; b. Cleve., Aug. 9, 1934; s. David and Anne Irene (Meisel) Marmorstein; children: Denise Lauren, David Marc. B.S. in Elec. Engring. (Union Carbide scholar), Case Inst. Tech., 1956, Ph.D., 1961; M.S. (Mpls. Honeywell fellow), MIT, 1957. Asst. prof. elec. engring. Case Inst. Tech., 1960-65; mem. tech. staff Bell Telephone Labs., Holmdel, N.J., 1965-66; mem. faculty Wayne State U., Detroit, 1966—; prof. elec. engring. Wayne State U., 1970—, acting chmn. dept., 1985-87; cons. in field. Author: Principles of Electromechanical Energy Conversion, 1966; also articles. Sr. mem. IEEE. Home: 156 Linden Rd Birmingham MI 48009-1609 Office: Wayne State U Dept Elec Engring Detroit MI 48202

MEISEL, JOHN, political scientist; b. Vienna, Austria, Oct. 23, 1923; s. Fryda and Ann M. BA, U. Toronto, 1948, MA, 1950; PhD in Polit. Sci., London Sch. Econs., 1959; LLD (hon.), Brock U., 1983, U. Guelph, 1985, Carleton U., 1990, U. Toronto, 1993; DU (hon.), U. Ottawa, 1983; D of Scis. Sociales, Laval U., 1988. Head dept. polit. studies Queen's U., Kingston, Ont., Can., 1963-67, Hardy prof. polit. sci., 1963-80; former chmn. Can. Radio-TV and Telecomms. Commn.; Sir Edward Peacock prof. polit. sci. emeritus Queens' U.; moderator symposia on finding common grounds for polit. issues confronting Yugoslavia, UN, Vienna, 1995. Author: The Canadian General Election of 1957, 1962, Papers on the 1962 Election, 1964, Ethnic Relations in Canadian Voluntary Associations, 1972, Working Papers on Canadian Politics, 1975; editor: Internat. Polit. Sci. Rev., 1979-95. Decorated officer Order of Can.; recipient Killam award Can Coun., 1968-73. Fellow Royal Soc. Can. (pres. 1992-95). Home: Colimaison, Tichborne, ON Canada K0H 2V0 Office: Queen's U, Kingston, ON Canada K7L 3N6

MEISEL, MARTIN, English and comparative literature educator; b. N.Y.C., Mar. 22, 1931; s. Joseph and Sally (Rössler) Mörsel; m. Martha Sarah Winkley, Dec. 22, 1957; children—Maude Frances, Andrew Avram, Joseph Stoddard. A.B., Queens Coll., 1952; M.A., Princeton U., 1957, Ph.D., 1960; postgrad., U. Rome, 1959. Instr. English Rutgers U., New Brunswick, N.J., 1957-58; instr., asst. prof., assoc. prof. Dartmouth Coll., Hanover, N.H., 1959-65; prof. English U. Wis., Madison, 1965-68; prof. English and comparative lit. Columbia U., N.Y.C., 1968—, Brander Matthews prof. dramatic lit., 1987—, chmn. dept., 1980-83, acting v.p. arts and scis., 1986-87, v.p. arts and scis., 1989-93; trustee Columbia U. Press, 1990-94. Author: Shaw and the 19th Century Theater, 1963, Realizations: Narrative, Pictorial, and Theatrical Arts in 19th Century England (George Freedley Meml. award Theater Libr. Assn. 1984, Barnard Hewitt award Am. Theatre Assn. 1984), 1983; mem. editorial and adv. bds. Jour. Victorian Studies, PMLA, Jour. Contemporary Lit., Bull. Rsch. in the Humanities, 19th Century Contexts. Served with U.S. Army, 1954-56. Fellow Guggenheim Found., 1963-64, 1987-88, Am. Council of Learned Socs., 1970-71, Inst. for Advanced Studies in the Humanities, Edinburgh, 1977, Huntington Library and Art Gallery, 1978, 80, 83, Nat. Humanities Ctr., 1983-84, Wilson Ctr., Smithsonian Instn., 1987-88. Mem. MLA, Acad. Lit. Studies, Am. Soc. Theatre Rsch. Home: 18 Bacon Hill Rd Pleasantville NY 10570-3502 Office: Columbia U 611 Philosophy Hall New York NY 10027

MEISEL, STEVEN, advertising photographer; b. 1954; s. Lenny and Sally. Student, Parsons Sch. Design. Illustrator Women's Wear Daily; advt. photographer The Gap, Revlon, Valentino, Anne Klein, Calvin Klein, Gianfranco Ferré, Prada, Dolce and Gabbana, Lancome, Barney's, Donna Karan, Versace; photographer Madonna's Sex, 1992; free-lance photographer Vogue, Harper's Bazaar. Recipient Spl. award Photography Coun. Fashion Designers Am., 1992, Internat. Fashion Photography award Festival Internat. de la Photo de Mode, 1994. Office: Steven Meisel Studio 64 Wooster St Fl 4 New York NY 10012-4350

MEISELAS, SUSAN CLAY, photographer; b. Balt., June 21, 1948; d. Leonard and Murrayl (Groh) M. BA, Sarah Lawrence Coll., 1970; EdM, Harvard U., 1971; DFA (hon.), Parsons Sch./New Sch., N.Y.C., 1988, Art Inst. of Boston, 1996. Photographic cons. Community Resources Inst., N.Y.C., 1972-74; artist-in-residence S.C. Arts Commn., 1974-75; photography tchr. New Sch., N.Y.C., 1975; free-lance photographer Magnum Photos, N.Y.C., 1976—, v.p., 1986-91. Author: Carnival Strippers, 1976, Nicaragua, 1981; co-editor: El Salvador, 1983; editor: Chile from Within, 1991; editor Learn to See, 1974; co-dir.: (film) Living at Risk, 1985, Pictures from a Revolution, 1991. Recipient Robert Capa gold medal Overseas Press Club, 1979, Leica award of excellence New Sch., 1981, Photojournalist of Yr. award Am. Soc. Mag. Photographers, 1981, award Nat Endowment for Arts, 1987, Hasselblad Found., 1994, Maria Moors Cabot prize Columbia U., 1994; MacArthur fellow, 1992. Office: Magnum Photos Inc 151 W 25th St New York NY 10001-7204

MEISELS, GERHARD GEORGE, academic administrator, chemist, educator; b. Vienna, May 11, 1931; came to U.S., 1951, naturalized, 1961; s. Leo and Adele Josefa Maria (Seehofer) M.; m. Sylvia Claire Knopsnider, June 28, 1958; 1 dau., Laura Germaine. Student, U. Vienna, 1949-51, 52-53; M.S., U. Notre Dame, Ind., 1952, Ph.D., 1956. Postdoctoral research assoc. U. Notre Dame, 1955-56; chemist Gulf Oil Corp., Pitts., 1956-59; part time instr. Carnegie Inst. Tech., Pitts., 1956-58; chemist nuclear div. Union Carbide Corp., Tuxedo, N.Y., 1959-63; asst. group leader Union Carbide Corp., 1964-65; assoc. prof. U. Houston, 1965-70, prof., 1970-75, dept. chmn., 1973-75; prof., chmn. dept. chemistry U. Nebr., Lincoln, 1975-81, dean Coll. Arts and Scis., 1981-88; provost, COO U. South Fla., Tampa, 1988-94; dir. Coalition Sci. Literacy, 1994—; cons. Union Carbide Corp., Gearhart-Owen Industries. Editor: spl. issue Jour. Radiation Physics and Chemistry, 1980; contbr. writings in field to profl. publs. Sec., pres. Ramsey (N.J.) Jr. C. of C., 1959-64; active All Children's Hosp. Rsch. Bd. Fulbright fellow, Smith-Mundt fellow, 1951-52; sr. fellow Sci. Research Council, Eng., 1976. Mem. Am. Chem. Soc. (com. chmn.), Am. Soc. for Mass Spectrometry (charter, com. chmn., v.p. 1984-86, pres. 1986-88, bd. dirs. 1988-90), Nebr. Acad. Scis., AAAS, Am. Phys. Soc., Coun. Sci. Soc. Pres. (exec. bd. 1989-92, chmn. elect 1990, chmn. 1991, chmn. com. on sci. priorities), Coun. for Chem. Rsch. (bd. dirs. 1982-85), Sigma Xi. Clubs: Houston Kennel (bd. dirs. 1968-70), Cornhusker Kennel (pres., bd. dirs., del. to Am. Kennel Club 1976-81), St. Petersburg Dog Fanciers Assn. (sec. 1996—). Home: 870 3rd Ave S Tierra Verde FL 33715-2223 Office: U South Fla 100 5th Ave S Saint Petersburg FL 33701-5010

MEISEN, AXEL, chemical engineering educator, university dean; b. Hamburg, Germany, Oct. 17, 1943; came to Can., 1966; s. Paul and Emmi (Schaaf) M.; children: Nadine Ramona, Kai Noel. B.Sc., Imperial Coll., 1965; M.Sc., Calif. Inst. Tech., 1966; Ph.D., McGill U., 1970. Registered profl. engr., B.C. Asst. prof. chem. engring. U. B.C., Vancouver, 1969-74, assoc. prof., 1975-79, assoc. dean, 1976-85, prof., 1979—, dean, 1985—; environ. engr. Imperial Oil Enterprise Ltd., Sarnia, Ont., 1974-75. Contbr. articles to profl. jours. Chmn. Can. Engring. Accreditation Bd., 1989-90. Fellow Chem. Inst. Can., Instn. Engrs. Ireland, Can. Acad. Engring.; mem. Can. Soc. Chem. Engrs. (pres. 1994), Assn. Profl. Engrs. B.C., Vancouver Club. Office: U BC Office of Dean, 2006-2324 Main Mall, Vancouver, BC Canada V6T 1Z4

MEISINGER, HENRY PETER, electronics engineer; b. N.Y., Mar. 24, 1921; s. Henry Paul and Sophie (Denenberg) M.; m. Jeane Alma Van Horn, June 1940 (dec. Aug. 1961); children: Shannon Peter, Daniel Claude, Mark Colin; m. Catherine C. Stephenson, Oct. 1962; 1 child, Mary Cover; m. Susan Barney Cushing, June 25, 1969. Registered profl. engr., D.C. Chief engr. U.S. Recording Co., Washington, 1940-41; engr. radio station WINX, Washington, 1940-42; engr. Recording Lab. Libr. Congress, Washington,

1941-42; engr. in charge Radio Sect. Dept. Interior, Washington, 1942-47; chief engr. U.S. Recording Co., Washington, 1947-54; dir. engr. Lab. Elec. Engring., Washington, 1954-58; pres. Versitron Inc., Washington, 1958-85; pres. elec. group Keene Corp., N.Y.C., 1982-85; cons. engr. Vienna, Va., 1985—; dir. NationsBank D.C., 1984-94; adv. Nat. Security Agy., Ft. Meade. Contbr articles to profl. jours. Pres. Cen. H.S. Alumni Assn., 1976-77. Capt. USMC, 1943-46, PTO, 1950-52, Korea. Fellow Audio Engring. Soc. (chmn. 1974-76); mem. Inst. Radio Engrs. (chmn. 1952-54, Disting. Svc. award 1962, sr.), Wash. Audio Soc. (pres. 1949-50), Ind. Telephone Pioneers (pres. 1973-74). Achievements include pioneer work in fiber optics, loudspeaker system design, and microgroove disk recording. Home and Office: 8618 Wolftrap Rd Vienna VA 22182-5025

MEISLICH, HERBERT, chemistry educator emeritus; b. Bklyn., Mar. 26, 1920; s. Isidore and Bessie (Rose) M.; m. Estelle Kalechstein, July 1, 1951; children—Mindy, Debrah, Susan. A.B., Bklyn. Coll., 1940; A.M., Columbia U., 1947, Ph.D., 1950. With Edgewood Arsenal, Md., 1942-44; asst. prof. chemistry CCNY, 1946-62, assoc. prof., 1963-68, prof., 1969-86, prof. emeritus, 1986—. Author: Introduction to Organic Chemistry, 1960, Fundamentals of Chemistry, 1966, 5th edit., 1980, Introduction to Chemistry, 1968, Schaum's Organic Chemistry, 1977, 2d edit., 1991, Schaum's 3000 Solved Problems in Organic Chemistry, 1993. Mem. New Milford (N.J.) Bd. Edn., 1967-81. Served to lt. (j.g.) USN, 1944-46. Sloan Kettering fellow, 1956. Mem. Am. Chem. Soc. (past chmn. N.Y. sect., councilor). Home: 338 Lacey Dr New Milford NJ 07646-1128 Office: CUNY Dept Chemistry Convent Ave # 138th St New York NY 10027

MEISLIN, HARVEY WARREN, emergency healthcare physician, professional society administrator; b. June 19, 1946; s. Milton M. and Celia (Weiner) M.; m. Loretta Marie Bielski, Apr. 30, 1977; children: Justin, Jonathan, Megan. BS in Chemistry, Purdue U., 1968; MD, Ind. U., 1972. Diplomate Am. Bd. Emergency Medicine, Am. Bd. Med. Spltys. (del. 1990, fin. com. 1992, exec. com. 1994); cert. cardiac life support, ACLS instr., advanced trauma life support instr. Intern U. Chgo. Hosps. and Clinics, 1973-75, resident, 1975-77, dir. div. emergency medicine, 1975-77; asst. prof. internal and emergency medicine UCLA Emergency Med. Ctr., 1977-80, resident dir. emergency medicine, 1977-80, assoc. dir., 1977-80; assoc. prof. dept. surgery emergency medicine Coll. Medicine, U. Ariz., Tucson, 1980-83, assoc. prof., 1983-85; assoc. head, dept. surgery U. Ariz., Tucson, 1995—; prof. Coll. Medicine, U. Ariz., Tucson, 1985—; chief emergency medicine U. Ariz., Tucson, 1980—; chief sect. emergency medicine dept. surgery Ariz. Health Scis. Ctr., Tuscon, 1980—, dir. emergency svcs. Univ. Med. Ctr., 1980—, dir. Ariz. Emergency Med. Rsch. Ctr., 1990—; med. dir. MEDTRAN-Aeromed. Ambulance Corp., 1985-88; mem. emergency med. svc. com. Mid-South Health Planning Orgn., Chgo., 1974; coord. Mid-South Disaster Plan, Chgo., 1974; mem. com. revision of Disaster Plan Billings Hosp., 1974-76; mem. faculty Am. Hosp. Assn. Inst. Disaster Preparedness, 1975; vis. prof. dept. emergency medicine Denver Gen. Hosp., 1977; bd. trustees Emergency Med. Found., 1978-81; mem. med. adv. com. L.A. City Fire Dept., 1979-80; chmn.-elect Tuscon Met. EMS Coun., 1983-84, chmn., 1984-85; chmn. Tuscon Pre-Hosp. Care Coun., 1981; mem. trauma steering com. So. Ariz. Regional Trauma Ctr., 1986-88; mem. ETHICON emergency physicians adv. panel Johnson & Johnson Co., 1987-92; presenter and lectr. in field. Editor: Purdue Rivet, 1971-72, abstract sect. Annals Emergency Medicine, 1982-90, EMS sect., 1989-90; guest editor: Topics in Emergency Medicine, 1979; sci. editor: Drug Therapy, 1984—; mem. editorial bd.: Annals Emergency Medicine, 1977-90, Emergency Dept. News, 1979-87, Emergency Dept. and Ambulatory Care News, 1987-90, Digest of Emergency Medicine Care, 1981-87; contbr. articles and revs. to profl. jours. Mem. select med. adv. com. City of Tucson, 1981, med. dir. emergency med. svcs., 1982-83, 84-85; bd. dirs. so. Ariz. divsn. Am. Heart Assn., 1985-90; mem. emergency cardiac care com. so. divsn. Ariz. Heart Assn., 1986-88; mem. med. dirs. commn., dept. health svcs. State of Ariz., 1992—, also mem. Mex. border commn., 1991—; mem. med. direction commn. State of Ariz. (appointed by gov.), 1993—. Recipient Pres. gavel and plaque Am. Bd. Emergency Medicine. Fellow Am. Coll. Emergency Physicians (State of Ill. chpt.): mem. sci. adv. com. 1975, mem. sci. edn. com. 1975-76, mem. grad./undergrad. edn. com. 1976-79, mem. ethics com. 1976-77, mem. surgery/trauma task force bd. cert. exam. 1976-77, bd. dirs. 1976-77, chmn. edn. com. 1976-77; State of Calif. chpt.: mem. hosp. and contract com. 1978-79, mem. EMS and legis. com. 1978-79, mem. spl. task force on emergency dept. distbn. 1979-80, mem. membership com. 1979-80, mem. legis. com. 1979-80, mem. sci. assembly planning com. 1980-81, bd. dirs. 1979-81, mem. rsch. com. 1981; State of Ariz. chpt.: bd. dirs. 1982-92, 92—, chmn. pub. rels. com. 1982-83, v.p. and sec. 1983-84, counselor 1984-87, mem. credentials com. 1986-91, chmn. 1987-90, mem. test com. 1986-87, mem. ad hoc com. for combined tng. 1987-88, chmn. task force on emergency medicine 1987-89, mem. exec. com. 1988—, mem. fin. com. 1988—, sec./treas. 1989-90, mem. EMS com. 1990—, pres.-elect 1990-91, pres. 1991-92, chair stds. com., mem. faculty Nat. Sci. Assembly 1974-76, Cert. Appreciation award 1990); mem. APHA, Am. Coll. Physician Execs., Am. Trauma Soc., Am. Bd. Med. Specialties (mem. fin. com. 1992, mem. exec. com. 1995—), Ariz. Med. Assn., Pima County Med. Soc. (bd. dirs. 1991—), Phi Rhions: racquetball, golf, skiing, automobiles. Office: U Ariz Med Ctr Sect Emergency Med 1501 N Campbell Ave Tucson AZ 85724-0001

MEISNER, GARY WAYNE, landscape architect; b. Terre Haute, Ind., Oct. 19, 1949; s. Ervin Gustav and Mary Lou (Maret) M.; children: Christopher Wayne, Kira Valora. BS in Landscape Architecture, Mich. State U., 1972. Lic. landscape architect, Ohio, Mich., Ind., Ill., Ky., W.Va. Designer Huron Clinton Metro Parks, Detroit, 1969, City of East Lansing, Mich., 1970, Fairfax County Park Authority, Annandale, Va., 1971; city design adminstr. Akron (Ohio) Dept. Planning and Urban Devel., 1972-79; prin. Bentley Meisner Assocs., Inc, Cin., 1979-94, Myers, Schmalenberger, Meisner Inc., Cin. and Columbus, Ohio, 1994—. Designer Akron Downtown Plan, 1978, King Sch. Plan, 1980 (honor award 1982), master plan Toyota Regional Office, 1983 (honor award 1987), Falls at Cumberland Hill, 1987 (honor award 1989), Cin. Mus. Ctr., 1990 (honor award 1990), Walk Across Am. Garden, 1990 (honor award 1991), Dayton Nat. Cemetery, 1993 (honor award 1994), Dayton Plaza of Flight (honor award 1995). Trustee Cin. Hillside Trust, 1987—, Capitol Square Renovation Found., Columbus, Ohio, 1987-93, Cin. Sculpture Coun., 1989-94, Hubbard Ednl. Trust, 1988—. Recipient gov.'s commendation State of Ohio, 1985, Ohio Arts Coun. fellow, 1992-93, Apple award Architecture Found. of Cin., 1995. Fellow Am. Soc. Landscape Architects (nat. trustee 1982-89, chmn. nat. cmty. assistance team program 1983-86, chmn. editorial bd. Garden Design mag. 1986-90, chmn. nat. publs. bd. 1988-92, Nat. Com. Assistance Team commendation 1986, Trustee commendation 1989); mem. Am. Soc. Botanic Garden and Arboretum, Urban Land Inst., Am. Underground Space Assn (treas. Ohio Roadside coun. 1985—). Mem. Unity Ch. Home: 4137 Jora Ln Cincinnati OH 45209-1406 Office: Myers Schmalenberger Meisner Inc 2011 Madison Rd Cincinnati OH 45208-3218

MEISNER, JUDITH ANNE, clinical social worker, marital and sex therapist, psychotherapist; b. Dayton, Ohio, Mar. 20, 1931; d. Lowell DeWight and Mary Elizabeth (Anderson) Richardson; m. S. Clair Varner, 1953 (div. 1964); m. Carl E. Meisner, Dec. 31, 1970; children: Christopher, Cynthia, Deborah, Catherine; stepchildren: Janet, Elizabeth, Barbara. BA, Oberlin Coll., 1952; MSW, Fla. State U., 1970; PhD, Inst. Advanced Study Human Sexuality, 1987. Cert. Acad. Cert. Social Workers; bd. cert. diplomate; lic. clin. social worker; lic. marriage and family therapist; diplomate Am. Bd. Sexology, Am. Coll. Sexologists, clin. supr. Am. Bd. Sexology. Psychiat. aide Inst. Living, Hartford, Conn., 1952-53; caseworker, supr. Div. Family Svcs., Dept. Health and Rehabilitative Svcs., St. Petersburg, Fla., 1964-66, 66-68; dir. standing com. on health and rehabilitative svcs. Fla. Ho. Reps. , Fla. State Legis., Tallahassee, 1970-72; adj. prof. grad. sch. social work Fla. State U., Tallahassee, 1972-73; family life cons. Family Counseling Ctr., St. Petersburg, 1973-75; coord. Teenage Info. Program for Students Pinellas County Sch. Bd., St. Petersburg, 1975-78, coord. Citizen's Task Force on Edn. for Family Living, 1978-80; psychotherapist Counseling & Cons. Svcs., St. Petersburg, 1975—; profl. adv. bd. Nat. Found. March of Dimes Pinellas chpt., Clearwater, Fla., 1976-85, Parents Without Ptnrs. chpt. 186, St. Petersburg, 1973—; mem. Family Life Edn. Coun. Pinellas County Sch. Bd., Clearwater, 1980-85. Bd. dirs. Neighborly Sr. Svcs., Clearwater, 1974-85, pres., bd. dirs., 1982, 83; bd. dirs. Marriage and Family Counseling of Pinellas County, Inc., 1993—. Fellow Am. Acad. Clin. Sexologists (life); mem. NASW, Am. Assn. for Marriage and Family Therapists (clin.), Pinellas Assn. for Marriage and Family Therapists (clin.), Am. Assn. Sex. Educators, Counselors and Therapists (life, cert. sex educator, sex therapist), Soc. for the Sci. Study of Sex, Fla. Soc. Clin. Social Workers, Soc. of Neuro-Linguistic Programming (cert. master practitioner), Harry Benjamin Internat. Gender Dysphoria Assn., Fla. Soc. of Clin. Hypnosis. Avocations: tennis, travel, jazz, singing, reading. Home: 7 Marina Ter Treasure Island FL 33706

MEISNER, MARY JO, editor; b. Chgo., Dec. 24, 1951; d. Robert Joseph and Mary Elizabeth (Casey) M.; 1 child, Thomas Joseph Gradel. BS in Journalism, U. Ill., 1974, MS in Journalism, 1976. Copy editor Wilmington (Del.) News Jour., 1975-76, labor and bus. reporter, 1975-79; labor and gen. assignment reporter Phila. Daily News, 1979, city editor, 1979-83, met. editor, 1983-85; PM city editor San Jose (Calif.) Mercury News, 1985-86, met. editor, 1986-87; city editor The Washington Post, 1987-90; mng. editor The Ft. Worth Star-Telegram, 1991-93; editor and v.p. The Milw. Jour., 1993-95; editor, sr. v.p The Milw. Jour. Sentinel, 1995—. Mem. AP Mng. Editors (bd. dirs. 1992-95), Am. Soc. Newspaper Editors, Internat. Press Inst. (bd. dirs. 1994—, Pulitzer prize juror 1994, 96). Office: The Milw Jour Sentinel 333 W State St Milwaukee WI 53201-0371

MEISSNER, ALICE MARTHA, real estate broker; b. Bklyn., June 30, 1926; d. Karl Frederick and Marta Alexandria (Kaipiainen) Nilsson; m. Charles Joseph Meissner, Mar. 31, 1952; children: Gregory, Christopher, Melissa. Diploma, Adelphi Coll., 1946; BS cum laude, Adelphi U., 1949; postgrad., NYU, 1950-51. RN, N.Y.; registered real estate broker, Fla. V.p. North Manor Constrn., Great Neck, N.Y., 1955-58; vol. ARC, Bradenton, Fla., 1960-66; owner, founder Meissner Real Estate, Bradenton, 1969—. Mem. AAUW, Nat. Assn. Realtors, Fla. Assn. Realtors, Manatee County Bd. Realtors, Manatee County Art League, Epsilon Sigma Alpha (v.p. 1970, pres. 1979). Presbyterian. Avocations: art, boating, travel, interior decorating. Home: 500 Palma Sola Blvd Bradenton FL 34209-3226 Office: Meissner Real Estate 4411 60th St W Bradenton FL 34210-2731

MEISSNER, DORIS, federal commissioner; b. Nov. 3, 1941; d. Fred and Hertha H. (Tromp) Borst; m. Charles F. Meissner, June 8, 1963; children: Christine M., Andrew D. BA, U. Wis., 1963, MA, 1969. Asst. dir. student fin. aid U. Wis., 1964-68; exec. dir. Nat. Women's Polit. Caucus, 1971-73; asst. dir. office policy and planning U.S. Dept. Justice, 1975, exec. dir. cabinet com. illegal aliens, 1976, dep. assoc. atty. gen., 1977-80, acting commr. immigration and naturalization svc., 1981, exec. assoc. commr. immigration and naturalization svc., 1982-86; sr. assoc., dir. immigration policy project The Carnegie Endowment for Internat. Peace, 1986-93; commr. immigration and naturalization svc., 1993; adv. coun. U.S./Mex. project Overseas Devel. Coun., 1981-86; trustee Refugee Policy Group, 1987-93; adv. bd. Program for Rsch. on Immigration Policy Rand Corp./Urban inst., 1988-92; cons. panel to comptroller gen. GAO, 1989-93; with Coun. Fgn. Rels., 1990—, Washington Office Latin Am., 1989-93. White Ho. fellow, 1973-74. Mem. Nat. Women's Polit. Caucus (nat. adv. bd. 1976—), White House Fellows Alumni Assn. and Found. (sec., exec. com. 1979-82, Assn. Governing Bds. Colls. and Univs. (panel higher edn. issues 1990-92), Phi Kappa Phi, Mortar Board, Alpha Chi Omega. Office: Dept Justice Immigration & Naturalization Svc 425 I St NW Rm 7100 Washington DC 20536

MEISSNER, DOROTHY THERESA, reading specialist; b. Jersey City, N.J., Apr. 20, 1932; d. John and Mary (Garofalo) Biondo; m. Carl Frederick Meissner; children: Kathleen Ann, Mary Gretl. BA summa cum laude, Jersey City State Coll., 1970, MA summa cum laude, 1974. Cert. tchr. of reading, reading specialist, supr. and adminstr. Metallographer Engelhard Industries, Newark, N.J., 1953-61; 2nd grade tchr. Rutherford (N.J.) Bd. Edn., 1970-74, 4th grade tchr., 1974, reading specialist, 1974-94, 94—; instr. Fairleigh Dickinson U., Rutherford, 1977; spl. edn. steering com. Kearny (N.J.) Pub. Schs., 1968-69; G&T adv. coun. Rutherford Pub. Schs., 1978-79; v.p. Union Fin. Chain, Rutherford, 1985-89, pres., 1989-92; adj. prof. reading dept. Jersey City State Coll. Contbr. articles to profl. jours.; designer sculpture; artist charcoal drawing (hon. mention 1987). Lector Roman Cath. Ch., Kearny, 1988—; coord. William Carlos Williams Project, Rutherford, 1984. Recipient Gov.'s Tchr.'s Recognition State of N.J., 1987; seminar grantee N.J. Coun. for Humanities, 1995. Mem. Internat. Reading Assn. (chair and presenter 1992-93, v.p. 1994-95, pres. 1995—, rec. sec. North Jersey coun. 1996—), Women's Coll. Club, Phi Delta Kappa, Kappa Delta Pi. Avocations: reading, tennis, gardening, art, theater. Home: PO Box 355 Kearny NJ 07032-0355

MEISSNER, EDWIN BENJAMIN, JR., real estate broker; b. St. Louis, Dec. 27, 1918; s. Edwin B. and Edna R. (Rice) M.; m. Nina Renard, Dec. 17, 1946; children: Edwin Benjamin III, Wallace, Robert, Donald. B.S., U. Pa., 1940. Joined St. Louis Car Co., 1934, asst. to pres., v.p., exec. v.p., 1950-56, pres., gen. mgr., 1956-61; pres. St. Louis Car div. Gen. Steel Industries, Inc., 1961-67; sr. v.p., dir. Gen. Steel Industries, Inc., 1968-74; v.p. Bakewell Corp., 1974-85; real estate broker, v.p. Hilliker Corp., St. Louis, 1985—; dir. First Ill. Bank. Mem. pres.' coun. St. Louis U.; bd. dirs. Washington U. Med. Ctr. Redevel. Corp., Barnard Free Skin and Cancer Hosp.; past bd. dirs. James S. McDonnell USO; trustee, bd. dirs. Washington U. Task Force; com., bd. dirs. St. Louis Symphony Youth Orch.; mem. exec. com., outreach com. St. Louis Symphony Soc.; pres., bd. dirs. Humane Soc. Mo.; bd. mgrs. Ctrl. Inst. for Deaf; v.p. Gateway Ctr. Met. St. Louis; chmn. Ladue (Mo.) Police and Fire Commn.; mem. Jefferson Nat. Expansion Meml. Commn., Mo. Arts Coun.; mil. affairs com. Regional Commerce. Mem. St. Louis Flood Assn. (dir.), Am. Ordnance Assn. (life), Internat. Assn. Chiefs of Police (assoc.), Mo. Assn. Chiefs of Police, Mo. Athletics Club, Westwood Country Club, Bridlespur Hunt Club, St. Louis Club, Beta Gamma Sigma. Home: 40 Roan Ln Saint Louis MO 63124-1480 Office: Ste 608 509 Olive st Saint Louis MO 63101-1855

MEISSNER, WILLIAM WALTER, psychiatrist, clergyman; b. Buffalo, Feb. 13, 1931; s. William Walter and Mary Emma (Glauber) M. BA, St. Louis U., 1956, PhL, 1957, MA, 1957; STL, Woodstock Coll., 1962; MD, Harvard U., 1967. Diplomate Am. Bd. Psychiatry and Neurology, Bd. Psychoanalysis. Entered S.J., 1951; intern Mt. Auburn Hosp., Cambridge, Mass., 1967-68; resident Mass. Mental Health Ctr., Boston, 1968-71; mem., instr. Boston Psychoanalytic Inst., 1971—, tng. and supervising analyst, 1980—; staff psychiatrist Mass. Mental Health Ctr., 1971-87, Cambridge (Mass.) Hosp., 1971-78; asst. clin. prof. psychiatry Harvard U. Med. Sch., 1973-76, assoc. clin. prof., 1976-81, clin. prof. psychiatry, 1981-87; prof. psychoanalysis Boston Coll., 1987—. Author: Annotated Bibliography in Religion and Psychology, 1961, Group Dynamics in the Religious Life, 1965, Foundations for a Psychology of Grace, 1966, The Assault on Authority-Dialogue or Dilemma, 1971, Basic Concepts in Psychoanalytic Psychiatry, 1973, The Paranoid Process, 1978, Internationalization in Psychoanalysis, 1981, The Borderline Spectrum, 1984, Psychoanalysis and Religious Experience, 1984, Psychotherapy and the Paranoid Process, 1986, Life and Faith: Psychoanalytic Perspectives on Religious Experience, 1987, Treatment of Patients in the Borderline Spectrum, 1988, What is Effective in Psychoanalytic Therapy, 1991, Ignatius of Loyola: The Psychology of a Saint, 1992; mem. editorial bd. Psychoanalytic Inquiry, 1983—, Jour. Geriatric Psychiatry, 1980—, Rev. of Psychoanalytic Books, 1980-84, Psychoanalytic Study of Society, 1981—, Theol. Studies, 1981-91, Dynamic Psychotherapy, 1982-89, Internat. Forum for Psychoanalysis, 1983—, Internat. Jour. Psychoanalytic Psychotherapy, 1984—, Psychoanalytic Edn., 1990—, Bull. of Menninger Clinic, 1985—, Jour. Am. Psychoanalytic Assn., 1995—, Psychoanalysis and Psychotherapy, 1989—, Internat. Series in Psychology of Religion, 1990—, Am. Jour. Psychotherapy, 1993—. Recipient Deutsch prize Boston Psychoanalytic Inst., 1969. Fellow Am. Psychiat. Assn. (task force on treatments of psychiat. disorders 1989, Oskar Pfister award 1989), Mass. Psychiat. Soc., Ctr. for Advancement Psychoanalytic Studies; mem. Am. Psychoanalytic Assn. (councilor-at-large 1980-84), Internat. Psycho-Analytical Assn., Boston Psychoanalytic Inst., Am. Psychotherapy Seminar Ctr. (mem. prof. adv. com. 1991—), Sigma Chi, Psi Chi. Office: Boston College Carney Hall 420 D Chestnut Hill MA 02167-3806

MEISTAS, MARY THERESE, endocrinologist, diabetes researcher; b. Grand Rapids, Mich., July 22, 1949; d. Frank Peter and Anne Therese (Karsokas) M. MD, U. Mich., 1975. Diplomate Am. Bd. Internal Medicine, Am. Bd. Endocrinology. Intern, then resident in internal medicine Cleve. Clinic Hosp., 1975-78, endocrinology fellow, 1978-79; fellow in pediatric endocrinology Johns Hopkins Hosp., Balt., 1979-81; diabetes researcher Joslin Diabetes Ctr., Boston, 1981-86; assoc. in medicine Brigham and Women's Hosp., Boston, 1981-86; asst. in medicine, diabetes researcher Mass. Gen. Hosp., Boston, 1986-92; staff endocrinologist Emerson Hosp., Concord, Mass., 1989—. Mem. ACP, Am. Diabetes Assn., Am. Fedn. Clin. Research, Endocrine Soc. Office: Emerson Hosp 747 Main St Ste 111 Concord MA 01742-3302

MEISTER, BERNARD JOHN, chemical engineer; b. Maynard, Mass., Feb. 27, 1941; s. Benjamin C. M. and Gertrude M. (Meister) M.; m. Janet M. White, Dec. 31, 1971; children: Mark, Martin, Kay Ellen. B.S. in Chem. Engring., Worcester Poly. Inst., 1962; Ph.D. in Chem. Engring., Cornell U., 1966. Engring. researcher Dow Chem. Co., Midland, Mich., 1966—, sr. rsch. specialist, 1978-81, assoc. scientist, 1981-85, sr. assoc. scientist, 1985-92, rsch. scientist, 1992—. Contbr. articles to profl. jours. Mem. Am. Inst. Chem. Engrs., Am. Chem. Soc., Soc. Plastics Engrs., Soc. Rheology, Sigma Xi. Mem. Ch. of Nazarene. Home: 2925 Chippewa Ln Midland MI 48640-4181 Office: Dow Chem Co 438 Bldg Midland MI 48640 *Free the mind of things you can't change, and let it focus on things you can accomplish.*

MEISTER, DORIS POWERS, investment management executive; b. Ames, Iowa, Sept. 12, 1954; d. James Phillip and Doris (Goess) P.; m. Gilbert Meister Jr., Oct. 18, 1980. AB, Smith Coll., 1976; MBA, U. Chgo., 1979. Mgr. currency Harris Trust & Savs. Bank, Chgo., 1976-78; sr. engagement mgr. McKinsey & Co. Inc., N.Y.C., London, 1979-84; dir., dept. head portfolio strategies dept., adminstrv. mgr. fixed income rsch. group C S First Boston, N.Y.C., 1984-90; exec. v.p., COO Christie, Manson & Woods Internat. Inc., N.Y.C., 1990-94; mng. dir. Copley Real Estate Advisors, Boston, 1994—. Bd. dirs. Arts Connection, 1990, Am. Women's Econ. Devel. Corp., 1994. Named one of "Top 40 under 40" Execs., Crain's N.Y., 1992. Mem. Fin. Women's Assn., Com. of 200, Women's Forum. Episcopalian. Office: Copley Real Estate Advisors 399 Boylston St Boston MA 02116-3305

MEISTER, MARK JAY, museum director, professional society administrator; b. Balt., June 26, 1953; s. Michael Aaron and Yetta (Haransky) M.; m. Carla Steiger, Aug. 7, 1977; children: Rachel, Kaitlin. AB, Washington U., St. Louis, 1974; MA, U. Minn., 1976; cert. mus. mgmt., U. Calif., Berkeley, 1983. Asst. lectr. St. Louis Art Mus., 1974; asst. coord. young people's program Mpls. Inst. Arts, 1975-76, coord. mobile program, 1976, coord. tchrs. resource svcs., 1976-77; dir. Mus. Art and History, Port Huron, Mich., 1978-79, Midwest Mus. Am. Art, Elkhart, Ind., 1979-81; exec. dir. Children's Mus., St. Paul, 1981-86; dir. Mus. Art, Sci. and Industry, Bridgeport, Conn., 1986-89; exec. dir. Archaeol. Inst. of Am., Boston, 1989—; adj. lectr. museology Kenyon Coll., Gambier, Ohio, 1977; adj. lectr. art history Ind. U., South Bend, 1980-81; regional reviewer Inst. Mus. Svcs., Washington, 1985-86, 89; treas., vice chmn. Minn. Assn. Mus., St. Paul, 1983-86; ex-officio trustee U.S. com. Internat. Coun. on Monuments and Sites, 1995—. Bd. dirs. Seaway Arts Coun., St. Clair County, Mich., 1978-79; mem. Mayor's Arts Adv. Com., Elkhart, 1981; mem. projects with industry bus. adv. coun. Goodwill Industries of Southwestern Conn., 1988-89; mem. exec. com., Conf. Adminstrv. Officers, Am. Coun. Learned Socs., 1994—. NEH museology fellow, Mpls. Inst. Arts, 1976-77, Kress fellow U. Minn. 1977-78, Bush leadership summer fellow, Bush Found., St. Paul, 1983; named One of Outstanding Young Men Am., 1981. Mem. Am. Assn. Mus., Am. Coun. Learned Socs., Conf. Adminstrv. Officers, Am. Soc. Assn. Execs. Office: Archaeol Inst of Am 656 Beacon St Boston MA 02215-2006

MEITZEN, MANFRED OTTO, religious studies educator; b. Houston, Dec. 12, 1930; s. Otto Hugo and Laura Emma (Munsch) M.; m. Fredrica Haden Kilmer, May 16, 1970. BA, Rice U., 1952; MDiv, Wartburg Sem., 1956; PhD, Harvard U., 1961. Assoc. prof. religious studies Rocky Mountain Coll., Billings, Mont., 1961-65; assoc. prof. religious studies, chmn. dept. W.Va. U., Morgantown, 1965-70, prof., chmn. religious studies, 1970—, prof. clin. psychiatry Med. Sch., 1991—, chmn. program humanities Coll. Arts and Scis., 1972-77, mem. senate, 1968-82, 84—; vis. scholar Christ Ch. Coll., Oxford (Eng.) U., 1973; columnist Morgantown Dominion-Post, 1975-76, 80-89. Contbr. articles to profl. jours. and chpts. to books. Harvard Div. Sch. scholar, 1957, fellow, 1958; Rockefeller fellow, 1959-60; Sheldon Traveling fellow, 1961; W.Va. U. Study grantee, 1970; recipient Outstanding Tchr. award W.Va. U., 1971-72, Coll. Arts & Scis., 1979-80, 87-88, Outstanding Educator Am. award, 1974-75, W.Va. Assocs. award, 1974-75, Golden Apple Tchg. award, 1995. Mem. Am. Guild Organists, Am. Acad. Religion, W.Va. Assn. for Humanities (pres. 1976-77), Harvard Alumni Assn., Univ. Profs. for Acad. Order (nat. 1st v.p. 1977-79, nat. pres. 1979, dir. 1974—, nat. sec.-treas. 1986-91), Nat. Assn. Scholars, Am. Rifle Assn., Rice U. Alumni Assn., Harvard Found. for Advanced Study and Rsch., Delta Phi Alpha. Lutheran. Home: 119 Forest Dr Morgantown WV 26505-2323 *It is very important, particularly in our times, not to sell one's own ideas and convictions short in face of the increasing pressure in academe and throughout society to comply with standardized opinion on moral, political and social issues.*

MEITZLER, ALLEN HENRY, electrical engineering educator, automotive scientist; b. Allentown, Pa., Dec. 16, 1928; s. Herbert Henry and Estella Irene (Wagner) M.; m. Joan Catherine Egan, June 13, 1953; children: Thomas Joseph, Peter Michael, David Christopher. B.S., Muhlenberg Coll., Allentown, Pa., 1951; M.S., Lehigh U., 1953, Ph.D., 1955. Mem. tech. staff Bell Labs., Whippany and Murray Hill, N.J., 1955-72; prin. research scientist, research staff Ford Motor Co., Dearborn, Mich., 1972-96, elec. engring. educator, 1996—; adj. prof. U. Mich.-Dearborn. Patentee ultrasonic and ferroelectric devices, automotive electronic devices and systems. Prof. Wackernagel scholar, 1947-51; Hood grad. fellow, 1954-55. Fellow IEEE, Acoustical Soc. Am.; mem. Am. Phys. Soc., Soc. Automotive Engrs., Am. Ceramic Soc. Republican. Home: 3055 Foxcroft St Ann Arbor MI 48104-2827 Office: Ford Motor Co Sci Rsch Staff PO Box 2053 Dearborn MI 48123-2053

MEIXSELL, BERRAE NEVIN (MIKE MEIXSELL), distribution executive; b. Palmerton, Pa., June 28, 1936; s. Earl Henry and Beatrice Ellen (Walk) M.; m. Hilda Elizabeth Landis, July 5, 1980; children: Berrae Jr., Tracy Young, Pamela Thomas, Gail Machella, Craig Horner, Michele Uterbach, Michael Meixsell. Diploma, Lehighton High Sch., 1954. Asst. mgr., then mgr. G.C. Murphy Co., 1952-64, W.T. Grant Co., 1964-67; mgr., buyer Norman Purchasing Corp., Silver Spring, Md., 1967-83; dir. purchasing Oscar Robbins Corp., Pitts., 1983-86; dist. sales mgr. Shakespeare Fishing Tackle Corp., Pitts., 1986-88; pres., CEO Nisito-Meixsell & Assocs., Ltd., Parker, Pa., 1988-96; pres., owner Mike Meixsell & Assocs., Parker, 1994—. Elected ofcl. Butler County, Butler, Pa., 1992-93. Recipient Eagle Scout award Boy Scouts Am., 1952, Silver award Boy Scouts Am., 1954, award of merit Am. Legion, 1950. Republican. Lutheran. Avocations: hunting, fishing. Home: RR 2 Box 311A Parker PA 16049-7908 Office: Nisito-Meixsell & Assocs RR 2 Box 311A Parker PA 16049-7908 also: Mike Meixsell & Assoc RR #2 Box 311A Parker PA 16049

MEJIA, PAUL ROMAN, choreographer, dancer; b. Lima, Peru, Oct. 29, 1947; s. Pablo Enrique and Romana (Kryzanowska) M.; m. Suzanne Farrell, Feb. 21, 1969. Student, Sch. Am. Ballet, 1959. Dancer N.Y.C. Ballet, 1965-70; dancer Ballet of the XX Century, Belgium, 1970-75; guest dir. Stars of Am. Ballet, Ballet Guatemala, 1977-79; assoc. artistic dir., dancer, choreographer Chgo. City Ballet, 1981-87; dir., artistic dir. Ft. Worth Ballet, 1987—; dir. Cedar Islands Ballet Summer Camp, 1980—. Office: Ft Worth Ballet 6845 Green Oaks Rd Fort Worth TX 76116-1713

MEKEEL, ROBERT K., lawyer; b. Ossining, N.Y., Mar. 21, 1950; s. Ira III and Carmen E. (Munson) M.; m. Martha J. Keller, Sept. 29, 1979; 1 child, Meryl Fox. BA, Wesleyan U., Middletown, Conn., 1972; JD, U. Puget Sound, 1978. Bar: N.H. 1978, N.Y. 1979, U.S. Dist. Ct. (so. dist.) N.Y. 1980, U.S. Ct. Appeals (2d cir.) 1981, U.S. Dist. Ct. N.H. 1983, U.S. Ct. Appeals (1st cir.) 1983. Asst. dist. atty. Westchester County N.Y. Dist. Atty., White Plains, N.Y., 1979-82; assoc. Craig Wenners & McDowell, Manchester, N.H., 1983-84; clk. ct. Coos County Superior Ct., Lancaster, N.H., 1985; ptnr. McKible & Mekeel, P.A., Concord, N.H., 1986-89, Cullity

Kelley & McDowell, Manchester, 1989-93, McDowell & Mekeel P.A., Manchester, 1994—; mem. mentor program Franklin Pierce Law Sch., Concord, 1992; lectr. Nat. Bus. Inst., Eau Claire, Wis., 1993-95; mem. Million Dollar Advocates forum; mediator N.H. Superior Cts.; panelist Am. Arbitration Assn. Mem. Am. Trial Lawyers Assn., N.H. Trial Lawyers Assn. (amicus com. 1986—), N.H. Bar Assn. (com. on cooperation with cts., lectr. evidence seminar 1994). Democrat. Unitarian. Avocations: running, biking, swimming, drawing, wood working. Home: 73 Main St Hopkinton NH 03229-2628 Office: McDowell & Mekeel PA 282 River Rd Manchester NH 03104-2423

MEKENNEY, C. ROBERT, management analyst, tax accountant; b. Chester, Pa., Nov. 30, 1944; s. William Hatred and Alfreda Frances (Laskoski) M.; m. Susan Mary Szollosi, Sept. 2, 1977; children: Jonathan, Christopher. BS in Bus. Mgmt., Pa. State U., 1966. Cert. tax specialist. Pers. mgmt. specialist Drug Enforcement Adminstrn., Phila., 1972-74; regional pers. officer Drug Enforcement Adminstrn., Kansas City, Mo., 1974-76; pers. mgmt. specialist Drug Enforcement Adminstrn., Washington, 1976-78; employee benefits specialist U.S. Customs Svc., Washington, 1978-80, employee benefits officer, 1980-90, mgmt. analyst, 1990—, inst. orgnl. mgmt., 1978—; participant Citizen Amb. Program teaching acctg. to Russian businessmen. Exec. treas. Boy Scouts Am., Falls Church, Va., 1993—. Served with USN, 1967-71. Mem. Nat. Assn. Tax Practitioners, Nat. Soc. Pub. Accts., Internat. Assn. for Fin. Planning, Nat. Soc. Tax Profls. Roman Catholic. Avocations: cooking.

MEKLER, ARLEN B., lawyer, chemist; b. N.Y.C., May 4, 1943; s. Lev A. and Ethel (Fox) M.; children from previous marriage: Jeffrey Arlen, Rebecca Ann, Ann-Marie Laura, Victoria Arlene, Lamar Adam, Lars Arlen; m. Molly L. Malone, Feb. 3, 1995. B.S. in Chemistry, Reed Coll.-San Jose State U., 1953; M.S. in Organic Chemistry, Iowa State U., 1955; Ph.D., Ohio State U., 1958; J.D., Temple U., 1972. Bar: Del. 1972, Pa. 1972, U.S. Supreme Ct. 1976. Sr. rsch. chemist E.I. du Pont de Nemours & Co., Wilmington, Del., 1958-69; ptnr. Mekler and Maurer, Wilmington, 1972—; chief appellate div. Office Pub. Defender, State of Del., 1973-77; pres. Del. Law Ctr., Wilmington, 1973—; instr. constl. law Wilmington Coll., 1976-80; dir. Bar Rev. Del., 1972—; mem. 3d Circuit Ct. Appeal Jud. Nominating Commn., 1977-81, 3d Circuit Ct. Appeals Jud. Conf. Contbr. monographs to legal publs. Pres. Mental Health Aux. for Gov. Bacon Health Ctr., 1964-66; mem. Citizens Conf. for Modernization of State Legislatures, 1964-68; state chmn., Reform Commn. for Modernization Polit. Party Rules, 1965-68; pres. Del. Citizens for Fair Housing, 1965-69; state commr. Nat. Conf. on Uniform State Laws, 1972—; pres. Democratic Forum Del., 1966-70; mem. Del. Dem. Platform Com., 1966, 68, 72, 76; research dir. Del. Citizens for Humphrey-Muskie, 1968, Citizens for Biden, 1972, 78, 84, Citizens for McDowell, 1986—, Biden for Pres., 1986—; del. Dem. Nat. Conv., 1980; mem. social action com. Unitarian Ch., Wilmington, 1962-68. Recipient Keyman award, 1964, 65; State Govtl. Affairs award, 1964, 65. Mem. ABA, Del. Bar Assn. (com. on rules of criminal procedure 1973-74, supreme ct. com. on revision of criminal law 1973—, supreme ct. com. on rules of evidence 1976—, com. on revised rules of evidence 1976—, com. on revised rules of Del. Supreme Ct. 1974—, family law com. 1979—, continuing legal edn. com. 1981—), Pa. Bar Assn., Am. Chem. Soc., N.Y. Acad. Scis., Chem. Soc. (London), AAAS, Catalyst Club Phila., Wilmington Organic Chemists Club, ACLU (bd. dirs.), Sigma Xi, Phi Alpha Delta. Home: Brandywine Hills 714 W Matson Run Pky Wilmington DE 19802-1912 Office: PO Box 2285 Wilmington DE 19899-2285

MEL, HOWARD CHARLES, biophysics educator; m. Nancy Helene Shenon, June. 18, 1949; children—Amélie Catherine, Stéphanie Frances, Bartlett Woolsey. Student electronics and physics, Bowdoin Coll., 1945; student humanities and music, U. Geneva,, Conservatoire de Musique, Geneva,, 1946-47; B.S. with honors, U. Calif.-Berkeley, 1948, Ph.D. in Phys. Chemistry, 1953; postgrad., U. Brussels, 1953-55. Traffic mgr. Calo Pet Food Co., Oakland, 1948-50; instr. chemistry U. Calif.-Berkeley, 1955, USPHS fellow, lectr. med. physics, 1955-60, asst. prof., assoc. prof. biophysics, 1960-74, prof. biophysics, 1974-93, prof. emeritus, 1993—, dir. Lawrence Hall of Sci., 1981-82; faculty sr. scientist Lawrence Berkeley Lab. U. Calif. Berkeley, 1960—; dir. U. Calif. Study Ctrs., Bordeaux, Pau, Poitiers, France, 1986-89; dir. tng. grants Nat. Inst. Gen. Med. Scis., 1972-82; maître de recherche INSERM, U. Paris, 1974-75. Organizer, editor: Aharon Katchalsky Meml. Symposium, 1977; editor for biophysics: Ency. Sci. and Tech., 4th edit., 1977; mem. editorial bd.: Blood Cells, 1974—, Cell Biophysics, 1978—, Rev. Sci. Instruments, 1975-78, Jour. Math. Biology, 1974-82; contbr. numerous articles to profl. jours.; patentee in field; researcher in cell membrane biophysics, hematopoiesis, biophys. instrumentation, and thermodynamic theory; inventor, developer stable-flow free-boundary method for analytical characterization & preparative separation of live cells and other particles, and of resistive pulse spectroscopy for characterization of geometrical, rheological, membrane-osmotic properties of cells, especially red blood cells. Former dir., mem. exec. com., chmn. music com. Oakland Symphony Orch. Assn.; v.p. Berkeleans for Acad. Excellence, 1970, Inverness Properties, Inc., 1965-75; bd. dirs. Pine Acres Homeowners Assn., 1983-86. Served to lt (j.g.) USNR, 1943-46. Recipient Prix du Rayonnement de la Langue Francaise Acad. Francais, 1993; Fulbright fellow to Brussels, 1953-55; NSF sr. postdoctoral fellow, 1965-66. Fellow AAAS, Assn. Claude Bernard, Sigma Xi; mem. Biophys. Soc. (coun. 1969-71, founding), Am. Chem. Soc., Am. Inst. Physics, Am. Assn. Physics Tchrs., Soc. Gen. Systems Rsch., Internat. Soc. Biorheology, Internat. Union Pure and Applied Biophysics, Assn. Sci. Tech. Ctrs., Phi Beta Kappa, Sigma Phi Epsilon. Clubs: Faculty U. Calif.-Berkeley (dir. 1979-80); Bohemian (San Francisco), Sierra (San Francisco); Amphion (Berkeley), Mosswood Investment (Berkeley) (pres. 1958). Office: U Calif MCB-CDB Donner Lab Berkeley CA 94720-3206

MELADY, THOMAS PATRICK, academic administrator, ambassador, author, public policy expert, educator; b. Norwich, Conn., Mar. 4, 1927; m. Margaret Judith Badum; children: Christina, Monica. BA, Duquesne U., 1950; MA, Cath. U. Am., 1952, PhD, 1954; hon. doctorates from 26 univs. Former mem. faculties Fordham and St. John's Univs.; founder Inst. African Affairs Duquesne U., 1957; cons. to founds., govts., corps., 1959-67; hon. doctorates from 27 univs. Africa Service Inst.; prof. Afro-Asian affairs, chmn. dept. Asian studies and NonWestern civilization Seton Hall U., South Orange, N.J., 1967-69, regent, 1987-90; prof. Afro-Asian affairs, dir. Office of Internat. Studies, 1973-74; exec. v.p., prof. politics St. Joseph's U., Phila., 1974-76; pres. Sacred Heart U., Fairfield, Conn., 1976-86, prof. polit. sci., 1976-86, pres. emeritus, 1986—; asst. sec. for postsecondary edn. U.S. Dept. Edn., Washington, 1981-82; amb. to Burundi, 1969-72, amb. to Uganda, 1972-73; sr. adviser to U.S. del. to 25 UN Gen. Assembly, 1970; chmn. Conn. Conf. Ind. Colls., 1979-81; pres., chief exec. officer Conn. Pub. Expenditures Coun., 1986-89; U.S. amb. to The Holy See, Vatican City, 1989-93, 94-95; exec. dir. Cath. Network of Vol. Svc., 1993-94; disting. vis. prof. George Washington U. and St. John's U., 1993-94; chmn. nat. com. Cath. Campaign for Am., 1994—; counsel Hayward Internat., 1994—. Author: Ambassadors Story: The United States and The Vatican in World Affairs, and 14 other books. Chmn. nat. com. Cath. Campaign for Am., 1993—; counsel Hayward Internat., 1994—. Knighted by Pope Paul VI, 1968 and by Pope John Paul II, 1983, 91; honored by 5 countries; recipient Native Son award. Mem. Order of Malta, The Sacred Mil. Constantinian Order of St. George.

MELAMED, ARTHUR DOUGLAS, lawyer; b. Mpls., Dec. 3, 1945; s. Arthur Charles and Helen Beatrix (Rosenberg) M.; m. Carol Drescher Weisman, May 26, 1983; children: Kathryn Henrie, Elizabeth Allyn. B.A., Yale U., 1967; J.D., Harvard U., 1970. Bar: D.C. 1970, U.S. Ct. Internat. Trade 1985, U.S. Ct. Appeals (9th cir.) 1971, U.S. Ct. Appeals (2d cir.) 1975, U.S. Ct. Appeals (D.C. cir.) 1978, U.S. Ct. Appeals (8th cir.) 1981, U.S. Ct. Appeals (fed. cir.) 1985, U.S. Ct. Appeals (4th cir.) 1989, U.S. Ct. Appeals (10th cir.) 1993, U.S. Supreme Ct. 1981. Law clk. U.S. Ct. Appeals for 9th Circuit, 1970-71; assoc. Wilmer, Cutler & Pickering, Washington, 1971-77, ptnr., 1978—; vis. prof. Georgetown U. Law Ctr., 1992-93, adj. prof., 1993-94. Contbr. articles to profl. jours. Class agt. Alumni Fund Yale U.; D.C. area chair Yale campaign, 1993—; mem. social scis. coun. com. Yale U., 1989-94; trustee Nat. Child Rsch. Ctr., 1990-93. Mem. ABA, D.C. Bar Assn., Am. Law Inst., Yale Club (N.Y.C.), Kenwood Country Club. Office: 2445 M St NW Washington DC 20037-1435

MELAMED, LEO, investment company executive; b. Bialystok, Poland, Mar. 20, 1932; came to U.S., 1941, naturalized, 1950.; s. Isaac M. and Fayga (Barakin) M.; m. Betty Sattler, Dec. 26, 1953; children: Idelle Sharon, Jordan Norman, David Jeffrey. Student, U. Ill., 1950-52; JD, John Marshall Law Sch., Chgo., 1955. Bar: Ill. 1955. Sr. ptnr. Melamed, Kravitz & Verson, Chgo., 1956-66; chmn., CEO Sakura Dellsher, Inc., Chgo., 1965—; mem. Chgo. Merc. Exch., 1953—, mem. bd. govs., 1967-91, chmn. bd., 1969-71, 75-77, chmn. exec. com. 1985-91, also spl. counsel; chmn. bd. Internat. Monetary Market, 1972-75, spl. counsel, 1976-91; mem. Chgo. Bd. Trade, 1969—; mem. corp. adv. bd. U. Ill., Chgo., 1991; mayor Chgo. Coun. Manpower and Econ. Advisors, 1972. Author: (sci. fiction novel) The Tenth Planet, 1987, Leo Melamed on the Markets, 1993; editor: The Merits of Flexible Exchange Rates, 1989. Trustee John Marshall Law Sch., 1991; coun. mem. U.S. Holocaust Meml. Mus. Named Man of Yr., Israel Bonds, 1975; recipient Am. Jewish Com. Human Rights medallion, 1991. Fellow Internat. Assn. Fin. Engrs. (sr.); mem. ABA, Am. Judicature Soc., Ill. Bar Assn., Chgo. Bar Assn., Nat. Bur. Econ. Rsch. (bd. dirs.), Econs. Club Chgo., Nat. Futures Assn. (chmn. 1982-89), Am. Contract Bridge League (life master), Union League Club, Chgo. Club, Standard Club. Avocations: writing, jogging. Office: Sakura Dellsher Inc 10 S Wacker Dr Chicago IL 60606-7402

MELAMID, ALEXANDER, economics educator; b. Freiburg, Germany, Mar. 28, 1914; s. Michael and Zinaida (Gruenholz) M.; m. Ruth Caro, Nov. 28, 1940 (dec. July 1968); m. Ilse Hoenigsberg, Apr. 15, 1975; children: Diane H.C. Melamid Michaels, Suzanna C. Melamid Portnoy. BSc in Econs., London Sch. Econs., 1939; PhD, New Sch. for Social Research, 1952. Asst. prof. New Sch. for Social Research, N.Y.C., 1953-57; assoc. prof. NYU, 1957-65, prof., 1965-87, prof. emeritus, 1987—; v.p. Am. Geog. Soc., N.Y.C., 1975. Author: Turkey, 1956, History of Iran, 1968, New York City Region, 1985. Fellow Am. Geog. Soc. (hon., mem. council, Morse medal 1991); mem. Middle East Studies Assn. Am. Avocations: skiing. Office: NYU Dept Econs Washington Sq N New York NY 10003

MELAMID, ALEXANDER, artist; b. Moscow, July 14, 1945. Student, Stroganov Inst. Art and Design, Moscow, 1967. Ptnr. Komar & Melamid Studio, N.Y.C., 1965—; instr. visual art Moscow Regional Art Sch., 1968-76. Exhibitions include Wadsworth Atheneum, Hartford, Conn., 1978, Mus. Modern Art, Oxford, Eng., Mus. Decorative Art, Paris, 1985, Neuen Gesellschaft für Gildende Kunst, Berlin, 1988, Bklyn. Mus., 1990, Alternative Mus., N.Y.C., 1994, Storefrong for Art and Arch., N.Y.C., 1995, Ukraine State Mus., Kiev, 1995, Mus. Modern Art, Cologne, Germany, 1996; exhibited in group shows Met. Mus. Art, N.Y.C., 1982, 84, Chrysler Mus., Norfolk, Va., 1983, Sydney, 1986, Kassel, Germany, 1987, Solomon R. Guggenheim Found., 1987, FIAC, Paris, 1989, Bklyn. Mus., 1990; represented in permanent collections Whitney Mus. Am. Art, N.Y.C., Stedelijk Mus., Amsterdam, The Netherlands, Guggenheim Mus., Mus. Modern Art, Met. Mus. Art; commns. include mural Unity, 1st Interstate Bank Bldg., L.A., 1993, murals Liberty as Justice, N.Y. Percent for Art Program, 1994. Grantee Nat. Endowment Arts, 1982.

MELANÇON, TUCKER LEE, judge; b. 1946. BS, La. State U., 1968; JD, Tulane U., 1973. Atty. Knoll & Knoll, 1973-75; pvt. practice Marksville, La., 1975-83; prin. Melancon & Rabalais, Marksville, 1984-94; judge U.S. Dist. Ct. (we. dist.) La., Monroe, 1994—; Mem. adv. bd. Catalyst Old River Hydroelectric Partnership, Vidalia, La., 1989-92, La. Workers Compensation, 1990-91; mem. com. Study Backlog in Cts. of Appeal, 1st and 3d Cirs., 1991; bd. dirs. Catalyst Vidalia Corp., N.Y.C., 1993-94. Active La. Pub. Broadcasting. Mem. Am. Judicature Soc., Am. Inns of Ct., La. State Bar Assn., Bar Assn. 5th Fed. Cir., New Orleans Track Club. Office: US Dist Ct 201 Jackson St Monroe LA 71201-7472

MELBINGER, MICHAEL S., lawyer; b. Chgo., Sept. 5, 1958; s. Donald G. and Joyce A. (Haynes) M.; m. Karen Mary Melbinger, June 16, 1984; children: Peter Donald, Charlotte Anna. BA, U. Notre Dame, 1980; JD, U. Ill., 1983. Bar: Ill. Assoc. McDermott, Will & Emery, Chgo., 1983-88, ptnr., 1989-93; ptnr., head employee benefits dept. Schiff, Hardin & Waite, Chgo., 1993—; author, speaker Coll. for Fin. Planning, Denver, 1990—. Mem. editorial bd. Taxation for Lawyers, N.Y.C., 1989—, Employee Benefits Counselor, 1993—, Pension Management, 1995—; contbr. articles to profl. jours. Precinct capt. Regular Rep. Orgn., Cook County, Ill., 1985—. Mem. Union League Club. Home: 623 W Campbell St Arlington Heights IL 60005-1419 Office: Schiff Hardin & Waite 7200 Sears Towers Chicago IL 60606

MELBY, ALAN KENNETH, linguist, educator; b. Murray, Utah, Mar. 25, 1948; s. Kenneth O. and Charolette (Bryner) M.; m. Ulla-Britta L. Sandholm, Aug. 14, 1970; children: Eric, Roland, Irene, Philippe, Yvette, Vivianne. BS, Brigham Young U., 1973, MA, 1974, PhD, 1976. Assoc. prof. linguistics Brigham Young U., Provo, Utah, 1977-94, prof. linguistics, 1994—, bd. dirs. TermNet, Vienna; chmn. translation rsch. group; pres. CMR Computer, Inc.; v.p. LinguaTech Internat., Inc.; vis. prof. Coll. de France, Paris, 1990. Mem. Am. Translators Assn. (chair translation & computers com.); editoral bd. (jour.) Machine Translation; contbr. articles to profl. jours. Mem. ACM, Linguistic Soc. Am., Assn. Computational Linguistics, Linguistic Assn. Can. and U.S., Am. Translators Assn. (accredited translator French to English). Republican. Mormon. Home: 1223 Aspen Ave Provo UT 84604-3617 Office: Brigham Young U Linguistics Dept Provo UT 84602

MELBY, EDWARD CARLOS, JR., veterinarian; b. Burlington, Vt., Aug. 10, 1929; s. Edward C. and Dorothy H. (Folsom) M.; m. Jean Day File, Aug. 15, 1953; children: Scott E., Susan J., Jeffrey T., Richard A. Student, U. Pa., 1948-50; D.V.M., Cornell U., 1954. Diplomate: Am. Coll. Lab. Animal Medicine. Practice veterinary medicine Middlebury, Vt., 1954-62; instr. lab. animal medicine Johns Hopkins U. Sch. Medicine, Balt., 1962-64; asst. prof. Johns Hopkins U. Sch. Medicine, 1964-66, assoc. prof., 1966-71, prof., dir. div. comparative medicine, 1971-74; prof. medicine, dean Coll. Vet. Medicine, Cornell U., Ithaca, N.Y., 1974-84; v.p. R & D SmithKline Beecham Animal Health, 1985-90, v.p. sci. and tech. assessment, 1990-91; ind. cons., 1992—; cons. VA, Nat. Research Council, NIH. Author: Handbook of Laboratory Animal Science, Vols. I, II, III, 1974-76. Served with USMC, 1946-48. Mem. Am., N.Y. State, Md., Pa. Veterinary Med. Assns., Am. Assn. Lab. Animal Sci., Am. Coll. Lab. Animal Medicine, AAAS, Phi Zeta. Home: PO Box 248 Charlotte VT 05445-0248 Office: 736 Lime Kiln Rd Charlotte VT 05445

MELBY, JOHN B., composer, educator; b. Whitehall, Wis., Oct. 3, 1941; s. John B. Sr. and Margaret (Edmundson) M.; m. Carol A. Wurtz, July 7, 1961 (div. 1977); 1 child, John; m. Jane H. Thompson, June 15, 1978; children: Kirsten, Charles. MusB, Curtis Inst., 1966; MA, U. Pa., 1967; MFA, Princeton U., 1971, PhD, 1972. Assoc. prof. West Chester (Pa.) U., 1971-73; prof. music U. Ill., Urbana, 1973—; assoc. U. Ill. Ctr. for Advanced Studies, 1989-90. Composer numerous mus. works for live performers, computer-synthesized tape, vocal, chamber and orchestral music, works pub. by Am. Composers Edit., Merion Music Co., Margun Music, Inc.; recs. on Composers Recs., Inc., New World Records, Advance Records, Centaur Records, Zuma Records. Recipient 1st prize 7th Internat. Electroacoustic Music Awards, Bourges, France, 1979, Am. Acad./Inst. Arts and Letters award, 1984; Guggenheim fellow, 1983. Mem. BMI, Am. Composers Alliance. Democrat. Avocations: railroading, cooking, herpetology. Office: U Ill Sch Music 2136 Music Bldg 1114 W Nevada St Urbana IL 61801-3859

MELBY, ORVILLE ERLING, retired banker; b. Butte, Mont., Oct. 9, 1921; s. Ole and Esther (Jacobsen) M.; m. Arvilla L. Underland, Nov. 24, 1956; children—Steve E., James E., Ann-Margaret. B.A. magna cum laude, U. Wash., 1949. C.P.A., Wash., Oreg. Treas. Boeing Co., 1956-66; sr. v.p. fin. Continental Airlines, Los Angeles, 1966; v.p. Bank of Am., San Francisco, 1967; treas. Bendix Corp., Detroit, 1968; v.p., treas. Vought Aeronautics, Dallas, 1969-70, Bonanza Internat., Dallas, 1971-74; vice chmn. Rainier Nat. Bank, Seattle, 1974-87; bd. dirs. Health Care Property Investors, Los Angeles. Served with USAAF, 1942-46. Mem. Fin. Execs. Inst., Phi Beta Kappa. Presbyterian. Club: Mason. Home: 9439 Lake Washington Blvd NE Bellevue WA 98004-5410

MELCHER, JERRY EUGENE, lawyer; b. Eugene, Oreg., June 26, 1945; s. Gordon Neil Wilcox and Irene Marie (Wagner) Melcher Mueller; m. Esther Donna Westby; children: Maureen Margit, Trenton Wilcox. BS, U. S.D., 1967; JD, Willamette U., 1970. Bar: Oreg. 1970, Alaska 1970, U.S. Dist. Ct. Alaska. Assoc. Hughes, Thorsness, Gantz, Powell & Brundin, Anchorage, Alaska, 1970-72, ptnr., 1972-89, prin. ptnr., 1980-89; ptnr. Heller, Ehrman, White & McAuliffe, Anchorage, 1989—. Mem. ABA, Oreg. State Bar Assn., Alaska State Bar Assn., Anchorage Bar Assn., Masons. Republican. Avocations: hunting, sports, fly fishing. Office: Bank of America Center 550 W 7th Ave Anchorage AK 99501-3510*

MELCHER, TRINI URTUZUASTEGUI, accounting educator; b. Somerton, Ariz., Dec. 1, 1931; d. Francisco Juan and Dolores (Barraza) Urtuzuastegui; m. Arlyn Melcher, Aug. 3, 1957 (div. Feb. 1972); children: Teresa Dolores, Michael Francis, Jocelyn Marie. BS, Ariz. State U., 1954; MBA, Kent State U., 1964; PhD, Ariz. State U., 1977. Acct. CPA firm, L.A., 1954-56; instr. L.A. Sch. Dist., 1956-58, Dolton (Ill.) Sch. Dist., 1958-61; asst. prof. Kent (Ohio) State U., 1962-72; prof. Calif. State U., Fullerton, 1976-89; founding faculty mem. Calif. State U., San Marcos, 1990—. Author: Intermediate Accounting Study Guide, 1984. Treas. Community Devel. Coun., Santa Ana, 1985-88, chmn. bd., 1989; mem. com. U.S. Dept. Labor, 1989—. Named Outstanding Educator, League of United Latin Am. Citizens, Stanton, Calif., 1987, Mex. Am. Women's Nat. Assn., Irvine, Calif., 1987; recipient Outstanding Faculty award Calif. State U. Sch. Bus., 1983, Pub. Svc. award Am. Soc. Women CPAs, San Antonio, 1989; Affirmative Action grantee, 1990. Mem. AICPA (editorial bd. The Woman CPA), Am. Acctg. Assn., Calif. Soc. CPAs (Merit award 1991), Hispanic CPAs. Avocations: music, travel. Home: 2024 Sequioa St San Marcoa CA 92069 Office: Calif State U San Marcos CA 92096-0001

MELCHERT, JAMES FREDERICK, artist; b. New Bremen, Ohio, Dec. 2, 1930; s. John Charles and Hulda Lydia (Egli) M.; m. Mary Ann Hostetler, June 18, 1954; children: Christopher, David, Renee. A.B., Princeton U., 1952; M.F.A., U. Chgo., 1957; M.A., U. Calif., Berkeley, 1961. Prof. art U. Calif., Berkeley, 1965-76, 81-84, 88-92, prof. emeritus, 1992—; dir. Am. Acad. in Rome, 1984-88; dir. Visual Arts Program, Nat. Endowment for Arts, Washington, 1977-81. Exhibited in one man shows at San Francisco Art Inst., 1970, San Francisco Mus. Modern Art, 1975, Holly Solomon Gallery, N.Y.C., 1991; group shows at Biennale de Paris, 1963, Whitney Mus., N.Y.C., 1966, 68, 70, Documenta 5, Kassel, Germany, 1972, Sydney (Australia) Biennal, 1976; commd. for Artwork (new Biology Bldg.) at MIT, 1993-94, Biomed. Rsch. Bldg. at Case Western Res. U., 1994. Recipient Adaline Kent award San Francisco Art Inst., 1970; Nat. Endowment for Arts artist fellow, 1973; hon. DFA, San Francisco Art Inst., 1984, Md. Inst. Coll. Arts, 1993. Home: 6077 Ocean View Dr Oakland CA 94618-1844

MELCONIAN, LINDA JEAN, state senator, lawyer; b. Springfield, Mass.; d. George and Virginia Elaine (Noble) Melconian. B.A., Mt. Holyoke Coll., 1970; M.A., George Washington U., 1976, J.D., 1978. Bar: Mass. Chief legis. asst. to Ho. of Reps. Speaker Thomas P. O'Neill, Jr., U.S. Congress, Washington, 1971-80; pros. atty. Hampden County Dist. Atty., Springfield, Mass., 1981-82; state senator Mass. Gen. Ct., Boston, 1983—; instr. Western New Eng. Coll., Springfield, 1978-82; Our Lady of the Elms Coll., Springfield, 1982-83. Chmn., Heart Fund Ball, Western Mass., 1983; incorporator Springfield Coll., 1982—; ex officio trustee Ella T. Grasso Found., Conn., 1982—; active Democratic State Com., Mass., 1983, Hampden County Dems. Recipient Appreciation award Vietnam Vets. of Greater Springfield, 1983; Equal Edn. for All Children award Bilingual Parents of Springfield, 1983; Appreciation award Vets.-Hampden County Council, 1984. Mem. Hampden County Bar Assn. Home: 257 Ft Pleasant Ave Springfield MA 01108-1521 Office: Mass State Senate Rm 213-b Boston MA 02133

MELCZEK, DALE J., bishop; b. Nov. 9, 1938. A.B., St. Mary Coll., Orchard Lake, Mich.; M.Div., St. John Sem., Plymouth, Mich.; M.A. in Edn., U. Detroit; postgrad., U. Notre Dame. Ordained priest Roman Cath. Ch., 1964, appointed aux. bishop, 1982. Assoc. pastor St. Sylvester Ch., Warren, Mich., 1964-70, co-pastor, 1970-72; pastor St. Christine Ch., Detroit, 1972-75; vicar West Detroit Vicariate, 1973-75; asst. vicar for parishes Archdiocese of Detroit, 1975-77, sec. to archbishop and vicar gen., 1977-82, archdiocesan consultor, 1972-83, aux. bishop, titular bishop of Trau, 1982-95; regional bishop Detroit N.W. Region, 1983-92; apostolic adminstr. Diocese of Gary, Ind., 1992-95; coadjutor Bishop of Gary Diocese of Gary, Ind., 1995-96; bishop of Gary Diocese of Gary, Ind., 1996—.

MELDMAN, CLIFFORD KAY, lawyer; b. Milw., July 27, 1931; s. Edward H. and Rose (Bortin) M.; children: Mindy, David, Linda, James, Noah. JD, Marquette U., 1956. Bar: Wis. 1956. Ptnr. Meldman & Meldman, Milw., 1956-73; pres. Meldman & Meldman S.C., Milw., 1973—. Contbr. articles to profl. jours., also editor. Fellow Am. Acad. Matrimonial Lawyers (pres. 1982); mem. Milw. Bar Assn. (bd. dirs. 1984-86, pres. 1986-87, chmn. family law sect.), Wis. Bar Assn. (chmn. family law sect.). Home: 170 W Cherokee Cir Milwaukee WI 53217-2716 Office: Meldman & Meldman SC PO Box 17397 Milwaukee WI 53217-0397

MELDMAN, ROBERT EDWARD, lawyer; b. Milw., Aug. 5; s. Louis Leo and Lillian (Gollusch) M.; m. Sandra Jane Setlick, July 24, 1960; children—Saree Beth, Richard Samuel. B.S., U. Wis., 1959; LL.B., Marquette U., 1962; LL.M. in Taxation, NYU, 1963. Bar: Wis. 1962, fla. 1987, colo. 1990, U.S. Ct. Fed. Claims, U.S. Tax Ct. 1963, U.S. Supreme Ct. 1970. Practice tax law Milw., 1963—; pres. Meldman, Case & Weine, Ltd., Milw., 1975-85; dir. tax div. Mulcahy & Wherry, S.C., Milw., 1985-90; shareholder Reinhart, Boerner, Van Deuren, Norris & Rieselbach, S.C., 1991—; adj. prof. taxation U. Wis., Milw., 1970—, mem. tax adv. coun., 1978—; sec. Profl. Inst. Tax Study, Inc., 1978—; bd. dirs. Wis. Bar Found., 1988-94. Co-author: Federal Taxation Practice and Procedure, 1983, 86, 88, 92, Practical Tactics for Dealing with the IRS, 1994, A Practical Guide to U.S. Taxation of International Transactions, 1996; editor Jour. Property Taxation; mem. editorial bd. Tax Litigation Alert, 1995—; contbr. articles to legal jours. Recipient Adj. Taxation Faculty award UWM Tax Assn., 1987; named Outstanding Tax Profl. 1992 Corp. Reports Wis. Mag. and UWM Tax Assn. Mem. ABA, Fed. Bar Assn. (pres. Milw. chpt. 1966-67), Milw. Bar Assn. (chmn. tax sect. 1970-71), Wis. Bar Assn. (bd. dirs. tax sect. 1964-78, chmn. 1973-74), Am. Coll. Tax Counsel, Internat. Bar Assn., The Law Assn. for Asia and the Pacific, Marquette U. Law Alumni Assn. (bd. dirs. 1972-77), Milw. Athletic Club, Wis. Club, Country Club of Wis., B'nai B'rith (trustee, Ralph Harris Meml. award Century Lodge 1969-70), Phi Delta Phi, Tau Epsilon Rho (chancellor Milw. chpt. 1969-71, supreme nat. chancellor 1975-76, v.p. Wis. chpt., tech. 1992—). Jewish (trustee congregation 1972-77). Home: 7455 N Skyline Ln Milwaukee WI 53217-3327 Office: Ste 2100 1000 N Water St Ste 2100 Milwaukee WI 53202-6025

MELDONIAN, SUSAN LUCY, elementary education educator; b. N.Y.C., Apr. 21, 1955; d. John Sarkis and Margaret (Avdoyan) M. BA in Elem. Edn., William Paterson Coll., Wayne, N.J., 1977, MEd in Reading, 1993. Cert. tchr. K-8, reading specialist, K-12, N.J. Basic skills tchr. K-4 Walter O. Krumbiegel Sch., Hillside, N.J., 1979; tchr. 1st grade Margaret L. Vetter Sch., Eatontown, N.J., 1979-88; tchr. 1st grade Cherry Hill Sch., River Edge, N.J., 1988-94, tchr. 3d grade, 1994—. Contbg. author: Moving Forward with Literature: Basals, Books and Beyond, 1993; contbr. articles to profl. jours. Mem. NEA, N.J. Edn. Assn., Internat. Reading Assn., Pi Lambda Theta. Mem. Armenian Apostolic Ch. Avocations: piano, singing, travel, bowling. Office: Cherry Hill Sch 410 Bogert Rd River Edge NJ 07661-1813

MELDRUM, HARVEY HERMAN, financial consultant; b. Point Pleasant, N.J., Oct. 15, 1956; s. Harvey A. and Mildred J. (Beyer) M.; m. Kristen R. Flipse, Nov. 25, 1989 (div. Apr. 1994). Student, Ocean County Coll., 1974-75, Trenton State Coll., 1975-76. Fin. advisor John Hancock Fin. Svcs., Manalapan, N.J., 1987-89; fin. cons. Meldrum Assocs., Manasquan, N.J., 1989-90; fin. cons., dir. ednl. planning divsn. E.P.A. Fin. Svcs., Toms River, N.J., 1990—; guest spkr. Nat. Assn. for the Edn. of Young Children, Sta. WADB, WOBM and WJRZ, Ocean and Monmouth Counties, N.J., 1993—. tchr. h.s. fin. planning program Coll. for Fin. Planning, , Denver, 1992-93. With U.S. Army, 1976-79. Mem. Internat. Assn. for Fin. Planning, Nat. Fin. Aid Practitioners Alliance, Nat. Assn. of Life Underwriters, Nat. Assn. of Student Fin. Aid Adminstrs. Republican. Avocations: high school official, recreational basketball, tennis and golf. Home: 2102 Barnegat Blvd Point Pleasant NJ 08742

MELDRUM, PETER DURKEE, venture capital/biotechnology company executive; b. Salt Lake City, June 26, 1947; s. Benjamin Nibley and Grace Natalie (Durkee) M.; m. Catherine Roper, June 16, 1970; children: Christopher Shawn. BS in Chem. Engring., U. Utah, 1970, MBA, 1974. Asst. to pres. Terra Tek, Inc., Salt Lake City, 1974-78; pres., chief exec. officer Resource Enterprises, Inc., Salt Lake City, 1978-81; pres., CEO, AgriDyne Techs., Salt Lake City, 1981-91, bd. dirs., 1979-93; pres., CEO, Founder's Fund Inc., 1991-95; pres., CEO Myriad Genetics Inc., Salt Lake City, 1992—; bd. dirs. Dairy Equipment Co. Utah, Salt Lake City, Paradigm Bioscis. Inc., Cognetix Inc., Sonix Techs. Inc., Vaxsys Corp. Vice chmn. fundraising Salt Lake Boy's Club, 1978-79; bd. dirs., vice chmn. ARC Golden Spike, Salt Lake City, 1980-90; mem. State of Utah Council Sci. and Tech., 1984-89; adv. bd. High Tech Mktg. Rev., Austin, Tex., 1986-88; mem. Gov.'s Task Force on Entrepreneurship; mem. rev. panel Utah Tech. Fin. Corp., Gov.'s Com. on Biomed. Industry, 1988-91; mem. bioengring. adv. bd. U. Utah, bus. adv. bd. Coll. Bus. Weber State U.; bd. arbitrators NASD, 1991—. Served to 1st lt. USAR, 1970-72. Mem. Utah Life Scis. Assn. (bd. dirs. 1995—), Tau Beta Pi, Phi Kappa Phi, Beta Gamma Sigma. Republican. Presbyterian. Avocations: skiing, backpacking, basketball, racquetball. Home: 1808 Mohawk Way Salt Lake City UT 84108-3363 Office: Founder's Fund 390 Wakara Way Salt Lake City UT 84108-1214

MELE, ALFRED R., philosophy educator; b. Detroit, May 22, 1951; s. Alfred Emil and Rosemary (Pardo) M.; m. Constance, July 18, 1970; children: Al, Nick, Angela. BA, Wayne State U., 1973; PhD, U. Mich., 1979. Asst. prof. Philosophy Davidson (N.C.) Coll., 1979-85, assoc. prof., 1985-91, prof., 1991-95, Vail prof., 1995—. Author: Irrationality, 1987, Springs of Action, 1992, Autonomous Agents, 1995; contbr. articles to profl. jours. Fellow NEH, 1985-86, 92-93, Nat. Humanities Ctr., Rsch. Triangle Park, N.C., 1992-93. Mem. Am. Philos. Assn., So. Assn. Philosophy and Psychology, N.C. Philos. Soc. (pres. 1987-89). Avocations: racquetball, tennis. Office: Davidson Coll PO Box 1719 Davidson NC 28036-1719

MELEIS, AFAF IBRAHIM, nurse sociologist, educator, clinician, researcher; b. Alexandria, Egypt, Mar. 19, 1942; d. Abdel Baki Ibrahim and Soad Hussein Hassan; m. Mahmoud Meleis, Aug. 21, 1964; children: Waleed, Sherief. BS magna cum laude, U. Alexandria, 1961; MS, UCLA, 1964, MA, 1966, PhD, 1968; D of Pub. Svc. (hon.), U. Portland, 1989. Instr. U. Alexandria, 1961-62; acting instr. UCLA, 1966-68, asst. prof. nursing, then assoc. prof., 1968-75; assoc. prof., dean Health Inst., Kuwait, 1975-77; prof. nursing U. Calif., San Francisco, 1977—, also dir. Study Immigrant Health and Adjustment; vis. prof. colls. in Sweden, Brazil, Japan, Saudi Arabia, Kuwait, Egypt; 1st Centennial prof. Columbia U., N.Y.C., 1992-94; cons., speaker in field. author: theoretical Nursing: Development & Progress, 1985 (Book of Yr., am. Jour. Nursing, 1985), 2d edit., 1991; contbr. articles to rsch. and profl. jours. Recipient Helen Hahm award U. Calif. Sch. Nursing, San Francisco, 1981, Teaching awards U. Calif., San Francisco, 1981, 85, Pres. Hosni Mubarak medal of Excellence, 1990; Kellogg Internat. fellow, 1986-89. Fellow Am. Acad. Nursing; mem. Coun. Nurse Researchers, Western Soc. Research in Nursing, Am. Nurses Assn. Avocations: jogging, symphony, reading, international affairs, women's issues. Home: 39 Corte Ramon Greenbrae CA 94904-1228 Office: U Calif San Francisco Sch Nursing N511Y San Francisco CA 94143-0608

MELENDEZ, JOAQUIN, orthopedic assistant; b. San Gabriel, Calif., Aug. 16, 1929; s. Guadalupe and Gudelia (Maldonado) M.; m. Lola Hester Harris, Sept. 3, 1954. BS, Instituto del Estado, Chihuahua, Mex., 1949; AA, Foothill Coll., Los Altos Hill, Calif., 1973. Enlisted U.S. Army, 1950, advanced through grades to sgt. 1st class, ret., 1971; orthopedic asst. St. Vrain Valley Orthopedics (name now Longmont Orthopedics and Sports Medicine Clinic), Longmont, Colo., 1973—; tchr. pub. spkg. and Spanish for med. office use. Author: (poems) Saturday Night, 1990, Reflections, 1991, Freedom, 1992. With U.S. Army, 1950-71. Decorated Bronze Star with V, Meritorious Svc. medal with V; recipient marathon awards. Mem. Nat. Assn. Orthopedic Technologist, Colo. Acad. Physician Assts., Nat. Assn. Parlimentarians, Toastmasters Internat. (named Outstanding Divsn. Gov. 1988-89, Silver Level of Recognition 1995, recipient speech awards), Internat. Soc. Poets. Republican. Roman Catholic. Avocations: pub. speaking, writing, photography, running, hist. rsch. Home: 3331 Mountain View Ave Longmont CO 80503-2155 Office: Longmont Orthopedics and Sports Medicine Clinic 1331 Linden St Longmont CO 80501-3208

MELENDEZ, SARA E., non-profit organization executive; b. San Juan, P.R., Jan. 20, 1941; d. Pablo and Lucia (Espinosa) M.; 1 child, Adam. BA, Bklyn. Coll., 1967; MS, L.I. U., 1974; EdD, Harvard U., 1981. Tchr. N.Y.C. Bd. of Edn., Bklyn.; asst. prof. U. Hartford (Conn.); dir. Spl. Minority Initiatives Am. Coun. on Edn., Washington; vice provost, dean arts and humanities U. Bridgeport (Conn.); pres. Ctr. for Applied Linguistics, Independent Sector, Washington. Author (book) Bilingual Education: A Sourcebook, 1987. Danforth fellow, Ford fellow. Mem. Soc. for Values in Higher Edn. (dir.). Office: Independent Sector 1828 L St, NW Washington DC 20036

MELENDY, DAVID RUSSELL, broadcast journalist; b. Corpus Christi, Tex., Oct. 19, 1948; s. Harold Orville and Marguerite Doris (Waller) M.; m. Lorna Sandra Katz, Mar. 19, 1972; children: Seth Howard, Andrew Scott. Student, George Washington U., 1966-70; BA magna cum laude, U. Hartford, 1972. News dir. Sta. WINY, Putnam, Conn., 1971-77; news anchor, reporter Sta. WPOP, Hartford, Conn., 1977-80; news dir. Sta. WNVR, Waterbury, Conn., 1980-81; news anchor Sta. WCBS-FM, N.Y.C., 1981; prodr., assignment editor, anchor, reporter AP Broadcast Svcs., Washington, 1981—; instr. journalism Briarwood Coll., Southington, Conn., 1977-81; mem. broadcast adv. com. Briarwood Coll., Southington, 1978-81. Prodr., writer, reporter (audio spl. report series) Star Wars: Strategic Defense Initiative, 1985, (daily audio feature) Flashback, 1986—. Publicity chmn. Woodstock (Conn.) Players Cmty. Theater, 1972-77; publicity chmn. Quinebaug Valley C.C. Found., Danielson, Conn., 1973-75, fundraising chmn., 1976; neighborhood coord. Am. Heart Assn., Washington, 1994; mem. Barker Found., Washington, 1983—. Mem. House and Senate Radio-TV Corr. Assn. Avocations: personal computers, photography, hiking, swimming. Office: AP Broadcast Svcs 1825 K St NW Washington DC 20006-1202

MELHORN, WILTON NEWTON, geosciences educator; b. Sistersville, W.Va., July 8, 1921; s. Ralph Wilton and Pauline (Jones) M.; m. Agnes Leigh Beck, Aug. 25, 1961; children—Kristina L., Kimberly M. B.S., Mich. State U., 1942, M.S., 1951; M.S., N.Y. U., 1943; Ph.D., U. Mich., 1955. Hydrogeologist Mich. Geol. Survey, Lansing, 1946-49; hydrologist U.S. Weather Bur., Indpls., 1949-50; asst., then asso. prof. engring. geology Purdue U., Lafayette, Ind., 1954-70; head dept. geoscis. Purdue U., 1967-70, prof., 1970-91, prof. emeritus, 1991—; vis. prof. U. Ill. at Urbana, 1960-61, U. Nev., Reno, 1971-72, adj. prof., 1973-82; geol. cons. Cook County Hwy Commn., Chgo., 1955-56, Martin-Marietta Corp., Balt., 1964-66, Calif. Nuclear, Inc., Lafayette, 1966-68. Contbr. articles to tech. jours. Served to maj. USAAF, 1942-46. Fellow Geol. Soc. Am., AAAS, Ind. Acad. Scis. (pres. 1988, exec. officer 1992-94); mem. Am. Assn. Petroleum Geologists, Soc. Econ. Geologists and Paleontologists, Speleological Soc., Mich. Acad. Arts, Sci. and Letters, Am. Meteorol. Soc., Explorers Club, Sigma Xi, Sigma Gamma Epsilon. Home: 2065 S 9th St Lafayette IN 47905-2168

MELICAN, JAMES PATRICK, JR., lawyer; b. Worcester, Mass., Sept. 8, 1940; s. James Patrick and Abigail Helen (Donahue) M.; m. Debra A. Burns, Dec. 2, 1978; children: Marlane, James P., David, Molly, Megan. BA, Fordham U., 1962; JD, Harvard U., 1965; MBA, Mich. State U., 1971. Bar: Mich 1966, Calif. 1983. Supervising atty. product liability sect. Gen. Motors Corp., Detroit, 1971-73; atty.-in-charge trade regulation Gen. Motors Corp., 1973-77, atty.-in-charge mktg. and purchasing, 1977-80, asst. gen. counsel, 1980-81; gen. counsel Toyota Motor Sales, U.S.A., Inc., Torrance, Calif., 1981-82, v.p., gen. counsel, 1982-84; v.p., gen. counsel Internat. Paper Co., N.Y.C., 1984-87, sr. v.p., gen. counsel, 1987-91; exec. v.p. legal and external affairs Internat. Paper Co., Purchase, N.Y., 1991—; bd. dirs. Nat. Assn. Mfrs., Scitex Corp., Ltd.; bd. trustees Fordham Prep. Sch. Mem. ABA, NAM (bd. dirs.), Am. Law Inst., Assn. Bar City of N.Y., Assn. Gen. Counsel, Industry Sector Adv. Com. on Paper and Paper Products for Trade Policy Matters; chair Lawyers' Adv. Com. to Bus. Roundtable Corp. Governance task force. Roman Catholic. Home: 46 Clearview Ln New Canaan CT 06840-3444 Office: Internat Paper Co 2 Manhattanville Rd Purchase NY 10577-2118

MELICHER, RONALD WILLIAM, finance educator; b. St. Louis, July 4, 1941; s. William and Lorraine Norma (Mohart) M.; m. Sharon Ann Schlarmann, Aug. 19, 1967; children: Michelle Joy, Thor William, Sean Richard. BSBA, Washington U., St. Louis, 1963; MBA, Washington U., 1965, DBA, 1968. Asst. prof. fin. U. Colo., Boulder, 1969-71, assoc. prof., 1971-76, prof. fin., 1976—, chmn. fin. div., 1978-86, 90; chmn. fin. and econ. div., 1993—; MBA/MS programs dir. U. Colo., Boulder, 1990-93, chmn. fin. and econ. div., 1993—; assoc. dir. space law bus. and policy ctr. U. Colo., 1986-87; rsch. cons. FPC, Washington, 1975-76, GAO, Washington, 1981, RCG/Hagler, Bailly, Inc., 1985—, Ariz. Corp. Commn., 1986-87, Conn. Dept. Pub. Utility Control, 1989, U.S. SEC, 1992—; cons. tech. edn. IBM Corp., 1985-91; dir. ann. Exch. Program for Gas Industry, 1975-94; instr. ann. program Nat. Assn. Regulatory Utility Commrs., Mich. State U., 1981—. Co-author: Real Estate Finance, 1978, 2d edit. 1984, 3d edit. 1989, Finance: Introduction to Markets, Institutions and Management, 1980, 84, 88, 92; assoc. editor Fin. Mgmt. Jour., 1975-80, The Fin. Rev., 1988-91. Recipient News Ctr. 4 TV Teaching award, 1987, MBA/MS Assn. Teaching award, 1988, Boulder Faculty Assembly Teaching award, 1988, Grad. Bus. Students Teaching award, 1995; grantee NSF, 1974, NASA, 1986, 87; scholar W.H. Baughn Disting., 1989—, U. Colo. Pres.'s Teaching, 1989—. Mem. Fin. Mgmt. Assn. (mem. com. 1974-76, regional dir. 1975-77, v.p. ann. mtg. 1985, v.p. program 1987, pres. 1991-92, exec. com. 1991-93, bd. trustees 1992—, chmn. 25th Anniversary com. 1994-95), Am. Fin. Assn. Western Fin. Assn. (bd. dirs. 1974-76), Fin. Execs. Inst. (acad. mem. 1975—), Ea. Fin. Assn., Southwestern Fin. Assn., Midwest Fin. Assn. (bd. dirs. 1978-80), Alpha Kappa Psi, Beta Gamma Sigma. Presbyterian. Home: 6348 Swallow Ln Boulder CO 80303-1456 Office: U Colo Coll Bus PO Box 419 Boulder CO 80303

MELICKIAN, GARY EDWARD, trade association executive; b. L.A., Apr. 2, 1935; s. Ara Harry Melickian and Virginia Anne (Gargan) Jardine; m. Greta Gail Rasbury, Aug. 20, 1955 (div. 1972); children: Mark Stanley, Lynn Anne; m. Sharon Anne McDaniel, July 28, 1989. Student, UCLA, 1953-55; EM, Colo. Sch. Mines, 1959; postgrad., U. So. Calif., 1961-67, Calif. Poly. Inst., 1969-71. Lic. geologist, Calif., Alaska, engrng. geologist, Calif.; cert. profl. geologist. Geologist Humble Oil & Refining Co., L.A., 1959; civil engr. L.A. County Flood Control Dist., L.A., 1960; geophysicist Dames & Moore, L.A., 1961, project geologist, 1962-64, mgr. pers., 1965-66, mgr. pub. rels., 1967-69, ptnr., 1970-84; dir. mining Dames & Moore, Denver, 1970-80; dir. tech. svcs. Dames & Moore, Bethesda, Md., 1980-84; pres., bd. dirs. Consultation Networks, Inc., Washington, 1985-90, Expert Witness Network, Washington, 1985-90; dir. indsl. mktg. Am. Gas Assn., Arlington, Va., 1990—; tech. project advisor Gas Rsch. Inst., Indsl. Gas Tech. Commercialization Ctr., Gas Tech. Can., Can. Gas Assn.; presenter in field. Contbr. articles to profl. jours. Fellow Geol. Soc. Am. (editor Engrng. Geology newsletter 1966-67); mem. NSPE, ASME, Am. Inst. Profl. Geologists (pres. Calif. sect. 1971, bd. dirs. 1972-73, sec.-treas. 1982, Cert. of Merit 1982, 83), Soc. Mining Engrs. (bd. dirs. 1972-74, chmn. Peele award com., publs. com., program com.), Assn. Engring. Geologists (del. Internat. Geol. Congress, Prague), Hist. Earth Sci. Soc., Am. Soc. Metals, Tech. Assn. Pulp and Paper Industry, Assn. Iron and Steel Engrs., Assn. Energy Engrs. Avocations: art history, mineral collecting, stamps, western U.S. history, collecting rare books. Office: Am Gas Assn 1515 Wilson Blvd Arlington VA 22209-2402

MELILLO, JOSEPH VINCENT, producer, performing arts; b. New Haven, Conn., Nov. 15, 1946; s. Vincent and Viola (Fucci) M. BA, Sacred Heart U., 1968; MFA, Cath. U. Am., 1972. Adminstr. City Ctr. Music and Drama, N.Y.C., 1972-75; mktg. dir. The Walnut St. Theatre, Phila., 1975-76; dir. FEDAPT, N.Y.C., 1976-80; gen. mgr. New World Festival of Arts, Miami, Fla., 1982; dir. Next Wave Festival, N.Y.C., 1983-89; artistic dir. N.Y. Internat. Festival, N.Y.C., 1990-91; producing dir. Bklyn. Acad. Music, 1991—; trustee EnGarde Arts, N.Y.C., 1991—; v.p., bd. dirs. Assn. Performing Arts Presenters, Washington, 1991-93; cons.-specialist Opera Am. Washington, 1991-93; cons. The Japan Found. "Performing Arts Japan", The Bush Found., St. Paul, Arts Internat., N.Y.C.; adj. prof. Theater Dept. Bklyn. Coll. Editor: Market the Arts, 1980. Democrat. Avocations: reading, travel.

MELIN, ROBERT ARTHUR, lawyer; b. Milw., Sept. 13, 1940; s. Arthur John and Frances Magdalena (Lanser) M.; m. Mary Magdalen Melin, July 8, 1967; children: Arthur Walden, Robert Dismas, Nicholas O'Brien, Madalyn Mary. B.A. summa cum laude, Marquette U., 1962, J.D., 1967. Bar: Wis. 1966, U.S. Dist. Ct. (ea. dist.) Wis. 1966, U.S. Ct. Appeals (7th cir.) 1966, U.S. Ct. Mil. Appeals 1967, U.S. Supreme Ct. 1975. Law clk. U.S. Dist. Ct. Eastern Dist. Wis., 1966; instr. bus. law U. Ga., Hinesville, 1968, also lectr. bus. law U. Md., Asmara, 1970; lectr. law Haile Selassie I U. Law Faculty, Addis Ababa, Ethiopia, 1971-72; mem. firm Walther & Halling, Milw., 1973-74, Schroeder, Gedlen, Riester & Moerke, Milw., 1974-82; ptnr. Schroeder, Gedlen, Riester & Melin, Milw., 1982-84, Schroeder, Riester, Melin & Smith, 1984—. lectr. charitable solicitations and contracts Philanthropy Monthly 9th Ann. Policy Conf., N.Y.C., 1985. Chmn. Milw. Young Democrats, 1963-64. Served to capt. JAGC, AUS, 1967-70. Mem. Wis. Acad. Trial Lawyers, ABA, Wis. Bar Assn., Milw. Bar Assn., Am. Legion, Friends of Ethiopia, Delta Theta Phi, Phi Alpha Theta, Pi Gamma Mu. Roman Catholic. Author: Evidence in Ethiopia, 1972; contbg. author to Annual Survey of African Law, 1974; contbr. numerous articles to legal jours. Home: 8108 N Whitney Rd Milwaukee WI 53217-2752 Office: 135 W Wells St Milwaukee WI 53203-1807 *Notable cases include: Anderson vs. Continental Ins. Co. 85 Wis. 2d 675, 271 NW 2d 368, 1978, new tort cause of action for insurer's bad-faith refusal to honor claim of 1st party insured; Allstate Ins. Co. vs. Met. Sewerage Commn. 80 wis. 2d 10, 258 N.W. 2d 148, 1977, broad application of remaining vestiges of mcpl. immunity doctrine in Wis. applied in favor of mcpl. client; Met. Sewerage Commn. vs. R.W. Constrn., Inc. 78 Wis 2d 451, 255 NW 2d 293, 1977, breach of sewer constrn. contract case.*

MELISSINOS, ADRIAN CONSTANTIN, physicist, educator; b. Thessaloniki, Greece, July 28, 1929; came to U.S., 1955, naturalized, 1970; s. Constantin John and Olympia (Abbott) M.; m. Mary Joyce Mitchell, June 7, 1960; children: Constantin John, Andrew William. Student, Royal Naval Acad., Greece, 1945-48; M.S., Mass. Inst. Tech., 1956, Ph.D., 1958. Naval cadet Greek Navy, 1945-48, commd. ensign, 1948, advanced through grades to lt., 1951; ret., 1954; teaching and research asst. Mass. Inst. Tech., 1955-58; instr. U. Rochester, N.Y., 1958-60; asst. prof. physics U. Rochester, 1960-63, assoc. prof., 1963-67, prof., 1967—, chmn. dept. physics and astronomy, 1974-77; vis. scientist CERN European Center for Nuclear Research, 1968-69, 77-78, 89-90; cons. Brookhaven Nat. Lab., 1970-72, 75-79. Author: Experiments in Modern Physics, 1966, (with F. Lobkowicz) Physics for Scientists and Engineers, 1975; (with A. Das) Quantum Mechanics, 1985, Principles of Modern Technology, 1990. Decorated Swedish Order of Sword. Fellow Am. Phys. Soc.; mem. Greek Nat. Acad. (corr.). Achievements include experimentation with elementary particles at most major high energy accelerators in the U.S. and Europe, experimentation with high power lasers. Home: 177 Whitewood Ln Rochester NY 14618-3223 Office: U Rochester Dept Physics Rochester NY 14627

MELKONIAN, HARRY G., lawyer, rancher; b. Bridgeport, Conn., June 18, 1949; s. Harry Artin and Hermina (Barsumian) M. BA, U. Rochester, 1971; JD cum laude, NYU, 1974. Bar: N.Y. 1975, Calif. 1977, U.S. Supreme Ct. 1984. Atty. Breed Abbott & Morgan, N.Y.C., 1974-76, Rifkind Sterling & Lockwood, Beverly Hills, Calif., 1976-78; atty. Buchalter Nemer Fields & Younger, L.A., 1978-81, ptnr., 1981-87; ptnr. White & Case, L.A., 1987—. Editor NYU Law Review, 1973-74. Trustee Project Literacy L.A., 1990-92; bd. govs. The Pilgrim Sch., L.A., 1992—; bd. dirs. HopeNet, L.A., 1990-91; chmn. bd. deacons 1st Congl. Ch. L.A., 1992-93, trustee, 1994—. Mem. Olympic Club, Calif. Club, Phi Alpha Delta. Republican. Avocations: fishing, hunting. Office: White & Case 633 W 5th St Fl 19 Los Angeles CA 90071-2005

MELLA, ARTHUR JOHN, insurance company executive; b. New York, N.Y., Sept. 25, 1937; s. Anthony Arthur and Angela Helen (Morrongiello) M.; m. Louise Vetere, May 5, 1962; children: Douglas James, Gregory Arthur. BS, Fordham U., 1959. CPCU. Supr. Liberty Mut. Ins. Co., N.Y.C., 1960-70; v.p. The Home Ins. Co., N.Y.C., 1970-80, Skandia Am. Reinsurance Co., N.Y.C., 1980-85; sr. v.p. Reliance Reinsurance Corp., Phila., 1985—. With USNG, 1960-63. Mem. Fedn. Ins. and Corp. Counsel, Excess Surplus Lines Claims (pres. 1988-89, v.p. 1987-88, bd. dirs. 1986-87), Broker and Reins. Underwriting, Soc. CPCU. Republican. Roman Catholic. Avocations: gardening, book collecting, golf. Office: Reliance Reinsurance Co 1 Penn Center Plz Philadelphia PA 19103-1821

MELLBERG, LEONARD EVERT, physicist; b. Springfield, Mass., Dec. 18, 1935; s. Evert and Dorothy (Baker) M. BS in Physics, U. Mass., 1961; MS in Physics, Trinity Coll., Hartford, Conn., 1968. Rsch. physicist Navy Underwater Sound Lab., New London, Conn., 1961-68, SACLANT Undersea Rsch. Ctr., LaSpezia, Italy, 1968-72, Office of Naval Rsch., London, 1968-72, Naval Underwater Systems Ctr., Newport, R.I., 1972-91; sr. scientist Marine Acoustics Inc., Newport, 1991-94; cons. sci. applications Internat. Corp., Newport, R.I., 1994—; mem. numerous govt. and profl. tech. adv. bds. and coms. Contbr. over 70 articles to profl. jours. Pres. Verdandi Swedish Cultural Found., Providence, 1992—; bd. dirs. Verdandi Chorus Am. Union Swedish Singers, Providence, 1992—. Recipient Naval Underwater Sys. Ctr. Excellence in Sci. award, 1977, 84, Civilian Navy Meritorious Svc. medal Dept. of Navy, 1991. Fellow Acoustical Soc. Am.; mem. IEEE (sr.), AIAA (svc. award 1977), Am. Geophys. Union. Achievements include research in ocean physics, ocean acoustic propagation, anti-submarine warfare acoustics, Arctic sea-ice ridges and lighter than air vehicles. Home: 20 Willow Ave Middletown RI 02842-4948

MELLEN, FRANCIS JOSEPH, JR., lawyer; b. Williamsport, Pa., Dec. 19, 1945; s. Francis Joseph and Mary Emma (Oberst) M.; m. Mary Wilder Davison, Aug. 2, 1975 (div. 1987); children: Elizabeth, Catherine, Robert, Christine. BA, U. Ky., 1967, MA, 1971; JD, Harvard U., 1973. Bar: N.Y. 1974, Ky. 1975, U.S. Dist. Ct. (so. dist.) N.Y. 1974, U.S. Dist. Ct. (ea. dist.) Ky. 1977, U.S. Dist. Ct. (we. dist.) Ky. 1978, U.S. Ct. Appeals (2d cir.) 1975, U.S. Ct. Appeals (6th cir.) 1982. Assoc. atty. Rogers & Wells, N.Y.C., 1973-75, Wyatt, Grafton & Sloss, Louisville, 1975-80; ptnr. Wyatt, Tarrant & Combs, Louisville, 1980—. Co-author: Kentucky Mineral Law, 1986, Kentucky Forms and Transactions, 1991. Contbr. articles to profl. jours. Mem. spl. study com. for Uniform Commercial Code, Ky. Legis. Rsch. Comsn., Frankfort, 1984-91. Lt. USNR, 1967-69, Vietnam. Bd. Dirs. Leaderships Louisville Found., Stage One: The Louisville Children's Theatre, Louisville-Jefferson County A.W.A.R.E. Coalition; Mem. ABA, Am. Arbitration Assn. (panel), Ky. Bar Assn. (Chmn. Com. profl. responsibility 1992-94, Ho. of delegates 1986-92) Jefferson Club, Filson Club, American Mensa, Louisville Bar Assn. Republican. Home: 429 Trinity Hills Ln Louisville KY 40207-2132 Office: Wyatt Tarrant & Combs 2800 Citizens Plz Louisville KY 40202

MELLENCAMP, JOHN (JOHN COUGAR), singer, songwriter; b. Seymour, Ind., Oct. 7, 1951; m. Vicky C. (div.); children: Michelle, Teddy Joe, Justice; m. Elaine Irwin, Sept. 5, 1992. Student, Vincennes U., Ind. Albums include Chestnut Street Incident, 1977, Biography, 1978, Johnny Cougar, 1979, Nothing Matters and What If It Did, 1980, Night Dancin, 1980, American Fool, 1982, Uh-huh, 1983, Scarecrow, 1985, The Lonesome Jubilee, 1988, Big Daddy, 1989, Whenever We Wanted, 1991, Human Wheels, 1993, Dance Naked, 1994; performed one song for Folkways: A Vision Shared (A Tribute to Woody Guthrie and Leadbelly), 1988; film actor, dir., soundtrack performer: Falling From Grace, 1992; TV appearance Bob Dylan: The 30th Anniversary Concert Celebration, 1993. Office: Champion Entertainment 130 W 57th St Apt 12B New York NY 10019

MELLETTE, M. SUSAN JACKSON, physician, educator, researcher; b. Raleigh, N.C., June 4, 1922; d. Donald Rudolph and Bessie Lou (Mull) Jackson; m. Peter A. Mellette, June 16, 1943; children: Susan E. Mellette Lederhouse, Peter Mason. AB, Meredith Coll., 1942; postgrad., U. N.C., 1942-43, U. Pa. Med. Sch., 1944; MD, U. Cin., 1947. Fels rsch. asst. U. N.C., Chapel Hill, 1942-43; intern Cleve. City Hosp., 1947-48; resident in internal medicine St. Barnabas Hosp., N.Y.C., 1949-51, Koch Hosp., St. Louis, 1952-54; rsch. assoc. U. Louisville, 1952; NIH rsch. fellow Med. Coll. Va., 1955-57, Damon Runyon cancer rsch. fellow, 1957-58; rsch. assoc. Med. Coll. Va., Richmond, 1958-60, asst. prof. internal medicine, 1960-69, assoc. prof., 1969-79, prof. internal and rehab. medicine, 1979-93, prof. emerita, 1993—, cancer coord., 1961-66, dir. Cancer Rehab. Program, 1974-93; mem. behavioral medicine study sect. NIH, Bethesda, Md., 1986-91; mem. cancer edn. com. Nat. Cancer Inst., NIH, 1974-78, mem. task force on rehab. rsch., 1990, mem. expert panel on advances in cancer treatment Nat Cancer Inst., 1992. Contbr. numerous articles and book chpts. on cancer treatment and rehab. to profl. publs. Mem. Commn. on Terminal Care Legislature Va., Richmond, 1982-83; adv. bd. Women's Bank, Richmond, 1979-81. Recipient Hoover award Va. Rehab. Assn., 1979, Nat. Brotherhood award NCCJ, 1987, Profl. of Yr. award Va. Assn. Professions, 1989. Fellow Am. Assn. Cancer Edn. (pres. 1975); mem. N.Y. Acad. Sci., Am. Congress Rehab. Medicine (chmn. cancer rehab. com. 1984-87), Am. Cancer Soc. (nat. svc. and rehab. com. 1982-92, nat. patient svcs. com. 1992-94, Profl. Edn. award Va. divsn. 1982), Am. Assn. Med. Colls., Med. Coll. Va. Alumni Assn. (named disting. prof. 1995), Alpha Omega Alpha. Home: 1502 Wilmington Ave Richmond VA 23227-4430 Office: Med Coll Va Richmond VA 23298

MELLI, MARYGOLD SHIRE, law educator; b. Rhinelander, Wis., Feb. 8, 1926; d. Osborne and May (Bonnie) Shire; m. Joseph Alexander Melli, Apr. 8, 1950; children: Joseph, Sarah Bonnie, Sylvia Anne, James Alexander. BA, U. Wis., 1947, LLB, 1950. Bar: Wis. 1950. Dir. children's code revision Wis. Legis. Coun., Madison, 1950-53; exec. dir. Wis. Jud. Coun., Madison, 1955-59; asst. prof. law U. Wis., Madison, 1961-66, assoc. prof., 1966-67, prof., 1967-84; Voss-Bascom prof. U. Wis., 1985-93, emerita, 1993—; assoc. dean U. Wis., 1970-72, rsch. affiliate Inst. for Rsch. on Poverty, 1980—; mem. spl. rev. bd. Dept. Health and Social Svcs., State of Wis., Madison, 1973—. Author: (pamphlet) The Legal Status of Women in Wisconsin, 1977, (book) Wisconsin Juvenile Court Practice, 1978, rev. edit., 1983, (with others) Child Support & Alimony, 1988, The Case for Transracial Adoption, 1994; contbr. articles to profl. jours. Bd. dirs. Am. Humane Assn., 1985-95. Named one of five Outstanding Young Women in Wis., Jaycees, 1961; rsch. grantee NSF, 1983; recipient award for Outstanding Contbn. to Advancement of Women in State Bar of Wis., award for Lifelong Contbn. to Advancement of Women in the Legal Prof., 1994. Fellow Am. Acad. Matrimonial Lawyers (exec. editor jour. 1985-90); mem. Am. Law Inst. (reporter, cons. project on law of family dissolution), Internat. Soc. Family Law (v.p.), Wis. State Bar Assn. (reporter family law sect.), Nat. Conf. Bar Examiners (chmn. bd. mgrs. 1989). Democrat. Roman Catholic. Avocations: jogging, swimming, collecting art. Home: 2904 Waunona Way Madison WI 53713-2238 Office: U Wis Law Sch Madison WI 53706

MELLINK, MACHTELD JOHANNA, archaeologist, educator; b. Amsterdam, Holland, Oct. 26, 1917; came to U.S., 1949; d. Johan and Machteld (Kruyff) M. B.A., U. Amsterdam, 1938, M.A., 1941; Ph.D., Utrecht (Netherlands) U., 1943; LLD (hon.), U. Pa., 1987, Anatolian U., Turkey, 1990. Faculty Bryn Mawr Coll., 1949-88, prof. classical and Near Eastern archaeology, 1962-88, chmn. dept., 1955-83; staff mem. excavations Tarsus, Turkey, 1947-49, Gordion, Turkey, 1950-74; field dir. excavations Karatas-Semayuk, Lycia, Turkey, 1963—; Troy, 1988—; research asso. U. Mus., U. Pa., 1955-82, con. scholar, 1982—. Author: A Hittite Cemetery at Gordion, 1956; author: (with Jan Filip) Frühe Stufen der Kunst-Propyläen Kunstgeschichte XIII, 1974; editor: Dark Ages and Nomads c. 1000 B.C., 1964, Troy and the Trojan War, 1986, Elmali-Karatas I, 1992, II, 1994; contbr. articles to profl. jours. Recipient Lucy Wharton Drexel medal U. Pa. Mus., 1994—. Fellow Am. Acad. Arts and Scis.; mem. Archaeol. Inst. Am. (pres. 1981-84, gold medal 1991), German Archaeol. Inst., Am. Oriental Soc., Am. Philos. Soc.; corr. mem. Royal Netherlands Acad. Scis., Austrian Archaeol. Inst. (corr.), Türk Tarih Kurumu (hon.), Am. Research Inst. Turkey (v.p. 1977-87, pres. 1988-92). Home: 264 Montgomery Ave Haverford PA 19041-1531

MELLINKOFF, DAVID, lawyer, educator; b. 1914. AB, Stanford U., 1935; LLB, Harvard U., 1939. Bar: Calif. 1939. Sole practice Calif., 1939-41, 46-64; lectr. UCLA Law Sch., 1964-65, prof., 1965-85, prof. emeritus, 1985—. Author: The Language of the Law, 1963, 12th printing, 1994, The Conscience of a Lawyer, 1973, 4th printing, 1978, Lawyers and the System of Justice, 1976, Legal Writing: Sense of Nonsense, 1982, 4th reprint, 1995,

Mellinkoff's Dictionary of American Legal Usage, 1992, 2d printing, 1993; also articles. Served to capt. U.S. Army, 1941-46. Home: 744 Holmby Ave Los Angeles CA 90024-3320 Office: UCLA Law Sch 405 Hilgard Ave Los Angeles CA 90024-1301

MELLINKOFF, SHERMAN MUSSOFF, medical educator; b. McKeesport, Pa., Mar. 23, 1920; s. Albert and Helen (Mussoff) M.; m. June Bernice O'Connell, Nov. 18, 1944; children: Sherrill, Albert. BA, Stanford U., 1941, MD, 1944; LHD (hon.), Wake Forest U., 1984, Hebrew Union Coll., L.A., 1988. Diplomate Am. Bd. Internal Medicine, Am. Bd. Gastroenterology, Am. Bd. Nutrition. Intern asst. resident Stanford U. Hosp., San Francisco, 1944-45; asst. resident Johns Hopkins Hosp., Balt., 1947-49, chief resident, 1950-51, instr. in medicine, 1951-53; fellow in gastroenterology Hosp. of U. Pa., Phila., 1949-50; from asst. prof. to prof. medicine UCLA Sch. of Medicine, L.A., 1962-86; dean UCLA Sch. Medicine, L.A., 1962-86, emeritus prof. of medicine, 1990—; disting. physician of VA Wadsworth VA Medical Ctr., L.A., 1990-93; mem. sci. adv. panel Rsch. to Prevent Blindness, Inc., N.Y.C., 1975-93; mem. program devel. com. Nat. Med. Fellowships, Inc., N.Y.C., 1984—. Editorial bd. The Pharos, 1986; contbr. articles to profl. jours. Apptd. by Gov. of Calif. to McCone Com., 1965. Capt. U.S. Army, 1945-47. Recipient Abraham Flexner award Assn. Am. Med. Colls., 1981, J.E. Wallace Sterling Disting. Alumnus award Stanford U. Sch. of Medicine, 1987. Master ACP; fellow Royal Coll. of Physicians; mem. Am. Gastroenterol. Assn. Assn., of Am. Physicians, Inst. of Medicine of NAS, Am. Acad. of Arts and Scis., The Johns Hopkins Soc. of Scholars. Avocations: reading, hiking. Office: UCLA Sch of Medicine Dept of Medicine 44-143 CHS Los Angeles CA 90024

MELLINS, HARRY ZACHARY, radiologist, educator; b. N.Y.C., May 23, 1921; s. David J. and Ray (Hoffman) M.; m. Judith Alice Weiss, Dec. 26, 1950; children—Elizabeth, William, Thomas. A.B., Columbia Coll., 1941; M.D., L.I. Coll. Medicine, 1944; M.S. in Radiology, U. Minn., 1951; A.M. (hon.), Harvard U., 1970. Intern Jewish Hosp., Bklyn., 1944-45, asst. resident in radiology, 1945-46; resident in radiology U. Minn., Mpls., 1948-50, instr. radiology, 1950-52, asst. prof., 1952-53; clin. asst. prof. radiology Wayne State U., Detroit, 1953-56; dir. radiology Sinai Hosp., Detroit, 1953-56; prof., chmn. dept. radiology SUNY, Coll. Medicine, N.Y.C., 1956-69; chief radiology Kings County Hosp. Center, Bklyn., 1956-69; radiologist-in-chief State Univ. Hosp., Bklyn., 1966-69; prof. radiology Harvard Med. Sch., Boston, 1969-91, prof. radiology emeritus, 1991—; dir. diagnostic radiology Peter Bent Brigham Hosp., 1969-79; dir. diagnostic radiology Brigham and Women's Hosp., 1980-87, dir. edn. and tng., dept. radiology, 1987-94; co-dir. edn. and tng. dept. radiology, 1994—; chief of radiology Harvard U. Health Svc., 1988—; nat. cons. in radiology to surgeon gen. U.S. Air Force, 1968-79; mem. radiation study sect. NIH, 1967-71; mem. subcom. for written exam. in diagnostic radiology Am. Bd. Radiology, 1970-75; mem. radiology tng. com. research tng. grants br. Nat. Inst. Gen. Med. Scis.; mem. diagnostic research adv. group div. cancer biology and diagnosis Nat. Cancer Inst., 1975-79; guest examiner Am. Bd. Radiology. Served to capt. M.C. USAAF, 1946-48. Mem. Bklyn. Radiol. Soc. (pres. 1965-66), N.Y. Roentgen Soc. (pres 1966-67), Assn. Univ. Radiologists (pres. 1969-70, Gold medal 1986), Soc. Uroradiology (pres. 1975-76), Am. Roentgen Ray Soc. (pres. 1977-79, Gold medal 1989), Radiol. Soc. N.Am., New Eng. Roentgen Ray Soc. (pres. 1986-87), Soc. Gastrointestinal Radiology, Alpha Omega Alpha. Office: Brigham and Women's Hosp 75 Francis St Boston MA 02115-6110

MELLINS, ROBERT B., pediatrician, educator; b. N.Y.C., Mar. 6, 1928; s. David J. and Ray H. (Hoffman) M.; m. Sue Mendelsohn, Apr. 19, 1959; children: Claude Ann, David Rustin. A.B., Columbia U., 1948; M.D., Johns Hopkins U., 1952. Intern Johns Hopkins Hosp., 1952-53; mem. epidemic intelligence svc, founder poison control ctr. Ctr. Disease Control, Chgo., 1953-55; resident in pediatrics N.Y. Hosp., 1955-56; resident in pediatrics Presbyn. Hosp., N.Y.C., 1956-57, dir. pediatric ICU, 1970-75; assoc. prof. pediatrics Columbia U., 1970-75, prof. pediatrics, 1975—, dir. Cystic Fibrosis Ctr., 1978-91, dir. pediatric pulmonary div., 1972—; founding mem. sect. on pulmonology Am. Bd. Pediatrics, 1985—; Christmas Seal prof. Can. Lung Assn., 1979-80; 1st Deans Disting. lectr. in clin. scis. Columbia U. Coll. P&S, 1982. Mem. editorial bd. Am. Rev. Respiratory Diseases, 1974-81, assoc. editor, 1984-90; contbr. articles to med. jours. Bd. dirs. Am. Lung Assn., 1981-93, nat. v.p., 1987-89, bd. dirs. N.Y. chpt., 1984—, v.p., 1994—; bd. dirs. L.A. Jonas Found., 1970-78, 90—, Syphony of UN, 1990—; chmn. steeering com. Multictr. Study of Heart and Lung Complications of HIV Infection in Children, NIH, 1989—. Recipient Career Devel. award NIH, 1966-71, Career Scientist award Health Rsch. Coun. N.Y.C. Health Rsch. Coun., 1975, Stevens Triennial award for rsch. Columbia U., 1980, Health Edn. Rsch. award Nat. Asthma Edn. Program, 1992, Will Ross medal Am. Lung Assn., 1996. Mem. Am. Pediatric Soc., Soc. Pediatric Rsch., Am. Physiol. Soc., Am. Soc. Pharmacology and Exptl. Therapeutics, Am. Acad. Pediat. (Med. Edn. Lay Edn. award 1995, Med. Edn. award 1995), Am. Thoracic Soc. (bd. dirs. 1975-75, 81-84, nat. pres. 1982-83, v.p., Disting. Achievement award 1996), Soc. Critical Care Medicine, Fleischner Soc. (pres. 1995—), Am. Acad. Allergy and Immunology, Alpha Omega Alpha. Home: 2 W 67th St New York NY 10023-6241 Office: Columbia U 630 W 168th St New York NY 10032-3702

MELLISH, GORDON HARTLEY, economist, educator; b. Toronto, May 3, 1940; came to U.S., 1958; s. Gordon Day and Catherine (Hartley) M.; m. Nancy Bernice Newsll (div. Nov. 1972); m. Diane Evelyn Bostow, Jan. 1, 1978; children: Jennie Bostow, Luke Bostow. BA, Rockford (Ill.) Coll., 1962; PhD, U. Va., 1965. Econs. educator U. South Fla., Tampa, 1965-89; pvt. practice Tampa, Fla., 1966—; vis. prof. U. Va., 1969, Hillsborough Jr. Coll., 1968; vis. lectr. U. Tampa, 1965, 74. Contbr. articles to profl. jours. Bd. dirs. Tampa Ballet. Mem. Tampa Yacht and Country Club, Tampa Club, Leadership Tampa Alumni. Democrat. Avocations: sailing, skiing. Home: 2510 W Shell Point Pl Tampa FL 33611-5033

MELLON, JOHN, publishing executive; b. 1940. Chmn. IPC mags., Reed Bus. Pub., Reed Regional Newspapers; CEO Reed Pub. Europe; dir. Reed Internat., 1990—, exec. dir., 1992—; mem. Reed Elsevier Exec. Committee, 1994—; mem. adv. com. on advt. for the Ctrl. Office of Info. Office: IPC Magazines rm 1701, King's Reach Tower Stamford Street, London SE1 9LS, England*

MELLON, PAUL, retired art gallery executive; b. Pitts., June 11, 1907; s. Andrew W. and Nora (McMullen) M.; m. Mary Conover, Feb. 2, 1935 (dec. Oct. 1946); children: Catherine Conover, Timothy; m. Rachel Lambert Lloyd, May 1, 1948. AB, Yale U., 1929, LHD (hon.), 1967; AB, Cambridge (Eng.) U., 1931, MA, 1938, LLD (hon.), 1983; Litt.D. (hon.), Oxford U., 1961; LL.D. (hon.), Carnegie Inst. Tech., 1967; DVM (hon.), Royal Vet. Coll., U. London, 1991. Pres. Nat. Gallery Art, Washington, to 1979; chmn. bd. trustees Nat. Gallery Art, 1979-85, hon. trustee, 1985—; trustee Andrew W. Mellon Found., N.Y.; assoc. fellow Berkeley Coll., Yale U.; hon. fellow Clare Coll., Cambridge, Eng., St. John's Coll., Annapolis; Benjamin Franklin fellow Royal Soc. Arts, London, 1969. Served from pvt. to 1st lt. Cav. AUS, 1941-43; 1st lt. to maj. overseas service with OSS, 1943-45. Recipient Yale medal award, 1953; Horace Marden Albright Scenic Preservation medal, 1957; award for distinguished service to arts Nat. Inst. Arts and Letters, 1962; Benjamin Franklin medal Royal Soc. Arts, London, 1965; Skowhegan Gertrude Vanderbilt Whitney award, 1972, Nat. Medal of Arts, 1985, Thomas Jefferson Meml. Found. medal in architecture, 1989, Hadrian award World Monuments Fund, 1989, medal disting. philanthropy Am. Assn. Mus., 1993; decorated hon. knight comdr. Order Brit. Empire, 1974; decorated Knight Grand Officer of the Order of Orange Nassau, 1982. Fellow AAAS; mem. Scroll and Key Soc., Am. Philos. Soc. (Benjamin Franklin award 1989); hon. mem. AIA. Clubs: Metropolitan (Washington); Racquet and Tennis (N.Y.C.), Grolier (N.Y.C.), Links (N.Y.C.), Knickerbocker (N.Y.C.), Jockey (N.Y.C.), Nat. Steeplechase and Hunt Assn. (N.Y.C.); Society of the Dilettanti (London), Roxburghe (London), Buck's (London), English Jockey (hon.). Office: Ste 1201 1140 Connecticut Ave NW Washington DC 20036-6000

MELLON, RICHARD PROSSER, charitable foundation executive; b. Chgo., May 19, 1939; s. Richard King and Constance Mary (Prosser) M.; m. Gertrude Alice Adams, Apr. 28, 1962 (div. 1976); children: Richard Adams, Armour Negley; m. 2d Katherine Woodward Hooker, Dec. 2, 1976. Student, U. Pitts, 1958-60; A.A. (hon.), Valley Forge Mil. Jr. Coll., 1970. Chmn. Richard King Mellon Found., Pitts., 1980—. Bd. dirs. Ducks Unltd. Found.; nat. trustee, mem. nat. exec. com. life mem. Ducks Unltd., Inc.; corporator Western Pa. Sch. for Blind. Served to 1st lt. USAR, 1958-67. Episcopalian. Clubs: Duquesne (Pitts.); Laurel Valley Golf (Ligonier), Rolling Rock (Ligonier), Rolling Rock-Westmoreland Hunt (Ligonier); Links (N.Y.C.); Nat. Steeplechase and Hunt Assn. (Ligonier). Home: Gen Delivery Ligonier PA 15658 Office: Mellon Found One Mellon Bank Center 500 Grant St Pittsburgh PA 15219-2502*

MELLON, SEWARD PROSSER, investment executive; b. Chgo., July 28, 1942; s. Richard King and Constance Mary (Prosser) Mellon Burrell; m. Karen Leigh Boyd, Sept. 10, 1966 (div. 1974); children—Catharine Leigh, Constance Elizabeth; m. Sandra Springer Stout, 1975. Grad., Choate Sch., 1960; B.A., Susquehanna U., 1965, DH, 1993. With Mellon Nat. Corp., Pitts., 1965-69; with T. Mellon & Sons, Pitts., 1969-71; pres. Richard K. Mellon & Sons, Ligonier, 1971—; bd. dirs. Mellon Bank N.A., Mellon Nat. Corp. Trustee Richard King Mellon Family Found.; trustee, pres. Richard King Mellon Found.; chmn. real estate com., chmn. bd. mem. fin. and exec. com. Valley Sch. Ligonier. Mem. Western Pa. Conservancy (life), LoyalHanna Assn. (pres.), Vintage Club (Palm Springs, Calif.), Duquesne Club (Pitts.), Laurel Valley Golf Club (Ligonier), Rolling Rock Club, Rolling Rock Hunt, Phi Mu Delta. Republican. Home: Huntland Downs Box K Ligonier PA 15658 Office: PO Box Rkm Ligonier PA 15658-0780

MELLON, THOMAS S., lawyer; b. Phila., Nov. 18, 1956. BA, Ohio Wesleyan U., 1978; JD cum laude, Vt. Law Sch., 1989. Bar: Pa. 1989, N.J. 1991, U.S. Dist. Ct. N.J., U.S. Dist. Ct. (ea. amd mid. dists.) Pa., U.S. Ct. Appeals (3d cir.). Atty. Krusen Evans and Byrne, Phila., 1990-94, Murphy & O'Connor, Phila., 1994—. Avocations: golf, squash, racketball, softball. Office: Murphy & O'Connor 2 Penn Center Plz Ste 1100 Philadelphia PA 19102-1721

MELLON, TIMOTHY, transportation executive. CEO Guilford Transp. Industries, North Billerica, Mass. Office: Guilford Transp Industries High St Iron Horse Pk North Billerica MA 01862*

MELLOR, JAMES ROBB, electronics executive; b. Detroit, May 3, 1930; s. Clifford and Gladys (Robb) M.; m. Suzanne Stykos, June 8, 1953; children: James Robb, Diane Elyse, Deborah Lynn. BS in Elec. Engring. and Math., U. Mich., 1952, MS, 1953. Mem. tech. staff Hughes Aircraft Co., Fullerton, Calif., 1955-58; pres. Data Systems divsn. Litton Industries, Van Nuys, Calif., after 1958; exec. v.p. Litton Industries, Inc., Beverly Hills, Calif.; pres., COO AM Internat., Inc., L.A., to 1981; exec. v.p., dir. Gen. Dynamics Corp., Falls Church, Va., 1981-90, pres., 1990—, COO, 1990-93, CEO, 1993-94, chmn., CEO, 1994—; bd. dirs. Bergen Brunswig Corp., Kerr, Computer Scis. Corp. Patentee in fields of storage tubes and display systems; contbr. articles to profl. publs. 1st lt., Signal Corps, AUS, 1953-55. Mem. IEEE, Am. Mgmt. Assn., Armed Forces Comm. and Electronics Assn. (bd. dirs.), Computer and Bus. Equipment Mfrs. Assn. (former chmn.), L.A. Country Club, Calif. Club, Eldorado Club, Congl. Country Club, Burning Tree Club, Sigma Xi, Tau Beta Pi, Eta Kappa Nu. Home: 7901 Sandalfoot Dr Potomac MD 20854-5449 Office: Gen Dynamics Corp 3190 Fairview Park Dr Falls Church VA 22042-4524

MELLOR, JOHN WILLIAMS, economist, policy consultant firm executive; b. Paris, Dec. 28, 1928; came to U.S., 1929; s. Desmond W. and Katherine (Beardsley) M.; m. Arlene Patton, June 15, 1950 (div. Sept. 1972); children: Michael, Brian, Mark (dec.); m. Uma Lele, Feb. 17, 1973 (div. Apr. 1992). BS, Cornell U., 1950, MS, 1951, PhD, 1954; Diploma, Oxford (Eng.) U., 1952. Prof. Cornell U., Ithaca, N.Y., 1953-75; chief economist USAID, Washington, 1975-77; dir. Internat. Food Policy Rsch. Inst., Washington, 1977-91; pres. John W. Mellor Assocs., Inc., Washington, 1991—; mem. bd. on agrl. NAS, 1989-92; mem. Agrl. Credit Commn., Res. Bank India, 1986-88. Author: Economics of Agricultural Development, 1966 (Am. Agrl. Econs. Assn. award 1976), Accelerating Food Production Growth in Sub-Saharan Africa, 1987, Agricultural Price Policy for Developing Countries, 1988 (hon. mention Am. Agrl. Econs. Assn. 1989). Mem. Internat. Commn. on Food and Peace, 1988—. Recipient Wihuri Internat. prize Wihuri Found., Helsinki, 1985, Presdl. End Hunger award The White House, 1987, Outstanding Alumni award Cornell U., 1987. Fellow AAAS, Am. Acad. Arts and Scis., Am. Agrl. Econs. Assn. (Best Pub. Rsch. award 1967). Avocations: sailing, skiing. Office: John Mellor Assocs Inc Ste PH18 801 Pennsylvania Ave NW Washington DC 20004-2615

MELLOR, MICHAEL LAWTON, lawyer; b. Yorkshire, Eng., July 20, 1922; came to U.S., 1922; s. Bethel and Carmen (Lawton) M.; m. Mary Gordon, May 17, 1952 (dec.); children—Wendy, Jane, Christie. A.B., U. Calif.-Berkeley, 1943, LL.B., 1950. Bar: Calif. 1951. Assoc., Thelen, Marrin, Johnson & Bridges, San Francisco, 1950-62, ptnr., 1962-90, of counsel, 1990-93; dir. various bus. cos. Bd. dirs. San Francisco Attic Theatre, 1979-83, Robinson Jeffers Tor House Found., Carmel, Calif., 1980-96, Pacific Vision Found., San Francisco, 1982—, Friends of San Francisco Pub. Libr., 1984-92, Dance Through Time, Kentfield, Calif., 1986-92, Internat. Visitors Ctr., 1990-96. 1st lt. U.S. Army, 1943-45, Philippines, Japan. Mem. ABA, Calif. State Bar, San Francisco Bar Assn. Democrat. Club: The Family (dir., sec.) (San Francisco). Home: 81 5th Ave San Francisco CA 94118-1307 Office: Thelen Marrin Johnson & Bridges Two Embarcadero Ctr San Francisco CA 94111

MELLOR, RONALD JOHN, history educator; b. Bklyn., Sept. 30, 1940; s. Ronald Green and Eleanor Teresa (Walsh) M.; m. Anne Tidaback Kostelanetz, June 7, 1969; 1 child, Ronald Blake. AB, Fordham Coll., 1962; cert., U. Louvain, Belgium, 1961; AM, Princeton U., 1964, PhD in Classics, 1968. Acting asst. prof. Classics Stanford (Calif.) U., 1965-68, asst. prof. Classics, 1968-75; assoc. prof. history UCLA, 1976-82, prof. history, 1982—, vice chair history, 1991-92, chair history, 1992—. Author: Thea Rhome, 1975, From Augustus to Nero: The First Dynasty of Imperial Rome, 1990, Tacitus, 1993, Tacitus and the Classical Tradition, 1995. Fellow NEH, 1969, Am. Coun. Learned Socs., 1972, Humanities Rsch. Ctr. Australian Nat. U., Canberra, Australia, 1990; hon. fellow U. Coll. London, Eng., 1969, 72, 83-85. Mem. Am. Hist. Assn., Am. Philol. Assn., Am. Inst. Archaeology, Assn. Ancient Historians, Soc. for the Promotion of Roman Studies. Democrat. Avocations: opera, travel, theater, tennis. Home: 2620 Mandeville Canyon Rd Los Angeles CA 90049-1004 Office: UCLA Dept History 405 Hilgard Ave Los Angeles CA 90095-1473

MELLORS, ROBERT CHARLES, physician scientist; b. Dayton, Ohio, 1916; s. Bert S. and Clementine (Steinmetz) M.; m. Jane K. Winternitz, Mar. 25, 1944; children: Alice J., Robert C., William K., John W. Ph.D., Western Res. U., 1940; M.D., Johns Hopkins, 1944. Diplomate Am. Bd. Pathology. Intern Nat. Naval Med. Ctr., Bethesda, Md., 1944-45; rsch. fellow medicine Meml. Center Cancer and Allied Diseases, N.Y.C., 1946-50; rsch. fellow pathology Meml. Ctr. Cancer and Allied Diseases, 1950-53, asst. attending pathologist, 1953-57, assoc. attending pathologist, 1957-58; sr. fellow Am. Cancer Soc., 1947-50; sr. clin. rsch. fellow Damon Runyon Meml. Fund, 1950-53; asst. attending pathologist Meml. Hosp., N.Y.C., 1953-57, assoc. attending pathologist, 1957-58; asst. attending pathologist Ewing Hosp., N.Y.C., 1953-57, assoc. attending pathologist, 1957-58; instr. biochemistry Western Res. U., 1940-42; rsch. assoc. Poliomyelitis Rsch. Ctr. and Dept. Epidemiology Johns Hopkins U. Sch. Hygiene, 1942-44; asst. prof. biology Meml. Ctr. Cancer and Allied Diseases, N.Y.C., 1952-53; asst. prof. pathology Sloan Kettering div. Cornell U., 1953-57, assoc. prof., 1957-58; prof. pathology Cornell U. Med. Coll., 1961-90, prof. emeritus, 1990—; assoc. attending pathologist N.Y. Hosp., 1961-72, attending pathologist, 1972-86; pathologist-in-chief, dir. labs., 1958-84, emeritus, 1984-85, hon. staff, 1986—; assoc. dir. rsch. Hosp. for Spl. Surgery, N.Y.C., 1958-69, dir. rsch., 1969-84, emeritus, 1984-85, scientist emeritus, 1986—; mem. rsch. adv. com. NIH, 1962-66; adv. com. Nat. Inst. Environ. Health Sci., 1966-69; com. nomenclature and classification of disease Coll. Am. Pathologists, 1960-64. Author: Analytical Cytology, 1955, 2d edit., 1959, Analytical Pathology, 1957. Served as lt. (j.g.), M.C. USNR, 1944-46. Recipient Kappa Delta award Am. Acad. of Orthopedic Surgeons, 1962. Fellow Royal Coll. Pathologists, Molecular Medicine Soc., Am. Soc. Clin. Pathology; mem. Am. Assn. Pathologists, Am. Assn. Immunologists, Am. Soc. Biochemistry and Molecular Biology, Am. Coll. Rheumatology, Am. Orthopedic Assn. (hon.). Home: 3 Hardscrabble Cir Armonk NY 10504-2222

MELLOTT, ROBERT VERNON, advertising executive; b. Dixon, Ill., Jan. 1, 1928; s. Edwin Vernon and Frances Rhoda (Miller) M.; m. Sarah Carolyn Frink, June 11, 1960; children: Lynn Mellott Finzer, Susan Mellott Dodge, David Robert. BA, DePauw U., 1950; postgrad. Grad. Sch., Ind. U., 1950-51, Law Sch., 1959-61, MA, 1983. TV producer, dir. Jefferson Standard Broadcasting Co., Charlotte, N.C., 1951-59; asst. dist. mgr. GM., Flint, Mich., Chgo., 1961-62; TV and radio comml. supr. NW Ayer & Son, Chgo., 1962-65; TV and radio producer Foote, Cone & Belding Advt. Inc., Chgo., 1965-67, mgr. midwest prodn., 1967-69, mgr. comml. coordination, 1969-74, v.p., mgr. comml. svcs., Chgo., 1974-93 (ret.); cons. speech and broadcasting comm. Mem. media adv. com. Coll. of Dupage, Glen Ellyn, Ill., 1971-82; chmn. Cub Scout Com., Wheaton, Ill., 1978-79; bd. dirs. Chgo. Unltd., 1969-71. Mem. Am. Assn. Advt. Agys. (broadcast adminstrn. policy com., broadcast talent union rels. ANA-AAAA joint policy com. 1984-93), World Communication Assn., Internat. Platform Assn., Phi Delta Phi, Alpha Tau Omega. Republican. Mem. Evang. Christian Ch. Clubs: DePauw U. Alumni Assn., Ind. U. Alumni. Home: 26w130 Tomahawk Dr Wheaton IL 60187-7823

MELLOY, MICHAEL J., federal judge; b. 1948; m. Jane Anne Melloy; children: Jennifer, Katherine, Bridget. BA, Loras Coll., 1970; JD, U. Iowa, 1974. With O'Conner & Thomas P.C. (formerly O'Conner, Thomas, Wright, Hammer, Bertsch & Norby, Dubuque, Iowa, 1974-86; judge U.S. Bankruptcy Ct. (no. dist.) Iowa, 1986-92; apptd. chief judge U.S. Dist. Ct. (no. dist.) Iowa, Cedar Rapids, 1992—. With U.S. Army, 1970-72, USAR, 1972-76. Mem. ABA, Comml. Law League Am., Nat. Conf. Bankruptcy Judges, Eighth Cir. Judicial Coun. (bankruptcy judge rep., bankruptcy com.), Iowa State Bar Assn. (coun. mem. bankruptcy and comml. law sect.), Ill. State Bar Assn., Dubuque County Bar Assn., Linn County Bar Assn., Mason L. Ladd Inn of Ct., Rotary. Office: US Dist Ct 101 1st St SE Ste 304 Cedar Rapids IA 52401-1202*

MELLUM, GALE ROBERT, lawyer; b. Duluth, Minn., July 5, 1942; s. Lester Andrew and Doris Esther (Smith) M.; m. Julie Murdoch Swanstrom, July 23, 1966; children: Eric Scott, Wendy Jane. BA summa cum laude, U. Minn., 1964, JD magna cum laude, 1968. Bar: Minn. 1968. Assoc. Faegre & Benson, Mpls., 1968-75, ptnr., 1976—; mem. mgmt. com. Faegre & Benson, 1986—; mem. adv. bd. Quali Tech Inc., Chaska, Minn., 1985—; bd. dirs. Edn. Alts. Inc., Mpls.; adv. bd. Excelsior-Henderson Motorcycle Mfg. Co., 1996—. Hockey chmn. LARC Bd., Mpls., 1980-85. Mem. ABA (fed. securities regulation com.), Minn. Bar Assn., Hennepin County Bar Assn. (securities regulation com.). Republican. Lutheran. Avocations: tennis, golf, snow and water skiing, handball, boating. Home: 4889 E Lake Harriet Pky Minneapolis MN 55409-2222 Office: Faegre & Benson 2200 Norwest Ctr 90 S 7th St Minneapolis MN 55402-3903

MELMON, KENNETH LLOYD, physician, biologist, pharmacologist, consultant; b. San Francisco, July 20, 1934; s. Abe Irving and Jean (Kahn) M.; m. Elyce Edelman, June 9, 1957; children: Bradley S., Debra W. AB in Biology with honors, Stanford U., 1956; MD, U. Calif. at San Francisco, 1959. Intern, then resident in internal medicine U. Calif. Med. Ctr., San Francisco, 1959-61; clin. assoc., surgeon USPHS, Nat. Heart, Lung and Kidney Inst., NIH, 1961-64; chief resident in medicine U. Wash. Med. Ctr., Seattle, 1964-65; chief div. clin. pharmacology U. Calif. Med. Ctr., 1965-78; chief dept. medicine Stanford U. Med. Ctr., 1978-84, Arthur Bloomfield prof. medicine, prof. pharmacology, 1978-86, prof. medicine and pharmacology, 1978—; assoc. dean postgrad. med. edn., 1994—; dir. tech. transfer program Stanford U. Hosp., 1986-93; assoc. dean post grad. med. edn. Stanford (Calif.) U., 1994—; mem. sr. staff Cardiovasc. Rsch. Inst.; chmn. joint commn. prescription drug use Senate Subcom. on Health, Inst. Medicine and HEW-Pharm. Mfrs. Assn.; mem. Nat. Bd. Med. Examiners, 1987—; pres. Bio 2000, Woodside, Calif., 1983-85; co-founder Immunologic, Waltham, Mass., 1988; sci. advisor Hoffman LaRoche, Microphobe, Vysis, others; cons. FDA, 1965-82, Office Tech. Assessment, 1974-75, Senate Subcom. on Health, 1975—; bd. dirs. Vysis, Chgo., Immologic, Boston, Microphobe, Seattle; cons. to govt.; founder Inst. Biol. and Clin. Investigation, Ctr. for Molecular and Genetic Medicine, Stanford Cmty. of Internists and Stanford Med. Group. Author articles, chpts. in books, sects. encys.; Editor: Clinical Pharmacology: Basic Principles in Therapeutics, 3d edit., 1992, Cardiovascular Therapeutics, 1974; assoc. editor: The Pharmacological Basis of Therapeutics (Goodman and Gilman), 1984; mem. editorial bd. numerous profl. jours. Surgeon USPHS, 1961-64. Burroughs Wellcome clin. pharmacology scholar, 1966-71; John Simon Guggenheim fellow Weizman Inst., Israel, 1971, NIH spl. fellow, Bethesda, 1971. Fellow AAAS (nat. coun. 1985-89); mem. Am. Fedn. Clin. Rsch. (pres. 1973-74), Am. Soc. Clin. Investigation (pres. 1978-79), Assn. Am. Physicians, Western Assn. Physicians (pres. 1983-84), Am. Soc. Pharmacology and Exptl. Therapeutics, Am. Soc. Clin. Pharmacology and Therapeutics (Oscar Hunter award in therapeutics 1994), Inst. Medicine of NAS, Am. Physiol. Soc., Calif. Acad. Medicine, Med. Friends of Wine, Phi Beta Kappa. Democrat. Jewish. Achievements include initiation of founding of Ctr. of Molecular and Genetic Medicine, The Integrated Ctr. for Clin. Immunology, Stanford, others. Home: 51 Cragmont Way Woodside CA 94062-2307 Office: Stanford U Med Ctr Dept Medicine # S025 Stanford CA 94305

MELNER, SINCLAIR LEWIS, insurance company executive, retired; b. Reno, Apr. 6, 1928; s. Abraham H. and Carol Rachel (Myers) M.; m. Roma F. Garner, Dec. 26, 1949; children: Catherine, Michael, Joan. B.S., U. Nev., 1949; M.S. in Internat. Affairs, George Washington U., 1969. Commd. 2d lt. U.S. Army, 1949; advanced through grades to lt. gen. U.S. Army, Ft. Benjamin Harrison, Ind., formerly comdg. gen.; later dep. chmn. NATO Mil. Command, Brussels; ret., 1984; v.p., corp. sec. Hudson Inst., 1984-88; sr. advisor Am. Amicable Life Ins. Co. Tex., 1989-95; ret., 1995. Decorated Silver Star with oak leaf cluster, Def. Superior Service medal, Def. D.S.M., Army D.S.M., Legion of Merit with oak leaf cluster. Home: 301 E Braeburn Dr Phoenix AZ 85022-3621

MELNGAILIS, IVARS, solid state research executive; b. Riga, Latvia, Nov. 13, 1933; came to U.S., 1949; s. Janis and Jakobine (Zile) M.; m. Valda Dreimanis, June 6, 1964; children: Nils, Zinta. BS, Carnegie-Mellon U., 1956, MS, 1957, PhD, 1961. Mem. staff. Lincoln Lab., MIT, Lexington, 1961-67, asst. group leader, 1967-71, group leader, 1971-75, assoc. div. head, 1975—. Fellow IEEE; mem. Am. Phys. Soc., Am. Optical Soc. Office: MIT Lincoln Lab Solid State Div 244 Wood St Lexington MA 02173-6426

MELNICK, DANIEL, film producer; b. N.Y.C., Apr. 21, 1932; 1 son, Peter. Partner Talent Assos.; v.p., then sr. v.p. charge worldwide prodn. M.G.M., 1972-76; ind. film producer, 1976-77, 79—; in charge worldwide prodn. Columbia Pictures Industries Inc., 1977-78, pres. motion picture div., 1978; now independent prodr. Indie Prodn. Co. Prodr. films: Straw Dogs, First Family, 1981, Making Love, 1982, Footloose, 1985, Quicksilver, 1986, Roxanne, 1987, Punchline, 1988, Mountains of the Moon, 1990, Air America, 1990, L.A. Story, 1991, The Quick and the Dead, 1994; exec. prodr. films: That's Entertainment, That's Entertainment II, All That Jazz, Altered States, Footloose. Recipient Nat. Acad. TV Arts and Scis. Emmy award for Death of a Salesman and The Ages of Man. Office: Tristar Bldg 10202 Washington Blvd # 211 Culver City CA 90232-3119

MELNICK, GILBERT STANLEY, radiologist, educator; b. N.Y.C., July 31, 1930; s. Haskel and Ida (Palter) M.; m. Iris Dorothy Cohen, June 19, 1955 (div. Jan. 1983); children: Daniel, David, Deborah, Jeffrey; m. Noreen E. Moore, Apr. 28, 1984. BA, Cornell U., 1980; MD, SUNY, Bklyn., 1954. Diplomate: Am. Bd. Radiology. Intern Meadowbrook Hosp., Hempstead, N.Y., 1954-57; fellow in radiology U. Minn., Mpls., 1957-61; instr., then asst. prof. Yale U. Sch. Medicine, New Haven, 1961-66; dir. radiology St. Michael's Med. Ctr., Newark, 1967-82; chmn. dept. radiology N.J. Med. Sch., Newark, 1982-86, clin. prof. radiology, 1982, prof. clin. radiology, 1982-86, clin. prof. radiology, 1986—; clin. prof. radiology Sch. Physicians and Surgeons, Columbia U., 1987-90; asst. attending radiologist Christ Hosp., Jersey City, 1990—; chmn. radiology Morristown Meml. Hosp., 1986-90. Capt. U.S. Army, 1955-57. Fellow Am. Coll. Radiology; mem. AMA, Radiol. Soc. N.Am., Radiol. Soc. N.J. (treas. 1982, sec. 1983, pres. 1985-86), Essex PSRO (sec. 1982-88), Met Pro (trustee 1985), Axiom Group (trustee, vice-chmn 1987—). Democrat. Jewish. Office: Christ Hosp Dept Radiology PO Box 8184 Jersey City NJ 07308-8184

MELNICK, JOSEPH L., virologist, educator; b. Boston, Oct. 9, 1914; s. Samuel and Esther (Melny) M.; m. Matilda Benyesh, 1958; 1 child, Nancy. AB, Wesleyan U., 1936; PhD, Yale U., 1939; DSc, Wesleyan U., 1971; MD (hon.), Charles U., Prague, Czech Republic, 1993. Asst. in physiol. chemistry Sch. Medicine Yale U., New Haven, 1937-39; Asst. in physiol. chemistry, Finney-Howell Research Found. fellow, 1939-41, NRC fellow in med. scis., 1941-42, rsch. asst. in preventive medicine with rank of instr., 1942-44, asst. prof., 1944-48, rsch. assoc., 1948-49, assoc. prof. microbiology, 1949-54, prof. epidemiology, 1954-57; chief virus labs. divsn. biologics stds. NIH, USPHS, 1957-58; prof., chmn. virology and epidemiology Coll. Medicine Baylor U., Houston, 1958-68; Disting. Svc. prof. Coll. Medicine Baylor U., 1974—, dean grad. scis., 1968-91, dean emeritus, 1992—; mem. com. on viral diseases WHO, 1957—, mem. internat. task force on hepatitis B immunization, 1992—, dir. Internat. Ctr. Enteroviruses, 1963-93, mem. cons. group on poliomyelitis vaccine, 1973—, dir. Collaborating Ctr. for Virus Reference and Rsch., 1970—; mem. com. on live poliovirus vaccines USPHS, 1958-61; mem. virus reference bd. NIH, 1962-70, mem. dir. adv. com. on DNA recombinants, 1976, mem. evaluation com. divsn. rsch. resources, 1975-76, mem. nat. adv. cancer coun., 1965-69; mem. human cancer virus task force Nat. Cancer Inst., NIH, USPHS, 1962-67; sec.-gen. Internat. Congresses Virology, Helsinki and Budapest, 1968-71; chmn. Internat. Conf. on Viruses in Water, Mexico City, 1974; mem. rsch. coun. Am. Cancer Soc., 1971-75; mem. com. on hepatitis NAS/NRC, 1972-77; lectr., cons. Chinese Acad. Med. Scis., 1978, 79, 93; mem. adv. com. Comparative Virology Orgn., 1978-86; chmn. adv. com. on viral hepatitis Ctr. fo Disease Control, 1989, 95, mem. adv. com. on respiratory and enteric viruses, 1991, mem. adv. com. on evaluation of U.S. polio cases, 1963-75, 76-84; cons. devel. program for health manpower and svcs. of Palestinian people UN, 1981-83. Author: Textbook of Medical Microbiology; editor: Progress in Medical Virology and Monographs in Virology, also over 1000 rsch. papers in virology; editor-in-chief ofcl. jour. virology Intervirology, Internat. Union Microbiol. Socs., 1972-85. Bd. dirs. Houston Acad. Medicine-Tex. Med. Ctr. Libr., 1967-90, chmn., 1988-89; trustee Albert B. Sabin Vaccine Found., 1994—; chmn. U.S. Commn. on Polio Eradication, 1994—. Univ. scholar Yale U., 1939; co-recipient Internat. medal for rsch. in immunity to poliolyelitis Argentinian Found. Against Infantile Paralysis, 1949, Indsl. Rsch.-100 award, 1971, 74; recipient Humanitarian award Jewish Inst. Med. Rsch., 1964, Modern Medicine Disting. Achievement award, 1965, Eleanor Roosevelt Humanities award, 1965, Inventor of Yr. award Houston Patent Law Assn., 1972, Gold medal South African Poliomyelitis Rsch. Found., 1979, Maimonides award State of Israel, 1980, Raymond E. Baldwin medal for Disting. Svc., Wesleyan U., 1986; named to Nat. Found.'s Polio Hall of Fame, 1958. Fellow AAAS, APHA, N.Y. Acad. Scis. (Freedom Found. award for rsch. in virology 1973), Am. Acad. Microbiology; mem. Am. Soc. Microbiology, Am. Soc. Virology, Soc. Exptl. Biology and Medicine (mem. coun. 1965-69), Am. Assn. Immunologists, Am. Epidemiol. soc., Am. Assn. Cancer Rsch. (pres. S.W. sect. 1968), Internat. Assn. Microbiol. Socs. (life, chmn. sect. on virology 1970-75, mem. exec. com. 1976-79, mem. internat. commn. on microbiol. ecology 1972-87, mem. internat. com. on taxonomy of viruses 1966—), Microbiol. Soc. Israel (hon.), Microbiol. Soc. Argentina (hon.), USSR Soc. Microbiologists and Epidemiologists (hon.), Chinese Soc. Med. Virology (hon.), Med. Soc. Bulgaria (hon.), Phi Beta Kappa, Sigma Xi.

MELNICK, ROBERT, dean. Dean architecture and applied arts U. Oreg., Eugene. Office: Architecture Dept Univ Oregon Eugene OR 97403*

MELNICK, VIJAYA LAKSHMI, biology educator, research center director; b. Kerala, India; came to U.S., 1959; m. Daniel Melnick, June 28, 1963; 1 child, Anil D. BS, Madras Agriculture Coll., India, 1959; MS, U. Wis., 1961, PhD, 1964, postgrad., 1964-66. Asst. prof. dept. biology Fed. City Coll., Washington, 1970-74; assoc. prof. dept. biology U. D.C., Washington, 1974-77, prof. biology, 1977—; dir. Ctr. for Applied Rsch. and Urban Policy, Washington, 1992—; sr. staff assoc. Internat. Ctr. Inter-Disciplinary Studies in Immunology Georgetown U. Med. Sch., 1978-85, assoc. dir. tech. transfer, edn. and community outreach Ctr. Inter-Disciplinary Studies in Immunology, 1985—; sr. rsch. scholar Ctr. for Applied Rsch. and Urban Policy, Washington, 1984-85; spl. asst. policy and bioethics Nat. Inst. Aging/NIH, Bethesda, Md., 1980-82; vis. prof., rsch. participant Carnegie program Oak Ridge Grad. Sch. Biomed. Sci., U. Tenn., 1974-78; vis. scientist Biology and Medicine Inst., Lawrence Livermore Labs., U. Calif., 1972-73; invited del. cell biologist to People's Republic of China, 1990, to Initiave on Edn. Sci. & Tech. to Republic South Africa, 1995; mem. health edn. adv. com. Internat. Med. Svc. for Health, Washington; mem. Nestle Infant Formula Audit Commn., 1981-91; mem. Mayor's Adv. Bd. on Infant and Maternal Health, 1987—; del. 1st Asian-Pacific Orgn. for Cell Biology Congress, Shanghai, 1990; mem. nat. coun. on rsch. in child welfare Child Welfare League Am., Inc., 1992—; mem. adv. coun. D.C. family policy seminar Georgetown U. Grad. Pub. Policy Program, 1993—; mem. adv. com. tng. program for postdoctoral program in devel. immunology Internat. Ctr. Interdisciplinary Studies in Immunology, Georgetown U. Med. Ctr., 1993—; mem. steering com. Nat. Consortium for African Am. Children, Nat. Commn. to Prevent Infant Mortality, 1993—; host scientist Science in American Life exhibition Nat. Mus. Am. Hist. The Smithsonian Inst., 1994—; del. Initiative for Edn., Sci., & Tech., South Africa, 1995. Invited del. initiative on edn., sci., and tech. to Republic of South Africa, 1995. Recipient Outstanding Svc. award March of Dimes, 1987; postdoctoral fellow U. Wis. Med. Sch., 1964-66. Mem. APHA, AAAS, Am. Soc. Cell Biology, Assn. for Women in Sci., Am. Polit. Sci. Assn., Nat. Assn. Minority Med. Educators (legis. com. 1977—), Nat. Assn. for Equal Opportunities in Higher Edn. (sci. and tech. adv. com. 1982), N.Y. Acad. Sci., Sigma Xi, Sigma Delta Epsilon. Office: U DC Ctr Applied Rsch 4200 Connecticut Ave NW Washington DC 20008-1174

MELNIK, ROBERT EDWARD, aeronautical engineer; b. N.Y.C., Nov. 19, 1933; s. Adam Edward and Anna Elizabeth (Petroccia) M.; m. Carol Joan Ceparano, Sept. 24, 1960; children: Joann, Christine. B.Aero.Engring., Poly. Inst. Bklyn., 1956, M.Aero. Engring., 1961, Ph.D., 1965. Research scientist Grumman Aerospace Corp., Bethpage, N.Y., 1956-66; head aerodynamics research group Grumman Aerospace Corp., 1966-73, dir. fluid mechanics, 1973-89; tech. mgr. Northrop Grumman Corp., Bethpage, 1994—. Assoc. editor: AIAA Jour, 1978-80; mem. editorial com.: Ann. Rev. Fluid Mechanics, 1982-87; contbr. articles to profl. jours. Bd. dirs. Family Service League of Suffolk, 1975—. Rsch. fellow, 1989-94. Fellow AIAA; mem. Am. Phys. Soc. Office: Northrop Grumman Corp Bethpage NY 11714

MELNUK, PAUL D., diversified financial services company executive; b. Winnipeg, Man., Can., May 24, 1954; s. Martin William and Rita Clarice (Cochrane) M.; m. Donna Sturko, Oct. 21, 1989; children: Jillian, Andrew, Bryan, Kevin. B in Comm., U. Man., 1976. Joined Touche Ross & Co., 1976-80; v.p., contr. Can. Comml. Bank, 1980-86; corporate fin. rep. Pemberton Securities Inc., 1986-87; pres. WFL Capital Corp., 1987-88; pres., CEO Clark Refining & Mktg. Inc., St. Louis, 1988-93; pres., COO The Horsham Corp., St. Louis, 1993—. Office: 8182 Maryland Ave Saint Louis MO 63105 also: 24 Hazelton Ave, Toronto, ON Canada M5R 2E2*

MELNYK, STEVEN ALEXANDER, business management educator; b. Hamilton, Ont., Can., Apr. 12, 1953; came to U.S., 1980; s. Stephen and Mary (Sahan) M.; m. Christine Ann Halstead, July 10, 1976; children: Charles Edward Phillip, Elizabeth Victoria Michaela. BA in Econs., U. Windsor, Ont., 1975; MA in Econs., U. We. Ont., London, 1976, PhD in Ops. Mgmt., 1981. Asst. prof. ops. mgmt. Mich. State U., East Lansing, 1980-85, assoc. prof., 1985-90, prof., 1990—. Author: Shop Floor Control, 1985, 87, Production Activity Control, 1987, Computer Integrated Manual, 1992, others. Recipient Tchr.-Scholar award Mich. State U., 1985, other awards. Mem. Am. Prodn. and Inventory Control Soc. (software editor 1991—, cons. 1980—, Paul Berkobile award 1992), Nat. Assn. Purchasing Mgrs., Decision Sci. Inst. (editor procs. 1991, Outstanding Theoretical Paper award 1982), Soc. Mfg. Engrs., Inst. Mgmt. Sci. Episcopalian. Avocations: Civil War history, baseball history, bicycling. Office: Mich State U N431 NBC East Lansing MI 48824-1122

MELNYKOVYCH, ANDREW O., journalist; b. Mpls., Aug. 23, 1952; s. George and Oksana (Demianchuk) M.; m. Debra Denise Mamigonian, May 24, 1986; children: Alexander Vartan, Anna Emilia. BS in Biology, Yale U., 1975, M in Forest Sci., 1977; postgrad., U. Wyo., 1978-82. Lab. instr. dept. biochemistry U. Wyo., Laramie, 1982-83; corr. Casper (Wyo.) Star-Tribune, 1982-83, environ. writer, 1983-86, Washington reporter, 1986-90; environ. writer Louisville Courier-Jour., 1990—; contbg. writer High Country News, Paonia, Colo., 1987-90, The Post-Register, Idaho Falls, Idaho, 1989-90. Recipient George S. Polk award L.I. U., N.Y., 1989, 2d pl. Barnet Nover award Standing Com. of Corrs., Washington, 1989. Mem. Soc. Environ. Journalists. Avocations: birding, photography. Office: Louisville Courier-Jour 525 W Broadway St Louisville KY 40202-2206

MELOAN, TAYLOR WELLS, marketing educator; b. St. Louis, July 31, 1919; s. Taylor Wells and Edith (Graham) M.; m. Anna Geraldine Leukering, Dec. 17, 1944 (div. 1974); children: Michael David, Steven Lee; m. Jane Innes Bierlich, Jan. 30, 1975. B.S. cum laude, St. Louis U., 1949; M.B.A., Washington U., St. Louis, 1950; D of Bus. Admin., Ind. U., 1953. Advt. mgr. Herz Corp., St. Louis, 1941-42; sales promotion supr. Liggett & Myers Tobacco Co., St. Louis, 1942-43; asst. prof. mktg. U. Okla., Norman, 1953; asst., then assoc. prof. mktg. Ind. U., Bloomington, 1953-59; prof., chmn. dept. mktg. U. So. Calif., Los Angeles, 1959-69, prof. mktg., 1969-92, Robert E. Brooker prof. mktg., 1970-79, Robert E. Brooker prof. mktg. emeritus, 1991—; dean Sch. Bus. Adminstrn. U. So. Calif., 1969-71, assoc. v.p. acad. adminstrn. and research, 1971-81; prof. bus. adminstrn. U. Karachi, Pakistan, 1962; vis. prof. mktg. Istituto Post U. Per Lo Studio Dell Organizzazione Aziendale, Turin, Italy, 1964, U. Hawaii, 1993, Madrid Bus. Sch., 1993; disting. vis. prof. U. Witwatersrand, Johannesburg, 1978, U. Hawaii, 1993; editl. advisor bus. adminstrn. Houghton Mifflin Co., Boston, 1959-73; cons. to industry and govt., 1953%; bd. dirs Inst. Shipboard Edn. Author: New Career Opportunities, 1978, Innovation Strategy and Management, 1979, Direct Marketing: Vehicle for Department Store Expansion, 1984, Preparing the Exporting Entrepreneur, 1986, The New Competition: Dilemma of Department Stores in the 1980's, 1987, Franchise Marketing: A Retrospective and Prospective View of a Contractual Vertical Marketing System, 1988; co-author: Managerial Marketing, 1970, Internationalizing the Business Curriculum, 1968, Handbook of Modern Marketing, contbg. author, 1986; co-author, co-editor: International and Global Marketing: Concepts and Cases, 1994; bd. editors Jour. Mktg., 1965-72. Trustee World Affairs Coun. Orange County, 1994—. Lt. (j.g.) U.S. Maritime Svc., 1943-46. Mem. Am. Mktg. Assn. (pres. L.A. chpt. 1963-64), Order of Artus, Beta Gamma Sigma, Delta Pi Epsilon, Calif. Yacht Club, Univ. Club, Rotary. Home: 59 Lakefront Irvine CA 92714-4683 Office: U So Calif Dept Mktg Los Angeles CA 90089-1421

MELODY, MICHAEL EDWARD, publishing company executive; b. Streator, Ill., Dec. 22, 1943; s. Giles Lambert and Rose Mary (Moreschi) M.; m. Carol Ann Weir, June 8, 1968 (div.); 1 dau., Alison Anne; m. Bonnie Kaye Binkert, Mar. 26, 1983. BA, Ala. Coll., 1966. Exec. editor, asst. v.p. Prentice-Hall, Inc., Englewood Cliff, N.J., 1974-79; v.p., editor-in-chief coll. div. Macmillan Pub. Co., N.Y.C., 1979-80, sr. v.p., pres. coll. div., 1980-87, pres. sch. div., 1987-88; v.p. higher edn. group Simon & Schuster, N.Y.C., 1988-90; sr. v.p. Houghton Mifflin Co., Boston, 1990-91, exec. v.p., 1991-95; prin. Michael E. Melody Cons., Boston, 1995-96; v.p., gen. mgr. info. prod. Inso Corp., Boston, 1996—; chmn. bd. dirs. Appleton & Lange, N.Y.C., 1989-90. Bd. overseers Huntington Theatre Co., Boston, 1993—. Served with USAR, 1967. Mem. Assn. Am. Pubs. (vice chmn. coll. divsn. 1981-83, chmn. coll. divsn. 1983-86, exec. com. sch. divsn. 1987-88, exec. com. higher edn. divsn. 1990—), Nat. Assn. Coll. Stores (trustee 1986-87, 94-95).

MELONAKOS, CHRISTINE MARIE, educational administrator; b. Shelby, Mich., Apr. 29, 1960; d. L.V. Charles and Dorothy June (Arman) Besemer; m. Paul W. Melonakos, May 31, 1983; children: Christian, Timothy, Kandice, Emerson. BS in Psychology, Brigham Young U., 1989. Presch. tchr. Minnieland, Manassas, Va., 1989-90; kindergarten tchr. Manassas Christian Sch., 1990-91; presch. owner Appleseed Presch., Manassas, 1991-92; pres., founder Applebrook Family Enrichment Network, Fremont, Mich., 1992-95, Applebrook Inst., Newaygo, Mich., 1994—; pub. spkr. various orgns., 1990-95; parent educator various orgns., Va. and Mich., 1989-95; creator (tchg. method) Interactive Assistance, 1992. Author: Starting Right, 1993, Cooperation Kit, 1993, Parenting Success Program, 1995; editor Motivated Mother Newsletter, 1990-91. Sec. PTA, Manassas, 1991-92; children's program dir. Parents Anonymous, Manassas, 1991. Recipient Va. Mother of Yr. award Am. Mothers Assn., 1992. Mem. ASCD, Interactive Parents Assn. (founder, pres. 1993—). Republican. Avocations: sewing, antiques, country line dancing, Victorian postcards. Office: Applebrook Inst PO Box 40 Fremont MI 49412

MELONE, JOSEPH JAMES, insurance company executive; b. Pittston, Pa., July 27, 1931; s. Dominick William and Beatrice Marie (Pignone) M.; m. Marie Jane DeGeorge, Jan. 23, 1960; children—Lisa, Carol. B.S., U. Pa., 1953, M.B.A., 1954, Ph.D. in Econs, 1961. C.L.U., 1963 C.P.C.U., 1964. Asso. prof. ins. U. Pa., 1959-66, mem. pension research council, 1961-66; research dir. Am. Coll. Life Underwriters, 1966-68; v.p. Prudential Ins. Co., Boston, 1969-76; sr. v.p. Prudential Ins. Co., Newark, 1976-81, exec. v.p., 1981-84, pres., 1984-90; pres., COO, bd. dirs. The Equitable Life Assurance Soc. U.S., 1990-94; pres., COO The Equitable Life Assurance Soc. of U.S., 1990-94, also bd. dirs.; pres., COO The Equitable Cos., Inc., 1992-96, also bd. dirs.; pres., CEO The Equitable Cos., Inc., N.Y.C., 1996—; chmn. The Equitable Life Assurance Soc. U.S., N.Y.C., 1994—; chmn., CEO Equitable Variable Life Ins. Co.; bd. dirs. Foster Wheeler Corp., Alliance Capital Mgmt., Donaldson, Lufkin & Jenrette, Equity and Law, AT&T Capital Corp., LICONY, ACLI. Author: Collectively Bargained Multi-Employer Pension Plans, 1961; co-author: Risk and Insurance, 1963, Pension Planning, 1966. Trustee Newark Mus.; chmn. ins. divsn. Cardinal's Commn. Laity N.Y. Archdiocese; ptnr. N.Y.C. Partnership; bd. overseers Wharton Sch. U. Pa.; bd. dirs. Am. Coll., Huebner Found.-U. Pa.; bd. dirs. Greater N.Y. couns. Boy Scouts Am. Mem. Am. Risk and Ins. Assn., Am. Soc. CLUs, Am. Coll. (trustee), Am. Inst. Property and Liability Underwriters (trustee), Pa. State U. Internat. Ins. Soc., Internat. Acad. Mgmt., Health Ins. Assn. Am. (bd. dirs., past chmn.), Health Ins. Assn. Am. (bd. dirs., past chmn.), U.S.-Korea Bus. Coun., Morris County Country Club, Baltruso Golf Club, Alpha Tau Omega. Home: 281 Hartshorn Dr Short Hills NJ 07078-1916 Office: Equitable Cos Inc 787 7th Ave New York NY 10019-6018

MELONI, ANDREW P., protective services official; b. Rochester, N.Y., Apr. 10, 1931; s. Andrew and Carrie (DeMaria) M.; m. Laura Ann Tiebe, June 28, 1952; children: Andrew, Michael, Philene Cromwell, Mary Therese Damiano, Stephen. BS, Empire State Coll., 1975. Desk dep. Monroe County Sheriff, Rochester, 1955-60, records sgt., 1960-63, records lt., 1963-65, asst. chief dep., 1965-68, undersheriff, 1968-73; pub. safety commr. Monroe County, Rochester, 1974-77; dir. security U. Rochester, 1977-79; sheriff Monroe County, Rochester, 1980—; commr. accreditation Commn. Accreditation Law Enforcement, Washington, 1993-94. Author: National Code of Ethics, 1991, National Standards for Sheriff & Deputy Sheriff, 1992. Mem. exec. com. Italian Charities, Rochester, 1981—, Rochester Fights Back Drug Com., 1990—. Staff sgt. U.S. Army, 1951-53. Recipient Hall of Fame award Aquinas Inst., 1993. Mem. Nat. Sheriffs Assn. (chmn. stds. and ethics com. 1983—), N.Y. State Sheriffs Ann. (mem. exec. com. 1981—). Republican. Roman Catholic. Avocations: coin collecting, jazz, golf. Office: Monroe County Sheriff's Office 130 Plymouth Ave S Rochester NY 14614-2209

MELOY, SYBIL PISKUR, lawyer; b. Chgo., Dec. 1, 1939; d. Michael M. and Laura (Stevenson) Piskur; children: William S., Bradley M. BS in Chemistry with honors, U. Ill., 1961; JD, Chgo. Kent Coll. Law, 1965. Bar: Ill. 1965, Fla. 1985, D.C. 1995, U.S. Dist. Ct. (no. dist.) Ill. 1965, U.S. Supreme Ct. 1972, U.S. Ct. Appeals (fed. cir.) 1983, U.S. Dist. Ct. (so. dist.) Fla. 1985, D.C. 1995. Patent chemist, patent atty., sr. atty., internat. counsel G.D. Searle & Co., Skokie, Ill., 1961-72; regional counsel Abbott Labs., North Chicago, Ill., 1972-78; pvt.practice, Arlington Heights, Ill., 1978-79; asst. gen. counsel Alberto Culver Co., Melrose Park, Ill., 1979-83; corp. counsel Key Pharms., Inc., Miami, Fla., 1983-86; assoc. Ruden, Barnett McCloskey, Smith, Schuster and Russell, Pa., 1987-89, ptnr., 1990-91; ptnr. Foley & Lardner, Miami, Washington 1991—; adj. prof. Univ. of Miami Sch. of Law, 1986—. Recipient Abbott Presdl. award, 1977; Bur. Nat. Affairs prize, 1965; Law Rev. prize for best article. Mem. ABA, Chgo. Bar Assn. (chmn. and vice chmn. internat. and fgn. law com.), Am. Patent Law Assn., Am. Chem. Soc., Licencing Execs. Soc., Phi Beta Kappa, Phi Kappa Phi. Patentee oral contraceptive, 1965; contbr. article on fertility control and abortion laws, book rev. on arbitration to law revs. Home: 1915 Brickell Ave Apt 1108C Miami FL 33129-1736 also: 1676 32nd St NW Washington DC 20007-2960 Office: Foley & Lardner 3000 K St NW Washington DC 20007-5109

MELROSE, BARRY JAMES, sportscaster, former professional hockey team coach; b. Kelvington, Sask., Can., July 15, 1956. Player various minor league teams, 1973-77, 82-83, 83-86, 86-87; player Cin. Stingers, 1976-79, Winnipeg Jets, 1979-81, Toronto Maple Leafs, 1981-82, 82-83, Detroit Red Wings, 1983-84, 85-86; former gen. mgr., head coach Adirondack Red Wings; now head coach L.A. Kings, 1992-94; sportscaster ESPN, 1995—. Office: care ESPN ESPN Plz Bristol CT 06010

MELROSE, KENDRICK BASCOM, manufacturing company executive; b. Orlando, Fla., July 31, 1940; s. Henry Bascom and Dorothy (Lumley) M.; children: Robert, Velia, Kendra. B.S. cum laude, Princeton U., 1962; M.Sc., MIT, 1965; M.B.A., U. Chgo., 1967. Mktg. mgr. Pillsbury Co., Mpls., 1967-69; dir. corp. planning Bayfield Techs., Inc., Mpls., 1969-70; with Toro Co. (mfrs. outdoor power equipment), Mpls., 1970—, exec. v.p. outdoor power equipment div., 1980-81, pres., 1981-88, chief exec. officer, 1988, also chmn. Congregationalist. Office: Toro Co 8111 Lyndale Ave S Minneapolis MN 55420-1136*

MELSHEIMER, MEL P(OWELL), consumer products business executive; b. Los Angeles, July 9, 1939; s. Oscar Merrill M.; m. Sara Sturdevant, Sept. 1, 1962; children: Heidi, Erich, Douglas. A.B. in Econs., Occidental Coll., 1961; M.B.A., U. So. Calif., 1965. With United Calif. Bank, Los Angeles, 1962-66; sr. fin. analyst Ford Motor Co., Newport Beach, Calif., 1966-67; v.p., chief fin. officer Pepsi Cola Co. Pepsico, Inc., Purchase, N.Y., 1968-75; exec. v.p., chief operating officer AZL Resources, Inc., 1975-84; chmn. bd., chief exec. officer PHX Pacific, Inc., 1984-89; pres., chief exec. officer MPM Capital Corp., 1987-89; exec. v.p. Finevest Foods, Inc., Greenwich, Conn., 1989-92; pres., CEO Land-O-Sun Dairies Inc., 1991-92, Atlanta Dairies, Inc., 1991-92; exec. v.p., sec., chief oper. officer Dairy Holdings, Inc., Johnson City, Tenn., 1992-94; exec. v.p., COO, CFO Sonex Internat. Corp., Brewster, N.Y., 1994; pres., CEO M.P. Melsheimer & Co., Ridgefield, Conn., 1995—; pres. NFX Corp., 1995—. Served with U.S. Army, 1961-62.

MELSHEIMER, WILLIAM C., principal; b. Chgo., Nov. 3, 1940; s. Raymond C. and Gladys (Janar) M.; m. Nancy S. Melsheimer, July 29, 1987; children: David, Elizabeth, Michael Clevenger, Ami Clevenger. BA, North Cen. Coll., Naperville, Ill., 1962; MS in Edn., No. Ill. U., 1967. Tchr. Social Studies, prin. Jr. High Sch. Gower Sch. Dist. #62, Hinsdale, Ill.; prin. Jr. High Sch. Wilmette (Ill.) Pub. Schs. Contbr. articles to profl. jours. Mem. ASCD, NAESP, NASSP, NSDC, ISDC.

MELSHER, GARY W., lawyer; b. Cleve., Mar. 8, 1939. BS, Ohio State U., 1961; JD, Case Western Reserve U., 1964. Bar: Ohio 1964. Ptnr. Jones, Day, Reavis & Pogue, Cleve. Mem. Order of Coif. Office: Jones Day Reavis & Pogue North Point 901 Lakeside Ave E Cleveland OH 44114-1116

MELSON, RENÉ HARBER, elementary school educator; b. Atlanta, Dec. 4, 1954; d. Talmon Eugene and June (Slaton) Harber; children: Presley, Cameron. BS in Elem. Edn., Ga. State U., 1977. Cert. tchr., Ga. Tchr. Greater Atlanta Christian Schs., Norcross, Ga., 1977-82, 88—. Republican. Ch. of Christ. Avocations: reading, quilting, cross stitch. Home: 445 Cambria Ln SW Lilburn GA 30247-3076 Office: Greater Atlanta Christian PO Box 277 Norcross GA 30091-0277

MELSOP, JAMES WILLIAM, architect; b. Columbus, Ohio, June 2, 1939; s. James Brendan and Juanita Kathryn (Van Scoy) M.; m. Sandra Lee Minnich, Sept. 21, 1957; children: Deborah Lee, Susan Elizabeth, Kathryn Anne. BArch, Ohio State U., 1964; MArch, Harvard U., 1965; MBA, U. Chgo., 1975. Reg. architect, profl. engr. Architect The Austin Co., Chgo., 1967-69, mgr. bus. devel., 1969-74, asst. dist. mgr., 1974-75; pres., mng. dir. Austin Brasil, Sao Paulo, 1975-78; asst. dist. mgr. The Austin Co., Roselle, N.J., 1978-80; dist. mgr. The Austin Co., 1980-81; v.p., dist. mgr. The Austin Co., Cleve., 1986, group v.p., dir., 1986—, exec. v.p. chief oper. officer, 1992, pres., CEO, 1992—, also bd. dirs. Mem. Am. Inst. Architects., Harvard Club, Presidents' Club, Ohio State U. Pres. Club (Disting. Alumnus award 1989). Home: 3165 Trillium Trail Cleveland OH 44124-5205 Office: Austin Co 3650 Mayfield Rd Cleveland OH 44121-1734

MELSTED, MARCELLA H., retired administrative assistant, civic worker; b. Mayville, N.D., Mar. 3, 1922; d. Hans Morris and Betsy (Stenerson) Hanson; m. Alvin K. Melsted, June 6, 1965 (dec. June 1994). BS in Commerce, U. N.D., 1946, postgrad. Sec. Off. Sci. R&D, Washington, 1943-45; adminstrv. asst. Am. Embassy (Marshall Plan), Oslo, 1948-50, Paris, 1950-52; adminstrv. asst. N.D. Geol. Soc., Grand Forks, 1953-65. Co-editor: Memories of Homemakers, 1988. Pres. Borg Home Auxiliary, 1984—; apptd. cons. rep. State Plumbing Bd.; chmn. needlepointing dining room chairs N.D. Gov.'s mansion; parliamentarian N.D. Extension Homemakers, Women of Evang. Luth. Ch. Am., v.p., bd. dirs., 1985-91; mem. N.D. Humanities Coun., 1985-91; bd. dirs. Friends of N.D. Mus.; mem. Quad County Cmty. Action Bd., 1995—. Mem. AAUW (parliamentarian N.D. State divsn., 2 fellowships, author branch history, state pres. 1962-64, nat. membership com. 1964-66), N.D. State Fedn. Garden Clubs (state pres., life, tree chmn. nat. bd., state treas. 1991—), Four Seasons Garden Club (sec.-treas. 1987—), Homemakers Clubs (various coms.), China Painters Guild (various coms.). Democrat. Avocations: antiques, china painting, stamp collecting. Home: 7862 127th Ave NE Edinburg ND 58227-9604

MELTEBEKE, RENETTE, career counselor; b. Portland, Oreg., Apr. 20, 1948; d. Rene and Gretchen (Hartwig) M. BS in Sociology, Portland State U., 1970; MA in Counseling Psychology, Lewis and Clark Coll., 1985. Lic. profl. counselor, Oreg.; nat. cert. counselor. Secondary tchr. Portland Pub. Schs., 1970-80; project coord. Multi-Wash CETA, Hillsboro, Oreg., 1980-81; coop. edn. specialist Portland C.C., 1981-91; pvt. practice career counseling, owner Career Guidance Specialists, Lake Oswego, Oreg., 1988—; mem. adj. faculty Marylhurst (Oreg.) Coll., 1989-93, Portland State U., 1994—; assoc. Drake Beam Morin Inc., Portland, 1993—; career cons. Occupational Health Svcs. Corp., 1994—, Career Devel. Svcs., 1990—, Life Dimensions, Inc., 1994—. Author video Work in America, 1981. Pres. Citizens for Quality Living, Sherwood, Oreg., 1989; mem. Leadership Roundtable on Sustainability for Sherwood, 1994-95. Mem. ASTD, Assn. for Psychol. Type, Nat. Career Devel. Assn., Oreg. Career Devel. Assn. (pres. 1990), Assn. for Quality Participation, Assn. for Humanistic Psychology, Willamette Writers. Avocations: walking, swimming, bicycling, cross-country skiing, photography. Home: 890 SE Merryman St Sherwood OR 97140-9746 Office: Career Guidance Specialists 15800 Boones Ferry Rd # C104 Lake Oswego OR 97035-3456

MELTON, AUGUSTUS ALLEN, JR., airport executive; b. New Bern, N.C., Feb. 18, 1942; s. Augustus Allen and Margaret (Tucker) M.; m. E. LaRhett Fagan, Oct. 27, 1995; children from previous marriage: Augustus Allen III, Harold David. B.S., Howard U., 1965. Ops. safety officer FAA, Washington, 1971-72; airport cert. and safety insp. FAA, Atlanta, 1972-75; airport cert. safety specialist FAA, Washington, 1976-79, airport mgr., 1980—. Office: Office of Airport Mgr Washington Nat Airport Washington DC 20001

MELTON, CHARLES ESTEL, physicist, educator; b. Fancy Gap, Va., May 18, 1924; s. Charlie Glenn and Ella (Ayers) M.; m. Una Faye Hull, Dec. 7, 1946; children—Sharon (Mrs. Lawrence Husch), Wayne, Sandra (Mrs. Glenn Allen). B.A., Emory and Henry Coll., 1952, D.Sc., 1967; M.S., Vanderbilt U., 1954; Ph.D., U. Notre Dame, 1964. Physicist Oak Ridge Nat. Lab., 1954-67; prof. chemistry U. Ga., Athens, 1967—; head dept. U. Ga., 1972-77. Author: Principles of Mass Spectrometry and Negative Ions, 1970, Ancient Diamond Time Capsules, Secrets of Life and the World, 1985, Primordial Petroleum, 1989; contbr. articles to profl. jours. Served with USNR, 1943-46. Recipient DeFriece medal Emory and Henry Coll., 1959, numerous research grants. Fellow AAAS; mem. Am. Phys. Soc., Am. Chem. Soc., Ga. Acad. Sci. Presbyterian. Home: 34 Glen Carrie Rd Hull GA 30646-9778 Office: Univ Georgia Dept Chemistry Athens GA 30602

MELTON, DAVID REUBEN, lawyer; b. Milw., Apr. 4, 1952; s. Howard and Evelyn Frances (Cohen) M.; m. Nancy Hillary Segal, May 22, 1981; children: Michelle, Hannah. BA, U. Wis., 1974; JD, U. Chgo., 1977. Bar: Ill. 1977, U.S. Dist. Ct. (no. dist.) Ill. 1977, U.S. Ct. Appeals (7th cir.) 1981, U.S. Supreme Ct. 1982. Assoc. Karon, Morrison & Savikas, Ltd., Chgo., 1977-83; ptnr. Karon, Morrison & Saviskas, Ltd., Chgo., 1983-87, Karon, Savikas & Horn, Ltd., Chgo., 1987-88, Keck, Mahin & Cate, Chgo., 1988—. Office: Keck Mahin & Cate 77 W Wacker Dr Ste 4900 Chicago IL 60601*

MELTON, EMORY LEON, lawyer, publisher, state legislator; b. McDowell, Mo. June 20, 1923; s. Columbus Right and Pearly Susan (Wise) M.; student Monett Jr. Coll., 1940-41, S.W. Mo. State U., 1941-42; LLB, U. Mo., 1945; m. Jean Sanders, June 19, 1949; children: Stanley Emory, John Russell. Admitted to Mo. bar, 1944; individual practice law, Cassville, Mo., 1947—; pres. Melton Publs., Inc., pub. 2 newspapers, 1959—; pros. atty. Barry county (Mo.), 1947-51; mem. Mo. Senate, 1973—. Chmn., Barry County Republican Com., 1964-68. Served with AUS, 1945-46. Recipient award for meritorious public service St. Louis Globe-Democrat., 1976. Mem. Mo. Bar Assn. Baptist. Clubs: Lions, Masons. Office: PO Box 488 Cassville MO 65625-0488

MELTON, FLORETTE JEANNE, realtor, marketing consultant; b. Newton, Iowa, Oct. 30, 1945; d. Floyd Leroy and Donna Jean (Engle) Mulbrook; m. James Francis Rittenmeyer (div.); 1 child, Matthew David Rittenmeyer; m. Charles Wade Melton; 1 child, Jennifer. Student, U. Iowa, 1964-66; BA, U. N.C., 1977, MA, 1983. Comm. cons. Booke & Co., Winston-Salem, N.C., 1977-78; pres. RCC, Winston-Salem, 1980-85; real estate agent Merrill Lynch, Winston-Salem, 1986-88, ReMax, Winston-Salem, 1988-92; broker, pres. Unique Properties of the Triad, Winston-Salem, 1992—; mktg. cons. Creative Advt. Active Triad Health Orgn., Greensboro, 1994—. Mem. Bd. Realtors. Avocations: travel, art, decorating, photography, movies. Office: Unique Properties of the Triad 112 Cambridge Plaza Dr Winston Salem NC 27104-3556

MELTON, GARY BENTLEY, psychology and law educator; b. Salisbury, N.C., June 4, 1952; s. Harold Sumner Jr. and Marion Adair (Reeves) M.; m. Julia Ann Young, Aug. 25, 1973; children: Jennifer Lynn, Stephany Beth. BA, U. Va., 1973; MA, Boston U., 1975, PhD, 1978. Lic. psychologist, Nebr. Asst. prof. psychology Morehead (Ky.) State U., 1978-79, U. Va., Charlottesville, 1979-81; from asst. prof. to full prof. psychology and law U. Nebr., Lincoln, 1981-87, Carl A. Happold prof. psychology and law, 1987-94; prof. neuropsychiatry, law, pediat. and psychology, dir. Inst. Families in Soc., U. S.C., Columbia, 1994—; dir. Consortium on Children, Families and the Law. Author: Child Advocacy: Psychological Issues and Interventions, 1993; co-author: Community Mental Health Centers and the Courts: An Evaluation of Community-Based Forensic Services, 1985, Psychological Evaluations for the Courts: A Handbook for Mental Health Professionals and Lawyers, 1987, Pediatric and Adolescent AIDS: Research Findings from the Social Sciences, 1992, Ethical and Legal Issues in AIDS Research, 1995; editor numerous books. Mem. U.S. Adv. Bd. on Child Abuse and Neglect, 1989-93, vice-chair, 1991-93. Recipient Frederick Howell Lewis award Psi Chi, 1993. Fellow APA (chmn. various coms., Disting. Contbn. to Psychology in Pub. Interest award 1985, Cert. of Recognition for Psychology in Pub. Interest 1981, Nicholas Hobbs award 1992, Harold Hildreth award 1992); mem. Am. Psychology-Law Soc. (pres. 1990-91), Nat. Com. to Prevent Child Abuse (Donna Stone award 1992). Democrat. Mem. Unitarian Ch. Office: Inst for Families in Soc Univ of SC Columbia SC 29208

MELTON, HOWELL WEBSTER, SR., federal judge; b. Atlanta, Dec. 15, 1923; s. Holmes and Alma (Combee) M.; m. Margaret Catherine Wolfe, Mar. 4, 1950; children—Howell Webster, Carol Anne. J.D., U. Fla., 1948. Bar: Fla. 1948. Mem. firm Upchurch, Melton & Upchurch, St. Augustine, 1948-61; judge 7th Jud. Circuit of Fla., St. Augustine, 1961-77, U.S. Dist. Ct. (mid. dist.) Fla., Jacksonville, 1977—; past chmn. Fla. Conf. Cir. Judges, 1974; past chmn. coun. bar pres.'s Fla. Bar. Trustee Flagler Coll., St. Augustine. Served with U.S. Army, 1943-46. Recipient Disting. Service award St. Augustine Jaycees, 1953. Mem. ABA, St. Johns County Bar Assn., Jacksonville Bar Assn., Fed. Bar Assn., Fla. Blue Key, Phi Delta Theta, Phi Delta Phi. Methodist (past chmn. bd. trustees). Clubs: Ponce de Leon Country (St. Augustine), Marsh Creek Country (St. Augustine Beach), St. Augustine Fla. Officer's. Lodges: Masons, Kiwanis (past pres.). Office: US Dist Ct PO Box 52957 Jacksonville FL 32201-2957

MELTON, JUNE MARIE, nursing educator; b. St. Louis, Oct. 16, 1927; d. Thomas Jasper and Alice Marie (Sloas) Hayes; m. Malcolm Adrian Essen, July 12, 1947 (dec. July 1978); children: Alison, William, Terrence, Mark, Cathleen, Melodie; m. Denver A. Melton, Sept. 6, 1989 (dec.). Grad., Jewish Hosp. Sch. Nursing, 1948; student, U. Mo., Lincoln U., U. Colo., Stephens Coll., U. S.W. RN, Mo.; nurse ARC. Instr. home nursing U. Mo., Columbia, 1948-49; acting dir. nurses, 1957-68; supr. instr., obstet. supr. Charles E. Still Hosp., Jefferson City, Mo.; supr. nurse ICU, primary nurse St. Mary's Health Ctr., Jefferson City; health dir. Algoa Correctional Instn., Jefferson City, 1979-83; home health vis. nurse A&M Home Health, Jefferson City, 1983—; mem. adv. bd. A&M Home Nursing, Jefferson City; instr. GED Lincoln U., Jefferson City; participant study of premature baby nursing U. Colo., 1964. Vol., instr. home nursing ARC, Belle-Rolla, Mo. Mem. U.S. Nurse Corps. Democrat. Lutheran. Avocations: fishing, sewing, reading, traveling. Home: 1753 Roberts St Holts Summit MO 65043 Office: A&M Home Health 1411 Southwest Blvd Jefferson City MO 65101-1503

MELTON, LYNDA GAYLE, reading specialist, educational diagnostician; b. Gatesville, Tex., Mar. 11, 1943; d. Dee and Myrtle (Dunlap) White; divorced; children: Melanie Gayle, William Matthew. BS, U. Tex., 1964; MA, U. North Tex., 1979, PhD, 1983, postgrad., 1993, 94; postgrad., Tex. Womans U., 1983. Cert. elem. tchr., spl. edn. tchr., supervision, spl. edn. supr., learning disabilities tchr., orthpedically handicapped tchr., reading specialist, Tex., adminstrs., ednl. diagnostician. Tchr. 2d and 4th grades, spl. edn. tchr. Irving (Tex.) Ind. Sch. Dist., 1964-79, tchr., 1982-83; 4th grade tchr. Northwest Ind. Sch. Dist., Justin, Tex., 1980-81; asst. prin. Grapevine-Colleyville Ind. Sch. Dist., Tex., 1983-87; tchr. reading improvement Carrollton (Tex.)-Farmers Branch Ind. Sch. Dist., 1988-89; cons. lang. arts Edn. Svc. Ctr. Region 10, Richardson, Tex., 1989-91; pvt. practice diagnostic reading and ednl. diagnostician Trophy Club, Tex., 1991—; reading clinician N.Tex. State U., Denton, 1980; instr. spl. edn. U. Tex., Dallas, 1983, U Tex., Arlington, 1988; vis. prof. Tex. Women's U., Denton, 1983, 84, 87-88. Contbr. Reading Rsch. Revisited, also revs. to Case Mgmt. Monthly Confs., Scottish Rite Hosp. and profl. jours. Mem. ASCD, Internat. Reading Assn. (North Tex. coun.), Learning Disabilities, Orton Disability Soc., Coun. for Exceptional Children, Phi Delta Kappa. Home: 30 Sonora Dr Trophy Club TX 76262 Office: 30 Sonora Trophy Club TX 76262

MELTON, MARIE FRANCES, university dean; b. Bayshore, N.Y.; d. Edward Kilgallon and Anne (Mohan) M. BS in Edn., St. John's U., Jamaica, N.Y., 1960, MS in Edn., 1975; MLS, Pratt Inst., Bklyn., 1961; EDD, St. John's U., Jamaica, N.Y., 1981. Dir. media ctr. Mater Christi High Sch., Astoria, N.Y., 1961-72; libr. sci. libr. St. John's U., Jamaica, N.Y., 1972-76, asst. dir., 1976-83, dir. Univ. Libr., 1983-89, dean Univ. Libr., 1989—. Mem., officer St. John's Prep Bd. of Trustees, Astoria, N.Y., 1980—, Holy Cross High Sch., Flushing, N.Y., 1979-89; chair Sunnyside Hist. Com., Sunnyside, N.Y., 1988-91. Mem. Am. Libr. Assn., Cath. Libr. Assn., N.Y. Libr. Assn., Council Nat. Libr. & Info. Assns. Roman Catholic. Office: St Johns Univ 8000 Utopia Pkwy Jamaica NY 11439

MELTON, PATRICIA ANN, cardiovascular nurse; b. Roanoke Rapids, N.C., Sept. 14, 1936; d. Dewey Paul and Bessie Mae (Thompson) Todd; m. Q. L. Melton, Aug. 19, 1970; children: Kenneth, Cindy, Patty, Debbie, Reginia, Shannon, Quinton. Lic. vocat. nurse, Pasadena Vocat. Sch. Nursing, 1976; student, Coll. of the Mainland, 1986-89; RN, ADN, Galveston Coll. Nursing, 1989; postgrad., U. Tex., 1992—. Nurses aid, lic. vocat. nurse Pasadena (Tex.) Bayshore Hosp., 1975-78; lic. vocat. nurse UpJohn Health Svcs., Pasadena, 1978-83; lic. vocat. staff nurse Jefferson Davis Hosp., Houston, 1981-83, King Fahad Nat. Guard Hosp., Riydh, Saudi Arabia, 1983-86; lic. vocat. staff nurse cardiothoracic care unit U. Tex. Med. Br., John Sealy Hosp., 1988-89, RN staff nurse cardiothoracic care unit, 1989; RN staff nurse, nurse clinician IV in cardio ICU recovery St. Luke's Episcopal Hosp., Houston Med. Ctr., 1989; vol. to pre-natal and post-natal care nurses and drs., Saudi Arabia, 1983. Recognition for vol. svcs. Saudi Arabia N.G. and Hosp. Corp. Am., 1983. Mem. AACN (historian Galveston chpt. 1991-92, head membership com. 1992-93, mem. Houston chpt.), Tex. Student Nurses Assn. (officer 1986-89), Assn. of Nurses Endorsing Transplantation, Phi Theta Kappa, Phi Beta Lambda. Baptist. Avocations: snorkling, sewing, oil painting. : Home: Rt 4 Box 1153 Houston TX 75938

MELTZER, ALLAN H., economist, educator; b. Boston, Feb. 6, 1928; s. George B. and Minerva I. (Simons) M.; m. Marilyn Ginsburg, Aug. 27, 1950; children: Bruce Michael, Eric Charles, Beth Denise. A.B., Duke U., 1948; M.A., UCLA, 1955, Ph.D., 1958. Univ. prof. polit. economy and pub. policy, 1991—; Lectr. econs. U. Pa., Phila., 1956-57; mem. faculty Carnegie Mellon U. Grad. Sch. Indsl. Adminstrn., Pitts., 1957—; prof. econs. Carnegie Mellon U. Grad. Sch. Indsl. Adminstrn., 1964—, Maurice Falk prof. econs. and social sci., 1970-80, John M. Olin univ. prof. polit. economy and pub. policy, 1980-91; Univ. prof. polit. economy and pub. policy Carnegie Mellon U. Grad. Sch. Indsl. Admisntrn., 1991—; vis. prof. U. Chgo., 1964-65, Fundacao Getulio Vargas, Rio de Janeiro, 1976-79, City U., London, 1979-86; vis. fellow Hoover Instn., 1977-78; vis. scholar Am. Enterprise Inst., Washington, 1989—; co-chmn. Shadow Open Market Com., 1974-89, chmn., 1989—; cons. U.S. Treasury, joint econ. com. U.S. Congress, 1960; com. on banking and currency U.S. Ho. of Reps., 1963-64; mem. Pres.'s Econ. Policy Adv. Bd., 1988-90; acting mem. Coun. Econ. Advisors, 1988-89; panel econ. advisors Congl. Budget Office, 1995—; cons., bd. govs. FRS, FDIC; dir. Cooper Tire & Rubber Co.; hon. advisor Inst. Monetary and Econ. Studies Bank of Japan, 1987—; bd. dirs. Sarah Scaife Found., Commonwealth Foun.; dir. Stillhalter Vision AG, Zurich, 1994—, Advanced Materials Group, 1994—. Author: Monetary Economics, 1989, Keynes's Monetary Theory: A Different Interpretation, 1988, (with Karl Brunner) Money and the Economy: Issues in Monetary Analysis, 1993, (with Alex Cukierman and Scott Richard) Political Economy, 1991; editor: (with Karl Brunner) Carnegie-Rochester Conf. Series, 1976-89, (with Charles Plosser), 1989-96; contbr. articles to profl. jours. Recipient award for Outstanding Achievement UCLA, 1983, Social Sci. Rsch. Coun. fellow, 1955-56; Ford Found. fellow, 1962-63; Man of Yr in Fin., Pitts., 1995-96. Fellow Nat. Assn. Bus. Economists; mem. Am. Econ. Assn. (v.p. 1990), Western Econ. Assn. (pres. 1985-86), Am. Fin. Assn., Phila. Soc. (v.p. 1981-83), Cosmos Club. Avocations: research in macroeconomics, money, political economy. Office: Carnegie Mellon U Dept Econs Pittsburgh PA 15213

MELTZER, BERNARD DAVID, legal educator; b. Phila., Nov. 21, 1914; s. Julius and Rose (Welkov) M.; m. Jean Sulzberger, Jan. 17, 1947; children: Joan, Daniel, Susan. A.B., U. Chgo., 1935, J.D., 1937; LL.M., Harvard U., 1938. Bar: Ill. 1938. Atty., spl. asst. to chmn. SEC, 1938-40; assoc. firm Mayer, Meyer, Austrian & Platt, Chgo., 1940; spl. asst. to asst. sec. state, also acting chief fgn. funds control div. dir. State 1941-43; asst. trial counsel U.S. stafff Internat. Nuremberg War Trials, 1945-46; from professorial lectr. to disting. svc. prof. law emeritus U. Chgo. Law Sch., 1946—; counsel Vedder, Price, Kaufman & Kamnholz, Chgo., 1954-55, Sidley and Austin, Chgo., 1987-89; hearing commr. NPA, 1952-53; labor arbitrator; spl. master U.S. Ct. Appeals for D.C., 1963-64; bd. publs. U. Chgo., 1965-67, chmn., 1967-68; mem. Gov. Ill. Adv. Commn. Labor-Mgmt. Policy for Pub. Employees in Ill., 1966-67, Ill. Civil Service Commn., 1968-69; cons. U.S. Dept. Labor, 1969-70. Author: Supplementary Materials on International Organizations, 1948, (with W.G. Katz) Cases and Materials on Business Corporations, 1949, Labor Law Cases, Materials and Problems, 1970, supplement, 1972, 75, 2d edit., 1977, supplements, 1980, 82 (with S. Henderson), 3d edit. (with S. Henderson), 1985, supplement, 1988; also articles. Bd. dirs. Hyde Park Community Conf., 1954-56, S.E. Chgo. Commn., 1956-57. Served to lt. (j.g.) USNR, 1943-46. Mem. ABA (co-chmn. com. devel. law under NLRA 1959-60, mem. spl. com. transp. strikes), Ill. Bar Assn., Chgo. Bar Assn. (bd. mgrs. 1972-73), Nat. Acad. Arbitrators, Am. Law Inst., Am. Acad. Arts and Scis., Order of Coif, Phi Beta Kappa. Home: 1219 E 50th St Chicago IL 60615-2908 Office: U Chgo Law Sch 1111 E 60th St Chicago IL 60637-2702

MELTZER, BERNARD N(ATHAN), sociologist, educator; b. N.Y.C., Oct. 17, 1916; s. Philip and Anna (Kemper) M.; m. Ida Wasserman, June 11, 1944; children: Iris Jean, William Jay. B.A., Wayne State U., 1943, M.A., 1944; Ph.D., U. Chgo., 1948. Research assoc. U. Chgo., 1948-49; asst. prof. sociology McGill U., 1949-51; mem. faculty Central Mich. U., Mt. Pleasant, 1951-87; prof. sociology Central Mich. U., 1955-87, chmn. dept., 1959-87, prof. emeritus, 1987—. Author: Education in Society: Readings, 1958, The Social Psychology of George Herbert Mead, 1959, Symbolic Interaction: A Reader in Social Psychology, 3d edit., 1978, Symbolic Interactionism: Genesis, Varieties and Criticism, 1975; contbr. articles to profl. periodicals and books. Chmn. Isabella County Civil Rights Com., 1959. Recipient citation Mich. Acad. Sci., Arts and Letters, 1969; Ascher fellow social sci. U. Chgo., 1944; Univ. fellow sociology, 1945; Marshall Field fellow sociology, 1946; grantee Can. Social Sci. Research Council, 1950. Fellow Am. Sociol. Assn.; mem. Mich. Sociol. Assn. (pres. 1961-62), North Central Sociol. Assn. (v.p. 1971-72), Soc. Study Symbolic Interaction. Home: 318 E Cherry St Mount Pleasant MI 48858-2606

MELTZER, BRIAN, lawyer; b. Chgo., Apr. 15, 1944; s. Maurice and Ethel (Goldstein) M.; m. Rosemary Labriola, Sept. 11, 1982; children: Stuart Joseph, Alan Phillip, Martin Angelo. BA in Math., Cornell U., 1966; JD, Harvard U., 1969. Bar: Ill. 1969. Assoc. atty. D'ancona & Pflaum, Chgo., 1969-72; assoc. then ptnr. Schwartz & Freeman, Chgo., 1972-88; ptnr. Keck, Mahin & Cate, Chgo., 1988-95, Meltzer, Purtill & Steele, Schaumburg, Ill., 1996—. Office: Meltzer Purtill & Steele 1515 E Woodfield Rd Schaumburg IL 60173-6046

MELTZER, DANIEL J., law educator; b. 1951. AB, Harvard U., 1972, JD, 1975. Bar: Ill. 1975, D.C. 1978, Mass. 1983. Law clk. to Hon. Carl McGowan, 1975-76, law clk. to Hon. Potter Stewart, 1976-77; spl. asst., sec. Dept. Health, Edn. and Welfare, 1977-78; assoc. Williams & Connolly, 1979-81; asst. prof. Harvard U., Cambridge, Mass., 1982-87, prof., 1987—, assoc. dean, 1989-93. Office: Law Sch Harvard U Cambridge MA 02138

MELTZER, DAVID, author, musician; b. Rochester, N.Y., Feb. 17, 1937; s. Louis and Rosamunde (Lovelace) M.; m. Christina Meyer, Apr. 1, 1958; children—Jennifer, Margaret, Amanda, Adam Benjamin ben David. Student, Los Angeles City Coll., 1955-56, U. Calif. at Los Angeles, 1956-57. Mem. cons. bd. Coordinating Coun. of Lit. Mags.; instr. M.A. program in poetics New Coll., San Francisco, 1980—, coord. writing and lit. program in undergrad. humanites program, 1987—. Author: numerous books of poetry, including Tens, Selected Poems, 1973, Six, 1976, Two-Way Mirror: Notebook on Poetry, 1977, The Art, The Veil, 1981, The Name: Selected oetry, 1973-83, 1983; editor: The San Francisco Poets, 1971, Birth, 1973, The Secret Garden: Anthology of the Classic Kabbalah, 1977, Birth: An Anthology of Ancient Texts, Songs, Prayers, and Stories, 1981, Death: An Anthology of Ancient Texts, Songs, Prayers and Stories, 1983, The Book Within the Book: Approaching the Kabbalah, 1990, Arrows: Selected Poetry: 1952-92, 1994, Reading Jazz, 1993, Writing Jazz, 1996, Tree; editor, pub. biann. jour. Writing Jazz, Orf, 1968, The Agency, 1968, The Agency Trilogy, 1994, Under, 1995, also Tree Books; song-writer: Serpent Power, 1968, Poet Song, 1970; soundtrack for Chance, 1978. Bd. dirs. Before Columbus Found., 1977—. Coordinating Coun. of Lit. Mags. grantee, 1973-74, 81, Nat. Endowment of Arts grantee for creative writing, 1974, for pub., 1975, Calif. Arts Coun. grantee, 1979; recipient Tombstone award for poetry John Ryan Morris Meml. Found., 1992. Office: PO Box 9005 Berkeley CA 94709-0005

MELTZER, DONALD RICHARD, treasurer; b. Boston, Sept. 1, 1932; s. Leo N. and Betty (Flesher) M.; m. Mary Douglas Seelye, Dec. 7, 1963; children: Kimberly, Christopher. AB, Dartmouth Coll., 1954, MBA, 1955. Mgr. Peat, Marwick, Mitchell & Co., Boston, 1955-67; asst. controller United Fruit Corp., Boston, 1968-69, controller, 1969-70, v.p., controller, 1970-73; v.p., chief acctg. office United Brands Co., N.Y.C., 1973-74, v.p. fin. and adminstrn., 1974-76; v.p. fin., treas. Instron Corp., Canton, Mass., 1976-88; v.p. fin. and adminstrn., treas., chief fin. officer Dialogue, Inc., Braintree, Mass., 1988-90; corp. fin. cons., Sudbury, Mass., 1988—. Overseer Children's Hosp. Med. Ctr., Boston, 1980-94; fin. com. Town of Sudbury, Mass., 1967; chmn. bd. trustees First Parish Ch., Sudbury, 1970-71, treas., 1991-93; pres. Mass. Parents Assn. for Deaf and Hard of Hearing, Boston, 1976-77, bd. dirs., 1973-86. Mem. AICPA, Mass. Soc. CPAs, Fin. Execs. Inst., Am. Assn. Indsl. Mgmt. (bd. dirs. 1980-85), Walk 'N Mass Volkssport Club (co-pres. 1993-95). Avocation: postal history, stamp collecting. Home: 341 Old Lancaster Rd Sudbury MA 01776-2035

MELTZER, HERBERT YALE, psychiatry educator; b. Bklyn., July 29, 1937; s. David and Estelle (Gross) M.; m. Sharon Rae Bittenson, June 12, 1960; children—David, Danielle. A.B., Cornell U., 1958; M.A., Harvard U., 1959; M.D., Yale U., 1963. Diplomate Am. Bd. Neurology and Psychiatry. Prof. U. Chgo., 1968-85; dir. biol. psychiatry lab. Ill. State Psychiat. Inst., Chgo., 1975-84; Bond prof. psychiatry Case Western Res. U., Cleve., 1985-96; dir. psychiat. research Univ. Hosp., Cleve., 1985-96; prof. psychiatry Vanderbilt U., Nashville, 1996—; dir., divsn. psychopharmacology, 1996—. Editor: Neuropsychopharmacology; contbr. articles to profl. jours. Recipient Efron prize Am. Coll. Neuropsychopharmacology, 1981, Noyes prize for schizophrenia rsch. Commonwealth of Pa., 1990, Sachar award Columbia U., gold medal Soc. Biol. Psychiatry, 1993, Dean prize Am. Coll. Psychiatry, 1996. Mem. NIMH, Am. Coll. Neuropsychopharmacology (pres. 1984-85), Am. Psychiat. Assn., Soc. Biol. Psychiatry (editorial bd.), Nat. Alliance Rsch. Schizophrenia Affective Disorders (Lieber prize 1992). Avocation: music. Office: 83 Altentann Nashville TN

MELTZER, JACK, consultant, retired college dean; b. Bayonne, N.J., Aug. 21, 1921; s. Louis and Debbie (Gold) M.; m. Rae Libin, June 26, 1944; children: Richard, Marc, Ellen. B.A., Wayne State U., 1941; M.A., U. Chgo., 1947. Dir. planning Michael Reese Hosp., Chgo., 1953-54; S.E. Chgo. Commn. and U. Chgo., 1954-58; propr. Jack Meltzer Assos. (planners), 1958-63; acting dir. Am. Soc. Planning Ofcls., 1967-68; prof., dir. Center Urban Studies, U. Chgo., 1963-71; prof. div. social scis., prof. Sch. Social Service Adminstrn., 1965-83; prof., dean Sch. Social Scis. U. Tex.-Dallas, 1983-86; pvt. practice cons., 1986—; cons. to govt. and industry, 1945—. Author book revs., articles, books. Village trustee, Park Forest, Ill., 1950-52, mem. plan commn., 1949; Served to capt. USAAF, World War II. Mem. AAUP, Am. Soc. Planning Ofcls. (past treas.), Am. Inst. Planners (past v.p. pvt. practice dept.), Nat. Assn. Housing and Renewal Ofcls., Am. Soc. Pub. Adminstrn. Home: 4550 N Park Ave Apt 803 Bethesda MD 20815-7237

MELTZER, JAY H., lawyer, retail company executive; b. Bklyn., Mar. 30, 1944; s. Solomon G. and Ethel L. (Kraft) M.; m. Bonnie R. Rosenberg, June 27, 1965; children: Wendy, Elizabeth, Jonathan. A.B., Dartmouth Coll., 1964; JD, Harvard U., 1967. Bar: N.Y. 1968, Mass. 1978, U.S. Dist. Ct. Mass. 1979. Law clk. to U.S. dist. judge, 1967-68; assoc. firm Shearman & Sterling, N.Y.C., 1968-72; with Damon Corp., Needham Heights, Mass., 1972-84; gen. counsel, sec. Damon Corp., 1973-84, v.p., 1979-84; v.p., corp. counsel The TJX Cos., Inc., Framingham, Mass., 1984-87, v.p., gen. counsel, sec., 1987-89, sr. v.p., gen. counsel, sec., 1989—. Dir. coun. Better Bus. Bur., 1990-93. Mem. ABA, Am. Soc. Corp. Secs., Am. Corp. Counsel Assn. (bd. dirs. N.E. chpt.), Retailers Assn. Mass. (bd. dirs., exec. com., sec.), New Eng. Corp. Counsel Assn. (bd. dirs.). Office: TJX Cos Inc 770 Cochituate Rd Framingham MA 01701-4657

MELTZER, MILTON, author; b. Worcester, Mass., May 8, 1915; s. Benjamin and Mary (Richter) M.; m. Hilda Balinky, June 22, 1941; children: Jane, Amy. Student, Columbia, 1932-36. adj. prof. history U. Mass., Amherst, 1977-80. Author: Mark Twain Himself, 1960; (with Walter Harding) A Thoreau Profile, 1962, Langston Hughes: A Biography, 1968, Bread and Roses, 1967, Brother, Can You Spare a Dime, 1968, Never to Forget: The Jews of the Holocaust, 1976, Dorothea Lange: A Photographer's Life, 1978; co-editor: Lydia Maria Child: Selected Letters, 1817-1880, 1982, The Terrorists, 1983, A Book About Names, 1984, The Black Americans, 1984, Ain't Gonna Study War No More, 1985, Mark Twain: A Writer's Life, 1985, Poverty in America, 1986, George Washington and the Birth of Our Nation, 1986, The Landscape of Memory, 1987, The American Revolutionaries, 1987, Benjamin Franklin: The New American, 1988, Rescue: The Story of How Gentiles Saved Jews in the Holocaust, 1988, Starting From Home: A Writer's Beginnings, 1988, Voices From the Civil War, 1989, Columbus and the World Around Him, 1990, The Bill of Rights: How We Got It and What It Means, 1990, Crime in America, 1990, Thomas Jefferson: Revolutionary Aristocrat, 1991, The Amazing Potato, 1992, Slavery: A World History, 1993, Lincoln: In His Own Words, 1993, Andrew Jackson and His America, 1993, Gold, 1993; (with Langston Hughes, C. Eric Lincoln, and Jon Michael Spencer) A Pictorial History of African-Americans, 1994, Cheap Raw Material: How Our Youngest Workers Are Exploited and Abused, 1994, Theodore Roosevelt, 1994, Who Cares? Millions Do: A Book About Altruism, 1994, Frederick Douglass: In His Own Words, 1995. Served with USAAF, 1942-46. Mem. Orgn. Am. Historians, Authors Guild, P.E.N. Address: 263 W End Ave New York NY 10023-2612

MELTZER, YALE LEON, economist, educator; b. N.Y.C., Nov. 3, 1931; s. Benjamin and Ada (Luria) M.; BA, Columbia U., 1954, postgrad. Sch. Law, 1954-55; MBA, NYU, 1966; m. Annette Schoenberg, Aug. 7, 1960; children: Benjamin Robert, Philippe David. Asst. to chief patent atty. Beaunit Mills, Inc., Elizabethton, Tenn., 1955-56, prodn. mgr., 1956-58, rsch. chemist N.Y. Med. Coll., N.Y.C., 1958-59; rsch. chemist H. Kohnstamm & Co., Inc., mfg. chemists, N.Y.C., 1959-66, mgr. comml. devel., market rsch., patents and trademarks, 1966-68; sr. security analyst Harris, Upham & Co., Inc., 1968-70; instr. dept. econs. N.Y. U., 1972-79; adj. asst. prof. dept. acctg., fin. and mgmt. Pace U., N.Y.C., 1974-80, adj. assoc. prof., 1980-84; lectr. dept. polit. sci., econs. and philosophy Coll. S.I., CUNY, 1977-82, asst. prof. dept. polit. sci., econs. and philosophy, 1983—; lectr. bus., fin., econs., sci. and tech.; presenter papers confs. Mem. AAAS, Am. Econ. Assn. Author: Soviet Chemical Industry, 1967; Chemical Trade with the Soviet Union and Eastern European Countries, 1967; Chemical Guide to GATT, The Kennedy Round and International Trade, 1968; Phthalocyanine Technology, 1970; Hormonal and Attractant Pesticide Technology, 1971; Urethane Foams: Technology and Applications, 1971; Water-Soluble Polymers: Technology and Applications, 1972; Encyclopedia of Enzyme Technology, 1973; Economics, 1974; Foamed Plastics; Recent Developments, 1976; Water-Soluble Resins and Polymers: Technology and Applications, 1976; Putting Money to Work: An Investment Primer, 1976; (with W.C.F. Hartley) Cash Management: Planning, Forecasting, and Control, 1979; Water-Soluble Polymers: Recent Developments, 1979; Putting Money to Work: An Investment Primer for the '80s, 1981, updated edit., 1984; Water-Soluble Polymers: Developments since 1978, 1981; Expanded Plastics and Related Products: Developments Since 1978, 1983. Contbr. articles to profl. publs. Translator, Russian, French and German tech. lit. Home: 14110 82nd Dr Jamaica NY 11435-1134 Office: Coll SI Rm 2N226 2800 Victory Blvd Staten Island NY 10314

MELVILLE, ROBERT SEAMAN, chemist; b. Worcester, Mass., Nov. 20, 1913; s. Carey Eyster and Maud Tesmer (Seaman) M.; m. Eleanor Elisabeth Vogel, Mar. 6, 1942; children: Robert Andrew, John Frederick, Margaret Ellen, Emily Jean, Martin Carroll. AB in Chemistry, Clark U., 1937; PhD in Biochemistry, State U. Iowa, 1950. Chief chemist St. Luke's Hosp., Chgo., 1950-54; chief biochemist VA Hosp., Iowa City, 1954-63; chief biochemist, lab. requirement specialist VA Cen. Office, Washington, 1963-65; health sci. adminstr. Nat. Inst. Gen. Med. Scis., NIH, Bethesda, Md., 1965-67, chief automated clin. lab. program, 1967-77, spl. asst. to dir. of biomed. engring., 1977-81; dir. In Vitro Diagnostic Device Standards div. Bur. Med. Devices, FDA, Silver Spring, Md., 1981-82; cons. in clin. scis., 1983—; clin. prof. pathology George Washington U. Med. Ctr., Washington, 1977—; pres. Trans-Tech. Biomed., 1983—. Contbr. articles on clin. lab. automation to profl. publs. With U.S. Army, 1942-46. Fellow AAAS, Am. Chem. Soc., Am.. Assn. Clin. Chemistry (Joseph H. Rowe award 1972, Nat. Fisher award 1976, pres. 1969-70), Instrument Soc. Am., Assn. for Advancement of Med. Instrumentation; mem. Am. Bd. Clin. Chemists (pres. bd. dirs. 1978-81), Am. Inst. Chemists (chmn. cert. commn. in chem. engring. and chemistry 1981-84, 87-91, cert. chemist 1989—), Alpha Chi Sigma (Profl. Chemist award 1990), Lambda Chi Alpha. Unitarian. Club: Cosmos. Lodge: Masons. Home and Office: 11112 Kenilworth Ave PO Box 56 Garrett Park MD 20896-0056

MELVILL-JONES, GEOFFREY, physician, educator; b. Cambridge, Eng., Jan. 14, 1923; emigrated to Can., 1961, naturalized, 1974; s. Benett and

Dorothy Laxton (Jotham) Melvill J.; m. Jenny Marigold Burnaby, June 21, 1953; children—Katharine F., Francis H., Andrew J., Dorothy H. B.A., Cambridge U., 1944, M.A., 1947, M.B.,B.Ch., 1949. House surgeon Middlesex (Eng.) Hosp., 1950; sr. house surgeon in otolaryngology Addenbrooke's Hosp., Cambridge, 1950-51; sci. officer Med. Research Council Gt. Britain, 1955-61; assoc. prof. physiology McGill U., Montreal, Que., Can., 1961-68; prof. McGill U., 1968-92, prof. emeritus, 1992—, Hosmer research prof., 1978-92, dir. aerospace med. research unit, 1961-89; adj. prof. dept. clin. neurosci., faculty medicine U. Calgary, 1992—; vis. prof. Stanford U., 1971-72, College de France, 1979, 95; Ashton Graybiel lectr. U.S. Naval Aerospace Lab., Fla. Author: Mammalian Vestibular Physiology, 1979, Adaptive Mechanisms in Gaze Control, 1985; contbr. numerous articles to profl. publs. Flying pers. med. officer RAF, 1951-55. Recipient SkyLab Achievement award NASA, 1974, Dohlman medal Toronto U., 1986, Wilbur Franks award Can. Soc. Aerospace Medicine, 1988. Fellow Can. Aero. and Space Inst., Aerospace Med. Assn. (Harry G. Armstrong Lectureship award 1968, Arnold D. Tuttle award 1971), Royal Soc. (London), Royal Soc. Can. (McLaughlin medal 1991), Royal Aero. Soc. (London) (Stewart Meml. award 1989, Buchanan Barbour award 1990); mem. U.K. Physiol. Soc., Can. Physiol. Soc., Can. Soc. Aviation Medicine, Internat. Collegium Otolaryngology, Soc. Neurosci., Bárány Soc. (Gold medal 1988). Office: U Calgary Dept Clin. Neuroscis, 3330 Hospital Dr NW, Calgary, AB Canada T2N 4N1

MELVIN, BEN WATSON, JR., petroleum and chemical manufacturing executive; b. Nashville, Mar. 27, 1926; s. Ben Watson and Virginia (Darden) M.; m. Elizabeth Cooper Hershey, May 10, 1952; children—Ben W., Landis Anne, Thomas C., Mark C. B.Chem. Engring., U. Del., 1950. With E. I. duPont de Nemours & Co., Inc., Wilmington, Del., 1950-91, ret., 1991. Served with USAAF, 1944-46. Mem. AICE, Soc. Plastics Engrs., So. Chem. Industry, Wilmington Country Club.

MELVIN, BILLY ALFRED, clergyman; b. Macon, Ga., Nov. 25, 1929; s. Daniel Henry and Leola Dale (Seidell) M.; m. Marcia Darlene Eby, Oct. 26, 1952; children: Deborah Ruth, Daniel Henry II. Student, Free Will Baptist Bible Coll., Nashville, 1947-49; B.A., Taylor U., Upland, Ind., 1951; postgrad., Asbury Theol. Sem., Wilmore, Ky., 1951-53; B.D., Union Theol. Sem., Richmond, Va., 1956; D.D., Azusa (Calif.) Coll., 1968; LL.D. (hon.), Taylor U., 1984; DD, Huntington Coll., 1995. Ordained to ministry Free Will Baptist Ch., 1951; pastor First Free Will Baptist Chs., Newport, Tenn., 1951-53, Richmond, 1953-57; pastor Bethany Ch., Norfolk, Va., 1957-59; exec. sec. Nat. Assn. Free Will Baptists, 1959-67; exec. dir. Nat. Assn. Evangelicals, 1967-95.

MELVIN, CHARLES EDWARD, JR., lawyer; b. Greensboro, N.C., July 13, 1929; s. Charles Edward and Mary Ruth (Plunkett) M.; m. Jacklyn McDaniel, Mar. 1, 1958; 1 child, Dana W. BS, U. N.C., 1951, JD with honors, 1956. Bar: N.C. 1956. Ptnr. Smith, Helms, Mulliss & Moore, L.L.P., Greensboro, 1958—. Capt. U.S. Army, 1952-54. Mem. N.C. Bar Assn. (chmn. real property sect. 1981), Am. Coll. Real Estate Lawyers, Greensboro C. of C. (pres. 1978). Office: Smith Helms Mulliss & Moore Ste 1400 PO Box 21927 300 N Greene St Greensboro NC 27420

MELVIN, JAY WAYNE, computer programmer; b. Oak Park, Ill., Feb. 3, 1946; s. Kendred Wayne and Margarita Alice (Pérez) M.; m. Linda Hansen, Dec. 10, 1980. MA in Urban Studies, Claremont (Calif.) Grad. Sch., 1975, postgrad., 1977. Hot line/prodn. mgr. Forth, Inc., Hermosa Beach, Calif., 1981-85; sr. software engr. Maxtor Corp., San Jose, Calif., 1986-88; computer programmer Tracor-Ultron Labs., San Jose, 1988-90, Comtech Labs., Palo Alto, Calif., 1990-92; programmer, team leader, mgr. software devel. lab. Omnipoint Corp., Colorado Springs, Colo., 1992-96; mgr. applications integration lab. Pacific Bell Mobile Svcs., Pleasanton, Calif., 1996—; cons. phenomenoLOGIC, La Honda, Calif., 1985-92, InfoPath, La Honda, 1990—. Contbr. articles to profl. jours. Peace Corps vol. U.S. State Dept., Begal, India, 1966-68; fire dept. vol. Calif. Dept. Forestry, Kings Mountain, 1986-88; fire dept. lt. Vol. Fire Brigade, La Honda, San Mateo, 1988-94; radio operator Mil. Affiliate Radio Svc., Jackson, Miss., 1962-64. Recipient Beyond War award, 1987; grad. fellowship Law Enforcement Adminstrn. Assn., 1975-77. Mem. Amateur Radio Relay League (life, radio amateur), Amateur Satellite Corp. (life), Forth Interest Group, Assn. of Computing Machinery, Pi Sigma Alpha. Avocation: amateur radio. Home and Office: PO Box 123 La Honda CA 94020-0123

MELVIN, JOHN LEWIS, physician, medical educator, administrator; b. Columbus, Ohio, May 26, 1935; s. John Harper and Ruth Eleanor (Wertenberger) M.; m. Carol Ann Pate, Apr. 10, 1991; children from a previous marriage: Megan Marie, Beth Anne, John Patrick, Mia Michelle. BS, Ohio State U., 1955, MD, 1960, M in Med. Sci., 1966. Rotating Intern Mt. Carmel Hosp., Columbus, 1960-61; resident in phys. medicine Univ. Hosp., Columbus, 1961, 63-66; asst. prof. Ohio State U., Columbus, 1966-69, assoc. prof., 1969-73; prof., chmn. dept. Med. Coll. Wis., Milw., 1973-91; prof., dep. chmn. dept. Temple U., Phila., 1992—; cons. to numerous U.S. govtl. agys., health care insts.; lectr. in field; research assoc. Ohio State Research Found., Columbus, 1966-68; assoc. coordinator Ohio State Regional Med. Program, Columbus, 1969-71; med. dir. Curative Rehab. Ctr., Milw., 1973-91; v.p. med. affairs Moss Rehab. Hosp., Phila., 1991—; dept. chmn. Einstein Med. Ctr., Phila., 1991—. Contbr. articles to profl. jours. Bd. dirs. Vis. Nurses Assn., Milw., 1974-83; mem. com. Mental Health Planning Council, Milw., 1974-75, Wis. Council Devel. Disabilities, Madison, 1979-80; mem. planning and evaluation com. Elizabethtown Hosp. for Children and Youth, Pa., 1977; advisor Nat. Multiple Sclerosis Soc., Milw., 1979-87; mem. Wis. Nicaragua Ptnrs., 1982-91; trustee Easter Seal Research Found., vice chmn., 1985, chmn. 1986-88. Served to capt. M.C., U.S. Army, 1961-63. Recipient cert. of appreciation Goodwill Industries, 1972, spl. recognition award Commn. Accreditation Rehab. Facilities, 1977, Performance award Wood VA Med. Ctr., 1978, Goldschmidt award Nat. Rehab. Hosp., 1990, cert. of appreciation Jour. Rehab. Adminstrn., 1982; Alumni Achievement award Ohio State U., 1985; grantee Rehab. Svcs. Adminstrn., 1979-91, Health Care Financing Adminstrn., 1984-85; Ford Found. fellow, 1951-53. Fellow Am. Acad. Cerebral Palsy and Devel. Medicine, Am. Acad. Phys. Medicine and Rehab. (sec. 1992—, Zeiter Lectr. award 1987); mem. Am. Bd. Phys. Medicine and Rehab. (Diplomate, chmn. 1988-93, chmn. residency Rev. Com. 1985-88), Am. Bd. Med. Specialists (exec. com. 1990-92), Med. Soc. Milw., Milw. Acad. Medicine, Wis. Soc. Phys. Medicine and Rehab., Am. Assn. Electromyography and Electrodiagnosis (pres. 1979-80), Am. Congress Rehab. Medicine (pres. 1987-88, gold medal 1971, 78, Gold Key award 1988), Am. Heart Assn., Am. Hosp. Assn. (sect. rehab. hosp., chmn. 1981), AMA (cert. of appreciation 1976, 82), Am. Paraplegia Soc., Assn. Acad. Physiatrists (pres. 1985-87), Internat. Fedn. Phys. Medicine and Rehab. (exec. com. 1980—, hon. sec. 1980-88, pres. elect 1995—), Internat. Rehab. Medicine Assn., Rehab. Internat. Med. Commn., Nat. Assn. Rehab. Facilities (pres. 1981-83, bd. dirs.), Coun. of Med. Splty. Socs. (pres. 1989-90), Alpha Omega Alpha. Home: 244 Delancey St Philadelphia PA 19106-4330 Office: Moss Rehab Hospital 1200 W Tabor Rd Philadelphia PA 19141-3019

MELVIN, RUSSELL JOHNSTON, magazine publishing consultant; b. New Castle, Pa., Nov. 16, 1925; s. Russell Conwell and Anna Katharine (Johnston) M.; m. Helen Margaret Connery, Aug. 6, 1949; children: Thomas Kirk, Meredith. B.A., U. Pa., 1949. Reporter Phila. Inquirer, 1949; copywriter, then asst. to circulation mgr. Time mag., 1949-53; with Newsweek mag., 1953-86, dir. Pacific edits., 1960-64, mng. dir. internat. edits., 1964-68, mng. editor internat. editorial service, 1969-86; cons. internat. affairs and profl. edn. Mag. Pubs. Am. (formerly Mag. Pubs. Assn.), N.Y.C., 1986—; v.p. Newsweek, Inc., 1965-85; founding editor The Journal, Tokyo, 1963; founding dir. Newsweek Feature Service, 1968; mem. UN Communications Adv. Coun. Served with USNR, 1942-46. Mem. Internat. Advt. Assn. (chmn., CEO 1980-85, exec. dir. Chgps. Corp. 1985-86, bd. dirs. 1988-91, mem. world coun. 1990), Internat. Fedn. Periodical Press (mem. exec. and mgmt. bd.), Univ. Club, Chappaqua Tennis Club. Episcopalian. Home: 153 Douglas Rd Chappaqua NY 10514-3104 Office: Mag Pubs Am 919 3rd Ave New York NY 10022

MELZACK, RONALD, psychology educator; b. Montreal, Que., Can., July 19, 1929; s. Joseph and Annie (Mandel) M.; m. Lucy Birch, Aug. 7, 1960; children: Lauren, Joel. BSc, McGill U., Montreal, 1950, MSc, 1951, PhD, 1954; DLitt (hon.), U. Waterloo, 1992. Lectr. Univ. Coll., London, 1957-58; assoc. prof. MIT, 1959-63; lectr. psychology McGill U., 1953-54; prof. McGill U., 1963—, E.P. Taylor prof., 1986. Author: The Day Tuk Became a Hunter, and Other Eskimo Stories, 1967, Raven, Creator of the World, 1970, The Puzzle of Pain, 1973, Why the Man in the Moon is Happy, and Other Eskimo Creation Stories, 1977, (with P.D. Wall) The Challenge of Pain, 1982, 2nd edit., 1988, Pain Measurement and Assessment, 1983, (with P.D. Wall) Textbook of Pain, 1984, 3rd edit., 1994, (with D.C. Turk) Handbook of Pain Assessment, 1992. Decorated Officer, Order of Can., 1995; recipient Molson prize Can. Coun., 1985, Gaston Labat award Am. Soc. Regional Anesthesia, 1989, J.J. Bonica award VI World Congress on Pain, 1990, Prix du Que. Marie-Victorin, 1994; recipient Disting. Contbn. award Can. Pain Soc., 1995. Fellow APA, AAAS, Royal Soc. Can., Can. Psychol. Assn. (Disting. Contbns. to Psychol. Sci. award 1986, hon. pres. 1988-89); mem. Internat. Assn. Study of Pain (hon., past pres.), Can. Pain Soc. (Award for Disting. Contbn. to pain rsch. and mgmt. in Can. 1995). Home: 51 Banstead Rd, Montreal, PQ Canada H4X 1P1

MEMORY, JASPER DURHAM, academic administrator, physics educator; b. Raleigh, N.C., Dec. 10, 1936; s. Jasper Livingston and Margaret Moore (Durham) M.; m. Carolyn Hofler, June 4, 1961; children—Margaret Carolyn, Jasper William. B.S. summa cum laude, Wake Forest U., 1956; Ph.D., U. N.C., 1960. Successively asst. prof., assoc. prof. physics U. S.C., Columbia, 1960-64; assoc. prof. N.C. State U., Raleigh, 1964-67, assoc. dean, physics and math. scis., 1973-82, prof., 1967—, vice-provost, grad. dean, 1982-86; v.p. for research U. N.C. System, Chapel Hill, 1986—; bd. govs. Research Triangle Inst., Research Triangle Park, N.C., 1983-84, Triangle Area rsch. dir., 1981—; cons. NASA Langley, Hampton, Va., 1970-74, Ohio Bd. Regents, 1993-95, Ark. Bd. Regents, 1987; N.C. State U. rep. Oak Ridge Associated Univs., 1982-85, Grad. Record Exam. Bd., 1985-90, chair, 1989, Policy Coun., Test of English as a Fgn. Lang., 1987-88, chair, 1988. Author: Quantum Theory of Magnetic Resonance Parameters, 1968; (with others) NMR of Aromatic Compounds, 1982, High Resolution NMR in the Solid State: Fundamentals of CP/MAS, 1994. Recipient Outstanding Tchr. award N.C. State U., 1967, Disting. Alumni Service award Wake Forest U., 1981. Fellow Am. Phys. Soc.; mem. Am. Assn. Physics Tchrs., Phi Beta Kappa, Sigma Xi. Democrat. Presbyterian. Home: 124 Talon Dr Cary NC 27511-8604 Office: Univ NC Gen Adminstrn Chapel Hill NC 27515-2688

MENAKER, RONALD HERBERT, banking executive; b. N.Y.C., Dec. 17, 1944; s. Harold L. Menaker and Gladys (Bleiberg) Ross; m. Kathleen Sager Thomas, Sept. 11, 1966; children: Meredith E., Kyri D. Student, Queen's Coll., 1965-66. Sr. v.p., head of corp. svcs. J.P. Morgan & Co., Inc., N.Y.C., 1966—; dir. J.P. Morgan Svcs., Wilmington, Del. Trustee, chmn. N.Y. Downtown Hosp., N.Y.C., 1991—; trustee NYU Med. Ctr., St. Huberts Giralda Animal Welfare and Edn. Ctr., Madison, N.J.; pres. The Dog Mus., St. Louis, 1989—. Mem. Westminster Kennel Club (show chmn. 1990—). Avocations: sporting art, judging dogs. Office: JP Morgan & Co Inc 60 Wall St New York NY 10260

MENAKER, SHIRLEY ANN LASCH, psychology educator, academic administrator; b. Jersey City, July 22, 1935; d. Frederick Carl and Mary Elizabeth (Thrall) Lasch; m. Michael Menaker, June 4, 1955; children: Ellen Margaret, Nicholas. BA in English Lit., Swarthmore Coll., 1956; MA, Boston U., 1961, PhD in Clin. Psychology, 1965. Adminstrv. asst. N.J. State Fedn. Dist. Bds. Edn., Trenton, 1956-59; trainee clin. psychology Mass. Mental Health Ctr., Boston, 1960-61; intern clin. psychology Thom Guidance Clinic for Children, Boston, 1961-62; research assoc. ednl. psychology U. Tex.-Austin, 1964-67, asst. prof. ednl. psychology, 1967-70. assoc. prof., 1970-79, assoc. dean grad. sch., 1975-77, psychology cons. Research and Devel. Ctr. for Tchr. Edn., 1965-67, faculty investigator, 1967-74; assoc. prof. counseling psychology U. Oreg., Eugene, 1979-85, prof., 1985-87 , assoc. dean grad. sch., 1979-84, acting dean grad. sch., 1980-81, 82-83, dean grad sch., 1984-87; assoc. provost for acad. support, prof. gen. faculty, U. Va., Charlottesville, 1987—. Bd. dirs. Nat. Grad. Record Exam. Bd. and Policy Council-Test of English as Fgn. Lang., Ednl. Testing Services, 1984-88. Contbr. articles to profl. jours. NIMH fellow, 1963-64. Office: U Va Adminstrn Madison Hall Charlottesville VA 22906-9014

MENARD, EDITH, English language educator, artist, poet, actress; b. Washington, Dec. 5, 1919; d. Willis Monroe and Edith Berncenia (Gill) M. BS summa cum laude, Miner Tchrs. Coll., Washington, 1940; MA in English, Howard U., 1942; postgrad., NYU, 1944-46; MA in Teaching English, Columbia U., 1952; postgrad. in edn., George Washington U., 1966-79, 89-92, doctoral candidate, 1992—. Instr. English and speech Howard U., Washington, 1946-53; high sch. tchr. English D.C. Pub. Schs., Washington, 1953-73; chmn. dept. English Woodrow Wilson High Sch., Washington, 1972-73; adj. asst. prof. English fundamentals U. D.C., 1988-90; founder, dir. Miss Menard's Exclusive English Tutorial Svc., 1991—; substitute tchr. D.C. and Montgomery County (Md.) pub. schs. Contbr. articles and poetry to various publs., including At Day's End, 1994. Reader poetry to civic orgns.; vol. Washington Nat. Cathedral Assn., 1993—. Recipient Golden Poet award World of Poetry, 1988, Silver Poet award, 1989, Editor's Choice award The Nat. Libr. of Poetry, 1994; Julius Rosenwald fellow Yale U., 1943-44. Mem. Internat. Soc. Poets (Disting. mem. 1995, Merit award 1995), Smithsonian Assocs. Episcopalian. Avocations: interior decorating and restoration, pub. speaking and politics, painting, writing. Home: Ste 916 6101 16th St NW Washington DC 20011-1766

MÉNARD, JACQUES EDOUARD, historian; b. Montreal, Que., Can., Feb. 21, 1923; s. Leon Paul and Alice Marie (LaFrance) M.; BA, lic. theology, U. Montreal, 1947, Dr. (hon.), 1978; ThD summa cum laude, U. Angelicum, Rome, 1948; lic. Bibl. scis. Bibl. Inst., Rome, 1950; diploma Ecole Pratique Hautes Etudes, Paris, 1960; D.Theology summa cum laude, U. Strasbourg, 1967; DEd (hon.) La Valette, Malta, 1988, Marquis Guiseppe Sciluna Internat. U. Found., 1990, PhD Albert Einstein Inst., 1993. Ordained priest Roman Cath. Ch., 1947; prof. N.T., U. Montreal Div. Sch., 1951-57; rsch. worker Can. Coun., 1957-61; rsch. asst. Centre Nat. Recherche Sci., France, 1961-65; mem. Faculty Cath. Theology, U. Scis. Humaines, Strasbourg, France, 1965—, ordinary prof. history of religions, 1973—, prof. emeritus, 1991; dir. Can. project integral French edit. Nag Hammadi texts, 1973—; dir. Cahiers de la Bibliothèque Copte; hon. dir. Revue des Scis. Religieuses; co-editor Bibliothèque Copte de Hammadi, Quebec, 1977—; co-editor Nag Hammadi Studies, 1970—. Mem. Societas Novi Testamenti Studiorum, Internat. Assn. Coptic Studies (bd., founding pres., hon.). Author: Les Dons du Saint Esprit chez Monsieur Olier (Theologica), 1951, 2d edit., 1987, L'Evangile de Vérité Rétroversion grecque et Commentaire, 1962, 2d edit., 1972, L'Evangile selon Philippe, 2d edit., 1967, 3d edit., 1988, Exégèse biblique et judaïsme, 1973, Le symbole, 1975, L'Evangile selon Thomas, 1975, Les textes de Nag Hammadi, 1975, La Lettre de Pierre à Philippe, 1977, L'Authentikos Logos, 1977; Le Traité sur la Résurrection, 1983; Ecritures et traditions dans la littérature Copte, 1984; L'Exposé valentinien: Fragments du Baptême et de l'Eucharistie, 1985; Gnose et Manichéisme, 1986, Introduction à l'Histoire des Religions, 1987, La Gnose de Philon d'Alexandrie, 1987, Le Chant de la Perle, 1991, La Pistis Sophia, 1st band, 1994, 2nd band, 1995, Memories, 1994; contbr. 400 articles and book revs. Home: Foyer de la Solitude 27 Rue Minard, 92130 Issy-les-Moulineaux France Office: Faculty Cath Theology Univ Scis Humaines, Palais Universitaire, 67084 Strasbourg France

MENARD, JOHN R., lumber company executive; b. 1940. Pres., ceo Menard Inc., Eau Claire, Wis., 1960—. Office: Menard Inc 4777 Menard Dr Eau Claire WI 54703-9604*

MENCER, GLENN EVERELL, federal judge; b. Smethport, Pa., May 18, 1925; s. Glenn Hezekiah and Ruth Leona (Rice) M.; m. Hannah Jane Freyer, June 24, 1950; children—Ruth Ann, Cora Jane, Glenn John. B.B.A., U. Mich., 1949, J.D., 1952. Bar: Pa. 1953, U.S. Dist. Ct. (we. dist.) Pa. 1953, U.S. Supreme Ct. 1958. Sole practice Eldred, Pa., 1953-64; dist. atty. McKean County, Pa., 1956-64; judge 48th Jud. Dist. Ct., Smethport, 1964-70, Commonwealth Ct. of Pa., Harrisburg, 1970-82, U.S. Dist. Ct., Erie, Pa., 1982—. Served with U.S. Army, 1943-45, ETO. Mem. Fed. Judges Assn., Pa. Bar Assn., McKean County Bar Assn. Republican. Methodist. Lodge: Masons (33 degree). Home: 30 W Willow St Smethport PA 16749-1524 Office: US Dist Ct Fed Courthouse PO Box 1820 Erie PA 16507-0820

MENCH, JOHN WILLIAM, retail store executive, electrical engineer; b. N.Y.C., Feb. 27, 1943; s. John William and Edna (Ilgen) M.; m. Rose Irene Miller, Aug. 12, 1962; 1 child, William Ilgen. BSEE, U. S.C., 1969; MBA, Ohio U., 1983; PhD, Calif. Coast U., 1994. Elec. engr. Uniroyal, Shelbyville, Tenn., 1969-74; facility engr. Kroger, Nashville, 1974-77; asst. mgr. facility engring. Kroger, Atlanta, 1977-79; Kroger mktg. area mgr. facility engring. Kroger, Columbus, Ohio, 1979-85; div. mgr. facility engring., v.p. Safeway Stores, Inc., Oakland, Calif., 1985-86; v.p. constrn., engring. Big V Supermarkets, Inc., Florida, N.Y., 1986-95; pres. Mench & Assocs. Inc., 1994—. Author tech. manuals in field. Trustee Meth. Ch., 1987-93; bd. dirs. Goshen Day Care Ctr., 1988-95; past v.p. Tri State V.W. Assn.; mem. exec. adv. bd. Ohio U. Coll. Bus. Adminstrn., 1992—; mem. bd. dirs. Elec. Distbn. Systems, 1993-94. Mem. IEEE (sr.), Assn. Energy Engrs. (sr.). Republican. Methodist. Avocation: Volkswagens.

MENCHACA, PEGGY SUE BEARD, energy company executive; b. San Angelo, Tex., Mar. 25, 1938; d. Rufus Arch and Laura Enola (Davis) Beard; m. Elias Menchaca Jr., Feb. 7, 1957; children: Dana Menchaca Barber, Michael T., David R., Jay A. Cert. in ct. reporting/legal stenography, Alvin (Tex.) Community Coll., 1984; BA in Liberal Arts, Our Lady of the Lake U., 1993. Sec. to city mgr. and city atty. City of San Angelo, 1956-58; legal sec. Hardeman, Smith & Foy, San Angelo, 1959-65; with Enron Corp. (formerly HNG/InterNorth and Houston Nat. Gas Corp.), 1965—, successively exec. sec. to v.p. and gen. counsel, exec. sec. to sr. v.p. and gen. counsel, adminstrv. asst. to pres. and COO, adminstrv. asst. to chmn. and CEO, adminstr. corp. contbns., corp. sec., now v.p., sec.; bd. dirs. Houston Downtown Mgmt. Corp.; mem. Supreme Ct. Tex. Task Force on Gender Bias in Jud. Sys., 1991-94. Trustee Enron Found., bd. dirs., 1984—. Mem. Tex. Bar Assn. (legal assts. div.), Am. Soc. Corp. Secs. (v.p. Houston regional group 1989-90, pres. 1990-91), Inwood Forest Golf (Houston) Club. Avocation: skiing. *

MENCHEL, DONALD, television executive; b. N.Y.C., Oct. 26, 1932; s. Abraham and Tessie (Green) M.; m. Barbara Winograd, Jan. 27, 1957; children: Pamela W., Terry G. B.A., Brandeis U., 1954. Film booker ABC Films, N.Y.C., 1956; with Telcom Assocs., N.Y.C., 1957-72; v.p. Telcom Assocs., 1961; exec. v.p. Telcom Assos., 1972; also dir.; dir. mktg. Time-Life TV, N.Y.C., 1972-75; v.p., dir. sales MCA TV, N.Y.C., 1975-77; exec. v.p. MCA TV, 1977-78, pres., 1978-89; pres. The Menchel Co., N.Y.C., 1989—. Trustee Brandeis U; bd. dirs. Literacy Vols. of N.Y.C. With U.S. Army, 1954-56. Mem. Internat. Radio and TV Soc.

MENCHER, BRUCE STEPHAN, judge; b. Washington, May 21, 1935; s. Emanuel and Bertha Miriam (Robbin) M.; m. Janet Patricia Whitfield, Nov. 24, 1974; children by previous marriage: Sean Robbin, Marc Nadzo. B.A., George Washington U., 1957, J.D. with honors, 1960. Bar: D.C. 1960, U.S. Supreme Ct. 1964. Gen. atty. Office Gen. Counsel, Dept. Agr., 1960-61; asst. corp. counsel for D.C., 1961-67; atty.-adviser Office Gen. Counsel, Bur. for Africa, AID, 1967-69; ptnr. Wilkes & Artis, Washington, 1969-75; assoc. judge Superior Ct. D.C., 1975-91; sr. judge, 1991—; presiding judge Family div. Superior Ct. D.C., 1988-90; professorial lectr. law George Washington U. Nat. Law Ctr., 1982-83; lectr. criminal justice Nat. Cathedral Sch./St. Albans Sch., 1985; faculty advisor Nat. Jud. Coll., 1995. Asst. rsch. editor George Washington Law Rev., 1959-60; contbr. articles to law revs. Mem. gen. alumni gov. bd. George Washington U., 1972-80; life mem. Nat. Children's Ctr.; bd. dirs. Nat. Child Support Enforcement Assn., 1994—, The Washington Savoyards Ltd., 1991—. Recipient Alumni Svc. award, 1975, Judge of Yr. award Assn. Plaintiffs Trial Attys., 1983, Samuel Green award for disting. svc. to Washington legal comty. and Phi Delta Phi, 1985, Disting. Alumni Achievement award George Washington U., 1987, also various appreciation and recognition awards local bar assns., D.C. and fed. govts. for work in area of family law and child support enforcement. Mem. Am., D.C. bar assns., George Washington Law Assn. (exec. com. 1972-77), The Barristers (exec. com. 1981), Phi Delta Phi (pres. Barrister Inn 1974-75). Office: Superior Ct DC 500 Indiana Ave NW Rm 5520 Washington DC 20001-2131 *While it may sound old-fashioned, I attribute my appointment to the bench, in large part, to hard work, dedication, a love of the law and respect for my fellow man. One should maintain his sense of balance, always try to understand the other person's position and, at all costs, maintain a sense of humor throughout.*

MENCHER, MELVIN, journalist, retired educator; b. Bklyn., Jan. 25, 1927; s. Peter and Theresa (Sherman) M.; m. Helen Chamberlain, Aug. 27, 1947; children: Thomas, Marianne, Nicholas. Student, U. N.Mex., 1943-44; B.A., U. Colo., 1947; postgrad. (Nieman fellow), Harvard, 1952-53. Reporter UP, 1947-50; state polit. corr. Albuquerque Jour., 1951-54; reporter Fresno (Calif.) Bee, 1954-58; asst. prof. journalism U. Kans., Lawrence, 1958-62; asst. prof. Columbia U., N.Y.C., 1962-65, assoc. prof., 1965-75, prof., 1975-90, assoc. dir. summer program for journalism edn. of minorities, 1971, prof. emeritus, 1990—. Contbg. author: Evaluating the Press, 1973; author: News Reporting and Writing, 1977, Basic Media Writing, 1983; editor: The FNMA Guide to Buying, Financing and Selling Your Home, 1973; contbr. articles to profl. jours. Mem. Soc. Profl. Journalists, Nat. Council Coll. Pubs. Advisers, Kappa Tau Alpha. Home: 450 Riverside Dr New York NY 10027-6821 Office: Grad Sch Journalism Columbia U New York NY 10027

MENCHER, STUART ALAN, sales and marketing executive; b. N.Y.C., Apr. 25, 1939; s. Meyer H. and Mildred B. (Finger) M.; m. Judith Leslie Schneider; children: Jane Lizabeth, Tracy Ellen. B in Mgmt. Engring., Rensselaer Poly. Inst., 1960; MBA, NYU, 1965. Sales rep. Sperry Rand Univac, Albany, N.Y., 1960-62; various sales and mktg. mgmt. positions IBM Corp., White Plains, N.Y., 1965-78; br. mgr. data processing div. IBM Corp., Harrison, N.Y., 1978-81; dr. mktg. ops. planning, bus. mktg. dept. AT&T, Basking Ridge, N.J., 1981-83; dir. market planning, sales and mktg. div. AT&T Info. Systems, Morristown, N.J., 1983; dir. data systems mktg. AT&T Info. Systems, Morristown, 1983-84, v.p. mktg., large bus. systems div., 1985-87; sr. v.p. sales and mktg. MCI Communications Corp., Washington, 1987-90; sr. v.p., gen. mgr. U.S. distbn. div. Motorola/Codex Corp., Mansfield, Mass., 1990-91; sr. v.p., gen. mgr. Teleport Communications, N.Y.C., 1992-93; sr. v.p. nat. sales and mktg., 1994—. Pres. Westfield Men's Coll. Scholarship Club, N.J., 1977; coach Westfield Young Soccer Assn., 1976-81; mem. budget rev. com. United Fund, Westfield, 1983-85; mem. adv. bd. N.Y.C. Tech. Coll., 1993; mem. Mayor's Telecomms. Mutual Aid and Restoration Com. N.Y.C., 1992-93. Lt. USCGR, 1962-65. Avocations: golf, soccer coaching, sailing. Office: Teleport Communications Group 2 Teleport Dr Staten Island NY 10311-1001

MENCHIK, PAUL LEONARD, economist, educator; b. N.Y.C., Sept. 16, 1947; s. Irving and Eleanor (Swedlow) M.; m. Bettie Ann Landauer, May 28, 1972; children: Daniel Aron, Jeremy Matthew. BA, SUNY, Binghamton, 1969; AM, U. Pa., 1971, PhD, 1976. Lectr. Rutgers Coll., New Brunswick, N.J., 1974-76; rsch. assoc. Inst. for Rsch. on Poverty, U. Wis., Madison, 1976-79; prof., chairperson dept. econs. Mich. State U., East Lansing, 1979—; sr. economist, econ. policy Office Mgmt. & Budget, Washington, 1990-91; acad. visitor Stanford (Calif.) U., 1980, London Sch. Econs., 1987-88; vis. assoc. prof. U. Pa., Phila., 1982-83; cons., advisor in field. Mem. editl. bd. Jour. Income Distbn., Amsterdam, 1992—; contbr. articles to profl. jours. Grantee NSF, Social Security Adminstrn., U.S. Dept. Health and Human Svcs.; recipient Best Article of Yr. award Econ. Inquiry, 1987. Mem. Am. Econ. Assn., Nat. Tax Assn., Nat. Bur. Econ. Rsch. Conf. on Income & Wealth. Avocations: bowling, softball, golf, ping-pong, camping. Office: Mich State U 101 Marshall Hall E Circle Dr East Lansing MI 48824

MENCHIN, ROBERT STANLEY, marketing executive; b. Kingston, N.Y., Oct. 31, 1923; s. Abraham H. and Gertrude (Gorlin) M.; m. Marylin Barsky, Dec. 26, 1949; children: Jonathan, Scott. BA, NYU, 1948. Account exec. DKG Advt., N.Y.C., 1949-51; dir. spl. projects Am. Visuals Corp., N.Y.C., 1952-59; dir. advt. and pub. rels. Arthur Wiesenberger & Co., N.Y.C., 1959-65; pres. Wall St. Mktg. Communications, Inc., N.Y.C., 1967-77; dir. mktg. communications Chgo. Bd. Trade, 1977-83, v.p. communication and member rels., 1983-87; pres. Wall Street Mktg., Chgo., 1987—. With AUS, 1942-45. Mem. Am. Mktg. Assn., Pub. Rels. Soc. Am., Fin. Planners Assn. Author: The Last Caprice, 1964, Where There's a Will, 1977, The Mature Market: A Strategic Marketing Guide to America's Fastest-Growing Population Segment, 1989, New Work Opportunities for Older Americans, 1993. Home: Lake Point Tower 505 N Lake Shore Dr Ste 1407-08 Chicago IL 60611-3427

MENDE, HOWARD SHIQEHARU, mechanical engineer; b. Hilo, Hawaii, Nov. 19, 1947; s. Tsutomu and Harue (Kubomitsu) M. BSME, U. Hawaii, 1969; MSME, U. So. Calif., 1975. Registered profl. engr., Calif. Mem. tech. staff I Rockwell Internat., Anaheim, Calif., 1970-71; mem. tech. staff I Rockwell Internat., L.A., 1971-73, mem. tech. staff II, 1973-77, mem. tech. staff IV, 1984-86; devel. engr. AiRsch. Mfg. Co., Torrance, Calif., 1977-83; mech. engr. Def. Contracts Mgmt. Dist. West, Santa Ana, Calif., 1987-94, electronics engr., 1994—; lectr. Pacific States U., L.A., 1974-75. Mem. ASME (assoc.). Democrat. Buddhist. Home: 1946 W 180th Pl Torrance CA 90504-4417 Office: Def Contracts Mgmt 2525 W 190th St Torrance CA 90504-6099

MENDE, ROBERT GRAHAM, retired engineering association executive; b. Newark, Dec. 4, 1926; s. Herman Ernest and Etta (Hillenbrand) M.; m. Joan B. Tamlyn, Apr. 12, 1958; children: Lisa Anne, Robert Graham Jr. Student, Mass. Inst. Tech., 1944-45; degree, N.Y. State Maritime Acad., 1947; B.S., Webb Inst. Naval Architecture, 1951. Project engr. Foster Wheeler Corp., N.Y.C., 1953-56; dist. mgr., naval architect Bird-Johnson Co., N.Y.C., 1956-62; sr. naval architect J.J. Henry Co., Inc., N.Y.C., 1962-69; exec. dir. Soc. Naval Architects and Marine Engrs., 1969-91; mem. marine engring. coun. Underwriters Labs., Inc., 1969-91; ad hoc vis. com. Engrs. Coun. for Profl. Devel., 1970-72. Bd. dirs. Friends of World Maritime U., 1987-91; trustee Webb Inst. Naval Architecture, 1987-91. Lt. USNR, 1951-53. Fellow Royal Inst. Naval Architects, Soc. Naval Architect and Marine Engrs. (hon. life v.p., chmn. N.Y. sect. 1968-69, Vice Admiral E.S. Jerry Land medal 1991, Robert G. Mende Bldg. hdqrs. bldg. named in his honor); mem. ASME, Am. Soc. Naval Engrs., Am. Soc. Assn. Execs., Coun. Engring. and Sci. Soc. Execs. (bd. dirs. 1988-91), Maritime Coll. Assn., N.E. Coast Inst. Engrs. and Shipbuilders, Webb Alumni Assn. (pres. 1970-72). *Hard work, perseverance, humility and a dash of deprivation almost always insure success. It also doesn't hurt to be in the right place at the right time.*

MENDEL, JERRY MARC, electrical engineering educator; b. N.Y.C., May 14, 1938; s. Alfred and Eleanor (Deutch) M.; m. Letty Susan Grossman, June 26, 1960; children: Jonathan, Aileen. BMechE cum laude, Poly. U., 1959, MEE, 1960, PhD in Elec. Engring., 1963. Registered profl. engr., Calif. Instr. elec. engring. Poly. Inst. Bklyn., 1960-63; engring. scientist and sect. chief McDonnell-Douglas Astronautics Co., Huntington Beach, Calif., 1963-74; prof. dept. elec. engring. systems U. So. Calif., L.A., 1974—, chmn. dept., 1984-91; dir. Signal and Image Processing Inst., L.A., 1991-94; pres., founder MENTECH, Culver City, Calif., 1983—; pres. United Signals and Systems, Inc., 1989—. Author: Discrete Techniques of Parameter Estimation: The Equation Error Formulation, 1973, Optimal Seismic Deconvolution: An Estimation Based Approach, 1983 (Phi Kappa Phi award 1984), Lessons in Digital Estimation Theory, 1987, Maximum-Likelihood Deconvolution, 1990, Lessons in Estimation Theory for Signal Processing, Communications and Control, 1995; editor: Prelude to Neural Networks: Adaptive and Learning Systems, 1994; co-editor: Adaptive Learning and Pattern Recognition Systems, 1970. Fellow IEEE (centennial medal 1984); Disting. mem. IEEE Control Systems Soc. (pres. 1986). Office: U So Calif Dept Elec Engring Systems EEB 438 Los Angeles CA 90089-2564

MENDEL, MAURICE, audiologist, educator; b. Colorado Springs, Colo., Oct. 6, 1942; married; 3 children. BA, U. Colo., 1965; MS, Washington U., 1967; PhD in Audiology, U. Wis., 1970. Asst. prof. audiology U. Iowa Hosp., 1970-74, assoc. rsch. scientist, 1975-76; assoc. prof. U. Calif., Santa Barbara, 1976-84, prof. audiology, 1984-88; chmn. dept. audiology and speech pathology Memphis State U., 1988-92; dean Sch. Audiology and Speech-Lang. Pathology U. Memphis, 1993—; program dir. speech and hearing sci. U. Calif., Santa Barbara, 1980-82. Fellow Am. Speech-Lang.-Hearing Assn., Soc. Ear Nose and Throat Advance in Children; mem. Am. Acad. Audiology, Internat. Elec. Response Audiology Study Group, Internat. Soc. Audiology, Tenn. Assn. Audiology and Speech-Lang. Pathologists, Sigma Xi. Achievements include research in middle components of the auditory evoked potentials and their subsequent clinical applications to hearing testing. Office: U Memphis CRISCI 807 Jefferson Ave Memphis TN 38105-5042

MENDELEJIS, LEONARDO NIERMAN, artist; b. Mexico City, Nov. 1, 1932; s. Chanel and Clara (Mendelejis) N.; m. Esther Ptak, Feb. 16, 1957; children: Monica, Daniel, Claudia. BS in Physics and Math, U. Mexico; degree in bus. adminstrn., U. Mex., 1959, degree in music, hon. degree, 1960; D (honoris causa), Concordia U., 1994. One-man shows, Proteo Gallery, 1958, 60, C.D.I. Gallery, 1956, Misrachi Gallery, 1964, Galeria Merkup, 1969, Mus. Modern Art, 1972, all Mexico City, Galeria Sudamericana, N.Y.C., 1958, Hammer Galleries, N.Y.C., 1960, I.F.A. Galleries, Washington, 1952, 62, 65, 68, 71, Edgardo Acosta Gallery, Beverly Hills, Calif., 1961, Art Collectors Gallery, Beverly Hills, 1966, Main St. Gallery, Chgo., 1961, Doll & Richard Gallery, Boston, 1963, Pucker Safrai Gallery, Boston, 1969, El Paso (Tex.) Mus Art, 1964, 71, Wolfard's Gallery, Rochester, N.Y., 1964, Pub. Library Rockville Center, N.Y., 1964, Little Gallery, Phila., 1964, Neusteters Gallery Fine Arts, Denver, 1965, Judah L. Magnes Meml. Mus., Berkeley, Calif., 1967, Galerie Katia Granoff, Paris, 1969, Little Gallery, Phila., 1970, Aalwin Gallery, London, 1970, Gallery Modern Art, Scottsdale, Ariz., 1971, Mus. Contemporary Arts, Bogota, Colombia, 1973, 74, Galerie Dresdnere, Ont., Can., Casa de la Cultura, Cucuta, Colombia, 1974, also mus., galleries, Haifa, Israel, Rome, Italy, Toronto, Ont., Can., Paris, France, 1962—; exhibited group shows mus., Caracas, Venezuela, 1958, Mexico City, 1958—, Havana, Cuba, 1959, Tokyo, Japan, 1963, Paris, France, 1961, Nagoya, Japan, 1963, Kyoto, Japan, 1963, Osaka, Japan, 1963, Bogota, 1963, Santiago, Chile, 1963, Buenos Aires, Argentina, 1963, Rio de Janeiro, Brazil, 1963, Costa Rica, 1963, Panama, 1963, Oslo, Norway, 1965, Warsaw, Poland, 1965, Madrid, Spain, 1965, Stockholm, Sweden, 1966, Brussels, Belgium, 1966; also exhibitions at the Mus. Contemporary Art, Bogota, Colombia (diploma d'honneur of fine arts in Monaco), 1976, B. Lewin Galleries, Los Angeles, 1977, I.F. A. Galleries, Washington, 1977, Merrill Chase Galleries, Chgo., 1977, Am. Mus., Hayden Planetarium, N.Y.C., 1978, Cumberland Mus. of Sci. Ctr., Nashville, 1978, Fernback Sci. Ctr., Atlanta, 1978, Nahan Galleries, New Orleans, 1980, Broward Galleries, Pompano Beach, Fla., 1980, Mus. Sci. and Industry, Chgo., 1980, Galeria de Arte Misrachi, Mexico City, 1982, Calif. Mus. Sci. and Industry, 1982, Museo de Arte e Historia, Ciudad Juarez, Mexico, 1984, Centro de Artes Visuales e Investigaciones Esteticas, Mexico, 1984, Barbara Gillman Gallery, Miami, 1984, MIT Mus., Boston, 1984, Merrill Chase Galleries, Chgo., 1987, Museo de Arte Costarricense, Art Ctr. Galleries Hawaii Inc., 1988, Maison de L'Amerique Latine de Monaco, Monte Carlo, 1990, Centro Cultural San Angel, Mex.; also exhibited Expo, 1958, also numerous mus., univs., Eastern and Western U.S., Can., 1958—; executed murals, Sch. Commerce University City, Mexico, 1956, Bank San Francisco, 1965, physics bldg., Princeton, 1969; also executed stained glass windows, Mexican synagogues, 1968-69; executed tapestries Concert & Opera House, Salzburg, 1989, Majestic Theatre, San Antonio 1989, Theatre An Der Wein, Austria; prin. sculptures in including at Birmingham (Ala.) Mus. Art, Mexican Nat. U., Yeshiva U., N.Y., Hebrew U. Jerusalem, Sherman Bldg. Mount Scopus, City of Monterrey, Mex., Eleanor Roosevelt Inst., Denver, Wichita (Kans.) Airport; represented in permanent collections, Mus. Modern Art in Mexico, Atlanta Mus., Mus. Modern Art Haifa, Gallery Modern Art, N.Y.C., Phoenix Art Mus., Pan Am. Union, Washington, Detroit Inst. Arts, Bogota Mus. Contemporary Arts, Mus. Contemporary Arts, Madrid, Acad. Fine Arts, Honolulu, Tucson Art Center, Tel-Aviv Mus., Israel Mus., Jerusalem, Kennedy Art Center, Washington, Boston Mus. Fine Arts, U. Va., No. Ill. Univ., Chgo. Art Inst., New Orleans Mus. Art, other mus. and galleries. (Recipient 1st prize Mexican Contemporary Art, Art Inst. Mexico 1964, Palme d'or Beaux Arts, Monaco 1969, gold medal Tomasso Camella Found. 1972). Patron Acad. St. Martin in the Fields, 1993—. Recipient Gold medal Internat. Parliament for Safety and Peace-U.S.A.-Italy, 1983; named Accademico D'Europe, Centro Studi di Ricerchi L'Accademia D'Europa, Italy; European Banner of Arts Prize, Italy, 1984, Oscar D'Italia, 1984; winner of world-wide competition to do a sculpture for U. Cen. Fla., Orlando, 1986. Life fellow Royal Soc. Arts (London, Eng.). Office: Reforma 16B San Angel, 01000 Mexico City 20, Mexico also: Str Reforma 16 Bis, Mexico City 20, Mexico also: Lublin Graphics 95 E Putnam Ave Greenwich CT 06830-5611

MENDELL, OLIVER M., banking executive; b. N.Y.C., Apr. 4, 1925; s. M. Lester and Malvina Mendell; grad. Washington and Lee U., 1950; postgrad. Columbia U. Exec. Course, 1969; m. Shelley R. Disick, Sept. 24, 1962; children—Steven, David. Asst. treas. Bankers Trust Co., N.Y.C., 1950-56; v.p., dir. Queens Nat. Bank, N.Y.C., 1956-58; sr. v.p. Chem. Bank, N.Y.C., 1958—; dir. Cartier, Inc., 1967-69. Pres., Fifth Ave. Assn., 1978-82, chmn., 1982-87; trustee Washington and Lee U. Alumni, vice chmn. alumni fund campaign; bd. dirs. Citizens Budget Commn. N.Y., SSS, 1962-76, JFK Internat. Synagogue, Park 86th Apt. Corp., 1966-71, Joint Distbn. Com.; bd. govs. Sch. Banking and Money Mgmt., Adelphi U., 1975-82; gov. USO World Bd. Govs.; chmn. USO of Met. N.Y.; co-treas., bd. dirs. United Jewish Appeal Greater N.Y., Inc.; mem. adv. bd. Regional Emergency Med. Services Council of N.Y.C.; bd. dirs., mem. exec. com. Am. Jewish Com.; trustee Bernard J. Moncharsh Found., Inc., Temple Shaaray Tefila, 1971-74, Fedn. Jewish Philanthropies, B'nai Brith Banking Lodge; mem. com. legacies and bequests ARC; trustee NYU Real Estate Inst.; vice-chmn. steering com., treas. N.Y. Bus. Council for Clean Air, 1966-71; fellow Brandeis U. Served as navigator USAF, 1943-46. Recipient numerous civic awards. Mem. Assn. for Better N.Y. (mem. exec. com.), Phi Epsilon Pi (nat. budget com.), Omicron Delta Kappa. Clubs: Harmonie (N.Y.C.); Rockrimmon Country (Stamford, Conn.). Home: 1040 Park Ave New York NY 10028-1032 Office: Chem Bank 270 Park Ave New York NY 10017-2014

MENDELS, JOSEPH, psychiatrist, educator; b. Cape Town, Republic of South Africa, Oct. 29, 1937; came to U.S., 1964; s. Max and Lily (Turecki) M.; m. Ora Kark, Jan. 22, 1960; children: Gilla Avril, Charles Alan, David Ralph. MB, ChB, U. Cape Town, 1960; MD, U. Witwatersrand, Johannesburg, Republic of South Africa, 1965. Asst. prof., assoc. prof. psychiatry and pharmacology U. Pa., Phila., 1967-73; prof. U. Pa. and VA Hosp., Phila., 1973-80; med. dir. Fairmount Inst., Phila., 1980-81; prof. psychiatry and human behavior Thomas Jefferson Med. Ctr., 1985—; med. dir. Therapeutics PC Phila. Med. Inst., Phila., 1981—; cons. NIMH, NIH, numerous pharm. cos., 1968—; lectr. to univs. and hosps. worldwide, 1968—. Author, editor: Concepts of Depression, 1971, Biological Psychiatry, 1973, Psychobiology of Affective Disorders, 1981; contbr. over 200 articles to med. jours. Fellow Internat. Coll. Neuropsychopharmacology, Am. Coll. Neuropsychopharmacology, Am. Coll. Clin. Pharmacology; mem. Am. Psychiat. Assn. (Lester N. Hofheimer prize 1976). Office: 9 E Laurel Rd Stratford NJ 08080

MENDELSOHN, DENNIS, chemical pathology educator, consultant; b. Johannesburg, Transvaal, South Africa, Nov. 20, 1927; s. Max and Rachel (Sacks) M.; m. Leah Zar, Dec. 12, 1958; 1 child, Michaela. M.B.Ch.B, Witwatersrand U., Johannesburg, 1954, MD, 1963. Jr. lectr. dept. chem. pathology Witwatersrand U., Johannesburg, 1955-56, lectr. dept. chem. pathology, 1956-66, sr. lectr. dept. chem. pathology, 1967-72, assoc. prof. dept. chem. pathology, 1973-82, prof., head dept. chem. pathology, 1982—; chief cons. 5 teaching hosps., Johannesburg, 1982—; mem. bd. faculty medicine Witwatersrand U., Johannesburg, 1972—. Author: Fats in Food, 1988; contbr. numerous articles to profl. jours. USPHS postdoctoral fellow NIH, Bethesda, Md., 1962-64; recipient numerous rsch. grants Med. Rsch. Coun., Witwatersrand U., 1964—. Fellow Royal Coll. Pathologists (London); mem. Am. Assn. Clin. Chemists. Achievements include patent for cholesterol-free, polyunsaturated fat milk powder used to lower blood cholesterol levels. Home: 78 Linden Rd Bramley, Johannesburg 2090, South Africa Office: U Witwatersrand Dept Chem Pathology, York Rd Parktown, Johannesburg 2193, South Africa

MENDELSOHN, EVERETT IRWIN, science history educator; b. Yonkers, N.Y., Oct. 28, 1931; s. Morris H. and May (Albert) M.; m. Mary B. Anderson, Sept. 14, 1974; children by previous marriage: Daniel Leeds, Sarah Ellicott, Joanna Moore; 1 stepson, Jesse Marshall Wallace. AB, Antioch Coll., 1953; postgrad., Marine Biol. Lab., Woods Hole, Mass., 1957; PhD, Harvard U., 1960; DHL (hon.), R.I. Coll., 1977. Rsch. assoc. sci. and pub. policy Grad. Sch. Pub. Adminstrn. Harvard U., 1960-65, assoc. prof. history of sci., 1965-69, prof. history of sci., 1969—, chmn. dept., 1971-78; overseas fellow Churchill Coll., U. Cambridge, Eng.; fellow Van Leer Jerusalem Inst., Israel, 1978; vis. fellow Zentrum für Interdizsciplinare Forschung, Bielefeld, W. Ger., 1978; fellow Wissenschafts Kolleg, Berlin, 1983-84; prof. invitée Conservatoire Nat. des Arts et Metiers, Paris, 1989, 90; dir. rsch. group on bio-med. scis. Program on Tech. and Soc. Harvard U., 1966-68; mem. Soc. Fellows, 1957-60; Olaf Palme prof. U. Sweden, 1994. Author/editor: Heat and Life: The History of the Theory of Animal Heat, 1964, Human Aspects of Biomedical Innovation, 1971, Topics in The Philosophy of Biology, 1976, The Social Production of Scientific Knowledge, 1977, The Social Assessment of Science, 1978, Sciences and Cultures, 1981, A Compassionate Peace: A Future for the Middle East, 1982, 89, Transformation and Transition in the Sciences, 1984; Nineteen Eighty Four: Science Between Utopia and Dystopia, 1984, Science, Technology and the Military, 1988, Technology, Pessimism and Post Modernism, 1993, Society as Biology, Biology as Society: Metaphors, 1994, Israeli-Palestinian Security: Issues in the Permanent Status Negotiations, 1995; editor: Jour. History Biology, 1967—; mem. editl. bd.: Sci., 1965-70, Social Studies of Sci., 1970-82, Ethics in Science and Medicine, 1973-80, Philosophy and Medicine, 1974-85, Sociology of Scis., 1976—, Social Sci. and Medicine, 1981-92, Sci. in Context, 1986-94, Social Epistemology, 1986—, Synthese, 1987—. Trustee Cambridge Friends Sch., The Sanctuary; bd. dirs. Inst. for Def. and Disarmament Studies; chmn. exec. com. Am. Friends Service Com. New Eng. regional office; mem. Commn. for Sci. and Cultural History of Mankind UNESCO; chmn. Harvard-Radcliffe Child Care Council.; mem. Cambridge Commn. for Nuclear Disarmament and Peace Edn.; pres. Inst. for Peace and Internat. Security. Fellow Swedish Collegium for Advanced Study in Social Scis., 1994; recipient Bowdoin prize, 1957, Tchg. award Phi Beta Kappa, 1996. Fellow AAAS (v.p., chmn. sect. L, com. on arms control and nat. security), Am. Acad. Arts and Scis. (chmn. program Middle East Security Studies; mem. Academie Internat. d'Histoire des Scis., History Sci. Soc. (council), Internat. Acad. History Medicine, Internat. Council Sci. Policy Studies (pres.), Am. Scandinavian Found. (fellowship com.). Home: 26 Walker St Cambridge MA 02138-2404

MENDELSOHN, HAROLD, sociologist, educator; b. Jersey City, Oct. 30, 1923; s. Louis and Bessie (Yulinsky) M.; m. Irene Sylvia Gordon, Apr. 10, 1949; 1 dau., Susan Lynn. B.S., CCNY, 1945; M.A., Columbia U., 1946; Ph.D., New Sch. Social Research, 1956. Sr. survey analyst U.S. Dept. State, Washington, 1951-52; research assoc. Bur. Social Sci. Research, Am. U., Washington, 1952-56; assoc. mgr. mktg. communications McCann-Erickson Advt., N.Y.C., 1956-58; assoc. dir. Psychol. Corp., N.Y.C., 1958-62; prof. dept. mass communications U. Denver, 1962-89, prof. emeritus, 1989—, chmn., 1970-78, dean faculty social scis., 1984-86, spl. asst. to chancellor, 1986-88; Morton vis. disting. prof. Ohio U., spring 1981; cons. FTC, Denver Rsch. Inst., U.S. Consumer Product Safety Commn., The Gallup Orgn., Ford Found., Fedn. Rocky Mountain States, CBS, ABC, Children's TV Workshop. (Emmy award Nat. Acad. TV Arts Scis. 1968, Gold Camera award U.S. Indsl. Film Festival 1972); Author: Mass Entertainment, 1966, (with David H. Bayley) Minorities and the Police: Confrontation in America, 1969, (with Irving Crespi) Polls, Television and the New Politics, 1970, (with others) Television and Growing Up: The Impact of Televised Violence, 1972, (with Garrett O'Keefe) The People Choose a President, 1976; editor: Mass Communications series, 1967-69; contbr. articles to profl. jours. Mem. Denver Coun. Pub. TV, 1970-78; mem. U.S. Surgeon Gen.'s Sci. Adv. Com. on TV and Social Behavior, 1969-71; bd. dirs. Nat. Safety Coun., 1963-69; mem. pub. affairs adv. bd. Air Force Acad. Found., 1972-76; mem. cancer control and rehab. adv. com. Nat. Cancer Inst., 1976-81; mem. adv. coun., prevention div. Nat. Inst. Alcoholism and Alcohol Abuse, 1977-82; trustee Colo. Med. Svc., Inc., 1973-78. Recipient award TV Bur. Advt., 1962, Met. Life award Nat. Safety Council, 1967; Gold Eagle award, 1973; Silver award Internat. Festival Film and TV, 1974. Fellow Am. Psychol. Assn., Am. Sociol. Assn.; mem. Am. Assn. Pub. Opinion Research (pres. 1973-74), AAAS, N.Y. Acad. Scis., Sigma Delta Chi, Omicron Delta Kappa. Club: Chicago Press. Home: 1451 E Cornell Pl Englewood CO 80110-3013 Office: U Denver Dept Mass Communications Denver CO 80208

MENDELSOHN, JOHN, oncologist, hematologist, educator; b. Cin., Aug. 31, 1936; s. Joe and Sarah (Feibel) M.; m. Anne Charles, June 23, 1962; children: John Andrew, Jeffrey Charles, Eric Robert. BA, Harvard U., 1958, MD, 1963. Diplomate Am. Bd. Internal Medicine, Am. Bd. Hematology, Am. Bd. Med. Oncology. Intern, resident Peter Bent Brigham Hosp., Boston, 1963-65, 67-68; fellow in hematology Washington U. Sch. Medicine, St. Louis, 1968-70; asst. prof. to prof. medicine U. Calif., La Jolla, 1970-85, Am. Cancer Soc. prof. clin. oncology, 1982-85, dir. Cancer Ctr., 1977-85; prof. medicine Cornell U. Med. Coll., N.Y.C., 1985-96; chmn. dept. medicine Meml. Sloan Kettering Cancer Ctr., N.Y.C., 1985-96; pres., prof. medicine U. Tex. M.D. Anderson Cancer Ctr., Houston, 1996—; mem. bd. sci. counselors divsn. cancer treatment Nat. Cancer Inst., 1986-90; bd. dirs. Am. Assn. Cancer Rsch.; cons. Hybritech, Genentech, Immunex, Im Clone, Prism, Bristol-Myers; founder, 1st dir. U. Calif. San Diego Cancer Ctr. Editor-in-chief: (textbook) The Molecular Basis of Cancer; mem. editl. bd. Jour. Immunology, Blood, Cancer Rsch., Jours. Clin. Oncology, Gworth Factors; editor-in-chief Clin. Cancer Rsch.; contbr. numerous articles in field of oncology to profl. jours. Mem. Gov.'s Cancer Adv. Coun., Calif., 1982-85; bd. dirs. Am. Cancer Soc., San Diego, 1981-85. Officer USPHS, 1965-67. Fulbright scholar U. Glasgow, Scotland, 1958-59; named Headliner of Yr. in Medicine, San Diego, 1985. Mem. Assn. Am. Physicians, Am. Soc. Clin. Investigation, Am. Soc. Clin. Oncology, Am. Assn. Cancer Rsch., Am. Soc. Hematology, Century Assn., Harvard Club N.Y., Phi Beta Kappa, Alpha Omega Alpha. Achievements include laboratory research establishing inhibition of tumor growth by antibodies against growth factor receptors. Avocations: tennis, music, history, hiking. Office: U Tex MD Anderson Cancer Ctr 1515 Holcombe Blvd Houston TX 77030

MENDELSOHN, LOUIS BENJAMIN, financial analyst; b. Providence, R.I., Mar. 26, 1948; s. Alvin Harold and Frances (Leitner) M.; m. Illyce Deborah Greenspan, Aug. 29, 1976; children: Lane Jeffrey, Ean Graham, Forrest Lee. BS, Carnegie Mellon U., 1969; MSW, SUNY, Buffalo, 1973; MBA with hons., Boston U., 1977. Rsch. asst. Mass. Gen. Hosp., Boston, 1969-71; regional health planner Comprehensive Health Planning Coun., Buffalo, 1973-74; adminstv. resident New Eng. Hosp., Boston, 1976; mgmt. specialist Humana Hosp. Bennett, Ft. Lauderdale, Fla., 1977-78; asst. exec. dir. Humana Women's Hosp., Tampa, Fla., 1978-80; pres. Mendelsohn Enterprises, Inc., Wesley Chapel, Fla., 1979—, Mendelsohn Trading Corp., Wesley Chapel, 1989—. Contbg. rschr.: The Encyclopedia of Technical Market Indicators, 1988; contbg. author: High Performance Futures Trading, 1990, Virtual Trading, 1995, Artifical Intelligence in the Capital Markets, 1995; editor (newsletter) Neural-Financial News, 1991; contbg. writer Tech. Analysis of Stocks and Commodities Mag.; developer (investment software) ProfitTaker, 1980-96, VantagePoint, 1988-96; contbr. articles to profl. jours. U.S Pub. Health Svc. fellow, 1975-77. Mem. Market Technicians Assn., Beta Gamma Sigma. Avocations: raising horses, antique collecting. Office: Mendelsohn Enterprises Inc 25941 Apple Blossom Ln Wesley Chapel FL 33544-5108

MENDELSOHN, ROBERT VICTOR, insurance company executive; b. N.Y.C., July 18, 1946; s. Harold Victor and Mary Ellen (Muldoon) M.; A.B., Georgetown U., 1968; J.D., Harvard U., 1971; Bar: N.Y. 1971. Atty. firm Willkie Farr & Gallagher, N.Y.C., 1971-74; pres., dir. W.R. Berkley Corp., Greenwich, Conn., 1974-93; CEO Royal Group, Inc., Charlotte, N.C.; dir. Royal Ins., plc, London; dir. Am. Ins. Assn., Nat. Assn. Casualty & Surety Execs., 1994—. Trustee Jose Limon Dance Found., 1979—. Clubs: Innis Arden Golf, N.Y. Athletic, Riverside (Conn.) Yacht. Office: PO Box 1000 9300 Arrowpoint Blvd Charlotte NC 28201-1000

MENDELSOHN, WALTER, lawyer; b. N.Y.C., Jan. 22, 1897; s. Sigmund and Paula (Stieglitz) M.; m. Josephine Becker, Mar. 31, 1927; children—Sue (Mrs. Robert Mellins), Paul Richard. A.B., Yale U., 1918, LL.B., 1921. Bar: N.Y. bar 1921. Ptnr. Proskauer Rose Goetz & Mendelsohn and predecessors, N.Y.C., 1926—; Bd. dirs. 150 Central Park S. Corp. Mem. bd. Surprise Lake Camp, Welfare and Health Council; exec., adminstrv. coms. Am. Jewish Com., 1942—; bd. visitors State Tng. Sch. for Boys; chmn. trustees, chmn. bd., past pres. Jewish Bd. Guardians; trustee, past chmn. com. communal planning Fedn. Jewish Philanthropies; hon. trustee, past pres. Camp Ramapo; past trustee Inst. Internat. Edn.; trustee, pres. Henry Kaufmann Found., Edward de Rothschild Found. Served as pvt. U.S. Army, World War I; from maj. to lt. col. AUS, World War II; liaison officer SSS to under sec. war. Recipient Disting. Community Service award Brandeis U., Naomi and Howard Lehman Meml. award, Joseph M. Proskauer award, Horace Mann-Barnard Disting. Achievement award, Felix M. Warburg Meml. award. Mem. ABA, N.Y. State Bar Assn., Assn. Bar City N.Y., New York County Lawyers Assn., Am. Judicature Soc., Yale U. Law Sch. Assn. N.Y. (bd. dirs.), Yale Club, Harmonie Club. Home: 150 Central Park S New York NY 10019-1566 also: High Up Purdy's Station NY 10578 Office: Proskauer Rose Goetz & Mendelsohn 1585 Broadway New York NY 10036-8200

MENDELSON, ALAN CHARLES, lawyer; b. San Francisco, Mar. 27, 1948; s. Samuel Mendelson and Rita Rosalie (Spindel) Brown; children: Jonathan Daniel, David Gary; m. Agnès Marie Barbariol. BA with great distinction, U. Calif., Berkeley, 1969; JD cum laude, Harvard U., 1973. Bar: Calif. 1973. Assoc. Cooley, Godward et al., San Francisco, 1973-80; ptnr. Cooley, Godward, Castro, Huddleson & Tatum, Palo Alto, Calif., 1980—; mng. ptnr. Cooley, Godward, Castro, Huddleson & Tatum, Palo Alto, 1990-95; sec., acting gen. counsel Amgen Inc., Palo Alto, 1990-91; bd. dirs. Isis Pharms. Inc., CoCensys, Inc., Senses Internat. Inc.; sec. Walker Interactive Sys., 1982—, Acuson, 1982-91, PetsMart, 1986—, Trans Ocean Ltd., 1988—, Arris Pharm. Corp., 1993—; mem. mgmt. com. Cooley, Godward, Castro, Huddleson & Tatum, 1986—; chmn. Cos. Practice Group, 1990—. Chmn. Piedmont (Calif.) Civil Svc. Commn., 1978-80; den leader Boy Scouts Am., Menlo Park, Calif.; fundraiser Crystal Springs Upland Sch., Hillsborough, Calif., 1981—; coach Menlo Park Little League, 1982-86; pres., mem. exec. com., bd. dirs. No. Calif. chpt. Nat. Kidney Found., 1986—. With USAR, 1969-75. Recipient Disting. Svc. award Nat. Kidney Found., 1992; named U. Calif. Berkeley Alumni scholar, 1966, Scaife Found. scholar, 1966. Mem. Harvard U. Law Sch. Alumni Assn. (area rep. funds com. 1978—), Bohemian Club, Phi Beta Kappa. Jewish. Avocations: golf, tennis, softball, basketball, photography. Home: 76 De Bell Dr Atherton CA 94027 Office: Cooley Godward Castro Huddleson & Tatum 5 Palo Alto Sq 3000 El Camino Real Palo Alto CA 94306-2122

MENDELSON, ELLIOTT, mathematician, educator; b. N.Y.C., May 24, 1931; s. Joseph and Helen (Bienstock) M.; m. Arlene Zimmerman, Jan. 25, 1959; children—Julia, Hilary, Peter. A.B., Columbia U., 1952; M.A., Cornell U., 1954, Ph.D., 1955. Instr. U. Chgo., 1955-56; jr. fellow Soc. Fellows, Harvard U., 1956-58; Ritt instr. Columbia U., 1958-61; mem. faculty Queens Coll., CUNY, 1961—, prof. math., 1965—; dir., instr. NSF math. program for high sch. students, 1964-71; researcher axiomatic set theory and math. logic, especially ind. various important propositions of axiomatic set theory, axiom of choice, axiom of restriction. Author: Introduction to Mathematical Logic, 1964, Boolean Algebra and Switching Circuits, 1970, Number Systems, 1973, Beginning Calculus, 1985, 3000 Solved Problems in Calculus, 1988, Differential and Integral Calculus, 1990; contbr. articles to profl. jours. Mem. Am. Math. Soc., Math. Assn. Am., Assn. for Symbolic Logic, Phi Beta Kappa. Home: 10 Pinewood Rd Roslyn NY 11576-2420 Office: Queens Coll Dept Math Flushing NY 11367

MENDELSON, HAIM, artist, educator, art gallery director; b. Siemiatycze, Bielsk, Poland, Oct. 15, 1923; s. David Cemach and Frieda (Konopiati) M.; m. Lita Joan Gordon, Mar. 30, 1955 (div. June 1966); children: Paul, Jan. Student, Am. Artists Sch., 1938-41, Saul Baizerman Sch. Art, 1940-43, Ednl. Alliance Art Sch., 1946. Tchr. Ednl. Alliance, N.Y.C., 1956-61; instr. CCNY, 1961-64; tchr. Columbia Grammar Sch., 1963-64, City and Country Sch., N.Y.C., 1964-91; dir. Hudson Guild Art Gallery, N.Y.C., 1971-94. One-man shows include Creative Galleries, N.Y.C., 1954, Caravan Gallery, N.Y.C., 1957, Chase Gallery, N.Y.C., 1960, Hudson Guild Art Gallery, N.Y.C., 1961, 76, 79, 82, 94, Yellow Poui Art Gallery, Grenada, W.I., 1973, 76, 79, 82, Ednl. Alliance, N.Y.C., 1976, Berkshire Artisans Gallery, Pittsfield, Mass., 1987, Hudson Guild, 1994; group shows include Mus. Modern Art, N.Y.C., 1940-41, Pa. Acad. Fine Arts, 1965, Butler Inst. Am. Art, Ohio, 1965, 67, St. Paul Art Ctr., 1961, 66, NAD, N.Y.C., 1965, 68, 75, 77, 90, Bronx Mus. Arts, 1976, Prints U.S.A., 1982, Gallery Assn. N.Y. State, 1975-78, Internat. Art Biennale, Malta, 1995; represented in permanent collections N.Y. Pub. Libr., Minn. Mus. Art, Edward Ulrich Mus., Wichita, Kans., St. Vincent Coll., Latrobe, Pa., Griffiths Art Ctr., Canton, N.Y., Manhattan Coll., Riverdale, N.Y., Flint (Mich.) Inst. Fine Arts; portfolio drypoint engravings Grass, 1963, The Artist and His Dead, 1975. Recipient numerous awards, prizes. Mem. Fedn. Modern Painters and Sculptors, Audubon Artists, Print Consortium, Am. Soc. Contemporary Artists. Home: 234 W 21st St # 63 New York NY 10011-3451 *Art is the avenue in which I express the significant experiences of my life. Out of feelings of expressive need, new forms and techniques spontaneously arise. The forms of the future are in life itself.*

MENDELSON, LEE M., film company executive, writer, producer, director; b. San Francisco, Mar. 24, 1933; s. Palmer C. and Jeanette D. (Wise) M.; m. Desiree Mendelson; children: Glenn, Linda, Jason, Sean. BA, Stanford U., 1954. With Sta. KPIX-TV, 1961-63; chmn. bd., pres. Lee Mendelson Film Prodns. Inc., Los Angeles and Burlingame, Calif., 1963—; guest instr. in communications Stanford U. Exec. producer, co-writer (miniseries) This Is America, Charlie Brown; producer: Charlie Brown, Cathy, Betty Boop, (TV spls.) John Steinbeck's Travels with Charley, American and Americans, The Fantastic Funnies, You Asked for It, Here Comes Garfield, (animated films) A Boy Named Charlie Brown, Snoopy Come Home, Race for Your Life Charlie Brown, Peanuts, Bon Voyage Charlie Brown (And Don't Come Back), Garfield and Friends, Mother Goose and Grim. Served to 1st lt. USAF, 1954-57. Recipient 7 Emmy awards, 3 Peabody awards. Mem. Writers Guild Am., Dirs. Guild Am. Office: 1440 Chapin Ave Ste 350 Burlingame CA 94010-4011

MENDELSON, LEONARD M., lawyer; b. Pitts., May 20, 1923; s. Jacob I. and Anna R. M.; m. Emily Solomon, Dec. 2, 1956; children: Ann, James R., Kathy S. AB, U. Mich., 1947; JD, Yale U., 1950. Bar: Pa. 1951, U.S. Supreme Ct. 1955. Mem. Hollinshead, Mendelson, Bresnahan & Nixon, P.C., Pitts., chmn. bd., 1974—; chmn. Lawyer-Realty Joint Com., Pitts., 1971-72. Mem. Pitts. Bd. Pub. Edn., 1975-76. Mem. ABA, Pa. Bar Assn., Allegheny County Bar Assn. Office: 820 Grant Bldg Pittsburgh PA 15219-2105

MENDELSON, RICHARD DONALD, former communications company executive; b. N.Y.C., Dec. 2, 1933; s. George and Martha (Goodman) M.; m. Marilyn Miller, July 28, 1956; children: Sandra, Kenneth. BS, Wharton Sch. U. Pa., 1955; JD, NYU, 1959. Bar: N.Y., 1960; CPA, N.Y. Asst. atty. gen. N.Y. State Dept. Law, N.Y.C., 1959-70; v.p., treas. Petry TV, N.Y.C., 1971-75; v.p., dir. corp. devel. Katz Communications, Inc., N.Y.C., 1975-77, sr. v.p. ops., 1977-79, sr. v.p., chief fin. officer, 1979-81, exec. v.p., chief operating officer, 1981-82, pres., chief oper. officer, 1982-89; free-lance writer, 1989—. Mem. Employee Stock Ownership Assn. Am. (pres. 1987-88, bd. dirs.). Home and Office: 71 Saint George Pl Palm Beach Gardens FL 33418-4024

MENDELSON, ROBERT ALLEN, polymer scientist, rheologist; b. Cleve., 1930; s. Julius and Theodora Anne (Bloch) M.; m. Lura Lauzon, 1971; children: John A. Blackstone, Marie L. Taylor. BS in Indsl. Chemistry, Case Inst. Tech., 1952, PhD in Phys. Chemistry, 1956. From sr. rsch. chemist to sci. fellow rsch. dept. Monsanto Co., Texas City, Tex., 1956-71; sci. fellow Monsanto Co., Springfield, Mass., 1972-89, sr. sci. fellow, 1989-91; rheology focus area leader Baytown (Tex.) Polymers Ctr. Exxon Chem., 1991-94; rheology principal investigator, 1995—; mem. com. for pub. policy Am. Inst. Physics, 1985-89; collaborator Univ. Rsch. Programs, Cornell U., 1989-91. Mem. editorial bd. Journal of Rheology, 1986—; contbr. articles to profl. jours.; patentee in field. Mem. Soc. Rheology (pres. 1989-91, v.p. 1987-89, sec. 1974-78), Am. Chem. Soc. (Arthur Doolittle award div. organic coatings and plastics 1982), Soc. Plastics Engrs., AAAS. Home: 16503 Scenic Peaks Ct Houston TX 77059-5554 Office: Exxon Chem Co 5200 Bayway Dr Baytown Polymers Ctr Baytown TX 77522

MENDELSON, SOL, physical science educator, consultant; b. Checonovska, Poland, Oct. 10, 1926; came to U.S., 1927; s. David C. and Frieda (Cohen) M. BME, CCNY, 1955; MS, Columbia U., 1957, PhD, 1961. Prof. engring. CCNY, 1955-58; sr. scientist Sprague Electric Co., North Adams, Mass., 1962-64, Airborne Instruments Lab., Melville, N.Y., 1964-65; phys. metallurgist Bendix Rsch. Lab., Southfield, Mich., 1966-67; cons., rschr., writer, N.Y.C. and Troy, Mich., 1968-72; adj. prof. phys. sci. CUNY, 1972-87. Contbr. numerous articles to sci. jours. Mem. Am. Phys. Soc., Fedn. Am. Scientists, Sigma Xi, Tau Beta Pi, Pi Tau Sigma. Achievements include research on theory and mechanisms of Martensitic transformations. *We have to keep reminding ourselves that data proclaims theory, but theory does not proclaim anything if it does not address crucial data. Many a scientist has gained prominence for a theory by exaggerating ambiguous data or unrealistic models, but those who succeed in solving a problem are able to develop a theory which accounts for crucial experimental data.*

MENDENHALL, CARROL CLAY, physician; b. Missouri Valley, Iowa, July 26, 1916; s. Clay and Maude (Watts) M.; student U. So. Calif., 1942-44, Chapman Coll., 1946-47, Los Angeles City Coll., 1947-48; D.O., Coll. Osteo. Physicians and Surgeons, 1952; M.D., Calif. Coll. Medicine, 1962; m. Lucille Yvonne Bonvouloir, June 14, 1946 (div. July 1957); 1 son, Gregory Bruce; m. 2d, Barbara Marilyn Huggett-Davis, Sept. 28, 1974. Intern, Los Angeles County Osteo. Hosp., 1952-53; gen. practice medicine, 1953-82, specializing in weight control, Gardena, Calif., 1961-74, specializing in stress disorders and psychosomatic medicine, Ft. Worth, 1974-78, specializing in integral medicine and surgery, Santa Clara, Calif., 1978—; med. dir. Green's Pharms., Long Beach, Calif., 1956-64; v.p. Internat. Pharm. Mfg. Co., Inc., San Pedro, Calif., 1965-66; pres. Chemico of Gardena, Inc., 1964-69; staff Gardena Hosp.; active staff O'Connor Hosp., San Jose, Calif., 1979—; tchr., lectr. biofeedback, prevention and treatment of stress, creative thought; founder, dir. Eclectic Weight Control Workshop, 1971-74, Longevity Learning, Longevity Learning Seminars, 1980; past mem. adv. bd. dirs. L.A. Nat. Bank. Cadre med. dir. Gardena Civil Def., 1953-54, asst. to chief med. dir., 1954-60, chief med. and first aid services, 1960-64. Served as pharmacist's mate USNR, 1944-46. Fellow Royal Soc. Health, Am. Acad. Med. Preventics, Am. Acad. Homeopathic Medicine; mem. Calif. Med. Assn., Santa Clara County Med. Soc., Acupuncture Research Inst. (also alumni assn.), Los Aficionados de Los Angeles (pres. 1964-66), Am. Soc. Clin. Hypnosis. Flamenco Soc. No. Calif. (bd. dirs. 1986—). Address: 1653 Milroy Pl San Jose CA 95124-4723

MENDENHALL, JOHN RYAN, retired lawyer, transportation executive; b. Des Moines, Jan. 17, 1928; s. Merritt Blake and Elizabeth M. (Ryan) M.; m. Joan Lois Schafer, June 20, 1953; children: Thomas, James, Jane, Julie, Robert, Jennifer. BS, U. Notre Dame, 1950; JD, Harvard U., 1953. Bar: Iowa 1953, U.S. Tax Ct. 1954, D.C. 1975, U.S. Ct. Claims 1975. Mem. tax staff Arthur Andersen & Co., Cleve., 1953-63, ptnr., 1963-66; dir. taxes Arthur Andersen & Co., Chgo., 1966-70; ptnr. Arthur Andersen & Co., Washington, 1970-74, Williams, Connolly & Califano, Washington, 1974-76; gen. tax counsel Union Pacific Corp., N.Y.C., 1977-80, v.p. taxes, 1980-93; bd. dirs. Empire Steel Castings, Reading, Pa. Co-author: Reforming the Tax Structure, 1973; contbr. articles on taxes to various jours. Bd. dirs. Cook County Hosp., Chgo., 1968-71, Inst. Rsch. on Econs. of Taxation, Washington, 1977-93, Burnside Plantation Inc., Bethlehem, Pa., 1989-93; trustee Convent of Sacred Heart, Greenwich, Conn., 1976-80; bd. govs. Bethlehem Area Found., 1989-93. With U.S. Army, 1946-47, Japan. Mem. ABA (tax sect., chmn. indexing com. 1985-86), Am. Coun. Capital Formation (bd. dirs. 1972-88), Bus. Roundtable (tax adv. group 1977-92), C. of C. U.S. (mem. tax com. 1972-92), Am. Law Inst. (tax adv. group 1974-88), Nat. Tax Assn. (pres. 1981-82), Nat. Chamber Found. (chmn. tax com. 1984-93), Chevy Chase (Md.) Club, Harvard Club (N.Y.C.), Met. Club (Washington), Belle Haven Club. Republican. Roman Catholic. Home: 47 Lafayette Pl Apt 6H Greenwich CT 06830-5401

MENDENHALL, ONIEL CHARLES, retail executive; b. Seiling, Okla., Aug. 21, 1922; m. Trinidad Vasquez, Dec. 28, 1977; children: Oniel C. Jr., Janice L., Warren, Mark O. Student, Southwestern Okla. State. Mgr., owner Mendenhall Grocery, Seiling; owner several Red Bud Stores Alva and Enid, Okla. and Wichita; founder, owner, vice chair Fiesta Mart, Inc., Houston, 1971—; ethnic foods cons. FMI-AMI, Washington, 1985. Mem. Houston Ballet. Recipient Cmty. Leadership award Nat. Hispanic Inst. Houston, 1985. Mem. Food Mktg. Inst., Food Pac (pres. club, spl. recognition award 1984, 85), Produce Mktg. Assn., United Fresh Fruit and Vegetable Assn. (bd. dirs. 1993), Houston C. of C., Coll. Colleagues Fine Arts Mus. Republican. Methodist. Avocations: golf, seasonal hunting. Office: Fiesta Mart Inc PO Box 7481 5235 Katy Fwy Houston TX 77007-2210*

MENDENHALL, ROBERT VERNON, mathematics educator; b. Geneva, Ind., Dec. 27, 1920; s. Carl and Lulu (Niswander) M.; m. Gay Dalrymple, Dec. 15, 1944; children—Lisa, Robin, Valerie. B.A. summa cum laude, Ohio State U., 1947, M.A., 1949, Ph.D., 1952. Instr. Ohio State U., 1951-53; sr. engr. N.Am. Aviation Corp., 1953-55; mathematician Vitro Labs., Inc., 1955; asst. prof. U. Miami, 1955-62; assoc. prof. Ohio Wesleyan U., 1962-66, prof. math., 1966-89, prof. emeritus, 1989—; cons. math Benares Hindu U., 1965, Andhra (India) U., 1966, U. Roorkee, India, 1970. Author: (with Herman Meyer) Techniques of Differentiation and Integration, 1966. Served with AUS, 1942-46, ETO. Mem. Am., Indian math. socs., Math. Assn. Am., Phi Beta Kappa, Sigma Xi. Home: 129 Oak Hill Ave Delaware OH 43015-2519

MENDEZ, ALBERT ORLANDO, industrialist, financier; b. Bogota, Colombia, Sept. 7, 1935; came to U.S., 1960; naturalized, 1968; s. Angelino Benjamin and Ana Isabel (Gutierre de Cetina) M.; children: Nicole C., Eric A. BS in Nuclear Physics, N.C. State U., 1961, MS in Nuclear Engring., 1963; MBA, U. Hartford, 1970. Physicist, mgr. mfg. Combustion Engring. Co., Windsor, Conn., 1963-67; mgr. corp. devel. and planning Gulf Oil Corp., Pitts., 1967-71; v.p. mktg., controller for Latin Am. Xerox Corp., Stamford, Conn., 1971-76; exec. v.p., CEO, chmn. ops. com., bd. dirs. Ogden Corp., N.Y.C., 1976-84; chmn., chief exec. officer, prin. shareholder Am. Indstl. Corp., Stamford, 1984—; chmn., chief exec. officer, prin. Argo-Tech Corp., Aerospace, Cleve., 1986-89; bd. dirs. Catalyst Energy Co., N.Y.C., 1st Prin. Corp., N.Y.C., Demag, AG, Hamburg, Germany; gen. ptnr. Agnem Holdings Ltd. Partnership, New Canaan, Conn., 1984—; pres., CEO, bd. dirs., prin. shareholder Agnem Investment Co., New Canaan, 1983—; pres., CEO, prin. shareholder AM World Trade Corp., West Palm Beach, Fla.; mem. Pres.'s Adv. Com. on Def. Preparedness and Intelligence, 1986-92. Contbr. articles to profl. jours. Mem. Internat. Platform Assn., Am. mgmt. Assn., Assn. of Corp. Dirs., The Conf. Bd., Am. Nuclear Soc., Palm Beach (Fla.) Polo Club. Office: 131 Pequot Ln New Canaan CT 06840-2023

MENDEZ, CELESTINO GALO, mathematics educator; b. Havana, Cuba, Oct. 16, 1944; s. Celestino Andres and Georgina (Fernandez) M.; came to U.S., 1962, naturalized, 1970; BA, Benedictine Coll., 1965; MA, U. Colo., 1968, PhD, 1974, MBA, 1979; m. Mary Ann Koplau, Aug. 21, 1971; children: Mark Michael, Matthew Maximilian. Asst. prof. maths. scis. Met. State Coll., Denver, 1971-77, assoc. prof., 1977-82, prof., 1982—, chmn. dept. math. scis., 1980-82; adminstrv. intern office v.p. for acad. affairs Met. State Coll., 1989-90. Mem. advt. rev. bd. Met. Denver, 1973-79; parish outreach rep. S.E. deanery, Denver Cath. Cmty. Svcs., 1976-78; mem. social ministries com. St. Thomas More Cath. Ch., Denver, 1976-78, vice-chmn., 1977-78, mem. parish council, 1977-78; del. Adams County Rep. Conv., 1972, 74, 1994, Colo. 4th Congl. Dist. Conv., 1974, Colo. Rep. Conv., 1982, 88, 90, 92, 96, Douglas County Rep. Conv., 1980, 82, 84, 88, 90, 92, 94, 96; alt. del. Colo. Rep. Conv., 1974, 76, 84, 5th Congl. dist. conv., 1976, mem. rules com., 1978, 80, precinct committeeman Douglas County Rep. Com., 1976-78, 89-92, mem. cen. com., 1976-78, 89-92; dist. 29 Rep. party candidate Colo. State Senate, 1990; mem. Colo. Rep. Leadership program, 1989-90, bd. dirs., 1990—; Douglas county chmn. Rep. Nat. Hispanic Assembly, 1989—; bd. dirs. Rocky Mountain Better Bus. Bur., 1975-79, Rowley Downs Homeowners Assn., 1976-78; trustee Hispanic U. Am., 1975-78; councilman Town of Parker (Colo.), 1981-84, chmn. budget and fin. com. 1981-84; chmn. joint budget com. Town of Parker-Parker Water and Sanitation Dist. Bds., 1982-84; commr. Douglas County Planning Commn., 1993—; dir. Mile High Young Scholars Program, 1995—. Recipient U. Colo. Grad. Sch. excellence in teaching award, 1965-67; grantee Benedictine Coll., 1964-65, Math. Assn. Am. SUMMA grantee Carnegie Found. N.Y., 1994, NSF, 1995—. Mem. Math. Assn. Am. (referee rsch. notes sect. Am. Math. Monthly 1981-82, gov. Rocky Mountain section 1993—, investment com. 1995—, devel. com. 1995—, task force on reps. 1994—), Am. Math. Soc., Nat. Coun. Tchrs. of Math., Colo. Coun. Tchrs. of Maths. (bd. dirs. 1994—), Colo. Internat. Edn. Assn., Assoc. Faculties of State Insts. Higher Edn. in Colo. (v.p. 1971-73). Republican. Roman Catholic. Assoc. editor Denver Metro. Jour. Math. and Computer Sci., 1993—; contbr. articles to profl. jours. including Am. Math. Monthly, Procs. Am. Math. Soc., Am. Math. Monthly, Jour. Personalized Instruction, Denver Met. Jour. Math. and Computer Sci., and newspapers. Home: 11482 S Regency Pl Parker CO 80134-7330 Office: PO Box 173362 Denver CO 80217

MENDIUS, PATRICIA DODD WINTER, editor, educator, writer; b. Davenport, Iowa, July 9, 1924; d. Otho Edward and Helen Rose (Dodd) Winter; m. John Richard Mendius, June 19, 1947; children: Richard, Catherine M. Graber, Louise, Karen M. Chooljian. BA cum laude, UCLA, 1946; MA cum laude, U. N.Mex., 1966. Cert. secondary edn. tchr., Calif., N.Mex. English teaching asst. UCLA, 1946-47; English tchr. Marlborough Sch. for Girls, L.A., 1947-50, Aztec (N.Mex.) High Sch., 1953-55, Farmington (N.Mex.) High Sch., 1955-63; chair English dept. Los Alamos (N.Mex.) High Sch., 1963-86; sr. technical writer, editor Los Alamos Nat. Lab., 1987—; adj. prof. English, U. N.Mex., Los Alamos, 1970-72, Albuquerque, 1982-85; English cons. S.W. Regional Coll. Bd., Austin, Tex., 1975—; writer, editor, cons. advanced placement English test devel. com. Nat. Coll. Bd., 1982-86, reader, 1982-86, project equality cons., 1985-88; book selection cons. Scholastic mag., 1980-82. Author: Preparing for the Advanced Placement English Exams, 1975; editor Los Alamos Arts Coun. bull., 1986-91. Chair Los Alamos Art in Pub. Places Bd., 1987-92; chair adv. bd. trustees U. N.Mex., Los Alamos, 1987-93; pres. Los Alamos Concert Assn., 1972-73, 95—; chair Los Alamos Mesa Pub. Libr. Bd., 1990-94, chair endowment com., 1995—. Mem. Soc. Tech. Communicators, AAUW (pres. 1961-63, state bd. dirs. 1959-63, Los Alamos coordinating coun. 1992-93, pres. 1993-94), DAR, Order Ea. Star, Mortar Bd., Phi Beta Kappa (pres. Los Alamos chpt. 1969-72, v.p. 1996-97), Phi Kappa Phi, Delta Kappa Gamma, Gamma Phi Beta. Avocations: swimming, reading, hiking, astronomy, singing. Home: 124 Rover Blvd Los Alamos NM 87544-3634 Office: Los Alamos Nat Lab Diamond Dr Los Alamos NM 87544

MENDONSA, ARTHUR ADONEL, retired city official; b. Wauchula, Fla., Apr. 5, 1928; s. Arthur Abner and Mamie (Swafford) M.; m. Beverly Glover, Sept. 6, 1951; children—Arthur Adonel, George Andrew; m. Suzanne Danzig, Sept. 7, 1980. B.A., Emory U., 1952; M. City Planning, Ga. Inst. Tech., 1954. Planning dir. Gainesville-Hall County (Ga.) Planning Commn., 1954-56, 57-60; sr. planner Charleston (S.C.) County Planning Commn., 1956-57; exec. dir. Savannah-Chatham (Ga.) County Met. Planning Commn., 1960-62; city mgr. Savannah, 1962-67, 71-95; dir. field svcs., asst. prof. Inst. Govt., U. Ga., Athens, 1967-69; exec. asst. to chmn. DeKalb County Bd. Commrs., Decatur, Ga., 1969-71; mem. Coastal Area Planning and Devel. Commn., 1972-90, chmn., 1983-85; mem. Ga. Gov.'s Adv. Council on Coastal Zone Mgmt., 1976-78, Ga. Coastal Mgmt. Bd., 1978-82. Author: Simplified Financial Management in Local Government, 1969. Recipient All-Pro City Mgmt. Team City and State mags., 1986, 87, 88. Mem. Am. Inst. Planners (bd. examiners), Am. Soc. Pub. Adminstrn., Internat. City Mgrs. Assn. (Outstanding Mgmt. Innovator award 1979), Ga. City-County Mgrs. Assn. (pres. 1974-75), Kiwanis.

MENDOZA, GEORGE, poet, author; b. N.Y.C., June 2, 1934; s. George and Elizabeth Mendoza; m. Ruth Sekora, 1967; children: Ashley, Ryan. BA, State Maritime Coll., 1953; postgrad., Columbia U., 1954-56. Author over 100 books for children and adults published worldwide; many included in Boston U.'s George Mendoza Collection, established 1984; children's books on display at the Centre Nat. d'Art et de Culture Georges Pompidou. Works include: And Amedeo Asked, How Does One Become a Man?, (illustrated by Ati Forberg), 1959, The Puma and the Pearl, 1962, The Hawk Is Humming: A Novel, 1964, A Piece of String, Astor-Honor, 1965, Gwot! Horribly Funny Hairticklers (illustrated by Steven Kellog), 1967, The Crack in the Wall and Other Terribly Weird Tales (illustrated by Mercer Mayer), 1968, Flowers and Grasses and Weeds (illustrated by Joseph Low), 1968, The Practical Man (illustrated by Imero Gobbato), 1968, Hunting Sketches (illustrated by Ronald Stein), 1968, A Beastly Alphabet (illustrated by J. Low), 1969, The Digger Wasp (illustrated by Jean Zallinger), 1969, Herman's Hat (illustrated by Frank Bozzo), 1969, The Starfish Trilogy (illustrated by Ati Forberg), 1969, (compiler) The World From My Window: Poems and Drawings (children's writings), 1969, Are You My Friend? (illustrated by F. Bozzo), 1970, The Marcel Marceau Alphabet Book, 1970, The Thumbtown Toad (illustrated by Monika Beisner), 1970, The Inspector, 1970, The Good Luck Spider & other bad luck stories, 1970, The Fearsome Brat (illustrated by F. Bozzo), 1971, Fish in the Sky (illutrated by Milton Glaser), 1971, Moonfish and owl scratchings, 1971, Moonstring, 1971, The Hunter, the Tick and the Gumberoo, 1971, The Marcel Marceau Counting Book, 1971, The Scarecrow Clock (illustrated by Eric Carle), 1971, Big Frog, Little Pond, 1971, The Scribbler, 1971, The Christmas Tree Alphabet Book, 1971, Shadowplay, 1974, Lord, Suffer me to Catch a Fish, 1974, Fishing the Morning Lonely, 1974, (with Carol Burnett) What I Want to Be When I Grow Up, 1975, (with Zero Mostel) The Sesame Street Book of Opposites, 1975, Norman Rockwell's Americana ABC (illustrated by N. Rockwell), 1975, Doug Henning's Magic Book, 1975, Lost Pony, 1976, Norman Rockwell's Boys and Girls at Play, 1976, Secret Places of a Trout Fisherman, 1977, Norman Rockwell's Diary for a Young Girl (illustrated by N. Rockwell), 1978, Magic Tricks, 1978, Mon livre de magic (French edit. of My Book of Magic), Norman Rockwell's Scrapbook for a Young Boy (illustrated by N. Rockwell), 1979, (with Andres Segovia) Segovia, My Book of the Guitar, 1979, Need a House? Call Ms. Mouse! (illustrated by Doris Susan Smith), 1981, Alphabet Sheep (illustrated by K. Reidy), 1982, The Sheepish Book of Opposites, 1982, Silly Sheep and other sheepish rhymes, 1982, Norman Rockwell's Four Seasons, 1982, Norman Rockwell's Happy Holidays, 1983, Henri Mouse (illustrated by Joelle Boucher), 1985, Henri La Souris, 1987, Norman Rockwell's Patriotic Times, 1985, (with Ivan Lendl) Hitting Hot, 1986, (with Sam Snead) Slammin' Sam, 1986, Norman Rockwell's Love and Remembrance, 1986, Top Tennis, 1987, L'Album des Noeuds, 1988, Norman Rockwell's Old Fashioned American Cookbook, 1988, Hairticklers (illustrated by Gahan Wilson), 1989, The Hunter I Might Have Been, reprint 1989, Were You a Wild Duck, Where Would You Go? (illustrated by Jane Osborn-Smith), 1990, Traffic Jam (illustrated by David Stoltz), 1990; also author screenplays for Petals from a Poem Flower, You Show Me Yours and I'll Show You Mine and scripts for Sesame Street; numerous others; over 15 books of poetry including The Hunter I Might Have Been (Lewis Carroll Shelf award 1968), The Mist Men, Goodbye, River, Goodbye; also dozens of articles in The N.Y. Times, Herald Tribune, Stern, Vogue, Harper's Bazaar, Ms., Esquire, Town & Country, Sports Afield, Men's Journal, Philadelphia Inquirer; special travel corr. Toronto Globe & Mail, 1991-94. Cited by Pres. Reagan for Norman Rockwell's Patriotic Times. Avocation: trout and salmon fishing. Worldwide fishing expeditions recorded for TV spls. *I believe we are living in a world where people no longer see each other as individuals. We have become invisible. It is necessary to save our souls. Go out to a field and pick up a fallen leaf. Look at the veins that river the leaf. Follow them until nothing else matters except for the leaf in your hand. Then you will become visible. You will see others and others will see you.*

MENDOZA, ROBERTO G., JR., banker; b. Cuba, 1945. BA, Yale U., 1967; MBA, Harvard U., 1974. With Morgan Guaranty Trust Co., N.Y.C., 1967—, formerly mng. dir.; vice chmn. J.P. Morgan & Co., N.Y.C., 1990—, also dir. for global mergers and acquisitions. Office: J P Morgan & Co 60 Wall St New York NY 10005-2807

MENDOZA, STANLEY ATRAN, pediatric nephrologist, educator; b. Pitts., May 7, 1940; s. Joseph William and Marian Ruth (Atran) M.; m. Carole Ann Klein, June 23, 1963; children: Daniel, Joseph. Student, Harvard U., 1957-59; B.A., Johns Hopkins U., 1961, M.D., 1964. Diplomate: Am. Bd. Pediatrics. Intern Johns Hopkins Hosp., Balt., 1964-65; jr. asst. resident dept. medicine Children's Hosp. Med. Ctr., Boston, 1965-66; asst. attending physician, dir. renal rsch. labs Children's Meml. Hosp., Chgo., 1969-71; asst. prof. pediatrics Sch. Medicine U. Calif., San Diego, 1971-73; assoc. prof. Sch. Medicine U. Calif., 1973-79, prof. pediatrics, dept. pediatrics, div. pediatric nephrology, 1979—, vice chmn. dept. pediatrics, 1986-87, chmn. dept. pediatrics, 1992—. Contbr. article in field to profl. publ. Served With USPHS, 1966-69. Fogarty Sr. Internat. fellow, 1978-79; Alan J. Wurtzburger research scholar, 1964; recipient Johns Hopkins Med. Soc. award, 1964, hon. mention Borden Undergrad. research award in medicine, 1964; Eleanor Roosevelt internat. fellow Internat. Union Against Cancer, 1984-85. Mem. Am. Fedn. Clin. Research, Am. Pediatric Soc., Am. Physiol. Soc., Am. Soc. Nephrology, Am. Soc. Pediatric Nephrology, Internat. Soc. Nephrology. Office: U Calif San Diego Dept Pediatrics 200 W Arbor Dr San Diego CA 92103-1911

MENEELEY, EDWARD STERLING, artist; b. Wilkes-Barre, Pa., Dec. 18, 1927; s. Edward Sterling and Louina Halter M. Student, Murray Art Sch., Wilkes-Barre, 1947-50, Sch. Visual Arts, N.Y.C., 1952-53. vis. lectr. Belleville Coll., St. Louis, Art Students League, N.Y.C.; lectr. Lehigh Valley Sch. System, 1987, Rogers College, Istanbul, Turkey, 1991; pres. ESM Documentations, N.Y.C.; fine arts cons. Arts Initiatives, Inc., N.Y.C.; founder Portable Gallery Press, 1957-67. One-man exhbs. include, Donovan Gallery, Phila., 1952, Parma Gallery, N.Y.C., 1962, Teuscher Gallery, N.Y.C., 1966, 68, Inst. Contemporary Arts, London, 1971, Victoria and Albert Mus., London, 1972, U. Sussex, Eng., 1972, Whitechapel Art Gallery, London, 1973, Demos Gallery, Athens, Greece, 1976, Frank Marino Gallery, N.Y.C., 1978, 79, 80, 81, 82, Sordoni Gallery, Wilkes (Pa.) Coll., 1981, Ericson Gallery, N.Y.C., 1980, Portfolio Gallery, Atlanta, 1983, Angela Flowers Gallery, London, 1985, J.T. Gallery, Jim Thorpe, Pa, 1987, 55 Mercer St., N.Y.C., 1987, Anita Shapolsky Gallery, N.Y.C., 1988, Bucknell U. Gallery Art, Lewisburg, 1988, Recent Painting & Sculptute, Coll. Misericordia, Dallas, Pa., 1989, Mixed Media, Craft Alliance Gallery, St. Louis, 1990, Provincetown (Mass.) Art Mus., 1993. Served with USNR, 1945-47, 50-52. Nat. Endowment Arts grantee; Pollock-Krasner Found. grantee, 1986, 90. Mem. Artist Club N.Y.C., Inst. Contemporary Arts London, Josiah White Soc., Weissport, Pa.

MENEFEE, SAMUEL PYEATT, lawyer, anthropologist; b. Denver, June 8, 1950; s. George Hardiman and Martha Elizabeth (Pyeatt) M. BA in Anthropology and Scholar of Ho. summa cum laude, Yale U., 1972; diploma in Social Anthropology, Oxford (Eng.) U., 1973, BLitt, 1975; JD, Harvard U., 1981; LLM in Oceans, U. Va., 1982, SJD, 1993; MPhil in Internat. Rels., U. Cambridge, Eng., 1995. Bar: Ga. 1981, U.S. Ct. Appeals (11th cir.) 1982, Va. 1983, La. 1983, U.S. Ct. Mil. Appeals 1983, U.S. Ct. Internat. Trade 1983, U.S. Ct. Claims 1983, U.S. Ct. Appeals (fed., 1st, 3d, 4th, 5th, 6th, 7th, 8th and 96h cirs.) 1984, D.C. 1985, Nebr. 1985, Fla. 1985, U.S. Supreme Ct. 1985, U.S. Ct. Appeals (D.C. cir.) 1986, Maine 1986, Pa. 1986. Assoc. Phelps, Dunbar, Marks, Claverie & Sims, New Orleans, 1983-85; of counsel Barham & Churchill PC, New Orleans, 1985-88; sr. assoc. Ctr. for Nat. Security Law U. Va. Sch. Law, 1985—; vis. asst. prof. U. Mo.-Kansas City, 1990; law clk. Hon. Pasco M. Bowman, U.S. Ct. Appeals (8th cir.), 1994-95; lectr. various nat. and internat. orgns. Author: Wives for Sale: An Ethnographic Study of British Popular Divorce, 1981; co-editor: Materials on Ocean Law, 1982; contbr. numerous articles to profl. jours. Recipient Katharine Briggs prize Folklore Soc., 1992; Bates traveling fellow Yale U., 1971, Ctr. for Oceans Law and Policy fellow Law Sch. U. Va., 1982-83, sr. fellow, 1985-89, Maury fellow, 1989—, Cosmos fellow Sch. Scottish Studies U. Edinburgh, 1991-92, IMB fellow, ICC Internat. Maritime Bur., 1991—, Regional Piracy Ctr. fellow, Kuala Lumpur, 1993—; Rhodes scholar, 1972. Fellow Royal Anthrop. Inst., Am. Anthrop. Assn., Royal Asiatic Soc., Royal Soc. Antiquaries of Ireland, Soc. Antiquaries (Scotland), Royal Geog. Soc., Soc. Antiquaries; mem. ABA (vice-chmn. marine resources com. 1987-90, chmn. law of the sea com. subcom. naval warfare, maritime terrorism and piracy 1989—, mem. working group on terrorism), Southeastern Admiralty Law Inst. (com. mem.), Maritime Law Assn. (proctor, com. mem., chmn. subcom. law of the sea 1988-91, vice chmn. com. internat. law of the sea 1991— , chair working group piracy 1992—), Marine Tech. Soc. (co-chmn. marine security com. 1991-95, chmn. 1995—), Selden Soc., Am. Soc. Internat. Law Internat. Law Assn. (com. mem., rapporteur Am. br. com. EEZ 1988-90, rapporteur Am. br. com. Maritime Neutrality 1992, observer UN conv. on Law of the Sea meeting of States Parties 1996), Am. Soc. Indsl. Security (com. mem.), U.S. Naval Inst., USN League, Folklore Soc., Royal Celtic Soc., Internat. Studies Assn., Royal Scottish Geog. Soc., Royal African Soc., Egypt Exploration Soc., Arctic Inst. N.Am., Internat. Studies Assn., Am. Hist. Soc., Nat. Eagle Scout Assn., Raven Soc., Jefferson Soc., Fence Club, Mory's Assn., Elizabethan Club, Leander Club, Cambridge Union, United Oxford and Cambridge Univ. Club, Yale Club (N.Y.C.), Paul Morphy Chess Club, Pendennis Club, Round Table Club (New Orleans), Phi Beta Kappa, Omicron Delta Kappa. Republican. Episcopalian. Avocations: anthropology, archaeology, social history, crew, hill walking. Office: U Va Ctr Nat Security Law 580 Massie Rd Charlottesville VA 22903-1789

MENENDEZ, ADOLFO, engineering company executive; m. Silvia Perez; children: José Adolfo, Mercedes Silvia. BSME, Manhattan Coll.; postgrad., Golden Gate U. Registered profl. engr. D.C., Va., Miss. Project mgr. internat. ops. Bechtel Power Corp.; pres., COO K & M Engrng. & Cons. Corp., Washington; bd. dirs. KMR Power Corp.; cons. Wold Bank, Internat. Fin. Corp., European Bank for Reconstruction and Devel., USAID, others. Mem. Georgetown Club, U. Club, Lakewood Country Club. Office: K & M Engrng & Consulting Corp 2001 L St NW Ste 500 Washington DC 20036-4910

MENENDEZ, CARLOS, financial executive, banker; b. Havana, Cuba, Apr. 16, 1938; s. Ramon and Rita (Leon) M.; m. Teresa Moran, Oct. 29, 1960; 1 child, Maria-Teresa. B.B.A., NYU, 1971. Asst. sec. Irving Trust Co., N.Y.C., 1970-72, asst. v.p., 1973-75, v.p., 1975-83; 2d v.p. Continental Bank, N.Y.C., 1972-73; sr. v.p., gen. mgr. Irving Trust Internat. Bank, Miami, Fla., 1983-87; sr. v.p. Latin Am. banking div. Irving Trust Co., 1987-88, Bank of N.Y., 1989-90; CFO, Pacific Group, N.Y.C., 1990—; pres. Intercredit Bank, N.A., Miami, Fla., 1992—, Galo Worldwide Travel & Tours, N.Y.C., 1992—, Intercredit Capital Markets, Miami, 1996—. Mem. Fla. Internat. Bankers Assn. (bd. dirs. 1985-87), Spain U.S.C. of C. (bd. dirs. 1985), Coun. of Ams. (corp. adv. bd. 1993—). Roman Catholic.

MENENDEZ, MANUEL, JR., judge; b. Tampa, Fla., Aug. 2, 1947; s. Manuel and Clara (Marin) M.; m. Linda Lee Stewart, Aug. 31, 1969; children: Jennifer Kay, Christine Marie. AA, U. Fla., 1967, BA, 1969, JD with Honors, 1972. Bar: Fla. 1972, U.S. Dist. Ct. (mid. dist.) Fla. 1973, U.S. Ct. Appeals (5th cir.) 1973, U.S. Ct. Claims 1974, U.S. Tax Ct. 1974, U.S. Ct. Customs and Patent Appeals 1974, U.S. Supreme Ct. 1976, U.S. Ct. Appeals (11th cir.) 1983, U.S. Ct. Appeals (D.C. cir.) 1984. Asst. U.S. atty. Dept. Justice, Jacksonville, Fla., 1973-77; chief asst. U.S. atty. Dept. Justice, Tampa, 1978-83; assoc. Law Office Jack Culp, Jacksonville, 1977-78; ptnr. Culp & Menendez, P.A., Jacksonville, 1978; county judge jud. br. State of Fla., Tampa, 1983-84, cir. judge jud. br., 1984—; dept. head, faculty mem. Fla. Coll. of Advanced Jud. Studies; faculty mem. pre-bench program Fla. New Judges Coll., 1993; faculty mem. Fla. Bar Prosecutor-Pub. Defender Advocacy Tng. Program, 1989-91, 94—; mentor judge coord. 13th Cir. Ct., 1995—; co-chair edn. steering com. Fla. Cir. Judge's Conf., 1996. Exec. editor U. Fla. Law Rev., 1971-72. Mem. adv. bd. Salvation Army, 1988-91. Recipient Pub. Service Meritorious Achievement award West Tampa Civic Clubs Assn., 1983. Mem. ABA, Fla. Bar Assn. (mem. criminal procedure rules com. 1988-94, chmn. 1991-92, chmn. rules and jud. adminstrn. com. 1995-96), Fed. Bar Assn. (v.p. Jacksonville chpt. 1974-75, pres. Tampa Bay chpt. 1980-85), Hillsborough County Bar Assn. (media law com. 1984—, trial lawyers sect. 1985—, Liberty Bell award selection com. 1991-93, jud. evaluation com. 1993), Am. Judicature Soc., Am. Judges Assn., Am. Inns of Ct. (master of bench, pres. 1991—), U. Fla. Alumni Assn., U. Fla. Law Ctr. Assn., First U.S. Calvary Regiment Rough Riders Inc., Propellor Club, Tampa Gator Club. Avocations: fishing, golf, Univ. Fla. athletics, coaching little league sr. girls softball. Office: Hillsborough County Courthouse 419 N Pierce St Ste 370 Tampa FL 33602-4025

MENENDEZ, ROBERT, congressman, lawyer; b. N.Y.C., Jan. 1, 1954; s. Mario and Evangelina (Lopez) M.; m. Jane Jacobsen, June 5; children: Alicia, Robert. BA, St. Peter's Coll., 1976; JD, Rutgers U., 1979. Bar: N.J. 1980. Sole practice Union City, N.J., 1980-92; mem. 103d-104th Cngresses from 13th Dist. N.J., Dem. whip at large; mem. Congl. Arts Caucus. Mayor of Union City, 1986-92; sec. Union City Bd. Edn., 1978-82, trustee, 1974-78; pres. Alliance civic Orgn., 1982-92; mem. Gov.'s Hispanic Adv. Com., Trenton, N.J., 1984—; mem. Gov.'s Ethnic Adv. Com., Washington, 1985—. Recipient Cmty. Svc. award Gran Logia del Norte, 1981, Outstanding Svc. award Hispanic Law Enforcement, 1981, Outstanding Cmty. Svc. Revista Actualidades, 1982, Disting. Citizen award U. Medicine and Dentistry N.J., 1994, Man of Yr. award Kiwanis, 1994. Mem. N.J. Hispanic Elected and Apptd Ofcls. (chair), Hoboken Elks Club. Democrat. Roman Catholic. Avocations: chess, racquetball. Office: 1730 Longworth Bldg Washington DC 20515-3013 also: 911 Bergen Ave Jersey City NJ 07306-4301*

MENES, PAULINE H., state legislator; b. N.Y.C., July 16, 1924; d. Arthur B. and Hannah H. Herskowitz; m. Melvin Menes, Sept. 1, 1946; children: Sandra Jill Menes Ashe, Robin Joy Menes Elvord, Bambi Lynn Menes Gavin. BA in Bus. Econs. and Geography, Hunter Coll., N.Y.C., 1945. Economist Quartermaster Gen. Office, Washington, 1945-47; geographer Army Map Service, Washington, 1949-50; chief clk. Prince George's County Election Bd., Upper Marlboro, Md., 1963; substitute tchr. Prince George's County H.S.s, Md., 1965-66; mem. Md. Ho. of Dels., Annapolis, 1966—, mem. judiciary com., 1979—, mem. com. on rules and exec. nominations, 1979-94, 95—, chmn. spl. com. on drug and alcohol abuse, 1986—, chmn. Prince George's County del., 1993-95, parliamentarian, 1995—. Mem. Md. Arts Coun., Balt., 1968-95, Md. Commn. on Aging, Balt., 1975-95; bd. dirs. Prisoner's Aid Assn., Balt., 1971-94. Recipient Internat. Task Force award Women's Yr., 1977; named to Hall of Fame Hunter Coll. Alumni Assn., 1986, Women's Hall of Fame Prince George County, 1989. Mem. NOW, Nat. Conf. State Legislators (com. on drugs and alcohol 1987), Md. NOW (Ann London Scott Meml. award for legis. excellence 1976), Nat. Order Women Legislators (pres. 1979-80), Women's Polit. Caucus, Bus. and Profl. Women. Avocations: theater, music, dance show attending, stamp collector. Home: 3517 Marlbrough Way College Park MD 20740-3925 Office: Md Ho of Reps Rm 210 Lowe State Office Bldg Annapolis MD 21401

MENG, JACK, food products executive. CEO Schreiber Foods. Office: Schreiber Foods PO Box 19010 Green Bay WI 54307-9010 Office: PO Box 19010 Green Bay WI 54307

MENGDEN, JOSEPH MICHAEL, investment banker; b. Houston, Sept. 28, 1924; s. Hippolyt Frederick and Amalia (Dittlinger) M.; m. Suzanne Miner, Sept. 30, 1950 (dec. July 1990); children: Anne Elise Mengden Giliberto, Amanda Mary, Michael Joseph, Charles Louis, Melissa Mary Mengden Bunker, Mary Miner Mengden Fitch; m. Dorothy Duggan, July 27, 1991. Ph.B., U. Notre Dame, 1949. V.p. Nat. Bank of Detroit, 1950-67; exec. v.p. First of Mich. Capitol Corp., Detroit, 1967-90, sr. cons., 1990-95, chmn. bd., 1994-95; bd. dirs. First of Mich. Captial Corp., Detroit, 1969—; bd. dirs. Saginaw (Mich.) Bay Broadcasting Corp. Served to 1st lt. USAAF, World War II. Decorated Air medal with 2 oak leaf clusters. Home: 321 Rivard Blvd Grosse Pointe MI 48230-1625

MENGE, RICHARD CRAMER, electric utility executive; b. Ann Arbor, Mich., Aug. 28, 1935; s. Walter Otto and Elsie Belle (Cramer) M.; m. Mary Carolyn Poe, July 1, 1961; children: David, Peter, Karen. BA, U. Mich., 1957, MBA, 1961. Bus. trainee Am. Elec. Power Co., N.Y.C., 1961-63; personnel supr. Ind. Mich. Power Co., Lawrenceburg, Ind., 1963-65; with Ind. Mich. Power Co., Fort Wayne, Ind., 1965—, sr. v.p., 1988-89, pres., 1989—; also bd. dirs.; bd. dirs. Ind. Ky. Elec. Co., Madison, Ind., Am. Elec. Power Svc. Corp., Columbus, Ohio, Ft. Wayne Nat. Bank. Treas. Fort Wayne YMCA, 1989; chmn. Jr. Achievement of No. Ind., 1992-94; 1st lt. U.S. Army, 1957-59. Mem. Ind. Elec. Assn. (chmn. 1989), Ft. Wayne Downtown Assn. (pres. 1980), Greater Ft. Wayne C. of C. (chmn. 1994), Quest Club, Summit Club (v.p.) Rotary (pres. Ft. Wayne chpt. 1978). Lutheran. Home: 4415 Brixworth Ct Fort Wayne IN 46835-4609 Office: Ind Mich Power Co 110 E Wayne St Fort Wayne IN 46802-2604*

MENGEDOTH, DONALD ROY, commercial banker; b. Naperville, Ill., Aug. 10, 1944; s. Orville Gustav and Bernice Lydia (Fries) M.; m. Stacy K. Halverson; children: Paul Bernard, Daniel Lawrence, Mary Bernice. BS, Marquette U., 1968, MBA, 1973. Ops. officer lst Bank, N.A.-Milw., 1968-69, asst. v.p., 1969-71, v.p., 1971-73, sr. v.p., 1973-79; v.p. lst Bank System, Inc., Mpls., 1979-82, sr. v.p., 1983-87; chmn., pres., chief exec. officer Community 1st Bankshares Inc., Fargo, N.D., 1987—; bd. dirs. Treasure Enterprises, Inc., Vail Banks Inc. Adv. bd. United Way Cass-Clay Campaign, Fargo, 1988-89; chmn. Cmty. 1st Polit. Action Com., Fargo, 1988-89; bd. dirs. Fargo Cath. Schs. Network Found., 1989-92; bd. dirs., vice chmn. Red River Zool. Soc., 1993-96; chmn. Diocesan God's Gift Appeals, Fargo, 1989. Mem. Am. Bankers Assn. (govt. rels. coun.), Am. Mgmt. Assn., N.D. Bankers Assn., S.D. Bankers Assn., Greater N.D. Assn., Fargo Country Club. Avocations: tennis, golf, hunting, reading. Office: Cmty 1st Bankshares 520 Main Ave Fargo ND 58124-0001

MENGEL, CHARLES EDMUND, physician, medical educator; b. Balt., Nov. 29, 1931; s. Charles LeRoy and Anna (Apgar) M.; m. Paula Padgett, June 5, 1978; children: Cheryl Lynn, Charles Edmund, Gregory John, Scott Alan, Carol Ann, Michael Daniel. A.B. in Chemistry, Lafayette Coll., 1953; M.D., Johns Hopkins U., 1957. Intern Johns Hopkins Hosp., 1957-58; resident Duke Hosp., 1958-59, 61-62; clin. assoc. NIH, 1959-61; mem. faculty Duke U. Med. Sch., 1961-65; Doan prof., dir. hematology and oncology Ohio State U., 1965-69; prof. medicine U. Mo., Columbia, 1969-82; chmn. dept. U. Mo., 1969-81; pvt. practive gen. medicine Moberly, Mo., 1982-88; prof. medicine Kans. U. Med. Ctr., Kansas City, 1988—. Author textbook; contbr. articles to med. publs. Served with USPHS, 1959-61. Markle scholar acad. medicine, 1963. Mem. ACP, Am. Fedn. Clin. Research, Am. Soc. Hematology, Am. Soc. Clin. Investigation. Home: 3221 Meadow Rd Leavenworth KS 66048-4764 Office: VA Med Ctr Chief Med Ctr Leavenworth KS 66048

MENGEL, CHRISTOPHER EMILE, lawyer, educator; b. Holyoke, Mass., Sept. 11, 1952; s. Emile Oscar and Rose Ann (O'Donnell) M.; m. Ellen Christine Creager, Dec. 6, 1991; children: Meredith Anne, Celia Claire; stepchildren: Cara Elizabeth Creager, Kristen Michelle Creager. Student, U. Notre Dame, 1970-71; BA, Holy Cross Coll., 1974; JD, Detroit Coll. Law, 1979. Bar: Mich. 1979, U.S. Dist. Ct. (ea. dist.) Mich. 1989, U.S. Ct. Appeals (6th cir.) 1990. Tchr. Holyoke Pub. Schs., 1974-76; assoc. Fried & Sniokaitis P.C., Detroit, 1980-82; prof. law Detroit Coll. Law, 1982-85; pvt. practice law Detroit, 1982-91; mng. ptnr. Berkley, Mengel & Vining, PC, 1992—. Mem. coun. St. Ambrose Parish, Grosse Pointe Park, Mich., 1985-88, pres. 1986-87. Matthew J. Ryan scholar, 1970. Mem. ABA, Mich. Bar Assn., Detroit Bar Assn. Democrat. Roman Catholic. Avocations: baseball, sailing, photography. Home: 1281 N Oxford Rd Grosse Pointe MI 48236-1857 Office: Berkley Mengel & Vining PC 3100 Penobscot Bldg Detroit MI 48226

MENGEL, DAVID BRUCE, agronomy and soil science educator; b. East Chicago, Ind., May 1, 1948; s. Bill M. and Thelma Lee (Miller) M.; m. Susan Kay Haverstock, Aug. 30, 1968; children: David, Erin. BS in Agricultural Edn., Purdue U., 1970, MS in Agronomy, 1972; PhD in Soil Sci., N.C. State U., 1975. Cert. profl. agronomist, soil scientist. Asst. prof. agronomy La. State U., Crowley, 1975-79; asst. prof. agronomy Purdue U., West Lafayette, Ind., 1979-82, assoc. prof., 1982-86; prof. agronomy Purdue U., West Lafayette, 1986—. Mem. Am Soc. Agronomy, Soil Sci. Soc. Am., Internat. Soil Sci. Soc., Sigma Xi, Gamma Sigma Delta, Epsilon Sigma Phi, Delta Tau Delta. Avocations: fishing, woodworking. Office: Purdue U Dept Agronomy West Lafayette IN 47906

MENGEL, PHILIP R(ICHARD), investment banker; b. Memphis, Oct. 30, 1944; s. John P. and Marjorie Ann M.; m. Jayne E. Frutig, Dec. 20, 1980; 1 child, Jill Kathryn. AB, Princeton U., 1968; cert., Woodrow Wilson Sch. Pub. & Internat. Affairs, 1968. With Fiduciary Trust Co. N.Y., N.Y.C., 1968-77, mem. exec. com., 1973-77, v.p., 1970-77; pres., dir. Fiduciary Investment Corp., N.Y.C., 1973-77; founder, pres., dir. Mengel & Co., Inc. (formerly Mengel, McCabe & Co., Inc.), N.Y.C., 1978—; chmn., pres. Mengel & Co., Inc., N.Y.C., 1983-90; pres., chief exec. officer Glen-Gery Corp., Wyomissing, Pa., 1990—, also bd. dirs.; bd. dirs. Brick Inst. Am., Ibstock Johnsen PLC (U.K.), Atlas Corp. Trustee St. Stephen's Sch., Rome, 1976-88, chmn. bd. 1978-82; co-chmn. Graham Windham Childcare Benefit, 1986-88. With USNR, 1962-64. Mem. Racquet and Tennis Club, U.S. Ct. Tennis Assn. (bd. dirs. 1993—), The Brook, Racquet Club of Phila., Tuxedo Club (gov. 1988—). Episcopalian. Office: 1166 Spring St Reading PA 19604-2238 also: 9 Three Kings Yard, London England

MENGELING, WILLIAM LLOYD, veterinarian, virologist, researcher; b. Elgin, Ill., Apr. 1, 1933; s. William Paul and Blanche Joyce (Wormwood) M.; m. Barbara Ann Kethcart, Aug. 23, 1958; children: Michelle, Michael. BS, Kans. State U., 1958, DVM, 1960; MS, Iowa State U., 1966, PhD, 1969. Diplomate M. Coll. Vet. Microbiologists (chmn. 1977-78, bd. dirs. 1975-77). Vet. clinician St. Francis Animal Hosp., Albuquerque, 1960-61; vet. med. officer Nat. Animal Disease Ctr., Ames, Iowa, 1961-69, rsch. leader, 1969—; rsch. leader U.S. Sr. Exec. Svc., 1991—; cons. numerous state, fed., pvt. U.S. and fgn. agys.; collaborative prof., mem. grad. faculty Iowa State U. Co-editor: Diseases of Swine, 5th, 6th, 7th editions; contbr. articles to jours., chpts. to books. With U.S. Army, 1953-55. Recipient cert. appreciation USDA, 1978, George Fleming award Brit. Vet. Jour., 1978, Disting. Svc. award USDA, 1984, Gov.'s medal sci. State of Iowa, 1985, Vet. Med. Rsch. award Am. Feed Industry Assn., 1989, Leadership Merit awards USDA, 1989, 90, 91, 93. Mem. AVMA (Vet. Med. Rsch. award 1989), U.S. Animal Health Assn., Conf. Rsch. Workers in Animal Disease (pres. 1987-88, coun. 1981-86), Kiwanis (pres. 1975-76). Methodist. Avocations: wilderness survival, canoeing, camping, fishing. Address: 4220 Phoenix St Ames IA 50014-3922

MENGES, CARL BRAUN, investment banker; b. N.Y.C., Sept. 17, 1930; s. Hermann and Alice (Braun) M.; m. Cordelia Sykes, Apr. 24, 1965; children: James C., Benjamin W., Samuel G. B.A., Hamilton Coll., 1951; M.B.A., Harvard U., 1953. Salesman Owens Corning Fiberglas Corp., 1954-59, mktg. mgr., 1959-63; with instl. sales dept. Model Roland Co., N.Y.C., 1963-65; with instnl. sales dept., syndicate mgr., dir. internat. Donaldson, Lufkin & Jenrette Inc., 1965-77, mng. dir., 1972—, chmn. fin. services group, 1984-87, vice chmn. of bd., 1987—; chmn. bd. dirs. Winthrop Focus Funds, 1986—; bd. dirs. Med. Indemnity Assurance Corp., The Greenwall Found., G-Tech Corp. Trustee Hosp. for Spl. Surgery, 1977—, Hamilton Coll., Clinton, N.Y., trustee 1985—; v.p., treas., trustee The Allen-Stevenson Sch., N.Y.C., 1979-86, bd. dirs. Boys Club of N.Y. Mem. Union Club, Maidstone Club (gov. 1969-86, pres. 1982-86), Nat. Golf Links Am., Regency Whist Club, Colony Club, Leash Club, L.I. Wyandanch Club. Office: Donaldson Lufkin & Jenrette Securities Corp 140 Broadway New York NY 10005-1101

MENGES, CHRIS, cinematographer, film director; b. Kington, Eng., Sept. 15, 1940. Began career as cameraman with British TV, 1963. Cinematographer: Poor Cow, 1967, Gumshoe, 1970, Kes, 1970, Blackjack, 1979, Warlords of the 21st Century, 1982, Danny Boy Angel, 1983, Local Hero, 1983, Comfort and Joy, 1984, The Killing Fields, 1984 (Acad. award 1984), Marie, 1985, A Sense of Freedom, 1985, The Mission, 1986 (Acad. award 1986), Walter and June, 1986, Shy People, 1987, High Season, 1988, Singing the Blues in Red, 1988; film dir.: A World Apart, 1988 (Grand prize Cannes Internat. Film Festival), Second Best, 1994. Office: Casarotto Co Ltd, Nat House, 60-66 Wardour St, London W1V 3HP, England

MENGES, JOHN KENNETH, JR., lawyer; b. Louisville, Sept. 23, 1957; s. John Kenneth and Barbara Jean (Vick) M. BSBA, Boston U., 1979; JD, Harvard U., 1982. Bar: Tex. 1982. Assoc. Akin, Gump, Strauss, Hauer & Feld, Dallas, 1982-89, ptnr., 1989—. Pres. Dallas County Young Dems., 1985-88, Dallas Dem. Forum, 1990-91, bd. dirs., 1986-89; pres. sch. mgmt. Boston U., 1987—, bd. trustees, 1995—; bd. dirs. Save the Children Adv. Coun., Friends of Fair Park; bd. trustees Boston U.; Dallas County chair North Tex. Clean Air Coalition. Mem. ABA, Tex. State Bar Assn., Dallas Bus. League (pres. 1989), Dallas Coun. on World Affairs, Dallas Assn. Young Lawyers, Harvard U. Law Sch. Assn. Tex. (bd. dirs. 1984-87, 90-91, pres. 1993), Boston U. Nat. Alumni Coun. (Young Alumni award 1987). Democrat. Methodist. Avocation: basketball. Office: Akin Gump Strauss Hauer & Feld 1700 Pacific Ave Ste 4100 Dallas TX 75201-4624

MENGES, PAMELA ANN, aerospace engineer, consultant; b. Northport, Mich.; d. Raymond Alfred and Margaret Carolyn (St. Amand) M. BS in Biomathematics, Thomas More Coll., 1985; PhD in Aerospace Engrng., Union Inst., Cin., 1995. Teaching asst. in physics Am. U. Paris, 1982-83; intern sci. writing Behringer-Crawford, Covington, Ky., 1984; specialist overseas prodn. GE, Evendale, Ohio, 1984; dir. project svcs., rsch. engineer, mgr. intern ops. Ray A. Menges and Assocs. (formerly RAM Assocs. Inc.), Cin., 1984-92; pres., CEO Menges Consulting, Inc., Cin., 1992—; postdoctoral rsch. assoc. NIS-8 Los Alamos (N.Mex.) Nat. Lab., 1995—; prin. investigator/project mgr. Nat. Air Intelligence Ctr., Wright-Patterson AFB, Ohio, 1996—. Mem. ASTM, AIAA (flight testing tech. com. assoc.), Am. Def. Preparedness Assn., Am. Phys. Soc. Avocations: flying, sculpting. Office: Menges Consulting Inc 2196 W North Bend Rd Cincinnati OH 45239-6858

MENGUY, RENE, surgeon, educator; b. Prague, Czechoslovakia, Feb. 4, 1926; came to U.S., 1951, naturalized, 1957; s. Auguste and Beatrice (Adam) M.; m. Emilie Rigacci, Aug. 10, 1950; children—John, Ghislaine. B.A., U. Hanoi, Indochina, 1944; M.D., U. Paris, France, 1951; Ph.D., U. Minn., 1957. Fellow gen. surgery Mayo Clinic, 1952-57; mem. faculty U. Okla. Med. Sch., 1957-61, U. Ky. Med. Center, 1961-65; prof. surgery, chmn. dept. U. Chgo. Med. Sch., 1965-71; prof. surgery U. Rochester Med. Sch., 1971—; surgeon Genesee Hosp., 1971—; Mem. clin. research tng. com. NIH, 1965-69; cons. VA, 1964—. Author: Peptic Ulcer, 1975; Mem. editorials bd. jours. in field.; Contbr. articles to profl. jours. Recipient citation French Expeditionary Corps, Hanoi, 1946; Fulbright travel grantee, 1951-52; recipient Alumni award meritorious research Mayo Found., 1956; John and Mary R. Markle scholar med. scis., 1958-63. Mem. A.C.S., Am. Fedn. Clin. Research, N.Y. Acad. Scis., Soc. Exptl. Biology and Medicine, Am. Assn. Cancer Research, Am. Gastroenterol. Assn., Soc. Univ. Surgeons, Soc. Surgery Alimentary Tract, Am. Physiol. Soc., Internat. Soc. Surgery, Surg. Biology Club, Soc. Clin. Surgery, Am. Surg. Assn., Acad. Chir. (Paris), Surg. Research Soc. So. Africa (corr.), Congrés Francais de Chirurgie (hon.), Sigma Xi. Home: 8 Highland Hts Rochester NY 14618-1116

MENHALL, DALTON WINN, lawyer, insurance executive, professional association administrator; b. Edgerton, Wis., Aug. 1, 1939; s. Joseph Laurence and Mary Winn (Dalton) M.; m. Lilian Marilyn Christie, Oct. 19, 1968; children: Dalton Winn, Rebecca Lynn, Katherine Elizabeth. B.A., Ill. Coll., 1962; J.D., Vanderbilt U., 1965. Bar: Wis. 1965. Staff asst. State Bar of Wis., Madison, 1965-72, dir., 1972-76, legis. counsel, dir. continuing legal edn., 1972-76; exec. dir. N.J. State Bar Assn., Trenton, 1976-86; nat. programs dir. Herbert L. Jamison & Co., 1987-91; trustee, cert. assn. exec. St. Patricks' Day Sch., 1994. Exec. v.p. Phi Alpha Delta Pub. Svc. Ctr., Washington, 1991-94; exec. dir. Phi Alpha Delta Law Frat. Internat., Granada Hills, Calif., 1992-94. Fellow Am. Bar Found.; mem. ABA (cons., youth edn. and citizenship com 1993—), Nat. Assn. Bar Execs. (pres. 1985-86), N.J. State Bar Assn., State Bar Wis., Am. Soc. Assn. Execs., Am. Judicature Soc., Nat. Assn. Bar Execs. (hon.), So. Calif. Soc. Assn. Execs.

MENINO, THOMAS M., mayor; b. Dec. 27, 1942; m. Angela Faletra; children: Susan, Thomas Michael, Jr. Degree in Community Planning, U. Mass., 1988; cert. in State and Local Govt. Program, Harvard U. Mem. City Coun., Boston, 1985—, pres., 1993; acting mayor Boston, 1993—; sr. rsch. asst. Joint Com. Urban Affairs, 1978-83. Contbr. articles to historic preservation jours. Regional chmn. Nat. Trust Historic Preservation; bd. dirs. Nat. League Cities, 1985—, mem. various coms. Office: Office of Mayor 1 City Hall Plaza 5th Fl Boston MA 02201*

MENIUS, ARTHUR CLAYTON, JR., former university dean; b. Salisbury, N.C., Apr. 30, 1916; s. Arthur Clayton and Maud Edna (Webb) M.; m. Lucille Clark Varner, Mar. 31, 1946; 1 son, Arthur Clayton III. A.B. in Physics and Math, Catawba Coll., 1937, D.Sc., 1969; Ph.D. in Physics, U. N.C., 1942. Sr. physicist Applied Physics Lab., Johns Hopkins, 1944-46, head battery group for proximity fuse project, 1945-46; prof. physics Clemson Coll., 1946-48; mem. faculty N.C. State U., Raleigh, 1949-81; prof. physics N.C. State U., 1949-55, head dept., 1956-60; dean N.C. State U. (Sch. Phys. and Math. Scis.), 1960-81; sec., v.p. Tharrington's Handcrafted 18th Century Furniture, Inc., 1984; cons. govt. agys. pvt. bus., 1950-81; Chmn. Gov. N.C. Sci. Adv. Com., 1961-69, Atomic Energy Adv. Com. N.C., 1963-71; mem. N.C. Sci. and Tech. Bd.; N.C. State council rep. Oak Ridge Asso. Univs., 1963-69, mem. bd., 1969-76; edn. rep. So. Interstate Nuclear Bd. Author numerous monographs, articles profl. jours. Bd. govs. Research Triangle Inst. Fellow Am. Phys. Soc.; mem. N.C. Acad. Sci., Am. Inst. Physics, Sigma Xi, Phi Kappa Phi. Presbyn. Home: 541 Hertford St Raleigh NC 27609-6905 *It has been exciting and rewarding to live in a period when so much as happened in the scientific field - space exploration, nuclear physics, computers, etc. Fortunately, I was involved with most of them.*

MENIUS, ESPIE FLYNN, JR., electrical engineer; b. New Bern, N.C., Mar. 5, 1923; s. Espie Flynn and Sudie Grey (Lyerly) M.; BEE, N.C. State U., 1947; MBA, U. S.C., 1973; adopted children: James Benfield, Ruben Hughes, James Sechler, Steve Walden. With Carolina Power & Light Co., 1947-63, asst. to dist. mgr., Raleigh, Henderson, N.C., Sumter, S.C., 1947-50, elec. engr., Asheville, Southern Pines, Dunn, N.C., 1950-52, dist. engr. Hartsville, S.C., 1952-63; sr. elec. engr. Sonoco Products Co., Hartsville, 1963-74, engrng. group leader, 1974-89, sr. profl. engr., 1989-91; profl. con., electrical engr., 1991—; instr. Florence-Darlington Tech. Ednl. Center. Mem. Hartsville Vol. Fire Dept., 1958—; Eagle Scout, Boy Scouts Am., 1938, scout troop leader New Bern, N.C., 1940-41, Raleigh, 1941-47, Henderson, 1948-49, Asheville, N.C., 1950, Southern Pines, N.C., 1951-52, Sumter, 1949-50, Hartsville, 1952-64; bd. mgrs. Nazareth Children's Home, Rockville, N.C., 1980—; chmn. bd. examiners City of Hartsville, 1980—; advocate Thornwell Children's Home, Clinton, S.C., 1990—; bd. dirs. Darlington (S.C.) County Youth Home, 1992—; active Hartsville Leadership Coun., 1993—. Served with AUS, 1943-46. Recipient Silver Beaver award Boy Scouts Am., 1959, Citizenship award S.C. State Firemen's Assn., 1993; named Hartsville's Citizen of Yr., Rotary, 1960; named to S.C. Fire Fighters Hall of Fame, 1995. Registered profl. engr., N.C., S.C., Tenn., Ga., Fla. Mem. IEEE, AAAS, VFW, Nat. Assn. Engrs., Am. Legion, Knight of St. Patrick, Scabbard and Blade, Eta Kappa Nu, Pine Burr, Phi Eta Sigma, Theta Tau, Beta Gamma Sigma. Presbyn. (elder, trustee, tchr. men's Bible class). Club: Civitan (past dir.). Author articles in field. Home and Office: 423 W Richardson Cir Hartsville SC 29550-5437

MENK, CARL WILLIAM, executive search company executive; b. Newark, Oct. 19, 1921; s. Carl William and Catherine Regina (Murray) M.; m. Elizabeth Cullum, May 30, 1947; children: Carl, Elizabeth (dec.), Mary, Paul. BSBA, Seton Hall U., 1943; MA, Columbia U., 1950. Sr. v.p. P. Ballantine & Sons, Newark, 1946-69; pres. Boyden Assocs., Inc., N.Y.C., 1969-84; chmn. Canny, Bowen, Inc., N.Y.C., 1984—; dir. Howard Savs. Bank, 1980-91. 2d Lt., pilot USAAF, 1943-46. Mem. Union League N.Y., Spring Lake Golf Club, Bent Pine Golf Club, John's Island Club, Knights of Malta, Internat. Exec. Svc. Corps. Republican. Roman Catholic. Home: 950 Beach Rd Johns Island Vero Beach FL 32963 Office: Canny Bowen Inc 200 Park Ave New York NY 10166-0005

MENKE, ALLEN CARL, industrial corporation executive; b. Huntingburg, Ind., Feb. 16, 1922; s. William Ernest and Clara (Moenkhaus) M.; m. Virginia Lee MacDonald, Apr. 14, 1944; children: Janet, William, Sarah. B.S. in Mech. Engrng. Purdue U., 1943, M.S., 1948. Instr. Purdue U., 1946-48; with Trane Co., 1948-68, v.p. sales, 1963-64, exec. v.p. sales, mfg. and engrng., 1964-68; v.p. Borg-Warner Corp., Chgo., 1969-76; chmn., pres., chief exec. officer Artesian Industries, Northbrook, Ill., 1976-88. Pres. Met. Housing Devel. Corp.; founder, pres. Winnetka Interch. Coun.; bd. dirs., chmn. Presbyn. Home; past chmn. dean's adv. coun. Krannert Sch. Mgmt. Purdue U.; bd. dirs. McCormick Sem., U. Chgo.; active Kenilworth Union Ch. Served to 1st lt. AUS, 1944-46. Named Disting. Alumnus, Purdue U., 1965, Outstanding Engr. Grad., 1991, mem. Purdue Hall of Fame. Mem. Sigma Chi (Significant award). Presbyterian (elder). Lodge: Mason. Home: 1420 Tower Rd Winnetka IL 60093-1629

MENKELLO, FREDERICK VINCENT, computer scientist; b. Boston, Mar. 22, 1942; s. Albert Frederick and Angelina Marie (Tecci) M. BS, Boston U., 1964, MEd, 1965; PhD, Tex. A&M U., 1975. Commd. 2d lt. USAF, 1966, advanced through grades to lt. col.; scientist Environ. Tech. Applications Ctr., Washington, 1967-69; rsch. scientist NASA, Greenbelt, Md., 1969-70; sect. chief Global Weather Cen., Offutt AFB, Nebr., 1973-77; div. chief Mil. Airlift command, Scott AFB, Ill., 1978-82; br. chief Office Sec. Def., Washington, 1982-85; dir. Computer Acquisition Ctr., Hanscom AFB, Mass., 1985-86; ret., 1986; prin. engr. for R & D, Vitro Corp., Silver Spring, Md., 1986—. Mem. Assn. for Computing Machinery, Soc. for Indsl. and Applied Math., Phi Kappa Phi, Upsilon Pi Epsilon. Avocations: weightlifting, jogging, theater, reading. Office: Vitro Corp 1601 Research Blvd Rockville MD 20850-3173

MENKEL-MEADOW, CARRIE JOAN, law educator; b. N.Y.C., Dec. 24, 1949; d. Gary G. and Margot (Sinn) Menkel; m. Robert Gary Meadow, Aug. 22, 1971. AB magna cum laude, Columbia U., 1971; JD cum laude, U. Pa., 1974; LLD (hon.), Quinnipiac Coll. Law, 1995. Bar: Pa. 1974, U.S. Ct. Appeals (3d cir.) 1975, Calif. 1979. Dir. legal writing U. Pa. Law Sch., Phila., 1974-75; clin. supt., lectr. U. Pa. Law Sch., 1976-79; staff atty. Cmty. Legal Svcs., Phila., 1975-77; prof. UCLA, 1979-96, prof. law, 1979—; prof. law Georgetown Law Ctr., Washington, 1996—; panel mem. NAS, Washington, 1986-87, NSF, Washington, 1987—; cons. ABA, Chgo., 1979-84; dir. UCLA Ctr. for Conflict Resolution, 1994—. Contbr. articles to profl. jours. Chairperson Ctr. for Study of Women, UCLA; bd. dirs. Western Ctr. on Law and Poverty, L.A., 1980-86; chair CPR Commn. on Ethics and ADR. Recipient Rutter award, 1992. Mem. Soc. Am. Law Tchrs. (trustee), Assn. Am. Law Schs. (alt. dispute resolution sect., law and social sci. sect., women in law sect., mem. accreditation com. 1987—), Ctr. for Law and Human Values (bd. dirs.), Law and Soc. Assn. (trustee), Am. Bar Found. (bd. dirs., exec. com. 1994—), Phi Beta Kappa. Democrat. Office: Georgetown Law Ctr 600 New Jersey Ave NW Washington DC 20001

MENKEN, ALAN, composer; b. 1949. Student, NYU. Composer, lyricist, performer Lehman Engel Mus. Theatre Workshop at BMI; ptnr. with Howard Ashman. Works include: (theatre) Off-Broadway debut God Bless You, Mr. Rosewater, (with Howard Ashman) Little Shop of Horrors, Kicks, The Apprenticeship of Duddy Kravitz, Diamonds, Personals, Let Freedom Sing, Weird Romance; (films) Little Shop of Horrors, 1986 (Acad. award nominee for best original score 1986), The Little Mermaid, 1988 (Acad. award for best original score 1989, Acad. award for best original song 1989), Beauty and the Beast, 1990 (Acad. award for best original score 1991, Acad. award for best original song 1991), Newsies, 1992, Aladdin, 1992, (Acad. award for best original score 1993, Acad. award best original song 1993, 3 Grammy awards 1994), Lincoln, 1992, Life With Mikey, 1993; (with Stephen Schwartz) Pocahontas, 1995 (Golden Globe award 1996, Acad. award for best original score 1996, Acad. award for best original song 1996). Office: The Shukat Co 340 W 55th St/Ste 1A New York NY 10019

MENKEN, JANE AVA, demographer, educator; b. Phila., Nov. 29, 1939; d. Isaac Nathan and Rose Ida (Sarvetnick) Golubitsky; m. Matthew Menken, 1960 (div. 1985); children: Kenneth Lloyd, Kathryn Lee; m. Richard Jessor, Nov. 13, 1992. A.B., U. Pa., 1960; M.S., Harvard U., 1962; Ph.D., Princeton U., 1975. Asst. in biostats. Harvard U. Sch. Pub. Health, Boston, 1962-64; math. statistician NIMH, Bethesda, Md., 1964-66; research assoc. dept. biostats., Columbia U., N.Y.C., 1966-69; mem. research staff Office of Population Research Princeton U., N.J., 1969-71, 75-87, asst. dir., 1978-86, assoc. dir., 1986-87, prof. sociology, 1980-82, prof. sociology and pub. affairs, 1982-87; prof. sociology and demography U. Pa., Phila., 1987—, UPS Found. prof. social scis., 1987—, dir. Population Studies Ctr., 1989-95; mem. social scis. and population study sect., NIH, Bethesda, Md., 1978-82, chmn., 1980-82, population adv. com. Rockefeller Found., N.Y.C., 1981-93, com. on population and demography, NAS, Washington, 1978-83, com. on population, 1983-85, com. nat. stats., 1983-89, com. on AIDS research, 1987-94, co-chair panel data and rsch. priorities for arresting AIDS in sub-Saharan Africa, 1994—, Commn. on Behavioral and Social Scis. and Edn., 1991—, sci. adv. com., Demographic and Health Surveys, Columbia, Md., 1985-90, Nat. Adv. Child Health and Human Devel. Council, 1988-91; cons. Internat. Centre for Diarrhoeal Disease Research, Bangladesh, Dhaka, 1984—. Author: (with Mindel C. Sheps) Mathematical Models of Conception and Birth, 1973; editor: (with Henri Leridon) Natural Fertility, 1979, (with Frank Furstenberg, Jr. and Richard Lincoln) Teenage Sexuality, Pregnancy and Childbearing, 1981, World Population and U.S. Policy: The Choices Ahead, 1986; contbr. articles to profl. jours. Bd. dirs. Alan Guttmacher Inst., N.Y.C., 1981-90, 93—. Nat. Merit scholar, 1957; John Simon Guggenheim Found. fellow, 1992-93, Ctr. for Advanced Study in Behavioral Scis. fellow, 1995-96. Fellow AAAS, Am. Statis. Assn.; mem. NAS, Am. Acad. Arts and Scis., Population Assn. Am. (Mindel Sheps award 1982, pres. 1985), Am. Pub. Health Assn. (Mortimer Spiegelman award 1975, program devel. bd. 1984-87), Am. Sociol. Assn., Soc. for Study of Social Biology, Internat. Union for Sci. Study of Population (coun. 1989—), Sociol. Research Assn. (exec. com. 1991—). Office: U Pa Population Studies Ctr 3718 Locust Walk Philadelphia PA 19104-6298

MENKES, JOHN HANS, pediatric neurologist; b. Vienna, Austria, Dec. 20, 1928; came to U.S., 1940; s. Karl and Valerie (Tupler) M.; m. Miriam Trief, Apr. 14, 1957 (div. Feb. 1978); m. Joan Simon Feld, Sept. 28, 1980; children: Simon, Tamara, Rafael C. AB, U. So. Calif., 1947, MS, 1951; MD, Johns Hopkins U., 1952. Diplomate Am. Bd. Pediatrics, Am. Bd. Neurology. Intern, jr. asst. resident Children's Med. Ctr., Boston, 1952-54; asst. resident pediatrics Bellevue Hosp., N.Y.C., 1956-57; resident neurology, trainee pediatric neurology Columbia-Presbyn. Med. Ctr., Neurological Inst. N.Y., N.Y.C., 1957-60; asst. prof. pediatrics Johns Hopkins U., Balt., 1960-63, assoc. prof., 1963-66, asst. prof. neurology, 1964-66, chief pediatric neurology div., 1964-66; prof. pediatrics and neurology UCLA, 1966-74, chief pediatric neurology div., 1966-70, prof. psychiatry, 1970-74; chief Neurology-Neurochem. Lab. Brentwood (Calif.) VA Hosp., 1970-74; clin. prof. psychiatry, neurology and pediatrics UCLA, 1974-77, clin. prof. pediatrics and neurology, 1977-84, prof. pediatrics and neurology, 1985-89, prof. emeritus pediatrics and neurology, 1989—; mem. metabolism study sect. NIH, 1968-70, project com., 1969-70; mem. adv. com. Nat. Inst. Child Health and Human Devel., 1985-87; mem. Dept. Health Svcs., Calif., 1980-87; mem. vaccine safety commn. Nat. Inst. Medicine, 1995—; mem. Coun. Child Neurology Soc., Dysautonomia Found., med. adv. bd. Nat. ORgn. Rare Diseases, Nat. Wilson's Disease Found.; trustee Dystonia Med. Rsch. Found., Vancouver, Can., 1985—. Author: Textbook of Child Neurology, 5th edit., 1995, (plays) The Last Inquisitor, 1985 (Drama-Logue Critics award 1985), The Salvation of Miguel Toruna, 1987, (screen plays) Miguel, Open Ward, 1989, The Countess of Silgo, 1992, Programmed Destinies, 1996; contbr. numerous articles to pediatric and neurol. jours. Served with USAF, 1954-56. Mem. Am. Acad. Neurology, Am. Acad. Pediatrics, Am. Chem. Soc., Soc. for Pediatric Rsch., Sociedad Peruana de Neuro-Psychiatra (hon.), Am. Neurochem. Soc., Am. Neurol. Assn., Am. Pediatric Soc., Child Neurology Soc. (Hower award 1980), Dramatist Guild, PEN. Jewish. Home: 1201 Park Way Beverly Hills CA 90210-3334 Office: 9320 Wilshire Blvd Beverly Hills CA 90212-3216

MENKIN, CHRISTOPHER (KIT MENKIN), leasing company executive; b. Manhattan, N.Y., Jan. 1, 1942; s. Lawrence and Columbia (Riland) M.; children: Dashiel, Tascha, Ashley. Student, Julliard Sch. of Music, 1960, Santa Monica Coll., 1959-61, UCLA, 1961-64. News editor, dir. Sta. KRFC Radio, San Francisco, 1964-67; adminstrv. asst. to assemblyman Leo J. Ryan South San Francisco, 1967-68; mng. editor Sta. KGO TV News, San Francisco, 1968-69; news producer west coast Sta. ABC TV, Los Angeles, 1969; city mgr. City of San Bruno (Calif.), 1970; owner Menkin & Assocs., Santa Clara, Calif., 1971—; sr. ptnr. Am. Leasing, Santa Clara, 1971—; ptnr. Medallon Leasing, Santa Clara, 1974-80; pres. Monte Sereno Wine Co., Santa Clara, 1978—; dir. Meridian Nat. Bank, 1982-84. Chmn. nominating com. San Jose (Calif.) Symphony, 1988—; sec. Salvation Army, Santa Clara, 1968—, bd. dirs., 1990—, bd. dirs. San Jose chpt., 1990, vice chmn. county adv. bd., 1992; bd. dirs. Cmty. Against Substance Abuse, Los Gatos, Calif., 1988—, Valley Inst. of Theater Arts, Saratoga, Calif., 1987-88, San Jose Trolley, 1988—. Mem. United Assn. Equipment Leasing (regional chmn. 1992-95, membership chmn. 1994-95, dir. 1996—), Credit Women Internat. (1st male pres.), Santa Clara Valley Wine Soc. (pres. 1988), Credit Profls. Santa Clara Valley (pres. 1990-91), Assn. Credit Grantors (past pres.), Santa Clara C. of C. (pres. 1973-76), Bay Area Exec. Club (sec.), Confrerie de la Chaine de Rotisseurs (charge de presse 1992-95), Royal Rose Soc. Gt. Britain (rep. No. Calif. 1990—). Democrat. Avocations: Rosarian, gardening, wine collecting, music, books. Office: Am Leasing 348 Mathew St Santa Clara CA 95050-3114

MENN, JULIUS JOEL, scientist; b. Danzig, Free City (now Poland), Feb. 20, 1929; came to U.S., 1950, naturalized, 1959; s. David Gregory and Regina (Ajzenstadt) M.; m. Alma R. Zito, Aug. 31, 1952 (div. 1981); children: Leslie, David (dec.), Diana (dec.); m. Dianne R. Sagner, Apr. 17, 1992. BS, U. Calif., Berkeley, 1953, MS, 1954, PhD, 1958. Dir. biochem. and insecticide rsch. Stauffer Chem. Co., Mountain View, Calif., 1957-79; dir. agrichem. research Zoecon Corp., Palo Alto, Calif., 1979-85; nat. program leader crop protection Agrl. Rsch. Svc., USDA, Beltsville, Md., 1985-88, assoc. dep. area dir. Beltsville Agrl. Rsch. Ctr., 1988-94, ret. 1994; internat. cons. crop protection & agr. biotechnology, 1994—; chmn. Gordon Rsch. Conf., 1989; adj. prof. environ. toxicology San Jose State U., Calif., 1979-84; adj. prof. entomology U. Md., College Park, 1986—, internat.cons. Crop Protection and Agrl. Biotech., 1994—; mem. U.S./USSR Team on Environ. Pollution, 1974-85; tech. expert UNIDO, 1995—. Editor: Insect Juvenile Hormones, 1972, Insect Neuropeptides, 1991, 10 other tech. books; contbr. over 125 articles to profl. jours.; pioneered pesticide metabolism studies and research on selective insect control agents including juvenile hormones and neuropeptides; patentee in field. Recipient Bussart Meml. award Eastern Br. Entomol. Soc. Am., 1990, Ciba-Geigy Recognition award, Eastern Br. Entomol. Soc. Am. 1991, 92. Mem. Am. Chem. Soc. (fellow pesticide chem. div. 1973, chmn. 1976, councilor 1981-89, adv. bd. books dept. 1991-94, Burdick & Jackson Internat. award for rsch. in pesticide chem. 1979, Internat. Soc. Study Xenobiotics (councilor 1983-86), Cosmos Club (Washington).

MENNA, CHRISTINE ANN, public relations executive; b. Johnstown, Pa., Dec. 4, 1955; d. Joseph and Cecilia (Wojnaroski) Pisczek; m. Thomas Menna, Oct. 20, 1984; 1 child, Elizabeth. BA in Journalism, U. Pitts., 1977. Copywriter, account exec. Accent-Midstate Advt., Johnstown, Pa., 1977-85; mgr. corporate comm. Crown Am. Realty Trust, Johnstown, 1985—, dir. corp. comm., 1995—; pub. rels. cons. Johnstown Chiefs, 1990—. Mem. adv. bd. Salvation Army, Johnstown, 1989—; bd. dirs. United Way, Johnstown, 1993—. Mem. Nat. Orgn. Underwater Instrs. (open water I diver), Internat. Coun. Shopping Ctrs. Avocations: sewing, ice skating, scuba diving. Office: Crown Am Realty Trust Pasquerilla Plz Johnstown PA 15901

MENNEL, TIMOTHY MCKISSON, magazine editor; b. Cambridge, Mass., May 17, 1968; s. Robert McKisson and Gisela Irmgard (Gebhart) Mennel-Bele. BA, Carleton Coll., Northfield, Minn., 1989. Editor Comico the Comic Co., Norristown, Pa., 1989-90; editl. asst. Princeton (N.J.) U. Press, 1990-91, prodn. editor, 1991-94; mng. editor Philosophy and Pub. Affairs, Princeton, 1993-94, Artforum Internat., N.Y.C., 1994—. Collaborator (performance art): Why Do People?, 1995. Figurehead The New Nothing, Bklyn., 1994—. Recipient Haldeman prize for notable misapprehension The New Nothing, 1995. Mem. Players Club. Avocations: cultural exploration, cooking, beer brewing, community outreach. Home: 134 Ft Greene Pl Brooklyn NY 11217 Office: Artforum Internat 65 Bleecker St New York NY 10012

MENNICKE, AUGUST THEODORE, church officer; b. Reeseville, Wis., July 4, 1931; s. Victor A.W. and Helen (Lau) M.; m. Joyce Scheidt, Aug. 21, 1954; children: Sheryll, Steven, David, Susan, Philip. Student, Concordia Coll., 1950; BA, St. Louis Concordia Sem., 1955; LittD (hon.), Concordia Coll., 1974; DD (hon.), Concordia Sem., 1974. Pastor St. John, Aitkin, Minn., 1955-62, Immanuel, Aitkin, Zion, Crosby, Minn., 1955-62, Prince of Peace, Ozark, Ala., 1962-63; exec. counselor Minn. North Dist., 1963-70, pres., 1970-86; 1st v.p. Luth. Ch.-Mo. Synod, St. Louis, 1986—. Author: My Devotions, 1978, Portals of Prayer, 1984, 90; contbr. essays and articles to jours.; mem. editl. com. for ofcl. publs., 1975-79. Mem. Coun. of Pres., 1970—, chmn., 1982-86; mem. steering com. Alive in Christ, 1984-86, Com. for Luth. Coop., 1986—; mem. bd. regents St. Louis and Ft. Wayne sems., 1986-92; bd. dirs. LSS of Minn., 1970-86; mem. steering com. Am. Bible Soc., 1994—. Office: 1333 S Kirkwood Rd Saint Louis MO 63122-7226

MENNINGER, EDWARD JOSEPH, public relations executive; b. N.Y.C., 1931; s. Edward Joseph and Pauline Loretta (Sessa) M.; m. Catherine Ann Giordano, Nov. 1, 1952 (div. 1978); children: Christopher, Catherine, Carl, Carolyn, Lisa; m. Ann Clementine Hunt, Jan. 5, 1979. B Social Sci. magna cum laude, Fordham U., 1952. Retail adv. sales promotion Sears, Roebuck and Co., N.Y.C., 1958-62; pub. rels. exec. Sears, Roebuck and Co., Chgo., N.Y.C., 1962-72; sr. buyer, buyer Sears, Roebuck and Co., N.Y.C., 1972-73; nat. mdse. mgr. Sears, Roebuck and Co., Chgo., N.Y.C., 1973-81; v.p., group mgr. Burson-Marsteller, N.Y.C., 1981-87, sr. v.p. consumer retail mktg., 1987-92, mng. dir., 1992-93, exec. v.p., 1993—, dir. employee devel. and tng. for N.Y. and Americas region; mem. comm. mgmt. adv. com., Syracuse U. Sch. Pub. Comm., 1996; mem. exec. bd. N.Y. Yeats Soc., 1996; lectr. in field. Contbr. articles to profl. jours. Mem. comms. mgmt. adv. com. Sch. Pub. Comms., Syracuse U., 1995. With M.I., U.S. Army, 1953-55. Mem. PRSA (accredited, edn. affairs commr. 1982-85, 87-88, v.p. Chgo. chpt. 1971-72, Chmn.'s Cert. of Recognition 1969, 73, 76, 84, 91, 92, Toth award Washington chpt. 1983, Silver Anvil award 1983, 89, 92, Big Apple award N.Y. chpt. 1991, 93, 94), Pub. Rels. Student Soc. Am. (profl. advisor 1983-84, Recognition award 1992), Am. Sch. Counselors Assn. (mem. bus. adv. bd. 1995). Office: Burson-Marsteller 230 Park Ave S New York NY 10003-1513

MENNINGER, ROSEMARY JEANETTA, art educator, writer; b. N.Y.C., Feb. 2, 1948; d. Karl Augustus and Jeanetta (Lyle) M. BA, Washburn U., 1983, BFA, 1984. Cert. tchr., Kans. Rsch. specialist, grant writer Navajo Tribe Navajo Community Coll., Many Farms, Ariz., 1969, 71; adminstrv. asst., counselor San Francisco Drug Treatment Program, 1972-73; exec. dir. Inst. Applied Ecology, San Francisco, 1973-80; coord. Calif. Community Gardening program Gov.'s Office State of Calif., Sacramento, 1976-80; editor Whole Earth Catalogs and CoEvolution Quar., Sausilito, Calif., 1973-80; editor, rsch. specialist Dept. Agr. Scis. Colo. State U., Ft. Collins, 1980-81; instr. Mulvane Art Ctr., Topeka, 1982-86, 90—; art tchr. Topeka Pub. Schs., 1985—. Author: Community Gardening in California, 1977; editor: (newspaper) California Green, 1977-80; contbr. articles to profl. jours. Mem. San Francisco Parks and Recreation Open Space Commn., 1975-78; mem. master plan task force Calif. State Fair, Sacramento, 1978-80; commr. Gov.'s Commn. on Children and Families, Topeka, 1988-89; bd. dirs. The Villages, Inc., 1989—. Democrat. Presbyterian. Avocations: painting, gardening, swimming. Home: 1819 SW Westwood Cir Topeka KS 66604-3269

MENNINGER, ROY WRIGHT, medical foundation executive, psychiatrist; b. Topeka, Oct. 27, 1926; s. William Claire and Catharine (Wright) M.; m. Beverly Joan Miller, Mar. 4, 1973; children: Heather, Ariel, Bonar, Eric, Brent, Frederick, Elizabeth. AB, Swarthmore (Pa.) Coll., 1947; MD, Cornell U., 1951; DHL, Ottawa (Kans.) U., 1977; LittD, William Jewell Coll., Liberty Mo., 1985. Diplomate Am. Bd. Psychiatry and Neurology, 1959. Intern N.Y. Hosp., 1951-52; resident in psychiatry Boston State Hosp., 1952-53, Boston Psychopathic Hosp., 1953-56; from resident psychiatrist to assoc. med. psychiatrist Peter Bent Brigham Hosp., Boston, 1956-61; teaching and rsch. fellow Harvard U. Med. Sch., Boston, 1956-61; staff psychiatrist Menninger Found., Topeka, 1961-63, dir. dept. preventative psychiatry, 1963-67, pres., CEO, 1967-93; chmn., 1991—; bd. dirs. Bank IV Topeka N.A., CML Corp., The New Eng., U.S. Behavioral Health; mem. Karl Menninger Sch. Psychiatry, Topeka, 1972—, Ind. Sector, 1990—; clin. prof. psychiatry U. Kans. Med. Ctr., Wichita, 1977—; cons. Colmery-O'Neil VA Med. Ctr., Topeka, 1979—. Author: Trends in American Psychiatry: Implication for Psychiatry in Japan; co-author: The Medical Marriage, 1988, The Psychology of Postponement in the Medical Marriage; cons. editor Jour. Medical Aspects Human Sexuality, 1967-90; editor adv. bd. Parents mag., 1966-80, Clin. Psychiatry News, 1973—; reviewer Am. Jour. Psychiatry, 1980—. Mem. sponsoring com. Inst. Am. Democracy, 1967-70; mem. adv. group Horizons '76 Am. Revolution Bicentennial Commn.; adv. bd., steering com. Topeka Inst. Urban Affairs, 1967-70; adv. bd. Highland Park-Pierce Neighborhood House, Topeka, 1967-70; bd. dirs. Shawnee council Campfire Girls, Topeka, 1962-69, A.K. Rice Inst., Washington, Sex Info. and Edn. Council U.S., 1972-73, mem. edn. com., long range planning com., 1972-73; bd. dirs. Goals for Topeka, Topeka Inst. Urban Affairs, 1969-74, v.p., 1973; med. adv. com. VA Hosp., 1972-78; mem. Gov.'s Com. on Criminal Adminstrn., 1971-74; trustee People-to-People, Kansas City, Mo., 1967-69, Baker U., 1968-72, Midwest Research Inst., 1967-1986, 86—, mem. exec. com., 1970-86; vis. lectr. Fgn. Service Inst., State Dept., 1963-66; chmn. social issues com. Group Advancement Psychiatry, 1972-82; community adv. bd. Kans. Health Workers Union, 1968-70; adv. com. to bd. dirs. New Eng. Mut. Life Ins. Co., 1968-70. With U.S. Army, 1953-55. Recipient Disting. Svs. citation U. Kans., 1985; Pacific Rim Coll. Psychiatry fellow. Fellow Am. Psychiat. Assn. (life), Joint Info. Svc. (exec. com.), Am. Coll. Psychiatry, Am. Orthopsychiat. Assn., Am. Coll. Mental Health Adminstrs.; mem. AAAS, Northeastern Group Psychotherapy (hon.), Physicians Social Responsibility, Kans. Psychiat. Soc., Greater Topeka C. of C. (dir.). Episcopalian. Avocations: stamp collecting, chamber music, microcomputers. Office: Menninger Found PO Box 829 Topeka KS 66601-0829

MENNINGER, WILLIAM WALTER, psychiatrist; b. Topeka, Oct. 23, 1931; s. William Claire and Catharine Louisa (Wright) M.; m. Constance Arnold Libbey, June 15, 1953; children: Frederick Prince, John Alexander, Eliza Wright, Marian Stuart, William Libbey, David Henry. A.B., Stanford U., 1953; M.D., Cornell U., 1957; LittD (hon.), Middlebury Coll., 1982; DSc (hon.), Washburn U., 1982; LHD (hon.), Ottawa U., 1986; LLD (hon.), Heidelberg Coll., 1993. Diplomate: Am. Bd. Psychiatry and Neurology, Am. Bd. Forensic Psychiatry. Intern Harvard Med. Service, Boston City Hosp., 1957-58; resident in psychiatry Menninger Sch. Psychiatry, 1958-61; chief med. officer, psychiatrist Fed. Reformatory, El Reno, Okla., 1961-63; assoc. psychiatrist Peace Corps, 1963-64; staff psychiatrist Menninger Found., Topeka, 1965—, coordinator for devel., 1967-69, dir. law and psychiatry, 1981-85, dir. dept. edn., dean Karl Menninger Sch. Psychiatry and Mental Health Scis., 1984-90, exec. v.p., chief of staff, 1984-93; pres., chief exec. officer Menninger Found., 1993—; clin. supr. Topeka State Hosp., 1969-70, sect. dir., 1970-72, asst. supt., clin., dir. residency tng., 1972-81; pres., chief exec. officer Menninger Clinic, Topeka, 1991—; staff Stormont-Vail Hosp., Topeka, 1984-94, assoc., 1994—; clin. prof. Kans. U. Med. Coll.; adj. prof. Washburn U., Wichita State U.; instr. Topeka Inst. for Psychoanalysis; mem. adv. bd. Nat. Inst. Corrections, 1975-88 , chmn., 1980-84; cons. U.S. Bur. Prisons; mem. Fed. Prison Facilities Planning Council, 1970-73; bd. dirs. Mercantile Bank Topeka (formerly Mchts. Nat. Bank, Topeka). Syndicated columnist: In-Sights, 1975-83; author: Happiness Without Sex and Other Things Too Good to Miss, 1976, Caution: Living May Be Hazardous, 1978, Behavioral Science and the Secret Service, 1981, Chronic Mental Patient II, 1987; editor: Psychiatry Digest, 1971-74; mem. editorial bd. Bull. Menninger Clinic, 1985—; contbr. chpts. to books, articles to profl. jours. Mem. nat. health and safety com. Boy Scouts Am., 1970-92, chmn., 1980-85, mem. nat. exec. bd., 1980-90, mem. nat. adv. coun., 1990—; mem. Kans. Gov.'s Adv. Commn. on Mental Health, Mental Retardation and Community Mental Health Svcs., 1983-90; bd. dirs. Nat. Com. for Prevention Child Abuse, 1975-83; mem. nat. adv. health coun. HEW, 1967-71; mem. Nat. Commn. Causes and Prevention Violence 1968-69, Kans. Gov.'s Penal Planning Coun., 1970; chmn. Kans. Gov.'s Criminal Justice Adv. Commn., 1991-94, rsch. adv. com. U.S. Secret Svc., 1990—; trustee Kenworthy-Swift Found., 1980—; ruling elder 1st Presbyn. Ch., Topeka, 1992-95; active Ks. Gov.'s Commn. on Crime Reduction and Prevention/Koch Commn. 1994—; dir. Police Found., Washington, 1996—; trustee Midwest Rsch. Inst., Kansas City, Mo., 1996—. With USPHS, 1959-64. Fellow ACP, Am. Psychiat. Assn. (chmn. com. on chronically mentally ill 1984-86, chmn. Guttmacher award bd. 1990-96), Am. Coll. Psychiatrists; mem. AAAS, AMA, Group for Advancement of Psychiatry (chmn. com. mental health svcs. 1974-77, 91—), Inst. Medicine NAS, Am. Psychoanalytic Assn. (chmn. com. on psychoanalysis, community and society 1984-93), Am. Acad. Psychiatry and Law, Stanford (Univ.) Assocs. Office: Menninger Found PO Box 829 Topeka KS 66601-0829

MENNIS, EDMUND ADDI, investment management consultant; b. Allentown, Pa., Aug. 12, 1919; s. William Henry and Grace (Addi) M.; m. Selma Adinoff, Sept. 25, 1945; children: Ardith Grace, Daniel Liam. B.A., CCNY, 1941; M.A., Columbia U., 1946; Ph.D., NYU, 1961. Security analyst Eastman, Dillon & Co., N.Y.C., 1945-46; sr. research asst. Am. Inst. Econ. Research, Great Barrington, Mass., 1946-50; security analyst Wellington Mgmt. Co., Phila., 1950-61; dir. research Wellington Mgmt. Co., 1958-61, v.p., mem. investment com., 1958-66, economist, 1953-66; sr. v.p., chmn. trust investment com. Republic Nat. Bank, Dallas, 1966-72; sr. v.p., chmn. investment policy com. Security Pacific Nat. Bank, Los Angeles, 1973-81; pres., dir. Bunker Hill Income Securities, Inc., 1973-81; chmn. bd. Security Pacific Investment Mgrs., Inc., 1977-81; ind. cons. to investment mgmt. orgns., 1982—; Tech. cons. Bus. Council, Washington, 1962-66, 72-77, 79-81; econ. adviser sec. commerce, 1967-68; mem. investment adv. panel Pension Benefit Guaranty Corp., 1981-83. Assoc. editor: Financial Analysts Jour., 1960-88; editor: C.F.A. Digest, 1971-86, Bus. Econs., 1985—, Bank Funds Mgmt. Report, 1993—; author or editor books, chpts., numerous articles in field of econs. and investments. Trustee Fin. Analysts Research Found., 1981-86. Served to 1st lt. USAAF, 1942-45; to capt. USAF, 1951-53. Fellow Nat. Assn. Bus. Economists (coun. 1967-69), Fin. Analysts Fedn. (dir. 1970-72, Graham and Dodd award 1972, Molodovsky award 1972); mem. Am. Econ. Assn., Am. Fin. Assn., N.Y. Soc. Security Analysts, L.A. Soc. Fin. Analysts, Conf. Bus. Economists (vice chmn. 1977, chmn. 1978), Inst. Chartered Fin. Analysts (pres. 1970-72, trustee 1968-74, C. Stewart Sheppard award 1978). Home: 721 Paseo Del Mar Palos Verdes Estates CA 90274 Office: PO Box 1146 Palos Verdes Estates CA 90274

MENO, JOHN PETER, chorepiscopus; b. Carlinville, Ill., Aug. 22, 1942; s. John Victor and Margaret Mary (Cena) M.; m. Rolanda A. Abyad, Sept. 14, 1968; 1 child, Peter James. MA, Am. U. Beirut, 1969; STM, Union Theol. Sem., 1972. Ordained priest Syrian Orthodox Ch. of Antioch, 1972, elevated to chorepiscopus, 1983. Gen. sec. Archdiocese of Syrian Orthodox Ch. in U.S. and Can., Lodi, N.J., 1972—; cathedral rector St. Mark's Syrian Orthodox Cathedral, Teaneck, N.J., 1975—; co-sec. Standing Conf. of Oriental Orthodox Chs. in Am., N.Y.C., 1973—; co-chmn. U.S. Roman Cath.-Oriental Orthodox Cons., 1989—. Editor: Hymns of the Syrian Orthodox Church of Antioch, 1976. Recipient Golden Cross of the Archdiocese of the Syrian Orthodox Ch. in U.S., and Can., 1992. Home: 263 Elm Ave Teaneck NJ 07666-2323 Office: St Marks Syrian Orthodox Cathedral 260 Elm Ave Teaneck NJ 07666-2323

MENO, LIONEL R., state education official. Commr. edn. Tex. Edn Agy., Austin; dist. supt. Board of Corp. Education Services, Angola, NY. Office: Board of Corp. Education Svcs 8685 Erie Rd Angola NY 14004*

MENOHER, PAUL EDWIN, JR., army officer; b. West Palm Beach, Fla., July 20, 1939; s. Paul E. and Gladys (Bingaman) M.; m. Kay I. Craddock; 1 child, Scott A.; m. Bebe Doris Etzler, Aug. 21, 1980. BA in Polit. Sci., U. Calif., Berkeley, 1961; MS in Internat. Rels., George Washington U., 1972. Commd. 2d lt. U.S. Army, 1961, advanced through grades to lt. gen., 1995; student USN Coll. Command and Staff, Newport, R.I., 1971-72, U.S. Army War Coll., Carlisle, Pa., 1977-78; chief plans br. Hdqrs. U.S. Army Forces Command, Ft. McPherson, Ga., 1978-79, chief combat intelligence div., 1979-81; chief collection div. Hdqrs. U.S Army Europe, Heidelberg, Fed. Republic Germany, 1981-82; G2 VII Corps, Stuttgart, Fed. Republic Germany, 1982-84; comdr. 501st Mil. Intelligence Brigade, Seoul, Republic of Korea, 1984-86; dir. U.S. Army Intelligence and Electronic Warfare Master Plan, Washington, 1986-89; comdg. gen. U.S. Army Intelligence Agy., Washington, 1987-89, U.S. Army Intelligence Ctr., Ft. Huachuca, Ariz., 1989-93, U.S. Army Intelligence and Security Command, Ft. Belvoir, Va., 1993-94; dep. chief of staff for intelligence Dept. Army, Washington, 1994—. Mem. Assn. U.S. Army, Armed Forces Comms. and Electronics Assn., Nat. Mil. Intelligence Assn., Assn. Old Crows. Avocations: tennis, jogging. Office: Dept Army Hdqs The Pentagon Washington DC 20310

MENON, MANI, urological surgeon, educator; b Trichur, Kerala, India, July 9, 1948; came to U.S., 1972, naturalized, 1977; s. Balakrishna and Sumathie Menon; m. Shameem Ara Begum, Oct. 17, 1972; children: Nisha, Roshen. MBBS, Madras U., India, 1971. Diplomate Am. Bd. Urology. Intern Bryn Mawr (Pa.) Hosp., 1973-74; resident Brady Urol. Inst., The Johns Hopkins Hosp., Balt., 1974-80; asst. prof. urology Washington U. Med. Ctr., St. Louis, 1980-83, assoc. prof., 1983; prof. urology, chmn. div. urology and transplant surgery U. Mass. Med. Ctr., Worcester, 1983—; prof. physiology, U. Mass. Med. Ctr., Worcester, 1986—. Mem. AAAS, Am. Assn. Genito Urinary Surgeons, Am. Urol. Assn. (Gold Cytoscope award 1990), Am. Fedn. Clin. Rsch., Am. Soc. Transplantation and Vascular Surgery, Rschrs. on Calculus Kinetics, Johns Hopkins Med. and Surg. Assn., Mass. Med. Soc., Mass. Soc. Med. Rsch. Avocations: tennis, puzzles, mystery fiction. Office: U Mass Med Ctr Div Urology Worcester MA 01655

MENOTTI, GIAN CARLO, composer; b. Cadegliano, Italy, July 7, 1911; came to U.S., 1928; s. Alfonso and Ines (Pellini) M. Grad. in composition, Curtis Inst. Music, 1933, Mus.B. (hon.), 1945. Tchr. Curtis Inst. Music, 1941-45. Writer chamber music, songs and operas; composer: (operas) Amelia al ballo, 1936, The Old Maid and the Thief, 1939, The Island God, 1942, The Medium, 1945 (Pulitzer Prize for music 1950), The Telephone,

1947, The Consul, 1949; Amahl and the Night Visitors, 1951, The Saint of Bleecker Street, 1954 (Pulitzer Prize for music 1955, Drama Critics' Circle Award 1955, New York Music Critics' Award 1955), Maria Golovin, 1958, The Last Savage, 1963, Labyrinth, 1963, Martin's Lie, 1964, Help, Help, the Globolinks, 1968, The Most Important Man, 1971, Arrival, 1973, Tamu-Tamu, 1973, The Egg, 1976, The Hero, 1976, The Trial of the Gypsy, 1978, Chip and His Dog, 1979, La loca, 1979, The Mad Woman, 1979, St. Teresa, 1982, A Bride from Pluto, 1982, The Boy Who Grew Too Fast, 1982, Goya, 1986, Giorino di Nozze, 1988; (symphonies/orchestral) Pastorale and Dance, 1934, (from Amelia al ballo) Prelude, 1937, (from The Old Maid and the Thief) Prelude, 1939, (from The Island God) Two Interludes, 1942, Piano Concert in F, 1945, Sebastian, 1945, Apocalypse, 1951, Introduction, March Shepherds' Dance, 1951, Violin Concerto, 1952, Triple Concerto a tre, 1970, Fantasia, 1975, Symphony No. 1: The Halcyon, 1976, Double Bass Concerto, 1983; (chamber/instrumental) Variations on a Theme of Schumann, 1931, Six Compositions, 1934, Four Pieces, 1936, Trio for a House-Warming Party, 1936, Poemetti per Maria Rosa, 1937, Ricercare e toccata, 1949, Suite, 1973, Cantilena scherzo, 1977; (vocal/choral) Baba's Aria, 1946, The Black Swan, 1946, Monica's Waltz, 1946, Lucy's Aria, 1947, Magda's Aria, 1950, Shepherd's Chorus, 1951, The Hero, 1952, The Death of the Bishop of Brindisi, 1963, Canti della lontananza, 1967, Landscapes and Remembrances, 1976, Missa o pulchritudo, 1979, Four Songs, 1981, Notturno, 1982, Muero porque no muero, 1982; (ballets) Sebastian, 1944, Errand in the Maze, 1947, The Unicorn, the Gorgon and the Manticore, or The Three Sundays of a Poet, 1956; writer own libretti.; Founder: Festival of Two Worlds, Spoleto, Italy, 1958; composer, artistic dir. Spoleto Festival USA, Charleston, S.C., 1988—. Recipient Guggenheim award, 1946, 47; Honary associate, Nat'l Inst. for Arts and Letters, 1953, Kennedy Ctr. award, 1984, N.Y.C. Mayor's Liberty award, 1986; George Peabody Medal, Johns Hopkins Univ., 1987; named Musician of Yr., Musical Am., 1991. Mem. ASCAP. Address: Yester House, Gifford East Lothian EH41 4JF, Scotland

MENSCHEL, RICHARD LEE, investment banker; b. N.Y.C., Jan. 6, 1934; s. Benjamin and Helen (Goldsmith) M.; m. Ronay Arlt, Aug. 21, 1974; children: Charis, Sabina, Celene. B.S., Syracuse U., 1955; M.B.A., Harvard U., 1959. Assoc. securities sales adminstr. Goldman, Sachs & Co., N.Y.C., 1959-67; v.p. Goldman. Sachs & Co., N.Y.C., 1967-69; ptnr. securities sales Goldman, Sachs & Co., N.Y.C., 1969-88, mgmt. com., 1980-88, ltd. ptnr., 1988—; bd. dirs. T. Rowe Price. Co-chmn. City of N.Y. Transitional Gov. Search Panel, 1977; pres., bd. dirs. Joffrey Ballet Found., 1977-79; bd. dirs. Nat. Corp. Fund for Dance, 1977-79; trustee Fed. Protestant Welfare Agys., 1978-81, The Hastings Ctr., Nightingale Bamford Sch., The Jewish Mus., Nantucket Conservation Found., Storm King Art Ctr.; mng. dir. Horace W. Goldsmith Found., 1980—; bd. dirs. Mcpl. Art Soc., 1980-92; trustee, mem. exec. com. George Eastman House, Rochester, N.Y., 1980-94, Vera Inst. Justice, 1989—, Pierpont Morgan Libr.; trustee, treas., mem. exec. com. N.Y. Acad. Medicine; mem. vis. com. Harvard Grad. Sch. Bus. Adminstrn., 1985-91; dean's coun. Harvard Sch. Pub. Health; mem. exec. com. on univ. resources, co-chair Harvard U. campaign; mem. adv. bd. Mus. Modern Art, Oxford, 1987—; co-chmn., trustee Hosp. for Spl. Surgery. 2d lt. USAF, 1955-56. Clubs: India House, Harvard. Home: 660 Park Ave New York NY 10021-5963 Office: Goldman Sachs & Co 85 Broad St New York NY 10004-2434

MENSCHEL, ROBERT BENJAMIN, investment banker; b. N.Y.C., July 2, 1929; s. Benjamin and Helen (Goldsmith) M.; m. Joyce Virginia Frank, Dec. 5, 1968; children: David F., Lauren E. BS, Syracuse U., 1951, LLD (hon.), 1991; postgrad., NYU, 1951-53. Mem. N.Y. Stock Exchange, N.Y.C., 1950-51; specialist HW Goldsmith and Co., N.Y.C., 1951-54; with Goldman, Sachs & Co., N.Y.C., 1954-66, gen. ptnr. instl. sales, 1966-78, ltd. ptnr., 1979—. V.p. bd. trustees, mem. fin. and exec. com. Temple Emanu-El, N.Y.; trustee Mus. Modern Art, mem. investment com., co-chmn. photography com.; trustee Inst. Advanced Study Princeton; trustee, exec. com. Syracuse U., Montefiore Hosp., N.Y., Guild Hall, East Hampton, past chmn. bd.; pres. bd. trustees, exec. com. Dalton Sch., N.Y.C.; past bd. advs. Grad. Sch. Inst. Internat. Bus. Pace U.; mem. exec. bd. N.Y. chpt. Am. Jewish Com.; bd. dirs., mem. fin. and budget com. N.Y. Pub. Library, N.Y.C.; bd. dirs. Parks Council; bd. dirs., v.p. Emanu-El Midtown YMHA; mng. dir. Horace W. Goldsmith Found.; bd. trustees Mus. Modern Art; bd. dirs. associated YM-YWHA; mem. Pres. Clinton's com. on the arts and the humanities. Recipient George Arents medal Syracuse U., 1984. Mem. Investment Assn. N.Y. Clubs: India House, City Athletic (N.Y.C.); Dunes Racquet (East Hampton, N.Y.). Home: 920 5th Ave New York NY 10021-4160 also: Further East Ln Amagansett NY 11930 Office: Goldman Sachs & Co 85 Broad St New York NY 10004-2434

MENSCHER, BARNET GARY, steel company executive; b. Laurelton, N.Y., Sept. 5, 1940; s. Samuel and Louise (Zaimont) M.; student Centenary Coll., 1958-59; B.B.A., U. Tex., 1963; m. Diane Elaine Gachman, June 12, 1966; children—Melissa Denise, Corey Lane, Scott Jay. Vice pres. mktg. Ella Gant Mfg., Shreveport, La., 1964-66; warehouse mgr., dir. material control Gachman Steel Co., Fort Worth, 1966-68, gen. mgr., Houston, 1968-70, v.p., sales mgr. Gulf Coast, 1971-76; pres. Menko Steel Service, Inc., Houston, 1979—; v.p., treas. Gachman Metal Co.; investment cons. D & L Enterprises, 1966—. Mem. solicitation com. United Fund, 1969-76; mem. Nat. Alliance of Businessmen Jobs Program, 1969—. Served with AUS, 1963-65. Mem. Tex. Assn. Steel Importers, Purchasing Agts. Assn. Houston, Credit Assn. Houston, Am. Mgmt. Assn., Assn. Steel Distbrs., Nat. Assn. Elevator Contractors, Phi Sigma Delta, Alpha Phi Omega. Home: 314 Tealwood Dr Houston TX 77024-6113 Office: PO Box 40296 Houston TX 77240-0296

MENSE, ALLAN TATE, research and development engineering executive; b. Kansas City, Mo., Nov. 29, 1945; s. Martin Conrad Mense and Nancy (Tate) Johnson; children from previous marriage: Melanie Georgia, Eileen Madelaine. BS, U. Ariz., 1968; MS, U. So. Ariz., 1970; PhD, U. Wis., 1976. Scientist Oak Ridge (Tenn.) Nat. Lab, 1976-79; mem. sr. staff Sci. and Tech. commn. U.S. Ho. Reps., Washington, 1979-81; sr. scientist McDonnell Douglas Astro. Co., St. Louis, 1981-85; dep. chief scientist Dept. Def. Strategic Def. Initiative Orgn., Washington, 1985-86, chief scientist, 1986-88; v.p. for rsch. Fla. Inst. Tech., Melbourne, 1988-92; pres. Advanced Tech. Mgmt., Inc., Arlington, Va., 1992-95; vis. scholar Sloan Sch., MIT, 1995—; bd. dirs. F.I.T. Aviation, Inc. Contbr. over 60 articles to profl. jours. Mem. AIAA (sr. mem.), IEEE (chmn. energy com. 1985—, sr. mem.), Am. Def. Preparedness Assn., Am. Phys. Soc., Am. Nuclear Soc., Fla. Com. Nat. Space Club (charter), Navy League, Sigma Xi, Theta Tau. Episcopalian. Home: Ste G1 16 Vandine St Cambridge MA 02141 Office: PO Box 410440 Cambridge MA 02141-0005

MENSES, JAN, artist, draftsman, etcher, lithographer, muralist; b. Rotterdam, Netherlands, Apr. 28, 1933; emigrated to Can., 1960, naturalized, 1965; s. Jan and Elisabeth Wilhelmina (Schwarz) M.; m. Rachel Régine Kadoch, Dec. 7, 1958; children: Salomon, Hnina Sarah, Nechamah Elisabeth Halo. Student, Acad. Fine Arts, Rotterdam, Officers Acad. Royal Dutch Air Force, 1953-55. lectr. in fine arts Concordia U., Montreal, 1973-76, others. One-man shows include Montreal Mus. Fine Arts, 1961, 65, 76, Isaacs Gallery, Toronto, Ont., Can., 1964, Delta Gallery, Rotterdam, 1965, Galerie Godard Lefort, Montreal, 1966, Gallery Moos, Toronto, 1967, Rotterdam Art Found., 1974, Galerie Mira Godard, Toronto, 1977, Montreal, 1978, Seasons Gallery, The Hague, 1980, U. B.C. Fine Arts Gallery, Vancouver, 1981, Galerie Don Stewart, Montreal, 1981, Mead Art Mus., Amherst, Mass., 1983, Agnes Etherington Art Mus., 1984, Blom and Dorn Gallery, N.Y.C., 1985, Marywood Coll. Mus., Scranton, Pa., 1985, Blom & Dorn Gallery, N.Y.C., 1986-93, Saraya-Wolfson Ctr., Safed, Israel, 1987, Mayanot Gallery, Jerusalem, 1987-88, Esperanza Gallery, Montreal, 1988, 89, Gallery Hamaayan Haradum, Safed, Israel, 1989-93, 94, 95, Blom & Dorn Gallery, Hartford, Conn., 1995, Nora Gallery, Jerusalem, 1995, Artist's Colony, Safed, Isreal; over 300 group shows include Montreal World Exhbn., 1967, Salon Internat. Art, Basel, Switzerland, 1972, 74, Can. Nat. Exhbn., 1972, Centennial Exhbn., Royal Can. Acad., Toronto, 1980, Que. Biennale I, II, III, Montreal, 1977, 79, 81, Foire Internat. D'Art Contemporain Paris and Internat. Fair Koln Germany, 1986, Migdal Ha-Emek, Israel, 1988, Group of 8 Israel, Toronto, 1990, Royal Can. Acad. Show, Toronto, 1991; represented in permanent exhbn. Gallery Hamaayan Haradum, Safed, Profl. Artists' Assn., Artists Colony, Safed; represented in permanent collections Museo Ciani di Villa Caccia, Lugano, Switzerland, The Art Gallery of Hamilton, Ont.,Can., David Giles Carter Collection, New Haven, Gallery of Nova Scotia-Halifax, Can, Jewish Public Libr. Collection, Montreal, Can., Cadillac Fairview Collection, Toronto, Can, Museum Modern Art, N.Y.C., Phila. Mus. Art, Solomon R. Guggenheim Mus., N.Y.C., Yivo Inst., N.Y.C., Bklyn. Mus., Art Inst. Chgo., Cleve. Mus. Art, Detroit Inst. Arts, Yale U., U. Montreal, Queens U., Kingston, Mead Art Mus., Amherst Coll., Jonathan Edwards Coll., New Haven, Victoria & Albert Mus., London, Vatican Mus., Rome, Quebec Art Bank, Concordia U., Montreal, Haifa Mus. Modern Art, Hebrew U., Jerusalem, Govt. of Que., Yad Vashem Holocaust Meml., Jerusalem, Mus. Boymans-van Beuningen, Rotterdam, Stedelijk Mus., Amsterdam, Rijksmuseum, Amsterdam, Nat. Gallery Can., Ottawa, Gallery Stratford, Montreal Mus. Fine Arts, Musée d'Art Contemporain, Montreal, Que. Provincial Mus., Que. Art Bank, Art Bank of the Can. Coun., Ottawa, Ariz. State Mus., Tucson, Hebrew U., Jerusalem, City of Safed-Israel, Holocaust Meml. Ctr., Toronto, Lavalin Mus. Coll, Montreal, Oshawa Mus., Ont., Dept. External Affairs Govt. Can., Ottawa, Can. Jewish Congress Mus., Montreal, Israel Mus., Jerusalem, McGill U., Montreal, Olympia & York Collection, Toronto, CBC Collection, Montreal, Kingston (Ont.) U. Mus. Collection, N.Y. Pub. Libr., Worcester (Mass.) Art Mus., Currier Gallery Art, Manchester, N.H., Art Gallery of U. N.H., Durham, Mus. Art. RISD, Providence, Olympia & York Collection, Toronto, Collection Rishon Le'Zion, Jerusalem, Rose Art Mus., Brandeis U., Waltham, Mass., C.I.L. Collection Montreal, Tel Aviv U., McGill U. Coll., Montreal, Can. Jewish Congress Mus., Montreal, Young Israel of Montreal (Coll.), Can., Confedn. Art Ctr., Charlottetown-Prince Edward Island, Can.; paintings include Klippoth Series, 1963-78, Kaddish Series, 1964-80, Hechaloth Series, 1973—, Tikkun Series, 1978—; mural for, Montreal Holocaust Meml. Center. Mem. Pres.'s Coun. of U. N.H. Served with Royal Dutch Air Force Res., 1953-55. Recipient 5 1st prizes Nat. Art Exhbn., Quebec, Que., 1960-65; Grand prize Concours Artistiques de la Province de Que., 1965; prize X and XI Winnipeg (Man., Can.) Shows, 1966, 68; prize IX Internat. Exhbn. Drawings and Prints, Lugano, 1966; prize Ofcl. Centennial Art Competition, Toronto; 1st prize Hadassah, 1969, 71, 82; Recipient Imago award U. Montreal, 1971; award Reeves of Can., 1969; Tigert award Ont. Soc. Arts, 1970; Loomis and Toles award, 1972; J. I. Segal award J. I. Segal Fund Jewish Culture, 1975; Gold medal Accademia Italia Delle Arte, Italy, 1980; Gold medal Internat. Parliament U.S.A., 1982; Gran Premio delle Nazioni, Italy, 1983, European Banner of Arts with Gold medal, 1984, Oscar d' Italia, 1985, 1st prize III Que. Biennale, 1981, OSA award of merit, Toronto, 1981, 82; World Culture prize Italy, 1984; Golden Flame of World Parliament (U.S.A.) award, 1986; Ish Shalom award Jerusalem, 1993; numerous others; Can. Council sr. arts fellow, 1969-70, 71-72, 81-82; grantee, 1966-67, 67-68; travel grantee, 1968, 73. Mem. Royal Can. Acad. Arts, Acad. Italia Arte e del Lavoro, Acad. Nazioni, Maestro Accademico-Accademia Bedriacense (Italy), Jewish Am. Acad. Arts and Scis., Israeli Art Assn. (Telaviv), Israel Assn. Profl. Artists Safed, Acad. Europa, Academician Italy, Israel Assn. Visual Art (Jerusalem). Jewish. Office: care Blom & Dorn Gallery 140 Huyshope Ave Hartford CT 06106 *My works have dealt with death, the eclipse of faith, exile, the Galut. They are shaped by my childhood experiences, real and imagined, in Nazi-occupied Europe; influenced by and rooted in my principles and standards of conduct as an Orthodox Jew in the post-holocaust/pre-Messianic era. They are an attempt to translate these experiences into visual contemporary terms (imagery conflicts and reconciliations of conflicts) in order to ascend from the personal/specific to the universal/general. They are a lament, an elegy, a denial and confirmation, an expression of the attitude of the soul in its debasement and dignity towards its Creator; a striving towards serenity in anticipation of the Redemption: a form of prayer.*

MENSON, RICHARD L., lawyer; b. Chgo., Nov. 10, 1943; s. John Lewis and Elizabeth Eileen (Carroll) M.; m. Lynne Patricia Lemke, Apr. 24, 1971; children: Melissa Lynne, Kristin Anne. BA, Ripon Coll., 1965; JD, Northwestern U., 1968; LLM in Taxation, George Washington U., 1973. Bar: Ill. 1968, U.S. Dist. Ct. (no. dist.) Ill. 1973, U.S. Ct. Mil. Appeals 1968, U.S. Ct. Claims 1973, U.S. Tax Ct. 1975. Commd. lt. U.S. Army, 1965, advanced through grades to capt., with JAG office, 1965-73, resigned, 1973; assoc. Gardner, Carton & Douglas, Chgo., 1973-77, ptnr., 1977—. Mem. bd. edn. Oak Grove Sch. Dist. #68, Libertyville, Ill., 1983-87; elder First Presbyn. Ch., Libertyville, 1979-83, mem. bd. deacons, 1975-79. Mem. ABA, Ill. State Bar Assn., Chgo. Bar Assn., Lake County Bar Assn., Legal Club Chgo., Conway Farms Golf Club, Army Navy Country Club, Profit Sharing Coun. Am. (legal and legis. com.). Presbyterian. Home: 1000 Ashley Ln Libertyville IL 60048-3813 Office: Gardner Carton & Douglas 321 N Clark St Chicago IL 60610-4714

MENTZ, HENRY ALVAN, JR., federal judge; b. New Orleans, Nov. 10, 1920; s. Henry Alvan and Lulla (Bridewell) M.; m. Ann Lamantia, June 23, 1956; children—Ann, Cahi, Hal, Frederick, George. B.A., Tulane U., 1941; J.D., La. State U., 1943. Bar: La. 1943, U.S. Dist. Ct. (ea. dist.) La. 1944. With legal dept. Shell Oil, New Orleans, 1947-48; pvt. practice Hammond, 1948-82; judge U.S. Dist. Ct. (ea. dist.) La., 1982—, sr. judge, 1992—. Editor: Combined Gospels, 1976. Pres. La. Soc. Music and Performing Arts, 1994—, L.A. Civil Service League, 1979-81; bd. dirs. Southeastern La. U. Found., Salvation Army; chmn. Tulane U. 50th Anniversary Reunion for 1991. Decorated 2 Battle Stars, Bronze Star; recipient Disting. Svc. award AMVETS, 1950. Mem. SAR, Royal Soc. St. George (pres.), Boston Club New Orleans, Delta Tau Delta. Republican. Episcopalian. Home: 2105 State St New Orleans LA 70118-6255 Office: US Dist Ct C-114 US Courthouse 500 Camp St New Orleans LA 70130-3313

MENTZER, JOHN RAYMOND, electrical engineer, educator; b. Arch Spring, Pa., June 16, 1916; s. Walter Ray and Katheryn Henderson (Barr) M.; m. Bernice Roslyn Simon, Feb. 17, 1945; children—Jacqueline Ferne, Richard Alan. B.S., Pa. State U., 1942, M.S., 1948; Ph.D., Ohio State U., 1952. Engr. Westinghouse Electric Corp., Balt., 1942-46, Ordnance Research Lab., 1946-48; research asso. Ohio State U., 1948-52; mem. staff Lincoln Lab., M.I.T., 1952-54; mem. faculty Pa. State U., 1954—, prof. engring. scis., 1956—, head dept. engring. sci. and mechanics, 1974-81, prof. emeritus engring. scis., 1981—. Author: Scattering and Diffraction of Radio Waves, 1955. Recipient Service award Pa. State U., 1979. Sr. mem. IEEE; mem. Am. Soc. Engring. Edn., AAAS, Sigma Xi. Home: 557 Clarence Ave State College PA 16803-3456 Office: 227 Hammond Bldg University Park PA 16802

MENUEZ, D. BARRY, religious organization administrator; b. Benton, Ohio, Feb. 28, 1933; s. Kyle LeRoy and Roxie Beulah (Rottman) M.; m. Mary Jane Sidley, Aug. 30, 1956 (div. 1974); children: Douglas, Stephanie, Jane, Ross; m. Jean Venable, June 30, 1989; 1 stepchild, Alan. BD, Kenyon Coll., 1955; MDiv, U. Chgo., 1971; LHD, Berkeley-Yale Div. Sch., 1990. Dir. office of ministries Episcopal Ch. Ctr., N.Y.C., dir. coun. for devel. of ministry, exec. edn. for mission and ministry, sr. exec. for missions ops., 1986—; v.p. Indsl. Areas Found., Garden City, N.Y., 1974—. 1st lt. USAF, 1955-57. Recipient Disting. Christian Svc. award Seabury-Western Theol. Sem., 1988. Home: 199 Davis Ave White Plains NY 10605-3215 Office: Episcopal Ch Ctr 815 2nd Ave New York NY 10017-4503

MENUHIN, YEHUDI, violinist; b. N.Y.C., Apr. 22, 1916; s. Moshe and Marutha M.; m. Nola Ruby Nicholas, May 26, 1938; children: Zamira, Krov; m. Diana Gould, Oct. 19, 1947; children: Gerard, Jeremy. Educated by pvt. tutors; studied music under, Sigmund Anker, Louis Persinger, San Francisco, Georges Enesco, Rumania and Paris, Adolph Busch, Switzerland; MusD (hon.), U. Oxford, 1962, Queen's U., Belfast, 1965, U. Leicester, 1965; LLD (hon.), U. St. Andrews, 1963, U. Liverpool, 1963, U. Sussex, 1966, U. Bath, 1969; LittD (hon.), U. Warwick, 1968; MusD (hon.), U. London, 1969, U. Cambridge, 1970. Pres. Halle Orch., 1992; Established Yehudi Menuhin Sch. at Stoke D'Abernon, Eng.; pres. Internat. Music Council of UNESCO, Folkestone Menuhin Internat. Violin Competition, Royal Philharmonic Orch., 1982—. Completed his first round-the-world concert tour, 1935; appearing in 110 concert engagements; has toured in Latin Am., S.Am., Australia, South Africa and Pacific Islands; played 22 concerts during 12 day tour in Israel; filmed series of complete concert programs; opened Japan to world concert artists, 1951, concert tours in India, 1952, 54, also charity concerts various instns.; has own yearly summer festival in Gstaad, Switzerland, 1957—; debut as condr. symphony orch. in Am. with Am. Symphony Orch., Carnegie Hall, 1966, dir., Bath Festival, Eng., 1958-68, Bath Festival Orch.; presented his first festival at Windsor, 1969; held over 500 concerts for armed forces, Red Cross, others; followed U.S. Army into, France and Belgium, first artist to play in liberated Paris, Brussels, Bucharest, Budapest and Antwerp, also first in Moscow after cessation of hostilities; prin. guest condr. English Sting Orch., 1988—; author: The Violin: Six Lessons by Yehudi Menuhin, 1971, Theme and Variations, 1972, The Violin and Viola, 1976, The King, the Cut, and the Fiddle, 1983, Life Class, 1986, The Compleat Violinist: Thoughts, Exercises and Reflections of a Humanist Violinist, 1986; autobiography Unfinished Journey, 1977; co-author: The Music of Man, 1979. Goodwill Amb. UNESCO, 1992. Decorated officer Legion of Honor; chevalier de L'Ordre des Arts et des Lettres (France); Order of Leopold (Belgium); Ordre de la Couronne (Belgium); Order of Merit (West German Republic); knight comdr. Order Brit. Empire (Gt. Britain); Royal Order Phoenix (Greece), Order of Merit (Gt. Britain); Gran Cruz de la Order del Gerito Civil (Spain); recipient Jawaharlal Nehru award for Internat. Understanding India, 1968, Mendelssohn prize, 1986, 10 Grammy awards, Golden Viotti prize, 1987, Glenn Gould prize Glenn Gould Found., 1990, Wolf prize in Arts, 1991. Fellow World Acad. Art and Sci.; mem. and/or officer numerous U.S., fgn. orgns. Research in expansion violin concert repertoire; introduced many rare and important works both classical and modern. Office: care Columbia Artists Mgmt 165 W 57th St New York NY 10019-2201 also: Menuhin Festival, Gstaad-Saanen/Alpengala, CH-3780 Gstaad Switzerland also: SYM Music Co, PO Box 6160, London SW1W OXJ, England

MENY, ROBERT, medical research administrator; b. Hackensack, N.J., Jan. 7, 1945; m. Janet Meny; children: Danielle, Ellen. BS, Tulane U., 1966; MD, Columbia U., 1971. Intern and resident in pediat. N.Y. Hosp., N.Y.C., 1971-73; fellow in neonatology U. Md. Hosp., Balt., 1975-77; mem. staff neonatal ctr. Rutgers Med. Sch., New Brunswick, N.J., 1977-80; dir. Hurley Neonatal Ctr., Flint, Mich., 1980-83; dir. Sudden Infant Death Syndrome Inst. U. Md., Balt., 1983—. Capt. USAFR. Mem. Am. Assn. Sudden Infant Death Prevention Physicians (pres.-elect 1995). Office: U Md SIDS Inst 22 S Greene St Rm N5W67 Baltimore MD 21201

MENYUK, PAULA, developmental psycholinguistics educator; b. N.Y.C., Oct. 2, 1929; d. Louis and Helen (Weissman) Nichols; m. Norman Menyuk, Mar. 5, 1950; children—Curtis R., Diane E., Eric D. B.S., NYU, 1951; Ed.M., Boston U., 1955, Ed.D., 1961. Chief lang. therapist Mass. Gen. Hosp., Boston, 1952-54; teaching fellow Boston U., 1957-60; NIMH postdoctoral fellow MIT, Cambridge, 1961-64, mem. research staff, 1964-72; prof. edn. Boston U., 1972, dir. div., vice chmn. faculty coun., 1981-87, chmn. faculty coun., 1990-91; cons. Children's Hosp., Boston, 1964-92, Kennedy Hosp., Boston, 1981-89, NIH, Bethesda, Md., 1972-80, 89-94, Nat. Found. March of Dimes, White Plains, N.Y., 1977-93; rsch. assoc. MIT, 1972-90. Author: Sentences Children Use, 1969, Acquisition and Development of Language, 1971, Language and Maturation, 1977, Language Development: Knowledge and Use, 1988, Early Language Development in Full-Term and Premature Infants, 1995. NIH fellow, 1958-64; Fulbright fellow, 1971, 88. Fellow Am. Speech, Lang. and Hearing Assn. (Disting. Svc. award 1976, highest honors 1992); mem. AAAS, Soc. Rsch. in Child Devel., Linguistic Soc. Am., Internat. Soc. Study Behavioral Devel., Am. Assn. Phonetic Scis. Home: 162 Mason Ter Brookline MA 02146-2772 Office: Boston U 605 Commonwealth Ave Boston MA 02215-1605

MENZEL, DIANA ANNA, small business owner; b. Trenton, N.J., Mar. 29, 1958; d. Rena (Paterra) M. Grad. high sch., West Trenton, N.J. Transit operator Ewing Bank & Trust, West Trenton, 1975-80; comms. operator N.J. State Police, Trenton, 1981-84; owner, mgr. Muscle Magic Fitness Ctr., Lambertville, N.J., 1984-86; carpenter Paul Raywood, Contractor, New Hope, Pa., 1987-90; head chef Marcella's Restaurant, Lambertville, 1984-87; chef, owner DeAnna's Restaurant, Lambertville, 1990—. Named N.J.'s Top 5 New Restaurants, N.J. Monthly mag., 1991, 3 1/2 Stars, Princeton Packet Restaurant Rev., 1991, My 50 Favorite Restaurants, Suzanne Goldenson, 1991, Top Restaurants in New Hope and Lambertville, N.J. Monthly mag., 1993. Mem. N.J. Police Acad., Lambertville C. of C. Avocations: skiing, surfing, carpentry weight lifting, snowboarding. Office: DeAnna s Restaurant 18 S Main St Lambertville NJ 08530-1827

MENZER, ROBERT EVERETT, toxicologist, educator; b. Washington, Dec. 21, 1938; s. Russell Ernest and Ora Taylor (Oates) M.; m. Sara Lee Gribbon, Dec. 29, 1962; children: R. Eric, Paul D., Joan Coleraine. B.S. in Chemistry, U. Pa., 1960; M.S., U. Md., 1962; Ph.D., U. Wis., 1964. Instr. U. Wis., Madison, 1964; mem. faculty U. Md., 1964-89, asst. prof. entomology, 1964-69, assoc. prof., 1969-73, prof., 1973-89, assoc. dean grad. studies and research, 1974-77, acting dean, 1977-80, chmn. grad. program marine-estuarine-environ. scis., 1978-89, dir. Water Resources Research Ctr., 1981-89; dir. environ. rsch. lab. EPA, Gulf Breeze, Fla., 1989-95; sr. sci. advisor EPA, Washington, 1995—; prof. emeritus U. Md., 1990—; chmn. hazardous substances data bank rev. panel Nat. Library Medicine, 1973—. Contbr. articles to profl. jours. Recipient U. Md. Alumni award, 1974. Fellow Washington Acad. Scis.; mem. AAAS, Am. Chem. Soc., Soc. Toxicology, Soc. for Environ. Toxicology and Chemistry, Sigma Xi, Phi Kappa Phi. Republican. Episcopalian. Club: Cosmos (Washington). Home: 1726 Seaton St NW Washington DC 20009-2626 Office: USEPA (8701) 401 M St SW Washington DC 20460

MENZIE, DONALD E., petroleum engineer, educator; b. DuBois, Pa., Apr. 4, 1922; s. James Freeman and Helga Josephine (Johnson) M.; m. Jane Cameron Redsecker, Nov. 6, 1946; children: Donald, William Lee, John Peter, Thomas Freeman. B.S in Petroleum and Natural Gas Engring., Pa. State U., 1942, M.S, 1948, Ph.D., 1962. Marine engr. Phila. Navy Yard, 1943-46; rsch. asst. air-gas dr. recovery Pa. State U., 1946-48, instr. petroleum and natural gas engring., 1948-51; asst. prof. petroleum engring. U. Okla., Norman, 1951-55, assoc. prof., 1955-64, prof., 1964-91, Kerr-McGee Centennial prof. Petroleum and Geol. Engring., 1991—, Halliburton Disting lectr., 1982-84; disting. lectr. Okla. U., 1986-87; dir. Sch. Petroleum and Geol. Engring U. Okla., Norman, 1963-72, petroleum engr. rsch. info. systems program, 1979-88, assoc. exec. dir. Energy Resources Ctr., 1988; assoc. exec. dir. Microbial Enhanced Oil Recovery Rsch. Project, Norman, 1982-; microbial enhanced oil recovery rsch. project U. Okla., 1982—; pres., owner Petroleum Engring. Educators, Norman, 1971—; cons. in field. Author: Reservoir Mechanics, 1954, Waterflooding for Engineers, 1968, Applied Reservoir Engineering for Geologists, 1971, New Recovery Techniques, 1975, Microbial Enhanced Oil Recovery, 1987, Dispersivity As An Oil Reservoir Rock Characteristic, 1989; contbr. articles to profl. jours. Mem. enhanced oil com. Interstate Oil and Gas Compact Commn., 1982-; commr., scoutmaster Last Frontier Coun. Boy Scouts Am., 1951-81; mem. adminstrv. bd. McFarlin United Meth. Ch., Norman, also sunday sch. tchr., pres. fellowship class, treas.; pres. Jackson PTA, Norman, 1962-68; treas. Cleveland County Rep. Com.; mem. Norman Park Commn., 1974-80; co-chmn., dir. Norman Parks Found., 1983-; mem. Cen. Com. U. Okla., 1987-. Mem. AIME, Am. Assn. Petroleum Geologists, Okla. Soc. Profl. Engrs., Nat. Soc. Profl. Engrs., Am. Soc. Engring. Edn., Soc. Petroleum Engrs., Am. Petroleum Inst., AAAS, Okla. Engring. and Tech. Guidance Coun., Okla. Anthopol. Soc., Soc. Petroleum Engrs. (recipient Nat. Disting. Achievement award for petroleum engring. faculty 1989), Sigma Xi, Pi Epsilon Tau, Alpha Chi Sigma, Phi Lamda Upsilon, Phi Kappa Phi. Clubs: Sportsmen of Cleve. County, Sooner Swim (dir. 1966-78). Lodge: Masons. Home: 1503 Melrose Dr Norman OK 73069-5366 Office: U Okla F314 The Energy Ctr Norman OK 73019

MENZIES, IAN STUART, newspaper editor; b. Glasgow, Scotland, Mar. 11, 1920; came to U.S., 1944, naturalized, 1948; s. John S. and Gertrude (Mephius) M.; m. Barbara Edith Newton, June 16, 1945; children: Marla Ann, Gillian Jean, Alexa Stuart, Deborah Newton. Student, Royal Tech. Coll., 1937-39; Nieman fellow, Harvard U., 1961-62; L.H.D., Salem State Coll., 1978. Reporter Boston Globe, 1948-57, sci. editor, 1957-63, fin. editor, 1963-65, mng. editor, 1965-70, assoc. editor, 1970-85; sr. fellow John McCormack Inst. Pub. Affairs, U. Mass., Boston, 1985—; vis. assoc. Joint Ctr. for Urban Studies, Mass. Inst. Tech.-Harvard, 1970-71. Mem. Hingham (Mass.) Sch. Com., 1962-68. Served to lt. Royal Naval Vol. Res., 1939-46. Decorated D.S.C.; recipient Pub. Service award Nat. Edn. Writers, 1961, Pub. Service award AAAS, 1963, Heywood Broun award, 1961, Sevellon Brown award, 1959, Rudolph Elie award, 1959, A.P. Big City award, 1958, U.P.I. award, 1959. Mem. Harvard Club, Hingham Yacht Club, Brit. Officers Club New Eng. Home: 479 Main St Hingham MA 02043-4705 Office: McCormack Inst U Mass Boston MA 02125

MENZIES, JOHN ALEXANDER, mechanical engineer; b. London, June 11, 1947; s. James and Rose (Howlett) M.; m. Jean Frances Kindell, Sept. 27, 1969; children: Cheryl Joanne, Heather Jean, Claire. Degree mech. engring., Harrow Coll., London, 1968; degree chem. engring., Southbank U., London, 1970. Piping designer M.W. Kellogg Co., London, 1963-68, mech. engr., 1968-70, project engr., 1970-71, process engr., 1971-73; project mgr. M.W. Kellogg Co., London and Houston, Tex., 1973-84; dir. proposals M.W. Kellogg Co., Houston, 1984-87, dir. ops., 1987-91, v.p. project mgmt., 1991—. Contbr. articles to profl. jours. Gov. Richmond Coll., London, 1990-91. Mem. AIChe, ASME, PMI. Avocations: tennis, golf, squash, fishing, bowling. Office: The MW Kellogg Co 601 Jefferson Houston TX 77210-4557

MEOLA, TONY, professional soccer player, actor; b. Belleville, N.J., Feb. 21, 1969; f. Vincent Meola m. Maria; w. Colleen. Student, U. Virginia, 1986-89. Goalkeeper CONCACAF World Cup Qualifying Games, 1989, U.S. World Cup Team, 1990, Brighton Football Club, England, 1990, Fort Lauderdale Strikers, Amer. Prof. Soccer League, 1991, U.S. Nat. Team, 1992-94, Long Island Roughriders, 1994-95, U.S. World Cup Team, 1994, NY-NJ MetroStars, Secaucus, 1996—; drafted ctr. fielder N.Y. Yankees; tried out as placekicker for N.Y. Jets, 1994. Appeared in play Tony N' Tina Wedding, 1995. Named Hermann Trophy winner, Mo. Athletic Club Player of Yr., 1989, MVP U.S. Cup, 1993. mem., N.J. State H.S. Soccer Champions, 1986, NCAA Division I Co-Champions, 1989. Office: care NY-NJ MetroStars One Harmon Plaza Secaucus NJ 07094*

MEOTTI, MICHAEL PATRICK, lawyer, former state legislator; b. New Britain, Conn., Oct. 30, 1953; s. Joseph John Sr. and Margaret Mary (O'Brien) M.; m. Pamela Goldman, June 16, 1990. BS in Fgn. Service cum laude, Georgetown U., 1975, JD cum laude, 1978. Atty. Updike, Kelly & Spellacy, P.C., Hartford, Conn., 1978-80; gen. counsel Ins. Assn. Conn., Hartford, 1980-85; counsel The Travelers Cos., Hartford, 1985-94; mem. Conn. State Senate, Hartford, 1987-95; ptnr. Shipman & Goodwin, Hartford, 1995—; chmn. environ. com. gen. assembly State of Conn., Hartford, 1987-89, transp. com., 1989-95. Mem. Bd. Edn., Glastonbury, Conn., 1979-83; mem. Town Council, Glastonbury, 1983-86, majority leader, 1985-86. Mem. Georgetown U. Alumni Club Conn. (pres. 1984-89). Democrat. Roman Catholic. Home: 56 Heather Glen Rd Glastonbury CT 06033-4161 Office: Shipman & Goodwin 1 American Row Hartford CT 06103-2833

MERACHNIK, DONALD, superintendent of schools. AB, Upsala Coll., 1951; MS, City Coll. of N.Y., 1952; PhD, N.Y. U., 1961. Supt. Union County Regional H.S., Springfield, N.J., 1971—. Named Nat. Supt. of Yr. for N.J., Am. Assn. Sch. Adminstrs., 1993. Office: Union Co Regional HSD Jonathan Dayton Regional HS Mountain Ave Springfield NJ 07081

MERAHN, STEVEN, communications executive; b. N.Y.C., Feb. 18, 1956; s. Alan George Davis and Elizabeth (Blumberg) Merahn; m. Nancy Groveman, May 18, 1980 (div. Jan. 1989); children: Alexander, David. BA, SUNY, New Paltz, 1977; MD, Albert Einstein Coll. Medicine, 1982. Instr. SUNY Coll. at New Paltz, 1976-78; cons., sr. specialist N.Y. City Dept. of Health, N.Y.C., 1985-91; pres. Cmty. Pediat. Inc., Yonkers, N.Y., 1988-91; sr. v.p. Burson-Marsteller, N.Y.C., 1991-93; mng. dir. Stratis Health Comm., N.Y.C., 1993—, Townhouse Comm. Group, Inc., N.Y.C., 1995—; exec. dir., founder Inst. for Health and Human Devel., N.Y.C., 1983-85; pediatrician-in-residence Bank Street Coll. Edn., N.Y.C., 1984; bd. advisors/mags. Childrens TV Workshop, N.Y.C., 1985-89; cons., media product devel. Scholastic Inc., N.Y.C., 1985-89; cons., trainer Fed. Region II Head Start, N.Y.C., 1986-91. Cons. Mayors Commn. on Early Childhood Edn., N.Y.C., 1989, N.Y.C. Bd. Edn. Adolescent Parenting Program. Office: Townhouse Comm Group 305 Madison Ave Ste 1166 New York NY 10165

MERANUS, ARTHUR RICHARD, advertising agency executive; b. Bklyn., May 27, 1934; s. Herbert and Dorothy (Newman) M.; m. Phyllis Ochitell, Sept. 21, 1958; children—Lisa, Leonard, Steven. Grad., Cooper Union, 1956. With Gaynor & Ducas, N.Y.C., 1961-63; with Norman, Craig & Kummel, Inc., N.Y.C., 1963-65; with Cunningham & Walsh Advt. Inc., N.Y.C., 1965-87, sr. v.p., 1978-87, creative dir., 1979-81, dir. creative svcs., 1981-87; mng. dir. creative svcs. N.W. Ayer, N.Y.C., 1987-88, exec. v.p., mng. dir. creative svcs., 1988—, also bd. dirs., 1988-96; creative dir. N.W. Ayer & Ptnrs., N.Y.C., 1996—. Served with USAR, 1956-57, 60-61. Recipient Clio award, Art Dirs. Club N.Y. award, One Show awards, Andy award, Effie award. Mem. Garden State Yacht Club (dir.). Office: NW Ayer & Ptnrs Inc Worldwide Plz 825 8th Ave Fl 35 New York NY 10019-7416

MERANUS, LEONARD STANLEY, lawyer; b. Newark, Jan. 7, 1928; s. Norman and Ada (Binstock) M.; m. Jane B. Holzman, Sept. 20, 1989; children: Norman, James M., David. LittB, Rutgers U., 1948; LLB, Harvard U., 1954. Bar: Ohio 1954. Assoc. Paxton & Seasongood, Cin., 1954-59, ptnr., 1959-85, pres., 1985-89; ptnr. Thompson, Hine and Flory, 1989—, ptnr.-in-charge Cin. office, 1989-91, mem. firm mgmt. com., 1991-93. Co-editor: Law and the Writer, 1978, 81, 85. Chmn. bd. dirs. Jewish Hosp., 1982-86; trustee Andrew Jergens Found., 1962—. Mem. ABA, Ohio Bar Assn., Internat. Bar Assn., Cin. Bar Assn., Am. Arbitration Assn. (Ohio, Ind., Ky. regional adv. com., chmn. comml. arbitration com., Ohio panel large, complex arbitration cases), Union Internationale des Avocats. Office: Thompson Hine & Flory 312 Walnut St Ste 14 Cincinnati OH 45202-4024

MÉRAS, PHYLLIS LESLIE, journalist; b. Bklyn., May 10, 1931; d. Edmond Albert and Leslie Trousdale (Ross) M.; BA, Wellesley Coll., 1955; MS in Journalism, Columbia U., 1954; Swiss Govt. Exchange fellow, Inst. Higher Internat. Studies, Geneva, 1957; m. Thomas H. Cocroft, Nov. 3, 1968. Reporter, copy editor Providence Jour., 1954-57, 59-61; feature writer Ladies Home Jour. mag., 1957-58; editor Weekly Tribune, Geneva, Switzerland, 1961-62; copyeditor, travel sect. N.Y. Times, 1962-68; mng. editor Vineyard Gazette, Edgartown, Mass., 1970-74, contbg. editor, 1974—; assoc. editor Rhode Islander, Providence, 1970-76; travel editor Providence Jour., 1976-95; editor Wellesley Alumnae mag., 1979—; assoc. in journalism U. R.I., 1974-75; adj. instr. Columbia U. Sch. Journalism, 1975-76. Author: First Spring: A Martha's Vineyard Journal, 1972, A Yankee Way With Wood, 1975, Miniatures: How to Make Them, Use Them, Sell Them, 1976, Vacation Crafts, 1978, The Mermaids of Chenonceaux and 828 Other Tales: An Anecdotal Guide to Europe, 1982, Exploring Rhode Island, 1984, Castles, Keeps and Leprechauns: Tales, Myths and Legends of Historic Sites in Great Britain and Ireland, 1988; co-author: Christmas Angels, 1979, Carry-out Cuisine, 1982, New Carry Out Cuisine, 1986, Eastern Europe: A Traveler's Companion, 1991, Rhode Island Explorer's Guide, 1995. Pulitzer fellow in critical writing, 1967. Mem. Soc. Am. Travel Writers. Home: Music St PO Box 215 West Tisbury MA 02575-9999 Office: Providence Jour 75 Fountain St Providence RI 02902-0050

MERAT, FRANCIS LAWRENCE, engineering educator; b. Frenchville, Pa., Aug. 22, 1949; s. Lawrence Clarence and Lucille Magdalen (DeMange) M. BSEE, Case Western Res. U., 1972, MSEE, 1975, PhDEE, 1978. Rsch. engr. Case Western Res. U., Cleve., 1978-79; asst. prof. engring. Case Western Res. U., Cleve., N.Y., 1979-85; assoc. prof. Case Western Res. U., Cleve., 1985—, exec. officer dept. elec. engring. and applied physics, 1994—; co-founder, sec./treas. PGM Diversified Industries, Inc., Parma Heights, Ohio, 1986—; fellow summer faculty program USAF, Griffiss AFB, N.Y., 1980, U.S. Army, Ft. Belvoir, Va., 1987; cons. ARTomation, Chagrin Falls, Ohio, NASA Lewis Rsch. Ctr.; mem. adv. bd. Cleve. Inst. Electronics. Contbr. articles to tech. jours. Named Disting. Advisor, Nat. Assn. Acad. Counseling and Advising, 1985. Mem. IEEE (sect. chmn. 1983-84, reviewer IEEE Robotics and Automation), Soc. Mfg. Engrs., Assn. Computing Machinery, Soc. Photo-optical Instrumentation Engrs., Sigma Xi. Roman Catholic. Avocations: photography, science fiction, movies. Home: 4398 Groveland Rd University Hgts OH 44118 Office: Case Western Res Univ 10900 Euclid Ave Cleveland OH 44106-7221

MERBAUM, MICHAEL, psychology educator, clinical psychologist; b. N.Y.C., Nov. 6, 1933; s. Max J. and Molly (Rubin) M.; m. Marta Ettinger, Nov. 18, 1962; children: Tal, Marc. BA, Drake U., 1954; MA, U. Mo., Kansas City, 1956; PhD, U. N.C., 1961. Diplomate Am. Bd. Clin. Psychology. Staff psychologist U. Chgo., 1961-64; asst. prof. Bowling Green (Ohio) State U., 1964-66; assoc. prof. Adelphi U., N.Y.C., 1966-72; prof. U. Haifa, Israel, 1972-78; prof., dir. clin. tng. Washington U., St. Louis, 1978—; corp. psychologist Wetterau, Inc., St. Louis, 1988—. Editor: Personality: Readings in Theory and Research, 1964, 3d edit., 1978, Behavior Change Through Self-control, 1973. Mem. Am. Psychol. Assn., Assn. for Advancement Behavior Therapy. Democrat. Jewish. Avocations: tennis, reading, music. Home: 825 Fairfield Lake Dr Chesterfield MO 63017-5926 Office: Washington U Dept Psychology Saint Louis MO 63130

MERCADANTE, ANTHONY JOSEPH, special education educator; b. Newark, N.J., Mar. 10, 1951; s. Anthony Joseph Jr. and Anna Rose (Cocuzzo) M.; m. Barbara Ferrari, May 27, 1979; children: Anthony, Lisa, David. BS in Edn., Seton Hall U., 1973; MA in Audiology and Communication Sci., Kean Coll., 1978; cert. in adminstrn. and supervision, U. S. Fla., 1987. Cert. audiologist, adminstr./supr., tchr. bus. edn., tchr. hearing impaired. Acctg. clerk supply div. U.S. Steel Corp., Newark, 1973-75; acctg. and bookkeeping instr. Sch. Data Programming, Union, N.J., 1976-78; bus. adminstrn. instr., curriculum coord. Roberts-Walsh Bus. Sch., Union, 1978-83; clin. audiologist Ea. Speech, Lang. and Hearing Ctr., Woodbridge, N.J., 1980-83; ednl. audiologist exceptional student edn. dept. Polk County Pub. Schs., Bartow, Fla., 1983—; advisor Fla. Audiologists in Edn., Orlando, 1987—; mem. multidisciplinary team Polk County Pub. Schs., 1983—; mem. planning com. Project Healthy Start, Polk County Pub. Schs., Bartow, 1994—. Baseball coach S. Lakeland Babe Ruth Baseball League, Lakeland, Fla., 1993, baseball mgr., 1994. Mem. Am. Speech, Lang. and Hearing Assn., Nat. Youth Sports Coaches Assn., Fla. Speech, Lang. and Hearing Assn., Scott Lake Elem. PTA. Avocations: tennis, golf, bowling, swimming, coaching. Home: 6122 Donegal E Lakeland FL 33813-3713 Office: Polk Life and Learning Ctr 1310 S Floral Ave Bartow FL 33830-6309

MERCER, DAVID ROBINSON, cultural organization administrator; b. Van Nuys, Calif., Aug. 14, 1938; s. Samuel Robinson and Dorothy (Lenox) M.; m. Joyce Elaine Dahl, Aug. 23, 1958; children: Steven, Michael, Kimberly. BA, Calif. State U., L.A., 1961. Exec. dir. YMCA of L.A., 1963-69, sr. v.p., 1969-80; reg. mgr. Am. City Bur., Hoffman Estates, Ill., 1980-82; pres. YMCA of San Francisco, 1982-90; nat. exec. dir. YMCA of USA, Chgo., 1990—; cons. fin. devel. YMCAs throughout U.S., 1975—. Mem. The Family, Rotary (bd. dirs. 1987-89). Republican. Methodist. Avocations: golf, bridge, flying, back packing. Office: YMCA of USA 101 N Wacker Dr Chicago IL 60606-1718

MERCER, DOUGLAS, lawyer; b. Sharon, Mass., Feb. 16, 1918; m. Pauline Loring Tobey, 4 children. AB, Harvard U., 1940, LLB, 1947. Bar: Mass. 1947. Ptnr. Ropes & Gray, Boston, 1957-90, of counsel, 1991—; moderator, panelist various Am. Law Inst.-ABA and other investment co. seminars. Former mem. and chmn. Planning Bd., Town of Weston, Mass., also former selectman, former mem. fin. com.; former trustee, treas. Social Law Library; chmn. Harvard Coll. Fund, 1975-77; chmn. Boston area Harvard Campaign for $350 Million; former mem. overseers resources com. Harvard U.; former trustee Groton Sch.; mem. corp. Belmont Hill Sch. Served to lt. comdr. USN, 1942-46, PTO. Mem. ABA, Boston Bar Assn. Clubs: The Country. Office: Ropes & Gray 1 Internat Pl Boston MA 02110-2624

MERCER, EDWIN WAYNE, lawyer; b. Kingsport, Tenn., July 19, 1940; s. Ernest LaFayette and Geneva (Frye) M. BBA, Tex. Tech U., 1963; JD, S. Tex. Coll. Law, 1971. Bar: Tex. 1971, U.S. Dist. Ct. (no. dist.) Tex 1975, U.S. Supreme Ct. 1976, U.S. Ct. Appeals (5th Cir.) 1979. Pvt. practice law Houston, 1971-73; gen. counsel, corp. sec. Alcon Labs., Inc., Ft. Worth, 1973-81; ptnr. Gandy Michener Swindle Whitaker Pratt & Mercer, Ft. Worth, 1981-84; v.p., gen. counsel, corp. sec. Pengo Industries, Inc., Ft. Worth, 1984-90, also bd. dirs. Bd. dirs. Soc. for Prevention Blindness, 1979—. Mem. ABA, State Bar Tex., Houston Bar Assn., Ft. Worth-Tarrant County Bar Assn., Coll. State Bar Tex., South Tex. Coll. Law Alumni Assn., Tex. Tech U. Ex-Assn., Ft. Worth Club, Delta Theta Phi, Phi Delta Theta. Methodist.

MERCER, LEE WILLIAM, lawyer, corporate executive, former government agency administrator; b. East Orange, N.J., July 16, 1943; m. Deborah Clare Robottom, Sept. 11, 1965 (div. Mar. 1980); children: James W., Charles A.; m. Deborah Anne O'Brien, Sept. 20, 1986; 1 child, Garrett W. BA, Dartmouth Coll., 1965; JD, Boston U., 1971, LLM in Tax, 1974. Ptnr. Sheehan, Phinney, Bass & Green, Manchester, N.H., 1971-80; counsel, legis. dir. U.S. Sen. Warren Rudman, Washington, 1981-84; v.p. The 1st Phillips Corp., Acton, Mass., 1985; dep. asst. sec. for trade adminstrn. U.S. Dept. Commerce, Washington, 1986-87, dep. under sec. for export adminstrn., 1887-89, dep. under sec. for tech., 1989-90; export mgr. Digital Equipment Corp., Washington, 1990-94; pres. U.S. Fiber Optics & Telecomms. Corp., 1994-95, Baraka Art & Frame Co., 1995-96, Nat. Assn. Small Bus. Investment Cos., 1996—. Served to cpl. USMC, 1966-68. Mem. N.H. Bar Assn. Republican. Office: NASBIC 1199 N Fairfax St Alexandria VA 22314

MERCER, LEONARD PRESTON, II, biochemistry educator; b. Ft. Worth, Jan. 16, 1941; s. Leonard Preston and Margie (Miller) M.; m. Diane Cottingham, Feb. 6, 1963; children: Cindy Louise, Timothy Clayton, Megan Hope. BS in Chemistry, U. Tex., 1968; PhD in Biochemistry, La. State U., 1971. NIH postdoctoral fellow U. Ala., Birmingham, 1971-73; instr. U. South Ala., Mobile, 1973-74, asst. prof., 1974-77; asst. prof. Oral Roberts U. Sch. Medicine, Tulsa, 1977-80, assoc. prof., 1980-84, prof., chmn. dept., 1984-90, assoc. dean biomed. scis., 1989-90; prof., chmn. dept. nutrition and food sci. U. Ky., Lexington, 1990—; cons. in math. modeling phys. responses and neurochemistry of appetite control. Contbr. articles to profl. jours., chapters in books. Fellow Am. Coll. Nutrition; mem. Am. Inst. Nutrition, Am. Chem. Soc., Am. Soc. for Biochemistry, Soc. Math. Biology. Avocations: reading, computer programming. Home: 4633 Spring Creek Dr Lexington KY 40515-1506 Office: U Ky 212 Funkhouser Bldg Lexington KY 40506

MERCER, MARGARET TEELE, medical and software marketing executive; b. Bronxville, N.Y., Sept. 10, 1962; d. William Earl Jr. and Judith (Forster) M.; m. Robert Mitchell Fromcheck, May 23, 1993. BS, U. Colo., 1985. Assoc. prodn. mgr. Prescription Products divsn. Fisons Pharms., Denver, 1988-92; mktg. mgr. HealthScan Products, Cedar Grove, N.J., 1992-93; account exec. Sandler Comm., N.Y.C., 1993-94; mktg. dir. Proctor Cos., Littleton, Colo., 1995—. Youth leader Calvary Ch., Denver, 1988-91. Mem. NAFE, Healthcare Bus. Assn. Avocations: athletics, travel, reading. Home: 2 Rose Clover Littleton CO 80127-2220

MERCER, MELVIN RAY, electrical engineer, educator; b. Lubbock, Tex., Sept. 5, 1946; s. Dixie Melvin and Ollie Faye (Sheppard) M.; m. Sharry Billene Cannon, Sept. 9, 1967; children: Rebecca Raylene, Elizabeth Anne. BSEE, Tex. Tech U., 1968; MSEE, Stanford U., 1971; PhD in Elec. Engring., U. Tex., 1980. Registered profl. engr., Tex. Rsch. and devel. engr. GTE Sylvania, Mountain View, Calif., 1968-73; mem. tech. staff Hewlett-Packard Labs., Palo Alto, Calif., 1973-77; lectr. U. Tex., San Antonio, 1977-80; mem. tech. staff Bell Labs., Murray Hill, N.J., 1980-83; asst. prof. elec. and computer engring. U. Tex., Austin, 1983-87, assoc. prof., 1987-91, prof., 1991-95; prof. computer engring. dept. elec. engring. Tex. A&M U., 1995—; lectr. Kilgore (Tex.) Jr. Coll., 1977; cons. Rothe Devel. Co., San Antonio, 1979, Lockheed Missiles and Space Co., Austin, 1983, IBM, Austin, 1984, 88-90, Harris Semiconductor, Dallas, 1983-86, State of Tex., Austin, 1984-85, CBS, N.Y.C., 1985-86, Teltech Resource Network, Mpls., 1986-93, Motorola Semiconductor, Austin, 1987-88, 91, TSSI, Beaverton, Ore., 1988—, MCC, Austin, 1989, Cimflex Teknowledge, Pitts., 1989-90, Integra-Test, L.I., N.Y., 1993, Teradyne, 1993-94, Sematech, 1994; advisor NSF, Washington, 1987-88, mem. engring. initiation awards evaluation panel, 1987, 1993; mem. program com. 1st MCC-Univ. Rsch. Symposium, 1987; lectr. in field. Contbr. articles to profl. jours.; patentee in field. Recipient Presdl. Young Investigator award NSF, 1986, rsch. award Office Naval Rsch., 1986-95, Advanced Projects Rsch. Adminstrn., 1992-95; Werner W. Dornberger Centennial tchg. fellow U. Tex., 1984-90, Engring. Found. endowed faculty fellow, 1990-91, Temple Found. endowed prof. engring., 1991-95; grantee Univ. Rsch. Inst., 1983, Bur. Engring. Rsch., 1984, AT&T Info. Sys., 1985-88, Microelectronics and Computer Tech. Corp., 1985-90, Internat. Test Found., 1986-89, Semicondr. Rsch. Corp., 1989-95, IBM, 1989-92, Tex. Advanced Tech. Program, 1990-92, Motorola, 1991-92. Fellow IEEE (editor Design and Test of Computers mag. 1985-88, mem. program com. design for testability workshop Vail, Colo. 1989—); mem. Computer Soc. of IEEE (vice chmn. Ctrl. Tex. chpt. 1983-85, chmn. 1985-86), Internat. Test Conf. (program com. 1986-89, program vice chmn. 1988, program chmn. 1989, steering com. 1988-93, mktg. vice chmn. 1990, planning chmn. 1992-93, best paper award 1982, hon. mention 1988), Internat. Conf. on CAD (program com. 1987), Design Automation Conf. (best paper award 1991), Austin C. of C. (recruitment resource 1983-87), Tau Beta Pi, Eta Kappa Nu, Phi Kappa Phi, Phi Eta Sigma. Avocations: racquetball, swimming, scuba. Office: Tex A&M U Dept Elec Engring 214 Zachry Bldg College Station TX 77843-3128

MERCER, RICHARD JOSEPH, retired advertising executive, freelance writer; b. Elizabeth, N.J., Mar. 29, 1924; s. George Washington and Margaret Elizabeth (Walsh) M.; m. Muriel Davis, June 24, 1945; children: Richard George, Karen, James Davis, Lesley Ann. L.B. in Journalism, Rutgers U., 1949. Announcer, copywriter, news reporter Sta. WCTC, New Brunswick, N.J., 1946-49; asso. creative dir., then v.p., dir. BBDO, Inc., N.Y.C., 1949-76; sr. v.p., creative exec. SSC&B, Inc., N.Y.C., 1977-83, exec. v.p. creative, 1983-85; sr. v.p., assoc. creative dir. McCann-Erickson, Inc., N.Y.C., 1985-87; part-time lectr. Rutgers U. Sch. Bus., New Brunswick, N.J., 1988-89; speaker in field. Chmn. Roselle (N.J.) Police Raise Referendum Com., 1958; promotion chmn. Cranford (N.J.) United Fund, 1960; publicity dir. Friends of Mendham (N.J.) Libr., 1974-75; bd. dirs. Friends of Nantucket Atheneum, 1991—; trustee Atheneum, 1993—. With A.C. USNR, 1943-45. Decorated Air medal.; Recipient 10 Clio awards, 2 Effie awards, also Silver Key award Advt. Writers Assn. N.Y.C. Mem. NATAS, Air Force Assn. (life), Col. Henry Rutgers Soc. Roman Catholic. Home: 24 Pleasant St Nantucket MA 02554-3374

MERCER, RONALD L., retired manufacturing executive; b. Camargo, Okla., Oct. 19, 1934; s. Joseph William and Lura (Dewald) M.; m. D. Yvonne Edwards, July 23, 1954; children: Gary D., Marla K., Lisa R., Michael D. BBA, So. Nazarene U., Bethany, Okla., 1970; HHD, So. Nazarene U., 1989; PMD, Harvard U., 1973. Br. sales mgr. Xerox Corp., Dallas, 1961-65; br. mgr. Xerox Corp., Oklahoma City, 1965-70; mgr. sales planning Xerox Corp., Rochester, N.Y., 1970-71; regional sales mgr. Xerox Corp., Chgo., 1971-74; regional v.p., gen. mgr. Xerox Corp., Greenwich, Conn., 1975-79; sr. v.p. Xerox Corp., Rochester, 1982-87; pres., chief exec. officer Xerox Can., Inc., Toronto, Ont., 1979-82; chmn., chief exec. officer Wilson Foods Corp. wholly owned subs. Doskocil Cos., Inc., Oklahoma City, 1988-89; pres., COO Doskocil Cos., Inc., 1989-91. Chmn. internat. Layman's Conf., Nashville, 1991; bd. dirs. So. Nazarene U., Internat. Ch. Nazarene, Kansas City, Kans; pres. Bethany (Okla.) Healthcare Corp. Republican. Mem. Ch. of Nazarene. Avocation: golf. Home: 7917 NW 38th St Bethany OK 73008-3141 Office: 3925 N Asbury Ave Bethany OK 73008-3329*

MERCEREAU, JAMES EDGAR, educator, physicist; b. Sharon, Pa., Apr. 3, 1930; s. James T. and S. Francis (Festermaker) M.; m. Gabriella Lengyel, Dec. 23, 1967; children: James A., Michael D., Steven F. B.A., Pomona Coll., 1953, Sc.D. (hon.), 1968; M.S., U. Ill., 1954; Ph.D., Calif. Inst. Tech., 1959. Research physicist Hughes Research Lab., 1954-59; asst. prof. physics Calif. Inst. Tech., 1959-62, prof., 1969—; prin. scientist Ford Sci. Lab., 1962-65; mgr. Ford Cryogenic Labs., 1965-69; Dir. R.A.I. Corp.; Mem. adv. com. NASA; mem. Nat. Acad. Com. Adv. to Nat. Bur. Standards. Contbr. articles profl. jours. Named one of America's 10 Outstanding Young Men U.S. Jr. C. of C., 1965; recipient achievement award in physics Am. Acad. Achievement, 1966. Fellow Am. Phys. Soc. Patentee in field. Home: 24652 El Camino Capistrano Dana Point CA 92629-3012 Office: 1201 E California Blvd Pasadena CA 91125-0001

MERCHANT, DONALD JOSEPH, microbiologist; b. Biltmore, N.C., Sept. 7, 1921; s. Oscar Lowell and Bess Lee (Clark) M.; m. Marian Adelaide Yeager, May 31, 1943; children—Nancy Adele, Barry Scott, Karen Ruth. A.B., Berea Coll., 1942; M.S., U. Mich., 1947, Ph.D., 1950. Instr. U. Mich., 1948-51, asst. prof., 1951-58, asso. prof., 1958-64, prof., 1964-69; dir., scientist W. Alton Jones Cell Sci. Center, Tissue Culture Assn., Lake Placid, N.Y., 1969-72; prof. U. Vt., 1969-72; prof., chmn. dept. microbiology and immunology Eastern Va. Med. Sch., Norfolk, 1973-86, prof. emeritus, 1986—; dir. Tidewater Regional Cancer Network, 1974-88; cons. U.S. Army Biol. Lab., 1966-68; mem. sci. adv. bd. Found. for Research on the Nervous System, Boston, 1965-69, Masonic Med. Research Lab., Utica, N.Y., 1970-75; mem. Nat. Prostatic Cancer Task Force, Nat. Cancer Inst., 1972-79, 83-86. Author: (with others) Handbook of Cell and Organ Culture, 1960, 2d edit., 1964; Editor: (with J.V. Neel) Approaches to the Genetic Analysis of Mammalian Cells, 1962, Cell Cultures for Virus Vaccine Production, 1968, (with others) Biology of Connective Tissues Cells, 1962; Contbr. (with others) chpts. to books, articles to profl. jours. Served with U.S. Army, 1944-46. Mem. Am. Acad. Microbiology, Am. Soc. Microbiology (past pres. Mich. br.), Soc. Exptl. Biology and Medicine, Am. Soc. Cell Biology, Tissue Culture Assn. (pres. 1964-68), Va. Acad. Sci., N.Y. Acad. Sci., Assn. Community Cancer Centers, Brit. Soc. Cell Biology, Royal Soc. Medicine. Presbyterian. Home: Apt 622 3100 Shore Dr Virginia Beach VA 23451

MERCHANT, ISMAIL NOORMOHAMED, film producer and director; b. Bombay, Dec. 25, 1936; arrived in U.S., 1958; s. Noormohamed and Hazrabi (Memon) Rehman. BA, St. Xavier's Coll., Bombay, 1958; MBA, NYU, 1960. V.p. Merchant Ivory Prodns. Inc., N.Y.C., 1962—. Prdor.: (Films) Creation of Woman, 1960, The Householder, 1963, Shakespeare Wallah, 1965, The Guru, 1969, Bombay Talkie, 1970, Adventures of a Brown Man in Search of Civilization, 1971, Savages, 1972, Helen, Queen of the Nautch Girls, 1973 (dir.), Mahtma and the Mad Boy, 1973, Autobiography of a Princess, 1975, The Wild Party, 1975, Sweet Sounds, 1976, Roseland, 1977, Hullabaloo Over Georgie and Bonnie's Pictures, 1978, The Europeans, 1979, The Five-Forty-Eight, 1979, Jane Austen in Manhattan, 1980, Quartet 1981, The Courtesans of Bombay, 1982, Heat and Dust, 1983, The Bostonians, 1984, A Room With A View, 1986, The Deceivers, 1988, Slaves of New York, 1988, Mr. and Mrs. Bridge, 1990, Howards End, 1992, The Remains of the Day, 1993, In Custody, 1993, Jefferson in Paris, 1995, The Proprietor, 1996; author: (books) Ismail Merchant's Indian Cuisine, 1986, The Making of the Deceivers, 1988, Ismail Merchant's Vegetarian Cuisine, 1991, Ismail Merchant's Florence, 1993, Ismail Merchant's Passionate Meals: The New Indian Cuisine for Fearless Cooks and Adventurous Eaters, 1994. Home: 400 E 52nd St New York NY 10022-6404 Office: 250 W 57th St Ste 1913A New York NY 10107

MERCHANT, KENNETH ALLEN, accounting educator; b. Troy, N.Y., Jan. 24, 1947; s. Reuben and Violet (Norden) M.; m. Gail Worth Merchant. AB, Union Coll., Schenectady, N.Y., 1968; MBA, Columbia U., 1969; PhD, U. Calif., Berkeley, 1978. CPA, Tex. Adminstr. Tex. Instruments, Inc., Dallas, 1970-73; cons. Ernst and Ernst, Dallas, 1973-74; assoc. U. Calif., Berkeley, 1976-77; cons. Donald Clark Assocs., San Francisco, 1976-77; asst. prof. Harvard U., Boston, 1978-85, assoc. prof., 1985—. Author: Control in Business Organizations, 1985, Fraudulent and Questionable Financial Reporting: A Corporate Perspective, 1987; contbr. articles to profl. jours. Peat Marwick Mitchell and Co. Found. grantee, 1979; Arthur Andersen and Co. Found. fellow, 1977-78. Mem. Am. Inst. CPA's, Am. Acctg. Assn., Fin. Execs. Inst., Nat. Assn. Accts., Beta Alpha Psi. Home: 2000 Derwood Dr La Canada CA 91011-1204 Office: Harvard U Grad Sch Bus Adminstrn Cotting 201 Boston MA 02163

MERCHANT, MYLON EUGENE, physicist, engineer; b. Springfield, Mass., May 6, 1913; s. Mylon Dickson and Rebecca Chase (Currier) M.; m. Helen Silver Bennett, Aug. 4, 1937; children: Mylon David (dec.), Leslie Ann Merchant Alexander, Frances Sue Merchant Jacobson. B.S. magna cum laude, U. Vt., 1936, D.Sc. (hon.), 1973; D.Sc., U. Cinn., 1941; D.Sc. (hon.), U. Salford, Eng., 1980; D of Engring (hon.), GMI Engring. and Mgmt. Inst., 1994. Research physicist Cinn. Milacron, Inc., 1940-48, sr. research physicist, 1948-51, asst. dir. research, 1951-57, dir. phys. research, 1957-63, dir. sci. research, 1963-69, dir. research planning, 1969-81, prin. scientist, mfg. research, 1981-83; dir. advanced mfg. research Metcut Research Assocs., Inc., 1983-90; sr. cons. Inst. Advanced Mfg. Scis., Cinn., 1990—; adj. prof. mech. engring. U. Cin., 1964-69; vis. prof. mech. engring. U. Salford, Eng., 1973—; hon. prof. U. Hong Kong, 1995—. Bd. dirs. Dan Beard council Boy Scouts Am., 1967-80, pres.'s council, 1980—. Recipient Georg Schlesinger prize City of Berlin, 1980; Otto Benedikt prize Hungarian Acad. Scis., 1981; ; named to Automation Hall of Fame, 1995. Fellow Soc.

Tribologists and Lubrication Engrs. (pres. 1952-53), Am. Soc. Metals Internat., Ohio Acad. Sci., Soc. Mfg. Engrs. (hon. mem., pres. 1976-77); mem. NAE, ASME (hon.), Internat. Instn. Prodn. Engring. Rsch. (hon., pres. 1968-69), Engrs. and Scientists of Cin. (pres. 1961-62), Fedn. Materials Socs. (pres. 1974), Phi Beta Kappa, Sigma Xi, Tau Beta Pi. Achievements include research on systems approach to manufacturing. Home: 3939 Erie Ave Apt 105 Cincinnati OH 45208-1913 Office: Inst of Advanced Mfg Scis 1111 Edison Dr Cincinnati OH 45216-2265

MERCHANT, ROLAND SAMUEL, SR., hospital administrator, educator; b. N.Y.C., Apr. 18, 1929; s. Samuel and Eleta (McLymont) M.; m. Audrey Bartley, June 6, 1970; children: Orelia Eleta, Roland Samuel, Huey Bartley. BA, NYU, 1957, MA, 1960; MS, Columbia U., 1963, MSHA, 1974. Asst. statistician N.Y.C. Dept. Health, 1957-60, statistician, 1960-63; statistician N.Y. TB and Health Assn., N.Y.C., 1963-65; biostatistician, adminstrv. coord. Inst. Surg. Studies, Montefiore Hosp., Bronx, N.Y., 1965-72; resident in adminstrn. Roosevelt Hosp., N.Y.C., 1973-74; dir. health and hosp. mgmt. Dept. Health, City of N.Y., 1974-76; from asst. adminstr. to adminstr. West Adams Community Hosp., L.A., 1976; spl. asst. to assoc. v.p. for med. affairs Stanford U. Hosp., Calif., 1977-82, dir. office mgmt. and strategic planning, 1982-85, dir. mgmt. planning, 1986-90; v.p. strategic planning Cedars-Sinai Med. Ctr., L.A., 1990-94; cons. Roland Merchant & Assocs., L.A., 1994—; clin. assoc. prof. dept. family, community and preventive medicine Stanford U., 1986-88, dept. health rsch. and policy Stanford U. Med. Sch., 1988-90. Served with U.S. Army, 1951-53. USPHS fellow. Fellow Am. Coll. Healthcare Execs., Am. Pub. Health Assn.; mem. Am. Hosp. Assn., Nat. Assn. Health Services Execs., N.Y. Acad. Scis. Home: 27335 Park Vista Rd Agoura Hills CA 91301-3639 Office: Roland Merchant & Assocs 27335 Park Vista Rd Agoura Hills CA 91301-3639

MERCIECA, CHARLES, philosophy and political science educator; b. Hamrun, Malta, Feb. 3, 1933; came to U.S. 1961; s. Carmelo and Julia (Brincat) M.; m. Sherry Jean Watson, May 15, 1950; children: Juliette, Alexander. BA in English, Loyola U., Malta, 1955; BA Philosophy, Aloisianum Coll., Varese, Italy, 1958; MS in Mgmt., Kans. State U., 1964; PhD, U. Kans., 1966. Prof. history, geography, philosophy and polit. sci. Ala. A&M U., Normal, 1967—; supr. Ala. A&M U., 1969-75, asst. to pres., 1987-91, dir. Inst. for Internat. Rels., 1988—; exec. v.p. Internat. Assn. of Educators for World Peace, Huntsville, Ala.; cons. UN, N.Y.C., 1973—, UNESCO, Paris, 1973—, Drug Rehab. prog., Montgomery, Ala., 1988—; vis. prof. Tver State U., Russia, 1992-93, U. Santa Ana, El Salvador, spring 1990. Author: Mismanagement in Higher Education, 1986 (citation 1987), Iscariots of Killversity, 1987 (citation 1988), Teaching Methods: On Making Classroom Instruction More Effective and Relevant, 1990, Education for Peace: What It Entails, 1991, Administrative Skills and the Development of the Human Potential, 1992, Perspective of Yeltsin's Russia: Problems and Challenges, 1994, A Malignant Tumor Develops on the United States Constitution, 1995. Recipient Ky. Col., 1983; Grand Cross of Honor & Merit, Federal Republic Germany, 1990; Albert Schweitzer Peace award, 1992. Mem. AAUP, NEA, Internat. Parliament for Safety and Peace (fed. magistrate 1987—), Internat. Assn. Educators for World Peace (sec.-gen. 1970-78, exec. v.p. 1978—), World Constn. and Parliament Assn. (trustee mem.). Office: Internat Assn Educators World Peace PO Box 3282 Huntsville AL 35810-0282

MERCIER, EILEEN ANN, management consultant; b. Toronto, Ont., Can., July 7, 1947; d. Thomas Sidley and Frances Katherine (Boone) Falconer; m. Ernest Cochrane Mercier, Jan. 29, 1980; children: Jenny, Sheelagh, Peter, Michael, Stuart. BA with honors, Waterloo Luth. U., 1968; MA, U. Alberta, 1969; fellow, Instn. Can. Bankers, 1975; MBA, York U., 1977. Mgr. corp. fin. Toronto-Dominion Bank, 1972-78, portfolio mgr. TD capital; dir., U.S. comm. ops. Canwest Capital Corp., Toronto, 1978-81; mgr. fin. strategy & planning Gulf Can. Ltd., Toronto, 1981-86, mgr. corp. fin.; v.p. The Pagurian Corp., Toronto, 1986-87; v.p., treas. Abitibi-Price, Inc., Toronto, 1987-88, v.p. corp. devel., 1989-90, sr. v.p., CFO, 1990-95; bd. dirs. C.I. Covington Fund, Inc., Reko Internat. Group Inc., Journey's End Corp., The CGI Group Inc., Winpak Ltd. Bd. dirs. Toronto Hosp. Found.; past chmn., mem. bd. govs. Wilfrid Laurier U., Waterloo, Ont. Recipient Outstanding Bus. Leader award Sch. Bus. & Econs., Wilfrid Laurier U., 1991. Office: Finvoy Mgmt Inc, 207 Queens Quay W Ste 680, Toronto, ON Canada M5J 2P5

MERCIER, FRANCOIS, lawyer; b. Paris, France, Apr. 13, 1923; s. Oscar and Jeanne (Bruneau) M.; m. Lucile Rouleau, May 25, 1946; children—Genevieve, Madeleine, Jean Francois, Helene. B.A., Loyola Coll., Montreal, Que., Can., 1942; LL.B., U. Montreal, 1945. Bar: Called to bar Que 1945. Since practiced in Montreal; sr. partner Stikeman, Elliott and predecessors, 1964—; lectr. ins. law U. Montreal, 1945-58. Pres. La Librairie Fernand Nathan Can. Ltée.; vice chmn. Société des Hôtels Méridien Can., Ltée. Decorated officer Order of Can. Fellow Am. Coll. Trial Lawyers; mem. Can. bar assns., Montreal bar assns. Home: One Spring Grove Crescent, Outremont, PQ Canada H2V 3H8 Office: Stikeman Elliott, 1155 Dorchester St, Montreal, PQ Canada

MERCORELLA, ANTHONY J., lawyer, former state supreme court justice; b. N.Y.C., Mar. 6, 1927; s. Sante and Josephine (Bozzuti) M.; m. Maria G. Delucia, June 16, 1956; children: Anne Mercorella Flynn, Susan Mercorella Creavin, Robert, Carole. B.A., L.I. U., 1949; LL.D., Fordham U., 1952. Bar: N.Y. Law asst. City Ct., City of N.Y., 1955-62; chief law asst. Civil Ct. City of N.Y., 1962-65; mem. N.Y. State Assembly, 1965-72; councilman City N.Y., 1973-75; judge Civil Ct. City of N.Y., 1975-79; justice Supreme Ct., N.Y.C., 1980-84; ptnr. Wilson, Elser, Moskowitz, Edelman & Dicker, N.Y.C., 1984—; currently arbitrator and mediator in various dispute resolution systems. Served with USN, 1945-46, Europe, Pacific. Mem. ABA (del. N.Y. State Bar Assn.), N.Y. State Bar Assn., Assn. of Bar of City of N.Y., Bronx County Bar Assn. (pres. 1971), Columbian Lawyers Westchester County (pres. 1984). Office: Wilson Elser Moskowitz Edelman & Dicker 150 E 42nd St New York NY 10017-5612

MERCOUN, DAWN DENISE, manufacturing company executive; b. Passaic, N.J., June 1, 1950; d. William S. and Irene F. (Micci) M. BS in Bus. Mgmt., Fairleigh Dickinson U., 1978. Personnel payroll coordinator Bentex Mills, Inc., East Rutherford, N.J., 1969-72; employment mgr. Inwood Knitting Mills, Clifton, N.J., 1972-75; gen. mgr. Consol. Advance, Inc., Passaic, 1975-76; v.p. human resources Gemini Industries, Inc., Clifton, 1976—; v.p., bd. dirs. Contact Morris-Passaic. Mem. Soc. for Human Resource Mgmt., Am. Compensation Assn., Internat. Found. Employee Benefits, Earthwatch Rsch. Team, IMA Mgmt. Assn. (bd. dirs., trustee 1996—), Daus. of the Nile (Maalas Temple No. 20, elective officer 1993-96, queen 1996—). Republican. Office: 179 Entin Rd Clifton NJ 07014-1424

MERCURIO, RENARD MICHAEL, real estate corporation executive; b. N.Y.C., June 22, 1947; s. Pasquale J. and Ann F. Mercurio; m. Abbie Gonzalez, June 29, 1968; children—Kristin, Allison. B.A., Queens Coll., N.Y.C., 1968; M.B.A., U. Rochester, 1969. CPA, N.Y.; lic. real estate broker, Calif. Sr. accountant Peat, Marwick & Mitchell, N.Y.C., 1969-73; mgr. Gulf & Western Industries, Inc., N.Y.C., 1973-78; v.p., treas. Famous Players Ltd., Toronto, Ont., Can., 1978-81; exec. v.p. Famous Players Realty Ltd., Toronto, 1981-84; v.p. Design Twenty-Seven Ltd., Toronto, 1984-87; pres. Renric Holdings, Ltd., 1987—; cranio sacral therapist Upledger Inst., 1995—. Mem. AICPA, N.Y. State Soc. CPAs, Calif. Assn. Mortgage Brokers, Calif. Assn. Realtors.

MERDEK, ANDREW AUSTIN, publishing/media executive, lawyer; b. Portland, Maine, Oct. 11, 1950; s. Philip and Eleanor (Weiss) M.; m. Jeanne Mullen, July 22, 1983; children: David, Jonathan. AB, Middlebury Coll., 1972; JD, U. Va., 1978. Bar: D.C. 1978, U.S. Dist. Ct. D.C. 1979, U.S. Ct. Appeals (D.C. cir.) 1979, U.S. Supreme Ct. 1982. Reporter, editor Portland Press Herald, 1973-75; assoc. Dow, Lohnes & Albertson, Washington, 1978-86, ptnr., 1986-87; v.p., gen. mgr. Atlanta Constitution and Journal, 1987-92; v.p. legal affairs, corp. sec. Cox Enterprises, Inc., Atlanta, 1993—. Mem. Order of Coif, Phi Beta Kappa. Home: 445 Mt Vernon Hwy NW Atlanta GA 30327-4313 Office: Cox Enterprises Inc 1400 Lake Hearn Dr NE Atlanta GA 30319-1464

MERDINGER, CHARLES JOHN, civil engineer, naval officer, academic adminstrator; b. Chgo., Apr. 20, 1918; s. Walter F. and Catherine (Phelan) M.; m. Mary McKelleget, Oct. 21, 1944; children: Anne, Joan, Susan, Jane. Student, Marquette U., 1935-37; BS, U.S. Naval Acad., 1941; BCE, Rensselaer Poly. Inst., 1945, MCE, 1946; DPhil (Rhodes scholar), Brasenose Coll., Oxford U., Eng., 1949; LHD (hon.), Sierra Nev. Coll., 1987; LLD (hon.), U. Nev., Reno, 1994. Registered profl. engr., Wis. Commd. ensign U.S. Navy, 1941, advanced through grades to capt., 1959; served aboard USS Nevada, USS Alabama Atlantic and Pacific, 1941-44; design, constrn. pub. works Panama, 1946-47, Washington, Bremerton, Wash., Adak, Alaska and Miramar, Calif., 1949-56; comdg. officer, dir. U.S. Naval Civil Engring. Lab., Port Hueneme, Calif., 1956-59; pub. works officer U.S. Fleet activities, Yokosuka, Japan, 1959-62; head English, history and govt. dept. U.S. Naval Acad., Annapolis, Md., 1962-65; asst. comdr. ops. & maintenance Naval Facilities Engring. Command, Navy Dept., 1965-67; pub. works officer Seabees (NSA), DaNang, Vietnam, 1967-68; comdg. officer Western div. Naval Facilities Engring. Command, San Bruno, 1968-70; pres. Washington Coll., Chestertown, Md., 1970-73; v.p. Aspen (Colo.) Inst. Humanistic Studies, 1973-74; dep. dir. Scripps Instn. Oceanography, La Jolla, Calif., 1974-80; dir. Avco, 1978—. Author: Civil Engineering Through the Ages, 1963; contbr.: articles to Ency. Britannica; others. Mem. Md., Calif., Oreg. and Nev. Selection Coms. for Rhodes Scholars, sec. Nev. Com., 1982-89; exec. vol. Boy Scouts Am.; sec., mem. exec. com. Md. Ind. Coll. and Univ. Assn., 1971-72; mem. So. Regional Edn. Bd, 1971-73, Nat. Com. History and Heritage of Am. Civil Engring., 1965-72; Alumni trustee U.S. Naval Acad., 1971-74; mem. coun. Rensselaer Poly. Inst., 1972—; trustee Found. for Ocean Rsch., 1976-80, Desert Rsch. Inst. Found., Nev., 1983-92, U. Nev. Reno Found., 1986-93; chmn. bd. trustees Sierra Nev. Coll., 1980-87, chmn. bd. emeritus, 1987; commr. N.W. Assn. Commn. on Colls., 1988-93. With Wis. Nat. Guard, 1935-37. Decorated Legion of Merit with combat V; named All-Am. in lacrosse, 1945, Papal Knoght Grand Cross Equestrian Order of Holy Sepulchre of Jerusalem, 1992; inducted into Rensselaer Athletic Hall of Fame, 1983; recipient Disting. Eagle Scout award, 1984. Fellow ASCE (Nat. History and Heritage award 1972), Explorers Club, Soc. Am. Mil. Engrs. (Toulmin medal 1952, 57, 61); mem. NSPE, Soc. History Tech., Am. Soc. Engring. Edn., Brasenose Soc., Pearl Harbor Survivors Assn., Nat. Eagle Scout Assn. (regent), Phalanx, Sigma Xi, Tau Beta Pi, Chi Epsilon. Roman Catholic. Clubs: Vincent's, Oxford. Home: 726 Tyner Way PO Box 7249 Incline Village NV 89452 also: 5538 Caminito Consuelo La Jolla CA 92037

MERDINGER, EMANUEL, retired chemistry educator; b. Suczawa, Austria, Mar. 29, 1906; came to U.S., 1947; s. Josef and Rosa (Stanger) M.; m. Raidie Poole, Mar 23, 1953. M of Pharmacology and Pharmacy, German U., Prague, 1931; D of Pharmacy, Ferrara (Italy) State U., 1934, D of Chemistry, 1935, D of Natural Scis., 1939. Assoc. prof. Ferrara State U., 1936-38, 45-47; prof. Roosevelt U., Chgo., 1947-72; rsch. assoc. U. Chgo., 1954-56; Disting. Lectr. Loyola U. Med. Sch., Maywood, Ill., 1972-76; sr. chemist rsch. Chem. & Bacteriological Lab., Gainesville, Fla., 1976-77; researcher U.S. Agrl. Lab., Gainesville, 1977-82; disting. prof. Dept. Entomol. Biochem. and Lang. Dept. U. Fla., Gainesville, 1978-91, U. Fla., 1980—; NAS exch. scientist to Romania, Bulgaria and Germany, 1971, 74, personal amb. to Romania; pres. Ill. State Acad. Sci., 1972-73, hon. mem.; head biochemistry sect. Roosevelt U. Mem. Am. Chem. Soc. (emeritus), Soc. Med. Balkanique (hon.), Union de Socs. (hon.), Med. Rumania (hon.). Avocations: playing the violin, composing little songs. Home: 4908 NW 16th Pl Gainesville FL 32605-3412

MEREDITH, BURGESS, actor; b. Cleve., Nov. 16, 1909; s. William George and Ida (Burgess) M.; m. Helen Berrian Derby, 1932 (div. 1935); m. Margaret H. Frueauff (Margaret Perry), 1936 (div. July 1938); m. Paulette Goddard, May 21, 1944 (div. July 1948); m. Kaja Sundsten, 1950; children: Jonathan Sanford, Tala Beth. Student, Amherst Coll., 1927-28, A.M. (hon.), 1939. Reporter, salesman, seaman, 1928-29; exec. dir. Actors Studio West, 1972—; artistic dir. Merle Oberon Theatre, L.A., 1972—; v.p. Actors Equity, 1938—, acting pres., spring 1938; chmn. adv. bd. Fed. Arts Projects, 1937. First small part with, Eva La Gallienne's Student Repertory Group, 1930; theatre appearances include Little Ol' Boy, 1933; She Loves Me Not, 1933, The Barretts of Wimpole Street, (with Katherine Cornell) Flowers of the Forest, 1935, Winterset, 1936 (Drama Critics award), High Tor, 1937 (Drama Critics award), Star Wagon, 1937, Five Kings, 1939, Liliom, 1941, Candida, 1942, Lincoln Portrait, 1943, The Playboy of the Western World, 1947, Winterset, 1947, Harvey, 1950, Let Me Hear the Melody, 1951, Lo and Behold! (dir.), 1951, The Remarkable Mr. Pennypacker, 1953, 58, Macbeth (dir.), 1954, Teahouse of the August Moon, 1955, Major Barbara, 1956, Speaking of Murder (producer), 1957, Ulysses in Nighttown (dir.), 1958, 74, Enrico IV, 1958, God and Kate Murphy (dir.), 1959, The Vagabond King, 1959, A Thurber Carnival (dir.), 1960, An Evening with Burgess Meredith, 1960, Midgie Purvis (dir.), 1961, A Whiff of Melancholy (dir.), 1961, Blues for Mr. Charlie (dir.), 1964, Park Your Car in Harvard Yard, 1984; motion pictures include Winterset, 1936; There Goes the Groom, 1937, Spring Madness, 1938, Idiot's Delight, 1938, Of Mice and Men, 1939, Castle on the Hudson, 1940, Second Chorus, 1941, San Francisco Docks, 1941, That Uncertain Feeling, 1941, Tom, Dick and Harry, 1941, The Forgotten Village, 1941, Street of Chance, 1942, Welcome to Britain, 1943, Salute to France, 1944, The Yank Comes Back, 1945, Story of G.I. Joe, 1945, The Diary of a Chambermaid, 1946, Magnificent Doll, 1946, On Our Merry Way, 1948, Mine Own Executioner, 1948, Jigsaw, 1949, The Man on the Eiffel Tower, 1950, The Gay Adventure, 1953, Joe Butterfly, 1957, Universe, 1961, Advise and Consent, 1962, The Cardinal, 1963, In Harm's Way, 1965, Madame X, 1966, The Crazy Quilt, 1966, A Big Hand for the Little Lady, 1966, Batman, 1966, Hurry Sundown, 1967, Fortune Garden, 1968, Stay Away Joe, 1967, Mackenna's Gold, 1967, There Was a Crooked Man, 1969, The Yin and the Yang (also writer, dir.), 1970, A Fan's Notes, 1970, The Clay Pidgeon, 1970, Such Good Friends, 1971, The Man, 1972, B for Murder, 1973, Golden Needles, 1973, Day of the Locust, 1973, The Hindenburg, 1974, 92 in the Shade, 1975, Burnt Offerings, 1975, Rocky, 1976 (Acad. award nomination), The Sentinel, 1977, Foul Play, 1978, Magic, 1978, The Manitou, 1978, Rocky II, 1979, The Day the World Ended, 1979, Clash of the Titans, 1979, Final Assignment, 1979, The Last Chase, 1979, When Time Ran Out, 1980, True Confessions, 1980, Rocky III, 1982, Wet Gold, 1984, Santa Claus-The Movie, 1984, Outrage, 1986, Mr. Corbett's Ghost, 1986, No Thing, 1988, Full Moon in Blue Water, 1988, State of Grace, 1990, Rocky V, 1990, Grumpy Old Men, 1993, Camp Nowhere, 1994, Tall Tale, 1994; producer, writer: Diary of a Chambermaid, 1946; producer, actor: On Our Merry Way, 1947; dir.: Man On The Eiffel Tower, 1948, The Latent Heterosexual, 1969; writer, dir., narrator: film Afterglow (on the life Robert Frost), 1986; various TV appearances, including World of Disney; dir. others; directed, N.Y. Symphony, Carnegie Hall, 1969; narrator numerous commls.; film Houdini, 1979; co-host: Those Amazing Animals, ABC-TV, 1980-81; filmed: documentary Myths of Ancient Greece, 1981; singer, narrator the dragon in Puff the Magic Dragon, Part II, 1979; appeared as Penguin in TV series Batman, 1965-66; author; So Far, So Good. Served with AUS, 1942-44, ETO. Episcopalian. Club: Players (N.Y.C.). *

MEREDITH, DALE DEAN, civil engineering educator, consultant; b. Centralia, Ill., Mar. 24, 1940; s. Leslie Edward Meredith and Beulah Marie (McClelland) Nattier; m. Linda Jean Hutson, July 3, 1965; children: Sarah Elizabeth, Laura Jane. AA, Centralia Twp. Jr. Coll., 1961; BS, U. Ill., 1963, MS, 1964, PhD, 1968. Registered profl. engr., N.Y., Ill. Asst. prof. U. Ill., Urbana, 1968-73; assoc. prof. civil engring. SUNY, Buffalo, 1973-79, prof., 1979—; chmn. Dept. Civil Engring., 1987—. Co-author: Design and Planning Engineering Systems, 1973, 2d edit., 1985; also over 50 articles. Vice pres. Baptist Conv. N.Y., Syracuse, 1982-84, 94-95, chmn. exec. bd., 1987. Grantee U.S. Office Water Research and Tech., 1966-73, 75-78, U.S. Dept. Interior, 1968-79, U.S. Dept. Commerce, 1976-79, various pvt. cos., 1979—, N.Y. State Agys., 1980—. Fellow ASCE (chmn. exec. com. Water Resources Planning and Mgmt. div., 1988, editor jour. Water Resources Planning and Mgmt. 1982-84); mem. Am. Geophys. Union, Am. Soc. Engring. Edn., Am. Water Resources Assn. (editor Water Resources Bull. 1990-91), Internat. Assn. Water Resources, Water Environ. Fedn. Office: SUNY Dept Civil Engring Buffalo NY 14260-4300

MEREDITH, ELLIS EDSON, association and business executive; b. Mobile, Ala., Sept. 5, 1927; s. Charles Elmer and Eleanor Emery (Ellis) M.; m. Alice Foley; children: Shane Snowdon, Kent Williamson, Scott Emery; stepchildren: Scott Corcoran, Candace Corcoran. AB, U. Chgo., 1948, George Washington U., 1950. Exec. dir. Allied Florists Assn. of Greater Washington, 1952-55; legis. dir. Am. Assn. Nurserymen, 1955-58; asst. mgr. assn. dept. C. of C. U.S., 1958-60; pres. Am. Apparel Mfrs. Assn., Arlington, Va., 1960-84; pres. Nat. Ctr. for Missing and Exploited Children, 1986-89, emeritus nat. dir., 1989—; chmn. bd. dirs., CEO Allied Realty Corp.; chmn. Newsletters Inc., Food Execs. Internat. Found., 1989—; pres. Orgn. Mgmt., Inc.; bd. dirs. Phillips Van Heusen Corp., Internat. Apparel Fedn.; mem. adv. bd. Prodn. Group Internat. Fin. chmn. Md. Rep. Party, 1977-78; bd. visitors Sch. Pub. Affairs, U. Md.; bd. dirs., chmn. U. Md. Found. Mem. Am. Soc. Assn. Execs. (chmn. 1980), Greater Washington Soc. Assn. Execs. (pres. 1965-66), Met. Club, Nat. Press Club, Bethesda Country Club, Capital Hill Club. Episcopalian.

MEREDITH, GEORGE DAVIS, advertising agency executive; b. Milw., Aug. 7, 1940; s. George Wade and Carol (Catcott) M.; m. Ruth Lawrence, 1964 (div. 1968); 1 child, Hilary; m. Elizabeth Lee, Feb. 8, 1969; children: Sean, Daniel, Lisa. Student U. Ariz., 1958-60; BA, Fla. So. U., 1962; postgrad., Ind. U., 1963-66. With Spencer Mktg., Inc., N.Y.C., 1967-68, Force, Inc., Paterson, N.J., 1968-70; v.p., creative dir. Keyes, Martin, Springfield, N.J., 1970-77; pres., creative dir. Gianettino and Meredith, Inc., Short Hills, N.J., 1977—; pres. Derring-do Press; mem. founder com. Advt. Hall of Fame; Author: (poetry) Two for You, One for Me, 1967; contbr. articles to profl. jours.; Trustee Bloomfield (N.J.) Coll., 1982—; bd. dirs. Unity Concerts, Montclair, 1983—; mem. adv. coun. Reading is Fundamental, Inc.; nat. co-chmn. Yogi Berra/Montclair State U. Stadium Fund. Named to N.J. Advt. Hall of Fame, 1987. Mem. New Jersey Advt. (bd. dirs. 1978-81), Pi Delta Epsilson, Sigma Tau Delta, Omicron Delta Kappa, Sigma Chi. Home: 159 Upper Mountain Ave Montclair NJ 07042-1905 Office: Gianettino & Meredith Inc 788 Morris Tpke Short Hills NJ 07078-2698

MEREDITH, GEORGE (MARLOR), association executive, writer; b. Somerville, N.J., Apr. 21, 1923; s. Gilbert Judson and Dorothea (Pope) M.; m. Mary Elizabeth Heilker, June 9, 1945 (div. 1955); 1 child, Gilbert Judson III; m. Elizabeth Jean Moore, Nov. 15, 1955; 1 child, Scott Arthur. Student, Columbia U., 1940-41. Indsl. engring. writer Johns-Manville Corp., 1942-44; mng. editor Mast, 1944-47; editor Premium Practice, 1947-55; ptnr., editorial dir. Meredith Assocs., 1956-67, pres., 1967-88, chmn., 1989-91; pres. Meredith Rsch. Corp., 1962-74; mng. dir. Meredith & Henry, 1977-92, chmn., 1992—; exec. sec. Assn. Incentive Mktg., 1957-67, exec. dir., 1967-74, pub. rels. dir., 1972—; mng. dir. Eastman Editorial Rsch., 1979-87; exec. sec. Nat. Assn. Food Equipment Mfrs., 1957-59; exec. dir. Nat. Premium Mfrs. Reps., 1963-66; dir. Mktg. New Bur., Red Bank, N.J., 1973-92; exec. dir. Trading Stamp Inst. Am., Assn. Retail Mktg. Svcs., 1979-91, editorial dir., 1991-92, pub. rels. dir., 1993—; mng. dir., Mktg. Comms. Execs. Internat., 1981-85, exec. dir. N.Y. chpt. 1981-82. Author: Effective Merchandising with Premiums, 1962, Creative Application of Sales Incentive Plans, 1972, (film) The Caine Coil, 1973, Incentives in Marketing, 1977, Incentives in Marketing & Motivation, 1996; editor: Premiums in Marketing, 1971; exec. editor, rsch. dir. Incentive Marketing Facts, 1968-87; rsch. dir. Incentive Mag., 1988-92; editor, pub. Sales Motivation Letter, 1973-74; editor The Register, 1979—, The Communicator, 1982-85, Creative Mktg. newsletter, 1989—; contbr. articles to profl. pub為ls. Coord., moderator Premiums and Incentives Conf. NYU, 1972; pub. rels. dir. Soc. Incentive Travel Execs., 1974-79. Recipient Premium Man of Yr. award Nat. Premium Mfrs. Reps., 1973, Nat. Premium Sales Execs. Past Pres.'s award, 1966, Disting. Achievement award Premium Advt. Assn. Am., 1963. Mem. Overseas Press Club, Am. Soc. Assn. Execs., Incentive Fedn. (vice chmn. 1984-88, 89-95, chmn. 1988-89), Assn. Incentive Mktg., Premium Mktg. Club N.Y., Am. Humanist Assn., Lions. Home: 3 Caro Ct Red Bank NJ 07701-2315

MEREDITH, KAREN ANN, accountant, financial executive; b. San Antonio, Sept. 30, 1954; d. Carroll J. and Doris J. (Calvin) Keller; m. William F. Meredith, July 6, 1974; children: Brian, Matthew. BBA in Acctg., U. North Tex., 1979. CPA, Tex.; CFP. Sr. acct. Deloitte Haskins & Sells, Dallas, 1979-82; CFO, sr. v.p. Commerce Savs. Assn., Dallas, 1982-86; exec. dir., chmn. bd. Am. Assn. Boomers, Irving, Tex., 1989-95; mng. ptnr. Meredith & Assocs., Irving, 1986—. Author various ednl. programs, 1991. Bd. dirs. Generations Found., N.Y.C., 1992. Recipient Fin. Edn. and Awareness award H.D. Vest Fin. Svcs., 1990. Mem. AICPA, Tex. Soc. CPAs (mem. Dallas chpt.), Internat. Assn. CFPs. Office: Meredith & Assocs 2621 W Airport Fwy Ste 101 Irving TX 75062-6069

MEREDITH, MICHAEL, science educator, researcher; b. London, Jan. 15, 1942; came to U.S., 1967.; s. Philip George and Dorothy Mary M.; married. BSc with honors, U. Birmingham, England, 1963; PhD, U. Pa., 1974. Rsch. assoc. Rockefeller U., N.Y.C., 1975-77, Worcester Found. Exptl. Biology, Shrewsbury, Mass., 1977-81; rsch. assoc. Fla. State U., Tallahassee, 1981-84, asst. prof., 1984-88, co-dir. program in neurosci., 1986—, assoc. prof., 1988-93, prof., 1993—; cons. site visits, grant revs. NIH, Washington, grant proposals, peer revs. NSF, Washington. Contbr. articles to profl. jours., chpts. to books. Pre-Doctoral Rsch. fellow NIH, 1970-73, Post-Doctoral Rsch. fellow, 1978-80; Rsch. grantee NIH, 1982-85, 88-91, 90-94, 94—, NSF, 1984-87, 87-90. Mem. Soc. Neurosci. (pres. local chpt. 1991-92, 94-95), Assn. Chemoreception Scis. (councillor 1981-83, chair membership 1986-88, program com. 1990-91, exec. chair 1996—), N.Y. Acad. Scis. Office: Fla State U Dept Biol Sci Tallahassee FL 32306-4075

MEREDITH, THOMAS C., academic administrator. Vice chancellor exec. affairs U. Miss., until 1988; pres. Western Ky. U., Bowling Green, 1988—. Office: Western Ky U Office of President Bowling Green KY 42101

MERENBLOOM, ROBERT BARRY, hospital and medical school administrator; b. Balt., July 13, 1947; Philip William and Florence Ruth (Surosky) M.; B.A., U. Md., 1969; M.S., Morgan State U., 1973; M.B.A., U. Balt., 1980. Mem. staff Mayor Balt. Office Manpower Resources, 1972-73; assoc. staff mem. Office Dean, U. Md. Med. Sch., 1976-80; adminstrv. officer rsch. and devel. Balt. VA Med. Ctr., 1974-80; assoc. adminstr. dept. medicine Sch. Medicine Johns Hopkins U., Balt., 1980-84, adminstr. dept. medicine Johns Hopkins Hosp., 1984-88, assoc. Sch. Hygiene and Pub. Health, 1984-88; lectr. dept. medicine Bowman Gray Sch. Medicine Wake Forest U., 1988-93, asst. chmn. dept. medicine, 1988-91, assoc. chmn. dept. medicine, 1991-93; vice chmn., asst. prof. medicine, clin. asst. prof. health adminstrn. & policy Med. U. S.C., Charleston, 1993—; instr. sociology U. Balt., 1973-76; adj. faculty Weekend Coll., Coll. Notre Dame, Balt., 1980—; assoc. mgmt. Babcock Grad. Sch. Bus. Wake Forest U. Exec. dir. J. Paul Sticht Ctr. on Aging. Recipient Hon. Corpsmen Leader award Office Mayor Balt., 1973; Outstanding Performance award Balt. VA Med. Ctr., 1975, Superior Performance award, 1980. Mem. Am. Gerontology Soc., So. Gerontology Soc., Soc. Rsch. Adminstrs., Nat. Coun. Univ. Rsch. Adminstrs., Adminstrs. Internal Medicine, Assn. Am. Med. Colls. (group on bus. affairs), Am. Hosp. Assn., Am. Pub. Health Assn., Am. Coll. Healthcare Adminstrs., Soc. Gen. Internal Medicine, Johns Hopkins Club, Piedmont Club, Harbour Club.

MERENDINO, K. ALVIN, surgical educator; b. Clarksburg, W.Va., Dec. 3, 1914; s. Biagio and Cira (Bivona) M.; m. Shirley Emojane Hill, July 6, 1943; children: Cira Anne Watts, Nancy Jane Napuunoa, Susan Hill Mitchell, Nina Francine Sarich, Maria King Merendino-Stillwell. BA, Ohio U., 1936, LLD (hon.), 1967; MD, Yale U., 1940; PhD, U. Minn., 1946. Diplomate Am. Bd. Surgery, Am. Bd. Thoracic Surgery. Intern Cin. Gen. Hosp., 1940-41; resident U. Minn. Hosp., Mpls., 1941-45; rsch. asst. Dr. Owen H. Wangensteen, 1942-43; trainee Nat. Cancer Inst., 1943-45; dir. program in postgrad. med. edn. in surgery Ancker Hosp., St. Paul, 1946-48; instr. dept. surgery U. Minn., Mpls., 1944-45, asst. prof. dept. surgery, 1945-48; assoc. prof. dept. surgery U. Wash., Seattle, 1949-55, dir. exptl. surgery labs., dept. surgery, 1950-72, prof. dept. surgery, 1955-81, prof. emeritus, 1981—, prof. and adminstrv. officer dept. surgery, 1957-64, prof., chmn., 1965-72; chmn. dept. surgery King Faisal Specialist and Rsch. Ctgr., Riyadh, Saudi Arabia, 1976, dir. med. affairs, 1976-79, dir. Cancer Therapy Inst., spl. cons. to Coun., supr. for exec. mgmt., assoc. dir. med. affairs, 1981-82; dir. ops. King Faisal Med. City, Riyadh, 1981-85; mem. adv. com. for med. rsch., Boeing Airplane Co., 1959-67, chmn., 1962l cons. Children's Orthopedic Hosp., Seattle, 1972-82; mem. adv. com. on heart disease and surgery for crippled children's svc., Wash. State Dept. Health and Div. Vocational Rehab., 1961; mem. surgery study sect. NIH, 1958-62, subcom. on prosthetic valves for cardiac surgery, chm. 1st Nat. Conf., 1960, mem. adv. com. 2d Nat. Conf. on

Prosthetic Heart Valves, 1969, Surgery A study sect. chmn., 1970-72, Nat. Heart and Lung Inst. Tng. Com., 1965-69; cons. VA, Seattle, 1949-59, 65-81; mem. adv. com. on hosps. and clinics, USPHS, 1963-66; mem. surgery test com. Nat. Bd. Med. Examiners, 1963-67; mem. surgery resident rev. com., Conf. Com. on Grad. Edn. in Surgery, 1963-73, vice-chmn., 1972-73; chmn. 2d Saudi Arabian Med. Conf., Riyadh, 1978; mem. com. on postgrad. med. edn., Kingdom of Saudi Arabia Ministry of Health, 1978-79. Editor in chief: Prosthetic Valves for Cardiac Surgery, 1961; assoc. editor: Prosthetic Heart Valves, 1969; mem. editorial bd. Am. Jour. Surgery,. 1958—, Jour. Surg. Rsch., 1961-69, Pacific Medicine and Surgery, 1964-68, King Faisal Hosp. Medicine Jour. (renamed Annals of Saudi Medicine), 1981-85; contbr. articles to profl. jours., chpts. to books; producer movies on surgery. Recipient cert. of merit Ohio U. Alumni Assn., 1957, Outstanding W.Va. Italian-Am. award W.Va. Italian Heritage Festival Inc., Clarksburg, W.Va., 1984, Spirit of Freedom award A. James Mancin, Sec. State W.Va., 1984, Disting. W. Virginian award State of W.Va., 1984, John Baird Thomas Meml. award Ohio U.; named Surgery Alumnus of Yr., U. Minn., 1981, Disting. Citizen Wash. State, Lt. Gov. John Cherberg, 1981; NIH grantee, 1951-76. Fellow ACS (numerous coms., bds.), Soc. of Univ. Surgeons (councilman at large 3 yrs.), Internat. Soc. Surgery; mem. Am. Surg. Assn. (adv. mem. com. 1959-64, v.p. 1972-73), Am. Assn. for Thoracic Surgery, Halsted Soc., Henry N. Harkins Surg. Soc., N. Pacific Coast Surg. Assn., Seattle Surg. Soc., So. Surg. Soc. (Arthur H. Shipley award 1972), Am. Bd. Surgery 1958-64 (vice chmn. 1962-63, chmn. 1963-64, emeritus 1964—); University Club, Seattle Golf Club, Phi Beta Kappa, Sigma Xi, Beta Theta Pi (sec., pres.), Phi Beta Pi (hon.). Republican. Episcopalian. Avocations: golf, fly fishing, bird hunting, gardening. Home: The Highlands Seattle WA 98177 Office: U Wash Sch Medicine Dept Surgery Seattle WA 98195

MERGLER, H. KENT, investment counselor; b. Cin., July 1, 1940; s. Wilton Henry and Mildred Amelia (Pulliam) M.; m. Judith Anne Metzger, Aug. 17, 1963; children: Stephen Kent, Timothy Alan, Kristin Lee. BBA with honors, U. Cin., 1963, MBA, 1964. Chartered fin. analyst, chartered investment counselor. Portfolio mgr. Scudder, Stevens & Clark, Cin., 1964-68, exec. v.p., Chgo., 1970-73; v.p. Gibraltar Rsch. and Mgmt., Ft. Lauderdale, Fla., 1968-70; ptnr., exec. v.p., pres., dir. and prin. Stein Roe & Farnham, Inc., Ft. Lauderdale, 1973-84, Chgo., 1984-91, also exec. com.; pres. Stein Roe Investment Trust; mng. ptnr. Loomis, Sayles & Co., L.P., Palm Beach Gardens, Fla., 1992—; bd. dirs. Gold Coast Mag., Inc., 1994—; arbitrator Nat. Assn. Security Dealers, Inc., 1976-82. Chmn. adminstrv. bd. Christ United Meth. Ch., Ft. Lauderdale, 1981-83; mem. fin. com. Kenilworth Union Ch., 1989-92, Broward Community Found. (Investment Com.), 1992—, chmn., 1994—, bd. dirs., 1995—, Martin County Econ. Coun., 1992—; bd. dirs. Pine Crest Prep. Sch., 1982-84, bd. advisors, 1984-87; mem. corp. adv. bd. U. Cin. Coll. Bus. Adminstrn., 1991-94; bd. dirs. Hibiscus House Children's Found., 1993—; bd. dirs. Coral Ridge Little League, 1976-84, pres., 1980-81. Mem. Fin. Analysts Soc. So. Fla. (bd. dirs. 1974-78, pres. 1975), Bond Club Ft. Lauderdale (dir. 1978-82), Tower Club (Ft. Lauderdale), Highlands Country Club (N.C.), Cullasaja Club (Highlands, N.C.), Sailfish Point Yacht and Country Club (Stuart, Fla.), City Club of Palm Beach, Beta Theta Pi, Beta Gamma Sigma. Republican. Home: 7036 SE Harbor Cir Stuart FL 34996 Office: 4400 Pga Blvd Ste 600 Palm Beach Gardens FL 33410

MERGLER, HARRY WINSTON, engineering educator; b. Chillicothe, Ohio, June 1, 1924; s. Harry Franklin and Letitia (Walburn) M.; m. Irmgard Erna Steudel, June 22, 1948; children—Myra A. L., Marcia B. E., Harry F. B.S., MIT, 1948; M.S., Case Inst. Tech., 1950, Ph.D., 1956. Aero. research scientist NACA, 1948-56; mem. faculty Case Inst. Tech., 1957—, prof. engring., 1962—, Leonard Case prof. engring. emeritus, 1973—; dir. Digital Systems Lab., 1959—; vis. scientist, USSR, 1958; vis. prof. Norwegian Tech. U., 1962; cons. to industry, 1957—; editor Control Engring. mag., 1956—; pres. Digital/Gen. Corp., 1968-72; cons. Exploratory Research div. NSF. Author: Digital Systems Engineering, 1961, also articles, chpts. in books. Served with AUS, 1942-45. Recipient Case gold medal for sci. achievement Case Inst. Tech., 1980. Fellow IEEE (bd. dirs. 1987-89, v.p. 1989, Lamme medal 1978, Centennial medal 1984); mem. NAE, Indsl. Electronic Soc. (pres. 1977-79), Cleve. Engring. Soc., N.Y. Acad. Scis., Blue Key, Sigma Xi, Tau Beta Pi, Theta Tau, Pi Delta Epsilon, Zeta Psi. Home: 9658-23 Halyards Ct Fort Myers FL 33919

MERHIGE, ROBERT REYNOLD, JR., federal judge; b. N.Y.C., Feb. 5, 1919; s. Robert Reynold and Eleanor (Donovan) M.; m. Shirley Galleher, Apr. 24, 1957; children: Robert Reynold III, Mark Reynold. LLB, U. Richmond, 1942, LLD (hon.), 1976; LLM, U. Va., 1982; LLD (hon.), Washington and Lee U., 1990, Wake Forest U., 1994. Bar: Va. 1942. Ptnr. Bremner Merhige Montgomery & Baber, Richmond, 1945-67; judge U.S. Dist. Ct., Richmond, 1967—; guest lectr. trial tactics Law Sch. U. Va., Ewald disting. prof. law, 1987-88; adj. prof. Law Sch. U. Richmond, 1973-87; appeal agt. Henrico County Draft Bd., 1954-67; mem. NCAA spl. com. on discipline rules; profl.-in-residence, Zambia, Africa, 1994. Co-author: Virginia Jury Instructions. Mem. Richmond Citizens Assn.; mem. citizens adv. com. San. Dist. A, Henrico County. Served with USAAF, World War II. Decorated Air medal with four oak leaf clusters; recipient Amara Civic Club award, 1968, Spl. award City of Richmond, 1967; named Citizen of the Yr., 3d Dist. Omega Psi Phi, 1972, Citizen of the Yr., Richmond Urban League, 1977, Richmonder of Yr. Style mag., 1984, 87, Citizen of Yr., 1986; recipient Disting. Alumni award U. Richmond, 1979, Disting. Svc. award Nat. Alumni Coun., U. Richmond, 1979, Herbert T. Harley award Am. Judicature Soc., 1982, Athenian Citizen medal, 1979, Torch of Liberty award Anti-Defamation League of B'nai Brith, 1982, T.C. Williams Sch. of Law Disting. Svc. award, 1983, Pres.'s award Old Dominion Bar Assn., 1986, William J. Brennan award, 1986, Merit Citation award NCCJ, 1987, William B. Green award for professionalism U. Richmond, 1989, Marshall-Wythe medallion (William & Mary Faculty award), 1989. Fellow Va. Law Found.; mem. Va. Bar Assn., Richmond Bar Assn. (pres. 1963-64, multi-dist. litigation panel 1990—, Hill-Tucker award 1991), Am. Law Inst. (faculty), Va. Trial Lawyers Assn. (chmn. membership com. 1964-65, Disting. Svc. award 1977), Jud. Conf. U.S., John Marshall Inns of Ct. (founding mem.), Omicron Delta Kappa. Office: Lewis F Powell Jr Courthouse Bldg Ste 307 1000 E Main St Richmond VA 23219-3525

MERIANOS, JOHN JAMES, medicinal chemist; b. Krokeai Sparta Laconia, Greece, Feb. 12, 1937; came to the U.S., 1957; s. Demetrios Nicholaos and Eleni (Patrianakos) M.; m. Stavroula P. Doumas, Apr. 21, 1974; children: Laura, Helen, Demetri. BS in Pharmacy magna cum laude, New Eng. Coll. Pharmacy, 1961; MS in Pharm. Chemistry, U. Wis., 1963, PhD in Medicinal Chemistry, 1966. Registered pharmacist, N.J. Rsch. chemist FMC Corp., Princeton, N.J., 1966-68; rsch. scientist, sr. rsch. scientist Millmaster Onyx Corp., Jersey City, N.J., 1968-87; sr. rsch. scientist GAF Corp., Wayne, N.J., 1987-92; rsch. fellow ISP Corp., Wayne, 1992-95; dir. R & D Sutton Labs., Chatham, N.J., 1992—; sr. rsch. fellow ISP Internat. Specialty Products, Chatham, N.J., 1992—; exec. dir. MerPan Chem. Cons. Diagnostic Reagents, Pharmaceutics, Middletown, N.J., 1974—. Contbr. chpt. to book: Disinfection, Sterilization and Preservation, 4th edit., 1991. Pres. Krokeai Soc., U.S. and Can., 1990-95. Recipient Kappa Psi gold key Kappa Psi Fraternity, Boston, 1961. Mem. Am. Chem. Soc., Am. Assn. Pharm. Scientist, Soc. Cosmetic Chemists, Soc. Indsl. Microbiology, N.J. Pharm. Assn. Greek Orthodox. Achievements include 95 patents in indsl. biocides and synergisms in cosmetic preservatives; inventor of Onamer M, Polyquaternium-1 Polyquad TM a preservative system for contact lens cleaners. Avocations: volleyball, soccer, bowling. Home: 32 Doherty Dr Middletown NJ 07748 Office: Sutton Labs/ISP Group Mem 116 Summit Ave Chatham NJ 07928-0837

MERIDEN, TERRY, physician; b. Damascus, Syria, Oct. 12, 1946; came to U.S., 1975; s. Izzat and Omayma (Aidi) M.; m. Lena Kahal, Nov. 17, 1975; children: Zina, Lana. BS, Sch. Sci., Damascus, 1968; MD, Sch. Medicine, Damascus, 1972, doctorate cum laude, 1973. Diplomate Am. Bd. Internal Medicine. Resident in infectious diseases Rush Green Hosp., Romford, Eng., 1973; house officer in internal medicine and cardiology Ashford (Eng.) Group Univ. Hosps., 1973-74; sr. house officer in internal medicine and neurology Grimsby (Eng.) Group Univ. Hosps., 1974; registrar in internal medicine and rheumatology St. Annes Hosp., London, 1974-75; jr. resident in internal medicine Shadyside Hosp., Pitts., 1975-76, sr. resident in internal medicine, 1976-77; fellow in endocrinology and metabolism Shadyside Hosp. and Grad. Inst., Pitts., 1976-77; clin. asst. prof. U. Ill., Peoria, 1979; pres. Am. Diabetes Assn., Peoria, 1982-84; dir. Proctor Diabetes Unit, Peoria, 1984—, 1984—; adviser to the Gov. of Ill. on Diabetes. Mem. editorial bd. Diabetes Forecast mag., Clin. Diabetes, 1990; contbr. articles to profl. jours. Fellow ACP, FACE, Am. Coll. Endocrinology; mem. AMA (Recognition award 1985, ADA (chmn. profl. edn. and rsch. 1980—, mem. editl. bd. and Spanish lit. bd. nat. bd. dirs. 1986—, vice chmn. nat. com. on diabetes edn. and affiliate svcs. 1986—, Outstanding Svc. award 1984, Outstanding Diabetes Educator award 1986), Am. Cancer Soc. (Life Line award 1983), Am. Assn. Clin. Endocrinology (founding), Am. Coll. Endocrinology, The Obesity Found. (Century award 1984, Recognition award 1985). Home: 115 E Coventry Ln Peoria IL 61614-2103 Office: 900 Main St Ste 300 Peoria IL 61602-1005

MERIDETH, FRANK E., JR., lawyer; b. 1944. BA, U. San Francisco, JD. Bar: Calif. 1970. Ptnr. Bryan Cave, Santa Monica, Calif. Office: Bryan Cave 120 Broadway Ste 500 Santa Monica CA 90401-2386*

MERIGAN, THOMAS CHARLES, JR., physician, medical researcher, educator; b. San Francisco, Jan. 18, 1934; s. Thomas C. and Helen M. (Greeley) M.; m. Joan Mary Freeborn, Oct. 3, 1959; 1 son, Thomas Charles III. BA with honors, U. Calif., Berkeley, 1955; MD, U. Calif., San Francisco, 1958. Diplomate: Am. Bd. Internal Medicine. Intern in medicine 2d and 4th Harvard med. services Boston City Hosp., 1958-59, asst. resident medicine, 1959-60; clin. assoc. Nat. Heart Inst., NIH, Bethesda, Md., 1960-62; asso. Lab. Molecular Biology, Nat. Inst. Arthritis and Metabolic Diseases, NIH, 1962-63; practice medicine specializing in internal medicine and infectious diseases Stanford, Calif., 1963—; asst. prof. medicine Stanford U. Sch. Medicine, 1963-67, assoc. prof. medicine, 1967-72, head div. infectious diseases, 1966-92, prof. medicine, 1972—, George E. and Lucy Becker prof. medicine, 1980—; dir. Diagnostic Microbiology Lab., Univ. Hosp., 1966-72, Diagnostic Virology Lab., 1969—, Ctr. AIDS Rsch. Stanford U., 1988—; hosp. epidemiologist, 1966-88; mem. microbiology rsch. tng. grants com. NIH, 1969-73, virology study sect., 1974-78; cons. antiviral substances program Nat. Inst. Allergy and Infectious Diseases, 1970—, mem. AIDS clin. drug devel. commn., 1986-94; mem. Virology Task Force, 1976-78, bd. sci. counselors, 1980-85; mem. U.S. Hepatitis panel U.S. and Japan Coop. Med. Sci. Program, 1979-90, AIDS subcom. Nat. Adv. Allergy and Infectious Diseases Coun., 1988-89; co-chmn. interferon evaluation Group Am. Cancer Soc., 1978-81; mem. vaccines and related biol. products adv. com. Ctr. for Drugs and Biols., FDA, 1984-88; mem. internat. adv. com. on biol. sci. Sci. Council, Singapore, 1985-88; mem. adv. com. J.A. Hartford Found., 1979-84; mem. Albert Lasker awards jury, 1981-84; mem. peer review panel U.S. Army Med. Rsch. and Devel. Com., 1986-88; nat. com. to rev. current procedures for approval New Drugs for Cancer and AIDS, 1989-90; mem. Com. to Study Use of Coms. within FDA, 1991-92. Contbr. numerous articles on infectious diseases, virology and immunology to sci. jours.; editor: Antivirals with Clinical Potential, 1976, Antivirals and Virus Diseases of Man, 1979, 2d edit., 1984, 3d edit., 1990, Regulatory Functions of Interferon, 1980, Interferons, 1982, Interferons as Cell Growth Inhibitors, 1986; assoc. editor: Virology, 1975-78, Cancer Research, 1987-91; co-editor: monograph series Current Topics in Infectious Diseases, 1975—, Cytomeglovirus Infect and Ganciclovir, 1988, Focus on Didanosine (ddI), 1990, Practical Diagnosis of Viral Infection, Textbook of AIDS Medicine, 1994, Surrogate Markers for HIV Infection, 1995; editl. bd.: Archives Internal Medicine, 1971-81, Jour. Gen. Virology, 1972-77, Infection and Immunity, 1973-81, Intervirology, 1973-85, Proc. Soc. Expt. Biology and Medicine, 1978-87, Reviews of Infectious Diseases, 1979-89, Jour. Interferon Research, 1980-89, Antiviral Research, 1980-86, Jour. Antimicrobial Chemotherapy, 1981-91, Molecular and Cellular Biochemistry, 1982-89, AIDS Research and Human Retroviruses, 1983—, Jour. Virology, 1984-89, Biotechnology Therapeutics, 1988—, Jour. Infectious Diseases, 1989—, Clinical Drug Investigation, 1989—, HIV: Advances in Research and Therapy, 1990—, Internat. Jour. Antimicrobial Agts. 1990—, The AIDS Reader, 1991—, AIDS, 1993, Clinical Immunotherapeutics, 1994—, Antiviral Therapy, 1996—. Recipient Borden award for Outstanding Rsch., Am. Assn. Med. Colls., 1973, Merit award, Nat. Inst. Allergy and Infectious Diseases, 1988, Maxwell Finland award Infectious Diseases Soc. Am., 1988; Guggenheim Meml. fellow, 1972. Fellow AAAS; mem. AMA, Assn. Am. Physicians, Western Assn. Physicians, Am. Soc. Microbiology, Am. Soc. Clin. Investigation (coun. 1977-80), Am. Assn. Immunologists, Am. Fedn. Clin. Rsch., Western Soc. Clin. Rsch., Soc. Exptl. Biology and Medicine (publ. com. 1985-89), Infectious Diseases Soc. Am., Am. Soc. Virology, inst. Medicine, Pan Am. Group for Rapid Viral Diagnosis, Internat. Soron Rsch. (coun. 1983-89), Calif. Med. Assn., Santa Clara County Med. Soc., Calif. Acad. Medicine, Royal Soc. Medicine, Alpha Omega Alpha. Home: 148 Goya Rd Menlo Park CA 94028-7307 Office: Stanford U Sch Medicine Div Infectious Diseases Stanford CA 94305

MERILAN, JEAN ELIZABETH, statistics educator; b. Columbia, Mo., Sept. 18, 1962; d. Charles Preston and Phyllis Pauline (Laughlin) M. AB summa cum laude, U. Mo., 1985, MA in Math., MA in Stats., 1987; postgrad., U. Ariz., 1987—. Grad. teaching asst. U. Mo., Columbia, 1985-87; grad. rsch. asst. U. Ariz., Tucson, 1988-89, grad. teaching asst., 1989—. Nat. Merit scholar, Univ. Curators scholar U. Mo., 1981-85, Grad. Acad. scholar U. Ariz., 1990—, Arts and Sci. Grad. scholar U. Mo., 1985-87; Gregory fellow U. Mo., 1985-87, Faculty of Sci. fellow U. Ariz., 1987-88. Mem. Am. Statis. Assn., Inst. Math. Stats., Soc. for Indsl. and Applied Math., Biometric Soc., Am. Math. Soc., Math. Assn. Am., Golden Key Nat. Honor Soc., Sigma Xi, Phi Beta Kappa, Phi Kappa Phi, Phi Eta Sigma, Pi Mu Epsilon. Office: U Ariz Dept Stats Tucson AZ 85721

MERIMEE, THOMAS JOSEPH, medical educator; b. Louisville, May 28, 1931; s. William McNeal and Christina (Homm) M.; m. Martha Ann Barksdale; children: Thomas Joseph Jr., Timothy Lee, Ruth Ann, William McNeal. BA, U. Louisville, 1952, MD, 1959. Intern, resident Louisville (Ky.) Hosp.; fellow in endocrinology John Hopkins U., Balt., 1962-66, instr. medicine, 1966-69; asst. prof. Boston U., 1969-71; program dir. Gen. Clin. Rsch. Ctr., Boston City Hosp., 1971-74; prof. medicine, chief div. endocrinology and metabolism, dept. medicine U. Fla., Gainesville, 1974—, dir. Clin. Rsch. Ctr., 1979-88; cons. FTC, 1970—. Author: African Pygmy, 1987; assoc. editor Jour. Metabolism, 1970—; mem. editorial bd. Jour. Diabetes, 1970—, Jour. Clin. Endocrinology and Metabolism, 1970—. Pres. Alachua County Youth Orch., Gainesville, 1983-85. Recipient Clin. Scis. Faculty Rsch. award U. Fla., 1987. Mem. Am. Diabetes Assn. (R & D award), Endocrine Soc., Am. Fedn. Clin. Rsch., Am. Soc. Clin. Investigation, Assn. Am. Physicians, Fla. Med. Assn. Republican. Roman Catholic. Office: U Fla Coll Medicine Div Endocrinology & Metab 1600 SW Archer Rd # 226J Gainesville FL 32608

MERIN, ROBERT GILLESPIE, anesthesiology educator; b. Glens Falls, N.Y., June 16, 1933; s. Joseph Harold and Jessie Louisa (Gillespie) M.; m. Barbara R. Rothe, Mar. 1, 1958; children: Michael, Jan, Sarah. BA, Swarthmore Coll., 1954; MD, Cornell U., 1958. Diplomate Nat. Bd. Med. Examiners, Am. Bd. Anesthesiology. From asst. prof. to prof. anesthesiology U. Rochester (N.Y.) Med. Ctr., 1966-81; prof. anesthesiology U. Tex. Health Sci. Ctr., Houston, 1981-92; prof Anesthesiology Med. Coll. Ga., Augusta, 1992—; mem. anesthetic life support drug com. FDA, Washington, 1982-87, spl. cons., 1987—; Murray Mendolsohn Meml. lectr. U. Toronto Sch. Medicine, 1976, Harry M. Shields Meml. lectr., 1988; Litchfield lectr. Oxford U., 1977, William and Austin Friend Meml. vis. prof. Queens U., 1981, Joseph F. Artusio endowed lectr. Cornell U. Med. Coll., N.Y.C., 1991, and others. Editorial bd. Anesthesiology, 1977-86; contbr. articles to Anesthesiology, Jour. Pharmacology and Exptl. Therapeutics. Capt. U.S. Army, 1961-63. Recipient Rsch. Career Devel. award NIH, 1972-77. Mem. Assn. Univ. Anesthesiologists (pres. 1987-88), Am. Soc. Pharmacology and Exptl. Therapeutics. Achievements include pioneering work in demonstrating effects of anesthetics on myocardial perfusion and metabolism; cardioactive drug interactions with anesthetic drugs. Office: Med Coll Ga Dept Anesthesiology 1120 15th St Augusta GA 30901-3157

MERINI, RAFIKA, foreign language and literature and women's studies educator; b. Fès, Morocco; came to U.S., 1972; d. Mohamed and Fatima (Chraibi) M. BA in English cum laude, U. Utah, 1978, MA in Romance Langs. and Lits., 1981; postgrad., U. Wash., 1980-82; cert. in translation, SUNY, Binghamton, 1988, PhD in Comparative Lit., 1992. Teaching asst. U. Utah, Salt Lake City, 1978-80, U. Wash., Seattle, 1980-82; adminstrv. asst., tchr. French, interpreter The Lang. Sch., Seattle, 1982-83; lectr. Pacific Luth. U., Tacoma, Wash., 1983; instr. Fort Steilacoom C.C. (now Pierre C.C.), 1983-85; teaching asst. dept. romance langs. SUNY, Binghamton, 1985-87, teaching asst. women's studies dept., 1988, teaching asst. comparative lit. dept., 1986-88; vis. instr. Union Coll., Schenectady, N.Y., 1988-89; vis. instr. dept. fgn. langs. and lits. Skidmore Coll., Saratoga Springs, N.Y., 1989-90; asst. prof. dept. fgn. langs. State U. Coll., Buffalo, 1990—; coord. Women's Studies Interdisciplinary unit State U. Coll., Buffalo, 1993—, adviser French Club, 1990-93; mem. French Circle, Buffalo, 1990—. Contbr. articles to profl. pubs.; presenter at seminars and workshops. Grantee Nat. Defense Student Award. Mem. MLA, Nat. Women's Studies Assn., Am. Assn. Tchrs. French, Conseil Internat. d'Etudes Francophones, Pi Delta Phi, Soc. Hon. Française, Kappa Theta (hon.). Home: PO Box 1063 Buffalo NY 14213-7063 Office: State Univ Coll-Buffalo Dept Fgn Langs 1300 Elmwood Ave Buffalo NY 14222-1004

MERIWETHER, HEATH J., newspaper publisher; b. Columbia, Mo., Jan. 20, 1944; s. Nelson Heath and Mary Agnes (Immele) M.; m. Patricia Hughes, May 4, 1979; children: Graham, Elizabeth. BA in History, BJ, U. Mo., 1966; MA in Teaching, Harvard U., 1967. Reporter Miami (Fla.) Herald, 1970-72, editor Broward and Palm Beach burs., 1972-77, exec. city editor, 1977-79, asst. mgr. editor news, 1979-80, mng. editor, 1981-83, exec. editor, 1983-87; exec. editor Detroit Free Press, 1987-95, publisher, 1996—. Trustee Greenhills Sch., 1995—; bd. dirs. Detroit Symphony Orch., 1996—. Served to lt. USNR, 1967-70. Journalism fellow Stanford U., 1980. Roman Catholic. Avocation: tennis. Office: Detroit Free Press 321 W Lafayette Blvd Detroit MI 48226-2705

MERIWETHER, JAMES BABCOCK, retired English language educator; b. Columbia, S.C., May 8, 1928; s. Robert Lee and Margaret (Babcock) M.; m. Nancy Anderson Callcott, July 29, 1955 (div. May 1992); children: Rebecca, Robert, George, Nicholas, Margaret; m. Anne M. Blythe, Nov. 14, 1992. BA, U. S.C., 1949; MA, Princeton U., 1952, PhD, 1958. Asst. prof. English U. Tex., Austin, 1958-59; asst. prof. English U. N.C., Chapel Hill, 1959-62, assoc. prof., 1962-64; prof. U. S.C., Columbia, 1964-70, McClintock prof. So. letters, 1970-90, dir. So. studies program, 1974-80, disting. prof. emeritus, 1990—; appointed Bd. Fgn. Scholarships, Washington, 1982, 86, vice chmn., 1984, chmn. 1984-87; Fulbright prof. U. Paris, 1970-71, U. Bonn, 1980, Chinese U. Hong Kong, 1993. Author: The Literary Career of William Faulkner, 1961, others; editor: Essays, Speeches and Public Letters of William Faulkner, others; contbr. articles to profl. jours. Served with U.S. Army, 1953-56. Fellow Am. Coun. Learned Socs., 1960-61, Guggenheim Found., 1963-64, Earhart Found., 1989-90. Mem. MLA, Bibliographical Soc. Am., Am. Studies Assn., South Atlantic Modern Lang. Assn., Phi Beta Kappa. Home: 2526 Monroe St Columbia SC 29205

MERK, FREDERICK BANNISTER, biomedical educator, medical researcher; b. Cambridge, Mass., Feb. 21, 1936; s. Frederick and Lois Alberta (Bannister) M.; m. Linda Jean Poole, Oct. 22, 1966 (dec. Dec. 1994); children: John F., R. Daniel. AB, Harvard Coll., 1958; PhD, Boston U., 1971. Asst. prof. pathology Boston U. Sch. Medicine, 1972-73; assoc. prof. pathology and anatomy Tufts U. Sch. Medicine, Boston, 1973—; also dir. electron microscopy facility, 1975-85; cons. electron microscopy Mass. Gen. Hosp., Boston, 1964-85; cons. toxicol. testing Transgenic Scis., Worcester, Mass., 1988-91. Contbr. articles to profl. jours. Trustee Broadway United Meth. Ch., Lynn, Mass., chmn. 1994—. Recipient grant NIH, 1994—. Mem. Am. Soc. Cell Biology, Fedn. Am. Soc. Exptl. Biology, Am. Assn. Anatomists, Microscopy Soc. Am., Sigma Xi. Avocations: photography, indoor gardening, swimming. Home: 17 Jefferson Rd Winchester MA 01890 Office: Tufts Univ Sch Medicine Dept Pathology 136 Harrison Ave Boston MA 02111

MERKEL, CHARLES MICHAEL, lawyer; b. Nashville, Nov. 2, 1941; s. Charles M. and Lila K. Merkel; m. Donna White, Jan. 7, 1967; children: Kimberly Dale, Charles M. III. BA, U. Miss., 1964, JD, 1966; LLM in Taxation, Georgetown U., 1969. Bar: Miss. Trial atty. U.S. Dept. Justice, Washington, 1966-70; ptnr. Dunbar & Merkel, Clarksdale, Miss., 1970-73, Holcomb Dunbar Connell & Merkel, Clarksdale, 1973-82, Merkel & Cocke, Clarksdale, 1982—; pres. Miss. chpt. Am. Bd. Trial Advs., 1989. Bd. dirs. Lula Rich Edn. Found., Clarksdale, 1983-89. Carrier scholar U. Miss. 1959-63. Fellow Miss. State Bar Found.; mem. ATLA, Am. Bd. Trial Advocates, Am. Coll. Trial Lawyers, Miss. Trial Lawyers Assn. (sec. 1985-87). Episcopalian. Avocations: hunting, tennis, skiing. Home: 101 Cypress Ave Clarksdale MS 38614-2603 Office: PO Box 1388 30 Delta Ave Clarksdale MS 38614-2718

MERKELO, HENRI, microelectronics and computer scientist; b. Borky, Ukraine, June 12, 1939; came to U.S., 1960; s. Alexander and Natalia (Niushko) M. Certificat d'Aptitude Professionnelle, Coll. Moderne et Tech., Reims, France, 1956; MS, U. Ill., 1962, PhD, 1966. Translator Russian-Am. Math. Soc., Providence, 1961-63, Am. Phys. Soc., Am. Math. Soc., 1962-64; research scientist physics and thermodynamics Douglas Aircraft Co., Santa Monica, Calif., 1962; faculty U. Ill., Urbana, 1966—, dir. quantum electronics ultra high speed digital electronics rsch. lab., 1973—; dir. picosecond digital electronics U. Calif., Santa Barbara, 1982—; cons. Sangamo/Schlumberger, Atlanta, 1977-80, AMP Inc., Harrisburg, Pa., 1983—, Stanfor Rsch. Inst., 1983, Hewlett Packard Corp., 1992; lectr. in field, U.S. and abroad. Fgn. editor, French translator Schlumberger, 1978-80; contbr. numerous articles to profl. jours.; patentee in field. Ford Found. fellow, 1960-62, RCA fellow, 1963, Kodak fellow, 1964; grantee NSF, 1970—, AMP, 1985—, IBM, 1988—, Hewlett-Packard, 1993—, other U.S. industries. Fellow IEEE (chmn. computer elements workshop 1988, 89); mem. Am. Inst. Physics, Am. Physics Soc., Am. Optical Soc., Sigma Xi, Tau Beta Pi. Research directed to development of high speed and ultra high speed logic devices and networks for high speed computing and communication. Modeling and numerical simulation of high speed digital electronic and photonic networks. Picosecond and femtosecond switching phenomena. Office: U Ill Quantum Electronics Ultrahigh Speed Digital Electronics 1406 W Green St Urbana IL 61801-2918

MERKER, STEVEN JOSEPH, lawyer; b. Cleve., Feb. 21, 1947; s. Steven Joseph and Laverne (Zamenik) M.; m. Janet L. Whyatt; children: Steven, Rena, Ashley. BS, Case Inst. Tech., 1968; MS, U. Fla., 1973. Bar: Ohio 1976, U.S. Dist. Ct. (no. dist.) Ohio, 1976, U.S. Dist. Ct. Colo. 1979, U.S. Ct. Appeals (10th cir.) 1979, U.S. Supreme Ct. 1989. Assoc. Jones, Day, Reavis & Pogue, Cleve., 1976-78; assoc. Davis, Graham & Stubbs, Denver, 1978-82, ptnr., 1983-96, chmn. labor and employment group, 1989-96; mem., chmn. litig. and labor and employment groups Merrick, Calvin & Merker, L.L.C., 1996—. Legal counsel Coloradans for Lamm-Dick campaign, Denver, 1982, Nancy Dick for U.S. Senate Com., Denver, 1984, Cantrell for Dist. Atty., Jefferson County, Colo., 1984; bd. dirs. Very Spl. Arts, Colo., 1994—. Served as capt. USAF, 1969-72. Mem. ABA, Colo. Bar Assn., Denver Bar Assn. Office: Merrick Calvin and Merker 600 17th St Ste 950S Denver CO 80202

MERKERT, GEORGE, visual effects producer. Formerly exec. producer, producer Colossal Pictures, San Francisco; now producer MetroLight Studios, L.A. Recent visual effects projects include 7 effects shots (film) Total Recall; title sequence (TV pilot) Moe's World; also Apple Computers promotional film. Office: MetroLight Studios 5724 W 3rd St Ste 400 Los Angeles CA 90036-3078

MERKIN, WILLIAM LESLIE, lawyer; b. N.Y.C., Apr. 30, 1929; s. Jules Leo Merkin and Rae (Levine) Lesser; children—Monica Jo, Lance Jeffrey, Tiffany Dawn. B.A., U. Tex., Austin, 1950; J.D., St. Mary's U., San Antonio, Tex., 1953. Bar: Tex. 1953, U.S. Ct. Mil. Appeals 1954, U.S. Dist. Ct. (we. dist.) Tex. 1957, U.S. Ct. Appeals (5th cir.) 1969, U.S. Supreme Ct. 1970. Pvt. practice, El Paso, Tex., 1956-71; sr. ptnr. firm Merkin & Gibson, El Paso, 1972-78, Merkin, Hines & Pasqualone, 1978-90, ret.; lectr. U. Tex., El Paso, 1978—; cons. in field. Served to capt. JAGC, U.S. Army, 1953-56. Mem. Tex. State Bar Assn., El Paso County Bar Assn., San Diego County Bar Assn., Soc. of Profls. in Dispute Resolution, Am. Trial Lawyers Assn., Tex. Trial Lawyers Assn., Common Cause, Internat. Wine and Food Soc. (pres. 1979-80), Am. Arbitration Assn. (part-time arbitrator), Del Norte Club (El Paso), B'nai B'rith (pres. 1961-62), Phi Delta Phi. Home: 1830 Ave del Mundo Ste 1208 Coronado CA 92118

MERLIS, GEORGE, television producer; b. Bklyn., Feb. 7, 1940; s. Martin Richard and Ethel (Pollack) M.; m. Susan Haviland Crane, Nov. 21, 1963; children: James Duncan, Andrew Richard. B.A., U. Pa., 1960; M.S.,

Columbia U. Grad. Sch. Journalism, 1961. Sports editor Rome (Italy) Daily Am., 1961; reporter N.Y. World-Telegram and Sun, N.Y.C., 1962-65; asst. city editor N.Y. World-Telegram and Sun, 1965-67; day city editor World Jour. Tribune, N.Y.C., 1967; supr. editorial tng. program N.Y. News, N.Y.C., 1967-68; dir. pub. relations ABC News, N.Y.C., 1967-72; field producer Reasoner Report, 1972-75; exec. producer Good Morning America, 1975-81, CBS Morning News, 1981-83, Entertainment Tonight, 1983-84, Dick Cavett, USA, 1985, Great Weekend, 1987-88; supervising producer ABC-TV's Home Show, 1988-91; exec. producer Willard Scott's Home and Garden Almanac, 1994-96, Kitty Bartholomew You're Home, 1994-96; pres. Jaand Prodns., Inc.; founder, chmn. J-Nex TV News Services, Inc.; chmn. Sunrise News Co. Author: V.P. a Novel of Vice Presidential Politics, 1971, (with Al Ubell) Al Ubell's Energy-Saving Guide for Homeowners, 1980; contbr. articles to TV Guide. Mem. Nat. TV Acad. Arts and Scis., Home Video Acad. Arts and Scis., Internat. Assn. Bus. Communicators, N.Y. Newspaper Guild.

MERLOTTI, FRANK HENRY, office furniture and hardware manufacturing company executive; b. Herrin, Ill., 1926; married. With Magic Chef Co., Chgo., 1950-53; with Whirlpool Corp., Benton Harbor, Mich., 1953-57, Steelcase, Inc., Grand Rapids, Mich., 1957—; v.p. Steelcase, Inc., from 1967, pres., chief oper. officer, dir., then pres., chief exec. officer, dir., until 1990, now chmn. exec. com., 1990—; dir. CMS Energy Corp., Consumer Power Co., Old Kent Fin. Corp. Office: Steelcase Inc PO Box 1967 CH5C Grand Rapids MI 49501 also: 901 44th St SE Grand Rapids MI 49508-7575

MERMANN, ALAN CAMERON, pediatrics educator, chaplain; b. Bklyn., June 23, 1923; s. William Joseph and Ada Fischer (McCree) M.; m. Constance Barnes, Sept. 4, 1948 (div. Mar. 1988); children: Edith, Constance, Sarah, Elizabeth; m. Cecily Allen Reynolds, Apr. 15, 1989. BA, Lehigh U., 1943; MD, Johns Hopkins U., 1947; MDiv, Yale U., 1979, MST, 1988. Diplomate Am. Bd. Pediatrics; med. license, Conn.; ordained to Christian ministry, United Ch. of Christ, 1979. Intern pediatrics Bellevue Hosp., N.Y.C., 1947-48, Johns Hopkins Hosp., Balt., 1948-49; sr. asst. resident pediatrician N.Y. Hosp., N.Y.C., 1949-50; resident pediatrician Meml. Hosp., N.Y.C., 1950-51; rsch. fellow Sloane-Kettering Inst., N.Y.C., 1953-54; pvt. practice pediatrics Guilford, Conn., 1954-82; clin. instr. pediatrics Yale Sch. Medicine, 1954-59, asst. clin. prof. pediatrics, 1959-71, assoc. clin. prof. pediatrics, 1971-79, clin. prof. pediatrics, 1979—; trustee New Eng. Coll., Henniker, N.H., 1969-91; fellow Branford Coll., Yale U., 1979—; mem. instnl. rev. bd. Union Carbide Corp., Danbury, Conn., 1991—; lectr. pastoral theology Yale Divinity Sch., 1979-82; asst. pastor First Congregational Ch., Guilford, 1979-82; assoc. pastor Ch. of Christ Congl., United Ch. of Christ, Norfolk, Conn., 1995—; chaplain Yale Sch. Medicine, 1982—, human investigation com., 1983-91, med. ctr. bioethics com., chair pediatrics ethics com., sch. medicine admissions com., com. on well-being of students. Contbr. articles to profl. jours. Lt. USNR, 1951-53. Fellow Am. Acad. Pediatrics. Democrat. Avocations: Dixieland, jazz, dancing, gardening. Home: 36 Eld St New Haven CT 06511-3816

MERMELSTEIN, ISABEL MAE ROSENBERG, senior citizen consultant; b. Houston, Aug. 20, 1934; d. Joe Hyman and Sylvia (Lincove) Rosenberg; m. Robert Jay Mermelstein, Sept. 6, 1953 (div. July 1975); children: William, Linda, Jody. Student U. Ariz., 1952, Mich. State U., 1974, Lansing (Mich.) C.C., 1975. Exec. dir. Shiawassee County YWCA, Owosso, Mich., 1975-78; real estate developer F&S Devel. Corp., Lansing, Mich., 1978-79, Corum Devel. Corp., Houston, 1979-81; adminstrv. fin. planner, sr. citizen cons. Investec Asset Mgmt. Group, Inc.; owner Ins. Filing Svcs. Sr. Citizens, 1985-96; guardian VA, 1990—. Author: For You! I Killed the Chicken, 1972. Mem. Older Women's League, Houston, 1st Ecumenical Council of Lansing, Nat. Mus. Women in Arts, Judaica Mus., Houston, Mus. Fine Arts, Houston, Mus. Natural Sci., Houston; docent Holocaust Mus., Houston. Recipient State of Mich. Flag, 1972, Key to City, City of Lansing, 1972-73. Mem. Nat. Assn. Claims Assistance Profls., Internat. Women's Pilot Orgn. (The 99's), Jewish Geneal. Soc., Internat. Directorate Disting. Leadership. Republican. Jewish. Lodges: Zonta, Licoma, B'nai B'rith, Hadassah, Nat. Fedn. Temple Sisterhoods. Flew All Women's Transcontinental Air Race (Powder Puff Derby), 1972, 73. Avocations: flying, gourmet cooking, needlepoint, knitting, snow skiing. Home: 4030 Newshire Dr Houston TX 77025-3921

MEROLLA, MICHELE EDWARD, chiropractor, broadcaster; b. Providence, Feb. 20, 1940; s. Joseph and Viola (Horne) M.; m. Ednamarie H.; children: Michele Edward II, Matthew Joseph, Samantha Joan, Alexandra Marie. BSc, Bryant Coll., 1961; DC, Chiropractic Inst. N.Y., 1965; LHD, Logan Chiropractic Coll., St. Louis, 1973. Owner chiropractic clinics, New Bedford, Taunton, Somerset, Seekonk, Attleboro and Westport, Mass., 1965—. Daily Network radio talk show host Holistic Hotline; owner radio sta. WARA-AM, Attleboro, Mass. Mem. Nat. Assn. Broadcasters, New Bedford City Coun., 1969-73, Airport Commn., 1972-75, Sch. Com., 1978-83, Recreation Commn., 1983-89; pres. New Bedford Aid Ctr., 1977; bd. dirs. Your Theatre Inc. Recipient Svc. award New England Chiropractic Coun., 1973. Mem. Southeastern Mass. Chiropractic Soc. (bd. dirs.), Mass. Chiropractic Soc., Am. Chiropractic Assn., N.Y. Acad. Sci., Fla. Chiropractic Soc., New Bedford Preservation Soc. (bd. dirs.). Editor: New England Jour. Chiropractic, 1965-75. Home: 62 Rear Manhattan Ave Fairhaven MA 02719 also: 3300 NE 23d Ave Lighthouse Point FL 33064 Office: 100 Bedford St New Bedford MA 02740-4839

MERON, THEODOR, law educator, researcher; b. Kalisz, Poland, Apr. 28, 1930; came to U.S., 1978, naturalized, 1984; s. Yhiel and Bluma (Lipschitz) Znamirowski; m. Monique Jonquet, Mar. 13, 1981; children: Daniel, Amos. M.J., Hebrew U., 1954; LL.M., Harvard U., 1955, S.J.D., 1957; diploma in Pub. Internat. Law, Cambridge U., Eng., 1957. Bar: Israel 1971, N.Y. 1984. Legal advisor to Fgn. Ministry of Israel, 1967-71; Israeli ambassador to Can., 1971-75; permanent rep. Geneva, 1977; prof. law Sch. Law, NYU, N.Y.C., 1978—; Carnegie lectr. Hague Acad. Internat. Law, 1980; Sir Hersch Lauterpacht Meml. lectr.; vis. fellow All Souls Coll., Oxford U., Eng., Max-Planck Inst., Heidelberg, Germany; vis. prof. Grad. Inst. Internat. Studies, Geneva, prof. law, 1991-95; pub. mem. U.S. Del. Conf. on Human Dimension Conf. on Security and Cooperation in Europe, Copenhagen, 1990. Author: Investment Insurance in International Law, 1976, The United Nations Secretariat, 1977, Human Rights Law-Making in the United Nations, 1986, Human Rights in Internal Strife: Their International Protection, 1987, Human Rights and Humanitarian Norms as Customary Law, 1989, Henry's Wars and Shakespeare's Laws, 1993; editor: Human Rights in International Law, 1984; editor in chief: Am. Jour. Internat. Law; contbr. articles to profl. publs. Bd. dirs. Helsinki Watch, Americas Watch, Internat. League of Human Rights. Rockefeller Found. fellow, 1975-76; Humanitarian Trust student Cambridge U., 1956-57. Mem. Am. Soc. Internat. Law (Cert. Merit 1987), French Soc. Internat. Law, Internat. Law Assn., Can. Coun. on Internat. Law, Coun. on Fgn. Rels., UN Assn. of the U.S. (hon.). Office: NYU Law Sch 40 Washington Sq S New York NY 10012-1005

MEROW, JAMES F., federal judge; b. Salamanca, N.Y., Mar. 16, 1932; s. Walter and Helen (Smith) M. AB, George Washington U., 1953, JD, 1956. Bar: Va. Trial atty. U.S. Dept. Justice, Washington, 1959-78; trial judge U.S. Ct. Claims, Washington, 1978-82, judge, 1982—. With JAGC, U.S. Army, 1956-59. Mem. ABA, Va. State Bar. Office: US Ct Fed Claims 717 Madison Pl NW Washington DC 20005-1011*

MEROW, JOHN EDWARD, lawyer; b. Little Valley, N.Y., Dec. 20, 1929; s. Luin George and Mildred Elizabeth (Stoll) M.; m. Mary Alyce Smith, June 19, 1957; 1 child, Alison. Student, UCLA, 1947-48; BS in Engring., U. Mich., 1952; JD, Harvard U., 1958. Bar: N.Y. 1958, U.S. Supreme Ct. 1971. Assoc. Sullivan & Cromwell, N.Y.C., 1958-64, ptnr., 1965—, vice chmn., 1986-87, chmn., sr. ptnr., 1987-94; bd. dirs. Seligman Group Investment Cos., Commonwealth Aluminum Corp.; chmn. bd. dirs. NYH Care Network, Inc.; bd. govs. N.Y. Hosp.; mem. joint bd. N.Y. Hosp.-Cornell Med. Ctr., chmn. adv. bd., 1990-95. Chmn. bd. dirs. Am.-Australian Assn.; bd. dirs. The U.S.-New Zealand Coun., Mcpl. Art Soc. N.Y.; chmn. Mcpl. Art Soc. Coun.; trustee, v.p. Am. Friends of Australian Nat. Gallery, Inc.; trustee, mem. exec. com. U.S. Coun. Internat. Bus.; bd. dirs., sec. Met. Opera Club, 1986-94; trustee N.Y. Downtown Hosp., 1991-95. Mem. ABA, Assn. of Bar of City of N.Y. (chmn. com. on securities regulation 1974-77), Am. Law Inst. (advisor corp. governance project 1978-92), Coun. on Fgn. Rels., Fgn. Policy Assn. (bd. govs.), Links Club, Pilgrims, Piping Rock Club, Down Town Assn., The Calif. Club, Union Club, Griffis Faculty Club. Home: 350 E 69th St New York NY 10021-5706 also: 51 Fruitledge Rd Brookville NY 11545-3316 Office: Sullivan & Cromwell 125 Broad St New York NY 10004-2498

MERRELL, JAMES LEE, religious editor, clergyman; b. Indpls., Oct. 24, 1930; s. Mark W. and Pauline F. (Tucker) M.; m. Barbara Jean Burch, Dec. 23, 1951; children: Deborah Lea Merrell Griffin, Cynthia Lynn Merrell Archer, Stuart Allen. A.B., Ind. U., 1952; M.Div., Christian Theol. Sem., 1956; Litt.D., Culver-Stockton Coll., 1972. Ordained to ministry Christian Ch., 1955; asso. editor World Call, Indpls., 1956-66; editor World Call, 1971-73; pastor Crestview Christian Ch., Indpls., 1966-71; editor The Disciple, St. Louis, 1974-89; sr. v.p. Christian Bd. Publ., 1976-89; sr. minister Affton Christian Ch., St. Louis, 1989-94; interim chaplain Culver-Stockton Coll., Canton, Mo., 1995; interim sr. pastor Friedens United Ch. of Christ, Warrenton, Mo., 1995—; bd. dirs. Horizons mag., 1995—. Author: They Live Their Faith, 1965, The Power of One, 1976, Discover the Word in Print, 1979, Finding Faith in the Headlines, 1985, We Claim Our Heritage, 1992. Chmn. bd. Kennedy Meml. Christian Home, Martinsville, Ind., 1971-73; trustee Christian Theol. Sem., 1978-81. Recipient Faith and Freedom award Religious Heritage of Am., 1983. Mem. Associated Ch. Press (award 1973, 79, 80, 81, 82, dir. 1974-75, 78-81, 1st v.p. 1983-85), Christian Theol. Sem. Alumni Assn. (pres. 1966-68), Religious Pub. Rels. Coun. (awards 1979, 80, 84, 87, 90, pres. St. Louis chpt. 1985-86), Sigma Delta Chi (award 1952), Theta Phi. Home: 5347 Warmwinds Ct Saint Louis MO 63129-3013 *As a religious communicator and as a pastor, I have always believed in applying the same standards in the sacred realm as in the secular. I have tried to pursue the truth, to keep my constituency informed, to celebrate the noble in life, to fight against those who would lie, distort and hide God's truth in the name of some supposed good.*

MERRELL, JESSE HOWARD, writer; b. Shelby, Ala., Dec. 9, 1938; s. James Walton and Emma Thelma (Davis) M.; m. Betsy Lee Davis, Jan. 11, 1964 (div. 1979); children: Sandra, Mark, Brad, Carolyn, Gwen. Grad., Shelby High Sch., Columbiana, Ala., 1957. Pitcher Cin. Redlegs, 1958-62; reporter, news dir. WHAP Radio, Hopewell, Va., 1963; writer/editor Hopewell News, 1963-65; state editor Daily Progress, Charlottesville, Va., 1965-68; assoc. editor Transport Topics, Washington, 1968-75; spl. asst. to pres. Am. Trucking Assn., Washington, 1975-76; editor Transport Topics, Washington, 1976-77; pres. Merrell Ent., Washington, 1977—; pub. rels. com. Am. Movers Conf., Washington, 1969-72; instr. Dale Carnegie courses, Washington, 1974-81, 1st pres., 1980-81; cons. Mid. Atlantic Conf., Riverdale, Md., 1981-82, Contract Carrier Conf., 1977-82; speechwriter ICC, Washington, 1982. Author: (novel) A Christmas Gift, 1979; syndicated columnist Religion and the Times, Washington Welter, (genealogy) The Merrells of Alabama, 1995. Mem. Nat. Trust for Hist. Preservation. With U.S. Army, 1960-62. Recipient Liberty award Congress of Freedom, Jackson, Miss., 1970, 71, Honor Cert., Freedoms Found., 1972, 1st place editorial writing Va. Press Assn., 1965, 1st place news writing, 1966. Mem. Nat. Press Club, Colonial Williamsburg Duke of Gloucester Soc. (charter mem.). Avocation: photography. Office: Merrell Ent 2610 Garfield St NW Washington DC 20008-4104

MERRELL, RONALD CLIFTON, surgeon, educator; b. Birmingham, Ala., June 18, 1946; s. Greene Lawrence and Florence (Jones) M.; m. Marsha Karen Cox, Dec. 24, 1966; children: Alexandria, Alison, R. Clifton. BS in Chemistry, U. Ala., 1967, MD, 1970. Diplomate Am. Bd. Surgery. Resident and fellow in surgery Wash. U., St. Louis, 1970-77; asst. prof. surgery Stanford (Calif.) U., 1979-84; assoc. prof. surgery U. Tex. Med. Sch., Houston, 1984-88, prof. surgery, 1988—; prof. surgery M.D. Anderson Cancer Ctr., Houston, 1988—; assoc. dean clin. affairs U. Tex. Med. Sch., Houston, 1988-92, vice dean, 1992—. Author 2 books; contbr. 61 articles to profl jours., 18 chpts. to books. Maj. U.S. Army, 1977-79. Recipient Basil O'Connor award March of Dimes, 1979, Rsch. Career Devel. award NIH, 1979-84, Henry J. Kaiser award Stanford U., 1982, 83, John P. McGovern Outstanding Tchr. award U. Tex. Med. Sch., 1988, Dean's Teaching Excellence award, 1983-89. Fellow ACS, Soc. Univ. Surgeons; mem. Am. Assn. Endocrine Surgery, Soc. Internat. de Chirurgie, Alpha Omega Alpha. Democrat. Episcopalian. Achievements include research in the transplantation of islets of Langerhans. Office: U Tex Med Sch 6431 Fannin St Ste 104 Houston TX 77030-1501

MERRELL, WILLIAM JOHN, JR., oceanography educator; b. Grand Island, Nebr., Feb. 16, 1943; s. William John and Dorothy Belle (Dye) M.; m. June Bearden, Oct. 12, 1970; children: Bethany Susan, Meredith Megan. BS, Sam Houston State U., 1965, MA, 1967; PhD, Tex. A&M U., 1971. Rsch. assoc. Dept. Oceanography, Tex. A&M U., 1970-71, 73-74, postdoctoral rsch. assoc., 1971-72, lectr., dep. dept. head, 1977-79, dep. dept. head, 1981-83, assoc. prof., 1981-85, prof., 1985—; co-investigator oceanography remote sensing project Tex. A&M U., 1969-70, dep. sea grant dir., 1977-78, asst. to dean geoscis., 1978-79, assoc. dir. Earth Resources Inst., 1978-79; dir. Earth Resources Inst. Coll. Geoscis., Tex. A&M U., 1983-84, assoc. dean, 1983-85, dir. div. atmospheric and marine scis., 1985; rsch. program mgmt. system officer Office Internat. Decade Ocean Exploration, NSF, 1972-73, exec. officer, 1974-77, asst. dir., 1985-87; oceanographer, mgr. Climate and Coastal Zone Br. Sci. Applications Inc., 1979-80; pres. Tex. A&M U., Galveston, 1987-91; v.p. rsch. policy Tex. A&M U., 1992-93; vice chancellor for strategic programs Tex. A&M U. System, Galveston, 1993-96; pres. Tex. Inst. Oceanography, 1989-91; program mgr. Gulf of Mex. Topographic Features Synthesis, 1981-83, prin. investigator ocean drilling program, 1983-85; mem. human exploration of space-space studies bd., chmn. ocean studies bd., mem. bd. on sustainable devel., mem. global change com., chmn. internat. spce programs com. NRC; pres. H. John Heinz Ctr. for Sci. Econs. and the Environment, Washington, 1995—; adv. com. on rsch. programs State of Tex.; adv. com. for Geosci. NSF. Contbr. articles to profl. jours. Bd. dirs. Galveston Hist. Fedn.; bd. govs. Galveston Econ. Devel. Corp.; bd. trustees Galveston Wharves. Recipient Disting. Svc. award NSF, 1987, Disting. Alumnus award Sam Houston State U., 1988, Disting. Achievement award Coun. for Geosciences and Earth Resources, 1990. Mem. The Oceanography Soc., Vanda Club (Antarctica), Sigma Xi (Disting. Mem. award 1987), Sigma Phi Sigma, Alpha Chi, Phi Kappa Phi. Office: Tex A&M U PO Box 1675 Galveston TX 77553-1675

MERRIAM, DWIGHT HAINES, lawyer, land use planner; b. Norwood, Mass., Apr. 20, 1946; s. Austin Luther and Lillian Diana (Olsen) M.; m. Cynthia Ann Hayes, May 21, 1966 (div. June 1992); children: Sarah Ann Leilani, Jonathan Hayes, Alexander Harlan; m. Susan Manning Standish, May 6, 1995. BA cum laude, U. Mass., 1968; M in Regional Planning, U. N.C., 1974; JD, Yale U., 1978. Bar: Conn. 1978, Mass. 1980, U.S. Dist. Ct. Conn. 1981, U.S. Dist. Ct. Hawaii 1984, U.S. Supreme Ct. 1990, U.S. Ct. Appeals (4th cir.) 1993. Land use planner Charles E. Downe, Newton, Mass., 1968; assoc. Byrne, Buck & Steiner, Farmington, Conn., 1978, Robinson, Robinson & Cole, Hartford, Conn., 1979-83; ptnr. Robinson & Cole, Hartford, 1984—; adj. prof. law Western New Eng. Coll., 1978-86, U. Conn., 1982, 84-87, U. Vt. Law Sch., 1994—; instr. planning U. Bridgeport, 1981-83, U. Conn., 1986-92; mem. faculty nat. Coll. Dist. Attys., 1983-87, Nat. Jud. Coll., 1994; instr. city and regional planning Memphis State U., 1989, 94; speaker in field. Co-editor: Inclusionary Zoning Moves Downtown, 1985; contbr. more than 50 articles and book revs. to profl. jours. Bd. dirs. Growth Mgmt. Inst., Washington, 1992—, Housing Edn. Resource Ctr., 1984-88, Housing Coalition for Capitol Region, Inc., 1984-86; bd. dirs. Conn. Fund for Environment, 1981-85, legal adv. com., 1985-88, legal adv. bd., 1978-81; mem. Environment 2000 environ. plan adv. bd. Conn. Dept. Environ. Protection, 1987-91; assoc. Environ. Law Inst., 1987—; mem. housing task force Conn. Dept. on Aging, 1981; mem. Gov.'s Housing Task Force, Conn., 1980-81. With USN, 1968-75, Vietnam; capt. USNR. Mem. ABA, Conn. Bar Assn. (exec. com. zoning & planning sect. 1985-87, 91—), Am. Planning Assn. (bd. dirs. 1988-90, chmn. planning & law divsn. 1984-86, exec. com. planning & law divsn. 1978-88, chmn. legis. com. Conn. chpt. 1978-80, editorial adv. bd. 1984-92), Nat. Inst. Mcpl. Law Officers (chmn. sect. on zoning, planning & land devel. 1988-89, sect. vice-chmn. 1987), Assn. State Floodplain Mgrs., Am. Inst. Cert. Planners (pres. 1988-90), Am. Coll. Real Estate Lawyers, U. N.C. Alumni Assn. Democrat. Unitarian. Avocations: sailing, skiing. Home: 1 Linden Pl Apt 410 Hartford CT 06106-1745 Office: Robinson & Cole 1 Commercial Plz Hartford CT 06103-3512

MERRIAM, JANET PAMELA, special education educator; b. L.A., Jan. 11, 1958; d. Allen Hugo and Linda (Teagle) Warren; m. Marshal Lockhart Merriam, Aug. 4, 1984 (div. June 1991); 1 child, Jennifer Elizabeth. BA, San Jose State U., 1981. Cert. tchr. learning handicapped, lang. devel. specialist, Calif. Asst. youth edn. dir. Christ Ch. Unity, San Jose, 1988-90; substitute tchr. Santa Clara (Calif.) Unified Sch. Dist., 1990; spl. day class tchr. Oak Grove Sch. Dist., San Jose, 1990—. Sunday sch. tchr. Christ Ch. Unity, San Jose, 1980-92. Mem. Coun. for Exceptional Children, Learning Disabilities Assn. Calif. Republican. Avocations: reading, knitting, Star Trek, old movies. Home: 1657 Glenville Dr San Jose CA 95124-3808 Office: 330 Bluefield Dr San Jose CA 95136-2100

MERRICK, BEVERLY CHILDERS, journalism, communications educator; b. Troy, Kans., Nov. 20, 1944; d. Horace Buchanan Merrick and Vola Yolantha (Clausen) Maul; m. John Douglas Childers, July 10, 1963; children: John Kevin, Pamela Christine, Jessica Faye. BA in Journalism with honors, Marshall U., 1980, BA in English with honors, 1980, M Journalism, 1982; M Creative Writing, Ohio U., 1986, cert. in Women's Studies, 1984, PhD in Comm. with honors, 1989. Reporter, photographer Ashland (Ky.) Daily Ind., 1981; tchr., instr. Albuquerque Pub. Schs., 1986-89; gen. assignment reporter, photographer Rio Rancho (N.Mex.) Observer, 1986; editor, rsch. cons. Ins. Pub. Law, Sch. of Law U. N.Mex., Albuquerque, 1990; asst. prof. Ga. So. U., Statesboro, 1991-94; assoc. prof. dept. mass comm. U. S.D., Vermillion, 1994-95; asst. prof. dept. journalism and mass comm. N. Mex. State U., Las Cruces, 1995—; part-time tchr., teaching assoc. Ohio U., Athens, 1981-84; part-time copy editor Albuquerque Tribune, 1991; vis. prof. East Carolina U., Greenville, N.C., 1989-90; adj. prof. Embry-Riddle U., Kirtland AFB, N.Mex., 1989, 91; organizer diversity conf., 1st amendment conf. Ga. So. U.; mem. session MIT, 1989. Author: (poetry) Navigating the Platte, 1986, Pearls for the Casting, 1987, Closing the Gate, 1993; contbr. poems to profl. publs., jours. and chpts. to books. Pub. rels. liaison Nat. Convention Bus. and Profl. Women, Albuquerque, 1988; pres. Albuquerque Bus. and Profl. Women, 1986-87, Rio Rancho Civic Assn., 1987-89, So. Ohio Improvement League, 1973-76; pres. bd. dirs. Pine Creek Conservancy Dist., 1976-83. Named Outstanding Citizen, N.Mex. Legislature, Truly Fine Citizen of Ohio, Ohio Gen. Assembly, 1973, Outstanding Homemaker of Ohio, Gov. of Ohio, 1974; grantee Reader's Digest, 1980, 83; John Houk Meml. grantee W.Va. Women's Conf., 1982; fellow Nat. Women's Studies Inst., Lilly Found., 1983, Freedom Forum Ethics, 1995, Am. Newspaper Inst., 1996; E.W. Scripps scholar, 1984; recipient Silver Clover award 4-H, Writing award Aviation/Space Writers Assn., 1981, 1st place open rsch competition Nat. Assn. Women's Dean's, Adminstrs. and Counselors, 1990; rsch. grantee N.Mex. State U., 1996. Mem. Soc. Profl. Journalists, Assn. for Edn. in Journalism and Mass Comm. (mem. nat. convention com. 1993-94, vice head mag. divsn. 1995-96, head mag. divsn., 1996-97), N.Mex. State Poetry Soc. (pres. 1987-89), Sigma Tau Delta. Office: N Mex State U Dept 3J, Box 30001 Las Cruces NM 88001-3001

MERRICK, DAVID (DAVID MARGULOIS), theatrical producer; b. St. Louis, Nov. 27, 1912; s. Samuel and Celia Margulois; m. Etan Aronson. B.A., Washington U., St. Louis; LL.B., St. Louis U. Produced plays on Broadway: Fanny, 1954, The Matchmaker, 1955, Look Back in Anger, Romanoff and Juliet, Jamaica, 1957, The Entertainer, The World of Suzie Wong, La Plume de ma Tante, Epitaph for George Dillon, 1958, Destry Rides Again, Gypsy, Take Me Along, 1958, Irma La Douce, A Taste of Honey, Becket (Tony award), Do Re Mi, 1960, Carnival, 1961, Sunday in New York, 1961, Ross, 1961, Subways are for Sleeping, 1961, I Can Get It For You Wholesale, Stop the World—I Want to Get Off, Tchin Tchin, Oliver, 1962, Rehearsal, Luther (Tony award), 110 in the Shade, Arturo Ui, 1963, Hello Dolly (Tony award), Oh, What A Lovely War, 1964, The Roar of the Greasepaint—The Smell of the Crowd, Inadmissible Evidence, Cactus Flower, 1965, The Persecution and Assassination of Jean Paul Marat as Performed by the Inmates of the Asylum of Charenton Under the Direction of the Marquis de Sade, 1965 (Tony award), Philadelphia, Here I Come, Don't Drink the Water, I Do I Do, 1966, Rosencrantz and Guildenstern Are Dead, 1967 (Tony award), Forty Carats, 1968, Promises, Promises, Play it Again Sam, Private Lives, 1969, Child's Play, 1970, Four in a Garden, 1971, A Midsummer Night's Dream, The Philanthropist, Mack and Mabel, Dreyfus in Rehearsal, 1974, Travesties (Spl. Tony award 1968), Red Devil Battery Sign, Very Good Eddy, 1975, 42nd Street, 1985-86 (Tony award 1980); produced films The Great Gatsby, 1974, Semi-Tough, 1977, Rough-Cut, 1980.

MERRICK, GEORGE BOESCH, aerospace company executive; b. Burlington, Iowa, Mar. 9, 1928; s. Dale McKeen and Marjorie May (Boesch) M.; m. Eleanor Gamble Moore, Sept. 1, 1951; children: Charles, Ellen, Elizabeth. B.S., U. Minn., 1949. With N.Am. Aviation (name changed to Rockwell Internat.), 1949; dir. Apollo Command and Service Module, Space div., 1966-72; v.p., program mgr. Apollo Program, 1972-74, v.p., program mgr. Space Shuttle Orbiter Program, 1974-76; pres. space div. Rockwell Internat., Downey, Calif., 1976-78; pres. space systems group Rockwell Internat., 1978-80, corp. v.p., 1980—. Recipient Pub. Service award NASA. Fellow Am. Astron. Soc., AIAA. Office: 2201 Seal Beach Blvd Seal Beach CA 90740-5603

MERRICK, ROSWELL DAVENPORT, educational association administrator; b. Kings County, N.Y., July 20, 1922; s. George Roswell and Marguerite Regina M.; m. Gladys K. Kinley, June 26, 1948; children—Gregory, Susan, Peter. B.S., Springfield Coll., 1944; M.A., N.Y. U., 1947; Ed.D., Boston U., 1953. Assoc. prof., head basketball coach Central Conn. Coll., New Britain, 1946-53; asst. dean (Coll. Edn.); dir. div. health, phys. edn., recreation and athletics So. Ill. U., Carbondale, 1953-58; exec. dir. Nat. Assn. Sport and Phys. Edn., Reston, Va., 1958-91, U.S. Fitness and Sport Coun., 1991—. Contbr. articles to profl. jours. Mem. U.S. Olympic Com. Served with USAAF, 1944-46. Mem. AAHPERD, Mt. Vernon Yacht Club. Methodist. Address: 4739 Neptune Dr Alexandria VA 22309-3132

MERRIER, HELEN, actress, writer; b. Chgo., Mar. 10, 1932; d. Miner Thompson and Helen (Hembree) Coburn; m. Tim Meier, Dec. 23, 1954; 1 child, William Frank. BA, Mills Coll., 1954; BS, Northwestern U., 1955. Actress (radio) Ma Perkins, One Man's Family, Standard School House of the Air, 1934-52, (stage) Lady Lucinda's Scrapbook, Edinburgh Fringe Festival, Scotland, 1996, New Am. Conservatory Theater, San Francisco, 1996, Time and the Conways, Remains Theater, 1991, Cinderella, Milw., 1991, Chgo. theatres including Second City ETC, Organic Theatre, Center Theatre, Court, Drury Lane Oakbrook, Hull House, Kingston Mines, other theatres, including Cleveland Play House, Coconut Grove Playhouse, Fla., Evergreen Stage Co., L.A., M & W Prodns., Milw., Guthrie Theatre, Mpls., (musicals) Woman of Year, Drury Lane, Evergreen Park, Ill., 1989, Sweeney Todd, Calo Theater, Chgo., 1991, Dreams of Defiance, N.Y.C., Chgo. and Ohio, Aristophanes' The Birds, Wisdom Bridge Theatre, Chgo., 1993, Dreams of Defiance, Theatre Bldg., Chgo., 1994, (film) Women in Treatment, 1990; dir. (stage) Center, Chgo., 1993. Women's bd. dirs. No. Ill. divsn. Salvation Army, 1965—; bd. dirs. Chgo. chpt. Prin. Found., 1972—, Women's Coll. Bd., 1956-66, Scottish Cultural Soc., 1976—; mem. Gaelic League, 1981-86, Celtic League, 1985—, Clan Irvine Assn., 1992—, Am. Anthrop. Soc., 1955-70, Am. Folklore Soc., 1955-70, Primitive Art Soc., 1975-85; mem. Apollo Chorus of Chgo., 1982-87, bd. mgmt., 1984-85. Mem. AFTRA, Actors Equity Assn. (Midwest adv. bd. 1983-84), Screen Actors Guild, Mills Coll. Club Chgo. (bd. dirs. 1962-81), Brit. Club Chgo., The Arts Club Chgo. Home: 915 Linden Ave Wilmette IL 60091-2712

MERRIFIELD, DONALD PAUL, university chancellor; b. Los Angeles, Nov. 14, 1928; s. Arthur S. and Elizabeth (Baker) M. B.S. in Physics, Calif. Inst. Tech., 1950; M.S., U. Notre Dame, 1951; A.M., Ph.L. in Philosophy, St. Louis U., 1957; Ph.D., MIT, 1962; S.T.M., U. Santa Clara, Calif., 1966; S.T.D. (hon.), U. So. Calif., 1969; D.H.L. (hon.), U. Judaism, 1984, Hebrew Union Coll.-Jewish Inst. Religion, 1986. Joined Soc. of Jesus, 1951; ordained priest Roman Cath. Ch., 1965; instr. physics Loyola U., Los Angeles, 1961-62; lectr. Engring. Sch., Santa Clara, 1965; cons. theoretical chemistry Jet Propulsion Lab., Calif. Inst. Tech., 1962-69; asst. prof. physics U. San Francisco, 1967-69; pres. Loyola Marymount U., Los Angeles, 1969-84, chancellor, 1984—. Mem. Sigma Xi. Home: Loyola Marymount U Xavier

Hall Los Angeles CA 90045 *In today's world, we all stand in need of that pragmatic hope which allows us to see the possibilities for building a more just society and meeting the challenges before us. Without such hope we are paralyzed before our difficulties. With a less realistic hope, too idealistic, we are continually overwhelmed by failures. But with an openness to possibilities, we can move ahead with determination.*

MERRIFIELD, DUDLEY BRUCE, business educator, former government official; b. Chgo., June 13, 1921; s. Fred and Anna (Marshall) M.; m. Paula Sorensen, June 8, 1949; children: Bruce, Robert, Marshall. AB in Chemistry, Princeton U., 1942; MS in Chemistry, U. Chgo., 1948, PhD in Chemistry, 1950. Sr. rsch. chemist Monsanto, St. Louis, 1950-56; mgr. polymer rsch. Tex.-U.S. Chem. Co., Parsippany, N.J., 1956-63; dir. rsch. and devel. Petrolite Corp., St. Louis, 1963-68; v.p. tech. and ventures Occidental Petroleum Co., Houston, 1968-77; v.p. tech. and venture mgmt. Continental Group, Stamford, Conn., 1977-82; asst. sec. for productivity, tech. and innovation Dept. Commerce, Washington, 1982-89; undersec. econ. affairs, 1986-87; Walter Bladstrom prof. emeritus U Pa., Phila., 1989-94; pres., CEO Pinnacle Rsch. Inst. Devel. Co., 1991—; mem. adv. bd. Binat Research and Devel. Found., U.S., Israel, France, India, 1979—. Contbr. articles to profl. jours.; patentee in field. Mem. exec. com. Episcopal Ch., 1973-79; chmn. Princeton Alumni Coun., 1968-72. With USMC, 1943-46. Fellow AAAS, Inst. for Chemists; mem. Am. Chem. Soc., Indsl. Rsch. Inst. (dir., pres.-elect 1977-82 M. Holland Best Article award), Am. Mgmt. Assn. (trustee, chmn. rsch. coun.), Dirs. Rsch., Sigma Xi. Republican. Episcopalian. Office: Pridco Mgmt Corp 1655 N Ft Meyer Dr Ste 700 Arlington VA 22209

MERRIFIELD, ROBERT BRUCE, biochemist, educator; b. Ft. Worth, Tex., July 15, 1921; s. George E. and Lorene (Lucas) M.; m. Elizabeth Furlong, June 20, 1949; children: Nancy, James, Betsy, Cathy, Laurie, Sally. B.A., UCLA, 1943, Ph.D., 1949. Chemist Park Research Found., 1943-44; research asst. Med. Sch., UCLA, 1948-49; asst. Rockefeller Inst. for Med. Research, 1949-53, assoc., 1953-57; asst. prof. Rockefeller U., 1957-58, assoc. prof., 1958-66, prof., 1966-92, John D. Rockefeller prof., 1984-92, emeritus prof., 1992—; Developed solid phase peptide synthesis; completed (with B. Gutte) 1st total synthesis of an enzyme, 1969. Assoc. editor: Internat. Jour. Peptide and Protein Research; contbr. articles to sci. jours. Recipient Lasker award biomed. rsch., 1969, Gairdner award, 1970, Intra-Sci. award, 1970, Nichols medal, 1973, Alan E. Pierce award Am. Peptide Symposium, 1979, Nobel prize in chemistry, 1984, Rudinger award European Peptide Soc., 1990, Chem. Pioneer award Am. Inst. Chemists, 1993. Mem. Am. Chem. Soc. (award creative work synthetic organic chemistry 1972, Hirschmann award in peptide chemistry 1990, Glenn T. Seaborg award 1993), NAS USA, Am. Soc. Biol. Chemists, Sigma Xi, Phi Lambda Upsilon, Alpha Chi Sigma. Office: Rockefeller Univ Dept Chemistry 1230 York Ave New York NY 10021-6307

MERRILL, ARTHUR ALEXANDER, financial analyst; b. Honolulu, June 17, 1906; s. Arthur Merton and Grace Graydon (Dickey) M.; m. Elsie Louise Breed, Aug. 17, 1929; 1 child, Anne Louise Merrill Breiling. B.S. in Elec. Engring, U. Calif., 1927; M.B.A., Harvard U., 1929. Mem. engring., statistics, and mgmt. depts. Gen. Electric Co., Schenectady, also N.Y.C., 1927-61; fin. writer and analyst, pres. Merrill Analysis Inc., Haverford, Pa., 1961—. Author: How Do You Use a Slide Rule, 1961, Behavior of Prices on Wall Street, 1985, Battle of White Plains, 1975, Seasonal Tendencies in Stock Prices, 1975, Filtered Waves, Basic Theory, 1977, Bias in Hourly, Daily and Weekly Wave Patterns, 1979, Remembering Names, 1985; editor: Tech. Trends, 1961-88. Mem. Market Technicians Assn. (chartered, Ann. award 1977), Fin. Analysts Fedn., N.Y. Soc. Security Analysts, Mensa, Intertel, Soc. Preservation and Encouragement Barber Shop Quartet Singing Am., Sigma Xi, Theta Chi, Tau Beta Pi, Eta Kappa Nu. Republican. Congregationalist. Home and Office: 3300 Darby Rd Apt 3325 Haverford PA 19041-1071

MERRILL, ARTHUR LEWIS, retired theology educator; b. Tura, Assam, India, Sept. 14, 1930; s. Alfred Francis and Ida (Walker) M.; m. Barbara Jean Mayer, Aug. 18, 1951 (dec. June 1978); children: Margaret Jean, Katherine Merrill Nelson, Robert L.; m. Margaret Z. Morris, Sept. 11, 1985. BA, Coll. of Wooster, 1951; BD with distinction, Berkeley Bapt. Div. Sch., 1954; PhD, U. Chgo., 1962. Ordained to ministry United Ch. of Christ, 1954. Asst. prof. Bapt. Missionary Tng. Sch., Chgo., 1957-58; assoc. prof. Mission House Theol. Sem., Plymouth, Wis., 1958-62; assoc. prof. United Theol. Sem. Twin Cities, New Brighton, Minn., 1962-67, prof., 1967-95, Piper prof. bibl. interpretation, 1993-95. Author: United Theological Seminary of the Twin Cities: An Ecumenical Venture, 1993; co-author: Biblical Witness and the World, 1967; co-editor: Scripture in History and Theology, 1977; contbr. articles to profl. publs. ATS-Lilly postdoctoral fellow, 1966-67. Mem. Soc. Bibl. Lit., Am. Schs. Oriental Rsch., Israel Exploration Soc., Minn. Theol. Libr. Assn. (pres. 1994-95). Home: 1601 Bessmore Park Rd Rochester IN 46975

MERRILL, CHARLES EUGENE, lawyer; b. San Antonio, Aug. 26, 1952; s. Charles Perry and Florence Elizabeth (Kupper) M.; m. Carol Ann Rutter, Apr. 28, 1984; children: Elizabeth C., Charles C. AB, Stanford U., 1974; JD, U. Calif., Berkeley, 1977. Bar: Mo. 1977, Calif. 1983, Ill. 1993. Ptnr. Husch & Eppenberger, St. Louis, 1977—. Mem. ABA, Bar Assn. of Met. St. Louis. Office: Husch & Eppenberger 100 N Broadway Ste 1300 Saint Louis MO 63102-2728

MERRILL, CHARLES MERTON, federal judge; b. Honolulu, Dec. 11, 1907; s. Arthur M. and Grace Graydon (Dickey) M.; m. Mary Luita Sherman, Aug. 28, 1931 (dec.); children: Julia Booth Stoddard, Charles McKinney. AB, U. Calif., 1928; LLB, Harvard, 1931. Bar: Calif. 1931, Nev. 1932. Sole practice Reno, 1932-50; judge Nev. Supreme Ct., 1951-59, chief justice, 1955-56, 59; judge U.S. Ct. of Appeals (9th cir.), San Francisco, 1959-74, sr. judge, 1974—. Mem. ABA, State Bar Nev. (gov. 1947-50), Am. Law Inst. (council 1960—). Office: US Ct of Appeals PO Box 547 San Francisco CA 94101*

MERRILL, DAVID NATHAN, ambassador; b. Balt.; s. Maurice B. and Ann (Nathanson) M.; m. Darlene J. Luke, 1976; four children. BA cum laude, Brandeis U., 1964; MA, Tufts U., 1965; MPA, Harvard U., 1974. Congl. liaison officer AID, 1976-79, rep. to Burma, 1979-83, deputy dir. legis. affairs, 1983-84, dir. East Asia affairs, 1984-87, mission dir. to Indonesia, 1987-90, dep. asst. adminstr., Europe Bur., 1990-94; U.S. amb. to Bangladesh, 1994—. Recipient Disting. Honor award AID, 1987, President's Meritorious Svc. award Dept. State, 1989. Mem. Am. Fgn. Svc. Assn. Office: Dhaka-DOS Washington DC 20521

MERRILL, EDWARD WILSON, chemical engineering educator; b. New Bedford, Mass., Aug. 31, 1923; s. Edward Clifton and Gertrude (Wilson) M.; m. Genevieve de Bidart, Aug. 19, 1948; children—Anne de Bidart, Francis de Bidart. AB, Harvard U., 1945; DSc, MIT, 1947. Research engr. Dewey & Almy div. W.R. Grace & Co., 1947-50; mem. faculty MIT, 1950—, prof. chem. engring., 1964—, Carbon P. Dubbs prof., 1973—; cons. in field, 1950—; cons. in biochem. engring. Harvard U. Health Services, 1982—. Author articles on polymers, rheology, med. engring. Pres. bd. trustees Buckingham Sch., Cambridge, 1969-74; trustee Browne and Nichols Sch., Cambridge, 1972-74, hon. trustee, 1974—. Recipient Alpha Chi Sigma award 1984. Fellow Am. Inst. for Med. and Biol. Engring., Am. Acad. Arts and Scis.; mem. AIChE (Charles M.A. Stine award 1993), Am. Chem. Soc., Soc. for Biomaterials. Patentee chem. and rheological instruments. Home: 90 Somerset St Belmont MA 02178-2010

MERRILL, GEORGE VANDERNETH, lawyer, investment executive; b. N.Y.C., July 2, 1947; s. James Edward and Claire (Leness) M.; m. Janice Anne Humes, May 11, 1985; 1 child, Claire Georgina. AB magna cum laude, Harvard U., 1968, JD, 1972; MBA, Columbia U., 1973. Bar: N.Y. 1973, U.S. Dist. Ct. (so. and ea. dists.) N.Y. 1974, U.S. Ct. Appeals (2d cir.) 1974. Assoc. Cleary, Gottlieb, Steen & Hamilton, N.Y.C., 1974-77, Hawkins, Delafield & Wood, N.Y.C., 1977-79; v.p. Irving Trust Co., N.Y.C., 1980-82; v.p., gen. counsel Listowel Inc., N.Y.C., 1982-84, bd. dirs., exec. v.p., gen. counsel, 1984-93, also bd. dirs. Pres. Arell Found., N.Y.C., 1985-93, also bd. dirs.; pres. Northfield Charitable Corp., N.Y.C., 1986-93; v.p., sec. Brougham Prodn. Co., N.Y.C., 1986-89, bd. dirs., sr. v.p., sec., 1990-93; v.p., sec. Marinetics Inc., N.Y.C., 1988-90, sr. v.p., sec., 1991-93, also bd. dirs., 1989-93; v.p. Sci. Design and Engring. Co., Inc., N.Y.C., 1987-88, bd. dirs., exec. v.p., 1989-93; v.p. Instl. Portfolio Mgmt., Shawmut Investment Advisors, 1993-95, v.p. Instl. Portfolio Mgmt., Fleet Investment Advisors, 1996—. Recipient Detur award Harvard U., 1968, John Harvard scholar. Mem. ABA, Am. Mgmt. Assn., Assn. of Bar of City of N.Y., The Brook, Union Club (N.Y.C.), Down Town Assn., Racquet and Tennis Club, Somerset Club (Boston), Pilgrims of U.S. Home: 60 Brenway Dr West Hartford CT 06117-3010 Office: Fleet Fin Group Inc 777 Main St Hartford CT 06115-2000

MERRILL, HARVIE MARTIN, manufacturing executive; b. Detroit, Apr. 26, 1921; s. Harvie and Helen (Nelson) M.; m. Mardelle Merrill; children—Susan, Linda. B.S. in Chem. Engring, Purdue U., 1942. Devel. engr. Sinclair Refining Co., 1946-47; research and gen. mgr. 3M Co., St. Paul, 1947-65; v.p. fabricated products Plastics div. Stauffer Chem. Co., N.Y.C., 1965-69; with Hexcel Corp., San Francisco, 1969-86, pres., chief exec. officer, 1969-86, chmn. bd., 1976-88; Calif.; bd. dirs. TIS Mortgage/Investment Co., Corp., San Francisco; adv. dir. Arrow Venture Ptnrs., N.Y.C. With USAF, 1942-46. Mem. Pacific-Union Club, Bohemian Club San Francisco, Villa Taverna (San Francisco), Burlingame Country Club. Home: 1170 Sacramento St San Francisco CA 94108-1943

MERRILL, JEAN FAIRBANKS, writer; b. Rochester, N.Y., Jan. 27, 1923; d. Earl Dwight and Elsie (Fairbanks) M. B.A., Allegheny Coll., 1944; M.A., Wellesley Coll., 1945. Feature editor Scholastic Mags., 1947-50; editor Lit. Cavalcade, 1956-57; publs. div. Bank St. Coll. Edn., 1964-65. Children's books include Henry, the Hand-Painted Mouse, 1951, The Woover, 1952, Boxes, 1953, The Tree House of Jimmy Domino, 1955, The Travels of Marco, 1956, A Song for Gar, 1957, The Very Nice Things, 1959, Blue's Broken Heart, 1960, Shan's Lucky Knife (Jr. Lit. Guild selection), Emily Emerson's Moon, 1960 (Jr. Lit. Guild selection), The Superlative Horse (Jr. Lit. Guild selection), 1961 (Lewis Carroll Shelf award 1963), Tell About the Cowbarn, Daddy, 1963, The Pushcart War (Lewis Carroll Shelf award), 1964 (Boys Club Am. Jr. Book award), High, Wide & Handsome, 1964 (Jr. Lit. Guild selection), The Elephant Who Liked to Smash Small Cars, 1967, Red Riding, 1968, The Black Sheep, 1969, Here I Come—Ready or Not!, 1970, Mary, Come Running, 1970, How Many Kids are Hiding on My Block?, 1970, Please, Don't Eat My Cabin, 1971, The Toothpaste Millionaire (Dorothy Canfield Fisher Meml. award 1975-76), 1972 (Sequoyah award 1977), The Second Greatest Clown in the World, 1972, The Jackpot, 1972, The Bumper Sticker Book, 1973, Maria's House, 1974, The Girl Who Loved Caterpillars, 1992; poetry books edited include A Few Flies and I, 1969; libretto for chamber opera Mary Come Running, 1983. Fulbright fellow India, 1952-53. Mem. N. Am. Mycol. Assn., Authors League, Vt. Arts Coun., War Resisters League, Vt. Inst. Natural Sci., Dramatists Guild, Vt. Nat. Resources Coun., Vt. League Writers, Soc. Children's Book Writers, Fulbright Assn., Sierra Club, Audobon Soc., Phi Beta Kappa. *My interest in writing children's books may have derived from the impact certain books had on me as a child, and a wish to recreate the quality of that experience. As to my general motivation as a writer, I would say that it is to celebrate those aspects of the human experience that affirm the creative and life-reverencing instinct in man. I always hope that my stories may be essentially liberating, opening the reader to emotional, as well as intellectual experience, and that they may be entertaining, encouraging the capacity for joy by evoking the free play of a reader's curiosity, humor and inventiveness.*

MERRILL, JOSEPH HARTWELL, religious association executive; b. Norway, Maine, Jan. 16, 1903; s. Wiggin L. and Ella M. (Porter) M. Grad. high sch. Head retouching dept. Bachrach, Inc. (photographers), Newton, Mass., 1937-61; sec. Mass. Assn. Spiritualists, 1953-61; exec. sec. Nat. Spiritualist Assn. Chs., Milw., 1961-71; v.p. Nat. Spiritualist Assn. Chs., 1971-73, pres., 1973-94; v.p. Internat. Spiritualist Fedn. Spiritualists, London, 1975-81; lectr. social legislation for oldsters Townsend Orgn. Served with AUS, 1942-43. Address: 13 Cleveland Ave Lily Dale NY 14752

MERRILL, KENNETH COLEMAN, retired automobile company executive; b. South Bend, Ind., Feb. 20, 1930; s. Kenneth Griggs and Helen Shapley (Coleman) M.; m. Helen Jean Tagtmeyer, June 10, 1956; children: Barry, Diane, John. B.A., Cornell U., 1953; M.B.A., Ind. U., 1956. With Ford Motor Co., Dearborn, Mich., 1956-91; asst. controller Ford Motor Co., Dearborn, 1967-71, gen. asst. controller, 1971-73, controller N.Am. automotive ops., 1973-79, exec. dir. parts ops., 1979-80, exec. dir. bus. planning and trust mgmt., 1980-87; pres. Ford Motor Credit Co., Dearborn, 1987-91, ret., 1991; bd. dirs. Am. Dental Techs., 1990—; v.p. Wadsworth (Ohio) Ford, 1992—. Pres. Plymouth (Mich.) Symphony Soc., 1969-70; vice chmn. bd. dirs. Detroit Inner City Bus. Improvement Forum, 1977-79; bd. dirs. Schoolcraft Coll. Found., 1982-94, pres., 1984-86; bd. dirs. Crossroads, 1992-94, 96—, treas., 1994. Mem. Fin. Execs. Inst., Greater Detroit C. of C. (bd. dirs. 1988-91, exec. com. 1990-91), Detroit Econ. Club, Barton Hills Country Club, Oaks Club (Sarasota, Fla.), Beta Gamma Sigma, Psi Upsilon. Episcopalian (treas. 1973-74, 79—). Home: 1450 Maple St Plymouth MI 48170-1516 also: Apt 306H 8779 Midnight Pass Rd Sarasota FL 34242-2850

MERRILL, LELAND GILBERT, JR., retired environmental science educator; b. Danville, Ill., Oct. 4, 1920; s. Leland Gilbert and May (Babcock) M.; m. Virginia Gilhooley, Sept. 14, 1949; children: Susan Jane, Alison Lee. B.S., Mich. State U., 1942; M.S., Rutgers U., 1948, Ph.D., 1949. Research asst. entomology Rutgers U., 1946-49; asst. prof. entomology Mich. State U., 1949-53; mem. faculty Rutgers U., 1953-82, research specialist entomology, 1960-61, dean agr., 1961-71, dir. Inst. Environ. Studies, 1971-76, prof. center coastal and environ. studies, 1976-82; exec. sec. N.J. Acad. Sci., 1984-92. Served to maj. AUS, 1942-46. Medallist, Wrestling XIV Olympiad, 1948. Mem. AAAS, Entomol. Soc. Am., Coastal Soc., Sigma Xi, Alpha Gamma Rho, Phi Kappa Phi, Alpha Zeta, Epsilon Sigma Phi. Home: 49 Gulick Rd Princeton NJ 08540-4111

MERRILL, MARTHA, instructional media educator; b. Anniston, Ala., Apr. 21, 1946; d. Walter James and Polly (McCarty) M. BA, Birmingham-So. Coll., 1968; MS, Jacksonville (Ala.) State U., 1974; PhD, U. Pitts., 1979. Social worker Tuscaloosa (Ala.) County Dept. Human Resources, 1968-71, Calhoun County Dept. Human Resources, Anniston, Ala., 1971-73; social scis./bus. libr. Jacksonville State U., 1974-86, prof. instrnl. media, 1987—. Mem. Friends of Libr. bd. Anniston-Calhoun County Pub. Libr., 1984—. Recipient Ala./SIRS Intellectual Freedom award, Intellectual Freedom Com., Ala. Libr. Assn., 1992. Mem. ALA (exec. bd., Intellectual Freedom Round Table 1987-93), Ala. Libr. Assn. (pres. 1990-91, Disting. Svc. award 1995), Ala. Assn. Coll. and Rsch. Librs. (pres. 1989-90), Southeastern Libr. Assn. (chair intellectual freedom com. 1986-88, chair resolutions com. 1990-92). Office: Jacksonville State U Dept Ednl Resources Coll Edn Jacksonville AL 36265

MERRILL, PHILIP, publisher; b. Balt.; m. Eleanor Merrill; children: Douglas, Catherine, Nancy. BA, Cornell U., 1955; PMD, Harvard Bus. Sch., 1963. Spl. asst. Dept. State, Deputy Sec. of State, Washington, 1961-68; counsellor undersec. of defense for policy Washington, 1981-83; asst. sec. gen. NATO, Brussels, Belgium, 1990-92; pub., chmn. Capital-Gazette Communications, Inc., Washingtonian Mag., Washington, 1968—; mem. policy bd. Dept. Defense, 1983-90. Del. USA Short Wave Treaty, USA Law of the Sea Treaty; trustee Cornell U., U. Md. Found., Aspen Inst.; bd. dirs. Ctr. Strategic and Internt. Studies, Johns Hopkins Sch. Advanced Internat. Studies; bd. dirs. Johnson Sch. Mgmt. Cornell U., Chesapeake Bay Found., Fed. City Coun., U. Md. Sch. Pub. Policy; mem. Gulf War Air Power Survey, 1991-92. Recipient Disting. Svc. medal U.S. Dept. Def., 1988. Mem. Coun. Fgn. Rels., Inst. Internat. Strategic Studies, Chief Execs. Orgn., World Pres. Orgn. Office: The Washingtonian Mag 1828 L St NW Washington DC 20036-5118

MERRILL, RICHARD JAMES, educational director; b. Milw., Apr. 15, 1931; s. Henry Baldwin and Doris (Lucas) M.; m. Kathleen Emden Keely, June 14, 1953 (dec. Jan. 1974); children—Wendy Ann, Vicki Louise, Robin Kay, Christina Suzanne; m. Terry Bradley Alt, Aug. 10, 1974 (div. 1976); m. Shannon Ann Lynch, June 19, 1977. B.S., U. Mich., 1953; M.A., Columbia U., 1957, Ed.D., 1960. Tchr. sci. Ramona High Sch., Riverside, Calif., 1958-62; secondary sci. coordinator Riverside city schs., 1960-62; exec. dir. chem. edn. material study Harvey Mudd Coll. and U. Calif. at Berkeley, 1962-65; curriculum specialist Mt. Diablo Unified Sch. Dist., Concord, Calif., 1965-91, dir. curriculum, 1980-81; assoc. dir. Inst. for Chem. Edn. and Project Phys. Sci., U. Calif., Berkeley, 1990-94; bd. dirs. San Francisco Bay Area Sci. Fair; mem. sci. adv. com. Calif. Assessment Program, 1983-89, also mem. assessment adv. com. to state supt., pub. instrn., 1984-86; dir. N. Calif. W. Nev. Jr. Sci. and Humanities Symposium, 1993—; lectr. Calif. State U., Hayward, 1996—. Author: (with David W. Ridgway) The CHEM Study Story, 1969; co-author: National Science Teachers Association Guidelines for Self-Assessment of Secondary Science Programs, 1975, Science Framework for California Public Schools, 1978, 84; co-author, editor: The Physical Science of Living in California, 1993. Bd. dirs. Ctr. for New Ams., Concord, Calif., 1984-91. Served from ensign to lt. (j.g.) USN, 1953-56. Mem. Nat. Sci. Tchrs. Assn. (past pres., past mem. exec. com.), Nat. Sci. Suprs. Assn., Elem. Sch. Sci. Assn. (coun. 1975-82, pres. 1983), Calif. Sci. Tchrs. Assn. (Disting. Svc. award 1990), Assn. Calif. Sch. Adminstrs., Acacia, Phi Delta Kappa. Home: 1862 2nd Ave Walnut Creek CA 94596-2553 Office: U Calif Lawrence Hall of Sci Berkeley CA 94720

MERRILL, ROBERT, baritone; b. Bklyn., June 4, 1919; s. Abraham and Lillian (Balaban) Miller; m. Marion Machno, May 30, 1954; children—David Robert, Lizanne. MusD (hon.), Gustavus Adolphus Coll., 1970. Ind. baritone N.Y.C. and on tour, 1945—. Baritone in concert, opera and on radio and TV; winner, Met. Auditions of the Air, 1945, debut in opera, 1945; operatic roles include Escamillo in Carmen, Germont in La Traviata, Valentine in Faust, Amonasro in Alda, Marcello in La Boheme, Don Carlo in La Forza del Destino, Sir Henry Ashton in Lucia de Lammermoor; sang in La Traviata condr. Arturo Toscanini over NBC network; singer with NBC, 1946—; opened Met. Opera season Rodrigo in Don Carlo, 1950; appeared in Toscanini's final opera performance and rec. as Renato in Un Ballo in Maschera; opened Met. season as Valentine in Faust, 1953, as Figaro in Barber of Seville, 1954, Rigoletto in Rigoletto; Barnaba in Gioconda, Scarpia in Tosca, Renato in Un Ballo in Maschera, Iago in Otello, Count di Luna in Il Trovatore, Tonio in Pagliacci, Gerard in Andrea Chenier, 1962, Sir Henry in Lucia, 1964, Valentine in Faust, 1965, Germont in La Traviata, 1966, Amonasro in Aida, 1969; also opened Met. Opera season, 1971; opened Royal Opera House-Covent Garden season as Germont in La Traviata, 1967, Met. Opera visit to Japan, Tokyo, 1975; appeared in concerts, London, Bournemouth, Geneva, Israel, 1975; rec. artist: RCA-Victor, Angel, London, Columbia labels; stage debut as Tevye in Fiddler on the Roof, 1970; author: (novel) The Divas, 1978, (autobiography) Once More From the Beginning, 1965, Between Acts, 1976. Mem. Nat. Council of the Arts, 1968-74. Recipient Music Ann. award for rec. Ah, Dite Alla Giovine, 1946, best opera rec. award NARAS, 1962, 64, Harriet Cohen Internat. Music award, 1961, Handel medal City of N.Y., 1970, medal Westchester C.C. Found., 1981, Nat. Medal of Arts, 1993, Internat. Dor L'Dor award B'nai B'rith, 1994, Lawrence Tibbett award Am. Guild Mus. Artists Relief Fund, 1996; named Father of Yr. in Music, 1980. Mem. Opera Guild, AFTRA, AGVA, Actors Equity Assn., Screen Actors Guild, Am. Guild Mus. Artists. Club: Friars (monk 1968—). Avocations: golf, baseball, fine art. Achievements: 1st Am. opera singer to give 500 performances at Met. Opera, N.Y.C., 1973; ofcl. singer New York Yankees, 1969—; performer for Pres. Roosevelt, Truman, Eisenhower, Kennedy, Johnson, Nixon, Ford, Carter, Reagan; only singer to perform before both houses of Congress at Roosevelt Meml. Office: Robert Merrill Assocs Inc 79 Oxford Rd New Rochelle NY 10804-3712 *If you honestly feel that you are doing your best, it makes good criticism even sweeter and bad criticism less painful.*

MERRILL, RONALD THOMAS, geophysicist, educator; b. Detroit, Feb. 5, 1938; s. Robert Able and Freda (Havens) M.; m. Nancy Joann O'Byrne, Sept. 1, 1962; children: Craig Elliot, Scott Curtis. BS in Math., U. Mich., 1959, MS in Math., 1961; PhD in Geophysics, U. Calif., Berkeley, 1967. Asst. prof. oceanography U. Wash., Seattle, 1967-72, assoc. prof. geophysics and oceanography, 1972-77, prof. geophysics and geol. sci., 1977—, chmn. dept. geophysics, 1985-92. Author: (with M.W. McElhinny) The Earth's Magnetic Field, 1984; contbr. numerous articles to profl. jours. Recipient numerous rsch. grants from NSF, other founds. Fellow Am. Geophys. Union (pres. geomagnetism and paleomagnetism sect. 1988-90); mem. AAAS, Soc. Geomagnetism (Japan). Avocations: skiing, hiking, scuba diving, dancing. Office: U Wash Dept Geophysics AK-50 Seattle WA 98195

MERRILL, STEPHEN, governor. Student, U. N.H., Georgetown U. Former personal counsel to Sec. Air Force, Pentagon; atty. gen. State of N.H., Concord, 1985-89; gov. State of N.H., 1993—; mem. N.H. task force on Child Abuse and Neglect, former pres., legal counsel. Served to capt., USAF. Fellow ABA; mem. Ea. Assn. Attys. Gen. (chmn.), Phi Beta Kappa. Office: Office of the Governor State Capitol Concord NH 03301*

MERRILL, STEVEN WILLIAM, research and development executive; b. Oakland, Calif., Aug. 6, 1944; s. David Howard and Etha Nadine (Wright) M. BA in Chemistry, Calif. State U., 1986. Lic. pyrotechnic, Calif. Apprentice Borgman Sales Co., San Leandro, Calif., 1960-64; assembler Calif. Fireworks Display, Rialto, Calif., 1970; pyrotechnician Hand Chem. Industries, Milton, Ont., Can., 1972-74; dir. R&D Pyrospectaculars, Rialto, 1988-92; pyrotechnic cons., 1993—; owner, dir. Merrill Prodns. Ordnance, Crestline; experimenter in field, 1958—; chief chemist Baron Blakesly Solvents, Newark, Calif., 1987-88; court expert San Francisco Superior Ct., 1971, Victorville (Calif.) Superior Ct. Counselor Xanthos, Inc., Alameda, Calif., 1970. Mem. AAAS, Am. Chem. Soc., Am. Stats. Assn., Am. Bd. Forensic Examiners, Internat. Platform Assn. Avocations: wood carving, sculpture, photography, electronics. Home: PO Box 676 Crestline CA 92325-0676 Office: Merrill Prodns Ordnance PO Box 3327 Crestline CA 92325

MERRILL, THOMAS WENDELL, lawyer, law educator; b. Bartlesville, Okla., May 3, 1949; s. William McGill and Dorothy (Glasener) M.; m. Kimberly Ann Evans, Sept. 8, 1973; children: Jessica, Margaret, Elizabeth. BA, Grinnell Coll., 1971, Oxford U., 1973; JD, U. Chgo., 1977. Bar: Ill. 1980, U.S. Dist Ct. (no. dist.) Ill. 1980, U.S. Ct. Appeals (5th cir.) 1982, U.S. Ct. Appeals (7th cir.) 1983, U.S. Ct. Appeals (9th and D.C. cirs.) 1984, U.S. Supreme Ct. 1985. Clk. U.S. Ct. Appeals (D.C. cir.), Washington, 1977-78, U.S. Supreme Ct., Washington, 1978-79; assoc. Sidley & Austin, Chgo., 1979-81, counsel, 1981-87, 90—; dep. solicitor gen. U.S. Dept. Justice, 1987-90; prof. law Northwestern U., Chgo., 1981—, John Paul Stevens prof., 1993—. Contbr. articles to profl. jours. Rhodes scholar Oxford U., 1971; Danforth fellow, 1971. Home: 939 Maple Ave Evanston IL 60202-1717 Office: Northwestern U Sch Law 357 E Chicago Ave Chicago IL 60611-3008

MERRILL, VINCENT NICHOLS, landscape architect; b. Reading, Mass., Apr. 28, 1912; s. Charles Clarkson and Bessie Louise (Nichols) M.; m. Anna Victoria Swanson, Jan. 20, 1943. AB, Dartmouth Coll., 1933; M in Landscape Architecture, Harvard U., 1937. Registered landscape architect, Mass. Office asst. Shurcliff & Shurcliff, Boston, 1937-42, 47-54, ptnr., 1954-58; ptnr. Shurcliff & Merrill and predecessors Shurcliff, Shurcliff & Merrill, Boston, Mass., 1958-81; prin. Shurcliff & Merrill, Cambridge, Mass., 1981-89. Founder, bd. dirs., pres. Charles River Watershed Assn., Auburndale, Mass., 1963-75; bd. dirs. Charles Basin Adv. Com., Boston, 1979-82; pres. Hubbard Ednl. Trust, Cambridge, 1981-89, bd. dirs., 1989-95. Capt. U.S. Army, 1942-46, ETO. Recipient Gold medal Mass. Hort. Soc., 1988. Fellow Am. Soc. Landscape Architects; mem. Boston Soc. Landscape Architects (pres. 1961-63), Hort. Club of Boston (pres. 1992-94). Avocation: home landscaping. Home and Office: 141 Old County Rd Lincoln MA 01773-3506

MERRILL, WILLIAM DEAN, retired architect, medical facility planning consultant; b. Portland, Oreg., June 1, 1915; s. Charles O. and Grace (Ruhl) M.; m. Bernice E. Wickham, Apr. 19, 1943; 1 child, Sue Ann Merrill Boardman. Student in Fine Arts and Forestry, Oreg. State U., 1936-38; student in Architecture, U. Oreg., 1939-42. Registered architect, Oreg., Calif. Prin. W.D. Merrill, Architect, Portland, 1959-64; architect, ptnr. Bissell & Merrill, Architects, Stockton, Calif., 1964-68; architect Kaiser Found. Hosps. design and constrn., 1968-81; pvt. practice hosp. design and constrn., residential design and constrn., Bay Area, 1981-91; hosp. and sch. constrn. insp. State of Calif., 1984-93; ret. 1996. Served as lt. (j.g.) USNR, 1942-44, PTO. Mem. AIA (emeritus). Republican. Address: 14349 SE Sieben Pky Clackamas OR 97015-6319

MERRILL, WILLIAM DICKEY, architect; b. Honolulu, Mar. 21, 1909; s. Arthur Merton and Grace (Dickey) M.; m. Evelyn Gregory Selfridge, Oct. 23, 1936; children: Elizabeth, Thomas Selfridge. BA, U. Calif., Berkeley, 1930; MArch, Harvard U., 1932; PhD, Edinburgh U., 1974. Staff achitect Am. Schs. Oriental Rsch., Jerusalem, 1933-35; assoc. C.W. Dickey, architect, Honolulu, 1936-42; ptnr. Merrill, Simms and Roehrig, architects, Honolulu, 1942-60; pres. Merrill, Roehrig, Onodera and Kinder, Inc., Honolulu, 1960-65; cons. architect Honolulu, 1965-81; mem. affiliate grad. faculty U. Hawaii, 1971. Prin. works include Neill Blaisdell Concert Hall, campus Mid-Pacific Inst., campus Kamehameha Elem. Sch., class rm. bldg. Kamehameha Girls Sch., Foremost Dairies, TH-3 Hawaii Housing Authority, other comml., indsl., ednl. and mil. structures, hosps. in Hawaii. Mem. com. mgmt. Armed Svcs. YMCA, 1952-69; bd. dirs. Hawaiian Humane Soc., 1954-65, Hawaiian Mission Children's Soc., 1945-64. Fellow AIA (past pres. Hawaii, mem. emeritus). Home: 8545 Carmel Valley Rd Carmel CA 93923-9556

MERRIMAN, ILAH COFFEE, financial executive; b. Amarillo, Tex., Mar. 22, 1935; d. Oran and Frances Elizabeth (Rocque) Coffee; children: Pamela, Michael. BS in Math., Tex. Tech. U. Cert. secondary tchr., Tex. Pres., chief exec. officer H&R Block Inc. of Houston; pres. H&R Block Inc., Tex.; exec. bd. Tex. Tech U. ex students assn., pres., 1989, past trustee; mem. steering com. Pres.'s Council, bd. dirs. Tex. Tech Double T Connection, Tex. Tech Found., Women's Basketball Tournament, Southwest Athletic Coun., past; mem. Tex. Tech U. enterprise fund Dallas Chpt.; dir. Cotton Bowl Assn. representing Tex. Tech U. Named Disting. Alumni, Texas Tech U., 1992; recipient Ernest T. Steward award Coun. Advancement and Support Edn., 1993. Mem. Dallas Mus. Fine Art, Dallas Shakespeare Festival, Dallas Symphony Assn., Dallas Hist. Soc., Cotton Bowl Assn. (exec. com.), Women's Basketball Coaches Assn. dir. nat. corp. bd.), Red Raider Club of Tex. Tech U. (past mem. exec. com.). Methodist.

MERRIMAN, JOHN ALLEN, lawyer, insurance executive; b. Knoxville, Iowa, Aug. 13, 1942; s. John W. and Doris (Henry) M.; m. Barbara Anne Beatty, Nov. 10, 1990. AB, Northwestern U., 1964; LLB, Columbia U., 1967. Bar: Iowa 1967, U.S. Dist. Ct. (no. and so. dists.) Iowa 1967. Assoc. Gamble, Riepe, Martin & Webster, Des Moines, 1967-69; counsel Equitable Life Ins. Co. Iowa, Des Moines, 1969-76; ptnr. Mumford, Schrage, Merriman & Zurek, P.C., Des Moines, 1976-86; assoc. gen. counsel Equitable of Iowa Cos., Des Moines, 1986-87, gen. counsel, sec., 1987—. Active state and local politics. Lt. USNR, 1968-79. Mem. Des Moines Club, Des Moines Golf and Country Club (dir. 1987-90). Republican. Avocations: golf, running. Office: Equitable of Iowa 604 Locust St Des Moines IA 50309-3705

MERRIN, SEYMOUR, computer marketing company executive; b. Bklyn., Aug. 13, 1931; s. Joseph and Esther Bella (Manelis) M.; m. Elaine Cohen, Sept. 4, 1960 (dec. May 1962); m. Elizabeth Jenifer Slack, Oct. 12, 1963 (dec. Mar. 1995); children: Charles Seymour, Marianne Jenifer Weights. BS, Tufts Coll., 1952; MS, U. Ariz., 1954; PhD, Pa. State U., 1962. Geologist Magma Copper Co., Superior, Ariz., 1954; geologist U.S. Geol. Survey, 1956-58; chemist IBM, Poughkeepsie, N.Y., 1962-64; mgr. package devel., mgr. reliability and failure analysis Sperry Semicondr. div. Sperry Rand, Norwalk, Conn., 1965-68; cons. materials tech. Fairfield, Conn., 1967-69; v.p., dir. Innotech Corp., Norwalk, 1969-74; div. mgr. Emdex div. Exxon Enterprises, Milford, Conn., 1974-78; chmn., dir. Computerworks, Westport, Conn., 1978-85; v.p., dir. personal computing service Gartner Group, Inc., Stamford, Conn., 1984-87; pres. Merrin Resources, Southport, Conn., 1987-89, Merrin Info. Svcs., Inc., Palo Alto, Calif., 1987—; bd. dirs. Micrografx Corp., Richardson, Tex.; mem. adv. panel Apple Computer Co., Cupertino, Calif., 1982-83; mem. adv. bd. Compaq Computer Corp., Houston, 1984-85, Computer and Software News, N.Y.C., 1984-89; mem. program adv. bd. Comdex, Boston, 1985—; lectr. in field. Contbr. numerous articles to profl. publs.; patentee in field. Served with U.S. Army, 1954-56. Fellow Geol. Soc. Am., Am. Inst. Chemists; Computing Tech. Industry Assn. (founder, pres. 1981-83, bd. dirs. 1981-84). Home: 143 Buckthorn Way Menlo Park CA 94025-3027 Office: 2275 E Bayshore Rd Palo Alto CA 94303-3220

MERRION, ARTHUR BENJAMIN, mathematics educator, tree farmer; b. Williamstown, N.J., Oct. 25, 1938; s. Anthony Robert and Eva May Merrion; m. Martha Jane Banse, Dec. 26, 1965 (div. May 1977); children: Benjamin Thomas, Elizabeth Jane. AB in Math., Pfeiffer Coll., 1965; MS in Numerical Sci., Johns Hopkins U., 1976. Navigations scientist Defense Mapping Agy. Hydrographic Ctr., Suitland, Md., 1966-78; fellow ops. rsch. analysis Sec. Army Pentagon, Washington, 1978-80; ops. rsch. analyst Asst. Sec. Army, Washington, 1980-86; tree farmer Huntingtown, Md., 1986—; instr. math. and stats. Embry-Riddle Aeronautical U., 1993-94; math. instr. Charles County C.C., 1990-91; tutor Literary Coun.; recruiter for cadets at West Point. Author: A Short Story By Edgar Allen Pooh. With U.S. Army, 1957-58. Mem. Md. Soc. SAR. Avocations: chess, violin, judo, wrestling, ice skating. Home: PO Box 395 Huntingtown MD 20639-0395 *The Bible says many different things to many different people. To Thomas Alva Edison it was a "Chemist's Handbook". To me it is the source of all man's creativity, directly from the greatest Creator of all. It is a source of inspiration, a solace for periods of depression, and a prescription when I'm in error.*

MERRISS, PHILIP RAMSAY, JR., corporate banker; b. N.Y.C., June 7, 1948; s. Philip Ramsay and Elisabeth (Paine) M.; m. Janet Henry Hylan, Oct. 27, 1973. AB in Econs. magna cum laude, Lafayette Coll., 1970, MBA with high distinction, Dartmouth Coll., 1972. Assoc. corp. fin. dept. A.G. Becker and Co. Inc., N.Y.C., 1972-73; fin. analyst corp. banking dept. Chase Manhattan Bank, 1973, asst. treas. N.Y.C. dist., 1974-75, 2d v.p. mining and metals div., 1976-78, 2d v.p. petroleum div., 1978-79, v.p. global petroleum div., 1979-86, client exec., v.p. pub. utilities component, 1986-87, client exec., v.p. global energy component, 1987-89, credit supervising officer, div. exec., v.p. U.S. pvt. banking, 1989-94; credit exec. Chase Manhatten Pvt. Bank, N.Y.C., 1994—. Served to capt. U.S. Army, 1978. Tuck scholar Dartmouth Coll., 1972. Mem. Am. Econ. Assn., Fin Mgmt. Assn., Aircraft Owners and Pilots Assn., N.Y. Road Runners Club, Weston Gun Club, Yale Club, Fairfield County Fish and Game Club, Phi Beta Kappa. Republican. Episcopalian. Home: 100 Hillspoint Rd Westport CT 06880-5111 Office: Chase Manhattan Bank 1211 Avenue Of The Americas New York NY 10036-8701

MERRITT, BRUCE GORDON, lawyer; b. Iowa City, Iowa, Oct 4, 1946; s. William Olney and Gretchen Louise (Kuever) M.; m. Valerie Sue Jorgensen, Dec. 28, 1969; children: Benjamin Carlyle, Alicia Marie. AB magna cum laude, Occidental Coll., 1968; JD magna cum laude, Harvard U., 1972. Bar: Calif. 1973, D.C., 1996. Assoc. Markbys, London, 1972-73; assoc. Nossaman, Krueger & Marsh, L.A., 1973-79, ptnr., 1979-81; asst. U.S. atty., L.A., 1981-85; ptnr. Hennigan & Mercer, L.A., 1986-88; ptnr. Debevoise & Plimpton, L.A., 1989-95, N.Y., 1996—. Bd. dirs. Inner City Law Ctr., 1991-96. Fellow Am. Coll. Trial Lawyers; mem. Calif. State Bar Assn. (exec. com. litigation sect. 1992-95), L.A. County Bar Assn. (del. state bar conf. 1984-86), Phi Beta Kappa. Office: Debevoise & Plimpton 875 3d Ave New York NY 10022

MERRITT, CAROLE ANNE, secondary school educator; b. Trenton, N.J., Oct. 30, 1943; d. Angelo Joseph and Katherin Paulline (Petruccio) Tramontana; 1 child, Stephen; m. John Howard Merritt, June 10, 1990. BA, Glassboro State U., 1965; MA, Salisbury State U., 1992. Tchr., class advisor Steinert H.S., Hamilton, N.J., 1965-70; tchr. Bode Sch., St. Joseph, Mo., 1971-84; mock trial coach, class advisor, cheerleader advisor Wicomico Sr. H.S., Salisbury, Md., 1992-95, cheerleader, advisor, 1985-87; Am. edn. week chairperson Parkside H.S., Salisbury, Md., 1987-94; tchr. Parkside H.S., Salisburg, Md., 1985—, mock trial coach, 1985-95; freshman class advisor Parkside H.S., 1993-94, sophomore class advisor, 1994-95, jr. class advisor, 1995-96. Contbr. articles to profl. jours., including Tchr., Sch. & Cmty. Vol. Crisis Ctr., Joseph House, Peninsular Med. Ctr., Salisbury Zoo, Salisbury Arts Coun. Mem. Delta Kappa Gamma, Kappa Delta Pi, Phi Delta Kappa. Avocations: swimming, exercise, reading, ceramics, travel. Home: 29822 Deer Harbour Dr Salisbury MD 21801-2505 Office: Parkside HS 1015 Beaglin Park Dr Salisbury MD 21801-9295

MERRITT, DORIS HONIG, pediatrics educator; b. N.Y.C., July 16, 1923; d. Aaron and Lillian (Kunstlich) Honig; children: Kenneth Arthur, Christopher Ralph. B.A., CUNY, 1944; M.D., George Washington U., 1952. Diplomate Am. Bd. Pediatrics, Nat. Bd. Med. Examiners. Pediatric intern Duke Hosp., 1952-53; teaching and rsch. fellow pediatrics George Washington U., 1953-54; pediatric asst. resident Duke U. Hosp., 1954-55, cardiovascular fellow pediatrics, 1955-56, instr. pediatrics, dir. pediatric cardiorenal clinic, 1956-57; exec. sec. cardiovascular study sect., gen. medicine study sect. div. rsch. grants NIH, 1957-60; dir. med. rsch. grants and contracts Sch. Medicine Ind. U., 1961-62, asst. prof. pediatrics Sch. Medicine, 1961-68, asst. dean med. rsch. Sch. Medicine, 1962-65, asst. dir. med. rsch., aerospace rsch. application ctr. Sch. Medicine, 1963-65, assoc. dir. med. rsch. Sch. Medicine, 1965-68, asst. dean for rsch., office v.p. rsch. and dean advanced studies Sch. Medicine, 1965-67, dir. sponsored programs, asst. to provost Sch. Medicine, 1965-68, assoc. dean for rsch. and advanced studies, office v.p. and dean for rsch. and advanced studies Sch. Medicine, 1967-71, assoc. prof. pediatrics Sch. Medicine, 1968-73, prof. Sch. Medicine, 1973-80, assoc. dean Sch. Medicine, 1987—, prof. pediatrics, assoc. dean Sch. Medicine, 1988—; spl. asst. to dir. NIH, 1978-87, rsch. tng. and rsch. resource officer, 1980-87, acting dir. Nat. Ctr. Nursing Rsch., 1986-87; acting dean Sch. Engring. and Tech. Purdue U., 1995—; bd. dirs. Ind. Health Industry Reform; cons. USPHS, NIH div. rsch. grants Div. Health Rsch. Facilities and Resources, Nat. Heart Inst., 1963-78, Am. Heart Assn., 1963-67, Ind. Med. Assn. Commn. Vol. Health Orgns., 1964-67, Bur. Health Manpower, Health Profession's Constrn. Program, 1965-71, Nat. Library Medicine, Health Ctr. Libr. Constrn. Program, 1966-72; dir. office sponsored programs Ind. U.-Purdue U. Indpls. Office Chancellor, 1968-71, dean rsch. and sponsored programs, 1971-79; mem. Nat. Library Medicine biomed. communications rev. com., 1970-74; mem. com. to study rsch. capabilities acad. depts. ob-gyn Inst. Medicine, 1990-91. Contbr. articles to profl. jours. Chmn. Indpls. Consortium for Urban Edn., 1971-75; v.p. Greater Indpls. Progress Com., 1974-79; mem. Community Svc. Council, 1969-75; bd. dirs. Bd. for Fundamental Edn., 1973-77, Ind. Sci. Edn. Found., 1977-78, Community Addiction Svc. Agy., Inc., 1972-74; trustee Marian Coll., 1977-78; exec. com. Nat. Council U. Rsch. Adminstrs., 1977-78; bd. regents Nat. Library Medicine, 1976-80; chmn. adv. screening com. for life scis. Council Internat. Exchange of Scholars, 1978-81; bd. dirs. Community Svc. Coun. Cen. Ind., 1989-94, Univ. Hosp. Consortium, Tech. Assessment Ctr., 1990-93; mem. Ind. Health Industry Forum, 1993—; chmn. scientific and tech. review bd. on biomedical and behavioral rsch. facilities NIH Ctr. for Rsch. Resources, 1994—. Served to lt. (j.g.) USNR. Fellow Am. Acad. Pediatrics; mem. AAAS, George Washigton U., Duke U. Med. Alumni Assns., Phi Beta Kappa, Alpha Omega Alpha., NIHNCRR (chair scientific and tech. rev. bd. on biomed. and biobehavioral rsch. facilities 1994-97). Office: Dean's Office ET 219 Purdue Sch E & T 799 W Michigan St Indianapolis IN 46202-5132 *The era in which I have lived and worked has been one of transition for women entering traditional male fields. What recognition and advancement I have achieved, have been due to maintaining high standards of performance on equal terms with my professional peers. I consider the three essential ingredients of success to be competence, optimistic tenacity of purpose and an enduring sense of humor.*

MERRITT, GILBERT STROUD, federal judge; b. Nashville, Tenn., Jan. 17, 1936; s. Gilbert Stroud and Angie Fields (Cantrell) M.; m. Louise Clark Fort, July 10, 1964 (dec.); children: Stroud, Louise Clark, Eli. BA, Yale U., 1957; LLB, Vanderbilt U., 1960; LLM, Harvard U., 1962. Bar: Tenn. 1960. Asst. dean Vanderbilt U. Law Sch., 1960-61, lectr., 1963-69, 71-75, assoc. prof. law, 1969-70; assoc. Boult Hunt Cummings & Conners, Nashville, 1962-63; city atty. City of Nashville, 1963-66; U.S. Dist. atty. for (mid. dist.) Tenn., 1966-69; ptnr. Gullett, Steele, Sanford, Robinson & Merritt, Nashville, 1970-77; judge U.S. Ct. Appeals (6th cir.), Nashville, 1977—; chief judge U.S. Ct. Appeals (6th cir.), 1989—; exec. sec. Tenn. Code Commn., 1977. Mng. editor: Vanderbilt Law Rev, 1959-60; contbr. articles to law jours. Del. Tenn. Constl. Conv., 1965; chmn. bd. trustees Vanderbilt Inst. Pub. Policy Studies. Mem. ABA, Fed. Bar Assn., Tenn. Bar Assn., Nashville Bar Assn., Vanderbilt Law Alumni Assn. (pres. 1979-80), Am. Law Inst., Order of Coif. Episcopalian. Office: US Ct Appeals 303 Customs House Nashville TN 37203*

MERRITT, HOWARD SUTERMEISTER, retired art educator; b. Ithaca, N.Y., June 12, 1915; s. Ernest and Bertha (Sutermeister) M.; m. Florence Sederquest Hill, June 27, 1941; children—Jessica, Stephen, Jonathan, James. B.A., Oberlin Coll., 1936; M.F.A., Princeton U., 1942, Ph.D., 1958. Mem. faculty U. Rochester, N.Y., 1946-80; prof. emeritus U. Rochester, 1980—; cons. 19th Century Am. Painting, 1960—. Contbr. articles to various publs. Served with AUS, 1942-45. Decorated Bronze Star; Nat. Endowment for Humanities summer grantee, 1966-68. Mem. Coll. Art Assn. Home: 85 Bellevue Dr Rochester NY 14620-2703 Office: Dept of Fine Arts University Rochester Rochester NY 14627

MERRITT, JACK NEIL, retired army officer; b. Lawton, Okla., Oct. 23, 1930; s. Theodore and Lovell Wood; m. Rosemary Ralston, Oct. 31, 1953; children—Stephen Cahill, Grover Wood, Roger William. B.S., U. Nebr., Omaha, 1959; M.B.A., George Washington U., 1965; grad., F.A. Officer Advance Course, 1961, Air Command and Staff Coll., 1965, Indsl. Coll. Armed Forces, 1970; PhD (hon.), The Citadel. Commd. 2d lt. U.S. Army, 1953, advanced through grades to gen., 1985; served in various command and staff assignments U.S., Korea, Germany, 1953-65; served with (Army Gen. Staff, Pentagon), 1965-66; mem. staff (Asst. Sec. Def. for Systems Analysis), Washington, 1966-68; bn. comdr. (Riverine Arty.), Vietnam, 1968-69; staff (Asst. to Pres. for Nat. Security Affairs, White House), 1970-73; div. arty. comdr. 1st Cavalry Divsn., Ft. Hood, Tex., 1973-74, chief of staff, 1974-75, asst. div. comdr., 1975-77; comdg. gen. U.S. Army F.A. Center and comdt. U.S. Army F.A. Sch., Ft. Sill, Okla., 1977-80; comdt. U.S. Army War Coll., Carlisle, Pa., 1980-82; comdg. gen. Ft. Leavenworth, Kans., 1982-83; dir. joint staff Joint Chiefs of Staff, 1983-85; U.S. Rep. NATO Mil. Com., 1985-87; ret., 1987; pres. Assn. U.S. Army, Arlington, Va., 1988—; chmn. mil. profl. devel. com. West Point Study, 1977; adj. fellow Ctr. Strategic and Internat. Studies; mem. Commn. on West Point Honor Code, 1988-89. Bd. dirs. Atlantic Coun. Marshall Found., Brassey's, Inc.; chmn. adv. com. The Citadel. Decorated D.S.M., Silver Star, Legion of Merit, D.F.C., Soldiers medal, Bronze Star, Air medal, Joint Commendation medal, Navy Commendation medal, Army Commendation medal; named to Okla. Hall of Fame. Mem. Internat. Inst. Strategic Studies, Inter-Univ. Seminar Armed Forces and Soc., Assn. U.S. Army, F.A. Assn., 1st Cavalry Div. Assn., 9th Inf. Div. Assn., Kappa Alpha. Office: Assn US Army 2425 Wilson Blvd Arlington VA 22201-3326

MERRITT, JAMES EDWARD, lawyer; b. Hickory, N.C., June 10, 1938; s. Eddy Schmidt and Dorothy (Hunt) M.; m. Joan L. Hiscock, June 14, 1960 (div. 1983); children: James Edward Jr., Catherine Hunt; m. Kristine McFadden, May 4, 1983. AB, Duke U., 1959; LLB, Harvard U., 1962. Bar: D.C. 1962, Calif. 1968; cert. tax specialist, Calif. Assoc. Pogue & Neal, Washington, 1962-64; trial atty. regional counsel IRS, San Francisco, 1964-68; assoc. Morrison & Foerster, San Francisco and Washington, 1968-72, ptnr., 1972—; lectr. Golden Gate U., San Francisco, 1970-74; cons. chief counsel IRS, Washington, 1983; mem. adv. bd. Tax Mgmt. Inc., N.Y.C., 1987—. Contbr. articles to profl. jours. Mem. Asia Soc., Washington, 1986—. Mem. Am. Coll. Tax Counsel (regent), ABA (coun., dir., sect. taxation 1990-93, mem. commn. on legal problems of elderly 1993—), Bar Assn. D.C., Bar Assn. San Francisco (Outstanding Tax Lawyer 1983), J. Edgar Murdock Inn of Ct. Avocations: travel, gardening, sports. Office: Morrison & Foerster 345 California St San Francisco CA 94104-2675

MERRITT, JAMES FRANCIS, biological sciences educator, administrator; b. Raleigh, N.C., July 21, 1944; s. Clifton and Emily (Rogers) M.; m. Sue Wall, Aug. 9, 1969; children—Ashley Grant, Bradley Gene, Carey Reid. B.S., E. Carolina U., 1966, M.S., 1968; Ph.D., N.C. State U., 1973. Asst. prof. biological scis. U. N.C., Wilmington, 1973-78, assoc. prof., chmn., 1978-89, dir. Ctr. Marine Scis. Rsch., Wilmington, 1989—. Contbr. articles to profl. jours. Chmn. PTA, Wilmington, 1983, Marine Expo Com., Wilmington, 1984—. E.G. Moss fellow N.C. State U., 1972. Mem. Am. Genetic Assn., N.C. Acad. Sci. (sect. chmn. 1975-76, vice pres. 1979-80), Chi Beta Phi (Outstanding Service award 1966). Avocations: fishing; woodworking. Home: 3523 Violet Ct Wilmington NC 28409-2541 Office: U NC at Wilmington Ctr Marine Sci Rsch 7205 Wrightsville Ave Wilmington NC 28403-7224

MERRITT, JOE FRANK, industrial supply executive; b. Paris, Tex., Dec. 9, 1947; s. Henry Grady and Margaret Leon (Murrell) M.; m. Barbara Jean Sands (div. May 1973); 1 child, Daniel Joe; m. Bonnie Louise McLure, Feb. 1, 1975; 1 stepchild, David Wright Dwyer. BA in Govt., U. Tex., Arlington, 1970. Cert. contractor Dept. Def. USA and Can. With purchasing A.F. Holman Boiler Works Inc., Dallas, 1970-77; supply salesman Stanco Indsl. Supply, Dallas, 1977-79, Tool Specialty Indsl. Supply, Dallas, 1979-80, Briggs-Weaver Indsl. Supply, Dallas, 1980-81; owner, pres. Joe F. Merritt & Co., Inc., Carrollton, Tex., 1981; v.p., gen. mgr. Abrasives & Buffs Co., Dallas, 1981-83; owner, pres. Buff, Polish & Grind Indsl. Supply Co., Inc., Argyle, Tex., 1984—; cons. The Broadway Collection, OLathe Kans., 1990, Ofenhauser Co., Houston, 1993, 94; Innovation Industries, Russellville, Ark., 1994; instr. buff, polish and grind methods quality control dept. Rsch. Facility, Peterbilt Motors Co., 1994. Creator State of the Art Rsch. and Tchg. Facility, 1984, 100% Virgin Lambswool Buffing Belt, 1987, spl. extra wide spindle buffers to be manufactured by Baldor Electric, Ft. Smith, Ark., 1995. Recipient Cert. of Appreciation, City of Carrollton, Tex., 1981. Mem. Soc. Mfg. Engrs. Republican. Methodist. Avocations: sailing, coin collecting, travel, animals, sports cars. Office: Buff Polish & Grind Indsl Supply 1907 Fm 407 E Argyle TX 76226-9447

MERRITT, JOSHUA LEVERING, JR., retired engineering executive, consultant; b. Balt., July 28, 1931; s. Joshua Levering Sr. and Sarah Ethel (Sparks) M.; m. Eleanor Grace Williams , June 26, 1954; children: Nancy Lynn Mann, Debra Sue Stevens, Steven Edward. BSCE, Lehigh U., 1952; MSCE, U. Ill., 1955, PhD in Engring., 1958. Registered civil, structural, geotech. engr., Calif.; registered civil and structural engr., Nev.; registered structural engr., Ill.; registered profl. engr., N.M. Rsch. asst., civil engr. U. Ill., Urbana, 1952-54, rsch. assoc., civil engr., 1954-58, asst. prof. civil engring., 1958-60, assoc. prof., 1960-66, prof., 1966-68; vis. prof. U. Ill., Urbana, Ill., 1968-69; mgr. hard rock silo devel. program TRW, 1968-70, mgr. facilities engring., 1970-71; pres. Merritt Cases, Inc., Redlands, Calif., 1971—; dir. Redlands ops. BDM Internat., Inc., 1986-91; mem. U.S. nat. com. on rock mechanics NRC, 1989-90; expert mem. panel on underground tech. devel. NRC, 1990; chmn. bd. appeal Dept. Bldg. and Safety, San Bernardino County, Calif.; cons. in field, Urbana, 1958-68, Yucaipa, 1991—. Author more than 70 articles and rsch. reports. Fellow ASCE (local and nat. com.); mem. Am. Underground Space Assn., Structural Engrs. Assn. So. Calif., Inst. for Shaft Drilling Tech. (charter mem.), Internat. Soc. for Rock Mechanics, Internat. Soc. for Soil Mechanics and Found. Engrs., Internat. Tunnelling Assn., Seismol. Soc. Am., Am. Concrete Inst., Earthquake Engring. Rsch. Inst., Sigma Xi, Phi Kappa Phi, Chi Epsilon. Presbyterian. Achievements include research in fields of structural dynamics, earthquake engineering and behavior of materials.

MERRITT, LAVERE BARRUS, engineering educator, civil engineer; b. Afton, Wyo., Mar. 11, 1936; s. Joseph M. and Lera (Barrus) M.; m. Jackie Call, Jan. 5, 1956; children: Teri F., Lynn T., Rachel R., Shaun S. BSCE, U. Utah, 1963, MSCE, 1966; PhD, U. Wash., 1970. Registered profl. engr., Utah. Prof. civil and environ. engring. Brigham Young U., Provo, Utah, 1970—, chmn. dept. civil engring., 1986-92; chmn. faculty senate, 1996-97; spl. cons. Utah Div. Health, Salt Lake City, 1973-74; cons. engring. firms, 1970—. Chmn. Provo Met. Water Bd., Utah, 1978-87. Named Utah Engring. Educator of the Yr. Utah Joint Enring. Coun., 1987. Mem. ASCE (nat. dir. 1982-85), Am. Acad. Environ. Engrs., Water Environment Fedn. (nat. dir. 1981-84, Bedell award), Am. Water Works Assn., Am. Soc. Engring. Edn., No. Am. Lake Mgmt. Soc., Sigma Xi. Republican. Mormon. Home: 562 E 3050 N Provo UT 84604-4264 Office: Brigham Young U 368 Cb Provo UT 84602-1021

MERRITT, LORETTA GAETANA, primary education educator; b. Passaic, N.J., Dec. 21, 1944; d. James A. and Rosalia (Ricci) Domino; m. Robert V. Merritt, Apr. 29, 1973. BA in Elem. Edn., William Paterson, 1966; MA in Edn. Adminstrn., Kean Coll. N.J., 1987; postgrad., various colls., 1984-90. Cert. early childhood/nursery sch. tchr., prin., supr. First grade, kindergarten and pre-kindergarten tchr. Roosevelt Sch. #10, Passaic, N.J., 1966—; acting asst. prin. Roosevelt Sch. #10, Passaic, 1993; adv. mem. pupil assistance coun. #10 Sch., Passaic, 1986—, chairperson site-based coun., 1992-94, mem.-advisor devel. kindergarten full-day curriculum com., 1992, mem.-advisor for devel. basic skills checklist test com., 1992, mem. dist. steering com., 1993-94. Recipient Gov.'s Convocation on Excellence in Tchg., N.J. State Dept. Edn., Trenton, 1987, Passaic County Tchr. of the Year, 1987-88. Mem. NEA, N.J. Edn. Assn., Edn. Assn. Passaic (rep. 1993—), Kindergarten Tchrs. Assn., PTO Dist. #10 (cons. 1994), Kappa Delta Phi. Avocations: arts and crafts, gardening, traveling.

MERRITT, NANCY-JO, lawyer; b. Phoenix, Sept. 24, 1942; d. Robert Nelson Meeker and Violet Adele Gibson; children: Sidney Kathryn, Kurt, Douglas. BA, Ariz. State U., 1964, MA, 1974, JD, 1978. Bar: Ariz. 1978, U.S. Dist. Ct. Ariz. 1978, U.S. Ct. Appeals (9th cir.) 1984. Assoc. Erlichman, Fagerberg & Margrave, Phoenix, 1978-79, Pearlstein & Margrave, Phoenix, 1979-81, Corwin & Merritt, P.C., Phoenix, 1982-87; with Nancy-Jo Merritt & Assocs., P.C., Phoenix, 1987-88; shareholder Bryan Cave, Phoenix, 1988—. Author: Understanding Immigration Law, 1993; contbr. articles to profl. jours. Active Ariz. Coalition for Immigration Representation, Phoenix, 1988—. Fellow Ariz. Bar Found.; mem. ABA, Am. Immigration Lawyers Assn. (chairperson Ariz. chpt. 1985-87, several coms., Pro Bono award), Am. Immigration Law Found. (trustee), Ariz. Bar Assn. (immigration sect.), Nucleus Club. Democrat. Avocations: modern literature, South American literature, hiking, scuba diving, gardening. Office: Bryan Cave 2800 N Central Ave Fl 21 Phoenix AZ 85004-1007

MERRITT, ROBERT EDWARD, lawyer, educator; b. San Francisco, Jan. 31, 1941; s. Robert Edward and June Adele (Reynolds) M.; m. Robin Susan Kragen, July 2, 1966; children: Kim, Kevin, Kristin, Kate. BA, Sacramento State U., 1963; JD, U. Calif., Berkeley, 1966. Bar: Calif. 1967. Ptnr. Steinhart & Falconer, San Francisco, 1968-82, McCutchen, Doyle, Brown & Enersen, San Francisco, 1982—; lectr. U. Calif. Extension, Berkeley, 1976—, U. Calif. Extension, Davis, 1980—, U. Calif. Boalt Hall, 1989; mem. subdiv. adv. com. Calif. Dept. Real Estate, 1984—; cons. real property law subcom. U. Calif. Continuing Edn. of Bar, 1983—; mem. planning com. Real Property Inst., 1984—; mem. editorial bd. Land Use and Environment Forum, U. Calif. Continuing Edn. of Bar, 1991-96. Author: Guide to Subdivision Sales Law, 1974, California Real Estate Forms and Commentaries Law and Business, Inc., 1985, California Subdivision Map Act Practice, 1987, Understanding Development Regulations, 1994; contbr. articles to profl. publs. Trustee Moraga (Calif.) Sch. Dist., 1977-89/. Named Citizen of Yr., Lesher Publs.-Moraga Kiwanis Club, 1983. Mem. ABA, State Bar Calif., Am. Coll. Real Estate Lawyers. Home: 227 Paseo Del Rio Moraga CA 94556-1628 Office: McCutchen Doyle Brown & Enersen 1331 N California Blvd Walnut Creek CA 94596-4537

MERRITT, SUSAN MARY, computer science educator, university dean; b. New London, Conn., July 28, 1946; d. Nelson Alfred and Mary (Cory) M. BA summa cum laude, Cath. U. Am., 1968; MS, NYU, 1969, PhD, 1982; Cert., Inst. for Edn. Mgmt., Harvard U., 1985. Joined Sisters of Divine Compassion, 1975; permanent cert. tchr., N.Y. Systems programmer Digital Equipment Corp., Maynard, Mass., 1969-70; tchr. Good Counsel Acad. High Sch., White Plains, N.Y., 1970-75; adj. instr. computer sci. Pace U., 1972-78; asst. prof. Pace U., White Plains, 1978-82, assoc. prof., 1982-85, prof., 1985—, chmn. dept., 1981-83, dean Sch. Computer Sci., 1983—; mem. gen. coun. Sisters Divine Compassion, 1988-92. Contbr. articles to profl. jours. Recipient Cert. of Appreciation IEEE, 1990. Mem. Assn. for Computing Machinery (edn. bd. 1988—), Phi Beta Kappa, Sigma Xi. Roman Catholic. Office: Pace U 1 Martine Ave White Plains NY 10606

MERRITT, THOMAS BUTLER, lawyer; b. Toledo, Apr. 3, 1939; s. George Robert and Bernice (Gerwin) M.; m. Mary Jane Bothfeld, July 23, 1966; children—Thomas Butler, Haidee Soule, Theodore Bothfeld. A.B. magna cum laude, Harvard U., 1961, LL.B. cum laude, 1966. Bar: Mass. 1966, U.S. Supreme Ct. 1974, N.H. 1994. Law clk. to assoc. justice Arthur E. Whittemore Supreme Jud. Ct. Mass., Boston, 1966-67; assoc. Nutter, McClennen & Fish, Boston, 1967-69, Palmer & Dodge, Boston, 1969-73; asst. counsel to Gov. Mass., 1973; reporter of decisions Supreme Jud. Ct. Mass., Boston, 1974-94; pvt. practice Hollis, N.H., 1994—. Mem. Conservation Commn. Town of Sherborn, Mass., 1969-74, chmn., 1972-74; mem. corp. Tenacre Country Day Sch., Wellesley, Mass., 1972-84, trustee, 1973-78. Served to 1st lt. U.S. Army, 1962-63, capt. USAR, 1963-69. Mem. Mass. Bar Assn., N.H.

Bar Assn., Fed. Bar Assn., Am. Law Inst., Am. Soc. Internat. Law, Internat. Law Assn. (Am. br.), Nat. Assn. Reporters of Jud. Decisions (pres. 1983-84). Episcopalian. Clubs: Union, Harvard (Boston). Office: PO Box 344 Hollis NH 03049-0344

MERRITT, WILLIAM ALFRED, JR., lawyer, telecommunications company executive; b. N.Y.C., Aug. 7, 1936; s. William Alfred and Florence Anne (O'Connor) M.; m. Christine Marie Cartnick, Sept. 27, 1969; children—William Tyler, Brian Edward, Elizabeth Cody. BA in Econs., Holy Cross Coll., Worcester, Mass., 1958; LLB, Harvard U., 1964. Bar: N.Y. 1965. Assoc. Olwine, Connelly, Chase, O'Donnell & Weyher, N.Y.C., 1964-68; atty., v.p. ops. and controls Bunge Corp., N.Y.C., 1968-81; exec. v.p. TIE/Communications Inc., Seymour, Conn., 1981-90; pres. Wiltel Communications Systems Inc, Rolling Meadows, Ill., 1991-92; gen. counsel Carolina Barnes Capital Inc., N.Y.C., 1992—; ptnr. Seaboard Equities Inc., Stamford, Conn., 1992—, Integrated Commn. Sys., Corp., Stamford, Conn., 1994—, Navigator Comms., LLC, Mt. Laurel, N.J., 1995—. Served to capt. USNR, 1958-80. Mem. Wee Burn Club. Avocations: skiing, boating, tennis. Home: 83 Brookside Rd Darien CT 06820-3505 Office: 2 Stamford Landing Ste 100 Stamford CT 06902

MERRY, ROBERT WILLIAM, publishing executive; b. Tacoma, Wash., Mar. 5, 1946; s. Robert Ellsworth and Carol Beatrice (Rasmussen) M.; m. Susan Diane Pennington, Sept. 20, 1969; children: Robert Ellsworth II, Johanna Lynn, Stephanie Ann. BA in Comms., U. Wash., 1968; MS in Journalism, Columbia U., 1972. Legis. reporter, gen. assignment reporter, copy editor Denver Post, 1972-74; reporter Nat. Observer Dow Jones & Co., Inc., 1974-77, reporter Wall St. Jour., 1977-86; exec. editor Roll Call, Newspaper of Capitol Hill, 1986-87; mng. editor Congl. Quar., Inc., Washington, 1987-89, exec. editor, 1990—, also bd. dirs.; appeared on CBS Face the Nation, NBC Meet the Press, ABC Good Morning Am., CNN Newsmakers, and Take Two, C-SPAN, numerous other local and Can. programs. Author: Taking On the World: Joseph and Stewart Alsop--Guardians of the American Century, 1996; contbr. chpt. to book. With U.S. Army, 1968-71. Avocations: jogging, biking, hiking, biography, movies. Office: Congl Quarterly Inc 1414 22nd St NW Washington DC 20037-1003

MERRYDAY, STEVEN D., federal judge; b. 1950. BA, U. Fla., 1972, JD, 1975. With Holland & Knight, Tampa, 1975-83; ptnr. Glenn, Rasmussen, Fogarty, Merryday & Russo, Tampa, 1983-91; federal judge U.S. Dist. Ct. (mid. dist.), Fla., 1992—. Mem. Fed. Bar Assn., The Fla. Bar, Hillsborough County Bar Assn. Office: US Courthouse 611 N Florida Ave Ste 310 Tampa FL 33602-4500*

MERSEL, MARJORIE KATHRYN PEDERSEN, lawyer; b. Manila, Utah, June 17, 1923; d. Leo Henry and Kathryn Anna (Reed) Pedersen; AB, U. Calif., 1948; LLB, U. San Francisco, 1948; m. Jules Mersel, Apr. 12, 1950; 1 son, Jonathan. Admitted to D.C. bar, 1952, Calif. bar, 1955; Marjorie Kathryn Pedersen Mersel, atty., Beverly Hills, Calif., 1961-71; staff counsel Dept. Real Estate State of Calif., Los Angeles, 1971—. Active L.A.-Guangzhou Sister City. Mem. Beverly Hills Bar Assn., L.A. County Bar Assn., Trial Lawyers Assn., So. Calif. Women Lawyers Assn. (treas. 1962-63), L.A.-Guangzhou Sister City Assn., Beverly Hills C. of C., World Affairs Coun., Current Affairs Forum, L.A. Athletic Club, Sierra Club. Home: 13007 Hartsook St Sherman Oaks CA 91423-1616 Office: Dept Real Estate 107 S Broadway Los Angeles CA 90012

MERSER, FRANCIS GERARD, manufacturing company executive, consultant; b. Boston, Jan. 23, 1930; s. Herbert Bartlett and Irene (Bonier) M.; m. Mary Elizabeth Snedeker, Aug. 8, 1936; children: Pamela Bartlett, Alison Gerrish. BS, Babson Coll., 1957; grad. Stanford exec. program, Stanford U., 1982. Product mgr. Dennison Mfg. Co., Framingham, Mass., 1960-70, mktg. mgr., 1970-75, div. gen. mgr., 1975-80, v.p., 1980-85, group v.p., 1985-90, ret., 1990; cons. Avery-Dennison Corp., Framingham, 1990—; overseer Myles Meml. Hosp., Damariscolta, Maine, 1979—. Approx. 35 patents in fastening methods. Served with USAF, 1951-55. Clubs: Cabadetis Boat, Cruising of Am., Manchester Yacht. Avocations: squash, racquetball, ocean racing. Office: Dennison Mfg Co Avery-Dennison Mfg Co 1 Clarks Hill Rd Framingham MA 01701-8163

MERSEREAU, HIRAM STIPE, wood products company consultant; b. Portland, Oreg., Aug. 4, 1917; s. E.W. and Ruth (Stipe) M.; m. Margaret Daggett, Dec. 25, 1937; children: Hiram Stipe, John Bradford, Timothy Daggett. Student, George Washington U., 1936-37, Harvard U., 1959. With Weyerhauser Timber Co., Klamath Falls, Oreg., 1937-38, Alexander-Yawkey Lumber Co., Prineville, Oreg., 1938-52; gen. mgr. lumber div. Crossett Co., Ark., 1954-62; corp. sr. v.p., gen. mgr. So. div. Ga.-Pacific Corp., 1963-82, cons., 1982—; past dir. Citizens & So. Nat. Bank, Augusta, Appalachian Hardwood Mfrs. Inc., Merry Cos., Inc., Augusta. Past bd. dirs. Young Life, Ga. Conservancy, Jr. Achievement Augusta; bd. dirs. Augusta br. Boys Clubs Am., Augusta Cancer Fund; trustee Paine Coll., Augusta. Mem. Nat. Forest Products Assn. (exec. com., dir.). Republican. Presbyterian (elder). Home: 6 Turnberry Ln Sea Pines Plantation Hilton Head Island SC 29928

MERSEREAU, JOHN, JR., Slavic languages and literatures educator; b. San Jose, Calif., Apr. 16, 1925; s. John Joshua and Winona Beth (Roberts) M.; m. Nanine Landell, July 11, 1953; children: Daryl Landell, John Coates. AB, U. Calif., 1945, MA, 1950, PhD, 1957. Teaching fellow, Slavic dept. U. Calif., Berkeley, 1950-52, research asst., 1953-54; instr. Slavic dept. U. Mich., Ann Arbor, 1956-59, asst. prof., 1959-61, assoc. prof., 1961-63, prof., 1963—, chmn. dept., 1961-71, 85-89, prof. emeritus, 1990—, dir. Residential Coll., 1977-85; mem. Joint Com. Eastern Europe of Am. Council Learned Socs./Social Sci. Research Council, 1971-74, chmn., 1973-74. Author: Mikhail Lermontov, 1962, Baron Delvig's Literary Almanac: Northern Flowers, 1967, Translating Russian, 1968, Russian Romantic Fiction, 1983, Orest Somov, 1989; assoc. editor Mich. Slavic Publs., 1962—; contbr. articles to profl. jours. Served to lt. (j.g.) USNR, 1943-46, PTO. Calmerton Slavic scholar U. Calif., Berkeley, 1954-55; Ford Found. fellow, London and Paris, 1955-56, Guggenheim fellow, 1972-73; recipient Disting. Service award U. Mich., Ann Arbor, 1961. Mem. Am. Assn. Advancement Slavic Studies, U. Mich. Research Club. Club: Waterloo Hunt (Grass Lake, Mich., sec. 1970-80); Commanderie de Bordeaux (Detroit). Avocations: flying, gourmet cuisine, raising horses. Office: U of Mich Slavic Dept Ann Arbor MI 48109

MERSEREAU, LORI MICHELLE, lawyer; b. Cin., Aug. 12, 1963; d. Leo and Sonya Ingrid (Rosenfeld) Roos; m. Richard Charles Mersereau, Nov. 20, 1988. BS, U. Calif., Davis, 1985; JD, U. So. Calif., 1989; LLM, Univ. of Pacific, 1992. Bar: Calif. 1989, U.S. Dist. Ct. (ea. dist.) Calif., U.S. Ct. Appeals (9th cir.), U.S. Tax Ct. Assoc. tax and corp. div. Weintraub, Genshlea, Hardy, Erich and Brown, Sacramento, 1989-90; pvt. practice Fair Oaks, Calif., 1990-91; atty. office of dist. counsel U.S. Dept. Treasury, Sacramento, 1991—; spl. asst. to U.S. atty. East and North Dists. Calif., Sacramento, 1994—; lectr. in tax law and internat. tax law U. Calif. Davis Law Sch. Sr. assoc. U. So. Calif. Law Rev., 1988-89; sr. editor Harvard Jour. Law and Pub. Policy, 1988. Bd. dirs. Protection and Advocacy, Inc., Sacramento, 1987-93; vol. atty. Vol. Legal Svcs., Sacramento, 1989—; chair fundraising Hadassah, Sacramento, 1990-91. Mem. Order of Coif, Phi Kappa Phi, Phi Alpha Delta. Republican. Jewish.

MERSEREAU, SUSAN S., clinical psychologist; b. Atlanta, Apr. 9, 1947; d. John Andy Jr. and Dorothy Grace (Smith) Smith; m. Peter Roland Mersereau, May 30, 1970; children: Barrett, Travis, Courtney. AB, Vassar Coll., 1969; MSEd, Elmira Coll., 1973; D in Psychology, Pacific U., 1989. Lic. psychologist, Oreg. Psychology intern Pacific Gateway Hosp., Portland, Oreg., 1987-88, Psychol. Svcs. Ctr., Hillsboro, Oreg., 1988-89; psychology resident Lee Doppelt, Beaverton, Oreg., 1990-91; staff Pac. Gateway Hosp., 1990—; pvt. practice psychologist Beaverton, 1991-93; dir. Pacific Ctr. for Attention and Learning, Beaverton, 1993—; registrant Nat. Register of Health Svc. Providers in Psychology. Tchr. Incentive grantee Guam Dept. Edn., 1979. Mem. APA, Oreg. Psychol. Assn., Nat. Register Health Svc. Providers, Vassar Club Oreg. (admissions com. 1984—, pres. 1984-88). Avocations: gardening, orchid growing. Office: Pacific Ctr Attention & Learning 3800 SW Cedar Hills Blvd Beaverton OR 97005-2027

MERSKEY-ZEGER, MARIE GERTRUDE FINE, retired librarian; b. Kimberley, South Africa, Oct. 10, 1914; came to U.S., 1960, naturalized, 1965; d. Herman and Annie Myra (Wigoder) Fine; m. Clarence Merskey, Oct. 8, 1939 (dec. 1982); children: Hilary Pamela Merskey Nathe, Susan Heather Merskey Sinistore, Joan Margaret Merskey Schneiderman; m. Jack I. Zeger, July 15, 1984. Grad. Underwood Bus. Sch., Cape Town, South Africa, 1934; BA, U. Cape Town, 1958, diploma librarianship, 1960. Sec. to Chief Rabbi Israel Abrahams, South Africa, 1945-49, Jewish Sheltered Employment Council, 1954-56; reference librarian New Rochelle Pub. Library, 1960-63; research librarian Consumers Union, Mt. Vernon, 1963-66; asst. readers services, head union catalog Westchester Library System, 1966-69, trustee, 1989-93, v.p., 1991; dir. Harrison (N.Y.) Pub. Library and West Harrison Br., 1969-84; acting dir. Mamaroneck (N.Y.) Free Library, 1987-88, also trustee, 1988-93. Pub. edn. officer USCG Aux. Flotilla 63. Author: History of the Harrison Libraries, 1980; editor: (cookbook) On Harrison's Table, 1976; Harrison Highlights and Anecdotes, 1989. Bd. dirs. Shore Acres Point Corp., Mamaroneck, 1985-89; program dir. Friends of the Mamaroneck Libr., N.Y., 1993—. Recipient Brotherhood award B'nai B'rith, 1974; named Woman of Yr., Harrison, 1984. Mem. ALA, Westchester Library Assn., N.Y. Library Assn. (adult edn. com. for continuing edn. 1971-75, adult services com. 1973-75, vice chmn., 1975, exec. bd. 1981-82), Pub. Library Dirs. Assn. (tech. services com. chmn. Westchester County 1971, exec. bd. 1974-75, vice chmn. 1975), Clubs: YMCA, Charles Dawson History Ctr. (bd. dirs., founder), Rye Womans Club. Contbr. articles to local newspapers. Home: 316 S Barry Ave Mamaroneck NY 10543-4201

MERSKY, ROY MARTIN, law educator, librarian; b. N.Y.C., Sept. 1, 1925; s. Irving and Rose (Mendelson) Mirsky; m. Deena Hersh, Feb. 3, 1951; children—Deborah, Lisa, Ruth. BS, U. Wis., 1948, JD, 1952, MALS, 1953. Bar: Wis. 1952, U.S. Supreme Ct. 1970, Tex. 1972, U.S. Ct. Appeals (5th cir.) 1981, N.Y. 1983. U.S. govt. documents cataloger U. Wis. Law Libr., 1951-52; reference asst. Madison (Wis.) Free Libr., 1952; pvt. practice law Wis., 1952-54; readers adv., reference and catalog libr., mcpl. reference libr. at City Hall, Milw. Pub. Libr., 1953-54; chief readers and reference svc. Yale Law Libr., 1954-59; dir. Wash. State Law Libr., 1959-63; exec. sec. Jud. Coun. Commn. Wash. Court Report, State of Wash., 1959-63; prof. law, law libr. U. Colo., Boulder, 1963-65; prof. law, dir. rsch. U. Tex., Austin, 1965-84, Atlas Family Centennial prof. law, 1984—, adj. prof. Grad. Sch. Libr. and Info. Sci., 1976—; vis. prof. law, dir. law libr. N.Y. Law Sch., N.Y.C., 1982-84; M.D. Anderson Found. vis. prof. law Queen Mary and Westfield Coll., U. London, 1994; interim dir. Jewish Nat. and Univ. Libr., Hebrew U., 1972-73; cons. to legal pubs. and law schs.; panelist various confs.; lectr. in field. Author: A Treasure in Jerusalem, 1974, (with J. Myron Jacobstein) Fundamentals of Legal Research, 1977, 5th edit., 1990, Legal Research Illustrated, an Abridgement of Fundamentals of Legal Research, 1977, (with Jackstein, Dunn) 6th edit. 1994, (with Albert P. Blaustein) The First One Hundred Justices: Statistical Studies on the Supreme Court of the United States, 1978, (with Gary R. Hartman) A Documentary History of the Legal Aspects of Abortion in the United States, 1990, (with Jacobstein) Reports on Successful and Unsuccessful Nominations, 1987, 90; contbr. articles to profl. jours., chpts. to books; editor numerous books in field. Bd. dirs. ACLU Cen. Tex. chpt., pres. Austin chpt., 1969; bd. advisors Anti-Defamation League Austin lodge, 1974-78; bd. dirs. Hillel Found., 1980-83; bd. dirs. Tex. Com. for Humanities, 1978-80, chair, 1980-82, conf. facilitator, 1982. With U.S. Army, 1944-46, ETO. Decorated Bronze Star. Fellow Am. Bar Found.; mem. ABA (com. sect. econs. of law practice 1982-86, Gavel com., various other coms.), AAUP (chmn. nominating com. 1979-80), Am. Trial Lawyers Assn. (chair law libr. com. 1984—), Am. Law Inst., Assn. Am. Law Schs. (various coms.), Internat. Assn. Lawyers and Jurists (bd. govs. Am. sect. 1980—), Coll. of Law Practice Mgmt., Nat. Bar Assn., Am. Assn. Law Librs. (chair various coms.), Am. Soc. Info. Sci. (pres. Tex./Okla. chpt. 1992-93), Scribes (bd. dirs. 1974—, book awards com. 1978-95, pres. 1991-93), Soc. Am. Law Tchrs. (bd. govs. 1979-88, nominations com. 1984), ALA, rsch. librs. group 1987, library edn. div.), Am. Soc. Indexers, Internat. Assn. Law Librs. (U.S. adv. council), Internat. Fedn. Libr. Assns., Nat. Librs. Assn. (pres. 1980-81), Spl. Libr. Assn., State Bar Tex. (com. Tex. Bar Jour. 1983-90), State Bar Wisc. (bd. mem. nonresident lawyers divsn. 1992—), Nat. Assn. Coll. and Univ. Attys., Tex. Assn. Coll. Tchrs., Tex. Humanities Alliance (bd. dirs. 1986—, pres. 1988), Tex. Supreme Ct. Hist. Soc. (bd. trustees 1988—), Order of Coif (mem. triennial book award com.), Am. Soc. of Inf. Sci. (pres. Tex./Okla. chpt. 1992-94). Home: 6412 Cascada Dr Austin TX 78750-8157 Office: U Tex Sch Law Tarlton Law Libr 727 E 26th St Austin TX 78705-3224

MERTE, HERMAN, JR., educator, mechanical engineer; b. Detroit, Apr. 3, 1929; s. Herman and Anna Marie (Mitterer) M.; m. Bernice Marie Brant, Sept. 17, 1952; children—Kenneth Edward, James Dennis, Lawrence Carleton, Richard Brant, Robert Paul. B.S. in Marine Engrng, U. Mich., Ann Arbor, 1950, B.S. in Mech. Engring, 1951, M.S., 1956, Ph.D., 1960. Mem. faculty U. Mich., 1959—, prof. mech. engring., 1967—; vis. prof. Tech. U. Munich, Germany, 1974-75. Served to lt. (j.g.) USNR, 1952-55. NSF sr. postdoctoral fellow, 1967-68. Mem. ASME, Am. Soc. Engring. Edn., Am. Assn. U. Profs. Home: 3480 Cottontail Ln Ann Arbor MI 48103-1706 Office: U Mich Heat Transfer Lab 2148 G G Brown Lab Ann Arbor MI 48109

MERTEN, ALAN GILBERT, academic administrator; b. Milw., Dec. 27, 1941; s. Gilbert Ervin and Ruth Anna (Ristow) M.; m. Sally Louise Otto; children: Eric, Melissa. BS, U. Wis., 1963; MS, Stanford U., 1964; PhD, U. Wis., 1970. Asst. prof. U. Mich., Ann Arbor, 1970-74, assoc. prof., 1974-81, prof., 1981-86, assoc. dean, 1983-86; dean U. Fla., Gainesville, 1986-89; dean Johnson Grad. Sch. of Mgmt. Cornell U., Ithaca, N.Y., 1989-96; pres. George Mason U., Fairfax, Va., 1996—; bd. dirs. Comshare, Inc., Ann Arbor, Tompkins County Trust Co., Ithaca, 1989-96; mem. inf. sys. adv. coun. Whirlpool Corp., Benton Harbor, Mich., 1987—; mem. Fla. Gov.'s Select Com. on Workforce 2000, 1988-89. Author: Internal Control in U.S. Corporations, 1980, Senior Management Control of Computer-Based Information Systems, 1983. Bd. dirs. Univ. Musical Soc., Ann Arbor, 1985-86, Common Sense Trust, Houston, 1990—, INDUS Group, Inc., San Francisco, 1995—, Washington Campus, 1993-96; mem. Airport Authority, Gainesville, Fla., 1986-89; mem. Speakers Adv. Com. on the Future, Tallahassee, Fla., 1987-88. Served to capt. USAF, 1963-67. Lutheran. Home: 11020 Popes Head Rd Fairfax VA 22030 Office: George Mason U Office of Pres Fairfax VA 22030-4444

MERTENS, JOAN R., museum curator, art historian; b. N.Y.C., Oct. 10, 1946; d. Otto R. and Helen H. M. B.A., Radcliffe Coll., 1967; Ph.D., Harvard U., 1972. Curatorial asst. Met. Mus. Art, N.Y.C., 1972-73, asst. curator, 1973-76, assoc. curator, 1976-81, curator Greek and Roman dept., 1981—; curator, adminstr. Met. Mus. Art, 1983-90, mem. editorial bd. Mus. Jour., 1976—; adj. prof. NYU, Inst. Fine Arts, 1992—. Author: Attic White-Ground—Its Development, 1977, Greek Bronzes in the Metropolitan Museum of Art, 1985. Mem. Archaeol. Inst. Am., German Archael. Inst. (corr. mem.). Home: 124 E 84th St New York NY 10028-0915 Office: Met Mus Art Fifth Ave at 82nd St New York NY 10028

MERTENS, THOMAS ROBERT, biology educator; b. Fort Wayne, Ind., May 22, 1930; s. Herbert F. and Hulda (Burg) M.; m. Beatrice Janet Abair, Apr. 1, 1953; children—Julia Ann, David Gerhard. B.S., Ball State U., 1952; M.S., Purdue U., 1954, Ph.D., 1956. Research assoc. dept. genetics U. Wis.-Madison, 1956-57; asst. prof. biology Ball State U., Muncie, Ind., 1957-62, assoc. prof., 1962-66, prof., 1966-93, dir. doctoral programs in biology, 1974-93, disting. prof. biology edn., 1988-93; prof. emeritus Ball State U., 1993—. Author: (with A. M. Winchester) Human Genetics, 1983 (with R.L. Hammersmith) Genetics Laboratory Investigations, 9th edit., 1991, 10th edit., 1995; contbr. numerous articles to profl. jours. Fellow NSF, 1963-64, Ind. Acad. Sci., 1969; co-recipient Gustav Ohaus award for Innovative Coll. Sci. Teaching, Nat. Sci. Tchrs. Assn., 1986; recipient Dist. Service to Sci. Edn. citation Nat. Sci. Tchrs. Assn., 1987. Fellow AAAS; mem. Nat. Assn. Biology Tchrs. (pres. 1985, hon. mem. 1988), Am. Genetic Assn., Genetics Soc. Am. Lutheran. Home: 2506 W Johnson Rd Muncie IN 47304-3066 Office: Ball State U Dept Biology Muncie IN 47306

MERTIN, ROGER, photographer; b. Bridgeport, Conn., Dec. 9, 1942; s. George and Margaret (Marcinko) M. B.F.A, Rochester Inst. Tech., 1965; M.F.A, Visual Studies Workshop, Rochester, 1972. Prof. art U. Rochester, N.Y., 1981—. Exhibited in group shows at Internat. Mus. Photography, Rochester, 1966, 67, Nat. Gallery Can., Ottawa, 1969, Fogg Art Mus., Harvard U., Cambridge, Mass., 1974, Ctr. Culturel Americain, Paris, 1976, U. Colo., Boulder, 1977, Mus. Modern Art, N.Y.C., 1978, Kunsthalle, Cologne, Fed. Republic Germany, 1980, Tampa (Fla.) Mus., 1983, Barbican Art Gallery, London, 1985; one-man shows include Internat. Mus. Photography, Rochester, 1966, U. Calif., Davis, 1969, Do Not Bend Gallery, London, 1970, Toronto (Can.) Gallery Photography, 1972, Light Gallery, N.Y.C., 1973, 75, 80, Galerie Stampa, Basel, Switzerland, 1974, Afterimage Gallery, Dallas, 1976, Ctr. for Contemporary Photography, Chgo., 1978, Visual Studies Workshop, Rochester, 1978, Sun Valley Ctr. for Arts and Humanities, Idaho, 1979, Rockwell Kent Gallery, Plattsburgh, N.Y., 1979, Light Work, Syracuse, N.Y., 1979, Friends of Photography, 1981; represented in permanent collections Mus. Modern Art, N.Y.C., Internat. Mus. Photography, Rochester, Visual Studies Workshop, Rochester, Mus. Fine Arts, Boston, Princeton (N.J.) U., Art Inst. Chgo., Mpls. Inst. Art, Bibliothèque Nat., Paris, Nat. Gallery Can., Ottawa, Australian Nat. Gallery, Canberra; author: Roger Mertin: Records 1976-78, 1978. Nat. Endowment Arts Photographer fellow, 1976; Photographers fellow Guggenheim Found., 1974, Creative Aritsts Pub. Service, 1974. Mem. Soc. Photog. Edn. Office: U Rochester Dept Art and Art History River Campus 424 Morey Hall Rochester NY 14627

MERTON, ROBERT C., economist, educator; b. N.Y.C., July 31, 1944; s. Robert K. and Suzanne (Carhart) M.; m. June Patricia Rose, June 4, 1966; children: Samantha June, Robert Frederick, Paul Jonathan. B.S. in Engring. Math., Columbia U., 1966; M.S. in Applied Math., Calif. Inst. Tech., 1967; Ph.D. in Econs., MIT, 1970; MA (hon.), Harvard U., 1989; LLD (hon.), U. Chgo., 1991; Prof. honoris causa degree, HEC Sch. Mgmt., Paris, 1995. Instr. econs. MIT, Cambridge, 1969-70; asst. prof. fin. Alfred P. Sloan Sch. Mgmt., 1970-73, assoc. prof., 1973-74, prof., 1974-80, J.C. Penney prof. mgmt., 1980-88; vis. prof. fin. Harvard U., Boston, 1987-88, George Fisher Baker prof. bus. adminstrn., 1988—; trsutee Coll. Retirement Equities Fund; rsch. assoc. Nat. Bur. Econ. Rsch., 1979—; prin., co-founder Long-Term Capital Mgmt., L.P., Greenwich Conn.; mem. itnerat. bd. sci. advisors Tinbergen Inst. Author: Continous-Time Finance, 1990, rev. edit., 1992; co-author: Casebook in Financial Engineering: Applied Studies of Financial Innovation, 1995, The Global Financial System: A Functional Perspective, 1995; editor: The Collected Scientific Papers of Paul A. Samuelson, vol. III, 1972, Finance Series, Basil Blackwell, 1987—; mem. editl. bd. Internat. Econ. Rev., 1972-77, Jour. Fin., 1973-77, Jour. Money, Credit and Banking, 1974-79, Jour. Fin. Econs., 1974-83, Jour. Banking and Fin., 1977-79, 92—, Fin. India, 1988—, Geneva Papers on Risk and Ins., 1989—, Jour. Fixed Income, 1991—, Fin. Rev., 1992—; mem. adv. bd. The New Palgrave Dictionary of Money and Finance, Math. Fin., Rev. Derivatives Rsch., Nihon Finance Gakkai; contbr. articles to profl. jours. Recipient Leo Melamed prize U. Chgo. Sch. Bus., 1983, Roger Murray prize Inst. for Quantitative Rsch. in Fin., 1985, 86, Disting. Scholar award Ea. Fin. Assn., 1989, Internat. INA-Nat. Acad. Lincei prize Nat. Acad. Lincei, Rome, 1993, FORCE award for fin. innovation Fuqua Sch. Bus., Duke U., 1993, Fin. Engr. of Yr. award Internat. Assn. Fin. Engrs., 1993. Fellow Internat. Assn. Fin. Engrs. (sr.), Econometric Soc., Am. Acad. Arts and Scis.; mem. NAS, Am. Fin. Assn. (dir. 1982-84, pres. 1986), Soc. for Fin. Studies (v.p. 1993), Tau Beta Pi, Sigma Xi. Office: Harvard U Grad Sch Bus Adminstrn Morgan 397 Soldiers Field Rd Boston MA 02163

MERTON, ROBERT K., sociologist, educator; b. Phila., July 4, 1910; s. Harry David and Ida (Rosoff) Schkolnick; m. Suzanne Carhart, 1934 (sep. 1968, dec. 1992); children: Stephanie, Robert C., Vanessa; companion Harriet Zuckerman, 1968-92, m. June, 1993. AB, Temple U., 1931, LLD (hon.), 1956; MA, Harvard U., 1932, PhD, 1936, LLD (hon.), 1980; LHD (hon.), Emory U., 1965, Loyola U., Chgo., 1970, Kalamazoo Coll., 1970, Cleve. State U., 1977, U. Pa., 1979, Brandeis U., 1983, SUNY-Albany, 1986, New Sch. Social Rsch., 1995, Long Island U., 1996; Dr. honoris causa, U. Leyden, 1965, Jagiellonian U., Cracow, Poland, 1989; LLD (hon.), Western Res. U., 1966, U. Chgo., 1968, Tulane U., 1971, U. Md., 1982; LittD (hon.), Colgate U., 1967, SUNY, 1984, Columbia U., 1985, SUNY, Albany, 1986, Oxford U., 1986; Dr. Social Sci. (hon.), Yale, 1968; DSC in Econ. (hon.), U. Wales, 1968; PhD (hon.), Hebrew U. of Jerusalem, 1980, U. Oslo, Norway, 1991; D of Polit. Sci. (hon.), U. Bologna, 1996. Tutor, instr. sociology Harvard U., 1936-39; prof., chmn. dept. Tulane U., 1939-41; from asst. prof. to prof. Columbia U., 1941-63, Giddings prof., 1963-74, univ. prof., 1974-79, spl. svc. prof., 1979-84, Univ. prof. emeritus, 1979—; assoc. dir. Bur. Applied Social Rsch., 1942-71; adj. faculty Rockefeller U., 1979—; George Sarton prof. hist. sci. U. Ghent, Belgium, 1986-88; adv. editor sociology Harcourt Brace [Jovanovich], 1947—; ednl. adv. bd. Guggenheim Found., 1963-79, chmn., 1971-79. Author: Science Technology and Society in 17th Century England, 2d edit., 1970, Mass Persuasion, 2d edit., 1971, Social Theory and Social Structure, rev. edit., 1968, On the Shoulders of Giants, 1965, vicennial edit., 1985, post-Italianate edit., 1993, on Theoretical Sociology, 1967, The Sociology of Science, 1973, Sociological Ambivalence, 1976, Sociology of Science: An Episodic Memoir, 1979, Social Research and the Practicing Professions, 1982;, co-author: the Focused Interview, rev. edit., 1956, 3d edit., 1990, Freedom to Read, 1957; co-editor, co-author: Continuities in Social Research, 1950, Social Policy and Social Research in Housing, 1951, Reader in Bureaucracy, 1952, The Student-Physician, 1957, Sociology Today, 1959, Contemporary Social Problems, 4th edit., 1976, The Sociology of Science in Europe, 1977, Toward a Metric of Science, 1978, Qualitiative and Quantitative Social Research: Papers in Honor of Paul F. Lazarsfeld, 1979, Sociological Traditions from Generation to Generation, 1980, Continuities in Structural Inquiry, 1981; co-editor Internat. Ency. of Social Scis., vol. 19, 1991, Social Sci. Quotations, 1992, Opportunity Structure, 1995, Social Structure and Science, 1996. Trustee Ctr. Advanced Study Behavioral Scis., 1952-75, Temple U., 1964-68, Inst. Sci. Info., 1968—; mem. bd. guarantors Italian Acad. for Advanced Studies in Am., 1992—. Recipient Commonwealth award for Disting. Svc. to Sociology, 1979, award Meml. Sloan-Kettering Cancer Ctr., 1981, Nat. Medal of Sci., 1994, Derek Prize award Scientometrics, 1995; disting. scholar in humanities Am. Coun. Learned Socs., 1962, Haskins lectr., 1994, Russell Sage Found. scholar, 1979—; NIH lectr. in recognition of Outstanding Sci. Achievement, 1964; Guggenheim fellow, 1962, MacArthur Prize fellow, 1983-88. Fellow Am. Acad. Arts and Scis. (Talcott Parsons prize 1979), Brit. Acad. (fgn., corr.); mem. NAS, Am. Philos. Soc., Sociol. Rsch. Assn. (pres. 1968), Nat. Acad. Edn., Nat. Inst. Medicine, Am. Sociol. Assn. (pres. 1957, Disting. Scholarship award 1980), Ea. Sociol. Soc. (pres. 1969), History of Sci. Soc., World Acad. Arts and Scis., Soc. Social Studies of Sci. (pres. 1975, Bernal prize), Royal Swedish Acad. Scis. (fgn.), Academia Europaea (fgn.). Home: 450 Riverside Dr New York NY 10027-6821

MERTZ, EDWIN THEODORE, biochemist, emeritus educator; b. Missoula, Mont., Dec. 6, 1909; s. Gustav Henry and Louise (Sain) M.; m. Mary Ellen Ruskamp, Oct. 5, 1936; children: Martha Ellen, Edwin T.; m. Virginia T. Henry, Aug. 1, 1987. B.A., U. Mont., 1931, D.Sc. (hon.), 1979; M.S. in Biochemistry, U. Ill., 1933, Ph.D. in Biochemistry, 1935; D.Agr. (hon.), Purdue U., 1977. Research biochemist Armour & Co., Chgo., 1935-37; instr. biochemistry U. Ill., 1937-38; research assoc. pathology U. Iowa, 1938-40; instr. agrl. chemistry U. Mo., 1940-43; research chemist Hercules Powder Co., 1943-46; prof. biochemistry Purdue U., West Lafayette, Ind., 1946-76; emeritus Purdue U., 1976—; vis. prof. U. Notre Dame, South Bend, Ind., 1976-77; cons. in agronomy Purdue U., 1977-94; affiliate prof. crops and soils Mont. State U., Bozeman, 1995—. Author: Elementary Biochemistry, 1969; author, editor: Quality Protein Maize, 1992. Recipient McCoy award Purdue U., 1967; John Scott award City of Phila., 1967; Hoblitzelle Nat. award Tex. Research Found., 1968; Congressional medal Fed. Land Banks, 1968; Disting. Service award U. Mont., 1973; Browning award Am. Soc. Agronomy, 1974; Pioneer Chemist award Am. Inst. Chemists, 1976. Mem. AAAS, AAUP, Nat. Acad. Scis., Am. Soc. Biol. Chemists, Am. Inst. Nutrition (Osborne-Mendel award 1972), Am. Chem. Soc. (Spencer award 1970), Am. Assn. Cereal Chemists. Lutheran. Co-discoverer high lysine corn, 1963. Office: Montana State Univ Dept Plant and Soils Bozeman MT 59717

MERTZ, FRANCIS JAMES, academic administrator; b. Newark, Sept. 24, 1937; s. Frank E. and Marian E. (Brady) M.; m. Gail Williams, Apr. 11, 1964; children: Lynn, Christopher, Suzanne, David, Amy, Jonathan. BA, St. Peter's Coll., 1958; JD, NYU, 1961; LLD (hon.), Felician Coll., 1984, Stevens Inst. Tech., Hoboken, N.J., 1988. Bar: N.J. 1967. Exec. v.p. St. Peter's Coll., Jersey City, 1972-78; v.p., CFO N.Y. Med. Coll., Valhalla,

1978-79; dir. adminstrn. Sage Gray Todd and Sims, N.Y.C., 1979-81; pres. Ind. Coll. Fund N.J., Summit, 1981-90, Assn. Ind. Colls. and Univs. N.J., Summit, 1982-90, Fairleigh Dickinson U., Teaneck, N.J., 1990—; bd. dirs. Summit Bancorp (formerly UJB Fin.), Princeton, N.J., United Jersey Bank. Trustee, sec. St. James Found., Westfield, N.J., 1987—; bd. dirs. Ready Found., Tri County Scholarship Fund, Paterson, N.J., 1992—, New Cmty. Found., Libr. Sci. Ctr. Mem. N.J. State Bar Assn., University Club. Home: 167 Stanie Brae Dr Watchung NJ 07060-6233 Office: Fairleigh Dickinson U 1000 River Rd Teaneck NJ 07666-1914

MERTZ, STUART MOULTON, landscape architect; b. Wayne, Pa., Dec. 4, 1915; s. Walter Smith and Elizabeth Armenia (Day) M.; m. Constance Coulter Buck, June 27, 1942 (dec. Mar. 17, 1978); children: Stuart Moulton, Maurice Walter; m. Theodora Lucks Hager, Oct. 13, 1979 (div. Dec. 1987); married, Sept. 13, 1988. B.S. in Landscape Architecture, Pa. State U., 1937; B.Landscape Architecture, Cornell U., 1938; travelling fellow, Am. Acad. Rome, 1938-40, fellow, 1940. With John Noyes, St. Louis, 1940-41; chief designer Harland Bartholomew & Assocs., St. Louis, 1941-49; pvt. practice landscape architecture St. Louis, 1949-83; sr. assoc. Austin Tao & Assocs., Inc., 1984-92; lectr. nurserymen's short course Tex. A & M Coll.; lectr. landscape architecture Iowa State U., also S.W. Park Tng. Inst., U. Kans., U. Ga., Mich. State U., others. Work includes 26 parks and playgrounds for City and County of St. Louis, St. John's Hosp., St. Lukes Hosp. West, Visitation Acad., Florissant Valley C.C., Bettendorf Stores, Meramec C.C., Barnwell Art and Garden Ctr., Shreveport, La. golf course and facilities design St. Andrew's Golf Club, St. Charles, Mo., site planning and recreational facilities design for Bellevive Country Club, Meadowbrook Country Club, Bogey Golf Club. Pres., People's Art Center Assn., 1960-62, bd. dirs., 1959-63; bd. dirs. Spirit of St. Louis Fund, 1960-62; mem. adv. council U. Mo. Sch. Forestry, Fisheries and Wildlife, 1974-83. Served to 2d lt. USAAF, 1943-45. Recipient Centennial medal for disting. achievement in landscape architecture Am. Acad. in Rome, 1994. Fellow Am. Soc. Landscape Architects (chmn. St. Louis 1960-63, trustee Missouri Valley chpt. 1954-60, nat. sec.-treas. 1963-67, nat. 2d v.p. 1967-69, chmn. Coun. of Fellows 1977-79, bd. soc. found. 1965-69, 71-75, sec.-treas. 1967-69); mem. Mo. Assn. Landscape Architects (pres. 1966-86), Sovestor's Investment Club (sec. 1988-92, pres. 1992-94), Cornell Club St. Louis (pres. 1955-56), Penn State Club, Chi Phi. Presbyterian. Home: 9009 Sedgwick Place Dr Saint Louis MO 63124-1890

MERTZ, WALTER, retired government research executive; b. Mainz, Germany, May 4, 1923; s. Oskar and Anne (Gabelmann) M.; m. Marianne C. Maret, Aug. 8, 1953. M.D., U. Mainz, 1951. Intern County Hosp., Hersfeld, Germany, 1952-53; resident Univ. Hosp., Frankfurt, Germany, 1953; vis. scientist NIH, Bethesda, Md., 1953-61; chief dept. biol. chemistry Walter Reed Army Inst. Research, Washington, 1961-69; mem. staff Nutrition Inst., Agrl. Research Service, Dept. Agrl., Beltsville, Md., 1969-72, chmn. inst., 1972-92; ret.; dir. Human Nutrition Research Ctr.; lectr. George Washington U. Med. Sch., 1963-73. Served with German Army, 1941-46. Recipient Osborne and Mendel award Am. Inst. Nutrition, 1971, Superior Performance award Dept. Agr., 1972, Lederle award in Human Nutrition, 1982, Internat. prize for Modern Nutrition, 1987, award for Disting. Svc., Dept. Agr., 1988. Mem. Am. Inst. Nutrition, Am. Soc. Biol. Chemists, Am. Soc. Clin. Nutrition. Home: 12401 St James Rd Rockville MD 20850-3744

MERVIS, LOUIS, school system administrator. Chmn. Ill. Bd. Edn., Springfield. Office: Bd Edn 100 N 1st St Springfield IL 62702-5199

MERWIN, DAVIS UNDERWOOD, newspaper executive; b. Chgo., June 22, 1928; s. Davis and Josephine (Underwood) M.; m. Nancy Snowden Smith Tailer, Nov. 14, 1958 (dec. Feb. 1995); children: Davis Fell, Laura Howell, James B. Tailer. AB, Harvard U., 1950; LLD (hon.), Ill. Wesleyan U., 1991. Pres. Evergreen Communications, Inc., Bloomington, Ill., 1969-80; pub. Daily Pantagraph, 1968-80; pres. Wood Canyon Corp., Tucson, 1989-93; bd. dirs. State Farm Growth, Balanced, Interim & Mcpl. Bond Funds, 1967, Crown C Cattle Co.; vice-chmn. Bloomington Broadcasting Corp. Bd. dirs., mem. exec. com. Adlai E. Stevenson Lectures; trustee emeritus Ill. Wesleyan U., Inland Daily Press Found., chmn. investment com., 1983-91; trustee Ill. Nature Conservancy. Recipient Disting. Service award U.S. Jaycees, 1959. Mem. Am. Newspaper Pubs. Assn., Inland Daily Press Assn. (pres. 1977, chmn. bd. 1978). Republican. Unitarian. Clubs: Harvard (Chgo.); Phoenix-SK, Hasty Pudding, Bloomington Country, Ristigouche Salmon. Office: 236 Greenwood Ave Bloomington IL 61704-7243 Mailing Address: PO Box 8 Bloomington IL 61702-0008

MERWIN, JOHN DAVID, lawyer, former governor; b. Frederiksted, St. Croix, V.I., Sept. 26, 1921; s. Miles and Marguerite Louise (Fleming) M.; m. Marjorie Davis Spaulding, Feb. 18, 1993. Student, U. Lausanne, Switzerland, 1938-39, U. P.R., 1939-40; BSc, Yale U., 1943; LLB, George Washington U., 1948. Bar: Conn., V.I. 1949. Practice law St. Croix, V.I., 1949-50, 1953-57, 67-85; gen. counsel, v.p. Rob't L. Merwin & Co., Inc., 1953-57; senator-at-large V.I. Legislature, 1955-57; govt. sec. for V.I., 1957-58, gov. V.I., 1958-61; rep. Chase Manhattan Bank, Nassau, Bahamas, 1961-65; exec. v.p. Equity Pub. Corp. Orford, N.H., 1965-67. Chmn. V.I. Port Authority, 1972-75; Rep. candidate for Pres. N.H. Primary Election, 1992; pres. The Nason Found., Cleve., 1981—. Served from 2d lt. to capt. F.A. AUS, 1942-46, 50-53. Decorated Bronze Star; Croix de Guerre with silver star. Mem. Conn., N.H., V.I. bar assns., Phi Delta Phi. Episcopalian. Clubs: Tennis of St. Croix (V.I.), Yale (N.Y.C.), Cosmos (Washington). Home and Office: PO Box 778 Franconia NH 03580-0778

MERWIN, WILLIAM CHARLES, academic administrator; b. La Crosse, Wis., June 25, 1939; s. Donald Francis and Effie Marie (Haggerty) M.; m. Patricia Ann Byrne, Jan. 28, 1961 (div. Mar. 1980); children: John, Michael, William B.; m. Debra Lee Davis, Aug. 8, 1987. BS, U. Wis., La Crosse, 1961, MA, 1965; EdD, U. Ga., 1972. Tchr., coach Onalaske (Wis.) High Sch., 1961-65; tchr. W. Salem (Wis.) High Sch., 1965-68; asst. prof. U. Wis., La Crosse, 1968-73; chmn. dept. U. No. Fla., Jacksonville, 1973-77, assoc. v.p., 1977-81; provost, v.p. acad. affairs U. North Fla., Jacksonville, 1981-85; pres. Mont. State U. Northern, Havre, 1985-89, SUNY, Potsdam, 1989—; bd. dirs. First Nat. Bank, Havre. Author: Studies in State and Local History, 1967, Developing Competencies in Social Studies, 1974, Handbook on Contemporary Education "The Inquiry Method," 1975. Fulbright scholar Japan, 1966. Mem. Phi Kappa Phi. Democrat. Roman Catholic. Lodge: Rotary. Office: SUNY-Potsdam Office of Pres Potsdam NY 13676

MERZ, JAMES LOGAN, electrical engineering and materials educator, researcher; b. Jersey City, Apr. 14, 1936; s. Albert Joseph and Anne Elizabeth (Farrell) M.; m. Rose-Marie Weibel, June 30, 1962; children: Kathleen, James, Michael, Kimarie. BS in Physics, U. Notre Dame, 1959; postgrad., U. Göttingen, Fed. Republic Germany, 1959-60; MA, Harvard U., 1961, PhD in Applied Physics, 1967; PhD (hon.), Lingköping U., Sweden, 1993. Mem. tech. staff Bell Labs., Murray Hill, N.J., 1966-78; prof. elec. engring. U. Calif., Santa Barbara, 1978-94, prof. materials, 1986-94, chmn. dept. elec. and computer engring., 1982-84, assoc. dean for rsch. devel. Coll. Engring., 1984-86, acting assoc. vice chancellor, 1988, dir. semiconductor rsch. corp. core program on GaAs digital ICs, 1984-89, dir. Compound Semiconductor Rsch. Labs., 1986-92, dir. NSF Ctr. for Quantized Electronic Structures, 1989-94; Freimann prof. elec. engring. U. Notre Dame (Ind.), 1994—, v.p. for grad. studies and rsch., 1996—; NATO Advanced Study Inst. lectr. Internat. Sch. Materials Sci. and Tech., Erice-Sicily, Italy, 1990; mem. exec. com. Calif. Microelectronics Innovation and Computer Rsch. Opportunities Program, 1986-92; mem. NRC com. on Japan, NAS/NAE, 1988-90; mem. internat. adv. com. Internat. Symposium on Physics of Semiconductors and Applications, Seoul, Republic of Korea, 1990, Conf. on Superlattices and Microstructures, Xi'an, China, 1992; participant, mem. coms. other profl. confs. and meetings. Contbr. numerous articles to profl. jours.; patentee in field. Fulbright fellow, Danforth Found. fellow, Woodrow Wilson Found. fellow. Fellow IEEE, Am. Phys. Soc.; mem. IEEE Lasers and Electro-Optics Soc. (program com. annual mtg. 1980), IEEE Electron Device Soc. (sec. 1994, 95), Am. Vacuum Soc. (exec. com. electronic materials and processing divsn. 1988-89), Electrochem. Soc., Materials Rsch. Soc. (editl. bd. jour. 1984-87), Soc. for Values in Higher Edn., Inst. Electronics, Info. and Comm. Engrs. (overseas adv. com.), Sigma Xi, Eta Kappa Nu. Achievements include research in field of optoelectronic materials and devices: semiconductors and ionic materials; optical and electrical properties of implanted ions, rapid annealing; semiconductor lasers, detectors, solar cells, other optoelectronic devices; low-dimensional quantum structures. Office: U Notre Dame Dept Elec Engring 275 Fitzpatrick Hall Notre Dame IN 46556-5637

MERZ, MICHAEL, federal judge; b. Dayton, Ohio, Mar. 29, 1945; s. Robert Louis and Hazel (Appleton) M.; m. Marguerite Logan LeBreton, Sept. 7, 1968; children: Peter Henry, Nicholas George. AB cum laude, Harvard U., 1967, JD, 1970. Bar: Ohio 1970, U.S. Dist. Ct. (so. dist.) Ohio 1971, U.S Supreme Ct. 1974, U.S. Ct. Appeals (6th cir.) 1975. Assoc. Smith & Schnacke, Dayton, Ohio, 1970-75, ptnr., 1976-77; judge Dayton Mcpl. Ct., 1977-84; magistrate U.S. Dist. Ct. (so. dist.) Ohio, 1984—; adj. prof. U. Dayton Law Sch., 1979—. Bd. dirs. United Way, Dayton, 1981-95; trustee Dayton and Montgomery County Pub. Libr., 1991—, Montgomery County Hist. Soc., 1995—. Mem. ABA, Fed. Bar Assn., Am. Judicature Soc., Fed. Magistrate Judges Assn., Ohio State Bar Assn., Dayton Bar Assn. Republican. Roman Catholic. Office: US Dist Ct 902 Federal Bldg 200 W 2nd St Dayton OH 45402-0758

MERZBACHER, EUGEN, physicist, educator; b. Berlin, Germany, Apr. 9, 1921; came to U.S., 1947, naturalized, 1953; s. Siegfried and Lilli (Wilmersdoerffer) M.; m. Ann Townsend Reid, July 11, 1952; children: Celia, Charles, Matthew, Mary. Licentiate, U. Istanbul, 1943; A.M., Harvard U., 1948, Ph.D., 1950; DSc (hon.), U. N.C., Chapel Hill, 1993. High sch. tchr. Ankara, Turkey, 1943-47; mem. Inst. Advanced Study, Princeton, N.J., 1950-51; vis. asst. prof. Duke U., 1951-52; mem. faculty U. N.C., Chapel Hill, 1952—; prof. U. N.C., 1961—, acting chmn. physics dept., 1965-67, 71-72, Kenan prof. physics, 1969-91, Kenan prof. physics emeritus, 1991—, chmn. dept., 1977-82; vis. prof. U. Wash., 1967-68, U. Edinburgh, Scotland, 1986; Arnold Bernhard vis. prof. physics Williams Coll., 1993; vis. rsch. fellow Sci. and Engring. Rsch. Coun., U. Stirling, 1986; chair Internat. Conf. on Physics of Electronic and Atomic Collisions, 1987-89, chair APS task force on jour. growth, 1994-95. Author: Quantum Mechanics, 2d edit, 1970; also articles. NSF Sci. Faculty fellow U. Copenhagen, Denmark, 1959-60; recipient Thomas Jefferson award U. N.C., 1972; Humboldt sr. scientist award U. Frankfurt, Germany, 1976-77. Fellow Am. Phys. Soc. (pres. 1990); mem. AAUP, Am. Assn. Physics Tchrs. (Oersted medal 1992), Sigma Xi. Achievements include research on applications of quantum mechanics to study atoms and nuclei. Home: 1396 Halifax Rd Chapel Hill NC 27514-2724

MESA, JOSE RAMON, professional baseball player; b. Azua, Dominican Republic, May 22, 1966. Grad., high sch., Dominican Republic. With Balt. Orioles, 1990-92; pitcher Cleve. Indians, 1992—. Mem. World Series Championship Team, 1995. Achievements include most saves (46) in American League, 1995, most consecutive saves (38) in American League history, 1995. Office: Cleve Indians 2401 Ontario St Cleveland OH 44115

MESA-LAGO, CARMELO, economist, educator; b. Havana, Cuba, Aug. 11, 1934; s. Rogelio M. and Ana Maria (Lago); m. Elena Mesa-Gross, Sept. 3, 1966; children: Elizabeth, Ingrid, Helena. LLB, U. Havana, 1956; LLD, U. Madrid, 1958; MA in Econs., U. Miami, 1965; PhD, Cornell U., 1968. Asst. prof. Cath U. Villanueva, Havana, Cuba, 1956-57, 59-61; research assoc. U. Miami, Fla., 1962-65; asst. prof. U. Pitts., 1968-71, assoc. prof., 1971-76, prof., 1976-81, disting. prof. econs. and Latin Am. affairs, 1981—; dir. Ctr. Latin Am. Studies, 1974-86; vis. prof. Oxford U., 1977, Mellon vis. prof. Fla. Internat. U., 1995, vis. prof. Inst. Univ. Ortega y Gasset, 1990-91; Bacardi chair U. Miami, 1994; regional advisor Econ. Commn. Latin Am., Santiago, Chile, 1983-84; rsch. assoc. Max-Planck-Inst., Munich, 1991-92; cons. in field. Author: Cuba in the 1970's, 1974, 2d edit. 1978, Social Security in Latin America, 1978, The Economy of Socialist Cuba, 1981 (A.P. Whitaker 1982), The Crisis of Social Security and Health Care: Latin American Experiences and Lessons, 1985, Ascent to Bankruptcy: Financing Social Security in Latin America, 1989, Health Care for the Poor in Latin America and the Caribbean, 1992, Cuba After the Cold War, 1993, Changing Social Security in Latin America, 1994 (Outstanding Book Choice award 1995), Are Economic Reforms Propelling Cuba To the Market?, 1994; former editor: Yearbook Cuban Studies. Recipient numerous rsch. grants, 1986—, Alexander von Humboldt sr. rsch. prize, 1990-91. Mem. Latin Am. Studies Assn. (pres. 1980), Caribbean Studies Assn. (eec. coun. 1973-74), Am. Econ. Assn., Assn. Comparative Econs., Internat. Assn. Labor Law and Social Security, Coun. on Fgn. Rels. and the Nat. Acad. of Social Ins., Spanish Club (Pitts., v.p.). Democrat. Roman Catholic. Office: U Pittsburgh Dept Econ 4M38 Forbes Quadrangle Pittsburgh PA 15260

MESCHAN, ISADORE, radiologist, educator; b. Cleve., May 30, 1914; s. Julius and Anna (Gordon) M.; m. Rachel Farrer, Sept. 3, 1943; children: David, Eleanor Jane Meschan Foy, Rosalind Weir, Joyce Meschan Lawrence. BA, Western Res. U., 1935, MA, 1937, MD, 1939; ScD (hon.), U. Ark., 1983. Instr. Western Res. U., 1946-47; prof., head dept. radiology U. Ark., Little Rock, 1947-55; prof., dir. dept. radiology Bowman Gray Sch. Medicine, Wake Forest U., Winston-Salem, N.C., 1955-77; now prof. emeritus Bowman Gray Sch. Medicine, Wake Forest U. Author: Atlas of Normal Radiographic Anatomy, 1951, Roentgen Signs in Clinical Diagnosis, 1956, (with R. Meschan) Synopsis of Roentgen Signs, 1962, Roentgen Signs in Clinical Practice, 1966, Radiographic Positioning Related Anatomy, 1969, 2d edit., 1978, Analysis of Roentgen Signs, 3 vols, 1972, Atlas of Anatomy Basic to Radiology, 1975, Synopsis of Analysis of Roentgen Signs, 1976, Synopsis of Radiographic Anatomy, 1978, 2d rev. edit., 1980, (with B.W. Wolfman) Basic Atlas of Sectional Anatomy, 2d edit.; co-author: Atlas of Cross-Sectional Anatomy, 1980, Roentgen Signs in Diagnostic Imaging, vol. 1, 1984, vol. 2, 1985, vol. 3, 1986, vol. 4, 1987; editor: The Radiologic Clinics of North America, 1965; contbr. articles to profl. jours. Recipient Disting. Alumnus award Case-Western Res. U. Sch. Medicine, 1984, Disting. Faculty Svc. Alumni award Wake Forest U. Bowman Gray Sch. Medicine, 1989. Fellow Am. Coll. Radiology (com. chmn., Gold medal 1978, Living Legends of Radiology 1986); mem. Am. Roentgen Ray Soc., AMA, Radiology Soc. N.Am., N.C. Radiol. Soc., So. Med. Assn., Soc. Nuclear Medicine, Assn. U. Radiologists, Phi Beta Kappa, Sigma Xi, Alpha Omega Alpha. Home: 305 Weatherfield Ln Kernersville NC 27284-8337

MESCHAN, RACHEL FARRER (MRS. ISADORE MESCHAN), obstetrics and gynecology educator; b. Sydney, Australia, May 21, 1915; came to U.S., 1946, naturalized, 1950; d. John H. and Gertrude (Powell) Farrer; m. Isadore Meschan, Sept. 3, 1943; children: David Farrer-Meschan, Jane Meschan Foy, Rosalind Meschan Weir, Joyce Meschan Lawrence. MB, BS, U. Melbourne (Australia), 1940; MD, Wake Forest U., 1957. Intern Royal Melbourne Hosp., 1942; resident Women's Hosp., Melbourne, 1942-43, Bowman-Gray Sch. Medicine, Wake Forest U., Winston-Salem, N.C., 1957-73, asst. clin. prof. dept. ob-gyn, 1973—; also marriage counselor. Co-author (with I. Meschan): Atlas of Radiographic Anatomy, 1951, rev., 1959; Roentgen Signs in Clinical Diagnosis, 1956; Synopsis of Roentgen Signs, 1962; Roentgen Signs in Clinical Practice, 1966; Radiographic Positioning and Related Anatomy, 1968; Analysis of Roentgen Signs in General Radiology, 1973; Roentgen Signs in Diagnostic Imaging, Vol. III, 1986, Vol. IV, 1987. Home: 305 Weatherfield Ln Kernersville NC 27284-8337

MESCHES, ARNOLD, artist; b. Bronx, N.Y., Aug. 11, 1923; s. Benjamin and Anna (Grosse) M.; m. Sylvia Snetsky, Apr. 8, 1945 (div. 1972); children: Paul Elliot, Susan Jean; m. Jill Karen Ciment, Mar. 19, 1983. Student, Art Ctr. Sch., 1943-45, Jepson's Art Inst., 1945, Chouinard's Art Inst., 1945. Instr. painting U. So. Calif., L.A., 1950; instr. painting and drawing Kann Inst. Art, L.A., 1950-55, New Sch. of Art, L.A., 1955-58, Otis Art Inst., L.A., 1963-67, U. Calif., L.A., 1972-77, Otis/Parsons Art Inst., L.A., 1975-84; instr. advanced painting and drawing Parsons Sch. Design, N.Y.C., 1986; guest prof. grad. painting Rutgers U., New Brunswick, N.J., 1985; instr. grad. painting NYU, N.Y.C., 1988—; art dir. Frontier mag., L.A., 1954-60; ct._rm. artist Walter Cronkite Program, CBS, L.A., 1968-70. One-man shows include L.A. Mcpl. Art Gallery, 1983, Civilian Warfare Gallery, N.Y.C., 1984, 85, Hallwalls, Buffalo, 1985, Haines Gallery, San Francisco, 1988, 91, 93, 96, Jack Shainman Gallery, Washington and N.Y.C., 1985, 86, 89, Castellani Art Mus. and Burchfield Art Ctr., Buffalo, 1988, Carlo Lamagna Gallery, N.Y.C., 1989, East Hampton Ctr. for Contemporary Art, 1990, Robert Berman Gallery, Santa Monica, 1990, E.M. Donahue Gallery, N.Y.C., 1991, 93, 94, 96, Inst. Contemporary Art, Phila., 1994. Grantee John F. and Anna Lee Stacey Sch. Fund, 1954, 56, NEA, 1982, N.Y. Found. for Arts, 1991; Ford Found. Faculty grantee, 1979-80; Altos de Chavon fellow Dominican Republic, 1994. Home: 254 E 7th St # 15-16 New York NY 10009-6053

MESCHKE, HERBERT LEONARD, state supreme court justice; b. Belfield, N.D., Mar. 18, 1928; s. G.E. and Dorothy E. Meschke; m. Shirley Ruth McNeil; children: Marie, Jean, Michael, Jill. B.A., Jamestown Coll., 1950; J.D., U. Mich., 1953. Bar: N.D. Law clk. U.S. Dist. Ct. N.D., 1953-54; practice law Minot, N.D., 1954-85; justice N.D. State Supreme Ct., 1985—; mem. N.D. Ho. of Reps., 1965-66, N.D. Senate, 1967-70. Mem. ABA, Am. Law Inst., Am. Judicature Soc., N.D. Bar Assn. Office: ND State Supreme Ct State Capitol 600 E Boulevard Ave Bismarck ND 58505-0660

MESCHUTT, DAVID RANDOLPH, historian, curator; b. N.Y.C., May 29, 1955; s. Philip Frederick and Mary Evelyn (Mahanes) M.; m. Sarah Caroline Bevan, July 14, 1990. BA in Journalism, Washington and Lee U., 1977; MA in History Mus. Studies, SUNY, Cooperstown, 1988. Rschr. Thomas Jefferson Meml. Found., Charlottesville, Va., 1977-78, Frick Art Reference Libr., N.Y.C., 1980-86; curator art West Point (N.Y.) Mus./U.S. Mil. Acad., 1988—; guest curator N.Y. State Hist. Assn., Cooperstown, 1986-87, Brandywine River Mus., Chadds Ford, Pa., 1992; cons. Curatorial Office, U.S. Dept. Treasury, Washington, 1988, Albany (N.Y.) Inst. History and Art, 1988. Author: A Bold Experiment: John Henri Isaac Browere's Life Masks of Prominent Americans, 1988; co-author: The Portraits and History Paintings of Alonzo Chappel, 1992; assoc. editor and contbr. Am. Nat. Biography, Oxford U. Press, 1994—; contbr. articles to profl. jours. Nourse Found. fellow, 1986-87, Nat. Endowment for Arts fellow, 1987, Soc. Colonial Wars fellow, 1988, Andrew W. Mellon fellow Va. Hist. Soc., 1992, Anne S.K. Brown fellow Brown U., 1993. Mem. Assn. Historians Am. Art, Historians Brit. Art, Herbert Howells Soc., Va. Hist. Soc., N.Y. State Hist. Assn. Methodist. Avocation: music. Office: West Point Mus US Mil Acad West Point NY 10996

MESCON, RICHARD ALAN, lawyer; b. Yonkers, N.Y., Oct. 14, 1945; s. Howard and Florence (Greenwald) M.; m. Eileen Etzi, Oct. 12, 1975 (div. 1984); children: Andrew, David; m. Veronica Day, May 6, 1988; 1 child, Hannah. BA, Cornell U., 1968; JD, Columbia U., 1972. Bar: N.Y. 1973, U.S. Dist. Ct. (so. and ea. dist.) N.Y. 1973, U.S. Ct. Appeals (2nd cir.) 1975, U.S. Ct. Internat. Trade 1983, U.S. Ct. Appeals (fed. cir.) 1984. Law clk. to Hon. David N. Edelstein U.S. Dist. Ct. (so. dist.), N.Y.C., 1972-73; assoc. Paul Weiss Rifkind Wharton & Garrison, N.Y.C., 1973-77; asst. U.S. atty. criminal divsn. so. dist. U.S. Dept. Justice, N.Y.C., 1977-83; ptnr. Kassel Neuwirth & Geiger, N.Y.C., 1983-85, Webster & Sheffield, N.Y.C., 1986-90, Morgan, Lewis & Bockius, N.Y.C., 1990—; adj. assoc. prof. law NYU, 1987-90. Mem. Assn. Bar City N.Y., Fed. Bar Coun. Office: Morgan Lewis & Bockius 101 Park Ave New York NY 10178*

MESELSON, MATTHEW STANLEY, biochemist, educator; b. Denver, Col., May 24, 1930; s. Hymen Avram and Ann (Swedlow) M.; m. Jeanne Guillemin, 1986; children: Zoe, Amy Valor. Ph.B., U. Chgo., 1951, D.Sc. (hon.), 1975; Ph.D., Calif. Inst. Tech., 1957; Sc.D. (hon.), Oakland Coll., 1964, Columbia, 1971, Yale U., 1987, Princeton U., 1988. From research fellow to sr. research fellow Calif. Inst. Tech., 1957-60; asso. prof. biology Harvard U., 1960—, prof. biology, 1964-76, Thomas Dudley Cabot prof. natural scis., 1976—. Recipient Eli Lilly award microbiology and immunology, 1964, Alumni medal U. Chgo., 1971; Lehman award 1975, Presidential award 1983, N.Y. Acad. Scis., 1975; Alumni Disting. Svc. award Calif. Inst. Tech., 1975; Leo Szilard award Am. Phys. Soc., 1978; MacArthur fellow, 1984-89. Fellow AAAS (Sci. Freedom and Responsibility award, 1990); mem. NAS (Molecular Biology prize 1963), Inst. Medicine, Am. Acad. Arts and Scis., Fedn. Am. Scientists (chmn. 1986-88, Pub. Svc. award 1972), Coun. Fgn. Rels., Accademia Santa Chiara, Am. Philos. Soc., Royal Society (London), Académie des Sciences (Paris), Genetics Soc. Am. (Thomas Hunt Morgan medal 1995). Office: Harvard U Fairchild Biochem Bldg 7 Divinity Ave Cambridge MA 02138-2019

MESERVE, RICHARD ANDREW, lawyer; b. Medford, Mass., Nov. 20, 1944; s. Robert William and Gladys Evangeline (Swenson) M.; m. Martha Ann Richards, Sept. 20, 1966; children: Amy, Lauren. BA, Tufts U., 1966; JD, Harvard U., 1975; PhD in Applied Physics, Stanford U., 1976. Bar: Mass. 1975, D.C. 1980, U.S. Supreme Ct. 1982. Law clk. Mass. Supreme Jud. Ct., Boston, 1975-76; law clk. to presiding justice U.S. Supreme Ct., Washington, 1976-77; legal counsel Pres. Sci. Adviser, Washington, 1977-81; ptnr. Covington & Burling, Washington, 1981—; chmn. com. to assess safety and tech. issues at Dept. Energy reactors, NAS, 1987-88, chmn. com. on fuel economy of automobiles and light trucks, 1991-92, chmn. com. on declassification of info. for Dept. Energy's environ. programs, 1994-95; co-chmn. AAAS-ABA Nat. Conf. Lawyers and Scientists, 1988-94; bd. dirs. Carnegie Instn., Washington. Fellow AAAS, Am. Phys. Soc., Am. Acad. Arts and Scis.; mem. Phi Beta Kappa, Sigma Xi. Democrat. Home: 708 Berry St Falls Church VA 22042-2402 Office: Covington & Burling PO Box 7566 1201 Pennsylvania Ave NW Washington DC 20004-2401

MESERVE, WALTER JOSEPH, drama studies educator, publisher; b. Portland, Maine, Mar. 10, 1923; s. Walter Joseph and Bessie Adelia (Bailey) M.; m. Mollie Ann Lacey, June 18, 1981; children by previous marriage—Gayle Ellen, Peter Haynes, Jo Alison, David Bryan. Student, Portland Jr. Coll., 1941-42; AB, Bates Coll., Lewiston, Maine, 1947; MA, Boston U., 1948; PhD, U. Wash., 1952. Instr. to prof. U. Kans., Lawrence, 1951-68; prof. dramatic lit. and theory Ind. U., Bloomington, 1968-88, assoc. dean rsch. and grad. devel., 1980-83, dir. Inst. for Am. Theatre Studies, 1983-88; disting. prof. grad. ctr. CUNY, N.Y.C., 1988-93, disting. prof. emeritus, 1993—; v.p. Feedback Svcs., N.Y.C., 1983—. Author: History of American Drama, 1965, rev. edit., 1994, Robert Sherwood, 1970, An Emerging Entertainment, 1977, Heralds of Promise, 1986, A Chronological Outline of World Theatre, 1992; editor: Plays of WD Howells, 1960, On Stage, America! A Selection of Distinctly American Plays, 1996; editor-in-chief Feedback Theatrebooks, 1985—; co-editor Jour. Am. Drama and Theatre, 1989-93; co-compiler: Who's Where in the American Theatre, 1990, 3d edit., 1992, Musical Theatre Cookbook, 1993, Playhouse America!, 1991, The Theatre Lover's Cookbook, 1992; mem. adv. bd. College Literature, 1990-95. With AC, U.S. Army, 1943-46. Fellow NEH, 1974-75, 83-84, 88-89, Rockefeller Found., 1979, Guggenheim Found., 1984-85. Mem. Cosmos Club.

MESERVE, WILLIAM GEORGE, lawyer; b. Medford, Mass., June 14, 1940; s. Robert William and Gladys Evangeline (Swenson) M.; m. Susan Mary Rycroft, Oct. 21, 1967; children: Daniel Scott, Susan Elizabeth, Jonathan Robert. BA, Tufts U., 1962; LLB, Harvard U., 1965; MSc, London Sch. Econs., 1966. Bar: Mass. 1966, U.S. Dist Ct. Mass. 1970, U.S. Ct. Appeals (1st cir.) 1973. Legal asst. to commr. FTC, Washington, 1966-67; staff counsel com. on commerce U.S. Senate, Washington, 1967-69; assoc. Ropes & Gray, Boston, 1970-76, ptnr., 1976—; geology field asst. McMurdo Sound, Antarctica, 1959-60, Inglefield Land, Greenland, summer 1965. Bd. visitors Fletcher Sch. Law and Diplomacy, Tufts U., Medford, 1971—; trustee Tufts U., 1979—, AFS Intercultural Programs Inc., N.Y.C., 1979-92, 93—, New Eng. Med. Ctr., Inc., Boston, 1988—; bd. dirs. United South End Settlements, Boston, 1979—; bd. govs. New Eng. Med. Ctr. Hosps., Boston, 1982-94, 95—. Fellow Am. Coll. Trial Lawyers; mem. ABA, Boston Bar Assn., Phi Beta Kappa. Democrat. Club: Appalachian Mountain (Boston) (rec. sec. 1977-78). Office: Ropes & Gray One International Pl Boston MA 02110

MESHBESHER, RONALD I., lawyer; b. Mpls., May 18, 1933; s. Nathan J. and Esther J. (Balman) M.; m. Sandra F. Siegel, June 17, 1956 (div. 1978); children: Betsy F., Wendy S., Stacy J.; m. Kimberly L. Garnaas, May 23, 1988; 1 child, Jolie M. BS in Law, U. Minn., 1955, JD, 1957. Bar: Minn. 1957, U.S. Supreme Ct. 1966. Prosecuting atty. Hennepin County, Mpls., 1958-61; pres. Meshbesher and Spence Ltd., Mpls., 1961—; lectr. numerous legal and profl. orgns.; mem. adv. com. on rules of criminal procedure Minn. Supreme Ct., 1971-91; cons. on recodification of criminal procedure code Czech Republic Ministry of Justice, 1994. Author: Trial Handbook for Minnesota Lawyers, 1992; mem. bd. editors Criminal Law Advocacy Reporter; mem. adv. bd. Bur. Nat. Affairs Criminal Practice Manual; contbr. numerous articles to profl. jours. Mem. ATLA (bd. govs. 1968-71), ABA, Minn. Bar Assn., Internat. Acad. Trial Lawyers, Am. Coll. Trial Lawyers,

Am. Bd. Trial Advs., Am. Bd. Criminal Lawyers (v.p. 1983), Am. Acad. Forensic Scis., Nat. Assn. Criminal Def. Lawyers (pres. 1984-85), Minn. Trial Lawyers Assn. (pres. 1973-74), Minn. Assn. Criminal Def. Lawyers (pres. 1991-92), Trial Lawyers for Pub. Justice, Calif. Attys. for Criminal Justice. Avocations: biking, photography, travel, flying. Home: 2010 Sugarwood Dr Orono MN 55356-9339 Office: Meshbesher & Spence 1616 Park Ave Minneapolis MN 55404-1631

MESHEL, HARRY, state senator, political party official; b. Youngstown, Ohio, June 13, 1924; s. Angelo and Rubena (Markakis) Michelakis; children: Barry, Melanie. BSBA, Youngstown Coll., 1949; MS, Columbia U., 1950; LLD (hon.), Ohio U.; Youngstown State U.; LLD (hon.), Ohio Coll. Podiatric Medicine; LHD (hon.), Youngstown State U. Exec. asst. to mayor City of Youngstown, Ohio, 1964-68; urban renewal dir. City of Youngstown, Ohio, 1969; mem. 33d district Ohio Senate, Columbus, 1971-93; Dem. minority leader Ohio Senate, 1981-82, 85-90, pres. and majority leader, 1983-84, com. mem. econ. develop., sci. & tech., state & local govt., ways & means, commerce & labor, controlling bd., state employment compensation bd., fin. chmn., 1974-81, rules chmn., 1983-84, com. mem. rules, reference & oversight, 1985-90; state chair Ohio Dem. Party, 1993—; real estate broker; adj. prof. polit. sci. Ohio U.; faculty mem. (limited svc.) Youngstown State U.; div. mgr. investment firm; Ohio Senate special com. mem. Task Force on Drug Strategies, Ohio Acad. Sci. Centennial Celebration Commn., Motor Vehicle Inspection & Maintenance Program, Legis. Oversight Com., Ohio Boxing Commn., Correctional Inst. Inspection Com., Ohio Small Bus. & Entrepreneurship Coun., Gov.'s Adv. Coun. Travel & Tourism, Legis. Svc. Commn., Capital Sq. Rev. & Adv. Bd., others. Past pres., past lt. gov. Am. Hellenic Ednl. Prog. Assn. (AHEPA); precinct committeeman Mahoning County Dem. Party, ward captain, mem. exec. com.; campaign mgr. local candidates, county campaign mgr. presdl. candidates; del. Dem. Mid-Term Conv., 1981; founder Great Lakes/N.E. Legis. Coalition; chmn., founder Nat. Dem. State Legis. Leaders Assn.; dir. State Legis. Leaders Found.; state/fed. assembly, mem. communications com. Nat. Conf. State Legis., legis. mgmt. com., govt. opers. com.; chair fiscal affairs com. Midwest Conf. Coun. State Govts., task force on econs. & fiscal affairs; del., exec. com. Dem. Nat. Com.; mem. Dem. Leadership Coun., State Dem. Exec. Com.; exec. com. Assn. State Dem. Chairs; bd. trustees Nat. Hall of Fame for Persons with Disabilities; mem. St. Nicholas Greek Orthodox Ch. With USN, 1943-46. Decorated two Bronze Battle Stars; recipient Dist. Svc. award Office of Pres., Top Legislator award Ohio Union Patrolmen Assn., Dist. Citizen award Med. Coll. Ohio, City of Hope Leadership award, 1993, Legis. Leadership award Ohio Coalition for Edn. of Handicapped Children, Phillips Medal of Pub. Svc., Ohio U., John E. Fogarty award Gov.'s Com. of Employment of Handicapped, Gov.'s award, 1992, U. Cin. Award for Excellence, Lamp of Learning award Ohio Edn. Assn., Black Cultural Soc. award East Liverpool, Mahoning Valley Man of Yr. award, Mahoning Valley Econ. Devel. Corp., Office Holder of Yr. award Truman-Johnson Dem. Women, Best Interest of Children award Fathers of Equal Rights, Founders Day award Circle of Friends Found., Helping Hand award Easter Seal Soc., Honorary Riverboat Captain award Mahoning County Dem. Party, Community Svc. and Special Svcs. awards Eastern Orthodox Men's Soc., Periclean award AHEPA, Academy of Achievement award Nat. AHEPA Ednl. Found., Nat. Svc. Dem. award AHEPA, 1994, Disting. Citizen award Youngstown State U. Alumni Assn., numerous appreciation and recognition awards; recipient Outstanding Legislator awards Ohio Acad. Trial Lawyers, Ohio Assn. Pub. Sch. Employees, Ohio Rehab. Assn., League Ohio Sportsmen; recipient Dist. Svc. awards Youngstown State U., Ohio Edn. Assn., Ohio Union Patrolmen Assn., Ohio Disabled Vets., AFL-CIO Ohio Barbers Union, AFL-CIO Nat. Assn. of Theatre Owners of Ohio; named Guardian of the Menorah, Youngstown B'nai B'rith, Outstanding Dem., Fairfield Dem. Club, 1993. Mem. (life) NAACP, ACLU, AMVETS (Legislator of Yr. 1993), VFW, Am. Legion, Cath. War Vets (Dist. Legislator award), Vet. Boxers Assn. Mercer County, Pa., Trumbull County Boxers' Legends of Leather (Man of Yr. award Hall of Fame), William Holmes McGuffey Hist. Soc., Buckeye Elks Lodge (hn.); mem. Kiwanis Internat., Urban League, Alliance C. of C., Southern Community Jaycees (hon.), Soc. for Preservation of Greek Heritage, Greek Am. Progressive Assn., Pan Cretan Assn., Arms Hist. Mus. Soc., Eagles, Moose, The Stambaugh Pillars.

MESHII, MASAHIRO, materials science educator; b. Amagasaki, Japan, Oct. 6, 1931; came to U.S., 1956; s. Masataro and Kazuyo M.; m. Eiko Kumagai, May 21, 1959; children: Alisa, Erica. BS, Osaka (Japan) U., 1954, MS, 1956; PhD, Northwestern U., 1959. Lectr., rsch. assoc. dept. materials sci. and engring. Northwestern U., Evanston, Ill., 1959-60, asst. prof., assoc. prof., then prof., 1960-88, chmn. dept. materials sci. and engring., 1978-82, John Evans prof., 1988—; vis. scientist Nat. Rsch. Inst. Metals, Tokyo, 1970-71; NSF summer faculty rsch. participant Argonne (Ill.) Nat. Lab., 1975; guest prof. Osaka U., 1985; Acta/Scripta Metallurgica lectr., 1993-95. Co-editor: Lattice Defects in Quenched Metals, 1965, Martensitic Transformation, 1978, Science of Advanced Materials, 1990; editor: Fatigue and Microstructures, 1979, Mechanical Properties of BCC Metals, 1982; contbr. over 225 articles to tech. publs. and internat. jours. Recipient Founders award Midwest Soc. Electron Microscopists, 1987. Fellow ASM (Henry Marion Howe medal 1968), Japan Soc. Promotion of Sci.; mem. AIME, Metallurgical Soc., Japan Inst. Metals (Achievement award 1972). Home: 3051 Centennial Ln Highland Park IL 60035-1017 Office: Northwestern U Dept Materials Sci Eng Evanston IL 60208

MESHKE, GEORGE LEWIS, drama and humanities educator; b. Yakima, Wash., Oct. 7, 1930; s. George Joseph and Marye Elizabeth (Lopas) M. BA, U. Wash., 1953, MA, 1959, PhD in Drama, 1972. Cert. tchr., Wash. Tchr. English and drama Zillah High Sch., Wash., 1955-58; tchr. English and drama high sch., Bellevue, Wash., 1958-60, Federal Way, Wash., 1960-70; dir., actor Old Brewery Theatre, Helena, Mont., 1962-66; prof. drama Yakima Valley C.C., Yakima, 1970—; casting dir., dir. summer seminar Laughing Horse Summer Theatre, Ellensburg, Wash., 1989—; lectr. Inquiring Mind series Wash. State Humanities, 1989-91; regional dir. Am. Coll. Theatre Festival, Washington, 1980-86; arts dialogue J.F. Kennedy Ctr., Washington, 1987—. Author, producer Towers of Tomorrow, 1985. Regional bd. dirs. Common Cause, Yakima, 1971-73; active Wash. State Commn. Humanities. With U.S. Army, 1953-55, Austria. Recipient Gold medallion Kennedy Ctr., 1985, Wash. State Humanities medal, 1983, NISAD medallion, 1989. Mem. ACLU, Wash. Edn. Assn., N.W. Drama Assn., Am. Edn. Theatre Assn., Am. Fedn. Tchrs., Phi Delta Kappa. Democrat. Avocations: travel, mountain climbing, skiing, reading. Home: 5 N 42nd Ave Yakima WA 98908-3214 Office: Yakima Valley CC 16th And Nob Hill Blvd Yakima WA 98907

MESINGER, JOHN FREDERICK, psychologist, special education educator; b. Indpls., July 17, 1929; s. William F. and Thelma E. (Harden) M.; m. Marguerite E. Rudolf, June 12, 1954; children: Karen Mesinger-Miller, Stuart F., Brian W.L. AB in Psychology, Hamilton Coll., 1951; MA in Psychology, Butler U., 1952; PhD in Experimental Child Psychology, Pudue U., 1955. Lic. psychologist, Va., clin. psychologist, Pa. Clin. psychologist, spl. edn. supr. Allegheny County, Pa. Schs., Pitts., 1958-64; prof. spl. edn. dept. curriculum, instruction and spl. edn. U. Va., Charlottesville, 1964-96, prof. emeritus, 1996; lectr. Sch. Edn., U. Pitts., 1959-63, Pa. State U., 1963-64, Syracuse U., 1966; mem. U. Va. Sch. Edn. Editl. Policy Bd., 1971; cons. Avonworth Union Sch. Dist., 1958-64, Easter Seal Soc., 1958-64; evaluator Allegheny County Juvenile Ct., 1958-64, Thornhill Instn., 1958-64, Oak Hill Sch., 1958-64; mem. staff Consultative Resource Ctr. Sch. Desegregation, U. Va., 1968-69; co-dir. Ctr. Youth and Family Svcs., 1977-80; dir. Va. Educateur Program, 1977-88, Beginning Tchr. Assistance Program, Region III, 1988-91; lectr. Internat. Conf. Children with Learning Disabilities, Washington, 1977, Nat. Adolescent Conf., Pensacola, Fla., 1984, Correctional Edn. Conf., San Francisco, 1987, Tri-State Optometric Conf. Reading, Pitts., 1963, Va. Mental Health Assn., 1965, Va. State Psychiat. Assn., 1972, Va. Assn. Sch. Psychologists, 1974, Va. State CEC Conf., Roanoke, 1977, Va. Optometric Assn., Norfolk, 1977, Va. State Conf. Adminstrs. Spl. Edn., 1991, Va. Assn. Correctional Educators, 1991, Villages Conf. Menninger Found., Topkea, Kans., 1991; bd. dirs. Charlottesville-Albemarle Mental Health Assn., 1965-69, mem. adv. bd.; bd. dirs. Charlottesville-Albemarle chpt. ACLU, 1975-80, Adventure Bound Sch., 1980-84; chmn. adv. bd. Va. Rehab. Sch. Authority, 1975-78; cons. Va. State Dept. Spl. Edn., 1965—; mem. rev. teams SEA, 1965—; cons. Peking Med. Union, 1988, Va. Dept. Edn. Task Force, 1989-91. Author: Children and Youth in Need of Care and Supervision, 1978; (with others) Problems and Issues in Education of Exceptional Children, 1971, Contemporary Issues in Educational Psychology, 1987; cons. editor Behavioral Disorders, 1981-93, The Jour. of Correctional Edn., 1984-96; contbr. 35 articles to profl. jours. Chmn. Pres.'s Com. Equal Ednl. and Employment Opportunities, Obligations and Rights, 1967-71. With U.S. Army, 1956-58. Grantee Bur. for Edn. of the Handicapped, 1964-65, NIMH, 1969, Law Enforcement Assistance Agy., 1973-75, Edwin Gould Found., 1981, Dept. Edn., 1981-83, Beginning Tchr. Assistance Program, 1989-90, 90-91. Mem. AAUP, Am. Orthopsychiat. Assn., Pa. PTA (life), Correctional Edn. Assn. (lectr. internat. convs. 1990, 91), Coun. for Children with Behavioral Disorders (pres. Va. chpt. 1986-87, editor Jour. 1986-91), Coun. Exceptional Children (lectr. internat. convs. 1968, 70, 72, 79, 88, lectr. Va. state chpt. 1979), Sigma Xi, Alpha Kappa Delta, Phi Delta Kappa. Avocations: photography, fishing, gunsmithing, gardening. Office: U Va Curry Sch Edn 405 Emmet St Charlottesville VA 22903

MESIROV, LEON ISAAC, lawyer; b. Phila., Jan. 19, 1912; s. Isaac and Zippa (Robbins) M.; m. Sylvia W. Portner, June 25, 1935; children: Joan C. Rondell Sparens, Judy Lynn, Jill P. AB, U. Pa., 1931, LLB, 1934. Bar: Pa. 1934, U.S. Dist. Ct. (ea. dist.) Pa. 1934, U.S. Ct. Appeals (3d and Fed. cirs.) 1948, U.S. Ct. Internat. Trade 1948. Pvt. practice law Phila., 1934—; ptnr. Mesirov, Gelman, Jaffe, Cramer & Jamieson, Phila., 1959-88, counsel, 1988—. Commr. Phila. Civil Svc., 1952-70; pres. Jewish Community Rels. Coun., 1952-55, hon. pres., 1955—; commr. Phila. Fellowship Commn., 1952—, counsel, 1959—; sec. Jewish Y's and Ctrs., 1967-71; Trustee Fedn. Jewish Ags., 1960-71, Com. of Seventy, 1972—. Mem. ABA, Pa., Phila. bar assns., Order of Coif, Beta Sigma Rho. Jewish. Home: 2131 Saint James Pl Philadelphia PA 19103-4804 Office: Mesirov Gelman Jaffe Cramer & Jamieson 1735 Market St Philadelphia PA 19103-7598

MESKILL, THOMAS J., federal judge; b. New Britain, Conn., Jan. 30, 1928; s. Thomas J. M.; m. Mary T. Grady; children—Maureen Meskill Heneghan, John, Peter, Eileen, Thomas. B.S., Trinity Coll., Hartford, Conn., 1950, LL.D., 1972; J.D., U. Conn., 1956; postgrad., Sch. Law, NYU; LL.D., U. Bridgeport, 1971, U. New Haven, 1974. Bar: Conn. 1956, Fla. 1957, D.C. 1957, U.S. Ct. Appeals (2d cir.) 1975, U.S. Supreme Ct. 1971. Former mem. firm Meskill, Dorsey, Sledzik and Walsh, New Britain; mem. 90th-91st Congresses 6th Conn. Dist.; gov. Conn., 1971-75; judge U.S. Ct. Appeals (2d cir.), New Britain, Conn., 1975—, chief judge, 1992-93. Pres. New Britain Council Social Agys.; Asst. corp. council City of New Britain, 1960-62, mayor, 1962-64, corp. counsel, 1965-67; mem. Constl. Conv., Hartford, 1965. Served to 1st lt. USAF, 1950-53. Recipient Disting. Svc. award Jr. C. of C., 1964, Jud. Achievement award ATLA, 1983, Learned Hand medal for Excellence in Fed. Juridprudence, Fed. Bar Coun., 1994. Mem. Fla. Bar Assn., Con. Bar Assn. (Henry J. Naruk Jud. award 1994), Hartford County Bar Assn., New Britain Bar Assn., KC. Republican. Office: US Ct Appeals OLD POST OFFICE PLAZA, STE 204 114 W Main St New Britain CT 06051-4223

MESKILL, VICTOR PETER, college president, educator; b. Albertson, N.Y., May 9, 1935; s. James Joseph and Ida May (Pfalzer) M.; m. Gail King Heidinger, 1986; children by previous marriage—Susan Ann, Janet Louise, Gary James, Glenn Thomas, Kenneth John, Matthew Adam. B.A., Hofstra U., 1961, M.A. (grad. scholar), 1962; Ph.D., St. John's U., 1967; postgrad. insts., Ohio State U., 1968, Harvard U., 1972; postgrad., NYU, 1973; DSc (hon.), Samara State Aerospace U., Russia, 1993; LHD (hon.), St. John's U., 1995; DCL (hon.), Moscow Internat. U., Russia, 1996, Moscow Internat. U., 1996. Lab. asst., instr. biology Hofstra U., 1960-62; N.Y. State teaching fellow St. John's U., 1962-63; instr. biology Nassau (N.Y.) Community Coll., 1963-64; tchr. sci. Central High Sch. Dist. 2, Floral Park, N.Y., 1963-64; lectr. biology C.W. Post Coll., Greenvale, N.Y., 1963-64, instr. biology, 1964-67, asst. prof., 1967-68, assoc. prof., 1968-74, assoc. dir. Inst. for Student Problems, supr. student tchrs., 1967-68, asst. dean Coll., dean summer sch., coordinator Admissions Office, coordinator adult and continuing edn. programs, 1968-69; dean adminstrn. C.W. Post Ctr. of L.I. U., 1969-70, v.p. adminstrn., 1970-77, prof. biology, 1975-77; pres. Dowling Coll., Oakdale, L.I., 1977—; hon. prof. Minjiang U., Fuzhou, Peoples Republic of China, 1994; cons. in edn. and biology; chem. technician, detective Tech. Rsch. Bur., Nassau County Police Dept., 1958-63, mem. sci. adv. com., 1970; mem. adv. coun. Aerospace Edn. Coun. Inc., 1968; trustee, mem. state legis. com. Commn. Ind. Colls. and Univs.; mem. evaluation teams Mid. States Assn., 1971—; mem. higher edn. adv. com. N.Y. State Senate; mem. Nassau-Suffolk Comprehensive Health Planning Coun.; chmn. Internat. and Mediterranean Studies Group Conf. Author book; contbr. articles to profl. jours. Founding mem., vice chmn. bd. trustees Nassau Higher Edn. Consortium; bd. dirs. Suffolk County coun. Boy Scouts Am.; mem. N.Y. State Energy Rsch. and Devel. Authority, Town of Islip Devel. Commn.; chmn. bd. trustees L.I. Regional Adv. Coun. Higher Edn.; chmn. L.I. Mid Suffolk Bus. Action; bd. dirs. Southside Hosp., N.Y.; v.p. L.I. Forum for Tech.; former commr. Suffolk County Vanderbilt Mus.; mem. Bus. Coun. N.Y.; hon. mem. U. Pau and Pays de l'Adour, Pau, France, 1994. NSF rsch. grantee, 1967-69; Named Tchr. of Year, Aesculapius Med. Arts Soc., C.W. Post Coll. of L.I. U., 1967; Disting. Faculty Mem. of Year, C.W. Post Ctr. L.I. U., 1977; recipient George M. Estabrook award Hofstra U., 1978, Higher Edn. Leadership award Corning Glass Works, 1987, Disting. Leadership award L.I., 1989. Mem. AAAS, Coun. Advancement and Support of Edn., Am. Assn. Collegiate Registrars and Admissions Officers, Am. Assn. Higher Edn., Am. Inst. Biol. Scis., Am. Soc. Zoologists, Am. Assn. U. Adminstrs., Nat. Assn. Biology Tchrs., Nat. Sci. Tchrs. Assn., Soc. Protozoologists, N.Y. Acad. Scis., Camilo Josè Cela Found. (hon.), Met. Assn. Coll. and Univ. Biologists (founder, mem. steering com.), Bus. Coun. N.Y., Oakdale C. of C. (founding mem., dir.), Univ. Club (N.Y.C.), Wings Club (N.Y.C.), Nat. Arts Club (N.Y.C.), L.I. Assn. Commerce and Industry (v.p. edn., dir.), Alpha Chi, Kappa Delta Pi, Phi Delta Kappa, Sigma Xi, Beta Beta Beta, Alpha Eta Rho, Delta Mu Delta, Kappa Delta Rho. Office: Dowling Coll Office of Pres Oakdale NY 11769

MESNIKOFF, ALVIN MURRAY, psychiatry educator; b. Asbury Park, N.J., Dec. 25, 1925; s. Nathan and Rachel (Feinberg) M.; m. Wendy Savin, June 15, 1952; children: Nathaniel, Rachel, Joel, Ann. A.B., Rutgers U., 1948; M.D., U. Chgo., 1954; cert. Psychoanalytic medicine, Columbia U., 1962. Diplomate: Am. Bd. Psychiatry and Neurology. Pvt. practice, 1958—; collaborating psychoanalyst Columbia U. Psychoanalytic Ctr. for Tng. and Rsch., N.Y.C., 1962—; dir. Washington Heights Community, N.Y. State Psychiat. Inst., N.Y.C., 1965-68; assoc. clin. prof. psychiatry Columbia U. Coll. Physicians and Surgeons, 1958-68; prof. psychiatry SUNY, Bklyn., 1968-81; dir. South Beach Psychiat. Ctr., S.I., N.Y., 1968-75; regional dir. N.Y. State Dept. Mental Health, N.Y.C., 1975-78, dep. commr. research, 1978-81; Marion E. Kenworthy prof. Psychiatry Columbia U. Sch. Social Work, 1981-89; lectr. Union Theol. Sem., N.Y.C., 1989-90; cons. St. Vincent's Hosp., S.I., 1970-76; attending psychiatrist S.I. Hosp., 1972-76; sr. attending psychiatrist St. Luke's/Roosevelt Hosp. Ctr., N.Y., 1987—; cons. Ford Found., N.Y.C., 1980-81. Contbr. chpts. to books, articles to profl. jours. Bd. dirs. Reality House, 1967-74; mem. task force med. sch. enrollment and physician manpower N.Y. State Bd. Regents, 1973-75; mem. task force on gen. and splty. hosp. care N.Y. State Health Planning Commn., 1973-74. Served with U.S. Army, 1943-45. Grantee Ford Found., 1982. Fellow Am. Psychiat. Assn. (life); mem. Am. Psychoanalytic Assn., Assn. Psychoanalytic Medicine, Am. Friends Tel Aviv U. (chmn. 1974-75), Phi Beta Kappa. Jewish. Office: 360 Central Park W New York NY 10025-6541

MESROBIAN, ARPENA SACHAKLIAN, publisher, editor, consultant; b. Boston; d. Aaron Harry and Eliza (Der Melkonian) Sachaklian; m. William John Mesrobian, June 22, 1940; children: William Stephen, Marian Elizabeth (Mrs. Bruce MacCurdy). Student, Armenian Coll. of Beirut, Lebanon, 1937-38; A.A., Univ. Coll., Syracuse (N.Y.) U., 1959, B.A. magna cum laude, 1971; MSsc, Syracuse U., 1993. Editor Syracuse U. Press, 1955-58, exec. editor, 1958-61, asst. dir., 1961-65, acting dir., 1965-66, editor, 1968-85, assoc. dir., 1968-75, dir., 1975-85, 87-88, dir. emeritus, 1985; dir. workshop on univ. press. pub. U. Malaysia, Kuala Lumpur, 1985; cons. Empire State Coll. Book rev. editor: Armenian Rev., 1967-75; mem. publs. bd. Courier, 1970-94; mem. adv. bd. Armenian Rev., 1981-83; contbr. numerous articles, revs. to profl. jours. Pres. Syracuse chpt. Armenian Relief Soc., 1972-74; sponsor Armenian Assembly, Washington, 1975; mem. mktg. task force Office of Spl. Edn., Dept. Edn., 1979-84, Adminstrn. of Developmental Disabilities, HHS; mem. publs. panel Nat. Endowment for Humanities, Washington; bd. dirs. Syracuse Girls Club, 1982-87; pres. trustees St. John the Bapt. Armenian Apostolic Ch. and Cmty. Ctr., 1991-95. Named Post-Standard Woman of Achievement, 1980; recipient Chancellor's award for disting. service Syracuse U., 1985; Nat. award U.S. sect. World Edn. Fellowship, 1986; N.Y. State Humanities scholar. Mem. Women in Communications, Soc. Armenian Studies (adminstrv. council 1976-78, 85-87, sec. 1978, 85-87), Syracuse U. Library Assocs. (v.p. 1983-88), Am. Univ. Press Services (dir. 1976-77), Armenian Lit. Soc., Armenian Community Center, Assn. Am. Univ. Presses (v.p. 1976-77), UN Assn. (bd. dirs. 1983-88, v.p. 1985), Phi Kappa Phi, Alpha Sigma Lambda. Mem. Armenian Apostolic Ch. (trustee). Club: Zonta of Syracuse (pres. 1979-80, 1st v.p. 1985-86, dist. historian Dist. 2 Zonta Internat. 1993). Home: 4851 Pembridge Cir Syracuse NY 13215-1023

MESSA, JOSEPH LOUIS, JR., lawyer; b. Phila., Mar. 24, 1962; s. Joseph Louis and Virginia (Ciaffoni) M. BS, Tulane U., 1984; JD, Temple U., 1988. Bar: Pa. 1988, N.J. 1988, U.S. Dist. Ct. (ea. dist.) Pa. 1990, U.S. Dist. Ct. (cen. dist.) N.J. 1988. Assoc. Duane Morris & Heckscher, Phila., 1988-90; ptnr. Ominsky, Welsh, Messa, Tanner & Giles, Phila., 1990—. Ward loader Rep. Party, Phila. 1985—, city com., 1985—, exec. com., 1985—. Mem. ATLA, ABA, Pa. Trial Lawyers (cons., seminar presenter, liability com.), Phila. Trial Lawyers. Roman Catholic. Avocations: physical fitness, bodybuilding, waterskiing, boating, traveling. Office: Ominsky Welsh Messa Tanner & Giles 1760 Market St 10th Fl Philadelphia PA 19103

MESSAM, LEROY ANTHONY, accountant; b. Kingston, Jamaica, West Indies, July 24, 1923; came to U.S., 1951; s. David A. and Irene Beatrice (Patterson) M.; m. Ruby Patricia Jackson, July 25, 1964; children: LeRoy Jr., Andrea, Conrad, Mahalia. BA in Bus. Adminstr., Bryant & Stratton, Boston, 1958; MEd, Cambridge Coll., 1983; DD, Free Anglican Ch. in Am., 1979; DBA, Southland (Lassell) U., Pasadena, Calif., 1986; grad., Harvard U., 1980. CPA; accredited Accreditation Coun. for Accountancy. Prin. Leroy A. Messam, Pub. Acct., Boston, 1962—; bishop St. John's Episcopal Ch., Mattapan, Mass., 1986—. Author: Resource Handbook for Black & Minority Entrepreneurs, 1983; co-author Pub. Adminstrn. of Our Nat. Economy, 1983. Treas. NAACP, Boston, 1962; coord. Boy Scouts Am., Boston, 1984—; del. White House Conf. on Small Bus., Washington, 1986; bd. dirs. Mass. Dept. Social Svcs., Boston, 1987; chmn. Jamaican Hurricane Relief, 1988—. Recipient Community Svcs. award Boston Soc. Vulcans Inc., Black Profl. Fire Fighters, 1989. Fellow Reg. Pub. Accts. of Jamaica (v.p. 1975-76); mem. Nat. Soc. Pub. Accts., Mass. Assn. Pub. Accts., Jamaican Culture Soc. (pres. 1962-73), The Friends of BOAF (sec. 1989—). Republican. Episcopalian. Office: 96 Greenfield Rd Mattapan MA 02126-3203

MESSEMER, GLENN MATTHEW, lawyer; b. Hartford, Conn., Jan. 7, 1947; s. Joseph M. and Mary S. Messemer; BSBA, Georgetown U., 1968; JD, U. Conn., 1971. Bar: Conn. 1972. Staff atty. Kaman Corp., Bloomfield, Conn., 1972-74, asst. sec., 1974-79, asst. v.p., 1979-81, v.p., sec., gen. counsel, 1981—; prof. bus. law Sch. Bus. Adminstrn., U. Hartford (Conn.), 1974-80; legal counsel Am. Helicopter Soc.; arbitrator Am. Arbitration Assn., 1978-82. Bd. dirs., trustee, regent U. Hartford, 1993—. Served with M.I., U.S. Army, 1969-75. Mem. ABA, Conn. Bar Assn. (founding; exec. com., sec.), Hartford County Bar Assn. Clubs: Hartford Golf, Hartford, Masons. Office: Kaman Corp Old Windsor Rd Bloomfield CT 06002

MESSENGER, GEORGE CLEMENT, engineering consultant; b. Bellows Falls, Vt., July 20, 1930; s. Clement George and Ethel Mildred (Farrar) M.; m. Priscilla Betty Norris, June 19, 1954; children: Michael Todd, Steven Barry, Bonnie Lynn. BS in Physics, Worcester Poly. U., 1951; MSEE, U. Pa., 1957; PhD in Engring., Calif. Coast U., 1986. Rsch. scientist Philco Corp., Phila., 1951-59; engring. mgr. Hughes Semicondr., Newport Beach, Calif., 1959-61; div. mgr. Transitron Corp., Wakefield, Mass., 1961-63; staff scientist Northrop Corp., Hawthorne, Calif., 1963-68; cons. engr., Las Vegas, Nev., 1968—; lectr. UCLA, 1969-75; v.p., dir. Am. Inst. Fin., Grafton, Mass., 1970-78; gen. ptnr. Dargon Fund, Anaheim, Calif., 1983—; v.p., tech. dir. Messenger and Assoc., 1987—, registered investment adviser, 1989—. Co-author: The Effects of Radiation on Electronic Systems, 1986; contbg. author: Fundamentals of Nuclear Hardening, 1972; contbr. numerous articles to tech. jours.; patentee microwave diode, hardened semicondrs. Recipient Naval Rsch. Lab. Alan Berman award, 1982; Best Paper award HEART Conf., 1983, Spl. Merit award HEART Conf., 1983, Goddard award for outstanding profl. achievement Worcester Polytechnic Inst., 1996; fellow IEEE, 1976, annual merit award 1986, Pete Haas award. HEART Conf., 1992. Mem. Rsch. Soc. Am., Am. Phys. Soc. Congregationalist. Home and Office: 3111 Bel Air Dr Apt 7F Las Vegas NV 89109-1510

MESSENGER, JAMES LOUIS, lawyer; b. Youngstown, Ohio, Oct. 18, 1942; s. William Robert and Georgette Elizabeth (Capehart) M.; m. Barbara Ann Vasslides, June 21, 1969; children: William, John. BBA, Ohio U., 1964; LLB, Syracuse U., 1967. Bar: Ohio 1967, U.S. Dist. Ct. (no. dist.) Ohio 1968, U.S. Ct. Appeals (6th cir.) 1976, U.S. Supreme Ct. 1982, U.S. Ct. Appeals (3d cir.) 1989. Assoc. Henderson, Covington, Stein & Donchess, Youngstown, 1967-74; ptnr./ Henderson, Covington, Stein, Donchess & Messenger, Youngstown, 1974-94, Henderson, Covington, Messenger, Newman & Thomas, Co., L.P.A., Youngstown, 1995—; bd. dirs. YSD Industries, Inc., Youngstown. Chmn., bd. dirs., founding mem. Ohio Coun. Sch. Bd. Attys., Columbus, Ohio, 1975—; active Civil Svc. Commn., Youngstown, 1991—. Mem. ABA, Ohio State Bar Assn., Mahoning County Bar Assn. (pres., award 1983). Republican. Episcopal. Avocations: thoroughbred horse racing, golf, handball. Home: 1811 Bears Den Rd Youngstown OH 44511 Office: 600 Wick Bldg Youngstown OH 44503-1473

MESSENGER, RON J., health facility administrator; b. 1944. MBA, U. So. Calif., 1968. Engr. CASH, L.A., 1968-73; v.p. Nat. Med. Enterprises, Santa Monica, Calif., 1973-84; pres. L.A. Cmty. Hosp., 1984—, Hollywood (Calif.) Cmty. Hosp., 1984—; pres., sec., CEO Paracelsus Healthcare Corp., Pasadena, Calif., 1984—. Office: Paracelsus Healthcare 155 N Lake Ave Ste 1100 Pasadena CA 91101-1857*

MESSENKOPF, EUGENE JOHN, real estate and business consultant; b. N.Y.C., Jan. 26, 1928; s. John Philip and Helen Bessie (Holden) M.; m. Martha Ann Crane, Jan. 29, 1955; children: Diane, Nancy, Eugene John, Susan. BBA, Iona Coll., 1950; MBA, NYU, 1956. CPA, N.Y. Sec.-treas. KLM Process Co., N.Y.C., 1952-54; acct. Am. Tobacco Co., N.Y.C., 1954-56; staff acct. Peat, Marwick & Mitchell, N.Y.C., 1956-60; exec. v.p. Donaldson, Lufkin & Jenrette, Inc., N.Y.C., 1960-84, pres., chief exec. officer real estate div., 1977-84; pres., chief exec. officer Meridian Investing and Devel. Corp., 1977-84; pvt. practice cons., 1984—; mem. adv. bd. NYU Real Estate Inst., 1981-85; mem. exec. coun. small scale devel. Urban Land Inst., 1983-90; chmn. Wall St. Tax Com., N.Y.C., 1965-68; bd. dirs. SIA Acctg. Div., N.Y.C., 1965-79. Trustee, chmn. fin. com. Mt. Vernon Hosp., 1982-87. Served as sgt. AUS, 1950-52, Korea. Recipient Brother Loftus award Iona Coll., 1976. Mem. AICPA, N.Y. State Soc. CPAs, Fin. Execs. Inst. Republican. Roman Catholic. Walked 2000 mile Appalachian Trail, 1987.

MESSER, DONALD EDWARD, theological school president; b. Kimball, S.D., Mar. 5, 1941; s. George Marcus and Grace E. (Foltz) M.; m. Bonnie Jeanne Nagel, Aug. 30, 1964; children: Christine Marie, Kent Donald. BA cum laude, Dakota Wesleyan U., 1963; M. Divinity magna cum laude, Boston U., 1966, PhD, 1969; LHD (hon.), Dakota Wesleyan U., 1977. Asst. to commr. Mass. Commn. Against Discrimination, Boston, 1968-69; asst. prof. Augustana Coll., Sioux Falls, S.D., 1969-71; assoc. pastor 1st United Meth. Ch., Sioux Falls, 1969-71; pres. Dakota Wesleyan U., Mitchell, S.D., 1971-81, Iliff Sch. Theology, Denver, 1981—. Author: Christian Ethics and Political Action, 1984, Contemporary Images of Christian Ministry, 1989, Send Me? The Intineracy in Crisis, 1991, The Conspiracy of Goodness, 1992, Caught in the Crossfire: Helping Christians Debate Homosexuality, 1994, Calling Church and Seminary Into the 21st Century, 1995, Unity, Liberty, and Charity: Building Bridges Under Icy Waters, 1996; contbr. articles to Face to Face, The Christian Century, The Christian Ministry. Active Edn. Commn. of U.S., 1973-79; co-chmn. Citizens Commn. Corrections, 1975-76; vice chmn. S.D. Commn. on Humanities, 1979-81. Dempster fellow, 1967-68; Rockefeller fellow, 1968-69. Mem. Soc. Christian Ethics, Am. Acad. Religion, Assn. United Meth. Theol. Schs. (v.p. 1986-91, pres. 1991-92). Democrat. Office: Iliff Sch Theology Office Pres 2201 S University Blvd Denver CO 80210-4707

MESSER, THOMAS MARIA, museum director; b. Bratislava, Czechoslovakia, Feb. 9, 1920; came to U.S., 1939, naturalized, 1944; s. Richard and Agatha (Albrecht) M.; m. Remedios Garcia Villa, Jan. 10, 1948. Exch. student, Inst. Internat. Edn., 1939; student, Thiel Coll., Greenville, Pa., 1939-41; BA, Boston U., 1942; degree, U. Sorbonne, Paris, 1947; MA, Harvard U., 1951; DFA (hon.), U. Mass., 1962, U. of Arts, Phila., 1988. Dir. Roswell (N.Mex.) Mus., 1949-52; asst. dir. Am. Fedn. Arts, N.Y.C., 1952-53, dir. exhbns., 1953-55, dir. fedn., 1955-56, trustee, 1972-75; dir. Inst. Contemporary Art, Boston, 1957-61, Solomon R. Guggenheim Mus., N.Y.C., 1961-88, Peggy Guggenheim Collection, Venice, Italy, 1980-88, Solomon R. Guggenheim Found., N.Y.C., trustee, 1980-90, dir. emeritus, 1990—; chief curator Schiin Kunsthalle, Frankfurt, 1994—; adj. prof. Harvard U., 1960, Barnard Coll., 1966, 71; prof. Hochschule fuer Angewandte Kunst, Vienna, Austria, 1984; prof. Goethe U., Frankfurt, 1991-92, 93-95; pres. Assn. Art Mus. Dirs., 1974-75; founding mem. exec. com. Am. Arts Alliance, Washington, 1978-81; pres. The MacDowell Colony Inc., 1977-78, 93-95; mem. adv. bd. Palazzo Grassi, Venice, 1986—; trustee Fontana Found., Milan, 1988—; sr. cultural advisor Am.'s Soc., 1988—; sr. advisor visual arts Caixa Found., 1991—; trustee Inst. Internat. Edn., 1991—; mem. coun. Nat. Gallery, Czech Republic, 1994—. Author: Edvard Munch, 1973; contbr. to mus. catalogues, art jours. Decorated chevalier Legion d'Honneur, France, 1980, Officier Legion d'Honneur, France, 1989; recipient Goethe medal Fed. Republic Germany; spl. fellow for study in Brussels Belgian-Am. Ednl. Found., 1953; sr. fellow Ctr. Advanced Studies, Wesleyan U., 1966. Mem. Internat. com. for Mus. and Collections Modern Art (hon. pres.), Met. Opera (N.Y.C.), Century Assn. (N.Y.C.). Home: 35 Sutton Pl New York NY 10022 Office: Americas Soc 680 Park Ave New York NY 10021-5009

MESSERLE, JUDITH ROSE, medical librarian, public relations director; b. Litchfield, Ill., Jan. 16, 1943; d. Richard Douglas and Nelrose B. (Davis) Wilcox; m. Darrell Wayne Messerle, Apr. 26, 1968; children: Kurt Norman, Katherine Lynn. BA in Zoology, So. Ill. U., 1966; MLS, U. Ill., 1967. Cert. med. libr. Libr., St. Joseph's Sch. Nursing, Alton, Ill., 1967-71, dir. med. info. ctr., 1971-76, dir. info. services, 1976-79, dir. ednl. resources and community relations, St. Joseph's Hosp., Alton, Ill., 1979-84; dir. Med. Ctr. Libr., St. Louis U., 1985-88; libr. Francis A. Countway Libr. for the Harvard Med. Sch. and Boston Med. Libr., 1989—; instr. Lewis and Clark Coll., 1975; cons. 1973—; instr. Med. Library Assn. Bd. dirs. Family Services and Vis. Nurses Assn., Alton, 1976-79. Mem. Med. Library Assn. (dir. 1981-84, pres. 1986-87, task force for knowledge and skills, 1988-92, Legis. task force 1986-90, nom. com. 1996, search com. for exec. dir. 1979), Ill. State Libr. Adv. Com., Midwest Health Sci. Libr. Network (dir. health sci. council), St. Louis Med. Librs., Hosp. Pub. Relations Soc. of St. Louis, Nat. Libr. Medicine (biomed. libr. rev. com. 1988-92), AMA (com. on allied health edn. and accreditation 1991-94), Assn. Acad. Health Sci. Libr. Dirs. (pres. 1993, joint legis. task force 1992—, editorial bd. for ann. stats. 1989-94, Region 8 Adv. Bd. 1992-93), Am. Med. Informatics Assn. (planning com. 1990, publications com. 1994-96, annual mtg. com. 1996—), OCLC (spl. libr. adv. com. 1994—). Office: Countway Libr of Medicine 10 Shattuck St Boston MA 02115-6011

MESSERSCHMIDT, GERALD LEIGH, pharmaceutical industry executive, physician; b. Vancouver, B.C., Can., Feb. 2, 1950; s. George Gus and Joan May (Chapman) M.; m. Donna Kay Mackinley, Sept. 29, 1990; children: Jacqueline Diane, Victoria Leigh, Jonathan Leigh. BS, Portland State U., 1972; MD, U. Oreg., Portland, 1976. Diplomate Am. Bd. Internal Medicine, Am. Bd. Med. Oncology, Am. Bd. Hematology. Resident in internal medicine Letterman Army Med. Ctr., San Francisco, 1976-79; fellow in oncology and hematology NIH, Bethesda, Md., 1979-82; head exptl. hematology Nat. Cancer Inst., NIH, Bethesda, Md., 1981-82; dir. bone marrow transplants for Dept. of Def. Wilford Hall Med. Ctr., San Antonio, 1982-88; dir. bone marrow transplants U. Mich. Med. Ctr., Ann Arbor, 1988-90; dir. med. affairs Ciba-Geigy Pharm., Summit, N.J., 1990-92, exec. dir. med. affairs, 1992-93; v.p. med. and regulatory affairs DNX Corp., Princeton, N.J., 1993-94; corp. v.p. C.R. Bard Inc., Murray Hill, N.J., 1994-95, sr. v.p., 1995-96; CEO, pres. Kimeragen, Inc., N.Y.C., 1996—. Maj. USAF, 1982-88. Fellow ACP; mem. Am. Soc. Med. Oncology, Am. Soc. Hematology. Home: 11 Glen Gary Dr Mendham NJ 07945-3030 Office: Kimeragen Inc 375 Park Ave New York NY 10052

MESSERSCHMITT, DAVID GAVIN, engineering educator; b. Denver, May 21, 1945; s. Darwin Erwin and Helen Marilla (Dentan) M.; m. Dorothy Margaret Seegers, May 2, 1970; 1 child, Laura Joanne. BS, U. Colo., 1967; MS, U. Mich., 1968, PhD, 1971. Mem. tech. staff Bell Labs., Holmdel, N.J., 1968-77; supr. Bell Labs., 1974-77; prof. dept. elec. engring. and computer sci. U. Calif., Berkeley, 1977—, chair dept., 1993-96; bd. dirs. Teknekron Communication Systems, Berkeley. Contbr. articles to profl. jours. Patentee in field. Recipient Pres.'s award U. Colo., 1967, named Outstanding Grad. Engr., 1967; NSF fellow, 1967. Fellow IEEE (bd. govs. communications soc. 1981-84); mem. NAE. Office: U Calif 231 Cory Hall Berkeley CA 94720

MESSIER, MARK DOUGLAS, professional hockey player; b. Edmonton, Alta., Can., Jan. 18, 1961. With Indpls. Racers, 1978, Cin. Stingers, 1979; with Edmonton Oilers, 1979-91, team capt., 1988-91; with N.Y. Rangers, 1991—; player NHL All-Star Game, 1982-84, 86, 88-92, 94, Stanley Cup Championship Game, 1984, 85, 87, 88, 90, 94. Recipient Conn Smythe trophy, 1984, Lester B. Pearson award, 1989-90, 91-92, Hart trophy, 1990, 92; named NHL Player of Yr., 1989-90, 91-92; named to Sporting News All-Star Team, 1981-82, 82-83, 89-90, 91-92. Office: NY Rangers 4 Pennsylvania Plz New York NY 10001*

MESSIER, PIERRE, lawyer, manufacturing company executive; b. Montreal, Que., Can., Mar. 3, 1945; s. Lionel and Anita (Caron) M.; m. Ginette Piche, July 11, 1970; 1 child, Mathieu. B.A., Coll. St. Viateur, Outremont, Que., 1964; LL.L., U. Montreal, 1968; D.S.A., Ecole Hautes Etudes Commerciales, Montreal, 1973. Bar: Que. 1969. Assoc. firm Lemay & Messier, Montreal, 1969-75; v.p., sec. gen. counsel Can. Cement Lafarge, Ltd., Montreal, 1975-84; v.p., sec. Lafarge Corp., 1983-84; v.p. bus. devel., legal affairs Norsk Hydro Can. Inc., Montreal, 1989—; v.p. Que. Bar Service Corp. Pres. Clinique Pedagogique de Montreal; bd. dirs. Coll. Jean de Brebeuf; pres. Greenfield Park Bd. Revision, 1973-74; bd. dirs. Societe Progres Rive Sud, Longueuil, Que., 1974-75. Mem. ABA, Can. Bar Assn. (pres. young lawyers sect. 1976, nat. exec. 1977-78), Montreal Jr. Bar (treas. 1972), Que. Mfrs. Assn. (bd. dirs.), St. Denis Club (Montreal). Office: Norsk Hydro Canada Inc, 2000 Peel # 700, Montreal, PQ Canada H3A 2W5

MESSINEO, KAREN, newspaper publishing executive. V.p. and cfo The New York Times, N.Y.C. Office: The NY Times 229 W 43rd St New York NY 10036-3913

MESSING, ARNOLD PHILIP, lawyer; b. N.Y.C., Sept. 2, 1941; s. Louis Messing and Ruth Aaron; m. Esther S. Buchman, Oct. 1, 1967; 1 child, Noah. BA magna cum laude, NYU, 1962; JD, Yale U., 1965. Bar: N.Y. 1966, Mass. 1976, Pa. 1985, U.S. Dist. Ct. (so. and ea. dists.) N.Y., U.S. Dist. Ct. Mass. 1976, U.S. Ct. Internat. Trade 1977, U.S. Ct. Appeals (1st, 2d, 6th and D.C. cirs.), U.S. Supreme Ct. 1977, U.S. Tax Ct. 1984. Assoc. Cravath, Swaine & Moore, N.Y.C., 1967-76; ptnr. Gaston & Snow and predecessor firm, Boston, 1976-91, Choate, Hall & Stewart, Boston, 1991—. Served to sgt. USAFR, 1965-71. Mem. ABA, Boston Bar Assn., Mass. Bar Assn. Jewish. Home: 271 Mill St Newton MA 02160-2438

MESSING, KAREN, biology educator; b. Springfield, Mass., Feb. 2, 1943. BA, harvard U., 1963; MSc, McGill U., 1970, PhD in Biology, 1975. Rsch. asst. biochemistry Jewish Gen. Hosp., Montreal, Can., 1970-71; NIH fellow genetics Boyce Thompson Inst. Plant Rsch., 1975-76; prof. women's occupl. health U. Quebec, Montreal, 1976—, dir. Ctr. Study Biol. Interactions & Environ. Health, 1990—; invited rschr. Inst. Cancer Montreal, 1983—; mem. bd. dirs. Quebec Sci. & Tech. Muc., 1984-86, Quebec Coun. Social Affairs, 1984-90. Editor Recherchee Feministes. Mem. AAAS, Am. Pub. Health, Genetics Soc. Can., Environ. Mutagenesis Soc. Office: Univ Quebec at Montreal, CP 8888 succursale A, Montreal, PQ Canada H3C 3P8*

MESSING, MARK P., advertising executive; b. Wellesley, Mass., Aug. 13, 1948; s. Richard F. and Gertrude (Walsh) M.; m. Tina M. Gallagher, Feb. 21, 1987; 1 child, Mark P. BA, Williams Coll., 1970. Account exec. Deutsch Shea & Evans, N.Y.C., 1970-72, Muller Jordan Herrick, N.Y.C., 1972-75, F. William Free & Co., N.Y.C., 1975; sr. v.p., mgmt. supr. Scali McCabe Sloves, Inc., N.Y.C., 1976-91; sr. v.p., mgmt. dir. J. Walter Thompson, N.Y.C., 1991-93; mng. dir. Young and Rubicam, N.Y.C., 1993—; bd. dirs. Southampton (N.Y.) Commons Bd. Avocations: cooking, tennis, music. Office: Young & Rubicam Madison Ave New York NY 10017

MESSINGER, CORA R., funeral director; b. Chickasha, Okla., Sept. 28, 1930; d. George Franklin and Addie (Jewett) Ross; m. Paul R. Messinger, Nov. 23, 1950;children: H. Kendrick, David William. Student, U. Ariz., 1957. Asst. control records dept. Valley Nat. Bank, Phoenix, 1948-50; engring. coord. Air Rsch. Mfg., Phoenix, 1954-56; owner Messinger Mortuary and Chapel, Scottsdale, Ariz., 1959—; owner, corp. sec., treas. Messinger Ins. Agy., Inc., Scottsdale, 1985—. Rep. dist. chmn., Scottsdale and East Phoenix, 1964-69; mem. Scottsdale Meml. Hosp. Aux., 1961—, YMCA bd., 1972-80, Scottsdale Indian Art bd., 1962-68. Mem. Boyce Thomson Arboretum, Desert Bot. Gardens, Arizona Club, Phoenix Art Mus., USTA. Republican. Roman Catholic. Avocations: tennis, gardening, Western art. Office: Messinger Mortuary Inc 7601 E Indian School Rd Scottsdale AZ 85251-3607

MESSINGER, SCOTT JAMES, advertising agency executive; b. Bklyn., Feb. 27, 1952; s. Nathaniel Bernard and Joy Black (Artson) M.; m. Michele Barbaro, Sept. 1988; children: Katherine Lydon, Zachary Ryan, Gabriella Lucia, Victoria Joy. BS in Journalism, Northwestern U., 1974, MS in Journalism, 1975. Asst. account exec. Ted Bates/N.Y., N.Y.C., 1977-78, account exec., 1978-79, account supr., 1979-80, v.p., account supr., 1980-84, sr. v.p., mgmt. rep., 1984-90, Scali McCabe Sloves, 1990—, exec. v.p. acct. dir., 1990—, dir. client svcs., 1991—, mng. dir., 1992-94; exec. dir. Lowe & Ptnrs./SMS, N.Y.C., 1994—. Roman Catholic. Avocations: running, skiing, tennis, squash. Home: 110 W 96th St Apt 11cd New York NY 10025-6413 Office: Lowe & Ptnrs/SMS 1111 Avenue Of The Americas New York NY 10036-6706

MESSITTE, PETER JO, judge; b. Washington, July 17, 1941; s. Jesse B. and Edith (Wechsler) M.; m. Susan P. Messitte, Sept. 5, 1965; children: Zachariah, Abigail. BA cum laude, Amherst Coll., 1963; JD, U. Chgo., 1966. Bar: Md. 1969, D.C. 1969, U.S. Ct. Appeals (4th cir.) 1977, U.S. Supreme Ct. 1973, U.S. Ct. Appeals (D.C. cir.) 1982, U.S. Ct. Appeals (5th cir.) 1983. Assoc. Zuckert, Scoutt & Rasenberger, Washington, 1968-71; solo practice, Chevy Chase, Md., 1971-75; mem. Messitte & Rosenberg, P.A., Chevy Chase, 1975-81, Peter J. Messitte, P.A., Chevy Chase, 1981-85; assoc. judge Cir. Ct. for Montgomery County, Md., Rockville, 1985-93; judge U.S. Dist. Ct. Md., 1993—. Bd. dirs. Cmty. Psychiat. Clinic, Montgomery County, Md., 1974-85, v.p., 1980-85, Peace Corps vol., Sao Paulo, Brazil, 1966-68; Md. del. Dem. Nat. Conv., N.Y.C., 1980. Recipient teaching citations Fed. Deposit Ins. Corp. Bank Exam. Sch., 1975, 79, Am. Inst. Banking, 1978; Elizabeth Scull award for Outstanding Svc. to Montgomery County, Md., 1993, Spl. citation Div. Roundtable Montgomery County, 1993, Contbr. Mental Health Cmty. Psychiat. Clinic, 1986. Mem. ABA, Fed. Bar Assn., Inter-Am. Bar Assn., D.C. Bar Assn., Md. Bar Assn., Montgomery County Bar Assn., Am. Law Inst., Fed. Bar Assn., Charles Fahy Inn of Ct. (master 1987-88), Montgomery County Inn of Ct. (pres. 1988-90), Jud. Inst. Md. (bd. dirs. 1989-93). Jewish. Office: US Courthouse 6500 Cherrywood Ln Greenbelt MD 20770-1249

MESSMAN, JACK L., oil executive; b. Clarksburg, W.Va., Mar. 13, 1940; s. Marvin C. and Betty L. (Jones) M.; m. Ellen Frances Stiggins, Sept. 5, 1965; children—Valerie Lynne, Kyle Andrew. B.Chem. Engring., U. Del.-Newark, 1962; M.B.A., Harvard U., 1968. Ptnr. Butcher & Singer, Phila., 1971-73; pres. Norcross, Inc., West Chester, Pa., 1973-80; v.p. corp. devel. UGI Corp., Valley Forge, Pa., 1980-81; exec. v.p. Safeguard Scientifics, King of Prussia, Pa., 1981-83; pres., chief exec. officer Novell Data Systems, Inc., Orem, Utah, 1981-83; exec. v.p., chief fin. officer Warner Amex, N.Y.C., 1983-86; chmn., chief exec. officer Somerset House Corp., Houston, 1986-88; chief exec. officer, bd. dirs. USPCI, Inc., Oklahoma City, 1988-91; pres., CEO, Union Pacific Resources, Inc., Ft. Worth, 1991—; bd. dirs. Wawa, Inc. (Pa.), Novell Inc., Utah. Served to 1st lt. U.S. Army, 1963-65. Republican. Episcopalian. Clubs: Aronimink Golf (Newtorn Square, Pa.), River Crest Country (Ft. Worth), Shady Oaks Country (Ft. Worth). Office: Union Pacific Resources Inc 801 Cherry St Fort Worth TX 76102-6803

MESSMER, DONALD JOSEPH, business management educator, marketing consultant; b. St. Louis, July 30, 1936; s. Edgar Louis and Lucille Louise (Straub) M.; m. Charlotte Jean Fox; 1 child, Angeline Charlotte. BSBA with honors, Washington U., St. Louis, 1969, PhD, 1974. Asst. mgr. M.A. Bell Co., St. Louis, 1956-61; dist. sales exec. U. S. Gypsum Co., St. Louis, 1962-65; br. sales exec. Victor Comptometer Corp., St. Louis, 1965-68; asst. prof. Coll. William and Mary, Williamsburg, Va., 1973-76, assoc. prof., 1976-81, prof., 1981—, J.S. Mack prof., 1982—, dir. exec. MBA program, 1988-91; pres. The Wessex Group, Ltd., Williamsburg, 1979—; bd. dirs. Williamsburg Winery, Ltd., Chateau Hotels, Ltd.; chmn. bd. dirs. Community Svcs. Coalition, Inc. Assoc. editor Decision Scis. jour., 1985-88; contbr. articles to profl. jours. Bd. dirs., treas. Community Action Agy., Williamsburg, 1984-91, United Way of Greater Williamsburg, 1985-91, pres., 1989. Mem. Decision Scis. Inst. (mktg. coord. 1985-86), Southeastern Decision Scis. Inst. (pres. 1985-86), Am. Mktg. Assn. (Dissertation award 1974), Rotary (bd. dirs. 1990-92), Alpha Mu Alpha, Beta Gamma Sigma. Republican. Avocations: fishing, golf. Office: Coll William and Mary Grad Sch Bus Williamsburg VA 23185-8795

MESSMORE, DAVID WILLIAM, construction executive, former psychologist; b. Indpls.; s. Max J. and Betty G. (Miller) M.; m. Sondra Renée Bastian, Aug. 22, 1981; children: Kristen Nicole, Eric Christian William David. AB in Social Sci., Calif. State Coll., Long Beach, 1968; PhD in Student Devel., Counseling and Clin. Psychology, Mich. State U., 1972. Lic. class A gen. contractor, Tex., Va.; lic. psychologist, Calif., Mich.; lic. sch. psychologist, Calif. Counselor Okemas (Mich.) Pub. Sch., 1970-72; psychologist Frederick Ctr. Day Hosp., Grand Rapids, Mich., 1972-73, Newport-Mesa Schs., Newport Beach, Calif., 1973-80; commr. Bd. Med. Quality Assurance, State of Calif. Psychol. com., Sacramento, 1980-82; pres. Bridgewater Constrn., Inc., Chesapeake, Va., 1987—; psychol. counselor Camp Highfields Residential Sch., Onondago, Mich., 1971; cons. The Open Door, Lansing, Mich., 1971-72, Juv. and Domestic Rels. Ct. of the Family Ct., State of Va., Chesapeake, 1989-91; pres. Bridgewater Consultation Svcs., Chesapeake, 1989-91; intern Counseling Ctr., Calif. State U., Long Beach, asst. prof. ednl. psychology, 1981; instr. Golden West Coll., Huntington Beach, Calif., 1977-78; advisor, counselor Dean of Students Mich. State U., 1969-71; coach City of Chesapeake, Parks/Recreation, commr. Transp./Safety, 1994—, vice chmn. Transp. and Safety, 1995—. Author: (manual) The Impact of Divorce on Families, 1989; designer sch. crest Long Beach City Coll., 1965. Active Gt. Bridge Conf. Com., Ehesapeake, 1987-91; treas. Paint Your Heart Out, Chesapeake, 1993; coach parks and recreation dept. City of Chesapeake, 1994—; mem. fin. com. city com. Chesapeake Rep. Com., vice chmn. programs, 1996—. With USMC, 1959-63. Recipient Cert. of Appreciation Chesapeake Vols. in Youth Svcs., Inc., 1989, Outstanding Svc. award, 1990, Gov.'s award State of Va., 1990. Mem. Nat. Youth Sports Coaches Assn., Rotary (bd. dirs. Chesapeake 1990-94, co-chmn. programs 1996—), Delta Tau Delta. Avocations: tennis, reading, investments.

MESSMORE, THOMAS ELLISON, asset management company executive; b. Monongahela, Pa., June 30, 1945; s. Lindsay Ellison and Margaret (Hoffmann) M.; m. Sharon Weaver, Aug. 19, 1966; children: Lauren, Beth, Benjamin, William. BS in Indsl. Engring., W.Va. U., 1967; MBA, Harvard U., 1969. Chartered fin. analyst. Asst. treas. State Street Bank and Trust Co., Boston, 1969-72; fin. product mgr. Interactive Data Corp., Waltham, Mass., 1972-75; sr. v.p. Keystone Custodian Funds, Inc., Boston, 1975-80; sr. v.p. and chief fin. officer Keystone Mass. Group, Boston, 1981-83; sr. v.p. The Travelers Ins. Co., Hartford, Conn., 1984-94; pvt. cons. Hartford, 1994-95; pres., CEO, UBS Asset Mgmt., N.Y.C., 1995—; dir. Energy BioSystems Corp. Mem. Assn. for Investment Mgmt. and Rsch. Home: 1090 Prospect Ave Hartford CT 06105-1125

MESSNER, HOWARD MYRON, professional association executive; b. Newark, June 10, 1937; s. Elias and Freda (Trachtenberg) M.; m. Aletha Bragg, 1960 (div. 1980); children: Jennifer, Linda, David; m. Melba June Meador, June 22, 1986. BA, Antioch Coll., 1960; MA, U. Mass., 1962. Mgmt. analyst Office Gov., Mass., 1960-61; staff asst. to adminstr. NASA, Washington, 1962-65; mgmt. analyst Bur. Budget, Washington, 1965-71; dir. adminstrn. EPA, Washington, 1971-75, asst. adminstr. for adminstrn., 1983-87; asst. dir. Congl. Budget Office, Washington, 1975-77, Office Mgmt. and Budget, Washington, 1977-83; controller Dept. Energy, Washington, 1983; exec. v.p., chief exec. officer Am. Cons. Engrs. Council, 1987—. Recipient William A. Jump Meml. award, 1971, Presdl. Disting. Exec. award, 1986, Outstanding Pub. Service award Nat. Capital chpt. Am. Soc. Pub. Adminstrn., 1986, Chancellor's medal U. Mass., 1988. Mem. Nat. Acad. Pub. Adminstrn., Am. Consortium for Internat. Pub. Adminstrn. (v.p.). Democrat. Jewish. Home: 1683 Justin Dr Gambrills MD 21054-2012 Office: Am Cons Engrs Coun 1015 15th St NW Washington DC 20005-2605

MESSNER, KATHRYN HERTZOG, civic worker; b. Glendale, Calif., May 27, 1915; d. Walter Sylvester and Sadie (Dinger) Hertzog; m. Ernest Lincoln, Jan. 1, 1942; children: Ernest Lincoln, Martha Allison Messner Cloran. BA, UCLA, 1936, MA, 1951. Tchr. social studies L.A. schs., 1937-46; mem. L.A. County Grand Jury, 1961. Mem. exec. bd. L.A. Family Svc., 1959-62; dist. atty.'s adv. com., 1965-71, dist. atty.'s adv. coun., 1971-82; mem. San Marino Community Coun.; chmn. San Marino chpt. Am. Cancer Soc.; bd. dirs. Pasadena Rep. Women's Club, 1960-62, San Marino dist. coun. Girl Scouts U.S.A., 1959-68, Am. Field Svc., San Marino, 1983—; pres. San Marino High Sch. PTA, 1964-65; bd. mem. Pasadena Vol. Placement Bur., 1962-68; mem. adv. bd. Univ. YWCA, 1956—; co-chmn. Dist. Atty.'s Adv. Bd. Young Citizens Coun., 1968-72; mem. San Marino Red Cross Coun., 1966—, chmn., 1969-71, vice chmn., 1971-74; mem. San Marino bd. Am. Field Svc.; mem. atty. gen.'s vol. adv. com., 1971-80; bd. dirs. L.A. Women's Philharm. Com., 1974-89, Beverly Hills-West L.A. YWCA, 1974-85, L.A. YWCA, 1975-84, L.A. Law Affiliates, 1974-89, Pacificulture Art Mus., 1976-80, Reachout Com., Music Center, Vol. Action Center, West L.A., Calif., 1980-85, Stevens House, 1980—, Pasadena Philharm. Com., 1980-85, Friends Outside, 1983—, Internat. Christian Scholarship Found., 1984—; hon. bd. dirs. Pasadena chpt. ARC, 1978-82. Recipient spl. commendation Am. Cancer Soc., 1961; Community Svc. award UCLA, 1981. Contbr. articles to profl. jours. Mem. Pasadena Philharmonic, Las Floristas, Huntington Meml. Clinic Aux., Nat. Charity League, Gold Shield (co-founder), Pi Lambda Theta (sec. 1983-89), Pi Gamma Mu, Mortar Bd., Prytanean Soc. Home: 1786 Kelton Ave Los Angeles CA 90024-5508

MESSNER, RICHARD STEPHEN, school system administrator; b. N.Y.C., Nov. 8, 1939; s. Blasius and Anna (Kuti) M.; m. Eugenia Mancuso, Oct. 22, 1968 (div. 1974); 1 child, Stephanie; m. Mary Theodorakis, May 28, 1976' stepchildren: Paul, Nicole. BS, Alderson-Broaddus Coll., 1961; MBA, Fairleigh Dickinson U., 1972; MEd, Rutgers U., 1980. Acctg. mgr. McGraw-Hill, Hightstown, N.J., 1968-71; bus. coord. Fairleigh Dickinson U., Rutherford, N.J., 1971-73; dep. treas. County of Somerset, Somerville, N.J., 1973-78; asst. dir. of adminstrv. svcs. Somerset County Vo-Tech, Bridgewater, N.J., 1978-82; dir. adminstrv. svcs. Somerset County Vocat. Tech., Bridgewater, 1982-85, asst. supt. for bus., 1985—, acting supt., 1987-88, supt. of schs., 1992—; bd. dirs. Edn. Svcs. Commn., Somerset County. Dep. mayor Franklin Twp., N.J., 1975, mayor, 1975-76; commr. Urban Enterprize Zone Authority, N.J., 1984—; treas. Somerset County Reps., 1985-91; bd. dirs. Somerset Alliance Future, 1992—, Greater Raritan Pvt. Industry Coun., 1992—; mem. Middlesex, Hunterdon, Somerset Pvt. Industry Coun., 1992—; co-chair Somerset ITV Consortium Inc.; bd. dirs. Greater Raritan Valley Workforce Investment Bd, Somerset County Workforce Investment Bd., 1992—; trustee Somerset/Hunterdon Bus.- Edn. Partnership, 1992—. With U.S. Army, 1962-64. Recipient Outstanding Bus. Person of the Yr., Somerset County C. of C., 1995. Mem. Am. Soc. Bus. Officers Internat. (chmn. purchasing com. Reston, Va. chpt. 1986-88, legis. com. 1988—), N.J. Assn. Bus. Ofcls. (chmn. legis. com. Bordentown, N.J. chpt. 1985—), N.J. Assn. Sch. Adminstrs., Somerset County Adminstrs., Somerset County Bus. Ofcls. (v.p. Somerville chpt. 1991—), N.J. Edn. Assn. (adv. com. 1984—), VFW, Masons, Phi Delta Kappa. Baptist. Avocations: sports, World War II history, golf. Home: 32 Pin Oak Rd Skillman NJ 08558-1320

MESSNER, ROBERT THOMAS, lawyer, banking executive; b. McKeesport, Pa., Mar. 27, 1938; s. Thomas M. and Cecilia Mary (McElhinny) M.; m. Anne Margaret Lux, Dec. 3, 1966; children: Megan Anne, Michael Thomas. A.B., Dartmouth Coll., 1960; LL.B., U. Pa., 1963. Bar: Pa. 1965. With firm Rose, Schmidt & Dixon, Pitts., 1965-68; with G.C. Murphy Co., McKeesport, 1968-86; corp. sec. G.C. Murphy Co., 1974—, gen. counsel, 1975-86, v.p., 1976-86; v.p., gen. counsel, corp. sec. Dollar Bank, Pitts., 1986—; dir. G.C. Murphy Found. Bd. dirs. McKeesport YMCA, Downtown Pitts. YMCA, Mon-Yough Heritage Found., 1981-83, Braddock's Field Hist. Soc., 1994—; mem. adv. bd. Pa. Human Rels. Commn., 1968, 69; Rep. candidate for Pa. Legis., 1986, fin. adv. bd. Wilkinsburg, Pa., 1988—. 1st lt. U.S. Army, 1963-65. Decorated Commendation medal. Mem. ABA, Pa. Bar Assn. (chmn. corp. law dept. com.), Allegheny County Bar Assn. (coun. on corp., banking and bus. law), Am. Soc. Corp. Secs. (pres. Pitts. regional group, dir.), Am. Mgmt. Assn., Pa. Assn. Savs. Instns. (chmn. legal com. 1989—), Am. Corp. Counsel Assn., Theta Delta Chi. Clubs: Dartmouth Western Pa; Rivers, Gateway Ctr. (Pitts.). Home: 1061 Blackridge Rd Pittsburgh PA 15235-2719 Office: Dollar Bank Three Gateway Ctr Pittsburgh PA 15222

MESSNER, THOMAS G., advertising executive, copywriter; b. N.Y.C., Jan. 26, 1944; s. Malcolm V. Messner and Virginia M. Burkard; m. Terry Carol Bonaccolta, Nov. 28, 1971; 1 child, Zachary. Letter carrier U.S. Post Office, N.Y.C., 1965-67; copywriter Occidental Life Calif., L.A., 1967-68; mail boy D'Arcy Advt., N.Y.C., 1968; copywriter BBDO, N.Y.C., 1968-69, Doyle Dane Bernbach, N.Y.C., 1969-72; creative dir. Ally and Gargano, N.Y.C., 1972—; ptnr. Messner Vetere Berger Carey Schmetterer, N.Y.C., 1986-92, Messner Vetere Berger McNamee Schmetterer Euro RSCG, N.Y.C., 1992—; bd. dirs. Council for Study of Pub. Choice, Fairfax, Va., N.Y. Club for Art and Copy. Copywriter Ronald Reagan, 1984 presdl. campaign, Republican Nat. Com., N.Y., 1984, Andrew O'Rourke for Gov., N.Y., 1986, George Bush 1988 presdl. campaign. Roman Catholic. Office: Messner Vetere Berger McNamee Schmetterer Euro RSCG 350 Hudson St New York NY 10014-4504*

MESTER, JORGE, conductor; b. Mexico City, Apr. 10, 1935; came to U.S., 1946, naturalized, 1968; s. Victor and Margarita (Knöpfler) M. BS, Juilliard Sch. Music, 1957, MS, 1958; studied conducting with, Jean Morel, Leonard Bernstein., Abert Wolff. Faculty Juilliard Sch. Music, 1956-68, chmn. conducting studies, 1980—. Also condr., Juilliard Theatre Orch., 1961-62, Beaux Arts Trio, 1961-65; mus. dir., Louisville Orch., Greenwich Village Symphony, 1961-62, mus. dir., condr., Louisville Orch., 1967-79, artistic adviser, Kansas City Philharmonic, 1971-72, then music dir., Kansas City Philharmonic, 1973-77, music dir., Aspen Music Festival, 1970—, Festival Casals, 1978-85; music dir. Pasadena Symphony, 1984—; prin. guest condr., St. Paul Chamber Orch., 1978-79, guest condr., Orquesta Sinfonica Nacional de Mexico, Philharmonica Triestina, Spoleto Festival Orch., Japan Philharmonic, Yomiuri Nippon Symphony, Boston Symphony, Pitts. Symphony, New Orleans Philharmonic, Indpls. Symphony, N.Y.C. Opera, Phila. Orch., London Royal Philharmonic, Denver Symphony, Bach Aria Group, Cin. Orch., Rochester Philharmonic, Utah Symphony, Oreg. Symphony, Cin. Symphony, others; condr. dance season, Spoleto Festival, Grant Park, Chgo., Tanglewood, Mass., Harkness Dance Festival, 1964, Cosi Fan Tutte, 1964, L'Elisir D'Amore, rec. with, Columbia, Vanguard, Mercury, Desto, CRI, Cambridge records, also, Louisville 1st Edit. Recs. Named Ky. col., 1967; recipient Naumburg award, 1968, Ditson Condrs. award, 1985.

MESTRALLET, GÉRARD, professional society administrator; b. Paris, Apr. 1, 1949; arrived in Belgium, 1991; s. Georges Julien Marie and Paule Andrée Augustine (Besnard) M.; m. Joëlle Emilienne Renée Arcens, Sept. 7, 1974; children: Stephanie, Caroline, Bastien. Student, Ecole Polytech., Paris, 1968, Ecole Aviation Civile, Paris, 1971, Inst. for Study of Politics, Toulouse, France, 1973, Ecole Nat. d'Adminstrn., Paris, 1978. Counsellor Minister Transp., Econs., Fins., & Budget, Paris, 1973-84; chargé de mission Suez,

Paris, 1984-86, dél. adjoint indsl. affairs, 1986-91, dir. gen. adjoint, 1991—; CEO Soc. Gen. de Belgique, Brussels, 1991; chmn., CEO Compagnie de Suez, Paris, 1995—; chmn. Banque Indosuez, Paris, 1995—. Office: Compagnie de Suez, 1 rue d'Astorg, 75008 Paris France

MESTRES, RICARDO A., III, motion picture company executive; b. N.Y.C., Jan. 23, 1958; s. Ricardo Angelo Jr. and Ann (Farnsworth) M.; m. Tracy Stewart; children: Alexander Carson, Carrie Ann. AB, Harvard U., 1980. Creative exec. Paramount Pictures, L.A., 1981-82, exec. dir. prodn., 1982-84, v.p. prodn., 1984-85; v.p. prodn. Walt Disney Pictures, Burbank, Calif., 1985-86, sr. v.p. prodn., 1986-88; pres. prodn. Touchstone Pictures, Burbank, Calif., 1988-89; pres. Hollywood Pictures, Burbank, Calif., 1989-94; co-founder Great Oaks Entertainment, Burbank, 1995—. Mem. Acad. Motion Picture Arts and Scis. Office: Great Oaks Entertainment 500 S Buena Vista St Burbank CA 91521-0001

MESTRES, RICARDO ANGELO, JR., lawyer; b. N.Y.C., Aug. 12, 1933; s. Ricardo Angelo and Anita (Gwynne) M.; m. Ann Farnsworth, June 18, 1955; children: Laura, Ricardo III, Lynn, Anthony. AB, Princeton U., 1955; LLB, Harvard U., 1961. Bar: N.Y. 1962, U.S. Supreme Ct. 1970. Assoc. Sullivan & Cromwell, N.Y.C., 1961-67, ptnr., 1968—, chmn., sr. ptnr., 1995—. Trustee Unitarian Ch. All Souls, N.Y.C., 1973-79, 84-87, Phillips Exeter Acad., 1989—. Served to lt. USN, 1955-58. Mem. ABA, N.Y. State Bar Assn., Assn. of Bar of City of N.Y. (corp. law, securities regulation law and state legis. coms.), Am. Law Inst., Phi Beta Kappa. Clubs: Downtown Assn., Links (N.Y.C.); Mill Reef (Antigua). Office: Sullivan & Cromwell 125 Broad St New York NY 10004-2400

MESZAR, FRANK, publishing executive, former army officer; b. East Chicago, Ind., Sept. 5, 1915; s. Frank Rach and Julia (Labois) M.; m. Carla Ruth Jorgensen, May 21, 1965; children—Frank, Sarah. B.S. in Civil Engring., U.S. Mil. Acad., 1940; grad., Army War Coll., 1955; M.B.A., Ga. So. Coll. Commd. 2d lt. U.S. Army, 1940, advanced through grades to brig. gen., 1965; chief aviation affairs Dept. Army, 1959-62; asst. dep chief staff ops. U.S. Army Europe, 1962-65; asst. dep. chief staff Continental Army Command, Ft. Monroe, Va., 1965-67; comdg. gen. Army Flight Tng. Center, Hunter AFB, Ga., 1967-68; asst. comdg. gen. 1st Cav. Div., 1969-70; ret., 1970; v.p. finance U.S. Medicine, Inc., Washington, 1970—; treas. Profl. Lithography, Inc., Washington. Pres. Savannah Symphony Soc., 1970-79, Savannah West Point Soc., 1972, Savannah Symphony Soc.; trustee Ga. Infirmary; hon. judge Chatham County, Ga.; vestryman , sr. warden St. John's Episc. Ch. Decorated D.S.M. with oak leaf cluster, Legion of Merit, D.F.C., Silver Star with oak leaf cluster, Bronze Star with 3 oak leaf clusters, Purple Heart with oak leaf cluster; Legion of Honor; Croix de Guerre France). Clubs: Oglethorpe, Rotary. Home: 302 E 46th St Savannah GA 31405-2257 Office: US Medicine 1155 21st St NW Washington DC 20036-3302

MÉSZÁROS, PETER ISTVAN, astrophysicist, researcher, astronomy educator; b. Budapest, Hungary, July 15, 1943; came to U.S., 1968; s. Istvan and Margit Ilona (Andronyi) M.; m. Deborah Ann Runde, Nov. 2, 1974; 1 child, Andor Istvan. MS in Physics, U. Buenos Aires, 1967; PhD, U. Calif., Berkeley, 1972. Rsch. assoc. Princeton (N.J.) U. Obs., 1972-73; rsch. fellow Inst. of Astronomy Cambridge (Eng.) U., 1973-75; staff scientist Max Planck Inst. for Astrophysics, Garching, Fed. Republic of Germany, 1975-83; assoc. prof. Pa. State U., University Park, 1983-87, prof., 1987—, head dept. astronomy and astrophysics, 1993—; vis. scientist NASA-Goddard Space Flight Ctr., Greenbelt, Md., 1980-82, Harvard-Smithsonian Ctr. for Astrophysics, Cambridge, 1982-83, 90; cons. Max Planck Inst. for Astrophysics, Garching, 1983-87, NASA, 1987—, Tokyo Met. U., 1990, Cambridge U., 1991, Inst. Theoretical Physics, U. Calif. Santa Barbara, 1995. Author: (monograph) High Energy Radiation From Magnetized Neutron Stars; contbr. articles to Astrophys. Jour., Phys. Rev., Astron & Astrophysics; contbr. over 130 articles to profl. jours. U. Calif. fellow, 1970-72, Irex fellow NRC, 1986, Smithsonian Inst. fellow, 1982, 83, 90, Royal Soc. Guest Rsch. fellow, 1991; recipient First prize Gravity Rsch. Found., 1976. Mem. Am. Phys. Soc., Am. Astron. Soc. (exec. com. 1987-89), Internat. Astron. Union. Achievements include discovery of growth rate of cold matter perturbations in radiation dominated cosmological models; development of radiative cross sections for cyclotron radiation in neutron stars; research in spherical accretion on black holes, the development of models of accreting pulsars and neutron stars, and development of models for cosmological gamma-ray burst sources. Office: Pa State U Dept Astron & Astrophysics 525 Davey University Park PA 16802

MESZNIK, JOEL R., investment banker; b. Beirut, Oct. 3, 1945; s. Hans and Eugenie (Bagdadi) M.; m. Lynne Gladstein, Mar. 25, 1979; children: Daniel, Jared, Kara. BS, CCNY, 1967; MBA, Columbia U., 1970. Engr. Ebasco Svcs., N.Y.C., 1967-70; banker Citibank, N.Y.C., 1970-71, Newhouse Capital, N.Y.C., 1971-72, Matthews & Wright, N.Y.C., 1972-76; mng. dir. Drexel Burnham Lambert, N.Y.C., 1976-89; pres. Mesco Ltd., 1990—. Office: 122 E 42nd St Ste 4906 New York NY 10168-0002

METALLO, FRANCES ROSEBELL, mathematics educator; b. Jersey City, N.J.; d. Vincenzo James and Lucille (Frank) M. BA in Math., Jersey City State Coll., 1985, MA in Math. Edn., 1987. Math. tchr. Emerson High Sch., Union City, N.J., 1990-92; math tchr. gifted/talented program Jefferson Annex Woodrow Wilson Sch. Dist. Union City, 1992-95; math tchr. Woodrow Wilson Sch., Dist. Union City, 1995—; adj. tchr. math. Hudson County C.C., 1987—, Jersey City State Coll., 1986—, tutor, 1983-86; reviewer for Nat. Coun. Tchrs. Math mag., A Plus for Kids Tchr. Network, 1994, grantee 1993, 96. Contbr. articles to profl. publs. Mem. Nat. Coun. Tchrs. Math., Assn. Math. Tchrs. of N.J., Alumni Assn. Jersey City State Coll., Math. Assn. Am., Am. Soc. Prevention of Cruelty to Animals, Assn. of Women in Math., Am. Math. Soc., Dozenal Soc., Kappa Delta Pi, Phi Delta Kappa. Avocations: developing classroom math. materials, crochet, embroidery, piano. Office: Union City Bd Edn Woodrow Wilson Sch Dist Union City 80 Hawkhurst Ave Weehawken NJ 07087

METCALF, ARTHUR GEORGE BRADFORD, electronics company executive; b. Boston, Nov. 1, 1908; s. Franklin B. and Emma A. (Maclachlan) M.; m. Mary G. Curtis, Feb. 22, 1935; children: Anne C., Helen C., Mary Lee, Hope S. Student, Mass. Inst. Tech., 1932; S.B., Boston U., 1935, LL.D., 1974; S.M., Harvard U., 1939; S.D., Franklin Pierce Coll., 1966. Engring. test pilot, 1930—; prof. math., physics Boston U., 1935; pres. Electronics Corp. Am., Cambridge, Mass., 1954—. Mil. editor: Strategic Rev; contbr. articles to profl. jours. Chmn. emeritus, bd. trustees, exec. com. Boston U.; bd. overseers Mus. Fine Arts, Boston; mem. trustee coun. Boston U. Med. Ctr.; chmn. U.S. Strategic Inst., Washington. Served to lt. col. AUS, WWII. Decorated Legion of Merit, Commendation medal.; Benjamin Franklin fellow Royal Soc. Arts London, 1972. Asso. fellow Royal Aero. Soc. (London), Inst. Aero. Scis.; mem. Am. Def. Preparedness Assn. (dir.), Phi Beta Kappa. Clubs: Harvard (Boston, N.Y.C.); Harvard Faculty (Boston), Algonquin (Boston); Edgartown (Mass.) Yacht; Army and Navy (Washington). Home: 45 Arlington St Winchester MA 01890-3732 Office: 125 Bay State Rd Boston MA 02215-1708

METCALF, BRUCE BARBER, visual artist, craft critic; b. Amherst, Mass., Sept. 30, 1949; s. Leroy Alfred and Catharine (Bartlett) M. BFA, Syracuse U., 1972; MFA, Tyler Sch. Art, Phila., 1977. Temporary instr. Colo. State U., Ft. Collins, 1977-78; instr. Mass. Coll. Art, Boston, 1979-80; asst. prof. art Kent (Ohio) State U., 1981-86, assoc. prof., 1986-91; sr. lectr. The Univ. of the Arts, Phila., 1994; lectr. in U.S., Can., Korea. Solo exhbns. include Heller Gallery, N.Y.C., 1982, Ind. U. Bloomington, 1985, CDK Gallery, N.Y.C., 1989, Contacto Directo Galeria, Lisbon, 1992, Jewelerswerk Galerie, Washington, 1985, 92, Perimeter Gallery, Chgo., 1987, 89, 93, Susan Cummins Gallery, Mill Valley, Calif., 1990, 92, 94, 96; exhibited in group shows Renwick Gallery, Washington, 1981, Am. Craft Mus., 1984, V&V Galerie, Vienna, 1988, Galerie Marzee, Nijmegen, Netherlands, 1989, Kunsthal Rotterdam, Netherlands, 1993, others; contbg. editor, mem. editl. adv. com. Metalsmith mag., 1981-95; author numerous articles on craft theory. Mass. Artists Found. fellow, 1980, Ohio Arts Coun. fellow, 1983, 84, 88, Fulbright teaching/rsch. fellow, Korea, 1990, Nat. Endowment for Visual Arts fellow, 1977, 92. Mem. Soc. N.Am. Goldsmiths (Disting. mem.). Home: 3586 Indian Queen Ln Philadelphia PA 19129

METCALF, ERIC QUINN, professional football player; b. Seattle, Jan. 23, 1968. Degree in liberal arts, U. Tex., 1990. With Cleve. Browns, 1989-94; wide receiver, kick returner, running back Atlanta Falcons, 1995—. Named to Sporting News Coll. All-Am. 2d team, 1987, named to Sporting News NFL All-Pro Team, 1993-94; selected to Pro Bowl, 1993-94. Office: Atlanta Falcons Complex 2745 Burnett Rd Suwanee GA 30174*

METCALF, JACK, congressman, retired state senator; b. Marysville, Wash., Nov. 30, 1927; s. John Read and Eunice (Grannis) M.; m. Norma Jean Grant, Oct. 3, 1948; children: Marta Jean, Gayle Marie, Lea Lynn, Beverlee Ann. Student U. Wash., 1944-45, 47; BA, BEd, Pacific Luth. U., 1951. Tchr., Elma (Wash.) pub. schs., 1951-52, Everett (Wash.) pub schs., 1952-81; mem. Wash. Ho. of Reps., 1960-64; mem. Wash. Senate, 1966-74, 80-92, U.S. congressman, Wash. 2nd Dist., 1995—; chmn. environment and natural resources com., 1988-92. Chmn. Honest Money for Am. Mem. Council State Govts., Wash. Edn. Assn. (dir. 1959-61), Wash. Assn. Profl. Educators (state v.p. 1979-81, state pres. 1977-79). Mem. Nat. Conf. State Legislatures, Western States Recycling Coalition, South Whidbey Kiwanis, Deer Lagoon Grange. Republican. Home: 3273 E Saratoga Rd Langley WA 98260-9694 Office: US House Reps House Office Bldg 507 Cannon Washington DC 20515-4702

METCALF, KAREN, foundation executive; b. Reading, Mass., Dec. 12, 1936; d. Albion Edmund and Natalie Viola (Ives) M. AB, Vassar Coll., 1958; MBA, Harvard U., 1968. CFA. Sec. Radio Liberty Com., N.Y.C., 1958-60; rsch. asst. Air Inc., Cambridge, Mass., 1960-64; sys. analyst Keydata Corp., Watertown, Mass., 1964-66; customer edn. cons. Interactive Data Corp., N.Y.C., 1968; portfolio mgr. Scudder, Stevens & Clark, N.Y.C., 1969-81; v.p. fin. and adminstrn. N.Y. Cmty. Trust, N.Y.C., 1981—. Episcopalian. Avocations: travel, opera. Office: NY Cmty Trust 2 Park Ave New York NY 10016-5603

METCALF, LAURIE, actress; b. Edwardsville, Ill., June 15, 1955; 1 child, Zoe. Student, Ill. State U. Off-Broadway appearances: Balm in Gilead (debut, Theatre World award), 1984; stage appearances: Who's Afraid of Virginia Woolf?, 1982, Coyote Ugly, 1985, Bodies Rest, and Motion, 1986, Educating Rita, 1987 (Joseph Jefferson award best performance by principal actress in a play), Little Egypt, 1987, Killers, 1988, My Thing of Love, 1995; films: Desperately Seeking Susan, 1984, Making Mr. Right, 1987, Stars and Bars, 1988, Candy Mountain, 1988, Miles from Home, 1988, Uncle Buck, 1989, Internal Affairs, 1989, Pacific Heights, 1990, Frankie and Johnny, 1991, JFK, 1991, Mistress, 1992, A Dangerous Woman, 1993, Blink, 1994; TV series: Saturday Night Live, 1981, Roseanne, 1988— (Emmy award, Outstanding Supporting Actress in a Comedy Series, 1993, 94); TV appearances: The Equalizer, 1986, The Execution of Raymond Graham, 1985. Address: care ICM 8942 Wilshire Blvd Beverly Hills CA 90211*

METCALF, ROBERT CLARENCE, architect, educator; b. Nashville, Ohio, Nov. 7, 1923; s. George and Helen May (Drake) M.; m. Bettie Jane Sponseller, Sept. 15, 1943. Student, Johns Hopkins U., 1943; B.Arch., U. Mich., 1950. Draftsman G.B. Brigham, Jr., Architect, Ann Arbor, Mich., 1948-52; pvt. practice architecture Ann Arbor, 1953—; lectr. architecture U. Mich., Ann Arbor, 1955-58; asst. prof. U. Mich., 1958-63, asso. prof., 1963-68, prof., 1968-91, chmn. dept., 1968-74; dean U. Mich. (Coll. Architecture and Urban Planning), 1974-86; Emil Lorch prof. emeritus U. MIch., 1991—, dean emeritus, 1991—; sec. Mich. Bd. Registration for Architects, 1975-79, chmn., 1980-82. Designer 127 bldgs., Ann Arbor, 1953—. Served with U.S. Army, 1943-46, ETO. Decorated Silver Star; recipient Sol King award for excellent teaching in architecture U. Mich., 1974; named Emil Lorch Professor of Architecture, 1989. Fellow AIA; mem. Mich. Soc. Architects, Assn. Collegiate Schs. Architecture, Phi Kappa Phi, Tau Sigma Delta. Home: 1052 Arlington Blvd Ann Arbor MI 48104-2816 Office: U Mich 2150 Art Architecture Bldg Ann Arbor MI 48109 also: 2211 Medford Rd Ann Arbor MI 48104-5004

METCALF, WILLIAM EDWARDS, museum curator; b. East Grand Rapids, Mich., Dec. 16, 1947; s. George Ellington and Ruthanne (Schnitzler) M.; m. Margaret Mary Finn, May 21, 1972 (annulled 1984); 1 son, Daniel F.; m. Jane Salinger, Oct. 26, 1991. B.A., U. Mich., 1969, M.A., 1970, Ph.D. in Classical Studies (Horace H. Rackham prize fellow), 1973. Asst. curator Roman and Byzantine coins Am. Numismatic Soc., N.Y.C., 1973-75; assoc. curator Am. Numismatic Soc., 1975-78, curator, dep. chief curator, 1978-79, chief curator, 1979—; adj. prof. art history and archaeology Columbia U., 1978; adj. prof. history, 1993; adj. prof. classics NYU, 1996. Author: The Cistophori of Hadrian, 1980, The Silver Coinage of Cappadocia, Vespasian-Commodus, 1995; editor: Studies in Early Byzantine Gold Coinage, 1988, America's Gold Coinage, 1990, Mnemata: Papers in Memory of Nancy M. Waggoner, 1991; mem. adv. com. Lexicon Iconographicum Mythologiae Classicae, 1979—; mem. adv. bd. Am. Jour. Archaeology, 1980; editor book revs. Am. Jour. Numismatics, 1989; contbr. articles on Roman and Byzantine coinage and revs. to profl. jours. NEA fellow for mus. profls., 1978; mem. Inst. for Advanced Study, 1988-89. Mem. Am. Numismatic Soc., Royal Numismatic Soc., Am. Philol. Assn. (subcom. on classical bibliography 1979-89), Archaeol. Inst. Am. (exec. com. N.Y. 1976-80), Columbia U. Seminar on Classical Civilization, Internat. Numismatic Commn. Office: Am Numismatic Soc Broadway & 155th St New York NY 10032-7598

METCALF, WILLIAM HENRY, (JR.), architect; b. Memphis, Feb. 9, 1928; s. William Henry and Mary Myrtle (Tittle) M.; m. Barbara Ann Keller, Oct. 8, 1955; children: Ramsay Katherine, Anne Louis; m. Evelyn Byrd Gates, June 6, 1980. B.A., Yale U., 1949, B.Arch., 1951, M.Arch., 1952. Fellow div. archtl. studies Nuffield Found., London, 1957-58; pvt. practice architecture Washington, 1958-66; partner Metcalf and Assos., Washington, 1966-89; ptnr. Metcalf Tobey & Ptnrs., Reston, Va., 1990-96; prin. Metcalf Assocs., McLean, Va., 1996—; vis. archtl. critic/lectr. Carnegie Inst. Tech., Howard U., Cath. U. Am., George Washington U., Tex. A&M U., Yale U. Prin. works include Health Centers, Lagos, Nigeria, 1964, Anne Arundel Gen. Hosp., Annapolis, Md., 1966, Fairfax Hosp., Falls Church, Va., 1967, Andrew Meml. Hosp., Tuskegee Inst., Ala., 1968, Montgomery Gen. Hosp., Olney, Md., 1969, Concentrated Care Center, Georgetown U., 1976; Am. embassy residence, also Cairo Am. Coll., 1977, St. Joseph's Hosp., Parkersburg, W.Va., 1977, Wilmington (Del.) Med. Center, 1977, Central Bank Bolivia, La Paz, 1978, Prospect Place, Washington, 1979, Intercultural Center, Georgetown U., 1980, Alleghany Valley Hosp., Natrona Heights, Pa., 1980, Smithsonian Instn. Mus. Support Center, Suitland, Md., 1981, Am. Embassy Office Bldg., Cairo, 1981, Phico Group corp. hdqrs., Mechanicsburg, Pa., 1985, Replacement Hosp., U. Va., Charlottesville, 1989, New Sci. Bldg., Va. Mil. Inst., Lexington, 1989. Bd. dirs. Innisfree Found. Served with USAF, 1953-56. Hopper fellow, 1951. Fellow AIA (Rehmann fellow 1957), Colegio de Arquitectos del Peru; mem. Am. Assn. Hosp. Planning, Internat. Hosp. Fedn. Presbyterian. Home and Office: 201 Chain Bridge Rd Mc Lean VA 22101-1908

METCALFE, DARREL SEYMOUR, agronomist, educator; b. Arkansaw, Wis., Aug. 28, 1913; s. Howard Lee and Mabel (De Marce) M.; m. Ellen Lucille Moore, May 16, 1942; children: Dean Darrel, Alan Moore. Tchr. cert., U. Wis. at River Falls, 1931; B.S. in Agronomy, U. Wis., 1941; M.S., Kans. State U., 1942; Ph.D., Iowa State U., 1950. From instr. to prof. agronomy Iowa State U., 1946-56, asst. dir. student affairs, 1956-58; assoc. dean, dir. resident instrn., asst. dir. agrl. expt. sta., agronomist U. Ariz., Tucson, 1958—; dean U. Ariz., 1978-82, dean emeritus, 1982—; Chmn. resident instrn. sect., div. agr. Nat. Assn. State Univs. and Land Grant Colls., 1958-59; mem. com. edn. agr. and natural resources Nat. Acad. Sci., 1966-70, mem. rev. panel for Egypt, 1980-83, mem. Inst. Internat. Edn. Com., Somalia and Kenya, 1980-82; U.S. rep. OECD Conf. Higher Edn. in Agr., Paris, 1963-65; trustee Consortium for Internat. Devel., 1978-82; mem. AID missions to Brazil, 1962, 64, 66, 69, 71, 72, 73, Sultan Qaboos U. Com., Oman, 1982-86. Co-author: Forages, 4th edit., 1985, Crop Production, rev. edits, 1957, 72, 80. Served with AUS, 1942-46, PTO. Named Hon. Alumnus U. Ariz., 1985. Fellow Am. Soc. Agronomy (Agronomic edn. award 1958, Agronomic Svc. award 1980, chmn. student activities sect. 1950-53, edn. div. 1956, editorial bd., tech. editor jour. 1961-65), Nat. Assn. Colls. and Tchrs. Agr. (E.B. Knight award 1967, pres. 1970-71, Disting. Educator award 1980, U. Ariz. Lifetime award), Sigma Xi, Phi Kappa Phi, Phi Eta Sigma, Gamma Sigma Delta, Alpha Tau Alpha, Delta Theta Sigma, Acacia (medallion of merit 1966). Home: 5811 E 9th St Tucson AZ 85711-3221

METCALFE, DEAN DARREL, medical research physician; b. Medford, Oreg., June 27, 1944; s. Darrell S. and Lucille E. (Moore) M.; m. Joan I. Peterson, Dec. 21, 1977; children: Justin, Jonathan, Elisabet. BS, No. Ariz. U., 1966; MS in Microbiology, U. Mich., 1968; MD, U. Tenn., 1972. Medicine residency Univ. Mich. Hosps., Ann Arbor, 1972-74; clin. assoc. NIH, Bethesda, Md., 1974-77; Rheum fellow Harvard Med. Sch. and Hosp., Boston, 1977-79; clin. investigator NIH, Bethesda, 1979-85; head mast cell physiology sect. lab. of clin. investigation Nat. Inst. of Allergy and Infectious Diseases, Bethesda, 1985-93; heal allergic diseases sect., 1994—; co-dir. Allergy-Immunology Tng. Program, NIAID/NIH, Bethesda, 1979—; dir. Am. Bd. Allergy-Immunology, Phila., 1990—; bd. dirs. Am. Acad. Allergy and Immunology. Capt. USPHS, 1979—. Recipient Commendation medal USPHS, 1985, Outstanding Svc. medal, USPHS, 1991. Fellow Am. Acad. Allergy and Immunology, Am. Rheumatism Assn.; mem. Am. Fedn. for Clin. Rsch., Am. Soc. for Clin. Investigators, Assn. Am. Physicians. Office: NIH Rm 11c205 Bethesda MD 20892

METCALFE, ROBERT DAVIS, III, lawyer; b. Bridgeport, Conn., July 2, 1956; s. Robert Davis Jr. and Barbara Ann (Peaslee) M. BA summa cum laude, U. Conn., 1978, JD, 1981; MA, Trinity Coll., 1982. Bar: Conn. 1981, U.S. Supreme Ct. 1986. Judge adv. USN, Norfolk, Va., 1982-85; spl. asst. U.S. atty. U.S. Dept. Justice, Norfolk, 1985; trial atty. U.S. Dept. Justice, Washington, 1985—. Instr. ARC, Hartford, Conn., 1976-80; legis. asst. Conn. Gen. Assembly, Hartford, 1977. Served to lt. USN, 1982-85. Mem. Fed. Bar Assn., Conn. Bar Assn., Judge Adv. Assn., Mensa, Phi Beta Kappa. Republican. Roman Catholic. Avocations: martial arts, reading, sailing, trap and skeet shooting, philately.

METCALFE, TOM BROOKS, chemical engineering educator; b. Smithville, Tex., Feb. 26, 1920; s. Joseph Franklin and Ethel Louise (Taylor) M.; m. Gwendolyn Imogene Soward, July 3, 1944; children: Gwendolyn Jean Metcalfe Ellis, Linda Gail Metcalfe Gallup, Marilyn Louise, Carolyn Marguerite Metcalfe Montiel. BS, U. Tex., 1941, MS, 1947; PhD, Ga. Inst. Tech., 1953. Registered profl. engr., Tex. Chemist Dow Chem. Co., Freeport, Tex., 1941-43; rsch. scientist U. Tex., 1947-50; rsch. engr. Ga. Inst. Tech., 1951-52, Shell Oil Co., Houston, 1952-62; asst. prof. U. Houston, 1953-56, rsch. prof., 1975; head dept. chem. engring. W.Va. Inst. Tech., 1962-63; prof., head dept. chem. engring. U. Southwestern La., 1963-82, Found. prof., 1982-85, adj. prof., 1985—; vis. prof. U. Tex., Austin, 1982; founder, pub. Pinehill Pub. Co.; cons. U.S. Bur. Public Rds.; U.S. Dept. Interior Office of Saline Water. Author: Radiation Spectra of Radionuclides, 1970, Chemical Engineering as a Career, 1966, Safe Handling of Radioactive Materials, 1964; Contbr. articles to profl. jours. Pres. Edgewood Civic Corp., 1954, 57, 59; mem. Houston Mayor's Com. on Zoning, 1958-60; chmn. bd. dirs. U. Southwestern La. Wesley Found., 1966-67; mem. ofcl. bd. area Meth. ch. Lt. USNR, 1943-46, PTO. Fellow AIChE (nat. chmn. acad. dept. heads 1967-69, 80); mem. Am. Soc. Engring. Edn., Masons, Sigma Xi, Phi Eta Sigma, Omega Chi Epsilon, Phi Lambda Upsilon, Tau Beta Pi. Home: 5907 Overlook Dr Austin TX 78731-4221 *Seek good and not evil; bless them who curse you; with God, all things are possible.*

METCALFE, WALTER LEE, JR., lawyer; b. St. Louis, Dec. 19, 1938; s. Walter Lee and Carol (Crowe) M.; Cynthia Williamson, Aug. 26, 1965; children—Carol, Edward. A.B., Washington U., St. Louis, 1960; J.D., U. Va., 1964. Bar: Mo. 1964. Ptnr. Armstrong, Teasdale, Kramer & Vaughan, St. Louis, 1964-81; sr. ptnr. Bryan Cave, St. Louis, 1982—, now chmn. Bd. dirs. Grand Ctr., Inc. chmn.,1994—; bd. dirs. New England Patriots Football Club; sec., bd. dirs. Masters & Johnson Inst., St. Louis Regional Health Care Corp. Mem. ABA, Mo. Bar Assn., St. Louis Bar Assn. Episcopalian. Club: Bogey, Noonday. Home: 26 Upper Ladue Rd Saint Louis MO 63124-1675 Office: Bryan Cave 1 Metropolitan Sq Saint Louis MO 63102-2750*

METEVIER, JAMES F., finance company executive; b. 1941. BSA, DePaul U., 1970. Asst. mgr., treas. ops. Standard Oil Co., 1962-66; asst. to treas. Pullman, Inc., 1966-68; fin. sales rep. Ford Motor Credit Co., 1968-70; pres. AFC Securities Inc., 1970-72; sr. v.p. corp. fin. Assocs. Corp. N.Am., 1972-81, exec. v.p., 1981-85, sr. v.p., 1985—. Office: Assocs Corp N Am PO Box 660237 250 E Carpenter Frwy Irving TX 75062*

METHANY, PAT, jazz musician. Recipient Best Contemporary Jazz Performance Grammy award, 1996. Office: Ted Kurland & Assocs 173 Brighton Ave Boston MA 02134*

METHENY, PATRICK BRUCE, musician; b. Lee's Summit, Mo., Aug. 12, 1954. Student, U. Miami, Fla. Instr. dept. music U. Miami; mem. faculty Nat. Stage Band Camps, Fla., Berklee Coll. Music, Boston. Guitarist with Gary Burton Quintet, 3 yrs, mus. dir. and guitarist, Pat Metheny Group, 1978—; performing tours in U.S., Europe, Can., Japan, USSR, S.Am.; rec. artist ECM Records, currently Geffen Records; composer for guitar and band: records include Bright Size Life, 1976, Watercolors, 1977, Pat Metheny Group, 1978, New Chautauqua, 1979, American Garage, 1980, 80/81, 1980, As Falls Wichita, So Falls Wichita Falls, 1981, Offramp, 1982, Travels, 1983, Rejoicing, 1983, Works, 1984, First Circle, 1984, Still Life (Talking), 1987, Works II, 1988, Letter From Home, 1989, (with Roy Haynes and Dave Holland, Grammy award Best Jazz Composition 1990) Question and Answer, 1990, Secret Story, 1992, The Road to You, 1993 (Jazz Instrumental Grammy award, 1994); (with Ornette Coleman) Song X, 1986 (Best Jazz Album award Downbeat mag. Readers' Poll, 1986, Downbeat Readers Poll Jazz Album of Yr., Guitarist of Yr., 1989, USA Today, 1986, Best Jazz Colloboration Album award Cashbox mag., 1986, John Pareles Top Albums of 1986 award N.Y. Times); composer film scores: (with David Bowie) The Falcon and the Snowman, 1984, Twice in a Lifetime, 1985. Nominated for Grammy award, 1980, 81; recipient 7 Grammy awards; Outstanding Jazz Album award Boston Music Awards, 1986; named Best Jazz Musician Jazziz Readers' Poll, Best Jazz Guitarist Downbeat mag., 1986, Guitar Player mag., 1986, Guitar Player mag. Gallery of Greats, 1982-86, Outstanding Guitarist Boston Music Awards, 1986, Outstanding Jazz Fusion Group Boston Music Awards, 1986. Office: care Ted Kurland Assocs Inc 173 Brighton Ave Allston MA 02134-2003

METHODIOS OF BOSTON See TOURNAS, METHODIOS

METIVIER, ROBERT EMMETT, mayor; b. Panama Canal Zone, Nov. 5, 1934; came to the U.S., 1956; s. William Henry and Loretta Jane (Rooney) M.; m. Carol Ann O'Brien, Aug. 16, 1958; 1 child, Michael E. (dec.). AA, Canal Zone Jr. Coll., 1954; student, U. Md., 1957-58; BS in Bus. Adminstrn., Bryant Coll., 1960. Bd. dirs. Pawtucket (R.I.) Credit Union, 1976-91, treas., mgr., 1977-87, pres., CEO, 1987-91; cons. R.I. Credit Union League, Providence, 1991; mayor City of Pawtucket, R.I., 1992—; past pres. credit Exec. Assn. SNE; bd. mem. Meml. Hosp. Pawtucket, Pawtucket Local Devel. Corp.; rep. of 911 Uniform Emergency Telephone Sys. Adv. Comm. With U.S. Army, 1954-56. Recipient Len Tune awards Nat. Credit Union Mgmt. Assn. Mem. NRI C. of C., To Kalon Club, Panama Canal Soc. Fla., R.I. League of Cities and Towns (pres.). Democrat. Roman Catholic. Home: 59 Woodside Ave Pawtucket RI 02861 Office: City of Pawtucket 137 Roosevelt Ave Pawtucket RI 02860

METREY, GEORGE DAVID, social work educator, academic administrator; b. Milw., July 23, 1939; s. Richard Joseph and Catherine (Evans) M.; m. Cheryl Ann Mosca, June 21, 1969; 1 child, Mary Beth. A.B., Marquette U., 1961; M.S.W., Fordham U., 1963; Ph.D., NYU, 1970. Lic. ind. clin. social worker, R.I., N.J. Social worker N.J. Diagnostic Ctr., Edison, 1963-64, asst. social work supr., 1964-66, dir. psychiat. social work, 1966-70; coordinator undergrad. social work program Kean Coll., N.J., 1970-73, assoc. prof. social work, 1970-74, prof., 1974-79, chmn. dept. sociology, anthropology and social work, 1973-77, dir. social work program, acting assoc. dean Sch. Arts and Sci., 1977-79; dean Sch. Social Work, prof. R.I. Coll., Providence, 1979—; field instr. Fordham U. Sch. Social Service, 1966-70, adj. prof., 1969-77; adj. assoc. prof. Rutgers U. Grad. Sch. Social Work, 1972-73. Mem. program com. R.I. affiliate Am. Heart Assn., 1980—, bd. dirs., 1983-89, chmn. program com., 1985-87, exec. com., 1985-87; sec. bd. dirs. Ocean State Adoption Resource Exch., 1987-89, pres. bd. dirs., 1989-92. Recipient

Fordham U. Grad. Sch. Social Svc. Outstanding Alumni, 1984, Spl. award disting. award R.I. Coll. Alumni Assn., 1996. Mem. NASW (N.J. Social Worker of Yr. 1977, pres. 1978-80, parliamentarian R.I. 1981—, treas. R.I. chpt. 1986-87, mem. nat. competence cert. commn. 1989-91, nat. 2d v.p. 1978-80, chair nat. program com. 1981-83), Coun. on Social Work Edn. (bd. dirs. 1979-82, mem. commn. on accreditation 1996—), Acad. Cert. Social Workers, Nat. Assn. Deans and Dirs. Schs. Social Work (nominating com. 1993—, program com. 1993—), Alpha Phi Omega, Gamma Pi Mu, Alpha Delta Mu (regional v.p.). Roman Catholic. Home: 540 Waverly Rd Wyckoff NJ 07481-1229 Office: RI Coll Sch Social Work Providence RI 02908

METROPOLIS, NICHOLAS CONSTANTINE, mathematical physicist; b. Chgo., June 11, 1915; s. Constantine Nicholas and Katharine (Ganas) M.; m. Patricia Hendrix, Oct. 15, 1955 (div. 1977); children: Katharine, Penelope, Christopher. BS, U. Chgo., 1936, PhD, 1941. Staff mem. Manhattan Project U. Chgo., 1942, asst. prof., 1946-48, prof., 1957-64; group leader Los Alamos Sci. Lab, Los Alamos, N.Mex., 1943-46, 1948-57, sr. fellow, 1965-85, emeritus, 1985—; cons. nat. labs. U. Ill. at Champaign-Urbana, 1970—; mem. com. for rsch. NSF, Washington, 1974-76; mem. tech. mission UN, Calcutta, India, 1961; mem. US-USSR Exch. State Dept., USSR, 1976; mem. 70th anniversary celebration Internat. Conf. on Quantum, Monte Carlo; J.R. Oppenheimer Meml. Lectr., Los Alamos, 1992; speaker 50th anniversary celebration Los Alamos Nat. Lab., 1993. Editor: J.R. Oppenheimer, 1984, The Los Alamos 40th Anniversary Vol.: New Directions in Physics; editor-author: History of Computing, 1980, Essays in Applied Math., 1976; editor, contbr. MIT publ. Daedalus, 1993; mem. editl. bds. profl. jours., 1970—; contbr. articles to profl. jours. Mem. J.R. Oppenheimer Meml. Com., Los Alamos, 1965—; trustee Santa Fe Inst., 1985-88, bd. advisors, 1988—; sec., bd. dirs. Global Pursuits, Inc., 1986—. U. Chgo. fellow, 1938-41; recipient Computer Pioneer medal IEEE, 1984. Fellow Am. Phys. Soc.; mem. AAAS, Am. Math. Soc., Soc. Indsl. and Applied Math., Am. Acad. Arts and Scis. (contbr. to Daedalus 1992). Home: 71 Loma Vista St Los Alamos NM 87544-3090 Office: Los Alamos Nat Lab Mail Stop B210 Los Alamos NM 87545

METSCH, JONATHAN MARTIN, health facility executive; b. Paterson, N.J., Mar. 28, 1945. BS in Polit. Sci., Queens Coll. CUNY, 1966; MPA, SUNY, Albany, 1967; DRPH, U. N.C., 1972. With med. svc. corps Wilford Hall USAF Med. Ctr., Lackland AFB, Tex., 1967-70; asst. prof. grad. program health care adminstrn. CUNY, N.Y.C., 1972-75; adminstr. Mt. Sinai Svcs., City Hosp. Ctr., Elmhurst, N.Y., 1975-79; sr. v.p. for adminstrn. Mt. Sinai Med. Ctr., N.Y.C., 1979-89; pres., CEO Jersey City Med. Ctr., Liberty HealthCare Sys., 1989—; CEO Greenville Hosp.; chmn. bd. trustees, CEO Liberty Health Plan, Inc.; CEO Meadowlands Hosp. Med. Ctr.; pres. bd. dirs. LHS Receivable Corp.; founder, vice chmn. bd. trustees Hudson Cradle, Inc.; adj. prof., preceptor Baruch Coll., N.Y.C., 1987—; adj. assoc. prof. health care mgmt. Mt. Sinai Sch. Medicine, N.Y.C., 1989—; adj. prof. Ctr. Pub. Svc. Seton Hall U., N.J., 1990—; clin. instr., preceptor NYU, 1992—. Office: Jersey City Med Ctr Exec Office 50 Baldwin Ave Jersey City NJ 07304-3154

METTINGER, KARL LENNART, neurologist; b. Helsingborg, Sweden, Nov. 1, 1943; came to the U.S., 1989; s. Nils Allan and Anna Katarina (Hallberg) M.; m. Chesne Maree Ryman, Jan. 27, 1979. MD, U. Lund, 1973; PhD, Karolinska Inst., 1982. Intern Stockholm Hosps., 1973-74; resident Karolinska Hosp., Stockholm, 1974-77, clin. neurologist, 1977-85; med. dir. Kabi Hematology, Stockholm, 1985-87; dep. gen. mgr. Kabi Cardiovascular, Stockholm, 1987-89; med. dir. Ivax/Baker Norton Pharms., Miami, Fla., 1989-93, sr. clin. rsch. dir., 1993—; assoc. prof. Karolinska Inst., Stockholm, 1983-91; cons. neurologist Odenplan Med. Ctr., Stockholm, 1984-89. Author: Cerebral Thromboembolism, 1982, Refaat-Myths and Billions in Biotech, 1987; editor: Coronary Thrombolysis: Current Answers to Critical Questions, 1988, Controversies in Coronary Thrombolysis, 1989. Lt. Swedish Army, 1979. Recipient Silver award Spanish Health Ministry, 1989, Classical Langs. award King Gustav V Found., 1963. Mem. Swedish Stroke Soc. (bd. dirs. 1979-89, pres. 1984-86), Swedish Med. Soc., Swedish Christian Med. Soc. (bd. dirs. 1972-88, pres. 1983-88), Am. Heart Assn., N.Y. Acad. Scis., Nat. Found. for Advancement of Arts, Internat. Assn. Christian Physicians (exec. com. 1975-86). Home: 5401 Collins Ave Apt 1022 Miami FL 33140-2535 Office: IVAX 4400 Biscayne Blvd Miami FL 33137

METTLER, GERALD PHILLIP, reliability engineer; b. Ft. Wayne, Ind., Oct. 24, 1936; s. Joseph Lucian and Dorothy Louise (Bixler) M.; m. Patricia Parent Mettler, May 23, 1959; children: James Anthony, Kenneth Joseph, Lisa Catherine, Charles Matthew. BS in Physics, Ill. Benedictine Coll. (now Benedictine U.), 1958; MS in Mgmt. Engring., George Washington U., 1972. Engr. Sperry Gyroscope Co., Great Neck, N.Y., 1958-66; reliability engr. ARINC Rsch. Corp. subs. Aero. Radio INC, Annapolis, Md., 1966-77; founder, pres. Reltem Rsch., Paw Paw, Mich., 1977-80; prin. reliability engr. Gould Ocean Systems, Cleve., 1980-83; staff reliability engr. Goodyear Aerospace divsn. Lockheed Martin, Akron, Ohio, 1983—; presenter in field. Contbr. articles to symposiums. Cath. youth orgn. advisor St. Pius X Ch., Ft. Worth, 1960-62; tchr. Sunday sch. Sacred Heart Ch., Warner Robins, Ga., 1962-65; instnl. rep. Boy Scouts Am., Bowie, Md., 1972-77. Mem. IEEE, Am. Soc. Qualtiy Control, Motivators Square Dance Club (pres. 1992—). Roman Catholic. Achievements include research in predictive technology. Office: Lockheed Martin 1210 Massillon Rd Akron OH 44315-0001

METYKO, MICHAEL JOSEPH, owner, manager development company; b. Port Arthur, Tex., Feb. 27, 1945; s. Frank Joseph and Rita Claire (Suavé) M.; m. Barbara Ann Neises, Dec. 29, 1967; 1 child, Christopher M. R. Student, Saint Thomas U., Houston, 1963-64, Pratt Inst., 1964-65, U. Houston, 1965-67; MFA, San Francisco Art Inst., 1972. Asst. to dir., assoc. curator Blaffer Gallery, Univ. Houston, 1973-78; dir. Craft and Folk Arts Adv. Com., Houston, 1978-80; owner W. Metyko & Co., Houston, 1967—; trustee, adminstr. Metyko Testamentary Trusts & Other Family Trusts, Houston, 1986—; mng. ptnr. Metyko Interests Partnership, Houston, 1991—; pres. Metyko Devel. Corp., Houston, 1992—; pres. of gen. ptnr. RSM Broad Oaks, Ltd., Houston, 1992—; owner Metyko Event Prodns., Inc., Houston, 1994—. Editor: (book, touring exhibition) Texas Crafts, 1978; editor (exhibitions and catalogs) Texas Sampler, 1979-81, Texas Treasures-- U.S. Olympic Festival, 1980; curator, artist numerous fine arts exhibits. Past co-chmn. Houston-Chiba Japan Sister City Com., Houston, 1985—; origami sensei Japan Am. Soc., Houston, 1985—. Mem. Tex. Forestery Assn. (Communicator of Yr. Lufkin 1992), Gulf Coast Agribus. Coun., Harris County Forest Landowners Assn. (pres., v.p., dir. comms.). Avocation: origami. Office: Metyko Family Interests PO Box 541068 Houston TX 77254-1068

METZ, CHARLES EDGAR, radiology educator; b. Bayshore, N.Y., Sept. 11, 1942; s. Clinton Edgar and Grace Muriel (Schienke) M.; m. Maryanne Theresa Bahr, July, 1967 (div. 1988); children: Rebecca, Molly. BA, Bowdoin Coll., 1964; MS, U. Pa., 1966, PhD, 1969. Instr. radiology U. Chgo., 1969-71, asst. prof., 1971-75, assoc. prof., 1976-80, dir. grad. programs in med. physics, 1979-85, prof., 1980—, prof. structural biology, 1984-86; mem. diagnostic rsch. adv. group Nat. Cancer Inst., 1980-81; mem. sci. com. Nat. Coun. on Radiation Protection and Measurements, 1982-95, Internat. Commn. on Radiation Units and Measurements, 1988—, chmn. sci. com., 1992—; cons. and lectr. in field. Assoc. editor Radiology jour., 1986-91, Med. Physics jour., 1992-95; mem. editl. bd. Med. Decision Making, 1980-84; contbr. over 150 articles to sci. jours. and chpts. to books. Mem. Radiol. Soc. N.Am., Am. Assn. Physicists in Medicine, Soc. Med. Decision Making, Assn. Univ. Radiologists, Phi Beta Kappa, Sigma Xi. Office: U Chgo Dept Radiology MC2026 5841 S Maryland Ave Chicago IL 60637-1463

METZ, CRAIG HUSEMAN, legislative administrator; b. Columbia, S.C., Aug. 26, 1955; s. Leonard Huseman and Annette (Worthington) M.; m. Karen Angela McCleary, Aug. 11, 1984; 1 child, Preston Worthington. BA, U. Tenn., 1977; JD, U. Memphis, 1986; cert., U.S. Ho. of Reps. Rep. Leadership Parlimentary Law Sch., 1987. Bar: S.C., D.C., U.S. Ct. Claims, U.S. Supreme Ct., U.S. Ct. Appeals (4th cir.). Canvass coord., liaison Campaign to Re-elect Congressman Floyd Spence, 1978; del., chmn. Shelby County Del. to 1983 Tenn. Young Rep. Fedn. Conv.; vice chmn. Shelby County Young Reps., 1983-84, chmn., 1984-85; Shelby County adminstr., asst. to Tenn. state exec. dir. Reagan-Bush Campaign, 1984; field rep. Campaign to Re-elect Congressman Floyd Spence, 1986; spl. asst. to Congressman Floyd Spence, 1986-88; counsel com. on labor and human resources U.S. Senate, 1988-90; commr.'s counsel U.S. Occupational Safety and Health Rev. Commn., Washington, 1990-91; dep. asst. sec. for congl. liaison U.S. Dept. Edn., Washington, 1991-93; asst. dir. Divsn. Congl. Affairs AMA, Washington, 1993; chief of staff Congressman Floyd Spence, Washington, 1993—. Judge nat. writing competition U.S. Constn. Bicentennial, S.C. 1987-88; mem. Ch. of the Ascension and Saint Agnes, Washington. Recipient award of merit Rep. Party of Shelby County, 1985, Outstanding Leadership award Shelby County Young Reps., 1985. Mem. ABA, Rep. Nat. Lawyers Assn. (state chmn. S.C. chpt. 1987-90), Federalist Soc., Freedoms Found. Valley Forge, Va. Hist. Soc., Assn. for Preservation Va. Antiquities, Va. Geneal. Soc., U. South Caroliniana Soc., Nat. Trust for Hist. Preservation (assoc. Capital region), SAR, St. David's Soc., St. Andrew's Soc. Washington, Mil. Soc. War of 1812, Vet. Corps Arty. State of N.Y., Gen. Soc. War of 1812, Mil. Order Loyal Legion of U.S., Order of St. John (hospitalier), Confederate Meml. Assn., SCV, Mil. Order Stars and Bars, Nat. Cathedral Assn., U. Tenn. Nat. Alumni Assn., Sigma Alpha Epsilon, Phi Alpha Delta (v.p. McKellar chpt., Outstanding Svc. award 1983). Republican. Episcopalian. Home: 8505 Westown Way Vienna VA 22182-2513 Office: 2405 Rayburn Bldg Washington DC 20515-4002

METZ, EMMANUEL MICHAEL, investment company executive, lawyer; b. Pitts., Sept. 19, 1928; s. Solomon and Gertrude (Krieger) M.; m. Janine Spaner, Apr. 3, 1964. BA, Dartmouth Coll., 1949; LLB, Harvard U., 1952; LLM, NYU, 1958. Bar: N.Y. 1952. Atty. ABC, N.Y.C., 1956-58; security analyst Standard & Poor's, N.Y.C., 1958-68; mng. dir. Oppenheimer & Co., Inc., N.Y.C., 1968—. Author: Street Fighting at Wall and Broad, 1982. Lt. USN, 1952-56. Home: 150 E 56th St New York NY 10022-3631 Office: Oppenheimer & Co Inc 200 Liberty St New York NY 10281-1003

METZ, FRANK ANDREW, JR., data processing executive; b. Winthrop, Mass., Jan. 28, 1934; s. Frank Andrew and Frances E. (Fallon) M.; married; children: Christopher, Lelia, Amy, Patrick, Joshua, Rebecca; m. Judith Ann Mapes, July 21, 1979. A.B., Bowdoin Coll., 1955. With IBM, 1955—; dir. fin. planning data processing group IBM, Harrison, N.Y., 1969-72; div. v.p. office products IBM, Franklin Lakes, N.J., 1972-75; asst. controller IBM, Armonk, N.Y., 1975-78, controller, 1978-80; v.p., asst. group exec. IBM, White Plains, N.Y., 1980-84, sr. v.p., group exec., 1984-86, sr. v.p., chief fin. officer, bd. dirs., 1986-93, ret., 1993; bd. dirs. Allegheny Power Systems, Monsanto Co., Norrell Corp. Trustee St. Luke's Roosevelt Hosp., N.Y.C., 1979—, chmn. 1994—; trustee Am. Mus. Natural History, 1986—. Served to 1st lt. Transp. Corps U.S. Army, 1956. Roman Catholic.

METZ, LAWRENCE ANTHONY, lawyer; b. Chgo., July 26, 1941; s. Florian Lawrence and Angeline M.; m. Lorraine Kutz, Aug. 14, 1965; children: Robert, Kathleen, Sandra, Diane, Jeanne. B.S.C., DePaul U., 1963, J.D., 1967. Bar: Ill. 1967. Atty. City Products Corp., Des Plaines, Ill., 1967-70; atty. Jewel Cos., Inc., Chgo., 1970-75, asst. sec., 1975-79, asst. gen. counsel, 1979-84; gen. counsel Osco Drug, Inc., Oak Brook, Ill., 1984-89, Jewel Food Stores, Melrose Pk., Ill., 1989-90, Jewel Cos., Inc., Chgo., 1990-93; sr. v.p., asst. gen. counsel Am. Stores Co., Chgo., 1993-94; sr. v.p., dep. gen. counsel Am. Stores Co., Salt Lake City, 1994—. Bd. dirs. United Way of Suburban Chgo., 1977-79. Served with U.S. Army, 1963. Roman Catholic. Office: 420 E South Temple Salt Lake City UT 84111-1319

METZ, MARILYN JOYCE, bank executive; b. Denver, Colo., Nov. 10, 1949; d. James C. and Lois M. (Roach) M.; m. Jack W. Calabrese, Apr. 15, 1977 (div. 1981); m. Frank C. Margowski, Oct. 13, 1986 (div.). Student, Colo. State U., 1968-72; diploma, Colo. Grad. Sch. Banking, 1983. With First Interstate Bank Denver, 1972-83; v.p., mgr. United Banks Colo., Denver, 1983-88; v.p., area mgr. First Interstate Bank Oreg., Portland, 1988-89; v.p., dist. mgr. 5 brs. 1st Interstate Bank Wash., Seattle, 1989-91; v.p., dist. mgr. 11 brs. 1st Interstate Bank, Bellevue, Wash., 1991—. Bd. dirs., Met. Child Dental Care Assn., 1985-87. Mem. Nat. Assn. Bank Women (state pres. Colo. 1986-87), Cherry Creek Commerce Assn., Seattle C. of C., Pres. Club Seattle. Republican. Avocations: travel, reading, skiing. Office: First Interstate Bank Bellevue Fin Ctr 225 108th Ave NE Bellevue WA 98004-5705

METZ, MARY HAYWOOD, sociologist; b. Zurich, Switzerland, Oct. 2, 1939; came to U.S., 1939; d. Richard Mansfield and Margaret Rider (Mowbray) Haywood; m. Donald Lehman Metz, July 31, 1965; children: David Haywood, Michael Lehman. AB, Radcliffe Coll., 1960; MA, U. Calif., Berkeley, 1966, PhD, 1971; postgrad., U. Freiburg, 1960-61. Author: Classrooms and Corridors, 1978, Different by Design, 1986. German Acad. Exch. Commn. fellow, Bonn, Germany, 1960-61, Woodrow Wilson fellow, Princeton, N.J., 1961-62, Kent fellow Danforth Found., St. Louis, 1965-69. Mem. Am. Edn. Rsch. Assn. (mem. coun. and exec. bd. 1991-94), Am. Sociol. Assn. (chair soc. edn. sect. 1985-86), Soc. Values Higher Edn. (bd. dirs. 1972-74). Mem. United Ch. of Christ. Home: 2952 N Stowell Ave Milwaukee WI 53211 Office: U Wis 1000 Bascom Mall 221 Edn Bldg Madison WI 53706

METZ, MARY SEAWELL, university dean, retired college president; b. Rockhill, S.C., May 7, 1937; d. Columbus Jackson and Mary (Dunlap) Seawell; m. F. Eugene Metz, Dec. 21, 1957; 1 dau., Mary Eugena. BA summa cum laude in French and English, Furman U., 1958; postgrad., Institut Phonetique, Paris, 1962-63, Sorbonne, Paris, 1962-63; PhD magna cum laude in French, La. State U., 1966; HHD (hon.), Furman U., 1984; LLD (hon.), Chapman Coll., 1985; DLT (hon.), Converse Coll., 1988. Instr. French La. State U., 1965-66, asst. prof., 1966-67, 1968-72, assoc. prof., 1972-76, dir. elem. and intermediate French programs, 1966-74, spl. asst. to chancellor, 1974-75, asst. to chancellor, 1975-76; prof. French Hood Coll., Frederick, Md., 1976-81, provost, dean acad. affairs, 1976-81; pres. Mills Coll., Oakland, Calif., 1981-90; dean of extension U. Calif., Berkeley, 1991—; vis. asst. prof. U. Calif.-Berkeley, 1967-68; mem. commn. on leadership devel. Am. Coun. on Edn., 1981-90, adv. coun. Stanford Rsch. Inst., 1985-90, adv. coun. Grad. Sch. Bus., Stanford U.; assoc. Gannett Ctr. for Media Studies, 1985—; bd. dirs. PG&E, Pacific Telesis, PacTel & PacBell, Union Bank, Longs Drug Stores, S.H. Cowell Found. Author: Reflets du monde francais, 1971, 78, Cahier d'exercices: Reflets du monde francais, 1972, 78, (with Helstrom) Le Francais a decouvrir, 1972, 78, Le Francais a vivre, 1972, 78, Cahier d'exercices: Le Francais a vivre, 1972, 78; standardized tests; mem. editorial bd.: Liberal Edn., 1982—. Trustee Am. Conservatory Theater. NDEA fellow, 1960-62, 1963-64; Fulbright fellow, 1962-63; Am. Council Edn. fellow, 1974-75. Mem. Western Coll. Assn. (v.p. 1982-84, pres. 1984-86), Assn. Ind. Calif. Colls. and Univs. (exec. com. 1982-90), Nat. Assn. Ind. Colls. and Univs. (govt. rels. adv. coun. 1982-85), So. Conf. Lang. Teaching (chmn. 1976-77), World Affairs Coun. No. Calif. (bd. dirs. 1984-93), Bus.-Higher Edn. Forum, Women's Forum West, Women's Coll. Coalition (exec. com. 1984-88), Phi Kappa Phi, Phi Beta Kappa. Address: PO Box 686 Stinson Beach CA 94970-0686

METZ, PHILIP JOHN, mathematics educator; b. Paterson, N.J., Aug. 22, 1939; s. Peter William and Clara (Ferraro) M.; m. Dorothy C. Miller, Aug. 1, 1970; children: Christine, Philip Jr. BA, St. Francis U., Bklyn., 1970; MEd, William Paterson U., 1980. Cert. elem. social studies, math. tchr., N.J. 6th grade tchr. Notre Dame Sch., New Hyde Park, N.Y., 1960-62; 7th and 8th grade tchr. St. Brigid's Sch., Bklyn., 1963-69; 6th and 7th grade tchr. St. Brendan's Sch., Clifton, N.J., 1970-72; 8th grade tchr. Holy Name Sch., Garfield, N.J., 1972-74; spl. edn. math. tchr. Passaic County Vocat. Tech. High Sch., Wayne, N.J., 1974-76; adj. instr. Passaic County C.C., Paterson, N.J., 1976-78, assoc. prof. math., 1978—; textbook reviewer Harper Collins Pub., Chgo., 1991-92, Scott Foresman, N.Y.C., 1989-90; cons. math. grants; active weekend programs for gifted and talented, Passaic County Community Coll., Paterson, 1988-90; presenter workshops in field. Reciepient plaque for Outstanding Svc. Passaic County Community Coll. Faculty Assn. Mem. Math. Assn. Am., N.J. Edn. Assn. (local treas. 1978—), Math. Assn Two Yr. Colls. N.J., William Paterson Alumni Assn., St. Francis Alumni Assn. Democrat. Roman Catholic. Avocations: fishing, coins, sports. Home: 536 Mcbride Ave West Paterson NJ 07424-2850

METZ, ROBERT ROY, publisher, editor; b. Richmond Hill, N.Y., Mar. 23, 1929; s. Robert Roy, Sr. and Mary (Kissel) M.; m. Susan Lee Blair, 1984; children: Robert Sumner, Christopher Roy. B.A., Wesleyan U., Middletown Conn., 1950. Copyboy N.Y. Times, 1951, asst. fgn. news desk, 1952; rewriteman cable desk I.N.S., 1953, overnight cable editor, 1954-56, asst. feature editor, 1956-58; asst. news editor Newspaper Enterprise Assn., 1958, news editor, 1959-63, mng. editor, 1963-66, exec. editor, 1966-68, v.p., 1967-71, editorial dir., 1968-71, pres., editor, dir., 1972-94; dir. Berkeley-Small Inc., 1974-77; chmn. Berkley-Small Inc., 1976-77; v.p., dir. United Feature Syndicate, 1976-77, pres., editor, 1978; pres., editor, dir. United Media, 1978-93, chmn., 1993-94; media cons., 1994—. Lutheran. Club: Union League (N.Y.C.). Home: 170 E 77th St New York NY 10021-1912

METZ, STEVEN WILLIAM, small business owner; b. Inglewood, Calif., Nov. 30, 1946; s. Glenn Ludwig and Kathleen Martha (Peterson) M.; m. Michelle Marie McArthur, Aug. 11, 1989; 1 child, Glenn Christian. Student, Fullerton Coll., Calif. Supt. Oahu Interiors, Honolulu, 1969-71, Hackel Bros., Miami, Fla., 1971-73; exec. v.p. Tru-Cut Inc., Brea, Calif., 1974-82; gen. mgr. The Louvre', Grass Valley, Calif., 1983-85; mfg. engring. mgr. Rexnord Aerospace, Torrance, Calif., 1986-87; pres., founder Metz/Calcoa Inc., Torrance, Calif., 1987—; mfg. rep. consul Orange County Spring, Anaheim, 1987—, Alard Machine Products, Gardena, Calif., 1988—, TALSCO, 1994—, Precision Resources, 1994—, GEMTECH, 1994—. Charter mem. Rep. Presdl. Task Force, 1991—; mem. L.A. Coun. on World Affairs, 1991-92. With U.S. Army, 1966-68. Recipient Appreciation awards DAV, 1968, Soc. Carbide & Tool Engrs., 1981, Soc. Mfg. Engrs., 1991. Fellow Soc. Carbide Engrs.; mem. Soc. Carbide & Tool Engrs. (chpt. pres. 1980-82), Rep. Presdl. Legion of Merit. Avocations: golf, swimming, riding, boating, church activities.

METZ, T(HEODORE) JOHN, librarian, consultant; b. Erie, Pa., Nov. 5, 1932; s. Theodore John and Dorothy Pearl (Schutte) M.; m. Dorothy Page Neff, June 11, 1955; 1 child, Margaret Elizabeth. Mus.B., Heidelberg Coll., 1954; M.A. in Music, Miami U., Oxford, Ohio, 1955; M.L.S., U. Mich., 1959. Librarian II U. Wis., Madison, 1959-61; asst. librarian Lawrence U., Appleton, Wis., 1961-67; dir. libraries U. Wis.-Green Bay, 1967-75; exec. dir. Midwest Region Library Network, Evanston, Ill., 1975-79; coll. librarian, assoc. prof. Carleton Coll., Northfield, Minn., 1979—; speaker, participant, coord. numerous confs. and insts., 1969—; chmn. several state libr. groups, 1971-76; mem. several nat. libr. adv. coms., 1974-80; bldg. cons. Carleton Coll., others, 1978—; mem. Citizen Amb. Rsch. Librs. del. to Ea. Europe, 1992. Author: MIDLNET Symposium Report, 1976. Chmn. Green Bay Symphony, 1971-76; mem. various bds. coms., relating to mus. activities; performer Green Bay and other orchs., 1955—. Library Service scholar U. Mich., 1957; Library Service fellow U. Mich., 1958. Mem. ALA, Assn. Coll. Rsch. Librs., Internat. Fedn. Libr. Assns. Avocations: musical activities; hunting; fishing; gardening. Home: 1200 Elm St Northfield MN 55057-2906 Office: Carleton Coll Libr Northfield MN 55057-4097

METZENBAUM, HOWARD MORTON, former U.S. Senator; b. Cleve., June 4, 1917; s. Charles I. and Anna (Klafter) M.; m. Shirley Turoff, Aug. 8, 1946; children: Barbara Jo, Susan Lynn, Shelley Hope, Amy Beth. B.A., Ohio State U., 1939, LL.D., 1941. Chmn. bd. Airport Parking Co. Am., 1958-66, ITT Consumer Services Corp., 1966-68; chmn. bd. ComCorp, 1969-74; mem. War Labor Panel, 1942-45, Ohio Bur. Code rev., 1949-50, Cleve. Met. Housing Authority, 1968-70, Lake Erie Regional Transit Authority, 1972-73, Ohio Ho. of Reps., 1943-46, Ohio Senate, 1947-50; chmn. anti-trust sub-com., labor sub-com. U.S. Senate; mem. intell com., budget com., environ. and pub. works com., judiciary com., labor and human resources, energy and natural resources, dem. policy com. Trustee Mt. Sinai Hosp., Cleve., 1961-73, treas, 1966-73; bd. dirs. Coun. Human Rels., United Cerebral Palsy Assn., Nat. Coun. Hunger and Malnutrition, Karamu House, St. Vincent Charity Hosp., Cleve., St. Jude Rsch. Hosp., Memphis; nat. co-chmn. Nat. Citizen's Com. Conquest Cancer; vice chmn. fellows Brandeis U.; chmn. Am. Friend Rabin Ctr., Tel Aviv, Israel; mem. Bd. Nat. Peace Garden Found. Mem. ABA, Ohio Bar Assn., Cuyahoga Bar Assn., Cleve. Bar Assn., Am. Assn. Trial Lawyers, Order of Coif, Phi Eta Sigma, Tau Epsilon Rho. Office: Consumer Federation of America 1424 16th St NW Ste 504 Washington DC 20036-2211

METZER, PATRICIA ANN, lawyer; b. Phila., Mar. 10, 1941; d. Freeman Weeks and Evelyn (Heap) M.; m. Karl Hormann, June 30, 1980. BA with distinction, U. Pa., 1963, LLB cum laude, 1966. Bar: Mass. 1966, D.C. 1972, U.S. Tax Ct. 1988. Assoc., then ptnr. Mintz, Levin, Cohn, Glovsky and Popeo, Boston, 1966-75; assoc. tax legis. counsel U.S. Treasury Dept., Washington, 1975-78; shareholder, dir. Goulston & Storrs, P.C., Boston, 1978—; lectr. program continuing legal edn. Boston Coll. Law Sch., Chestnut Hill, Mass., spring 1974; mem. adv. com. NYU Inst. Fed. Taxation, N.Y.C., 1981-87; mem. practitioner liaison com. Mass. Dept. Revenue, 1985-90; spkr. in field. Author: Federal Income Taxation of Individuals, 1984; mem. adv. bd. Review Corp. Tax and Bus. Planning Review, 1996—; mem. editl. bd. Am. Jour. Tax Policy, 1995—; contbr. articles to profl. jours., chpts. to books. Bd. mgrs. Barrington Ct. Condominium, Cambridge, Mass., 1985-86; bd. dirs. University Road Parking Assn., Cambridge, 1988—; trustee Social Law Libr., Boston, 1989-93. Mem. ABA A(tax sect., chmn. subcom. allocations and distbns. partnership com. 1978-82, vice chmn. legis. 1991-93, chmn. 1993-95, com. govt. submissions, vice liaison 1993-94, liaison 1994-95, North Atlantic region, co-liaison 1995-96, N.E. region, regional liaison meetings (com.), Mass. Bar Assn., Boston Bar Assn., (coun. 1987-89, chmn. tax sect. 1989-91), Fed. Bar Assn. (coun. on taxation, chmn. corp. taxation com. 1977-81, chmn. com. partnership taxation 1981-87), Boston Estate Planning Coun. (exec. com. 1975, 79-82), Am. Coll. Tax Counsel. Avocation: vocal performances (as soloist and with choral groups). Office: Goulston & Storrs PC 400 Atlantic Ave Boston MA 02110-3333

METZGER, BARRY, lawyer; b. Newark, June 11, 1945; s. William and Dorothy (Bagoon) M.; m. Jacqueline Sue Ivers, June 26, 1966; children: Darren Thomas, Rebecca Lynne. AB magna cum laude, Princeton U., 1966; JD cum laude, Harvard U., 1969. Bar: D.C. 1970. Asst. to Prin. Ceylon Law Coll., Colombo, 1969-71; dir. Asian programs Internat. Legal Ctr., N.Y.C., 1971-74; ptnr. Coudert Brothers, N.Y.C., 1974-76, resident in Hong Kong, 1976-84, Sydney, 1984-89, London, 1989-95; gen. counsel Asian Devel. Bank, Manila, 1995—; mem. New South Wales Atty. Gen.'s Commn. on Comml. Dispute Resolution, Com. for Econ. Devel. Australia; arbitrator ICC Ct. Arbitration.; v.p. Internat. Legal Aid Assn., 1972-80; pres. Harvard Legal Aid Bur., 1968-69; trustee Princeton-in-Asia. Editorial advisor: Internat. Fin. Law Rev.; editor: Legal Aid and World Poverty, 1974; contbr. articles to profl. jours. Sheldon Meml. fellow, 1969. Mem. ABA, Assn. Bar City N.Y., Internat. Bar Assn. Democrat. Home: 3 Flame Tree Place, South Forbes Park Manila The Philippines Office: Office Gen Counsel Asian Devel Bank, PO Box 789, 0980 Manila The Philippines

METZGER, BOBBIE ANN, public relations executive; b. N.Y.C., June 10, 1948. BA in Journalism, Calif. State U., San Diego, 1970; MA in Internat. Rels., Calif. State U., Sacramento, 1980. Reporter, writer, producer Sta. KFMB-TV, San Diego, 1970-73; sr. cons., press liaison Assembly Retirement Com., Sacramento, 1973-76; press sec. for Gov. Jerry Brown Sacramento, 1976-80; press sec., assembly speaker Willie Brown Jr., Sacramento, 1980-84; pres., ptnr. Stoorza, Ziegaus, Metzger & Hunt, Sacramento, 1984—. Recipient Cappie award Sacramento chpt. Pub. Rels. Soc. Am., 1986, 92, Cappie Silver award, 1990, 92, Cappie Gold award, 1993, Silver Anvil award, 1989, Cipra award Inside PR, 1993. Mem. Internat. Assn. Bus. Communicators (Crystal award 1990, 92, 93, award of merit 1986, 90, award of excellence 1988), Sacramento Press Club, Bldg. Industry Assn. Superior Calif., Calif. Bldg. Assn., Sacramento Met. C. of C., Sacramento Area Commerce and Trade Orgn., Capitol Club. Avocations: travel, tennis. *

METZGER, BRUCE MANNING, clergyman, educator; b. Middletown, Pa., Feb. 9, 1914; s. Maurice Rutt and Anna Mary (Manning) M.; m. Isobel E. Mackay, July 7, 1944; children—John Mackay, James Bruce. A.B., Lebanon Valley Coll., 1935, D.D., 1951; Th.B., Princeton Theol. Sem., 1938, Th.M., 1939; A.M., Princeton U., 1940, Ph.D., 1942; L.H.D., Findlay U., 1962; D.D., St. Andrews U., Scotland, 1964; D.Theol., Münster U., Fed. Republic Germany, 1970; D.Litt., Potchefstroom U., South Africa, 1985. Ordained to ministry Presbyn. Ch., 1939. Teaching fellow N.T. Princeton Theol. Sem., 1938-40, mem. faculty, 1940—, prof. N.T. lang. and lit., 1954-64, George L. Collord prof. N.T. lang. and lit., 1964-84, emeritus, 1984—; vis. lectr. Presbyn. Theol. Sem. South, Campinas, Brazil, 1952, Presbyn. Theol. Sem. North, Recife, Brazil, 1952; mem. Inst. Advanced Study, Princeton, 1964-65, 73-74; scholar-in-residence Tyndale House, Cambridge, 1969; vis. fellow Clare Hall, Cambridge, 1974, Wolfson Coll., Oxford U., 1979, Macquarie U., Sydney, Australia, 1982, Caribbean Grad. Sch. of Theology, Jamaica, 1990, Seminario Internacional Teológico Bautista, Buenos Aires, 1991, Griffith Thomas Lectrs., Dallas Theol. Sem., 1992; mem. mng. com. Am. Sch. Classical Studies, Athens, Greece; mem. Standard Bible com. Nat. Coun. Chs., 1952—, chmn., 1975—; mem. seminar N.T. studies Columbia U., 1959-80; mem. Kuratorium of Vetus-Latina Inst., Beuron, Germany, 1959—; adv. com. Inst. N.T. Text Rsch., U. Münster, 1961—, Thesaurus Linguae Graecae, 1972-80; Collected Works of Erasmus, 1977—; chmn. Am. com. versions Internat. Greek N.T., 1950-88; participant internat. congresses scholars, Aarhus, Aberdeen, Bangor, Basel, Bonn, Brussels, Budapest, Cairo, Cambridge, Dublin, Exeter, Frankfurt, Heidelberg, London, Louvain, Manchester, Milan, Munich, Münster, Newcastle, Nottingham, Oxford, Praque, Rome, St. Andrews, Stockholm, Strasbourg, Toronto, Trondheim, Tübingen; mem. Presbytery, N.B. Author: The Saturday and Sunday Lessons from Luke in the Greek Gospel Lectionary, 1944, Lexical Aids for Students of New Testament Greek, 1946, enlarged edit., 1955, A Guide to the Preparation of a Thesis, 1950, An Introduction to the Apocrypha, 1957, Chapters in the History of New Testament Textual Criticism, 1963, The Text of the New Testament, Its Transmission, Corruption, and Restoration, 1964, 3d enlarged edit., 1992, (with H.G. May) The Oxford Annotated Bible with the Apocrypha, 1965, The New Testament, Its Background, Growth, and Content, 1965, Index to Periodical Literature on Christ and the Gospels, 1966, Historical and Literary Studies, Pagan, Jewish, and Christian, 1968, Index to Periodical Literature on the Apostle Paul, 1970, 2nd edit., A Textual Commentary on the Greek New Testament, 1971, 2d edit., 1994, The Early Versions of the New Testament, 1977, New Testament Studies, 1980, Manuscripts of the Greek Bible, 1981, The Canon of the New Testament, 1987, (with Roland Murphy) The New Oxford Annotated Bible with the Apocrypha, 1991, (with M.D. Coogan) The Oxford Companion to the Bible, 1993, Breaking the Code-Understanding the Book of Revelation, 1993; mem. editorial com.: Critical Greek New Testament, 1956-84; chmn. Am. com., Internat. Greek New Testament Project, 1970-88; sec. com. translators: Apocrypha (rev. standard version); editor: New Testament Tools and Studies, 19 vols, 1960-94, Oxford Annotated Apocrypha, 1965, enlarged edit., 1977; Reader's Digest Condensed Bible, 1982; co-editor: United Bible Societies Greek New Testament, 1966, 4th edit., 1993; compiler: Index of Articles on the New Testament and the Early Church Published in Festschriften, 1951, supplement, 1955, Lists of Words Occurring Frequently in the Coptic New Testament (Sahidic Dialect), 1961, Annotated Bibliography of the Textual Criticism of the New Testament, 1955, (with Isobel M. Metzger) Oxford Concise Concordance to the Holy Bible, 1962 (with R.C. Dentan and W. Harrelson), The Making of the New Revised Standard Version of the Bible, 1991; contbr. articles to jours. Chmn. standard bible com. Nat. Coun. Chs., 1977—. Recipient cert. Disting. Svc. Nat. Coun. Chs., 1957, Disting. Alumnus award Lebanon Valley Coll. Alumni Assn., 1961, citation of appreciation Laymen's Nat. Bible Assn., 1986, Disting. Alumnus award Princeton Theol. Sem., 1989, lit. competition prize Christian Rsch. Found., 1955, 62, 63, E.T. Thompson award, 1991. Mem. Am. Philos. Soc., Soc. Bibl. Lit. (pres. 1970-71, past del. Am. Coun. Learned Socs.), Am. Bible Soc. (bd. mgrs. 1948—, chmn. com. transls. 1964-70), Am. Philol. Assn., Studiorum Novi Testamenti Societas (pres. 1971-72), Cath. Bibl. Assn., N.Am. Patristic Soc. (past pres.), Soc. Textual Scholarship (pres. 1995), Am. Soc. Papyrologists; hon. fellow, corr. mem. Higher Inst. Coptic Studies, Cairo; corr. fellow Brit. Acad. (Burkitt medal in Bibl. studies 1994). Republican. Home: 20 Cleveland Ln Princeton NJ 08540 Office: Princeton Theol Sem Mercer St Princeton NJ 08542

METZGER, ERNEST HUGH, aerospace engineer, scientist; b. Nurnberg, Germany, Oct. 22, 1923; came to U.S., 1939, naturalized, 1943; s. Paul Arthur and Charlotte Babette (Kann) M.; m. Sarah Temple Grinnell, Nov. 19, 1956; children: Lisa Metzger Dunning, Charlotte Bennett, George Grinnell. B.S., CCNY, 1949; M.S., Harvard U., 1950. Automatic control engr. Bell Aerospace Co. div. Textron, Buffalo, 1950-54, tech. dir. inertial nav. systems, 1954-60, chief engr., inertial instruments, 1960-70, chief engr., gravity gradiometer systems, 1970-83, dir. gravity sensor systems, 1983-86, exec. dir. engring., 1986-89, cons., 1989—; mem. panel future navigation systems Nat. Acad. Sci., com. on geodesy NRC, 1988-89, accelerator criteria com. NASA, tech. com. navigation guidance and control, AIAA, 1989—; vis. lectr. dept. aernautics and astronautics Stanford U., 1990. Contbr. articles to profl. jours.; patentee in field. Served with AUS, 1943-46. Recipient Aerospace Pioneer award Niagara Frontier sect. AIAA, 1977; named to Niagara Frontier Aviation Hall of Fame, 1992. Mem. IEEE, Inst. Navigation (Thurlow award for outstanding contbn. to sci. navigation 1983), AAAS, Air Force Assn., N.Y. Acad. Scis., Explorers Club, Sigma Xi, Tau Beta Pi, Eta Kappa Nu. Clubs: Harvard, Buffalo Ski. Home: 90 High Park Blvd Buffalo NY 14226-4209 Office: Bell Aerospace Co PO Box 1 Buffalo NY 14240-0001

METZGER, FRANK, management consultant; b. Mainz, Fed. Republic Germany, Feb. 27, 1929; came to U.S., 1938; s. Paul Alfred and Anna (Daniel) M.; m. Lore Lichter, Dec. 21, 1952; children: Peter D., Mark S. BS in Indsl. Edn., N.Y. State Tchrs.'s Coll., 1951; MS in Psychology, Carnegie Mellon U., 1953, PhD in Indsl. Psychology, 1954. Lic. psychologist, N.Y., Ill. Supr. tech. adminstrn. Gen. Electric., Lynn., Mass., 1956-58; dir. mgmt. devel. Raytheon, Newton, Mass., 1958-59; asst. dir. personnel ITT, N.Y.C., 1959-69; sr. v.p. adminstrn. Nytronics Inc., Pelham, N.Y., 1969-71; sr. v.p. corp. and orgn. devel. CNA Fin. Corp., Chgo., 1971-75; pres. Metzger and Co. Inc., Chgo., 1975-76; sr. v.p. adminstrn. Bairnco Corp., N.Y.C., 1976-88; prin. Metzger & Co., Rye, N.Y., 1988—; bd. dirs. Genlyte Group Inc., Secaucus, N.J. Contbr. articles to profl. jours. Mem. Pres. Com. on Equal Opportunity, Washington, 1962-65. Served with signal corps. U.S. Army, 1954-56. Office: Metzger & Co 16 Norman Dr Rye NY 10580-2250

METZGER, HENRY, federal research institution administrator; b. Mainz, Germany, Mar. 23, 1932; came to U.S., 1938; naturalized, 1945; s. Paul Alfred and Anne (Daniel) M.; m. Deborah Stashower, June 16, 1957; children: Eran D., Renée V., Carl E. MD, Columbia U., 1957. Chief chem. immunology sect. Nat. Inst. Arthritis & Musculoskeletal & Skin Disease/NIH, Bethesda, Md., 1973—; br. chief USPHS, Bethesda, 1983-94, sci. dir., 1987—, med. officer grade VI, 1975—; Carl Prausnitz Meml. lectr., 1982; Ecker Meml. lectr. Case Western Res. U., Cleve., 1984; Harvey Soc. lectr., 1984; Eli Nadel Meml. lectr. St. Louis U., 1987; Rodney Porter Meml. lectr., 1993; Burroughs-Wellcome lectr., 1994; R.E. Dyer lectr.; mem. health rsch. coun. BMFT, German Govt., 1994—. Editor: Fc Receptors & the Action of Antibodies, 1990; assoc. editor Ann. Rev. Immunology, 1982—; contbr. numerous articles to profl. jours.; mem. editorial bd. numerous sci. jours. Recipient Meritorious Svc. award USPHS, 1978, Disting. Svc. award, 1985, Joseph Mather Smith prize Columbia U., 1984. Fellow AAAS, Am. Acad. Allergy and Immunology; mem. NAS, Am. Assn. Immunologists (pres. 1991-92), Am. Soc. Biol. Chemists, Am. Soc. Cell Biology, Am. Rheumatism Assn., Internat. Union Immunol. Soc. (pres. 1992-95), Found. for Advanced Edn. in the Scis. (pres. 1990-92), Alpha Omega Alpha. Home: 3410 Taylor St Bethesda MD 20815-4024 Office: NIH 9000 Rockville Pike Rm 9n228 Bethesda MD 20892-0001

METZGER, H(OWELL) PETER, writer; b. N.Y.C., Feb. 22, 1931; s. Julius Radley and Gertrude (Fuller) M.; m. Frances Windham, June 30, 1956 (div. July 1987); children: John, James, Lisa, Suzanne; m. Valerie A. Farnham, Jan. 12, 1990 (div. Sept. 1995). B.A., Brandeis U., 1953; Ph.D., Columbia U., 1965. Mgr. advanced programs Ball Bros. Research Corp., Boulder, 1968-70; research assoc. Dept. Chemistry, U. Colo., Boulder, 1966-68; sr. research scientist N.Y. State Psychiat. Inst., N.Y.C., 1965-66; syndicated columnist N.Y. Times Syndicate, 1972-74, Science Critic, Newspaper Enterprise Assn., 1974-76; sci. editor Rocky Mt. News, Denver, 1973-77; mgr. public affairs planning Public Service Co. Colo., Denver, 1977-96; cons. Environ. Instrumentation, 1970-72; dir. Colspan Environ. Systems, Inc., Boulder, Colo., 1969-72. Author: The Atomic Establishment, 1972; contbr. articles in field to profl. jours., nat. mags. Pres. Colo. Com. for Environ. Info., Boulder, 1968-72; mem. Colo. Gov.'s State Health Planning Coun., 1969-72, Colo. Gov.'s Adv. Com. on Underground Nuclear Explosions, 1971-74; mem. spl. project on energy policy mgmt. Heritage Found., 1980; mem. 1981 U.S. Presdl. Rank Rev. Bd., U.S. Office Pers. Mgmt., 1981; bd. dirs. Wildlife-2000, 1970-72, Colo. Def. Coun., 1972-75. USPHS fellow, 1959-65; prin. investigator, 1968; archivee Hoover Instn. Stanford U., 1982. Mem. ACLU (state bd. dirs. 1968-71), Am. Alpine Club, Sigma Xi, Phi Lambda Upsilon. Address: 2595 Stanford Ave Boulder CO 80303-5332

METZGER, MARK KAVANAUGH, public relations company executive; b. Bethlehem, Pa., Aug. 13, 1951; s. A. Richard and Lucile (Kavanaugh) M.; m. Wendy J. Strothman, Nov. 25, 1978; children: Andrew R., Margaret A. BA, Brown U., 1973. Reporter The Express, Easton, Pa., 1973-76; newsman AP, Chgo., 1977-78; assoc. editor Crain Comm., Chgo., 1978-80, editor, 1980-83; sr. editor Inc. mag., Boston, 1983-85; account supr. Miller Comm. Inc., Boston, 1985-88, v.p., 1989-90, sr. v.p., 1990-94, exec. v.p., 1994-96; prs. Shandwick Spiderworx, Boston, 1996—. Trustee Beacon Hill Nursery Sch., Boston, 1987-88. Recipient news writing award Pa. Newspaper Pubs. Assn., 1979. Avocation: sailing. Home: 1099 Massachusetts Ave Lexington MA 02173 Office: Shandwick Spiderworx Four Copley Pl Boston MA 02116

METZGER, ROBERT STREICHER, lawyer; b. St. Louis, Sept. 27, 1950; s. Robert Stanley and Jean Harriet (Streicher) M.; m. Stephanie Joy Morgan, Nov. 16, 1980; children: Michael, Kristen, Marisa. BA, Middlebury Coll., 1974; JD, Georgetown U., 1977. Bar: Calif. 1978, D.C. 1978. Legis. aide U.S. Rep. Robert F. Drinan, Washington, 1972-73; legis. asst. U.S. Rep. Michael J. Harrington, Washington, 1973-75; rsch. fellow Ctr. for Sci. and Internat. Affairs Harvard U., Cambridge, Mass., 1977-78; assoc. Latham & Watkins, L.A., 1978-84, ptnr., 1984-90; ptnr. Kirkland & Ellis, L.A., 1990-93, Troop, Meisinger, Steuber & Pasich and predecessor, L.A., 1993—; cons. Congl. Rsch. Svc., Washington, 1977-78. Contbr. articles to profl. jours. Mem. ABA (litigation pub. contracts sect.), Internat. Inst. for Strategic Studies, Jonathan Club. Office: Hill Wynne Troop & Meisinger 10940 Wilshire Blvd Los Angeles CA 90024-3915

METZGER, VERNON ARTHUR, management educator, consultant; b. Baldwin Park, Calif., Aug 13, 1918; s. Vernon and Nellie C. (Ross) M.; BS, U. Calif., Berkeley, 1947, MBA, 1948; m. Beth Arlene Metzger, Feb. 19, 1955; children: Susan, Linda, 1 step-son, David. Estimating engr. C. F. Braun & Co., 1949; prof. mgmt. Calif. State U. at Long Beach, 1949-89, prof. emeritus, 1989—, founder Sch. Bus.; mgmt. cons., 1949-89. Mem. Fire Commn. Fountain Valley, Calif., 1959-60; pres. Orange County Dem. League, 1967-68; mem. State Dept. mgmt. task force to promote modern mgmt. in Yugoslavia, 1977; mem. State of Calif. Fair Polit. Practices Commn., Orange County Transit Com. Served with USNR, 1942-45. Recipient Outstanding Citizens award Orange County (Calif.) Bd. Suprs. Fellow Soc. for Advancement of Mgmt. (life; dir.); mem. Acad. Mgmt., Orange County Indsl. Rels. Rsch. Assn. (v.p.), Beta Gamma Sigma, Alpha Kappa Psi, Tau Kappa Upsilon. Home: 1938 Balearic Dr Costa Mesa CA 92626-3513 Office: 1250 N Bellflower Blvd Long Beach CA 90840-0006

METZKER, RAY K., photographer; b. Milw., Sept. 10, 1931; s. William Martin and Marian Helen (Krueger) M. B.A., Beloit Coll., 1953; M.S., Inst. Design, Ill. Inst. Tech., 1959. Mem. faculty photography-film dept. Phila. Coll. Art, 1962-81, prof., chmn. dept., 1978-79; vis. assoc. prof. U. N.Mex., 1970-72; vis. adj. prof. R.I. Sch. Design, spring 1977; adj. Columbia Coll., Chgo., 1980-83; Smith Disting. vis. prof. art George Washington U., 1987-88. Author: Sand Creatures, 1979; one-man exhbns. include, Art Inst. Chgo., 1959, Mus. Modern Art, N.Y.C., 1967, Milw. Art Ctr., 1970, The Picture Gallery, Zurich, Switzerland, 1974, Marion Locks Gallery, Phila., 1978, 83, Internat. Ctr. Photography, N.Y.C., 1978, Light Gallery, N.Y.C., 1979, Shadai Gallery, Tokyo Inst. Polytechnics, 1992, Turner/Krull Gallery, L.A., 1992, Zelz Lieberman Gallery, Chgo., 1995, Lawrence Miller Gallery, 1984, 85, 87, 88, 90, 92, 94; represented in permanent collections, Mus. Modern Art, N.Y.C., Art Inst. Chgo., Smithsonian Inst., Washington, Met. Mus. Art, N.Y.C., Phila. Mus. Art, Bibliotheque Nat., Paris: 25 Yr. Retrospective, Mus. Fine Art, Houston and six other U.S. mus.; subject of monograph: Unknown Territory: Ray K. Metzker, 1984. Served with U.S. Army, 1954-56. Guggenheim fellow, 1966, 79; Nat. Endowment Arts fellow, 1974, 88; residency LaNapoule Art Found., France, 1989. Home: 733 S 6th St Philadelphia PA 19147-2109

METZLER, CYNTHIA A., federal agency administrator, lawyer. BA, Purdue U., 1970; JD, U. Ind., 1974; MS in Human Resources Devel. with distinction, Am. U. Atty., asst. dir. litigation Legal Svcs. Orgn. Ind., Indpls., 1979; from exec. asst. to spl. asst. to chmn. for new initiatives and programs Fed. Labor Rels. Authority, 1987—; assoc. dir. presdl. personnel The White House, Washington; assoc. adminstr. for adminstrn. Gen. Svcs. Adminstrn. U.S. Dept. Labor, asst. sec. adminstrn. and mgmt., 1994—. Mem. Clinton/Gore Transition Team. Office: Dept of Labor Adminstrn 200 Constitution Ave NW Washington DC 20210-0001

METZLER, DWIGHT FOX, civil engineer, retired state official; b. Kans., Mar. 25, 1916; s. Ross R. and Grace (Fox) M.; m. Lela Ross, June, 1941; children: Linda Diane, Brenda Lee, Marilyn Anne, Martha Jeanne. BSCE, Kans. U., 1940, CE, 1947; SM, Harvard U., 1948. Registered profl. engr., Kans., N.Y.; diplomate Am. Acad. Environ. Engrs. Asst. engr. Kans. Bd. Health, 1940-42, san. engr., 1946-48; chief engr. Topeka, 1948-62; assoc. prof. dept. civil engring. U. Kans., 1948-59, prof., 1959-66; exec. sec. Kans. Water Resources Bd., Topeka, 1962-66; dep. commr. N.Y. State Dept. Health, Albany, 1966-70, N.Y. State Dept. Environ. Conservation, Albany, 1970-74; sec. Kans. Dept. Health and Environment, Topeka, 1974-79, dir. water supply devel., 1979-84, retired, 1984; cons. san. engring. Fed. Pub. Housing Authority, USPHS, 1943-46; housing cons. Chgo.-Cook County Health Survey, 1946; cons. water supply and water pollution control USPHS, 1957-66; adviser Govt. of India, 1960; mem. ofcl. exchange to USSR on environ.health research and practice, 1962; adviser WHO, 1964-84; cons., expert witness Occidential Chem. Co., Love Canal, 1990-91; mem. Water Pollution Bd., Internat. Joint Commn., 1967-74, Assembly of Engring. NRC, 1977-80. Editor Internat. Jour. Water Pollution Rsch.; contbr. articles to profl. jours. Chmn. Kans. Bible Chair Bd., 1957-66; chmn. com. for new bldg. U. Kans. Sch. Religion. Recipient Disting. Service award U. Kans., 1970, Disting. Engring. Service award U. Kans., 1984. Fellow Royal Soc. Health Gt. Britain (hon.), Am. Pub. Health Assn. (former mem. governing council, exec. bd., pres., chmn. action bd., Centennial award 1972, Sedgwick medal 1981), ASCE (sec. sanitary engring. div. 1959-61, chmn. 1963); mem. Am. Water Works Assn. (Fuller award 1954, Purification div. award 1958), Water Pollution Control Fedn. (Bedell award 1963, hon. mem. 1983), Kans. Pub. Health Assn. (Crumbine award 1965), Kans. Engring. Soc. (Outstanding Engr. award 1978), Nat. Acad. Engring., Kans. Rural Water Assn. (Conger award 1990), Sigma Xi, Tau Beta Pi. Home: 900 SW 31st St Apt 325 Topeka KS 66611-2196

METZLER, GLENN ELAM, minister; b. Lititz, Pa., Nov. 22, 1945; s. Elam B. and Anna Mary (Martin) M.; m. Esther G. Stoltzfus, July 1, 1967; children: Gwenda L., Millie E., Danita K., Laurel M. BA in Family Counseling, U. Maine, Augusta and Farmington, 1981. Ordained to ministry Mennonite Ch., 1985. Dir. voluntary svc. Mennonite Ch., Hallowell, Maine, 1972-74; pastor Mennonite Ch., Augusta, 1975—; chmn. New Eng. Fellowship of Mennonite Chs., 1986—; carpenter, Augusta, 1979—. Bd. mem. Maine Interfaith Flood Recovery Inc., Waterville, Maine, 1987-88. Mem. Augusta Clergy Assn. Home: RR 1 Box 338 Readfield ME 04355-9733

METZLER, ROGER JAMES, JR., lawyer; b. East Orange, N.J., Feb. 4, 1945; s. Roger James and Dorothy Marie (Clark) M.; m. Marilyn Carol Schick, Apr. 19, 1969; children: Andrea C., Maria N. BS, Brown U., 1967; JD, Santa Clara U., 1975. Ptnr. Farrand, Cooper, Metzler & Bruiniers, San Francisco, 1975-88, McQuaid, Bedford, Clausen & Metzler, San Francisco, 1988-89, Keck, Mahin & Cate, Chgo. and San Francisco, 1990—. Avocation: soccer referee. Office: Keck Mahin and Cate 1 Maritime Plz Fl 23 San Francisco CA 94111-3404*

METZNER, CHARLES MILLER, federal judge; b. N.Y.C., Mar. 13, 1912; s. Emanuel and Gertrude (Miller) M.; m. Jeanne Gottlieb, Oct. 6, 1966. A.B., Columbia U., 1931, LL.B., 1933. Bar: N.Y. 1933. Pvt. practice, 1934; mem. Jud. Council State N.Y., 1935-41; law clk. to N.Y. supreme ct. justice, 1942-52; exec. asst. to U.S. atty. Gen. Herbert Brownell, Jr., 1953-54; mem. firm Chapman, Walsh & O'Connell, 1954-59; judge U.S. Dist Ct. (so. dist.) N.Y., 1959—; Mem. Law Revision Commn. N.Y. State, 1959; chmn. com. adminstrn. magistrates system U.S. Jud. Conf., 1970-81; chmn. Columbia Coll. Coun., 1965-66. Pres. N.Y. Young Republican Club, 1941; Trustee Columbia U., 1972-84, trustee emeritus, 1984—; bd. dirs. N.Y.C. Ctr. Music and Drama, 1969-74. Recipient Lawyer Div. of Joint Def. Appeal award, 1961, Columbia U. Alumni medal, 1966, Founders award Nat. Coun. U.S. Magistrates, 1989. Mem. ABA, Am. Law Inst., Fed. Bar Coun. (cert. Disting. Jud. Svc. 1989).

METZNER, RICHARD JOEL, psychiatrist, psychopharmacologist, educator; b. L.A., Feb. 15, 1942; s. Robert Gerson and Esther Rebecca (Groper) M.; children: Jeffrey Anthony, David Jonathan; m. Leila Kirkley, June 26, 1993. BA, Stanford U., 1963; MD, Johns Hopkins U., 1967. Intern, Roosevelt Hosp., N.Y.C., 1967-68; resident in psychiatry Stanford U. Med. Center, 1968-71; staff psychiatrist div. manpower and tng. NIMH-St. Elizabeths Hosp., Washington, 1971-73; chief audiovisual edn. system VA Med. Center Brentwood, L.A., 1973-79, chmn. VA Dist. 26 Ednl. Task Force, 1976-78; asst. prof. psychiatry UCLA Neuropsychiat. Inst., 1973-80, assoc. clin. prof., 1980—, lectr. Sch. Social Welfare, 1975-84; pvt. practice medicine specializing in psychiatry, Bethesda, Md., 1972-73, L.A., 1973—; dir. Western Inst. Psychiatry, L.A., 1977—; pres. Psychiat. Resource Network, Inc., 1984—; Served with USPHS, 1968-71. Recipient 6 awards for film and videotape prodns., 1976-80; diplomate Am. Bd. Psychiatry and Neurology (cons. 1974-78, producer audiovisual exam. programs 1975-77). Fellow Am. Psychiat. Assn.; mem. So. Calif. Psychiat. Soc., Mental Health Careerists Assn. (chmn. 1972-73), Phi Beta Kappa. Democrat. Jewish. Contbr. numerous articles to profl. publs., 1963—; producer, writer numerous ednl. films and videotapes, 1970—.

MEULEMAN, ROBERT JOSEPH, banker; b. South Bend, Ind., May 1, 1939; s. Joseph and Louise (Dutrieux) M.; m. Judith Ann Mc Comb, July 1, 1961; children Joseph, Jennifer, Rachel. BA, U. Notre Dame, 1961; MBA, Mich. State U., 1962. Investment analyst Nat. Bank of Detroit, 1965-68, Heritage Investment Advisors, Milw., 1968-72; sr. investment officer St. Joseph Bank and Trust Co., South Bend, 1972-81; pres., CEO Amcore Bank N.Am., Rockford, Ill., 1981—; bd. dirs. Amcore Fin. Bd. dirs. Swedish Am. Hosp. Found., Rockford, 1986—, Rockford Pro-Am., 1986—, Rockford YMCA, 1993. Served to 1st lt. U.S. Army, 1963-65. Mem. Chartered Fin. Analysts, Milw. Fin. Analysts, Rockford C. of C. (bd. dirs. 1985). Republican. Roman Catholic. Club: Rockford Country. Avocations: skiing, golf, tennis. Home: 5329 Gingeridge Ln Rockford IL 61114-5333 Office: Amcore Bank NA Rockford 501 7th St Rockford IL 61104-1242

MEUNIER, JOHN CHARLES CHRISTOPHER, architecture educator, university dean; b. Nottingham, Eng., June 17, 1936; came to U.S., 1976; s. Stanislass and Louie (Naylor) M.; m. Dorothy Elizabeth Donnelly, Feb. 6, 1960; children: Matthew John, Elizabeth Ann. BArch with 1st class honours, Liverpool (Eng.) U., 1959; MArch, Harvard U., 1960; MA, Cambridge (Eng.) U., 1962. Registered architect, U.K., Ariz. Archtl. asst. Buro Fred Angerer, Munich, 1960-62; asst. lectr. Cambridge U., 1962-66, lectr., 1966-76; head architecture dept. U. Cin., 1976-79, dir. Sch. Architecture and Interior Design, 1979-87; prof. architecture, dean Ariz. State U. Coll. Architecture and Environ. Design, Tempe, 1987—; prin. John Meunier Architect, Cambridge, 1962-76, Gasson & Meunier Architects, Cambridge, 1964-74, Cambridge Design Coop., 1974-76. Contbr. numerous articles to profl. jours. in Eng., U.S., Japan, Germany; prin. works include Burrell Mus., Glasgow, Scotland, 1972-83 (1st prize 1972). Mem. Urban Design Rev. Bd., Cin., 1985-87, Cen. City Bd. Archtl. Rev., Phoenix, 1989—, Phoenix Community Alliance, 1988—, Phoenix Little Theatre, 1988-90. Frank Knox fellow Harvard U., 1959. Fellow Royal Soc. Arts; mem. AIA (bd. dirs. Nat. Archtl. Accrediting Bd., 1994—), Royal Inst. Brit. Architects (bd. edn. and practice 1970-76), Assn. Collegiate Schs. Architecture (bd. dirs. 1989-92, pres. 1990-91). Avocations: tennis, travel, theatre, photography. Home: 6744 N 63rd Pl Paradise Vly AZ 85253-4279 Office: Ariz State U Coll Arch-Environ Design Tempe AZ 85287

MEUNIER, ROBERT RAYMOND, research electrical engineer, optical engineer; b. Hollywood, Calif., Mar. 27, 1957; s. Raymond Robert and Anna Marie (Rapp) M. ASD in Laser Electro-Optics, Pasadena (Calif.) City Coll., 1984; BS in Mgmt., Pepperdine U., 1993. Lab. asst. Jet Propulsion Lab., Pasadena, Calif., 1984-85; rsch. engr. satellite sys. Rockwell Internat., Seal Beach, Calif., 1985-89; electro-optical engr. Cymbolic Scis. Internat., Irvine, Calif., 1989-90; project engr. OCA Applied Optics, Garden Grove, Calif., 1990-92; owner, program mgr. Integrated Scientific, Mission Viejo, Calif., 1992—; sr. sys. test engr. Rocketdyne Corp., Granada Hills, Calif., 1994—. Mem. Laser Inst. Am., Soc. Photo-optical Instrumentation Engrs., L.A. Collegiate Coun. (alumnus), Inter Orgnl. Coun. (founder, chmn. 1981-82), Nat. Mgmt. Assn., Internat. Platform Assn., Lions Club, Inventors Forum, Sigma Pi. Republican. Roman Catholic. Office: Rockwell Internat 2600 Westminster Blvd PO Box 3644 Seal Beach CA 90740

MEURLIN, KEITH W., airport terminal executive. Mgr. Wash. Dulles Internat. Airport. Office: Washington Dulles Intl Airport PO Box 17045 Washington DC 20041-0045*

MEUSER, FREDRICK WILLIAM, retired seminary president, church historian; b. Payne, Ohio, Sept. 14, 1923; s. Henry William and Alvina Maria (Bouyack) M.; m. Jeanne Bond Griffiths, July 29, 1951; children: Jill Martha, Douglas Griffiths. AB, Capital U., 1945, BD, 1948, DD (hon.), 1989; STM, Yale U., 1949, MA, 1953, PhD, 1956; DD (hon.), Tex. Luth. Coll., 1980, Capital U., 1989; LHD (hon.), Augustana Coll., 1985. Ordained to ministry Am. Lutheran Ch., 1948; asst. pastor 1st Luth. Ch., Galveston, Tex., 1948, Christ Luth. Ch., North Miami, Fla., 1949-51; campus minister Yale U., 1951-53; prof. ch. history Luth. Theol. Sem., Columbus, Ohio, 1953-78, dean grad. studies, 1963-69, pres., 1971-78; pres. Trinity Luth. Sem., Columbus, 1978-88; exec. sec. div. theol. studies Luth. Council in U.S.A., 1969-71; del. World Council Chs., 1968, Luth. World Fedn., 1970; v.p. Am. Luth. Ch., 1974-80; mem. Commn. for a New Luth. Ch., 1982-86; asst. pastor St. Paul Luth. Ch., Westerville, Ohio, 1995—. Author: The Formation of the American Lutheran Church, 1958, Luther the Preacher, 1983; author: (with others) Church in Fellowship, 1963, Lutherans in North America, 1975; translator: (with others) What Did Luther Understand by Religion, 1977, The Reconstruction of Morality, 1979; editor: (with others) Interpreting Luther's Legacy, 1967. Recipient Disting. Churchman's award Tex. Luth. Coll., 1972, Joseph Sittler award Trinity Luth. Sem., 1990; named Outstanding Alumnus Capital U., 1977; Am. Assn. Theol. Schs. fellow, 1961-62. Mem. Am. Soc. Ch. History. Home: 6392 Claypool Ct Columbus OH 43213-3435 Office: 2199 E Main St Columbus OH 43209-3913

MEVERS, FRANK CLEMENT, state archivist, historian; b. New Orleans, Oct. 10, 1942; s. Lloyd F. and Mary Ashley (Collins) M.; m. Kathryn Ann Hayes, Dec. 23, 1967; children: John F., Lauren K. BA in History, La. State U., 1965; PhD in Am. History, U. N.C., 1972; MA, La. State U., 1967. Editor Papers of James Madison, Charlottesville, Va., 1972-74, Papers of Josiah Bartlett, Concord, N.H., 1974-77, Papers of William Plumer, Concord, 1977-79; state archivist State of N.H., Concord, 1979—. Editor, author: New Hampshire: State That Made US a Nation, 1989. Mem. Pub. Libr. Bd. Trustees, Concord, 1979—. With U.S. Army, 1967-69, Korea. Episcopalian. Avocation: stamp collecting. Home: 29 Bradley St Concord NH 03301-6432 Office: NH State Archives 71 S Fruit St Concord NH 03301-2410

MEW, THOMAS JOSEPH, III (TOMMY MEW), artist, educator; b. Miami, Fla., Aug. 15, 1942; s. Thomas Joseph and Maude Edith (Perry) M.; m. Mary Ann Kelley, June 17, 1966; 1 son, Thomas Joseph. B.S., Fla. State U., 1962, M.A., 1964; Ph.D., N.Y. U., 1966. Grad. instr. Fla. State U., 1963; asst. prof. art Troy State U., 1966-68, Jacksonville U., 1968-70; prof., chmn. dept. art Berry Coll., 1970—, Dana prof. art; juror art shows: vis. artist; lectr. in field, cons. art; dir. Fluxus West/Southeast. Exhibited in one-man shows Parkway Gallery, Miami, 1962-63, 319 Gallery, N.Y.C., 1968, Meridian (Miss.) Mus., 1976, C.D.O. Gallery, Parma, Italy, 1978, Calif. State U., Sacramento, 1979, Miss. Mus. Art, Jackson, 1979, Art Inst. for Permian Basin, ITex, Arte Studio, Bergamo, Italy; group shows include High Mus., Atlanta, 1971, 72, 74, New Reform Gallery, Aalst, Belgium, 1975, U. Guelph, Ont., Can., 1975, Neuberger Mus., Purchase, N.Y., 1978, Arte Fiera, Bologna, Italy, 1979; represented in permanent collections, Kansas City Art Inst., Mildura Art Centre, Australia, Wichita Art Mus., Jacksonville (Fla.) Art Mus., Macon Mus. Art, AT&T, Harn Mus., U. Iowa; host: Cable TV show Art: The Mew View, 1978—; Filmmaker, 1966-69; contbr. articles to profl. jours. Bd. dirs. Rome Arts Council, 1984—; bd. dirs. Interface. Recipient Gellhorn award N.Y. U., 1966; Cowperthwaite grantee, 1972; Lilly Found. grantee, 1975; Gulf Life grantee, 1977. Mem. Southeastern Coll. Art Conf., Coll. Art Assn. Am., Am. Fedn. Arts, Nat. Art Edn. Assn., Am. Assn. Art Dealers. Home: 100 Saddle Trl Rome GA 30161-6841 Office: Berry Coll Art Dept Mount Berry GA 30149 *I've always moved in the direction of my dreams . . . always tried to make the great dream a reality.*

MEWHINNEY, BRUCE HARRISON NICHOLAS, publisher; b. Charlottesville, Va., Apr. 15, 1949; m. Elyse Tager, June 5, 1982. BA, Antioch Coll., 1971. Editorial prodn. mgr. Computer Currents Mag., Emeryville, Calif., 1988-90; assoc. editor MacUser Mag., Foster City, Calif., 1990-93; pub., majority stockholder Diosa Corp., Alameda, Calif., 1993—; tech. mgr. Am. Online forum of Preview Media, San Francisco, 1995—; forum mgr. in "eWorld" online svc., Apple Computer, Cupertino, Calif., 1993-94. Author, photographer: Down Below: Aboard the World's Classic Yachts, 1980. Avocations: sailing, boatbuilding, multimedia devel. Office: Diosa Corp 3028 Alta Vista Alameda CA 94502

MEYAART, PAUL JAN, distilling company executive; b. Berchem, Belgium, Mar. 6, 1943; came to U.S., 1965; s. Joseph and Leonie (Devreese) M.; m. Mary-Ann Mota, Mar. 18, 1967; children—Peter, Antoine, Danielle. B.Commerce, U. Antwerp, Belgium, 1965; M.B.A. (Ford internat. fellow 1965-67, Fulbright grantee 1965-67), U. Chgo., 1967. Fin. planning mgr. Sinclair Belgium S. A., Brussels, 1967-70; controller-treas. Knoll Internat. Inc., N.Y.C., 1971-74; v.p. fin., treas. Boyle Midway div. Am. Home Products Co., N.Y.C., 1974-78; v.p. fin. and adminstrn., treas. Am. Distilling Co. Inc., N.Y.C., 1978—. Mem. Fin. Execs. Inst. Home: 897 Franklin Lake Rd Franklin Lakes NJ 07417 Office: 245 Park Ave New York NY 10167-0002

MEYBERG, BERNHARD ULRICH, entrepreneur; b. Norden, Germany, Aug. 29, 1917; s. Peter Bernhard and Katharine (v. Oterendorp) M.; m. Lotte Essig, Apr. 1949; children: Horst Eugen, Ursula Eugenie, Gabriele Christine. Student, U. Greifswald/Pommern, 1943-45. Apprentice Savingsbank, Norden, 1935-37, employee, 1937-38; collaborator Eug Essig, Ludwigsburg, Fed. Republic Germany, 1948-70; pvt. practice Möglingen, Fed. Republic Germany, 1970—. Contbr. essays to newspapers. 1st lt. German Air Force, 1938-45, prisoner of war, 1945-47. Mem. Internat. Furniture-Carpet-Purchase Assn. (mem. exec. com.), Chamber Industry and Trade (mem. com.), Italian Chamber Trade for Germany (mem. com.). Lutheran. Avocations: sports, tennis, sailing. Home: Max-Ostheimerstrasse 6, 87534 Oberstaufen Germany Office: Eugen Essig, DaimlerstraBe 62, Möglingen Germany

MEYBURG, ARNIM HANS, transportation engineer, educator, consultant; b. Bremerhaven, W. Ger., Aug. 25, 1939; came to U.S., 1965; s. Friedel and Auguste (Kleeberg) M.; m. Ruth Meyburg; 1 child, Jennifer Susan. Student, U. Hamburg, 1960-62, Free U. Berlin, 1962-65; M.S. (Fulbright travel grantee), Northwestern U., 1968, Ph.D., 1971. Research assoc. Transp. Center, Northwestern U., 1968-69; asst. prof. transp. engring. Cornell U., 1969-75, assoc. prof., 1975-78, prof., 1978—, acting chmn. dept., 1977-78, chmn. dept., 1980-85, dir. Sch. Civil and Environ. Engring., 1988—, chmn. bd. Univ. Transp. Rsch. Ctr., 1992-95; dir. Transp. Infrastructure Rsch. Consortium, 1995—; vis. mem. faculties U. Calif., Irvine, Tech. U. Munich, Germany, (Fulbright lectr.) U. Sao Paulo, Brazil, 1984, Tech. U. Brunswick, W. Ger., 1985-86; Humboldt Found. research fellow, 1978-79; prin. investigator projects Dept. Transp., NSF, Nat. Coop. Hwy. Research Program, N.Y. State Dept. Transp., U.S. Dept. Transp. Author: (with others) Urban Transportation Modeling and Planning, 1975, Transportation Systems Evaluation, 1976, Survey Sampling and Multivariate Analysis for Social Scientists and Engineers, 1979, Survey Methods for Transport Planning, 1995; co-editor: (with others) Behavioral Travel-Demand Models, 1976, New Horizons in Travel-Behavior Research, 1981, Selected Readings in Transport Survey Methodology, 1992; contbr. articles to profl. jours., chpts. to books. NSF Research Initiation grantee, 1973; recipient Humboldt U.S. Sr. Scientist award, 1984, Fulbright sr. lectr. award, 1984. Mem. ASCE, AAUP, Transp. Rsch. Bd., Transp. Rsch. Forum, Sigma Xi, Chi Epsilon. Office: Cornell U 220 Hollister Hall Ithaca NY 14853-3501

MEYE, ROBERT PAUL, retired seminary administrator, writer; b. Hubbard, Oreg., Apr. 1, 1929; s. Robert and Eva (Pfau) M.; m. Mary Cover, June 18, 1954; children: Marianne Meye Thompson, Douglas, John. BA, Stanford U., 1951; BD, Fuller Theol. Sem., 1957, ThM, 1959; DTheol magna cum laude, U. Basel, Switzerland, 1962; DD Eastern Bapt. Theol. Sem., 1990. Prof. No. Bapt. Theol. Sem., Lombard, Ill., 1962-77, dean, 1971-77; dean Sch. Theology, Fuller Theol. Sem., Pasadena, Calif., 1977-90, dean emeritus, 1992—, assoc. provost for Ch. Rels. and Christian Community, 1990-92, prof. N.T. interpretation, 1977-92, prof. emeritus, 92—. Author: Jesus and The Twelve;1968, co-editor: Studies in Old Testament Theology; 1992—, contbr. articles to profl. jours., dictionaries and encys. Served to lt. (j.g.) USN, 1946-47, 51-54, Korea. Am. Assn. Theol. Schs. grantee, 1970-71; 75-76. Mem. Nat. Assn. Bapt. Profs. of Religion, Studiorum Novi Testamenti Societas, Chgo. Soc. Bibl. Res., Soc. Bibl. Lit., Inst. Bibl. Research. Republican. Home: 1170 Rubio St Altadena CA 91001-2027 Office: Fuller Theol Sem 135 N Oakland Ave Pasadena CA 91182-0001

MEYER, ALBERT JAMES, educational researcher; b. Cleve., Sept. 24, 1929; s. Jacob Conrad and Esther Agnes (Steiner) M.; m. Mary Ellen Yoder, Aug. 21, 1954; children: Richard, Anne, Kathryn, Barbara, Elaine. BA, Goshen Coll., 1950; MA, Princeton U., 1952, PhD, 1954. Asst. in teaching and rsch. Princeton (N.J.) U., 1950-53; fellow U. Basel, Switzerland, 1953-54, rsch. assoc., 1956-57; dir. for France, rep. European peace sect. Mennonite Ctrl. Com., 1954-57; asst. prof. physics Goshen (Ind.) Coll., 1958-61, prof., rsch. prof., 1967-89, adj. rsch. prof., 1989—; acad. dean, prof. Bethel Coll., North Newton, Kans., 1961-66, Menno Simons lectr., 1993; exec. sec., pres. Mennonite Bd. Edn., Elkhart, Ind., 1967-95; vis. fellow Princeton (N.J.) U., 1995-96; exec. for secretariat Puidoux Theol. Confs., 1955-57; former mem. staff Mennonite Student Svcs. Com.; former coord. com. on liberal arts edn. North Ctrl. Assn. Colls. and Secondary Schs.; vis. rsch. scientist U. Paris, 1974-75; vis. rschr. New Coll. Berkeley, 1986-87; presenter in field; former cons. Conrad Grebel Coll., U. Waterloo, Ont., Can.; mem. peace and social concerns com. Mennonite Ch., 1959-71; former mem. Continuation Com. of Hist. Peace Chs. Contbr. articles to denominational periodicals and sci. jours. Princeton U. exch. fellow and Charles Foster Kent fellow Nat. Coun. for Religion in Higher Edn., 1935-54. Mem. Denominational Execs. for Ch.-Related Higher Edn. (chmn. 1984-86), Am. Assn. for Higher Edn., Am. Assn. Physics Tchrs. Avocations: tennis, hockey, hiking. Home: 708 Emerson St Goshen IN 46526-3904 Office: Mennonite Bd Edn 500 S Main St Elkhart IN 46516-3207

MEYER, ALDEN MERRILL, environmental association executive; b. Buffalo, Mar. 21, 1952; s. Arthur Merrill Meyer and Susan (Rogers) Meyer Markle. BA, Yale U., 1975; MS, Am. U., 1990. Energy policy analyst Conn. Citizen Action Group, Hartford, 1975-78, Environ. Action Found., Washington, 1979-82; exec. dir. Environ. Action, Inc., 1983-85, League Conservation Voters, Washington, 1985-88; dir. climate change and energy policy Union of Concerned Scientists, Washington, 1989-92, legis. dir., 1992-95, dir. govt. rels., 1995—; bd. dirs. Ams. for Environment, Washington, 1983-87, chmn., 1985-87; bd. dirs. Urban Environment Conf., Washington, 1984-87, Zero Population Growth, 1989—; pres. bd. dirs. Safe Energy Communication Council, Washington, 1980-85; chmn. U.S. Climate Action Network, 1990—; mem. adv. coun. Nat. Renewable Energy Lab., 1993—; mem. state and local adv. bd. U.S. Dept. Energy, 1994—. Mem. Yale Whiffenpoofs, 1975. Democrat. Avocations: hiking; camping; skiing; singing. Home: 15 Montgomery Ave Takoma Park MD 20912-4614 Office: Union of Concerned Scientis 1616 P St NW Washington DC 20036-1434

MEYER, ALICE VIRGINIA, state official; b. N.Y.C., Mar. 15, 1921; d. Martin G. and Marguerite Helene (Houzé) Kliemand; m. Theodore Harry Meyer, June 28, 1947; children: Robert Charles, John Edward. BA, Barnard Coll., 1941; MA, Columbia U., 1942. Tchr. pub. schs. Elmont, N.Y., 1942-43; tchr. Fairlawn (N.J.) High Sch., 1943-47; office mgr., sales rep. N.Y.C., 1948-55; substitute tchr. Pub. Schs., Easton, Conn., 1965-72; state rep., asst. minority leader Conn. State Legislature, Hartford, 1976-93; mem. Ct. Bd. of Govs. for Higher Edn., 1993—, vice-chair. Mem. bd. trustees Discovery Mus., 1980—, United Way Regional Youth Substance Abuse Project, Bridgeport, 1983-93; bd. dirs. 3030 Park, 1993—, Fairfield County Lit. Coalition, Bridgeport, 1988-94; vice chmn. Easton Rep. Town Com., 1970-78; mem. strategic planning com. Town of Easton, 1993—; vice-chmn. ct. adv. coun. on intergovtl. rels., 1988—; mem. Conn. Commn. on Quality Edn., 1992-93; supporter of Conn. Small Towns, 1988; mem. lt. gov.'s commn. on mandate reduction, 1995; sec. Easton Free Sch. Scholarship Fund, 1980—. Named Legislator of Yr. Conn. Libr. Assn., 1985; Guardian Small Bus. grantee Nat. Fedn. Ind. Bus., 1987; honoree Fairfield YWCA Salute to Women, 1988; named grant to AAUW Fellowship Fund, Bridgeport Br., 1970, Conn. State AAUW, 1974. Mem. AAUW (past local pres. 1976, bd. dirs. 1982), LWV, Bus. and Profl. Women, Nat. Order Women Legislators (regional dir. 1987—, past pres. Conn. chpt.). Congregationalist. Avocations: swimming, sailing, bridge. Home: 18 Lantern Hill Rd Easton CT 06612-2218

MEYER, ANDREW W., publishing executive; b. Phila., July 29, 1941; s. John O. and Katherine (Wachter) M.; m. Helen Hope Hogan, Oct. 1963; children: Kelly Ann, Michael, Melissa, Suzanne, Jennifer. BS in Accounting, St. Joseph's U., Phila., 1963; MBA in Finance, U. Conn., 1973. CPA. Sr. accountant Jenkins Fetterolf, Phila., 1963-67; asst. treas. PA & S Small Co., York, 1967-71; v.p. finance Xerox Pub. Group, Greenwich, Conn., 1971-82, R.R. Bowker, N.Y.C., 1982-94; COO Reed Reference Pub., New Providence, N.J., 1995—. Office: Reed Reference Publishing 121 Chanlon Rd New Providence NJ 07974-1541*

MEYER, ANTHONY ANDREW, surgeon; b. Melrose, Minn., Apr. 24, 1948. MD, U. Chgo., 1977. Diplmate Am. Bd. Surgery. Intern U. Calif., San Francisco, 1977-78, resident in surgery, 1978-82; staff U. N.C. Hosps., Chapel Hill, 1982—; prof. surgery U. N.C., Chapel Hill, 1982—. Mem. ACS. Office: U NC Dept Surgery Box 7210 164 Burnett Womack Bldg Chapel Hill NC 27599

MEYER, ARMIN HENRY, retired diplomat, author, educator; b. Ft. Wayne, Ind., Jan. 19, 1914; s. Armin Paul and Leona (Buss) M.; m. Alice James, Apr. 23, 1949; 1 dau., Kathleen Alice. Student, Lincoln (Ill.) Coll., 1931-33; A.B., Capital U., 1935, LL.D., 1957; M.A., Ohio State U., 1941, LL.D., 1972; LL.D., Wartburg Coll., S.D. Sch. Mines and Tech., 1972. Faculty Capital U., Columbus, Ohio, 1935-41; staff OWI, Egypt, Iraq, 1942-46; U.S. pub. affairs officer Baghdad, Iraq, 1946-48; pub. affairs adviser U.S. Dept. State, 1948-52; sec. Am. embassy, Beirut, Lebanon, 1952-55; dep. chief mission Kabul, Afghanistan, 1955-57; dep. dir. Office South Asian Affairs Dept. State, 1957-58, dep. dir. Office Near Eastern Affairs, 1958-59, dir. Office Nr. Ea. Affairs, 1959-61, dep. asst. sec. of state for Nr. Ea. and South Asian Affairs, 1961; U.S. ambassador to Lebanon, 1961-65, Iran, 1965-69, Japan, 1969-72; spl. asst. to sec. state, chmn. Cabinet Com. to Combat Terrorism, 1972-73; vis. prof. Am. U., 1974-75; dir. Ferdowsi project Georgetown U., 1975-79, adj. prof. diplomacy, 1975-86; dir. Internat. Affairs Ecology and Environ. Inc.; Woodrow Wilson vis. fellow, 1974—; cons. internat. bus. and environment, 1975—. Author: Assignment Tokyo: An Ambassador's Journal, 1974; co-author: Education in Diplomacy, 1987. Hon. mem. Lincoln Sesquicentennial Commn., 1959; bd. dirs. Washington Inst. Fgn. Affairs, 1979—, pres., 1988—. Recipient Meritorious Svc. award Dept. State, 1958, Superior Honor award, 1973; decorated Order of Rising Sun, 1st class (Japan), 1982; inducted into Hall of Excellence Ohio Fedn. Ind. Colls., 1989. Mem. Sigma Psi. Lutheran. Home: 4610 Reno Rd NW Washington DC 20008-2941 *Faith in God; where there is a will there is a way; if a job is worth doing it is worth doing well; and the Golden Rule.*

MEYER, AUGUST CHRISTOPHER, JR., broadcasting company executive, lawyer; b. Champaign, Ill., Aug. 14, 1937; s. August C. and Clara (Rocke) M.; m. Karen Haugh Hassett, Dec. 28, 1960; children: August Christopher F., Elisabeth Hassett. BA cum laude, Harvard U., 1959, LLB, 1962. Bar: Ill. 1962. Ptr. Meyer, Capel, Hirschfeld, Muncy, Jahn and Aldeen, Champaign, Ill., 1962-77, of counsel, 1977—; owner, dir., officer Midwest TV, Inc., Sta. KFMB-TV-AM-FM, San Diego, Sta. WCIA-TV, Champaign, Ill. , Sta. WMBD-TV-AM, WMXP, Peoria, Ill., 1968—; pres. Sta. KFMB-TV-AM-FM, San Diego, Sta. WCIA-TV, Champaign, Ill. , Sta. WMBD-TV-AM, WMXP, 1976—; bd. dirs. BankIll.; spl. asst. atty. gen. State of Ill., 1968-76. Chmn. bd. trustees Carle Found. Hosp., Urbana, Ill. Mem. Ill. Bar Assn., Champaign County Bar Assn. Club: Champaign Country. Home: 1408 S Prospect Ave Champaign IL 61820-6837 Office: Midwest TV Inc PO Box 777 509 S Neil St Champaign IL 61820-5219 also: Sta KFMB PO Box 85888 7677 Engineer Rd San Diego CA 92111-1515

MEYER, BERNARD STERN, lawyer, former judge; b. Balt., June 7, 1916; s. Benjamin and Josephine Meyer; m. Elaine Strass, June 25, 1939 (div.); children: Patricia, Susan; m. Edythe Birnbaum, Apr. 18, 1975; m. Hortense Fox, Oct. 29, 1991. B.S., Johns Hopkins U., 1936; LL.B., U. Md., 1938; LL.D., Hofstra U., 1980, Western State U. Coll. Law, 1982, Union U., 1984. Bar: Md. 1938, D.C., N.Y. 1947. Assoc. Fisher & Fisher, Balt., 1938-41; with Office Gen. Counsel Treasury Dept., Washington, 1941-43; pvt. practice, N.Y.C., 1948-54; ptnr. Meyer, Fink, Weinberger & Levin, N.Y.C., 1954-58; justice N.Y. State Supreme Ct., 1959-72; of counsel Fink, Weinberger, Fredman & Charney, P.C., N.Y.C., 1973-79; ptnr. Meyer, English & Cianciulli, P.C., Mineola, N.Y., 1975-79; assoc. judge N.Y. Ct. Appeals, Albany, 1979-86; dep. atty. gen. in charge spl. Attica investigation State of N.Y., 1975; ptnr. Meyer, Suozzi, English & Klein P.C., Mineola, 1987—; assoc. spl. counsel Moreland Commn. To Study Workmen's Compensation Adminstrn. and Costs, 1955-57; mem. com. on govt. integrity State of N.Y., 1987-90. Contbr. articles to profl. jours. Founder United Fund L.I.; former mem. adv. bd. Commn. Law and Social Action, Am. Jewish Congress; chmn. Task Force on Permanency Planning for Foster Children, 1986-91; past pres., bd. dirs. Health and Welfare Coun. Nassau County; former mem. bd. dirs. Nassau-Suffolk region NCCJ, Nassau County coun. Boy Scouts Am., Nat. Ctr. for State Cts.; mem. Coalition for Effective Govt., 1991—. Lt. USNR, WWII. Recipient Disting. Svc. award L.I. Press, Presdl. medal Hofstra U., Disting. Svc. award Legal Aid Soc. Nassau County, N.Y., Johns Hopkins U. Disting. Alumnus award. Mem. ABA, Am. Bar Found., Am. Coll. Trial Lawyers, Am. Law Inst., N.Y. Bar Assn. (chmn. jud. sect., com. on legis. policy), N.Y. Bar Found., Bar of City of N.Y. (chmn. libr., matrimonial, election law com.), Nassau County Bar Assn. (Disting. Svc. medallion 1982), Nat. Conf. State trial Judges (exec. com., past chmn.), Nat. Coll. State Jud. (bd. dirs.), Assn. Supreme Ct. Judges (past pres., chmn. pattern jury instrn. com. 1962-79), Supreme Ct. Hist. Soc., Com. Modern Cts., Nassau County Lawyers Assn. (award), Scribes, Order of Coif, Omicron Delta Kappa. Office: Meyer Suozzi English & Klein PC 1505 Kellum Pl Mineola NY 11501-4811

MEYER, BILL, newspaper publisher, editor; b. Pratt, Kans., Aug. 6, 1925; s. Otto William and Ruth Clarinda (Jones) M.; m. Joan Aileen Wight, Sept. 11, 1949; 1 child, Eric Kent. BS in Journalism, U. Kans., 1948. News editor Marion County Record, Hoch Pub Co., Inc., Marion, Kans., 1948-67, editor, pub., 1967—; owner Cottonwood Valley Agy., Marion, 1990—; editor 99th Inf. Divsn. Assn., Marion, 1971—; lectr. media law Wichita (Kans.) State U., 1985; polit. interviewer St. KPTS-TV, Wichita, 1983-91; bd. dirs. Ctrl. Nat. Bank, Junction City, Kans.; mil. cons., travel agt. Battlefield Tours, Slidell, La., 1990—. Passt pres. Marion Sch. dist. Bd. Edn., Marion County Hosp. Dist.; bd. dirs. Marion Manor Nursing Home, Kans. Hist. Soc., 1985-94; trustee, past pres. William Allen White Found., Lawrence, Kans.; mem. selection com. for judges, 8th Jud. Dist., 1994—. With U.S. Army, 1943-45, ETO. Recipient commendation Kans. Ho. of Reps., 1982, 99th Inf. Div. Assn., 1986, 89, named Hon. Col. Kans. Calvary, 1987, Hon. Ky. Col., 1990. Mem. Nat. Newspaper Assn., Kans. Press Assn. (pres. 1982-83, Boyd Community Svc. award 1979), Marion C. of C. (past bd. dirs.), Marion Country Club, Masons, Shriners, Kiwanis (pres. Marion 1957), Sigma Delta Chi. Republican. Methodist. Avocations: military vehicle restoration, flying, military history. Home: PO Box 99 Marion KS 66861-0099 Office: Hoch Pub Co Inc 117 S 3rd St Marion KS 66861-0278

MEYER, BILLIE JEAN, special education educator; b. Kansas City, Mo., July 27, 1943; d. Charles William and Dorothy Ellen (Alt) Emerson; m. Kenneth Lee Morris, Aug. 24, 1963 (div. Oct. 1985); 1 child, Darla Michelle Morris Stewart; m. Gordon Frederick Meyer, June 1, 1986 (dec. May 1994); stepchildren: Ardith Helmer, Susan Stanford, Gary, Geneace, Patti Draughon, Shari Mohr. BS in Edn., Northeastern State U., 1965, M in Tchg., 1968. Cert. tchr., Okla.; cert. visually impaired, Braille. Substitute tchr. Muskogee (Okla.) Pub. Schs., 1965; elem. tchr. Okla. Sch. for the Blind, Muskogee, 1965-67, elem. tchr., computer tchr., 1969—; adj. lectr. Northeastern State U., Tahlequah, summers 1990-92, 94, 95-96; on-site team mem. Nat. Accreditation Coun., 1987; mem. com. revision cert. stds., State of Okla., 1982. Author: A Sequential Math Program for Beginning Abacus Students, 1979. Mem. Assn. of Edn. and Rehab. of the Blind and Visually Impaired, Okla. Assn. of Ednl. Rehab. of the Blind and Visually Impaired (pres.-elect 1985-86, pres. 1986-87, sec. 1993-96), Computer Using Educators, Epsilon Sigma Alpha (state pres. 1981-82, Girl of Yr. 1971). Avocations: stained glass, photo preservation, gardening, traveling, bird watching. Office: Okla Sch for the Blind 3300 Gibson St Muskogee OK 74403-2811

MEYER, BRUD RICHARD, pharmaceutical company executive; b. Waukegan, Ill., Feb. 22, 1926; s. Charles Lewis and Mamie Olive (Broom) M.; m. Betty Louise Stine (dec. 1970); children: Linda (Mrs. Gary Stillabower), Louise (Mrs. Donald Knochel), Janet (Mrs. Gerald Cockrell), Jeff, Karen, Blake, Amy; m. Barbara Ann Hamilton, Nov. 26, 1970. B.S., Purdue U., 1949. With Eli Lilly & Co., Indpls., 1949-87, indsl. engr., 1949-56, supr. indsl. engr., 1956-59, sr. personnel rep., 1960-64; personnel mgr. Eli Lilly & Co., Lafayette, Ind., 1964-67; asst. dir. Eli Lilly & Co., Lafayette, 1967-69, dir. adminstrn., 1969-79, dir. personnel and public relations, 1980-87, ret., 1987. Bd. dirs. Lafayette Home Hosp., 1977—, Hanna Community Ctr., 1983—, Tippecanoe Hist. Corp., 1985—; bd. dirs. United Way Tippecanoe County, 1970-76, pres., 1974; bd. dirs. Legal Aid Soc. Tippecanoe County, 1973—, Jr. Achievement, pres., 1979; bd. dirs. Lilly Credit Union, 1969-75, pres., 1973-74; mem. Citizen's Com. on Alcoholism, 1966-72; bd. dirs. Greater Lafayette Community Centers, 1975-79, pres., 1977-78; mem., mng. dir. Battle Tippecanoe Outdoor Drama Bd. Served with USAAF, 1943-45. Mem. Pi Tau Sigma, Lambda Chi Alpha, C. of C. Greater Lafayette (bd. dirs., v.p. 1969-73), Battleground Hist. Soc. Methodist. Home: 4217 Trees Hill Dr Lafayette IN 47905-3451 Office: Eli Lilly & Co PO Box 7685 Lafayette IN 47903-7685

MEYER, CAROL FRANCES, pediatrician, allergist; b. Berea, Ky., June 2, 1936; d. Harvey Kessler and Jessie Irene (Hamm) Meyer; m. Daniel Baker Cox, June 5, 1955 (div. Apr. 1962). AA, U. Fla., 1955; BA, Duke U., 1957; MD, Med. Coll. Ga., 1967. Diplomate Am. Bd. Pediatrics, Am. Bd. Allergy and Immunology. Intern in pediatrics Med. Coll. Ga., Augusta, 1967-68; resident in pediatrics Gorgas Hosp., Canal Zone, 1968-69; fellow in pediatric respiratory disease Med. Coll. Ga., 1969-71, instr. pediat., 1971-72; med. officer pediatrics Canal Zone Govt., 1972-79; med. officer pediatrics Dept. of Army, Panama, 1979-82, med. officer allergy, 1982-89, physician in charge allergy clinic, 1984-89; asst. prof. pediatrics and medicine Med. Coll. Ga., Augusta, 1990—; mem. Bd. of Canal Zone Merit System Examiners, 1976-79. Contbr. articles to profl. jours. Mem. First Bapt. Ch. Orch., 1992—; founding mem., violoncello Curundu Chamber Ensemble, 1979-89. Recipient U.S. Army Exceptional Performance awards, 1985, 86, 89, Merck award Med. Coll. Ga., 1967; U. Fla. J. Hillis Miller scholar, 1954. Mem. AAAS, Am. Coll. Rheumatology, Allergy and Immunology Soc. Ga., Hispanic-Am. Allergy and Immunology Assn., Ga. Pediatric Soc., Pan Am. Med. Assn., Soc. Leukocyte Biology, Am. Coll. Allergy, Asthma and Immunology, Am. Acad. Allergy, Asthma and Immunology, Am. Acad. Pediat., Am. Med. Women's Assn., Panama Canal Soc. Fla., Ga. Ornithol. Soc., Ga. Thoracic Soc., Am. Lung Assn. (Ga. East Ctrl. br. exec. bd.), Am. Assn. Ret. Persons, Nature Conservancy, Royal Soc. for Preservation Birds, Nat. Assn. Ret. Fed. Employees, Nat. Audubon Soc., Panama Audubon Soc., Willow Run Homeowner's Soc. (pres.), Alpha Omega Alpha. Office: Med Coll Ga BG 232 1120 15th St Augusta GA 30912

MEYER, CATHERINE DIEFFENBACH, lawyer; b. Seattle, Mar. 27, 1951; d. Patrick Andrew and Hope Dieffenbach; m. Michael E. Meyer, Nov. 21, 1982; children. AB, Bryn Mawr Coll., 1973; JD, Northwestern U., 1979. Bar: Calif. 1979, U.S. Dist. Ct. (cen. dist.) Calif., 1979, U.S. Ct. Appeals (9th cir.) 1982, U.S. Dist. Ct. (ea., no. and so. dists.) Calif. 1987. Assoc. Lillick, McHose & Charles, L.A., 1979-85, ptnr., 1985-88; ptnr. Lillick & McHose, L.A., 1988-90, Pillsbury Madison & Sutro, L.A., 1990—. Office: Pillsbury Madison & Sutro 725 S Figueroa St Ste 1200 Los Angeles CA 90017-5443

MEYER, CHARLES APPLETON, former retailing executive; b. Boston, June 27, 1918; s. George von Lengerke and Frances (Saltonstall) M.; m. Suzanne Seyburn, June 15, 1940; children: Brooke M. Gray, Nancy M. Hovey. BA, Phillips Acad.; B.A., Harvard, 1939. With Sears, Roebuck & Co., 1939-69; beginning in New Haven store, successively mail order buyer Sears, Roebuck & Co., Boston; asst. buyer hdqrs. orgn., staff asst. fgn. stores, mgr. fgn. adminstrn., pres. Sears, Roebuck & Co. (Sears subsidiary), Bogota, Colombia, 1953-55; v.p. fgn. ops. Sears, Roebuck & Co., 1955-60; v.p., dir. southwestern ter. Sears, Roebuck & Co. (Sears subsidiary), 1960-66, v.p., dir. Eastern ter., 1966-69, v.p. corp. planning, 1973-78, sr. v.p. public affairs, 1978-81; ret., 1980; asst. sec. state for inter-Am. affairs, 1969-73; bd. dirs. Addison Capital Shares. Life trustee Children's Meml. Hosp. Chgo., Art Inst. Chgo., Lake Forest (Ill.) Coll.; trustee emeritus Phillips Acad., Andover, Mass. Capt. AUS, World War II. Clubs: Harvard (N.Y.C.); Racquet (Chgo.); Old Elm (Ft. Sheridan, Ill.); Shoreacres (Lake Bluff, Ill.); Metropolitan (Washington). Home: 1320 N Sheridan Rd Lake Forest IL 60045-1444 Office: 135 S La Salle St Chicago IL 60603-4105

MEYER, DANIEL JOSEPH, machinery company executive; b. Flint, Mich., May 31, 1936; s. John Michael and Margaret (Meehan) M.; m. Bonnie Harrison, June 22, 1963; children—Daniel P., Jennifer. B.S., Purdue U., 1958; M.B.A., Ind. U., 1963. C.P.A., N.Y. Mgr. Touche, Ross & Co., Detroit, 1964-69; contr. Cin. Milacron, Inc., 1969-77, v.p. fin., treas., 1977-83, exec. v.p. fin. and adminstrn., 1983-86, pres., chief operating officer, 1987-90, pres., chief exec. officer, 1990-91, chmn., chief exec. officer, 1991-92, also bd. dirs.; bd. dirs. E.W. Scripps Inc., Hubbell Inc., Star Bank Corp. Served with U.S. Army, 1959. Mem. Am. Inst. C.P.A.'s. Club: Kenwood Country (Cin.). Home: 8 Grandin Ln Cincinnati OH 45208-3304 Office: Cin Milacron Inc 4701 Marburg Ave Cincinnati OH 45209-1025

MEYER, DANIEL KRAMER, real estate executive; b. Denver, July 15, 1957; s. Milton Edward and Mary (Kramer) M. Student, Met. State Coll., Denver, 1977-78, U. Colo., 1978-80. Ptnr., developer RM & M II (Ltd. Partnership), Englewood, Colo., 1981-87; pres. Centennial Mortgage and Investment, Ltd., Englewood, Colo., 1984-87; prin. Capriole Properties, Greenwood Village, Colo., 1983—. Alumni mem. bd. trustees Kent Denver Country Day Sch., 1981-83; sec. dist. 37 ctrl. and vacancy com. Colo. Ho. of Reps., 1991-92. Recipient Pamela Davis Beardsley devel. award Kent Denver Sch., 1995. Mem. Greenwood Athletic Club. Republican. Avocations: climbing, rollerblading, political economy, 20th century English lit., metaphysics.

MEYER, DENNIS IRWIN, lawyer; b. Dayton, Ohio, Oct. 20, 1935; s. Luther Edward and Mary (McGee) M.; m. Rita Murray, June 23, 1962; children: Matthew, Michael, Rita Catherine, Peter, Denise, Abigail. BS, U. Dayton, 1957; LLB, Georgetown U., 1960, LLM, 1962. Bar: Ohio 1960, D.C. 1962. Atty.-advisor U.S. Tax Ct., Washington, 1960-62; ptnr. Baker & McKenzie, Washington, 1965—; bd. dirs. United Fin. Banking Cos., Vienna, Va., Splty. Retailing, College Park, Md., Oakwood Homes, Greensboro, N.C., Daily Express, Inc., Carlisle, Pa.; gen. ptnr. Potomac Investment Assoc., Md., 1976—. Mem. ABA, Internat. Fiscal Assn., Met. Club, 1925 F Street Club of Washington, Belle Haven Country Club, Avenel Golf Club, Robert Trent Jones Golf Club. Roman Catholic. Office: Baker & McKenzie 815 Connecticut Ave NW Washington DC 20006-4004

MEYER, DONALD GORDON, college dean, educator; b. St. Louis, Nov. 5, 1934; s. William Gordon and Grace Frances (Picraux) M.; m. Marilyn Lee Nathan, June 9, 1956; children: Wayne, Kathleen. BA, Blackburn Coll., 1956; MA, Northwestern U., 1959, PhD, 1965. Instr. econs. Oberlin (Ohio) Coll., 1959-60; lectr. Northwestern U., Evanston, Ill., spring 1960; mem. faculty Loyola U., Chgo., 1961—, assoc. prof. mktg., 1967-70, prof., chmn. dept., 1970—; dir. Loyola U. Grad. Sch. Bus., Chgo., 1975-77; dean Loyola U. Sch. Bus. Adminstrn., Chgo., 1977—; rsch. cons. Lerner Newspapers,

1964-72; mem. adv. bd. regional econ. seminars Ill. Bell Telephone Co., 1968-69; bd. dirs. Binks Mfg. Co. Trustee Blackburn Coll., Carlinville, Ill., 1973-82. Scholar Northwestern U., 1956-57; fellow, 1957-58; rsch. fellow, 1958-59; recipient Wall St. Jour. award, 1956. Mem. Am. Mktg. Assn., Am. Econs. Assn., Am. Inst. Decision Scis. (editor Mktg. Insights 1969). Home: 1868 Grove St #G Glenview IL 60025 Office: Loyola U Sch Bus Adminstrn 820 N Michigan Ave Chicago IL 60611-2103

MEYER, DONALD RAY, psychologist, brain researcher; b. Rhineland, Mo., July 31, 1924; s. Julius Caesar and Annie Laurie (Wagner) M.; m. Patricia Lee Morgan, Dec. 31, 1957; 1 child, Julia Catherine. A.B., U. Mo., 1947; M.S., U. Wis., 1948, Ph.D., 1950. Asst. prof. psychology Ohio State U., Columbus, 1950-51, assoc. prof. psychology, 1951-57, prof. psychology, 1957-85, prof. emeritus, 1985—; dir. lab. comparative and physiol. psychology Ohio State U., Columbus, 1958-85. Consulting editor to various jours.; contbr. articles to profl. jours. Served with USAF, 1943-46. Fellow AAAS, APA (pres. div. comparative and physiol. psychology 1975), Midwestern Psychol. Assn. (pres. 1971), Soc. Exptl. Psychologists, Am. Psychol. Soc., Phi Beta Kappa, Sigma Xi. Republican. Calvinist. Achievements include participation in Project Mercury, 1st manned space program. Avocation: arborist. Home: 476 Overbrook Dr Columbus OH 43214-3127 Office: Dept Psychology Ohio State U 1885 Neil Ave Columbus OH 43210-1222

MEYER, DONALD ROBERT, banker, lawyer; b. Phoenix, June 4, 1942; s. Donald Duncan and Eleanor M.; m. Virginia Whitesel, Sept. 3, 1966; 2 children. AB, U. Calif., Berkeley, 1964, JD, 1967; postgrad. Harvard U. Sch. Bus. Adminstrn., 1968. Bar: Calif. 1972. Lectr. Seoul Nat. Univ., Korea, 1969-70; assoc. Graham & James, San Francisco, 1971-76; asst. sec. Calif. First Bank (name now Union Bank), San Francisco, 1973-76, v.p., 1976-78, gen. counsel, 1976-96, sr. v.p., 1978-96; corp. sec., exec. v.p. gen. counsel Union Bank Cal Corp., 1996—. Contbr.: Intro to the Law & Legal System of Korea, 1983. Mem. World Affairs Council, San Francisco, Sierra Club; co-chmn. San Francisco/Seoul Sister City Com., 1980-90; trustee Asian Art Found. of San Francisco, 1985-92; commr. Asian Art Mus., San Francisco, 1985-91. Recipient Key to Seoul, Korea, 1984. Mem. ABA, San Francisco Bar Assn., Am. Bankers Assn. (v.p. Calif. State 1982-83), Calif. Bankers Assn. (chmn. legal affairs com. 1982-84, svc. award 1989), Korean-Am. C. of C. (dir. San Francisco sec., bd. dirs. 1974-93), Soc. Calif. Pioneers, Univ. Club of San Francisco, Bohemian Club. Republican. Episcopalian. Office: Union Bank 350 California St San Francisco CA 94104-1402

MEYER, EDMOND GERALD, energy and natural resources educator, resources scientist, entrepreneur, former chemistry educator, university administrator; b. Albuquerque, Nov. 2, 1919; s. Leopold and Beatrice (Ilfeld) M.; m. Betty F. Knobloch, July 4, 1941; children: Lee Gordon, Terry Gene, David Gary. B.S. in Chemistry, Carnegie Mellon U., 1940, M.S., 1942; Ph.D., U. N.Mex., 1950. Chemist Harbison Walker Refractories Co., 1940-41; instr. Carnegie Mellon U., 1941-42; asst. phys. chemist Bur. Mines, 1942-44; chemist research div. N.Mex. Inst. Mining and Tech., 1946-48; head dept. sci. U. Albuquerque, 1950-52; head dept. chemistry N.Mex. Highlands U., 1952-59; dir. Inst. Sci. Rsch., 1957-63; dean Grad. Sch., 1961-63; dean Coll. Arts and Sci., U. Wyo., 1963-75, v.p., 1974-80, prof. energy and natural resources, 1981-87, prof. and dean emeritus, 1987—; exec. cons. Diamond Shamrock Corp., 1980; bd. dirs. Carbon Fuels Corp., First Nat. Bank, Laramie; sci. adviser Gov. of Wyo., 1964-90; pres. Coal Tech. Corp., 1981—; cons. Los Alamos Nat. Lab., NFS, HHS, GAO, Wyo. Bancorp; contractor investigator Rsch. Corp., Dept. Interior, AEC, NIH, NSF, Dept. Energy, Dept. Edn.; Fulbright exch. prof. U. Concepcion, Chile, 1959. Co-author: Chemistry-Survey of Principles, 1963, Legal Rights of Chemists and Engineers, 1977, Industrial Research & Development Management, 1982; contbr. articles to profl. jours.; patentee in field. Chair, Laramie Regional Airport Bd., 1989-93, treas., 1994—. Lt. comdr. USNR, 1944-46, ret. Recipient Disting. Svc. award Jaycees; rsch. fellow U. N.Mex., 1948-50. Fellow AAAS, Am. Inst. Chemists (pres. 1992-93, chmn. 1994-95); mem. Assoc. Western Univs. (chmn. 1972-74), Am. Chem. Soc. (councilor 1962-90, chmn. Wyo. sect. 1997), Biophys. Soc., Coun. Coll. Arts and Scis. (pres. 1971, sec.-treas. 1972-75), dir. Washington office 1973), Laramie C. of C. (pres. 1984), Sigma Xi. Home: 1058 Colina Dr Laramie WY 82070-5015 Office: U Wyo Dept Energy & Natural Resources Laramie WY 82071-3825

MEYER, EDWARD HENRY, advertising agency executive; b. N.Y.C., Jan. 8, 1927; s. I.H. and Mildred (Driesen) M.; m. Sandra Raabin, Apr. 26, 1957; children: Margaret Ann, Anthony Edward. B.A. with honors in Econs, Cornell U., 1949. With Bloomingdale's div. Federated Dept Stores, 1949-51, Biow Co. (agy.), 1951-56; with Grey Advt., Inc., N.Y.C., 1956—; exec. v.p. Grey Advt., Inc., 1963-68, pres., chief exec. officer, 1968—, chmn. bd., 1970—; bd. dirs. May Dept. Stores co., Ethan Allan Interiors Inc., Harman Internat. Industries, Inc., Bowne & Co., Inc.; bd. dirs., trustee various mut. funds Merrill Lynch Asset Mgmt., Inc. Trustee Am. Mus. Natural History, Guggenheim Mus.; bd. dirs. NYU Med. Ctr., Film Soc. of Lincoln Ctr. With USCGR, 1945-47. Mem. Econ. Club (N.Y.C.), Century Country Club, Harmonie Club (N.Y.C.), Univ. Club (N.Y.C.). Office: Grey Advt Inc 777 3rd Ave New York NY 10017

MEYER, EDWARD N., lawyer; b. Bklyn., Mar. 8, 1939. BS, U. Wis., 1960; LLB, Columbia U., 1963. Bar: N.Y. 1964, U.S. Dist. Ct. (so. and ea. dists.) N.Y. 1970, U.S. Supreme Ct. 1976. Ptnr. Winston & Strawn, N.Y.C. Mem. ABA, N.Y. State Bar Assn., N.Y. County Lawyers Assn. Office: Winston & Strawn 200 Park Ave New York NY 10166-4193

MEYER, EDWARD PAUL, advertising executive; b. Chgo., May 23, 1949; s. Edward and Eleanor Kathryn (DeJong) M.; m. Marsha L. Tower, Aug. 10, 1974; children: Paul Edward, Sarah Linnea. BA in Econs. and Bus. Adminstrn., Wheaton (Ill.) Coll., 1971, MA in Comm., 1983. Asst. dir. Wheaton Coll. Alumni Assn., 1972-81; v.p. corp. comm. The Yarmouth Group, Inc. (formerly Richard Ellis Co.), Chgo., 1981-88, sr. v.p., 1988—; cons. mktg. Service Auto Glass, Lombard, Ill., 1979—. Active with Coll. Ch. Wheaton, 1974—; pres., bd. dirs. Crusader Club Wheaton Coll., 1985-88; bd. dirs. Christian Svc. Brigade, Wheaton, 1985—, chmn., 1991—. Mem. Pub. Rels. Soc. Am., Internat. Assn. Bus. Communicators. Republican. Home: 1303 E Harrison Ave Wheaton IL 60187-4422 Office: The Yarmouth Group Two Prudential Pla Ste 1300 Chicago IL 60601

MEYER, EDWIN DALE, SR., school system administrator; b. Peoria, Ill., Sept. 2, 1943; s. Dale Lorenzo and Alice Eva (Bell) M.; m. Sharon Anne Allen, Dec. 26, 1966; children: Wendy Kimryn Meyer Rathmell, Edwin Dale II, John C. BS in Edn., Peru (Nebr.) State Coll., 1965; MS in Edn., U. Nebr., Kearney, 1974; EdS, U. Nebr., Omaha, 1985; EdD, Drake U., 1992. Tchr. Red Oak (Iowa) Community Sch. Dist., 1965-66, Bellevue (Nebr.) Pub. Schs., 1966-67, 69-78, Hildreth (Nebr.) Pub. Sch., 1968-69; grad. instr. ctrl. office adminstrn. Kearney State Coll., 1967-69; prin. Woodbine (Iowa) Ctrl. Sch. Dist., 1978-82; supr. schs. Sheffield (Iowa)-Chapin Ctrl. Sch. Dist., 1982-86, Missouri Valley (Iowa) Ctrl. Sch. Dist., 1986-93; supt. schs. Richland (Wis.) Sch. Dist., 1993—; presenter in field. Mem. Bellevue City Coun., 1976-79; bd. dirs. Monona Svcs. Industries, Missouri Valley, 1991-93; pres. Missouri Valley Devel. Coun., 1988-93; mem. Iowa Bus. and Edn. Task Force Com., 1987; active Boy Scouts Am. Doctoral fellow Iowa Scottish Rite, 1991. Mem. Masons, Kiwanis (pres.), Phi Delta Kappa. Republican. Roman Catholic. Avocations: beekeeping, rescue squad. Home: RR 3 Box 80-a-i Richland Center WI 53581-9803

MEYER, EUGENE CARLTON, retired editor; b. McGregor, Iowa, Dec. 10, 1923; s. Gilbert Nelson and Christine Winnifred (Henkes) M.; m. Maxine Beth Mallory, June 1, 1947; children—Bruce, Mary Lynn, John. B.S., Iowa State U., 1946. Farm news editor Sta. WHO, Des Moines, 1947-48; assoc. editor Hoard's Dairyman, Fort Atkinson, Wis., 1948-72, mng. editor, 1972-88. Trustee Fort Atkinson Meml. Hosp., 1966-81, pres. bd. trustees, 1976-81. Navigator, USAAF. Recipient Disting. Service award Am. Dairy Sci. Assn., 1980, Disting. Grad. award Iowa State Dairy Sci. Club, Iowa State U., 1981, Agrl. Leadership award Alpha Gamma Rho, 1982, Award of Distinction U. Wis.-Madison, 1982, Disting. Citizen of Agr. Nat. Milk Producers, 1988, Henry A. Wallace award Iowa State U., 1989, Richard E. Lyng award, 1989; named Industry Person of Yr. World Dairy Expo, 1988. Mem. Nat. Dairy Shrine (pres. 1980, Guest of Hon. 1986). Republican. Methodist. Home: 524 Jackson St Fort Atkinson WI 53538-1356

MEYER, F. WELLER, bank executive; b. Washington, Dec. 15, 1942; s. Martin William and Sallie Rita (Weller) M.; m. Brenda Burton, Sept. 27, 1972; children: F. Weller Jr., Brandon Michael. BS, U. Md., 1977. V.p. W.S. Steed Mortgage Co., Wheaton, Md., 1970-73; asst. dir. Mortgage Bankers Assn., Washington, 1973-77; mng. dir. Mortgage Systems Corp., Bethesda, Md., 1977-83; pres., chief executive officer Westmark Mortgage Corp., Rockville, Md., 1983-87, Acacia Fed. Savs. Bank, Falls Church, Va., 1987—; dir. Acacia Federal Svcs. Bank, Acacia Svc. Corp., Falls Church, Calvert Group Ltd., Am.'s Cmty. Bankers, Va. Bankers Assn. Co-author: Residential Mortgage Underwriting, 1981, Consturction Lending—Residential, 1981, Construction Lending—Residential Income Property, 1981, Income Property Underwriting, 1981. Dir. Make-A-Wish Found. of the Mid-Atlantic, No. Va. Comty. Found., Fairfax, Va., 1989; mem. Citizen's Housing Adv. Com., Montgomery County, Md., 1988-90. 1st lt. U.S. Army, 1967-70, Vietnam. Mem. Optimists (pres. Washington 1978-79). Republican. Roman Catholic. Avocations: golf, hunting, jogging. Home: 9809 Kendale Rd Rockville MD 20854-4246

MEYER, FRANCES MARGARET ANTHONY, elementary and secondary school educator, health education specialist; b. Stella, Va., Nov. 15, 1947; d. Arthur Abner Jr. and Emmie Adeline (Murray) Anthony; m. Stephen Leroy Meyer, Aug. 2, 1975. BS, Longwood Coll., 1970; MS, Va. Commonwealth U., 1982, PhD, 1996. Cert. tchr., Va. Health, phys. edn., and dance tchr. Fredericksburg (Va.) City Pub. Schs., 1970-89; AIDS edn. coord. Va. Dept. Edn., Richmond, 1989-90, health edn. specialist, 1990-94, comprehensive sch. health program specialist, 1994—. Author: (with others) Elementary Physical Education: Growing through Movement--A Curriculum Guide, 1982; health editor Va. Jour., 1994—; contbr. articles to profl. jours. Mem. pub. edn. coun., comprehensive sch. health edn. team Va. affiliate, Am. Cancer Soc., Richmond, 1990—; dir. Va. Children's Dance Festival, Hist. Fredericksburg Found., Inc., 1981—; vol. ARC, Fredericksburg, 1976-84. Mem. AAUW (com. 1989-90), ASCD, NEA, AAPHERD (past v.p., chmn. divsn. 1970—, mem. Nat. Mid. Sch. Assn., So. Dist. Honor award 1995), Va. Edn. Assn., Va. Mid. Sch. Assn., Va. Alliance for Arts Edn., Internat. Coun. for Health, Phys. Edn., Recreation, Sport and Dance, Va. Health Promotion and Edn. Coun. (bd. dirs. 1990—), Soc. State Dirs. Health, Phys. Edn. and Recreation (legis. affairs com. 1994—), Longwood Coll. Alumni Coun. (bd. dirs. 1987-90), Nat. Network for Youth Svcs. (rev. panel, adv. bd. 1994—), Am. Coll. Health Assn. (curriculum and tng. rev. panel 1992-94), Va. Alliance for Arts Edn. (adv. bd. 1980-83, 89-90, 95—), Va. Assn. for Health, Phys. Edn., Recreation and Dance (past pres., various coms. 1970—, Tchr. of Yr. 1983), Delta Kappa Gamma (pres. Beta Eta chpt. 1988-90), Nat. Dance Assn. (bd. dirs. 1996—). Baptist. Avocations: traveling, dancing, swimming, reading, attending theatrical performances.

MEYER, FRED JOSEF, advertising executive; b. Zurich, Switzerland, Jan. 1, 1931; came to U.S., 1959; s. Josef and Claire (Lehmann) M.; m. Beverly Ruth Carter, Apr. 9, 1961 (div. Feb. 1975); children: Fred Jay, Marcus Clinton, Michael Josef; m. Marie-Noelle Vigneron, Oct. 30, 1975. MS, Fed. Inst. Tech., Zurich, 1956; MBA, Harvard U., 1961; LLD (hon.), Sacred Heart U., 1981. Vice pres. plannng and adminstrn. Sandoz Inc., Hanover, N.J., 1971-73, exec. v.p., chief fin. officer, 1973-78; pres., chief exec. officer Sandoz U.S., Inc., Greenwich, Conn., 1978-81; mng. dir., chief exec. officer Wander Ltd., Berne, Switzerland, 1981-82; sr. v.p., chief fin. officer CBS Inc., N.Y.C., 1982-88; chief fin. officer, bd. dirs. Omnicom Group, Inc., N.Y.C., 1988—; bd. dirs. Zurich-Am. Ins. Cos., Ill., SoGen Internat. Fund, Inc., N.Y.C., SoGen Funds, Inc., N.Y.C., Sandoz Corp., SyStemix, Inc., Palo Alto, Calif. Mem. Fin. Execs. Inst., Econ. Club, Harvard Club (N.Y.C.), Greenwich Country Club. Republican. Presbyterian. Office: Omnicom Group Inc 437 Madison Ave New York NY 10022-7001

MEYER, FRED WILLIAM, JR., memorial parks executive; b. Fair Haven, Mich., Jan. 7, 1924; s. Fred W. and Gladys (Marshall) M.; m. Jean Hope, Aug. 5, 1946; children—Frederick, Thomas, James, Nancy. AB, Mich. State Coll., 1946. Salesman Chapel Hill Meml. Gardens, Lansing, Mich., 1946-47; mgr. Roselawn Meml. Gardens, Saginaw, Mich., 1947-49; dist. mgr. Sunset Meml. Gardens, Evansville, Ind., 1949-53; pres., dir. Memory Gardens Mgmt. Corp., Indpls., Hamilton Meml. Gardens, Chattanooga, Covington Meml. Gardens, Ft. Wayne, Ind., Chapel Hill Meml. Gardens, Grand Rapids, Mich., Forest Lawn Memory Gardens, Indpls., Lincoln Memory Gardens, Indpls., Sherwood Meml. Gardens, Knoxville, Tenn., Chapel Hill Meml. Gardens, South Bend, Ind., White Chapel Meml. Gardens, Springfield, Mo., Nebo Meml. Park, Martinsville, Ind., Mercury Devel. Corp., Indpls., Quality Marble Imports, Indpls., Quality Printers, Indpls., Am. Bronze Craft, Inc., Judsonia, Ark. Mem. C. of C., A.I.M., Am. Cemetery Assn., Sigma Chi, Phi Kappa Delta. Clubs: Columbia, Meridian Hills Country, Woodland Country. Home: 110 E 111th St Indianapolis IN 46280-1051 Office: 3733 N Meridian St Indianapolis IN 46208-4305

MEYER, G. CHRISTOPHER, lawyer; b. Fremont, Nebr., Mar. 27, 1948; s. Gerald William and Mildred Ruth (Clausen) M.; m. Linda Haines, Dec. 27, 1969; children: Katie, Stacy, Jon, Robert. Student, Grinnell (Iowa) Coll., 1966-69; BA, U. Kans., 1970; JD, U. Pa., 1973. Bar: Ohio 1973, U.S. Dist. Ct. (no. dist.) Ohio 1975, U.S. Ct. Appeals (6th cir.) 1982. Assoc. Squire, Sanders & Dempsey, Cleve., 1973-82, ptnr., 1982—. Mem. ABA, Ohio State Bar Assn., Greater Cleve. Bar Assn. Office: Squire Sanders & Dempsey 4900 Society Ctr 127 Public Sq Cleveland OH 44114-1304

MEYER, GEORGE GOTTHOLD, psychiatrist, educator; b. Frankfurt, Germany, Nov. 13, 1931; came to U.S., 1941, naturalized, 1946; s. Hans and Hilda (Lesser) M.; m. Paula Saslaw, June 17, 1953; children: Bruce Alan, Brian Lee, Barry Dale. B.A., Johns Hopkins U., 1951; M.D., U. Chgo., 1955. Diplomate: Am. Bd. Psychiatry and Neurology (asst. examiner 1979—). Intern USPHS Hosp., Staten Island, N.Y., 1955-56; resident in psychiatry U. Chgo. Hosps. and Clinics, 1958-60, chief resident, 1960-61, chief psychiat. inpatient service, 1966-69; mem. faculty U. Chgo. Med. Sch., 1961-69, assoc. prof. psychiatry, 1968-69; assoc. prof. psychiatry U. Tex. Med. Sch., San Antonio, 1969-71; prof. U. Tex. Health Sci. Ctr., San Antonio, 1971—, clin. prof., 1982—; dir. N.W. San Antonio Mental Health Ctr., 1969-74; mem. exec. bd. Crisis Ctr., San Antonio, 1971-75; cons. VA Hosp., San Antonio and Kerrville, Tex., Kerrville State Hosp., San Antonio State Hosp., Santa Rosa Hosp., Santa Rosa Children's Hosp., Jewish Family Svc., 1980-86, Cath. Family Svcs.; active staff Villa Rosa Hosp., Meth. Hosp.; courtesy staff Regional Hosp., Charter Real Hosp., Mission Fiesta Hosp., Univ. Hosp.; psychiat. cons. Dallas Office, NIMH, 1970-81; also psychiatry edn. br., 1978-82; med. dir. Mex. Am. Unity Coun., San Antonio, 1970-80; vis. lectr. psychiatry U. Edinburgh (Scotland) Med. Sch., 1966; vis. prof. psychiatry U. Man. (Can.) Winnipeg, 1977; mem. med. adv. bd. for driver licensing Tex. Dept. Health, 1973-78. Author 4 books; contbr. numerous articles to med. jours. Bd. dirs., cons. Ecumenical Ctr. Religion and Health San Antonio, 1974-86; bd. dirs. Cmty. Guidance Ctr. of Bexar County, 1979-81; bd. dirs., cons. Jewish Family Svc., San Antonio, 1980-86. Served with USPHS, 1955-58. NIMH career tchr. grantee, 1961-63; recipient Okie award Gov. Okla., 1969. Fellow APA, Am. Psychiat. Assn. (life); mem. Tex. and Bexar County Med. Assns., Tex., Bexar County and World Psychiat. Assns., Am. Coll. Psychiatrists, Biofeedback Soc. Tex. (dir. 1980-82), Sigma Xi, Alpha Omega Alpha, Phi Lambda Upsilon. Home: 2907 Marlborough Dr San Antonio TX 78230-4427 Office: 4499 Medical Dr Ste 267 San Antonio TX 78229-3712

MEYER, GEORGE HERBERT, lawyer; b. Detroit, Feb. 19, 1928; s. Herbert M. and Agnes F. (Eaton) M.; m. Carol Ann Jones, 1958 (div. 1981) children: Karen Ann, George Herbert Jr.; m. Katherine Palmer White, Nov. 12, 1988. A.B., U. Mich., 1949; J.D., Harvard U., 1952; cert., Oxford (Eng.) U., 1955; LL.M. in Taxation, Wayne State U., 1962. Bar: D.C. bar 1952, Mich. bar 1953. Assoc. firm Fischer, Franklin & Ford, Detroit, 1956-63; mem. firm Fischer, Franklin & Ford, 1963-74; established firm George H. Meyer, 1974-78; sr. mem. firm Meyer and Kirk, 1978-85; sr. mem. Meyer, Kirk, Snyder & Safford PLLC, Bloomfield Hills and Detroit, Mich., 1985—; curator Step Lively exhibit Mus. Am. Folk Art, N.Y.C., 1992; lectr. Am. Folk Art. Author: Equalization in Michigan and Its Effect on Local Assessments, 1963, Folk Artists Biographical Index, 1986, American Folk Art Canes: Personal Sculpture, 1992. Chmn. Birmingham (Mich.) Bd. Housing Appeals, 1964-68; vice chmn. Birmingham Bd. Zoning Appeals, 1966-69; mem. Birmingham Planning Bd., 1968-70; trustee, Bloomfield Village, Mich., 1976-80, pres., 1979-80; trustee Mus. Am. Folk Arts, N.Y.C., 1987—; mem. exec. bd. Detroit Area coun. Boy Scouts Am., 1976—, counsel, 1986—; mem. nat. adv. bd. Folk Art Soc. Am., 1994—; trustee Detroit Sci. Ctr., 1985—. 1st lt. JAG, USAF, 1952-55, maj. Res. ret. Recipient Silver Beaver award Detroit Area coun. Boy Scouts Am., 1989. Mem. ABA, Detroit Bar Assn., Oakland County Bar Assn., State Bar Mich., Harvard Law Sch. Assn. Mich. (dir. 1959—, pres. 1970-78), Detroit Sci. Mus. Soc. (pres. 1961-74, chmn. 1974—), Am. Folk Art Soc., Prismatic Club, Scarab Club, Harvard Club (N.Y.C.), Detroit Club, Masons, Rotary, Phi Beta Kappa, Alpha Phi Omega. Republican. Unitarian. Home: Meyer Kirk Snyder & Stafford PLLC Ste 100 100 W Long Lake Rd Bloomfield Hills MI 48301-2242 Office: Meyer Kirk Snyder & Stafford 100 W Long Lake Rd Ste 100 Bloomfield Hills MI 48304-2773

MEYER, GRACE TOMANELLI, lawyer; b. Bklyn., Aug. 7, 1935; d. Cosmo and Grace (Giabia) Tomanelli; m. Heinz Meyer, May 26, 1956; children: Kenneth, Carolyn, Christa, Karla. BA, Ramapo Coll. of N.J., 1975; JD, Seton Hall U., 1978. Bar: N.J. 1978, U.S. Supreme Ct. 1983, N.Y. 1988. Adminstrv. sec. U.S. Atomic Energy Commn., N.Y.C., 1955-58; assoc. lawyer Beattie & Padovano, Montvale, N.J., 1978-80; counselor Grace T. Meyer Law offices, River Vale, N.J., 1980—; adj. prof. Ramapo Coll., 1980, 81, Nyack Coll., 1994, 95; facilitator Pressing Onward, Pascack Bible Ch., Hillsdale, 1991—. Contbr. various articles to profl. jours. Honored for pro bono work by Bergen County Legal Svcs., 1993. Mem. N.J. Bar Assn., Bergen County Bar Assn., Christian Legal Soc., Rutherford Inst., Concerned Women for Am., Am. Family Assn. Republican. Avocations: writing, counseling, walking, arts and crafts. Office: Grace T Meyer Law Offices 669 Westwood Ave Ste H River Vale NJ 07675-6336

MEYER, GREG CHARLES, psychiatrist; b. Bismarck, N.D., Aug. 17, 1935; s. Oscar Clarence and Agnes Josephine (Pearson) M. Degree in profl. engring., Colo. Sch. Mines, 1958, Alexander Hamilton Bus. Inst., 1960; MME, U. So. Calif., 1965; MD, Marquette U., 1970. Diplomate Am. Bd. Psychiatry and Neurology. Engr. Minuteman-Thiokol, Brigham City, Utah, 1958-61; sr. engr. Saturn S-II N.Am. Aviation, Downey, Calif., 1962-65; design specialist Titan-Martin, Denver, 1965-66; rotating intern Weld Country Gen. Hosp., Greenly, Colo., 1970-71; psychiatric resident Ariz. State Hosp., Phoenix, 1971-74, psychiatrist, 1974-76; pvt. practice Mesa, Ariz., 1975-94; psychiatrist Ariz. Ctrl. Med. Ctr., 1994—; psychiatrist Ariz. Ctrl. Med. Ctr.; chmn. psychiatry Desert Samaritan Hosp., Mesa, 1982-86, 90-94, chmn. joint mental health, 1981-83, mem. edn. com., 1979-82, quality assurance com., 1979; mem. exec. com. Desert Vista Hosp., Mesa, 1988-94, chief of staff, 1989; chmn. psychiatry Mesa Luth. Hosp., 1984-85, mem. exec. com., 1984-85; mng. ptnr. Desert Samaritan Med. Bldg. II, Mesa, 1985-86; rsch., edn. com. East Valley Camel Back Hosp., 1989-90, quality assurance com., 1985; psychiatrist Ctrl. Ariz. Med. Ctr., 1995. Co-discoverer Larson-Meyer Transform. Coach Pop Warner Football, 1974. With USMCR, 1953-59. Mem. AMA, Am. Psychiatric Assn., Ariz. Med. Assn., Ariz. Psychiatric Assn., Phoenix Psychiatric Coun., Maricopa County Med. Assn., Christian Med./Dental Assn., Triple Nine Soc. Republican. Lutheran. Avocations: multi engine instrument pilot, sailing, computers, canoeing, photography.

MEYER, GREGORY TOBIN, city official, public administration executive; b. L.A., June 12, 1942; s. Glenn Harold and Kathryn Gertrude (Lyons) M.; m. Susan L. Rehshaw, Aug. 27, 1971 (div. 1992). BA in Pub. Adminstrn., Calif. State U., L.A., 1964; MS in Pub. Adminstrn., 1967; cert. in Urban mgmt., MIT, Cambridge, 1977. Cert. cmty. coll. tchr., Calif. Adminstrn. intern City of Pasadena, Calif., 1963-64; adminstrn. aide City of Alhambra, Calif., 1965-66; asst. to city mgr. City of Pasadena, Calif., 1966-72; deputy city mgr. City of Torrance, Calif., 1972-79; city mgr. City of Coachella, Calif., 1979-81, City of Hermosa Beach, Calif., 1981-87; deputy adminstr. Cmty. Redevelelopment Agy., City of L.A., 1987—. Author: Total Compensation Costing in California Cities, 1976, Orienting Elected Officials in California Cities, 1977. Pres. Greater Pasadena (Calif.) Kiwanis, 1970; pres., exec. dir. Nat. Coun. on Sexual Addiction and Compulsivity, Tucson, 1990-91; pres. Men's Guild, St. George's Episc. Ch., Hawthorne, 1994-95, Episc. lay eucharist min.. Staff sgt. U.S. Army, 1966-71. Named Com. Chmn. of Yr. Pasadena (Calif.) Jaycees, 1969. Mem. Bus. Profl. Assn. L.A., Gay Fathers, Lambda Alumni UCLA and USC, South Coast Chorale. Avocations: choral singing, camping, hiking, swimming. Home: 1515 Prospect Ave Hermosa Beach CA 90254-3334

MEYER, HARRY MARTIN, JR., retired health science facility administrator; b. Palestine Tex., Nov. 25, 1928. s. Harry Martin and Marjory Isabel (Griffin) M.; m. Mary Jane Martin, Aug. 19, 1949 (div. 1966); children: Harry, Mary, David; m. Barbara Story Chalfort, Nov. 21, 1966. BS Hendrix Coll., 1949, MD U. Ark., 1953; Diplomate Am. Bd. Pediatics, 1960. instr. biology Little Rock Coll., 1949, intern. Walter Reed Army Hosp., Washington, 1953-54, med. officer dep. virus and rickettsial diseases, Walter Reed Army Inst. Rsch., 1954-57, asst. resident dep. pediatrics, N.C. Meml. Hosp., Chapel Hill, 1957-59, head virology sect. div. biologics standards, NIH, Bethesda, Md., 1959-64, chief lab. of viral immunol., div. biologics standards, NIH, 1964-72, dir. bur. biologics FDA, Bethesda, 1972-82, dir. Ctr. for Drugs & Biologics FDA, Rockville, Md., 1982-86, pres. med. research div. Am. Cyanamid Co., Pearl River, N.Y., 1986-93; retired 1993. Served to rear admiral USPHS, 1959-86, capt. U.S. Army, 1953-57. Mem. AMA, Am. Epidemiol. Soc., Am. Acad. Pediatrics, Am. Pediatric Soc. Protestant. Avocations: sailing, scuba diving, skiing, back packing. Conbr. articles to profl. jours.; patentee in field.

MEYER, HARVEY KESSLER, II, retired academic administrator; b. Carlisle, Pa., Feb. 6, 1914; s. Harvey Kessler and Frances May (Shultz) M.; m. Jessie Irene Hamm, Feb. 22, 1935; children: Carol Frances, Harvey Kessler III, Howard Madison. BA, Berea (Ky.) Coll., 1936; MA, Eastern Ky. U., 1942; D Edn., U. Fla., Gainesville, 1951. Surveyor Wash. State Hwy. Engrs., 1932; furniture designer Berea Woodwork, 1932-36; lic. contractor Bailey Constrn. Co., Seattle, Wash., 1935, Alachua County, Fla., 1948-50.; instr. U. Fla., Ocala, 1936-37; supr. Nat. Youth Adminstrn., Jacksonville, Fla., 1937-38; vocat. tchr. Richmond (Ky.) City Schs., 1938-40; asst. prof. Eastern Ky. U., Richmond, 1940-43; tchr. P.K.Yonge Lab. Sch., Gainesville, Fla., 1946-47, prin., 1947-48; assoc. prof. U. Fla., Gainesville, 1948-51, prof., 1951-65; assoc. dean acad. affairs Fla. Atlantic U., Boca Raton, 1965-68, grad. prof., 1968-73; dir. Indsl. Arts and Vocat. Edn., Managua, Nicaragua, 1955-57; founder Instituto Nacional Educacion Vocacional, Nicaragua; dir., trustee Moravian Theol. Sem., Bethlehem, Pa., 1976; dean radio and TV Fla. Inst. for Continuing Univ. Studies, 1962-65; adminstrv. cons. Brit.-Am. Investment Fund, Luxembourg City, Europe, 1969-71; owner, design Plantation Glen, Alachua County, 1948-77, Hacienda Ocotlan, Clay County, N.C., 1975-78. Author: Technical Eduction in Nicaragua, 1958, Historical Dictionary Nicaragua, 1972, Historical Dictionary Honduras, 1976, rev. edit., 1994. Pres. Fla. dist. Moravian Ch., 1970-73, Melrose (Fla.) Library Assn., 1983—, pres., 1984-90, 92—; trustee Moravian Coll. and Sem., 1966-78. Comdr. USNR, ret.; naval aviation observer. Named Disting. Alumnus Berea Coll., 1986. Mem. Berea Coll. Alumni Assn. (pres. 1990-91), Rotary, Phi Kappa Phi, Phi Delta Kappa, Epsilon Pi Tau (trustee 1950—). Democrat. Avocations: boating, architecture, pistol shooting, furniture design and building, archaeology. Home: Quinta la Maya Atlán 2805 NW 83d St #405C Gainesville FL 32606-6288

MEYER, HELEN (MRS. ABRAHAM J. MEYER), retired editorial consultant; b. Bklyn., Dec. 4, 1907; d. Bertolen and Esther (Greenfield) Honig; m. Abraham J. Meyer, Sept. 1, 1929; children—Adele Meyer Brodkin, Robert L. Grad. pub. schs. With Popular Sci., McCall's mag., 1921-22; pres., dir. Dell Pub. Co., Inc., N.Y.C., 1923-57, Dell Distbg., Inc., from 1957, Dell Internat., Inc., from 1957; pres. Dell Pub. Co., Inc., Montville Warehousing Co., Inc.; chmn. bd. Noble & Noble Pubs., Inc.; v.p. Dellprint, Inc., Dunellen, N.J.; pres. Dial Press.; later editorial cons. Doubleday & Co., N.Y.C.; cons. Fgn. Rights, N.Y.C. Bd. dirs. United Cerebral Palsy. Named to Pub.'s Hall of Fame, 1986. Mem. Assn. Am. Pubs. (dir.). Home: 1 Claridge Dr Apt 608 Verona NJ 07044-3054

MEYER, HORST, physics educator; b. Berlin, Germany, Mar. 1, 1926. BS, U. Geneva, 1949; PhD in physics, U. Zurich, 1953. Fellow Swiss Assn. Rsch. Physics and Math. Studies, Oxford, Eng., 1953-55; Nuffield fellow Clarendon Lab. U. Oxford, 1955-57; lectr., rsch. assoc. dept. engring. and applied physics Harvard U., Cambridge, Mass., 1957-59; from asst. prof. to prof. Duke U., Durham, N.C., 1959-84, Fritz London prof. physics, 1984—;

vis. prof. Technische Hochschule, Federal Republic of Germany, 1965, Tokyo U., 1980, 81, 83; traveling fellow Japanese Soc. for Promotion Sci., 1971, vis. scientist, 1979; guest scientist Inst. Laue-Langevin, France, 1974, 75; Yamada Found. fellow, Japan, 1986; guest scientist USSR Acad. Sci., 1988; chmn. Gordon Conf. on Solid H2, 1990; western chmn. conf. quantum crystals, Almaty, Kazakhstan, 1995. Editor Jour. Low Temperature Physics, 1992—, mem. editorial bd., 1988-92; contbr. articles to profl. jours. Alfred P. Sloan fellow, 1961-65. Fellow Am. Phys. Soc. (Jesse Beams prize, 1982, Fritz London prize 1993). Exptl. rsch. on the properties of liquid and solid helium, solid hydrogen and deuterium, magnetic insulators, critical phenomena. Office: Duke U Dept Physics PO Box 90305 Durham NC 27708-0305

MEYER, IRWIN STEPHAN, lawyer, accountant; b. Monticello, N.Y., Nov. 14, 1941; s. Ralph and Janice (Cohen) M.; children: Kimberly B., Joshua A. BS, Rider Coll., 1963; JD, Cornell U., 1966. Bar: N.Y. 1966; CPA, N.J. Tax mgr. Lybrand Ross Bros. & Montgomery, N.Y.C., 1966-71; mem. Ehrenkranz, Ehrenkranz & Schultz, N.Y.C., 1971-74; prin. Irwin S. Meyer, 1974-77, 82—; mem. Levine, Honig, Eisenberg & Meyer, 1977-78, Eisenberg, Honig & Meyer, 1978-81, Eisenberg, Honig, Meyer & Fogler, 1981-82. With U.S. Army, 1966-71. Mem. ABA, N.Y. Bar Assn., Am. Assn. Atty.-CPA, N.Y. Assn. Atty-CPA, N.J. Soc. CPA. Office: 1 Blue Hill Plz Ste 1006 Pearl River NY 10965-3104

MEYER, J. THEODORE, lawyer; b. Chgo., Apr. 13, 1936; s. Joseph Theodore and Mary Elizabeth (McHugh) M.; m. Marilu Bartholomew, Aug. 16, 1961; children: Jean, Joseph. B.S., John Carroll U., 1958; postgrad. U. Chgo.; J.D., DePaul U., 1962. Bar: Ill. 1962, U.S. Dist. Ct. (no. dist.) Ill. 1962. Ptnr. Bartholomew & Meyer, Chgo., 1963-83; mem. Ill. Gen. Assembly, House of Rep., 28th Legis. Dist., 1966-72, 74-82, chmn. House environ. study com., 1968; chmn. energy environ. com. and natural resources com.; mem. appropriations and exec. com.; chmn. Joint House/Senate com. to review state air and water plans, 1968; mem. Fed. State Task Force on Energy; chmn., founder Midwest Legis. Coun. on Environ., 1971; mem. State of Ill. Pollution Control Bd., Chgo., 1983—; mem. Joint Legis. Com. on Hazardous Waste in Lake Calumet Area, 1987; lectr. in field. Recipient Appreciation award Ill. Wildlife Fedn., 1972, Environ. Quality award Region V, EPA, 1974, Pro Bono Publico award Self-Help Action Ctr., 1975, Merit award Dept. Ill. VFW, 1977, Environ. Legislator of Yr. award Ill. Environ. Coun., 1978-79; Disting. Lawyer Legislator of Yr.; commd. hon. lt. aide-de-camp Ala. State Militia; commd. Hon. Tex. Citizen. Fellow Chgo. Bar Found.; mem. ABA, Ill. Bar Assn., Chgo. Bar Assn., Nat. Rep. Legis. Assn., Nat. Trust Hist. Preservation, Nat. Wildlife Fedn., Ill. Hist. Soc., Beverly Tennis Club, Beverly Hills Univ. Club. Republican. Roman Catholic. Office: State of Ill Ctr 100 W Randolph St Ste 11500 Chicago IL 60601-3220

MEYER, JACKIE MERRI, publishing executive; b. Phila., Oct. 19, 1954; d. George Gilbert Meyer and Sylvia Magerman; m. W. Scot Carouge, May 23, 1982. BFA, The Cooper Union, N.Y.C., 1977. Art dir. Macmillan Pub. Co., N.Y.C., 1980-85; v.p., creative dir. Warner Books, N.Y.C., 1985—; pub. Warner Treasures, An Imprint of Warner Books, 1995; tchr. Parsons Sch. Design, N.Y.C., 1984-85; lectr. Fashion Inst. Tech., N.Y.C., 1984-85, Am. Illustration, N.Y.C., 1984. Co-author: I Loathe New York, 1981. Fundraiser The Cooper Union, N.Y.C., 1977—. Recipient numerous profl. awards, orgns. including Advt. Club, Desi awards, Art Direction mag., Print mag., Graphis, Comm. Arts. Mem. AFTRA, Soc. Illustrators (bd. dirs. 1988—), Am. Inst. Graphic Arts (awards), Art Dirs. Club (awards). Avocations: photography, gardening, painting. Office: Warner Books Inc 1271 Avenue Of The Americas Fl 9 New York NY 10020

MEYER, JAROLD ALAN, oil company research executive; b. Phoenix, July 28, 1938; s. Lester M. and Anita (Walker) M.; m. Diane Louise Wheeler; children: Ronald Alan, Sharon Lynne. BSChemE, Calif. Inst. Tech., 1960, MS, 1961. Mgr. process devel. Chevron Rsch., Richmond, Calif., 1978-82; tech. mgr. Chevron U.S.A., El Segundo, Calif., 1982-84; v.p. process rsch. Chevron Rsch., Richmond, 1984-86, pres., 1986—; sr. v.p. Chevron Rsch. and Tech., Richmond, 1990-93; ret., 1993; prin. J.A. Meyer Assocs., Martinez, Calif., 1993—; bd. dirs. Solvent Refined Coal Internat., Inc., San Francisco; mem. adv. bd. Surface Sci. and Catalysis Program Ctr. for Advanced Materials, Lawrence Berkeley Lab., 1988-91; mem. adv. coun. Lawrence Hall Sci., 1989-94; indsl. advisor Accreditation bd. for Engring. and Tech. Inventor petroleum catalysts; contbr. articles to profl. jours. Bd. visitors U. Calif., Davis, 1986-93, trustee found., 1989—. Mem. Nat. Acad. Engring., Am. Chem. Soc., Nat. Petroleum Refining Assn., Indsl. Rsch. Inst., Conf. Bd. Internat. Rsch. Mgmt. Coun., Accreditation Bd. for Engring. and Tech. Indsl. Advisor, Sigma Xi, Tau Beta Pi. Avocations: electronics design and constrn., photography. Home and Office: 849 Corte Briones Martinez CA 94553-5950

MEYER, JEAN-PIERRE GUSTAVE, mathematician, educator; b. Lyon, Rhone, France, Aug. 5, 1929; s. Jules and Germaine (Becker) M.; m. Marily Noan Pettit, 1959; children: David, Susan, Steven, Alison, Nadine, Nicholas; m. Roselyne Fischer-LaVerton, 1996. BA, Cornell U., 1950, MS, 1951, PhD, 1954. Asst. prof. math. Syracuse (N.Y.) U., 1956; research assoc. math. Brown U., Providence, R.I., 1956-57; from asst. to assoc. to prof. Johns Hopkins U., Balt., 1957—, chmn. dept. math., 1985-90; dir. Japan-U.S. Math. Inst., 1992—. Co-author: Fundamental Structures of Algebra, 1963; contbr. articles to profl. jours. Served with U.S. Army, 1954-56. Grad. fellow NSF, 1953. Mem. Am. Math. Soc. Avocations: mineral collecting, archaeology. Home: 3601 Greenway Baltimore MD 21218-9999 Office: Johns Hopkins U Dept Math Baltimore MD 21218

MEYER, JEROME J., diversified technology company executive; b. Caledonia, Minn., Feb. 18, 1938; s. Herbert J. and Edna (Staggemeyer) M.; m. Sandra Ann Beaudoin, June 18, 1960; children—Randall Lee, Lisa Ann, Michelle Lynn. Student, Hamline U., 1956-58; B.A., U. Minn., 1960. Devel. engr. Firestone Tire & Rubber Co., Akron, Ohio, 1960-61; v.p., gen. mgr. Sperry Univac, St. Paul, 1961-79; group v.p. Honeywell, Inc., Mpls., 1979-84; pres., chief operating officer Varian Assocs., Palo Alto, Calif., 1984-86, also bd. dirs.; pres., chief exec. officer Honeywell Inc., 1986-90; from pres. to chmn., CEO Tektronix Inc., Beaverton, Oreg., 1990—; bd. dirs. Portland Gen. Corp., Esterline Tech., Oregon Bus. Coun., AMP. Trustee Oreg. Grad. Inst., Willamette U., Oreg. Children's Found. Mem. Oregon Golf Club. Avocation: golf. Office: Tektronix Inc PO Box 1000 26600 S W Pky Wilsonville OR 97070

MEYER, JOHN, church administrator. Acting dir. Dept. of Stewardship of the Lutheran Church MO Synod International Ctr., St. Louis. Office: The Lutheran Church MO Synod Intl 1333 S Kirkwood Rd Saint Louis MO 63122-7226

MEYER, JOHN BERNARD, public relations executive; b. St. Louis, July 22, 1933; s. Bernard Charles and Virginia Marie (Hetherington) M.; m. Alberta Ruth Krohn, June 13, 1957; children: Margaret, Chrystal, Kathleen, Jennifer, Victoria. Student, So. Meth. U., 1951-53. TV network news corr. CBS News, Washington, 1962-75; anchor, corr. Mut. Radio Network, Washington, 1975-77; nat. dir. communications Gen. Aviation Mfrs. Assn., Washington, 1977-81; dir. corp. pub. relations Gates-Lear Jet Corp., Wichita, Kans., 1981-85; mgr. corp. pub. relations The Garrett Corp., L.A., 1985-87; mgr. mktg. comm. Allied Signal Controls and Accessories Divsn., Tucson, 1987-93; area dir. pub. affairs Allied Signal Inc., South Bend, Ind., 1993—; Editor: Civil Aviation-Fuel Crisis CBS News, 1974 (Aviation/Space Writers award 1975); producer: General Aviation Benefits CBS News, 1978 (Aviation/Space Writers award 1979). Bd. dirs. Tucson-Pima Arts Coun., 1987-93, pres., 1990-92; bd. edirs. Ariz. Coun. Econ. Edn., Tucson, 1987-93, Tucson Symphony Orch., 1988-90, Metro YMCAs of Tucson, 1989-93; bd. dirs. Project Future, South Bend, Ind., 1994—, No. Ind. Pub. TV Commn., 1994—. Mem. Aviation/Space Writers Nat. Found. (v.p., bd. dirs. 1987-93, pres. 1993—, Golden Quill award 1988), Pub. Rels. Soc. Am. (pres. Tucson chpt. 1985), Tucson Met. C. of C. (vice chmn., bd. dirs. 1990-93), St. Joseph County (Ind.) C. of C. (bd. dirs. 1995—). Democrat. Lutheran. Avocation: comml. aviation. Home: 17913 Sable Ridge Dr South Bend IN 46635-1035

MEYER, JOHN EDWARD, nuclear engineering educator; b. Pitts., Dec. 17, 1931; s. Albert Edward and Thelma Elizabeth (Brethauer) M.; m. Gracyann Lenz, June 13, 1953; children: Susan Meyer Heydon, Karl, Karen Meyer Gleasman, Thomas. B.S., Carnegie Inst. Tech., 1953, M.S., 1953, Ph.D. (ASME Student award 1955), 1955. Engring. and mgmt. positions Westinghouse Bettis Atomic Power Lab., West Mifflin, Pa., 1955-75; vis. lectr. U. Calif., Berkeley, 1968-69; prof. nuclear engring. M.I.T., 1975—; cons. in field. Author papers in field. Recipient Bettis Disting. Service award, 1962, Outstanding Tchr. award nuclear engring. M.I.T., 1979, Alumni Merit award Carnegie Mellon U., 1987. Fellow Am. Nuclear Soc.; mem. ASME, Sigma Xi. Office: Room 24-202 77 Massachusetts Ave Rm 24-202 Cambridge MA 02139-4301

MEYER, JOHN FREDERICK, engineering and computer science educator, researcher, consultant; b. Grand Rapids, Mich., July 26, 1934; s. Frederick Albert and Harriet (Stibbs) M.; m. Nancy Shaw Briggs, July 4, 1959; children: John, Patricia, James. B.S., U. Mich., 1957; M.S., Stanford U., 1958; Ph.D., U. Mich., 1967. Data systems engr. Douglas Aircraft Corp., Santa Monica, Calif., 1957; research engr. Caltech, Jet Propulsion Lab., Pasadena, Calif., 1958-67; asst. prof. U. Mich., Ann Arbor, 1968-71, assoc. prof., 1971-76, prof. elec. engring. and computer sci., 1976—; dir. Computing Research Lab. U. Mich., 1984-89; cons. Calif. Inst. Tech. Jet Propulsion Lab., 1979—, Indsl. Tech. Inst., Ann Arbor, 1985—, CIMSA, Paris, 1992, Bendis Advanced Tech. Ctr., Columbia, Md., 1977-85, Thomson CSF, Paris, 1975, Italtel, Milan, 1990—, Applied Scis. Corp., Reading, Mass., 1993. Patentee Time Division Multiplexer, 1963 (NASA Inventions award 1964). Precinct chmn. 3d ward Democratic Party, Ann Arbor, 1971-74. Recipient Disting. Service Award U. Mich., 1964; IBM fellow, 1957. Fellow IEEE; mem. IEEE Computer Soc. (Cert. of Appreciation 1981, 95, Meritorious Svc. award 1985), AAAS, Assn. Computing Machinery. Home: 1946 Ridge Ave Ann Arbor MI 48104-6306 Office: U Mich 2114B EECS Bldg Ann Arbor MI 48109-2122

MEYER, JOHN ROBERT, economist, educator; b. Pasco, Wash., Dec. 6, 1927; s. Philip Conrad and Cora (Kempter) M.; m. Lee Stowell, Dec. 17, 1949; children: Leslie Karen, Ann Elizabeth, Robert Conrad. Student, Pacific U., 1945-46; BA, U. Wash., 1950; PhD (David A. Wells prize), Harvard U., 1955. Jr. fellow Harvard U., 1953-55, asst. prof., 1955-58, assoc. prof., 1958-59, prof. econs., 1959-68, prof. transportation and logistics, 1973-83; prof. Yale U., 1968-73; Harpel prof. capital formation and econ. growth Harvard U., 1983—; dir. Dun & Bradstreet, Rand McNally; vice chmn. Union Pacific Corp., 1982-83, now dir.; trustee Mut. Life. Ins. Co. N.Y., Pacific U. Author: (with others) The Investment Decision—An Empirical Inquiry, 1957, Economics of Competition on the Telecommunications Industry, 1980, Autos, Transit and Cities, 1981, Deregulation and the Future of Intercity Passenger Travel, 1987, Going Private: The International Experience with Transport Privatization, 1993, other books; contbr. articles to profl. jours. Mem. Presdl. Task Forces on Transp., 1964, 80, Presdl. Commn. on Population Growth and Am. Future, 1970-72; pres. Nat. Bur. Econ. Research, 1967-77. Served with USNR, 1946-48. Guggenheim fellow, 1958. Fellow Am. Acad. Arts and Scis., Econometric Soc.; mem. Am. Econ. Assn. (mem. exec. com. 1971-73), Council Fgn. Relations, Econ. History Assn. Home: 138 Brattle St Cambridge MA 02138-2202 Office: Harvard U Ctr Bus & Govt 79 Jfk St Cambridge MA 02138-5801

MEYER, JON KEITH, psychiatrist, psychoanalyst, educator; b. Springfield, Ill., May 6, 1938; s. Samuel Barclay and Finela Hermoine (Roehl) M.; m. Eleanor Fumie Yamashita, June 6, 1964; children: David Christopher, Laura Tamiko. AB summa cum laude, Dartmouth Coll., 1960; MD, Johns Hopkins U., 1964; grad., Washington Psychoanalytic Inst, 1980. Intern internal medicine Johns Hopkins Hosp., Balt., 1964-65, resident in psychiatry, 1965-67, 69; resident in psychiatry St. Elizabeth's Hosp., Washington, 1968; spl. asst. to dir. NIMH, Bethesda, Md., 1969-71; asst. prof. psychiatry Johns Hopkins Med. Sch., Balt., 1971-76, assoc. prof., 1976-83; prof. psychiatry Med. Coll. Wis., Milw., 1983—, prof. psychoanalysis in psychiatry, 1987—, prof. family medicine, 1990—; tng. and supervising analyst Chgo. Inst. for Psychoanalysis, 1987—; vice chmn. Dept. of Psychiatry, 1993—; chief psychiatry Froedtert Meml. Luth. Hosp., Milw., 1994—; med. dir. Wis., Psychoanalytic Found., Milw., 1987-91, sec. bd. dirs., 1988-91; bd. dirs. DePaul Hosp. Author books; contbr. chpts. to books, numerous articles to profl. jours. Comdr. USPHS, 1967-71. Daniel Webster Nat. scholar Dartmouth Coll., 1960, sr. fellow, 1959-60, Dennison rsch. fellow Johns Hopkins Med. Sch., 1964; Erik Erikson scholar-in-residence Austen Riggs Ctr., Stockbridge, Mass., 1991-92. Fellow Am. Psychiat. Assn.; mem. Internat. Psychoanalytic Assn., Am. Psychoanalytic Assn., (exec. councilor 1993—, chmn. com. on coun. structure and function 1995—), Internat. Acad. Sex Rsch., Am. Coll. Psychiatrists, Am. Coll. Psychoanalysts, Wis. Psychoanalytic Soc. (founding pres. 1989-91). Avocations: photography, hiking, kayaking. Office: Med Coll Wis 2321 E Stratford Ct Milwaukee WI 53211-2631

MEYER, KARL ERNEST, journalist; b. Madison, Wis., May 22, 1928; s. Ernest Louis and Dorothy (Narefsky) M.; m. Sarah Nielsen Peck, Aug. 12, 1959 (div. 1972); children—Ernest, Heather, Jonathan; m. Shareen Blair Brysac, Jan. 6, 1989. B.A., U. Wis., 1951; M.P.A., Princeton U., 1953, Ph.D., 1956. Reporter N.Y. Times, N.Y.C., 1952, mem. editorial bd., 1979—; editorial writer Washington Post, 1956-65, chief London Bur., 1965-70, N.Y.C. corr., 1970-71; Washington corr. New Statesman, 1961-65; sr. editor, TV critic Saturday Rev., N.Y.C., 1975-79; corr. in residence Fletcher Sch. Law and Diplomacy, Tufts U., 1979; vis. journalist fellow Duke U., Durham, N.C., 1988; vis. prof. Yale U., 1983, 90, McGraw prof. in writing Princeton (N.J.) U., 1993-94. Author: The New America, 1961, (with Tad Szulc) The Cuban Invasion, 1962, Fulbright of Arkansas, 1963, The Pleasures of Archaeology, 1971, The Plundered Past, 1973, Teotihuacán, 1975, The Art Museum: Power, Money, Ethics, 1979, Pundits, Poets and Wits: An Omnibus of American Newspaper Columns, 1990. Recipient citation for excellence Delta Chi, 1963; George Foster Peabody Broadcasting award 1983, Disting. Achievement award Sch. Journalism, U. Wis., 1985; Davenport Coll. of Yale U. fellow; Wisenschaftskolleg Inst. Adv. Studies (Berlin) fellow, 1994-95, Reuter fellow Oxford (Eng.) U., 1996-97. Mem. PEN Club Internat., Coun. on Fgn. Rels., NYU Soc. Fellows, Century Assn. Home: 50 W 96th St New York NY 10025 Office: NY Times 229 W 43rd St New York NY 10036-3913

MEYER, KARL WILLIAM, retired university president; b. Ft. Wayne, Ind., May 8, 1925; s. K.W. and L. (Hofacker) M.; m. Margery R. Hamman, Apr. 15, 1950; children—Mary, William, Frederick, Ann, Jean. A.B., Valpariaso U., 1948; M.F.S., U. Md., 1949; Ph.D., U. Wis., 1953; postgrad., U. Basel, Switzerland, 1948-49; postdoctoral fellow, U. Mich., 1958-59. Faculty Valparaiso U., 1952-53, Augustana Coll., 1953-55, Wis. State U., 1955-58; dean instrn., dir. grad. studies Wayne State Coll., 1959-63; asst. dir. bd. regents Wis. State Colls., Madison, 1963-64; pres. U. Wis.-Superior, 1964-87. Author: Karl Liebknecht: Man Without a Country, 1957; Contbr. articles to profl. jours. Served with USAAF, 1943-46, ETO. Home: 7012 S Maple Creek Rd Lake Nebagamon WI 54849-9220

MEYER, KATHLEEN MARIE, English educator; b. St. Louis, Oct. 29, 1944; d. Richard Henry and Leonora (Moser) Bailey; m. Thomas A. Meyer, Dec. 26, 1966; children: Richard, Amy, Mindy, Heidi. BA, Webster Coll., Webster Groves, Mo., 1966; MA, Fla. Atlantic U., 1981; postgrad., No. Ill. U., 1982—. Cert. secondary tchr., Mo., Ill. Tchr. English Notre Dame High Sch., St. Louis, 1966-67; tchr. English, chmn. dept. Rosary High Sch., Aurora, Ill., 1981-91; instr. English DeKalb Coll., Decatur, Ga., 1992—; mem. adv. bd. Univ. High Sch.; mem. joint enrollment coun. DeKalb Coll. Mem. ASCD, Nat. Coun. Tchrs. English.

MEYER, KENNETH MARVEN, academic administrator; b. Chgo., Nov. 27, 1932; s. Kenneth M. and Lorraine B. (Reiff) M.; m. Carol Jean Ebner, June 12, 1953; children: Keith, Kevin, Caryn. BD, Trinity Coll., 1954, MDiv, 1956; DMin., Luther Rice, 1978. Pastor Crystal Evang. Free Ch. in Am., Mpls., 1959-66, also bd. dirs.; pastor 1st Free Ch., Rockford, Ill., 1969-74; pres. Trinity Evangelical Div. Sch. and Coll., Deerfield, Ill., 1974-95, chancellor, 1995—; bd. dirs. Firstar Ill.; CEO Radio WMCU, Miami, Fla. Author: Guide to Financial Planning, 1987, (monograph) Turning Point Psalms, 1981. Mem. Nat. Assn. Evangelicals. Mem. Evangelical Free Ch. Avocations: money mgmt., reading. Office: Trinity Internat Univ Office of Chancellor 2065 Half Day Rd Deerfield IL 60015-1241

MEYER, KERSTIN, mezzo-soprano, music educator; b. Stockholm, Apr. 3, 1928; d. J.O. and Anna (Eriksson) M.; m. Björn Bexelius. Student, Royal Conservatory, Stockholm, Accademia Chigiana, Siena, Italy, Mozarteum, Salzburg, Austria. Chmn. Jussi Bjoerling Meml. Fund, Royal Opera Found., Sch. Svanholm Fund, Kerstin Meyer Fund for young opera singers; prin. Swedish State Acad. Opera, Stockholm; dir. Swedish State Concert Bur., Royal Swedish Acad. Music, Swedish State Music Collections, European Cultural Found. in Amsterdam, Benjamin Britten Soc., Swedish Performing Rights Soc., Danish Conservatory of Music; prof. Mozarteum Salzburg; master tchr. Britten-Perce Sch. Advanced Mus. Studies, U.K. Debut in Il Trovatore, Stockholm, 1952; appeared with opera cos. in Buenos Aires, Salzburg, Vienna, Brussels, Vancouver, Copenhagen, Helsinki, Paris, London, Glyndebourne, Cardiff, Salzberg, Bayreuth, E. and W. Berlin, Hamburg, Tokyo, Munich, Cologne, Glasgow, Mexico City, Milan, Rome, Oslo, Edinburgh Festival, Moscow, Riga, Taschkent, N.Y.C., San Francisco, Santa Fe, San Diego, New Orleans, Boston, Tulsa, Cologne, Venice, Hong Kong, others, also maj. orchs. in, U.S., Europe, Australia, New Zealand, Far East; numerous radio TV appearances, recs.; translator opera librettos; producer various operas. Decorated Comdr. Order Brit. Empire, officer Italian Order of Merit, medal Litteris et Artibus; named Royal Ct. singer; recipient Swedish Wasa Order, Norwegian Royal medal, Bundesverdienstkrutz 1 Klasse, Germany. Mem. Royal Acad. Music (Prof. of Yr.). Office: Operahögskolanr, Strändvagen 82, S-11527 Stockholm Sweden

MEYER, L. DONALD, retired agricultural engineer, researcher, educator; b. Concordia, Mo., Apr. 14, 1933; s. Lawrence Dick and Florence Malinda (Uphaus) M.; m. Loretta Lou Bush, Dec. 26, 1954; children: Dan W., James B., David J. Student, Cen. Coll., Fayette, Mo., 1950-51; BS in Agrl. Engring., U. Mo., 1954, MS in Agrl. Engring., 1955; PhD, Purdue U., 1964. Cert. profl. soil erosion and sediment control specialist; registered profl. engr., Ind. Agrl. engr. Agrl. Rsch. Svc., USDA, West Lafayette, Ind., 1955-73; agrl. engr. Nat. Sedimentation Lab., USDA, Oxford, Miss., 1973-93; asst. prof., assoc. prof. Purdue U., West Lafayette, 1965-73; adj. prof. agr.-biol. engring. Miss. State U., Starkville, 1975—. Contbr. articles to profl. jours. Recipient Outstanding Performance award USDA Agrl. Rsch. Svc., 1959, 88, 89, 90, 91. Fellow Am. Soc. Agrl. Engrs. (dir. publs. 1968-69, chmn. soil and water div. 1972-73, Hancor award 1985), Soil and Water Conservation Soc.; mem. Soil Sci. Soc. Am.

MEYER, LASKER MARCEL, retail executive; b. Houston, Jan. 8, 1926; s. Lasker M. and Lucille (Dannenbaum) M.; m. Beverly Jean Goldberg; children: Lynn Meyer Brown, Susan Meyer Sellinger. Student, Rice U., 1942-43. Pres. Foley's, Houston, 1979, chmn., chief exec. officer, 1982-87; chmn., chief exec. officer Abraham and Straus, Bklyn., 1980-81; vice chmn. bd. Splty. Retailers, Inc., Houston, 1989-93; bd. dirs. BookTronics, Inc., Houston. Past chmn. bd. United Way Tex. Gulf Coast. Mem. Bentwater Yacht and Country Club. Jewish.

MEYER, LAWRENCE GEORGE, lawyer; b. East Grand Rapids, Mich., Oct. 2, 1940; s. George and Evangeline (Boerma) M.; children from previous marriage: David Lawrence, Jenifer Lynne; m. Linda Elizabeth Buck, May 31, 1980; children: Elizabeth Tilden, Travis Henley. BA with honors, Mich. State U., 1961; JD with distinction, U. Mich., 1964. Bar: Wis., 1965, Ill. 1965, U.S. Supreme Ct. 1968, D.C. 1972. Assoc. Whyte, Hirschboeck, Minahan, Hardin & Harland, Milw., 1964-66; atty. antitrust div. U.S. Dept. Justice, Washington, 1966-68; legal counsel U.S. Senator Robert P. Griffin, Mich., 1968-70; dir. policy planning FTC, Mich., 1970-72; ptnr. Patton, Boggs & Blow, Washington, 1972-85, Arent, Fox, Kintner, Plotkin & Kahn, Washington, 1985-96, Gadsby & Hannah, 1996—. Contbr. articles on antitrust and trial practice to law jours.; asst. editor. U. Mich. Law Rev., 1960-61. Bd. dirs. Hockey Hall of Fame, Toronto, 1993—. Recipient Disting. Svc. award FTC, 1972. Mem. ABA, D.C. Bar Assn., Wis. Bar Assn., Ill. Bar Assn., U.S. Senate Ex S.O.B.s Club, City Tavern Club, Congl. Country Club. Home: 8777 Belmart Rd Potomac MD 20854-1610

MEYER, LAWRENCE ROBERT, journalist; b. Chgo., Nov. 27, 1941; s. Fernando Kolomon and Gertrude M.; m. Aviva Sagalovitch, June 15, 1968; children: Ariel David, Evan Asher, Noa Anne. BA, U. Mich., 1963; MA, Columbia U., 1965, MS, 1965. Reporter Times-Herald Record, Middletown, N.Y., 1965-66, Louisville Times, 1968-69; reporter Washington Post, 1969-87, editor Nat. Weekly Edit., 1987—. Author: A Capitol Crime, 1977, False Front, 1979, Israel Now: Portrait of a Troubled Land, 1982. Sgt. USMC, 1966-68. Jewish. Home: 3311 Ross Pl NW Washington DC 20008-3332 Office: Washington Post 1150 15th St NW Washington DC 20071-0001

MEYER, LEONARD B., musician, educator; b. N.Y.C., Jan. 12, 1918; s. Arthur S. and Marion (Wolff) M.; m. Janet M. Levy; children: Marion L., Carlin, Erica Cecile. Student, Bard Coll., 1936-37; BA, Columbia, 1940, MA, 1948; PhD, U. Chgo., 1954; LHD, Grinnell Coll., Loyola U., Chgo., Bard Coll., U. Chgo. Faculty U. Chgo., 1946-75, head humanities sect., 1958-60, prof. music, 1961-75, chmn. music dept., 1961-70, Phyllis Fay Horton disting. svc. prof., 1972-75; Benjamin Franklin prof. music U. Pa., 1975-88, Benjamin Franklin prof. emeritus, 1988—; fellow Ctr. for Advanced Studies, Wesleyan U., Middletown, Conn., 1960-61, Ctr. for Advanced Study in Behavioral Scis., Stanford, Calif., 1994; Ernest Bloch prof. music U. Calif., Berkeley, 1971, sr. fellow Sch. Criticism and Theory, 1975-88; resident scholar Bellagio Study and Conf. Ctr., 1982; Tanner lectr. Stanford U., 1984; Patten lectr. Ind. U., 1985. Author: Emotion and Meaning in Music, 1956, (with G.W. Cooper) The Rhythmis Structure of Music, 1960, Music, the Arts and Ideas, 1967, Explaining Music: Essays and Explorations, 1973, Style and Music: Theory, History and Ideology, 1994; gen. editor: Studies in the Criticism and Theory of Music, 1980-96; mem. editorial bd. Critical Inquiry, 1974—, Misoc Perception, 1983; contbr. articles to profl. jours. Guggenheim fellow, 1971-72. Fellow AAAS, Am. Acad. Arts and Scis.; mem. Am. Musicological Soc. (hon.), Soc. Music Theory, Soc. Music Perception and Cognition (bd. dirs.), Phi Beta Kappa. Home: 165 W End Ave Apt 23M New York NY 10023-5513 Office: U of Pa Dept of Music Philadelphia PA 19104

MEYER, LESLEY ANNE, nurse recruiter, nursing administrator; b. Beaufort, S.C., Nov. 8, 1944; d. Andrew M. and Helen Margaret (Mark) Olesak; m. Gary B. Glick, DDS, July 1983; 1 child Gregory Andrew Meyer. Diploma in nursing, L.A. County-U. So. Calif. Med. Ctr., 1965; BSN magna cum laude, Pepperdine U., 1979. RN, CAlif., N.J.; cert. in nursing adminstrn. Charge nurse Kaiser Found. Hosp., San Diego, 1976-81, nurse recruiter, 1981-83; N.E. recruitment cons. So. Calif. region Kaiser Permanente Med. Group, Pasadena, 1983-86; mgr. nurse recruitment and retention Morristown (N.J.) Meml. Hosp., 1986-96; employment svcs. mgr. Mountainside (N.J.) Hosp., 1996—; mgr. nurse recruitment and retention Atlantic Health Sys.; shared governance coordinating coun. facilitator; speaker to local and nat. groups. Contbr. articles to profl. jours. Mem. ANA, N.J. State Nurses Assn., Nat. Assn. Healthcare Recruitment, N.J. Assn. Hosp. Recruiters (2d v.p., corr. sec. 1988-90), Morristown Bus. Edn. Adv. Coun. Home: 3 Fern Ct Flanders NJ 07836-9140

MEYER, LOUIS B., superior court judge, retired state supreme court justice; b. Marion, N.C., July 15, 1933; s. Louis B. and Beulah (Smith) M.; m. Evelyn Spradlin, Dec. 29, 1956; children: Louis B. III, Patricia Shannon, Adam Burden. B.A., Wake Forest U., 1955, J.D., 1960; LLM, U. Va., 1992. Bar: N.C. 1960, U.S. Dist. (ea. dist.) N.C. 1960, U.S. Ct. Appeals (4th cir.) 1960, U.S. Supreme Ct. 1962. Law clk. Supreme Ct. N.C., Raleigh, 1960; spl. agent FBI, 1961-62; atty. Lucas, Rand, Rose, Meyer, Jones & Orcutt P.A., Wilson, N.C., 1962-81; assoc. justice Supreme Ct. N.C., Raleigh, 1981-95, ret., 1995; spl. judge Superior Ct., 1995—. Former county chmn. Wilson County Dems., N.C.; former mem. N.C. State Exec. Com. Dem. Party. Served to 1st lt. U.S. Army, 1955-57. Mem. Wilson County Bar Assn. (former pres.), 7th Jud. Dist. Bar Assn. (former pres.), N.C. Bar Assn. (former v.p.), Masons. Baptist.

MEYER, M. HOLT, judge; b. Hong Kong, Sept. 28, 1930; s. Clarence E. and Thresa (Heidecke) M.; m. Catherine Dindia, Sept. 2, 1956; children: Christopher M., Holt V. BA, Harvard U., 1952; LLB, Columbia U., 1957. Bar: N.Y. 1958, U.S. Dist. Ct. (so. and ea. dists.) N.Y. 1963. Atty. Webster & Sheffield, N.Y.C., 1959-66; asst. to mayor City of N.Y., 1966-73; judge N.Y. State Family Ct., Staten Island, 1973-95; sr. judge N.Y. State Supreme Ct., Richmond County, 1996—. Cpl. U.S. Army, 1952-54, Germany. Mem.

N.Y. State Family Ct. Judges Assn. (pres. 1990-91), N.Y.C. Family Ct. Judges Asns. (pres. 1985-86). Office: NY State Supreme Ct County Court House Staten Island NY 10301

MEYER, MARA ELLICE, special education educator, consultant; b. Chgo., Oct. 28, 1952; d. David and Harriett (Lazar) Einhorn; m. Leonard X. Meyer, July 20, 1986; children: Hayley Rebecca, David Joseph. BS in Speech and Hearing Sci., U. Ill., 1974, MS in Speech Pathology, 1975, postgrad. in Pub. Policy Analysis, 1990—. Cert. speech and lang. pathologist, spl. edn. tchr., reading tchr. Speech and lang. pathologist Macon-Piatt Spl. Edn. Dist., Decatur, Ill., 1975-76; speech and lang. pathologist, reading specialist, learning disabilities coord. Community Consolidated Sch. Dist. # 59, Arlington Heights, Ill., 1976-87; test cons. Psychol. Corp., San Antonio, 1987-89; adj. prof. Nat.-Lewis U., Evanston, Ill., 1985-87; ednl. cons. Am. Guidance Svc., Circle Pines, Minn., 1989-94; pvt. practice ednl. cons. Deerfield, Ill., 1994—; project dir. Riverside Pub. Co., Chgo., 1993-94; mem. adv. coun. to Headstart, Dept. Human Svsc., City of Chgo., 1990—; cons. Spl. Edn. Dist. of Lake County, 1995—. Area coord. Dem. Party, Lake County, Ill., 1978—; pres. Park West Condo Assn., Lake County, 1983-88. Mem. NEA, ASCD, Am. Speech-Lang. and Hearing Assn., Internat. Reading Assn., Coun. on Exceptional Children. Avocations: family, golf, skiing, leisure reading, technical reading. Home: 1540 Central Ave Deerfield IL 60015-3963

MEYER, MARGARET ELEANOR, microbiologist, educator; b. Westwood, Calif., Feb. 8, 1923; d. Herman Henry and Eleanor (Dobson) M. B.S., U. Calif., Berkeley, 1945; Ph.D., U. Calif., Davis, 1961. Pub. health analyst USPHS, Bethesda, Md., 1945-46; swine Brucellosis control agt. Dept. Agr., Davis, 1946-47; bacteriologist U. Calif., Davis, 1947-61; research microbiologist U. Calif. (Sch. Vet. Medicine), 1961-77, prof. vet. pub. health and microbiologist exptl. sta., 1977—; research microbiologist U. Calif. Med. Sch., Los Angeles, 1961-77; supr. Brucella identifications lab. WHO, U. Calif.-Davis, 1964—, prof. vet. pub. health, 1973—; also dir. M.A. program in preventive vet. medicine; cons. subcom. on Brucella Internat. Com. Bacterial Taxonomy, 1962—, mem., 1966—; mem. 5th Pan Am. Congress Veterinary Medicine, Venezuela, 1966; mem. Internat. Congress Microbiology, Moscow, 1966, Mexico City, 1970, Munich, Ger., 1978, mem., officer, Eng., 1986; mem. Internat. Conf. Culture Collections, Tokyo, 1968; mem. adv. com. to Bergey's Manual Determative Bacteriology, 1967; cons. in resident Pan Am. Health Orgn., Zoonoses Lab., Buenos Aires, 1968; mem. brucellosis tech. adv. com. U.S. Animal Health Assn., 1977; FAO cons. on brucellosis control in dairy animals, Tripoli, Libya, 1981, mem. 3d internat. brucellosis symposium, Algiers, 1983; cons. Alaska Dept. Fish and Game, 1976, FAO, Libya, 1981, Bering Straits Reindeer Herders Assn., Nome, Alaska, 1981; invited speaker Internat. Symposium on Advances in Brucellosis Rsch., Tex. A&M U., 1989, Internat. Bison Conf.; resident cons. on brucellosis control in sheep and goats Am. Near East Refugee Aid, East Jerusalem, 1989; cons. on brucellosis in Yellowstone Nat. Pk., Nat. Pk. Svc., 1991—; invited mem. nat. symposium on brucellosis in the Greater Yellowstone Area, Jackson Hole, Wyo., 1994; cons. on brucellosis control in livestock for Armenia, 1994—. Contbr. articles to profl. jours. Bd. dirs. Carmichael Park and Recreation Dist., Calif., 1975. Recipient Research Career Devel. award USPHS-NIH, 1963. Fellow Am. Pub. Health Assn., Am. Acad. Microbiology; mem. Soc. Am. Microbiologists, N.Am. Conf. Animal Disease Research Workers, Am. Coll. Vet. Microbiologists (hon. affiliate), U.S. Animal Health Assn. (chmn. brucellosis tech. advisory com. 1978-79), Internat. Assn. Microbiol. Socs. (mem. 1st intersect. congress 1974), AAUW, No. Calif. Women's Golf Assn., U. Calif. Alumni Assn., Sigma Xi. Clubs: U. Calif. Faculty (Davis); El Dorado Royal Country (Shingle Springs, Calif.); Reno Women's Golf. Home: 5611 Fair Oaks Blvd Carmichael CA 95608-5503 Office: U Calif Sch Vet Medicine Dept Epidemiology & Preventive Medicine Davis CA 95616

MEYER, MARION M., editorial consultant; b. Sheboygan, Wis., July 14, 1923; d. Herman O. and Viola A. (Hoch) M. BA, Lakeland Coll., 1950; MA, NYU, 1957. Payroll clk. Am. Chair Co., Sheboygan, 1941-46; tchr. English and religion, dir. athletics Am. Sch. for Girls, Baghdad, Iraq, 1950-56; mem. edn. and publ. staff United Ch. Bd. for Homeland Ministries, United Ch. Press/Pilgrim Press, 1958-64, sr. editor, 1965-88, ret., 1988; cons. to individuals and orgns. on editorial matters and copyrights. Editor Penney Retirement Cmty. Newsletter, 1990—; contbr. articles to various publs.; writer hymns Look to God, Be Radiant, 1989, Be Still, 1990, Come, God, Creator, 1992, Something New! (extended work), 1993, Our Home is PRC, 1996. Incorporating mem. Contact Phila., Inc., 1972, bd. dirs., 1972-75, v.p., chmn. com. to organize community adv. bd., chmn. auditing com., editor newsletter, 1972-74, pres., 1974-75, assoc. mem., 1977—; mem. ofcl. bd. Old First Reformed Ch., Phila., 1984-89; deacon United Ch. Christ, 1984—, Mid.-East Com. of Pa. SE Conf. United Ch. Christ, 1986-88. Honored as role model United Ch. of Christ, 1982, 85. Mem. AAUW, NOW, Nat. Mus. Women in the Arts (charter mem.), Nat. Trust for Hist. Preservation. Home: PO Box 656 Penney Farms FL 32079-0656

MEYER, MARY COELI, management consultant; b. Brighton, Mass.; d. Herbert Walter and Eleanor Louise (Beecher) M. BEd, Nat. Coll. Edn., 1965; MBA, Calif. Western U., 1977; PhD, Calif. Coast U., 1982. Educator pub./pvt. schs., univs., Ohio, Ind., Ill., 1965-72; pub. rels. Watts, Lamb, Kenyon & Herrick, Chagrin, Ohio, 1973; rsch. asst. Addressograph Multigraph, Cleve., 1973; supr. personnel AMI Brunging Divsn., Schaumber, Ill., 1974, mgr. human resources, 1975, acting dir. strategic manpower planning, tng., devel., 1976; pres. Cheshire Ltd., Chgo., Atlanta, 1977—; speaker in field. Author: Personnel Records Management, 1985, Time, Mind and Achievement, 1993, (with I. Berchtold, J. Oestreich, F. Collins) Sexual Harrassment, 1981, (with I. Berchtold) Getting the Job: How To Interview Successfully, 1982, (ednl. materials) So You Think It's Time To Change Jobs, 1976, Creative Guide to Finding Scholarships, 1977, How to Avoid an Unemployment Crisis, 1982, The Small Business Guide to Marketing, 1984, (videos) Power Pinch, 1981, The Leadership Link, 1985, Sexual Harrassment, 1985; (audio-cassette porgrams) Getting the Job: How to Interview, 1981, Demotivation/Remotivation, 1981. Avocation: mushroom hunting. Office: Cheshire Ltd 1601 Shadowbrook Dr NE Acworth GA 30102-2447

MEYER, MARY-LOUISE, art gallery executive; b. Boston, Feb. 21, 1922; d. Alonzo Jay and Louise (Whitledge) Shadman; m. Norman Meyer, Aug. 9, 1941; children: Wendy C., Bruce R., Harold Alton, Marilee, Laurel. BA, Wellesley Coll., 1943; MS, Wheelock Coll., 1965. Head tchr. Page Sch., Wellesley Coll., Mass., 1955-60; instr. early childhood edn. Pine Manor Coll., Brookline, Mass., 1960-65; chaplain/counselor Charles St. Jail, Boston, 1974-79; Christian Sci. practitioner, Wellesley, Mass., 1974—; owner Alpha Gallery, Boston, 1972-87; cons. Living & Learning Centers, Boston, 1966-69; 2d reader Christian Sci. Ch., 1979-82. Contbr. articles to profl. jours. Overseer Sturbridge Village, 1981—, trustee, 1986; visitor Am. Decorative Arts dept. Mus. Fine Arts, Boston, 1973—; chmn. Wellesley Voters Rights Com., 1983-84; state organizer Ednl. Channel 2 Group, Boston, 1960; cofounder Boston Assn. for Childbirth Edn., 1950; overseer Strawberry Banke Living Mus., 1987; trustee Maine Coast Artists, Rockport, Maine, 1991, v.p. Friends of Montpelier (Knox Mansion-Thomaston), 1994-96, pres. 1996—; trustee Bay Chamber Concerts, Rockport, 1990. Mem. Mus. Trustees Assn., Farnsworth Mus., Waldoboro Hist. Soc., Soc. for Pres. New Eng. Antiquities (mem. Maine coun.), Wellesley Coll. Club.

MEYER, MAURICE WESLEY, physiologist, dentist, neurologist; b. Long Prairie, Minn., Feb. 13, 1925; s. Ernest William and Augusta (Warnke) M.; m. Martha Helen Davis, Sept. 3, 1946; children—James Irvin, Thomas Orville. B.S., U. Minn., 1953, D.D.S., 1957, M.S., 1959, Ph.D., 1961. Teaching asst. U. Minn. Sch. Dentistry, 1954-55, USPHS fellow, 1955-56, rsch. fellow, 1956-57, mem. faculty, 1960—; prof. physiology, dentistry and neurology U. Minn., 1976-88, prof. emeritus, 1988—; investigator Ctr. Rsch. and Cerebral Vascular Disease, 1969—; dir. lab. Center Research and Cerebral Vascular Disease, 1975—; postdoctoral research fellow Nat. Inst. Dental Research, 1957-60, research fellow, 1958-61, mem. faculty, 1961—, asso. prof. neurology, 1974-80, mem. grad. faculty, 1973—; trainee Inst. Advanced Edn. in Dental Research, 1964—; vis. asso. prof., also vis. research fellow dept. physiology and Sch. Dentistry Cardiovascular Research Inst., U. Calif., San Francisco, 1971. Contbr. articles to profl. jours. Served to col. Dental Corps AUS, 1943-50. Decorated D.F.C., Air medal with 3 oak leaf clusters. Fellow AAAS; mem. ADA, Minn. Dental Soc., Internat. Assn. Dental Research (pres. Minn. sect. 1967-68), Soc. Exptl. Biology and Medicine, Am. Physiol. Soc., Microcirculatory Soc., Am. Assn. Dental Schs. (chmn. 1972-73), Can. Physiol. Soc., Sigma Xi, Omicron Kappa Upsilon. Club: Masons. Home: 560 Rice Creek Ter NE Minneapolis MN 55432-4472 Office: U Minn 6-255 Millard Minneapolis MN 55455

MEYER, MAX EARL, lawyer; b. Hampton, Va., Oct. 31, 1918; s. Earl Luther and Winifred Katherine (Spacht) M.; m. Betty Maxwell Dodds, Sept. 22, 1945; children—Scott Maxwell, Ann Culliford. AB, U. Nebr., 1940, JD, 1942. Bar: Nebr. 1942, Ill. 1946. Assoc. firm Lord, Bissell & Brook, Chgo., 1945-53; ptnr. Lord, Bissell & Brook, 1953-85; chmn. Chgo. Fed. Tax Forum, 1965, U. Chgo. Ann. Fed. Tax Conf., 1972; mem. Adv. Group to Commr. of IRS, 1967; lectr. in field. Bd. dirs. Music Acad. of the West, chmn. 1993-94. Mem. ABA (mem. council tax sec. 1969-72), Ill. Bar Assn. (mem. council tax sect. 1973-76), Nebr. Bar Assn., Chgo. Bar Assn. (chmn. taxation com. 1959-61), Am. Coll. Tax Counsel. Republican. Presbyterian. Clubs: Legal, Law (Chgo.); Valley Club of Montecito, Birnam Wood Golf. Lodge: Masons.

MEYER, MELISSA, artist; b. N.Y.C., 1947. BS, NYU, 1968, MA, 1975. Artist; teaching positions include Syracuse (N.Y.) U., 1985, 86, Art Inst. Chgo., 1985, U. Buffalo, 1986, Columbia U., N.Y.C., 1989, R.I. Sch. Design, Providence, 1982, 84, Ringling Sch. Art, Sarasota Fla., 1994, Vt. Studio Ctr., 1992, 94, Sch. Visual Arts, N.Y.C., 1993—. Solo exhbns. include Frank Marino Gallery, N.Y.C., 1979, Jane Steinberg Gallery, San Francisco, 1985, R.C. Erpf Gallery, N.Y.C., 1986, 87, J.L. Becker/East End Gallery, Provincetown, Mass., 1988, Ellen Miller Fine Art, Boston, 1991, Holly Solomon Gallery, N.Y.C., 1991, 93, 96, Galerie Renee Ziegler, Zurich, 1993, Miller/Block Gallery, Boston, 1994, Allezles Filles, Columbus, Ohio, 1995, Montgomery Glasoe Fine Art, Mpls., 1993, 96; group shows include Touchstone Gallery, N.Y.C., Loeb Student Ctr./NYU, Grand-Palais, Paris, Frank Marino Gallery, Calif. State Coll., Stanislaus, Nina Freudenheim Gallery, Buffalo, Ruth Siegel Gallery, N.Y.C., Exit Art, N.Y.C., Aldrich Mus. Contemporary Art, Ridgefield, Conn., Tibor de Nagy Gallery, N.Y.C., U. Maine Mus. Art, Orono, Butler Inst. Art, Youngstown, Ohio, Nat. Gallery Art, Washington, HollySolomon Gallery, Alta. Gallery Art, Calgary, Galerie Renee Ziegler, Zurich, U. Ala., Tuscaloosa, Rosenberg & Kaufman Fine Art, N.Y.C.; subject of numerous articles. Grantee Provincetown Workshop, 1972, 73, 74, Edward F. Albee Found., Montauk, N.Y., 1979, 80, Am. Acad. in Rome, 1980-81, N.Y. Found. for the Arts, 1992, NEA, 1983-84, 93, others. Office: care Holly Solomon Gallery 172 Mercer St New York NY 10012-3206

MEYER, MICHAEL EDWIN, lawyer; b. Chgo., Oct. 23, 1942; s. Leon S. and Janet (Gorden) M.; m. Catherine Dieffenbach, Nov. 21, 1982; children: Linda, Mollie, Patrick, Kellie. BS, U. Wis., 1964; JD, U. Chgo., 1967. Bar: Calif. 1968, U.S. Supreme Ct. 1973. Assoc. Lillick & McHose, L.A., 1967-73, ptnr., 1974-90, mng. ptnr., 1986-87; ptnr. Pillsbury Madison Sutro, 1990—, mem. mgmt. com., 1990-92; judge pro tem Beverly Hills Mcpl. Ct., Calif., 1976-79, Los Angeles Mcpl. Ct., 1980-86; lectr. in field. Bd. dirs. Bldg. Owners and Mgrs. Assn. of Greater L.A., L.A. Coun. Boy Scouts Am.; pub. counsel United Way Greater L.A. Recipient Good Scout award L.A. coun. Boy Scouts Am., 1992. Mem. ABA, Am. Arbitration Assn. (arbitrator), Calif. Bar Assn., L.A. Bar Assn., U. Chgo. Alumni Assn. So. Calif. (pres. 1980-82), Calif. Club, U. L.A. Club (dir. 1979-85, pres. 1984-85), L.A. Country Club. Jewish. Home: 4407 Roma Ct Marina Dl Rey CA 90292-7702 Office: Pillsbury Madison Sutro 725 S Figueroa St Los Angeles CA 90017-5524

MEYER, MICHAEL LOUIS, lawyer; b. Buffalo, Dec. 17, 1940; s. Bernard H. and Florence (Nusbaum) M.; m. Jo Ann Ackerman, Sept. 21, 1990. AB, Princeton U., 1962; LLB, Harvard U., 1965. Bar: Ill. 1965, D.C., 1978. Assoc. Schiff Hardin & Waite, Chgo., 1965-72, ptnr., 1972—. Lt. USN, 1965-68. Mem. ABA (mem. fed. regulation of security com.), Chgo. Bar Assn., Chgo. Coun. Lawyers, Chgo. Yacht Club, Metropolitan Club. Office: Schiff Hardin & Waite 7200 Sears Towers Ste 1200 Chicago IL 60606

MEYER, MILTON EDWARD, JR., lawyer, artist; b. St. Louis, Nov. 26, 1922; s. Milton Edward and Jessie Marie (Hurley) M.; m. Mary C. Kramer, Nov. 5, 1949; children: Milton E. III, Melanie M. Meyer Francis, Daniel K., Gregory N. B.S. in Bus. Adminstrn, Washington U., 1943; LL.B., St. Louis, U., 1950; LL.M., N.Y. U., 1953. Bar: Mo. 1950, Colo. 1956. Trust adminstr. Mississippi Valley Trust Co., St. Louis, 1946-50; assoc. firm Burnett, Stern & Liberman, St. Louis, 1953-56; founding partner firm Hindry & Meyer, Denver, 1956-79; chmn. bd. Hindry & Meyer, 1970-79; spl. counsel Schmidt, Elrod & Wills, and predecessors, 1979-83, pres., 1980-82; sec. C.A. Norgren Co., Littleton, Colo., 1960-78; dir. C.A. Norgren Co., 1971-78. Contbr. articles to profl. jours. Bd. dirs. Nat. Club Assn., 1971-91, pres., 1976-78; bd. dirs., pres. Denver Community Concert Assn., 1960-64; bd. dirs. Sewall Rehab. Ctr., Denver, 1965-68, Carl A. Norgren Found., 1960-70, Denver Leadership Found., 1983-93; bd. dirs. Found. Colo. Women's Coll., 1982-86, chmn., 1984-86; bd. dirs. Conf. Pvt. Orgns., 1982-89, chmn., 1984-88; chmn. Denver Rotary's Artists of Am. Exhbn., 1990-92. With airborne inf. U.S. Army, 1943-46, 50-52. Mem. ABA, Colo. Bar Assn., Denver Bar Assn., Greater Denver Tax Counsels Assn. (founder, chmn. 1957, Denver Estate Planning Coun. (founder, pres. 1958), Am. Coll. Probate Counsel, Knickerbocker Artists, Am. Coll. Probate Counsel, Pastel Soc. Am., Pastel Soc. West Coast (Disting. Pastellist award), Internat. Assn. Pastel Socs. (founder, dir. 1994—), Cherry Hills Country Club, Pinehurst Country Club (pres. 1979-80), Denver Execs. Club, Hundred Club Denver, Rotary (bd. dirs. 1991-93), Phi Eta Sigma, Beta Gamma Sigma, Omicron Delta Kappa, Beta Theta Pi. Republican. Roman Catholic. Home and Studio: 5784 E Oxford Ave Cherry Hills Village CO 80111

MEYER, NICHOLAS, screenwriter, director; b. N.Y.C., Dec. 24, 1945; s. Bernard Constant and Elly (Kassman) M. B.A. in Theatre and Film, U. Iowa, 1968. Assoc. publicist Paramount Pictures, N.Y.C., 1968-69; story editor Warner Bros., N.Y.C., 1970-71. Writer, dir.: (films) Time After Time, 1979 (Avoriaz Film Festival grand prize, Academy of Science Fiction, Fantasy, and Horror Films award), Company Business, 1991, Star Trek VI: The Undiscovered Country, 1991; writer: (films) Invasion of the Bee Girls, 1973, The Seven-Per-Cent Solution, 1976 (Academy award nomination best adapted screenplay 1976), Sommersby, 1993, (TV movies) Judge Dee, 1974, Please Stand By, 1975, The Night That Panicked America, 1975; dir.: (films) Startrek II: The Wrath of Khan, 1982, Volunteers, 1985, The Deceivers, 1988, (TV movies) The Day After, 1983; playwright, dir.: Loco Motives; author: (nonfiction) The Love Story, 1971, (novels) Target Practice, 1974 (Mystery Writers Guild award), The Seven-Percent Solution: Being a Reprint from the Reminiscences of John H. Watson, M.D., 1974 (Gold Dagger award British Crime Writers Assn.), The West End Horror: A Posthumous Memoir of John H. Watson, M.D., 1976, (with Barry J. Kaplan) Black Orchid, 1977, Confessions of a Homing Pigeon, 1981, The Canary Trainer, 1993. Recipient Anne Radcliffe award Count Dracula Soc. Mem. Authors Guild, Writers Guild. Democrat. Home: 2109 Stanley Hills Dr Los Angeles CA 90046-1529 Office: Creative Artists Agy 9830 Wilshire Blvd Beverly Hills CA 90212-1804

MEYER, PATRICIA MORGAN, neuropsychologist, educator; b. Delaware, Ohio, June 23, 1934; d. Thomas Wendell and Ceola (Drummond) Morgan; m. Donald Ray Meyer, Dec. 31, 1957; 1 dau., Julia Catherine. A.B., Ohio Wesleyan U., 1956; M.A., Ohio State U., 1958, Ph.D., 1960. Research assoc. Ohio State U., Columbus, 1960-76, prof. psychology, 1976-85, prof. psychology emeritus, 1985—. Editor Physiol. Psychology jour., 1980-85. Recipient Career Devel. award NIMH, Ohio State U., 1966-76. Fellow Am. Psychol. Assn. (bd. sci. affairs 1973-76), Midwestern Psychol. Assn., Psychonomic Soc., Soc. for Neuroscis. Republican. Methodist. Avocation: videography. Home: 476 Overbrook Dr Columbus OH 43214-3127 Office: Ohio State U Dept Psychology 1885 Neil Ave Columbus OH 43210-1222

MEYER, PAUL JOSEPH, lawyer; b. Oak Park, Ill., Nov. 27, 1942; s. Paul Gilbert and Frances Marie (O'Shea) M. B.A. summa cum laude, U. Minn., 1964; J.D. cum laude, U. Notre Dame, 1967. Bar: Ill. 1967, Ariz. 1970, U.S. Tax Ct. 1975, U.S. Supreme Ct. 1980. Law clk. to Hon. Walter V. Schaefer, Ill. Supreme Ct., 1967-68; sr. law clk. to Hon. Earl Warren U.S. Supreme Ct., Washington, 1968-69; assoc. Snell & Wilmer, Phoenix, 1969-71; mem. Meyer, Hendricks, Bivens & Moyes, Phoenix, 1971-96; exec. v.p., gen. counsel Eller Media Co., 1996—. Trustee Ariz. Heart Inst. Found., U. Minn., 1986-96; bd. dirs. Ariz. Coalition for Tomorrow, Phoenix Cmty. Alliance. Ill. State scholar, 1960; Weymouth Kirkland scholar, 1964; William J. Brennan Law scholar, 1964. Mem. Am. Law Inst., ABA, Ariz. Bar Assn., Maricopa County Bar Assn., Notre Dame Law Assn. (bd. dirs.). Club: Phoenix Country, Arizona (Phoenix). Home: 1101 Crystal Point 3129 E San Juan Phoenix AZ 85016 Office: 2850 E Camelback Rd Phoenix AZ 85016

MEYER, PAUL WILLIAM, arboretum director, horticulturist; b. Cin., Aug. 30, 1952; s. Edward F. and Dorothy (Schroeder) M.; m. Debra L. Rodgers, May 16, 1990. BSc, Ohio State U., 1973; MSc, U. Del., 1976; diploma, U. Edinburgh, 1988. Curator Morris Arboretum U. Pa., Phila., 1976-91, dir., 1991—. Bd. dirs. The Henry Found., 1992-93; chair Springfield Twp. planning com., Montgomery County, Pa., 1993. Mem. Am. Assn. Botanical Gardens and Arboreta (bd. dirs. Montgomery County Land Trust), The John Bartram Assn. (bd. dirs., v.p. 1984-85). Avocations: bicycling, swimming, backpacking, gardening. Office: Morris Arboretum of Univ Pa 9414 Meadowbrook Ave Philadelphia PA 19118-2624

MEYER, PAUL WILLIAM, biblical literature educator emeritus; b. Raipur, India, May 31, 1924; s. Armin Frederick and Hulda Dorothea (Klein) M.; m. Mary Louise Yonker, Sept. 3, 1948; children: Katherine Priode, Elizabeth Cooper. BA, Elmhurst Coll., 1945; BD, Union Theol. Sem., 1949, ThD, 1955. Instr. Union Theol. Sem., N.Y.C., 1952-54; asst. prof. Div. Sch., Yale U., New Haven, 1954-62; assoc. prof. Div. Sch., Yale U., 1962-64; prof. N.T. interpretation Colgate Rochester (N.Y.) Div. Sch., 1964-70; prof. N.T. Div. Sch., Vanderbilt U., Nashville, 1970-78; Helen H.P. Manson prof. N.T. lit. Princeton (N.J.) Theol. Sem., 1978-89, prof. emeritus, 1989—; adj. prof. dept. religious studies Univ. N.C., Chapel Hill, 1989—. Served with U.S. Army, 1943-45. Morse fellow Yale U., 1961-62; Fulbright research grantee U. Gottingen, W. Ger., 1961-62. Mem. Soc. Bibl. Lit. and Exegesis, Studiorum Novi Testamenti Societas, Am. Theol. Soc., AAUP. Presbyterian.

MEYER, PEARL, executive compensation consultant; b. N.Y.C.; d. Allen Charles and Rose (Goldberg) Weissman; m. Ira A. Meyer. BA cum laude, NYU, postgrad. Statis. specialist, exec. comp. div. Gen. Foods Corp., White Plains, N.Y.; exec. v.p. and cons. Handy Assocs., Inc., N.Y.C.; founder, pres. Pearl Meyer & Ptnrs., N.Y.C., 1989—; lectr. on exec. compensation at confs. and seminars. Contbr. numerous articles to profl. jours. Recipient Entrepreneurial Woman award Women Bus. Owners N.Y., 1983. Mem. Am. Mgmt. Assn., Am. Compensation Assn., Soc. for Human Resources Mgmt. (cert. accredited pers. diplomate), Women's Econ. Roundtable, Pers. Accreditation Inst., Women's Forum, Sedgewood Club, Atrium Club, Sky Club, Phi Beta Kappa, Pi Mu Epsilon, Kappa Pi Sigma. Clubs: Sedgewood, Bd. Rm., Atrium, Sky. Office: Pearl Meyer & Partners Inc 300 Park Ave 21st Fl New York NY 10022-7402*

MEYER, PETER, physicist, educator; b. Berlin, Jan. 6, 1920; came to U.S., 1952, naturalized, 1962; s. Franz and Frida (Lehmann) M.; m. Luise Schützmeister, July 20, 1946 (dec. 1981); children: Stephan S., Andreas S.; m. Patricia G. Spear, June 14, 1983. Dipl.Ing., Tech. U., Berlin, 1942; Ph.D., U. Goettingen, Germany, 1948. Faculty U. Goettingen, 1946-49; fellow U. Cambridge, Eng., 1949-50; mem. sci. staff Max-Planck Inst. fuer Physik, Goettingen, 1950-52; faculty U. Chgo., 1953—, prof. physics, 1965-90, prof. emeritus, 1990—, chmn. Dept. Physics, 1986-89; dir. Enrico Fermi Inst., 1978-83; cons. NASA, NSF; mem. cosmic ray commn. Internat. Union Pure and Applied Physics, 1966-72; mem. space sci. bd. Nat. Acad. Scis., 1975-78. Recipient Alexander von Humboldt Sr. U.S. Scientist award, 1984, Llewellyn John and Harriet Manchester Quantrell award, 1971. Fellow Am. Phys. Soc. (chmn. div. cosmic physics 1972-73), AAAS; mem. NAS, Am. Astron. Soc., Am. Geophys. Union, Max Planck Inst. fuer Physik und Astrophysik (fgn.), Sigma Xi. Office: 933 E 56th St Chicago IL 60637-1460

MEYER, PHILIP EDWARD, journalism educator; b. Deshler, Nebr., Oct. 27, 1930; s. Elmer Edward and Hilda Grace (Morrison) M.; m. Sue Quail, Aug. 5, 1956; children: Caroline, Katherine, Melissa, Sarah. BS, Kans. State U., 1952; MA, U. N.C., 1963. Asst. state editor Topeka (Kans.) Daily Capital, 1954-56; reporter Miami (Fla.) Herald, 1958-62; Washington corr. Akron Beacon Jour., 1962-66; nat. corr. Knight-Ridder, Inc., Washington, 1967-78; dir. news research Knight-Ridder, Inc., Miami, 1978-81; William Rand Kenan Jr. prof. journalism U. N.C., Chapel Hill, 1981-93; Knight prof., 1993—. Author: Precision Journalism, 1973 (Sigma Delta Chi Disting. Service award 1974), The Newspaper Survival Book, 1985, Ethical Journalism, 1987, The New Precision Journalism, 1991; co-author: To Keep the Republic, 1975. Project dir. Russell Sage Found., N.Y.C., 1969-70. Served with USNR, 1952-54. Recipient Disting. Contbns. to Journalism award Nat. Press Found., 1994, Disting. Contbns. to Media and Media Studies award Freedom Forum Media Studies Ctr., 1995; Nieman fellow Harvard U., 1966-67, fellow Freedom Forum Ctr. for Media Studies, 1985. Mem. Am. Assn. for Pub. Opinion Rsch. (pres. 1989-90), World Assn. for Pub. Opinion Rsch. (pres. 1994-95), Assn. for Edn. in Journalism and Mass Comm., Nat. Press Club (Washington). Democrat. Episcopalian. Avocation: photography. Home: 610 Croom Ct Chapel Hill NC 27514-6706 Office: UNC Sch Journalism & Mass Comm Howell Hall CB3365 Chapel Hill NC 27599

MEYER, PRISCILLA ANN, Russian language and literature educator, writer, translator; b. N.Y.C., Aug. 26, 1942; d. Herbert Edward and Marjorie Rose (Wolff) M.; m. William L. Trousdale, Sept. 15, 1974; 1 dau., Rachel V. B.A., U. Calif.-Berkeley, 1964; M.A., Princeton U., 1966, Ph.D., 1971. Lectr. in Russian lang. and lit. Wesleyan U., Middletown, Conn., 1968-71, asst. prof., 1971-75, assoc. prof., 1975-88, prof., 1988—; vis. asst. prof. Yale U., 1973; tchr. John Lyman Elem. Sch., Middlefield, Conn., 1982, 83. Editor: Dostoevsky and Gogol, 1979; Life in Windy Weather (by Andrei Bitov), 1986; Find What The Sailor Has Hidden: Vladimir Nabokov's Pale Fire, 1988; co-editor: Essays on Gogol: Logos and the Russian Word, 1992; translator stories; contbr. articles to profl. jours. Sr. scholar exchange Internat. Research and Exchange Bd., 1973; Ford Found. grantee, 1964-68, 70. Mem. Am. Council Tchrs. Russian (dir. 1983-86), Am. Assn. Tchrs. Slavic and East European Langs., Am. Assn. for Advancement of Slavic Studies, Vladimir Nabokov Soc., Tolstoi Soc., Dostoevsky Soc., Conn. Acad. Arts and Scis. Office: Russian Dept Wesleyan U Middletown CT 06459

MEYER, PUCCI, newspaper editor; b. N.Y.C., Sept. 1, 1944; d. Charles Albert and Lollo (Offer) M.; m. Thomas M. Arma, Sept. 16, 1979. BA, U. Wis., 1966. Asst. editor Look mag., N.Y.C., 1970-71; editorial asst. Look mag., Paris, 1967-69; reporter Newsday, Garden City, L.I., N.Y., 1971-73; style editor N.Y. Daily News Sunday Mag., N.Y.C., 1974-76, assoc. editor, 1977-82, editor, 1983-86; sr. editor Prodigy, White Plains, N.Y., 1987; spl. projects editor N.Y. Post, N.Y.C., 1988-89, style editor, 1990-92, food editor, 1992-93, assoc. features editor, 1993—, travel editor, 1994—. Contbr. articles to various nat. mags. Recipient Pulitzer prize as mem. Newsday investigative team that wrote articles and book The Heroin Trail, 1973. Office: NY Post 1211 6th Ave New York NY 10036

MEYER, RACHEL ABIJAH, foundation director, artist, theorist, poet; b. Job's Corners, Pa., Aug. 18, 1963; d. Jacob Owen and Velma Ruth (Foreman) M.; children: Andrew Carson, Peter Franklin. Student, Lebanon Valley Coll., 1982-84. Restaurant owner Purcy's Place, Ono, Pa., 1985-87; restaurant mgr. King's Table Buffet, Citrus Heights, Calif., 1987-89; product finalizer TransWorld Enterprises, Blaine, Wash., 1989-91; dir., support svcs. adminstr. Tacticar Found., Sacramento, 1991—; tchr. Tacticar Inst., 1995; chair Conirems, Sacramento, 1996—. Author: Year of the Unicorn, 1994. Avocations: researching, writing, painting. Home and Office: 2052 Janice Ave Sacramento CA 95821-1519

MEYER, RANDALL, retired oil company executive; b. Mt. Union, Iowa, Jan. 19, 1923; s. Carl Henry and Edythe (Stuck) M.; m. Barbara Swetman, Nov. 29, 1958; children: Warren, Gretchen, Kirsten. B.S. in Mech. Engring, U. Iowa, 1948; LL.D. (hon.), Iowa Wesleyan Coll., 1977. With Exxon Co. U.S.A. div. Exxon Corp., 1948-88; with tech. and mgmt. depts. Exxon Co. U.S.A., Baton Rouge and Houston, 1948-66; exec. asst. to pres. Exxon Corp., N.Y.C., 1966-67; sr. v.p., dir. Exxon Co. U.S.A., Houston, 1967-72, pres., 1972-88; bd. dirs., exec. com. Greater Houston Partnership; bd. dirs., chmn. Exec. Svc. Corps Houston; dir. M.D. Anderson Cancer Ctr. Outreach Corp. Trustee, mem. exec. com. Kinkaid Sch.; mem. bd. visitors U. Tex. M.D. Anderson Cancer Ctr. Found.; bd. dirs., pres. Greater Houston Cmty. Found.; bd. dirs. U. Iowa Found., Tex. So. U. Found. Mem. Am. Petroleum Inst. (bd. dirs.), Tex. Rsch. League, Sigma Xi, Tau Beta Pi, Omicron Delta Kappa, Pi Tau Sigma. Methodist.

MEYER, RAYMOND JOSEPH, former college basketball coach; b. Chgo., Dec. 18, 1913; s. Joseph E. and Barbara (Hummel) M.; m. Margaret Mary Delaney, May 27, 1939 (dec. 1985); children—Barbara (Mrs. Gerald Starzyk), Raymond Thomas, Patricia (Mrs. Thomas Butterfield), Merianne (Mrs. James McGowan), Joseph, Robert. A.B., U. Notre Dame, 1938. Asst. coach U. Notre Dame, 1941-42; basketball coach DePaul U., Chgo., 1942—. Author: How To Play Winning Basketball, 1960, Basketball as Coached by Ray Meyer, 1967, Ray Meyer, 1 Coach, 1980, Coach, 1987. Named Coach of Yr. Chgo. Basketball Writers, 1943, 44, 48, 52, Coach of Yr. Nat. Assn. Basketball Coaches, 1978-79, Sportwriters Coach of Yr., 1978, Salvation Man of Yr., 1990; recipient Marine Corps Sportsman of Yr. award, 1979, Bunn award, 1981, Victor award, 1981, Lincoln Acad. award, 1988, Nat. Basketball Coach's Golden Jubilee award; inducted into Basketball Hall of Fame, 1979, Basketball Hall of Fame Chgo., 1981, Basketball Hall of Fame Ill., Golden Anniversay award Nat. Basketball Coaches, 1992. Mem. Nat. Basketball Coaches Assn. Roman Catholic. Home: 2518 W Cedar Glen Dr Arlington Heights IL 60005-4336 Office: 1011 W Belden Ave Chicago IL 60614-3205

MEYER, RICHARD CHARLES, microbiologist; b. Cleve., May 2, 1930; s. Frederick Albert and Tekla Charlotte (Schrade) M.; m. Carolyn Yvonne Patton, Apr. 6, 1963; children: Frederick Gustav, Carl Anselm. B.Sc., Baldwin-Wallace Coll., 1952; M.Sc., Ohio State U., 1957, Ph.D., 1961. Teaching and research asst. Ohio State U., 1956-61, research assoc., 1961-62; microbiologist Nat. Cancer Inst., NIH, Bethesda, Md., 1962-64; asst. prof. vet. pathology and hygiene and microbiology U. Ill., Urbana-Champaign, 1965-68; assoc. prof. U. Ill., 1968-73, prof., 1973-89, prof. emeritus, 1989—. Served with C.E. U.S. Army, 1952-54. Mem. Am. Acad. Microbiology, AAAS, Am. Inst. Biol. Sci., Am. Soc. Microbiology, Gamma Sigma Delta, Phi Zeta. Republican. Lutheran. Home: 1504 Buckthorn Ln Mahomet IL 61853-3632 Office: Dept Vet Pathobiology U Ill at Urbana-Champaign Urbana IL 61801

MEYER, RICHARD JONAH, broadcast executive, consultant; b. Bklyn., Feb. 15, 1933; s. Max and Evelyn (Berman) M.; m. Sylvia R. Marshall, Feb. 21, 1956 (div. 1974); children: Adina, Mahlon, Rachel; m. Susan Diane Harmon, Apr. 9, 1983. BA, Stanford U., 1954, postgrad., 1954, 60, MA, 1960; PhD, NYU, 1967; postgrad., Harvard U., 1978. Prodn. asst. Sta. KQED-TV, San Francisco, 1961; dir. ednl. TV Wichita (Kans.) State U., 1961-64; v.p. Sta. WNET-TV, N.Y.C., 1965-72; gen. mgr. Sta. KCTS-TV, Seattle, 1972-82; pres., gen. mgr., chief exec. officer Stas. KERA-FM-TV, KDTN-TV, Dallas, Ft. Worth, Denton, Tex., 1982—; cons. SUNY-Albany, 1967-68, UNESCO, Paris, 1970—, Corp. for Pub. Broadcasting, Washington, 1971—, USIA, Washington, 1972—; broadcaster-in-residence, sr. fellow East-West Ctr., 1989; adj. prof. U. North Tex., 1990, U. Tex., Dallas, 1994. Contbr. chpts. to books; exec. producer (TV series) Communications and Edn., 1967. Bd. dirs. NAEB, 1971-73, Henry Art Gallery, Seattle, 1974, PBS, 1979-84, Nat. Mus. Comm.; trustee Va. Mason Rsch. Ctr., 1979, Goals for Dallas, 1988; v.p. bd. dirs. Silent Film Festival, San Francisco, 1995—. Russell Sage fellow Columbia U., 1968. Mem. Nat. Assn. Underwater Instrs., Internat. Brecht Soc. Jewish. Club: City (Dallas). Office: Sta KERA-TV 3000 Harry Hines Blvd Dallas TX 75201-1012

MEYER, RICHARD SCHLOMER, food company executive; b. Rapid City, S.D., Dec. 31, 1945; s. Harm Henry Schlomer and Marie Charolette (Hoffman) Meyer; m. Bonnie June Francis, July 15, 1970; children: Jennifer June, Christina Francis, Robert Schlomer. BS, Wash. State U., 1968, MS, 1970; PhD, Cornell U., 1974. Sr. scientist Nestle Co., New Milford, Conn., 1974-76; mgr. research and devel. Armour & Co., Scottsdale, Ariz., 1976-81; v.p. and tech. mgr. research and devel. Griffith Labs., Alsip, Ill., 1981-82; v.p. tech. dir. research and devel. Kitchens of Sara Lee, Deerfield, Ill., 1982-84, Nalley's Curtice-Burns div. Agway, Tacoma, 1984-88; tech. v.p. Western regional lab. Curtice-Burns, Tacoma, 1988-95; v.p. tech. McCain Foods, Inc., Oak Brook, Ill., 1995—; strategic planning com. N.W. Food Processor's Assn., Portland, Oreg., 1985—; pres. agrl. mktg. adv. bd. State of Wash., gov. coun. on agr. and environ., 1994—; pres. adv. bd. Wash. State U. Coll. Agr. and Home Econs., bd. trustees, 1992—; mem. U.S. Trade Mission to Indonesia, 1992; adj. prof. Wash. State U., Oreg. State U.; adv. coun. on food processing Elec. Power Rsch. Inst., 1994—; adv. com. food sci. dept. Cornell U., 1994—. Contbr. articles to profl. jours.; holder 24 patents in field. Mem. exec. com. Cornell U., 1973-74, mem. adv. bd. food sci. dept., 1994; mem. bd. edn. New Milford Pub. Schs., 1975-81; bd. regents Wash. State U., 1969-70, trustee, 1992—, pres. Coll. Agr. and home econs. adv. bd., mem. food svc. and human nutrition adv. bd.; Rep. state committeeman and precinct capt., Phoenix, 1979-81; mem. indsl. food coun., food sci. dept. Oreg. State U., 1990—; mem. food engring. adv. coun. U. Calif., Davis, 1990—; mem. agrl. mktg. adv. bd. Wash. State U., 1991—; food industry rep. WSU-Kellogg Found. Edn. Sys. for U.S. Food Industry, 1994. NIH fellow, 1971, 72. Mem. Inst. Food Technologists, Internat. Rsch. Inst., Nutrition Today Soc., Wash. Agr. and Forestry Found., Can. Inst. Food Sci. and Tech., Am. Meat Sci. Assn., Coll. of Agr. and Home Econs. Alumni Assn. (pres. 1990-92), World Poultry Sci. Assn., Shriner, Masons, Phi Kappa Phi, Alpha Zeta. Mem. Christian Ch. Office: McCain Foods Inc 2905 Butterfield Rd Oak Brook IL 60521-1106

MEYER, ROGER JESS CHRISTIAN, pediatrics educator; b. Olympia, Wash., May 14, 1928; s. Paul Eugene and Martha Bell Rogers Meyer; m. Joyce Langley, Mar. 14, 1959; children: Paul, John, William, Douglas, Nancy, Liz. BS in Chemistry, U. Wash., Seattle, 1951; MD, Washington U., St. Louis, 1955; MPH, Harvard U., 1959. Cert. pediatric bds. eligible rehab., preventive medicine, family practice. Instr. pediatrics Harvard Med. Sch., Boston, 1959-62; asst. prof. U. Vt. Coll. Medicine, Burlington, 1962-65; assoc. prof. U. Va. Sch. Medicine, Charlottesville, 1965-68; assoc. prof. pediatrics Northwestern U., Chgo., 1968-76; asst. dean U. Ill. Sch. Pub. Health, Chgo., 1974-76; prof. pediatrics and pub. health Sch. Medicine U. Wash., Seattle, 1976—; with U.S. Army Res. Med. Corps, 1982; advanced through grades to col. U.S. Army, 1986; chair, bd. dirs. community pediatrics sect. Am. Acad. Pediatrics, Evanston, Ill,, 1973-74; pres. Child and Family Health Found., 1976—; bd. dirs. Nat. Com. Prevention Child Abuse, Chgo., 1974-76. Author 140 books and articles. Bd. dirs. N.W. orgn. ARC, Miller Bay Estates and Indianola Land Trust, Unitarian Universalist Ch., Bainbridge; chief pub. health Pacific Rim, U.S. Army Med. Corps 364 Civil Affairs, 1986-93; staff Madigan Army Med. Ctr.; faculty Def. Dept. JMRTC. Decorated Army Achievement medal (2) for disting. svc. 1988-89; recipient NIMH Social Sci. in Medicine award Harvard U., 1961, Children's Hosp. Ann. award, Boston, 1959; Shaller scholar U. Wash., 1950-51, NIMH Health scholar U. Rochester, 1957-58; Oxford fellow, 1992. Mem. APHA, Am. Acad. Pediat. (sect. on child devel., ethics, pediat. mil.), Marine Sci. Soc. Pacific N.W. (N.W. global epidemiology com., pres.), N.W. Pediat. Soc., Res. Officers Assn., Harvard U. Alumni Assn., Washington U. Alumni Assn. Home: 22125 Apollo Dr NE Poulsbo WA 98370-7719

MEYER, RON, agent; b. 1944; m. Kelly Chapman; children, Jennifer, Sarah, Carson. With Paul Kohner Agency, 1965-1970; agent William Morris Agency, Beverly Hills, CA, 1970-1975; co-founder, pres. Creative Artists Agency, Inc., Beverly Hills, CA, 1975-95; pres., ceo Universal City Studios Inc., Universal City, 1995—. Served with USMC. Office: Universal City Studios Inc 100 Universal City Plz Universal City CA 91608*

MEYER, RUSSEL WILLIAM, JR., aircraft company executive; b. Davenport, Iowa, July 19, 1932; s. Russell William and Ellen Marie (Matthews) M.; m. Helen Scott Vaughn, Aug. 20, 1960; children: Russell William, III, Elizabeth Ellen, Jeffrey Vaughn, Christopher Matthews, Carolyn Louise. B.A., Yale U., 1954; LL.B., Harvard U., 1961. Bar: Ohio 1961. Mem. firm Arter & Hadden, Cleve., 1961-66; pres., chief exec. officer Grumman Am. Aviation Corp., Cleve., 1966-74; exec. v.p. Cessna Aircraft Co., Wichita, Kans., 1974-75; chmn. bd., chief exec. officer Cessna Aircraft Co., 1975—; bd. dirs. Western Resources, Boatman's Bancorp, Vanguard Airlines; presdl. appointee Aviation Safety Commn., 1987—; mem. Pres.' Airline Commn., 1993. chmn. bd. trustees 1st Bapt. Ch., Cleve., 1972-74; bd. dirs. United Way, Wichita and Sedgwick County, Wichita State U. Endowment Assn.; trustee Wesley Hosp. Endowment Assn., Wake Forest univ.; bd. govs. United Way Am., 1993—. Served with USAF, 1955-58. Recipient Collier trophy Nat. Aeronautic Assn., 1986, George S. Dively award Harvard U., 1992, Wright Bros. Meml. trophy, 1995. Mem. ABA, Ohio Bar Assn., Kans. Bar Assn., Cleve. Bar Assn., Gen. Aviation Mfrs. Assn. (chmn. bd. dirs. 1973-74, 81-82, 93-94), Wichita C. of C. (chmn. 1988—, bd. dirs.). Clubs: Wichita, Wichita Country, Castle Pines, Isleworth, Latrobe Country. Home: 600 N Tara Ct Wichita KS 67206-1830 Office: Cessna Aircraft PO Box 7704 1 Cessna Blvd Wichita KS 67215-1400

MEYER, RUTH KRUEGER, museum administrator, educator, art historian; b. Chicago Heights, Ill., Aug. 20, 1940; d. Harold Rohe and Ruth Halbert (Bateman) Krueger; m. Kenneth R. Meyer, June 15, 1963 (div. 1978); 1 child, Karl Augustus. B.F.A., U. Cin., 1963; M.A., Brown U., 1968; Ph.D., U. Minn., 1980. Lectr. Walker Art Ctr., Mpls., 1970-72; instr. U. Cin., 1973-75; curator Contemporary Arts Ctr., Cin., 1976-80; dir. Ohio Found. Arts, Columbus, 1980-83, Taft Mus., Cin., 1983-93; prof. Miyazaki (Japan) Internat. Coll., 1994—; adj. prof. The Union Inst., Cin., 1994. Pub. Dialogue Mag., Columbus, 1980-83; author: (exhbn. catalogues) Sandy Rosen Vestal Vases, 1986, Oblique Illusion: An Installation by Rick Paul, 1986, David Black an American Sculptor, 1985, Brad Davis: The Pines, 1984, The American Weigh, 1983, New Epiphanies, 1982, (with others) The Tafts Collection: The First Ten Years of Its Development, 1988, The Tafts of Pike St., 1988, (exhbn. catalogue) The History of Travel: Paintings by William Wegman, 1985-90, 1990, The Artist Face to Face: Two Centuries of Self-Portraits from the Paris Collection of Gerald Shurr, 1989, Tributes to the Tafts, 1991, The Taft Museum: Its Collection and Its History, 1995; contbr. articles to profl. jours. Recipient rsch. award Kress Found., 1967, 76; named Chevalier in the Order of Arts and Letters, Govt. of France, 1989. Mem. Internat. Assn. Art Critics, Coll. Art Assn. Democrat. Office: Miyazaki Internat College, 1405 Kano Kiyotake-Cho, Miyazaki 88916, Japan

MEYER, SANDRA W(ASSERSTEIN), bank executive, management consultant; b. N.J., Aug. 20, 1937; children—Jenifer Anne Schweitzer, Samantha Boughton Schweitzer. Student, U. Mich.; B.A. cum laude, Syracuse U., 1957; postgrad., London Sch. Econs., 1958. Advt. account exec. London Press Exchange, 1959-63; product mgr. Beecham Products Inc., Clifton, N.J., 1963-66; with Gen. Foods Co., White Plains, N.J., 1966-76; mktg. mgr. coffee div. Gen. Foods Co., 1973-74, dir. corp. mktg. planning, 1975-76; with Am. Express Co., N.Y.C., 1976-84; pres. communications div. Am. Express Co., 1980-84; mng. dir. Russell Reynolds Assocs., N.Y.C., 1985-89; sr. corp. officer corp. affairs Citicorp, N.Y.C., 1989-93; sr. partner Clark & Weinstock, N.Y.C., 1993—. Trustee Met. Opera Guild, East Hampton Guild Hall; mng. dir. Met. Opera Assn.; bd. dirs. St. Luke's Orch. Office: Clark & Weinstock 52 Vanderbilt Ave New York NY 10017-3808

MEYER, SCOTT D., public relations firm executive; b. Mpls., Oct. 7, 1949. BA in Journalism, U. Minn., 1972; postgrad., N.Y. Inst. of Fin. Asst. v.p., corp. rels. Piper, Jaffray & Hopwood, 1976-77; mgr. investor rels. Internat. Multifoods, 1977-79; dir. pub. rels. First Nat. Bank of Mpls., 1979-80; gen. mgr. pub. rels. Control Data Corp., 1980-84; exec. v.p. Dorn Pub. Rels., 1984-85, pres., from 1985; chmn., chief operating officer Mona, Meyer & McGrath, Mpls.; now vice chmn. Mona, Meyer, McGrath & Gavin, Inc., Mpls. Office: Mona Meyer McGrath & Gavin Inc Ste 500 8400 Normandale Lake Blvd Bloomington MN 55437-1080*

MEYER, SHELDON, publisher; b. Chgo., June 8, 1926; s. Arthur Christof and Hester Truslow (Sheldon) M.; m. Margaret Mary Kirk, July 29, 1964; children: Arabella Christina, Andrew Kirk. A.B. summa cum laude, Princeton U., 1949; MA (hon.), U. Oxford, 1993. With Funk & Wagnalls Co., 1951-55; assoc. editor Grosset & Dunlap, 1955-56; with Oxford Univ. Press, N.Y.C., 1956—; editor Oxford Univ. Press, 1956-70; exec. editor Trade Books, 1970-82, v.p., 1974-79, sr. v.p., 1979—. Mem. Am. Assn. Univ. Presses (bd. dirs. 1969-71, 79-82, v.p. 1979-80), Am. Hist. Assn., Orgn. Am. Historians, Inst. Early Am. History and Culture (bd. dirs. 1985-87), So. Hist. Assn., Am. Studies Assn., Am. Musicol. Assn., Century Assn., Phi Beta Kappa. Home: 180 Riverside Dr New York NY 10024-1021 Office: Oxford U Press Inc 198 Madison Ave New York NY 10016-3903

MEYER, SUSAN E., publisher; b. N.Y.C., Apr. 22, 1940; d. Ernest L. and Dorothy (Narefsky) M. BA, U. Wis., 1962. Asst. editor Collier Books, N.Y.C., 1962; mng. editor Watson-Guptill Publs., N.Y.C., 1963-70; editor-in-chief Am. Artist mag., N.Y.C., 1971-79; editorial dir. Am. Artist, Art and Antiques, Interiors, Residential Interiors, 1979-81; co-pub. Roundtable Press, Inc., 1981—; dir. Ednl. Solutions, Inc., 1969-70; draft counselor Village Peace Ctr., 1967-70; tutor Empire State Coll., 1975-76; adj. prof. Union Grad. Sch., 1976-78; adj. prof. summer program NYU, 1995—. Author: (with Kent) Watercolorists at Work, 1972, Three Generations of the Wyeth Family, 1975, James Montgomery Flagg, 1974, 40 Watercolorists and How They Work, 1976, America's Great Illustrators, 1978, You Can Renovate Your Own Home, 1978, Norman Rockwell's People, 1981, Pasteups and Mechanicals, 1982, Treasury of the Great Children's Book Illustrators, 1983, How to Draw in Pen and Ink, 1985, Mary Cassatt, 1990, Norman Rockwell's World War II, 1991, Edgar Degas, 1994; editor: (with Guptill) Watercolor Painting Step-by-Step, 1966, (with Kent) 100 Watercolor Techniques, 1968, (with Kinstler) Painting Portraits, 1971, 87, (with Craig) Designing with Type, 1971, (with Guptill) Rendering in Pen and Ink, 1976, Rendering in Pencil, 1977, 20 Landscape Painters and How They Work, 1977, 20 Oil Painters and How They Work, 1978, 20 Figure Painters and How They Work, 1979; photographer: (with Buchman) Stage Makeup, 1971, Film and Television Makeup, 1973. Trustee Artists Fellowship, 1978-84, Little Red Sch. House Inc., 1990-92, 92-94, Art Table Inc., 1981-84. Mem. Am. Book Producers Assn. (treas. 1984-89).

MEYER, SUSAN MOON, speech language pathologist, educator; b. Hazleton, Pa., Mar. 8, 1949; d. Robert A. and Jane W. (Walters) Moon; m. John C. Meyer Jr., Feb. 16, 1989; children: Chris, Scott. BS, Pa. State U., 1971, MS, 1972; PhD, Temple U., 1983. Cert. tchr., Pa. Speech-lang. pathologist, instr. Elmira (N.Y.) Coll., 1973-74; speech-lang. pathologist Arnot-Ogden Hosp., Elmira, 1973-74; supr. Sacred Heart Hosp. Speech and Hearing Ctr., Allentown, Pa., 1974-75; speech-lang. pathology instr. Kutztown (Pa.) U., 1975-78, asst. prof., 1978-82, assoc. prof., 1982-85, prof., 1985—; owner Speech and Lang. Svcs., Allentown, 1975-87; cons. Vis. Nurses Assn., Allentown, 1975-85, Home Care, Allentown, 1975-85. Mem. Am. Speech-Lang.-Hearing Assn. (cert., councilor 1986-89, Continuing Edn. award 1982, 85, 88, 91, 93, 94, 95), Pa. Speech-Lang.-Hearing Assn. (cert., v.p. profl. preparation 1985-89, Appreciation award 1987, 88, 89), Northeastern Speech and Hearing Assn. Pa. (pres. 1984-86, Outstanding Dedication award 1985), Coun. Suprs. Speech-Lang. Pathology and Audiology. Avocations: family activities, cross-country skiing, British sports cars, reading. Office: Kutztown U Dept Speech-Lang Kutztown PA 19530

MEYER, SYLVAN HUGH, editor, magazine executive, author; b. Atlanta, Oct. 7, 1921; s. David Norman and Ray (Levinsohn) M.; m. Annemie Heineman, Jan. 19, 1947; children: Erica, David, Jason. A.B. in Journalism, U. N.C., 1943; D.H.L. (hon.), Oglethorpe U., 1973; DL (hon.), Fla. Internat. U., 1994. Editor The Times, Gainesville, Ga., 1950-69; editor Miami (Fla.) News, 1969-73; editor, pres. Miami/South Fla. Mag., 1975-87; pub. South Florida Home & Garden Mag., 1984-87; pub. cons., 1988—; disting. vis. prof. Fla. Internat. U., Miami, 1973-75; project dir. Commn. on Future of South, 1974; chmn. 3d Century U.S.A., Bicentennial Commn. Dade County, 1973-76; chmn., Ga. adv. com. U.S. Commn. Civil Rights, 1958-65; mem. nat. adv. coun. ACLU, 1959—; mem. adv. bd. Pulitzer prize, 1968-73, bd. dirs., 1966-73; adv. com. sch. of communications FIU, 1985—; adj. prof. journalism, U. Miami, 1986-87. Author: (with Seymour C. Nash) Prostate Cancer: Making Survival Decisions, 1994. Mem. So. Growth Policy Bd., 1980-88; mem. exec. com. So. Regional Coun., 1980-86, 92—; mem. Speaker Ho. Rep. Com. on Future of Fla., 1985-89; chair Edn. for Info. Age campaign Fla. Internat. U. Lt. USNR, 1943-46. Nieman fellow Harvard U., 1951; recipient Disting. Svc. Editorial Writing award, 1957, award Sidney Hillman Found., 1961, Dept. of Army Patriotic Civilian Svc. award, 1961, Nat. Jour. award Am. Soc. Planning Ofcls., 1961, Civic award Miami Area Jewish Com. Human Rels., 1989. Mem. City/Regional Mag. Assn. (bd. dirs. 1983-88, pres. 1986-87, Lifetime Achievement award 1991), Am. Coun. on Edn. in Journalism, Greater Miami C. of C. (bd. govs. 1970-74), U. N.C. Alumni Assn. (bd. dirs. 1973), Chattahoochee Country Club, La Gorce Country Club, Sigma Delta Chi, Tau Epsilon Phi. Home and Office: 5500 Collins Ave Apt 901 Miami FL 33140 Address: Long Branch Rd Dahlonega GA 30355

MEYER, THOMAS J., chemistry educator; b. Dennison, Ohio, Dec. 3, 1941; s. Harold Arthur and Sybil (Reece) M.; m. Sandra L. Meyer, June 5, 1963; children: Tyler, Justin. BS, Ohio U., 1963; PhD, Stanford U., 1966. NATO postdoctoral research fellow U. Coll. London, 1967; asst. prof. chemistry U. N.C., Chapel Hill, 1968-72; assoc. prof. chemistry U. N.C., 1972-75, prof. chemistry, 1975—, M.A. Smith prof. chemistry, 1982-86, Kenan prof. chemistry, 1986—, chmn. dept. chemistry, 1985-90, dir. Curriculum in Applied Scis., 1991-94, vice chancellor for grad. studies and rsch., 1994—; ednl. cons. Dillard U., New Orleans, 1974; mem. exec. com. Material Research Ctr., U. N.C., 1974-77; mem. NATO ASI com. on mixed valence compounds in chemistry, physics and biology, Oxford U., 1979; mem. chem. dynamics rev. NSF, 1980; adv. com. proram in molecular biology and biotechnology U. N.C., 1986—, faculty indsl. relations com. Sch. Medicine, 1986—; mem. dept. chemistry Haverford Review Com., 1986; mem. chemistry rev. com. Dept. Energy-SERI, 1986-88, chmn., 1987-88; mem. rev. com. for chemistry Argonne Nat. Lab., U. Chgo., 1987; chmn. outside rev. panel U. Rochester Sci. and Tech. Ctr., 1989-94, rev. com. for chemistry Brookhaven Nat. Lab., 1990-94. Bd. editors Inorganic Chemistry Jour., Am. Chem. Soc., 1985, Accounts Chem. Rsch., 1990—. Mem. N.C. Bd. Sci. and Tech., 1995—; bd. dirs. N.C. Biotech. Ctr., 1994—, Triangle Univs. Ctr. for Advanced Study, Inc., 1995—; bd. trustees Assoc. Univs. Inc., 1995—. Woodrow Wilson fellow, 1963-64; NSF grad. fellow, 1965-66, NATO postdoctoral fellow, 1967, Alfred P. Sloan fellow, 1975-77, Guggenheim fellow, 1983, Erskine fellow, 1985; recipient Tanner award for teaching excellence U. N.C., 1972, Dwyer medal U. NSW, Australia, 1989, Centenary medal Royal Soc. Chemistry, 1991, N.C. Disting. Chemist award N.C. Inst. of Chemists divsn. Am. Inst. Chemists, Inc., 1993. Fellow AAAS, NAS, Am. Acad. Arts and Scis.; mem. AAUP, Am. Chem. Soc. (exec. com. divsn. inorganic chemistry 1982-84, chair 1994, Charles H. Stone award Piedmont sect. 1982, Monsanto Co. award in inorganic chemistry 1990, So. Chemist of Yr. award Memphis sect. 1992, chair divsn. inorganic chemistry 1994). Office: U NC Dept Chemistry Cb 3290 Venable Hall Chapel Hill NC 27599

MEYER, THOMAS JAMES, editorial cartoonist; b. Fort Benning, Ga., May 8, 1955; s. Edward Charles and Carol (McCunniff) M. B.A., U. Mich., 1977. Congl. aide U.S. Ho. of Reps., Washington, 1977-79; free lance cartoonist, illustrator Washington Post, Fed. Times, Bus. Rev. of, Washington, 1979-81; editorial cartoonist San Francisco Chronicle, 1981—. Co-illustrator: The Church In A Democracy: Who Governs?, 1981. Mem. Am. Assn. Editorial Cartoonists. Roman Catholic. Office: San Francisco Chronicle 901 Mission St San Francisco CA 94103-2988

MEYER, TODD KENT, secondary school educator; b. Spencer, Iowa, Sept. 3, 1964; s. Cleber Daniel and Marlys Elaine (Fie) M.; m. Lynette Elizabeth Frohrip, Jan. 1, 1994. BA in Comm./Theater Arts, U. No. Iowa, 1987, BA in Social Sci. Edn., 1990; MA in History, U. S.D., 1995. Tchr. Am. history Waterloo East (Iowa) H.S., 1990; tchr. Am. studies Watertown (S.D.) H.S., 1990—; drama dept. dir. Watertown H.S., 1993-95. Contbr. articles to local newspapers. Vol. ARC, Cedar Falls, Iowa, 1985-90, Spl. Olympics, Cedar Falls, 1985-90; bd. dirs. Watertown Town Players Cmty. Theater, 1992-95. NEH Thomas Jeffer Seminar fellow, 1992, Monticello-Stratford Hall Summer Seminar, Thomas Jefferson Meml. Found., 1993, James Madison Meml. Found. fellow, 1993—. Mem. S.D. Social Studies Coun. (pres. 1993-94). Home: 521 4th St NE Watertown SD 57201-2547 Office: Watertown High Sch 200 9th St NE Watertown SD 57201-2863

MEYER, URSULA, library director; b. Free City of Danzig, Nov. 6, 1927; came to U.S., 1941; d. Herman S. and Gertrud (Rosenfeld) M. BA, UCLA, 1949; M.L.S., U. So. Calif., 1953; postgrad., U. Wis., 1969. Librarian Butte County (Calif.) Library, 1961-68; asst. pub. libraries div. library devel. N.Y. State Library, Albany, 1969-72; coordinator Mountain Valley Coop. System, Sacramento, 1972-73; chmn. 49-99 Coop. Library System, Stockton, Calif., 1974-85; dir. library services Stockton-San Joaquin County Pub. Library, 1974-94. Higher Edn. Title II fellow, 1968-69. Active Freedom to Read Found. Mem. ALA (council 1979-83, chmn. nominating com. 1982-83, legis. com. 1985-87), Calif. Library Assn. (pres. 1978, council 1974-82), Am. Assn. Pub. Adminstrs., Sierra Club. AAUW, LWV, Common Cause. Lodges: Rotary, Soroptimists.

MEYER, WILLIAM DANIELSON, retired department store executive; b. Mpls., May 5, 1923; s. J.A. and Florence (Danielson) M.; m. Betty Ann McBride, May 28, 1950; children—Patricia Ann, Janet Elizabeth, Jean Louise. BS, UCLA, 1947. With actuarial dept. Prudential Ins. Co. Am., L.A., 1948-53; with Carter Hawley Hale Stores, Inc., L.A., 1953-93; ret. L.A., 1993; asst. sec. Carter Hawley Hale Stores, Inc., 1962-64, sec., 1964-73, dir. employee benefits, asst. sec., 1973-93. Bd. dirs. Profit Sharing Coun., chmn., 1984-86; bd. dirs. Travelers Aid Soc., L.A., pres., 1976-77; trustee Profit Sharing Rsch. Found.; v.p. U.S. Diving Found., 1982-84, 90-94, trustee, 1994—. Mem. Am. Soc. Corp. Secs., Personnel and Indsl. Relations Assn., Los Angeles C. of C., Gold Key, Sigma Pi (Founder's award 1992), Alpha Kappa Psi, Phi Phi. Republican. Presbyterian. Home: 1725 Durklyn Ct San Marino CA 91108-2035

MEYER, WILLIAM F., church administrator. Exec. dir. Higher Edn. Svc. of the Lutheran Ch. MO Synod Internat. Ctr., St. Louis. Office: Luth Ch Mo Synod Internat Ctr 1333 S Kirkwood Rd Saint Louis MO 63122-7226

MEYER, WILLIAM MICHAEL, mortgage banking executive; b. Fort Wayne, Ind., Oct. 21, 1940; s. Henry and Lola Mae (Leedy) M.; m. Phyllis Ann Ruetschilling, Aug. 12, 1961; children: Michael Dean, Blaine Aaron, Nathan Daniel, Andrea Rene. Degree in Bus., Ind. U., 1970. V.p. Waterfield Mortgage Corp., Fort Wayne, 1963-73, First Nat. Bank, Colorado Springs, Colo., 1973-78, Underwood Mortgage Co., Lawrenceville, N.J., 1978-79, Data Link Systems, South Bend, Ind., 1979-82; sr. v.p. Inland Mortgage Corp., Indpls., 1982—; bd. dirs. Ctrl. Ind. Quality Leadership Forum, Indpls. Mem. Mortgage Bankers Assn. (mem. com. 1979—), Ind. Mortgage Bankers (bd. dirs. 1992—), Rotary (Zionsville bd. dirs. 1990-93). Republican. Roman Catholic. Avocations: skiing, gardening, swimming, golf. Home: 3216 S 975 E Zionsville IN 46077-8915

MEYER-BAHLBURG, HEINO F. L., psychologist, educator; b. Hamburg, Germany, Feb. 26, 1940; came to U.S., 1969; s. Wilhelm and Marie Luise Meyer-B. Vordiplom in Psychology, U. Hamburg, 1963, Diplom Psychology, 1966; Dr.rer.nat., U. Duesseldorf, 1970. Sci. asst. U. Duesseldorf, 1970; rsch. asst., then rsch. assoc. prof. psychiatry and pediatrics SUNY Med. Sch., Buffalo, 1970-77; rsch. scientist N.Y. State Psychiat. Inst., N.Y.C., 1977—; from assoc. clin. prof. med. psychology to prof. clin. psychology in psychiatry Columbia U. Coll. Physicians and Surgeons, 1978—; pediatric behavioral endocrinologist in psychiatry svc., then full prof., psychologist Presbyn. Hosp., N.Y.C., 1978—. Contbr. numerous articles to profl. publs. Recipient Disting. Sci. Achievement award Soc. for Sci. Study of Sex, 1993; grantee NIMH. Mem. AAAS, APA, German Psychol. Soc., Soc. Pediatric Psychology, Internat. Acad. Sex Rsch., Internat. Soc. Rsch. on Agression, German Sexual Rsch. Soc., Internat. Soc. Psychoneuroendocrinology, Soc. Sci. Study Sex, Soc. Rsch. Child Devel., Soc. Sexual Therapy and Rsch., Lawson Wilkins Pediatric Endocrine Soc., Harry Benjamin Internat. Gender Dysphoria Assn., Internat. AIDS Soc. Office: Columbia U. Dept Psychiatry 722 W 168th St Unit 10 New York NY 10032-2603

MEYER-BORDERS, JANET LOUISE, artist; b. Shreveport, La., June 20, 1955; d. Russell Barton Meyer and Shirley Ann (Emerson) Rydberg; m. Steven Fredric Cogliano, Apr. 21, 1975 (div. Apr. 1981); 1 child, Jeremy Steven Borders; m. Douglas Harold Borders, June 26, 1982; 1 child, Heather Nicole Borders. AA, Coll. of the Desert, 1983; student, Saddleback Coll., 1990; BA in Art and Art History, U. Calif., Santa Cruz, 1993. docent, artist Long Marine Lab., Santa Cruz, 1992—. Tchr. Lawndale (Calif.) Unified Schs., 1976-77; with Employment Devel. Dept., Mammoth Lakes, Calif.,

1978-79, Standard Mortgage Co., Palm Desert, Calif., 1980-82, IBM, Gilroy, Calif., 1983-84, Holidy Host RV Ctr., Scotts Valley, Calif., 1985-86; sec. Classic Framing Constrn. Co., Irvine, Calif., 1988-89; co-owner Santa Cruz Constrn., 1993—. One woman shows include Bridge Gallery, 1992, St. George Expresso, S.C., 1994; Group shows include Saddleback Coll., Calif., 1990, Rt. 66 Gallup, N.Mex., 1990, UCSC Student Ctr., Calif., 1991, 92, 93, Squid Festival, Santa Cruz, Calif., 1991. Mem. Western Arts Assn. Conservators. Democrat. Roman Catholic. Avocations: oil painting, etching, drawing, matting and framing art, collecting art. Home: 213 Continental St Santa Cruz CA 95060-6065 Office: Wildflowers Studio PO Box 2228 Silverdale WA 98383-2228

MEYERHOFF, ERICH, librarian, administrator; b. Braunschweig, Germany, Nov. 24, 1919; came to U.S., 1935; s. Karl and Irma Meyerhoff; m. Inge Zuber; children—Tina, C. Michael. B.S., CCNY, 1943; M.S., N.Y. Sch. Social Work, 1949; M.S.L.S., Columbia U., 1951, cert. advanced librarianship, 1974. Social worker various orgns., to 1951; reference librarian Columbia U. Med. Library, N.Y.C., 1951-57; librarian, asst. prof. Downstate Med. Ctr., SUNY, Bklyn., 1957-61; dir. Med. Library Ctr. N.Y., 1961-67; librarian Health Scis. Library, SUNY-Buffalo, 1967-70; librarian Cornell U. Med. Coll., N.Y.C., 1970-86, asst. dean, 1977-86; chief library service VA Med. Ctr., N.Y.C., 1986-88; archives librarian NYU Med. Ctr., 1980-91; adj. instr. biomed. communications Columbia U., 1976-81; cons. U. Mich., Ann Arbor, 1968, N.Y. Met. Reference and Research Library Agy., 1968-69, Coll. Physicians of Phila., 1969-70. Fellow Med. Library Assn. (cert., bd. dirs. 1972-76, chmn. various coms. 1968-72, 78-81, Inst. for Sci. Info. award 1981-82, Janet Doe lectr. 1977), N.Y. Acad. Medicine; mem. AAAS, AAUP, Spl. Libraries Assn., N.Y. Met. Sect. History of Sci. Soc., Archons of Colophon. Avocations: skiing; hiking; camping. Home: 90 La Salle St New York NY 10027-4719 Office: NYU Med Ctr Archives 550 1st Ave New York NY 10016-6481

MEYERHOFF, JACK FULTON, financial executive; b. Joliet, Ill., May 15, 1926; s. Charles F. and Helen (Ferguson) M.; m. Mary Margaret Williams, Jan. 2, 1949; children—Keith F., Greg H., Deborah S., Todd C. B.S., Miami U., Oxford, Ohio, 1947; postgrad., Ohio Wesleyan U., 1944-45; grad. Advanced Mgmt. Program, Harvard U., 1968. C.P.A., Ohio, Ill. Mgr. Arthur Andersen & Co., Chgo., Cin., Cleve., 1947-59; treas. MacGregor Sports, Cin., 1959-63; v.p., corp. controller Brunswick Corp., Chgo., 1963-77; chief fin. officer Brunswick Corp., 1972-77, v.p. corp. affairs, 1977-80, v.p. human resources, 1980-81; chmn., chief exec. officer MarJac Assocs., Nokomis, Fla., 1981—; pres., dir. Charles Oxford Corp., Nokomis, 1984—; bd. dirs. Sherwood Med. Industries, Inc., Old Orchard Bank & Trust Co., Tech: Time Inc., Nokomis; organizer, vice chmn. bd. trustees Caldwell Trust Co. and Trust Cos. Am., Venice, Fla., 1993—. Treas., bd. dirs. Cove Schs.; bd. dirs., pres. Skokie Valley Cmty. Hosp., No. Ill. Indsl. Assn.; v.p., bd. dirs. Jr. Achievement; bd. dirs. Chgo. Responsibility Growth, Gulf Area Med. Properties; chmn. bd. Bon Secours-Venice Hosp., Venice Hosp. Found.; bd. dirs. J. Clifford MacDonald Handicapped Ctr. of Tampa, Sarasota Com. of 100, Triangle Econ. Devel. Coun., Manatee Cmty. Coll. Found.; mem. adv. coun. Miami U., Georgetown U., U. So. Fla. With USNR, 1944-46. Mem. Am. Inst. C.P.A.s, Ohio Soc. C.P.A.s, Ill. Soc. C.P.A.s, Fin. Execs. Inst., Nat. Assn. Accts., Harvard Bus. Sch. Alumni Assn., Miami U. Exec. Alumni Council (bd. dirs., treas.), Venice Area C. of C. (bd. dirs.), Sigma Alpha Epsilon, Delta Sigma Pi, Beta Alpha Psi, Beta Gamma Sigma. Methodist. Clubs: Venice Yacht, Mid America, Economic, Misty Creek Country, Saddlebrook Country. Lodges: Masons, Rotary. Home: 20 Inlets Blvd Nokomis FL 34275-4108 Office: MSW Assocs PO Box 1326 Nokomis FL 34274-1326

MEYERHOFF, JAMES LESTER, medical researcher; b. Phila., Dec. 12, 1937; s. Lester Bacharach and Natalie Hatch (Rosenberg) M. BA, U. Pa., 1962, MD, 1966. Diplomate Nat. Bd. Med. Examiners, Am. Bd. Psychiatry and Neurology; lic. physician, Md. Intern Misericordia Hosp., Phila., 1966-67; resident U. Chgo. Hosp., 1967-70; postdoctoral fellow Johns Hopkins U., 1970-71; rsch. assoc. Walter Reed Army Inst. Rsch. and Med. Ctr., Washington, 1971-72, head neurochemsitry sect., 1972-74, chief dept. neuroendocrinology, 1974-76, chief neuroendocrinology and neurochemistry bd., 1976—; rsch. prof. psychiatry Uniformed Svcs. U. Health Scis., 1978; clin. assoc. prof. psychiatry Georgetown U., 1977. Contbr. numerous articles to profl. jours. Maj. M.C., U.S. Army, 1969-72. Fellow APA, Acad. Behavioral Medicine; mem. Am. Psychosomatic Soc., Soc. for Neurosci. Office: Walter Reed Army Inst Rsch & Med Ctr Washington DC 20307-5100

MEYEROWITZ, ELLIOT MARTIN, biologist, educator; b. Washington, May 22, 1951; s. Irving and Freda (Goldberg) M.; m. Joan Agnes Kobori, June 17, 1984; 2 children. AB, Columbia U., 1973; MPhil, Yale U., 1975, PhD, 1977. Rsch. fellow Stanford U., Calif., 1977-79; asst. prof. biology Calif. Inst. Tech., Pasadena, 1980-85, assoc. prof. 1985-89, prof., 1989—, exec. officer, 1995—. Mem. editl. bd. Trends in Genetics, Current Biology, Cell, Devel.; contbr. articles to profl. jours., 1978—. Jane Coffin Childs Meml. Fund fellow, 1977-79, Sloan Found. fellow, 1980-82. Fellow AAAS; mem. NAS, Am. Acad. Arts and Scis., Am. Soc. Plant Physiologists (Gibbs medal), Bot. Soc. Am. (Pelton award), Genetics Soc. Am., Internat. Soc. Developmental Biology (bd. dirs.), Internat. Soc. for Plant Molecular Biology (pres.). Office: Calif Inst Tech Div Biology Pasadena CA 91125

MEYERS, ABBEY S., foundation administrator; b. Bklyn., Apr. 11, 1944; d. Herbert and Blossom (Ruben) Feldman; m. Jerrold B. Meyers, Oct. 23, 1966; children: David, Adam, Laura. AAS, N.Y.C. Community Coll., 1962. Comml. artist various advt. agys., N.Y.C., 1962-65; dir. patient svcs. Tourette Syndrome Assn., Bayside, N.Y., 1980-85; exec. dir., founder Nat. Org. for Rare Disorders, New Fairfield, Conn., 1985-95, pres., CEO, 1995—; U.S. commr. Nat. Commn. on Orphan Diseases, Washington, 1986-89; mem. subcom. Human Gene Therapy NIH, Bethesda, Md., 1989-92; mem. recombinant DNA adv. com. NIH, 1992-96; mem. Health Care Payor Adv. Commn. on Conn. Commn. on Hosps. and Health Care, 1992-94. Author: (with others) Orphan Drugs and Orphan Diseases: Clinical Reality and Public Policy, 1983, (with others) Cooperative Approaches to Research and Development of Orphan Drugs, 1985, (with others) Tourette Syndrome: Clinical Understanding and Treatment, 1988, (with others) Physicians Guide to Rare Diseases, 1992. Bd. dirs. Nat. Orphan Drug and Device Found., N.Y.C., 1982-85; leader Coalition to Pass Orphan Drug Act of 1983, 1979-82. Recipient Pub. Health Svc. award HHS, 1985, Commr.'s Spl. citation FDA, 1988. Mem. Nat. Health Coun. (bd. dirs. 1989-94), Alliance of Genetic Support Groups (bd. dirs. 1987-89). Avocations: reading, horseback riding. Office: Nat Org for Rare Disorders PO Box 8923 Fairwood Profl Bldg New Fairfield CT 06812

MEYERS, ALBERT IRVING, chemistry educator; b. N.Y.C., Nov. 22, 1932; s. Hyman and Sylvia (Greenberg) M.; m. Joan Shepard, Aug. 10, 1957; children—Harold, Jill, Lisa. BS, NYU, 1954, PhD, 1957. Rsch. chemist Cities Svc. Oil Co., Cranbury, N.J., 1957-58; asst., assoc. prof., prof. La. State U., New Orleans, 1958-70, Boyd prof., 1969; prof. Wayne State U., Detroit, 1970-72; prof. Colo. State U., Fort Collins, 1972—, disting. prof., 1986—, John K. Stille prof. chemistry, 1993—; spl. postdoctoral fellow Harvard U., Cambridge, 1965-66; cons. G.D. Searle Co., Skokie, Ill., 1972-84, Mid-West Rsch. Inst., Kansas City, Mo., 1974-77, NIH, Bethesda, Md., 1977-79, 85-89, Bristol-Myers Squibb Co., 1983-95, Roche Bioscience, 1989—, Smith Kline Beecham Co., 1994—. Editor Jour. Am. Chem. Soc., 1979-85, Jour. Organic Chemistry, 1990-95, Tetrahedron, 1990—; contbr. over 400 articles to profl. jours. Recipient Alexander von Humboldt award Fed. Republic of Germany, 1984, Disting. Alumni award NYU, 1990; named Man of Yr., New Orleans Jaycees, 1968, Boyd Prof. La. State U., 1969. Fellow AAAS, Nat. Acad. Sci.; mem. Royal Soc. Chemistry (silver medalist 1982), Phila. Organic Chemistry Soc. (Allan Day award 1987). Home: 1500 Hepplewhite Ct Fort Collins CO 80526-3822 Office: Colorado State Univ Dept Chemistry Fort Collins CO 80523

MEYERS, ANN ELIZABETH, sports broadcaster; b. San Diego, Mar. 26, 1955; d. Robert Eugene and Patricia Ann (Burke); m. Donald Scott Drysdale, Nov. 1, 1986; children: Donald Scott Jr., Darren John, Drew Ann. Grad., UCLA, 1978. Profl. basketball player N.J. Gems, 1979-80; profl. basketball player Ind. Pacers NBA, 1979; sports broadcaster Ind. Pacers, 1979-80; sportscaster men's basketball U. Hawaii, Honolulu, 1981-82; sportscaster men's and women's basketball UCLA, 1982-84, 89—; sportscaster volleyball, basketball, softball, tennis ESPN, 1981—; sportscaster Olympic Games ABC, L.A., 1984; sportscaster volleyball, softball, tennis, basketball, soccer Sportsvision, 1985-87; sportscaster volleyball, basketball, softball Prime Ticket, 1985—; sportscaster CBS-TV, 1991—; sportscaster Goodwill Games, WTBS, 1986, 90. Winner Silver medal Montreal Olympics, 1976, Gold medal Pan Am. Games, 1975, Silver medal, 1979, All-Am. UCLA, 1975, 76, 77, 78; 1st woman named to Hall of Fame UCLA, 1987; named to Women's Sports Hall of Fame, 1987, Orange County Sports Hall of Fame, 1985, Calif. H.S. Hall of Fame, 1990, Basketball Hall of Fame, 1993, Nat. H.S. Hall of Fame, 1995, NBC Hoop It Up, 1995, Cath. Youth Org. Hall of Fame, 1996. Office: c/o Lampros and Roberts 16615 Lark Ave # 101 Los Gatos CA 95030-2439

MEYERS, ARTHUR SOLOMON, library director; b. N.Y.C., Dec. 14, 1937; s. Nathan and Selma (Leeser) M.; m. Marcia Indianer, June 11, 1961; children: Naomi, Ruth. AB in History, U. Miami, 1959; MS in LS, Columbia U., 1961; MA in English, U. Mo., St. Louis, 1980; MA in History, Ball State U., Muncie, Ind., 1987. Cert. libr. I, Ind. Young adult libr. N.Y. Pub. Libr., N.Y.C., 1959-61; adult and young adult libr. Detroit Pub. Libr., 1963-67; adult and young adult specialist Enoch Pratt Free Libr., Balt., 1967-73; mgr. brs. and cmty. svc. St. Louis Pub. Libr., 1973-80; dir. Muncie Pub. Libr., 1980-86, Hammond (Ind.) Pub. Libr., 1986—; past pres. Ednl. Referral Ctr., Lake County, Ind.; condr. workshops and insts. in field; presenter in field; past pres. N.W. Ind. Area Libr. Svcs. Authority: mem. Libr. Svcs. to Aging Population Com., Reference and Adult Svcs. Divsn. Contbr. articles to profl. jours. Sec. Calumet Ethnic Heritage Alliance, Lake County, panelist Ind. Humanities Coun., Ind. Arts Commn. With U.S. Army, 1961-63. Mem. ACLU, NAACP, ALA (pres. reference and adult svcs. divsn. 1989-90), Ind. Libr. Fedn. (fed. leg. coord.), Ind. Jewish Hist. Soc. (past pres.), Ind. Hist. Soc., Freedom To Read Found., Democrat. Jewish. Avocations: local and family history research, ethnic heritage research, reference book reviewing. Home: 6537 Kansas Ave Hammond IN 46323-1746 Office: Hammond Pub Libr 564 State St Hammond IN 46320-1532

MEYERS, CANDICE R., television executive; b. Chgo., Aug. 15, 1952; d. Edward A. and Phyllis (Peskind) M.; m. Jonathan Foster King, May 26, 1991; 1 child, Lily. Student, Chgo. Art Inst., 1971, Stanford U., 1973; BA in History, Washington U., St. Louis, 1974. News writer KMOX-TV, St. Louis, 1973-74; writer, prodr. WLS TV, Chgo., 1974-77; news exec. prodr. KPIX TV, San Francisco, 1977-80, programming prodr., 1984-90, exec. news prodr., 1990-95, exec. prodr. programming, new media, 1995—; news exec. prodr. KGO TV, San Francisco, 1980-84. Mem. NATAS (3 No. Calif. Emmy awards 1986, Nat. Emmy award for Cmty. Svc. 1988). Avocations: reading, internet, family. Office: KPIX TV 855 Battery San Francisco CA 94111

MEYERS, CHRISTINE LAINE, marketing and media executive, consultant; b. Detroit, Mar. 7, 1949; d. Ernest Robert and Eva Elizabeth (Laine) M.; 1 child, Kathryn Laine; m. Oliver S. Moore III, May 12, 1990. BA, U. Mich., 1968. Editor, indsl. relations Diesel div. Gen. Motors Corp., Detroit, 1968; nat. advt. mgr. J.L. Hudson Co., Detroit, 1969-76, mgr. internal sales promotion, 1972-73, dir. pub., 1973-76; nat. advt. mgr. Pontiac Motor div., Mich., 1976-78; pres., owner Laine Meyers Mktg. Cos., Inc., Troy, Mich., 1978—; dir. Internat. Inst. Met. Detroit, Inc. Contbr. articles to profl. publs. Mem. bus. adv. council Cen. Mich. U., 1977-79; mem. pub. adv. com. on jud. candidates Oakland County Bar Assn.; mem. adv. bd. Birmingham Community Hosp., bd. dirs. YMCA, Mich., 1992—; Named Mich. Ad Woman of Yr., 1976, one of Top 10 Working Women Glamour mag., 1978, one of 100 Best and Brightest Advt. Age, 1987, one of Mich.'s top 25 female bus. owners Nat. Assn. Women Bus. Owners, One of Top 10 Women Owned Bus., Mich., 1994; recipient Vanguard award Women in Communications, 1986. Mem. Internat. Assn. Bus. Communicators, Adcraft Club, Women's Advt. Club (1st v.p. 1975), Women's Econ. Club (pres. 1976-77), Internat. Women's Forum Mich. (pres. 1986—), Internat. Inst. of Detroit (bd. dirs. 1986-89), Detroit C. of C., Troy C. of C., Mortar Board, Quill and Scroll, Pub. Relations Com. Women for United Found., Founders Soc. Detroit Inst. Arts, Fashion Group, Pub. Relations Soc. Am., First Soc. Detroit (exec. com. 1970-71), Kappa Tau Alpha. Home: 1780 Kensington Rd Bloomfield Hills MI 48304-2428 Office: Laine Meyers Marketing Companies Inc 3645 Crooks Rd Troy MI 48084-1642

MEYERS, DALE (MRS. MARIO COOPER), artist; b. Chgo.; d. Walter Herman and Gertude (Pettee) Wetterer; m. Mario Cooper, Oct. 11, 1964; children: Dale (Mrs. John F. Hellegers), Steven R. Student, Glendale Coll., Corcoran Gallery Sch. Art, Washington, 1962-63, Art Student's League, N.Y.C., 1964-78. Instr. Art Students League, 1979—; ofcl. artist NASA, USCG.; lectr. Parson's Sch. Design, Nat. Acad. Sch. Author The Sketchbook, 1983; contbr.: Watercolor Bold and Free, Am. Artist mag, Diversion mag.; solo exhbns. include, West Wing Gallery, Ringwood (N.J.) State Park, 1970, Manor Club, Pelham Manor, N.Y., 1970, Apollo Art Gallery, Oklahoma City, 1972, Quadrangle Gallery, Dallas, 1972, Galveston Ctr. for Arts, 1974, Fla. Gulf Coast Art Ctr., 1977, 86, Okura Hotel, Tokyo, Japan, 1977, Owensboro Mus. Art, 1983, Salmagundi Club, 1986, 88, Stehle-Reed Gallery, Midland, Tex., 1987, others; artist-in-residence, Galveston Arts Ctr., 1974, Owensboro Mus. Art, 1983, Asilomar, Calif., 1983, 84; group exhbns. include Two Hundred Years of Watercolor Painting in Am, Met. Mus. Art, 1966, Eyewitness to Space, Nat. Gallery Art, Washington, 1969, Smithsonian Instn., 1961-63, Corcoran Gallery, 1963, Museo de la Acuarela, Mexico City, 1968, 89, London (Ont., Can.) Mus. Art, 1971-72, Art Gallery Hamilton, Ont., Can., 1971-72, Ont. Inst. Edn., 1971-72, Butler Inst. Art, 1962—, Frye Mus., 1962—; represented in permanent collections, Calif. Palace of Legion of Honor, San Francisco, Nat. Acad. N.Y.C., Avon Fine Arts Collection, NASA, EPA, Museo de la Acuarela, Schumacher Gallery, Columbus, Ohio, Slater Mus., Conn., Portland (Maine) Mus., U. Utah Fine Arts Collection, Frye Mus., Seattle, Owensboro Mus. Art, Coll. Misericordia, Dallas, Pa, Canton Art Inst., Ohio, Arnot Mus., Elmira, N.Y.; internat. watercolor exhbn. Can., U.S., Gt. Britain, 1991-94, Chung Cheng Gallery, Taipei, 1994. Recipient Henry W. Ranger award Nat. Acad. Design, 1968, Samuel F.B. Morse medal, 1973, Anna Hyatt Huntington Bronze medal, 1971, Knickerbocker Artists Gold medal, 1981, 88, Allied Artists Am. award, 1969, Gold medal honor Nat. Arts Club, 1972, Anna Hyatt Huntington Gold medal, 1974, Adolf and Cara Obrig award Nat. Acad., 1974, 81, Walter Biggs award, 1976, Allied Arts Gold medal, 1978, Audubon ARtists Silver medal, 1984. Fellow Royal Soc. Arts (Grumbocher Gold medals 1988, 90); mem. Am. Watercolor Soc. (pres. 1993—, editor jours. 1962-79, Bronze medal honor award 1968, awards 1970, 72, 78, 79, 81, 82, 83, 85, 87, 89, 93), Nat. Acad. (academician), Allied Artists Am. (pres. 1975-78), Knickerbocker Artists, Art Students League N.Y., La. Watercolor Soc. (hon.), Ky. Watercolor Soc., Ohio Watercolor Soc. (hon.), Watercolor Soc. Mex., Fla. Watercolor Soc. (hon.), Audubon Artists, Salimagundi Club (medal of honor 1994). Address: 1 W 67th St New York NY 10023-6200

MEYERS, DOROTHY, education consultant, writer; b. Chgo., Jan. 9, 1927; d. Gilbert and Harriet (Levitt) King; m. William J. Meyers, Oct. 9, 1947; children: Lynn, Jeanne. BA, U. Chgo., 1945, MA, 1961, postgrad.; postgrad. Columbia U., New Sch. Social Rsch., Northwestern U. Instr. sr. adults, Chgo. Bd. and/City Colls. Chgo., 1961-78; coord. pub. affairs forum and health maintenance program City Colls. Chgo.-Jewish Community Ctrs., Chgo., 1975-78; lectr. adult program City Colls. Chgo., 1984; tchr. Dade County Adult Edn. Program, Miami, Fla., 1983-85; discussion leader Brandeis U. Adult Edn., 1985-86; cons., lectr. in field. Contbr. articles to profl. jours. Chmn. legis. PTA; discussion leader Great Decisions, 1984-86; chmn. civic assembly Citizens Sch. Com.; v.p. community rels. Womens Fedn. and Jewish United Fund; discussion leader LWV, Gt. Decisions, Fgn. Policy Assn.; program chmn. Jewish Community Ctrs., 1966-67, mem. sr. adult com.; bd. dirs. coun. Jewish Elderly, Open U.; mem. art and edn. com. Chgo. Mayor's Com. for Sr. Citizens and Handicapped; mem. com. on media Met. Coun. on Aging; active Bon Secour's Villa Maria Hosp.; founder Mt. Sinai Hosp., Miami Beach; sponsor Miami Heart Inst.; active Royal Notable Alzheimer Care Unit-Douglas Home Miami; com. mem. March of Dimes; amb. Project Newborn U. Miami Pre Natal Unit. Recipient Prima Donna award Men's Opera Guild-Fla., 1995. Mem. ASA, Gerontol. Assn., Nat. Coun. Aging, Nat. Coun. Jewish Women, Women's Auxiliary Jewish Community Ctr., Chgo. Met. Sr. Forum (media com.), Coun. Women Chgo. Real Estate Bd., Women in Communications, Chgo. Real Estate Bd., Nat. Assn. Real Estate Bds., Cultural Ctr. (Miami, Fla.), Mus. Art Ft. Lauderdale, Miami Internat. Press Club, Gastrointestinal Rsch. Found., Brandeis U., Art Inst. Chgo., Mus. Contemporary Art (life), Mus. Art Boca Raton, Brandeis Women's Auxiliary, Circumnavigator Club (Chgo. and Fla. chpts.). Office: 77 W Washington St Chicago IL 60602-2801

MEYERS, EDWARD, photographer, writer, publisher; b. Flushing, N.Y., Nov. 2, 1934; s. Gerson G. and Hester (Noble) M.; m. Marcia Rothman, June 29, 1958; children: Beth, Adam, Rosemarie. BFA, Rochester (N.Y.) Inst. Tech., 1957. Tech. editor Modern Photography mag., N.Y.C., 1957-66; photographer-writer N.Y.C., 1966-70; exec. editor Popular Photography mag., N.Y.C., 1971-86; assoc. pub. Silver Halide Press, N.Y.C., 1986—; lectr. Sch. Visual Arts, 1968—; U.S. corr. FotoPro Reflex mag., Italy, FotoVideo, Spain. Editor: Modern Photography Photo Almanac, 1967, 69; co-editor: The Official Depth of Field Tables, 1962. Served with U.S. Army, 1957-58. Recipient Alumni Achievement award Rochester Inst. Tech., 1972, Art Dir.'s Gold award, 1986. Mem. N.Y. Press Photographers Assn., Am. Soc. Picture Profls., Internat. Assn. Panoramic Photographers, N.Y.C. Audubon Soc., Joint Ethics Com., Nat. Writers Union. Home: 61-68 77th St Middle Village NY 11379

MEYERS, ERIC MARK, religion educator; b. Norwich, Conn., June 5, 1940; s. Karl D. and Shirlee M. (Meyer) M.; m. Carol Lyons, June 25, 1964; children: Julie Kaete, Dina Elisa. AB, Dartmouth Coll., 1962; MA, Brandeis U., 1964; PhD, Harvard U., 1969. Prof. religion, archeology, biblical studies, ancient hist. Duke U., Durham, N.C., 1969—; dir. Annenberg Inst., Phila., 1991-92; pres. Am. Schs. of Oriental Rsch., Balt., 1990-96. Author 8 books; editor-in-chief The Oxford Encyclopedia of Archaeology in the Near East, 5 vols., 1996; contbr. over 250 articles to profl. jours. Jewish. Avocation: singing (baritone). Home: 3202 Waterbury Dr Durham NC 27707-2416 Office: Duke U PO Box 90964 Bldg Durham NC 27708-0964

MEYERS, GEORGE EDWARD, plastics company executive; b. N.Y.C., June 26, 1928; s. Sol and Ethel (Treppel) M. Student, Sampson Coll., 1948-49, Columbia U., 1949-50; m. Marianna Jacobson, Dec. 8, 1955; children: Deborah Lynn, Joanne Alyssa. Technician Manhattan Project, 1944; tech. rep. Mearl Corp., 1952-56; sales mgr. Rona Labs., Bayonne, N.J.1956-59; v.p. Dimensional Pigments Corp., Bayonne, 1959-60; pres. Plastic Cons. Internat., Inc., Dix Hills, N.Y., 1959—, Tech. Machinery Corp., Plainview, N.Y., 1963-69; pres. Extrudyne, Inc., Amityville, N.Y., 1970-77, also bd. dirs.; bd. dirs. rsch. and devel. Homeland Industries, Bohemia, N.Y., 1977-80; bd. dir. ops. Aqua-Sol, Inc., Deer Park, N.Y., 1980-85; tchr., staff cons. N.Y.C. Bd. Higher Edn., Bronx C.C., 1966-70; lectr. NYU, Technion, Haifa, Israel; lectr. in field. Patentee in field; contbr. articles to profl. jours. Served with CIC, AUS, 1946-48. Mem. Soc. Plastics Engrs. (sr. mem., v.p. N.Y. sect. 1967-68), Soc. Plastics Industry (profl. mem.), Am. Ordnance Assn., Aircraft Owners and Pilots Assn, NRA (life mem., cert. instr.), Am. Chem. Soc., Internat. Assn. Housing Sci. (charter mem.), Internat. Assn. Soilless Culture, Army Counter-Intelligence Corps Assn., U.S. Constabulary Assn. Seminar conductor in plastics and hydroponics and seminar leader Modern Plastics Mag. courses. Avocations: flying, numismatics, pistol shooting, antique collector, tech. expert to legal firms and qualified expert witness in state and federal courts. Home and Office: 25 Penn Dr Dix Hills NY 11746-8532

MEYERS, GERALD A., metal products executive. With Logan Aluminum Inc., Bowling Green, Ky., Alcan & Logan, U.S. and Canada; now pres., coo Ravenswood Aluminum Corp., W.Va. Office: Ravenswood Aluminum Corp RR 2 Ravenswood WV 26164-9802*

MEYERS, GERALD CARL, management consultant, author, educator, lecturer, former automobile company executive; b. Buffalo, Dec. 5, 1928; s. Meyer and Berenice (Meyers) M.; m. Barbara Jacob, Nov. 2, 1958. BS, Carnegie Inst. Tech., 1950, MS with distinction, 1954. With Ford Motor Co., Detroit, 1950-51, Chrysler Corp., Detroit and Geneva, 1954-62; with Am. Motors Corp., Detroit, 1962—; v.p. Am. Motors Corp., 1967-72, group v.p. product, 1972-75, exec. v.p., 1975-77, pres., 1977—, chief operating officer, 1977, chief exec. officer, 1977—, chmn., 1978-82; pres. Gerald C. Meyers Assocs., Inc., West Bloomfield, Mich.; Ford disting. prof. Carnegie Mellon U. Grad. Sch. Indsl. Adminstrn.; prof. Grad. Sch. Bus. Adminstrn., U. Mich., Ann Arbor. Served as 1st lt. USAF, 1951-53. Decorated French Legion of Honor. Mem. Econ. Club Detroit, Tau Beta Pi, Phi Kappa Phi, Omicron Delta Kappa. Office: 5600 W Maple Rd Ste 216B West Bloomfield MI 48322-3704

MEYERS, HAROLD VERNON, chemist; b. New Orleans, Feb. 21, 1961; s. Albert Irving and Joan (Shepard) M.; m. Jane Allin Bybee, Aug. 9, 1986; 1 child, Kimberly Allin. BS, Colo. State U., 1982; PhD, Yale U., 1988. Postdoctoral fellow Columbia U., N.Y.C., 1988-89; scientist Vertex Pharms., Cambridge, Mass., 1989-93; head Cambridge rsch. Sphinx-Cambridge div. Eli Lilly & Co., 1993—. Editor Dodecahedron Abstracts, Yale U., 1984-85, Chem. Highlights, Columbia U., 1988-89; contbr. articles to profl. jours. Univ. fellow Yale U., 1982-86. Mem. ACS (div. medicinal chemistry, div. organic chemistry). Achievements include patents on chemical methods or composition of matter. Home: 46 Van Ness Rd Belmont MA 02178-3405 Office: Sphinx-Cambridge 840 Memorial Dr Cambridge MA 02139-3771

MEYERS, HOWARD L., lawyer; b. Dec. 22, 1948. BS, U. Del., 1970; JD, U. Va., 1973. Bar: Pa. 1973. Mng. ptnr., sr. ptnr. in bus. and fin. sect. Morgan, Lewis & Bockius, Phila. Mem. ABA, Pa. Bar Assn., Phila. Bar Assn., Greater Phila. C. of C. (mem. exec. com., bd. dirs., gen. counsel). Office: Morgan Lewis & Bockius 2000 One Logan Sq Philadelphia PA 19103

MEYERS, JAN, congresswoman; b. Lincoln, Nebr., July 20, 1928; m. Louis Meyers; children: Valerie, Philip. A.A. in Fine Arts, William Woods Coll., 1948; B.A. in Communications (hon.), U. Nebr.-Lincoln, 1951; LittD, William Woods Coll., 1986; LLD (hon.), Baker U., 1993. Mem. Overland Park (Kans.) City Coun., 1967-72; pres. Overland (Kans.) Park City Council; mem. Kans. Senate, 1972-84, chmn. pub. health and welfare com., local govt. com.; mem. 99th-103rd Congresses from 3rd Kans. Dist., 1985—, mem. com. internat. rels., chmn. sml. bus. com., mem. com. on econ. and ednl. opportunities. 3rd Dist. co-chmn. Bob Dole for U.S. Senate, 1968; chmn. Johnson County Bob Bennett For Gov., 1974; mem. Johnson County Cmty. Coll. Found.; bd. dirs. Johnson County Mental Health Assn. Recipient Outstanding Elected Ofcl. of Yr. award Assn. Cmty. Mental Health Ctrs. Kans., Woman of Achievement Matrix award Women in Communications, Disting. Service award Bus. and Profl. Women Kansas City, William Woods Alumna award of distinction, Cmty. Svc. award Jr. League Kansas City, 1st Disting. Legislator award Kans. Assn. C.C.s, Outstanding Svc. award Kans. Library Assn., United Community Services, Kans. Pub. Health Assn., award Gov.'s Conf. Child Abuse and Neglect, Outstanding Legislator award Kans. Action for Children, Friend award Nat. Assn. County Park and Recreation Ofcls., 1987, Disting. Alumna award, 1991, numerous others. Mem. LWV (past pres. Shawnee Mission). Methodist. Office: US Ho of Reps 2303 Rayburn Bldg Ofc Washington DC 20515-0005*

MEYERS, JOHN ALLEN, magazine publisher; b. Winnetka, Ill., Feb. 21, 1929; s. Fred W. and Ruth B. (Burras) M.; m. Jane Bowers, Sept. 18, 1954; children: Jennifer, Katherine, John. B.A., Mich. State U., 1951, Litt.D. (hon.), 1978; postgrad., Columbia U., 1965. Mgr. Cleve. Time mag., 1960-63, mgr. Chgo., 1963-65; mgr. Time mag., N.Y.C., 1965-68, worldwide advt. sales dir., 1968-72; v.p. Time, Inc., publisher Sports Illustrated mag., 1972-78; pub. Time mag., 1978-85; chmn. Time Inc. Mag. Co., 1985-88; chmn. emeritus Time Inc., 1988—; appointed presdl. bd. adv. on Pvt. Sector Initiatives; chmn. J.A.M. Enterprises; bd. dirs. Tambrands. Editor-in-chief Constitution mag. Pres., Found. for the U.S. Constn. Served with USMC, 1951-53. Decorated Purple Heart. Office: Time & Life Bldg 1221 Avenue Of The Americas New York NY 10020-1001

MEYERS, JUDITH ANN, education educator; b. Scranton, Pa., Aug. 5, 1946; d. Paul Meyers and Elaine Jenkins; m. Stuart M. Olinsky, July 10, 1977; children: Seth, Noah. BA with honors, Rutgers U., 1969; MA in Early Childhood Edn., Kean Coll., 1973. Cert. tchr. early childhood K-8, N.J., Pa. Tchr. Tchr.'s Corp., Newark, 1970-71; head tchr. Arlington Ave. Presch., East Orange, N.J., 1972-75, ednl. dir., 1976-78, exec. dir., 1979-81;

program developer for early childhood program, instr. early childhood Williamsport (Pa.) Area C.C./Penn Tech., 1987-89; community mem. curriculum rev. com. Penn Tech. C.C., Williamsport, 1990-91; parent mem. West Branch. Sch., tchr. selection com., 1991-93, tchr. evaluation com., 1991-93, curriculum devel. com., 1993. Author, program developer early childhood edn. courses. Chmn. Victorian Williamsport Preservation Com., 1993-94; bd. dirs. Community Theatre, Williamsport, 1993-94. Avocation: painting. Home: 150 Selkirk Rd Williamsport PA 17701-1869

MEYERS, KAREN DIANE, lawyer, educator, corporate officer; b. Cin., July 8, 1956; d. Willard Paul and Camille Jeannette (Schutte) M.; m. William J. Jones, Mar. 27, 1982. BA summa cum laude, Thomas More Coll., 1974; MBA, MEd, Xavier U., 1978; JD, U. Ky., Covington, 1978. Bar: Ohio 1978, Ky. 1978; CLU; CPCU. Clk. to mgr. Baldwin Co., Cin., 1970-78; adj. prof. bus. Thomas More Coll., Crestview Hill, Ky., 1978—; asst. sec., asst. v.p., sr. counsel The Ohio Life Ins. Co., Hamilton, 1978-91; prin. KD Meyers & Assocs., 1991; v.p. Benefit Designs, Inc., 1991—. Bd. dirs. ARC, Hamilton, 1978-83, vol., 1978—; bd. dirs. YWCA, Hamilton, 1985-91; v.p. Benefit Designs Inc., 1991—. Gardner Found. fellow, 1968-71; recipient Ind. Progress award Bus. & Profl. Women, 1990. Fellow Life Mgmt. Inst. Atlanta; mem. ABA, Soc. Chartered Property Casualty Underwriters (instr. 1987—), Cin. Bar Assn., Butler County Bar Assn., Ohio Bar Assn., Ky. Bar Assn. Roman Catholic. Avocations: aerobics, jogging, crafts. Home: 7903 Hickory Hill Dr Cincinnati OH 45241-1363

MEYERS, MARLENE O., hospital administrator; m. Eugene Meyers; children: Lori, Lisa, Dean. BSc, U. Sask., 1962; MSc, U. Calgary, Alta., Can., 1976. Instr., chair Mount Royal Coll. Allied Health, Calgary, 1969-82; asst. exec. dir. Rockyview Hosp., Calgary, 1982-85; v.p. patient svcs. Calgary Gen. Hosp., 1985-91, pres., CEO, 1991-95; pres., CEO Meyers and Assocs. Health Care Mgmt. Cons., Calgary, 1995—; surveyor Can. Coun. on Health Facilities Accreditation, 1986—. Rotary Intl. Named Calgary Woman of Yr. in field of Health, 1982; recipient Heritage of Svc. award, 1992. Mem. Alta. Assn. RNs. (hon. mem., 1996), Can. Coll. Health Svcs. Org., Can. Exec. Svcs. Org. Office: Meyers and Assocs, 139 Coleridge Rd NW, Calgary, AB Canada T2K 1X5

MEYERS, MARY ANN, writer, college administrator; b. Sodus, N.Y., Sept. 30, 1937; d. Harold Galpin and Clarice Mildred (Daniel) Dye; m. John Matthew Meyers, Aug. 22, 1959; children: Andrew Christopher, Anne Kathryn. BA magna cum laude, Syracuse U., 1959; MA, U. Pa., 1965, PhD, 1976. Editorial asst. Ladies' Home Jour., Phila., 1959-62; editor, asst. dir. news bur. U. Pa., Phila., 1962-65, asst. to pres., 1973-75, univ. sec., lectr. Am. civilization, 1980-90; contbg. writer The Pennsylvania Gazette, Phila., 1965—; dir. coll. rels., editor Haverford Horizons, lectr. in religion Haverford (Pa.) Coll., 1977-80; pres. The Annenberg Found., St. Davids, Pa., 1990-92; v.p. for external affairs Moore Coll. Art and Design, Phila., 1995—. Author: A New World Jerusalem, 1983; contbg. author: Death in America, 1975, Gladly Learn, Gladly Teach, 1978, Coping with Serious Illness, 1980, Religion in American Life, 1987; contbr. articles to profl. jours. Judge recognition program Coun. for Advancement and Support Edn., Washington, 1977-78, chair creative editing and writing workshop, 1978; mem. Picker Found. Program on Human Qualities in Medicine, N.Y.C. and Phila., 1980-83; del. Phila.-Leningrad Sister Cities Project, 1986; trustee U. Pa. Press, 1985—, vice chmn. U. Pa., 250th Anniversary Commn., 1987-90, mem. steering com. of bd. trustees, U. Pa., Annenberg Sch. for Communication, 1990-92, mem. adv. bd. U. Pa., Annenberg Ctr. for the Performing Arts, 1990—; mem. bd. overseers, U. Pa., Sch. Arts and Scis., 1990—; mem. steering com. of bd. trustees Annenberg Ctr. for Communication, U. So. Calif., L.A., 1990-92, The Annenberg Washington Program in Communications Policy Studies of Northwestern U., Washington, 1990-92; trustee Am. Acad. Polit. and Social Sci., 1992—, World Affairs Coun. Phila., 1990-95; dir. Diagnostic and Rehab. Ctr., Phila., 1993—. Recipient Excellence award Women in Communications, Inc., 1973-74, award for pub. affairs reporting Newsweek/Coun. for Advancement and Support Edn., 1977, Silver medal Coun. for Advancement and Support Edn., 1986. Mem. Cosmopolitan Club, Sunday Breakfast Club, Phi Beta Kappa (mem. steering com. Delaware Valley chpt. 1995—). Roman Catholic. Avocations: reading, theater, classical music, biking. Home: 217 Gypsy Ln Wynnewood PA 19096-1112

MEYERS, MORTON ALLEN, physician, radiology educator; b. Troy, N.Y., Oct. 1, 1933; s. David and Jeanne Sarah (Dunn) M.; m. Beatrice Applebaum, June 1, 1963; children—Richard, Amy. M.D., SUNY, Upstate Med. Coll., 1959. Diplomate: Am. Bd. Radiology. Intern Bellevue Hosp., N.Y.C., 1959-60; resident in radiology Columbia-Presbyn. Med. Ctr., N.Y.C., 1960-63; fellow Am. Cancer Soc., 1961-63; prof. dept. radiology Cornell U. Med. Center, N.Y.C., 1973-78; prof., chmn. dept. radiology SUNY Sch. Medicine, Stony Brook, 1978-91; prof. dept. radiology SUNY Sch. Medicine, 1991—; vis. investigator St. Mark's Hosp., London, 1976; spkr. Radiol. Soc. N.Am., 1986. Author: Diseases of the Adrenal Glands: Radiologic Diagnosis, 1963, Dynamic Radiology of the Abdomen: Normal and Pathologic Anatomy, 1976, 4th edit., 1994, Iatrogenic Gastrointestinal Complications, 1981; series editor: Radiology of Iatrogenic Disorders, 1981-86; editor: Computed Tomography of the Gastrointestinal Tract: Including the Peritoneal Cavity and Mesentery, 1986; founding editor in chief Abdominal Imaging, 1976—; mem. editorial bd. Iatrogenics, Surg. and Radiol. Anatomy; contbr. chpts. to med. textbooks, articles to med. jours.; speaker in field. Served to capt. M.C. U.S. Army, 1963-65. Fellow Am. Coll. Radiology; mem. AAAS, Am. Coll. Gastroenterology, Radiol. Soc. N.Am., Am. Roentgen Ray Soc., Am. Gastroenterol. Assn., Soc. Uroradiology, Soc. Gastrointestinal Radiologists, Assn. Univ. Radiologists, N.Y. Roentgen Ray Soc., N.Y. Acad. Gastroenterology, Phila. Roentgen Soc., Harvey Soc., N.Y. Acad. Scis., L.I. Radiologic Soc., Alpha Omega Alpha. Home: 14 Wainscott Ln East Setauket NY 11733-3816 Office: SUNY Health Scis Ctr Sch Medicine Dept Radiology Stony Brook NY 11794

MEYERS, NANCY JANE, screenwriter, producer; b. Phila., Dec. 8, 1949; d. Irving H. and Patricia (Lemisch) M. BA, Am. U., Washington, 1971. Co-writer, prodr.: (films) Private Benjamin (Acad. award nominee, Writers Guild award 1980), Irreconcilable Differences, 1984, Baby Boom, 1987, Father of the Bride, 1991, I Love Trouble, 1994, Father of the Bride Part II, 1995. Mem. ASCAP, Acad. Motion Picture Arts and Scis., Writers Guild Am. West. Office: Starr & Co 350 Park Ave Flr 9 New York NY 10022

MEYERS, PETER L., banker; b. Syracuse, N.Y., Mar. 19, 1939; s. Edwin Clark and Phyllis (Schiess) M.; m. Teresa Maley, Mar. 2, 1963; children: Gary, Gregory, Cheryl. BBA, Syracuse U., 1974. With Merchants Nat. Bank & Trust Co., Syracuse, N.Y., 1963-92, v.p., comml. loan officer, 1975-78, v.p., sr. loan officer, 1978-79, sr. v.p., 1979, exec. v.p., 1980-88, exec. v.p., COO, 1988, pres., CEO, 1988-92; vice chmn. OnBank & Trust Co., Syracuse, 1993—; dir. Security Mutual Life Ins. Co.; chmn. bd. dirs. N.Y. Bus. Devel. Corp. Bd. dirs. Met. Devel. Assn., Syracuse, YMCA; chmn. Syracuse Housing Partnership; chmn. United Way Ctrl. N.Y., Mus. Sci. and Tech. Found.; trustee Erie Canal Mus.; bd. regents LeMoyne Coll.; active Syracuse Onondaga County Youth Bd., Onondaga Lake Mgmt. Conf. Mem. Am. Inst. Banking, Syracuse U. Alumni Assn., Onondaga Golf and Country Club. Avocations: golf, fishing. Office: OnBank & Trust Co 101 S Salina St PO Box 4983 Syracuse NY 13221

MEYERS, RICHARD JAMES, landscape architect; b. Columbus, Ohio, Jan. 25, 1940; s. Ralph Joseph and Margaret Mary (Kruse) M.; m. Mary Igoe, Jan. 12, 1963; children: Gregory James, Helen Marie, Andrew James. B.Landscape Arch., Ohio State U., 1961. Registered landscape architect, Ohio, Mich., Fla., Ind.; cert. Council Landscape Archtl. Registration Bds. Jr. planner Columbus Planning Commn. (Ohio), 1960-62; landscape architect Behnke-Nes & Assocs., Cleve., 1962-65, Arthur Hills & Assocs., Toledo, 1965-67; ptnr. Mortensen-Meyers Assocs., Toledo, 1967-69; prin. MMSS Inc., Toledo, 1969-71, The Collaborative, Inc., Toledo, 1973—; bd. dirs., past pres. Council Landscape Archtl. Registration Bd., Syracuse, N.Y., 1978-86, Ohio Bd. Landscape Architect Examiners, 1975-83. Mem. St. Vincent Hosp. and Med. Ctr. Assocs., Toledo, 1978-83; bd. dirs. Family Svcs. Greater Toledo, 1977-82; com. mem. Toledo Met. Area Coun. of Govt., 1972-79, 87-89, Toledo Bot. Gardens Design Rev. Bd., 1988-90, Downtown Toledo Vision, Inc., 1988—; vice-chmn. Toledo Lucas County Plan Commn., 1989—, Toledo Adminstrv. Bd. Zoning Appeals, 1994—, Met. Parks Com. of 25, 1991; chmn. campaign divsn. United Way, 1991; mem. adv. bd. U. Toledo-Stranahan Arboretum, 1994—. Dumbarton Oaks Jr. summer scholar, 1960; recipient First Honor Design award Am. Assn. Nurserymen, 1974. Fellow Am. Soc. Landscape Architects (merit design award Ohio chpt. 1975, 81, 83, 85, Outstanding Svc. to Profession award 1983, Ohio Chpt. medal 1984); mem. AIA, Ohio Chpt. of Am. Soc. Landscape Architects (v.p. 1974-76), Urban Land Inst., Soc. for Coll. and Univ. Planning, Am. Forestry Assn., Am. Planning Assn., Rails to Trails Conservancy, Ohio Pks. and Recreation Assn., Heatherdowns Country Club (bd. dirs. 1983). *I am fortunate to be part of a profession dedicated to improving and beautifying our physical environment through the preservation and protection of our natural resources and by the sensitive blending of economic and social needs with these natural systems. Landscape architecture provides me with a great deal of personal satisfaction.*

MEYERS, RICHARD STUART, college president; b. Chgo., Sept. 6, 1938; m. Yasuko Kamata, Sept. 15, 1965; children—Anne Akiko, Toni Takiko. BM, DePaul U., 1961; MS, U. So. Calif., 1963, PhD, 1971. With Inglewood Unified Sch. Dist., Calif., 1967-68; with Dept. Def. Overseas Sch. System, Tokyo, 1964-67; jr. and sr. high sch. tchr. Palos Verdes Peninsula Unified Sch. Dist., Palos Verdes, Calif., 1962-64; instr. media coordinator Grossmont Coll., El Cajon, Calif., 1968-72; dean instrn. Cerro Coso Community Coll., Ridgecrest, Calif., 1972-75, pres., 1975-78; sec. to bd. trustees, supt. and pres. Pasadena City Coll., Calif., 1978-83; pres. Western Oreg. State Coll., Monmouth, 1983—; speaker; cons. Contbr. articles to profl. jours. Bd. dirs. United Way, Salem, Oreg., 1984-89; mem. Oreg. Internat. Trade Commn., 1983-86, bd. dirs. Oreg. Symphony Assn., 1985-90, pres., 1909—. Fulbright scholar, Egypt, 1975. Fellow Am. Leadership Forum; mem. Am. Assn. State Colls. and Univs., Pi Gamma Mu , Phi Delta Kappa. Republican. Lodge: Rotary. Home: 5290 Waterman Ave Apt 4W Saint Louis MO 63108-1161 Office: Western Oreg State Coll 345 Monmouth Ave N Monmouth OR 97361-1314

MEYERS, SHELDON, engineering company executive; b. N.Y.C., Sept. 6, 1929; s. Charles and Charlotte (Farb) M.; m. Anne Catherine Dietzel, Apr. 14, 1962; children—James, John, Catherine, Peter, Paul. B.Engring., SUNY, 1952; M.S.E., U. Mich., 1955; M.B.A., N.Y. U., 1967. Engr. Cities Svc. Oil Co., N.Y.C., 1955-56, Westinghouse Co., Pitts., 1957-58, Argonne (Ill.) Nat. Lab., 1958-69; engr., div. dir. AEC, N.Y.C., 1970-78; office dir., dep. asst. adminstr. EPA, dir. Office Air Quality Planning and Standards, 1982-83, dep. asst. adminstr. Office Air and Radiation, 1983-84; dep. asst. sec. Office of Nuclear Waste Mgmt., Dept. Energy, Washington, 1978-82; dir. Office Radiation, Washington, 1983-87; assoc. adminstr. internat. activities, 1987-88; v.p. Jacobs Engring., 1988—. Princeton U. fellow, 1964-65. Mem. ASME. Home: 3506 Dundee Dr Chevy Chase MD 20815-4741 Office: Jacobs 1300 N 17th St Ste 602 Arlington VA 22209

MEYERS, TEDSON JAY, lawyer; b. Bayonne, N.J., May 6, 1928; s. Irving and Norma Miriam (Anson) M.; m. Patricia Elizabeth Sullivan, Apr. 10, 1965 (div. Apr. 1978); children: Mary, John, Katherine; m. Lynn Scholz, Aug. 6, 1978 (div. Oct. 1992). Student, Ohio State U., 1945-47; BA, NYU, 1949, MA, 1950; JD, Harvard U., 1953. Bar: D.C. 1953, N.Y. 1957, U.S. Supreme Ct. 1971. Asst. counsel Office Gen. Counsel, Dept. Navy, Washington, 1955-56; assoc. Liebman, Eulau & Robinson, N.Y.C., 1956-58; staff counsel for govt. regulations ABC, N.Y.C., 1958-61; adminstrv. asst. to chmn. FCC, Washington, 1961-62; asst. to dir., dir. overseas ednl. TV projects Peace Corps, Washington, 1962-68; pvt. practice Washington, 1968-70; ptnr. Sullivan Beauregard Meyers & Clarkson, Washington, 1970-74, Peabody Lambert & Meyers, Washington, 1974-84, Reid & Priest, Washington, 1984-96, Coudert Brothers, Washington, 1996—; adj. prof. comm. San Diego State U., 1993—; founding pres. Harvard Legis. Rsch. Bur., 1952-53; mem. White House Task Force on Ednl. TV Overseas, 1966-68, adv. panel on internat. telecomm. law U.S. State Dept., 1987—; bd. govs. Internat. Coun. on Computer Comm., 1986—; bd. dirs. Internat. Ctr. for Comms. Contbr. conf. papers and articles to profl. publs. Mem. City Coun. Washington, 1972-75; bd. govs. Met. Washington Coun. Govts., 1973-75; chmn. Bicycle Fedn. of Am., 1977—; bd. dirs. U.S. Coun. for World Comm. Yr. 83, 1982-84; dir. The Arthur C. Clarke Found. of the U.S. Inc., 1987—. Lt. USMC, 1953-55, Korea. Rsch. fellow Carnegie Found., 1949. Mem. ABA (co-founder and chmn. internat. telecomm. com., sect. sci. and tech. 1982-85, coun. mem. sect. sci. and tech. 1983-87), Fed. Comm. Bar Assn., Internat. Inst. Comm., Royal TV Soc., Pacific Telecomm. Coun., Soc. Satellite Profls., Cosmos Club (pres. 1988-90), Cosmos Club Found. (trustee, chmn. 1985-88, 90—), Potomac Boat Club, Alpha Epsilon Pi. Avocations: computers, sculling, bicycling, motorcycling, military music. Office: Coudert Brothers Ste 1200 1627 I St NW Washington DC 20006

MEYERS, WAYNE MARVIN, microbiologist; b. Huntingdon County, Pa., Aug. 28, 1924; s. John William and Carrie Venca (Weaver) M.; m. Esther Louise Kleinschmidt, Aug. 26, 1953; children: Amy, George, Daniel, Sara. BS in Chemistry, Juniata Coll., 1947; diploma, Moody Bible Inst., 1950; M.S. in Med. Microbiology, U. Wis., 1953, Ph.D. in Med. Microbiology, 1955; M.D., Baylor Coll. Medicine, 1959; DSc (hon.), Juniata Coll., 1986. Instr. Baylor Coll. Medicine, 1955-59; intern Conemaugh Valley Meml. Hosp., Johnstown, Pa., 1959-60; staff physician Berrien Gen. Hosp., Berrien Ctr., Mich., 1960-61; missionary physician Am. Leprosy Missions, Burundi and Zaire, Africa, 1961-73; prof. pathology Sch. Medicine U. Hawaii, Honolulu, 1973-75; chief microbiology divsn. Armed Forces Inst. Pathology, Washington, 1975-89, chief mycobacteriology, 1989—, registrar leprosy registry, 1975—; mem. leprosy panel U.S.-Japan Coop. Med. Sci. Program, 1976-83; mem. sci. adv. bd. Leonard Wood Meml., 1981-85, sci. cons. dir., 1985-87, sci. dir., 1987-90; cons., 1990—; rsch. affiliate Tulane U., 1981—; corp. bd. dirs. Gorgas Meml. Inst. Tropical and Preventive Medicine, Inc. Bd. dirs. Internat. Jour. Leprosy, 1978—; contbr. numerous chpts. and articles on tropical medicine to textbooks and jours. Adv. bd. Damien-Dutton Soc. for Leprosy Aid, Inc., 1983—, Am. Leprosy Missions, Inc., 1979-88, chmn. bd., 1985-88, program cons. to bd., mem. bd. reference, 1988—; mem. Hansen's Disease Ctr., Carville, La., 1983-85; chmn., 1985—. With U.S. Army, 1944-46. Allergy Found. Am. fellow, 1957, 58; WHO rsch. grantee, 1978-87. Mem. Internat. Leprosy Assn. (councillor 1978-88, pres. 1988-93), Internat. Soc. Tropical Dermatology, Am. Soc. Tropical Medicine and Hygiene, Am. Soc. Microbiology, Binford-Dammin Soc. Infectious Disease Pathologists (sec.-treas. 1988-91, pres. 1995-96), Internat. Soc. Travel Medicine, Sigma Xi. Achievements include researching human and experimental leprosy. Office: Armed Forces Inst Pathology Washington DC 20306-6000

MEYERS, WILLIAM HENRY, economics educator; b. Souderton, Pa., Nov. 24, 1941; s. Isaac Claude and Mary (Wismer) M.; m. Dalisay Honorata Cuento, Jan. 1, 1972; children: Naila-Jean, Celina-Beth. BA in Math. and Physics, Goshen (Ind.) Coll., 1963; MS in Agrl. Econs., U. of The Philippines, Los Banos, 1972; PhD in Agrl. Econs., U. Minn., 1977. Team leader Internat. Vol. Svc., Can Tho, Vietnam, 1966-67; VEP coord. United Meth. Ch., Washington, 1968; rsch. fellow Internat. Rice Rsch. Inst., Los Banos, 1971-72; grad. asst. U. Minn., St. Paul, 1972-77; agrl. economist USDA, Washington, 1977-79; prof. econs. Iowa State U., Ames, 1979—; co-dir. Food and Agr. Policy Rsch. Inst., Ames, 1984—; assoc. dir. Ctr. for Agrl. and Rural devel., Ames, 1985—; exec. dir. MATRIC, Ames, 1987—; agr. policy cons. World Bank, Washington, 1992—; ad hoc group of experts East/West, OECD, Paris, 1993—; vis. prof. Inst. Agrl. Econs., Christian-Albrechts U., Kiel, Germany, 1991; agrl. economist Forecast Support Group and Food and Agrl. Policy Br., Econ. Rsch. Svc., USDA, Washington, 1977-79; rsch. fellow Internat. Rice Rsch. Inst., 1971-72; lectr. in field; cons. in field. North Am. editor: Agrl. Econs., 1991-94; editor: Iowa Ag Rev., 1995-96; editl. bd. Agrl. Econs., 1989-91; assoc. editor Am. Jour. Agrl. Econs., 1987-90; article referee Agrl. Econs. Rsch., Am. Jour. Agrl. Econs., North Ctrl. Jour. Agrl. Econs., Western Jour. Agrl. Econs., Can. Jour. Agrl. Econs.; contbr. numerous articles to profl. jours., chpts. to books. Mem. coun. of founders Baltic Mgmt. Found., Vilnius, Lithuania, 1991—. Rsch. grantee Mo. Valley Rsch. Assocs., 1982-83, USDA, 1982-83, Iowa Soybean Promotion Bd., 1984-86, Nat. Corn Devel. Found., 1982-86, Coop. State Rsch. Svc./USDA, 1983-95, ERS/USDA, 1986, US AID, 1984-87, 89-90, U.S. Feed Grains Coun., 1986-88, Iowa Lottery Funds, 1987-88, U.S. Agy. for Internat. Devel., 1988-90, Nat. Ctr. for Food and Agrl. Policy, Resources for Future, 1990-91, Agrl. Can., 1988-95, Asian Devel. Bank, 1990-92, Farm Credit Svc., 1992-93, Pioneer Hi-Bred Internat., 1994-95, others. Mem. Ames C. of C., Am. Agrl. Econs. Assn. (Disting. Policy Contbn. award 1991, Quality of Comm. award 1991), Assn. for Advancement of Baltic Studies, Am. Econs. Assn., Am. Assn. for Advancement of Slavic Studies, European Assn. Agrl. Economists, Internat. Agrl. Trade Rsch. Consortium, Internat. Assn. Agrl. Economists, Internat. Agribus. Mgmt. Assn., Western Agrl. Econs. Assn. (1994 Published Rsch. award), Gamma Sigma Delta, Phi Kappa Phi, Phi Beta Delta. Office: FAPRI Iowa State Univ 578 Heady Hall Ames IA 50011

MEYERSON, ADAM, magazine editor, foundation executive; b. Phila., Aug. 2, 1953; s. Martin and Margy Ellin (Lazarus) M.; m. Nina Hope Shea, Sept. 13, 1986; children: Thomas Abraham, William Ulysses, Henry Elijah. BA, Yale U., 1974; student, Harvard U., 1977-79. Mng. editor The Am. Spectator, Bloomington, Ind., 1974-77; editorial writer Wall St. Jour., N.Y.C., 1979-83; editor Policy Rev. The Heritage Found., Washington, 1983—, v.p. ednl. affairs, 1993—. Co-editor: The Wall Street Journal on Management, 1985. Mem. bd. selectors Am. Inst. Pub. Svc., Washington, 1989—; mem. Coun. Fgn. Rels., 1980-85; bd. dirs. PERC, Bozeman, Mont. Mem. Phila. Soc. Home: 3714 Ingomar St NW Washington DC 20015-1820 Office: Heritage Foundation 214 Massachusetts Ave NE Washington DC 20002-4958

MEYERSON, MARTIN, university executive, professor, city planner; b. N.Y.C., Nov. 14, 1922; s. Samuel and Etta (Berger) M.; m. Margy Ellin Lazarus, Dec. 31, 1945; children: Adam, Laura (dec.), Matthew. BA, Columbia U., 1942; MCP, Harvard U., 1949; LLD, U. Pa., 1970; LLD (hon.), Queen's U., Can., 1968, Shiraz U., Iran, 1973, U. Edinburgh, 1976; also 17 other hon. doctorates including ScD, Ph D, LHD, LittD, 1967-94. Mem. staff Michael Reese Hosp., Chgo., 1945-47; asst. prof. coll. and grad. social scis. U. Chgo., 1948-52; assoc. Com. on Nat. Policy, Yale U., 1948; assoc. prof., city and regional planning U. Pa., 1952-56, prof., 1956-57, pres., 1970-81, pres. emeritus, 1981—, chmn. bd. dirs. U. Pa. Press, Inst. for Rsch. on Higher Edn. Fels Ctr. Govt., bd. dirs. Inst. Contemporary Art, Mahoney Inst. Neurosciss., Lauder Inst. Mgmt. and Internat. Studies, co-chmn. Commn. for U. Pa. 250th Anniversary, 1987-90; Univ. prof. U. Pa. Found., 1977—, chmn., 1981—; exec. dir. Am. Council to Improve Our Neighborhoods, 1955-56, vice chmn., 1956-66; Frank Backus Williams prof. city planning and urban research Harvard U., 1957-63, acting dean Grad. Sch. Design,, 1963; founding dir. Joint Center for Urban Studies, MIT and Harvard U., 1958-63; dean, prof. urban devel. Coll. Environ. Design, U. Calif., Berkeley, 1963-66; interim chancellor U. Calif., Berkeley, 1965; pres., prof. public policy SUNY, Buffalo, 1966-70; dir. visitor Inst. for Advanced Study, Princeton, N.J., 1983-84; pres. Found. for Internat. Exchange of Sci. and Cultural Info. by Telecommunications, Switzerland-U.S., 1986—; dir. Real Estate Research Corp., 1961-67, Marine Midland Bank, 1966-70, 1st Fidelity Bancorp., Scott Paper Co., Penn Mut. Life, Saint Gobain Corp., Certain Teed, Norton, Avatar, Universal Health Services; cons. to govts., pvt. firms U.S. and abroad, UN missions to, Japan, Indonesia, Yugoslavia, 1958-65; sr. advisor Arthur D. Little, Inc., 1958-66, Taylor Internat., 1989—; cons. Sears Roebuck Found., 1958-69, Ford Found., various times; chmn. bd. Western N.Y. Nuclear Research Center, 1966-70; mem. adv. com. U.S. Census, 1958-61; adv. com. NASA, 1960-65; White House Office Sci. and Tech., 1962-66, White House task forces, 1960-69; mem. council Electric Power Research Inst., 1973-77; mem. U.S. del. UN Conf. on Sci. and Tech. for Less Developed Areas, 1963. Author: (with E. C. Banfield) Politics, Planning and the Public Interest, 1955, Housing, People and Cities, 1962, Face of the Metropolis, 1963, Boston, 1966, Gladly Learn and Gladly Teach, 1978; editor: Conscience of the City, 1970, McGraw-Hill Series; mem. editorial bd. Ency. Britannica, 1980—, Daedalus, 1972-90. Mem. Air Conservation Commn., 1962-66; mem. Bay Area Conservation and Devel. Commn., 1965-66; chmn. Assembly Univ. Goals and Governance, 1969-73; commr. N.Y. State Commn. on Post-Secondary Sch. Edn., 1976-77; hon. prof. Nat. U. Paraguay, 1969—; bd. dirs. Phila. Bicentennial Corp., 1970-76, Greater Phila. Partnership, 1973-81, Afro-Am. Film Found., 1966-70, Niagara U., 1968-70, Center for Community Change, 1968-72, Acad. Religion and Mental Health, 1970-78, Center for Ednl. Devel., 1967-70, Phila. Mus. Art, 1974—, Nat. Urban Coalition, 1969-78; trustee, Am. Coll., 1982-92, Curtis Inst. Music, 1987-94, Armand Hammer United World Coll.N. Mex., 1984—, Am. Schs. Oriental Rsch., 1985—, Tel Aviv U., Coll. Bd., 1986-92, Hebrew U., Internat. House Ctr., Monell Chem. Senses Ctr., chmn., 1993—, Fgn. Policy Rsch. Inst., 1981—, Panasonic Found., 1982—, Ctr. for Visual History, U.S. Com. on the Constl. System; founding dir. Internat. Centre for Study East Asian Devel. Japan; Inst. for Internat. Edn., 1971—, chmn., 1981-85; bd. dirs. Internat. Council Ednl. Devel., 1971—, Am. Council Financial Aid to Edn., 1975-81, Open Univ. Found., U.K., 1979-82; chmn. council pres. Nat. Accelerator Lab., 1972-73; co-chmn. Images (French TV), 1976-79, Salzburg Seminar Bd., 1978—, Marconi Fellowship Council, chair exec. com., 1978—; nter Environ. Studies, London, 1966-84; mem. sr. exec. council Conf. Bd., 1970-77; trustee Aspen. Inst., 1976—; chair adv. group for UN Centre for Regional Devel., Nagoya, Japan, 1983-93; chair internat. selection commn. Phila. Liberty Medal, 1988—; bd. overseers Koc Univ., Bosphorus, Turkey, 1994—; bd. dirs. Internat. Literacy Inst., 1995—. Decorated Commendatore Order of Merit (Italy); chevalier de l'Ordre Nat. de Mérite (France); Order of the Rising Sun, Gold and Silver Star (Japan); recipient Einstein medal Am. Technion Soc., 1976, Disting. Achievement award U. Calif. Berkeley, 1984, John Jay award Columbia U., keynoter Academia Lincei, Rome, 1995, Disting. Educator award Assn. Collegiate Schs. of Planning, 1996; overseas fellow Churchill Coll., Cambridge U., 1983; hon. fellow Soc. for Tech. Communication, 1988; Meyerson Hall named in his honor U. Pa. Grad. Sch. Fine Arts; Meyerson Professorship named in his honor U. Pa. Fellow Am. Acad. Arts and Scis., Royal Soc. Arts (Franklin fellow), Am. Philos. Soc. Nat. Acad. Edn.; mem. Am. Soc. Planning Ofcls. (past dir.), Am. Inst. Planners (past gov., award winner), Internat. Assn. Univs. Paris (Am. dir. 1975—, v.p., interim pres. 1981-85, hon. pres. 1985—), Council Fgn. Relations, European Acad. Arts, Scis. and Letters (academician), Phi Beta Kappa (hon.). Clubs: Philadelphia, Century (N.Y.C.); Cosmos (Washington). Office: Univ Pa 225 Van Pelt Library Philadelphia PA 19104

MEYERSON, SEYMOUR, retired chemist; b. Chgo., Dec. 4, 1916; s. Joseph and Rena (Margulies) M.; m. Lotte Strauss, May 22, 1943; children: Sheella, Elana. SB, U. Chgo., 1938, postgrad., 1938-39, 47-48; postgrad., George Williams Coll., 1939-40; DSc (hon.), Valparaiso Univ., Ind., 1995. Chemist Deavitt Labs., Chgo., 1941-42; inspector powder & explosives Kankakee Ordnance Works, Joliet, Ill., 1942; from chemist to rsch. cons. Standard Oil Co. (Ind.) Rsch. Dept., Whiting, Ind.-Naperville, Ill., 1946-84; mem. indsl. adv. coun. chemistry dept. U. Okla., Norman, 1967-69, Frontiers in Chemistry lectr. Wayne State U., 1965; invited spkr. James L. Waters Symposium, Pitts. Conf., Chgo., 1995. Charter mem. editl. adv. bd. Organic Mass Spectrometry, 1968-87, Mass Spectromony Revs., 1980-87; author, co-author 190 sci. publs. 2d lt. AUS, 1943-46, ETO. Mem. emeritus Am. Chem. Soc. (Frank H. Field and Joe L. Franklin award for outstanding achievement in mass spectrometry 1993), Am. Soc. for Mass Spectrometry. Achievements include many contributions to systematic chemistry of gas-phase organic ions; 2 patents in field. Home: 650 N Tippecanoe St Gary IN 46403-2262

MEYLER, WILLIAM ANTHONY, financial executive; b. Newark, Oct. 29, 1944; s. Raymond Francis and Margaret (Loveless) M.; BS, St. Joseph's Coll., 1966; MBA, Fairleigh Dickinson U., 1974; m. Dana Irene Brennan, May 3, 1975; children: Daniel, Diana. CPA, N.J. Sr. acct. Ernst & Young, Trenton, N.J., 1970; dir. acctg. Baker Industries, Inc., Parsippany, N.J., 1971-72; mgr. corp. acctg. Witco Chem. Corp., N.Y.C., 1973-75, asst. to controller, 1976-79, asst. controller world-wide ops., 1977-82, asst. controller mgmt. info. systems, 1982-84; ptnr. Letters, Meyler & Co., CPAs, 1984-91; cons., exec. v.p. Investment Techs., Inc., Edison, N.J., 1985-91, also bd. dirs.; pvt. practice, Middletown, N.J., 1991—; exec. v.p., CFO Gateways to Space, Inc., 1994—, also bd. dirs.; adj. prof. Monmouth Coll., 1983-85. Fellow N.J. Soc. CPA's; mem. Am. Inst. CPA's, Am. Acctg. Assn., Middletown C. of C., Rotary. Home: 30 Southview Ter S Middletown NJ 07748-2415 Office: One Arin Park 1715 Highway 35 Middletown NJ 07748

MEYSENBURG, MARY ANN, principal; b. L.A., Sept. 16, 1939; d. Clarence Henry and Mildred Ethel (McGee) Augustine; m. John Harold Meysenburg, June 17, 1967; children: Peter Augustine, Amy Bernadette. BA magna cum laude, U. So. Calif., 1960; MA Pvt. Sch. Adminstrn. magna cum laude, U. San Francisco, 1995. Cert. elem. tchr., Calif. Auditor, escrow officer Union Bank, L.A., 1962-64; v.p., escro mgr. Bank of Downey, Calif., 1964-66; cons., tchr. Santa Ana (Calif.) Coll. Bus., 1964-66; elem. tchr. St.

Bruno's Sch., Whittier, Calif., 1966-70, Pasadena (Calif.) Unified Sch. Dist., 1971-84, Holy Angels Sch., Arcadia, Calif., 1985-89; vice prin., computer coord. Our Mother of Good Counsel, L.A., 1989-93; prin. St. Stephen Martyr, Monterey Park, Calif., 1993—; master catechist religious edn. L.A. Archdiocese, 1988—. Author: History of the Arms Control and Disarmament Organization, 1976; organizer, editor newsletter Cath. Com. for Girl Scouts and Campfire. Eucharistic min. Our Mother of Good Counsel, 1989-95; sec. of senatus Legion of Mary, 1980-85; counselor Boy Scouts Am., 1985—; mem. Cath. com. for Girl Scouts U.S.A. and Campfire, vice chmn. acad. affairs L.A. Archdiocese, 1985-90. Recipient Pius X medal L.A. Archdiocese, 1979, St. Elizabeth Ann Seton award Cath. Com. for Girl Scouts, 1988, St. Anne medal Cath. Com. for Girl Scouts, 1989, Bronze Pelican award Cath. Com. for Boy Scouts, 1989; grantee Milken Family Found., 1989, 92. Mem. Phi Beta Kappa, Phi Delta Kappa (historian 1991-92, founds. rep. 1992-93, treas. 1993-94, 1st v.p. 1994-95, pres. 1995—), Phi Kappa Phi. Avocations: tennis, walking, swimming, reading. Home: 6725 Brentmead Ave Arcadia CA 91007 Office: 119 S Ramona Ave Monterey Park CA 91754-2802

MEYSKENS, FRANK LOUIS, JR., hematologist, oncologist, educator; b. San Francisco, Sept. 3, 1945; m. Alice Covell; children: Moriah, Covell, Desiree. BS, U. San Francisco, 1967; MD, U. Calif., San Francisco, 1972. Prof. medicine and biol. chemistry U. Calif. Irvine, Orange, 1989—; chief hematology/oncology, co-dir. cancer program, dir. Clin. Cancer Ctr., U. Calif. Irvine, 1989—; co-chairperson conf. on minorities Nat. Cancer Inst., 1990; Hamilton lectr. U. Rochester Cancer Ctr., 1989; active various profl. adv. and cons. bds. Contbr. over 200 articles to sci. jours. Recipient Grace A. Goldsmith award Am. Coll. Nutrition, 1989, Yr. 2000 award Nat. Cancer Inst., 1990. Office: Univ Calif Irvine 101 The City Dr S Bldg 44 Orange CA 92668-3201

MEZA, CHOCO GONZALEZ, federal agency administrator; b. Zaragoza, Coahuila, Mexico, May 16, 1952. BBA in Phys. Edn., St. Mary's U., 1977. CEO YWCA, San Antonio, 1983-90; demographic and polit. mgmt. cons. Tex. Legis., 1981-83; rsch. dir. S.W. Voter Registration Edn. Project, 1977-81; exec. dir. Partnership for Hope, San Antonio, 1990-93; dep. asst. sec. intergovtl. rels. U.S. Dept. Housing and Urban Devel., Washington, 1993—. Named San Antonio Trend Setter, San Antonio Assn. for Bilingual Bicultural Edn., 1983; named to San Antonio Womens Hall of Fame, 1989; one of People Most Likely to Change Our Lives, San Antonio Express-News, 1990. Office: Dept Housing & Urban Devel Congression & Intergov Relations 451 7th St SW Washington DC 20410-0001

MEZEY, ROBERT, poet, educator; b. Phila., Feb. 28, 1935; s. Ralph and Clara (Mandel) M.; m. Olivia Simpson (div.); children: Naomi, Judah, Eve. Student, Kenyon Coll., 1951-53; BA, U. Iowa, 1959; postgrad., Stanford U., 1960-61. Lectr. Western Res. U., Cleve., 1963-64, Franklin & Marshall Coll., Lancaster, Pa., 1965-66; asst. prof. Fresno (Calif.) State U., 1967-68, U. Utah, Salt Lake City, 1973-76; prof., poet-in-residence Pomona Coll., Claremont, Calif., 1976—. Author: (poems) White Blossoms, 1965, The Lovemaker, 1960 (Lamont award), The Door Standing Open, 1970, Selected Translations, 1981, Evening Wind, 1988 (Bassine citation, PEN prize 1989); editor Naked Poetry, 1968, Poems from the Hebrew, 1973, Collected Poems of Henri Coulette, 1990; translator: Tungsteen (César Vallejo), 1987. With U.S. Army, 1953-55. Fellow Ingram Merrill, 1973, 89, Guggenheim Found., 1977, Stanford U., 1960, NEA, 1987; recipient Poetry prize Am. Acad. Arts and Letters, 1982. Avocations: tennis, chess. Home: 1663 Chattanooga Ct Claremont CA 91711-2917 Office: Pomona Coll Dept English 140 W 6th St Claremont CA 91711

MEZVINSKY, EDWARD M., lawyer; b. Ames, Iowa, Jan. 17, 1937; m. Marjorie Margolies; 11 children. BA, U. Iowa, 1960; MA, U. Calif., Berkeley, 1963, JD, 1965. State rep. Iowa State Legislature, 1969-70; U.S. congressman 1st Dist., Iowa, 1973-77; U.S. rep. UN Commn. on Human Rights, 1977-79; chmn. Pa. Dem. State Com., Narberth, Pa., 1981-86. Contbr. articles to law jours. Mem. Pa. Bar Assn., Omicron Delta Kappa. Office: 815 Woodbine Ave Narberth PA 19072

MEZZACAPPA, DALE VERONICA, journalist; b. Jersey City, Feb. 1, 1951; s. Santo Michael and Eleanor Veronica (Dixon) Z.; 1 child, Matthew. AB, Vassar Coll., 1972. Staff reporter Suburbanite, Englewood, N.J., 1972-73, Ridgewood (N.J.) Newspapers, 1973-74; staff writer Bergen Record, Hackensack, N.J., 1974-79; N.J. corr. Phila. Inquirer, 1979-81, Trenton bur. chief, 1981-82, Washington corr., 1982-86, edn. reporter, 1986—. Nieman fellow Harvard U., 1990-91. Roman Catholic. Avocations: tennis, travel, reading. Office: Phila Inquirer 400 N Broad St Philadelphia PA 19130-4015

MEZZULLO, LOUIS ALBERT, lawyer; b. Balt., Sept. 20, 1944; m. Judith Scales, Jan. 2, 1970. BA, U. Md., 1967, MA, 1976; JD, T.C. Williams Law Sch., 1976. Bar: Va. 1976. Sales rep. Humble Oil (name now Exxon), Richmond, Va., 1970-72; acctg. Marcoin, Inc., Richmond, 1972-73; pvt. practice bookkeeping, tax preparation Richmond, 1973-76; assoc. McGuire, Woods, Battle and Boothe, Richmond, 1976-79; dir. Mezzullo & McCandlish, Richmond, 1979—. Contbr. articles to profl. jours. Bd. dirs. Richmond Symphony; former pres. Southampton Citizens Assn., Richmond, 1986. Served with USAR, 1969-75. Mem. ABA (tax sect.), Internat. Acad. Estate and Trust Law, Am. Coll. Trust and Estate Counsel, Am. Coll. Tax Counsel, Va. State Bar (tax sect.), Va. Bar Assn., Am. Bar Found., Va. Law Found., Estate Planning Coun. Richmond, Trust Adminstrs. Coun., Willow Oaks Country Club. Home: 2961 Westchester Rd Richmond VA 23225-1842 Office: Mezzullo & McCandlish PO Box 796 Richmond VA 23218

MFUME, KWEISI, congressman; b. Balt., Oct. 24, 1948; divorced; children: Donald, Kevin, Keith, Ronald, Michael. BS, Morgan State U.; MA, Johns Hopkins U., 1984. Mem. Balt. City Council, 1979-87, 100th-104th Congresses from 7th Md. dist., 1987—; former chmn. congl. black caucus, ranking minority mem., mem. banking and fin. svcs. subcom. on gen. oversight and investigations, mem. small bus. com., mem. joint econ. com.; former adj. prof. polit. sci. Morgan State U., Balt. Baptist. Office: US Ho of Reps 2419 Rayburn HOB Washington DC 20515-2007

MIAMIS, JAMES D., retail grocery chain executive; b. 1927. With Demoulas Supermarkets Inc., Tewksbury, Mass., 1948—, now exec. v.p. meat ops. Office: Demoulas Supermarkets Inc 875 East St Tewksbury MA 01876-1469

MIAN, FAROUK ASLAM, chemical engineer, educator; b. Lahore, Punjab, Pakistan, Aug. 10, 1944; came to U.S., 1969; s. Mohd Aslam and Qureshia Mian; m. Zahida Perveen, July 16, 1970; children: Shoaib F., Sophia F. BS in Chem. Engring., Inst. Chem. Tech., Punjab U., Lahore, 1964, MS in Chem. Engring., 1965; postgrad., Ill. Inst. Tech., Chgo., 1972-74. Registered profl. engr., Tex., Calif., Colo., La., Miss., Wis., Wyo.; registered environ. engr.; diplomate Am. Acad. Environ. Engrs. Chem. engr. Kohinoor/Didier-Werke, 1965-69, Nuclear Data, Inc., Palatine, Ill., 1969-71; prodn. supr. Searle Corp., Arlington Heights, Ill., 1971-74; lead process engr. Austin Co., Des Plaines, Ill., 1974-76, Crawford and Russell, Inc., Houston, 1976-77; supr. process Bechtel, Inc., Houston, 1977-80; process mgr. Litwin Corp., Houston, 1980; mgr. chems., product mgr. line Brown and Root, Inc., Houston, 1980—; chmn.'s adviser U.S. Congl. Adv. Bd., Am. Security Coun. Found., Washington, 1983-84. Contbr. articles to profl. publs. Mem. AICE, NSPE, Technologists. Achievements include engring. design/rsch. in petrochemicals, petroleum refining, inorganic/organic chemicals, specialty and fine chemicals, polymers, petroleum refining and coal gasification processes, chlor-alkali and electro-chemicals, food/pharmaceuticals; advisor, cons. to fin. instns. and investment banks on the major transactions in the chlor-alkali (chlorine caustic) soda ash, speciality chemicals, vinyl chemicals, petrochemicals, and related finished products. Office: Brown and Root Inc PO Box 4574 Houston TX 77210-4574

MIAN, GUO, electrical engineer; b. Shanghai, Feb. 6, 1957; came to U.S., 1987; s. Wenseng Mian and Guorong Sun; m. Ann Wang, Nov. 1, 1989. BS in Physics, Shanghai U. Sci. & Tech., 1982; MS in Physics, Western Ill. U., 1989; DSc in Elec. Engring., Washington U., 1992. Mgr. Rec. Media Lab. Magnetic Rec. Ctr., Shanghai (China) Ctrl. Chem. Ltd., 1982-85; vis. scientist materials sci. lab. Keio U., Yokohama, Japan, 1985-87; sr. rsch. elec. engring. Quantum Corp., Milpitas, Calif., 1992-93, Conner Peripherals, San Jose, Calif., 1993-95; sr. mgr. HDD R&D Ctr. Samsung Info. Sys. Am., San Jose, Calif., 1995—. Contbr. articles to Jour. Materials Sci., IEEE Trans. Magnetics, Jour. Magnetism & Magnetic Materials, Jour. Applied Physics, Japanese Jour. Applied Physics, Jour. Japanese Magnetic Soc. Recipient C & C Promotion award Found. for C & C Promotion, Tokyo, 1986. Mem. IEEE, IEEE Magnetics Soc., IEEE Computer Soc., Am. Phys. Soc. Achievements include discovery of transverse correlation length in magnetic thin film media, a linear relationship between correlation function of media noise and an off track displacement of a recording head, an algorithm to determine a signal to noise ratio for an arbitratry data sequence in time domain, an algorithm to determine a nonlinear bit shift in high density magnetic storage by a time domain correlation analysis which has been implemented in Lecory 7200 and 9350 digital scopes, an in-situ measurement of exchange coupling of magnetic thin film, mechanism of residual stress forming and releasing in electronic ceramics processing; inventor in field. Home: 105 Serra Way # 362 Milpitas CA 95035-5206

MIANO, LOUIS STEPHEN, advertising executive; b. N.Y.C., July 28, 1934; s. Louis Clyde and Zefira (Palombo) M. BA, Dartmouth Coll., 1955; MA, Columbia U., 1958. Writer Look Mag., N.Y.C., 1960-61; editor Show Mag., N.Y.C. and L.A., 1961-63; assoc. producer ABC-TV, N.Y.C. and L.A., 1963-66; vice-chmn., dir. creative services AC&R Advt., N.Y.C., 1966-90; sec. EEE Theatrical Ventures, N.Y.C., 1974—; cons. in field. Co-producer plays: Design for Living, Corpse, The Seagull, Legends, Inner Voices, 1974-86. Trustee Marymount Manhattan Coll., N.Y.C., 1980—; cons. Home Box Office, 1991-92; bd. dirs. The Nat. Bd. of Rev. of Motion Pictures, 1995—; bd. dirs. Circle-in-the Square. Mem. N.Y. Athletic Club. Home and Office: 430 E 57th St New York NY 10022-3061

MIASKIEWICZ, THERESA ELIZABETH, secondary education educator; b. Salem, Mass., Aug. 29, 1933; d. Chester and Anastasia (Zmijewski) M. BA, Emmanuel Coll., Boston, 1954. Cert. tchr., Mass.; lic. real estate broker, Mass. Tchr. fgn. lang. dept. Salem Sch. Dept., 1954-94; head tchr. Salem High Sch., 1954-94; ret., 1994; vol. Salem Hosp., 1979-88, Salem Hosp. Aux., 1980—; playground instr. City of Salem summers, 1951-54; mem. vis. com. New Eng. Assn. Secondary Schs. and Colls., Salem Sch. Com., 1996—, Mass. Assn. Sch. Coms., 1996—. Vol. Salem Hosp., 1979-88, House of Seven Gables, Salem, summers, 1987-89; active North Shore Med. Ctr. Aux.; mem. com. Salem Sch., 1996. Mem. Am. Assn. Ret. Persons (NRTA divsn.), Ret. State, County and Mcpl. Employees Assn., Nat. Ret. Tchrs. Assn., New Eng. Assn. Secondary Schs. and Colls., Mass. Ret. Tchrs. Assn., Mass. Fedn. Polish Women's Clubs (v.p. 1988-89, regional chmn. scholarship com.), Polish Bus. and Profl. Women's Club Greater Boston (past corr. sec., chmn. scholarship com.,pres. 1988-89). Avocations: travel, floral design, cooking, reading, arts and crafts.

MICA, JOHN L., congressman; b. Binghamton, N.Y., Jan. 27, 1943; s. John and Adeline Resciniti M.; m. Patricia Szymanek, 1972; children: D'anne, Clark. AA, Miami (Fla.)-Dade C.C., 1965; BA, U. Fla., 1967. Chief of staff U.S. Senate; v.p. Winter Park (Fla.) Antique Mall; pres. M.K. Devel. Corp., Winter Park, Fla.; mem. Fla. Ho. of Reps., 1976-80; mem. appropriations com., mem. ethics com., mem. elections com., mem. community affairs com.; mem. transp. and infrastructre com., govt. reform and oversight com., chmn. civil svc. com. 103d Congress from 7th Fla. Dist., 1993—. Author: Factor affecting local government reorganization efforts in Florida, Urban and Environmental Issues. Active Beth Johnson Mental Health Bd., PTA Bd., Zora Neale Hurston Meml. Com. Recipient Outstanding Svc. award Fla. Conservative Union, Outstanding Svc. award Fla. Cancer Soc., Outstanding Svc. award Sertoma, Outstanding Young Men of Am. award; named as one of five outstanding Young Men in Fla. Mem. C. of C., Kiwanis, Winter Park Jaycees (Good Govt. award 1972), Fla. Jaycees Statewide (Good Govt. award 1973), Tiger Bay, Crime Line Bd. Republican. Episcopal. Office: PO Box 756 Winter Park FL 32790-0756 Office: 336 Cannon Washington DC 20515*

MICCICHE, SALVATORE JOSEPH, retired journalist, lawyer; b. Everett, Mass., Jan. 27, 1928; s. Calogero and Marianna M.; m. Theresa Ellen Miraglia, Oct. 11, 1953; children: Charles M., Marlene, Marcia E. B.S. in Journalism, Boston U., 1950; LL.B., Suffolk U., 1968. Bar: Mass. 1968, U.S. Dist. Ct. Mass. 1977. Reporter Portsmouth (N.H.) Herald, 1953-55; with Boston Globe, 1955-90, editorial writer, 1969-70, Washington bur., 1970-75, asst. to editor, 1975-77, mng. editor for adminstrn., 1977-80, ombudsman, 1980-82, assoc. editor for editorial dept. legal matters, 1982-85, asst. exec. editor, 1985, ret., 1990. Served with U.S. Army, 1950-52. Mem. Mass. Bar (bar-press com. 1975-90), Boston Bar Assn., Orgn. Newspaper Ombudsmen (past dir.), Am. Soc. Newspaper Editors. Roman Catholic. Home: PO Box 152 33 Martha's Ln South Harwich MA 02661

MICCIO, G. KRISTIAN, law educator; b. N.Y.C., Dec. 14, 1951; d. Guy Joseph and Lucille (D'Andrea) M.; m. Peri L. Rainbow, June 18, 1993. BA, Marymount Coll., Tarrytown, N.Y., 1973; MA, SUNY, Albany, 1975; JD, Antioch U., Washington, 1985; postgrad., Columbia U. Bar: N.Y. 1986, U.S. Dist. Ct. (so. and ea. dists.) N.Y., 1986, U.S. Ct. Appeals (2d cir.) 1986, U.S. Supreme Ct. 1989. Asst. dist. atty. Bronx (N.Y.) Dist. Atty.'s, 1985-87; prof. law CUNY, Queens, 1987-91; adj. prof. law CUNY, N.Y.C., 1990-92; adj. prof. N.Y. Law Sch., 1990-93; clin. prof. Albany (N.Y.) Law Sch., Albany, N.Y., 1993-96; sr. rsch. assoc., dir. project for domestic violence studies Ctr. for Women in Govt., Rockefeller Inst., U. N.Y., Albany, 1996—; prof. law and pub. policy U. N.Y., Albany, 1996—; lectr. in field. Contbr. articles to profl. and law jours. Founding dir., atty.-in-charge Ctr. for Battered Women's Legal Svcs., N.Y.C., 1988-93; pres. bd. Coalition of Battered Women's Advs., N.Y.C., 1989—; bd. dirs. Prisoners Legal Svcs., N.Y.C., 1990-93, N.Y.C. Adv. Bd. for N.Y. Police Dept. on Gay and Lesbian Affairs, 1991-93; chair domestic violence com. N.Y.C. Commn. on Status of Women, 1992-93, mayoral appointee, 1992-93; faculty mem. N.Y. State Jud. Inst. Recipient Susan B. Anthony award NOW, 1991, Atty. of Yr. award Kings County D.A.'s Office, 1993, Making Waves award NOW Albany Chpt., 1996; named Outstanding Lawyer of the Yr. on Behalf of Women and Children of the City of New York, CUNY Law Sch. at Queens Coll., 1991. Mem. N.Y. Bar Assn. (task force on family law 1993—), N.Y. County Lawyers Assn (Outstanding Pub. Svc. award 1991, Pro-Bono award 1992), Assn. of Bar of City of N.Y. (Pub. Interest Lawyer award 1993). Office: Albany Law Sch 80 New Scotland Ave Albany NY 12208

MICCIO, JOSEPH V., business educator, consultant; b. Bklyn., May 1, 1915; s. Salvatore and Marian (Lauro) M.; m. Lillian Teves Pratt, Oct. 12, 1957; children: Kathryn, Michael. B.B.A. cum laude (econ. award), St. John's U., 1938; M.A. cum laude, NYU, 1940, Ed.D., 1965; LL.D., Fairleigh Dickinson U., 1963. C.P.A., N.Y. Accountant Rockwood & Co., Bklyn., 1932-39; controller Lightfoot, Schultz Co., N.J., 1939-42; controller, asst. to financial v.p. Republic Aviation Corp., L.I., 1942-45; controller-treas. Air-cooled Motors, Inc., Syracuse, N.Y., 1945-50; gen. mgr. electronics div. Curtiss-Wright Corp., 1951-54, v.p. corp., 1953-64; pres., gen. mgr. Curtiss-Wright Corp. (Wright Aero. div.), Wood-Ridge, N.J., 1954-64, sr. v.p., 1964-66, gen. mgr. plastics div., 1953-54; gen. mgr., exec. v.p. Columbia Protektosite Co. (wholly-owned subs.), 1951-54; chmn. bd. Redel Corp., Anaheim, Calif.; adj. prof. Fairleigh Dickinson U.; instr. NYU; prof. mgmt. and bus. policy U. Hawaii, 1966-69, prof., 1969—, chmn. Grad. Sch. Bus., 1966-69, assoc. dean Coll. Bus. Adminstrn., 1966-69; founder, chmn. bd., CEO, Hawaii Biotech. Group, Inc.; mgr. Hawaiian State Kitechs Bus. Incubator Facility in Honolulu; mem. state com. on employee stock ownership plans, Hawaii Govs. Task Force on Internat. Bus.; bd. dirs. Sun Fashions Inc., Cen. Pacific Supply Inc., IMUA Builders,, Grace Pacific Corp., Hawkins Audio Comm., Inc.; adviser SBA; Hawaii del. Pres.'s Conf. Small Bus., 1980, 87; advisor Hawaii State Com. on E.S.O.P.'s, Hawaii State Spaceport Com. Contbr. articles to profl. jours. Trustee N.J. Symphony; bd. fellows Fairleigh Dickinson U.; mem. coun. St. John's U.; bd. regents Chaminade U., Honolulu. Recipient award of merit Aircraft War Prodn. Coun.; Founders award NYU; Profl. Mgr. award Soc. Advancement Mgmt., 1975; Outstanding Educator award and Excellence in Teaching award U. Hawaii Coll. Bus. Adminstrn., 1985, U. Pres. Citation for Teaching Excellence U. Hawaii, 1986, Bus. Advocate award for Region IX (Calif., Ariz., Nev., Hawaii) U.S. SBA, 1988. Fellow Soc. Advancement of Mgmt.; mem. N.Y. State Soc. CPAs, Fin. Execs. Inst., Am. Arbitration Assn., Am. Mgmt. Assn., Fin. Execs. Inst., Aerospace Industries Assn., Acad. Mgmt., Am. Inst. C.P.A.s, AIAA, Navy League U.S., Conquistadores del Cielo, Honolulu C. of C., Phi Delta Kappa, Phi Delta Epsilon, Beta Gamma Sigma (adv. com. to Hawaii Crime Com.). Clubs: Economic (N.Y.C.); Outrigger Canoe. Address: 2943 Kalakaua Ave Honolulu HI 96815-4269

MICEK, ERNEST S., food products executive; b. Arcadia, Wis., Feb. 18, 1936; m. Sally; 4 children. BS in Chem. Engring., U. Wis., 1959. Mgr. Cargill, Inc., Mpls., 1959, Spain; asst. v.p., gen. mgr. corn milling dept. Cargill, Inc., Mpls., 1973, v.p. milling divsn., 1978, pres. corn milling divsn., 1981, pres. food sector, 1992, exec. v.p., 1993, pres., 1994—, chmn., CEO, 1995—; Bd. dirs. Cargill, Inc., Schneider Nat.; mem. bd. overseers Carlson Sch. Mgmt.; mem. vis. com. chem. engring. dept. U. Wis., mem. indsl. liaison coun.; past mem. com. on trade rels. U.S./Can. C. of C.; past chmn. Corn Refiners Assn. Bd. dirs. United Way Mpls.; hon. bd. dirs. Viking Coun. Boy Scouts Am. Recipient Disting. Svc. citation U. Wis. Dept. Engring., 1991. Mem. Nat. Assn. Mfrs. (chmn. trade tech. policy group, bd. dirs.). Office: Adminstrv office Cargill Inc PO Box 5724 Minneapolis MN 55440

MICH, CONNIE RITA, mental health nurse, educator; b. Nebr., Feb. 5, 1926; d. Henry B. and Anna (Stratman) Redel; m. Richard Mich. BSN, Alverno Coll.; postgrad., Marquette U.; MSN, Cath. U. Am. Asst. clin. dir. in-patient svcs. Fond du Lac (Wis.) County Health Ctr., 1974-78; head nurse, program coord. acute psychiat. unit St. Agnes Hosp., Fond du Lac, 1979-83; mental health clinician Immanuel Med. Ctr., Omaha, 1984-89; instr., clin. supr., asst. prof. psychiat. mental health Coll. St. Mary, Omaha, 1989-93; med. programs dir. Inst. Computer Sci. Ltd., 1989—; program dir. med. programs Gateway Coll., Omaha, 1995; chairperson Examining Coun. on RNs; writer items State Bd. Test Pool Exam.; pres. Milw. Coun. Cath. Nurses; vice chairperson Wis. Conf. Group Psychiat. Nursing Practice. Mem. Sigma Theta Tau, Pi Gamma Mu.

MICHA, DAVID ALLAN, chemistry and physics educator; b. Argentina, Sept. 12, 1939; came to U.S., 1966, naturalized, 1974; s. Simon David and Catalina (Cohen) M.; m. Rebecca Stefan, 1991; children: Michael F., Anna K. MS, U. Cuyo, Bariloche, Argentina, 1962; DSc, U. Uppsala, Sweden, 1966. Rsch. assoc. Theoretical Chemistry Inst. U. Wis., Madison, 1966-67; asst. rsch. physicist Inst. Pure and Applied Sci. U. Calif., La Jolla, 1967-69; assoc. prof. chemistry and physics U. Fla., Gainesville, 1969-74, prof., 1974—, dir. Ctr. Chem. Physics, 1982-91; vis. prof. U. Gothenburg, Sweden, 1970, Harvard U., 1972, 90, Max-Planck Inst., Göttingen, Germany, 1976, Imperial Coll., London, 1977, U. Calif., Santa Barbara, 1982, U. Colo. and Weizmann Inst., Israel, 1983, U. Buenos Aires, 1988, 95, Supercomputer Inst., Fla. State U., 1991; mem. adv. panel div. advanced sci. computing NSF, 1990-92. Mem. editl. bd. Internat. Jour. Quantum Chemistry, 1979-88, Few-Body Systems, 1985—; editor Finite Systems and Multiparticle Dynamics, 1990—, symposium procs.; contbr. several book chpts., numerous articles to sci. jours. Recipient U.S. Sr. Scientist award A. Von Humboldt Found., 1976, Sr. Faculty Rsch. award Sigma Xi, 1985; Alfred P. Sloan Found. fellow, 1971-74; Nat. Bur. Standards JILA fellow, 1983. Fellow Am. Phys. Soc. (vice chmn. topical group on few body sys. and multi-particle dynamics 1986-88, chmn. 1988-89); mem. Am. Chem. Soc. Office: U Fla 366 Williamson Hall Gainesville FL 32611-8435

MICHAEL, ALFRED FREDERICK, JR., physician, medical educator; b. Phila.; s. Alfred Frederick and Emma Maude (Peters) M.; children: Mary, Susan, Carol. M.D., Temple U., 1953. Diplomate: Am. Bd. Pediatrics (founding mem. sub-bd. pediatric nephrology, pres. 1977-80). Diagnostic lab. immunology and pediatric nephrology intern Phila. Gen. Hosp., 1953-54; resident Children's Hosp. and U. Cin. Coll. Medicine, 1957-60; postdoctoral fellow dept. pediatrics Med. Sch., U. Minn., Mpls., 1960-63; asso. prof. Med. Sch., U. Minn., 1965-68, prof. pediatrics, lab. medicine and pathology, 1968—, dir. pediatric nephrology, Regents' Prof., head Dept. Pediatrics, 1986—; established investigator Am. Heart Assn., 1963-68. Mem. editorial bd. Internat. Yr. Book of Nephrology, Kidney Internat., Am. Jour. Nephrology, Kidney Internat., Am. Jour. Nephrology, Clin. Nephrology, Am. Jour. Pathology; contbr. articles to profl. jours. Served with USAF, 1955-57. Recipient Alumni Achievement award in clin. scis. Temple U. Sch. Medicine, 1988; NIH fellow, 1960-63; Guggenheim fellow, 1966-67; AAAS fellow, 1995. Mem. AAAS, AMA, Am. Acad. Pediat., Am. Soc. Clin. Investigation, Assn. Am. Physicians, Am. Pediat. Soc., Soc. for Pediat. Rsch., Am. Assn. Investigative Pathology, Am. Soc. Cell Biology, Ctrl. Soc. for Clin. Rsch., Am. Soc. Nephrology (coun., pres.-elect 1992—, pres. 1993), Internat. Soc. Nephrology, Soc. for Exptl. Biology and Medicine, Am. Fedn. Clin. Rsch., Minn. Med. Assn. Congregationalist. Office: U Minn Hosp Dept Pediatrics PO Box 391 Minneapolis MN 55455

MICHAEL, DONALD NELSON, social scientist, educator; b. Chgo., Jan. 24, 1923; s. Albert Abraham and Jean (Lewis) M.; m. Margot Jean Murphy, Apr. 7, 1956; 1 child, Geoffrey William. S.B., Harvard U., 1946, Ph.D., 1952; M.A., U. Chgo., 1948; D.Sc. (hon.), Marlboro Coll., 1964. Staff social scientist Weapons Systems Evaluation Group U.S., Joint Chiefs Staff, Washington, 1953-54; adviser Office Spl. Studies NSF, Washington, 1954-56; sr. research asso. Dunlap & Assos., Stanford, Conn., 1956-59; sr. staff mem. Brookings Instn., Washington, 1959-61; dir. Peace Research Inst., Washington, 1961-63; resident fellow Inst. Policy Studies, Washington, 1963-66; prof. planning and pub. policy, program dir. Center Research Utilization Sci. Knowledge, Inst. Social Research, prof. psychology U. Mich., Ann Arbor, 1966-82, prof. emeritus, 1982—; rsch. assoc. Inst. Urban and Regional Design, U. Calif., Berkeley, 1980—; lectr. 10th Ann. Lecture John Dewey Soc., 1967; mem. Commn. Study Orgn. Peace, 1965-74; sr. mgmt. cons. SRI Internat., 1980-88; spl. rschr. Shanghai Inst. for Sci. of Sci., 1988—; adj. faculty Saybrook Inst., San Francisco, 1983-91. Author: Proposed Studies on the Implications of Peaceful Space Activities for Human Affairs, 1961, Cybernation: The Silent Conquest, 1962, The Next Generation, 1965, The Unprepared Society, 1968, On Learning to Plan —And Planning to Learn, 1973. Founding mem. nat. bd. U.S. Assn. for Club of Rome, 1978-81; mem. nat. bd. Citizen Involvement Network, 1975; mem. nat. bd. dirs. Girl Scouts U.S.A., 1969-72, Congl. Inst. for Future; mem. exec. bd. Wash. Assn. Scientists, 1961-66, chmn., 1963-64; founding bd. dirs., mem. adv. bd. Rollo May Ctr. for Humanistic Studies, San Francisco, 1988—; bd. dirs. San Francisco chpt. UN Assn., 1989-92; mem. adv. bd. Resource Renewal Inst., Sausalito, Calif., 1991—; adv. bd. Commonweal, Bolinas, Calif., 1993—. NIMH spl. rsch. fellow, 1968-70, vis. fellow Inst. Internat. Studies U. Calif., Berkeley, 1972-73, fellow Sch. Mgmt. and Strategic Studies We. Behavioral Sci. Inst., La Jolla, Calif., 1981-92; first recipient Aurelio Peccei prize L'eta Verde, Rome, 1987; named hon. rsch. prof. Rsch. Ctr. Econ., Tech. and Social Devel. of State Coun., Shanghai, 1988. Fellow AAAS, APA, Inst. Soc. Ethics Life Scis., Soc. for Psychol. Study Social Issues, World Acad. Art and Sci.; mem. Am. Soc. Cybernetics (founding bd. 1964-68), Internat. Soc. for Panetics (founding mem., founding bd. govs. 1991-94), N.Y. Acad. Scis., Fedn. Am. Scientists, Meridian Internat. Inst. (founding bd. 1992—), Club of Rome, Cosmos Club, Sigma Xi.

MICHAEL, ERNEST ARTHUR, mathematics educator; b. Zurich, Switzerland, Aug. 26, 1925; came to U.S., 1939; s. Jakob and Erna (Sondheimer) M.; m. Colette Verger Davis, 1956 (div. 1966); children: Alan, David, Gerard; m. Erika Goodman Joseph, Dec. 4, 1966; children: Hillary, Joshua. B.A., Cornell U., 1947; M.A., Harvard U., 1948; Ph.D., U. Chgo., 1951. Mem. faculty dept. math. U. Wash., Seattle, 1953—; asst. prof. U. Wash., 1953-56, assoc. prof., 1956-60, prof., 1960-93, prof. emeritus, 1993—; mem. Inst. for Advanced Study, Princeton, 1951-52, 56-57, 60-61, 68, Math. Research Inst., E.T.H., Zürich, 1973-74; vis. prof. U. Stuttgart, Ger., 1978-79, U. Munich, Fed. Republic Germany, 1987, 88, 92-93. Editor: Procs. Am. Math. Soc., 1968-71, Topology and Its Applications, 1972-94; contbr. articles to profl. jours. Served with USNR, 1944-46. Grantee AEC; Grantee Office Nav. Research; Grantee NSF; Grantee Guggenheim Found.; Grantee Humboldt Found. Mem. Am. Math. Soc., Math. Assn. Am., ACLU, Amnesty Internat. Jewish. Home: 16751 15th Ave NW Seattle WA 98177-3842

MICHAEL, GARY G., retail supermarket and drug chain executive; b. 1940; married. BS in Bus., U. Idaho, 1962. Staff acct. Ernst & Ernst, CPA's, 1964-66; with Albertson's, Inc., Boise, Idaho, 1966—, acct., 1966-68, asst. controller, 1968-71, controller, 1971-72, v.p., controller, 1972-74, sr. v.p. fin., treas., 1974-76, exec. v.p., 1976-84, vice chmn., CFO, corp. devel. officer,

1984-91, chmn., CEO, 1991—; also dir. Albertson's, Inc. Served to 1st lt. U.S. Army, 1962-64. Office: Albertson's Inc 250 Parkcenter Blvd Boise ID 83706*

MICHAEL, GEORGE (GERGIOS KYRIAKOU PANAYIOTOU), musician, singer, songwriter; b. London, Eng., June 25, 1963; s. Jack and Lesley Panayiotou. Formed group The Executive with Andrew Ridgeley, 1979, band became Wham!, 1980-86. Albums with Wham! Fantastic, 1982, Make it Big, 1984, Music From the Edge of Heaven, 1985; album (with Queen) Five Live, 1993; solo releases Faith, 1987 (best dir. MTV Video award 1988, Best Pop Male Vocalist Am. Music award, 1989, best soul R&B vocalist Am. Music award 1989, best soul R&B album Am. Music award 1989), Listen Without Prejudice, Vol. I, 1990; contbr. albums Two Rooms: Celebrating the Songs of Elton John and Bernie Taupin, 1991, Red, Hot & Dance, 1992, A Very Special Christmas II, 1992; duet (with Aretha Franklin) I Knew You Were Waiting For Me, 1987 (Grammy award best duo R&B 1987); prodr., writer Trojan Souls. Recipient Best New Video Artist award Am. Video Awards, 1985, Grammy nomination Wham! best pop performance by duo, 1985.

MICHAEL, HAROLD LOUIS, civil engineering educator, consultant; b. Columbus, Ind., July 24, 1920; s. Louis Edward and Martha (Armuth) M.; m. Elsie Marie Ahlbrand, Aug. 15, 1943 (dec. Sept. 1951); m. Elizabeth Annette Welch, Dec. 12, 1954 (dec. Jan. 30, 1989); stepchildren: Betty, Ellen, Harold, Thomas Williams; 1 child, Edward Michael. BSCE with highest distinction, Purdue U., 1950, MSCE, 1951, DEng (hon.), 1992. Registered profl. engr., Ind. Grad. asst. Purdue U., 1950-51; dir. urban transp. studies Ind. State Hwy. Commn., 1951-54; research asst., instr. Purdue U., West Lafayette, Ind., 1952-54, asst. prof. hwy. engring., asst. dir. joint hwy. research project, 1954-56, assoc. prof. hwy. engring., assoc. dir. joint hwy. research project, 1956-61, prof. hwy. engring., head transp. and urban engring., assoc. dir. joint hwy. research project, 1961-78, head Sch. Civil Engring., prof. hwy. engring., dir. joint hwy. research project, 1978-91, prof. emeritus, 1991—; chmn. exec. com. Transp. Rsch. Bd., NRC, 1976, mem. exec. com., 1973-79, chmn. or mem. adv. panels for Nat. Coop. Hwy. Research Programs, 1971-79; mem. adv. bd. Hwy. Extension and Research Program for Ind. Counties, 1971-91; chmn. Nat. Com. on Uniform Traffic Control Devices, 1971-74, mem., 1969—; chmn. Nat. Com. on Uniform Traffic Laws and Ordinances, 1990-95, vice chmn. com. on ops., 1973-90; mem. adv. panel on nat. accident sampling system Nat. Hwy. Traffic Safety Adminstrn., 1978-80; mem. exec. res. U.S. Dept. Transp., 1967-83; mem. com. on transp. NRC, 1976-80; mem. bd. cons. Eno Found. Transp., 1978-82; chmn. Traffic Commn., West Lafayette, Ind., 1956—, chmn. transp. tech. com., Greater Lafayette, 1965—. Served to capt. U.S. Army, 1942-46, ETO; with USAR, 1946-64, ret. lt. col. Decorated Bronze Star; recipient citation for Disting. Service State Ind., 1967, Service award Ind. Soc. Profl. Engr., 1969, Disting. Service award Transp. Research Bd., 1976, Roy W. Crum award Transp. Research Bd., 1978, award in recognition of disting. service Ind. Soc. Profl. Engrs., 1978, Theodore M. Matson award, 1979, George S. Bartlett award Am. Assn. Hwy. and Transp. Ofcls., Am. Rd. and Transp. Builders Assn. and Transp. Research Bd., 1982; named Engr. of Yr., Ind. Soc. Profl. Engrs., 1972; Sagamore of Wabash, Ind. Fellow Inst. Transp. Engrs. (pres. 1974-75, Marsh award 1984), ASCE (hon., mem. ABET visitors com. 1978-83, G. Brooks Earnest Lecture award Cleve. sect. 1981, Laurie Prize 1981, Wilbur S. Smith award 1991); mem. NAE, NSPE (nat. dir. 1964-78), Am. Rd. and Transp. Builders. Assn. (life, vice chmn. 1978-80, chmn. hwys. adv. council 1981-94, Disting. Svc. award 1994), Ind. Constructors, Inc. (hon. life), Am. R.R. Engring. Assn. (chmn. subcom. hwys. 1970-87), Am. Soc. Engring. Edn., Am. Pub. Works Assn. (trustee Research Found. 1976-79), Inst. Transp. Engrs. (hon., Wilbur S. Smith Disting. Transp. Engring. Career Educator 1994), Rotary (dist. gov.), Theta Xi. Avocations: gardening; golf; stamp collecting; coin collecting. Home: 1227 N Salisbury St West Lafayette IN 47906-2415 Office: Purdue U Civil Engring Bldg West Lafayette IN 47907

MICHAEL, HENRY N., geographer, anthropologist; b. Pitts., July 14, 1913; s. Anthony M. and Albina (Dubska) M.; m. Ida Nemez, June 18, 1943; children: Susan Shelley, Richard Carleton, Andrew Paul. B.A., U. Pa., 1948, M.A., 1951, Ph.D., 1954. Instr. geography U. Pa., 1948-54; faculty Temple U., 1958-80, prof. geography, chmn. dept., 1965-73, prof., 1965-80; research assoc. Univ. Mus., Phila., 1959-82, sr. fellow, 1982—; mem. Bi-Nat. Commn. on Social Scis. and Humanities, Am. Council Learned Socs./Acad. Scis. USSR, 1975—. Editor: Anthropology of the North, 1959-72; editor, author: Dating Techniques for the Archaeologist, 1971, 73, 82; translator, editor various archaeol. and ethnographic works; mem. adv. publs. com. Mus. Applied Sci. Ctr. for Archaelogy, U. Pa., Anthropology and Archaeology of Eurasia-A Jour. of Transls., Alaska-Siberia Rsch. Ctr.; mem. editorial bd. Expedition-The Univ. Mus. Mag. Archaeology and Anthropology, U. Pa.; contbr. articles to profl. jours. Served to 1st lt. AUS, 1942-45. Decorated Purple Heart. Fellow Am. Anthrop. Assn., Arctic Inst. N.Am.; mem. Phila. Anthrop. Soc. (coun. 1954-90), Delaware Valley Assn. Geographers, Assn. Am. Geographers, Sigma Xi. Home: 2712 Pine Valley Ln Ardmore PA 19003-1719 Office: Univ Museum U Pa Philadelphia PA 19104

MICHAEL, JAMES HARRY, JR., federal judge; b. Charlottesville, Va., Oct. 17, 1918; s. James Harry and Reuben (Shelton) m. Barbara E. Puryear, Dec. 18, 1946; children: Jarrett Michael Stephens, Victoria von der Au. B.S., U. Va., 1940, LL.B., 1942. Bar: Va. 1942. Sole practice Charlottesville; ptnr. Michael & Musselman, 1946-54, J.H. Michael, Jr., 1954-59, Michael & Dent, 1959-72, Michael, Dent & Brooks Ltd., 1972-74, Michael & Dent, Ltd., 1974-80; assoc. judge Juvenile and Domestic Relations Ct., Charlottesville, 1954-68; judge U.S. Dist. Ct., Charlottesville, 1980—; mem. Va. Senate, 1968-80; exec. dir. Inst. Pub. Affairs, U. Va., 1952; chmn. Council State Govts., 1975-76, also mem. exec. com.; chmn. So. Legis. Conf., 1974-75. Mem. Charlottesville Sch. Bd., 1951-62; bd. govs. St. Anne-Belfield Sch., 1952-76. Served with USNR, 1942-46; comdr. Res. ret. Wilton Park fellow Wilton Park Conf., Sussex, Eng., 1971. Fellow Am. Bar Found.; mem. ABA, Va. Bar Assn. (v.p. 1956-57), Charlottesville-Albermarle Bar Assn. (pres. 1966-67), Am. Judicature Soc., 4th Jud. Conf., Va. Trial Lawyers Assn. (Va. disting. svc. award 1993), Assn. Trial Lawyers Am., Raven Soc., Sigma Nu Phi, Omicron Delta Kappa. Episcopalian (lay reader). Office: US Dist Ct 255 W Main St Rm 320 Charlottesville VA 22902-5058

MICHAEL, JERROLD MARK, public health specialist, former university dean, educator; b. Richmond, Va., Aug. 3, 1927; s. Joseph Leon and Esther Leah M.; m. Lynn Y. Simon, Mar. 17, 1951; children: Scott J., Nelson L. B.C.E., George Washington U., 1949; M.S.E., Johns Hopkins U., 1950; M.P.H., U. Calif., Berkeley, 1957; Dr. P.H. (hon.), Mahidol U., 1983; Sc.D. (hon.), Tulane U., 1984. Commd. ensign USPHS, 1950, advanced through grades to rear adm., asst. surgeon gen., 1966; ret., 1970; dean Sch. Pub. Health, U. Hawaii, Honolulu, 1971-92, prof. pub. health, 1971-95; emeritus prof. pub. health U. Hawaii, Honolulu, 1995—; bd. dirs. Nat. Health Coun., 1967-78, Nat. Ctr. for Health Edn., 1977-90; mem. nat. adv. coun. on health professions edn., 1978-81; chmn. bd. dirs. Kuakini Med. Ctr., Honolulu; sec., treas. Asia-Pacific Acad. Consortium Pub. Health; vis. prof. U. Adelaide, 1993, George Washington, 1994; hon. prof. Beijing Med. U., 1994. Contbr. articles to profl. jours.; assoc. editor Jour. Environ. Health, 1958-80, Asia-Pacific Jour. of Pub. Health, 1986-95. Served with USNR, 1945-47. Decorated D.S.M., comdr. Royal Order of Elephant (Thailand); recipient Walter Mangold award, 1961, J.S. Billings award for mil. medicine, 1964, gold medal Hebrew U. Jerusalem, 1982, San Karcil gold medal Govt. of Malaysia, 1989, Disting. Svc. award Gov. of Hawaii, 1989, Assn. Schs. Pub. Health, 1992, recognition of svc. award Pacific Island Health Officers Assn., 1992, USPHS awards, also others. Fellow Am. Public Health Assn.; mem. Am. Acad. Health Adminstrn., Am. Soc. Cert. Sanitarians, Nat. Environ. Health Assn., Am. Acad. Environ. Engrs. Democrat. Jewish. Club: Masons. Office: George Washington U 23rd & Eye St NW Washington DC 20037

MICHAEL, JOAN YVONNE JOHNSON, dean, psychologist; b. Pomona, Calif., Jan. 1, 1935; d. William Frank and Madge Garnet (Simkins) Johnson; m. William Burton Michael, Aug. 26, 1966. AB, U. So. Calif., L.A., 1964, MS, 1965, PhD, 1967. Lectr. in ednl. psychology Immaculate Heart Coll., L.A., 1965-69, U. So. Calif., L.A., 1966; asst. prof. in ednl. psychology San Fernando Valley State Coll., Northridge, Calif., 1967-68; asst. prof. in ednl. psychology Calif. State U., Long Beach, 1968-70, assoc. prof., 1970-75, prof., 1975-83, assoc. dean grad. studies and rsch., 1977-83; dean Sch. Edn. U. Houston at Clear Lake, 1983-89, dean Coll. Edn. and Psychology N.C. State U., Raleigh, 1989—, dir. Lit. Sys. Ctr., 1989-94; chair task force prep for tchr. edn. Assn. Colls. and Schs. of Edn. in State Univ. and Land Grant Colls., 1993—; mem. task force assessing math. and sci. edn. in N.C. Glaxo Found. and N.C. Pub. Sch. Forum, Raleigh, 1995. Author chpt. to book, test manuals; asst. editor Ednl. and Psychology Measurement, 1965-85, assoc. editor, 1985-95; adv. editor Jour. Ednl. Measurement, 1983-84; contbr. articles to profl. jours. Mem. APA, Am. Psychol. Soc., Am. Edn. Rsch. Assn. Avocations: pvt. pilot, swimming, travel. Home: 123 Lochwood West Cary NC 27511 Office: NC State U Coll Edn and Psychology 208 Poe Hall, Box 7801 Raleigh NC 27695

MICHAEL, JONATHAN EDWARD, insurance company executive; b. Columbus, Ohio, Mar. 19, 1954; s. James Franklin and Mary Manetta (McCloud) M.; m. Lori Jeanette Fry, Sept. 1, 1973 (div. Feb. 1985); children: Amber Nicole, Jonathan Andrew. BA, Ohio Dominican Coll., 1977. CPA, Ohio. Acct. Coopers & Lybrand, Columbus, Ohio, 1977-82; chief acct. RLI Ins. Co., Peoria, Ill., 1982-84, controller, 1984-85, v.p. fin., CFO, 1985—, exec. v.p., 1991-94, pres., 1994—. Mem. Am. Inst. CPA's, Ins. Acctg. and Systems Assn. Cen. Ill. (treas. 1985, sec. 1986). Roman Catholic. Club: Mt. Hawley Country (Peoria). Avocation: golf. Home: 12706 Georgetowne Rd Dunlap IL 61525-9462 Office: RLI Ins Corp 9025 N Lindbergh Dr Peoria IL 61615-1431*

MICHAEL, LARRY PERRY, sportscaster, broadcasting company executive; b. Chgo., Sept. 1, 1956; s. Perry Peter and Voula (Sakalleris) M.; m. Darlene Faith Coskey, Oct. 15, 1988; children: Olivia Diane, Anjelica Sharon, Nicholas Parker. BA, U. Md., 1979. Producer MBS, Arlington, Va., 1980-82, mgr. sports ops., 1982-86, dir. sports, 1986-87; dir. sports Westwood One Inc., Arlington, 1987—; exec. prodr. football Notre Dame U., 1984—; play-by-play announcer George Washington U., Washington, 1991-95, Home Team Sports Basketball TV, 1995; host TV Sport Edge...Play-by-Play, Westwood, 1990—, Washington Redskins Radio Network, 1995. Recipient gold medal for 1988 summer Olympic coverage Internat. Radio Festival N.Y., 1989. Mem. Laconian Soc. Democrat. Greek Orthodox. Avocations: weightlifting, sports collecting, golf. Office: Westwood One Sports 1755 Jefferson Davis Hwy Arlington VA 22202-3509

MICHAEL, M. BLANE, federal judge; b. Charleston, S.C., Feb. 17, 1943. AB, W.Va. U., 1965; JD, NYU, 1968. Bar: N.Y. 1968, U.S. Dist. Ct. (so. and ea. dists.) N.Y. 1968, W.Va. 1973, U.S. Ct. Appeals (4th cir.) 1974, U.S. Dist. Ct. (no. dist.) W.Va. 1975, U.S. Dist. Ct. (so. dist.) W.Va. 1981. Counsel to Gov. W.Va. John D. Rockefeller IV, 1977-80; atty. Jackson & Kelly, Charleston, W.Va., 1981-93; fed. judge U.S. Ct. Appeals (4th cir.), Charleston, W.Va., 1993—; active 4th Jud. Conf. Mem. ABA, W.Va. Bar Assn., Kanawha County Bar Assn., Phi Beta Kappa.

MICHAEL, MARY AMELIA FURTADO, retired educator, freelance writer; m. Eugene G. Michael; children: David, Douglas, Gregory. BA, Albertus Magnus Coll.; MS, U. Bridgeport, 1975; CAS, Fairfield U., 1982. Cert. secondary sch. sci. tchr., ednl. adminstr. Housemaster, sci. tchr. Fairfield (Conn.) Pub. Schs., adminstrv. housemaster, sci. tchr., sci. dept. coord., 1992, retired, 1992; freelance fin. rsch. and investment writer and cons., 1994—. Author: The Art and Science of Cooking, 1996; contbr. articles to profl. jours. Mem. Discovery Mus., Conn. Arts & Sci. Mus. Mem. AAUW, LWV, Conn. Assn. Suprs. and Curriculum, Fairfield Sch. Adminstrs. Assn., Retired Educators of Fairfield, Fairfield Hist. Soc. Avocations: collecting antiques, gourmet cooking, collecting old cookbooks and recipes, photography, writing. Home: 942 Valley Rd Fairfield CT 06432-1671

MICHAEL, SANDRA DALE, reproductive endocrinology educator, researcher; b. Sacramento, Calif., Jan. 23, 1945; d. Gordon G. and Ruby F. (Johnson) M.; m. Dennis P. Murr, Aug. 12, 1967 (div. 1974). BA, Calif. State Coll., Sonoma, 1967; PhD, U. Calif., Davis, 1970. NIH predoctoral fellow U. Calif., Davis, 1967-70, NIH postdoctoral fellow, 1970-73, asst. rsch. geneticist, 1973-74; asst. prof. SUNY, Binghamton, 1974-81, assoc. prof., 1981-88, prof. reproductive endocrinology, 1988—, dept. chair, 1992—; adj. prof. dept. ob-gyn. SUNY Health Scis. Ctr., Syracuse; mem. NIH Reproductive Endocrinology Study Sect., 1991—; cons., presenter in field; grant reviewer NIH, NSF, USDA and others. Contbr. articles to profl. jours. Vice chair Tri Cities Opera Guild, Binghamton, 1987-90, chair, 1990-92; mem. Harpur Forum, Binghamton, 1987—, SUNY Found., Binghamton, 1990-96. Fulbright Sr. scholar Czech Republic, 1994; grantee NIMH, 1976-79, Nat. Cancer Inst., 1977-80, 83-87, Nat. Inst. Environ. Health Scis., 1979-80, NSF, 1981-83, NIH, 1987—. Mem. Endocrine Soc., Soc. for the Study of Reprodn., Soc. for Study of Fertility, Am. Soc. for Immunology of Reprodn., Women in Endocrinology (sec.-treas. 1992-95), Soc. for Exptl. Biology and Medicine, N.Y. Acad. Sci., Sigma Xi. Avocations: golf, skiing, bridge, opera, literature. Office: State Univ of NY Dept Biol Scis Binghamton NY 13902

MICHAEL, TAMARA, postmaster; b. Allentown, Pa., June 29, 1949; d. Leo Franklin and Gloria Anna (Kuhns) M.; m. Paul Edwin Stauffer Jr., Mar. 7, 1970 (div. Oct. 1981); 1 child, Sean Michael Stauffer. BA in Art History, Moravian Coll., 1973. Postmaster U.S. Postal Svc., Sumneytown, Pa., 1982-85; dist. women's program coord. U.S. Postal Svc., Cherry Hill, N.J., 1985-86; assoc. office coord. U.S. Postal Svc., New Orleans, 1986-87, supr. delivery and vehicle programs, 1987-90; postmaster U.S. Postal Svc., Gulf Shores, Ala., 1990—. Mem. fin. com. Gulf Shores Meth. Ch., 1993-94; vol. Baldwin County Family Violence Project. Mem. Nat. Assn. Postmasters, Emmaus Jr. Woman's Club (pres. 1984-85). Republican. Avocations: golf, foreign and domestic travel, reading. Home: PO Box 747 Gulf Shores AL 36547-0747 Office: US Postal Svc 2149 W 1st St Gulf Shores AL 36542-9998

MICHAEL, WILLIAM BURTON, psychologist, educator; b. Pasadena, Calif., Mar. 6, 1922; s. William Whipple and Helen Augusta (Schultz) M.; m. Martha Walker Hennessey, Aug. 30, 1947 (dec. 1959); m. Joan Yvonne Johnson, Aug. 26, 1966. A.B., UCLA, 1943; M.S. in Edn., U. So. Calif., Los Angeles, 1945, M.A. in Psychology, 1946, Ph.D., 1947. Lic. psychologist Calif. Lectr. engring. math. Calif. Inst. Tech., Pasadena, 1942-45; asst. prof. psychology Princeton U., N.J., 1947-50; research assoc. Rand Corp., Santa Monica, Calif., 1951-52; dir. testing bur. U. So. Calif., Los Angeles, 1952-62, prof. edn. and psychology, 1957-62, 1967—; prof. edn. and psychology U. Calif., Santa Barbara, 1962-67; cons. in field; lectr. math, psychology and edn. U. So. Calif., 1944-47, others. Author: Teaching for Creative Endeavor, 1967; co-author: Psychological Foundations of Learning and Teaching, 2d edit., 1974, Handbook in Research and Evaluation, 3d edit., 1995 (standardized tests) Study Attitudes and Methods Survey, Dimensions of Self-Concept; editor Ednl. and Psychol. Measurement, 1985-95; cons. editor Jour. Pers. Evaluation in Edn., Ednl. Rsch. Quar.; contbr. chpts. to books and articles to profl. jours. Mem., bd. dirs. Neuro-Psychiat. Clinic, Los Angeles and Pasadena, 1958—; mem. Los Angeles Philharmonic Assn., 1965—; advisor Sch. of Communication, Arcadia, Calif., 1981—. Fellow APA, mem. Am. Ednl. Rsch. Assn. (exec. com., editor Rev. Edn. Rsch. 1962-65), Western Psychol. Assn., Northeastern Ednl. Rsch. Assn., Nat. Coun. on Measurement in Edn., Calif. Ednl. Rsch. Assn. (pres. 1965), Phi Beta Kappa, Sigma Xi, Phi Kappa Phi, Psi Chi, Phi Delta Kappa. Independent. Congregationalist. Avocations: Music; travel; reading; ice cream gourmet. Home: 325 Callita Pl San Marino CA 91108-2311 Office: U So Calif Sch Edn 3470 University Ave Los Angeles CA 90089-0031

MICHAELIDES, CONSTANTINE EVANGELOS, architect, educator; b. Athens, Greece, Jan. 26, 1930; came to U.S., 1955, naturalized, 1964; s. Evangelos George and Kalliopi Constantine (Kefallonitis) M.; m. Maria S. Canellakis, Sept. 3, 1955; children: Evangelos Constantine, Dimitri Canellakis. Diploma in Architecture, Nat. Tech. U., Athens, 1952; M.Arch., Harvard U., 1957. Practice architecture Athens, 1954-55, St. Louis, 1963—; asso. architect Carl Koch, Jose Luis Sert, Hideo Sasaki, Cambridge, Mass., 1957-59, Doxiadis Assos., Athens and Washington, 1959-60, Hellmuth, Obata & Kassabaum, St. Louis, 1962; instr. Grad. Sch. Design Harvard U., 1957-59, Athens Inst. Tech., 1959-60; asst. prof. architecture Washington U., St. Louis, 1960-64, assoc. prof., 1964-69, prof., 1969-94, assoc. dean Sch. Architecture, 1969-73; dean Washington U., Sch. Architecture, 1973-93, dean emeritus, 1993—; Ruth and Norman Moore vis. prof. Washington U., St. Louis, 1995; vis. prof. (Sch. Architecture), Ahmedabad, India, 1970; counselor Landmarks Assn. St. Louis., 1975-79. Author: Hydra: A Greek Island Town: Its Growth and Form, 1967; contbr. articles to profl. jours. Mem. Municipal Commn. on Arts, Letters, University City, Mo., 1975-81. Served to lt. Greek Army Res., 1952-54. Fellow AIA (Rsch. award 1963-64, Presdl. Citation 1992); mem. Tech. Chamber of Greece, Soc. Archtl. Historians, Modern Greek Studies Assn., Hellenic Soc. St. Louis (pres. 1991, 95, 96). Home: 735 Radcliffe Ave Saint Louis MO 63130-3139 Office: Washington U Sch Architecture 1 Brookings Dr Saint Louis MO 63130-4862

MICHAELIS, ELIAS K., neurochemist; b. Wad-Medani, Sudan, Oct. 3, 1944; came to U.S., 1962; married, 1967; 1 child. BS, Fairleigh Dickinson U., 1966; MD, St. Louis U. Med. Sch., 1969; PhD in Physiology and Biophysics, U. Ky., 1973. Spl. fellow rsch. dept. physiology and biophysics U. Ky., 1972-73, from asst. prof. to prof. depts. human devel. and biochemistry, 1982-87; chair pharmacology and toxicology U. Kans., Lawrence, 1988—; dir. ctr. biomed. rsch. and Higuchi bioscis. rsch. ctr. U. Kans., 1988—. Mem. AAAS, Am. Soc. Neurochemistry, Am. Soc. Biochemistry and Molecular Biology, Internat. Soc. Biomedical Rsch. on Alcoholism, Soc. Neuroscience, N.Y. Acad. Sci. Achievements include research in characterization of L-glutamate receptors in neuronal membranes, in membrane protein isolation and chemical analysis, in characterization of membrane transport systems for amino acids, sodium, potassium, and calcium, in neuronal membrane biophysics, in molecular neurobiology.

MICHAELIS, KAREN LAUREE, law educator; b. Milw., Mar. 30, 1950; d. Donald Lee and Ethel Catherine (Stevens) M.; m. Larry Severtson, Aug. 12, 1980 (div. Aug. 1982); 1 child, Quinn Alexandra Michaelis. BA, U. Wis., 1972, BS, 1974; MA, Calif. State U., L.A., 1979; PhD, U. Wis., 1988, MS, 1985, JD, 1989. Bar: Wis., U.S. Dist. Ct. (we. dist.) Wis. Asst. prof. law Hofstra U., Hempstead, N.Y., 1990-93; assoc. prof. law Ill. State U., Normal, 1993-95; asst. prof. law Wash. State U., Pullman, 1995—. Author: Reporting Child Abuse: A Guide to Mandatory Requirements for School Personnel, 1993; editor Ill. Sch. Law Quarterly, 1993-95; mem. editl. bd. Nat. Assn. Profs. of Ednl. Adminstrn., 1994-95, Planning and Changing, 1993-95, Jour. Sch. Leadership, 1991—, People & Education: The Human Side of Edn., 1991-96. Mem. ABA, Nat. Coun. Profs. Ednl. Adminstrn. (program com. 1994-95, morphet fund com. 1993—), Nat. Orgn. Legal Problems in Edn. (publs. com. 1993—, program com. 1995), Wis. Bar Assn. Office: Wash State U Cleveland Hall 351 Pullman WA 99164-2136

MICHAELIS, MICHAEL, management and technical consultant; b. Berlin, June 8, 1919; s. George and Martha (Bluth) M.; m. Diana Ordway Tead, Sept. 11, 1954; children: Ordway Peter, David Tead; m. Cintra McIlwain Williams, Mar. 19, 1966 (div. Nov. 1975); m. Caroline Crutcher Bishop, Mar. 17, 1984. B.Sc. in Engring., U. London, 1941. Research asst., group leader Research Labs. Gen. Electric Co., Ltd., U.K., 1935-45; staff physicist and cons. Gen. Electric Co., Ltd., 1945-49; dir. physics div. Radiochem. Centre, U.K. Atomic Energy Authority, 1949-51; cons. Arthur D. Little, Inc., Cambridge, Mass., 1951-52; staff cons. Arthur D. Little, Inc., 1952-61, sr. asso., 1957-61, head nuclear mgmt. cons. services, 1956-61, internat. bus. devel. services, 1959-61, policy adviser to several large corps, 1954-61, mgr. Washington ops., 1963-72, sr. cons., 1972-81; pres., chief exec. officer Partners In Enterprise, Inc., 1981—; cons. to Pres.'s Spl. Asst. Sci. and Tech., 1961-63; exec. sec. The White House Panel on Civilian Tech., 1961-63; exec. dir. rsch. mgmt. adv. panel, com. on sci. and tech. U.S. Ho. of Reps., 1963-67; dep. coord. then Pres.-elect Carter's Task Force on Sci. and Tech. Policy, 1976; mem. tech. adv. bd. to U.S. Sec. Commerce, 1978-81; mem. citizens adv. coun. Congl. Caucus for Sci. and Tech., 1983-86; mem. nat. com. Am. Goals and Resources, Nat. Planning Assn., 1964-67, mem. adv. com. sci., tech. and economy, 1966-68; vice chmn. com. internat. affairs Atomic Indsl. Forum, 1958-60; assoc. with Anglo-Am. Radar Rsch. Project, World War II. Editor, project dir.: Federal Funding of Civilian Research and Development, 1976; Contbr. articles to publs., periodicals. Fellow AAAS (chmn. engring. sect. 1980-82, exec. dir. sr. scientists and engrs. program 1989-90); mem. IEEE (sr.), Sci. Film Assn. (founder 1943, sec. 1943-48, v.p. 1948-51), Am. Nuclear Soc., Boston Com. Fgn. Rels., Royal Inst. Physics and Phys. Soc., Soc. Internat. Devel., Royal Instn. Elec. Engrs., Assn. Hosp. Physicists, Nat. Planning Assn., World Future Soc. (dir.), U.S. C. of C. (chmn. com. on govt.-industry rels. in sci. and tech. 1963-64), Interdisciplinary Comm. Assocs. Inc. (dir. 1969-79), Am. Econ. Assn., Am. Soc. Cybernetics, Am. Soc. for Pub. Adminstrn., Atlantic Coun. U.S., Cosmos Club (Washington; sec. 1994—), Harvard Faculty Club. Home and Office: 6812 Meadow Ln Chevy Chase MD 20815-5018 *The Constitution of the U.S. diffuses power so as to better secure liberty. But it also intends that practice will integrate the dispersed powers into a workable government. It confers upon its branches autonomy but also reciprocity, separateness but also interdependence. It is incumbent on each of us to help make this system work, and to make it responsive to the human needs of our country and the world.*

MICHAELIS, PAUL CHARLES, engineering physicist executive; b. Bronx, N.Y., June 18, 1935; s. Paul Fredrick and Rose (Landsbury) M.; m. Geraldine A. DeCuollo, June 29, 1958; 1 son, Paul Charles. B.S. in Elec. Engring, Newark Coll. Engring., 1964, M.S. in Physics, 1967. With AT&T Bell Labs., Whippany, N.J., 1953—; assoc. mem. tech. staff Bell Telephone Labs., 1963-67, mem. tech. staff, 1967-82, tech. mgr., 1982—; lectr. USSR Acad. Scis., 1972. Contbr. articles to profl. jours.; patentee in optics, magnetics, mechanics and electronics. Mem. IEEE (Morris N. Liebmann award 1975), Am. Phys. Soc., AAAS, U.S. Naval Inst. Clubs: Watchung Lions (past pres.), Raritan Yacht (sec.). Home: 103 High Tor Dr Watchung NJ 07060-5408 Office: Bell Labs PO Box 903 67 Whippany Rd Whippany NJ 07981-1406

MICHAELS, ALAN RICHARD, sports commentator; b. Bklyn., Nov. 12, 1944; s. Jay Leonard and Lila Ruth (Ross) M.; m. Linda Anne Stamaton, Aug. 27, 1966; children—Steven, Jennifer. BA, Ariz. State U., 1966. TV/radio play-by-play announcer Cin. Reds, 1971-73, San Francisco Giants, 1974-76; sports commentator ABC TV Network, N.Y.C., 1976—. Recipient Nat. Sportscaster of Yr. award Nat. Sportscasters and Sportswriters Assn., 1980, 83, 86, Emmy award, 1987. Avocations: reading; tennis. Office: ABC Sports Inc 47 W 66th St New York NY 10023-6201

MICHAELS, CINDY WHITFILL (CYNTHIA G. MICHAELS), educational services consultant, telecommunications services representative; b. Plainview, Tex., Aug. 31, 1951; d. Glenn Tierce and Ruby Jewell (Nichols) Whitfill; m. Terre Joe Michaels, July 16, 1977. BS, W. Tex. State U., 1972; MS, U. Tex., Dallas, 1976; postgrad. cert., E. Tex. State U., 1982. Registered profl. ednl. diagnostician, Tex.; cert. supr. (gen. and spl. edn.), elem. edn. tchr., K-8 English tchr., spl. edn. tchr. (generic and mental retardation), Tex. Gen. and spl. edn. tchr. Plano (Tex.) Ind. Sch. Dist., 1972-76; dependents' sch. tchr. U.S. Dept. Def., Office of Overseas Edn., Schweinfurt, West Germany, 1976-77; asst. dir. edn. dept. spl. edn. Univ. Affiliated Ctr., U. Tex., Dallas, 1977-80; asst. to acting dir. edn., dept. pediatrics, Southwestern Med. Sch. Univ. Affiliated Ctr., U. Tex. Health Sci. Ctr., Dallas, 1980-82; dir. Collin County Spl. Edn. Coop., Wylie, Tex., 1982-89; dir. spl. svcs. Terrell (Tex.) Ind. Sch. Dist., 1989-92; cons. for at-risk svcs. instrnl. svcs. dept. Region 10 Edn. Svc. Ctr., Richardson, Tex., 1992-93, cons. for staff devel., 1993-95; cons. Title I Svcs., 1995-96; ind. rep. Am. Communications Network, 1995—; owner Strategic Out Source Svcs., Garland, Tex., 1996—; regional cons. presenter and speaker Region 10 Adminstrs. Spl. Edn., Dallas, 1982-92; state conf. presenter and speaker Tex. Assn. Bus. Sch. Bds., Houston, 1991, Tex. Edn. Agy., Austin, 1992, grant reviewer, 1984; cons. S.W. regional tng. program educators U. So. Miss., 1992-93; regional coord. H.S. mock trial competition State Bar Tex., 1993; regional liaison Tex. Elem. Mentor Network, 1993—; state presenter Tex. Vocat. Educators Conf., 1994. Active Dance-A-Thon for United Cerebral Palsy, Dallas, 1986; area marcher March of Dimes, Dallas, 1990, Park Cities Walkathon for Multiple Sclerosis, 1994, 95. Grantee Job Tng. & Partnership Act, 1991, Carl Perkins Vocat. Program, 1991, Tex. Edn. Agy., 1990, 91, 92; named Outstanding Young Woman in Am., Outstanding Young Women in Am., 1981. Mem. AAUW, Assn. Compensatory Educators of Tex. (state conf. com. 1996), Tex. Assn. for Improvement of Reading, Tex. Assn. Sect. 504 Coords. and Hearing Officers, Nat. Coun. Adminstrs. Spl. Edn., Coun. Exceptional Children (chpt. pres. 1973-74), Tex. Assn. Supervision & Curriculum Devel. (mem. leadership team Project Pathways 1992-93), Tex. Coun. Adminstrs. Spl. Edn. (region 10 chairperson 1985-87, state conf. presenter 1989, 92), Tex. Ednl. Diagnosticians Assn. (Dal-Metro v.p., state conf. program chair 1982-83, state conf. presenter 1983), Internat. Reading Assn., Nat. Assn. Supervision and Curriculum Devel., Alpha Delta Pi (Richardson alumnae, philanthropy chair 1988, v.p. 1989, 90, 91, v.p./sec. 1993-94, v.p. 1994-95). Avocations: aerobics, snow skiing, travel, dancing. Home and Office: 2613 Oak Point Dr Garland TX 75044-7809 also: 232 Broadmoor Alto NM 88312

MICHAELS, GENEVA LANE, lay worker, retired elementary school administrator; b. Dayton, Ohio, June 27, 1929; d. William Bert and Ethel Lee (Jackson) O'Neal; m. James Edward Michaels, Oct. 6, 1951 (dec. Mar. 1989); children: Ethel Adeline, Geneva Lee, Jamie Bert. Student, Cedarville Coll., 1952-54, Zola Levitt Jewish Christian Inst., Dallas, 1990-91, Liberty Bible Home Inst., Lynchburg, Va., 1991. Dir. youth, tchr. Bible, musician Ft. McKinley (Ohio) Bapt. Ch., 1952-56; dir. youth, musician Sidney (Ohio) Bapt. Ch., 1957-59; tchr. Bible, musician Hope Bapt. Ch., Kettering, Ohio, 1959-64; dir. youth Liberty Bapt. Ch., Xenia, Ohio, 1978—, tchr. Bible, head of music, Gospel soloist, musician, 1978—; sec. Huffman Elem. Sch., Dayton, 1966-80, pres., 1965-70. Pres. PTA, 1965-70. Recipient cert. and blue ribbon Ohio State PTA, 1964-65, 67. Mem. Smithsonian Instn. Republican. Home: 417 Huffman Ave Dayton OH 45403-2505 Office: Liberty Bapt Ch PO Box 641 Xenia OH 45385-0641 *As a teenager, I was presented with the statement, "In later life, I'll win or lose, depending on how, now I choose." I believe life is a trust from Almighty God, and my life is either a stepping stone or a stumbling block, thereby touching lives along the way. I have chosen to be a stepping stone as I pass through life, and hope others can say they are blessed for having known me.*

MICHAELS, JAMES WALKER, magazine editor; b. Buffalo, June 17, 1921; s. Dewey and Phyllis (Boasberg) M.; m. Jean A. Briggs, June 1985; children: Robert Matthews, James Walker, Anne Phyllis. B.S. cum laude, Harvard U., 1942. Ambulance driver Am. Field Service, India and Burma, 1943-44; with USIS, New Delhi, Bangkok, 1944-46; fgn. corr. UP; bur. mgr. UP, New Delhi, 1946-50; with Forbes mag., N.Y.C., 1954—; mng. editor Forbes mag., 1956-61, editor, 1961—. Contbr. articles to mags. Office: Forbes Inc 60 5th Ave New York NY 10011-8802

MICHAELS, JENNIFER ALMAN, lawyer; b. N.Y.C., Mar. 1, 1948; d. David I. and Emily (Arnow) Alman; 1 child, Abigail Elizabeth. BA, Douglas Coll., 1969; JD, Cardozo Sch. of Law, 1990. Ptnr. Alman & Michaels, Highland Park, N.J., 1990—. Author, composer: (record) Music for 2's and 3's, 1981; producer, writer: (film) Critical Decisions in Medicine, 1983. Mem. ABA, Middlesex County Bar Assn., N.J. State Bar Assn., Am. Trial Lawyers Assn., Phi Kappa Phi. Avocations: aviculture, sailing. Office: Alman and Michaels 611 S Park Ave Highland Park NJ 08904-2928

MICHAELS, JENNIFER TONKS, foreign language educator; b. Sedgley, England, May 19, 1945; d. Frank Gordon and Dorothy (Compston) Tonks; m. Eric Michaels, 1973; children: Joseph, David, Ellen. MA, U. Edinburgh, 1967, McGill U., 1971; PhD, McGill U., 1974. Teaching asst. German dept. Wesleyan U., 1967-68; instr. German dept. Bucknell (Pa.) U., 1968-69; teaching asst. German dept. McGill U., Can., 1969-72; prodn. asst. Pub. TV News and Polit. program, Schenectady, N.Y., 1974-75; from asst. prof. to assoc. prof. Grinnell (Iowa) Coll., 1975-87, prof., 1987—; vis. cons. German dept. Hamilton Coll., 1981; cons. Modern Lang. dept. Colby Coll.; panelist NEH, 1985; spkr. in field. Author: D.H. Lawrence, The Polarity of North and South, 1976, Anarchy and Eros: Otto Gross' Impact on Germany Expressionist Writers, 1983, Franz Jung: Expressionist, Dadaist, Revolutionary and Outsider, 1989, Franz Werfel and the Critics, 1994; contbr. numerous articles, revs. to profl. jours. Mem. MLA, Am. Assn. Tchrs. of German, Soc. Exile Studies, German Studies Assn. (sec. treas. 1991-92, v.p. 1992-94, pres. 1995—, numerous coms.). Democrat. Avocations: music, travel, reading. Office: Grinnell Coll German Dept PO Box 805 Grinnell IA 50112-0805

MICHAELS, KEVIN RICHARD, lawyer; b. Buffalo, Feb. 9, 1960; s. Richard Ronald and Marlene Constance (Mnich) M.; m. Beatrice Mary Szeliga, Jan. 15, 1983; 1 child, Jaena René. BS in Govt., U. Houston, 1987; JD, South Tex. Coll. Law, 1992. Bar: Tex. 1992. Ct. coord. Harris County Dist. Clk., Houston, 1985-88; paralegal O'Quinn, Kerensky, McAninch & Laminack, Houston, 1988-92, atty., 1992—. Mem. Assn. Trial Lawyers Am. (Tex. gov. New Lawyers div. 1994—). Avocations: golf, camping. Office: O'Quinn Kerensky McAninch and Laminack 440 Louisiana St Ste 2300 Houston TX 77002-1636

MICHAELS, LORNE, television writer, producer; b. Toronto, Ont., Can.. Grad., U. Toronto, 1966. Chmn. bd. Broadway Video, N.Y.C. Creator, exec. producer: Saturday Night Live, NBC, 1975-80, 85—, Late Night with Conan O'Brien, 1993—; writer, co-producer 3 Lily Tomlin spls., Paul Simon spl.; exec. producer: (HBO spl.) Simon and Garfunkel, Concert in the Park, Paul Simon Born at the Right Time in Cen. Park, 1991, (ABC-TV spl) Rolling Stone's 30 Years of Rock 'n' Roll, 1988; writer, producer: (movie) Three Amigos; exec. producer (TV series) Night Music, NBC, Kids in the Hall, HBO, (spl.) Stones Retro., HBO; exec. producer and producer (spl.) Saturday Night 15th Anniversary Spl., 1989; producer I(spl.), Wayne's World; producer, co-writer Steve Martin's Best Show Ever 81. Recipient 4 awards Writers Guild Am., 8 Emmy awards Nat. Acad. TV Arts and Scis. Office: Broadway Video 1619 Broadway New York NY 10019-7412

MICHAELS, PATRICK FRANCIS, broadcasting company executive; b. Superior, Wis., Nov. 5, 1925; s. Julian and Kathryn Elizabeth (Keating) M.; AA, U. Melbourne, 1943; BA, Golden State U., 1954; PhD, London U., 1964; m. Paula Naomi Bowen, May 1, 1960; children—Stephanie Michelle, Patricia Erin. War corr. CBS; news editor King Broadcasting, 1945-50; war corr. Mid-East Internat. News Service, 1947-49; war corr. MBS, Korea, 1950-53; news dir. Sta. WDSU-AM-FM-TV, 1953-54; fgn. corr. NBC, S. Am., 1954-56; news dir. Sta. KWIZ, 1956-59; commentator ABC, Los Angeles, 1959-62; fgn. corr. Am. News Services, London, 1962-64; news commentator McFadden Bartell Sta. KCBQ, 1964-68; news commentator ABC, San Francisco, 1968-70; news dir. Sta. KWIZ, Santa Ana, Calif., 1970-74, station mgr., 1974-81; pres. Sta. KWRM, Corona, Calif., Sta. KQLH, San Bernardino, Calif., 1981-88; chmn. Michaels Media, Huntington Beach, Calif., 1988—. Bd. dirs. Econ. Devel. Corp. Mem. Nat. Assn. Broadcasters (bd. dirs.), Calif. Broadcasters Assn. (v.p.), Am. Fedn. TV and Radio Artists, Orange County Broadcasters Assn. (pres.), Sigma Delta Chi (ethics com.). Republican. Clubs: Rotary, Balboa Bay (bd. govs.), South Shore Yacht, Internat. Yachting Fellowship of Rotarians (staff commodore). Home: PO Box 832 Corona Del Mar CA 92625

MICHAELS, WILLARD A., retired broadcasting executive; b. Omaha, May 13, 1917; s. Gus M. and Bessie (Kerstine) M.; m. Helen Louise Mintel, Nov. 20, 1938; children: Marcella, Lawrence Richard, Betty Michaels Westbrook. BA, Trinity U., 1940. Asst. sports editor San Antonio Express, 1937-40; sports announcer, sales mgr., gen. mgr. KABC, San Antonio, 1940-53; gen. mgr. KGBS-TV, 1954; v.p. WJBK-TV, Detroit, 1955-61; dir. Storer Broadcasting Co., Miami Beach, Fla., 1960-85; TV v.p. Storer Broadcasting Co., 1961-66, exec. v.p., 1966-67, pres., 1967-74, chmn., 1974-82, ret., 1982; chmn. New Boston Garden Corp. (Boston Bruins), 1972-75; dir., mem. exec. com. Northeast Airlines, 1965-72, pres., 1970-72; dir. Delta Airlines, 1972-90, adv. dir., 1990—. Bd. trustees Storer Found. Home: 12419 Winding Br San Antonio TX 78230-2771

MICHAELSON, ARTHUR M., lawyer; b. N.Y.C., May 16, 1927; s. Samuel H. and Augusta L. M.; m. Arline L. Kahn, June 30, 1957; children: Barbara L., Sarah E., David N. A.B., Columbia U., 1947; LL.B., Yale U., 1950. Bar: N.Y. 1950, U.S. Supreme Ct 1964. Partner Wachtel & Michaelson, N.Y.C., 1957-66; v.p. McCrory Corp., N.Y.C., 1966-68, Glen Alden Corp., N.Y.C., 1968-73; partner Miller, Singer, Michaelson & Raives, N.Y.C., 1973-84; counsel Hofheimer Gartlir & Gross, 1984—. Author: (with J. Blattmachr) Income Taxation of Estates and Trusts, 1980, 85, 89, 95. Bd. dirs., mem. exec. com. Amnesty Internat. of U.S.A., Inc., 1972-81, vice chmn., 1975-76. Served with USN, 1945-46. Mem. ABA, Assn. Bar City N.Y. Office: 633 3rd Ave New York NY 10017

MICHAELSON, MARTIN, lawyer; b. Boston, Apr. 12, 1943; s. Eliot D. and Charlotte (Selib) M.; m. Anne Taylor, Aug. 30, 1987; children: Andrew M., Daniel M.; stepchildren: Rachel T., Hannah T. BA, U. Chgo., 1965; JD, Boston Coll., 1968. Bar: N.Y. 1968, D.C. 1973, U.S. Supreme Ct. 1973, Mass. 1983, U.S. Dist. Ct. N.Y. 1969, D.C. 1973, U.S. Ct. Appeals (1st, 2d, 3d, 4th, 9th cirs.). Atty. Cravath, Swaine & Moore, N.Y.C., 1968-71; legis. asst. Congressman Robert F. Drinan, Washington, 1971-73; atty. Hogan & Hartson, Washington, 1973-76, ptnr., 1976-83, 89—; dep. gen. counsel Harvard U., Cambridge, Mass., 1983-88, univ. counsel, 1989. Office: Hogan & Hartson Columbia Square 555 13th St NW Washington DC 20004-1109

MICHAELSON, RICHARD AARON, health science facility administrator; b. Newton, Mass., Feb. 7, 1952; s. Eliot David and Charlotte Natalie (Selib) M.; m. Allyn Joan Shaloff, Apr. 11, 1981; 1 child, David Benjamin. BA in Psychology, U. Rochester, 1973; MS in Mgmt., MIT, 1977. Research asst. MIT Ctr. Info. Systems Research, Cambridge, Mass., 1976-77; analyst IBM Biomed. Systems Group, Mt. Kisco, N.Y., 1977-79; staff fin. analyst IBM Gen. Bus. Group, White Plains, N.Y., 1979-80; dir. fin. planning MetPath, Inc., Teterboro, N.J., 1980-82, dir. fin. services, 1982-84, v.p. fin., chief fin. officer, 1984-86, v.p. corp. devel., 1986—. Bd. dirs. United Jewish Assn. Fedn. of North N.J., 1987—. Club: MIT Sloan (N.Y.C.) (regional gov. 1986—). Home: 11-18 Fairhaven Pl Fair Lawn NJ 07410-1683 Office: Unilab Corp 18448 Oxnard St Tarzana CA 91356-1504*

MICHAK, HELEN BARBARA, educator, nurse; b. Cleve., July 31; d. Andrew and Mary (Patrick) M. Diploma Cleve. City Hosp. Sch. Nursing, 1947; BA, Miami U., Oxford, Ohio, 1951; MA, Case Western Res. U., 1960. Staff nurse Cleve. City Hosp., 1947-48; pub. health nurse Cleve. Div. Health, 1951-52; instr. Cleve. City Hosp. Sch. Nursing, 1952-56; supr. nursing Cuyahoga County Hosp., Cleve., 1956-58; pub. information dir. N.E. Ohio Am. Heart Assn., Cleve., 1960-64; dir. spl. events Higbee Co., Cleve., 1964-66; exec. dir. Cleve. Area League for Nursing, 1966-72; dir. continuing edn. nurses, adj. assoc. prof. Cleve. State U., 1972-86; asst. regional cons. Ohio Bd. Nursing, 1991—. Trustee N.E. Ohio Regional Med. Program, 1970-73; mem. adv. com. Dept. Nursing Cuyahoga C.C., 1967-87; mem. long term care com. Met. Health Planning Corp., 1974-76, plan devel. com. 1977; mem. policy bd. Ctr. Health Data N.E. Ohio, 1972-73; mem. Rep. Assembly and Health Planning and Devel. Commn., Welfare Fedn. Cleve., 1967-72, Cleve. Cmty. Health Network, 1972-73, United Appeal Films and Speakers Bur., 1967-73; mem. adv. com. Ohio Fedn. Lic. Practical Nurses, 1970-73; mem. tech. adv. com. No. Ohio Lung Assn., 1967-74, 90-93; mem. Ohio Commn. on Nursing, 1971-74; mem. citizens com. nursing homes Fedn. Community Planning, 1973-77; mem. com. on home health services Met. Health Planning Corp., 1973-75; mem. profl. adv. com. on home care Fairview Gen. Hosp., 1987-91. Mem. Nat. League Nursing (mem. com. 1970-72), Am. Nurses Assn. (accreditation visitor 1977-78, 83-88) Ohio Nurses Assn., (com. continuing edn. 1974-79, 82-87, 89-92, chmn. 1984-86), Greater Cleve. (joint practice com. 1973-74, Greater Cleve. Nurses Assn. (trustee 1975-76) , Cleve. Area Citizens League for Nursing (trustee 1976-79, v.p. 1988-90), Zeta Tau Alpha, Sigma Theta Tau. Home and Office: 4686 Oakridge Dr North Royalton OH 44133

MICHAL, RONALD JAMES, physicist; b. Compton, Calif., Oct. 26, 1953; s. James Victor and Joy Aileen (Rogers) M.; m. Monica Jewel Anderson, Feb. 9, 1974 (div. Jan. 1983); children: Kenneth James, Debra Jewel, Michal; m. Valerie Jean Lowe, Oct. 19, 1984; children: Katherine Marie, Christopher Paul Miller. AA Physics, Fullerton (Calif.) C.C., 1976; BA Physics, Calif. State U., Fullerton, 1978; MA Physics, Calif. State U., Long Beach, 1981. Cert. community coll. tchr., Calif. Engr./scientist McDonnell Douglas, Huntington Beach, Calif., 1978-88; sr. engr. Smith Industries, Grand Rapids, Mich., 1988-90; engr. specialist Litton Guidance and Control, Woodland Hills, Calif., 1991—; instr. Fullerton Coll., 1981-88. Contbr. articles to profl. jours. Mem. Astron. Soc. Pacific, Planetary Soc., Internat. Planetarium Soc., High-Desert Astron. Soc. Republican. Achievements include patents for apparatus for reducing magnetic field effects in fiber optic gyros; fiber-optic senor, optical fiber sensing systems having acoustical modulation, reciprocally switched four modulator systems. Home: PO Box 152 1016 Apple St Wrightwood CA 92397 Office: Litton Guidance and Control 5500 Canoga Ave Woodland Hills CA 91367

MICHALAK, EDWARD FRANCIS, lawyer; b. Evanston, Ill., Sept. 6, 1937; s. Leo Francis Michalak and Helen Sophie (Wolinski) Krakowski; m. Margaret Mary Minx, Jan. 2, 1978. BSBA, Northwestern U., 1959; LLB, Harvard U., 1962. Bar: Ill. 1962. Assoc. McDermott, Will & Emery, Chgo., 1963-69, ptnr., 1969—. Served to sgt. USAR, 1962-68. Mem. Ill. Bar Assn., Chgo. Bar Assn., Beta Gamma Sigma, Beta Alpha Psi. Roman Catholic. Club: Mid-Day (Chgo.). Avocations: golf, opera. Home: 3409 Summit Ave Highland Park IL 60035-1111 Office: McDermott Will & Emery 227 W Monroe St Chicago IL 60606-5016

MICHALAK, JANET CAROL, reading education educator; b. Buffalo, Mar. 22, 1949; d. Theodore and Thelma Ruth (Roesch) Vukovic; m. Gerald Paul Michalak, June 19, 1971; children: Nathan, Justin. BS in Edn., SUNY Coll. at Buffalo, Buffalo, 1970; MS in Edn., SUNY, Buffalo, 1971, EdD, 1981. Cert. tchr. nursery, kindergarten, grades 1-6, reading tchr., English tchr. grades 7-12, N.Y. Reading tchr. Tonawanda (N.Y.) Sch. System, 1971-80; instr. Niagara County C.C., Sanborn, N.Y., 1980-82, asst. prof., 1982-85, assoc. prof., 1985-91, prof., 1991—; adj. lectr. SUNY, Buffalo, 1990-91. Recipient Pres.'s award for Excellence in Teaching, Niagara County C.C., 1990, Nat. Inst. for Staff & Orgnl. Devel. Excellence award, 1991, SUNY Chancellor's award for Excellence in Teaching, 1991. Mem. Coll. Reading Assn., Internat. Reading Assn., N.Y. Coll. Learning Skills Assn., Niagara Frontier Reading Coun. (bd. dirs. 1986-88). Republican. Presbyterian. Avocation: reading. Home: 184 Montbleu Dr Getzville NY 14068-1329 Office: Niagara County CC 3111 Saunders Settlement Rd Sanborn NY 14132-9487

MICHALEK, SUZANNE M., biology educator; b. Chgo., July 19, 1944. BS, Ill. State U., 1967, MS, 1968; PhD in Microbiology, U. Ala., 1976. Rsch. asst. microbiology and immunology Nat. Inst. Dental Rsch. NIH, Bethesda, Md., 1972-76, fellow microbiology and immunology, 1977-79; investigator Inst. Dental Rsch. U. Ala., Birmingham, 1980-85, scientist, 1985—, sr. investigator Rsch. Ctr. Oral Biology, 1988—. Mem. Am. Soc. Microbiology, Am. Assn. Immunologists, Internat. Assn. Dental Rsch., Am. Assn. Dental Rsch., Soc. Exptl. Biology and Medicine. Office: U Ala at Birmingham Rsch Ctr in Oral Biology BBRB 258 845 S 19th St Birmingham AL 35294*

MICHALIK, JOHN JAMES, legal educational association executive; b. Bemidji, Minn., Aug. 1, 1945; s. John and Margaret Helen (Pafko) M.; m. Diane Marie Olson, Dec. 21, 1968; children: Matthew John, Nicole, Shane. BA, U. Minn., 1967, JD, 1970. Legal editor Lawyers Coop. Pub. Co., Rochester, N.Y., 1970-75; dir. continuing legal edn. Wash. State Bar Assn., Seattle, 1975-81, exec. dir., 1981-91; asst. dean devel. & cmty. rels. Sch. of Law U. Wash., 1991-95; exec. dir. Assn. Legal Adminstrs., 1995. Mem. Am. Soc. Assn. Execs., Nat. Assn. Bar Execs., Am. Mgmt. Assn., Nat. Trust Hist. Preservation, Ninth Jud. Cir. Hist. Soc., Coll. Club Seattle. Lutheran. Office: Assn Legal Adminstrs 175 E Hawthorn Pky Vernon Hills IL 60061-1428

MICHALKO, JAMES PAUL, library association administrator; b. Cleve., May 13, 1950; s. Paul James and Lillian (Fanta) M.; 1 child, Alexandra. BA, Georgetown U., 1971; MLS, MBA, U. Chgo., 1974. Asst. to v.p., adminstrn. Technicare Inc. (formerly BCC Industries), Cleve., 1971-72; asst dir., administrn. U. Pa. Librs., Phila., 1974-80; dir. bus. and fin. Rsch. Librs. Group, Stanford, Calif., 1980-85, v.p. fin. and administrn., 1985-87, acting pres., 1988-89; pres. Rsch. Librs. Group, Mountain View, Calif., 1989—. Contbr. to Libr. Quar., Coll. & Rsch. Librs.; reviewer for Libr. Quar., Coll. & Rsch. Librs., Acad. of Mgmt. Rev., Jour. Acad. Librarianship, Jour. Libr. Adminstrn. Office: Rsch Librs Group Inc 1200 Villa St Mountain View CA 94041-1106*

MICHALS, DUANE, photographer; b. McKeesport, Pa., Feb. 18, 1932; s. John Ambrose and Margaret Cecilia (Matik) M. B.A., U. Denver, 1953. Comml. photographer with works appearing in Life Magazine, Esquire mags., N.Y. Times and others; comml. clients include Eli Lilly Co., Revlon, Estee Lauder, Elizabeth Arden. One person shows: Museum fur Kunst und Gewerbe Hamburg, Germany, Galerie John A. Schweitzer, Montreal, Can., 1990, San Francisco Mus. of Modern Art, Internat. Mus. of Photography at George Eastman House, Rochester, 1991, Sidney Janis Gallery, N.Y.C.,1985; represented in permanent collections, Mus. of Modern Art, N.Y.C., Chgo. Art Inst., George Eastman House, Folkwang Mus., Essen, Fed. Republic Germany, Internat. Mus. Photography, Smithsonian Instn., Mus. N.Mex., U. N.Mex., UCLA, Norton Simon Mus., Calif., Mus. Ludwig, Cologne. Author: Sequences, 1970, The Journey of the Spirit After Death, 1971, Things Are Queer, 1973, Take One and See Mt. Fujiyama, 1976, Real Dreams, 1977, Merveilles d'Egypte, Homage to Cavafy, 1981, Duane Michals: Photographs with Written Text, Changes, A Visit with Magritte, 1982, Duane Michals Photographs de 1958 a 1982, Duane Michals: Sleep and Dream, Duane Michals Photographs/Sequences/Texts, 1958-84, The Nature of Desire, 1988, Portraits, 1990, Now Becoming Then. Served with U.S. Army, 1953-55. Nat. Endowment for the Arts grantee, 1976. Office: care Sidney Janis Gallery 110 W 57th St New York NY 10019-3319

MICHALS, GEORGE FRANCIS, investment and business development executive; b. Hungary, Sept. 14, 1935; came to Can., 1956, naturalized, 1961; s. Todor and Ilona (Sinkovich) Mihalcsics; m. Patricia Elizabeth Hoffman, June 18, 1971; children: Katherine, Julie, Elizabeth, Georgina. BComm, Sir George Williams U., Montreal, 1961; CA, McGill U., 1963. Chartered acct. McGill U., Montreal, 1963. Acct. Coopers & Lybrand, Montreal, 1963-68; from treas. to exec. v.p. Dominion Textile Co. Ltd., 1969-74; v.p. fin., sr. v.p., then exec. v.p. Genstar Corp., San Francisco, 1974-86; exec. v.p., chief fin. officer Can. Pacific Ltd., Montreal, 1987-90; pres. Baymont Capital Resources Inc., Toronto, 1990—; chmn. Phargo Group Inc. Home: RR 5, Orangeville, ON Canada L9W 2Z2 Office: Baymont Capital Resources, 141 Adelaide St W Ste 1506, Toronto, ON Canada M5H 3L5

MICHALS, LEE MARIE, retired travel agency executive; b. Chgo., June 6, 1939; d. Harry Joseph and Anna Marie (Monaco) Perzan; children: Debora Ann, Dana Lee, Jami. BA, Wright Coll., 1959. Cert. travel specialist and cons., destination specialist. Internat. travel sec. E.F. MacDonald Travel, Palo Alto, Calif., 1963-69; pres. Travel Experience, Santa Clara, Calif., 1973-88; ptnr. Cruise Connection, Mountain View, Calif., 1983-85; travel specialist Allways Travel, Sunnyvale, Calif., 1992—; former stars rep. Hertz, Ritz Carlton, Marriott Hotels, various airlines and tour cos. Mem. Am. Soc. Travel Agts., Inst. Cert. Travel Agts., Bay Area Travel Assn., Pacific Area Travel Agts., San Jose Women in Travel (organizing pres. 1971, 1st v.p. 1989). Office: Allways Travel 139 S Murphy Ave Sunnyvale CA 94086-6113

MICHALSKI, CAROL ANN, medical, surgical and psychiatric nurse, writer, poet; b. Balt., Feb. 21, 1955; d. John B. Rassa and Genevieve J. Ryncewicz; m. Martin Joseph Michalski, June 21, 1976; children: Matthew, Nathan. RN, Grand View Hosp., Sellersville, Pa., 1976; BS in Health Care Adminstrn., Pacific Western U., 1986, PhD in Religious Studies/Ministry, 1987. RN; ordained to ministry Christian Ch., 1983. Staff nurse Md. Gen. Hosp., Balt., 1974-75, Union Meml. Hosp., Balt., 1975-77; head nurse Levindale Chronic Hosp., Balt., 1977-79; charge staff nurse Franklin Sq. Hosp. Ctr., Balt., 1979—, pain mgmt. liaison, 1993—; head procedure com. Levindale Chronic Hosp., Balt., 1978-79; min. Faith Seed Ministries, Balt., 1983—; Bible Coll. adminstr. L.W. Christian Ctr., Balt., 1987-89. Author: Don't Blame God-Making Sense Out of Tragedy and Suffering, 1995; contbr. articles and poetry to profl. jours. and anthologies. Asst. youth activities Ridgeleigh Cmty. Assn., Balt., 1980; block capt. Woodcroft Civic Assn., Balt.; coord. Churchville Christian Sch., 1993-94; Christian Home Educator's Network group coord. Teen Boys Group, 1995—. Recipient Nursing Achievement award Johnston Sch.-Union Meml. Hosp., 1984, Ministry Recognition Certs. Gospel Tabernacle Balt., 1990, 91, poetry awards. Mem. Md. League Nursing, Nat. Author's Registry, Internat. Soc. Poets. Avocations: art, crafts, writing, hiking, water sports.

MICHALSKI, MARK MARIAN MATEUSZ, consulting company executive; b. Slomniki, Poland, Apr. 5, 1955; came to U.S., 1979; s. Jozef and Helena (Jurek) M.; m. Judith Anders, July 21, 1979; children: Sarah, Emily, Anders, Peter. AB, Acad. Econ., Krakow, 1975, Stockholm U., 1979; postgrad., Cath. U. Am., 1984; MBA, Southeastern U., 1985; PhD in Telecom Policy, GW U., 1995, MPhil in Pub. Policy, 1995. Rsch. economist World Bank, Washington, 1982-87; sr. trade advisor Australian Embassy, Washington, 1987-90; project dir. Nat. Telephone Coop. Assn., Washington, 1990-91; cons. European Bank, London, 1992; asst. prof. Jagiellonian U., Krakow, Poland, 1993—; cons. World Bank, Washington, 1991—; pres. Michalski & Assocs., Washington, 1984—; v.p. Polish-Am. Congress, Washington, 1984-86, sec., 1982-84; economist Am. Enterprise Inst., Washington, 1981-82; UNDP cons. and advisor to local govt. in Poland, 1994-96. Contbr. chpts. to books; corr. Nowy Dziennik (Polish Daily News), N.Y.C., 1982-86; asst. editor Perspectives Jour., 1987-89. Sabre Found. fellow, 1991. Mem. Polish Inst. Arts & Scis., Assn. Pub. Policy Analysis & Mgmt., Phi Beta Kappa. Democrat. Roman Catholic. Avocations: swimming, poetry, philosophy. Home: 517 5th St SE Washington DC 20003-4206

MICHALSKI, THOMAS JOSEPH, city planner, developer; b. Waukesha, Wis., Jan. 28, 1933; s. Thomas and Anna (Benca) M. B.Arch., U. Mich., 1956, M.City Planning, 1959; postgrad., Magdalene Coll., U. Cambridge, Eng., 1988—. Urban renewal planner City of Milw., 1956-57; land planner, urban designer Baltimore County, Md., 1959-60; planning cons. City of N.Y., 1961-77; project mgr. Yanbu Indsl. Complex, Royal Comm., Saudi Arabia, 1980-83; cons. UN Ctr. for Human Settlements, Habitat Nairobi, Kenya, 1984—; bd. Community Housing Initiative Trust, 1993—; faculty U. Mich., 1994—; mem. faculty NYU, 1965-66, CUNY, 1970-71, Rollins Coll., 1992—; town planning cons. new town in Iran, 1977; mem. Community Bd. 8, N.Y.C., 1972-76, chmn. landmarks com.; cons. Islamic Devel. Bank, 1989—, Fla. Solar Energy Ctr. Affordable Living Conf., 1991. Author: In Search of Purpose: Essays on Planning the Human Environment, 1961, Human Values and the Emerging City, 1967. Founding mem. Friends of Cen. park; 1000 Friends of Fla., 1987—; pres. Brevard 21 Inc., 1988—; bd. govs. Coll. Architecture and Urban Planning, U. Mich., 1984-88; bd. ACLU, 1993—. Wis. Architects Found. scholar, 1953-56; Vincent Astor Found. grantee, 1971, World Wildlife Fund Successful Communities grantee, 1991. Fellow Am. Hort. Soc.; mem. Am. Planning Assn. (charter), Am. Inst. Cert. Planners, Royal Town Planning Inst., Town and Country Planning Assn., Internat. Fedn. Housing and Planning, Nat. Trust for Historic Preservation, Wis. Soc. Archtl. Historians, Mich. Urban Planning Alumni Soc. (bd. dirs. 1984-88), Audubon Soc. Fla. (chmn. conservation com. 1987-91), Assn. for Asian Studies, Worldwatch Inst., English-Speaking Union (London), Brevard County (Fla.) Democratic exec. com., U. Mich. Club (N.Y.C.), Delta Chi (Morrey Outstanding Alumnus award 1984). Roman Catholic. Address: 3325 Rivercrest Dr Melbourne FL 32935 *The educated person prepares mightily to do something constructive about that which is displeasing, to sustain that which is good, and to discriminate the one from the other.*

MICHALSKI, (ŻUROWSKI) WACŁAW, adult education educator; b. Pierzchnica, Poland, Sept. 14, 1913; came to the U.S., 1951; s. Antoni and Józefa (Skrybuś) M.; m. Urszula Lewandowska, Nov. 12, 1959 (dec. 1986); 1 child, Anthony Richard. MA, Tchr.'s Coll., Poland, 1934; grad., Officer's Mil. Sch., Poland, 1934-35; postgrad., U. Wis. M.A.T.C., 1951-55. Lic. real estate broker, Wis. Tchr. jr. high sch. Poland, 1936-39; mgr. acctg. Ampco Metal Co., Milw., 1951-84; tchr., educator Marquette U., U. Wis. Ext., Milw., 1962-90, Milw. Area Tech. Coll., 1963—; real estate agt. Wauwatosa Realty Co., Milw., 1955—. Contbr. articles to profl. jours. Archivist Holy Cross Brigade and Nat. Armed Forces of Poland, 1991—. With underground resistance, Poland, 1939-45; officer Holy Cross Brigade, Poland, 1944-55, which joined U.S. 3rd Army, Czechoslovakia, 1945; Polish guard U.S. Army, Germany, 1945-47; officer Internat. Refugee Orgn., Germany, 1947-51. Recipient Polish Heritage award Pulaski Coun. Milw., 1992, Cert. of Appreciation State Hist. Soc. Wis., 1987, Vol. Svc. award Inner Agy. Coun. Volunteerism, 1986, Cert. of Commendation for Exemplary Work as an Older Worker in Our Community Milw. Com. for Nat. Older Work Week, 1995. Mem. Polish Am. Congress, N.Am. Polish Ctr. Study, Polish Western Assn. Am. (Diploma of Merit 1988), Vets. Orgns. WWI, WWII. Roman Catholic. Avocations: chess, bridge. Home: 5505 Bentwood Ln Greendale WI 53129-1314 Office: Wauwatosa Realty Co 5300 S 108th St Hales Corners WI 53130-1368

MICHAUD, GEORGES JOSEPH, astrophysics educator; b. Que., Can., Apr. 30, 1940; s. Marie-Louis and Isabelle (St. Laurent) M.; m. Denise Lemieux, June 25, 1966. BA, U. Laval, Que., 1961, BSc, 1965; PhD, Calif. Tech. Inst., Pasadena, 1970. Prof. Universite de Montreal, Can., 1969—; dir. Centre du Recherche en Calcul Appliqué, 1992-96. Recipient Steacie prize NRC, 1980, Medaille Janssen, Academie des Sciences, Paris, 1982, Prix Vincent, ACFAS, 1979; Killam fellow Conseil des Arts, 1987-89. Office: Universite de Montreal, Dept de Physique, Montreal, PQ Canada H3C 3J7

MICHAUD, HOWARD HENRY, conservation educator; b. Berne, Ind., Oct. 12, 1902; s. Justin Album and Bertha Amelia (Baumgartner) M.; m. Ruth M. Hefner, Aug. 19, 1928; 1 child, Ted C. AB, Bluffton Coll., 1925; MA, Ind. U., 1930. High sch. tchr. Ft. Wayne, Ind., 1925-45; chief naturalist Ind. State Parks, 1934-45; prof. conservation Purdue U., 1945-71, prof. emeritus, 1971—; head program of conservation edn. Pub. Sch. Ind., 1945-71; dir. Conservation Edn. Camp for Tchrs., 1946-59; del. conf. Internat. Union for Conservation of Nature and Natural Resources Conf., N.Y., 1949, Lucerne, Switzerland, 1966. Editor: (pamphlets on conservation) Ind. Dept. Pub. Instrn.; contbr. articles to profl. jours. Past mem. Bd. Pks. and Recreation, West Lafayette. Recipient Purdue Conservation award, 1945-71, Chase S. Osborn Wildlife award Purdue U., 1959, Sagamore of the Wabash award Gov. of Ind., 1991, Theodore Roosevelt award U.S. EPA, 1993; NSF grantee, 1960-61. Mem. Nat. Assn. Biology Tchrs. (pres. 1948), Ind. Audubon Soc. (past pres., Earl Brooks Conservationist of Yr. award 1986), Conservation Edn. Assn. (pres. 1956-57, v.p. 1953-55, Key Man award 1967), Ind. Acad. Sci. (pres. 1963), Soil Conservation Soc. Am. (hon.), Izaak Walton League Am. (div. pres. 1953), Am. Nature Study Soc., Am. Assn. Interpretive Naturalists (founder), Environ. Edn. Assn. Ind. Inc. (pres. 1972-73, editor newsletter 1972-88), Nat. Wildlife Fedn., Ind. Park and Recreation Assn. (Outstanding Svc. award 1984), Nat. Recreation and Park Assn., Pi Kappa Phi, Xi Sigma Pi. Democrat. Presbyterian. Lodge: Lafayette Noon Optimists (Optimist of Yr. award 1986). Avocations: travel, photography, lapidary. Home: 2741 N Salisbury St Lafayette IN 47906

MICHAUD, MICHAEL ALAN GEORGE, diplomat, writer; b. Hollywood, Calif., Aug. 22, 1938; s. George Emile and Nathalie Adele (Neagles) M.; m. Carmen Yvonne Mitchell, Sept. 1960 (div. 1963); m. M. Grace Russo, June 5, 1965 (div. 1996); children: Jon C., Cassandra M., Jason M., Joshua M. B.A., UCLA, 1960, M.A., 1963; postgrad., Georgetown U., 1978-79. Commd. fgn. service officer Dept. State, 1963; consular officer Dacca, East Pakistan, 1963-65; analyst Bur. Intelligence and Research/Dept. State, Washington, 1965-66; staff asst. Bur. Near Eastern and South Asian Affairs Dept. State, Washington, 1966-67; polit. officer Am. Embassy, Tehran, 1967-68, econ. officer, 1968-70; info. officer USIS, Bombay, India, 1970-72, co-dir., 1971-72; country officer for Iran Dept. State, 1972-74, country officer Australia, Papua New Guinea and Solomon Islands, Bur. East Asian Affairs, 1974-76; dep. dir. Office Internat. Security Policy, Bur. Politico-Mil. Affairs, 1976-78; trainee Georgetown U., Washington, 1978-79; officer-in-charge U.K. and Bermuda Affairs, Bur. European Affairs Dept. State, 1979-80; consul gen. Am. Consulate Gen. Belfast, No. Ireland, 1980-83; Una Chapman Cox fellow Fgn. Service Inst. Dept. State, 1983-84, div. chief fgn. service counseling and assignments, 1984-85, spl. asst. for space policy, 1985-86, dir. Office Advanced Tech., 1986-89; counselor sci., tech. and environ. affairs Am. Embassy, Paris, 1989-93; minister-counselor environ. sci. and tech. Am. Embassy, Tokyo, 1993-95; mgr. Am. Ctr. Geneva, 1996—. Author: Reaching for the High Frontier, 1986; editor: Flotsam and Jetsam lit. ann., 1956; founding editor: Open Forum, 1974-76 (Honor award 1976); mem. editorial bd.: Fgn. Service Jour., 1977-79; contbr. numerous articles, papers, book revs., short stories to various publs. Recipient Superior Honor award Dept. State, 1966; recipient Meritorious Honor award Dept. State, 1976; Scott fellow, 1962. Fellow Brit. Interplanetary Soc.; mem. Internat. Inst. Strategic Studies, Internat. Inst. Space Law, Internat. Acad. Astronautics, AAAS, AIAA, Royal Soc. Asian Affairs, Planetary Soc., Nat. Space Soc., Am. Astron. Soc. Home and Office: care Arbuthnot USTR Geneva Dept State Washington DC 20521

MICHAUD, NORMAN PAUL, association administrator, logistics consultant; b. Fall River, Mass., June 28, 1931; s. Amedee and Mary Veronica (Simcoe) M.; m. Helen P. Pettine, Oct. 11, 1952; children: Marianne, Norman, Elizabeth, Robert, Virginia. Cert. in Engring., U. Mass; student, Queens Coll., 1958-61. Joined U.S. Army, 1948, advanced through grades to master sgt., 1958, ret., 1958; field engr. Raytheon Co., 1958-67; dept. mgr. Raytheon Svc. Co., Burlington, Mass., 1968-92; exec. dir. Soc. Logistics Engrs., Hyattsville, Md., 1992-95; pvt. practice logistics cons. Chelmsford, Mass., 1995—. Editor (tech. jour.) Logistics Spectrum, 1992-95, (newsletter) Soletter, 1992-95; contbr. articles to profl. jours. Pres. Chelmsford (Mass.) PTA, 1968-71, mem. coun., 1969-70. Fellow Soc. Logistics Engrs. (cert. profl. logistician, bd. dirs. 1985-96, exec. bd. 1986-92, Pres.'s award for merit 1992-93, Tech. Field award 1985). Roman Catholic. Home: 21 Radcliffe Rd North Chelmsford MA 01863-2320

MICHAUDON, ANDRÉ FRANCISQUE, physicist; b. Cavaillon, Vaucluse, France, May 14, 1929; s. Maurice Louis and Jeanne Francoise (Chatal) M.; children: Claire Hello, Helene Caron. Engring. degree, Ecole Supérieure Ingenieurs Arts et Métiers, Paris, 1951, Ecole Supérieure Electricite, Paris, 1953; DSc, U. Paris, 1964. Rsch. engr. Le Materiel Teléphonique, Boulogne, France, 1954-56; group leader Commissariat à Energie Atomique, Cen Saclay, France, 1956-64, 65-72; theorist MIT, Cambridge, 1964-65; div. head Commissariat à Energie Atomique, Bruyeres le Chalel, France, 1972-79; dept. dept. head Commissariat à l'Energie Atomique, Limeil, France, 1979-83; French co-dir. Inst. Laue Langevin, Grenoble, France, 1983-89; prof. Inst. Nat. des Scis. et Techniques Nuclèaires, Saclay, Orsay, France, 1969-84; physicist Los Alamos Nat. Lab., 1989—; mem. exec. coun. European Sci. Found., Strasbourg, France, 1987-90; mem. adv. coun. Cen. Bur. for Nuclear Measurements EU, Geel, Belgium, 1990-95; cons. Orgn. for Econ. Cooperation and Devel., Paris, 1989-92. Author, editor: Nuclear Fission, 1981; co-gen. editor: Neutron Sources, 1983, Neutron Radiative Capture, 1984, Probability & Statistics, 1991; contbr. articles to profl. jours. Lt. French Navy, 1953-54. Recipient written congratulations Minister of the Navy, France, 1954, award Acad. des Sciences, Paris, 1980; named knight Order of Merit, Paris, 1984. Fellow Am. Phys. Soc., Am. Nuclear Soc.; mem. Soc. Francaise de Physique, N.Y. Acad. Scis. Avocations: music, tennis, skiing, golf, hiking. Home: 211 W Water Sante Fe NM 87501 Office: Los Alamos Nat Lab Physics Divsn P-23 MS H803 Los Alamos NM 87545

MICHEL, ANTHONY NIKOLAUS, electrical engineering educator, researcher; b. Rekasch, Romania, Nov. 17, 1935; came to U.S., 1952; s. Anton Michel and Katharina (Metz) Malsam; m. Leone Lucille Flasch, Aug. 17, 1957; children: Mary Leone, Katherine Jean, John Peter, Anthony Joseph, Patrick Thomas. B.S.E.E., Marquette U., 1958, M.S. in Math., 1964, Ph.D. in Elec. Engring., 1968; D.Sc. in Math., Tech. U. Graz (Austria), 1973. Registered profl. engr., Wis. Engr. in tng. U.S. Army C.E., Milw., 1958-59; project engr. AC Electronics div. Gen. Motors Corp., Milw., 1959-62, sr. research engr., 1962-65; asst. prof. elec. engring. Iowa State U., Ames, 1968-69, assoc. prof., 1969-74, prof., 1974-84; prof. and chmn. dept. elec. engring. U. Notre Dame, Ind., 1984-87, Frank M. Freimann prof. engring., chmn. dept. elec. and computer engring., 1987-88, dean coll. engring., 1988—; cons. Houghton Mifflin Co., 1975, Acad. Press, 1983; cons. editor William C. Brown Co. Pubs., Dubuque, Iowa, 1982-83. Author: (with others) Qualitative Analysis of Large Scale Dynamical Systems, 1977, Mathematical Foundations in Engineering and Science, 1981, Ordinary Differential Equations, 1982, Applied Linear Algebra and Functional Analysis, 1993, (with Derong Liu) Dynamical Systems with Saturation Nonlinearities, 1993, (with Kaining Wang) Qualitative Theory of Dynamical Systems, 1994; contbr. articles to profl. jours., chpts. to books. Research grantee NSF, 1972—; research grantee Dept. Def., 1968-72; Fulbright fellow Tech. U. Vienna, Austria, 1992. Fellow IEEE (mng. editor Trans. on Cirs. and Sys. 1981-83, Best Trans. Paper award 1978, 83, 93, Centennial medal 1984); mem. IEEE Cirs. and Sys. Soc. (pres.s 1989, Myril B. Reed Outstanding Paper award 1993, Tech. Achievement award 1995), Russian Acad. Engring. (hon.), Sigma Xi, Eta Kappa Nu, Pi Mu Epsilon, Phi Kappa Phi. Home: 17001 Stonegate Ct Granger IN 46530-6948 Office: U Notre Dame Coll Engring Notre Dame IN 46556

MICHEL, CLIFFORD LLOYD, lawyer, investment executive; b. N.Y.C., Aug. 9, 1939; s. Clifford William and Barbara Lloyd (Richards) M.; m. Betsy Shirley, June 6, 1964; children: Clifford Fredrick, Jason Lloyd, Katherine Beinecke. A.B. cum laude, Princeton U., 1961; J.D., Yale U., 1964. Bar: N.Y. 1964, U.S. Dist. Ct. (so. dist.) N.Y. 1968, U.S. Ct. Appeals (2d cir.) 1967, U.S. Supreme Ct. 1972. Assoc. Cahill Gordon & Reindel, N.Y.C., 1964-67, Paris, 1967-69, N.Y.C., 1969-71; ptnr. Cahill Gordon & Reindel, Paris, 1972-76, N.Y.C., 1976—; bd. dirs. Alliance Capital Mgmt. Mut. Funds, Placer Dome Inc., Tempo Tech. Corp. Bd. dirs. Jockey Hollow Found., Michel Found., St. Mark's Sch., Morristown Meml. Hosp., Meml. Health Found., Atlantic Health Sys. Mem. ABA, FBA, N.Y. State Bar Assn., New York County Lawyers Assn., Am. Soc. Internat. Law, City Midday Club, Racquet and Tennis Club, River Club, The Links, Shinnecock Hills olf Club, Somerset Hills Country Club, Essex Hunt Club (N..), Sankaty Head Golf Club (Mass.), Golf de Morfontaine Club, Travellers Club (Paris), Loch Lomond Club (Scotland. Republican. Office: Cahill Gordon & Reindel 80 Pine St New York NY 10005-1702

MICHEL, DAVID J., metallurgist, crystallographer; b. Denison, Tex., July 24, 1942; married, 1966; 2 children. BS in Metall. Engring., U. Mo., 1964; MS in Metallurgy, Pa. State U., 1966, PhD in Metallurgy, 1968. Rsch. metallurgist U.S. Naval Rsch. Lab, Washington, 1972-73, head high temperature metals sect., 1973-91, assoc. supr. materials sci. & tech. divsn., 1991—; asst. metallurgist Homer Rsch. Lab., Bethlehem Steel Co., 1964; rsch. asst. in metallurgy Pa. State U., 1964-68, fellow, 1968-69; metallurgist rsch. divsn. US AEC, 1969-71; rsch. asst. prof. materials sci. U. Cin., 1971-72; prof. George Washington U., 1979—; vis. scientist Carnegie-Mellon U., 1984-85. Recipient Nat. Capital award for Profl. Achievement Engring., Washington Coun. Engring. & Archtl. Soc., 1978. Fellow Am. Soc. Metals Internat. (George Kimball Burgess Meml. award 1993-94), Am. Inst. Mining, Metall. and Petroleum Engrs., Am. Crystallographers Assn., Internat. Metallurgists Soc. Achievements include research in radiation effects in materials, mechanical behavior of materials, intermetallic compounds, x-ray crystallography, alloy theory, phase equilibria, phase transformations in solids, electron microscopy, semiconductor alloys. Office: Naval Rsch Lab 4555 Overlook Ave SW # 6300 Washington DC 20375-0001

MICHEL, DONALD CHARLES, editor; b. Ventura, Calif., Nov. 17, 1935; s. Charles J. and Esther Caroline (Heilert) M.; m. Loretta Perron, May 4, 1963; children: Edwin, Robert, Christopher. B.A., UCLA, 1958, M.S., 1959. Editor San Fernando (Calif.) Sun, 1958-60; successively reporter, weekend editor, mng. editor Valley Times Today, North Hollywood, Calif., 1960-63; feature editor Houston Chronicle, 1963-68; asst. mng. editor features Chgo. Daily News, 1968-77; exec. v.p., editor Chgo. Tribune-N.Y. News Syndicate, 1977-84; v.p. adminstrn. and editl. devel. L.A. Times Syndicate, 1984-93, dir. book devel., 1993—. Mem. Am. Assn. Sunday and Feature Editors, Features Coun., Sigma Delta Chi. Home: 3000 Adornos Way Burbank CA 91504-1609 Office: Los Angeles Times Syndicate Times Mirror Sq Los Angeles CA 90012

MICHEL, HARRIET R., association executive; b. Pitts., July 5, 1942; d. John and Vida (Fish) Richardson; m. Yves Michel, Apr. 13, 1968; children: Christopher, Gregory. BA, Juniata Coll., 1965; LHD (hon.), Baruch Coll., 1990. Dir. spl. projects Nat. Scholarship Svcs. & Fund for Negro Students, N.Y.C., 1971; asst. to Mayor Lindsay City of N.Y. for Anti-Drug Efforts, 1971-72; exec. dir. N.Y. Found., 1972-77; dir. Cmty. Youth Employment Program U.S. Dept. Labor, Washington, 1977-79; established Women Against Crime Found. John Jay Coll., N.Y.C., 1980-81; cons. U.S. Dept. Housing & Urban Devel., Washington, 1982; pres., CEO N.Y. Urban League, 1983-88; pres. Nat. Minority Supplier Develop. Coun., N.Y.C., 1988—; bd. dirs. Ctr. for Advance Purchasing Studies, Phoenix, Maxima Corp., Balt., N.Y.C. Partnership; mem. nat. adv. coun. U.S. SBA, Washington, 1993—; lectr., cons. in field; U.S. rep. Ditchley Found. Confs., London. Vice chair N.Y.C. Charter Revision Commn., 1986-91; bd. dirs. African Am. Inst., N.Y.C., 1985—, Citizens Com. of N.Y., 1984—, Juniata Coll., Huntington, Pa., 1989—, Trans Africa Forum, Washington, 1988—. Recipient 1st Non-Profit Leadership award new Sch. Social Rsch., 1988, Women on the Move award Anti-Defamation League of B'nai B'rith, 1990, Appreciation award Pres. Commn. Minority Bus. Devel., 1992, Bus. Advocate award Mayor of N.Y.C., 1993, Black Entrepreneurial award Wall St. Jour., 1994, others; named one of 50 Outstanding Internat. Bus. and Profl. Women by Dollars and Sense Mag., 1987. Mem. Assn. Black Found. Execs. (founder), Coun. on Founds. (bd. dirs.). Office: Nat Minority Supplier Devel Coun 15 W 39th St Fl 9 New York NY 10018-3806

MICHEL, HENRY LUDWIG, civil engineer; b. Frankfurt, Germany, June 18, 1924; s. Maximilian Frederick and Loschka (Hepner) M.; m. Mary Elizabeth Strolis, June 5, 1954; children—Eve Musette, Ann Elizabeth. B.S.C.E., Columbia U., 1949. Registered profl. engr., Pa., N..Y. Pres., CEO, Parsons Brinckerhoff, Inc., 1975-90, chmn., 1990-94; chmn. Parsons Brinckerhoff, Internat., N.Y.C., 1975-96; guest lectr. NYU, Columbia U., Colo. State U., Cornell U., MIT; vice chmn. Bldg. Futures Coun., 1980—; instrumental in devel. and mgmt. of maj. transp. and pub. works project in U.S. and abroad; mem. Nat. Acad. Engrs., 1995—. Contbr. numerous articles on mgmt. and transp. engring. to engring. jours. Fellow ASCE, Soc. Am. Mil. Engrs., Instn. Civil Engrs.; mem. Internat. Rd. Found. (chmn. 1989-92, bd. dirs. 1977—), Constrn. Industry Pres. Forum (chmn. 1990-91), Civil Engring. Rsch. Found. (chmn. 1992—), Columbia U. Engring. Sch. Alumni Assn. (Egelston medal 1992, Alumni medal 1991), Am. European Cmty. Assn. (bd. dirs. 1993—), Spain-U.S. C. of C. (bd. dirs. 1993—). Home: 35 Sutton Pl New York NY 10022-2464 Office: Parsons Brinckerhoff Internat Inc 1 Penn Plaza New York NY 10119

MICHEL, JAMES H., ambassador, lawyer; b. St. Louis, Aug. 25, 1939; s. Paul J. and Margaret K. (Scheitlin) M.; m. Conception L. Trejo, Sept. 10, 1960; children—Mark, Kurt, Linda, Paul. J.D., St. Louis U., 1965. Bar: Mo. 1965, D.C. 1973. Atty. Dept. State, Washington, 1965-74, asst. legal adviser, 1974-78, dep. legal adviser, 1978-83, dep. asst. sec. for Inter-Am. affairs, 1983-87; ambassador to Guatemala, 1987-89; asst. adminstr. Latin Am. and Carribbean Bur. AID, Washington, 1990-93; pres. devel. assistance com. OECD, Paris, 1994—. Pres. St. Thomas More Fed. Credit Union, Arlington, Va., 1970-87. Recipient Superior awards Dept. State, 1971, 76, 83, Meritorious Exec. award, 1980, 87, Disting. award, 1981, Disting. Exec. award, 1982, 92. Mem. Fed. Bar Assn. (Tom C. Clark award 1982), D.C. Bar Assn., Mo. Bar Assn., Am. Soc. Internat. Law, Inter-Am. Bar Assn. Roman Catholic. Office: 2 rue Andre Pascal, Paris 75116, France

MICHEL, MARY ANN KEDZUF, nursing educator; b. Evergreen Park, Ill., June 1, 1939; d. John Roman and Mary (Bassar) Kedzuf; m. Jean Paul Michel, 1974. Diploma in nursing, Little Company of Mary Hosp., Evergreen Park, 1960; BS in Nursing, Loyola U., Chgo., 1964; MS, No. Ill. U., 1968, EdD, 1971. Staff nurse Little Co. of Mary Hosp., 1960-64; instr. Little Co. of Mary Hosp. (Sch. Nursing), 1964-67, No. Ill. U., DeKalb, 1968-69; asst. prof. No. Ill. U., 1969-71; chmn. dept. nursing U. Nev., Las Vegas, 1971-73; prof. nursing U. Nev., 1975—, dean Coll. Health Scis., 1973-90; pres. PERC, Inc.; mgmt. cons., 1993—; mgmt. cons. Nev. Donor Network, 1993; mem. So. Nev. Health Manpower Task Force, 1975; mem. manpower com. Plan Devel. Commn., Clark County Health Sys. Agy., 1977-79, mem. governing body, 1981-86; mem. Nev. Health Coordinating Coun., Western Inst. Nursing, 1971-85; mem. coordinating com. assembly instnl. adminstrs. dept. allied health edn. and accreditation AMA, 1985-88; mem. bd. advisors So. Nev. Vocat. Tech. Ctr., 1976-80; sec.-treas. Nev. Donor Network, 1988-89, bd. dirs., 1986-90, chmn. bd., 1988-90. Contbr. articles to profl. jours. Trustee Desert Spring Hosp., Las Vegas, 1976-85; bd. dirs. Nathan Adelson Hospice, 1982-88, Bridge Counseling Assocs., 1982, Everywoman's Ctr., 1984-86; chmn. Nev. Commn. on Nursing Edn., 1972-73, Nursing Articulation Com., 1972-73, Yr. of Nurse Com., 1978; moderator Invitational Conf. Continuing Edn., Am. Soc. Allied Health Professions, 1978; active Nev. Donor Network, Donor Organ Recovery Svc., Transplant Recipient Internat. Orgn., S.W. Eye Bank, S.W. Tissue Bank. Named Outstanding Alumnus, Loyola U., 1983; NIMH fellow, 1967-68. Fellow Am. Soc. Allied Health Professions, 1991, (chmn. nat. resolutions com. 1981-84, treas. 1988-90, sec's. award com. 1982-83, 92-93, nat. by-laws com. 1985, conv. chmn. 1987); mem. AAUP, Am. Nurses Assn., Nev. Nurses Assn. (dir. 1975-77, treas. 1977-79, conv. chmn. 1978), So. Nev. Area Health Edn. Coun., Western Health Deans (co-organizer 1985, chair, 1988-90), Nat. League Nursing, Nev. Heart Assn., So. Nev. Mem. Hosps. (mem. nursing recruitment com. 1981-83, mem. nursing practice com. 1983-85), Las Vegas C. of C. (named Woman of Yr. Edn.) 1988, Slovak Catholic Sokols, Phi Kappa Phi (chpt. sec. 1981-83, pres.-elect 1983, pres. 1984, v.p. Western region 1989-95, editl. bd. jour. Nat. Forum 1989-93), Alpha Beta Gamma (hon.), Sigma Theta Tau, Zeta Kappa. Office: U Nev Las Vegas 4505 S Maryland Pky Las Vegas NV 89154-9900

MICHEL, PAUL REDMOND, federal judge; b. Philadelphia, Pa., Feb. 3, 1941; s. Lincoln M. and Dorothy (Kelley) M.; m. Sally Ann Clark, 1965 (div. 1987); children: Sarah Elizabeth, Margaret Kelley; m. Elizabeth Morgan, 1989. BA, Williams Coll., 1963; JD, U. Va., 1966. Bar: Pa. 1967, U.S. Supreme Ct., 1970. Asst. dist. atty. Dist. Atty's Office, Phila., 1967-71, dep. dist. atty. for investigations, 1972-74; asst. spl. prosecutor Watergate investigation Dept. Justice, Washington, 1974-75, dep. chief pub. integrity sect., Criminal div. and prosecutor "Koreagate" investigation, 1976-78, assoc. dep. atty. gen., 1978-81, acting dep. atty. gen., 1979-80; asst. counsel intelligence com. U.S. Senate, 1975-76, counsel and adminstrv. asst. to Sen. Arlen Specter, 1981-88; judge U.S. Ct. Appeals (Fed. cir.), Washington, 1988—; instr. appellate practice and procedure George Wash. U. Nat. Law Ctr., 1991—, appellate advocacy John Marshall Law Sch., Chgo. 2d lt. USAR, 1966-72. Office: US Ct Appeals Fed Cir 717 Madison Pl NW Ste 808 Washington DC 20439-0001

MICHEL, ROBERT CHARLES, retired engineering company executive; b. N.Y.C., July 14, 1927; s. Charles John and Helen Carolyn (Wagner) M.; m. Alice Virginia Kraissl, June 16, 1951; children: Richard Charles, Ann Florence, Susan Jean. SB in Chem. Engring., MIT, 1950, SM in Chem. Engring., 1951. Registered profl. engr., N.J. Chmn., pres. The Kraissl Co., Inc., Hackensack, N.J., 1986-92. Pres. Bd. Edn., River Edge, N.J., 1968-72. With USNR, 1945-46. Mem. Am. Inst. Chem. Engrs., ASME, ASM, Bergen County Soc. Profl. Engrs. (pres. 1960-61), U.S. Power Squadron, Palisades Power Squadron (comdr. 1982-83), Elks, Tau Beta Pi, Sigma Xi. Home: 470 Prospect St Glen Rock NJ 07452-1909 Office: The Kraissl Co Inc 299 Williams Ave Hackensack NJ 07601-5225

MICHEL, THOMAS MARK, internal medicine educator, scientist, physician; b. Portland, Oreg., July 14, 1955. AB in Biochem. Scis., Harvard U., 1977; PhD in Biochemistry, Duke U., 1983, MD, 1984. Diplomate Am. Bd. Internal Medicine, Am. Bd. Cardiovasc. Disease. House officer, jr. and sr. resident in medicine Brigham and Women's Hosp., Boston, 1984-87, clin. and rsch. fellow in medicine cardiovasc. div., 1987-88, assoc. physician, staff physician cardiovasc. div., 1988—; clin. fellow in medicine Harvard U. Med. Sch., Boston, 1984-87, rsch. fellow dept. genetics, 1988-90, instr. medicine, 1988-89, asst. prof., 1989-95, assoc. prof., 1995—; tutor in biochem. scis. Harvard Coll., Harvard U., Cambridge, Mass., 1990—; lectr. molecular mechanisms of disease Harvard Med. Sci.-MIT health scis. and tech. program, 1990—; speaker at seminars, confs. and univs.; vis. lectr. U. Alta., U. Calgary, U. Alcala, Madrid, St. Bartholomew's Hosp., London; Cecilie Greig vis. prof. Hammersmith Hosp., Royal Postgrad. Med. Sch., London; plenary lectr., Nitric Oxide Forum, Tokyo. Contbr. articles to med. jours. Recipient John J. Abel award in Pharmacology Am. Soc. for Pharmacology Therapeutics, 1995, young scholar's award Am. Soc. Hypertension, 1991; Harvard nat. scholar Harvard U., 1973-77; fellow NIH, 1977-84. Fellow Am. Coll. Cardiology; mem. ACP, Am. Fedn. for Clin. Rsch., Henry Christian award for excellence in rsch. 1992, 93), Am. Heart Assn. (Established Investigator award 1993—, Clinican-Scientist award 1988-93), Am. Soc. for Biochemistry and Molecular Biology, Mass. Med. Soc. Office: Brigham & Women's Hosp Harvard Med Sch 75 Francis St Boston MA 02115-6110

MICHEL, VICTOR JAMES, JR., retired librarian; b. St. Louis, Feb. 2, 1927; s. Victor James and Bernadette (Fox) M.; m. Margaret A. Renaud, Feb. 3, 1951; children: Dennis W., Daniel J., Catherine A., Denise M.; student St. Louis U., 1946-48. Asst. librarian McDonnell Aircraft Corp., St. Louis, 1948-55; mgr. Anaheim (Calif.) Information Center, Electronics Ops., Rockwell Internat. Corp., 1955-84; pres. V.J. Michel Inc., Grass Valley, Calif., 1986—; sec. Placentia Devel. Co., 1964-71. Charter mem. Placentia-Tlaquepaque Sister City Orgn., 1964-84; founder, pres. Placentia chpt. St. Louis Browns Fan Club. Planning commr., Placentia, Calif., 1957-60, city councilman, 1960-70, vice-mayor, 1960-64, mayor, 1964-68. Trustee Placentia Library Dist., 1970-79, pres., 1974-79; city historian, Placentia, 1976-84, city treas., 1980-84; chmn. Placentia Fine Arts Commn., 1978-80. Served from pvt. to staff sgt. AUS, 1945-46. Named Placentia Citizen of Yr., 1979. Mem. Placentia C. of C. (v.p. 1960), Placentia Jaycees (hon. life), Calif., Orange County (pres. 1976) library assns. Democrat. Roman Catholic. Club: West Atwood Yacht (hon. yeoman emeritus with citation 1970, ship's librarian). Author: Pictorial History of the West Atwood Yacht Club, 1966; Placentia—Around the World, 1970; also articles in profl. jours. Home: 909 Jack Rabbit Ct Saint Peters MO 63376

MICHELI, CHRISTOPHER MICHAEL, lawyer; b. Sacramento, Mar. 14, 1967; s. Paul Lothar and Vima Nina (de Marchi) M.; m. Liza Marie Hernandez, Sept. 4, 1994; 1 stepchild, Morgan. Attended, George Washington U., 1985-86; BA in Polit. Sci. and Pub. Svc., U. Calif., Davis, 1989; JD, McGeorge Sch. Law, 1992. Bar: Calif. 1992, U.S. Dist. Ct. (no. and cen. dists.) 1993, (ea. dist.) 1992, U.S. Ct. Appeals (D.C. and 9th cirs.) 1993. Assoc. Bell & Hiltachk, Sacramento, 1992-93; gen. counsel Calif. Mfrs. Assn., Sacramento, 1993-94; atty., legis. advocate Carpenter, Snodgrass & Assocs., Sacramento, 1994—; mem. editl. adv. bd. State Income Tax Alert, Fla., 1995—; mem. legis. com. Inst. Govtl. Advocates, Sacramento, 1994—. Columnist The Daily Recorder, 1994—; contbr. articles to newspapers and profl. jours. Bd. dirs. Jesuit High Sch. Alumni Assn., Sacramento, 1992-95; soccer referee and coach Del Dayo Sch., Carmichael, Calif., 1994. Scholar William D. James Found., 1989. Mem. ABA, State Bar Calif., Sacramento County Bar Assn., Phi Delta Phi. Democrat. Roman Catholic. Avocations: politics, martial arts, travel, soccer. Home: 5511 Ivanhoe Way Carmichael CA 95608 Office: Carpenter Snodgrass Assocs 1121 L St # 210 Sacramento CA 95814

MICHELI, FRANK JAMES, lawyer; b. Zanesville, Ohio, Mar. 23, 1930; s. John and Theresa (Carlini) M.; m. Doris Joan Clum, Jan. 9, 1954; children: Michael John, James Carl, Lisa Ann, Matthew Charles. Student, John Carroll U., Cleve., 1947-48, Xavier U., Cin., 1949-50; LL.D., Ohio No. U., Ada., 1953. Bar: Ohio 1953. Since practiced in Zanesville; partner Leasure & Micheli, 1953-65, Kincaid, Micheli, Geyer & Ormond, 1965-75, Kincaid, Cultice, Micheli & Geyer (and predecessor), 1982-92; ptnr. Micheli, Baldwin, Bopeley & Northrup, 1992—; Instr. bus. law Meredith Bus. Coll., Zanesville, 1956; lectr. on med. malpractice, hosp. and nurse liability. Dir. Public Service for, City of Zanesville, 1954. Mem. Internat. Assn. Ins. Counsel, Def. Rsch. Inst., Ohio Def. Assn., Am. Ohio bar assns., Am. Judicature Soc., Am. Arbitration Assn. (mem. nat. panel), Am. Bd. Trial Advs. (bd. dirs. Ohio chpt. 1991-95). Club: Elk. Home: 160 E Willow Dr Zanesville OH 43701-1249 Office: PO Box 2687 2806 Bell St Zanesville OH 43701

MICHELMAN, FRANK I., lawyer, educator; b. 1936. BA, Yale U., 1957; LLB, Harvard U., 1960. Bar: N.Y. 1961, Mass. 1967. Law clk. to assoc. justice William J. Brennan, U.S. Supreme Ct., Washington, 1961-62; asst. to asst. atty. gen., Tax Div., Dept. Justice, 1962-63; asst. prof. Harvard U., Cambridge, Mass., 1963-66, prof., 1966-93, Robert Walmsley Univ. prof., 1993—; cons. HUD, 1966; cons. Boston Model City Program, 1968-69; mem. Boston Home Rule Commn., 1969-71; mem. Gov.'s Task Force on Met. Devel., 1974-75. Mem. Am. Soc. for Polit. and Legal Philosophy, Am. Assn. Arts and Scis. Author: (with Sandalow) Materials on Government in Urban Areas, 1970. Office: Law Sch Harvard U Cambridge MA 02138

MICHELS, EUGENE, physical therapist; b. Cin., May 16, 1926; s. Joseph and Anna (Bauer) M.; m. Genevieve Wilma Readinger, June 28, 1947; children: Karen, Timothy, Donald, Marian, Monica, Martha, David, Ann. B.S., U. Cin., 1950; cert. phys. therapy, U. Pa., 1951, M.A., 1965; Litt.D. (hon.), Thomas Jefferson U., 1985. Phys. therapist Grad. Hosp., U. Pa., Phila., 1951-58, mem. faculty dept. phys. therapy, 1965—, asst. prof., 1969-75, asso. prof., 1975-77; dir. phys. therapy Magee Meml. Hosp., Phila., 1958-65; assoc. exec. v.p. Am. Phys. Therapy Assn., 1977-88. Served with USNR, 1944-46. Recipient Lindback Found. Disting. Tchg. award, 1972; Pa. Phys. Therapy Assn. ann. achievement award named Carlin-Michels Achievement award in honor of Eleanor J. Carlin and Eugene Michels. Mem. Pa. Phys. Therapy Assn. (past pres.), Am. Phys. Therapy Assn. (past pres., Dorothy Briggs Meml. Sci. Inquiry award 1971, Golden Pen award 1977, Mary McMillan lectr. 1984, Catherine Worthingham fellow 1986, Eugene Michels New Investigator award established in his honor 1989, John Maley award sect. rsch. 1994), World Confedn. Phys. Therapy (pres. 1974-82). Democrat. Roman Catholic. Home: 7608 Wellesley Dr College Park MD 20740-3040

MICHELS, ROBERT, psychiatrist, educator; b. Chgo., Jan. 21, 1936; s. Samuel and Ann (Cooper) M.; m. Verena Sterba, Dec. 23, 1962; children—Katherine, James. BA, U. Chgo., 1953; MD, Northwestern U., 1958. Intern Mt. Sinai Hosp., N.Y.C., 1958-59; resident in psychiatry Columbia Presbyn.-N.Y. State Psychiat. Inst., N.Y.C., 1959-62; mem. faculty Coll. Physicians and Surgeons, Columbia U., N.Y.C., 1964-74; assoc. prof. Coll. Physicians and Surgeons, Columbia U., 1971-74; psychiatrist student health service Columbia U., 1966-74; supervising and tng. analyst Columbia U. Center for Psychoanalytic Tng. and Research, 1972—; attending psychiatrist Vanderbilt Clinic, Presbyn. Hosp., N.Y.C., 1964-74; Barklie McKee Henry prof. psychiatry Cornell U. Med. Coll., N.Y.C., 1974-93, prof. psychiatry, 1993—, chmn. dept. psychiatry, 1974-91; Stephen and Suzanne Weiss dean Cornell U. Med. Coll., 1991-96; provost for med. affairs Cornell U., 1991-96, Walsh McDermott U. prof. of medicine, 1996—; psychiatrist-in-chief N.Y. Hosp., 1974-91, attending psychiatist, 1991—; attending psychiatrist St. Luke's Hosp. Ctr., N.Y.C., 1966—. Co-author: The Psychiatric Interview in Clinical Practice, 1971; contbr. articles to profl. jours. Served with USPHS, 1962-64. Mem. Am. Psychiat. Assn., Am. Coll. Psychiatrists, N.Y. Psychiat. Soc., Royal Medico-Psychol. Assn., Psychiat. Rsch. Soc., Assn. Rsch. in Nervous and Mental Diseases, Assn. Acad. Psychiatry, Am. Psychoanalytic Assn., Internat. Psychoanalytic Assn., Ctr. Advanced Psychoanalytic Studies, N.Y. Acad. Scis., Alpha Omega Alpha. Office: Cornell U Med Coll 1300 York Ave New York NY 10021-4805

MICHELSEN, CHRISTOPHER BRUCE HERMANN, surgeon; b. Boston, Aug. 18, 1940; s. Jost Joseph and Ingeborg Elizabeth (Dilthey) M.; BA, Bowdoin Coll., 1961; MD, Columbia U., 1969; m. Amy Lee; children: Heidi Elizabeth, Matthew Christopher, Joshua Jost. Intern Columbia Presbyn. Med. Center, N.Y.C., 1969-70, resident, 1970-71; orthopedic resident N.Y. Orthopedic Hosp., N.Y.C., 1971-73, jr. Anne C. Kane fellow, 1973-74, sr. Anne C. Kane fellow and hip fellow, 1974-75, traveling fellow, 1975-76; internat. A-O fellow, postgrad. fellow in biomechanics, instr. biomed. engring. Case-Western Res. U.; assoc. prof. clin. orthopaedic surgery Columbia Coll. Physicians and Surgeons; co-dir. combined orthopaedic neuro surg. spine svc.; chief orthopaedic spine surgery svc., chief orthopaedic svc. Allen Pavillion, CPMC, 1994; chief orthopaedic svc. Individual Mobilization Designee, Fitzsimmons Army Med. Coll., 1995—. Col. USAR, 1961—. Diplomate Am. Bd. Orthopaedic Surgery. Fellow ACS, N.Y. Acad. Medicine, Am. Assn. for Surgery of Trauma, Am. Orthopaedic Assn., N.Am. Spine Soc., Am. Acad. Orthopaedic Surgeons, Internat. Coll. Surgeons; mem. AMA, Am. Coll. Physician Execs., Am. Coll. Physician Execs., Orthopaedic Research Soc., Am. Soc. Bone & Mineral Rsch., Royal Soc. Medicine (affiliate). Home: 102-57 Shearwater Ct E Jersey City NJ 07305 Office: 5141 Broadway New York NY 10034-1159

MICHELSEN, W(OLFGANG) JOST, neurosurgeon, educator; b. Amsterdam, Holland, Aug. 20, 1935; came to U.S., 1936; s. Jost Joseph and Ingeborg Mathilde (Dilthey) M.; m. Constance Richards, Sept. 21, 1963 (div. 1987); children: Kristina, Elizabeth, Ingrid; m. Claude Claire Grenier, Mar. 30, 1988 (div. Oct. 1992). AB magna cum laude, Harvard U., 1959; MD, Columbia U., 1963. Diplomate Am. Bd. Neurol. Surgery. Intern in surgery Case Wester Res. U. Hosps., Cleve., 1963-64; asst. resident in neurology Mass. Gen. Hosp., Boston, 1964-65; asst. resident, then chief resident neurol. surgery Columbia-Presbyn. Med. Ctr., N.Y.C., 1965-69; from instr. to assoc. prof. neurosurgery Columbia U. Coll. Physicians and Surgeons, N.Y.C., 1969-89, prof. clin. surgery, 1990—; fellow in neurosurgery Presbyn. Hosp., N.Y.C., 1969-71, dir. neuro vascular surgery, 1989-90; dir. neurosurgery St. Luke's Roosevelt Hosp. Ctr., N.Y.C., 1990—; prof. and chmn. dept. neurological surgery Albert Einstein Coll. Medicine, Bronx, N.Y., 1992—; dir. neurosurgery Montefiore Med Ctr, Bronx, 1992—; asst. attending in neurosurgery, St. Luke's Hosp. Ctr., 1970—; cons. neurosurgeon Nyack (N.Y.) Hosp., 1972—, Englewood (N.J.) Hosp., 1972—; vis. prof. neurosurgery Tufts U., 1975, Emery U., 1977, Presbyn.-St. Luke's Hosp. Ctr., Chgo., 1978, Yale U., 1980; guest faculty Northwestern U., 1977, 78, U. Chgo., 1977, Colby Coll., 1980; mem. numerous panels on neurosurgery. Contbr. articles to profl. publs. 1st lt. U.S. Army, 1954-57. Grantee NIH, USPHS. Fellow ACS, Am. Heart Assn.; Mem. AMA, Am. Assn. Neurol. Surgeons (mem. sect. pediatric neurosurger), Neurosurg. Soc. Am. (v.p. 1984-85, pres. 1987-88), Congress Neurol. Surgeons, N.Y. Neurosurg. Soc., Neurosurg. Soc. State N.Y., N.Y. Acad. Scis., Assn. Rsch. in Nervous and Mental Diseases, Internat. Neurosurg. Soc., Internat. Pediatric Neurosurg. Soc., Explorers Club, N.Y. State Med. Soc., N.Y. County Med. Soc. Office: Montefiore Med Ctr 111 E 210th St Bronx NY 10467-2490

MICHELSON, EDWARD J., journalist; b. Northampton, Mass., Apr. 3, 1915; s. Isadore Henry and Fannie (Avrich) M.; m. Dorothea Adair Pohlman, Feb. 3, 1938; children—Kathleen (Mrs. Howard J. Connolly), Paul, Emily (Mrs. Thomas D. Crews). B.A., Williams Coll., 1937. Reporter St. Louis Post-Dispatch, 1937-38; sci. writer Westinghouse Electric Co., 1939-40; day editor, internat. shortwave news div. CBS, 1941-44; spl. asst. Office Sec. War, 1946; mem. hist. sect. strategic services unit War Dept., 1946; asso. Robert S. Allen (syndicated columnist), 1946-50; Washington corr. N.Am. Newspaper Alliance, also New Eng. dailies, 1946—; Washington editor Forbes mag., 1956-63, Printer's Ink mag., 1958-63; mag. editor Ocean Sci. News, 1958-63, 1968; Washington editor Sci. and Tech. mag., 1969—; Exec. Enterprises Publs.; Research dir. pub. works subcom. on water resources U.S. Ho. of Reps., 1951. Contbr. to gen., financial, spl. bus. periodicals.; Editor: (Wright Patman) Our American Government, 1948. Served with OSS, AUS, 1944-46. Mem. White House Corrs. Assn., Gargoyle Soc. Club: Cosmos. Home: #C-302 2300 Indian Creek Blv W Vero Beach FL 32966

MICHELSON, GAIL IDA, lawyer; b. N.Y.C., Sept. 19, 1952; d. Max and Virginia (Seames) M. BA, Columbia U., 1984; JD, W.Va. U., 1993. Bar: W.Va. 1993, U.S. Dist. Ct. (so. dist.) W.Va. Assoc. Kopelman & Assocs., Charleston, W.Va., 1994; asst. atty. gen. Atty. Gen. State of W.Va., Charleston, 1995—. Actor: (soap operas) Another World, Guiding Light, All My Children, 1976-79. Dir./staff Am. Theatre of Actors, N.Y.C., 1985-90. Mem. ABA, W.Va. Bar Assn., W.Va. Trial Lawyers Assn., ACLU. Home: 300 Park Ave Charleston WV 25302 Office: Atty Gen State of W Va Capitol Complex Charleston WV 25305

MICHELSON, GERTRUDE GERALDINE, retired retail company executive; b. Jamestown, N.Y., June 3, 1925; d. Thomas and Celia Rosen; m. Horace Michelson, Mar. 28, 1947; children: Martha Ann (dec.), Barbara Jane. B.A., Pa. State U., 1945; LL.B., Columbia U., 1947; LLD with honors, Adelphi U., 1981; DHL with honors, New Rochelle Coll., 1983; LLD with honors, Marymount Manhattan Coll., 1988. With Macy's N.Y., N.Y.C., 1947—; mgmt. trainee Macy's N.Y., 1947-48, various mgmt. positions, v.p. employee personnel, 1963-70, sr. v.p. for labor and consumer relations, 1970-72, dir., mem. exec. com., 1970—; sr. v.p. pers. labor and consumer rels. Macy & Co., Inc., 1972-79, sr. v.p. external affairs, 1979-80; sr. v.p. external affairs R.H. Macy & Co., Inc., 1980-92, sr. advisor, 1992-94; retired, 1995; bd. dirs. Chubb Corp., GE Co., Stanley Works, Inc., Goodyear Tire & Rubber Co.; bd. dirs., trustee Rand Corp.; former dep. chmn. N.Y. Fed. Res. Bank; gov. Am. Stock Exch. Chmn. Helena Rubinstein Found; dir. Markle Found.; chmn. emeritus bd. trustees Columbia U.; life trustee Spelman Coll.; mem. adv. coun. Catalyst. Recipient Disting. Svc. medal Pa. State U., 1969. Mem. N.Y. City C. of C. (bd. dirs., mem. exec. com., vice chmn.), N.Y.C. Ptnrship. (vice chmn.), Women's Forum, Econ. Club N.Y. Home: 70 E 10th St New York NY 10003-5102 Office: Federated Dept Stores Inc 151 W 34th St New York NY 10001-2124

MICHELSON, HAROLD, production designer; b. N.Y.C., Feb. 15, 1920; s. Max and Gussie (Reichel) M.; m. Lillian Farber, Dec. 14, 1947; children: Alan Bruce, Eric Neil, Dennis Paul. Student, Pratt Inst., 1938, NYU, 1939, Art Students League, N.Y.C., 1945-47, Calif. Sch. Art, L.A., 1947-49. Illustrator Columbia Pictures, L.A., 1949-52; illustrator Paramount Pictures, L.A., 1953-58, art dir., prodn. designer, 1959-95; illustrator Warner Bros., Burbank, Calif., 1959-89; art dir. 20th Century Fox, Beverly Hills, Calif., 1959-89, visual cons., 1990-91; ind. prodn. designer, Hollywood, Calif., 1959-95; visual cons. Metro-Goldwyn-Mayer, Hollywood, 1992—; lectr. U. So. Calif., L.A., 1988-95; instr. UCLA, 1989-90, Maine Photog. Workshop, Rockport, Maine, 1991; mem. faculty Am. Film Inst., L.A., 1992-95. Exhibited in group show Storyboard-Le Cinema Dessiná, 1992. 1st lt. USAAF, 1941-45, ETO. Decorated Air medal with 7 oak leaf clusters. Mem. Soc. Motion Picture Art Dirs. (exec. bd. 1985-95), Acad. Motion Picture Arts and Scis. (membership bd. 1975—, 2 Acad. award nominations 1978, 84).

MICHELSON, LILLIAN, motion picture researcher; b. Manhattan, N.Y., June 21, 1928; d. Louis and Dora (Keller) Farber; m. Harold Michelson, Dec. 14, 1947; children: Alan Bruce, Eric Neil, Dennis Paul. Vol. Goldwyn Libr., Hollywood, Calif., 1961-69; owner Former Goldwyn Rsch. Libr., Hollywood, Calif., 1969—; ind. location scout, 1973—. Bd. dirs Beverlywood After Care Ctr., L.A., 1988—; mem. Friends of L.A. Pub. Libr. Office: care Dreamworks SKG 100 Universal Plz Lakeside Bldg #601 Universal City CA 91608

MICHENER, CHARLES DUNCAN, entomologist, researcher, educator; b. Pasadena, Calif., Sept. 22, 1918; s. Harold and Josephine (Rigden) M.; m. Mary Hastings, Jan. 1, 1941; children: David, Daniel, Barbara, Walter. B.S., U. Calif., Berkeley, 1939, Ph.D., 1941. Tech. asst. U. Calif., Berkeley, 1939-42; asst. curator Am. Mus. Natural History, N.Y.C., 1942-46; assoc. curator Am. Mus. Natural History, 1946-48, research assoc., 1949—; assoc. prof. U. Kans., 1948-49, prof., 1949-89, prof. emeritus, 1989—, chmn. dept. entomology, 1949-61, 72-75, Watkins Disting. prof. entomology, 1959-89, acting chmn. dept. systematics, ecology, 1968-69, Watkins Disting. prof. systematics and ecology, 1969-89; dir. Snow Entomol. Museum, 1974-83, state entomologist, 1949-61; Guggenheim fellow, vis. research prof. U. Paraná, Curitiba, Brazil, 1955-56; Fulbright fellow U. Queensland, Brisbane, Australia, 1958-59; research scholar U. Costa Rica, 1963; Guggenheim fellow, Africa, 1966-67. Author: (with Mary H. Michener) American Social Insects, 1951, (with S.F. Sakagami) Nest Architecture of the Sweat Bees, 1962, The Social Behavior of the Bees, 1974, (with M.D. Breed and H.E. Evans) The Biology of Social Insects, 1982, (with D. Fletcher) Kin Recognition in Animals, 1987, (with R. McGinley and B. Danforth) The Bee Genera of North and Central America, 1994; contbr. articles to profl. jours.; editor: Evolution, 1962-64; Am. editor: Insectes Sociaux, Paris, 1954-55, 62-90; assoc. editor: Ann Rev. of Ecology and Systematics, 1970-90. Served from 1st lt. to capt. San. Corps AUS, 1943-46. Fellow Am. Entomol. Soc., Entomol. Soc. Am., Am. Acad. Arts and Scis., Royal Entomol. Soc. London, AAAS; mem. NAS, Linnean Soc. London (corr.), Soc. for Study Evolution (pres. 1967), Soc. Systematic Zoologists (pres. 1969), Am. Soc. Naturalists (pres. 1978), Internat. Union for Study Social Insects (pres. 1977-82), Kans. Entomol. Soc. (pres. 1950), Brazilian Acad. Scis. (corr.). Home: 1706 W 2nd St Lawrence KS 66044-1016

MICHENER, JAMES ALBERT, author; b. N.Y.C., Feb. 3, 1907; s. Edwin and Mabel (Haddock) M.; m. Patti Koon, July 27, 1935 (div.); m. Vange Nord, Sept. 2, 1948 (div.); m. Mari Yoriko Sabusawa, Oct. 23, 1955 (dec. 1994). A.B. summa cum laude, Swarthmore Coll., 1929; A.M., U. No. Colo., 1937; research study, U. Pa., U. Va., Ohio State U., Harvard U., U. St. Andrews, Scotland, U. Siena, Italy, Brit. Mus. London; research study (Lippincott Traveling fellow), 1930-33, numerous hon. degrees. Tchr. Hill Sch., 1929-31, George Sch., Pa., 1933-36; prof. Colo. State Coll. Edn., 1936-41; vis. prof. Harvard U., 1939-40; asso. editor Macmillan Co., 1941-49; mem. adv. com. on arts State Dept., 1957; mem. adv. council NASA, 1980-83; mem. U.S. Adv. Commn. on Info., 1971; mem. Citizen's Adv. Stamp Com., 1982-87; mem. Bd. for Internat. Broadcasting. Author: Unit in the Social Studies, 1940, Tales of the South Pacific, 1947 (Pulitzer prize), The Fires of Spring, 1949, Return to Paradise, 1951, The Voice of Asia, 1951, The Bridges at Toko Ri, 1953, Sayonara, 1954, Floating World, 1955, The Bridge at Andau, 1957, Rascals in Paradise, (with A. Grove Day), 1957, Selected Writings, 1957, The Hokusai Sketchbook, 1958, Japanese Prints, 1959, Hawaii, 1959, Report of the County Chairman, 1961, Caravans, 1963, The Source, 1965, Iberia, 1968, Presidential Lottery, 1969, The Quality of Life, 1970, Kent State, 1971, The Drifters, 1971, A Michener Miscellany, 1973, Centennial, 1974, Sports in America, 1976, Chesapeake, 1978, The Covenant, 1980, Space, 1982, Poland, 1983, Texas, 1985, Legacy, 1987, Journey, 1988, Alaska, 1988, Caribbean, 1989; (with John Kings) Six Days in Havana, 1989, The Novel, 1991, The World Is My Home, 1991, Writer's Handbook, 1992, Mexico, 1992, My Lost Mexico, 1992, Creatures of the Kingdom: Stories of Animals and Nature, 1993, Literary Reflections: Michener on Michener, Hemingway, Capote, and Others, 1993, Recessional, 1994, Miracle in Seville, 1995; editor: Future of Social Studies for N.E.A, 1940. With USNR, 1944-46. Recipient U.S. Medal of Freedom, Disting. Svc. medal NASA, Golden Badge of Order of Merit, 1988. Mem. Phi Beta Kappa. Democrat. Mem. Soc. of Friends. Office: Tex Ctr for Writers PCL 3.102 Mail Code S5401 Austin TX 78713

MICHENER, JAMES LLOYD, medical educator; b. Dec. 19, 1952; m. Gwendolyn Curtis Murphy; children: Rebecca Liane, Joshua Kieran. BA, Oberlin (Ohio) Coll., 1974; MD, Harvard Med. Sch., 1978. Diplomate Am. Bd. Family Practice. Resident in family medicine Duke U. Med. Ctr., Durham, N.C., 1978-81, Kellogg fellow, 1981-82, clin. prof. dept. cmty. and family medicine, 1994—, chmn. dept. cmty. and family medicine, 1994—; v.p. Durham Health Care, Inc., 1985-86. Co-author: Nutrition in Practice, 1990, 2d edit., 1992; contbr. numerous articles to med. pubs. including Academic Medicine, The Jour. of Family Practice, Medical Care, others; mem. editl. bd. Rx Nutrition, 1989-91; presenter in field. Bd. dirs. N.C. Med. Soc. Found., 1995—; STFM rep. resource com. on nutrition edn. Am. Acad. Family Practice Found., 1987-91. Grantee The Fullerton Found., Inc., The Josiah Macy, Jr. Found., U.S. Dept. Health and Human Svcs. Mem. AMA, Assn. Tchrs. of Preventive Medicine, Am. Acad. of Family Physicians Found., Am. Heart Assn. (del. Nat. Cholesterol Edn. Program 1987), N.C. Acad. Family Physicians (bd. dirs. 1995—). Home: 4011 Duck Pond Trail Chapel Hill NC 27514 Office: Duke U Med Ctr Box 2914 Durham NC 27710

MICHENFELDER, JOHN DONAHUE, anesthesiology educator; b. St. Louis, Apr. 13, 1931; s. Albert A. and Ruth J. (Donahue) M.; m. Margaret Grey Nick, Oct. 22, 1955 (dec. Nov. 1971); children: Carol, David, Joseph, Paul, Matthew, Laura; m. Mary Monica Milroy, Aug. 11, 1972; 1 child, Patrick. BS, St. Louis U., 1951, MD, 1955. Diplomate Am. Bd. Anesthesiology. Intern Presbyn. St. Luke's Hosp., Chgo., 1955-56; resident in internal medicine Presbyn. St. Luke's Hosp., 1956; resident in anesthesiology Mayo Clinic, Rochester, Minn., 1958-61, cons. in anesthesiology, 1961-91; prof. anesthesiology Mayo Med. Sch., Rochester, 1976-93, emeritus prof., 1993—. Author: Anesthesia and the Brain, 1988, Clinical Neuroanesthesia, 1990. Lt. USN, 1956-58. NIH grantee, 1966-89, 91-95; Faculty Anaesthetists of Royal Coll. Surgeons Ireland fellow, 1982, Faculty Anaesthetists Royal Coll. Surgeons Eng. fellow, 1988. Mem. Am. Soc. Anesthesiologists (Excellence in Rsch. award 1990, Disting. Svc. award 1990), Inst. Med., Assn. Univ. Anesthetists (councilman 1975-78). Avocations: upland game bird hunting, gardening, reading, writing. Home: 325 1st Ave NW Oronoco MN 55960-1410 Office: Mayo Clinic Dept of Anesthesiology 200 1st St SW Rochester MN 55905-0001

MICHENFELDER, JOSEPH FRANCIS, public relations executive; b. Webster Groves, Mo., Mar. 30, 1929; s. Albert Aloysius and Ruth Josephine (Donahue) M.; m. Audrey Laurine Glynn, Aug. 8, 1970. BA, N.Y. State U., N.Y.C., 1951, STB, 1954, MRE, 1955; MS in Journalism, Columbia U., 1958. Projects dir. Maryknoll Headquarters, Ossining, N.Y., 1955-57; communications dir. Maryknoll Headquarters, Ossining, 1958-62; dir., chief exec. officer Noticias Aliadas, S.A., Lima, Peru, 1962-69; pub. rels. dir. Pub. Affairs Analysts, Inc., N.Y.C., 1970-72; exec. v.p. Pub. Affairs Analysts, Inc., 1973-89; sr. v.p. Napolitan Assocs./PAA, Inc., N.Y.C., 1989-95; pres., CEO, 1995—; pres. IDOC/N.Am., Inc., N.Y.C., 1976—. Mng. Editor (polit. quarterly) POLITEIA, 1970-73; co-producer: TV documentary A Quiet Revolution, 1987. Trustee The Fund for Peace, 1994—, Coun. on Hemispheric Affairs, Washington, 1980—; cons. UNESCO WHO, Bogota, Lima, 1964-66; bd. dirs. Jobs for Youth, Inc., N.Y.C., 1978-84. Mem. Internat. Pub. Relations Assn., Internat. Assn. Polit. Cons., Columbia U. Journalism Alumni Fed. (pres. 1971-74), Ovrses Press Club, Columbia Club. Democrat. Avocations: theater arts, film, creative writing, ecology, Third World affairs. Office: Napolitan Assocs/PAA Inc 55 5th Ave New York NY 10003-4301

MICHERO, WILLIAM HENDERSON, retired retail trade executive; b. Fort Worth, June 19, 1925; s. William Alvin and Lela Belle (Henderson) M.; m. Nan Elaine Henderson, July 9, 1948; children—Jane Elaine Michero Christie, William Sherman, Thomas Edward. B.S. in Commerce, Tex. Christian U., 1948. Sec. Tandy Corp., Fort Worth, 1960-75; v.p. Tandy Corp., 1970-75; with Tandycrafts, Inc., Fort Worth, 1975-90; sr. v.p., sec., dir. Tandycrafts, Inc., 1979-83, chmn. bd., 1983-90, ret., 1990; Sec. B.F. Johnston Found., Fort Worth, 1962-90. Bd. dirs. David L. Tandy Found., Fort Worth, 1978—, Oakwood Cemetery Assn., 1979-89, Panther Boys Club, 1974-78, Fort Worth Mus. Sci. and History, 1973-75, pres. 1975, United Way; chmn. Distributive Edn. Council, 1970. Served with U.S. Navy, 1943-46. Clubs: Fort Worth, Colonial Country. Home: 4705 Shady Ridge Ct Fort Worth TX 74109-1803 Office: 550 Bailey Ave Fort Worth TX 76107-2155

MICHNA, ANDREA STEPHANIE, real estate agent and developer; b. Chgo., Nov. 4, 1948; d. Andrew Stephen and Ann Barbara (Ciesla) M. Student, Northwestern U., 1984-86. Travel cons. Internat. Sporting Travel, Chgo., 1975-77; office mgr., legal asst. Law Office of J.A. Rosin, Chgo., 1977-83; asst. to pres. Mt. Sinai Hosp., Chgo., 1983-85; exec. v.p. real estate Continental Fin., Ltd., Northbrook, Ill., 1985—. Avocations: tng. and showing of dressage horses. Office: Continental Financial Ltd 555 Skokie Blvd Ste 285 Northbrook IL 60062-2833

MICK, HOWARD HAROLD, lawyer; b. Newton, Kans., Oct. 21, 1934; s. Marvin Woodrow and Edith (Bergen) M.; m. Susan Siple, Sept. 5, 1957; children: Martha, Julie, Elizabeth. Student, U. Okla., 1952-54; BS, LLB, U. Colo., 1958. Bar: Colo. 1958, Mo. 1959. Assoc. Stinson, Mag & Fizzell, Kansas City, Mo., 1959-62; ptnr. Stinson, Mag & Fizzell, Kansas City, 1962—. Bd. dirs. Ctr. Mgmt. Assistance, Kansas City, Mo., 1984-88; mem. adv. coun. Kansas City Salvation Army, 1987—. Mem. ABA, Lawyers Assn. Kansas City, Kansas City Bar Assn., Rotary, Kansas City Club, Indian Hills Country. Democrat. Presbyterian. Avocations: golf, tennis, boating. Office: Stinson Mag & Fizzell PO Box 419251 Kansas City MO 64141-6251

MICKEL, EMANUEL JOHN, foreign language educator; b. Lemont, Ill., Oct. 11, 1937; s. Emanuel John and Mildred (Newton) M.; m. Kathleen Russell, May 31, 1959; children: Jennifer, Chiara, Heather. BA, La. State U., 1959; MA, U. N.C., 1963, PhD, 1965. Asst. prof. U. Nebr., Lincoln, 1965-67, assoc. prof., 1967-68; assoc. prof. Ind. U., Bloomington, 1968-73, prof., 1973—, dir. Medieval Studies Inst., 1976-91, chmn. French and Italian, 1984-95; cons. NEH; French advisor Soc. Rencesvals, 1995—; adv. bd. mem. Nineteenth Century French Studies, 1995—. Author: Marie de France, 1974, Eugene Fromentin, 1982, Ganelon Treason and the Chanson de Roland, 1989, Jules Vernes Complete Twenty Thousand Leagues Under the Sea, 1992. Capt. U.S. Army, 1963-65. Grantee NEH, Washington, 1978-84; Lilly Open fellow Lilly Found., Indpls., 1981-82. Avocations: music, theater, sports, travel, ancient literature. Office: French & Italian Dept Indiana Univ 642 Ballantine Bloomington IN 47405

MICKEL, JOSEPH THOMAS, lawyer; b. Monroe, La., Nov. 12, 1951; s. Toufick and Ruth Ella (Phelps) M.; m. Carlene Elise Nickens, Dec. 10, 1981 (div.); children: Thomas, Matthew. BA, La. State U., 1975; postgrad., Tulane U., 1977-78; JD, So. U., 1979. Bar: La. 1979, U.S. Dist. Ct. (mid. dist.) La. 1981, U.S. Ct. Appeals (5th cir.) 1981, U.S. Dist. Ct. (we. dist.) La. 1983, U.S. Ct. Mil. Appeals 1985, U.S. Supreme Ct. 1985. Staff atty. Pub. Defenders Office, Baton Rouge, La., 1979-80; assoc. Law Offices of Michael Fugler, Baton Rouge, 1981; asst. dist. atty. La. 4th Jud. Dist. Atty.'s Office, Monroe, 1982-84, 85-89; ptnr. Bruscato, Loomis & Street, Monroe, 1984-85; asst. U.S. atty. Western Dist. State of La., Lafayette, 1989—; adj. prof. Northeast La. U., Monroe, 1988; mem. U.S. Dept. Justice Organized Crime Drug Task Force, 1992-93. Mem. ABA. Republican. Presbyterian. Avocations: trapshooting, skeetshooting, bird hunting, fishing. Home: PO Box 91961 Lafayette LA 70509-1961 Office: US Atty Office 600 Jefferson St Ste 1000 Lafayette LA 70501

MICKELSON, ARNOLD RUST, consultant, religious denominational official; b. Finley, N.D., Jan. 8, 1922; s. Alfred B. and Clara (Rust) M.; m. Marjorie Arveson, June 8, 1944; 1 son, Richard. BA, Concordia Coll., Moorhead, Minn., 1943, LLD (hon.), 1972; LLD (hon.), Calif. Luth. U., 1983, Luther Coll., 1987. Owner, mgr. Luther Book Store, Decorah, Iowa, 1946-48; credit supr. Gen. Motors Acceptance Corp., Fargo, N.D., 1948-53; mgr. Epko Film Service, Fargo, 1953-58; asst. to pres. No. Minn. dist. Evang. Luth. Ch., 1958-61, No. Minn. dist. Am. Luth. Ch., 1961-66; gen. sec. The Am. Luth. Ch., Mpls., 1967-82; coordinator Commn. for a New Luth. Ch., Mpls., 1982-87; pres. A.M. Cons., Amery, Wis., 1987—; councilor Luth. Council in U.S.A., 1966-82, sec., 1969-72, pres., 72-75; mem. U.S.A. Nat. Com. Luth. World Fedn., 1966-82, sec., 1966-69, 72-75, v.p., 1979-81, pres., 1981-82; mem. Consultation on Luth. Unity, 1970-76, sec., 1970-73, chmn., 1974-76; mem. Com. on Luth. Unity, 1976-82; del. 4th Assembly World Coun. Chs., Uppsala, Sweden, 1968, 5th Assembly, Nairobi, Kenya, 1975; chmn. Faith-in-Life Dialogue, Fargo-Moorhead, 1964, observer-trainer, Duluth, 1965; gen. sec. emeritus Am. Luth. Ch., 1982—; pres. Ctrl. Luth. Ch., Mpls., 1992-93. Mem. Mpls.-St. Paul Town Meeting Coun., 1968-76, Conf. on Inflation, 1974; bd. dirs. Midwest League, 1979—; mem. bd. mgrs. Am. Bible Soc., 1979—; trustee Suomi Coll., 1981—; mem. com. on hearing officers Evang. Luth. Ch. in Am., 1993—; pres. Luth. Leadership Inst., 1994-95, Luth. Resources Network, 1995—. With AUS, 1943-46. Recipient Civic Service award Eagles, 1965, Ch. award Suomi Coll., 1987, Judge Graven Lay Leadership award Wartburg Coll., 1990. Mem. Ch. Staff Workers Assn. (past pres.), Concordia Coll. Alumni Assn. (past pres.), Mpls. Athletic Club, Alpha Phi Gamma, Zeta Sigma Pi. Home: 1235 Yale Pl Apt 409 Minneapolis MN 55403-1944 Office: AM Cons 1232 Marina Dr Amery WI 54001-5132

MICKELSON, SIG, broadcasting executive, educator; b. Clinton, Minn., May 24, 1913; s. Olaf and Harriet (Reinholdson) M.; m. Maybelle Brown, June 8, 1940 (dec. Apr., 1985); children: Karen Ann (Mrs. Christiaan De Brauw), Alan; m. Elena Mier y Teran, June 14, 1986. B.A., Augustana Coll., 1934, LLD, 1987; M.A., U. Minn., 1940. With CBS, N.Y.C., 1943-61; pres. CBS News, 1954-61; v.p., dir. Time-Life Broadcast, Inc., N.Y.C., 1961-70, Ency. Brit. Ednl. Corp., Chgo., 1970-72; prof., chmn. editorial dept. Medill Sch. Journalism, Northwestern U., Evanston, Ill., 1972-75; pres. RFE/RL, Inc., Washington, 1975-78; Disting. vis. prof. San Diego State U., 1978-79, exec. dir. Ctr. for Communications, 1979-82, adj. prof, 1984-90, Van Deerlin prof. communications, 1989-90; pres. San Diego Communications Coun., 1989-90; Manship prof. journalism La. State U., 1991-93, disting. prof. comm., 1994—; rsch. fellow Hoover Instn., 1981—; advisor Nat. News Coun., 1973-80; ex-officio Bd. Internat. Broadcasting, 1975-78; dir. Stauffer Comms. Inc., 1979-95. Author: The Electric Mirror, 1972, America's Other Voice, 1983, The First Amendment: The Challenge of New Technology, 1989, From Whistle Stop to Sound Bite, 1989, The Northern Pacific Railroad and the Selling of the West, 1993. Bd. regents Augustana Coll., 1983-95. Mem. Radio TV News Dirs. Assn. (founder, v.p. 1946-48, pres. 1948-49), Internat. Inst. for Comm. (founder, chmn. 1970-71, chmn. exec. com. 1967-70, 71-73), Coun. on Fgn. Rels. Clubs: Century Assn. (N.Y.C.); Cosmos (Washington). Home: 6443 Pasatiempo Ave San Diego CA 92120-3823

MICKEY, PAUL F(OGLE), JR., lawyer; b. Washington, Sept. 25, 1949; s. Paul Fogle and Margaret Snowden (Stanley) M.; m. Carol Lynne Forsyth, Mar. 19, 1977; children: Alison Langlands, Suzanne Snowden, Scott Forsyth. A.B. summa cum laude, Princeton U., 1971; J.D., U. Va., 1974. Bar: D.C. 1975, U.S. Supreme Ct. 1982. Law clk. to George E. MacKinnon, U.S. Ct. Appeals, D.C. Circuit, 1974-75; with office of legal adv. U.S. Dept. State, Washington, 1975-77; asso. firm Covington & Burling, Washington, 1977-79; v.p., gen. counsel Nat. R.R. Passenger Corp. (Amtrak), Washington, 1979-83, exec. v.p. law and pub. affairs, 1983-85; ptnr. Shaw, Pitman, Potts & Trowbridge, Washington, 1985-95, mng. ptnr., chmn., 1995—. Contbr. articles to legal revs. Mem. bd. govs. Nat. Cathedral Sch.; mem. corp. bd. dirs. Children's Hosp., Nat. Med. Ctr.; bd. dirs. St. Francis Ctr. Mem. ABA, D.C. Bar Assn., Am. Arbitration Assn. (arbitrator), Met. Club, Chevy Chase Club. Episcopalian. Office: 2300 N St NW Washington DC 20037-1122

MICKIEWICZ, ELLEN PROPPER, political science educator; b. Hartford, Conn., Nov. 6, 1938; d. George K. and Rebecca (Adler) Propper; m. Denis Mickiewicz, June 2, 1963; 1 son, Cyril. B.A., Wellesley Coll., 1960; M.A., Yale U., 1961, Ph.D., 1965. Lectr. dept. polit. sci. Yale U., 1965-67; asst. prof. dept. polit. sci. Mich. State U., East Lansing, 1967-69; assoc. prof. Mich. State U., 1969-73, prof., 1973-80; prof. dept. polit. sci. Emory U., Atlanta, 1980-88; dean Grad. Sch. Arts and Scis. Emory U., 1980-85, Alben W. Barkley prof. polit. sci., 1988-93; James R. Shepley prof. pub. policy, prof. polit. sci. Duke U., Durham, N.C., 1994—, dir. DeWitt Wallace Ctr. for Comm. and Journalism Terry Sanford Inst. Pub. Policy, 1994—; vis. prof. Kathryn W. David Chair Wellesley Coll., 1978; vis. com. dept. Slavic lang. and lit. Harvard U., 1978-85, vice chmn. vis. com. Russian Rsch. Ctr., Harvard U., 1986-92; mem. subcom. on comms. and society Am. Coun. Learned Socs./Soviet Acad. Scis., 1986-90; mem. com. on internat. security studies, Am. Acad. Arts and Scis., 1988-90; fellow The Carter Ctr., 1985—, dir. Commn. on Radio and TV Policy; mem. area adv. com. for Ea. Europe and USSR, Coun. for Internat. Exch. Of Scholars, 1987-90; mem. acad. adv. coun. The Kennan Inst. for Advanced Russian Studies, 1989-93; mem. bd. overseers Internat. Press Ctr., Moscow, 1995; dir., commr. Commn. Radio and TV Policy, 1990. Author: Soviet Political Schools, 1967, Media and the Russian Public, 1981, Split Signals: Television and Politics in the Soviet Union, 1988 (Electronic Book of Yr. award Nat. Assn. Broadcasters and Broadcast Edn. Assn. 1988); co-author: Television and Elections, 1992, Television/Radio News and Minorities, 1994; editor: Soviet Union Jour., 1980-90; co-editor: International Security and Arms Control, 1986, The Soviet Calculus of Nuclear War, 1986; editor, contbr.: Handbook of Soviet Social Science Data, 1973; mem. editl. bd. Jour. Politics, 1985-88, Harvard Internat. Jour. Press/Politics, 1995—, Polit. Comms., 1996—. Founder, 1st chmn. bd. dirs. Opera Guild of Greater Lansing, Inc., 1972-74. Recipient Outstanding Svc. to Promote Dem. Media in Russia award Journalists Union of Russia, 1994; Ford Found. Fgn. Area Tng. fellow, 1962-65, Guggenheim fellow, 1973-74; Sigma Xi grantee, 1972-74, John and Mary R. Markle Found. grantee, 1984-88, 94-96, 95—, Ford Found. grantee, 1985, 88-91, 92—, Rockefeller Found. grantee, 1985-87, W. Alton Jones Found. grantee, 1987-88, Eurasia Found. grantee, 1993-94, Carnegie Corp. of N.Y. grantee, 1996—. Mem. Am. Assn. for Advancement Slavic Studies (bd. dirs. 1978-81, mem. awards com., mem. endowment com. 1984-86, pres. 1987-88), Am. Polit. Sci. Assn.,Internat. Studies Assn. (v.p. N.Am. 1983-84), Dante Soc. Am., So. Conf. Slavic Studies (exec. com. 1983-84), Counc. Fgn. Rels. Office: Sanford Inst Pub Policy PO Box 90241 Duke U Durham NC 27708-0241

MICKLITSCH, CHRISTINE NOCCHI, health care administrator; b. Hazleton, Pa., Oct. 23, 1949; d. Nicholas Edmund and Matilda Nocchi; m. Wayne D. Micklitsch, May 20, 1972; children: Sarah N., Emily M. BS, Pa. State U., State College, 1971; MBA, Boston U., 1979. Blood bank med. technologist The Deaconess Hosp., Boston, 1971-73; sr. blood bank med. technologist Tufts New Eng. Med. Ctr., Boston, 1973-76, environ. svcs. coord., 1976-78; adminstrv. resident Joslin Diabetes Found., Boston, 1978-79; sr. analyst Analysis, Mgmt. & Planning, Inc., Cambridge, Mass., 1979-80; adminstrv. dir. Hahnemann Family Health Ctr., Worcester, Mass., 1980-84; exec. dir. Swampscott (Mass.) Treatment & Trauma Ctr., 1984-85; dir. practice mgmt., instr. U. Mass. Med. Ctr., Worcester, 1985-91; dir. adminstrv. svcs. The Fallon Clinic, Worcester, 1991-94; mgr. physician network devel. The Fallon healthcare Sys., Worcester, 1994—. Incorporator, pres. Newton (Mass.) Highlands Cmty. Devel. Corp., 1981-82; treas. Patriot's Trail coun. Girl Scouts U.S., Newton, 1993—; Christian edn. instr. Newton Highlands Congl. Ch., 1987-94. Kellogg fellow Ctr. for Rsch. in Ambulatory Health Care Adminstrn., Denver, 1979; grantee in grad. tng. in family medicine HHS, U. Mass. Med. Sch., Worcester, 1989. Fellow Am. Coll. Med. Practice Execs. (state coll. forum rep. 1989—, ea. sect. coll. forum rep. 1993—); mem. Am. Coll. Med. Practice Execs. (mem. chair 1995-96), Mass. Med. Group Mgmt. Assn. (pres. 1987-89, newsletter editor 1984—), Boston U. Health Care Mgmt. Program Alumni Assn., Alpha Omicron Pi (parlimentarian Epsilon Alpha chpt. 1969-70). Avocations: classic cars, real estate. Home: 320 Lake Ave Newton MA 02161-1212 Office: Fallon Healthcare Sys Chestnut Pl 10 Chestnut St Worcester MA 01608-2804

MICKO, ALEXANDER S., financial executive; b. Munich, May 8, 1947; came to U.S., 1952, naturalized, 1957; s. Zygmunt and Maria (Huber) M.; m. Sharon E. Judge, June 7, 1969; 1 child, Brian A. BS, LaSalle U., 1969. CPA, N.J., Pa. Audit mgr. Price Waterhouse, Phila., 1970-77; asst. chief fin. investigations div. of Casino Gaming Enforcement, State of N.J., Trenton, 1977-79; v.p. fin. TeleScis., Inc., Mt. Laurel, N.J., 1979-87; v.p. fin., chief fin. officer, asst. sec. Dechert, Price & Rhoads, Phila., 1987-89; v.p. fin., treas., sec. NET Atlantic, Inc., Thorofare, N.J., 1989-92; v.p., contr. AAA Mid-Atlantic, Inc., Phila., 1992—; owner AM Fin. Services, Medford, N.J., 1986—; cons. United Computer Services, Berlin. N.J., 1982—; lectr. in field. Bd. dirs. Forest Hills Civic Assn., Williamstown, N.J., 1976. With USMC, 1969-75. Recipient Michael A. DeAngelis Outstanding Profl. Achievement award, LaSalle U., Phila., 1985. Mem. AICPA, N.J. Soc. CPAs, Pa. Inst. CPAs, Fin. Execs. Inst., Nat. Assn. Accts. Roman Catholic. Avocations: skiing, golf. Home: 5 Huntington Cir Medford NJ 08055-3315 Office: AAA Mid Atlantic Inc 2040 Market St Philadelphia PA 19103-3302

MICKS, DON WILFRED, biologist, educator; b. Mt. Vernon, N.Y., Nov. 23, 1918; s. Wilfred Wallace and Bernice (Barbour) M.; m. Martha Millican, Feb. 15, 1944; children—Donald Frederick, Stephen Alan, Marjorie Ellen, Carol Jeanne. B.S., N. Tex. State U., 1940, M.S., 1942; Sc.D., Johns Hopkins, 1949. Faculty Med. Br. U. Tex., Galveston, 1949-86; prof., chmn. preventive medicine, community health Med. Br. U. Tex., 1966-86; prof. emeritus, 1993—; Scientist-biologist div. Environmental Health, WHO, Geneva, Switzerland, 1958-59; cons. WHO, Pakistan, 1969. Contbr. articles to profl. jours. Chmn. bd. St. Vincent's House, 1969-70; mem. adv. bd. Tex. Air Control Bd. Served to lt. USNR, 1942-45, PTO. Named Disting. Alumnus North Tex. State U., 1970; Fulbright sr. rsch. scholar U. Pavia, Italy, 1953-54; recipient Excellence in Teaching award, 1991; named suite dedication Ewing Hall, Dept. Preventive Medicine and Cmty. Health. Fellow Am. Pub. Health Assn., Royal Soc. Tropical Medicine and Hygiene, AAAS; mem. Assn. Tchrs. Preventive Medicine, Soc. Exptl. Biology and Medicine, Am. Soc. Tropical Medicine and Hygiene, Internat. Soc. Toxinology, Entomol. Soc. Am., Am. Mosquito Control Assn., Sigma Xi. Episcopalian (vestryman 1968-70, 74-76).

MICOZZI, MARC STEPHEN, health executive, physician, educator; b. Norfolk, Va., Oct. 27, 1953; s. Edio Dominic and Huguette (Picon) M.; m. Carole Ann O'Leary, Oct. 8, 1982; 1 child, Alicia Madeleine. Cadet, USAF Acad., 1971-72; BA, Pomona Coll., 1974; MD, U. Pa., 1979, PhD, 1986. Diplomate Am. Bd. Pathology. Rsch. fellow City of Hope Nat. Med. Ctr., Duarte, Calif., 1973; chem. engr. Gould Corp., El Monte, Calif., 1974; Luce Found. scholar Mindanao, The Philippines, 1976-77; clin. applications chemist McDonnell-Douglas Corp., Pasadena, Calif., 1978; postdoctoral fellow Allied Inst. Environ. Health, Princeton, N.J., 1979; resident in pathology Pa. Hosp., Phila., 1980-83; med. examiner Dade County Med. Examiner's Office, Miami, Fla., 1983-84; sr. investigator Nat. Cancer Inst., Bethesda, Md., 1984-86; dir. Nat. Mus. Health and Medicine, Washington, 1986-95; exec. dir. Coll. Physicians' of Phila., 1995—; adj. prof. Uniformed Svcs. U. Health Scis., Bethesda, 1986-95, U. Pa. Sch. Medicine, 1996—; vis. lectr. Georgetown U. Sch. Medicine, Washington, 1986—, Johns Hopkins U. Sch. Medicine, Balt., 1988—; adj. prof. dept. phys. medicine U. Pa., 1996—. Editor: Nutrition and Cancer, 1989; assoc. editor Health Care, Jour. Human Orgn., 1983-89; contbr. chpts. to books and numerous articles to profl. jours. Del. White House Conf. on Youth, Estes Park, Colo., 1971, UN Conf. on Human Environ., Stockholm, 1972, NATO Advanced Study Inst., Brussels, 1982; mem. Calif. Gov.'s Adv. Com., 1972-74. Fellow Human Biology coun., Soc. for Applied Anthropology, Am. Anthrop. Assn.; Am. Acad. Forensic Scis., Am. Pub. Health Assn., N.Y. Acad. Scis. Roman Catholic. Office: Coll Physicians 19 S 22nd St Philadelphia PA 19103

MICZEK, KLAUS ALEXANDER, psychology educator; b. Burghausen, Bavaria, Germany, Sept. 28, 1944; came to U.S., 1967; s. Erich and Irene (Wirthl) M.; m. Christiane Baerwaldt, Aug. 8, 1970; 1 child, Nikolai A. Tchrs. cert., Paedagogische Hochschule, Berlin, 1966; PhD, U. Chgo., 1972. Asst. prof. Carnegie-Mellon U., Pitts., 1972-74, assoc. prof., 1974-79; assoc. prof. Tufts U., Medford, Mass., 1979-83, prof., 1983-93, Moses Hunt prof. psychiatry, psychology, pharmacology, 1993—; cons. Duphar v.b., Weesp, The Netherlands, 1984—, Nat. Inst. Drug Abuse, Rockville, Md., 1984—; Boerhaave prof. U. Leiden, The Netherlands, 1987; mem. panel on violence, NAS, 1989-92. Editor: Ethopharmacology, 1983, Ethopharmacological Aggression Research, 1984; field editor, coord. editor Behavioral Pharmacology, Jour. Psychopharmacology; contbr. articles on psychopharmacology, 1973—. Rsch. grantee Nat. Inst. Drug Abuse, 1973—, Nat. Inst. Alcoholism and Alcohol Abuse, 1981—; recipient Solvay-Duphar award APA, 1993. Fellow Am. Psychol. Assn. (program chmn. 1981, pres. div. psychopharmacology 1990-91), Behavioral Pharmacological Soc. (pres. 1992-94), Internat. Soc. for Rsch. on Aggression (councilor 1987); mem. Soc. Neurosci., N.Y. Acad. Scis., Internat. Primatol. Soc. Office: Tufts U Dept Psychology 490 Boston Ave Medford MA 02155-5532

MIDANEK, DEBORAH HICKS, portfolio manager, director; b. N.Y.C., Nov. 30, 1954; d. Frederick Stevens and Mary Leavenworth (Barnes) H.; m. James Ira Midanek, Sept. 29, 1985; children: Benjamin Abraham, Thomas Hicks. AB, Bryn Mawr Coll., 1975; MBA, U. Pa., 1980. Asst. dir. admissions Bryn Mawr (Pa.) Coll., 1975-78; asst. v.p. Bankers Trust, N.Y.C., 1980-84; v.p. Drexel Burnham Lambert, N.Y.C., 1984-90; CEO Solon Asset Mgmt. Corp., 1990—; mng. dir. mutual funds Montgomery Asset Mgmt., San Francisco, 1992-93; bd. dirs. Drexel Burnham Lambert Group, 1990-92, Std. Brands Paint Co., chmn. compensation com., 1993—, chmn. of the bd., 1995—. Trustee, treas. New St. Found., 1992-94; bd. dirs. Pelham (N.Y.) Art Ctr., 1989-91, Mgmt. Decision Lab. Stern Sch. Bus., NYU, 1990-93, United Way of Pelham, 1990-93; mem. exec. bd. exploring divsn. Greater N.Y. coun. Boy Scouts Am., 1991-93; trustee Warren Wilson Coll., Asheville, N.C., 1993—. Mem. N.Y. Soc. Securities Analysts, Bryn Mawr Coll. Club of N.Y. (pres. 1991-93), Econ. Club of N.Y. Republican. Home: 375 La Casa Via Walnut Creek CA 94598-4842 Office: Solon Asst Mgmt LP 1981 N Broadway Ste 325 Walnut Creek CA 94596-3852

MIDDAUGH, ROBERT BURTON, artist; b. Chgo., May 12, 1935; s. John Burton and Mae Knight (Crooks) M. Student, U. Chgo., 1960-64; BFA, Art Inst. Chgo., 1964. curator art collection 1st Nat. Bank Chgo., 1971-83. Designed, executed ednl. display, Prehistoric Project at Oriental Inst. of U. Chgo., 1968; One-man shows include, Kovler Gallery, Chgo., 1965, 67, 69, Martin Schweig Gallery, St. Louis, 1970, 72, 79, 83, U. Wis., 1976, 81, 82, Fairweather Hardin Gallery, Chgo., 1977, 80, 83, 85, Rockford Art Mus., 1987, Zaks Gallery, Chgo., 1992, 93; group shows, including, Art Inst. Chgo., 1964, 66, 78, 79, Evanston (Ill.) Art Center, 1966, Joslyn Art Mus., Omaha, 1968, U. Notre Dame, 1969, Va. Mus. Fine Arts, Richmond, 1966; represented in permanent collections, Art Inst. Chgo., Boston Mus. Fine Arts, Fine Art Mus. of South, Mobile, Ala., Los Angeles County Mus., Phoenix Art Mus., Worcester (Mass.) Art Mus., Ill. State Mus., Springfield. Served with U.S. Army, 1958-60. Mem. Arts Club Chgo.

MIDDELKAMP, JOHN NEAL, pediatrician, educator; b. Kansas City, Mo., Sept. 29, 1925; s. George H. and Clara M. (Ordelheide) M.; m. Roberta Gill, Oct. 3, 1949 (div. 1970); children—Sharon Ann, Steven Neal, Susan Jean, Scott Alan; m. Lois Harper, Mar. 1, 1974. B.S., U. Mo., 1946; M.D., Washington U., St. Louis, 1948. Diplomate Am. Bd. Pediatrics. Intern D.C. Gen. Hosp., Washington, 1948-49; resident St. Louis Children's Hosp., 1949-50, 52-53; instr. pediatrics Washington U., 1953-57, asst. prof. pediatrics, 1957-64, assoc. prof., 1964-70, prof., 1970—; dir. ambulatory pediatrics St. Louis Children's Hosp., 1974-91. Author: Camp Health Manual, 1984; contbr. articles, chpts. to profl. publs. Served to comdr. M.C., USNR, 1943-66. NIH postdoctoral fellow, 1961-62. Mem. Am. Acad. Pediatrics, Am. Soc. Microbiology, Infectious Diseases Soc. Am., Am. Pediatric Soc., Ambulatory Pediatric Assn., Sigma Xi, Alpha Omega Alpha. Home: 8845 Paragon Cir Saint Louis MO 63123-1114 Office: 1 Childrens Pl Saint Louis MO 63110

MIDDENDORF, JOHN HARLAN, English literature educator; b. N.Y.C., Mar. 31, 1922; s. George Arlington and Margaret (Hofmann) M.; m. Beverly Bruner, July 14, 1943 (dec. 1983); children: Cathie Jean Middendorf Hamilton, Peggy Ruth Middendorf Brindisi; m. Maureen L. MacGrogan, Jan. 31, 1986. AB, Dartmouth Coll., 1943; AM, Columbia U., 1947, PhD, 1953. Lectr. English CCNY, 1946, Hunter Coll., 1946-49; faculty Columbia, 1947—, prof. English, 1965-89, prof. emeritus, 1990—, dir. grad. studies, 1971-74, vice-chmn., 1976-80; chmn. English test com. Coll. Entrance Exam. Bd., 1967-69. Contbr. articles, revs. to profl. jours.; Editor: English Writers of the Eighteenth Century, 1971; asst. editor: Johnsonian News Letter, 1950-58; co-editor, 1958-78, editor, 1978-90; asso. editor: Yale edit. Works Samuel Johnson, 1962-66; gen. editor, 1966—. Served to lt. (j.g.) USNR, 1943-46. Faculty fellow Fund Advancement Edn., 1951-52; grantee Coun. Rsch. Humanities, 1958-59, Am. Philos. Soc., 1962, Am. Coun. Learned Socs., 1962, NEH, 1976-88. Mem. Johnsonians (sec.-treas. 1958-68, chmn. 1969, 79), Univ. Seminar on 18th Century European Culture (chmn. 1973-75, 85-87), Oxford Bibliog. Soc., Grolier Club, English Inst. (mem. supervisory com. 1963-66), Modern Lang. Assn., Conf. Brit. Studies, Soc. Textual Scholarship (adv. bd.), Am. Soc. 18th Century Studies, Phi Beta Kappa. Home: 404 Riverside Dr New York NY 10025-1861 Office: Columbia U Dept English New York NY 10027

MIDDENDORF, WILLIAM HENRY, electrical engineering educator; b. Cin., Mar. 23, 1921; s. William J. and Mary J. (Frommeyer) M.; m. Evelyn B. Taylor, Nov. 20, 1946; children—Judith A., Mark E., Jeffrey W., Craig A., Susan A. B. Elec. Engring., U. Va., 1946; M.S., U. Cin., 1948; Ph.D., Ohio State U., 1960. Mem. faculty U. Cin., 1948-91, prof. elec. engring., 1960-91, assoc. head. dept., 1986-91; prof. emeritus, 1991—; with Wadsworth Elec. Mfg. Co., Covington, Ky., 1966-90, dir. engring. and research, 1966-86, sr. cons., 1986-90; dir. research Cin. Devel. and Mfg. Inc., 1960-66. Author: Electric Circuit Analysis, 1956, Introductory Network Analysis, 1966, Engineering Design, 1969; author: Invention, 1981, Design of Devices and Systems, 1986, 2d edit., 1990; co-author: Product Liability, 1979; editor book series: Marcel Dekker, Inc. (85 vols.), Continuing Edn. Series (30 vols.); contbr. to profl. publs.; holder 27 patents. Trustee St. Elizabeth Hosp., Covington, 1967-83, pres. bd., 1977-80. With USNR, 1943-46. Recipient Herman Schneider award Tech. Socs. of Cin., 1978, U. Cin. Public Service award, 1981, Rieveschl award for scholarly and creative works U. Cin., 1989; NSF fellow, 1958-59. Fellow IEEE (life); mem. Am. Soc. Engring. Edn. Home: 1941 Provincial Ln Covington KY 41011-1816

MIDDLEBROOK, DIANE WOOD, English language educator; b. Pocatello, Idaho, Apr. 16, 1939; d. Thomas Isaac and Helen Loretta (Downey) Wood; m. Jonathan Middlebrook, June 15, 1963 (div. 1972); 1 child, Leah Wood Middlebrook; m. Carl Djerassi, June 21, 1985. BA, U. Wash., 1961; MA, Yale U., 1962, PhD, 1968. Asst. prof. Stanford (Calif.) U., 1966-73, assoc. prof., 1973-83, prof., 1983—, D, dir. Ctr. for Rsch. on Women, 1977-79. Author: Walt Whitman and Wallace Stevens, 1974, Worlds into Words: Understanding Modern Poems, 1980, Anne Sexton, A Biography, 1991, (poems) Gin Considered as a Demon, 1983; editor: Coming to Light: American Women Poets in the Twentieth Century, 1985. Founding trustee Djerassi Resident Artists Program, Woodside, Calif., 1980-83, chair, 1994; trustee San Francisco Art Inst., 1993. Ind. study fellow NEH, 1982-83, Bunting Inst. fellow Radcliffe Coll., 1982-83, Guggenheim Found. fellow, 1988-89, Rockefeller Study Ctr. fellow, 1990; recipient Yale Prize for Poetry; finalist Nat. Book award, 1991. Mem. MLA. Avocations: collecting art, theater. Home: 1101 Green St Apt 1501 San Francisco CA 94109-2016 Office: Stanford U Dept English Stanford CA 94305-2087

MIDDLEBROOK, ROBERT DAVID, electronics educator; b. England, May 16, 1929. BA, Cambridge U., England, 1952, MA, 1956; MS, Stanford U., 1953, PhD in Elec. Engring., 1955. Sr. tech. instr., mem. trade testing bd. Radio Sch. No. 3, Royal Air Force, Eng., 1947-49; asst. prof. electrical engring. Calif. Inst. Tech., Pasadena, 1955-58; assoc. prof. Calif. Inst. Tech., Pasedena, 1958-65, prof. electronics, 1965—; mem. hon. editorial adv. bd. Solid State Electronics, 1960-74; mem. WESCON tech. program com., 1964; lectr. 23 univs. and cos. in Eng., The Netherlands, Germany, 1965-66; mem. rsch. and tech. adv. coun. com. on space propulsion and power, NASA, 1976-77; gen. chmn. Calif. Inst. Tech. Indsl. Assocs. Conf. Power Electronics, 1982; cons. in field. Author: An Introduction to Transistor Theory, 1957, Differential Amplifiers, 1963, (with S. Cuk) Advances in Switched-Mode Power Conversion, Vols. I and II, 1981, 2d edit., 1983, Vol. III, 1983; mem. editorial bd. Internat. Jour. Electronics, 1976-82; presented 77 profl. papers; patentee in field. Recipient Nat. Profl. Group Indsl. Engrs. award, 1958, Indsl Rsch. 100 award Indsl. Rsch. Mag., 1980, award for the Best Use of Graphics Powercon 7, 1980, Powercon 8, 1981, William E. Newell Power Electronics award Inst. Elec. & Electronics Engrs., 1982, PCIM award for Leadership in Power Electronics Edn., 1990, Edward Longstreth Medal Franklin Inst., 1991. Fellow IEEE (exec. com. San Gabriel Valley sect. 1964-65, treas. 1977-78, gen. chmn. power electronics specialists conf. 1973, AES-S elec. power/energy systems panel 1977-87, program chmn. applied electronics conf. 1986, 87), Instn. Elec. Engrs. (Eng.); mem. Sigma Xi. Achievements include research in new solid state devices, their development, representation and application; electronics education (design-oriented analysis techniques); power conversion and control. Office: Calif Inst Tech 136-93 Engring Applied Sci Pasadena CA 91125

MIDDLEBROOK, STEPHEN BEACH, lawyer. BA, Yale U., 1958, LLB, 1961. Bar: Conn. 1961. Counsel Aetna Life and Casualty Co., Hartford, Conn., 1969-71, asst. gen. counsel, 1971-78, corp. sec., 1973-83, v.p., gen. counsel, 1981-88, sr. v.p., gen. counsel, 1988-90, sr. v.p., exec. counsel, 1990-94; spl. counsel Day, Berry & Howard, Hartford, 1995—; vis. fellow Rand, Santa Monica, Calif., 1994, cons., 1995—. Office: Day Berry & Howard City Place I Hartford CT 06103-3499

MIDDLEBROOKS, EDDIE JOE, environmental engineer; b. Crawford County, Ga., Oct. 16, 1932; s. Robert Harold and Jewell LaVerne (Dixon) M.; m. Charlotte Linda Hardy, Dec. 6, 1958; 1 child, Linda Tracey. B.C.E., U. Fla., 1956, M.S., 1960; Ph.D., Miss. State U., 1966. Diplomate: Am. Acad. Environmental Engrs.; registered profl. engr., Ariz., Miss., Utah; registered land surveyor, Fla. Asst. san. engr. USPHS, Cin., 1956-58; field engr. T.T. Jones Constrn. Co., Atlanta, 1958-59; grad. teaching asst. U. Fla., 1959-60; research asst. U. Ariz., 1960-61; asst. prof., assoc. prof. Miss. State U., 1962-67; research engr., asst. dir. San. Engring. Research Lab., U. Calif.-Berkeley, 1968-70; prof. Utah State U., Logan, 1970-82, dean Coll. Engring., 1974-82; Newman chair natural resources engring. Clemson U., 1982-83; provost, v.p. acad. affairs Tenn. Tech. U., 1983-88; provost, v.p. acad. affairs U. Tulsa, 1988-90, prof. chem. engring., 1988-92, Trustees prof. chem. engring., 1990-92, acting pres., 1990; prof. civil engring. U. Nevada, Reno, 1992—; mem. nat. drinking water adv. council EPA, 1981-83; cons. EPA, UN Indsl. Devel. Orgn., Calif. Water Resources Control Bd., also numerous indsl. and engring. firms. Author: Modeling the Eutrophication Process, 1974, Statistical Calculations-How To Solve Statistical Problems, 1976, Biostimulation and Nutrient Assessment, 1976, Water Supply Engineering Design, 1977, Lagoon Information Source Book, 1978, Industrial Pollution Control, Vol. 1: Agro-Industries, 1979, Wastewater Collection and Treatment: Principles and Practices, 1979, Water Reuse, 1982, Wastewater Stabilization Lagoon Design, Performance and Upgrading, 1982, Reverse Osmosis Treatment of Drinking Water, 1986, Pollution Control in the Petrochemicals Industry, 1987, Natural Systems for Waste Management and Treatment, 1988, 2d edit., 1995; mem. editl. adv. bd. Lewis Pubs. Inc., Environment Internat., Environ. Abstracts; contbr. tech. articles to profl. jours. Fellow ASCE; mem. AAAS, Water Environment Fedn. (dir. 1979-81, 91-92), Eddy medal 1969), Assn. Environ. Engring. Profs. (pres. 1974), Utah Water Pollution Control Assn. (pres. 1976), Internat. Assn. on Water Quality, Am. Soc. Engring. Edn., Am. Acad. Environ. Engrs. (trustee 1992-95, v.p. 1995), Sigma Xi, Omicron Delta Kappa, Phi Kappa Phi (Disting. mem.), Tau Beta Pi, Sigma Tau. Home: 3855 Skyline Blvd Reno NV 89509-5661 Office: U Nevada Dept Civil Engring Reno NV 89557

MIDDLEDITCH, BRIAN STANLEY, biochemistry educator; b. Bury St. Edmunds, Suffolk, Eng., July 15, 1945; came to U.S., 1971; s. Stanley Stafford and Dorothy (Harker) M.; m. Patricia Rosalind Nair, July 18, 1970; 1 child, Courtney Lauren. BSc, U. London, 1966; MSc, U. Essex, 1967; PhD U. Glasgow, 1971. Rsch. asst. U. Glasgow, Scotland, 1967-71; vis. asst. prof. Baylor Coll. Medicine, Houston, 1971-75; asst. prof. U. Houston, 1975-80, assoc. prof., 1980-89, prof., 1989—; hon. prof. Eurotechnical Rsch. U. Author: Mass Spectrometry of Priority Pollutants, 1981, Analytical Artifacts, 1989, Kuwaiti Plants, 1991; editor: Practical Mass Spectrometry, 1979, Environmental Effects of Offshore Oil Production, 1981. Grantee Nat. Marine Fisheries Service 1976-80, Sea Grant Program, 1977-81, NASA, 1980-90, IBM, 1985-88, NIH, 1988—, Tex. Advanced Rsch. Program, 1988—, Nat. Dairy Coun., 1991—. Mem. Am. Chem. Soc., Am. Soc. Mass Spectrometry, World Mariculture Soc. Home: 4101 Emory St Houston TX 77005-1920 Office: U Houston Dept Biochemistry Houston TX 77204

MIDDLEDITCH, LEIGH BENJAMIN, JR., lawyer, educator; b. Detroit, Sept. 30, 1929; s. Leigh Benjamin and Hope Tiffin (Noble) M.; m. Betty Lou Givens, June 27, 1953; children: Leigh III, Katherine Middleditch McDonald, Andrew B. BA, U. Va., 1951, LLB, 1957. Bar: Va. 1957. Assoc. James H. Michael, Jr., Charlottesville, Va., 1957-59; ptnr. Battle, Neal, Harris, Minor & Williams, Charlottesville, 1959-68; legal adviser U. Va., Charlottesville, 1968-72; ptnr. McGuire, Woods, Battle & Boothe, Charlottesville, 1972—; lectr. Grad. Bus. Sch., U. Va., Charlottesville, 1958—, lectr. Law Sch., 1970-90. Co-author: Virginia Civil Procedure, 1978, 2d edition, 1992; contbr. articles to profl. jours. Pres. Ellen Bayard Weedon Found., 1984—; chmn. U. Va. Health Svcs. Found., 1988—; bd. mgrs. U. Va. Alumni, 1994—; bd. dirs. Va. Health Care Found., 1992—; trustee Claude Moore Found., 1991—; mem. Va. Health Planning Bd., 1989—; bd. visitors U. Va., 1990-91; trustee Thomas Jefferson Meml. Found., Monticello, 1994—. Fellow Am. Bar Found., Va. Bar Found., Am. Coll. Tax Counsel; mem. ABA, Va. State Bar (coun., chmn. bd. govs. various sects.), Charlottesville-Albemarle Bar Assn. (pres. 1979-80), U. Va. Law Sch. Alumni Assn. (pres. 1979-81), Va. C. of C., Omicron Delta Kappa. Episcopalian. Office: McGuire Woods Battle & Boothe PO Box 1288 Charlottesville VA 22902-1288

MIDDLEKAUFF, ROBERT LAWRENCE, history educator, administrator; b. Yakima, Wash., July 5, 1929; s. Harold and Katherine Ruth (Horne) M.; m. Beverly Jo Martin, July 11, 1952; children: Samuel John, Holly Ruth. B.A., U. Wash., 1952; Ph.D., Yale U., 1961. Instr. history Yale U., New Haven, Conn., 1959-62; asst. prof. history U. Calif.-Berkeley, 1962-66, assoc. prof., 1966-70, prof., 1970-80, Margaret Byrne prof. history, 1980-83; dir. Huntington Library, Art Gallery and Bot. Gardens, San Marino, Calif., 1983-88; prof. history U. Calif., Berkeley, 1988-92, Preston Hotchkiss prof., 1992—; mem. council Inst. Early Am. History and Culture, Williamsburg, Va., 1974-76, 85-88. Author: Ancients and Axioms, 1963, The Mathers, 1971, The Glorious Cause: The American Revolution, 1763-1789, 1982. Served to 1st lt. USMC, 1952-54, Korea. Recipient Bancroft prize, 1972; recipient Commonwealth Club Gold medal, 1983; fellow Am. Council Learned Socs., 1965, NEH, 1973, Huntington Library, 1977. Fellow Am. Acad. Arts and Scis.; mem. Am. Hist. Assn., Orgn. Am. Historians, Soc. Am. Historians, Am. Antiquarian Soc., Assocs. Early Am. History and Culture (mem. exec. com.), Colonial Soc. Mass. (corr.). Home: 5868 Ocean View Dr Oakland CA 94618-1535 Office: Univ Calif Dept History Berkeley CA 94720

MIDDLETON, ANTHONY WAYNE, JR., urologist, educator; b. Salt Lake City, May 6, 1939; s. Anthony Wayne and Dolores Caravena (Lowry) M.; m. Carol Samuelson, Oct. 23, 1970; children: Anthony Wayne, Suzanne, Kathryn, Jane, Michelle. BS, U. Utah, 1963; MD, Cornell U., 1966. Intern, U. Utah Hosps., Salt Lake City, 1966-67; resident in urology Mass. Gen. Hosp., Boston, 1970-74; practice urology Middleton Urol. Assos., Salt Lake City, 1974—; mem. staff Primary Children's Hosp., staff pres., 1981-82; mem. staff Latter-Day Saints Hosp., Salt Lake Regional Med. Ctr.; assoc. clin. prof. surgery U. Utah Med. Coll., 1977—; vice chmn. bd. govs. Utah Med. Self-Ins. Assn., 1980-81, chmn. 1985-87; med. dir. Uroquest Co., 1996—. Bd. dirs. Utah chpt. Am. Cancer Soc., 1978-86; bishop, later stake presidency Ch. Jesus Christ Latter-day Saints; vice chmn. Utah Med. Polit. Action Com., 1978-81, chmn., 1981-83; chmn. Utah Physicians for Reagan, 1983-84; mem. U. Utah Coll. Medicine Dean's Search Com., 1983-84; bd. dirs. Utah Symphony, 1985—, Primary Children's Found., 1989—. Capt. USAF, 1968-70. Editor (monthly pub.) AACU-FAX, 1992—, Millenial Star Brit. LDS mag. 1960-61. Mem. ACS, Utah State Med. Assn. (pres. 87-88, disting. svc. award 1993), Am. Urologic Assn. (socioecons. com. 1987—, chmn. western sect. socioecons. com. 1989—, western. sect. health policy com. chmn., 1990—), AMA (alt. del. to House of Dels. 1989-92, 94, 96—), Salt Lake County Med. Assn. (sec. 1965-67, pres. liaison com. 1980-81, pres.-elect 1981-83, pres. 1984), Utah Urol. Assn. (pres. 1976-77), Salt Lake Surg. Soc. (treas. 1977-78), Am. Assn. Clin. Urologists (bd. dirs. 1989-90, nat. pres. elect 1990-91, pres. 1991-92, nat. bd. chmn. urologic polit. action com.

UROPAC, 1992—), Phi Beta Kappa, Alpha Omega Alpha, Beta Theta Pi (chpt. pres. Gamma Beta 1962). Republican. Contbr. articles to profl. jours. Home: 2798 Chancellor Pl Salt Lake City UT 84108-2835 Office: 1060 E 1st St Salt Lake City UT 84102-4147

MIDDLETON, CHARLES RONALD, history educator; b. Hays, Kans., Sept. 16, 1944; s. Charles Buster and Dorothy Bryant (Parsons) M.; m. Sandra Leigh Paulson, Dec. 19, 1964 (dec. 1986); children: Charles Christopher, Kevin Andrew, Kathryn Gillian. AB with honors, Fla. State U., 1965; MA, Duke U., 1967, PhD, 1969. Asst. prof. U. Colo., Boulder, 1969-77, assoc. prof., 1977-85, asst. dean, 1979-80, prof. history, 1985—, assoc. dean Coll. Arts and Scis., 1980-88, dean Coll. Arts and Scis., 1988-96; v.p. acad. affairs Bowling Green (Ohio) State U., 1996—. Contbr. articles to profl. jours. Bd. dirs. Found. for World Health, Denver and Boulder, 1985-87, Boulder County AIDS Project (hon.), 1990—, The Consenting Adults Theatre Co., Washington, 1992—. Recipient Faculty Teaching Excellence award U. Colo., Boulder, 1978; research grantee Am. Philos. Soc., 1977, U. Colo., 1972. Fellow Royal Hist. Soc.; mem. N.Am. Conf. on Brit. Studies, Western Conf. on Brit. Studies (pres.-elect 1985-86, pres. 1986-87), Western Humanities Conf. (bd. dirs. 1990-95), Am. Hist. Assn. (mem. com. gay and lesbian history), Am. Com. for Irish Studies, Brit. Politics Group, So. Conf. on Brit. Studies, Rotary, Coun. of Colls. and Arts and Scis. (bd. dirs. 1993—), Phi Beta Kappa, Phi Eta Sigma. Democrat. Avocations: fishing, cooking, travel, cycling. Office: Bowling Green State U 230 McFee Ctr Bowling Green OH 43403

MIDDLETON, CHRISTOPHER, Germanic languages and literature educator; b. Truro, Cornwall, Eng., June 10, 1926; came to U.S., 1966; s. Hubert Stanley and Dorothy May (Miller) M. BA, U. of Oxford, Eng., 1951, PhD, 1954. Lectr. King's Coll., London, 1955-65; prof. Germanic langs. and lit. U. Tex., Austin, 1966—. Author: Selected Writings, 1989, Andalusian Poems, 1993, The Balcony Tree, 1992, Intimate Chronicles, 1996. Recipient trans. prize Schlegel-Tieck/Govt. Fed. Republic Germany, 1985, Anglo-Swiss Cultural Rels. prize Max Geilinger Stiftung, Zurich, Switzerland, 1987; Guggenheim Found. poetry fellow, 1974-75, NEA poetry fellow, 1980. Mem. Akademie der Künste Berlin. Office: U Tex Dept Of Germanic Langs Austin TX 78712

MIDDLETON, DAVID, physicist, applied mathematician, educator; b. N.Y.C., Apr. 19, 1920; s. Charles Davies Scudder and Lucile (Davidson) M.; m. Nadea Butler, May 26, 1945 (div. 1971); children: Susan Terry, Leslie Butler, David Scudder Blakeslee, George Davidson Powell; m. Joan Bartlett Reed, 1971; children: Christopher Hope, Andrew Bartlett, Henry H. Reed. Grad., Deerfield Acad., 1938; AB summa cum laude, Harvard U., 1942, AM, 1945, PhD in Physics, 1947. Teaching fellow electronics Harvard U., Cambridge, Mass., 1942, spl. rsch. assoc., Radio Rsch. Lab., 1942-45, NSF predoctoral fellow physics, 1945-47, rsch. fellow electronics, 1947-49, asst. prof. applied physics, 1949-54; cons. physicist Cambridge, 1954—, Concord, Mass., 1957-71, N.Y.C., 1971—; adj. prof. elec. engring. Columbia U., 1960-61; adj. prof. applied physics and communication theory Rensselaer Poly. Inst., Hartford Grad. Ctr., 1961-70; adj. prof. communication theory U. R.I., 1966—; adj. prof. math. scis. Rice U., 1979-89; U.S. del. internat. conf. Internat. Radio Union, Lima, Peru, 1975; lectr. NATO Advanced Study Inst., Grenoble, France, 1964, Copenhagen, 1990, Luneburg, Germany, 1984; mem. Naval Rsch. Adv. Com., 1970-77; mem., cons. Inst. Def. Analyses; mem. sci. adv. bd. Supercomputing Rsch. Ctr., 1987-91; cons. physicist since 1946, orgns. including Johns Hopkins U., SRI Internat., Rand Corp., USAF, Cambridge Rsch. Ctr., Comm. Satellite Corp., Lincoln Lab., NASA, Raytheon, Sylvania, Sperry-Rand, Office Naval Rsch., Applied Rsch. Labs., U. Tex., GE, Honeywell Transp. Sys. Ctr. of Dept. Transp., Dept. Commerce Office of Telecom., NOAA, Office Telecom. Policy of Exec. Office Pres., Nat. Telecom. and Info. Adminstrn., Sci. Applications Inc., Naval Undersea Warfare Ctr., Lawrence Livermore Nat. Labs., Planning Rsch. Corp., Applied Physics Labs. U. Wash., 1992—, Kildare Corp., 1995—, others. Author: Introduction of Statistical Communication Theory, 1960, 3d edit., 1996, Russian edit. Soviet Radio Moscow, 2 vols., 1961, 62, Topics in Communication Theory, 1965, 87, Russian edit., 1966; sci. editor English edit. Statistical Methods in Sonar (V.V. Ol'shevskii), 1978; mem. editl. bd. Info. and Control, Advanced Serials in Electronics and Cybernetics, 1972-82; contbr. articles to tech. jours. Recipient award (with W.H. Huggins) Nat. Electronics Conf., 1956; Wisdom award of honor, 1970; First prize 3d Internat. Symposium on Electromagnetic Compatibility Rotterdam, Holland, 1979; awards U.S. Dept. Commerce, 1978. Fellow AAAS, IEEE (life, awards 1977, 79), Am. Phys. Soc., Explorers Club, Acoustical Soc. Am., N.Y. Acad. Scis.; mem. Am. Math. Soc., Author's Guild Am., Electromagnetics Acad. MIT, Harvard Club (N.Y.C.), Cosmos Club (Washington), Dutch Treat (N.Y.C.), Phi Beta Kappa, Sigma Xi. Achievements include research in radar, telecommunications, underwater acoustics, oceanography, seismology, systems analysis, electromagnetic compatibility, communication theory; pioneering research in statistical communication theory. Home and Office: 127 E 91st St New York NY 10128-1601 Also: MIND 48 Garden St Cambridge MA 02138-1561 Also: 13 Harbor Rd Harwich Port MA 02646-2409

MIDDLETON, DAWN E., education educator; b. Pottstown, Pa.; d. William H. and Sara G. Bowman; m. Stephen R. Mourar, June 1983; children: William Middleton, Shelly Mourar. AA in Early Childhood Edn., Montgomery Community Coll., 1972; BS in Elem. Edn., West Chester State Coll., 1974; MA in Edn. Curriculum and Instrn. Edn., Pa. State U., 1982, DEd, 1984. Instr. Continuing Edn. Pa. State U., University Park; dir. specialized early childhood programs and svcs. Wiley House, Bethlehem, Pa.; dir. Children's Sch. of Cabrini Coll., Radnor, Pa.; dept. chmn., assoc. prof. edn. Cabrini Coll., Radnor. Home: 208 Bethel Rd Spring City PA 19475-3200

MIDDLETON, ELLIOTT, JR., physician; b. Glen Ridge, N.J., Dec. 15, 1925; s. Elliott and Dorothy (Thoman) M.; m. Elizabeth Blackford, Sept. 25, 1948; children: Elliott III, Ellen Alice, Blackford, James Jay. A.B., Princeton U., 1947; M.D., Columbia U., 1950. Diplomate: Am. Bd. Internal Medicine, Am. Bd. Allergy and Immunology. Intern Presbyn. Hosp., N.Y.C., 1950-51; resident in medicine Presbyn. Hosp., 1951-52; asst. in medicine immunochem. lab. Coll. Physicians and Surgeons, Columbia U., 1952-53; clin. assoc. Nat. Heart Inst., 1953-55; fellow in allergy R.A. Cooke Inst. Allergy, Roosevelt Hosp., N.Y.C., 1955-56; practice medicine Montclair, N.J., 1956-69; dir. clin. services and research Children's Asthma Research Inst. and Hosp., Denver, 1969-76; assoc. clin. prof. medicine U. Colo., 1969-76; prof. medicine and pediatrics, dir. allergy div. Sch. Medicine, SUNY, Buffalo, 1976-92; emeritus prof. medicine SUNY, Buffalo, 1995; hon. staff physician Buffalo Gen. Hosp.; prof. medicine emeritus, 1995. Editor-in-chief Allergy: Principles and Practice, 1978, 4th edit., 1993; editor Jour. Allergy and Clin. Immunology, 1983-88; contbr. numerous articles to jours. chpts. to books. Served with M.C. USNR, 1944-50; Served with M.C. USPHS, 1950-55. Fellow Am. Acad. Allergy and Immunology (pres. 1972, Disting. Svc. award 1991), Am. Coll. Physicians; mem. AAAS, Am. Assn. Immunologists. Episcopalian. Home: RR 1 Box 596 Chebeague Island ME 04017 Office: Buffalo Gen Hosp 100 High St Buffalo NY 14203-1126

MIDDLETON, GEORGE, JR., clinical child psychologist; b. Houston, Feb. 26, 1923; s. George and Bettie (McCrary) M.; m. Margaret MacLean, Nov. 17, 1953. BA in Psychology, Birmingham-Southern Coll., 1948; MA in Psychology, U. Ala., Tuscaloosa, 1951; PhD in Clin. Psychology, Pa. State U., 1958. Lic. psychologist, La. Asst. clin. psychology Med. Coll. Ala., Birmingham, 1950-52; dir. dept. psychology Bryce Hosp., Tuscaloosa, 1952-54; instr. counseling Coll. Bus. Adminstrn. Pa. State U., 1956-58; asst. prof. spl. edn. McNeese State U., 1962-65, assoc. prof. spl. edn., 1962-65; dir. La. Gov.'s Program for Gifted Children, 1963—; prof. spl. edn. McNeese State U., 1965-73, prof. psychology, 1973-74; pvt. practice clin. psychology and neuropsychology, 1974—; cons. psychologist Calcasieu Parish Sch. Bd., 1975—; cons. Charter Hosp. Adolescent Psychiat. Unit, dir. psychol. svcs., 1990-95. Mem. Am. Psychol. Assn., Nat. Acad. Neuropsychology, Internat. Neuropsychol. Soc., La. Psychol. Assn. (pres. 1973-74), La. Sch. Psychol. Assn., S.W. La. Psychol. Assn. (pres. 1965, 73, 84), La. State Bd. Examiners Psychologists (chmn. 1977-78), Coun. for Exceptional Children, Assn. for the Gifted. Episcopalian. Home and Office: 2001 Southwood Dr Ste A Lake Charles LA 70605-4139

MIDDLETON, HARRY JOSEPH, library administrator; b. Centerville, Iowa, Oct. 24, 1921; s. Harry J. and Florence (Beauvais) M.; m. Miriam Miller, Oct. 29, 1949; children—Susan, Deborah, James Miller, Jennifer. Student, Washburn U., 1941-43; B.A., La. State U., 1947. Reporter AP, N.Y.C., 1947-49; news editor Archtl. Forum mag., N.Y.C., 1949-52; writer March of Time, N.Y.C., 1952-54; free lance writer, author, film dir., 1954-66; staff asst. to Pres. Lyndon B. Johnson, Washington, 1966-69; spl. asst. Pres. Lyndon B. Johnson, Austin, Tex., 1969-70; dir. Lyndon Baines Johnson Libr., U. Tex., Austin, 1970—. Author: Compact History of the Korean War, 1965, LBJ: The White House Years, 1990, Lady Bird Johnson: A Life Well-Lived, 1992. Mem. Am. Battle Monuments Commn., 1968—. Served with AUS, 1943-46, 50-52. Mem. Sigma Delta Chi. Home: 2201 Exposition Blvd Austin TX 78703-2209 Office: Lyndon Baines Johnson Libr & Mus 2313 Red River St Austin TX 78705-5702

MIDDLETON, HERMAN DAVID, SR., theater educator; b. Sanford, Fla., Mar. 24, 1925; s. Arthur Herman and Ruby Elmerry (Hart) M.; m. Amelia Mary Eggart, Dec. 1, 1945; children—Herman David, Kathleen Hart. B.S., Columbia U., 1948, M.A., 1949; Ph.D., U. Fla., 1964; postgrad., N.Y. U., 1950, Northwestern U., 1951. Instr., dir. drama and speech Maryville (Tenn.) Coll., 1949-50; instr., designer, tech. dir. theatre U. Del., 1951-55; asst. prof., head dept. drama U. N.C., Greensboro, 1956-59; assoc. prof., head dept. drama and speech U. N.C., 1959-65, prof., head dept., 1965-74, prof., 1974-79, Excellence Fund prof. dept. communication and theatre, 1979-90, prof. emeritus, 1990; designer Chucky Jack, Great Smokey Mountains Hist. Soc., Gatlinburg, Tenn., 1956, designer, dir., 1957; communications cons. N.C. Nat. Bank, 1968, Jefferson Standard Life Ins. Co., Greensboro, N.C., 1969, Gilbarco, Inc., Greensboro, 1969-70, 73. Drama critic, columnist: Sunday Star, Wilmington, Del., 1952; theatre editor: Players Mag, 1959-61; theatre columnist: Sunday editions Greensboro Daily News, 1959-62; contbr. articles to profl. jours. Mem. N.C. Arts Council Commn., 1964-66, Guilford County Bi-Centennial Celebration Commn., 1969-70; pres. Shanks Village Players, Orangeburg, N.Y.C., 1947-48, Univ. Drama Group, Newark, Del., 1954-55; bd. dirs. Broadway Theatre League Greensboro, 1958-60, Greensboro Community Arts Council, 1964-67, 69-72, Greensboro Community Theatre, 1983-86, Carolina Theatre Commn., 1990—; organizer-cons. The Market Players, West Market St. United Meth. Ch., 1979-82. Served with USN, 1943-46. Recipient O. Henry award Greensboro C. of C., 1966, Gold medallion Amoco Oil Co., 1973, Suzanne M. Davis award Southeastern Theatre Conf., 1975, Marian A. Smith Disting. Career award N.C. Theatre Conf., 1990. Mem. Am. Nat. Theatre and Acad. (organizer, exec. v.p. Piedmont chpt. 1957-60), Am. Theatre Assn. (chmn. bd. nominations 1971-72), Am. Coll. Theatre Festival (regional festival dir. 1973, 80, regional dir., mem. nat. com. 1978-80), Assn. for Theatre in Higher Edn. (founding mem. 1986-87), Speech Communication Assn. Am., Nat. Collegiate Players, Southeastern Theatre Conf. (bd. dirs. 1963-68, 87-92, pres. 1965, pres. pro-tem 1966), Carolina Dramatic Assn. (bd. dirs. 1958-59), N.C. Drama and Speech Assn. (pres. 1966-67), N.C. Theatre Conf. (co-organizer 1971, bd. dirs. 1984-92, pres. 1987-88), Assn. for Theater in Higher Edn., Phi Delta Kappa, Phi Kappa Phi, Theta Alpha Phi, Alpha Psi Omega. Democrat. Methodist. Home: 203A Village Ln Greensboro NC 27409-2502

MIDDLETON, JACK BAER, lawyer; b. Phila., Jan. 13, 1929; s. Harry C. and Mildred Cornell (Baer) M.; m. Ann Dodge, Aug. 22, 1953; children: Susan D., Jack B. Jr., Peter C. AB, Lafayette Coll., 1950; JD cum laude, Boston U., 1956. Bar: N.H. 1956, U.S. Dist. Ct. Vt. 1988, U.S. Ct. Appeals (1st cir.) 1957, U.S. Supreme Ct. 1972. Assoc. McLane, Graf, Raulerson & Middleton, Manchester, N.H., 1956-62; ptnr., dir. McLane, Graf, Raulerson & Middleton, Manchester, 1962—; spl. justice Merrimack (N.H.) Dist. Ct., 1964-87; bd. dirs. Greater Manchester Devel. Corp., 1983-95; commr. Uniform State Laws, 1971-74; trustee New Eng. Law Inst., 1977-80. Author: (with others) Summary of New Hampshire Law, 1964, Compendium of New Hampshire Law, 1969, Trial of a Wrongful Death Action in New Hampshire, 1977; editor Boston U. Law Rev., 1954-56; contbr. articles to legal jours. Mem. Mt. Washington Commn., 1969—, Bedford (N.H.) Sch. Bd., 1960-66; mem. adv. bd. Merrimack Valley Coll.; trustee, sec. Mt. Washington Obs., 1957—; chmn. bd. trustees White Mountain Sch., 1976-79; campaign chmn. United Way Greater Manchester, 1987, bd. dirs., 1986-92, chmn., 1990-91; bd. dirs. N.H. Pub. Radio, 1988-91, gov., 1994—; bd. govs. N.H. Pub. TV, 1994—. Sgt. USMCR, 1950-52. Fellow Am. Coll. Trial Lawyers (chmn. N.H. sect. 1988-90), Am. Bar Found. (life); mem. ABA (ho. dels. 1984—, bd. govs. 1996—), New Eng. Bar Assn. (bd. dirs. 1977-88, pres. 1982-83), N.H. Bar Assn., N.H. Bar Found. (bd. dirs. 1979-92, chair 1983-90), Nat. Conf. Bar Found. (trustee 1985-92, pres. 1989-90), Nat. Conf. Bar Pres. (exec. coun. 1987-95, pres. 1993-94), N.H. Bus. and Industry Assn. (bd. dirs. 1988—, sec. 1990—), Manchester C. of C. (bd. dirs. 1967-89, chmn. 1984-85), New Eng. Coun. (bd. dirs. 1991—). Office: McLane Graf Raulerson & Middleton 900 Elm St Manchester NH 03101-2007

MIDDLETON, JAMES ARTHUR, oil and gas company executive; b. Tulsa, Mar. 15, 1936; s. James Arthur and Inez (Matthews) M.; m. Victoria Middleton; children: Robert Arthur, James Daniel, Angela Lynn. B.A., Rice U., 1958, B.S. in Mech. Engring., 1959. With Atlantic Richfield Co., 1959—; design engr. Dallas, 1962-67; tech. planner, 1967-69; mgr. shale devel. Grand Junction, Colo., 1969-72; mgr. engring. dept. Los Angeles, 1972-74; mgr. Prudhoe Bay project Pasadena, Calif., 1974-80; v.p., mgr. corp. planning Los Angeles, 1980-81; pres. ARCO Coal Co., Denver, 1981-82; sr. v.p. ARCO Oil and Gas Co., Dallas, 1982-85, pres., 1985—, sr. v.p. parent co., 1981-87, exec. v.p. parent co., 1987—, also bd. dirs.; bd. dirs. Tex. Utilities Co., Dallas. Corp. rep. Circle Ten coun. Boy Scouts Am.; bd. dirs. L.A. coun. Boy Scouts Am., United Way Met. Dallas, Dallas Coun. on World Affairs, Jr. Achievement So. Calif. 2d lt. C.E., AUS, 1959-60. Recipient ASME Petroleum div. Oil Drop award. Mem. Soc. Petroleum Engrs. of AIME, Tex. Mid-Continent Oil and Gas Assn., Am. Petroleum Inst., Rocky Mountain Oil and Gas Assn., We. States Petroleum Assn. (bd. dirs.), L.A. C. of C. (bd. dirs.), L.A. Music Ctr. Founders, Ctr. for Strategic and Internat. Studies (CSIS)-Dallas Round Table, Am. Enterprise Forum Chief Execs. Round Table, Dallas Petroleum Club, Tower, Northwood, Calif. Club, Bel-Air Country Club, L.A. Country Club. Office: Arco 574 Chapala Dr Pacific Palisades CA 90272

MIDDLETON, JOHN EDISON, management consultant; b. Sunnyside, Wash., May 1, 1947; s. John Willbey Middleton and Marion (Brignic) Hoage; m. Virginia Louise Bishop, Nov. 5, 1957; children: William Arthur, Rose Marie, Rachel Ranee. BBA, UCLA, 1968; MBA, NYU, 1989, PhD, 1987; PhD (hon.), Oxford (Eng.) U., 1988. Dir. Ramic Prodn., N.Y.C., 1973-75; v.p. Nelson Berry, N.Y.C., 1975-79, CEO, 1984-87; exec. v.p. Investment Internat., N.Y.C., 1980-84, Am. Video, N.Y.C., 1987-89; pres. JBL Assocs., N.Y.C., 1989-92; CEO LBJ Assocs. Ltd., N.Y.C., 1992—. Col. U.S. Army, 1968-72. Named Big Brother of Yr. Big Bros. N.Y., 1979. Mem. Assn. Pub. Pay Phones (pres. 1991—), Masons, Scottish Rite, Shriners, Am. Purple Heart. Republican. Jewish. Avocations: scuba diving, sky diving. Office: Zrzen Beret 2374 81st St Brooklyn NY 11214

MIDDLETON, LINDA JEAN GREATHOUSE, lawyer; b. Poplar Bluff, Mo., Sept. 22, 1950; d. Casper Scott and Anna Garnelle (Qualls) Greathouse; m. Roy L. Middleton, Sept. 27, 1969. BS cum laude, Ark. State U., 1972; JD, Baylor U., 1974. Bar: Tex., 1974; CPCU, CLU. Asst. v.p., asst. sec., atty. Equitable Gen. Ins. Co., Ft. Worth, 1977-81; gen. counsel, corp. sec. Chilton Corp., Dallas, 1981-83; asst. corp. sec., sr. atty., mgr. pub. affairs Fina Oil and Chem., Dallas, 1983-85; sec. Parliamentarian, Dallas, 1985—. Sec. Homeowners Assn., Dallas, 1981—. Mem. Tex. Bar Assn., Dallas Bar Assn. Baptist. Avocations: oil painting, sewing, piano. Office: Fina Inc 8350 N Ctrl Expwy PO Box 2159 Dallas TX 75221

MIDDLETON, MARY, secondary education educator; b. Lackawana, N.Y., Nov. 13, 1942; d. Arthur Jordan and Kathryn (Sternburg) M. BS in Edn., Ohio State U., 1965; postgrad., Akron U., 1970, Cleve. State U., 1981-84. Profl. cert. in edn. Tchr. Columbus (Ohio) Schs., 1966-68, Brooklyn (Ohio) Schs., 1968—; co-dir. C.A.R.E. (Chem. Abuse Reduced through Edn.), Brooklyn (Ohio) City, 1986—, Englist dept. chair, acad. team advisor Brooklyn (Ohio) Schs., 1987—; mem. dimensions of learning task force Bklyn. Schs., Advisor: English hon. 1990—. Contbr. articles to profl. jours. Campaign worker North Olmsted (Ohio) Dem. club, 1988, 92, 96; recreation dir. Country Club Condominiums, 1992—. Recipient N.E. Ohio Writing Project fellowship Martha Holden Jennings, Cleve. State U., 1985. Mem. ASCD, NEA, AAUW, Ohio Edn. Assn., Brooklyn (Ohio) Edn. Assn. (sec.), Ohio Coun. Tchrs. English and Lang. Arts, Cinnamon Woods Condominiums Assn. (bd. dirs.), Re-elect the Pres. Com., Ohio State U. Alumni Assn., Phi Mu. Methodist. Avocations: swimming, reading, traveling. Home: 7127 Bayberry Cir North Olmsted OH 44070-4765 Office: Brooklyn City Schs 9200 Biddulph Rd Brooklyn OH 44144-2614

MIDDLETON, NORMAN GRAHAM, social worker, psychotherapist; b. Jacksonville, Fla., Jan. 21, 1935; s. Norman Graham and Betty (Quina) M.; m. Judy Stephens, Aug. 1, 1968; stepchildren: Monty Stokes, Toni Stokes. BA, U. Miami (Fla.), 1960; MSW, Fla. State U., 1962. Casework counselor Family Svc., Miami, 1962-64; psychiat. social worker assoc. firm Drs. Warson, Steele, Wiener, Sarasota, Fla., 1964-66; psychotherapist, Sarasota, 1966—. Instr. Manatee Jr. Coll., Bradenton, Fla., 1973-76. Author: The Caverns of My Mind, 1985, Imaginative Healing, 1993. Pres. Coun. on Epilepsy, Sarasota, 1969-70. Served with USAF, 1954-58. Fellow Fla. Soc. Clin. Social Work (pres. 1978-80); mem. Am. Group Psychotherapy Assn., Am. Assn. Sex Educators and Counselors (cert. sex educator). Democrat. Episcopalian. Home: 16626 Winburn Dr Sarasota FL 34240-9221 Office: 1257 S Tamiami Trl Sarasota FL 34239-2208

MIDDLETON, TIMOTHY GEORGE, writer; b. Alton, Ill.; s. Elbert George and Freda Margaret Middleton; m. Joyce Elaine Rhea; children: Brendan Mansfield, Michael Travis, Margaret Hart. BA, So. Ill. U. Reporter, copy editor Wall St. Jour., 1981-84; dep. mng. editor Crain's N.Y. Bus., 1984-92. Author: Corporate and Foundation Fundraising, 1982, Grass Roots Fundraising, 1982; writer for Reader's Digest, N.Y. Times, Bus. Week, Money Mag., Computer Life, Field and Stream; editl. cons.; radio personality WCBS-AM N.Y. Fellow U. Mo., 1977. Mem. Outdoor Writers Assn. Am., Am. Soc. Journalists and Authors, KC. Roman Catholic. Avocations: fishing, hunting. Home: 34 Pine Ter E Short Hills NJ 07078-2548

MIDELFORT, HANS CHRISTIAN ERIK, history educator; b. Eau Claire, Wis., Apr. 17, 1942; s. Peter Albert and Gerd (Gjems) M.; m. Corelyn Forsyth Senn, June 16, 1965 (div. Dec. 1981); children: Katarina, Kristian; m. Cassandra Clemons Hughes, May 25, 1985 (div. April 1996); children: Sanford, Raphael, Lucy. BA, Yale U., 1964, MPhil, 1967, PhD, 1970. Instr. Stanford (Calif.) U., 1968-70; asst. prof. U. Va., Charlottesville, 1970-72, assoc. prof., 1972-87, prof., 1987—, Charles Julian Bishko prof. history, 1996—; vis. prof. Harvard U., Cambridge, Mass., 1985, Univ. Stuttgart, Germany, 1988, Univ. Bern, Switzerland, 1988; prin. Brown Coll., U. Va., 1996—. Author: Witch Hunting in Southwestern Germany, 1972 (Gustave Arlt prize 1972), Mad Princes of Renaissance Germany, 1991 (Roland H. Bainton prize 16th Century Studies Conf. 1995); translator: Revolution of 1525 (Peter Bickle), 1981, Imperial Cities and the Reformation (Bernd Moeller), 1972. Mem. Soc. Reformation Rsch. (pres. 1992-93). Office: U Va Dept History Charlottesville VA 22903

MIDGLEY, A(LVIN) REES, JR., reproductive endocrinology educator, researcher; b. Burlington, Vt., Nov. 9, 1933; s. Alvin Rees and Maxine (Schmidt) M.; m. Carol Crossman, Sept. 4, 1955; children: Thomas, Debra, Christopher. B.S. cum laude, U. Vt., 1955, M.D. cum laude, 1958. Intern U. Pitts., 1958-59, resident dept. pathology, 1959-61; resident dept. pathology U. Mich., Ann Arbor, 1961-63, instr. pathology, 1963-64, asst. prof., 1964-67, assoc. prof., 1967-70, prof., 1970—, dir. Reproductive Scis. Program; chmn. BioQuant of Ann Arbor, Inc., 1985-89. Contbr. articles to med. jours. Recipient Parke-Davis award, 1970; Ayerst award Endocrine Soc., 1977; Smith Kline Bio-Sci. Labs. award, 1985; NIH grantee, 1960—; Mellon Found. grantee, 1979-91. Mem. Soc. Study Reprodn. (pres. 1983-84), Endocrine Soc., Am. Assn. Pathology, Am. Physiol. Soc. Home: 3600 Tubbs Rd Ann Arbor MI 48103-9437 Office: U Mich Reproductive Scis Program 300 N Ingalls St Fl 11 Ann Arbor MI 48109-2007

MIDKIFF, DONALD WAYNE, program manager; b. Post, Tex., Sept. 26, 1940; s. Colvert Crockett Midkiff and Judy M. (Poss) Hinckley; m. Olga Maria Androvitch, June 21, 1961 (div. 1968); m. Manbeth Jean Crowell, Apr. 29, 1979. BS in Tech. Mgmt., Denver Tech. Coll., 1988; MS in Mgmt., Colo. Tech. U., 1994. With USAF, 1960, advanced through grades to sgt., 1968; electronics supr. Lockheed Aircraft, Jidda, Saudi Arabia, 1969-71; site mgr. Kentron Hawaii, Ltd., Pleiku, South Vietnam, 1971-73; supr. Kentron, Kwajalein, Marshall Islands, 1973-80, range ops. engr., 1980-84; ops. supr. Kentron PRC, Maui, Hawaii, 1984-85; ops. mgr. Kentron PRC, Colorado Springs, Colo., 1985-87; div. security mgr. PRC, Colorado Springs, Colo., 1987-89; program mgr. PRC Inc., Colorado Springs, Colo., 1989—; advisor Denver Tech. Coll., Colorado Springs, 1991—. CPR instr. Am. Red Cross, 1980-86; pres. Kwajalein Dive Club, 1981-83, Kwajalein Tennis Club, 1978-80. Recipient Group Achievement award NASA, 1992. Mem. AFCEA, Mensa, Nat. Contract Mgmt. Assn., Profl. Assn. Diving Instrs. (dive master). Republican. Avocations: golf, tennis, trap shooting, scuba diving, reading. Office: PRC Inc Ste 260 985 Space Ctr Dr Colorado Springs CO 80915-3695

MIDKIFF, ROBERT RICHARDS, financial and trust company executive, consultant; b. Honolulu, Sept. 24, 1920; s. Frank Elbert and Ruth (Richards) M.; m. Evanita Sumner, July 24, 1948; children: Mary Lloyd, Robin Starr, Shelley Sumner, Robert Richards Jr., David Wilson. BA, Yale U., 1942; grad. Advanced Mgmt. Program, Harvard U., 1962. Asst. sec. Hawaiian Trust Co., 1951-56, asst. v.p., 1956-57, v.p., 1957-65; dir. Am. Factors, Ltd., 1954-65; v.p. Amfac, Inc., 1965-68; exec. v.p., dir. Am. Security Bank, Honolulu, 1968-69, pres., dir., 1969-71; pres., chief exec. officer, dir. Am. Trust Co. Hawaii, Honolulu, 1971-93; chmn. bd. Bishop Trust Co. Ltd., Honolulu, 1984-93; pres., chief exec. officer Am. Fin. Svcs. of Hawaii, 1988-93; bd. dirs. Persis Corp., Honolulu. Co-chmn. Gov.'s Archtl. Adv. Com. on State Capitol, 1960-65; co-chmn. Gov.'s Adv. Com. on Fine Arts for State Capitol, 1965-69; past chmn., bd. dirs. Hawaii Visitors Bur.; past pres., bd. dirs. Downtown Improvement Assn., Lahaina Restoration Found., Hawaii Cmty. Found.; bd. dirs., pres. Atherton Family Found.; past chmn. Profit Sharing Rsch. Found.; bd. dirs. Coun. on Founds. Mem. Coun. on Founds., Profit Sharing Coun. Am. (bd. dirs.), Employee Stock Ownership Plan Assn. Am. (bd. dirs.), Small Bus. Coun. Am. (bd. dirs.), Pacific Club, Waialae Golf Club, Oahu Country Club, Phi Beta Kappa. Democrat. Episcopalian. Office: 4477 Kahala Ave Honolulu HI 96816-4924

MIDLARSKY, MANUS ISSACHAR, political scientist, educator; b. N.Y.C., Jan. 28, 1937; s. Max and Rachel (Potechin) M.; m. Elizabeth Steckel, June 25, 1961; children—Susan, Miriam, Michael. B.S., CUNY, 1959; M.S., Stevens Inst. Tech., 1963; Ph.D. (Ford Found. fellow), Northwestern U., 1969. Instr. polit. sci. U. Colo., Boulder, 1967-68, asst. prof., 1968-71, assoc. prof., 1971-74, prof., 1974-89, dir. Ctr. Internat. Relations, 1983-89; Moses and Annuta Back prof. internat. peace and conflict resolution Rutgers U., New Brunswick, N.J., 1989—; cons. USAF, 1968. Author: On War: Political Violence in the International System, 1975, The Disintegration of Political Systems: War and Revolution in Comparative Perspective, 1986, The Onset of World War, 1988; editor: Inequality and Contemporary Revolutions, 1986, Handbook of War Studies, 1989, 93, The Internationalization of Communal Strife, 1992, (with J. Vasquez and P. Gladkov) From Rivalry to Cooperation: Russian and American Perspectives on the Post-Cold War Era, 1994. Faculty fellow Richardson Inst. Conflict and Peace Research, London, 1977-78; faculty fellow Council Research and Creative Work, U. Colo., 1977-78; NSF grantee, 1973-76, 81-83, 83-85, 86-89; Nat. Endowment Humanities grantee, 1980, 83. Mem. Am. Polit. Sci. Assn. (pres. conflict processes sect. 1985-88) Internat. Studies Assn. (pres. West 1980-81, v.p. 1986-87), Am. Soc. Polit. and Legal Philosophy, Inter-Univ. Seminar in Armed Forces and Soc. Office: Rutgers U Dept Polit Sci Hickman Hall New Brunswick NJ 08903

MIDLER, BETTE, singer, entertainer, actress; b. Honolulu, Dec. 1, 1945; m. Martin von Haselberg, 1984; 1 child, Sophie. Student, U. Hawaii, 1 year. Debut as actress film Hawaii, 1965; mem. cast Fiddler on the Roof, N.Y.C., 1966-69, Salvation, N.Y.C., 1970, Tommy, Seattle Opera Co., 1971; night-club concert performer on tour, U.S., from 1972; appearance Palace Theatre, N.Y.C., 1973, Radio City Music Hall, 1993; TV appearances include The Tonight Show, Bette Midler: Old Red Hair is Back, 1978, Gypsy, 1993 (Golden Globe award best actress in a mini-series or movie made for television 1994, Emmy nomination, Lead Actress - Special, 1994), Seinfeld, 1995;

appeared Clams on The Half-Shell Revue, N.Y.C., 1975; recs. include The Divine Miss M, 1972, Bette Midler, 1973, Broken Blossom, 1977, Live at Last, 1977, The Rose, 1979, Thighs and Whispers, 1979, Songs for the New Depression, 1979, Divine Madness, 1980, No Frills, 1984, Mud Will Be Flung Tonight, 1985, Beaches (soundtrack), 1989, Some People's Lives, 1990; motion picture appearances include Hawaii, 1966, The Rose, 1979 (Academy award nomination best actress 1979), Divine Madness, 1980, Jinxed, 1982, Down and Out in Beverly Hills, 1986, Ruthless People, 1986, Outrageous Fortune, 1987, Oliver and Company (voice), 1988, Big Business, 1988, Beaches, 1988, Stella, 1990, Scenes From a Mall, 1991, For the Boys, 1991 (Academy award nomination best actress 1991), Hocus Pocus, 1993; appeared in cable TV (HBO) prodn. Bette Midler's Mondo Beyondo, 1988; author: A View From A Broad, 1980, The Saga of Baby Divine, 1983. Recipient After Dark Ruby award, 1973; Grammy awards, 1973, 1990; spl. Tony award, 1973; Emmy award for NBC Spl., Ol' Red Hair is Back, 1978; 2 Golden Globe awards for The Rose, 1979, Golden Globe award for The Boys, 1991; Emmy award The Tonight Show appearance, 1992. Office: care Atlantic Records 75 Rockefeller Plz New York NY 10019-6908

MIDORI (MIDORI GOTO), classical violinist; b. Osaka, Japan, Oct. 25, 1971. Attended, Juilliard Sch. Music; grad., Profl. Childrens Sch., 1990. Performer worldwide, 1981—. Recordings on Philips, Sony Classical, Columbia Masterworks; performed with N.Y. Philharmonic Orch., Boston Symphony Orch.; worldwide performances include Berlin, Chgo., Cleve., Phila., Montreal, London; recordings include Encore, Live at Carnegie Hall. Named Best Artist of Yr. by Japanese Govt., 1988; recipient Dorothy B. Chandler Performing Arts award, L.A. Music Ctr., 1989, Crystal award Ashani Shimbun Newspaper contbn. arts, Suntory award, 1994. Office: Sony Classical Sony Music Entertainment Inc 550 Madison Ave New York NY 10022-3211

MIEL, GEORGE JOSEPH, computer scientist, mathematician, system engineer; b. Paris, Sept. 7, 1943; s. Joseph and Josephine (Modlinska) M. BS, U. Ill., 1964, MS, 1965; PhD, U. Wyo., 1976. Mem. tech. staff Bellcomm, 1967-69, NASA, 1967-69; cons. Siemens A.G., Munich, 1969-70; computer scientist Applied Rsch. Labs., Ecublens, Switzerland, 1970-73; assoc. prof. U. Nev., Las Vegas, 1978-85; researcher Hughes Aircraft Co., Malibu, Calif., 1985—; prof. U. Nev., Las Vegas, 1991—; cons. on computer modeling and parallel processing Las Vegas, 1994—, rsch. on environ. engring. and modeling, 1995—; vis. asst. prof. U. Calgary, Can., 1976-78; vis. assoc. prof. Ariz. State U., Tempe, 1983-84. Contbr. numerous articles to profl. jours. Recipient numerous rsch. grants, Chauvenet prize Math. Assn. Am., 1986. Mem. IEEE, AIAA (vice chmn. com. on software sys. 1993—), Aerospace Industries Assn. (chmn. computational sci. com. Washington 1989-91), Soc. Indsl. Applied Math. Office: 220 E Flamingo Rd Apt 324 Las Vegas NV 89109-0305 Office: PO Box 72226 Las Vegas NV 89170-2226

MIELE, ALFONSE RALPH, former government official; b. N.Y.C., Jan. 6, 1922; s. Angelo and Alesia (Laudadio) M.; m. Gloria I. Litrento, Nov. 22, 1942 (dec. Dec. 1977); children: Richard Lynn, Barbara Jo, Steven Arnold; m. Ann Carlino Valerio, Mar. 31, 1979 (dec. June 1988); m. Dorothy A. McGowan, July 7, 1990. AB in Litteris Gallicis with honors, Fordham U., 1942; postgrad., U. Nancy, France, 1945; MA, Columbia U., 1947, PhD, 1958. Commd. 2nd lt. U.S. Army, 1942; advanced through grades to col. USAF, 1961; served in 377th Automatic Weapons Bn., 1942-45; ret., brig. gen.; instr. French and pub. speaking Fordham Prep. Sch., N.Y.C., 1946-47; asst. prof. French and Russian U.S. Naval Acad., 1949-52; exec. officer to NATO comdrs., 1953-55; teaching asst. Columbia U., 1955-58; assoc. prof. French USAF Acad., 1958-60, prof., head dept. fgn. langs., 1960-67, assoc. dean, chmn. divsn. humanities, 1967-68; exec. v.p. Loretto Heights Coll., Denver, 1968-70; pres. Coll. St. Rose, Albany, 1970-72; prof. gen. edn. Schenectady County C.C., Schenectady, N.Y., 1972-73; dep. asst. adminstr. internat. aviation affairs FAA, Washington, 1973-75, edn. specialist, 1976—; 1968; asst. dir. pub. affairs U.S. Dept. Interior, Washington, 1975-76; chief negotiator civil aviation tech. agreement with USSR, 1973-75; project dir. Nat. Aviation Edn. Program for Am. Indians, 1978; asst. dir. Union County (N.J.) Coord. Agy. for Higher Edn., 1979-82; rep. Eckhart Assocs., 1983-88; relocation specialist Bradley/Wildman Co., Monument, Colo., 1989-92. Mem. Westfield (N.J.) Bd. Edn., 1985-88; bd. dirs. Pike's Peak chpt. ARC, 1990-93; pres. Colorado Springs World Affairs Coun., 1993-95. Decorated Bronze Star, Legion of Merit; chevalier Palmes Academiques France; recipient Encaenia award Fordham Coll., 1962. Mem. Monument C. of C. (bd. dirs. 1992-94). Home: PO Box 321 Monument CO 80132-0321 *Be ever curious and willing to dare. The sweet becomes even sweeter when the bitter is overcome. Each living moment is a learning experience and adds to the anticipation of better tomorrows. The journey of life is exciting—live with that thought in mind.*

MIELE, ANGELO, engineering educator, researcher, consultant, author; b. Formia, Italy, Aug. 21, 1922; came to U.S., 1952, naturalized, 1985; s. Salvatore and Elena (Marino) M. D.Civil Engring., U. Rome, Italy, 1944, D.Aero. Engring., 1946; DSc (hon.), Inst. Tech., Technion, Israel, 1992. Asst. prof. Poly. Inst. Bklyn., 1952- 55; prof. Purdue U., 1955-59; dir. astrodynamics Boeing Sci. Research Labs., 1959-64; prof. aerospace scis., math. scis. Rice U., Houston, 1964-88, Foyt Family prof. engring., 1988-93, Foyt prof. emeritus engring., aerospace scis., math. scis., 1993—; cons. Douglas Aircraft Co., 1956-58, Allison divsn. GM Corp., 1956-58, U.S. Aviation Underwriters, 1987, Boeing Comml. Airplane Co., 1989; Breakwell Meml. lecturership Internat. Astron. Fedn., 1994. Author: Flight Mechanics, 1962; editor: Theory of Optimum Aerodynamic Shapes, 1965, Math. Concepts and Methods in Science and Engineering, 1994; editor-in-chief Jour. Optimization Theory and Applications, 1966—; assoc. editor Jour. Astronautical Scis., 1964-93, Applied Math. and Computation, 1975—, Optimal Control Applications and Methods, 1979—; mem. editl. bd. RAIRO-Ops. Rsch., 1990—; mem. adv. bd. AIAA Edn. Series, 1991—; contbr. numerous articles on aerospace engring., windshear problems, hypervelocity flight, math. programming, optimal control theory and computing methods to sci. jours. Pres. Italy in Am. Assn., 1966-68. Decorated knight comdr. Order Merit Italy, 1972; recipient Levy medal Franklin Inst. of Phila., 1974, Brouwer award AAS, 1980, Schuck award Am. Automatic Control Coun., 1988. Fellow AIAA (Pendray award 1982, Mechanics and Control of Flight award 1982), Am. Astronautical Soc., Franklin Inst.; mem. NAE, Russian Acad. Scis. (fgn.), Internat. Acad. Astronautics, Acad. Scis. Turin (corr.). Home: 3106 Kettering Dr Houston TX 77027-5504 Office: Rice Univ MS-322 Aero-Astronautics Group PO Box 1892 Houston TX 77251-1892

MIELE, ANTHONY WILLIAM, retired librarian; b. Williamsport, Pa., Feb. 12, 1926; s. Harry John and Louise Casale (Troyano) M.; m. Ruth Cassidy, Jan. 29, 1955; children—Terri Ann, Anthony William, Robert John, Elizabeth Ann. B.S. in Bus. Adminstrn, Marquette U., Milw., 1951; M.L.S., U. Pitts., 1966. Partner, mgr. restaurant Williamsport, 1960-66; dir. Elmwood Park (Ill.) Pub. Libr., 1967-68; asst. dir. Oak Park (Ill.) Pub. Libr., 1968-70; asst. dir. tech. services Ill. State Libr., Springfield, 1970-75; state librn. Ala. Pub. Libr. Service, Montgomery, 1975-86; coord. Libr. Svcs. and Constrn. Act, 1986-87; dir. library extension div. Ariz. Dept. Libr., Archives and Pub. Records, Phoenix, 1987-95; ret.; exec. dir. Ill. Nat. Libr. Week, 1970, ALA Nat. Libr. Week Commn., 1971-74; mem. Pub. Printer's Adv. Coun. Depository Librs., 1975-78, vice chmn., 1977-78; mem. CLSI Nat. Adv. Com., 1983-87; reader NEH, 1987; exhibits chair for confs. Mountain Plains Libr. Assn., Ariz. State Libr. Assn., Ariz. Edn. Media Assn., 1992; cochair ASLA/AEMA Annual Conf., 1993. Assoc. editor Govt. Publs. Rev., 1974-85; contbr. articles to profl. publs. Mayor Arrowhead Community, 1984; bd. dirs. Amigos Libr. Network, 1990-94. Recipient cert. of appreciation Am. Libr. Trustee Assn., 1986. Mem. ALA (chmn. govt. documents round table 1974-76, chair state libr. agy. sect. 1992-93, mem. coun. 1994-98), Ill. Libr. Assn., Ala. Libr. Assn. (Exceptional Svc. citation 1986), Ariz. State Libr. Assn. (pres. award of recognition 1993, mem-at-large 1995-98), Nat. Microfilm Assn., Spl. Libr. Assn., Chief Officers State Libr. Agys. (sec. 1978-80). Roman Catholic.

MIELE, JOEL ARTHUR, SR., civil engineer; b. Jersey City, May 28, 1934; s. Jene Gerald Sr., and Eleanor Natale (Bergida) M.; m. Faith Roseann Trombetta, July 21, 1952 (div. 1954); m. 2d Josephine Ann Cottone, Feb. 14, 1959; children: Joel Arthur, Jr., Vita Marie, Janet Ann. B.C.E., Poly. Inst. Bklyn., 1955. Registered profl. engr. N.Y., n.J., Fla.; profl. planner N.J. Civil engr. Yudell & Miele, Queens, N.Y., 1955-57; chief engr. Jene G. Miele Assocs., Queens, 1960-68; prin., CEO Miele Assocs., Queens, 1968-94; commr. N.Y.C. Planning Commn., 1990-94; commr. of bldgs. City of N.Y., 1994—. Patentee masonry wall constrn. Commr. N.Y.C. Planning Commn., 1990-94; bd. visitors Creedmoor State Hosp., 1978—, pres., 1979—; bd. dirs. Peninsula Hosp. Ctr., 1984—, pres., 1990—; bd. dirs. Peninsula Nursing Home, 1984—, pres., 1990—; bd. dirs. Cmty. Bd. 10, Queens, 1973-90, chmn., 1978-90; trustee, treas. Queens Pub. Comm. Corp., 1983—; trustee Queens Borough Pub. Libr., 1979—, pres., 1995—; bd. dirs. Queen County Overall Econ. Devel. Corp., 1989-94, pres., 1992-94; exec. v.p. Queens coun. Boy Scouts Am., 1991—. Lt. (j.g.) USN, 1957-60; capt. USNR, 1960-88. Named Italian-Am. of Yr. Ferrini Welfare League, Queens, 1980, Hon. Mem. of Queens Chpt. AIA, 1994, Prof. Affiliated Mem. (Hon.), N.Y. Soc. Architects, 1994; recipient Outstanding Cmty. Leader award Boy Scouts Am., 1987, Pride of Queens award, 1990, Pub. Servant Extraordinaire award United Cerebral Palsy of Queens, 1994, Good Scout award Greater N.Y. Coun. Boy Scouts Am., 1994. Fellow ASCE; mem. ASTM, NSPE (trustee polit. action com. 1988—), N.Y. State Soc. Profl. Engrs. (v.p. 1984-86, pres. 1988-89, nat. dir. 1987-90, Engr. of Yr. 1983, pres. Queens chpt. 1980-82), Soc. Am. Mil. Engrs., N.Y. State Assn. of Professions (founding), Ozone Howard C. of C. (pres. 1980-84, 86-91), Am. Parkinson Disease Assn. (dir. 1985—, exec. com. 1987—). Democrat. Congregationalist. Office: City of New York Dept of Buildings 60 Hudson St New York NY 10013-3315

MIELKE, CLARENCE HAROLD, JR., hematologist; b. Spokane, Wash., June 18, 1936; s. Clarence Harold and Marie Katherine (Gillespie) M.; m. Marcia Rae, July 5, 1964; children: Elisa, John, Kristina. BS, Wash. State U., 1959; MD, U. Louisville, 1963. Intern, San Francisco Gen. Hosp., 1963-64; resident in medicine Portland VA Hosp., 1964-65, San Francisco Gen. Hosp., 1965-67; fellow in hematology U. So. Calif., 1967-68; teaching fellow, asst. physician, instr. Tufts-New Eng. Med. Ctr. Hosps., Boston, 1968-71; sr. scientist Med. Rsch. Inst., San Francisco, 1971-90; chief hematology Presbyn. Hosp., San Francisco, 1971-82; asst. clin. prof. medicine U. Calif. Sch. Medicine, San Francisco, 1971-80, assoc. clin. prof., 1979-90, bd.92—dirs. Inst. Cancer Rsch.; trustee, bd. dirs. Med. Rsch. Inst. San Francisco, Sacred Heart Hosp. Found., 1994—. NIH grantee, 1973-88; dir. emeritus Inst. Cancer Rsch.; trustee emeritus, bd. dirs. Med. Rsch. Inst., 1988—; dir. Health Rsch. and Edn. Ctr., Wash. State U., 1989—, prof. pharmocology, 1989—, prof. vet. medicine, 1989—, assoc. dean rsch., 1992—. Fellow ACP, Internat. Acad. Clin. & Applied Thrombosis & Hemostasis, Internat. Soc. Hematology, Am. Coll. Angiology; mem. Am. Soc. Internal Medicine, Internat. Soc. Thrombosis and Hemostasis, Am. Heart Assn., N.Y. Acad. Scis., AMA, San Francisco Med. Soc., Am. Thoracic Soc., AAAS, Internat. Soc. Angiology. Editor emeritus, Jour. Clin. Apheresis, 1981; contbr. chpts. to books, articles to med. jours. Office: Wash State U Health Rsch & Edn Ctr West 601 First Ave Spokane WA 99204-0399

MIELKE, FREDERICK WILLIAM, JR., retired utility company executive; b. N.Y.C., Mar. 19, 1921; s. Frederick William and Cressida (Flynn) M.; m. Lorraine Roberts, 1947; children: Bruce Frederick, Neal Russell. AB, U. Calif., 1943; JD, Stanford U., 1949. Bar: Calif. 1950. Law clk. to Assoc. Justice John W. Shenk, Calif. Supreme Ct., 1949-51; with Pacific Gas and Electric Co., San Francisco, 1951-86; exec. v.p. Pacific Gas and Electric Co., 1976-79, chmn. bd., chief exec. officer, 1979-86; bd. dirs. The Bay Area Coun., Edison Electric Inst., 1979-82; dir. emeritus SRI Internat. Trustee Stanford U., 1977-87, Golden Gate U., 1977-79; mem. adv. coun. Stanford Grad. Sch. Bus., 1984-90; bd. dirs. Calif. C. of C., 1979-85, San Francisco C. of C., 1977-79, Ind. Colls. No. Calif., 1969-79; chmn. bd. dirs. United Way of Bay Area, 1986-88. With USN, 1943-46. Mem. Calif. Bar Assn. Office: Pacific Gas and Electric Co PO Box 770000 Mail Code H17 123 Mission St # 7F San Francisco CA 94105-1551

MIELKE, PAUL WILLIAM, JR., statistician; b. St. Paul, Feb. 18, 1931; s. Paul William and Elsa (Yungbauer) M.; m. Roberta Roehl Robison, June 25, 1960; children: William, Emily, Lynn. BA, U. Minn., 1953, PhD, 1963; MA, U. Ariz., 1958. Teaching asst. U. Ariz., Tucson, 1957-58; teaching asst. U. Minn., Mpls., 1958-60, statis. cons., 1960-62, lectr., 1962-63; from asst. to assoc. prof. dept. statistics Colo. State U., Fort Collins, 1963-72, prof. dept. statistics, 1972—. Contbr. articles to Am. Jour. Pub. Health, Jour. of Statis. Planning and Inference, Ednl. and Psychol. Measurement, Biometrika, Earth-Sci. Revs. Capt. USAF, 1953-57. Recipient Banner I. Miller award Am. Meteorological Assn., 1994. Fellow Am. Statis. Assn.; mem. Am. Meteorol. Soc. (Banner I. Miller award 1993), Biometric Soc. Achievements include proposal that common statistical methods (t test and analysis of variance) were based on counter intuitive geometric foundations and provided alternative statistical methods which are based on appropriate foundations. Home: 736 Cherokee Dr Fort Collins CO 80525-1517 Office: Colo State U Dept Stats Fort Collins CO 80523-1877

MIERCORT, CLIFFORD ROY, coal mining company executive; b. Denver, Jan. 13, 1940; s. Frederic E. and Olga S. (Schlaepfer) M.; m. Barbara Dolan, Aug. 22, 1964; children: David Butler, Jennifer Dolan. BS in Archtl. Engring., U. Colo., 1964; MCE, U. Ill., 1966; advanced mgmt. program, Harvard U., 1983. Registered profl. engr., Colo., Kans., Mont., N.Mex., Tex. Supr. offshore oil drilling and production Shell Oil Co., New Orleans, 1966-69; oil production engr. Denver, 1969-71, staff engr., 1971-73; project mgr. mining venture Houston, 1973-76; asst. to pres. N.Am. Coal Corp., Cleve., 1976-77; v.p. SW div. N.Am. Coal Corp., Dallas, 1977-81, pres. SW div., 1981-87, pres., 1987—, CEO, 1988—; bd. dirs. Bellaire Corp., The Coteau Properties Co., The Falkirk Mining Co., N.Am. Coal Royalty Co., The Sabine Mining Co. Mem. AIME, Nat. Mining Assn. (bd. dirs. 1987), Nat. coal Coun. (mem. coal policy com., mem. fin. and exec. coms.), Soc. Profl. Engrs. Avocations: reading, traveling, gardening, refurbishing houses, golf. Office: N Am Coal Corp 14785 Preston Rd Ste 1100 Dallas TX 75240-7889*

MIEUX, DONNA MARIE, special education educator; b. L.A., Feb. 10, 1949; d. Donald Lee and Alma Olivia (Johnson) Troy; m. Isom (Ike) Mieux, June 9, 1972; children: Kendra Desiree, Andre Donald. BA in Sociology, U. Calif., Santa Barbara, 1971; MA in Spl. Edn., U. Akron, 1976; EdD, Nova Southeastern U., 1993. Cert. spl. edn.; cert. tchr. Lang. enrichment tchr. L.A. Unified Sch. Dist., 1972-74; resource specialist Whittier (Calif.) City Sch. Dist., 1976-79; resource specialist Hacienda La Puente (Calif.) Unified Sch. Dist., 1979—, mentor. tchr., 1993—, tchr. severely handicapped, 1989-92, artist-of-the-month developer, stamp club sponsor, 1988-90; developer, coord. before sch. tutorial program for at-risk students, 1990—; adj. faculty psychology The Union Inst., L.A., 1994—; instr. writing Mt. San Antonio Coll., Walnut,' Calif., 1994—. Sunday sch. tchr. United Ch. of Christ, Claremont, Calif., 1989-93; mem. PTA, La Puente, 1972—; vol. Rancho Los Amigos Hosp., Brownies, Girl Scouts USA, various sports activities, 1969—. Recipient scholarship Compton Tchrs. Assn., 1967, Martin Luther King scholarship Calif. Tchrs. Assn., 1990; fellow Occidental Coll., 1971. Mem. Nat. Tchrs. Assn., Calif. Tchrs. Assn. Democrat. Avocations: sculpturing, writing, viewing high quality foreign movies, tennis. Office: Palm Elem Sch 14740 Palm Ave Hacienda Heights CA 91745

MIFFLIN, FRED J., Canadian government official; b. Bonavista, Nfld., Can., 1938; m. Gwenneth Davies; children: Cathy, Mark, Sarah. Grad., Can. Navy's Venture Tng. Program, U.S. Naval War Coll., Nat. Def. Coll., Kingston, Ont. Enlisted Can. Navy, 1954, advanced through ranks to rear admiral, 1985, head nat. def. secretarian; mem. parliament Canadian Govt., 1988-96, parliamentary sec. to min. nat. def. & vet. affairs, 1993, min. fisheries & oceans, 1996—. Avocations: jogging, country music, gourmet cooking, raising golden retrievers. Office: Fisheries & Oceans, Stn 1570 200 Kent St, Ottawa, ON Canada K1A 0E6*

MIGALA, LUCYNA JOZEFA, broadcast journalist, arts administrator, radio station executive; b. Krakow, Poland, May 22, 1944; d. Joseph and Estelle (Suwala) M.; came to U.S., 1947, naturalized, 1955; student Loyola U., Chgo., 1962-63, Chicago Conservatory of Music, 1963-70; BS in Journalism, Northwestern U., 1966. Radio announcer, producer sta. WOPA, Oak Park, Ill., 1963-66; writer, reporter, producer NBC news, Chgo., 1966-69, 1969-71, producer NBC local news, Washington, 1969; producer, coord. NBC network news, Cleve., 1971-78, field producer, Chgo., 1978-79; v.p. Migala Communications Corp., 1979—; program and news dir., on-air personality Sta. WCEV, Cicero, Ill., 1979—; lectr. City Colls. Chgo., 1981, Morton Coll., 1988. Columnist Free Press, Chgo., 1984-87. Founder, artistic dir., gen. mgr. Lira Ensemble (formerly The Lira Singers), Chgo., 1965—; mem., chmn. various cultural coms. Polish Am. Congress, 1970-80; bd. dirs. Nationalities Svcs. Ctr., Cleve., 1973-78; bd. dirs., v.p. Cicero-Berwyn Fine Arts Coun., Cicero, Ill.; mem. City Arts I and II panels Chgo. Office of Fine Arts, 1986-89, 94; v.p. Chgo. chpt. Kosciuszko Found., 1983-86; bd. dirs. Polish Women's Alliance Am., 1983-87, Ill. Humanities Coun., 1983-89, mem. exec. com., 1986-87; bd. dirs. Ill. Arts Alliance, 1989-92; founder, gen. chmn. Midwest Chopin Piano Competition (now Chgo. Chopin Competition), 1984-86; founding mem. ethnic and folk arts panel Ill. Arts Coun., 1984-87, 92-94. Recipient AP Broadcasters award, 1973, Emmy award NATAS, 1974, Cultural Achievement award Am. Coun. for Polish Culture, 1990, Award of Merit Advocates Soc. Polish Am. Attys., 1991, Human Rels. Media award City of Chgo., 1992, Outstanding Achievement in Polish Culture award Minister of Fgn. Affairs, Rep. of Poland, 1994; Washington Journalism Ctr. fellow, spring 1969. Mem. Soc. Profl. Journalists. Office: Sta WCEV 5356 W Belmont Ave Chicago IL 60641-4103 also: The Lira Ensemble 6525 N Sheridan Rd # SKY 905 Chicago IL 60626

MIGDEN, CHESTER L., professional society administrator; b. N.Y.C., May 21, 1921; s. Albert and Louise (Jawer) M.; m. Dina Vohl, July 22, 1944; children: Barbara, Ann, Amy. B.A., CCNY, 1941; LL.B., Columbia U., 1947. Bar: N.Y. State 1947. Atty. NLRB, N.Y.C., 1947-51; various positions Screen Actors Guild Inc., Hollywood, 1952-81; nat. exec. sec. Screen Actors Guild Inc., 1973-81; v.p. Internat. Fedn. Actors, 1973-81, Calif. Labor Fedn., 1974-81, Associated Actors and Artistes Am., 1973-81; exec. dir. Assn. Talent Agts., 1982-94; ret., 1994; officer, trustee Producers-Screen Actors Guild pension, welfare plans, 1960-81; v.p. Motion Picture and TV Fund, 1975—; instr. extension program UCLA. Contbr. articles to profl. jours. Mem. Acad. Motion Picture Arts and Scis., Am. Arbitration Assn. (arbitrator), Labor Rels. Cons. Democrat.

MIGEON, CLAUDE JEAN, pediatricics educator; b. Lievin, Pas-De-Calais, France, Dec. 22, 1923; came to U.S., 1950, naturalized, 1967; s. André and Pauline (Descamps) M.; m. Barbara Lou Ruben, Apr. 2, 1960; children: Jacques, Jean-Paul, Nicole. M.D., Sch. Medicine, U. Paris, 1950. Fellow dept. pediatrics Sch. Medicine, Johns Hopkins U., 1950-52, asst. prof., 1954-60, asso. prof., 1960-71, prof. pediatrics, 1971—; instr. biochemistry U. Utah, 1952-54; pediatrician Johns Hopkins Hosp., 1954—; mem. diabetes and metabolism tng. grants com. NIH, 1963-67, gen. clin. research centers com., 1968-71, mem. endocrinology study sect., 1974-78; cons. Med. Research Council Can., 1969-85, others; vis. prof. Maadi Armed Forces Hosp., Cairo, 1985, Guy's Hosp., London, 1986. Co-editor: (textbook) The Diagnosis and Treatment of Endocrine Disorders in Childhood and Adolescence, 4th edit., 1994; mem. editl. bd.: Johns Hopkins Med. Jour., 1970-72, Jour. Clin. Endocrinology and Metabolism, 1971-77, Hormone Rsch., 1979—; contbr. articles to profl. jours. Fulbright fellow, 1950; Am. Field Service fellow, 1950-51; Andre and Bella Meyer fellow, 1951-52; recipient research career award NIH, 1964-85. Fellow AAAS; mem. Endocrine Soc. (coun. 1971-74, chmn. pub. affairs com. 1974-91, Ayerst award, Williams award), Soc. Pediatric Rsch. (emeritus), Am. Pediatric Soc., Lawson Wilkins Pediatric Endocrine Soc. (founding pres. 1972), Am. Soc. Clin. Investigation (emeritus), Am. Physiol. Soc., Japanese Pediatric Endocrine Soc. (hon.), Found. for Am. Meml. Hosp. (bd. dirs. 1985—), Soc. Francaise d'Endocrinologie (fgn. corr. mem.). Home: 502 Somerset Rd Baltimore MD 21210-2720 Office: CMSC 3-110 Johns Hopkins Hosp Baltimore MD 21205

MIGHELL, KENNETH JOHN, lawyer; b. Schenectady, N.Y., Mar. 17, 1931; s. Richard Henry and Ruth Aline (Simon) M.; m. Julia Anne Carstarphen, Aug. 24, 1961; children: Thomas Lowry, Elizabeth Anne. BBA, U. Tex., 1952, JD, 1957. Bar: Tex. 1957. Assoc. Scurry, Scurry, Pace & Wood, Dallas, 1957-61; asst. U.S. Atty. Justice Dept., Dallas, 1961-77; 1st asst. No. Dist. Tex., 1972-77; U.S. Atty. No. Dist., Tex., 1977-81; ptnr. Cowles & Thompson, 1981—. Chmn. bd. mgmt. Downtown Dallas YMCA, 1974-76; pres. Dallas Area Am. Lung Assn., 1985-87; bd. dirs. YMCA Met. Dallas, 1987—; chmn. adv. bd. Southwestern Law Enforcement Inst., 1994—. With USN, 1952-54; capt. USNR, 1954-78. Mem. ABA, Fed. Bar Assn., Dallas Bar Assn. (bd. dirs. 1984-89, chmn. 1989, v.p. 1990-91, pres. 1993), State Bar Tex. (bd. dirs. 1994-95), Nat. Assn. Former U.S. Attys. (pres. 1995). Democrat. Methodist. Office: 4000 Nations Bank Plz Dallas TX 75202

MIGHT, THOMAS OWEN, newspaper company executive; b. Fort Walton Beach, Fla., Apr. 22, 1951; s. Gerald William and Rosina (Bugner) M.; m. Sept. 22, 1973; children—Matthew, Daniel. B.S. in Indsl. Engring., Ga. Tech. U., 1972; M.B.A., Harvard Bus. Sch., 1978. Asst. to pub. Washington Post, 1978-80, mgr. plant, 1980-81, v.p. prodn., v.p. marketing; now pres., COO, divsn. Post-Newsweek cable The Washington Post Co., Phoenix. Served to capt. U.S. Army, 1972-76. Roman Catholic. Office: Washington Post Co Divsn Post-Newsweek Cable 4742 N 24th St Ste 270 Phoenix AZ 85016-4860

MIGIELICZ, GERALYN, photojournalist; b. St. Louis, Feb. 15, 1958; d. Edward J. and Mary Ann (McCarthy) M. BJ, U. Mo., 1979. Photographer Emporia (Kans.) Gazette, 1979-80; chief photographer St. Joseph (Mo.) News-Press & Gazette, 1980-83; photo editor, photographer Seattle Times, 1984; picture editor Rocky Mountain News, Denver, 1985-86; graphics editor San Jose (Calif.) Mercury News, 1986-92, dir. photography, 1992—. Recipient Individual Editing awards Soc. Newspaper Designers, 1988-92, Editing awards, 91-92; named for Overall Excellence in Editing, Picture of Yr. Contest, U. Mo., 1993. Office: San Jose Mercury News 750 E Ridder Park Dr San Jose CA 95190

MIGL, DONALD RAYMOND, optometrist, pharmacist; b. Houston, Tex., Sept. 18, 1947; s. Ervin Lawrence and Adele Marie (Boenisch) M.; m. Karen S. Coale, Mar. 23, 1974; children: Christopher Brian, Derek Drew, Monica Michelle. BS in Pharmacy, U. Houston, 1970, BS, 1978, OD, 1980, postgrad., 1992; postgrad., U. Ala. Med. Ctr., Birmingham, 1974-76, Stephen F. Austin State U., Nacogdoches, Tex., 1987-88. Registered pharmacist; cert. Nat. Bds. Examiners Optometry, Treatment & Mgmt. Ocular Disease; cert. therapeutic optometrist. Pharmacist Tex. Med. Ctr., Houston, 1967-69, St. Luke's and Tex. Childrens Hosp., 1967-69, Meml. Hosp., 1969-70, Ben Taub (Harris County) Hosp., 1970-71, Shades Mountain Pharmacy, Birmingham, 1974-76, Westbury Hosp., Houston, 1976-81; instr. pharmacology lab. Coll. Optometry U. Houston, 1980; pvt. practice, Nacogdoches, Tex., 1981—; mem. interdisciplinary health teams, 1977; charter advisor publ. Contact, CIBA Vision Corp., 1988-89. Judge health sci. div. Houston Area Sci. Fair, 1970. Recipient svc. award Houston Community Interdisciplinary Health Screening Programs, 1977, Spl. Academic Achievement award in pharmacy and optometry U. Houston, 1980. Mem. Am. Optometric Assn. (Optometric recognition award 1985-94), Tex. Optometric Assn. (recognition cert. 1979), Piney Woods Optometric Soc. (pres. 1984), Am. Pharm. Assn. (recognition cert. 1970), Tex. Pharm. Assn., Am. Soc. Hosp. Pharmacists, U.S. Jaycees, Gold Key, Omicron Delta Kappa. Methodist. Lodge: Rotary (Paul Harris Fellow 1987, Pres. award Outstanding Svc., 1991-92). Office: Eagle Eye 20/20 Plus Vision PO Box 632730 Nacogdoches TX 75963-2730

MIGLIARO, MARCO WILLIAM, electrical engineer; b. N.Y.C., Mar. 29, 1948; s. Marco Salvatore and Anna (Dalton) M.; children: Kristen Marie, Meredith Anne, Marie Angela, Marco Thomas; m. Jasoda Badlu, Nov. 19, 1988. BEE, Pratt Inst., 1969; postgrad., N.J. Inst. Tech., 1970-72. Registered profl. engr., N.Y., N.J., Pa., Mass., Fla. Engr. Am. Electric Power, N.Y.C., 1969-78; staff engr. Gibbs & Hill, Inc., N.Y.C., 1978-81; sr. cons. engr. Ebasco Svcs., Inc., N.Y.C., 1981-88; tech. mgr. ABB Impell Corp., Melville, N.Y., 1988-90; sr. staff specialist for nuclear engring. Fla. Power & Light, Juno Beach, 1990—; developer seminar on stationary batteries, 1987. Contbg. author: Handbook of Power Calculations, 1984; also articles. Recipient Meritorious Svc. award Am. Nat. Standards Inst., 1994. Fellow IEEE (bd. dirs. 1990-92, fin. com. 1990-92, dir. stds. 1990-91, mem. exec. com. 1992, v.p. stds. activities, 1992, Stds. medal 1986, Stds. Bd. Disting. Svc. award 1993, Charles Proteus Steinmetz award 1996); mem. IEEE Power Engring. Soc. (Disting. Svc. award 1988, 92). Avocations: fishing, travel. Home: PO Box 9253 Jupiter FL 33468-9253 Office: Fla Power & Light PO Box 14000 (JPN/JB) Juno Beach FL 33408-0420

MIGLIO, DANIEL JOSEPH, telecommunications company executive; b. Phila., June 23, 1940; s. Daniel Joseph and Eleanor (Zucca) M.; children: Paige Leslie, Marcus Daniel. BS in Econs., U. Pa., 1962. With So. New Eng. Telephone Co, 1962-84; acct. New Haven, Conn., 1962-67; budget coordinator New Haven, 1967-69; dist. traffic mgr. New London, Conn., 1969-72; gen. acctg. mgr. New Haven, 1972-74; div. ops. mgr. Hartford, Conn., 1974-78; gen. mgr. corp. planning New Haven, 1979-83, v.p. corp. planning and regulatory matters. 1983-84; sr. v.p. fin. and planning So. New Eng. Telecommunications Corp., New Haven, 1984—; now chmn. & ceo So. New England Telecommunications Corp.; bd. dirs. 1st Constn. Bank, New Haven. Charter mem., bd. dirs. Clinton (Conn.) Jaycees, 1967-68; chmn. allocations com., bd. dirs. United Way, New Haven, 1973-74, New Haven Symphony Orch., 1990—; bd. dirs., v.p., pres. Gateway Counseling, Essex, Conn., 1975-86; bd. govs. Old Saybrook (Conn.) Hist. Soc., 1979-80; trustee Rector's Concern, Old Saybrook, 1980-88; chmn. So. New Eng. Telephone Co. Polit. Action Com., New Haven, 1987—. Mem. U.S. Telephone Assn. (bd. dirs., exec. com. 1984—), Conn. Joint Coun. on Econ. Edn. (fin. chmn. 1988—), U. Pa. Club Greater Hartford, Univ. Club Hartford, Kappa Alpha. Republican. Episcopalian. Avocations: cross country skiing, hiking, golf, tennis. Office: So New England Telecom Corp 227 Church St Fl 15 New Haven CT 06510-1801*

MIGNANELLI, JAMES ROBERT, manufacturing executive; b. Lawrence, Kans., May 20, 1932; s. Giacomo Mignanelli and Ida (Longo) Wlodyka; divorced; children: James T., Karen S., Suzanne J. Sales/mktg. AT&T, N. Andover, Mass., 1955-61; asst. sales engr. Transitron Corp., Wakefield, Mass., 1961-64; mgr. customer service ITT Corp., Lawrence, 1964-66, mgr. export and govt. sales, 1966-68, product mktg. engr., 1968-75; v.p. Plastronic Engring. Corp., Haverhill, Mass., from 1975, now exec. v.p. Served in USN, 1951-54. Roman Catholic. Home: 7 Greenlawn Ave Methuen MA 01844-6223 Office: Plastronic Engring Corp 35 Walnut St Haverhill MA 01830-5605

MIGNON, PAUL KILLIAN, laboratory executive; b. Manchester, Conn., Nov. 26, 1960; s. Charles William and Mary Anne (Killian) M.; m. Kimberly Anne Ray, Dec. 6, 1956; children: Rudolph, Sophia, Frank. AAS in Environ. Lab. Tech., S.E. C.C., Lincoln, 1983; BS in Chemistry, Doane Coll., 1996. Analytical lab. technician Hoskins-Western-Sonderegger, Inc., Lincoln, 1983-87; mgr. analytical svcs. divsn. HWS Cons. Group, Inc., Lincoln, 1987—; seminar leader Nebr. Wastewater Operators Conf., 1991-92, 95, Govt. Refuse Collection and Disposal Assn., Nebr., 1988; conf. presenter in field. Mem. ASTM, Am. Chem. Soc., Water Environment Fedn. Avocations: golf, hiking, camping. Home: RR 1 Box 95 Martell NE 68404-9750 Office: HWS Cons Group Inc 825 J St Lincoln NE 68508-2958

MIGNONE, MARIO B., Italian studies educator; b. Benevento, Italy, July 26, 1940; came to U.S., 1960; s. Roberto and Palmina (Iannace) M.; m. Lois Dolores Pontillo, June 29, 1968; children: Pamela Anne, Cristina Maria, Elizabeth Maria. BA, CCNY, 1967; MA, Rutgers U., 1969, PhD, 1972. Prof. Italian lang. SUNY, Stony Brook, 1970—, dir. undergrad. studies, 1976-83, dir. grad. studies, 1983-87; founder, exec. dir. Ctr. for Italian Studies, chmn. French and Italian dept., Stony Brook, 1988—. Author: The Theater of Eduardo De Filippo, 1974, Abnormality and Anguish in the Narrative of Dino Buzzati, 1981, Eduardo De Filippo, 1984, Pirandello in America, 1988, Columbus: Meeting of Cultures, 1993, Italy Today: A Country in Transition, 1995; assoc. mng. editor Forum Italicum, 1986-94, editor, 1994—; contbr. articles to profl. jours. Mem. Am. Assn. Tchrs. Italian (pres. 1982-84). Home: 26 Hopewell Dr Stony Brook NY 11790-2339 Office: SUNY Dept French Italian Stony Brook NY 11794

MIGUE, JEAN LUC, economics educator; b. Montreal, Que., Can., Apr. 13, 1933; s. Joseph Alfred and Marie Laurence (Venne) M.; m. Renee Caron, Sept. 13, 1958; children—Paule, Pascal, Nicolas. B.A. in Econs, U. Montreal, 1953, M.A., 1956; Ph.D. in Econs, Am. U., 1968. Researcher Bank of Can., 1957-58; prof. Laval U., 1962-70; prof. econs. Nat. Sch. Public Adminstrn., Quebec, 1970—; mem. staff Econ. Council Can., 1973-74. Author: The Price of Health, 1974, Le Prix du Transport, 1978, Nationalistic Policies of Canada, 1979, L'Economiste et La chose Publique, 1979, The Public Monopoly of Education, 1989, Federalism and Free Trade, 1993. Massey Found. fellow, 1956. Fellow Royal Soc. Can.; mem. Am. Econ. Assn., Can. Econ. Assn., Public Choice Soc. Roman Catholic. Office: 945 Wolfe, Quebec, PQ Canada G1V 3J9

MIGUEL DESOUSA, LINDA J., critical care nurse, nursing educator; b. Honolulu, Dec. 6, 1946; d. Gregory and Irene N. (Calasa) Furtado; children: Joseph H. Miguel Jr., Brett A. Miguel. ADN, Maui Community Coll., Kahului, Hawaii, 1980; BSN, U. Hawaii, 1987, MS, 1990. RN, Hawaii. Charge nurse ICU-CCU Maui Meml. Hosp., Wailuku; nursing instr. Maui Community Coll., Kahului; unit supr.-coronary care Straub Clinic and Hosp., Honolulu; nursing instr. Kapiolani Community Coll., Honolulu; edn. dir. Waianae Health Acad.; researcher in field. Contbr. articles to profl. jours. Outer Island Students Spl. Nursing scholar, 1988-90, Rsch. scholarship, 1989. Mem. AACN, Hawaii Nurses Assn., Hawaii Soc. for Cardiovascular and Pulmonary Rehab., Assn. Am. Women in C. C.s, Sigma Theta Tau. Home: 98-402 Koauka Loop #1202 Aiea HI 96701

MIHALAS, DIMITRI MANUEL, astronomer, educator; b. Los Angeles, Mar. 20, 1939; s. Emmanuel Demetrious and Jean (Christo) M.; m. Alice Joelen Covalt, June 15, 1963 (div. Nov. 1974); children: Michael Demetrious, Genevieve Alexandra; m. Barbara Ruth Rickey, May 18, 1975 (div. Dec. 1992). B.A. with highest honors, UCLA, 1959; M.S., Calif. Inst. Tech., 1960, Ph.D., 1964. Asst. prof. astrophys. scis. Princeton U., 1964-67; asst. prof. physics U. Colo., 1967-68; asso. prof. astronomy and astrophysics U. Chgo., 1968-70, prof., 1970-71; adj. prof. astrogeophysics, also physics and astrophysics U. Colo., 1972-80; sr. scientist High Altitude Obs., Nat. Center Atmospheric Research, Boulder, Colo., 1971-79, 82-85; prof. astronomy U. Ill., 1985—; astronomer Sacramento Peak Obs., Sunspot, N.Mex., 1979-82; cons. Los Alamos Nat. Lab, 1981—; vis. prof. dept. astrophysics Oxford (Eng.) U., 1977-78; sr. vis. fellow dept. physics and astronomy Univ. Coll., London, 1978; mem. astronomy adv. panel NSF, 1972-75. Author: Galactic Astronomy, 2d edit, 1981, Stellar Atmospheres, 1970, 2d edit., 1978, Theorie des Atmospheres Stellaires, 1971, Foundations of Radiation Hydrodynamics, 1984; assoc. editor Astrophys. Jour, 1970-79, Jour. Computational Physics, 1981-87, Jour. Quantitative Spectroscopy, 1984—; mem. editorial bd. Solar Physics, 1981-89. NSF fellow, 1959-62; Van Maanen fellow, 1962-63; Eugene Higgins vis. fellow, 1963-64; Alfred P. Sloan Found. Research fellow, 1969-71; Alexander von Humboldt Stiftung sr. U.S. scientist awardee, 1984. Mem. U.S. Nat. Acad. Sci., Internat. Astron. Union (pres. commn. 36 1976-79), Am. Astron. Soc. (Helen B. Warner prize 1974), Astron. Soc. Pacific (dir. 1975-77). Home: 1924 Blackthorn Dr Champaign IL 61821-6300 Office: Dept Astronomy U Ill 1002 W Green St Urbana IL 61801-3074

MIHALY, EUGENE BRAMER, corporate executive, consultant, writer, educator; b. The Hague, The Netherlands, Nov. 11, 1934; s. Eddy and Cecile (Bramer) Kahn; stepson of Eugene Mihaly; m. Stacey Beth Pulner, Apr. 21, 1996; children: Lisa Klee, Jessica. AB magna cum laude, Harvard U., 1956; PhD, London Sch. Econs. and Polit. Sci., 1964. Aviation/space editor Hartford (Conn.) Courant, 1960-61; internat. economist AID, Washington, 1964-65; dep. dir. Peace Corps, Tanzania, 1966, dir., 1967-68; dep. dir. East Asia/Pacific bur. Peace Corps, Washington, 1969, dir. office program devel., evaluation and rsch., 1969-70; assoc. dir. Inst. Internat. Studies, U. Calif., Berkeley, 1970-72; pres. Mihaly Internat. Corp., 1972—; chmn. bd. Mihaly Internat. Can., Ltd., 1992—; pres., CEO MI Energy Ptnrs., L.P., 1995—; sr. lectr. Haas Sch. Bus. U. Calif., Berkeley, 1991-95. Author: Foreign Aid and Politics in Nepal: A Case Study, 1965; contbr.: Political Development in Micronesia, 1974, Management of the Multinationals, 1974; also articles to various publs. Vice chmn. bd. dirs. Childreach (Plan Internat. U.S.A.); bd. dirs. Plan Internat., Inc.; trustee World Without War Coun.; chmn. emeritus Calif.-S.E. Asia Bus. Coun.; mem. Dist. Export Coun. No. Calif.; mem. adv. bd. World Resources Inst.; mem. U.S. nat. com. Pacific Econ. Coop. Mem. Coun. on Fgn. rels., Signet Soc. Home: 153 Rumstick Rd Barrington RI 02806

MIHAN, RICHARD, retired dermatologist; b. L.A., Dec. 20, 1925; s. Arnold and Virginia Catherine (O'Reilly) M.; student U. So. Calif., 1945; MD, St. Louis U., 1949. Rotating intern Los Angeles County Gen. Hosp., 1949-51, resident in dermatology, 1954-57; practice medicine specializing in dermatology, Los Angeles, 1957-95; emeritus clin. prof. dept. medicine, dermatology and syphilology U. So. Calif. Served as lt. (j.g.) M.C., USNR, 1951-53, ret. as lt. comdr. Diplomate Am. Bd. Dermatology. Fellow ACP; mem. Internat. Soc. Dermatology, Soc. Investigative Dermatology, Pacific Dermatologic Assn. (exec. bd. 1971-74), Calif. Med. Assn. (chmn. dermatologic sect. 1973-74), AMA, Los Angeles Dermatol. Soc. (pres. 1975-76), Am. Acad. Dermatology, L.A. Acad. Medicine (pres. 1988-89), Order of St. Lazarus (comdr.); Club: Calif. Roman Catholic.

MIHICH, ENRICO, medical researcher; b. Fiume, Italy, Jan. 4, 1928; came to U.S., 1957; s. Milan and Rosina (Lenaz) M.; m. Renata Marisa Mustacchi, Sept. 25, 1954; 1 child, Sylvia. B.S., U. Milan, Italy, 1944, M.D., 1951, docent, 1962; MD (honoris causa), U. Marseille, 1986. Research asst. Inst. Pharmacology U. Milan, Italy, 1951, asst. prof., 1954-56; vis. research fellow Sloan Kettering Inst. Cancer Research, N.Y.C., 1952-54; head pharmacology lab. Valeas Pharm. Industry, Milan, 1954-56; sr. cancer research scientist dept. exptl. therapeutics Roswell Park Cancer Inst., Buffalo, 1957-59, assoc. cancer research scientist, 1959-66, prin. scientist, 1966-71, dir. dept. exptl. therapeutics and Grace Cancer Drug Ctr., 1971—, v.p. for sponsored programs, 1987—; prof. pharmacology SUNY-Buffalo, 1960—, research asst., 1960-66, research assoc., 1966-68, research prof. pharmacology, 1968-69, chmn. dept. pharmacology, 1969—; assoc. prof. biochem. pharmacology Sch. of Pharmacy, 1963-68, adj. prof. biochem. pharmacology, 1968—; cons., lectr. in field; participant numerous symposia; sci. advisor govt. agys., pvt. industry; mem. Nat. Cancer Adv. Bd., 1984-90. Author more than 230 books, articles, chpts. in books; editor-in-chief for N.Am. and Japan, Cancer Immunology and Immunotherapy; mem. editorial bd. Advances in Cancer Chemotherapy, Internat. Jour. Immunopharmacology, Cancer and Metastasis Revs., others; adv. editor Oncology Rsch., Selective Cancer Therapeutics jours. Recipient numerous grants for med. rsch.; Fulbright travel fellow, 1952-53, Sloan Found. fellow, 1953-54; recipient Lifetimw Sci. award Inst. Advanced Studies in Immunology and Aging, 1994; named Myron Karon Meml. lectr., 1981. Office: Grace Cancer Drug Ctr Roswell Park Cancer Inst Elm And Carlton St Buffalo NY 14263-0001

MIHM, MICHAEL MARTIN, federal judge; b. Amboy, Ill., May 18, 1943; s. Martin Clarence and Frances Johannah (Morrissey) M.; m. Judith Ann Zosky, May 6, 1967; children—Molly Elizabeth, Sarah Ann, Jacob Michael, Jennifer Leah. B.A., Loras Coll., 1964; J.D., St. Louis U., 1967. Asst. prosecuting atty. St. Louis County, Clayton, Mo., 1967-68; asst. state's atty. Peoria County, Peoria, Ill., 1968-69; asst. city atty. City of Peoria, Ill., 1969-72; state's atty. Peoria County, Peoria, Ill., 1972-80; sole practice Peoria, Ill., 1980-82; U.S. dist. judge U.S. Govt., Peoria, Ill., 1982—; chief U.S. dist. judge U.S. Dist. Ct. (ctrl. dist.) Ill., 1991—; chmn. com. internat. jud. rels. U.S. Jud. Conf., 1994-96, mem. exec. coun., 1995—;, mem. com. jud. br., 1987-93; adj. prof. law John Marshall Law Sch., 1990—. Past mem. adv. bd. Big Brothers-Big Sisters, Crisis Nursery, Peoria; past bd. dirs. Salvation Army, Peoria, W.D. Boyce council Boy Scouts Am., State of Ill. Treatment Alternatives to Street Crime, Gov.'s Criminal Justice Info. Council; past vice-chmn. Ill. Dangerous Drugs Adv. Council; trustee Proctor Health Care Found., 1991—. Recipient Good Govt. award Peoria Jaycees, 1978. Mem. Peoria County Bar Assn. (former bd. dirs., past chmn. entertainment com.). Roman Catholic. Office: US Dist Ct 204 Federal Bldg 100 NE Monroe St Peoria IL 61602-1003

MIHRAN, THEODORE GREGORY, retired physicist; b. Detroit, June 28, 1924; s. Miro Krikor and Zaroohi (Mesrobian) M.; m. Hermine Misirian, July 26, 1953 (dec. 1980); children: Gregory Charles, Joyce Hermine, Richard Theodore; m. Jean Wilson, Aug. 22, 1981; stepchildren: Mark Whitcomb, Susan Rebecca. A.B., Stanford U., 1944, M.S., 1947, Ph.D. (Fortescue fellow, 1948-49), 1950. Physicist Rsch. and Devel. Ctr,, Gen. Electric Co., Schenectady, 1950-92; ret., 1992; vis. prof. elec. engring. dept. Cornell U., Ithaca, N.Y., 1963-64; adj. prof. Union Coll., Schenectady, 1960-61; lectr. Chalmers Inst., Gothenburg, Sweden, 1965; cons. in field. Contbr. articles to profl. publs. Pres., bd. dirs. Schenectady Symphony, 1962-63. Served with USN, 1944-46. Fellow IEEE (editor Trans. on Electron Devices 1970-73); mem. Am. Phys. Soc., Inst. Microwave Power, Sigma Xi, Phi Beta Kappa, Tau Beta Pi. Mem. Niskayuna Reformed Church. Patentee. Home: 898 Ash Tree Ln Niskayuna NY 12309-1723

MIIKE, LAWRENCE HIROSHI, public health officer; m. Kiliwehi Kono, 1993; 3 stepchildren, Kapono, Nainoa, Makana. BS in Chemistry, Amherst Coll., 1962; MD, U. Calif., San Francisco, 1966; JD, UCLA, 1972. Intern Phila. Gen. Hosp., 1966-67; with Nat. Ctr. Health Svcs. Rsch. and Devel., Washington, 1972-73; faculty Health Policy Program Sch. Medicine U. Calif., San Francisco, 1973-75, Med. Sch. Georgetown U., Washington, 1977-89; sr. assoc. Office of Tech. Assessment, U.S. Congress, Washington, 1977-89; founder, exec. dir. Papa Ola Lōkahi, Hawaii, 1989-92; prof. family prace and cmty. health U. Hawaii, Honolulu, 1989-92; med. dir. Hawaii QUEST Program, Honolulu, 1993-95; dir. Dept. Health, State of Hawaii, Honolulu, 1996—. With USAF, 1967-69. Office: 1250 Punchbowl St Honolulu HI 96813

MIILLER, SUSAN DIANE, artist; b. N.Y.C., June 10, 1953; d. Elwood Charles and Alyce Mary (Gebhardt) Knapp; m. Dennis Miiller, May 22, 1982. MA, Queens Coll., 1980; BFA, SUNY, 1988; MFA, U. North Tex., 1992. Palynologist Phillips Petroleum Co., Bartleville, Okla., 1980-85; scenic designer Forestburgh (N.Y.) Playhouse, 1989; rsch. asst. Lamont-Doherty Geol. Observatory, Palisades, N.Y., 1990; adj. prof. Tex. Christian U., Ft. Worth, 1992-94; lectr. U. Tex., Dallas, 1995-96; treas. mem. 500X Gallery, Dallas, 1991-92. One-woman shows include 500X Gallery, 1992, Milam Gallery, 1992, Bath House Cultural Ctr., 1992, Western Tex. Coll., 1993, Brazos Gallery, Richland Coll., 1993 Women and Their Work Gallery, 1995, A.I.R. Gallery, 1996; gallery representation: Milagros Contemporary Art, Sotto Gallery, Pentimento Gallery, Volkman/Bertow. Recipient 4th Nat. Biennial Exhbns., Grand Purchase award, 1991, Mus. Abilene award, 1992, Lubbock Art Festival Merit award, 1992, 2d pl. award Matrix Gallery, 1995, Hon. Mention award 3d Biennial Gulf of Mex. Exhbn., 1995, 1st place award Soho Gallery, 1996. Mem. Dallas Mus. Art, Coll. Art Assn., D-Art Visual Art Ctr., D.A.R.E., Women and Their Work. Home: 449 Harris St # J102 Coppell TX 75019-3224 Studio: 3309 Elm St # 3E Dallas TX 75226-1637

MIJARES, PERCIVAL S., beverage distribution company executive; b. Manila, Jan. 27, 1949; came to U.S., 1973; s. Jose M. and Paz (Samson) M.; m. Cecilia La Torre, Sept. 15, 1973; children: Cheryl, Philip. BBA, U. St. Tomas, Manila, 1968; M in Bus. Mgmt., Asian Inst. Mgmt., Makati, Philippines, 1972. CPA, The Philippines. Sr. auditor Sycip, Gorres, Velayo & Co., Manila, 1968-72; fin. mgr. TWA, Manila, 1973; contr. Norton Simon Communications, N.Y.C., 1973-76; v.p. Guinness Am., N.Y.C., 1977-88; CFO Blair Importers Ltd., N.Y.C., 1989-94, Conn. Distributors, Stratford, 1994—; lectr. N.Y. World Trade Inst. FX Mgmt. Seminar. Bd. dirs. PTA St. Sebastian Sch., N.Y.C., 1983. Sycip, Gorres, Velayo and Co. scholar, 1967-72. Mem. N.Am. Shippers Assn. (bd. dirs. 1990—). Avocations: golf, skiing, photography, oenology. Home: 9 Bayberry Ave Garden City NY 11530-1708 Office: Conn Distributors 333 Lordship Blvd Stamford CT 06904

MIKA, JOSEPH JOHN, library educator, consultant; b. McKees Rocks, Pa., Mar. 1, 1948; s. George Joseph and Sophie Ann (Stec) M.; children: Jason-Paul Joseph, Matthew Douglas, Meghan Leigh. BA in English, U. Pitts., 1969, M.L.S., 1971, Ph.D. in L.S., 1980. Asst. librarian, instr. Ohio State U., Mansfield, 1971-73; asst. librarian, asst. prof. Johnson State Coll. (Vt.), 1973-75; grad. asst., teaching fellow Sch. Libr. and Info. Sci. U. Pitts., 1975-77; asst. dean, assoc. prof. libr. svc. U. So. Miss., Hattiesburg, 1977-86, dir. libr. and info. sci. program, Wayne State U. Libr. and Info. Sci. program, 1986-94, prof., 1994—; cons. to libraries. Served to lt. col. USAR. Decorated D.S.M., Army Res. Components Achievement medal, Meritorius Svc. medal, Army Commendation medal. Mem. ALA (councilor 1983-86, chmn. constn. and bylaws com. 1985-86), Assn. Libr. and Info. Sci. Edn., (chmn. membership com. 1982-83, chmn. nominating com. 1982, exec. bd. 1986), Miss. Libr. Assn. (pres.-elect 1985), Mich. Libr. Assn. (chair libr. edn. com. 1989), Leadership Acad. (oversight com. 1989—), Assn. Coll. and Rsch. Librs. (chmn. 1982-83, chmn. budget com. 1982-83), Soc. Miss. Archivists (treas., exec. bd. 1981-83), Mich. Ctr. for The Book (chair 1994—), Beta Phi Mu (pres.-elect 1987-89, pres. 1989-91), Phi Delta Kappa. Lodge: Kiwanis (Hattiesburg). Contbr. articles to profl. jours. Home: 4332 Hillside Dr Ann Arbor MI 48105-2787 Office: Wayne State U Libr and Info Sci Program 106 Kresge Library Detroit MI 48202

MIKALOW, ALFRED ALEXANDER, II, deep sea diver, marine surveyor, marine diving consultant; b. N.Y.C., Jan. 19, 1921; m. Janice Brenner, Aug. 1, 1960; children: Alfred Alexander, Jon Alfred. Student Rutgers U., 1940; MS, U. Calif., Berkeley, 1948; MA, Rochdale U. (Can.), 1950. Owner Coastal Diving Co., Oakland, Calif., 1950—, Divers Supply, Oakland, 1952—; dir. Coastal Sch. Deep Sea Diving, Oakland, 1950—; capt. and master rsch. vessel Coastal Researcher I; mem. Marine Inspection Bur., Oakland. marine diving contractor, cons. Mem. adv. bd. Medic Alert Found., Turlock, Calif., 1960—. Lt. comdr. USN, 1941-47, 49-50. Decorated Purple Heart, Silver Star. Mem. Divers Assn. Am. (pres. 1970-74), Treasury Recovery, Inc. (pres. 1972-75), Internat. Assn. Profl. Divers, Assn. Diving Contractors, Calif. Assn. Pvt. Edn. (no. v.p. 1971-72), Authors Guild, Internat. Game Fish Assn., U.S. Navy League, U.S. Res. Officers Assn., Tailhook Assn., U.S. Submarine Vets. WWII, Explorer Club (San Francisco), Calif. Assn. Marine Surveyors (pres. 1988—), Soc. Naval Archs. and Marine Engrs. (assoc.), Masons, Lions. Author: Fell's Guide to Sunken Treasure Ships of the World, 1972; (with H. Rieseberg) The Knight from Maine, 1974. Office: 320 29th Ave Oakland CA 94601-2104

MIKALSON, JON DENNIS, classics educator; b. Milw., Aug. 1, 1943; s. John Martin and Evelyn Kathryn (Heuser) M.; m. Mary Helen Villemonte, Aug. 28, 1966; children: Melissa, Jacquelyn. BA, U. Wis., 1965; postgrad., Am. Sch. Classical Studies, Athens, Greece, 1968-69; PhD, Harvard U., 1970. Asst. prof. classics U. Va., Charlottesville, 1970-75, assoc. prof., 1975-84, prof., 1984—, chmn. dept. classics, 1978-90; vis. scholar Corpus Christi Coll., Cambridge, Eng., 1977-78; mem. Inst. for Advanced Study, Princeton, N.J., 1984-85; Whitehead prof. Am. Sch. Classical Studies, 1995-96. Author: The Sacred and Civil Calendar of the Athenian Year, 1975, Athenian Popular Religion, 1983, Honor Thy Gods: Popular Religion in Greek Tragedy, 1991; contbr. articles to profl. and scholarly jours. James Rignall Wheeler fellow Am. Sch. Classical Studies, 1968-69, NEH fellow, 1977-78, Herodotus fellow Inst. for Advanced Study, 1984-85. Mem. Am. Philol. Assn., Am. Sch. Classical Studies, Archeol. Inst. of Am., Classical Assn. of Middle West and South (pres. so. sect. 1988-90), Classical Assn. of Va., Phi Beta Kappa, Phi Eta Sigma, Phi Kappa Phi. Club: Lions. Home: PO Box 664 Crozet VA 22932-0664 Office: University of Virginia Dept of Classics 146 Cabell Hall Charlottesville VA 22903-3196

MIKE, DEBORAH DENISE, systems software, quality assurance engineer; b. Norfolk, Va., Oct. 19, 1959; d. William A. and Mophecia (Cook) Brickhouse. BA in Math., U. Va., 1981; postgrad., Johns Hopkins U., 1982-83; MS in Computer Systems Mgmt., U. Md., 1994. Primary systems engr. GTE Govt. Systems Corp., Rockville, Md., 1984-85, Vienna, Va., 1985-87; computer analyst Info. Systems and Networks Corp., Arlington, Va., 1987-88; realtor Mount Vernon Realty, Chevy Chase, Md., 1988-89; primary systems engr. Grumman Corp., McLean, Va., 1988-91, J.G. Van Dyke & Assocs., Alexandria, Va., 1991-93; systems engr. Pulse Engring., Inc., Beltsville, Md., 1993-94; sr. systems software quality assurance engr. Unisys at NASA, Greenbelt, Md., 1995—; owner DDM Enterprises, Designs by Debbie. Active Smithsonian Resident Assoc. Program, 1988; mem. Friends of the Kennedy Ctr. Mem. NAFE (bd. dirs. Reston chpt. 1986), Nat. Assn. Realtors, Md. Assn. Realtors, Montgomery County Bd. Realtors, N.Y. Inst. Photography, U. Va. Alumni Assn., U. Va. Club Washington. Avocations: sewing and fashion planning, photography, sketching, painting, designing jewely.

MIKEL, SARAH ANN, librarian; b. Bklyn., Aug. 29, 1947; d. Robert H. and Sarah A. (Saver) Whalen; m. John R. Mikel, Oct. 21, 1977; 1 dau., Katherine Ann. B.A., U. Miami, 1969; M.A., U. Fla., 1971; M.A.L.S., Rosary Coll., River Forest, Ill., 1973. Editorial researcher Field Ednl. Enterprises, Chgo., 1971-72; librarian Purdue U., West Lafayette, Ind., 1973-75, U.S. Army Corps of Engrs., Rock Island, Ill., 1975-76, chief librarian, Washington, 1976-87, major command librarian, 1987-91; libr. dir. Nat. Def. Libr., Washington, 1991—; chmn. FEDLINK Users Group, 1980-83; mem. exec. adv. coun. FEDLINK, 1988-90; program chmn. Fed. Interagy. Field Librs. Workshop, 1983-84; mem. com. Fed. Libr. and Info. Ctr., 1992-95; mem. mil. edn. coordinating com. Libr. Group. Mem. Spl. Libr. Assn. (chmn. mil. librs. 1978-79), Army Libr. Inst. (chmn. 1988, 94, Army dep. functional chiefs rep. 1992-94). Home: 3343 Reservoir Rd NW Washington DC 20007-2312 Office: Nat Def Univ Ft Leslie J McNair 4th & P St SW Washington DC 20319

MIKEL, THOMAS KELLY, JR., laboratory administrator; b. East Chicago, Ind., Aug. 27, 1946; s. Thomas Kelly and Anne Katherine (Vrazo) M.; BA, San Jose State U., 1973; MA, U. Calif.-Santa Barbara, 1975. Asst. dir. Santa Barbara Underseas Found., 1975-76; marine biologist PJB Labs., Ventura, Calif., 1976-81; lab. dir. CRL Environ., Ventura, 1981-88; lab. dir. ABC Labs, Ventura, 1988—; instr. oceanography Ventura Coll., 1980-81. Chair joint task group, section author 20th edit. Std. Methods Examination Water & Wastewater APHA, 1996. With U.S. Army, 1968-70. Mem. Assn. Environ. Profls., Soc. Population Ecologists, ASTME (rsch. contbr. 10th ann. symposium 1986), Soc. Environ. Toxicology and Chemistry. Biol. coord. Anacapa Underwater Natural trail U.S. Nat. Park Svc., 1976; designer ecol. restoration program of upper Newport Bay, Orange County, Calif., 1978; rsch. contbr. 3d Internat. Artificial Reef Conf., Newport Beach, Calif., 1983, Ann. Conf. Am. Petroleum Inst., Houston. Democrat.

MIKELS, J(AMES) RONALD, bank executive; b. Knoxville, Tenn., Nov. 21, 1937; s. Jesse R. and Virginia L. (Walters) M.; m. Norma Jean Weatherly, Jan. 8, 1966; 1 child, J. Richard. M in Graphoanalysis, Internat. Graphoanalysis Soc., Chgo., 1961; BS, U. Tenn., 1980; MRE, Bethany Theol. Sem., 1993. Cert. human resources profl. Electronic data processing auditor Park Nat. Bank, Knoxville, 1956-78; retirement specialist U. Tenn., Knoxville, 1979-80; dir. pers. Home Fed. Bank, Knoxville, 1980—; instr. U. Tenn., Knoxville, 1972-77; mem. adv. coun. Pellissippi State Coll., Knoxville, 1986-88; ct. handwriting expert, 1968—. Contbr. articles to mags. and jours. Campaign coord. United Way, Knoxville, 1985-96; cons. Jr. Achievement, Knoxville, 1990, 92, 93, 94. Mem. Full Gospel Businessmen's Fellowship Internat., Tenn. League Savs. Instns. (bd. dirs. 1989). Wesleyan Methodist. Office: Home Fed Bank 515 Market St Knoxville TN 37902-2145

MIKESELL, MARVIN WRAY, geography educator; b. Kansas City, Mo., June 16, 1929; s. Loy George and Clara (Wade) M.; m. Reine-Marie de France, Apr. 1, 1957. B.A., UCLA, 1952, M.A., 1953; Ph.D., U. Calif.-Berkeley, 1959. Instr. to prof. geography U. Chgo., 1958—, chmn. dept. geography, 1969-74, 83-86; del. U.S. Nat. Commn. for UNESCO. Author: Northern Morocco, 1961; editor: Readings in Cultural Geography, 1962, Geographers Abroad, 1973, Perspectives on Environment, 1974. Fellow Am. Geog. Soc. (hon.); mem. Assn. Am. Geographers (pres. 1975-76, Disting. Career award 1995). Club: Quadrangle. Home: 1155 E 56th St Chicago IL 60637-1530 Office: Com Geog Studies 5828 S University Ave Chicago IL 60637-1515

MIKESELL, RAYMOND FRECH, economics educator; b. Eaton, Ohio, Feb. 13, 1913; s. Otho Francis and Josephine (Frech) M.; m. Desyl De-Lauder, July 6, 1937 (div.); children: George DeLauder and Norman De-Lauder (twins); m. Irene Langdoc, Feb. 18, 1956. Student, Carnegie Inst. Tech., 1931-33; BA cum laude, Ohio U., 1935, MA, 1935, PhD, 1939. Asst. prof. econ. U. Wash., 1937-41; economist OPA, Washington, 1941-42, U.S. Treasury Dept., 1942-46; rep. U.S. Treasury Dept., Cairo, Egypt, 1943-44; cons. U.S. Treasury Dept., 1946-47; on Middle East affairs FOA, 1953; chief fgn. minerals div. Pres.'s Materials Policy Commn., 1951-52; mem. staff Fgn. Econ. Policy Com. (Randall Com.), 1953-54; mem. U.S. Currency Mission to Saudi Arabia, 1948; spl. U.S. rep. to Israel, summer 1952; mem. U.S. mission to Israel, Ethiopia, summer 1953; prof. econs. U. Va., 1946-57; W.E. Miner prof. econs. U. Oreg., 1957-87, prof. econs., 1987—; dir. Inst. Internat. Studies and Overseas Adminstrn., 1958-60; assoc. dir. Inst. Internat. Studies and Overseas Adminstrn. U. Oreg., 1960-68; vis. prof. Grad. Inst. Internat. Studies, Geneva, 1964; sr. staff mem. Council Econ. Advisers, Exec. Office of Pres., 1955-56, cons. to Council Econ. Advisers, 1956-57; cons. Pan Am.

Union, 1954-63, Dept. State, 1947-53, 63-67, 71-83, Ford Found., 1962, Dept. Commerce, 1962-64, ICA, 1952-53, 61-62, OAS, 1963-73, AID, 1964-71; mem. UN Econ. Commn. for Latin Am. working group on regional market, 1958; cons. Senate Fgn. Relations Com., 1962, 67, World Bank, 1968, Inter-Am. Devel. Bank, 1968-75; mem. panel advisers Sec. Treasury, 1965-69; sr. fellow Nat. Bur. Econ. Research, 1972-73. Author: U.S. Economic Policy and International Relations, 1952, Foreign Exchange in the Postwar World, 1954, The Emerging Pattern of International Payments, 1954, Foreign Investments in Latin Am, 1955, Promoting United States Private Investment Abroad, 1957, Agricultural Surpluses and Export Policy, 1958, (with H. Chenery) Arabian Oil, 1949, (with M. Trued) Postwar Bilateral Payments Agreements, 1955, (with J. Behrman) Financing Free World Trade with the Sino-Soviet Bloc, 1958, Public International Lending for Development, 1966, (with R.W. Adler) Public External Financing of Devel. Banks, 1966, Public Fgn. Capital for Private Enterprises in Developing Countries, 1966, The Economics of Foreign Aid, 1968, Financing World Trade, 1969, (with others) Foreign Investment in the Petroleum and Mineral Industries, 1971; Editor: U.S. Private and Government Investment Abroad, 1962, (with H. Furth) Foreign Dollar Balances and the International Role of the Dollar, 1974, Foreign Investment in the Copper Industry, 1975, The World Copper Industry, 1979, New Patterns of World Mineral Development, 1979, The Economics of Foreign Aid and Self-Sustaining Development, 1983, Foreign Investment in Mining Projects, 1983, Petroleum Company Operations and Agreements in the Developing Countries, 1984, Stockpiling Strategic Materials, 1986, Nonfuel Minerals: Foreign Dependence and National Security, 1987; (with John W. Whitney) The World Mining Industry: Investment Strategy and Public Policy, 1987, The Global Copper Industry: Problems and Prospects, 1988, (with Lawrence F. Williams) International Banks and the Environment, 1992, Economic Development and the Environment, 1992, The Bretton Woods Debates, 1994; mem. editorial adv. bd. Middle East Jour., 1947-58; mem. bd. editors: Am. Econ. Rev., 1953-55. Home: 2290 Spring Blvd Eugene OR 97403-1860

MIKESELL, RICHARD LYON, lawyer, financial counselor; b. Corning, N.Y., Jan. 29, 1941; s. Walter Ray and Clara Ellen (Lyon) M.; m. Anna May Creese, Mar. 16, 1973; 1 child, Joel. BSChemE, U. Calif., Berkeley, 1962; LLB, Duke U., 1965; BA in Liberal Studies, UCLA, 1977. Bar: U.S. Supreme Ct., Ohio, Calif., U.S. Ct. Appeals (9th and 2d cirs.), U.S. Patent Office. Patent atty. Procter & Gamble, Cin., 1965-66, Rocketdyne divsn. N.Am. Aviation, L.A., 1966-69; pvt. practice law L.A., 1969-81; prin. Law Offices of R.L. Mikesell, L.A., 1981—; fin. counselor L.A. Police Dept., 1986—; arbitrator Am. Arbitration Assn., L.A., 1980—. Pres. San Fernando Valley Fair Housing Coun., L.A., 1969-72, Valley Women's Ctr., L.A., 1990; line res. officer L.A. Police Dept., 1969-72. Named Res. Officer of Yr. L.A. Police Dept., 1990. Avocation: high power rifle shooting. Office: 14540 Hamlin St Ste B Van Nuys CA 91411-1626

MIKI, ARATA, law educator; b. Mifune, Kumamoto, Japan, Jan. 15, 1928; s. Gunji Yamashita and Chiyo M.; m. Michiko Kogure, May 9, 1959. LLB, Nagoya (Japan) Law Sch., 1953; postgrad., Nagoya Grad. Sch. Law, 1956. Prof. faculty law Kyoto (Japan) Sangyo U., 1969-79, leading prof. Grad. Sch. Law, 1972-79, prof., leading prof. faculty law Grad. Sch. Law, 1980—; fellow Japan Found., Tokyo, 1979-80; Japan Found. vis. fellow Rheinische Friedrich Wilhelms U. Bonn, Germany, 1979-80; sr. assoc. mem. governing body St. Anthony's Coll., U. Oxford, Eng., 1980; vicarious exec. dir. Inst. World Affairs, Tokyo, 1974-76; dean faculty law Kyoto Sangyo U., 1982-88, pres. Grad. Sch. Law, 1982-88; trustee Found. Kyoto Sangyo U., 1985-89. Author: Systematic Motivation to the Philosophy of Law, 1974; joint chmn./joint author: What is Law to Japanese?, 1974; proponent/joint editor: Acta Humanistica Scientifica Universitatis Sangio Kyotiensis, 1977, 78, 79; contbr. articles to profl. jours. Mem. Assn. Music, Opera and Culture, Tokyo, 1975—, Tokyo Round Table, 1985-95, Japan Com. for East Asia Econ. Cmty., Tokyo, 1992—, Japan Philanthropic Assn., Tokyo, 1992—. Named Hon. Citizen of Huntsville (Ala.), 1973. Mem. Internat. Assn. Philosophy Law and Social Philosophy, Inst. Nat. Politics, St. Anthony's Soc. U. Oxford. Avocations: walking, Japanese traditional Noh play, classical music, opera, pictures. Office: c/o Kyoto Sangyo U, 36 Kamigemo Motoyama Kitaku, Kyoto 603, Japan 113

MIKITA, JOSEPH KARL, broadcasting executive; b. nr. Richmond, Va., Oct. 3, 1918; s. John and Catherine (Wargofcak) M.; m. Mary Therese Benya, Nov. 26, 1942; children: Patty-Jane Mikita Cashman, Michael, M. Noël Mikita Garagiola. BS, Fordham U., 1939; MS, Columbia U., 1940. Treas., controller Capital Cities Broadcasting Co., Albany, N.Y., 1955-58; controller Westinghouse Broadcasting Co., Inc., N.Y.C., 1958-60, v.p. fin., 1960-64, v.p. fin. and adminstrn., 1964-65, sr. v.p., 1965-69, 1975—; also dir., exec. v.p. Westinghouse Electric Corp. for Broadcasting, Learning and Leisure Activities, N.Y.C., 1969-75; dir. Sutro Tower, Inc. Author: (with others) The Business of Broadcasting, 1964. Bd. dirs. Fordham U. Council, Albany County Workshop, Albany County Heart Assn., Citizens For Reasonable Growth, Boca Raton; chmn. bd. Instructional TV. Served to maj. AUS, 1940-45, ETO. Recipient Order of Merit (Silver), Westinghouse Electric Corp., Disting. Service Alumni award Fordham U., 1969. Mem. AICPA, Internat. Radio and TV Soc., N.Y. Soc. CPAs, Fin. Execs. Inst. (dir., past pres. Manhattan chpt.), Inst. Broadcasting Fin. Mgmt. (past dir.), Town Club, Westchester Country Club, Boca Raton Club, M.G.A. Club, JDM Country Club, Royal Palm Yacht and Country Club, Rotary (1st v.p. N.Y. club). Home: 3125 NE 7th Dr Boca Raton FL 33431-6906 Office: 90 Park Ave New York NY 10016

MIKITKA, GERALD PETER, investment banker, financial consultant; b. Chgo., July 7, 1943; s. Michael and Helen (Cuprisin) M.; m. Nancy Lee Parker, Mar. 6, 1977; children: Richard, Jeffrey, Jennifer. B.S.B.A. in Fin., Roosevelt U., 1966, postgrad., 1967. Diplomate: registered investment advisor. Sr. investment exec. Shearson-Hayden, Stone, Chgo., 1967-73; chmn., pres. Capital Directions, Inc., Chgo., 1973—; pres. CDI Fin. Advisors, Chgo., 1974—, CDI Properties, Chgo., 1974—, CDI Communications, Inc., Chgo., 1978—, A.B. Properties Inc., Chgo., 1986—, Am. Eagle Realty Inc., Chgo., 1988—, Grand Caribbean Properties Inc., Chgo., 1988, Cain Estates Inc., Chgo., 1988—, Caribbean Sea Properties Inc., Chgo., 1989—. Served with U.S. Army, 1967-69. Mem. Nat. Assn. Securities Dealers, Securities Investment Protection Assn., Broadcast Fin. Mgmt. Assn., Nat. Radio Broadcast Assn., Internat. Assn. Fin. Planning. Lodge: Rotary.

MIKKELSON, DEAN HAROLD, geological engineer; b. Devils Lake, N.D., July 25, 1922; s. John Harold and Theodora (Eklund) M.; m. Delphene Doss, May 30, 1946; 1 child, Lynn Dee Hoffman. Student, N.D. State Coll., 1940-41; midshipman, U.S. Naval Acad., 1942-45; BS in Geological Engring., U. N.D., 1956. Registered profl. engr., Okla. 2d officer U.S. Lines, Quaker Lines-States Lines, Portland, Oreg., 1945-48; ptnr. J.I. Case Farm Machinery & Packard Automobile Franchises, Devils Lake, N.D., 1948-52; oil and gas lease broker Devils Lake, N.D., 1952-54; geologist Sohio Petroleum Co., Oklahoma City, 1956-58; geol. engr. Petrobras, Belem do Para, Brazil, 1958-60; pvt. practice Oklahoma City, 1961-78; pres., owner Dogwatch Petroleum, Inc., Oklahoma City, 1978—; agrl. pilot, N.D., Mont., Tex., N.Mex., summers, 1952-56. Author: (as Dee Geo) Danny; contbr. articles to profl. jours. Candidate Okla. Rep. State Legislature, Oklahoma City, 1958; del. various county and state conv., N.D. and Okla., 1948-68. With N.D. N.G., 1938-40, U.S. Army Air Corps., 1942. Mem. Oklahoma City Geol. Soc., Masons, Shriners, Jesters, Am. Legion, Sportsmans Country Club. Republican. Avocations: hunting, fishing, golf, oil painting, singing. Office: Dogwatch Petroleum Inc Ste H 4430 NW 50 St Ste H Oklahoma City OK 73112-2295

MIKLASZEWSKI, JAMES ALAN, television news correspondent; b. Milw., July 8, 1949; s. Bernard Anthony Miklaszewski and LaVerne Dorothy (Venus) Montagano; m. Cheryl Ann Heyse; children: James Alexander, Jeffrey Alan. Reporter WISM Radio, Madison, Wis., 1970-71; new dir. WIZM Radio, LaCrosse, Wis., 1971-72; reporter WBAP Radio, Ft. Worth, 1972-75; news dir. KRXV Radio, Ft. Worth, 1975-80; corr. CNN, Dallas, N.Y.C., 1980-83; White House corr. CNN, Washington, 1983-84, nat. corr., 1984-85; Pentagon corr. NBC TV News, Washington, 1985-88, White House corr., 1988—. Recipient ACE award Nat. Cable Acad., 1983, Edward R. Murrow award Bnai Brith, 1985, Pres.' award Wesley Coll., 1994. Mem. White House Corrs. Assn. Methodist. Avocations: ornithology, golf. Office: NBC News Washington Bur 4001 Nebraska Ave NW Washington DC 20016-2733

MIKLOSHAZY, ATTILA, bishop. Ordained priest Roman Cath. Ch., 1961, consecrated bishop, 1989. Titular bishop Castel Minore; bishop Apostolate to Hungarians, Scarborough, Ont., Can., 1989—. Mem. Jesuit Soc. Office: St Augustine's Sem, 2661 Kingston Rd, Scarborough, ON Canada M1M 1M3

MIKOLYZK, THOMAS ANDREW, librarian; b. Kenosha, Wis., Sept. 9, 1953; s. Andrew John and Charlotte Elaine (McIver) M.; m. Ann J. Moyer, May 26, 1973 (div. June 1981); children: Kari, Emily; m. Amy L. Kessel, Sept. 4, 1982; 1 child, Alice; 1 stepchild, David. BA in English and Elem. Edn., Beloit (Wis.) Coll., 1982; MA in Libr. Sci., U. Chgo., 1986; cert. in advanced study, Concordia U., 1995. Libr. asst. Beloit Coll., 1980-82; sports writer Beloit Daily News, 1981-83; tchr. Turner Mid. Sch., Beloit, 1983; tchr., libr. Horizon's Edge Sch., Canterbury, N.H., 1983-85; libr. U. Ill., Chgo., 1985-86, Lake Forest (Ill.) Coll., 1986-89, Dist 62, Des Plaines, Ill., 1989-93; libr., dir. summer program Avery Coonley Sch., Downers Grove, Ill., 1993—. Author: Langston Hughes-A Bio-Bibliography, 1990, Oscar Wilde: An Annotated Bibliography, 1993. Campaign mgr. United Way, Delavan, Wis., 1978-79; deacon 1st Congregation Ch., Des Plaines, 1990. Mem. ASCD, Ill. Sch. Libr. Assn., Ind. Sch. Assn. Ctrl. States, U.S. Chess Fedn. Avocations: chess, bibliography, book collecting, sailing. Home: 7361 Prescott Ln Countryside IL 60525-5037 Office: Avery Coonley Sch 1400 Maple Ave Downers Grove IL 60515-4828

MIKULAS, JOSEPH FRANK, graphic designer, educator, painter; b. Jacksonville, Fla., Sept. 15, 1926; s. Joseph and Marina (Zeman) M.; m. Joyce Gregory Haddock, Sept. 29, 1946; children—Joyce Marina Mikulas Abney, Juliana Claire Mikulas Catlin. Student Harold Hilton Studios, 1942-50. Art dir. Peeples Displays, Inc., 1945-50, 53-56, Douglas Printing Co. Inc., 1950-53, 56-59; ptnr., graphic design exec. Benton & Mikulas Assocs., Inc., Jacksonville, 1960-67; pres. Mikulas Assocs., Inc., Jacksonville, 1968-92, exec. graphic designer, retired dir. communications, adj. prof. advt. design Jacksonville U.; mem. adv. bd. Pub. TV. Chmn. Youth Resources Bur.; chmn. Mayor's Medal Com. Served with USAAF, 1945. Recipient Gold medal Am. Advt. Fedn., 4th dist., 1971; numerous other awards, 1960-81. Mem. Advt. Fedn. of Jacksonville (past pres. 1970), Jacksonville Watercolor Soc. Republican. Episcopalian. Clubs: San Jose Country, River, Art Dirs. of Jacksonville (past pres.). Lodges: Masons, Rotary (past pres. S. Jacksonville 1970, Paul Harris fellow), Torch of Jacksonville (past pres. 1977). Creator over 40 trademarks for local, regional, nat. and internat. use by corps. based in Jacksonville. Home: 2014 River Rd Jacksonville FL 32207-3906 Office: 3886 Atlantic Blvd Jacksonville FL 32207-2035

MIKULSKI, BARBARA ANN, senator; b. Balt., July 20, 1936; d. William and Christine (Kutz) M. BA, Mt. St. Agnes Coll., 1958; MSW, U. Md., 1965; LLD (hon.), Goucher Coll., 1973, Hood Coll., 1978, Bowie State U., 1989, Morgan State U., 1990, U. Mass., 1991; DHL (hon.), Pratt Inst., 1974. Tchr. Vista Tng. Ctr. Mount St. Mary's Sem., Balt.; social worker Balt. Dept. Social Services, 1961-63, 66-70; mem. Balt. City Council, 1971-76, 95th-99th Congresses from 3d Md. Dist., 1977-87; U.S. senator from Md., 1987—, sec. Dem. Conf. 104th Congress; adj. prof. Loyola Coll., 1972-76. Bd. visitors U.S. Naval Acad. Recipient Nat. Citizen of Yr. award Buffalo Am.-Polit. Eagle, 1973, Woman of Yr. Bus. & Profl. Women's Club Assn., 1973, Outstanding Alumnus U. Md. Sch. Social Work, 1973, Govt. Social Responsibility award, 1991. Mem. LWV. *

MIKULSKI, PIOTR WITOLD, mathematics educator; b. Warsaw, Poland, July 20, 1925; came to U.S., 1957; s. Julian and Zofia (Zalewska) M.; m. Barbara H. Mikulski, Sept. 2, 1960; 1 son, Antony F. B.S., Sch. Stats., Warsaw, Poland, 1951, M.S., 1952; Ph.D., U. Calif.-Berkeley, 1961. Adj. Sch. Stats., 1950-57, Inst. Math., Warsaw, Poland, 1952-57; teaching and research asst. U. Calif.-Berkeley, 1957-61; asst. prof. math. U. Ill., Urbana, 1961-62; asst. prof. U. Md., College Park, 1962-66, assoc. prof., 1966-70, prof., 1970. Assoc. editor: Am. Jour. Math. and Mgmt. Sci., 1982—; contbr. articles to profl. jours. Mem. Inst. Math. Stats., Polish Inst. Arts and Scis. Am. Home: 2525 Sandy Run Ct Annapolis MD 21401-7371 Office: U Md Dept Math College Park MD 20742

MIKURIYA, MARY JANE, educational agency administrator; b. Pitts., Oct. 8, 1934; d. Tadafumi and Anna (Schwenk) M.; m. J. Anton Jungherr, June 8, 1977 (div. Dec. 1992); children: Anna Schwenk Mikuriya Jungherr, Anton Jungherr Jr. BA, Brown U., 1956; MA, San Francisco State U., 1970. Cert. tchr. and adminstr., Calif. Tchr. Castilleja Sch. for Girls, Palo Alto, Calif., 1958-60, Mpls. Pub. Schs., 1961-62; tchr. San Francisco Unified Sch. Dist., 1963-68, evaluator, 1968-71, dir. Emergency Sch. Assist. Program, 1971-73; HEW fellow U.S. Dept. of Edn., Washington, 1973-74, edn. program specialist, 1974-76; special asst. to assoc. supt. San Francisco Unified Sch. Dist., 1976-78, grant writer, facilitator, Dept. State & Fed. Projects, 1978—; adv. bd. mem. Far West Lab., San Francisco, 1977-81, Ednl. Testing Svc., Princeton, N.J., 1974-75; cons. U.S. Dept. of Edn., Washington, 1978, 80, 81, 91. Interviewer, bd. dirs. U.S. Servas, 1978—; active Unitarian Ch., 1978—; host Internat. Visitor Ctr., 1985—; area rep. George Sch., Pa., 1988—. Mem. Japanese-Am. Citizens League. Avocations: international travel, camping. Home: 361 Mississippi St San Francisco CA 94107-2925 Office: San Francisco Unified Sch Dist 2550 25th Ave San Francisco CA 94116-2901

MIKUS, ELEANORE ANN, artist; b. Detroit, July 25, 1927; d. Joseph and Bertha (Englot) M.; m. Richard Burns, July 6, 1949 (div. 1963); children: Richard, Hillary, Gabrielle. Student, Mich. State U., 1946-49, U. Mex., summer 1948; B.F.A., U. Denver, 1957, M.A., 1967; postgrad., Art Students League, 1958, NYU, 1959-60. Asst. prof. Cornell U., Ithaca, N.Y., 1979-80, assoc. prof., 1980-92, prof. art, 1992-94, prof. emerita, 1994—; asst. prof. art Monmouth Coll., West Long Branch, N.J., 1966-70, prof. Cornell, Rome, 1989; vis. lectr. painting Cooper Union, N.Y.C., 1970-72, Central Sch. Art and Design, London, 1973-77, Harrow (Eng.) Coll. Tech. and Art, 1975-76. Exhibited in 14 one-person shows at, Pace Gallery, N.Y.C. and O.K. Harris Gallery, N.Y.C., Baskett Gallery, Cin., 1982, 84, 85; represented in permanent collections including, Mus. Modern Art, N.Y.C., Whitney Mus., N.Y.C., Los Angeles County Mus., Cin. Mus., Birmingham (Ala.) Mus. Art, Indpls. Mus. Art, Nat. Gallery Art, Washington, Victoria and Albert Mus., London, Library of Congress, Washington; subject of book Eleanore Mikus, Shadows of the Real (by Robert Hobbs and Judith Bernstock), 1991. Guggenheim fellow, 1966-67; Tamarind fellow, summer 1968; MacDowell fellow, summer 1969; grantee Cornell U., 1988. Mem. AAUP. Home: PO Box 6586 Ithaca NY 14851-6586 Office: Cornell U Dept Art Tjaden Hall Ithaca NY 14853 *I have always adhered in my paintings to an almost classic simplicity of expression; it is the simplicity of the child as seen through the eyes of the artist—impulsive, dramatic and yet close to the rhythm of childlike expression, born of an innocence which is all the more sophisticated for being so. It doesn't pretend—it just is.*

MIKVA, ABNER JOSEPH, lawyer, retired federal judge; b. Milw., Jan. 21, 1926; s. Henry Abraham and Ida (Fishman) M.; m. Zoe Wise, Sept. 19, 1948; children: Mary, Laurie, Rachel. JD cum laude, U. Chgo., 1951; DL (hon.), U. Ill., Am. U., Northwestern U., Tulane U.; DHL (hon.), Hebrew U.; DHL (Hon.), U. Wis. Bar: Ill. 1951, D.C. 1978. Law clk. to U.S. Supreme Ct. Justice Sherman Minton, 1951; ptnr. firm Devoe, Shadur, Mikva & Plotkin, Chgo., 1952-68, D'Ancona, Pflaum, Wyatt & Riskind, 1973-74; lectr. Northwestern U. Law Sch., Chgo., 1973-75, U. Pa. Law Sch., 1983-85, Georgetown Law Sch., 1986-88, Duke U. Law Sch., Durham, N.C., 1990-91, U. Chgo. Law Sch., 1992-93; mem. Ill. Gen. Assembly from 23d Dist., 1956-66, 91st-92d Congresses from 2d Dist. Ill., 94th-96th Congresses from 10th Dist. Ill., ways and means com., judiciary com.; chmn. Dem. Study Group; resigned, 1979; judge U.S. Circuit Ct. Appeals D.C., 1979-91, chief judge, 1991-94; counsel to the President The White House, Washington, 1994-96; vis. prof., Walter Schaefer chair in pub. policy U. Chgo., 1996—. Author: The American Congress: The First Branch, 1983, The Legislative Process, 1995. Served with USAAF, World War II. Recipient Page One award Chgo. Newspaper Guild, 1964; Best Legislator award Ind. Voters Ill., 1956-66, Alumni medal U. Chgo., 1996; named one of ten Outstanding Young Men in Chgo., Jr. Assn. Commerce and Industry, 1961. Mem. ABA, Chgo. Bar Assn. (bd. mgrs. 1962-64), D.C. Bar Assn., Am. Law Inst., U.S. Assn. Former Mems. Congress, Order of Coif, Phi Beta Kappa. Home: 442 New Jersey Ave SE Washington DC 20003-4008

MILAM, JOHN DANIEL, pathologist, educator; b. Kilgore, Tex., May 22, 1933; s. Ott G. and Effie (White) M.; m. Carol Jones Milam, Aug. 1, 1959; children: Kay, Beth, John Jr., Julie. BS, La. State U., 1955, MS, 1957, MD, 1960. Attending pathologist St. Luke's Episcopal Hosp., Houston, 1967-89; cons. in pathology Tex. Children's Hosp., Houston, 1979—; prof. lab. medicine M.D. Anderson Cancer Ctr., U. Tex., Houston, 1990—; prof. pathology and lab. medicine U. Tex. Med. Sch., Houston, 1989—; chief pathology Lyndon B. Johnson Gen. Hosp., Houston, 1995—. Contbr. numerous articles to profl. jours., chpts., abstracts to books. Trustee Am. Bd. Pathology, 1985—, pres., 1995; bd. dirs. Harris County chpt. ARC, 1978—. Mem. Am. Assn. Blood Banks (pres. 1984, Disting. Svc. award 1988), Tex. Soc. Pathologists (George T. Caldwell award 1981). Republican. Baptist. Home: 11927 Arbordale Ln Houston TX 77024-5001 Office: U Tex Houston Med Sch Dept Pathology 6431 Fannin St Rm 2022 Houston TX 77030-1501

MILAM, WILLAM BRYANT, diplomat, economist; b. Bisbee, Ariz., July 24, 1936; s. Burl Vivian and Alice Vera (Pierce) M.; m. Faith Adele Handley; step-children: Erika, Fred. AB, Stanford U., 1959; MA, U. Mich., 1970; postgrad., Am. U., 1973. Polit. officer Dept. of State, Washington, 1967-69; fin. economist Dept. of State, Washington and, U.S. Embassy, London, 1970-75; energy economist Dept. of State, Washington, 1975-77, dep. office dir., 1977-80, office dir., 1980-83; dep. chief of mission U.S. Embassy, Yaounde, Cameroon, 1983-85; dep. asst. sec. Dept. of State, Washington, 1985-90; U.S. amb. to Bangladesh, 1990-93; spl. negotiator Oceans Environ. Sci. Dept. State, Washington, 1993-95; chief of mission U.S. Embassy, Monrovia, Liberia, 1995—. Calif. State scholar, 1956-59; recipient James Clement Dunn award Dept. of State, 1981, Superior Honor award, 1983, Pres.'s Meritorious Svc. award U.S. Govt., 1990, Pres. Outstanding Svc. award, 1991. Avocations: reading, golf. Home and Office: Embassy of Monrovia Dept of State Washington DC 20521-8800

MILAN, MARJORIE LUCILLE, early childhood education educator; b. Ludlow, Colo., June 24, 1926; d. John B. and Barbara (Zenonian) Pinamont; m. John Francis Milan, June 18, 1949; children: Barbara, J. Mark, Kevin. BA, U. Colo., 1947, MA, 1978; PhD, U. Denver, 1983. Cert. tchr., adminstr., supt., Colo. Tchr. Boulder (Colo.) Pub. Schs., 1947-49, Denver Pub. Schs., 1949-51, 67—; adminstr. T. Tot Kindergarten, Denver, 1951-55; tchr. Colo. Women's Coll., Denver, 1956-57; adminstr. Associated Schs., Denver, 1956-67; adv. bd. George Washington Carver Nursery, Denver, 1960-85. Mem. Assn. Childhood Edn. (state bd. 1960—, Hall of Excellence 1991), Rotary (pres. chpt. 1994-95), Philanthropic Ednl. Orgn., Phi Delta Kappa, Delta Kappa Gamma. Avocations: swimming, music. Home: 1775 Lee St Lakewood CO 80215-2855

MILAN, THOMAS LAWRENCE, accountant; b. Balt., Md., Nov. 23, 1941; s. Lawrence Francis and Mary Elizabeth (Feeley) M.; m. Mary Agnes LaCoste; children: Thomas Brian, Kathrine Mary. BS, U. Balt., 1965; attended Darden Sch. U. Va., 1987. CPA, Md., Va., Washington. With Ernst & Young, Balt., 1965-80, ptnr., 1976-80, Ernst & Young, Richmond, Va., 1980-88, regional dir. acctg. and auditing, Washington, 1988—; nat. dir. SEC practice Ernst & Young, 1989—. Dir. U. Balt. Edn. Found. Mem. AICPA (chmn. SEC regulations com. 1994—), Annapolis Yacht Club, Commonwealth Club, TPC at Avenel, Beta Alpha. Republican. Roman Catholic. Avocations: boating, waterfowling, tennis. Home: 9721 Meyer Point Dr Rockville MD 20854-5420

MILANDER, HENRY MARTIN, educational consultant; b. Northampton, Pa., Apr. 17, 1939; s. Martin Edward and Margaret Catherine (Makovetz) M.; children: Martin Henry, Beth Ann. BS summa cum laude, Lock Haven U., Pa., 1961; MA, Bowling Green (Ohio) State U., 1962; EdS (Future Faculty fellow 1964), U. No. Iowa, 1965; EdD, Ill. State U., Normal, 1967. Instr. Wartburg Coll., Waverly, Iowa, 1962-64; asst. prof. Ill. State U., 1966-67; dean instrn. Belleville (Ill.) Area Coll., 1967-69; v.p. acad. affairs Lorain County Community Coll., Elyria, Ohio, 1969-72; pres. Olympic Coll., Bremerton, Wash., 1972-87, Northeastern Jr. Coll., Sterling, Colo., 1988-95; ednl. cons., 1995—; pres. Bremers, Inc., 1986-87. Contbr. articles to profl. jours. Pres. Kitsap County Comprehensive Health Planning Council, 1975-76; pres. Logan County Colo. United Way, 1992-93. Recipient Faculty Growth award Wartburg Coll., 1963, Community Service award, 1975, Chief Thunderbird award, 1985. Mem. Am. Assn. C.C., Am. Assn. Sch. Adminstrs., N.W. Assn. Cmty. and Jr. Colls., Wash. Assn. C.C. (pres. 1984-85), Wash. C.C. Computing Consortium (chmn. bd. dirs. 1985-87), Puget Sound Naval Bases Assn. (pres. 1982-86), Wash. Assn. C.C. Pres. (pres. 1984-85), Bremerton Area C. of C. (pres. 1977-78), Colo. Assn. C.C. Pres. (pres. 1993-94), Rotary (pres. Sterling Club 1992-93), Kappa Delta Pi, Phi Delta Kappa. Lutheran. Home: 12779 Vista Dr NE Bainbridge Island WA 98110

MILANICH, JERALD THOMAS, archaeologist, museum curator; b. Painesville, Ohio, Oct. 13, 1945; s. John Joseph and Jean Marie (Bales) M.; m. Maxine L. Margolis, Dec. 20, 1970; 1 child, Nara Bales. BA, U. Fla., 1967, MA, 1968, PhD, 1971. Cert. Soc. Profl. Archaeologists, 1975. Post doctoral fellow Smithsonian Inst., Washington, 1971-72; asst. prof. anthropology U. Fla., Gainesville, 1972-75; asst. curator Fla. Mus. Natural History, 1975-77; assoc. curator, 1977-81, chmn. dept. anthropology, 1981-83, 91—, curator, 1981—. Author: (with Samuel Proctor) Tacachale—Essays on the Indians of Florida and Southeastern Georgia during the Historic Period, 1978; (with Charles Fairbanks) Florida Archaeology, 1980; McKeithen Weeden Island, 1984; Early Prehistoric Southeast, 1985; (with Susan Milbrath) First Encounters, Spanish Explorations in the Caribbean and the United States, 1492-1570, 1989; The Hernando de Soto Expedition, 1990; Earliest Hispanic-Native America Interactions in the Greater American Southwest, 1991, (with Charles Hudson) Hernando de Soto and the Indians of Florida, 1993, Archaeology of Precolumbian Florida, 1994, Florida Indians and the Invasion of Europe, 1995, The Timucuas, 1996. Recipient Ripley P. Bullen awards, 1980, Rembert Patrick Book award, 1994, 95; grantee NSF, 1970-71, 73-75, 77-81, 82, Wentworth Found., 1976-77, 81-84, 91, NEH, 1985, 87-89. Mem. Am. Anthrop. Assn., Soc. Am. Archaeology (exec. bd. 1990-93), Soc. Profl. Archeologists (pres. 1981-82), So. Anthrop. Soc., S.E. Archeol. Conf. (pres. 1986-88), Explorers Club. Office: Fla Mus Natural History Gainesville FL 32611

MILANOVICH, NORMA JOANNE, occupational educator, training company executive; b. Littlefork, Minn., June 4, 1945; d. Lyle Albert and Loretta (Leona) Drake; m. Rudolph William Milanovich, Mar. 18, 1943; 1 child, Rudolph William Jr. BS in Home Econs., U. Wis., Stout, 1968; MA in Curriculum and Instrn., U. Houston, 1973, EdD in Curriculum and Program Devel., 1982. Instr. human svcs. dept. U. Houston, 1971-75; dir. videos project U. N.Mex., Albuquerque, 1976-78, dir. vocat. edn. equity ctr., 1978-88, asst. prof. tech. occupational edn., 1982-88, coord. occupational vocat. edn. programs, 1983-88, dir. consortium rsch. and devel. in occupational edn., 1984-88; pres. The Alpha Connecting Tng. Corp., Albuquerque, 1988—; adj. instr. Cen. Tng. Acad., Dept. Energy, Wackenhut; mem. faculty U. Phoenix; mem. adj. faculty So. Ill. U., Lesley Coll., Boston. Author: Model Equitable Behavior in the Classroom, 1983, Handbook for Vocational-Technical Certification in New Mexico, 1985, We, The Arcturians, 1990, Sacred Journey to Atlantis, 1991, The Light Shall Set You Free, 1996, A Vision for Kansas: Systems of Measures and Standards of Performance, 1992, Workplace Skills: The Employability Factor, 1993; editor: Choosing What's Best for You, 1982, A Handbook for Handling Conflict in the Classroom, 1983, Starting Out. . .A Job Finding Handbook for Teen Parents, Going to Work. . .Job Rights for Teens; author, editor: Majestic Raise newsletter, 1996, Celestial Voices newsletter, 1991-96. Bd. dirs. Albuquerque Single Parent Occupational Scholarship Program, 1984-86; del. Youth for Understanding Internat. Program, 1985-90; mem. adv. bd. Southwestern Indian Poly. Inst., 1984-88; com. mem. Region VI Consumer Exch. Com., 1982-84; ednl. lectures, tng., tour dir. internat. study toursto Japan, Austria, Korea, India, Nepal, Mex., Eng., Greece, Egypt, Australia, New Zealand, Fed. Republic Germany, Israel, Guatemala, Peru, Bolivia, Chile, Easter Island, Tibet, China, Hong Kong, Turkey, Italy, Russia, Ukraine, Sweden, Norway, 1984-95. Grantee N.Mex. Dept. Edn., 1976-78, 78-86, 83-86, HEW, 1979, 80, 81, 83, 84, 85, 86, 87, JTPA Strategic Mktg. Plan. Mem. ASTD, Am. Vocat. Assn., Vocat. Edn. Equity Coun., Nat. Coalition for Sex Equity Edn., Am. Home Econs. Assn., Inst. Noetic Scis., N.Mex. Home Econs. Assn., N.Mex. Vocat. Edn. Assn., N.Mex. Adv. Coun. on Vocat.

Edn., Greater Albuquerque C. of C., NAFE, Phi Delta Kappa, Phi Upsilon Omicron, Phi Theta Kappa. Democrat. Roman Catholic.

MILAVSKY, HAROLD PHILLIP, real estate executive; b. Limerick, Sask., Can., Jan. 25, 1931; s. Jack and Clara M. B in Commerce, U. Sask., Saskatoon, Can., 1953; LLD (hon.), U. Sask., 1995, U. Calgary, 1995. Chief acct., treas., controller Loram Internat. Ltd. div. Mannix Co. Ltd., Calgary, Alta., Can., 1956-65; v.p., chief fin. officer Power Corp. Devels. Ltd., Calgary, Alta., Can., 1965-69; exec. v.p., bd. dirs. Great West Internat. Equities Ltd. (name now Trizec Corp. Ltd.), Calgary, Alta., Can., 1976-94; pres. Trizec Corp. Ltd., Calgary, Alta., Can., 1976-86, bd. dirs., 1976-94, chmn., 1986-93; chmn. Quantico Capital Corp., Calgary, 1994—; bd. dirs. Brascan Ltd., Toronto, Can., Toronto, London Life Ins. Co., London Ins. Group Ltd., London Reins. Group, Wascana Energy Inc., Regina, Nova Corp. Alberta, Calgary, Amoco Can., Calgary, Telus Corp., Edmonton, Encal Energy, Inc., Calgary. Past dir. Terry Fox Humanitarian Award Program; past dir. Conf. Bd. Can.; past. gov. Acctg. Edn. Found. Alta.; hon. col. 14th Svc. Battalion, Calgary. Recipient Commemorative medal B'nai Brith, 1992. Fellow Inst. Chartered Accts. Alta.; mem. Inst. Chartered Accts. Sask., Can. Inst. Pub. Real Estate Cos. (past pres., bd. dirs.), Can. C. of C. (past chmn.), Internat. Profl. Hockey Alumni (founding dir.), Petroleum Club, Ranchmen's Club. Avocations: skiing, tennis, horseback riding. Office: Quantico Capital Corp, 1920-855 Second St SW, Calgary, AB Canada T2P 4J7

MILAZZO, THOMAS GREGORY, lawyer; b. New Orleans, Sept. 18, 1957; s. Anthony Joseph and Lucille Catherine (Fontana) M.; m. Robyn Denise Sanders, Jan. 31, 1987; children: Jordan Thomas, Devin Thomas. BA in Broadcast Journalism, La. State U., 1979; JD, Loyola U., 1982. Bar: La. 1982, U.S. Dist. Ct. (ea. dist.) La. 1983, U.S. Dist. Ct. (mid. and we. dists.) La. 1987, U.S. Ct. Appeals (5th cir.) 1993. Assoc. Francipane, Regan & St. Pé, Metairie, La., 1982-87; ptnr. Regan, St. Pé & Milazzo, Metairie, 1987-91, St. Pé & Milazzo, Metairie, 1991-95, LeBlanc, Miranda & deLaup, Metairie, 1995—. Mem. Def. Res. Inst., La. Assn. Def. Counsel, Jefferson Parish Bar Assn. Office: LeBlanc Miranda & deLaup The Pelican Bldg 2121 Airline Hwy Ste 601 Metairie LA 70001

MILBANK, JEREMIAH, foundation executive; b. N.Y.C., Mar. 24, 1920; s. Jeremiah and Katharine (Schulze) M.; m. Andrea Hunter, July 19, 1947 (dec. Oct. 1982); children: Jeremiah III, Victoria Milbank Whitney, Elizabeth Milbank Archer, Joseph H.; m. Rose Jackson Sheppard, May 4, 1991. B.A., Yale U., 1942; M.B.A., Harvard U., 1948; L.H.D. (hon.), Ithaca (N.Y.) Coll., 1976, Sacred Heart U., Conn.; LL.D., Manhattan Coll. With J.M. Found., N.Y.C.; pres. J.M. Found., 1971—; pres. Cypress Woods Corp., 1972—. Author: First Century of Flight in America, 1942. Chmn. emeritus Boys and Girls Clubs Am.; hon. pres. Internat. Ctr. for the Disabled, 1991—; fin. chmn. Rep. Nat. Com., 1969-72, 75-77. Lt. USNR, 1943-46. Mem. Brook Club, River Club (N.Y.C.), Round Hill Club (Greenwich), Yale Club. Republican. Home: 535 Lake Ave Greenwich CT 06830-3831 Office: 60 E 42nd St New York NY 10165

MILBOURNE, WALTER ROBERTSON, lawyer; b. Phila., Aug. 27, 1933; s. Charles Gordon and Florie Henderson (Robertson) M.; m. Georgena Sue Dyer, June 19, 1965; children: Gregory Broughton, Karen Elizabeth, Walter Robertson, Margaret Henderson. A.B., Princeton U., 1955; LL.B., Harvard U., 1958. Bar: Pa. 1959. Assoc. firm Pepper, Hamilton & Sheetz, Phila., 1959-65, Obermayer, Rebmann, Maxwell & Hippel, Phila., 1965-67; ptnr. Obermayer, Rebmann, Maxwell & Hippel, 1968-84, Saul, Ewing, Remick & Saul, 1984—; bd. dirs. Pa. Lumbermen's Mut. Ins. Co., Phila. Reins. Corp.; co-chmn. Nat. Conf. Lawyers and Collection Agys., 1979-90; chmn. bus. litigation com. Def. Rsch. Inst., 1986-89, mem. law instsn. com., 1989-95. Chmn. mental health budget sect. Phila. United Fund, 1967-70. Served with Army N.G., 1958-64. Fellow Am. Coll. Trial Lawyers (mem. advancing the rule of law abroad com. 1992—); mem. ABA, Pa. Bar Assn., Phila. Bar Assn., Internat. Assn. Def. Counsel (exec. com. 1985-88), Assn. Def. Counsel, Union League, Merion Cricket Club, Princeton Club, Idle Hour Tennis Club (pres. 1968-68, Phila. Lawn Tennis Assn. (pres. 1969-70). Republican. Home: 689 Fernfield Cir Wayne PA 19087-2002 Office: Saul Ewing Remick & Saul 3800 Centre Sq W Philadelphia PA 19102

MILBRATH, ROBERT HENRY, retired petroleum executive; b. Apr. 17, 1912; s. Paul and Mabel (Volkman) M.; m. Margaret Ripperger, Jan. 19, 1940; children: Robert S., Constance, Susan. B.S., U.S. Naval Acad., 1934. With Standard Oil Co. N.J., 1934-74; v.p., gen. mgr. Esso Sociedad Anonima Petrolera Argentina, 1938-42, 45-50; area contact East Coast South Am., mktg. coordination, 1950-52; dir. Internat. Petroleum Co., 1954—, v.p., 1956; v.p., dir. Esso Export Corp. N.Y., 1957-59, exec. v.p., dir., 1959-61; pres., dir. chmn. exec. com. Esso Internat., Inc. (formerly Esso Export Corp.), 1961-66; exec. v.p. Esso Europe, 1966-68; logistics coordinator Standard Oil Co. (N.J.) (now Exxon Corp.), 1968-69, dir., v.p., 1969-70, dir., sr. v.p., 1970-73, ret., 1974. Cons. Boys Clubs Am., 1978-84. Served to lt. comdr. USNR; asst. naval attache 1942, Buenos Aires; chief Latin Am. sect. Army-Navy Petroleum Bd. 1943-45, Washington. Mem. U.S. Naval Acad. Alumni Assn. Republican. Clubs: Univeristy (N.Y.C.), Ponte Vedra Club. Home: 214 Pablo Ct Ponte Vedra Beach FL 32082-1802

MILBURN, HERBERT THEODORE, federal judge; b. Cleveland, Tenn., May 26, 1931; s. J.E. and Hazel (Shanks) M.; m. Elaine Dillow, Aug. 23, 1957; children: Blair Douglas, Elizabeth Elaine. Student, U. Chattanooga, 1949-50, Boston U., 1950-51; BS, East Tenn. State U., 1953; JD, U. Tenn., 1959. Bar: Tenn. 1959, U.S. Supreme Ct. 1971. Assoc. Folts, Bishop, Thomas, Leitner & Mann, Chattanooga, 1959-63; ptnr. Bishop, Thomas, Leitner, Mann & Milburn, Chattanooga, 1963-73; judge Hamilton County Cir. Ct., Chattanooga, 1973-83, U.S. Dist. Ct. (ea. dist.) Tenn., Chattanooga, 1983-84, U.S. Ct. Appeals (6th cir.), Chattanooga, 1984—; mem. faculty Nat. Jud. Coll. U. Nev., Reno, 1980, Tenn. Jud. Acad., Vanderbilt U., Nashville, 1982. Pres. Hamilton County Young Reps., Chattanooga, 1965; mem. Chancellor's Roundtable U. Tenn., Chattanooga, 1983-86; pres. Lakeside Kiwanis, 1964. With U.S. Army Security Agy., 1953-56. Recipient award Chattanooga Bd. Realtors, 1987, Outstanding Alumnus award East Tenn. State U., 1988; named Outstanding Young Rep., Hamilton County Young Reps., 1965. Mem. ABA, Tenn. Bar Assn. (commr. 1971-73, mem. profl. ethics and grienvance com.), Chattanooga Bar Assn. (sec.-treas. 1967), Fed. Bar Assn. (chairperson U.S. jud. conf. com. on adminstrv. office of U.S. cts. 1994—), Am. Legion, East Tenn. State U. Found., Signal Mountain Golf and Country Club, Univ. Club Cin., Kiwanis. Republican. Episcopalian. Office: US Ct Appeals PO Box 750 Chattanooga TN 37401-0750

MILBURN, RICHARD ALLAN, aerospace company executive; b. Washington, May 30, 1933; s. Robert Andrew and Anna Janet (Schmidtman) M.; m. Joan (Frances) Hurst, Oct. 15, 1955; children: Jennifer Leigh, Michele Lynn. BS in Aeronautic and Space Engring. with honors, Okla. U., 1964, MS in Aerospace Engring. with honors, 1965. Commd. 2d lt. USAF, 1954, advanced through grades to col., 1980, interceptor pilot Aerospace Def. Command, 1955-64; designer, supr. constrn. ultra low speed wind tunnel Okla. U. Rsch. Inst., 1964-65, project engr. Aerospace Def. Command, 1965-68, chief weapons system div. Joint Chiefs of Staff, 1968-71; asst. air attache, chief Fgn. Tech. Office Okla. U. Rsch. Inst., London, 1971-75; deputy chief East Asia divsn., chief east and south Asia Defense Security Agy. Dept. Def., 1975-77; chief Mut. Def. Assistance Office Am. Embassy, Tokyo, 1977-80; chief rsch., devel., and systems acquisition Mgmt. Policy div. Hdqrs. USAF, 1980, ret., 1980; dir. def. programs Grumman Internat., Inc., 1980-82, v.p. def. programs, 1982-85, v.p. Washington ops., 1985-87, sr. v.p., 1987-94; v.p. policy, plan and industrial corp. Northrop Grumman Internat., Arlington, Va., 1994—; chmn. fin. and compensation com., mem. exec. com. US/ROC Econ. Coun.,1991 chmn. NATO Industrial adv. group, Brussels, 1996—; bd. dirs. Robert C. Byrd Nat. Aviation Edn. and Tng. Ctr., 1990—. Fellow AIAA (assoc.); mem. Nat. Security Industries Assn. (bd. dirs. Washington), Am. Def. Preparedness Assn. (bd. dirs. Washington), Am. League Export and Security Assistance (chmn., pres. 1994—), Royal Aero. Soc., Aerospace Industries Assn. (mem. internat. coun.), Order of Daedalians. Methodist. Home: 2200 Hunter Mill Rd Vienna VA 22181-3025 Office: Northrop Grumman Internat 1000 Wilson Blvd Ste 2400 Arlington VA 22209-3901

MILBURN, RICHARD HENRY, physics educator; b. Newark, June 3, 1928; s. Richard Percy and Lucy Elizabeth (Karr) M.; m. Nancy Jeannette Stafford, Aug. 25, 1951; children—Sarah Stafford, Anne Douglas. A.B., Harvard U., 1948, A.M., 1951, Ph.D., 1954. Instr. Harvard U., Cambridge, Mass., 1954, 56-57, asst. prof., 1957-61; assoc. prof. physics Tufts U., Medford, Mass., 1961-65, prof., 1965—, John Wade prof., 1990—; Fulbright lectr., India, 1984. Trustee Cambridge Friends Sch., 1989-95. With U.S. Army, 1954-56. Sheldon travelling fellow, 1948-49; NSF fellow, 1952-53; Guggenheim fellow, 1960. Fellow Am. Phys. Soc. (past chmn. New Eng. sect.); mem. Am. Assn. Physics Tchrs., AAAS, AAUP. Research on high energy and elementary particles physics. Home: 1 Plymouth Rd Winchester MA 01890-3620 Office: Tufts Univ Medford MA 02155

MILCHAN, ARNON, film producer; b. Dec. 6, 1944. Prodr.: (plays) Tomb, It's So Nice To Be Civilized, Amadeus (Paris prodn.), (TV) MASADA, 1981, (films) The Medusa Touch, 1978, The King of Comedy, 1983, Once Upon a Time in America, 1984, Brazil, 1985, Stripper, 1986, Legend, 1986, Man on Fire, 1987, The Adventures of Baron Munchausen, 1989, Who's Harry Crumb, 1989, The War of the Roses, 1989, Big Man on Campus, 1990, Pretty Woman, 1990, Q&A, 1990, Guilty by Suspicion, 1991, JFK, 1991, The Mambo Kings, 1992, Memoirs of an Invivsible Man, 1992, The Power of One, 1992, Under Siege, 1992, Sommersby, 1993, Falling Down, 1993, Made in America, 1993, Free Willy, 1993, The Nutcracker, 1993, That Night, 1993, Heaven and Earth, 1993, The New Age, 1993, Striking Distance, 1993, Six Degrees of Separation, 1993, Second Best, 1994, Boys on the Side, 1994, The Client, 1994, Bogus, 1995, A Time to Kill, 1996. Office: Regency Enterprises 4000 Warner Blvd Bldg 66 Burbank CA 91522-0001*

MILDE, LESLIE NEWBERG, anesthesiologist, educator; b. Rochester, N.Y., Aug. 17, 1943; d. Frederick Johnson and Frances Stevenson Newberg; m. James Hans Milde, Dec. 31, 1984; children: Steven, Craig, Jade, Peggy Sue. AB, U. Rochester, 1965; MD, U. Calif., San Francisco, 1977. Diplomate Nat. Bd. Med. Examiners, Am. Bd. Anesthesiology. Cardiopulmonary technician Boston Children's Hosp., Harvard U., 1965-67, U. Calif., San Francisco, 1968-73; resident in internal medicine Kaiser Permanente Hosp., San Francisco, 1977-78; resident in anesthesiology Mass. Gen. Hosp., Harvard U., Boston, 1978-80, fellow in critical care medicine, 1980-81; fellow in neuroanesthesiology Mayo Grad. Sch. Medicine, Rochester, Minn., 1981-82; cons. anesthesiologist Mayo Clinic, Rochester, 1982-94, Scottsdale, Ariz., 1994—; prof. anesthesiology Mayo Med. Sch., Scottsdale, 1992—; assoc. examiner Am. Bd. Anesthesiology, 1989—. Editor: Clinical Anesthesia Procedures of Massachusetts General Hospital, 1982, Anesthesia Review, 1991; editor Jour. Neurosurg. Anesthesia. Mem. Assn. Univ. Anesthesiologists (sci. adv. bd. 1985—). Avocations: refinishing antique furniture. *

MILDREN, JACK, lieutenant governor; b. Kingsville, TX, Oct. 10, 1949; s. Larry J. and Mary Glynne (Lamont) M.; m. Janis Susan Butler, Jan. 14, 1972; children: Leigh, Lauren, Drew. BBA, U. Okla., 1972. Cert. petroleum landman. Mem. Balt. Colts Football Club, 1972-73, New England Patriots Football Club, 1974; v.p. Saxon Oil Co., 1972-79; co-founder, pres. Regency Exploration Inc., 1977-88; ind. oil oper., 1988-90; lt. gov. State of Okla., Oklahoma City, 1990-95; pres., ceo Pre-Paid Lgl Svcs Inc., Ada, OK, 1995. Bd. dirs. Children's Med. Rsch. Found., Arts Coun. Oklahoma City, Nat. Football League Players Found. and Hall of Fame, State Ctr. Com., Jim Thorpe Club; mem. Leadership Okla., Leadership Oklahoma City; mem. Com. to Devel. Biotech. Industry in Okla. Named All-Am. Football Player, 1971, Acad. All-Am., 1971, NAt. Football Found. Hall Fame, 1971, Most Valuable Player Sugar Bowl, 1972. numerous other athletic awards. Mem. Beta Gamma Sigma, Phi Delta Theta (past pres., bd. dirs.). Meth. Home: 1701 Guilford Oklahoma City OK 73120 Office: Pre-Paid Legal Services Inc. 321 E. Main St. Ada OK 74820*

MILDVAN, DONNA, infectious diseases physician; b. Phila., June 20, 1942; d. Carl David and Gertrude M.; m. Rolf Dirk Hamann; 1 child, Gabriella Kay. AB magna cum laude, Bryn Mawr Coll., 1963; MD, Johns Hopkins U., 1967. Diplomate Am. Bd. Internal Medicine and Infectious Diseases. Intern, resident Mt. Sinai Hosp., N.Y.C., 1967-70, fellow, infectious diseases, 1970-72; asst., assoc. prof. clin. medicine Mt. Sinai Sch. Medicine, N.Y.C., 1972-87; prof. clinical medicine Dept. Medicine, Mt. Sinai Sch. Medicine, N.Y.C., 1987-88, prof. medicine, 1988-94; physician-in-charge infectious diseases Beth Israel Med. Ctr., N.Y.C., 1972-79, chief, div. infectious diseases, 1980—; prof. medicine Albert Einstein Coll. of Medicine, N.Y.C., 1994—; mem. AIDS charter rev. com., NIH/Nat. Inst. Allergy and Infectious Diseases, Bethesda, 1987—; cons. FDA, Rockville, 1987—, Ctrs. for Disease Control, Atlanta, 1985-86; among first to describe AIDS, "Pre-AIDS", AIDS Dementia, 1982, among first to study AZT, 1986; Keynote speaker, II Internat. Conf. on AIDS, Paris, 1986 and other achievements in field; Sophie Jones Meml. lectr. in infectious diseases U. Mich. Hosps., 1984. Contbr. numerous articles to profl. jours; co-editor two books, several book chpts. and abstracts on infectious diseases and AIDS. Grantee N.Y. State AIDS Inst., 1986-87; Henry Strong Denison scholar Johns Hopkins U. Sch. Medicine, 1967; recipient Woman of Achievement award AAUW, 1987; contract for antiviral therapy in AIDS, Nat. Cancer Inst./Nat. Inst. Allergy and Infectious Diseases, 1985-86, subcontract Nat. Inst. Allergy and Infectious Diseases, ACTU, 1987—. Fellow Infectious Diseases Soc. Am.; mem. Am. Soc. Microbiology, AAAS, Harvey Soc., Internat. AIDS Soc. Democrat. Jewish. Avocation: old movies. Office: Beth Israel Med Ctr 1st Ave New York NY 10003-7903

MILEDI, RICARDO, neurobiologist; b. Mexico City, Sept. 15, 1927; m. Ana Mela Garces, Dec. 17, 1955; 1 child, Rico. B.Sc., Instituto Cientifico y Literario, Chihuahua, Mex., 1945; M.D., U. Nacional Autónoma de Mex., 1955, Doctor Honoris Causa Universidad del Pais Vasco, 1992. Researcher Instituto Nacional de Cardiologia, Mex., 1954-56; fellow John Curtin Sch. Med. Res., Canberra, Australia, 1956-58; mem. faculty U. Coll., London, 1959-85, Foulerton research prof. of Royal Soc., 1975-85, head dept. biophysics, 1978-85; Disting. prof. dept. psychobiology U. Calif., Irvine, 1984—. Fellow Royal Soc. London, Am. Acad. Arts and Scis.; mem. AAAS, NAS, 3d World Acad. Scis., (titular) European Acad. Arts, Scis., Humanities, N.Y. Acad. Scis., Hungarian Acad. Scis. (hon.), Mex. Acad. Scis., Mex. Acad. Medicine. Home: 9 Gibbs Ct Irvine CA 92715-4032 Office: U Calif Dept Psychobiology Lab Cellular and Molecular Neurobiology Irvine CA 92717-4550

MILES, ARTHUR J., financial planner, consultant; b. N.Y.C., Sept. 2, 1920; s. Levi and Rachel Goldsworthy (Hiscock) M.; m. Pearl Cooper, Nov. 27, 1947; children: Beverly Miles Kerns, Douglas Robert. B.B.A., Pace U., 1958; M.B.A., NYU, 1963. With Dime Savs. Bank, N.Y.C., 1938-81, exec. v.p., treas., 1975-78, sr. exec. v.p., treas., 1978-81; pres. AJM Assocs., Floral Park, N.Y., then Sarasota, Fla., 1981—; newscaster Sta. WUSF-FM, Tampa, Fla.; bd. dirs. Cultural Instns. Retirement System, N.Y.C., 1968—; fin. cons. Bklyn. Inst. Arts and Scis., 1972—. Trustee, nat. treas. Alcoholics Anonymous, N.Y.C., 1970-79; tech. adviser N.Y.C. Fin. Liason Com., 1975-76. Served to sgt., inf. U.S. Army, 1942-45, Philippines. Fellow Fedn. Fin. Analysts; mem. Nat. Assn. Bus. Economists, Internat. Assn. Fin. Planners, NYU Club, Marco Polo Club (N.Y.C.), Tournament Players Club. Republican. Office: AJM Assocs 8325 Shadow Pine Way Sarasota FL 34238-5624

MILES, ELLEN GROSS, art historian, museum curator; b. N.Y.C., July 28, 1941; d. Mason Welch and Julia (Kernan) Gross; m. Nathan Reingold. BA, Bryn Mawr Coll., 1964; MPhil, Yale U., 1970, PhD, 1976. Registrar Corcoran Gallery Art, Washington, 1965-66; asst. to dir. Nat. Portrait Gallery, Washington, 1971-77, assoc. curator, 1977-84, curator dept. painting and sculpture, 1984—; guest curator Iveagh Bequest, Kenwood, London, 1979; vis. lectr. dept. Am. studies George Washington U., 1982. Co-author: American Colonial Portraits: 1700-1776, 1987; editor: The Portrait in 18th Century America, 1993; author: Saint-Mémin and the Neoclassical Profile Portrait in America, 1994, American Paintings of the Eighteenth Century, 1995. Rsch. grantee Smithsonian Instn., 1973-74, 79, 82, 87. Mem. Assn. Historians Am. Art, Am. Soc. for Eighteenth-Century Studies, Coll. Art Assn. Office: Nat Portrait Gallery 8th and F Sts NW Washington DC 20560

MILES, ELSIE, counselor, educator; b. Washington; d. James O. and Annie (Wint) M. BS, U. D.C.; MA, Howard U., Washington, Cath. U., Washington; postgrad., U. Wis., 1977, U. Mich., 1984. Lic. profl. counselor; nat. cert. counselor. Tchr., guidance counselor Washington, D.C. Pub. Schs., 1967-85; program planner, presenter and del. profl. confs. Editor (newsletter) D.C. Elem. Sch. Counselors Assn., D.C. Sch. Counselors Assn.; editor Assn. for Specialists in Group Work Govt. Rels. Communique; contbr. articles to profl. jours. & bulls. Civic and cmty. activist for civil and human rights. Recipient award Assn. for Multicultural Counseling and Devel. Am. Counseling Assn., C. Harold McCully Recognition award, 1992. Mem. ACA (awards), Am. Psychol. Soc., Am. Mental Health Counselors Assn. (award), D.C. Mental Health Counselor Assn. (pres. 1993-94, exec. bd. dirs., editor newsletter), D.C. Counseling Assn. (pres. 1987-88, award), D.C. Sch. Counselors Assn. (exec. bd. dirs., editor newsletter, award), D.C. Assn. for Specialists in Group Work (pres. 1984-85, govt. rels. chair 1985-91, exec. bd. dirs., editor newsletter), Internat. Assn. for Marriage and Family Therapists, Am. Orthopsychiat. Assn., World Future Soc., Nat. Orgn. of Victim's Assistance, Am. Bus. Women's Assn. (sec. Adams Morgan Civic Assn., Federal City chpt., program chair 1994-96), Chi Sigma Iota, others.

MILES, FRANK CHARLES, retired newspaper executive; b. Detroit, Jan. 1, 1926; s. Nelson and Ethel Jane (Mennill) M.; m. Catharine Estelle Coleman, Sept. 4, 1948; children—Barbara Ann, Diana Estelle. Student, Westervelt Bus. Coll., 1947-48. With Thomson Newspapers Ltd., Des Plaines, Ill., 1950—, Cambridge, Ont., 1950-52, 54-55; bus. mgr. Sarnia (Ont.) Obs., 1952-54; gen. mgr. Pembroke (Ont.) Obs., 1956-58, Moose Jaw (Sask) Times-Herald, 1958-62; pub. Austin (Minn.) Daily Herald, 1962-66; sr. v.p., gen. mgr. Thomson Newspapers Inc., Des Plaines, Ill., 1966-89; exec. v.p. acquisitions, 1990-91; ret.; also dir. Thomson Newspapers Inc., Des Plaines, Ill. Vol. assignments Internat. Media Fund, Baltics, Albania, 1992-93; Knight fellowship Moscow 1994; Ctr. for Ind. Journalism, Bucharest, Romania, Spring, 1995. With USNR, 1943-46. Mem. Am. Newspaper Pubs. Assn., Inland Daily Press Assn., Sigma Delta Chi. Republican. Mem. United Ch. of Christ. Home: 4 Duxbury St Rolling Meadows IL 60008-1918

MILES, JACK (JOHN RUSSIANO), journalist, educator; b. Chgo., July 30, 1942; s. John Alvin and Mary Jean (Murphy) M.; m. Jacqueline Russiano, Aug. 23, 1980; 1 child, Kathleen. LittB, Xavier U., Cin., 1964; PhB, Pontifical Gregorian U., Rome, 1966; student, Hebrew U., Jerusalem, 1966-67; PhD, Harvard U., 1971. Asst. prof. Loyola U., Chgo., 1970-74; asst. dir. Scholars Press, Missoula, Mont., 1974-75; postdoctoral fellow U. Chgo., 1975-76; editor Doubleday & Co., N.Y.C., 1976-78; exec. editor U. Calif. Press, Berkeley, 1978-85; book editor L.A. Times, 1985-91, mem. editl. bd., 1991-95; dir. Humanities Ctr. Claremont (Calif.) Grad. Sch., 1995—; contb. editor Atlantic Monthly, 1995—. Author: Retroversion and Text Criticism, 1984, God: A Biography, 1995; contbr. learned and popular articles to various periodicals; book reviewer. Recipient Pulitzer prize for biography, 1996; Guggenheim fellow, 1990-91. Mem. PEN, Nat. Book Critics Circle (pres. 1990-92), Am. Acad. Religion, Amnesty Internat. Episcopalian. Home: 3568 Mountain View Ave Pasadena CA 91107-4616 Office: Grad Humanities Ctr Claremont Grad Sch Claremont CA 91711

MILES, JEANNE PATTERSON, artist; b. Balt.; d. Walter and Edna (Webb) M.; m. Frank Curlee, Dec. 31, 1935 (dec.); m. Johannes Schiefer, Feb. 11, 1939 (div.); 1 child, Joanna. BFA, George Washington U.; postgrad., Philips Meml. Gallery Sch., Atelier Gromaire, Grand Chaumiere, Paris. One-woman shows include Betty Parsons Gallery, N.Y.C., 1945, 52, 55, 56, 59, 77, 82, Grand Central Moderns, N.Y.C., 1968, Wesbeth Galleries, N.Y.C., 1972; group shows include N.Y. Rome Found., 1957, Walker Art Gallery, Mpls., 1954, Corcoran Biennial, Yale U. Mus., 1957, Chateau Gagnes, France, 1938, Whitney Mus., 1963, Nat. Fedn. Am. Art, 1963, Mus. Modern Art, 1966, Riverside Mus., N.Y.C., 1964, Guggeheim Mus., 1965-66, Geodok Am. Women Show, Hamburg and Berlin, 1972, Springfield (Mass.) Art Mus., 1975, Hunterton Art Center, Clinton, N.J., 1975, Betty Parsons Gallery, 1977, 82, Sid Deutch, 1978, 79, Marlyn Pearl Gallery, N.Y.C., 1986, 88, Bronx Mus. Art, 1986, George Washington, 1989, 55 Mercer St, N.Y.C., 1989, Marlyn Pearl Gallery, N.Y.C., 1991, Anita Shapalsky Gallery, N.Y.C., 1994, Shapalsky Gallery, 1993; represented in permanent collections NYU, Santa Barbara (Calif.) Mus., Muson Proctor Mus., Utica, N.Y., Rutgers Coll., U. Ariz., Guggenheim Mus., Cin. and Newark museums, White Art Mus., N.Y. State U. at Purchase, Cornell U., Ecumenical Inst., Garrison, N.Y., Graymoor, Garrison, Springfield Art Mus., Weatherspoon Art Mus., U. N.C., Wichita (Kans.) Mus., Mus. of Wichita, Mus. of St. Mary's (Md.) Coll., L.A. County Mus., Alexander Mus., La., also pvt. collections, N.Y.C. and France; traveling exhibits; poster and cover for catalogues, 1987-92; video tape showing of exhibits on cable TV, N.Y.C., 1989. Charles C. Ladd painting scholar Tahiti, 1938, 56, traveling scholar France, 1937-48; grantee Am. Inst. Arts and Letters, 1968, Mark Rothko Found., 1970-73, Pelham von Stoeffler Art Fund, 1974; invited residency (award) to Yaddo Art Colony, Saratoga Springs, N.Y., 50s and 60s, MacDowell Colony, N.H. Mem. Abstract Artists Am., George Washington U. Alumni Assn. (Disting. Achievement award 1987). *My paintings, I find, come out successfully when I keep a steady grip on an interior focus.*

MILES, JESSE MC LANE, retired accounting company executive; b. De Funiak Springs, Fla., June 17, 1932; s. Percy Webb and Dora (Pippin) M.; m. Catherine Rita Eugenio, July 18, 1959; children—Jesse Jr., Catherine, Teresa, John, Thomas, Robert. B.S.B.A., U. Fla., 1954. C.P.A., N.Y. Mem. staff, mgr., prin. Arthur Young & Co., N.Y.C., 1954-63, ptnr., 1963-89, dep. chmn.-internat., 1985-89; chmn. Arthur Young Internat., 1985-89; ptnr. Ernst & Young, 1989-92; co-chmn. Ernst & Young Internat., 1989-92; ret., 1992. Mem. AICPA, N.Y. Inst. CPAs, Burning Tree Country Club (Greenwich, Conn.), Blind Brook Club (Rye Brook, N.Y.), Boca Pointe Country Club (Boca Raton, Fla.), Adios Golf Club (Coconut Creek, Fla.). Home: 18 Red Coat Ln Greenwich CT 06830-3432

MILES, JIM, state official. Prof. of law Greenville Tech. Coll.; sec. of state S.C. Mem. Soc. Internat. Bus. Office: Sec of State PO Box 11350 Columbia SC 29211-1350*

MILES, JOHN FREDERICK, retired manufacturing company executive; b. Fredericton, N.B., Can., Aug. 13, 1926; s . Ralph Edward and Hazel Jean (Young) M.; m. Frances Power, Oct. 2, 1950; children: John F., Robert D., Dalyce J., Leytha J. Sr. Matric, U. N.B., 1944; B.Sc. in Chem. Engring., Queen's U., Kingston, Ont., Can., 1948. Prodn. mgr. Dominion Steel & Coal Corp. Ltd., 1948-65, jr. engr., 1948-49, battery foreman coke ovens, 1949-51, gen. foreman coke ovens, 1951-56, rsch. engr. coke ovens and blast furnaces, 1956-57, asst. supt. blast furnace dept., 1957-58, asst. to gen. supt., 1958-60, asst. works mgr. Sidney Works, 1960-62, gen. mgr. Etobicoke Works, 1962-65; works mgr. Slater Steels—Hamilton Splty. Bar Div. (div. Slater Industries), Hamilton, Ont., Can., 1965-66, 1966-71, v.p. mfg., 1971-86, div. pres., 1986-91, pres., CEO, 1991-93, bd. dirs., 1991—. Mem. Assn. Profl. Engrs. Ont., Assn. Iron and Steel Engrs.

MILES, JOHN KARL, marketing executive; b. Indpls., June 17, 1937; s. Louis John and Rachel Anna (Robbins) M.; m. Nancy Margaret McCay, Aug. 22, 1959; children—John Karl, Ann McCay, James Vance. B.A., DePauw U., 1959; B.F.A., U. Ill., 1965, M.F.A., 1966. Design mgr. Arvin Industries Inc., Columbus, Ind., 1966-72; dir. design and mktg. Gen. Housewares Corp., Atlanta, 1972-77; exec. v.p. Homecrest Industries Inc., Wadena, Minn., 1977-88; pres. Crestmark Internat., Atlanta, 1988—; pres. bd. advisors Dallas Market Ctr., 1983-86; bd. dirs. Garden Window Network, Summer Casual Furniture Mfrs. Assn., pres. 1990-92, chair bd. 1993—, Atlantic Market Center Accessories Center, 1992. Inventor, designer electric heater, shoe buffer, bowling game table, electric scissors. Del. Wadena County Republican Conv., 1980-84; pres. Wadena Devel. Authority, 1986-87; mem. United Meth. Ch. Dist. Com. on Superintendency, 1985-88; lay leader Wadena United Meth. Ch., 1987; bd. dirs. Wadena Econ. Devel. Council, Community Edn. Adv. Com., Wadena. Served to 1st lt. USAF, 1959-62. Recipient Exec. of Yr. award Nat. Secs. Assn., Wadena, 1980. Mem. Summer and Casual Furniture Mfrs. Assn. (pres. bd. dirs. 1984—), Nat. Home Furnishings Coun. (bd. dirs. 1988—), Nat. Furnishings Coun. (bd. dirs. 1994), Wadena C. of C. (bd. dirs. 1985, pres. 1987, Citizen of Yr. 1988), Elks, Rotary. Methodist. Avocations: antiques, reading, drawing. Home: 601 Old Post Rd Madison GA 30650-1852 Office: Homecrest/Crestmark Internat 240 Peachtree St NW Atlanta GA 30303-1302

MILES, LELAND WEBER, university president; b. Balt., Jan. 18, 1924; s. Leland Weber and Marie (Fitzpatrick) M.; m. Mary Virginia Geyer, July 9, 1947; children: Christine Marie, Gregory Lynn. AB cum laude, Juniata Coll., 1946; MA, U. N.C., 1947, PhD, 1949; postgrad., Duke U., 1949; DLitt (hon.), Juniata Coll., 1969; LHD (hon.), Rosary Hill Coll., 1970; LLD (hon.), Far East U., 1979; DHC (hon.), U. Guadalajara (Mex.), 1984; Order of Merit, Alfred U., 1986. Assoc. prof. English Hanover Coll., 1949-50, prof., chmn. English dept., 1950-60; assoc. prof., asst. to head English dept. U. Cin., 1960-63, prof., 1963-64, founder humanities reading program for engrs., 1961; dean Coll. Arts and Scis., U. Bridgeport, Conn., 1964-67; pres. U. Bridgeport, 1974-87, founder Sch. Law, 1977, pres. emeritus, 1987—; pres. Alfred U., 1967-74; bd. dirs. United Illuminating, 1978-94, chmn. audit com., 1992-94, Grolier, 1984-88, Wright Managed Investment Funds, 1988—, Internat. Peace Acad., 1982-90, mem. adv. coun., 1990—; mem. adv. coun. Internat. Exec. Svc. Corps, 1993—; Danforth scholar Union Theol. Sem., 1956; Lilly fellow Sch. Letters Ind. U., 1959; Am. Council Learned Socs. fellow Harvard, 1963-64; Sr. Fulbright Research scholar Kings Coll. U. London, 1964, vis. scholar, 1972; seminar leader, deans and presidents insts. Am. Council on Edn., 1973-79; chmn. bd. Acad. Collective Bargaining Info. Service, Washington, 1977-79; producer, moderator Casing the Classics CBS Sta. WHAS-TV, Louisville, 1958-61; moderator Aspen (Colo.) Inst. for Humanistic Studies, 1969-70; lectr. Keedick Lecture Bur., N.Y.C., 1956-83. Author: John Colet and the Platonic Tradition, 1961; editor: St. Thomas More's Dialogue of Comfort Against Tribulation, 1966; sr. editor: (with Stephen Graubard and later Stephen B. Baxter) Studies in British History and Culture, 1965-79; contbg. editor Nat. Forum, 1983-91, editorial advisor, 1991-94; contbr. articles to learned jours. Trustee Western N.Y. Nuclear Rsch. Ctr., 1967-73; chmn. bd. Coll. Ctr. Finger Lakes, 1968-71; vice chmn. bd. Empire State Found., 1969-71, chmn., 1971-73; mem. New Eng. Bd. Higher Edn., 1985-87, Ambs. Roundtable, 1986-92, Fuld Found./Nat. League Nursing Adv. Coun. on Accreditation, 1986-88; chmn. Ettinger scholarship com. ednl. Found. Am., 1987-93; bd. dirs. Conn. Grand Opera, 1978-89, Bridgeport Bus. Coun., 1982-88, Save the Children, 1988-95; chmn. adv. coun. Save the Children, 1990-94, mem. adv. coun., 1995—. 1st lt. USAAF, 1944-45; capt. USAFR. Decorated DFC with oak leaf cluster, Crown Decoration of Honor 3rd Order Iran, 1978; chevalier l'Ordre des Palmes Académique (France), 1984; recipient Rosa and Samuel Sachs prize Cin. Inst. Fine Arts, 1961, Cultural medal Republic of China, 1983, Disting. Svc. award Greater Bridgeport Bar Assn., 1986, Outstanding Civilian Svc. medal Dept. Army, 1988. Fellow Royal Soc. Arts (life); mem. Renaissance Soc. Am., English Speaking Union, Internat. Assn. Univ. Pres. (pres. 1981-84, pres. emeritus 1984—, chief UN mission 1988—, World Peace award 1987, chmn. commn. on arms control edn. 1991—, mem. coun. sr. advisers 1992—), Knights of Malta (order of the Orthodox Knights Hospitaller of St. John of Jerusalem, Russian orthodox br.), Phi Kappa Phi. Episcopalian. Clubs: Univ. (N.Y.C.); Country of Fairfield (Conn.). Office: 2425 Post Rd Southport CT 06490-1217

MILES, RAYMOND EDWARD, former university dean, organizational behavior and industrial relations educator; b. Cleburne, Tex., Nov. 2, 1932; s. Willard Francis and Wilma Nell (Owen) M.; m. Lucile Dustin, Dec. 27, 1952; children: Laura, Grant, Kenneth. B.A. with highest honors, N. Tex. State U., 1954, M.B.A., 1958; Ph.D., Stanford U., 1963. Clk. Santa Fe R.R., Gainesville, Tex., 1950-55; instr. mgmt. Sch. Bus. N. Tex. State U., Denton, 1958-60; asst. prof. organizational behavior and indsl. relations Sch. Bus. Adminstrn. U. Calif.-Berkeley, 1963-68, assoc. prof., 1968-71, prof., 1971—, assoc. dean Sch. Bus. Adminstrn., 1978-81, dean, 1983-90; dir. Inst. Indsl. Relations, 1982-83; cons. various pvt., pub. orgns. Author: Theories of Management, 1975, (with Charles C. Snow) Organization Strategy, Structure and Process, 1978, (with Charles C. Snow) Fit, Failure, and the Hall of Fame, 1994; co-author: Organizational Behavior: Research and Issues, 1976; co-editor, contbg. author: Organization by Design: Theory and Practice, 1981. Served to 1st. lt. USAF, 1955-58. Mem. Indsl. Relations Research Assn., Acad. Mgmt. Democrat. Unitarian. Home: 8640 Don Carol Dr El Cerrito CA 94530-2733 Office: U Calif-Berkeley Walter A Haas Sch Bus Berkeley CA 94720

MILES, RICHARD, diplomat; b. Little Rock, Ark., 1937; m. Sharon O'Brien, June 18, 1960; children: Richard, Elizabeth. AA, Bakersfield Coll., 1960; AB, U. Calif., Berkeley, 1962; MA, Ind. U., 1964; grad., U.S. Army Russian Inst., Garmisch-Partenkirchen, Germany. With voter registration, political leadership tng. S.C. Voter Edn. Project, 1964-67; with Fgn. Svc., Oslo, Moscow, Belgrade, 1967-88; consul gen. Leningrad, 1988-91; prin. officer U.S. Embassy Office, Berlin, 1991-92; with Soviet, East European, Yugoslav Affairs, Politico-Military Bureau State Dept., amb. to Azerbaijan, 1992-93; dep. chief mission Am. Embassy, Moscow, 1993-96; chief of mission Am. Embassy, Belgrade, 1996—. With USMC, 1954-57. Am. Polit. Sci. fellow for Sen. Ernest F. Hollings, 1983-84; fellow Harvard U. Ctr. Internat. Affairs, 1987-88. Office: Belgrade Dept of State Washington DC 20521-5070

MILES, RICHARD BRYANT, mechanical and aerospace engineering educator; b. Washington, July 10, 1943; s. Thomas Kirk and Elizabeth (Bryant) M.; m. Susan McCoy, May 14, 1983; children: Thomas, Julia. BSEE, Stanford U., 1966, MSEE, 1967, PhD in Elec. Engring., 1972. Rsch. assoc. elec. engring. dept. Stanford (Calif.) U., summer 1972; asst. prof. mech. and aerospace engring. dept. Princeton (N.J.) U., 1972-78, assoc. prof., 1978-82, prof., 1982—, chmn. engring. physics program, 1980—; lectr. Northwestern Poly. U., Xian, China, 1987; rsch. scientist CNRS; vis. prof. U. Marseilles, France, spring, 1995. Contbr. articles to profl. publs., chpt. to book Advances in Fluid Mechanics Measurements, 1989; patentee in field. Bd. dirs. Fannie and John Hertz Found., Livermore, Calif., 1989—. Fannie and John Hertz Found. fellow, 1969-72; NSF summer trainee, 1972. Mem. AIAA (sr.), IEEE (sr.), Am. Phys. Soc., Optical Soc. Am. Office: Princeton U Mech & Aerospace Engring D-414 Eng Quad Olden St Princeton NJ 08544

MILES, RICHARD ROBERT, art historian, writer; b. Tokyo, Apr. 1, 1939; s. Robert Henri and Eleanor Alfrida (Child) Perreau-Saussine. BA, UCLA, 1972. Novelist, screenwriter various, 1965-72; dir. Meilinki Enterprises Ltd., 1980—; pres. Burbank (Calif.) Tchrs. Assn., 1984-85; bd. dirs. Balcom Trading Co., Tokyo, 1979-82. Author: That Cold Day in the Park, 1965 (Dell Book award 1965), Angel Loves Nobody, 1967 (Samuel Goldwyn award UCLA, 1969); (art history) Prints of Paul Jacoulet, 1982, Elizabeth Keith-The Prints, 1989, The Watercolors of Paul Jacoulet, 1992, others. Mem. Internat. Soc. of Fine Art Appraisers, New Eng. Appraisers Assn., Writers Guild of Am. West, Acad. of Am. Poets. Office: Meilinki Enterprises Ltd 214 N Bowling Green Way Los Angeles CA 90049-2816

MILES, ROBERT HENRY, management consultant, educator; b. Norfolk, Va., Mar. 10, 1944; s. Henry Bateman and Mildred Verda (Cuthrell) M.; m. Jane Irving Calfee, Aug. 27, 1966; children: Alexander Bateman, Holen Irving. BS, U. Va., 1967; MBA, Old Dominion U., 1969; PhD, U. N.C., 1974. Ops. analyst Ford Motor Co., Norfolk, 1968; project mgr. Advanced Rsch. Projects Agy. Office Sec. Def., Washington, 1970-71; asst. prof., co-founder Inst. Pub. Welfare Mgmt., U. Ala. Grad. Sch. Bus., Tuscaloosa, 1974-75; asst. prof. Sch. Orgn. and Mgmt. Yale U., New Haven, 1975-78; assoc. prof. Harvard Bus. Sch., Boston, 1978-85; vis. prof. Stanford Exec. Inst., 1985; Isaac Stiles Hopkins prof. orgn. and mgmt. Emory U. Bus. Sch., Atlanta, 1987—, dept. dean, 1989-91, dean faculty, 1991-93, Hopkins fellow, 1995—; mem. sec.'s adv. bd. U.S. Dept. Energy, Washington, 1993—; mem. adv. bd. orgn. effectiveness programs The Conf. Bd., N.Y.C., 1994—; mem. adv. bd. McIntire Sch. Commerce, U. Va., Charlottesville, 1987—. Author: Macro-Organizational Behavior, 1980, (with J.R. Kimberly) The Organizatoinal Life Cycle: Issues in the Creation, Transformation, and Decline of Organizations, 1980, Managing the Corporate Social Environment: A Grounded theory, 1987, Corporate Comeback: The Transformation of National Semiconductor, 1996; (in collaboration with K.S. Cameron) Coffin Nails and Corporate Strategies, 1982, (with A. Bhambri) The Regulatory Executives, 1983, (with W.A. Randolph) The Organization Game: A Simulation, 1979, 83, 93; mem. edit. bd. Adminstrv. Sci. Quar., 1978-86, Mgmt. Sci., 1979-82. 1st lt. U.S. Army, 1969-71. Recipient Disting. Svc. award Emory U., 1993; Hopkins fellow, 1994—. Mem. APA, Acad. Mgmt. (chmn. orgn. and mgmt. theory divsn. 1984-85), Strategic Mgmt. Soc., Harvard Club (Boston), Commerce Club (Atlanta), Cherokee Town Club (Atlanta), Beta Gamma Sigma. Unitarian Universalist. Avocations: boating, tennis. Home and Office: 3414 Habersham Rd NW Atlanta GA 30305 Home (summer): 177 Fox Hill Rd Chatham MA 02633

MILES, RUBY WILLIAMS, secondary education educator; b. Petersburg, Va., Jan. 19, 1929; d. Richard Allen and Elizabeth (Penny) Williams; m. John Oscar Miles, Jan. 7, 1950 (div. 1966); children: Karen Jonnia Miles George, Steven Ricardo. BA, Va. State Coll., Petersburg, 1971, MA, 1977. Cert. high sch. tchr., Va. Tchr. English Dinwiddie (Va.) Sch., 1971-78, Clarksville (Tenn.) Sch., 1978-80; tchr. English Petersburg Pub. Schs., 1982—, head English dept., 1991—; instr. St. Paul's Coll., Lawrenceville, Va., 1981-82; asst. prof. St. Leo Coll., Ft. Lee, Va., 1988; tchr., counselor Upward Bound project Va. State U., summer, 1974; tchr. Hopewell Pub. Schs., Va. summer 1983—; adj. prof. John Tyler C.C., Fort Lee Va., 1992—. Bd. dirs. Playmaker Fellows Ltd., Petersburg, 1983; co-dir. Exclusively Youth Models, 1984-85. Recipient Leadership award Va. Edn. Assn., 1985. Mem. Petersburg Edn. Assn. (past pres.), Am. Bus. Women's Assn., Nat. Orgn. for Women, Nat. Assn. Female Execs., NEA, Nat. Coun. Tchrs. English, Delta Sigma Theta. Avocations. writing, traveling. Home: 2733 Rollingwood Rd Petersburg VA 23805-2317

MILES, SAMUEL ISRAEL, psychiatrist, educator; b. Munich, Mar. 4, 1949; came to U.S., 1949; s. Henry and Renee (Ringel) M.; m. Denise Marie Robey, June 26, 1977; children: Jonathan David, Justin Alexander. BS, CCNY, 1970; MD, N.Y. Med. Coll., 1974; PhD, So. Calif. Psychoanalytic Inst., 1986. Diplomate Am. Bd. Psychiatry and Neurology with added qualifications in forensic psychiatry. Intern D.C. Gen. Hosp., Washington, 1974-75; resident in psychiatry Cedars-Sinai Med. Ctr., Los Angeles, 1975-78; practice medicine specializing in psychiatry Los Angeles, 1978—; ind. med. examiner Calif. Dept. Indsl. Relations, 1984-91, qualified med. examiner, 1991—; asst. clin. prof. psychiatry UCLA Sch. Medicine, 1978—; attending psychiatrist Cedars-Sinai Med. Ctr., 1978—; attending psychiatrist Brotman Med. Ctr., Culver City, Calif., 1978—; mem. faculty So. Calif. Psychoanalytic Inst., 1986—; mem. psychiat. panel Superior Ct. Los Angeles County, 1990—, Fed. Ct., 1990—. Fellow Am. Acad. Psychoanalysis, Am. Orthopsychiat. Assn.; mem. Acad. Psychiatry and the Law, Am. Coll. Legal Medicine, Calif. Psychiat. Assn. (mem. managed care com. 1991—), So. Calif. Psychiat. Soc. (coun. rep. 1985-88, 92-95, chairperson pvt. practice com. 1988-92, sec. 1991-92, mem. worker's compensation com. 1992—), So. Calif. Psychoanalytic Inst. (pres. clin. assocs. orgn. 1981-82, mem. admissions com. 1988—, mem. ethics stds. com. 1991-92, chairperson ethics stds. com. 1993—, mem. exec. com. 1993—). Jewish. Avocations: aviation, swimming. Office: 8631 W 3rd St Ste 425E Los Angeles CA 90048-5908

MILES, THOMAS CASWELL, aerospace engineer; b. Atlanta, Mar. 21, 1952; s. Franklin Caswell and Eugenia Frances (Newsom) M.; m. Linda Susan Duggleby, Aug. 10, 1980. BMET, So. Tech. Inst., 1977; postgrad., Troy State U., 1978-80. Assoc. engr. aircraft design Lockheed Martin Aero. Sys., Marietta, Ga., 1980-82; engr., aircraft design Lockheed Aero. Systems Co., Marietta, Ga., 1982-85, sr. engr., aircraft design, 1985-89, group engr., 1989-90, specialist engr., 1990—; mem. SAE-A-6 Mil. Aircraft & Helicopter Panel, 1987-91. Mem. AIAA (sr.), ASME, ASTM, Nat. Mgmt. Assn., Lockheed Ga. Mgmt. Assn. (bd. dirs. 1996), Soc. Automotive Engrs. (SAE co. rep., SAE Atlanta sect. vice chmn. aircraft), Oxygen Standardization Coord. Group Assn. Fraternity Advisors (affiliate), Wick's Lake Homeowners Assn. (pres. 1995, v.p. 1996), Tau Kappa Epsilon (dist. pres. 1987-88, dist. v.p. 1984—, chpt. advisor 1980-87, key leader 1985, 90, So. Order of Honor 1989). Avocations: sailing, scuba diving, screen printing. Home: 1926 Wicks Ridge Ln Marietta GA 30062-6777 Office: Lockheed Martin Aero Sys Dept 73-05 cc-34 Marietta GA 30063-0199

MILES, VIRGINIA (MRS. FRED C. MILES), marketing consultant; b. N.Y.C., Apr. 20, 1916; d. Samuel and Jeanette (Shalet) Goldman; m. Fred C. Miles, Mar. 24, 1940; 1 dau., Erica. B.A., Wellesley Coll., 1936; M.A., Columbia, 1938, Ph.D., 1940. Asso. dir. research R.H. Macy & Co., N.Y.C., 1940-46; instr. dept. psychology Coll. City N.Y., 1946-48; advt. research dir. Alexander Smith & Co., Yonkers, N.Y., 1948-50; v.p., research dir. McCann-Erickson Advt. Agy., N.Y.C., 1950-60; v.p. spl. planning Young & Rubicam, Inc., N.Y.C., 1960-71; sr. v.p. new product devel. Young & Rubicam, Inc., 1971-75; mktg. cons. Englewood, N.J., 1975—. Contbr. articles to profl. jours., trade mags. Active Urban Coalition. Mem. Advt. Women of N.Y., Am. Assn. Pub. Opinion Rsch., Am. Mktg. Assn., Internat. Advt. Assn., Sigma Zi. Democrat. Jewish. Avocations: reading, music, gardening, travel. Home and Office: 91 Glenbrook Pky Englewood NJ 07631-2105

MILES, WENDELL A., federal judge; b. Holland, Mich., Apr. 17, 1916; s. Fred T. and Dena Del (Alverson) M.; m. Mariette Bruckert, June 8, 1946; children: Lorraine Miles, Michelle Miles Kopinski, Thomas Paul. AB, Hope Coll., 1938, LLD (hon.), 1980; MA, U. Wyo., 1939; JD, U. Mich., 1942; LLD (hon.), Detroit Coll. Law, 1979. Bar: Mich. Ptnr. Miles & Miles, Holland, 1948-53, Miles, Mika, Meyers, Beckett & Jones, Grand Rapids, Mich., 1961-70; pros. atty. County of Ottawa, Mich., 1949-53; U.S. dist. atty. Western Dist. Mich., Grand Rapids, 1953-60; U.S. dist. judge Western Dist. Mich., 1974—, chief judge, 1979-86, sr. chief judge, 1986—; cir. judge 20th Jud. Cir. Ct. Mich., 1970-74; instr. Hope Coll., 1948-53, Am. Inst. Banking, 1953-60; adj. prof. Am. constl. history Hope Coll., Holland, Mich., 1979—; mem. Mich. Higher Edn. Commn.; apptd. Fgn. Intelligence Surveillance Count, Washington, 1989—. Pres. Holland Bd. Edn., 1952-63. Served to capt. U.S. Army, 1942-47. Recipient Liberty Bell award, 1986. Fellow Am. Bar Found.; mem. ABA, Mich. Bar Assn., Fed. Bar Assn., Ottawa County Bar Assn., Grand Rapids Bar (Inns of Ct. 1995—), Am. Judicature Soc., Torch Club, Rotary Club, Masons. Office: US Dist Ct 236 Fed Bldg 110 Michigan Ave NW Grand Rapids MI 49503-2313

MILES-LAGRANGE, VICKI LYNN, federal judge; b. Oklahoma City, Sept. 30, 1953; d. Charles and Mary (Greenard) Miles. BA, Vassar Coll., 1974; LLB, Howard U., 1977. Congl. aide Speaker of the Ho., Rep. Carl Albert, 1974-76; formerly grad. fellow, trial atty. U.S. Dept. Justice, 1979-82; mem. Okla. Senate from Dist. 48, 1987-93; U.S. atty. U.S. Dept. of Justice, Oklahoma City, Okla., 1993-94; judge U.S. Dist. Ct. (we. dist.) Okla., Oklahoma City, 1994—. Democrat. Baptist.

MILETICH, DON, engineering executive; b. Luzane, Yugoslavisa, Nov. 23, 1951; s. Miodrag and Zorka (Ganic) M.; m. Slavica Miletich, July 10, 1974; children: Nikola, Angelina. BS in Applied Engring. Scis., U. Wis., 1973. Registered profl. engr., Wis. Sr. project engr. Jacabson Textron, Racine, Wis., 1973-80; product engr. Seaman Parson Co., Milw., 1980-81; dir. engring. Cooper Lighting, Elk Grove, Ill., 1981—. Mem. Illuminating Engrs. Soc. of N. Am., Soc. of Automotive Engrs. Home: 1595 Burning Bush Ln Hoffman Estates IL 60195 Office: Cooper Lighting 400 Busse Rd Elk Grove Village IL 60007

MILETICH, IVO, library and information scientist, bibliographer, educator, linguist, literature research specialist; b. Pucisca, Yugoslavia, Apr. 18, 1936; came to U.S., 1966, naturalized, 1972; s. Josip and Mandina (Bagich) M.; m. Mira Pilja, Mar. 11, 1967; children: George Edward, Marina Julie. AB, Acad. Edn., Split, Yugoslavia, 1960; AM in History, U. Skopje, Macedonia, Yugoslavia, 1966; cert. advanced study, English Inst., Chgo., 1969; MA in Libr. Sci., Rosary Coll., River Forest, Ill., 1971. Cert. libr., Va. Tchr. various schs. Yugoslavia, 1959-65; asst. bibliographer Slavic langs. and lit. Joseph Regenstein and Sam Harper Librs., U. Chgo., 1967-71; tchr. Croatian lang. co-edn. YMCA Community Coll., Chgo., 1969-71, 74—; bibliographer Old Dominion U., Norfolk, Va., 1971-74; assoc. prof. libr. sci., bibliographer Chgo. State U., 1974—; translator, interpreter English, Latin, Croatian, Serbian, Macedonian, Bulgarian, Old Ch. Slavic, Slovene, 1969—; interpreter Berlitz Trans. Ctr. Sch. Langs.; lectr. South Slavonic langs., lit., history and culture, Balkan states culture, heritage and folk lit., transl. techniques. Contbr. various confs., seminars, workshops, jours., transl. of articles, studies, work on dictionary, Berlitz Transl. Svc. transl. and interpretion. Recipient cert. of appreciation YMCA C.C., Chgo., 1976, cert. Beta Phi Mu, U. Pitts., 1972, Am. Translators Assn., 1980, Assn. Coll. and Rsch. Librs., 1986. Mem. ALA, Am. Fedn. Tchrs., Assn. Coll. and Rsch. Librs., Chgo. Acad. Libr. Coun. Libr. of Congress (assoc.), Beta Phi Mu. Home: 618 Exchange Ave Calumet City IL 60409-3903 Office: Chgo State U Rm Lib 203 95th St at King Dr Chicago IL 60628

MILEWSKI, BARBARA ANNE, pediatrics nurse, neonatal intensive care nurse; b. Chgo., Sept. 11, 1934; d. Anthony and LaVerne (Sepp) Witt; m. Leonard A. Milewski, Feb. 23, 1952; children: Pamela, Robert, Diane, Timothy. ADN, Harper Coll., Palatine, Ill, 1982; BS, Northern Ill. U., 1992; postgrad., North Park Coll. RN, Ill.; cert. CPR instr. Staff nurse Northwest Community Hosp., Arlington Heights, Ill., Resurrection Hosp., Chgo.; nurse neonatal ICU Children's Meml. Hosp., Chgo.; day care cons. Cook County Dept. Pub. Health; CPR instr. Stewart Oxygen Svcs., Chgo.; instr., organizer parenting and well baby classes and clinics; vol. Children's Meml. Hosp.; health coord. CEDA Head Start; cons. day care Cook County Dept. Pub. Health. Vol. first aid instr. Boy Scouts Am.; CPR instr. Harper Coll., Children's Meml. Hosp.; dir. Albany Park Comm. Ctr. Head Start, Chgo.; day care cons. Cook County Dept. Pub. Health. Mem. Am. Mortar Bd., Sigma Theta Tau.

MILEWSKI, STANISLAW ANTONI, ophthalmologist, educator; b. Bagrowo, Poland, June 16, 1930; s. Alfred and Sabina (Sicinska) M.; came to U.S., 1959, naturalized, 1967; BA, Trinity Coll., U. Dublin (Ireland), 1954, MA, 1959, B. Chir., M.B., B.A.O., 1956; m. Anita Dobiecka, July 11, 1959; children: Andrew, Teresa, Mark. House surgeon Hammersmith Hosp. Post-grad. Sch. London, 1958; intern St. Raffael Hosp., New Haven, 1960-61; resident in ophthalmology Gill Meml. Hosp., Roanoke, Va., 1961-64; practice medicine specializing in surgery and diseases of the retina and vitreous; mem. staff Manchester (Conn.) Meml. Hosp., 1964-71, chief of ophthalmology, sr. attending physician St. Francis Hosp., Hartford, Conn., 1971—; asst. clin. prof. ophthalmology U. Conn., 1972—. Clin. fellow Montreal (Que., Can.) Gen Hosp., McGill U., 1971-72, Mass. Eye and Ear Infirmary, Harvard Med. Sch., Boston, 1974; diplomate Am. Bd. Ophthalmology. Fellow ACS; mem. AMA, New England Ophthal. Soc., Conn. Soc. Eye Physicians, Vitreous Soc. Republican. Roman Catholic. Home: 127 Lakewood Cir S Manchester CT 06040-7086 Office: 191 Main St Manchester CT 06040-3556 also: 43 Woodland St Ste 100 Hartford CT 06105-2339

MILEY, GEORGE HUNTER, nuclear engineering educator; b. Shreveport, La., Aug. 6, 1933; s. George Hunter and Norma Angeline (Dowling) M.; m. Elizabeth Burroughs, Nov. 22, 1958; children: Susan Miley Hibbs, Hunter Robert. B.S. in Chem. Engring., Carnegie-Mellon U., 1955; M.S., U. Mich., 1956, Ph.D. in Chem.-Nuclear Engring., 1959. Nuclear engr. Knolls Atomic Power Lab., Gen. Electric Co., Schenectady, 1959-61; mem. faculty U. Ill., Urbana, 1961—; prof. U. Ill., 1967—, chmn. nuclear engring. program, 1975-86, dir. Fusion Studies Lab., 1976—, fellow Ctr. for Advanced Study, 1985-86; dir. rsch. Rockford Tech. Assocs. Inc., 1990-94; vis. prof. U. Colo., 1967, Cornell U., 1969-70, U. New South Wales, 1986, Imperial Coll. of London, 1987; mem. Ill. Radiation Protection Bd., 1988—; mem. Air Force Studies Bd., 1990-94; chmn. tech. adv. com. Ill. Low Level Radioactive Waste Site, 1990—; chmn. com. on indsl. uses of radiation Ill. Dept. Nuclear Safety, 1989—. Author: Direct Conversion of Nuclear Radiation Energy, 1971, Fusion Energy Conversion, 1976; editor Jour. Fusion Tech., 1980—; U.S. assoc. editor Laser and Particle Beams, 1982-86, mng. editor, 1987-91, editor-in-chief, 1991—; U.S. editor Jour. Plasma Physics, 1995—. Served with C.E. AUS, 1960. Recipient Western Electric Tchg.-Rsch. award, 1977, Halliburton Engring. Edn. Leadership award, 1990, Edward Teller medal, 1995; NATO sr. sci. fellow, 1975-76, Guggenheim fellow, 1985-86, Japanese Soc. Promotion of Sci. fellow, 1994. Fellow IEEE, Am. Nuclear Soc. (dir. 1980-83, Disting. Svc. award 1980, Outstanding Achievement award Fusion Energy divsn. 1992), Am. Phys. Soc.; mem. Am. Soc. Engring. Edn. (chmn. energy conversion com. 1967-70, pres. U. Ill. chpt. 1973-74, chmn. nuclear divsn. 1975-76, Outstanding Tchr. award 1973), Sigma Xi, Tau Beta Pi. Presbyterian. Achievements include research on fusion, energy conversion, reactor kinetics. Office: U Ill 214 Nuclear Engring Lab 103 S Goodwin Ave Urbana IL 61801-2901 *My professional goal has been to insure that future generations have a plentiful supply of economical, readily available energy such as offered by fusion. Not only should this insure a continued improvement in the standard of living for persons in all nations, but it should help maintain peace which is threatened by the struggle to obtain and control limited natural sources of energy.*

MILFORD, FREDERICK JOHN, retired research company executive; b. Cleve., July 1, 1926; s. Frederick Charles and Florence M.; m. Jean Irene Olson, Sept. 8, 1951; 1 child, Cheryl Lynn. B.S. in Physics, Case Inst. Tech., 1949; Ph.D. in Physics, M.I.T., 1952. Instr. Case Inst. Tech., Cleve., 1952-56; asst. prof. Case Inst. Tech., 1956-59; div. cons. Battelle Columbus Labs., 1959-62, div. chief, 1962-64, sr. fellow, 1964-66, dir. research in phys. scis., 1966-73, scientist, 1973, dept. mgr., 1973-76, assoc. dir., 1976-85, chief scientist, 1985-87, v.p. spl. programs, 1987-89, ret., 1989; vis. prof. physics U. Wash., 1969. Author: (with J.R. Reitz) Foundations of Electromagnetic Theory, 1960, 4th edit., 1993. Mem. adv. bd. Central Ohio Salvation Army. Served with USNR, 1945-46. George Eastman fellow, 1951-52; Focke scholar, 1948-49. Fellow Am. Phys. Soc.; mem. Masons, Army and Navy Club, Kit Kat Club. Home: 1411 London Dr Columbus OH 43221-1543

MILFORD, MURRAY HUDSON, soil science educator; b. Honey Grove, Tex., Sept. 29, 1934; s. Murray Lane and Vivian Ione (Hudson) M.; m. Marsha Ann Rasmussen, July 21, 1961; children: Rebecca Ione, Murray Daniel. BS in Agronomy, Tex. A&M, 1955, MS in Agronomy, 1959; PhD in Soil Science, U. Wis., 1962. Cert. profl. soil scientist. Rsch. assoc. Cornell U., Ithaca, N.Y., 1962-63; asst. prof. Cornell U., Ithaca, 1963-68, assoc. prof., 1968; assoc. prof. Tex. A&M U., College Station, 1968-74, prof., 1974—. Author: (lab. manual) Soils and Soil Science-Lab. Exercises, 1970. 1st lt. USAR, 1955-57. Recipient so. region award for excellence in coll. and univ. tchg. in food and agrl. scis., 1995. Fellow AAAS, Am. Soc. Agronomy (pres. Tex. chpt. 1982-83, Resident Edn. award 1978), Soil Sci. Soc. Am. (Edn. award 1988); mem. Soil and Water Conservation Soc. (pres. Tex. coun. of chpts. 1987). Democrat. Presbyterian. Home: 3606 Tanglewood Dr Bryan TX 77802-3320 Office: Tex A&M Univ Soil & Crop Scis Dept College Station TX 77843-2474

MILGRAM, JEROME H., marine and ocean engineer, educator; b. Phila., Sept. 23, 1938; s. Samuel J. and Fannie M. BSEE, MIT, 1961, BS in Naval Architecture and Marine Engring., 1961, MS, 1962, PhD in Hydrodynamics, 1965. Registered profl. engr., Mass. With Scripps Inst. Oceanography, San Diego, summer 1961; project engr. Block Assocs., Cambridge, Mass., 1961-67; asst. prof. MIT, Cambridge, 1967-70, assoc. prof., 1970-77, prof. ocean engring., 1977-89, William I. Koch prof. marine tech., 1989—; rsch. assoc. in biophysics Harvard U. Med. Sch., 1974-76; vis. prof. in naval architecture and marine engring. U. Mich., 1988-89; design dir. Am. 3 Found., 1991-95. Contbr. articles to profl. jours. Recipient Am. Bur. Shipping award, 1961, Alan Berman Outstanding Rsch. Publ. award U.S. Naval Rsch. Lab., 1990, AT&T Design Innovation award, 1992. Mem. Soc. Naval Archs. and Marine Engrs. (life), Nat. Acad. Engring. (life). Patentee in field. Home: 322 Ridge St Arlington MA 02174-1703 Office: MIT 77 Massachusetts Ave Rm 5-318 Cambridge MA 02139-3594

MILGRAM, RICHARD MYRON, music school administrator; b. Moultrie, Ga., Nov. 9, 1943; s. Bernard Byron and Libbie Elaine M.; m. Judith Lee Milgram, Nov. 26, 1964; children: Rhonda Beth, Gary David. MusB, Berklee Coll. Music, Boston, 1966; MusM, Boston U., 1973. Cert. tchr. Mass., Conn. Tchr. Norwood (Mass.) Pub. Schs., 1969-72; asst. prof. Merrimack Coll., North Andover, Mass., 1972-75; tchr. Guilford (Conn.) Pub. Schs., 1975-77; pres., co-founder Shoreline Sch. Art and Music, Branford, Conn., 1978—; mem. music edn. coun./student tchr. practicum com. Westfield (Mass.) State Coll., 1978-81, New Haven Arts Coun., 1979; judge various music competitions; clarinet soloist. Contbr. revs. to music jours. Mem. Music Educators Nat. Conf., Conn. Music Educators Assn., Phi Mu Alpha Sinfonia. Office: Shoreline Sch Art and Music 482 E Main St Branford CT 06405-2919

MILGRIM, FRANKLIN MARSHALL, merchant; b. N.Y.C., Aug. 24, 1925; s. Charles and Sally (Knobel) M.; m. Carol E. Kleinman, Sept. 2, 1945; children: Nancy Ellen, Catherine. Grad. with honors, Woodmere (N.Y.) Acad., 1943; B.S. in Econs. with honors, Wharton Sch. U. Pa., 1949. Asst. mgr. Milgrim, Cleve., 1949-50; merchandiser, buyer H. Milgrim Bros., Inc., N.Y.C., 1950-52; v.p., dir., gen. merchandiser H. Milgrim Bros., Inc., 1952-57; pres., dir. Milgrim, Inc., Cleve. and Columbus, Ohio, 1957—; v.p., dir. Milgrim, Inc. (Mich.), Detroit, 1962-66, The 9-18 Corp., Cleve., 1969—; pres., treas., dir. Milgrim Suburban, Inc., 1963—, Milo, Inc., Columbus, 1966—, The Milgrim Co., Cleve., 1966—; pres., dir. Frankly Paul Bailey Inc., Cleve., 1965—; Dir., v.p. M and M Receivers Assn., Cleve., 1959-68. Pres. Severance Center Mchts. Assn., Cleveland Heights, 1963-66; Pres., bd.

dirs. Greater Cleve. Area chpt. Nat. Council on Alcoholism, 1973—; chmn. bd. Alcoholism Services of Cleve., 1977—; fin. chmn. adv. council Salvation Army Harbor Light Complex, 1976—, chmn. bd. adv. council, 1981—; mem. Greater Cleve. adv. bd. Salvation Army, 1981—; founding bd. dirs. Sister Mary Ignatia Gavin Found.; foreman Cuyahoga County Grand Jury, 1986. Served with USNR, 1943-46. Mem. Oakwood Country Club (Cleve.), Cleve. Mid-Day Club, City Club (Cleve.), Cleve. Playhouse, Turnberry club (North Miami Beach, Fla.). Home: 4000 Towerside Terr #1908 Miami FL 33138 also: 1 Bratenahl Pl # 807 Cleveland OH 44108-1181 also: 1 Bratenahl Pl Apt 807 Cleveland OH 44108-1154

MILGRIM, ROGER MICHAEL, lawyer; b. N.Y.C., Mar. 22, 1937; s. Isreal and Iola (Lash) M.; m. Patricia Conway, July 10, 1971; children: Justin, Alex. BA, U. Pa., 1958; LLB, NYU, 1961, LLM, 1962. Bar: N.Y., U.S. Supreme Ct. Assoc. Baker & McKenzie, Paris, 1963-65, Nixon Mudge et al, N.Y.C., 1965-68; mem. Milgrim Thomajan & Lee P.C., N.Y.C., 1968-92; ptnr. Paul, Hastings, Janogsky & Walker, N.Y.C., 1992—; adj. prof. sch. law NYU, N.Y.C., 1974—. Author: Milgrim on Trade Secrets, 1968, supplement, 1996, Milgrim on Licensing, 1990, supplement, 1996. Trustee Coll. Wooster, 1994—, Bklyn. Hosp., 1982-91. Mem. Knickerbocker Club, Phila. Cricket Club. Republican. Home: 14 Sutton Pl S New York NY 10022-3071 Office: Paul Hastings Janofsky & Walker 399 Park Ave New York NY 10022-4697

MILGROM, FELIX, immunologist, educator; b. Rohatyn, Poland, Oct. 12, 1919; came to U.S., 1958; naturalized, 1963; s. Henryk and Ernestyna (Cyryl) M.; m. Halina Miszel, Oct. 15, 1941; children: Henry, Martin Louis. Student, U. Lwow, Poland, 1937-41, U. Lublin, Poland, 1945; MD, U. Wroclaw, Poland, 1947; MD (hon.), U. Vienna, Austria, 1976, U. Lund, Sweden, 1979, U. Heidelberg, Fed. Republic Germany, 1979, U. Bergen, Norway, 1980; DSc (hon.), U. Med. Dent., N.J., 1991. Rsch. assoc., prof. dept. microbiology Sch. Medicine U. Wroclaw, 1946-54, chmn. dept., 1954; prof., head dept. microbiology Sch. Medicine, Silesian U., Zabrze, Poland, 1954-57; rsch. assoc. Svc. de Chime Microbienne, Pasteur Inst., Paris, 1957; rsch. assoc. prof. dept. bacteriology and immunology U. Buffalo Sch. Medicine, 1958-62; assoc. prof., then prof. and disting. prof. microbiology Sch. Medicine, SUNY, Buffalo, 1962—, chmn. dept., 1967-85. Author: Studies on the Structure of Antibodies, 1950; co-editor: International Convocations on Immunology, 1969, 75, 79, 85, Principles of Immunology, 1973, 2d edit., 1979, Principles of Immunological Diagnosis in Medicine, 1981, Medical Microbiology, 1982; editor in chief Internat. Archives of Allergy and Applied Immunology, 1965-91; contbg. editor Vox Sanguinis, 1965-76, Transfusion, 1966-73, Cellular Immunology, 1970-83, Transplation, 1975-78; contbr. numerous articles to profl. jours. Recipient Alfred Jurzykowski Found. prize, 1986, Paul Ehrlich and Ludwig Darmstaedter prize, 1987. Mem. Am. Assn. Immunologists, Transplantation Soc. (v.p. 1976-78), Am. Acad. Microbiology, Coll. Internat. Allergologicum (v.p. 1970-78, pres. 1978-82, hon. mem. 1990—), Polish Acad. Learning, Sigma Xi. Achievements include research on the serology of syphillis, Tb, rheumatoid arthritis, organ and tissue specificity including blood groups, transplantation and autoimmunity. Home: 474 Getzville Rd Buffalo NY 14226-2555

MILGROM, PAUL ROBERT, economics educator; b. Detroit, Apr. 20, 1948; s. Abraham Isaac and Anne (Finkelstein) M.; m. Jan Thurston, Dec. 10, 1977; children: Joshua, Elana. AB in Math. with high honors, U. Mich., 1970; MS in Stats., Stanford U., 1978, PhD in Bus., 1979; MA (hon.), Yale U., 1983. Actuarial trainee Met. Life Ins. Co., 1970-71; conulting actuary Nelson and Warren, Inc., 1972-75; asst. prof. dept. managerial econs. and decision scis. Kellogg Grad. Sch. Mgmt. Northwestern U., 1979-81, assoc. prof., 1981-82, prof., 1982-83; prof. econs. and mgmt. Yale U., 1983-85, Williams Bros. prof. mgmt. studies, prof. econs., 1985-87; prof. econs. Stanford U., 1987-93; Ely prof. econs. Yale U., 1993—; dir. Stanford Inst. Theoretical Econs. Stanford U., 1989-91; vis. rsch. assoc. econs. Stanford U., 1981; vis. prof. Yale U., 1982-83; Ford vis. prof. econs. U. Calif. Berkeley, 1986-87; IBM rsch. chair Northwestern U., 1981; Williams Bros. chair mgmt. studies Yale U., 1985; Olin disting. lectr. Princeton U., 1988; past cons. So. New Eng. Telephone Co., Rand Corp., Arctic Slope Regional Corp., Ga. Pacific, Exxon, Pacific Telesis, Bell Atlantic, Govt. of Mex., others; lectr. in field. Author: (with John Roberts) Economics, Organization and Management, 1992, (with John Roberts), Instructor's Manual for Economics, Organization and Management, 1992; assoc. editor Jour. Econ. Theory, 1983-87, Rand Jour. Econs., 1985-89, Econometrica, 1987-90, Jour. Fin. Intermediation, 1989-92, Games and Econ. Behavior, 1990-92; co-editor Am. Econ. Review, 1990-93; contbr. over 50 articles to profl. jours. Recipient Leonard J. Savage Meml. Thesis award, 1980, Rsch. grant NSF, 1980, 82, 85, 88-91, 89, 91, Rsch. award Actuarial Edn. and Rsch. Fund, 1983, John Simon Guggenheim fellowship, 1986, Best Paper of Yr. award, 1987, Rsch. grant Ctr. Econ. Policy, 1988, 90. Fellow Am. Acad. Arts and Scis., Econometric Soc. (plenary lectr. 5th World Congress 1985), Morse Coll., Inst. Advanced Studies Hebrew U. Jerusalem, Ctr. Advanced Study in Behavioral Scis., Soc. Actuaries (Triennial Paper prize 1976); mem. Am. Econ. Assn. Office: Stanford Univ Dept Econs Stanford CA 94305

MILHAVEN, JOHN GILES, religious studies educator; b. N.Y.C., Sept. 1, 1927; s. John Michael and Rose (Burns) M.; m. Anne Teresa Lally, May 21, 1970; 1 child, Shelly. B.A., Woodstock Coll., 1949, M.A. in Teaching, Licentiate in Philosophy, 1950; Licentiate in Theology, Facultés Théologiques de la Compagnie de Jésus d'Enghien, Belgium, 1957; Ph.D. in Philosophy, U. Munich, Germany, 1962. Instr. philosophy Canisius Coll., Buffalo, 1951-53; asst. prof. philosophy Fordham U., N.Y.C., 1961-66; assoc. prof. moral theology Woodstock Coll., Md., 1966-70; assoc. prof. religious studies Brown U., Providence, 1970-76; prof. religious studies Brown U., 1976—; lectr. med. ethics Georgetown U. Med. Sch., Washington, 1966-68. Author: Towards a New Catholic Morality, 1970, Good Anger, 1989, Hadewijch and Her Sisters: Other Ways of Loving and Knowing, 1993; contbr. articles to various publs. Mem. Am. Acad. Religion, Soc. Christian Ethics, Cath. Theol. Soc. Am. Roman Catholic. Home: 20 Penrose Ave Providence RI 02906-5620 Office: Brown U Dept Religious Studies Providence RI 02912 *I believe I succeeded when I effectively shared with others something of my evasive but persistent experience of human life as important.*

MILHORAT, THOMAS HERRICK, neurosurgeon; b. N.Y.C., Apr. 5, 1936; s. Ade Thomas and Edith Caulkins (Herrick) M.; children: John Thomas, Robert Herrick. BA, Cornell U., 1957, MD, 1961. Intern, asst. resident in gen. surgery N.Y. Hosp.-Cornell Med. Ctr., 1961-63; clin. assoc., dept. surg. neurology Nat. Inst. Neurol. Diseases and Blindness, Bethesda, 1963-65; asst. resident, chief resident in neurosurgery N.Y. Hosp.-Cornell Med. Ctr., 1965-68, asst. neurosurgeon NIH, 1968-71; assoc. prof. neurol. surgery, assoc. prof. child health and devel. George Washington U. Sch. Medicine, Washington, 1971-74; prof. child health and devel. George Washington U., Washington, 1974-81, prof. neurol. surgery, 1974-81; chmn. dept. neurosurgery Children's Hosp. Nat. Med. Ctr., Washington, 1971-81; prof. neurol. surgery, dept. chmn. SUNY Health Sci. Ctr., Bklyn., 1982—; neurosurgeon-in-chief Kings County Hosp. Ctr.; regional chmn. neurol. surgery L.I. Coll. Hosp., 1986—, Coney Island Hosp., 1986—; program dir. Neurosurgery Rsch. Tng. Program, 1982—; mem. Nat. Coun. Scientists, NIH, 1969-82. Author: Hydrocephalus and Cerebrospinal Fluid, 1972, Pediatric Neurosurgery, 1978, Cerebrospinal Fluid and the Brain Edemas, 1987 (with M.K. Hammock) Cranial Computed Tomography in Infancy and Childhood, 1981; contbr. 220 articles to sci. publs. and chpts. to books. Chmn. bd. Internat. Neurosci. Found., pres. 1986—; chmn. med. adv. bd. Am. Spingomyelia Alliance Project, 1996—. Lt. commdr. USPHS, 1963-65. Recipient 1st prize in pathology, Cornell U. Med. Sch. Dept. Ob-Gyn., 1960, Charles L. Horn prize Cornell Med. Sch., 1961, Best Paper award ann. combined meeting N.Y. Acad. Medicine/N.Y. Neurosurg. Soc., 1965, Pudenz award for Excellence in CSF Physiology, 1994; named one of N.Y.'s Best Doctors, N.Y. Mag., 1992. Mem. AAAS, Internat. Soc. Pediat. Neurosurgery, Am. Assn. Neurol. Surgery (pediat. sect.), Am. Acad. Pediat. (surg. sect.), Soc. Pediat. Rsch., N.Y. Acad. Medicine, N.Y. Soc. Neurosurgery (pres. 1988-90), Bklyn. Neurologic Soc. (pres. 1988-95), Soc. Neurosci., Internat. Soc. Neurosci., Soc. Neurol. Surgeons, Med. Club Bklyn., Sigma Xi. Avocations: golf, billiards, gardening. Office: SUNY Health Sci Ctr Bklyn 450 Clarkson Ave PO Box 1189 Brooklyn NY 11203

MILHOUSE, PAUL WILLIAM, bishop; b. St. Francisville, Ill., Aug. 31, 1910; s. Willis Cleveland and Carrie (Pence) M.; m. Mary Frances Noblitt, June 29, 1932; children: Mary Catherine Milhouse Hauswald, Pauline Joyce Milhouse Vermillion, Paul David. A.B., U. Indpls. (formerly Ind. Cen. U.), 1932; D.D., U. Ind. (formerly Ind. Cen. U.), 1950; B.D., Am. Theol. Sem., 1937, Th.D., 1946; L.H.D., Westmar Coll., 1965; S.T.D., Oklahoma City U., 1969; D.D., So. Meth. U., 1969. Ordained to ministry United Brethren Ch., 1931; pastor Birds, Ill., 1928-29, Elliott, Ill., 1932-37, Olney, Ill., 1937-41; pastor 1st Ch., Decatur, Ill., 1941-51; asso. editor Telescope-Messenger, 1951-58; exec. sec. gen. council Evang. United Brethren Ch., 1959-60, bishop, 1960-68; bishop United Meth. Ch., 1968—; presiding bishop Southwestern Area, Evang. United Brethren Ch., 1960-68; presiding bishop Okla., 1968-80; pres. Coun. United Meth. Bishops, 1977-78; bishop-in-residence Oklahoma City U., 1980-91, U. Indpls., 1992—; mem. commn. to unite Evang. United Brethren Ch. and Meth. Ch., 1960-68. Author: Enlisting and Developing Church Leaders, 1946, Come Unto Me, 1946, Lift Up Your Eyes, 1955, Doorways to Spritual Living, 1950, Except the Lord Build the House, 1949, Christian Worship in Symbol and Ritual, 1953, Laymen in the Church, 1957, At Life's Crossroads, 1959, Phillip William Otterbein, 1968, Nineteen Bishops of the Evangelical United Brethren Church, 1974, Organizing for Effective Ministry, 1980, Theological and Historical Roots of United Methodists, 1980, Detour Into Yesterday, 1984, Okla. City U., Miracle at 23d and Blackwelder, 1984, Transforming Dollars into Service, A History of Methodist Manor, 1987, St. Lukes of Oklahoma City, 1988; also articles; editor: Facing Frontiers, 1960. Trustee Westmar Coll., 1960-68, Western Home, 1960-68, So. Meth. U., 1968-80, Oklahoma City U., 1968-80, hon. life trustee, 1980—, Francis E. Willard Home, 1968-80, Meth. Manor, 1968-80, Boys Ranch, 1968-80, Last Frontier coun. Boy Scouts Am., 1968-80; hon. life trustee United Theol. Sem. Recipient Disting. Alumnus award Ind. Ctrl. U. (now U. Indpls.), 1978, Disting. Friend award Oklahoma City U., 1979, Disting. Svc. award Oklahoma City U., 1980, Top Hand award Oklahoma City C. of C., 1980, Bishop Paul W. Milhouse award Oklahoma City U., 1990, Disting. Svc. award for contbns. to United Meth. history Gen. Commn. on Archives and History, 1996. Mem. Mark Twain Writers Guild, Epsilon Sigma Alpha, now Alpha Chi. *Life is a gift to be lived in harmony with the purpose of God, who holds us accountable.*

MILIC, LOUIS TONKO, English educator; b. Split, Yugoslavia, Sept. 5, 1922; came to U.S., 1936, naturalized, 1945; s. Tonko L. and Helen (Gross) M.; m. Patricia A. Langwell, May 27, 1950 (div. Sept. 1960); 1 dau., Barbara; m. Ann Mulford Boyer, Sept. 24, 1960 (div. Oct. 1970); children: Pamela, Antonia, Byrd Jones; m. Jan Louise Lundgren, Nov. 20, 1970. A.B., Columbia U., 1948, M.A., 1950, Ph.D., 1963. Instr., Mont. State Coll., 1952-54; lectr. Columbia U., 1955-58, instr., 1958-63, asst. prof., 1963-67, assoc. prof. Tchrs. Coll., 1967-69; prof. English, Cleve. State U., 1969-91, prof. emeritus, 1991—, chmn. dept., 1969-78. Author: A Quantitative Approach to the Style of Jonathan Swift, 1967, Style and Stylistics: An Analytical Bibliography, 1967, Stylists on Style, 1969; co-author: The English Language: Form and Use, 1974; editor: Modernity of the Eighteenth Century, 1971, The Gamut, 1983-92; gen. editor: New Humanistic Research series, 1972-80; book rev. editor Computers and the Humanities, 1966-72; compiler The Augustan Prose Sample, The Century of Prose Corpus. Served with USAAF, 1943-46. Am. Council Learned Socs. and IBM fellow, 1967; NEH fellow, 1980. Mem. Internat. Assn. Univ. Profs. English, Assn. Computers in Humanities, Am. Soc. 18th Century Studies, Midwest MLA (exec. com. 1972-75), Henry Sweet Soc., Dictionary Soc. N.Am. (sec.-treas. 1990—), Assn. for Lit. and Linguistic Computing, Rowfant Club. Home: 3111 Chelsea Dr Cleveland OH 44118-1220 *The world is a lucky accident. Its chance opportunities for the inquisitive mind are limitless. I have always found it hard to avoid studying everything, because of this richness, which is tantalizing and yet without permanent meaning.*

MILIC-EMILI, JOSEPH, physician, educator; b. Sezana, Slovenia, May 27, 1931; arrived in Can., 1963; s. Joseph Milic-Emili and Giovanna Milic-Emili Perhavec; m. Ann Harding, Nov. 2, 1957; children: Claire, Anne-Marie, Alice, Andrew. MD, U. Milan, 1955. Asst. prof. physiology and exptl. medicine McGill U., Montreal, Que., Can., 1963-65, assoc. prof., 1965-69, prof., 1970—, dir. Meakins-Christie Labs., 1979-94; vis. prof. Lab. de Physiologie Faculte de Medecine Saint-Antoine, Paris, Svc. de Pneumologie Hosp. Beaujon, Paris, 1978-79, 94-95, chmn. dept. physiology, 1973-78; vis. cons. medicine Royal Postgrad. Med. Sch., London, 1969-70; vis. cons. aeronautics Imperial Coll. Tech., London, 1969-70; asst. prof. physiology U. Liege, Belgium, 1958-60; asst. prof. U. Milan, 1956-58. Mem. editl. bd. Jour. Applied Physiology, 1970-76, Rev. Française des Maladies Respiratories, 1979—, Rivista de Biologia, 1979-86, Am. Rev. Respiratory Disease, 1982-89, Reanimation, Soins Intensifs, Medicine d'Urgence, 1984—. Mem. applied physiology and bioengring. study sect. NIH, 1975-78. Decorated Order of Can.; recipient Gold medal C. Forlanini U. Pavia, Italy, 1982, Am. Coll. Chest Physicians medal, 1984, Harry Wunderly medal Thoracic Soc. Australia, 1988; named Dr. Honoris Causa U. Louvain, Belgium, 1987, Kunming Med. Coll., China, 1987, U. Montpelier, France, 1994; author one of 100 most-cited articles in clin. rsch. of 1960s; named on of 1,000 most-cited contemporary scientists, 1965-78. Fellow Royal Soc. Can., Slovenian Acad. Scis. (fgn. corr.); mem. Soc. Belge de Physiologie, Assn. Physiologistes de Langue Française, Am. Physiol. Soc., Can. Physiol. Soc., Can. Soc. for Clin. Investigation (assoc. editor Clin. Investigative Medicine 1981-86), Italian Physiol. Soc., Can. Thoracic Soc., Med. Rsch. Coun. (mem. grants com. 1980), Soc. Pneumologie Belge (hon.), Brazilian Physiol. Soc. (hon.). Home: 4394 Circle Rd, Montreal, PQ Canada H4W 1Y5 Office: McGill U Meakins-Christie Labs, 3626 St Urbain St, Montreal, PQ Canada H2X 2P2

MILIORA, MARIA TERESA, chemist, psychotherapist, psychoanalyst, educator; b. Somerville, Mass., June 29, 1938; d. Andrew and Maria Civita (Gallinaro) Migliorini. BA cum laude, Regis Coll., 1960; PhD, Tufts U., 1965; MSW, Boston U., 1985. Rsch. asst. Tufts U., Medford, Mass., 1960-64; rsch. assoc. Tufts U., 1965-66; assoc. prof. Suffolk U., Boston, 1965-68; asso. prof. Suffolk U., 1968-71, prof., 1971—, chmn. dept. chemistry, 1972-84, mem. presdl. search com., 1980; faculty rep. univ. strategic planning com. Suffolk U., Boston, 1992—; faculty Boston Inst. for Psychotherapy, 1992—; faculty mem. Tng. and Rsch. Inst. for Self Psychology, N.Y.C., 1994—; research asso. Bio-Research Inst., Cambridge, Mass., 1968. Contbr. articles to profl. jours. Faculty rep. to trustees Joint Coun. on Univ. Affairs, Suffolk U., 1973-77, 79-81; convenor Pres.'s Commn. on Status of Women, 1974-78, speaker ednl. policy com., 1972-73; chair cultural diversity CLAS Curriculum, 1991—. Mem. AAUP (chpt. pres. 1970), NASW, Am. Chem. Soc. (alt. councillor 1976-79, 82—, councillor 1979-82, bd. dirs. Northeastern sect. 1976—, chmn. pub. rels. sect. 1977-79), Mass. Acad. Clin. Social Work, Nat. Assn. for Advancement Psychoanalysis, Nat. Membership Com. on Psychoanalysis, Sigma Xi (chpt. pres. 1972-73), Sigma Zeta (chpt. sect. 1970—), Alpha Lambda Delta, Delta Epsilon Sigma. Home: 41 Irving St Newton MA 02159-1611 Office: Suffolk University Beacon Hill Boston MA 02114

MILIUS, JOHN FREDERICK, film writer, director; b. St. Louis, Apr. 11, 1944; s. William Styx and Elizabeth (Roe) M.; 3 children. Ed., U. So. Calif. instr. motion pictures script analysis U. So. Calif., fall 1973, advanced motion picture script analysis, spring 1974. Films include: (screenwriter) Devil's 8, 1969, Evel Knievel, 1971, Jeremiah Johnson, 1972 (Heritage Wrangler Award), The Life and Times of Judge Roy Bean, 1973, Magnum Force, 1973, Apocalypse Now, 1979 (with Francis Ford Coppola, Academy Award nominee Best screenplay), Clear and Present Danger, 1994; (story) Extreme Prejudice, 1987; (dir., screenwriter) Dillinger, 1973, The Wind and the Lion, 1975 (National Bell Ringers ednl. award, Writers Guild nom. for Best Orig. Screenplay), Big Wednesday, 1978, Conan the Barbarian, 1981, Red Dawn, 1984, Farewell to the King, 1989, Flight of the Intruder, 1991; (exec. prodr.) Hardcore, 1979, Used Cars, 1980; (exec. prodr., co-screenwriter) 1941, 1979; (co-screenwriter, story) Geronimo: An American Legend, 1993. Recipient Nat. Student Film Festival award U. So. Calif., 1968; numerous gun shooting awards; honored by Winchester for The Wind and the Lion. Office: care Jeff Berg International Creative Mgmt 8942 Wilshire Blvd Beverly Hills CA 90211

MILIUS, RICHARD A., organic chemist; b. Lawrence, Mass., Nov. 10, 1950; s. Leo and Teresa (Liehr) M.; m. Amy L. Dingley, Sept. 29, 1979; children: James, Elena. BS, Marquette U., 1972; PhD, Northeastern U., 1981. Rsch. chemist Miles Labs., Inc., Elkhart, Ind., 1972-74; chemist New Eng. Nuclear Corp., Boston, 1974-77; rsch. assoc. Harvard Med. Sch., Boston, 1981-84; tech. dir. Rsch. Biochems. Internat., Natick, Mass., 1984-94; dir. sponsored rsch. Rsch. Biochems. Internat., Natick, 1994—; chmn. small bus. rsch. rev. com. NIMH, Washington, 1991-93; instr. Univ. Coll. Northeastern U., Boston, 1988-92. Co-chmn. Norwood/Brockton chpt. Open Door Soc. Mass., 1989-90. Recipient Marie Curie award European Assn. Nuclear Medicine, 1992. Mem. AAAS, Am. Chem. Soc., Soc. Neurosci., Soc. Nuclear Medicine. Achievements include patents for astatinated organic compounds, iodinated neuroprobe for mapping monoamine reuptake sites. Office: Rsch Biochems Internat 1 Strathmore Rd Natick MA 01760-2418

MILKMAN, ROGER DAWSON, genetics educator, molecular evolution researcher; b. N.Y.C., Oct. 15, 1930; s. Louis Arthur and Margaret (Weinstein) M.; m. Marianne Friedenthal, Oct. 18, 1958; children: Ruth Margaret, Louise Friedenthal, Janet Dawson Milkman Lussenhop, Paul David. A.B., Harvard U., 1951, A.M., 1954, Ph.D., 1956. Student, asst., instr., investigator Marine Biol. Lab., Woods Hole, Mass., 1952-72, 88-96; instr., asst. prof. U. Mich., Ann Arbor, 1957-60; assoc. prof., prof. Syracuse U., N.Y., 1960-68; prof. biol. scis. U. Iowa, Iowa City, 1968—, chmn. univ. genetics PhD program, 1992-93; vis. prof. biology Grinnell (Iowa) Coll., 1990; mem. genetics study sect. NIH, 1986-87; NSF panelist, 1996—. Translator: Developmental Physiology, 1970; editor: Perspectives on Evolution, 1982, Experimental Population Genetics, 1983, Evolution jour., 1984-86; mem. editl. bd. Molecular Phylogenetics and Evolution; contbr. articles to profl. jours. Sec. Soc. Gen. Physiologists, 1963-65, Am. Soc. Naturalists, 1980-82; alumni rep. Phillips Acad., Andover, Mass., 1980-94. NSF grantee, 1959—; USPHS grantee, 1984-87. Fellow AAAS; mem. Am. Soc. for Microbiology, Genetics Soc. Am., Corp. Marine Biol. Lab., Soc. for Gen. Microbiology (U.K.), Soc. Study Evolution, Soc. Molecular Biology and Evolution, Internat. Soc. for Molecular Evolution. Jewish. Avocation: mountain hiking. Home: 12 Fairview Knoll NE Iowa City IA 52240-9147 Office: U Iowa Dept Biol Scis 138 Biology Building Bldg Iowa City IA 52242-1324

MILLANE, LYNN, town official; b. Buffalo, N.Y. Oct. 14, 1928; d. Robert P. Schermerhorn and Justine A. (Ross) m. J. Vaughan Millane, Jr.; Aug. 16, 1952 children: Maureen, Michele, John, Mark, Kathleen. EdB, U. Buffalo, 1949, EdM, in Health Education 1951. Mem. Amherst Town Bd., 1982—, dep. town supr., 1990—; pres., E. J. Meyer Hosp. Jr. Bd., 1962-64; pres. Aux. to Erie County Bar Assn., 1966-68; pres. Women's Com. of Buffalo Philharm. Orch., 1976-78, v.p. adminstrn., 1975-76, v.p. pub. affairs, 1974-75, chmn. adv. bd., 1979-82; v.p. Buffalo Philharm. Orch. Soc., Inc., 1976-78, mem. coun., trustee, 1979-87, bd. overseers, 1987-92; dir. 8th judicial dist. N.Y. State Assn. of Large Towns, 1989-90, 90-91; bd. dirs. oper. bd. Millard Fillmore Suburban Hosp., 1992-2001; 1st v.p. Fans for 17, 1980-82; 1st. v.p. Friends of Baird Hall, SUNY-Buffalo, 1980-82; exec. bd. mem. Longview Protestant Home for Children, 1979-85, 2d v.p., 1982-85; bd. dirs. ARC, Town of Amherst br., 1982-91, by-laws com., 1981, 84, chmn. sr. concerns com., 1982-91, liaison code of ethics com., 1987-89; bd. dirs. Amherst Symphony Orch. Assn., 1981-87, roster chmn., 1982-84, nominating chmn., 1985-86, vice-chmn. 50th anniversary com. 1994—; nat. music com. Women's Assn. for Symphony Orchs. in Am. and Can., 1977-79; coun. mem. Am. Symphony Orch. League; sec. Amherst Sr. Citizen's Adv. Bd., 1980-81, liaison from Amherst Town Bd., 1982—; founder, liaison 1st adult day svcs. adv. bd. Town of Amherst, 1988; liaison to ad hoc cable TV com., 1992—, liaison to Amherst C. of C., 1993—, mem. 1st records mgmt. adv. bd., liaison ethics bd. Town of Amherst, 1994—, dep. supr. 1990—; liaison to the Alternate Fuel and Clean Cities Com., 1994-96; dir.-at-large community adv. coun. SUNY-Buffalo, 1981-91; co-assoc. chmn. maj. gift div. capital campaign Daeman Coll., 1983-84; co-chmn. Women United Against Drugs Campaign, 1970-72; founding mem. Lunch and Issues, Amherst, 1981—; mem. edn. com. Network in Aging of Western N.Y., Inc., 1982-89, bd. dirs., 1982-89, housing com., 1987-89; bd. dirs. Amherst Elderly Transp. Corp., 1982—; committeeman dist. Town of Amherst Republican Com.; treas. Town and Country Rep. Club, 1980-81; mem. nominating com. Fedn. Rep. Women's Clubs Erie County, 1980; exec. bd. mem. Women's Exec. Coun. of Erie County Rep. Com., 1969-71; dir. Amherst Rep. Women's Club, 1963-65; delegate N.Y. State Govs. Conf. on Aging, 1995, White House Conf. on Aging, 1995, named mem. aging svcs. adv. com. N.Y. State Office of the Aging Gov. George Pataki, 1996. Named Homemaker of Yr., Family Circle Mag., 1969; Woman of Substance, 20th Century Rep. Women, 1983; Woman of Yr., Buffalo Philharm. Orch. Soc., Inc., 1982; Outstanding Woman in Community Svc., SUNY-Buffalo, 1985; recipient Good Neighbor award Courier Express, 1978; Merit award Buffalo Philharm. Orch., 1978; award Fedn. Rep. Women's Clubs Erie County, 1982; Disting. Svc. award Town of Amherst Sr. Ctr., 1985; Susan B. Anthony award Interclub Coun. of Western N.Y., 1991, Community Svc. award Amherst Rep. Com., 1991, D.A.R.E. award Town of Amherst Police Dept., 1994, Disting. Svc. award Amherst Adult Day Care and Vis. Nurses Assn., 1994. Mem. Amherst C. of C. (VIP dinner com. 1984), LWV, SUNY-Buffalo Alumni Assn. (life, presdl. advisor 1977-79), Zonta (pres. Amherst chpt. 1986-88, Zontian of Yr. 1992), Pi Lambda Theta (hon.). Office: 5583 Main St Buffalo NY 14221-5409

MILLAR, GORDON HALSTEAD, mechanical engineer, agricultural machinery manufacturing executive; b. Newark, Nov. 28, 1923; s. George Halstead and Dill E. (McMullen) M.; m. Virginia M. Jedryczka, Aug. 24, 1957; children—George B., Kathryn M., Juliet S., John G., James H. B.M.E., U. Detroit, 1949, D.Sc. (hon.), 1977; Ph.D., U. Wis., 1952; L.H.D., West Coast U., 1984; D.Sc. (hon.), Western Mich. U., 1986. Registered profl. engr., Fla., Ill., Iowa, Mich., Minn., Ohio. Supr. new powerplants Ford Motor Co., 1952-57; engring. mgr. Meriam Instrument Co., Cleve., 1957-59; dir. new products McCulloch Corp., Los Angeles, 1959-63; with Deere & Co., 1963-84; v.p. engring. Deere & Co., Moline, Ill., 1972-84; exec. assoc. Southwest Research Inst., 1987; mem. Fed. Adv. Com. Indsl. Innovation, 1979; chmn. West Ctrl. Ill. Ednl. Telecom. Corp.; pres. Accreditation Bd. for Engring. and Tech., 1983-85; pres., fellow Accreditation Bd. for Engring. and Tech. Contbr. articles to profl. jours.; patentee in field. Chmn. Quad Cities chpt. United Way, 1976-77; bd. dirs.; adv. council Bradley U. Coll. Engring. and Tech.; mem. exec. com. Illowa council Boy Scouts Am., 1977-79. Served with U.S. Army, World War II. Decorated Purple Heart; recipient Alumnus of Year award U. Detroit, 1976, Comdrs. medal for pub. svc. Dept. Army, 1989. Fellow ASME (hon. life mem.), Soc. Automotive Engrs. (pres. 1984, bd. dirs. 1984-86, mem. nat. nominating com.); mem. NAE, NSPE, Engrs. Joint Coun., Indsl. Rsch. Inst., Engring. Soc. Detroit, Am. Soc. Agrl. Engrs., Ill. Soc. Profl. Engrs., Moline C. of C., Aviation Coun. Home: 1840 Wiley Post Trl Daytona Beach FL 32124-6756

MILLAR, JAMES ROBERT, economist, educator, university official; b. San Antonio, Tex., July 7, 1936; s. James G. and Virginia M. (Harrison) M.; m. Gera Ascher, July 4, 1965; children: Leo Schaeg (dec.), Mira Gail. B.A., U. Tex., 1958; Ph.D. in Econs, Cornell U., 1965. Asst. prof. dept. econs. U. Ill., Urbana, 1965-70, assoc. prof., 1970-72, prof., 1973-89, assoc. vice chancellor for acad. affairs, 1984-89, dir. internat. programs and studies, 1984-89; prof. econs. and internat. affairs George Washington U., Washington, 1989—, dir. Inst. for European, Russian and Eurasian Studies, 1989—, assoc. dean Elliott Sch. Internat. Affairs, 1989-95, acting dean, 1994; mem. acad. coun. Kennan Inst. Advanced Russian, 1975-84; young faculty exchangee Moscow State U., 1966; cons. to congressmen and various U.S. govt. depts., 1972—; dir. Soviet Interview Project, 1981-88; sec., bd. dirs. Midwest Univs. Consortium for Internat. Activities, 1984-88, chmn. bd., 1988-89. Author: The ABCs of Soviet Socialism, 1981, The Soviet Economic Experiment, 1990; editor, contbr. The Soviet Rural Community, 1971; editor: Slavic Rev., Am. Quar. Soviet and East European Studies, 1975-80; editor, contbr. Politics, Work and Daily Life, A Survey of Former Soviet Citizens, 1987; editor, contbr. Cracks in the Monolith: Party Power in the Brezhnev Era, 1992, The Social Legacy of Communism, 1994; contbr. articles on studies on Soviet/Russian economy and econ. history to scholarly jours. Served with Q.M.C. U.S. Army, 1960. Ford Found. fgn. area fellow, 1961-64; sr. scholar rsch. travel grantee to USSR, 1972; Am. Coun. Learned Socs./USSR Acad. Scis. travel exchangee, 1979; fellow Woodrow Wilson Internat. Ctr. for Scholars, 1988-89, Guggenheim fellow, 1995-96; IREX advanced rsch. grantee, 1996. Mem. AAAS, Econ. History Assn., Assn. Evolutionary Econs., Am. Assn. Slavic Studies (del. Am. Coun. Learned Soc. 1992—), Am. Coun. Learned Soc. (treas., bd. dirs. 1996—, sec. 1995-96, mem. exec. com. del., chair 1993-95, mem. joint com. with Social Sci. Rsch. Coun. 1990-95), Am. Assn. Pub. Opinion Rsch., N.Y. Acad. Sci. Home: The Westchester 4000 Cathedral Ave NW Apt 143B Washington DC 20016-

5249 Office: George Washington U Inst Eur Russ Eurasian Studies 2130 H St NW Ste 601 Washington DC 20037-2521

MILLAR, JEFFERY LYNN, columnist; b. Houston, July 10, 1942; s. Daniel Lynn Millar and Betty Ruth (Shove) Coons; m. Lynne McDonald, Dec. 21, 1964 (div. Aug. 1983); m. Peggy V. Watson, Apr. 1, 1994. BA, U. Tex., 1964. Reporter Houston Chronicle, 1964-65, film critic, 1965—, columnist, 1972—. Writer, co-creator: (comic strip) Tank McNamara, Universal Press Syndicate, Kansas City, 1974—. Office: Houston Chronicle PO Box 4260 Houston TX 77210-4260

MILLAR, JOHN DONALD, occupational and environmental health consultant, educator; b. Newport News, Va., Feb. 27, 1934; s. John and Dorothea Virginia (Smith) M.; m. Joan M. Phillips, Aug. 17, 1957; children: John Stuart, Alison Gordon, Virginia Taylor. B.S., U. Richmond, 1956; M.D., Med. Coll. Va., 1959; D.T.P.H., London Sch. Hygiene and Tropical Medicine, 1966; D of Pub. Svc. (hon.), Greenville (Ill.) Coll., 1994. Cert. specialist in Gen. Preventive Medicine, 1969. Intern U. Utah Affiliated Hosps., Salt Lake City, 1959-60, asst. resident in medicine, 1960-61; chief Epidemic Intelligence Svc., Ctr. for Disease Control, USPHS, HEW, Atlanta, 1961-63, dep. chief surveillance sect. epidemiology br., 1962-63, chief smallpox unit, 1963-65, dir. smallpox eradication program, 1966-70, dir. Bur. State Svcs., 1970-78, asst. dir. Ctr. for Disease Control for Pub. Health Practice, 1979-80; dir. Ctr. for Environ. Health Atlanta, 1980-81; dir. Nat. Inst. for Occupation Safety and Health, Atlanta, 1981-93; pres. Don Millar & Assocs., Inc., Atlanta, 1993—; adj. prof. occupational and environ. health Sch. Pub. Health Emory U., Atlanta; cons. on smallpox, smallpox eradication, immunization programs and occupational and environ. health WHO; mem. WHO expert adv. panel on occupational health. Contbr. articles to profl. jours. Recipient Surgeon Gen's. Commendation medal, 1965, Okeke prize London Sch. Hygiene and Tropical Medicine, 1966, Presdl. award for mgmt. improvement, 1972, W.C. Gorgas medal Assn. Mil. Surgeons U.S., 1987, Lucas lectr. Faculty Occupational Medicine Royal Coll. Physicians, London, 1987, Outstanding Med. Alumnus award Med. Coll. Va., 1988; also recipient Equal Employment Opportunity award, 1975, Medal of Excellence, 1977, Joseph W. Mountin lectr. award, 1986, all from Ctrs. for Disease Control, Disting. Svc. medal USPHS, 1983, 88, Exemplary Svc. medal Surgeon Gen. U.S., 1988, Giants in Occupational Medicine lectr. U. Utah, 1989, William S. Knudsen award Am. Coll. Occupational Medicine, 1991, presdl. citation APA, 1991, William Steiger Meml. award Am. Conf. Govtl. Indsl. Hygienists, 1993, Health Watch award for outstanding contbns. toward improving health of minority popyulations, 1992, Award of Merit Minerva Edn. Inst., 1993, Alumni Disting. Svc. award U. Richmond, 1993; named to Order Bifurcated Needle, World Health Orgn., 1978, Faculty Occupational Medicine, Royal Coll. Physicians, London, 1990. Office: Don Millar & Assocs Inc Ste 201 3243 Wake Robin Trail Atlanta GA 30341-5721

MILLAR, JOHN FRANCIS, industrial products company executive; b. Teaneck, N.J., Jan. 23, 1936; m. Doris Connolly; children: Michael R., Cynthia A. BS in Fin., Fairleigh Dickinson U., 1961. Sr. auditor Hurdman & Cranstoun CPAs, NYC, 1961-64; dir. treas. ops. Keuffel & Esser Co., Morristown, N.J., 1964-76; treas., chief fin. officer Batt Bates & Co., Washington, 1976-77, Joseph Dixon Crucible Co., Jersey City, 1977-83, Dixon Ticonderoga Co., Vero Beach, Fla., 1983-85; exec. v.p. chief ops. officer indsl. products Dixon Ticonderoga Co., Lakehurst, N.J., 1985-90; bd. dirs. Dixon Ticonderoga Co., Vero Beach. Served with U.S. Army, 1954-56. Mem. Am. Chem. Soc., Am. Powder Metal Inst., Metal Powder Prodrs. Assn. (bd. dirs.), Nat. Assn. Accts., Ind. Lubricants Mfrs. Assn. Republican. Roman Catholic. Home: 1780 Rolling Ridge Ln Toms River NJ 08755-1004 Office: Dixon Ticonderoga Co Ridgeway Blvd Lakehurst NJ 08733

MILLAR, RICHARD WILLIAM, JR., lawyer; b. L.A., May 11, 1938. LLB, U. San Francisco, 1966. Bar: Calif. 1967, U.S. Dist. Ct. (cen. dist.) Calif. 1967, U.S. Dist. Ct. (no. dist.) Calif. 1969, U.S. Dist. Ct. (so. dist.) Calif. 1973, U.S. Supreme Ct. Assoc. Iverson & Hogoboom, Los Angeles, 1967-72; ptnr. Eilers, Stewart, Pangman & Millar, Newport Beach, Calif., 1973-75, Millar & Heckman, Newport Beach, 1975-77, Millar, Hodges & Bemis, Newport Beach, 1979—. Fellow Am. Bar Found.; mem. ABA (litigation sect., trial practice com., ho. of dels. 1990—), Calif. Bar Assn. (lectr. CLE), Orange County Bar Assn. (chmn. bus. litigation sect. 1981, chmn. judiciary com. 1988-90), Balboa Bay Club, Bohemian Club (San Francisco). Home: 2546 Crestview Dr Newport Beach CA 92663-5625 Office: Millar Hodges & Bemis One Newport Pl Ste # 900 Newport Beach CA 92660

MILLAR, SALLY GRAY, nurse; b. Madison, Wis., Dec. 8, 1946; d. William Llewellyn and Janet Josephine (Dean) M. Student, U. Iowa, 1964-65; R.N., St. Joseph Hosp. Sch. Nursing, 1968; M.B.A., Simmons Coll. Grad. Sch. Mgmt., 1985. Staff nurse Bryn Mawr (Pa.) Hosp., 1968-69; team leader, cardiac surg. intensive care unit Mass. Gen. Hosp., Boston, 1969-78, head nurse, respiratory/surg. intensive care unit, 1978-81, clin. nurse leader, intensive care nursing service, 1981-85, project dir. patient classification system, 1985-86, dir. nursing info. systems, 1986—. Editor: Focus on Critical Care, 1978-80; editor-in-chief: Methods in Critical Care, 1980, Procedure Manual for Critical Care, 1985. Mem. Am. Assn. Critical Care Nurses (pres. 1980-81, dir. 1976-82), Soc. Critical Care Medicine. Republican. Roman Catholic. Home: 849 Boston Post Rd E Apt 3-e Marlborough MA 01752-3727 Office: Mass Gen Hosp 32 Fruit St Boston MA 02114-2620

MILLARD, CHARLES WARREN, III, museum director, writer; b. Elizabeth, N.J., Dec. 20, 1932; s. Charles Warren and Constance Emily (Keppler) M. A.B. magna cum laude, Princeton U., 1954; M.A., Harvard U., 1963, Ph.D., 1971. Asst. to dir. Fogg Art Mus. Harvard U., Cambridge, Mass., 1963-64; asst. to dir. Dumbarton Oaks, Washington, 1965-66; dir. Washington Gallery Modern Art, 1966-67; teaching fellow Harvard U., 1968-69; curator 19th Century European art Los Angeles County Mus. Art, 1971-74; chief curator Hirshhorn Mus. and Sculpture Garden Smithsonian Instn., Washington, 1974-86; adj. prof. Johns Hopkins U., Balt., 1983-86; dir. Ackland Art Mus. U. N.C., Chapel Hill, 1986-93, adj. prof., 1986-93; chmn. vis. com. to fine arts dept. Boston U., 1977-80. Author: The Sculpture of Edgar Degas, 1977; art editor Hudson Rev., 1972-87; contbr. articles to profl. jours. Served with USN, 1956-59.

MILLARD, JOHN ALDEN, lawyer; b. Buenos Aires, Argentina, Nov. 4, 1940; s. Alden Shultz and Lois (Guthrie) M.; m. Carey Barbara French, Sept. 7, 1966; children—John Alden, James Guthrie, Alexander French. B.A., Harvard U., 1963, LL.B., 1967. Bar: N.Y. 1968. Assoc., Shearman & Sterling, N.Y.C., 1967-75, ptnr., 1976—. Served with U.S. Army, 1963-64. Mem. Assn. Bar City N.Y.*

MILLARD, NEAL STEVEN, lawyer; b. Dallas, June 6, 1947; s. Bernard and Adele (Marks) M.; m. Janet Keast, Mar. 12, 1994; 1 child, Kendall Layne. BA cum laude, UCLA, 1969; JD, U. Chgo., 1972. Bar: Calif. 1972, U.S. Dist. Ct. (cen. dist.) Calif. 1973, U.S. Tax Ct. 1973, U.S. Ct. Appeals (9th cir.) 1987, N.Y. 1990. Assoc. Willis, Butler & Schiefly, Los Angeles, 1972-75; ptnr. Morrison & Foerster, Los Angeles, 1975-84, Jones, Day, Reavis & Pogue, Los Angeles, 1984-93, White & Case, L.A., 1993—; instr. Calif. State Coll., San Bernardino, 1975-76; lectr. Practising Law Inst., N.Y.C., 1983-90, Calif. Edn. of Bar, 1987-90; adj. prof. USC Law Ctr., 1994—. Citizens adv. com. L.A. Olympics, 1982-84; trustee Altadena (Calif.) Libr. Dist., 1985-86; bd. dirs. Woodcraft Rangers, L.A., 1982-90, pres., 1986-88; bd. dirs. L.A. County Bar Found., 1990—; mem. Energy Commn. of County and Cities of L.A. Mem. ABA, Calif. Bar Assn., N.Y. State Bar Assn., L.A. County Bar Assn. (trustee 1985-87), Pub. Counsel (bd. dirs. 1984-87, 90-93), U. Chgo. Law Alumni Assn. (bd. dirs. So. Calif. chpt. 1981—), Calif. Club, Phi Beta Kappa, Pi Gamma Mu, Phi Delta Phi. Office: White and Case 633 W 5th St Ste 1900 Los Angeles CA 90071-2017

MILLARD, PETER TUDOR, English language educator; b. Treorchy, Rhondda, Wales, U.K., July 21, 1932; s. Percival and Catherine (Davies) M. B.A. with hons., McGill U., Montreal, 1959, Oxford (Wadham Coll.), Eng., 1961; D.Phil., Oxford U. (Linacre Coll.), Eng., 1970. Lectr. U. of Sask., Saskatoon, 1964-70, asst. prof., 1970-74, assoc. prof., 1974-86, prof., 1986—, head Dept. of English, 1985—, pres. Faculty Assn., 1987-88. Author: Dmytro Stryjek: Trying the Colours, 1988, (short stories) The Malahat Review, 1985-87; editor: Roger North's Life of Dr. John North, 1984; contbg. editor Inuit Art Quar.; contbr. articles to various jours. Trustee Mendel Art Gallery, Saskatoon, 1971-74; pres. Saskatoon Human Rights Assn., 1980-83, Saskatoon Gay Community Ctr., 1974-75. Can. Coun. fellow, 1968; Social Scis. and Humanities Rsch. Coun. fellow, 1979 and rsch. grantee, 1985. Avocation: art. Office: 308 Skyline Dr Box 1372, Gibsons, BC Canada V0N 1V0

MILLARD, RICHARD STEVEN, lawyer; b. Pasadena, Calif., Feb. 6, 1952; s. Kenneth A. and Kathryn Mary (Paden) M.; m. Jessica Ann Edwards, May 15, 1977; children: Victoria, Elizabeth, Andrew. AB, Stanford U., 1974; JD magna cum laude, U. Mich., 1977. Bar: Calif. 1977, Ill. 1985. Assoc. Heller, Ehrman, White & McAuliff, San Francisco, 1977-81; assoc. Mayer, Brown & Platt, Chgo., 1982-83, ptnr., 1984—. Mem. ABA, Order of Coif. Office: Mayer Brown & Platt 190 S La Salle St Chicago IL 60603-3410

MILLARD, STEPHENS FILLMORE, electronics company executive; b. Balt., Dec. 5, 1932; s. Lyman Clifford and Frances Louise (Stephens) M.; m. Suzanne Taylor, Nov. 2, 1957 (div. 1990); children: Anne, Stephens, William; m. Linda Dyer, 1995. BS in Econs., U. Pa., 1955; MBA, Northwestern U., 1963. Dist. sales mgr. Olin Mathieson Chem. Corp., Chgo., 1958-63; Western Sales mgr. Champion Papers, Inc., San Francisco, 1963-70; U.S. sales mgr. MacMillan Bloedel, Ltd., Vancouver, B.C., Can., 1970-72; dir. new product devel. Crown Zellerbach Corp., San Francisco, 1972-75; Midwestern sales mgr. paper group Internat. Paper Co., Chgo., 1975-79; v.p. mktg. Mead Corp., Dayton, Ohio, 1979-83; co-founder, sr. v.p. Packet Techs., Inc. (now Stratacom, Inc.), Cupertino, Calif., 1983-86; co-founder, Cable Data, Inc., Equatorial Communications, Telebit, Inc., Metricom, Inc., Com-21; assoc. prof. mgmt. Golden Gate U., 1970-75; vis. lectr. Simon Frasier U., 1973; bd. adv. Sch. of Bus. San Francisco State U., 1995—. Dir. alumni ann. giving Northwestern U.; trustee Severn Prep. Sch., Severna Park, Md.; chmn. devel. com. Santa Fe Inst., 1993; bd. visitors Nat. Def. U., Ft. McNair, Washington, 1994— (Nat. War Coll., Armed Forces Staff Coll., Industrial Coll. of the Armed Forces); adv. bd. Bionomics Inst., San Rafael, Calif., 1995—. Recipient Rolland Marshall Teel award Severn Sch., 1994. Served to 1st lt., U.S. Army, 1955-57. Mem. Northwestern U. Grad. Sch. Bus. Alumni Assn. (nat. pres. 1967-68), Wharton Sch. Alumni Assn. (v.p.), Active Core Execs., The February Group. Republican. Episcopalian. Home: 5 Fremontia St Portola Valley CA 94028

MILLBERG, JOHN C., lawyer; b. New London, Conn., Jan. 4, 1956; s. Melvin Roy and Dorothy (Van Zandt) M.; m. Lori Bruce Millberg, Oct. 18, 1981; children: Kathryn Faye, Rebecca Ann, Melvin Roy III. BA, Bowling Green State U., 1977; JD, Wake Forest U., 1980. Bar: Tex. 1980, N.C. 1986, U.S. Dist. Ct. (so. dist.) Tex. 1981, U.S. Dist. Ct. (ea., mid. and we. dists.) N.C. 1986, U.S. Ct. Appeals (4th cir.) 1986, U.S. Ct. Appeals (5th and 11th cir.) 1981. Assoc. Crain Caton James & Womble, Houston, 1981-85; assoc., dir. Maupin, Taylor, Ellis & Adams, Raleigh, N.C., 1985-94; mng. ptnr. Millberg & Gordon, Raleigh, N.C., 1994—; mem. bar candidate com. N.C. Bd. Law Examiners, 1988-90. Scholar Wake Forest U. Sch. Law, 1977-80. Mem. N.C. Assn. Def. Attys., Nat. Assn. R.R. Trial Counsel. Office: Millberg & Gordon 1030 Washington St Raleigh NC 27605

MILLER, ALAN B., hospital management executive; b. N.Y.C., Aug. 17, 1937; s. Daniel and Mary (Blumenthal) M.; m. Jill K. Stein, Oct. 5, 1968; children: Marc Daniel, Marni Elizabeth, Abby Danielle. BA, Coll. William and Mary, 1958; MBA, U. Pa., 1960. V.p. Young & Rubicam, Inc., N.Y.C., 1964-69; sr. v.p. Am. Medicorp., Inc., L.A., 1970; pres., chief exec. officer Am. Medicorp., Inc., Phila., 1973-77, chmn. bd., 1977; chmn. bd. Hosp. Underwriting Group, 1977-78; founder, pres., chmn. bd. Universal Health Svcs., King of Prussia, Pa., 1978—; chmn., founder UHT-Real Estate Trust, King of Prussia, 1986—; formerly health care adviser Fed. Mediation and Conciliation Svc.; bd. mem. Leonard Davis Inst. U. Pa.; past mem. adv. bd. Temple U. Sch. Bus.; chmn., pres. Universal Health Svcs. Real Estate Investment Trust, N.Y. Stock Exch., 1986—; bd. dirs. Genesis Health, GMIS, Inc. Trustee Penn Mut. Life; former trustee Coll. of William and Mary; bd. dirs. Penjerdel Coun., pres. Opera Co. of Phila. Capt. USAR. Mem. Phila. C. of C. (bd. dir.). Home: 57 Crosby Brown Rd Gladwyne PA 19035-1512 Office: Universal Health Svcs Inc 367 S Gulph Rd King Of Prussia PA 19406

MILLER, ALAN GERSHON, lawyer; b. Boston, Feb. 24, 1931; s. Harold Louis and Etta (Futransky) M.; m. Maxine Schreiber, July 2, 1951 (div. 1971); m. Natalie Cohen, Oct. 6, 1977; 1 child, Geoffrey Paul. AB, U. Ill., 1952; JD, Harvard U., 1955. Bar: Mass. 1955, U.S. Dist. Ct. Mass. 1956, Fla. 1978. Assoc. Morrison, Mahoney & Pearlman, Boston, 1955-59; ptnr. Morrison, Mahoney & Miller, Boston, 1959—. Co-author: Business Interruption Insurance, 1986. Mem. ABA, Internat. Bar Assn., Boston Bar Assn., Fedn. Ins. Corp. & Counsel, Def. Rsch. Inst., Fla. Bar Assn., Soc. of CPCU's. Office: Morrison Mahoney & Miller 250 Summer St Boston MA 02210-1134

MILLER, ALAN JAY, financial consultant, author; b. Bklyn., July 11, 1936; s. Louis and Claire (Maltz) M.; m. Susan Ruth Morris, Oct. 29, 1961; children—Laurie Ann, Adam Louis. B.A., Cornell U., 1957. Chartered fin. analyst. Pres. Analysis-in-Depth Inc., N.Y.C., 1965-67; mng. editor Value Line Investment Survey, N.Y.C., 1967-68; research dir. Emanuel Deetjen & Co., N.Y.C., 1968-69; exec. v.p., dir. Intersci. Capital Mgmt. Corp., N.Y.C., 1969-71; pres., dir. ICM Equity Fund Inc., N.Y.C., 1970-71, ICM Fin. Fund Inc., N.Y.C., 1970-71; v.p., assoc. research dir. Bache & Co., Inc., N.Y.C., 1972, G.H. Walker & Co., Inc., N.Y.C., 1972-73; 1st v.p., assoc. research dir. Blyth Eastman Dillon & Co. Inc., N.Y.C., 1974-76; dir. research E.F. Hutton & Co., Inc., N.Y.C., 1976-81, sr. v.p., 1976-80, exec. v.p., 1981-88; dir. Hutton Investment Mgmt., 1976-88; mng. dir. SLH Asset Mgmt. Shearson Lehman Hutton, Inc, N.Y.C., 1988-90; sr. v.p. Martin E. Segal Co., N.Y.C., 1990-92; adj. assoc. prof. Columbia U. Grad. Sch. Bus., 1978-79; mem. faculty N.Y. Inst. Fin., 1977—; adj. prof. Adelphi U. Coll., 1993—. Author: Socially Responsible Investing: How to Invest with Your Conscience, 1991, Standard and Poor's 401(k) Planning Guide, 1995. Mem. N.Y. Soc. Security Analysts, Fin. Analysts Fedn.

MILLER, ALAN M., editor, educator, writer; b. N.Y.C., July 24, 1934; s. Philip and Sylvia (Lubash) M.; m. Roberta F. Brody, Sept. 2, 1956 (div. 1977); children: Neil, Peter, Stephanie, Douglas; m. Ferne Mayer Steckler, Jan. 13, 1978 (div. 1985). AB, Syracuse U., 1955, LLB, 1958, JD, 1968. Commr., Village of Woodsburgh, N.Y., 1980; asst. counsel 3 joint legis. coms. N.Y. State Legislature, 1968-70; counsel to minority Nassau County Bd. Suprs., 1974-75; legal editor Info. Pub. Group, Westbury, N.Y., 1985—; adj. prof. Hofstra U. Sch. Law, 1978-85, Emory U. Sch. Law, 1982, Touro Coll. Law, 1983-85; N.E. regional faculty mem., sect. leader Nat. Inst. Trial Advocacy, 1978-85, mem. nat. teaching team, 1982; adj. faculty N.Y. State Inst. Tech., 1974-75, Nassau C.C., 1978-80; anchor, regular panelist Joe Franklin TV Show, WWOR-TV and cable, 1990-93; mem. adj. faculty screenwriting and writing Hofstra U., 1990—, Discovery Ctr., 1990-94, N.Y. Inst. Tech., Old Westbury, 1987-89. Presenter 2d Internat. Conf. Law and Psychiatry, Israel, 1986. Columnist South Shore Record, Woodmere, N.Y., Another Viewpoint, 1985— (awards N.Y. Press Assn. 1988, 89, 94, Best Column award 1992), Single-Minded, 1991-92, N.Y. Bowler, 1991-93 (Bowling Mag. awards 1990-93, Best Column award 1992), Nostalgia Mag., 1990-91, Never Too Late, Writer's Digest (award winning screenplay 1992), Paradox, (Screenplay awards 1994-95, Maui Writing Conf., Nicholls Screenwriting fellow); contbr. numerous articles to various publs. including N.Y. Times, Newsday, Newsday Mag., Mpls. Star-Tribune, Nat. Press. Assembly dist. leader N.Y. State Democratic Com., 1965-76. Recipient awards for coverage of Persian Gulf War from Israel, 1991, Nat. Coun. Jewish Women, 1991, 5 town's Sr. Coun's. Mem. Nat. Writer's Club, Am. Film Inst. Jewish. Office: 860 E Broadway # 3-0 Long Beach NY 11561-4756 also: 615 Merrick Ave Westbury NY 11590

MILLER, ALAN STANLEY, ecology center administrator, law educator; b. Detroit, Dec. 22, 1949; s. Ralph and Ruth (Leeman) M.; m. Susan O'Hara, Aug. 25, 1973; 1 child, Joanna. AB in Goverment, Cornell U., 1971; JD, U. Mich., 1974, M of Pub. Policy, 1974. Bar: Mich. 1974, D.C. 1975. Rsch. atty. Environ. Law Inst., Washington, 1974-77; atty. ABA, Washington, 1978-79, Natural Resources Def. Coun., Washington, 1979-84; assoc. World Resources Inst., Washington, 1984-86; asst. prof. law Widener U., Wilmington, Del., 1988-89; exec. dir. Ctr. Global Change, College Park, Md., 1989-96; prof. Vermont Law School, South Royal, Vt., 1991-93; exec. dir. Renewable Energy Policy Project Univ. Md., 1996—; head EPA Transition Team for Pres. Clinton Wash. D.C. 1992, Energy Task Force State of Md. Annapolis, Md. 1991-92; bd. dirs. Environmental Exchange; adjunct prof. Maryland Law Sch. 1989—; vis. asst. prof. U. Iowa Coll. of Law 1979, Wash. Coll. of Law Am. U., Wash., D.C. 1986, Duke U. N.C. 1990, Vt. Law Sch 1991, 92; mem. adv. bd. Office Tec. Assessment, Washington, 1989. Co-author: (book) International Regulation Flourocarbons, 1980, Green Gold, 1994; monographs) Growing Power, The Sky is the Limit, 1985, Environmental Regulation, 1992. Bd. dirs. Solar Light Fund, 1988, Renewable Energy Inst., 1995—. Fulbright scholar Macquarie Univ., Australia, 1977-87, Fulbright scholar Tokyo Univ. Law Sch., Japan, 1987-87; Stratospheric Ozone Protection award U.S. EPA Washington, D.C. 1992. Mem. ABA (global climate com. 1992-93, chair 1993-94). Avocations: jogging white-water rafting, writing. Office: Univ of Maryland Dept Gov't & Politics 3140 Tydings Hall College Park MD 20742

MILLER, ALBERT JAY, retired librarian, educator; b. Beaver Falls, Pa., Dec. 7, 1927; s. Joseph Jefferson and Alberta Fae (Shaffer) M. B.S., Geneva Coll., 1952; M.L.S., Rutgers U., 1958; postgrad., U. Chgo., 1960-61, U. Pitts., 1963-68, U. Mich., 1969. Librarian West Allegheny Jr. High Sch., Imperial, Pa., 1959-60, Butler (Pa.) Area Sr. High Sch., 1962-67; librarian Pa. State U., New Kensington, 1969-89, tchr.-librarian continuing edn. dept., 1970-89, ret., 1989. Author: A Selective Bibliography of Existentialism in Education and Related Topics, 1969, Confrontation, Conflict and Dissent, 1972, Death: A Bibliographical Guide, 1977; book and media rev. editor: Learning Today, 1978—, mem. editorial bd., 1979—. Instr. water safety ARC, New Kensington, 1969—, Citizens Gen. Hosp., 1971-72; active Boy Scouts Am., 1970—; bd. dirs. Westmoreland County, Butler County mental health assns.; mem. Allegheny-Kiski Human Relations Council, 1976-77; bd. dirs. Allegheny-Kiski Sr. Citizens Center, 1976-77, fund raising chmn., 1989-90; bd. corporators Geneva Coll., Beaver Falls, Pa., 1987—; Sunday Sch. tchr. Manchester Ref. Presbyn. Ch., 1970—, elder, 1984—, clk. of session, 1984—, Sabbath Sch. supt., 1990; mem., pub. rels. dir. Twirling Unltd, Akron, OHio; baton twirler Kensington Firemens Band; mem. Alle-Kiski Revitalization Corp. Mem. NEA, Pa. Edn. Assn., ALA, Pa. Library Assn. Democratic. Home: 417 Charles Ave New Kensington PA 15068-5335

MILLER, ALLAN JOHN, lawyer; b. Beachwood, Ohio, Oct. 17, 1921; s. Carl Frederick and Rhoda (Warren) M.; m. Marjorie Hewitt Pirtle, Aug. 10, 1946; children: James W., Patricia Anne. B.B.A., Fenn Coll., 1946; LL.B., Western Res. U., 1948; D. (hon.), Dyke Coll., Cleve., 1986. Bar: Ohio 1948. With Standard Oil Co., Ohio, 1948-77; treas. Standard Oil Co., 1967-77; mem. firm Kiefer, Knecht, Rees, Meyer & Miller, Cleve., 1977-81; dir. United Screw & Bolt Corp. Chmn. bd. dirs. Luth. Med. Ctr., Cleve., 1967-82; pres. Luth. Med. Ctr. Med. Staff Found., 1979-85; bd. dirs. Christian Residencies Found., 1972-77, St. Luke's Hosp. Assn., 1973-84; chmn. bd. trustees Dyke Coll., Cleve., 1971-86. With AUS, 1943-46, PTO. Mem. Cleve. Treas.'s Club, Cleve. Soc. Security Analysts. Presbyterian. Club: Capri Isles Golf Club (Venice, Fla.). Home: 1364 Capri Isles Blvd Venice FL 34292-4459

MILLER, ANDREW PICKENS, lawyer; b. Fairfax, Va., Dec. 21, 1932; s. Francis Pickens and Helen (Hill) M.; m. Penelope Farthing, Nov. 18, 1990; children: Julia Lane, Andrew Pickens, Elise Givhan, Winfield Scott, Lucia Holcombe. AB magna cum laude, Princeton U., 1954; postgrad., New Coll., Oxford (Eng.) U., 1954-55; LLB, U. Va., 1960. Bar: Va. 1960, U.S. Supreme Ct. 1967, D.C. 1979. Asso. Penn, Stuart & Stuart, 1960-62; partner Penn, Stuart & Miller, Abingdon, Va., 1963-69; atty. gen. Va., 1970-77; partner Mays, Valentine, Davenport & Moore, Richmond, Va., 1977-78, Dickstein, Shapiro & Morin, LLP, Washington, 1979—. Pres., Young Democratic Clubs Va., 1966-67; chmn. Washington County Dem. Com., 1967-69; Dem. nominee for U.S. Senate from Va., 1978; bd. dirs. Barter Found., 1962-69; trustee King Coll., 1966-74; mem. adv. bd. Ams. for Effective Law Enforcement, 1973-77, Center for Oceans Law and Policy, 1975-79; vice-chmn. Va. Bd. Corrections, 1983-86. Served to 1st lt. AUS, 1955-57. Fellow Am. Bar Found.; mem. ABA (ho. dels. 1971-76, mem. action commn. to reduce ct. costs and delay 1979-84, chmn. pub. election law com. 1986-87, commn. on pub. understanding about the law 1992-95, co-chair program devel. com., govt. and pub. lawyers divsn. 1993-94), So. Conf. Attys. Gen. (vice chmn. 1972-73, chmn. 1973-74), Nat. Assn. Attys. Gen. (exec. com. 1973-74), Nat. Assn. Attys. Gen. (exec. com. 1973-74, chmn. antitrust com. 1971-76, Wyman Meml. award 1976), Va. Bar Assn. (chmn. young lawyers sect. 1967-68, exec. com. 1985-88), Am. Judicature Soc. on the Cin. (Va. standing com. 1986-89, 93—, asst. sec., 1992-95, sec. gen. 1995—), The John Marshall Found. (pres. 1987-89), Phi Beta Kappa, Omicron Delta Kappa. Presbyn. Home: 1503 35th St NW Washington DC 20007-2729 Office: Dickstein Shapiro & Morin LLP 2101 L St NW Washington DC 20037-1526

MILLER, ANTHONY BERNARD, physician, medical researcher; b. Woodford, Eng., Apr. 17, 1931; married, 1952; 5 children. BA, U. Cambridge, 1952, MB, BChir, 1955. House officer Oldchurch Hosp., Romford, Eng., 1955-57; med. registrar Luton and Dunstable Hosp., Eng., 1959-62; mem. sci. staff Med. Research Council Tb and Chest Disease Unit, London, 1962-71; assoc. prof. preventive medicine and biostats. U. Toronto, 1972-76, prof., 1976—, chmn. dept., 1992-96, dir. grad. program in epidemiology, 1986-91; dir. epidemiology unit Nat. Cancer Inst. Can., Toronto, 1971-86; dir. Nat. Breast Screening Study, 1980—, WHO Collaborating Ctr. on Evaluation of Screening for Cancer, 1991—; Nat. Health scientist, 1988-93; mem. working cadre Bladder Cancer Project, U.S., 1973-75; mem. epidemiology com. Breast Cancer Task Force, U.S., 1973-77, chmn., 1975-77; mem. Fed. Task Force Cervical Cytol. Screening, Can., 1974-76, 80-81, Union Internat. Contre le Cancer com., controlled therapeutic trials, 1978-82, Multidisciplinary project breast cancer, 1978-82, chmn. project on screening, 1982-93; mem. sci. council Internat. Agy. Research Cancer, Lyon, 1981-85, chmn., 1985; mem. com. on diet, nutrition and cancer NRC of U.S., 1980-83, mem. oversight com. radioepidemiologic tables, 1983-84, com. on diet and health, 1986-89, com. on dietary guidelines implementation, 1988-91, chmn. com. on environmental epidemiology, 1990-94; chmn. Ont. Task Force on Primary Prevention of Cancer, 1994-95. Served with RAF, 1957-59. Mem. Can. Oncology Soc. (sec.-treas. 1975-79, pres. 1980-81), Soc. Epidemiology Research, Internat. Epidemiology Assn., Am. Soc. Preventive Oncology (pres. 1983-85), Am. Coll. Epidemiology (bd. dirs. 1987-89). Office: U Toronto Dept Preventive, Medicine and Biostats, McMurrich Bldg, Toronto, ON Canada M5S 1A8

MILLER, ANTHONY G., advertising executive; b. Sydney, Australia, Aug. 25, 1942; s. Gordon James and Patricia (Fuller) M.; m. Karen Frances Wilson, Oct. 14, 1967; children: Ryan, Adam, Kelly Ann. Mgmt. trainee McCann-Erickson, Sydney, 1963-65; with J. Walter Thompson, N.Y.C., 1969-73, v.p., 1970-73; with MacLaren Advt., Toronto, 1966-69, 73—; gen. mgr. MacLaren Advt., Montreal, 1973-79; exec. v.p., gen. mgr. MacLaren Advt. Ltd., Toronto, 1979-80, pres., CEO, from 1980; now chmn. MacLaren Lintas Inc., Toronto; chmn., CEO Lintas: N.Y., N.Y.C., 1991—. Liberal. Mem. Ch. of England. Office: MacLaren Lintas Inc, 20 Dundas St, Toronto, ON Canada M5G 2H1

MILLER, ARJAY, retired university dean; b. Shelby, Nebr., Mar. 4, 1916; s. Rawley John and Mary Gertrude (Schade) M.; m. Frances Marion Fearing, Aug. 18, 1940; children: Kenneth Fearing, Ann Elizabeth (Mrs. James Olstad). B.S. with highest honors, UCLA, 1937; LL.D. (hon.), 1964; postgrad., U. Calif.-Berkeley, 1938-40; LL.D. (hon.), Washington U., St. Louis; LL.D., Whitman Coll., 1965, U. Nebr., 1965, Ripon Coll., 1980. Teaching asst. U. Calif. at Berkeley, 1938-40; research technician Calif. State Planning Bd., 1941; economist Fed. Res. Bank San Francisco, 1941-43; asst. treas. Ford Motor Co., 1946-53, controller, 1953-57, v.p., controller, 1957-61, v.p. finance, 1961-62, v.p. of staff group, 1962-63, pres., 1963-68, vice chmn., 1968-69; dean Grad. Sch. Bus., Stanford U., 1969-79, emeritus, 1979—; former chmn. Automobile Mfrs. Assn., Econ. Devel. Corp. Greater Detroit; councillor The Conf. Bd.; past chmn., life trustee Urban Inst.; mem. Public Adv. Commn. on U.S. Trade Policy, 1968-69, Pres.'s Nat. Commn. on Productivity, 1970-74. Trustee Internat. Exec. Svc. Coirps.; hon. trustee The Brookings Instn.; dir. emeritus S.R.I. Internat.; chmn. Pub. Policy Inst. Calif.; former pres. Detroit Press Club Found.; former chmn. Boy Area

Coun. Capt. USAAF, 1943-46. Recipient Alumnus of Year Achievement award UCLA, 1964; Distinguished Nebraskan award, 1968; Nat. Industry Leader award B'nai B'rith, 1968. Fellow Am. Acad. Arts and Scis. Presbyterian. Clubs: Pacific Union, Bohemian.

MILLER, ARLYN JAMES, oil and gas company executive; b. LeMars, Iowa, Aug. 31, 1940; s. Clarence Theodore and Irene (DeSmet) M.; m. Loyola E. Valdes, Nov. 11, 1978. BBA, U. Iowa, 1962. CPA, Colo. Staff acct. Peat, Marwick, Mitchell & Co., Denver, 1962-65; acct. Hamilton Bros. Oil Co., Denver, 1965-69, treas., 1969—, v.p., 1978-80, sr. v.p., 1980-81, exec. v.p., CFO, 1981—; bd. dirs. Luth. Community Health Svcs., Wheat Ridge, Colo., Tejas Gas Corp., Houston, Luth. Med. Ctr. and Luth. Hosp., Wheat Ridge. Mem. AICPA. Republican. Roman Catholic. Clubs: Lakewood Country (Colo.), Denver Petroleum. Home: 1682 Montane Dr E Golden CO 80401-8092 Office: Hamilton Oil Co Inc 1560 Broadway Ste 2100 Denver CO 80202-5133

MILLER, ARNOLD, electronics executive; b. N.Y.C., May 8, 1928; s. Sam and Mina (Krutalow) M.; m. Beverly Shayne, Feb. 5, 1950; children: Debra Lynn, Marla Jo, Linda Sue. BS in Chemistry, UCLA, 1948, PhD in Phys. Chemistry, 1951. Registered profl. engr., Calif. Rsch. phys. chemist Wrigley Rsch. Co., Chgo., 1951; supr. phys. chemistry Armour Rsch. Found., Chgo., 1951-54, mgr. chemistry and metals, 1954-56; chief materials sci. dept. Borg-Warner Rsch. Ctr., Des Plaines, Ill., 1956-59; dir. rsch. Rockwell Corp., Anaheim, Calif., 1959-66, dir. microelec. ops., 1967-68; group exec. materials ops. Whittaker Corp., L.A., 1968-70; pres. Theta Sensors, Orange, Calif., 1970-72; mgr. xeroradiography Xerox Corp., Pasadena, Calif., 1972-75; corp. dir. rsch. and adv. devel. Xerox Corp., Stamford, Conn., 1975-78; corp. dir. rsch. and adv. devel. Xerox Corp., El Segundo, Calif., 1978-81, v.p. electronics div., 1981-84, pres. electronics div., 1984-87; corp. officer Xerox Corp., Stamford, 1984-87; pres. Tech. Strategy Group, Fullerton, Calif., 1987—; bd. dirs. Spectro Diode Labs, San Jose, Calif., Semicondr. Rsch. Corp., Colorep Inc., Carlsbad, Calif.; bd. dirs., chair audit com. Merisel Computer Products, El Segundo, Calif., lead dir.; mem. vis. com. on materials sci. U. So. Calif., L.A., 1966-68; mem. State of Calif. Micro Bd., 1984—. Editorial adv. bd. Advances in Solid State Chemistry; co-editor Electronics Industry Development; contbr. numerous articles to profl. jours. and monographs; patentee in field. Mem. civilian adv. group Dept. Commerce, 1959-60; mem. 5th decade com., also adv. com. on engring. and mgmt. program UCLA, 1984—; mem. com. on scholarly commn. with People's Republic of China, Tech. Transfer Task Force, Nat. Acad. Sci., Washington, 1985; bd. dirs. Orange County Pacific Symphony, Fullerton, Calif., 1982—; mem. univ.'s adv. bd. Calif. State U.-Fullerton, 1986—, chair, 1991—; v.p., bd. dirs. Heritage Pointe Home for the Aging, 1987—; trustee So. Calif. Coll. Optometry; chmn. Indsl. Assocs. sch. engring. and computer sci. Calif. State U., 1987—, trustee continuing learning ctr., 1993—; mem. Overseas Devel. Coun., 1988—; mem. Nat. Com. U.S.-China Rels., 1990—. Recipient Sci. Merit award Navy Bur. Ordnance/Armour Rsch. Found., 1952, IR-100 award, 1964, 69; named hon. alumnus Calif. State U., Fullerton, 1996. Fellow AAAS; mem. IEEE, AIME, Am. Chem. Soc., So. Calif. Coalition Edn. Mfg. Engring. (bd. dirs. 1994—), Soc. Photog. and Instrumentation Engrs. and Scientists, Elec. Industry Assn. (past chmn. microelectronics), Phi Beta Kappa, Sigma Xi, Phi Lamda Upsilon. Home: 505 E Westchester Pl Fullerton CA 92635-2706 Office: Tech Strategy Group PO Box 5769 Fullerton CA 92635-0769

MILLER, ARTHUR, playwright, author; b. N.Y.C., Oct. 17, 1915; s. Isadore and Augusta (Barnett) M.; m. Mary Grace Slattery, Aug. 5, 1940 (div. 1956); children: Jane Ellen, Robert; m. Marilyn Monroe, June 1956 (div. 1961); m. Ingeborg Morath, Feb. 1962; children: Rebecca Augusta, Daniel. AB, U. Mich., 1938, LHD, 1956; LittD (hon.), Oxford U., 1995. Assoc. prof. drama U. Mich., 1973-74. Author: (plays) Honors at Dawn, 1936 (Avery Hopwood award for playwriting U. Mich. 1936), No Villain: They Too Arise, 1937 (Avery Hopwood award for playwriting U. Mich. 1937), Man Who Had All the Luck, 1944 (Nat. prize Theatre Guild 1944), That They May Win, 1944, All My Sons, 1947 (N.Y. Drama Critics Circle award 1947, Tony award best play 1947, Donaldson award 1947), Death of a Salesman, 1949 (N.Y. Drama Critics Circle award 1949, Tony award best play 1949, Donaldson award 1949, Pulitzer prize in drama 1949), The Crucible, 1953 (Tony award best play 1953, Donaldson award 1953, Obie award 1958), A View from the Bridge, 1955, A Memory of Two Mondays, 1955, After the Fall, 1964, Incident at Vichy, 1964, The Price, 1968, Fame, 1970, The Reason Why, 1970, The Creation of the World and Other Business, 1972, Up From Paradise, 1974, The Archbishop's Ceiling, 1976, The American Clock, 1980, Some Kind of Love Story, 1983, Elegy for a Lady, 1983, Playing for Time, 1986, Danger: Memory!, 1986, The Last Yankee, 1990 (BBC Best Play award 1992), The Ride Down Mt. Morgan, 1991, Broken Glass, 1994 (Olivier award Best Play London 1995); (play adaptation) Enemy of the People (Ibsen), 1950; (screenplays) The Story of G.I. Joe, 1945, The Misfits, 1961, The Hook, 1975, Everybody Wins, 1990, The Crucible, 1995; (teleplays) Death of a Salesman, 1966, The Price, 1971, Fame, 1978, Playing for Time, 1980 (George Foster Peabody award 1981, Outstanding Writing Emmy award 1981), All My Sons, 1987, An Enemy of the People, 1990, The American Clock, 1994; author: Situation Normal, 1944, Focus, 1945, Jane's Blanket, 1963, I Don't Need You Anymore, 1967, In Russia, 1969, In the Country, 1977, The Theatre Essays of Arthur Miller, 1978, Chinese Encounters, 1979, Salesman in Beijing, 1987, Timebends: A Life, 1987, The Misfits and Other Stories, 1987, (novella) Homely Girl, 1994; exec. prodr. Death of a Salesman, 1985 (Outstanding Drama/Comedy Spl. Emmy award 1985). Recipient Bur. New Plays prize Theatre Guild, 1938, Nat. Assn. Ind. Schs. award, 1954, Gold Medal for drama Nat. Inst. Arts and Letters, 1959, Anglo-Am. award, 1966, Creative Arts award Brandeis U., 1970, Lit. Lion award N.Y. Pub. Libr., 1983, John F. Kennedy Lifetime Achievement award, 1984, Algur Meadows award So. Meth. U., 1991. Home: Tophet Rd Roxbury CT 06783

MILLER, ARTHUR HAWKS, JR., librarian, consultant; b. Kalamazoo, Mar. 15, 1943; s. Arthur Hawks and Eleanor (Johnson) M.; m. Janet Carol Schroeder, June 11, 1967; children: Janelle Aileen, Andrew Hawks. AB, Kalamazoo Coll., 1965; student U. Caen, Calvados, France, 1963-64, Lake Forest Grad. Sch. Mgmt., 1990-91; AM in English, U. Chgo., 1966, AM in Librarianship, 1968; PhD, Northwestern U., 1973. Reference libr. Newberry Libr., Chgo., 1966-69, asst. libr. pub. svcs., 1969-72; coll. libr. Lake Forest (Ill.) Coll., 1972-94, archivist and libr. for spl. collections, lectr. English dept., 1993—; mem. Ill. Libr. Computer Sys. Policy Coun., Chgo., 1982-87, 92-94. Pres. Lake Forest/Lake Bluff Hist. Soc., 1982-85, Lake County Hist. Soc., 1985—, Ill. Ctr. for Book Bd., 1992-93, v.p. 1993—; trustee Ragdale Found., 1986—, sec., 1987-92, pres., 1992-93, v.p., 1993-94, bd. dirs., 1990—. Mem. ALA (chmn. history sect. 1982-83, chmn. coll. sect. 1986-87), Melville Soc. Am., Ill. Libr. Assn. (chmn. pub. policy com. 1988-90), Pvt. Acad. Librs. of Ill. (v.p. 1988-90, pres. 1990-92), Caxton Club (pres. 1978-80, coun. mem. 1988-91). Presbyterian. Home: 169 Wildwood Rd Lake Forest IL 60045-2462 Office: Lake Forest Coll Donnelley Library 555 N Sheridan Rd Lake Forest IL 60045-2338

MILLER, ARTHUR MADDEN, investment banker, lawyer; b. Greenville, S.C., Apr. 10, 1953; s. Charles Frederick and Kathryn Irene (Madden) M.; m. Roberta Beck Connolly, Apr. 17, 1993. AB in History, Princeton U., 1973; MA in History, U. N.C., 1976; JD with distinction, Duke U., 1978; LLM in Taxation, NYU, 1982. Bar: N.Y. 1979, U.S. Dist. Ct. (so. dist.) N.Y. 1979. Assoc. Mudge Rose Guthrie Alexander & Ferdon, N.Y.C., 1978-85; v.p. pub. fin. Goldman, Sachs & Co., N.Y.C., 1985—. mem. adv. bd. Mary Baldwin Coll., Staunton, Va., 1982-86; trustee Princeton U. Rowing Assn., N.J., 1980—, pres., 1986-95; trustee Rebecca Kelly Dance Co., N.Y.C., 1984-86. Mem. ABA (tax sect. com. on tax exempt financing 1985—), Nat. Assn. Bond Lawyers (lectr. 1985—), Pub. Securities Assn. (cons. 1985—), Practising Law Inst. (lectr. 1980, editor/author course materials 1980), Bond Attys. Workshop (editor/author course material 1983—, lectr. 1983—), Princeton Club. Office: Goldman Sachs & Co 85 Broad St New York NY 10004-2434

MILLER, ARTHUR RAPHAEL, legal educator; b. N.Y.C., June 22, 1934; s. Murray and Mary (Schapin) M.; m. Ellen Monica Joachim, June 8, 1958 (div. 1978); 1 child, Matthew Richard.; m. Marilyn Tarmy, 1982 (div. 1988.); m. Sandra L. Young, 1992. AB, U. Rochester, 1955; LLB, Harvard U., 1958; student, Bklyn. Coll., 1952, 55, CCNY, 1955. Bar: N.Y. 1959, U.S. Supreme Ct. 1959, Mass. 1983. With Cleary, Gottlieb, Steen & Hamilton, N.Y.C., 1958-61; assoc. dir. Columbia Law Sch. Project Internat. Procedure, N.Y.C., 1961-62; instr. Columbia U. Law Sch., 1961-62; assoc. prof. U. Minn. Law Sch., 1962-65; prof. law U. Mich. Law Sch., 1965-72; vis. prof. Harvard U. Law Sch., 1971-72, prof., 1972-86, Bruce Bromley prof., 1986—; rsch. assoc. Mental Health Research Inst., 1966-68; dir. project computer assisted instn. Am. Assn. Law Schs., 1968-75; spl. rapporteur State Dept. concerning chpt. II of Hague Conv., 1967; del. U.S.-Italian Conf. Internat. Jud. Assistance, 1961, 62; chmn. task force external affairs Interuniv. Communications Council, 1966-70; mem. law panel, com. sci. and tech. info. Fed. Council Sci. and Tech., Pres.'s Office Sci. and Tech., 1969-72; mem. adv. group Nat. Acad. Sci. Project on Computer Data Banks, 1970-78; mem. spl. adv. group to chief justice Supreme Ct. on Fed. Civil Litigation; mem. com. on automated personal data systems HEW, 1972-73; chmn. Mass. Security and Privacy Council, Mass. Commn. on Privacy; mem. U.S. Commn. New Technol. Uses Copyrighted Works, 1975-79; reporter U.S. Supreme Ct.'s Adv. Com. on Civil Rules, 1978-86, mem. 1986-91; faculty Fed. Jud. Ctr.; reporter study on complex litigation Am. Law Inst.; bd. dirs. Research Found. on Complex Litigations, 1975-80. Author: The Assault on Privacy: Computers, Data Banks, and Dossiers, 1971, Miller's Court, 1982; (with others) New York Civil Practice, 8 vols., Civil Procedure Cases and Materials, 6th edit., 1993, Federal Practice and Procedure: Civil, 32 vols., 1969—, CPLR Manual, 1967; host syndicated TV shows in Context, Miller's Law, Miller's Court, Headlines on Trial; legal expert Good Morning America. Served with AUS, 1958-59. Recipient Nat. Emmy award for The Constitution, That Delicate Balance. Mem. Am. Law Inst. Office: Harvard U Law Sch Cambridge MA 02138 Also: Good Morning Am 147 Columbus Ave New York NY 10023-5900

MILLER, B. JACK, investment company executive; b. N.Y.C., Mar. 1, 1945; s. Bertram Jackson and Charlotte (Kea) M.; m. Lynsie Schaberg; children: Molly, Andrew. AB, Princeton U., 1966; MBA, U. Mich., 1968. Various positions Eli Lilly and Co., Indpls., 1968-80, dir. benefit plan investments, 1980-88; v.p. benefit investments Philip Morris Cos. Inc., N.Y.C., 1988-89, v.p., corp. contr., 1989-92; v.p. J.P. Morgan Investment Mgmt., N.Y.C., 1992—. Served with M.I., USAR, 1968-74. Mem. Fin. Execs. Inst., Princeton Club N.Y. Avocations: golf, bridge. Office: JP Morgan Investment Mgmt 522 5th Ave New York NY 10036-7601

MILLER, BARBARA KAYE, lawyer; b. Omaha, Aug. 21, 1964; d. Carl Reuben and Sandra Jean (Matthews) Wright; m. Julius Anthony Miller, May 4, 1991. BA, U. Iowa, 1987, JD, 1990. Bar: Ohio 1990, U.S. Dist. Ct. (no. dist.) Ohio 1991. Assoc. Fuller & Henry, Toledo, Ohio, 1990-92; law clk. to Hon. John W. Potter U.S. Dist. Ct. (no. dist.) Ohio, Toledo, 1992-93; asst. prosecutor Lucas County Prosecutor's Office, Toledo, 1994-95; ptnr. Wise People Mgmt., Toledo, 1994—, Ryan, Wise & Miller, 1995—; adj. prof. Lourdes Coll., Sylvania, Ohio, 1994—. Bd. dirs. Toledo Ballet Assn., 1992-94, Hospice, Toledo, 1992-94. Martin Luther King scholar, 1987; named to Profl. Women in Christ, 1992. Mem. ABA, Lucas County Bar Assn., Toledo Bar Assn. (mem. grievance com. 1994—), Thurgood Marshall Law Assn. (v.p. 1993-94), Lawyers Roundtable of Toledo (mem. steering com., recruiting program com. 1994—). Avocations: tennis, biking, swimming. Office: Wise People Mgmt Ste 333 151 N Michigan St Toledo OH 43624 also: Ryan Wise & Miller Ste 333 151 N Michigan St Toledo OH 43624

MILLER, BARNEY E., biochemist; b. Chattanooga, Tenn., Apr. 3, 1952; s. Gilbert R. and Marcella (Wear) M.; m. Merry A. Noel, June 11, 1983; Children: Corwin Andrew, Melanie Kay. BA in chemistry, U. Tenn., Chattanooga, 1975; PhD in biochemistry, U. Tenn., Memphis, 1983; post doctoral in biochemistry, Duke U., 1985. Rsch. assoc. Duke U. Hughes Med. Inst., Durham, N.C., 1985-88; project leader Abbott Labs, North Chgo., 1988-90, sr. sci., 1990-92; lab chief Molecular Geriat., Lake Bluff, Ill., 1992-94; sec. Neurosci. Cons. Inc., Libertyville, Ill., 1992—; v.p. rsch. Nymox Labs, Johnson City, Tenn., 1994—, Med. Toolworks, Inc., Evanston, Ill., 1995—; adj. prof. East Tenn. State U., Johnson City, 1994—; cons. Med. Toolworks, 1994—, Neurosci. Cons., Libertville, 1992—. Contbr. articles to profl. jours. Mem. Am. Assn. for the Advancement of Sci., N.Y. Acad. of Sci., Am. Chem. Soc., Soc. for Neurosci. Republican. Methodist. Avocations: rafting, animation, computer programing. Home: 504 W Maple St Johnston City TN 37604 Office: East Tenn State U W Memorial Ctr Rm 213 University Dr Johnson City TN 37614

MILLER, BARRY, research administrator, psychologist; b. N.Y.C., Dec. 25, 1942; s. Jack and Ida (Kaplan) M.; m. Susan Hallermeier; children: Eric, Arianne, Kristina, Barrie. BS in Psychology, Bklyn. Coll., 1965; MS in Psychology, Villanova U., 1967; PhD in Psychiatry, Med. Coll. Pa., 1971. Instr. psychology Villanova (Pa.) U., 1971-73; asst. dir. dept. behavioral sci., med. rsch. scientist Ea. Pa. Psychiatric Inst., Phila., 1971-73, sr. med. rsch. scientist, 1973-80; dir. Pa. Bur. Rsch. and Tng., Harrisburg, 1973-81; asst. prof. psychology U. Pa. Med. Sch., Phila., 1975-78, clin. prof. psychology, 1978—; assoc. prof. psychiatry Med. Coll. Pa., Phila., 1981-90, rsch. assoc. prof. medicine, 1983-90, assoc. dean for rsch., 1981-90; dir. for rsch. devel. Albert Einstein Healthcare Network, Phila., 1990-95; dir. The Permanente Med. Group Rsch. Inst., Oakland, Calif., 1995—; adj. assoc. prof. psychiatry Med. Coll. Pa., Phila., 1990—; rsch. assoc. prof. psychiatry Temple U. Sch. Med., Phila., 1990—; mem. sci. and tech. task force Pa. Econ. Devel. Partnership, Harrisburg, 1987-88, adv. com. Clin. Rsch. Ctr. Psychopathology of Elderly, Phila., 1985-88; mem. cancer control prgram Pa. Dept. Health, 1994; vis. rsch. assoc. prof. Med. Coll. Pa., Phila., 1991—. Contbr. articles to profl. jours.; mem. editorial bd. Jour. Mental Health Adminstrn., 1988—, assoc. editor, 1989—. Bd. dirs. Community Mental Health Ctr. 6A, Phila., 1969-73, Northwest Jewish Youth Ctrs., Phila., 1974-75; mem. Lafayette Hill Civic Assn., 1973-86, Citizens Coun. Whitemarsh (Pa.) Twp., 1975-86. Grantee HHS, NIH. Fellow Pa. Psychol. Assn.; mem. AAAS, Am. Psychol. Assn., Assn. Mental Health Adminstrs., Assn. Univ. Tech. Mgrs., Soc. Rsch. Adminstrs. Avocation: tennis. Office: The Permanente Med Group 1800 Harrison St Oakland CA 94612-3429

MILLER, BENJAMIN K., state supreme court justice; b. Springfield, Ill., Nov. 5, 1936; s. Clifford and Mary (Luthyens) M. BA, So. Ill. U., 1958; JD, Vanderbilt U., 1961. Bar: Ill. 1961. Ptnr. Olsen, Cantrill & Miller, Springfield, 1964-70; prin. Ben Miller-Law Office, Springfield, 1970-76; judge 7th jud. cir. Ill. Cir. Ct., Springfield, 1976-82, presiding judge Criminal div., 1977-81, chief judge, 1981-82; justice Ill. Appellate Ct., 4th Jud. Dist., 1982-84, Ill. Supreme Ct., Springfield, 1984—; chief justice Ill. Supreme Ct., 1991-93; adj. prof. So. Ill. U., Springfield, 1974—; chmn. Ill. Cts. Commn., 1988-90; mem. Ill. Gov.'s Adv. Coun. on Criminal Justice Legis., 1977-84, Ad Hoc Com. on Tech. in Cts., 1985—. Mem. editorial rev. bd. Illinois Civil Practice Before Trial, Illinois Civil Trial Practice. Pres. Cen. Ill. Mental Health Assn., 1969-71; bd. govs. Aid to Retarded Citizens, 1977-80; mem. Lincoln Legals Adv. Bd., 1988—. Lt. USNR, 1964-67. Mem. ABA (bar admissions com. sect. of legal edn. and admissions to bar 1992—), Ill. State Bar Assn. (bd. govs. 1970-76, treas. 1975-76), Sangamon County Bar Assn., Women's Bar Assn. of Ill., Ctrl. Ill. Women's Bar Assn., Am. Judicature Soc. (bd. dirs. 1990-95), Abraham Lincoln Assn. (bd. dirs. 1988—). Office: Supreme Ct Ill 1st Of America Ste 560 Springfield IL 62701

MILLER, BENNETT, physicist, former government official; b. N.Y.C., Jan. 18, 1938; s. Meyer Leon and Henrietta (Abramowitz) M.; m. Patricia Dawn Schoenhut, June 3, 1961; children: Beth Ann, Jeffrey Martin. A.B. magna cum laude (U.S. Rubber Co. scholar), Columbia U., 1959, M.A. (Eugene Higgins fellow), 1961, Ph.D., 1965. Research assoc. plasma physics lab. Columbia U., 1965-69, adj. asst. prof. physics, 1969; adj. assoc. prof. physics Fairleigh Dickinson U., 1967-69; asst. prof. nuclear engring. Ohio State U., cons. Battelle Meml. Inst, Columbus, Ohio, 1969-70; physicist div. controlled thermonuclear research U.S. Dept. Energy (formerly AEC and ERDA), Washington, 1970-74; dep. asst. dir. for research, acting chief exptl. plasma research br. U.S. Dept. Energy (formerly AEC and ERDA), 1974-75, asst. dir. research, 1975-76; dir. Office Plans, Budget and Program Implementation Solar, Geothermal and Advanced Energy Systems, U.S. Dept. Energy, 1976-78, program dir. solar, geothermal, electric and storage systems, 1978-80, dep. asst. sec. solar energy, 1980-81; v.p. energy programs McLaren Hart Inc. (formerly Fred C. Hart Assocs., Inc.), 1981-83; pres. Alternate Gas, Inc., Washington, 1983—, Miller Energy Corp., 1987—; v.p. tech. Kira, Inc., 1992—. Assoc. editor Jour. Solar Engring, 1980-84; contbr. articles to profl. jours. Pres. Columbia Coll. Class of 1959 Alumni, 1965-69, 84-89; v.p. Watkins Mill Elem. Sc. PTA, Gaithersburg, Md., 1970-71, pres., 1972-73. Finalist White House Fellows Program, 1966; recipient Spl. Achievement certificate AEC, 1973; Exceptional Service award Dept. Energy, 1979; Presdl. citation for meritorious service, 1980; hon. Woodrow Wilson fellow, 1960. Mem. Nat. Wood Energy Assn. (v.p., vice chmn. 1983-84, chmn. 1984-85, bd. dirs. 1983-87), Phi Beta Kappa. Home and Office: 7805 Fox Gate Ct Bethesda MD 20817-4100

MILLER, BERNARD JOSEPH, JR., advertising executive; b. Louisville, July 31, 1925; s. Bernard J. Sr. and Myrtle (Herrington) M.; m. Jayne Hughes, Aug. 7, 1948 (div. Oct. 1970); children: Bernard J. III, Jeffrey, Janet Marie.; m. Brita Naujok, Nov. 24, 1970; 1 child, Brian. BS, Ind. U., 1949. Merchandising mgr. Brown-Forman Distillers, Inc., Louisville, 1949-54; v.p. Phelps Mfg. Co., Terre Haute, Ind., 1954-60; pres. Columbian Advt. Inc., Chgo., 1960-87, chmn., 1987—. 2d lt. USAF, 1943-46, PTO. Mem. Point of Purchase Advt. Inst. (dir. 1970-73), Saddle and Cycle Club (bd. dirs. 1987-90). Avocations: tennis, downhill skiing, collecting first edition autographed books. Office: Columbian Advt Inc 201 E Ohio St Chicago IL 60611-3202

MILLER, BEVERLY WHITE, academic administrator; b. Willoughby, Ohio; d. Joseph Martin and Marguerite Sarah (Storer) White; m. Lynn Martin Miller, Oct. 11, 1945 (dec. 1986); children: Michaela Ann, Craig Martin, Todd Daniel, Cass Timothy, Simone Agnes. AB, Western Res. U., 1945; MA, Mich. State U., 1957; PhD, U. Toledo, 1967; LHD (hon.), Coll. St. Benedict, St. Joseph, Minn., 1979; LLD (hon.), U. Toledo, 1988. Chem. and biol. researcher, 1945-57; tchr. schs. in Mich., also Mercy Sch. Nursing, St. Lawrence Hosp., Lansing, Mich., 1957-58; mem. chemistry and biology faculty Mary Manse Coll., Toledo, 1958-71; dean grad. div. Mary Manse Coll., 1968-71, exec. v.p., 1968-71; acad. dean Salve Regina Coll., Newport, R.I., 1971-74; pres. Coll. St. Benedict, St. Joseph, Minn., 1974-79, Western New Eng. Coll., Springfield, Mass., 1980—; cons. U.S. Office Edn., 1980; mem. Pvt. Industry Count./Regional Employment Bd., exec. com., 1982-94; cons. in field. Author papers in field. Corporator Mercy Hosp., Springfield, Mass. Recipient President's citation St. John's U., 1979; also various service awards. Mem. AAAS, Am. Assn. Higher Edn., Assn. Cath. Colls. and Univs. (exec. bd.), Internat. Assn. Sci. Edn., Nat. Assn. Ind. Colls. and Univs. (govt. rels. adv. com., bd. dirs. 1990-93, exec. com. 1991-93, treas. 1992-93), Nat. Assn. Biology Tchrs., Assn. Ind. Colls. and Univs. of Mass. (exec. com. 1981—, vice chmn. 1985-86, chmn. 1986-87), Nat. Assn. Rsch. Sci. Teaching, Springfield C. of C. (bd. dirs.), Am. Assn. Univ. Adminstrs. (bd. dirs. 1989-92), Delta Kappa Gamma, Sigma Delta Epsilon. Office: Western New Eng Coll Office of the President 1215 Wilbraham Rd Springfield MA 01119-2654

MILLER, BRIAN KEITH, airline executive; b. Cin., Aug. 12, 1958; s. Charles Eugene and Vera Adeline (Garrison) M.; m. Victoria Lee Vaughan, Oct. 20, 1990. BBA, Tex. A&M U., 1980. CPA, Tex. From audit staff to audit mgr. Ernst and Young, Dallas, 1980-86; corp. controller and treas. Metro Airlines, Inc., Dallas, 1986-90, v.p. controller and treas., 1990-91, sr. v.p., chief fin. officer, sec., treas., 1991-92, pres., 1992—; v.p., CFO Lone Star Airlines, Ft. Worth, 1994-95. Mem. steering com. Dallas Bus. Forum, 1989-92; active The 500, Inc., Dallas, 1983-86; bd. dirs. Partnership for Arts, Culture and Edn. Inc., 1996—. Mem. AICPA, Treasury Mgmt. Assn., Fin. Execs. Inst., Tex. Soc. CPAs. Avocation: travel. Office: 6452 Waggoner Dr Dallas TX 75236

MILLER, BRUCE RICHARD, employee benefits executive; b. Hazleton, Pa., Mar. 16, 1944; s. Robert Joseph and Marguerite Marie (Fritz) M.; BA in Polit. Sci., Pa. State U., 1971. Supr. salary adminstrn. Govt. Employees Ins. Co., Chevy Chase, Md., 1971-73; asst. to personnel dir. MCI Telecommunications, Inc., Washington, 1973-74; wage and salary adminstr. Kay Jewelers, Inc., Alexandria, Va., 1974, dir. personnel, 1974-84, div. v.p. personnel, 1981-85; founder, pres., chief exec. officer Employee Benefits Corp. Am., Fairfax, 1984-89, McLean, Va., 1989—. Pa. State U. Presdl. assoc.; contbr. articles to profl. jours. Mem. Alexandria Human Rights Commn., 1982-85, Active Back the Lions Club. Served with U.S. Army, 1966-70. Mem. Soc. Human Resource Mgmt., Pa. State U. Alumni Assn., Pa. State U. Nittany Lion Club (bd. dirs., mem. adv. council), Pa. State U. Club of Greater Washington, Nat. Capital Area Nittany Lion (pres.), Nat. Assn. Life Underwriters, Nat. Assn. Health Underwriters, No. Va. Assn. Life Underwriters, Assn. Health Ins. Agts. Home: 12312 Blair Ridge Rd Fairfax VA 22033-1800 Office: 1420 Spring Hill Rd Ste 620 Mc Lean VA 22102-3006

MILLER, BURTON LEIBSLE, sales executive; b. L.A., July 17, 1944; s. Kenneth Wilbur and Dorothy (Leibsle) M.; m. April Suydam, Dec. 22, 1969 (div. 1983); children: Brandon, Gregory; m. Linda L. Reynolds, Aug. 11, 1990. BSCE, San Jose State U., 1968; MS in Engring., U. So. Calif., 1977. Civil engr. USN, San Bruno, Calif., 1968-74; cost engr. Bechtel Corp., L.A., 1974-79; supr. Bechtel Corp., Saudi Arabia, 1979-81; project mgr. Bechtel Corp., San Francisco, 1981-84, Bay Area Contractors, San Francisco, 1984—; dist. sales mgr. ISC, San Francisco, 1994—; cons. KMD/Kimco Mgmt. Co., San Francisco, 1989-90. Mem. World Affairs Coun., San Francisco, 1991, C. of C., San Francisco, 1986. Recipient Commendation, V.P. Dan Quayle, 1992, Cert. of Appreciation, Pres. George Bush, 1989, Cert. of Appreciation, Congressman Bob Mitchel, 1991. Mem. Commonwealth Club of Calif., Olympic Club, Project Mgmt. Inst. Republican. Avocations: snow skiing, scuba diving, real estate investment. Home: 1035 Cabrillo St San Francisco CA 94118

MILLER, C. ARDEN, physician, educator; b. Shelby, Ohio, Sept. 19, 1924; s. Harley H. and Mary (Thuma) M.; m. Helen Meihack, June 26, 1948; children—John Lewis, Thomas Meihack, Helen Lewis, Benjamin Lewis. Student, Oberlin Coll., 1942-44; M.D. cum laude, Yale, 1948. Intern, then asst. resident pediatrics Grace-New Haven Community Hosp., 1948-51; faculty U. Kans. Med. Center, 1951-66, dir. childrens rehab. unit, 1957-60, dean Med. Sch., dir., 1960-66; prof. pediatrics and maternal and child health U. N.C., Chapel Hill, 1966—, vice chancellor health scis., 1966-71, chmn. dept. maternal and child health, 1977-87; chmn. exec. com. Citizens Bd. Inquiry into Health Services for Am., 1968-71. Mem. editorial bd.: Jour. Med. Edn, 1960-66; Author numerous articles in field. Trustee Appalachian Regional Hosps., 1974-84, Alan Guttmacher Inst., Planned Parenthood Fedn. Am. Markle scholar in med. scis., 1955-60; recipient Robert H. Felix Distinguished Service award St. Louis U., 1977, Martha Mae Eliot award in pub. health, 1984, Sedgewick Meml. medal Am. Pub. Health Assn., 1986, O. Max Gardner award U. N.C., 1987. Fellow Royal Soc. Health (hon.), Clare Hall Cambridge (Eng.) U. (life); mem. Am. Pub. Health Assn. (chmn. action bd. 1972-75, pres. 1974-75), Soc. Pediatric Research, Assn. Am. Med. Colls. (v.p. 1965-66), Inst. of Medicine of Nat. Acad. Sci., Sigma Xi, Alpha Omega Alpha, Delta Omega. Home: 908 Greenwood Rd Chapel Hill NC 27514-3910

MILLER, CALVIN FRANCIS, geology educator; b. Escondido, Calif., Aug. 6, 1947; s. Wells Wait and Alice Atherton (Bakeman) M.; m. Molly Beth Fritz, Apr. 19, 1971; children: Spring Alice, Zachary Fritz. BA, Pomona Coll., 1969; MS, George Washington U., 1973; PhD, UCLA, 1977. Instr. Pomona Coll., Claremont, Calif., 1976-77; asst. prof. Vanderbilt U., Nashville, 1977-84, assoc. prof., 1984-89, prof., 1989—, chair dept. geology, 1991—; vis. rsch. assoc. prof. Rensselaer Polytechnic Inst., Troy, N.Y., 1984-85. Assoc. editor Jour. Geophys. Rsch., Washington, 1995—. Lt. USCG, 1969-73. Grantee NSF, 1978—. Mem. Am. Geophys. Union, Geol. Soc. Am. (assoc. editor Bull. 1989-94), Mineral. Soc. Am. Achievements include understanding the growth histories and geochemical significance of accessory minerals in the crust, the origins of peraluminous granites, and the history of the crust of Ea. Calif. and So. Nev. Home: 6744 Pennywell Dr Nashville TN 37205 Office: Vanderbilt U Dept Geology Box 6028, Sta B Nashville TN 37235

MILLER, CANDICE S., state official; b. May 7, 1954; m. Donald G. Miller; 1 child, Wendy Nicole. Student, Macomb County C.C., Northwood Inst. Sec., treas. D.B. Snider, Inc., 1972-79; trustee Harrison Twp., 1979-80, supr., 1980-92; treas. Macomb County, 1992-95; sec. of state State of Mich., Lansing, 1995—; chair Mich. State Safety Commn., 1995—; mem. M-59 Task Force Strategy Com. Mem. community coun. Selfridge Air Nat. Guard Base. Mem. Boat Town Assn., Ctrl. Macomb C. of C., Harrison Twp. Indsl. Corridor. Avocations: boating, yachting. Office: Treasury Building 430 W Allegan, 1st Fl Lansing MI 48918-9900

MILLER, CARL CHET, business educator; b. Richmond, Va., June 23, 1961; s. Carl Chester and Nancy Ellis (Peters) M.; m. Laura Bridget Cardinal, Dec. 28, 1982. BA summa cum laude, U. Tex., 1982, PhD, 1990. Shift mgr. Frontier Enterprises, Austin, Tex., 1983; instr. Ind. U., Bloomington, 1983-84; tchg. asst. U. Tex., Austin, 1984-85, instr., 1985, rsch. assoc., 1985-89; asst. prof. bus. Baylor U., Waco, Tex., 1989-95, assoc. prof. bus., 1995—; mem. faculty senate, 1996—; reviewer Acad. Mgmt. Jour., Briarliff Manor, N.Y., 1991—, Mgmt. Sci., Providence, 1987, 88, 93—, Orgn. Sci., Providence, 1990, 94, 95. Contbr. articles to profl. jours., chpts. to books; author numerous conf. papers; liaison Tex. Conf. on Orgns., Austin, 1989—. Bd. dirs. Windridge Home Owners Assn., Dallas, 1993—; pres. Assn. Mgmt., Austin, 1985-87; bd. advs. Cin. Glory Drum and Bugle Corps, 1995—. Recipient Outstanding Young Rschr. award Hankamer Sch. Bus., 1992; grantee Hankamer Sch. Bus., 1990, 91, 92, 94, 95, 96, Bohham Meml. Rsch. Fund grantee Grad. Sch. Bus. U. Tex., 1985, 89. Mem. Acad. Mgmt. (divsnl. regional liaison 1994-96, reviewer ann. meeting 1987, 88, 93—), Inst. Mgmt. Scis., Phi Beta Kappa (chpt. scholarship chair 1992-94), Phi Beta Kappa, Phi Kappa Phi. Avocations: sailing, reading, golf. Office: Baylor U Hankamer Sch Bus PO Box 98006 Waco TX 76798

MILLER, CARL GEORGE, manufacturing executive; b. Milw., Oct. 3, 1942; s. Carl Conrad and Agnes Frances (Patla) M.; m. Patricia Ann Smith, Apr. 27, 1968; children: Gregory, Brian. BS, St. Louis U., 1964. CPA, Mo. Audit mgr. Ahrens & McKeon, CPAs, St. Louis, 1967-73; supr. internal audit Gen. Dynamics Corp., St. Louis, 1973-75, mgr. fin. analysis, 1975-78, dir. fin. analysis, 1978-80; v.p., contr. Quincy (Mass.) Shipbldg. div. Gen. Dynamics Corp., 1980-86; v.p. fin. Cessna Aircraft Co., Wichita, Kans., 1986-88; v.p., contr. Ft. Worth div. Gen. Dynamics Corp., Ft. Worth, 1988-90; v.p., contr. TRW, Inc., Cleve., 1990-96, exec. v.p., CFO, 1996—. Mem. adv. coun. So. U. and A&M Bus. Sch., Case Western Reserve U. Acctg. Dept. Mem. AICPA, Fin. Execs. Inst. (com. on corp. reporting), Mfr. Alliance for Productivity and Innovation (fin. coun. II), Mo. Soc. CPA, Mayfield Country Club, Delta Sigma Pi (pres. 1963-64). Republican. Lutheran. Avocations; traveling, reading. Office: TRW Inc 1900 Richmond Rd Cleveland OH 44124-3719

MILLER, CAROL A., health administrator, government official, consultant; b. Bayonne, N.J., Apr. 5, 1932; d. John J. and Antoinette (DeLuca) Pagano; m. Charles H. Miller, Aug. 29, 1953 (dec. Apr. 1977); children: Charles, Toni. Diploma, Monmouth Meml. Hosp., Long Branch, N.J., 1952; BA, Monmouth Coll., 1981. RN, N.J., N.Y. Office mgr. cardiologist West Long Branch, N.J., 1965-71; asst. adminstr. Monmouth Coll. Student Health, West Long Branch, 1972-79; occupl. health nurse Gateway Young Adult C.C., Sandy Hook, N.J., 1979-81, Gateway Job Corps/CCC, Bklyn., 1981-85; nurse cons., DON Office of Job Corps U.S. Dept. Labor, Washington, 1985—; bd. dirs., sec. New Hope Found., Marlboro, N.J., 1979-81. Contbr. articles to profl. jours. Mem. APHA, DAV, Gold Star Wives of Am. Roman Catholic. Avocations: piano, tennis, arts and crafts, poetry. Office: US Dept Labor Office of Job Corps 200 Constitution Ave NW Washington DC 20210-0001

MILLER, CAROLE ANN LYONS, editor, publisher, marketing specialist; b. Newton, Mass., Aug. 1; d. Markham Harold and Ursula Patricia (Foley) Lyons; m. David Thomas Miller, July 4, 1978. BA, Boston U., 1964; bus. cert., Hickox Sch., Boston, 1964; cert. advt. and mktg. profl. UCLA, 1973; cert. retail mgmt. profl. Ind. U., 1976. Editor Triangle Topics, Pacific Telephone, L.A.; programmer L.A. Cen. Area Speakers' Bur., 1964-66; mng. editor/mktg. dir. Teen mag., L.A. and N.Y.C., 1966-76; advt. dir. L.S. Ayres & Co., Indpls., 1976-78; v.p. mktg. The Denver, 1978-79; founder, editor, pub. Clockwise mag., Ventura, Calif., 1979-85; mktg. mgr., mgr. pub. rels. and spl. events Robinson's Dept. Stores, L.A., 1985-87, exec. v.p., dir. mktg. Harrison Svcs., 1987-93; pres. divsn. Miller & Miller Carole Ann Lyons Mktg., Camino, Calif., 1993—; instr. retail advt. Ind. U., 1977-78. Recipient Pres.'s award Advt. Women of N.Y., 1974; Seklemian award 1977; Pub. Svc. Addy award, 1978. Mem. Advt. Women N.Y., Calif. Videographers Assn., Fashion Group Internat., Bay Area Integrated Mktg., San Francisco Fashion Group, San Francisco Direct Mktg. Assn. UCLA Alumni Assn., Internat. TV Videographer's Assn. (Sacramento chpt.). Editor: Sek Says, 1979. Home: 3709 Carson Rd Camino CA 95709-9593

MILLER, CAROLINE, editor-in-chief. Exec. editor Variety mag., N.Y.C., 1989-92; editor-in-chief Lear's mag., N.Y.C., 1992-94, Seventeen mag., N.Y.C., 1994—. Office: Seventeen 850 3rd Ave New York NY 10022-6222*

MILLER, CARROLL GERARD, JR. (GERRY MILLER), lawyer; b. San Antonio, Tex., Dec. 12, 1944; s. Carroll Gerard Sr. and Glyn (Roddy) M.; m. Sylvia Louise Mertins, Mar. 7 1971 (dec. 1982); children: Glyn Marie Bennett, Roddy Gerard, Gina Louise. AS, Del Mar Coll., 1965; BS, U. Houston, 1967; JD, Tex. Tech. U., 1970. Bar: Tex. Ct. Criminal Appeals 1970, U.S. Dist. Ct. (so. dist.) Tex. 1971, U.S. Ct. Appeals (5th cir.) Tex. 1973, U.S. Supreme Ct. 1974, U.S. Ct. Appeals (D.C. 1986), Colo. 1987, D.C. 1989. Assoc. Allison, Madden, White & Brin, Corpus Christi, Tex., 1970-71; asst. city atty. City of Corpus Christi, 1971; asst. dist. atty. Nueces County Dist. Attys. Office, Corpus Christi, 1971-73; asst. city atty. civil div. City of Corpus Christi, 1973-74; atty. Corpus Christi Police Dept.-City of Corpus Christi, 1974-77; pvt. practice Corpus Christi, 1973—; adj. prof. Bee County Coll., Beeville, Tex., 1973-74, Tex. A & I U., Corpus Christi, 1975-76. Past treas. and diaconate First Presbyn. Ch., Corpus Christi; bd. dirs., incorporator Iron Curtain Outreach; 20/20 coun. Open Doors. Mem. SAR, SCV, Assn. Trial Lawyers Am., Tex. Criminal Def. Lawyers Assn., Nat. Criminal Def. Lawyers Assn., Coll. State Bar Tex., Sons of Republic Tex., Crime Stoppers, Inc. (past dir.), Bay Yacht Club (dir.). Republican. Avocations: sailing, scuba diving, photography. Home: 1209 Sandpiper Dr Corpus Christi TX 78412-3821 Office: 1007 Kinney Corpus Christi TX 78401

MILLER, CARROLL LEE LIVERPOOL, educational researcher; b. Washington, Aug. 20, 1909; s. William and Georgie E. (Liverpool) M. B.A. magna cum laude, Howard U., 1929, M.A., 1930; Ed.D., Columbia U., 1952. Instr. Miles Coll., 1930-31; mem. faculty Howard U., 1931—, prof. edn., 1957-88, chmn. dept., 1961-68, assoc. dean Coll. Liberal Arts, 1961-64, acting dean Grad. Sch., 1964-66, dean Grad. Sch., 1966-74, prof. higher edn., 1974-88, prof. emeritus edn., 1988—, cons. sch. social work, 1987—, adv. bd. sch. continuing edn., 1987—, coord. Grad. Internat. Programs, 1980-88, dir. summer session, 1964-70; chmn. Charles H. Thompson Lecture/Symposium, 1984—; instr. social studies D.C. pub. schs., evenings 1933-40; summer 1934; research asst. Commonwealth Va., 1938-39; Mem. adv. com. Nat. Conf. Problems Rural Youth Okla., 1963; participant conf. Commn. Civil Rights, 1962; mem. exec. council Episcopal Diocese Washington, 1964-66, mem. dept. coll. work, 1957-67, mem. standing com., 1967-68, chmn. Interracial Task Force, 1969-70, mem. Commn. on Ministry, 1971-72, mem. Rev. Bd., 1973-76; mem. Episcopal Council Overseas Students and Visitors, 1960-63; mem. adv. com. Anglican/Episcopal Ministry, Howard U., 1988—; coord. Ch. Bros., St. Augustine's Episcopal Ch., and Riverside Bapt. Ch., 1985-89; steering com. LEAD-Leadership in Ednl. Adminstrn.-D.C. Pub. Schs., 1990-93; bd. dirs. Samaritan Ministry of Greater Washington, 1990—; coord. The Role Model Forum, Christian Youth Report, Seminarian's Lay Com., Ch. of Holy Communion, 1990-94, lay eucharistic minister, 1995—; mem. field work adv. com. Va. Theol. Sem., 1991—, Grad. Record Exams. Bd., 1965-70; exec. com. Council Grad. Schs. U.S., 1968-71; mem. com. grad. deans African-Am. Inst. Author: Role Model Blacks: Known But Little Known, 1982; mem. editorial bd. Jour. Negro Edn; contbg. editor Profiles; contbr. to ednl. jour. Bd. dirs. D.C. Tb Assn., 1953-59, 65-71, D.C. Episcopal Center for Children, 1964-76; bd. dirs. New Ednl. Ways, 1977-87 , pres., 1980-81; trustee Absalom Jones Theol. Inst.; cons. Nigerian Univs. Commn., 1981. Mem. Am. Assn. for Counseling and Devel. (del. assembly 1963-65, 68-69, bd. dirs. 1972), Consortium of Univs. of Washington Met. Area (adminstrv. com. 1964-88), Am. Assn. Colls. Tchr. Edn. (liaison rep. D.C. 1963-65), Am. Coll. Personnel Assn., Nat. Career Devel. Assn., Assn. for Humanistic Edn. and Devel. (pres. 1971-72), Nat. Soc. Study Edn., Assn. for Multicultural Counseling and Devel., Soc. Profs. Edn., AAAS, So. Regional Council, Nat. Guild of Churchmen, Columbia Tchrs. Coll. Alumni Council, Am. Ednl. Studies Assn., Nat. Cath. Assn., Phi Delta Kappa, Kappa Delta Pi. Home: 1301 Delaware Ave SW North 406 Washington DC 20024-3929

MILLER, CECELIA SMITH, chemist; b. Tyron, N.C., Apr. 3, 1965; d. Thad Lewis Jr. and Johnnie Lucille (Staley) Smith; m. Ronnie Edward Miller, Apr. 16, 1988; children: Joshua Edward, Jaylin. BA in Chemistry, Converse Coll., 1987. Lab. technician Groce Labs., Greer, S.C., 1988; quality assurance technician Baxter Pharmaseal, Spartanburg, S.C., 1988-89; lab. dir. CAPSCO, Inc., Greenville, S.C., 1989, quality assurance mgr., 1989—. Mem. Am. Soc. Quality Control, S.C. Lab. Mgmt. Soc. Democrat. Baptist. Avocations: cooking, reading, music. Home: 3017 Southfield St Inman SC 29349-9190 Office: CAPSCO Inc 1101 W Blue Ridge Dr Greenville SC 29609-3350

MILLER, CHARLES, business management research and measurements consultant; b. Crowley, La., Nov. 1, 1959; s. Rufus Paul and Rose (Lacombe) M.; m. Monica Lynn Habetz, Aug. 10, 1985. BS, La. State U., 1981, MS, 1985; PhD, Ohio State U., 1989. Rsch. asst. horticulture dept. La. State U., Baton Rouge, 1977-78, La. State Soil Testing Lab., Baton Rouge, 1978-81; rsch. assoc. La. Rice Rsch. Sta., Crowley, 1982; agriculture tchr. Acadia Parish Sch. Bd., Crowley and Iota, 1982-87; rsch. assoc. Ohio State U., Columbus, 1987-89, asst. prof., 1989-92; sr. cons., mgr. measurements Shaffer Sherman Sperry & Swaddling, Inc., Westerville, Ohio, 1992—. Minister, lector St. John Neumann Ch., Sunbury, Ohio, 1992—. Recipient project grant for tchr. prep. program U.S. Dept. Edn., 1990, Am. Farmer award Nat. Future Farmers Am., 1979. Mem. Am. Soc. for Quality Control, Omicron Tau Theta (editor 1991-92, Outstanding Svc. award 1992), Phi Delta Kappa, Gamma Sigma Delta, Alpha Zeta. Democrat. Roman Catholic. Avocation: woodworking. Office: Shaffer Sherman Sperry & Swaddling Inc 575 Copeland Mill Rd Westerville OH 43081-8977

MILLER, CHARLES A., lawyer; b. Oakland, Calif., Feb. 7, 1935; s. Frank and Janice (Greene) M.; m. Jeanette Segal, Sept. 27, 1964; children: Jennifer Fay, Charlotte Irene Marvin, Ira David. AB, U. Calif., Berkeley, 1955, LLB, 1958. Law clk. to assoc. justice U.S. Supreme Ct., Washington, 1958-59; assoc. Covington & Burling, Washington, 1959-67, ptnr., 1967—; mem. criminal justice coordinating bd., Washington, 1977-78; chmn. hearing com. Bd. on Profl. Responsibility, Washington, 1980-86. Pres. U. Calif. Alumni Club, Washington, 1962-70; mem. various coms. and adv. bds. Washington Pub. Sch. System, 1972-79; chmn. lawyers com. Washington Performing Arts Soc., 1984-86; bd. dirs. Dumbarton Concert Series, Washington, 1986—, chmn., 1990—. Fellow Am. Coll. Trial Lawyers; mem. ABA, D.C. Bar Assn., U. Calif. Alumni Assn. (trustee 1989-92). Democrat. Jewish. Club: Burning Tree (Bethesda, Md.). Office: Covington & Burling 1201 Pennsylvania Ave NW PO Box 7566 Washington DC 20044

MILLER, CHARLES DALY, self-adhesive materials executive; b. Hartford, Conn., 1928; married. Grad., Johns Hopkins U. Sales and mktg. mgr. Yale & Towne Mfg. Co., 1949-59; assoc. Booz, Allen & Hamilton, 1959-64; with Avery Internat. Corp., Pasadena, Calif., 1964—; v.p., mng. dir. Materials Europe, 1965-68; v.p. Fasson Internat. Ops., 1968; group v.p. materials group Avery Internat. Corp., Pasadena, 1969-75, pres., bd. dirs., COO, 1975-77, pres., CEO, 1977-83; chmn., CEO Avery Dennison Corp. (formerly Avery Internat. Corp.), Pasadena, 1983—. Office: Avery Dennison Corp PO Box 7090 Pasadena CA 91109-7090

MILLER, CHARLES E., judge; b. Washington, Sept. 26, 1944; s. Charles Edward Miller and Mary (Cox) M.; divorced; 1 child, Samantha McGill Cox. BA, So. Meth. U., 1971, JD, 1972. Bar: Tex. 1972. Assoc., Roseborough & Curlee, Dallas, 1972-77; judge County Criminal Ct. #7, Dallas, 1977-82, Ct. Criminal Appeals, Austin, Tex., 1983-94; state judge at large, 1995—; adj. prof. criminal law So. Meth. U. Law Sch., Dallas, 1980-82. Author and lectr. in field. Mem. nat. adv. coun. Nat. Victim Ctr., N.Y.C. and Washington; mem. nat. steering com. Victims Constitutional Amendment Network; mem. adv. bd. Victims Organized to Ensure Rights and Safety; mem. victim assistance com. Tex. Young Lawyers Assn.; parliamentarian state exec. bd. People Against Violent Crime. Served with U.S. Army, 1966-70. Named Disting. Mil. Grad., Officer Candidate Sch., Ft. Sill., Okla., 1968, Best Dallas Misdemeanor Ct. Judge, Dallas Bar Assn., 1982, Best Dallas Criminal Ct. Judge, Dallas County Criminal Bar Assn., 1982; decorated Army Commendation medal, 1970; recipient Sunny von Bulow Nat. Victim Advocacy Ctr. Appreciation cert., 1987, U.S. Dept. Justice Victims of Crime Appreciation cert., 1992, Victims Organized to Ensure Rights and Safety Advocate for Justice award, 1993, People Against Violent Crime Appreciation cert., 1993. Mem. SAR, State Bar Tex. (chmn. criminal law sect. 1981-82, course dir. advanced criminal law course 1990, chmn. crime victim com. 1992-94, crime victim & witness, 1994, cert. specialist in criminal law), Coll. State Bar Tex., Tex. Bar Found. Republican. Home and Office: 1705 Wild Basin Ldg Austin TX 78746-2820

MILLER, CHARLES EDMOND, library administrator; b. Bridgeport, Conn., Aug. 3, 1938; s. Edmond and Irene Ovelia (Boudreaux) M.; m. Alice Ann Phillips, June 2, 1962; children—Alison, Charles Edmond, Catherine, Susan. Student, U. Hawaii, 1957-58; B.A., McNeese State U., 1964; M.S. in L.S, La. State U., 1966. Tchr. Lake Charles (La.) High Sch., 1964-65; mem. staff La. State U. Library, Baton Rouge, 1966-69; asso. dir. Tulane U. Library New Orleans, 1969-73; dir. Fla. State U. Library, Tallahassee, 1973—; vis. coms. So. Assn. Colls. and Schs.; bd. dirs. SOLINET, 1979-81, 85-86, corp. v.p., vice chmn., 1980-81; cons. in field; adv. com. State Libr. Fla.; bd. dirs. Ctr. for Rsch. Librs., 1976-77, 91—, sec., 1993-96; mem. policy bd. Fla. Libr. Network; pres. Assn. Southeastern Rsch. Librs., 1982-84; mem. rsch. libr. adv. com. OCLC, 1993-96. Asst. editor: La. Library Assn. Bull, 1967; contbr. articles to library sci. jours.; book revs. to Southeastern Librarian. Served with USMCR, 1956-59. Mem. ALA, Fla. Libr. Assn. (dir. 1979-81), Southeastern Libr. Assn., Assn. Coll. and Rsch. Librs., Assn. Rsch. Librs. (bd. dirs. 1985-90, v.p., pres.-elect 1987-88, pres. 1988-89), Fla. Ctr. Libr. Automation (chmn. bd. dirs. 1985-96), Rsch. Librs. Group (exec. com. 1988-90, bd. dirs. 1991-94), Phi Kappa Phi, Beta Phi Mu, Sigma Tau Delta.

MILLER, CHARLES HAMPTON, lawyer; b. Southampton, N.Y., Jan. 25, 1928; s. Abraham E. and Ethel (Simon) M.; m. Mary Fried, Aug. 26, 1956; children—Cathy Lynn, Steven Scott, Jennifer Lee. B.A., Syracuse U., 1949; LL.B., Columbia U., 1952. Bar: N.Y. 1952, Republic Korea 1954, U.S. Ct. Appeals (2d cir.) 1958, U.S. Supreme Ct. 1969, U.S. Ct. Appeals (3d cir.) 1972, U.S. Ct. Appeals (7th cir.) 1973, U.S. Ct. Appeals (9th cir.) 1995; cert. mediator and early neutral evaluator (so. and ea. dists.) N.Y., 1994—, mediator Supreme Ct. N.Y. County, 1996—. Asst. counsel Waterfront Commn. N.Y. Harbor, 1954-56; asst. atty. U.S. Atty. for So. Dist. N.Y., 1956-58; assoc. Cole & Deitz, N.Y.C., 1958-61; assoc. Marshall Bratter Greene Allison & Tucker, N.Y.C., 1961-64, ptnr., 1964-82; ptnr. Hess Segall Guterman Pelz Steiner & Barovick, N.Y.C., 1982-86, Loeb and Loeb, N.Y.C., 1986—; mem. faculty Continuing Legal Edn. Columbia U. Law Sch., 1976-82. Served with U.S Army, 1952-54. Fellow Am. Bar Found.; mem. ABA, N.Y. State Bar Assn. (chmn. fed. ct. com. 1976-79, vice chmn. com. on specialization 1976-79, mem. fin. com. 1980-81), Assn. Bar City N.Y., Fed. Bar Council. Home: 171 Ralph Ave White Plains NY 10606-3813 Office: Loeb and Loeb 345 Park Ave New York NY 10154-0004

MILLER, CHARLES LESLIE, civil engineer, planner, consultant; b. Tampa, Fla., June 5, 1929; s. Charles H. and Myrle Iona (Walstrom) M.; m. Roberta Jean Pye, Sept. 9, 1949; children—Charles Henry, Stephen, Jonathan, Matthew. BCE, MIT, 1951, MCE, 1958. Registered profl. engr., Mass., Fla., Tenn., N.H., R.I., P.R. Successively field engr., project engr., exec. engr. Michael Baker, Jr., Inc. (cons. engrs.), Rochester, Pa., 1951-55; asst. prof. surveying, dir. photogrammetry lab. Mass. Inst. Tech., 1955-59, asso. prof. civil engring., head data engring. div., 1959-61, prof. civil engring., 1961-77, head dept., 1961-70, dir. urban systems lab., 1968-75, dir. civil engring. systems lab., 1961-65, dir. inter-Am. program civil engring., 1961-65, asso. dean engring., 1970-71; cons. engr., 1955—; chmn. bd., sr. cons., pres. CLM Systems, Inc., C.L. Miller Co., Inc.; adviser Commonwealth of P.R; dir. Geo-Transport Found.; Chmn. Pres.-elect's Task Force on Transp., 1968-69. Author: The COGO Book, 1990; contbr. articles to tech. jours. Recipient Outstanding Young Man of Greater Boston award. Fellow ASCE, Am. Acad. Arts and Scis.; mem. Am. Inst. Cons. Engrs., Am. Soc. Engring. Edn. (George Westinghouse award), Am. Soc. Photogrammetry, Am. Congress Surveying and Mapping, Am. Rd. Builders Assn., Transp. Rsch. Bd., Assn. Computing Machinery, Sigma Xi, Chi Epsilon, Tau Beta Pi. Originator of DTM, COGO, ICES, CEAL computer systems. Office: CL Miller Co 4315 Beachway Dr Tampa FL 33609-3416

MILLER, CHARLES MAURICE, lawyer; b. L.A., Sept. 7, 1948; s. Samuel C. and Sylvia Mary Jane (Silver) M.; m. Terri Lee Senesac, Mar. 25, 1979; children: Samuel Mark, Seth Michael. BA cum laude, UCLA, 1970; postgrad., U. So. Calif., L.A., 1970-71; JD, U. Akron, 1975. Bar: Ohio 1975, Calif. 1978, U.S. Dist. Ct. (cen. dist.) Calif. 1978, U.S. Ct. Appeals (9th cir.) 1978, U.S. Supreme Ct. 1981. Gen. atty. U.S. Immigration & Naturalization Svc., U.S. Dept. Justice, L.A., 1976-79; ptnr. Miller Law Offices, L.A., 1979—; adj. prof. law U. West L.A., 1989-90. Co-editor: The Visa Processing Guide: Process and Procedures at U.S. Consulates and Embassies, 3d edit., 1995; articles editor U. Akron Law Rev., 1974-75. Mem. Calif. Bd. Legal Specialization, San Francisco, 1988-89. Mem. Bar of Calif. (chmn. immigration splty. 1988-89, commr. immigration splty. 1987-90), Am. Immigration Law Found. (bd. trustees 1995—), Am. Immigration Lawyers Assn. (chair So. Calif. chpt. 1993-94, co-chair membership 1989-90, co-chair mentor program 1990-91, co-chair visa office liaison 1991-92, vice chair 1994—, co-chair consular rev. task force 1993-95, Jack Wasserman Meml. award for excellence in immigration litigation 1995). Office: Miller Law Offices 12441 Ventura Blvd Studio City CA 91604-2407

MILLER, CHARLES Q., engineering company executive; b. 1945. BA, Balt. Polytechnic Inst., 1963; BS in Mech. Engring. and Math., U.S. Naval Acad., Annapolis, 1967; MS in Applied Mechanics, Stanford U., 1970; JD, Rutgers U., 1980. Ensign US Navy, 1967-74; with Raytheon Engineers and Constructors, Phila., 1974—, now CEO. Office: Raytheon Engrs & Constructors 141 Spring St Lexington MA 02173-9999

MILLER, CHARLES RICKIE, thermal/fluid systems analyst, engineering manager; b. New Albany, Ind., Oct. 4, 1946; s. Marshall Christian and Thelma Virginia (Martin) M.; m. Janel Howell, Nov. 24, 1968; children: Kimberly, Brian, Audrey, Rachel. BA in Physics, DePauw U., 1969; postgrad., Rice U., 1969-70, U. Houston, 1972-76. Tech. editor ITT/Fed. Electric Corp., Houston, 1970-71, LTV/Svc. Tech. Corp., Houston, 1971; sys. safety engr. Boeing Aerospace Corp., Houston, 1971-76; thermal analyst space sys. divsn. Rockwell Internat. Corp., Houston, 1976-89; mgr. thermal and fluid sys. for space shuttle payloads Space Shuttle Program, Office NASA/L.B. Johnson Space Ctr., Houston, 1989—; mem. edtl. team Apollo 14, 15 preliminary sci. reports, 1971-72; mem. sys. integration negotiating team for Space Shuttle to Mir Space Sta. rendezvous and docking missions, 1993—, chmn. negotiating team for Space Shuttle to Mir Space Sta. water preparation and transfer, 1994—. Bd. dirs. Space City Aquatic Team, Houston, 1990-91. Rector scholar DePauw U., 1964-68; Rice fellow Rice U., 1969-70. Mem. AIAA, ASME, Nat. Space Soc., Air Force Assn., Am. Inst. Physics, Sigma Pi Sigma. Avocations: children's sports, jogging, science fiction, military history. Home: 806 Walbrook Dr Houston TX 77062 Office: Nat Aeronautic & Space Admn L B Johnson Space Ctr Houston TX 77058

MILLER, CHARLES S., clergy member, church administrator. Exec. dir. Division for Church in Society of the Evangelical Lutheran Church in America, Chicago, Ill. Office: Evangelical Lutheran Church Am 8765 W Higgins Rd Chicago IL 60631-4101

MILLER, CHRISTINE MARIE, marketing executive; b. Williamsport, Pa., Dec. 7, 1950; d. Frederick James and Mary (Wurster) M.; m. Robert M. Ancell, Mar. 30, 1985. BA, U. Kans., 1972; MA, Northwewstern U., 1978, PhD, 1982. Pub. rels. asst. Bedford County Commr., Bedford, Pa., 1972-73; teaching asst. Northwestern U., Evanston, Ill., 1977-80; asst. prof. U. Ala., Tuscaloosa, 1980-82, Loyola U., New Orleans, 1982-85; vis. prof. Ind. U. Sch. Journalism, Bloomington, 1985-86; mktg. dir. Nat. Inst. Fitness & Sport, Indpls., 1986-88; program dir. Nat. Entrepreneurship Acad., Bloomington, 1986-88; mgmt. assoc. community and media rels. Subaru-Isuzu Automotive, Inc., Lafayette, Ind., 1988-91; dir. pub. rels. Giddings & Lewis, Fond Du Lac, Wis., 1991-93; v.p. comm. and enrollment mgmt. Milton Hershey (Pa.) Sch., 1993-94, dir. adminstrn., 1994-95; mktg. comms. mgr. MCI Govt. Markets, McLean, Va., 1995—; USNR., 1977—, (commd.). Co-author: The Biographical Dictionary of World War II, General and Flag Officer, contbr. articles to profl. jours. Bd. dirs. Indpls. Entrepreneurship Acad., 1988-91, Area IV Agy., Greater Lafayette Mus. Art, 1989-91. With USN, 1973-77, comdr. USNR. Mem. Pub. Rels. Soc. Am., Naval Order of the U.S., Naval Res. Assn., Res. Officers Assn. Presbyterian. Avocations: cooking, swimming, reading, travel, diving. Home: 7406 Salford Ct Alexandria VA 22315 Office: MCI Govt Markets 6th Fl 8200 Greensboro Ave Mc Lean VA 22102

MILLER, CHRISTINE ODELL COOK, federal judge; b. Oakland, Calif., Aug. 26, 1944; d. Leo Marshall and Carolyn Grant (Odell) Cook; m. Dennis F. Miller, Sept. 10, 1994. BA, Stanford U., 1966; JD, U. Utah, 1969. Bar: Utah 1969, D.C. 1972, Calif. 1982. Clk. to chief judge U.S. Ct. Appeals (10th cir.), 1969-70; trial atty. U.S. Dept. Justice, Washington, 1970-72, Fed. Trade Commn., Washington, 1972-74; litigation Hogan & Hartson, Washington, 1974-76; spl. counsel Pension Benefit Guaranty Corp., Washington, 1976-78; asst. gen. counsel U.S. Ry. Assn., Washington, 1978-80; litigation Shack & Kimball P.C., Washington, 1980-83; judge U.S. Ct. of Fed. Claims, Washington, 1983—. Mem. State Bar Assn. Calif., D.C. Bar Assn., Order of Coif. Republican. Presbyterian. Club: University. Avocation: gemology. Office: US Ct of Fed Claims 717 Madison Pl NW Washington DC 20005-1011*

MILLER, CHRISTINE TALLEY, physical education educator; b. Wilmington, Del., Sept. 11, 1959; d. Willard Radley and Anna Rose (Oddo) Talley; m. Jeffrey Lynch Miller, Nov. 14, 1987; children: Radley Edward, Rebecca Anna. BS in Phys. Edn., U. Del., 1981, MS in Phys. Edn., 1984. Cert. phys. edn. tchr., Del. Phys. edn. tchr. Pilot Sch. Inc., Wilmington, 1981-85; EKG technician Med. Ctr. Del., Newark, 1978-88; phys. edn. tchr. Red Clay Consol. Sch. Dist., Wilmington, 1985—; mem. stds. revision com. Del. Dept. Pub. Instrn., 1991; mem. stds. rev. com. Red Clay Consol. Sch. Dist., 1993-94, curriculum revision com., 1988-92; coach spl. olympics, 1985-88. Contbg. author: A Legacy of Delaware Women, 1987. Jump Rope for Heart coord. Am. Heart Assn., Newark, 1994—; mem. Gov.'s Coun. for Lifestyles and Fitness, State of Del., 1991-93. Recipient Gov.'s Cup award for outstanding phys. edn. program Gov. Mike Castle, Del., 1991. Mem. AAHPERD, Del. Assn. for Health, Phys. Edn., Recreation and Dance (sec. 1981-86, v.p. health, Outstanding Phys. Edn. Tchr. of Yr. 1986). Home: 1206 Arundel Dr Wilmington DE 19808-2137

MILLER, CLAIRE ELLEN, periodical editor; b. Milw., July 17, 1936; d. Emil George Benjamin and Phyllis Dorothy (Rahn) Holtzen; m. Gerald Ray Miller, June 21, 1958; children: Karin Miller O'Callaghan, Russell Bruce Miller. BS in Edn., Concordia U., 1961. Catalog clk. U. Ill. Libr., Urbana, 1960-61; tchr. Grace Episcopal Day Sch., Silver Spring, Md., 1971-77, The Norwood Sch., Bethesda, Md., 1977-79; title I tchr. Rock Creek Forest Elem., Silver Spring, 1979-80; writer Media Materials, Balt., 1980; project editor Ednl. Challenges, Alexandria, Va., 1981; asst. mng. editor Ranger Rick Mag., Nat. Wildlife Fedn., Vienna, Va., 1981-87, mng. editor, 1988—. Author numerous activity books for presch. thru jr. high, 1979-80; project editor 6 vocabulary books, 1981; author numerous children's stories to mag. Mem. Ednl. Press. Assn. of Am., Md. Ornithol. Soc. Democrat. Lutheran. Avocation: birding. Home: 17501 Kirk Ln Rockville MD 20853-1033 Office: Nat Wildlife Fedn Ranger Rick Mag 8925 Leesburg Pike Vienna VA 22182-1742

MILLER, CLIFFORD ALBERT, merchant banker, business consultant; b. Salt Lake City, Aug. 6, 1928; s. Clifford Elmer and LaVeryl (Jensen) M.; m. Judith Auten, Sept. 20, 1976; 1 child, Courtney; children by previous marriage, Clifford, Christin, Stephanie. Student, U. Utah, 1945-50, UCLA, 1956. Pres. Braun & Co., L.A., 1955-82, chmn., 1982-87; exec. v.p. Gt. Western Fin. Corp., Beverly Hills, Calif., 1987-91; chmn. Clifford Group, Inc., bus. cons., 1992—; mng. dir. Shamrock Holdings, Inc., 1992—, Shamrock Capital Advisors, L.P., 1992—; bd. dirs. First Am. Corp., First Am. Bankshares, Inc., Washington, Shamrock Broadcasting , Inc., Burbank, Calif., L.A. Gear, Inc., Santa Monica, Calif.; cons to White House, 1969-74. Trustee Harvey Mudd Coll., Claremont, Calif., 1974—, chmn. bd. trustees, 1991; chmn. bd. dirs. L.A. Master Chorale, 1989-93, chmn. emeritus, 1993;

mem. chmn.'s coun. Music Ctr. Unified Fund Campaign. Mem. UCLA Chancellor's Assocs., Skull and Bones, The Lakes Country Club, Calif. Club, Wilshire Country Club, Jeremy Golf and Country Club, Pi Kappa Alpha. Office: Shamrock Holdings Inc PO Box 7774 4444 W Lakeside Dr Burbank CA 91510-7774

MILLER, CURTIS HERMAN, bishop; b. LeMars, Iowa, May 3, 1947; s. Herman Andrew and Verna Marion (Lund) M.; m. Sharyl Susan Vander-Tuig, June 2, 1969; children: Eric, Nathan, Paul. BA, Wartburg Coll., 1969; MDiv., Wartburg Sem., 1973; DD (hon.), Wartburg Coll., 1987. Assoc. pastor Holy Trinity Luth. Ch., Dubuque, Iowa, 1973-75; pastor St. Paul Luth. Ch., Tama, Iowa, 1975-82; coord. for congl. life Am. Luth. Ch. Iowa dist., Storm Lake, 1982-87; bishop Western Iowa Synod Evang. Luth. Ch. in Am., Storm Lake, 1987—. Bd. regents Waldorf Coll., Forest City, Iowa, 1987—; bd. dirs. Luth. Social Svcs. of Iowa, Des Moines, 1987. Office: Evang Luth Ch Am Western Iowa Synod PO Box 1145 Storm Lake IA 50588-1145

MILLER, DAN, congressman; b. Mich., 1943; m. Glenda Darsey; children: Daniel, Kathryn. Grad., U. Fla., 1964; MBA, Emory U.; PhD, La. State U. Ptnr. Miller Enterprises, Bradenton, Fla.; restaurant owner Memorial Pier, Fla., 1977—; instr. Ga. State U., U. South Fla., Sarasota; mem. 103d-104th Congresses from 13th Fla. Dist., 1993—; mem. appropriations com., mem. budget com. Active Rep. Leader's Task Force on Health. Mem. Manatee C. of C. Episcopalian. Office: US Ho of Reps 117 Cannon HOB Washington DC 20515-0913*

MILLER, DANIEL NEWTON, JR., geologist, consultant; b. St. Louis, Aug. 22, 1924; s. Daniel Newton and Glapha (Shuhardt) M.; m. Esther Faye Howell, Sept. 9, 1950; children: Jeffrey Scott, Gwendolyn Esther. B.S. in Geology, Mo. Sch. Mines, 1949, M.S., 1951; Ph.D., U. Tex., 1955. Intermediate geologist Stanolind Oil and Gas Co., 1951-52; sr. geologist Pan Am. Petroleum Corp., 1955-60, Monsanto Chem. Co., 1960-61; cons. geologist Barlow and Haun, Inc., Casper, Wyo., 1961-63; prof. geology, chmn. dept. So. Ill. U., 1963-69; state geologist, exec. dir. Wyo. Geol. Survey, 1969-81; adj. prof. geology U. Wyo., 1969-81; asst. sec. energy and minerals Dept. Interior, 1981-83; geol. cons., 1983-89; dir. Anaconda Geol. Documents Collection U. Wyo., 1989-92; mem. Interstate Oil Compact Commn., 1969-81. Co-editor: Overthrust Belt of Southwestern Wyoming, 1960; gen. editor: Geology and Petroleum Production of the Illinois Basin, 1968; Contbr. articles to profl. jours. Served with USAAF, 1942-46. Decorated Air medal; recipient award merit So. Ill. U., 1967. Mem. Assn. Am. State Geologists (pres. 1979-80, chmn. govt. liaison com. 1970-71), Am. Assn. Petroleum Geologists (pres. Rocky Mountain sect. 1987, Pub. Svc. award), Am. Inst. Profl. Geologists (pres. 1992, Ben H. Parker Meml. medal 1993, Martin Van Couvering Meml. award 1994), Assn. Am. State Geologists (pres. 1979-80, hon. mem. 1982), Rocky Mountain Assn. Geologists (Disting. Pub. Svc. award). Achievements include patent for exhausto-port for automobiles. Home: 402 Colony Woods Dr Chapel Hill NC 27514-7908 *Use everything you know, in everything you do, all the time.*

MILLER, DAVID, lawyer, advertising executive; b. Fort Worth, Dec. 12, 1906; s. Max and Tillie (Hoffman) M.; m. Rosalie Agress, Jan 31, 1929; children—Allan David, Martha Sally. A.B. cum laude, U. Tex., 1926; LL.B. cum laude, Harvard, 1929. Bar: N.Y. State bar 1931. With law firm of Jones, Clark & Higson, N.Y. City, 1929-33; pvt. practice with Harold W. Newman, Jr., 1937-44; mem. law firm of Engel, Judge & Miller, 1944-74; counsel RFC, Washington, 1933-34; asst. gen. counsel Md. Casualty Co., Balt., 1934-36; with Office of Gen. Counsel, Securities & Exchange Commn., 1936-37; v.p. and gen. counsel Young & Rubicam, Inc. (Advt. agy.), 1951-71, sec., dir., sr. v.p., 1971; counsel Squadron, Ellenoff & Plesent, 1974—; v.p., sec., gen. counsel The Music Project for TV, Inc., 1973—; Trustee Motion Picture Players Welfare Fund, Am. Fedn. TV & Radio Artists Pension and Welfare Fund.; Cons. joint policy com. Am. Assn. Advt. Agys.-Assn. Nat. Advertisers. Lecturer on radio and TV law for professional groups.; Editor: Harvard Law Review, 1927-29. Mem. Am. Bar Assn., Assn. Bar City N.Y., N.Y. County Lawyers' Assn., Am. Assn. Advt. Agencies (cons. broadcast business affairs com.), Phi Beta Kappa. Club: Harvard (N.Y.). Home: 30 Arleigh Rd Great Neck NY 11021-1327 Office: 551 5th Ave New York NY 10176

MILLER, DAVID ANDREW BARCLAY, physicist; b. Hamilton, Scotland, Feb. 19, 1954; came to U.S., 1981; s. Matthew Barclay and Martha Sanders (Dalling) M.; m. Patricia Elizabeth Gillies, Aug. 13, 1976; children: Andrew Donald, Susan Rachel. BS, St. Andrews U., Scotland, 1976; PhD, Heriot-Watt U., Edinburgh, Scotland, 1979. Postdoctoral rsch. assoc. Heriot-Watt U., 1979-80, lectr., 1980-81; mem. tech. staff AT&T Bell Labs., Holmdel, N.J., 1981-87, head photonics switching device rsch. dept., 1987-92, head advanced photonics rsch. dept., 1993—. Contbr. 170 articles to profl. jours.; holder 30 patents. Recipient Prize of Internat. Commn. for Optics, 1991. Fellow Royal Soc. London, Optical Soc. Am. (Adolph Lomb medal 1986, R.W. Wood prize 1988), Am. Phys. Soc., IEEE (pres. lasers and electroptics soc. 1995). Avocations: playing clarinet and saxophone. Home: 64 Hance Rd Fair Haven NJ 07704-3210 Office: AT&T Bell Labs Rm 4B401 101 Crawfords Corner Rd Holmdel NJ 07733-1900

MILLER, DAVID ANTHONY, lawyer; b. Linton, Ind., Oct. 6, 1946; s. Edward I. and Jane M. (O'Hern) M.; m. Carol E. Martin, Aug. 9, 1970; 1 child, Jennifer Rose. Student, Murray State U., 1965; BS, Ind. State U., 1969; JD, Ind. U., Indpls., 1973. Bar: Ind. 1973, U.S. Dist. Ct. (so. dist.) Ind. 1973, U.S. Supreme Ct. 1981, U.S. Ct. Appeals (7th cir.) 1982. Dep. atty. gen. State of Ind., Indpls., 1973-76, dir. consumer protection divsn. office atty. gen., 1976-93, asst. atty. gen., 1977-80, chief counsel office atty. gen., 1981-93; prin. Hollingsworth, Meek, Miller and Minglin, Indpls., 1993—. Youth dir. Emmanuel Luth. Ch., Indpls., 1981-85, exec. dir., 1988-90; chmn. bd. Chambers Found., 1994—; mem. bd. Lutheran H.S. Mem. ABA, Ind. State Bar. Assn., Indpls. Bar Assn., Ind. State U. Alumni Assn., Columbia Club, Lambda Chi Alpha. Republican. Avocations: numismatics, golfing. Home: 5320 E Fall Creek Pky North Dr Indianapolis IN 46220-5737 Office: Ste 100 9202 N Meridian St Indianapolis IN 46260

MILLER, DAVID EDMOND, physician; b. Biscoe, N.C., June 6, 1930; s. James Herbert and Elsie Dale (McGlaughon) M.; m. Marjorie Willard Penton, June 4, 1960; children: Marjorie Dale, David Edmond. AB, Duke U., 1952, MD, 1956. Diplomate Am. Bd. Internal Medicine (subspecialty bd. cardiovasular disease). Internmed. ctr. Duke U., Durham, N.C., 1956-57, resident in internal medicine, 1957-58, 59, 60, research fellow cardiovascular disease, 1958-59, 61, assoc. internal medicine and cardiology, 1963-79, clin. asst., prof. medicine cardiology, 1979—; practice medicine specialising in internal medicine Durham, 1964—; attending physician internal medicine div. cardiology Watts Hosp., Durham, 1964-76, chief medicine, 1975-76; attending physician cardiology divsn. internal medicine Durham Regional Hosp. (formerly Durham County Gen. Hosp.), 1976—, chmn. dept. internal medicine, 1976-82, pres. med. staff, 1980-81; adv. com. Duke Med. Ctr. Contbr. articles to profl. jours. Council clin. cardiology N.C. chpt. Am. Heart Assn., 1963—. Served to lt. comdr. USNR, 1961-63. Fellow ACP, Am. Coll. Cardiology, Royal Soc. Medicine, Royal Soc. Health; mem. AMA, So. Med. Assn., N.C. Med. Soc. (del. ho. of dels. 1981, 82, 83), N.C. Durham-Orange County Med. Soc., Am. Soc. Internal Medicine, N.C. Soc. Internal Medicine (exec. coun. 1984-92), Am. Fedn. Clin. Rsch. Methodist. Clubs: Capitol, Hope Valley Country, Univ., Duke Faculty, Carolina Yacht. Home: 1544 Hermitage Ct Durham NC 27707-1680 Office: 2609 N Duke St Ste 403 Durham NC 27704-3048

MILLER, DAVID EMANUEL, physics educator, researcher; b. Bethel, Vt., Aug. 30, 1943; s. Manuel Southworth and Lucille (Shurtleff) M. BA, U. Vt., 1965; MA, SUNY, Stony Brook, 1967, PhD, 1971; Habilitation in Theoretical Physics, U. Bielefeld, Fed. Republic Germany, 1978. Instr. physics SUNY, Stony Brook, 1970-71; Wissenschaftlicher asst. Freie U., Berlin, 1972-75; scientist U. Bielefeld, 1975-78, Heinrich-Hertz Stipendium, 1977-78; privat dozent U. Bielefeld, 1978-83, univ. prof., 1987—; asst. prof. of physics Pa. State U., Hazelton, 1983-86, assoc. prof., 1986-92, prof., 1992—. Recipient Heinrich-Hertz stipendium, 1977-78. Mem. Am. Phys. Soc., Am. Assn. Physics Tchrs., Deutsche Physikalische Gesellschaft, Deutscher Hochschulverband, N.Y. Acad. Sci., Am. Math. Soc., Phi Beta Kappa, Sigma Xi. Home: PO Box 611 Conyngham PA 18219-0611 Office: Pa State U High Acres Hazleton PA 18201

MILLER, DAVID EUGENE, soil scientist, researcher; b. Scipio, Utah, July 31, 1926; s. Henry and Josie (Peterson) M.; m. Jo Ann Peterson, Mar. 17, 1950; children: Ross H., Dale E., Diane. BS, Utah State U., 1950; MS, Colo. State U., 1953; PhD, Wash. State U., 1959. Cert. agronomy, crops and soils profl. Asst. agronomist Colo. State U., Grand Junction, 1950-53; soil scientist USDA Agrl. Rsch. Svc., Grand Junction, 1953-54; rsch. soil scientist USDA Agrl. Rsch. Svc., Prosser, Wash., 1958-89, ret., 1989; acting instr. soils Wash. State U., Pullman, 1954-58. Contbr. numerous articles to profl. jours. Sgt. U.S. Army, 1944-46, ETO. Fellow Am. Soc. Agronomy, Soil Sci. Soc. Am. (chair S-6 1982-83); mem. Western Soc. Soil Sci. (pres. 1979-80), Internat. Soc. Soil Sci., Soil and Water Conservation Soc. Mem. LDS Ch. Avocations: camping, sports, gardening, travel. Home: 965 Campbell Dr Prosser WA 99350-1307

MILLER, DAVID HEWITT, environmental scientist, writer; b. 1918; m. Enid Woodson Brown; 1 child. AB cum laude, UCLA, 1939, MA, 1944; PhD, U. Calif., Berkeley, 1953; DLitt (hon.), U. Newcastle, 1979. Meteorologist U.S. Corps Engrs., 1941-43; forecaster TWA, 1943-44; climatologist Quartermaster Gen.'s Office, 1944-46; meteorologist, hydrologist Coop. Snow Investigations, San Francisco, 1946-53; geographer U.S. Natick (Mass.) Labs., 1953-59; meteorologist, hydrologist U.S. Forest Svc., 1959-64; prof. geography U. Wis., Milw., 1964-75, prof. atmospheric scis., 1975—; sr. acad. meteorologist NOAA, 1981-82; Fulbright lectr., Australia, 1966, 71, 79; exchange scientist Acad. Scis., Moscow, 1969; mem. adv. com. climatology Nat. Acad. Scis., 1958-64. Author: Snow Cover and Climate, 1955, (with others) Snow Hydrology, 1956, Heat and Water Budget of Earth's Surface, 1965, Energy at the Surface of the Earth, 1981, Water at the Surface of the Earth, 1982; editor: Climate and Life (M.I. Budyko), 1974. NSF fellow, 1952-53. Fellow AAAS (life); mem. Am. Geophys. Union (life, transl. bd. 1972-76), Am. Meteorol. Soc. (profl. life), Ecol. Soc. Am., Assn. Am. Geographers, Inst. Australian Geographers, Internat. Assn. Landscape Ecology, We. Snow Conf., Phi Beta Kappa, Sigma Xi. Office: Univ Wis Dept Geoscis PO Box 413 Milwaukee WI 53201-0413

MILLER, DAVID W., lawyer; b. Indpls., July 1, 1950; s. Charles Warren Miller and Katherine Louise (Beckner) Dearing; m. Mindy Miller, May 20, 1972; children: Adam David, Ashley Kay, Amanda Katherine Kupfer. BA, Ind. U., Bloomington, 1971; JD summa cum laude, Ind. U., Indpls., 1976. Bar: Ind. 1977. Investigator NLRB, Indpls., 1971-76; assoc. Roberts & Ryder, Indpls., 1977-80, ptnr., 1981-86; ptnr. Baker & Daniels, Indpls., 1986—; bd. dirs. Everybody's Oil Corp., Anderson, Ind. Mem. Ind. Bar Assn. (chmn. labor law sect. 1981-82). Republican. Office: 300 N Meridian St Ste 2700 Indianapolis IN 46204-1755

MILLER, DAVID WILLIAM, historian, educator; b. Coudersport, Pa., July 9, 1940; s. Arthur Charles and Kathryn Marie (Long) M.; m. Margaret Vick Richardson, Aug. 22, 1964; 1 child, Roberta Neal. BA, Rice U., 1962; MA, U. Wis., 1963; PhD, U. Chgo., 1968. Instr. history Carnegie Mellon U., Pitts., 1967-68, asst. prof., 1968-73, assoc. prof., 1973-80, prof., 1980—; dir. Ctr. for Hist. Info. Sys. and Analysis, 1994—. Author: Church, State and Nation in Ireland, 1898-1921, 1973, Queen's Rebels: Ulster Loyalism in Historical Perspective, 1978; editor: Peep o'Day Boys and Defenders: Selected Documents on the Disturbances in County Armagh, 1784-1796, 1990; assoc. editor: New Dictionary of National Biography, 1994—; mem. editl. bd.: Hist. Methods, 1991-93; prin. developer: (interactive atlas) Great American History Machine, 1994. Sr. research fellow Inst. Irish Studies Queen's U., Belfast, Northern Ireland, 1975-76. Mem. Am. Hist. Assn., Am. Conf. for Irish Studies. Democrat. Presbyterian. Avocations: walking, singing. Office: Carnegie Mellon Univ Dept of History Schenley Park Pittsburgh PA 15213

MILLER, DEANE GUYNES, salon and cosmetic studio owner; b. El Paso, Tex., Jan. 12, 1927; d. James Tillman and Margaret (Brady) Guynes; degree in bus. adminstrn. U. Tex., El Paso, 1949; m. Richard George Miller, Apr. 12, 1947; children: J. Michael, Marcia Deane. Owner four Merle Norman Cosmetic Studios, El Paso, 1967—; pres. The Velvet Door, Inc., El Paso, 1967—; dir. Mountain Bell Telephone Co. Pres. bd. dirs. YWCA, 1967; v.p. Sun Bowl Assn., 1970; bd. dirs. El Paso Symphony Assn.; bd. dirs., treas. El Paso Mus. Art, pres., trustee, 1990, pres., 1991—; chmn. bd. El Paso Internat. Airport; bd. dirs., sec. Armed Services YMCA, 1987, 1st v.p., 1990. Named Outstanding Woman field of civic endeavor, El Paso Herald Post. Mem. Women's C. of C. (pres. 1969), Pan Am. Round Table (dir., pres. 1987). Home: 1 Silent Crest Dr El Paso TX 79902-2160 Office: 4150 Rio Bravo Ste 110 El Paso TX 79902

MILLER, DEBORAH JEAN, computer training and document consultant; b. Elmhurst, Ill., Oct. 2, 1951; d. Thomas Francis and Ruthe Conn (Johnston) M. BFA, Ill. Wesleyan U., 1973; MA, Northwestern U., 1974. Pres. Miller & Assocs., Evanston, Ill., 1980—. Mem. AAUW, NOW, Internat. Interactive Comm. Soc., Soc. Tech. Comm., Ind. Writers Chgo. (bd. dirs. 1985-86), Chgo. Coun. Fgn. Rels., Internat. Soc. Performance and Instrn. (Chgo. chpt.), Northwestern U. Alumni Assn. Office: 814 Mulford St Evanston IL 60202-3331

MILLER, DECATUR HOWARD, lawyer; b. Balt., June 29, 1932; s. Lawrence Vernon and Katherine Louise (Baum) M.; m. Sally Burnam Smith, Nov. 23, 1963; 1 dau., Clemence Mary Katherine. B.A., Yale U., 1954; LL.B., Harvard U., 1959. Bar: Md. 1959. Assoc. Piper & Marbury, Balt., 1959-62, 1963-66, assoc., ptnr., 1967-94, mng. ptnr., 1974-87, chmn., 1987-94; Md. Securities commr., 1962-63. Trustee Enoch Pratt Free Libr., 1975—, v.p., 1977-85, pres., 1985-89; bd. dirs. Balt. Symphony Orch., 1970—, v.p., 1978-86, 88-90, pres., 1990-92; trustee Calvert Sch., 1976-89, pres., 1982-87; trustee Walters Art Gallery, 1987-91; bd. dirs. United Way Ctrl. Md., 1988-91, The Leadership, 1990-93, Empower Balt. Mgmt. Corp., 1995—; bd. dirs. Coll. Bound Found., 1990—, chmn., 1994-96; bd. dirs. Greater Bapt. Com., 1988-96, chmn., 1992-94; mem. bd. sponsors Sellinger Sch. Bus. and Mgmt. Loyola Coll., 1990—; mem. Mayor's Bus. Adv. Coun., 1993—; mem. bd. visitors U. Md. Baltimore County, 1994—; mem. bus. sch. adv. coun. Morgan State U., 1994—. With U.S. Army, 1954-56. Mem. ABA, Md. Bar Assn., Balt.Bar Assn., Am. Law Inst., Am. Bar Found., Md. Bar Found., Elkridge Club, 14 W. Hamilton St. Club, Ctr. Club, Elizabethan Club, Lawyers Round Table. Home: 26 Whitfield Rd Baltimore MD 21210-2928 Office: Piper & Marbury 36 S Charles St Baltimore MD 21201-3020

MILLER, DENNIS, comedian; b. Pitts., Nov. 3, 1953; m. Ali Espley, 1988; 2 children, Holden, Marlon. BA, Point Park Coll. Stand-up comic, cast mem. Saturday Night Live, 1985-91; prodr., writer, host Dennis Miller Show, 1992; exec. prod., writer, host Dennis Miller Live, 1994—. HBO spls. include: Mr. Miller Goes to Washington, 1988, host 13th Annual Young Comedians Show, 1989, (also prodr., writer) Black & White, 1990, They Shoot HBO Specials, Don't They?, 1993; host Freedomfest: Nelson Mandela's 70th Birthday Celebration, The America's Choice Awards, 1990, 43d Annual Primetime Emmy Awards Presentation, 1991; albums include The Off-White Album, 1989; film appearances include: Disclosure, 1994, The Net, 1995, Tales From the Crypt Presents: Bordello of Blood, 1996; TV series include NewsRadio, 1995. Recipient Best Writing Emmy award for a Variety/Music Program for Dennis Miller Live, 1994, 1995. Address: Internat Creative Mgmt Inc 8899 Beverly Blvd Los Angeles CA 90048-2412 also: Internat Creative Mgmt Inc 8942 Wilshire Blvd Beverly Hills CA 90211-1934*

MILLER, DENNIS EDWARD, corporate executive; b. Detroit, Dec. 21, 1951; m. Deborah Ann Keith, Feb. 12, 1977. BS, Austin Peay State U., 1973; MBA, U. South Fla., 1981. CPA. Chief exec. officer Hosp. Corp. of Am., Bennettsville, S.C., 1976-84; div. v.p. Westworld Community Healthcare, Waco, Tex., 1984-86; group v.p. Nat. Healthcare, Inc., Dothan, Ala., 1986-87; COO Healthcare Connections, Brentwood, Tenn., 1988; cons. VHA Physician Svcs., Inc., Dallas, 1988-90; asst. adminstr., CFO Clarksville (Tenn.) Meml. Hosp., 1990; Franklin, Tenn., 1990; sr. v.p., COO Eastside Ventures, Inc., Birmingham, Ala., 1990-93; sr. v.p. Ea. Health System, Inc., Birmingham, 1993—; chmn. Minority Leadership Task Force, Ea. Health System, Inc., 1994-95. Sec. Ala. Health Svcs. Bd.; mem. Literacy Coun. Ala., Ala. Hosp. Assn. State Legis. Com., future directions com.; chmn. Birmingham Regional Healthcare Exec. Forum; chmn. friends of scouting campaign Boy Scouts Am., 1996. Fellow Am. Coll. Healthcare Execs. (chmn diplomate credentials com., Ala. Regent's award for exec. excellence 1995), Hosp. Fin. Mgmt. Assn. (Follmer Bronze Merit award for outstanding svc.); mem. AICPA, Tenn. Soc. CPAs, Ala. Soc. CPAs (chmn. state legis. com.), Ala. Hosp. Assn. (future directions com.), Birmingham C. of C. (chmn. memberhsip com.), Birmingham East Rotary Club (pres., chmn. membership com.), Mensa, Shriners, Masons, Birmingham Touchdown Club, Sigma Chi. Avocations: hunting, fishing, gardening, antique collecting. Office: Ea Health System Inc 48 Medical Park Dr E Birmingham AL 35235-3400

MILLER, DIANE WILMARTH, human resources director; b. Clarinda, Iowa, Mar. 12, 1940; d. Donald and Floy Pauline (Madden) W.; m. Robert Nolen Miller, Aug. 21, 1965; children: Robert Wilmarth, Anne Elizabeth. AA, Colo. Women's Coll., 1960; BBA, U. Iowa, 1962; MA, U. No. Colo., 1994. Cert. tchr., Colo.; vocat. credential, Colo.; cert. sr. profl. in human resources. Sec.-counselor U. S.C., Myrtle Beach AFB, 1968-69; instr. U. S.C., Conway, 1967-69; tchr. bus. Poudre Sch. Dist. R-1, Ft. Collins, Colo., 1970-71; travel cons. United Bank Travel Svc., Greeley, Colo., 1972-74; dir. human resources Aims Community Coll., Greeley, 1984—; instr. part-time Aims Community Coll., Greeley, 1972—. Active 1st Congl. Ch., Greeley. Mem. Coll. Univ. Pers. Assn., Coll. Univ. Pers. Assn. Colo., No. Colo. Human Resources Assn., Soc. Human Resource Mgmt., Philanthropic Ednl. Orgn. (pres. 1988-89), Women's Panhellenic Assn. (pres. 1983-84), Scroll and Fan Club (pres. 1985-86), WTK Club, Questers. Home: 3530 Wagon Trail Pl Greeley CO 80634-3405 Office: Aims Cmty Coll 5401 20th St PO Box 69 Greeley CO 80634-3002

MILLER, DON ROBERT, surgeon; b. Highland, Kans., July 6, 1925; s. Pleasant V. and Lucy Anna (Hammond) M.; m. Geraldine Ellen Nelson, Sept. 6, 1947; children: Don R., Laurie, Todd, Marcia, Kristen, Felicia. A.B., Westminster Coll., 1944; M.D., U. Kans., 1948. Mem. faculty U. Kans., Kansas City, 1957-73; prof. surgery U. Kans., 1970-73; prof. surgery U. Calif. Irvine, 1973-92, prof. emeritus, 1992—, vice chmn., chief dept. surgery, pres. med. staff, 1989-91; dir. surgery Orange County (Calif.) Med. Center, 1973-77. Contbr. articles to profl. jours. Gov. 1988-92. Served with USNR, 1943-45, 50-52. Spl. research fellow Zurich, Switzerland, 1965-66. Fellow A.C.S., Am. Coll. Cardiology; mem. Am. Soc. Univ. Surgeons, Am. Surg. Assn., Soc. Vascular Surgery, Am. Assn. Thoracic Surgery, Am., Central, Western surg. assns., Internat. Cardiovascular Soc., Sigma Xi, Alpha Omega Alpha. Research extracorporeal circulation, myocardial function. Home: 743 Louisiana St Lawrence KS 66044-2339

MILLER, DON WILSON, nuclear engineering educator; b. Westerville, Ohio, Mar. 16, 1942; s. Don Paul and Rachel (Jones) M.; m. Mary Catherine Thompson, June 25, 1966; children: Amy Beth, Stacy Catherine, Paul Wilson Thompson. BS in Physics, Miami U., Oxford, Ohio, 1964, MS in Physics, 1966; MS in Nuclear Engring., Ohio State U., 1970, PhD in Nuclear Engring., 1971. Rsch. assoc. Ohio State U., Columbus, 1966-68, univ. fellow, 1968-69, tchg. assoc., 1969-71, asst. prof. nuclear engring., 1971-74, assoc. prof., 1974-80, chmn. nuclear engring. program, 1977—, prof., 1980—, dir. nuclear reactor lab., 1977—; sec., treas. Cellar Lumber Co., Westerville, Ohio, 1972-84, 85—; cons. Monsanto Rsch. Corp., Miamisburg, Ohio, 1979, NRC, Washington, 1982-84, Scantech. Corp., Santa Fe, 1984-95, Neoprobe Corp., Columbus, 1990, Electric Power Rsch. Inst., Palo Alto, Calif., 1992-94; mem. adv. com. on reactor safeguards, 1995—. Patentee in field; contbr. articles to profl. jours. Mem. Westerville Bd. Edn., 1976-91, pres., 1977-78, 86-88; mem. Ohio Sch. Bd.'s Assn., Columbus, 1976-91; mem. fed. rels. com. Nat. Sch. Bd.'s Assn., Washington, 1984-86. With USAR, 1960-68. Named Tech. Person of Yr. Columbus Tech. Coun., 1979; named to All Region Bd. Ohio Sch. Bd's. Assn., 1981, 86; recipient Coll. of Engring Rsch. award Ohio State U., 1984, Achievement award Mid Ohio Chpt Multiple Sclerosis Soc., 1988. Fellow Am. Nuclear Soc. (chmn. edn. divsn. 1986-87, bd. dirs. 1989-91, chair human factors divsn. 1993-94, v.p./pres. elect 1995, cert. appreciation 1991); mem. IEEE, Am. Soc. Engring. Edn. (chmn. nuclear engring. divsn. 1978-79, Glenn Murphy award 1989), Instrument Soc. Am. (sr. mem.), Nuclear Dept. Heads Orgn. (chmn. 1985-86), Westerville Edn. Assn. (Friend of Edn. award 1992), Rotary (Courtright Cmty. Svc. award 1989), Kiwanis, Hoover Yacht Club, Alpha Nu Sigma (chmn. 1991-93). Avocations: sailing, Am. history, traveling, amateur radio (extra class license). Home: 172 Walnut Ridge Ln Westerville OH 43081-2464 Office: Ohio State U Dept Mech Engring Nuclear Engring Program 206 W 18th Ave Columbus OH 43210-1189

MILLER, DONALD, art critic; b. Pitts., Dec. 21, 1934; s. LeRoy Gatskell and Alyse G. (McFarland) M. B.A., U. Pitts., 1956, M.A., 1975. Art critic Pitts. Post-Gazette, 1956—; instr. Carnegie-Mellon U., Pitts., 1979-80; lectr. Community Coll. Allegheny County, 1973, Westmoreland Mus. Art, 1973; art critic Sta. KDKA-TV, 1970-71. Author: (with others) Organic Vision: The Architecture of Peter Berndtson, 1980 (Merit award Pa. Soc. Architects 1981), Malcolm Parcell Wizard of Moon Lorn, 1985. Contbr. articles to profl. jours., also chpts. to various books. Chmn. Art and Antiques auction, Sta. WQED-TV, 1975. Recipient Golden Quill award Pitts. Press Club, 1980, 87, Forbes medal Ft. Pitt Mus., 1986. Assoc. Artists Pitts. (hon.), 100 Friends of Pitts. Art, Pitts. Bibliophiles, Phi Beta Kappa. Democrat. Office: Pitts Post-Gazette 50 Blvd Of The Allies Pittsburgh PA 15222-1220

MILLER, DONALD EUGENE, minister, educator; b. Dayton, Ohio, Dec. 2, 1929; m. Phyllis Gibbel, Aug. 19, 1956; children: Bryan Daniel, Lisa Kathleen, Bruce David. Student, Manchester Coll., 1947-49; MA, U. Chgo., 1952; postgrad., United Theol. Sem., 1955-56; BD, Bethany Theol. Sem., 1958; PhD, Harvard U., 1962; postgrad., Yale U., 1968-69, Cambridge (Eng.) U., 1975-76. Ordained minister Ch. of the Brethren, 1957. Dir. material aid Brethren Svc. Commn. in Europe, 1952-54; tchr. Madison Twp. High Sch., Trotwood, Ohio, 1954-55; social worker Dayton, 1954-56; tchr. Gregory Sch., Chgo., 1957-58; interim pastor Salem Ch. of the Brethern, Dayton, 1959; assoc. prof. Christian Edn. and Ethics Bethany Theol. Sem., Oak Brook, Ill., 1961-70, prof., 1970-82, dir. grad. studies, 1973-86, Brightbill prof. ministry studies, 1982-86; gen sec. Ch. of the Brethren Gen. Bd., Elgin, Ill., 1986—; lectr. Pastoral Psychotherapy Inst., Park Ridge, Ill., U. Chgo., Princeton Theol. Seminary, Princeton, N.J.; guest tchr. Theol. Coll. No. Nigeria, 1983. Author: A Self Instruction Guide Through Brethren History, 1976, The Wingfooted Wanderer: Conscience and Transcendence, 1977, The Self Study of the Chicago Cluster of Chicago Schools, 1981, Story and Context: An Introduction to Christian Education, 1986, The Gospel and Mother Goose, 1987; (with Warren F. Groff) The Shaping of Modern Christian Thought, 1968; (with Jack L. Seymour) Marking Choices, 1981, Contemporary Approaches to Christian Education, 1982, Theological Approaches to Christian Education, 1990; (with Robert W. Neff and Graydon F. Snyder) Using Biblical Stimulations, vol. 1, 1973, vol. 2, 1975; (with James N. Poling) Foundation for a Practical Theology of Ministry, 1985; designer programs include Edn. for A Shared Ministry, 1976-86, Tng. in a Ministry, 1984; TV host Christianity and the Arts, 1963. Mem. faith and order commn. Nat. Counc. Chs., 1976-81; del. to Russian Orth. Chs., 1967. Fellow Case Study Inst., 1972; rsch. fellow U. Chgo., 1951-52; teaching fellow Harvard U., 1960-61; faculty fellow Am. Assn. Theol. Schs. Faculty, 1968-69. Mem. Assn. for Profl. Edn. for Ministry (editor yearbook 1972, pres. 1976), Assn. Profs. and Researchers in Religious Edn. (pres. 1968), Am. Theol. Soc., Am. Soc. Christian Ethics., Religious Edn. Assn. Office: Ch of the Brethren 1451 Dundee Ave Elgin IL 60120-1674

MILLER, DONALD EUGENE, aerospace electronics executive; b. Providence, Mar. 20, 1947; s. Meyer Samuel and Beatrice (Wattman) M.; m. Deborah Neary Miller, Mar. 14, 1987. BA, Boston U., 1968; JD, U. Pa., 1972. Law clk. Assoc. Justice Alfred H. Joslin Supreme Ct., Providence, 1972-73; prin., lawyer Temkin, Marolla & Zurier, Providence, 1973-81, Temkin & Miller, Ltd., Providence, 1981-91; sr. v.p., gen. counsel The Fairchild Corp., Chantilly, Va., 1991—. Author: (treatise) Buying and Selling a Small Business, 1987. Mem. R.I. Bar Assn., Mass. Bar Assn. Avocations: dog breeding, table tennis. Home: 10704 Riverwood Dr Potomac MD 20854-1332 Office: Fairchild Corp PO Box 10804 300 W Service Rd Chantilly VA 22094

MILLER, DONALD KEITH, venture capitalist, asset management executive; b. Akron, Ohio, Feb. 2, 1932; s. Clinton Raymond and Hazel Elizabeth

(Curl) M.; m. Barbara Dewees Duff, Sept. 25, 1971 (div. 1983); children: Prescott Clinton, Barclay St. John; m. Priscilla Corwith Barker, Sept. 17, 1988. BS, Cornell U., 1954; MBA, Harvard U., 1959. Asst. treas. Chase Manhattan Bank, N.Y.C., 1959-62; asst. to v.p. Electric Bond & Share, N.Y.C., 1962-66; gen. ptnr. G.H. Walker & Co. Inc., N.Y.C., 1966-74; sr. v.p. White Weld & Co., N.Y.C., 1974-77; mng. dir. Blyth Eastman Paine Webber Inc., N.Y.C., 1978-86; chmn. Greylock Fin., N.Y.C., 1987—, Christensen Boyles Corp., Salt Lake City, 1987-95; dir. Layne Christensen, 1995—; chmn., CEO Thomson Adv. Group L.P., Stamford, Conn., 1990-93, vice chmn., 1993-94; pres., CEO PIMCO Inc., 1994—; bd. dirs. PIMCO Advisors L.P., Newport Beach, Calif.; dir. Layne Christensen Co., 1996—; bd. dirs. Fibreboard Corp., Walnut Creek, Calif.; bd. dirs. chmn. audit com. RPM, Inc., Medina, Oho, 1972—, Huffy Corp., Dayton, Ohio, 1988—. 1st lt. U.S. Army, 1954-57. Avocation: tennis, squash. Home: 588 Round Hill Rd Greenwich CT 06831-2724 Office: Greylock Fin 399 Park Ave Fl 28 New York NY 10022-4614

MILLER, DONALD LESESSNE, publishing executive; b. N.Y.C., Jan. 10, 1932; s. John H. and Mamie (Johnson) M.; m. Ann Davie, Aug. 12, 1951 (div. 1981); children: Lynn, Mark; m. Gail Aileen Wallace, June 27, 1981. BA, U. Md., 1967; cert., Harvard Grad. Sch. Bus. Adminstrn., 1969. Enlisted U.S. Army, 1948, advanced through grades to maj., 1966, ret., 1968; spl. asst. to pres., mgr. corp. recruitment Inmont Corp., N.Y.C., 1968-70; v.p. indsl. relations Seatrain Shipbldg. Corp., N.Y.C., 1970-71; dep. asst. sec. def. U.S. Dept. Def., Washington, 1971-73; v.p. personnel mgmt. Columbia U., N.Y.C., 1973-78; dir. personnel devel. and adminstrn. Internat. Paper, N.Y.C., 1978-79; v.p. employee relations Consol. Edison N.Y., N.Y.C., 1979-86, Dow Jones & Co., Inc., N.Y.C., 1986-95; CEO, pub. Out World News, LLC; bd. dirs. Bank of N.Y. and Bank of N.Y. Co., N.Y.C. Author: An Album of Black Americans in the Armed Forces, 1969. Chmn. bd. emeritus Associated Black Charities, N.Y.C., 1982-94; trustee Pace U., 1979—. Decorated Legion of Merit; decorated Commendation Medal; recipient Disting. Civilian Service medal Dept. Def., 1973, Disting. Alumnus award U. Md., 1977. Mem. Alpha Sigma Lambda, Pi Sigma Alpha, Phi Kappa Phi, Alpha Phi Alpha, Sigma Pi Phi. Office: Our World News LLC Two Hopkins Plaza Ste 500 Baltimore MD 21201

MILLER, DONALD MORTON, physiology educator; b. Chgo., July 24, 1930; s. Harry Madison and Anna Loraine (Zeller) M.; 1 son, Tad Michael. A.B. in Zoology, U. Ill., Urbana, 1960, M.A. in Physiology, 1962, Ph.D. (NIH fellow), 1965; NIH postgrad. fellow, UCLA, 1965-66. Insp. Buick Jet div. Gen. Motors Corp., Willow Springs, Ill., 1953-55; sci. asst. Organic Chemistry Lab., U. Ill., 1960-62, counselor residence halls, 1960-63, teaching asst. physiology, 1960-64; mem. faculty So. Ill. U., Carbondale, 1966—, prof. physiology, 1976-94, retired, 1995, vis. prof., 1995; adj. prof. McKendree Coll., Lebanon, Ill., 1986-88, Queensland U. of Tech., Brisbane, Australia, 1989; Damon lectr., 1973-74; lectr. trauma edn. Ill. Hwy. Div., So. Ill. Health Manpower Consortium, Critical Care Nurse Program; judge Ill. Jr. Acad. Sci; vis. instr. Nakajo, Japan, 1992. Contbr. articles to profl. jours. Treas. Jackson County chpt. ARC, 1973-79; active CAP, 1968-79. Served with USAF, 1955-59. USPHS summer grantee, 1962, 73, NIH grantee, 1968-80, NASA grantee, 1973-85, Coll. Sea Grant Program grantee, 1983-88, U.S. Army Med. Rsch. Inst. grantee, 1987-92. Mem. Am. Physiol. Soc., Biophys. Soc., Am. Microscopic Soc., Neurosci. Soc., Am. Soc. Zoologists, N.Y. Acad. Scis., Am. Soc. Photobiology (charter), Am. Soc. Parasitologists (ednl. policies com.), Am. Midwest Conf. of Parasitologists (pres. 1980-81 sec.-treas. 1985-93), Am. Trauma Soc., Sigma Xi (past chpt. pres.), Chi Gamma Iota. Clubs: Elks, Lions. Home: 9 New Swan Lake Rd Murphysboro IL 62966-5539

MILLER, DONALD MUXLOW, accountant, administrator; b. Luverne, Minn., Feb. 21, 1924; s. Henry Clay and Mildred Eva (Muxlow) M.; m. Eunice Jean Gibson, Feb. 19, 1944; children: SueRilla M., Donna Jean Eichten, Patsy Ann Pushee. Student, Metro State, St. Paul, Minn., 1973-84. Lic. pub. acct. Mgr. Hines & Paulus, CPA, Worthington, Minn., 1952-65; commandant Minn. Vets. Home, Mpls., 1965-68; prin. D.M. Miller, Acct., 1968-70, 76-78; asst. sec. Minn. State Senate, St. Paul, 1970-72; comptr. Western Oil Co., Mpls., 1972-76; commr. Dept. Vet. Affairs, State of Minn., St. Paul, 1978-81; prin. D.M. Miller & Assoc., Ltd., Mpls., 1981—; chief exec. officer MARD, Inc., Mpls., 1985-95; v.p. Miller, Micketts & Assocs. Ltd., Mpls., 1993—. Trustee Heart Professorship Found., 1987-91; pres. Legionville Sch. Patrol Camp, Brainerd, Minn., 1963-64; pres. bd. govs. Big Island Vets. Camp, Mpls., 1986-88. 2nd lt. USAAC, 1942-46; 1st lt. USAF, 1951-52. Recipient Volunteer of the Year award Kidney Found., 1975. Mem. VFW, Nat. Soc. Pub. Accts., Minn. Assn. Pub. Accts., Nat. Assn. State Vets. Homes (hon. life mem., reg. v.p. 1967-68), Nat. Assn. State Dirs. Vets Affairs (reg. v.p. 1978-79), Minn. Gaming Assn. (exec. sec. 1987-92), Am. Legion (hon life mem., comdr. Minn. 1962-63, com. chmn. 1980-84, pres. Minn. Found. Bd. 1990-91), Masons, Shriners. Presbyterian. Avocation: golf. Office: Miller Micketts & Assocs Ltd 9033 Lyndale Ave S Ste 201 Minneapolis MN 55420-3537

MILLER, DONALD ROSS, management consultant; b. Huntington, N.Y., Aug. 5, 1927; s. George Everett and Ethel May (Ross) M.; m. Constance Higgins, 1948 (div. 1955); children: Donald Ross Jr., Cynthia Lynn, Candace Lee; m. Janet Heyman Behr, Apr. 15, 1965; children: Jeffrey Lawrence, Wendy Lorraine. BS/BEA, MIT, 1950. Cert. mgmt. cons. Inst. of Mgmt. Cons. Staff engr. Stop & Shop, Inc., Boston, 1950-56; v.p., dir. Cresap, McCormick and Paget, Inc., N.Y.C., 1956-76; mng. dir. Donald R. Miller Mgmt. Cons., Forest Hills, N.Y., 1977—; bd. dirs. Nash Finch Co., Mpls., chmn. bd. dirs., 1995—; bd. dirs. Michael Anthony Jewelers, Inc., Mt. Vernon, N.Y. Author: Management Practices Manual, 3 vols., 1963, (booklet) Management of Managerial Resources, 1969. Bd. dirs. Queens Mus. Art, Flushing, N.Y., 1982-93, pres., 1988-92; pres. Lexington House, Forest Hills, 1984—. With U.S. Maritime Svc., 1945-46, ETO, U.S. Army, 1946-48. Mem. Nat. Assn. Corp. Dirs., Inst. Mgmt. Cons. (cert. com. 1986—), Sky Club. Episcopal. Avocations: tennis, reading. Home: 68-10 108th St Forest Hills NY 11375-3367 Office: PO Box 649 Forest Hills NY 11375-0649

MILLER, DONNA PAT, library administrator, consultant; b. Lindale, Tex., Dec. 13, 1948; d. Donald Edward and Patsy Ruth (Dykes) Pool; m. James D. Miller, Aug. 17, 1991; children: James Jr., John, Julie, Jaynie. BS in Music, Tex. Woman's U., 1971, MA in Music, 1976; MLS, U. North Tex., 1987. Cert. music and learning resources tchr. Band dir. Grapevine (Tex.) Mid. Sch., 1971-77; pvt. music tchr. Mesquite, Tex., 1978-79; band dir. T.W. Browne Mid. Sch., Dallas, 1979-84, Vanston Mid. Sch., Mesquite, 1984-86; elem. libr. McKenzie Elem. Sch., Mesquite, 1986-90, Reinhardt Elem. Sch., Dallas, 1990-91, Range Elem. Sch., Mesquite, 1991-92; dir. libr. svcs. Mesquite Ind. Sch. Dist., 1992-95; libr. dir. Craig-Moffat County Pub. Libr., Craig, Colo., 1995—; adj. prof. Tex. Woman's U., Denton, 1993—; mem. sci. adv. bd. Gale Rsch., Inc., Detroit, 1993—; cons. Region V Edn. Svc. Ctr., Beaumont, Tex., 1994—. Author: Developing an Integrated Libr. Program Reviewer Booklist Mag., 1986—, The Book Report Mag., 1992—; contbr. articles to mags. Mem. ALA, ASCD, Tex. Libr. Assn., Phi Delta Kappa, Beta Phi Mu. Avocations: running, reading, writing, music. Office: Craig-Moffat County Libr 570 Green St Craig CO 81625

MILLER, DOROTHY ANNE SMITH, cytogenetics educator; b. N.Y.C., Oct. 20, 1931; d. John Philip and Anna Elizabeth (Hellberg) Smith; m. Orlando Jack Miller, July 10, 1954; children: Richard L., Cynthia K., Karen A. BA in Chemistry magna cum laude, Wilson Coll., Chambersburg, Pa., 1952; PhD in Biochemistry, Yale U., 1957. Rsch. assoc. dept. ob-gyn Columbia U., N.Y.C., 1964-72, from rsch. assoc. to asst. prof. dept. human genetics-devel., 1973-85; prof. depts. molecular biology and genetics and pathology Wayne State U., Detroit, 1985-94, prof. dept. pathology, 1985—, prof. Ctr. for Molecular Medicine and Genetics, 1994—; vis. scientist clin. and population cytogenetics unit Med. Rsch. Coun., Edinburgh, Scotland, 1983-84; vis. prof. dept. genetics and molecular biology U. la Sapienza, Rome, 1988; vis. disting. fellow La Trobe U., Melbourne, Australia, 1992. Contbr. numerous articles to sci. jours. Grantee March of Dimes Birth Defects Found., 1974-93, NSF, 1983-84. Mem. Am. Soc. Human Genetics, Genetics Soc. Am., Genetics Soc. Australia, Phi Beta Kappa. Presbyterian. Home: 1915 Stonycroft Ln Bloomfield Hills MI 48304-2339 Office: Wayne State U 540 E Canfield St Detroit MI 48201-1928

MILLER, DOROTHY ELOISE, education educator; b. Ft. Pierce, Fla., Apr. 13, 1944; d. Robert Foy and Aline (Mahon) Wilkes. BS in Edn., Bloomsburg U., 1966, MEd, 1969; MLA, Johns Hopkins U., 1978; EdD, Columbia U., 1991. Tchr. Cen. Dauphin East High Sch., Harrisburg, Pa., 1966-68, Aberdeen (Md.) High Sch., 1968-69; asst. dean of coll., prof. Harford C. C., Bel Air, Md., 1969—; owner Ideas by Design, 1995—; mem. accreditation team Mid. States Commn., 1995, 96. Editor: Renewing the American Community Colleges, 1984; contbr. articles to profl. jours. Pres. Harlan Sq. Condominium Assn., Bel Air, 1982, 90—, Md. internat. divsn. St. Petersburg Sister State Com., 1993—; edn. liaison AAUW, Harford County, Md., 1982-92; cen. com. mem. Rep. Party, Harford County, 1974-78; crusade co-chair Am. Cancer Soc., Harford County, 1976-78; mem. faculty adv. com. Md. Higher Edn. Commn., 1993—; mem. people's adv. coun. Harford County Coun., 1994—. Recipient Nat. Tchg. Excellence award Nat. Inst. for Staff and Orgn. Devel., U. Tex.-Austin, 1992. Charter mem. Nat. Mus. Women in the Arts. Republican. Methodist. Avocations: skiing, swimming, reading, image consulting, interior design, writing, travel. Office: Harford Community Coll 401 Thomas Run Rd Bel Air MD 21015-1627

MILLER, DOUGLAS ANDREW, lawyer; b. Chgo., May 10, 1959; s. Walter William and Jean (Johnson) M.; m. Birgitte Jorgensen, Aug. 4, 1984. BS, Boston Coll., 1981; JD, Ill. Inst. Tech. Chgo., 1986. Bar: Fed. Trial, Ill., U.S. Dist. Ct. (no. dist.) Ill. Legal asst. Lupel & Amari, Chgo., 1984-86; assoc. Bresnahan, Garvey, O'Halloran & Colman, Chgo., 1986-90, Williams & Montgomery, Ltd., Chgo., 1990—. Contbr. articles to profl. jours. Mem. ABA, Ill. State Bar Assn. (civil practice sect., torts sect.), Chgo. Bar Assn. (vice-chmn. bench and bar com., trial techniques sect., ins. law sect.), Ill. Assn. of Def. Trial Counsel. Avocation: distance running. Office: Williams & Montgomery Ltd 20 N Wacker Dr Ste 2100 Chicago IL 60606-3003

MILLER, DUANE KING, health and beauty care company executive; b. N.Y.C., Mar. 1, 1931; s. Henry Charles and Helen Marion (King) M.; A.B. in Econs. and Fin., NYU, 1951; m. Nancy L. Longley, June 6, 1954; children—Cheryl L., Duane L. Vice pres. mktg. Warner-Chilcott div. Warner Lambert Co., Morris Plains, N.J., 1970-72, pres. div., 1973-77, exec. v.p. Am. Optical div. and pres. Am. Optical Internat. div., Southbridge, Mass., 1978; pres. biol. and proprietary products divs., v.p. Revlon Health Care Group, Revlon Corp., Tuckahoe, N.Y., 1978-80, pres. ethical, proprietary and vision care divs., 1981-82, corp. v.p. parent co., 1982, pres. Revlon Health Care Group, 1983-92, corp. exec. v.p. parent co., 1984-92, pres. Revlon Health Beauty Care and Internat. Group, 1988-92, ret., 1992; pres. DKL Properties, health care cons. Promedex Techs., 1992—. Mem. Republican Nat. Com. Mem. Am. Mgmt. Assn., Am. Mktg. Assn. (pres. N.J. chpt. 1967-68), Sales Exec. Club N.Y. Clubs: Princeton N.Y.; Cripple Creek (Del.) Golf; Masons, Shriners. Author: (with others) Marketing Planning for Chief Executives and Planners, 1966. Home: 8 Western Dr Colts Neck NJ 07722-1271 Office: 1 Bethany Rd Ste 44 Hazlet NJ 07730-1662

MILLER, DWIGHT RICHARD, cosmetologist, corporate executive, hair designer; b. Johnstown, Pa., Jan. 24, 1943. Grad., Comer & Doran Sch., San Diego; DSci. (hon.), London Inst. for Applied Rsch., 1973. Cert. aromatherapist; lic. cosmetologist., instr.; Brit. Mastercraftsman. Styles dir. Marinello-Comer, Hollywood, Calif., 1965-67; expert Pivot Point Internat., Chgo., 1967-68; styles dir. Lapins, L.A., 1969; dir. Redken, L.A., 1970, Vidal Sassoon, London, 1971-74; world amb. Pivot Point, New Zealand and Australia, 1974-75; internat. artistic dir. Pivot Point, Chgo., 1975-78; internat. dir., co-founder Hair Artists Inst. & Registry, 1978-81; internat. artistic dir. Zotos Internat., Darien, Conn., 1981-87, Matrix Essentials, Inc., Solon, Ohio, 1987-92; bd. dirs., v.p. creative, internat. artistic dir. Anasazi Exclusive Salon Products, Inc., Dubuque, Iowa, 1992—; judge hairdressing competitions including Norwegian Masters, Australian Nat. Championships; pres. Intercrimpers, London, 1974-75. Author: Sculptic Cutting Pivot Point 75, Prismatics, 1983; prod., dir. 15 documentaries, numerous tech. and industry videos; contbr. articles, photographs to popular mags.; developer several profl. product lines including Vidal Sassoon-London, Design Freedom, Bain de Terre, Ultra Bond, Vavoom!, Systeme Biolage, Anasazi. With USMC, 1960-64. Named Artistic Dir. Yr. Am. Salon mag.; presented with Order of White Elephant, 1976; recipient London Gold Cup for Best Presentation London Beauty Festival, 1982, Dr. Everett G. McDonough award for Excellence in Permanent Waving, World Master award Art and Fashion Group, 1992. Mem. Cercle des Arts et Techniques de la Coiffure, Intercoiffure, Haute Coiffure Franchaise, Soc. Cosmetic Chemists, Hair Artists Great Britain, Internat. Assn. Trichogists, Nat. Cosmetologists Assn. (HairAmerica), Am. Soc. Phytotherapy and Aromatherapy, HairChicago (hon.), Art and Fashion Group (pres. 1993), 'Dressers MC (pres. 1990—), London's Alternative Hair Club (patron). Address: 13900 Watt Rd Novelty OH 44072-9741

MILLER, E. HITE, banker, holding company executive. Pres. First Citizens Bancorp of S.C., Columbia, First Citizens Bank TR of S.C., Columbia; chmn., CEO First Citizens Bank of S.C. (now First Citizens Bancorporation), Columbia. Office: First Citizens Bancorp 1230 Main St Columbia SC 29201-3213*

MILLER, E. WILLARD, geography educator; b. Turkey City, Pa., May 17, 1915; s. Archie Howard and Tessie Bernella (Master) M.; m. Ruby Skinner, June 27, 1941. MA, U. Nebr., 1939; PhD, Ohio State U., 1942. Instr. Ohio State U., 1941-43; asst. prof. geography and geology Western Res. U., 1943-44; asso. prof. geography Pa. State U., University Park, 1945-49; prof. Pa. State U., 1949—, chief div. geography, 1945-53, head dept. geography, 1954-63; asst. dean for resident instrn. Coll. Earth and Mineral Scis., 1964-72, asst. dean, 1972-80, assoc. dean for resident instrn. and continuing edn., 1967-69; dir. Acad. Year Inst., Earth Scis., NSF, 1967-71; geographer OSS, Washington, 1944-45; spl. research on Arctic environ. problems for Q.M. Gen., U.S. Army, 1947-50; geographic adviser Thomas Y. Crowell Co., hon. chmn. Nat Coun. Geog. Edn. (Disting. Mentor award, 1995) 21st Century Endowment Fund, 1994—. Author: Careers in Geography, 1948 (rev. 1955), (with others) The World's Nations: An Economic and Regional Geography, 1958, A Geography of Manufacturing, 1962, An Economic Atlas of Pennsylvania, 1964, (with G. Langdon) Exploring Earth Environments: A World Geography, 1964, Energy Resources of the United States, 1968, Mineral Resources of the United States, 1968, A Geography of Industrial Location, 1970, A Socio-Economic Atlas of Pennsylvania, 1974, Manufacturing: A Study of Industrial Location, 1977, Industrial Location: A Bibliography, 1978, Physical Geography: Earth Systems and Human Interactions, 1985, Pennsylvania: A Keystone to Progress, 1986, (with Ruby M. Miller) During Business In and With Latin America, 1987, (with Ruby M. Miller) Economic, Political and Regional Aspects of the World's Energy Problems, 1979, The Third World: Natural Resources, Economics, Politics and Social Conditions, 1981, Africa: A Bibliography on the Third World, 1981, The American Coal Industry: Economic, Political and Environmental Aspects, 1980, Manufacturing in Nonmetropolitan Pennsylvania, 1980; (with Ruby M. Miller) Latin America: A Bibliography on the Third World, 1982, South America: A Bibliography in the Third World, 1982, Middle America: A Bibliography on the Third World, 1982, Industrial Location and Planning: Theory, Models and Factors of Localization: A Bibliography, 1984, Industrial Location and Planning: Localization, Growth and Organization: A Bibliography, 1984, Industrial Location and Planning: Regions and Countries: A Bibliography, 1984; Pennsylvania: Architecture and Culture: A Bibliography, 1985, United States' Foreign Relation: Western Europe, 1987, United States' Foreign Relations: Soviet Union and Eastern Europe, 1987, United States' Foreign Relations: United States and Canada, 1987, Industrial Parks, Export Processing Zones, and Enterprise Zones: A Bibliography, 1987, The 1976 Presidential Elections: A Bibliography, 1987, The 1980 Presidential Election: A Bibliography, 1987, The 1984 Presidential Election: A Bibliography, 1987, The Third World: Economic Development, 1988, The Third World: Government and Political Relations, Social Conditions, Population, Urbanization, Education, and Communications, 1988, The Third World: Economic Activities, 1988, Natural Resources and Commerical Policy, 1988, others; editl. dir.: Earth and Mineral Scis. Bull, 1967-69; editor: (with S.K. Majumdar) Pennsylvania Coal: Resources, Technology and Utilization, 1983, Hazardous and Toxic Wastes: Management and Health Effects, 1984, Solid and Liquid Wastes: Managment Methods and Socioeconomic Considerations, 1984, Management of Radioactive Materials and Wastes: Issues and Progress, 1985, Environmental Consequences of Energy Production, 1987, Ecology and Restoration of the Delaware River Basin, 1988, A Geography of Pennsylvania, 1995; (with S.K. Majumdar, R.F. Schmalz) Management of Hazardous Materials and Wastes: Treatment, Minimization and Environmental Impacts, 1989, (with Ruby M. Miller) Environmental Hazards: Air Pollution, 1989, (with S.K. Majumdar and R.R. Parizek) Water Resources in Pennsylvania, 1990, (with S.K. Majumdar and R.F. Schmalz) Environmental Radon, 1990; (with Ruby M. Miller) Environmental Hazards: Radioactive Wastes and Materials, 1990, Environmental Hazards: Toxic Materials and Hazardous Wastes, 1991; (with S.K. Majumdar, L.M. Rosenfeld, P.A. Rubba and R.F. Schmalz) Science Education in the United States, Issues, Crises and Priorities, 1991; (with S.K. Majumdar and John Cahir) Air Pollution, 1991, (with G. Forbes, R.F. Schmalz and S.K. Majumdar) Natural and Technological Disasters, 1992, (with S.K. Majumdar, L.S. Kalkstein, B.M. Yarnal, and L.M. Rosenfeld) Global Climatic Change: Implications Challenges and Mitigation Measures, 1992, (with Ruby M. Miller) Water: Quality and Availability, 1993, (with S.K. Majumdar, L.S. Kalkstein, B.M. Yarnal and L.M. Rosenfeld) Global Climatic Change: Implications, Challenges and Mitigation Measures, 1992, (with S.K. Majumdar et al) Conservation and Resource Management, 1993, (with S.K. Majumdar, D.E. Baker, E.K. Brown, J.R. Pratt and R.F. Schmaltz) Conservation and Resource Management, 1993, (with Ruby M. Miller) Energy and American Society, 1993, (with others) Biological Diversity: Problems and Challenges, 1994, (with Miller) America's International Trade, 1995; assoc. editor The Pennsylvania Geographer, Jour. of Pa. Acad. Scis.; media materials editor: Jour. Geography, 1981-84; contbg. editor: Producers Monthly Mag; editor Middle States Geographer, 1991-94; contbr. articles to sci. jours. Recipient cert. of merit from OSS, Whitbeck award Nat. Coun. Geog. Edn., 1950, Pa. Gov.'s citation for Contbn. to Commonwealth, 1975, Pa. Dept. Commerce Sec.'s Meritorious Svcs. award, 1975, Disting. Alumnus Clarion U., 1989; named Hon. Alumnus Pa. State U., 1991. Fellow AAAS, Am. Geog. Soc., Explorers Club, Nat. Coun. Geog. Edn.; mem. Am. Inst. Mining, Metall. and Petroleum Engrs., Am. Soc. Profl. Geographers (sec, 1945-48, pres. 1948), Assn. Am. Geographers (Honors award 1990), Pa. Geog. Soc. (pres. 1962-63, dir. 1965—, Meritorious Service award 1974, 84, 93), Pa. Acad. Sci. (pres. 1966-68, editorial bd. Procs. 1985—, Spl. Services award 1976, 87, Appreciation award 1992), Obelisk Soc., Mount Nittany Soc. of Pa. State U., Pres.'s Club of Pa. State U., George Atherton Soc. Pa. State U., Sigma Xi, Pi Gamma Mu, Beta Gamma Sigma. Home: 845 Outer Dr State College PA 16801-8234

MILLER, EDMOND TROWBRIDGE, civil engineer, educator, consultant; b. Pitts., Dec. 9, 1933; s. George Ellsworth and Billie Sue (Watson) M.; m. Nancy Lee Cooper, July 21, 1956; children: Carol Anne, Nancy Ruth, Laura Elizabeth. B.C.E., Ga. Inst. Tech., 1955, M.S.C.E., 1957; C.E., MIT, 1963; Ph.D., Tex. A&M U., 1967. Registered profl. engr., Ala., Fla. Asst. prof. civil engring. U. Ala., Tuscaloosa, 1963-64, assoc. prof., 1967-71, prof., 1971-75; v.p. William S. Pollard Cons., Memphis, 1976-77; chmn. dept. civil engring. U. Louisville, 1977-81; prof. U. Ala., Birmingham, 1981-96, chmn. dept. civil engring., 1981-90, interim dean Sch. Engring., 1984; ret., 1996; instr. civil engring. Tex. A&M U., 1964-67. Served to capt. C.E. AUS, 1956-57. Automotive Safety Found. fellow, 1964-65; recipient Outstanding Achievement in Edn. award Ky. Soc. Profl. Engrs., 1980. Fellow ASCE (dist. 9 council 1978-80), Inst. Transp. Engrs.; mem. Am. Soc. Engring. Edn., Transp. Research Bd., Sigma Xi, Phi Kappa Phi, Tau Beta Pi, Chi Epsilon. Christian Scientist. Home: 2566 Dalton Dr Pelham AL 35124-1448 Mailing Address: PO Box 158 Pelham AL 35124-0158

MILLER, EDMUND KENNETH, retired electrical engineer, educator; b. Milw., Dec. 24, 1935; s. Edmund William and Viola Louise (Ludwig) M.; m. Patricia Ann Denn, Aug. 23, 1958; children: Kerry Ann, Mark Christopher. BSEE, Mich. Tech. U., 1957; MS in Nuclear Engring., U. Mich., 1958, MSEE, 1961, PhD in Elec. Engring., 1965. Rsch. assoc. U. Mich., Ann Arbor, 1965-68; sr. scientist MB Assocs., San Ramon, Calif., 1968-71; group leader engring. rsch. div. Lawrence Livermore Lab., Livermore, Calif., 1971-78, leader engring. rsch. div., 1978-83, leader nuclear energy systems div., 1983-85; regents prof. elect. and computer engring. U. Kans., 1985-87; mgr. electromagnetics Rockwell Sci. Ctr., Thousand Oaks, Calif., 1987-88; dir. electromagnetics rsch. operation Gen. Rsch. Corp., Santa Barbara, Calif., 1988-89; group leader MEE div. Los Alamos (N.Mex.) Nat. Lab., 1989-93, ret., 1993. Stocker vis. prof. of elec. and computer engring., Ohio U., Athens, 1994-95. Editor: Time Domain Measurements in Electromagnets, 1986; past assoc. editor Radio Sci.; assoc. editor IEEE Potentials, 1985-91, editor, 1992—; assoc. editor IEEE AP-S mag.; co-editor (with L. Medgyesi-Mitschang and E.H. Newman) Computational Electromagnetics, 1991; editorial bd. Internat. Jour. Numerical Modeling, 1990—, Computer Applications in Engring. Edn., 1992—; editor: Jour. Electromagnetic Waves and Applications, 1991—, Jour. of Applied Computational Electromagnetics Soc., IEEE Computer Soc. Mag. Computational Sci. and Engring., 1994—; contbr. 100 articles to profl. jours. Singer Lyra Male Chorus, Ann Arbor, Mich., 1966-68, Livermore Civic Chorus, 1969-71. Fellow IEEE (mem. press. bd. 1991—), mem. Am. Phys. Soc., Optical Soc. Am., Acoustical Soc. Am., Am. Soc. Engring. Edn., Electromagnetics Soc. (past bd. dirs.) Internat. Sci. Radio Union (past chmn. U.S. Commn. A), Applied Computational Electromagnetics Soc. (past pres.). Home: 3225 Calle Celestial Santa Fe NM 87501

MILLER, EDWARD BOONE, lawyer; b. Milw., Mar. 26, 1922; s. Edward A. and Myra (Munsert) M.; m. Anne Harmon Chase Phillips, Feb. 14, 1969; children by previous marriage: Barbara Miller Anderson, Ellen Miller Gerkens, Elizabeth Miller Lawhun, Thomas; stepchildren: T. Christopher Phillips, Sarah Phillips Parkhill. B.A., U. Wis., 1942, LL.B., 1947; student, Harvard Bus. Sch., 1942-43. Bar: Wis. 1947, Ill. 1948. With firm Pope, Ballard, Shepard & Fowle, Chgo., 1947-51, 52-70, ptnr., 1953-70, 75-93, mng. partner, 1979-82, chmn. labor and employment law dept., 1975-76, 87-88, 90-91; of counsel Seyfarth, Shaw, Fairweather, and Geraldson, Chgo., 1994—; mem. adv. com. Ctr. for Labor Mgmt. Dispute Resolution, Stetson U., 1984—, Inst. Indsl. Rels., Loyola U., 1987-91, Kent Pub. Employee Labor Rels. Conf., 1988—, Ill. Ednl. Labor Rels. Bd., 1988—; exec. asst. to industry mems. Regional Wage Stblzn. Bd., Chgo., 1951-52, industry mem., 1952; chmn. NLRB, Washington, 1970-74; mem. panel of labor law experts Commerce Clearing House, 1987—; dir. Chgo. Wheel & Mfg. Co., 1965-70, 75-88, Andes Candies, Inc., 1965-68, 75-80. Mem. Gov. Ill. Commn. Labor-Mgmt. Policies for Pub. Employees, 1966-67; chmn. Midwest Pension Conf., 1960-61; mem. labor relations com. Ill. C. of C., 1953-70; bd. dirs. Am. Found. Continuing Edn., 1960-69. Served to lt. USNR, 1943-46. Mem. ABA (NLRB practice and procedures com., internat. labor law com.), Ill. Bar Assn., Wis. Bar Assn., Chgo. Assn. Commerce and Industry (chmn. labor relations com. 1980-86, bd. dirs. 1987—), Am. Employment Law Coun. (mem. adv. bd. 1995—), Order of Coif. Republican. Congregationalist. Clubs: Legal (Chgo.), Law (Chgo.), Cliff Dwellers (Chgo.); North Shore Country (curling mem.). Home: 632 Chatham Rd Glenview IL 60025-4402 Office: 55 E Monroe St Chicago IL 60603-5702

MILLER, EDWARD DANIEL, banker; b. 1940; married. Grad., Pace U. With Mfrs. Hanover Trust Co., N.Y.C., 1959—, former sr. v.p. consumer credit, sr. v.p., dep. gen. mgr. br. banking group, 1980-82, exec. v.p., head retail banking div., 1982-85, sector exec. v.p. retail banking, 1985-88; vice chmn. Mfrs. Hanover Corp. and Mfrs. Hanover Trust Co., 1988—; vice chmn. Chem. Banking Corp., N.Y.C., 1992-93, pres., 1994—, also bd. dirs.; sr. vice chmn., bd. dirs. Chase Manhattan Corp., 1996—. Office: Chase Manhattan Corp 270 Park Ave New York NY 10000

MILLER, EDWARD DORING, JR., anesthesiologist; b. Rochester, N.Y., Feb. 1, 1943; s. Edward D. and Natalie (Sidam) M.; m. Leslie Coombs, June 15, 1968 (dec. Apr. 1987); children: Sara Davenport, Katherine Coombs; m. Lynne Perkins, Apr. 30, 1988. AB, Ohio Wesleyan U., 1964; MD, U. Rochester, 1968. Diplomate Am. Bd. Anesthesiology, Am. Coll. Anesthesiology; cert. critical care medicine. Surg. intern University Hosp., Boston, 1968-69; anesthesia resident Peter Bent Brigham Hosp., Boston, 1969-71; fellow in physiology Harvard Med. Sch., Boston, 1971-73; dir. anesthesia research Brooke Army Med. Ctr., Ft. Sam Houston, Tex., 1973-75; asst. prof. anesthesiology U. Va. Med. Ctr., Charlottesville, Va., 1975-79, assoc. prof. anesthesiology, 1979-82, prof. anesthesiology, 1982-83, prof. anesthesiology, surgery, 1983-86; E.M. Papper prof. anesthesiology, chmn. dept. Columbia U. Coll. Physicians and Surgeons, N.Y.C., 1986-94; Mark C. Rogers prof., chmn. dept. anesthesiology Johns Hopkins U., Balt., 1994-96, interim dean med. faculty, v.p. medicine Sch. Medicine, 1996—; sr. scientist physiology, pharmacology Hosp. Necker, Paris, 1981-82; examiner Am. Bd. Anesthesiology; v.p. clin. faculty U. Va., 1983-85, pres. 1985-86. Editor Anesthesia and Analgesia, 1982-92; contbr. numerous articles to profl. jours. Pres. Barracks-Rugby-Preston Neighborhoods, Va., 1977-79; vestry Christ Episc. Ch., Va., 1985-86. Served to maj. M.C., U.S. Army, 1973-75. Recipient Research Career Devel. award Nat. Inst. Gen. Med. Scis., 1978-83; NIH grantee, 1977-87, Inst. Nat. de la Recherche Medicale grantee, 1981-82. Mem. Assn. U. Anesthetists (sec. 1984-87), Am. Soc. Anesthesiologists, Am. Physiol. Soc., Internat. Anesthesia Research Soc. (trustee 1988—), Soc. Critical Care Medicine, Soc. Cardiovascular Anesthesiologists, Assn. Univ. Anesthesiologists (pres. 1990-92), Found. for Anesthesia Edn. and Rsch. (bd. dirs. 1986—), Up Med. Bd. Presbyn. Hosp. Home: 15 Meadow Rd Baltimore MD 21212-1022 Office: Johns Hopkins U Sch Med Blalock #1415 600 N Wolfe St Baltimore MD 21287-4965

MILLER, ELDON EARL, corporate business publications consultant, retired manufacturing company executive; b. Hutchinson, Kans., Jan. 1, 1919; s. Robert Dewalt and Martha Velva (Stauffer) M.; m. Margaret Borgsdorf, Mar. 26, 1950. B.A., UCLA, 1941. Formerly newspaper editor, mag. editor, pub. relations cons., polit. writer; with Purex Industries, Inc., Lakewood, Calif., 1950-85; asst. sec. Purex Industries, Inc., 1971-72, v.p. corp. relations, 1972-85, cons. bus. publs., corp. relations, 1985—. Republican. Presbyterian. Home and Office: 26685 Westhaven Dr Laguna Hills CA 92653-5767

MILLER, ELLIOTT CAIRNS, retired bank executive, lawyer; b. Cambridge, Mass., May 4, 1934; s. James Wilkinson and Mary Elliott (Cairns) M.; m. Mary Killion, July 2, 1960; children: Jonathan Vaill, Stephen Killion. Grad., Matthew Whaley Sch., Williamsburg, Va., 1952; A.B., Harvard Coll., 1956; J.D., U. Mich., 1961; LL.M., Boston U., 1970. Bar: Conn. 1962. Assoc. Robinson & Cole, Hartford, Conn., 1961-66, ptnr., 1967-72; v.p., counsel Soc. for Savs., Hartford, Conn., 1972-73, sr. v.p., 1973-78, exec. v.p., 1978, pres., chief exec. officer, dir., 1979-90; pres., chief exec. officer Soc. for Savs. Bancorp Inc., 1987-90; bd. dirs. nat. council Savs. Inst., Washington, 1984-88. Trustee, chmn. Kingswood-Oxford Sch., West Hartford, 1977-87; trustee Coordinating Coun. on Founds., 1987-90; bd. dirs. Downtown Coun., Hartford, 1975-90; trustee Greater Hartford Arts Coun., 1980-88; trustee Wadsworth Atheneum, 1990—; trustee Hartford Stage Co., 1973-85, hon. trustee, 1985—; corporator Hartford Hosp., Mt. Sinai Hosp., Inst. of Living, Hartford Pub. Libr. With U.S. Army, 1956-58. Mem. Conn. Bar Assn. Home: 4 Stratford Rd West Hartford CT 06117-2838

MILLER, EMANUEL, retired lawyer, banker; b. N.Y.C., Jan. 22, 1917; s. Mayer and Helen (Stein) M.; m. Ruth Marcus, Jan. 3, 1942; children—Linda Alice, Henry Ward, Marjorie Joan. B.A., Bklyn. Coll., 1937; LL.B., St. Lawrence U., Bklyn., 1941. Bar: N.Y. bar 1942. With Harold W. Zeamans, Flushing, N.Y., 1950-51; firm White & Case, N.Y.C., 1951-53; with Bankers Trust Co., N.Y.C., 1953-89; v.p., counsel Bankers Trust Co., 1976-89, ret., dir. various affiliates; lectr. in field. Contbr. legal publs. Served with U.S. Army, 1942-45. Mem. Am., N.Y. State bar assns., Iota Theta. Club: Indian Spring Golf (Boynton Beach, Fla.). Home: 6370 Evian Pl Boynton Beach FL 33437-4909 *Never let the poetry of evil doctrine or thought, regardless of its literary artistry and excellence, debase our staunch adherence to our principles of righteousness, morality, justice and love of America.*

MILLER, EMILIE F., former state senator; b. Chgo., Aug. 11, 1936; d. Bruno C. and Etta M. (Senese) Feiza; m. Dean E. Miller; children: Desireé M., Edward C. BS in Bus. Adminstrn., Drake U., 1958. Asst. buyer Jordan Marsh Co., Boston, 1958-60, Carson, Pirie, Scott & Co., Chgo., 1960-62; dept. mgr., asst. buyer Woodward & Lothrop, Washington, 1962-64; state labor coord. Robb Davis Daliles Joint Campaign; legis. aide Senator Adelard Brandt, Va., 1980-83; fin. dir. Saslaw for Congress, 1984; legis. cons. Va. Fedn. Bus. Profl. Women, 1986-87; senator Va. Gen. Assembly, Richmond, 1988-92; apptd. by Gov. Wilder to bd. dirs. Innovative Tech. Authority, 1992, Ctr. for Innovative Tech., 1992; cons., 1992—; mem. Edn. and Health com., Gen. Laws com., Local Gov. com., Rehab. and Social Scis. com.; bus. tng. seminars Moscow, Nizhny Novgorod, Russia, 1993, Novgorod, St. Petersburg, 1995; cons. in field. Guest editorial writer No. Va. Sun, 1981; host, producer weekly TV program, Channel 61. Mem. State Ctrl. Com. Dem. Party Va., Richmond, 1974-92, Fairfax County Dem. Com., 1968—, Presdl. Inaugural Com., 1977, 1992 Dem. Nat. Platform Com., Va. mem. on temp. coms., Dem. Adv. Com. Robb-Spong Commn., 1978-79; founder, chmn. Va. Assoc. Dem. County and City Chmn., 1976-80, Fairfax County Dem. Com., 1976-80; security supr. 1980 Dem. Nat. Conv.; v.p. Va. Fedn. Dem. Women, 1992—; bd. dirs. Stop Child Abuse Now, 1988, Ctr. Innovative Tech., 1992-94, Ct. Apptd. Spl. Advs., 1993—; mem. nat. alumni bd. J.A. Achievement, BRAVO adv. com. for the first Gov.'s Awards for Arts in Va., 1979-80; lay tchr. St. Ambrose Cath. Ch., 1963-80; del. to White House Conf. on Children, 1970; chmn. Va. Coalition for Mentally Disturbed, 1992-94. Recipient Disting. Grad. award Jr. Achievement, 1973, Woman of Achievement award Fairfax (Va.) Bd. Suprs. and Fairfax County Commn. for Women, 1982, Cmty. Svc. award Friends of Victims Assistance Network, 1988, Founders award Fairfax County Coun. of Arts, 1989, Mental Health Assn. of Northern Va. Warren Stambaugh award, 1991, Ann. Svc. award Va. Assn. for Marriage and Family Therapy, 1991, Psychology Soc. of Washington Cmty. Svc. award, 1993. Mem. NOW, Nat. Mus. Women in the Arts, Va. Assn. Female Execs. (mem. adv. bd., bd. dirs., v.p. 1992—), Va. Assn. Cmty. Svc. Bds. (chmn. 1980-82), North Va. Assn. Cmty. Bds. (chmn. 1978-79), Fairfax County Coun. Arts (v.p. 1980—, mem. exec. com. internat. children's festival, Founders award 1989), Fairfax County C. of C. (mem. legis. com.), Greater Merrifield Bus. and Profl. Assn., Mental Health Assn. No.Va. (bd. dirs.), Ctrl. Fairfax C. of C., Bus. and Profl. Women's Fedn. Va., Mantua Citizen's Assn. (mem. exec. bd.), Tower Club (Fairfax), Bus. and Profl. Women's Club (pres. Falls Church chpt. 1994-96, Woman of Yr. award 1990), Women's Nat. Dem. Club (past v.p., mem. bd. govs.), Downtown Club (Richmond), Phi Gamma Nu. Roman Catholic. Avocations: Cubs fan, tennis, art. Home: 8701 Duvall St Fairfax VA 22031-2711

MILLER, ERNEST CHARLES, management consultant; b. Bronx, N.Y., July 14, 1925; s. Ernest Philip and Elizabeth (Hellwig) M.; m. Edith Grosvenor Porterfield, Nov. 11, 1947 (div. Oct. 3, 1963); children: Laura Lee, Marcy Rogers, Ernest Charles; m. Tung-fen Lin, Jan. 8, 1985. A.B., Yale U., 1945; M.A., U. Pa., 1949. Lic. psychologist, N.Y. Instr. U. Pa., 1947-51, cons., 1950-53; br. mgr., bd. dirs. Richardson, Bellows, Henry & Co., Inc., 1953-55; mgr. personnel tech. Am. Standard, Inc., 1955-59; mng. prin. Hellwig, Miller & Assos., Westport, Conn., 1959-61; sr. assoc. Cresap, McCormick & Paget, Inc., N.Y.C., 1961-63; with Am. Mgmt. Assns., N.Y.C., 1964-83; pres. AMACOM div. Am. Mgmt. Assns., 1978-81, group v.p. AMA Publs. Group, 1981-83; pres. Miller, Hellwig Assocs., 1984—. Author works in strategic planning, orgn. devel., human resources, exec. compensation and mgmt. Bd. dirs. La Jolla Inst. for Allergy and Immunology; mem. Columbia U. All-Univ. Seminar, China Internat. Bus. Orgn. and Mgmt. NEH fellow, 1980. Mem. Am. Psychol. Assn., Japan Soc., Soc. Indsl. and Orgnl. Psychology, Inc. Episcopalian. Office: Miller Hellwig Assocs 150 W End Ave New York NY 10023-5713

MILLER, EUGENE, business executive, university official; b. Chgo., Oct. 6, 1925; s. Harry and Fannie (Prosterman) M.; m. Edith Sutker, Sept. 23, 1951 (div. Sept. 1965); children: Ross, Scott, June; m. Thelma Gottlieb, Dec. 22, 1965; stepchildren: Paul Gottlieb, Alan Gottlieb. BS, Ga. Inst. Tech., 1945; AB magna cum laude, Bethany Coll., 1947, LLD, 1969; diploma, Oxford (Eng.) U., 1947; MS in Journalism, Columbia U., 1948; MBA, NYU, 1959; postgrad., Pace U., 1973—. Reporter, then city editor Greensboro (N.C.) Daily News, 1948-52; S.W. bur. chief Bus. Week mag., Houston, 1952-54; asso. mng. editor Bus. Week mag., N.Y.C., 1954-60; dir. pub. affairs and communications McGraw-Hill, Inc., 1960-63, v.p., 1963-68; sr. v.p. pub. rels. and investor rels., exec. com. N.Y. Stock Exch., N.Y.C., 1968-73; sr. v.p. CNA Fin. Corp., Chgo., 1973-75; chmn. Eugene Miller & Assos., Glencoe, Ill., 1975-77; v.p. USG Corp., Chgo., 1977-82, sr. v.p., 1982-85, mem. mgmt. com., 1982-91, exec. v.p., chief fin. officer, 1985-87, elected vice chmn., chief fin. officer, 1987-91, mem. exec. com., also bd. dirs.; prof., asst. dean Coll. Bus., Fla. Atlantic U., 1991—; chmn., CEO Ideon Group, Inc., Jacksonville, Fla., 1996—; adj. prof. mgmt. NYU, 1963-65; prof. bus. adminstrn. Fordham U., 1969-75; prof. fin., chmn. dept. Northeastern Ill. U., 1975-78; lectr. to bus. and ednl. groups; bd. dirs. MRFI, Inc., Chgo., Teletech Holding Inc., Denver; bd. dirs., mem. adv. bd. dirs. Nationwide Acceptance Corp., Chgo.; cons. to sec. Dept. Commerce, 1961-66; editor-in-residence U. Oreg., 1992; exec.-in-residence U. Ill., 1991, U. Wis., 1991, U. Toronto, 1992; exec.-in-residence, POHL fellow U. Wyo., 1992; mem. adv. bd. CFO mag., 1991—. Author: Your Future in Securities, 1974, Barron's Guide to Graduate Business Schools, 1977, 9th edit., 1995; contbg. editor: Public Relations Handbook, 1988, Boardroom Reports, 1986—; writer syndicated bus. column., 1964-86. Trustee Bethany Coll.; mem. alumni bd. Columbia U. Sch. Journalism. Comdr. USNR, World War II, ret. Recipient outstanding achievement award Bethany Coll., 1963, 50th anniversary award Sch. Journalism Columbia U., also honors award, 1963, Sch. Journalism Ohio U., 1964, disting. svc. award in investment edn. Nat. Assn. Investment Clubs, 1980, Roalman award Nat. Investor Rels. Inst., 1987. Fellow Pub. Rels. Soc. Am.; mem. Nat. Assn. Bus. Economists, Soc. Am. Bus. Editors and Writers (founder), Fin. Execs. Inst., Arthur Page Soc., Mid-Am. Club, St. Andrew's Country Club, Sigma Delta Chi, Alpha Sigma Phi. Home: 7351 Ballantrae Ct Boca Raton FL 33496-1423 Office: Fla Atlantic U 777 Glades Rd Boca Raton FL 33431-0991 Office: Ideon Group Inc 7596 Centurion Pkwy Jacksonville FL 32256

MILLER, EUGENE ALBERT, banking executive; married. B.B.A., Detroit Inst. Tech., 1964; grad., Sch. Bank Adminstrn., Wis., 1968. With Comerica Bank-Detroit (formerly The Detroit Bank, then Detroit Bank & Trust Co.), 1955—, v.p., 1970-74, controller, 1971-74, sr. v.p., 1974-78, exec. v.p., 1978-81, pres., 1981-89, chief exec. officer, 1989—, chmn., 1990—; with parent co. Comerica Inc. (formerly DETROITBANK Corp.), 1973—, treas., 1973-80, pres., 1981—, chief exec. officer, 1989-92, chmn. bd., 1990-92; pres., COO Comerica Inc. (merger with Manufacturers Nat. Corp.), Detroit, 1992—; also bd. dirs. Comerica Inc. (formerly DETROITBANK Corp.); chmn., CEO Comerica Bank (merged with Manufacturers Nat. Corp.), Detroit, 1993—; chmn., CEO Comerica Inc., Detroit, 1993—, also bd. dirs. Office: Comerica Inc 500 Woodward Ave Detroit MI 48226-3423*

MILLER, EVA MARY, hospital administrator; b. Canon City, Colo., June 10, 1943; d. Nicholas A. and Ellen G. (Shaeffer) Herniak; m. Gary L. Miller, Aug. 14, 1964; children: Christopher, Timothy, Joseph. RN diploma, Wichita-St. Joseph Sch Nursing, 1964; BS in Psychology/Mgmt., U. Md., 1988. With Hellenikon Air Base, Greece, 1973-77, ARC Vol Svcs., Bitburg Air Base, Germany, 1985-88; charge nurse Paxton Community Hosp., Ill., 1977-80, Val Verde Meml. Hosp., Tex., 1981; pub. health nurse Tex. State Dept. Health, 1981-82, Wayne County, N.C., 1982-85; quality assurance coord. USAF, Bitburg AFB, Fed. Republic of Germany, 1985-88, Georgetown U. Hosp., Washington, 1989; dir. quality assurance U.S. Naval Hosp., Charleston, S.C., 1989-95; performance improvement coord. U.S. Naval Acad. Clinic, Annapolis, Md., 1995—. Mem. Nat. Assn. Healthcare Quality (cert.). Home: 889 Willys Dr Arnold MD 21012

MILLER, EWING HARRY, architect; b. Toledo, Ohio, Oct. 5, 1923; s. Ewing Harry and Esther Alice (Graves) M.; m. Gladys Jacquelyn Good, Dec. 18, 1948 (dec.); children: Victoria Alice, Paul Ewing. B.A., U. Pa., 1947, M.A., 1948. Draftsman Harbeson, Hough, Livingston & Larson, Phila., 1948; designer Nolen & Swinburne, Phila., 1950-52; project architect Gilboy & O'Malley, London, 1953-55; partner Miller, Vrydagh & Miller, Terre Haute, Ind., 1955-65; pres. Ewing Miller Partnership, Terre Haute, 1965-70; pres. Archonics Corp., 1970-76, chmn. bd., 1976-79; sr. ptnr. for design Archonics Design Partnership, Indpls., 1979-84; assoc. ptnr. architecture eastern region U.S. Howard Needles, Tammen & Bergendoff, 1985-92; archtl. cons. Design & Bldg. Industry, 1992—; gen. ptnr. Lockerbie Devel. Co., 1978-86, Lockerbie Glove Devel. Co., 1983-86, East St. Devel. Co., 1979-86. Contbr. articles to profl. jours.; archtl. critic Indpls. Monthly Mag.; major archtl. works include: various bldgs. Ind. U., including grad. biology lab., Ind. State U., master plan and edn. bldgs., residence halls and power ctr., Southwestern Ind. U., master plan and edn. bldgs., Ind. and Ohio Laborers Tng. Ctr., Prairie Elem. Sch., Indpls. Westin Conv. Hotel; various office parks, Indpls. Pub. Transp. Corp. facility, addition to Duesenberg Factory; master plan Ind. State Govt. Complex, State of Ind. and design of new state office bldg.; prin. in charge printing facility Ho. of Rep. Architect of the Capitol, prin. in charge of Prospectus Devel. Study for design and restoration of Old Exec. Office Bldg., Washington; master plan for remodeling The Pentagon, Washington; prin. in charge design for remodeling Dept. of State, Washington; prin. in charge design for remodeling Midwest Direct Mktg. Ctr., Bing, Inc., N.Y. Mem. Ind. Gov.'s Commn. on Aging, 1959-62; pres. Gov.'s Commn. on Comprehensive Health Planning, Ind., 1970-75, Behavioral Research Found., 1965-85; bd. mgrs. Sheldon Swope Art Gallery, 1965-80, pres., 1965-73; bd. dirs. Center for Exploration of Values and Meaning, 1978-85, Herron Art Gallery, 1980-88; chmn. Indpls. Arts and Cultural Alliance, 1983. Recipient design citation, biennial awards program Ind. Soc. Architects; Honor awards, triennial design awards East Central Region AIA; Archtl. award of excellence Am. Inst. Steel Constrn.; 1st Honor award and winner Internat. Competition for Housing, Indpls.; award of excellence for univ. bldgs. Am. Sch. and Univ. Mag., 1985; Ind. Soc. Architects Honor award restoration of Circle Theater, various office bldgs., 1985, 86. Fellow AIA (mem. com. on design, chmn. com. on architecture for edn., mem. Vision 2000 study, architecture in coming decade), Lambda Alpha Hon. Soc. Home and Office: 2230 Birch Rd Port Republic MD 20676-2640 also: The Pennsylvania Apts #1201 601 Pennsylvania Ave NW Washington DC 20004-2601

MILLER, FRANCES SUZANNE, historic site curator; b. Defiance, Ohio, Apr. 17, 1950; d. Francis Bernard Johnson and Nellie Frances (Holder) Culp; m. James A. Batdorf, Aug. 7, 1970 (div. Aug. 1979); 1 child, Jennifer Christine Batdorf; m. Rodney Lyle Miller, Aug. 8, 1982 (div. Apr. 1987). BS in History/Museology, The Defiance Coll., 1990; AS in Bus. Mgmt., N.W. Tech. Coll., 1986. With accts. receivable dept. Ohio Art Co., Bryan, Ohio, 1984-87; leasing agent Williams Met. Housing Authority, Bryan, 1987-91; curator, property mgr. James A. Garfield Nat. Historic Site, Mentor, Ohio, 1991—. Mem. AAUW (pres. 1993-95, treas. 1995-97), Nat. Trust Hist. Preservation, Ohio Mus. Assn., Ohio Assn. Host. Socs. and Mus., Cleve. Restoration Soc., Phi Alpha Theta. Avocations: needlework, reading. Office: James A Garfield Nat Historic Site 8095 Mentor Ave Mentor OH 44060-5753

MILLER, FRANCIE LORADITCH, college recruiter; b. Avilton, Md., Apr. 18, 1937; d. John William and Agnes Wilda (Broadwater) Loraditch; m. George Aloys Miller, Feb. 27, 1965; children: Peter Raymond, Sandra Patricia. Student, Kent State U., 1955-57; BA in English, Calif. State U., Dominguez Hills, 1978, Ma in English, 1980. Flight attendent Western Airlines, L.A., 1957-65; lectr. English Calif. State U., Carson, 1980-82, asst. coord. learning assistance ctr., 1979-84, asst. dir. univ. outreach svcs., 1984—. Editor Campus Staff Newsletter, 1992—. Mem. edn. com. Palos Verdes (Calif.) C. of C., 1994—; vol. Olympic Games, L.A., 1984; campus rep. Statewide Alumni Coun., Sacramento, 1982-84; participant Civic Chorale, Torrance, Calif., 1993—; apptd. statewide campus adv. com. Project Assist, 1996. Acad. scholar Kent State U., 1955. Mem. Calif. Intersegmental Articulation Coun. (newsletter editor 1993—, vice chair 1995—), Western Assn. Coll. Admission Counselors, South Coast Higher Ednl. Coun., Phi Kappa Phi (chpt. pres. 1992—, mem. nat. comm. com. 1996). Republican. Roman Catholic. Avocations: singing, dancing, golf. Office: Calif State U Dominguez Hills 1000 E Victoria St Carson CA 90747-0001

MILLER, FRANK L., JR., army officer; b. Atchinson, Kans., Jan. 27, 1944; s. Frank L. and Evelyn (Wilson) M.; m. Paulette Duncan, Sept. 28, 1968; children: Frank L. III, Michael W., Toni K. BA, U. Wash., 1973; MS, Troy State U., Eng., 1979. Commd. 2d lt. U.S. Army, 1966, advanced through grades to maj. gen., 1992; disting. grad. student U.S. Army Command and Gen. Staff Coll., Ft. Leavenworth, Kans., 1977, Naval War Coll., Newport, R.I., 1984; chief of staff Free World's Ctr. for Fire Support, Ft. Sill, Okla., 1988-89; comdg. gen. III Corps Arty., Ft. Sill, 1989-92; dir. ops. Forces Command, Ft. McPherson, Ga., 1992-94; DCG III Corps, Ft. Hood, Tex., 1994-95; asst. chief of staff Install. Mgmt., HQ DA, Pentagon, Washington, 1995—. Decorated DFC, Legion of Merit with two oak leaf clusters, Bronze Star with two oak leaf clusters, Meritorious Svc. medal, Air medal with 19 oak leaf clusters; Cross of Gallantry with silver star (Vietnam). Mem. Assn. U.S. Army, F.A. Assn.

MILLER, FRANK WILLIAM, legal educator; b. Appleton, Wis., May 15, 1921; s. Frank Paul and Ruth Margaret (Arft) M.; m. Lucille Gloria Rinnan, Sept. 8, 1945; children: Deborah Lynn, Patricia Elizabeth. B.A., U. Wis., 1946, LL.B., 1948, S.J.D., 1954. Bar: Wis. 1948. Mem. faculty Washington U., St. Louis, 1948-91, Coles prof. criminal law and adminstrn., 1962-64, James Carr prof. criminal jurisprudence, 1964-91, prof. emeritus, 1991—; Dan Hopson Disting. prof. So. Ill. U., Carbondale, 1992; summer vis. prof. law U. Ark., 1952, 54, 56, Stetson U., 1955, U. Wis., 1957, U. Tex., 1975, 85; vis. prof. law So. Ill. U. at Carbondale, 1973-74, summers 1976-81; chmn. round table council criminal law Assn. Am. Law Schs., 1961; chmn. Pub. Defender Adv. Com. St. Louis County, 1962. Author: (with A.C. Becht) Factual Causation in Negligence and Strict Liability Cases, 1961, Prosecution: The Decision to Charge a Suspect with a Crime, 1969; editor: (with R.O. Dawson, George E. Dix, Raymond I. Parnas) Criminal Justice Administration, 1976, 4th edit., 1991, (with Dawson, Dix, Parnas) The Police Function, 1982, 5th edit., 1991, Sentencing and The Correctional Process, 1976, The Juvenile Justice Process, 1976, 3d edit., 1985, The Mental Health Process, 1976, Prosecution and Adjudication, 1982, 4th edit., 1991. Served with AUS, 1942-45. Recipient citation for outstanding teaching Washington U. Alumni Fedn., 1965, Washington U. Law Alumni Assn., 1991. Mem. ABA, Am. Law Inst. (Guttmacher award 1977), Order of Coif. Democrat.

MILLER, FREDERICK, pathologist; b. N.Y.C., Apr. 5, 1937; s. Alex and Sarah M.; m. Emilie J. Kronish, June 2, 1962; children: David, Allison. B.S., U. Wis., 1956; M.D., N.Y. U., 1961. Diplomate: Am. Bd. Pathology. Intern Bellevue Hosp., N.Y.C., 1961-62, resident, 1962-63; practice medicine specializing in pathology, 1965—; clin. assoc., attending physician Nat. Inst. Arthritis and Metabolic Diseases, 1963-65; resident chief pathology dept. NYU Med. Ctr., 1965-67; attending pathologist Bellevue and Univ. Hosps., N.Y.C., 1967; asst. prof. pathology NYU, 1967-70, assoc. prof., 1970; assoc. prof. SUNY, Stony Brook, 1970-75, prof., 1975—, chmn. dept. pathology, 1977—, Marvin Kuschner prof. pathology, 1991, dir. lab. for arthritis and related diseases, 1976—; dir. labs. Univ. Hosp., Stony Brook, 1978—, pathologist-in-chief, 1979—; mem. Nat. Bd. Med. Examiners in Pathology, 1996—. Contbr. articles to med. jours. Served with USPHS, 1963-65. Recipient Bausch and Lomb medal for rsch., 1961; Pres.'s award SUNY, Stony brook, 1990, Chancellor's award, 1990, Aesculapius award, 1993; Golden Apple award ASMA, 1995; NIH grantee, 1963-87. Mem. AAAS, Harvey Soc., Soc. Clin. Immunology, Am. Soc. Investigative Pathology, Am. Soc. Clin. Pathologists (award 1961), Internat. Acad. Pathology, N.Y. Acad. Sci., Am. Assn. Immunologists, Assn. Pathology Chairmen, Suffolk Orchid Soc. (pres.), Sigma Xi, Alpha Omega Alpha. Hort. authority on roses and orchids. Home: 46 Manchester Ln Stony Brook NY 11790-2826 Office: SUNY Stony Brook Dept Pathology Hsc Stony Brook NY 11794

MILLER, FREDERICK N., pharmacology educator. PhD in Pharmacology, U. Cin., 1971. Assoc. prof. cardiovascular physiology U. Louisville Health & Sc. Ctr., Louisville, 1981—. Office: Univ Louisville Applied Microcirculatory Rsch Health Sciences Ctr Rm 1115 Louisville KY 40292*

MILLER, FREDERICK POWELL, agronomy educator; b. Springfield, Ohio, Oct. 17, 1936; s. Edwin S. and Marcella (Powell) M.; m. Marilyn Ellen Miller (dec. Dec. 1991); m. Jann M. Ricchetti, Mar. 12, 1993. Student, Wittenberg Coll., Springfield,Ohio, 1954-56; B.Sc., Ohio State U., 1958, M.S., 1961, Ph.D., 1965. Cert. prof. soil scientist, Am. Registry of Cert. Profls. in Agronomy, Crops, Soils. Asst. prof. dept. agronomy U. Md., College Park, 1965-69, assoc. prof., 1969-74, prof., 1974-82; head and prof. dept. agronomy U. Ark., Fayetteville, 1982-86; prof., chmn. dept. agronomy Ohio State U., 1986-94, dir., prof., Sch. Natural Resources, 1994—; vis. assoc. prof. dept. soil sci. U. Calif.-Davis, 1972-73; vis. prof. U. Fla., Gainesville, 1980. Fellow AAAS, Am. Soc. Agronomy, Soil Sci. Soc. Am. (div. chmn. 1979-80, pres. 1991, past pres. 1992); mem. Soil Conservation Soc. Am. Office: Ohio State U Sch of Natural Resources 2021 Coffey Rd Columbus OH 43026

MILLER, FREDERICK ROBESON, banker; b. Oakland, Calif., Oct. 11, 1927; s. Charles Lennon and Juliet Robeson (Chamberlain) M.; m. Nancy McDaniel, July 19, 1952; children: Susan Chase Miller Clark, Stephen Robeson, Elizabeth Rockwell. B.A., Yale U., 1952. With J.P. Morgan & Co., Inc., 1952-54; v.p. Phila. Nat. Bank, 1954-69; pres. Waterbury Nat. Bank, Conn., 1969-71, City Nat. Bank, Bridgeport, Conn., 1971-72, Conn. Nat. Bank, Bridgeport, 1973-83; also chief exec. officer, vice chmn. Conn. Nat. Bank; vice chmn. Hartford Nat. Corp., until 1984. Served with U.S. Army, 1946-47. Mem. Tubac Valley Country Club. Republican. Episcopalian. Home: PO Box 1503 Tubac AZ 85646-1503

MILLER, FREDERICK STATEN, music educator, academic administrator; b. Lima, Ohio, Dec. 12, 1930; s. Donald Frederick and Esther Lillian (Moore) M.; m. Florence Dorothy Mistak, June 20, 1959; children: Jennifer Leigh, John Staten. B of Music Edn., Northwestern U., 1957, M in Music, 1958; D of Music Performance, U. Iowa, 1974. Mem. music faculty U. Ark., Fayetteville, 1958-64; asst. dir. bands Northwestern U., Evanston, Ill., 1964-70, assoc. dean, sch. music, 1970-76; dean, sch. music DePaul U., Chgo., 1976-95; bd. dirs. Concertante de Chgo., 1985—; accreditation evaluator North Cen. Assn., Boulder, Colo., 1982—, Nat. Assn. Schs. Music, Washington, 1981—. Composer/arranger numerous pub. works for band; editor music publs. Served with USN, 1948-52. Mem. ASCAP, Nat. Assn. Schs. Music (hon. life, regional chmn. 1982-84, instl. rep., treas. 1984-88, v.p. 1988-91, pres. 1991-94), Pi Kappa Lambda (bd. regents 1970-74), Phi Kappa Phi. Roman Catholic. Clubs: University (Chgo.); Sheridan Shore Yacht (Wilmette, Ill.). Avocations: sailing, cooking, jazz performance. Home: 1322 Greenwood Ave Wilmette IL 60091-1624 Office: DePaul Univ Sch Music 804 W Belden Ave Chicago IL 60614-3214

MILLER, FREDERICK WILLIAM, publisher, lawyer; b. Milw., Mar. 18, 1912; s. Roy W. and Kathryn (Oehlers) M.; m. Violet Jane Bagley, Mar. 31, 1939. B.A., U. Wis., 1934, LLB, 1936. Bar: Wis. 1936. Assoc. Tenney & Davis, Madison, 1935-36; atty. State of Wis., Madison, 1936-77; pub. The Capital Times Co., Madison, 1979—, also dir.; dir. Madison Newspaper, Inc., 1970—, chmn. bd., 1980—; dir. Evjue Found., Inc., Madison, 1957—. Trustee Evjue Charitable Trust, Madison, 1970—. Mem. Wis. Bar Assn. Clubs: Madison Club, Univ. Club. Home: 2810 Arbor Dr Madison WI 53711-1826 Office: Capital Times Co PO Box 8056 1901 Fish Hatchery Rd Madison WI 53713-1248

MILLER, GABRIEL LORIMER, physicist, researcher; b. N.Y.C., Jan. 18, 1928; s. Hugh Lorimer and Olga (Katzin) M.; m. Natalie Coffin, May 20, 1962; children: Matthew, Jonathan, Katharine. BS in Physics, London U., 1949, MS in Math., 1952, PhD in Physics, 1957. Sr. demonstrator Birkbeck Coll. London U., 1953-57; physicist Brookhaven Nat. Lab., Upton, L.I., N.Y., 1957-63; mem. tech. staff AT&T Bell Labs., Murray Hill, N.J., 1963-82, head dept. interactive systems rsch., 1982—; vis. prof. U. Aarhus, Denmark, 1969-70, Rutgers U., New Brunswick, N.J., 1972-73; mem. vis. coms. Oak Ridge, Lawrence Berkeley and Brookhaven nat. labs. Contbr. numerous publs. on instrumentation, measurement and sensors; holder over 30 patents; past assoc. editor Rev. Sci. Instruments. Fellow IEEE (mem. nuclear instruments com. 1960—, Centennial medal 1984), Am. Phys. Soc.; mem.IEEE Indsl. Electronics Soc. (assoc. editor Robotics 1985—), Bohmische Phys. Soc. Home: 614 Boulevard Westfield NJ 07090-3210

MILLER, GAIL ANN, elementary school educator; b. Buffalo, Apr. 10, 1955; d. John F. and Joan M. (Simon) Holtz; m. Robert G. Miller Jr., Aug. 25, 1979; children: John Robert, Brianna Lynne. BS in Edn., St. Bonaventure U., Olean, N.Y., 1977; MS in Reading, SUNY, Fredonia, 1979. Faculty reading SUNY, Fredonia, 1992; title I reading tchr. Dunkirk (N.Y.) Pub. Sch. #3, 1979—, team tchr. pilot multi-age grades 2-3, 1994—; co-dir. Sch. # variety show; presenter/lectr. various confs. Co-editor Celebrations newsletter. Coord. Vacation Bible Sch., First United Presbyn. Ch., Silver Creek, N.Y., 1985-91, Sunday sch. tchr., elder, clk of session and mem. edn. com. Named Tchr. of Month, Dunkirk Rotary, 1993. Mem. Internat. Reading Assn. (Chautauqua coun.). Republican. Avocations: writing, reading, golf. Home: 1845 Lake Rd Silver Creek NY 14136-9725 Office: Dunkirk Public School #3 Lamphere St Dunkirk NY 14048

MILLER, GALE TIMOTHY, lawyer; b. Kalamazoo, Sept. 15, 1946; s. Arthur H. and Eleanor (Johnson) M.; m. Janice Lindvall, June 1, 1968; children: Jeremy L., Amanda E., Timothy W. AB, Augustana Coll., 1968; JD, U. Mich., 1971. Bar: Mich. 1971, Colo. 1973, U.S. Dist. Ct. Colo. 1973, U.S. Ct. Appeals (10th cir.) 1979. Trial atty. FTC, Washington, 1971-73; assoc. Davis, Graham & Stubbs, L.L.C., Denver, 1973-77, ptnr., mem., 1978—. Bd. dirs. Sr. Housing Options, Inc., 1980-93; chair Colo. Lawyers Com., 1989-91, bd. dirs. 1987—, Individual Lawyer of Yr. 1994. Mem. ABA (antitrust sect. task force on model civil antitrust jury instrns. 1984—), Colo. Bar. Assn. (chair-elect antitrust sect. 1996—), Denver Bar Assn. Democrat. Lutheran. Office: Davis Graham & Stubbs LLC PO Box 185 Denver CO 80201-0185

MILLER, GARY EVAN, psychiatrist, mental health services administrator; b. Cleve., Aug. 19, 1935; s. Henry M. and Mollie (Price) M.; m. Karen Ann Marie Barrett, Sept. 16, 1972; children: Anna Charis, Rebecca Elizabeth. MD, U. Tex., Galveston, 1960. Diplomate in psychiatry, addiction psychiatry, and geriatric psychiatry Am. Bd. Psychiatry and Neurology. Intern Montefiore Hosp., N.Y.C., 1960-61; resident in psychiatry Univ. Hosps. Cleve., 1961-62, Austin (Tex.) State Hosp., 1963-65; dep. commr. mental health services Tex. Dept. Mental Health and Mental Retardation, 1967-70; dir. Rio Grande State Center for Mental Health and Mental Retardation, Tex. Dept. Mental Health, Harlingen, 1966-67; asst. commr., dir. Rochester regional office N.Y. State Dept. Mental Hygiene, 1970-72; clin. asst. prof. psychiatry U. Rochester Sch. Medicine and Dentistry, 1970-72; asst. clin. prof. psychiatry SUNY, Buffalo, 1970-72; cons. mental health Ga. Dept. Human Resources, Atlanta, 1972; dir. div. mental health Ga. Dept. Human Resources, 1972-74; clin. prof. psychiatry Emory U. Sch. Medicine, Atlanta, 1972-74; vice chmn. Ga. State Planning and Adv. Council for Devel. Disabilities Services and Constrn., 1972-73; cons. mental health services orgn. and adminstrn., 1974-76; dir. mental health and devel. services State of N.H. Concord, 1976-82; commr. Tex. Dept. Mental Health and Mental Retardation Austin, 1982-88; clin. prof. psychiatry U. Tex. Health Sci. Ctr., Houston; adj. assoc. prof. psychiatry U. Tex. Health Sci. Ctr., San Antonio, 1984-95; dir. profl. svcs. HCA Gulf Pines Hosp., Houston, 1988-94, chief of staff, 1993; clin. dir. adult psychiatry Cypress Creek Hosp., Houston, 1994—, pres. med. staff, 1996; assoc. clin. psychiatry Post Oak Psychiatry Assocs., Houston, 1988-90; pres. Alternative Svcs. Network, Houston, 1990—; clin. dir. adult psychiatry Cypress Creek Hosp., Houston, 1994—, pres.-elect med. staff, 1995, pres., 1996—; dir. state alcoholism program in Ga., 1972-74, also, South Tex. region, 1966-67; mem. faculty U. S.C. Sch. Alcohol and Drug Studies, 1975; bd. dirs. nat. patient rights policy research project NIMH, 1981; Bd. dirs. Genessee Regional Health Planning Council, Rochester, 1970-72. Contbr. articles to profl. jours. Served as capt. M.C., U.S. Army, 1962-63. Recipient Cert. of Recognition, Ga. Psychol. Assn., 1973. Fellow Am. Psychiat. Assn. (cert. in adminstrv. psychiatry 1983); mem. AMA, Am. Soc. Addiction Medicine (cert. alcoholism and other drug dependencies 1993), N.H. Psychiat. Soc. (pres. 1981-82), Nat. Assn. State Mental Health Program Dirs. (bd. dirs. 1984-88, sec. 1986-88), N.H. Med. Soc., Am. Acad. Psychiatry and the Law, Am. Assn. Psychiat. Adminstrs. (pres. Tex. chpt.), Tex. Med. Assn., Tex. Soc. Psychiat. Physicians, Mental Health Assn. Houston and Harris County (bd. dirs. 1989-95, v.p. advocacy 1990-95), Alpha Omega Alpha. Home: 5314 Westminister Ct Houston TX 77069-3338 Office: 530 Wells Fargo Dr Ste 110 Houston TX 77090-4026

MILLER, GARY J., political economist; b. Urbana, Ill., Jan. 2, 1949; s. Gerald J. and Doris Elaine (Miner) M.; m. Anne Colberg, Jan. 29, 1971; children: Neil, Ethan. BA, U. Ill., 1971; PhD, U. Tex., 1976. Asst. prof. Calif. Inst. Tech., Pasadena, 1976-79; assoc. prof. Mich. State U., East Lansing, 1979-86; Taylor prof. of polit. economy Washington U., St. Louis, Mo., 1986—; assoc. dean for acad. affairs Olin Sch. Bus. Washington U., St. Louis, 1995—. Author: Cities by Contract, 1981, Reforming Bureaucracy, 1987, Managerial Dilemmas, 1992. NSF grantee, 1981, 83, 92. Mem. Phi Beta Kappa, Phi Kappa Phi (Disting. Faculty award 1994). Democrat. Office: Washington U Sch of Bus 1 Brookings Dr Saint Louis MO 63130-4862

MILLER, GENE EDWARD, newspaper reporter and editor; b. Evansville, Ind., Sept. 16, 1928; m. Electra Sonia Yphantis, Apr. 13, 1952 (dec. May 1993); children: Janet Irene, Theresa Jean, Thomas Raphael, Roberta Lynn. A.B. in Journalism, Ind. U., 1950, LL.D. (hon.), 1977; Nieman fellow, Harvard U., 1967-68. Reporter Jour.-Gazette, Ft. Wayne, Ind., 1950-51, Washington Bur. Wall St. Jour., 1953-54, Richmond (Va.) News Leader, 1954-57, Miami (Fla.) Herald, 1957—. Author: Invitation To A Lynching, 83 Hours Till Dawn. Served with AUS, 1951-53. Recipient Pulitzer prize for local reporting, 1967, 76. Office: 1 Herald Plz Miami FL 33132-1609

MILLER, GENEVIEVE, retired medical historian; b. Butler, Pa., Oct. 15, 1914; d. Charles Russell and Genevieve (Wolford) M. AB, Goucher Coll., 1935; MA, Johns Hopkins U., 1939; PhD, Cornell U., 1955. Asst. in history of medicine Johns Hopkins Inst. of History of Medicine, Balt., 1943-44, instr., 1945-48, rsch. assoc., 1979-94; asst. prof. history of medicine Sch. Medicine, Case Western Res. U., Cleve., 1953-67, assoc. prof., 1967-79, assoc. prof. emeritus, 1979—; research assoc. in med. history Cleve. Med. Library Assn., 1953-62, curator Howard Dittrick Mus. of Hist. Medicine, 1962-67, dir. Howard Dittrick Mus. Hist. Medicine, 1967-79. Author: William Beaumont's Formative Years: Two Early Notebooks 1811-1821, 1946; The Adoption of Inoculation for Smallpox in England and France (William H. Welch medal Am. Assn. for History of Medicine 1962), 1957; Bibliography of the History of Medicine of the U.S. and Canada, 1939-1960, 1964; Bibliography of the Writings of Henry E. Sigerist, 1966; Letters of Edward Jenner and Other Documents Concerning the Early History of Vaccination, 1983; assoc. editor Bull. of History of Medicine, 1944-48, acting editor, 1948, mem. adv. editorial bd. 1960-92; mem. bd. editors Jour. of History of Medicine and Allied Scis., 1948-65; editor Bull. of Cleve. Med. Library, 1954-72; editor newsletter Am. Assn. for History of Medicine, 1986-96; contbr. articles in field to profl. jours. Am. Council Learned Socs. fellow, 1948-50; Dean Van Meter fellow, 1953-54. Alumna trustee Goucher Coll., Balt., 1966-69; trustee Judson Retirement Cmty., Cleve., 1993—. Hon. fellow Cleve. Med. Library Assn.; mem. Am. Assn. for History of Medicine (pres. 1978-80, mem. council 1960-63), Am. Hist. Assn., Internat. Soc. for History of Medicine, Soc. Archtl. Historians, Phi Beta Kappa; corr. mem. fgn. socs. for history of medicine. Democrat. Home and Office: Judson Manor 1890 E 107th St Apt 816 Cleveland OH 44106-2245 *The desire to see as much of the world as possible and to retrace its past adds enormously to the richness and pleasure of life.*

MILLER, GEOFFREY PARSONS, law educator; b. Princeton, Oct. 17, 1950; s. Robert Parsons and Daphne (Haynes) M.; m. Joan R. Falk; children: Jason, Forrest. AB, Princeton U., 1973; JD, Columbia U., 1978. Bar: D.C. Law clk. to Hon. Carl McGowan Washington, 1978-79, law clk. to Hon. Byron R. White, 1979-80; atty., advisor U.S. Dept. Justice, Washington, 1980-82; assoc. atty. Ennis, Friedman, Bersoff & Ewing, Washington, 1982-83; asst. prof. U. Chgo., 1983-87, prof. law, assoc. dean, 1987-89, Kirkland and Ellis prof., 1989—; prof. of law New York University, N.Y.C., NY. Contbr. articles to profl. jours. Office: NYU Law School 40 Washington Square S New York NY 10012*

MILLER, GEORGE, mayor; b. Detroit; m. Roslyn Girard; 4 children. BA, U. Ariz., 1947, MEd, 1952. Tchr. high schs., owner, prin. painting contracting co., until 1989; mayor City of Tucson, 1991—. Active mem. Dem. Party So. Ariz., 1960—, treas. Pima County div., state chmn. Presdl. Del. Selection Reform Commn.; bd. dirs. Tucson Jewish Community Ctr., Anti-Defamation League of B'nai B'rith; councilman Tucson City Coun., 1977-91, also vice mayor. With USMC, WWII. Decorated Purple Heart; recipient Recognition award United Way, Cmty. Svcs. Support award Chicano Por La Causa (2), Met. Edn. Commn. Crystal Apple award, cert. appreciation San Ignacio Yaqui Coun., Old Pasqua, Dr. Martin Luther King Jr. Keep the Dream Alive award, 1995; named Father of Yr. 1995, Man of Yr. So. Ariz. Home Builders Assn., Outstanding Pub. Ofcl. Ariz. Parks and Recreation Assn., 1995. Office: Office of Mayor PO Box 27210 Tucson AZ 85726-7210

MILLER, GEORGE, film director; b. Brisbane, Australia, Mar. 3, 1945. MD, U. NSW, Australia, 1970. Former physician St. Vincent's Hosp., Sydney, Australia. Films include: dir., writer: Violence in the Cinema, Part I, 1971, Mad Max, 1979, The Road Warrior-Mad Max II, 1982, Mad Max: Beyond the Thunderdome, 1985, Lorenzo's Oil, 1992, 40, 000 Years of Dreaming, 1996; dir.: Devil in Evening Dress, 1973, Twilight Zone: The Movie, 1983, The Witches of Eastwick, 1987; editor Frieze, an Underground Film, 1973; assoc. prodr.: Chain Reaction, 1980; prodr.: The Year My Voice Broke, 1988, Dead Calm, 1989, Flirting, 1990, Video Fool For Love, 1996; prodr., writer: Babe, 1995 (Acad. award nominee for best film and for best screenplay 1996). Office: Kennedy Miller Prodns, 30 Orwell St Kings Cross, Sydney 2011, Australia

MILLER, GEORGE, congressman; b. Richmond, Calif., May 17, 1945; s. George and Dorothy (Rumsey) M.; m. Cynthia Caccavo, 1964; children: George, Stephen. B.A., San Francisco State Coll., 1968; J.D., U. Calif., Davis, 1972. Legis. counsel Calif. senate majority leader, 1969-73; mem. 94th-104th Congresses from 7th Calif. dist., 1975—; chmn. subcom. on oversight and investigations, 1985—, chmn. subcom. on labor stds., 1981-84, chmn. select com. on children, youth and families, 1983-91, chmn. com. on natural resources, 1991-94; mem. com. on edn. and lab., dep. majority whip, 1989-94; vice chair Dem. Policy Com., 1995—. Mem. Calif. Bar Assn. Office: House of Representatives 2205 Rayburn Bldg Washington DC 20515-0005*

MILLER, GEORGE ARMITAGE, psychologist, educator; b. Charleston, W.Va., Feb. 3, 1920; s. George E. and Florence (Armitage) M.; m. Katherine James, Nov. 29, 1939; children: Nancy, Donnally James. BA, U. Ala., 1940, MA, 1941; AM, Harvard U., 1944, PhD, 1946; Doctorat honoris causa, U. Louvain, 1976; D Social Sci. (hon.), Yale U., 1979; DSc honoris causa, Columbia U., 1980; DSc (hon.), U. Sussex, 1984, New Sch. Social Rsch., 1993; LittD (hon.), Charleston U., 1992. Instr. psychology U. Ala., 1941-43; research fellow Harvard Psycho-Acoustic Lab., 1944-48; asst. prof. psychology Harvard U., 1948-51, assoc. prof., 1955-58, prof., 1958-68, chmn. dept psychology, 1964-67, co-dir. Ctr. for Cognitive Studies, 1960-67; prof. Rockefeller U., N.Y.C., 1968-79; adj. prof. Rockefeller U., 1979-82; prof. psychology Princeton U., 1979-90, James S. McDonnell Disting. Univ. prof. psychology, 1982-90, James S. McDonnell Disting. Univ. prof. psychology emeritus, 1990—, program dir. McDonnell-Pew Program in Cognitive Neurosci., 1989-94; assoc. prof. MIT, 1951-55; vis. Inst. for Advanced Study, Princeton, 1972-76, 82-83, mem., 1950, 70-72; vis. prof. Rockefeller U., 1967-68; vis. prof. MIT, 1976-79, group leader Lincoln Lab., 1953-55; fellow Ctr. Advanced Study in Behavioral Scis., Stanford U., 1958-59; Fulbright research prof. Oxford (Eng.) U., 1963-64; Sesquicentennial prof. U. Ala., 1981. Author: Language and Communication, 1951, (with Galanter and Pribram) Plans and the Structure of Behavior, 1960, Psychology, 1962, (with Johnson-Laird) Language and Perception, 1976, Spontaneous Apprentices, 1977, Language and Speech, 1981, The Science of Words, 1991; editor Psychol. Bulletin, 1981-82. Recipient Disting. Service award Am. Speech and Hearing Assn., 1976, award in behavioral scis. N.Y. Acad. Scis., 1982, Hermann von Helmholtz award Cognitive Neurosci. Inst., 1989, Nat. Medal Sci. NSF, 1991, Gold Medal Am. Psychological Found. 1990, Nat. Medal of Sci. 1991, Louis E. Levy medal Franklin Inst., 1991; Guggenheim fellow, 1986, William James fellow Am. Psychological Soc., 1989; Fondation Fyssen Priz Internat. for cognitive sci., 1992. Fellow Brit. Psychol. Assn. (hon.); mem. NAS, AAAS (chmn. sect. J 1981), Am. Psychol. Assn. (pres. 1968-69, Disting. Scientific Contbn. award 1963, William James Book award divsn. gen. psychology 1993), Eastern Psychol. Assn. (pres. 1961-62), Acoustical Soc. Am., Linguistic Soc. Am., Am. Statis. Assn., Am. Philos. Soc., Am. Physiol. Soc., Psychometric Soc., Soc. Exptl. Psychologists (Warren medal 1972), Am. Acad. Arts and Scis., Psychonomic Soc., Royal Netherlands Acad. Arts and Scis. (fgn.), Sigma Xi. Home: 753 Prospect Ave Princeton NJ 08540-4080 Office: Princeton Univ Dept Psychology Green Hall Princeton NJ 08544

MILLER, GEORGE DAVID, retired air force officer, marketing consultant; b. McKeesport, Pa., Apr. 5, 1930; s. George G. and Nellie G. (Cullen) M.; m. Barbara Aex; 1 child from previous marriage: George David Jr. BS, U.S. Naval Acad., 1953; MS in Aerospace Engring, Air Force Inst. Tech., 1966; postgrad., Nat. War Coll., 1970-71. Commd. 2d lt. U.S. Air Force, 1953, advanced through grades to lt. gen., 1981; ops. officer, comdr. 22d Spl. Ops. Squadron, Nakhon Phanom Royal Thai AFB, Thailand, 1970-71; dep. comdr. for ops., vice comdr., comdr. 55th Strategic Reconnaissance Wing, Offutt AFB, Nebr., 1971-74; comdr. 17th Air div., 307th Strategic wing, U-Tapao Airfield, Thailand, 1974-75; comdr. 57th A Div. Minot AFB, N.D., 1975-76; asst. dep. chief staff ops. hdqrs. SAC, Offutt AFB,, Nebr., 1976-77; dep. dir. single integrated operational plan Joint Strategic Target Planning Staff, Joint Chiefs of Staff, 1977-79; dir. plans, dep. chief of staff ops., plans and readiness Hdqrs. USAF, Washington, 1979-80; asst. dep. chief staff ops., plans and readiness Hdqrs. USAF, 1980-81; vice comdr.-in-chief SAC, Offutt AFB, Nebr., 1981-84; sec.-gen. U.S. Olympic Com., 1984-87; cons. Sports Mktg. and Def. Programs, 1984—. Pres., exec. dir. Morris Animal Found., 1989-92; pres., CEO Nat. Fire Protection Assn., 1992—, chmn. bd. NRPA Rsch. Found.; trustee U.S. Naval Acad. Found. Decorated D.S.M., Def. D.S.M., Legion of Merit, D.F.C. with 3 oak leaf clusters, Air medal with 18 oak leaf clusters, others. Mem. Air Force Assn., Am. Legion, Masons, Scottish Rite, Shriners, Daedalians. Republican. Lutheran. Home: 20 Phillips Pond Natick MA 01760-5643 Office: NFPA PO Box 9101 1 Batterymarch Pk Quincy MA 02269-9101

MILLER, GEORGE DEWITT, JR., lawyer; b. Detroit, Aug. 20, 1928; s. George DeWitt and Eleanor Mary Miller; m. Prudence Brewster Saunders, Dec. 28, 1951; children: Margaret DeWitt, Joy Saunders. BA magna cum laude, Amherst Coll., 1950; JD with distinction, U. Mich., 1953. Bar: Mich. 1953, U.S. Dist. Ct. (so. dist.) Mich. 1953, U.S. Ct. Appeals (6th cir.) 1960, U.S. Tax Ct. 1960. Assoc. Bodman, Longley & Dahling, Detroit, 1957-61, ptnr., 1962—. Trustee, mem. Matilda R. Wilson Fund, 1993—; trustee Maplegrove Ctr./Kingswood Hosp., Henry Ford Health Sys., 1995—. Capt. USAF, 1953-56. Recipient Commendation medal. Mem. ABA, State Bar Mich., Detroit Bar Assn., Detroit Club, Detroit Athletic Club, Orchard Lake Country Club, Order of Coif, Phi Beta Kappa. Episcopalian. Avocations: yacht racing, shooting. Home: 320 Dunston Rd Bloomfield Hills MI 48304-3415 Office: Bodman Longley & Dahling 100 Renaissance Ctr Ste 34 Detroit MI 48243-1003

MILLER, GEORGE H., historian, educator; b. Evanston, Ill., Aug. 5, 1919; s. Donald Crandon and Janet Gordon (Hall) M. BA, U. Mich., 1941, MA, 1946, PhD in History, 1951; MA, Harvard U., 1949; LHD (hon.), Ripon Coll., 1985. Instr. history U. Mich., Ann Arbor, 1951-54; from asst. prof. to prof. Ripon (Wis.) Coll., 1954-81; ret., 1981; bd. curators State Hist. Soc. Wis., Madison, 1980—, pres., 1989-91; dir. Wis. History Found., Madison, 1989—. Author: Railroads and the Granger Laws, 1971; co-author: Ripon College: A History, 1990; editor: A History of Ripon, Wisconsin, 1964. Mem., pres. Ripon Hist. Soc., 1962—; bd. dirs. Wis. Humanities Commn., Madison, 1973-79. With AUS, 1941-45. Recipient honor medal DAR, 1986; fellow Ford Found., 1951. Mem. Univ Club (Chgo.). Home: Unit J 778 Hillside Ter Ripon WI 54971

MILLER, G(EORGE) WILLIAM, merchant banker, business executive; b. Sapulpa, Okla., Mar. 9, 1925; s. James Dick and Hazle Deane (Orrick) M.; m. Ariadna Rogojarsky, Dec. 22, 1946. BS in Marine Engring., U.S. Coast Guard Acad., 1945; JD, U. Calif., Berkeley, 1952; hon. degree, Babson Coll, Boston U., Brown U., Bryant Coll., Fairfield U., Fla. State U., R.I. U. Bar: Calif. 1952, N.Y. 1953. Asst. sec. Textron Inc., 1956-57, v.p., 1957-60, pres., 1960-74, COO, 1960-67, CEO, 1967-74, chmn., CFO, 1974-78; chmn. Fed. Res. Bd., Washington, 1978-79; sec. of Treasury Washington, 1979-81; chmn. G. William Miller & Co. Inc., Washington, 1981—; chmn., CEO Federated Dept. Stores, Inc., 1990-92; chmn. bd. Waccamaw Corp., 1995—; bd. dirs. Repligen Corp., GS Industries, Inc., Kleinwort Benson Australian Income Fund, Inc., De Bartolo Realty Corp.; chmn. supervisory com. Schroder Venture Trust; past chmn. adv. coun. Pres.'s Com. EEO, 1963-65; mem. coun. Nat. Found. Humanities, 1966-67; bd. dirs. USCG Acad. Found., 1969-78, pres., 1973-77, chmn., 1977-78; chmn. U.S. Indsl. Payroll Savs. Bond Com., 1977, Pres.'s Com. HIRE, 1977; co-chmn. Polish-U.S. Econ. Coun., 1977-78, U.S.-USSR Trade and Econ. Coun., 1977-78, Pres.'s Cir. NAS, 1989-92. Bd. dirs. Washington Opera, Wolf Trap Found. Officer USCG, 1945-49. U. Calif. fellow, Berkeley. Mem. State Bar Calif., Nat. Alliance Businessmen (bd. dirs. 1968-78, chmn. 1977-78), Conf. Bd. (trustee 1972-78, chmn. 1977-78), Bus. Coun., Lyford Cay Club (Nassau), Acoaxet Club (Westport, Mass.), Brook Club (N.Y.C.), Burning Tree Club, Chevy Chase Club, Order of Coif, Phi Delta Phi. Office: 1215 19th St NW Washington DC 20036-2401

MILLER, GEORGIA ELLEN, business owner; b. Seattle; d. George Rynd Sr. and Mary Edith (Martin) M. BE, UCLA, 1934, MEd, 1956. Tchr. Punahou Sch., Honolulu, 1948-74; owner Miller's Bus. Svcs., Honolulu, 1975—. Bd. dirs. Waikiki Improvement Assn., Honolulu, 1980—, Waikiki Cmty. Ctr., Honolulu, 1992-95; pres. Waikiki Residents Assn., Honolulu, 1978—; sec. Waikiki Neighborhood Bd., 1980-86, v.p., 1990—, acting chair, 1992-93; county chmn. Oahu (Hawaii) Rep. Party, 1976; founding mem. Waikiki Neighbook Bd., officer; lobbyist Waikiki Residents Assn. Recipinet Kilohana award for Outstanding Vol. Svc. Gov. Coyetano, 1996. Mem. Bus. and Profl. Women (pres. 1973, legis. chair 1980, 88, state lobbyist 1988—), AAUW, Alpha Chi Omega, Pi Lambda Theta. Mem. United Ch. of Christ. Avocations: gardening, historic preservation. Home: 2415 Ala Wai Blvd Apt 1603 Honolulu HI 96815-3409 Office: Millers Bus Svcs Ste B4c 1720 Ala Moana Blvd Apt B4C Honolulu HI 96815-1347

MILLER, GERALD E., bishop. Bishop Allegheny dist. Evang. Luth. Ch. in Am., Altoona, Pa. Office: Evang Luth Ch in Am 701 Quail Ave Altoona PA 16602-3010

MILLER, GERRI, magazine editor, writer; b. Bklyn., Mar. 2, 1954; d. Norman and Isobel (Rand) M. BA, SUNY, Binghamton, 1976. Assoc. editor Sixteen Mag., N.Y.C., 1977-80; editor, then exec. editor Sterling/Macfadden, N.Y.C., 1981—. Avocations: travel, reading, rock concerts, crossword puzzles. Office: Metal Edge TV Picture Life Sterling/Macfadden 233 Park Ave S New York NY 10003-1606

MILLER, G(ERSON) H(ARRY), research institute director, mathematician, computer scientist, chemist; b. Phila., Mar. 2, 1924; m. Mary Alexa Heath, Jan. 28, 1961; children: Byron, Alexandra. BA, Pomona Coll., 1949; MEd in Counseling and Pers., Temple U., 1951; PhD. in Ednl. Psychology, U. So. Calif., 1957; MS in Math., U. Ill., 1982, postgrad., 1963-65. Jr. high sch. and jr. coll. instr. math. L.A. Sch. Dist., 1953-57; assoc. prof. Western Ill. U., Macomb, 1957-60; prof. Towson State U., Balt., Md., 1960-61; prof. math. and edn. Parsons Coll., Fairfield, Iowa, 1961-65; prof. Tenn. Technol. U., Cookeville, 1966-89; prof. math. and computer sci. Edinboro (Pa.) U., 1968-71, 81-89, asst. dir. Institutional Rsch., 1972-80; dir. Studies On Smoking, Inc and SOS Stop Smoking Clinic, Edinboro, 1972—; spkr. state, nat. and internat. profl. meetings; condr. seminars on smoking and health London, Fed. Republic Germany, Alaska, New Brunswick, N.J., Chgo., Costa Rica; dir. Nat. Study Math. Requirements for Scientists and Engrs., 1966-73. Contbr. numerous articles to profl. jours. Pres. Edinboro YMCA, 1972-83; bd. dirs. Common Cause, Harrisburg, Pa., 1975-80; Sgt. USAAF, 1943-46, PTO. Grantee U.S. Office Edn., 1968, 70, No Other World, 1973, NAS, 1980, ITT Life Ins. Corp., 1983, Erie Community Found., 1987. Fellow Am. Inst. Chemists (cert. profl. chemist); mem. AAAS, APHA, Am. Assn. World Health, Am. Chem. Soc., Am. Soc. Engring. Edn., Internat. Assn. Pure and Applied Chemists, Internat. Soc. for Preventive Oncology, Math. Assn. Am., Am. Diabetes Assn., Nat. Coun. Tchrs. Math., Sch. Sci. and Math. Assn., N.Y. Acad. Scis. (hon.), Acad. Sr. Profls. (hon.). Home and Office: Studies on Smoking Inc 125 High St Edinboro PA 16412-2552 also: 25 Crescent Pl S Saint Petersburg FL 33711

MILLER, GORDON K., lawyer; b. Madison, Wis., Oct. 17, 1949. BBA, U. Wis., 1971, JD, 1974. Bar: Wis. 1974. Mem., ptnr. Michael, Best & Friedrich, Milw. Mem. ABA. Office: Michael Best & Friedrich 100 E Wisconsin Ave Milwaukee WI 53202-4108*

MILLER, H. TODD, lawyer; b. Buffalo, N.Y., Sept. 19, 1947; s. Henry Opel and Irene Teresa (Hauck) M.; m. June Diehl Lancaster, Aug. 1, 1970; children: Catharine Maclay, Todd Lancaster, Peter Hanes. BA, SUNY, Buffalo, 1969; JD, Duke U., 1971. Bar: N.C. 1971, D.C. 1973. Jud. clerk to Hon. Charles R. Simpson U.S. Tax Ct., Washington, 1971-73; assoc. atty. Hogan & Hartson, Washington, 1973-78, ptnr., 1979—. Mem. Phi Beta Kappa, Order of the Coif. Episcopalian. Office: Hogan & Hartson Columbia Sq 555 13th St NW Washington DC 20004-1109

MILLER, HAINON ALFRED, lawyer, investor; b. Kosciusko, Miss., Oct. 9, 1930; s. J. Wesley and Louise (Johnston) M.; m. Lillian Henderson, June 4, 1956; children: Nadalyn, Philip, Kendall, Melissa, Lyon. BA, Miss. Coll., 1951; LLB, Tulane U., 1954. Bar: Miss. 1954, U.S. Dist. Ct. (no. and so. dists.) Miss. 1954, U.S. Ct. Appeals (5th cir.) 1972. Sole practice Greenville, Miss., 1954-92; mem. Miss. Senate, Jackson, 1987-95. Mem. Miss. Ho. of Reps., 1968-83; sec. Washington County Dem. Exec. Com., 1955-60. Recipient Disting. Service award U.S. Jr. C. of C., 1957, Humanized Edn. award Miss. Assn. Educators, Jackson, 1979. Mem. Kiwanis (lt. gov. dist. 1959). Baptist.

MILLER, HARBAUGH, lawyer; b. Wilkinsburg, Pa., July 23, 1902; s. Charles Shively and Ella (Harbaugh) M.; m. Ruth M. Davis, Nov. 8, 1952. B.S., U. Pitts., 1922, J.D., 1925. Bar: Pa. 1925. Ptnr. Miller & Entwisle, Pitts., 1949-95. Pres. Goodwill Industries, 1958-61, YMCA Pitts., 1956-58; trustee U. Pitts., 1945-60, 66-72, trustee emeritus, 1973—; trustee Western Theol. Sem., 1955-58. Fellow Am. Bar Found., Am. Coll. Trust & Estate Counsel; mem. ABA (ho. of dels.), Am. Law Inst., Am. Judicature Soc., Pa. Bar Assn., Allegheny County Bar Assn. (pres. 1955), Pitts. Coun. Chs. (pres. 1951-53), SAR (pres. Pitts. 1940), U. Pitts. Alumni Assn. (pres. 1940), Univ. Club, Duquesne Club, Masons, Shriners, Pitts. Athletic Assn., Phi Delta Theta, Omicron Delta Kappa, Beta Gamma Sigma, Phi Delta Phi. Presbyterian. Home: 154 N Bellefield Ave Pittsburgh PA 15213-2655 Office: 614 Oliver Bldg Pittsburgh PA 15222-2404

MILLER, HAROLD ARTHUR, lawyer; b. St. Marie, Ill., Aug. 18, 1922; s. Arthur E. and Luletta (Noé) M.; m. Michele H. Rogivue, Nov. 23, 1947; children: Maurice H., Jan Leland, Marc Richard. BS in Acctg., U. Ill., 1942, JD, 1950. Bar: Ill. 1950, U.S. Dist. Ct. Ill. 1950, U.S. Tax Ct. 1950. Fgn. svc. officer U.S. State Dept., Paris, France, 1945-48; ptnr. Filson, Williamson & Miller, Champaign, Ill., 1950-60, Williamson & Miller, Champaign, 1960-72, Miller & Hendren, Champaign, 1972—; atty. Christie Clinic Assn., Champaign, 1960-88; atty. pub. schs. dists., Champaign & Vermilion Counties, Ill., 1960—; atty. for municipalities in Champaign County, Ill., 1970—. Author: Estate Planning for Doctors, 1961. Bd. dirs., officer Urbana Sch. Dist., 1957-69; chmn., trustee Parkland Coll., Champaign, 1971-91; founding bd. mem. CCDC Found., Champaign-Urbana Ednl. Found., Moore Heart Found., Christie Found.; life mem. PTA. With inf. U.S. Army, 1942-45, ETO. Mem. ABA, Am. Judicature Soc., Ill. and Local Bar Assns., Ill. Trial Lawyers Assn., Alpha Kappa Psi. Presbyterian. Office: Miller & Hendren Attys 30 E Main St # 300 Champaign IL 61820-3629

MILLER, HAROLD EDWARD, retired manufacturing conglomerate executive, consultant; b. St. Louis, Nov. 23, 1926; s. George Edward and Georgenia Elizabeth (Franklin) M.; m. Lilian Ruth Gantner, Dec. 23, 1949; children—Ellen Susan, Jeffrey Arthur. B.S.B.A., Washington U., St. Louis, 1949. Vice pres. Fulton Iron Works Co., St. Louis, 1968-71; pres. Fulton Iron Works Co., 1971-79, chmn. bd., 1979-90; v.p. Katy Industries Inc., Elgin, Ill., 1976-77; exec. v.p. Katy Industries Inc., 1978-90, also dir., to 1990; pres. HM Consulting, Palatine, Ill., 1990—; dir. Vigel Machine Tool Co., Tecumseh, Ont., Can.; internat. cons. Vigel Spa, Italy. Served with U.S. Army, 1945-46. Mem. Sugar Equipment and Service Exporters Assn., Internat. Machine Tool Builders Assn., Cutting Tool Mfrs. Assn. Presbyterian. Clubs: Barrington Tennis, Inverness Golf.

MILLER, HARRIET SANDERS, art center director; b. N.Y.C., Apr. 18, 1926; d. Herman and Dorothy (Silbert) S.; m. Milton H. Miller, June 27, 1948; children—Bruce, Jeffrey, Marcie. B.A., Ind. U., 1947; M.A., Columbia U., 1949; M.S., U. Wis., 1962, M.F.A., 1967. Dir. art sch. Madison Art Ctr., Wis., 1963-72; acting dir. Center for Continuing Edn., Vancouver, B.C., 1975-76; mem. fine arts faculty Douglas Coll., Vancouver, 1972-78; exec. dir. Palos Verdes Arts Center, Calif., 1978-84; dir. Junior Arts Center, Los Angeles, 1984—; one woman exhibits at Gallery 7, Vancouver, 1978, Gallery 1, Toronto, Ont., 1977, Linda Farris Gallery, Seattle, 1975, Galerie Allen,

Vancouver, 1973. Mem. Calif. Art Edn. Assn., Museum Educators of So. Calif., Arts and Humanities Symposium. Office: Junior Arts Ctr 4814 Hollywood Blvd Los Angeles CA 90027-5302

MILLER, HARRY BRILL, scenic designer, director, acting instructor, lyricist, interior designer; b. Jersey City, Jan. 26, 1924; s. Max Joseph Miller and Lillian (Hirsch) Grodjesk. BA, U. Mich., 1946; MA, Smith Coll., 1948. Set designer, asst. scenic designer various Broadway, Off Broadway and summer shows, N.Y.C., 1948-72; scenic designer NBC-TV, N.Y.C., 1950-63; art dir. MPO-Video Prodns., N.Y.C., 1962; scenic designer CBS-TV, N.Y.C., 1963-91; indsl. show designer Norelco, Thompson CSF, Engelhard, N.Y.C., 1958-75; interior designer Interior Comml. Constrn. Assocs., Hialeah, Fla., 1969-70; dir., writer Miramar Minstrels, N.Y.C., 1979-96; dir. PACT Theatre, N.Y.C., 1995; acting tchr. Emmanuel Midtown Young Men and Young Women's Hebrew Assn., N.Y.C., 1989-90. Set designer (TV shows) Princeton '54, '55, '56 (Peabody 1954, 55), The Price is Right, 1962-63, Jackie Gleason Show, 1969-70, CBS News and Special Events, 1986-91, (mus. show) Nashville at the Garden, 1972; art dir. (TV show) Guiding Light, 1978-86 (2 Emmys 1984, 85), The Edge of Night, 1964-69; prodn. designer TV show Captain Kangaroo, 1970-78 (various Peabody awards); set design asst. (Broadway mus.) Funny Girl, 1964, (Broadway play) Sign in Sidney Brustein's Window. Sgt. U.S. Army, 1943-46. Recipient Teaching Assistanship French Govt., Paris, 1948. Mem. United Scenic Artists, Miramar Ski Club (trip chair 1991-93). Avocations: skiing, dancing, swimming, painting, acting. Address: 333 W 56th St Apt 7B New York NY 10019-3770

MILLER, HARRY GEORGE, education educator; b. Waukesha, Wis., Feb. 15, 1941; s. Harry Fricke and Ethel Ruth (D'Amato) M.; m. Mary Frances Shugrue, June 20, 1964; children: Alicia, Michael, Anne, Dierdre, Courtney. B.A., Carroll Coll., 1963; M.Ed., U. Nebr., 1967, Ed.D., 1970. Tchr. Westside Community Schs., Omaha, 1964-67; demonstration tchr. East Edn. Complex, Lincoln (Nebr.) Pub. Schs., 1967-68; instr. curriculum research Tchrs. Coll., U. Nebr., Lincoln, 1968-70; faculty So. Ill. U., Carbondale, 1970—; asso. prof. edn., dept. secondary edn. So. Ill. U., 1972—, chmn. dept. secondary edn., 1973-75, prof., chmn. dept. ednl. leadership, 1975—; dean, prof. Coll. Tech. Careers, 1980-89; assoc. v.p. acad. affairs So. Ill. U., 1989-92; dean, prof. Ctr. Adult and Continuing Edn. The Am. U., Cairo, 1992—; rsch. prof. Ministry Edn., Thailand, 1978; vis. prof. Ministry Edn., Sabah, East Malaysia, 1980, Korea, 1985; vis. prof. Vladimir State U., Russia, 1989; vis. prof. PRC, 1991; cons. to various orgns. and instns., 1969-74. Author: Beyond Facts: Objective Ways to Measure Thinking, 1976, Adults Teaching Adults, 1977, Responsibility Education, 1977, The Adult Educator: A Handbook for Staff Development, 1978, An Introduction to Adult and Continuing Education, 1979, The Education of Adults, 1981, The Life-long Learning Experience, 1986, Grassroots, 1992, Veiled Voices, 1993; also monographs; mem. editorial bd. Traning, 1976. Mem. Ill. Migrant Council, 1974; Adv. bd. Evaluation and Devel. Center, Rehab. Inst., Carbondale, 1974-80; bd. dirs. St. Joseph's Hosp. Fulbright grantee Republic of Togo, 1982. Mem. Pub. Adult and Continuing Edn. Assn., Rural Edn. Assn., Ill. Coun. for Social Studies (hon.), Community Svcs. Assn. Cairo (bd. dirs. 1994—), Greater Cleve. Coun. for Social Studies (hon.), Ednl. Coun. fo 100 Inc., Coll. of Cons. Democrat. Roman Catholic. Club: K.C. Office: The Am U Ctr for Adult and Con Edn, PO Box 2511 113 Sharia Kass Aini, Cairo Egypt

MILLER, HARVEY ALFRED, botanist, educator; b. Sturgis, Mich., Oct. 19, 1928; s. Harry Clifton and Carmen (Sager) M.; m. Donna K. Hall, May 9, 1992; children: Valerie Yvonne, Harry Alfred, Timothy Merk, Tanya Merk. B.S., U. Mich., 1950; M.S., U. Hawaii, 1952; Ph.D., Stanford U., 1957. Instr. botany U. Mass., 1955-56; instr. botany Miami U., 1956-57, asst. prof., 1957-61, assoc. prof., curator herbarium, 1961-67; prof., chmn. program in biology Wash. State U., 1967-69; vis. prof. botany U. Ill., 1969-70; prof., chmn. dept. biol. scis. U. Cen. Fla., 1970-75, prof., 1975-94; v.p. Marine Research Assocs. Ltd., Nassau, 1962-65; assoc. Lotspeich & Assocs., natural systems analysts, Winter Park, Fla., 1979—; botanist U. Mich. Expdn. to Aleutian Islands, 1949-50; prin. investigator Systematic and Phytogeographical Studies Bryophytes of Pacific Islands, NSF, 1959, Miami U. Expdn. to Micronesia, 1960; dir. NSF-Miami U. Expdn. to Micronesia and Philippines, 1965; prin. investigator NSF bryophytes of So. Melanesia, 1983-86; research assoc. Orlando Sci. Ctr., Orlando; vis. prof. U. Guam, 1965; cons. tropical botany, foliage plant patents, also designs for sci. bldgs.; adj. prof. botany Miami U., 1985—, vis. prof. botany, 1994—; field researcher on Alpine meadows in Irian Jaya, 1991, 1992. Author: (with H.O. Whittier and B.A. Whittier) Prodromus Florae Muscorum Polynesiae, 1978, Prodromus Florae Hepaticarum Polynesiae, 1983; Field Guide to Florida Mosses and Liverworts, 1990; editor: Florida Scientist, 1973-78; contbr. articles to sci. jours. Mem. exec. bd. and chem. scholarship and grant selection com. Astronauts Scholarship Found. (formerly Mercury Seven Found.), 1985—. Recipient Acacia Order of Pythagoras; recipient Acacia Nat. award of Merit; Guggenheim fellow, 1958. Fellow AAAS, Linnean Soc. London; mem. Pacific Sci. Assn. (chmn. sci. com. for botany 1975-83), Assn. Tropical Biology, Am. Inst. Biol. Scis., Am. Bryol. Soc. (v.p. 1962-63, pres. 1964-65), Brit. Bryol. Soc., Bot. Soc. Am., Internat. Assn. Plant Taxonomists, Internat. Assn. Bryologists, Mich. Acad. Sci. Arts and Letters, Hawaiian Acad. Sci., Am. Soc. Plant Taxonomists, Fla. Acad. Sci. (exec. sec. 1976-83, pres. 1980), Nordic Bryol. Soc., Acacia, Explorers Club, Sigma Xi, Phi Sigma, Beta Beta Beta. Home: PO Box 6004 Oxford OH 45056-6004 Office: Miami U Dept Botany Oxford OH 45056

MILLER, HARVEY R., lawyer, bankruptcy reorganization specialist; b. Bklyn., Mar. 1, 1933; married;. Grad., Columbia U. Law Sch., 1959. Ptnr. Weil Gotshal and Manges, N.Y.C. Office: Weil Gotshal & Manges 767 5th Ave New York NY 10153

MILLER, HARVEY S. SHIPLEY, foundation trustee; b. Phila., Sept. 28, 1948; s. Frank Leroy and Betty Charlotte (Elfont) M. BA, Swarthmore Coll., 1970; JD, Harvard U., 1973. Bar: N.Y. 1973. Assoc. Debevoise & Plimpton, N.Y.C., 1973-75; curator and dir. dept. collections and spl. exhbns. Franklin Inst., Phila., 1975-81; v.p. Energy Solutions, Inc., N.Y.C., 1982-84; pres., chief exec. officer, dir. Daltex Med. Scis., Inc., N.Y.C., 1983-86, dir. exec. com., 1983-94, chief operating officer, vice chmn., 1986-91, pres., chief operating officer, 1991-93; trustee The Judith Rothschild Found., N.Y.C., 1993—. Author: Milton Avery: Drawings and Paintings, 1976, It's About Time, 1979; author, editor: New Spaces: Exploring the Aesthetic Dimensions of Holography, 1979; co-author: Rapid Inactivation of Infectious Pathogens by Chlorhexidine-coated Gloves, 1992; contbr. articles to profl. jours. Mem. vis. com. on photography George Eastman House, Rochester, N.Y., 1976-78; trustee Milton and Sally Avery Arts Found., N.Y.C., 1983—, sec., 1996—; trustee The Franklin Inst., Phila., 1993-95, Phila. Mus. Art, 1985—, exec. com., 1993—; assoc. trustee U. Pa., 1981-95; bd. govs. Print Club, Phila., 1976-87; bd. overseers U. Pa. Sch. Nursing, 1981—, Edith C. Blum Art Inst. Bard Coll., 1984-87; bd. dirs., mem. corp. MacDowell Colony, N.Y.C., 1982-85; exec. bd. dirs. Fabric Workshop, Phila., 1976-86; mem. prints and drawings and photographs trustees adv. com. Phila. Mus. Art, 1974—, trustee, 1985—, investment com., 1989-95, exec., devel. and exhbn. coms., 1993—; bd. assocs. Swarthmore Coll. Librs., Phila., 1978-86; treas., dir. Arcadia Found., Norristown, Pa., 1981—; chmn. adv. bd. Inst. Contemporary Art U. Pa., 1982-84; trustee, vice chmn. coms. on instrn. Pa. Acad. Fine Arts, 1982-91, trustee emeritus, 1991—, chmn. collections and exhbns. com., 1985-87; trustee N.Y. Studio Sch., 1974-80, U. of the Arts, 1979-86; mem. exec. bd. Citizens for Arts in Pa., 1980; bd. dirs. Once Gallery, Inc., 1974-75, Wildlife Preservation Trust Internat., Inc., 1990-95; mem. Mayor's Cultural Adv. Coun., Phila., 1987-91; chair Mayor's Art-in-City Hall Program, Phila., 1992-94; trustee coun. Nat. Gallery Art, Washington, 1995—; mem. collections com. Hist. Soc. Pa., 1991-93, councilor trustee, 1992-93; mem. vis. com. photographs Met. Mus. Art, 1996—. Mem. ABA, Assn. of Bar of City of N.Y., Athenaeum, Libr. Co. Phila., Am. Philos. Soc., Hist. Soc. Pa., Phila. Art Alliance, Union League of Phila., Harvard Club of N.Y.C., Swarthmore Club Phila., Phi Sigma Kappa. Republican. Home: Moorhope Mathers Ln Fort Washington PA 19034 Office: 1110 Park Ave New York NY 10128-1201

MILLER, HASBROUCK BAILEY, financial and travel services company executive; b. Gloversville, N.Y., Aug. 1, 1923; s. Edward Waite and Lorraine (Taylor) M.; m. Elizabeth J. Wilson, Jan. 5, 1949; children: Kimberly Elizabeth, Stacey Wilson, Hasbrouck Bailey, Sloan Taylor. B.A., Hamilton Coll., 1944; postgrad., U. Lausanne, Switzerland, 1946, Sch. Advanced Internat. Studies, Washington, 1947, Stanford Grad. Sch. Bus., 1961. With Am. Express Co. (and subsidiaries), 1948—, v.p., sec., 1964-65, sr. v.p., 1965-68, exec. v.p., 1968-83; exec. v.p. Am. Express Internat., Inc., 1960-83; ret., 1983. Served with OSS, AUS, 1942-45. Mem. Morris County Golf Club (Convent Station, N.J.). Home: Fox Hollow Rd Morristown NJ 07960

MILLER, HENRY FORSTER, architect; b. Sept. 16, 1916; s. Rutger Bleecker and Dorothy (Forster) M.; m. Maria Stockton Bullitt, Apr. 6, 1942; children: Maria, Andrew, Dorothy, Steven, Henry Jr. BA, Yale U., 1938, MArch, 1948. Registered architect, Conn., R.I., Mass. Instr. archtl. design Yale Sch. Architecture, New Haven, 1948-49; assoc. dir. facilities planning office Yale U., New Haven, 1974-90; assoc. Harold H. Davis Architect, New Haven, 1949-56; ptnr. Davis, Cochran & Miller, New Haven, 1956-69, Davis, Cochran, Miller, Baerman, Noyes, New Haven, 1969-74; pvt. practice Orange, Conn., 1990—; pres. Conn. Bldg. Congress, 1957-58. Prin. works include Booth Meml. Boys Club Bldg. (Archtl. Design award 1971), Columbus Sch. New Haven (HUD Design Excellence award 1970). Mem. bd. govs. New Haven Boys and Girls Club, 1956-93; v.p. Comty. Coun. Greater New Haven, 1964-66; apptd. mem. State Housing Commn., Conn., 1970-72; mem. Conn. Rev. Bd. for Nat. Register of Hist. Places, 1974-81; founding dir. Conn. Trust for Hist. Preservation, 1975-86, pres., 1975-77; bd. dirs. New Haven Preservation Trust. Maj. F.A. AUS, 1941-46, ETO. Fellow AIA (Conn. state preservation coord. 1965-90, exec. com. 1967-69), Mory's Assn. Democrat. Roman Catholic. Avocations: tennis, hiking, drawing, painting. Home and Office: 30 Derby Ave Orange CT 06477-1403

MILLER, HENRY FRANKLIN, lawyer; b. Phila., May 19, 1938; s. Lester and Bessie (Posner) M.; m. Barbara Ann Gendel, June 20, 1964; children: Andrew, Alexa. AB, Lafayette Coll., 1959; LLB, U. Pa., 1964. Bar: Pa. 1965. Law clk. U.S. Dist. Ct. Del., Wilmington, 1964-65; assoc. Wolf, Block, Schorr & Solis-Cohen, Phila., 1965-71, ptnr., 1971—. Pres. Soc. Hill Synagogue, Phila., 1978-79, Big Brothers/Big Sisters Assn. of Phila., 1980-81, Jewish Family & Children's Agy., Phila., 1986-88. 1st lt. U.S. Army, 1959-60. Mem. Am. Coll. Real Estate Lawyers. Avocations: swimming, hiking, reading. Office: Wolf Block Schorr & Solis-Cohen 12th Fl Packard Bldg 15th And Chestnut St Philadelphia PA 19102-2625

MILLER, HERBERT DELL, petroleum engineer; b. Oklahoma City, Sept. 29, 1919; s. Merrill Dell and Susan (Green) M.; BS in Petroleum Engring., Okla. U., 1941; m. Rosalind Rebecca Moore, Nov. 23, 1947; children: Rebecca Miller Friedman, Robert Rexford. Field engr. Amerada Petroleum Corp., Houston, 1948-49, Hobbs, N.Mex., 1947-48, dist. engr., Longview, Tex., 1949-57, sr. engr., Tulsa, 1957-62; petroleum engr. Moore & Miller Oil Co., Oklahoma City, 1962-78; owner Herbert D. Miller Co., Oklahoma City, 1978—. Maj., F.A., AUS, 1941-47; ETO. Decorated Bronze Star with oak leaf cluster, Purple Heart (U.S.); Croix de Guerre (France). Registered profl. engr., Okla., Tex. Mem. AIME. Republican. Episcopalian (pres. Men's Club 1973). Clubs: Oklahoma City Golf, Country. Home and Office: 6708 NW Grand Blvd Oklahoma City OK 73116-6016

MILLER, HERBERT ELMER, accountant; b. DeWitt, Iowa, Aug. 11, 1914; s. Elmer Joseph and Marian (Briggs) M.; m. Lenore Snitkey, July 1, 1938; 1 dau., Barbara Ruth. A.B., State U. Iowa, 1936, M.A., 1937; Ph.D., U. Minn., 1944; Dr. h.c., Free U. Brussels, 1982; D.H.L. (h.c.), De Paul U., 1983. C.P.A., Iowa. Acctg. prof. U. Minn., U. Mich., Mich. State U., 1938-70; ptnr. Arthur Andersen & Co., Chgo., 1970-78; dir. Sch. Acctg., U. Ga., Athens, 1978-83. Co-author: Finney-Miller accounting series, 1950-70; editor, contbr.: C.P.A. Rev. Manual, 1951-79. Mem. AICPA (bd. dirs. 1968-70), Am. Acctg. Assn. (pres. 1965-66), Federated Schs. Acctg. (pres. 1982), Beta Gamma Sigma, Beta Alpha Psi (nat. pres. 1961-62). Home: 145 S Stratford Dr Athens GA 30605-3025

MILLER, HERBERT JOHN, JR., lawyer; b. Mpls., Jan. 11, 1924; s. Herbert John and Catherine (Johnson) M.; m. Carey Kinsolving, Apr. 3, 1948; children—John Kinsolving William Grady. Student, U. Minn., 1941-43; B.A., George Washington U., 1948, LL.B., 1949. Bar: D.C. 1949. Asso. Kirkland, Fleming, Green, Martin & Ellis, Washington, 1949-58; partner Kirkland, Ellis, Hodson, Chaffetz and Masters, 1958-61; asst. atty. gen., criminal div. Dept. Justice, 1961-65; partner Miller, Cassidy, Larroca & Lewin, Washington, 1965—; chmn. U.S. del. Conferees Attys. Gen. Ams., Mexico City, 1963, Mins. of Govt., Interior and Security of Cen. Am., Panama, and U.S., 1964, 65; chmn. Pres.'s Commn. on D.C. Crime, 1965-67. Capt. AUS, 1943-46. Mem. ABA, Am. Coll. Trial Lawyers, D.C.Bar Assn. (pres. 1970-71), Order of Coif, Phi Delta Phi, Alpha Delta Phi. Club: Congressional (Washington). Home: 17017 Whites Store Rd Boyds MD 20841-9665 Office: Miller Cassidy Larroca & Lewin 2555 M St NW Washington DC 20037-1302

MILLER, HERMAN LUNDEN, retired physicist; b. Detroit, Apr. 23, 1924; s. Josiah Leonidas and Sadie Irene (Lunden) M.; m. Dorothy Grace Sack, Sept. 15, 1951. BS in Engring. Physics, U. Mich., 1948, MS in Physics, 1951. Registered profl. engr., Mich. Physicist Ethyl Corp., Ferndale, Mich., 1948-49, Dow Chem. Co., Denver, 1950-55; mem. project rsch. staff Princeton (N.J.) U., 1955-65; physicist Bendix Aerospace, Ann Arbor, Mich., 1965-72; nuclear engr. Commonwealth Assocs., Jackson, Mich., 1973-80. Contbr. articles to profl. jours. With USAF, 1943-46, PTO, lt. col. Res. Mem. IEEE, Am. Phys. Soc., Am. Nuclear Soc.

MILLER, HOPE RIDINGS, author; b. Bonham, Tex.; d. Alfred Lafayette and Grace (Dupree) Ridings; m. Clarence Lee Miller, Sept. 26, 1932 (dec. Jan. 1965). B.A., U. Tex.; M.A., Columbia; D.Litt., Austin Coll. Society editor Washington Post, 1938-45; Washington corr. Town and Country mag., 1944-46, The Argonaut mag., 1945-49; Washington columnist Promenade mag., 1945-51; syndicated column McNaught, 1945-50; asso. editor Diplomat mag., 1952-55, editor in chief, 1956-66; television prodn. staff Metromedia, Inc., 1966-70; Washington editor Antique Monthly, 1976-89; mem. editorial adv. bd. Horizon mag., 1978-89. Author: Embassy Row: The Life and Times of Diplomatic Washington, 1969, Great Houses of Washington, 1969, Scandals In The Highest Office: Facts and Fictions in the Private Lives of Our Presidents, 1973; script for cassette tape Circling Lafayette Square, 1976. Mem. women's bd. Columbia Hosp., Friends of the Folger Library, Washington Heart Assn. Mem. Nat. Press Club, Hist. Soc. Washington, Friends of LBJ Libr., Am. News women's Club, The Circle of the Nat. Gallery of Art, Stephen F. Austin Soc., Am. Archives of Art, Smithsonian Assocs., Nat. Mus. Women in the Arts, Sulgrave Club. Home: 1868 Columbia Rd NW Washington DC 20009-5183

MILLER, HUGH THOMAS, computer consultant; b. Indpls., Mar. 22, 1951; s. J. Irwin and Xenia S. Miller; m. Linda Anderson, 1975 (div. 1987); 1 child, Jonathan William; m. Katherine McLeod, 1988 (div. 1995). BA, Yale U., 1976; SM in Mgmt., MIT, 1985. Owner Hugh Miller Bookseller, New Haven, 1976-83, Hugh Miller Cons., New Haven; ind. cons. microcomputers, 1981-85; supr. decision technologies divsn. Electronic Data Sys., Inc., Troy, Mich., 1985-86, supr. product and mfg. engring. divsn., 1986-90; product mgr. Indsl. Bus. Devel. Electronic Data Sys., Inc., Troy, supr. Packard Electric Acct., 1990-92, acct. mgr. GM Chassis Sys. Ctr., 1992-93; with mfg. profl. devel. program Electronic Data Sys., Inc., Troy, Mich., 1993, requirements mgr. Consistent Engring. Environ., 1994—. Editor, ptnr. The Common Table, pub. firm. Bd. dirs. Irwin-Sweeney-Miller Found., Columbus, Ind.,1972—; bd. of govs. MIT Sloan Sch. Mgmt., 1989-94; IT adv. com. Yale U., 1996—. Mem. IEEE, Assn. Computing Machinery, Am. Mensa Ltd. Home: 1173 Lake Angelus Rd Lake Angelus MI 48326-1028 Office: EDS Ste 200 3310 W Big Beaver Rd Troy MI 48084

MILLER, I. GEORGE, physician, educator, researcher; b. Chgo., Apr. 18, 1937; s. Irving George and Florence (Levy) M.; m. Arlette Goldmuntz, Mar. 25, 1962; children: Lisa, John, David. A.B., Harvard U., 1958, M.D., 1962. Intern Univ. Hosp., Western Res, U., Cleve., 1962-63; resident Univ. Hosp., Western Res., U., Cleve., 1963-64; epidemiology intelligence oficer Communicable Disease Ctr. USPHS, Atlanta, 1964-66; research fellow in medicine Harvard U. Med. Sch., Boston, 1966-69; asst. prof. pediatrics, epidemiology, biophysics and biochemistry Yale Sch. Medicine, New Haven, 1969-72, J.F. Enders prof., 1979—; mem. exptl. virology study sect. NIH, 1974-77; mem. sci. adv. com. damon Runyon Fund, 1979-85, dir., 1985-94; Leukemia Soc. Am., 1976-81. Contbr. numerous articles, chpts. to profl. publs.; editl. bd. Jour. Virology, 1981-87, Virology, 1982-86. Recipient epidemic Intelligence Service Alumni Assn. prize, 1967; Macy faculty scholar, 1977, Am. Cancer Soc. scholar, 1990; Howard Hughes Med. Inst. investigatorship, 1972-80. Fellow Infectious Diseases Soc. (Squibb award 1982, Enders award 1989); mem. Am. soc. Clin. Investigation, Am. Pediatric Soc., Am. Soc. Virology, Assn. Am. Physicians. Jewish. Home: 95 Alden Ave New Haven CT 06515-2718 Office: Yale U Sch Medicine Pediatrics Infectious Diseases PO Box 208064 New Haven CT 06520-8064*

MILLER, IRVING FRANKLIN, chemical engineering educator, academic administrator; b. N.Y.C., Sept. 27, 1934; s. Sol and Gertrude (Rochkind) M.; m. Baila Hannah Milner, Jan. 28, 1962; children: Eugenia Lynne, Jonathan Mark. BS in Chem. Engring., NYU, 1955; MS, Purdue U., 1956; PhD, U. Mich., 1960. Research scientist United Aircraft Corp., Hartford, 1959-61; from asst. prof. to prof., head chem. engring. Poly. Inst. Bklyn., 1961-72; prof. bioengring., head bioengring. program U. Ill., Chgo., 1973-79, acting head systems engring. dept., 1978-79, assoc. vice chancellor for research, dean Grad. Coll., 1979-85, prof. chem. engring., head chem. engring., 1986-95, dir. Ctr. for Advanced Edn. and Rsch., 1989-90, dir. Office of Spl. Projects, 1990-92, dir. bioengring. program, 1992-95; dean Coll. Engring. U. Akron, Ohio, 1995—; cons. to industry, also Nat. Acad. Scis., NIH. Editor: Electrochemical Bioscience and Bioengineering, 1973; Contbr. articles profl. jours. Mem. Am. Inst. Chem. Engrs., Am. Chem. Soc., AAAS, Biomed. Engring. Soc., N.Y. Acad Scis. Home: 23299 Shaker Blvd Shaker Heights OH 44122 Office: ASEC 201 Akron OH 44325-3901

MILLER, ISRAEL, rabbi, university administrator; b. Balt., Apr. 6, 1918; s. Tobias and Bluma (Bunchez) M.; m. Ruth Joan Goldman, Oct. 16, 1945; children: David, Michael, Deborah, Judith. B.A. magna cum laude, Yeshiva Coll., 1938, D.D., 1967; M.A., Columbia U., 1949. Ordained rabbi, 1941. Rabbi Kingsbridge Heights Jewish Center, Bronx, 1941-68; rabbi emeritus Kingsbridge Heights Jewish Center, 1968—; asst. to pres. Yeshiva U., N.Y.C., 1968-70; v.p. Yeshiva U., 1970-80, sr. v.p., 1980-94, sr. v.p. emeritus, 1994—; counselor B'nai B'rith Hillel Found., Hunter Coll., Bronx, 1951-60; lectr. homiletics Yeshiva U., 1954-55; prof. applied rabbinics Rabbi Isaac Elchanan Theol. Sem., 1968—. Editor: Sermon Manual, 1951. V.p. Bronx Coun. Am. Jewish Congress, 1954-60, Bronx Coun. Jewish Edn., 1964-68; pres. Rabbinical Coun. Am., 1964-66, hon. pres., 1966-68; mem. exec. com. World Zionist Orgn., 1971-76; chmn. Am. Jewish Conf. on Soviet Jewry, 1965-67, Am. Zionist Council, 1967-70; pres. Am. Zionist Fedn., 1970-74, hon. pres., 1974—; v.p. Religious Zionists Am., 1966-68; religious cons., retreat master Dept. Def. in, Europe, 1954, 63-64, Alaska, 1958, Japan, 1960; Vice chmn. Conf. Pres.'s Am. Jewish Orgns., 1969-74; chmn. Conf. Pres.'s Major Am. Jewish Orgns., 1974-76; vice chmn. N.Y. Jewish Community Rels. Coun., 1976—; exec. com. Bronx coun. Boy Scouts Am., 1951-58; mem. Nat. Citizens Com. Community Rels., 1946—; bd. dirs. Nat. Jewish Welfare Bd., v.p., 1969—; chmn. Commn. Jewish Chaplaincy, 1962-65; bd. dirs. Bd. Jewish Edn. N.Y.C., Nat. Jewish Community Relations, United Israel Appeal, 1968—; bd. dirs., acting pres. Conf. on Jewish Material Claims Against Germany, 1983, pres., 1984—; pres. Conf. on Jewish Material Claims Against Austria, 1984—; sec. Meml. Found. for Jewish Culture, 1973-94, mem. bd. dirs. ad personam, 1994—; bd. govs. Jewish Agy. for Israel, 1971-76; vice chmn. Am. Israel Pub. Affairs Com., 1983-91; mem. Jerusalem Com., 1990—; bd. dirs. The Jerusalem Found., 1985—; hon. chmn. Jewish Nat. Fund. Served as chaplain USAAF, 1945-46. Recipient Bernard Revel award Yeshiva Coll. Alumni Assn., 1961, Nat. Rabbinic Leadership award Union of Orthodox Jewish Congregations, 1966, 81, Shofar award Boy Scouts Am., 1965, Frank L. Weill award Nat. Jewish Welfare Bd., 1972, Louis Lipsky Meml. award Am. Jewish League for Israel, 1993, Dr. Harris J. Levine award B'nai Zion, 1979, Lifetime Achievement award Rabbinical Coun. Am., 1996; named Man of Yr. Nat. Coun. Young Israel, 1976. Mem. Am. Zionist Youth Found. (life), Jewish War Vets. (nat. chaplain 1962-63), Assn. Jewish Chaplains Armed Forces (pres. 1955-56), Rabbinic Alumni Yeshiva U. (pres. 1960-62). Home: 2619 Davidson Ave Bronx NY 10468-4103 Office: Yeshiva U 2540 Amsterdam Ave New York NY 10033-2807 *In life I have found the verbs more important than the nouns and adjectives. We show who we are by how we act, respond, love or hate.*

MILLER, J. PHILIP, television producer, director, educator; b. Barberton, Ohio, July 10, 1937; s. Cloy M. and Mary (Yoder) M.; children—Kimberly Lowell, Marc Cloy. B.A., Haverford Coll., 1959; EdM, Harvard U., 1960. Tchr. public schs. Newton and Lexington, Mass., 1959-63; dir., lead guitarist profl. folksinging trio Boston, 1963-66; prodn. coordinator, prodn. asst. Candid Camera, N.Y.C., 1966-67; unit mgr., assoc. producer NBC-TV, N.Y.C., 1967-73; instr. TV prodn. NYU; freelance producer, dir. N.Y.C., 1973—; exec. producer Miller Greenewood Prodns., N.Y.C., 1982-83; sr. spls. producer WCVB-TV, Boston, 1983-85; asst. prof. broadcasting and film Coll. Communication Boston U., 1985-89, assoc. prof., 1989—; dir., writer, head writer Kids-TV series showtime, N.Y.C., 1989-90. Programs include Go Show, 1973-75, Special Treat, 1975, 77, First Tuesday, 1970-71, Tonight Show, 1969, Christmastime with Mr. Rogers, 1978, 3-2-1 Contact, 1979, The Bloodhound Gang, 1979, Getting the Most Out of Television, 1980. Recipient Emmy awards, 1976, 84, 86; Peabody award, 1975; Ohio State award, 1985, 86; Chgo. Internat. Film Festival Cert., 1975, Silver Circle award Nat. Acad. TV Arts and Scis., 1994. Mem. Dirs. Guild Am., Writers Guild Am., Nat. Acad. TV Arts and Scis., Assn. Ind. Video and Filmmakers, Phi Delta Kappa. Avocations: photography, tennis. Home: 161 W Newton St Boston MA 02118-1204 Office: Boston U Coll of Communication 640 Commonwealth Ave Boston MA 02215-2422

MILLER, JACK DAVID R., radiologist, physician, educator; b. Johannesburg, South Africa, Apr. 15, 1930; s. Harold Lewis and Inez (Behrman) M.; m. Miriam Sheckter, Dec., 1988. B.Sc., M.B., Ch.B., U. Witwatersrand, Johannesburg, 1956. Diplomate: Am. Bd. Radiology. Intern Coronation Hosp., Johannesburg, 1957-58; resident in radiology Passavant Meml. Hosp., Chgo., 1959-62, Wesley Meml. Hosp., Chgo., 1959-62; fellow in radiology Northwestern U. Med. Sch., 1962-63; chmn. dept. radiology U. Hosp., Edmonton, Alta., Can., 1971-83; clin. prof. radiology U. Alta., 1971—. Fellow Royal Coll. Physicians Can., Am. Coll. Radiology. Office: U Alberta Dept Radiology, Edmonton, AB Canada

MILLER, JACQUELINE WINSLOW, library director; b. N.Y.C., Apr. 15, 1935; d. Lynward Roosevelt and Sarah Ellen (Grevious) W.; 1 child, Percy Scott. BA, Morgan State Coll., 1957; MLS, Pratt Inst., 1960; grad. profl. seminar, U. Md., 1973. Cert. profl. librarian. With Bklyn. Pub. Library, 1957-68; head extension services New Rochelle (N.Y.) Pub. Library, 1969-70; br. adminstr. Grinton Will Yonkers (N.Y.) Pub. Libr., 1970-75; dir. Yonkers Pub. Library, 1975-96; mem. adj. faculty grad. libr. studies Queens Coll., CUNY, 1989, 90. Mem. commr.'s com. Statewide Libr. Devel., Albany, N.Y., 1980; mem. N.Y. Gov.'s Commn. on Librs., 190, 91; bd. dirs. Community Planning Coun., Yonkers, N.Y., 1987; mem. Yonkers Black Women's Polit. Caucus, 1987; pres. bd. Literacy Vols. of Westchester County, 1991-92. Recipient Yonkers Citizen award Ch. of Our Saviour, 1980, 2d Ann. Mae Morgan Robinson award Yonkers chpt. Westchester Black Women's Polit. Caucus, 1992, 3d Ann. Equality Day award City of Yonkers, 1992, African-Am. Heritage 1st award YWCA, 1994; named Outstanding Profl. Woman Nat. Assn. Negro Bus. and Profl. Women's Clubs Inc., 1981. Mem. ALA (councilor 1987-91), N.Y. State Libr. Assn., Pub. Libr. Dirs. Assn. (exec. bd.), N.Y. State Pub. Libr. Dirs. Assn., Westchester Libr. Assn., Yonkers C. of C. (bd. dirs. 1992-95), Rotary (Yonkers chpt.). Office: Yonkers Pub Libr 7 Main St Yonkers NY 10701-2711

MILLER, JAMES, construction company executive; b. Scotland, Sept. 1, 1934; s. Sir James and Lady Ella Jane M.; m. Kathleen Dewar, 1959; 3 children; m. 2d, Iris Lloyd Webb, 1969; 1 child. MA in Engring. Sci., Oxford (Eng.) U., 1958. With Miller Group Ltd. (formerly James Miller & Ptnrs.), Edinburgh, Scotland, 1958—; chmn. Miller Group Ltd. (formerly James Miller & Ptnrs.), 1970—; chmn. Fedn. Civil Engring. Contractors, 1985-86, pres., 1990-93; bd. dirs. Brit. Linen Bank Ltd., Bank of Scotland; mem. Scottish adv. bd. Brit. Petroleum, 1990—. Chmn. Ct. Heriot-Watt U., 1990-96. Mem. City Livery Club, Merchants of City of Edinburgh (master 1992-94). Avocation: shooting. Office: Miller Group Ltd Miller Hse, 18 S Groathill Ave, Edinburgh EH4 2LW, Scotland

MILLER, JAMES A., wholesale grocery executive. Pres. Alliant Food Svc. Inc., Deerfield, Ill. Office: Alliant Food Svc Inc 1 Parkway N Deerfield IL 60015

MILLER, JAMES ALEXANDER, oncologist, educator; b. Dormont, Pa., May 27, 1915; s. John Herman and Emma Anna (Stenger) M.; m. Elizabeth Cavert, Aug. 30, 1942; children: Linda Ann, Helen Louise; m. Barbara Butler, Dec. 21, 1988. B.S. in Chemistry, U. Pitts., 1939; M.S., U. Wis., 1941, Ph.D. in Biochemistry, 1943; D.Sc. (hon.), Med. Coll. Wis., 1982, U. Chgo., 1991. Finney-Howell fellow in cancer research U. Wis., Madison, 1943-44; instr. oncology U. Wis., 1944-46, asst. prof., 1946-48, asso. prof., 1948-52, prof., 1952-85, Wis. Alumni Research Found. prof. oncology, 1980-82, Van Rensselaer Potter prof. on oncology, 1982-85, prof. emeritus, 1985—; mem. advisory coms. Nat. Cancer Inst., Am. Cancer Soc., 1950—. Contbr. numerous articles on chemical carcinogenesis and microsomal oxidations to profl. jours. Recipient awards (with E.C. Miller); Langer-Teplitz award Ann Langer Cancer Research Found., 1962; Lucy Wortham James award James Ewing Soc., 1965; G.H.A. Clowes award Am. Assn. Cancer Research, 1969; Bertner award M.D. Anderson Hosp. and Tumor Inst., 1971; Papanicolaou award Papanicolaou Inst. Cancer Research, 1975; Rosenstiel award Brandeis U., 1976; award Am. Cancer Soc., 1977; Bristol-Myers award in cancer research, 1978; Gairdner Found. ann. award Toronto, 1978; Founders award Chem. Industry Inst. Toxicology, 1978; 3M Life Sci. award Fedn. Am. Socs. Exptl. Biology, 1979; Freedman award N.Y. Acad. Sci., 1979; Mott award Gen. Motors Cancer Research Found., 1980, Noble Found. Research award, 1986, 1st E. C. Miller and J. A. Miller Disting. Lectureship in Exptl. Oncology award Rutgers U., 1989. Fellow Am. Acad. Arts and Scis., Wis. Acad. Scis., Arts and Letters; mem. Am. Assn. for Cancer Research (hon.), Am. Soc. Biol. Chemists, AAAS, Japanese Cancer Soc. (hon.), Am. Chem. Soc., Soc. Toxicology, Soc. for Exptl. Biology and Medicine, Nat. Acad. Scis. Home: 5517 Hammersley Rd Madison WI 53711-3556 Office: U Wis Mcardle Lab Madison WI 53706

MILLER, JAMES CHRISTOPHER, paper industry information systems specialist; b. Augsburg, Germany, Oct. 20, 1951; came to U.S., 1955, naturalized, 1969; s. William Edwin and Martha (Isele) M.; B.S. in Acctg., Pa. State U., 1973; M.S. in Computer Sci., Rensselaer Poly. Inst., 1975; M.B.A., U. New Haven, 1980; m. Lynette Marie Murri, Aug. 25, 1973; children—Meghan Leigh, Margo Elizabeth. Fin. and EDP auditor United Techs. Corp., Hartford, Conn., 1973-74, fin. systems analyst, 1974-76, asst. mgr. corp. acctg., 1976-77; sr. analyst The Upjohn Co., North Haven, Conn., 1977-79; cons. bus. systems Am. Can Co., Greenwich, Conn., 1980-81, mgr. systems planning, 1981-82, assoc. dir. systems support, 1982; mgr. mgmt. info. systems James River Corp., Richmond, Va., 1983, dir. mgmt. info. systems, 1984-86, v.p. mgmt. info. systems, 1986-90, v.p. info. tech., 1990-93; v.p. info. tech. Hallmark Cards, Inc., Kansas City, Mo., 1993—; instr. info. systems Conn. Tech. Colls., Waterbury and Thames Valley; instr. bus. adminstrn. Western Conn. State U., Ancell Sch. Bus.; chmn. MIS adv. coun. Bloch Sch. Bus. U. Mo., Kansas City. Republican. Roman Catholic. Home: 3405 W 132nd St Leawood KS 66209-4120 Office: Hallmark Cards Mail Drop 511/2501 McGee Box 419580 Kansas City MO 64141

MILLER, JAMES CLIFFORD, III, economist; b. Atlanta, June 25, 1942; s. James Clifford and Annie (Moseley) M.; m. Demaris Humphries, Dec. 22, 1961; children: Katrina Demaris, John Felix, Sabrina Louise. BBA, U. Ga., 1964; PhD in Econs., U. Va., 1969. Asst. prof. Ga. State U., Atlanta, 1968-69; economist U.S. Dept. Transp., Washington, 1969-72; assoc. prof. econs. Tex. A&M U., College Station, 1972-74; economist U.S. Coun. Econ. Advs., Washington, 1974-75; asst. dir. U.S. Council Wage and Price Stability, Washington, 1975-77; resident scholar Am. Enterprise Inst., 1977-81; adminstr. Office Info. and Regulatory Affairs, Office Mgmt. and Budget and exec. dir. Presdl. Task Force on Regulatory Relief, Washington, 1981; chmn. FTC, Washington, 1981-85; dir. Office Mgmt. and Budget, Washington, 1985-88; disting. fellow, chmn., counsellor Citizens for a Sound Economy, 1988—; disting. fellow Ctr. for Study of Pub. Choice George Mason U., 1988—; pres., chmn. bd. Econ. Impact Analysts, Inc., 1978—. Author: Why the Draft?: The Case for a Volunteer Army, 1968, Economic Regulation of Domestic Air Transport: Theory and Policy, 1974, Perspectives on Federal Transportation Policy, 1975, Benefit-Cost Analyses of Social Regulation: Case Studies from the Council on Wage and Price Stability, 1979, Reforming Regulation, 1980, The Economist as Reformer, 1989, Fix the U.S. Budget: Urgings of an "Abominable No-Man," 1994. Thomas Jefferson fellow, 1965-66, DuPont fellow, 1966-67, Ford Found. fellow, 1967-68. Mem. Am. Econ. Assn., Pub. Choice Soc., So. Econ. Assn. (exec. com. 1980-81, v.p. 1990-91), Adminstrv. Conf. U.S. (vice chmn. 1987-88). Republican. Presbyterian. Office: Citizens for Sound Economy 1250 H St NW Washington DC 20005-3952

MILLER, JAMES EDWARD, computer scientist, educator; b. Lafayette, La., Mar. 21, 1940; s. Edward Gustave and Orpha Marie (DeVilbis) M.; m. Diane Moon, June 6, 1964; children—Deborah Elaine, Michael Edward. B.S., U. La.-Lafayette, 1961, Ph.D., 1972; M.S., Auburn U., 1964. Systems engr. IBM, Birmingham, Ala., 1965-68; asst. prof. U. West Fla., Pensacola, 1968-70, chmn. systems sci., 1972-86; grad. researcher U. La.-Lafayette, 1970-72; computer systems analyst EPA, Washington, 1979; prof., chmn. computer sci. and stats. U. So. Miss., Hattiesburg, 1986-92; prof. U. So. Miss., 1992—; program evaluator Computer Sci. Accreditation Commn., 1986-92, cons., lectr. in field; co-dir. NASA/Am. Soc. Engring. Edn. Summer Faculty Fellowship Program-Stennis Space Flight Ctr., 1990—. Author numerous articles for tech. publs. Mem. Computer Soc. of IEEE, Assn. Computing Machinery (editor Computer Sci. Edn. spl. interest group bull. 1982—), Data Processing Mgmt. Assn. (dir. edn. spl. interest group 1985-86), Info. Systems Security Assn., Internat. Assn. Math. and Computer Modeling. Democrat. Methodist. Avocations: Research on parallel computing, computer sci. edn. and optimal sensor deployment. Office: U So Miss Computer Sci & Stat PO Box 5106 Hattiesburg MS 39406-5106

MILLER, JAMES EDWIN, JR., English language educator; b. Bartlesville, Okla., Sept. 9, 1920; s. James Edwin and Leona (Halsey) M.; m. Barbara Anderson, July 3, 1944 (dec. 1981); children: James E. III, Charlotte Ann; m. Kathleen Farley, Mar. 15, 1990. B.A., U. Okla., 1942; M.A., U. Chgo., 1947, Ph.D., 1949. Asst. prof. English U. Nebr., Lincoln, 1953-56; prof., chmn. dept. U. Nebr., 1956-62, Charles J. Mach Regents prof. English, 1961-62; prof. English U. Chgo., 1962—, chmn. dept., 1978-84, Helen A. Regenstein prof. lit., 1983-90, prof. emeritus, 1990—; vis. prof. Northwestern U., 1962, U. Hawaii, 1964, The Sorbonne, Paris, 1984-85, 86, Beijing, China, 1994; Fulbright lectr., Italy, 1958-59, Kyoto, Japan, 1968, Australia, 1976; Otto Salgo prof. Am. studies, Budapest, Hungary, 1991-93. Author: A Critical Guide to Leaves of Grass, 1957, (with Bernice Slote and Karl Shapiro) Start with the Sun, 1960, Walt Whitman, 1962, rev. 1990, Reader's Guide to Herman Melville, 1962, F. Scott Fitzgerald: His Art and His Technique, 1964, J.D. Salinger, 1965, Quests Surd and Absurd: Essays in American Literature, 1967, Word Self, Reality: The Rhetoric of Imagination, 1972, T.S. Eliot's Personal Waste Land, 1977, The American Quest for a Supreme Fiction: Whitman's Legacy in the Personal Epic, 1979, Leaves of Grass: America's Lyric-Epic of Self and Democracy, 1992; Editor: Complete Poetry and Selected Prose of Walt Whitman, 1959, Myth and Method: Modern Theories of Fiction, 1960, Dimensions of Poetry, 1962, Dimensions of the Short Story, 1964, Whitman's Song of Myself: Origin, Growth, Meaning, 1964, Dimensions of Literature, 1967, The Arts and The Public, 1967, Theory of Fiction: Henry James, 1972, Heritage of American Literature, 2 Vols., 1991. Capt. U.S. Army, 1942-46, 50-52. Recipient Walt Whitman award Poetry Soc. Am., 1958, Poetry Chap Book award, 1961; Distinguished Service award Nat. Council Tchrs. English, 1975; Guggenheim fellow, 1969-70; Nat. Endowment for Humanities sr. fellow, 1974-75. Mem. Modern Lang. Assn., Nat. Council Tchrs. of English (editor Coll. English 1960-66, pres. 1970), Am. Studies Assn., Assn. Depts. English (exec. council 1981-84, pres. 1984); AAUP (council 1964-67), Midwest Modern Lang. Assn. (pres. 1961-62), Phi Beta Kappa. Home: 5536 S Blackstone Ave Chicago IL 60637-1834

MILLER, JAMES GEGAN, research scientist, physics educator; b. St. Louis, Nov. 11, 1942; s. Francis John and Elizabeth Ann (Caul) M.; m. Judith Anne Kelvin, Apr. 23, 1966; 1 child, Douglas Ryan. A.B., St. Louis U., 1964; M.A., Washington U., 1966, Ph.D., 1969. Asst. prof. physics Washington U., St. Louis, 1970-72, assoc. prof., 1972-77, prof. physics, 1977—, dir. lab. for ultrasonics, 1987—, research asst. prof. medicine, 1976-81, research assoc. prof. medicine, 1981-88, research prof. medicine, 1988—. Contbr. articles to profl. jours.; patentee in field. Recipient I-R 100 award Indsl. Research Devel. Mag., 1974, 78; NIH, NASA grantee. Fellow Am. Inst. Ultrasound in Medicine, Acoustical Soc. Am.; mem. IEEE (gov. com. Ultrasonics, Ferroelectrics and Frequency Control Soc. 1978-80, 86-88, 92-94), Am. Phys. Soc., Sigma Xi (nat. lectr. 1981-82). Home: 444 Edgewood Dr Saint Louis MO 63105-2016 Office: Washington U Box 1105 Dept Physics Saint Louis MO 63130

MILLER, JAMES L., food products executive; b. 1948. Grad., Cornell U., 1972. V.p. sales, pres., gen. mgr Sysco Corp., Houston, 1972-83; v.p., gen. mgr., exec. v.p., COO no. divsn. PYA/Monarch, Inc., Balt., 1983-89; pres., COO J.P. Foodservice, Inc., Hanover, Md., 1989—. Office: J P Foodservices Inc 9830 Patuxent Woods Dr Columbia MD 21046*

MILLER, JAMES LYNN, lawyer; b. Fairmont, W.Va., June 1, 1951; s. Robert Ogden Jr. and Dora Alice (Ward) M.; m. Maureen Clancy, Apr. 16, 1983; children: James Clancy, Bailey Ward. BA, Calif. State U., Humboldt, 1973; JD, U. Calif., Berkeley, 1976. Bar: Calif. 1976, Hawaii 1988. From assoc. to ptnr. Brobeck, Phleger & Harrison, San Francisco, 1976-95; with antitrust divsn. U.S. Dept. Justice, San Francisco, 1995—. Republican. Avocation: fishing. Office: Dept of Justice Antitrust Divsn 450 Golden Gate Ave San Francisco CA 94102-3478

MILLER, JAMES ROBERT, lawyer; b. McKeesport, Pa., Aug. 2, 1947; s. Robert Charles and Ethel Margaret (Yahn) M.; m. Kathleen Ann Galka, June 6, 1975; children: Jesse J., Cassidy A. BA, NYU, 1969; JD, Duquesne U., 1972. Bar: Pa. 1972, U.S. Dist. Ct. (we. dist.) Pa. 1974, U.S. Ct. Appeals (3d cir.) 1978, U.S. Ct. Appeals (11th cir.) 1989, U.S. Supreme Ct. 1990. Law clerk to Hon. James C. Crumlish, Jr. Commonwealth Ct. of Pa., Phila., 1972-74; shareholder Dickie, McCamey & Chilcote, Pitts., 1974—. Mem. ABA, Am. Coll. Trial Lawyers, Pa. Bar Assn., Acad. Trial Lawyers. Avocation: sports. Office: Dickie McCamey & Chilcote Two PPG Pl Ste 400 Pittsburgh PA 15222

MILLER, JAMES RUMRILL, III, finance educator; b. Phila., Dec. 21, 1937; s. James Rumrill and Elizabeth Pleasants (King) M.; m. Bettie M. Studer, May 1, 1989; children from previous marriage: Elizabeth, Katharine, Kerry. A.B., Princeton U., 1959; M.B.A. (Woodrow Wilson fellow), Harvard U., 1962; Ph.D., M.I.T., 1966. Systems analyst MITRE Corp., Bedford, Mass., 1962-67; asst. prof. bus. adminstrn. Stanford U., 1967-69, asso. prof., 1970-73, prof., 1973—, Walter and Elise Haas prof. bus. adminstrn., 1977—; asso. dean Stanford U. (Bus. Sch.), 1974-76; cons. in field. Author: Professional Decision Making, 1970; contbr. numerous articles to profl. jours. Mem. Phi Beta Kappa. Republican. Episcopalian. Office: Stanford U Bus Sch Stanford CA 94305

MILLER, JAMES VINCE, university president; b. Waynetown, Ind., July 16, 1920; s. J. Vince and Hazel B. (Spore) M.; m. Mildred Mae Hockersmith, June 13, 1943; children: Maryllyn Jean, Rachel Katherine. B.A. in Philosophy and English, U. Indpls., 1942; M.Div. in History and Lit., United Sem., Dayton, Ohio, 1945; postgrad., Earlham Coll., 1945-46; Ph.D. in Philosophy, Boston U., 1955; LL.D. (hon.), Otterbein Coll., 1971, U. Indpls., 1979. Ordained to ministry Evang. United Brethren Ch., 1945; pastor Greensfork, Ind., 1944-46, Stow, Mass., 1946-48; faculty dept. philosophy and religion Bates Coll., Lewiston, Maine, 1950-64; prof. Bates Coll., 1960-64, chmn. dept., 1958-64; acad. dean Otterbein Coll., Westerville, Ohio, 1964-68; v.p. for acad. affairs, acad. dean Otterbein Coll., 1968-71; pres. Pacific U., Forest Grove, Oreg., 1971-83, pres. emeritus, 1983—; pres. Nat. Coll. of Naturopathic Medicine, Portland, Oreg., 1989-93, pres. emeritus, 1993—; adj. prof. Union Grad. Sch., 1970-78, San Francisco Theol. Sem., 1979-86; chmn. N.W. Assn. Pvt. Colls. and Univs., 1974-76; treas. Oreg. Ind. Coll. Assn., 1974-75, 76-78, chmn., 1978-79; adv. com. Oreg. Ednl. Coordinating Commn., 1976-79; chmn. council for higher edn. United Ch. Bd. Homeland Missions, 1975-76; former mem. adv. com. Gov.'s Listening Post; former mem. spl. com. on future of edn. in Oreg., Oreg. Ednl. Coordinating Commn.; mem. Oreg. Bd. Optometry, 1988-92; bd. dirs. Terwilliger Plz., Inc. Methodist. Lodge: Rotary.

MILLER, JAN DEAN, metallurgy educator; b. Dubois, Pa., Apr. 7, 1942; s. Harry Moyer and Mary Virginia (McQuown) M.; m. Patricia Ann Rossman, Sept. 14, 1963; children: Pamela Ann, Jeanette Marie, Virginia Christine. B.S., Pa. State U., 1964; M.S., Colo. Sch. of Mines, 1966, Ph.D., 1969. Research engr. Anaconda Co., Mont., 1966, Lawrence Livermore Lab., Calif., 1972; asst. prof. metallurgy U. Utah, Salt Lake City, 1968-72, assoc. prof., 1972-78, prof., 1978—; cons. on processing of mineral resources to various cos. and govt. agys. Editor: Hydrometallurgy, Research, Development, and Plant Practice, 1983. Contbr. over 200 articles to profl. jours. First commercial plant using air-sparged hydrocyclone tech. for deinking flotation in wastepaper recycling plant, 1992, 24 patents. Bethelehem Steel fellow, 1964-68; recipient Marcus A. Grossman award Am. Soc. Metals, 1974; Van Diest Gold medal Colo. Sch. Mines, 1977; Mellow Met award U. Utah, Salt Lake City, 1978, 82, 94, Stefanko award coal divsn. Soc. Mining Engrs., 1988, Extractive Metallurgy Tech. award, Metall. Soc., 1988, Richards award Am. Inst. Mining, Metall. and Petroleum Engrs., 1991, Extractive and Processing Lectr. award The Minerals, Metals and Materials Soc., 1992, Disting. Achievement medal Colo. Sch. of Mines, 1994. Mem. Soc. Mining, Metallurgy and Exploration (chmn. mineral processing div. 1980-81, Disting. mem. Antoine M. Gaudin award 1992), Fine Particle Soc., AIME (Henry Krumb lectr. 1987), NAE, Am. Chem. Soc., Soc. Mining Engrs. (bd. dirs. 1980-83, program chmn. 1982-83, Taggart award, 1986), Metall. Soc. Baptist. Clubs: Salt Lake Swim and Tennis; U. Utah Faculty. Office: U Utah 412 WBB Dept Metallurgy Salt Lake City UT 84112

MILLER, JANEL HOWELL, psychologist; b. Boone, N.C., May 18, 1947; d. John Estle and Grace Louise (Hemberger) Howell; BA, DePauw U., 1969; postgrad. Rice U., 1969; MA, U. Houston, 1972; PhD, Tex. A&M U., 1979; m. C. Rick Miller, Nov. 24, 1968; children: Kimberly, Brian, Audrey, Rachel. Asso. sch. psychologist Houston Ind. Sch. Dist., 1971-74; research psychologist VA Hosp., Houston, 1972; asso. sch. psychologist Clear Creek Ind. Sch. Dist., Tex., 1974-76; instr. psychology, counseling psychology intern Tex. A. and M. U., 1976-77; clin. psychology intern VA Hosp., Houston, 1977-78; coordinator psychol. services Clear Creek Ind. Sch. Dist., 1978-81, assoc. dir. psychol. services, 1981-82; pvt. practice, Houston, 1982—; faculty U. Houston-Clear Lake, 1984—; adolescent suicide cons., 1984—. DePauw U. Alumni scholar, 1965-69; NIMH fellow U. Houston, 1970-71; lic. clin. psychologist, sch. psychologist, Tex. Mem. APA, Tex. Psychol. Assn., Houston Psychol. Assn. (media rep. 1984-85), Am. Assn. Marriage and Family Therapists, Tex. Assn. Marriage and Family Therapists, Houston Assn. Marriage and Family Therapists, Soc. for Personality Assessment. Home: 806 Walbrook Dr Houston TX 77062-4030 Office: Southpoint Psychol Svcs 11550 Fuqua St Ste 450 Houston TX 77034-4537

MILLER, JASON, playwright; b. Scranton, Pa., Apr. 22, 1939; s. John and Mary M.; m. Linda Gleason, 1963 (div. 1973); children: Jennifer, Jason, Jordan, Joshua. Student, Cath. U.; B.A., U. Scranton, 1961. Author: (plays) Lou Gehrig Did Not Die of Cancer, 1967, Perfect Son, 1967, The Circle Lady, 1967, Nobody Hears a Broken Drum, 1970, That Championship Season, 1971 (Pulitzer prize for drama 1973, Tony award best play 1973, N.Y. Drama Critics Circle award best play 1972), It's a Sin to Tell a Lie; (poetry) Stone Step, 1968, (teleplays) The Reward, 1980, Marilyn: The Untold Story, 1980; dir., writer: (film) That Championship Season, 1982; actor: (theatre) Pequod, 1969, The Happiness Cage, 1970, Subject to Fits, 1971, Long Day's Journey into Night, 1971, Juno and the Paycock, 1971, That Championship Season, 1987, (films) The Exorcist, 1973 (Academy award nomination best supporting actor 1974), The Nickel Ride, 1975, The Ninth Configuration, 1980, Monsignor, 1982, Toy Soldiers, 1984, Light of Day, 1987, The Exorcist III, 1990, Rudy, 1993, (TV movies) A Home of Our Own, 1975, F. Scott Fitzgerald in Hollywood, 1976, The Dain Curse, 1978, Vampire, 1979, Henderson Monster, 1980, The Best Little Girl in the World, 1981, A Touch of Scandal, 1984, Deadly Care, 1987, A Mother's Courage: The Mary Thomas Story, 1989. Office: Mickey Freiberg/Rich Shepard The Artists Agy 10000 Santa Monica Blvd Ste 305 Los Angeles CA 90067-7007

MILLER, JAY ALAN, civil rights association executive; b. Cleve., Feb. 8, 1928; s. Herbert Phillip Miller and Ruth Weisbach; m. Joyce Dannen, Feb. 1, 1952 (div. Oct. 1964); children: Joshua, Adam, Rebecca; m. Maryanne Carol Dust, Jan. 1, 1989; stepchild, Joshua Kalin. Student, Roosevelt U., 1948; BSc, U. Ill., 1950. Organizer Amalgamated Clothing Workers, Chgo., 1950-52; bus. agt., edn. dir. Amalgamated Clothing Workers, Wilkes-Barre, Pa., 1956-61; organizer United Packing House Workers, Chgo., 1952-53; reporter Cleve. Press, 1954-56; peace edn. dir. Am. Friends Svc. Com., Chgo., 1961-65; exec. dir. ACLU of Ill., Chgo., 1965-71, 78—, ACLU of No. Calif., San Francisco, 1971-74; assoc. dir. legis. office ACLU, Washington, 1975-78. Pres. AFL-CIO Labor Coun., Hazelton, Pa., 1959-61, mem. trade union delegation to USSR, 1960; chmn. Turn Toward Peace, Chgo., 1962-64; coord. Com. for a Test Ban Treaty, Ill. and Wis., 1962-63; dep. dir. Ill. Rally for Civil Rights, Chgo., 1964. With U.S. Army, 1946-48, PTO. Home: 2573 N Clark St Chicago IL 60614-1717 Office: ACLU 203 N La Salle St Ste 1405 Chicago IL 60601-1210

MILLER, JEAN PATRICIA SALMON, art educator; b. Little Falls, Minn., Sept. 28, 1920; d. Albert Michael and Wilma (Kaestner) Salmon; m. George Fricke Miller, Sept. 8, 1951 (dec. Apr. 1991); children: Victoria Jean, George Laurids. BS, St. Cloud State Tchrs. Coll., 1942; MS, U. Wis., Whitewater, 1976. Lic. cert. secondary English, art, Wis. Tchr. elem. and secondary art Pub. Schs. Sauk Center, Minn., 1943; tchr. secondary art Bd. Edn., Idaho, 1945; tchr. elem. and secondary art Elkhorn (Wis.) Area Schs., 1950-78; tchr. art adult edn. Kenosha Tech. Coll., Elkhorn, Wis., 1969; cooperating tchr., supr. art majors in edn. U. Wis., Whitewater, 1970-77; coord. Art Train Project, Madison. Represented in permanent collections Irwin L. Young Auditorium, Fern Young Ter., U. Wis., Whitewater. Sec. Walworth County Needs of Children and Youth, Williams Bay, Wis., 1956-57; co-chair, sponsor Senate Bill 161-art requirement for h.s. grad., 1988-89. Recipient Grand award painting Walworth County Fair, 1970, 3rd award painting Geneva Lake Art Assn., Lake Geneva, Wis., Acrylic Painting award Badlants Art Assn., 1994. Mem. Nat. Art Edn. Assn., Wis. Women in the Arts, Wis. Art Edn. Assn., Wis. Regional Artists Assn. (co-chair Wis. regional art program 1992, 93, corr. sec. 1992—), Walworth County Art Assn. (bd. dirs. 1979-94, pres. 1986-87), Alpha Delta Kappa (pres. Theta chpt. Wis. 1968-70). Home and Office: 671 24th St W Apt 8 Dickinson ND 58601

MILLER, JEANNE-MARIE ANDERSON (MRS. NATHAN J. MILLER), English language educator, academic administrator; b. Washington, Feb. 18, 1937; d. William and Agnes Catherine (Johns) Anderson m. Nathan John Miller, Oct. 2, 1960. BA, Howard U., 1959, MA, 1963, PhD, 1976. Instr. dept. English Howard U., Washington, 1963-76, asst. prof., 1976-79, assoc. prof., 1979-92, prof., 1992—, also asst. dir. Inst. Arts and Humanities, 1973-75, asst. acad. planning, office v.p. for acad. affairs, 1976-90; cons. Am. Studies Assn., 1972-75, Silver Burdett Pub. Co., Nat. Endowment for Humanities, 1978—; adv. bd. D.C. Libr. for Arts, 1973—, John Oliver Killens Writers Guild, 1975—, Afro-Am. Theatre, Balt., 1975—. Editor, Black Theatre Bull., 1977-86; Realism to Ritual: Form and Style in Black Theatre, 1983; assoc. editor Theatre Jour., 1980-81; contbr. articles to profl. jours. Mem. Washington Performing Arts Soc., 1971—, Friends of Sta. WETA-TV, 1971—, Mus. African Art, 1971—, Arena Stage Assos., 1972—, Washington Opera Guild, 1982—, Wolf Trap Assocs., 1982—, Drama League N.Y., 1995—. Ford Found. fellow, 1970-72, So. Fellowships Fund fellow, 1973-74; Howard U. rsch. grantee, 1975-76, 94-95, ACLS grantee, 1978-79, NEH grantee, 1981-84. Mem. AAUP, ACLU, MLA, Nat. Coun. Tchrs. English, Coll. English Assn., Am. Studies Assn., Assn. for Theatre in Higher Edn., D.C. LWV, Common Cause, Am. Acad. Polit. and Social Sci., Coll. Lang. Assn., Am. Assn. Higher Edn., Nat. Assn. Women Deans, Adminstrs. and Counselors, Friends of Kennedy Ctr. for Performing Arts, Pi Lambda Theta. Democrat. Episcopalian. Home: 504 24th St NE Washington DC 20002-4818

MILLER, JEFFREY CLARK, lawyer; b. Boston, Aug. 17, 1943; s. Andrew Otterson and Jeanne (White) M.; m. Susanne Jackson, Oct. 23, 1970; children: Gordon, Andrew, Katharine, Eric. BA, Yale U., 1965; JD, Cornell U., 1968. Bar: N.Y. 1970. Assoc. Miller, Montgomery, Spalding & Sogi, N.Y.C., 1968-69; sec. Jamaica Water & Utilities Inc., Greenwich, Conn., 1969-72; assoc. Reid & Priest, N.Y.C., 1972-86, ptnr., 1986-93; asst. gen. coun. Northeast Utilies Svc. Co., Berlin, Conn., 1993—. Bd. dirs. Wilson Point Property Owners Assn., Norwalk, Conn., 1972-74, pres., 1988-92; trustee St. Luke's Sch., New Canaan, Conn., 1992—, chmn., 1995—; sec. Yale U. Class 1965, 1990—. Mem. ABA, N.Y. State Bar Assn. (sec. pub. utility com. 1983-87). Home: 1 Valley Rd Norwalk CT 06854-5010 Office: Northeast Utilities Svc Co PO Box 270 Hartford CT 06141-0270

MILLER, JEFFREY GRANT, law educator; b. Muncie, Ind., Aug. 15, 1941; s. Robert G. and Virginia (Bell) M.; m. Georgia Callahan, Feb. 19, 1988; children: Elizabeth, Scott. AB, Princeton U., 1963; LLB, Harvard U., 1967. Bar: Mass. 1968, D.C. 1982. Rsch. asst. Harvard Law Sch., Cambridge, Mass., 1976-78; assoc. Bingham, Dana & Gould, Boston, 1968-71; enforcement br. chief U.S. EPA, Boston, 1971-73, dir. enforcement div., 1973-75; dep asst. adminstr. for water enforcement U.S. EPA, Washington, 1975-79, acting asst. adminstr. for enforcement, 1979-81; ptnr. Bergson, Borkland, Margolis & Adler, Washington, 1981-86, Verner, Liipfert, Washington, 1986-87; of counsel Perkins Coie, Washington, 1987—; prof. law Pace U., White Plains, N.Y., 1987—; bd. dirs. EnviroSource, Inc., Stamford, Conn.; sec.-treas. Environ. Law Inst., 1987-90. Author: Citizen Suits: Private Enforcement of Federal Pollution Control Laws, 1987, (with T. Colosi) Fundamentals of Negotiation, 1989; mem. editl. adv. bd. Environ. Law Reporter, 1983—. Mem. ABA (chmn. water quality com. 1986-88). Avocations: backpacking, hiking, white water canoeing.

MILLER, JEFFREY VEACH, biochemist, researcher; b. Schenectady, N.Y., Apr. 11, 1955; s. Ray H. and Donna L. (Veach) M. BA, U. Calif., Berkeley, 1978. Biochemist Syva Co., Palo Alto, Calif., 1979-81, Genentech Inc., South San Francisco, 1981-83, Genencor Inc., South San Francisco, 1983-88, U. Calif., Santa Cruz, 1988. Contbr. articles to profl. jours.; patentee in field. Avocation: yacht racing.

MILLER, JERI L. HULL, counselor; b. Quincy, Ill., Mar. 5, 1954; d. Gerald Edward and Ronda Juanita (Nothern) Hull; children: Jennifer Jean, Jaime Terese. BA magna cum laude, Quincy Coll., 1980; MA, Sangamon State U., 1993. Cert. counselor; cert. clin. mental health counselor; nat. bd. cert. counselor; lic. profl. clin. counselor, Ill. Probation officer Adams County Probation Office, Quincy, 1980-81; caseworker Ill. Dept. Pub. Aid, Quincy, 1984-86; truancy officer Adams County Supt. of Schs., Quincy, 1989-91; sch. guidance counselor Quincy Sch. Dist., 1991—; clin. counselor Luth. Child and Family Svcs., Quincy, 1993—. Field worker Am. Cancer Soc., Muscular Dystrophy Assn.; leader Girl Scouts U.S.A. Mem. ACA, Am. Sch. Counselors Assn., Nat. Bd. Cert. Counselors, Chi Sigma Iota. Methodist. Avocations: painting, reading, skiing. Home: 908 Pawn Ave Quincy IL 62301-4738 Office: Berrian Alternative Sch 1327 S 8th St Quincy IL 62301-7245 also: Luth Child and Family Svcs 431 Hampshire St Quincy IL 62301-2927

MILLER, JEROME GILBERT, criminologist; b. Breckenridge, Minn., Dec. 8, 1931; s. George Ernest and Beatrice Irene (Butts) M.; m. Charlene Elizabeth Coleman, June 9, 1968; 1 child, Patrick. BA, Mary Knoll Coll., 1954; MSW, Loyola U., 1957; DSW, Cath. U. Am., 1964. Lic. clin. social worker, Va. Commd. officer USAF, 1957, advanced through grades to capt.; psychiat. social work officer USAF, Sheppard AFB, Tex., 1957-59; chief social work USAF, various locations, U.S., Eng., 1959-68; ret. USAF, 1968; assoc. prof. Ohio State Univ., Columbus, 1968-69; commr. Mass. Dept. Youth Svcs., Boston, 1969-73; dir. Ill. Dept. Children and Family Svcs., Springfield, 1973-75; commr. Pa. Office Children and Youth, Harrisburg, 1975-79; founder, pres. Nat. Ctr. on Instns. and Alternatives, Alexandria, Va., 1979—. Author: Last One Over the Wall, 1991; contbr. articles to profl. jours. Named Social Worker of Yr., New Eng. Chpt. NASW, Bostonk, 1972; recipient award in recognition of nat. contbn. to criminal justice adminstrn. Am. Soc. Pub. Adminstrn., 1975, Karl Menninger award Fortune Soc., N.Y., 1977, August Villmer award Am. Soc. Criminology, Montreal, 1987. Office: Nat Ctr on Instn & Alts 635 Slaters Ln Alexandria VA 22314-1177

MILLER, JERRY HUBER, retired university chancellor; b. Salem, Ohio, June 15, 1931; s. Duber Daniel and Ida Claire (Holdereith) M.; m. Margaret A. Setter, 1958; children: Gregory, Joy, Carol, Beth, David. BA, Harvard U., 1953; MDiv., Hamma Sch. Theology, 1957; DD (hon.), Trinity Luth. Sem., 1981. Ordained to ministry Luth. Ch., 1957. Research assoc., intern Cornell U., Ithaca, N.Y., 1955-56; instr. Wittenberg U., Springfield, Ohio, 1956-57; parish pastor Ch. of Good Shepherd, Cin., 1957-62; asst. to pres. Ohio Synod Luth. Ch. Am., 1962-66; sr. campus pastor, dir. campus ministry U. Wis., Madison, 1966-69; regional dir. Nat. Luth. Campus Ministry, Madison, 1969-76; exec. dir. Nat. Luth. Campus Ministry, Chgo., 1977-81; pres. Calif. Luth. U., Thousand Oaks, 1981-92, chancellor, 1992-94, pres. emeritus, 1994—; ret. Ventura County Maritime Mus., Channel Islands Harbor, Calif., 1993-95; chmn. Los Robles Bank, Thousand Oaks; mem. exec. com. Coun. Ind. Colls., Washington, Assn. Ind. Calif. Colls. and Univs., 1981-92, Coun. Luth. Colls., Luth. Ednl. Conf. N.Am., 1977-94. Editor: The Higher Disciplines, 1956; contbr. articles to profl. jours. Bd. dirs. Wittenberg U., Augustana Coll., Rock Island, Ill., United Way, Thousand oaks, Ventura County chpt. ARC, Thousand Oaks, YMCA; chmn. bd. dirs. Los Robles Hosp. Named Man of Yr., Salem, 1975; Siebert Found. fellow, 1975. Mem. Am. Assn. Higher Edn., Council Advancement and Support Edn., Harvard Alumni Assn., Western Coll. Assn. (bd. dirs.), Conejo Valley C. of C. (bd. dirs.), Conejo Symphony Orch. (bd. dirs.). Club: Harvard (Ill., Ohio, Wis., Calif.), YMCA (regional bd. dirs.), Rotary. Avocations: skiing, golfing, hiking, travelling.

MILLER, JESSE D., lawyer; b. Chgo., June 13, 1930; s. Jesse B. and Rose Veronica (Jasnoch) M.; m. Geraldine Rae Richardson, Apr. 7, 1967; children: Nancy, Craig, Cynthia, Steven, Traci, Christian. BS summa cum laude, UCLA, 1956; JD cum laude, Harvard U., 1959. Bar: Wis. 1959, Calif. 1965, U.S. Supreme Ct. 1966. Assoc. Foley, Sammond & Lardner, Milw., 1959-64, Keatinge & Sterling, L.A., 1964-65; ptnr. Iverson & Hogoboom (now Iverson, Hatch & Miller), L.A., 1965-69, Law Offices of Jesse D. Miller, L.A., 1969-74, Miller & Mandel, L.A., 1974-82; mng. ptnr. Pepper Hamilton & Scheetz, L.A., 1982-89, Fulbright & Jaworski, L.A., 1990—; lectr. bus. law UCLA Grad. Sch. Mgmt., 1965-67; affiliated Stanford Ctr. Conflict and Negotiation, 1989—; mem. adv. com. Ctr. Pub. Resources, 1983—; ptnr. gambling casino, Cripple Creek, Colo.; owner Standardbred racehorse. With US Army, 1951-53. Mem. ABA (chmn. litigation sect. litigation mgmt. subcom. 1989—), Calif. Dental Assn. (hon.), Phi Beta Kappa, Beta Gamma Sigma. Avocation: golf.

MILLER, JIM, film editor. Editor: (TV pilots) Feel the Heat, 1993, The Wizard, 1986, (TV movies) Two Fathers' Justice, 1985, Alice in Wonderland, 1985, (films) (with Dede Allen) The Breakfast Club, 1985, Blue City, 1986, (with Allen) The Milagro Beanfield War, 1988, (with Allen) Let It Ride, 1990, (with Allen) The Addams Family, 1991, (with Arthur Schmidt) Addams Family Values, 1993, For Love or Money, 1993. Office: 3926 Corte Cancion Thousand Oaks CA 91360-6915

MILLER, JO ANN, education educator, college official; b. Shelbyville, Mo., June 13, 1940; d. Carl Edward and Mary Lillian (Wood) Willey; m. Robert William Miller, Mar. 1, 1961; children: David William, Mariann Denise. BA in English, Mo. Bapt. Coll., St. Louis, 1979; MEd, U. Mo., St. Louis, 1981; PhD in Higher Edn. Adminstrn., St. Louis U., 1992. Cert. English, libr. sci. and adult edn. tchr., Mo. Instr. adult edn. Jefferson Coll., Hillsboro, Mo., 1976-82; tchr. English, De Soto (Mo.) Sch. Dist., 1981-84; dean students Mo. Bapt. Coll., 1984-88, assoc. prof. edn., chmn. div. edn., asst. acad. dean, 1988—, seminar presenter and facilitator, 1993—; adj. prof. S.W. Bapt. U., Bolivar, Mo., 1994—; mem. Mo. Task Force for Tchr. Edn. Stds., 1993. Contbr. articles to profl. jours. Mem. resolutions com. So. Bapt. Conv., Nashville, 1989; mem. program com. Jefferson Bapt. Assn., 1992—. Named Parkway Outstanding Educator of Yr., 1992; ednl. policy fellow Mo. Fellows, 1993. Mem. ASCD, AAUW, Mo. Bapt. Coll. Alumni Assn., Phi Lambda Theta, Sigma Tau Delta. Avocations: needlepoint, travel, collecting antiques. Home: PO Box 411642 Saint Louis MO 63141-1642 Office: Mo Bapt Coll One College Park Dr Saint Louis MO 63141-8613

MILLER, JOEL STEVEN, solid state scientist; b. Detroit, Oct. 14, 1944; s. John and Rose (Schpok) M.; m. Elaine J. Silverstein, Sept. 20, 1970; children: Stephen D., Marc A., Alan D. BS in Chemistry, Wayne State U., 1967; PhD, UCLA, 1971. Mgr. rsch. Occidental Rsch. Corp., Irvine, Calif., 1979-83; supr. rsch. Cen. R & D Lab. E. I. Du Pont Nemours & Co., Wilmington, Del., 1983-93; prof. chemistry U. Utah, 1993—, adj. prof. Materials Sci.; adj. prof. materials sci., 1994—; assoc. Inorganic Synthesis Corp., Chgo.; vis. prof. U. Calif., Irvine, 1980, Weizmann Inst., Rehovot, Israel, 1985, U. Pa., Phila., 1988, U. Paris-Sud, 1991. Editor 9 books; mem. adv. bd. Jour. Chemistry Materials, 1990—, Jour. Materials Chemistry, 1991—, Advanced Materials, 1994—; contbr. over 250 articles to sci. jours. Indsl. fellow in material sci. Northwestern U., 1991-93. Mem. Am. Chem. Soc. (chmn. solid state subdiv. 1989). Achievements include discovery and development of molecular-based conductors and magnets. Office: U Utah Dept Chemistry Salt Lake City UT 84108

MILLER, JOHN A., JR., public relations executive. Chmn., CEO Miller Comms., Boston. *

MILLER, JOHN ALBERT, university administrator, consultant; b. St. Louis County, Mo., Mar. 22, 1939; s. John Adam and Emma D. (Doering) M.; m. Eunice Ann Timm, Aug. 25, 1968; children: Michael, Kristin. AA, St. Paul's Coll., 1958; BA with high honors, Concordia Sr. Coll., 1960; postgrad., Wash. U., St. Louis, 1960-64; MBA, Ind. U., 1971, D.B.A. in Mktg., 1972. Proofreader, editor Concordia Pub. House, St. Louis, 1960-62, periodical sales mgr., 1964-68; asst. prof. Drake U., Des Moines, 1971-74; cons. FTC, Washington, 1974-75; vis. assoc. prof. Ind. U., Bloomington, 1975-77; assoc. prof. U. Colo., Colorado Springs, 1977-79, prof., 1977-86, prof. mktg., resident dean, 1980-84; v.p. market devel. Peak Health Care Inc., Colorado Springs, 1984-85; dean, prof. mktg. Valparaiso (Ind.) U., 1986—; cons. and rschr. govt. and industry; dir. health maintenance orgn.; bd. dirs. Ind. Acad. Social Scis., 1988-90; adv. bd. N.W. Ind. Small Bus. Devel. Ctr., 1989-91; consulting dean USIA project to form Polish Assn. of Bus. Schs., 1995. Author: Labeling Research The State of the Art, 1978; contbr. articles to profl. jours. Mem. Colorado Springs Symphony Orch. Coun., 1980-86; cons. Citizens Goals of Colorado Springs, 1985-86, Jr. League Colorado Springs, 1981-82; bd. dirs. Christmas in April-Valparaiso, 1991—. With U.S. Army, 1962-64. U.S. Steel fellow, 1970-71. Mem. Assn. Consumer Rsch. (chmn. membership 1978-79), Am. Mktg. Assn. (fed. govt. liaison com. 1975-76), Am. Acad. Advt., Ind. Acad. Social Scis. (bd. dirs. 1988-90), Greater Valparaiso C. of C. (accreditation com. 1991, planning com. 1989-92, chair 1992), Am. Assembly Collegiate Schs. Bus. (internat. affairs com. 1991-93, mem. peer rev. team 1994, 96, com. mem., seminar leader, faculty mem., program chair for New Deans seminar and other workshops 1992—), Beta Gamma Sigma, Alpha Iota Delta. Lutheran. Avocations: racquetball, jogging, walking. Home: 1504 Del Vista Dr Valparaiso IN 46383-3322 Office: Valparaiso U Dept Mktg Valparaiso IN 46383

MILLER, JOHN DAVID, agronomist; b. Todd, N.C., Aug. 9, 1923; s. Reuben Patterson and Chessie (Graham) M.; B.S., N.C. State U., 1948, M.S., 1950; Ph.D., U. Minn., 1953; m. Frances McCollum, June 9, 1946 (dec.); children—John David, Glenn, Mary; m. 2d Jimmie Heard, Mar. 24, 1984. Research fellow U. Minn., 1953; asst. prof. Kans. State Coll., 1953-57; research agronomist Agrl. Research Service, U.S. Dept. Agr., Blacksburg, Va. and Tifton, Ga., 1957-75, research leader, 1972-79, sr. agronomist, 1975-91. Dist. commr. Boy Scouts Am., 1971-74. Served with AUS, 1943-46. Decorated Bronze Star medal. Mem. Am. Soc. Agronomy, Phi Kappa Phi, Gamma Sigma Delta, Sigma Xi. Clubs: Toastmasters, Lions. Home: 801 E 12th St Tifton GA 31794-4115 Office: USDA Coastal Plain Sta Agrl Rsch Svcs Tifton GA 31793

MILLER, JOHN EDDIE, lawyer; b. Wayne, Mich., Nov. 14, 1945; s. George Hayden and Georgia Irene (Stevenson) M.; m. Nancy Carol Sanders, Jan. 7, 1968; children: Andrea Christine, Matthew Kit. BA, Baylor U., 1967; JD, Memphis State U., 1973; LLM, U. Mo., 1980. Bar: Mo. 1974, U.S. Dist. Ct. (we. dist.) Mo. 1974, Tex. 1982. Asst. prof. Central Mo. State U., Warrensburg, 1973-74; sole practice, Sedalia, Mo., 1974-79; sr. contract adminstr. Midwest Research Inst., Kansas City, Mo., 1979-81; sr. contract adminstr Tracor Inc., Austin, Tex., 1981-84; contract negotiator Tex. Instruments, Austin, 1984-86; sr. contract adminstr., Tracor Aerospace Inc., Austin, 1986-87, Radian Corp., Austin, 1987—; corp. sec. Radian Southeast Asia Ltd., Bangkok, 1995—, Radian Sys. Corp., Austin, 1995—; instr., bus. law State Fair Community Coll., Sedalia, 1974-79, Austin Community Coll., 1983-84. Bd. dirs. Legal Aid Western Mo., 1977-79, Boy's Club, Sedalia, 1974-79, Austin Lawyers Care, 1987—. Served with U.S. Army, 1968-71. Mem. Mo. Bar Assn. (mem. internat. law com., mem. computer law com.), Tex. Bar Assn. (intellectual property law section, internat. law section), Coll. of the State Bar of Tex., Nat. Contract Mgmt. Assn., Travis County Bar Assn., Austin Young Lawyers Assn., U.S. Tennis Assn., Phi Alpha Delta. Baptist. Club: AM Tennis (Austin). Office: Radian Corp 8501 North Mo-Pac Blvd PO Box 201088 Austin TX 78720-1088

MILLER, JOHN EDWARD, army officer, educational administrator; b. Paragould, Ark., May 8, 1941; s. Wardlow Knox and Anna Mae (Danford) M.; m. Joan Carolyn Capano, Oct. 5, 1968; children: C. Claire, J. Andrew, JoAnna M., Mary Ellen. BS in Math., S.W. Mo. State U., 1963; MS in Ops. Rsch., Ga. Inst. Tech., 1971; postgrad., Yale U., 1991. Commd. 2d lt. U.S. Army, 1963, advanced through grades to lt. gen., 1993; student U.S. Army Command and Gen. Staff Coll., Ft. Leavenworth, Kans., 1974; bn. comdr. 4th Brigade, 4th Inf. Div., Wiesbaden, Fed. Republic Germany, 1977-79; ops. officer 8th Inf. Div., Badkreuznach, Fed. Republic Germany, 1979-81; student U.S. Army War Coll., Carlisle, Pa., 1982; div. chief Office Dep. Chief of Staff for Rsch. Devel. and Acquisition, Dept. Army, Washington, 1982-84; brigade comdr., chief of staff 9th Inf. Div., Ft. Lewis, Wash., 1984-87; asst. for combat devels. U.S. Army Tng. and Doctrine Command, Ft. Monroe, Va., 1987-88; asst. div. comdr. 8th Inf. Div., Baumholder, Fed. Republic Germany, 1988-89; dep. comdt. U.S. Army Command and Gen. Staff Coll., Ft. Leavenworth, 1989-91; comdr. 101st Airborne Div., Ft. Campbell, Ky., 1991-93; U.S. army command, gen. staff coll. U.S. Army, Ft. Leavenworth, 1993-95; dep. comdg. gen. U.S. Army Tng. and Doctrine Command, Ft. Monroe, Va., 1995—. Recipient Outstanding Alumni award, S.W. Mo. State U., 1993. Mem. Assn. U.S. Army, Army Aviation Assn. Am., 101st Airborne Divsn.Assn. Republican. Avocations: tennis, skiing, sailing. Office: HQ TRADOC Fort Monroe VA 23651

MILLER, JOHN FRANCIS, association executive, social scientist; b. Canton, Ill., Aug. 3, 1908; s. Frank Lewis and Minnie Grace (Eyerly) M.; m. Ruth Roby, May 29, 1937; children: Joan, Kent R., Dana R. AB, U. Ill., 1929, AM, 1930; postgrad., Columbia U., 1930-31, 34-35; German-Am. student exch. fellow, U. Frankfurt on Main, 1931-33. Staff Commn. Inquiry on Pub. Svc. Pers., 1934-35, Regent's Inquiry Character and Cost Pub. Edn., 1936; cons. Pres.'s Com. on Adminstrv. Mgmt., 1936-37, Com. Civil Svc. Improvement, 1939, Inst. Pub. Adminstrn., 1937-38, Pub. Adminstrn. Clearing House, 1938; chief field svc. Nat. Resources Planning Bd., 1938-43; asst. dir. Nat. Planning Assn., 1943-50, asst. chmn., 1951-77, exec. sec., 1951-71, pres., 1971-79, vice chmn., 1977-89; trustee Nat. Planning Assn., Washington, 1977—; sec. Canadian-Am. Com., 1957-76, N.Am. sec. Brit.-N.Am. Com., 1969-85. Author: Veteran Preference in the Public Service, 1935. Trustee, mem. adv. com. Nat. Conf. on Family, 1946-49; mem. adv. council social security Senate Com. on Finance, 1947-48. Mem. The Planning Forum, Am. Econ. Assn., Am. Polit. Sci. Assn., Am. Hist. Assn., Phi Beta Kappa, Cosmos Club (Washington), Univ. Club (N.Y.). Home: Washington Hill Rd Chocorua NH 03817 Office: Nat Planning Assn 1424 16th St NW Ste 700 Washington DC 20036-2211

MILLER, JOHN GRIDER, magazine editor; b. Annapolis, Md., Aug. 23, 1935; s. John Stanley and Ruby Corinne (Young) M.; m. Susan Bradner Bailey, Oct. 26, 1974; children: Kerry, John, Alison. BA, Yale U., 1957. Commd. 2d lt. USMC, 1957, advanced through grades to col., inf./ops. advisor Vietnamese Marine Corps., 1970-71; prin. speechwriter for Commandant USMC, Washington, 1971-76; commd. officer Battalion Landing Team USMC, 1977-78; asst. chief of staff ops. and plans III Amphibious Force USMC, Okinawa, 1982-83; dep. dir. Marine Corps History USMC, Washington, 1983-85; ret. USMC, 1985; mng. editor Procs. and Naval History U.S. Naval Inst., Annapolis, Md., 1985—. Author: The Battle to Save the Houston, 1985, Pocket Books edit., 1992, the Bridge at Dong Ha, 1989, 90, Punching Out: A Guide to Post-Military Transition, 1994. Decorated Legion of Merit with oak leaf cluster, Bronze Star with combat V, Cross of Gallantry, Vietnamese Marine Corps.; recipient Author of Yr. award Naval Inst., 1990. Mem. Marine Corps. Hist. Found. (bd. dirs., Gen. Wallace M. Greene Jr. Book award 1989), Mil. Order of World Wars (past chpt. comdr., mem. nat. mag. com.), Civitan Internat. (past chpt. pres.), Washington Naval and Maritime Corrs.' Cir., New Providence Club. Avocations: music, piano, choral singing, boating. Home: 21 Sands Ave Annapolis MD 21403 Office: US Naval Inst 118 Maryland Ave Annapolis MD 21402-5035

MILLER, JOHN HENRY, clergyman; b. Ridgeway, S.C., Dec. 3, 1917; s. Fletcher and Frances Helo (Turner) M.; BA, Livingstone Coll., 1941; M. Div., Hood Theol. Sem., 1945; postgrad. Hartford Theol. Sem. Found., 1954; m. Bernice Frances Dillard, June 27, 1945; children: George Frederick, John Henry. Ordained to ministry, AME Zion Ch., 1939-40; ordained bishop, 1972. Bishop, 10th Dist., 1972-80, 8th Dist., Dallas, 1980-84, 7th Dist., 1984-88, 5th Dist., 1988—, ret.; mem. Gov.'s Advocacy Com. on Children and Youth, 1985—; chmn. bd. AME Zion Ch. Trustee Livingstone Coll.; former chmn. bd. Lomax-Hannon Jr. Coll.; chmn. bd. Black Reps. N.C., 1985—; chmn. hon. degrees com. L.C. Mem. NAACP, World Meth. Council, Alpha Phi Alpha. Republican. Clubs: Masons, Elks. Office: African Meth Episcopal Zion Ch 8605 Caswell Ct Raleigh NC 27613-1101

MILLER, JOHN LAURENCE, professional golfer; b. San Francisco, Apr. 29, 1947; s. Laurence O. and Ida (Meldrum) M.; m. Linda Strouse, Sept. 17, 1969; children: John Strouse, Kelly, Casi, Scott, Brent, Todd. Student, Brigham Young U., 1965-69. Profl. golfer, 1969—; Pres. Johnny Miller Enterprises, Inc. Author: Pure Golf, 1976, Johnny Miller's Golf for Juniors, 1987. Named PGA Player of Yr., 1974. Winner U.S. Open at Oakmont County Club, 1973, Otago Golf Classic; New Zealand, 1972, Lancome Trophy tournament, Paris, 1973, Dunlop Phoenix, Japan, 1974, World Cup individual and team titles, 1973, 75, So. Open, 1971, Los Angeles Open, 1981, Inverrary Classic, 1980, 83, Los Angeles Open, 1981, Crosby Nat., Heritage and Tournament of Champions, 1974, Westchester Classic, World Open and Kaiser Internat., 1974 Brit. Open, Bob Hope Classic, Tucson Open, 1974-76, 81, San Diego Open, 1982, Chrysler Team Invitational, 1983, AT&T Nat. Pro Am., 1987, 94; NBC commentator for golf. Office: PO Box 2260 Napa CA 94558-0060*

MILLER, JOHN PATRICK, secondary education educator; b. Lebanon, Pa., June 10, 1947; s. Victor V. and Florence A. (Coleman) M.; m. Linda L. Loose, Aug. 26, 1967; children: Suzanne L., Kelly E., Ryan P., John B., Steven K. BS, Millersville U., 1969, MA, 1974. Cert. secondary education social sci. H.S. instr., social studies dept. chmn. Palmyra (Pa.) Area Sch. Dist., 1969—; baseball coach Palmyra (Pa.) Area Sch. Dist., 1969-74, football announcer, 1971-91; football announcer state playoffs Pa. State Interscholastic Athletic Assn., Harrisburg, 1991. Author: Immigration in Lebanon County, 1974. Dir. Annville (Pa.)-Cleona Recreation Assn., 1976-94. Named Outstanding Educator, Lebanon County Ednl. Soc., Lebanon, 1979, Rotary Club Palmyra, Pa., 1994. Mem. NEA, Pa. State Edn. Assn., Palmyra Edn. Assn. (pres. 1971, 80, 84, 93, 94, 95, 96), Pa. State Hall of Fame. Republican. Roman Catholic. Avocations: softball, volleyball, studying history, baseball, travel. Home: 720 Pearl St Annville PA 17003-2223 Office: Palmyra Area Sch Dist 1125 Park Dr Palmyra PA 17078-3447

MILLER, JOHN RICHARD, interior designer; b. Washington, Feb. 11, 1927; s. John Henry and Helen (Vermillion) M.; m. Audrey Gene Owens, Nov. 6, 1946; children: Pamela Dawn, Felicity Amanda, Timothy John. Diploma in interior design, Colbert Inst., Washington, 1950. Designer Hollidge Interiors, Washington, 1950-51; pres. Miller's Interiors Inc., Temple Hills, Md., 1951—; bd. dirs. St. Barnabas Venture, Temple Hills. Author: Training for Design Related Trades, 1976; columnist Washington Star, 1971-79. Mem. Pres.'s Com. on Employment of Handicapped, 1978-82, White House Design Com., 1969-74, Presdl. Barrier Free Design Com., 1972-80. With USN, 1944-46, PTO. Fellow Am. Soc. Interior Designers (pres. Potomac chpt. 1973-80, nat. dir. 1960-74, chmn. opportunity guidance coun. 1972-74); mem. Nat. Soc. Interior Designers (pres. Potomac chpt. 1974-76), Tantallon Country Club (Oxon Hill, Md.). Democrat. Episcopalian. Avocations: tennis, reading. Home: 13710 Piscataway Dr Fort Washington MD 20744 Office: Millers Interiors Inc PO Box 441711 Fort Washington MD 20749

MILLER, JOHN ROBERT, environmental recycling company executive; b. Lima, Ohio, Dec. 28, 1937; s. John O. and Mary L. (Zickafoose) M.; m. Karen A. Eier, Dec. 30, 1961; children: Robert A., Lisa A., James E. BSChE with honors, U. Cin., 1960, D.Comml. Sc. hon., 1983. With Standard Oil Co., Cleve., 1960-86, dir. fin., 1974-75, v.p. fin., 1975-78, v.p. transp., 1978-79, sr. v.p. tech. and chems., 1979-80, pres., COO, 1980-86; bd. dirs. Cleve.; pres., CEO TBN Holdings, Pepper Pike, Ohio, 1986—; bd. dirs. Am. Waste Svcs., Inc., Eaton Corp.; former chmn. Fed. Res. Bank, Cleve. Mem. Pepper Pike Club, Chagrin Valley Hunt Club, Country Club, Nat. Assn. Chem. Recyclers (bd. dirs.), Tau Beta Pi. Office: 3550 Lander Rd Cleveland OH 44124-5727

MILLER, JOHN T., JR., lawyer, educator; b. Waterbury, Conn., Aug. 10, 1922; s. John T. and Anna (Purdy) M.; children: Kent, Lauren, Clare, Miriam, Michael, Sheila, Lisa, Colin, Margaret. AB with high honors, Clark U., 1944; JD, Georgetown U., 1948; Docteur en Droit, U. Geneva, 1951; postgrad., U. Paris, 1951. Bar: Conn. 1949, D.C. 1950, U.S. Ct. Appeals (3d cir.) 1958, U.S. Ct. Appeals (D.C. cir.) 1952, U.S. Ct. Appeals (5th cir.) 1957, U.S. Supreme Ct. 1952. With Econ. Cooperation Adminstn. Am. Embassy, London, 1950-51; assoc. Covington & Burling, 1952-53, Gallagher, Connor & Boland, 1953-62; pvt. practice Washington, 1962—; adj. prof. law Georgetown U. Law Ctr., Washington, 1959—; mem. Panel on Future of Internat. Ct. Justice. Co-author: Regulation of Trade, 1953, Modern American Antitrust Law, 1948, Major American Antitrust Laws, 1965; author: Foreign Trade in Gas and Electricity in North America: A Legal and Historical Study, 1970, Energy Problems and the Federal Government: Cases and Material, 8th edit., 1996; contbr. articles, book revs. to legal publs. Trustee Clark U., 1970-76, De Sales Sch. of Theology, 1993—; bd. advisors Georgetown Visitation Prep. Sch., 1978-94, bd. trustees, 1994—; former fin. chmn. troop 46 Nat. Capital Area coun. Boy Scouts Am. Served to 1st lt. U.S. Army, 1943-46, 48-49. Recipient 10 yr. teaching award Nat. Jud. Coll., 1983. Mem. ABA (coun., chmn. adminstrv. law sect. 1972-73, ho. dels. 1991-93), AAUP, D.C. Bar Assn., Fed. Energy Bar Assn. (pres. 1990-91), Internat. Bar Assn., Internat. Law Assn., Congl. Country Club, Army and Navy Club, DACOR, Prettyman-Leventhal Am. Inn of Ct. (master, pres.), Sovereign Mil. Order of Malta (knight). Republican. Roman Catholic. Home: 4721 Rodman St NW Washington DC 20016-3234 Office: 1001 Connecticut Ave NW Washington DC 20036-5507

MILLER, JOHN ULMAN, minister, author; b. N.Y.C., Dec. 9, 1914; s. Clarence James and Edythe Gladys (Shaffer) M.; m. Marcella E. Hubner, June 12, 1937; children: John U., Mark C. (dec.), Mary Kay (Mrs. Charles Bolin, dec.), Gretchen (Mrs. Ernest Micka). BA cum laude, Taylor U., 1937; MA, Butler U., 1942; DD, Geneva (Wis.) Theol. Coll., 1968. Ordained to ministry Bapt. Ch., 1937; pastor First Bapt. Ch., Bluffton, Ind., 1946-49, Boston, 1949-56; pastor Tabernacle Ch., Utica, N.Y., 1956-63, United Ch. of Christ, Hagerstown, Ind., 1963-66, St. John's Evang. Ch., Louisville, 1967-77; Participant Churchmen Weigh News, WNAC, Boston, 1953-56; preacher Meml. Chapel; instr. religion N.Y. Masonic Home, Utica, 1957-62; broadcast weekly services WKBV, Richmond, Ind., 1965-66; preacher Fellowship Chapel WHAS, Louisville, 1967-77; maintains 24 hour Dial-A-Prayer, Louisville, 1968-77; minister Royal Poinciana Chapel, Palm Beach, Fla., 1978-84; ret., 1984. Author: Only to the Curious, The Voice of St. John, Providence on Pilgrimage, Two Wonders I Confess, Stop! Look! Listen!, He Opened the Book, Christian Ethic in the Sermon on the Mount, Windows on the Agony, Prayers Under Pressure, 1989. Chmn. Campaigns Crippled Children, Tb, U.S.O., 1946-49. Capt. USAAF, 1942-45, PTO. Named Community Leader Am. News Pub. Co., 1969. Mem. Ind.-Ky. Conf. United Ch. of Christ, Bach Soc. Louisville. Home: 4409 Green Pine Dr Louisville KY 40220-1542 *Reverence is my name—the unwritten law of the universe, the invisible order of time, the cardinal virtue of life. Call me sovereign, for so I am, the gift of God to the world of man. Follow me, if you will, and I will disclose to you the life of God in the affairs of man. Charity is my attitude—the most pure of all gifts in the world, the ever redemptive spirit of time, the reconciling power of life. Call me sovereign, for so I am, the gift of God to the world of man. Seek me, if you will, and I will disclose to you the blessings of the eternal in the world of the temporal. Justice is my goal—the incredible design of the universe, the rightness of all things, the inescapable oughtness of life. Call me sovereign, for so I am, the gift of God to the world of man. Pursue me if you will and I will disclose to you the triumph of right amid the shadows of wrong.*

MILLER, J(OHN) WESLEY, III, lawyer, author; b. Springfield, Mass., Oct. 3, 1941; s. John Wesley Jr. and Blanche Ethel (Wilson) M. AB, Colby Coll., 1963; AM, Harvard U., 1964, JD, 1981. Bar: Mass. 1984, U.S. Dist. Ct., 1984, U.S. Supreme Ct. 1993. Instr. English Heidelberg Coll., Tiffin, Ohio, 1964-69, U. Wis., 1969-77; real estate broker, 1977-84; founder Miller-Wilson Family Papers, U. Vt., Madison (Wis.) People's Poster and Propaganda Collection, St. Hist. Soc. Wis. Author: History of Buckingham Junior High School, 1956, The Millers of Roxham, 1958, Giroux Genealogy, 1958, Symphonic Heritage, 1959, Community Guide to Madison Murals, 1977, Aunt Jennie's Poems, 1986; founding editor: Hein's Poetry and the Law Series, 1985—; editor: The Curiosities and Law of Wills, 1989, The Lawyers Alcove, 1990, Famous Divorces, 1991, Legal Laughs, 1993; founding editor: Law Libr. Microform Consortium Arts Law Letters Collection, 1991—; exhibitor A Salute to Street Art, State Hist. Soc. Wis., 1974; represented in permanent collections U. Vermont, Colby Coll. Archives, State Hist. Soc. Wis., Boston Pub. Libr.; contbr. The Poems of Ambrose Philips, 1969, Dictionary of Canadian Biography, 1980, Collection Building Reader, 1992; also numerous articles on Am. street lit., bibliography, ethics, history, edn., law, religion, librarianship, mgmt. of archives. Mem. MLA, Am. Philol. Assn., Milton Soc., New Eng. Historic Geneal. Soc., Vt. Hist. Soc., Wis. Acad. Scis., Arts & Letters, Social Law Library, Pilgrim Soc., Ancient and Hon. Arty. Co., Mayflower Soc., Soc. Colonial Wars, Sons and Daus. of the Victims of Colonial Witch Trials, Mensa. Recipient Cmty. Activism award Bay State Objectivist, 1993, 94, 95. Office: 5 Birchland Ave Springfield MA 01119-2708 *The advancement of learning is my goal. Professionalism is the standard, and nothing else will do.*

MILLER, JOHN WILLIAM, JR., bassoonist; b. Balt., Mar. 11, 1942; s. John William and Alverta Evelyn (Rodemaker) M.; m. Sibylle Weigel, July 12, 1966; children: Christian Desmond, Andrea Jocelyn, Claire Evelyn. BS, M.I.T., 1964; MusM with highest honors, New Eng. Conservatory, 1967, Artist's Diploma, 1969. Instr. bassoon Boston U., 1967-71, U. Minn., 1971—; prin. bassoonist, founding mem. Boston Philharmonia Chamber Orch., 1968-71; prin. bassoonist Minn. Orch., Mpls., 1971—; dir. Boston Baroque Ensemble, 1963-71, John Miller Bassoon Symposium, 1984—; mem. Am. Reed Trio, 1977—; faculty Sarasota Music Festival, 1986—, Affinis Seminar, Japan, 1992; vis. faculty Banff Ctr. for Arts, 1987. Soloist on recs. for Cambridge, Mus. Heritage Soc., Pro Arte; featured guest artist 1st Internat. Bassoon Festival, Caracas, Venezuela, 1994. Recipient U.S. Govt. Fulbright award, 1964-65, Irwin Bodky award Cambridge Soc. Early Music, 1968. Mem. Internat. Double Reed Soc., Minn. Bassoon Assn. (founder). Home: 706 Lincoln Ave Saint Paul MN 55105-3533 Office: 1111 Nicollet Mall Minneapolis MN 55403-2406

MILLER, JONATHAN WOLFE, theater and film director, physician; b. London, July 21, 1934; s. Emanuel Miller; m. Helen Rachel Collet, 1956; 3 children. Ed. St. John's Coll., Cambridge U.; MB, BCh, Univ. Coll. Hosp. Med. Sch., London, 1959; DLitt (hon.), U. Leicester, 1981; Dr. (hon.), Open U., 1983. Dir. Nottingham Playhouse, 1963-69; assoc. dir. Nat. Theatre, 1973-75; mem. Arts Council, 1975-76; vis. prof. drama Westfield Coll., U. London, 1977-78; artistic dir., Old Vic, 1988-90. Co-author, actor in Beyond the Fringe, 1961-64; dir. Under Plain Cover, Royal Ct. Theatre, 1962, The Old Glory, N.Y.C., 1964, Prometheus Bound, Yale Drama Sch., 1967, Oxford and Cambridge Shakespeare Co. prodn. of Twelfth Night, on tour in U.S., 1969; dir. for Nat. Theatre, London: The Merchant of Venice, 1970, Danton's Death, 1971, The School for Scandal, 1972, The Marriage of Figaro, 1974; other prodns. include: The Tempest, London, 1970, Prometheus Bound, London, 1971, The Taming of the Shrew, Chichester, Eng., 1972, The Seagull, Chichester, 1973, The Malcontent, Nottingham, Eng., 1973, The Family in Love, 1974, The Importance of Being Earnest,

1975, All's Well That Ends Well, Measure For Measure, Greenwich Season, 1975, Three Sisters, 1977; dir. operas Arden Must Die, 1973, Sadler's Well Theatre, 1974, The Cunning Little Vixen, Glyndebourne, 1975, 77, Marriage of Figaro, Vienna State Opera, 1991, Robert Deveureux, Monte Carlo, 1992, Die Gezeichnete, Zurich, 1992, Maria Stuarda, Monte Carlo, 1993, The Secret Marriage, Opera North, 1993; dir. for English Nat. Opera: The Marriage of Figaro, 1978, The Turn of the Screw, 1979, 91, Arabella, 1980, Othello, 1981, Rigoletto, 1982, 85 (also at Met. Opera, N.Y.C.), Fidelio, 1982, 83, Don Giovanni, 1985, The Magic Flute, 1986, Tosca, 1986, The Mikado, 1986, 88, The Barber of Seville, 1987, Cosí fan Tutte, 1995, Carmen, 1995; dir. for Kent Opera: Cosí Fan Tutte, 1975, Rigoletto, 1975, Orfeo, 1976, Eugene Onegin, 1977, La Traviata, 1979, Falstaff, 1980, 81, Fidelio, 1982, 83, 88; dir. for La Scala Milan: La Fanciulla del West, 1991, Manon Lescaut, 1992; dir for Maggio Musicale, Florence: Don Giovanni, 1990, Cosí fan Tutte, 1991, 94, Marriage of Figaro, 1992, La Bohème, 1994; dir Met. Opera, N.Y.: Katya Kabanova, 1991, Pelléas et Mélisande, 1995; dir. in co-prodn. with L.A. Music Ctr. and Houston Grand Opera House Der Rosenkavalier, 1994 dir. Broadway play Long Day's Journey Into Night, 1986, The Taming of the Shrew at Royal Shakespeare Co., Stratford, 1987, Andromache, One Way Pendulum, Bussy D'Ambois, all at Old Vic, 1988, The Tempest, 1988, Turn of the Screw, 1989, King Lear, 1989, The Liar, 1989; films include: Take a Girl Like You, 1969; TV films include: Whistle and I'll Come to You, 1967, Alice in Wonderland, 1967, The Body in Question series, 1978, Henry the Sixth, part one, 1983, States of Mind series, 1983; exec. producer Shakespeare TV series, 1979-81; author: McLuhan, 1971, The Body in Question, 1978, States of Mind, The Human Body, The Facts of Life, Subsequent Performances, 1986; editor: Freud: The Man, His World, His Influence, 1972, The Don Giovanni Book, 1990. Decorated Order Brit. Empire; named dir. of Yr., Soc. West End Theatre Awards, 1976; recipient Silver medal Royal TV Soc., 1981; fellow Univ. Coll. London; hon. fellow St. John's Coll., Cambridge U.; research fellow in history of medicine Univ. Coll., London U., 1970-73. Office: care IMG Artists, Media House 3 Burlington Ln, London W4 2TH, England

MILLER, JOSEF M., otolaryngologist, educator; b. Phila., Nov. 29, 1937; married, 1960; 3 children. BA in Psychology, U. Calif., Berkeley, 1961; PhD in Physiology and Psychology, U. Wash., 1965; MD (hon.), U. Göteborg, Sweden, 1987; MD (h.c.), U. Turku, Finland, 1995. USPHS fellow U. Mich., 1965-67; rsch. assoc., asst. prof. dept. Psychology U. Mich., Ann Arbor, 1967-68, prof., dir. rsch. dept. Otolaryngology, dir. Kresge Hearing Rsch. Inst., 1984—; asst. prof. depts. Otolaryngology, Physiology and Biophysics U. Wash., Seattle, 1968-72, rsch. affiliate Regional Primate Rsch. Ctr, 1968-84, assoc. prof., 1972-76, acting chmn. dept. Otolaryngology, 1975-76, prof., 1976-84; mem. study sect. Nat. Inst. Neurol. and Communicative Disorders and Stroke, NIH, 1978-84, ad hoc bd. dirs. sci. counselors, 1988; sci. rev. com. Deafness Rsch. Found., 1978-83, chair, 1983—; mem. faculty Nat. Conf. Rsch. Goals and Methods in Otolaryngology, 1982; adv. com. hearing, bio-acoustics and biomechanics Commn. Behavioral and Social Scis. and Edn., Nat. Rsch. Coun., 1983—; hon. com. Orgn. Nobel Symposium 63, Cellular Mechanisms in Hearing, Karlskoga, Sweden, 1985; cons. Otitis Media Rsch. Ctr., 1985-89, Pfizer Corp., 1988; faculty opponent U. Gôteborg, Sweden, 1987; rsch. adv. com. Galludet Coll., 1987; chair external sci. adv. com. House Ear Inst., 1988-91; author authorizing legis. Nat. Inst. Deafness and Other Comm. Disorders, NIH, 1988, co-chair adv. bd. rsch. priorities com., bd. dirs. Friends adv. coun., 1989—, chair rsch. subcom., 1990-93, treas., bd. dirs., 1996—; grant reviewer Mich. State Rsch. Fund, NSF, VA; reviewer numerous jours. including Acta Otolaryngologica, Jour. Otology, Physiology and Behavior, Science. Mem. editorial bd. Am. Jour. Otolaryngology, 1981—, AMA, Am. Physiology Soc., Annals of Otology, Rhinology and Laryngology, 1980—, Archives of Oto-Rhino-Laryngology, 1985-93, Hearing Rsch., Jour. Am. Acad. Otolaryngology-Head and Neck Surgery, 1990—. Bd. dirs. Internat. Hearing Found., 1985—. Fellow U. Wash., 1962-65, Kresge Hearing Rsch. Inst., U. Mich., 1965-67; recipient award Am. Acad. Otolaryngology; grantee Deafness Rsch. Found., U. Wash., 1969-71; rsch. grantee NIH, 1969-73. Mem. AAAS, Am. Acad. Otolaryngology and Head and Neck Surgery (com. rsch. in otolaryngology 1971-82, continuing edn. com. 1975-79, NIH liaison com. 1988—, program steering com. jour. 1990), Am. Auditory Soc., Am. Otological Soc., Am. Neurotological Soc., Am. Otologic Honor Soc., Acoustical Soc. Am. (com. rsch. psychol., physiol. acoustics 1969-78), Fedn. Am. Physiological Soc., Fedn. Am. Socs. Experimental Biology, Soc. Neurosci., Assn. Rsch. Otolaryngology (sec.-treas. 1979-80, pres. elect 1981, pres. 1982. program dir. mtg. 1983, award of merit com. 1985, 95-96, chair 1988, program dir., pres. symposium homeostatic mech. of inner ear 1993), Sigma Xi. Office: U Mich Kresge Hearing Rsch Inst 1301 E Ann St # R5032 Ann Arbor MI 48109-0500

MILLER, JOSEPH CALDER, history educator, historical consultant, editor; b. Cedar Rapids, Iowa, Apr. 30, 1939; s. John William and Harriet Eleanor (Calder) M.; m. Mary Catherine Wimer; children: Julia Carolyn, John Russell, Laura Andrée. BA, Wesleyan U., 1961; MBA, Northwestern U., 1963; MA, U. Wis., 1967, PhD, 1972. Asst. prof. U. Va., Charlottesville, 1972-75, assoc. prof., 1975-82, prof., 1982-89, Commonwealth prof., 1989-96, T. Cary Johnson prof., 1996—, dean Coll. Arts and Scis., 1990-95. Author: Way of Death, 1988 (Herskovitz prize, spl. citation Conf. Latin Am. Historians 1988), Kings and Kinsmen, 1976; editor: The African Past Speaks, 1980; compiler Slavery: Worldwide Bibliography, 1985, Slavery and Slaving in World History: A Bibliography, 1900-1991, 1993; editor Jour. African History, 1990-96. NEH fellow, 1978-79, 85. Mem. Am. Coun. Learned Socs. (study fellow 1974-75), Soc. Sci. Rsch. Coun. (rsch. grant 1977), African Studies Assn. (treas. 1988-93, bd. dirs. 1986-89), Am. Hist. Assn. (rsch. div. 1987-89), Can. Assn. African Studies. Avocations: theater, music, roadrunning. Office: U Va Corcoran Dept History Randall Hall Charlottesville VA 22903

MILLER, JOSEPH IRWIN, automotive manufacturing company executive; b. Columbus, Ind., May 26, 1909; s. Hugh Thomas and Nettie Irwin (Sweeney) M.; m. Xenia Ruth Simons, Feb. 5, 1943; children: Margaret Irwin, Catherine Gibbs, Elizabeth Ann Garr, Hugh Thomas, II, William Irwin. Grad., Taft Sch., 1927; AB, Yale U., 1931, MA (hon.), 1959, LHD (hon.), 1979; MA, Oxford (Eng.) U., 1933; LLD, Bethany Coll., 1956, Tex. Christian U., Ind. U., 1958, Oberlin Coll., Princeton, 1962; LL.D., Hamilton Coll., 1964, Columbia, 1968, Mich. State U., 1968, Dartmouth, 1971, U. Notre Dame, 1972, Ball State U., 1972, Lynchburg Coll., 1985; L.H.D. (hon.), Case Inst. Tech., 1966, U. Dubuque, 1977; Hum.D., Manchester U., 1973, Moravian Coll., 1976. Assoc. Cummins Engine Co., Inc., Columbus, Ind., 1934—; v.p., gen. mgr. Cummins Engine Co., Inc., 1934-42, exec. v.p., 1944-47, pres., 1947-51, chmn. bd., 1951-77, chmn. exec. com., 1977-95; dir., 1995—; pres. Irwin-Union Bank & Trust Co., 1947-54, bd. dir., 1937—, chmn., 1954-75; chmen. exec. com. Irwin Union Corp., 1976-90; bd. dirs. Irwin Fin. Corp., 1990—; mem. Commn. Money and Credit, 1958-61, Pres.'s Com. Postal Reorgn., 1968, Pres.'s Com. Urban Housing, 1968; chmn. Pres.'s Com. on Trade Rels. with Soviet Union and Eastern European Nations, 1965, Nat. Adv. Commn. on Health Manpower, 1966; vice chmn. UN Commn. on Multinat. Corps., 1974; adv. council U.S. Dept. Commerce, 1976; mem. Study Commn. on U.S. Policy Toward So. Africa, 1979-81. Pres. nat. Coun. Chs. of Christ U.S.A., 1960-63; trustee Nat. Humanities Ctr., 1978-90, Carnegie Instn., Washington, 1988-91; mem. cen. and exec. coms. World Coun. Chs., 1961-68; trustee Ford Found., 1961-79, Yale Corp., 1959-77, Urban Inst., 1966-76, Mayo Found., 1977-82; fellow Branford Coll. Recipient Rosenberger award U. Chgo., 1977, 1st MacDowell Colony award, 1981; hon. fellow Balliol Coll., Oxford (Eng.) U.; Benjamin Franklin fellow Royal Soc. Arts. Fellow Am. Acad. Arts and Scis., Royal Inst. Brit. Architects (hon.); mem. AIA (hon.), Am. Philos. Soc., Ind. Acad., Bus. Coun., Conf. Bd. (sr.), Phi Beta Kappa, Beta Gamma Sigma. Mem. Christian Ch. Office: 301 Washington St Columbus IN 47201-6743

MILLER, JOSEPH S., astronomy researcher; b. L.A., Sept. 7, 1941; s. William George and Bertha Florence (Standard) M.; m. Nina Armstrong Parker, Dec. 22, 1971; children: Miriam Q., Samuel A. BA, UCLA, 1963; MA, U. Wis., 1966, PhD, 1967. Dir. U. Calif. Lick Observatory, Santa Cruz, Calif., 1967-68; prof. astronomy Lick Obs., Santa Cruz, 1968—, dir., 1991—. Fellow Am. Acad. Arts and Scis. Office: Lick Obs Univ Calif Santa Cruz CA 95064

MILLER, JUDITH, federal official. BS summa cum laude, Beloit Coll., 1972; JD, Yale U., 1975. Bar: U.S. Supreme Ct., U.S. Ct. Appeals (D.C. cir.), U.S. Ct. Appeals (armed forces cir.). Clk. to presiding justice Harold Leventhal U.S. Ct. of Appeals (D.C. cir.); clk. to assoc. justice Potter Stewart Supreme Ct. of U.S.; asst. to sec. and dep. sec. of def. Office of the Spl. Asst., 1977-79; mem. adv. bd. on the investigative capability Dept. of Def., gen. counsel, 1994—; mem. civil justice reform act adv. group U.S. Dist. Ct. D.C.; mem. jud. conf. D.C. Cir. Recipient Vol. Recognition award Nat. Assn. of Attys. Fellow Am. Bar Found.; mem. ABA (litigation sect.), Am. Law Inst. *

MILLER, JUDITH ANN, retired financial executive; b. Chgo., Sept. 8, 1941; d. Frank G. and Kathryn M. (Stocklin) Bell; m. William J. Shrum, Aug. 3, 1958 (div. 1976); children: Steven W., Vickie L. White, Lisa A. Rhodes, Mark A., Brian D.; m. William L. Miller Jr., Nov. 28, 1976. Student, Ind. Cen. Coll., 1959-60, DePaw U., 1964-65. Lic. minister Christian Ch. (Disciples of Christ). Office cashier, mgr. G.C. Murphy Co., Indpls., 1967-70; asst. treas., office mgr. Missions Blvd. Fed. Credit Union, Indpls., 1970-72; treas., office mgr. Bd. Higher Edn., Christian Ch. (Disciples of Christ), Indpls. and St. Louis, 1972-77; dir. fin. Mt. Olive United Meth. Ch., Arlington, Va., 1978-79; exec. dir. Interfaith Forum on Religion, Art and Architecture, Washington, 1979-82; devel. assoc. Nat. Benevolent Assn., Des Moines, Iowa, 1982-85; adminstrv. asst. Davis, Hockenberg, Wine, Brown, Koehn & Shors, Des Moines, 1985-88; fin. officer Episcopal Diocese of Iowa, Des Moines, 1988-93; ret., 1993; owner Cakes by Judy, Manteo, N.C., 1996—. Mem. citizen adv. coun. Parkway Schs., St. Louis, 1976-77; county rep., mem. Fairfax County Sch. Bd. adv. coun., Springfield, Va., 1979-81; treas. congl. campaign Des Moines, 1983-85; mem. exec. St. Louis Children's Home, 1976-78; v.p., treas. Emmaus Fellowship Project on Aging, Washington, 1980-82; bd. dirs. Urban Mission Coun., Des Moines, 1983-86, Pre-Trial Release Prog., Des Moines, 1984-87; mem. steering com. Iowa Interfaith Network on AIDS, Des Moines, 1989-94; chmn. Cancer Awareness Sunday, Am. Cancer Soc., 1990; mem. pub. rels com. Dare County Librs., 1996—. Named Vol. of Yr., Iowa Victorian Soc., 1985, Our Community Kitchen, 1986. Mem. Nat. Soc. Fund Raising Execs. (chpt. sec. 1985-87), Nat. Assn. Ch. Bus. Adminstrs., NAFE. Democrat. Mem. Christian Ch. (Disciples of Christ). Avocations: camping, sewing, knitting, reading, cooking. Home: PO Box 194 Manteo NC 27954-0194

MILLER, JUDITH ANN, elementary education educator; b. Chgo., Dec. 16, 1956; d. Clarence William and Jean E. Miller; children: Carey Michael, Rachael Marie. BA, Nat. Coll. Edn., 1978. Cert. tchr., Ill. Buyer, mgr. Learning Village Store, Chgo., 1977-80; adminstrv. and tech. cons. Chatham Bus. Assn., Chgo., 1980-81; adminstrv. asst. Chatham-Avalon Local Devel. Corp., Chgo., 1981-82; dir. Devel. Inst., Chgo., 1983-85; sub-tchr. Chgo. Bd. Edn., 1985-87; cadre tchr. John J. Pershing Magnet Sch., Chgo., 1987-88; tchr. Charles N. Holden Sch., Chgo., 1988—; master tchr. Columbia Coll. Sci. Inst., Chgo., 1992—. V.p. parent aux. bd. Link Unltd., Chgo., 1992-94. Mem. Chgo. Tchrs. Union, Ill. Fedn. Tchrs., Alpha Kappa Alpha. Roman Catholic. Office: Charles N Holden Sch 1104 W 31st St Chicago IL 60608-5602

MILLER, JUDSON FREDERICK, lawyer, former military officer; b. Tulsa, Dec. 5, 1924; s. Herbert Frederick and Martha (Davidson) M.; m. June Hirakis, Aug. 4, 1967; children by previous marriage: Kathleen, Shelley, Douglas, Judson Frederick. BS, U. Md., 1961; postgrad., Army War Coll., 1961-62; MA, George Washington U., 1962; JD, U. Puget Sound, 1980. Bar: Wash. 1981. Commd. 2d lt. U.S. Army, 1943, advanced through grades to maj. gen., 1975; platoon leader, co. comdr. 4th Cav. Group, Europe, 1944-46, 82d Airborne Div., 1947-50; with 187th Airborne RCT and Hdqrs. 8th Army, 1950-52; instr. Armored Sch., 1953-56; bn. comdr. 14th Armored Cav., 1958-60; with Hdqrs. U.S. Strike Command, 1963-65; brigade comdr., chief of staff 4th Inf. Div., Vietnam, 1966-67; mem. gen. staff Dept. Army, 1967-68; dep. comdg. gen. Ft. Ord, Cal., 1968-69; asst. chief of staff Hdqrs. Allied Forces Central Europe, 1969-71; asst. comdr. 3d Inf. Div., Germany, 1971-73; chief of staff I Corps Group, Korea, 1973-75; dep. comdg. gen. VII Corps, Germany, 1975-77; ret., 1977; assoc. F.G. Enslow and Assocs., Tacoma, 1981—. Decorated Silver Star, Legion of Merit, Bronze Star with V device and oak leaf cluster, Joint Service Commendation medal, Air medal with 8 oak leaf clusters, Purple Heart, Vietnamese Gallantry Cross with palm; named to Okla. Mil. Acad. Hall of Fame, 1988. Mem. ABA, Assn. U.S. Army. Club: Tacoma Country, Lakewood Racquet. Home: 8009 75th St SW Tacoma WA 98498-4817 Office: Tacoma Mall Office Bldg 4301 S Pine St Ste 205 Tacoma WA 98409-7205

MILLER, KAREN LYNN, clinical social worker; b. Trenton, Mo., Mar. 3, 1956; d. Arthur Leon and JoAnn (Ellis) Sawyer; m. Stuart W. Miller, May 31, 1975; children: Matthew A., and Michael A. AA, Longview C.C., Lees Summit, Mo., 1992; BSW, Ctrl. Mo. State U., 1994; postgrad. in social work, U. Kans., 1994—. Accts. payable clk. Panhandle Ea. Pipeline, Kansas City, Mo., 1975-81; hairdresser The Hairdresser, Independence, Mo., 1984-87; self employed hairdresser Independence, 1987-93, 94-95; case mgr. intern Hope House, Independence, 1994; clin. social worker, intern Heart Am. Family Svcs., Kansas City, 1994—, Western Mo. Mental Health Ctr., Kansas City, 1989—; vol. hotline Hope House Battered Women's Shelter, Independence, 1989—; mem. adv. bd. home econs. dept. Independence Schs., 1990—. Vol. Juvenile Family Ct., Kansas City; sec. Assn. S.W. Students Ctrl. Mo. State U., 1992-93. Mem. Nat. Assn. S.W., Phi Alpha (sec. 1994—), Phi Theta Kappa. Avocations: reading, bowling, walking, piano, sports. Home: 4815 S Kendall Dr Independence MO 64055-5344

MILLER, KEN LEROY, religious studies educator, consultant, writer; b. San Antonio, July 29, 1933; s. Eldridge and Paskel Dovie (Vick) M.; m. Eddie Juanell Crawford, June 14, 1953 (dec. Apr. 1981); children: Kimberly Miller Stern, Kerry, Karen Miller Davis; m. Carolyn Gayle Jackson, May 4, 1982; children: Sheila Stanley, Keith Conatser. BA, Abilene Christian U., 1958; MEd, Trinity U., 1965; EdD, Ariz. State U., 1975. Cert. tchr., Tex. Tchr. SAn Antonio Ind. Sch. Dist., 1957-58; tchr., adminstr. N.E. Ind. Sch. Dist., San Antonio, 1958-69; min. edn. MacArthur Park Ch. of Christ, San Antonio, 1960-69; prin. Ralls (Tex.) Ind. Sch. Dist., 1969-70; minister of edn. S.W. Ch. of Christ, Phoenix, 1970-74; adminstr., tchr. Lubbock (Tex.) Christian Sch./U., 1974-77; minister of edn. Sunset Ch. of Christ, Lubbock, 1977-87; prof. religious edn. Harding U., Searcy, Ark., 1987—; curriculum cons. Sweet Pub. Co., Ft. Worth, 1988-91; leader internat. and nat. religious edn. workshops and seminars. Author: Moral and Religious Stages of Development, 1975, (curriculum) Old Testament Personalities, 1980, Organization, Administration, Supervision of the Bible School, 1993, Recruiting, Training, Retaining Teachers in the Bible School, 1993, Curriculum for the Bible School, 1993; editor: Recipes for Living and Teaching, 1982, (curiculum) Growing in Knowledge, 1977-90, The MINNITH series, 1991-95; guest editor, contbr. Christian Family 1984. With U.S. Army, 1954-56. Mem. Christian Educators, Christian Edn. Assn., Religious Edn. Assn., Assn. Secondary Schs. and Colls., Alpha Psi Omega, Sigma Tau Delta. Republican. Mem. Ch. of Christ. Avocations: fishing, hunting, reading, travel, writing, poetry readings. Home: 111 Water Oak Searcy AR 72143-4551 Office: Harding U 900 E Center Ave Box 792 Searcy AR 72149-0001

MILLER, KENNETH EDWARD, sociologist, educator; b. N.Y.C., June 17, 1929; s. Joseph F. and Irene (Edersheim) M.; m. Andrée Nora Barthelemy, Feb. 14, 1959 (div. Nov. 1984); children: Jennifer Andrée, Christopher Kenneth; m. Janet Sue Daniels, May 21, 1990. B.A., U. Ala., 1953, M.A., 1956; Ph.D., Duke, 1965; MS, Drake U., 1986. Asst. to pres., dir. devel. Jacksonville (Fla.) U., 1957-60; dir. Health Council, asso. dir. Community Planning Council, Birmingham, Ala., 1960-62; asst. prof. sociology Emory U., Atlanta, 1966-70; acting chmn. dept. Emory U., 1969-70; prof. sociology Drake U., Des Moines, 1970—; chmn. dept. Drake U., 1970-79, 82-88, asst. to dean for grad. studies, 1991-92; Research sociologist U. Ala., 1956-57; research asso. U.S. Civil Service Commn., summer 1968. Served with USN, 1946-48. Postdoctoral research fellow Duke, 1965-66. Mem. Midwest Sociol. Soc. Home: 2129 NW 140th St Clive IA 50325-8730 Office: Drake Univ Dept Sociology Des Moines IA 50311

MILLER, KENNETH GREGORY, retired air force officer; b. Bryan, Tex., July 28, 1944; s. Max Richard and Catherine Mae (Sultzman) M.; m. Ann Marguerite Perpich, Nov. 25, 1966; children: Keith G., Deborah J., Craig S. BS in Aero. Engring., Purdue U., 1966; MS in Systems Mgmt., U. So. Calif., 1970; grad., Nat. War Coll., Washington, 1986; postgrad., U. Va., 1988. Commd. 2d lt. USAF, 1966, advanced through grades to brig. gen., 1990; with Office Sec. Def., Washington, 1980-81; various positions to dir. field ops. F-16 System Program Office, Wright-Patterson AFB, Ohio, 1981-86; chief engring. div. Sacramento Air Logistics Ctr., McClellan AFB, Calif., 1986-87; dir. materiel mgmt. Ogden (Utah) Air Logistics Ctr., Ga., 1987-89; vice comdr. Acquisition Logistics Div., Wright-Patterson AFB, 1989-90; comdr. contract mgmt. div. Air Force Systems Command, Kirtland AFB, N.Mex., 1990; comdr. western dist. Def. Contract Mgmt. Command, L.A., 1990-91; dir. C-17 Program Office, Wright-Patterson AFB, 1991-93; dep. asst. sec. of AF for acquistion Washington, 1993-94; dir. supply Hdqs. USAF, Washington, 1994-95; v.p. for gulf ops. BDM Fed., 1995—. Decorated Disting. Svc. medal, Legion of Merit (2), Def. Superior Svc. medal; recipient award of merit Freedom Found. Mem. Nat. Contract Mgmt. Assn. (bd. advisors 1990-92), Soc. Logistics Engrs. Office: BDM Fed 1501 BDM Way Mc Lean VA 22102-3204

MILLER, KENNETH MERRILL, computing services company executive; b. Lowell, Mass., Dec. 13, 1930; s. Harry Dow and Marjorie Louise (Morris) M.; m. Mary Jo Putnam, June 8, 1952 (div. Aug. 1979); children: Debra, Pamela, Carol; m. Eileen Anne Durnin, Feb. 4, 1980; 1 child, Andrew. BS, Am. U., 1964; MBA, Syracuse U., 1966. Commd. 2d lt. U.S. Army, 1953, advanced through grades to col., 1974; assigned to France, Fed. Republic Germany, Korea, Vietnam; ret., 1978; v.p. Robert W. Baird & Co., Inc., Milw., 1978-79; sr. v.p. Automatic Data Processing, Inc., Roseland, N.J., 1979—. Decorated Legion of Merit with three oak leaf clusters, Bronze Star, Purple Heart. Mem. Ont. Club (Toronto). Office: ADP Inc, 4 King St W, Toronto, ON Canada M5H 1B6

MILLER, KENNETH MICHAEL, electronics executive; b. Chgo., Nov. 20, 1921; s. Matthew and Tillie (Otto) M.; student Ill. Inst. Tech., 1940-41, UCLA, 1961; m. Dolores June Miller, Jan. 16, 1943 (dec. Dec. 1968); children: Barbara Anne Reed, Nancy Jeanne Hathaway, Kenneth Michael, Roger Allan; m. Sally J. Ballingham, June 20, 1970. Electronics engr. Rauland Corp., Chgo., 1941-48; gen. mgr. Lear, Inc., Santa Monica, Calif., 1948-59; v.p., gen. mgr. Motorola Aviation Electronics, Inc., Culver City, Calif., 1959-60; v.p., gen. mgr. Instrument div. Daystrom, Inc., Los Angeles, 1961; gen. mgr. Metrics div. Singer Co., Bridgeport, Conn. and Los Angeles, 1962-65; v.p., gen. mgr. Lear Jet Corp., 1965-66; pres., dir. Infonics Inc., 1967-68; v.p., gen. mgr. Computer Industries, Inc., 1968-69; dir. ops., tech. products group Am. Standard Corp., McLean, Va., also v.p., gen. mgr. Wilcox Electric div., Kansas City, Mo., 1969-71; pres. Wilcox Electric, Inc. subs. Northrop Corp., Kansas City, 1971-72, v.p., dir. World Wide Wilcox, Inc. subs., McLean, Va., 1971-72; pres., chief exec. officer Penril Corp., Rockville, Md., 1973-86, dir. 1973-86, pres. K-M Miller and Assocs., Rockville, Md., 1986—; dir., mem. investment com. Palmer Nat. Bank, Washington. Mem. regional planning coun. Community Mental Health Svcs., Bridgeport, 1964; mem. Bridgeport Capital Fund Com.; trustee Park City Hosp.; vice dir. Montgomery County Arts Council; bd. dirs. U. Bridgeport; mem. Md. State Com. High Tech. Recipient Job Makers award Mfrs. Assn. Bridgeport, 1963. Fellow Radio Club Am. (dir., chmn. grants-in-aid com.); mem. AIAA. IEEE, Aircraft Owners and Pilots Assn., Am. Mgmt. Assn., Armed Forces Communications and Electronics Assn. (life), Electronic Industries Assn., Instrument Soc. Am. (life), Nat. Aero. Assn., Soc. Non-Destructive Testing, Soc. Automotive Engrs., Air Force Assn., Am. Radio Relay League (life), Amateur Satellite Corp. (life), Am. Def. Preparedness Assn. (life), Aero. Elec. Soc. (life), Nat. Capital DX Assn. (pres. 1987-88), Assn. Old Crows (life), Mfrs. Assn. Bridgeport (dir.), Bridgeport Engring. Inst., Bridgeport C. of C. (pres, 1964), Quarter Century Wireless Assn. (life, Disting. Svc. award 1994), Soc. Wireless Pioneers. Clubs: Rolling Hills Country (Wichita); Algonquin (Bridgeport). Mem. adv. bd. Washington Bus. Jour.; contbr. articles to profl. jours. Home and Office: 16904 George Washington Dr Rockville MD 20853-1128

MILLER, KENNETH ROY, management consultant; b. Uniontown, Pa., Oct. 22, 1902; s. Franklin Pierce and Annabelle (Darby) M.; m. Mary E. Hunnicutt, June 14, 1930; 1 son, Stephen Goodrich. Student, Emerson Inst., 1922-23, George Washington U., 1923-25; LL.D., Lebanon Valley Coll., 1957, Fla. Atlantic U., 1975. Dir. conservation dept. Acacia Mut. Life Ins. Co., Washington, 1926-28; asst. supt. agencies Occidental Life Ins. Co., Raleigh, N.C., 1928-31; cons. Life Ins. Agy. Mgmt. Assn., Hartford, 1931-38; supt. agencies Atlantic Life Ins. Co., Richmond, Va., 1938-41; mng. dir. Nat. Fed. Sales Execs., N.Y.C., 1941-42; asst. to program vice chmn., dir. ops. analysis WPB, Washington, 1942-43; with NAM, N.Y.C., 1943-64; asst. to exec. v.p., asst. treas., treas., bus. mgr., sr. v.p. NAM, 1943-55, mng. dir., 1955-57, gen. mgr., 1957-62, group v.p., 1962-63, sr. v.p., adviser, 1963-64; prin. Kenneth R. Miller & Assos. (mgmt. and fin. cons.), Boca Raton, Fla., from 1964. Bd. dirs., past pres., dir. emeritus Fla. Atlantic U. Found., Boca Raton; founder, sponsor dept. ocean engring. Fla. Atlantic U.; former mem. Boca Raton Airport Authority; retired chmn. bd. Caldwell Theatre Co.; former chmn. adv. council Music Guild of Boca Raton.; mem. Friends of Caldwell Playhouse; former moderator Congl. Ch. of Boca Raton; citizens adv. com. Boca Raton Downtown Redevel. Agy. Mem. Economic Roundtable (treas., exec. com.), English-Speaking Union (past pres. Boca Raton br.), Phi Sigma Kappa, Pi Delta Epsilon. Club: Bankers (Boca Raton) (past pres.). Address: 699 SW 5th St Boca Raton FL 33486-4615

MILLER, KENNETH WILLIAM, holding company executive, financier; b. Albany, N.Y., Sept. 25, 1947; s. Kenneth Carpenter and Rose May (Chatfield) M.; m. Barbara Ann Tortorici, Aug. 5, 1967; children: Justin Carpenter, Jason Chatfield. BBA, SUNY, Albany, 1970. Exec. v.p., chief operating officer Texgas Corp., Houston, 1981-84; chief exec. officer The Edge Group, Inc., Houston, 1984—, Edge Mgmt. Group, Inc., Houston, 1984—, Superior Energy Group, Ltd., Houston, 1985-94, Gulf Butane Co., Houston, 1985-89, Auto-Quip Leasing Co., Houston, 1986—, MetroGas Corp., Mpls., 1986-89, MetroGas Supply Corp., Houston, 1986—, TRICO, Inc., Savannah, Ga., 1986-90, Tri-County Gas & Appliance Co., Tifton, Ga., 1986-90, Delta Storage and Distbn. Co., Hattiesburg, Miss., 1987-94, Edge Fin. Group, Inc., Atlanta, N.Y.C. and Houston, 1989—, Edge Realty Group, Inc., Houston, 1991—, AMC Funding, Inc., Houston, Little Rock, 1992—; Edge Ins. Holdings, Houston, 1993—, Edge Transp. Group, Inc., Houston, 1994-95; CEO Harper Energy Group, Atlanta, 1994—; DaVinci Sci. Corp., L.A., 1995—; mem. adv. commn. N.Y. Cotton Exch., N.Y.C., 1984-87; del. to USSR Am. People Amb. Program, 1989, Western Europe, 1990; bd. dirs. ProLine Golf Corp., Cardio Dynamics Internat. Pres. Hidden Dunes Community Assn., Destin, Fla., 1988-90. With USAR, 1968-74. Mem. Nat. Propane Gas Assn. (bd. dirs. 1984-95), Gov.'s Club, Pine Forest Country Club, West Side Tennis Club. Avocations: tennis, water sports, scuba diving, golf, skiing. Office: The Edge Group Inc 16225 Park Ten Pl Ste 380 Houston TX 77084-5138

MILLER, KENNETH WILLIAM, II, business consultant, educator; b. Cleve., May 11, 1951; s. Kenneth William and Margaret Mary (Leonard) M.; m. Joan Ellen Pattillo, Aug. 12, 1972 (div. Oct. 1992); children: Kenneth William III, Victoria Joan, Christopher John. BSEE, MIT, 1974, MS in Mgmt., 1983; postgrad., Cornell U., Am. U. of Paris, 1994—. Programmer Fed. Res. Bank, Boston, 1972-74; various Corning (N.Y.) Glass Works, 1974-81; mgr. product devel. Duracell, Tarrytown, N.Y., 1983-85; with Lucent Technologies, 1985; cons. Zacks Investment Rsch., 1991—; mgr. AT&T Tech. Systems, 1985; with Idea Disclosure Program AT&T, 1992—; with Intellogistics, 1989; cons. Zachs Imvestment Rsch., 1991—; guest lectr. Ohio State U., 1988. Mem. Greensboro Ctr. for Leadership, 1987. Mem. IEEE (cand. for state rep. 1988, city coun. 1989), Ohio Acad. Sci. (life), Mus. Broadcasting (Chgo.), Amnesty Internat., Boston Mus. of Fine Arts, Eagle Scout Assn. (life), Internat. Telecomms. Union (Geneva). Republican. Methodist. Lodge: Rotary.

MILLER, KEVIN D., security executive; b. Chgo., Feb. 7, 1949; s. Donald D. and Anna Agnes (Long) M.; m. Patricia D. Hallberg, Sept. 5, 1995; children: Angela Christy, Jenny Lynne Hallberg, Julie Anne Judd, Suzanne Michelle. BSBA cum laude, Upper Iowa U., 1984. Cert. info. sys. security profl., cert. disaster recovery planner. Detective Dolton (Ill.) Police Dept., 1970-78; systems analyst United Airlines, Chgo., 1978-88; mgr. info. security and bus. continuance Apollo Travel Svcs., Rolling Meadows, Ill., 1989—. Mem. Am. Soc. Indsl. Security, Info. Sys. Security Assn. (past pres. Chgo.

chpt.). Avocations: traveling, reading, comedy writing, acting. Home: 236 Skylark Ct Bartlett IL 60103-2024

MILLER, KIRK EDWARD, lawyer, health foundation executive; b. San Jose, Calif., June 9, 1951; s. Edward R. and Katherine Miller; children: Anja, Jenny. BA in Polit. Sci., U. Calif., Riverside, 1973; JD, Syracuse U., 1976. Bar: Colo. 1976, Calif. 1980, Tex. 1993. Assoc. Hughes & Dorsey, Denver, 1977-78; v.p., assoc. gen. counsel Am. Med. Internat., Inc., Dallas, 1979-88, v.p., sec., gen. counsel, 1988-91; with McGlinchey Stafford Lang, Dallas, 1991-94; sr. v.p., sec., gen. counsel Kaiser Found. Health Plan, Inc., Kaiser Found. Hosps., Inc., Oakland, Calif., 1994—; instr. Syracuse U., 1975-76. Mem. ABA (co-vice chair com. health care fraud and abuse). Office: Kaiser Found Health Plan 1 Kaiser Plz Oakland CA 94612

MILLER, L. MARTIN, accountant, financial planning specialist; b. N.Y.C., Sept. 17, 1939; s. Harvey and Julia (Lewis) M.; m. Judith Sklar, Jan. 21, 1962; children: Philip, Marjorie. BS, Wharton Sch., U. Pa., 1960. CPA; CFP; accredited fin. planning specialist. Jr. acct. Deloitte, Haskins & Sells, N.Y.C., 1960-62, sr. acct., Phila., 1962-64; mng. partner Cogen, Sklar LLP, Phila., 1964—; treas. Coronet Container Co., Inc., Phila., Val Mar Realty Corp., N.Y.C.; dir. Penn Internat. Trading Co., Phila.; mng. dir. CPA Tax Forum, 1966-69; underwriting mem. Lloyds of London, 1978-95, chmn. Mid-Atlantic region, 1991-92; mem. faculty Wharton Sch. U. Pa., 1992—; lectr., discussion leader on fin. and taxation; columnist Montgomery and Bucks County Dental News. Mem. Phila. Rep. com., 1963-67; chmn. Lower Merion Twp. scholarship fund, 1975-78; bd. dirs. Penn Valley Civic Assn., 1973-79, Gladwyne Civic Assn., 1992-95; mem. Lower Merion Planning Commn., 1978-82, Gov.'s Tax Study Commn.; pres. Mensa Edn. and Rsch. Found., 1984-86; mem. SEC Forum on Small Bus. Capital Formation, 1983, Pa. Impact, 1995; apptd. to Pa. State Bd. Accountancy, 1985-94, chmn., 1990-91; elected sch. bd. dir. Lower Merion Twp., 1993—, also chmn. fin. com. Served with U.S. Army, 1961-62. Recipient Outstanding Achievement award Germantown Civic Assn., 1965. Mem. Pa. Inst. CPAs (edn. com. 1975-78, bd. dirs. 1979-81, by-laws chmn. 1980-83), Nat. Assn. State Bds. Accountancy (edn. com. 1987, nominating com. 1989, experience com. 1990, continuing edn. com. 1995—), Cert. Fin. Planner (bd. ethics 1995—), AICPAs (nat. tax commn. 1979-82, exec. com. self regulation div. for CPA firms 1984-87, acctg. and rev. svcs. com. 1985-88, ethics div. 1985-88, specialization bd. 1989-90, ethics exec. com. 1990-93, mem. curriculum and acctg. edn. 1993—, chmn. fin. assistance task force 1995), Little 10 Acctg. Assn. (edn. chmn. 1980-84), Main Line C. of C. (govt. affairs com. 1991—), Mensa (internat. fin. officer 1970-74), Beta Alpha Psi. Clubs: Masons (past master) Plays and Players (treas. 1978-79). Author: Accountants Guide to S.E.C. Filings, 1968; contbr. articles to profl. jours. Home: 204 Dove Ln Haverford PA 19041-1902 Office: Cogen Sklar LLP 150 Monument Rd Bala Cynwyd PA 19004-1725

MILLER, LARRY D., broadcasting executive; b. Chadron, Nebr., June 14, 1943; s. John and Lettie Leota (Maiden) M.; m. Karen Eva Galey, Dec. 28, 1963; children: Bradley James, Jill Marie. BA in History, Chadron State Coll., 1969; MSc in Journalism, Iowa State U., 1974. News dir. sta. KCSR, Chadron, 1966-67; asst. mgr., news dir. sta. KDUH-TV Duhamel Broadcasting Co., Scottsbluff, Nebr., 1967-69; news dir. sta. KMA May Broadcasting Co., Shenandoah, Iowa, 1969-70; news dir., instr. sta. KOSU Okla. State U., Stillwater, 1971-7e; dir. news and pub. affairs sta. KLRN/KUT U. Tex., Austin, 1973-76; asst. prof., sta. mgr. Okla. State U., Stillwater, 1977-80; sta. mgr. Okla. Edn. TV Authority, Tulsa, 1980-85; dep. exec. dir. S.D. Pub. Broadcasting, Vermillion, 1985-93; exec. dir. Miss. Authority Edn. TV, Jackson, 1993—; pres., CEO EdNet Inst., Inc., Jackson, 1993—. Bd. dirs. Internat. Ballet competition, Miss. Rural Econ. Devel. coun. Commdr. U.S. Naval Res., 1962—. Named Outstanding Young Man, U.S. Jaycees, 1978, Ambassador Good Will, Indep. Order Foresters, 1984. Mem. Found. Pub. Broadcasting (bd. dirs.), Naval Res. Assn. (pres. Tulsa chpt. 1984), Oil Capital C. of C. (pres. 1983), Metro C. of C. (bd. dirs. 1983). Methodist. Avocations: genealogy, amateur radio, photography. Home: 140 Pinevale St Brandon MS 39042-8356 Office: 3825 Ridgewood Rd Jackson MS 39211-6463

MILLER, LARRY H., professional sports team executive, automobile dealer; b. Salt Lake City; m. Gail Miller; 5 children. Formerly with auto parts bus., Denver and Salt Lake City; now owner auto dealerships, Salt Lake City, Albuquerque, Denver and Phoenix; part-owner Utah Jazz, NBA, Salt Lake City, 1985-86, owner, 1986—. Office: care Utah Jazz 301 W South Temple Salt Lake City UT 84101-1216 Office: Larry H Miller Group 5650 South State St Murray UT 84107*

MILLER, LAWRENCE EDWARD, lawyer; b. Trenton, N.J., May 18, 1944; s. Lawrence William and Cathryn (Brennan) M.; m. Michele Bongiovanni. Mar. 4, 1978; children: Lawrence Michael, Kristin Michele. BA, Villanova U., 1966; JD, Boston Coll., 1969; diploma Pvt. Internat. Law, The Hague, Netherlands, 1969; MA, Princeton U., 1970. Bar: N.J. 1969, N.Y. 1972, U.S. Supreme Ct. 1973. Assoc. Donovan Leisure Newton & Irvine, N.Y.C., 1971-76; sec., asst. gen. counsel Asarco, Inc., N.Y.C., 1977-86; v.p., sec., gen. counsel Lac d'Amiante du Que. Ltee, Que., Can., 1982-86; ptnr. LeBoeuf, Lamb, Greene & MacRae, N.Y.C., 1986—. Contbr. articles to profl. jours. Mem. ABA, Fed. Bar Assn. N.J. (v.p.), Bedens Brook Club (Skillman, N.J.). Democrat. Roman Catholic. Office: LeBoeuf Lamb Greene & MacRae 125 W 55th St New York NY 10022-3502 also: One Riverfront Plz Newark NJ 07102

MILLER, LELAND BISHOP, JR., food processing and financial consultant; b. Bloomington, Ill., June 17, 1931; s. Leland Bishop and Nellie (Jolly) M.; m. Alice P. Elder; children: Susan Elizabeth, James Bishop, Steven Robert. B.S. in Chem. Engring, U. Ill., 1954, M.S. in Chem. Engring, 1955, M.B.A., 1978. Research engr. Exxon Research & Engring., Linden, N.J., 1955-58; research asst. Purdue U., 1958-59; with A. E. Staley Mfg. Co., Decatur, Ill., 1959-85; dir. corp. planning A. E. Staley Mfg. Co., 1971-73, asst. treas., 1973-77, corp. treas., 1977-81, v.p., treas., 1981-85; v.p., treas. Staley Continental Inc., Rolling Meadows, Ill., 1985-88; exec. v.p., chief fin. officer MultiFresh Systems, Inc., Hoffman Estates, Ill., 1989-90; exec. v.p. MWT Ltd., Inc., Barrington, Ill., 1990-93; fin. cons., 1993—; pres. Indsl. Devel. Research Council, 1973-74. State v.p. United Cerebral Palsy of Ill., 1971-72; pres. United Cerebral Palsy of Macon County, Ill., 1972-73; bd. dirs. Progress Resource, Inc., Decatur. Served to 1st lt. U.S. Army, 1955-57. Mem. Am. Mgmt. Assn. (fin. council), Fin. Mgmt. Assn., Nat. Assn. of Corp. Treas., Alpha Chi Sigma, Phi Lambda Upsilon, Sigma Chi.

MILLER, LENORE, labor union official; b. Union City, N.J., Mar. 10, 1932; d. Louis and Lillian (Bergen) Shapiro; m. Louis Miller, Dec. 25, 1952; 1 child, Jessica. BA, Rutgers U., 1952; postgrad., Purdue U., 1952-56, New Sch. Social Research, 1957. Sec., asst. to pres. Panel of Ams.; sec., asst. to pres. Retail, Wholesale & Dept. Store Union, AFL-CIO, CLC, N.Y.C., 1958-78, v.p., 1978-80, sec.-treas., 1980-86, pres., 1986—; vice chair civil rights com. AFL-CIO, 1990—; exec. bd. AFL-CIO Indsl. Union Dept., Washington, 1980-82, AFL-CIO Food & Beverage Trades Dept., Washington, 1980—, Maritime Trades Dept., 1986; v.p. Transp. Trades Dept. AFL-CIO, 1992—; vice-chmn. Nat. Trade Union Coun. for Human Rights, N.Y.C., 1980—; mem. Nat. BD. Workers Def. League, N.Y.C., 1980—, Pres. Commn. Tariff & Trade, 1994—; mem. com. Am. Trade Union Coun. for Histadrut & Afro-Asian Inst., N.Y.C., 1980—; bd. dirs. Health Security Action Coun., 1986; chmn. RWDSU Welfare and Pension Plan, 1986. Mem. adv. com. AFL-CIO Com. on Polit. Edn., Washington, 1978—, Frontlash, 1978—; bd. dirs. A. Philip Randolph Ednl. Fund, 1988, Cen. Labor Rehab. Coun. N.Y.; charter trustee Rutgers U., 1988-94; pres. Jewish Labor Com., 1989; mem. platform com. Dem. Nat. Conv., 1992; mem. Pres. Commn. on Family and Med. Leave, 1993—. Named to Acad. of Women Achievers YWCA, 1987. Mem. AFL-CIO (v.p. 1987—, mem. exec. coun.), Douglass Soc. Office: Retail Wholesale & Dept Store Union AFL-CIO CLC 30 E 29th St Fl 4 New York NY 10016-7925

MILLER, LEONARD DAVID, surgeon; b. Jersey City, July 8, 1930; s. Louis Abner and Esther (Levy) M.; children—Steven Lawrence, Jason Lloyd. A.B., Yale U., 1951; M.D., U. Pa., 1955. Intern Hosp. of U. Pa., Phila., 1955-56; resident Hosp. of U. Pa., 1956-57, 59-65; practice medicine, specializing in surgery Phila., 1965—; vice chmn. dept. research and surgery U. Pa., 1972-75, acting chmn., 1975-78, John Rhea Barton prof., 1978-83, chmn. dept. surgery, 1978-83; dir. Harrison Dept. Surgery. Mem. editorial bd.: Annals of Surgery, 1973—. Served to capt., M.C. USAF, 1957-59. Recipient Lindback award for disting. teaching, 1969, Student award for clin. teaching, 1965. Mem. Am. Surg. Assn., AAAS, Soc. for Surgery of Alimentary Tract, Nat. Soc. Med. Research (rep.), Soc. Univ. Surgeons, Am. Soc. Surgery of Trauma, Coll. Physicians of Phila., N.Y. Acad. Sci., Sigma Xi, Alpha Omega Alpha. Office: Univ Pa Hosp Dept Surgery 4 Silverstein 3400 Spruce St Philadelphia PA 19104

MILLER, LEROY BENJAMIN, architect; b. Cleve., Dec. 24, 1931; s. Harry Simon and Carol Jane (Goldberg) M.; m. Sue Firestone, July 1, 1956; children: Laurie, Janet, David, Matthew. BArch, U. Mich., 1956. Registered architect, Calif. From assoc. to v.p. Daniel Dworsky & Assocs., L.A., 1958-66; prin., pres. Leroy Miller Assocs., L.A., Santa Monica, Calif., 1966—; tchr. Calif. State Poly. Coll., Pomona, 1971-72. Exhibited in group shows, 1976, 84, 94. Pres. Leo Baeck Temple, L.A., 1991-93. Cpl. U.S. Army, 1956-58. Fellow AIA (Design awards L.A. chpt. 1966, 69, 72, 89). Democrat. Jewish. Avocations: writing, music, skiing, racquetball. Office: Leroy Miller Assocs 2800 Olympic Blvd Santa Monica CA 90404-4119

MILLER, LEROY PAUL, JR., secondary English educator; b. Holyoke, Mass., Feb. 21, 1949; s. Leroy Paul Sr. and Rose Marie (Danehey) M. AA, Northampton (Mass.) Jr. Coll., 1972; BA, U. New Eng., Biddeford, Maine, 1974; MEd, Springfield (Mass.) Coll., 1977; postgrad., Am. Internat. Coll., Springfield. Cert. elem. tchr., history/English tchr., guidance counselor, Mass. Sch. adjustment counselor Holyoke Pub. Schs., 1978-79, ednl. programmer, 1979-80, tutor Chpt. I, 1980-81; tutor Amherst (Mass.) Pub. Schs., 1982-84; tchr. West Springfield (Mass.) Pub. Schs., 1985-86; tchr. English Springfield Pub. Schs., 1986—; fund raiser M. Marcus Kiley Mid. Sch.; alumni counselor U. New Eng., 1977—. Alumni counselor U. New Eng., 1990—. Mem. NEA, ASCD, Nat. Coun. Tchrs. English, Mass. Tchrs. Assn., Springfield Edn. Assn. (faculty rep. 1986—), U. New Eng. Alumni Assn. (v.p. 1990—), Elks, Psi Chi. Democrat. Roman Catholic. Avocations: reading, bowling. Home: 2 Gerard Way Holyoke MA 01040-1204 Office: M Marcus Kiley Mid Sch 180 Cooley St Springfield MA 01128-1108

MILLER, LESLEY JAMES, JR., state representative; b. Tampa, Fla., Apr. 21, 1951; s. Lesley James and Shaddie Alice (Robinson) M.; m. Gwendolyn Martin, Nov. 27, 1982; children: Le'Jean Michelle, Lesley James III. BA in Polit. Sci., U. South Fla., 1978. Customer rels. rep. Tampa Electric Co., 1978-87; pres. Lesley Miller Cons., Tampa, 1988-89; v.p., COO Greater Tampa Urban League, 1989-90; human resources recruiter Time Customer Svc., Inc., Tampa, 1990-91; mem. City of Tampa City Coun., 1991; mem Fla. Ho. of Reps., Tampa, 1992—; pres. Miller, Miller and Assocs., Tampa, 1990—. Mem. Fla. Commn. on Mental Health, Tallahassee, 1993—, Planning Commn., Hillsborough County, Fla., 1987-91, City Conv. Facilities Bd., Tampa, 1987-91, City County Cable TV Bd., Tampa, 1981-91; dir. Tampa Hillsborough Urban League, 1977—. With USAF, 1971-74. Recipient Milestone award Tampa Hillsborough Urban League, 1993, Achievement award Charmettes, Inc., 1993, Outstanding Support award Fla. Consortium Urban Leagues, 1993, Disting. Alumnus award U. South Fla., 1985. Mem. Masons (32d degree), Kappa Alpha Psi (life). Democrat. Baptist. Avocations: singing, reading, travel. Home: 2505 E 38th Ave Tampa FL 33610-7617 Office: Fla Ho of Reps PO Box 5993 Tampa FL 33675-5993

MILLER, LESLIE ANNE, lawyer; b. Franlin, Ind., Nov. 4, 1951; d. G. Thomas and Anne (Gaines) Miller; m. Richard B. Worley, Feb. 14, 1987. AB cum laude, Mt. Holyoke Coll., South Hadley, Pa., 1973; MA in Polit. Sci., Eagle Inst. Politics, New Brunswick, N.J., 1974; JD, Dickinson Sch. of Law, Carlisle, Pa., 1977; LLM with honors, Temple U., 1994. Bar: Pa. 1977, U.S. Dist. Ct. (ea. dist.) Pa. 1977, U.S. Ct. Appeals (3d cir.) 1980, U.S. Dist. Ct. (ea. dist.) Pa. 1987. Assoc. LaBrum & Doak, Phila., 1977-81; ptnr. LaBrum & Doak, 1982-86, Goldfein & Joseph, Phila., 1986-95, McKissock & Hoffman, P.C., Phila., 1995—; mem. Jud. Inquiry and Rev. Bd., 1990-94, chair, 1993. Chmn. Com. on Jud. Selection and Retention, Phila., 1987-89; mem. Open Space Task Force Com., Lower Merion Twp., Pa., 1990—, Lower Merion Conservancy, 1995—; bd. dirs. Med. Coll. Pa., 1985—, sec., 1987-92, chair presdl. search com., 1993, chair presdl. inauguration, 1987, chair com. on acad. affairs, 1989—, chair dean's search com., 1994—, Allegheny Health Edn. and Rsch. Found., 1993—, Med. Coll. Pa./Hahnemann U. Med. Sch., 1994—, United Hosps., 1991-94, St. Christopher's Hosp. for Children, 1991-94, vice chair, 1992—. Recipient Mary Lyon award, Mt. Holyoke Alumni Assn., 1985, Alumnae Medal of Honor, 1988, Hon. Alumnae award, 1989, Pres.'s award, 1993; named to Pa. Honor Roll of Women, 1996. Fellow Am. Bar Found., Pa. Bar Found.; mem. ABA, Phila. Bar Assn. (bd. govs. 1990-93), gender bias task force 1993, chair com. on jud. selection and retention 1987-89, chair Andrew Hamilton Ball 1989, trustee Phila. Bar Found. 1990—), Pa. Bar Assn. (ho. dels. 1981—, bd. govs. 1980-83, 84-87, 91-93, chair young lawyers divsn. 1982-83, sec. 1984-87, chair ho. dels. 1991-93, chair com. on status of women in the profession 1993, v.p. 1996-97), Pa. Bar Inst., Phila. Assn. Def. Counsel, Def. Rsch. Inst. Democrat. Lutheran. Avocations: collecting Am. antiques, gardening, running. Office: McKissock & Hoffman PC 1700 Market St Ste 3000 Philadelphia PA 19103-3930

MILLER, LEVI, publishing administrator; b. Millersburg, Ohio, Sept. 15, 1944; s. Andrew A. and Mattie (Schlabach) M.; m. Gloria E.; children: Jakob, Hannah, Elizabeth. Student, Kent State U., 1963-64; BA in English/History, Malone Coll., 1968; MA in English, Bowling Green State U., 1976. Tchr. English pub. schs. Orocovis, P.R., 1968-71; editor Mennonite Pub. House, Scottdale, Pa., 1971-82, dir. congl. lit. divsn., 1990—; tchr., pastor Eastern Mennonite Bd. Missions, Caracas, Venezuela, 1982-84; program dir. Laurelville Mennonite Ch. Ctr., Mt. Pleasant, Pa., 1984-90; sec. Allegheny Mennonite Conf., 1976-79. Contbr. articles to profl. jours.; author: Ben's Wayne, 1989, Our People, 1983, 2d edit. 1992; editor Allegheny Conf. News, 1979-82; editor Found. Series for Youth and Adults, Mennonite Pub. House, 1981-83. Mem. sch. bd. Southmoreland Sch. Dist., Scottdale, 1989-93. Home: 903 Arthur Ave Scottdale PA 15683-1543 Office: Mennonite Pub House 1600 Walnut St Scottdale PA 15683

MILLER, LEWIS NELSON, JR., banker; b. 1944. BA, Washington and Lee U., 1966; postgrad., U. Va., 1972. With 1st & Mchts. Nat. Bank, 1969-70; planning mgr. Cen. Fidelity Bank N.A., Richmond, Va., 1972-73, planning officer, then asst. v.p., 1973-75, v.p., 1975-76, sr. v.p., mgr. fin. group, 1976-78, chief fin. officer, 1978-79, exec. v.p., 1979-82, exec. v.p., chief adminstrv. officer, from 1982; with Cen. Fidelity Banks Inc., Richmond, 1972—, sr. v.p., 1980-82, corp. exec. officer, 1982-83; exec. v.p. Cen. Fidelity Banks Inc., Richmond, Va., 1983-84; pres., later also treas., bd. dirs. Cen. Fidelity Banks Inc., Richmond, from 1984; now chmn., pres., chief exec. officer Cen. Fidelity Banks, Richmond. Lt. USN, 1966-69. Office: Cen Fidelity Banks Inc PO Box 27602 1021 E Cary St Richmond VA 23219-4000*

MILLER, LINDA B., political scientist; b. Manchester, N.H., Aug. 7, 1937; d. Louis and Helene (Chase) M. A.B. cum laude, Radcliffe Coll., 1959; M.A., Columbia U., 1961, Ph.D., 1965. Asst. prof. Barnard Coll., 1964-67; research asso. Princeton U., 1966-67; research asso. Harvard U., 1967-71, 76-81, lectr. polit. sci., 1968-69; assoc. prof. Wellesley (Mass.) Coll., 1969-75, prof. polit. sci., 1975—, chmn. dept., 1985-89. Author: World Order and Local Disorder: The United Nations and Internal Conflicts, 1967, Dynamics of World Politics: Studies in the Resolution of Conflicts, 1968, Cyprus: The Law and Politics of Civil Strife, 1968; co-author, co-editor: Ideas and Ideals: Essays on Politics in Honor of Stanley Hoffmann, 1993; also articles and monographs. Internat. Affairs fellow Coun. Fng. Rels., 1973-74, Rockefeller Found. fellow, 1976-77, Oceanographic Instn. sr. fellow, 1979-80, 82-83, NATO social sci. rsch. fellow, 1982-83. Mem. Inst. Strategic Studies, Internat. Studies Assn., Coun. Fgn. Rels., Phi Beta Kappa. Home: PO Box 415 South Wellfleet MA 02663-0415 Office: Wellesley Coll Dept Polit Sci Wellesley MA 02181

MILLER, LLOYD DANIEL, real estate agent; b. Savannah, Mo., May 25, 1916; s. Daniel Edward and Minnie (Wiedmer) M.; m. Mabel Gertrude Kurz, June 9, 1939; children: Sharon Miller Schumacher, Donna Miller Bodinson, Rosemary Rae Dixon, Jeffrey Lloyd. B.S. in Agrl. Journalism, U. Mo., 1941. Reporter, feature writer, photographer, market editor Corn Belt Farm Dailies, Chgo., Kansas City, Mo., 1941-43; asst. agrl. editor U. Mo., 1946; dir. pub. relations Am. Angus Assn., Chgo., 1946-67, St. Joseph, Mo., 1967; asst. sec., dir. pub. relations Am. Angus Assn., 1968, exec. sec., 1968-78, sr. cons., 1978-81; realtor The Prudential Summers Realtors, 1978—; mem. U.S. Agrl. Tech. Adv. Com. on Livestock and Livestock Products for Trade Negotiations, 1975-79. Bd. dirs. Mo. Western State Coll. Found., 1976-82, pres., 1978-79; deacon Wyatt Park Bapt. Ch.; chmn. Heartland Ctr., Heartland Hosp. West, 1987-89, bd. dirs. 1987-95. With AUS, 1943-45. Recipient Silver Anvil award Pub. Relations Soc. Am., 1962, Faculty-Alumni award U. Mo.-Columbia, 1975. Mem. Nat. Assn. Realtors, St. Joseph Area C. of C. (pres. 1969, dir., chmn. agri-bus. coun. 1971), St. Joseph Regional Bd. Realtors (pres. 1986), Realtors Land Inst. (v.p. Mo. chpt. 1987-90), Am. Angus Heritage Found., Masons (32 deg.), Shriners, Kiwanis, Sigma Delta Chi. Home: 3208 Miller Rd Saint Joseph MO 64505-1532 Office: 1007 E Saint Maartens Dr Saint Joseph MO 64506-2993

MILLER, LOUIS H., lawyer; b. Lampeter, U.K., Apr. 22, 1945; m. Diane Matuszewski, Dec. 31, 1973; children: Margaret, Anthony. BA in History, Rutgers Coll., 1967; JD, Temple U., 1970. Bar: N.J. 1970, U.S. Dist. Ct. N.J. 1970, U.S. Supreme Ct. 1996. Law clk. to Judge Thomas Beetel Hunterdon County Ct., Flemington, N.J., 1970-71; law clk. to Judge Baruch Seidman Superior Ct. N.J. Chancery, Trenton, N.J., 1971-72; assoc. Jefferson, Jefferson & Vaida, Flemington, 1972-75; ptnr. Vaida & Miller, Flemington, 1975-78; pvt. practice Flemington, 1978-81, 88—; judge Superior Ct. N.J., Flemington, 1981-88; of counsel Levinson Axelrod Wheaton & Grayzel, Flemington, 1990—; spl. dep. atty. gen. N.J. Hunterdon County Prosecutor Office, Flemington, 1972-73; condemnation commr. Appt. Superior Ct. N.J., Flemington, 1988—, assembly spkrs. commr.; commr. N.J. State Commn. Investigation, Trenton, 1993—. Twp. committeeman Alexandria Twp. Com., R.D. Milford, N.J., 1978-81. Mem. Am. Judges Assn., Am. Judicature Soc., N.J. State Bar Assn. (mem. dist. ethics com. 1980-81), Hunterdon County Bar Assn., Warren County Bar Assn., Welsh Am. Geneal. Soc. Republican. Avocations: paleontology, traveling, hiking. Office: PO Box 850 124 Rte 31 Flemington NJ 08822

MILLER, LOUIS HOWARD, biologist, researcher; b. Balt., Feb. 4, 1935; s. David and Daisy (Arenson) M.; m. Nancy Jo Harned, Sept. 26, 1959; 1 child, Jennifer. BS, Haverford Coll., 1956; MD, Washington U., St. Louis, 1960; MS in Parasitology, Columbia U., 1964. Asst. prof. then assoc. prof. Coll. of P & S, Columbia U., N.Y.C., 1967-71; head malaria sect. NIAID, NIH, Bethesda, Md., 1971-92, chief lab. parasitic diseases, 1992—. Contbr. articles to profl. jours. Capt. U.S. Army, 1965-67. Recipient Paul Ehrlich/Ludwig Darmstaedter prize, 1989. Fellow Royal Soc. Tropical Med. Hygiene, Queensland Inst. Med. Rsch., ACP; mem. Am. Soc. Tropical Medicine & Hygiene (pres. 1988), NAS, Inst. of Medicine, Assn. Am. Physicians. Office: NIH Building 4 Rm 126 Bethesda MD 20892*

MILLER, LOUIS RICE, lawyer; b. Frankfort, Ind., Feb. 28, 1914; s. Louis A. and Josephine (Rice) M.; m. Jean Preston Russell, Feb. 1, 1941; 1 child, Mary Melissa. A.B., U. Chgo., 1935, J.D., 1937. Bar: Ill. 1938. Assoc. Gardner, Carton & Douglas, Chgo., 1937-40; atty. Armour & Co., Chgo., 1940-71, Phoenix, 1971-79; v.p., chief legal officer Armour & Co., (acquired by Greyhound Corp. 1970), 1967-79; v.p., gen. counsel Greyhound Corp. (now The Dial Corp.), Phoenix, 1972-79. Served with AUS, 1941; Served with USNR, 1942-45. Mem. ABA, Assn. Gen. Counsel. Club: Paradise Valley Country (Phoenix). Home: 7541 N Shadow Mountain Rd Paradise Vly AZ 85253-3311 Office: Dial Corp Phoenix AZ 85077-2212

MILLER, LOWELL DONALD, pharmaceutical company research executive; b. Chgo., Jan. 20, 1933; s. Nick William and Ottilie M.; m. Marian N. Couranz, Aug. 22, 1959; children—Lowell Donald, Jeanette L. B.S., U. Mo., 1957, M.S. in Biochemistry, 1958, Ph.D. in Biochemistry, 1960. Dir. biol. sci. Neisler Labs., Decatur, Ill., 1960-69; assoc. dir. biomed. sci. Warren-Teed, Columbus, Ohio, 1969-71; pres. Lab. Exptl. Biology, St. Louis, 1971-73; sci. dir. Marion Labs., Kansas City, Mo., 1973-78, corp. v.p. research and devel., 1978-87, sr. v.p. research and devel., 1987-89; cons., 1989—; bd. dirs. Air Methods. Contbr. numerous articles to profl. jours. Bd. dirs. Kansas City Eye Bank, 1981-90. Served with U.S. Army, 1953-55. Fellow Am. Inst. Chemists; mem. Soc. Toxicology, Am. Soc. Clin. Chemists, Am. Chem. Soc.

MILLER, LOYE WHEAT, JR., journalist, corporate communications specialist; b. Knoxville, Tenn., Mar. 20, 1930; s. Loye Wheat and Sara Vance (Davis) M.; children: Lissa Wethey, Loye Wheat. AB, Dartmouth Coll., 1951; MS in Journalism, Columbia U., 1952. Mem. staff Charlotte (N.C.) observer, 1955-59, asst. city editor, 1959; corr. Washington bur. Time mag., 1959-64, 69-70; chief Midwest news bur. Time-Life mags., 1964-69; corr. Washington bur. Knight-Ridder Newspapers, 1970-77; chief Washington bur. Chgo. Sun-Times, 1977-78; corr. Washington Bur. Gannett Newspapers, 1978-79; chief polit. writer Newhouse Newspapers, 1979-85; dir. pub. affairs U.S. Dept. Edn., Washington, 1985-88, U.S. Dept. Justice, Washington, 1988-89; dir. pub. info. Northrop Corp., Arlington, Va., 1989-94. Lt. (j.g.) USNR, 1952-55. Home: 1672D Beekman Pl NW Washington DC 20009-4009

MILLER, LYLE G., bishop. Bishop Sierra Pacific dist. Evang. Luth. Ch. in Am., Oakland, Calif. Office: Evang Luth Ch in Am 401 Roland Way Ste 215 Oakland CA 94621-2034

MILLER, M. JOY, financial planner, real estate broker; b. Enid, Okla., Dec. 29, 1934; d. H. Lee and M.E. Madge (Hatfield) Miller; m. Richard L.D. Berlemann, July 21, 1957 (div. Nov. 1974); children: Richard Louis, Randolph Lee. BSBA, N.Mex. State U., 1956. Cert. fin. planner; grad. Realtors Inst. Tchr. of bus. and mathematics Alamogordo (N.Mex.), Las Cruces (N. Mex.) and Omaha Pub. Schs., 1956-63; tchr., dir. Evelyn Wood Reading Dynamics Southern N.Mex. Inst., 1967-68; registered rep. Westamerica Fin. Corp., Denver, 1968-76; gen. agt. Security Benefit Life, Topeka, 1969—, Delta Life & Annuity, Memphis, 1969—; registered rep. Am. Growth Fund Sponsors, Inc., Denver, 1976—; pres., broker Fin. Design Corp. R.E., Las Cruces, 1977—; official goodwill ambassador of U.S. Treasury, U.S. Savs. Bond Div., Washington, 1966-70. Contbr. articles to profl. jours. Vice pres. Dona Ana County Fedn. Rep. Women. Recipient Top Sales Person award Investment Trust and Assurance, 1976-77. Fellow Life Underwriting Tng. Coun.; mem. Nat. Assn. Realtors, Nat. Assn. Life Underwriters, Internat. Bd. CFP's, Internat. Assn. Registered Fin. Planners, S.W. N.Mex. Assn. Life Underwriters (treas. 1990-91, pres.-elect 1991-92, pres. 1992-93), Las Cruces City Alumnae Panhellenic, Altrusa, Order Ea. Star, Delta Zeta Alumnae. Presbyterian. Home: 1304 Wolf Trl Las Cruces NM 88001-2357 Office: Fin Design Corp PO Box 577 Las Cruces NM 88004-0577

MILLER, MALCOLM LEE, retired lawyer; b. Canton, Ohio, Jan. 4, 1923; s. Thomas Maxwell and Margaret (Unkefer) M.; m. Laura Washburn; children: Stephen Washburn, Ann Mayo. JD, Ohio State U., 1949. Bar: Ohio 1950. Assoc. Law Office of Paul R. Gingher, Columbus, Ohio, 1950-53; assoc. Gingher & Christensen, Columbus, 1953-58, ptnr., 1958-86; of counsel Baker & Hostetler, Columbus, 1986-87; asst. counsel legal dept. Columbus Mut. Life Ins. Co., 1987-89, Columbus Life Ins. Co., 1989-90. Bd. dirs. Columbus Area chpt. ARC, 1972-94. 2d lt. USAAF, 1943-45. Mem. Sigma Chi, Phi Delta Phi. Home: 1427 London Dr Columbus OH 43221-1543

MILLER, MARGARET HAIGH, librarian; b. Ashton-under-Lyne, Lancashire, Eng., Feb. 26, 1915; came to U.S., 1915, naturalized, 1919; d. Errwood Augustus and Florence (Stockdale) Savage; m. Mervin Homer Miller, June 30, 1940; children: Nancy Elaine Reich, Edward Stockdale, Jane Elizabeth Miller-Dean. B.S. in Edn., Millersville U. (Pa.), 1937; M.S. in L.S., U. So. Calif., 1952; postgrad. in supervision Calif. State U.-Northridge, 1957-59. Jr. high sch. librarian Phoenixville Sch. Dist. (Pa.), 1937-40; jr. high sch. librarian Los Angeles Unified Sch. Dist., 1952-55, coordinating librarian, 1955-62, coll. head librarian, 1959-62, supr. library services, 1962-83; lectr. children's lit. U. So. Calif., Los Angeles, 1959-76, advisor Sch. Library and Info. Sci., 1980-83; resource person Nat. Council for Accreditation Tchr. Edn., Washington, 1976-85; cons. Pied Piper Prodns., Glendale, Calif., 1978—, David Sonnenshein Assocs., Los Angeles, 1983-85, Baker & Taylor Co., Inc., N.Y.C., 1979-83, H.W. Wilson Co., N.Y.C., 1975—, Mook & Blanchard, La Puente, Calif., 1985—, Enslow Pub., Inc., Hillside, N.J, 1986—. Mem. Los Angeles area planning com. Library of Congress Yr. of the Young Reader, 1989. Editor: Book List for Elementary School Libraries, 1966; Books for Elementary School Libraries, 1969; Children's Catalog, 13th edit., 1976; Multicultural Experiences in Children's Literature, Grades K-6, 1978; Periodicals for School Libraries, Grades K-12, 1977; Multicultural Experiences in Literature for Young People, Grades 7-12, 1979; Baker & Taylor School Selection Guide, K-12, 1980, 81, 82, 83; Supplement to Multicultural Experiences in Children's Literature, 1982; Special Books for Special People: A Bibliography about the Handicapped, 1982. Bibliographer: Concepts in Science, Levels 1 through 6 students' edits. (P. Brandwein et al), 1972; Concepts in Science Teacher's Education, 1972. Columnist, book reviewer Los Angeles Times, various jours. Recipient Dorothy McKenzie award for disting. contbn. outstanding svc. in field of children's literature. Mem. Los Angeles Sch. Library Assn. (cons. 1952-83), Calif. Assn. Sch. Librarians (pres. So. sect. 1971-72, state pres. 1975-76, many coms. 1952-77), Calif. Media and Library Educators Assn. (various coms. 1977-95), ALA (many coms.), Young Adult Svcs., Am. Assn. Sch. Librarians, Assn. Library Service to Children, Friends Children and Lit. (dir. 1979—, pres. 1987-88), So. Calif. Council on Lit. for Children and Young People (dir. 1961—, pres. 1973-74, 1st v.p. 1986, 3d v.p. 1987-88, awards chair 1989, 90, 91), Calif. Sch. Library Assn., Young Adult Reviewers Booklist Com. (sec. 1995), Assn. Adminstrs. Los Angeles Unified Sch. Dist., Women's Nat. Book Assn (Los Angeles chpt.), Beta Phi Mu (dir. 1977-79, 84-86, pres. 1979-80), Pi Lambda Theta (chpt. pres. 1964-66, 91-92), Delta Kappa Gamma (chpt. sec. 1962-64), Phi Delta Kappa (contest essay judge). Republican. Home: 4321 Matilija Ave Sherman Oaks CA 91423-3659

MILLER, MARGARET JOANNE, pediatrics nurse; b. Rolette, N.D., Apr. 12, 1939; d. William J. and Nora (Slaubaugh) Graber; m. Ervin S. Miller, June 16, 1962; children: Charlene, Angela, Lisa. ASN, Vincennes U., 1960; student, St. Mary's-of-the-Woods Coll., Terre Haute, Ind., 1986-87, Ind. U., South Bend, 1989, Regents Coll., 1995-96. RN, Ind., Tex. Head nurse St. Joseph Mem. Hosp., Kokomo, Ind., 1975-77; asst. dir. Mennonite Mutul Aid, 1982-84; staff nurse Meml. Hosp., South Bend, Ind., 1984-87, asst. head nurse, 1987-89, asst. unit dir., 1989-91; unit dir. for pediatrics Med. Ctr. Hosp., Odessa, Tex., 1992—. Mem. Soc Pediatric Nurses. Home: 3411 Rocky Lane Rd Odessa TX 79762-5046

MILLER, MARGERY K., lawyer; b. Phila., Jan. 16, 1947. BA, Smith Coll., 1968; JD cum laude, U. Pa., 1972. Bar: Pa. 1972. Ptnr. Reed Smith Shaw & McClay, Phila. Office: Reed Smith Shaw & McClay 2500 1 Liberty Pl Philadelphia PA 19103*

MILLER, MARGERY SILBERMAN, psychologist, speech and language pathologist, higher education adminstrator; b. Roslyn, N.Y., May 7, 1951; d. Bernard and Charlotte (Schatzberg) Silberman; m. Donald F. Moores; children—Kip Lee, Tige Justice. Lic. speech pathologist, N.Y., Md.; cert. tchr. nursery-6th grades, spl. edn., N.Y., advanced profl. tchr. speech and hearing, Md.; cert. sch. psychologist, Md. B.A., Elmira Coll., 1971; M.A., NYU, 1972; Ed.S., M.S., SUNY-Albany, 1975; M.A. Towson State U., 1987, Ph.D Georgetown U., 1991. Speech and lang. pathologist Mental Retardation Inst., Flower and Fifth Ave. Hosp., N.Y.C., 1971-72; community speech/lang. pathologist N.Y. State Dept. Mental Hygiene, Troy, dir. speech and hearing services, 1972-74; instr. communication disorders dept. Coll. of St. Rose, Albany, N.Y., 1975-77; clin. supr. U. Md., College Park, 1978; speech/lang. pathologist Md. Sch. for Deaf, Frederick, 1978-84; auditory devel. specialist Montgomery County Pub. Schs., Rockville, Md., 1984-87; coordinator Family Life program Nat. Acad. Gallaudet U., Washington, 1987-88, interim dir., 1988-89, dir. Counseling & Devel. Ctr. N.W. Campus, 1989-93; adj. assoc. prof. psf. psychology Gallaudet U., 1993—; instr. sign lang. program Frederick Community Coll.; dance instr. for deaf adolescents; diagnostic cons. on speech pathology; mem. editorial rev. com. Gov.'s Devel. Disabilities Council of Md., 1984; presenter at confs. Author: It's O.K. To Be Angry, 1976; contbr. chpt. to Cognition, Education, and Deafness: Directions for Research and Instruction, 1985; contbr. articles to profl. jours. Vol., choreographer Miss Deaf Am. Pageant, 1984. Office of Edn. Children's Bur. fellow, 1971. Mem. Am. Speech, Lang. and Hearing Assn. (cert. clin. competence in speech/lang. pathology), Md. Speech, Lang. and Hearing Assn., D.C. Speech, Lang. and Hearing Assn., Nat. Assn. of Deaf, Nat. Assn. Sch. Psychologists, Am. Psychol. Assn. Jewish. Home: 9807 Meriden Rd Potomac MD 20854-4311 Office: Gallaudet U 800 Florida Ave NE Washington DC 20002-3660

MILLER, MARILYN LEA, library science educator. AA, Graceland Coll., 1950; BS in English, U. Kans., 1952; AMLS, U. Mich., 1959, PhD of Librarianship and Higher Edn., 1976. Bldg.-level sch. libr. Wellsville (Kans.) High Sch., 1952-54; tchr.-libr. Arthur Capper Jr. High Sch., Topeka, Kans., 1954-56; head libr. Topeka High Sch., 1956-62; sch. libr. cons. State of Kans. Dept. of Pub. Instrn., 1962-67; from asst. to assoc. prof. Sch. Librarianship Western Mich. U., Kalamazoo, 1967-77; assoc. prof. libr. sci. U. N.C., Chapel Hill, 1977-87; prof., chair dept. libr. and info. studies U. N.C., Greensboro, 1987-95, prof. emeritus, 1996—; vis. faculty Kans. State Tchrs., Emporia, 1960, 63, 64, 66, U. Minn., Mpls., 1971, U. Manitoba, Winnipeg, Can., 1971; vis. prof. Appalachian State U., Boone, N.C., 1987; mem. adv. bd. sch. libr. media program Nat. Ctr. for Ednl. Stats., 1989, mem. user rev. panel, 1990; chair assoc. dean search com. Sch. Edn., 1988, coord. Piedmont young writers conf., 1989-94, chair race and gender com., 1990-93, SACS planning and evaluation com., 1990, 91, learning resources ctr. adv. com., 1991-93; hearing panel for honor code U. N.C. Greensboro, 1988-91, assn. women faculty and administrv. staff, 1987—, faculty coun., 1987—, univ. libr. com., 1987-88, com. faculty devel. in race and gender scholarship, 1990-92; lectr. and cons. numerous confs., seminars in field. Mem. editorial bd. The Emergency Librarian, 1981—, Collection Building: Studies in the Development and Effective Use of Library Resources, 1978—; contbr. numerous chpts. to books, and articles to profl. jours., procs. and revs. Selected as one of four children's libr. specialists to visit Russian sch. and pub. librs., book pubs., Moscow, Leningrad, Tashkent, 1979; hon. del. White House Conf. on Libr. and Info. Svcs., Washington, 1991; head del. Romanian Summer Inst. on Librarianship in U.S., 1991; citizen amb. People to People Internat. Program, People's Republic of China, 1992, Russian and Poland, 1992, Russia, 1994, Barcelona, 1995. Recipient Freedom Found. medal, 1962, Disting. Svc. to Sch. Librs. award Kans. Assn. Sch. Librs., 1982, Disting. Svc. award Graceland Coll., 1992, Disting. Alumnus award Sch. Libr. and Info. Studies, U. Mich., 1988; Delta Kappa Gamma scholar, 1972. Mem. ALA (chair rsch. com., exec. dir. 1994, pres. 1992-93, adv. com. Nat. Ctr. Ednl. Stats. 1984, standing com. libr. edn. 1987-91, chair 1989-90, chair Chgo. conf. resolutions 1972, awards com. 1971-72, chair 1973-75, resolutions com. 1976-78, yearbook adv. com. 1988-90, Disting. Svc. award Am. Assn. Sch. Librs. 1993, other coms.), Am. Assn. Sch. Librs. (nominating com. 1980, pub. com. 1981-82, v.p.-pres.-elect 1985-86, chair search com. exec. dir. 1985, pres. 1986-87), Assn. for Ednl. Comms. and Tech., Assn. for Libr. and Info. Sci. Edn., Assn. of Libr. Svc. to Children (bd. dirs. 1976-81, pres. 1979-80, rsch. com. 1982-85, chair 1984-85, chair nominating com. 1984, other coms.), N.C. Libr. Assn. (edn. libr. com. 1978-80, 82-86, exec. bd. status of women roundtable 1989—), N.C. Assn. Sch. Librs., Southeastern Libr. Assn. (chair libr. educators sect. 1990-92), So. Assn. of Colls. and Schs. (mem. accreditation team 1988).

MILLER, MARK, newspaper editor. BA in English, Grinnell Coll., 1976. Mng. editor Crain's Chgo. Bus., 1983-89, editor, 1989-93; dep. mng. editor, columnist Chgo. Sun-Times, 1993—; mem. exec. com. Com. on Fgn. Affairs. Guest radio and TV shows including Chicago Tonight with John Callaway, Sta. WTTW. Office: Chgo Sun Times 401 N Wabash Ave Chicago IL 60611-3532

MILLER, MARK KARL, journalist; b. Meadville, Pa., Aug. 5, 1953; s. Richard Karl and Ellener Louise (Zimber) M. BA in Comms. and Journalism, Shippensburg U. of Pa., 1975. Editl. asst. Broadcasting mag., Washington, 1975, staff writer, 1976-77, asst. editor, 1977-80, sr. news editor, 1980-87, asst. mng. editor, 1987-91; mng. editor Broadcasting & Cable mag., Washington, 1991—; mem. editl. adv. bd. Shippensburg U. of Pa., 1989-94, mem. profl. adv. bd. comm./journalism dept., 1994—. Recipient Outstanding Alumnus award Shippensburg U., 1992. Mem. Soc. Profl. Journalists, Art Deco Soc. of Washington (bd. dirs., publs. chair 1986—), Nat. Press Club. Home: 2425 Valley Way Cheverly MD 20785 Office: Broadcasting & Cable 1705 De Sales St NW Washington DC 20036

MILLER, MARSHALL LEE, lawyer; b. Chattanooga, Tenn., Oct. 18, 1942. BA, Harvard U., 1964; student, Oxford U., Eng., Heidelberg U., Germany; JD, Yale U., 1970. Bar: D.C. 1971, Va. 1979, U.S. Supreme Ct. 1979. Spl. asst. to adminstr. U.S. EPA, 1971-73; assoc. dep. atty. gen. U.S. Dept. Justice, 1973-74; asst. sec. labor (acctg.), dep. adminstr. OSHA, 1975-76; ptnr. Baise & Miller, Washington; bd. dirs. Electronic Warfare Assocs. Bd. editors: Yale Law Jour.; Soviet Mil. editor: Armed Forces Jour., 1983-87; author books internat. and environ. topics. Bd. dirs. Bulgarian-Am. Enterprise Fund, Electronic Warfare Assocs., Am. Coun. of Internat. Living. Office: Baise & Miller 815 Connecticut Ave NW Ste 620 Washington DC 20006-4004

MILLER, MARVIN EDWARD, building materials company executive; b. Far Rockaway, N.Y., Jan. 28, 1929; s. Philip J. and Dorothy B. (Verby) M.; m. Beverly Kolikof, June 7, 1953; children: Lisa, Deborah, James. BS, Ind. U., 1949; MS, Columbia U., 1950. Salesman M. Verby Co., Jamaica, N.Y., 1953-56; pres. Miller Supply Corp., White Plains, N.Y., 1956-74, chmn. bd., 1975—; pres. Grip-Rite Ltd., Hong Kong, 1979—; chmn., co-chief exec. officer PrimeSource, Inc., 1990—. Bd. dirs., v.p. Westchester Jewish Community Svcs., Hartsdale, N.Y., 1985. With AUS, 1951-53. Mem. Masons, Shriners. Republican. Avocation: tennis. Home: 17153 Ericarose Ct Boca Raton FL 33496-5939 Office: PrimeSource Inc 1800 John Connally Dr Carrollton TX 75006-5403

MILLER, MARY ANDREA, nursing administrator; b. Tomahawk, Wis., Mar. 26, 1947; d. Andrew Herman and Martha (Wild) Kleppe; m. James Allen Snedden, Aug. 19, 1965 (div. July 1982); children: Roxanne L., Dawn C., Jason J., Sarah C. Snedden; m. Roger D. Miller, Nov. 12, 1983 (dec. Apr. 1990). ADN, Fox Valley Tech. Coll., 1985; BBA, Marion Coll., 1995. RN, Wis.; ACLS, BLS. Nursing asst. Iola (Wis.) Nursing Home, 1981-85; nurse Bethany Home, Iola Hosp., Waupaca and Iola, Wis., 1985-90; oper. rm. nurse Iola Hosp., 1988-90, emergency rm. nurse, hosp. supr., 1988-90, quality assurance coord., 1988-90; DON Iola Nursing Home, 1990—, also bd. dirs. Bd. dirs. SAFE-T of Waupaca County, 1984-90; co-organizer Domestic Abuse Task Force, Waupaca, 1984-90; mem. Hospice Adv. Bd., Waupaca County, 1994. Recipient Spl. Recognition award for svc./assistance during med. emergency U.S. Dept. of Interior, 1988. Mem. Wis. DON. Lutheran. Avocations: canoeing, dancing, listening to music. Office: Iola Nursing Home PO Box 237 185 S Washington St Iola WI 54945

MILLER, MARY HELEN, retired public administrator; b. Smiths Grove, Ky., June 30, 1936; d. Walter Frank and Lottie Belle (Russell) Huddleston; m. George Ward Wilson, Sept. 12, 1958 (div. Sept. 1973); children: Ward Glenn, Amy Elizabeth Huddleston; m. Francis Guion Miller Jr., June 6, 1981. BA, Western Ky. U., 1958. Tchr. Fayette County Schs., Lexington, Ky., 1958-60, Seneca High Sch., Louisville, 1960-63, Shelby County High Sch., Shelbyville, Ky., 1963-69; rsch. analyst Legis. Rsch. Com., Frankfort, Ky., 1973-79, asst. dir., 1979-83, 90-91; chief exec. asst. Office Gov., Frankfort, 1983-87, 93-95, legis. liaison, 1991-93; cabinet sec. Natural Resources and Environ. Protection Cabinet, Frankfort, 1987-88; sales assoc. W. Wagner, Jr. Comml. Real Estate, Louisville, 1989-91; ret., 1996. Author: (constl. revision) Citizens Guide To/Perspective, 1978, (booklet) A Look at Kentucky General Assembly, 1979, A Guide to Education Reform, 1990, (handbook) Gubernatorial Transition in Kentucky, 1991. Active Leadership Ky. Alumni, Frankfort, 1986, Waterfront Devel. Corp. Bd., Louisville, 1986-87, Greater Louis Partnership Econ. Devel., 1988-92, Shelbyville 2000 Found. Bd., 1991-92; mem., sec. Regional Airport Authorty Bd., Louisville, 1986-89; pres. Shelby County Cmty. Theatre Bd., Shelbyville, 1989-90; active Ky. Long Term Policy Bd., 1992—, chair, 1995; active Ky. Hist. Properties Commn., 1995—; chair Shelby County Cmty. Found., 1995; active Ky. Applachian Commn., 1995-96. Mem. Pendennis Club, Jefferson Club. Democrat. Episcopalian. Avocations: reading, theatre, gardening, antiques. Home: 1116 Main St Shelbyville KY 40065-1420

MILLER, MARY JEANNETTE, office management specialist; b. Washington, Sept. 24, 1912; d. John William and David Evengeline (Hill) Sims; m. Cecil Miller, June 17, 1934 (dec.); children: Sylvenia Delores Doby, Ferdi A., Cecil Jr. (dec.). Student, Howard U., 1929-30, U. Ill., 1940-42, Dept. Agr. Grad. Sch., 1957-59, U. Md., 1975; cert. in Vocat. Photography, Prince George's C.C., 1986. Chief mail processing unit Bur. Reclamation, Washington, 1940-57; records supr. AID, Manila, Korea, Mali, Guyana, Dominican Republic, Indonesia, Laos, 1957-71; office engr. Bechtel Assocs., Washington, 1976-79; real estate assoc; tchr. English as 2d lang. Ministry of Edn., Seoul, Korea, 1960-61, Ministry of Fin., Laos, 1968-70; cons. to Ministry of Fin. Royal Lao Govt., 1971-74; cons. AID missions to Yemen, Sudan, Somalia, 1982; records mgmt. cons. AID, Monrovia, Liberia, 1980-81, Sri Lanka, 1984; docent Mus. African Art Smithsonian Inst., Washington, 1986-89; circulation asst. Prince George County Meml. Libr. System, Hyattsville, Md., 1987-91, ret.; mem. Friends of Internat. Edn. Com., 1985-92; sec./treas., bd. dirs. Miller Transitional, Inc., 1993—. Author handbooks on office mgmt. Mem. AARP, NAFE, Mayor's Internat. Adv. Coun. Mem. Soc. Am. Archivists, Am. Mgmt. Assn., Montgomery County Bd. Realtors, Am. Fgn. Svc. Assn., Nat. Trust Hist. Preservation, Assn. Am. Fgn. Svc. Women's Writer Group, Consumer Mail Panel, Zeta Phi Beta. Roman Catholic. Home: 14200 Pimberton Dr Hudson FL 34667-8542

MILLER, MARY LOIS, nurse midwife; b. Altoona, Pa., Feb. 21, 1933; d. Isaac Emory and Lucinda Jane (Brumbaugh) Miller. Diploma, West Suburban Hosp. Sch., 1953; BSN, Wheaton (Ill.) Coll., 1955; MRE, Grace Theol. Sem., 1957; nurse midwife, Frontier Nursing Svc., 1959. Cert. nurse midwife. Nurse obstetrics Delnor Hosp., St. Charles, Ill., 1953-55; head nurse McDonald Hosp., Warsaw, Ind., 1955-57; med. missionary Fgn. Missionary Soc. Grace Brethren Ch., Winona Lake, Ind., 1959-79; cert. nurse midwife Lewistown (Pa.) Hosp., 1979—; adj. faculty dept. ob-gyn. Phila. Coll. Osteopathic Medicine. Mem. APHA, Am. Coll. Nurse Midwives (sec.), Nat. Perinatal Assn., Pa. Perinatal Assn., Nat. Assn. Childbearing Ctrs. Home: 4 Townhouse Taylor Dr Reedsville PA 17084

MILLER, MAURICE JAMES, lawyer; b. Barron, Wis., May 14, 1926; s. James Martin and Fern (Harvey) M.; m. Marguerite Joyce Mielke, Nov. 1, 1952; children: Maureen J., Mark J. B.B.A., U. Wis., 1951, J.D., 1955. Bar: Ill., Wis. 1955, .; C.P.A., Wis. Assoc. Sidley & Austin, Chgo., 1955-62, ptnr., 1963-90, counsel, 1991—. Trustee William H. Miner Found., 1994—. With U.S. Army, 1944-46. Mem. ABA, Chgo. Bar Assn., Phi Alpha Delta. Republican. Methodist. Clubs: Chicago, Mid-Day. Home: 925 Brand Ln Deerfield IL 60015-3403 Office: Sidley & Austin 1 First Nat Plz Chicago IL 60603

MILLER, MAX DUNHAM, JR., lawyer; b. Des Moines, Oct. 17, 1946; s. Max Dunham and Beulah (Head) M.; m. Melissa Ann Dart, Jan. 10, 1969 (div. July 1975); 1 child, Ann Marie Victoria; m. Caroline Jean Armendt, Sept. 19, 1981; children: Alexander Bradshaw, Benjamin Everett. BS with high honors, Mich. State U., 1968; postgrad., George Washington U., 1970-71; JD, U. Md., 1975. Bar: Md. 1976, U.S. Dist. Ct. Md. 1976, U.S. Ct. Appeals (4th cir.) 1981, U.S. Supreme Ct. 1982. Engr. U.S. Dept. of Def., Aberdeen Proving Ground, Md., 1968-72; law clk. to presiding judge Md. Cir. Ct., Higinbothom in Bel Air, Md., 1975-76; asst. county atty. Harford County, Bel Air, 1976-79; assoc. Lentz & Hooper P.A., Balt., 1979-81; ptnr. Miller, Olszewski & Moore, P.A., Bel Air, 1981-94; prin. Law Offices of Max D. Miller, P.A., 1994—; county atty. Harford County, Md., 1983-88. Mem. Md. Bar Assn., Assn. Trial Lawyers Am., Md. Trial Lawyers Assn., Harford County Bar Assn., Phi Kappa Phi, Phi Eta Sigma. Avocations: carpentry, sailing, canoeing. Home: 308 Whetstone Rd Forest Hill MD 21050-1332 Office: Law Office Max D Miller PA 5 S Hickory Ave Bel Air MD 21014-3732

MILLER, MAYNARD MALCOLM, geologist, educator, research foundation director, explorer, state legislator; b. Seattle, Jan. 23, 1921; s. Joseph Anthony and Juanita Queena (Davison) M.; m. Joan Walsh, Sept. 15, 1951; children: Ross McCord, Lance Davison. BS magna cum laude, Harvard U., 1943; MA, Columbia U., 1948; PhD (Fulbright scholar), St. John's Coll., Cambridge U., Eng., 1957; student, Naval War Coll., Air War Coll., Oak Ridge Inst. Nuclear Sci.; D of Sci. (hon.), U. Alaska, 1990. Registered profl. geologist, Idaho. Asst. prof. naval sci. Princeton (N.J.) U., 1946; geologist Gulf Oil Co., Cuba, 1947; rsch. assoc., coordinator, dir. Office Naval Rsch. project Am. Geog. Soc., N.Y.C., 1948-52; staff scientist Swiss Fed. Inst. for Snow and Avalanche Rsch., Davos, 1952-53; instr. dept. geography Cambridge U., 1953-54, 56; assoc. producer, field unit dir. film Seven Wonders of the World for Cinerama Corp., Europe, Asia, Africa, Middle East, 1954-55; rsch. assoc. Lamont Geol. Obs., N.Y.C., 1955-57; sr. scientist dept. geology Columbia U., N.Y.C., 1957-59; asst. prof. geology Mich. State U., East Lansing, 1959-61, assoc. prof., 1961-63; prof. Mich. State U., Lansing, 1963-75; dean Coll. Mines and Earth Resources U. Idaho, Moscow, 1975-88, prof. geology, dir. Glaciological and Arctic Scis. Inst., 1975—; dir., state geologist Idaho Geol. Survey, 1975-88; elected rep. Legislature of State of Idaho, Boise, 1992—; prin. investigator, geol. cons. sci. contracts and projects for govt. agys., univs., pvt. corps., geographic socs., 1946—; geophys. cons. Nat. Park Svc., NASA, USAF, Nat. Acad. Sci.; organizer leader USAF-Harvard Mt. St. Elias Expdn., 1946; chief geologist Am. Mt. Everest Expdn., Nepal, 1963; dir. Nat. Geographic Soc. Alaskan Glacier Commemorative Project, 1964-74; organizer field leader Nat. Geographic Soc. Joint U.S.-Can. Mt. Kennedy Yukon Meml. Mapping Expdn., 1965, Muséo Argentino de Ciencias Naturales, Patagonian expdn. and glacier study for Inst.. Geologico del Peru & Am. Geog. Soc., 1949-50, participant adv. missions People's Republic of China, 1981, 86, 88, geol. expdns. Himalaya, Nepal, 1963, 84, 87, USAF mission to Ellesmere Land and Polar Sea, 1951; organizer, ops. officer USN-LTA blimp geophysics flight to North Pole area for Office Naval Rsch., 58; prin. investigator U.S. Naval Oceanographic Office Rsch. Ice Island T-3 Polar Sea, 1967-68, 70-73; dir. lunar field sta. simulation program USAF-Boeing Co., 1959-60; co-prin. investigator Nat. Geographic Soc. 30 Yr. Remap of Lemon & Taku Glaciers, Juneau Icefield, 1989-92; exec. dir. Found. for Glacier and Environ. Rsch., Pacific Sci. Ctr., Seattle, 1955—, pres., 1955-85, trustee, 1960—, organizer, dir. Juneau (Alaska) Icefield Rsch. Program (JIRP), 1946—; cons. Dept. Hwys. State of Alaska, 1965; chmn., exec. dir. World Ctr. for Exploration Found., N.Y.C., 1968-71; dir., mem. adv. bd. Idaho Geol. Survey, 1975-88; chmn. nat. coun. JSHS program U.S. Army Rsch. Office and Acad. Applied Sci., 1982-89; sci. dir. U.S. Army Rsch. Office-Nat. Sci. and Humanities Symposia program, 1991—; disting. guest prof. China U. Geoscis., Wuhan, 1981-88, Changchun U. Earth Scis., People's Republic of China, 1988—; affiliate prof. U. Alaska, 1986—. Author: Field Manual of Glaciological and Arctic Sciences; co-author books on Alaskan glaciers and Nepal geology; contbr. over 200 reports, sci. papers to profl. jours., ency. articles, chpts. to books, monographs; prodr., nat. lectr. 16 mm films and videos. Past mem. nat. exploring com., nat. sea exploring com. Boy Scouts Am.; mem. nat. adv. bd. Embry Riddle Aero. U.; bd. dirs. Idaho Rsch. Found.; pres. state divsn. Mich. UN Assn., 1970-73; mem. Centennial and Health Environ. Commns., Moscow, Idaho, 1987-96. With USn, 1943-46, PTO. Decorated 11 battle stars; named Leader of Tomorrow Seattle C. of C. and Time mag., 1953, one of Ten Outstanding Young Men U.S. Jaycees, 1954; recipient commendation for lunar environ. study USAF, 1960, Hubbard medal (co-recipien Mt. Everest expdn. team) Nat. Geog. Soc., 1963, Elisha Kent Kane Gold medal Geog. Soc. Phila., 1964, Karo award Soc. Mil. Engrs., 1966, Franklin L. Burr award Nat. Geog. Soc., 1967, Commendation Boy Scouts Am., 1970, Disting. Svc. commendation plaque UN Assn. U.S., Disting. Svc. commendation State of Mich. Legis., 1975, Outstanding Civiclian Svc. medal U.S. Army Rsch. Office, 1977, Outstanding Leadership in Minerals Edn. commendations Idaho Mining Assn., 1985, 87, Nat. Disting. Tchg. award Assn. Am. Geographers, 1996; recipient numerous grants NSF, Nat. Geog. Soc., others, 1948—. Fellow Geol. Soc. Am., Arctic Inst. N.Am., Explorers Club; mem. councilor AAAS (Pacific divsn. 1978-88), AIME, Am. Geophys. Union, Internat. Glaciological Soc. (past councilor), ASME (hon. nat. lectr.), Am. Assn. State Geologists (hon.), Am. Assn. Amateur Oarsmen (life), Am. Alpine Club (past councilor, life mem.), Alpine Club (London), Appalachian Club (hon. corr.), Brit. Mountaineering Assn. (hon., past v.p.), The Mountaineers (hon.), Cambridge U. Mountaineering Club (hon.), Himalyan Club (Calcutta), English Speaking Union (nat. lectr.), Naval Res. Assn. (life), Dutch Treat Club, Circumnavigators Club (life), Adventurers Club N.Y. (medalist), Am. Legion, Harvard Club (N.Y.C. and Seattle), Sigma Xi, Phi Beta Kappa (pres. Epsilon chpt. Mich. State U. 1969-70), Phi Kappa Phi. Republican. Methodist. Avocations: skiing, mountaineering, photography. Home: 514 E 1st St Moscow ID 83843-2814 Office: U Idaho Coll Mines & Earth Resources Mines Bldg Rm 204 Moscow ID 83843 also: House of Reps Idaho State House Boise ID 83720 also: Found for Glacier & Environ Rsch 4470 N Douglas Hwy Juneau AK 99801-9403

MILLER, MERTON HOWARD, finance educator; b. Boston, Mass., May 16, 1923; s. Joel L. and Sylvia F. (Starr) M. AB, Harvard U., 1943; PhD, Johns Hopkins U., 1952. With Treasury Dept., 1944-47, Fed. Res. Bd., 1947-49; asst. lectr. London Sch. Econs., 1952; asst. prof., then assoc. prof. Grad. Sch. Indsl. Adminstrn., Carnegie Inst. Tech., Pitts., 1958-61; prof. banking and fin. Grad. Sch. Bus. U. Chgo., 1961—. Co-author: Theory of Finance, 1972, Macroeconomics, 1974, Financial Innovation and Market Volatility, 1991. Recipient Nobel prize in econs., 1990. Fellow Econometric Soc.; mem. Am. Fin. Assn. (pres. 1976), Am. Econ. Assn., Am. Statis. Assn. Office: U Chgo Grad Sch Bus 1101 E 58th St Chicago IL 60637-1511*

MILLER, MICHAEL, publishing executive. V.p., editor in chief PC Mag., N.Y.C. Office: PC Mag-Ziff Davis Publ Co One Park Ave New York NY 10016

MILLER, MICHAEL EVERETT, chemical company executive; b. Indiana, Pa., Sept. 4, 1941; s. Everett Michael and Elizabeth Mary (Becker) M.; m. Eleanor Ann Flyn, June 19, 1965; children: Elizabeth Anne, Christopher. BS in History, St. Louis U., 1963, MS in History, 1965; grad. Advanced Mgmt. Program, Stanford U., 1982. Tchr. Ferguson/Florissant Sch. System, St. Louis, 1965; sales rep. inorganic chems. div. Monsanto Chem. Co., St. Louis, 1965, dir. mktg., cycle-safe, 1976-77, dir. mktg., detergents and phosphates, 1977-80, comml. dir., water treatment chems., 1980-83, gen. mgr., detergent materials, 1983-86, v.p., gen. mgr., detegents div., 1986-88, v.p. rubber chems. and instruments div. and Asia Pacific, 1988-89, corp. v.p. adminstrn., 1989-93; sr. v.p. ops. The Chem. Group, 1993, group v.p. indsl. products, 1993, pres. splty. products, 1995—; bd. dirs. Watlow Electric Mfg. Co., St. Louis, Group Health Plan; adv. bd. Emerson Electric Ctr. for Bus. Ethics, St. Louis U. Vice chmn. bd. trustees Fontbonne Coll., St. Louis, 1990. Mem. Algonquin Golf Club. Avocations: golf, skiing, racquetball, restoration of early model Corvettes. Office: Monsanto Company 800 N Lindbergh Blvd Saint Louis MO 63141-7843

MILLER, MICHAEL I., lawyer; b. Chgo., Apr. 9, 1937. BA, Northwestern U., 1957, JD, 1960. Bar: D.C. 1960, Ill. 1960. Ptnr. Sidley & Austin, Chgo. Office: Sidley & Austin 1 First Nat Plz Chicago IL 60603*

MILLER, MICHAEL JON, survey engineer, local government manager; b. Parkers Prairie, Minn., Mar. 17, 1950; s. Buford Kenneth and Gretchen Cena (Sharp) M.; m. Terry Lynn Peck, May 20, 1972; children: Livia Mica, David Peter. BS, U. Wis., Platteville, 1972; M of Pub. Adminstrn., Ariz. State U., 1988. Cert. profl. land surveyor, Wis., Ariz., soil tester, Wis. Chief of surveys Hovelsrud Cons. Assn., Richland Ctr., Wis., 1972-78; ops. mgr. Tech. Advisors, Inc., Phoenix, 1978-82; profl. surveyor Coe and Van Loo, Inc., Phoenix, 1982-83; survey engr. City of Phoenix, 1983—; land surveyor mem. Ariz. Bd. Tech. Registration, sec., 1990-91, vice chmn., 1991, chmn., 1991-92, vice chmn. 1993-94, chmn. 1994-95. Contbr. articles to profl. jours. Dep. registrar Dem. Party of Ariz., Phoenix, 1983-94; clk. Phoenix Friends Meeting, 1985-86; recording clk. Intermountain Yearly Meeting of Religious Soc. of Friends, 1984-85. Fellow Congress Surveying and Mapping (membership chmn. 1987-88); mem. Nat. Soc. Profl. Surveyors (gov. for Ariz. 1985-89), Western Fedn. Land Surveyors (state del. 1988-89), Ariz. Profl. Land Surveyors (sec. 1983-84, pres. 1985-86, Outstanding award 1981, life mem. award 1996), Nat. Coun. Examiners for Engrs. and Surveyors, Am. Pub. Works Assn., Am. Soc. for Pub. Adminstrn., World Clown Assn., Internat. Jugglers Assn., Greater Ariz. Bicycle Assn. Democrat. Avocations: hist. research, writing, juggling, bicycling. Home: 4026 E Campbell Ave Phoenix AZ 85018-3709

MILLER, MICKEY LESTER, retired school administrator; b. Albuquerque, July 26, 1920; s. Chester Lester and Myra Easter (Cassidy) M.; m. Louise Dean Miller, Aug. 30, 1946; children: Linda Miller Kelly, Lee Miller Parks, Lynne Miller Carson. BS, U. N.Mex., 1944; MS, Columbia U., 1949. Coach, tchr. math. Jefferson Jr. H.S., Albuquerque, 1946-49; coach, dept. chair, athletic dir. Highland H.S., Albuquerque, 1949-64, asst. prin., 1964-70; dist. program coord. Albuquerque Pub. Schs., 1970-90; ret., 1990. Author:

Guide to Administration of Secondary Athletics, 1990; author brochures, handbooks, articles. Pub. mem. N.Mex. Bd. Dentistry, 1992—; recommending scout Pitts. Pirates Baseball, 1985—. With USN, 1942-46. Recipient Honor award S.W. Dist. Am. Alliance Health, Phys. Edn., Recreation and Dance, 1971, N.Mex. Coaches Assn., 1981, Hall of Fame award N.Mex. Activities Assn., 1985; named Retiree of Yr., S.W. Dist. Am. Alliance Health, Phys. Edn., Recreation and Dance, 1994; named to U. N.Mex. Alumni Lettermen Hall of Honor, 1994; named to Albuquerque Sports Hall of Fame, 1995. Mem. AAHPERD (life, budget/nominating rep. 1985), U. N.Mex. Alumni Assn., U. N.Mex. LOBO Lettermen Club (pres., treas. 1972). Democrat. Methodist. Avocations: golf, travel, baseball scouting. Home: 1201 Richmond Dr NE Albuquerque NM 87106

MILLER, MILDRED, opera singer, recitalist; b. Cleve.; d. William and Elsa (Friedhofer) Mueller; m. Wesley W. Posvar, Apr. 30, 1950; children: Wesley, Margot Marina, Lisa Christina. MusB, Cleve. Inst. Music, 1946; hon. doctorate, Cleve. Ins. Music, 1983; artists' diploma, New England Conservatory Music, 1948, hon. doctorate, 1966; MusD (hon.), Bowling Green State U., 1960; hon. doctorate, Washington and Jefferson U., 1988. Founder, pres., artistic dir. Opera Theater of Pitts., 1978—; mem. music faculty Carnegie-Mellon U., 1996. Operatic debut in Peter Grimes, Tanglewood, 1946; appeared N.E. Opera Theater, Stuttgart State Theater, Germany, 1949-50, Glyndebourne Opera, Edinburgh Festival; debut as Cherubino in Figaro, Met. Opera, 1951; 23 consecutive seasons Met. Opera; radio debut Bell Telephone Hour; TV debut Voice of Firestone, 1952; appeared in films including Merry Wives of Windsor (filmed in Vienna), 1964; Vienna State Opera debut, 1963, appearances with San Francisco, Chgo. Lyric, Cin. Zoo, San Antonio, Berlin, Munich, Frankfurt, Pasadena, Ft. Worth, Kansas City, Pitts., Tulsa and St. Paul operas. Bd. dirs. Gateway to Music. Recipient Frank Huntington Beebe award for study abroad, 1949, 50, Grand Prix du Disque, 1965, Outstanding Achievements in Music award Boston C. of C., 1959, Ohioana Career medal, 1985, Outstanding Achievement in Opera award, Slippery Rock U., 1985, YWCA Ann. Tribute to Women award, 1989, Keystone Salute award Pa. Fedn. Music Clubs, 1994; named one of outstanding women of Pitts., Pitts. Press-Pitts. Post-Gazette, 1968, Person of Yr. in Music, Pitts. Jaycees, 1980. Mem. Nat. Soc. Arts and Letters (pres. 1989-90, Gold medal 1984), Disting. Daus. Pa. (pres. 1991-93), Tuesday Mus. Club, Phi Beta Kappa, Phi Delta Gamma, Sigma Alpha Iota. Office: PO Box 110108 Pittsburgh PA 15232-0608

MILLER, MILTON ALLEN, lawyer; b. Los Angeles, Jan. 15, 1954; s. Samuel C. and Sylvia Mary Jane (Silver) M.; m. Mary Ann Toman, Sept. 10, 1988; 1 child, Mary Ann. AB with distinction and honors in Econs., Stanford U., 1976; JD with honors, Harvard U., 1979. Bar: Calif. 1979, U.S. Ct. Appeals (9th cir.) 1979, U.S. Dist. Ct. (cen., no. and so. dists.) Calif., U.S. Supreme Ct. 1989. Law clk. U.S. Ct. Appeals (9th cir.), Sacramento, 1979-80; assoc. Latham & Watkins, L.A., 1979-87, ptnr., 1987—. chmn. ethics com. Latham & Watkins. Author: Attorney Ethics; articles editor Harvard Law Rev., 1978-79. Mem. Am. Cancer Soc., L.A. Mem. ABA, Calif. State Bar Assn. (com. on profl. responsibility), L.A. County Bar Assn. (chmn. profl. responsibility and ethics com.), Assn. Trial Lawyers Am., Phi Beta Kappa. Office: Latham & Watkins 633 W Fifth St Ste 4000 Los Angeles CA 90071 *Notable cases include Raquel Welch vs. MGM Corp.; served as trial and insurance counsel in San Juan Dupont Plaza Hotel Fire litigation.*

MILLER, MILTON HOWARD, psychiatrist; b. Indpls., Sept. 1, 1927; came to Can., 1971; s. William and Helen L. (Lefkovits) M.; m. Harriet Sanders, June 27, 1948; children—Bruce, Jeffrey, Marcie. B.S., Ind. U., 1946, M.D., 1950; diploma in psychiatry, Menninger Sch., Topeka, 1953. Intern Indpls. Gen. Hosp., 1950-51; resident Menninger Sch. Psychiatry, Topeka, 1951-53; with dept. psychiatry Univ. Hosps., U. Wis., Madison, 1955-71; prof. Univ. Hosps., U. Wis., 1961-71, chmn., 1962-71; dir. Wis. Psychiat. Inst., 1962-71; vis. prof. Nat. Taiwan U., Taipei, 1969-70; prof. psychiatry U. B.C., Vancouver, 1972-78; head dept. psychiatry U. B.C., 1972-78; dir. WHO-U. B.C. Mental Health Tng. Centre, Vancouver, 1974-78; dep. dir coastal region Dept. of Mental Health, L.A. County, 1978-86; chmn. dept. psychiatry Harbor-UCLA Med. Ctr., Torrance, Calif., 1978—; prof., vice chmn. dept. psychiatry UCLA, 1978—; dep. med. dir. Dept. of Mental Health, L.A., 1986—; cons. in field. Author: Psychiatry: A Personal View, 1981; Contbr. articles to profl. jours. Fellow Am. Psychiat. Assn., Royal Coll. Psychiatry; mem. Can. Psychiat. Assn., Royal Coll. Physicians and Surgeons (examiner 1973—), Can. Med. Assn., World Fedn. for Mental Health (mem. exec. bd. 1973—). Home: 1321 Paseo Del Mar San Pedro CA 90731 Office: Harbor-UCLA Med Ctr Dept Psychiatry Torrance CA 90509-2910 *For many years I worked hard for my parents and myself. Later I worked hard for my wife, children, friends and self. These last years I've been including strangers and it's better.*

MILLER, MORGAN LINCOLN, textile manufacturing company executive; b. New Rochelle, N.Y., Feb. 11, 1924; s. Harry H. and Belle M.; m. Marjorie Leff, June 8, 1952; children—Betsy, Harry Robert, Amy, Cindy. B.A., Lehigh U., Bethlehem, Pa., 1947. With Nat. Spinning Co., Inc., 1959—; exec. v.p. Nat. Spinning Co., Inc., N.Y.C., from 1964; now vice chmn. Nat. Spinning Co., Inc.; pres. Jr. Accent Dress Mfg. Co., 1956—; pres. Nat. Yarn Crafts subs. Coquet Bathing Suit Mfg. Co., 1954—; Bd. dirs. BHC Comm., Inc. V.p. Westchester (N.Y.) Reform Temple, 1971, Westchester Jewish Cmty. Svcs., White Plains, N.Y., 1970; trustee Beth Israel Med. Ctr.; pres. Craft Youth Coun. Am. With USNR, 1942-45. Named Industry Man of Year United Jewish Appeal, 1980. Mem. Craft Yarn Coun. Am., Beach Point Club. Republican. Office: 183 Madison Ave New York NY 10016-5113

MILLER, MORRIS FOLSOM, banker; b. Omaha, Mar. 17, 1919; s. Max Arnold and Phebe (Folsom) M.; m. Nancy Keegan, July 26, 1952 (dec. Jan. 1977); children: Jay, Louise, Paul; m. Barbara Osborne Cunningham, Feb. 12, 1978 (dec. June 1986); m. Kathryn Klok Lewis, June 20, 1987. A.B., U. Mich., 1940. With Gering (Nebr.) Nat. Bank, 1946, Am. Nat. Bank, Kimball, Nebr., 1946-47, Boone (Iowa) State Bank, 1947-51; with Omaha Nat. Bank, 1951-80, asst. v.p., 1953-54, v.p., 1954-58, exec. v.p., 1958-62, pres., 1962-70, chmn., 1969-77, vice chmn., 1977-80, also past dir. Past dir. Creighton U., Omaha Pub. Power Dist.; past chmn. and past bd. dirs. Health Future Found., 1986-88; past receiver Midlands Community Hosp. Served with AUS, 1941-46; with USAF, 1951-52. Mem. Mid Am. Bankcard Assn. (past chmn., dir.), Omaha C. of C. (past pres.). Home: PO Box 454 Dubois WY 82513-0454 Office: First Bank PO Box 3443 Omaha NE 68103-0443

MILLER, NAN LOUISE, museum director; b. Atlanta, Aug. 6, 1948; d. William Mitchell and Harriet Irene (Wilkie) Schotanus; B.S., Kans. State U., 1970; postgrad. UCLA, 1979-80, Media Communications, 1981, Weist Barron Sch. TV, 1982, East Tenn. State U., 1982-83; m. Robert W. Miller Jr., Oct. 31, 1981. Buyer, Jones Store Co., Kansas City, Mo., 1971-75, Harzfeld's, Kansas City, 1975-76; exec. sales rep. Monet, Los Angeles, 1976-80; mgr. corp. buying offices Trifari, N.Y.C., 1980-82, field mktg. coordinator and media pub. relations rep., 1981-82; co-owner, v.p. mktg. Devel. Resources Corp., Kingsport, Tenn., 1982-89; exec. dir. Hands On! Regional Mus., Johnson City, Tenn., 1989-93, Richmond (Va.) Children's Mus., 1993—. Mem. Nat. Soc. Fundraising Execs., Assn. Youth Mus. (bd. dirs. nat. coun.), Am. Assn. Mus., S.E. Mus. Conf., Va. Assn. Mus., Nat. Coun. Assn. Youth Mus. (treas.), Jr. League of Richmond, Rotary Club Richmond, Chi Omega. Presbyterian. Home: 3600 Noble Ave Richmond VA 23222-1834 Office: Richmond Children's Mus 740 Navy Hill Dr Richmond VA 23219-1418

MILLER, NANCY ELLEN, computer consultant; b. Detroit, Aug. 30, 1956; d. George Jacob and Charlotte M. (Bobroff) M. BS in Computer and Comm. Sci., U. Mich., 1978; MS in Computer Sci., U. Wis., 1981. Product engr. Ford Motor Co., Dearborn, Mich., 1977; computer programmer Unique Bus. Systems, Inc., Southfield, Mich., 1978; tchg. asst. computer sci. dept. U. Wis., Madison, 1978-82; computer scientist Lister Hill Nat. Ctr. for Biomed Comm. Nat. Libr. Medicine, NIH, Bethesda, Md., 1984-88; knowledge engr. Carnegie Group, Inc., Dearborn, 1989; computer cons. West Bloomfield, Mich., 1993—. Mem. Nat. Abortion and Reproductive Rights Action League, Washington, 1984—, Nat. Women's Polit. Caucus, 1984—, Jewish Fedn. Met. Detroit, 1991—. Recipient Jour. of Am. Soc. for Info. Sci. Best Paper award, 1988. Mem. IEEE Computer Soc., Assn. for Computing Machinery (sec. S.E. Mich. spl. interest group on artificial intelligence 1993-94), Am. Assn. for Artificial Intelligence and Spl. Interest Groups in Mfg. and Bus., Assn. for Logic Programming, U. Wis. Alumni Club (life), U. Mich. Alumni Club (life). Democrat. Jewish. Home and Office: 6220 Village Park Dr #104 West Bloomfield MI 48322

MILLER, NAOMI, art historian; b. N.Y.C., Feb. 28, 1928; d. Nathan and Hannah M. B.S., CCNY, 1948; M.A., Columbia U., 1950, NYU, 1960; Ph.D., NYU, 1966. Asst. prof. art history R.I. Sch. Design, 1963-64; asst. prof. U. Calif.-Berkeley, 1969-70; asst. to assoc. prof. Boston U., 1964—, prof. art history, 1981—; vis. prof. U. B.C., Vancouver, 1967, Hebrew U., Jerusalem, 1980, U. Padua, 1990; vis. scholar I Tatti, 1984-85. Author: French Renaissance Fountains, 1977, Heavenly Caves, 1982, Renaissance Bologna, 1989; co-author: Fons Sapientiae: Garden Fountains in Illustrated Books, 16th-18th Centuries, 1977, Boston Architecture 1975-90, 1990; book rev. editor: Jour. Soc. Archtl. Historians, 1975-81, editor, 1981-84; articles, catalogues. Jr. fellow NEH, 1972-73; sr. fellow Dumbarton Oaks, 1976-77, 83-89; vis. sr. fellow Ctr. for Advanced Study in Visual Arts, 1988, 95. Mem. Coll. Art Assn., Soc. Archtl. Historians, Renaissance Soc. Office: 725 Commonwealth Ave Boston MA 02215-1401

MILLER, NEAL ELGAR, psychologist, emeritus educator; b. Milw., Aug. 3, 1909; s. Irving E. and Lily R. (Fuenfstueck) M.; m. Marion E. Edwards, June 30, 1948; children: York, Sara. B.S., U. Wash., 1931; M.S., Stanford U., 1932; Ph.D., Yale U., 1935; D.Sc., U. Mich., 1965, U. Pa., 1968, St. Lawrence U., 1973, U. Uppsala, Sweden, 1977, LaSalle Coll., 1979, Rutgers U., 1985. Social sci. research fellow Inst. Psychoanalysis, Vienna, Austria, 1935-36; asst. research psychologist Yale U., 1933-35; instr., asst. prof., research asst. psychol. Inst. Human Relations, 1936-41, assoc. prof., research assoc., 1941-42, 46-50, prof. psychology, 1950-52, James Rowland Angell prof. psychology, 1952-66; fellow Berkeley Coll., 1955—; prof. Rockefeller U., N.Y.C., 1966-81; prof. emeritus Rockefeller U., 1981—; research affiliate Yale U., 1985—; expert cons. Am. Inst. Research, 1946-62; spl. cons. com. human resources Research and Devel. Bd., Office Sec. Def., 1951-53; mem. tech. adv. panel Office Asst. Sec. Def., 1954-57; expert cons. Ops. Research Office and Human Resources Research Office, 1951-54; bd. of sci. counsellors Nat. Inst. of Aging, 1987-90; bd. gov.s and mem. of exec. com. N.Y. Acad. of Scis., 1987. Author: (with J. Dollard et al) Frustration and Aggression, 1939, (with Dollard) Social Learning and Imitation, 1941, Personality and Psychotherapy, 1950, Graphic Communication and the Crisis in Education, 1957, N.E. Miller: Selected Papers, 1971; contbr. chpts. to psychol. handbooks; editor: Psychological Research on Pilot Tng., 1947. Chmn. bd. sci. dirs. Roscoe B. Jackson Meml. Lab., Bar Harbor, Maine, 1962-76, hon. trustee, 1980—; bd. sci. counsellors NIMH, 1957-61; fellowship com. Founds. Fund for Research in Psychiatry, 1956-61; mem. central council Internat. Brain Research Orgn., 1964; v.p. bd. dirs. Foote Sch., 1964-65; chmn. NAS/NRC Com. on Brain Scis., 1969-71; bd. sci. counsellors Nat. Inst. Child Health and Human Devel., 1969-72; v.p. Inst. for Advancement of Health, 1982-90. Maj. USAAC, 1942-46; officer in charge research, Psychol. Research Unit 1, Nashville 1942-44; dir. psychol. research project Hdqrs. Flying Tng. Command, Randolph Field, Tex. 1944-46. Recipient Warren medal for exptl. psychology, 1954, Newcomb Cleveland prize, 1956, Nat. medal of sci., 1964, Kenneth Craik Rsch. award U. Cambridge, 1966, Wilbur Cross medal Yale U., 1966, Alumnus Summa Laude Dignitatus U. Wash., 1967, Disting. Alumnus award Western Wash. State Coll., Gold medal award Am. Psychol. Found., 1975, Mental Health Assn. rsch. achievement award, 1978, Inst. for Advancement of Health Sci. and Art of Health award, 1988, Disting. Scholar award Internat. Soc. for Behavioral Medicine, 1990. Fellow Am. Acad. Arts and Scis. (coun. 1979-83), Brit. Psychol. Soc. (hon. fgn.), Internat. Soc. Rsch. on Aggression (life); mem. Am. Philos. Soc., N.Y. Acad. Scis. (hon. life), Spanish Soc. Psychology (hon.), APA (coun. reps. 1954-58, pres. exptl. divsn. 1952-53, pres. 1960-61, pres. divsn. health psychology 1980-81, Disting. Sci. Contbn. award 1959, award for Disting. Contbns. to Knowledge 1983, citation for Outstanding Lifetime Contbn. to Psychology, 1991, establishment of Neal E. Miller Disting. Lectr. in Neurosci. 1995—, Divsn. Health Psychology Centennial award for outstanding achievement 1992), Eastern Psychol. Assn. (pres. 1952-53), NRC (divsn. anthropology and psychology 1950-53, chmn. 1958-60), Nat. Acad. Sci. (chmn. sect. psychology 1965-67, chmn. com. brain sci. 1969-71, sr. fellow Inst. of Medicine 1983—, bd. mental health and behavioral medicine 1980-85), German Soc. Behavioral Medicine and Behavior Modification (hon.), Soc. Exptl. Psychologists, AAAS, Soc. Neurosci. (pres. 1971-72, pres. award for Career of Outstanding Neurosci. Rsch. Teaching and Svc. 1994), Biofeedback Soc. Am. (pres.-elect 1983, pres. 1984, Outstanding Rsch. award 1987, Disting. Rsch. award 1995), Acad. Behavioral Medicine Rsch. (pres. 1978-79, Neal E. Miller New Investigator award establish 1989), Mory's Grad. Club (New Haven), Grad. Club Assn., Sigma Xi (pres. Rockefeller U. chpt. 1968-69), Phi Beta Kappa. Office: Yale U Dept Psychology PO Box 208-205 New Haven CT 06520-8205

MILLER, NEIL AUSTIN, biology educator; b. Grand Rapids, Mich., Apr. 9, 1932; s. Kennith C. and Marjorie (Linsenmeyer) M.; m. Sally Bond, June 23, 1961; children: Anne C., Mary Leigh. AS, Grand Rapids Jr. Coll., 1956; BS, Mich. State U., 1958; MS, Memphis State U., 1964; PhD, So. Ill. U., 1968. Asst. prof. Western Ky. Coll., Bowling Green, 1964-65; fellow So. Ill. U., Carbondale, 1965-68; prof. The Univ. Memphis, 1968—; Disting. prof. U. Memphis, 1984; ecologist Hall, Blake and Assocs.; cons. Continental Engring., Inc., B.F.I., Inc., wetland ecologist cons.; environ. cons. Republic of Estonia. With USCG, 1950-53. Named Tenn. Conservation Educator of Yr., 1983. Baptist. Home: 6898 Trowbridge Cv Memphis TN 38138-1822 Office: The Univ Memphis Biology Dept Life Sci 225 Memphis TN 38152

MILLER, NEIL STUART, financial officer, advertising executive; b. N.Y.C., July 30, 1958; s. Irving Israel Maltz and Lenore (Goldstein) M.; m. Karen Joyce Salomon, Nov. 22, 1987; children: Lindsay Alexandra, Jacqueline Olivia. BS, SUNY, Buffalo, 1980; MBA, SUNY, Binghamton, 1982. CPA, N.Y. Staff auditor Peat Marwick Mitchell & Co., N.Y.C., 1982-83; ops. auditor Gulf & Western Industries, N.Y.C., 1983-84; spl. projects acct. Mickelberry Comms., N.Y.C., 1984-86; v.p. fin. Ptnrs. & Shevack Inc. (subs. Mickelberry Comms. Inc.), N.Y.C., 1986-87; sr. v.p. fin. Ptnrs. & Shevack Inc., N.Y.C., 1987-89, exec. v.p., CFO, 1989—. Mem. AICPA, Am. Mgmt. Assn., N.Y. State Soc. CPA's (past mem. com. CFOs and advt.), Advt. Agy. Fin. Mgmt. Group. Avocations: skiing, motorcycling. Home: 594 W Saddle River Rd U Saddle Riv NJ 07458-1115 Office: Ptnrs & Shevack Inc 1211 Ave of Americas New York NY 10036-8701

MILLER, NEWTON EDD, JR., communications educator; b. Houston, Mar. 13, 1920; s. Newton Edd and Anastasia (Johnston) M.; m. Edwina Whitaker, Aug. 30, 1942; children: Cathy Edwina, Kenneth Edd. B.S., U. Tex., 1939, M.A., 1940; Ph.D., U. Mich., 1952; LL.D., U. Nev., Reno., 1974. Tutor U. Tex., Austin, 1940-41; instr. U. Tex., 1941-45, asst. prof. speech, 1945-47; research asst. Navy Conf. Research, 1947-52; mem. faculty U. Mich., Ann Arbor, 1947-65; successively lectr., instr., asst. prof. speech U. Mich., 1947-55, assoc. prof., 1955-59, prof., 1959-65, asst. dir. summer session, 1953-57, assoc. dir., 1957-63, asst. to v.p. acad. affairs, 1963-65; chancellor U. Nev., Reno, 1965-68; pres. U. Nev., 1968-73, U. Maine, Portland-Gorham, 1973-78; chmn. communications dept. No. Ky. U., 1978-87, emeritus, 1987—, interim gen. mgr. Sta. WNKU, 1985-86; mem. adv. com. to commr. of edn. U.S. Office of Edn., Accreditation and Instl. Eligibility, 1976-79, acting chmn., 1977-78; mem. Judicial Edn. Study Group Am. Univ. Law Inst., 1977-78; mem. Nat. Accreditation Commn. for Agys. Serving Blind and Physically Handicapped, 1988—, pres., 1991-92. Author: Post War World Organization, Background Studies, 1942, (with J.J. Villareal) First Course in Speech, 1945, (with W.M. Sattler) Discussion and Debate, 1951, Discussion and Conference, 2d edit., 1968, (with Stephen D. Boyd) Public Speaking: A Practical Handbook, 1985, 2d edit., 1989; co-editor: Required Arbitration of Labor Disputes, 1947. Pres. bd. dirs. Perry Nursery Sch., 1956-57, Sierra Community Orch., 1989-94; mem. Ann Arbor Bd. Edn., 1959-65, Washtenaw County Bd. Edn.; sec. bd. dirs. Behringer Crawford Mus.; bd. dirs. Sierra Arts Found., 1992—; pres. Reno/Sparks Theater Cmty. Coalition, 1994—; mem. Nev. Humanities Com., 1994—. Mem. Mich. Assn. Sch. Bds. (dir.), N.W. Assn. Colls. and Secondary Schs. (chmn. higher commn. 1971-73), Am. Forensic Assn. (pres. Midwest sect. 1950-53), Central States Speech Assn. (pres. 1958-59), Mich. Speech Assn. (exec. sec. 1950-55), Speech Communication Assn. (chmn. fin. bd.), Assn. Western Us. (chmn. 1971-72), Delta Sigma Rho (nat. v.p. 1948-52), Phi Kappa Phi. Address: 1480 Ayershire Ct Reno NV 89509-5248

MILLER, NICOLE JACQUELINE, fashion designer; b. Ft. Worth, Tex., Mar. 20, 1951; d. Grier Bovey and Jacqueline (Mahieu) M. BFA, RISD, 1973; cert. de coursspeciale, École de la Chambre Syndicale de la Couture Parisienne, Paris, 1971. Asst. designer Clovis Ruffin, N.Y.C., 1974; designer Raincheetahs, N.Y.C., 1974-75, P.J. Walsh, N.Y.C., 1975-82, Nicole Miller, N.Y.C., 1982—; mem. Sports Commn. of N.Y., Commn. of Status of Women; bd. trustees R.I. Sch. of Design. Bd. dirs. Smith's Food and Drug. Recipient Dallas Fashion award, 1991, Earnie award for children's wear, Michael award for fashion. Mem. Fashion Group, Fashion Roundtable, Coun. of Fashion Designers of Am., N.Y. Athletic Club. Avocations: skiing, ice skating, waterskiing, wind surfing. Office: 525 7th Ave Fl 20 New York NY 10018-4901*

MILLER, NORMAN, psychology educator, researcher; b. N.Y.C., Nov. 29, 1933; s. Arthur and Pearl (Doudera) M.; divorced 1975; 1 dau., Carrie Ellen. B.A., Antioch Coll., Yellow Springs, Ohio, 1956; M.S., Northwestern U., 1957; Ph.D., 1959. Asst. prof. Yale U., New Haven, 1959-65; assoc. prof. U. Calif., Riverside, 1966-68; assoc. prof. U. Minn., Mpls., 1966-68, prof., 1968-70; prof. psychology U. So. Calif., Los Angeles, 1970—, now Mendel B. Silberberg prof. Editor: Jour. Personality and Social Psychology, Interpersonal Rels. and Group Processes. Jame McKeen Cattell fellow, 1978; Guggenheim fellow, 1984-85; Fulbright Research fellow Bar-Ilan U. Israel, 1984-85. Office: U Southern Calif Dept Psychology 3620 Mc Clintock Ave Los Angeles CA 90007-4010

MILLER, NORMAN CHARLES, JR., newspaper editor; b. Pitts., Oct. 2, 1934; s. Norman Charles and Elizabeth (Burns) M.; m. Mollie Rudy, June 15, 1957; children—Norman III, Mary Ellen, Teri, Scott. B.A., Pa. State U., 1956. Reporter Wall Street Jour., San Francisco, 1960-63; reporter Wall Street Jour., N.Y.C., 1963-64; bur. chief Wall Street Jour., Detroit, 1964-66; Washington corr. Wall Street Jour., 1966-72, Washington Bur. chief, 1973-83; nat. editor Los Angeles Times, 1983—. Author: The Great Salad Oil Swindle, 1965. Served to lt. (j.g.) USN, 1956-60. Recipient Disting. Alumnus award Pa. State U., 1978; George Polk Meml. award L.I. U., 1963; Pulitzer Prize, 1964. Roman Catholic. Club: Gridiron (Washington). Avocation: tennis. Office: Los Angeles Times Times Mirror Sq Los Angeles CA 90012

MILLER, NORMAN RICHARD, diversified manufacturing company executive; b. Balt., Mar. 7, 1922; s. Samuel and Tobie Hildreth (Engleman) M.; m. Nancy Lee Rosenthal, 1967; children: Hilary S., Dana A. B.S. in Indsl. Engring., Ga. Inst. Tech., 1947; M.B.A., Harvard U., 1950. Indsl. cons. George S. Armstrong & Co., Inc., N.Y.C., 1950-51; ind. mgmt. cons. Italy, 1952-56; founder Italian Postgrad. Bus. Sch., Turin, 1953-55; dir. analysis and bus. planning RCA, 1957-61, v.p. div. bus. planning, 1962-68, v.p., gen. mgr. Graphic Systems Div., 1968-71; cons. Office Sci. and Tech., 1971-72; pres., chief exec. officer, dir. Lynch Corp., N.Y.C., 1972-73; exec. v.p., dir. Radiation Dynamics, Inc., Westbury, N.Y., 1973-76; v.p. Diebold Group, N.Y.C., 1976-82; pres., dir. Conn. Corridor Cellular Communications Cos., Inc., West Hartford, Conn., 1982-87, Broadcast Enterprises Inc., N.Y.C., 1985-92; pres. Twenver, Inc., Denver, 1986-93, Continental Divide PCS Ltd., 1993—. Pres. Merce Cunningham Dance Found., 1976-83; trustee Phila. Mus. Art, 1967-89; trustee, mem. exec. com. Am. Fedn. Arts, 1982-90; mem. Boulder County Cultural Com., 1993—, Sci. and Cultural Facilities Dist., Denver, 1993—, Denver Found. Arts and Culture, 1994—. 2d lt. AUS, 1943-46. Mem. Inst. Aero. Scis., Ga. Tech. Alumni Assn., Harvard Club (N.Y.C.), Tau Beta Pi, Omicron Delta Kappa, Phi Delta Epsilon, Phi Epsilon Pi. Home: 5411 Sunshine Canyon Dr Boulder CO 80302-9777

MILLER, ORLANDO JACK, physician, educator; b. Oklahoma City, Okla., May 11, 1927; s. Arthur Leroy and Iduma Dorris (Berry) M.; m. Dorothy Anne Smith, July 10, 1954; children: Richard Lawrence, Cynthia Kathleen, Karen Ann. B.S., Yale U., 1946, M.D., 1950. Intern St. Anthony Hosp., Oklahoma City, 1950-51; asst. resident in obstetrics and gynecology Yale-New Haven Med. Center, 1954-57, resident, instr., 1957-58; vis. fellow dept. obstetrics and gynecology Tulane U. Service, Charity Hosp., New Orleans, 1958; hon. research asst. Galton Lab., Univ. Coll., London, 1958-60; instr. Coll. Physicians and Surgeons Columbia U., N.Y.C., 1960, asso. dept. obstetrics and gynecology, 1960-61, asst. prof., 1961-65, asso. prof., 1965-69, prof. dept. human genetics and devel., dept. obstetrics and gynecology, 1969-85; asst. attending obstetrician, gynecologist Presbyn. Hosp., N.Y.C., 1964-65, assoc., 1965-70, attending obstetrician and gynecologist, 1970-85; prof. molecular biology, genetics and ob-gyn. Wayne State U. Sch. Medicine, Detroit, 1985-94, prof. Ctr. for Molecular Medicine and Genetics, 1994—, chmn. dept. molecular biology and genetics, 1985-93, dir. Ctr. for Molecular Biology, 1987-90; bd. dirs.Am. Bd. Med. Genetics, 1983-85, v.p., 1983, pres., 1984, 85; mem. human genome Study Sect. NIH, 1991-94. Editor: Cytogenetics, 1970-72; assoc. editor: Birth Defects Compendium, 1971-74, Cytogenetics and Cell Genetics, 1972—; mem. editl. bd. Cytogenetics, 1961-69, Am. Jour. Human Genetics, 1969-74, 79-83, Gynecologic Investigation, 1970-77, Teratology, 1972-74, Cancer Genetics and Cytogenetics, 1979-84, Jour. Exptl. Zoology, 1989-92, Chromosome Rsch., 1994—; mem. editl. bd. com. Genomics, 1987-93, assoc. editor, 1993-96; mem. adv. bd. Human Genetics, 1978—; cons. Jour. Med. Primartolgoy, 1977-94; contbr. chpts. to textbooks and articles to med. and sci. jours. Mem. sci. adv. com. on rsch. Nat. Found. March of Dimes, 1967-96, mem. sci. com., 1996—; mem. sci. rec. com. Basil O'Connor starter grants, 1973-77, 86-94; mem. human embryology and devel. study sect. NIH, 1970-74, chmn., 1972-74; mem. com. for study of inborn errors of metabolism NRC, 1972-74; mem. sci. adv. com. virology and cell biology Am. Cancer Soc., 1974-78, mem. sci. adv. com. cell and devel. biology, 1986-90; U.S. rep. permanent com. Internat. Congress of Human Genetics, 1986-91. With AUS, 1951-53. James Hudson Brown Jr. fellow Yale U., 1947-48; NRC fellow, 1953-54; Population Council fellow, 1958-59; Josiah Macy Jr. fellow, 1960-61; NSF sr. postdoctoral fellow U. Oxford, 1968-69; vis. scientist U. Edinburgh, 1983-84; Disting. vis. fellow, Fogarty Internat. fellow LaTrobe U., Melbourne, Australia, 1992. Fellow AAAS; mem. AAAS, Am. Genetic Assn., Am. Soc. Cell Biology, Am. Soc. Human Genetics (bd. dirs. 1970-73, 86-90), Genetics Soc. Am., Genetics Soc. Australia, Am. Soc. Microbiologists, Human Genome Orgn., Acad. Scholars, Wayne State U. (life), Sigma Xi. Presbyterian. Home: 1915 Stonycroft Ln Bloomfield Hills MI 48304-2339 Office: 540 E Canfield St Detroit MI 48201-1928

MILLER, PAMELA GUNDERSEN, city official; b. Cambridge, Mass., Sept. 7, 1938; d. Sven M. and Harriet Adams Gundersen; A.B. magna cum laude, Smith Coll., 1960; m. Ralph E. Miller, July 7, 1962; children—Alexander, Erik, Karen. Feature writer Congressional Quar., Washington, 1962-65; dir. cable TV franchizing Storer Broadcasting Co., Louisville, Bowling Green, Lexington, and Covington, Ky., 1978-80, 81-82; mem. 4th Dist. Lexington, Fayette County Urban Council, 1973-77, councilwoman-at-large, 1982-93, vice-mayor, 1984-86, 89-93, mayor, 1993—; dep. commr. Ky. Dept. Local Govt., Frankfort, 1980-81; pres. Pam Miller, Inc., 1984—, Community Ventures Corp., 1985—. Mem. Fayette County Bd. Health, 1975-77, Downtown Devel. Commn., 1975-77; alt. del. Dem. Nat. Conv., 1976; bd. dirs. YMCA, Lexington, 1975-77, 85-90, Fund for the Arts, 1984-93, Council of Arts, 1978-80, Sister Cities, 1978-80; treas. Prichard Com. for Acad. Excellence, 1983—. Named Woman of Achievement YWCA, 1984, Outstanding Woman of Blue Grass, AAUW, 1984. Mem. LWV (dir. 1970-73), Profl. Women's Forum, NOW, Land and Nature Trust of the Bluegrass. Home: 140 Cherokee Park Lexington KY 40503-1304 Office: 200 E Main St Lexington KY 40507-1315

MILLER, PATRICIA LOUISE, state legislator, nurse; b. Bellefontaine, Ohio, July 4, 1936; d. Richard William and Rachel Orpha (Williams) Miller; m. Kenneth Orlan Miller, July 3, 1960; children: Tamara Sue, Matthew Ivan. RN, Meth. Hosp. Sch. Nursing-Indpls., 1957; BS, Ind. U., 1960. Office nurse A.D. Dennison, MD, 1960-61; staff nurse Meth. Hosp., Indpls., 1959, Community Hosp., Indpls., 1958; representative, State of Ind., Dist. 50, Indpls., 1982-83, senator, State of Ind., Dist. 32, Indpls., 1983—, mem. edn. com., 1984-90, health welfare and aging com. 1983-90, labor and pension com. 1983-94, legis. apportionment and elections coms., chmn. interim study com. pub. health and mental health Ind. Gen. Assembly, 1986; chair Senate Environ. Affairs, 1990-92, Health and Environ. Affairs, 1992—; mem. election com., 1992—; mem. budget subcom. Senate Fin. Com., 1995— . Mem. Bd. Edn., Met. Sch. Dist. Warren Twp., 1974-82, pres., 1979-80, 80-81; mem. Warren Twp. Citizens Screening Com. for Sch. Bd. Candidates, 1972-74, 84,

Met. Zoning Bd. Appeals, Div. I, appointed mem. City-County Council, 1972-76; bd. dirs. Central Ind. Council on Aging, Indpls., 1977-80; mem. State Bd. of Voc. and Tech. Edn., 1978-82, sec., 1980-82; mem. Gov.'s Select Adv. Commn. for Primary and Secondary Edn., 1983; precinct committeeman Republican Party, 1968-74, ward vice chmn., 1975-78, ward chmn., 1978-85, twp. chmn., 1985-87; vice chmn. Marion County Rep., 1986—; del. Rep. State Conv., 1968, 74, 76, 80, 84, 86, 88, 90, 92, 94, sgt. at arms, 1982, mem. platform com., 1984, 88, 90, 92, co-chmn. Ind. Rep. Platform Com., 1992; del. Rep. Nat. Conv., 1984, alternate del., 1988, Rep. Presdl. Elector Alternate, 1992; active various polit. campaigns; bd. dirs. PTA, 1967-81; pres. Grassy Creek PTA, 1971-72; state del. Ind. PTA, 1978; mem. child care adv. com. Walker Career Center, 1976-80, others; bd. dirs. Ch. Fedn. Greater Indpls., 1979-82, Christian Justice Center, Inc., 1983-85, Gideon Internat. Aux., 1977—; mem. United Meth. Bd. Missions Aux. of Indpls., 1974-80, v.p., 1974-76; bd. dirs. Lucille Raines Residence, Inc., 1977-80; exec. com. S. Ind. Conf. United Meth. Women, 1977-80, lay del. S. Ind. Conf. United Meth. Ch., 1977—, fin. and adminstrn. com., 1979-88, planning and research com., 1980-88, co-chmn. law adv. com., chmn. health and welfare, conf. council ministries, also mem. task force, bd. ordained ministry, also panel, chmn. com. on dist. superintendency, dist. council on ministries; sec. Indpls. S.E. Dist. Council on Ministries, 1977-78, pres., 1982; chmn. council on ministries Cumberland United Meth. Ch., 1969-76; chmn. stewardship com. Old Bethel United Meth. Ch., 1982-85, fin. com., 1982-85, adminstrv. bd., mem. council on ministries, 1981-85; co-chair Evangelism Com., 1994—; jurisdictional del. United Meth. Ch., 1988, 92; alternate del. United Meth. Ch. Gen. Conf., 1988, delegate, 1992; mem. health and human svcs. com. Midwest Legis. Conf., 1995. Recipient Phi Lambda Theta Honor for outstanding contbr. in field of edn., 1976; Woman of the Year, Cumberland Bus. and Profl. Women, 1979; Ind. Voc. Assn. citation award, 1984, others. Mem. Indpls. Dist. Dental Soc. Women's Aux., Ind. Dental Assn. Women's Aux., Am. Dental Assn. Women's Aux., Council State Govt. (intergovtl. affairs com.), Nat. Conf. State Legislatures (health com. vice chmn. 1994—), Warren Twp. Rep. Franklin Rep., Lawrence Rep., Center Twp. Rep., Fall Creek Valley Rep., Marion County Council Rep. Women, Ind. Women's Rep., Indpls. Women's Rep., Ind. Fedn. Rep. Women, Nat. Fedn. Rep. Women, Beech Grove Rep., Perry Twp. Rep. Home: 1041 Muessing Rd Indianapolis IN 46239-9614

MILLER, PATRICK DWIGHT, JR., religion educator, minister; b. Atlanta, Oct. 24, 1935; s. Patrick Dwight and Lila Morse (Bonner) M.; m. Mary Ann Sudduth, Dec. 27, 1958; children: Jonathan Sudduth, Patrick James. AB, Davidson Coll., 1956; BD, Union Theol. Sem., Va., 1959; PhD, Harvard U., 1964. Ordained to ministry Presbyn. Ch., 1963. Pastor, minister Trinity Presbyn. Ch., Traveler's Rest, S.C., 1963-65; asst. prof. Bibl. studies Union Theol. Sem., Richmond, Va., 1966-68, assoc. prof., 1968-73, prof., 1973-84, dean of faculty, 1979-83; prof. of Old Testament Theology Princeton (N.J.) Theol. Sem., 1984—. Author: The Divine Warrior in Early Israel, 1973, The Hand of the Lord, 1977, Sin and Judgment in the Prophets, 1982, Interpreting the Psalms, 1986, Deuteronomy, 1990, They Cried to the Lord, 1994; editor: Theology Today, 1990—. Mem. Soc. of Bibl. Lit. (sec.-treas. 1987-88), Colloquium for Bibl. Rsch. (rev. standard version translation com. 1974—). Democrat. Presbyterian. Home: 89 Mercer St Princeton NJ 08540-6826 Office: Princeton Theol Sem PO Box 821 Princeton NJ 08542-0803*

MILLER, PATRICK WILLIAM, research administrator, educator; b. Toledo, Sept. 1, 1947; s. Richard William and Mary Olivia (Rinna) M.; m. Jean Ellen Thomas, Apr. 5, 1974; children: Joy, Tatum, Alex. BS in Indstrl. Edn., Bowling Green State U., 1971, MEd in Career Edn. and Tech., 1973; PhD in Indstrl. Tech. Edn., Ohio State U., 1977. Tchr. Montgomery Hills Jr. High Sch., Silver Spring, Md., 1971-72, Rockville (Md.) High Sch., 1973-74; asst. prof. Wayne State U., Detroit, 1977-79; assoc. prof., grad. coord. indstrl. edn. and tech. Western Carolina U., Cullowhee, N.C., 1979-81; assoc prof. U. No. Iowa, Cedar Falls, 1981-86; dir. grad. studies practical arts and vocat.-tech. edn. U. Mo., Columbia, 1986-89; devel. editor Am. Tech. Pubs., Homewood, Ill., 1989-90; proposal mgr. Nat. Opinion Rsch. Ctr. U. Chgo., 1990—; pres. Patrick W. Miller and Assocs., Munster, Ind., 1981—; presenter, advisor and cons. in field. Author: Nonverbal Communication: Its Impact on Teaching and Learning, 1983, Teacher Written Tests: A Guide for Planning, Creating, Administering and Assessing, 1985, Nonverbal Communication: What Resarch Says to the Teacher, 1988, How To Write Tests for Students, 1990; mem. editl. bd. Jour. Indsl. Tchr. Edn., 1981-88, Am. Vocat. Edn. Rsch. Jour., 1981-85, 94—, Tech. Tchr., 1982-84, Jour. Indsl. Tech., 1984—, Jour. Vocat. and Tech. Edn., 1987-90, Human Resource Devel. Quar., 1989—; also articles. Sec. U. No. Iowa United Faculty, Cedar Falls, 1983-84, pres., 1984-86. Lance cpl. USMC, 1966-68, Vietnam. Recipient editl. recognition award Jour. Indsl. Tchr. Edn., 1984, 86, 88; named One of Accomplished Grads. of Coll. Tech., Bowling Green State U., 1995. Mem. ASTD, Am. Ednl. Rsch. Assn., Am. Vocat. Assn., Am. Vocat. Edn. Rsch. Assn., Nat. Assn. Indsl. Tech. (chmn. rsch. grants 1982-87, pres. industry div. 1991-92, chmn. exec. bd. 1992-93, past pres. 1993-94, Leadership award 1992, 93), Nat. Assn. Indsl. and Tech. Tchr. Educators (pres. 1988-89, past pres. 1989-90, trustee 1990-93, Outstanding Svc. award 1988, 90), Nat. Assn. Vocat. Edn. Spl. Needs Pers., Internat. Tech. Edn. Assn., Coun. Tech. Tchr. Edn., Epsilon Pi Tau, Phi Delta Kappa. Office: Univ Chgo Nat Opinion Rsch Ctr 1155 E 60th St Chicago IL 60637-2745

MILLER, PAUL AUSBORN, adult education educator; b. East Liverpool, Ohio, Mar. 22, 1917; s. Harry A. and Elizabeth (Stewart) M.; m. Catherine Spiker, Dec. 9, 1939 (dec. Dec. 1964); children—Paula Kay, Thomas Ausborn; m. Francena Lounsbery Nolan, Jan. 15, 1966. B.S., U. W.Va., 1939; M.A., Mich. State U., 1947, Ph.D., 1953. County agrl. agt. in W.Va., 1939-42; extension specialist sociology and anthropology Mich. State U., East Lansing, 1947-55; asst. prof. Mich. State U., 1947-52, asso. prof., 1953, prof., 1953-61, provost, 1959-61; pres. W.Va. U., Morgantown, 1962-66; asst. sec. for edn. HEW, 1966-68; disting. prof. edn., dir. univ. planning studies U. N.C., Charlotte; prof. adult edn. N.C. State U. at Raleigh, 1968-69; pres. Rochester (N.Y.) Inst. of Tech., 1969-79, pres. emeritus, 1979—, prof., 1979-93; sr. program cons. W.K. Kellogg Found., 1979-83; adj. prof. rural sociology U. Mo.-Columbia, 1994—. Author: Community Health Action, 1953; co-author: Patterns for Lifelong Learning, 1973; contbr. to publs. in field. Mem. Colombian Commn. Higher Edn., 1960-61. Served as 1st lt. USAAF, 1942-46. Fellow Am. Sociol. Assn.; mem. Rural Sociol. Soc., Phi Kappa Phi, Epsilon Sigma Phi. Home: 1909 Walden Ct Columbia MO 65203-5407

MILLER, PAUL DEAN, breeding consultant, geneticist, educator; b. Cedar Falls, Iowa, Apr. 4, 1941; s. Donald Hugh and Mary (Hansen) M.; m. Nancy Pearl Huser, Aug. 23, 1965; children: Michael, Steven. BS, Iowa State U., 1963; MS, Cornell U., 1965, PhD, 1967. Asst. prof. animal breeding Cornell U., Ithaca, N.Y., 1967-72; v.p. Am. Breeders Svc., DeForest, Wis., 1972-95; pres. Windsor (Wis.) Park Inc., 1985—; adj. prof. U. Wis., Madison, 1980—. Contbr. articles to profl. jours. Mem. Beef Improvement Fedn. (disting. service award 1980), Am. Soc. Animal Sci., Am. Dairy Sci. Assn., Nat. Assn. Animal Breeders (dir. 1983, v.p. 1986). Republican. Home: 3665 Windsor Rd De Forest WI 53532-2727 Office: Windsor Park Inc 3671 Windsor Rd De Forest WI 53532

MILLER, PAUL FETTEROLF, JR., retired investment company executive; b. Phila., 1927; s. Paul Fetterolf and Katharine Mills (Thompson) M.; m. Ella Warren Shafer, June 14, 1952; children: Ella Warren, Katharine Shafer, Paul Fetterolf III. BS, U. Pa., 1950, LLD (hon.), 1982; LLD (hon.), Washington & Lee U., 1988. Chartered fin. analyst. Founding ptnr. Miller, Anderson & Sherrerd, West Conshohocken, Pa.; bd. dirs. Mead Corp., Rohm & Haas Co., Hewlett-Packard. Trustee U. Pa., Ford Found., 1982-94, Colonial Williamsburg; trustee Sci. Ctr. of N.H.; mem. bd. overseers Wharton Sch. Mem. Fin. Analysts Phila., World Wildlife Fund (dir.), Merion Golf Club, Merion Cricket Club, Philadelphia Club, Useppa Island Club, Beta Theta Pi. Home: 115 Maple Hill Rd Gladwyne PA 19035-1305 Office: One Tower Bridge West Conshohocken PA 19428

MILLER, PAUL GEORGE, computer company executive; b. Louisville, Dec. 13, 1922; s. George Moore and Pauline Louise (Koob) M.; m. Doris Kahl Ingram, Feb. 17, 1979; children: George, James, Randolph. B.M.E., Purdue U., 1948; B.S., U.S. Naval Acad., 1946; B.S. in Electronics Engring., Mass. Inst. Tech., 1949, postgrad. in Nuclear Sci., 1949. Gen. mgr. control systems div. Daystrom (later acquired by Control Data Corp.), La Jolla, Calif., 1957-65; v.p., gen. mgr. communications and spl. systems group Control Data Corp., Mpls., 1965-67; v.p., group gen. mgr. computer systems and devel. Control Data Corp., 1967-69, sr. v.p., mktg. group exec., 1970-72, sr. v.p., 1973—; pres. Control Data Mktg. Co.; chmn., chief exec. officer Comml. Credit Co., 1977-83; bd. dirs. Merrill Corp., Bon Secours Health System; chmn. and treas. LSC, Inc. Served to lt. USN, 1946-57. Recipient Distinguished Alumnus award Purdue U., 1968. Mem. IEEE (sr.), Sigma Xi, Tau Beta Pi, Eta Kappa Nu, Delta Tau Delta. Home: 11203 Falls Rd Lutherville MD 21093 Office: PO Box 725 Brooklandville MD 21022-0725

MILLER, PAUL J., lawyer; b. Boston, Mar. 27, 1929; s. Edward and Esther (Kalis) M.; children—Robin, Jonathan; m. Michal Davis, Sept. 1, 1965; children—Anthony, Douglas. B.A., Yale U., 1950; LL.B., Harvard U., 1953. Bar: Mass. 1953, Ill. 1957. Assoc. Miller & Miller, Boston, 1953-54; assoc. Sonnenschein Nath & Rosenthal, Chgo., 1957-63, ptnr., 1963—; bd. dirs. Oil-Dri Corp. Am., Chgo. Trustee Latin Sch. of Chgo., 1985-91. 1st lt. JAGC, U.S. Army, 1954-57. Fellow Am. Bar Found.; mem. Tavern Club, Saddle and Cycle Club, Law Club, Phi Beta Kappa. Avocations: jogging; sailing. Office: Sonnenschein Nath & Rosenthal 233 S Wacker Dr Ste 8000 Chicago IL 60606-6404

MILLER, PAUL JAMES, coffee company executive; b. San Mateo, Calif., Aug. 23, 1939; s. Paul and Rita M.; m. Patricia Ann Deruette, Aug. 22, 1964; children—Mike, Britt, Brian. B.S. in Bus. Adminstrn. with honors, San Jose (Calif.) State U., 1962; M.B.A. in Mktg, Santa Clara (Calif.) U., 1964. With Hills Bros. Coffee, Inc., San Francisco, 1964—, advt. mgr., then dir. mktg., 1971-75, pres., 1975-83, chmn. bd., 1983-89, pres., chief exec. officer, dir., 1989-91; pres., chief exec. officer Nestle Beverage Co., San Francisco, 1991—. Mem. Am. Mgmt. Assn., Grocery Mfrs. Assn. Am., Better Bus. Bur. San Francisco, Conf. Board, U.S. C. of C., Calif. C. of C. Clubs: World Trade, Olympic. Office: Nestle Beverage Co 345 Spear St San Francisco CA 94105-1673*

MILLER, PAUL LUKENS, investment banker; b. Phila., Dec. 6, 1919; s. Henry C.L. and Elsie (Groff) M.; m. Adele Olyphant, Nov. 4, 1950; children: Paul L. (dec.), Hilary, Beverly, Leslie. Student, William Penn Charter Sch., Phila., 1937; A.B., Princeton U., 1941. With First Boston Corp., N.Y.C., 1946—; v.p. First Boston Corp., 1955-64, dir., 1959-78, pres., 1964-78, sr. advisor, 1978—. Served to maj., F.A. AUS, 1941-46. Clubs: Ivy (Princeton); Links, River (N.Y.C.). Office: First Boston Corp Park Ave Plaza 55 E 52 St New York NY 10055

MILLER, PAUL MCGRATH, JR., executive search consulting company executive; b. Bowling Green, Ky., Oct. 31, 1935; s. Paul McGrath and Lena D. (Carr) M.; m. Charlene F. Russnak, Sept. 12, 1970 (div.); children: Andrew McGrath, Christopher Paul; m. C. Sue Whitehouse, Aug. 12, 1989. B. Mech. Engring., Cornell U., 1958; M.B.A., Harvard U., 1966. Foreman, Procter & Gamble, Cin., 1958-60; market analyst United Aircraft Co., Sunnyvale, Calif., 1963-64; asst. to chmn. bd. Boise Cascade Corp. (Idaho), 1966, gen. mktg. mgr. Insulite div., 1966-67, nat. sales mgr. Lumber and Plywood, 1967-68, asst. to exec. v.p. Paper Group, 1968-69; group dir. mktg. Am. Standard, Inc., N.Y.C., 1969-71; dir. corp. communications Indian Head, Inc., N.Y.C., 1971-74; v.p. mktg. Ball & Socket Mfg. Co., Cheshire, Conn., 1975; v.p. mktg. Cory Coffee Service, Chgo., 1976, v.p., gen. mgr., 1977-80; v.p., ptnr. Korn/Ferry Internat., Chgo., 1980-87; ptnr. Lamalie Assocs. Inc., Chgo., 1987—. Mem. Winnetka Caucus (Ill.), 1980. Served to capt. USAF, 1960-63. Episcopalian. Clubs: Racquet Chgo., Harvard N.Y.C., Harvard Bus. Sch. Chgo. (dir.). Office: Lamalie Amrop Internat 225 W Wacker Dr Chicago IL 60606-1229

MILLER, PAUL SAMUEL, lawyer; b. Paterson, N.J., Apr. 8, 1939; s. Louis and Etta (Wolff) M.; m. Carol Plesser, Mar. 26, 1961; children: Nicole F., Margo H., Jason E. BA, Rutgers U., 1960, JD magna cum laude, 1962. Bar: N.Y. 1963. Assoc. Kaye, Scholer, Fierman, Hayes & Handler, N.Y.C., 1962-63, Rubin, Baum & Levin, N.Y.C., 1964; ptnr. Fishman, Miller & Zimet, N.Y.C., 1964-70; counsel Leasing Cons., Inc., Rosyln, N.Y., 1970-71; with Pfizer Inc., N.Y.C., 1971—, assoc. gen. counsel, v.p., gen. counsel, 1986—; sr. v.p., gen. counsel, 1992—; official corr. Pharm. Mfrs. Assn., mem., chmn. exec. com. law sect., 1989-90. Mem. United Jewish Appeal Com., Essex County, 1981-83, co-chmn. Livingston sect., 1982; mem. bus. adv. coun. Touro Law Sch., Northwestern Sch. Law; bd. dirs. Mgmt. Decision Lab. NYU Sch. Bus. Adminstrn., 1982—, Citizens Crime Commn. of N.Y.C., Inc., Jewish Conciliation Bd. Am., Inc., Nat. Com. for Furtherance of Jewish Edn., Lawyers for Civil Justice. Mem. ABA (antitrust law sect., corp. banking and bus. law sect., natural resources law sect., sci. and tech. sect., mem. health law forum com.), N.Y. State Bar Assn. (antitrust law sect., food and drug law sect., mem. internat. trade com., mem. long range policy proposals com.), Nat. Inst. Dispute Resolution (bd. dirs.), U.S. C. of C. (mem. govt. and regulatory affairs com.). Avocations: golf, tennis. Office: Pfizer Inc 235 E 42nd St New York NY 10017-5703

MILLER, PEGGY FERGUESON, nursing administrator; b. Nashville, Apr. 7, 1946; d. David Shannon and Helen Beatrice (Hale) Fergueson; m. David Wayne Miller, Dec. 17, 1966; children: Christopher W., Julie A. RN, Nashville Gen. Hosp. Sch., 1967. Staff nurse Nashville Gen. Hosp., 1967-68; svcs. dir. Cheatham County Rest Home, Ashland City, Tenn., 1968-79, dir. nursing, 1986-91; sch. nurse Cheatham County Bd. Edn., Ashland City, 1976-86; shift supr. Cheatham Med. Ctr., Ashland City, 1991-93, dir. nursing, 1993—. County dir. Cheatham County Area Easter Seals Summer Camp, Ashland City, 1981-85; county coord. Cheatham County Spl. Olympics, Ashland City, 1980-86; chairperson Cheatham County Interagy. Network, Ashland City, 1989-90. Recipient Outstanding Svc. award Civitans Club, Cheatham County, 1987. Mem. Tenn. Orgn. Nurse Execs. Democrat. Mem. Ch. of Christ. Avocations: acoustic guitar, ornamental horticulture. Office: Cheatham Med Ctr 313 N Main St Ashland City TN 37015-1319

MILLER, PEGGY MCLAREN, management educator; b. Tomahawk, Wis., Jan. 12, 1931; d. Cecil Glenn and Gladys Lucille (Bame) McLaren; m. Richard Irwin Miller, June 25, 1955; children: Joan Marie, Diane Lee, Janine Louise. BS, Iowa State U., 1953; MA, Am. U., 1959; MBA, Rochester Inst. Tech., 1979; PhD, Ohio U., 1987. Instr. Beirut Coll. for Women, 1953-55, U. Ky., Lexington, 1964-66, S.W. Tex. State U., San Marcos, 1981-84; home economist Borden Co., N.Y.C., 1955-58; cons. Consumer Cons., Chgo., Springfield, Ill., 1972-77; sr. mktg. rep. N.Y. State Dept. Agr., Rochester, 1978-79; asst. prof., coord. bus. and mgmt. Keuka Coll., Keuka Park, N.Y., 1979-81; lectr. mgmt. Ohio U., Athens, 1984—. Co-editor: Fifty States Cookbook, 1977; contbr. articles to profl. jours. Mem. Soc. for Advancement of Mgmt. (advisor campus chpt.), Mortar Bd., Phi Kappa Phi. Home: 17 Briarwood Dr Athens OH 45701-1302 Office: Ohio U Copeland Hall Athens OH 45701

MILLER, PENELOPE ANN, actress; b. Jan. 13, 1964; d. Mark and Beatrice (Ammidown) M. Studies with Herbert Berghof. Appeared in (plays) The People From Work, 1984, Biloxi Blues, 1984-85, Moonchildren, Our Town (Tony Award nom.), (TV shows) The Guiding Light, 1984, As the World Turns, 1984, The Popcorn Kid, (films) Adventures in Babysitting, 1987, Biloxi Blues, 1988, Big Top Pee-Wee, 1988, Miles From Home, 1988, Dead-Bang, 1989, Downtown, 1990, The Freshman, 1990, Kindergarten Cop, 1990, Awakenings, 1990, Other People's Money, 1991, Year of the Comet, 1992, The Gun in Betty Lou's Handbag, 1992, Chaplin, 1992, Carlito's Way, 1993 (Golden Globe nom.), The Shadow, 1994. Mem. Actors' Equity Assn., AFTRA. *

MILLER, PHILIP BOYD, retail executive; b. Balt., June 4, 1938; s. Robert Boyd and Claire Elise (Hossfeld) M.; m. Anne Gorman, Dec. 23, 1985; 1 child, Philip Graham; children from previous marriage: Laura, Brandt, Heather. Student, McDonogh Sch., Tulane U., John Hopkins U. Divisional mdse. mgr. Filene's, Boston, 1962-70; v.p. and gen. mgr. Wallach's, N.Y.C., 1970-73, Bloomingdale's, N.Y.C., 1975-77; vice chmn. Lord & Taylor, N.Y.C., 1977-83; pres. Neiman-Marcus, Dallas, 1979-83; chief exec. officer, chmn. bd. Marshall Field and Co., Chgo., 1983-90; chmn., CEO Saks Fifth Ave., N.Y.C., 1990—, COO, 1993, CEO, 1993—. Mem. Chgo. Urban League Bus. Adv. Council, 198690, Mid-Am. Com., Chgo., 1985-90, Chgo. Cen. Area Com., 1984-90, Econ. Devel. Corp., Chgo., 1986-90; bd. dirs. Rehab. Inst., 1986-87, Lyric Opera Chgo., 1984—, Dallas Opera, 1980—. Mem. Nat. Retail Merchants Assn., Ill. Retail Merchants Assn., Greater State Stree Council (chmn. 1986-87), Northwestern Univ. Assocs. Clubs: Econ. (Chgo.), Chicago. Office: Saks Fifth Avenue 12 E 49th St New York NY 10017-1028*

MILLER, PHILIP EFREM, librarian; b. Providence, Feb. 18, 1945; s. Jacob and Natalie (Rouslin) M.; m. Zenia Weiner, Dec. 20, 1969; 1 son, Paul Jeremy. B.S.L., Georgetown U., 1967; M.S., U. Mich., 1968, A.M.L.S., 1973; Ph.D., NYU, 1984. Asst. libr. Hebrew Union Coll., N.Y.C., 1973-76, acting libr., 1976-78, librarian, 1978—. Author: Karaite Separatism in 19th Century Russia, 1993. Mem. Assn. Jewish Libraries (pres. 1982-84), Jewish Book Coun. (exec. bd. 1977—), Am. Soc. for Jewish Music (exec. bd. 1990—), Assn. Jewish Studies. Home: 56 Truman Dr Marlboro NJ 07746-1122 Office: Hebrew Union Coll-Jewish Inst of Religion Klau Libr 1 W 4th St New York NY 10012-1105

MILLER, PHILIP NICHOLSON, engineering and technology educator, consultant; b. Providence, Feb. 22, 1947; s. Arthur Phillip and Mildred May (Brown) M.; m. Sandra Veronica Green; children: Stephanie, Spencer, Erik, Brian, Philip, Adrian, Vonya. AS in Mech. Engring. Tech., Roger Williams Coll., 1968, BS in Indsl. Tech., 1970; MBA, Providence Coll., 1976; MS in Indsl. Engring., U. R.I., 1986. Process engr. Corning Glass Works, Providence, 1970; methods engr. Raytheon, North Dighton, Mass., 1970-72; stds. engr. Kaiser Aluminum, Bristol, R.I., 1973; methos/mfg. engr. submarine div. Raytheon, Portsmouth, R.I., 1974-79; sr. mgmt. engr. Roger Williams Hosp., Providence, 1979-80; indsl. engr. Bostitch Textron, East Greenwich, R.I., 1980-85; mgr. tng. and devel. Stanley-Bostitch, East Greenwich, R.I., 1985-86; asst. prof. engring. Cmty. Coll. R.I., Warwick, 1986-92, assoc. prof. engring., 1992—; cons. Antaya Inc., Providence, 1991. Pentacostal. Avocations: tennis, basketball. Home: 299 Willard Ave Providence RI 02907

MILLER, PHILLIP EDWARD, environmental scientist; b. Waterloo, Iowa, May 29, 1935; s. Joe Monroe and Katherine Elva (Groom) M.; m. Cathy Ann Love, Sept. 15, 1962; children: Eric Anthony, Bryan Edward, Stefan Patrick, Gregory Joseph. BA in Sci. Edn., U. No. Iowa, 1961; MA in Sci. Edn., U. Iowa, 1964; postgrad., U. Wis., 1966-68. Physics and chemistry tchr. Millersburg (Iowa) Community High Sch., 1961-62; supervising tchr. NSF Insvc. Inst. U. Iowa, Iowa City, 1962-64; instr. biology, area coord. Office Equal Opportunity Western Ky. U., Bowling Green, 1964-66; sci. editor, journalism instr.-sci. and tech. Mich. State U., East Lansing, 1968-74; asst. prof. agr., forestry and home econs. U. Minn., St. Paul, 1974-77; sr. editor atomic energy div. E.I. du Pont de Nemours and Co., Aiken, S.C., 1977-89; sr. scientist environ. protection dept. Westinghouse Savannah River Co., Aiken, 1989—; pres. Agy. for Book Authors, Collectors and Understanding of Sci., Aiken, 1994—; panelist 26th Internat. Tech. Comm. Conf., L.A., 1979; participant Dept. Energy/Westinghouse Sch. for Environ. Excellence, Cin., 1991; invited contbr. to proceedings of the 1st Tatarstan Symposium on Energy, Environment and Econs., Kazan, Tatarstan, Russia, 1992. Mem. publs. com. Cen. Assn. Sci. and Math. Tchrs., Iowa City, 1969-72; editor Nat. Task Force on Agrl. Energy R&D, Washington, 1976; editor, contbr. Minn. Sci. Mag., 1974-77; contbr. several hundred med., sci. and engring. articles including to Procs. of Iowa Acad. Sci., Sch. Sci. and Math., Am. Biology Tchrs., Procs. of Internat. Communication Conf., and Procs. of Westinghouse Computer Symposium. Pres. Savannah River Rifle & Pistol Club, Aiken, 1981-82, Aiken Toastmasters, 1984; judge speech contests Optimist and 4-H Club Contests, Aiken, 1985-86. Sgt. U.S. Army, 1955-58. Decorated Disting. Marksman Badge gold medal; recipient 1st place sci. writing Argonne Labs. Assn., 1973, Profl. Achievement Permanent Profl. cert. Iowa State Bd. of Pub. Instrn., 1974, Blue Ribbon, Am. Assn. Agrl. Coll. Editors, Tex. A&M, 1976. Mem. AAAS, N.Y. Acad. Scis., Am. Chem. Soc., Phi Delta Kappa, Sigma Xi. Achievements include research in the causes and timing of pre-adolescent initial interest in science; discovery that low-zinc root environment causes delay of development and acceleration of senescence in tobacco plants; creation of publicity for the MSU discovery of platinum drugs-now among the most widely used cancer drugs and new models for future drugs to destroy tumors by locking onto cancer DNA. Office: Westinghouse Savannah River Co Environ Protection Dept Aiken SC 29801

MILLER, PHOEBE AMELIA, marketing professional; b. Jan. 13, 1948; d. William Prescott and Elizabeth Helen (Lucker) M.. BA in Math., U. Wis., 1970; postgrad., Stanford U., 1973, Golden Gate U., 1975-76. Engr. Bechtel, San Francisco, 1972-77; asst. mgr. Rand Info. Systems, San Francisco, 1977-79; sr. mktg. rep. Computer Sci. Corp., San Francisco, 1979-81; mgr. distbr. sales COGNOS Corp., Walnut Creek, Calif., 1981-86; owner, mgr. P.A. Miller & Assocs., San Francisco, 1986—. Office: PA Miller & Assocs 1750 Montgomery St San Francisco CA 94111-1003

MILLER, RALPH BRADLEY, lawyer, former state legislator; b. Fayetteville, N.C., May 19, 1953; s. Nathan David and Margaret Virginia (Hale) M.; m. Esther Susan Hall, Dec. 19, 1981. BA, U. N.C., 1975; MSc, London Sch. Econs., 1978; JD, Columbia U., 1979. Bar: N.C. 1979, U.S. Dist. Ct. (ea. dist.) N.C. 1980, U.S. Ct. Appeals (4th cir. 1980), U.S. Dist. Ct. (mid. dist.) N.C. 1983. Law clk. to Hon. J. Dickson Phillips Jr. U.S. Ct. Appeals (4th cir.), 1979-80; assoc. Allen, Steed & Allen, Raleigh, N.C., 1980-82, Barringer, Allen & Pinnix, Raleigh, N.C., 1982-84, LeBoeuf, Lamb, Leiby & MacRae, Raleigh, N.C., 1985-88; prin. Nichols, Miller & Sigmon, Raleigh, N.C., 1988-90; pvt. practice Raleigh, N.C., 1991—; mem. N.C. Ho. of Reps., Raleigh, 1993-94. Chmn. Wake County Dem. Com., 1985-87; mem. state exec. com. N.C. Dem. Com., 1985-89, 91—; mem. N.C. Environ. Rev. Commn., 1994-95. Mem. ATLA, N.C. Bar Assn., Wake County Bar Assn., N.C. Acad. Trial Lawyers, Am. Judicature Soc., Raleigh Civitan Club. Democrat. Episcopalian. Home: 3211 Coleridge Dr Raleigh NC 27609-7201 Office: 4006 Barrett Dr Raleigh NC 27609-6604

MILLER, RALPH MENNO, minister, religious organization administrator; b. Hubbard, Oreg., Mar. 22, 1925; s. Samuel S. and Catherine (Hooley) M.; m. Evelyn Irene Whitfield, Feb. 23, 1947; children: Judith Karen, Donna Joyce. D of Ministry, Internat. Bible Inst. and Sem., 1985. Owner, operator M & M Logging, Sweet Home, Oreg., 1952-56; support person Children's Farm Home, Palmer, Alaska, 1956-58; pastor North Pole (Alaska) Assembly of God, 1959-68, Sitka (Alaska) Assembly of God, 1968-78; pioneer pastor Sand Lake Assembly of God, Anchorage, 1978-84; sec., treas. Alaska Dist. Assemblies of God, Anchorage, 1978—, presbyter, 1964—; gen. presbyter Gen. Council Assemblies of God, Springfield, Mo.; exec. presbyter Alaska Assemblies of God, Anchorage, 1978—; exec. dir. Alaska Ch. Builders, 1984—, Revolving Loan Fund, Anchorage, 1984—, Little Beaver Camp, Big Lake, Alaska, 1984-90. Pres. PTA, North Pole, 1964-66. Republican. Avocations: flying, sports, woodworking, gardening. Home: 12630 Galleon Cir Anchorage AK 99515-3652 Office: Alaska Dist Assemblies of God 1048 W Internat Airport Rd # 101 Anchorage AK 99518

MILLER, RAYMOND EDWARD, computer science educator; b. Bay City, Mich., Oct. 9, 1928; s. Martin Theophil and Elizabeth Charlotte (Zierath) M.; m. Marilyn Lueck, June 18, 1955; children: Patricia Ann, Laura Jean, Donna Lyn, Martha Eileen. BS in Mech. Engring., U. Wis., 1950; BEE, U. Ill., 1954, MS in Math., 1955, PhD in Elect. Engring., 1957. Design engr. IBM, Endicott, Poughkeepsie, N.Y., 1950-51; mem. rsch. staff IBM, Yorktown Heights, N.Y., 1957-81; dir., prof. Ga. Inst. Tech., Atlanta, 1980-89, prof. emeritus, 1989—; dir. Ctr. Excellence in Space Data and Info. Scis. NASA, Greenbelt, Md., 1988-93; prof. U. Md., College Park, 1989—; pres. Computing Scis. Accreditation Bd., N.Y.C., 1985-87. Author: Switching Theory, Vols. I and II, 1965; editor: (with J.W. Thatcher) Complexity of Computer Computation, 1972; patentee in field. Lt. USAF, 1951-53. Fellow AAAS, IEEE; Assn. for Computing Machinery, IEEE Computer Soc. (v.p. edn. acts 1991-92). Lutheran. Avocations: tennis, fishing. Office: U Md Dept of Computer Sci A V Williams Bldg College Park MD 20742

MILLER, RAYMOND JARVIS, agronomy educator; b. Claresholm, Alta., Can., Mar. 19, 1934; came to U.S., 1957, naturalized, 1975; s. Charles Jarvis and Wilma Macy (Anderson) M.; m. Frances Anne Davidson, Apr. 28, 1956; children—Cheryl Rae, Jeffrey John, Jay Robert. B.S. (Fed. Provincial grantee 1954-56, Dan Baker scholar 1954-56), U. Alta., Edmonton, 1957; M.S., Wash. State U., 1960; Ph.D., Purdue U., 1962. Mem. faculty N.C. State U., 1962-65, U. Ill., 1965-69; asst. dir., then asso. dir. Ill. Agrl. Expt.

Sta., 1969-73; dir. Idaho Agrl. Expt. Sta., 1973-79; dean U. Idaho Coll. Agr., 1979-85, v.p. for agr.; dean Coll. Agr. and Coll. Life Sci. U. Md., College Park, 1986-89, vice chancellor agr. and natural resources, 1989-91; pres. Md. Inst. for Agrl. and Natural Resources, 1991-93, prof. agronomy, 1986—; internat. expert in areas of agrl. sci. and edn. with spl. emphasis on Russia, former Soviet Union, East Europe. Author numerous papers in field. Pres. Idaho Rsch. Found., 1980-85; bd. govs. Agrl. Rsch. Inst., 1979-80; chmn. legis. subcom. Expt. Sta. Com. on Policy, 1981-82; chmn. bd. div. agr. Land Grant Assn., 1985-86; co-chmn. Nat. Com. Internat. Sci. Edn. Joint Coun., USDA, 1991-94; bd. dirs. C.V. Riley Found., 1985-93; chmn. budget com. Bd. Agr., Nat. Assn. State Univs. and Land Grant Colls., 1993. Grantee Internat. Congress Soil Sci., 1960, Purdue U. Research Found., summers 1960, 61. Fellow AAAS, Am. Soc. Agronomy, Soil Sci. Soc. Am.; mem. Internat. Soc. Soil Sci., Clay and Clay Minerals Soc., Am. Chem. Soc., Am. Soc. Plant Physiolotists, Elks, Lions, Sigma Xi, Phi Kappa Phi, Gamma Sigma Delta, Alpha Zeta. Home: 3319 Gumwood Dr Hyattsville MD 20783-1934 Office: HJ Patterson Hall Univ Md College Park College Park MD 20742

MILLER, REED, lawyer; b. Fairmont, W.Va., Dec. 1, 1918; s. Maurice Entler and Lillian Moore (Reed) M.; m. Emilie Morrison Crawford, Feb. 20, 1943; children: Michael Reed, George Crawford, Richard Clinton. AB, W.Va. U., 1939, LLB, 1941. Bar: W.Va. 1941, N.Y. 1945, D.C. 1946. Assoc. Arnold & Fortas, 1946-47; assoc. Arnold, Fortas & Porter, Washington, 1947-59, ptnr., 1959-65; ptnr. Arnold & Porter, Washington, 1965—; ret., 1995; mem. vis. com. Coll. Law, W.Va. U., 1981-86. Trustee N.Y. Ave. Presbyn. Ch., Washington, 1967-69, 88-91. Served to maj. U.S. Army, 1941-46. Mem. ABA, Fed. Communications Bar Assn. (pres. 1976, mem. exec. com.), Army Navy Country Club (Arlington, Va.), Columbia Country Club, Kenwood Golf and Country Club, Phi Beta Kappa, Beta Theta Pi. Avocation: skiing.

MILLER, REGINALD WAYNE, professional basketball player; b. Riverside, Calif., Aug. 24, 1965. Student, UCLA. Basketball player Indiana Pacers, 1987—. Named to NBA All-Star Team, 1990, 94, Dream Team II, 1994. Holder NBA Playoff record most three-point field goals in one quarter (5), 1994, co-holder NBA Playoff record most three-point field goals in one half (6), 1994, 95. Office: Indiana Pacers 300 E Market St Indianapolis IN 46204*

MILLER, RENE HARCOURT, aerospace engineer, educator; b. Tenafly, N.J., May 19, 1916; s. Arthur C. and Elizabeth M. (Tobin) M.; m. Marcelle Hansotte, July 16, 1948 (div. 1968); children: Christal L., John M.; m. Maureen Michael, Nov. 20, 1973. B.A., Cambridge U., 1937, M.A., 1954. Registered profl. engr., Mass. Aero. engr. G.L. Martin Co., Balt., 1937-39; chief aero. and devel. McDonnell Aircraft Corp., St. Louis, 1939-44; mem. faculty aero. engring. MIT, Cambridge, 1944—, prof., 1957-86, Slater prof. flight transp., 1962-86; head dept. aeros. and astronautics MIT, 1968-78, prof. emeritus, 1986—; v.p. engring. Kaman Aircraft Corp., Bloomfield, Conn., 1952-54; mem. tech. adv. bd. FAA, 1964-66; mem. Aircraft panel Pres.'s Sci. Adv. Com., 1960-72, Army Sci. Adv. Panel, 1966-73; chmn. Army Aviation Sci. Adv. Group, 1963-73; mem. Air Force Sci. Adv. Bd., 1959-70; com. on aircraft aerodynamics NASA, 1960-70. Contbr. articles to profl. jours. Recipient U.S. Army Decoration for Meritorious Civilian Service, 1967, 70; recipient L.B. Laskowitz award N.Y. Acad. Scis., 1976. Fellow Am. Helicopter Soc. (hon. tech. dir. 1957-59, editor jour. 1957-59, Klemin award, Hon. Nikolski lectr. 1983), AIAA (hon., pres. 1977-78, Sylvanus Albert Reed award), Royal Aero. Soc. (Great Britain); mem. Nat. Acad. Engring., Internat. Acad. Astronautics, Academie National de L'Air et de L'Espace France. Home: San Jose New Rd, Penzance Cornwall TR18 4PN, England Office: MIT Dept Aeros and Astronautics 33-411 Cambridge MA 02139

MILLER, REUBEN GEORGE, economics educator; b. Phila., Mar. 28, 1930; s. George and Edna (Fuchs) M.; m. Sylvia Raigla, June 9, 1955. B.A., LaSalle Coll., 1952; diploma, U. Stockholm, 1954; M.A., U. Mont., 1956; Ph.D., Ohio State U., 1966. Asst. instr. Ohio State U., 1954-57; acting asst. prof. Oberlin (Ohio) Coll., 1957-58; asst. prof. U. Mass., Amherst, 1959-67; assoc. prof. econs. Smith Coll., Northampton, Mass., 1967-70; Charles A. Dana prof. econs., chmn. dept. Sweet Briar Coll., 1970—, chmn. div. social scis.; mem. adv. staff Computer Sci. Corp., Washington; cons. Dept. Def.; Fulbright-Hayes lectr. econs. Coll. Law, Nat. Taiwan U., Republic China, 1965-66. Contbr. articles to profl. jours. Am.-Scandinavian Found. fellow, 1952-53; Research Tng. fellow Social Sci. Research Council, 1958-59. Mem. Am. Econ. Assn., Am. Fin. Assn., Royal Econ. Soc. Office: Sweet Briar Coll Dept Econs Sweet Briar VA 24595

MILLER, RICHARD ALAN, lawyer, former merger and acquisition and forest products company executive; b. Cleve., July 29, 1939; s. Joshua Spencer and Martha (Harris) M.; m. Virginia Bell McCully, June 23, 1962; children: Cynthia Lynn (dec.), Alexander James. B.B.A., U. Mich., 1961, J.D., 1964. Bar: Ariz. 1964, Ill. 1989, Wis. 1989, Fla. 1994; lic. real estate broker, Ill., Wis. Assoc. Fennemore, Craig, von Ammon and Udall (now Fennemore Craig), Phoenix, 1964-69; ptnr. Fennemore, Craig, von Ammon and Udall (now Fennemore Craig), 1970-71; exec. v.p. Southwest Forest Industries, Inc., Phoenix, 1972-86; pres., chief exec. officer Knox Lumber Co., St. Paul, 1986; v.p. F.H. Fin. Corp., Milw., 1987-88; owner Hammett, Williams & Miller, Delavan, Wis., 1989-91; of counsel Brennan, Steil, Basting & MacDougall, S.C., Delavan, 1991—. Mem. Ariz. Bar Assn., Ill. Bar Assn, Wis. Bar Assn., Fla. Bar Assn.

MILLER, RICHARD ALAN, economist, educator; b. Springfield, Ohio, Feb. 25, 1931; s. Ross and Beatrice Miller; m. Joan Taylor Walton, July 7, 1956; children: Carol Elizabeth, Jean Anne, Eric Ross. B.A., Oberlin Coll., 1952; M.A., Yale U., 1957; MA (hon.), Wesleyan U., 1972; PhD, Yale U., 1962. Mem. faculty Wesleyan U., Middletown, Conn., 1960—, chmn. dept. econs., 1968-69, 71-73, 75-76, 92-94, Andrews prof., 1995—; vis. lectr. Yale U., New Haven, 1961-62, vis. assoc. prof., 1967-68, vis. prof., 1973, 83, 85, 95; vis. assoc. prof. U. Calif., Berkeley, 1969-70; vis. prof. U. Adelaide, Australia, 1981; vis. lectr econs. U. Conn., Storrs, 1983; economist Econ. Policy Office, Antitrust Div., U.S. Dept. Justice, Washington, 1973-74, cons., 1974-75; cons. antitrust sect. State Conn., 1980, 82; dir. Kawanhee, Inc., Maine, 1975-81, 82-86. Contbr. articles on indsl. orgn. and antitrust econs. to profl. jours. Mem. cert. adv. coun. Dept. Edn., State Conn., 1982-86; mem. coms. Bd. for State Acad. Awards. State Conn., 1978—; dean faculty of Cons. Examiners., 1985-87; trustee Conn. Joint Coun. Econ. Edn., 1982-85. Served to lt. (j.g.) USNR, 1952-55. Ford Found. fellow Yale U., 1958-59; NSF fellow MIT, 1964-65, Wesleyan U., 1965-69; Shelby Cullom Davis Found. grantee Wesleyan U., 1979-82; Fulbright fellow N.Z. Inst. Econ. Research, 1986, 88. Mem. Am. Econs. Assn., Am. Law and Econs. Assn., Indsl. Orgn. Soc., So. Econ. Assn. Congregationalist. Home: 83 Paterson Dr Middletown CT 06457-5138 Office: Wesleyan U Dept Econs Middletown CT 06459

MILLER, RICHARD DWIGHT, professional association executive; b. Topeka, Jan. 21, 1929; s. Amzie Keith and Josephine Amelia (Reese) M.; m. Phyllis Ann Pease, June 11, 1949; children: Rebecca Lynn Miller Shanahan, Susan Kay Barker. BS, Ind. U., 1951, MS, 1958; PhD, Purdue U., 1963. Prin. Jimtown High Sch., Elkhart, Ind., 1958-60; asst. supt. schs. Elkhart Community Schs., 1961-62, supt., 1973-83; asst. supt. schs. Richmond (Ind.) Community Schs., 1962-64; supt. Baugo Community Schs., Elkart, 1964-65, Logansport (Ind.) Community Schs., 1965-69, East Allen County Schs., New Haven, Ind., 1969-73, Elkhart Community Schs., 1973-83; dep. exec. dir. Am. Assn. Sch. Adminstrs., Arlington, Va., 1983-85, exec. dir., 1985-94. Served to sgt. U.S. Army, 1952-54. Mem. Am. Soc. Assn. Execs., Am. Assn. Sch. Adminstrs. (pres. 1980-81), Greater Washington Soc. Assn. Exec. *

MILLER, RICHARD HAMILTON, lawyer, broadcasting company executive; b. Cleve., July 18, 1931; s. Ray Thomas and Ruth (Hamilton) M.; m. Ernestine Bowman, Aug. 25, 1985; children: James M., Suanne R., Elizabeth M., Judith K., William P., Matthew W. A.B., U. Notre Dame, 1953, J.D., 1955. Bar: Ohio 1955. Since practiced in Cleve. as mem. firm Miller & Miller; asst. prosecutor Cuyahoga County, 1957-60; pres. Cleve. Broadcasting, Inc., 1966-70, Searles Lake Chem. Corp., Los Angeles, 1966-69, Miller Broadcasting Co., Cleve., 1970-87, Hollywood Bldg. Systems, Inc., Meridian, Miss., 1974-86; mng. partner Miller & Co., Cleve., 1974—; former owner, dir. Cleve. Profl. Basketball Co., Cleve. Baseball, Inc. Dir. gen. counsel Mail Marketing Inc., 1974—, R.W. Sidley, Inc., 1966—; gen. chmn. N.E. Ohio March of Dimes, 1971-73; adv. council Catherine Horstman Home Retarded Children, 1969-73; mem. Cuyahoga Democratic Exec. Com., 1955-66. Served to capt. AUS, 1956-57. Named Irishman of the Yr., City Counsel of Cleve., 1995. Mem. Ohio, Cuyahoga County, Cleve. bar assns., Cleve. Citizens League. Clubs: K.C. (Cleve.), Variety (Cleve.), Notre Dame (Cleve.) (pres. 1964-65), Cleve. Athletic (Cleve.) (dir. 1971-74); Shaker Heights (Ohio) Country. Office: The Park 1700 E 13th St Ste 20T Cleveland OH 44114-3238

MILLER, RICHARD IRWIN, education educator, university administrator; b. Fairbury, Nebr., Feb. 1, 1924; s. Carl W. and Iva Mae (Wilburn) M.; m. Peggy J. McLaren, June 25, 1955; children: Joan Marie, Diane Lee, Janine Louise. B.S., U. Nebr., 1947; M.Ed., Springfield Coll., 1948; Ed.D., Columbia U., 1958. Instr. Pa. State U., 1957-58; observer UN, 1958-60; assoc. dir. project on instrn. NEA, 1960-63; assoc. dir. Ctr. Study of Instrn., 1963-64; prof. edn. U. Ky., Lexington, 1964-69, chmn. dept. social philosophy Founds. in Edn., 1967-69, dir. program for ednl. change, 1964-69; v.p. acad. affairs, dean Baldwin-Wallace Coll., Berea, Ohio, 1970-72; assoc. dir. Ill. Bd. Higher Edn., Springfield, 1972-77; prof. higher edn., v.p. for ednl. services SUNY, Brockport, 1977-80; vis. fellow Cornell U., Ithaca, N.Y., 1980-81; v.p. for acad. affairs, prof. S.W. Tex. State U., San Marcos, 1981-84; prof., coordinator higher edn. Ohio U., Athens, 1984—; ednl. advisor ABA, 1959-63; mem. adv. bd. Ctr. for Info. on Am., 1965-70; dir. nat. evaluation program Elem. and Secondary Edn. Act Title III, 1967-68; exec. sec. Pres.'s Nat. Adv. Council Supplementary Ctrs. and Services, 1968-69; cons. Com. Econ. Devel., U.S. Office Edn., 1967-70; cons. edn. Mead Ednl. Service, Inc. div. Mead Corp., also coordinator spl. ednl. seminars. Author: Dag Hammarskjod and Crisis Diplomacy, 1961, Education in a Changing Society, 1963, Teaching About Communism, 1966; editor: (with Ole Sand) Schools for the Sixties, 1963, ESEA Title III: Catalyst for Change, 1967, The Nongraded School, 1968, Perspectives on Educational Change, 1967, Evaluating Faculty Performance, 1972, Developing Programs for Faculty Evaluation, 1974, Assessment of College Performance, 1979, Institutional Assessment for Self-Improvement, 1981, Evaluating Faculty for Promotion and Tenure, 1987, (with Ed Holzapfel) Issues in Personnel Management, 1988; editor: Evaluating Major Components in Two-Year Colleges, 1988, Major American Higher Education Issues and Challenges in the Nineties, 1990; editor, chpt. contbr.: Applying the Deming Method to Higher Education, 1991. Served with USAF, 1942-43. Recipient Nat. Pacesetter award in edn. Nat. Coun. Supplementary Ctrs. and Svcs., 1968, Kathryn G. Moore award Coll. and Personnel Assn., 1994. Mem. Am. Assn. Higher Edn. (nat. planning group), Nat. Council Social Studies (research council 1967-70), Am. Assn. Univ. Adminstrs. (bd. dirs. 1972), Phi Delta Kappa. Presbyn. Club: Cosmos (Washington). Lodge: Rotary. Home: 17 Briarwood Dr Athens OH 45701-1302

MILLER, RICHARD JEROME, bank executive; b. Erie, Pa., May 8, 1939; s. Richard A. and Irene (Strahl) M.; children by previous marriage: Edward Scott, Lisa Ann, Sondra Lynn; m. Suzanne Marie Johnson, Oct. 22, 1983. BS, Lehigh U., 1961; MA, New Sch. N.Y.C., 1964; postgrad. NYU, 1964-68. With Chase Manhattan Bank, N.Y.C., 1961-82, v.p., 1974-82; v.p. E.F. Hutton Credit Corp./Chrysler Capital Corp., Greenwich, Conn., 1982-88, The CIT Group, N.Y.C., 1988-90; dir. Miller/Davis & Assocs., N.Y.C., 1991—; v.p. Nat. Westminster Bank, N.Y.C., 1991—. Mem. Waldwick Bd. Edn., N.J., 1968-72, v.p., 1971-72; pres. Columbia Condominium. Mem. Am. Econ. Assn., Western Fin. Assn., Fin. Mgmt. Assn. Republican. Roman Catholic. Office: Miller/Davis & Assocs 60 E 42nd St Ste 1440 New York NY 10165-2199

MILLER, RICHARD KEITH, engineering educator; b. Fresno, Calif., June 12, 1949; s. Albert Keith and Gloria Mae (Pittman) M.; m. Elizabeth Ann Parrish, July 10, 1971; children: Katherine Elizabeth, Julia Anne. BS in Aerospace Engring., U. Calif., Davis, 1971; MS in Mech. Engring., MIT, 1972; PhD in Applied Mechanics, Calif. Inst. Tech., Pasadena, 1976. Asst. prof. mech. engring. U. Calif., Santa Barbara, 1975-79; assoc. prof. civil engring. U. So. Calif., L.A., 1979-85, prof., 1985-92, assoc. dean engring., 1989-92; prof., dean Coll. Engring., U. Iowa, 1992—; cons. Astro Aerospace Corp., The Aerospace Corp., Jet Propulsion Lab. Contbr. numerous articles to sci. and profl. jours. Mem. ASCE, Am. Soc. Engring. Edn. Office: U Iowa Coll Engring Office of Dean 3100 EB Iowa City IA 52242-1527

MILLER, RICHARD KIDWELL, artist, actor, educator; b. Fairmont, W.Va., Mar. 15, 1930; s. Maurice Entler and Lillian (Reed) M.; m. Teresa Marie Robinson, Apr. 27, 1957. Student, Pa. Acad. Fine Arts, 1948-49; BA, Am. U., Washington, 1953; MFA, Columbia U., 1956. Instr. painting Scarsdale (N.Y.) Community Sch., 1970-75; asst. prof. Kansas City Art Inst., 1968-69. Participated extensively in profl. theater as actor and singer including roles in Broadway Prodn. Baker Street; actor stock cos. including Fiddler on the Roof; one man art shows include Trans-Lux Gallery, Washington, 1951, Bader Gallery, Washington, 1954, Balt. Mus. Art, 1955, Graham Gallery Ltd., N.Y.C., 1960, 62, 65, Argas Gallery, Madison, N.J., 1966, Jefferson Place Gallery, Washington, 1966, Albrecht Gallery Art, St. Joseph, Mo., 1969, L.I. U., 1973, Aaron Berman Gallery N.Y.C., 1983, Westbeth Gallery, N.Y.C., 1982; group shows include Corcoran Gallery Art., 1950-51, 53, Pa. Acad. Fine Arts, 1951, 64, Carnegie Internat., 1961, Salon de National, Paris, 1954, Whitney Mus., 1958, U. Nebr., 1963, Martha Jackson Gallery, N.Y.C., 1973, Nat. Acad. Design, N.Y.C., 1996, Art of the Northeast, New Caanan, Conn., 1996, others; represented in permanent collections Hirshorn Mus. and Sculpture Garden, Washington, Phillips Collection, Washington, Rochester Mus. Art, Albrecht Gallery U. Ariz., also numerous private collections; featured in Jan. edit. Am. Artist Mag., 1988, Christian Sci. Monitor, 1990,, World Artists (Claude Marks), 1991. Washington Times Herald scholar, 1944, 45, 46; Gertrude Whitney scholar, 1948-53, 55-56; Fulbright fellow, 1953-54. Address: 222 West 83d St Apt 8C New York NY 10024 *I have an insatiable need to express myself—I suppose I was born with it. I was given more than one talent to satisfy this need, and for that I thank God. I have endeavored to use these talents to the absolute best of my ability. I can do no more than that. Some times I have succeeded, and many times I have failed, but the real joy and meaning is in the doing. All the pain has been worth it.*

MILLER, RICHARD L., architectural executive; b. Salina, Kans., Jan. 31, 1941; s. L. William and Inez Corine (DeMars) M.; m. Sharalena Miller, June 22, 1963; children: Lora Miller Vinson, Scott Miller. Student, Kansas Wesleyan U., 1959-61; BArch, U. Kans., 1966, postgrad., 1966-67. Registered architect, 38 states and V.I. Assoc. Earl Swensson Assocs., Nashville, 1967-73, pres., 1973—; mem. hosp. licensure task force State of Tenn. Dept. Pub. Health, 1975, Ambulatory Surg. Treatment Ctr. Act Task Force, 1976-77, SCARAB, Hon. Archtl. Frat., Nursing Home Task Force, 1977-78; participant Internat. Pub. Health Seminar, Budapest, 1984; speaker Fla. HRS seminars, 1986, 90; mem. ann. faculty health care forum on health facilities design, 1990; speaker numerous confs. in field, including World Workplace, 1995, NeoCon '95 World's Trade Fair, 1995, Health Facility Inst. Fifth Ann. Conf., 1994. Co-author: New Directions in Hospital and Healthcare Facility Design, 1995. Mem. Leadership Nashville, 1993-94. Mem. Am. Inst. Architects (mem. com. architecture for health 1980), Tenn. Soc. Architects (mem. ad hoc fire com. 1975). Mem. Christian Ch. Avocations: golfing, kite flying, sailing. Office: Earl Swensson Assocs 2100 W End Ave Ste 1200 Nashville TN 37203-5225

MILLER, RICHARD MCDERMOTT, sculptor; b. New Philadelphia, Ohio, Apr. 30, 1922; s. J. Harry and Clela Belle (McDermott) M.; m. Audrey F. Miller, 1942; 1 dau., Sue Ann (Mrs. Kenneth Hartz); m. Gloria B. Bley, Mar. 18, 1961. Student, Cleve. Inst. Art, 1940-42, 49-51. Prof. emeritus Queens Coll., CUNY. One man shows include Peridot Gallery, N.Y.C., 1964, 66, 67, 69, Washburn Gallery, N.Y.C., 1971, 74, 75, 77, Canton (Ohio) Art Inst., 1980, 20-yr. retrospective Artists Choice Mus., N.Y.C., 1984, Springfield (Mo.) Mus. Art, 1985, Friends of Figurative Sculpture Gallery, N.Y.C., 1987-94, Philharm. Ctr., Naples, Fla., 1991; represented in numerous pub. and pvt. collections; author: Figure Sculpture in Wax and Plaster, 1971. Served with AUS, 1942-46. Mem. NAD (pres. 1989-92), Sculptors Guild, Nat. Sculpture Soc., Century Assn. Address: 53 Mercer St New York NY 10013-2617

MILLER, RICHARD SHERWIN, legal educator; b. Boston, Dec. 11, 1930; s. Max and Mollie (Kruger) M.; m. Doris Sheila Lunchick, May 24, 1956; children: Andrea Jayne Armitage, Matthew Harlan. B.S.B.A., Boston U., 1951, J.D. magna cum laude, 1956; LL.M., Yale U., 1959. Bar: Mass. 1956, Mich. 1961, Hawaii 1977. Pvt. practice law Boston, 1956-58; assoc. prof. law Wayne State U., Detroit, 1959-62, prof., 1962-65; prof. Ohio State U., Columbus, 1965-73, dir. clin. and interdisciplinary program, 1971-73; prof. U. Hawaii, Honolulu, 1973-95, prof. emeritus, 1995—, dean, 1981-84; vis. prof. law USIA/U. Hawaii, Hiroshima U. Affiliation Program, Japan, fall 1986, Victoria U., Wellington, N.Z., spring 1987; del. Hawaii State Jud. Conf., 1989-92. Author: Courts and the Law: An Introduction to our Legal System, 1980; editor: (with Roland Stanger) Essays on Expropriations, 1967; editor-in-chief: Boston U. Law Rev., 1955-56; contbr. articles to profl. jours. Mem. Hawaii Substance Abuse Task Force, 1994-95. 1st lt. USAF, 1951-53. Sterling-Ford fellow Yale U., 1958-59; named Lawyer of Yr. Japan-Hawaii Lawyers Assn., 1990. Mem. ABA, Hawaii State Bar Assn., Hawaii ACLU, Am. Inn of Ct. IV (founding mem., master of the bench), Am. Law Inst., Honolulu Cmty-Media Coun. (pres. 1994—). Office: U Hawaii Richardson Sch Law 2515 Dole St Honolulu HI 96822-2328

MILLER, RICHARD STEVEN, lawyer; b. Mt. Vernon, N.Y., Dec. 5, 1951; s. Norman and Mildred (Curtis) M. BA, U. Pa., 1974; JD, NYU, 1977. Bar: N.Y. 1978, U.S. Dist. Ct. (so. and ea. dists.) N.Y. 1978, U.S. Ct. Appeals (2d cir.) 1978. Asst. dist. atty. Kings County, N.Y., 1977-79; with Hahn & Hessen, N.Y.C., 1979-82, Levin & Weintraub & Crames, N.Y.C., 1982-87; counsel, then ptnr. Rogers & Wells, N.Y.C., 1987-91; ptnr. Dewey Ballantine, N.Y.C., 1991—. Mem. ABA, Internat. Bar Assn., Am. Bankruptcy Inst. Office: Dewey Ballantine 1301 Avenue Of The Americas New York NY 10019-6022

MILLER, RICHARD ULRIC, business and industrial relations educator; b. N.Y.C., Sept. 6, 1932; s. Luther Cedric and Frances Elizabeth (Wells) M.; m. Louise Elaine O'Donnell, Jan. 6, 1954; children: Elizabeth Louise, Richard Christopher. B.B.A. cum laude, U. Miami, Coral Gables, Fla., 1958; M.S., Cornell U., 1960, Ph.D., 1966. Instr. U. Ariz., Tucson, 1960-62; asst. prof. SUNY-Buffalo, 1965-66; vis. prof. U. Tex., Austin, 1971-72; from asst. prof. to prof. bus. and indsl. relations U. Wis.-Madison, 1966-94; assoc. dean. sch. bus. U. Wis., Madison, 1994—; now assoc. dean masters program U. Wis. School of Bus., Madison; dir. Indsl. Rels. Rsch. Inst., 1973-77, 90-93; arbitrator Am. Arbitration Assn., Fed. Mediation and Conciliation Svc., Wis. Employment Rels. Commn., 1978—. Co-author: Collective Bargaining in Hospitals, 1978, Labor Relations in Urban Transit, 1977, Canadian Labour in Transition, 1971. Served with USN, 1951-55. Doherty fellow, 1964; Latin Am. studies fellow Cornell U., 1965. Mem. Indsl. Relations Research Assn. (sec.-treas. 1973-77), Phi Kappa Phi, Beta Gamma Sigma. Office: U Wis Grad Sch Bus 4106 Grainger Hall 975 University Ave Madison WI 53706-1324

MILLER, RITA, personnel consultant, diecasting company executive; b. Bklyn., Jan. 15, 1925; d. Joseph and Etta M.; BA, Bklyn. Coll., 1947; MA, Boston U., 1949; children: Erika Greenwald, Roy Barnet Glickman. Personnel officer, sec. to pres. Marine Elec. Corp., Bklyn., 1943-47; script writer Song Debut, Boston, 1949-50; dir. Writers' Workshops, interviewer pub. opinion surveys, New Rochelle, N.Y., 1962-64; mgr. employee relations Dynacast div. Coats & Clark, Inc., Yorktown Heights, 1966-89. Mem. Am. Soc. Personnel Adminstrn., Westchester Personnel Mgmt. Assn. (dir.), Personnel Council New Rochelle, Bus. and Profl. Women U.S.A., Nat. Sociology Hon. Soc. Editor: The Management Consultant (George Kenning), 1965; contbr. articles to profl. jours. Home: 16 Congress St New Rochelle NY 10801-1902

MILLER, ROBERT, advertising executive; b. N.Y.C., June 2, 1923; s. Samuel and Adele (Elswit) M.; m. Frances Fitzgerald, June 10, 1944 (dec. 1978); children: Marc Robert, William Fitzgerald, Daniel Bates, Ellen Minette (Mrs. John Meyer); m. Sandra Gold Patelmo, 1980. Student, NYU, 1940-42, Syracuse U., 1943. Newsroom employee N.Y. Daily Mirror, 1942; with Miller Advt. Agy., Inc., N.Y.C., 1946—, v.p., 1948-54, chmn. bd., 1954-57, pres., 1958—; pres. Miller Advt. Service Corp., 1956-62; pres. Miller Advt. Agy. Ill., Inc., 1965-73, also bd. dirs.; bd. dirs. Hereford Ins. Co., Inc., 1988-94. Contbg. editor Madison Avenue mag., 1975-78. Bd. govs. Roslyn Democratic Club, 1957-61, 68-73; mem. Nassau County Dem. Com., 1958-61, 68-73; Bd. dirs. Shalom Peace Found. Served to 1st lt. USAAF, 1942-46. Mem. Am. Legion. Home: 301 E 52nd St New York NY 10022-6319 also: 17 Shelly Dr Ellenville NY 12428-1809 Office: Miller Advt Agy Inc 71 Fifth Ave New York NY 10003-3004

MILLER, ROBERT ALLEN, hotel executive; b. Chgo., Nov. 26, 1945; s. Jerome David and Leah Ester (Pollack) M.; m. Diana Marie Hall, Dec. 29, 1967; children: David, Allison, Brian. BSBA, U. Fla., 1967. CPA, Fla. Auditor, acct. Arthur Young & Co., Tampa, Fla., 1967-72; chief fin. officer Fleetwing Corp., Lakeland, Fla., 1972-78; pres. Am. Resorts Corp., Lakeland, 1978-84; v.p. Marriott Corp., Bethesda, Md., 1984—. Office: Marriott Ownership Resorts PO Box 890 Lakeland FL 33802-0890

MILLER, ROBERT ARTHUR, state supreme court chief justice; b. Aberdeen, S.D., Aug. 28, 1939; s. Edward Louis and Bertha Leone (Hitchcox) M.; m. Shirlee Ann Schlim, Sept. 5, 1964; children: Catherine Sue, Scott Edward, David Alan, Gerri Elizabeth, Robert Charles. BSBA, U. S.D., 1961, JD, 1963. Asst. atty. gen. State of S.D., Pierre, 1963-65; pvt. practice law Philip, S.D., 1965-71; state atty. Haakon County, Philip, 1965-71; city atty. City of Philip, 1965-71; judge State of S.D. (6th cir.), Pierre, 1971-86, presiding judge, 1975-86; justice S.D. Supreme Ct., Pierre, 1986—, now chief justice; bd. dirs. Nat. Conf. of Chief Justices; trustee S.D. Retirement Sys., Pierre, 1974-85, chmn., 1982-85; mem. faculty S.D. Law Enforcement Tng. Acad., 1975-85. Mem. S.D. State Crime Commn., 1979-86; mem. adv. commn. S.D. Sch. for the Deaf, 1983-85, Communications Svcs. to Deaf, 1990—; cts. counselor S.D. Boy's State, 1986—. Mem. State Bar of S.D., S.D. Judges' Assn. (pres. 1974-75). Roman Catholic. Lodge: Elks. Avocations: golf, hunting. Office: SD Supreme Ct 500 E Capitol Ave Pierre SD 57501-5070*

MILLER, ROBERT BRANSON, JR., retired newspaper publisher; b. Battle Creek, Mich., Aug. 10, 1935; s. Robert Branson and Jean (Leonard) M.; m. Patricia E. Miller; children: Melissa Ann, Gregory Allen, Jennifer Lynn, Jeffrey William. Grad., Hotchkiss Sch., Lakeville, Conn., 1953; BA, Mich. State U., 1959. Advt. salesman State Jour., Lansing, Mich., 1959-61; circulation sales rep. State Jour., 1961-62, reporter, 1962-65, nat. advt. mgr., 1965-66; asst. to pub. Idaho Statesman, Boise, 1966-69, pub., 1971-79; pub. Daily Olympian, Olympia, Wash., 1969-71; pub. Battle Creek Enquirer, 1979-90, chmn., 1990-91. Mem. adv. bd. Battle Creek chpt. ARC, Big Bros./Big Sisters, Neighborhoods Inc.; sr. advisor United Way; trustee Cheff Ctr. for Handicapped, Miller Found., Battle Creek. With USNR, 1956-58.

MILLER, ROBERT CARL, library director; b. May 9, 1936. BS in History and Philosophy, Marquette U., 1958; MS in Am. History, U. Wis., 1962; MA in Libr. Sci., U. Chgo., 1966. Head telephone reference Library of Congress, Wash., 1959-60; reference librarian Marquette U., Milw., 1960-62, acquisition librarian, 1962-66; head tech. services/librarian Parsons Coll., Fairfield, Iowa, 1966-68; head acquisitions dept. U. of Chgo. Library, Ill., 1968-71; assoc. dir (reader services) U. of Chgo. Library, 1971-73; assoc dir (gen. service) U. of Chgo., 1973-75; dir. of libraries U. Mo., St. Louis, 1975-78; dir of libraries U. of Notre Dame, Ind., 1978—; vis. prof. IBIN-U. Warsaw, Poland, 1992, 93. Contbr. to prof. jour. Fellow Woodrow Wilson Found. (sr.), Coun. on Libr. Resources; mem. ALA, Polish Inst. of Arts and Letters of Am. Roman Catholic. Home: 17650 Tanager Ln South Bend IN 46635-1315 Office: U Notre Dame U Library 221 Theodore M Hesburgh Notre Dame IN 46556

MILLER, ROBERT CARMI, JR., microbiology educator, university administrator; b. Elgin, Ill., Aug. 10, 1942; s. Robert C. and Melba I. (Steinke) M.; m. Patricia A. Black, Aug. 29, 1964; children: Geoffrey T., Christopher J. BS in Physics, Trinity Coll., Hartford, Conn., 1964; MS in Biophysics, Pa. State U., 1965; PhD in Molecular Biology, U. Pa., 1969. USPHS trainee U. Pa., Phila., 1966-69; postdoctoral fellow U. Wis., Madison, 1969-70; rsch. assoc., Am. Cancer Soc. postdoctoral fellow MIT, Cambridge, 1970-71; asst. assoc. prof. U. B.C., Vancouver, 1971-79, prof. microbiology, 1980—, head dept. microbiology, 1982-85, dean sci., 1985-88, v.p. rsch., 1988-95, univ. senate, 1985-88; assoc. vice provost for rsch., dir. technology transfer U. Wash., Seattle, 1995—; vis. prof. Inst. Molecular Biology, U. Geneva, Switzerland, 1976; mem. grants com. on genetics Med. Rsch. Coun., 1980-82; mem. Grants Panel A Nat. Cancer Inst., 1981-85; biotech. com. B.C. Sci. Coun., 1981-87, univ./industry program grant com., 1987-92; biotech. com. Med. Rsch. Coun., 1983; assoc. com. for biotech. NRC, 1983-86; strategic grant com. biotech. NSERC, 1985-87; bd. dirs. Paprican, Discovery Found., Sci. Coun. B.C., TRIUMF. Assoc. editor Virology, 1974-85, Jour. Virology, 1975-84; contbr. 100 articles to profl. jours.; author research papers. Recipient gold medal Nat. Sci. Coun. B.C., 1993; grantee Natural Sci. and Engring. Rsch. Coun., 1971—, Med. Rsch. Coun., 1981, 86-89, Nat. Cancer Inst., 1982-86. Office: Office Technology Transfer Univ Wash 1107 NE 45th St Seattle WA 98105

MILLER, ROBERT CHARLES, retired physicist; b. State College, Pa., Feb. 2, 1925; s. Lawrence P. Miller and Eva Mae (Gross) Wiedemann; m. Virginia Callaghan, Aug. 30, 1952; children: Robin Kingon Storey, Jeffrey Lawrence Miller, Lauren Wray Lynch. AB, Columbia U., 1948, MA, 1952, PhD, 1956. Staff mem. Johns-Manville Research Ctr., Finderne, N.J., 1948-49; teaching asst. in physics Columbia U., N.Y.C., 1949-51, lectr. in physics, 1951-53; mem. tech. staff Bell Telephone Labs., Murray Hill, N.J., 1954-63, head solid state spectroscopy research dept., 1963-67; staff mem. Inst. Defense Analyses, Arlington, Va., 1967-68; head optical elec. research dept. Bell Telephone Labs., Murray Hill, 1968-77; mem. tech. staff AT&T Bell Labs., Murray Hill, 1977-84, disting. mem. tech. staff, 1984-88, ret., 1988; cons. Office of Sec. Def., Arlington, Va., 1968-75. Inventor (with Dr. J.A. Giordmaine) Optical Parametric Oscillator, 1965 (co-recipient R.W. Wood prize, 1986); contbr. articles to profl. jours. Served with U.S. Army, 1943-46, ETO. RCA predoctoral fellow Columbia U., 1953-54. Fellow Am. Phys. Soc.; mem. AAAS, N.Y. Acad. Scis., Sigma Xi. Avocations: sailing, sports cars, tennis. Home: 65 Eaton Ct Cotuit MA 02635-2908

MILLER, ROBERT DANIEL, lawyer; b. Houston, May 3, 1960; s. Robert Thomas and Joyce (Danielson) M.; m. Lisa Anne Davis, May 23, 1987. BA, Rice U., 1982; JD, U. Tex., Austin, 1985. Bar: Tex. 1985. Legis. aide Senator Don Henderson, Austin, Tex., 1983; assoc. Liddell, Sapp, Zivley, Hill & LaBoon, L.L.P., Houston, 1985-91, ptnr., 1992—; sec., treas. Com. for Jud. Merit Election, Tex., 1987-89. Chmn. Battleship Tex. Adv. Bd., 1988-92; mem. fin. com. Houston Conv. Fund, 1991-95, Leadership Houston Class X, 1991-92; bd. dirs. Citizens Commn. on Tex. Judiciary, 1991-95, Greater Houston Preservation Alliance, 1994—, Tex. Lyceum, 1994—, Vote Tex., 1995—, Met. Transit Authority, 1996—. Named one of Five Outstanding Young Houstonians, Jaycees, 1992. Mem. State Bar Tex., Houston Bar Assn., Tex. Assn. Bank Counsel, Houston Club, Order of Coif, Phi Delta Phi, Omicron Delta Epsilon. Republican. Office: Liddell Sapp Zivley Hill & LaBoon LLP 3400 Texas Commerce Twr Houston TX 77002

MILLER, ROBERT EARL, engineer, educator; b. Rockford, Ill., Oct. 4, 1932; s. Leslie D. and Marcia V. (Jones) M. B.S., U. Ill., 1954, M.S., 1955, Ph.D., 1959. Asst. prof. theoretical and applied mechanics U. Ill., Urbana, 1959-61; asso. prof. U. Ill., 1961-68, prof., 1968-94, prof. emeritus, 1994—; cons. in field to industry U.S. Army; in various positions in industry, summers, 1963-68. Contbr. articles to profl. jours. Mem. AIAA, Am. Soc. Engring. Edn. (Disting. Engring. award 1991), ASCE. Office: U Ill 216 Talbot Lab 104 S Wright St Urbana IL 61801-2935

MILLER, ROBERT FRANCIS, physiologist, educator; b. Eugene, Oreg., Nov. 30, 1939; s. Irvin Lavere and Ettie (Graham) M.; m. Rosemary F. Fish, June 12, 1968; children: Derek, Drew. MD, U. Utah, 1967. Head neurophysiology Naval Aerospace Med. Rsch. Lab., Pensacola, Fla., 1969-71; asst. prof. physiology SUNY, Buffalo, 1971-76, assoc. prof. physiology, 1976-78; assoc. prof. ophthalmology Washington U. Sch. Medicine, St. Louis, 1978-83, prof. ophthalmology, 1983-88; 3M Cross prof., head physiology dept. U. Minn., Mpls., 1988—; Mem. VISA 2 NEI study sect. NIH, 1986—. Mem. editorial bd. Jour. Neurophysiology, 1986—. Lt. comdr. USN, 1969-71. Recipient Merit award NIH, 1988, award for med. rsch. Upjohn, 1967, Rsch. to Prevent Blindness Sr. Scientists award, 1988; James S. Adams scholar, 1982, Robert E. McCormick scholar, 1977-78. Mem. AAAS, Assn. Rsch. in Vision and Ophthalmology, Assn. Chmn. Depts. Physiology, N.Y. Acad. Scis., Neurosci. Soc. Achievements include discovery of major new excitatory amino acid receptor, discovery that the electroretinogram in generated by glia. Home: 4613 Golf Ter Edina MN 55424-1512 Office: U Minn Dept Physiology 6-255 MIllard Hall 435 Delaware St SE Minneapolis MN 55455-0347

MILLER, ROBERT FRANK, retired electronics engineer, educator; b. Milw., Mar. 30, 1925; s. Frank Joseph and Evangeline Elizabeth (Hamann) M.; m. La Verne Boyle, Jan. 10, 1948 (dec. 1978); children: Patricia Ann, Susan Barbara, Nancy Lynn; m. Ruth Winifred Drobnic, July 26, 1980. BSEE, U. Wis., 1947, MSEE, 1954, PhD in Elec. Engring., 1957. Profl. engr., Wis. Instr. physics Milw. Sch. Engring., 1949-53; sr. engr. semicondr. Delco Electronics/GMC, Kokomo, Ind., 1957-67, asst. chief engr., 1967-70, mgr. product assurance, 1970-73, dir. quality control, 1973-85; asst. prof. elec. engring. tech. Purdue U., Kokomo, 1986-90; ret., 1990; ind. cons., Kokomo, 1990—; mem. Ind. Microelectronics Commn., Indpls., 1987—. Author tech. papers; co-author lab. manuals. Bd. dirs. Howard Community Hosp. Found., Kokomo, 1974—; trustee YMCA, Kokomo, 1990—, bd. dirs., 1967-90. Named Disting. Alumnus U. Wis., Madison, 1980, 90. Mem. IEEE (life), Am. Soc. Quality Control (bd. dirs. sect. 0918, advisor Cen. Ind. sect. bd. 1988—), Sigma Xi, Tau Beta Pi, Phi Kappa Phi, Eta Kappa Nu. Presbyterian. Home: 3201 Susan Dr Kokomo IN 46902-7506

MILLER, ROBERT G., retail company executive; b. 1944. With Albertson's Inc., 1961-89, exec. v.p. retail ops., 1989-91; chmn. bd., CEO Fred Meyer Inc., Portland, Oreg., 1991—. Office: Fred Meyer Inc 3800 SE 22nd Ave Portland OR 97202-2918*

MILLER, ROBERT H., university extension director; b. Fremont, Wis., Sept. 19, 1933; married, 1957; 3 children. BS, Wis. State U., 1958; MS, U. Minn., 1961, PhD in Soil Microbiology, 1964. From asst. to full prof. agronomy Ohio State U., 1964-81; head and prof. dept. soil sci. N.C. State U., 1982-89; dean coll. of resource devel. U. R.I., Kingston, 1989-95, dir. coop. extension, 1995—; Fulbright lectr., 1974-75. Fellow AAAS, Am. Soc. Agronomy (bd. dirs. 1978-81), Soil Sci. Soc. Am.. (bd. dirs. 1978-81); mem. Am. Soc. Microbiology, Sigma Xi. Achievements include research on plant rhizosphere microorganisms and their interactions with plants; ecology and physiology of Rhizobium japonicum; chemistry of soil organic matter; recycling of organic wastes in soil; international development. Office: U RI Cooperative Extension Kingston RI 02881

MILLER, ROBERT HAROLD, otolaryngologist, educator; b. Columbia, Mo., July 2, 1947; s. Harold Oswald and Ruth Nadine (Ballew) M.; m. Martha Guillory, Apr. 18, 1981; children: Morgan Guillory, Reed Thurston. BS in Biology, Tulane U., 1969, MD, 1973; cert. in otolaryngology-head/neck surg., UCLA Med. Ctr., 1978; MBA, Tulane U., 1996. Diplomate Am. Bd. Otolaryngology. From asst. prof. to assoc. prof. otolaryngology-HNS Baylor Coll. Medicine, Houston, 1978-87; prof., chmn. otolaryngology-HNS Tulane Sch. Medicine, New Orleans, 1987—; bd. dirs. Am. Bd. Otolaryngology; chief of staff Tulane Hosp., 1995—. Mem. editl. bd. Archives of Otolaryngology, 1986—, Head & Neck Surgery, 1987—. Named Outstanding Young Man, Houston C. of C., 1980. Fellow ACS, Am. Soc. Head & Neck Surgery, Am. Acad. Oto-Head & Neck Surgery (Disting. Svc. award 1994, Honor award 1991), Triological Soc. (exec. sec. 1992—). Avocations: tennis, computers. Home: 205 Brockenbraugh Ct Metairie LA 70005-3319 Office: Tulane U Sch Medicine 1430 Tulane Ave New Orleans LA 70112-2699

MILLER, ROBERT HASKINS, retired state chief justice; b. Columbus, Ohio, Mar. 3, 1919; s. George L. and Marian Alice (Haskins) M.; m. Audene Fausett, Mar. 14, 1943; children: Stephen F., Thomas G., David W., Stacey Ann (dec.). A.B., Kans. U., 1940, LL.B., 1942; grad., Nat. Coll. State Trial Judges, Phila., 1967. Bar: Kans. 1943. Practice in Paola, 1946-60; judge 6th Jud. Dist. Kans., Paola, 1961-69; U.S. magistrate Kans. Dist., Kansas City, 1969-75; justice Kans. Supreme Ct., Topeka, 1975-88, chief justice, 1988-90, ret., 1990; chmn. Kans. Jud. Coun., 1987-88. Contbg. author: Pattern (Civil Jury) Instructions for Kansas, 2d edit, 1969. Served with AUS, 1942-46. Mem. Kans. Bar Assn., Wyandotte County Bar Assn., Shawnee County Bar Assn., Am. Legion, Phi Gamma Delta, Phi Delta Phi. Presbyterian. Office: Supreme Ct Kans-Jud Ctr 301 SW 10th Ave Topeka KS 66612-1502

MILLER, ROBERT HENRY, English educator; b. Defiance, Ohio, Aug. 10, 1938; s. Richard Carl and Elizabeth Jane (Sowers) M.; m. Diane Sue Partee, June 5, 1960; children: Rebecca, Rachel, Amy. BA, Bowling Green State U., 1960, MA, 1961; PhD, Ohio State U., 1968. Instr. Mich. Tech. U., 1961-64; prof., chmn. Renaissance lit. and culture, modern novel U. Louisville, 1968—. Author: Understanding Graham Greene, 1990, Handbook of Literary Research, 1987, 95; editor: Harington's Catalogue of Bishops, 1979; contbr. poems to poetry mags. and articles to scholarly mags. Mem. AAUP, MLA, ACLU. Democrat. Roman Catholic. Avocations: fishing, baseball, bicycling. Home: 2440 Saratoga Dr Louisville KY 40205-2023 Office: U Louisville Dept English Louisville KY 40292

MILLER, ROBERT JAMES, educational association administrator; b. Mansfield, Ohio, Jan. 27, 1926; s. Dennis Cornelius and Mabel (Snyder) M.; m. Jerri Ann Burran, June 5, 1952; children: Robert James Jr., Dennis Burran. Student, Heidelberg Coll., 1946-47; BS, U. N.Mex., 1950, MA, 1952; postgrad., Miami U., Oxford, Ohio, 1951-55; MBA, Fla. Atlantic U., 1978. Asst. exec. sec. Phi Delta Theta Hdqrs., Oxford, 1951-54, adminstrv. sec., 1954-55, exec. v.p., 1955-91; pres. Phi Delta Theta Found., Oxford, 1984—; bus. mgr. The Scroll, Oxford, 1955-91; dir. Interfrat. Found., 1995—. Editor: Phikeia—The Manual of Phi Delta Theta, 1951, 19 edits., 1989, Phis Sing, 1958, Constitution and General Statutes of Phi Delta Theta, Fraternity Education Foundations, 1962, Directory of Phi Delta Theta, 1973. Chmn. United Appeal, Oxford, 1960; bd. dirs. U. N.Mex. Alumni Assn., 1961-68; pres. Fedn. of Clubs, Oxford, 1964, McGuffey PTA, 1971, Miami U. Art Mus., 1993-94, McCullough-Hyde Hosp., Oxford, 1966, chmn. endowment adv. com., 1988-89; vol. leader Boy Scouts Am., Oxford, 1966-79. Recipient citizen of yr. award City of Oxford, 1968, citation Theta Chi, 1967, Order of Interfrat. Svc. Lambda Chi Alpha, 1994, interfrat. leadership award Sigma Nu, 1994, accolate for intrafraternity svc. Kappa Alpha, meritorious svc. award Boy. Scouts Am., 1977, others; Interfrat. Inst. fellow Ind. U., 1988. Mem. Nat. Intrafraternity Conf. (various coms. 1954—, cert. of svc. 1981, 85, gold medal 1992), Am. Soc. Assn. Execs. (cert.), Cin. Soc. Assn. Execs., Fraternity Execs. Assn. (pres. 1962-63, svc. citations 1980, 85, 90, disting. svc. award 1991), Edgewater Conf. (pres. 1978-79), Summit Soc., Country Club Oxford (bd. dirs.), Order of Symposiarchs, Order of Omega, Rotary (founder Oxford club 1965, pres. 1966, merit award 1974, dist. gov. S.W. Ohio 1978-79, study group exch. leader South Africa 1992), Blue Key, Phi Delta Kappa, Omicron Delta Kappa. Home: 170 Hilltop Rd Oxford OH 45056-1572 Office: Phi Delta Theta Ednl Found 2 S Campus Ave Oxford OH 45056-1801

MILLER, ROBERT JAMES, lawyer; b. Dunn, N.C., Jan. 14, 1933; s. Robert James and Edith (Crockett) M.; m. Patricia L. Shaw, Sept. 29, 1984; children: Patricia Ann, Susan Ballantine, Nancy Crockett. B.S., N.C. State U., 1956; M.F., Yale U., 1962, M.S., 1965, Ph.D., 1967; J.D., N.C. Central U., 1984. Registered land surveyor. Forester W.Va. Pulp & Paper Co., 1956-59, Tilghman Lumber Co., 1959-61; asst. in instrn. and research Yale U., New Haven, 1962-65; assoc. prof. biology Radford (Va.) Coll., 1965-67, prof., chmn. biology dept., 1967-68, dean div. natural scis., 1968-71, v.p. for acad. affairs, 1971-73; prof. law, dean of coll. St. Mary's Coll., Raleigh, N.C., 1973-85; atty. Patton, Boggs & Blow, Raleigh, N.C., 1985-89; pvt. practice, 1989—; mediator N.C. Gen. Ct. of Justice; ecol. cons.; arbitrator Am. Arbitration Assn., Better Bus. Bur.; lectr. comml. law Tomsk (Russia) State U. Author: The Assimilation of Nitrogen Compounds by Tree Seedlings, 1967, Some Ecological Aspects of Dry Matter Production, 1962, Liberal Arts and the Individual, 1972, Liberal Arts: An Educational Philosophy, 1973, Laboratory Notebook: General Biology, 1976, Educational Malpractice, 1984, Issues in International Commercial Mediation, 1995. Mem. Am. Soc. Plant Physiologists, Ecol. Soc. Am., ABA, Am. Immigration Lawyers Assn., N.C. Acad. Trial Lawyers, N.C. Bar Assn., Sigma Xi, Phi Kappa Phi, Xi Sigma Pi. Episcopalian. Lodges: Masons; Shriners. Home: 3404 Lake Boone Trl Raleigh NC 27607-6756

MILLER, ROBERT JOSEPH, governor, lawyer; b. Evanston, Ill., Mar. 30, 1945; s. Ross Wendell and Coletta Jane (Doyle) M.; m. Sandra Ann Searles, Oct. 17, 1949; children: Ross, Corrine, Megan. BA in Polit. Sci., U. Santa Clara, 1967; JD, Loyola U., Los Angeles, 1971. First legal advisor Las Vegas (Nev.) Met. Police Dept., 1973-75; justice of the peace Las Vegas Twp., 1975-78; dep. dist. atty. Clark County, Las Vegas, 1971-73, dist. atty., 1979-86; lt. gov. State of Nev., 1987-89, acting gov., 1989-90, gov., 1991—. Chmn. Nev. Commn. on Econ. Devel., Carson City, 1987-91, Nev. Commn. on Tourism, Carson City, 1987-91; mem. Pres. Reagan's Task Force on Victims of Crime, 1982; chmn. Nev. divsn. Am. Cancer Soc., 1988-90. Mem. Nat. Dist. Attys. Assn. (pres. 1984-85), Western Govs. Assn. (chmn. 1993-94), Nat. Govs. Assn. (vice chmn. exec. com. 1995-96, chmn. 1996-97, past chmn. com. on justice and pub. safety, chmn. legal affairs com. 1992-94, lead gov. on transp. 1992—), Nev. Dist. Attys. Assn. (pres. 1979, 83). Democrat. Roman Catholic. Home: Gov Mansion 606 N Mountain St Carson City NV 89703-3955 Office: State of Nev Office of Gov Capitol Bldg Carson City NV 89710

MILLER, ROBERT L., JR., federal judge; b. 1950; m. Jane Woodward. BA, Northwestern U., 1972; JD, Ind. U., 1975. Law clk. to presiding justice U.S. Dist. Ct. (no. dist.) Ind., 1975; judge St. Joseph Superior Ct., South Bend, Ind., 1975-86, chief judge, 1981-83; judge U.S. Dist. Ct. (no. dist.) Ind., South Bend, Ind., 1985—. Office: US Dist Ct 325 Fed Bldg 204 S Main St South Bend IN 46601-2122*

MILLER, ROBERT LOUIS, university dean, chemistry educator; b. Chgo., Jan. 26, 1926; s. Sam P. and Ida (Reich) M.; m. Virginia Southard, Oct. 26, 1947 (dec. Sept. 1973); children: Ruth, Stephen, Martin, Andrew; m. Bonnie Seay Berard, Nov. 28, 1975; children: Edouard, Derek. Ph.B., U. Chgo., 1947, B.S., 1949, M.S., 1951; Ph.D., Ill. Inst. Tech.; Ph.D. (NSF Sci. faculty fellow), 1963. Mem. faculty U. Ill. Chgo. Circle Campus, 1953-67, asst. dean Coll. Liberal Arts and Scis., 1963-65, assoc. dean Coll. Liberal Arts and Scis., 1965-67; prof. chemistry U. N.C.-Greensboro, 1968—, dean arts and scis., 1968-85, acting dean Grad. Sch., 1989-91, spl. asst. to the provost, 1993-94; acting assoc. provost, 1994—; Am. Council Edn. adminstrv. intern SUNY-Binghamton, 1967-68. Mem. exec. com. of com. environ. affairs Piedmont Council Govts., 1971-76; mem. Greensboro Task Force on Energy; chmn. residential and transp. subcom Greensboro Energy Commn.; mem. Bd. Edn., Oak Park, Ill., 1965-66; bd. dirs. Hospice at Greensboro, 1981-87, pres., 1982-84, vol. 1988-89; vol., mem. bd. dirs. Cities in Schs., 1988-92; bd. dirs. Gilbert Pearson Audubon Soc., Greensboro Civil Liberties Union, Weatherspoon Gallery, 1981-85. Served with AUS, 1944-46, ETO. Mem. AAAS, Sigma Xi (treas. chpt.). Home: 1702 Natchez Trce Greensboro NC 27455-3226

MILLER, ROBERT NOLEN, lawyer; b. Monmouth, Ill., May 30, 1940; s. Robert Clinton and Doris Margaret (Nolen) M.; m. Diane Wilmarth, Aug. 21, 1965; children: Robert Wilmarth, Anne Elizabeth. BA, Cornell Coll., Mt. Vernon, Iowa, 1962; JD, U. Colo., 1965. Bar: Colo. 1965. Assoc. firm M. Quiat, Denver, 1965-66, Fischer & Beaty, Ft. Collins, Colo., 1969-70; dist. atty. Weld County Dist. Atty's. Office, Greeley, Colo., 1971-81; U.S. atty. U.S. Dept. Justice, Denver, 1981-88; chief counsel litigation and security US West Inc., Englewood, Colo., 1988-93; of counsel Patton, Boggs & Blow, Denver, 1993-94, LeBoeuf, Lamb, Greene & Mac Crae, Denver, 1994—; instr. bus. law Am. U., U. S.C., Myrtle Beach, 1966-69. Co-author: Deathroads, 1978. Bd. dirs. Boys Club, Greeley, 1974-78, 1st Congl. Ch., Greeley, 1975-78; Rep. candidate for atty. gen. Colo., 1977-78. Capt. USAF, 1966-69. Recipient Citizen of Yr. award Elks Club, Greeley. Mem. Fed. Bar Assn. (pres. Colo. chpt. 1983-84), Colo. Dist. Atty's Coun. (pres. 1976-77), Colo. Bar Assn., Weld County Bar Assn., Rotary (pres. local chpt. 1980-81). Republican. Avocations: fishing, hunting, golf, tennis, reading. Office: LeBoeuf Lamb Greene MacRae Ste 1975 633 17th St Ste 2800 Denver CO 80202

MILLER, ROBERT STEVENS, JR., finance professional; b. Portland, Oreg., Nov. 4, 1941; s. Robert Stevens and Barbara (Weston) M.; m. Margaret Rose Kyger, Nov. 9, 1966; children: Christopher John, Robert Stevens, Alexander Lamont. AB with distinction, Stanford U., 1963; LLB, Harvard U., 1966; MBA, Stanford U., 1968. Bar: Calif. bar 1966. Fin. analyst Ford Motor Co., Dearborn, Mich., 1968-71; spl. studies mgr. Ford Motor Co., Mexico City, 1971-73; dir. fin. Ford Asia-Pacific, Inc., Melbourne, Australia, 1974-77, Ford Motor Co., Caracas, Venezuela, 1977-79; v.p., treas. Chrysler Corp., Detroit, 1980-81, exec. v.p. fin., 1981-90, vice chmn., 1990-92; sr. ptnr. James D. Wolfensohn, Inc., N.Y.C., 1992-93; chmn. bd. dirs. Morrison Knudsen Corp., 1995—; bd. dirs. Fed.-Mogul, Fluke, Polk & Talbot, Coleman, Symantec.

MILLER, ROBERT WILEY, educational foundation executive; b. Linden, Calif., June 8, 1928; s. Raymond Wiley and Florence Estelle (Burke) M.; m. Betty Ruth Brown, Nov. 15, 1953; children—Janet Ruth, Stephen Wiley. B.A., Coll. of Pacific, Stockton, Calif., 1950; M.B.A., Harvard U., 1956; LL.D. (hon.), Lincoln Meml. U., 1978; L.H.D. (hon.), Samford U., 1978; Litt.D. (hon.), Rider Coll., 1981. Dir. program in pub. relations Columbia U., 1960-65; dir. bus.-govt. relations program, dir. Center Study Pvt. Enterprise, Am. U., 1965-70; dir. Office Domestic Bus. Policy, Dept. Commerce, 1970-71; exec. dir. White House Conf. Indsl. World Ahead, 1971-72; asst. dir. Council Internat. Econ. Policy, White House, 1972-73; spl. asst. for Bicentennial affairs White House, 1973-74; sr. asst. adminstr. Am. Revolution Bicentennial Adminstrn., 1974-75; pres. Freedoms Found. at Valley Forge, Pa., 1975-94, pres. emeritus, 1994—; mem. pres.'s Adv. Council Pvt. Sector Initiatives, 1983-85. Vice chmn. pub. relations com. Nat. council Boy Scouts Am., 1965-76; trustee Am. U., 1976-82, Valley Forge Mil. Acad. and Jr. Coll., 1991—. Served with AUS, 1951-53. Recipient Medal of Honor D.A.R., 1978; Silver Helmet Americanism award AMVETS, 1978; named Alumnus of Year U. Pacific, 1976. Mem. Cosmos Club (Washington), Union League (pres. 1995—), Phila. Country Club, Masons. Office: Union League of Phila 140 S Broad St Philadelphia PA 19102-3003

MILLER, ROBERT WILLIAM, personal property appraiser, writer; b. Phila., Apr. 28, 1922; s. Stuart Parmalee and Ruth Anne (Mills) M.; m. Judith Bayard Wood, Sept. 1948 (div. Feb. 1951); m. Bettie Lucy Hays, Apr. 28, 1962. Student, NYU, 1945-46, Fenster Sch. Writing, N.Y.C., 1945-47, Dickinson Coll., 1948-49. Copywriter Ruthraff & Ryan, N.Y.C., 1944-46; writer various publs., 1944-60; ind. personal property appraiser N.W. Fla., 1960—; writer Wallace-Homestead Book Co., Des Moines, 1971-86; lectr., mus. cons. on antiques, Gt. Britain, France, Italy, Fed. Republic Germany, 1963—; cons. McClung Mus., Knoxville, Tenn., 1968-72, Houston Mus., Chattanooga, 1970-78. Host TV talk show Antiques and Collectibles, PBS, 1968-72; author 34 books on antiques and collectibles. Dir. Swim Program for Handicapped, Oak Ridge, Tenn., 1954-68; scoutmaster, cubmaster Boy Scouts of Am. Troop #120, Oak Ridge, 1962-68. Vol. Am. Field Svc., 1943-44, CBI. Decorated 1939-45 Star, Burma Star, War Medal (Gt. Britain); recipient Nat. award Nat. Recreation Assn., 1960. Mem. Appraisers Assn. Am., Nat. Geog. Soc. Presbyterian. Avocations: scuba diving, fishing, collecting antique cars. Home: 100 Greenwood Dr Panama City Beach FL 32407

MILLER, ROBERTA BALSTAD, science administrator; b. Mpls., June 25, 1940; d. Gerhard Oliver and Laverne K. (Anderson) Balstad; m. Gary David Lange, Nov. 26, 1959 (div. 1968); m. Floyd John Miller, June 15, 1969; 1 child, Aaron Gerhard. BA, U. Minn., 1964, MA, 1970, PhD, 1973. Rsch. assoc. AIA, Washington, 1974; staff assoc. Social Sci. Rsch. Coun., Washington, 1975-81; exec. dir. Consortium Social Sci. Assns., Washington, 1981-84; divsn. dir. NSF, Washington, 1984-93; pres., CEO Consortium for Internat. Earth Sci. Info. Network (CIESIN), University Center, Mich., 1993—; adj. prof. natural resources policy and behavior U. Mich., 1993—; guest scholar Woodrow Wilson Internat. Ctr. Scholars, 1994; sr. assoc. mem. St. Anthony's Coll., U. Oxford, Eng., 1991-92; mem. chmn. NATO adv. panel on Advanced Sci. Insts./Advanced Rsch. Workshops, Brussels, 1988-91; mem. exec. com. Space Studies Bd. Nat. Rsch. Coun., 1995—; mem. U.S. Nat. Com. IIASA, 1995—; chmn. adv. bd. Luxembourg Income Survey, 1987-91. Author: City and Hinterland, 1979; editor (with Harriet Zuckerman) Scientometrics, 1979; contbr. articles to profl. jours.; translator poetry of Jorge Luis Borges, 1989, 90, 91. Bd. trustees Newport Schs., Kensington, Md., 1986-91, St. Anthony's Coll. Trust, 1994—; adv. trustee Environ. Rsch. Inst. Mich., 1995—. Recipient NSF Meritorious Svc. award, 1993. Mem. AAAS (com. mem., chmn. 1987—), U.S. Man in the Bioshphere Program (mem. com., chmn. 1989-91), Internat. Social Sci. Coun. (mem. com. 1991—, v.p. 1992-94), Am. Hist. Assn., Am. Lit. Translators Assn., Coun. on Fgn. Rels., Cosmos Club. Lutheran. Home: 3909 Jocelyn St NW Washington DC 20015-1905 Office: CIESIN 2250 Pierce Rd University Center MI 48710

MILLER, ROBERTA DAVIS, editor; b. Oklahoma City, Aug. 18, 1931; s. Robert Rutter and Lenora (Baldwin) Davis; children: Wendy, Jane, Elisabeth. Student, Okla. U., 1948-50, Central State U., 1950-51. Editor Golden Books, Western Pub. Co., 1963-71; pub. Sesame St. Mag., Electric Co. Mag., Children's TV Workshop, N.Y.C., 1971-76; editor-in-chief Pizzazz Mag., Cadence Pub. Co., N.Y.C., 1976-78; v.p., dir. lit. properties United Media, N.Y.C., 1978-85, v.p. internat. pub., 1986-93, v.p., dir. pub., 1993-94; prin. Roberta D. Miller Assoc., N.Y.C., 1994—. Mem. Authors Guild, Newswomen's Club N.Y. Office: 42 E 12th St New York NY 10003-4640

MILLER, ROBIN DAVIS, professional society administrator; b. Phila., May 22, 1962; d. Neil Monas and Julia (Kraft) Davis; m. Stephen Michael Miller, Apr. 17, 1993; 1 child, Benjamin Preston. BA, U. Pa., 1983; MA, U. Coll., Oxford, Eng., 1985; JD, U. Pa., 1988. Bar: N.Y. 1989, Pa. 1991. Litigator Rogers & Wells, N.Y.C., 1988-90, Kornstein Veisz & Wexler, N.Y.C., 1990-91, Drinker Biddle & Reath, Phila., 1991-93; exec. dir. Authors Guild Found., N.Y.C., 1993—, Authors League Am., N.Y.C., 1993—, Authors Guild, N.Y.C., 1993—; bd. dirs. Copyright Clearance Ctr., Danvers, Mass. Bd. dirs. Ralston House, Phila., 1992-93; del. Libr. of Congress ACCORD com. on Copyright Law, Washington, 1993-94. Mem. N.Y. Bar Assn., Pa. Bar Assn., Authors Registry, Inc. (bd. dirs.). Jewish. Office: Authors League of Am 330 W 42d St 29th Fl New York NY 10036

MILLER, RONALD ALFRED, family physician; b. Orange, Calif., Sept. 27, 1943; s. Alfred Casper and Inez Geraldine (Gunderson) M.; m. Jean Ilene Andrews, June 18, 1966; children: Jon, Lauri, Bryan. BA, Pacific Luth. U., 1965; MD, U. Wash., 1969. Diplomate Am. Bd. Family Practice (bd. dirs. 1985-90, pres. bd. 1989-90). Intern in medicine Parkland Meml. Hosp., Dallas, 1969-70; gen. practice residency USPHS Gallup Indian Med. Ctr., Gallup, N.Mex., 1970-72; prin. Medical Doctor Family Physicians' Clinic, Whitefish, Mont., 1972—; assoc. clin. prof. U. Wash., Seattle, 1975—; coord. community clin. unit in family medicine, U. Wash., Whitefish, 1975—; bd. dirs. Utah Med. Ins. Assn., Salt Lake City, 1987—. Bd. dirs. Whitefish Housing Authority, 1977-82; mem. alumni bd. Pacific Luth. U., Tacoma, 1976-81, pres., 1979-80; mem. Glacier Community Chorale, Whitefish, 1984—, bd. dirs., 1990—. Lt. comdr. USPHS, 1970-72. Mem. Am. Acad. Family Physicians (com. on continuing med. edn. 1977-81, com. on edn. 1984-89, Mead Johnson award Grad. Edn. in Family Practice 1972), Mont. Acad. Family Physicians (bd. dirs., sec./treas., v.p., pres. 1982-83, del. nat. congress 1978-84), Rotary, Alpha Omega Alpha. Republican. Lutheran. Avocations: hunting, fishing, skiing, backpacking, choral singing. Home: 721 Iowa Ave Whitefish MT 59937-2338 Office: Family Physicians Clinic 401 Baker Ave Whitefish MT 59937-2435*

MILLER, RONALD BAXTER, English language educator, author; b. Rocky Mount, N.C., Oct. 11, 1948; s. Marcellus Cornelius and Elsie (Bryant) M.; m. Jessica Garris, June 5, 1971; 1 child, Akin Dasan. BA magna cum laude, N.C. Ctrl. U., 1970; AM, Brown U., 1972, PhD, 1974. Asst. prof. English Haverford Coll., Haverford, Pa., 1974-76; assoc. prof. English, dir. Black lit. program U. Tenn., Knoxville, 1977-81, prof. English, dir. Black lit. program, 1982-92, Lindsay Young prof. liberal arts and English, 1986-87; prof. English, dir. Inst. for African Am. Studies U. Ga., Athens, 1992—; instr. summer sch. Roger Williams Coll., Bristol, R.I., 1973; lectr. SUNY, 1974; Mellon prof. Xavier Univ., New Orleans, 1988; Irvine Found. visiting scholar Univ. San Francisco, 1991. Author: (reference guide) Langston Hughes and Gwendolyn Brooks, 1978, The Art and Imagination of Langston Hughes, 1989 (Am. Book award, 1991), (monograph) Southern Trace in Black Critical Theory: Redemption of Time, 1991; editor, contbr.:

Black American Literature and Humanism, 1981, Black American Poets Between Worlds, 1940-60, 1986; co-editor: Call and Response The Riverside Anthology of African American Literary Experience, 1996; mem. editl. bd. Tenn. Studies in Lit., 1991-93, Black Fiction Project (Yale-Cornell-Duke-Harvard), 1985—, U. Ga. Press, 1994—; contbr. numerous articles and revs. to profl. jours. Recipient award Am. Coun. of Learned Socs., 1978, Golden Key Faculty award Nat. Golden Key, 1990, 95, Alpha award for disting. svc. U. Ga. Athens, 1993; Lilly Sr. Teaching fellow U. Ga. Athens, 1994, Nat. Rsch. Coun. sr. fellow, 1986-87, NDEA fellow, 1970-72, Ford Found. fellow, 1972-73, NEH fellow, 1975; Nat. Fellowships Fund dissertation grantee, 1973-74, others. Mem. MLA (exec. com. Afro-Am. Lit. Discussion Group 1980-83, chair 1982-83, mem. del. assembly 1984-86, com. on langs. and lits. of Am. 1993—, chair 1996), Langston Hughes Soc. (pres. 1984-90). Office: U Ga Inst African Am Studies Athens GA 30602

MILLER, RONALD GRANT, journalist; b. Santa Cruz, Calif., Feb. 28, 1939; s. Fred Robert and Evelyn Lenora (Mosher) M.; m. Darla-Jean Irene Rode, Nov. 2, 1963. AA, Monterey Peninsula Coll., 1958; BA, San Jose State U., 1961. Reporter Santa Cruz (Calif.) Sentinel, 1959-62; reporter, chief news bur. San Jose (Calif.) Mercury News, 1962-77, editor T.V., 1977—; syndicated TV columnist Knight Ridder Syndicate, 1978—; commentator, critic Sta. KLOK, San Jose, 1981-83; panelist, guest speaker various orgns., 1978—; nat. judge Cableace awards, 1987. Author: (foreword) Les Brown's Encyclopedia of Television, 1992; co-author: Masterpiece Theatre, 1995, Author: Mystery! A Celebration, 1996; contbr. articles and short fiction to various mags. Recipient Nat. Spot News Photo award Sigma Delta Chi, 1961, Outstanding Alumnus award San Jose State U. Dept. Journalism and Mass Comm., 1985, Nat. Headline award Press Club Atlantic City, 1994. Mem. TV Critics Assn. (nat. pres. 1981). Democrat. Home and Office: 1554 Arbor Ave Los Altos CA 94024-5913

MILLER, RONALD M., manufacturing executive; b. Bklyn., Aug. 30, 1944; s. Samuel L. and Kitty M.; m. Carole J. Schaps, June 9, 1966; children: Elisa, Deborah. BSEE, Poly. Inst., Bklyn., 1966, MS in Ops. Rsch., 1969. Sr. electronic engr. Grumman Aerospace Corp., Bethpage, N.Y., 1966-72; dir. program mgmt. Gould Inc., Simulation Systems div., Melville, N.Y., 1972-81; v.p. ops. EMS Devel., Farmingdale, N.Y., 1981-85; pres., chief exec. officer Marks Polarized Corp., Deer Park, N.Y., 1985-89, also chmn. bd. dirs., 1985—; pres., chief exec. officer Marks Polarized Corp., Hauppauge, N.Y., 1989—; pres., chmn. bd. dirs. Upward Tech. Corp., 1989-92, sec., COO, bd. dirs., 1989—; pres. Image Analytics Corp., 1992—; adj. lectr. Hofstra U. Hempstead, N.Y., 1969-70; bus. cons. Aerospace Industry, Long Island, N.Y., 1978—. Sr. arbitrator Better Bus. Bur., Farmingdale, 1981—; arbitrator Am. Arbitration Assn., Garden City, N.Y., 1980—. Mem. L.I. Forum for Tech. (v.p., bd. dirs. 1987—), Navy League of U.S. (life), Am. Def. Preparedness Assn. (life). Avocations: amateur radio. Home: 38 Fairfield Dr Dix Hills NY 11746-7137 Office: Marks Polarized Corp 275 Marcus Blvd # D Hauppauge NY 11788-2022

MILLER, RONALD WRIGHT, pharmaceutical scientist; b. Pottstown, Pa., Dec. 8, 1947; s. Wright Reninger and Marcelle (Scholler) M.; m. Carol Catherine Grove, Mar. 27, 1971. BS in Chemistry, Lebanon Valley Coll., 1970; MBA, Temple U., 1977, PhD in Pharmaceutics, 1988. Asst. to prodn. mgr. Glenbrook Labs. Divsn., Sterling Drug, Trenton, 1971-74; asst. prodn. mgr. Elkins-Sinn Co., Cherry Hill, N.J., 1974-75; sr. compounding supr. Richardson-Merrell Co., Hatboro, Pa., 1975-80; sr. rsch. scientist Whitehall Labs. Divsn., Am. Home Products, Hammonton, N.J., 1980-88; assoc. dir. Worldwide Pharm. Tech. Bristol-Myers Squibb Co., New Brunswick, N.J., 1988—. Lt. col. USAR, 19770-95, ret. Mem. Am. Chem. Soc. (cert.), Am. Assn. Pharm. Scientists. Achievements include patents for coated aspirin tablets decomposition inhibited by incorporation of citric, alginic and glutamic acid mixtures thereof, for enteric coated aspirin tablets rendered shock-insensitive by providing a protective coat of hydroxypropyl methylcellulose of at least 1.5% by weight of the tablet core. Home: 126 Fox Hollow Dr Langhorne PA 19053 Office: Bristol-Myers Squibb 1 Squibb Dr PO Box 191 New Brunswick NJ 08903-0191

MILLER, ROSEMARY MARGARET, accountant; b. Jersey City, Jan. 3, 1935; d. Joseph John and Marguerite (Delatush) Corbin; m. James Noyes Orton, 1956 (div. 1977); m. Julian Allen Miller, Oct. 14, 1978 (dec. 1993); children: Alexandria Lynn Hayes, Jennifer Ann Orton Cole. Student Barnard Coll., 1953-54, Rutgers U., Newark, 1954-56, Howard U., 1962-63, No. Va. Community Coll., 1976-83; AA, Thomas A. Edison State Coll., 1981; BS in Acctg., U. Md., 1987; cert. H & R Block, 1981; cert. tax profl. Am. Inst. Tax Studies. Bookkeeper Gen. Electronics, Inc., Washington, 1970-73; cost acct. Radiation Systems, Inc., Sterling, Va., 1973-80; acct. Bilsom Internat., Inc., Reston, Va., 1980-83; sales mgr. Bay Country Homes, Inc., Fruitland, Md., 1984; sr. staff acct. Snow, Powell & Meade, Salisbury, Md., 1985-86; acct. Meadows Hydraulics, Inc., Fruitland, Md., 1987-88; acct. Porter & Powell CPAs, Salisbury, 1988-93; owner, prin. RCOM Cons., acctg., bookeeping, taxes, Princess Anne, Md. Mem. Accreditation Council for Accountancy (accredited 1981), Nat. Soc. Public Accts., Inst. Mgmt. Accts., Nat. Soc. Tax Profls. (cert. tax profl. 1994). Democrat. Lutheran. Home and Office: 30531 Bardwell Dr Princess Anne MD 21853-2868

MILLER, ROSS HAYS, retired neurosurgeon; b. Ada, Okla., Jan. 30, 1923; s. Harry and Helen (Rice) M.; m. Catherine Railey, May 2, 1943; children—Terry Hays, Helen Stacy. B.S., East Central State Coll., Ada, 1943; M.D., U. Okla., 1946; M.S. in Neurosurgery, U. Minn., 1952. Diplomate: Am. Bd. Neurol. Surgery (chmn. exam. com. 1978-84). Intern St. Luke's Hosp., Cleve., 1946-47; fellow in neurosurgery Mayo Clinic, Rochester, Minn., 1950-54; instr. in neurosurgery Mayo Med. Sch., 1954-63, asst. prof. neurosurgery, 1963-73, asso. prof., 1973-75, prof., chmn. dept. neurosurgery, from 1975, now ret.; vis. prof. neurol. surgery Med. U. S.C., Med. Coll. Ga., Augusta. Contbr. numerous articles to med. publs. Trustee East Central State U. Found. Served as capt., M.C. U.S. Army, 1947-49, Korea. Named to Okla. Hall of Fame, 1977, Athletic Hall of Fame, East Central U. Okla., 1977; recipient Disting. Alumnus award East Central U. Okla., 1974, Mayo Found. Disting. Alumnus award, 1992. Mem. AMA, ACS, Am. Assn. Neurol. Surgeons (chmn. com. profl. practice 1976-79, dir. 1976-79, v.p. 1979, rep. to Council Med. Splty. Socs. 1980-84), Congress Neurol. Surgeons (exec. com. 1963-65), Minn. Soc. Neurol. Scis., Neurosurg. Soc. Am. (v.p. 1975), Soc. Neurol. Surgeons (v.p. 1983), Sigma Xi.

MILLER, RUSH GLENN, JR., university dean, librarian; b. Atlanta, Mar. 13, 1947; s. Rush Glenn and Gene (Ramsey) M.; m. Johnnye Mize, July 21, 1967; children: Lisa, Glenn, John, Edward. BA in History, Delta State Coll., Cleveland, Miss., 1969; MA in History, Miss. State U., 1971, PhD in medieval History, 1973; MLS, Fla. State U., 1974. Asst. prof. U. Miss., Oxford, 1974-75; dir. libr. svcs. Delta State U., 1975-82; dir. libr. Sam Houston State U., Huntsville, Tex., 1982-86; dean librs. Bowling Green (Ohio) State U., 1986-94; dir. univ. libr. sys. U. Pitts., 1994—; del. White House Conf. on Librs., Washington, 1979; del. to users coun. Online Computer Libr. Ctr., Inc., Dublin, Ohio, 1992-94. Contbg. author: Diversity and Multiculturalism in Libraries, 1994, also others; editor Miss. Librs., 1982-84; contbr. articles to profl. jours. Recipient Past President's award Miss. Libr. Assn., 1976. Mem. ALA (various coms. 1976—), Southeastern Libr. Assn. (exec. bd. 1976-82), Acad. Libr. Assn. Ohio. Democrat. Methodist. Avocations: golf, reading. Office: U Pitts Hillman Libr Pittsburgh PA 15260

MILLER, SAM SCOTT, lawyer; b. Ft. Worth, July 26, 1938; s. Percy Vernon and Mildred Lois (MacDowell) M.; m. Mary Harrison FitzHugh, May 10, 1969. BA, Mich. State U., 1960; JD, Tulane U., 1964; LLM, Yale U., 1965. Bar: La. 1965, N.Y. 1966, Minn. 1969. Assoc. Simpson Thacher & Bartlett, N.Y.C., 1965-68; sr. counsel Investors Diversified Services, Mpls., 1968-73; ptnr. Ireland Gibson Reams & Miller, Memphis, 1973-74; gen. counsel Paine Webber Group, Inc., N.Y.C., 1974-87, sr. v.p., 1976-87; ptnr. Orrick, Herrington & Sutcliffe, N.Y.C., 1987—; adj. prof. NYU Law Sch., 1986-90; vis. lectr. Yale Law Sch., 1980-85, Inst. for Internat. Econs. and Trade, Wuhan, China, 1983, U. Calif., 1986; mem. dean's coun. Tulane U. Law Sch., 1979—; trustee Omni Mut., Inc., 1988—; ombudsman Kidder Peabody Group, 1988—, Charles Schwab & Co., 1991—, Gruntal & Co., 1995—. Contbr. articles to profl. jours.; editor-in-chief: Tulane Law Rev, 1964-65; bd. editors Securities Regulation Law Jour., 1982—. Bd. dirs. Guthrie Theatre Found., Mpls., 1971-74; bd. dirs. Minn. Opera Co., 1971-74, Yale U. Law Sch. Fund., 1981—; bd. govs. Investment Co. Inst., 1980-87. Mem. ABA (vice chmn. com. fed. regulation of sec. 1995—, chmn. subcom. market regulation 1985-93), Assn. Bar City N.Y. (treas., mem. exec. com. 1994-96, chmn. broker-dealer investment co. and regulations subcom. 1982-83), Internat. Bar Assn., Securities Industry Assn. (chmn. fed. regulation com. 1976-78), Down Town Assn., Knickerbocker Club, Order of Coif, Omicron Delta Kappa. Democrat. Baptist. Office: Orrick Herrington et al 666 Fifth Ave New York NY 10103

MILLER, SAMUEL MARTIN, apparel company finance executive; b. N.Y.C., Jan. 31, 1938; s. Irving Nathaniel and Estelle (Furman) M.; m. Kay Shapiro, Dec. 23, 1963; children: Jennifer, Suzanne. BBA magna cum laude, CCNY, 1964. With Coopers & Lybrand, N.Y.C., 1964-72; supervising sr. acct. Coopers & Lybrand, 1968-69, audit mgr., 1969-72; corp. controller Manhattan Industries, Inc., Glen Rock, N.J., 1972-74; v.p., corp. controller Manhattan Industries, Inc., 1974-76, v.p., treas., controller, 1976-83, v.p., sec.-treas., controller, 1983-88; sr. v.p. fin., CFO, mem. policy com. Liz Claiborne Inc., North Bergen, N.J., 1988—. Served with USN, 1957-59. Recipient Haskin's award N.Y. State Uniform C.P.A. Exam. Mem. AICPA, Am. Arbitration Assn., Am. Apparel Mfrs. Assn. (chmn. fin. mgmt. com.), Fin. Execs. Inst. (CFO adv. com.), Nat. Assn. Accts., N.Y. State Soc. CPAs (chief fin. officer com.), Beta Gamma Sigma, Beta Alpha Psi. Office: Liz Claiborne Inc One Claiborne Ave North Bergen NJ 07047

MILLER, SANDRA PERRY, middle school educator; b. Nashville, Aug. 3, 1951; d. James Ralph and Pauline (Williams) Perry; m. William Kerley Miller, June 22, 1974. BS, David Lipscomb U., 1973; MEd, Tenn. State U., 1983, cert. in spl. edn., reading splty., 1986. Cert. tchr., Tenn. Tchr. Clyde Riggs Elem. Sch., Portland, Tenn., 1973-86; tchr. social studies Portland Mid. Sch., 1986—; adv. bd. tech. and comm. in edn. Sumner County Sch. Bd., Gallatin, Tenn., 1990—; co-dir., cons. Tenn. Students-at-Risk, Nashville, 1991—; assoc. edn. cons. Edn. Fgn. Inst. Cultural Exch., 1991-92; fellow World History Inst., Princeton (N.J.) U., 1992—; awards com. Tenn. Dept. Edn., Nashville, 1992; U.S. edn. amb. E.F. Ednl. Tours, Eng., France, Germany, Belgium, Holland, 1991; ednl. cons. HoughtonMifflin Co., Boston; apptd. Tenn. Mini-Grants award com., Tenn. 21st Century Tech. Com.; mem. Tenn. Textbook Com., 1995, Think-Tank on 21st Century Edn., Tenn. and Milliken Nat. Educator Found.; apptd. to Gov.'s Task Force Commn. on 21st Schs., Gov.'s Task Force for Anti-Drug and Alcohol Abuse Among Teens; mem. nat. com. for instnl. tech. devel. Milken Family Found. Nat. Edn. Conf., 1996; apptd. to Instrnl. Tech. Devel.-Project Strand, 1996 Milken Family Found., Nat. Edn. Conf. Author curriculum materials; presenter creative crafts segment local TV sta., 1990-93; producer, dir. documentary on edn. PBS, Corona, Calif., 1990. Performer Nashville Symphony Orch., 1970-73; leader Sumner County 4-H Club, 1976-86; mem. Woodrow Wilson Nat. Fellowship Found. on Am. History, Princeton U., 1994; nat. com. Instructional Tech. Devel. Project Strand of the 1996 Milken Family Found. Nat. Edn. Conf., L.A., 1996. Recipient Excellence in Teaching award U. Tenn., 1991-92, 92-93, award for Outstanding Teaching in Humanities Tenn. Humanities Coun., 1994; named Tchr. of Yr. Upper Cumberland dist. Tenn. Dept. Edn., 1991-92, 92-93, Mid. Tenn. Educator of Yr. Tenn. Assn. Mid. Schs., 1991, Tenn. Tchr. of Yr. Tenn. Dept. Edn., 1992, Nat. Educator of Yr. Milken Family Found., 1992; recipient grant Tenn. Dept. Edn. for Devel. of Model Drop Out Prevention Program, 1996. Mem. NEA, ASCD, Sumner County Edn. Assn. (sch. rep. 1973—, Disting. Tchr. of Yr. 1992), Tenn. Edn. Assn. (rep. 1973—), Nat. Geographic Tenn. Alliance (rep. 1990—, grantee 1990), Tenn. Humanities Coun. (rep. 1990—), Nat. Coun. Social Studies. Baptist. Avocations: crafts, doll collecting, reading, music, fashion modeling. Office: Portland Mid Sch 922 S Broadway Portland TN 37148-1624

MILLER, SARAH PEARL, librarian; b. Wilkensburg, Pa., Aug. 31, 1938; d. Samuel Henry and Anna Deborah (Shirley) Lyons; m. Paul Victor Miller, Apr. 15, 1989; children: Cheryl, Michael, Daniel, Lorel. BS, Indiana U. of Pa., 1960; MREM, Denver Conservative Bapt. Sem., 1965; MA, U. Denver, 1966. Libr. Denver Conservative Bapt. Sem., 1966—. Mem. Am. Theol. Libr. Assn. (bd. dirs. 1978-81, 90-91, index bd. 1983-90). Home: 15707 E Grand Ave Aurora CO 80015-1708

MILLER, SHELBY ALEXANDER, chemical engineer, educator; b. Louisville, July 9, 1914; s. George Walter and Stella Katherine (Cralle) M.; m. Jean Adele Danielson, Dec. 26, 1939 (div. May 1948); 1 son, Shelby Carlton; m. Doreen Adare Kennedy, May 29, 1952 (dec. Feb. 1971). B.S., U. Louisville, 1935; Ph.D., U. Minn., 1943. Registered profl. engr., Del., Kans., N.Y. Asst. chemist Corhart Refractories Co., Louisville, 1935-36; teaching, rsch. asst. chem. engring. U. Minn., Mpls., 1935-39; devel. engr., rsch. chem. engr. E.I. duPont de Nemours & Co., Inc., Wilmington, Del., 1940-46; assoc. prof. chem. engring. U. Kan., Lawrence, 1946-50; prof. U. Kan., 1950-55; Fulbright prof. chem. engring. King's Coll. Durham U., Newcastle-upon-Tyne, Eng., 1952-53; prof., chem. engring. U. Rochester, 1955-69, chmn., 1955-68; assoc. lab. dir. Argonne (Ill.) Nat. Lab., 1969-74; dir. Ctr. Ednl. Affairs, 1969-79, sr. chem. engr., 1969-84; ret. sr. chem. engr., cons., 1984—; vis. prof. chem. engring. U. Calif., Berkeley, 1967-68; vis. prof. U. of Philippines, Quezon City, 1986. Editor: Chem. Engring. Edn. Quar, 1965-67; sect. editor: Perry's Chem. Engring. Handbook, 5th edit., 1973, 6th edit., 1984; contbr. articles to tech., profl. jours. Sec. Kans. Bd. Engring. Examiners, 1954-55; mem. adv. com. on tng. Internat. Atomic Energy Agy., 1975-79; treas. Lawrence (Kans.) League for Practice Democracy, 1950-52; sec. Argonne Credit Union, 1994—. Fellow AAAS, Am. Inst. Chemists, Am. Inst. Chem. Engrs. (past chmn. Kansas City sect.); mem. Am. Chem. Soc. (past chmn. Rochester sect.), Soc. Chem. Industry, Am. Soc. Engring. Edn. (past chmn. grad. studies div.), Am. Nuclear Soc., Filtration Soc., Triangle, Sigma Xi, Sigma Tau, Phi Lambda Upsilon, Tau Beta Pi, Alpha Chi Sigma. Presbyn. Home: 825 63rd St Downers Grove IL 60516-1962 Office: Argonne Nat Lab Chem Tech Divsn Argonne IL 60439

MILLER, SHELDON IRVIN, psychiatrist, educator; b. Cleve., June 29, 1938; s. Edward A. and Evelyn Miller; m. Sarah Johnston, June 18, 1861; children: Lynne, David. AB, Oberlin Coll., 1960; MD, Tufts U., 1964. Diplomate Am. Bd. Psychiatry and Neurology. Prof. psychiatry Case Western Res. U. Sch. Medicine, Cleve., 1979-81; clin. prof. psychiatry U. Calif., Irvine, 1982-84; dir. acute inpatient svc. Sheppard & Enoch Pratt Hosp., Towson, Md., 1983-86; clin. prof. psychiatry U. Md., Balt., 1984-86; prof., chmn. of psychiatry U. Medicine and Dentistry, N.J. U. Hosp., Newark, 1986-91; chief of svc. psychiatry St. Barnabas Med. Ctr., Livingston, N.J., 1987-91; dir. Stone Inst. Psychiatry Northwestern Meml. Hosp., Chgo., 1991—; prof., chmn. psychiatry Northwestern U. Med. Sch., Chgo., 1991—; mem. psychiatry residency rev. com. Editor: Clinical Text Addictive Disorders, 1991, (jour.) Am. Jour. Addictions, 1990—; contbr. articles to sci. and psychiat. jours. Bd. dirs. Mental Health Assn., Ill., 1992—; advisor Abraham Low Inst., Ill., 1990-91; pres., bd. trustees Essex County Nat. Coun. Alcoholism, N.J., 1990-91. Lt. commdr. USPHS, 1968-70. Alcohol dependence grantee NIMH, 1990; fetal alcohol syndrome grantee Nat. Inst. on Alcohol Abuse and Alcoholism, 1983. Fellow ACP, Am. Psychiat. Assn. (com. mem. practice guidelines com.); mem. The Am. Acad. of Psychiat. on Alcohol and Addictions (exec. com., pres. 1987-89), Assn. Acad. Psychiatrists, Rsch. Soc. on Alcoholism, Am. Assn. Chairs. Depts. of Psychiatry, Am. Bd. Psychiatry & Neurology (bd. dirs. 1991—), Sigma Xi. Avocations: photography, biking, hiking. Office: Northwestern U Med Sch 303 E Superior #561 Chicago IL 60611

MILLER, STANFORD, reinsurance executive, arbitrator, lawyer; b. Kansas City, Mo., Nov. 15, 1913; s. Hugh and Gertrude Anna (Kraft) M.; m. Gloria Goble, July 11, 1942 (div. 1958); 1 child, Hans Hugh; m. Beverly Breuer, Apr. 19, 1962; 1 son, Bradford Channing. B.A., U. Kans., 1934; J.D., U. Chgo., 1938. Bar: Mo. 1938. lectr. in field. Author: (with Robert D. Brown) Health Insurance Underwriting, 1962; also articles. Bd. dirs. Kansas City, Boy Scouts Am., Community Living Opportunities; trustee emeritus U. Kansas City. Mem. Mo. Bar Assn., Reins. Assn. Am. (past chmn.), Health Ins. Assn. Am. (former sec., dir.), Am. Arbitration Assn. (panel of arbitrators), Phi Alpha Delta, Alpha Tau Omega. Clubs: Rotary, Profl. Men's, Mission Hills Country. Home: 2709 Tomahawk Rd Shawnee Mission KS 66208-1827 Office: 6700 Antioch Rd Ste 400 Shawnee Mission KS 66204-1200

MILLER, STANLEY CUSTER, JR., physicist, retired educator; b. Kansas City, Mo., July 30, 1926; s. Stanley Custer and Verda (Storer) M.; m. Elene G. Josephson, Nov. 27, 1957 (dec.); children: Gloria Diane, James Kenneth, Richard Eric (dec.). BS in Engring. Physics, U. Colo., 1948; PhD in Physics, U. Calif. at Berkeley, 1953. Mem. faculty U. Colo., Boulder, 1953-90; prof. physics U. Colo., 1961-90. Author: Principles of Physics, 2 vols, 1966, Irreducible Representations of Space Groups, 1967, Principles of Modern Physics, 1970, Kronecker Product Tables, 1979. Served with USNR, 1944-46. Mem. Am. Phys. Soc. Home: 2570 S Dayton Way Apt 306A Denver CO 80231-3944

MILLER, STEPHEN RALPH, lawyer; b. Chgo., Nov. 28, 1950; s. Ralph and Karin Ann (Olson) M.; children: David Williams, Lindsay Christine. BA cum laude, Yale U., 1972; JD, Cornell U., 1975. Bar: Ill. Assoc. McDermott, Will & Emery, Chgo., 1975-80, income ptnr., 1981-85, equity ptnr., 1986—, mgmt. com. mem., 1992-95; mem. spl. task force on post-employment benefits Fin. Acctg. Standards Bd., Norwalk, Conn., 1987-91. Contbr. articles to profl. jours. Mem. Chgo. Coun. on Fgn. Rels., 1978—; trustee police pension bd., Wilmette, Ill., 1992—; bd. trustees Seabury We. Theol. Sem., Evanston, Ill., 1994—. Mem. ABA, Ill. Bar Assn., Midwest Benefits Coun., Yale Club Chgo., Mich. Shores Club, Chgo. Athletic Assn., Hundred Club Cook County, Legal Club of Chgo. Avocations: sailing, water skiing, cross-country skiing. Office: McDermott Will & Emery 227 W Monroe St Ste 3100 Chicago IL 60606-5018

MILLER, STEVEN H., museum diector; b. Phila., 1947; m. Jane McClure Pelson; children: Andrew Steven, Katherine Ann. BA, Bard Coll., 1970; cert. in conservation sci., Internat. Ctr. for Study of Preservation and Restoration of Cultural Property, Rome, 1978. Asst. to sr. curator Mus. of City of N.Y., N.Y.C., 1971-72, asst. curator paintings, prints and photographs, 1973-77, curator prints and photographs, 1977-79, curator, dept. head fine art collections, history and spl. collections, 1979-85, sr. curator, 1985-87; asst. dir. Maine State Mus., 1987-91; dir. of mus. Western Res. Hist. Soc., Cleve., 1991-95; exec. dir. The Bennington (Vt.) Mus., 1995—; adj. prof. mus. studies Case Western Res. U., 1991-94; lectr. NYU, 1978-87, Columbia U., N.Y.C., 1981, 82, New Sch. for Social Rsch., N.Y.C., 1978, 83, Maine State Mus., 1987-91. Author catalogs; contbr. articles to profl. jours. Bd. govs. Bard-St. Stephen's Alumni Assn.; mem. fellowship gift com., bd. trustees Hist. Deerfield, Mass.; bd. dirs. Vt. Mus. and Gallery Alliance; former mem. landmarks preservation com. Shaker Heights, Ohio; charter and former mem. hist. preservation com. City of Gardiner, Maine; former mem. adv. com. Blaine House Restoration, Maine; former mem., art adv. com. Gracie Mansion Conservancy, N.Y.C.; former mem. adv. coun. Mus. Moving Image, Astoria, N.Y. Mem. Am. Assn. Mus. (mem. mus. advocacy team, mem. mus. accreditation vis. com.), Maine Assn. Mus. (co-founder, charter coun. mem.), Nat. Arts Club. Home: 5 Appletree Ln Bennington VT 05201-2210

MILLER, STEVEN MAX, humanities educator; b. Portland, Ind., Feb. 9, 1950; s. J. Max and Belva Kathryn (Kitty Booher) M.; m. Fran Felice Koski, May 30, 1985 (div. Aug. 7, 1992). BA in Eng., Coll. of William and Mary, 1972; MA in English Lang. and Lit., Ind. U., 1975, PhD in English Lang. and Lit., 1985. Sr. libr. asst. cataloger rare books and spl. collections Lilly Libr., Bloomington, Ind., 1972-76; assoc. instr. English Ind. U., Bloomington, 1975-82; asst. prof. English Millersville (Pa.) U., 1985-94; assoc. prof. English Millersville (Pa.) U., 1994—; faculty sponsor Iota Phi chpt. Sigma Tau Delta Millersville (Pa.) U., 1986—; asst. prof. English Murray (Ky.) State U., 1989-90; cons. women writers project Brown U., Providence, 1990-95; reader nat. tchg. exam. Ednl. Testing Svc., Princeton, N.J., 1990-92. Editor (Re)Soundings jour.; contbr. articles to profl. jours. Grantee NEH, 1991, 92. Mem. MLA, John Donne Soc. Am., Spenser Soc., English Assn. Pa. State Univs. (nominating com. 1987), Bibliog. Soc. Am. Episcopalian. Avocation: gardening. Office: Millersville U Dept English Chryst Bldg Millersville PA 17551

MILLER, STEVEN SCOTT, lawyer; b. N.Y.C., May 28, 1947; s. Stanley Irwin and Corinne (Mass) M.; m. Nina Catherine Augello, Apr. 24, 1983. BA cum laude, U. Pa., 1967; JD cum laude, NYU, 1970. Bar: N.Y. 1971, U.S. Dist. Ct. (so. and ea. dists.) N.Y. 1972, U.S. Ct. Appeals (2d cir.) 1974. Law clk. to judge U.S. Dist. Ct. (so. dist.) N.Y., N.Y.C., 1970-71; assoc. Proskauer Rose Goetz & Mendelsohn, N.Y.C., 1971-78; assoc. Rosenman & Colin, N.Y.C., 1978-81, ptnr., 1981-92; v.p., asst. gen. counsel Chemical Bank, N.Y.C., 1992—. Editor NYU Law Rev., 1968-70. Mem. N.Y. State Bar Assn. Home: 135 E 83rd St New York NY 10028-2408 Office: Chemical Bank 270 Park Ave Fl 39 New York NY 10017-2014

MILLER, SUSAN HEILMANN, publishing executive; b. Yuba City, Calif., Jan. 13, 1945; d. Paul Clay and Helen Christine (Sterud) Heilmann; m. Allen Clinton Miller III, June 24, 1967. BA, Stanford U., 1966; MS, Columbia U., 1969; PhD, Stanford U., 1976. Info. officer Montgomery County Schs., Rockville, Md., 1970-71, Palo Alto Schs., Calif., 1969-70, 71-73; news-features editor Bremerton Sun, Wash., 1976-80; night city editor Peninsula Times Tribune, Palo Alto, 1980-81; exec. editor News-Gazette, Champaign, Ill., 1981-85; dir. editorial devel. Scripps Howard Newspapers, Cin., 1985-90, v.p. editorial, 1990-93; pres., editor The Monterey (Calif.) County Herald, 1993—. Contbr. articles to profl. jours. Bd. dirs. Vol. Illini Projects, U. Ill., 1983-85, Washington Journalism Ctr., 1985-90, New Directions for News, 1988-91; mem. Pulitzer Prize Nominating Jury, 1986-87, accrediting com. Accrediting Council on Journalism and Mass Communication, 1986-89. Mem. Am. Soc. Newspaper Editors (bd. dirs. 1985-92), Newspaper Assn. Am., Nat. Press Found. (assoc.), Internat. Newspaper Fedn. Newspaper Pub. (mem. newspaper mktg. bureau), Assoc. Press Mng. Editors (bd. dirs.1984-91), Ill. AP Mng. Editors (bd. dirs. 1984-85). Clubs: Executive (Champaign, Ill.) (bd.dirs. 1984-85). Office: PO Box 271 8 Upper Ragsdale Dr Monterey CA 93940-0271

MILLER, SUZANNE MARIE, law librarian, educator; b. Sioux Falls, S.D., Feb. 25, 1954; d. John Gordon and Dorothy Margaret (Sabatka) M.; 1 child, Altinay Marie. B.A. in English, U. S.D., 1975; M.A. in Library Sci., U. Denver, 1976; postgrad. in polit. sci. U. LaVerne, 1980, postgrad. in law, 1984. Librarian II, U. S.D. Sch. of Law, Vermillion, 1977-78; law libr. U. LaVerne, Calif., 1978-85, instr. in law, 1980-85; asst. libr. tech. svcs. McGeorge Sch. Law, 1985—, prof. advanced legal rsch., 1994—. Co-author (with Elizabeth J. Pokorny) U.S. Government Documents: A Practical Guide for Library Assistants in Academic and Public Libraries, 1988; contbr. chpt. to book, articles to profl. jours. Recipient Am. Jurisprudence award Bancroft Whitney Pub. Co., 1983. Mem. Am. Assn. Law Librs., So. Calif. Assn. Law Libs. (arrangements com. 1981-82), Innovacq Users Group (chairperson, 1986-88), No. Calif. Assn. Law Librs. (mem. program com., inst. 1988), Western Pacific Assn. Law Librs. (sec. 1990-94, pres. elect 1994-95, pres. 1995—). Roman Catholic. Home: 4030 Jeffrey Ave Sacramento CA 95820-2551 Office: McGeorge Sch Law Library Univ of the Pacific 3200 Fifth Ave Sacramento CA 95817

MILLER, TAMARA DEDRA, psychologist; b. Cleve., Jan. 13, 1961; d. Taswill Taylor and Ethel (Midgett) M.; stepd. Gwendolyn (Hicks) M. BA in Psychology, Wittenberg U., 1982; D in Psychology, Wright State U., 1987. Lic. clin. psychologist, Ohio. Chief psychol. svc. USAF, Altus, Okla., 1987-89; chief psychol. testing USAF, Dayton, Ohio, 1989-92; dir. PTSD program Dept. VA, Dayton, 1992—; clin. prof. Wright State U., Dayton, 1992—; cons. Jackson County Youth, Altus, 1987-89, Ctr. for Retardation, Altus, 1987-89; adj. prof. Ctrl. State U., Wilberforce, 1991—; mem. panel Women's Fed. Program, Dayton, 1991; clin. advisor Les Femmes Concerned Citizens for Cancer, Dayton, 1992—. Consulting editor: Professional Psychology: Research and Practice, 1994. Capt. USAF, 1986-89. Mem. Nat. Coun. Negro Women Inc., VA Psychologists, Delta Sigma Theta. Avocations: reading, theatre, dance, aerobics, modeling. Home: 5670 Olive Tree Dr Dayton OH 45426-1313 Office: Dept VA Affairs Med Ctr 4100 E 3rd St Dayton OH 45403-2244

MILLER, TERRY ALAN, chemistry educator; b. Girard, Kans., Dec. 18, 1943; s. Dwight D. Miller and Rachel E. (Detjen) Beltram; m. Barbara Hoffmann, July 16, 1966; children: Brian, Stuart. BA, U. Kans., 1965; PhD, Cambridge (Eng.) U., 1968. Disting. tech. staff Bell Telephone Labs, 1968-84; vis. asst. prof. Princeton U., 1968-71; vis. lectr. Stanford U., 1972; vis. fgn. scholar Inst. Molecular Sci., Okazaki, Japan, summer 1983; Ohio eminent scholar, prof. chemistry Ohio State U., Columbus, 1984—; chair Molecular Spectroscopy Symposium, Columbus, 1992—. Me. editorial bd.

Jour. Chem. Physics, 1978-81, Jour. Molecular Spectroscopy, 1982-87, Laser Chemistry, 1986—, Rev. of Sci. Instruments, 1986-89, Jour. Phys. Chemistry, 1989-95, Jour. Optical Soc. Am., 1989-95, Chemtracts, 1989-90, Ann. Revs. Phys. Chemistry, 1989-94; contbr. more than 250 articles to profl. jours. Marshall fellow Brit. Govt., 1965-67, NSF fellow, 1967-68; William F. Meggard Awd., 1993, Optical Soc. Am. Fellow Optical Soc. Am. (Meggars award 1993), Am. Phys. Soc.; mem. Am. Chem. Soc. (councilor), Coblentz Soc. (Bomen-Michaelson award 1995). Office: Ohio State U 120 W 18th Ave Columbus OH 43210-1106

MILLER, TERRY MORROW, lawyer; b. Columbus, Ohio, Mar. 11, 1947; s. Robert E. and Elizabeth Jane (Morrow) M.; m. Martha Estella Johnson, Mar. 20, 1976; 1 child, Timothy. BS, Ohio State U., 1969, JD, 1975. Bar: Ohio 1975, U.S. Ct. Appeals (6th cir.) 1979, U.S. Supreme Ct. 1980. Asst. atty. gen. State of Ohio, Columbus, 1975-77; ptnr. Miller & Noga, Columbus, 1977-81; assoc. Vorys, Sater, Seymour and Pease, Columbus, 1981-85; ptnr. Vorys, Sater, Seymour & Pease, Columbus, 1986—. Sgt. U.S. Army, 1969-71, Okinawa. Mem. Ohio State Bar Assn., Columbus Bar Assn. Avocations: golf, Ohio history. Home: 288 E North Broadway Columbus OH 43214-4114 Office: Vorys Sater Seymour et al PO Box 1008 52 E Gay St Columbus OH 43215-3161

MILLER, TEVIE, supernumary justice, academic administrator; b. Edmonton, Alta., Can., Jan. 1, 1928; s. Abe William and Rebecca (Griesdorf) M.; m. Arliss June Toban, June 24, 1951; children: Catherine Dolgoy, Joshua Miller, Lisa Shadlyn. BA, U. Alta., 1949, LLB, 1950, LLD (hon.), 1991; LLD (hon.), U. Alta., 1991. Bar: Alta. 1951. Sr. ptnr. Miller, Miller, Witten, Edmonton, 1974; judge Alta. Dist. Ct., 1974; dep. judge N.W. territories, 1976; appointed to trial div. Supreme Ct. Alta., 1976; dep. judge Yukon territory, 1978; judge Ct. of Queen's Bench of Alta., 1974-84, assoc. chief justice, 1984-93; chancellor U. Alta., Edmonton, 1986-90; sessional lectr. law U. Alta., bd. govs., 1986-90; chmn. bd. Banff (Alta.) Sch. Advanced Mgmt., 1982-92. Former pres., former conv. chmn. Edmonton Liberal Assn.; liberal candidate Edmonton West Fed. Riding, 1968. Served to sub-lt. Royal Can. Navy. Recipient Torch of Learning award Hebrew U. of Jerusalem, 1992; honoree Edmonton Jewish Community Negev Dinner, 1972, Faculty Club of U. Alta. Avocations: sailing, travel. Office: Law Cts Bldg 6th Floor, 1A Sir Winston Churchill Sq, Edmonton, AB Canada T5J 0R2*

MILLER, THEODORE NORMAN, lawyer; b. Chgo., Oct. 9, 1942; s. Alexander Hyman and Bertha Helen (Swidler) M.; m. Marylyn Sue Zax, June 21, 1964; children—Henry, Amy. B.A., U. Mich., 1964; LL.B., Yale U., 1967. Bar: Ill. 1967, U.S. Dist. Ct. (no. dist.) Ill. 1967, U.S. Ct. Appeals (7th cir.) 1968, U.S. Supreme Ct. 1972. Law clk. U.S. Ct. Appeals (7th cir.), 1967-68; assoc. Sidley & Austin, Chgo., 1968-73, ptnr., 1973—. Mem. ABA, Chgo. Bar Assn., Chgo. Council Lawyers. Office: Sidley & Austin 1 First Nat Plz Chicago IL 60603*

MILLER, THEODORE ROBERT, surgeon, educator; b. Phila., Mar. 13, 1907; s. Robert and Regina (Ramspacher) M.; m. Helen E. Reiser, July 31, 1934. Student, Swarthmore Coll., Yale, Stockholm U.; MD, Temple U., 1933. Diplomate Am. Bd. Surgery. Intern Hackensack (N.J.) Hosp., 1933-34, resident, 1934-36, asst. attending surgeon, chief tumor clinic, 1936-39, adj. cons. neoplastic diseases, 1947-52, cons. in surgery, 1959—; asst. attending surgeon City Hosp., N.Y.C.; asst. resident, fellow Meml. Hosp., N.Y.C., 1939-42; clin. asst. surgeon gastric and mixed tumor services Meml. Hosp., 1947-49, asst. attending surgeon, gastric and mixed tumor services, 1949-59, asso. attending surgeon, 1959-64, attending surgeon chief bone tumor service, 1964-74, sr. attending surgeon, 1974-77, emeritus surgeon, 1977—, chief spl. surgery service, 1964-70; fellow Am.-Scandinavian Found., 1946-47; assoc. surgeon Pack Med. Group, N.Y.C., 1947-69; instr. surgery Cornell U. Med. Coll., 1952-62, clin. asst. prof., 1962-64, clin. assoc. prof. surgery, 1964-70, clin. prof. surgery, 1970-78, emeritus clin. prof., 1978—; clin. prof. surgery Rutgers U. Med. Coll. Contbr. articles to profl. publs. Served from capt. to lt. col. M.C. AUS, 1942-46. Fellow ACS, AMA, AAAS, N.Y. Acad. Medicine; mem. N.Y. State, County N.J. State, Middlesex County med. socs., Am. Radium Soc. (pres. 1959-60), N.Y. Cancer Soc., Del. Valley Ornithol. Club, N.Y. Surg. Soc., James Ewing Soc. (pres. 1967-68), N.Y. Acad. Scis., Academia Peruana de Cirguia (corr.), Sociedad Venezolana de Cirugia (corr.), Academia de Zulia (Venezuela) (corr.), Yale Club (N.Y.C. and Princeton), Phi Sigma Kappa. Home: 3-311 David Brainerd Dr Jamesburg NJ 08831

MILLER, THOMAS HULBERT, JR., former marine corps officer; b. San Antonio, June 3, 1923; s. Thomas Hulbert and Dora S. (Bartlett) M.; m. Ida Mai Giddings, May 11, 1943; children: Jacqueline Mai, Jo Ann. Student, U. Tex. Lic. comml. single and multi-engine pilot; lic. flight instr. Commd. 2d lt. USMC, 1943, designated naval aviator, 1943, advanced through grades to lt. gen., 1975; service in Pacific, Korea; chief staff 3d Amphibious Force Vietnam, 1970; comdg. gen. 2d Marine Aircraft Wing, 1972; dep. comdr., later comdg. gen. Fleet Marine Forces Pacific, 1975; dep. chief staff aviation Hdqrs. USMC, 1975-79, ret., 1979; cons. Applied Physics Lab., Johns Hopkins U., Nat. Acad. Sci., Def. Sci. Bd.; mem. FAA Blue Ribbon Panel on Civil Pilot and Maintenance Pers. Availability. Chmn. joint bd. U.S. Space Camp and Mercury Seven Found.; chmn. exec. bd. Mercury Seven Found.; mem. exec. bd. Washington Airports Task Force, Air & Space Heritage Coun. Decorated D.S.M., Legion of Merit (2), D.F.C. (4), Air medal (15), Navy Commendation medal; recipient Grey Eagle award; Silver Hawk award; Am./Brit. John Curtis Wilkinson Sword award for Anglo/Am. aerospace contbn.; Paul E. Haueter award Am. Helicopter Soc.; named one of Va.'s Pioneers of Aviation. Mem. Soc. Exptl. Test Pilots, Marine Corps Aviation Assn., Assn. Naval Aviation, Naval Aviation Mus. Found., Daedalians, Golden Eagles, Am. Radio Relay League, Masons. Presbyterian. Holder 500 kilometer closed course world speed record F4H-1 Phantom II aircraft, 1960; first American to fly British Harrier aircraft, 1968. Home: 3689 N Harrison St Arlington VA 22207-1843 *I believe a balanced life must include equal emphasis on moral, professional (work) and recreational activity. This activity must be guided by a strong Christian faith, moral and professional integrity, loyalty and a humble recognition of others rights. And, although we all are imperfect, we should strive to achieve perfection in these characteristics and never accept or receive those things that we do not work for.*

MILLER, THOMAS J., state attorney general; b. Dubuque, Iowa, Aug. 11, 1944; s. Elmer John and Betty Maude (Kross) M.; m. Linda Cottington, Jan. 10, 1981; 1 child, Matthew. B.A., Loras Coll., Dubuque, 1966; J.D., Harvard U., 1969. Bar: Iowa bar 1969. With VISTA, Balt., 1969-70; legis. asst. to U.S. rep.John C. Culver, 1970-71; legal edn. dir. Balt. Legal Aid Bur., also mem. part-time faculty U. Md. Sch. Law, 1971-73; pvt. practice McGregor, Iowa, 1973-78; city atty. McGregor, 1975-78, Marquette, Iowa; atty. gen. of Iowa, 1979-91, 95—; ptnr. Faegre & Benson, Des Moines, 1991-95. Pres. 2d Dist. New Democratic Club, Balt., 1972. Mem. Am. Bar Assn., Iowa Bar Assn., Common Cause. Roman Catholic. Office: Office of the Atty Gen Hoover State Office Bldg 2nd Fl Des Moines IA 50319

MILLER, THOMAS L., insurance company executive. Pres., ceo, Blue Cross Blue Shield of Kans., Topeka, 1983—. Office: Blue Cross Blue Shield of Kans 1133 SW Topeka Blvd Topeka KS 66629-0001*

MILLER, THOMAS MARSHALL, air transportation executive; b. Mineral Wells, Tex., Oct. 19, 1910; s. Van Dorn and Ida (Crockett) M.; m. Edith Mae Blake, July 8, 1936; children: Kay (Mrs. Robert Amick), Thomas Marshall, Robert, Philp, James. LL.B., Houston Law Sch., 1935. Office mgr. Dun & Bradstreet, Inc., Houston, 1936-42; v.p. traffic and sales Chgo. & So. Air Lines, Inc., Memphis, 1942-53; sr. v.p. mktg., dir. Delta Air Lines, Inc., Atlanta, 1973-87, mktg. cons., 1973-91, adv. dir., 1987—. Pres. Air Traffic Conf. Am., 1964. Mem. Am., Ga. bar assns., Inst. Cert. Travel Agts. (vice chmn. emeritus). Republican. Episcopalian. Home and Office: One Yonah Dr NE Atlanta GA 30309

MILLER, THOMAS ROBBINS, lawyer, publisher; b. Chgo., Mar. 8, 1938; s. William Whipple and Helen (Robbins) M.; m. Tran Tuong Nhu, July 3, 1974; children: Toby, Teddy, Nathalie, Gabriella. BA, Yale U., 1960; LLB, Stanford U., 1965; cert., Parker Sch. Fgn. and Comparative Law, Columbia U., 1966. Bar: N.Y. 1966, Calif. 1974. Assoc. Webster & Sheffield, N.Y.C., 1965-68; sole practice N.Y.C., 1968-74, Berkeley, 1974-89; pub. Lancaster Miller Pubs., Berkeley, 1974-89; sr. ptnr. Thomas R. Miller, A Profl. Law Corp., Oakland, Calif., 1989—; founder, pres. Internat. Children's Fund, Berkeley, 1974—; cons. Peace Corps, Washington, 1961, Ctr. for Constl. Rights, UNICEF, N.Y.C., 1973-76; dep. dir. Calif. Rural Legal Assistance, San Francisco, 1977-79. Named 1 of 10 Outstanding Young Men in U.S., U.S. Jaycees, 1974. Democrat. Office: 725 Washington St Oakland CA 94607-3924

MILLER, THOMAS WILLIAMS, former university dean; b. Pottstown, Pa., July 2, 1930; s. Franklin Sullivan and Margaret (Williams) M.; m. Edythe Edwards, Dec. 20, 1952; children: Theresa, Thomas, Christine, Stefanie. B.S. in Music Edn, West Chester (Pa.) State Coll., 1952; M.A., East Carolina U., Greenville, N.C., 1957; Mus.A.D. (Univ. fellow), Boston U., 1964. Dir. instrumental music Susquenita (Pa.) High Sch., 1955-56; instr. trumpet East Carolina U., 1957-61; asst. dean East Carolina U. (Sch. Music), 1962-68, dean, 1969-71; vis. prof. U. Hawaii, Honolulu, 1968; dean Sch. Music Northwestern U., Evanston, Ill., 1971-89; dean emeritus Northwestern U., Evanston, Ill. Contbr. articles to profl. jours. Assoc. Nat. Arts, 1989. Served with AUS, 1952-55. Named Distinguished Alumnus West Chester State Coll., 1975. Mem. Nat. Arts Assn., Music Educators Nat. Conf. (life), Nat. Assn. Schs. Music (hon. life, grad. commr. 1974-79, v.p. 1979-82, pres. 1982-85, chmn. grad. com. 1985-86, bd. dirs. 1986-89), Coll. Music Soc., Pi Kappa Lambda (hon. life regent, nat. pres. 1976-79), Phi Mu Alpha Sinfonia (hon. mem., Orpheus award 1989), Sigma Alpha Iota. Home: 3121 Walden Ln Wilmette IL 60091-1139 Office: Sch of Music Northwestern U Evanston IL 60208

MILLER, THORMUND AUBREY, lawyer; b. Pocatello, Idaho, July 14, 1919; s. Roy Edmund and Lillian (Thordarson) M.; m. Hannah A. Flansburgh, Feb. 10, 1946; children: Karen Lynette Van Gerpen, Christine Alison Westall. BA, Reed Coll., 1941; LLB, Columbia U., 1948; grad., Advanced Mgmt. Program, Harvard Bus. Sch., 1961. Bar: Calif. 1949, D.C. 1951, U.S. Supreme Ct. 1960. Assoc. McCutchen, Thomas, Matthews, Griffiths & Greene, San Francisco, 1948-50; atty. So. Pacific Transp. Co., Washington, 1950-56; asst. gen. atty. So. Pacific Transp. Co., 1956-59, gen. atty., 1959-66; sr. gen. atty. So. Pacific Transp. Co., San Francisco, 1966-75, gen. solicitor, 1975-79, gen. commerce counsel, 1979-83, dir., mem. exec. com., 1983-87, v.p., gen. counsel, 1983-89; gen. counsel So. Pacific Communications Co., San Francisco, 1970-79, dir., 1970-81; pvt. practice law Atherton, Calif., 1989—. Pres. Wood Acres Citizens Assn., Bethesda, Md., 1955-56; mem. exec. com. Holbrook Palmer Recreation Park Found., 1979—, pres., 1982-84; bd. dirs. Atherton Civic Interest League, 1981—, pres., 1992-94; mem. Atherton Park and Recreation Commn., 1991-95; mem. alumni bd. Reed Coll., 1971-72, trustee, 1987—, campaign com., 1995—; bd. dirs. Assocs. of U. Calif. Press, 1994—. Mem. ABA, Calif. Bar Assn., Assn. Transp. Law, Logistics and Policy, World Trade Club. Presbyterian.

MILLER, TIMOTHY ALDEN, plastic and reconstructive surgeon; b. Inglewood, Calif., Dec. 11, 1938; s. Henry Bernard and Florence Algena (Maddock) M.; 1 child, Matthew Christopher. Student, U. Calif., Berkeley; MD, UCLA, 1963. Diplomate Am. Bd. Surgery, Am. Bd. Plastic Surgery (bd. dirs. 1991—). Intern Vanderbilt U. Hosp., Nashville, 1963-64; resident in surgery, dept. surg. pathology UCLA, 1966-67, resident, then chief resident gen. and thoracics sugery, 1967-69, acting asst. prof., 1969-70, prof. surgery, 1981—; asst. surg. resident John Hopkins Hosp., 1967; fellow plastic and reconstructive surgery U. Pitts., 1970-72; chief plastic surgery West L.A. VA Med. Ctr., 1973—; dir. Am. Bd. Plastic Surgery, 1991—. Author: (novel) Practice to Deceive, 1991; assoc. editor Jour. Plastic & Reconstructive Surgery, 1987-93, co-editor, 1994—. Trustee Children's Inst. Internat., 1995—. Capt. U.S. Army, 1964-66, Vietnam. Decorated Bronze Star; recipient Thomas Symington award Pitts. Acad. Medicine, 1971. Mem. Am. Soc. for Plastic Surgery (co-editor Jour. Plastic and Reconstructive Surgery), Am. Soc. for Aesthetic Plastic Surgery (bd. dirs. 1990-95), Plastic Surgery Ednl. Found. (bd. dirs. 1991—); trustee Children's Inst. Internat. Avocations: tennis, novel writing. Office: UCLA Med Ctr 200 Medical Plz Ste 669 Los Angeles CA 90095-6960

MILLER, TOM POLK, retired architect; b. Houston, Nov. 17, 1914; s. Enoch Lester and Willie Elvie (Chumley) M.; m. Isabel Mount, Aug. 10, 1947; children: Crispin Mount, Abigail Mount. BA, Rice U., 1936, BS in Arch., 1937. Registered architect, Tex., Calif. Draftsman, designer Salisbury & McHale, Houston, 1937-38, Nunn & NcGinty, Houston, 1939-40, Robert & Co., Corpus Christi, Tex., 1940-41; assignee Civilian Pub. Service, Ark., Calif., Ind., Fla. and Oreg., 1942-46; draftsman, designer Kemper Nomland, Los Angeles, 1946-47, 48-49, Frick & Frick, Pasadena, Calif., 1950-51, Walter Reichardt, Los Angeles, 1951-52, De Witt & Swank, Dallas, 1952-54; prin. Mount-Miller, Houston, 1947-48, Denton, Tex., 1954-89; prin. Mount Miller McCain, Denton, 1989—. Editor The Illiterati and The Untide Press, 1945-52, The Denton Voice, 1970-74, Arkwork Rev., 1979-83; contbr. articles to profl. jours. Mem. Denton County Dem. Com., 1960-67; mem. Denton Hist. Landmark Commn., 1980-92, vice chmn., 1980-82; mem. The Fine Arts at Waldport, 1944-46, exec. sec. 1945, Am. Inst. Architects, 1957—, Anthropology Group Dallas, 1953—, The Forum, Denton, 1968—. Recipient Community Arts Recognition award Greater Denton Arts Council, 1982, State Service Recognition award Tex. Civil Liberties Union, 1986. Mem. AIA (emeritus), Interfaith Forum for Religion Art and Architecture (emeritus), Soc. Archtl. Historians, Nat. Trust for Hist. Preservation, Am. Solar Energy Soc., ACLU, War Resisters League, Fellowship of Reconciliation, Nat. Ataxia Found. Democrat. Unitarian Universalist. Avocations: music, piano, writing, travel, photography. Home and Office: 711 W Sycamore St Denton TX 76201-5919

MILLER, VERNON DALLACE, minister; b. McClure, Ill., Sept. 27, 1932; s. Homer Lee and Marie Kathleen (White) M.; m. Alice Elizabeth Wright, July 25, 1954; children: Ronald, Philip, Elizabeth, Annette, Douglas. Student, Moody Bible Inst., 1950-53, S.E. Mo. State, 1954, So. Ill. U., 1956-57; BA, Cedarville Coll., 1963, LittD, 1988. Ordained to min. Bapt. Ch., McClure, 1953. Pastor Camp Creek Bapt. Ch., Murphysboro, Ill., 1953-54, Bible Fellowship Bapt. Ch., Carterville, Ill., 1954-57, Faith Bapt. Ch., Mattoon, Ill., 1957-60, Immanuel Bapt. Ch., Arcanum, Ohio, 1961-63; editor, bus. mgr. Regular Bapt. Press, Chgo., 1963-70; pres. Ch. Bldg. Cons., Chgo., 1971-87; exec. editor, treas. Gen. Assn. of Regular Bapt. Chs., Schaumburg, Ill., 1987—; mem. exec. bd. Awana Youth Assn., Streamwood, Ill., 1965-83, Grand Rapids (Mich.) Bapt. Coll. and Sem., 1981-91, Shepherds Bapt. Ministries, Union Grove, Wis., 1965-96. Editor: (mag.) The Baptist Bulletin, 1987—. Del. Ill. Small Bus. Com., Springfield, Ill., 1984. Mem. Christian Ministries Mgmt. Assn. Republican. Office: Regular Bapt Press 1300 N Meacham Rd Schaumburg IL 60173-4806

MILLER, VICTORIA LOREN, designer, art director; b. San Francisco, May 25, 1957; d. Leon and Malvina (Hoffman) M. BFA, UCLA, 1979; postgrad., Art Ctr. Coll. Design, Pasadena, Calif., 1979, 80, UCLA, 1980-82, Otis/Parsons, L.A., 1981. Designer Bright and Assocs., L.A., 1979-80, Richard Runyon Design, L.A., 1980-83; art dir. Grey Entertainment Media, Santa Monica, Calif., 1984; prin. Victoria Miller Design, Santa Monica, Calif., 1984—; freelance art dir. Backer Spielvogel Bates, L.A., 1987-88; designer Sussman/Prejza & Co., Santa Monica, 1984, The Mednick Group, L.A., 1988-89. Label designer for Grand Cru Vineyards (Clio award 1985); designs represented in permanent collection Libr. Congress; pub. in Print Regional Ann., ADLA Ann., Am. Corp. Identity, Letterheads 5, Vision mag.; contbr. articles to profl. publs. Mem. Am. Inst. Graphic Arts, Mus. Contemporary Art (photography coun.), Art Dirs. Club. Jewish. Avocations: contemporary art, photography, dance, tennis, cycling. Home and Office: 10650 Kinnard Ave # 311 Los Angeles CA 90024-5983

MILLER, WALTER NEAL, insurance company consultant; b. N.Y.C., Nov. 26, 1929; s. Morton and Kathryn (Gersten) M.; m. Nancy Louise Clapp, Sept. 11, 1954; children—Scott, Timothy, David, Kathryn, Amy. B.A., Swarthmore Coll., 1951. With N.Y. Life Ins. Co., N.Y.C., 1951-86; v.p., actuary Prudential Ins. Co., Newark, 1986-93; sr. v.p., chief actuary Prudential Preferred Fin. Svcs., Liberty Corner, N.J., 1993-94; pvt. practice cons., 1994—. Author: (with others) Analysis of Actuarial Theory for Variable Life Insurance, 1969; contbr. (with others) articles to profl. jours. Mem. Soc. Actuaries, Am. Acad. Actuaries. Home: 470 Grandview Ave Wyckoff NJ 07481-2546

MILLER, WARREN, bishop. Bishop Ch. of God in Christ, Cleve. Office: Ch of God in Christ 3618 Beacon Dr Cleveland OH 44122-6009

MILLER, WARREN EDWARD, political scientist; b. Hawarden, Iowa, Mar. 26, 1924; s. John Carroll and Mildred Ovedia (Lien) M.; m. Ruth S. Jones, May 1981; children by previous marriage: Jeffrey Ralph, Jennifer Louise. B.S., U. Oreg., 1948, M.S., 1950; Ph.D., Maxwell Sch. Citizenship and Public Affairs, Syracuse U., 1954; Ph.D. (hon.), U. Goteborg, Sweden, 1972. Asst. study dir. Survey Research Ctr., Inst. Social Research, U. Mich., 1951-53, study dir., 1953-56, research assoc., 1956-59, program dir., 1959-68, research coordinator polit. behavior program, 1968-70, prin. investigator nat. election studies, 1977—; dir. Ctr. Polit. Studies, Inst. Social Research, 1970-81; program dir. Ctr. Polit. Studies, 1982-93; asst. prof. polit. sci. Ctr. Polit. Studies, Inst. Social Research, 1956-58, asso. prof., 1958-63, prof., 1963-93, Arthur W. Bromage prof. polit. sci., 1981-82; prof. polit. sci. Ariz. State U., 1981—; fellow Ctr. Advanced Study in Behavioral Scis., 1961-62; exec. dir. Inter-univ. Consortium for Polit. and Social Rsch., 1962-70, assoc. dir., 1978—; vis. prof. U. Tilburg, Netherlands, 1973, U. Geneva, 1973, European U. Inst., Florence, Italy, 1979; vis. Disting. prof. Ariz. State U., 1981; trustee Inst. Am. Univs., 1970—; Regents' prof., Ariz. State U., 1988—. Author: (with others) books including The Voter Decides, 1954, American Voter, 1960, Elections and the Political Order, 1966, (with T.E. Levitin) Leadership and Change: Presidential Elections from 1952-1976, 77, (with M.K. Jennings) Parties in Transition, 1986, Without Consent, 1988, (with others) The American National Election Studies Data Sourcebook, 1952-1978, 80, The American National Election Studies Data Sourcebook, 1952-86, 89; (with J. Merrill Shanks) The New American Voter, 1996; contbr. (with others) articles to profl. publs.; editl. bd.: (with others) Am. Polit. Sci. Rev, 1966-71, Computers and the Humanities, 1969-71, Social Science History, 1976-91, Social Science Rev., 1973; editorial adv. bd.: (with others) Sage Electoral Studies Yearbook, 1974. Served with USAAF, 1943-46. Recipient Disting. Alumnus award Maxwell Sch. Citizenship and Public Affairs, Syracuse U., 1974, Disting. Faculty Achievement award U. Mich., 1977; honored in the creation of the Warren E. Miller award for Intellectual Accomplishment and Svc. Am. Polit. Sci. Assn. sect. on Elecions, Pub. Opionion and Voting Behavior, 1995, creation of the Warren E. Miller award for Meritorious Svc. to Social Scis. Inter-Univ. Consortium for Polit. and Social Rsch., 1993. Fellow Am. Acad. Arts and Scis.; mem. AAAS, Am. Polit. Sci. Assn. (pres. 1979-80), Internat. Polit. Sci. Assn. (coun. 1969-73), M.W. Polit. Sci. Assn., Internat. Soc. Polit. Psychology, So. Polit. Sci. Assn., Social Sci. History Assn. (pres. 1979-80), Norwegian Acad. Sci. and Letters. Office: Ariz State U Dept Polit Sci Tempe AZ 85287

MILLER, WARREN LLOYD, lawyer; b. Bklyn., July 18, 1944; s. Allan and Ella (Faecher) M.; m. Jana Lee Morris, May 13, 1978; children: Lindsey Beth, Alan Gregory, William Brett. BA with high univ. honors, Am. U., 1966; JD with honors, George Washington U., 1969. Bar: Va., 1969, D.C., 1969, U.S. Supreme Ct., 1981. Law clk. to Hon. Edward A. Beard Superior Ct. D.C., 1968-69; asst. U.S. atty. for D.C., 1969-74; ptnr. Stein, Miller & Brodsky, 1974-85; pres. Warren L. Miller, P.C., 1986—; of counsel Reed, Smith, Shaw & McClay, 1986-93; lectr. Georgetown U. Law Sch., 1970-71, Am. U., 1971-72; guest spkr. various TV programs and legal forums; mem. Jud. Conf. D.C. Cir., 1984—; pres. Asst. U.S. Attys. Assn. of D.C., 1983-48. contbr. articles to profl. jours. Parliamentarian credentials and rules coms. Rep. Nat. Conv., 1984, mem. D.C. Law Revision Commn., 1987-91 (apptd. by Pres. Reagan), U.S. Commn. for Preservation of Am.'s Heritage Abroad, 1992— (apptd. by Pres. Bush); pres. Asst. U.S. Atty.'s Assn. of D.C., 1983-84; fundraiser Rep. Nat. Com. and Pres. Bush, 1988-92; co-chmn. dinner for V.P. Bush, 1988; vice-chmn. Pres.'s Dinner, 1989; co-chmn. Pres.'s Club, Washington, 1990-92; co-chmn. fundraiser for U.S. Senator Christopher Bond, 1992;, bd. dirs. Found. for Buchenwald and Mittelbau-Dora Memls., 1994—; spkr. Ceremonies at Buchenwald, Germany, 1995, Commemorative the 50th Ann. of its Liberation; spkr. U.S. Holocaust Meml. Mus., 1995. Mem. Congl. Country Club (Bethesda, Md.), Phi Delta Phi, Omicron Delta Kappa, Pi Gamma Mu. Office: 2300 N St NW Ste 600 Washington DC 20037-1122

MILLER, WENDELL SMITH, chemist, consultant; b. Columbus, Ohio, Sept. 26, 1925; s. Wendell Pierce and Emma Josephine (Smith) M.; m. Dorothy Marie Pagen, Aug. 18, 1949; children: William Ross, Wendell Roger. BA, Pomona Coll., 1944; MS, UCLA, 1952. Chemist U.S. Rubber Co., Torrance, Calif., 1944; sr. chemist Carbide & Carbon Chemicals Corp., Oak Ridge, 1944-48; ptnr. Kellogg & Miller, Los Angeles, 1949-56; patent coordinator Electro Optical Systems, Inc., Pasadena, Calif., 1956-59; v.p. Intertech. Corp. optical and optoelectronic system devel., North Hollywood, Calif., 1960-66, dir., 1966—; assoc. Ctr. for Study Evolution and Origin of Life, UCLA. Commr. Great Western Council Boy Scouts Am., 1960-65. Served with AUS, 1944-46. Decorated Army Commendation medal. Mem. Los Angeles Patent Law Assn., IEEE, AAAS, 20th Century Round Table, Sigma Xi, Phi Beta Kappa, Pi Mu Epsilon. Numerous patents in field. Home: 1341 Comstock Ave Los Angeles CA 90024-5314

MILLER, WILBUR HOBART, business diversification consultant; b. Boston, Feb. 15, 1915; s. Silas Reuben and Muriel Mae (Greene) M.; m. Harriett I. Harmon, June 20, 1941; children: Nancy Iber Miller Harray, Warren Harmon, Donna Sewall Miller Davidge. B.S., U. N.H., 1936, M.S., 1938; Ph.D., Columbia U., 1941. Rsch. chemist Am. Cyanamid Co., Stamford, Conn., 1941-49, Washington tech. rep., 1949-53, dir. food industry devel., 1953-57; tech. dir. products for agr. Cyanamid Internat. Am. Cyanamid Co., N.Y.C., 1957-60; sr. scientist Dunlap & Assos., Darien, Conn., 1960-63, sr. assoc., 1963-66; coord. new product devel. Celanese Corp., N.Y.C., 1966-67, mgr. comml. rsch., 1967-68, dir. corp. devel., 1969-84; bus. diversification cons., 1984—; lectr. on bus. and soc. Western Conn. State Coll., 1977-79. Contbr. sci. papers to profl. jours.; patentee in field. Chmn. Stamford Forum for World Affairs, 1954-87, hon. chmn., 1987—; mem. adv. bd. Ctr. for Study of Presidency, 1980—; bd. dirs. Stamford Symphony, 1974-80, v.p., 1978-80; bd. dirs. Stamford Hist. Soc., 1988, v.p., 1991-92, pres., 1993-95; pres. Coun. for Continuing Edn. Stamford, 1963, bd. dirs., 1960-70; elder United Presbyn. Ch., nominating com., 1960-63; pres. Interfaith Coun. of Stamford, 1973; internat. fellow U. Bridgeport, 1985-88; mem. pres.'s coun. U. N.H., 1982—. Recipient outstanding achievement award Coll. Tech., U. N.H., 1971, Am. Design award, 1948, Golden Rule Award J.C. Penney & Co., 1986; Univ. fellow Columbia U., 1940-41. Fellow AAAS, Am. Inst. Chemists (councillor N.Y. chpt. 1984-85); mem. Am. Chem. Soc. (news svc. adv. bd., 1948-53), N.Y. Acad. Scis., Société de Chimie Industrielle (v.p. fin. Am. sect. 1980-84, dir. 1984—), Inst. Food Tech., Soc. for Internat. Devel., Am. Acad. Polit. and Social Scis., Stamford Hist. Soc., Chemists Club (N.Y.C., treas. 1982-84), Sigma Xi, Alpha Chi Sigma, Phi Kappa Phi. Home: 19 Crestview Ave Stamford CT 06907-1906

MILLER, WILBUR RANDOLPH, retired university educator and administrator; b. Elsberry, Mo., Nov. 12, 1932; s. Charles Clifton and Pauline Jean (Dryden) M. Student, SE Mo. U., 1951-53; BEd, U. Mo., 1954, MEd, 1955, EdD, 1960. Cert. secondary tchr., Mo. Tchr. indsl. arts Hazelwood Sch. Dist., St. Louis, 1955-56, U. Lab. Sch., Columbia, Mo., 1956-60; indsl. tchr. educator Purdue U., West Lafayette, Ind., 1960-63; asst. prof. U. Mo., Columbia, 1963-67, assoc. prof. and chmn. dept. coll. edn., 1967-76, prof. and assoc. dean coll. edn., 1976-86, dean coll. edn., 1986-91, prof., dean emeritus, 1992; chmn. adv. coun. Fed. Rsch. Ctr. in Vocat. Edn., Ohio State U., Columbus, 1981-84; internat. edn. cons. 1992—; edn. adv. bd. DeVry Inc., Evanston, Ill., 1986—; mem. pvt. tech. sch. accreditation commn., 1994—. Author: Teaching Children Through Construction Activities, 1985, Instructors and Their Jobs, 1990, The Golf Primer, 1991, Handbook for College Teaching, 1995; editor: (series) Basic Industrial Arts, 1978; contbr. more than 40 articles to profl. jours. Pres., bd. dirs. Lenoir Inc., Columbia, 1977-84; mem. Woodhaven Sch. Bd., Columbia, 1982-83. With USNR, 1955-63. Recipient U. Faculty/Alumni award, 1985. Mem. Nat. Assn. Indsl. Tchr. Educators (pres., officer 1965-74), Am. Indsl. Arts Assn. (v.p. 1980), Mo. Vocat. Assn. (pres. 1974-75), Mo. Assn. Colls. for Tchr. Edn. (pres. 1987-90), Am. Vocat. Assn. (Outstanding Svc. award 1979). Mem. Disciples of Christ Ch. Club: Faculty (Columbia) (officer 1977-82). Lodge: Kiwanis. Avocations: golf, travel, home maintenance. Office: PO Box 2683 Auburn AL 36831

MILLER, WILLARD, JR., mathematician, educator; b. Ft. Wayne, Ind., Sept. 17, 1937; s. Willard and Ruth (Kemerly) M.; m. Jane Campbell Scott,

June 5, 1965; children—Stephen, Andrea. S.B. in Math., U. Chgo., 1958; Ph.D. in Applied Math, U. Calif.-Berkeley, 1963. Vis. mem. Courant Inst. Math. Scis., NYU, 1963-65; mem. faculty U. Minn., 1965—, prof. math., 1972—, head Sch. Math.,, 1978-86; co-prin. investigator Inst. Math. and its Applications, 1980-94, assoc. dir., 1987-94; assoc. dean Inst. of Tech., 1994—; acting dean Inst. of Tech., 1995. Author: Lie Theory and Special Functions, 1968, Symmetry Groups and Their Applications, 1972, Symmetry and Separation of Variables, 1977; assoc. editor Jour. Math. Physics, 1973-75, Applicable Analysis, 1978-90. Mem. AAAS, Soc. Indsl. and Applied Math. (mng. editor Jour. Math. Analysis 1975-81), Am. Math. Soc., Sigma Xi. Home: 4508 Edmund Blvd Minneapolis MN 55406-3629 Office: Univ Minn Sch Math Minneapolis MN 55455

MILLER, WILLIAM ALVIN, clergyman, author; b. Pitts., Jan. 1, 1931; s. Christ William and Anna Ernestine (Wilhelm) M.; m. Marilyn Mae Miller, Aug. 8, 1953; children: Mark William, Eric Michael. BA, Capital U., 1953; MDiv, Luth. Theol. Sem., Columbus, Ohio, 1957; MST, Andover Newton Theol. Sch., Newton Centre, Mass., 1958, D of Ministry, 1974. Ordained to ministry Luth. Ch.; lic. marriage & family therapist, Minn. Pastor St. James Luth. Ch., Balt., 1958-66; chaplain Fairview Hosp., Mpls., 1966-73, dir. dept. religion & health, 1973-87; instr. Fairview Sch. Nursing, Mpls., 1967-75, Luther Northwestern Theol. Sem., St. Paul, 1973-85; pres. Woodland Pub. Co., Wayzata, Minn., 1979—; dir. Woodland Pastoral Assocs., Mpls., 1987—; assoc. pastor Cen. Luth. Ch., Mpls., 1989-94; chair bd. dirs. Luth. Social Svcs. Md., Balt., 1963-65; adminstr. Dialogue 88, Mpls., 1987-88. Author: Why Do Christians Break Down?, 1973, Big Kids' Mother Goose, 1976, When Going to Pieces Holds You Together, 1976, You Count, You Really Do!, 1976, Mid Life, New Life, 1978, Conversations, 1980, Make Friends With Your Shadow, 1981, Prayers at Mid Point, 1983, The Joy of Feeling Good, 1986, Your Golden Shadow, 1989, 91, Meeting the Shadow, 1991; assoc. editor Jour. Pastoral Care, Decatur, Ga., 1984-88; contbr. articles to profl. jours. Chaplain, Jr. C. of C., Randallstown, Md., 1962-64; bd. dirs. Am. Protestant Health Assn., Schaumburg, Ill., 1983-89. Fellow Coll. Chaplains (pres. 1985-87), Assn. Mental Health Clergy (Anton T. Boisen award 1989); mem. Assn. Clin. Pastoral Edn. (supr.), Am. Assn. Marriage & Family Therapy. Avocations: cabinetmaking, skiing, publishing, construction. Home and Office: 2005 Xanthus Ln N Minneapolis MN 55447-2053

MILLER, WILLIAM CHARLES, lawyer; b. Jacksonville, Fla., Aug. 6, 1937; s. Charles and Mary Elizabeth (Kiger) M.; m. Hadmut Gisela Larsen, June 10, 1961; children: Monica Lee, Charles Andreas. BA, Washington and Lee U., 1958, LLB, 1961; LLM, N.Y. U., 1963; postgrad., Harvard U., 1978. Bar: Fla. 1961, Calif. 1984, Ind. 1987, U.S. Supreme Ct. 1968. Counsel to electrochem., elastomers and internat. depts. E.I. duPont de Nemours & Co., Wilmington, Del., 1963-66; counsel S. Am. ops. Bristol-Myers Co., N.Y.C., 1967-69; internat. counsel Xerox Corp., Stamford, Conn., 1969-79; assoc. gen. counsel Xerox Corp., Stamford, 1979-80; v.p., gen. counsel, sec. Max Factor & Co., Hollywood, Calif., 1981-85, Boehringer Mannheim Corp., Indpls., 1985-92; v.p., gen. counsel Collagen Corp., Palo Alto, Calif., 1992-95, Gen. Probe Inc., 1995—. Bd. dirs. Southwestern Legal Found., 1975-85. Fulbright scholar, 1959-60; Ford Found. fellow, 1961-62; Hague Acad. fellow, 1963; German Govt. grantee, 1962-63; Kappa Sigma scholar, 1959. Mem. Internat. Bar Assn., ABA, Calif. Bar Assn., Fla. Bar Assn., Ind. Bar Assn., Masons, Elks, Phi Beta Kappa, Phi Eta Sigma, Delta Theta Phi. Republican. Mem. Christian Ch. Home: 3516 Villanova Ave San Diego CA 92122-2313

MILLER, WILLIAM CHARLES, college dean, architect; b. San Francisco, May 11, 1945; s. Francis Leland and Ethel Lorene (Britt) M.; m. Beverly Jean McConnell, Dec. 22, 1968; children: Britt A., David A. BArch, U. Oreg., 1968; MArch, U. Ill., 1970. Registered architect, Ariz., Kans., Utah. Architect various firms, San Francisco, Sacramento, Calif., Tucson and Oak Harbor, Wash.; asst. prof. Coll. Architecture U. Ariz., Tucson, 1970-73, 74-77; assoc. prof. dept. architecture Kans. State U., Manhattan, 1977-86, prof., 1986-92, head dept., 1990-92; dean, prof. Grad. Sch. Architecture U. Utah, Salt Lake City, 1992—; guest lectr. over 36 schs. architecture; presenter to more than a dozen profl. socs. and orgns.; dir. west ctrl. region Assn. Collegiate Schs. Architecture, 1988-91, chair theme paper sessions ann. meeting, San Francisco, 1990, chair regional paper sessions ann. meeting, Washington, 1991, co-chair adminstrv. conf., Milw., 1995; bd. dirs. Nat. Archtl. Accrediting Bd., 1996—. Author: Alvar Aalto: An Annotated Bibliography, 1984; co-editor: The Architecture of the In-Between, 1990, Architecture: Back to Life, 1991; contbr. articles to profl. jours., chpts. to books. Bd. dirs. Assist, Inc., Contemporary Arts Group. Recipient Svc. awards Assn. Collegiate Schs. Architecture, Nat. Coun. Archtl. Registration Bds. Mem. AIA (architects in edn. com., com. on design, Kans. profl. edn. com., pres-elect Flint Hills, treas. Utah, exec. com., treas., exec. com. Western Mountain region), Am.-Scandinavian Found., Soc. for Advancement Scandinavian Studies, Tau Sigma Delta. Office: U Utah Grad Sch Architecture Salt Lake City UT 84112

MILLER, WILLIAM ELWOOD, mining company executive; b. Bend, Oreg., May 9, 1919; s. Harry Adelbert and Sarah (Heyburn) M.; B.A., Stanford, 1941, M.B.A., 1947; m. Constance Alban Crosby, July 2, 1955; children: William, Constance, Harold, Mary, Sarah Crosby, Charles Crosby, Helen, Harry. Owner and operator Central Oregon Pumice Co., Bend, 1948—; pres. The Miller Lumber Co., Bend, The Miller Ranch Co., Bend, Miller Tree Farm. Commr., City of Bend, 1959-62, mayor, 1960. Bd. dirs. Central Oreg. Coll.; pres. Central Oreg. Coll. Found., 1956-57; dir. Central Oregon Coll. Area Ednl. Dist., 1961-65, chmn., 1964-65; bd. govs. Ore. Dept. Geology and Mineral Industries, 1971-75. Served with A.C., USNR, 1942-45. Decorated D.F.C., Air medal. Mem. Central Oreg. (v.p. 1954), Bend (pres. 1954) C. of C., Bend Golf Club, Rotary (dir. Bend 1955-56), Kappa Sigma. Republican. Episcopalian. Home: 527 NW Congress St Bend OR 97701-2509 Office: 1 NW Greenwood Ave Bend OR 97701-2028

MILLER, WILLIAM FREDERICK, research company executive, educator, business consultant; b. Vincennes, Ind., Nov. 19, 1925; s. William and Elsie M. (Everts) M.; m. Patty J. Smith, June 19, 1949; 1 son, Rodney Wayne. Student, Vincennes U., 1946-47; BS, Purdue U., 1949, MS, 1951, PhD, 1956; D.Sc., 1972. Mem. staff Argonne Nat. Lab., 1955-64, assoc. physicist, 1956-59, dir. applied math. div., 1959-64; prof. computer sci. Stanford U., Palo Alto, Calif., 1965—; Herbert Hoover prof. pub. and pvt. mgmt. Stanford U., 1979—, assoc. provost for computing, 1968-70, v.p. for research, 1970-71, v.p., provost, 1971-78; mem. Stanford Assocs., 1972—; pres., chief exec. officer SRI Internat., Menlo Park, Calif., 1979-90; chmn. bd., chief exec. officer SRI Devel. Co., Menlo Park, David Sarnoff Research Ctr., Inc., Princeton, N.J.; chmn. bd. dirs. Borland Internat., Inc., 1996—; professiorial lectr. applied math. U. Chgo., 1962-64; vis. prof. math. Purdue U., 1962-63; vis. scholar Ctr. for Advanced Study in Behavioral Scis., 1976; bd. dirs. Wels Fargo and Co., Gemini-McKenna, Inc., Scios-Nova, Inc.; mem. adv. coun. BHP Internat.; mem. computer sci. and engring bd. NAS, 1968-71; mem. Nat. Sci. Bd., 1982-88; mem. corp. com. computers in edn. Brown UU., 1971-79; mem. policy bd. EDUCOM Planning Coun. on Computing in Edn., 1974-79, chmn., 1974-76; mem. ednl. adv. bd. Guggenheim Meml. Found., 1976-80; mem. com. postdoctoral and doctoral rsch. staff NRC, 1977-80, mem. computer sci. and telecom. bd. Nat. Inst. Stds. Tech. Bd. Assessment; mem. internat. adv. panel Nat. Sci. and Tech. Bd., Singapore. Assoc. editor: Pattern Recognition Jour, 1968-72, Jour. Computational Physics, 1970-74. Served to 2d lt. F.A. AUS, 1943-46. Recipient Frederic B. Whitman award United Way Bay Area, 1982. Fellow IEEE, Am. Acad. Arts and Scis., AAAS; mem. Am. Math. Soc., Am. Phys. Soc., Soc. Indsl. and Applied Math., Assn. Computing Machinery, Nat. Acad. Engring., Sigma Xi, Tau Beta Pi. Office: Stanford U Grad Sch Bus Stanford CA 94305

MILLER, WILLIAM GREEN, ambassador; b. N.Y.C., Aug. 15, 1931; m. Suzanne Lisle; 2 children. BA, Williams Coll., Oxford U., U.K.; MA, Oxford U., U.K.; postgrad., Harvard U. With Fgn. Svc., 1959; vice consul, polit. officer Isfahan, Iran, 1959; polit. officer Tehran, Iran, 1962-64; line officer, exec. secretariat Dept. of State, 1965-66; mem. Sr. Interdepartmental Group, 1966-67; spl. asst. fgn. affairs and def. Senator John Sherman Cooper, 1967-72; staff dir. Senate Select Com. Emergency Powers, 1973-75, Senate Select Com. to Study Govtl. Ops. with Respect to Intelligence Communities, 1975-76, Senate Select Com. Intelligence, 1976-81; assoc. dean, adj. prof. internat. politics Fletcher Sch. Law and Diplomacy, 1981-82, rsch. assoc., 1983-85; faculty assoc. Harvard Ctr. Middle Eastern Studies, 1983-86; pres. Am. Com. U.S.- Soviet Rels., 1986-92; U.S. amb. to Ukraine, 1993—; cons. D.H. Sawyer and Assocs., Ltd., N.Y.C., 1985; bd. dirs. Internat. Found., pres. 1986-92; pres. Com. Am.- Russian Rels., cons. Catherine T. MacArthur Found., 1992-93. Contbr. articles to profl. jours. Rsch. fellow Harvard Ctr. Sci. and Internat. Affairs, 1984-86, John F. Kennedy Sch. of Govt. fellow Harvard U., 1986. Mem. Nat. Acad. Pub. Diplomacy, Nat. Acad. Pub. Adminstrn., Internat. Inst. Strategic Studies, Coun. Fgn. Rels., Children of the 21st Century, Middle East Inst. Office: 10 Yuria Kotsyubinskovo, 252053 Kiev 53, Ukraine

MILLER, WILLIAM H., public relations executive; b. Cin., Jan. 27, 1941. BA, U. Pa., 1963; MBA, U. Cin., 1965. Fin. analyst Ford Motor Co., 1965-67; fin. specialist Booz Allen Hamilton, 1967-69; dir. midwest fin. commn. liaison Fin. Rels. Bd., Chgo., 1969-71, sr. v.p., 1971-73, exec. v.p., 1976-81, assoc. mng. ptnr., 1981—. Office: Fin Rels Bd John Hancock Ctr 875 N Michigan Ave Chicago IL 60611-1803*

MILLER, WILLIAM HUGHES, theoretical chemist, educator; b. Kosciusko, Miss., Mar. 16, 1941; s. Weldon Howard and Jewel Irene (Hughes) M.; m. Margaret Ann Westbrook, June 4, 1966; children: Alison Leslie, Emily Sinclaire. B.S., Ga. Inst. Tech., 1963; A.M., Harvard U., 1964, Ph.D., 1967. Jr. fellow Harvard U., 1967-69; NATO postdoctoral fellow Freiburg (Germany) U., 1967-68; asst. prof. chemistry U. Calif., Berkeley, 1969-72, assoc. prof., 1972-74, prof., 1974—, dept. chmn., 1989-93; fellow Churchill Coll., Cambridge (Eng.) U., 1975-76; hon. prof. Shandong U., People's Republic of China, 1994. Alfred P. Sloan fellow, 1970-72; Camille and Henry Dreyfus fellow, 1973-78; Guggenheim fellow, 1975-76, Christensen fellow St. Catherine's Coll., Oxford, 1993; recipient Alexander von Humboldt-Stiftung U.S. Sr. Scientist award, 1981-82, Ernest Orlando Lawrence Meml. award, 1985, Hirschfelder prize in theoretical chemistry, U. Wis., 1996. Fellow AAAS, Am. Acad. Arts and Scis., Am. Phys. Soc. (Irving Langmuir award 1990); mem. NAS, Am. Chem. Soc. (theoretical chemistry award 1994), Internat. Acad. Quantum Molecular Sci. (Ann. prize 1974). Office: U Calif Dept Chemistry Berkeley CA 94720

MILLER, WILLIAM JONES, lawyer; b. Cleve., Apr. 20, 1938; s. William John and Virginia Katheryn (Harris) M.; divorced; children: Cheray, Jason. BA, Yale U., 1960; JD, U. Miami, 1965. Bar: Fla. 1965, Ohio 1967. Assoc. Grimditch & Assoc., Pompano Beach, Fla., 1965-67; ptnr. Arter & Hadden, Cleve., 1967-81; shareholder Carlton, Fields, Ward, Emmanuel, Smith & Cutler, Tampa, Fla., 1981-95. Chmn. editorial com. Cleve. Bar Jour., 1973-74. Chmn. Yale U. Alumni Cleve., 1978-81; mem. exec. bd. Fed. Bar Assn. Middle Dist. Fla., Tampa. Sgt. USAR, 1963-68, then col. Mem. ABA, Maritime Law Assn. U.S., Propeller Club of Tampa Bay (pres. 1990-91), The Author's Guild. Republican. Presbyterian. Avocations: writing, golf, reading.

MILLER, WILLIAM LAWRENCE, government official; b. Medford, Oreg., May 12, 1937; s. Oliver William Miller and Ida Lucile Lowry; m. Jo Anne Carmen Clifton, Jan. 29, 1961; children: William Scott, Douglas Britton. B.S. in Chemistry, U. Calif.-Davis, 1963, M.S. in Geology, 1967. Assoc. chemist Aerojet Gen. Corp., Sacramento, 1963-64; chemist Bur. of Mines, Reno, 1966-70; program analysis officer U.S. Dept. Interior, Washington, 1970-71; staff metallurgist Bur. Mines, Washington, 1971-77; chief div. metallurgy Bur. Mines, 1977-79, chief research directorate staff, 1979-82, asst. dir. minerals and materials research, 1982-87, chief office regulatory projects coordination, 1988-91; chief div. regulatory and policy analysis, 1991-95; dir. office mineral issues analysis Washington, 1995—; alt. mem. coordinating com. on materials research and devel. Fed. Council Sci. and Tech., Washington, 1969. Recipient Meritorious Service award and silver medal U.S. Dept Interior, 1982. Mem. Am. Chem. Soc., Metall. Soc., AIME, Geol. Soc. Washington, Mining and Metall. Soc. Am., Sr. Execs Assn. Office: US Dept of Interior Bur of Mines 810 7th St NW Washington DC 20241-0002

MILLER, WILLIAM LEE, JR., minister; b. Mammoth Spring, Ark., Dec. 27, 1926; s. William L. and Janie Katherine (Murrell) M.; m. Marion Evelyn O'Neal, Mar. 23, 1947 (div. 1976); children: Georgia Katherine Miller Beach, William Lee III; m. Judith Ann Bell, Nov. 28, 1977. AB, Phillips U., 1950, LittD, 1968; postgrad., U. Ark., 1951-52, Tex. Christian U., 1958, U. Ky., 1961; BD, Lexington Theol. Sem., 1961. Ordained to ministry Christian Ch. (Disciples of Christ), 1950. Pastor 1st Christian Ch., Rogers, Ark., 1952-59; v.p. Bd. Higher Edn., Indpls., 1962-68; pres. Bd. Higher Edn. Christian Ch. (Disciples of Christ), 1968-77; v.p. devel. Nat. City Christian Ch. Corp., Washington, 1977-82; upper Midwest regional min., pres. Christian Ch. (Disciples of Christ), Des Moines, 1982-93; pres. Miller Devel. Assocs.; dir. Christian Ch. Found., Indpls., 1968-77, 84-93; trustee Bethany Coll., W.Va., 1972-85, Culver Stockton Coll., 1970-77, 82—, Tougaloo Coll., Jackson, Miss., 1970-76, Christian Theol. Sem., Indpls., 1987-94. Precinct committeeman Dem. Party, Indpls., 1968-72; mem. Reagan First Inaugural Religious Com.; bd. dris. St. Louis Christian Home, 1956-59; chmn. Coop. Coll. Registry, Washington, 1963-70; mem. Disciples of Christ Ch., Disciples Soc. for Faith & Reason; bd. dirs., exec. com. Christian Ch. D.C., N.C., 1995—. Mem. Disciples of Christ Hist. Soc., Coun. Christian Unity (exec. com. 1968-77), Nat. Evangelitic Assn. (bd. dirs. 1983-86), Am. Assn. Higher Edn., Masons, KT, Sigma Chi. Home: 113 Kellam Ct Manteo NC 27954 Office: Miller Devel Assocs PO Box 194 Manteo NC 27954-0194

MILLER, WILLIAM NAPIER CRIPPS, lawyer; b. Long Branch, N.J., June 7, 1930; adopted s. Julia (Erwin) M.; m. Carolyn Anderson, Jan. 19, 1951 (div. 1963); children: Bruce Douglass, Jennifer Erwin; m. Hannelore Steinbeck, Dec. 4, 1970;. A.A., Coll. Marin, 1949; student, U. Calif.-Berkeley, 1949-51, J.D., 1955. Bar: N.Y., Calif. 1956, U.S. Supreme Ct. 1983. Assoc. Mudge, Stern, Baldwin & Todd, N.Y.C., 1955-58; assoc. Pillsbury, Madison & Sutro, San Francisco, 1959-65, ptnr., 1966—; staff NYU Law Sch., 1957-58; ct. adv. com. Calif. State Assembly Judiciary Com., 1979-80. Bd. dirs. Laguna Honda Hosp., San Francisco, 1966—; bd. visitors U. Calif.-Hastings Law Sch. Served with USAF, 1951-52. Recipient Bur. Nat. Affairs award U. Calif.-Hastings, 1955; recipient Thurston Soc. award, 1953. Fellow Am. Coll. Trial Lawyers; mem. ABA, San Francisco Bar Assn., Order of Coif, St. Francis Yacht Club, Silverado Country Club. Home: 16 George Ln Sausalito CA 94965-1890 Office: Pillsbury Madison & Sutro PO Box 7880 San Francisco CA 94120-7880

MILLER, WILLIAM RICHEY, JR., lawyer; b. Oklahoma City, Apr. 4, 1947; s. William Richey and Edna Rosalind (Nielsen) M.; m. Susan Hammond, Aug. 2, 1970; children: Brooke, Karen. BA, Pomona Coll., Claremont, Calif., 1969; MA, Claremont Grad. Sch., 1972; JD, Lewis and Clark Coll., 1975. Bar: Oreg. 1975, U.S. Dist. Ct. Oreg. 1976, U.S. Ct. Appeals (9th cir.) 1976. Staff atty. Oreg. Ct. Appeals, Salem, 1975-76; with firm Griffith, Bittner, Abbott & Roberts, Portland, Oreg., 1976-83; ptnr. Davis Wright Termaine, Portland, 1983—; adj. prof. Lewis and Clark Law Sch., 1975-78. Bd. dirs. Portland Civic Theatre, 1988-91, Am. Lung Assn. Oreg., Portland, 1985-88, Oreg. Bus. Com. for the Arts, Portland, 1991-93. Mem. Oreg. State Bar (sect. chair 1990-91), Comml. Fin. Assn., Oreg. Bankers Assn., Lewis and Clark Alumni Assn. (bd. dirs. 1989-92). Presbyterian. Home: 843 Lakeshore Rd Lake Oswego OR 97034-3704 Office: Davis Wright Tremaine 1300 SW 5th Ave Ste 2300 Portland OR 97201-5630

MILLER, WILLIAM VENCILL, medical administrator; b. Kansas City, Mo., Feb. 21, 1940; s. John Pearse and Joy (Vencill) M.; m. Jeanne Wilmes Miller, Aug. 17, 1984; children: Joyce, John, Daniel, Mitchell. BA, U. Mo., 1962, MD, 1966. Diplomate Am. Bd. Pathology. Intern U. Rochester, N.Y., 1966-67; clin. assoc. NIH, Bethesda, Md., 1967-69; resident and fellow U. Mo., 1969-71; asst. prof. dept. pathology U. Ky., 1971-73; clin. prof. Washington U., 1973-91, St. Louis U., 1973-91, U. Tex., 1992—; dir. histocompatibility lab. U. Mo. Med. Ctr., 1969-71; dir. Cen. Ky. Blood Ctr., Lexington, 1971-73, U. Ky. Hosp. Blood Bank, Lexington, 1971-73; med. dir. U. Ky. Med. Ctr., 1971-73; dir. blood bank St. Louis U. Hosps., 1974-80; blood bank cons. Cardinal Glennon Hosp. for Children, 1977-80; dir. labs. St. Louis U. Hosps. for Children, 1977-81; pres., chief exec. BloodCare, Dallas, 1991—; mem. med. adv. bd. Primus Corp. Inc., Kansas City, Mo., 1991-95; dir. Biorelease Inc., 1989-93, Biocyte Inc., 1992-94. Author: HLA Without Tears, 1979; sr. editor: Transfusion Therapy, 1983, 86. bd. dirs. Sta. KWMU Pub. Radio, St. Louis, 1983-85, Nat. Mus. of Transport, St. Louis, 1987-91; chmn. Mayor's Task Force on Homeless, St. Louis, 1983-85; lt. comdr. USPHS, 1967-69. Recipient Dist. Citizen award St. Louis Jaycees, 1976, Dist. Alumnus award U. Mo., 1991. Mem. AMA, FDA (adv. com. on blood and blood products 1979-85, chmn. 1984-85, cons. 1986), Am. Nat. Red Cross (mem. pres. adv. com., chmn. nat. com. histocompatable blood transfusion, spl. com. bd. govs. plasma fractionation facility, chmn. spl. com. on blood resource sharing), Am. Assn. Blood Banks (chmn. com. tech. manual 1970-78, com. standards 1971-83), Am. Blood Commn. (bd. dirs. 1979-83, pres. 1983-85), Am. Soc. Clin. Pathologists, Am. Soc. Hematology, Am. Assn. Tissue Banks, Am. Coun. Transplantation (founding dir. 1984-85), Am. Soc. Histocompatibility and Immunogenetics (founding dir.), Internat. Soc. Blood Transfusion, South Central Assn. Blood Banks, AIDS Found. St. Louis (dir. 1988-91), U.S. Sailing Assn., Nat. Corvette Restorers Soc., Fort Worth Boat Club. Avocations: Sailing, Automobile Restoration, Folk and Bluegrass Music, Photography and Contemporary Art. Office: BloodCare 9000 Harry Hines Blvd Dallas TX 75235-1720

MILLER, YVONNE BOND, state senator, educator; b. Edenton, N.C.; d. John and Pency Bond. BS, Va. State Coll., Petersburg, 1956; postgrad., Va. State Coll., Norfolk, 1966; MA, Columbia U., 1962; PhD, U. Pitts., 1973; postgrad., CCNY, 1976. Tchr. Norfolk Pub. Schs., 1956-68; asst. prof. Norfolk State U., 1968-71, assoc. prof., 1971-74, prof., 1974-88, head dept. early childhood/elem. edn., 1984-87; mem. Va. Ho. Dels., Richmond, 1984-87, mem. edn. com., health, welfare and instns. com., militia and police com., 1983-87; mem. Va. Senate, Richmond, 1987—; now mem. commerce and labor com., gen. laws com., transp. com., rehab. and social svcs. com. Va. Senate, now chair rehab. and social svcs. com., mem. rules com.; Va. Dems. vice chair; mem. Nat. Dem. Com.; cons. to chs., parent orgns. and community groups. Commr. Ea. Va. Med. Authority; adv. bd. Va. Div. Children; active C.H. Mason Meml. Ch. of God in Christ. 1st black woman to be elected to Va. Legislature, 1983, 1st black woman to be elected to Va. Senate, 1987. Mem. Nat. Alliance Black Sch. Educators (bd. dirs.), Va. Assn. for Early Childhood Edn., Nat. Assn. Dem. Chairs, Zeta Phi Beta (past officer). Office: 960 Norchester Ave Norfolk VA 23504-4038 also: Norfolk State U 2401 Corprew Ave Norfolk VA 23504-3907 also: Va Senate Gen Assembly Bldg Rm 365 Richmond VA 23219

MILLER, ZELL BRYAN, governor; b. Young Harris, Ga., Feb. 24, 1932; s. Stephen Grady and Birdie (Bryan) M.; m. Shirley Carver, Jan. 14, 1954; children: Murphy Carver, Matthew Stephen. Student, Young Harris Coll.; AB, MA, U. Ga. Dir. Ga. Bd. Probation, 1965-66; dep. dir. Ga. Dept. Corrections, 1967-68; exec. sec. to gov. Ga., 1968-71; mem. State Bd. Pardons and Paroles, Atlanta, 1973-75; lt. gov. State of Ga., 1975-90, gov., 1990—; prof. polit. sci. and history U. Ga., Young Harris Coll., 1959-64. Author: The Mountains Within Me, Great Georgians, They Heard Georgia Singing. Mem. Ga. Senate, 1960-64; mayor Young Harris, 1959; exec. dir. Democratic Com. Ga., 1971-72; pres. Coun. State Govts., 1991—; vice chmn. So. Gov.'s Assn., 1991—; bd. dirs. Towns County Hosp. Authority. Served with USMC, 1953-56. Mem. Ga. Sch. Food Services Assn. (life), Ga. Peace Officers Assn. (life), Gridiron Soc. U. Ga., Blue Key, Lions Club. Methodist. Office: Office of Governor State Capitol Rm 203 Atlanta GA 30334

MILLER, ZOYA DICKINS (MRS. HILLIARD EVE MILLER, JR.), civic worker; b. Washington, July 15, 1923; d. Randolph and Zoya Pavlovna (Klementinovska) Dickins; m. Hilliard Eve Miller, Jr., Dec. 6, 1943; children: Jeffrey Arnot, Hilliard Eve III. Grad. Stuart Sch. Costume Design, Washington, 1942; student Sophie Newcomb Coll., 1944, New Eng. Conservatory Music, 1946, Colo. Coll., 1965; grad. Internat. Sch. Reading, 1969. Instr. Stuart Summer Sch. Costume Design, Washington, 1942; fashion coord. Julius Garfinckel, Washington, 1942-43; fashion coord., cons. Mademoiselle mag., 1942-44; star TV show Cowbelle Kitchen, 1957-58, Flair for Living, 1958-59; model mags. and comml. films, also nat. comml. recs., 1956—; dir. devel. Webb-Waring Inst. for Biomedical Rsch., Denver, 1973—. Contbr. articles, lectures on health care systems and fund raising. Mem. exec. com., bd. dirs. El Paso County chpt. Am. Lung Assn., Colo., 1954-63; mem. exec. com. Am. Lung Assn. Colo., 1965-84, bd. dirs. 1965-87, chmn. radio and TV coun., 1963-70, mem. med. affairs com., 1965-70, pres., 1965-66, procurer found. funds, 1965-70; developer nat. radio ednl. prodns. for internat. use Am. Lung Assn., 1963-70, coord. statewide pulmonary screening programs Colo., other states, 1965-72; chmn. benefit fund raising El Paso County Cancer Soc., 1963; co-founder, coord. Colorado Springs Debutante Ball, 1967—; coord. Nat. Gov.'s Conf. Ball, 1969; mem. exec. com. Colo. Gov.'s Comprehensive Health Planning Coun., 1967-74, chmn., 1971-72; chmn. Colo. Chronic Care Com., 1969-73, chmn. fund raising, 1970-72, chmn. spl. com. congl. studies on nat. health bills, 1971-73; mem. Colo.-Wyo. Regional Med. Program Adv. Coun., 1969-73; mem. Colo. Med. Found. Consumers Adv. Coun., 1972-78; mem. decorative arts com. Colorado Springs Fine Arts Ctr., 1972-75; founder, state coord. Nov. Noel Pediatrics Benefit Am. Lung Assn., 1973-87; founder, state pres. Newborn Hope, Inc., 1987—; mem. adv. bd. Wagon Wheel Girl Scouts, 1991—, Cmty. in Schs., 1995. Zoya Dickins Miller Vol. of Yr. award established Am. Lung Assn. of Colo., 1979; recipient James J. Waring award Colo. Conf. on Respiratory Disease Workers, 1963, Nat. Pub. Rels. award Am. Lung Assn., 1979, Gold Double Bar Cross award, 1980, 83, Jefferson award Am. Inst. Pub. Svc., 1991, Recognition award So. Colo. Women's C. of C., 1994, Silver Spur Community award Pikes Peak Range Riders, 1994, Silver Bell award Assistance League Colorado Springs, 1996; named Humanitarian of Yr., Am. Lung Assn. of Colo., 1987, One of 50 Most Influential Women in Colorado Springs by Gazette Telegraph Newspaper, 1990, One of 6 Leading Ladies Colo. Homes & Lifestyles Mag., 1991. Lic. pvt. pilot. Mem. Colo. Assn. Fund Raisers, Denver Round Table for Planned Giving, Nat. Soc. Fund Raising Execs., Nat. Cowbell Assn. (El Paso county pres. 1954, TV chmn., chmn. nat. Father of Yr. contest Colo. 1956-57), Broadmoor Garden Club. Home: 74 W Cheyenne Mountain Blvd Colorado Springs CO 80906-4336

MILLER-CHERMELY, DOROTHY L., sales executive; b. Hof, Bavaria, Germany, Nov. 30, 1947; d. Furman C. and Hilde (Weigold) Alderman; m. Kenneth Eugene Miller, Oct. 8, 1966 (div. 1972); m. Ronald Joseph Chermely, Feb. 14, 1993. AAS in Bus. Adminstrn., Corning Community Coll., 1973; BS in Indsl. and Labor Rels., Cornell U., 1975. Lic. real estate broker, Fla. Exec. sec. Corning (N.Y.) Bldg. Co., 1967-73; personnel adminstr. Xerox Corp., Rochester, N.Y., 1975-77; supt., constrn. mgr. U.S. Home Corp., Port Richey, Fla., 1979-80, sales cons., 1981-82, exec. v.p., 1982-83, v.p., sales mgr., 1990-94, v.p. project mgr., 1995—; constrn. supt. Charles Rutenberg Corp., Clearwater, Fla., 1983-85. Vol., mem. self-sufficiency subcom. Health and Rehab. Svcs., Port Richey, Fla., 1993. Mem. NOW, Fla. Trust for Hist. Preservation, Nat. Trust for Hist. Preservation, Pasco C. of C. (rep. 1990-93), Pasco Builders Assn. (rep. 1990-93), Optimist Club (sec. 1993-94, v.p. 1994—). Avocations: arts and crafts, antiquing, historic preservation, travel. Home: 8806 Planters Ln New Port Richey FL 34654-4200 Office: US Home Corp 2368 Fairskies Dr Spring Hill FL 34606-7259

MILLER-LANE, BARBARA See LANE, BARBARA MILLER

MILLER-YOUNG, CORRIENE CALHOUN, nursing educator; b. N.Y.C., Oct. 22, 1959; d. Timothy E. Calhoun and Suzetta Franklin; children: Christopher, Jeremy, James. BSN, Rutgers U., Newark, 1982; postgrad., Memphis State U., 1992—. RN, N.J., Tenn. Staff nurse Muhlenberg Hosp., Plainfield, N.J., 1981-86, Kimberly Nurses, Union, N.J., 1986-89; health coord. Neighborhood House, Plainfield, 1989-91; staff nurse/nurse clinician Bapt. Meml. Hosp., Memphis, 1991—; LPN instr. Tenn. Tech. Ctr., Memphis, 1994—. Named Nurse of Month, Kimberly Nurses, 1987. Mem. ANA, Kappa Delta Pi.

MILLETT, KATE (KATHERINE MURRAY MILLETT), political activist, sculptor, artist, writer; b. St. Paul, Sept. 14, 1934; m. Fumio Yoshimura, 1965. BA magna cum laude, U. Minn., 1956; postgrad. with 1st class honors, St. Hilda's Coll. Oxford, Eng., 1956-58; PhD with distinction, Columbia U., 1970. Instr. English U. N.C. at Greensboro, 1958; file clk. N.Y.C., kindergarten tchr., 1960-61; sculptor, Tokyo, 1961-63; tchr. Barnard Coll., 1964-70; tchr. English Bryn Mawr (Pa.) Coll., 1970; disting. vis. prof. Sacramento State Coll., 1972-73; founder Women's Art Colony Farm,

Poughkeepsie, N.Y. Author: Sexual Politics, 1970, The Prostitution Papers, 1973, Flying, 1974, Sita, 1977, The Basement, 1979, Going to Iran, 1982, The Loony Bin Trip, 1990, The Politics of Cruelty, 1994, A.D., 1995; co-prodr., co-dir. film Three Lives, 1970; one-woman shows Minami Gallery, Tokyo, Judson Gallery, N.Y.C., 1967, Noho Gallery, N.Y.C., 1976, 79, 80, 82, 84, 86, 93, Women's Bldg., L.A., 1977; drawings Andre Wanters Gallery, Berlin, 1980, Courtland Jessup Gallery, Provincetown, Mass., 1991, 92, 93, 94, 95. Mem. Congress of Racial Equality; chmn. edn. com. NOW, 1966; active supporter gay and women's liberation groups, also mental patients liberation and political prisoners. Mem. Phi Beta Kappa. Office: 295 Bowery New York NY 10003-7104

MILLETT, RALPH LINWOOD, JR., retired newspaper editor; b. Memphis, Oct. 30, 1919; s. Ralph Linwood and Alice (Campbell) M.; m. Mary Virgina Smith, Dec. 10, 1944; children—Mary Jo, Alice Virginia, Jan Vasco, Ralph Linwood III. Student, U. Wyo., 1938-40; B.J., U. Mo., 1942. Copy reader, copy desk chief, news editor Knoxville (Tenn.) News-Sentinel, 1947-66, editor, 1967-84; ret., 1984. Served to lt. USNR, 1942-45. Mem. Am. Soc. Newspaper Editors, Sigma Chi, Sigma Delta Chi, Kappa Tau Alpha. Presbyterian. Club: Cherokee.

MILLEY, JANE ELIZABETH, academic administrator; b. Everett, Mass., May 20, 1940; d. Walter R. and Florence (Leach) M. MusB, Boston U., 1961; MA in Music, Columbia U., 1966; PhD in Higher/Post Sec. Edn.-Adminstrn., Syracuse (N.Y.) U., 1977. Coord., founder, pianist Elmira (N.Y.) Coll. Fine Arts Trio, 1967-75; instr. music Elmira Coll., 1967-70, asst. prof. music, 1970-75, dir. arts and scis. program, 1974-75; rsch. assoc. Syracuse U., 1975-76, adminstrv. asst. to dean Coll. Arts and Scis., 1976-77; div. dean humanities and fine arts Sacramento City Coll., 1977-80; assoc. dean sch. fine arts, prof. music Calif. State U., Long Beach, 1980-81, interim dean, sch. fine arts, prof. music, 1981-82, dean, sch. fine arts, prof. music, 1982-84; arts advisor to chancellor Calif. State Univ. System, 1983-84; chancellor N.C. Sch. Arts U. N.C., Winston-Salem, 1984-89; cons. to pres. Sonoma State U., Rhonert Park, Calif., 1989-90; sr. fellow Am. Assn. State Colls. and Univs., Santa Rosa, Calif., 1989-90; provost, v.p. acad. affairs SUNY, Oswego, 1990-94; provost Simmons Coll., Boston, 1994—; speaker, cons. in field. Author: (with J. Sturnick and C. Tisinger) Women at the Helm, 1991; contbr. articles to profl. jours. Ex officio bd. dirs. Regional Arts Found., 1982-84, N.C. Scenic Studios, 1984-89, N.C. Dance Theatre, 1984-89, N.C. Shakespeare Festival, 1984-89; bd. dirs. Sacramento Film Festival, 1979-80, Long Beach Grand Opera, 1980; charter mem., founder Sacramento Exptl. Theatre, 1978-84. Commendation for outstanding svc. Los Rios Community Coll. Bd. Trustees, 1980, Sacramento City Coll., 1980. Mem. AAUW (found. adv. com. 1987-89), Am. Assn. State Colls. and Univs. (chmn. arts com. 1986-89), Nat. Assn. State Univs. and Land Grant Colls. (U. N.C. rep. commn. on arts 1986-89), Internat. Coun. Fine Arts Deans, N.C. Women's Forum, N.Y. Edn. Consortium, N.Y. State Sea Grant Inst. (bd. govs. 1991—), Oswego County Opportunities (bd. dirs. 1991—), Kappa Delta Pi, Pi Kappa Lambda. Office: 300 Fenway Boston MA 02115-5820

MILLGATE, JANE, language professional; b. Leeds, Eng., June 8, 1937; d. Maurice and Marie (Schofield) Barr; m. Michael Millgate, Feb. 27, 1960. B.A. with honors, Leeds U., Eng., 1959, M.A., 1963; Ph.D., U. Kent, Eng., 1970. Instr. U. Toronto, Ont., 1964-65, lectr., 1965-70, asst. prof., 1970-72, assoc. prof., 1972-77, prof. English, 1977—, vice-dean arts and scis., 1983-87; mem. bd. regents Victoria U., Toronto, 1981-86. Author: Macaulay, 1973, Walter Scott, 1984, 2d edit., 1987, Scott's Last Edition: A Study in Publishing History, 1987. Editor: Editing 19th Century Fiction, 1978. Contbr. articles to profl. jours. Doctoral fellow Can. Council, 1968-70; research fellow Can. Council, 1972, 74-75, Social Scis. and Humanities Research Council Can., 1980-81, 85-87, 88-90, 91-94, 95—, Connaught Rsch. fellow, 1995-96. Fellow Royal Soc. Can., Royal Soc. Edinburgh; mem. Victorian Studies Assn. (pres. 1978-80), Assn. Can. Univ. Tchrs. English (pres. 1980-82), Can. Fedn. for Humanities (exec. 1981-83, 95—), Assn. Scottish Studies, Soc. for History of Authorship, Reading and Pub., Bibliog. Soc. Home: 75 Highland Ave, Toronto, ON Canada M4W 2A4 Office: Victoria Coll, U Toronto, Toronto, ON Canada M5S 1K7

MILLGATE, MICHAEL (HENRY), retired English educator; b. Southampton, Eng., July 19, 1929; arrived in Can., 1964; s. Stanley and Marjorie Louisa (Norris) M.; m. Jane Barr, Feb. 27, 1960. BA, Cambridge U., 1952, MA, 1956; postgrad., U. Mich., Ann Arbor, 1956-57; PhD, U. Leeds, 1960. Tutor Workers' Ednl. Assn., Eng., 1953-56; lectr. English lit. U. Leeds, 1958-64; prof., chmn. dept. English York U., Ont., Can., 1964-67; prof. English U. Toronto, 67-94, univ. prof., 87-94; Carpenter lectr. Ohio Wesleyan U., 1978; vis. scholar Meiji U., 1985. Author: William Falulkner, 1961, American Social Fiction, 1964, The Achievement of William Faulkner, 1966, Thomas Hardy: His Career as a Novelist, 1971, Thomas Hardy: A Biography, 1982, Testamentary Acts: Browning, Tennyson, James, Hardy, 1992; editor: Tennyson: Selected Poems, 1963, Thomas Hardy: The Life and Work of Thomas Hardy, 1985, William Faulkner Manucripts, 20 (4 vols.), 21 (2 vols.), 22 (4 vols.), 23 (2 vols.), 1986, New Essays on Light in August, 1987, Thomas Hardy: Selected Letters, 1990, Letters of Emma and Florence Hardy, 1996; co-editor: Transatlantic Dialogue, 1966, Lion in the Garden, 1968, The Collected Letters of Thomas Hardy, Vol. I, 1978, Vol. II, 1980, Vol. III, 1982, Vol. IV, 1984, Vol. V, 1985, Vol. VI, 1987, Vol. VII, 1988, Thomas Hardy's Studies, Specimens, Etc. Notebook, 1994. Can. Coun. leave fellow, 1968-69, S.W. Brooks fellow U. Queensland, 1971; Killam sr. rsch. scholar, 1974-75; Guggenheim Meml. fellow, 1977-78, Connaught sr. fellow, 1979-80; Social Sci. and Humanities Rsch. Coun. Can. leave fellow, 1981-82, grantee, 1977—; Can. Coun. grantee, 1973-77; Killam rsch. fellow, 1986-88. Fellow Royal Soc. Lit., Royal Soc. Can.; mem. MLA (adv. com. Ctr. for Edit. Am. Authors 1971-74, com. on scholarly edits. 1985-89), Victorian Studies Assn. Ont. (pres. 1970-72), Thomas Hardy Soc. (v.p. 1973—), Bibliog. Soc. Am., Soc. for Study So. Lit. (exec. coun. 1972-76, 81-83), Soc. Textual Scholarship, Tennyson Soc. Home: 75 Highland Ave, Toronto, ON Canada M4W 2A4

MILLHAUSER, GLENN L., biochemist, educator; b. L.A., Mar. 1, 1956. BS in Chemistry with honors, Calif. State U., 1980; MS in Chemistry, Cornell U., 1982, PhD of Phys. Chemistry, 1985. Postdoctoral fellow NIH Cornell U., Ithaca, N.Y., 1985-88; asst. prof. chemistry and biochemistry U. Calif. Santa Cruz, 1988-93, assoc. prof., assoc. dean natural scis., 1993—; lectr. in field. Contbr. articles to profl. jours. Mem. AAAS, Am. Chem. Soc., Biophys. Soc. Home: 1606 King St Santa Cruz CA 95060 Office: Dept Chemistry & Biochem Univ California Santa Cruz CA 95064

MILLIAN, KENNETH YOUNG, public policy consultant; b. Washington, Sept. 29, 1927; s. John Curry and Myrtle (Young) M.; m. Alva Randolph Clarke, Sept. 10, 1949; children: John R., Kenneth Y. Jr., Kathleen M. Gilbert, Elizabeth W. Allen. BA, U. Md., 1951; MA in Internat. Rels., George Washington U., 1969; Diploma, Nat. War Coll., Washington, 1969; MS in Bus., Columbia U., 1980. Officer U.S. Fgn. Svc., 1951-76; corp. exec. W.R. Grace & Co., N.Y.C., 1976-93; corp. v.p., dir. govt. rels. W.R. Grace & Co., Washington, 1982-88; corp. v.p., dir. environ. policy W.R. Grace & Co., N.Y.C., 1988-93; ret., 1993; pres. Millian Assocs., Washington, 1993—; exec. dir. Global Environ. Mgmt. Initiative, Washington, 1995—; pres. Found. for Pres. Pvt. Sector Survey on Cost Control, 1986-92. Labor columnist Japan Times, 1955-57. Bd. govs. Wesley Sem., Washington, 1988—. Democrat. Methodist. Avocations: sailing, golf. Office: Millian Assocs 11 Dupont Circle NW Ste 300 Washington DC 20036-1207

MILLICHAP, JOSEPH GORDON, neurologist, educator; b. Wellington, Eng., Dec. 18, 1918; came to U.S., 1956, naturalized, 1965; s. Joseph P. and Alice (Flello) M.; m. Mary Irene Fortey, Feb. 25, 1946 (dec. Oct. 1969); children: Martin Gordon, Paul Anthony; m. Nancy Melanie Kluczynski, Nov. 7, 1970; children: Gordon Thomas, John Joseph. M.B. with honors in Surgery, St. Bartholomew's Med. Coll., U. London, Eng., 1946, M.D. in Internal Medicine, 1951, diploma child health, 1948. Diplomate: Am. Bd. Pediatrics, Am. Bd. Neurology and Child Neurology, Am. Bd. Electroencephalography. Intern, resident St. Bartholomew's Hosp., 1946-49, Hosp. Sick Children, London, 1951-53, Mass. Gen. Hosp., Boston, 1958-60; pediatric neurologist NIH, 1955-56; USPHS fellow neurology Mass. Gen. Hosp., Boston, 1958-60; cons. pediatric neurology Mayo Clinic, 1960-63; pediatric neurologist Children's Meml. Hosp., Northwestern Med. Center, Chgo., 1963—; prof. neurology and pediatrics Northwestern U. Med. Sch., 1963—; Cons. surgeon gen. USPHS; mem. med. adv. bds. Ill. Epilepsy League, Muscular Dystrophy Found., Cerebral Palsy Found., 1963—; vis. prof. Gt. Ormond St. Hosp., U. London, 1986-87. Author: Febrile Convulsions, 1967, Pediatric Neurology, 1967, Learning Disabilities, 1974, The Hyperactive Child with MBD, 1975, Nutrition, Diet and Behavior, 1985, Dyslexia, 1986, Progress in Pediatric Neurology, 1991, Vol. II, 1994, Environmental Poisons in Our Food, 1993, A Guide to Drinking Water, Hazards and Health Risks, 1995; editor Jour. Pediatric Neurology Briefs; contbr. articles to profl. jours., chpts. to books. Chmn. research com. med. adv. bd. Epilepsy Found., 1965—. Served with RAF, 1949-51. Named New Citizen of Year in Met. Chgo., 1965; recipient Americanism Medal D.A.R., 1972; USPHS research grantee, 1957. Fellow Royal Coll. Physicians; mem. Am. Neurol. Assn., Am. Pediatric Soc., Am. Soc. Pediatric Research, Am. Acad. Neurology, Am. Soc. Pharmacology and Exptl. Therapeutics, Soc. Exptl. Biology and Medicine, Am. Bd. Psychiatry and Neurology (asst. examiner 1961—), A.M.A. Episcopalian. Home: PO Box 11391 Chicago IL 60611-0391 Office: Northwestern Meml Med Ctr PO Box 11391 Chicago IL 60611-0391

MILLIGAN, ARTHUR ACHILLE, retired banker; b. Oxnard, Calif., Oct. 29, 1917; s. John Leslie and Julia (Levy) M.; m. Jeanne Welch, Dec. 12, 1942; children: Michael S., Marshall C. B.A., Stanford U., 1938. Pres., CEO Bank of A. Levy, Oxnard, Calif., 1955-82, chmn. bd., 1982-87, chmn. exec. com., 1988-95; dir. Oxnard Frozen Foods Corps., Oxnard, 1958-90; chmn. Real Estate Investment Trust of Calif., Santa Monica, 1968-87. Served to lt. USN, 1942-45. Mem. Ind. Bankers So. Calif. (pres., 1958), Western Ind. Bankers (pres. 1961), Calif. Bankers Assn. (pres. 1964), Am. Bankers Assn. (pres. 1978). Republican. Club: Valley (dir. 1969-73, 1985-87, 88—, pres. 1990-92) (Montecito). Lodges: Elks, Rotary (pres. 1949—).

MILLIGAN, FRANK DENNIS, museum director; b. Toronto, Ont., Can., Apr. 7, 1952; s. Frank Joseph and Mary Doris (McParland) M.; m. Nancy Louise Heather; children: Julie, Carrolyn, Heather. BA with honors, U. Guelph, Ont., 1976; MA, U. Western Ont., London, 1978; PhD in History, U. Alta., Edmonton, Can., 1987. Edn. officer Huronia Hist. Parks, Midland, Ont., 1978-82; regional mgr. historic sites and mus. Historic Sites and Archives Svc./Alta. Culture, Edmonton, 1983-89; dir. New Brunswick Mus., St. John, Can., 1992—. Mem. Am. Assn. Mus., Can. Mus. Assn. Avocations: squash, jogging, reading, learning. Home: 43 Queensbury Dr, Rothesay, NB Canada E2E 4W3 Office: New Brunswick Museum, 277 Douglas Ave, Saint John, NB Canada E2K 1E5

MILLIGAN, GLENN ELLIS, psychologist; b. Emporia, Kans., Nov. 12, 1919; s. Ellis S. and Clara (Kriete) M.; m. Phyllis Eaton, Aug. 26, 1945 (div.); children: Douglas, Gregory, David; m. Janice Barron Dawes, Oct. 10, 1970; 1 step-dau., Virginia. BS, Kans. State Tchrs. Coll., 1941, MS, 1942; postgrad., U. Chgo., 1943-44; Ed.D., Colo. State Coll., 1951. Head dept. edn. Findlay (Ohio) Coll., 1946-55; psychologist Columbus (Ohio) Pub. Schs., 1955-56; asso. prof. edn. Ohio Wesleyan U., Delaware, 1956-60; exec. dir. Am. Assn. Mental Deficiency, Columbus, 1960-65; cons. mental retardation Vocat. Rehab. Adminstrn., HEW, 1965-67; psychologist spl. edn. Montgomery County Pub. Schs., Rockville, Md., 1967—; Lectr. Catholic U. Am. Editor: (1st) Mental Retardation, 1963-64, (with others) Directory of Residential Facilities for the Mentally Retarded, 1965. Fellow Am. Assn. Mental Deficiency; mem. Am. Psychol. Assn., NEA (life). Home: 5208 Elsmere Ave Bethesda MD 20814-5731 Office: Montgomery County Pub Schs Spring Mill Field Office 11721 Kemp Mill Rd Silver Spring MD 20902-1722

MILLIGAN, JOHN DRANE, historian, educator; b. N.Y.C., Oct. 11, 1924; s. Carl Glover and Hazel Gray (Drane) M.; m. Joyce Mary Jervis, Nov. 16, 1946; children: Jacqueline M., Paula J., Mary M., Elizabeth Y. BA, U. Mich., 1952, MA, 1953, PhD, 1961. Tchg. asst. U. Mich., 1951-52, tchg. fellow, 1954-56; from asst. prof. to prof. history SUNY, Buffalo, 1962—, dir. grad. programs in history, 1963-68, 94-95, dir. undergrad. programs in history, 1979-86, acting dept. chmn., summers, 1977, 78-80, 88; vis. prof. McMaster U., Hamilton, Ont., Can., summer 1964, 69-70. Author: Gunboats Down the Mississippi, 1965, From the Fresh-Water Navy, 1861-1864, 1970; also chpts. in books, articles in jours., encys. Mem. Ann Arbor chpt. NAACP, exec. bd., 1956-61; mem. ACLU, exec. bd., 1959-61; mem. campaign coms. for various candidates for local and nat. office, 1960-76; mem. Buffalo NAACP, Buffalo Housing Opportunities Made Equal, Citizens Council on Human Relations, Physicians for Social Responsibility, Common Cause, Amnesty Internat.; faculty chmn. United Fund dr., 1977; active Foster Parents Plan, 1955—; adoptive parent Internat. Social Services; founder charitable trust for minority coll. scholarships. Served with USAAF, 1943-46, USAFR, 1946-56. James B. Angell scholar U. Mich.; grantee Research Found. SUNY; grantee U.S. Naval Inst.; Citation of Civil War Round Table; Moncado Award of Am. Mil. Inst. Mem. Am. Hist. Assn., Assn. Am. Historians, So. Hist. Assn., Buffalo and Erie County Hist. Soc., Afro-Am. Hist. Soc., Soc. Civil War Historians, Buffalo Coun. for Responsibility in Fgn. Policy (founding), Soaring Soc. Am., Aircraft Owners and Pilots Assn., Niagara Soaring Club, Cambria Flying Soc., Silver Wings Assn., Civil War Round Table, SUNY Buffalo Pres.'s Assocs., SUNY Buffalo Founders' Soc., Tau Sigma Delta, Phi Kappa Phi, Phi Alpha Theta. Home: 21 Allenhurst Rd Buffalo NY 14214-1201 Office: SUNY History Dept Buffalo NY 14260 *If an individual cannot influence for the better the course of humankind, one can sometimes influence for the better the life of another individual.*

MILLIGAN, LAWRENCE DRAKE, JR., consumer products executive; b. Lake Forest, Ill., Apr. 6, 1936; s. Lawrence Drake Sr. and Mary Catherine (Cliggit) M.; m. Lucy Shepard, Oct. 20, 1962; children: Michael D., Carolyn S. BA, Williams Coll., 1960. Nat. sales mgr. Bar Soap and Household Cleaning Products div. Procter & Gamble, Cin., 1974-78; gen. mgr. spl. products Procter & Gamble, Cin., 1979-80, gen. mgr. food service and lodging products, 1980-84, v.p. food service and lodging products, 1984, v.p. food products, 1984-87, v.p. sales in Europe, 1987-89, v.p. sales, customer devel. internat., 1989—; sr. v.p. worldwide sales Procter & Gamble, 1990—. Served as sgt. USMC, 1955-58. Republican. Home: 7475 Old Hickory Ln Cincinnati OH 45243-1454 Office: Procter & Gamble Co 1 Procter Gamble Plz Cincinnati OH 45202

MILLIGAN, MANCIL WOOD, mechanical and aerospace engineering educator; b. Shiloh, Tenn., Nov. 21, 1934; s. Mancil Abernathy and Ivy (Wood) M.; m. Arlys Joyce Cushman, Sept. 15, 1956; children: Mancil Wood, Matthew Wayne. B.S., U. Tenn., 1956, M.S., 1958, Ph.D., 1963; postgrad., U. Wash., 1958, Stanford U., 1964. Research engr. Boeing Co., Seattle, 1956-57, 58-59; instr. mech. engring. U. Tenn., Knoxville, 1957-58; prof. mech. and aerospace engring. U. Tenn., 1959—, head mech. and aerospace engring., 1973-82; cons. to more than 100 industries, 1959—. Mem. ASME, AIAA, Am. Soc. Engring. Edn., Tech. Soc. Knoxville, Pi Tau Sigma, Tau Beta Pi, Sigma Gamma Tau. Home: 10214 Emory Rd Luttrell TN 37779-2942

MILLIGAN, SISTER MARY, theology educator, religious consultant; b. Los Angeles, Jan. 23, 1935; d. Bernard Joseph and Carolyn (Krebs) M. BA, Marymount Coll., 1956; Dr. de l'Univ., U. Paris, 1959; MA in Theology, St. Mary's Coll., Notre Dame, Ind., 1966; STD, Gregorian U., 1975; D. honoris causa, Marymount U., 1988. Tchr. Cours Marymount, Neuilly, France, 1956-59; asst. prof. Marymount Coll., Los Angeles, 1959-67; gen. councillor Religious of Sacred Heart of Mary, Rome, 1969-75, gen. superior, 1980-85; asst. prof. Loyola Marymount U., Los Angeles, 1977-78, provost, 1986-90, prof., 1990—, dean liberal arts, 1992—; pres. bd. dirs. St. John's Sem., Camarillo, Calif., 1986-89; mem. exec. com. Internat. Union Superiors Gen., Rome, 1983-85; mem. planning bd. spiritual renewal program Loyola Marymount U., Los Angeles, 1976-78. Author: That They May Have Life, 1975; compiler analytical index Ways of Peace, 1986; contbr. articles to profl. jours. Vis. scholar Grad. Theol. Union, Berkeley, 1986. Mem. Calif. Women in Higher Edn., Coll. Theology Soc., Cath. Biblical Assn. Democrat. Roman Catholic. Office: Loyola Marymount U 7900 Loyola Blvd Los Angeles CA 90045-8319*

MILLIGAN, MICHAEL EDWARD, insurance services company executive; b. Fullerton, Calif., Aug. 28, 1952; s. Edward Scott Milligan and Patricia Ann (Shirk) Madson; m. Diane Marie Mascaro, June 21, 1974; children: Robert Michael, Lauren Alicia, Stefanie Diane. BS, U.S. Mil. Acad., 1974; MS, U. So. Calif., 1979. Commd. 2d lt. U.S. Army, 1974, advanced through grades to capt., 1979; comdr. U.S. Army, Europe, 1974-79; resigned, 1979; various positions to group leader product devel. Procter & Gamble, Cin., 1979-85; mgr. product devel. and tech. svcs., then div. mgr. engring. Pepsi Cola USA, Purchase, N.Y., 1985-87; div. mgr. stratetic planning ops. Pepsi Cola Co., Somers, N.Y., 1987-88; dir. mktg., sales and devel. Gen. Analysis Corp., Norwalk, Conn., 1988-89; dir. market planning and devel. Ins. Svcs. Office subs. ISOTEL, N.Y.C., 1989-91; asst. v.p. product devel. and planning Ins. Svcs. Office, Inc., N. Y.C., 1991—. Republican. Roman Catholic. Avocation: golf. Home: 14 Patti Pl Hopewell Junction NY 12533-6814 Office: Ins Svcs Office Inc 7 World Trade Ctr New York NY 10048-1102

MILLIKAN, CLARK HAROLD, physician; b. Freeport, Ill., Mar. 2, 1915; s. William Clarance and Louise (Chamberlain) M.; m. Gayle Margaret Gross, May 2, 1942 (div. Apr. 1966); children: Terri, Clark William, Jeffry Brent; m. Janet T. Holmes, July 21, 1966 (div. Dec. 1987); m. Nancy Futrell, Dec. 28, 1987. Student, Parsons (Kans.) Jr. Coll., 1935; MD, U. Kans., 1939. Diplomate Am. Bd. Psychiatry and Neurology. Intern St. Luke's Hosp., Clev., 1939-40, asst. resident medicine, 1940-41; from resident neurology to asst. prof. neurology State U. Iowa, Iowa City, 1941-49; staff Mayo Clinic, Rochester, Minn., 1949—, cons. neurology, 1958—; dir. Mayo Center for Clin. Research in Cerebrovascular Disease; prof. neurology Mayo Sch. Medicine; physician-in-chief pro tem Cleve. Clinic, 1970; prof. neurology U. Utah Sch. Medicine, Salt Lake City, 1976-87, U. Miami (Fla.) Sch. Medicine, 1987-88; scholar in residence, dept. neurology Henry Ford Hosp., Detroit, 1988-92; prof. neurology Sch. of Medicine Creighton U., Omaha, 1992-94; clin. prof. neurology Med. Coll. Ohio, Toledo, 1994—; Asst. chmn., editor trans. 2d Princeton Conf. Cerebrovascular Disease, 1957, chmn. confs., 1961, 64; chmn. com. classification and nomenclature cerebrovascular disease USPHS, 1955-69; mem. council Nat. Inst. Neurologic Diseases and Blindness, NIH, USPHS, 1961-65, div. regional med. program, 1965-68; A.O.A. lectr. Baylor U., Waco, Tex., 1952; James Mawer Pearson Meml. lectr., Vancouver, B.C., Can., 1958; Conner Meml. lectr. Am. Heart Assn., 1961; Peter T. Bohan lectr. U. Kans., 1965, 73. Editor: Jour. Stroke, 1970-76, assoc. editor, 1976—. Recipient Outstanding Alumnus award U. Kans., 1973. Fellow ACP, Am. Acad. Neurology (founding chmn. sect. on stroke and vascular neurology 1994), Royal Soc. Medicine; mem. AMA, AAUP, AAAS, Assn. Rsch. Nervous and Mental Disease (pres. 1961), Am. Neurol. Assn. (1st v.p. 1969-70, pres. 1973-74), Minn. Med. Assn., Four County Med. Soc. South Minn., Cen. Neuropsychiat. Assn., N.Y. Acad. Sci., Am. Heart Assn. (chmn. coun. cerebrovascular disease 1967-68, Gold Heart award 1976, Spl. Merit award 1981), Nat. Stroke Assn. (pres. 1986, editor Jour. Stroke and Cerebrovascular Disease 1990—), Sigma Xi.

MILLIKAN, LARRY EDWARD, dermatologist; b. Sterling, Ill., May 12, 1936; s. Daniel Franklin and Harriet Adeline (Parmenter) M.; m. Jeanine Dorothy Johnson, Aug. 27, 1960; children: Marshall, Rebecca. B.A., Monmouth Coll., 1958; M.D., U. Mo., 1962. Intern Great Lakes Naval Hosp., Ill., 1962-63; housestaff in tng. U. Mich., Ann Arbor, 1967-69, chief resident, 1969-70; asst. prof. dermatology U. Mo., Columbia, 1970-74, assoc. prof., 1974-81; chmn. dept. dermatology Tulane U., New Orleans, 1981—; cons. physician Charity Hosp., New Orleans, Tulane U. Hosp., New Orleans, Huey B. Long Hosp., Pineville; mem. bd. trustees Sulzberger Inst. for Dermatological Edn.; chmn. cont. med. edn. com. La. State Med. Soc., 1994-95. Assoc. editor Internat. Jour. Dermatology, 1980—; mem. editorial bd. Current Concepts in Skin Disorders, Am. Jour. Med. Scis., Postgrad. Medicine; contbr. articles to med. jours. Mem. bd. trustees Sulzberger Inst. for Dermatol. Edn. With USN, 1960-67. Recipient Andres Bello awrd Govt. of Venezuela, 1989, citation of merit Sch. Medicine, U. Mo., 1993; named Disting. Alumnus, Monmouth Coll., 1990; Nat. Cancer Inst. grantee, 1976-84. Fellow ACP; mem. AAAS, AMA, Am. Acad. Dermatology (bd. dirs. 1986-90), Am. Dermatol. Assn., Am. Dermatol. Soc. for Allergy and Immunology (pres., bd. dirs.), Soc. for Investigative Dermatology (past pres. South sect.), So. Med. Assn. (vice chmn. dermatology sect. 1984, chmn. 1994), Coll. Physicians Phila., Assn. Profs. Dermatology (bd. dirs. 1984-86), Orleans Parish Med. Soc., La. Med. Soc., Pam Am. Med. Assn., Internat. Soc. Dermatology (asst. sec. gen. 1989—), Mo. Allergy Assn. (past pres.), Am. Coll. Cryosurgery, Assn. Acad. Dermatol. Surgeons, Internat. Soc. Dermatol. Surgery, Dermatol. Found. Leaders Soc. (state chmn. 1993-96). Office: Tulane Univ Sch Medicine Dept of Dermatology 1430 Tulane Ave Ste 3551 New Orleans LA 70112-2699

MILLIKEN, CHRISTINE TOPPING, legal association administrator, lawyer. BA in Polit. Sci., George Washington U., 1970; JD, Cath. U. Am., 1976. Bar: D.C., U.S. Supreme Ct. Legislative cons. Harvard U., 1976-77; v.p. and gen. counsel Nat. Assn. Ind. Colls. and Univs., 1977-86; exec. dir. and gen. counsel Nat. Assn. of Attys. Gen., 1986—; 010legis. cons. mem. The Washington Ctr., 1982—, chair 1987-94; mem. Ind. Sector Founding Bd., Ethics Task Force, Mgmt. Com., chair Govt. Rels. Com. Office: Nat Assn Attys Gen 444 N Capitol St NW Washington DC 20001-1512

MILLIKEN, JOHN GORDON, research economist; b. Denver, May 12, 1927; s. William Boyd and Margaret Irene (Marsh) M.; m. Marie Violet Machell, June 13, 1953; children: Karen Marie, Douglas Gordon, David Tait, Anne Alain. BS, Yale U., 1949, BEng, 1950; MS, U. Colo., 1966, PhD, 1969. Registered profl. engr., Colo. Engr. U.S. Bur. Reclamation, Denver, 1950-55; asst. to plant mgr. Stanley Aviation Corp., Denver, 1955-56; prin. mgmt. engr., dept. mgr. Martin-Marietta Aerospace Div., Denver, 1956-64; mgmt. engr. Safeway Stores, Inc., Denver, 1964-66; sr. rsch. economist, prof., assoc. div. head U. Denver Rsch. Inst., 1966-86; pres. Univ. Senate, 1980-81; prin. Milliken Chapman Rsch. Group, Inc., Littleton, Colo., 1986-88, Milliken Rsch. Group, Inc., Littleton, 1988—; vis. fellow sci. policy rsch. unit U. Sussex, Eng., 1975-76; bd. dirs. Sci. Mgmt. Corp.; cons. mgmt. engr. Author: Aerospace Management Techniques, 1971, Federal Incentives for Innovation, 1974, Recycling Municipal Wastewater, 1977, Water and Energy in Colorado's Future, 1981, Metropolitan Water Management, 1981, Technological Innovation and Economic Vitality, 1983, Water Management in the Denver, Colorado Urban Area, 1988, Benefits and Costs of Oxygenated Fuels in Colorado, 1990, Water Transfer Alternatives Study, 1994, Colorado Springs Water Resources Plan Alternative Assessment Study, 1995; contbr. articles to profl. jours. Bd. dirs. Southeast Englewood Water Dist., 1963—, South Englewood San. Dist., 1965—; bd. dirs. South Suburban Park and Recreation Dist., 1971-96, chmn., 1990-92; chmn. Dem. Com. of Arapahoe County, 1969-71, 5th Congl. Dist. Colo., 1972-73, 74-75; mem. exec. com. Colo. Faculty Adv. Coun., 1981-85; mem. Garrison Diversion Unit Commn., 1984; trustee Colo. Local Govt. Liquid Asset Trust, 1986—, chmn., 1991-93; bd. dirs. Colo. Spl. Dist. Assn. Property and Liability Pool, 1989—. With M.C., U.S. Army, 1945-46. Recipient Adlai E. Stevenson Meml. award, 1981, hon. title "Amicus Universitatis," U. Denver, 1994, Disting. Svc. award Spl. Dist. Assn. Colo., 1995. Mem. Acad. Mgmt., Nat. Assn. Bus. Economists, Yale Sci. and Engring. Assn., Am. Water Works Assn., Sigma Xi, Tau Beta Pi, Beta Gamma Sigma, Sigma Iota Epsilon. Congregationalist. Home and Office: 6502 S Ogden St Littleton CO 80121-2561

MILLIKEN, ROGER, textile company executive; b. N.Y.C., Oct. 24, 1915; s. Gerrish and Agnes (Gayley) M.; m. Justine V. R. Hooper, June 5, 1948; children: Justine, Nancy, Roger, David, Weston. Student, Groton Sch., 1929-33; A.B., Yale U., 1937; LL.D. (hon.), Wofford Coll., Rose-Hulman Inst. Tech., Phila. Coll. Textiles and Sci., Brenau Coll., The Citadel; D. Textile Industry (hon.), Clemson U.; D.H.L. (hon.), Converse Coll. CEO Milliken & Co., N.Y.C., 1947-83, chmn., chief exec. officer, 1983—; bd. dirs. Merc. Stores Co., W.R. Grace & Co.; chmn. bd. Inst. Textile Tech., 1948—; bd. dirs. Am. Textile Mfrs. Inst., S.C. Textile Mfrs. Assn. Chmn. Greenville-Spartanburg Airport Commn.; trustee Wofford Coll., S.C. Found. Ind. Coll. Mem. Bus. Council, Textile Inst. (Eng.) (companion mem.). Clubs: Union League, Links, Augusta Nat. Golf, Yeamans Hall. Office: Milliken & Co 1045 6th Ave New York NY 10018

MILLILI, JOHN JOSEPH, chemiluminescence executive, surgeon; b. Phila., Sept. 21, 1954; s. John Joseph Millili; m. Susan Anne Meskill, July 30, 1983; children: John J. III, Elizabeth, Judy. BS in Biology, Moravian Coll., 1976; MD, U. Pa., 1979. Resident surgery Grad. Hosp., Phila., 1979-84; chief divsn. gen. surgery Underwood (N.J.) Meml. Hosp., 1987-93, attending surgeon, 1984—; clin. asst. prof. surgery U. Pa., Phila., 1987—; attending surgeon, asst. dir. surg. edn. Presbyn. Hosp., Phila., 1989—, program dir. transitional internship, 1992—; dir. Clin. Chemiluminescence Lab., Phila., 1993—; co-dir. Biologic Oxidation Rsch. Group, Phila., 1993—. Contbr. articles to profl. publs. V.p. Paul Nemir Surg. Found., Phila., 1988—; mem. Founder's Soc., Gloucester County United Way, Deptford, N.J., 1991—; mem. Friends of Libr., Deptford, 1993—. Fellow ACS; mem. AAAS, Oxygen Soc., Internat. Fedn. for Free Radical Rsch., Soc. for Surgery in the Alimentary Tract. Achievements include defining optical field variations in human urine in different pathologic conditions. Home: 217 Turbridge Ct Deptford NJ 08096-4202 Office: 52 W Red Bank Ave Woodbury NJ 08096

MILLIMET, ERWIN, lawyer; b. N.Y.C., Oct. 7, 1925; s. Maurice and Henrietta (Cohen) M.; m. Mary Malia; children: Robert, James, Rachel, Sarah. BA magna cum laude, Amherst Coll., 1948; LLB cum laude, Harvard U., 1951. Bar: N.Y. 1952. Formerly sr. ptnr., chmn. exec. com. Stroock & Stroock & Lavan, N.Y.C., ret. 1991. Mem. bd. visitors U. San Diego Law Sch.; active Nat. Support Group for Africa; founder Citizens for Am., Washington, 1984; mem. Rep. Presdl. Task Force; mem. Rep. Club, N.Y.C. and Washington. Served with inf. U.S. Army, 1943-46. Mem. N.Y. State Bar Assn., Assn. of Bar of City of N.Y., Fed. Bar Assn., Phi Beta Kappa.

MILLIMET, JOSEPH ALLEN, retired lawyer; b. West Orange, N.J., July 23, 1914; s. Morris and Dorothy (McBlain) M.; m. Elizabeth Gray Gingras, Jan. 10, 1942 (dec. 1995); children: Madlyn Ann (Mrs. Angus Deming), Lisa Gray (Mrs. Silas Little, III), Rebecca Allen, Peter Joseph (dec.). A.B., Dartmouth Coll., 1936; LL.B., Yale U., 1939; LLD (hon.), U. N.H., 1992. Bar: N.H. 1939. Pvt. practice Concord and Manchester, N.H.; sr. ptnr. Devine, Millimet, Stahl & Branch, and predecessors (now Devine Millimet & Branch), Manchester, 1947-93, ret.; with FCC, 1941-42. Mem. N.H. Bd. Bar Examiners, 1953-61, legislative counsel to, gov. N.H., 1963-66; chmn. Commn. to Revise N.H. Constn., 1964, 74, 84; mem. Commn. Uniform State Laws, 1965-73. Served with USCG, 1942-45. Fellow Am. Coll. Trial Lawyers; mem. N.H. Bar Assn. (pres. 1962-63), ABA. Democrat. Home: 1655 N River Rd Manchester NH 03104 Office: Devine Millimet & Branch 111 Amherst St Manchester NH 03105-0719

MILLING, BERT WILLIAM, JR., federal judge; b. Mobile, Ala., Mar. 5, 1946; s. Bert William and Marjorie Ann (Smith) M.; m. Priscilla Pitman, Apr. 15, 1966; children: Brooks Pitman, Jeremy Bacon, Maran Celeste. AB in Philosophy, Coll. William and Mary, 1968; JD, U. Ala., 1971. Bar: Ala. 1971. Legal officer 212th Arty. Group, Fort Lewis, Wash., 1971-72; legal asst. officer Judge Advocate Gen.'s Office, Ft. Sill, Okla., 1972-74; spl. asst. atty. gen. Dist. Atty.'s Office, Mobile, 1974-75, asst. dist. atty., 1977-78; assoc. Sintz, Pike, Campbell & Duke, Mobile, 1975-77; ct. referee Juvenile Div. of Cir. Ct., Mobile, 1978-81; counsel U.S. Senate Com. on Jud., Subcom. on Security & Terrorism, Washington, 1981-83; asst. U.S. atty. Justice Dept., Mobile, 1983-86; U.S. magistrate judge U.S. Dist. Ct. So. Dist. Ala., Mobile, 1986—. Capt. U.S. Army, 1971-74. Mem. Ala. Bar Assn., Mobile Bar Assn. Episcopalian. Avocations: jogging, reading. Office: US Courthouse 113 Saint Joseph St Mobile AL 36602-3606

MILLING, MARCUS EUGENE, SR., geologist; b. Galveston, Tex., Oct. 8, 1938; s. Robert Richardson and Leonora Mildred (Curney) M.; m. Sandra Ann Dunlay, Sept. 21, 1959; 1 child, Marcus Eugene Jr. BS in Geology, Lamar U., 1961; MS in Geology, U. Iowa, 1964, PhD in Geology, 1968. Cert. petroleum geologist. Rsch. geologist Exxon Prodn. Rsch. Co., Houston, 1968-76; prodn. geologist Exxon Co. U.S.A., Kingsville, Tex., 1976-78; dist. exptl. geologist Exxon Co. U.S.A., New Orleans, 1978-80; mgr. geol. rsch. Arco Oil and Gas Co., Plano, Tex., 1980-86; chief geologist Arco Oil and Gas Co., Dallas, 1986-87; assoc. dir. Bur. Econ. Geology U. Tex., Austin, 1987-92; exec. dir. Am. Geol. Inst., Alexandria, Va., 1992—; vice-chmn. Offshore Tech. Conf., Dallas, 1984-87; dir. Geosci. Inst. for Oil and Gas Recovery Rsch., Austin, 1988-91. NSF fellow, 1966. Fellow Geol. Soc. Am. (councilor 1986-89); mem. Am. Assn. Petroleum Geologists, Soc. Petroleum Engrs., Am. Inst. Profl. Geologists, Blue Key, Sigma Xi. Home: 11457 Hollow Timber Ct Reston VA 22094-1980 Office: Am Geol Inst 4220 King St Alexandria VA 22302-1507

MILLING, R(OSWELL) KING, bank executive, lawyer; b. New Orleans, Aug. 7, 1940; s. Robert E. and Claudia (Pipes) M.; m. Anne McDonald, June 20, 1964; children—Roberts Clay II, Roswell King Jr., Michael Delery. BA, Washington and Lee U., 1962; LLB, Tulane U., 1965. Bar: La. 1965, U.S. Dist. Ct. (ea. dist.) La. 1965, U.S. Ct. Appeals (5th cir.) 1965, U.S. Sup. Ct. 1979, U.S. Ct. Appeals (11th cir.) 1981. Assoc. Milling, Saal, Saunders, Benson & Woodward (now Milling, Benson, Woodward, Hillyer, Pierson & Miller), New Orleans, 1965-69, ptnr., 1969-84; pres. Whitney Nat. Bank, New Orleans, 1984—, also bd. dirs.; pres. Whitney Holding Corp., New Orleans; past pres. Bur. Govtl. Research, New Orleans. mem. Met. Area Com.; La. Civil Service League; past chmn. Upper Pontalba Bldg Commn.; bd. trustees Dillard U., N.O. Marine Inst.; bd. dirs. Downtown Devel. Dist., L.A. Civil Svc. League. Mem. La. State Bar Assn., New Orleans Bar Assn., ABA. Office: Whitney Nat Bank 228 Saint Charles Ave New Orleans LA 70130-2615*

MILLION, RODNEY REIFF, radiologist; b. Idaville, Ind., 1929. MD, Ind. U., 1954. Diplomate Am. Bd. Radiology. Intern Harbor Gen. Hosp., Torrance, 1954-55; resident in radiology Ind. U., 1958-60; resident in radiol. therapy MD Anderson Hosp., Houston, 1960-62; mem. staff Shands Tchg. Hosp., Gainesville, Fla.; prof. radiol. oncology U. Fla., Gainesville. Mem. ARS, ASTRO, Am. Coll. Radiology. Office: Shands Tchg Hosp Dept Radiology Gainesville FL 32602-0385*

MILLIS, ROBERT LOWELL, astronomer; b. Martinsville, Ill., Sept. 12, 1941; married, 1965; 2 children. BA, Ea. Ill. U., 1963; PhD in Astronomy, U. Wis., 1968. Astronomer Lowell Obs., Flagstaff, Ariz., 1967-86, assoc. dir., 1986-90, dir., 1990—. Mem. Am. Astron. Soc., Astronomy Soc. Pacific, Internat. Astronomy Union, Divsn. Planetary Sci. (sec.-treas. 1985-88, chmn. 1994-95). Achievements include research in planetary satellites and ring systems; occultation studies of solar system objects; research on comets. Office: Lowell Observatory 1400 W Mars Hill Rd Flagstaff AZ 86001-4470

MILLMAN, BRUCE RUSSELL, lawyer; b. Bronx, N.Y., June 4, 1948; s. Meyer and Garie (Solomon) M.; m. Lorrie Jan Liss, Aug. 12, 1973; children—Noemi, Avi. A.B., Princeton U., 1970; J.D., Columbia U., 1973. Bar: N.Y. 1974, U.S. Dist. Ct. (ea. and so. dists.) N.Y. 1975, U.S. Ct. Appeals (2d cir.) 1978, U.S. Supreme Ct. 1978. Assoc. Rains & Pogrebin and predecessors Rains, Pogrebin & Scher, Mineola, N.Y., 1973-79, ptnr., 1980—; arbitrator Nassau County Dist. Ct., Mineola, 1981-83. Contbr. to: Labor and Employment Law for the Corporate Counselor and General Practitioner, 1994, Updating Issues in Employment Law, 1986, Public Sector Labor and Employment Law, 1988. Bd. dirs. West Side Montessori Sch., N.Y.C., 1984-90, sec. 1985-87, pres. 1987-90. Harlan Fiske Stone scholar Columbia U. Law Sch., N.Y.C., 1971, 73. Mem. ABA, N.Y. State Bar Assn. (chair-elect labor & employment law sect.), Nassau County Bar Assn., Indsl. Relations Research Assn. (bd. dirs. L.I. chpt. 1984—, pres. 95—). Home: 60 Riverside Dr New York NY 10024-6108 Office: Rains & Pogrebin PC 210 Old Country Rd Mineola NY 11501-4218 also: 375 Park Ave New York NY 10152

MILLMAN, JODE SUSAN, lawyer; b. Poughkeepsie, N.Y., Dec. 28, 1954; d. Samuel Keith and Ellin Sadenberg (Bainder) M.; m. Michael James Harris, June 20, 1982; children: Maxwell, Benjamin. BA, Syracuse U., 1976, JD, 1979. Bar: N.Y. 1980, U.S. Dist. Ct. (so. and ea. dists.) N.Y. 1982, U.S. Supreme Ct. 1983. Asst. corp. counsel City of Poughkeepsie, 1979-81; assoc. Law Office of Lou Lewis, Poughkeepsie, 1981-85; pvt. practice Poughkeepsie, 1985—; staff counsel City of Poughkeepsie Office of Property Devel., 1990—; gen. mgr. WCZX-Communicatons Corp. Contbg. author: Kaminstein Legislative History of the Copyright Law, 1979. Pres. Dutchess County (N.Y.) Vis. Bur., 1980-82; bd. dirs. Poughkeepsie Ballet Theater, 1982, Jewish Cmty. Ctr., 1988; mem. assigned counsel program Dutchess County Family Ct., 1985—; trustee Greater Poughkeepsie Libr. Dist., 1991-94, Poughkeepsie Day Sch., 1995—. Mem. ABA, N.Y. State Bar Assn., Dutchess County Bar Assn. (chmn. pub. rels. 1991—), Mid-Hudson Women's Bar Assn., Poughkeepsie Area C. of C. (econ. devel. com. 1994—). Democrat. Jewish. Office: 97-99 Cannon St Poughkeepsie NY 12601-3140

MILLMAN, RICHARD GEORGE, architect, educator; b. St. Johns, Mich., Feb. 12, 1925; s. Harold Fildew and Elizabeth Hill (Van Deusen) M.; m. Mary Louise Manley, June 17, 1950; childen: John Richard, Ruth Barbara. BArch, U. Mich., 1951, MArch, 1962. Registered architect, Mich., Ohio, Ala. Job capt. Smith Hinchman & Grylls, Detroit, 1951-52; designer assoc. Eliot Robinson, AIA, Birmingham, Mich., 1952-55; designer Eero Saarinen Assocs., Bloomfield Hills, Mich., 1955-56; assoc. Chas. W. Lane Assocs. Inc., Ann Arbor, Mich., 1956-59; prin. Kainlauri, MacMullan, Millman, Ann Arbor, 1959-62; assoc. prof. Ohio U., Athens, 1962-68; prof. Auburn (Ala.) U., 1968—, head architecture dept., 1968-73, 84-85, head indsl. design dept., 1988-89; prof. Mid. East Tech. U., Ankara, Turkey, 1966-67,King Faisal U., Dammam, Saudi Arabia, 1979-81. One man shows include Dhahran Art Group, Saudi Arabia, 1981, Peet Gallery, Auburn U., 1983, 91; author: Washtenaw Community Coll., 1962, Auburn U. Tour Guide, 1990. With U.S. Army, 1943-46, ETO, PTO. Recipient Cert. of Honor Ala. Hist. Commn., 1977; Alumni scholar U. Mich., 1961; Fulbright lectr. Exch. Com., Mid. East Tech. U., 1966. Mem. AIA (treas. Ala. coun. 1969, v.p. 1970, pres. 1972, emeritus 1990, Auburn chpt. pres. 1970, emeritus), Nat. Coun. Archtl. Registration Bd. (cert.), Auburn Arts Assn. Avocations: painting, photography. Home: 736 Brenda Ave Auburn AL 36830-6038 Office: Auburn U Architecture Dept 104 Dudley Hall Auburn AL 36849-5121

MILLNER, ROBERT B., lawyer; b. N.Y.C., Apr. 20, 1950; s. Nathan and Babette E. (Leventhal) M.; m. Susan Brent, June 5, 1983; children: Jacob, Daniel, Rebecca. BA, Wesleyan U., 1971; JD, U. Chgo., 1975. Bar: Ill. 1975. Law clk. to Hon. George C. Edwards U.S. Ct. Appeals for 6th Cir., Cin., 1975-76; with Sonnenschein Nath & Rosenthal, Chgo., 1976—, ptnr., 1982—; mem. Panel of Bankruptcy Trustees, Chgo., 1992—. Editorial bd. Jour. Corp. Disclosure and Confidentiality, 1989-92; contbr. articles to profl. jours. Trustee Anshe Emet Synagogue, Chgo., 1990-93; mem. gov. coun. Am. Jewish Cong. midwest region, 1989—. Fellow Am. Bar Found.; mem. ABA (co-chair bankruptcy and insolvency com. litigation sect. 1992-95), Am. Bankruptcy Inst., Shakespearean Assn. Am. (v.p. Stratford chpt. 1992—), Chgo. Bar Assn., Comml. Bar Assn. (hon. overseas mem.), Legal Club, Std. Club, Wesleyan Alumni Club Chgo. (pres. 1988-90), Phi Beta Kappa. Office: Sonnenschein Nath & Rosenthal 8000 Sears Towers Chicago IL 60606

MILLNER, THOMAS, manufacturing and holding company executive. P-res. The Pilliod Cabinet Co., High Point, N.C., Pilliod Holding Co., Swanton, Ohio, Remington Arms Co., Madison, WI. Office: Remington Arms Co. 870 Remington Rd PO Box 700 Madison NC 27025-0700*

MILLNER, WALLACE B., III, banker; b. Charlotte, N.C., Aug. 1, 1939; s. Wallace B. and Virginia (Reed) M.; m. Nancy Jean Bost, Aug. 25, 1961; children—Wallace Michael, Christopher Bost. AB, Davidson Coll., N.C., 1961; MBA, U. N.C., Chapel Hill, 1962. Asst. v.p., dir. investment rsch. Bank of Va. Co., Richmond, 1971-72, treas., 1973-74, v.p., treas., 1974-76, sr. v.p., treas., 1976-80, chief fin. officer, 1980-85; exec. v.p., chief fin. officer Signet Banking Corp., 1985-88, sr. exec. v.p., chief fin. officer, 1988—; bd. dirs. Westminster Canterbury Corp. Chmn. bd. dirs. Family and Children's Svcs., 1984-86; pres. Richmond (Va.) Symphony. 1st lt. U.S. Army, 1962-64. Decorated Army Commendation medal. Mem. Richmond Soc. Fin. Analysts (pres. 1984-85), Inst. Chartered Fin. Analysts, Fin. Analysts Fedn. (bd. dirs. 1986-91, chmn. 1990), Bankers Roundtable, Assn. Investment Mgmt. and Rsch. (bd. govs. 1990-91), Country Club of Va., Commonwealth Club. Republican. Episcopalian. Avocations: tennis, art. Home: 314 Summit Ln Richmond VA 23221-3711 Office: Signet Banking Corp PO Box 25970 Richmond VA 23260-5970

MILLO, APRILE ELIZABETH, opera singer; b. N.Y.C., Apr. 14, 1958; d. Giovanni and Margarita (Girosi) M. Grad., Hollywood High Sch., 1976. Operatic debut in Aida, Utah Opera , Salt Lake City, 1980; European debut in Aida, Karlsruhe Opera House, 1982; appeared in Ernani, La Scala Teatro, Milan, 1982, Simon Boccanegra, Met. Opera, N.Y.C., 1984; prin. artist, Met. Opera, 1984—; appeared as Elizabetta in Don Carlo, Teatro a Bologna, Italy, 1987, Aida, Met. Opera, 1989; recs. include A Recital with Eugene Kohn, 1986, Aida Sony Classical, 1990, Lusia MIller Classical, 1991, Il Trovatore Sony Classical, 1991; video Deuctle Grammaphone Un Ballo in Maschera, 1991. Recipient Voce Verdiane award Verdian Voice Competition, Busetto, Italy, 1978, Monserrat Caballe Verdi award Francisco Viñas Competition. Barcelona, Spain, 1979, Richard Tucker Found. award, N.Y.C., 1985, Maria Callas award Maria Callas Found., Frankfurt, Fed. Republic Germany, 1986, Showstopper award N.Y. Woman mag., 1987. Roman Catholic. Avocations: tennis, sports, reading. Office: Met Opera Assn Inc Lincoln Ctr New York NY 10023 also: Columbia Artists Mgt Inc Crittenden Anson Div 165 W 57th St New York NY 10019-2201

MILLON, HENRY ARMAND, fine arts educator, architectural historian; b. Altoona, Pa., Feb. 22, 1927; s. Henri Francois and Louise (de Serent) M.; m. Emily Dees, June, 1953; m. Judith Rice, Dec. 27, 1966; children: Henri, Hadrian, Phoebe, Aaron. BA, Tulane U., 1947, BS, 1949, BArch, 1953; AM, Harvard U., 1954, MArch, 1955, PhD, 1964; LHD (hon.), Tulane U., 1995. Asst. prof. MIT, Cambridge, 1960-69, prof., 1969-80, vis. prof., 1981—, pres. univ. Film Study Ctr., 1972-73, trustee Film Study Ctr., 1967-73; dean Ctr. for Advanced Study in Visual Arts, Nat. Gallery Art, Washington, 1979—; mem. bd. visitors Fine Arts Sch. Boston Mus., 1972-78; mem. rsch. grants panel NEH, 1972-73, rsch. tools panel, 1983; dir. Am. Acad. in Rome, 1974-77, trustee, 1977—, vice chmn., 1982—; mem. adv. coun. Sch. Architecture, Princeton U., 1970-73, adv. coun. dept. art and archeology, 1972-73, 80-84; mem. cons. com. Nat. Survey Historic Sites and Bldgs., Nat. Pk. Svc. div. U.S. Dept. Interior, 1969-80; vice chmn. Boston Landmarks Commn., 1970-73; panelist Gladys Kriebel Delmas Found., 1979—; chmn. adv. bd. architecture and design TV series Guggenheim Prodns., 1980-88; vis. com. Dept. Fine Arts Harvard U., 1982-84, Sch. Hist. Studies Inst. Advanced Study, 1978, Arthur M. Sackler Gallery Smithsonian Instn., 1986-92; mem. U.S. Nat. Com. History of Art, 1980—; alt. del. Internat. Com. History of Art, 1981-85, del., 1985—, sci. sec. working group Thesaurus Artis Universalis, 1983-89; hon. mem. Boston Archtl. Ctr., 1982—; chmn. sr. fellows com. history of landscape architecture program Dumbarton Oaks, 1983-89, convenor archtl. drawing adv. group, 1983—; mem. adv. com. Getty Art Hist. Info. Program, 1983-91, mem. internat. repertory of lit. of art history, 1985-90, adv. com. Bibliography of the History of Art, 1986—; vice chmn. Coun. Am. Overseas Rsch. Ctrs., 1984-90; pres. Found. for Documents of Architecture, 1987-93; trustee Nat. Bldg. Mus., 1988-94. Author: Baroque and Rococco Architecture, 1962, Key Monuments of the History of Architecture, 1964, Filippo Juvarra: Drawings from the Roman Period, 1704-1714, 1984, (with Craig H. Smyth) Michelangelo Architect, 1988; editor: (with Linda Nochlin) Art and Architecture in the Service of Politics, 1978, Studies in Italian Art and Architecture 15th through 18th Centuries, 1980; co-editor: The Renaissance From Brunellschi to Michelangelo: The Representation of Architecture, 1994. With USNR, 1944-46. Recipient citation for excellence Internat. Archtl. Book Publ., AIA, 1994, Prix Hercule Catenacci, Inst. de France, 1995, A.H. Barr award Coll. Art Assn., 1996, Centennial medal Am. Acad. in Rome, others; named Hon. Mem. Accademia di San Luca, 1995; Fulbright fellow, Italy, 1957, Am. Acad. Rome fellow, 1957-60. Mem. Soc. Archtl. Historians (pres. 1968-70), Coll. Art Assn. (bd. dirs. 1982-85), AIA Found. (mem. octagon com. 1986-88), Renaissance Soc., Am. Acad. Arts and Scis., Am. Philos. Soc., Deputazione Subalpina di Storia Patria, Soc. Preservation New Eng. Antiquities, Am. Inst. Archeology, Am. Soc. 18th Century Studies, Academia delle Scienze di Torino. Home: 8051 Parkside Ln NW Washington DC 20012-2252

MILLS, AGNES EUNICE KARLIN, artist, printmaker, sculptor; b. N.Y.C., Apr. 2, 1915; d. Herman Karlin and Celia (Ducoffe) Karlin; m. Saul Mills, May 10, 1910 (dec. Nov. 1993); children: Karen, Marghe Mills Thysen. Grad., Cooper Union Art Sch., N.Y.C., 1938; BFA, Pratt Inst., 1975; student, NYU. One-woman shows include Carus Gallery, N.Y.C., Unitarian Soc., Manhasset, N.Y., Harbor Gallery, Cold Spring Harbor, N.Y., North Truro Art Gallery, Cape Cod, Mass., Alfredo Valente Gallery, N.Y.C., Robbins Gallery, East Orange, N.J., Nuance Galleries, Tampa, Friends of Tampa Ballet, Graphic Eye Coop Gallery, Pt. Washington, N.Y., City Ctr. Gallery, N.Y.C., Lincoln Ctr. Art Gallery, N.Y.C., North Shore Cmty. Arts Ctr., Great Neck, N.Y., Delray Beach Works in Progress Gallery, Boca Raton Cmty. Ctr., Palm Beach Pub. Libr.; exhibited in group shows at Alfredo Valente Gallery, N.Y.C., Audubon Soc., N.Y.C., Bowdoin Coll. Mus. Art, Brunswick, Maine, Brandeis U., Waltham, Mass., Bklyn. Mus. Art, Brown U., Providence, Butler Inst. Am. Art, Youngstown, Ohio, Colgate U. Libr., Hamilton, N.Y., Cornell U., Ithaca, N.Y., East Hampton (N.Y.) Guild Artists, Gallery K, Woodstock, N.Y., Graphic Eye Coop Gallery, Port Washington, N.Y., Heckscher Mus., Huntington, N.Y., Hunterdon County Mus., Clinton, N.J., Joan Avnet Gallery, Great Neck, N.Y., Lincoln Ctr. Libr. Performing Arts, N.Y.C., Madison Gallery, N.Y.C., Boca Raton City Hall, Boca Raton Cmty. Ctr., Boca Raton Libr.; represented in permanent collections at Boca Raton Mus. Art, Nat. Women in the Arts Mus. Home: Ste L 9 144 8903 Glades Rd Boca Raton FL 33434-4019 Studio: 9763 Majorca Pl Boca Raton FL 33434-3713

MILLS, BELEN COLLANTES, early childhood education educator; s. Ricardo and Epifania (Tomines) C.; children: Belinda Mills Keiser, Roger A. BSE, Leyte Normal Coll., Tacloban, Leyte, Philippines, 1954; MS in Edn., Ind. U., 1955, EdD, 1967. Prof. early childhood edn. Fla. State U., Tallahassee; early childhood cons. to ednl. agys. and orgns. Author books on early childhood edn. and acad. readiness computer programs; contbr. articles to profl.jours. Smith-Mundt Fulbright scholar. Mem. Nat. Assn. for the Edn. of Young Children, Nat. Assn. of Early Childhood Tchr. Edn., World Coun. for Curriculum and Instruction, Assn. of Childhood Edn. Internat. Home: PO Box 20023 Tallahassee FL 32316-0023

MILLS, BRADFORD, merchant banker; b. N.Y.C., Dec. 16, 1926; s. Dudley Holbrook and Louise (Morris) M.; m. Cheryl Ann Di Paolo; children: Elizabeth Lee, Bradford Alan, Barbara Louise, Ross Dudley. BA cum laude in Econs, Princeton U., 1948; postgrad., Oxford (Eng.) U., 1950-51. Asst. to dir. overseas ters. div. ECA, Paris, 1948-50; assoc. corp. fin. dept. F. Eberstadt & Co., N.Y.C., 1954-62; ptnr. F. Eberstadt & Co., 1960-62; mng. ptnr. N.Y. Securities Co., 1962-70; chmn., dir. Specialized Svcs., Inc., Atlanta, 1968-85; pres., CEO Overseas Pvt. Investment Corp., Washington, 1971-73; dir. Overseas Pvt. Investment Corp., 1971-75; chmn. bd., dir. F. Eberstadt & Co. Internat., 1973-74; mng. ptnr. Bradford Assocs., 1974-92; ltd. ptnr. Bradford Investment Ptnrs. Ltd., 1992—; past chmn. Diamond Glass, MMX Corp., HWC Corp., Chgo. Stock Tab Corp., Filtration Scis.; chmn., CEO Overseas Pvt. Investors Ltd., Overseas Pvt. Equities, Overseas Equity Investors, Inc., U.S. Precision Glass Inc.; bd. dirs. Papel Freelance, Inc., DentureCare, Inc., The Princeton Packet, Futronix Corp. Pres. Mills Found.; trustee, treas. Millbrook (N.Y.) Sch., 1978—; trustee Med. ctr. Princeton. Mem. Coun. Fgn. Rels., Blooming Grove Club (Pa.), Links Club, Leash Club, Anglers Club N.Y., Nassau Club, Bedens Brook Club. Home: 15 Van Kirk Rd Princeton NJ 08540-4214 Office: Bradford Investment Ptnrs 44 Nassau St Princeton NJ 08542-3719

MILLS, CAROL MARGARET, business consultant, public relations consultant; b. Salt Lake City, Aug. 31, 1943; d. Samuel Lawrence and Beth (Neilson) M.; BS magna cum laude, U. Utah, 1965. With W.S. Hatch Co., Woods Cross, Utah, 1965-87, corp. sec., 1970-87, traffic mgr., 1969-87, dir. publicity, 1974-87; cons. various orgns., 1988—; dir. Hatch Service Corp., 1972-87, Nat. Tank Truck Carriers, Inc., Washington, 1977-88; bd. dirs. Intermountain Tariff Bur. Inc., 1978-88, chmn., 1981-82, 1986-87; bd. dirs. Mountainwest Venture Group. Fund raiser March of Dimes, Am. Cancer Soc., Am. Heart Assn.; active senatorial campaign, 1976, gubernatorial campaign, 1984, 88, congl. campaign, 1990, 92, 94, vice chair voting dist., 1988-90, congressional capmpaing, 1994; chmn. 1990-92, chmn. party caucus legis. dist.; witness transp. com. Utah State Legislature, 1984, 85; apptd. by gov. to bd. trustees Utah Tech. Fin. Corp., 1986—, corp. sec., mem. exec. com., 1988—. Recipient service awards W. S. Hatch Co., 1971, 80; mem. Pioneer Theatre Guild, 1985—; V.I.P. capt. Easter Seal Telethon, 1989, 90, recipient Outstanding Vol. Svc. award Easter Seal Soc. Utah, 1989, 90. Mem. Nat. Tank Truck Carriers, Transp. Club Salt Lake City, Am. Trucking Assn. (public relations council), Utah Motor Transport Assn. (dir. 1982-88), Internat. Platform Assn., Beta Gamma Sigma, Phi Kappa Phi, Phi Chi Theta. Home and Office: 77 Edgecombe Dr Salt Lake City UT 84103-2219

MILLS, CELESTE LOUISE, hypnotherapist, professional magician; b. L.A., May 16, 1952; d. Emery John and Helen Louise (Bradbury) W.; m. Robert Richardson Feigel, Apr. 11, 1971 (div. 1973); m. Peter Alexander Mills, June 12, 1991. (div. 1992). BBA, Western State U., Doniphan, Mo., 1987; PhD in Religion, Universal Life Ch. Univ., 1987; grad., Hypnotism Tng. Inst., Glendale, Calif., 1990. Cert. hypnotherapist. Credit mgr. accounts receivable Gensler-Lee Diamonds, Santa Barbara, Calif., 1973-74, Terry Hinge and Hardware, Van Nuys, Calif., 1975-78; credit mgr., fin. analyst Peanut Butter Fashions, Chatsworth, Calif., 1978-82; personal mgr. Charter Mgmt. Co., Beverly Hills, Calif., 1982-83; co-owner, v.p. Noreen Jenney Communicates, Beverly Hills, 1983-85; corp. credit mgr., fin. analyst Cen. Diagnostic Lab., Tarzana, Calif., 1985-89; credit mgr., fin. analyst Metwest Clin. Lab., Inc., Tarzana, Calif., 1989-90; pvt. practice, 1990—; cons. Results Now, Inc., Tarzana, 1986-87. Prodr., host (TV) Brainstorm, 1993—. Media spokesperson Am. Cancer Soc., 1990—. Mem. NAFE, NOW, Nat. Assn. Credit Mgmt., Credit Mgrs. Assn. So. Calif., Credit Ednl. Found., Nat. Humane Ednl. Found., Credit Mgrs. Assn. Trade Groups (bd. govs. 1988-89), Nat. Clin. Lab. Trade Group (chmn. 1988-89), Med. and Surg. Suppliers Trade Group (vice chmn. 1988-89, chmn. 1989-90), Soc. Am. Magicians, Acad. Magical Arts, Internat. Brotherhood of Magicians, Assn. Advanced Ethical Hypnosis, Am. Coun. Hypnotist Examiners. Avocations: scuba diving, sailing.

MILLS, CHARLES G., photography company executive; b. 1935; married. Grad., Auburn U., 1960. With Olan Mills, Inc., Chattanooga, Tenn., 1962—, now treas., also bd. dirs. Served with U.S. Army, 1962-63. Office: Olan Mills Inc 4325 Amnicola Hwy Chattanooga TN 37406-1014*

MILLS, CHARLES GARDNER, lawyer; b. Griffin, Ga., Feb. 29, 1940; s. Charles G. and Marguerite (Powell) M. AB, Yale U., 1962; JD, Boston Coll., 1967. Bar: N.Y. 1967, U.S. Dist. Ct. (so. and ea. dists.) 1972, U.S. Ct. Appeals (2d cir.) 1975, U.S. Supreme Ct., 1977, U.S. Ct. Claims 1991, U.S. Ct. Veteran's Appeals 1996. Assoc. Smart & McKay, N.Y.C., 1967-68, Smart & Mills, N.Y.C., 1969-71, Eaton & VanWinkle, N.Y.C., 1971-82, Payne, Wood & Littlejohn, Glen Cove, Melville, N.Y., 1982-91. With U.S. Army, 1962-64, ETO. Mem. N.Y. State Bar Assn., Assn. Bar City N.Y., Nassau County Bar Assn., Rotary (pres. Glen Cove Club 1989-90), Am. Legion (comdr. Locust Valley, N.Y. post 1988-90, comdr. Nassau County com. 1995-96), Soc. Colonial Wars, SCV, Order of the Arrow. Republican. Roman Catholic. Office: 56 School St Glen Cove NY 11542-2512

MILLS, CYNTHIA SPRAKER, professional society asministrator; b. Williamsburg, Va., June 11, 1962; d. Charles E. and Marceil H. (Harris) S.; m. John E. Mills, Oct. 18, 1986. BA in History and Psychology, Queens Coll., 1984; MA in Medieval Studies, U. of York, Eng., 1986. Fin. aid officer Rutledge Edn. Sys., Charlotte, N.C., 1987-88; assoc. dir. Programming & Sys., Inc., Charlotte, 1988-90; asst. exec. dir. Nat. Assn. Coll. Aux. Svcs., Staunton, Va., 1990-93; exec. dir. Pilot Internat. & Pilot Internat. Found., Macon, Ga., 1993—; presenter in field. Contbr. articles to profl. publs. Chair Pacesetters divsn. United Way of Staunton/West Augusta County, 1992; mem. adv. bd. Edn. Exch., Ind., 1991-93; mem. Commonwealth/Cmty. Alliance for Drug Rehab. and Edn. of Staunton/Augusta County, Inc., 1991-93. Rotary Found. scholar, 1984-85, Queens Coll. Presdl. scholar, 1980-84. Mem. Ga. Soc. Assn. Execs. (membership com. 1991—, staff mgmt. com. 1994-96, chair tech. spl. interest group 1994-95, bd. dirs. 1995—), Am. Soc. Assn. Execs. (cert., membership com. 1991—, Notable Accomplishment award 1991, mem. Chmn.'s Honor Roll 1992, mem. Chmn.'s Round Table for Membership Recruitment 1994), Am. Biog. Inst. (rsch. bd. advisors), Nat. Ctr. for Nonprofit Bds., Svc. Club Leaders Conf. Republican. Lutheran. Office: Pilot Internat & Found PO Box 4844 244 College St Macon GA 31213

MILLS, DANIEL QUINN, business educator, consultant, author; b. Houston, Nov. 24, 1941; s. Daniel Monroe and Louise (Quinn) M.; divorced; children: Lisa Ann, Shirley Elizabeth. BA, Ohio Wesleyan U., 1963; MA, Harvard U., 1965, PhD, 1968. Prof. MIT, Cambridge, 1968-75, Harvard Bus. Sch., Boston, 1976—; impartial umpire Plan to Settle Disputes in Constrn., 1973-79, Trans-Alaska Pipeline, 1975-78, AFL-CIO Internal Disputes Plan, 1975-82; commr. Nat. Commn. on Employment Policy, Washington,

1982-86. Author: Industrial Relations in Construction, 1971, Labor, Government and Inflation, 1975, Labor-Management Relations, 1978, 5th edit., 1993, Construction Industry, 1979, The New Competitors, 1985, Not Like Our Parents: The Baby-Boom Generation, 1987, The IBM Lesson, 1988, The Rebirth of the Corporation, 1990, The GEM Principle, 1994, Broken Promises: What Went Wrong at IBM, 1996. Mem. Am. Econ. Assn., Indsl. Relations Research Assn., Phi Beta Kappa. Mem. United Ch. of Christ. Office: Harvard U Harvard Bus Sch Soldiers Field Rd Allston MA 02134-1805

MILLS, DAVID HARLOW, psychologist, association executive; b. Marshalltown, Iowa, Dec. 26, 1932; s. Harlow Burgess and Esther Winifred (Brewer) M.; m. Janet Louise Anderson, June 15, 1957 (div. 1984); children: Ross Harlow, Anne Louise; m. Susan S. Greene, Aug. 3, 1984. BS, Iowa State U., 1955, MS, 1957; PhD, Mich. State U., 1964. Postdoctoral fellow USPHS U. Ill., Champaign, 1964-65; asst. prof. psychology Iowa State U., Ames, 1965-68; assoc. prof. Iowa State U., 1968-69; asst. dir. Iowa State U. (Counseling Center), 1967-69; mem. faculty U. Md., College Park, 1969-81; prof. psychology U. Md., 1972-81, asst. dir. counseling center, 1969-81; adminstrv. officer Am. Psychol. Assn., Washington, 1981-86; pvt. practice Bangor, Maine, 1989—, Blue Hill, Maine, 1990—; cons. Iowa Women's Reformatory, 1966-69, VA, Rockwell City, Iowa, 1966-69; rsch. assoc. Nat. Register Health Svcs. Providers in Psychology; mgmt. cons. Ctr. Creative Leadership U. Md., 1980—; mem. Maine Bd. Psychologists; mem. examination com. Assn. State and Provincial State Psychology Bds., 1995—. Contbr. articles to profl. jours. Pres. Woodmoor-Pinecrest Citizens Assn., Silver Spring, Md., 1973-74; mem. com. higher edn. Allied Civic Group Montgomery County, 1974, sr. fellow Consortium of Univs. of the Washington D.C. Met. Area., 1987—. Served with U.S. Army, 1957-61. Fellow APA (bd. dirs. 1986-90, dir. ethics 1986—, ethics cons. 1990—); mem. Internat. Assn. Counseling Svcs. (accrediting bd. 1972-74, v.p. 1975-77, pres. 1977-79). Democrat. Unitarian. Home: RR 1 Box 323A Little Deer Isle ME 04650-9714 Office: 277 State St Ste 214 Bangor ME 04401-5439

MILLS, DON HARPER, pathology and psychiatry educator, lawyer; b. Peking, Republic of China, July 27, 1927; came to U.S., 1928; s. Clarence Alonzo and Edith Clarissa (Parrett) M.; m. Lillian Frances Snyder, June 11, 1949; children: Frances Jo, Jon Snyder. BS, U. Cin., 1950, MD, 1953; JD, U. So. Calif., 1958. Diplomate Am. Bd. Law in Medicine. Intern L.A. County Gen. Hosp., 1953-54, admitting physician, 1954-57, attending staff pathologist, 1959—; pathology fellow U. So. Calif., L.A., 1954-55, instr. pathology, 1958-62, asst. clin. prof., 1962-65, assoc. clin. prof., 1965-69, clin. prof., 1969—, clin. prof. psychiatry and behavioral sci., 1986—; asst. in pathology Hosp. Good Samaritan, L.A., 1956-65, cons. staff, 1962-72, affiliating staff, 1972-91; dep. med. examiner Office of L.A. County Med. Examiner, 1957-61; instr. legal medicine Loma Linda (Calif.) U. Sch. Medicine, 1960-66, assoc. clin. prof. humanities, 1966-95; cons. HEW, 1972-73, 75-76, Dept. of Def., 1975-80; bd. dirs. Am. Bd. Law in Medicine, Inc., Chgo., 1980-86; med. dir. Profl. Risk Mgmt. Group, 1989—. Column editor Newsletter of the Long Beach Med. Assn., 1960-75, Jour. Am. Osteopathic Assn., 1965-77, Ortho Panel, 1970-78; exec. editor Trauma, 1964-88, mem. editl. bd., 1988—; mem. editl. bd. Legal Aspects of Med. Practice, 1972-90, Med. Alert Comms., 1973-75, Am. Jour. Forensic Medicine and Pathology, 1979-87, Hosp. Risk Control, 1981-96; contbr. numerous articles to profl. jours. Bd. dirs. Inst. for Med. Risk Studies, 1988—. Recipient Ritz Heerman award Calif. Hosp. Assn., 1986, Disting. fellow Am. Acad. Forensic Scis., 1993, Genesis award Pacific Ctr. for Health Policy and Ethics, 1993, Founder's award Am. Coll. Med. Quality, 1994. Fellow Am. Coll. Legal Medicine (pres. 1974-76, bd. govs. 1970-78, v.p. 1972-74, chmn. malpractice com. 1973-74, jour. editl. bd. 1984—), Am. Acad. Forensic Sci. (gen. program chmn. 1966-67, chmn. jurisprudence sect. 1966-67, 73-74, exec. com. 1971-74, 84-88, v.p. 1984-85, pres. 1986-87, ethics com. 1976-86, 91—, chmn. ethics com. 1994—, strategic planning com. 1990—, jour. editl. bd. 1965-79); mem. AMA (jour. editl. bd. 1973-77), AAAS, ABA, Calif. Med. Assn., L.A. County Med. Assn., L.A. County Bar Assn., Am. Judicature Soc., Am. Soc. Hosp. Attys., Calif. Soc. Hosp. Attys. Home: Ste 2606 700 E Ocean Blvd Unit 2606 Long Beach CA 90802-5039 Office: Ste 250 911 Studebaker Rd Ste 250 Long Beach CA 90815-4900

MILLS, DONALD MCKENZIE, librarian; b. Virden, Man., Can., Feb. 25, 1946; s. Earl Townsend and Mable Elizabeth (Davies) M.; m. Kathrine Ann Richards, Aug. 26, 1968; children—Jennifer, Susan. B.A., U. Winnipeg, Man., Can., 1968; M.L.S., U. B.C., Vancouver, Can., 1972. Chief librarian St. Albert Pub. Library, Alta., Can., 1972-75; children's coordinator Kamloops Pub. Library, B.C., Can., 1975-78; chief librarian West Vancouver Pub. Library, B.C., Can., 1978-82, Winnipeg Pub. Library, Man., Can., 1982-87, Mississagua (Ont.) Pub. Library, 1987—. Mem. ALA, Can. Library Assn., Ontario Libr. Assn. Office: Mississauga Libr Sys, 301 Burnham Thorpe Rd, Mississauga, ON Canada L5B 3Y3

MILLS, DONNA, actress; b. Chgo., Dec. 11, 1945. Student, U. Ill. Began career with stage prodns. Chgo. area; appeared on Broadway in Don't Drink the Water; regular in TV series The Secret Storm, Dan August, The Good Life, 1971-72, Knots Landing, 1980-89, Love Is a Many Splendored Thing, 1967; appeared in various TV films including Haunts of the Very Rich, 1972, Rolling Man, 1972, Night of Terror, 1972, The Bait, 1973, Live Again, Die Again, 1974, Who is the Black Dahlia?, 1975, Beyond the Bermuda Triangle, 1975, Look What's Happened to Rosemary's Baby, 1976, Smash-Up on Interstate 5, 1976, Fire!, 1977, Curse of the Black Widow, 1977, The Hunted Lady, 1977, Superdome, 1978, Doctors' Private Lives, 1978, Waikiki, 1980, He's Not Your Son, 1984, Outback Round, 1988, The Lady Regrets, 1989, The World's Oldest Living Bridesmaid, 1990, Runaway Father, 1992, False Arrest, 1991, The President's Child, 1992; actress, co-prodr. In My Daughter's Name, 1992; mini series Hanging By a Thread, 1979, Bare Essence, 1982, Intimate Encounters, 1986; motion pictures (debut) The Incident, 1967, Play Misty for Me, 1971.

MILLS, DOROTHY ALLEN, investor; b. New Brunswick, N.J., Dec. 14, 1920; d. James R. and Bertha Lovilla (Porter) Allen; m. George M. Mills, Apr. 21, 1945; children: Dianne, Adele, Dorothy L. BA, Douglass Coll., New Brunswick, N.J., 1943. Investment reviewer Cen. Hanover Bank, N.Y.C., 1943-44; asst. to dir. of admissions and sec. undergrad. yrs. Douglass Coll., New Brunswick, 1944-45; sec., regional dir. O.P.A., Ventura, Calif., 1945-46; corp. sec. George M. Mills Inc., Highland Park, N.J., 1946-75; pvt. investor N. Brunswick, N.J., 1975—. Sr. v.p. Children Am. Revolution, N.J., 1965; active alumni com. Douglass Coll., 1990—. Recipient Douglass Alumni award, 1992. Mem. AAUW, New Brunswick Hist. Soc., DAR, English Speaking Union, Rutgers Alumni Faculty Club, Princeton-Douglass Alumni Club, N. Brunswick Women's Club, Auxiliary Robert Wood Johnson Hosp. and Med. Sch. Republican. Mem. Dutch Reformed Ch. Avocations: travel, gardening, bridge. Home: 1054 Hoover Dr New Brunswick NJ 08902

MILLS, EDWIN SMITH, economics educator; b. Collingswood, N.J., June 25, 1928; s. Edwin Smith and Roberta (Haywood) M.; m. Barbara Jean Dressner, Sept. 2, 1950; children: Alan Stuart, Susan Dorinda; m. Margaret M. Hutchinson, Jan. 22, 1977. B.A., Brown U., 1951; Ph.D., U. Birmingham, Eng., 1956. Asst. lectr. Univ. Coll. North Staffordshire, Eng., 1953-55; instr. Mass. Inst. Tech., 1955-57; mem. faculty Johns Hopkins, Balt., 1957-70; prof. econs. Johns Hopkins, 1963-70, chmn. dept. econs., 1966-69; prof. econs. and pub. affairs, Gerald L. Phillippe prof. urban studies Princeton U., 1970-75, prof. econs., 1975-87, chmn. dept., 1975-77; Gary Rosenberg prof. real estate and fin. Kellog Sch. Mgmt. Northwestern U., Evanston, Ill., 1987—; vis. research fellow Cowles Found., Yale, 1961; sr. profl. staff Council Econ. Advisers, 1964-65. Author: The Burden of Government, 1986. Served to 2d lt. AUS, 1946-48. Mem. Am. Econ. Assn., Phi Beta Kappa. Home: 430 W Roslyn Pl Chicago IL 60614-2713 Office: Northwestern U Ctr Real Estate Rsch Kellogg Graduate School 2001 Sheridan Rd Evanston IL 60208-0814

MILLS, ELIZABETH ANN, librarian; b. Cambridge, Mass., Apr. 1, 1934; d. Ralph Edwin and Sylvia Elizabeth (Meehan) McCurdy; m. Albert Ernest Mills, July 6, 1957; 1 child, Karen Elizabeth. BA, Duke U., 1956; MS, Simmons Coll., 1973; postgrad. Boston Coll., Framingham State U., Bridgewater State U. Sec. Lowell House, Harvard U., Cambridge, Mass., 1956-57; substitute libr., tchr. Wellesley (Mass.) H.S., 1972-73, Needham (Mass.) H.S., 1972-73; libr. Tucker Sch. Media Ctr., Milton (Mass.) Pub. Schs., 1973-94, chmn. comput curriculum com., 1982, mem. computer study com., 1988-91, bldg. coordinator gifted program, 1981-94; libr. Milton (Mass.) H.S., 1994—. Contbr. articles to profl. jours. Active Girl Scouts U.S.A., U.S. Power Squadron, Gt. Blue Hill, Mass., 1974—. Mem. ALA, Am. Assn. Sch. Librarians, Assn. Library Service Children, Mass. Assn. Ednl. Media, Mass. Sch. Libr. Assn., Beta Phi Mu, Kappa Delta, Delta Kappa Gamma. Republican. Episcopalian. Home: 177 Jarvis Cir Needham MA 02192-2034 Office: Milton HS 451 Centre St Milton MA 02186-4118

MILLS, EUGENE SUMNER, college president; b. West Newton, Ind., Sept. 13, 1924; s. Sumner Amos and Lela (Weatherly) M.; m. Dorothy Frances Wildman, Oct. 22, 1945; children: David Walden, Sara Anne. A.B., Earlham Coll., 1948; M.A., Claremont Grad. Sch., 1949, Ph.D., 1952; Specialist Postdoctoral Auditor, Harvard, 1958-59; LLD (hon.), N.H. Coll., 1979, U. N.H., 1988; LHD (hon.), Earlham Coll., 1987. Instr. psychology Whittier (Calif.) Coll., 1950, asst. prof., chmn. dept., 1952-55, assoc. prof., chmn. dept., 1955-60, prof. psychology, chmn. dept., 1960-62; faculty U. N.H., Durham, 1962-79; prof. psychology U. N.H., 1962-79, chmn. dept., 1962-65, dean Grad. Sch., coordinator research, 1963-67; dean U. N.H. (Coll. Liberal Arts), 1967-70, acad. v.p., 1970-71, provost, 1971-74, provost, acting pres., 1974, pres., 1974-79; pres. Whittier (Calif.) Coll. and Whittier Coll. Sch. of Law, 1979-89; prof. psychology Whittier (Calif.) Coll., 1979-89, emeritus prof. psychology, pres. emeritus, 1989—; vis. prof. U. Victoria, B.C., summers 1958, 60; bd. dirs. Elderhostel, Inc., 1977—, chmn., 1984-90; bd. dirs. Fedco Inc., 1988—, vice-chmn., 1996—; interim pres. Earlham Coll., 1996—; bd. dirs. New Eng. Bd. Higher Edn., 1974-79; mem. N.H. Psychol. Assn., 1962-79, pres., 1969-70, bd. dirs., 1967-70; trustee Earlham Coll., 1966-69. Author: George Trumbull Ladd: Pioneer American Psychologist, 1969, The Story ofElderhostel, 1993; contbr. articles to profl. jours. Danforth Found. grantee; NSF grantee. Fellow Am. Psychol. Assn.; mem. Western Psychol. Assn., Sigma Xi, Phi Kappa Phi., Omicron Delta Kappa. Mem. Soc. of Friends.

MILLS, FREDERICK VANFLEET, art educator, watercolorist; b. Bremen, Ohio, June 5, 1925; s. Frederick William and Juanita Ellen (VanFleet) M.; m. Lois Jean Rademacher; children: Mark Steven (dec.), Michael Sherwood, Mollie Sue, Merre Shannon, Randal Dean, Susan Lynn, Todd Patrick, Shondra Marie. BS, Ohio State U., 1949; MS, Ind. U., 1951, EdD, 1956; postgrad., U.S. Army Staff and Command Coll., 1973-76. Tchr. art, supr. Celina (Ohio) Pub. Schs., 1949-51; instr. univ. h.s. Ind. U., 1951-55; prof. art, art edn., chmn. dept. art edn. Ind. U., Bloomington, 1959-65; vis. prof. U. Tex.-Austin, 1965; chmn. dept. related arts, crafts and interior design U. Tenn., Konxville, 1966-68; prof. art, chmn. dept. art Ill. State U., 1968-85, prof. emeritus, 1985—; prof. art Lincoln Coll., Normal, 1986—; rsch. reader humanities HEW, 1968-69; resource person arts, edn. and Ams. panel Rockefeller Report Am Coun. Arts in Edn., 1977-78; cons. Latin Am. Fulbright Scholarship Program Harvard U., 1981-82; mem. com. Ill. Fine Arts Rev. for Capital Devel. Bd., 1987—, planning com. Nat. Inst. Advanced Studies in Art and Design and Archives of Am. Art Sch., 1988—, rsch. com. Nat. Sch. Art and Design. One-man shows include McLean County Arts Ctr., Bloomington, Ill., Lincoln (Ill.) Coll., Ill. Agriculture Assn. Credit Union Art Exhbn. Series, Bloomington, Suzette Schochet Gallery, Newport, R.I.; represented in permanent collections Wonderlin Gallery, Normal, Ill., State Farm Ins. Co., Kemper Fin. Securities/Kemper Fin. Fund, First of Am. Bank, Ill., Diamond Star Motors Corp., Easter Seal Assn., City of Vladimir, Russia, City of Asahikawa, Hokkaido, Japan, County of McLean, City of Bloomington, Town of Normal; author, editor: The Status of the Visual Arts in Higher Education, 1976, New Perspectives in Visual Arts Administration, 1977, Issues in the Administration of Visual Arts, 1978, Politics and the Visual Arts, 1979, The Visual Arts in the Ninth Decade, 1980; editor Western Arts Bull., 1958-62; featured in 12 part ser. As An Artist Sees local pub. access; contbr. to profl. jours. Pres. Ill. Alliance Art Edn., 1975-77, Ill. Task Force for Arts Edn. in Gen. Edn., 1976-77; mem. Tenn. Arts Commn., 1967-68, Nat. Alliance Arts Edn./Kennedy Ctr., 1975-77; charter trustee Ill. Summer Sch. for Arts, v.p., v.p. Found. Bd., 1988-94; bd. dirs., co-founder Sugar Creek Arts Festival, Normal, 1985—; chair major gifts com. Normal Theater Restoration Project, 1992—; bd. dirs., v.p. McLean County Arts Ctr., Bloomington, 1980-90, sponsor Skilled Crafts award, 1968—. Served to maj. USAR; Col. Ill. Militia. Recipient Recognition award Alliance for Arts Edn., 1984, Outstanding Svc. award Ill. Alliance Arts Edn., 1984, 1994 Ornament of Yr./Artist of Yr. award; subject articles, TV interviews. Mem. Nat. Council Art Adminstrs. (charter, sr. rsch. editor bd. dirs. 1973-81), Nat. Assn. Schs. Art (instnl. del. 1974-84, nominating com. 1977-78, rsch. com. 1976-77), Western Arts Assn. (pres. 1962-64), Coll. Art Assn., Nat. Art Edn. Assn. (dir. 1964-66), Scabbard and Blade, Phi Delta Kappa, Delta Tau Delta, Delta Phi Delta. Club: Rotary Internat. Home: K 162 Lake Bloomington RR 2 Box 60 A Hudson IL 61748 *As I reflect on my life and career up to this point, I feel that consistency and humaneness are two words that come to mind. It seems extremely important to be consistent when a person relates to others, and if that is coupled with humaneness and consideration of the value of others, being aware of their strengths and weaknesses, their likes and dislikes, it becomes easier to relate to them in this most complex world of ours.*

MILLS, GARY BERNARD, history educator; b. Marshall, Tex., Sept. 10, 1944; s. Harold Garland and Hazel Cecilia (Rachal) M.; m. Elizabeth Shown; children: Clayton Bernard, Donna Rachal, Daniel Garland. BA in History and Bus. Adminstrn., Delta State U., 1967; MA in History, Miss. State U., 1969, PhD in History, 1974. Instr. history McNeese State U., Lake Charles, La., 1969-72, U. Ctr., Jackson, Miss., 1972-75; asst. prof. U. Ala., Gadsden, 1976-79, assoc. prof., 1979-82; assoc. prof. U. Ala., Tuscaloosa, 1982-83, prof. history, 1984—; cons. in field. Author numerous books; coeditorr Nat. Geneal. Soc. Quar., 1987—; contbr. numerous articles to profl. jours. Del. Am.-Russian Archival Adv., Washington, Moscow, Minsk, 1989-91; mem. adv. bd. Archive Am. Minority Cultures, U. Ala., 1983-90. Fellow Huntington Libr., San Marino, Calif., 1988. Mem. Nat. Geneal. Soc., Am. Hist. Assn., Ala. Hist. Assn., La. Hist. Assn. (bd. dirs. 1972-94), Orgn. Ala. Historians, So. Hist. Assn. (various coms. 1981-86), St. George Tucker Soc. (fellow 1992). Independent. Roman Catholic. Avocations: music, genealogy. Home: 1732 Ridgedale Dr Tuscaloosa AL 35406-1942 Office: U Ala PO Box 870212 Tuscaloosa AL 35487

MILLS, GEORGE ALEXANDER, retired science administrator; b. Saskatoon, Sask., Can., Mar. 20, 1914; s. George Robison and Leafa (Johnson) M.; m. Roberta Walker Mills, June 15, 1940; children: Richard, Sandra, Marilyn, Janice. B.Sc., U. Sask., 1934, M.Sc., 1936; Ph.D., Columbia U. Instr., Dartmouth Coll., 1939-40; with Houdry Process Co., 1940-68; with U.S. Bur. Mines, 1968-75, chief coal div., 1968-75; dir. fossil energy research ERDA, 1975-77; dir. internat. programs fossil energy Dept. Energy, Washington, 1977-81; exec. dir. Ctr. Catalytic Sci. and Tech., U. Del., Newark, 1981-84, sr. scientist Ctr. Catalytic Sci and Tech., 1984-95. Contbr. numerous articles to profl. jours. Mem. Nat. Acad. Engring., Am. Inst. Chemists (Pioneer award), Am. Chem. Soc. (Storch award, Murphree award), AAAS, Am. Inst. Chem. Engring., Catalysis Soc. Presbyterian. Patentee in field. Home: Cokesbury Village # 48 726 Loveville Rd Hockessin DE 19707-1515

MILLS, GEORGE MARSHALL, insurance and financial consultant; b. Newton, N.J., May 20, 1923; s. J. Marshall and Emma (Scott) M.; m. Dorothy Lovilla Allen, Apr. 21, 1945; children: Dianne (Mrs. Thomas McKay III), Dorothy L.A. (Mrs. Edward Sphatt). BA, Rutgers U., 1943; MA, Columbia U., 1951. CLU, CPCU; chartered fin. cons.; cert. govt. fund mgr. Pres. George M. Mills Inc., North Brunswick, N.J., 1946-75; pres. CORECO, Inc., Newark, 1960-78; risk mgr. N.J. Hwy. Authority, Woodbridge, 1976-95; pres. Assoc. Risk Mgmt., North Brunswick, N.J., 1995—; cons. Govs.'s Com. on Bus. Efficiency in Pub. Schs., 1979-80; cons. Risk Mgmt. Ins., Real Estate. Bd. dirs. Alpha Chi Rho Endl. Found., vice-chmn. 1991—; workshop Easter Seal Soc.; mem. Gov.'s Task Force on Sound Mcpl. Govt., 1981-82; pres. Nat. Interfrat. Conf., 1979-80. With USNR, 1943-46. Mem. Am. Coll. Life Underwriters, Am. Coll. Property Liability Underwriters, Internat. Bridge Tunnel and Turnpike Assn. (chmn. risk mgmt. com. 1980-95, mem. bus. ins. risk mgmt. bd. 1988-95, Matthew J. Lenz Jr. medal 1989, Paul K. Addams award 1992), New Brunswick Hist. Soc., English Speaking Union, Rutgers U. Alumni-Faculty Club, Alpha Chi Rho (nat. councillor 1964-70, nat. pres. 1970-73, nat. treas. 1975-78), Kappa Kappa Psi, Tau Kappa Alpha, Phi Delta Phi. Mem. Reformed Ch. Am. Home: 1054 Hoover Dr North Brunswick NJ 08902-3244

MILLS, JAMES SPENCER, author; b. Milw., May 20, 1932; s. Ralph Erskine and Elisabeth Amsden (Stevens) M. Student, Erskine Coll., 1950-51; BA, Princeton U., 1956. Reporter Worcester (Mass.) Telegram and Evening Gazette, summer 1955, Corpus Christi (Tex.) Caller Times, 1958, UPI, 1959; reporter, corr., writer, editor Life mag., 1960-66. Author: The Panic in Needle Park, 1966, The Prosecutor, 1969, Report to the Commissioner, 1972, One Just Man, 1974, On the Edge, 1975, The Seventh Power, 1976, The Truth about Peter Harley, 1979, The Underground Empire: Where Crime and Governments Embrace, 1986, The Power, 1990, Haywire, 1995. Served with USNR, 1956-58. Address: care Marvin Kalickstein 2547 Joel Pl Oceanside NY 11572-1331

MILLS, JAMES STEPHEN, medical supply company executive; b. Chgo., Sept. 29, 1936; s. Irving I. and Beatrice (Shane) M.; m. Victoria L. Krisch, Mar. 23, 1973; children: Charles, Donald, Margaret. B.S. in Bus., Northwestern U. Vice pres. sales Mills Hosp. Supply Co., Chgo., 1961-66; pres. Medline Industries Inc., Northbrook, Ill., 1966-75, chmn. bd., 1975—. Served with AUS, 1958-64. Jewish. Home: 500 N Green Bay Rd Lake Forest IL 60045-2146 Office: Medline Industries Inc 1 Medline Pl Mundelein IL 60060-4485*

MILLS, JERRY WOODROW, lawyer; b. Springfield, Mo., July 17, 1940; s. Woodrow Wilson and Billie Louise M.; m. Marion Cargile, Mar. 27, 1964; children: Eric E., Brendon W. BSEE, Tex. A&M U., 1963; JD, Georgetown U., 1967. Bar: Tex. 1967, U.S. Patent Office 1967. Ptnr. Richards, Harris & Hubbard, Dallas, 1970-82, Baker, Mills & Glast, Dallas, 1982-90; sr. ptnr. Baker & Botts, Dallas, 1990—; adj. prof. So. Meth. U. Law Sch., 1994—. Bd. dirs. Dallas Legal Svcs. Project, 1972-75. Fellow Tex. Bar, Dallas Bar; mem. ABA, Tex. State Jr. Bar Assn. (treas. 1975, dir.), Dallas Jr. Bar Assn. (pres. 1971, Outstanding Young Lawyer award 1975), Dallas Bar Assn. (bd. dirs. 1983-85). Methodist. Home: 5316 Montrose Dr Dallas TX 75209 Office: Baker & Botts 800 Trammell Crow Ctr 2001 Ross Ave Dallas TX 75201-8001

MILLS, JON K., psychologist, educator. AS in Criminal Justice, Parkland Coll., 1985; BS in Psychology with honors, So. Ill. U., 1987, MA in Rehab. Counseling with honors, 1988; D in Clin. Psychology, Ill. Sch. Profl. Psychology, 1992; postgrad., Vanderbilt U., 1992. Cert. rehab. counselor. Crisis intervention trainer, hotline supr. Synergy Crisis Intervention Agy., Carbondale, Ill., 1986-87, individual and family counselor, 1987; individual and group therapist Evaluation and Devel. Ctr., Carbondale, Ill., 1987-88, Youth Options: Substance Abuse Svcs., Marion, Ill., 1988; intern Jackson County Community Mental Health Ctr., Carbondale, 1988; diagnostic extern Elgin (Ill.) State Mental Health Ctr., 1989-90; staff therapist Davis Ctr. for Emotional Devel., Glen Ellyn, Ill., 1989-90; therapy extern Roosevelt U., Chgo., 1990—; counselor coord. Copley Weight Mgmt. Copley Meml. Hosp., Aurora, Ill., 1989—; predoctoral intern Michael Reese Hosp. and Med. Ctr., Chgo., 1991; asst. prof. dept. psychology Lewis U., Romeoville, Ill., 1992—; staff psychologist Inst. for Behavioral Svcs., Oak Brook, Ill., 1993—; teaching asst. for tests and measurements Rehab. Inst., So. Ill. U., 1987-88; teaching asst. Ill. Sch. of Profl. Psychology, Chgo., 1989-90; adj. faculty dept. of psychology Waubonsee Community Coll., Sugar Grove, Ill., 1990—, Coll. of Dupage, Naperville, 1989—; faculty mem. social sci. dept. Joliet (Ill.) Jr. Coll., 1990—. Contbr. numerous articles to profl. jours. Vol. Crisis Hotline Jackson County Community Mental Health Ctr., Carbondale, 1987. Recipient numerous scholarships; Tchg. fellow Vanderbilt U. Dept. Philosophy, Nashville, 1994—. Mem. APA, Ill. Group Psychotherapy Soc., Chgo. Assn. for Psychoanalytic Psychology, Phi Kappa Phi, Gamma Beta Phi. Avocations: vocal, guitar, harmonica. Home: 301 31st Ave N Apt C-2 Nashville TN 37203-1231

MILLS, KEVIN LEE, government executive; b. Frederick, Md., Oct. 21, 1951; s. John Lee and Doris Jean (Comer) M.; m. Karen June Davis, Dec. 30, 1972; children: Colin Walter, Elizabeth Anne. BS in Polit. Sci. and Econs., Frostburg (Md.) State U., 1973; MS in Tech. Mgmt., Am. U., 1979; PhD in Info. Tech., George Mason U., 1996. Sr. computer analyst System Devel. Corp., McLean, Va., 1976-81; project mgr. Tesdata Systems Corp., McLean, 1981-82; computer scientist Nat. Bur. of Stds., Gathersburg, Md., 1982-84; group leader Nat. Bur. of Stds., Gathersburg, 1984-87; divsn. chief Nat. Inst. Stds. and Tech., Gathersburg, 1987-95; program mgr. Def. Advanced Rsch. Projects Agy., Arlington, Va., 1996—; cons. in field, 1980-82. Contbr. articles to profl. jours. Capt. USMC, 1972-78. Mem. IEEE (sr.), Assn. for Computing Machinery. Avocations: hiking, writing, reading.

MILLS, KEVIN PAUL, lawyer; b. Detroit, Oct. 1, 1961; s. Raymond Eugene and Helene Audry M.; m. Holly Beth Fechner, June 15, 1986. BA, Oberlin Coll., 1983; JD, U. Mich., 1987. Bar: Mich. 1988. High sch. tchr., asst. dir. summer environ. inst. The Storm King Sch., Cornwall-on-Hudson, N.Y., 1983-84; staff atty. E. Mich. Environ. Action Coun., Birmingham, Mich., 1987-90; assoc. Tucker & Rolf, Southfield, Mich., 1988-89; sr. atty., pollution prevention program dir. Environ. Def. Fund, Washington, 1990—; founder Pollution Prevention Alliance, 1991, co-founder Great Printer's Project, 1992—, staff to co-chair eco-efficiency Pres. Coun. Sustainable Devel., 1993-95, Auto Pollution Prevention adv. group, 1994—, EPA Auto Mfr. CSI, 1994—; low-level radioactive waste cons. State Mich., Lansing, 1988. Contbr. articles to profl. jours. Bd. dirs., v.p. Ea. Mich. Environ. Action Coun., Birmingham, 1985-87; pres. Environ. Law Soc., Ann Arbor, Mich., 1986-87. Mem. State Bar Mich. Office: Environ Def Fund 1875 Connecticut Ave NW # 1016 Washington DC 20009-5728

MILLS, LAWRENCE, lawyer, business and transportation consultant; b. Salt Lake City, Aug. 15, 1932; s. Samuel L. and Beth (Neilson) M. BS, U. Utah, 1955, JD, 1956. Bar: Utah 1956, ICC 1961, U.S. Supreme Ct. 1963. With W.S. Hatch Co. Inc., Woods Cross, Utah, 1947-89, gen. mgr., 1963-89, v.p., 1970-89, also dir.; bd. dirs. Nat. Tank Truck Carriers, Inc., Washington, 1963—, pres., 1974-75, chmn. bd., 1975-76; mem. motor carrier adv. com. Utah State Dept. Transp., 1979—; keynote speaker Rocky Mountain Safety Suprs. Conf., 1976. Contbr. articles to legal publs. Del. to County and State Convs., Utah, 1970-72; v.p. Utah Safety Coun., 1979-82, bd. dirs., 1979—, pres., 1983-84; mem. Utah Gov's Adv. Com. on Small Bus.; capt. Easter Seal Telethon, 1989, 90; state vice chmn. High Frontier, 1987—; mem. adv. com. Utah State Indsl. Commn., 1988—, chmn. com. studying health care cost containment and reporting requirements 1990—. Recipient Safety Dir. award Nat. Tank Carriers Co., 1967, Outstanding Svc. and Contbn. award, 1995, Trophy award W.S. Hatch Co., 1975, Disting. Svc. award Utah State Indsl. Commn., 1992, Outstanding Svc. award Utah Safety Coun., 1994. Mem. Salt Lake County Bar Assn., Utah Motor Transport Assn. (dir. 1967—, pres. 1974-76, Outstanding Achievement Award 1989), Utah Hwy. Users Assn. (dir. 1981—), Indsl. Rels. Coun. (dir. 1974—), Salt Lake City C. of C., U.S. Jaycees (life Senator 1969—, ambassador 1977—, pres. Utah Senate 1979-80, Henry Giessenbier fellow 1989), Nat. Petroleum Coun., Utah Associated Gen. Contractors (assoc. 1975-77, 88—), Silver Tank Club. Home and Office: 77 Edgecombe Dr Salt Lake City UT 84103-2219 *Personal philosophy: Excessive government regulation stifles individual initiative. We should learn from the downfall of communism.*

MILLS, LINDA S., public relations executive; b. San Antonio, June 26, 1951; d. Frank M. and Betty A. (Young) M. BA, St. Mary's U., 1971. Asst. dir. Paseo Del Rio Assn., San Antonio, 1971-74; mktg. officer Frost Nat. Bank, San Antonio, 1974-79; account exec. Fleishman-Hillard Inc., St. Louis, 1979-81, v.p., sr. ptnr., 1981-85, exec. v.p., sr. ptnr., 1985—, dir. corp. planning, 1986—; bd. dirs. Fleishman-Hillard U.K. Ltd., London, Fleishman-Hillard France, Paris. Mem. adv. bd. St. John's Mercy Med. Ctr. Mem. Pub. Relations Soc. Am., Noonday Club. Office: Fleishman Hillard Inc 200 N Broadway Saint Louis MO 63102-2730

MILLS, LISTON OURY, theology educator; b. Wilmington, N.C., Aug. 7, 1928; s. Leonard Liston and Ruby Preston (Oury) M.; m. Jennie Ellen Windsor, Dec. 28, 1962; 1 child, Sarah Elizabeth. BA, Davidson Coll., 1950; BD, So. Bapt. Theol. Sem., 1953, ThM, 1957, ThD, 1964. Ordained to ministry So. Bapt. Conv., 1953. Asst. pastor 5th Ave. Bapt. Ch., Huntington, W.Va., 1957-58; pastor Kent (Ind.) Bapt. Ch., 1960-62; successively instr, asst. prof., assoc. prof. Vanderbilt U. Div. Sch., Nashville, Oberlin

Alumni prof. pastoral theology and counseling, 1962—, Alexander Heard disting. svc. prof., 1991-92, acting dean, 1989; vis. prof. Earlham Grad. Sch. Theology, Richmond, Ind., 1965, St. Luke's Sch. Theology, Sewanee, Tenn., 1972, 73, 74, 85, So. Bapt. Theol. Sem., 1980, Lexington (Ky.) Theol. Sem., 1981; vis. lectr. Yale U. Div. Sch., New Haven, 1969; cons. Tenn. Dept. Mental Health, Nashville, 1964-65, Tenn. Personnel Dept., Nashville, 1967-68, VA Med. Ctr., Nashville, 1972—, Chief of VA Chaplains, Washington, 1975, 78; Ingersoll lectr. Harvard U., Cambridge, Mass., 1971; Upperman lectr. Tenn. Technol. U., Cookeville, 1973; Stringfellow lectr. Drake U., Des Moines, 1974. Editor: Perspectives on Death, 1969; assoc. editor: Dictionary of Pastoral Care and Counseling, 1990; editor Pastoral Psychology, 1974-82; contbr. articles to jours. Bd. dirs. Family and Children's Svc., Nashville, 1978-81, Tenn. Pastoral Counseling Ctrs., Nashville, 1984-91, 93—, St. Thomas Home Health Care, Nashville, 1986-89. 1st lt. U.S. Army, 1953-55. Recipient Obert Kempson award for disting. svc. S.E. Region Assn. for Clin. Pastoral Edn., 1994; named Alumni Educator of Yr., Vanderbilt U., 1984, Pastoral Theologian of Yr., Pastoral Psychology Jour., 1994; fellow So. Bapt. Theol. Sem., 1959-62, Assn. Theol. Schs., 1968-69. Mem. Soc. for Sci. Study of Religion, Assn. for Profl. Edn. for Ministry (pres. 1972-74), Assn. for Clin. Pastoral Edn., Soc. for Pastoral Theology, Omicron Delta Kappa. Office: Vanderbilt U Div Sch Nashville TN 37240

MILLS, LOIS JEAN, company executive, former legislative aide, former education educator; b. Chgo., Oct. 20, 1939; d. Martin J. and Annabelle M. (Hrabik) Rademacher; m. Frederick V. Mills, Dec. 1, 1974; children: Todd, Susan, Randal, Merre, Mollie, Michael, Mark (dec.). BS in Edn., Ill. State U., Normal, 1962, MS in Edn., 1969. Lectr. elem. curriculum Ill. State U.; in-svc. advisor for elem., gifted, critical thinking and study skills, coop. learning Title I State Bd. Edn., Springfield, Ill.; elem. tchr., supr. Metcalf Lab. Sch. Ill. State U.; legis. aide to Asst. Majority Leader Senator John Maitland, Jr., Ill. Gen. Assembly, 1991-95; pres., ptnr. Mills Design Assocs.; mem. state rep. Dan Rutherford's house task force for statute repeal, adv. roundtable, legis. task force for cmty. residential svcs. deaf adults; campaign coord. Asst. Majority Leader Senator John Maitland, Jr.; county campaign ccord. for Ill. Comptroller Loleta Didrickson. Contbr. articles to profl. jours. Pres. Leadership Ill.; past pres. governing bd. Lake Bloomington Assn.; mem. mgmt. com. McLean County 21st Century commn., commr. McLean County Regional Planning cmmn. (vice chair 1994-95); bd. govs. Ill. Lincoln Excellence in Pub. Svc. Series, other civic activities. Recipient Exemplary Tchr. awards Ill. State U. Student Elem. Edn. Bd., Women of Distinction award YWCA of McLean County. Mem. NAFE, Ill. State U. Alumni Assn. (bd. dirs., past pres.), McLean County Rep. Women's Club (past pres.), Ill. Rep. Committeewoman's Roundtable, Ill. Fedn. Rep. Women, Nat. Fedn. Rep. Women, Internat. Platform Assn. Home: K-162 Lake Bloomington RR 2 Box 60A Hudson IL 61748-9414

MILLS, MARGIE BATLEY, home health care executive; b. Gloster, Miss., Apr. 13, 1939; d. Charlie James and Celia Dee (Pettis) Batley; m. Robert Jackson Mills, Nov. 26, 1958; children: David Glen, Angela Denise Mills Dobson, Joel Vincent. Diploma, Mobile Gen. Hosp. Sch. Nursing, 1961; BS, St. Joseph's Coll., 1985. Assoc. dir. nurses D.W. McMillan Hosp., Brewton, Ala., 1961-63; head nurse burn unit Mobile (Ala.) Gen. Hosp., 1963-65, instr. Sch. Nursing, 1965-67; dir. nurses Twin Oaks Nursing Home, Mobile, 1968-70; field nurse Bur. Crippled Children, Panama City, Fla., 1970-72; dir. nurses Mary and Joseph Home of Elderly, New Orleans, 1972-73; Medicare coord. Eastwood Hosp., El Paso, Tex., 1973-76; dir. nurses ABC Home Health of Jacksonville, Fla., 1976-77; pres., COO, owner First Am. Home Care (formerly ABC Home Health Svcs., Inc.), Brunswick, Ga., 1977—. Author: Homebound, 1994. Pres. Glynn County Crisis Ctr., 1989; bd. dirs. Brunswick unit Am. Cancer Soc., 1991-92, pres., 1995—; bd. dirs. Am. Heart Assn., 1991-92, Salvation Army, 1994; bd. dirs. Brunswick United Way, 1992, pres. 1993-94; cmty. svc. chair Brunswick Kiwanis, 1991-92, pres., 1994; mem. vocat. adv. bd. Brunswick Coll., 1992; 2d v.p. United Way of Glynn, 1992. Recipient Top Ten Bus. Women of Yr. nomination Am. Bus. Womens Assn., 1996. Mem. ANA, Nat. League Nursing, Am. Fedn. Home Health (pres. 1987-91), Ga. Assn. Home Health (pres. 1980-82, 86-88). Methodist. Avocations: golf, needlework, reading. Home: 2660 Frederica Rd Saint Simons Is GA 31522-1917 Office: First Am Home Care 3528 Darien Hwy Brunswick GA 31525

MILLS, MARTHA ALICE, lawyer; b. Lansing, Mich., May 11, 1941; d. Edward Lucien and Muriel (Eastman) M.; m. A. Patrick Papas, Mar. 17, 1940. BA cum laude, Maclester Coll., St. Paul, 1964; JD cum laude, U. Minn., 1965. Bar: U.S. Ct. Appeals (5th cir.) 1967, U.S. Ct. Appeals (7th cir.) 1970, (6th cir.) 1987, U.S. Supreme Ct., 1970. City atty. Fayette, Miss., 1969; chief counsel Lawyer's Com. for Civil Rights Under Law, Cairo, Ill., 1969-71, Lawndale Legal Svcs. Office, Chgo. Legal Svcs., 1971; assoc. Schiff, Hardin and Waite, Chgo., 1971-75; instr. IIT Chgo. Kent Coll. of Law, 1976-82; owner Martha A. Mills, Ltd., 1976-79; ptnr. Cotton, Watt, Jones and King, Chgo., 1980-86, Foss, Schuman, Drake and Barnard, Chgo., 1986-88, Gottlieb and Schwartz, Chgo., 1989-90; of counsel Schaefer, Rosenwein & Fleming, Chgo., 1990-92, Smith, Williams & Lodge, Chgo., 1992-95; judge Cir. Ct. Cook County, Chgo., 1995—; adj. prof. law Northwestern U., Evanston, Ill., 1995—; fed. defender panel, U.S. Dist. Ct. for the No. Dist. Ill., Ea. Divsn., 1974-95. Contbr. articles to legal publs. Fellow Am. Coll. Trial Lawyers; mem. ABA (governing coun. litigation sect. 1979-84, Chgo. Bar Assn., 7th Cir. Bar Assn.), Womens Bar Assn. Ill. Avocations: reading, computers, languages, telecommunications. Home: 1021 W Bryn Mawr Ave Chicago IL 60660-4643

MILLS, MICHAEL JAMES, architect; b. Streator, Ill., Feb. 18, 1951; s. Harry Nelson and Ruth Ludia (Piel) M.; m. Kathryn Louise Brewington, June 6, 1974 (div. Feb. 1977); m. Beverly Jane Ballard, Mar. 14, 1981; children: Kevin Charles, Jeffrey Ross, Caroline Ruth. BA, Princeton U., 1973; cert., ICCROM, 1979; MS, Columbia U., 1980. Registered architect, N.J., S.C., N.Y., D.C., Pa., Mich.; lic. profl. planner, N.J. Draftsman John Milner Assocs., West Chester, Pa., 1973-74, John Diehl & Assocs., Princeton, N.J., 1974-75; project mgr. Heritage Studies, Princeton, N.J., 1975-76; draftsman Short and Ford Architects, Princeton, N.J., 1976-78; apprentice architect The Ehrenkrantz Group, N.Y.C., 1979-80; apprentice architect Short & Ford & Ptnrs., Princeton, 1980-83, assoc., 1983-87; partner Short & Ford & Ptnrs. (name changed to Ford, Farewell, Mills and Gatsch Architects 1992), Princeton, 1987-92, 1992—; cons. Burlington County Hist. Dist. Commn., Burlington, N.J., 1983-93. Contbr. articles to profl. jours. Chmn. Hopewell Planning Bd., 1985-89. Excellence in Architecture N.J. Soc. Architects, 1989, 92, hon. mention, 1983. Mem. AIA, Assn. Preservtion Tech., Nat. Trust for Hist. Preservation, N.J. Soc. Architects, U.S.-Internat. Coun. on Monuments and Sites. Presbyterian. Avocations: guitar, photography, tennis. Office: Ford Farewell Mills and Gatsch Architects 864 Mapleton Rd Princeton NJ 08540-9538

MILLS, MIKE, popular musician; b. Macon, Ga.. Student, U. Ga. Bass guitarist R.E.M., 1980—. Rec. albums include Chronic Town, 1982, Murmur, 1983 (Gold record, Rolling Stone Critics Poll Best Album of Yr. 1983), Reckoning, 1984 (Gold record), Fables of the Reconstruction, 1985 (Gold record), Life's Rich Pageant, 1986 (Gold record), Dead Letter Office, 1987 (Gold record), Document, 1987 (Platinum record), Eponymous, 1988 (Platinum record), Green, 1988 (Platinum record), Out of Time, 1991 (Platinum record, 7 Grammy nominations, Best Pop Vocal Group Grammy award 1992), Automatic for the People, 1993 (4 Grammy nominations), Monster, 1994; appeared on Robbie Robertson's album, Storyville, 1991; perfomed on "Backbeat" soundtrack, 1994. Named Rolling Stong Artist of Yr., 1992.

MILLS, NANCY ANNE, elementary education educator; b. Madisonville, Ky., Oct. 2, 1937; d. Leslie Owen and Ruby A. (Baker) Hawkins; m. Orton Leroy Mills, May 11, 1957; children: Charles Leroy, Roy Leslie. BS in Edn. Ind. U., South Bend, 1970, MS in Edn., 1972; Edml. Specialist dergree, Ind. U., 1978. Cert. elem. tchr., Ind. Tchr. elem. South Bend Schs., 1972—; gifted cadre' Purdue U-For Ind., Lafayette, 1988—; presenter workshops; cons. econ. edn. Chmn. new ch. com. Nazarene Ch., South Bend, 1990; supr. students with Student Exch., France, 1991-95. Named Woman of Yr., Profl. and Bus. Womans Club, 1989; Inst. for Chem. Edn. grantee, 1989. Mem. Ind. Coun. Econ. Edn. (cons. 1987—, Tchr. of Yr. for State of Ind. 1992), Delta Kappa Gamma. Avocations: sewing, travel. Home: 16320 Wellington Pky Granger IN 46530-8309 Office: Muessel Sch 1213 California Ave South Bend IN 46628-2701

MILLS, NANCY STEWART, chemistry educator; b. Osceola, Nebr., Mar. 31, 1950; d. Robert Lees and Margaret Eva (Stewart) M.; m. Mark Alan Hurd, Aug. 20, 1977; children: Caroline Margaret Mills Hurd, William Clark Mills Hurd. BA, Grinnell Coll., 1972; PhD, U. Ariz., 1976. Asst. prof. Carleton Coll., Northfield, Minn., 1977-79; asst. prof. Trinity U., San Antonio, 1979-83, assoc. prof., 1983-89, prof., 1979—, chmn. chemistry dept., 1990-93; mem. dept. rev. team Bowdoin Coll., Brunswick, Maine, 1986, Macalester Coll., St. Paul, 1989, Albion Coll., 1991, Hamilton Coll., 1996; mem. Coun. on Undergrad. Rsch., 1991—, chair chemistry divsn., 1996—. Contbr. articles to profl. jours. Grantee NSF, Welch Found., Petroleum Rsch. Fund, Rsch. Corp., 1977—; Camille and Henry Dreyfus Found. scholar, 1994; recipient Outstanding Teaching and Campus Leadership award Sears Roebuck Found., 1990, Z.T. Scott Fellowship for outstanding teaching Trinity U., 1992. Mem. AAUP, Sigma Xi. Avocations: backpacking, reading, sewing, singing. Home: 137 Alta Ave San Antonio TX 78209-4508 Office: Trinity U 715 Stadium Dr San Antonio TX 78212-3104

MILLS, OLAN, II, photography company executive; b. 1930; married. Grad., Princeton U., 1952. With Olan Mills, Inc., Chattanooga, 1950—, now chmn., sec., also bd. dirs. Office: Olan Mills Inc PO Box 23456 Chattanooga TN 37422*

MILLS, RICHARD, state education official. Commr. edn. Vermont; now commr. edn. New York, Albany. Office: NY Dept Edn Education Bldg. 89 Washington Ave Rm 111 Albany NY 12234*

MILLS, RICHARD HENRY, federal judge; b. Beardstown, Ill., July 19, 1929; s. Myron Epler and Helen Christine (Greve) M.; m. Rachel Ann Keagle, June 16, 1962; children: Jonathan K., Daniel Cass. BA, Ill. Coll., 1951; JD, Mercer U., 1957; LLM, U. Va., 1982. Bar: Ill. 1957, U.S. Dist. Ct. Ill. 1958, U.S. Ct. Appeals 1959, U.S. Ct. Mil. Appeals 1963, U.S. Supreme Ct. 1963. Legal advisor Ill. Youth Commn., 1958-60; state's atty. Cass County, Virginia, Ill., 1960-64; judge Ill. 8th Jud. Cir., Virginia, 1966-76, Ill. 4th Dist. Appellate Ct., Springfield, Ill., 1976-85, U.S. Dist. Ct. (cen. dist.) Ill., Springfield, 1985—; adj. prof. So. Ill. U. Sch. Medicine, 1985—; mem. adv. bd. Nat. Inst. Corrections, Washington, 1984-88, Ill. Supreme Ct. Rules Com., Chgo., 1963-85. Contbr. articles to profl. jours. Pres. Abraham Lincoln coun. Boy Scouts Am., 1978-80. With U.S. Army, 1952-54, Korea, col. res.; maj. gen. Ill. Militia. Recipient George Washington Honor medal Freedoms Found., 1969, 73, 75, 82, Disting. Eagle Scout Boy Scouts Am., 1985. Fellow Am. Bar Found.; mem. ABA (joint com. profl. sanctions), Ill. Bar Assn., Chgo. Bar Assn., Cass County Bar Assn. (pres. 1962-64, 75-76), Sangamon County Bar Assn., 7th Cir. Bar Assn., Am. Law Inst., Fed. Judges Assn., Army and Navy Club (Washington), Sangamo Club, Masons (33 degree). Republican. Home: 2112 Augusta Dr Springfield IL 62704-3103 Office: US Dist Ct 319 US Courthouse Springfield IL 62701

MILLS, RICHARD P., state agency administrator. BA with honors, Middlebury Coll., 1966; MA in Am. History, Columbia U., 1967, MBA, 1975, EdD, 1977. Planning assoc. N.J. Dept. of Edn., 1975-78, dir. policy analysis, 1978-80, dep. asst. commr., 1980-82, spl. asst. to the commr., 1982-84; spl. asst. to Gov. Thomas H. Kean of N.J., 1984-88; commr. of edn. State of Vt., 1988-95, State of N.Y., 1995—; adj. asst. prof. Columbia Univ. Tchrs. Coll., 1977; adj. assoc. prof. Rider Coll., N.J., 1979; cons. task force to oversee fiscal reform in Newark, 1975; tchr. The Dalton Sch., N.Y.C., 1967-71, Elizabeth Seeger Sch., N.Y.C., 1971-73; mem. Carnegie Task Force on Learning in the Primary Grades; chair mgmt. group Nat. Alliance for Restructuring Edn.; bd. New Stds. Project; mem. bd. Nat. Ctr. on Edn. and the Economy. Contbr. articles to profl. jours. U.S. rep. to standing com. European Ministers of Edn., 1987. Office: Univ of the State of NY NY State Edn Dept Edn Bldg Washington Ave Albany NY 12234*

MILLS, ROBERT A., lawyer; b. Kansas City, Mo., Jan. 20, 1934; s. William N. and Mary Aileene (Arnold) M.; m. Jan. 14, 1956 (div. Apr. 1978); children: Thomas B., James A., John M.; m. Anita Hickey, Feb. 12, 1983; 1 child, Christopher Robert. BS, U. Mo., 1955; LLB, Washington U., St. Louis, 1960. Bar: Calif. Trial atty. U.S. Dept. Justice, Washington, 1960-62; assoc. Lewis & Roca, Phoenix, 1962-65, McCutchen Doyle Brown & Enersen, San Francisco, 1965-70; ptnr. McCutchen Doyle Brown & Enersen, 1970—; Editorial cons. Calif. Legal Systems, Wills and Trusts, 1983—. Served to 1st lt. U.S. Army, 1955-57. Fellow Am. Coll. Trust & Estate Counsel; mem. ABA, State Bar of Calif. (chmn. probate and trust law com. 1975-76), Fed. Bar Assn. (chpt. pres. 1964), Internat. Acad. Estate and Trust Law (Pres. 1988-90), The Pacific-Union Club, Olympic Club of San Francisco. Home: 15 Rancheria Rd San Rafael CA 94904-2833 Office: McCutchen Doyle Brown & Enersen 3 Embarcadero Ctr San Francisco CA 94111-4003

MILLS, ROBERT HARRY, church administrator; b. Moncton, N.B., Can., Mar. 3, 1933; s. Harry Earl and Evelyn Perl (Cosman) M.; m. Karen Barbara Keirstead, Dec. 26, 1953 (dec. June 1991); children: Deborah Karen, Michael Robert, Stephen Gordon, David Richard, Katrina Marie; m. Helga Kutz-Harder, July 1, 1995. BA, Mt. Allison U., Sackville, N.B., 1954; diploma in theology, Pine Hill Divinity Hall, Halifax, N.S., Can., 1956. Ordained to ministry United Ch. Can., 1956. Minister religion Port Mouton (N.S.) Pastoral Charge, 1956-59, Tatamagouche (N.S.) Pastoral Charge, 1959-65, St. Andrew's United Ch., Wolfville, N.S., 1965-67, Bridgewater (N.S.) United Ch., 1967-75, Wesley United Ch., St. John's, Nfld., Can., 1975-82, Fairview United Ch., Halifax, N.S., 1982-89; exec. sec. maritime conf. United Ch. Can., Sackville, 1989-95; interim gen. sec. Can. Coun. Chs., Toronto, Ont., 1995—; sec. settlement com. maritime conf. United Ch. Can., 1963-67, chmn., 1967-71, chmn. transfer com. gen. coun., 1970-71, chmn. staff com. Newfound and Labrador conf., 1978-82, sec. Halifax Presbyn., 1983-87. Avocation: music. Office: 40 St Clair Ave E Ste 201, Toronto, ON Canada M4T 1M9

MILLS, ROBERT LEE, president emeritus; b. Erlanger, Ky., Nov. 13, 1916; s. John Clifford and Dixie Lee (Morris) M.; m. Mildred Sizer, June 24, 1942; children: Robert Lee, Dixie Louise, Barbara Jean. A.B. in Math. and Physics, U. Ky., 1938, M.A. in Edml. Adminstrn. 1941, Ed.D., 1951; LLD, William Jewell Coll., 1971. Tchr. Covington (Ky.) pub. schs., 1938-41; head hydraulics br. Air Force Tech. Sch., Lincoln, Nebr., 1942-44; mem. supervisory staff electromagnetic plant Oak Ridge, 1944-48; research asst. U. Ky., Lexington, 1948-51; dean admissions, registrar U. Ky., 1954-57; dir. research, head bur. adminstrn. and finance Ky. Dept. Edn., 1951-54; chmn. dept. edml. adminstrn. U. Tex., Austin, 1957-59; pres. Georgetown (Ky.) Coll., 1959-78, chancellor, 1978-86, pres. emeritus, 1987—; exec. sec. Ky. Adv. Commn. Edml. Policy, 1952-54; v.p. Ky. Assn. Colls. and Secondary Schs., 1962-63, exec. com., 1959-64, pres., 1963-64; chmn. exec. com. Ky. Ind. Coll. Found.; mem. Ky. Commn. on Higher Edn., 1967-70, Ky. Govt. Council, 1968-72; adviser Texas Assn. Sch. Bds., 1957-59. Contbr. articles to profl. jours. Cons. Pres.' Com., White House Conf. Edn., 1955; mem. Ky. Devel. Council, 1961-65, Ky. Constn. Revision Assembly, 1964-66. Recipient Distinguished Alumni award U. Ky., 1963, Centennial award, 1964. Mem. Nat., Ky. edn. assns., Newcomen Soc., So. Assn. Bapt. Colls. (pres. 1965-66), Bapt. World Alliance (chmn. men's dept. 1965-67), So. Assn. Colls. and Schs. (commn. on colls. 1971-77), Kappa Delta Pi, Phi Delta Kappa, Phi Kappa Tau. Democrat. Baptist. Lodge: Kiwanis.

MILLS, RUSSELL ANDREW, newspaper publisher; b. St. Thomas, Ont., Can., July 14, 1944; s. Gerald Armond and Phyllis Marie (Hulse) M.; m. Judith Elizabeth Zimmerman, Mar. 25, 1967; children: Lara, Colin, Patrick. BA, U. Western Ont., London, 1967, MA, 1968. Reporter London (Ont.) Free Press, 1964-67; city editor The Oshawa (Ont.) Times, 1970; asst. city editor, night editor, asst. mng. editor The Ottawa (Ont.) Citizen, 1971-85, exec. editor, 1975-76, editor, 1977-84, gen.mgr., 1984-86, pub., 1986-89, pres., publ., 1992—; pres. Southam Newspaper Group, Toronto, Ont., 1989-92. Office: Ottawa Citizen, 1101 Baxter Rd, Ottawa, ON Canada K2C 3M4

MILLS, S. LOREN, product safety manager, engineer; b. Manassas, Va., Oct. 31, 1946; s. James Bryan and Charlatta Ruth (Holland) M.; m. Nancy Jane Mathews, Apr. 7, 1979; children: Tyler, Mitchell, Molly. BS, Western Mich. U., Kalamazoo, 1975. Cert. product safety mgr. Internat. Product Safety Mgmt. Cert. Bd. Sr. staff engr. Clark Equipment Co., Battle Creek, Mich., 1966-86; engring. mgr. Hayes Machine Co., Marshall, Mich., 1986-88; product safety cons. Mills Cons., Marshall, Mich., 1988-89; product safety mgr. Van Dorn Demag Corp., Strongsville, Ohio, 1989—; v.p., bd. dirs. Insulation Wholesale Supply Co., Battle Creek, 1981—. Co-author: Product Safety Management Handbook, 1994. Mem. Nat. Safety Coun., 1995—. With U.S. Army, 1968-74. Mem. ASME (mem. ANSI B56.1 stds. devel. com. 1981—), Soc. Plastics Industry (chmn. risk mgmt. com. 1992—), Assn. Mfg. Tech. (mem. capital goods stds. coalition U.S. Tag ISO/TC199 com. 1992—), Am. Soc. Plastics Industry (mem. ANSI B151.1 stds. devel. com. 1989—, mem. ANSI B151.27 stds. devel. com. 1991—), Nat. Elec. Mfrs. Assn. (mem. ANSI Z535 stds. devel. com. 1991—), Soc. Automotive Engrs., Am. Soc. Safety Engrs. Avocations: tennis, boating, fishing. Home: 19813 Winding Trl Strongsville OH 44136-8741 Office: Van Dorn Demag Corp 11794 Alameda Dr Strongsville OH 44136-3011

MILLS, SAMUEL DAVIS, JR., professional football player; b. Neptune, N.J., June 3, 1959. Student, Montclair State U. With Cleve. Browns, 1981, Toronto Argonauts, CFL, 1982, Phila. Stars, USFL, 1982; linebacker New Orleans Saints, 1986-95, Carolina Panthers, 1995—. Named USFL All-Star Team Inside Linebacker by Sporting News, 1983, 85, NFL All-Pro Team Inside Linebacker by Sporting News, 1991-92. Played in Pro Bowl, 1987, 88, 91, 92. Office: Carolina Panthers 227 W Trade St Ste 1600 Charlotte NC 28002

MILLS, STEPHEN NATHANIEL, computer software company executive; b. Boston, Apr. 18, 1942; s. Nathaniel and Alice Mary (Lerner) M.; m. Lorraine Hill Ransom, Mar. 27, 1966 (div. Apr. 1993); children: Nathaniel Stephen, George Robert, Beman Ransom (dec.), Priscilla Alden; m. Patricia Punch Meadows, Mar. 5, 1994 (div. Dec. 1995); stepchildren: James Christopher, Katherine Alexandra. Student, MIT, 1959-61; BS, Regents Coll., 1989. Programmer analyst Cambridge (Mass.) Computer Assocs., 1966-68; sr. programmer, analyst Computer Fulfillment, Winchester, Mass., 1968-69; pres. Software Engring., Inc., Norton, Mass., 1969-73; product devel. mgr. Pecan Software Corp., Roswell, Ga., 1987-88; pres. Software Eclectics, Inc., Alpharetta, Ga., 1988—; cons. in field; mem. Lang. Test Mgmt. Coun., Inst. Cert. Computer Profls., Des Plaines, Ill., 1994—; adj. faculty Gwinnett Tech. Inst., Lawrenceville, Ga., 1992, Chattahoochee Tech. Inst., Marietta, Ga., 1992. Sgt. USAR, 1964-70. Mem. IEEE Computer Soc., Southeastern Software Assn., Data Processing Mgmt. Assn. (Atlanta bd. dirs. 1992-93), Assn. Computing Machinery, Mensa (Boston chpt. pres. 1967-68, Little Rock newsletter editor 1978). Avocation: aviation. Office: Software Eclectics Inc Ste 401 10945 State Bridge Rd Alpharetta GA 30202-5676

MILLS, SYLVIA JANET, education educator; b. Chgo., Oct. 5, 1954; d. Clarence Thomas and Janet Lucille (Curry) Mills; children: Ean O'Harrel Gay Mills, Raymond Ear Echols II. BA in Journalism, Columbia Coll., Chgo., 1979; MA in Instructional Design, U. Iowa, 1993, secondary tchg. cert. in journalism, 1996. Edn. Beat reporter Chgo. Daily Defender Newspapers, 1979-80; tech. writer/editor, data mgmt. supr., ops./planning analyst Sonicraft, Inc., Chgo., 1983-88; sec. and pub. rels. officer Female Entrepreneurs of Chgo., 1988-89; adminstrv. asst./editor Student Devel. Office, City Colls. of Chgo., 1989-91; rsch. intern Am. Coll. Testing, Inc., Iowa City, Iowa, 1991-93; grad. asst. U. Iowa Grad. Coll., Iowa City, 1993-95; rsch. asst. Ctr. for Evaluation and Assessment, U. Iowa, 1995—. Bd. dirs. All in a Kid's Day Summer Immersion Program, Iowa City, 1994; mem. PTA Beasley Acad. Ctr., Chgo., 1988-90, PTO, Iowa City, 1992-93. Mem. ASCD, Alpha Kappa Alpha (treas., dean of pledges 1973—). Avocations: reading, writing. Home: 457 Hawkeye Dr Iowa City IA 52246-2611

MILLS, THEODORE MASON, sociologist, educator; b. Fairfield, Ind., May 6, 1920; s. Charles S., Sr. and Pearl (Mason) M.; m. Mary Jane Seaman, June 21, 1947; children: Duncan Kimball, Peter Benjamin, Sarah Jane. A.B., Guilford Coll., 1941; M.A., Haverford Coll., 1942; Ph.D., Harvard U., 1952. Lectr. sociology, also research assoc. Lab. of Social Relations of Harvard U., 1952-55, asst. prof. sociology and gen. edn., 1956-60; assoc. prof. sociology, dir. interaction lab. Yale U., 1960-68; prof. SUNY, Buffalo, 1968—, chmn. dept. sociology, 1968-72, prof. emeritus, 1989; also dir. Social Scis. Interaction Lab.; cons. USN, Family Service N.Y., Niagara Internat. Inst., A.K. Rice Inst., Prentice-Hall pubs.; Mem. Math. Seminar for Social Scientists, 1950; vis. Fulbright prof. U. Oslo, 1955-56, vis. prof., 1973-74; fellow Ctr. Advanced Study in Behavioral Scis., Social Sci. Research Council, 1951-52. Author: (with others) Group Structure and the Newcomer, 1957, Group Transformation: an Analysis of a Learning Group, 1964, The Sociology of Small Groups, 1967, 2d edit., 1984, translations Japanese, German, Spanish, Indonesian, and Danish, (with Stan Rosenberg) Readings on the Sociology of Small Groups, 1970; (with Michael P. Farrell and Dan Gilbertson) film Fathers and Sons; A Study in Group Dynamics, 1972; Assoc. editor: Sociometry, 1963-66, Personality and Social Systems. Mem. Guilford (Conn.) Dem. Com., 1962-65. Served with Am. Friends Service Com. China Convoy, 1942-46. Mem. Am. Sociol. Assn., Am. Anthrop. Assn., Soc. Exptl. Psychology, Am. Psychol. Assn., Sociol. Research Assn., Eastern Sociol. Soc. Home: 156 Mariner St Buffalo NY 14201-1413 Office: Social Scis Interaction Lab Ellicott Complex SUNY Amherst NY 14261

MILLS, WILLIAM HAROLD, JR., construction company executive; b. St. Petersburg, Fla., July 24, 1939; s. William Harold and Caroline (Bonfoey) M.; m. Sylvia Ludwig, Jan. 4, 1962 (div. 1975); children—William Harold III, Robert Michael, Leslie Anne; m. Kimberly Keyes, May 4, 1985 (div. 1988); m. Gigi Alice Schmidt, Aug. 1, 1990. Grad., Woodberry Forest Sch., 1954-57; B.S. in Civil Engring., U. Fla., 1961. Cert. Class A gen. contractor, Fla. V.P. bus. devel. Mills & Jones Constrn., St. Petersburg, Fla., 1964-68; v.p. Wellington Corp., Atlanta, 1968-71; exec. v.p. Mills & Jones Constrn., St. Petersburg, Fla., 1971-79; pres., chmn. Federal Constrn. Co., St. Petersburg, 1979-88, vice chmn., 1988—; pres., chair Univ. Housing Svcs., Inc., St. Petersburg; mem. adv. com. St Petersburg Port, 1993—. Pres. St. Petersburg Progress, Inc., 1986-87; active mem. Suncoasters, St. Petersburg, 1974—, St. Anthony's Devel. Found., St. Petersburg, 1983-86; past chmn. Pinellas Marine Inst., St. Petersburg, Blue Ribbon Zoning Com., City of St. Petersburg; former mem. Pinellas County Constrn. Licensing Bd., Tampa Bay Aviation Adv. Com., United Fund Pinellas County; former mem. U. South Fla. Campus Adv. Bd. Named Hon. Royal Navy Liaison Officer Her Majesty's Royal Navy, 1984—. Mem. ASCE, NSPE, Am. Mgmt. Assn., Mensa, St. Petersburg Area C. of C. (bd. govs. 1983-85), Fla. Sports Adv. Coun., Order of Salvador/Salvador Dali Mus., St. Petersburg Yacht Club, Dragon Club, Les Ambassadeurs Club (London), Vinoy Croquet Club (pres.), Annabel's Club (London), Useppa Island Club (bd. govs.), Sigma Alpha Epsilon, U.S. Croquet Assn., Univ. Fla. Pres.'s Coun. (life). Republican. Episcopalian. Home: 1260 Brightwaters Blvd NE Saint Petersburg FL 33704-3728 Office: Ste 201 1325 Snell Isle Blvd Saint Petersburg FL 33704

MILLS, WILLIAM HAYES, lawyer; b. Gordo, Ala., Mar. 30, 1931; s. Early S. and Bama (Cameron) M. LL.B., U. Ala., 1956. Bar: Ala. 1956. Since practiced in Birmingham; partner Rogers, Howard, Redden & Mills, 1961-79, Redden, Mills & Clark, 1979—; arbitrator Fed. Mediation and Conciliation Service, Am. Arbitration Assn. Served with AUS, 1948-50, 50-51. Mem. ABA, Ala., Birmingham bar assns., Am., Ala. trial lawyers assns. Baptist. Home: 2105 Williamsburg Way Birmingham AL 35223-1740 Office: Redden Mills & Clark 940 1st Alabama Bank Bldg Birmingham AL 35203

MILLS (KUTZ-HARDER), HELGA, religious organization executive. BA (hon.), U. Western Ont., 1959; MA, U. B.C., Vancouver, 1965; PhD in English Renaissance Lit., U. N.C., 1976. Specialist instr. English, German Fisher Pk. H.S., Ottawa, Can., 1959-63; sessional instr. to instr. dept. English U. B.C., 1964-67; sessional instr. to prof. dept English U. Windsor, Windsor, Ont., 1970-78, 82-85; missionary United Ch. Can., Tokyo, 1978-82; United Ch. Can.; program cons. United Ch. Can., Windsor, 1985-91; exec. sec. United Ch. Can. Toronto Conf., 1991-94; prin. St. Paul's United Coll., U. Waterloo, Ont., 1994—. Contbr. to articles to religious mags. Gov. Gen. Gold medalist, 1959; Deutsche Acad. Austauschdienst scholar, 1961, Can. Coun. scholar, 1963, U. B.C. grad. scholar, 1964. Office: U Waterloo, St Paul's United Coll, Westmount Rd, Waterloo, ON Canada N2L 3G5

MILLSAPS, FRED RAY, investor; b. Blue Ridge, Ga., Apr. 30, 1929; s. Samuel Hunter and Ora Lee (Bradshaw) M.; m. Audrey Margaret Hopkins, June 22, 1957; children: Judith Gail, Stephen Hunter, Walter Scott. A.B., Emory U., 1951; postgrad., U. Wis. Sch. Banking, 1955-57, Harvard Bus. Sch., 1962; LLD, Fla. So. Coll., 1991. Auditor Fed. Res. Bank, Atlanta, 1953-58, asst. v.p., 1958-62, v.p., 1962-64; fin. v.p. Fla. Power & Light Co., 1965-69; pres., dir. First Nat. Bank of Ft. Lauderdale, Fla., 1969-73; chmn., pres. Landmark Banking Corp. of Fla., Ft. Lauderdale, 1971-78; chmn. Landmark Union Trust Bank of St. Petersburg, Fla., 1976-78; bd. dirs. Templeton Mut. Funds, , Shipp Corp., Toronto, Ont. Chmn. com. of 100 Broward County Indsl. Devel. Bd., 1972-77; chmn. South Fla. Coordinating Coun., 1976-78, WPBT Community TV Found. of South Fla., 1973-75, Fla. So. Coll., Lakeland, Broward Performing Arts Authority, Honda Classic, Broward Workshop, Holy Cross Health Corp.; mem. Fla. Coun. of 100. Mem. Tower Club, Inverrary Club, Coral Ridge Country Club. Methodist.

MILLSAPS, RITA RAE, elementary school educator; b. Magdalena, N.Mex., Jan. 14, 1937; d. Samuel Thomas Martin and Geneva Opal (Nicholson) Martin Freeman; m. Daryl Ray Millsaps, June 26, 1955; children: Michael (dec.), Kathleen, Marian, Larry. Student, Delta Community Coll., 1981-82; BA, Calif. State U., Sacramento, 1986, MEd in Curriculum and Instrn., 1993. Cert. elem. educator, Calif. Mem. ASCD, Internat. Reading Assn. Home: PO Box 1413 San Andreas CA 95249-1413

MILLS-GOLDSTEIN, BETH HELEN, psychotherapist; b. Phoenix, Feb. 14, 1952; d. William and Marietta (Dawdy) Rumper; 1 child, Sara Elizabeth. BS, Barry U., 1986, MS, 1989. Lic. clin. social worker, Fla. Supr. intake South County Mental Health Ctr., Delray Beach, Fla., 1980-89; psychotherapist Coral Ridge Hosp., Ft. Lauderdale, Fla., 1990-92, Ctr. for Family Svc., Boca Raton, Fla., 1992—; pvt. practice cons., Boca Raton, 1992. Editor: (newspaper) The Voice, 1994. Fellow NOW; mem. NASW (state bd. mem.). Democrat. Jewish. Avocations: reading, collecting, studying different therapies. Office: Ctr for Family Svcs 5499 N Federal Hwy Boca Raton FL 33487-4963

MILLSPAUGH, MARTIN LAURENCE, real estate developer, urban development consultant; b. Columbus, Ohio, Dec. 16, 1925; s. Martin Laurence and Elisabeth (Park) M.; m. Meredith Plant, May 10, 1952; children: Elisabeth, M. Laurence, Meredith, Thomas. AB summa cum laude, Princeton U., 1949. Reporter, columnist Richmond News Leader, Va., 1949-53; urban affairs writer Balt. Evening Sun, 1953-57; asst. commr. Urban Renewal Adminstrn., Washington, 1957-60; dep. gen. mgr. Charles Ctr., Balt., 1960-65; pres., chmn., chief exec. officer Charles Ctr.-Inner Harbor Mgmt., Inc., 1965-85; exec. v.p., pres., vice chmn. Enterprise Devel. Co., Columbia, Md., 1985—, also bd. dirs.; pres. Enterprise Internat. Devel. Co., Columbia, 1988-91, vice chmn., 1991—; cons. to pvt. developers and local pub. agys., Mass., Va., S.C., Fla., Calif., Sydney, 1981—; conducted seminars in Nagasaki and Kagoshima, Japan, 1991-92; lectr. Columbia U., Princeton U., Johns Hopkins U., U. Md., U. New Orleans, NYU, Acad. Polit. Sci., AAAS, Lambda Alpha Internat., 1991, 95, U.K. Inst. Travel and Tourism, 1993, Can. Water Resources Assn., 1991, Nat. Bldg. Mus., 1995, Internat. Property Market, Cannes, 1996, and numerous other profl. confs. and seminars; appeared on USIA Worldnet TV Dialogue, Montevideo, Uruguay, 1990, Recife and Rio de Janeiro, 1995. Author: (with others) The Human Side of Urban Renewal, 1958; author, editor (monograph) Baltimore's Charles Center, 1964; author (newspaper series) Design for Living (hon. mention Heywood Broun award 1957); profl. appearances include VOA, 1994, CBS Sunday News, 1994; contbr. articles to profl. jours. Trustee Enoch Pratt Free Libr., Balt., 1965-85, Gilman Sch., 1975-80, Bryn Mawr Sch. for Girls, 1978-81; bd. dirs. Planned Parenthood Assn. Md., 1962-65, Roland Park Civic League, 1962-64, sec., 1963-64, Blue Cross of Md., Inc., 1970-80, Balt. Symphony Orch. Assn., 1974-78, YMCA of Greater Balt. area, 1977-81; Md. Internat. Coun., Balt., 1992—, mem. long range planning com., 1994—; mem. chair nominating com., mem. task force Twentieth Century Fund, N.Y.C., 1984-85; mem. adv. coun. real estate devel. program Columbia U. Grad. Sch. Architecture and Planning, 1985-94; mem. bd. advisors Fight-Blight Fund, Balt., 1961-62, Waterfront Ctr., Washington, 1987-90; mem. adv. bd. Nat. Aquarium, Balt., 1988—, Sch. Bus. Mgmt. Morgan State U., Real Estate Inst., Sch. Continuing Studies Johns Hopkins U., 1994—; mem. pres.'s adv. bd. U. Md. Balt. County, 1989-94; mem. adv. panel Ctr. Strategic and Internat. Studies, Washington, 1993-94; active U.S. Senate Productivity Award Selection Com. for Md., 1987. Served to sgt. USAF, 1944-46, PTO. Recipient Disting. Svc. award U.S. Housing and Home Fin. Agy., Washington, 1960, Urban Planning award The Waterfront Ctr., 1995. Mem. Urban Land Inst. (exec. group internat. coun., 1989—, vice chmn. internat. coun. 1995—, award of excellence, 1980, chair adv. panel for city of Harrisburg, Pa., 1984, internat. com. 1987-88, Balt. dist. coord. 1987-91, vice-chmn. dist. coun. com. 1991-94; mem. adv. panel for Oklahoma City, 1995), Greater Balt. Com. (urban affairs coun. 1982-84, J. Jefferson Miller award for civic accomplishment 1981), Coun. on Urban Econ. Devel., Internat. Downtown Assn., Internat. New Town Assn. (mem. adv. panel for waterfront devel. for City of Malmo, Sweden 1987), World Trade Ctr. Inst., Phi Beta Kappa, Lambda Alpha. Democrat. Episcopalian. Clubs: Center, Balt., 14 W Hamilton St (Balt.); Ivy (Princeton, N.J.). Home: 203 Ridgewood Rd Baltimore MD 21210-2538 Office: Enterprise Devel Co 600 American City Bldg Columbia MD 21044

MILLSTEIN, IRA M., lawyer, lecturer; b. N.Y.C., Nov. 8, 1926; s. Harry M. and Birdie E. (Rosenbaum) M.; m. Diane G. Greenberg, July 3, 1949; children: James Eliot, Elizabeth Jane. B.S., Columbia U., 1947, LL.B., 1949. Bar: N.Y. 1949, U.S. Supreme Ct. 1973. Atty. antitrust div. Dept. Justice, Washington, 1949-51; assoc. firm Weil Gotshal & Manges, N.Y.C., 1951-57, ptnr., 1957—; chmn. bd. advisors Ctr. for Law and Econ. Studies, Columbia U., 1987—; fellow faculty govt. John F. Kennedy Sch. Govt., Harvard U., 1983-87; disting. faculty fellow Yale U. Sch. of Mgmt., 1980-82, Sloan fellow, 1982-83, Disting. fellow Yale U.Sch. Orgnl. Mgmt., 1992—; mem. coun. Adminstrv. Conf. U.S., 1978-81. Author: (with Katsh) The Limits of Corporate Power, 1981; contbr. articles to profl. jours. Mem. Nat. Commn. on Consumer Fin., 1969-72, chmn., 1971-72; chmn. N.Y.C.'s Spl. Com. on Inquiry into Energy Failures, 1977-82, N.Y. State Energy Planning Bd., 1978-82, Gov. Cuomo's Task Force on Pension Fund Investment, 1988—; vice chmn. bd. overseers Albert Einstein Coll. Medicine, Yeshiva U., Bronx, N.Y., 1981—; chmn. bd. trustees Cen. Pk. Conservancy. Decorated chevalier Nat. Order of Merit, France. Fellow Am. Acad. Arts and Scis.; mem. ABA (chmn. antitrust law sect. 1977-78, chmn. antitrust law sect.'s task force report on antitrust div. 1988-89), N.Y. State Bar Assn. (chmn. antitrust law sect. 1967-68), Nat. Assn. Corp. Dirs. (bd. dirs. 1994—), Met. Club, Quaker Ridge Golf Club. Home: 1240 Flagler Dr Mamaroneck NY 10543-4601 Office: Weil Gotshal & Manges 767 5th Ave New York NY 10153

MILLSTONE, DAVID J., lawyer; b. Morgantown, W.Va., 1946. AB, Johns Hopkins U., 1968; JD, U. W.Va., 1971. Bar: W.Va. 1971, Ohio 1971, Fla. 1980. Ptnr. Squire, Sanders & Dempsey, Cleve. Mem. ABA (internat. coord. labor and employment practice). Office: Squire Sanders & Dempsey 4900 Society Ctr 127 Public Sq Cleveland OH 44114-1216*

MILMAN, DORIS HOPE, pediatrics educator, psychiatrist; b. N.Y.C., Nov. 17, 1917; d. Barnet S. and Rose (Smoleroff) Milman; m. Nathan Kreeger, June 15, 1941; 1 child, Elizabeth Kreeger Goldman. BA, Barnard Coll., 1938; MD, NYU, 1942. Diplomate Am. Bd. Pediats.; lic. physician, N.Y. Intern Jewish Hosp., Bklyn., 1942-43, resident, 1944-46, fellow in pediat., 1946-47; postgrad. extern in psychiatry Bellevue Hosp., N.Y.C., 1947-49; attending pediat. psychiatrist Jewish Hosp., Bklyn., 1950-56; asst. prof. pediat. Health Sci. Ctr. at Bklyn. SUNY, 1956-67, assoc. prof., 1967-73, prof., 1973-93, prof. emeritus, 1993—, acting chmn. dept. pediat., 1973-75, 82; pvt. practice child and adolescent psychiatry, Bklyn., 1950-90; vis. prof. Ben Gurion U. of the Negev, Beersheva, Israel, 1977. Mem. adv. bd. N.Y. Assn. for the Learning Disabled, N.Y.C., 1975-80. Recipient Disting. Alumna award Barnard Coll., 1986, Solomon R. Berson Achievement award NYU Sch. Medicine, 1991; Grace Potter Rice fellow Barnard Coll., 1938-39. Fellow Am. Acad. Pediat. (emeritus), Am. Psychiat. Assn. (life); mem. AAAS, Am. Orthopsychiat. Assn. (life), Am. Pediat. Soc. (emeritus), N.Y. Pediat. Soc. (emeritus). Home: 126 Westminster Rd Brooklyn NY 11218-3444 Office: Health Sci Ctr at Bklyn SUNY Box 49 450 Lenox Rd Brooklyn NY 11203-2020

MILMOE, PATRICK JOSEPH, lawyer; b. Oct. 2, 1939; s. Hugh A. Milmoe and Mary Frances (O'Connell) Steenken; m. Carolyn Mann, Nov. 30, 1963; children: Mary Kaye Chryssicas, Caroline Peugh, Hugh. BA, Coll. William and Mary, 1959; JD, U. Va., 1962. Bar: N.Y. 1962, Va. 1962, Fla. 1989. With Davis & Polk, N.Y.C., 1965-72; ptnr. Hunton & Williams, Richmond, Va., 1972—; chmn. DARE Marina, Inc., Grafton, Va., 1992—, States Roofing Corp., Norfolk, Va., 1994—, Virginia Beach Marlin Club, Inc., 1980—. Trustee Village of Atlantic Beach, N.Y., 1965-72; bd. dirs. St. Joseph's Villa, Richmond, Va., 1985-91. Capt. U.S. Army, 1963-65. Mem. Am. Coll. Real Estate Lawyers. Avocations: boating, fishing. Office: Hunton & Williams 951 E Byrd St Richmond VA 23219-4074

MILNE, JAMES, secretary of state; b. Barre, Vt., July 8, 1950; m. Judith Garigliano; children: Honah Lee, Heather, Joseph, Elizabeth. BS in Pharmacy, Mass. Coll. Pharmacy, 1974. City clk., treas. City of Barre (Vt.), 1988-94; sec. of state State of Vt., 1995—; pharmacist, mgr. Allan Milne Pharmacy, 1974-88. Mem. Aldrich Pub. Libr. (bd. trustees), Nat. Ski Patrol, Mutuo, Inc.; chair Barre Basketball Tournament Com.; dir. Granite Mutual Ins. Co. Mem. Vt. Municipal Clks. and Treas. Assn., Vt. Jaycees (pres. 1979-80), U.S. Jaycees (nat. v.p. 1980-81), Barre Elks Lodge, Barre Country Club, Barre Rotary Club (pres. 1985-86). Republican. Office: PO Box 992 Barre VT 05641 also: Off of Sec of State 109 State St Montpelier VT 05609-1101*

MILNER, BRENDA ATKINSON LANGFORD, neuropsychologist; b. Manchester, Eng., July 15, 1918; emigrated to Can., 1944; d. Samuel and Leslie (Doig) Langford. BA, Cambridge (Eng.) U., 1939, MA, 1949, ScD, 1972; PhD, McGill U., 1952; DSc (hon.), 1991;, LLD (hon.), Queen's U., 1980; ScD (hon.) U. Manitoba, 1982, U. Lethbridge, 1986, Mt. Holyoke Coll., 1986, U. Laval, 1987, U. Toronto, 1987; LHD (hon.), Mt. St. Vincent U., 1988; Hon. D. U. de Montréal, 1988; DSc (hon.) Wesleyan U., 1991, Acadia U., 1991, U. St. Andrews, 1992. Exptl. officer U.K. Ministry of Supply, 1941-44; prof. agrégé Institut de Psychologie, Université de Montréal, 1944-52; rsch. assoc. psychology dept. McGill U., Montreal, 1952-53, lectr. dept. neurology and neurosurgery, 1953-60, asst. prof., 1960-64, assoc. prof., 1964-70, prof. psychology, 1970-93; Dorothy J. Killam prof. Montreal Neurological Inst., 1993—; head neuropsychology rsch. unit Montreal Neurol. Inst., 1953-90; Clothworkers fellow Girton Coll., Cambridge, 1972-73. Mem. editorial bd. Neuropsychologia, 1973-93, Behavioral Brain Rsch., 1980-88, Hippocampus, 1990—. Decorated officer Order of Can., officier l'Ordre Nat. du Que., 1985; Career investigator Med. Rsch. Coun. Can., 1964—; recipient Kathleen Stott prize Newnham Coll., 1971, Karl Spencer Lashley award Am. Philos. Soc., 1979, Izaak Walton Killam Meml. prize Can. Coun., 1983, Hermann Von Helmholtz prize Cognitive Neuroscience Inst., 1984, Penfield award Can. league Against Epilepsy, 1984, William James fellow Am. Psychol. Soc., 1989, Wilder Penfield prize Province of Quebec, 1993; named Great Montrealer, 1987. Fellow APA (Disting. Contbn. award 1973), AAAS, Royal Soc. London, Royal Soc. Can. (McLaughlin medal 1995), Can. Psychol. Assn.; mem. NAS (fgn. assoc.), Am. Epilepsy Soc. (William G. Lennox award 1974, 95), Am. Neurol. Assn., Association de Psychologie Scientifique de Langue Française, Brit. Soc. Exptl. Psychology, Exptl. Psychol. Soc., Psychonomic Soc., Eastern Psychol. Assn., Internat. Neuropsychology Symposium, Internat. Brain Rsch. Orgn. (exec. sec. 1993—), Soc. Neurosci. (Ralph W. Gerard prize 1987), Am. Acad. Neurology (assoc.), Assn. Rsch. in Nervous and Mental Diseases (assoc.), Royal Soc. Medicine (affiliate), Sigma Xi. Office: Montreal Neurol Inst, 3801 University St, Montreal, PQ Canada H3A 2B4

MILNER, CLYDE A., II, historian; b. Durham, N.C., Oct. 19, 1948; s. Charles Fremont and Eloyse (Sargent) M.; m. Carol Ann O'Connor, Aug. 14, 1977; children: Catherine Carol, Charles Clyde. AB, U. N.C., 1971; MA, Yale U., 1973, MPhil, 1974, PhD, 1979. Admissions counselor Guilford Coll., Greensboro, N.C., 1968-70; acting instr. Yale U., New Haven, Conn., 1974-75; research fellow McNickle Ctr., Chgo., 1975-76; instr. Utah State U., Logan, 1976-79, asst. prof., 1979-82, assoc. prof., 1982-88, prof., 1988—; reader of manuscripts History Book Club, Inc., 1986—. Author: With Good Intentions, 1982; editor: Major Problems in the History of the American West, 1989; assoc. editor The Western Hist. Quar., 1984-87, co-editor, 1987-89, editor, 1990—; co-editor: Churchmen and the Western Indians, 1985, Trails: Toward a New Western History, 1991, Oxford History of the American West, 1994 (Western Heritage award for non-fiction Nat. Cowboy Hall of Fame 1994, Caughey Western History Assn. award for best book on history of Am. West 1995). Recipient Paladen Writing award The Montana Mag. Western History, 1987, Faculty Svc. award Associated Students Utah State U., 1987, Outstanding Social Science Researcher award Utah State U., 1983, (with Carol A. O'Connor) Charles Redd prize Utah Acad. Scis., Arts and Letters, 1996. Mem. Western History Assn., Orgn. Am. Historians, Phi Alpha Theta, Phi Beta Kappa. Society of Friends. Home: 1675 E 1400 N Logan UT 84341-2975 Office: Utah State U Dept of History Logan UT 84322

MILNER, HAROLD WILLIAM, hotel executive; b. Salt Lake City, Nov. 11, 1934; s. Kenneth W. and Olive (Schoettlin) M.; m. Susan Emmett, June 19, 1959 (div. 1976); children—John Kenneth, Mary Sue; m. Lois Freimuth, Aug. 14, 1977; 1 dau., Jennifer Rebecca. B.S., U. Utah, 1960; M.B.A., Harvard, 1962. Instr. Brigham Young U., Provo, Utah, 1962-64; v.p. Gen. Paper Corp., Mpls., 1964-65; dir. finance Amalgamated Sugar Co., Ogden, Utah, 1965-67; corp. treas. Marriott Corp., Washington, 1967-70; pres., chief exec. officer, trustee Hotel Investors, Kensington, Md., 1970-75; pres., chief exec. officer Americana Hotels Corp., Chgo., 1975-85, Kahler Corp., Rochester, Minn., 1985—. Author: A Special Report on Contract Maintenance, 1963. Served as lt. AUS, 1960. Mem. Minn. Bus. Partnership (dir. 1991—). Mem. Ch. Jesus Christ Latter-day Saints. Home: 4010 Mayowood Rd SW Rochester MN 55902-4255 Office: Kahler Corp 20 2nd Ave SW Rochester MN 55902-3013

MILNER, HOWARD M., real estate developer, international real estate financier; b. L.A., Sept. 21, 1937; s. David Daniel and Rose (Devron) M.; m. Shirley Glogow, Oct. 24, 1964 (div. 1978); children: Mara Lynn, Debra Faye. AA in Architecture, L.A. City Coll., 1960; cert. real estate, UCLA, 1962; Doctorate (hon.), London Inst. Applied Rsch., 1994; PhD in Philanthropy, Pepperdine U., 1995. Sr. store planner Broadway Dept. Stores, L.A., 1959; exec. v.p. Palm Properties Inc., Van Nuys, Calif., 1959-69; v.p. Network Cinema Corp., L.A., 1969-79, Hesa Global Investments Ltd., Beverly Hills, Calif., 1979-86; pres., chief exec. officer Lyons Internat. Realty and Devel. Inc., L.A., 1986-87, Howard M. Milner and Assocs., North Hollywood, Calif., 1987—; sr. cons. Swiss-Am. Investment Trust, North Hollywood, 1979—; adj. sr. assoc. Visa Enterprises Inc., Beverly Hills, 1986—; sr. assoc. cons. AMF Roadmaster Mfg. Co., North Hollywood, 1986—; developed nat. expansion Internat. House Pancakes, Copper Penny Coffee Shops, Fotomat Corp., Jerry Lewis Cinema Theatres, K-Mart Shopping Ctrs.; lectr. in field. Contbr. articles on real estate to profl. jours. Life mem., fin. sec. City of Hope, L.A.'s mem. Mayor's Comml. Devel. Com., Brea, Calif., Mayor's Redevel. Com., L.A. and Hollywood; active City of Hope Cancer Rsch. Found., Duarte, Calif. With U.S. Army, 1957-59. Recipient Eagle Scout award Boy Scouts Am., 1952, Disting. Citizen award and Disting. Eagle award Boy Scouts Am., Civic Appreciation award Mayor of L.A., 1987; Architecture scholar Ford Motor Co., 1954, Architecture scholar East L.A. Coll., 1955. Mem. AIA, Am. Inst. Indsl. Engrs., Am. Inst. Plant Engrs., Am. Soc. Mil. Engrs., Calif. Apt. and Motel Mgrs. Assn., Calif. Notary Assn., Calif. Real Estate Assn., Constrn. Specifications Inst., Inst. Real Estate Mgmt., Internat. Coun. Shopping Ctrs., Internat. Real Estate Fedn., Nat. Home Builders Assn. Am., Nat. Franchise Assn. Am., Real Estate Cert. Inst., Young Home Builders Coun. Am., L.A. C. of C., San Fernando C. of C., Saugus-Newhall C. of C., Van Nuys C. of C., Toastmasters, Masons, Shriners. Democrat. Jewish. Avocations: walking, jogging, racquetball, golf, cooking. Office: 1st Interstate Bank Bldg 4605 Lankershim Blvd # 413 North Hollywood CA 91602-1818

MILNER, IRVIN MYRON, lawyer; b. Cleve., Feb. 5, 1916; s. Nathan and Rose (Spector) M.; m. Zelda Winograd., Aug. 15, 1943. A.B. cum laude, Western Res. U. (now Case Western Res. U.), 1937, J.D., 1940, LL.M., 1970. Bar: Ohio 1940, U.S. Dist. Ct. (no. dist.) Ohio 1946. Pvt. practice Cleve., 1946—; exec. sec., counsel Men's Apparel Club Ohio, Cleve., 1947-48; adj. instr. Sch. Law, Case Western Res. U., 1965-66; spl. counsel Ohio Office Atty. Gen., 1960-70; legal counsel Korean Am. Assn. Greater Cleve., 1973-95. Mem. Cleve. Fgn. Consular Corps., 1970—, hon. consul Rep. of Korea for Cleve., 1970—; bd. dirs. Internat. Human Assistance Programs, Inc., 1973-79, voting corp. mem., 1980-88. Served with U.S. Army, 1941-45, ETO. Decorated Order Diplomatic Svc. Merit-Heung-in medal (Republic of Korea), 1975; named to Disting. Alumni Hall of Fame, Cleveland Heights (Ohio) High Sch., 1983. Fellow Internat. Consular Coll., Ohio Bar Found.; mem. ABA (small bus. com., corp. bus. law sect. 1971-74), Greater Cleve. Bar Assn., Cuyahoga County Bar Assn. (pres. 1975-76, co-chmn. jud. standards com. 1987-88, life trustee, award of Special Merit 1976, Pres.' award 1988), Ohio State Bar Assn. (coun. dels., 1976-86, com. on legal ethics and profl. conduct 1984—), Cuyahoga County Bar Found. (sec.-treas. 1980-84, bd. dirs. 1984—), Cuyahoga County Coun. Ohio VFW (comdr. 1958, Merit award 1958), Am. Security Coun. (nat. adv. bd.), Cleve. Coun. on World Affairs, Western Res. Coll. Alumni Assn. (bd. dirs. 1982-88). Tau Epsilon Rho (chancellor Cleve. Grad. chpt. 1987-88), Delta Phi Alpha. Republican. Jewish. Club: Cleve. City. Lodges: Masons 32 degree, Rotary. Office: Standard Bldg #1148 1370 Ontario St Cleveland OH 44113-1701

MILNER, MAX, food and nutrition consultant; b. Edmonton, Alta., Can., Jan. 24, 1914; came to U.S., 1939, naturalized, 1944; s. Morris Abram and Rose (Lertzman) M.; m. Elizabeth Banen, Aug. 9, 1942; children—Ruth Sharon, Marcia Ann. B.Sc., U. Sask., 1938; LL.D. (hon.), 1979; M.S., U. Minn., 1941, Ph.D., 1945. Research chemist Pillsbury Mills Inc., Mpls., 1939-40; prof. grain sci. and industry Kans. State U., Manhattan, 1947-59; sr. food technologist UNICEF, N.Y.C., 1959-71; chief nutrition br. AID, 1966-67; dir. secretariat protein calorie adv. group UN, 1971-75; assoc. dir. internat. nutrition program M.I.T., 1975-78; exec. officer Am. Inst. Nutrition, Bethesda, Md., 1978-84; mem. U.S. Wheat Industry Council, 1980-83; mem. expert evaluation panel Bd. Internat. Food and Agrl. Devel., 1983—; chmn. Gordon Research Conf. Food and Nutrition, 1968; Gen. Food Co. (Can.) disting. internat. lectr., 1975. Co-author: Protein Resources and Technology, 1978, Postharvest Biology and Biotechnology, 1978; Editor: Protein-enriched Cereal Foods for World Needs, 1969, Nutrition Improvement of Food Legumes by Breeding, 1975; Contbr. articles to profl. jours., chpts. to monographs. Bd. dirs., exec. com. Meals for Million/Freedom From Hunger Found., 1975-83, cons. in field. Fellow AAAS, Inst. Food Technologists (Internat. award 1968, lectr. sci. series 1971-72, Disting. Food Service award N.Y. sect. 1975), Am. Inst. Nutrition; mem. Am. Chem. Soc., Am. Assn. Cereal Chemists. Home: 10401 Grosvenor Pl Apt 721 Rockville MD 20852-4635 *As a child of immigrant parents with minimal formal education, my career, like that of many Americans with this kind of background, is a testimonial to the unique role of the Canadian and American system of open higher education, available to all able to qualify for admission. It is to such institutions that I owe a profound debt.*

MILNER, PETER MARSHALL, psychology educator; b. Silkstone Common, Eng., June 13, 1919; s. David William and Edith Anne (Marshall) M.; m. Susan Walker, Oct. 13, 1970; 1 son, David Elliot. B.S., Leeds U., 1941; M.S., McGill U., Ph.D., 1954. Sr. sci. officer U.K. Ministry Supply, 1941-48; research assoc. physics McGill U., 1948-50, research asst., prof. dept. psychology, 1950-92, prof. emeritus, 1992—, chmn. dept., 1980-83. Author: Physiological Psychology. Fellow Am. Psychol. Assn., Canadian Psychol. Assn.; mem. Sigma Xi. Home: 1050 Amesbury Ave #729, Montreal, PQ Canada H3H 2S5 Office: McGill U Dept Psychology, 1205 Dr Penfield Ave, Montreal, PQ Canada H3A 1B1

MILNER, THIRMAN L., mayor; b. Hartford, Oct. 29, 1933; s. Marshall Henry and Grace (Allen) M.; children by previous marriage—Theresa, Gary. Mem. Conn. Ho. of Reps., 1979-81, Democratic whip, 1979-81, sec. Conn. legis. black caucus, 1979-81, chmn. mcpl. affairs and home rule subcoms., 1979-81; mayor City of Hartford, 1981-87; state senator, Conn., 1987—. formerly minority bussings acct. rep. Oasis Oil Co.; pub. relations dir. and exec. asst. Community Renewal Team; exec. asst. N.Y.C. Against Poverty. Weekly columnist Northend Agt., 1974-80. Bd. dirs. St. Francis Hosp., Hartford Hosp. Mem. NAACP (life), Nat. Conf. Mayors, Conn. Govt. Assn. Methodist. Address: 19 Colebrook St Hartford CT 06112-1522

MILNES, ARTHUR GEORGE, electrical engineer, educator; b. Heswall, Eng., July 30, 1922; came to U.S., 1957, naturalized, 1964; s. George and Marion (Teasdale) M.; m. Mary Laverne Wertz, Dec. 4, 1955; children: Sheila Rae, Brian George, John Teasdale. BSc, U. Bristol, Eng., 1943, MSc, 1947, DSc, 1956. With Royal Aircraft Establishment, 1943-57, prin. sci. officer, 1952-57; mem. faculty Carnegie-Mellon U., Pitts., 1957-87; prof. elec. engring. Carnegie-Mellon U., 1960-87, assoc. head dept., 1966-69, Buhl prof., 1973-87; prof. emeritus Carnegie-Mellon U., Pitts., 1987—; cons. to industry on semiconductor devices, 1957. Author: Transductors and Magnetic Amplifiers, 1957, (with D.L. Feucht) Heterojunctions and Metal-Semiconductor Junctions, 1972, Deep Impurities in Semiconductors, 1973, Semiconductor Devices and Integrated Electronics, 1979; contbr. articles to profl. jours. FOA rsch. fellow NAS-Royal Soc. London, 1954. Fellow IEEE (J.J. Ebers award 1982, van der Ziel award 1993), Am. Phys. Soc., Instn. Elec. Engrs. (London). Home: 1417 Inverness St Pittsburgh PA 15217-1157

MILNES, SHERRILL EUSTACE, baritone; b. Downers Grove, Ill., Jan. 10, 1935; s. James Knowlton and Thelma (Roe) M.; children by previous marriage—Eric, Erin; m. Nancy Denise Stokes, Sept. 28, 1969; 1 son, Shawn. Student, North Central Coll., Ill.; B in Music Edn., Drake U., 1957, M in Music Edn., 1958; postgrad., Northwestern U., 1958-61; studied with Boris Goldovsky, Rosa Ponselle, Andrew White, Hermanes Baer; postgrad. hon. degree, Ripon Coll., Drake U., Coe Coll., Westminster Choir Coll., SUNY, Potsdam. Operatic debut Goldovsky Opera Co., N.Y.C., 1960; leading baritone N.Y.C. Opera Co., Met. Opera Co., 1964—; European debut in Macbeth, Vienna, 1970; appearances major world opera cos. including Covent Garden, London, L'Opera, Paris, Staasoper, Vienna, Austria, Teatro Colon, Argentina, La Scala, Milan, Hamburg, Munich, Salzburg, Frankfurt, Berlin, Zurich, as well as continued appearances in the U.S. in San Antonio, Cin., Miami, Houston, Pitts., Chgo., Balt.; numerous TV, concerts, recitals, recordings (RCA, Deutsche Grammophon, Angel/EMI, London, Decca, Philips, CBS). Recipient Order of Merit, Comdr. of the Rep. of Italy, 1984; Ford Found. award, 1962. Mem. Affiliate Artists, Inc. (past pres., chmn. devel. com. 1966—, chmn. emeritus), Tucker Found. (v.p.), Phi Mu Alfa Sinfonia (life). Office: care Herbert Barrett 1776 Broadway Ste 584 New York NY 10019-2002

MILNES, WILLIAM ROBERT, JR., insurance company executive; b. St. Louis, Jan. 11, 1946; s. William Robert and Patricia June (Hargate) M.; m. Rebecca Jane Richards, Oct. 14, 1983; children: Bill, Julie, Kristen, David. BSBA in Acctg., U. Mo., 1968, MBA in Fin., 1971. CPA 1980. Budget analyst Chrysler Corp., St. Louis, 1968; plant acctg. supr., acctg. analyst Monsanto Chem. Co., St. Louis, 1971-74; mgr., cost & budget Mo. Hosp. Svcs. Inc., St. Louis, 1974-76; dir. fin., controller Mo. Hosp. Svcs. Inc., 1976-78, v.p. fin., 1978-82; corp. sr. v.p. Hosp. care Corp., Cin., 1982-84; group sr. v.p., treas., chief fin. officer fin. svcs. Community Mutual Ins. Co., Cin., 1984-91, exec. v.p. corp. svcs., chief fin. officer, 1991—; s.r. v.p. Anthem, Inc., Indpls.; bd. dirs. Health Plans Capital Svcs. Corp., Chgo., Blue Cross Blue Shield Assn., Nat. Employee Benefits Com., Chgo.; bd. dirs., chmn. audit com. Exec. & Employee Benefits Plans Inc., Columbus, Ohio, 1990—; bd. dirs., sec., treas. CMIC Holding Co., Cin., 1986—; bd. dirs., chmn. investment com. Community Nat. Assurance Co., Columbus, 1983—. Chmn. Anderson Twp. Bicentennial, 1991—; bd. dirs. Nat. Employee Benefits Bd., Chgo. With USMC, 1968-70. Mem. Fin. Exec. Inst. Avocations: golf, bicycling, hiking. Office: Anthem Inc 120 Monument Circle Indianapolis IN 46204-4124*

MILNIKEL, ROBERT SAXON, lawyer; b. Chgo., Aug. 17, 1926; s. Gustav and Emma Hazel (Saxon) M.; m. Virginia Lee Wylie, July 26, 1969; children: Robert Saxon Jr., Elizabeth Wylie. AB, U. Chgo., 1950, JD, 1953. Bar: Ill. 1953, U.S. Dist. Ct. 1954. Assoc. Traeger, Bolger & Traeger, Chgo., 1953-57, Heineke, Conklin & Schrader, Chgo., 1958-66; ptnr. Peterson & Ross, Chgo., 1966—. With USN, 1944-46, PTO. Mem. Beta Theta Pi (pres. chpt. and alumni assn.), Cliffdwellers Club (bd. dirs. Arts Found.). Republican. Lutheran. Home: 601 Ridge Rd Kenilworth IL 60043-1042 Office: Peterson & Ross 200 E Randolph St # 7300 Chicago IL 60601-6436

MILNOR, WILLIAM ROBERT, physician; b. Wilmington, Del., May 4, 1920; s. William Robert and Virginia (Sterling) M.; m. Gabriella Mahaffy,

Aug. 19, 1944; children—Katherine Alexander, William Henry. A.B., Princeton U., 1941; M.D., Johns Hopkins U., 1944. Diplomate: Am. Bd. Internal Medicine. Intern, resident Johns Hopkins Hosp., 1944-46; research fellow Nat. Heart Inst., 1949-51; physician-in-charge heart sta. Johns Hopkins Hosp., 1951-60, physician, 1952—; mem. faculty Johns Hopkins Med. Sch., 1951—, prof. physiology, 1969—; vis. fellow St. Catherine's Coll., Oxford (Eng.) U., 1968; mem. med. adv. panel Am. Inst. Biol. Scis., 1971—; assessor Nat. Med. Research Council of Australia, 1976—. Author: Hemodynamics, 2d edit., 1989, Cardio-vascular Physiology, 1990; contbr. articles to med. textbooks, med. jours. Served to capt. M.C. USAAF, 1946-48. Fellow A.C.P.; mem. Am. Physiol. Soc., Am. Fedn. Clin. Research, Biomed. Engring. Soc., Am. Heart Assn. (chmn. research com. 1966), Heart Assn. Md. (past pres.). Clubs: L'Hirondelle, Princeton, 14 W Hamilton St. Office: Johns Hopkins Med Sch 725 N Wolfe St Baltimore MD 21205-2105

MILONAS, MINOS, artist, designer, poet; b. Heraklion, Crete, Greece, Apr. 28, 1936; came to U.S., 1964, naturalized, 1968; s. Stavros and Maria (Kaplantzis) M.; m. Arlene Watson, Dec. 23, 1963 (div. 1970); m. Sarah Brown, Dec. 1973 (div. 1974); m. Elaine Mauceli, May 26, 1988. BA, Calif. State U., Northridge, 1970; MFA with hons., U. Wash., Seattle, 1972. Freelance writer and poet Athens, 1960-64; freelance artist L.A., 1964-66; instr. U. Wash., 1971-72, Studio Milonas, Seattle, 1972-76; artist Studio Milonas, N.Y.C., 1977—, textile designer, 1984-94. One man shows include Second Story Gallery, Seattle, 1971, Henry Art Gallery, Seattle, 1972, Polly Friedlander Gallery, Seattle, 1973, Stavrakakis Gallery, Crete, Greece, 1977, West Broadway Gallery, N.Y.C., 1979, 81, 82, Heraklion Art Gallery, Crete, 1983, Kreonides Gallery, Athens, 1983, 84, Doma Gallery, N.Y.C., 1988, Hellenic Cultural Ctr., N.Y., 1990, 93, Cypriot Consulate, N.Y.C., 1990; exhibitions in group shows at Calif. State U., Northridge, 1968-69, Mcpl. Art Gallery, L.A., 1969, U. Wash. Libr., Seattle, 1971, 72, Panaca Gallery, Bellevue, Wash., 1973, Mercer Island Art Gallery, Seattle, 1973, Henry Art Gallery, Seattle, 1973, Tacoma Art Mus., 1973, 75, N.W. Watercolor Soc., 1974, Gordon Woodside Gallery, Seattle, 1974, Coll. of the Cisciyous, Calif., 1975, Laguna Gloria Art Mus., Austin, Tex., 1975, Redmonds (Wash.) Arts Festival, 1975, Univ. Dist. Arts Festival, Seattle, 1976, Bellevue Art Mus., 1976, Sunne Savage Gallery, Boston, 1976, Cretan Artists, Stavrakakis Gallery, Heraklion, Crete, 1978, Internat. Drawing Biennale, Cleveland, Eng., 1981-82, Bowes Mus., Barnard Castle, Eng., 1982, Shipley Art Gallery, Gateshed, Eng., 1982, House of Commons, London, 1982, Haggin Mus., Stockton, Calif., 1985-86, U. N.D., Grand Forks, 1987, Greek Cultural Ctr., Springfield, Mass., 1987, 89, Del Bello Gallery, Toronto, Ont., Can., 1987, Ball State U., Muncie, Ind., 1989, Morin-Miller Galleries, N.Y.C., 1989-90, Columbia (Md.) Coll., 1989, Grand Prospect Hall, Bklyn., 1990, Kenneth Raymond Gallery, Boca Raton, Fla., 1993-96; author: The Small Caravan, 1962; author of short stories; author of numerous poems; videos include Multimedia Artist, 1988, 500 Definitions--Art Is, 1991. Recipient 4 Sculpture awards Summer Art Festivals, 1970-76, 2 Merit awards Greek Cultural Ctr., 1987; U. Wash. grantee, 1970; U. Wash. scholar, 1971. Mem. Nat. Artists Equity Assn., Inc., N.Y. Artists Equity Assn., Inc., Poetry Soc. Am., Greek-Am. Writers Assn. Democrat. Home and Office: 790 11th Ave Apt 39A New York NY 10019-3521

MILONE, ANTHONY M., bishop; b. Omaha, Sept. 24, 1932. Grad., North American Coll. (Rome). Ordained priest Roman Catholic Ch., 1957. Ordained titular bishop of Plestia and aux. bishop Diocese of Omaha, 1982; apptd. bishop Mont. Diocese, Great Falls-Billings, 1987—. Office: PO Box 1399 121 23rd St S Great Falls MT 59403*

MILONE, FRANCIS MICHAEL, lawyer; b. Phila., June 18, 1947; s. Michael Nicholas and Frances Theresa (Fair) M.; m. Maida R. Crane, Nov. 25, 1991; children: Michael, Matthew. BA, LaSalle Coll., 1969; MS, Pa. State U., 1971; JD, U. Pa., 1974. Bar: Pa. 1974, U.S. Dist. Ct. (ea dist.) Pa. 1974, U.S. Dist. Ct. (mid. dist.) Pa. 1979, U.S. Dist. Ct. (ea. dist.) Mich. 1983, U.S. Ct. Appeals (3d cir.) 1978, U.S. Ct. Appeals (4th and 5th cirs.) 1979, U.S. Supreme Ct. 1979. Assoc. Montgomery, McCraken, Walker & Rhoads, Phila., 1974-77; ptnr. Morgan, Lewis & Bockius, Phila., 1977—. Mem. ABA (labor and litigation sects.), Pa. Bar Assn., Phila. Bar Assn. Home: 1020 Cedar Knl Newtown Square PA 19073-2808 Office: Morgan Lewis & Bockius 2000 One Logan Sq Philadelphia PA 19103*

MILONE, JAMES MICHAEL, environmental/occupational health-safety scientist and risk manager, engineer; b. Welfare Island, N.Y., Sept. 1, 1942; s. Michael James and Winifred Patricia (Rhenos) M.; m. Lois Esther Polinsky, Sept. 30, 1967; 1 child, Michelle Elena Milone Suchy. ABA, St. John's U., 1963; MPH Engring., MS in Environ. Scis., La Salle U., 1993, PhD in Indsl. Hygiene and Environ. Policy, 1994. Registered indsl. hygienist, constrn./re-engring. occupl. health & safety engr., occupational health & safety engr., Integrated Pest Mgmt. expert; cert. environ. auditor/insp., environ./food sanitarian, enviro/hazardous waste mgmt. cons., econ./biol. entomologist; lic. air sample technologist, remediation supr., project monitor, mgmt. planner, integrated pest mgmt. cons.; cert. comml. applicator, profl. mgr. bldgs. and grounds. Sales and mktg. cons., sales mgr. Profl. Porter Svc., Lynbrook, N.Y., 1963-69; dir. environ. svcs. Cross and Brown Co., N.Y.C., 1969-71; v.p., gen. mgr. Cert. Bldg. Maintenance Corp., N.Y.C., 1971-76; gen. mgr. Orkin Ext. Co., Inc., L.I., N.Y., 1976-80; sr. v.p., gen. mgr. environ.-occupational health-safety Envirotronics Ltd., Wilmington, Del., 1980—, human resources mentor, trainer; adj. faculty/prof. Nat. and Internat. Diplomate for LaSalle U., Kent Coll., Southland Law Sch., Nova U., LaSalle U. Internat. Practical Tng. Program U.S. Dept. Edn., Coun. on Post Secondary Christian Edn.; cons. Fed. Govt., Gen. Svcs. Adminstr., Dept. VA, Ben Gilman House of Reps., Sen. Joseph Holland/N.Y., others; corp. risk mgr., profl. cons. Author/lectr.: Integrated Pest Management Systems In A Government Hospital Metroplex, 1994. Served with U.S. Army, 1961-69. Mem. Am. Indsl. Hygiene Assn., Am. Soc. Safety Engrs., Environ. Mgmt. Assn., Entomol. Soc. Air and Waste Mgmt., Am. Assn. for Standards and Testing of Materials, Products, Svcs. and Systems, numerous other environ. assns. and orgns. Roman Catholic. Achievements include invention of non-toxic biodegradeable odor counteractant and the development of an inter-disciplinary building maintenance green building system. Home: 161-51 Jewel Ave Flushing NY 11365-4353

MILORO, FRANK PROTOPRESBYTER, church official, religious studies educator; b. Wilmington, Del., Jan. 26, 1947; m. Constance Ann Evanisko, Apr. 20, 1969; children: Alexandra, Stephanie, Christopher. Grad. summa cum laude, Saviour Sem., 1969; grad. with high honors, St. Vincent Coll., 1972; attended, U. Pitts. Ordained to Diaconate and Priesthood, 1969. Assigned St. John's Ch., Ligonier, Pa., 1969-72, St. Stephen's Ch., Latrobe, Pa., 1969-72, St. John's Ch., Rahway, N.J., 1972-76; dir. Camp Nazareth, diocesan dir. youth, 1976-86; dean Christ the Saviour Sem.; elevated to dignity of Very Rev., 1985; assoc. pastor Christ the Saviour Cathedral; sec. to bishop, instr. homiletics and parish administrn.; diocesan chancellor Am. Carpatho-Russian Orthodox Diocese, 1990—; chaplain Ea. Orthodox residents Polk Ctr., Commonwealth Pa., established chapel; sr. spiritual advisor A.C.R.Y. Assoc. editor The Ch. Messenger. Office: 312 Garfield St Johnstown PA 15906-2122

MILOSH, EUGENE JOHN, international trade association executive; b. N.Y.C., Nov. 18, 1933; s. John Peter and Natalie (Stack) M.; children: Wendy, Dara. AB, Dickinson Coll., 1955; postgrad. in acctg., U. N.C., 1957; MA in Internat. Econ., New Sch. for Social Rsch., 1962. Mgr. market devel. Union Carbide Corp., Danbury, Conn., 1957-73; v.p. US-USSR Trade and Econ. Coun., N.Y.C., 1973-80; pres. Am. Assn. Exporters and Importers, N.Y.C., 1980—; adv. bd. World Trade Inst., N.Y.C., 1982—; mem. adv. com. Com. on Customs Ops., Dept. Treasury, Washington, 1987—, Com. on Retailing, Dept. Commerce, Washington, 1986—; mem. steering com. Retail Industry Trade Action Com., Wshington, 1988—; Congl. testimony on trade related matters. Contbr. articles to profl. jours. 1st Lt. M.I., 1955-57. Mem. Chem. Assn. Execs. Coun. (steering com.). Republican. Episcopalian. Avocations: writing, home repair, tennis, sailing. Home: 145 Jonathan Rd New Canaan CT 06840-2117 Office: American Assn of Exporters And Importers 11 W 42nd St New York NY 10036-8002

MILOSZ, CZESLAW, poet, author, educator; b. Lithuania, June 30, 1911; came to U.S., 1960, naturalized, 1970; s. Aleksander and Weronika (Kunat) M. M Juris, U. Wilno, Lithuania, 1934; LittD (hon.), U. Mich., 1977; honoris causa, Brandeis U., 1985, Harvard U., 1989, Jaqellonian U., Poland, 1989, U. Rome, Italy, 1992. Programmer Polish Nat. Radio, 1935-39; diplomatic service Polish Fgn. Affairs Ministry, Warsaw, 1945-50; vis. lectr. U. Calif., Berkeley, 1960-61; prof. Slavic langs. and lits. U. Calif., 1961-78, prof. emeritus, 1978—. Author: The Captive Mind, 1953, Native Realm, 1968, Post-War Polish Poetry, 1965, The History of Polish Literature, 1969, Selected Poems, 1972, Bells in Winter, 1978, The Issa Valley, 1981, Separate Notebooks, 1984, The Land of Ulro, 1984, The Unattainable Earth, 1985, Collected Poems, 1988, Provinces, 1991, Beginning With My Streets, 1992, A Year of the Hunter, 1994, Facing the River, 1995. Recipient Prix Littéraire Européen Les Guildes du Livre, Geneva, 1953, Neustadt Internat. prize for lit. U. Okla., 1978, citation U. Calif., Berkeley, 1978, Nobel prize for lit., 1980, Nat. Medal of Arts, 1990; Nat. Culture Fund fellow, 1934-35; Guggenheim fellow, 1976. Mem. AAAS, Am. Acad. Arts and Scis., Am. Acad and Inst. Arts and Letters, Polish Inst. Letters and Scis. in Am., PEN Club in Exile. Office: U Calif Dept Slavic Langs Lits Berkeley CA 94720

MILSOM, ROBERT CORTLANDT, banker; b. Butler, Pa., Dec. 15, 1924; s. Robert C. and M. Ethel (Leyland) M. BS, John Carroll U., 1948. With PNC Bank (formerly Pitts. Nat. Bank), 1948-90; asst. sec., asst. cashier customer relations div. PNC Bank, 1953-56, asst. v.p. loan div., 1956-60, v.p. charge comml. loan group, 1960-65, sr. v.p. charge comml. banking div., 1965-68, exec. v.p., 1968-72, pres., 1972-85, chmn., CEO, 1985-90, also bd. dirs., 1972—; vice chmn., dir. PNC Bank Corp, 1972-90; bd. dirs. PNC Bank N.A., PNC Equity Mgmt. Corp., Exec. Svc. Corps., Foxwall Med. Svc.; chmn. bd. trustees Mercy Hosp. Pitts., 1994—. Bd. dirs. Pitts. Mercy Health System, Inc., Pitts. Ballet Theatre, Regional Indsl. Devel. Corp.; hon. trustee John Carroll U., Cleve.; mem. adv. bd. Mon Valley Renaissance program California U. Pa. Mem. Duquesne Club of Pitts., Fox Chapel Golf Club of Pitts., Laurel Valley Golf Club, Rolling Rock Club. Office: PNC Bank 5th Ave & Wood St Pittsburgh PA 15222

MILSOME, DOUGLAS, cinematographer. Cinematographer: (TV movies) Family of Spies, Hollywood Detective, Spies, Diana: Her True Story, Following the Heart, TV mini-series) Great Expectations, Dirty Dozen, Lonesome Dove, Lonesome Dove II-The Return, Old Curiosity Shop, Buffalo Girls, (cable movie) Seasons of the Heart, (films) Race for the Yankee Zephyr, Wild Horses, Full Metal Jacket (British Critics Cir. award 1987, Oscar nomination 1987), Hawks, The Beast, Desperate Hours, If Looks Could Kill-Teenagent, Robin Hood-Prince of Thieves, Last of the Mohicans, Sunset Grill, Body of Evidence, Rumpelstulskin, Sunchaser. Office: Smith/ Gosnell/Nicholson & Assoc PO Box 1166 1515 Palisades Dr Pacific Palisades CA 90272

MILSTED, AMY, medical educator. BSEd, Ohio State U., 1967; PhD, CUNY, 1977. Lectr. Hunter Coll./CUNY, 1970-76; instr. Carnegie-Mellon U., Pitts., 1976-77; postdoctoral fellow Muscular Dystrophy Assn./Carnegie-Mellon U., Pitts., 1978-79; rsch. assoc. Case Western Res. U., Cleve., 1979-82; rsch. chemist VA Med. Ctr., Cleve., 1982-87; project staff The Cleve. Clin. Found., 1987-89; asst. staff dept. brain and vascular rsch. Cleve. Clinic Found., 1989-93; grad. faculty Sch. Biomed. Scis. Kent (Ohio) State U., 1989-93, grad. faculty, 1995—; assoc. prof. dept. biology U. Akron, Ohio, 1993—; adj. faculty biology dept. Cleve. State U., 1991—. Contbr. articles to profl. jours. Mem. Am. Heart Assn., Am. Soc. Cell Biology, Am. Chem. Soc., Endocrine Soc., AAAS. Office: 302 Buchtel Commons Akron OH 44325

MILSTEIN, ALBERT, lawyer; b. Germany, Dec. 29, 1946. BA magna cum laude, Yeshiva U., 1969; JD, U. Chgo., 1972. Bar: Ill. 1972. Ptnr. Winston & Strawn, Chgo. Mem. Chgo. Bar Assn., Ill. State Bar Assn. Office: Winston & Strawn 35 W Wacker Dr Chicago IL 60601-1614*

MILSTEIN, ELLIOTT STEVEN, legal educator, academic administrator; b. Hartford, Conn., Oct. 19, 1944; s. Samuel M. and Mildred K. Milstein; m. Bonnie Myrun, Oct. 1, 1967 (div. Oct. 1992); 1 child, Jacob. BA, U. Hartford, 1966; JD, U. Conn., 1969; LLM, Yale U., 1971. Bar: Conn. 1969, D.C. 1972, U.S. Dist. Ct. Conn. 1969, U.S. Ct. Appeals (D.C.) 1972. Lectr. in law U. Conn. Clin. Program. 1969-70; staff atty. New Haven Legal Assistance Assn., 1971-72; asst. prof. law, dir. clin. programs Washington coll. law Am. U., 1972-74, assoc. prof., dir. clin. programs, 1974-77, prof., dir. clin. programs, 1977-88, interim dean, 1988-90, dean, 1990—, assoc. dean Law Sch., 1977-78, interim pres., 1993-94; dean. Washington Coll. Law Am. Univ., 1994-95, prof. law, 1995—; co-dir. Nat. Vets. Law Ctr., 1978-84; cons. Calif. Bar Bd. of Bar Admissions, Nat. Conf. of Bar Examiners, lawyer tng. Practising Law Inst., N.Y.C.; chmn. D.C. Law Students in Ct. Program, 1982-83; mem. Law Tchrs. for Legal Svcs. Bd. dirs. Alliance for Justice, 1996—. Ford Urban Law fellow, 1971-72. Mem. Soc. Am. Law Tchrs., Assn. Am. Law Schs. (chmn. sect. clin. edn. 1982, mem. accreditation com. 1984-86, chmn. standing com. clin. edn. 1993—, exec. com. 1996—), ABA (skills tng. com. 1983-85, govt. rels. com. 1992—), ACLU. Democrat. Home: 3216 Brooklawn Ct Bethesda MD 20815-3941 Office: Am U Washington Coll Law 4400 Massachusetts Ave NW Washington DC 20016-8001

MILSTEIN, LAURENCE BENNETT, electrical engineering educator, researcher; b. Bklyn., Oct. 28, 1942; s. Harry and Sadie (Kaplan) M.; m. Suzanne Barbara Hirschman, Oct. 3, 1969; children—Coreen Roxanne, Renair Marissa. B.E.E., CUNY, 1964; M.S.E.E., Poly. Inst. Bklyn., 1966, Ph.D. in Elec. Engring., 1968. Mem. tech. staff Hughes Aircraft Co., El Segundo, Calif., 1968-69, staff engr., 1969-72, sr. staff engr., 1972-74; asst. prof. Rensselaer Poly. Inst., Troy, N.Y., 1974-76; asst. prof. U. Calif.-San Diego, La Jolla, 1976-79, assoc. prof., 1979-82, prof. elec. engring., 1982—, chmn. dept., 1984-88; cons. Hughes Aircraft Co., Culver City, Calif., 1976-78, Lockheed Missiles & Space Co., Sunnyvale, Calif., 1978-93, Motorola Satellite Comm., 1992—, InterDigital Comm. Corp, 1992—, various govt. agys., pvt. cos., 1975—. Co-editor: Tutorials in Modern Communications, 1983; Spread Spectrum Communications, 1983; contbr. articles to profl. jours. Recipient Outstanding Tchr. award Warren Coll., U. Calif.-San Diego, La Jolla, 1982; grantee Army Rsch. Office, 1977-80, 81-84, 86-89, 91-94, 95—, Office of Naval Rsch., Arlington, Va., 1982—, TRW, San Diego, 1983-89, 92-95, NSF, 1993—. Fellow IEEE, IEEE Coms. Soc. (bd. govs. 1983, 85-87, 93-95, v.p. for tech. activities 1990-91), IEEE Info. Theory Soc. (bd. govs. 1989-94). Jewish. Office: U Calif-San Diego Dept Elec and Computer Engring La Jolla CA 92093

MILSTEIN, MONROE GARY, retail executive; b. N.Y.C., Jan. 14, 1927; s. Abe Herman and Ann Ethel (Isaacs) M.; m. Henrietta Haas, Dec. 22, 1949; children—Lazer, Andrew, Stephen. B.S., NYU, 1946. Pres. Monroe G. Milstein Inc., N.Y.C., 1947—; chmn. bd., pres., chief exec. officer Burlington Coat Factory Warehouse Corp., N.J., 1972—; dir. Fidelity Bank & Trust Co. of N.J., 1972—. Trustee, pres. bd. Long Beach Pub. Library, N.Y., 1967-76; pres. bd. trustees Nassau Library System, Roosevelt Field, N.Y., 1971-73. Recipient Man of Yr. awards Coat and Suit Buyers Assn., 1984, Long Beach C. of C., Youth Service award B'nai B'rith. Mem. Am. Gen. Mdse. Assn., U.S. C. of C. Jewish. Clubs: Dads (Long Beach) (pres. 1969). Lodge: B'nai B'rith (v.p. 1960-62). Avocations: fishing; reading; music. *

MILSTEIN, RICHARD SHERMAN, lawyer; b. Westfield, Mass., May 9, 1926; s. Abraham and Sarah (Yudman) M. BA, Harvard U., 1948; JD, Boston U., 1952. Bar: Mass. 1952, U.S. Supreme Ct. 1959. Ptnr. Ely & King, Springfield, Mass., 1954-95, Chaplin & Milstein, Boston, 1984-91; of counsel Robinson, Donovan, Madden & Barry P.C., Springfield, 1995—; dir. Mass. Continuing Legal Edn., 1969-80; cons. dir., 1980—. Commr. Springfield Parking Authority, 1984-90; trustee Comty. Music Sch., Springfield, 1994-96, Springfield Symphony Orch., 1995—, Springfield Libr. Mus. Assn.; overseer Mass. Supreme Jud. Ct. Hist. Soc., 1995—; trustee, life mem. Sta. WGBY-TV, pub. TV, Springfield; mem. adv. com. Springfield Fine Art Mus., 1988—, chmn., 1988-90; trustee Baystate Hosp., v.p., 1995—; vice chmn. Westfield Acad.; chmn. Horace Smith Fund, 1977-93. Lt. comdr. USCGR, 1952-64. Fellow Am. Coll. Trust and Estate Counsel, Mass. Bar Found. (life); mem. Am. Law Inst. (life), Am. Bar Found. (life). Home: 47 Mattoon St Springfield MA 01105-1715 Office: Robinson Donovan et al 1500 Main St Springfield MA 01115 also: Mass Continuing Legal Edn 10 Winter Pl Boston MA 02108-4751

MILSTEN, DAVID RANDOLPH, lawyer; b. Coalgate, Okla., Sept. 29, 1903; s. Morris and Etta (Goldstein) M.; m. Minnie Gottlieb, Nov. 16, 1930 (dec. June 1991); children: Donald E., Suzanne Parelman. BA, U. Okla., 1925, LLB, 1928; postgrad., Yale Law Sch., 1926. Bar: Okla. 1928. Practiced in Tulsa, 1928—; asst. county atty. Tulsa County, 1930-32. Author: An Appreciation of Will Rogers, 1935, Howdy Folks (Official State of Okla. poem about Will Rogers), 1938; (poetry) Before My Night, 1962, The Morning After, 1968, Thomas Gilcrease, 1969, Will Rogers, The Cherokee Kid, 1987. Pub. spkr., lectr.; founder, chmn. Benevolent and Welfare Fund and conceived establishment of Juvenile Ct. of Tulsa County, 1934; mem. Will Rogers Commn. Okla., 1978-93; chmn. bd. Tulsa Salvation Army, 1954-55; pres. Tulsa Opera, 1953-55, bd. dirs., 1951—; pres. Thoms Gilcrease Inst. Am. History and Art, Tulsa, 1967-68, chmn. bd., 1969-70, bd. dirs., 1954-72, life bd. dirs. emeritus, 1972—. Recipient Commendation Okla. Hist. Soc., Disting. Svc. award Okla. Heritage Assn. for State of Okla., 1990; inductee Hall of Fame, Tulsa Hist. Soc., 1994. Mem. Sigma Alpha Mu (nat. historian, past supreme prior). Jewish (bd. dirs., past pres. Temple Israel, hon. life pres.), Mason (33 deg., past potentate, Shriner). Home and Office: 3905 S Florence Pl Tulsa OK 74105-3731 *Throughout my adolescent and adult life my credo has been that there is no right way to do a wrong thing and there is no wrong way to do a right thing, and there is no compromise with efficiency.*

MILSTEN, ROBERT B., lawyer; b. Tulsa, Nov. 6, 1932; s. Travis I. and Regina (Jankowsky) M.; m. Jane Herskowitz, June 24, 1956; children: Stuart Paul, Leslie Jane. B.S., Ind. U., 1954; LL.B., U. Okla., 1956; postgrad., So. Meth. U., 1959. Bar: Okla. 1956, U.S. Ct. of Appeals 1956, U.S. Tax Ct 1956. Practiced in Oklahoma City, 1962—; govt. atty. Office Chief Counsel, IRS, 1958-62; atty. Fuller, Smith, Mosburg & Davis, 1962-63; atty. Andrews, Davis, Legg, Bixler, Milsten & Price, Inc. (and predecessor firm), 1964—, mem. firm, 1966—, dir., 1977-82; mem. S.W. region IRS/Bar Liaison Com., 1994—. Past pres., trustee Temple B'nai Israel. Served as lt., JAGC USAF, 1956-58. Mem. ABA (com. civil and criminal tax penalties sect. taxation 1962—), Okla. Bar Assn., Oklahoma County Bar Assn., Fed. Bar Assn. (2d v.p. local chpt. 1976), Econ. Club Okla., Quail Creek Golf and Country Club, Men's Dinner Club , Phi Delta Phi (treas. 1955-56). Office: 500 W Main St Oklahoma City OK 73102-2220

MILTON, CATHERINE HIGGS, public service entrepreneur; b. N.Y.C., Jan. 6, 1943; d. Edgar Homer and Josephine (Doughty) Higgs; m. A. Fenner Milton (div.); m. Thomas F. McBride, Aug. 25, 1974; children: Raphael McBride, Luke McBride. BA, Mt. Holyoke Coll., 1964, PhD (hon.), 1992. Reporter, travel writer Boston Globe, 1964-68; with Internat. Assn. Chiefs Police, Washington, 1968-70; asst. dir. Police Found., Washington, 1970-75; spl. asst. U.S. Treasury Dept., Washington, 1977-80; project staff Spl. Com. Aging/Senate, Washington, 1980-81; spl. asst. to pres., founder/exec. dir. Stanford (Calif.) U. Haas Ctr. for Public, 1981-91; exec. dir. Commn. for Nat. and Cmty. Svc., Washington, 1991-93; v.p. Corp. for Nat. Svc., Washington, 1993-95; exec. dir. Presidio Leadership Ctr., 1995-96; exec. dir. U.S. Programs Save the Children, Westport, Conn., 1996—; mem. U.S. Atty. General's Task Force on Family Violence, 1981-82; chair nat. forum Kellogg Found., 1990. Author: Women in Policing, 1972, Police Use of Deadly Force, 1976; co-author: History of Black Americans, 1965, Team Policing, Little Sisters and the Law, 1970. Bd. mem. Youth Svc. Calif., L.A., 1986-91, Trauma Found., San Francisco, 1982-90; spl. advisor Campus Compact, 1986-91. Nat. Kellogg Found. fellow, Battle Creek, Mich., 1985-88; recipient Dedication and Outstanding Efforts award Bd. Suprs., Santa Clara, Calif., 1989, Outstanding Vol. Contbn. award Strive for Five, San Francisco, 1991, Dinkelspiel award Stanford U., 1991; named Outstanding Campus Adminstr. COOL, 1987. Avocations: backpacking, skiing, hiking, travel. Home: 837 Cedro Way Stanford CA 94305-1034 Office: Save the Children Presidio Leadership Ctr PO Box 950 Westport CT 06881

MILTON, CHAD EARL, lawyer; b. Brevard County, Fla., Jan. 29, 1947; s. Rex Dale and Mary Margaret (Peacock) M.; m. Ann Mitchell Bunting, Mar. 30, 1972; children: Samuel, Kathleen, Kelsey. BA, Colo. Coll., 1969; JD, U. Colo., 1974; postgrad., U. Mo., 1976-77. Bar: Colo. 1974, Mo. 1977, U.S. Dist. Ct. Colo. 1974, U.S. Dist. Ct. (we. dist.) Mo. 1977. Counsel Office of Colo. State Pub. Defender, Colo. Springs, 1974-76; pub. info. officer, counsel Mid-Am. Arts Alliance, Kansas City, Mo., 1977-78; claims counsel Employers Reinsurance Corp., Kansas City, Mo., 1978-80; sr. v.p., asst. gen. counsel Media/Profl. Ins., Kansas City, Mo., 1981—; reporter, photographer, editor Golden (Colo.) Daily Transcript, 1970; investigator, law clk. Office of Colo. State Pub. Defender, Denver, Golden, 1970-74; assoc. Gage, Tucker, Hodges, Kreamer, Kelly & Varner (now Lathrop & Gage), Kansas City, 1973; participant Annenberg Project on the Reform of Libel Laws, Washington, 1987-88; adj. prof., comm. and advt. law Webster U., 1989-93; lectr. in field. Pres. bd. dirs. Folly Theater, 1992-94. Mem. ABA (chair intellectual property law com. of the torts and ins. practice sect., forum com. on comm. law), Mo. Bar Assn., Kansas City Met. Bar Assn., Libel Def. Resource Ctr. (editorial bd., exec. com.). Avocations: tennis, golf, skiing, sailing, antique maps. Home: 8821 Alhambra St Shawnee Mission KS 66207-2357 Office: Media/Profl Ins 2 Pershing Sq 2300 Main St Ste 800 Kansas City MO 64108-2415

MILTON, CHRISTIAN MICHEL, insurance executive; b. London, Nov. 13, 1947; came to U.S., 1978; s. Frank Harry and Gismonde Marie Susini; m. Rana Nikpour, Mar. 31, 1985. Claims clk. Stewart Smith Co., London, 1966-67; mgr. reins. claims Henry Head & Co., London, 1967-73; asst. v.p. reins. div. Airco, Hamilton, Bermuda, 1974-78, Nat. Union Fire Ins. Co., Pitts., 1980-81; asst. v.p. reins. div. Am. Internat. Group Inc., N.Y.C., 1978-80, 81-85, v.p. reins. div., 1985—; bd. dirs. Nat. Union Fire Ins. Co., N.Y.C., Am. Home Ins. Co., N.Y.C.; lectr. reins. Ins. Soc. N.Y., 1988—. Avocation: reading. Office: Am Internat Group Inc 70 Pine St New York NY 10270-0002

MILTON, JOHN CHARLES DOUGLAS, nuclear physicist; b. Regina, Sask., Can., June 1, 1924; s. William and Frances Craigie (McDowall) M.; m. Gwendolyn Margaret Shaw, Oct. 10, 1953; children: Bruce F., Leslie J.F., Neil W.D., Theresa M. A.M. in Music, U. Man., 1943, B.Sc. with honors, 1947; M.A., Princeton U., 1949, Ph.D. in Physics, 1951. Asst. research officer Atomic Energy Can., Ltd., Chalk River, Ont., 1951-57; assoc. research officer Atomic Energy Can., Ltd., 1957-62, sr. research officer, 1962-70, prin. research officer, 1970—, head nuclear physics br., 1967-83, dir. physics div., 1983-85, v.p. physics and health scis., 1986-90, researcher emeritus, 1990—; vis. scientist Lawrence Berkeley Lab., 1960-62, Centre de Recherches, Strasbourg & Bruyeres-le-Chatel, 1975-76; chmn. nuclear physics grants Natural Sci. and Engring. Research Council, 1977-82. Fellow Royal Soc. Can., Am. Phys. Soc.; mem. Can. Assn. Physicists (pres. 1992). Home: 3 Alexander Pl, Deep River, ON Canada K0J 1P0 Office: Chalk River Nuclear Lab, Chalk River, ON Canada K0J 1J0

MILTON, JOSEPH PAYNE, lawyer; b. Richmond, Va., Oct. 24, 1943; s. Hubert E. and Grace C. M.; children: Michael Payne, Amy Barrett, David King.; m. Cela Cabler Milton, Apr. 8, 1989. BS in Bus. Adminstrn., U. Fla., 1967, JD, 1969. Bar: Fla. 1969, U.S. Ct. Appeals (5th cir.) 1971, U.S. Supreme Ct. 1972, U.S. Ct. Appeals (11th cir.) 1981. Assoc. Toole, Taylor, Moseley & Gabel, Jacksonville, 1969-70; ptnr. Toole, Taylor, Moseley, Gabel & Milton, Jacksonville, 1971-78, Howell, Liles, Braddock & Milton, Jacksonville, 1978-89; Milton & Leach, Jacksonville, 1990-95; Milton, Leach & D'Andrea, Jacksonville, 1996—. Mem. Mayor's Blue Ribbon Task Force; pres. Civic Round Table of Jacksonville, 1980-81; campaign chmn. NE Fla. chpt. March of Dimes, 1973-74, v.p., 1974-75; pres. Willing Hands, 1974-75; chmn. attys.' div. United Way, 1977; mem. exec. com. Jacksonville Area Legal Aid, Inc., 1982-83; mem. Law Center Coun., U. Fla. Coll. Law, 1972-78; chmn. pvt. bar involvement com. Legal Aid Bd. dirs., 1982-83. Recipient Outstanding Service award for Individual Contbns. in Support of Legal Services for the Poor, 1981. Fellow Am. Bar Found., Internat. Soc. Barristers; mem. ABA, Am. Bd. Trial Advocates (charter, pres.-elect Jacksonville chpt. 1996), Jacksonville Bar Assn. (pres. 1980-81, pres. young lawyers sect. 1974-75), Fla. Bar (4th jud. cir. nominating comm. 1980-82, grievance com. 1975-77, chmn. 1976, mem. exec. coun. for trial sect. 1982—, chmn.-elect 1986-87, chmn. voluntary bar liaison com. 1982-83, bd. govs. 1988-90), Jacksonville Assn. Def. Counsel (pres. 1981-82, lectr. CLE programs, guest lectr. U. Fla., NARTC), Fla. Coun. Bar Assn. Pres. (exec. com. 1982-88, v.p. 1984, pres. 1985-86), Nat. Assn. R.R. Trial Counsel (v.p. southeastern region 1984-86, exec. com. 1979—, pres. elect 1989-90, pres. 1990-91), Maritime Law Assn. U.S., Acad. Fla. Trial Lawyers, Assn. Trial Lawyers Am., Judicature Soc. Republican. Clubs: San Jose Country (Jacksonville), University, Gulf Life Tower (Jacksonville). Home: 4655 Corrientes Cir N Jacksonville FL 32217 Office: Milton Leach & D'Andrea 1660 Prudential Dr Ste 200 Jacksonville FL 32207-8185

MILTON, RICHARD HENRY, retired diplomat, children's advocate; b. Bowling Green, Ky., Sept. 30, 1938; s. Lester Thomas and Rose Ann (Jesse) M.; m. Evy M. Miller, Aug. 28, 1964; children: Christopher, Ann. Student, W.Va. U., 1956-57; BA, Marshall U., 1960, MA, 1964. Tchr. Columbus, Ohio, 1960-61; tchr. Sidney, Ohio, 1964-65; fgn. svc. officer U.S. Dept. State, Washington, 1965-94; dep. asst. dir. ACDA, Washington, 1982-83; consul gen. U.S. consulate gen., Guayaquil, Ecuador, 1984-87; polit. advisor U.S. Space Command, Peterson AFB, Colo., 1987-90, 92-94; v.p. Am. Fgn. Svc. Assn., U.S. Dept. State, Washington, 1990-91; vis. prof. USCG Acad., New London, Conn., 1979-81. Pres. Community Welfare Assn., Warsaw, Poland, 1975; mem. gifted edn. com. Ledyard Pub. Schs., Conn., 1980. Served to 1st lt. U.S. Army, 1961-63. Congl. fellow Am. Polit. Sci. Assn., 1974-75. Mem. Am. Fgn. Svc. Assn., Consular Officers Assn. (pres. 1983-84), Sr. Fgn. Svc. Assn. Avocation: antique automobiles. Home: 2022 Devon St Colorado Springs CO 80909-1618

MILTON, ROBERT MITCHELL, chemical company executive; b. St. Joseph, Mich., Nov. 29, 1920; s. Clare Leon and Frances Thornton (Mitchell) M.; m. Mary Wills Bridges, June 22, 1946; children: Mrs. M. Gillian Sanders (dec.), Mrs. Suzanne M. Padilla, David Wills. B.A., Oberlin Coll., 1941; M.A., Johns Hopkins U., 1943, Ph.D., 1944. C.Y. War Project Johns Hopkins U., Balt., 1943-45, rsch. assoc., 1945-46; with Union Carbide Corp., 1946-85, rsch. chemist, 1946-51, rsch. supr., 1951-54, mgr. devel. lab., 1954-58, asst. mgr. new products, 1958-59, asst. dir., then dir. rsch. Linde div., 1959-73, exec. v.p. Showa UNOX, Showa Union Gosei div., 1973-77, dir. agrl. bus. devel., v.p. Keystone Seed Co. div., 1977-79; assoc. corp. dir. product safety and liability Union Carbide Corp., Danbury, Conn., 1980-85; pres. R. Milton Assocs., Inc., 1986—; cons. U.S. Naval Tech. Mission to Europe, 1945; mem. adv. bd. hyperbaric medicine SUNY, 1966-73; mem. NRC panel on environ. protection, safety and hazardous materials of Com. on Chem. Engrng. Frontiers, 1985-87. Inventor Linde molecular sieve adsorbents and catalysts, hi-flux tubing; patentee in field. Mem. AAAS, Am. Chem. Soc. (Jacob F. Schoellkopf medal 1963), Am. Inst. Chemists (dir.-at-large 1982-87, pres. elect 1988-89, pres. 1990-91, chmn. bd. dirs. 1992-93, Chem. Pioneer award 1980), Wawashkamo Golf Club (pres. emeritus), Mackinac Island Yacht Club, Johns Hopkins Club, Phi Beta Kappa, Sigma Xi. Home and Office: # 310 19800 US Hwy # 1 Tequesta FL 33469 also: PO Box 326 Mackinac Island MI 49757-0326

MILUM-WOOD, JOAN, hospital administrator; b. Miami, Fla., Nov. 25, 1937; d. James R. and Ruth K. (Still) Worline; married; children: Jenine M. Milum Weaver, Elizabeth J. Milum Eddington. BSN, Capital U., 1959. Cert. nursing adminstr. advanced. Dir. nursing Wyandot Manor ECR, Upper Sandusky, Ohio; asst. dir. nursing Lima (Ohio) Meml. Hosp.; v.p. nursing Candler Gen. Hosp, Savannah, Ga., Gwinnett Hosp. System, Lawrenceville, Ga.; dir. comty. outreach, parish nurse programs Promina Gwinnett Hosp. Sys.; Appt. by Gov. Joe Frank Harris Access to Health Care Commn., 1989-90. Mem. Ga. Orgn. Nurse Exec., Am. Holistic Nurses Assn., Health Ministry Assn. (greater Atlanta area pres.). Home: 3703 Madrid Cir Norcross GA 30092-4542

MILUNAS, J. ROBERT, health care organization executive; b. Aug. 7, 1947; s. Joseph John M.; m. Glenetta Graham; children: Amy, Joseph, Anna Kate. BS, Tulane U., 1969; postgrad., Samford U., 1973; MBA, Ga. State U., 1977. Mgr. internal and govt. reporting, corp. contr.'s staff Arvin Industries Inc., Columbus, Ind., 1977-80; mgr. consol. acctg., corp. contr.'s staff Mattel Inc., Hawthorne, Calif., 1980-82; asst. contr. Times Mirror Cable TV Inc., Irvine, Calif., 1982-83; Western Div. contr. SCA, Santa Ana, Calif., 1983-84; v.p., corp. contr. Tchrs. Mgmt. Investment Corp., Newport Beach, Calif., 1984-86; v.p., chief fin. officer Beech St. Inc., Irvine, 1987-89; v.p. fin. and adminstrn. ConsumerHealth Inc., Newport Beach, Calif., 1989-93; pres. Aegis Consulting Svcs., Laguna Niguel, Calif., 1993—. 1st lt. U.S. Army Transp. Corps., 1969-71. Decorated Bronze Star. Home: 28331 Las Cabos Laguna Niguel CA 92677 *Life is a precious gift to be nurtured daily through interaction with friends and family and helping others achieve their potential.*

MIMS, ROBERT PRICE, air force officer; b. Canton, Miss., Sept. 9, 1946; s. Robert Percy and Virginia (Price) M.; m. Diane Dotson, Apr. 12, 1969; 1 child, Robert David. BS in Indsl. Engring., Miss. State U., 1969; MS in Opts. Mgmt., U. Ark., 1977. Lic. comml. pilot FAA. Indsl. engr., 1968-70; commd. USAF, 1970—, advanced through grades to col.; tactical airlift dir. Hdqrs. Mil. Airlift Command, Scott AFB, Ill., 1979-84; officer US Pacific Command, Camp Smith, Hawaii, 1984-87; ops. officer 772 Tactical Airlift Squadron, Dyess AFB, Tex., 1987-89, comdr., 1989-91; commandant USAF Air Mobility Sch., Scott AFB, 1991-93; chief strategic planning and doctrine divsn. Directorate of Plans, Hdqrs. Air Mobility Command, Scott AFB, 1993—. Decorated Air Force Commendation medal. Mem. Air Force Assn., Tanker Airlift Assn., Jaycees, Order of Ark., Daedeleons. Baptist. Avocations: physical fitness, tennis. Home: 1102 Elisabeth Dr O'Fallon IL 62269

MIMS, WILLIAM CLEVELAND, state legislator, lawyer; b. Harrisonburg, Va., June 20, 1957; s. David Lathan and Lurleen Shirley (Stovall) M.; m. Jane Ellen Rehme, Dec. 20, 1980; children: Katherine Grace, Emily Anne, Sarah Joy. AB, Coll. of William & Mary, 1979; JD, George Washington U., 1984; LLM, Georgetown U., 1986. Bar: Va. Legis. asst. Congressman Paul Trible, Washington, 1981-82; dep. legis. dir. Senator Paul Trible, Washington, 1983-85; chief of staff Congressman Frank Wolf, Washington, 1986-87; atty. Hazel & Thomas, P.C., Leesburg, Va., 1987-91, Worcester, Mims & Atwill, P.C., Leesburg, 1993—; mem. Va. Gen. Assembly, Richmond, 1991—; Va. Housing Study Commn., 1994—. Bd. dirs. Dulles Area Transp. Assn., Herndon, Va., 1994—, Marshall Home Preservation Fund, Leesburg, 1992—, Youth for Tomorrow, 1995—; treas., bd. dirs. Loudoun Bar Assn., Leesburg, 1988-89; chmn. Loudoun Rep. Com., Leesburg, 1988-91; dist. rep. Nat. Eagle Scout Assn., 1992—. Recipient commendation Com. for Dulles, 1986; named outstanding local chmn. Rep. Party of Va. 1991, Flemming fellow, 1995-96. Mem. Va. Bar Assn., Va. Trial Lawyers Assn., Christian Legal Soc., Loudoun C. of C. Republican. Episcopalian. Office: Worcester Mims & Atwill PC PO Drawer 741 Leesburg VA 22075-2820

MIN, NANCY-ANN, federal agency administrator; b. Rockwood, Tenn.. BA with highest honors, U. Tenn.; BA in Politics and Econs., Balliol Coll.; MA in Polits. and Econs., Oxford U.; JD, Harvard U., 1983. Staff asst. Sarah Weddington, Pres. Carter's Asst. for Polit. Liaison; jud. intern to Mark Cannon Adminstrv. Asst. to Chief Justice Warren Burger Supreme Ct.; law clk. Chief Judge Gilbert Merritt, U.S. Ct. Appeals 6th Cir.; comml. litigation ptnr. Bass, Berry & Sims, Nashville; cabinet mem. Commr. of the Dept. Human Svcs., Tenn.; lawyer Covington & Burling, Washington; assoc. dir. health Office of Mgmt. Budget, Washington, 1993—; adj. prof. Vanderbilt U. Office: Health & Personnel Old Executive Ofc Bldg Washington DC 20503

MINAHAN, DANIEL FRANCIS, manufacturing company executive, lawyer; b. Orange, N.J., Dec. 3, 1929; s. Alfred A. and Katherine (Kelly) M.; m. Mary Jean Gaffney, May 2, 1953; children: Daniel F. Jr., John A. AB magna cum laude, U. Notre Dame, 1951; JD magna cum laude, U. Conn., 1964; grad., Advanced Mgmt. Program, Harvard, 1975. Bar: Conn. 1964, U.S. Supreme Ct 1964, U.S. Ct. of Appeals (2d cir.), U.S. Dist. Ct. Conn. 1967. Mgr. indsl. engring. Uniroyal, Inc., Naugatuck, Conn., 1952-59, mgr. indsl. relations, 1959-64; dir. labor relations Uniroyal, Inc., N.Y.C., 1964-66; v.p. indsl. relations and labor counsel Phillips Van Heusen Corp., N.Y.C., 1966-69; v.p. personnel-adminstrn. Broadway-Hale Stores, Inc., Los Angeles, 1969-70; v.p. employee relations, sec. Magnavox-N.Am., Philips Corp., 1970-73, v.p. ops., group exec., 1973-83, sr. v.p. adminstrn., 1984-89, exec. v.p., 1989-93, vice chmn., 1991-93; vice chmn. nat. found. bd. Robert Anderson Sch. Mgmt., U. N.Mex., 1993—; mem. trustees adv. coun., Fairfield U. Coauthor: The Developing Labor Law, 1971. Chmn. bd. Internat. Fedn. Keystone Youth Orgns., London and Chgo., 1984-88; trustee U. Conn. Law Sch.; vice-chmn. nat. found. bd. Anderson Sch. Mgmt., U. N.Mex., 1993—. With USMC. Mem. ABA, Conn. Bar Assn., NAM, Rsch. Inst. Am., Harvard Advanced Mgmt. Assn., Bur. Nat. Affairs, Internat. Platform Assn., Stanford Rsch. Inst. Internat., Washington Internat. Corp. Circle, Harvard Club, Club Internat. (Chgo.), Belfrey Club (London). Office: c/o Office of the Dean U N Mex Robert Anderson Sch Bus Albuquerque NM 87131

MINAHAN, JOHN ENGLISH, author; b. Albany, N.Y., Apr. 30, 1933; s. John English and Constance Madeline (Langdon) M.; m. Verity Ann Hill, Apr. 27, 1966. Student, Cornell U., 1955-57, Harvard U., 1958-59, Columbia U., 1959-60. Staff writer Time mag., 1960-61; chief TV writer J. Walter Thompson Co., N.Y.C., 1961-65; free-lance writer N.Y.C., 1965-73, L.A., 1976-79, Miami, 1981-95; editor, pub. American Way mag., N.Y.C., 1973-76; contbg. editor L.A. mag., 1978-79; dir. corp. comms. The Wackehut Corp., Coral Gables, Fla., 1990-95; free-lance writer Palm Springs, Calif., 1995—; cons. Universal-MCA Inc., 1976-79; instr. novel writing workshop Harvard U. Ctr. Lifelong Learning, 1987-89. Author: (novels) A Sudden Silence, 1963, The Passing Strange, 1965, Jeremy, 1973, Sorcerer, 1977, Nine/Thirty/Fifty-Five, 1977, Almost Summer, 1978, Nunzio, 1978, The Complete American Graffiti, 1979, Eyewitness, 1981, The Great Hotel Robbery, 1982, The Great Diamond Robbery, 1984, Mask, 1985, The Face Behind the Mask, 1986, The Great Pyramid Robbery, 1987, The Great Harvard Robbery, 1988, The Great Grave Robbery, 1989; (biographies) The Dream Collector, 1972, The Quiet American: A Biography of George R. Wackenhut, 1994; translation from French: The Fabulous Onassis, 1972; screenplays: A Sudden Silence, 1965, The Passing Strange, 1979; TV play: First Flight, 1968; contbg. editor book and theater revs., Miami Herald, 1983-95; also articles in N.Y. Times, Saturday Rev., Time-Life Spl. Reports. Recipient Doubleday award, 1960. Mem. Nat. Soc. Lit. and Arts, Alpha Delta Phi. Club: Harvard of Miami, Faculty of Harvard U.

MINAKER, GEORGE, Canadian provincial official; b. Morris, Manitoba, Can.. BSEE, U. Manitoba, 1960. Numerous engring. positions Winnipeg, 1961-84; mem. for Winnipeg-St. James House of Commons, 1984-88; mem. Nat. Transp. Agy., Ottawa, Ont., Can., 1990—; mem. fin. com. House of Commons, energy, mines and resources com. Mem. city coun. St. James, St. James-Assiniboia and Winnipeg, 1967-73; mem. Manitoba Legislative Assembly, St. James, 1973-81, Min. of Cmty. Svcs. and Corrections. Mem. Assn. Profl. Engrs. Ont. and Manitoba. Office: Nat Transp Agy, Ottawa, ON Canada K1A 0N9

MINARD, EVERETT LAWRENCE, III, journalist, magazine editor; b. Seattle, Nov. 19, 1949; s. Everett Lawrence Jr. and Nancy M.; m. Elizabeth Anne Bailey, Sept. 15, 1979. BA in Econs., Trinity Coll., Hartford, Conn., 1972; postgrad., New Sch. for Social Rsch., 1972-74. Reporter, staff writer, mgr. European, West Coast/Asia burs. Forbes mag., 1974-89; mng. editor Forbes mag., N.Y.C., 1989—. Mem. Seattle Yacht Club, Heights Casino Club, Lawrence Beach Club. Office: Forbes Inc 60 5th Ave New York NY 10011-8802

MINARIK, JOSEPH JOHN, economist, researcher; b. Lancaster, Pa., July 27, 1949; s. Joseph John and Helen Elizabeth (Mikus) M.; m. Eileen Marie Dowds; children: Mara Christina, Sara Elizabeth. B.A., Georgetown U., 1971; M.A., Yale U., 1972, M.Phil., 1973, Ph.D., 1974. Rsch. assoc. Brookings Instn., Washington, 1974-81; dept. asst. dir. Congl. Budget Office, Washington, 1981-84; sr. rsch. assoc. Urban Inst., Washington, 1984-88; exec. dir. Joint Econ. Com. U.S. Congress, Washington, 1988-90; exec. dir. for policy, chief economist House Budget Com., 1991-93; assoc. dir. econ. policy Office Mgmt. and Budget, 1993—. Author: Making Tax Choices, 1985, Making America's Budget Policy, 1989; contbr. articles to profl. jours. Fellow NSF, 1971-74, Yale U., 1971. Mem. Am. Econ. Assn., Nat. Tax Assn. Democrat. Home: 11656 Mediterranean Ct Reston VA 22090-3401 Office: Economic Policy 244 Old Executive Bldg Washington DC 20503

MINASI, ANTHONY, software company executive; b. N.Y.C., July 9, 1948; s. Dominic A. and Mary (De Rosa) M.; m. Patricia Ann Gallagher, Oct. 3, 1976; children: Christopher, Marie Elizabeth. BA, Hunter Coll., 1971; MBA with distinction, Pace U., 1982, postgrad., 1988. Bus. analyst Am. Internat. Group, N.Y.C., 1971-75; systems mgr., officer Fiduciary Trust Co., N.Y.C., 1975-79; systems mgr. Flexivan Leasing, N.Y.C., 1979-84; group mgr., v.p. Drexel Burnham, N.Y.C., 1984-89; mng. dir. tech. Vista Concepts, Inc., N.Y.C., 1989-93; sr. prin., mgr. N.Am. investment industry sales/svc. Am. Mgmt. Systems, Inc., N.Y.C., 1994-95; practice mgr. Investment Industry Group, N.Y.C., 1996—. Avocations: photography, tennis, woodworking. Office: American Management Sys 1 Chase Plz New York NY 10005

MINC, HENRYK, mathematics educator; b. Lodz, Poland, Nov. 12, 1919; came to U.S., 1960, naturalized, 1966; s. Izrael and Haja (Zyngler) M.; m. Catherine Taylor Duncan, Apr. 16, 1943; children: Robert Henry, Ralph Edward, Raymond. MA with honors, Edinburgh U. (Scotland), 1955, PhD, 1959. Tchr. Morgan Acad., Dundee, Scotland, 1956-58; lectr. Dundee Tech. Coll., Scotland, 1957-58, U. B.C., Vancouver, Can., 1958-59, asst. prof., 1959-60; assoc. prof. U. Fla., Gainesville, 1960-63; vis. prof. Technion Israel Inst. Tech., Haifa, 1969-80; prof. U. Calif.-Santa Barbara, 1963-90, emeritus, 1990—; referee and reviewer for math. jours. Author: A Survey of Matrix Theory and Matrix Inequalities, 1964, translated into Russian, 1972, Chinese, 1990; Introduction to Linear Algebra, 1965, translated into Spanish, 1968; Modern University Algebra, 1966; Elementary Linear Algebra, 1968, translated into Spanish, 1971; New College Algebra, 1968; Elementary Functions and Coordinate Geometry, 1969; Algebra and Trigonometry, 1970; College Algebra, 1970; College Trigonometry, 1971; Integrated Analytic Geometry and Algebra with Circular Functions, 1973; Permanents, 1978, translated into Russian, 1980, Chinese, 1991; Nonnegative Matrices, 1988, trans. into Chinese, 1991; contbr. over 80 research papers to profl. jours. 2d. lt. Polish Army, 1940-48. France, U.K. Recipient Lester Ford award Math. Assn. Am., 1966, rsch. contract Office Naval Rsch., 1985-88. Air Force Office Sci. Rsch. grantee, 1960-83, Lady Davis fellow, 1975, 78. Fellow Soc. Antiquaries of Scotland; mem. Am. Math Soc., Internat. Linear Algebra Soc., Inst. Antiquity and Christianity, Scottish Soc. Santa Barbara (past chieftain), Scots Lang. Soc., Saltire Soc., Assn. for Scottish Lit. Studies, Coll. of Piping, Burns Fedn., James Hogg Soc., Santa Barbara Elks Lodge, Clan Fraser Soc. N.Am. Democrat. Home: 4076 Naranjo Dr Santa Barbara CA 93110-1213 Office: U Calif Dept Math Santa Barbara CA 93106

MINCER, JACOB, economics educator; b. Tomaszow, Poland, July 15, 1922; came to U.S., 1948; s. Isaac and Dora (Eisen) M.; m. Flora Kaplan, 1951; children—Deborah, Carolyn. B.A., Emory U., 1950; Ph.D., Columbia U., 1957; LLD honoris causa, U. Chgo., 1991. Asst. prof. CUNY, 1954-59; assoc. prof. Columbia U., N.Y.C., 1960-62; prof. econs. Columbia U., 1962—; Mem. research staff Nat. Bur. Econ. Research, N.Y.C., 1960—. Author: Schooling, Experience and Earnings, 1974, Studies in Human Capital, ;882, Studies in Labor Supply, 1993; author, editor: Economic Forecasts and Expectations, 1969. Contbr. numerous articles to profl. publs. Postdoctoral fellow U. Chgo., 1957-58; Guggenheim fellow, N.Y.C., 1971. Fellow Am. Statis. Assn., Econometric Soc., Am. Econ. Assn. (Disting.); mem. Am. Acad. Arts and Scis., Nat. Acad. Edn. Home: 448 Riverside Dr New York NY 10027-6818 Office: Columbia U Dept Econs 118th St at Amsterdam Ave New York NY 10027

MINCHEY, SAMUEL BONE, research scientist; b. Nashville, July 7, 1955; s. Ruth Minchey. BA, U. Tenn., 1973, MS, 1975, PhD, 1978. Postdoctoral fellow NIH, Bethesda, Md., 1978-81; scientist Liposome Co., Princeton, N.J., 1981-83, sr. scientist in animal studies, 1983-85, dir. membrane rsch., 1985-91, exec. dir. rsch., 1991—. Contbr. over 39 articles to profl. jours. Mem. Biophys. Soc., N.Y. Acad. Scis. Democrat. Lutheran. Achievements include 10 U.S. and 12 international patents in field. Office: Liposome Co 1 Research Way Princeton NJ 08540

MINCKLEY, CARLA BETH, lawyer; b. N.Y.C., Mar. 3, 1957; d. Jerome J. and Estelle (Franklin) Landsman; m. Steven D. Minckley, May 10, 1985; children: Taylor F., Amanda K. BA magna cum laude, U. Albany, N.Y., 1979; JD, U. Denver, 1987. Bar: Colo. 1988, U.S. Dist. Ct. Colo. 1988, U.S. Ct. Appeals (10th cir.) 1992. Asst. compliance officer Integrated Resources Equity Corp., Englewood, Colo., 1981-85; law clk. Tallmadge, Tallmadge, Wallace & Hahn, P.C., Denver, 1985-88; assoc. Law Office of Fay Matsukage, Denver, 1988-90, Brega & Winters, P.C., Denver, 1990-95; pvt. practice Englewood, Colo., 1995—. Mem. Colo. Women's Agenda, Denver, 1995, Planned Parenthood Assn., Denver, 1992—, ACLU, Denver, 1992—. Recipient Am. Jurisprudence awards in corps., legislation, trusts and estates, 1986-87. Mem. ABA, Colo. Bar Assn., Denver Bar Assn. Democrat. Avocations: aerobics instruction, skiing, boating. Office: 3470 W Tufts Ave Englewood CO 80110

MINCY, HOMER F., school system administrator. Supt. Upper Arlington (Ohio) City Sch. Dist. State finalist Nat. Supt. Yr. award, 1992. Office: Upper Arlington City Sch Dist 1950 N Mallway Dr Upper Arlington OH 43221-4398

MINDELL, EARL LAWRENCE, nutritionist, author; b. St. Boniface, Man., Can., Jan. 20, 1940; s. William and Minerva Sybil (Galsky) M.; came to U.S., 1965, naturalized, 1972; BS in Pharmacy, N.D. State U., 1963; PhD in Nutrition, Pacific We. U., 1985; m. Gail Andrea Jaffe, May 16, 1971; children: Evan Louis-Ashley, Alanna Dayan. Pres. Adanac Mgmt. Inc., 1979—; instr. Dale Carnegie course; lectr. on nutrition, radio and TV. Mem. Beverly Hills, Rancho Park, Western Los Angeles (dir.) regional chambers commerce, Calif., Am. pharm. assns., Am. Acad. Gen. Pharm. Practice, Am. Inst. for History of Pharmacy, Am. Nutrition Soc., Internat. Coll. Applied Nutrition, Nutrition Found., Nat. Health Fedn., Am. Dieticians Assn., Orthomolecular Med. Assn., Internat. Acad. Preventive Medicine. Clubs: City of Hope, Beverly Hills Rotary, Masons, Shriners. Author: Earl Mindell's Vitamin Bible, Parents Nutrition Bible, Earl Mindell's Quick and Easy Guide to Better Health, Earl Mindell's Pill Bible, Earl Mindell's Shaping Up with Vitamins, Earl Mindell's Safe Eating, Earl Mindell's Herb Bible, Newsletter The Mindell Letter, Mindell's Food as Medicine, Earl Mindell's Soy Miracle, 1995, Anti-Aging Bible, 1996; columnist Let's Live mag., The Vitamin Supplement (Can.), The Vitamin Connection (U.K.), Healthy N' Fit; contbr. articles on nutrition to profl. jours. Home: 244 S El Camino Dr Beverly Hills CA 90212-3809 Office: 107 S Beverly Dr Beverly Hills CA 90212-3020

MINDELL, EUGENE ROBERT, surgeon, educator; b. Chgo., Feb. 24, 1922; s. Leon and Tillie (Rosenthal) M.; m. June A. Abrams, Sept. 19, 1945; children: Barbara, Ruth, David, Douglas. BS, U. Chgo., 1943, MD, 1945. Diplomate Am. Bd. Orthopaedic Surgery (bd. dirs. 1977-84, pres. 1983-84). Resident in orthopaedic surgery U. Chgo. Clinics, 1948-52; instr. U. Chgo., 1952; mem. faculty dept. orthopaedic surgery Sch. Medicine SUNY, Buffalo, 1953—, prof. Sch. Medicine, 1964—; chmn. dept. SUNY Sch. Medicine, Buffalo, 1964-88, dir. orthopaedic oncology Sch. Medicine, 1988—; mem. bd. mgrs. Erie County Med. Ctr., 1990-96. Assoc. editor Jour. Bone and Joint Surgery, 1984-88, trustee, 1991—; contbr. articles to profl. jours. Lt. (j.g.) M.C. USNR, 1946-48. Eugene R. Mindell Chair of Orthopaedic Surgery established in his honor SUNY, Buffalo, 1996; recipient Disting. Svc. award Alumni U. Chgo. Sch. Medicine, 1990; NRC fellow, 1949-50/. Fellow ACS; mem. Am. Acad. Orthopaedic Surgeons (bd. dirs. 1991), Am. Orthopaedic Assn. (v.p. 1990-91), Assn. Orthopaedic Chmn., Am. Assn. Surgery of Trauma, Am. Orthopaedic Rsch. Soc. (pres. 1972-73, residency rev. com. 1985-91), Musculoskeletal Tumor Soc. (pres. 1989-90), Coun. Musculoskeletal Specialty Socs. (chmn. elect 1991, chmn. 1992). Jewish. Home: 85 Depew Ave Buffalo NY 14214-1509 Office: 100 High St Buffalo NY 14203-1126

MINDES, GAYLE DEAN, education educator; b. Kansas City, Mo., Feb. 11, 1942; d. Elton Burnett and Juanita Maxine (Mangold) Taylor; BS, U. Kans., 1964; MS, U. Wis., 1965; EdD, Loyola U., Chgo., 1979; m. Marvin William Mindes, June 20, 1969 (dec.); 1 son, Jonathan Seth. Tchr. pub. schs., Newburgh, N.Y., 1965-67; spl. educator Ill. Dept. Mental Health, Chgo., 1967-69; spl. edn. supr. Evanston (Ill.) Dist. 65 Schs., 1969-74; lectr. Northeastern Ill. U., Chgo., 1974, Loyola U., Chgo., 1974-76, Coll. St. Francis, Joliet, Ill., 1976-79, North Park Coll., Chgo., 1978; cons. Chgo. Head Start, 1978-79; asst. prof. edn. Oklahoma City U., 1979-80; vis. asst. prof., rsch. assoc. Roosevelt U. Coll. Edn., Chgo., 1983-87, prof., dir. R&D, dir. tchr. edn., dir. early childhood, dir. grad. edn. ctr., Roosevelt U. Coll., Albert A. Robin campus, 1993; prof. sch. edn. De Paul U., 1993—, assoc. dean sch. edn., 1996—; chair Roosevelt U. Senate, 1986-89; co-chair ILAEYC Bldg. Bridges; cons. Ill. Resource Ctr., Arts Coun. Oklahoma City, Indian Affairs Commn., 1979-80, Bensenville Pub. Schs., Lincolnwood (Ill.) Pub. Schs., Chgo. Pub. Schs., Atwood Sch. Dist, Chgo. Assn. Retarded Citizens, Nat. Assn. Tech. Tng. Schs., Ill. State Bd. Edn., Itasca Pub. Schs., Decatur Pub. Schs., Robin Scholarship Found., 1982—, Rasho Media, Ill. Facilities Fund for Childcare; alt. rep. faculty coun. Sch. Edn. DePaul U., mem. faculty adv. com. to univ. plan. and info. tech., also mem. panel on grievances, 1995—, mem. comprehensive pers. devel. com., 1995—; mem. tng. sub-com. adv. Ill. Dept. Children & Family Svcs., 1993-95; mem. panel of advisers comprehensive pers. devel. sys. Ill. State Bd. Edn., 1995—; mentor, cons. to partnerships project tng. early intervention svcs. U. Ill., Champaign; early childhood panelist Ill. Initiative for Articulation between Ill. Bd. Higher Edn. and Ill. Cmty. Coll. Bd.; education panelist for Early Childhood Assessment System. Assoc. editor Ill. Sch. R & D; Ill. Div. Early Childhood Edn. Adv. Com. to Ill. Bd. Edn.; co-chair early childhood panelist for early childhood assessment system, Bansenville Pub. Schs.; meditor: Depaul U. Sch. Edn. Newsletter. Co-author: Planning a Theme Based Curriculum for 4's or 5's, 1993, Assessing Young Children, 1996; assoc. editor Jour. Rsch. in Childhood Edn., 1996—; contbr. articles to profl. jours. Bd. dirs. North Side Family Day Care, 1981; northside affiliates Mus. Contemporary Art, 1991-96; trustee Roosevelt U., 1987-93; mem. edn. adv. com. Okla. Dept. Edn., 1979-80; mem. adv. bd. bilingual early childhood program Oakton Community Coll.; mem. adv. bd. early childhood tech. assistance project Chgo. Pub. Schs., Lake View Mental Health, 1986-90; mem. planning com. Lake View Citizens Coun. Day Care Ctr., 1978-79, local planning coun. Ill. Dept. Child and Family Svcs., childcare block grant tng. sub. com.; co-chair Ill. Assn. for Edn. Young Children Building Bridges Project; chmn. teen com. Florence G. Heller JCC, membership com.; mem. adv. bd. Harold Washington Coll. Child Devel., regional tech. assistance grant LICA; mem. parents com. Francis W. Parker Sch. Cerebral Palsy Assn. scholar, 1965; U. Wis. fellow in mental retardation, 1964-65; U. Kans. scholar, 1960. Fellow Am. Orthopsychiat. Assn.; mem. AAUP, ASCD, AAUW, Assn. Children with Learning Disabilities, Nat. Assn. for Edn. Young Children (tchr. edn. bd. 1990—), Am. Ednl. Rsch. Assn., Coun. for Exceptional Children, Ill. Coun. for Exceptional Children (mem. multicultural affairs com. divsn. early childhood), Ill. Assn. for Edn. Young Children, Coun. for Adminstrs. Spl. Edn., Am. Assn. U. Women, Coun. on Children with Behavioral Disorders, Soc. for Rsch. in Child Devel., Foun. for Excellence in Teaching (selection com. Golden Apple 1989-94), Alpha Sigma Nu, Phi Delta Kappa, Pi Lambda Theta. Office: DePaul Univ Sch Of Edn Chicago IL 60614

MINDLIN, PAULA ROSALIE, reading educator; b. N.Y.C., Nov. 27, 1944; d. Simon S. and Sylvia (Naroff) Bernstein; m. Alfred Carl Mindlin, Aug. 14, 1965; 1 child, Spencer Douglas. BA in Edn., Bklyn. Coll., 1965; MS in Edn., Queens Coll., 1970, Specialist Sch. Adminstrn, 1973. Tchr. Dist. 16 Pub. Sch., Bklyn., 1965-68; reading tchr. Dist. 29 Pub. Sch. and Dist. 16, Bklyn., 1968-85; instr. insvc. courses Comty. Sch. Dist. 29, Queens Village, N.Y., 1984-93; reading coord. Reading/Comms. Arts Program Comty. Sch. Dist. 29, Queens, N.Y., 1985-90; dir. reading Cmty. Sch. Dist. 29, Queens Village, N.Y., 1990-94;, 1993-95; adj. lectr. York Coll., 1989; dir. chpt. 1 program U.S. Sec. Edn., 1993 (Nat. Recognition award). Recipient Educator of Yr. award Queensboro Coun. Reading. Mem. ASCD, Internat. Reading Assn., Nassau Reading Coun., Queensboro Reading Coun. (pres. 1994-96, Educator of Yr. award 1994), Phi Delta Kappa. Avocations: reading, gardening, boating. Office: Dist 29 Queens 1 Cross Island Plz Rosedale NY 11422-1484

MINDLIN, RICHARD BARNETT, market research executive; b. Kansas City, Mo., Apr. 9, 1926; s. Harold Saul and Ann (Copeland) M.; m. Susan Dorothy Weinberg, Feb. 6, 1954; children: Steven, Edward, Andrew. Student, U. of South, 1943-46, Columbia U., 1947-48. Mdse. mgr. Kaufmann's Dept. Store, Pitts., 1951-54; founder, pres. Coach House Stores, Kansas City, Mo., 1955-76, Richard B. Mindlin Assocs., mktg. and new product research and devel., Shawnee Mission, Kans., 1963—. Author books and articles to profl. jours. Chmn. bd. dirs. Bacchus Charity, 1960; bd. dirs. Kaw council Boy Scouts Am., 1964-66; pres. bd. trustees Kansas City Mus. History and Sci.; trustee Menorah Med. Center, Kansas City, Mo. Served to lt. (j.g.) USNR, 1943-45. Club: Oakwood Country (Kansas City,

Mo.) (dir. 1981-84). Home and Office: 4101 W 90th St Shawnee Mission KS 66207-2325

MINE, KATSUTOSHI, instrumentation educator; b. Fukuoka-ken, Japan, Apr. 28, 1928; s. Tsuneo and Chiyoko (Yoshimura) M.; m. Kazuko Yamauchi, Feb. 5, 1956; 1 child, Satoshi. Diploma, Meiji Tech. Coll., Kitakyushu, Japan, 1949; D of Engring., Kyoto (Japan) U., 1978. Engr. Mitsubishi Chem. Co. Ltd., Kitakyushu, 1949-50, Dantani Plywood Co. Ltd., Kitakyushu, 1955-56; assoc. prof. Ube (Japan) Tech. Coll., 1962-72, prof., 1972-80; prof. Kyushu Inst. Tech., Kitakyushu, 1980-92, Kyushu Kyoritsu U., Kitakyushu, 1992—. Author: T.EMC, IEEE, 1994; inventor in field. Recipient Acad. award Fukuhara Gakuen U. Consortium, Kitakyushu, 1993. Mem. IEEE (reviewer indsl. electronics 1992), IEEE Japan, Soc. Instrumentation and Control Engrs. (bd. dirs. 1990-92), Japan Soc. Med. and Biol. Engrs. (gen. chmn. 6th conf. 1991-92, bd. dirs. 1993—, congress 1992), Kitakyushu Med. and Engring. Coop. Assn. (pres. 1989-93), Kitakyushu Techno-coop. Assn. (bd. dirs. 1992—), N.Y. Acad. Sci. Avocations: classical music, skiing, hiking. Home: 296-2 Mushiozu, Onga-cho Fukuoka-ken 811-43, Japan Office: Kyushu Kyoritsu Univ, 1-8 Jiyugaoka Yahatanishiku, Kita-Kyushu 807, Japan

MINEAR, ROGER ALLAN, chemist, educator; b. Seattle, June 19, 1939; s. Herbert Russell M. and Iris Ione (Merrill) Patterson; m. Carol Louise English, Aug. 12, 1966; children: Meredith Edin, Melinda Erin. BS, U. Wash., 1964, MS in Engring., 1966, PhD, 1971. Assoc. prof. dept. civil engring. U. Tenn., Knoxville, 1973-77, prof., 1977-82, Armour T. Granger prof., 1983-84; prof., dir. inst. for environ. studies U. Ill., Urbana, 1985—; sr. scientist Radian Corp., Austin, Tex., 1980-81; sr. devel. staff mem. environ. sci. div. Oak Ridge (Tenn.) Nat. Lab., 1983-84; dir. office solid waste rsch. U. Ill., 1987—; mem. scientific adv. com. hazardous waste rsch. ctr. La. State U., Baton Rouge, 1989-91; bd. scientific counselors Agy. for Toxic Substances and Disease Registry, Atlanta, 1988-93; mem. bd. environ. sci. and tech. Nat. Rsch. Coun., Washington, 1983-86. Editor: Water Chlorination, Vol. 6, 1989, Water Analysis, Vols. 1, 2, 3, 1982, 84; contbr. articles to profl. jours. Mem. Am. Water Works Assn., Assn. Environ. Engring. Profs. (pres. 1980-81, Disting. Svc. award 1984), Am. Chem. Soc. (councilor 1989—, Disting. Svc. award 1985), ASCE, Water Environ. Fedn. Home: 1003 Eliot Dr Urbana IL 61801-6823 Office: U Ill Inst Environ Studues 1101 W Peabody Dr Urbana IL 61801-4723

MINER, A. BRADFORD, journalist; b. Columbus, Ohio, Oct. 30, 1947; s. Robert Bradford and Margaret L. (Earnhart) M.; m. Sydny H. Weinberg, Apr. 29, 1984; children: Robert Bradford II, Jonathan Frederick. BA, Ohio U., 1970. Mgr., Gaylord Enterprises, Columbus, 1974-77; sales planning mgr. Bantam Books, N.Y.C., 1977-80, sr. editor, 1980-84; editor hardcover and paperback books Harper & Row, N.Y.C., 1984-86; nat. sales mgr. Sea-Tex Inc. div. Balson-Hercules Group, N.Y.C., 1987-89; lit. editor National Review, 1989-91; co-editor Nat. Rev. Coll. Guide, 1991, rev. 1993; Olin prof. Adelphi U., 1994—. Editor Good Order, 1994; author: Concise Conservative Encyclopedia, 1996; pres. Religion Pub. Group, N.Y.C., 1983-84. Mem. Fulton J. Sheen Soc. (trustee). Republican. Roman Catholic. Club: N.Y. Athletic.

MINER, EARL HOWARD, retired trust banker; b. Donnellson, Iowa, Jan. 26, 1923; s. T. Ralph and Carrie T. (Talbot) M.; m. Marian Aumann, May 30, 1944; children: Marcia, Susan, Scott. B.A., Iowa Wesleyan Coll., 1947; J.D., U. Iowa, 1948. Bar: Iowa 1948, Mich. 1965. Atty. Mt. Pleasant, Iowa, 1948-55; trust officer Nat. Bank Burlington, Iowa, 1955-57; v.p. 1st Trust Co., St. Joseph, Mo., 1957-62; investment editor Trusts & Estates Mag., N.Y.C., 1962-64; v.p., trust officer Chem. Bank, Midland, Mich., 1964-70; v.p., sr. trust officer Old Kent Bank and Trust Co., Grand Rapids, Mich., 1970-72; sr. v.p. Old Kent Bank and Trust Co., 1972-79, Citizens Trust Co., Ann Arbor, Mich., 1979-88; ret., 1988; instr. Iowa Wesleyan Coll., part-time 1949-50; county atty., Henry County, Iowa, 1951-55. Chmn. bd. dirs. Mary Free Bed Hosp., Grand Rapids, 1977-79; pres. Green Valley Cmty. Coordinating Coun., 1995—. With USAAF, World War II. Decorated D.F.C., Air medal with 2 oak leaf clusters. Mem. Iowa Bar Assn., State Bar Mich., Mich. Bankers Assn. (chmn. trust div. 1970-71, 86-87), Lambda Chi Alpha, Phi Alpha Delta. Republican. Presbyterian (elder). Home: 1473 W Via De La Gloria Green Valley AZ 85614-5009

MINER, EARL ROY, literature educator; b. Marshfield, Wis., Feb. 21, 1927; s. Roy Jacob and Marjory M.; m. Virginia Lane, July 15, 1950; children: Erik Earl, Lisa Lane. B.A. summa cum laude, U. Minn., 1949, M.A., 1951, Ph.D., 1955. Instr. English Williams Coll., 1953-55; mem. faculty dept. English UCLA, 1955-72, prof., 1964-72; prof. English Princeton U., 1972-74, Townsend Martin Class of 1917 Prof. English and comparative lit., 1974—; vis. fellow U. Canterbury, 1985; mem. joint com. for Japanese Studies Social Sci. Rsch. Coun., 1979-83; disting. vis. prof. Emory U., 1989; vis. prof. UCLA, 1990, Stanford U., 1994; mem. Com. on Scholarly Communications with Peoples Republic China, 1983-87. Author numerous books including The Japanese Tradition in British and American Literature, 1958, The Metaphysical Mode from Donne to Cowley, 1969, The Restoration Mode from Milton to Dryden, 1974, The Princeton Companion to Classical Japanese Literature, 1985, Comparative Poetics, 1991; co-author: Literary Transmission and Authority, 1993; assoc. editor: The New Princeton Ency. of Poetry and Poetics, 1993; assoc. gen. editor: Calif. edit. Works of John Dryden, 1964-72, editor 3 vols.; author articles. Am. Coun. Learned Socs. fellow, 1962-63; Guggenheim Found. fellow, 1977-78; fellow Woodrow Wilson Internat. Ctr. for Scholars, 1982-83, U. Calif. Humanities Res. Inst. fellow, 1990; vis. prof. Internat. Rsch. Ctr. for Japanese Studies, 1993-94; recipient Yamagata Banto Prize Osaka Prefectural Govt., 1987, Koizumi Yakumo prize, 1991; decorated Order of the Rising Sun with Gold Rays and Neck Ribbon Japanese Govt., 1994. Mem. Am. Soc. for 18th Century Studies (pres. 1981-82), Milton Soc. Am. (pres. 1982-83), Am. Comparative Lit. Assn. (adv. bd. 1977-80, 86-89), Internat. Comparative Lit. Assn. (exec. coun. 1986-88, pres. 1988-91). Office: Princeton U 22 Mccosh Cir Princeton NJ 08540-5627

MINER, JACQUELINE, political consultant; b. Mt. Vernon, N.Y., Dec. 10, 1936; d. Ralph E. and Agnes (McGee) Mariani; B.A., Coll. St. Rose, 1971, M.A., 1974; m. Roger J. Miner, Aug. 11, 1975; children: Laurence, Ronald Carmichael, Ralph Carmichael, Mark. Ind. polit. cons., Hudson, N.Y.; instr. history and polit. sci. SUNY, Hudson, 1974-79. Rep. county committeewoman, 1958-76; vice chmn. N.Y. State Ronald Reagan campaign, 1980; candidate for Rep. nomination for U.S. Senate, 1982; co-chair N.Y. state steering com. George Bush for Pres. campaign, 1986-88; vice chmn. N.Y. State Rep. Com., 1991-93; del. Rep. Convention, 1992; chmn. Coll. Consortium for Internat. Studies; mem. White House Outreach Working Group on Central Am.; co-chmn. N.Y. State Reagan Roundup Campaign, 1984-86; mem. nat. steering com. Fund for Am.'s Future, 2d cir. Hist. Com. Mem. U.S. Supreme Ct. Hist. Soc., P.E.O. Address: 1 Merlin's Way Camelot Heights Hudson NY 12534

MINER, JOHN BURNHAM, industrial relations educator, writer; b. N.Y.C., July 20, 1926; s. John Lynn and Bess (Burnham) M.; children by previous marriage: Barbara, John, Cynthia, Frances; m. Barbara Allen Williams, June 1, 1979; children: Jennifer, Heather. AB, Princeton U., 1950, PhD, 1955; MA, Clark U., 1952. Lic. psychologist, N.Y. Rsch. assoc. Columbia U., 1956-57; mgr. psychol. svcs. Atlantic Refining Co., Phila., 1957-60; faculty mem. U. Oreg., Eugene, 1960-68; prof., chmn. dept. orgnl. sci. U. Md., College Park, 1968-73; rsch. prof. Ga. State U., Atlanta, 1973-87; pres. Orgnl. Measurement Systems Press, Eugene, Oreg., 1976—; prof. Human Resources SUNY, Buffalo, 1987-94; chmn. dept. orgn. and human resources, 1989-92; profl. practice Eugene, Oreg., 1995—; cons. McKinsey & Co., N.Y.C., 1966-69; vis. lectr. U. Pa., Phila., 1959-60; vis. prof. U. Calif., Berkeley, 1966-67, U. South Fla., Tampa, 1972; researcher on orgnl. motivation, theories of orgn., human resource utilization, bus. policy and strategy, entrepreneurship. Author many books and monographs including Personnel Psychology, 1969, Personnel and Industrial Relations, 1969, 73, 77, 85, The Challenge of Managing, 1975, (with Mary Green Miner) Policy Issues Personnel and Industrial Relations, 1977, (with George A. Steiner) Management Policy and Strategy, 1977, James A. Hamilton-Hosp. Adminstrs. Book award 1982, 86), (with M.G. Miner) Employee Selection Within the Law, 1978, Theories of Organizational Behavior, 1980, Theories of Organizational Structure and Process, 1982, People Problems: The Executive Answer Book, 1985, The Practice of Management, 1985, Organizational Behavior: Performance and Productivity, 1988, Industrial-Organizational Psychology, 1992, Role Motivation Theories, 1993, (with Donald P. Crane) Human Resource Management: The Strategic Perspective, 1995, The 4 Routes to Entrepreneurial Success, 1996; contbr. numerous articles, papers to profl. jours. Served with AUS, 1944-46, ETO. Decorated Bronze Star, Combat Infantryman's Badge; named Disting. Prof. Ga. State U., 1974. Fellow APA, Acad. of Mgmt. (editor Jour. 1973-75, pres. 1977-78), Soc. for Personality Assessment, Am. Psychol. Soc.; mem. Soc. for Human Resource Mgmt., Indsl. Rels. Rsch. Assn., Internat. Coun. for Small Bus., Strategic Mgmt. Soc., Internat. Pers. Mgmt. Assn., Human Resource Planning Soc. Republican. Home and Office: 34199 Country View Dr Eugene OR 97408

MINER, JOHN RONALD, bioresource engineer; b. Scottsburg, Ind., July 4, 1938; s. Gerald Lamont and Alice Mae (Murphy) M.; m. Betty Katheron Emery, Aug. 4, 1963; children—Saralena Marie, Katherine Alice, Frederick Gerald. B.S. in Chem. Engring, U. Kans., 1959; M.S.E. in San. Engring, U. Mich., 1960; Ph.D. in Chem. Engring. and Microbiology, Kans. State U., 1967. Lic. profl. engr., Kans., Oreg. San. engr. Kans. Dept. Health, Topeka, 1959-64; grad. research asst. Kans. State U., Manhattan, 1964-67; asst. prof. agrl. engring. Iowa State U., 1967-71, assoc. prof., 1971-72; assoc. prof. agrl. engring. Oreg. State U., 1972-76, prof., 1976—, head dept., 1976-86, acting assoc. dean Coll. Agrl. Sci., 1983-84, assoc. dir. Office Internat. Research and Devel., 1986-90, extension water quality specialist, 1991—; environ. engr. FAO of UN, Singapore, 1980-81; internat. cons.; cons. to livestock feeding ops., agrl. devel. firms. Co-author book on livestock waste mgmt.; author 3 books of children's sermons; contbr. numerous articles on livestock prodn., pollution control, control of odors associated with livestock prodn. to profl. publs. Mem. Am. Soc. Agrl. Engrs. (bd. dirs. 1985-87), Water Pollution Control Fedn., Sigma Xi, Gamma Sigma Delta, Alpha Epsilon, Tau Beta Pi. Presbyterian. Office: Oreg State U Dept Bioresource Engring Corvallis OR 97331

MINER, MARY ELIZABETH HUBERT, secondary school educator; b. Provident City, Tex., Mar. 25, 1921; d. Fred Edward and Charlotte Alice (Haynes) Hubert; m. Daniel Bowen Miner, Jan. 29, 1945 (dec. Aug. 1979); children: Charlotte Martelia Miner Williams, Daniel Bowen Jr., Mary Elizabeth Miner Martinez, Joseph Frederick, William McKinley. BA, Rice U., 1942; postgrad., U. Houston, East Tenn. State U., 1959, U. Tenn., 1961. Cert. tchr. math., English, French, history, Tex., 8th grade, math., English, French, Am. history grades 9-12. Math. tchr. Crosby (Tex.) H.S., 1942-43; office mgr. Uvalde Rock Asphalt, Houston, 1943-44; tchr. math., English, health Rogersville (Tenn.) H.S., 1947-49, 55-78; tchr. math., English, French Ch. Hill. (Tenn.) H.S., 1949-51, 53-55; tchr. 8th grade Rogersville (Tenn.) City Schs., 1951-53; tchr. math. Cherokee Comprehensive H.S., Rogersville, 1978-84; chmn. math. and sci. planning com., Hawkins County, Tenn., 1977-79; pvt. tutor, Rogersville. Tchr. ladies Bible class Rogersville United Meth. Ch., 1952—, mem. choir, 1979—, sec., 1967-94, sec. adminstr. bd. dirs.; blood donor ARC, Rogersville, 1974-75. Lt. Women's Corps USNR, 1944-47. Recipient Apple award Sta. WKGB, 1956. Mem. NEA (life), Tenn. Edn. Assn. (life), Rogersville Bus. and Profl. Women (pres. 1953-55, treas. 1948-53), Am. Legion Aux. (pres.), Delta Kappa Gamma (Alpha Iota chpt. pres.). Republican. Avocations: bridge playing, playing piano, teaching, sewing, visiting children.

MINER, MICHAEL E., neurosurgery educator; b. Louisville, July 25, 1943; s. Gerald Lamont and Alice Mae (Murphy) M.; m. Mildred Elizabeth Kennedy, 1972 (dec. July, 1978); children: Caroline, Matthew, Amanda, Nicholas; m. Mary Ann Bruton, 1980 (dec. Dec., 1992). BS, U. Kans., Lawrence, 1965; MD, U. Kans., Kansas City, 1969, PhD, 1975. Diplomate in neurological surgery Am. Bd. Psychiatry and Neurology. Prof. U. Tex. Med. Sch., Houston, 1975—, dir. divsn. neurosurgery, 1984—; neurosurg. dir. Por Cristo, Boston, 1983—. Author: Neurotrauma, 1986; contbr. articles on neurosurg. disorders to profl. jours. Chmn. Houston Child-Safe Com., 1986—. Served to capt. U.S. Army, 1965-75. Grantee NIH, 1983-87; named Outstanding Tchr., U. Tex., 1984. Mem. Peruvian Surg. Soc., Am. Assn. Neurol. Surgeons (cert.), Soc. Neurol. Surgeons, Ohio State Neurosurg. Soc. (pres. 1995-96). Avocations: running, Civil War history. Office: Univ of Tex Med Sch at Houston Dept of Immunology & Organ Transplant 6431 Fannin St # 148 Houston TX 77030-1501 Office: Ohio State Univ Hosps Neurol Dept Columbus OH 43210

MINER, ROBERT GORDON, creative promotional consultant, auctioneer, writer, publisher, actor, educator; b. Blue Island, Ill., Jan. 29, 1923; s. Glen Ernest and Catherine (Leytze) M.; m. Betty Anne Clegg, May 23, 1944; children: Patricia L. Miner Jolin, Stephen C., David N. Student, Knox Coll., 1941-42; M.B.A., U. Chgo., 1950; grad., U.S. Army Command and Gen. Staff Coll., 1968. Payroll auditor Employers Group Ins. Cos., 1946-49; advt. salesman Cole & Mason (pubs. reps.), 1949-54, partner, 1955-56; asst. pub. Flower Grower mag., Williams Press, 1956-61, pub., 1961-67; owner Media Design Assos., Westport, Conn., 1967-71; pres. Early Am. Soc., Inc. (pub. Early Am. Life), Harrisburg, Pa., 1971-81; owner, pub. Old Main Books, 1981-87; creative promotional cons., auctioneer, appraiser St. Thomas, V.I., 1987-94; adj. prof. humanities U. V.I., 1994—. Author: Handbook of Gardening, 1966; Complete Gardening Guide, 1969, Flea Market Handbook, 1981, rev., updated edit., 1990; columnist Virgin Islands Daily News, Bus. Jour., 1994-95; film appearances: My Father the Hero, 1993, Kawasaki Jet Ski Promo film and German TV program; contbr. articles to profl. jours. Served from 2d lt. to capt. AUS, 1942-46; col. Res. ret. Decorated Bronze Star. Republican. Episcopalian. Clubs: St. Thomas Yacht, Navy League. Home: 8-24 Estate Nazareth 6501 Red Hook Plz Ste 201 Saint Thomas VI 00802

MINER, ROGER JEFFREY, federal judge; b. Apr. 14, 1934; s. Abram and Anne M.; m. Jacqueline Mariani; 4 children. BS, SUNY; LLB cum laude, N.Y. Law Sch., 1956, LLD (hon.), 1989; postgrad., Bklyn. Law Sch., Judge Advocate Gen.'s Sch., U. Va.; LLD (hon.), Syracuse U., 1990. Bar: N.Y. 1956, U.S. Ct. Mil. Appeals 1956, Republic of Korea 1958, U.S. Dist. Ct. (so. and ea. dists.) N.Y. 1959. Ptnr. Miner & Miner, Hudson, N.Y., 1959-75; justice N.Y. State Supreme Ct., 1976-81; judge U.S. Dist. Ct. (no. dist.) N.Y., 1981-85, U.S. Ct. Appeals (2d cir.), Albany, N.Y., 1985—; corp. counsel City of Hudson, 1961-64; asst. dist. atty. Columbia County, 1964, dist. atty., 1968-74; adj. assoc. prof. criminal law State U. System, N.Y., 1974-79; adj. prof. law N.Y. Law Sch., 1986—; lectr. state and local bar assns.; lectr. SUNY-Albany, 1985; N.Y. Law Sch. Bd. Trustees; mem. jud. coun. 2d Cir.; 2d Cir. Com. on Hist. and Commemorative Events, 1989-94; Cameras in the Courtroom Com., No. Dist. Hist. Com., 1981-85; State, Fed. Jud. Coun. of N.Y., 1986-91, chmn., 1990-91; Jud. Conf. of U.S. com. on fed.-state jurisdiction, 1987-92; trustee Practicing Law Inst. Mng. editor N.Y. Law Sch. Law Rev.; contbr. articles to law jours. 1st lt. JAGC, U.S. Army, 1956-59, capt. USAR ret. Recipient Dean's medal for Disting. Profl. Svc., N.Y. Law Sch., Disting. Alumnus award, Charles W. Froessel award for Valuable Contbn. to Law. Albany Jewish Fedn. award, Abraham Lincoln award, Community Svc. award Kiwanis, others; named Columbia County Man. of Yr., 1984, Ellis Island medal of Honor. Mem. ABA, N.Y. State Bar Assn., Assn. of Bar of City of N.Y., Columbia County Bar Assn., Am. Law Inst., Am. Judicature Soc., Fed. Judges Assn., Fed. Bar Coun., Am. Soc. Writers on Legal Subjects, Assn. Trial Lawyers Am., Columbia County Magistrates Assn., Supreme Ct. Hist. Soc., Columbia County Hist. Soc., N.Y. Law Sch. Alumni Assn. (hon. mem., bd. dirs.), B'nai Brith, Elks (past exalted ruler). Jewish. Office: US Ct Appeals 445 BROADWAY, STE 414 Albany NY 12207-0858

MINER, THOMAS HAWLEY, international entrepreneur; b. Shelbyville, Ill., June 19, 1927; s. Lester Ward and Thirza (Hawley) M.; m. Lucyna T. Minciel, July 22, 1983; children: Robert Thomas, William John. Student, U.S. Mil. Acad., 1946-47; BA, Knox Coll., 1950; JD, U. Ill., 1953. Bar: Ill. 1954. Atty. Continental Ill. Nat. Bank & Trust Co., Chgo., 1953-55; pres. Harper-Wyman Internat. (S.A.), Venezuela and Mex., 1955-58, Hudson Internat. (S.A.), Can. and Switzerland, 1958-60, Thomas H. Miner & Assoc., Inc., Chgo., 1960—; chmn. Miner, Fraser & Gabriel Pub. Affairs, Inc., Washington, 1982-88, Miner Systems, Inc., 1981—; bd. dirs. Lakeside Bank; chmn. Ill. dist. export coun. U.S. Dept. Commerce, 1971-76; sec. Consular Corps Chgo., 1986-88. Chmn. bd. dirs. Sch. Art Inst. Chgo., 1977-81; bd. govs., life mem., sustaining fellow Art Inst. Chgo.; former chmn. UN Assn., Chgo.; founder, chmn. Mid-Am. Com., 1968—; former mem. bd. dirs. UNICEF, NAM, Internat. Trade Policy Com. and Working Group on Commonwealth of Ind. States and Ea. Europe; trustee 4th Presbyn. Ch., Chgo.; bd. advisors Mercy Hosp.; vice chmn. Chgo. Sister Cities; mem. adv. bd. Internat. Inst. Edn.; bd. dirs. Internat. Sister Cities. With USNR, 1945-46; mem. Pres. Coun. U. Ill. Found. Capt. U.S. Army, 1946-47. Decorated commendatore Ordine al Merito della Repubblica Italiana; recipient Alumni Achievement award Knox Coll., 1974, Gold Medallion award Internat. Visitors Ctr. Chgo., 1989; named One of Chgo.'s 10 Outstanding Young Men, 1962, Chicagoan of Year Chgo. Assn. Commerce and Industry, 1968, Alumni of Month Coll. Law U. Ill., Nov. 1970, Aug. 1984; hon. consul Republic of Senegal, 1970-88. Mem. Am. Mgmt. Assn., Chgoland C. of C., Mid-Am. Arab C. of C. (founder, former pres.), Chgo. Bar Assn., Chgo. Com., Chgo. Coun. Fgn. Rels. (past dir.), Coun. of the Ams., Internat. Trade Club (past dir., pres.), Japan-Am. Soc., Nat. Coun. U.S.-China Trade, Nat. Acad. Scis. (pres. coun.), English Speaking Union (dir., past chmn.) Trade and Econs. Coun. USA-CIS (dir.), U.S.-Russia Bus. Coun., Mus. Contemporary Art, Newcomen Soc. N.Am., U.S.-Arab C. of C. (bd. dirs.), U.S.-Mex. C. of C. (bd. dirs.), Thomas Minor Soc., Chgo. Club, Econ. Club, Grant Park Concerts Soc., Chgo. Farmers Club, Mid-Am. Club, Univ. Club (Washington), Desiree Club, Univ. Club (Milw.), Hillsboro Club (Fla.), Tryall Golf and Beach Club (Jamaica), Rotary, Phi Delta Phi, Phi Gamma Delta. Office: 150 N Michigan Ave Chicago IL 60601 also: 2400 Virginia Ave NW Washington DC 20037-2612 also: Miner Farms Shelbyville IL 62565

MINES, HERBERT THOMAS, executive recruiter; b. Fall River, Mass., Jan. 30, 1929; s. Abraham and Fanny (Lepes) M.; B.S. in Econs., Babson Coll., 1949; M.S. in Indsl. and Labor Relations, Cornell U., 1954; m. Barbara Goldberg, Oct. 23, 1960; 1 child, Susan. Supr., asst. buyer, employment supr. G. Fox & Co., Hartford, Conn., 1949-52; adminstr. div. tng.-exec. devel. and orgn. planning R.H. Macy & Co., N.Y.C., 1954-66; v.p. personnel Neiman Marcus Co., Dallas, 1966-68, sr. v.p. personnel, 1968-70; v.p. personnel Revlon, Inc., N.Y.C., 1970-73; pres. Bus. Careers, Inc., 1973-78, chmn., 1978-81; pres. Exec. Search and Cons. Div., Wells Mgmt. Corp., 1978-81; pres. Herbert Mines Assocs., Inc., 1981-93, chmn., CEO 1993—. Bd. dirs. Fashion Inst. Tech., Am. Jewish Com., Assn. of Exec. Cons. Contbr. articles to trade publs. Office: 815 Pirates Cv Mamaroneck NY 10543-4718

MINETA, NORMAN YOSHIO, aerospace transportation executive, former congressman; b. San Jose, Calif., Nov. 12, 1931; s. Kay Kunisaku and Kane (Watanabe) M.; m. Danealia; children: David, K., Stuart S. B.S., U. Calif.-Berkeley, 1953; D of Pub. Svc., Santa Clara U., 1989; HHD (hon.), Rust Coll., 1993. Agt./broker Mineta Ins. Agy., San Jose, 1956-89; mem. adv. bd. Bank of Tokyo in Calif., 1961-75; mem. San Jose City Council, 1967-71; vice mayor City of San Jose, 1969-71, mayor, 1971-75; mem. 94th-104th Congresses from 13th (now 15th) Calif. dist., 1975-95; subcom. surface transp., 1989-92, former dep. Dem. whip, ranking minority mem. transp. and infrastructure com.; sr. v.p., mng. dir. transp. sys. & srvs. Lockheed Martin, Washington, 1995—; chmn. fin. com. Santa Clara County (Calif.) Council Chs., 1960-62; commr. San Jose Human Relations Commn., 1962-64, San Jose Housing Authority, 1966—. Precinct chmn. Community Theater Bond Issue, 1964; mem. spl. gifts com. Santa Clara County council Boy Scouts Am., 1967; sec. Santa Clara County Grand Jury, 1964; bd. dirs. Wesley Found., San Jose State Coll., 1956-58, Pacific Neighbors, Community Council Cen. Santa Clara County, Japan Soc., San Francisco, Santa Clara County chpt. NCCJ, Mexican-Am. Community Services Agy.; mem. exec. bd. No. Calif.-Western Nev. dist. council Japanese Am. Citizens League, 1960-62, pres. San Jose chpt., 1957-59; bd. regents Smithsonian Instn., 1979—; chmn. Smithsonian vis. com. for Freer Gallery, 1981—; mem. bd. regents Santa Clara U. Served to lt. AUS, 1954-56. Mem. Greater San Jose C. of C., Nat. Assn. Indsl. Ins. Agts., Calif. Assn. Indsl. Ins. Agts., San Jose Assn. Ind. Ins. Agts. (dir. 1960-62), North San Jose Optimists Club (pres. 1956-58), Jackson-Taylor Bus. and Profl. Assn. (dir. 1963). Methodist. Office: Lockheed Martin 1200 K St NW Fl 12 Washington DC 20005 *Personal philosophy: My two greatest responsibilities are accountability and accessibility to everyone I represent, and to anyone who comes to me for help.*

MING, SI-CHUN, pathologist, educator; b. Shanghai, China, Nov. 10, 1922; came to U.S., 1949, naturalized, 1964; s. Sian-Fan and Jan-Teh (Kuo) M.; m. Pen-Ming Lee, Aug. 17, 1957; children—Carol, Ruby, Stephanie, Michael, Jeffrey, Eileen. M.D., Nat. Central U. Coll. Medicine, China, 1947. Resident in pathology Mass. Gen. Hosp., Boston, 1952-56; assoc. pathologist Beth Israel Hosp., Boston, 1956-67; asst. prof. pathology Harvard U. Med. Sch., 1965-67; assoc. prof. U. Md., 1967-71; prof. Temple U., Phila., 1971-93, prof. emeritus, 1993—, acting chmn. dept. pathology, 1978-80, dep. chmn. dept. path., 1980-86; mem. Internat. Study Group on Gastric Cancer; mem. coun. Internat. Gastric Cancer Assn.; U.S. rep. WHO Collaborating Ctr. for Primary Prevention, Diagnosis and Treatment of Gastric Cancer; hon. prof. Tianjin Med. Coll., Shanghai Second Med. U., Fourth Mil. Med. U., China, 1988—. Author: Tumors of the Esophagus and Stomach, 1973, supplement, 1985, Precursors of Gastric Cancer, 1984, Pathology of the Gastrointestinal Tract, 1992. Nat. Cancer Inst. sr. fellow Karolinska Inst. Stockholm, 1964-65; named hon. prof. Tianjin Med. U., Shanghai Second Med. U. and Fourth Mil. Med. U., China, 1988—. Mem. AAAS, U.S. Canadian Acad. Pathology, Am. Soc. Investigative Pathology, Am. Gastroenterol. Assn., N.Y. Acad. Scis. Achievements include development of classification method for stomach carcinoma based on the growth pattern of the cancer. Office: 3400 N Broad St Philadelphia PA 19140-5196

MINGE, DAVID, congressman, lawyer, law educator; b. Clarkfield, Minn., 1942; m. Karen Aaker; children: Erik, Olaf. BA in History, St. Olaf Coll., 1964; JD, U. Chgo., 1967. Atty. Faegre & Benson, Mpls., 1967-70; prof. law U. Wyo., 1970-77; atty. Nelson, Oyen, Torvik, Minge & Gilbertson, 1977-93; mem. 103d-104th Congresses from 2nd Minn. Dist., 1993—; mem. agrl. com.; cons. Ho. Jud. Com., Subcom. Adminstrv. Law U.S. Congress, 1975; formerly atty. Minn. Valley Coop. Light and Power Assn., 1984-93; chair Agrl. Law Sect., Minn. State Bar Assn. 1990-92, adv. bd. Western Minn. Legal Svcs., 1978-84; bd. dirs. Legal Advice Clinics, Ltd., Hennepin County, Western Minn. Vol. Atty. Program. Clk. Montevideo Sch. Bd., 1989-92; dir. Montevideo Community Devel. Corp.; steering com. Clean Up the River Environ., 1992 ; co-coord. Montevideo area CROP Walk for the Hungry, Multi-church Vietnamese Refugee Resettlement Com., Montevideo, 1978-90; bd. dirs. Montevideo United Way, Model Cities Program, Kinder Kare; chair AFS Montevideo chpt. Mem. Minn. Bar Assn., Chippewa County Bar Assn. (chair), Montevideo C. of C., Kiwanis (pres.). Office: 1415 Longworth HOB Washington DC 20515-2302*

MINGER, TERRELL JOHN, public administration institute executive; b. Canton, Ohio, Oct. 7, 1942; s. John Wilson and Margaret Rose M.; m. Judith R. Arnold, Aug. 7, 1965; 1 child, Gabriella Sophia. BA, Baker U., 1966; MPA, Kans. U., 1969; Urban Exec. Program, MIT, 1975; Loeb fellow Harvard U., 1976-77; Exec. Devel. Program, Stanford U., 1979; MBA, U. Colo., 1983. Asst. dir. admissions Baker U., 1966-67; asst. city mgr. City of Boulder, Colo., 1968-69; city mgr. City of Vail, Colo., 1969-79; pres., chief exec. officer Whistler Village Land Co., Vancouver, B.C., Can., 1979-81; v.p., gen. mgr. Cumberland S.W. Inc., Denver, 1981-83; exec. asst., dep. chief of staff to Gov. Colo., 1983-87; pres., chief exec. officer Sundance (Utah) Inst. for Resource Mgmt., 1986—; pres., chief exec. officer Sundance Enterprises Ltd., 1988-91; adj. prof. grad. sch. pub. affairs U. Colo., 1983—, Sch. Bus. U. Denver, 1992—; bd. dirs. Colo. Open Lands, Inc., 1986—; participant UN Conf. on Environment and Devel., Rio de Janeiro, 1992; chmn. environ. adv. bd. Wal-Mart, Inc., 1990—. Editor: Greenhouse/Glasnost—The Global Warming Crisis, 1990. Spl. del. UN Habitat Conf. Human Settlements, spl. rep. to UN Environment Program, 1992, coord. UN Global Youth Forum, 1993, 94, co-chmn. conf. on environment and marketing, N.Y.C., 1993; founder Vail Symposium; co-founder, bd. dirs. Colo. Park Found., 1985—; founding mem. Greenhouse/Glasnost U.S./USSR Teleconf. with Soviet Acad. Scis., 1989—; mem. pres. task force Commn. on Sustainable Devel., 1994—; co-chmn. Golf and Environ. Conf., Pebble Beach, Calif., 1995. Nat. finalist White House Fellowship, 1978; named one of B.C.'s Top Bus. Leaders for the '80's, 1980. Mem. Urban Land Inst., Colo. Acad. Pub. Adminstrn. (charter, founding mem. 1988), Colo. City Mgmt. Assn., Internat. City Mgrs. Assn. (Mgmt. Innovation award 1974-76), Western Gov.'s Assn. (staff coun., chmn. adv. com. 1985-86), Flatirons Athletic Club. Editor: Vail Symposium Papers, 1970-79; author, editor: Growth Alternatives for Rocky Mountain West, 1976; Future of Human Settlements in the West, 1977. Home: 785 6th St Boulder CO 80302-7416 Office: Ctr for Resource Mgmt 1410 Grant St Ste 307C Denver CO 80203-1846

MINGLE, JAMES JOHN, lawyer. AB in English, St. Joseph's Coll., Phila., 1968; JD, U. Va., 1973. Bar: Md. 1974, Va. 1990. Asst. to pres. Frostburg State Coll., 1973-77, adj. prof. bus. law, 1975-77; asst. atty. gen. State of Md., 1977-89; chief counsel U. Md., Balt., 1981-89; gen. counsel U. Va., Charlottesville, 1989-95, lectr. law Cornell U., Ithaca, N.J., 1995—; adj. prof. law U. Md., 1984-88; asst. to bus. mgr. Phila. 76ers NBA Club, 1968-69; city atty. City of Frostburg, Md., 1974-76. Mem. Nat. Assn. Coll. and Univ. Attys.

MINGLE, JOHN ORVILLE, engineer, educator, lawyer, consultant; b. Oakley, Kans., May 6, 1931; s. John Russell and Beulah Amelia (Johnson) M.; m. Patricia Ruth Schmitt, Aug. 17, 1957; children: Elizabeth Lorene, Stephen Roy. B.S., Kans. State U., Manhattan, 1953, M.S., 1958; Ph.D., Northwestern U., 1960; J.D., Washburn U., 1980. Bar: Kans., Wyo., U.S. Patent Office; registered profl. engr., Kans. Tng. engr. Gen. Electric Co., Schenectady, 1953-54; mem. faculty Kans. State U., 1956-90, prof. nuclear engring., 1965-90, prof. emeritus, 1990—, Black & Veatch Disting. prof., 1973-78; dir. Inst. Computational Research in Engring., 1969-88; exec. v.p., patent counsel Kans. State U. Research Found., 1983-88; instr. Northwestern U., 1958-59; vis. prof. U. So. Calif., 1967-68; cons. to govt. and industry. Author: The Invarient Imbedding Theory of Nuclear Transport, 1973; also articles. Bd. dirs. Laramie Regional Airport, 1994—. Officer AUS, 1954-56. Mem. ABA (chairperson sci. and tech. phys. scis. com. 1982-92), NSPE (sect. exec. com. 1985-87, chmn. 1985-86), Am. Nuclear Soc. (sect. pres. 1976-77), Am. Inst. Chem. Engrs. (profl. devel. com. 1982-95), Am. Soc. Engring. Edn. (chmn. Midwest sect. 1984-87, exec. com. 1984-87), Profl. Engrs. in Edn. (vice chmn. 1978-80, workshop chairperson 1983), Kans. Engring. Soc. (past chpt. pres.), Kans. Bar Assn., Licensing Execs. Soc., Sigma Xi (past chpt. pres., lectr.), Soc. Univ. Patent Adminstrs. (exec. com. 1985-87, v.p. cen. region 1985-87). Home: 1409 Downey St Laramie WY 82070-1867 *The "workaholic" doctrine has been highly chastised by our modern society which seems to place great emphasis upon leisure; however those who are most slothful appear to be its loudest critics. Yet, this doctrine still remains one of the most viable methods for the dedicated person to make a lasting contribution to our society.*

MINGO, JAMES WILLIAM EDGAR, lawyer; b. Halifax, N.S., Can., Nov. 25, 1926; s. Edgar Willard and Lila Theresa (McManus) M.; m. Edith Peppard Hawkins, July 6, 1953; children: Sarah M. (Mrs. J.P. Camus), James A., Johanna E., Nancy S., Charles H. B.A., Dalhousie U., Halifax, 1947, LL.B., 1949; LL.M., Columbia U., 1950; LL.D. (hon.), St. Mary's U., 1981. Bar: N.S. 1950, Queen's counsel 1966. Ptnr. Stewart, McKelvey, Stirling & Scales (and predecessors), Halifax, 1958—, assoc., 1950-57, chmn. exec. com., 1979-92; pres., dir. Canning Investment Corp. Ltd., Halifax; dir. Sun Life Assurance Co. Can., Toronto, Ont., Maritime Tel&Tel Co. Ltd., Halifax, Eastern Telephone & Telegraph Co., Halifax, Minas Basin Pulp & Power Co. Ltd., Hantsport, N.S., Minas Basin Holdings Ltd., Hantsport, The Great Eastern Corp. Ltd., Charlottetown, P.E.I. and Halifax, Onex Corp., Toronto, Crossley Carpet Mills Ltd., Truro, N.S., Oxford Frozen Foods Ltd., Oxford, N.S., CBA Law for the Future Fund; trustee Forum for Young Canadians, Found. for Legal Research. Mem. Halifax-Dartmouth Port Commn., 1955-83, chmn., 1960-83; chmn. Halifax Grammar Sch., 1971-73; mem. Halifax Port Authority, 1972-84; chmn. nat. treasury com. Liberal Party Can., 1976-85; dir. N.S. Legal Aid, 1977-80; mem. Med. Research Council Working Group on Human Experimentation, 1977-78. Mem. Can. Bar Assn. (exec. com. 1973-76, spl. com. on legal ethics 1969-75, 84-87), N.S. Barristers Soc. (pres. 1975-76), Law Found. N.S. Clubs: Halifax, Saraguay, Royal N.S. Yacht Squadron. Office: Box 997 Tower I, Purdy's Wharf, Halifax, NS Canada B3J 2X2

MINGO, JOE LOUIS, elementary school educator; b. Kershaw, S.C., Nov. 14; s. John L. and Ella (Wilson) M. BA in Elem. Edn., U. S.C., 1980, MEd, 1982, postgrad., 1994—. Cert. tchr. elem. edn., early childhood edn. Singer operator Springs Industries, Lancaster, S.C., 1972-79; with BJH Realty, Columbia, S.C., 1980-81, Carabo Inc., Columbia, 1980-85; tchr. 3d grade Sumter County (S.C.) Sch. Dist. #2, 1982-86, tchr. 4th grade, 1986-94, tchr. math, 1994—; lead tchr. math Shaw Heights Elem. Sch., Shaw AFB, S.C., 1993—; Author poetry in New Voices in Am. Poetry, 1986, 88. With USAF, 1984—, Desert Storm. Avocation: writing. Office: Shaw Heights Elem Sch 5121 Frierson Rd Shaw AFB SC 29152

MINHAS, FAQIR ULLAH, aerospace engineer; b. Shadiwal, Pakistan, Dec. 4, 1924; came to U.S. 1962; s. Ata M. and Sakeena (Khokhar) M.; m. Dolly Patricia Testa, Jan. 4, 1987. BA, Panjab U., Lahore, 1952; MA in Math., Panjab U., 1957; MASc, Laval U., Que., 1965; DSc, Laval U., 1973; MEngr., McGill U., Montreal, Que., 1984. Mechanic Rwy. Workshops, Lahore, 1943-47; instr. Govt. Sch. Engring., Rasul, 1952-53, Govt. Coll., Rawal Kot, 1954-55; devel. engr. John Inglis, Toronto, Ont., 1963-64; head transp. phenomena br. Dominion Engring., Montreal, 1966-80; sys. engr. Canadair, Montreal, 1980-83; sys. engr. aerodynamics Reflectone, Tampa, Fla., 1984-85; fellow MIT, Cambridge, 1985-86; rschr. U. Toronto, 1987-89; computer specialist U. Hawaii, 1990-93. Contbr. articles to profl. jours. Edn. officer Pakistan Air Force, 1958-61. Mem. AIAA. Avocation: sports. Home: 4024 N Ashland Ave # 210 Chicago IL 60613-2543

MINICHELLO, DENNIS, lawyer; b. Cleve., June 9, 1952; s. Ernest Anthony and Mary Theresa (Rocci) M.; m. Janine Stevens, Feb. 14, 1987. BA in Econs., Ohio U., 1974, MA in Econs., 1974; JD, Northwestern U., 1978. Bar: U.S. Dist. Ct. (no. dist.) Ill., U.S. Ct. Appeals (7th cir.), Supreme Ct. Ill., U.S. Supreme Ct. Assoc. Haskell & Perrin, Chgo., 1978-84; ptnr. Tribler & Marwedel, Chgo., 1984-89, Keck, Mahin & Cate, Chgo., 1989—. Contbr. articles to profl. jours. Bd. dirs. Great Lakes Naval and Maritime Mus. Fulbright scholar, 1974-75. Mem. ABA, Ill. State Bar Assn., Chgo. Bar Assn. (mem. transp. com.), Maritime Law Assn. (proctor), Casualty Adjusters Assn. Chgo., The Propeller Club U.S. (pres. 1983-84), Port Chgo., Met. Club. Roman Catholic. Avocations: sailing, reading, running. Office: Keck Mahin & Cate 77 W Wacker Dr Chicago IL 60601-1629

MINICK, MICHAEL, publishing executive; b. Albany, N.Y., Mar. 26, 1945; s. Jason and Ruth Isabelle (Solomon) M. Student, U. Va., 1963-66; BA in History, L.I. U., 1968. Editorial dir. Mag. Mgmt., N.Y.C., 1969-73; mng. editor Gentlemen's Quarterly, N.Y.C., 1975-76; pub., ptnr. Beauty Digest, N.Y.C., 1978-90; pub. Pa. Ofcl. Wine and Liquor Quar., N.Y.C., 1985—, Ohio Liquor Quar., 1990—. Author: The Kung Fu Exercise Book-Health Secrets of Ancient China, 1974, The Wisdom of Kung Fu, 1974; contbr. numerous articles to popular mags. Mem. 25 Yr. Club of Ind. Distbrs., Pa. Wine and Spirit Assn. Democrat. Home: 24 5th Ave Apt 930 New York NY 10011-8819 Office: Wine and Liquor Quars Inc 24 5th Ave Apt 930 New York NY 10011-8819

MINICUCCI, RICHARD FRANCIS, lawyer, former hospital administrator; b. N.Y.C., Jan. 16, 1947; s. Daniel Michael and Marie Felice (Trotta) M.; m. Nancy Jean Moran, Aug. 16, 1969; children: Jonathan, Elizabeth, Richard. BA, Rutgers Coll., 1969; MHA, Duke U., 1971; JD, Memphis State U., 1976. Bar: Tenn. 1977, N.Y. 1978. Adminstrv. asst. Duke Hosp., Durham, N.C., 1971; health planner Mid-South Med. Ctr. Coun., Memphis, 1971-73; dir. adminstrn. Memphis & Shelby County Hosp. Authority, 1973-77; assoc. Hayt Hayt & Landau, Great Neck, N.Y., 1977-81, ptnr., 1981-89; ptnr. Nixon Hargrave Devans & Doyle, Garden City, N.Y., 1989—; lectr. various health law assns. Editor: New York Environmental Law Handbook, 2d edit.; author: Residency Training Program Accreditation, 1st-5th edits.; editor-in-chief Accreditation Alert. Co-chmn. fund raising Luth. High Sch., Brookville, N.Y., 1991. Capt. U.S. Army, 1971-79. Mem. Am. Acad. Hosp. Attys., N.Y. State Bar Assn., Nassau Bar Assn., Nat. Health Lawyers Assn. Republican. Roman Catholic. Avocations: tennis, skiing, hockey, travel. Office: Nixon Hargrave Devans & Doyle 990 Stewart Ave Garden City NY 11530-4838

MINICUCCI, ROBERT A., business executive; b. Waterbury, Conn., May 7, 1952; s. Arnold A. and Mary (Garafola) M.; m. Jill Hanau, June 18, 1988; children: Robert A. Jr., Alexandra H. BA, Amherst (Mass.) Coll., 1975; MBA, Harvard U., 1979. CPA. Staff acct. Price Waterhouse, Boston, 1975-77; assoc. Lehman Bros., N.Y.C., 1979-82; v.p. Lehman Bros., 1982-85, sr. v.p., 1985-88, mng. dir., 1988-91; sr. v.p., treas. Am. Express Co., 1991-92; CFO First Data Corp., N.Y.C., 1992-93; gen. ptnr. Welsh, Carson, Anderson & Stowe, N.Y.C., 1993—; bd. dirs. Attachmate Corp., Global Knowledge Network Inc., Servantis Sys. Inc., Strategic Mortgage Svcs., Inc., Seer Techs., Inc. Home: 7 Hilltop Rd S Norwalk CT 06854-5001 Office: Welsh Carson Anderson Stowe Ste 3601 One World Financial Ctr New York NY 10281

MINISH, ROBERT ARTHUR, lawyer; b. Mpls., Dec. 25, 1938; s. William Arthur and Agnes Emilia (Olson) M.; m. Marveen Eleanor Allen, Sept. 16, 1961; 1 children: Roberta Ruth. BA, U. Minn., 1960, JD, 1963. Bar: Minn. 1963. Assoc. Popham, Haik, Schnobrich & Kaufman, Ltd., Mpls., 1963-67, ptnr., 1967—; bd. dirs. Braas Co., Mpls. Mem. ABA, Minn. Bar Assn. Avocations: fishing, traveling. Home: 331 Pearson Way NE Minneapolis MN 55432-2418 Office: Popham Haik Schnobrich & Kaufman 3300 Piper Jaffray Tower 222 S 9th St Minneapolis MN 55402

MINISI, ANTHONY JOSEPH, cardiologist, educator; b. Phila., May 9, 1954; m. Margaret Joan Conroy, May 23, 1980; children: John Anthony, Karen Margaret. BA cum laude, U. Pa., 1976, MD, 1980. Diplomate Am. Bd. Internal Medicine, Am. Bd. Cardiovascular Disease, Nat. Bd. Med. Examiners. Intern in internal medicine Med. Coll. Va., Richmond, 1980-81, resident, 1981-83, clin. fellow cardiology div., 1984-86, clin. instr. dept. medicine, 1983-84, instr., 1987-88, asst. prof., 1989—; mem. clin. attending staff cardiology div. McGuire VA Med. Ctr., Richmond, 1986-87, clin. attending in cardiology-Cardiac Catheterization Lab., 1987-88, attending staff, 1988-90, assoc. dir. Cardiac Catheterization Lab., 1989-93; dir. Cardiac Catheterization Lab., Richmond, 1993—. Co-author: (with others) Reflex Control of the Circulation, 1991, Cardiovascular Reflex Control in Health and Disease, 1993, Cardiovascular Reflex Control in Health and Disease, 1993; contbr. articles to profl. jours. Tng. grantee NIH, 1986. Fellow Am. Coll. Cardiology; mem. Am. Fedn. Clin. Rsch., Am. Heart Assn. Home: 7609 Dell Dr Richmond VA 23235-6303 Office: McGuire VA Med Ctr Div Cardiology Box 111J-1 1201 Broad Rock Blvd Richmond VA 23249-0001

MINISI, ANTHONY S., lawyer; b. Newark, Sept. 18, 1926; s. Anthony F. and Leonora (Petoia) M.; m. Rita Marie Hentz, Jan. 8, 1949; children: Claire, Anthony J., Joseph J., Brian A. BS, U. Pa., 1948, JD, 1952. Player, N.Y. Giants, NFL, 1948; law clk. to presiding judge Ct. of Common Pleas #6, Phila., 1952-54; sr. ptnr. Wolf, Block, Schorr and Solis-Cohen, Phila., 1954—; past pres., vice chmn. Robert E. Maxwell Meml. Football Club, Eastern Assn. Intercoll. Football Ofcls. Past chmn. Com. of Seventy, Phila.; former mem., past pres. Bd. of Edn., Tredyffrin/Easttown Joint Sch. Dist.; mem., past chmn. bd. supr. Easttown Twp.; past v.p. Cmty. Svcs. Planning Coun., Phila.; trustee U. Pa.; trustee, mem. exec. com. U. Pa. Health Sys.; mem. Clin. Care Assocs. U. Pa. Health Sys.; former mem., vice-chmn. Pa. State Bd. Law Examiners. Served to maj. USAR. Mem. ABA (ho. of dels.), Pa. Bar Assn., Phila. Jr. Bar Assn. (past pres.), Def. Lawyers Am., Assn. Trial Attys. Am., Phila. Bar Assn. (bd. of govs., past chmn.), Phila. Trial Lawyers Assn., Fed. Bar Assn., Phila. Trial Lawyers Assn. Republican. Roman Catholic. Clubs: Lawyers (past pres.), Justinian Soc., Union League (Phila.). Office: Wolf Block Schorr & Solis-Cohen SE Corner 15th & Chestnut Sts Philadelphia PA 19102

MINISTER, MICHAEL E., lawyer; b. Athens, Ohio, Feb. 14, 1944. BS, Ohio State U., 1966; JD, Capital U., 1974. Bar: Ohio 1974. Dir. adminstrn. City of Worthington, Ohio, 1970-73, city mgr., 1974, dir. law, 1975—; ptnr. Baker & Hostetler, Columbus, Ohio. Lt. (j.g.) USN, 1967-69. Mem. ABA. Office: Baker & Hostetler 65 E State St Ste 2100 Columbus OH 43215-4213*

MINK, ERIC P., newspaper columnist; b. St. Louis, Dec. 15, 1947; s. Joseph and Ida (Novack) M.; m. Claudia Eve Gellman, Mar. 22, 1970. BA, George Washington U., 1969. Consumer affairs editor, mng. editor The Midwest Motorist, St. Louis, 1973-77; consumer reporter, columnist St. Louis Post Dispatch, 1977-79, TV critic, 1979—; critic-at-large, commentator KSD-FM/KUSA Gannett Radio, St. Louis, 1987—; juror Banff (Alta., Can.) TV Festival, 1989, Alfred I. duPont-Columbia U. awards in broadcast journalism, N.Y.C., 1989—. Recipient Citation for excellence in consumer reporting Nat. Press Club, Washington, 1978, Lowell Mellett award citation Pa. State U. Sch. Communications, 1987. Office: St Louis Post Dispatch 900 N Tucker Blvd Saint Louis MO 63101-1069

MINK, JOHN ROBERT, dental educator; b. Peru, Ill., Sept. 8, 1927; s. Monte Franklin and Marcella (White) M.; m. Barbara Joanne Merrell, June 21, 1952; children: Sarah, Teresa, Kathleen, Mary, James, Elizabeth. BA, Ind. U., 1951; DDS with honors, 1956, MS in Pedodontics, 1961. Diplomate Am. Bd. Pedodontics (bd. examiners). Instr. Ind. U., Indpls., 1957-60, asst. prof., 1960-62; dir. dental Clinic Handicapped Children, James Whitcomb Riley Hosp. for Children, Indpls., 1957-62; mem. faculty U. Ky., Lexington, 1962—, chmn. dept. pedodontics, 1962-74, prof. pedodontics, 1966—, asst. dean clin. affairs Coll. Dentistry, 1974-80, assoc. dean clin. affairs, 1980-85; prof., chmn. dept. pediatric dentistry U. Ky. and U. Louisville, 1985-88; dir. U. Ky. Med. Plaza Dental Clinic, 1985-89; cons. pedodontics USPHS, 1969-72, U.S. Army, Fort Knox, 1969—, ADA, 1972—, Ft. Jackson, 1987—, Ft. Lewis, 1989. Pres. Vols. Bur. Lexington, Ky., 1972-73; bd. dirs. Vol. Action Ctr., 1978—; bd. dirs. Margaret Hall Sch., Versailles, Ky., chmn. bd., 1976—; pres. Margaret Hall Found., 1980—. Served with AUS, 1946-47. Fellow Am. Acad. Pedodontics, Internat. Coll. Dentists (dep. regent 1990—); mem. Am. Soc. Dentistry for Children (pres. Ky. chpt. 1967—), Ky. Assn. Pediat. Dentists (sec.-treas. 1979—), Am. Assn. Dental Schs., Blue Grass Dental Soc. (pres. 1985-86), Pierre Fauchard Acad., Ind. U. Pediat. Dentistry Alumni Assn. (pres. 1993—), Delta Upsilon, Delta Sigma Delta (Delta Epsilon chpt. sec.-treas. 1992-94, pres.-elect 1994, pres. 1995), Omicron Kappa Upsilon. Home: 5411 Parkers Mill Rd Lexington KY 40513-9711 Office: U Ky Coll Dentistry Chandler Med Ctr Lexington KY 40504

MINK, PATSY TAKEMOTO, congresswoman; b. Paia, Maui, Hawaii, Dec. 6, 1927; d. Suematsu and Mitama (Tateyama) Takemoto; m. John Francis Mink, Jan. 27, 1951; 1 child, Gwendolyn. Student, Wilson Coll., 1946, U. Nebr., 1947; BA, U. Hawaii, 1948; LLD, U. Chgo., 1951; DHL (hon.), Chaminade Coll., 1975, Syracuse U., 1976, Whitman Coll., 1981. Bar: Hawaii. Pvt. practice Honolulu, 1953-65; lectr. U. Hawaii, 1952-56, 59-62, 79-80; atty. Territorial Ho. of Reps., 1955; mem. Hawaii Ho. of Reps., 1956-58, Ter. Hawaii Senate, 1958-59, Hawaii State Senate, 1962-64, 89th-94th Congresses from 2nd Hawaii dist., 101st-104th Congresses from 2d dist. Hawaii, 1989—; mem. econ. and ednl. opportunity com., mem. budget com.; mem. U.S. del. to UN Law of Sea, 1975-76, Internat. Woman's Yr., 1975, UN Environ. Program, 1977, Internat. Whaling Commn., 1977; asst. sec. of state U.S. Dept. State, 1977-78. Charter pres. Young Dem. Club Oahu, 1954-56, Ter. Hawaii Young Dems., 1956-58; del. Dem. Nat. Conv., 1960, 72, 80; nat. v.p. Young Dem. Clubs Am., 1957-59; v.p. Ams. for Dem. Action, 1974-76, nat. pres., 1978-81; mem. nat. adv. com. White House Conf. on Families, 1979-80; mem. nat. adv. coun. Federally Employed Women. Recipient Leadership for Freedom award Roosevelt Coll., Chgo., 1968, Alii award 4-H Clubs Hawaii, 1969, Nisei of Biennium award, Freedom award Honolulu chpt. NAACP, 1971, Disting. Humanitarian award YWCA, St. Louis, 1972, Creative Leadership in Women's Rights award NEA, 1977, Human Rights award Am. Fedn. Tchrs., 1975, Feminist of Yr. award Feminist Majority Found., 1991, Margaret Brent award ABA, 1992. Office: US Ho of Reps 2135 Rayburn HOB Washington DC 20515*

MINKEL, HERBERT PHILIP, JR., lawyer; b. Boston, Feb. 11, 1947; s. Herbert Philip and Helen (Sullivan) M. AB, Holy Cross Coll., 1969; JD, NYU, 1972. Bar: Mass. 1973, N.Y. 1976, U.S. Dist. Ct. Mass. 1973, U.S. Dist. Ct. (so. dist.) N.Y. 1976. Law clk. U.S. Dist. Ct. Mass., Boston, 1972-73; assoc. Milbank, Tweed, Hadley & McCloy, N.Y.C., 1973-79; ptnr. Fried, Frank, Harris, Shriver & Jacobson, N.Y.C., 1979-94; adj. assoc. prof. NYU Law Sch., 1987-94; mem. adv. com. on bankruptcy rules Jud. Conf. U.S., 1987-93. Contbg. editor 5 Collier on Bankruptcy, 15th edit. 1979-95; contbr. articles to profl. jours.; co-author American Bankers Association Bankruptcy Manual, 1979. Root-Tilden scholar, NYU, 1969-72. Mem. ABA, Nat. Bankruptcy Conf., N.Y. Bar Assn., Assn. of Bar of City of N.Y.. Home: 85 E India Row Boston MA 02110 Office: Ste 3200 Exch Pl 53 State St Boston MA 02109

MINKEL, L. STEVEN, manufacturing executive, light. CFO Nimbus Mfg. Inc., Ruckersville, Va., Nimbus CD Internat., Inc., Ruckersville, Va. Office: Nimbus CD Internat Inc PO Box 7427 Charlottesville VA 22096 also: Nimbus CD Internat Inc Rt 629 Ruckersville VA 22968 also: PO Box 7427 Charlottesville VA 22906

MINKER, JACK, computer scientist, educator; b. Bklyn., July 4, 1927; s. Harry and Rose (Lapuck) M.; m. Rita Goldberg, June 24, 1951 (dec. Oct. 11, 1988); children: Michael Saul, Sally Anne. B.A. cum laude with honors in Math., Bklyn. Coll., 1949; M.S. in Math., U. Wis., 1950; Ph.D. in Math., U. Pa., 1959. Grad. teaching asst. U. Wis., 1949-50; tchr. math. Erasmus Hall High Sch., Bklyn., 1950-51; engr. Bell Aircraft Corp., Buffalo, 1951-52; mgr. info. tech. sect. RCA, Bethesda, Md., 1952-63; dir. tech. staff Auerbach Corp., Washington, 1963-67, tech. cons., 1967-72; mem. Faculty NIH Grad. Sch., 1965-66; vis. mem. faculty U. Md., 1967-68, assoc. prof. computer sci., 1968-71, prof., 1971—, 1st chmn. dept. computer sci., 1974-79; cons., speaker, lectr. in field; cons. NSF, 1979-82, chmn. adv. bd. on computer sci., 1980-82; prof. Inst. Advanced Computer Studies, 1986—; vice-chmn. Com. Concerned Scientists, 1973—; past mem. U.S. Nat. Com. for Fedn. Info. Documentalists. Author: (with H. Gallaire and J.M. Nicolas) Logic and Data Bases a Deductive Approach, 1984; editor: (with H. Gallaire and J.M. Nicholas) Advances in Data Base Theory, vol. 1, 1980, vol. 2, 1984, (with H. Gallaire) Logic and Data Bases, 1978, Foundations of Deductive Databases and Logic Programming, 1988, (with J. Lobo and A. Rajasekar) Foundations of Disjunctive Logic Programming, 1992; contbr. numerous articles to profl. publs.; publs. reviewer. Vice chmn. Com. Concerned Scientists, 1972—. With U.S. Army, 1945-46. Nat. Bur. Standards investigator, 1970-73, grantee, 1975-76; grantee NASA, 1969-81, NSF, 1971—, Air Force Office of Sci. Rsch., 1982-94, Army Rsch. Office, 1985-90. Fellow AAAS, ACM, IEEE (mem. editorial bd. Expert Info. Systems jour.), Am. Assn. Artificial Intelligence (founding); mem. Assn. Computing Machinery (chmn. nat. program com. 1968-69, vice chmn. com. on sci. freedom and human rights 1979-89, Outstanding Contbn. award Assn. Computer Machines, 1995, vice chmn. com. concerned scientists, 1972—). Jewish. Office: U Md Dept Computer Sci Inst Advanced Computer Studies College Park MD 20742

MINKOFF, JACK, economics educator; b. N.Y.C., Jan. 29, 1925; s. Isidore and Yetta (Fine) M.; m. Anne B. Johnson, June 19, 1948; children—Ellen, Paul. A.B., Cornell U., 1948; A.M., Columbia U., 1950, Ph.D. (Ford Found. fellow), 1960. Instr. econs. Western Res. U., 1952-53; instr. econs. Sarah Lawrence Coll., 1959-60; prof. econs., chmn. dept. social sci. Pratt Inst., Bklyn., 1960—; acting dean Sch. Liberal Arts and Scis. Pratt Inst., 1985-86, dean, 1986-93, acting provost, 1993-95; prof. econs., 1996—. Served with USAAF., 1943-45. Fellow Social Sci. Research Council, 1950-51. Mem. Phi Beta Kappa. Home: 57 Ruxton Rd Great Neck NY 11023-1528 Office: Pratt Inst Brooklyn NY 11205

MINKOWITZ, MARTIN, lawyer, former state government official; b. Bklyn.; s. Jacob and Marion (Kornblau) M.; 1 son from previous marriage, Stuart Allan. AA, Bklyn. Coll., 1959, BA, 1961; JD, Bklyn. Law Sch., 1963, LLM, 1965. Bar: N.Y. 1963, U.S. Supreme Ct. 1967, U.S. Tax Ct. 1974, all four U.S. Dist. Cts. N.Y. Ptnr. firm Minkowitz, Hagen & Rosenbluth, N.Y.C., 1964-76; gen. counsel State of N.Y. Workers' Compensation Bd., N.Y.C., 1976-81; gen. counsel, dep. supt. State of N.Y. Ins. Dept., N.Y.C., 1981-88; instr. CUNY, 1975; ptnr. Stroock & Stroock & Lavan, N.Y.C., 1988—; mem. adv. bd. Coll. Ins., 1987-90; adj. prof. law N.Y. Law Sch., N.Y.C., 1982—; lectr. ABA, N.Y. C. of C., Practicing Law Inst., N.Y. State Bar Assn., Nat. Assn. Ins. Commrs., Nat. Conf. Ins. Legis.; hearing officer N.Y.C. Transp. Dept., 1970-75; cons. City Council, N.Y.C., 1969. Author: (with others) Rent Stabilization and Control, 1973; (with others) Handling the Basic Workers' Compensation Law Case, 1982, 85, 87; co-author: Workers Compensation Insurance and Law Practice-The Next Generation, 1989; commentaries to McKinney's Consol. Laws, 1982—; mem. editorial bd. Jour. Occupational Rehabilitation U. Rochester, 1991—; contbr. numerous articles to profl. jours. Bd. dirs., sec. Kingsbay YM-YWHA, Bklyn., 1978—; pres. bd. dirs. Shore Terrace Co-op., Bklyn., 1982-83; co-chmn. exec. bd., met. council, nat. v.p. Am. Jewish Congress, N.Y.C., 1983-91; bd. dirs. Met. Coord. Coun. on Jewish poverty, 1993—, Nat. Conf. Christians and Jews (bd. dir. N.Y. divsn. 1994, nat. bd. trustees 1995—). Recipient cert. meritorious service Bklyn. Law Sch., 1963, Outstanding Pub. Service award Ind. Ins. Agts. Assn., 1988, citation outstanding performance State of N.Y. Workers' Compensation Bd., 1981, Disting. Leadership award N.Y. Claims Assn., 1986, City of Peace award State of Israel Bonds, 1986, Brotherhood award NCCJ, 1994. Mem. N.Y. County Lawyers Assn. (chmn. unlawful practice of law com. 1982-86, mem. profl. ethics com. 1985-91, chair worker's compensation com. 1988-91), N.Y. State Bar Assn. (chmn. unlawful practice of law com. 1981-83, mem. com. on profl. ethics 1981-84, chmn. com. profl. discipline 1988-92, Sustaining Mem. of Yr. award 1995), Soc. Ins. Recievers, Bklyn. Law Sch. Alumni Assn. (v.p. bd. dirs. 1984-92, pres. elect 1993-94, pres. 95—). Office: Stroock Stroock & Lavan 7 Hanover Sq New York NY 10004-2616

MINKOWYCZ, W. J., mechanical engineering educator; b. Libokhora, Ukraine, Oct. 21, 1937; came to U.S., 1949; s. Alexander and Anna (Tokan) M.; m. Diana Eva Szandra, May 12, 1973; 1 child, Liliana Christine Anne. B.S. in Mech. Engring., U. Minn., 1958, M.S. in Mech. Engring., 1961, Ph.D. in Mech. Engring, 1965. Asst. prof. U. Ill., Chgo., 1966-68, assoc. prof., 1968-78, prof., 1978—; cons. Argonne Nat. Lab, Ill., 1970-82, U. Hawaii, Honolulu, 1974—. Founding editor-in-chief Jour. Numerical Heat Transfer, 1978—; editor Internat. Jour. Heat and Mass Transfer, 1968—, Internat. Communications in Heat and Mass Transfer Jour., 1974—; editor book series: Computational and Physical Processes in Mechanics and Thermal Sciences, 1979—, Advances in Numerical Heat Transfer, 1996—; editor: Rheologically Complex Fluids, 1972, Handbook of Numerical Heat Transfer, 1988; contbr. articles to profl. jours. Recipient Silver Circle for Excellence in Teaching, U. Ill.-Chgo., 1975, 76, 81, 86, 90, 94, Harold A. Simon award Excellence in Teaching, 1986, Ralph Coats Roe Outstanding Tchr. award Am. Soc. Engring. Edn., 1988, U. Ill. Disting. Tchr. award, 1989. Fellow ASME (Heat Transfer Meml. award 1993); mem. Sigma Xi, Pi Tau Sigma. Republican. Ukrainian Catholic. Office: U Ill Dept Mech Engring Mail Code 251 842 W Taylor St Chicago IL 60607-7021

MINKUS, RAYMOND DAVID, communications and public relations executive; b. Chgo., Aug. 8, 1953; s. Fred and Roslyn Minkus; BS in Journalism, U. Mo., Columbia, 1975; m. Sara Anthony, June 26, 1977; children: Stephanie Raye, Evan Andrew. Reporter, asst. sect. editor Fairchild Publs., N.Y.C., 1975, Chgo.-Midwest editor, 1976; fin. news columnist Milw. Sentinel, 1976-78; sr. communications specialist, mgr. media rels. Miller Brewing Co. Milw., 1978-81; pres. Weiser Minkus Walek Communications, 1981-91; pres. Minkus & Dunne Communications, Inc., 1992—. Bd. dirs. Future Milw., 1980-81; mem. mktg. com. Milw. United Performing Arts Fund, 1980-81; communication task force Chgo. Area Cen. Com., 1984—; legis. asst. Mo. Ho. of Reps., 1974-75; bd dirs. Mental Health Assn. Ill., 1993—, Cystic Fibrosis Found., 1986-92. Recipient Outstanding Corp. Publ. award Bus. and Profl. Adv. Assn. Milw. Mem. Chgoland C. of C. (bd. dirs.), Pub. Rels. Soc. Internat. Assn. Bus. Communicators. Am., Chgo. Assn. Commerce and Industry (communications com., bd. dirs., exec. coms., div. v.p., Vol. of Yr. 1988). Contbr. articles to Common Stock Reporter, Women's Wear Daily, Chgo. Tribune, Commerce Mag., Prentice-Hall Exec. Action Report, others. Home: 2292 Sheridan Rd Highland Park IL 60035-2015 Office: Minkus & Dunne COmmunications, Inc. 150 S Wacker Dr Chicago IL 60606-4103

MINNELLI, LIZA, singer, actress; b. Los Angeles, Mar. 12, 1946; d. Vincente and Judy (Garland) M.; m. Peter Allen, 1967 (div. 1972); m. Jack Haley, Sept. 15, 1974 (div.); m. Mark Gero, Dec. 4, 1979 (div. 1992). Appeared in Off-Broadway revival of Best Foot Forward, 1963; recorded You Are For Loving, 1963, Tropical Nights, 1977, Liza Minelli at Carnegie Hall, 1987; appeared with mother at London Palladium, 1964; appeared in Flora, the Red Menace, 1965 (Tony award), The Act, 1977 (Tony award), The Rink, 1984; nightclub debut at Shoreham Hotel, Washington, 1965; films include Charlie Bubbles, 1967, The Sterile Cuckoo, 1969, Tell Me That You

Love Me, Junie Moon, 1970, Cabaret, 1972 (Oscar award), That's Entertainment, 1974, Lucky Lady, 1975, A Matter of Time, 1976, Silent Movie, 1976, New York, New York, 1977, Arthur, 1981, Rent A Cop, Arthur on the Rocks, 1988, Stepping Out, 1991; albums include: Results, 1989; appeared on TV in own spl. Liza With a Z, 1972 (Recipient Emmy award); other TV appearances include Goldie and Liza Together, 1980, Baryshnikov on Broadway, 1980, The Princess and the Pea, Showtime, 1983, A Time to Live, 1985, Sam Found Out, 1988, Liza Minnelli Live from Radio City Music Hall, PBS (Emmy nomination, Music Program Performance, 1993); internat. tour with Frank Sinatra, Sammy Davis Jr., 1988. Awarded the Brit. equivalent of the Oscar for Best Actress, 1972, Italy's David di Donatello award (twice), the Valentino award. Office: care PMK 1776 Broadway Fl 8 New York NY 10019-2002

MINNER, RUTH ANN, state senator; b. Milford, Del., Jan. 17, 1935; m. Roger Minner. Student Del. Tech. and Community Coll. Office receptionist Gov. of Del., 1972-74; mem. Del. Ho. of Reps., 1974-82; mem. Del. Senate, 1982-92; lt. gov. State of Del., Dover, 1993—; mem. Dem. Nat. Com., 1988. Home: RD 3 Box 694 Milford DE 19963 Office: Office Lt Gov Tatnall Bldg 3rd Fl Dover DE 19901*

MINNERLY, ROBERT WARD, headmaster; b. Yonkers, N.Y., Mar. 21, 1935; s. Richard Warren and Margaret Marion (DeBrocky) M.; m. Sandra Overmire, June 12, 1957; children: Scott Ward, John Robert, Sydney Sue. AB, Brown U., 1957; MAT, U. Tex., Arlington, 1980. Tchr., coach Rumsey Hall Sch., Washington, Conn., 1962-64; tchr., coach Berkshire Sch., Sheffield, Mass., 1964-70, asst. head, 1969-70, headmaster, 1970-76; dir. Salisbury (Conn.) Summer Sch. Reading and English, 1970; prin. upper sch. Ft. Worth Country Day Sch., 1976-86; headmaster Charles Wright Acad., Tacoma, Wash., 1986-96; cons. Tarrant County Coalition on Substance Abuse, 1982-84; mem. mayor's task force Tacoma Edn. Summit, 1991-92. Contbr. articles to profl. jours. Bd. dirs. Tacoma/Pierce County Good Will Games Art Coun., 1989; mem. exec. com. Am. Leadership Forum, 1991-95; mem. Broadway Ctr. for Performing Arts, Tacoma, 1988-94, mem. exec. com., 1990-93. Named Adminstr. of Yr. Wash. Journalism Edn. Assn., 1991. Mem. Pacific N.W. Assn. Ind. Schs. (chmn. long-range planning com. 1989-92, exec. com. 1990-92, 91, v.p. 1994). Republican. Presbyterian. Home: 4214 39th Avenue Ct NW Gig Harbor WA 98335-8029 Office: Charles Wright Acad 7723 Chambers Creek Rd W Tacoma WA 98467-2099

MINNICH, DALE E., religious administrator. Assoc. gen. sec. Gen. Svcs. Commn. Office: Ch of the Brethren 1451 Dundee Ave Elgin IL 60120-1674

MINNICH, JOSEPH EDWARD, tourist railway consultant; b. Swanton, Ohio, Sept. 13, 1932; s. Charles and Leila (Gaiman) M.; m. Frances Katherine Searcy, Feb. 6, 1977; children: Christopher, Susan, Teresa. Student, U. Toledo, 1956-58, Am. U., 1969. Ins. broker Wright Russell & Bay Co., 1961-67; ch. adminstr. St. Paul's Luth. Ch., Toledo, 1968-80; pres. Toledo Lake Erie & Western R.R., 1978-81, Heritage R.R. Co., 1981-83; exec. v.p. Centennial Rail, Ltd., Denver, 1981—; v.p. Airpower West Ltd., 1992-95. Author: Steam Locomotives in the United States, 1985, Historic Diesels in the United States, 1988; editor Trainline mag., 1979—. V.p. Airpower West, Ltd., 1992-95. Sgt. USAF, 1951-55. Nat. Assn. Ch. Bus. Adminstrs. fellow, 1971. Mem. Tourist Ry. Assn. (bd. dirs. 1984-95, Disting. Svc. award 1991), Colo. Ry. Mus. Republican. Lutheran. Home: 3641 S Yampa St Aurora CO 80013-3527 Office: Centennial Rail Ltd PO Box 460393 Aurora CO 80046-0393

MINNICH, VIRGINIA, retired medical researcher, educator; b. Zanesville, Ohio, Jan. 24, 1910; d. Rufus Humphrey and Ollie (Burley) M.; m. Jerry Hajek, Oct. 23, 1987. BS in Home Econs, Ohio State U., 1937; MS in Nutrition, Iowa State Coll., 1938; ScD (hon.), Williams Woods Coll., Fulton, Mo., 1972. Research asst., then research assoc. medicine, div. hematology Washington U. Sch. Medicine, St. Louis, 1939-78; mem. faculty Washington U. Sch. Medicine, 1958—, prof. medicine, 1974-78, prof. emeritus, 1978—. Contbr. articles to profl. jours. Recipient Alumni award home econs. Ohio State U., 1975; named St. Louis Woman of Achievement Group Action Council, 1947; award for founder of thalassemia research in Thailand, Mahidol U. Bangkok, 1985; Fulbright-Hays grantee Turkey, 1964. Mem. Am. Fedn. Clin. Research, Soc. Exptl. Biology and Medicine, Internat., Am. socs. hematology, Sigma Xi, Omicron Nu, Phi Upsilon Omicron. Office: Washington U Med Sch Dept Medicine Saint Louis MO 63110 *I discovered at an early age that there are many obstacles on the road to success. My friends and family helped me over the hurdles and they were the ones who were instrumental in the achievement of my goals.*

MINNICK, CARLTON PRINTESS, JR., bishop; b. Greensboro, N.C., Sept. 8, 1927; s. Carlton Printess and Catherine (Johnson) M.; m. Mary Ann Adams, Sept. 5, 1946; children: Mary Ann, Gregory Carlton, Patte Carroll, Jonathan Allan. Student, U. Va., 1944-45; BA, Lynchburg Coll., 1954; BD, Union Theol Sem. in Va., 1957, MTh, 1958. On trial Va. Conf., 1954, ordained deacon United Meth. Ch., 1955, full connection, 1956, elder, 1957. Pastor Mt. Airy charge United Meth. Ch., 1951-54, pastor Goochland charge, 1954-58; pastor St. James Meth. Ch. United Meth. Ch., Ferrum, 1958-1963; pastor Westhampton Meth. Ch. United Meth. Ch., Richmond, 1963-67; pastor Mt. Olivet United Meth. Ch. Arlington, 1973-78; supt. Alexandria Dist. United Meth. Ch., 1978-80, bishop, 1980—, resident bishop Jackson, Miss. area, 1980-84; bishop United Meth. Ch., Raleigh, N.C., 1984&. Office: United Meth Ch PO Box 10955 Raleigh NC 27605-0955

MINNICK, MALCOLM DAVID, lawyer; b. Indpls., July 5, 1946; s. Malcolm Dick and Frances Louise (Porter) M.; m. Heidi Rosemarie Klein, May 24, 1972. BA, U. Mich., 1968, JD, 1972. Bar: Calif. 1972, U.S. Dist. Ct. (cen. dist.) Calif. 1972, U.S. Ct. Appeals (9th cir.) 1984, U.S. Dist. Ct. (no. dist.) Calif. 1986, U.S. Supreme Ct. 1986. Assoc. Lillick McHose & Charles, Los Angeles, 1972-78; ptnr. Lillick & McHose, Los Angeles, 1978-91, Pillsbury, Madison & Sutro (formerly Lillick & McHose), San Francisco, 1991—; group mgr. Creditors Rights and Bankruptcy Group, 1993—; panelist Calif. Continuing Edn. of Bar, L.A., 1982-86, 88, Practicing Law Inst., 1992, 93, 94; bd. govs. Fin. Lawyers Conf., L.A., 1981-84; mem. exec. com. Lillick & McHose, 1982-85. Co-author: Checklist for Secured Commercial Loans, 1983. Mem. ABA (corp., banking and bus. law sect.), Calif. Bar Assn. (Uniform Comml. Code com. 1983-86), L.A. County Bar Assn. (exec. com. comml. law and bankruptcy sect. 1987-90), Bar Assn. San Francisco (comml. law and bankruptcy sect.), L.A. County Club, Univ. Club (bd. dirs. 1983-86, pres. 1985-86). Avocation: golf. Office: Pillsbury Madison & Sutro 235 Montgomery St Fl 14 San Francisco CA 94104-2902

MINNICK, MALCOLM L., JR., clergy member, church administrator. Exec. dir. Division for Outreach of the Evangelical Lutheran Church in America, Chicago, Ill. Office: Evangelical Lutheran Church Am 8765 W. Higgins Rd Chicago IL 60631-4101

MINNICK, WALTER CLIFFORD, building materials company executive; b. Walla Walla, Wash., Sept. 20, 1942; s. Walter Lawrence and Dorothy (Waldron) M.; children from previous marriage: Amy Louise, Adam Wade; m. A.K. Lienhart. BA summa cum laude in Econs., Whitman Coll., 1964; MBA with high distinction, Harvard U., 1966, JD magna cum laude, 1969. Bar: Oreg. and Wash. bars. Assoc. firm Davies, Biggs, Strayer, Stoel & Boley, Portland, Oreg., 1969-70; staff asst. to pres. Domestic Council, Washington, 1971-72; dep. asst. dir. Office Mgmt. and Budget, Washington, 1972-73; with T.J. Internat., Boise, Idaho, 1974-95, v.p. div. ops., 1976-79, pres., COO, 1979-95, pres., CEO, 1986-95, also past chmn. bd. dirs., trustee; pvt. investigator, 1995—; bd. dirs. Eljer Corp., MacMillan Bloedel, Ltd. Trustee, past chmn. Albertson Coll. of Idaho; past chmn. bus. adv. coun. Boise State U. Sch. Bus., bus. com. Coll. Idaho; mem. exec. com. Idaho Bus. Coun.; mem. Gov. Coun. of the Wilderness Soc. With U.S. Army, 1970-72. Named Idaho Bus. Leader of Yr., 1992. Mem. Wash. State Bar Assn., Oreg. State Bar Assn., Idaho Conservation League, Nature Conservancy, Boise Fgn. Affairs Soc. (mem. exec. com.), Bogus Basin Recreation Assn. (past chmn.). Unitarian. Office: T J Internat Inc Box 65 380 E Parkcenter Blvd Boise ID 83706-3962

MINNIGH, JOEL DOUGLAS, library director; b. Greenville, Pa., Apr. 9, 1949; s. Wendell Ellsworth and Frances Alene (Hyde) M.; m. Margaret Beth Crowther, Dec. 26, 1972; children: Bradley Dean, Douglas Knox. BA, Allegheny Coll., 1971; MLS, U. Pitts., 1975. Cert. libr., Pa. Asst. libr. Wilkinsburg (Pa.) Pub. Libr., 1976-77, head libr., 1977—. Bd. dirs. Goodwill Industries Pitts., 1980-90; vice chmn. bd. dirs. Bach Choir Pitts., 1984-87; sec., bd. dirs. United Meth. Ch. Union, Pitts., 1987-88; elder, deacon Fox Chapel Presbyn. Ch., 1987—; v.p. Friends of Music Libr.-Carnegie Libr., 1988—. Recipient honor Goodwill Industries Pitts., 1990, citation Pa. Senate, 1991. Mem. Pa. Libr. Assn. (treas. S.W. chpt. 1988-89), Allegheny County Libr. Assn. Republican. Avocations: travel, cooking, gardening, music, reading. Home: 1009 Blackridge Rd Pittsburgh PA 15235-2719 Office: Wilkinsburg Pub Libr 605 Ross Ave Pittsburgh PA 15221-2145

MINNIX, BRUCE MILTON, television and theatre director; b. Hendersonville, N.C., Apr. 26, 1923; s. Bruce Milton and Jane Irene (Leverett) M.; m. Corinne McClure, Aug. 5, 1950; 1 child, Tracy Logue. B.A., U. N.C., 1948. mem. faculty New Sch., N.Y.C., 1977-80; adj. prof., Bklyn., 1985; AT&T sales tng. program, 1987. Dir. numerous TV shows including: U.S. Steel Hour, 1961-62, Merchant of Venice, 1962, Essay on Doors, 1963, Never Too Young, 1965-66, On Being Black, 1969, The Haggadah Oratorio, 1981, Search for Tomorrow, 1968-74, All My Children, 1978-79, Another World, 1981, Texas, 1981-82, Body Talk, 1983, As the World Turns, 1985-86; The Cradle Will Rock, 1986 (Emmy nomination), Minolta Tng. series Minolta Info. Network, 1980-81; dir. Citibank, 1984, N.J. Bell (AT&T), 1985; dir. Victorian Cape May A Video Visit to a Town out of Time, 1988 (Bronze medal Houston Film Festival), dir. Pitney Bowes Copier Intro 1992, Time Warner Cable 1991; producer, writer: Mt. Washington Valley, A Video Visit in Four Seasons, 1990; Actor: Music Video by Little Texas What Might Have Been, 1993. Mayor, City of Cape May, N.J., 1972-76; founding mem., 3-term pres. Mid-Atlantic Center for Arts. Served with USN, 1943-45. Mem. Dirs. Guild Am.

MINOCHA, ANIL, physician, educator, researcher; b. India, Feb. 4, 1957; Came to U.S., 1982; s. Ram Saroop and Kamla Devi M. Pre-med. diploma, Punjab U., India, 1974; MD, Med. Coll., Rohtak, India, 1980; postgrad. studies in pharmacology, Baylor Coll. Medicine, 1982-84. Diplomate Am. Bd. Internal Medicine, Am. Bd. Gastroenterology, Am. Bd. Forensic Medicine. House officer depts. ophthalmology and dermatology Med. Coll. Hosp., Rohtak, India, 1980-81; med. officer State Health Svcs. Govts. of Punjab and Haryana, India, 1981-82; rsch. asst. Baylor Coll. Med., Houston, 1982-84; fellow clin. pharmacology U. Va., Charlottesville, 1984-86; resident physician Franklin Square Hosp., Balt., 1986-89; fellow gastroenterology Mich. State U., East Lansing, 1989-91; asst. prof. U. Louisville, 1991-95; assoc. prof. medicine U. Okla., Oklahoma City, 1995—; instr. dept. medicine Mich. State U., 1989-91; staff physician dept. medicine VAA Med. Ctr., Louisville, 1991-95; mem. credentials com. Humana Hosp., U. Louisville, 1992, other coms., 1992-94; mem. R&D com. VA Hosp., 1992-95; presenter in field. Contbr. numerous articles to profl. jours. Prin. investigator Gulf Biosystems, Charlottesville, 1985; biomed. rsch. grantee Mich. State U., 1990; sch. medicine rsch. grantee U. Louisville, 1993. Fellow Am. Coll. Physicians, Am. Coll. Gastroenterology; mem. Am. Gastroenterol. Assn., Am. Assn. for Study of Liver Disease.

MINOGUE, JOHN P., academic administrator, priest, educator; b. Chgo.. B in Philosophy, St. Mary's Sem.; MDiv, Deandreis Inst. Theology, 1972; M in Theology, DePaul U., 1975; D in Ministry, St. Mary of the Lake Sem., 1987. Ordained Vincentian priest, 1972. Vincentian priest Congregation of the Mission; instr. theology, dir. clin. pastoral placement programs St. Thomas Sem., Denver, 1972-76; instr. grad. theology, asst. then acad. dean DeAndreis Inst., 1976-83; pres. DePaul U., Chgo., 1993—; trustee DePaul U., 1991—; bd. mems. DePaul U. Corp., 1981-91; adj. prof. Sch. New Learning DePaul U., 1984—, instr. law and med. ethics Coll. Law DePaul U., 1989—; asst. prof. clin. ob.-gyn. Northwestern U.; instr. health care ethics St. Joseph Coll. Nursing, Joliet, Ill., Northwestern Sch. Nursing, Chgo.; cons. nat. heatlh care ethics, patient decision-making. Office: De Paul U 25 E Jackson Blvd Chicago IL 60604-2218

MINOGUE, ROBERT BROPHY, retired nuclear engineer; b. Covington, Ky., Jan. 31, 1928; s. Joseph and Catherine Ann (Brophy) M.; m. Marie Joan Clarke, June 12, 1954; children: Patrick, Margaret, Marie, Francis. B.S., Thomas More Coll., 1949; M.S., U. Cin., 1951; grad., Oak Ridge Sch. Reactor Tech., 1952. Registered profl. engr., Calif. Nuclear engr., then head nuclear tech. sect. naval reactors br. AEC, Washington, 1952-56; head research reactor design and enngring., then head nuclear power plant engring. sect. Gen. Atomic div. Gen. Dynamics Corp., 1957-67; chief spl. projects br. div. reactor standards AEC, Washington, 1967-72, asst. dir., then dep. dir. regulatory standards, 1972-74; dir. office standards devel. Nuclear Regulatory Commn., Washington, 1975-80, dir. office research, 1980-86; pvt. practice Temecula, Calif., 1986—; U.S. mem. sr. adv. group Safety Standards IAEA, 1974-86; mem. Com. on Interagy. Radiation Research and Policy Coordination, 1982-86. Author: Reactor Shielding Design Manual, 1956; patentee: Triga Research Reactor. Served with AUS, 1946-48. Recipient Bernard F. Langer award, ASME, 1982. Mem. ASTM (dir. 1975-76, 77-80). Roman Catholic. Home and Office: 29743 Marhill Cir Temecula CA 92591-1809

MINOR, CHARLES DANIEL, lawyer; b. Columbus, Ohio, May 28, 1927; s. Walter Henry and Helen Margaret (Bergman) M.; m. Mary Jo Klinker, Dec. 27, 1950; children: Elizabeth, Daniel, Amy. B.S. in Bus. Adminstrn, Ohio State U., 1950, J.D. summa cum laude, 1952. Bar: Ohio 1952. Mem. firm Vorys, Sater, Seymour and Pease, Columbus, 1952—, ptnr., 1957-93, of counsel, 1993—; bd. dirs. Inland Products, Inc., Worthington Industries, Inc. Served with USNR, 1945-46. Mem. Columbus, Ohio State bar assns., The Columbus Club, Double Eagle Club, Scioto Country Club. Republican. Office: Vorys Sater Seymour & Pease 52 E Gay St Columbus OH 43215-3108

MINOR, GEORGE GILMER, III, drug and hospital supply company executive; b. 1940; married. BA, Va. Mil. Inst., 1963; MBA, U. Va., 1966. With Owens & Minor, Inc., Richmond, Va., 1963—, mgr. sales Acme Candy Co. div., 1966-68, mgr. retail mktg., 1968-73, div. mgr. wholesale drug br., 1973-77, v.p., 1977-80, exec. v.p., 1980-81, pres., chmn., CEO, 1981—, also bd. dirs. Office: Owens & Minor Med Inc 4800 Cox Rd Richmond VA 23060*

MINOR, JOSEPH EDWARD, civil engineer, educator; b. Corpus Christi, Tex., June 2, 1938; s. William Smoot Jr. and Irene (Schiller) M.; m. Treva Ann Edmiston, Sept. 3, 1960; children: Joseph Edward Jr., Sharon Diane. BSCE, Tex. A&M U., 1959, M of Engring., 1960; PhD, Tex. Tech U., 1974. Registered profl. engr., Tex., Mo., Fla. Sr. rsch. engr. Southwest Research Inst., San Antonio, 1962-69; P. Whitfield Horn prof. Tex. Tech U., Lubbock, 1969-88; Thomas Reese prof., chmn. dept. civil engring. U. Mo., Rolla, 1988-93, rsch. prof., 1993—; pres. Insulating Glass Cert. Council, N.Y., 1986-89. Contbr. articles to profl. jours. Served with USAR. Recipient Disting. Engr. award Tex. Tech U., 1989; Nat. Def. fellow, 1959-60; Fulbright scholar, 1978. Fellow ASCE (pres. Tex. sect. 1984-85); mem. Nat. Soc. Profl. Engrs., Am. Meteorol. Soc. Presbyterian. Avocation: fishing. Office: Joseph E Minor PE Consulting Engineer PO Box 603 Rockport TX 78381-0603

MINOR, RALEIGH COLSTON, management consultant; b. Charlottesville, Va., June 3, 1936; s. Charles Venable and Louise (Minetree) M.; m. Nancy Ettinger, Oct. 12, 1963; children: Eves Scott Minetree, Catherine Colston. BA in Econs., U. Va., 1958, MBA in Fin., 1960. Cert. mgmt. cons.; cert. turnaround profl. With NCNB Charlotte, N.C., 1961-63; sales rep. IBM, Balt., 1963-65; various positions C&O/B&O R.R., Clev., Balt., 1965-69; v.p., CFO Info. Industries, Inc., Phila., 1969-71; CFO Quechee (Vt.) Lakes Corp., 1971-73, Hope Products, Inc., Fitchburg, Mass., 1973-75; pres. Standard Pyroxoloid Corp., Fitchburg, 1975-76; prin. Pace Cons. Group, Hartford, Conn., 1976-86; prin., founder, treas. Allomet Ptnrs. Ltd., N.Y., Ga., 1986—; COO, Cuisinarts, Stamford, 1989-90; guest lectr. Darden Sch. U. Va., 1986—. Contbr. articles to profl. jours. Mem. Turnaround Mgmt. Assn. (founder), Inst. Mgmt. Cons., Newcomen Soc. U.S., The Landings Club. Episcopalian. Avocations: reading, bridge, tennis, golf. Office: Allomet Ptnrs Ltd 325 E 77th St New York NY 10021-2257

MINOR, ROBERT ALLEN, lawyer; b. Washington, Oct. 20, 1948; s. Robert Walter and Joan (Allen) M.; m. Sue Ellyn Blose, June 13, 1981; children: Robert Barratt, Sarah Allen. AB in English, Duke U., 1970; JD, Ohio State U., 1975. Bar: Ohio 1975, U.S. Dist. Ct. (so. dist.) Ohio 1976, D.C. 1979. Assoc. Vorys, Sater, Seymour & Pease, Columbus, Ohio, 1975-82, ptnr., 1982—. Author seminar articles. With U.S. Army, 1970-72. Mem. ABA, Ohio Bar Assn., Columbus Bar Assn., Athletic Club Columbus, Scioto Country Club. Republican. Presbyterian. Office: Vorys Sater Seymour & Pease PO Box 1008 52 E Gay St Columbus OH 43216-1008

MINOR, RONALD RAY, minister; b. Aliceville, Ala., Nov. 3, 1944; s. Hershel Ray and Minnie Ozell (Goodson) M.; m. Gwendolyn Otella Newsome, July 25, 1970; 1 child, Rhonda Rene. BA in Ministerial, Southeastern Bible Coll., 1971, BA in Secondary Edn., 1973; DDiv, Southern Bible Coll., 1984. Ordained to ministry Pentecostal Ch. of God, 1968. Gen. sec. Pentecostal Ch. of God, Joplin, Mo., 1979—; dist. supt. Pentecostal Ch. of God, Philadelphia, Miss., 1975-79; pastor Pentecostal Ch. of God, Bartow, Fla., Orient Park Tabernacle, Tampa, Fla.; pres. Pentecostal Young People's Assn., Fla. and Miss.; sec. Gen. Bd. Pentecostal Ch. of God, Joplin, 1979; bd. dirs. Nat. Assn. Evangs., Wheaton, Ill., 1981-96; adv. coun. Am. Bible Soc., N.Y.C., 1979—; sec. Commn. Chaplains, Washington, 1991-95. Home: 2625 E 13th St Joplin MO 64801-5353 Office: Pentecostal Ch of God 4901 Pennsylvania Ave Joplin MO 64804-4947

MINOR, RUTH EMALINE, library media specialist; b. Leeton, Mo., Aug. 15, 1933; d. Russell Cooper and Katherine May (Butcher) Miller; m. William Marion Minor, Nov. 14, 1952; children: Christine E. Minor McMenemy, Kathleen E. Minor Sternecker. BS in Edn., Ctrl. Mo. State U., 1969; MA in Edn. with emphasis in libr. sci., U. Mo., Kansas City, 1974. Elem. tchr. Valley Grove Sch., Windsor, Mo., 1952-53, Adams Sch., Warrensburg, Mo., 1953-54; sec., bookkeeper 1st Bapt. Sch., Odessa, Mo., 1962-64, Presbyn. Ch., Clinton, Mo., 1964-66; libr. aide Clinton (Mo.) Pub. Schs., 1966-67; elem. tchr. Garden City (Mo.) Elem. Sch., 1969-70, Faubion and Nashua-North Kansas City Schs., Kansas City, 1970-78, Harrisonville (Mo.) McEowen Sch., 1978-84; libr. media specialist Harrisonville Elem. Sch., 1984-95; ret., 1995; grad. tchr. LaVerne (Calif.) U., 1978-80. Mem. AAUW (v.p.), Mo. Assn. Sch. Librs., Mo. Nat. Edn. Assn. (treas. local chpt.), Internat. Reading Assn., Cass County Hist. Soc., Johnson County Hist. Soc., Mo. Fedn. Women's Clubs (pres.), Women's Club William Jewell Coll., Alpha Delta Kappa (v.p.). Democrat. Baptist. Avocations: genealogy, antiques. Home: 1901 Thunderbird Dr Harrisonville MO 64701-1563

MINOW, JOSEPHINE BASKIN, civic worker; b. Chgo., Nov. 3, 1926; d. Salem N. and Bessie (Sampson) Baskin; m. Newton N. Minow, May 29, 1949; children: Nell, Martha, Mary. BS, Northwestern U., 1948. Asst. to advt. dir. Mandel Brothers Dept. Store, Chgo., 1948-49; tchr. Francis W. Parker Sch., Chgo., 1949-50; vol. in civil and charitable activities, 1950—; bd. dirs. Juvenile Protective Assn., Chgo., 1958—; pres. Juvenile Protective Assn., 1973-75; bd. dirs. Parnham Trust, Beaminster, Dorset, Eng. Founder, coord. Children's div. Hospitality and Info. Svc., Washington, 1961-63; mem. Caucus Com., Glencoe, Ill., 1965-69; co-chmn. spl. study on juvenile justice Chgo. Community Trust, 1978-80; chmn. Know Your Chgo., 1980-83; bd. dirs. Chgo. Coun. Fgn. Rels.; trustee Chgo. Hist. Soc., Ravinia Festival Assn.; mem. women's bd. Field Mus., U. Chgo.; founding mem., v.p. women's bd. Northwestern U., 1978; bd. govs. Chgo. Symphony, 1966-73, 76—; mem. Citizens Com. Juvenile Ct. of Cook County; exec. com. Northwestern U. Libr. Coun., 1974—. Recipient spl. award Chgo. Sch. and Workshop for Retarded, 1975, Children's Guardian award Juvenile Protective Assn., 1993. Mem. Hebrew Immigrant Aid Soc. (bd. dirs. 1977—, award 1988), Casino Club, Friday Club, Northmoor Country Club. Democrat. Jewish. Office: Chgo Hist Soc Clark St at North Ave Chicago IL 60614

MINOW, MARTHA LOUISE, law educator; b. 1954. AB, U. Mich., 1975; EdM, Harvard U., 1976; JD, Yale U., 1979. Bar: Mass. 1981. Law clk. to Judge David L. Bazelon U.S. Ct. Appeals (D.C. cir.), 1979-80; law to Assoc. Justice Thurgood Marshall U.S. Supreme Ct., 1980-81; asst. prof. Harvard U., Cambridge, Mass., 1981-86, prof., 1986—; trustee William T. Grant Found.; bd. dirs. Judge David L. Bazelon Ctr. for Mental Health Law, The Covenant Found. Trustee emeritus Judge Baker Children's Ctr.; bd. dirs. ABF, 1985-94; mem. Harvard Project on Schooling and Children. Sr. fellow Ethics and Professions Harvard U. Mem. Law and Soc. Assn. Office: Harvard Law Sch Cambridge MA 02138

MINSHALL, DREXEL DAVID, retired manufacturing company executive; b. Bridgeport, Nebr., Nov. 1, 1917; s. Charles D. and Minnie C. (Nordell) M.; m. Betty Jane Tesdell, Feb. 12, 1938 (dec. June 1971); children—Drexel David, Carol J. Minshall Preston; m. Roylynn Hurlburt McAllister, Apr. 19, 1974. Student, Colo. U., 1934-38. Sales mgr. Gates Rubber Co., Denver, 1939-61; v.p. mktg. Perfect Circle Corp., Hagerstown, Ind., 1961-65; pres. Dana Parts Co. div. Dana Corp., Toledo, Ohio, 1965-67, group v.p., 1967-73, sr. group v.p., 1973-79; pres. Service Parts Worldwide, 1979-81; chmn. bd. Dana Western Hemisphere Trade Corp., Toledo, 1970-81; dir. Dana World Trade Corp., Ludwig Motors Corp., Corp. HZ, Caracas, Venezuela, Arcamsa, Rosario, Argentina, Brown Bros. Ltd., London, Eng.; pres. Double D Mktg. Corp. Bd. dirs. Community Chest, 1972-75; trustee Toledo Boys Club, 1967-82. Mem. Automotive Service Industries Assn. (past pres.), Automotive Hall of Fame (past chmn.), Automotive Acad., Nat. Inst. Automotive Service Excellence (bd. dirs. 1972-86, past chmn.), Nat. Automotive Parts Assn. (bd. dirs. mfrs. council 1971-81, past chmn.), Motor and Equipment Mfrs. Assn. (product v.p. 1972-75), Alpha Tau Omega. Clubs: Toledo, Inverness; Atlantis Golf (Fla.). Lodges: Masons, Shriners. Contbr. articles to profl. jours. Home: 620 Estates Way Atlantis FL 33462

MINSKER, ROBERT STANLEY, consultant, former industrial relations executive; b. Pitts. Jan. 1, 1911; s. Theodore Kühne and Isabella Lavinia (Trumbor) M.; BS, U. Ill., 1934; postgrad. Pa. State U., 1938-39; m. Marion Elizabeth Warner, May 29, 1937; children: Norma (Mrs. Leo Jerome Brown II), Robert S., James. D. With Owens-Ill., Inc., Toledo, Ohio, 1934-76, pers. dir. Clarion (Pa.) plant, 1936-40, per. dir. Columbus (Ohio) plant, 1940-44, mgr. indsl. rels. Alton, 1945-72, adminstr. workmen's compensation, safety and health Ill. and pub. affairs Ill. Plants, 1972-76; dir. Germania Fin. Corp., 1963-82, Germania Bank 1953-82, hon. dir., 1982-91; assoc. faculty So. Ill. U., 1959-64; bd. dirs., chmn., CEO Midwestern Comm. Inc. Lectr., cons. Chmn. Madison County Savs. Bond Campaign, 1959-61; active Boy Scouts Am.; pres. Piasa Bird Coun., 1949-51, mem. exec. bd., 1945-90; mem. grievance com. panel State of Ill. Dept. Pers., 1967-80; vice chmn. Higher Edn. Coordinating Coun. Met. St. Louis, 1966-70; founder Board Pride, Inc., 1966—. Mem. Bd. Edn., 1957-70, pres. 1961-70. Bd. dirs., treas., sec., exec. com. Alton Meml. Hosp., 1969-88, dir. emeritus 1988—, bd. dirs. Alton Meml. Hosp. Found., 1986-91; Jr. Achievement, United Fund.; bd. dirs. Cmty. Chest, v.p., 1949-54, 61-66, gen. chmn., 1949-50; adminstr., sec., vice chmn. Alton Found., 1955—; trustee Lewis and Clark C.C., sec. bd., 1970-77; bd. dirs. McKendree Coll., 1981—; mem. pres. coun. U. Ill. Found., Alton Police Chief Adv. Com., 1994—. Recipient Silver Beaver award Boy Scouts of Am., 1951, Achievement award U.S. Treasury Dept., 1951, Hall of Fame award Piasa Bird Coun., 1969, Alton Citizens' award, 1988, Southwestern Ill. Leadership Coun. award, 1989, Lovejoy Human Rights award, 1989, Pride Outstanding Citizen award, 1988; named to Lewis and Clark Hall of Fame, 1977, Impact Cmty. Svc. award, 1992, Ill. State Bd. Edn. Cmty. mem. award of excellence, 1995, Marquett H.S. Svc. Leadership award, 1995, Boys & Girls Club Man and Youth award, 1996, Urban League chmn.'s award, 1996. Mem. Alton C. of C. (chmn. pub. rels. 1951-54), U. Ill. Varsity "I" Assn., U. Ill. Alumni Assn., Nature Conservation Assn. (a founder), Acacia, Alpha Phi Omega. Methodist. Clubs: Masons, (32 deg.), K.T., Shriners. Home: 2018 Chapin Pl Alton IL 62002-4631

MINSKY, BRUCE WILLIAM, lawyer; b. Queens, N.Y., Sept. 28, 1963; m. Jill R. Heinter, May 1992; 1 child, Aryeh Hanan. BA in Polit. Sci., Boston U., 1985; JD, Southwestern U., 1988; postgrad., Boston U., 1989. Bar: Calif. 1988, Conn. 1989, N.Y. 1990, U.S. Dist. Ct. (ea. and so. dist.), U.S. Ct. Appeals. Assoc. Quirk & Bakalar, N.Y.C., 1989-91; house counsel Banco Popular de P.R., N.Y.C., 1991—, Banco Popular, FSB, N.J., 1995—. Atty. Monday Night Law Pro Bono Svcs., N.Y.C. Mem. Assn. of Bar of City of N.Y. (young lawyers com. 1993-95). Avocations: music, sports, literature. Office: Banco Popular de PR 7 W 51st St New York NY 10019

MINTER, DAVID LEE, English literature educator; b. Midland, Tex., Mar. 20, 1935; s. Kenneth Cruse and Frances (Hennessey) M.; m. Cynthia Caroline Sewell, Dec. 22, 1957; children: Christopher Sewell, Frances Elizabeth. B.A., N. Tex. State U., 1957, M.A., 1959; B.D., Yale U., 1961, Ph.D., 1965. Univ. lectr. Hamburg (W. Ger.) U., 1965-66; lectr. Yale U., 1966-67; asst. prof. Rice U., Houston, 1967-69, assoc. prof., 1969-74, prof., 1974-80; prof. English Emory U., Atlanta, 1981-89, Asa G. Candler prof. Am. lit., 1989-90, dean Coll. Arts and Scis., 1981-90, v.p. arts and scis., 1984-90; Libbie Shearn Moody prof. English Rice U., Houston, 1990—. Author: The Interpreted Design as a Structural Principle in American Prose, 1969, William Faulkner: His Life and Work, 1980, 82, 91, A Cultural History of the American Novel: Henry James to William Faulkner, 1994, 96; editor: Twentieth-Century Interpretations of Light in August, 1969, The Norton Critical Edit. of The Sound and the Fury, 1987, 93; co-editor: The Harper American Literature, 1986, 93, The Columbia Literary History of the United States, 1987; also articles and revs. Fulbright Travel fellow, 1966; Nat. Endowment for Humanities fellow, 1969-70; Am. Council Learned Socs. grantee, 1975; Fred Harris Daniels fellow, 1980. Mem. MLA, Am. Lit. Group, Am. Studies Assn., Phi Beta Kappa. Methodist. Home: 5 Sunset Blvd Houston TX 77005-1836 Office: Rice U Dept English PO Box 1892 Houston TX 77251-1892

MINTER, JERRY BURNETT, electronic component company executive, engineer; b. Ft. Worth, Oct. 31, 1913; s. Claude Joe and Roxie (Ayers) M.; m. Monica Rose Hanlon, Mar. 2, 1940; children: Claude, Mark (dec.), Bryon, Claire, Maureen. BSEE, MIT, 1934. Engr., Boonton (N.J.) Radio Corp., 1935-36, Ferris Instruments Co., Boonton, 1936-39; v.p., chief engr. Measurements Corp., Boonton, 1939-53; pres. Components Corp., Denville, N.J., 1946—. Contbr. numerous articles to tech. jours.; patentee in field. Pilot, CAP, Morristown, N.J., 1947-50. Fellow IEEE (life, past chmn. no. N.J. sect.), Audio Engring. Soc. (past pres.), Radio Club Am. (life, pres. emeritus, past pres., Armstrong Medal 1968); mem. Am. Soc. for Metals (life), Am. Inst. Aero. and Astronautics, N.Y. Acad. Scis., Soc. Motion Picture TV Engrs. (life), Internat. Soc. Photo-Optical Instrumentation Engrs., Quiet Birdmen. Home: 48 Normandy Heights Rd Morristown NJ 07960-4613 Office: Components Corp 6 Kinsey Pl Denville NJ 07834

MINTER, JIMMIE RUTH, accountant; b. Greenville, S.C., Sept. 28, 1941; d. James C. and Lois (Williams) Jannino; BS Acctg., U. S.C., 1962; m. Charles H. Minter, Nov. 3, 1972; 1 child, Regina M.; stepchildren: Rhonda, Julie, Gregg; adopted child, Michael Minter. Asst. controller Package Supply & Equipment Co., Greenville, 1964-70, Olympia Knitting Mills, Spartanburg, S.C., 1970-72; controller Diacou Knitting Mills, Spartanburg, 1972-74; adminstr. Atlanta Med. Specialists, P.C., Riverdale, Ga., 1974-79; adminstr., corp. sec. David L. Cooper, M.D. P.C., Riverdale, 1979-89; acct. Ted L. Griffin Enterprises, Jonesboro, Ga., 1988-93; chief tax acct. Clayton County Tax Commn., Jonesboro, 1993—. Program chmn. 4th of July Celebration and Beauty Pageant, City of Riverdale; mem. exec. com. Clayton County Dem. Party, 1987—; Ga. State Dem. treas.; active Clinton Campaign Com.; active local and state election campaign fund raising; bd. dirs. Clayton County Human Rels. Coun. Mem. Am. Bus. Women's Assn. (chpt. Bus. Woman of Yr. 1969), Nat. Assn. Female Execs. Am. Cancer Soc. (silent auction com.), Clayton County Alzheimers Assn. (bd. dirs.). Home: 1244 Branchfield Ct Riverdale GA 30296-2148 Office: PO Box 1119 Riverdale GA 30274-1119

MINTER, PHILIP CLAYTON, retired communications company executive; b. Sydney, Australia, Aug. 9, 1928; cme to U.S., 1957; s. Roy Dixon and Adeline Claire (Bradly) M.; m. Mary Bashford Schettler, Jan. 24., 1959; children: Elizabeth C., Margaret S. BSc with honors, U. Sydney, 1951; MS, U. Wyo., 1958; PhD, U. Wis., 1960. Tchr. King's Sch., Parramatta, Australia, 1951-57; mng. dir. Motivational Rsch. Assocs., Sydney, 1960-62; dir. rsch. Nat. Fund Raising Coun., Sydney, 1962-65; project dir. USDA, Ft. Collins, Colo., 1965-67; chief info. pesticides program USPHS, Atlanta, 1967-68; mgr. data bases div. Pa. Rsch. Assocs., Phila., 1968-70; pres. Ednl. Communications Inc., King of Prussia, Pa., 1970-94; pres. Svc. Tng. Ltd., Kenilworth, Eng., 1976-88; cons. Westinghouse Learning Corp., 1972. Author: Handbook for Pesticide-Chemicals Program Coordinators, 1967. Recipient Terry Magill award Australia Soc., N.Y., 1994. Mem. Soc. Automotive Engrs., Sci. Rsch. Soc. Am., Royal Heritage Soc. (bd. dirs.), U. Wis. Alumni Assn. (bd. dirs. Delaware Valley br.), Australian/Am. C. of C. Phila. (exec. dir.), Union League, Brit. Officers Club Phila. (pres. 1992-93), Sloane Club (London), Sigma Xi. Republican. Episcopalian. Home: RR 5 Box 352 Malvern PA 19355-9800 Office: PO Box 902 Southeastern PA 19399-0902

MINTER, ROBERT, lawyer; b. Hollywood, Calif., Jan. 7, 1943; s. Ralph L. and Jaynelle (Adwon) M.; m. Karen K. Gregory, Aug. 14, 1966; children: Vincent R., Aimee L. BA, Friends U., 1965; JD, Washburn U., 1968. Bar: Kans. 1968. Ptnr. Wichita, Kans.; bd. dirs. Andover State Bank, Kans.; adv. dir. State Bank of Burden, Kans., Howard State Bank, Kans.; sec./bd. dirs. Elk Bancshares. Mem. ABA, Kansas Bar Assn., Wichita Bar Assn. Republican. Methodist. Avocations: antiques, gardening, construction. Office: Minter Case Zimmerman 212 N Market Ste 102 Wichita KS 67202

MINTON, DWIGHT CHURCH, manufacturing company executive; b. North Hills, N.Y., Dec. 17, 1934; s. Henry Miller and Helen Dwight (Church) M.; m. Marian Haven Haines, Aug. 4, 1956; children: Valerie Haven, Daphne Forsyth, Henry Brewster. B.A., Yale U., 1959; M.B.A., Stanford U., 1961. With Church & Dwight Co., Inc., Princeton, N.J., 1961—; asst. v.p. Church & Dwight Co., Inc., 1964-66, v.p., 1966-67, pres., 1967-81, chief exec. officer, 1969—, chmn., 1981—, dir., 1966—; bd. dirs. Crane Corp., Medusa Cement Corp., First Brands Corp. Trustee Atlanta U., 1971-88, Morehouse Coll., 1971—, Spelman Coll., 1971-80; v.p., bd. dirs. Greater Yellowstone Coalition, 1991—. With U.S. Army, 1956-57. Mem. Chem. Mfrs. Assn. (bd. dirs. 1980-83), Grocery Mfrs. Am. (dir. 1983-87). Clubs: Seawanhaka Corinthian Yacht, Racquet and Tennis, Yale, Lotos. Office: Church & Dwight Co Inc 469 N Harrison St Princeton NJ 08540-3510

MINTON, JERRY DAVIS, lawyer, former banker; b. Ft. Worth, Aug. 13, 1928; s. Robert Bruch and Anna Elizabeth (Davis) M.; m. Martha Drew Fields, Nov. 28, 1975; children: Marianne, Martha, John Morgan. B.B.A., U. Tex., Austin, 1949, J.D., 1960; grad. cert., Nat. Trust Sch., Northwestern U., 1960. Of counsel Michener, Larimore, Swindle, Whitaker, Flowers et al., 1991—; vice chmn. 1st Nat. Bank Ft. Worth, 1982-84; chmn. & CEO 1st City Bank Ft. Worth, 1986-91. Mem. Ft. Worth Air Power Council. Pilot USAF, 1951-55, pilot Tex. Air N.G., 1955-57; capt. USAFR Ret.). Decorated D.F.C., Air medal with 3 oak leaf clusters. Mem. SAR, State Bar Tex., Tarrant County Bar Assn. (former chmn.), Ft. Worth C. of C. Found., Mil. Order World Wars, Soc. Descendants of George Washington's Army at Valley Forge, Mil. Order Stars and Bars, Sons of Confederate Vets., City Club, River Crest Country Club, Breakfast Club, Sigma Iota Epsilon, Phi Delta Phi. Episcopalian. Home: 5404 El Dorado Dr Fort Worth TX 76107-3236 Office: 301 Commerce St Ste 3500 Fort Worth TX 76102-4135

MINTON, JOHN DEAN, historian, educator; b. Cadiz, Ky., July 29, 1921; s. John Ernest and Daisy Dean (Wilson) M.; m. Betty Jo Redick, June 8, 1947; children—John Dean, James Ernest. A.B. in Edn, U. Ky., 1943, M.A. in History, 1947; Ph.D., Vanderbilt U., 1959. Instr. history U. Miami, Fla., 1951; tchr. Broward County Pub. Sch. System, U. Miami evening div., 1951-53; prin. Trigg County (Ky.) High Sch., 1953-58; prof. history Western Ky. U., Bowling Green, 1958-86, ret., dean Grad. Coll., 1964-71, v.p. for adminstrv. affairs, 1970-79, interim pres., 1979, v.p. for student affairs, 1981-86, part-time prof., 1986—. Author: The New Deal in Tennessee, 1932-1938, 1979; contbr. articles to profl. jours. Mem. Gen. Bd. Discipleship, United Meth. Ch.; mem. Louisville Bd. Discipleship; lay speaker Louisville Conf. Meth. Ch.; bd. dirs. Higher Edn. Found., Meth. Ch., Jesse Stuart Found. Served with USNR, 1943-46. Mem. NEA, Ky. Edn. Assn., So. Hist. Assn., Ky. Hist. Soc., Bowling Green C. of C. (bd. dirs.), Civitan Club (pres. Cadiz 1956), Phi Alpha Theta, Phi Eta Sigma, Kappa Delta Pi. Home: 645 Ridgecrest Way Bowling Green KY 42104-3818

MINTON, JOSEPH PAUL, retired safety organization executive; b. Houston, Oct. 20, 1924; s. Joseph Marion and Stella (Fite) M.; m. Nancy Fettig, June 19, 1948; children: Joan M., Michael J., Jean A., Mary B., John E., Diane C. BS in Air Transp., Purdue U., 1949; Grad., U.S. Air Force Air Command and Staff Coll., 1958. Commd. 2d lt. USAF, 1944, advanced through grades to col., 1966; combat USAF, Burma, World War II; assignments in crew, staff and command USAF, ret., 1967; v.p. Purdue Airlines Inc., Lafayette, Ind., 1967-68, pres., CEO, 1969-71; mng. dir., chief exec. officer Saber Air Ltd., Singapore, 1971-73; sr. v.p. Brit. Caledonian Airways, N.Y.C., 1974-76; mng. dir. Nat. Transp. Safety Bd., Washington, 1977-78; exec. dir. Nat. Safety Coun., Washington, 1978-88. Decorated D.F.C. with oak leaf cluster, Air medal with 3 oak leaf clusters, 3 battle stars, Air Force Commendation medal with oak leaf cluster. Republican. Roman Catholic. Address: 1720 Lake Shore Crest # 15 Reston VA 22090

MINTON, TORRI, journalist; b. San Rafael, Calif., Oct. 7, 1956; d. John and Mary. BA in Ethnic Studies, U. Calif., Berkeley, 1983; M of Journalism, Columbia U., 1984. Reporter Associated Press, San Francisco, 1984, Bay City News Svc., San Francisco, 1984-86, San Francisco Chronicle, 1986—; vice chmn. San Francisco Chronicle Northern Calif. Newspaper Guild, 1992; rep. assembly del., 1992, 93, 94, 95, 96. Community devel. vol. Oper. Crossroads Africa, Tiriki, Kenya, 1979. Mem. Phi Beta Kappa. Office: San Francisco Chronicle 901 Mission St San Francisco CA 94103-2905

MINTON, YVONNE FAY, mezzo-soprano; b. Sydney, Australia; d. Robert Thomas and Alice Violet M.; m. William Barclay, Aug. 24, 1965; children—Malcolm Alexander, Alison Elizabeth. Ed., Sydney Conservatorium of Music, 1960-61. Mezzo-soprano with all maj. orchs. in, Australia, 1958-61; moved to, London, 1961, joined, Royal Opera House, Covent Garden, 1965-70, guest artist, Cologne (W. Ger.) Opera, 1969—, U.S. debut as Octavian in Der Rosenkavalier, 1970; appeared, with Lyric Opera, Chgo., 1970, Met. Opera, N.Y.C., 1973, San Francisco Opera, 1974, Paris Opera, 1974, Bayreuth, 1974, Salzburg, 1978; sings regularly with maj. symphony orchs. throughout world, 1968—; recs. include The Knot Garden, 1970, Cosi Fan Tutte, 1971, Lulu, 1979; maj. vocal works include Mahler songs with, Chgo. Symphony. Comdr. Order Brit. Empire, 1980. Hon. mem. Royal Acad. Music. Office: care Ingpen & Williams, 14 Kensington Ct, London England W85DN

MINTS, GRIGORI EFROIM, specialist in mathematical logic; b. Leningrad, USSR, June 7, 1939; s. Efroim B. and Lea M. (Novick) M.; m. Maryanna Rozenfeld, July 21, 1987; 1 child, Anna. Diploma, Leningrad U., 1961, PhD, 1965, ScD, 1989. Rsch. assoc. Steklov Inst. Math., Leningrad, 1961-79; with Nauka Pubs., Leningrad, 1979-85; sr. rsch. assoc. Inst. Cybernetics, Tallinn, Estonia, 1985-91; prof. dept. philosophy Stanford (Calif.) U., 1991—; mem. adv. bd. Jour. Symbolic Logic, 1987-90; mem. editorial bd. Jour. Symbolic Computation, 1983—, Jour. of Functional Programming, 1990—; mem. program orgn. com. Logic in Computer Sci., 1991-94, Conf. on Automated Deduction, Logic Programming and Automated Reasoning. Editor: Mathematical Investigation of Logical Deduction, 1967, COLOG-88, 1989, Journal of Logic and Computation, 1991—; contbr. articles to profl. jours. Mem. Assn. Symbolic Logic (mem. coun. 1990-93), Internat. Union History and Philosophy and Sci. (assessor 1991-95), Annals of Pure and Applied Logic (mem. editorial bd. 1980-89).

MINTZ, ALBERT, lawyer; b. New Orleans, Oct. 19, 1929; s. Morris and Goldie (Goldblum) M.; m. Linda Barnett, Dec. 19, 1954; children—John Morris, Margaret Anne. B.B.A., Tulane U., 1948, J.D., 1951. Bar: La. bar 1951. Since practiced in New Orleans; ptnr. Montgomery, Barnett, Brown, Read, Hammond & Mintz, Hurwitz-Mintz Realty Cos., New Orleans.; bd. dirs. Sublet Mfg., Inc., Strauss Distbrs., Avrico, Inc. Mem. adv. bd. Law Sch. Tulane U.; chmn., dir. adv. bd. Tulane Summer Lyric Theater; bd. dirs. Tulane Ctr. Stage Talent and Shakespearean Theatre; bd. dirs. Jewish Cmty. Ctr., New Orleans, 1965-72, Jewish Fedn., 1968—, Home for Jewish Aged, 1968-71, Jewish Family Svc., New Orleans, 1968-72; trustee, bd. mgrs. Touro Infirmary Hosp. and Found.; trustee Jewish Endowment Found.; charter mem. La. Hist. Assn. Mem. ABA, La. Bar Assn. (lectr., publ. on corp., tax, real estate law), New Orleans Bar Assn. (exec. com. 1971-74), Am. Law Inst., U.S. Hist. Assn., New Orleans C. of C. (chmn. com. civic affairs and state legis. 1968-69), Internat. House Club, Plimsoll of Internat. Trade Mart Club, City Energy Club, Phi Delta Phi, Omicron Delta Kappa, Zeta Beta Tau. Jewish. Home: 2017 Jefferson Ave New Orleans LA 70115-5618 Office: 3200 Energy Ctr 1100 Poydras St New Orleans LA 70163-1100

MINTZ, DANIEL HARVEY, endocrinologist, educator, academic administrator; b. N.Y.C., Sept. 16, 1930; s. Jacob A. and Fannie M.; m. Dawn E. Hynes, Jan. 15, 1961; children: David, Denise, Debra. B.S. cum laude, St. Bonaventure Coll., 1951; M.D., N.Y. Med. Coll., 1956. Diplomate: Am. Bd. Internal Medicine. Intern Henry Ford Hosp., Detroit, 1956-57; resident Georgetown med. div. D.C. Gen. Hosp., Washington, 1957-59, Georgetown U. Hosp., Washington, 1958-59; fellow medicine Nat. Inst. Arthritis and Metabolic Diseases, 1959-60, Am. Diabetes Assn., 1960-61; practice medicine, specializing in internal medicine Miami, Fla.; asst. prof. medicine Georgetown U. Sch. Medicine, 1963-64; assoc. prof. medicine U. Pitts. Sch. Medicine, 1964-69; prof. medicine U. Miami Sch. Medicine, 1969—, Mary Lou Held prof. medicine, 1981—, chief div. endocrinology and metabolism, dept. medicine, 1969-80, Sci. dir. Diabetes Research Inst., 1980—; chief of service Georgetown U. Med. div. D.C. Gen. Hosp., Washington, 1963-64; chief of medicine Magee-Women's Hosp., Pitts., 1964-69; chief div. endocrinology and metabolism, dept. medicine Jackson Meml. Hosp., Miami; guest prof. U. Geneva, 1976-77. Contbr. articles to profl. jours. Fellow ACP; mem. Endocrine Soc., Am. Diabetes Assn. (program dir. 1972), Am. Fedn. Clin. Research, Am. Soc. Clin. Investigation, Central Soc. Clin. Investigation, So. Soc. Clin. Investigation., Am. Assn. Physicians. Office: U Miami Diabetes Rsch Inst PO Box 016960 R-134 Miami FL 33101-6960

MINTZ, DONALD EDWARD, psychologist, educator; b. N.Y.C., July 19, 1932; s. Irving and Pauline Lynore (Arenson) M.; children: Peter Graham, Hayley Ilana. AB, Columbia U., 1954, PhD, 1961. Rsch. assoc. Princeton U., 1959-63; asst. prof. psychology City Coll., CUNY, 1963-67, assoc. prof., 1967-73, chmn. dept., 1971-74, prof., 1973-95, prof. emeritus, 1995—, acting dean Sch. Architecture and Environ. Studies, 1982-85; pvt. practice psychotherapy N.Y.C., 1979—. Author: Dynamics of Response, 1965; contbr. articles to profl. jours. Served to lt. USN, 1954-57. NSF predoctoral fellow, 1957. Fellow N.Y. Acad. Sci.; mem. Am. Psychol. Assn., AAAS, Psychonomic Soc., Assn. Advancement Behavior Therapy, Eastern Psychol. Assn., N.Y. Acad. Scis., Phi Beta Kappa, Sigma Xi. Democrat. Jewish. Club: Stuyvesant Yacht. Home: 10 W 15th St New York NY 10011-6838 Office: CCNY New York NY 10031

MINTZ, JEFFRY ALAN, lawyer; b. N.Y.C., Sept. 15, 1943; s. Aaron Herbert and Lillian Betty (Greenspan) M.; m. Susan Politzer, Aug. 22, 1979; children: Jennifer, Melanie, Jonathan. AB, Tufts U., 1964; LLB, Rutgers U., 1967; postgrad. U. Pa. Law Sch., 1968-70. Bar: D.C. 1968, N.Y. 1970, U.S. Supreme Ct. 1972, N.J. 1973, Pa. 1983. Law clk. to judge U.S. Ct. Appeals, New Orleans, 1967-68; asst. defender Defender Assn. Phila., 1968-70; asst. counsel NAACP Legal Def. and Ednl. Fund, N.Y.C., 1970-74; dir. Office Inmate Advocacy, N.J. Dept. Pub. Advocate, Trenton, 1974-81; pvt. practice Haddonfield and Medford, N.J., 1982; ptnr. Stein & Shapiro, Medford, 1982-83, Cherry Hill, N.J., 1983-84, Mesirov, Gelman, Jaffe, Cramer & Jamieson, Cherry Hill, also Phila., 1984-90, Schlesinger, Mintz & Pilles, Mt. Holly, N.J., 1990-92; pvt. practice atty., Mt. Holly, 1992—. Trustee Congregation M'Kor Shalom, Cherry Hill, 1990—; Mem. Burlington County and Mt. Laurel Dem. Coun. Com., 1993-95; chair Moorestown Dem. Com., 1995—. Mem. ABA, ATLA, N.J. Bar Assn. (del., gen. coun. 1986-88, 89-91), Pa. Bar Assn., D.C. Bar Assn., Camden County Bar Assn., Burlington County Bar Assn. (trustee 1989-92), Assn. Trial Lawyers N.J. (bd. govs. 1990-95). Jewish. Home: 224 Quakerbridge Ct Moorestown NJ 08057-2823 Office: 129 High St Mount Holly NJ 08060-1401 *Notable cases include: Piechotta vs. Kanther, Md. Superior Ct. N.J., Burlington County, a med. malpractice case involving use of anti-psychotic drugs by multiple physician defendants; Lugo vs. Schwartz, Md. Superior Ct. N.J., Cumberland County, a med. malpractice case involving birth injury by obstetrician and lack of follow-up by pediatricians; Hak vs. L & M Bakery, Superior Ct. N.J., Burlington County, which involved injury to 5-yr.-old that caused a mild learning disability.*

MINTZ, M. J., lawyer; b. Phila., Oct. 29, 1940; s. Arthur and Lillian (Altenberg) M.; children: Robert A., Christine L.; m. Judith E. Held. B.S., Temple U., 1961, J.D., 1968. Bar: D.C.; C.P.A., Pa., D.C. Atty. adv. to judge U.S. Tax Ct., Washington, 1968-70; asst. gen. counsel Cost of Living Council, Washington, 1971-73; ptnr. Dickstein, Shapiro & Morin, Washington, 1973—; adj. prof. George Mason U. Law Sch., Va., 1974-78; adv. Employee Retirement Income Security Act of 1974, Adv. Council, Washington, 1982-85. Contbr. articles to profl. jours. Apptd. by Pres. Reagan to advisory com. Pension Benifit Guaranty Corp., 1987; reapptd. and designated chmn. by Pres. George Bush; rep. candidate Fairfax County Bd. of Suprs., 1971. Fellow Nat. Assn. Watch & Clock Collectors; mem. ABA, Am. Inst. C.P.A.s, Antuquarian Horological Soc. (London). Clubs: Cosmos, Belle Haven Country, Met. Club of Washington. D.C., Chappaquiddick Beach. Avocations: antiquarian horologist.

MINTZ, MARSHALL GARY, lawyer; b. Detroit, May 28, 1947. BA, UCLA, 1968, JD, 1971. Bar: Calif. 1972. Law clk. appellate dept L.A. County Superior Ct., 1971-72; ptnr. Kelly & Lytton, L.A., Calif., 1995—; moderator, panelist Calif. Continuing Edn. of Bar, 1980—; mem. arbitration adminstrv. com. L.A. County Superior Ct., 1979, mem. 1984 Olympics spl. settlement panel. Mem. ABA, State Bar Calif., L.A. County Bar Assn. (arbitrator arbitration and client rels. com. 1978-90), Assn. Bus. Trial Lawyers (bd. govs. 1976-77, program chmn. 1976). Office: Kelly & Lytton Ste 1450 1900 Avenue Of The Stars Los Angeles CA 90067-4405

MINTZ, MORTON ABNER, author, former newspaper reporter; b. Ann Arbor, Mich., Jan. 26, 1922; s. William and Sarah (Solomon) M.; m. Anita Inez Franz, Aug. 30, 1946; children—Margaret Ruth, Elizabeth Diane (dec.), Roberta Joan, Daniel Robert. A.B. in Econs, U. Mich., 1943. Reporter St. Louis Star-Times, 1946-50; reporter, asst. city editor St. Louis Globe-Democrat, 1951-58; reporter Washington Post, 1958-88. Author: The Therapeutic Nightmare, 1965, By Prescription Only, 1967, The Pill: An Alarming Report, 1969, At Any Cost: Corporate Greed, Women, and the Dalkon Shield, 1985, (with Jerry S. Cohen) America, Inc.: Who Owns and Operates the United States, 1971, Power, Inc.; Public and Private Rulers and How to Make Them Accountable, 1976, (with others) In the Name of Profit: Profiles in Corporate Irresponsiblity, 1972, More Bucks, Less Bang: How the Pentagon Buys Ineffective Weapons, 1983. Recipient Heywood Broun, Raymond Clapper, George Polk awards for journalism, 1962, A.J. Liebling award, 1974, Worth Bingham Meml. award, 1976, Columbia Journalism award, 1983, Hugh M. Hefner First Amendment award for lifetime achievement, 1996.

MINTZ, NORMAN NELSON, investment banker, educator; b. N.Y.C., Sept. 18, 1934; s. Alexander and Rebecca (Nelson) M.; m. Marcia Lynn Belford, Aug. 27, 1960; children: Geoffrey Belford, Douglas Nelson. AB, Bucknell U., 1955; PhD, NYU, 1966. Asst. gen. mgr. Ross Products Inc., N.Y.C., 1957-59; media analyst Benton & Bowles Inc., N.Y.C., 1960; asst. prof. fin. Syracuse U., 1965-69; asst. prof. econs. Columbia U., N.Y.C., 1968-72; assoc. dean Grad. Sch. Arts and Scis. Columbia U., 1972-77, dep. provost, 1977-80, acting provost, 1978-79, sr. v.p., 1980-82, exec. v.p. for acad. affairs, 1982-89, exec. v.p., ret., 1990—; mng. dir. Loeb Ptnrs. Corp., 1990—; economist U.S.-P.R. Commn. on Status of P.R., 1965-66; bd. dirs. Sr. Network, Inc., Inncom, Inc., Comm. Mgmt. Sys., Inc., Exxel/Atmos, Inc., Gladwin Corp., Atlantic Eagle, Inc., Evare, Ltd. Author: Monetary Union and Economic Integration, 1970; contbr. articles to profl. jours. Dir. Conf. on Jewish Social Studies, 1975-94, N.Y.C. Coun. on Econ. Edn., 1993—. Served with Signal Corps U.S. Army, 1955-57. Earhart Found. fellow, 1963-65. Mem. Am. Econ. Assn., Am. Fin. Assn., Royal Econ. Soc., India House Club, Phi Beta Kappa, Omicron Delta Epsilon. Office: care Loeb Ptnrs 61 Broadway New York NY 10006

MINTZ, PATRICIA POMBOY, secondary education educator; b. N.Y.C., Sept. 1, 1934; d. Emil and Bertha (Armel) Pomboy; m. Edward A. LeVay Jr.; 1 child from previous marriage, Peter Graham Mintz. AB in History with honors, Barnard Coll., 1956; AM in English, Tchrs. Coll., N.Y.C., 1967, EdD, 1980. Cert. English tchr., adminstr. and supr. dist. level. English, history tch. Fieldston Sch., N.Y.C., 1960-67; English chmn. Byram Hills Schs., Armonk, N.Y., 1967-72; supr. dist. English/lang. arts North Shore Schs., Glen Head, N.Y., 1972—; instr. English Columbia U., 1966; dir. Upward Bound English Program, Fieldston Sch., 1967; program chmn. L.I. Writing Conf., 1984-90; program chair N.Y. State English Coun. Conf., 1993. Editor: America, The Melting Pot Anthology, 1969; author: Film Guides for Educational Films, 1972-73. N.Y. Found. for Arts grantee, 1988—, Title III Matching Grant, Writing Program for North Shore Schs., 1977-78. Mem. ASCD, Nat. Coun. Tchrs. English, N.Y. State English Coun., L.I. Lang. Arts Coun., Coun. Adminstrs. and Suprs.

MINTZ, RICHARD I., federal official; b. Bklyn., Aug. 10, 1961; s. Walter and Sandra (Ullman) M.; m. Helaine Greenfeld, Sept. 1, 1991. BA in Internat. Rels., Union Coll., 1983. Assoc. prodr. CBS News, 1983-85; press. sec. N.E.-Midwest Congrl. Coalition, 1985-86; media dir. Nat. Abortion Rights Action League, 1986-88; v.p. Ogilvy, Adams & Rinehart, 1988-91; dir. staff Hillary Rodham Clinton, dep. mgr. Clinton-Gore Campaign, Calif., 1991-92; dir. comm. Presdl. Inaugural Com., 1992-93; dir. pub. affairs Dept. Transp., Washington, 1993—; s.r. v.p. Ogilvy, Adams & Rinehart, Washington. Office: Ogilvy, Adams & Rinehart 1901 L St NW Ste 300 Washington DC 70036*

MINTZ, SEYMOUR STANLEY, lawyer; b. Newark, Mar. 7, 1912. A.B., George Washington U., 1933, J.D., 1936. Bar: D.C. 1936. Atty. Office of Undersec. of Treasury, 1937-38, Office of Chief Counsel, IRS, 1938-42; assoc. Hogan & Hartson, Washington, 1946-49; ptnr. Hogan & Hartson, 1949-84, counsel, 1985—. Contbr. articles to profl. jours. Fellow Am. Coll. Tax Counsel; mem. ABA, D.C. Bar Assn., Am. Law Inst., Order of Coif. Office: Hogan & Hartson 555 13th St NW Washington DC 20004-1109

MINTZ, SHLOMO, conductor, violist, violinist; b. Moscow, Oct. 30, 1957; came to U.S., 1974; s. Abraham and Eve (Labko) M.; m. Corina Ciacci; children: Eliav David, Alexander. Diploma, Juilliard Sch. Music, 1979. Violin solo recordings include Violin Concertos by Mendelssohn and Bruch (Grand prix du Disque Diapason d'or), 1981, Complete Sonatas and Partitas for Solo Violin by J.S. Bach, The Miraculous Mandarin-Two Portraits (with Abbado/Chicago Symphony Orchestra) by Bartok, Compositions and Arrangements (with Clifford Benson, piano) by Kreisler, Violin Concerto; also Bruch: Violin Concerto Number 1 (with Abbado/Chgo. Symphony Orchestra) by Mendelssohn, Twenty-Four Caprices by Paganini, Two Violin Concertos (with Abbado/London Symphony Orchestra) by Prokofiev, The Four Seasons (with Stern, Perlman, Mehta) by Vivaldi, Vivaldi violin concertos, Vols. I & II (with Israel Chamber Orch.), 1992, Collection String Symphonies, Vol. III to X, (with Israel Chamber Orch., 1992, Violin and Viola Sonatas by Chostakovich (with V. Postnikova); apptd. music advisor, chief condr., soloist Israel Chamber Orch., 1989—. Recipient Premio Accademia Musicale, Chigiana Siena, Italy, 1984. Uses Zahn violin made by Stradivarius, and a Carlo-Guiseppe Testrove viola. Office: ICM Artists Inc 40 W 57th St New York NY 10019-4001

MINTZ, SIDNEY WILFRED, anthropologist; b. Dover, N.J., Nov. 16, 1922; s. Solomon and Fromme Leah (Tulchin) M.; m. June Mirken, May 1952 (div. Dec. 1962); children: Eric Daniel, Elizabeth Rachel; m. Jacqueline Wei, June 6, 1964. BA, Bklyn. Coll., 1943; PhD, Columbia U., 1951; MA, Yale U., 1963. Mem. faculty dept. anthropology Yale U., New Haven, 1951-74; prof. Yale U., 1963-74; prof. anthropology Johns Hopkins U., Balt., 1974—; vis. prof. anthropology MIT, 1964-65, Princeton U., 1975-76; directeur d'études associé E.P.H.E., Paris, 1970-71; professeur associé. Coll. de France, Paris, 1988; editor Yale U. Press Caribbean Series, 1957-74; Lewis Henry Morgan lectr. U. Rochester, 1972; Christian Gauss lectr. Princeton U., 1979; Harry Hoijer lectr. UCLA, 1981; Duijker Found. lectr., Amsterdam, 1988; Rodney lectr. U. Warwick, 1993. Author: (with others) People of Puerto Rico, 1956, Worker in the Cane, The Life History of a Puerto Rican Sugar Cane Worker, 1960, Caribbean Transformations, 1974, Sweetness and Power, 1985, (with Richard Price) The Birth of African-American Culture, 1992. Served with USAAF, 1943-46. Recipient William Clyde DeVane medal Yale U., 1972, Huxley medalist Royal Anthropol. Inst., 1994; named Social Sci. Rsch. Coun. Faculty Rsch. fellow, 1958-59, Guggenheim fellow, 1957, Fulbright fellow, 1966-67, 70-71, NEH fellow, 1978-79, Smithsonian Inst. Regents' fellow, 1986-87. Fellow Am. Anthrop. Assn.; mem. Am. Ethnol. Soc. (v.p., pres.-elect 1967-68), Royal Anthrop.

Soc. Gt. Britain and Ireland, Am. Acad. Arts and Scis., Sigma Xi. Office: Johns Hopkins U Dept Anthropology Baltimore MD 21218

MINTZ, STEPHEN ALLAN, real estate company executive, lawyer; b. N.Y.C., May 21, 1943; s. Irving and Anne (Medwick) M.; m. Dale Leibson, June 19, 1966; children: Eric Michael, Jaclyn Leibson. AB, Cornell U., 1965; JD cum laude, Harvard U., 1968. Bar: N.Y. 1969. Assoc. Proskauer, Rose, Goetz & Mendelsohn, N.Y.C., 1968-76, ptnr., 1976-80; v.p. Integrated Resources, Inc., N.Y.C., 1980-84, 1st. v.p., 1984-86, sr. v.p., 1986-89, exec. v.p., 1989-94; chmn. Resources Hotel Mgmt. Svc. Inc., 1986-94; pres. Resources High Equity, Inc., 1991-94, Stemin Assocs., Rye, N.Y., 1994—. Mem. ABA, N.Y. State Bar Assn. Democrat. Jewish. Home: 11 Eve Ln Rye NY 10580-4113 Office: 11 Eve Ln Rye NY 10580-4113

MINTZ, SUSAN ASHINOFF, menswear manufacturing company executive; b. N.Y.C., Dec. 7, 1949; d. Lawrence Lloyd and Thelma B. (Rubens) A.; m. Robert Beier Mintz, June 18, 1983; children: Geoffrey Harrison, Tyler Edward Richard. BA, Finch Coll., 1971; MPA, NYU, 1977. Menswear advt. asst. New Yorker Mag., N.Y.C., 1971-72; assoc. Staub, Warmbold & Assocs., Inc., exec. search co., N.Y.C., 1972-80; exec. v.p. Muhammad Ali Sportswear, Ltd., N.Y.C., 1980-81; pres. Forum Sportswear, Ltd., N.Y.C. and Portsmouth, Va., 1981—; group v.p. Coronet Casuals, Inc., Portsmouth, 1985—, also bd. dirs. Trustee Dean Jr. Coll. Named to Outstanding Young Women Am., U.S. Jaycees, 1980. Mem. Nat. Assn. Men's Sportswear Buyers, Men's Apparel Guild Calif., Beacon Hill Club. Office: 2615 Elmhurst Ln Portsmouth VA 23701-2736

MINTZ, WALTER, investment company executive; b. Vienna, Austria, Feb. 23, 1929; came to U.S., 1938, naturalized, 1945; s. Maximilian and Ilse (Schueller) M.; m. Sandra Jane Earl, Aug. 27, 1971. B.A., Reed Coll., 1950; postgrad. in econs, Columbia, 1950-51, 53-54. Asso. editor Barrons mag., 1951-53, 54-56; with Shearson Hammill Co., 1956-70, dir. research, 1962-69, exec. v.p. charge investment div., 1965-70; partner Cumberland Assocs., investment mgmt., 1970-85; spl. ltd. ptnr. Cumberland Ptnrs., investment ptnrship., 1982—; bd. dirs. Merrill Lynch Phoenix Fund, Merrill Lynch Fed. Securities Trust, Merrill Lynch Retirement Series Fund. Trustee Reed Coll., 1971—, vice chmn. bd. trustees, 1991—; trustee Manhattan Inst., 1990—, vice chmn., 1994—; bd. dirs. Citizens Union of N.Y.C., 1980—. Mem. N.Y. Soc. Security Analysts (bd. dirs. 1969-75). Home: 2 E 88th St New York NY 10128-0555 Office: Cumberland Assocs 1114 Avenue Of The Americas New York NY 10036-7703

MINTZBERG, HENRY, management educator, researcher, writer; b. Montreal, Que., Can., Sept. 2, 1939; s. Myer and Irene M.; children: Susan, Lisa. B.Eng., McGill U., 1961; B.A., Sir George Williams U., 1962; S.M., M.I.T., 1965, Ph.D., 1968; hon. degree, U. Venice, 1983, U. Lund, 1989, U. Lausanne, 1991, U. Montreal, 1993, U. Geneva, 1995, U. Liege, 1996. Operational research analyst Can. Nat., 1961-63; mem. faculty mgmt. McGill U., Montreal, 1968—, INSEAD, Fontainebleau, France, 1994—; vis. prof. Carnegie-Mellon U., 1973, Universite d'Aix-Marseille, 1974-76, Ecole des Hautes Etudes Commerciales de Montreal, 1977-78, London Bus. Sch., 1990, INSEAD, France, 1992, 93-94. Author: The Nature of Managerial Work, 1973, The Structuring of Organizations, 1979, Power In and Around Organizations, 1983, The Strategy Process, 1988, Mintzberg on Management, 1989, The Rise and Fall of Strategic Planning, 1994, The Canadian Condition, 1995; contbr. articles to profl. jours. Fellow Royal Soc. Can., Acad. Mgmt., Internat. Acad. Mgmt.; mem. Strategic Mgmt. Soc. (pres. 1988-91). Office: McGill U Faculty Mgmt, 1001 Sherbrooke W, Montreal, PQ Canada H3A 1G5

MINTZER, DAVID, physics educator; b. N.Y.C., May 4, 1926; s. Herman and Anna (Katz) M.; m. Justine Nancy Klein, June 26, 1949; children: Elizabeth Amy, Robert Andrew. B.S. in Physics, Mass. Inst. Tech., 1945, Ph.D., 1949. Asst. prof. physics Brown U., 1949-55; research asso. Yale U., 1955-56, assoc. prof., dir. lab. marine physics, 1956-62; prof. mech. engring. Northwestern U., Evanston, 1962-91, prof. physics and astronomy, 1968-91, prof. emeritus mech. engring., prof emeritus physics and astronomy, 1991—; assoc. dean McCormick Sch. Engring. and Applied Sci., 1970-73, acting dean, 1971-72, v.p. for rsch., dean sci., 1973-86, spl. asst. to pres., 1986-87, prof. emeritus mech. engring., physics and astronomy, 1991—; mem. mine adv. com. Nat. Acad. Sci.-NRC, 1963-73; mem. Ill. Gov.'s Commn. on Sci. and Tech., 1987-88; mem. adv. bd. Applied Rsch. Lab. Pa. State U., 1976-82, chmn., 1980-81. Contbr. numerous chpts. to books, papers to profl. publs. Trustee EDUCOM interuniv. communications coun., 1975-83, vice chmn., 1977-78, chmn., 1978-81; trustee Adler Planetarium, 1976-92, life trustee, 1992—; bd. dirs. Rsch. Park, Inc., Evanston, 1986-92, treas., 1986-91; trustee Ill. Math. and Sci. Acad., 1986—, mem. exec. com., 1989-95, chmn. alliance coun., 1991-93; chmn. bd. dirs. Heartland Venture Capital Network, Inc., 1987-90; bd. dirs. Tech. Innovation Ctr., Inc., 1990-92, treas., 1990-92. Fellow Am. Phys. Soc., Acoustical Soc. Am.; mem. ASME, Am. Astron. Soc., Sigma Xi, Tau Beta Pi, Pi Tau Sigma. Research on underwater acoustics and rarefied gas dynamics. Office: Northwestern U 990 N Lake Shore Dr #16A Chicago IL 60611-1343

MINUDRI, REGINA URSULA, librarian, consultant; b. San Francisco, May 9, 1937; d. John C. and Molly (Halter) M. BA, San Francisco Coll. for Women, 1958; MLS, U. Calif.-Berkeley, 1959. Reference libr. Menlo Park (Calif.) Pub. Libr., 1959-62; regional libr. Santa Clara County (Calif.) Libr., 1962-68; project coord. Fed. Young Adult Libr. Svcs. Project, Mountain View, Calif., 1968-71; dir. profl. services Alameda County (Calif.) Libr., 1971, asst. county libr., 1972-77; libr. dir. Berkeley Pub. Libr., 1977-94; lectr. U. San Francisco, 1970-72, U. Calif., Berkeley, 1977-81, 91-93; lectr. San Jose State U., 1994—; cons., 1975—; adv. bd. Miles Cutter Ednl., 1992—. Bd. dirs. No. Calif. ACLU, 1994-96, Cmty. Memory, 1989-91, Berkeley Cmty. Fund, 1994—, chair youth com., 1994—, Berkeley Pub. Libr. Found. Bd., 1996—; mem. bd. mgrs. cen. br. Berkeley YMCA, 1988-93. Recipient proclamation Mayor of Berkeley, 1985, 86, 94, Citation of Merit Calif. State Assembly, 1994; named Woman of Yr. Alameda County North chpt. Nat. Women's Polit. Caucus, 1986, Outstanding Alumna U. Calif. Sch. Libr. and Info. Scis., Berkeley, 1987. Mem. ALA (pres. 1986-87, exec. bd. 1980-89, coun. 1979-88, 90-94, Grolier award 1974), Calif. Libr. Assn. (pres. 1981, coun. 1965-69, 79-82), LWV (dir. Berkeley chpt. 1980-81, v.p. comm. svcs. 1995—). Author: Getting It Together, A Young Adult Bibliography, 1970; contbr. articles to publs. including School Libr. Jour., Wilson Libr. Bull. Office: Reality Mgmt 836 The Alameda Berkeley CA 94707-1916

MINYARD, LIZ, food products executive. BBA, Tex. Christian U., 1975. CEO Minyard Food Stores, Coppell, Tex., 1976—; dir. consumer affairs Minyard Food Stores Inc., Coppell, Tex., v.p. consumer affairs, 1980, v.p. corp. rels., 1983, also vice-chmn. bd. dirs., also co-chmn. bd. dirs. Chmn. United Way Dallas and Tarrant Counties, 1978, 83-95, Tarrant County sect. chmn., 1983-84, merchants divsn. chmn. Dallas County, 1987, Dallas County bd. dirs., 1995; bd. mem. Goodwill Industries of Dallas, Inc., 1981-94, mem. exec. com., 1987-88, 93-95, vice-chmn., 1992-94, chmn., 1995; mem. YWCA Dallas campaign drive spring 1982, chmn. campaign, 1983-85, co-chmn. of capital campaign, 1995, mayor's summer youth employment commn. co-chmn., 1994, chmn., 1995, bd. dirs., 1995; v.p. Dallas Urban League, 1989-91, bd. dirs., 1985-95, chmn. bd. dirs., 1992-93, bldg. com. chmn., 1995; mem. Dallas Citizens Coun., 1988-94, bd. dirs. exec. com., 1992-95; bd. dirs. Leukemia Assn. of North Ctrl. Tex., 1988-95; mem. Dallas Assembly, 1989-95; bd. dirs. Baylor Hosp. Found., 1989-95; mem. Dallas Summit, 1992-95, Dallas Together Forum, 1993-95, Dallas Women's Forum, 1994-95; bd. dirs. Zale Lipshy Hosp., 1993-95, Am. Heart Assn., 1991-94; chmn. City of Dallas Bond Program, 1995; nat. trustee Boys and Girls clubs of Am., 1995, and numerous others. Recipient Dallas/Ft. Worth Dist. Women in Bus. Advocate of Yr. award U.S. Small Bus. Adminstrn., 1995, Tex. Family Bus. of Yr.-Cmty. Involvement award Tex. Inst. Family Bus., 1995, Bus. award for Cmty. Involvement Martin Luther King, Jr. Cmty. Ctr., 1995, Contbrs. award Black State Employees Assn. of Tex., 1995, Art of Achievement award Nat. Fedn. of Women Bus. Owners, 1995. Mem. Food Mktg. Inst. (mem. consumer coun. 1977-88, mem. steering com. 1982, mem. pub. affairs com. 1989-90, bd. dirs. 1991-95), Tex. Food Mktg. Assn. (v.p. 1981-82, pres. 1982-84), North Tex. Food Bank (founding bd. mem., sec. 1981-83, bd. mem. 1982-95, pres. 1984, v.p. devel. 1987, chmn. hunger link program 1989-90), Second Harvest (Chgo., bd. dirs. 1992-95), CIES The Food Bus. Forum (ann. congress com. mem. 1996), North Tex. Commn. (bd. dirs. 1992-95), Greater Dallas C. of C. (mem. leadership program 1982-83, bd. dirs. 1994-95, bd. dirs. 1987-90, mem. women's bus. issues exec. com. 1994-95, women's convenant diamond cutters award 1995). Office: Minyard Food Stores Inc PO Box 518 Coppell TX 75019-0518 Office: PO Box 518 Coppell TX 75019

MIRABAL, ANGELA PRINCE, special education educator; b. Tuscaloosa, Ala., Jan. 25, 1967; d. Bennie Andrew and Mary Clara (McCollum) Prince; m. Daniel Mirabal. BS in Specific Learning Disabilities, U. Ala., 1991; MA in Reading, Nova Southeastern U., Ft. Lauderdale, Fla., 1994; EdS in Ednl. Leadership, Nova U., Ft. Lauderdale. Tchr. Coral Springs (Fla.) Mid. Sch., 1991-95; ESE specialist Ft. Lauderdale H.S., 1995—; trainer N.J. Writing Project of Tex., Ft. Lauderdale, 1994—; dept. head exceptional student edn. Coral Springs Mid. Sch., 1994-95. Mem. ASCD, Nat. Reading Assn., Fla. Reading Assn. Democrat. Baptist. Avocations: reading, listening to music, travel. Home: 6811 Bayfront Cir Margale FL 33063-7031 Office: Fort Lauderdale HS 1600 NE 4th Ave Fort Lauderdale FL 33305

MIRABELLA, GRACE, magazine publishing executive; b. Maplewood, N.J., June 10, 1929; d. Anthony and Florence (Belfatto) M.; m. William G. Cahan, Nov. 24, 1974. BA, Skidmore Coll., 1950. Mem. exec. tng. program Macy's, N.Y.C., 1950-51; mem. fashion dept. Saks Fifth Ave., N.Y.C., 1951-52; with Vogue mag., N.Y.C., 1952-54, 56-88; assoc. editor Vogue mag., 1965-71, editor-in-chief, 1971-88; founder, publ. dir. Mirabella Mag., 1988—; mem. pub. relations staff Simonetta & Fabiani, Rome, Italy, 1954-56; hon. bd. dirs. Catalyst; lectr. New Sch. Social Rsch.; adv. bd. mem. Columbia Grad. Sch. Journalism, Leeds Castle, London. Mem. Meml. Sloat-Kettering Cancer Ctr. Women's Soc., bd. adv. Harvard Sch. Pub. Health Ctr. for Cancer Prevention. Decorated cavalier Order of Merit Republic of Italy; recipient Outstanding Grad. Achievement award Skidmore Coll., 1972, Coty Fashion Critics award, 1980, Fashion Critics award Parsons Sch. Design, 1985; Woman of Distinction award Birmingham-So. Coll., 1985, Girl Scouts Am. Leadership award, 1987, Excellence in Media award Susan G. Komen Found., 1987, Equal Opportunity award NOW, 1987; officer Order of Merit, Republic of Italy, 1987; Mary Ann Magnin award, 1988; Achievement award Am. Assn. Plastic and Reconstructive Surgery, 1988; Spl. Merit award Coun. Fashion Designers Am., 1989, Life and Breath award N.Y. Lung Assn., 1990, Matrix award Assn. Edn. in Journalism Mass Comm., 1991, AEJMC award, 1992, St. Francis Cabrini Humanitarian award, 1992, Heart of N.Y. award Am. Heart Assn., N.Y.C. Meals-on-Wheels honor, 1994, Nat. Italian-Am. Found. hon., 1994, Barnard award, 1995, Neiman Marcus award, 1995. Mem. Women's Forum N.Y. Office: Mirabella Mag 1633 Broadway New York NY 10019

MIRABELLI, MARIO V., lawyer; b. Elizabeth, N.J., July 5, 1939. AB, Georgetown U., 1961; LLB, Am. U., 1964. Bar: D.C. 1966. Trial atty. Bur. Deceptive Practices, FTC, Washington, 1967-69, Divsn. Corp. Fin., Br. Adminstrv. Proceedings, SEC, Washington, 1969-73; ptnr. Baker & Hostetler, Washington. Office: Baker & Hostetler Washington Sq 1050 Connecticut Ave NW Washington DC 20036-5303*

MIRABELLO, FRANCIS JOSEPH, lawyer; b. Ft. Lauderdale, Fla., Mar. 2, 1954; s. Frank Guy and Mary (Sorce) M.; m. Marianna Hay O'Neal, Aug. 5, 1978; children: Diana H., A. Paul. BS in Civil Engring., Princeton U., 1975; JD, Harvard U., 1978. Bar: Calif. 1978, Pa. 1981, Fla. 1983. Assoc. Irell & Manella, Los Angeles, 1978-81; ptnr. Morgan, Lewis & Bockius, Phila., 1981—; lectr. law Villanova (Pa.) U. Law Sch., adj. prof. law U. Pa., Phila. Mem. ABA (chmn. tax sect. subcom.). Club: Martins Dam, Merion Cricke. Avocation: tennis. Office: Morgan Lewis & Bockius 2000 One Logan Sq Philadelphia PA 19103

MIRABELLO, MARK LINDEN, history educator; b. Toledo, May 6, 1955; s. Paul Joseph and Regina Joan (Baranski) M. BA, U. Toledo, 1977; MA, U. Va., 1979; PhD, U. Glasgow (Scotland), 1988. Instr. honors program U. Toledo, 1984-87; sr. instr. European history Shawnee State U., Portsmouth, Ohio, 1987-88, asst. prof. European history, 1988-93, chair honors program, 1990—, assoc. prof. European History, 1993—; vis. assoc. prof. European history Nizhni Novgorod State U., Russia, 1994; dir. Ian B. Cowan Award for Outstanding Work in Hist. Studies, Shawnee State U., Portsmouth, 1990—; cons. The Open Air, Shawnee State U. newspaper, Portsmouth, 1992—, The Univ. Chronicle Shawnee State Univ. Newspaper, Portsmouth, 1992—; co-founder, advisor Ar Tyr Ar Fraternity Shawnee State U., Portsmouth, 1992—. Author: The Odin Brotherhood: A True Narrative of a Dialogue with a Mysterious Secret Society, 1992. Co-founder, adviser Delta Tau Omega fraternity, Shawnee State U., Portsmouth, 1992—. Mem. Am. Hist. Assn., Ohio Acad. History, Fortean Soc. (London), Internat. Fortean Orgn., Planetary Soc. Avocation: Fortean research. Home: 940 2nd St Portsmouth OH 45662 Office: Dept History Shawnee State U Portsmouth OH 45662

MIRABILE, CAROLYN ROSE, lawyer; b. Norristown, Pa., June 12, 1966; d. Paul Joseph and Norma Jean (DiFerdinando) M.; m. Richard Lawrence Giles, Sept. 26, 1992. BA in Polit. Sci., Villanova U., 1988, JD, 1991. Bar: Pa. 1991, N.J. 1991. Assoc. Gultanoff & Lynch, Norristown, 1992-93, Gultanoff Lynch & Tornetta, Norristown, 1993-94; ptnr. Lynch Tornetta & Mirabile, Norristown, 1994—; assoc. Montgomery County Family Law Com., 1991—, Doris Jonas Freed Am. Inn. of Ct., 1994—; co-chair Montgomery County Law Day, Norristown, 1993, 94, 95, family law practicum, 1996. Avocation: golf. Office: Lynch Tornetta & Mirabile 617 Swede St Norristown PA 19401-4739

MIRACLE, DONALD EUGENE, elementary school educator; b. Pineville, Ky., Jan. 4, 1952; s. Oliver Eugene and Ruth Edna (Borah) M.; m. Peggy Sifton; children: Mark Buis, David Buis. BS in Edn., Cumberland Coll., 1975; cert., Ea. Ky. U., 1984. Cert. tchr. Ky. Tchr. Bell County Bd. Edn., Pineville, 1975—; Ky. Ednl. Reform Act Fellows Cohort II, Frankfort, Ky., 1993—. Mem. adminstrv. coun. Covenant United Meth. Ch., Middlesboro, Ky., 1994-96, mem. choir, 1992—; tchr. leader Ky. Mid. Grades Math. Tchr. Network. Mem. NEA, Nat. Coun. Tchrs. Math., Ky. Edn. Assn., Cumberland Coun. of Tchrs. of Math. (exec. coun., advisor 1993-94, pres.-elect 1995-96). Avocations: gemology, fishing, motorcycling, bowling. Home: PO Box 222 Middlesboro KY 40965-0222 Office: Bell County Mid Sch Rte 1 Box 87C Pineville KY 40977

MIRACLE, GORDON ELDON, advertising educator; b. Olympia, Wash., May 28, 1930; s. Gordon Tipler and Corine Adriana (Orlebeke) M.; m. Christa Stoeter, June 29, 1957; children: Gary, Gregory, Glenn. BBA, U. Wis., 1952, MBA, 1958, PhD, 1962. Case officer, civilian intelligence analyst U.S. Army, Fed. Republic Germany, 1955-57; instr. commerce U. Wis. Grad. Sch. Bus., Madison, 1958-60; instr., then asst. prof. mktg. U. Mich., Ann Arbor, 1960-66; assoc. prof. advt. Mich. State U., East Lansing, 1966-70, chmn. PhD program in mass media, 1973-74, chmn. dept., 1974-80, prof. advt., 1970—; vis. prof. mktg. mgmt. N. European Mgmt. Inst., Oslo, 1972-73; cons., lectr. in field. Author: Management of International Advertising, 1966; co-author: International Marketing Management, 1970, Advertising and Government Regulation, 1979, Instructor's Manual for International Marketing Management, 1971, European Regulation of Advertising: Supranational Regulation of Advertising in the European Economic Community, 1986, Voluntary Regulation of Advertising: A Comparative Analysis of the United Kingdom and the United States, 1987, (in Korean) Cultures in Advertising: Advertising in Cultures, 1990; contbr. articles to scholarly and profl. jours.; editor: Marketing Decision Making: Strategy and Payoff, 1965, Sharing for Understanding, Proc. Ann. Conf. Am. Acad. Advt., 1977. Served with AUS, 1952-55. Recipient first Biennial Excellence in Advt. award, U. Ill., 1995; Ford Found. fellow, 1961-62, 64, Am. Assn. Advt. Agys. fellow Marsteller, Inc., 1967, Advt. Ednl. Found. fellow McCann-Erickson Hakuhodo, 1985, Fulbright rsch. fellow Waseda U., Tokyo, 1985; recipient numerous grants. Fellow Am. Acad. Advt. (treas., exec. com. 1978-79); mem. Acad. Internat. Bus. (sec., exec. com. 1973-75), Am. Mktg. Assn., Internat. Advt. Assn. (ednl. accreditation com. 1993-95), Adcraft Club Detroit. Home: 10025 Oak Island Dr Laingsburg MI 48848-8718 Office: Mich State U Dept Advt East Lansing MI 48824

MIRACLE, ROBERT WARREN, retired banker; b. Casper, Wyo.; m. Maggie Zanoni; children—Mark, John. BS in Law, U. Wyo., 1951; grad. with honors, Pacific Coast Banking Sch., 1960. With Wyo. Nat. Bank (now Norwest Bank Casper N.A.), 1954-91; exec. v.p. Wyo. Nat. Bank of Casper, 1967; pres., chief exec. officer Wyo. Nat. Bank of Casper (now Norwest Bank Casper N.A.)ú, 1968-87; chmn. Wyo. Nat. Bank of Casper (formerly Norwest Bank Casper N.A.), 1983-91, also bd. dirs.; pres., chief exec. officer, dir. Wyo. Nat. Bancorp. (formerly Affiliated Bank Corp Wyo.), Casper, 1970-91; instr. bank mgmt. U. Colo., 1971-75. Bd. dirs. United Fund of Natrona County, Wyo., 1963-85, campaign co-chmn., 1973-78; trustee The Myra Fox Skelton Found., 1963—, Goodstein Found., 1992—; bd. dirs., pres. Investment in Casper, 1967-70; Wyo. treas. Radio Free Europe, 1967-72; trustee Casper Coll. Foun., 1967-91, pres., 1973-75, 85-91; trustee U. Wyo. Found., 1972-87; chmn. Casper Downtown Improvement Assn., 1974-75; bd. dirs. Cen. Wyo. Fair Bd., 1974-79, pres., 1977-78; dir. Mountain States Employers Coun., 1979-91. Capt. USMC, 1951-53. Recipient James C. Scarboro Meml. award Colo. Sch. Banking., 1977; Disting. Service in Bus. award U. Wyo. Coll. Commerce and Industry, 1980. Mem. Wyo Bankers Assn. (chmn. legis. com. 1969-80, pres. 1974-75), Am. Bankers Assn. (mem. governing coun. 1974-75, 81-83), Am. Mgmt. Assn., Rocky Mountain Oil and Gas Assn., Newcomer Soc. in N.Am., Casper C. of C. (pres. 1965-66, Disting. Svc. award 1981), VFW, Casper Petroleum Club, Casper Country Club (pres. 1993-94), Masons, Lions.

MIRAGEAS, EVANS JOHN, record company executive; b. Ann Arbor, Mich., Nov. 17, 1954; s. Xenophon John and Constance (Collins) M. BA, U. Mich., 1976. Producer WUOM, Ann Arbor, Mich., 1973-82; sr. prodr. WFMT, Chgo., 1982-89; artistic adminstr. Boston Symphony, 1989-94; sr. v.p. artists and repertoire Decca Records Ltd., London, 1994—. Bd. mem. Classical Action, N.Y.C., 1992—. Greek Orthodox. Office: Decca Records Ltd, 347-353 Chiswick High Rd, London W4 4HS, England

MIRAND, EDWIN ALBERT, medical scientist; b. Buffalo, July 18, 1926; s. Thomas and Lucy (Papier) M. B.A., U. Buffalo, 1947, M.A., 1949; Ph.D., Syracuse (N.Y.) U., 1951; D.Sc. (hon.), Niagara (N.Y.) U., 1970, D'Youville Coll., Buffalo, 1974. Successively undergrad. asst., grad. asst., instr. U. Buffalo, 1946-48; teaching fellow Syracuse U., 1948-51; instr. Utica (N.Y.) Coll., 1950; mem. staff Roswell Park Meml. Inst., Buffalo, 1951—; head W. Seneca labs., 1961—, assoc. inst. dir., head dept. edn., 1967—, dir. cancer rsch., 1968-73, head dept. viral oncology, 1970-73, head dept. biol. recources, 1973—; rsch. prof. biology Grad. Sch., prof. biochem. pharmacology Sch. Pharmacy, SUNY, Buffalo, 1955—, dean Roswell Park grad. div. SUNY, 1967—; rsch. prof. biology Grad. Sch.; mem. human cancer virus task force, clin. cancer edn. com. NIH. Mem. editorial bd. Jour. Surg. Oncology, Cancer Rsch., Jour. Cancer Edn., Cancer jour.; contbr. articles to profl. jours. Mem. U.S. nat. com. Union Internat. Contra Cancer; profl. edn. com. cancer control Nat. Cancer Inst; liaison mem. Pres.'s Nat. Cancer Adv. Bd.; mem. N.Y. State Health Research Council; mem. Gov.'s AIDS Adv. Council, 1982—; sec. N.Y. State Cancer Programs, Inc., 1984—; bd. dirs. Network in Aging of Western N.Y., Inc., 1986—. Recipient Billings Silver medal AMA, 1963, Margaret Hays Edwards award in edn., SUNY, Buffalo, 1993, Citation award in sci. coll. arts and scis., 1964, award sci. rsch. mammalian tumor viruses Med. Soc. State N.Y., 1963. Life mem., fellow N.Y. Acad. Sci.; fellow AAAS; mem. Am. Cancer Soc. (state pub. edn. com. 1982—, nat. adv. com. on research personnel 1985—), Assn. Gnotobiotics (pres. 1968-69, dir. 1975-78), Internat. Assn. for Gnotobiology (pres. 1981-84), Assn. Am. Cancer Insts. (sec.-treas. 1968—), Am. Assn. Cancer Research, Radiation Research Soc., Am. Soc. Zoologists, Soc. Exptl. Biology and Medicine, Am. Assn. for Cancer Edn., Buffalo Acad. Medicine, Am. Soc. Hematology, Internat. Soc. Hematology, Pub. Health Cancer Assn. Am., Internat. Union Against Cancer (chmn. U.S. nat. com. 1979—, sec.-gen. 13th Internat. Cancer Congress), Hematology Soc., Am. Soc. Preventive Oncology, Buffalo Hist. Soc. (life), Buffalo Fine Arts Acad. (life), Sigma Xi. Home: S-6178 Hunters Creek Rd South Wales NY 14139 Office: Roswell Park Meml Inst 666 Elm St Buffalo NY 14263-0001

MIRANDA, CONSTANCIO FERNANDES, civil engineering educator; b. Raia-Goa, India, Dec. 4, 1926; came to U.S., 1960, naturalized, 1966; s. Alex Fernandes and Maria Marcelina (Viegas) M.; m. Joan Mary Menezes, Mar. 3, 1957; children: Steven Alex, Christopher Gerard, Kenneth Michael, Marie Lynn. Student, Karnatak Coll., Dharwar, 1944-46; B Engring. (civil), U. Bombay, 1949; MS in Civil Engring, U. Notre Dame, 1962; PhD in Structural Engring, Ohio State U., 1964; MA in Math, U. Detroit, 1974. Registered profl. engr., Ind., N.C. With civil engring. projects Govt. Bombay, 1950-60; teaching asst., then instr. U. Notre Dame, 1960-62; instr., rsch. assoc. Ohio State U., 1962-64; mem. rsch. staff U. N.Mex., 1964-65; mem. faculty U. Detroit, 1965-88, prof. civil engring., 1966-88, chmn. dept., 1965-72, prof. structural and systems engring., 1973-88, assoc. dean Coll. Engring., acting dean, 1972-73, ret., 1989; cons. civil, structural, systems engring., applied maths. and computer applications, 1989—; bd. dir. Profl. Adv. Svc. Ctr., 1973-75; staff engr. EPA, N.C., 1976-77. Contbr. profl. jours. Named Engring. Tchr. of Yr. Engring. Joint Coun., U. Detroit, 1967, 76; Distinguished Alumnus Ohio State U., 1973. Mem. ASCE, Am. Soc. Engring. Edn., Sigma Xi, Chi Epsilon, Tau Beta Pi, Pi Mu Epsilon. Home: 100 Silvercliff Trl Cary NC 27513-2803

MIRANDA, ROBERT NICHOLAS, publishing company executive; b. Bklyn., July 9, 1934; s. John and Florence Miranda; m. Marilyn H. Pils, May 25, 1958; children: Marilyn, Robert, Susan, Lori, Jennifer. A.A. in Acctg. and Bus. Adminstrn., SUNY-Farmingdale. Pres. Pergamon Press, Inc., Elmsford, N.Y., 1965-92; chmn., chief exec. officer Cognizant Communication Corp., Elmsford, 1992—; bd. dirs., exec. v.p., vice chmn. Soc. and Assoc. Svc. Corp., McLean, Va., 1979-82; bd. dirs., chmn. electronics com. Copyright Clearance Ctr., 1984-93. Pub. Acupuncture and Electro Therapeutics Research, Analgesia, Bird Behavior, Cancer Prevention International, Festival Management and Event Tourism, Gene Expression, Life Support and Biosphere Science, Tourism Analysis and Research, Technology: Jour. of Franklin Inst., Failure & Lessons Learned in Information Technology, Pacific Tourism Review, SSA Jour.-Jour. of Semi-Conductor Safety Assn. Served with USNR, 1954-59. Mem. Council Sci. Editors, Internat. Soc. Intelligent Systems (founder, bd. dirs., fin. dir. 1992—). Avocations: hunting; fishing; horseback riding. Office: Cognizant Comm Corp PO Box 217 Croton On Hudson NY 10520-0217

MIRCHANDANEY, ARJAN SOBHRAJ, mathematics educator; b. Hydrabad, Sind, India, Aug. 13, 1923; s. Sobhraj Gurmukhdas and Jamuna Mohanlal (Advani) M.; m. Padma Kalachand Lalwani, Oct. 20, 1958; 1 child, Haresh. BS, U. Bombay, India, 1943; MS, U. Bombay, 1946; PhD, U. Conn., 1984. Asst. prof. math. D.G. Nat. Coll., U. Bombay, 1943-47; lectr. Jai Hind Coll. U. Bombay, 1949-60, lectr. postgrad. classes, 1953-78, prof. math. Jai Hind Coll., 1960-69, prof., head dept. math. Jai Hind Coll., 1969-78; asst. prof. math. No. Ill. U., DeKalb, 1979-80, Knox Coll., Galesburg, Ill., 1982-85; prof. math. Defiance (Ohio) Coll., 1986—; coord. math. coll. sci. improvement program for Bombay colls., 1971-74; vis. prof. math. St. Lawrence U., Canton, N.Y., 1978; vis. asst. prof. Cornell U., Ithaca, N.Y., 1985-86; postgrad. lectr. U. Bombay, 1953-78; external examiner Shivaji U., Kolhapur, India, 1972-74; presenter Internat. Congress on Relativity and Gravitation, Munich, 1988, Internat. Congress History of Sci., Munich, 1989. Author: A Course in Elementary Trigonometry, 1954, 3d edit., 1965; contbr. to profl. jour. and book. Mem. Nat. Ctr. for Performing Arts, Bombay, 1969-78. Grantee Defiance Coll., 1989. Mem. Am. Math. Soc., Math. Assn. Am. Achievements include research in field theory of electromagnetics and photic field theory. Home: 700 Ralston Ave Apt 36 Defiance OH 43512-1567 Office: Defiance Coll 701 N Clinton St Defiance OH 43512-1610

MIRELS, HAROLD, aerospace engineer; b. N.Y.C., July 29, 1924; s. Hyman and Lily (Efron) M.; m. Nell Segal, Oct. 4, 1953; children: Lily, Laurence Franklin, Jeremy Mark. BSME, Cooper U., 1944; MSME, Case Inst. Tech., 1949; PhD in Aero. Engring., Cornell U., 1953. Sect. head NACA, Cleve., 1944-57; br. chief NASA, Cleve., 1957-61; dept. head Aerospace Corp., El Segundo, Calif., 1961-78, assoc. dir., 1978-84, prin. scientist, 1984-93; cons., 1993—. Co-inventor continuous wave chem. laser. Recipient Tech. Achievement award Cleve. Tech. Socs., 1960. Fellow AIAA (Fluid and Plasmadynamics award 1988), Am. Phys. Soc.; mem. Nat. Acad. Engring. Home: 3 Seahurst Rd Palos Verdes Peninsula CA 90274-3700

MIRICH, DAVID GAGE, secondary education language educator; b. Rock Springs, Wyo., June 17, 1956; s. John Jack and Kay Marie (Garvin) M. Student, U. de Filologia, Sevilla, Spain, 1981-82; BA in Psychology,

Dakota Western U., 1981; teaching cert., U. Colo., 1989; postgrad., U. de Complutense, Madrid, 1991, Universidad de Salamanca, Spain, 1993; MA in Bilingual/Spl. Edn., U. Colo., 1995; postgrad., 1994—. Pvt. practice tchr., interpreter Sevilla, 1981-83; tchr. bilingual Horace Mann Middle Sch., Denver (Colo.) Pub. Schs., 1989-92; tchr. bilingual/ESOL coord. North High Sch., Denver (Colo.) Pub. Schs., 1992—; tchr. on spl. assignment, secondary bilingual and ESOL edn. Denver Pub. Schs., 1994-95. Founder, chmn. Boulderiety Conv., Boulder, Colo., 1989-92; candidate Boulder Valley Sch. Bd., 1989; founder, pres. Front Range Children's Orthodontic Fund, Denver, 1991-92. With USN, 1974-75. Named Vol. of Week., Vol. Boulder (Colo.) County, 1987, Hero of the Week, Rocky Mountain News, 1994. Mem. Nat. Assn. Bilingual Edn. (Nat. Bilingual Tchr. of Yr. 1994), Colo. Assn. Bilingual Edn. (v.p. 1993-95, Colo. Bilingual Tchr. of Yr., 1994). Avocations: horses, breeding dogs, languages, travel, real estate restoration. Home: 2224 Hooker St Denver CO 80211 Office: West HS 9th and Elati Sts Denver CO 80203

MIRICK, HENRY DUSTIN, architect; b. Washington, Aug. 6, 1905; s. Henry Brown and Blanche Mitchell (Swope) M.; m. Marion Winsor, June 24, 1933; children: Marion Mirick Dick, Henry Dustin, Heath Mirick Kennedy, Richard. B.A., Princeton, 1927; B. Arch., U. Pa., 1930, M. Arch., 1931. Ptnr. Mirick, Pearson, Batcheler, Phila., 1935—. Works include monograph on large baths Hadrians Villa, Trivoli, Italy; works include Pennwalt, Nat. Bd. Med. Examiners bldgs., Friends Cen. Shipley Sch., Agnes Irwin Sch., Haverford Sch., Episcoal Schs., Pa. State U. natatorium and labs., Bryn Mawr Hosp., Lankeneau Hosp., Jefferson Hosp., U. Pa. Hosp., Medford Leas, Dunwoody, Cathedral Village retirement communities, Mus. Dr. Albert Barnes, Phila., Nat. Scis. Phila. auditorium and labs., James Murphy House, Episcopal Acad., St. Christopher's Ch., Parish House, Ch. of the Redeemer, Bryn Mawr, Humming Bird house, African Plains, Bear Mountain, Phila. Zoo, Sunnybrook, Buena Vista and Whitemarsh country clubs. Pres. Lower Merion Bd. Hist. Review, 1963-66; mem. Lower Merion Planning Commn., 1955-69; Trustee Acad. Natural Scis., 1965-78, emeritus, 1985—; bd. dirs. Pa. Environ. Council, Phila. Zool. Soc., 1963—Harriton Assn., Wharton Community Center, 1951-63; bd. dirs., treas. Phila. com. World Wildlife Fund; treas. Conservation Projects Inc.; chmn. bd. Montgomery Country Day Sch., 1965-67; bd. dirs. Dunwoody Retirement Community, 1976-82, emeritus, 1986—; mem. vestry Ch. of the Redeemer, Bryn Mawr, 1977-80; overseer Strawbery Banke, Portsmouth, N.H., 1981-84. Served to lt. col. AUS, 1942-45 (commendation medal). Recipient Rome prize in architecture, 1930, AIA merit citations; fellow Am. Acad. Rome, 1933. Fellow AIA (pres. Phila. 1970, chmn. Phila. charitable trust 1971-74); mem. Pa. Soc. Architects, Phila. C. of C. (bd. dirs. 1970-75), Pa. Hort. Soc. (pres. 1959-62), Pa. Soc. Promoting Agr. (v.p. 1980-83, pres. 1983-84), Am. Arbitration Assn., Shakspere Soc., Delaware Valley Ornithol. Club, Tau Sigma Delta, Delta Psi. Clubs: Merion Cricket, Philadelphia, Rittenhouse, Art Alliance Phila., Princeton, Pohoqualine Fish Assn., Wilderness (Phila.); Quadrangle (Princeton), Am. Alpine Club. Home: 101 Cherry Ln Ardmore PA 19003

MIRISCH, LAWRENCE ALAN, motion picture agent; b. Los Angeles, CA, Oct. 10, 1957; s. Walter and Patricia (Kahan) M. BA Radio & TV, Film, Calif. State U., Northridge, 1980. Apprentice film editor, 1975-77, 2nd asst. dir., 1978-81; agent The Gersh Agency, Los Angeles, CA, 1982-84, Adams, Ray & Rosenberg, Los Angeles, CA, 1984, Triad Artists, Los Angeles, CA, 1984-92; pres. The Mirisch Agency, Los Angeles, CA, 1992—; mem. Mot. Picture Editors Guild, 1975; Directors Guild of Amer., 1978; Academy of Motion Pictures Arts & Sciences, 1987; Amer. Cinema Editors, 1988; adv. bd., Amer. Film Inst., 1990; special products comm., Dir. Guild of Amer., 1991. bd. of governors, Cedars Sinai Hosp., 1991. Office: The Mirisch Agency 10100 Santa Monica Blvd Suite 700 Los Angeles CA 90067

MIRISCH, MARVIN ELLIOT, motion picture producer; b. N.Y.C., Mar. 19, 1918; s. Max and Josephine (Urbach) M.; m. Florene Smuckler, Dec. 28, 1941; children—Donald, Carol, Lynn. B.A., Coll. City N.Y., 1940. With contract and print depts., then office mgr. Grand Nat. Films, Inc., N.Y.C., 1936-40; organized theatre concession bus. Theatres Candy Co., Inc., Milw., 1940; exec., corporate officer Allied Artists Pictures Corp., Hollywood, Calif., 1953-57; co-organizer Mirisch Co., Inc. (motion picture producers), Hollywood, Calif., 1957; v.p.,, dir. Mirisch Co., Inc. (motion picture producers), 1957—; chmn., chief exec. officer Mirisch Prodns., Inc., 1968—; Chmn. permanent charities com. Motion Picture and TV Industries. (Recipient Best Picture of Year award Acad. Motion Picture Arts and Scis. for The Apartment, 1961, West Side Story, 1962, In the Heat of the Night 1968, Producer of Year award Nat. Assn. Theatre Owners 1972). Bd. govs. Cedars-Sinai Med. Ctr. Mem. Assn. Motion Picture and TV Producers Am. (dir., vice-chmn.), Los Angeles Art Inst., Acad. Motion Picture Arts and Scis. (bd. govs., 1st v.p.). Jewish. Clubs: Motion Picture Pioneers, Hillcrest Country. Office: Office 100 Universal C Plz North Hollywood CA 91606

MIRISCH, WALTER MORTIMER, motion picture producer; b. N.Y.C., Nov. 8, 1921; s. Max and Josephine (Urbach) M.; m. Patricia Kahan, Oct. 11, 1947; children: Anne, Andrew, Lawrence. Student, CCNY, 1938-40; BA, U. Wis., 1942, LHD (hon.), 1989; I.A., Harvard Grad. Sch. Bus., 1943. Producer, exec. producer Allied Artists Pictures Corp., 1946-57; producer, v.p. charge prodn. Mirisch Co., Inc., Los Angeles, 1957—; pres.-exec. head prodn. Mirisch Corp., Inc., 1969—. Prodns. include The Magnificent Seven, In the Heat of the Night (Acad. award for best picture of yr. 1968), Two for the Seesaw, The Hawaiians, The Organization, Toys in the Attic, Mr. Majestyk, Midway, Gray Lady Down, Same Time Next Year, Romantic Comedy, Prisoner of Zenda, 1979, Dracula, 1979, Some Like It Hot, West Side Story, The Apartment, The Great Escape, The Pink Panther, Fiddler on the Roof, others. Pres., bd. dirs. Motion Picture Permanent Charities, 1960-61; bd. dirs. Ctr. Theatre Group, L.A., Cedars-Sinai Med. Ctr.; bd. govs. The L.A. Music Ctr. Decorated Order Arts et Lettres (France); recipient UCLA medal, 1989. Mem. Acad. Motion Picture Arts and Scis. (pres. 1973-77, gov. 1964-70, 72—, Motion Picture Acad. Jean Hersholt award 1983, Motion Picture Acad. Irving Thalberg award 1977), Producers Guild Am. (pres., dir. 1959-62), Motion Picture Assn. Am. (dir. 1961—), Wis. Alumni Assn. (dir. 1967-73).

MIRISOLA, LISA HEINEMANN, air quality engineer; b. Glendale, Calif., Mar. 25, 1963; d. J. Herbert and Betty Jane (Howson) Heinemann; m. Daniel Carl Mirisola, June 27, 1987; 1 child, Ian Cataldo. BSME, UCLA, 1986. Cert. engr.-in-tng., Calif. Air quality engr. South Coast Air Quality Mgmt. Dist., Diamond Bar, Calif., 1988—. Chancellor's scholar UCLA, 1981. Mem. ASME, NSPE, Soc. Women Engrs. Office: South Coast Air Quality Mgmt Dist 21865 Copley Dr Diamond Bar CA 91765-4178

MIRKIN, ABRAHAM JONATHAN, surgeon; b. Flushing, N.Y., Aug. 17, 1910; s. Samuel and Anna (Jaffe) M.; m. Miriam G. Klawan, Jan. 26, 1936; children: Louise, Lawrence Stanley. A.B., Cornell U., 1931; M.D., NYU, 1935. Diplomate: Am. Bd. Surgery. Intern, then resident Sinai Hosp., Balt., 1935-41; mem. surg. staff Meml. and Sacred Heart hosps., both Cumberland, Md; pres. med. staff Meml. Hosp., 1966-67; instr. Traffic Inst., Northwestern U., 1964, 68, 72, 74, 76, 78, 80, 82; med. adv. bd. Fla. Dept. Hwy. Safety and Motor Vehicles, 1977—; mem. Com. on Uniform Laws and Ordinances, 1969-72. Gen. chmn. Nat. Conf. on Aging Drivers, 1974. Served to maj. M.C. AUS, 1942-46. Fellow A.C.S. (chmn. hwy. safety com. Md. chpt. 1967-68), Southeastern Surg. Congress; mem. AMA (past chmn. med. aspects automotive safety), Allegany County Med. Soc. (pres. 1947-48), Assn. for Advancement of Automotive Medicine (bd. dirs. 1957-60, 79-81, pres. 1957-59), Soc. Automotive Engrs. (com. on automotive safety), Med.-Chirurg. Faculty Md. (subcom. on traffic safety 1970-76), Fla. Med. Assn., Palm Beach County Med. Soc., Allegany County (Md.) Med. Soc. (pres. 1948-50). Home and Office: 2003 N Ocean Blvd Ph 203 Boca Raton FL 33431-7854

MIRKIN, BERNARD LEO, clinical pharmacologist, pediatrician; b. Bronx, N.Y., Mar. 31, 1928; s. Max and Esther M.; m. Phyllis Korduner, Aug. 1954 (dec. 1982); children: Lisa Mia, Mara Rebecca; m. Sarah Solotaroff, 1986; stepchildren: Jennifer, Rachel, Jacob. AB, NYU, 1949; PhD, Yale U., 1953; MD, U. Minn., 1964. Asst. prof. pharmacology SUNY, Downstate Med. Center, 1954-60; Ford Found. postdoctoral fellow Karolinska Inst., Stockholm, 1960-61; USPHS post-doctoral fellow Yale U., 1961-62; resident in pediatrics U. Minn. Hosp., Mpls., 1964-66; asst. prof. U. Minn. Med. Sch., Mpls., 1966-67; asso. prof. U. Minn. Med. Sch., 1967-72; prof. pediatrics and pharmacology, dir. div. clin. pharmacology U. Minn. Health Sci. Ctr., 1972-89; prof. pediatrics and pharmacology Northwestern U. Med. Sch., Chgo., 1989—; head, dir. rsch. Children's Meml. Inst. for Edn. and Rsch., Children's Meml. Hosp., Chgo., 1989—; assoc. dean Rsch. Northwestern U. Med. Sch., 1994—; cons. NIH, Office of Technology Assessment, U.S. Congress, WHO, U.S. Pharmacopeia, Pharm. Mfrs. Assn. Found.; vis. fellow Jesus Coll., Oxford U., 1974. Author: Perinatal Pharmacology and Therapeutics, 1976, Clinical Pharmacology: A Pediatric Perspective, 1978. postdoctoral fellow Karolinska Inst. Stockholm 1960-61. Served with M.C. U.S. Army, 1954-56. Mem. Am. Fedn. Clin. Research, Soc. Pediatric Rsch., Am. Assn. Cancer Rsch., Am. Pediatrics Soc., Am. Soc. Pharm. Exptl. Therapeutics. Home: 427 Greenleaf St Evanston IL 60202-1328 Office: Childrens Meml Inst Edn and Rsch Mailcode # 117 2300 N Childrens Plz Chicago IL 60614-3318

MIRKIN, DAVID, television producer; b. Phila.. Exec. prodr., writer, dir. Newhart, 1984-88 (Emmy award for writing 1987); exec. prodr., co-creator, dir. Get A Life, 1990-92; writer The Tracey Ullman Show; exec. prodr. The Simpsons, 1990— (Emmy award 1995). Office: Fox Broadcasting Co PO Box 900 Beverly Hills CA 90213

MIRMAN, IRVING R., scientific adviser; b. Syracuse, N.Y., July 29, 1915; s. Saniel I. and Rebecca (Raichlin) M.; m. Beatrice Wolff, Aug. 14, 1942; children—Robert, Marsha, Kenneth. B.E.E., N.Y. U., 1942; postgrad., Harvard-Mass. Inst. Tech., 1942-43, Poly. Inst. Bklyn., 1947-51, Air U., 1952, 56, 59, George Washington U., 1956, Colgate U., 1957, Syracuse U., 1958, Am. U., 1964-65. Registered profl. engr., Mass. Elec. engr. Central N.Y. Power Co., Syracuse, 1937-41; project engr. Watson Labs., Red Bank, N.J., 1946-50; mem. tech. staff Rome Air Devel. Ctr., N.Y., 1950-51; chief program staff Rome Air Devel. Ctr., 1951-55, asst. sci. dir., 1955-57, assoc. dir. R & D, 1957-59; dir. tech. planning and ops. Capehart Corp., N.Y., 1959-60; v.p. Capehart Corp., 1960-63; sci. cons. Anser Corp., Baileys Cross Roads, Va., 1963; sci. adviser, dep. chief staff research and devel. in sci. and tech. Dept. Air Force, Washington, 1963-66; sci. adviser S.E. Asia matters Dept. Air Force, 1966-72; spl. asst. to comdr. Hdqrs. Air Force System Command, 1966-76; dep. dir. SHAPE Tech. Center, The Hague, Netherlands, 1976-80; pres. Decision Process Systems, Washington, 1980—. Served to capt. USAF, 1942-46. Recipient Meritorious Civilian award Dept. Air Force, 1958, also Distinguished Civilian award, 1976. Fellow A.A.A.S.; sr. mem. IEEE; mem. Am. Inst. Aeros. and Astronautics, N.Y. Acad. Sci., Research Engring. Soc. Am. Home: 5729 Fairway Park Dr # 20203 Boynton Beach FL 33437-1764

MIRMAN, JOEL HARVEY, lawyer; b. Toledo, Dec. 3, 1941; s. Benjamin and Minnie (Krapifko) M.; m. Denise M. Dembinski, June 12, 1982; children: Lisa, Julie, Benjamin. BBA, Ohio U., 1963; JD, Ohio State U., 1966. Bar: Ohio 1966, U.S. Dist. Ct. (so. dist.) Ohio 1966, U.S. Supreme Ct. 1972. Ptnr. Topper, Alloway, Goodman, DeLeone & Duffey, Columbus, Ohio, 1966-85, Benesch, Friedlander, Coplan & Aronoff, 1986-93; shareholder Buckingham, Doolittle & Burroughs, Columbus, Ohio, 1994—; lectr. Ohio CLE Inst., Columbus, 1972—. Author direct examination CLE materials; contbr. articles to profl. jours. Mem. Ohio Elections Commn., 1976-80, vice-chmn. 1980. Mem. Capital Club, Worthington Hills Country Club, Worthington Hills Civic Assn. (pres. 1992-93), Assn. Trial Lawyers Am. (chmn. family law sects. 1993-94). Office: Buckingham Doolittle & Burroughs 88 E Broad St Ste 1600 Columbus OH 43215-3506

MIROCZNIK, SARA YITA, mathematician; b. Bklyn., Apr. 4, 1970; d. Aron and Frimit (Rosenbaum) M. BS in Math., Bklyn. Coll., 1991, MA in Math. Edn., 1994. Tchr. math. Midwood High Sch., Bklyn., 1991—; adj. lectr. Bklyn. Coll., 1994—. Recipient Citibank Incentive award, 1989, Prof. George W. Booth award Bklyn. Coll., 1991. Mem. Phi Beta Kappa, Sigma Xi. Avocations: racquetball, reading. Office: Bklyn Coll 2900 Bedford Ave Brooklyn NY 11236

MIROJNICK, ELLEN, costume designer; b. N.Y.C., July 7, 1949; d. Abe and Sunny (Schneider) Schneid; 1 child, Lili. Student, Sch. Visual Arts, N.Y.C., 1967-68, Parsons Sch. Design, N.Y.C., 1968-70. Head designer Happy Legs Inc., N.Y.C., 1970-76; freelance costume designer, 1976—. Costume designer: (films) French Quarter, 1977, Reckless, 1984, The Flamingo Kid, 1984, Remo Williams: The Adventure Begins, 1985, Nobody's Fool, 1986, Fatal Attraction, 1987, Wall Street, 1987 (Cutty Sark Men's Wear award for contbn. to menswear 1988), Cocktail, 1988, Talk Radio, 1988, Black Rain, 1989, Always, 1989, Narrow Margin, 1990, Jacob's Ladder, 1990, Switch, 1991, Mobsters, 1992, Basic Instinct, 1992, Chaplin, 1992 (Brit. Acad. award nomination 1993), Cliffhanger, 1993, Intersection, 1993, Speed, 1994; asst. costume designer: (films) Endless Love, 1981, Fame, 1984. Mem. Acad. Motion Picture Arts and Scis. Avocation: painting.

MIRONE, DAWN MARIE, secondary school educator, journalism educator; b. Mt. Vernon, N.Y., Sept. 21, 1963; d. Robert and Joann (Perrotta) M.; m. Greg Bartz; children: Shaun, Patrick John. BA in Journalism and Speech Comm., U. R.I., 1985; MA in Social Sci. Edn., Columbia U., 1987; cert. in social scis. and English, Calif. State U., Long Beach, 1991; postgrad., U. Mass., 1995—. Cert. tchr., Calif, N.Y. Reporter Std. Times, North Kingstown, R.I., 1984-85; tchg. asst. Greenwich (Conn.) H.S., 1985-86; journalism and English tchr. Evander Childs H.S., Bronx, 1986-88; dir. edn. Bellwood Med. Health Ctr., Bellflower, Calif., 1988-89; social sci. and English tchr. Regency H.S., Long Beach, 1989-90; social sci., English, speech, and journalism tchr. Laguna Beach (Calif.) H.S., 1990—, activities dir., 1992-95, mem. scholarship com., 1991, 94; journalism instr. Saddleback Coll., Mission Viejo, Calif., 1994—; cultural diversity coord. Laguna Beach (Calif.) H.S., 1993—. Mem. citywide youth violence commn. City of Laguna Beach/Sch. Dist., 1992-94; sch. coord. Close Up Washington, Laguna Beach, 1991—. Recipient Nat. Svc. award PTA, 1993; grantee Laguna Beach City Coun., 1992, Recognition award for Journalism, 1994. Mem. Nat. Coun. Tchrs. English, Nat. Forensics League, Am. Scholastic Press Assn. (1st pl. award 1994, 95), Journalism Education Assn., Quill & Scroll Soc. (Internat. 1st pl. award 1994). Avocations: motor cross racing, skiing, rollerblading. Office: Laguna Beach HS 625 Park Ave Laguna Beach CA 92651-2340

MIROW, SUSAN MARILYN, psychiatry educator; b. Manhattan, N.Y., Feb. 15, 1944. BA in Biology, Temple U., 1964; PhD in Anatomy, N.Y. Med. Coll., 1970; MD, Med. Coll. Pa., 1973. Diplomate Nat. Bd. Med. Examiners, Am. Bd. Psychiatry and Neurology. Intern in medicine and psychiatry Temple U. Hosp., Phila., 1973-74, resident in psychiatry, 1973-75; pvt. practice psychiatry Salt Lake City, 1976—; clin. asst. prof. psychiatry U. Utah Sch. Medicine, Salt Lake City, 1976—; clin. asst. prof. psychiatry Neuropsychiat. Inst. U. Utah; mem. staff Salt Lake Regional Med. Ctr., 1976—, Latter Day Saints Hosp., 1985—; prin. investigator Marine Biol. Lab., Woods Hole, Mass., 1968; research investigator Temple U., Dept. Biology, summer 1971, Hosp. Joint Diseases, N.Y.C., 1969-70; clin. dir. Utah State Hosp., Provo, 1980-82; psychiat. extern Phila. Child Guidance Clin, 1973, neurology clk. Med. Coll. Pa. Dept. Neurology, 1973, cons. psychiatrist Adolescent Residential Treatment Ctr., Salt Lake City, 1976-77; vis. prof. St. George's U., Grenada, 1990—; psychiat. cons. Divsn. Youth Corrections, Salt Lake City, 1992—; lectr. in field. Contbr. articles to profl. jours. NSF fellow 1965-69; grantee John Polachek Rsch. Found., 1969-70; recipient Weisman award Excellence Child Psychiatry, 1973. Fellow Am. Psychiat. Assn.; mem. AAAS, AMA, Utah State Med. Assn. (impaired physician's com. 1983), Salt Lake County Med. Soc., N.Y. Acad. Scis., Soc. Clin. and Exptl. Hypnosis, Internat. Soc. Clin. Hypnosis, Utah Soc. Clin. Hypnosis (sec. 1982-83), Am. Soc. Clin. Hypnosis, The Internat. Soc. for Traumatic Stress Studies. Office: 73 G St Salt Lake City UT 84103-2951

MIROWSKI, PHILIP EDWARD, economics educator; b. Jackson, Mich., Aug. 21, 1951; s. Edward and Elizabeth (Kapusinski) M.; m. Pamela Margaret Cook, June 14, 1986. BA, Mich. State U., 1973; MA in Econs., U. Mich., 1976, PhD in Econs., 1979. Asst. prof. U. Santa Clara, Calif., 1978-81; asst. prof. Tufts U., Medford, Mass., 1981-84, assoc. prof. econs., 1984-90; Carl Koch prof. econs. and history and philosophy of sci. U. Notre Dame, Ind., 1990—; vis. assoc. prof. Yale U., New Haven, 1987-88; vis. prof. Tinbergen Inst., Erasmus U., Rotterdam, Holland, 1991. Author: Reconstruction of Economic Theory, 1986, Against Mechanism, 1988, More Heat Than Light, 1989; Rowman & Littlefield series editor Studies in Worldly Philosophy; editor: Natural Images in Economics, 1994, Edgeworth on Chance, 1994; mem. editorial bd. History Polit. Econ., Duke U., 1986—, Social Concept, 1988-94, Review of Polit. Economy, 1994—; contbr. articles to profl. jours. Mem. Am. Econs. Assn., History Sci. Soc., History Econs. Soc., Soc. for Social Studies of Sci. Office: U Notre Dame Dept Econs Notre Dame IN 46556

MIRREN, HELEN, actress; b. London, 1946. First appeared with Nat. Youth Theatre; appeared as Cleopatra in Antony and Cleopatra, Old Vic, 1965; joined Royal Shakespeare Co., 1967; appeared as Castiza in The Revenger's Tragedy and Diana in All's Well That Ends Well; other roles include: Cressida in Troilus and Cressida, Royal Shakespeare Co., Stratford, Eng., 1968; Hero in Much Ado About Nothing, Stratford, 1968; Win-the-Fight Littlewit in Bartholomew Fair, Aldwych, 1969; Lady Anne in Richard III, Stratford, Ophelia in Hamlet, Julia in The Two Gentlemen of Verona, Stratford, 1970 (last part also at Aldwych); Tatyana in Enemies, Royal Shakespeare Co., Aldwych, 1971; title role in Miss Julie, Elynae in The Balcony, The Place, 1971; with Peter Brook's Centre Internationale de Recherches Theatrales, Africa and U.S., 1972-73; Lady Macbeth, Royal Shakespeare Co., Stratford, 1974, and Aldwych, 1975; Maggie in Teeth 'n' Smiles, Royal Ct., 1975; Nina in The Seagull and Ella in The Bed Before Yesterday, Lyric for Lyric Theatre Co., 1975, Antony and Cleopatra, The Roaring Girl, Henry VI-Parts 1, 2, 3, 1977-78, Measure for Measure, 1979, The Duchess of Malfi, 1980-81, Faith Healer, 1981, Royal Shakespeare Co., Barbican, 1983, Extremities, 1984, Madame Bovary, 1987, Two Way Mirror, 1988, Sex Please We're Italian, 1991, A Month in the Country, 1994 (Tony nominee - Lead Actress in a Play, 1995); films include: Age of Consent, 1969, Savage Messiah, O Lucky Man!, 1973, Caligula, 1977, The Long Good Friday, Excalibur, 1981, Cal, 1984 (Best Actress award Cannes Film Festival 1984), 2010, 1984, White Knights, 1984, Heavenly Pursuits, 1985, The Mosquito Coast, 1986, Pascali's Island, 1987, When The Whales Came, 1988, Bethune, Making of a Hero, 1988, The Cook, The Thief, His Wife, and Her Lover, 1989, The Comfort of Strangers, 1990, Where Angels Fear to Tread, 1991, The Gift, 1991, The Hawk, 1991, The Prince of Jutland, 1991, The Madness of King George, 1994 (Acad. award nominee for Best Supporting Actress), Prime Suspect; TV appearances include: Behind the Scene, Cousin Bette, Coffin for the Bride, Jackanory, The Changeling, Bellamira, The Philanthropist, Mussolini And Claretta Petacci, The Collection, The Country Wife, Blue Remembered Hills, The Serpent Son, Quiz Kids, Midsummer Night's Dream, After the Party, Cymbeline, Coming Through, Cause Celebre, Miss Julie, The Apple Cart, The Little Minister, As You Like It, Mrs. Reinhardt, Soft Targets, 1982, Heavenly Pursuits, 1985, Red King White Knight, 1988, Prime Suspect, 1991 (Best Actress award BAFTA 1991), Prime Suspect 2, 1992, Prime Suspect 3, 1993 (Emmy award, 1994), Prime Suspect 4, 1994, Chase in Losing Chase, 1995, Some Mothers Son, 1995, A Month in the Country, 1995. Mem. PTO. Office: Ken McReddie Ltd, 91 Regent St, London WIR 7TB, England

MIRRER, LOUISE, educator in Spanish and Portuguese; b. N.Y.C., Apr. 27, 1953; d. Gerald Paul and Mildred (Friedelbaum) M.; m. Philip Singer, Sept. 1, 1974 (div. Nov., 1984); 1 child, Philip Mirrer-Singer; m. David Halle, Mar. 6, 1947; children: Carla, Malcolm. BA, U. Pa., 1973; Diploma in Linguistics, Cambridge U., Eng., 1975; MA, Stanford U., 1977, PhD, 1980. Asst. prof. Spanish and Portugese Fordham U., N.Y.C., 1979-86, assoc. prof., 1986-91, prof. and dept. chair, 1991-94; prof. and dept. chair U. Minn., Mpls., 1994—; bd. advisors Medieval Feminist Newsletter, 1991—; project dir. Japan Found. Grant, 1992-94. Recipient McKnight fellowship, U. Minn., 1995; grantee Littauer Found., 1993, N.Y. Coun. for Humanities, 1994. Mem. MLA (chmn. exec. com. sephardic studies 1988-91, del. 1988-91), Am. Assn. Tchrs. of Spanish and Portugese (chmn. sephardic studies group 1989), Internat. Assn. Hispanists, Soc. for Medieval Feminism (bd. dirs. 1991—). Achievements include application of sociolinguistic methodology to orally composed texts; feminist approaches to medieval Spanish literature. Office: U Minn Dept Spanish & Portugese 34 Folwell H 9 Pleasant St SE Minneapolis MN 55455

MIRRIELEES, JAMES FAY, III, publishing executive; b. Cin., Nov. 2, 1939; s. James Fay and Alicia Lucille (Beatty) M.; m. Gillian C. Hanlon, July, 1986; 1 child, Hillary Evan, from previous marriage. BA, U. Cin. Editorial dir. McGraw-Hill Coll. Pub. Co., N.Y.C., 1975-77; v.p. Holt-Rinehart & Winston, N.Y.C., 1977-79; pres. CBS Coll. Pub., N.Y.C., 1979-81, 83-85, CBS Internat. Pub., 1981-83; mng. dir. European ops. Ashton-Tate, London, 1985-86; pres. Somerset House Edn. and Profl. Pubs., 1986-87; chief exec. officer Raintree Pub. Inc., 1987-88; chmn., pres. Raintree I Ltd. Partnership, 1988-91; pres. Coronet/MTI Film & Video, Deerfield, Ill., 1991-93; v.p. mktg. Edunetics Corp., Arlington, Va., 1993-95; v.p. bus. devel. Jennings & Keefe Media, 1995—. Democrat. Home: 2175 N Pierce St Arlington VA 22209-2505 Office: 2175 N Pierce St Arlington VA 22209-2505

MIRRO, RICHARD ALLEN, bank executive; b. Pitts., Oct. 9, 1951; s. Amaria Joseph and Agnes Elizabeth (Kassa) M.; m. Candace West. BA in Math. and Econs., St. Vincent Coll., 1972; MA in Math. Econs., Duquesne U., 1975. Mktg. officer Mellon Bank, Pitts., 1972-75; mgr. computer systems CACI, Inc., Roslyn, Va., 1976; banking ins. sales mgr. GE Info. Svc. Co., Rockville, Md., 1976-78; v.p. Transaction Tech., Inc., N.Y.C., 1978-81; prin. Booz Allen & Hamilton, N.Y.C., 1981-82; sr. v.p. Marine Midland Bank, N.A., N.Y.C., 1982-85; v.p. First Boston Capital Group, Tarrytown, N.Y., 1985-86; pres. Chase Home Mortgage Co., Tampa, Fla., 1986-89; sr. v.p. Chase Manhattan Bank, 1989—; COO Chase Manhattan MortgageCorp., Tampa, Fla., 1996—. Republican. Avocations: home remodeling, automobile restoration. Office: Chase Manhattan Home Mortgage Corp 4915 Independence Pky Tampa FL 33634-7540*

MIRSE, RALPH THOMAS, former college president; b. Carrsville, Ky., Aug. 8, 1924; s. Ralph Thomas and Rubye Catherine (Morris) M.; m. Blanche Allen, May 10, 1945; children: Ralph Allen, Deborah Lynn, Sally Ann. BA, Asbury Coll., Wilmore, Ky., 1943; ThM, Asbury Theol. Sem., 1946; PhD, Boston U., 1962; LHD (hon.), Lakeland Coll., Sheboygan, Wis., 1977; LLD (hon.), Buena Vista Coll., Storm Lake, Iowa, 1978; LittD (hon.), Heidleberg Coll., Tiffin, Ohio, 1981; DEd (hon.), Sungshin Women's U., Seoul Korea, 1983; DFA (hon.), Columbia Coll., 1988; DD (hon.), Oklahoma City U., 1988. Ordained to ministry United Methodist Ch., 1947; pastor Meth. Chs., in Ky., 1947-57; exec. sec. New Eng. Conf. United Meth. Ch., 1960-65, exec. sec. nat. div., 1965-70; v.p. Baker U., Baldwin, Kans., 1970-74; pres. Lakeland Coll., 1974-77, Columbia Coll., 1977-88, ret., 1989; part-time dir. ednl. devel. U. S.C., Hilton Head, 1989—; mem. Gov. S.C. Adv. Bd. Social Services, S.C. Adv. Council Pvt. Colls.; chmn. bd. S.C. Ptnrs. of Ams. Author: The Methodist Minister, 1960, The Self-Image of the Methodist Minister, 1962, The Changing Face of New England, 1964, Community Planning Studies, 1970. Decorated Order of the Palmetto, 1986. Mem. Am. Assn. Higher Edn., Counc. Advancement and Support Edn., Am. Acad. Polit. and Social Sci., Nat. Conf. Small Pvt. Colls. (pres., dir.), S.C. Found. Pvt. Colls., S.C. Coll. Counc., Internat. Assn. Univ. Pres.' (exec. com.), Am. Coun. on Edn. Republican. Clubs: Forest Lake, Summit (Columbia); Univ. (N.Y.C.); Hyannis (Mass.) Yacht. Lodges: Rotary, Shrine. Office: 10 Office Park Rd Hilton Head Island SC 29928-7535

MIRSKY, ARTHUR, geologist, educator; b. Phila., Feb. 8, 1927; s. Victor and Dorothy M.; m. Patricia Shorey, Dec. 22, 1961; 1 dau., Alexis Catherine. Student, Bklyn. Coll., 1944-45, 46-48; B.A., U. Calif., 1950; M.S., U. Ariz., 1955; PhD., Ohio State U., 1960. Cert. geologist, Ind. Field uranium geologist AEC, S.W. U.S., 1951-53; consulting uranium geologist Albuquerque, 1955-56; asst. dir. Inst. Polar Studies, Ohio State U., 1960-67; adj. asst. prof., 1964-67; asst. prof. geology Ind. U.-Purdue U., Indpls., 1967-70, asso. prof., 1970-74; prof. Ind. U.-Purdue U., Indpls., 1974-94; prof. emeritus Ind. U.-Purdue U., Indpls., 1994—, coord. geology, 1967-69, chmn. dept. geology, 1969-93. Contbr. articles to profl. jours. Served with USN, 1945-46. Mem. AAAS, AAUP, Am. Inst. Profl. Geologists, Geol. Soc. Am., Nat. Assn. Geosci. Tchrs., Am. Geol. Inst., Soc. Sedimentary Geology, Ind. Acad. Sci., Sigma Xi. Office: Indiana U-Purdue U Dept Geology 723 W Michigan St Indianapolis IN 46202-5132

MIRSKY, PHYLLIS SIMON, librarian; b. Petach Tikva, Israel, Dec. 18, 1940; d. Allan and Lea (Prizant) Simon; m. Edward Mirsky, Oct. 21, 1967; 1 child, Seth. BS in Social Welfare, Ohio State U., 1962; postgrad., Columbia

U., 1962-63; AMLS, U. Mich., 1965. Caseworker field placement Children's Aid Soc., N.Y.C., 1962-63; hosp. libr. hosp. and instns. divsn. Cleve. Pub. Libr., 1963-64; reference libr. UCLA Biomed. Libr., 1965-68, reference/acquisitions libr., 1968-69, head cons./continuing edn. Pacific S.W. Regl. Med. Libr. Sv., 1969-71, asst. dir. Pacific S.W. Regl. Med. Libr. Sv., 1971-73, faculty coord. Biomed. Libr. program Cen. San Joaquin Valley Area Health Edn. Ctr., 1973-77, assoc. dir. Pacific S.W. Regl. Med. Libr. Sv., 1973-79; head reference sect., coord. libr. assoc. program Nat. Libr. of Medicine, Bethesda, Md., 1979-81; asst. univ. libr., scis. U. Calif.-San Diego, La Jolla, 1981-86, acting univ. libr., 1985, 92-93, asst. univ. libr. adminstrv. and pub. svcs., 1986-87, assoc. univ. libr. adminstrv. and pub. svcs., 1987-92, assoc. univ. libr., 1993-95; dep. univ. libr., 1995—; guest lectr. Libr. Schs. UCLA and U. So. Calif., 1967-78, Grad. Sch. Libr. Sci. Cath. U., Washington, 1980, Grad. Sch. Libr. and Info. Sci. UCLA, 1984; mem. task force on role of spl. libr. nationwide network and coop. programs Nat. Commn. on Libr. and Info. Svcs./Spl. Libr. Assn., 1981-83; facilitator AASLD/MLA Guidelines Scenario Writing Session, L.A., 1984; mem. users coun. OCLC Online Computer Libr. Ctr., Inc., 1991-94; U. Calif.-San Diego rep. Coalition for Networked Info., 1992—; instr. Assn. Rsch. Librs., Office Mgmt. Studies, Mgmt. Inst., 1987; peer reviewer Coll. Libr. Tech. and Cooperation Grant Program U.S. Dept. Edn., 1988—; cons. Nat. Libr. Medicine, Bethesda, Md., 1988, San Diego Mus. Contemporary Art Libr., La Jolla, Calif., 1993, Salk Inst., 1995; mem. Libr. of Congress Network Adv. Com., 1994—, chair steering com., 1995—. Contbr. articles to profl. jours. and bulls. NIH fellow Columbia U., 1962-63; sr. fellow UCLA/Coun. on Libr. Resources, 1987. Mem. ALA (site visitors panel com. on accreditation 1990-92, libr. adminstrn. and mgmt. assn. 1990-92), Med. Libr. Assn. (bd. dirs. 1977-80), Med. Libr. Group Soc. Calif. and Ariz. (sec. 1970-71, v.p. 1971-72, pres. 1972-73), Documentation Abstracts, Inc. (bd. dirs. 1985-90, vice chair bd. dirs. 1988-90), Med. Libr. Assn. (pres. 1984-85), U. Mich. Sch. Libr. Sci. Alumni Assn. Office: U Calif-San Diego Univ Libr 0175G 9500 Gilman Dr La Jolla CA 92093-5003

MIRSKY, SONYA WOHL, librarian, curator; b. N.Y.C., Nov. 12, 1925; d. Louis and Anna (Steiger) Wohl; m. Alfred Ezra Mirsky, Aug. 24, 1967 (dec. June 1974). B.S. in Edn., CCNY, 1948; M.S.L.S., Columbia U., 1950. Asst. libr. Rockefeller U., N.Y.C., 1949-60, assoc. libr., 1960-77, univ. libr., 1977-91, univ. libr. emeritus, 1991—; trustee Med. Libr. Ctr. N.Y., 1965-91, v.p., 1980-88; cons. libr. mgmt. Mem. Bibliog. Soc. Am., Bibliog. Soc. Can., Bibliog. Soc. Gt. Britain, Soc. Bibliography of Natural History. Home: Sutton Ter 1161 York Ave Apt 4F New York NY 10021-7945 Office: Rockefeller U Libr 1230 York Ave New York NY 10021-6300

MIRZA, DAVID BROWN, economist, educator; b. Dayton, Ohio, Feb. 28, 1936; s. Youel Benjamin and Althea (Brown); m. Leona Lousin, June 20, 1965; children: Sara Anush, Elizabeth Ann. AB, Earlham Coll., 1958; PhD, Northwestern U., 1973. Instr. Dartmouth Coll., Hanover, N.H., 1961-63, Kalamazoo (Mich.) Coll., 1963-69; assoc. prof. econs. Loyola U., Chgo., 1969—, chmn. dept. econs., 1978—, dir. Inst. Futures Trading, 1973—. Trustee Earlham Coll., Richmond, Ind., 1988-95, mem. found. bd., 1991—. Mem. Am. Econ. Assn. Mem. Soc. of Friends. Home: 795 Lincoln Ave Winnetka IL 60093-1920 Office: Loyola Univ Chgo 820 N Michigan Ave Chicago IL 60611-2103

MIRZA, JEROME, lawyer; b. Chgo., Nov. 3, 1937. BS, Wesleyan U., 1960; LLB, U. Ill., 1963. Bar: Ill. 1972, U.S. Supreme Ct. 1980, U.S. Ct. Appeals (7th cir.). With Jerome Mirza and Assocs., Chgo. and Bloomington, Ill. Contbr. articles to profl. jours. Bd. dirs. Ill. Inst. Continuing Legal Edn., 1986-88. Fellow Internat. Soc. Barristers, Internat. Acad. Trial Lawyers; mem. ABA (ho. of dels. 1985-89), Ill,. State Bar Assn. (3d v.p. 1985-86, 2d. v.p. 1986-87, pres.-elect 1987-88, pres. 1988-89, co-editor Tort Trends jour. 1972, editor 1973-76), Ill. Trial Lawyers Assn. (bd. of mgrs. 1967-78, chmn. amicus curiae 1975-78, exec, com. 1975-77, v.p. 1978-80, pres.-elect 1980-81, pres. 1981-82, dir., prin. instr. 1980-89 Coll. Advocacy, editor Trial Lawyers Jour.1977-81), Assn. Trial Lawyers Am. (bd. govs. 1972-75, 81-89), Am. Bd. Trial Advocates, Trial Lawyers Pub. Justice (founder, lifetime mem.), Inner Circle Advocates. Office: Jerome Mirza and Assocs 3 1st Nat Plaza PO Box 308 Chicago IL 60602

MIRZA, MUHAMMAD ZUBAIR, product development company executive, researcher, engineering consultant, inventor; b. Jhelum, Punjab, Pakistan, Nov. 13, 1949; came to U.S., 1971; s. Muhammad Siddique and Shehr (Bano) M.; m. Tahira Beena, Aug. 12, 1977; children: Sarah, Nadia, Sana. Grad., Cadet Coll., Hasan Abdal, Pakistan, 1967; A in Respiratory Therapy, St. Joseph/VA Hines Hosps., Chgo., 1974; BS in Biology, Sangamon State U., Springfield, Ill., 1976; MS in Product Design, U. Ill., Chgo., 1978. Respiratory therapist St. Joseph Hosp., Chgo., 1974-79; assoc. engr. J.G.G. & Assocs., Woodbridge, N.J., 1979; product devel. engr. Becton-Dickinson Respiratory Sys., Lincoln Park, N.J., 1979-82; biomed. product devel. cons. Zubair Mirza Cons., Saddle Brook, N.J., 1982-86; v.p. R&D, bd. dirs. Critichem, Inc., Little Falls, N.J., 1982-86; mgr. advanced devel. engring. Becton-Dickinson, Critichem Group, Fairlawn, N.J., 1986-88; dir. biomed. engring./tech. and equipment planning Shifa Internat. Hosp., Islamabad, Pakistan, 1989-90; pres. Zubair Mirza Cons., Wyckoff, N.J., 1988—, Ameer, Natural Solutions, Inc., Wyckoff, 1991—; rsch. asst. Sch. Medicine, So. Ill. U., Springfield, 1976; rsch. assoc. Office of Spl. Edn., Springfield, 1975-76; rsch. assoc. to sr. cons. WHO, Geneva, 1977-78. Author: Islamization of Business, 1994; patentee on respiratory monitor, 1992, respiratory monitoring device, 1993, trocar system, 1994; patents pending on electronic spirometer, surg. (laparotomy) trocar and insertion sys. Trustee, v.p. Islamic Edn. Found. N.J., 1995—. Islam. Avocations: inventing, writing, reading, camping. Office: 570 Farview Ave Wyckoff NJ 07481-1140

MIRZA, SHAUKAT, engineering educator, researcher, consultant; b. Bhopal, India, Aug. 1, 1936; s. Mirza Afaq Beg and Birjees Jehan; m. Ferzana Beg, June 24, 1967; children: Sabah Jehan, Mazin. BS in Engring., Aligarh U., 1956; MS in Civil Engring., U. Wis.-Madison, 1960, PhD in Engring. Mechanics, 1962. Sr. lectr. Delhi Coll. Engring., India, 1962-64; prof. Indian Inst. Tech., New Delhi, 1964-69; prof. mech. engring. U. Ottawa, Ont., Can., 1969—, vice dean R & D faculty engring, 1991-94; vis. engr. Westinghouse Nuclear Europe, Brussels, 1976-77; vis. engr. Def. Rsch. Establishment, Ottawa, 1987-88; cons. Govt. of India, New Delhi, 1967-68, Atomic Energy Can., 1974-80, Bell No. Research, Ottawa, 1981-82. Vis. prof. Worcester (Mass.) Polytech. Inst., 1994-95, Ecole Nat. Superieur d'Ingeneur de Const. Aero., Toulouse, France, 1994. Invited keynote speaker various internat. profl. confs.; contbr. rsch. articles, tech. reports to publs. Recipient Pres.'s gold medal, Roorkee U., India, 1958. Mem. ASME, Assn. Profl. Engrs. Ont. Office: U Ottawa Faculty Engring, 770 King Edward Ave, Ottawa, ON Canada K1N 6N5

MISA, KENNETH FRANKLIN, management consultant; b. Jamaica, N.Y., Sept. 24, 1939; s. Frank J. and Mary M. (Soszka) M.; BS cum laude in Psychology, Fairfield U., 1961; MS in Psychology, Purdue U., 1963; PhD in Psychology (Fellow 1963-66), St. John's U., 1966. Staff psychologist Rohrer, Hibler & Replogle, Los Angeles, 1966-67; assoc. A.T. Kearney, Inc., Los Angeles, 1968-71, sr. assoc., 1972-74, prin., 1975-78, v.p., partner, 1979-86; pres. HR Cons. Group, 1987—. Cert. mgmt. cons.; lic. psychologist, Calif. Mem. Am. Psychol. Assn., Am. Psychol. Soc., Calif. State Psychol. Assn., Soc. for Human Resources Mgmt., Human Resources Planning Soc., Indsl. Rels. Rsch. Assn., Soc. for Indsl. and Organizational Psychology, World Affairs Coun. of L.A., Town Hall of So. Calif., Glendale C. of C., Jonathan Club. Republican. Roman Catholic. Home: 924C S Orange Grove Blvd Pasadena CA 91105-1741 Office: HR Cons Group 100 N Brand Blvd Ste 200 Glendale CA 91203-2614

MISAWA, MIWA, pharmacology educator; b. Toyama, Japan, Feb. 3, 1946; d. Bunji and Fumiko (Takata) Yamatake; m. Sachiko Misawa, Nov. 16, 1974; children: Tamako, Moko. BS, U. Tokyo, 1968, MS, 1970, PhD, 1973. Lic. pharmacist, Japan. Postdoctoral fellow Kans. Univ. Med. Ctr., 1979-81; prof. applied pharmacology Hoshi U., Tokyo, 1986-92, prof. pharmacology, 1992—; Mem. Japan Pharmacists Edn. Ctr., 1994—; vis. researcher Nat. Inst. Environ. Studies, 1990—; vis. prof. Beijing Med. U., China, 1993; mem. nat. evaluation team for Burma Drug Devel. Ctr., 1985. Author: Japanese Scientific Terms - Pharmacy and Pharmaceutical Sciences, 1993—. Recipient Iwaki award Iwaki Found., Tokyo, 1986. Fellow Japanese Pharmacol. Soc. (editl. bd. 1996—), Japanese Soc. Allergology, Japanese Soc. History of Pharmacy. Office: Hoshi Univ Dept Pharmacology, 2-4-41 Ebara Shinagawa, Tokyo 142, Japan

MISCHER, DONALD LEO, television director and producer; b. San Antonio, Mar. 5, 1940; s. Elmer Frederick and Lillian Alma. B.A., U. Tex., 1961, M.A., 1963. Mem. faculty U. Tex., 1962-63; producer/dir. USIA, Washington, 1965-68; with Charles Guggenheim Prodns., 1969-71; pres. Don Mischer Prodns., pres. Mischer Enterprises, Inc., Beverly Hills, Calif., prodr., dir., and program packager for network television programs, 1971—. Television programs include: The Kennedy Center Honors: A Celebration of the Performing Arts (Emmy Awards 1981,87); The Tony Awards (Emmy Awards 1987-88); Michael Jackson's Super Bowl XXVII Halftime Show; Baryshnikov by Tharp (Emmy Award 1985); Gregory Hines, Tap Dance America; Carnegie Hall: Live at 100; It's Garry Shandling's Show; Mowtown 25: Yesterday, Today, Tomorrow (Emmy Award 1983); The Muppets Celebrate Jim Henson; Motown Returns to the Apollo (Emmy Award 1985); Baryshnikov in Hollywood, Goldie and Liza Together, Shirley MacLaine—Illusions, Making Television Dance with Twyla Tharp, An Evening with Robin Williams, Am. Film Inst. Salute to Gene Kelly; producer additional programs with Bob Hope (Bob Hope: The First 90 Years - Emmy award Outstanding Variety, Music or Comedy Special, 1993), Barbara Walters, Goldie Hawn, others. Recipient: Primetime Emmy awards (10), Director's Guild awards for Outstanding Directorial Achiement (8), NAACP Image awards (3), Peabody award, Golden Rose of Montreux award, Gabriel award, Ohio State award. Mem. Dirs. Guild Am., Nat. Acad. TV Arts and Scis. Gov., Am. Film Inst. Office: Brillstein-Grey Entertainment 9150 Wilshire Blvd Ste 350 Beverly Hills CA 90212-3430

MISCHER, WALTER M., JR., health facility administrator; b. 1950. Grad., U. Tex., 1973. With Mischer Corp., Houston, 1974—, pres.; chmn. bd., pres., CEO Herman Hosp., Inc., Houston, 1991—; pres Southern Investors, Houston. Office: Southern Investors 2727 N Loop West Ste 200 Houston TX 77008*

MISCHKE, CARL HERBERT, religious association executive, retired; b. Hazel, S.D., Oct. 27, 1922; s. Emil Gustav and Pauline Alvina (Polzin) M.; m. Gladys Lindloff, July 6, 1947; children: Joel, Susan Mischke Blahnik, Philip, Steven. B.A., Northwestern Coll., Watertown, Wis., 1944; M.Div., Wis. Luth. Sem., Mequon, 1947. Ordained to ministry Evang. Lutheran Ch. Parish pastor Wis. Synod, 1947-79; pres. Western Wis. Dist. Evang. Luth. Ch., Juneau, 1964-79; v.p. Wis. Luth. Synod, Milw., 1966-79, pres., 1979-93; retired, 1993.

MISCHKE, CHARLES RUSSELL, mechanical engineering educator; b. Glendale, N.Y., Mar. 2, 1927; s. Reinhart Charles and Dena Amelia (Scholl) M.; m. Margaret R. Bubeck, Aug. 4, 1951; children: Thomas, James. BSME, Cornell U., 1947, MME, 1950; PhD, U. Wis., 1953. Registered mechanical engr. Iowa, Kans. Asst. prof. mech. engring. U. Kans., Lawrence, 1953-56; assoc. prof. mech. engring. U. Kans., 1956-57; prof., chmn. mech. engring. Pratt Inst., N.Y.C., 1957-64; prof. mech. engring. Iowa State U., Ames, 1964—, Alcoa Found. prof., 1974. Author: Elements of Mechanical Analysis, 1963, Introduction to Computer-Aided Design, 1968, Mathematical Model Building, 1972; editor: Standard Handbook of Machine Design, 1986, 1996, Mechanical Engineering Design, 5th edit., 1989, 8 Mechancal Designers Workbooks, 1990, Fundamentos de Diseno Mechanico, 4 vols., 1994. Scoutmaster Boy Scouts Am., Ames. With USNR, 1944-75, mem. Res. ret. Recipient Ralph Teetor award Soc. Automotive Engrs., 1977, best book award Am. Assn. Pubs., 1986, Legis. Teaching Excellence award Iowa Assembly, 1990, Ralph Coates Roe award Am. Soc. for Engring. Edn., 1991. Fellow ASME (life, Machine Design award 1990); mem. Am. Soc. Engring. Edn. (Centennial cert. 1993), Am. Gear Mfrs. Assn., Scabbard and Blade, Cardinal Key, Sigma Xi, Phi Kappa Phi, Pi Tau Sigma. Avocations: model bldg., railway history. Office: Iowa State U Dept Mech Engring Ames IA 50011

MISCHKE, FREDERICK CHARLES, manufacturing company executive; b. Benton Harbor, Mich., Sept. 21, 1930; s. Fred William and Clara Adeline (Ruhno) M.; m. Kathleen Ann Schultz, Nov. 19, 1955 (dec. Aug. 1980); children: Stephanie Ann, Michael Frederick, Eric William; m. Lori Ann Leonard, Dec. 23, 1983. AA, Lake Mich. Coll., 1956; BBA, Western Mich. U., 1958. CPA, Ind., Mich. Staff acct. Lybrand, Ross Bros. & Montgomery, Chgo., 1958-63; supr. acctg. Lybrand, Ross Bros. & Montgomery, Niles, Mich., 1963-65; v.p., treas. Skyline Corp., Elkhart, Ind., 1965-91, ret., 1991. Vol. Svc. Corps. Ret. Execs., 1992—, local v.p., 1993—; chmn. Meml. Endowment Fund Luth. Ch., 1995—. Mem. AICPA, Ind. Assn. CPAs (Civic Achievement award, 1976), Mich. Assn. CPAs, Fin. Execs. Inst. (Michiana chpt. pres. 1974-75), Nat. Assn. Accts., U.S. Power Squadron. Republican. Lutheran. Club: Elcona Country (pres. 1975). Lodge: Rotary (local pres. 1976-77). Avocations: photography, boating, golf, bowling. Home: 23322 Greenleaf Blvd Elkhart IN 46514-4508

MISCHLER, PAUL, grain company executive. Exec. v.p.-finance Garnac Grain Co. Inc., Shawnee Mission, Knas., 1958—. Office: Garnac Grain Co Inc 7101 College Blvd Ste 800 Shawnee Mission KS 66210-1891*

MISER, HUGH JORDAN, systems analyst, operations researcher, consultant; b. Fayetteville, Ark., May 23, 1917; s. Wilson Lee and Nellie (Pyle) M.; m. Josephine Spence Lehmann, June 24, 1944; children: James Spence, Wendel Lee, Andrew Lehmann, Emily Margaret. BA magna cum laude, Vanderbilt U., 1938; MS, Ill. Inst. Tech., 1940; PhD, Ohio State U., 1946. Tchr. math. Ill. Inst. Tech., Chgo., 1938-40, 42-44, Ohio State U., Columbus, 1940-42, 45-46; acting chmn. dept. math. Lawrence Coll., Appleton, Wis., 1944; ops. analyst Hdqrs. 20th Air Force, Washington and Guam, 1945; asst. prof. math. Williams Coll., Williamstown, Mass., 1946-49; ops. analyst Hdqrs. USAF, Washington, 1949-59, dep. asst. ops. analysis, 1951-59, acting asst. for ops. analysis, 1958-59; dir. operational scis. lab. Rsch. Triangle Inst., Durham, N.C., 1959-60; dir. applied sci. div. ops. evaluation group MIT, Cambridge, Mass., 1960-62; asst. to dir. systems planning and rsch. Mitre Corp., Bedford, Mass., 1962-65; v.p. Travelers Rsch. Ctr., Inc., Hartford, Conn., 1965-69; with U. Mass., Amherst, 1969—, prof. indsl. engring. and ops. rsch., 1969-80, acting head dept. indsl. engring. and ops. rsch., 1975-76, head dept., 1976-79, prof. emeritus, 1980—; leader craft of systems analysis, exec. editor publs. Internat. Inst. Applied Systems Analysis, Laxenburg, Austria, 1979-82, acting head communications, 1980-81; cons., sec., chief of staff USAF, 1967-68; cons. ops. analysis office hdqrs. USAF, 1968-71; mem. NAS Evaluation Panel for Inst. Applied Tech., Nat. Bur. Standards, 1969-72, Evaluation Panel for Tech. Analysis Div., 1967-69, 72-73, chmn. 1969-72; mem. commerce tech. adv. bd. Panel on Noise Abatement, 1968-71; cons. info. systems programs NSF Office Sci. Info. Svc., 1969-74, Ctr. for the Environment and Man Inc., Hartford, 1970-79, Rensselaer Poly. Inst. of Conn., Hartford, 1970, Am. Acad. Arts and Scis., Cambridge, 1983-85; chmn. rsch. adv. com. Ins. Inst. for Hwy. Safety, Washington, 1967-69; cons., mem. systems and program analysis panel Gen. Acctg. Office, Washington, 1972-76. Co-author: Basic Mathematics for Engineers, 1944, Basic Mathematics for Science and Engineering, 1955; co-editor: Handbook of Systems Analysis, Vol. 1, 1985, Vol. 2, 1988; editor: Vol. 3, 1995. Moderator First Ch. of Christ, Congl., Farmington, Conn., 1986-88; pres. New World Chamber Ensemble, Inc., Simsbury Conn., 1986-88, 90-92, 93-94. Recipient Arthur S. Flemming award U.S. Jr. C. of C., 1952. Fellow AAAS; mem. Ops. Rsch. Soc. Am. (founding mem. 1952, sec. 1958-61, v.p. 1961-62, pres. 1962-63, rep. to NRC 1967-73, editor Bull. 1959-61, editor Ops. Rsch. 1968-74, George E. Kimball medal 1975), Inst. Mgmt. Scis., Can. Operational Rsch. Soc. (Harold Larnder prize 1990), Am. Math. Soc., Math. Assn. Am., Soc. for Indls. and Applied Math., Inst. Math. Stats., Am. Statis. Assn., Conn. Acad. Sci. and Engring. (founding mem. 1976), Ops.-Rsch./Mgmt.-Sci. Found. Inc. (pres. 1987-91), Operational Rsch. Soc., Assn. Pub. Policy and Mgmt., Phi Beta Kappa, Sigma Xi. Home and Office: 199 South Rd Farmington CT 06032-2522

MISETICH, IONE HOZENDORF, business services company executive, enrolled agent, financial planner, accountant; b. Jackson, Miss., Sept. 19, 1937; d. Glenn Frederick and Ione Belle (Lowry) Hozendorf; m. Francis John Reget, Jan. 17, 1967 (div. 1986); m. Charles Drago Misetich, May 28, 1993; children: Diane Michele, Philip Francis, Michael Trahern. BA cum laude, U. Minn., 1959. CFP; CPA, Calif. Pres., Ea. Sierra Bus. Svcs., Inc., Bishop, Calif., 1980—; sec.-treas. Meyer Cookie Co., Inc. Soprano, Bishop Cmty. Chorus, 1974-78; treas. Calvary Bapt. Ch., Bishop, 1975—, choir dir., 1980—; chmn. Civic Arts Commn., City of Bishop, 1984-87; bd. dirs. Inyo Council for the Arts, 1987-90; pres. Bishop Com. Concert Assn., 1989—. Mem. Nat. Assn. Enrolled Agts., Calif. Soc. Enrolled Agts., Calif. Assn. Ind. Accts., Internat. Assn. Fin. Planners, Inst. CFP, Aircraft Owners and Pilots Assn., DAR, Mensa, Playhouse 395, Bishop Toastmasters Club, Bishop Rotary Club. Republican. Home: 146 North St RR 1 Bishop CA 93514-0728 Office: 130 Short St Bishop CA 93514-0728 Address: PO Box 728 Bishop CA 93515-0728

MISH, FREDERICK CRITTENDEN, editor; b. Hagerstown, Md., Feb. 11, 1938; s. Joseph Dubbs and Edith Louise (Crittenden) M.; m. Judith Elizabeth Solberg, Mar. 15, 1969; children—Stephen Crittenden, Andrew Dubbs, David Rogneby. BA, Yale U., 1959; MA, U. Minn., 1967, PhD, 1973; LHD (hon.), York Coll., 1995. Instr. English, Severn Sch., Severna Park, Md., 1959-61; chmn. dept. English Severn Sch., 1963-65; teaching assoc. U. Minn., Mpls., 1965-71; asst. editor G & C Merriam Co., Springfield, Mass., 1973-74, assoc. editor, 1974, sr. editor, 1974-75, joint editorial dir, 1975-78; editorial dir. Merriam-Webster Inc., 1978-93, v.p., editor-in-chief, 1993—. Editor-in-chief: The Merriam-Webster Book of Word Histories, 1976, 6,000 Words: A Supplement to Webster's Third, 1976, Webster's School Dictionary, 1980, Webster's Beginning Dictionary, 1980, Webster's Vest Pocket Dictionary, 1981, Webster's Ninth New Collegiate Dictionary, 1983, Merriam Webster's Collegiate Dictionary, 10th Edit., 1994, 9,000 Words: A Supplement to Webster's Third, 1983, 12,000 Words: A Supplement to Webster's Third, 1986, Webster's Intermediate Dictionary, 1986, Webster's Word Histories, 1989, The New Merriam Webster Dictionary, 1989, Addenda Section 1993: A Supplement to Webster's Third, The Merriam-Webster Dictionary, 1994. Advisor Noah Webster Found., 1979—; trustee Davis and Elkins Coll., 1986-95. With U.S. Army, 1961-63. S. H. Monk teaching fellow, 1971-72. Mem. MLA, Nat. Coun. Tchrs. English (commn. on English lang. 1981-83), Linguistic Soc. Am., Am. Dialect Soc., Am. Name Soc., Dictionary Soc. N.Am. Home: 45 Harwich Rd Longmeadow MA 01106-1207 Office: Merriam Webster Inc 47 Federal St PO Box 281 Springfield MA 01102-0281

MISHELL, DANIEL R., JR., physician, educator; b. Newark, May 7, 1931; s. Daniel R. and Helen Mishell; m. Carol Goodrich; children: Sandra, Daniel III, Tanya. BA, Stanford U., 1952, MD, 1955. Diplomate Am. Bd. Ob-Gyn. (examiner 1975—, bd. dirs., dir. subspecialty divsn. reproductive endocrinology 1985-89, pres. 1986-90, chmn. 1990-94). Intern L.A. County Harbor Gen. Hosp., Torrance, 1955-56; resident in ob-gyn. Bellevue Hosp., N.Y.C., 1956-57, UCLA-Harbor Gen. Hosp., Torrance, 1959-63; rsch. fellow Univ. Hosp., Uppsala, Sweden, 1961-62; asst. prof. dept. ob-gyn. Sch. Medicine, UCLA, 1963-68, assoc. prof., 1968-69; prof. U. So. Calif., L.A., 1969—, assoc. chmn. dept., 1972-78, chmn. dept., 1978—. Editor in chief Contraception, 1969—; editor Jour. Reproductive Medicine, 1982—, Year Book of Obstetrics and Gynecology, 1987—, Year Book of Infertility, 1989—; adv. com. Core Jours. in Obs-gyn., 1982—; mem. editorial bd. New Trends in GYN and OB, 1985—. Capt. USAF, 1957-59. Recipient Lester T. Hibbard award U. So. Calif., L.A., 1983, Joseph Bolivar DeLee Humanitarian award Chgo. Lying-In Hosp., 1985, Arthur and Edith Wippman Sci. Rsch. award Planned Parenthood Fedn. Am., 1992, Disting. Scientist award Soc. Gynecologic Investigation, 1994. Mem. Am. Gyn-Ob Soc., Am. Fertility Soc., Am. Coll. Obstetricians and Gynecologists, Am. Fedn. Clin. Rsch., Endocrine Soc., Soc. for Gynecologic Investigation (pres. 1985-86), L.A. Lb-Gyn. Soc. (v.p. 1984-85, pres. 1985-86), Assn. Profs. Gynecology and Obstetrics (exec. coun. 1982-85), Pacific Coast Fertility Soc. (pres. 1973-74), Salerni Collegium, L.A. Athletic Club, Phi Beta Kappa, Alpha Omega Alpha. Avocations: tennis, fishing. Office: U So Calif Dept Ob-Gyn 1240 N Mission Rd Los Angeles CA 90033-1078

MISHER, ALLEN, college president, retired; b. Feb. 12, 1933; m. Patricia Ann Kelley, Jan. 5, 1956; children: Robert, Lynda, David, Karen. BSc in Pharmacy, Phila. Coll. Pharmacy and Sci., 1959; PhD in Physiology, U. Pa., 1964. V.p. rsch. Smith, Kline & French, Inc., Phila., 1971-77, v.p. mfg., 1977-78; pres. Smith Kline Med. Diagnostics Co., Phila., 1978-82; sr. v.p. Nat. Med. Care, Boston, 1982-84; pres. Phila. Coll. Pharmacy and Sci., 1984—; bd. dirs. U.S. Health Care, U.S. Biosci., G.D. Searle, Inc., Cortech Inc. and Litmus Concepts.

MISHKIN, JEFFREY ALAN, lawyer; b. N.Y.C., Sept. 7, 1948; s. Arthur Lawrence Mishkin and Bette (Beraha) Jaffe; m. Janet Paula Steel, Dec. 26, 1971; children: Paul Steel, Douglas William. BA, State U. of N.Y., Albany, 1969; JD, Cornell U., 1972. Bar: N.Y. 1973, U.S. Dist. Ct. (no. dist.) N.Y. 1973, U.S. Dist. Ct. (so. and ea. dists.) N.Y. 1974, U.S. Ct. Appeals (2d cir.) 1974, U.S. Supreme Ct. 1980, U.S. Ct. Appeals (9th cir.) 1986, U.S. Ct. Appeals (3d cir.) 1988, U.S. Ct. Appeals (4th cir.) 1987, U.S. Ct. Appeals (1st and 7th cirs.) 1990, U.S. Ct. Appeals (DC circuit), 1992. Staff atty. Legal Aid Soc. N.Y., N.Y.C., 1972-73; assoc. Proskauer, Rose, Goetz & Mendelsohn, N.Y.C., 1973-80, ptnr., 1980-92; sr. v.p. legal and bus. affairs Nat. Basketball Assn., N.Y.C., 1993—; adj. prof. law Cardozo Law Sch., N.Y.C., 1984-89. Mem. ABA, N.Y. State Bar Assn., Assn. of Bar of City of N.Y. Home: 2 E End Ave Apt 4F New York NY 10021-1151 Office: NBA 645 5th Ave New York NY 10022-5910*

MISHKIN, MORTIMER, neuropsychologist; b. Fitchburg, Mass., Dec. 13, 1926; married; 2 children. AB, Dartmouth Coll., 1946; MA, McGill U., Montreal, Can., 1949, PhD, 1951. Asst. in research and physiology and psychiatry Yale U. Med. Sch., New Haven, Conn., 1949-51; research assoc. Inst. of Living, Hartford-Conn. and NYU Bellevue Med. Ctr., N.Y.C., 1951-55; research psychologist, sect. on neuropsychology NIMH, Bethesda, Md., 1955-75, research physiologist, Lab. of Neuropsychology, 1976-78, chief, sect. on cerebral mechanisms, Lab. of Neuropsychology, 1979-80, chief Lab. of Neuropsychology, 1980—, assoc. dir. basic rsch. DIRP, 1994—; part-time instr. psychology Howard U., 1956-58; vis. scientist Nencki Inst. Exptl. Biology, Warsaw, Poland, winter 1958, 68, Tokyo Met. Inst. Neuroscis., summer 1978, Oxford U. Dept. Exptl. Psychology, summer 1979; mem. psychol. scis. panel NIH, 1959-61, exptl. psychology study sect., 1965-69; mem. NIMH Assembly of Scientists Council, 1962-64, 72-74; mem. NIMH Scientist Promotion Rev. Com., 1984-86; mem. adv. com. Cognitive Neurosci. Inst., 1982-86; mem. NIH Fogart Internat. Scholars-in-Residence Adv. Panel, 1985-89; adv. bd. McDonnell-Pew Program Cognitive Neurosci., 1989-94; review com. Brain rsch., Human Frontier Sci. program, 1992-94, chmn. 1993—. Cons. editor Jour. Comparative and Physiol. Psychology, 1963-73, Exptl. Brain Rsch., 1965—, Brain Rsch., 1974-78, Neuropsychologia, 1963, mem. editl. bd., 1963-92; mem. editl. bd. Human Neurobiology, 1981-87, Exptl. Brain Rsch., 1965—, Brain Rsch., 1974-78, Human Neurobiology, 1981-87, Jour. Cognitive Neurosci., 1989—, Jour. NIH Rsch., 1989—, Cerebral Cortex, 1990-95, Advances in Neurobiology, 1990—, Handbook Behavioral Neurology, 1991—, Behavioral and Neural Biology, 1992—; reviewing editors Sci., 1985-93; assoc. editor Neuroreport, 1990—; contbr. numerous articles to profl. jours., also abstracts and book revs. Served to lt. (j.g.) USNR. Fellow AAAS (chair-elect 1990-91, chair 1991-92, past chair 1992-93), Am. Psychol. Assn. (officer, mem. at large 1964-66, coun. rep. 1967-69, pres. 1968-69); mem. NAS (officer, chmn. 1989-92), Ea. Psychol. Assn., Internat. Brain Research Orgn. (officer, rep.-at-large governing coun. 1993—), Internat. Neuropsychol. Soc., Internat. Neuropsychol. Symposium, Internat. Primatological Soc., Internat. Soc. Neuroethology, Soc. Exptl. Psychologists, Soc. Neurosci. (officer, pres.-elect 1985-86, pres. 1986-87, past pres. 1987-88), Sigma Xi, Phi Beta Kappa. Achievements includes research in behavioral and cognitive neuroscience in primates. Office: NIMH Lab Neuropsychology Bldg 49 Rm 1B80 49 Convent Dr MSC 4415 Bethesda MD 20892-4415

MISHKIN, PAUL J., lawyer, educator; b. Trenton, N.J., Jan. 1, 1927; s. Mark Mordecai and Bella (Dworetsky) M.; m. Mildred Brofman Westover; 1 child, Jonathan Mills Westover. AB, Columbia U., 1947, JD, 1950; MA (hon.), U. Pa., 1971. Bar: N.Y. State bar 1950, U.S. Supreme Ct. bar 1958. Mem. faculty Law Sch. U. Pa., Phila., 1950-72; prof. law U. Calif., Berkeley, 1972-75, Emanuel S. Heller prof., 1975—; Cons. City of Phila., 1953; reporter study div. jurisdiction between state and fed. cts. Am. Law Inst., 1960-65; mem. faculty Salzburg Seminar in Am. Studies, 1974; Charles Inglis Thompson guest prof. U. Colo., 1975; John Randolph Tucker lectr., 1978, Owen J. Roberts Meml. lectr., 1982; vis. fellow Wolfson Coll., Cambridge

U., 1984; vis. prof. Duke U. Law Sch., 1989. Author: (with Morris) On Law in Courts, 1965, (with others) Federal Courts and the Federal System, 2d edit, 1973, 3d edit, 1988; contbr. articles to profl. jours. Trustee Jewish Publ. Soc. Am., 1966-75; mem. permanent com. Oliver Wendell Holmes Devise, 1979-87. With USNR 1945-46. Rockefeller Found. rsch. grantee, 1956; Center for Advanced Study in Behavioral Scis. fellow, 1964-65. Fellow Am. Acad. Arts Scis., Am. Bar Found.; mem. Am. Law Inst., Order of Coif, Phi Beta Kappa. Home: 91 Stonewall Rd Berkeley CA 94705-1414 Office: U Calif Sch Law Boalt Hall Berkeley CA 94720

MISHLER, CLIFFORD LESLIE, publisher; b. Vandalia, Mich., Aug. 11, 1939; s. Nelson Howard and Lily Mae (Young) M.; m. Sandra Rae Knutson, Dec. 21, 1963 (dec. July 8, 1972); m. Sylvia M. Leer, Feb. 27, 1976; children: Sheila, Sharon, Susan. Student, Northwestern U., 1957-58. Author, pub. ann. edits. Ann. Studies U.S. and Can. Commemorative Medals and Tokens, 1958-63; assoc. editor Numismatic News, Krause Publs., Iola, Wis., 1963-64; editor Numismatic News, Krause Publs., 1964-66, numismatic editor all publs., 1966-75, exec. v.p., pub. all numismatic publs., 1975-78, exec. v.p., pub. all products, 1978-88, sr. v.p., pub. all Numismatic products, 1988-89, sr. v.p. ops., 1989-90; pres. Krause Publs., Iola, Wis., 1991—; bd. dirs. First State Bank Iola, 1972-83, Scandinavia Telephone Co., 1981—; ex-officio dir. Iola Old Car Show, Inc., 1985—; mem. coins and medals adv. panel Am. Revolution Bicentennial Commn., 1970-75; mem. ann. assay commn. U.S. Mint, 1973. Co-author: Standard Catalog of World Coins, ann. 1972—; contbr. articles New Book Knowledge, ann. 1969-81. Bd. dirs. William R. Higgins, Jr. Found., 1991—. Fellow Am. Numismatic Soc. (life mem.); mem. Am. Numismatic Assn. (life mem., medal of merit 1983, Farran Zerbe meml. disting svc. award 1984, Glen Smedley meml. dedicated svcs. award 1991), Token and Medal Soc. (life mem., pres. 1976-78, editor jour. 1964-68, disting. svc. award 1966, 80), Numismatists Wis. (life mem., pres. 1974-76, meritorious svc. award 1972), Soc. Internat. Numismatics (award of excellence 1981), Blue Ridge Numismatic Assn. (life mem., hall of fame 1994), Tex. Numismatic Assn. (life mem., hall of fame 1993), Ind. State Numismatic Assn. (life mem., founders award 1993), Ctrl. States Numismatic Soc. (life mem., medal of merit 1984), Iola Lions. Home: 100 Island Dr Iola WI 54945-9485 Office: 700 E State St Iola WI 54990-0001

MISHLER, JACOB, federal judge; b. N.Y.C., Apr. 20, 1911; s. Abraham and Rebecca M.; m. Lola Mishler, Sept. 1, 1936; m. Helen Mishler, Aug. 26, 1970; children: Alan, Susan Lubitz; stepchildren: Bruce Shillet, Gail Shillet Unger. Degree, NYU, 1931, JD, 1933. Pvt. practice L.I. City, N.Y., 1934-50; ptnr. Mishler & Wohl, 1950-59, 60; judge N.Y. State Supreme Ct., 1959; sr. judge U.S. Dist. Ct. (ea. dist.), Uniondale, N.Y., 1961—; mem. U.S. Jud. Conf., Dist. Judge Rep., 2nd cir., 1974-77. Office: US Dist Ct LI Courthouse 2 Uniondale Ave Uniondale NY 11553

MISHLER, JOHN MILTON (YOCHANAN MENASHSHEH BEN SHAUL), natural sciences educator, academic administrator; b. Cairo, Ill., Sept. 25, 1946; s. John Milton and Mary Jane (Woodbury) M.; m. Mary Therese Stember, Apr. 15, 1972 (div. Nov. 1981); m. Sigrid Ruth Elizabeth Fischer, Dec. 15, 1981; 1 child, Joshua Evan. AA with honors, Orange Coast Coll., Costa Mesa, Calif., 1966; AB in Molecular Biology, U. Calif., San Diego, 1969, ScM in Engring. Scis., 1971; DPhil in Immunohematology, St. John's Coll., Oxford U., 1978. Cert. community coll. instr., Calif. Clin. coord. McGaw Labs., Costa Mesa, 1972-78; rsch. fellow Royal Postgrad. Med. Sch., Eng., 1977-78, Med. U., Cologne, Fed. Republic Germany, 1978-80; br. chief Nat. Heart, Lung and Blood Inst. NIH, Bethesda, Md., 1980-82; prof. med., basic life scis. and pharmacol. U. Mo., Kansas City, 1983-89, asst. vice chancellor, 1983-85, dir. div. basic med. scis., 1985-86, assoc. vice chancellor, 1985-89; prof. nat. scis. U. Md. Ea. Shore, Princess Anne, 1989-94, dean grad. studies and rsch., 1989-91; prof. biology Delaware Valley Coll. Sci. and Agrl., Doylestown, Pa., 1994—, dean of Coll., 1994-95; frequent nat. and internat. lectr.; chmn. 13 nat. and internat. meeting sects. Author: Pharmacology of Hydroxyethyl Starch. Use in Therapy and Blood Banking, 1982; editor or co-editor 6 sci. monographs; mem. editorial rev. bd. Jour. Soc. Rsch. Adminstrs., 1987-91; book rev. editor Grants Mag., 1987-89; contbr. more than 100 articles to profl. jours. Bd. dirs. Ctr. for Bus. Innovation, Inc., 1987, Bucks Assn. for Retarded Citizens, 1995—. Sr. rsch. fellow Alexander von Humboldt Foun. (West Germany), 1978-80; recipient Outstanding Adminstrn. Svc. award U. Mo., Kansas City, 1987, Excellence award Soc. Rsch. Adminstrn., 1989, Cert. Appreciation, 1991. Fellow Internat. Soc. Haematology, Royal Coll. Pathologists; mem. Am. Soc. Hematology, German Soc. Hematology, Nat. Coun. Univ. Rsch. Adminstrn., Nat. Assn. State Univs. and Land-Grant Colls. (mem. exec. com. coun. on rsch. policy and grad. edn. 1990-91), Coun. Grad. Schs., N.Y. Acad. Scis., Sigma Xi. Jewish. Avocations: reading, writing, music. Home: 475 North Street Apt 6-F Doylestown PA 18901 Office: Delaware Valley Coll 700 E Butler Ave Doylestown PA 18901-2697

MISHLER, WILLIAM, II, political science educator; b. Miami, Fla., Oct. 14, 1947; s. William Thomas Earle and Marie Katheryn (Schmitz) M.; m. Mary Catherine Tanner, Aug. 5, 1972. BA, Stetson U., 1969; MA, Duke U., 1972, PhD, 1973. Asst. prof. Duke U., Durham, N.C., 1972-78; assoc. prof. SUNY, Buffalo, 1978-82, prof., chmn., 1984-86; dir. polit. sci. program NSF, Washington, 1982-84; prof., chmn. U. S.C., Columbia, 1986-89, prof., 1989—, James F. and Maude B. Byrnes prof. govt., 1995—; vis. prof. U. Strathelyde, Glasgow, Scotland, 1976-77; vis. scientist, dir. polit. sci. program NSF, Washington, 1990-91. Author: Influence in Parliament, Political Participation in Canada, Representative Democracy in the Canadian Provinces, Resurgence of Conservatism, Controversies in Political Economy; mem. editorial bds. Jour. Politics, 1982-88, Legis. Studies Quar., 1988-91. Capt. U.S. Army, 1972. Mem. Am. Polit. Sci. Assn., So. Polit. Sci. Assn., Midwest Polit. Sci. Assn., Can. Polit. Sci. Assn., Internat. Studies Assn., Assn. Can. Studies (U.S. chpt.). Office: Dept Govt & Internat Studies U SC Columbia SC 29208

MISHRA, VISHWA MOHAN, communications educator, consultant, priest; b. Hilsa, Patna, India, Nov. 12, 1937; s. Pandit Sheo Nath and Pandita Nitya (Rani) M.; came to U.S., 1956, naturalized, 1964; BA with honors, Patna U., 1954, MA, 1956; MA, U. Ga., 1958; PhD, U. Minn., 1968; M Theol. Studies, St. John's, 1987; m. Sally Schroeder, June 18, 1977; children—Aneil Kumar, Allan Kumar, Anand Kumar, Jennifer Kumari, Andrew Kumar, Alexander Kumar. Staff reporter, Hindusthan Samachar, Ltd., Patna, India, 1950-56; exec. dir. India for Christ, Inc., Mpls., 1960-64; research fellow, instr. Sch. Journalism and Mass Communication, U. Minn., 1964-68; asst. prof. U. Okla., 1968-69; asso. prof. Mich. State U., East Lansing, 1969-87, prof., 1987—, adjunct grad. prof. Ctrl. Mich. Univ., 1992—; dir. market and communication research Panax Corp., East Lansing, 1975-76; adminstrv. asst., research cons. to pres. Lansing (Mich.) Community Coll., 1976—, pres. Communications Cons. Internat., Inc., 1987—; Episcopal chaplain, State Mich. House Reps. and Senate; rector Episcopal Ch. of the Advent, 1988—. Vice chmn. Eaton-Ingham Substance Abuse Commn. Recipient NSF award, 1969; Bihar Rastrabhasha Parishad Lit. award, 1st prize, 1954. Mem. Am. Mgmt. Assn., Am. Statis. Assn., Am. Pub. Opinion Research Council, Newspaper Research Council, Radio and TV News Dirs. Assn., Assn. Edn. in Journalism, Internat. Communication Assn., Am. Platform Assn., Smithsonian Instn. Assos., Kappa Tau Alpha, Sigma Delta Chi. Clubs: East Lansing Rotary (dist. gov. Rotary Internat. dist. 6360), University. Author: Communication and Modernization in Urban Slums, 1972; The Basic News Media and Techniques, 1972; Law and Disorder; co-editor Dynamics of Information Management, 1987; also monographs. Contbr. articles to scholastic jours. Home: 3911 Hemmingway Dr Okemos MI 48864-3758

MISKIEWICZ, SUSANNE PIATEK, elementary education educator; b. Elizabeth, N.J., Nov. 19, 1947; d. Edward Walter and Charlotte Teresa (Kardel) Piatek; m. Randall Lee Grover; 1 child, Michelle Lee Grover Domenico; m. Raymond Richard Miskiewicz, July 11, 1977; children: Lisa Marie, Raymond Edward. BA, Newark State Coll., 1972; MA, Kean Coll., 1976. Cert. prin./supr., supr., reading specialist, elem. edn., nursery sch., N.J. Tchr. Linden (N.J.) Bd. Edn., 1973-79, 87-90; tchr. Linden Adult Sch., 1981-88, dir., 1988-90; tchr. Roselle (N.J.) Bd. Edn., 1991, New Providence (N.J.) Bd. Edn., 1991—; cons., trainer N.J. Dept. Edn., Trenton, 1987-90; cons. Am. Guidance Svc., Minn., 1979—; mem. bd. edn. Linden, 1991-94, v.p., 1993-94; presenter NJEA Conv., 1976, Edn. Fair, Washington, 1973. Reviewer: Prep, Keymath, You and Your Small Wonder, Books 1 and 2, 1979-88. sec., treas., v.p. PTA, Linden, 1984-92; mem., v.p. Gen. Pulaski Com., Linden, 1985—; mem., sec., v.p., treas. Linden Summer Theatre, 1978-85; trustee St. Teresa' Ch., Linden, 1970-73; advisor St. Elizabeth's Ch. Altar Server Soc., 1994—; leader Girl Scouts Am., Linden, 1987-91. Mem. ASCD, Internat. Reading Assn., N.J. Reading Assn., N.J. Edn. Assn., NEA, New Providence Edn. Assn. (pres. 1995—). Roman Catholic. Avocations: reading, crafts, golf. Home: 43 Palisade Rd Linden NJ 07036-3828 Office: New Providence Bd Edn 80 Jones Dr New Providence NJ 07974-1121

MISKOWSKI, LEE R., retired automobile executive; b. Stevens Point, Wis., Mar. 27, 1932; s. Paul P. and Marie Grace (Glazer) M.; m. Billie Poulson, 1963; children: Christine, Katherine. BBA, U. Wis., 1954, MBA, 1957. V.p. Ford of Europe Ford Motor Co., Cologne, Fed. Republic Germany, 1977-80; gen. mktg. mgr. Ford div. Ford Motor Co., Dearborn, Mich., 1980-83, v.p., gen. mgr. parts and svc. div., 1989-91, v.p., gen. mgr. Lincoln-Mercury div., 1991-94; ret. Ford Motor Co., 1994; bd. dirs. Autocraft, Inc., Adco Techs., Inc., Lear Seating. Trustee Hospice of S.E. Mich., Detroit, 1988-94, chmn.; chmn. Hospice of Mich., 1996; chmn. bd. dirs. Mich. Parkinson Found., Detroit, 1992-94. With U.S. Army, 1954-56. Mem. Oakland Hills Country Club. Roman Catholic. Avocations: tennis, snow skiing, reading, extensive travel.

MISKUS, MICHAEL ANTHONY, electrical engineer, consultant; b. East Chicago, Ind., Dec. 10, 1950; s. Paul and Josephine Miskus; BS, Purdue U., 1972; AAS in Elec. Engring. Tech., Purdue U., Indpls., 1972; cert. mgmt. Ind. U., 1972, Ind. Central Coll., 1974. Cert. plant engr.; registered environ. assessor REA, Calif. Service engr. Reliance Electric & Engring. Co., Hammond, Ind., 1972-73; maintenance supr., maintenance mgr. Diamond Chain Co./AMSTED Industries, Indpls., 1973-76; primary and facilities elec. engr. Johnson & Johnson Baby Products Co., Park Forest South, Ill., 1976-81; prin. Miskus Cons., indsl./comml. elec. cons., 1979—; plant and facilities engring. mgr. Sherwin Williams Co., Chgo. Emulsion Plant, Chgo., 1981-85; with Miscon Assocs., Riverside, Calif., 1985—; acting dir. plant and facilities engring. Bourns Inc., 1982-90; facility mgr. Cardiovascular Devices Inc., 3M Healthcare, 1990—; mgr. Metrology and Corp. Metrology Lab & ISO 9000, 3M, St. Paul; instr., lectr. EET program Moraine Valley C.C., Palos Hills, Ill., 1979; instr. cert. program plant engring. U. Calif.; lectr. energy engring., bldg. automation systems Prairie State Coll., Chicago Heights, Ill., 1980—; mem. adj. faculty, faculty adv. bd. Orange Coast Coll., Costa Mesa, Calif.; commr., chmn. Riverside Energy Commn., 1988—; mem. Elec. Industry Evaluation Panel. Mem. faculty adv. bd. Moraine Valley C.C., 1980—. Mem. IEEE, Am. Inst. Plant Engrs. (pres. Pomona chpt. 1989—, chmn. western region VI membership, chmn. nat. coun. stds. labs. region II Twin Cities sect. 1995—), Assn. Energy Engrs., Assn. Energy Engrs. (sr., So. Calif. chpt.), Assn. Profl. Energy Mgrs. (bd. dirs. Orange County chpt. 1992), Illuminating Engring. Soc. N.Am., Internat. Platform Assn., 3M Global plant engring. steering com., ops. subcom.; Riverside C. of C. Club: Purdue of L.A. Office: PO Box 25252 Woodbury MN 55125-0252

MISLOW, KURT MARTIN, chemist, educator; b. Berlin, Germany, June 5, 1923; came to U.S., 1940, naturalized, 1946; s. Max and Ida (Bingen) M.; m. Jacqueline Ford, 1966; children: Christopher, John. B.S., Tulane U., 1944, D.Sc. (hon.), 1975; Ph.D., Calif. Inst. Tech., 1947; D. honoris causa, Free U., Brussels, 1974, Uppsala U., 1977; Düsseldorf U., 1994. Instr. NYU, 1947-51, asst. prof., 1951-56, asso. prof., 1956-60, prof., 1960-64; Hugh Stott Taylor prof. chemistry Princeton, 1964-88, chmn. dept. chemistry, 1968-74, prof. emeritus, 1988—; vis. prof. Stanford U., 1960, Calif. Inst. Tech., 1994; M.S. Kharasch vis. prof. U. Chgo., 1989; Univ. lectr. U. London, 1965; J.A. McRae Meml. lectr. Queen's U., 1967; H.A. Iddles lectr. U. N.H., 1972; Solvay lectr. and medalist Free U. Brussels, 1972; E.C. Lee lectr. U. Chgo.; A.A. Vernon lectr. Northeastern U., 1976; PPG lectr. Ohio U., 1977; J. Musher Meml. lectr. Hebrew U. Jerusalem, 1978; North Country lectr., 1978; Honor lectr. Ariz. State U., 1981; E. Ritchie meml. lectr. Sydney U., 1983; Fuson lectr. U. Nev., 1983; Research Scholar lectr. Drew U., 1983; McGregory lectr. Colgate U., 1984; Sandia lectr. U. Alta., 1984; Purves lectr. McGill U., 1985; Arnold lectr. So. Ill. U., 1985; Bergmann lectr. Yale U., 1986; H.C. Brown lectr. Purdue U., 1988; Irvine lectr. U. St. Andrews, 1988; Eyring lectr. Ariz. State U., 1989; Disting. Scientist lectr. Bard Coll., 1991; Syntex Disting. lectr. Colo. State U., 1991; Disting. scientist lectr. Bard Coll., 1991; J.W.T. Spinks lectr. U. Saskatchewan, 1992; Bristol-Myers-Squibb disting. lectr. Syracuse U., 1992; Churchill fellow Cambridge U., 1974-75; mem. adv. panel chemistry NSF, 1963-66; mem. panel medical and organic chemistry NIH, 1963-66. Author: Introduction to Stereochemistry, 1965; also numerous articles; bd. editors: Jour. Organic Chemistry, 1965-70; mem. editl. adv. bd. Monatshefte für Chemie, Topics in Stereochemistry, Accounts of Chem. Rsch., Chem. and Engring. News, Bull des Sociétés Chimiques Belges, Symmetry, Jour. Math. Chemistry. Recipient Prelog medal, ETH Zurich, 1986, W.H. Nichols medal, 1987, Sci. Achievement award medal CCNY, 1988, Disting. Alumni award Calif. Inst. Tech., 1990, Chirality medal, 1993, Arthur C. Cope Scholar award Am. Chem. Soc. 1995; Guggenheim fellow, 1957-58, 74-75, Alfred P. Sloan fellow, 1959-63, Sherman Fairchild disting. scholar Calif. Inst. Tech., 1990, 91, 94. Fellow AAAS, Am. Acad. Arts and Scis.; mem. Nat. Acad. Scis., Am. Chem. Soc. (James Flack Norris award 1975), Chem. Soc. London, AAUP, Phi Beta Kappa, Sigma Xi, Phi Lambda Upsilon.

MISNER, CHARLES WILLIAM, physics educator; b. Jackson, Mich., June 13, 1932; s. Francis deSales and Madge B. (Mee) M.; m. Susanne Elisabeth Kemp, June 13, 1959; children: Benedicte Elisabeth, Francis Frithjof, Timothy Charles, Christopher Kemp. B.S., U. Notre Dame, 1952; M.A., Princeton U., 1954, Ph.D., 1957. Instr. Princeton U., (N.J.), 1956-59, asst. prof., 1959-63; assoc. prof. physics U. Md., College Park, 1963-66, prof., 1966—; vis. fellow Inst. for Theoretical Physics, U. Calif., Santa Barbara, 1980-81, All Souls Coll., Oxford, Eng., 1973; vis. faculty Calif. Inst. Tech., 1972, Princeton U., 1969. Author: (with Wheeler and Thorne) Gravitation, 1973, (with Patrick J.Cooney) Spreadsheet Physics, 1991; contbr. articles to profl. jours. Recipient Sci. Centennial award U. Notre Dame, 1965, Dannie Heineman prize (with R. Arnowitt and S. Deser) for math. physics Am. Phys. Soc., 1994; NSF sr. postdoctoral fellow, 1966-67; Guggenheim fellow, 1972-73; Einstein Centennial lectr., 1979. Fellow Am. Phys. Soc., Royal Astron. Soc., AAAS; mem. Philosophy of Sci. Assn., Am. Math. Soc. Fedn. Am. Scientists. Democrat. Roman Catholic. Office: U Md Dept Physics College Park MD 20742-4111

MISNER, CHARLOTTE BLANCHE RUCKMAN, community organization administrator; b. Gifford, Idaho, Aug. 30, 1937; d. Richard Steele and Arizona (Hill) Ruckman; m. G. Arthur Misner, Jr., Aug. 29, 1959; children: Michelle, Mary, Jennifer. BS in Psychology, U. Idaho, 1959. Vol. numerous orgns. India, Mexico, The Philippines, 1962-70; sec., v.p., pres., trustee St. Luke's Hosp., Manila, 1970-84; founding mem., 3d v.p., pres. Am. Women's Club of Philippines, 1980-84; exec. adminstr. Friends of Oakland (Calif.) Parks and Recreation, 1986-92, exec. dir., 1992—. Active Lincoln Child Ctr., Oakland, 1984—. Recipient Vol. Svc. award Women's Bd. St. Luke's Hosp., 1977, Mid. Sch. Vol. award Internat. Sch.-Manila, 1980. Me. Alpha Gamma Delta (alumnae treas., pres. East Bay 1985-89, province dir. alumnae 1989—), Cum Laude Soc. (hon.). Home: 481 Ellita Ave Oakland CA 94610-4808 Office: Friends of Oakland Parks & Recreation 1520 Lakeside Dr Oakland CA 94612-4521

MISNER, MICHAEL RICHARD, financial planner; b. Bellville, Ill., June 15, 1955; s. Richard and Alice J. Misner; m. Nancy Beth Misner, Sept. 19, 1987; children: Kenneth, Mary Beth. BBA, U. Tex., 1977; MBA, U. Tex., San Antonio, 1978. CFP, CLU. Acct. Shell Oil Co., Houston, 1978-80; fin. analyst, auditor Enterprise Products Co., Houston, 1980-83; stockbroker, planner Rauscher Pierce Refsnes, Houston, 1983-88, Oppenheimer & Co., Houston, 1988-90; sr. fin. planner, mem. advanced planner group Am. Express Fin. Advisors Inc., Houston, 1990—; mem. adv. bd. IDS Cert Co. Columnist Money Talks, 1987-88. Mem. Internat. Assn. Fin. Planners (bd. dirs. membership com. 1992-93), Am. Soc. CLUs and ChFCs, Houston Estate & Fin. Forum, C. of C. (amb., com. mem.). Avocations: golf, bowling, fishing. Home: 3 Robin Run Dr The Woodlands TX 77381-4326 Office: Am Express Fin Advisors Inc # 600 400 N Sam Houston Pky E Ste 600 Houston TX 77060-3540

MISONO, KUNIO, medical educator; b. Hiroshima, Japan, Nov. 21, 1946; married; 2 children. BS in Chemistry, Saitama U., Urawa, Japan, 1969; MS in Biochemistry, Osaka State U., Sakai, Japan, 1971; PhD in Biochemistry, Vanderbilt U., 1978; postdoctoral tng. in microbiology, Duke U., 1978-80. Chemist Ministry of Welfare, Tokyo, 1971-72; rsch. asst. in biochemistry Vanderbilt U. Sch. Medicine, Nashville, 1972-74; rsch. assoc. in microbiology Duke U. Sch. Medicine, Durham, N.C., 1978-80; rsch. instr. in biochemistry Vanderbilt U. Sch. Medicine, 1981-82, rsch. asst. prof. biochemistry, 1983-86; prin. scientist, group leader, rsch. divsn. Schering-Plough Corp., 1986-87; assoc. staff Cleve. Clinic Found. Rsch. Inc., 1987—, dir. protein and peptide chemistry core facility, 1988—; adj. assoc. prof. dept. biology Case Western Reserve U., Cleve., 1992—. Contbr. numerous articles to profl. jours. Recipient NIH nat. rsch. svc. award 1979-80. Mem. Am. Chem. Soc., Am. Peptide Soc., Endocrine Soc., Protein Soc., Am. Heart Assn. (High Blood Pressure Rsch. Coun. fellow 1989, Tenn. affiliate rsch. fellow 1980-81, Investigatorship award 1982-84), Am. Soc. Biochemistry and Molecular Biology, Sigma Xi. Office: Cleveland Clinic Found Dept Molecular Cardiology 9500 Euclid Ave FF3-02 Cleveland OH 44195-5071

MISRA, JAYADEV, computer science educator; b. Cuttack, Orissa, India, Oct. 17, 1947; s. Sashibhusan and Shanty (Kar) M.; m. Mamata Das, Nov. 30, 1972; children: Amitav, Anuj. B Tech, Indian Inst. Tech., Kanpur, 1969; PhD, Johns Hopkins U., 1972. Staff scientist IBM, Gaithersburg, Md., 1973-74; from asst. prof. to prof. computer sci. U. Tex., Austin, 1974—, Regents chair in computer sci., 1992—; vis. prof. Stanford (Calif.) U., 1983-84; cons. on software and hardware design. Contbr. articles to profl. jours. Guggenheim fellow, 1988-89. Fellow IEEE, Assn. Computing Machinery (Samuel N. Alexander Meml. award 1970). Office: Univ Tex Dept Computer Sci Austin TX 78712-1188

MISRA, RAGHUNATH PRASAD, physician, educator; b. Calcutta, W. Bengal, India, Feb. 1, 1928; came to U.S., 1964; s. Guru Prasad and Anandi M.; m. Therese Rettenmund, Sept. 13, 1963; children: Sima, Joya, Maya, Tara. BSc with honors, Calcutta U., 1948; MBBS, Med. Coll., Calcutta, 1953; PhD, McGill U., Montreal, Que., 1965. Diplomate Am. Bd. Anatomical and Clin. Pathology. Asst. prof., dir. kidney lab. U. Louisville Sch. Medicine, 1964-68; asso. investigator and dir. kidney lab Mt. Sinai Hosp., Cleve., 1968-73; asst. prof. Case Western Reserve Med. Sch., Cleve., 1973-76; asst. prof., dir. kidney lab. La. State U., Sch. Medicine, Shreveport, 1976-80, assoc. prof., 1980-86; prof. La. State U., Sch. of Medicine, Shreveport, 1986—, dir. Ocular Pathology Lab., 1988—; cons. VA Med. Ctr., Shreveport, 1977—, EA Conway Meml. Hosp., Monroe, La., 1980—. Author: Atlas of Skin Biopsy, 1983. Pres. India Assn. of Shreveport, 1979, 81. Recipient Tallisman Fellowship, Mt. Sinai Hosp., 1970-73. Fellow Am. Coll. Pathologists, Am. Soc. Clin. Pathologists, U. Calcutta Med. Alumni Assn. Am. (pres. 1992-93), Sigma Xi (pres. 1987-89). Democrat. Hindu. Avocations: photography, travel. Office: La State U Sch Medicine 1501 Kings Hwy Shreveport LA 71130-3932

MISRA, RAJ PRATAP, engineering educator, electrical engineer; b. Chhaperpur, India, Dec. 23, 1919; came to U.S., 1948; SB, MIT, 1941; MEE, Cornell U., 1945, PhD in Elec. Engring. & Indsl. Mgmt., 1955. Gen. mgr., chief engr. Hamara Radio & Gen. Industries Ltd., Delhi, India, 1947-50; instr. elec. engring. Cornell U., Ithaca, N.Y., 1950-52; mgr. reliability and high frequency Philco Corp., Lansdale, Pa., 1952-58; mgr. reliability rsch. and devel. Tex. Instruments, Dallas, 1958-62; emeritus prof. reliability N.J. Inst. Tech., Newark, 1962—; cons. Tex. Instruments, 1962-93, Soletron Inc., N.Y., Fla., 1966-69, Kertron, Reriera Beach, Fla., 1969-80; cons. reliability Astro Electronics Divsn. Westinghouse, Calif., 1962-65, Autonetics, Calif., 1965-66; vis. prof. U.S. Acad. Sci. to Romanian Acad., 1988-89. Fulbright scholar; Fulbright fellow Coun. Internat. Exch. Scholars, 1991-92. Fellow Indian Assn. Engrs.; mem. IEEE (chmn. reliability group 1965-68), ASTE (chmn. ref. planar diode task force 1955-59), Sigma Xi. Office: NJIT Ctr for Reliability Rsch 323 Martin Luther KingJr Blvd Newark NJ 07102*

MISRACH, RICHARD LAURENCE, photographer; b. L.A., July 11, 1949; s. Robert Laskin and Lucille (Gardner) M.; m. Debra Bloomfield, Jan. 18, 1981 (div. 1987); 1 son, Jacob Luke; m. Myriam Weisang, Apr. 17, 1989. A.B. in Psychology, U. Calif., Berkeley, 1971. Instr. Assoc. Students Studio, U. Calif., Berkeley, 1971-77; vis. lectr. U. Calif.-Berkeley, 1982; lectr. U. Calif.-Santa Barbara, 1984; juror Nat. Endowment Arts, 1986, Whitney Biennial, 1991. Exhbns. include Musée d'Art Moderne, Paris, 1979, Mus. Modern Art, N.Y.C., 1978, Whitney Mus. Am. Art, N.Y.C., 1981, Grapestake Gallery, San Francisco, 1979, 81, Young-Hoffman Gallery, Chgo., 1980, Oakland Mus., 1982, 87, San Franciso Mus. Modern Art, 1983, Centre Georges Pompidou, Paris, 1983, L.A. County Mus. Art, 1984, Fraenkel Gallery, San Francsico, 1985, 89, 91, 95, Min Gallery, Tokyo, 1975-87, Univ. Art Mus., Berkeley, Curt Marcus Gallery, 1995, James Danziger Gallery, 1995, Melbourne Internat. Festival, Australia, 1995, numerous others; one person exhbns. at Art Inst. Chgo., 1988, Milw. Art Mus., 1988, Carpenter Ctr., Harvard U., 1988, Fotomanm, Inc., N.Y., 1989, 91, Photographers Gallery, 1990, Parco Gallery, Tokyo, 1990, Arles Festival, France, 1990, Jan Kesner Gallery, 1990, 91, 94; art commn. cover Time mag., July 4, 1988; books include Telegraph 3 A.M., 1974, Grapestake Gallery, 1979, (A Photographic Book), 1979, Hawaii protfolio, 1980, Graecism dye-transfer portfolio, 1982, Desert Cantos, 1987, (Internat. Ctr. of Photography award 1988), Bravo 20: The Bombing of the americna West, 1990 (Pen Ctr. U.S. A. West award for nonfiction 1991), Houston Ctr. for Photography, 1985, Light Gallery, N.Y.C., 1985, Richard Misrach, Minn. Gallery, 1988, Violent Legacies, Aperture, 1992, Crimes and Splendors, 1996. Guggenheim fellow, 1978; Ferguson grantee, 1976; NEA grantee, 1973, 77, 84, 92; AT&T commn., 1979; Eureka fellow, 1991; NEA fellow, 1992-93; recipient Koret Israel prize, 1992. *Photographs are the shadows of reality much like dreams. On the one hand, they appear to literally transcribe the real world, while on the other, they defy our linear concept of time and meaning. Because the primary illusion of photography is fact, it is the most powerful art medium of our time.*

MISSAN, RICHARD SHERMAN, lawyer; b. New Haven, Oct. 5, 1933; s. Albert and Hannah (Hochberg) M.; m. Aileen Louise; children: Hilary, Andrew, Wendy. B.A., Yale U., 1955, J.D., 1958. Bar: N.Y. 1959, U.S. Dist. Ct. (so. and ea. dists.) N.Y. 1979, U.S. Ct. Appeals (2d cir.) N.Y. 1993. Assoc. Kaye, Scholer, Fierman, Hays & Handler, N.Y.C., 1962-67; ptnr. Schoenfeld & Jacobs, N.Y.C., 1968-78, Walsh & Frisch, N.Y.C., 1979-80, Gersten, Savage & Kaplowitz, N.Y.C., 1980-87, v.p., gen. counsel, Avis, Inc., 1987-88; pvt. practice, N.Y.C., 1988—; spl. prof. law Hofstra U., 1988—; mem. panel of mediators U.S. Dist. Ct. (ea. dist.) N.Y. Revision author: Corporations, New York Practice Guide (Business and Commercial). Mem. ABA, N.Y. State Bar Assn., Fed. Bar Council, Assn. of Bar of City of N.Y. (com. on corrections, chmn. subcom. on legis., com. on juvenile justice, chmn. subcom. on juvenile facilities, past com. corrections, com. on atomic energy, mem. com. on mcpl. affairs, com. on housing and urban devel.), Yale Club.

MISSAR, CHARLES DONALD, librarian; b. Cleve., July 16, 1925; s. Charles Frank and Genevieve Catherine (Buechele) M.; m. Margaret Mary du Fief, Feb. 17, 1962; children: Charles David, Stephen du Fief. Student, Sacred Heart Sem., Detroit, 1943-45, St. Mary's Sem., Cleve., 1945-49; BA, John Carroll U., 1951; MLS, Cath. U. Am., 1960. Referral specialist Libr. of Congress, Washington, 1963-66; ERIC info. specialist U.S. Office Edn., Washington, 1966-72; head Ednl. Reference Ctr. Nat. Inst. Edn., Washington, 1973-78, supervisory libr., 1978-85; sr. libr. U.S. Dept. Edn., 1985-86; sr. editor Computer Scis. Corp. Profl. Svcs. Group, 1986-94, Missar Assocs., Washington, 1994—; agy. rep. Fed. Libr. Com., Washington, 1978-86; ann. lectr. Fed. Libr. Resources Workshop, Catholic U. Am., Washington, 1981—. Editor: Management of Federally Sponsored Libraries: Case Studies and Analysis, 1995; editor monthly jour. Tech. Abstract Bull., 1958-60; mem. editorial bd. Online Mag., 1977-80. Recipient Superior Svc. Group award U.S. Office Edn., 1968, Superior Performance award Nat. Inst. Edn., 1974, 84; inductee Spl. Libraries Assn. Hall of Fame, 1991. Mem. ALA, D.C. Libr. Assn. (treas. 1972-74), Spl. Librs. Assn. (chmn. edn. divsn. 1980-81, chmn. 1989-90), Am. Soc. Info. Sci. (chmn. info. svcs. for edn. group 1984-86), John Carroll Soc., Cleve. Club, Serra Club (pres. 1992-93, 94—). Roman Catholic. Home: 5617 32nd St NW Washington DC 20015-1622 Office: Missar Assocs 5617 32nd St NW Washington DC 20015-1622

MISSIMER, THOMAS MICHAEL, geologist; b. Lancaster, Pa., Mar. 10, 1950; s. Jacob M. and Lorraine L. (Bilodeau) M.; A.B. in Geology, Franklin and Marshall Coll., 1972; M.S. in Geology, Fla. State U., 1973; PhD in Marine Geology and Geophysics, 1995. Hydrologist, U.S. Geol. Survey, Ft. Myers, Fla., 1973-75; research asso. sedimentology U. Miami, Coral Cables, Fla., 1975-76; pres. Missimer & Assocs., Inc., Cape Coral, Fla., 1976-91; vice chmn. ViroGroup, Inc., 1991-93; pres. Missimer Internat., Inc., 1993—, bd. Fla. Profl. Geologists, 1991-95, vice chmn. 1993, chmn. 1994, 95; vice chmn. tech. adv. com. Govs.' Com. for a Substantial South Fla., 1995—. Mem. citizens planning adv. com. Bd. Lee County (Fla.), 1981-82, chmn., 1982-83. Registered profl. geologist, Fla., Ga., Ind. Mem. Geol. Soc. Am., Am. Inst. Profl. Geologists (cert. profl. geol. scientist), Am. Water Resources Assn., Am. Water Works Assn., AAAS, Am. Inst. Hydrology (cert. profl. hydrogeologist), Am. Soc. Groundwater Engrs. and Scientists (cert. hydrogeologist), Fla. Acad. Scis. (chmn. earth and planetary sci. sect. 1973-74, 1995), Southeastern Geol. Soc. Republican. Author Water supply development for membrane water treatment facilities, 1994; contbr. hydrogeol. and geol. studies of Southeastern U.S. to sci. jours. RecipientBest Paper award, Internat. Desalination Assoc., D.C., World Conf. on Desalination, 1991. Home: 3214 Mcgregor Blvd Fort Myers FL 33901-6723 Office: Missimer Internat Inc 8140 McGregor Blvd Fort Myers FL 33914

MISTACCO, VICKI E., foreign language educator; b. Bklyn., Nov. 18, 1942; d. Anthony Sebastian and Lucia (Lalli) M. BA, NYU, 1963; MA, Middlebury Coll., 1964; M Philosophy, Yale U., 1968, PhD, 1972. Instr. French, Wellesley Coll., Mass., 1968-72, asst. prof. French, 1972-78, assoc. prof. French, 1978-84, prof. French, 1984—, chmn., 1978-81; mem. nat. adv. bd. Sweet Briar Jr. Yr. in France, Va., 1978—. Contbr. articles to profl. jours. Fulbright fellow, 1963-64; Woodrow Wilson fellow, 1964-65, 1966-67; NEH fellow, 1983-84, 94-95. Mem. MLA, N.E. MLA, Am. Assn. Tchrs. French, Phi Beta Kappa. Democrat. Roman Catholic. Avocations: photography; travel. Office: Wellesley Coll Dept French 106 Central St Wellesley MA 02181-8209

MISTHAL, HOWARD JOSEPH, accountant, lawyer; b. Bklyn., Feb. 16, 1940; s. Max and Evelyn (Glass) M.; m. Angela Marie Giorgio, May 7, 1975; children: Barry Jay, Robin Lyn, Sara Ann. BBA cum laude, CCNY, 1961; LLB cum laude, NYU, 1967, LLM, 1972. CPA, N.Y.; bar: N.Y. 1968. From staff mem. to sr. tax ptnr. David Berdon & Co., LLP, CPAs, N.Y.C., 1961—; dir., chmn. audit and loan com. The Apple Bank for Savs.; lectr. Sch. of Law Summer Continuing Ednl. Program, NYU, 1990-95. Mem. AICPAs (tax sect.), N.Y. State Soc. CPAs, N.Y. State Bar Assn. (trust and estates sect.). Avocations: bicycling, hiking, swimming, travel. Office: David Berdon & Co LLP 415 Madison Ave New York NY 10017-1178

MISUREC, RUDOLF, physician, surgeon; b. Dobre Pole, Czechoslovakia, June 27, 1924; came to U.S., 1967; s. Gustav and Hilda (Safar) M.; m. Miluse Kisil, 1951 (div. 1978); children: Peter Clyde, Rudolph Carl; m. Stanislava Coufal, 1978. MD, Masaryk's U., Brno-Czechoslovakia, 1950. Diplomate Am. Bd. Urology, gen. surgery (Czechoslovakia), thoracic surgery (Czechoslovakia). Intern U. Ill., Chgo., 1967-68, resident in urology, 1968-71, clin. asst. prof. urology, 1975—. Mem. Rep. Presdl. Task Force, 1984, Rep. Presdl. Legion of Merit, 1992. Capt. Czechoslovakia Army, 1950-55. Recipient Cert. of Achievement U.S. Army, 1967, Letter of Appreciation, 1967. Fellow ACS, Internat. Coll. Surgeons, Am. Urol. Assn.; mem. AMA, Chgo. Med. Soc., N.Y. Acad. Scis., Czechoslovak Soc. Arts and Scis. (U.S.). Roman Catholic. Office: 3340 Oak Park Ave Berwyn IL 60402-3420

MITAU, LEE R., bank executive; b. St. Paul, 1948. AB cum laude, Dartmouth Coll., 1969; JD magna cum laude, U. Minn., 1972. Bar: Minn. 1972, N.Y. 1973. Law clk. to Hon. George E. MacKinnon U.S. Ct. Appeals (D.C. cir.), 1972-73; ptnr. Dorsey & Whitney, Mpls.; exec. v.p. gen. counsel First Bank, Mpls.; adj. prof. law William Mitchell Coll. Law, 1982-83. Office: First Bank 601 2nd Ave Ste 3000 Minneapolis MN 55402*

MITBY, NORMAN PETER, college president; b. Cashton, Wis., May 21, 1916; s. Chester M. and Margaret (Murray) M.; m. Luvern J. Jensen, June 15, 1941; children: John C., Margaret N. BS, Whitewater (Wis.) State Coll., 1938; postgrad., U. Wis., 1947-48; MS, Stout State U., 1949. Tchr. high sch., vocat. sch. Cornell, Wis., 1938-41, Antigo, Wis., 1941-46; asst. dir. LaCrosse (Wis.) Vocat. and Adult Schs., 1946-54; dir. vocat. and adult sch. Oshkosh, Wis., 1954-55, Green Bay, Wis., 1955-60, Madison, Wis., 1960-67; dist. dir. tech. and adult edn. dist. Madison Area Tech. Coll., 1967, pres., 1967-88; prof. Stout State U. Grad. Sch., Menomonie, Wis.; mem. adv. council U. Wis. Schs. Edn., Madison and Milw., 1961-64; cons., examiner North Central Assn. Colls. and Secondary Schs., 1970-88; mem. pres.'s adv. com. Assn. Community Coll. Trustees, 1978-79; mem. joint adminstrv. com. on acad. programs U. Wis. Vocat., Tech. and Adult Edn. System, 1985-88. Mem. Community Welfare Council Madison, 1960-63, mem. needs and priorities com., 1964; sponsor Wis. Heart Assn.; chmn. pub. employees div. Cancer Fund drive, 1963; mem. Mayor's Com. for Employment Handicapped, 1964-68, Nat. Adv. Com. on Health Occupations Tng., 1964-68; chmn. gov.'s adv. com. Title I, Higher Edn. Act, 1965-74; mem. adv. council Midwest Community Coll., Leadership Council, 1968-73; mem. Wis. Gov.'s Adv. Council on Vocat. Edn., 1969-74, Wis. Gov.'s Health Planning and Policy Task Force, 1971-73; adv. com. Wis. State Bd. Nursing, 1972-74; mem. Wis. Council Safety, 1960-73; bd. dirs. Madison Civic Music Assn., 1960-88, Oakwood Found. Inc., 1990—. Recipient Disting. Svc. Alumni award U. Wis.-Whitewater, Spl. award NAACP, 1987, cert. recognition Phi Delta Kappa-U. Wis. chpt., 1987, Rotary Sr. Svc. award, 1992; named to Madison Area Tech. Coll. Athletic Hall of Fame, 1989. Mem. Am. Assn. Community and Jr. Colls. (dir. 1975-78, Leadership award 1988), Am. Vocat. Assn. Merit award Region 3 1988), Wis. Assn. for Vocat. and Adult Edn. (Disting. Svc. award 1988), Wis. Assn. Dirs. Vocat. and Adult Edn. (pres. 1960-61), Sigma Tau Gamma, Epsilon Pi Tau, Delta Pi Epsilon. Clubs: Rotarian, Elk, Nakoma Golf. Home: 4413 Waite Ln Madison WI 53711-2845

MITCH, WILLIAM EVANS, nephrologist; b. Birmingham, Ala., July 22, 1941; s. William Evans and Mary Elizabeth (Ackerman) M.; m. Frances Alexandra Fisher, Aug. 21, 1965; children: Eleanor Baylor, William Armistead. BA, Harvard Coll., 1963; MD, Harvard Med. Sch., 1967. Intern Brigham & Women's Hosp., Boston, 1967-68; resident Brigham & Women's Hosp., 1968-69; clin. assoc. Nat. Inst. Health, Bethesda, Md., 1969-72; resident Johns Hopkins Hosp., Balt., 1972-73, Brigham & Women's Hosp., 1973-74; asst. prof., assoc. prof. Johns Hopkins U. Dept. Pharm., Balt., 1974-78; assoc. prof. medicine Harvard Med. Sch., Boston, 1978-87; prof. medicine Emory U. Sch. Medicine, Atlanta, 1987—; pres. region II Nat. Kidney Found., 1990-92; sec., treas. Internat. Soc. Metabolism, 1988—; study sect. NIH, 1988-92; chmn. Am. Heart Assn., 1992-94. Editor: The Progressive Nature of Renal Disease, 1986, 2d edit., 1992, Nutrition and the Kidney, 1988, 2d edit., 1993. With USPHS, 1969-72. Grantee NIH, 1979—. Mem. Am. Soc. Clin. Investigation, Assn. Am. Physicians. Office: Emory U Sch Medicine 1364 Clifton Rd NE Atlanta GA 30322-1059

MITCHAM, JULIUS JEROME, accountant; b. Pine Bluff, Ark., Jan. 2, 1941; s. James Vernon and Bertha Lee (Robertson) M.; m. Janet Claire Berry, Mar. 31, 1970 (div. Sept. 1981); m. Marsha Lee Henderson, Oct. 22, 1983; 1 child, Timothy John. BBA, U. Cen. Ark., 1971. CPA, Ark.; cert. healthcare fin. mgr. Br. mgr. Comml. Nat. Bank, Little Rock, 1961-66; auditor, acctg. supr. Ark. Blue Cross and Blue Shield, Little Rock, 1971-77; controller Riverview Hosp., Little Rock, 1977-81; pvt. practice acctg. Little Rock, 1981-82; controller Henryetta (Okla.) Med. Ctr., 1982-83; fin. report supr. Am. Med. Internat., Houston, 1983; dir. corp. acctg. Ft. Myers (Fla.) Community Hosp., 1984-86; controller Med. Ctr. of Southeast Okla., Durant, 1986-87; chief fin. officer Gulf Coast Community Hosp./Qualicare of Miss., Inc., 1987-88; asst. adminstr. fin. S.W. Gen. Hosp., San Antonio, 1988-89; pvt. practice San Antonio, 1989-90; chief fin. officer Bapt. Meml. Hosps. of Mississippi County, Blytheville, Ark., 1991-94; CFO Med. Arts Hosp., Texarkana, Tex., 1994-96; asst. dir. healthcare fin. mgmt. U. Tex. Med. Br., Galveston, 1996—. Served with USN, 1959-61. Mem. AICPA, Ark. Soc. CPAs, Healthcare Fin. Mgmt. Assn. (cert. fellow), Lions (sec. 1985-86, 2d v.p. 1995-96), Masons. Republican. Baptist. Office: 301 University Blvd 7 122 John Sealy Annex Galveston TX 77555-0518

MITCHEL, F(REDERICK) KENT, retired food company executive; b. Orange, N.J., June 2, 1927; s. E. Kent and Arlene (Lee) M.; m. Elizabeth L. Rich, June 25, 1955 (div. 1990); children: Pamela, Peter; m. Susan Holden Colcock, 1990. AB, Dartmouth Coll., 1950; postgrad., Harvard U., 1970. With Gen. Foods Corp., 1950-86; v.p. mktg., then v.p. corp. comm. Gen. Foods Corp., White Plains, N.Y., 1970-79; v.p. mktg. staffs Gen. Foods Corp., 1979-86; pres. Mktg. Sci. Inst., Cambridge, Mass., 1987-89, chmn., 1990-91; pres. Fair Tide Assocs. Ltd., Sandwich, N.H., 1987-95; past chmn. Assn. Nat. Advertisers; trustee Mktg. Sci. Inst., chmn., 1990-91; past chmn. Nat. Advt. Rev. Coun., Advt. Coun. Bd. dirs. Squam Lakes Assn., 1989-91. Mem. Univ. Club (N.Y.C.), Harvard Club Boston. Episcopalian.

MITCHELHILL, JAMES MOFFAT, civil engineer; b. St. Joseph, Mo., Aug. 11, 1912; s. William and Jeannette (Ambrose) M.; BS, Northwestern U., 1934, CE, 1935; m. Maurine Hutchason, Jan. 9, 1937 (div. 1962); children: Janis Maurine Mitchelhill Johnson, Jeri Ann Mitchelhill Riney; m. 2d, Alicia Beuchat, 1982; Engring. dept. C., M., St. P. & P.R.R. Co., Chgo. and Miles City, Mont., 1935-45; asst. mgr. Ponce & Guayama R.R. Co., Aguirre, P.R., 1945-51, v.p., gen. mgr., 1969-70; mgr. Cen. Cortada, Santa Isabel, P.R., 1951-54; r.r. supt. Braden Copper Co., Rancagua, Chile, 1954-63; staff engr. Coverdale & Colpitts, N.Y.C., 1963-64; asst. to exec. v.p. Central Aguirre Sugar Co., 1964-67; v.p., gen. mgr. Coddea, Inc., Dominican Republic, 1967-68; asst. to gen. mgr. Land Adminstrn. of P.R., La Nueva Central Aguirre, 1970-71, for Centrals Aguirre Lafayette and Mercedita, 1971-72; asst. to gen. mgr. Corporacion Azucarera de P.R., 1973-76, asst. to exec. dir., 1977-79, asst. exec. dir. for environ., 1979-82; engring. cons., 1982-92; Kendall County engr., 1985-96. Registered profl. engr., Mont., P.R., Tex. Fellow ASCE; mem. Am. Ry. Engring. Assn., Colegio de Ingenieros y Agrimensores de P.R., Explorers Club, Circumnavigators Club, Travellers Century Club, Sigma Xi, Tau Beta Pi. Home: PO Box 506 Boerne TX 78006-0506 Office: 12 Staudt St Boerne TX 78006-1820

MITCHELL, ADA MAE BOYD, legal assistant; b. Nov. 23, 1927; d. Allen T. Boyd and Marjorie (Bigger) Boyd Mills; 1 child, Joseph W. Student, NYU, 1972-73. Supr. Faberge, Inc., Mahwah, N.J.; mgr. Demostration Svcs. and Promotional Monies; mgr. accounts receivables, credit mgr. Faberge, Inc., Mahwah, N.J.; legal asst. Wright Patterson Med. Ctr., Dayton, Ohio, 1990—. Pres. Urban League Guild, Bergen County, N.J., 1982—, bd. dirs., 1982-83; treas. Bethany Presbyn. Ch., Englewood, N.J., 1975, fin. sect., 1966-67, chairperson bldg. and renovation com., 1978-81, choir mem., elder, 1979—; 1st Black woman moderator Presbytery of Palisades-Presbyn. Ch., 1986; mem. self devel. of people com. Presbyn. Ch. Miami Presbytery, Dayton; dtr. Isis Akbar Ct. # 33, 1995—. Mem. NAFE, NAACP, Order Eastern Star (Queen of Sheba chpt. 4, Worthy Matron 1972-73).

MITCHELL, ALLAN EDWIN, lawyer; b. Okemah, Okla., May 13, 1944; m. Neva G. Ream; children: Brian, Amy. BA in Mass. Comm., Northwestern Okla. State U., Alva, 1991; JD, U. Okla., 1994. Bar: Okla. 1994, U.S. dist. ct. (we. and no. dists.) 1994. Asst. state mgr. Oklahomans for Right to Work, Oklahoma City, 1967-68; exec. dir. London Sq. Village, Oklahoma City, 1968-73; dist. mgr. Farmland Ins. Svc., Oklahoma City, 1974-80, Nat. Farmers Union, Oklahoma City, 1980-85; dist. agt. Prudential Ins., Cherokee, Okla., 1985-89; atty. Hughes & Grant, Oklahoma City, 1994—. Mem. Cherokee Bd. Edn., 1985-90; mem. fin. com. Rep. Party of Okla., 1995; scoutmaster, 1981-86; adult advisor Girl Scouts Am.; pres. United Way Cherokee, 1984; mem. Okla. Sch. Bd. Mems. Legis. Network, 1985-90. Mem. Ch. of the Nazarene. Avocations: public speaking, politics, civic activities. Home: 801 S Kansas Ave Cherokee OK 73728-3511 Office: Hughes & Grant 5801 Broadway Ext Ste 302 Oklahoma City OK 73118-7489

MITCHELL, ANDREA, journalist; b. N.Y.C., Oct. 30, 1946; d. Sydney and Cecile Mitchell. B.A., U. Pa., 1967. Polit. reporter KYW Newsradio, Phila., 1967-76; polit. corr. Sta. KYW-TV, Phila., 1972-76; corr. Sta. WTOP-TV, Washington, 1977-78; gen. assignment and energy corr. NBC News, Washington, 1978-81; White House corr. NBC News, 1981-88, chief congl. corr., 1989-92, chief White House corr., 1993-94; chief fgn. affairs corr. NBC News, Washington, 1995—, 1994—; instr. Gt. Lakes Colls. Assn., 1974-76; co-anchor Summer Sunday, USA, NBC-TV News, 1984, substitute anchor Meet the Press, 1988—. Overseer, Sch. of Arts and Scis., U. Pa., 1989-95, trustee, 1995—; mem. nat. adv. bd. Girl Scouts U.S. Recipient award for pub. affairs reporting Am. Polit. Sci. Assn., 1969, Pub. Affairs Reporting award AP, 1976, AP Broadcast award, 1977; named Communicator of the Yr., Phila. chpt. Women in Comms., 1976, Woman of the Yr., Phila. chpt. Am. Women in Radio and TV, 1989, Lucretia Mott award Woman's Way, 1991. Mem. White House Corrs. Assn. Office: NBC News 4001 Nebraska Ave NW Washington DC 20016-2733

MITCHELL, ARTHUR, dancer, choreographer, educator; b. N.Y.C., Mar. 27, 1934; s. Arthur and Willie Mae M. Student, Sch. Am. Ballet.; D. Arts (hon.), Columbia Coll., Chgo., 1975; cert. of competence, Peter U., 1978; DFA (hon.), City Coll., CUNY, 1979, N.C. Sch. Arts, 1981, L.I. U. Sch. Bus. Pub. Adminstrn., 1982, Fordham U., 1983, Princeton U., 1986, Williams Coll., 1986, Juilliard Sch., 1990; DHS (hon.), Urbana Coll., 1979; DA (hon.), Harvard U., 1987. With William Dollar's Ballet Theatre Workshop, 1954, John Butler Co., 1955; prin. dancer N.Y.C. Ballet, 1955-72; artistic dir., founder Am. Negro Dance Co., N.Y.C., 1966—; founder, dir., choreographer Dance Theatre of Harlem, N.Y.C., 1969—; former resident choreographer, artistic dir. Nat. Ballet Co., Brazil; tchr. dance Karel Shook Studio, Melissa Hayden Sch., Cedarhurst, L.I., Jones-Haywood Sch. Ballet, Washington. dancer in Kiss Me, Kate, Orpheus, Carmen Jones, Allegro, Creation of the World, Episodes, House of Flowers, numerous others; choreographer (with Rod Alexander) Newport Jazz Festival, Rhythmetron, 1971, Ode to Otis, 1969, Lil' Gal, 1969, Tones, 1970, Biosfera, 1970, Fun and Games, 1970, Holberg Suite, 1970, Manifestations, 1975, Concerto for Jazz Band and Orch., 1971, Fête Noire, 1971, Spiritual Suite: Dance In Praise of His Name, 1976, Breezin', 1977, The Greatest, 1977, El Mar, 1977, Doin' It, 1978, Porgy and Bess, 1985, Phoenix Rising, 1987, John Henry, 1988, Ribbon In The Sky, 1990, Bach Passacaglia, 1993; co-choreographer Broadway prodn. Shinbone Alley; dancer, choreographer, actor: Spoleto Festival of Two Worlds, 1960; TV prodns. A Streetcar Named Desire dance prodn., PBS, Songs of Mahler, Dance in America: Dance Theatre of Harlem, PBS, Stravinsky's Firebird, PBS, Creole Giselle, NBC, Fall River Legend, A&E. Active Nat. Conf. on Social Welfare, 1973, U.S. Dept. State Dance Adv. Panel, Pres. Task Force on Arts and Humanities, 1981, Commn. for Cultural Affairs, N.Y.C., 1982, Arts and Entertainment Adv. Bd. N.Y.C. Partnership, Inc., 1983, Nat. Coun. of Arts, 1987; named to Pres. Commn. on White House Fellowships, 1991. Recipient Changers award Mademoiselle Mag., 1970, North Shore Commn. Arts Ctr. award 1971, Capezio Dance award, 1971, Ann. Excellence award John F. Kennedy Ctr. for Performing Arts, 1980, Am. Dance Guild award, 1982, Ebony Mag. Am. Black Achievement award, 1983, Pres.'s Cabinet award U. Detroit, 1982, Paul Robeson award Actors Equity Assn., 1986, Lion of the Performing Arts award N.Y. Pub. Libr., 1986, Arnold Gingrich Meml. award, 1987, Banquet of Golden Plate, 1989, Harkness Disting. Artist award Adelphi U., 1990, Disting. Svc. to Arts award Am. Acad. of Arts and Letters, 1994, Zenith award for Fine Arts, 1994, Handel Medallion, City of New York, 1993, Barnard Medal of Distinction Barnard Coll., 1994, Lifetime Achievement award Sch. Am. Ballet, 1995, Nat. Medal of Arts Nat. Endowment for the Arts, 1995, Living Landmarks award N.Y. Landmarks Conservancy, 1995; named to NAACP Image Awards Hall of Fame, 1986; Kennedy Ctr. Honor for Lifetime Achievement, 1993; Conroy fellow St. Paul's Sch., Concord, N.H., 1982, MacArthur fellow, 1994. Office: Dance Theatre Harlem 466 W 152nd St New York NY 10031-1814

MITCHELL, ARTHUR HARRIS, newspaper columnist; b. St. John, N.B., Can., Nov. 8, 1916; s. Stuart Campbell and Marjorie (Harris) M.; m. Mary Moliawko, Nov. 6, 1944; children: John Stuart, Marjorie Starr. Student, Columbia Sch. Journalism, 1945-46. Travelling freelance writer various U.S., Can. mags., 1946-48; syndicated newspaper columnist, 1971—; editor Mitchell Press Ltd., Vancouver, B.C.; founding editor Can. Pulp and Paper Industry mag., Western Homes & Living mag., 1948-66; editor Can. Homes mag., Southstar Publs. Ltd., Toronto, Ont., 1967-80; Can. cons. Time-Life Books, N.Y.C., 1976-82. Author: You Wanted to Know, 1971, Easy Furniture Finishing, 1974, The Basement Book, 1977. Served with Brit. and U.S. Mcht. Marine, 1940-45. Home: TH28 270 Timberbank Blvd, Scarborough, ON Canada M1W 2M1

MITCHELL, BERT BREON, literary translator; b. Salina, Kans., Aug. 9, 1942; s. John Charles and Bernita Maxine (Breon) M.; m. Lynda Diane Fink, July 21, 1965; children—Kieron Breon, Kerry Archer. B.A., U. Kans., 1964; Ph.D., Oxford U., 1968. Asst. prof. German and comparative lit. Ind. U., Bloomington, 1968-71, assoc. prof., 1971-78, prof., 1978—, assoc. dean Coll. Arts and Scis., 1975-77, chmn. comparative lit., 1977-85, dir. Wells Scholars Program, 1988—. Author: James Joyce and the German Novel, 1922-1933, 1976, Beyond Illustration; The Livre d'Artiste in the Twentieth Century, 1976, The Complete Lithographs of Delacroix's Faust and Manet's The Rave, 1981; editor: Literature and the Other Arts, 1978, Metamorphosis and the Arts, 1979, Paul Morand, Fancy Goods/Open All Night, 1984; translator: Hearstop (Martin Grzimek), 1984, Selected Stories (Siegfried Lenz), 1989, The Musk Ceer and Other Stories (Vilas Sarang), 1990, Looking Back (Lou Andreas-Salomé), 1991, Shadowlife (Martin Grzimek), 1991, Laura's Skin (J.F. Federspiel), 1991, The Color of the Snow (Rüdiger Kreme), 1992, Knife Edge (Ralf Rothmann) 1992, In the Kingdom of Enki (Vilas Sarang), 1993, On the Glacier (Jürgen Kross), 1996, The Silent Angel (Heinrich Böll), 1994. Rhodes scholar, 1964-68; Danforth fellow, 1964-68, Woodrow Wilson fellow, 1964, Alexander-von-Humboldt fellow, 1971, Translation fellow Nat. Endowment for Arts, 1989; recipient Frederic Bachman Lieber Meml. award for disting. teaching, 1974, hon. citation Columbia Translation Ctr., 1990, Theodore Christian Hoepfner award So. Humanities Rev., 1995. Mem. MLA (chair William Riley Parker prize selection com. 1994), Am. Comparative Lit. Assn., Am. Lit. Translators Assn. (pres. 1985-87, Alta prize for disting. translation 1992), Am. Translators Assn. (com. lit. transl. 1983-84, German Lit. prize for disting. translation 1987, chmn. honors and awards com. 1995), P.E.N., James Joyce Found., Franz Kafka Soc., Samuel Beckett Soc., So. Comparative Lit. Assn., Brit. Comparative Lit. Assn., Internat. Comparative Lit. Assn. Office: BH402 Indiana University Bloomington IN 47405

MITCHELL, BERTIE N., accounting firm executive; b. 1938. BA, CCNY, 1963, MBA, 1968. CPA. Chmn., CEO Mitchell & Titus, L.L.P., N.Y.C., 1974—. Office: Mitchell & Titus One Battery Park Plz New York NY 10004

MITCHELL, BETTIE PHAENON, religious organization administrator; b. Colorado Springs, Colo., June 6, 1934; d. Roy William and Laura Lee (Costin) Roberts; m. Gerald Mitchell, May 3, 1952; children: Michelle Smith, Laura Sweitz, Jennie Grenzer, Mohammad Bader. BS in Edn., Lewis & Clark Coll., 1954; postgrad., Portland State U., 1962-72; MA in Religion summa cum laude, Warner Pacific Coll., 1979. Cert. counselor, Oreg. Elem. tchr. Quincy Sch. Dist., Clatskanie, Oreg., 1955-56; substitute tchr. Beaverton (Oreg.) and Washington County Schs., 1956-77; tchr. of the Bible Portland (Oreg.) C.C., 1974-92; counseling and healing ministry, 1977-79; founder, exec. dir. Good Samaritan Ministries, Beaverton, 1979-88, founder, internat. exec. dir., 1988—; tchr. Christian Renewal Ctr. Workshops, 1977-85; speaker, presenter in field; leader tours in the Mid. East; developing counselor edn. programs Pakistan, Ukraine, Jordan, Egypt, Kenya, Uganda, Tanzania, Zambia, Malawi, South Africa, Nigeria, Burundi, Sierra Leone. Author: Who Is My Neighbor? A Parable, 1988, The Power of Conflict and Sacrifice, A Therapy Manual for Christian Marriage, 1988, Good Samaritan Training Handbook, 1989, Be Still and Listen to His Voice, The Story of Prayer and Faith, 1990, A Need for Understanding - International Counselor Training Manual, 1993. Mem. Israel Task Force, Portland, 1974-80; Leader Camp Fire Internat., 1962-73, elem. sch. coord., 1962-68; asst. dir. Washington County Civil Def., 1961-63; precinct committeewoman Rep. Party, 1960; bd. dirs. Beaverton Fish, 1966-74; v.p. NCCJ, Portland, 1983-85; chmn., speaker's bur. Near East Task Force for Israel; chmn. fire bond issue campaign City of Beaverton, mgr. mayoral campaign, 1960; sunday sch. tchr., speaker, organizer Sharing and Caring program Bethel Ch., 1974-79. Mem. ACA, Christian Assn. for Psychol. Studies, Oreg. Counseling Assn. Republican. Avocations: historical research, writing, photography, Biblical archaeology, correspondence. Home: 6550 SW Imperial Dr Beaverton OR 97008 Office: Good Samaritan Ministries 7929 SW Cirrus Dr # 23 Beaverton OR 97008

MITCHELL, BEVERLY ANN BALES, agency owner, women's rights advocate; b. Fremont, Nebr., July 27, 1944; d. Richard Lee Roy Stillwell Bales and Thelma May (Nelson) Lemen (dec.). BA, Midland Luth. Coll., 1967; postgrad., U. Iowa, 1970, 71. Reporter, film columnist, entertainment sect. editor Fremont (Nebr.) Daily Guide and Tribune, 1961-66; tchr. H.S. English Cedar Bluffs (Nebr.) Valley PUb. Schs., 1967-71; dir. quality control, dir. field ops. Frank N. Magid Assocs., Marion, Iowa, 1971-76; employment specialist U.S. Dept. Labor, Cedar Rapids, Iowa, 1976-78; owner, gen. agy. Mitchell Ins., Cedar Rapids, 1978—. Founder, editor: (monthly periodical) Lilith Speaks, 1971-76, 88—; contbr.: Strong Minded Women, 1992. Cofounder, pres. Cedar Rapids (Iowa) Womens Caucus, 1971-76; commr. Cedar Rapids Civil Rights Commn., 1976-80, Cedar Rapics Charter Commn., 1995-96; pres. Linn County (Iowa) Women's Polit. Caucus, 1977-79; mem. Linn County Bd. Condemnation and Compensation, 1994—. Recipient Creighton By-Line award Creighton U., Omaha, 1963, Best Editorial award Nebr. Press Assn., Lincoln, 1963; named Women of the Yr., Cedar Rapids (Iowa) Women's Orgns., 1977. Mem. NAACP, NRA, NOW (coord. Iowa state divsn. 1973-76, pres. Cedar Rapids chpt. 1994—), Bus. and Profl. Women (bd. dirs. 1994-95), Dodge County Humane Soc. Lutheran. Unitarian. Office: Mitchell Ins 1000 Maplewood Dr NE Cedar Rapids IA 52402-3807

MITCHELL, BRIAN KEITH, professional football player; b. Ft. Polk, La., Aug. 18, 1968. Student, Southwestern La. U. Kick returner Washington Redskins, 1990—. Mem. Super Bown XXVI Championship Team, 1991; holds NFL single season record for most yards by combined kick return, 1994. Office: Washington Redskins Dulles Airport PO Box 17247 Washington DC 20041

MITCHELL, BRIANE NELSON, lawyer; b. Seattle, July 4, 1953; s. Robert Max and Frances Marie (Nelson) M.; m. Suzanne Harmatz; children: Brianne Nelson, Brittany Suzanne. AB, Columbia U., 1975; JD, U. Idaho, 1978. Law clk. U.S. Ct. Appeals (9th cir.), 1978-80; assoc. Debevoise & Plimpton, N.Y.C., 1980-84; assoc. Paul, Hastings, Janofsky & Walker, L.A., 1984-86, ptnr., 1986-93; ptnr. McCambridge, Deixler & Marmaro, L.A., 1993—. Mem. ABA, Idaho Bar Assn., N.Y. State Bar Assn., Calif. Bar Assn. *

MITCHELL, BRUCE TYSON, lawyer; b. San Francisco, Nov. 6, 1928; s. John Robert and Lorraine C. (Tyson) M.; m. Adrienne Means Hiscox, Oct. 14, 1951; 1 son, Mark Means. AB with great distinction, Stanford U., 1949, JD, 1951. Bar: Calif. 1952, U.S. Dist. Ct. (no. dist.) Calif 1952, U.S. Ct. Appeals (9th cir.) 1952, U.S. Supreme Ct. 1971. Estate adminstr. Crocker Nat. Bank, San Francisco, 1955-57; atty. Utah Internat. Inc., San Francisco, 1957-87; sec. Utah Internat. Inc., 1974-87, sr. counsel, 1961-87; mem. nonsecurities panel arbitrators N.Y. Stock Exch., Pacific Stock Exchange, NASD Bd. Arbitrators. Chmn. San Mateo County Rep. Cen. Com., 1964-70; mem. Calif. Rep. Central Com., 1964-74, 77-83; alt. del. Rep. Nat. Conv., 1968; co-chmn. San Mateo (Calif.) County Pres. Ford Com., 1976; mem. bd. visitors sch. law Stanford U., 1980-83; exec. v.p., bd. dirs. San Francisco Jr. C. of C., 1961; bd. dirs. No. Calif. chpt. Arthritis Found., 1972-85, 1987-92, St. Francis Hosp. Found., San Francisco. Lt. (j.g.) USNR, 1952-55, Japan. Mem. ABA, Calif. Bar Assn., San Francisco Bar Assn., Am. Judicature Soc., Am. Soc. Corp. Secs. (v.p. 1976-77, dir. 1976-79), Assn. Former Intelligence Officers, Commonwealth Club of Calif. (pres. San Francisco 1973), Pacific Union Club, Olympic Club, Capitol Hill Club, Travelers Century Club, Masons. Congregationalist. Home: 165 Redwood Dr Hillsborough CA 94010-6971 Office: 400 Montgomery St Ste 1002 San Francisco CA 94104-1224

MITCHELL, BURLEY BAYARD, JR., state supreme court chief justice; b. Oxford, N.C., Dec. 15, 1940; s. Burley Bayard and Dorothy Ford (Champion) M.; m. Mary Lou Willett, Aug. 3, 1962; children: David Bayard, Catherine Morris. BA, N.C. State U., 1966, DHL (hon.), 1995; JD, U. N.C., 1969. Bar: N.C. 1969, U.S. Ct. Appeals (4th cir.) 1970, U.S. Supreme Ct. 1972. Asst. atty. gen. State of N.C., Raleigh, 1969-72, dist. atty., 1973-77, judge Ct. Appeals, 1977-79, sec. crime control, 1979-82; justice Supreme Ct. N.C., Raleigh, 1982-94; chief justice Supreme Ct. of N.C., Raleigh, 1995—. Served with USN, 1958-62, Asia. Recipient N.C. Nat. Guard Citizen Commendation award, 1982. Mem. ABA, VFW, N.C. Bar Assn.,

Mensa, Am. Legion. Democrat. Methodist. Home: 820 Glen Eden Dr Raleigh NC 27612-5038 Office: Supreme Ct NC PO Box 1841 Raleigh NC 27602-1841

MITCHELL, CAROL ANN, nursing educator; b. Portsmouth, Va., Aug. 31, 1942; d. William Howell and Eleanor Bertha (Wesarg) M.; m. David Alan Friedman, June 17, 1971 (div. 1988). Diploma, NYU, 1963; BS, Columbia U., 1968, MA, 1971, EdM, 1974, EdD, 1980; MS, SUNY, Stony Brook, 1990. Charge nurse Nassau County Med. Ctr., East Meadow, N.Y., 1963-65; staff nurse Meml. Hosp., N.Y.C., 1965-68; head nurse, supr. Community Hosp. at Glen Cove (N.Y.), 1969-71; assoc. prof. dept. nursing Queensborough Community Coll. CUNY, Bayside, 1971-80; assoc. prof. Marion A. Buckley Sch. Nursing Adelphi U., Garden City, N.Y., 1981-88; ednl. cons. Nat. League for Nursing, N.Y.C., 1980-81; prof. sch. nursing SUNY, Stony Brook, 1988-92, chmn. adult nursing, 1988-92; prof. chair Coll. Nursing East Tenn. State U., 1992-95, mem faculty, 1995—; mem. faculty Regents Coll. degrees in nursing program USNY, Albany, 1978-91, cons., 1978—; faculty cons. geriatrics Montefiore Med. Ctr., 1991-93. Editor emeritus: Scholarly Inquiry in Nursing Practice, 1983—; contbr. articles to profl. jours. Robert Wood Johnson clin. nurse scholar postdoctoral fellow U. Rochester (N.Y.), 1983-85. Mem. Am. Nurses Assn., Nat. League for Nursing, Gerontol. Soc. Am., N.Am. Nursing Diagnosis Assn., Soc. for Research in Nursing Edn. Avocations: reading, gardening, cycling, travel, cooking.

MITCHELL, CAROLYN COCHRAN, college official; b. Atlanta, Dec. 27, 1943; d. Clemern Covell and Agnes Emily (Veal) Cochran; m. W. Alan Mitchell, Aug. 30, 1964; 1 child, Teri Marie. AB magna cum laude, Mercer U., 1965, M in Svc. Mgmt., 1989. Caseworker Ga. Dept. Family & Children Svcs., Macon, 1965-67, Covington, 1967-69; presch. dir. Southwestern Theol. Sem., Ft. Worth, 1969-70; presch. tchr., dir. Noah's Ark Day Care, Bowden, Ga., 1970-72, First Bapt. Ch., Bremen, Ga., 1972-75, Roebuck Park Bapt. Ch., Birmingham, Ala., 1975-79; freelance office mgr. and bookkeeper Macon, 1979-84; asst. to pres. Ga. Wesleyan Coll., Macon, 1984—; exec. dir. Ga. Women of Achievement, 1991-95; dir. Macon Arts Alliance, 1987-91; mem. Cultural Plan Oversight Com., 1989-90. Mem. Get Out the Vote Task Force, Macon, 1981—, Macon Symphony Guild, 1986-91; dep. registrar Bibb County Bd. Elections, Macon, 1981-95. Mem. AAUW (bd. dirs. Ga. chpt., v.p. 1991-93, chair coll.-univ. rels. com. 1993-94, bylaws com. 1996-97, v.p., treas., historian, Macon chpt., Named Gift Honoree 1988), NAFE, NOW, Women's Network for Change, Am. Mgmt. Assn., Presdl. Assts. in Higher Edn., Women's Polit. Orgn. Macon, Sigma Mu. Democrat. Unitarian. Office: Ga Wesleyan Coll 4760 Forsyth Rd Macon GA 31210-4407

MITCHELL, CHARLES ARCHIE, financial planning consultant, engineer; b. Kodia Kanal, Madras, India, May 3, 1926; came to U.S., 1932; s. Charles Archie and Ethel Blanche (Nutter) M.; m. Betty Louise Johnson, June 15, 1947; children: Cynthia E., Charles Archie Jr., Susan L. BSEE, Worcester (Mass.) Poly. Inst., 1946; MBA, Harvard U., 1954; CFP, Coll. of Fin. Planning, 1974. Sales engr. Johnson Steel & Wire Co., Worcester, 1947-50; dist. sales mgr. GE, Plainville, Conn., 1954-61; v.p. mktg. Dictograph Co., Danbury, Conn., 1962-63; dir. corp. planning GCA Corp., Bedford, Mass., 1963-65; div. mgr. Polaroid Corp., Cambridge, Mass., 1965-66; rep. Hayden Stone, Inc., Boston, 1966-69; div. mgr. Westamerica Fin. Corp., Boston, 1971-77; officer, dir. MHA Mgmt. Corp., Braintree, Mass., 1977-89; pres., dir. Mitchell Fin. Corp., Falmouth, Mass., 1989—. Contbr. articles to profl. jours. Instr. Northeastern U., Boston, 1962-66, Mass. Dept. of Edn., Cambridge, 1966-69. Lt. USN, 1943-47, 51-53, Korea. Mem. Internat. Assn. Fin. Planners (treas., bd. dirs. 1975-76), Inst. Cert. Fin. Planners (ea. v.p. nat. bd. dirs. 1974-79), Nat. Assn. Life Underwriters, Cape Cod Estate Planning Coun., Cape Cod Curling Club, Woods Hole Golf Club, Woods Hole Yacht Club, Masons, Shriners. Avocations: sailing, curling, golf. Office: PO Box 550 Falmouth MA 02541-0550

MITCHELL, CHARLES F., lawyer; b. Washington, Oct. 18, 1963; s. John Joseph and Duane (Schwertner) M.; m. Sherrie Ilyse Braude, June 7, 1986; children: Matthew Ryan, Sydni Paige. BA, U. Md., 1985; JD, Georgetown U., 1989. Bar: Md. 1989, D.C. 1991, U.S. Ct. Md. 1990, U.S. Ct. Appeals (4th and fed. cirs.) 1991, U.S. Ct. Fed. Claims 1991. Assoc. Holland & Knight (formerly Dunnells & Duvall), Washington, 1989-93; gen. counsel John J. Kirlin, Inc., Rockville, Md., 1993—. Contbr. articles to profl. jours. Mem. Am. Inns of Ct., ABA (vice-chmn. subcontracts com. for constrn. industry 1995, mem. public contract law/litigation sects.). Avocations: golf, tennis. Home: 9814 Bald Cypress Dr Rockville MD 20850 Office: John J Kirlin Inc 643 Lofstrand Ln Rockville MD 20850

MITCHELL, CLAYBOURNE, JR., retired utilities executive; b. Chgo., Jan. 13, 1923; s. Claybourne and Ethel Emma (Osby) M.; m. Isabella Ophelia Skerrett; 1 dau., Mary Faith. Assoc. in Engring. Sci., Flint Jr. Coll., 1948; B.S. in Physics, U. Mich., 1950, M.S. in Physics, 1959. Dir. research Controlled Power Corp., Farmington, Mich., 1968-74; gen. dir. engring. research dept. Detroit Edison, 1974-77, mgr. personnel services, 1977-79, asst. v.p. planning and research, 1979-80, v.p. planning and research, 1980-88. Inventor, patentee: system for periodically reversing elec. energy through a load; co-inventor photon detector sliderule; co-patentee resolution voltage controllable interferometer, micromeasurement apparatus, apparatus for infrared scanning. Served to master sgt. USAAF, 1943-46, PTO. Mem. Engring. Soc. Detroit, Detroit Sci. Ctr. Mem. Unity Ch.

MITCHELL, DAVID WALKER, lawyer; b. Oakland, Calif., Nov. 11, 1935; s. Theodore Boyd and Helen Louise (Walker) M.; m. Carolyn Hilliard Graves, July 29, 1961; children: Sarah M. Meyer, Betsy M. Kinney. AB in History, Stanford U., 1957; JD, Harvard U., 1960. Bar: Calif. 1961. Assoc. Kindel & Anderson, L.A., 1961-65, Weir, Hopkins, Donovan, San Jose, Calif., 1965-68; ptnr. Hopkins, Mitchell & Carley, San Jose, 1968-87, McCutchen, Doyle, Brown & Enersen, San Jose, 1987-93, Hoge, Fenton, Jones & Appel, San Jose, 1993—. Bd. dirs. Peninsula Open Space Trust, Menlo Park, Calif., 1982—, pres., 1984-92; bd. dirs. Santa Clara Community Found., San Jose, 1977-94; chair bd. trustees United Way Santa Clara County, 1983-85. Fellow Am. Bar Found., Am. Leadership Forum (sr.); mem. Santa Clara County Bar Assn. (trustee 1972-75), San Jose C. of C. (bd. dirs. 1975-80). Mem. United Ch. of Christ. Avocations: music, hiking. Office: Hoge Fenton Jones Appel Ste 1400 60 S Market St San Jose CA 95113-2396

MITCHELL, DENNIS A., Olympic athlete, track and field; b. Feb. 20, 1966. Student, U. Fla. Olympic runner Barcelona, Spain, 1992. Recipient 4x100m relay Track and Field Gold medal, 100m Bronze medal, Olympics, Barcelona, 1992. Office: US Olympic Com 1750 E Boulder St Colorado Springs CO 80909-5724*

MITCHELL, DONALD E., rehabilitation counselor, transition counselor; b. Kansas City, Mo., Jan. 19, 1948; s. Rosa E. Mitchell. BA, Southwestern Coll., 1970; MS in Community Counseling, Emporia State U., 1983, MS in Vocat. Rehab. Counseling, 1986; postgrad., U. Kans., Pitts. State U., Emory U. Svc. technician, sales and sheet metal installer Lee's Cooling and Heating, Independence, Kans., 1976-82; dir. partial hosp. facility, case mgr. Iroquis Ctr. for Human Devel., Greensburg, Kans., 1983-85; job coach Kans. Social Rehab. Svc., Topeka, 1985-86; title IV counselor Independence Community Coll., 1986-87; vocat., rehab. counselor II, transition counselor Kans. Rehab. Svcs., Chanute, 1988—; program dir. Magdeline Group Home, Kans. City, 1995—. Bd. dirs. Helping Hearts Heal. Mem. Nat. Eagle Scout Assn., Helping Hearts Heal (bd. dirs.), Kans. Vocat. Evaluator and Assessment Assn. (membership chmn., pres.), Nat. Rehab. Assn., Kans. Rehab. Assn., Chi Sigma Iota.

MITCHELL, DONALD J., former congressman; b. Ilion, N.Y., May 8, 1923; m. Margaretta Wilson Levee, 1945; children: Gretchen, Cynthia, Allen. Student, Hobart and William Smith Coll., 1946-47, LLD (hon.); BS in Optometry, Columbia U., 1949, MA in Edn., 1950; LLD (hon.), Pa. Coll. Optometry; D Ocular Scis. (hon.), So. Coll. Optometry. Optometrist; mem. 93d-97th Congresses from, N.Y.; Councilman Town of Herkimer, 1954-56; mayor Village of Herkimer, 1956-59; mem. sr. assoc. faculty Nat. Emergency Tng. Ctr.; pres. Mohawk Valley Conf. Mayors, 1959; mem. N.Y. State Assembly, 1965-72, majority whip, 1968-72; bd. dirs. Comml. Travelers Mut. Ins. Co. Bd. dirs. Herkimer chpt. Cub Scouts, Cen. N.Y. Assn. for the Blind, Herkimer County United Fund, ea. chpt. Nature Conservancy. With USNR, 1942-45, 51-53. Named Optometrist of Yr. N.Y. State Optometric Assn., 1971; recipient Pub. Svc. award, 1965, award of distinction SUNY State Coll. Optometry Alumni Assn., Patriot of Yr. award N.Y. Res. Officers Assn., Nat. Security award U.S. Civil Def.; Jimmy Doolittle fellow Aerospace Edn. Found. of Air Force Assn. Mem. Nat. Soc. State Legis. (gov. 1971), Am. Civil Def. Assn. (pres. 1988—), Am. Legion, VFW. Republican. Methodist. Clubs: Rod and Gun, Masons, Elks, Kiwanis. Home: Herkimer NY 13350

MITCHELL, EARL NELSON, physicist, educator; b. Centerville, Iowa, Aug. 30, 1926; s. Earl Nelson and Nina (Swank) M.; m. Marlys Marie Panning, July 23, 1955. AB magna cum laude, U. Iowa, 1949, MS, 1951; PhD, U. Minn., 1955. Research scientist Sperry Rand Corp., St. Paul, 1955-58; asst. prof., then assoc. prof. physics U. N.D., Grand Forks, 1958-62; vis. assoc. prof., then assoc. prof. and prof. physics U. N.C., Chapel Hill, 1962-91, prof. emeritus, 1991—, asst. chmn. dept., 1968-76; lectr. Hamline U., 1956, 57; cons. Sperry Rand Corp., 1958-62. Contbr. articles to profl. jours.; author textbooks. Mem. Chapel Hill Planning Bd., 1970-71; pres. Chapel Hill Concert Series, 1967-70; mem. bd. for missions to deaf Luth. Ch. Mo. Synod, 1958-64. Served in USNR, 1945-46. Mem. AAAS, Am. Phys. Soc., Am. Assn. Physics Tchrs., Am. Soc. Enologists (bd. dirs. ea. sect. 1984-91, pres. elect 1988, pres. 1989, past pres. 1990), Soc. Wine Educators, N.C. Grape Coun., N.C. Wine Growers Assn. (pres. 1994—), Phi Beta Kappa, Sigma Xi, Phi Eta Sigma. Democrat. Office: U NC Physics Dept Chapel Hill NC 27599

MITCHELL, EARL WESLEY, clergyman; b. Excelsior Springs, Mo., Mar. 16, 1931; s. Earl Van and Ora Leah (Butterfield) M.; m. Mary Lou Bell, June 8, 1956; children: Susan Yvonne, Randall Bruce. Ordained to ministry Christian Union Ch., 1971. Min. Vibbard (Mo.) Christian Union Ch., 1962-69, Liberty (Mo.) Christian Ch., 1969-77, Barwick Christian Union Ch., Cameron, Mo., 1977-80, Independence (Mo.) Christian Union Ch., 1980-95; assoc. pastor Flack Meml. Christian Union Ch., Excelsior Springs, Mo., 1995-96; mem. state exec. bd. Christian Union Mo.; area rep. Mo. Christian Union USA; former mem. gen. exec. bd., former editor C.U. Witness. Sgt. USAF, 1951-55. Avocations: music, woodworking, painting, photography. Home and Office: 618 Henrie St Excelsior Springs MO 64024

MITCHELL, EDWARD FRANKLIN, utility company executive; b. Harrisonburg, Va., Dec. 23, 1931; s. Charlotte Elaine M. m. Suzanne S. Sublette, Aug. 20, 1955; children: Karen Mitchell Holland, Brian. B.E.E., U. Va., 1956; M.E.A., George Washington U., 1960. Registered profl. engr., D.C. With Potomac Electric Power Co., Washington, 1956—, v.p. elec. engring., 1971-76, sr. v.p. system engring. and ops., 1976-80, exec. v.p., chief operating officer, 1980-83, former pres., former chief operating officer, also dir.; chief exec officer Potomac Electric Power Co., Washington, DC, 1989—, also chmn., 1993—; mem. bd. visitors U. Md. Engring. Coll.; dir. Acacia Mut. Life. Mem. Vienna (Va.) Town Council, 1963-66; mem. Vienna Planning and Zoning Commn., 1963-66; elder Vienna Presbyterian Ch.; active Md. Bus. Coun., Met. Washington Bd. Trade.; bd. dirs. Nat. Rehab. Hosp. Served with USN, 1950-52. Home: 9409 Duxford Ct Potomacle MD 20854 Office: Potomac Electric Power Co 1900 Pennsylvania Ave NW Washington DC 20068-0001*

MITCHELL, EDWARD JOHN, economist, retired educator; b. Newark, Aug. 15, 1937; s. Edward Charles and Gladys (Werner) M.; m. Mary Josephine Osborne, June 14, 1958; children: Susan, Edward. B.A. summa cum laude, Bowling Green State U., 1960; postgrad. (Social Sci. Research Council fellow), Nuffield Coll., Oxford U., Eng., 1963-64, Ph.D. in Econs. (NDEA fellow 1960-63, NSF fellow 1964-65), 1966. Lectr. in econs. Wharton Sch., U. Pa., 1964-65; economist Rand Corp., 1965-68; mem. Inst. Advanced Study, Princeton, N.J., 1968-69; sr. economist Pres.'s Council Econ. Advs., Washington, 1969-72; vis. assoc. prof. econs. Cornell U., 1972-73; assoc. prof. bus. econs. U. Mich., 1973-75, prof., 1975-88, prof. emeritus bus. econs. and pub. policy, 1988—; pres. Edward J. Mitchell Inc., Ann Arbor, 1977—; dir. nat. energy project Am. Enterprise Inst., 1974-76; pres. Fountainhead Investment Co., 1984—. Author: U.S. Energy Policy: A Primer, 1974, Dialogue on World Oil, 1974, Financing the Energy Industry, 1975, Vertical Integration of the Oil Industry, 1976, The Deregulation of Natural Gas, 1983; contbr. articles to profl. jours. Home: 310 Penny Ln Santa Barbara CA 93108-2601 Office: Grad Sch Bus U Mich Ann Arbor MI 48109

MITCHELL, EHRMAN BURKMAN, JR., architect; b. Harrisburg, Pa., Jan. 25, 1924; s. Ehrman Burkman and Alice (DeCevee) M.; m. Hermine Strickler, Sept. 25, 1948; children: Eric Ehrman, Marianne. AB, U. Pa., 1947, BArch, 1948; LHD (hon.), Spring Garden Coll., 1989. Asso. architect Bellante & Clauss, 1951-58; partner Mitchell/Giurgola, Assocs., Phila., 1958-85; dir. Wyck Assn.; lectr. Ohio State U., U. Ariz., U. Utah, Cath. U. Am., Washington U., St. Louis, U. Notre Dame, Dartmouth Coll., U. Ky., U. Md., Temple U.; Phila. lectr. U. Nebr.; lectr. Calif. Poly. State U., U. Brasilia, Boston Archtl. Ctr., Pa. State U., Clemson U., Cornell U.; bd. overseers Temple U. Arch. Sch., U. Pa. Grad. Sch. Fine Arts; arch. design panels U. Pa. Prin. works Nat. hdqrs. Am. Coll. Life Underwriters, Bryn Mawr, Pa. also, Adult Learning Research Center; office bldg. Penn Mut. Life Ins. Co., Phila., Ins. Co. N.Am., Phila.; U. Wash. Law Sch. and Library, Seattle, USIS Cultural Center, Brasilia, Brazil, A.B. Volvo Co. mfg. plant, Chesapeake, Va., New Parliament House, Canberra, Australia. Pres. Citizens Coun. Whitemarch Twp., Montgomery County, Pa., 1963-65, dir., 1963-67; mem. Del. Valley Citizens Transp. Com., 1964—, Citizens Coun. Montgomery County, 1964—; mem. archtl. rev. panel U.S. Fed. Res. System; bd. regents Am. Archtl. Found. With USNR, 1943-46. Recipient Gold medal Artists Guild Phila., Hazlett award Pa. Coun. Arts, 1985, plaque honor Mexican Fedn. Architects; fellow U. Pa. Mus. Fellow Royal Archtl. Inst. Can. (hon.), Royal Australian Inst. Architects; mem. AIA (chpt. dir. Phila. 1965-68, coll. fellows 1969—, nat. dir. 1973-75, v.p. 1977, 1st v.p. 1978, pres. 1979, gold medal Phila. chpt. 1964, 72, 74, silver medal 1973, Nat. Honor award 1974, 75, archtl. firm award 1976), Pa. Soc. Architects (dir. 1966—, sec. 1966, v.p. 1967, pres. 1967, silver medal 1974, 75, 77), Am. Inst. Mgmt. (pres.'s coun. 1967), Pa. Acad. Fine Arts, Pan Am. Fedn. Architects, Nat. Acad. Designs, Societe Arquitecto Mexicanos, Beta Theta Pi. Clubs: Philadelphia, Carpenter's Co., St. Andrew's Soc. (Phila.). Home: 600 E Cathedral Rd ENI Philadelphia PA 19128-1933

MITCHELL, ELIZABETH MARELLE, nursing educator, medical, surgical nurse; b. Bemis, Tenn., Dec. 2, 1937; d. William Columbus and Ruth Marelle (Wadley) Latham; m. Thomas Alton McNatt, June 20, 1953 (dec. Mar. 1984); children: Glenn McNatt, Craig McNatt, Chris McNatt; m. Charles Leon Mitchell, Sept. 7, 1985; stepchildren: Melanie Campbell, Mike, Allyson Flanagan. AA in Nursing, Union U., 1965; BSN, U. Tenn., Martin, 1994; MSN, FNP, U. Tenn., Memphis, 1996. RN, Tenn.; CNOR; cert. BCLS, BCLS instr., BCLS instr. trainer, ACLS, ACLS instr. Staff nurse med.-surg. units Jackson (Tenn.)-Madison County Gen. Hosp., 1965-66; physician 1st asst. Jackson Clinic Surgeons, 1966-74; nursing instr. Jackson Area Vo-Tech Sch., 1974-78, nursing instr. supr., 1978-81; supr. oper. rm. Jackson Splty. Hosp. (acquired by Jackson-Madison County Gen. Hosp. 1983), 1981-85; instr. nurse edn. Jackson-Madison County Gen. Hosp., 1985—; mem. nursing adv. bd. Jackson Area Vo-Tech Sch., 1987—; mem. task force nursing asst. curriculum devel. State of Tenn., Nashville, 1992; clin. skills judge Health Occupations Student Assn. Tenn. State Competition, Nashville, 1992. Tchr. Sunday sch. Malesus (Tenn.) Bapt. Ch., 1975-86. Mem. Assn. Oper. Rm. Nurses (del. to congress 1992, mem. program com. 1993, 94), Am. Soc. Healthcare Edn. and Tng. (svc. rep. West Tenn. 1988, Outstanding Regional Rep. Tenn. chpt. 1988), West Tenn. Healthcare Edn. and Tng. Conf. Group (pres. 1987, regional rep. 1988, sec. 1994), U. Tenn. Martin Nursing Honor Soc., Phi Theta Kappa. Avocations: reading, swimming, handicrafts. Home: RR 3 Box 378 Linden TN 37096-9544 Office: Jackson-Madison County Gen Hosp 708 W Forest Ave Jackson TN 38301-3901

MITCHELL, GARY EARL, physicist, educator; b. Louisville, July 5, 1935; s. Earl Raymond and Delma Kathlene (Lockard) M.; m. Carolyn Fey Stutz, Aug. 4, 1957; children: Scott Frederick, Karen Lee (dec.). BS, U. Louisville, 1956; MA, Duke U., 1958; PhD, Fla. State U., 1962. Research assoc. Columbia U., N.Y.C., 1962-64, asst. prof., 1964-68; assoc. prof. N.C. State U., Raleigh, 1968-74, prof. physics, 1974—, assoc. head physics dept., 1982—. Contbr. numerous articles to sci. publs. Sr. scientist Alexander Von Humboldt Found., Bonn, Fed. Republic Germany, 1975. Recipient Alumni Disting. Prof. award N.C. State U. Fellow Am. Phys. Soc.; mem. numerous sci. assns. Avocation: history. Home: 2913 Harriman Dr Durham NC 27705-5423 Office: NC State U Dept Physics PO Box 8202 Raleigh NC 27695-8202

MITCHELL, GEOFFREY CHRISTOPHER, physician, software developer, financial consultant; b. Columbus, Ohio, May 27, 1953; s. Earnest Edward Mitchell and Martha Joan (Kellough) Mitchell-Noe; m. Margaret Mary Zuber, Sept. 12, 1972; children: Matthew, Andrew, Kevin. BS, Ohio State U., 1974; MD, Med. Coll. Ohio, 1981. Diplomate Am. Bd. Emergency Medicine. Intern, resident Riverside Meth. Hosp., Columbus, 1981-84; attending physician St. Ann's Hosp., Westerville, Ohio, 1984-91; founding ptnr. IHA Inc., St. Ann's, Westerville, 1987-91; attending physician Riverside Meth. Hosp., 1991—; founder, pres. Smart Chart (med. software), Columbus, 1994—; course dir. Emergency Medicine Rev., Columbus, 1993; portfolio mgr. for pvt. clients, 1994; mem. faculty 1st Internat. Conf. on Emergency Medicine, Tegucigalpa, Honduras, 1993. Contbg. author: Photo and Xray Stimuli in Emergency Medicine, 1994; author/developer med. software, computerized stock and mut. fund selection; author suture technique Vertical Figure 8, 1987. Mem. short-term med. missions Christian Med. Soc., Honduras, 1981, 84, 89, Project Amazon, Manaus, Brazil, 1993. Recipient 2d Place award U.S. Investing Championship, L.A., 1991, 6th Place, 1993. Fellow Am. Coll. Emergency Physicians; mem. Ohio State Med. Assn., Christian Med. Soc. Home: 3847 Olentangy Blvd Columbus OH 43214-3533 Office: Riverside Meth Hosp Dept Emergency Medicine 3535 Olentangy River Rd Columbus OH 43214-3925

MITCHELL, GEORGE ERNEST, JR., animal scientist, educator; b. Duoro, N.Mex., June 7, 1930; s. George Ernest and Alma Thyrza (Hatley) M.; m. Billie Carolyn McMahan, Mar. 14, 1952; children: Leslie Dianne, Karen Leigh, Cynthia Faye. B.S., U. Mo., 1951, M.S., 1954; Ph.D., U. Ill., 1956. Asst. prof. animal sci. U. Ill., 1956-60; assoc. prof. U. Ky., Lexington, 1960-67; prof. U. Ky., 1967—, dir. grad. studies in animal scis., 1964—, coord. beef cattle and sheep, 1974-90. Contbr. articles to profl. jours. Served with USAF, 1951-53. Fulbright research scholar New Zealand, 1973-74; Rsch. scholar Japan Soc. for Promotion of Sci., Japan, 1989. Mem. Am. Soc. Animal Sci. (sec. 1969-70, v.p. 1970-71, pres. So. sect. 1971-72, rsch. fellow 1989, Disting. Svc. award 1994), Am. Dairy Sci. Assn., Am. Inst. Nutrition, AAAS, Council for Agrl. Sci. and Tech., Sigma Xi, Alpha Zeta, Gamma Sigma Delta, Omicron Delta Kappa. Democrat. Methodist. Home: 690 Hill N Dale Rd Lexington KY 40503-2164 Office: So U Ky 809 W P Garrigus Bldg Lexington KY 40546

MITCHELL, GEORGE HALL, lawyer; b. Houston, Oct. 24, 1939; s. David Eaton and Adelia Eveline (Hall) M.; m. Nancy Duffey, June, 1962; children: Cathleen McRoberts, Bradley Duffey. BA, U. Ariz., 1962, JD, 1965. Bar: Ariz. 1965, U.S. Dist Ct. Ariz. 1965, U.S. Supreme Ct. 1972. Atty.-at-law O'Connor, Cavanagh, Phoenix, 1965—; bd. dirs. State Capital Law Firm Group, Raleigh, N.C. Legal Counsel Theodore Roosevelt coun. Boy Scouts Am., Phoenix, 1988-93, pres. Grand Canyon coun., 1994-96 (Silver Beaver award); precinct committeeman Rep. Party, Dist. 25, Phoenix, 1991; dist. rep. Rep. State Com., Ariz., 1991; past chmn. bd. All Sts. Episcopal Day Sch.; past sr. warden All Sts. Episcopal Ch. James E. West fellow, 1994. Mem. ABA, State Bar Ariz., Maricopa County Bar Assn., Internat. Assn. Def. Counsel (chmn. property ins. com. 1989-91, mem. exec. com.), Ariz. Town Hall, Theodore Roosevelt Rough Riders (pres. 1986), Phoenix Country Club, Rotary (pres. Club No. 100 1985, Paul Harris fellow). Avocations: study of World War II, golf. Office: O'Connor Cavanagh 1 E Camelback Rd Ste 1100 Phoenix AZ 85012-1656

MITCHELL, GEORGE P., gas and petroleum company executive; b. Galveston, Tex., 1919; married. BS, Tex. A&M U., 1940. Exploration engr., geologist Amoco Prodn. Co., 1940-41, cons. geologist, engr., 1940-41; pres. Mitchell Energy & Devel. Corp., 1947-72, chmn. bd. dirs., CEO, 1972—; with Mitchell Energy & Devel. Corp., The Woodlands, Tex., 1947—, chmn., pres., 1972—, chief exec. officer, from 1972, also bd. dirs.; pres. George Mitchell & Assocs. Served to maj. U.S. Army, 1942-46. Recipient Michel T. Halbouty Human Needs award, Am. Assn. Petroleum Geologists 1994. Office: Mitchell Energy & Devel PO Box 4000 The Woodlands TX 77387*

MITCHELL, GEORGE WASHINGTON, JR., physician, educator; b. Balt., Apr. 30, 1917; s. George Washington and Katharyne Eugenia (Diggs) M.; m. Anne Jenkins Shriver, Dec. 19, 1942 (div. 1954); children: Beverly Shriver, George Washington III, Anne Jenkins, Edward Diggs; m. Mary Elizabeth McKay, Sept. 14, 1957; children—Bruce McKay, Katharyne Wilcox. A.B., Johns Hopkins, 1938, M.D., 1942. Diplomate: Am. Bd. Ob-Gyn (dir.). Intern Johns Hopkins Hosp., 1942, resident, 1946-49; gynecologist in chief New Eng. Med. Center Hosp., Boston, 1950-81; prof. ob-gyn Tufts U. Sch. Med., 1954-81, prof. emeritus, 1981—, chmn. dept., 1956-81; prof. ob-gyn U. Tex., San Antonio, 1981—; chief of gynecology U. Tex. Health Scis. Center, San Antonio, 1981-92; cons. Surgeon Gen. Navy. Served with USNR, 1943-46. Recipient Pub. Svc. award USN, 1977; named to Soc. Scholars Johns Hopkins U., 1991. Fellow ACS, ACOG, Am. Gynecol. and Obstet. Soc.; mem. AMA, Am. Fertility Soc., Soc. Pelvic Surgeons, Mass. Med. Soc., Obstet. Soc. Boston, New Eng. Ob-Gyn. Soc., Soc. Gynecol. Oncologists, So. Atlantic, Tex. Ob-Gyn. Soc., N.Am. Ob-Gyn. Soc., S.W. Ob-Gyn. soc., Johns Hopkins Med. and Surg. Assn., Soc. of Scholars Johns Hopkins U. Office: Dept Obstetrics and Gynecology U Texas Health Sci Center San Antonio TX 78284

MITCHELL, GLORIA JEAN, elementary school principal, educator; b. Plant City, Fla., Oct. 14, 1945; d. Jessie Mae (Anderson) Smith; m. Thero Mitchell, Sept. 19, 1969; children: Tarra Shariss Patrick, Thero Jr. BS, Bethune-Cookman Coll., 1967; MA, U. Detroit, 1974; postgrad., U. Wash., 1990. Cert. tchr., adminstr. Wash. Tchr. Dade County Schs., Miami, Fla., 1967-71, Agana (Guam) Presch., 1971-72, Detroit Pub. Schs., 1973-76, Prince Williams Schs., Dale City, Va., 1976-81; counselor/tchr. State of Alaska, Ketchikan, 1981-84; tchr. Bellevue (Wash.) Schs., 1985-90, prin., 1992—; bd. dirs. YMCA Bothell, Wash., chair sustaining drive, 1994-95; bd. dirs. Cascadia C.C., Bothell. Recipient Golden Acorn award PTA-Lake Hills Schs., 1986, Golden Apple award KCTS TV, Seattle, 1994-95; named West Field Vol. of Yr., YMCA, Bothell, Wash., 1987, Woman of Yr., Woodinville (Wash.) Region II Prin. of Yr., Bellevue, 1994. Mem. ASCD, Nat. Alliance Black Sch. Educators, Wash. Alliance Black Sch. Educators,. Avocations: needle point, golf, comty. volunteerism. Office: Bellevue Pub Schs 14220 NE 8th St Bellevue WA 98007-4103

MITCHELL, GRAHAM RICHARD, government engineering executive; b. Oxford, Eng., Sept. 14, 1938; came to U.S., 1968; s. David and Doris (Clarke) M.; m. Patricia Mary Garside, Jan. 11, 1963; children: Claire Helen, Iain Andrew. BSc, U. Westminster, London, 1962, PhD, 1968. Mgr. rsch., bus. devel. and engring. GE, Phila., 1968-76; cons. GE Corp. R&D Ctr., Schenectady, N.Y., 1976-80; dir. planning & forecasting GTE Labs., Waltham, Mass., 1980-93; asst. sec. for tech. policy U.S. Dept. Commerce, Washington, 1994—; bd. dirs. Indsl. Rsch. Inst. Contbr. articles to books and profl. jours.; patentee in field. Recipient Ayerton Premium Inst. of Elec. Engring., London, Maurice Holland award IRI, 1993. Mem. IEEE, Am. Mgmt. Assn. (mem. mgmt. coun. 1990—), Internat. Assn. for Mgmt. of Tech. (bd. dirs.). Home: 3909 Highwood Ct NW Washington DC 20007-2132 Office: US Dept Commerce Rm 4814C 14th & Constitution Ave NW Washington DC 20230-0002

MITCHELL, HAROLD, insurance executive. Prin. William Mercer, Inc. Office: 400 Renaissance Ctr Detroit MI 48243

MITCHELL, HERBERT HALL, former university dean, educational consultant; b. New Market, Ala., Dec. 10, 1916; s. Walter Hall and Vera Pearl (Johnston) M.; m. Audrey Elizabeth Taylor, Oct. 30, 1942; children: William Hall, Robert Michael, Richard Lee, Mary Ann. B.S., U. Ala., 1939, M.S., 1950; Ph.D., U. N.C., 1954. Asst. to dean of men U. Ala., 1939-42, asst. dean of men, 1942-43, asst. to dean of students, 1946-48; instr. U. N.C.,

1948-51; asst. prof. Ala. Poly. Inst., 1951-55, assoc. prof., 1955-56; prof., head dept. bus. adminstrn. Miss State U., 1956-60; prof., chmn. dept. bus. adminstrn. Va. Poly. Inst., 1960-61, dean Sch. Bus., 1961-81, dean emeritus, 1981—; dean Coll. Commerce and Bus. Adminstrn. U. Ala., 1981-86, dean emeritus, 1986—; ednl. cons. and lectr., 1986—; vis. prof. finance grad. program in England and Germany U. Ark., 1972; mem. adv. bd. Intercollegiate Case Clearing House, Harvard U., 1973-76, 77-78. Contbr. articles to jours. Bd. dirs. Ala. Council Econ. Edn., 1982—; trustee Joint Council on Econ. Edn., 1982-86. Capt. Transp. Corps, AUS, 1943-46, col. Res., ret. Edn. fellow Joseph T. Ryerson & Son, Inc., Chgo., summer 1956. Mem. So Bus. Adminstrn. Assn. (pres. 1968-69), Am. Assembly Collegiate Schs. Bus. (dir. 1973-80, v.p. 1977, pres. 1978), Anderson Soc., Ret. Officers Assn., Univ. Club, West Ala. Ret. Officers Club (pres. 1989), Indian Hills Country Club, Phi Eta Sigma, Delta Sigma Pi, Beta Alpha Psi, Omicron Delta Epsilon, Beta Gamma Sigma (nat. bd. govs. 1980-84), Omicron Delta Kappa (G. Burke Johnston award 1981), Mu Kappa Tau, Gamma Iota Sigma. Methodist. Home: 82 The Highlands Tuscaloosa AL 35404-2915

MITCHELL, HOWARD ESTILL, human resources educator, consultant; b. Indpls., Aug. 13, 1921; s. Estill and Emma (Howard) M.; m. Nadine Wilson Harris, July 21, 1946; 1 son, Howard Estill Jr. B.S., Boston U., 1943; Ph.D., U. Pa., 1950; D.F.A., Phila. Coll. Art, 1969. Asst. chief clin. psychologist VA Mental Hygiene Clinic, Phila., 1953-57; chief psychologist Lankenaw Hosp., Phila., 1957-59; asst. prof. family study in psychiatry U. Pa. Sch. Medicine, Phila., 1955-66; dir. U. Pa. Human Resources Ctr., 1964-84; prof. human resources U. Pa. Grad. Sch. Fine Arts, Phila., 1966-67, 1907 Found. Prof. urbanism and human resources, 1967-73; UPS prof. mgmt. and human resources Wharton Sch. U. Pa., 1974-92, emeritus UPS prof. mgmt. and human resources, 1992—; dir. U. Pa. Univ. Ctr. Transit Research and Mgmt. Devel., 1981-84; chmn. bd. Change Technologies, Inc., Phila., 1981-85; pres. Mitchell and Mitchell Assn., Phila, 1983—; cons. Barton-Aschman Assocs., Evanston, Ill., 1982—, IBM Human Resources Forum, Armonk, N.Y., 1983, Squibb Corp., 1984—, Skadden, Arps, 1985—, Ford Motor Co., 1986—, Gen. Motors Corp., 1986—, Covington & Burling, 1987—, others. Mem. bd. Com. of Seventy, Phila, 1975-78; mem. vestry Old Christ Ch., 1978—; chieftain Segamores of the Wabash, State of Ind., 1989. Served to 1st lt. U.S. Army, 1943-46. Named Albert Hill Cup Prof. of Yr., Sigma Kappa Phi, 1983, 91; named to Hall of Fame, Boston U., 1996; W.T. Grant Found. fellow, 1950-51. Fellow Am. Psychol. Assn.; mem. Pa. Psychol. Assn. (pres. 1959-60, 50th Anniversary past pres. award 1983), Am. Acad. Mgmt., Am. Soc. Tng. and Devel., Am. Pub. Transp. Assn., Friars Sr. Soc. U. Pa. (hon. mem.). Democrat. Episcopalian. Club: Franklin Inn (Phila.). Office: Mgmt Dept Wharton Sch U Pa 3620 Locust Walk Philadelphia PA 19104-6302

MITCHELL, JAMES AUSTIN, insurance company executive; b. Cin., Dec. 16, 1941; s. James Austin and Jeannette Louise (Stiles) M.; 1 child, J. David. A.B., Princeton U., 1963. CLU; chartered fin. cons.; FSA. Various positions Conn. Gen. Life Ins. Co., Hartford, 1963-73, v.p., controller, 1973-77; v.p., chief fin. officer Aetna Ins. Co., Hartford, 1977-82; pres. Cigna RE Corp., Hartford, 1982-84; chmn., CEO IDS Life Ins. Co., Mpls., 1984—; dir. IDS Fin. Services and Affiliated Cos., Mpls. Mem. exec. com. Mpls. Inst. Arts, 1987—; bd. dirs. Mpls. YMCA. With U.S. Army, 1964-70. Fellow Soc. Actuaries; mem. Soc. C.L.U.s. Republican. Presbyterian. Club: Minneapolis. Avocations: tennis; skiing; reading. Home: #3404 3404 Morqueal Ave Minneapolis MN 55403 Office: IDS Life Ins Co 2900 IDS Tower 10 Minneapolis MN 55474

MITCHELL, JAMES KENNETH, civil engineer, educator; b. Manchester, N.H., Apr. 19, 1930; s. Richard N. and Henrietta (Moench) M.; m. Virginia D. Williams, Nov. 24, 1951; children: Richard A., Laura K., James W., Donald M., David L. B.C.E., Rensselaer Poly. Inst., 1951; M.S., M.I.T., 1953; D.Sc., 1956. Mem. faculty U. Calif., Berkeley, 1958-93, prof. civil engring., 1968-89, chmn. dept., 1979-84, Edward G. and John R. Cahill prof. civil engring., 1989-92, Edward G. and John R. Cahill prof. civil engring. emeritus, 1993—; Berkeley citation, 1993; Via prof. civil engring. Va. Poly. Inst. and State U., Blacksburg, 1994—, Univ. Disting. prof., 1996—; geotech. cons., 1960—. Author: Fundamentals of Soil Behavior, 1976, 2d edit., 1993; contbr. articles to profl. jours. Asst. scoutmaster Boy Scouts Am., 1975-82; mem. Moraga (Calif.) Environ. Rev. Com., 1978-80. Served to 1st lt. AUS, 1956-58. Recipient Exceptional Sci. Achievement medal NASA, 1973, Berkeley Citation, 1993. Mem. ASCE (hon., Huber prize 1965, Middlebrooks award 1962, 70, 73, Norman medal 1972, 95, Terzaghi lectr. 1984, Terzaghi award 1985, pres. San Francisco sect. 1986-87); mem. Nat. Acad. Engring., Am. Soc. Engring. Edn. (We. Electric Fund award 1979), NRC (geotech. bd. chmn. 1990-94, bd. on infrastructure and constrn. environ. 1994—, transp. rsch. bd. exec. com. 1983-87), Internat. Soc. Soil Mechanics and Found. Engring. (v.p. N.Am. 1989-94), Earthquake Engring. Rsch. Inst., Brit. Geotech. Soc. (Rankine lectr. 1991), Sigma Xi, Tau Beta Pi. Office: Va Tech Dept Civil Engring Blacksburg VA 24061-0105

MITCHELL, JAMES LOWRY, lawyer, former government official; b. Evanston, Ill., May 20, 1937; s. David B. and Sara (McGinn) M.; children: Caitlin, Andrew. BA, Cornell U., 1959; LLB, Yale U., 1962. Bar: Ill. 1962, D.C. 1977, N.Y. 1985. Assoc. Mayer, Brown & Platt, Chgo., 1966-69, ptnr., 1970-72, 77-84; spl. asst. to sec. for policy devel. U.S. Dept. Commerce, Washington, 1972-73; gen. counsel HUD, Washington, 1973-74, under sec., 1974-75; assoc. dir. Office Mgmt. and Budget, Washington, 1975-77; dep. gen. counsel Citicorp/Citibank, N.Y.C., 1984-90; exec. v.p., gen. counsel 1st Fidelity Bancorp, Newark, 1990—. Lt. USN, 1962-66. Mem. ABA, Assn. of Bar of City of N.Y., Capitol Hill Club. Office: 1st Fidelity Bancorp 550 Broad St Newark NJ 07102-4517

MITCHELL, JOHN ADAM, III, banker; b. Wilmington, Del., May 26, 1944; s. John Adam and Carolyn Brown (Shomo) M.; m. Elizabeth Lenta Love, July 17, 1976; children—Christina Love, Jacqueline Elizabeth. B.S. in Elec. Engring., N.C. State U., 1966; M.B.A., U. N.C., 1968. Dir. market research Br. Banking & Trust Co., Wilson, N.C., 1968-70, regional credit adminstr., 1970-73, v.p., city exec., Lexington, 1974-76, sr. v.p., Wilson, N.C., 1977-79; exec. v.p. First Tulsa Bancorp., 1980-82; group exec. v.p. Northwestern Fin. Corp., North Wilkesboro, N.C., 1983-85; dir. advanced mgmt. program N.C. Sch. Banking, Chapel Hill, 1984-89; exec. v.p. First Union Nat. Bank, Greenville, S.C., 1986-87; dir. human resources First Union Corp., 1988-89; pres. First Union Nat. Bank, Jacksonville, Fla., 1990-92, also bd. dirs. 1990—, chmn. 1993—. Chmn. Mayor's commn. on housing, Jacksonville, 1990-93; bd. dirs. INROADS, Inc., Jacksonville, 1992—, chmn. 1992—; chmn. bd. dirs. Jacksonville Zool. Soc., 1995—; pres. bd. trustees Country Day Sch., Jacksonville, 1996—. Author: A General Credit Model: A Tool for Loan Officer Training and Decision Making, 1976. Bd. dirs. Jr. Achievement Tulsa, 1982; v.p. N.C. Phys. and Math. Scis. Found., Raleigh, 1984. Mem. Am. Bankers Assn. (banking advisor 1980-84), N.C. Bankers Assn. (dir. comml. lending com. 1983-84). Republican. Baptist. Office: First Union Nat Bank PO Box 2080 Jacksonville FL 32231

MITCHELL, JOHN CHARLES, business executive; b. Bedford, Ind., May 25, 1947; s. John Lewis and Mary Ellen (Rowe) M.; m. Marie Elizabeth Bruland, Aug. 21, 1971; 1 child, Allison Anne. BA in Econs., Va. Mil. Inst., 1969; MBA, Ind. U., 1975, JD, 1975. Bar: Ind., 1975, Fed. Cts., 1975. Brand mgr. Procter and Gamble Co., Cin., 1975-82; group product mgr. RJR/Del Monte, San Francisco, 1982-84; dir. mktg. RJR/Nabisco, Parsippany, N.J., 1984-87, v.p. mktg., 1987-88, v.p., gen. mgr., 1988-90, pres. sales and logistics Co., 1991-94; pres. planters, lifesavers co. RJR/Nabisco, Winston-Salem, N.C., 1994—. 1st lt. US Army, 1969-71. Inductee Va. Mil. Inst. Sports Hall of Fame, 1981. Mem. ABA. Republican. Methodist. Avocations: golf, skiing. Office: Planters Lifesavers Co 1100 Reynolds Blvd Winston Salem NC 27102-0064

MITCHELL, JOHN CHARLES, secondary education educator; b. Balt., Sept. 18, 1947; s. Albert Gray and Helen Clark (Northrop) M.; m. Beverly Adele Nutt, Dec. 20, 1969; children: David Alan, Donna Christine, Steven Charles. BA, Calif. State U., Long Beach, 1969. Cert. tchr., Calif. Tchr. Riverside (Calif.) Unified Sch. Dist., 1970-73; tchr., dist. coord. Glendora (Calif.) Unified Sch. Dist., 1973-76; tchr. math., basketball coach Sierra Plumas Joint Unified Sch. Dist., Downieville, Calif., 1976—; instrumental music judge, So. Calif. Sch. Band and Orch. Assn., Pasadena, 1974-76; music festival judge, Calif. Music Edn. Assn., Chester, 1982. Author curriculum guide. Chmn. bd. dirs., Sierra County Waterworks Dist., Calpine, Calif., 1980—; chief, Calpine Vol. Fire Dept., 1982. Mem. Sierra Plumas Tchrs. Assn. (pres. 1981-83), Riverside County Music Educators Assn. (pres. 1971-73), Nat. Coun. Tchrs. Math., NRA, Sierra Valley Fish and Game Club (sec.-treas. 1976-79). Republican. Avocations: golf, deer hunting, softball, coaching youth sports. Home: PO Box 9 Calpine CA 96124-0009

MITCHELL, JOHN DIETRICH, theatre arts institute executive; b. Rockford, Ill., Nov. 3, 1917; s. John Dennis Royce and Dora Marie (Schroeder) M.; m. Miriam Pitcairn, Aug. 25, 1956; children: John Daniel, Lorenzo Theodore, Barbarina Mitchell Heyerdahl. BSS, Northwestern U., 1939, MA, 1941; EdD, Columbia U., 1956; HHD (hon.), Northwood U., 1986. Dir., producer Am. Broadcasting Co., N.Y.C., 1942-46; assoc. editor Samuel French, Publ., N.Y.C., 1946-48; assoc. prof. Manhattan Coll., N.Y.C., 1948-58; pres. Inst. for Advanced Studies in the Theatre Arts, N.Y.C., 1958—; founder, pres. Eaton St. Press, Key West, Fla., 1994; bd. dirs. Beneficia Found., Jenkintown, Pa. Author: Staging Chekhov, 1990, Actors Talk, 1991, Gift of Apollo, 1992, Staging Japanese Theatre: Noh and Kabuki, 1995, Men Stand on Shoulders, 1995; author: (aka Jack Royce) The Train Stopped at Domodossola, 1993, Murder at the Kabuki, 1994, Dressed to Murder, Death at the Towers of Silence, 1995. Trustee Northwood U., Midland, Mich., 1972-91; patron Met. Opera, N.Y.C.; mem. Cmty. Ch. Key West. Named Hon. conch Key West (Fla.) Commrs., 1994. Mem. Met. Mus., Key West Arts and Hist. Soc., Tennessee Williams Fine Arts Ctr. (founder), Key West Literary Seminar (emeritus), Nippon Club N.Y.C., N.Y. Athletic Club. Avocations: Tai Chi Chuan, swimming, collecting musical recordings, books. Home: 703 Eaton St Key West FL 33040-6843 also: Eaton Street Press 524 Eaton St # 30 Key West FL 33040-6881 Office: Inst Advanc Studies Theater 703 Eaton St Key West FL 33040

MITCHELL, JOHN HENDERSON, retired army officer, management consultant; b. Atlanta, Sept. 9, 1933; s. William Lloyd and Jessie (Henderson) M.; m. Joan Ann Cameron, Apr. 8, 1961; children: John Cameron, Christopher Lloyd, Colin MacKenzie. BABA, St. Bonaventure U., 1956, PhD in Sci., 1991; MA in Pub. Adminstrn., Shippensburg State U., 1973. Commd. 2nd lt. U.S. Army, 1956, advanced through grades to maj. gen., 1982; comdr. 8th Bn., 6th Arty., 1st Inf. divsn. U.S. Army, Vietnam, 1968; chief officer assignments Field Arty. br. Officer Pers. Directorate, U.S. Army, Washington; chief of staff 8th divsn. U.S. Army, 1973-75; asst. dept. chief of staff for personnel, Hdqrs. U.S. Army Europe and 7th Army U.S. Army, Heidelberg, Germany, 1975-77; comdr. Arty. divsn., chief of staff 1st Inf. divsn. U.S. Army, Ft. Riley, Kans., 1977-79; comdr., Field Command, Def. Nuclear Agy. U.S. Army, Kirtland AFB, N.Mex., 1979-81; dir. Human Resources Devel. Office, dept. chief staff for pers. U.S. Army, Washington; U.S. comdr. Berlin, 1984-88; ret., 1989; pres. Intersys., Inc., Englewood, Colo., 1989-94, Pease, Orr, Mitchell Enterprises, Colorado Springs, Colo., 1994—. Bd. dirs. Nat. Safety Coun., 1982-84. Decorated D.S.M. with oak leaf cluster, Legion of Merit with oak leaf cluster, D.F.C. with oak leaf cluster, Bronze Star with oak leaf cluster and V., Air medals. Mem. Assn. U.S. Army, VFW, Army Navy Club, Army War Coll. Alumni, Soc. of First Inf. Div. Republican. Roman Catholic. Avocations: tennis, history, reading. Home: 375 Hidden Creek Dr Colorado Springs CO 80906-4386

MITCHELL, JOHN MCKEARNEY, manufacturing company executive; b. N.Y.C., Sept. 20, 1938; s. James William and Genevieve (McKearney) M.; AB, Dartmouth Coll., 1960; MBA, Amos Tuck Sch. Bus., 1961; m. Melinda Marsters, Aug. 25, 1962; children: Peter Marsters, Jeffrey Dewing. Acct., Ernst & Whinney, N.Y.C., 1962-64; asst. MIS mgr., mgr. acctg. Sperry Corp., Univac Internat. Div., N.Y.C., Bluebell, Pa., 1964-68; planning analyst, mgr. treas. ops., asst. contr. Sybron Corp., Rochester, N.Y., 1968-80; corp. contr. Condec Corp., Old Greenwich, Conn., 1980-83; exec. v.p. Powell Duffryn (U.S.A.) Ltd., 1983-86; pres. 1986-88; pres. Vt. Marble Co., Proctor, 1988-89, Pluess-Staufer Ind. Inc., 1990—; bd. dirs. Canadiagua Enterprises., Park Ridge Hosp., Greese, N.Y., 1971-80, Assoc. Ind. of Vt., 1990—; chmn. bd. dirs. Conn. Ballet Theatre, Stamford, Conn., 1983-88. 1st lt., inf., U.S. Army, 1961-62. Mem. Fin. Execs. Inst. Republican. Home: Otis Ho RR 1 Box 257B Danby VT 05739-9754

MITCHELL, JOHN NOYES, JR., electrical engineer; b. Pownal, Maine, Dec. 16, 1930; s. John Noyes and Frances (Small) M.; m. Marilyn Jean Michaelis, Sept. 1, 1956; children: Brian John, Cynthia Lynn Mitchell Tumbleson, Stephanie Lee Mitchell Judson. BSEE, Milw. Sch. Engring., 1957. Registered profl. engr., Ohio. Elec. rsch. engr. Nat. Cash Register Co., Dayton, Ohio, 1957-65; sr. engr. Xerox Corp., Rochester, N.Y., 1965-70, area mgr., 1970-73; area mgr. Xerox Corp., Dallas, 1973-76; area mgr. Xerox Corp., El Segundo, Calif., 1976-79, tech. program mgr., 1979-85, competitive benchmarking mgr., 1985-92, quality mgr., 1992—. With USN, 1949-53. Mem. IEEE, Mason. Republican. Episcopalian. Home: 11300 Providencia St Cypress CA 90630-5351 Office: Xerox Corp ESC1-16W 101 Continental Blvd El Segundo CA 90245-4806

MITCHELL, JONI (ROBERTA JOAN ANDERSON), singer, songwriter; b. Ft. Macleod, Alta., Can., Nov. 7, 1943; d. William A. and Myrtle M. (McKee) Anderson; m. Chuck Mitchell (div.); m. Larry Klein, Nov. 21, 1982. Student, Alta. Coll. Albums include Song to a Seagull, Clouds, Ladies of the Canyon, Blue, For the Roses, Court and Spark, 1974, Miles of Aisles, The Hissing of Summer Lawns, 1975, Hejira, 1976, Don Juan's Reckless Daughter, Mingus (Jazz Album of Year and Rock-Blues Album of Year, Downbeat mag. 1979), Shadows and Light, 1980, Wild Things Run Fast, 1982, Dog Eat Dog, 1985, Chalk Mark in a Rainstorm, 1988, Night Ride Home, 1991, Turbulent Indigo, 1994. Recipient Grammy award for Best Folk Performance, 1969, Grammy award for Best Arrangement Accompanying Vocalists (with Tom Scott), 1974.

MITCHELL, JOSEPH PATRICK, architect; b. Bellingham, Wash., Sept. 29, 1939; s. Joseph Henry and Jessie Delila (Smith) M.; student Western Wash. State Coll., 1957-59; BA, U. Wash., 1963, BArch, 1965; m. Marilyn Ruth Jorgenson, June 23, 1962; children: Amy Evangeline, Kirk Patrick, Scott Henry. Assoc. designer, draftsman, project architect Beckwith Spangler Davis, Bellevue, Wash., 1965-70; prin. J. Patrick Mitchell, AIA & Assoc./ Architects/Planners/Cons., Kirkland, Wash., 1970—. Chmn. long range planning com. Lake Retreat Camp, 1965-93; bldg. chmn. Northshore Baptist Ch., 1980—, elder, 1984-90; mem. bd. extension and central com. Columbia Baptist Conf., 1977-83; Northshore Bapt. Ch. del. Bapt. World Alliance 16th Congress, Soul Korea, 1990, 17th Cong., Buenos Aires, Argentina, 1995; trustee Bakke Libr./Cultural Ctr., 1994—; vice moderator Columbia Baptist Conf., 1995-96, moderator, 1996—. Recipient Internat. Architectural Design award St. John Vianney Parish, 1989. Cert. Nat. Council Archtl. Registration Bds. Mem. AIA, Constrn. Specification Inst., Interfaith Forum Religion, Art, and Architecture, Nat. Fedn. Ind. Bus., Christian Camping Internat., Wash. Farm Forestry Assn., Rep. Senatorial Inner Circle, Woodinville C. of C., Kirkland C. of C. Republican. Office: 12620 120th Ave NE Ste 208 Kirkland WA 98034-7511 *Personal philosophy: Look to God for inspiration and direction; pursue higher education; be a strong family person; plan wisely for today and the future; work hard yet take time to smell the roses; be firm yet kind; do it right the first time; take care of the details, and the big things will take care of themselves.*

MITCHELL, JOSEPH (QUINCY), writer; b. Fairmont, N.C., July 27, 1908; s. Averette Nance and Elizabeth Amanda (Parker) M.; m. Therese Dagny Engelsted Jacobsen, Feb. 27, 1931 (dec. Oct. 1980); children: Nora (Mrs. John L.R. Sanborn), Elizabeth (Mrs. Henry Curtis). Student, U. N.C., 1925-29. Reporter N.Y. World, N.Y.C., 1929-30, N.Y. Herald Tribune, 1930-31, N.Y. World Telegram, 1931-38; writer New Yorker, N.Y.C., 1938-96. Author: My Ears Are Bent, 1938, McSorley's Wonderful Saloon, 1943, Old Mr. Flood, 1948, The Bottom of the Harbor, 1960, Joe Gould's Secret, 1965, (with Edmund Wilson) Apologies to the Iroquois, With a Study of the Mohawks in High Steel, 1960, Up in the Old Hotel, 1992. Vestryman Grace Ch., N.Y.C., 1978-84; mem. N.Y.C. Landmarks Preservation Commn., 1982-87; mem. restoration com. South Street Seaport Mus., 1972-80. Recipient Gold medal for lit. State N.C., 1984, Disting. Alumnus award U. N.C., 1993, Brendan Gill prize Mcpl. Art Soc., 1993, Amb. Book award English-Speaking Union, 1993. Mem. Am. Acad. Arts and Letters, Soc. Archtl. Historians, Soc. Indsl. Archeology, Friends of Cast-Iron Architecture, James Joyce Soc., Gypsy Lore Soc. Club: Century Assn. (N.Y.C.). *Died May 24, 1996.*

MITCHELL, KENNETH D., physiologist, medical educator; b. Musselburgh, Scotland, Mar. 5, 1959; m. Maria Heavens, Sept. 30, 1995. BSc with upper 2d class honors, U. Edinburgh, Scotland, 1981, PhD in Physiology, 1986. Physiology tutor Univ. Med. Sch., Edinburgh, 1981-84; rsch. assoc. Dept. Physiology and Biophysics Nephrology Rsch. and Tng. Ctr. U. Ala., Birmingham, 1984-86, postdoctoral rsch. fellow, 1986-87, rsch. instr., 1987-88, scientist I, 1987-88; asst. prof. Dept. Physiology Tulane U. Sch. Medicine, New Orleans, 1988-95, assoc. prof., 1995—. Contbr. articles to profl. jours. Nat. Heart, Lung and Blood Inst. grantee, 1995—. Mem. Am. Physiological Soc., Am. Soc. Nephrology, Am. Heart Assn. (fellow Coun. High Blood Pressure Rsch. 1993—, established investigator 1995—), Internat. Soc. Nephrology. Office: Dept Physiology SL39 1430 Tulane Ave New Orleans LA 70112

MITCHELL, LANSING LEROY, federal judge; b. Sun, La., Jan. 17, 1914; s. Leroy A. and Eliza Jane (Richardson) M.; m. Virginia Jumonville, Apr. 18, 1938; children—Diane Mitchell (Mrs. Donald Lee Parker), Lansing Leroy. B.A., La. State U., 1934, LL.B., 1937. Bar: La. 1937. Pvt. practice Pontchatoula, 1937-38; spl. agt. FBI, 1938-41; atty. SEC, 1941-42; asst. U.S. atty. Eastern Dist. La., 1946-53; also engaged in pvt practice; ptnr. Deutsch, Kerrigan & Stiles., New Orleans, 1953-66; U.S. dist. judge Eastern Dist. La., 1966—. Chmn. nat. security com. New Orleans C. of C., 1963-66; vice chmn. New Orleans Armed Forces Day, 1964, 65, New Orleans Heart Fund campaign, 1959-60; mem. New Orleans Municipal Auditorium Adv. Com., 1957-61, New Orleans Municipal Com. Finance, 1955-67, Small Bus. Adv. Council La., 1963-66; pres. Camp Fire Girls Greater New Orleans, 1965-67; La. chmn. Lawyers for Kennedy-Johnson, 1960. Served to lt. col. AUS, 1942-46; col. Res. (ret.). Decorated Royal Order St. George Royal Order Scotland. Mem. ABA, Inter-Am. Bar Assn., La. Bar Assn., New Orleans Bar Assn., Maritime Law Assn. U.S., Judge Adv. Assn., Soc. Former Spl. Agts. FBI, Am. Legion, Mil. Order World Wars, V.F.W., Navy League, Assn. U.S. Army (pres. La. 1964-65, pres. New Orleans 1961-64, v.p. 4th Army region 1963-66), Soc. Mayflower Descendants in State of La. (assoc.), Scabbard and Blade, SAR, S.R., Soc. War 1812 La., Pi Kappa Alpha, Phi Delta Phi, Theta Nu Epsilon. Clubs: Mason (33 degree, New Orleans) (Shriner), Press (New Orleans), Paul Morphy Chess (New Orleans), Southern Yacht (New Orleans), Bienville, Pendennis (New Orleans); Tchefuncta Country (Covington, La.). Office: US Dist Ct C-508 US Courthouse 500 Camp St New Orleans LA 70130-3313 *To serve my country as a soldier, praying that I need never be called to arms again; to serve the people as a jurist, knowing that I too shall someday be judged; to serve my family as a shepherd, finding that my love for them begets greater loving.*

MITCHELL, LEE MARK, communications executive, investment fund manager, lawyer; b. Albany, N.Y., Apr. 16, 1943; s. Maurice B. and Mildred (Roth) M.; m. Barbara Lee Anderson, Aug. 27, 1966; children: Mark, Matthew. A.B., Wesleyan U., 1965; J.D., U. Chgo., 1968. Bar: Ill. 1968, D.C. 1969, U.S. Supreme Ct. 1972. Assoc. Leibman, Williams, Bennett, Baird & Minow, Chgo. and Washington, 1968-72; assoc. Sidley & Austin, Washington, 1972-74, ptnr., 1974-84, 92-94; exec. v.p. and gen. counsel Field Enterprises, Inc., Chgo., 1981-83, pres. and chief exec. officer, 1983-84; pres., chief exec. officer Field Corp., 1984-92; prin. Golder, Thoma, Cressey, Rauner, Inc., Chgo., 1994—; bd. dirs. Paging Network, Inc., Washington Nat. Corp., Chgo. Stock Exch., Inc., PTN Pub. Co.; chmn. Learning Scis. Corp., NOTIS Systems, Inc., 1987-91. Author: Openly Arrived At, 1974, With the Nation Watching, 1979; co-author: Presidential Television, 1973. Mem. LWV PResdl. Debates Adv. Com., Washington, 1979-80, 82; U.S. del. Brit. Legis. Conf. on Covt. and Media, Ditchley Park, Eng., 1974; bd. visitors U. Chgo. Law Sch., 1984-86, Medill Sch. Journalism, Northwestern U., 1984-91; bd. govs. Chgo. Met. Planning Coun., pres., 1988-91; mem. midwest regional adv. bd. Inst. Internat. Edn., 1987—; trustee Ravinia Festival Assn., Northwestern U. Mem. ABA, Fed. Comm. Bar Assn., Econ. Mid-Am. Club (trustee), Chgo. Club, Comml. Club Chgo. Home: 135 Maple Hill Rd Glencoe IL 60022-1252 Office: Golder Thoma Cressey Rauner Inc 6100 Sears Tower Chicago IL 60606-6402

MITCHELL, LEONA PEARL, soprano; b. Enid, Okla., Oct. 13, 1949; d. Hulon and Pearl Olive (Leatherman) M.; married. BA, Oklahoma City U., 1971, MusD (hon.), 1979. With San Francisco Opera, spring, 1973, fall, 1974, 77. Appeared at Edinburgh (Scotland) Festival, 1977, Sacria Umbria Festival, Perugia, Italy, 1977, on concert tour, Australia, 1978; has sung with most maj. symphonies throughout U.S.; European debut Barcelona, Spain, 1974; Met. Opera debut as Micaela, 1975; also appeared films and TV shows; recs. include Porgy and Bess with Cleve. Orch., 1975. Winner San Francisco Opera auditions, 1971; named Ambassadress of Enid, 1978, Okla. Hall of Fame, 1983. Mem. Am. Guild Musicians Assn. Sigma Alpha Iota, Alpha Kappa Alpha. Mem. Ch. of God in Christ. Performed for Pres. Ford, 1976, Pres. Carter, 1978, 79. Office: Orgn Internat Opera et Concert, 19,rue Vignon, F-7 5008 Paris France

MITCHELL, MARTIN MORGAN, JR., advertising executive; b. N.Y.C., Aug. 14, 1937; s. Martin Morgan and Helen (Flood) M.; BA, Holy Cross Coll., 1959; MBA, N.Y. U., 1967; postgrad. in advanced mgmt. Harvard U., 1968; m. Ann Fogarty, Mar. 23, 1964; children: Martin, Leeann, Marguerite. Product mgr. Colgate Palmolive Co., N.Y.C., 1960-63; account exec. J. Walter Thompson Co., N.Y.C., 1963-68; acoount exec. Wells Rich Greene, N.Y.C., 1968-81, v.p., account supr., 1969-72, v.p., mgmt. supr., 1972-75, sr. v.p., 1975-80; pres. WRG Can., 1980-81; exec. v.p., gen. mgr. Sawdon and Bess div. Ted Bates Worldwide, N.Y.C., 1981-83, pres., COO, 1983-87; vice chmn. AC&R, 1987-94; pres., COO Burkhardt & Christy (name changed to Christy, MacDougall & Mitchell), N.Y.C., 1994—; assoc. prof. mktg. Pace U., pres. Collegiate Info. Svcs. 1994—; tchr. seminars various univs. Mem. communications bd. Jr. Achievement, 1977-80; pres. Philharmonic Virtuosi, 1987-90, chmn.,1990-94. Served with U.S. Army, 1959-60. Roman Catholic. Club: Westchester Country. Home: 118 Winfield Ave Harrison NY 10528 Office: Christy, MacDougal & Mitchell 304 E 45th St New York NY 10017

MITCHELL, MAURICE B., publishing executive, educator; b. N.Y.C., Feb. 9, 1915; s. Jacob and Beatrice (Weinstein) M.; m. Mildred Roth, Mar. 1937; 1 child, Lee Mark; m. Mary V. Rowles, Nov. 1951; children: Keith Edward, Deborah Irene; m. Linda Merry Stewart, Nov. 1991. Student, NYU, 1932-35; LLD (hon.), U. Denver, 1958, W.Va. Wesleyan U., 1978; LHD (hon.), Nat. Coll. Edn., 1969, Nat. U., San Diego, 1986; LittD (hon.), Colo. State U., 1971. With N.Y. Times, 1935-36; editor Gouverneur (N.Y.) Press, 1936-37; asst. pub. Ogdensburg (N.Y.) Jour., 1938-39, Rochester (N.Y.) Times-Union, 1940; nat. advt. mgr. Albany (N.Y.) Knickerbocker-News, 1941-43; with CBS, Washington, also N.Y.C., 1945-48, Nat. Assn. Broadcasters, Washington, 1948-49; mng. dir. Broadcast Advt. Bur./TVB, N.Y.C., 1949-50; with NBC, 1950; v.p., assoc. program service div. Muzak Corp., N.Y.C., 1950-53; dir. Muzak Corp., 1953-58; pres., dir. Ency. Brit. Films, Inc., 1953-62; pres. Ency. Brit., Inc. (Chgo. and all subs.), 1962-67; dir. Ency. Brit. Ednl. Corp., 1977-94; chancellor U. Denver, 1967-77, emeritus, 1978—; pres. Ctr. for Study Dem. Instns./Fund for Republic, 1977-78; chmn. Pacific Basin Inst., Santa Barbara, Calif., 1978—; dir. Washington program com. policy studies Annenberg Found., 1983-85, cons., 1986-92; chmn. Internat. Acad., Santa Barbara, 1988-93, dir. Ctr. for Study of the Environment, Santa Barbara,1993—; co-founder, chmn. Westview Press, Boulder, Colo., 1975-83; chmn. Denver Br. Fed. Res. Bank, 1971-76; bd. dirs. Fed. Res. Bank of Kansas City. Contbr. articles on edn. and communications to profl. jours. Mem. U.S. Commn. on Civil Rights, 1968-74; chmn. Calif. Ednl. Tech. adv. com., 1981-83, Denver Community Edn. Council on Integration Pub. Schs., 1974-76; trustee Freedoms Found.; chmn. Colo. com. Rhodes Scholarship Trust, 1974-77, Calif. Commn., 1978-80; citizens bd. U. Chgo.; mem. adv. com. U.S. Army Command and Gen. Staff Coll., Dept. Army, 1975-78; chmn. Western Regional Judges Truman Scholarships, 1976-82; dir. Nat. Public Radio, 1977-82, chmn., 1979-80; bd. assos. Nat. Coll. Edn.; trustee Com. Econ. Devel., 1957-62; bd. dirs. Fgn. Policy Assn., World Affairs Center and Nat. Citizens on Internat. Coop., 1966-71, chmn., 1980; bd. dirs., Inst. Internat. Edn., 1978-85, African Student Aid Fund; trustee Nat. U., San Diego. Recipient George Washington medal Freedoms Found., 1969; VFW medal of Merit, 1970; Cert. of Recognition for disting. service to edn. Phi Delta Kappa, 1971; Golden Plate award Am. Acad. Achievement, 1972; Civis Princeps award Regis Coll., Denver, 1973; Meritorious award Denver Met. NAACP, 1973; Malcolm Glenn Wyer award Adult Edn. Council Met. Denver, 1975; B'nai B'rith award, 1976; Human Relations award Beth Joseph Synagogue, Denver, 1976; award NCCJ, 1974. Mem. Colo. State Hist. Soc. (dir.), Phi Beta Kappa, Beta Alpha Psi, Omicron

Delta Kappa, Beta Gamma Sigma, Alpha Kappa Psi, Cosmos Club (Washington), Chgo. Club, Mid-Am. Club (Chgo.), Santa Barbara Club, La Cumbre Country Club, Masons (32 deg., Knight Commdr., Ct. of Honor). Home: 1455 E Mountain Dr Santa Barbara CA 93108-1216

MITCHELL, MAURICE MCCLELLAN, JR., chemist; b. Lansdowne, Pa., Nov. 27, 1929; s. Maurice McClellan and Agnes Stewart (Kerr) M.; m. Marilyn M. Badger, June 14, 1952. BS in Chemistry, Carnegie-Mellon U., 1951, MS in Chemistry, 1957, PhD in Phys. Chemistry, 1960. Group leader rsch. and devel. U.S. Steel Corp., Pitts., 1951-61; br. head phys. chemistry rsch. and devel. Melpar Inc., Falls Church, Va., 1961-64; group leader rsch. and devel. Atlantic Richfield Co., Phila., 1964-73; dir. rsch. and devel. Houdry div. Air Products and Chems., Inc., 1973-81; dir. rsch. and devel. Ashland (Ky.) Oil Inc., 1981-86, v.p. rsch. and devel., 1986-93; vis. lectr. dept. chem. Coll. Arts and Scis. Ohio U. Southern Campus, Ironton, 1993—. Contbr. articles to profl. jours.; patentee in field. Fellow Am. Inst. Chemists; mem. Am. Chem. Soc., Am. Inst. Chem. Engrs., Catalysis Soc. N.Am. (pres. 1985-89), AAAS, Sigma Xi. Home: 2380 Hickory Ridge Dr Ashland KY 41101-3604

MITCHELL, MICHAEL KIEHL, elementary and secondary education educator, minister; b. Phila., Pa., Oct. 27, 1932; s. Robert Bartow and Louise Room (Keyser) M.; m. Gloria (Nell) Wilburn, Nov. 12, 1960; children: Donald Kiehl, Robert Alan. B in Edn., U. Miami, 1955; MEd, Tex. A&M U., 1975, PhD, 1978; grad., Internat. Sch. Christian Comm. Cert. elem. and secondary edn., Fla., Tex., Alaska; lic. comml. pilot. Tchr. math. Dade County Pub. Schs., Miami Springs, Fla., 1955-60; tchr. elem. Greenwood Sch. Dist., Midland, Tex., 1961-63; from tchr. social studies, English to tng. coord. Midland (Tex.) Sch. Dist., 1963-75; prin. rsch. investigator Tex. A&M U., College Station, 1977-78; project dir. Edn. Profl. Devel. Consortium, Richardson, Tex., 1978-79; sr. rsch. scientist Am. Airlines, Dallas, 1979-83; pres. North Rsch. Inc., Anchorage, Alaska, 1983-84; vocat. edn. curriculum specialist Anchorage Sch. Dist., 1984-87; sci. tchr., dept. head McLaughlin Youth Ctr. Anchorage (Alaska) Sch. Dist., 1987—; adj. prof. U. Alaska, Anchorage, 1987-89; evaluation team N.W. Accreditation Assn., Anchorage, 1985; asst. min. United Meth. ch., 1990-94; min. Christian Cmty. Fellowship, 1994—; instr. Flight and Ground Sch. Dir., v.p. Anchorage Comty. Theater, 1984-89; marriage commr. 3d Jud. Dist. Alaska, Anchorage, 1989-93; vol. United Way, Anchorage, 1984-90, Tony Knowles for Gov. Campaign, Anchorage, 1990, 94, Mark Begich for Mcpl. Assembly Campaign, 1991, Cheryl Clementson for Mcpl. Assembly Campaign, 1993. With U.S. Army, 1946-47. Tex. Edn. Agy. fellow, Austin, 1975, Ednl. Profl. Devel. fellow, 1975-78. Mem. Am. Correctional Edn. Assn., Alaska Airmans Assn. (bd. dirs. 1983-89), Screen Actors Guild, Mensa, Am. Legion, Clowns of Am., Nat. Sci. Tchrs. Assn., Alaska Sci. Tchrs. Assn., Alaskan Aviation Safety Found., Tex. Assn. Aerospace Tchrs., Phi Delta Kappa, Phi Kappa Phi. Avocations: commercial pilot, professional acting, FAA accident prevention counselor. Home: 6626 Foothill Dr Anchorage AK 99504-2620 Office: McLaughlin Youth Cen High 2600 Providence Dr Anchorage AK 99508-4613 *Life has taught me: 1) Regret not the past. 2) Fear not the future. 3) Enjoy the moment.*

MITCHELL, MILTON, lawyer; b. Rochester, N.Y., Apr. 6, 1916; s. Mark and Pauline (Amberg) M.; m. Marion Irene Lieberman, Nov. 1, 1942; children: Mark, Martha. J.D. with honors, George Washington U., 1942. Bar: D.C. 1941, U.S. Supreme Ct. 1966. Atty. Bur. Customs, Washington, 1945-50; asst. chief protocol Dept. State, Washington, 1950-64, sr. atty., 1964-69; lectr., prof. internat. law Nat. Law Ctr., George Washington U., Washington, 1964-80; professional lectr. diplomatic and consular law; gen. counsel Accuracy in Media, Inc., Washington, 1973-90. Bd. dirs. Community Action Council, Rossmoor Leisure World, Silver Spring, Md., 1979-85. Served to lt. USNR/World War II. Mem. Fed. Bar Assn., D.C. Bar Assn., Am. Acad. Philately (dir., pres.), Soc. Philatelic Americans, Royal Philatelic Soc. Can. Republican. Clubs: Lawyer (Washington); Diplomatic and Consular Assn, Aspen Hill Tennis. Address: 3401 Hallaton Ct Silver Spring MD 20906-1833 *I have always felt that one of cardinal principles of my life was to 'tell it like it is'— to have the courage to present my views on important subjects, no matter whether they met with agreement or disagreement. It was never my policy to curry favor with important people just to please them or to advance my station in life. I have always felt I first have to live with myself, and I have found that most people valued my sincerity, whether or not they agreed with my position.*

MITCHELL, MITCH, business owner; b. N.Y.C., July 18, 1940; s. Issac Allen Mitchell and Frances (Rosen) Jacobs; m. Louis Aug (div.); m. Martine Marie-Odile Fournier, Oct. 31, 1973; children: Ronnie, Jamie. Student, Syracuse (N.Y.) U., 1958-62. Sales mgr. United Transporter Corp., N.Y.C., 1962-64; co-owner Gary Lynn Realty, Inc., Miami Beach, Fla., 1987-94. Vice chmn. Surfside (Fla.) Zoning & Planning Bd.; commr. Town of Surfside, 1990-92; trustee Hope Ctr., Miami. Mem. NRA (life), Miami Beach Bd. Realtors (bd. dirs. 1985-89, 94—), Fla. Assn. Realtors (bd. dirs. Orlando chpt. 1985-89, 93—), Mt. Sinai Hosp. Young Pres.'s Club, Zool. Soc. (trustee Miami chpt.), Kiwanis (pres.). Republican. Jewish. Home: 8919 Hawthorne Ave Miami FL 33154-3331 Office: Gary Lynn Realty Inc 17800 W Dixie Hwy Miami FL 33160-4822

MITCHELL, ORLAN E., clergyman, former college president; b. Eldora, Iowa, Mar. 13, 1933; s. Frank E. and Alice G. (Brown) M.; m. Verlene J. Huehn, June 10, 1952; children: Jolene R., Stephen M., Nadene A., Timothy M., Mark E. B.A., Grinnell Coll., 1955; B.D., Yale U., 1959, M.Div., 1965; D.Min., San Francisco Theol. Sem., 1976. Ordained to ministry United Ch. of Christ, 1959; pastor chs. Sheridan Twp., Iowa, 1954-55, New Preston, Conn., 1956-59, Clarion, Iowa, 1959-69, Yankton, S.D., 1969-77; pres. Yankton (S.D.) Coll., from 1977; now conf. minister Iowa Conf. United Ch. Christ. Mem. Sch. Bd., Clarion, Iowa, 1965-69, mem., Yankton, S.D., 1973-77, pres., 1976; bd. dirs. Lewis and Clark Mental Health Center. Mem. S.D. Found. Pvt. Colls., S.D. Assn. Pvt. Colls., Colls. of Mid-Am. Democrat. Lodges: Kiwanis; Masons. Office: 600 42nd St Des Moines IA 50312-2701

MITCHELL, OTIS CLINTON, JR., history educator; b. Spearville, Kans., Jan. 10, 1935; s. Otis Clinton and Joeanna Esther (Woodring) M.; m. Darlene Foley, Aug. 20, 1966. A.B., Wichita U., 1957; M.A., Kans. State Coll., 1960; Ph.D., U. Kans., 1964. Instr. history Wichita State U., 1963-64; mem. faculty U. Cin., 1964—, prof. history, 1975—, also chmn. dept. history. Author: Two Totalitarians, 1965, The Western Cultural Way, 1965, A Concise History of Western Civilization, 2d edit, 1976, Fascism: An Introductory Perspective, 1978, The Great European Revolutionary Era of 1789-1815, 1979, A Concise History of Brandenburg-Prussia to 1786, 1980; co-author: The World Since 1919, 1971; editor, contbr.: Nazism and the Common Man, 2d edit, 1981, Hitler Over Germany, 1983, Two German Crowns, 1985, Hitler's Nazi State, 1987, Otto von Bismarck: Germany's Iron Chancellor, 1992; editor: Studies in Historical Europe, 1986, Thirty Year's War, 1993, Blood Purge, 1993, A German History, 3 Vols., 1994. Dir. civic com. Hidden Valley Lake, Ind., 1975; bd. dirs. Hidden Valley Lake P.O.A., 1978-79. Served with AUS, 1957-59. Grantee Taft Fund Fellowship, 1969-74, 77, 82, 89; recipient Outstanding Tchr. award Ohio Acad. History, 1983, Excellence in Teaching award U. Cin., 1985, Nat. Excellence in Teaching award Am. Assn. Higher Edn., 1989. Mem. Phi Alpha Theta. Home: Hidden Valley Lake 19912 Longview Dr Lawrenceburg IN 47025-9061 Office: Univ Cin Dept History Cincinnati OH 45221

MITCHELL, PAMELA ANN, airline pilot; b. Otis AFB, Mass., May 6, 1955; d. Gene Thomas and Rose Margaret (Jones) Mitchell; m. Robert Carroll Stephens, May 26, 1984 (div. Dec. 1992). BFA, Colo. State U., 1975; postgrad., Webster Coll., 1981. Lic. pilot Ill., comml. instr., airline transport pilot, jet rating, Boeing 747 and 727, Boeing 747-400. Flight attendant United Airlines, Chgo., 1976-80; charter pilot Air Aurora, Sugar Grove, Ill., 1978-80; owner, operator Deliverance, Unltd. Ferry Co., Aurora, Ill., 1978-81; flight test pilot Cessna Aircraft Co., Wichita, Kans., 1981-82, nat. spokeswoman, 1982-83; airline pilot Rep. Airlines, Mpls., 1983-84, Northwest Airlines, Mpls., 1985—; pres., ptnr., artist Aerographics Jacksonville, Fla., 1986-90. Mem. Safety Coun. Airline Pilots Assn., 99's Internat. Women Pilots Assn., Mooney Aircraft Pilots Assn., Internat. Soc. Women Airline Pilots (bd. dirs. 1994-96), Nat. Aviation Club, N.W. Airline Ski Team (capt. 1989-94), Kappa Kappa Gamma. Republican. Presbyterian. Avocations: piano, snow skiing, tennis, travel, golf. Home: 12502 Mission Hills Cir Jacksonville FL 32225 Office: Northwest Airlines Minn/St Paul Internat Airport Saint Paul MN 55111

MITCHELL, PATSY MALIER, religious school founder and administrator; b. Greenwood, Miss., Aug. 28, 1948; d. William Lonal and Lillian (Walker) Malier; m. Charles E. Mitchell, Apr. 20, 1970; children: Christopher, Kara, Angela. BS in Edn., Delta State U., 1970, MEd, 1974, Edn. Specialist, 1979; MA in Ch. Ministries, Ch. of God Sch. Theology, 1990; PhD in Psychology and Counseling, La. Bapt. U., 1994; D in Edn. Christian Sch. Adminstrn., Baptist Christian U., 1992. Cert. sch. adminstr. Youth, Christian edn. dir. Ch. of God, Minter City, Miss., 1975—; teen talent dir. Ch. of God, Minter City, 1983—, missions rep., 1975—; dist. Christian edn. dir. Ch. of God, Cleveland, Miss., 1983-85; sch. adminstr. Ch. of God, Cleveland, 1985—; del. Ch. of God Edn. Leadership, Cleveland, Tenn., 1990; del., speaker Christian Schs. Internat., Chattanooga, Tenn., 1991. Contbr. articles to profl. jours. Dir. St. Jude Children's Hosp., Memphis, 1991; vol. 4-H Club, Greenwood, Miss., 1985-91. Named to Outstanding Young Women of Am., 1983; recipient Community Pride award Chevron, 1988, Internat. Woman of Yr. award, 1993. Mem. Christian Sch. Adminstrs., Christian Schs. Internat., Ch. of God Edn. Assn., Delta State Alumni Assn., Ch. of God Sch. of Theology Alumni Assn, Gospel Music Assn. Republican. Home: RR 1 Box 72A Minter City MS 38944-9714 *The greatest gift that God has given mankind is the capacity to love and encourage others. It is God's gift to us and our gift to others.*

MITCHELL, PAULA RAE, nursing educator; b. Independence, Mo., Jan. 10, 1951; d. Millard Henry and E. Lorene (Denton) Gates; m. Ralph William Mitchell, May 24, 1975. BS in Nursing, Graceland Coll., 1973; MS in Nursing, U. Tex., 1976; EdD in Ednl. Adminstrn., N.Mex. State U., 1996. RN, Tex., Mo.; cert. childbirth educator. Commd. capt. U.S. Army, 1972; ob-gyn. nurse practitioner U.S. Army, Seoul, Korea, 1977-78; resigned, 1978; instr. nursing El Paso (Tex.) C.C., 1979-85, dir. nursing, 1985—, acting div. chmn. health occupations, 1985-86, div. chmn., 1986—, curriculum facilitator, 1984-86; ob-gyn. nurse practitioner Planned Parenthood, El Paso, 1981-86, mem. med. com., 1986—; cons. in field. Author: (with Grippando) Nursing Perspectives and Issues, 1989, 93; contbr. articles to profl. jours. Founder, bd. dirs. Health-C.R.E.S.T., El Paso, 1981-85; mem. pub. edn. com. Am. Cancer Soc., El Paso, 1983-84, mem. profl. activities com., 1992-93; mem. El Paso City-County Bd. Health, 1989-91; mem. Govt. Applications Rev. Com., Rio Grande Coun. Govts., 1989-91; mem. collaborative coun. El Paso Magnet H.S. for Health Care Professions, 1992-94. Decorated Army Commendation medal, Meritorious Svc. medal. Mem. Nat. League Nursing (mem. resolutions com. Assocs. Degree coun. 1987-89, accreditation site visitor, AD coun. 1990—, mem. Tex. edn. com. 1991-92, Tex. 3rd v.p. 1992-93), Am. Soc. Psychoprophylaxis Obstetrics, Nurses Assn. Am. Coll. Obstetricians & Gynecologists (cert. in ambulatory women's health care; chpt. coord. 1979-83, nat. program rev. com. 1984-86, corr. 1987-89), Advanced Nurse Practitioner Group El Paso (coord. 1980-83 legis. committee 1984), Am. Phys. Therapist Assn. (commn. on accreditation, site visitor for phys. therapist assistant programs 1991—), Orgn. Assoc. Degree Nursing (Tex. membership chmn. 1985-89, chmn. goals com. 1989—, mem nat. bylaws com., 1990—), Am. Vocat. Assn., Am. Assn. Women Community & Jr. Colls., Tex. Orgn. Nurse Execs., Nat. Coun. Occupational Edn. (mem. articulation task force 1986-89, program standards task force 1991-93), Nat. Coun. Instructional Adminstrs., Tex. Soc. Allied Health Profls., Tex. Nurses Assn., Nat. Soc. Allied Health Profls. (mem. edn. com. 1993—), Sigma Theta Tau, Phi Kappa Phi. Mem. Christian Ch. (Disciples of Christ). Home: 4616 Cupid Dr El Paso TX 79924-1726 Office: El Paso C C PO Box 20500 El Paso TX 79998-0500

MITCHELL, PETER KENNETH, JR., educational consultant, association administrator; b. Bklyn., June 12, 1949; s. Peter Kenneth and Joan Marie (Hayes) M.; m. Susan Veitch Mitchell, June 25, 1983; 1 child, Elyse Alexandra. BA, SUNY, Geneseo, 1970; MS in French, L.I. U., 1975; cert. of French lang. proficiency, U. de Neuchatel, Switzerland, 1969. Tchr. French and Spanish Middle Country Sch. Dist., Selden, N.Y., 1972-81; tech. asst. to dir. internat. affairs dept. Am. Fedn. Tchrs., Washington, 1981-82; asst. to gen. sec. Internat. Fedn. of Free Tchrs. Unions, Amsterdam, 1982-90; exec. dir. Internat. Reading Assn., Newark, Del., 1990-91; owner Insights Out Assocs., Newark, Del., 1992—; dir. mktg. Jr. Achievement Del., 1994—. Author numerous ednl. publs. Mem. ACLU, Am. Soc. Assn. Execs., Blue and Gold Club, Washington U. Club, Amnesty Internat. Avocations: reading, music, tennis. Office: Insights Out Assocs PO Box 9652 Newark DE 19714-9652

MITCHELL, RICHARD BOYLE, advertising executive; b. St. Louis, June 20, 1947; s. Samuel West and Blair (Boyle) M.; m. Deborah Mead Boas, June 1, 1968; children: Rebecca, Jessica. BS in Media, NYU, 1969. Account exec. D.L. Blair Corp., N.Y.C., 1967-70, NW Ayer Advt. Agy., N.Y.C., 1970-74; sr. account exec. Ted Bates Agy., N.Y.C., 1974-75; sr. v.p. DKG Advt., N.Y.C., 1975-81, McCaffrey/McCall, N.Y.C., 1981-86; pres., CEO Marshall Jaccoma Mitchell Advt., N.Y.C., 1986-96; sr. ptnr. Poppe Tyson Advt., N.Y.C., 1996—. Commr. Wilton (Conn.) Police Dept., 1984—. Served with USAR, 1969-75. Democrat. Roman Catholic. Club: Wilton Riding. Avocations: mil. history, running, weight lifting. Home: 43 Collinswood Rd Wilton CT 06897-1811 Office: Poppe Tyson Advt 41 Madison Ave New York NY 10010-2202

MITCHELL, RICK, journalist, writer; b. San Jose, Calif., Nov. 27, 1952; s. Maurice Dale Mitchell and Mary Margaret (Woody) Gron; m. Lori Sumako, May 3, 1987; 1 child, Chelsea Pearl. BA in Am. Studies, Calif. State U., Fullerton, 1974. Music critic Oreg. Jour., Portland, 1978-82, Willamette Week, Portland, 1983, The Oregonian, Portland, 1984-85; music critic, sports columnist Willamette Week, 1986; freelance writer L.A., 1987; arts and entertainment reporter The Bakersfield Californian, 1988; music critic Houston Chronicle, 1989—. Author: Garth Brooks: One of A Kind, Workin' on A Full House, 1993; jazz columnist Request Mag., 1990—; contbr. New Country Music Mag., 1994—. Mem. adv. com. Houston Blues Soc. Mem. Amnesty Internat. Avocations: athletics, reading.

MITCHELL, ROBERT ARTHUR, college president; b. N.Y.C., Jan. 19, 1926; s. George P. and Vera A. (Duffy) M. A.B. (summa cum laude), Woodstock Coll., 1949, AB summa cum laude, 1950; STL magna cum laude, Facultes S.J. de Louvain, Belgium, 1957; ThD, U. Strasbourg, France, 1965; (hon.), Le Moyne Coll., 1990, Loyola U., 1991; U. Detroit, 1992. Joined S.J., 1943, ordained priest, Roman Cath. Ch., 1956. Instr. in philosophy LeMoyne Coll., 1950-53, asst. prof. theology, 1958-59, acad. dean, 1959-63, assoc. prof. theology, acad. dean, 1965-66; pres. Loyola Coll., Shrub Oak, 1966; provincial N.Y. State Province (S.J.), 1966-72; pres. Jesuit Conf., chmn. Am. Jesuit Provincials, Washington, 1972-76; dir. Woodstock Theol. Ctr., 1976-79; pres. U. Detroit, 1979-90, chancellor, 1990-92; consultant, Higher Education to Jesuit U.S. Provincials, 1992—; acting pres. Le Moyne Coll., Syracuse, N.Y., 1993-94, pres., 1994—; bd. dirs. Economic Club of Detroit, 1979-92, Detroit Econ. Growth Corp., 1983-92, Detroit Symphony Orchestra, 1981-89, Woodstock Theological Ctr., 1977-83, Georgetown U., 1976-82, 1983-92; bd. trustees, Loyola Marymount U., 1986, St. Peter's Coll., 1992, U. Detroit, 1979, Sta. WTVS/Channel 56, 1979-86, 1988-92, Michigan Cancer Foundation, 1985-92, New Detroit, Inc., 1979-92, Fordham U., 1966-74, Le Moyne Coll., 1977-83, Boston Coll., 1966-90. Office: Le Moyne College Office of the Pres Syracuse NY 13214

MITCHELL, ROBERT DALE, consulting engineer; b. Worthington, Minn., Aug. 2, 1910; s. Karl V. and Margaret Dumont (Steigleder) M.; m. Carol Sherman Northrop, June 17, 1939; children—Constance Remington, Robert Brown. B.S., S.D. State U., 1932; S.M. (grad. fellow), Harvard U., 1939. Engr. J. Emberg, Madison, S.D., 1932-35; instr. S.D. State U., 1935-37; engr. Malcolm Pirnie, N.Y.C., 1939-42; project engr., partner Malcolm Pirnie, 1945-70, sr. v.p., sec., chief engr., 1970-75, cons., 1975—. Served to maj. San. Corps AUS, 1942-45. Recipient Distinguished Engr. award S.D. State U., 1977. Mem. ASCE, Am. Water Works Assn., Am. Cons. Engrs. Council, New Eng. Water Works Assn. (Commemorative award 1963). Home: 487 Brackett Rd Rye NH 03870-2204 Office: 2 Corporate Park Dr White Plains NY 10602

MITCHELL, ROBERT EDWARD, urban planner, international development specialist, educator; b. Detroit, May 16, 1930; s. Arthur and Elizabeth (Wayne) M.; m. Sylvia Ann Sheppard, Aug. 26, 1950 (div. 1993); children: Anthony Edward, Maude Wayne, Adam Arthur. BA in Oriental Civilizations, U. Mich., 1952; M.A., Harvard U., 1955; Ph.D. in Sociology, Columbia U., 1962. Instr., project dir. Bur. Applied Social Research, Columbia U., 1956-62; coord. internat. rsch. program, dep. dir. Survey Research Center, U. Calif.-Berkeley, 1962-66; dir. Hong Kong Urban Family Life Survey, dir. Social Survey Research Centre, Chinese U., Hong Kong, 1966-69; chief tech. market rsch. adviser Grant Advt. of Hong Kong, 1967-70; prof. urban and regional planning, dir. Survey Data Center Fla. State U., Tallahassee, 1969-78; pvt. internat. devel. cons., 1995—; exec. dir. Fla. Gov.'s Task Force on Housing and Cmty. Devel., 1971-73; mem. UN Ad Hoc Meeting Experts on Social Aspects of Housing in Urban Areas, 1970; mem. tech. mission to Jordan Dept. State, 1973; behavioral sci. adv. urban devel. Nr. East Bur., Office Tech. Support, AID, Dept. State, Washington, 1979—, devel. ofcl., 1980-95; AID duty tours, Egypt, Yemen and Guinea-Bissau; cons. in field. Author: The Needs of Hong Kong Manufacturing Industry for Higher Level Manpower, 1968, Levels of Emotional Strain in Southeast Asian Cities: A Study of Individual Responses to the Stresses of Urbanization and Industrialization, Family Life in Urban Hong Kong, 1972, Pupil, Parent and School, 1972, Housing, Urban Growth, and Economic Development, 1972; Contbr. articles to profl. jours. Mem. Am. Sociol. Assn.

MITCHELL, ROBERT EVERITT, lawyer; b. Port Washington, N.Y., June 14, 1929; s. Everitt and Alice (Fay) M.; m. Anne Nordquist, Nov. 2, 1957; children: Anne C. Mitchell Coneys, Maura A. Kelly, Michael E. BS, U. Mich., 1952; JD, Georgetown U., 1956. Bar: N.Y. 1957, U.S. Dist. Ct. (so. dist.) N.Y. 1958, U.S. Supreme Ct. 1966. Assoc. Sullivan & Cromwell, N.Y.C., 1956-63; v.p., sec., gen. counsel Lambert & Co. Inc., N.Y.C., 1963-65; ptnr. Campbell & Mitchell, Manhasset, N.Y., 1965-80; asst. gen. counsel J.P. Stevens & Co. Inc., N.Y.C., 1980-82, gen. counsel, 1982-88; pvt. practice Peconic, N.Y., 1988—. Atty. Village Baxter Estates, Port Washington, 1967-83; Counsel Mobilized Community Resources, Roslyn, N.Y., 1969-80; asst. scout master Troop 1001 Boy Scouts Am., Port Washington, 1976-79; justice Village Sands Point, N.Y., 1966-85. Served to lt. USNR, 1952-55. Mem. ABA. Republican. Roman Catholic. Clubs: Manhasset Bay Yacht (Port Washington) (commodore 1972-73); N.Y. Yacht (N.Y.C.). Avocations: sailing, fishing, camping, platform tennis, music. Home and Office: 3905 Wells Rd Peconic NY 11958-1738

MITCHELL, ROBERT GREENE, industrial manufacturing executive, consultant; b. Abington, Pa., July 20, 1925; s. James Henry and Nellie Edna (Greene) M.; m. Alma Maerker Honsberger, Mar. 6, 1948; children: Scott Craig, Donna Lynn, Sandra Lee. B.S., Drexel U., 1948. Cert., CPIM. Dept. mgr. Internat. Playtex, Dover, Del., 1949-52, quality control mgr., 1952-59, mfg. mgr. Indsl. div., 1959-60; v.p. ops. The Wool "O" Co., Phila., 1960-65; mfg. mgr. Plymouth Rubber, Canton, Mass., 1965-68; chief indsl. engr., spl. projects Vanity Fair Mills, Monroeville, Ala., 1968-75; v.p. materials mgmt. The H.W. Gossard Co., Chgo., 1975-76; v.p. adminstrn., 1977; v.p. adminstrn., mem. exec. com. Knickerbocker Toy Co., Middlesex, N.J., 1977-79; pres. H&R Block, Prince Frederick, Md., 1979-85; sr. mfg. cons. Sperry Corp. (now UNISYS Corp.), Lutherville, Md., 1980-87, Hunt Valley, Md., 1987-89; ret., 1989. 1st lt. USAF, 1943-46. Mem. Am. Soc. Quality Control (cert. quality engr., chmn. textile div. 1959-60), Am. Prodn. and Inventory Control Soc. Lodge: Lions (dir. 1954-56, pres. 1955-56). Patentee in field. Home and Office: 22 Hillside Ct Huntingtown MD 20639-9406

MITCHELL, ROGER LOWRY, agronomy educator; b. Grinnell, Iowa, Sept. 13, 1932; s. Robert T. and Cecile (Lowry) M.; m. Joyce Elaine Lindgren, June 26, 1955; children: Laura, Susan, Sarah, Martha. B.S. in Agronomy, Iowa State Coll., 1954; M.S., Cornell U., 1958; Ph.D. in Crop Physiology, Iowa State U., 1961. Mem. faculty Iowa State U., 1959-69, prof. agronomy, 1966-69, prof. charge farm operation curriculum, 1962-66; prof. agronomy, chmn. dept. U. Mo., Columbia, 1969-72, 81-83; dean agr., dir. expt. sta. U. Mo., 1983—, dean extension, 1972-75; v.p. agr. Kans. State U., Manhattan, 1975-80; exec. dir. Mid-Am. Internat. Agrl. Consortium, 1981; exec. bd. divsn. agr. Nat. Assn. State Univs. and Land Grant Colls., 1978-80, 85-90, chmn., 1988-89; mem. bd. agr. NRC/NAS, 1983-86. Author: Crop Growth and Culture, 1970; co-author: Physiology of Crop Plants, 1985. Served to 2d lt. USAAF, 1954-56. Danforth fellow, 1956-61; Acad. Adminstrn. fellow Am. Council Edn., 1966-67. Fellow AAAS (chmn. sect. O 1980-81), Am. Soc. Agronomy (pres. 1979-80), Crop Sci. Soc. (pres. 1975-76); mem. Soil Sci. Soc. Am., Coun. Agrl. Sci. and Tech., Sigma Xi, Gamma Sigma Delta, Alpha Zeta, Phi Kappa Phi. Home: 502 W Lathrop Rd Columbia MO 65203-2804

MITCHELL, RONNIE MONROE, lawyer; b. Clinton, N.C., Nov. 10, 1952; s. Ondus Corneilius and Margaret Ronie (Johnson) M.; m. Martha Cheryl Coble, May 25, 1975; children: Grant Stephen, Mitchell, Meredith Elizabeth Mitchell. BA, Wake Forest U., 1975, JD, 1978. Bar: N.C. 1978, U.S. Dist. Ct. (ea. dist.) N.C. 1978, U.S. Ct. Appeals (4th cir.) 1983, U.S. Supreme Ct. 1984. Assoc. atty. Brown, Fox & Deaver, Fayetteville, N.C., 1978-81; ptnr. Harris, Sweeny & Mitchell, Fayetteville, 1981-91, now Harris, Mitchell & Hancox, 1991—; adj. prof. law Norman Adrian Wiggins Sch. of Law, Campbell U; bd. dirs. Mace, Inc. Contbr. chpts. to books. Chmn. Cumberland County Bd. Adjustment, 1985—, Cumberland County Rescue Squad, 1986-93; bd. dirs. Cumberland County Rescue Squad, Fayetteville, 1983-91. Recipient U.S. Law Week award Bur. Nat. Affairs, 1978. Mem. ABA, ATLA, Twelfth Judicial Dist. Bar Assn. (pres. 1988-89), N.C. Bar Assn. (councillor Young Lawyers divsn. 1982-85), N.C. Legis. Rsch. Commn. (family law com. 1994), Cumberland County Bar Assn. (mem. family law com., N.C. State Bar Bd. legal specialization), N.C. Acad. Trial Lawyers, Fayetteville Ind. Light Infantry Club, Dem. Men's Club (pres. 1993-94), Moose, Masons. Home: RR 23 Box 108C Fayetteville NC 28301-9125 Office: Harris Mitchell & Hancox 308 Person St Fayetteville NC 28301-5736

MITCHELL, ROY DEVOY, industrial engineer; b. Hot Springs, Ark., Sept. 11, 1922; s. Watson W. and Marie (Stewart) M.; m. Jane Caroline Gibson, Feb. 14, 1958; children: Michael, Marilyn, Martha, Stewart, Nancy. BS, Okla. State U., 1948, MS, 1950; B of Indsl. Mgmt., Auburn U., 1960. Registered profl. engr., Ala., Miss. Instr. Odessa (Tex.) Coll., 1953-56; prof. engrng. graphics Auburn (Ala.) U., 1956-63; field engr. HHFA, Community Facilities Adminstrn., Atlanta and Jackson, Miss., 1963-71; area engr. Met. Devel. Office, HUD, 1971-72, chief architecture and engrng., 1972-75, chief program planning and support br., 1975, dir. archtl. br., Jackson, 1975-77, chief archtl. br. and engrng. br., 1977-84, community planning and devel. rep., 1984-88; prin. Mitchell Mgmt. and Engrng., 1988—; cons. Army Ballistic Missile Agy., Huntsville, Ala., 1957-58, Auburn Research Found., NASA, 1963; mem. state tech. action panel Coop. Area Manpower Planning System; elected pub. ofcl., chmn. Bd. of Election Commrs., Rankin County, Miss. Mem. Cen. Miss. Fed. Personnel Adv. Council; mem. House and Home mag. adv. panel, 1977; trustee, bd. dirs. Meth. Ch., 1959-60. Served with USNR, 1943-46. Recipient Outstanding Achievement award HUD, Commendation by Sec. HUD. Mem. NSPE, Am. Soc. for Engrng. Edn., Miss. Soc. Profl. Engrs., Nat. Assn. Govt. Engrs. (charter mem.), Jackson Fed. Execs. Assn., Cen. Miss. Safety Council, Am. Water Works Assn., Iota Lambda Sigma. Club: River Hills (Jackson). Home and Office: HUD 706 Forest Point Dr Brandon MS 39042-6220

MITCHELL, ROY SHAW, lawyer; b. Sherwood, N.Y., Jan. 16, 1934; s. Malcolm Douglas and Ruth Landon (Holland) M.; m. Nancy Elizabeth Bishop, Aug. 27, 1955; children: Mark E., Jeffrey B., Jennifer R. BS, Cornell U., 1957; JD with honors, George Washington U., Washington, D.C., 1959. Bar: D.C. 1959, Ohio 1960, Va. 1967, U.S. Fed. Claims Ct. 1963, U.S. Supreme Ct. 1965. Atty. Squire, Sanders & Dempsey, Cleve., 1960-61, Hudson & Creyke, Washington, 1961-67, Lewis, Mitchell & Moore, Vienna, Va., 1967-87, Morgan, Lewis & Bockius, Washington, 1987—; vice-chmn. Ameribanc Savs. Bank, Annandale, Va., 1980-95; trustee Ameribanc Investors Group, Annandale, 1980-95. Co-author: (with others) Handbook of Construction Law and Claims, 1982, 89; contbr. numerous articles to profl. jours. Fellow ABA (pub. contract law sect.), Am. Coll. Construction Lawyers, Va. Bar Assn., D.C. Bar Assn. Presbyterian. Avocation: boating. Home: 5 Jefferson Run Rd Great Falls VA 22066-3227 Office: Morgan Lewis & Bockius 1800 M St NW Washington DC 20036-5802

MITCHELL, RUSSELL HARRY, dermatologist; b. Erie, N.D., Oct. 19, 1925; s. William John and Anna Lillian (Sögge) M.; B.S., B.A., U. Minn., Mpls., 1947, B.M., M.D., 1951; postgrad. U. Pa. Med. Sch., 1968-69; m. Judith Lawes Douvarjo, May 24, 1968; children: Kathy Ellen, Gregory Alan, Jill Elaine, Crystal Anne. Intern, Gorgas Hosp., C.Z., 1951-52; resident in dermatology U.S. Naval Hosp., Phila., 1967-70; asst. chief out-patient dept. Gorgas Hosp., 1955-64; chief med. and surg. wards Ariz. State Hosp., Phoenix, 1965; commd. lt. (j.g.) M.C., U.S. Navy, 1953, advanced through grades to capt., 1968; svc. in Vietnam; ret., 1981; pvt. practice specializing in dermatology, Leesburg, Va., 1978—; mem. staff Loudoun Meml. Hosp., 1975—; dermatologist Nat. Naval Med. Center, Bethesda, Md., 1973-81; asst. prof. Georgetown U. Med. Sch., 1975-85. Pres. Archaeol. Soc. Panama, 1962-64. Decorated Bronze Star with combat V; Vietnam Gallantry Cross with palm and clasp; Condecoratión Vasco Nuñez de Balboa in orden de Caballero (Panama); diplomate Am. Bd. Dermatology. Fellow Am. Acad. Dermatology, Am. Acad. Physicians, Explorers Club; mem. AMA, Assn. Mil. Surgeons, Assn. Mil. Dermatologists (life), Am. Soc. Contemporary Medicine and Surgery, Soc. Am. Archaeology, Royal Soc. Medicine, Pan Am. Med. Assn., Loudoun County Med. Soc., Dermatology Found., Marine's Meml. Club (assoc.), Internat. Platform Soc., Phi Chi. Contbr. articles to med. and archaeol. publs. Home: 18685 Woodburn Rd Leesburg VA 20175-9008 Office: 823J S King St Leesburg VA 20175-3910

MITCHELL, T. L., medical educator; b. Columbia, La., Feb. 24, 1962; m. Janet Tornelli; children: Mary Katherine, Oliver Charles, Christopher Tornelli. Student, Kilgore (Tex.) Jr. Coll., 1980-81; BS in Biology, Stephen F. Austin State U., Nacogdoches, Tex., 1983; MD, U. Tex., Galveston, 1987. Diplomate Am. Bd. Internal Medicine, cert. of added qualification sports medicine; lic physician, Tex. Intern internal medicine U. Tex. Med. Br., Galveston, 1987-88, resident, 1988-90, chief resident, 1990-91; staff physician The Cooper Clinic, Dallas, 1991—; med. dir. The Cooper Wellness Program, Dallas, 1991—. Contbr. articles to profl. jours. Capt., M.C., U.S. Army. Mem. ACP, AMA, Am. Coll. Sports Medicine, Tex. Med. Assn., Dallas County Med. Soc. Home: 3224 Lovers Ln University Park TX 75225 Office: Cooper Clinic 12200 Preston Rd Dallas TX 75230*

MITCHELL, TERENCE EDWARD, materials scientist; b. Haywards Heath, Sussex, Eng., May 18, 1937; came to U.S., 1963, naturalized, 1978; s. Thomas Frank and Dorothy Elizabeth (Perrin) M.; m. Marion Wyatt, Dec. 5, 1959; children: Robin Norman, Jeremy Neil. BA, St. Catharine's Coll., Cambridge (Eng.) U., 1958, MA, 1962, PhD in Physics, 1962; ScD, U. Cambridge, 1994. Research fellow Cavendish Lab., Cambridge, 1962-63; asst. prof. metallurgy Case Inst. Tech., 1963-66; assoc. prof. Case Western Res. U., 1966-75, prof., 1975-87, adj. prof., 1987—, chmn. dept., 1983-86, dir. high voltage electron microscopy facility, 1970-82, co-dir. materials research lab., 1982-83; vis. scientist NASA at Ames Lab., Stanford U. and Electric Power Research Inst., Palo Alto, Calif., 1975-76; scientist Ctr. Materials Sci. Los Alamos (N.Mex.) Nat. Lab., 1987—, lab fellow, 1991—; lab fellows chair Los Alamos (N.Mex.) Nat. Lab., 1993-95; chmn. steering com. Electron Microscopy Ctr. Argonne (Ill.) Nat. Lab., 1979-83; cons. in field; mem. vis. com. metals and ceramics div. Oak Ridge Lab., 1987-91; vis. com. solid state scis. div. Ames Lab., 1987-89; sci. adv. com. Sci. and Tech. Ctr. for Superconductivity, 1989-93. Materials sci. editor Microscopy Rsch. and Technique, 1986—; sr. editor North Am., 1994—; contbr. articles to profl. jours. Pres. Cleve. Ethical Soc., 1970-72; bd. dirs Am. Ethical Union, 1972-74; steward Los Alamos Unitarian Ch., 1992-94; mem. policy com. Univ. Materials Coun., 1986-89; mem. policy com. Argonne Electron Microscopy Steering Com., chmn. 1978-82. Electric Power Research Inst. fellow, 1975-76; NSF grantee, 1966-88; Dept. Energy grantee, 1970-86, 87—; NIH grantee, 1969-72; NASA grantee, 1974-77, 81-87; USAF Office Sci. Research grantee, 1974-85; U.S. Army Research Office grantee, 1970-75, 79-83, EPRI grantee, 1986-89. Fellow Am. Soc. Metals, Am. Phys. Soc., Am. Ceramics Soc. (assoc. editor jour.), Los Alamos Nat. Lab.; mem. Metall. Soc. (editl. bd. 1981—), Electron Microscopy Soc. Am. (program chmn. 1981-82, dir. 1984-86, pres.-elect 1994, pres. 1995), Materials Rsch. Soc., Soc. Francaise de Microscopie Electronique (sci. com. 1982-90). Office: Los Alamos Nat Lab Ctr Materials Sci Ms # K-765 Los Alamos NM 87545

MITCHELL, THEODORE R., dean, education educator; b. San Rafael, Calif., Jan. 29, 1956; s. Theodore Robert and Genevieve Dolores (Doose) M.; m. Christine Marie Beckman, July 8, 1995. BA, Stanford U., 1978, MA, 1980, PhD, 1983. Asst. prof. Dartmouth Coll., Hanover, N.H., 1981-86, assoc. prof., 1986-87, chair dept. edn., 1987-91; dep. to pres. and provost Stanford U., 1991-92; dean Sch. Edn. and Info. Studies UCLA, 1992—; trustee Stanford U., 1985-90, Thetford (Vt.) Acad., 1989-91; bd. dirs. L.A. Edn. Partnership, L.E.A.R.N., L.A. Author: Political Education, 1985. Bd. dirs. Children Now, Oakland, Calif., 1994—. Office: UCLA Sch Edn & Info Studies 405 Hilgard Ave Los Angeles CA 90024

MITCHELL, THOMAS EDWARD, JR., communications cabling executive; b. Sacramento, Apr. 12, 1946; s. Thomas Edward and Violet Mae (Southall) M.; m. Terri Kathleen Vance, Apr. 20, 1969; children: Anthony E., Brian C. BA, Nat. U., 1987, MBA, 1988. Enlisted USMC, 1966, advanced through grades to maj., 1980, retired, 1989; sr. exec. Nat. Decision Sys., Encinitas, Calif., 1989-90, Equifax Mktg. Decision Sys., San Dieto, 1990-93; pres., COO Holocomm Sys. Inc., San Diego, 1993—; bd. dirs. Cal-Pacific Steel Structure Inc., Hawaii, Calif. Contbr. articles to profl. jours.; patentee in field. Dir. Toys for Tots, L.A./ORange Counties, Calif., 1974-77. Recipient Silver Star medal U.S. Pres., 1968, Meritorious Svc. medal, Joint Chiefs of Staff Commendation medal, others. Mem. World Trade Assn. (assoc. 1989—), Am. Legion, Internat. Platform Assn. Avocations: restoring old cars, racquetball, golf, history. Home: 3264 Chase Ct Oceanside CA 92056-3809 Office: Holcomm Sys Inc 6640 Lusk Blvd Ste D-211 San Diego CA 92121

MITCHELL, TONJA KEASHAVEL, physical education educator, nutritional consultant; b. Miami, Fla., Dec. 15, 1963; d. Harold and Barbara-Jean (Underwood) King; m. Vernon Ray Lofton, Mar. 3, 1984 (div. 1991); 1 child, Shatana Mailis Lofton; m. Marco Antonio Mitchell, July 27, 1991; 1 child, Dominique Amir Mitchell. BS in Bus., Fla. Internat. U., 1989; BSN in Nutrition, Am. Coll. Nutrition, Birmingham, Ala., 1993. Mgr. Amoco minimart, Miami, 1983-84; nail technician TKL Nails, Miami, 1988-90; office clk. Inst. Med. Specialties, Miami, 1990-91; nutritional cons. Quick Weight Loss Inc., Houston, 1993-95; assoc. Nature's Sunshine Products, Houston, 1993-94, Heart to Heart Nutritional Svc., 1995—, The Cottage Elem. Sch., 1995—. Mem. NAFE, Am. Naturopathic Med. Assn. Baptist. Avocations: reading, traveling, arts & crafts, music. Home: 16510 Rainbow Lake Rd Houston TX 77095-4066

MITCHELL, VIRGINIA BRINKMAN, office manager; b. New Brunswick, NJ, Jan. 20, 1949; d. Douglas Haig and Mary Alice (Cullinane) Brinkman; divorced; 1 child, Michael Joseph Mitchell. Cert., Durham Bus. Coll., Houston; student, Brevard C.C., Cocoa, Fla. Cert. profl. sec. Sec. ITT-Fed. Electric, Houston, 1968, Mullins Investments, Houston, 1968-69; exec. sec. U. Houston, 1969-79; adminstrv. asst. Tex. A&M U., Corpus Christi, 1979-88; sales coord. Hewlett-Packard, Corpus Christi, 1988-89; exec. sec., visitors svc. mgr. Tex. State Aquarium, Corpus Christi, 1989-91; office mgr. Unified Svcs., Inc., Kennedy Space Ctr., Fla., 1992—. Mem. Nat. Mgmt. Assn., Profl. Secs. Internat., Space Coast Pet Therapy Program, Phi Theta Kappa. Episcopalian. Avocations: landscaping, sailing, scuba diving, pet therapy. Home: 5575 Broad Acres Dr Merritt Island FL 32953-7507 Office: Unified Services Inc PO Box 21082 Kennedy Space Center FL 32815

MITCHELL, W. J. T., English language, literature and visual arts educator, editor; b. Anaheim, Calif., Mar. 24, 1942; s. Thomas Miles and Leona Marie (Gaertner) M.; m. Janice Misurell, Aug. 11, 1968; children: Carmen, Gabriel. B.A., Mich. State U., 1963; M.A., Johns Hopkins U., Ph.D., 1968. Asst. prof. Ohio State U., Columbus, 1968-73, assoc. prof., 1974-77; prof. English, art, and design U. Chgo., 1977-89, Gaylord Donnelley Disting. Svc. prof., 1989—, chair English dept., 1989-91; prof. Sch. Criticism and Theory Northwestern U., Evanston, Ill., 1983, Dartmouth Coll., 1990; vis. prof. Canterbury U., New Zealand, 1987, Beijing Fgn. Studies U., 1988, Aarhus (Denmark) U., 1995; editor Critical Inquiry U. Chgo. Press, 1978—. Author: Blake's Composite Art, 1978, Iconology, 1986, Picture Theory, 1994; editor: Language of Images, 1980 (outstanding issue of a learned jour. Conf. Editors Learned Jours. 1981), On Narrative, 1982, Politics of Interpretation, 1983, Against Theory, 1985, Art and the Public Sphere, 1992, Landscape and Power, 1994. Nat. Endowment Humanities fellow, 1976, 86; Guggenheim fellow, 1982; Am. Philos. Soc. grantee, 1967, 72; Fairchild Disting. scholar Calif. Inst. Tech., 1993; recipient Morey prize Coll. Art Assn., 1996. Mem. MLA, Am. Soc. 18th Century Studies, Conf. Editors Learned Jours., Johnson Soc., PEN (Poets, Editors, and Novelists), Acad. Lit. Studies. Democrat. Club: Quadrangle (Chgo.). Office: Critical Inquiry U Chgo 1050 E 59th St Chicago IL 60637-1512

MITCHELL, WAYNE LEE, health care administrator; b. Rapid City, S.D., Mar. 25, 1937; s. Albert C. and Elizabeth Isabelle (Nagel) M.; m. Marie Galletti; BA, U. Redlands (Calif.), 1959; MSW, Ariz. State U., 1970, EdD, 1979. Profl. social worker various county, state, and fed. agys., 1962-70, Bur. Indian Affairs, Phoenix, 1970-77, USPHS, 1977-79; asst. prof. Ariz. State U., 1979-84; with USPHS, Phoenix, 1984—. Bd. dirs. Phoenix Indian Cmty. Sch., 1973-75, ATLATL, 1995; bd. dirs. Phoenix Indian Ctr., 1974-79, Cmty. Svc. award, 1977; mem. Phoenix Area Health Adv. Bd., 1975; mem. Community Behavioral Mental Health Bd., 1976-80; mem. bd. trustees Heard Mus. of Anthropology, Phoenix, Ariz., 1996; mem. bd. dirs. Partnership for Cmty. Devel. Ariz. State U.-West, 1996—; lectr. in field. Bd. dirs. Cen. Ariz. Health Systems Agy.; mem. Fgn. Rels. Com. Phoenix. Served with USCG, 1960-62. Recipient Cmty. Svc. award Ariz. Temple of Islam, 1980, Ariz. State U., 1996, Dir. Excellence award Phoenix Area IHS Dir., 1992, 93. Mem. NASW, UN Assn., Am. Hosp. Assn., Am. Orthopsychiat. Assn., NAACP, Internat. Platform Assn., Asia Soc., U.S.-China Assn., Kappa Delta Pi, Phi Delta Kappa, Chi Sigma Chi, Nucleus Club. Congregationalist. Democrat. Contbr. articles to pubs. Home: PO Box 9592 Phoenix AZ 85068-9592 Office: 3738 N 16th St Phoenix AZ 85016-5947

MITCHELL, WILLIAM ALLEN, air force officer, political geography educator; b. Waco, Tex., Apr. 21, 1940; m. Joan Mary Woodill, May 31, 1958; children: Bill, Jim, John, Brian. BS in Geography and Bus., East Tex. State U., 1965; MA in Geography, UCLA, 1969; PhD in Geography, U. Ill., 1974. Commd. 2d lt. USAF, 1965, advanced through grades to col., 1986, ret., 1991; dir. intercultural edn. USAF Acad., 1980-83, prof., head geography, 1985-86, prof. nat. security affairs, 1986-88; seminar dir. Am. War Coll., 1987, Air War Coll.; assoc. prof. Baylor U., Waco, Tex., 1993; adj. faculty U. Md., 1970, U. Colo., Colorado Springs, 1975-80, Troy State U., Montgomery, 1979-80. Author: (with John Kolars) The Euphrates River and The Southeast Anatolia Development Project, 1991; contbr. articles to profl. jours. Decorated U.S. Legion of Merit, Bronze Star, Humanitarian award for Kurdish Relief Effort, Orgn. Excellence award, Vietnam Cross of Gallantry with bronze palm, Humanitarian award for Armenian Earthquake relief, Spl. Rsch. award for intercultural edn. Dept. Air Force; named Outstanding Young Man of Am., 1976; recipient rsch. and travel grants NSF Quick Response to Earthquakes, 1978, 80, 84, 92, 95, Inst. Turkish Studies, 1985, Atlantic Coun. of the U.S.-NATO DIscussion Series Assoc. to Brussels, 1988, German Marshall fund grant to Turkey, 1988, others. Mem. Phi Kappa Phi. Baptist. Home: 501 Brint Ln Waco TX 76706-6207 Office: Baylor Univ PO Box 97276 Waco TX 76798-7276

MITCHELL, WILLIAM B., electronics company executive; b. 1935; married. BSME, Lamar State Coll. Tech., 1958; MEEE, So. Meth. Univ., 1965. With Gen. Dynamics, Ft. Worth, 1958-61; system design engr. Tex. Instruments Inc., 1961-68, with advanced weapon design, 1968-76, with HARM missile design, 1976-77, mgr. HARM missile program, 1977-80, mgr. def. suppression, 1980-84, v.p., pres. def. system and electronic group, 1984-87, exec. v.p., pres. def. system and electronic group, 1987—; now vice chmn. office of the chief exec. Tex. Instruments; also bd. dirs. Tex. Instruments Inc. Office: Tex Instruments Inc 13500 N Central Expy Dallas TX 75243-1108*

MITCHELL, WILLIAM J., dean, architecture educator. BArch, U. Melbourne, Victoria, Australia, 1967; M of Environ. Design, Yale U., 1969; MA, U. Cambridge, Eng., 1977. Architect Yuncken-Freeman Architects, Melbourne, Australia, 1967-68; asst. prof. architecture, urban design UCLA, 1970-74, head architecture, urban design program, 1973-77, assoc. prof. architecture, urban design, 1974-80, prof. architecture, urban design, program headž, 1980-86; pres. The Urban Innovations Group, L.A., 1973-74; founding ptnr. The Computer-Aided Design Group, Marina Del Rey, Calif., 1978-91; prof. architecture Harvard U., Cambridge, Mass., 1986-89, dir. Master in Design Studies Program, 1986-92, G. Ware and Edythe M. Travelstead prof. architecture, 1989-92; prof. architecture and media arts & scis. MIT, Cambridge, Mass., 1992—, dean Sch. of Architecture and Planning, 1992—; vis. critic Yale U., New Haven, 1970-75, Tulane U., New Orleans, 1981; lectr. dept. architecture U. Cambridge, Eng., 1978-80; vis. prof. U. Calif., Berkeley, 1982, Carnegie-Mellon U., Pitts., 1979-83, U. Sydney, NSW, Australia, 1985; disting. vis. scholar U. Adelaide, South Australia. Author: (book) Computer-Aided Architecture Design, 1983, (with others) The Art of Computer Graphics Programming, 1987, (with others) The Poetics of Gardens, 1988, (with others) The Electronic Design Studio: Architectural Knowledge and Media in the Computer Era, 1990, The Logic of Architecture: Design, Computation and Cognition, 1990, The Reconfigured Eye: Visual Truth in the Post-Photographic Era, 1992, (with others) Digital Design Media, 2d edit., 1991, City of Bits: Space, Place, and the Infobahn, 1995; contbr. numerous articles to profl. jours. Fellow Royal Australian Inst. Architecture. Office: MIT 77 Massachusetts Ave Cambridge MA 02139-4301*

MITCHELL-CHAVEZ, BETTIANNE (BA MITCHELL-CHAVEZ), franchise executive; b. Washington, Nov. 27, 1952; d. Noriar and Marylou (Lenk) Pahigian; m. John J. Stabers (div.); 1 child, John Chad; m. Robert Franklin Chavez, Mar. 11, 1991; stepchildren: Andrea, Julia. BS in English cum laude, Suffolk U. Cert. Wilson sales trainer; cert. in Brian Tracy sales and sales mgmt. instrn.; cert. instr. internat. bus., sales mgmt. Sr. account rep. Letter Men Inc., pub., mktg., advt., Burlington, Mass., 1978-82; mgr. Boston sales br. The Boston Herald, 1982-83; telemktg. ter. mgr. Compugraphic Corp. div. AGFA Corp., Wilmington, Mass., 1983-85; pres., mktg. cons. Advance Inc., mktg., recruitment and search co., Marlboro, Mass., 1985-88; dir. sales devel. AlphaGraphics Printshops of Future Inc. affiliate R.R. Donnelly and Sons, Tucson, v.p. tng. and support, 1991-93, v.p. franchise devel., 1993-94; COO, software developer and licensor INVZN, 1994—; adj. bus. prof. Pima C.C.; presenter in field. Mem. ASTD, NAFE, AAUW, Ariz. Franchisor and Licensor Assn. (bd. dirs., program chairperson 1994—, licensor, liaison to Internat. Franchisor Assn. 1993—, pres.-elect, bd. dirs.), The Consortium, Inc. (CEO, founder). Avocations: networking, public speaking, travel, scuba diving, golf. Office: AlphaGraphics 3760 N Commerce Dr Tucson AZ 85705-6907 Address: 1338 N Palmsprings Dr Gilbert AZ 85234-8511

MITCHELSON, MARVIN M(ORRIS), lawyer; b. Detroit, May 7, 1928; s. Herbert and Sonia (Knoppow) M.; m. Marcella Ferri, Dec. 19, 1961; 1 child, Morgan. BA, UCLA, 1953; JD, Southwestern U., 1956. Bar: Calif. 1957, U.S. Supreme Ct. 1962. Pvt. practice law Beverly Hills, Calif., 1957-67, L.A., 1967—; numerous appearances as expert in family law on nat. TV, at bar assns. and law schs. Author: Made in Heaven, Settled in Court, 1976, Living Together, 1980. With USN, 1946-47. Mem. ABA, Century City Bar Assn., Assn. Trial Lawyers Am., Calif. Trial Lawyers Assn., Optimists Club (past pres. Hollywood). Jewish.

MITCHEM, MARY TERESA, publishing executive; b. Atlanta, Aug. 31, 1944; d. John Reese and Sara Letitia (Marable) Mitchem. BA in History, David Lipscomb Coll., 1966. Sch. and library sales mgr. Chilton Book Co., Phila., 1972-79; dir. market devel. Baker & Taylor Co. div. W.R. Grace, N.Y.C., 1979-81; dir. mktg. R.R. Bowker Co. div. Xerox Corp., N.Y.C, 1981-83, dir. mktg. research, 1983-85; mktg. mgr. W.B. Saunders Co. div. Harcourt, Brace & Jovanovich, Phila., 1985-87; mktg. dir. Congl. Quarterly Inc., Washington, 1987-89; dir. mktg. rsch. and devel. Bur. Nat. Affairs, Inc., Washington, 1990-96; account exec. Hughes Rsch. Corp., Rockville, Md., 1996—. Mem. Book Industry Study Group, Inc. (chairperson stats. com. 1984-86), Mktg. Research Assn., Soc. Competitive Intelligence Profls. Home: 4625 Tilden St NW Washington DC 20016-5617 Office: Hughes Rsch Corp 4 Research Pl Ste 140 Rockville MD 20850

MITCHUM, ROBERT CHARLES DURMAN (CHARLES MITCHUM), actor; b. Bridgeport, Conn., Aug. 6, 1917; m. Dorothy Spence, Mar. 16, 1940; children: Jim, Petrine, Chris. Ed., N.Y.C. pub. schs. Motion picture debut in Hopalong Cassidy film, 1944; producer, actor motion pictures including Nightkill, Thunder Road; film appearances include The Story of G.I. Joe, 1945, Undercurrent, 1946, Till the End of Time, 1946, Pursued Locket, 1947, Til the End of Time, 1946, Desire Me, 1947, Crossfire, 1947, Out of the Past, 1947, Rachel and the Stranger, 1948, Blood on the Moon, 1948, Red Pony, 1949, Where Danger Lives, 1950, My Forbidden Past, 1951, The Racket, 1951, Macao, 1952, The Lusty Men, 1952, One Minute to Zero, 1952, Angel Face, 1953, River of No Return, Track of the Cat, She Couldn't Say No, 1954, Not as a Stranger, 1955, The Night of the Hunter, 1955, The Man with the Gun, 1955, Bandido, 1956, Foreign Intrigue, 1956, Heaven Knows Mr. Allison, 1957, Fire Down Below, 1957, The Enemy Below, 1957, Thunder Road, 1958, The Hunters, 1958, The Angry Hills, 1959, The Wonderful Country, 1959, Home from the Hill, 1960, A Terrible Beauty, 1960, The Grass is Greener, 1960, The Sundowners, 1960, The Longest Day, 1962, Cape Fear, 1962, Two for the Seesaw, 1962, The List of Adrian Messenger, 1963, Rampage, 1963, Man in the Middle, 1964, What a Way to Go, 1964, Mr. Moses, 1965, The Way West, 1967, El Dorado, 1967, Anzio, 1968, Five Card Stud, 1968, Secret Ceremony, 1968, Villa Rides, 1968, Young Billy Young, 1969, The Good Guys and the Bad Guys, 1969, Ryan's Daughter, 1971, Wrath of God, 1972, The Friends of Eddie Coyle, 1973, The Yakusa, 1974, Battle of Midway, 1975, Farewell My Lovely, 1975, The Amsterdam Kill, 1975, The Last Tycoon, 1976, The Big Sleep, 1977, Matilda, 1978, That Championship Season, 1982, Breakthrough, 1984, The Ambassador, 1984, Maria's Lovers, 1985, Mr. North, 1988, Scrooged, 1988, Cape Fear (Martin Scorsese remake) 1991, Tombstone, 1994; TV appearances include The Hearts and Davies Affiar, Reunion at Fairborough, Promises to Keep, Thompson's Lost Run, Brotherhood of the Rose, 1989, Jake Spanner, Private Eye, 1989; starring role in TV mini-series The Winds of War, 1983, War and Remberance, 1988; TV series: A Family for Joe, 1990, Family Man, 1990. Subject of book: It Sure Beats Working, 1972. Office: Taylor and Lieberman 10866 Wilshire Blvd Los Angeles CA 90024-4300*

MITFORD, JESSICA, author; b. Batsford Mansion, Eng., Sept. 11, 1917; d. Lord and Lady Redesdale; m. Esmond Romilly, June 1937; 1 dau., Constancia; m. Robert Treuhaft, June 21, 1943; 1 son, Benjamin. Author: Life itselfmanship, 1956, Daughters and Rebels, 1960, The American Way of Death, 1963, The Trial of Dr. Spock, 1969, Kind and Usual Punishment-The Prison Business, 1973, A Fine Old Conflict, 1977, Poison Penmanship: The Gentle Art of Muckraking, 1979, Faces of Philip: A Memoir of Philip Toynbee, 1984, Grace Had an English Heart: The Story of Grace Darling, Heroine and Victorian Superstar, 1988, The American Way of Birth, 1992.

MITGANG, HERBERT, author, journalist; b. N.Y.C., Jan. 20, 1920; s. Benjamin and Florence (Altman) M.; m. Shirley Kravchick, May 13, 1945; children: Esther, Lee, Laura. LLB, St. John's Law Sch., 1942. Bar: N.Y. 1942. Sports stringer Bklyn. Eagle, 1938-39; screen writer Universal-Internat. Pictures, 1945; copy editor, reviewer N.Y. Times, N.Y.C., 1945-54; supervising editor Sunday Times drama sect., 1955-62; editorial writer, mem. editorial bd. N.Y. Times, 1963-64, 67-76, publishing, cultural corr., book critic, 1976-94; asst. to pres., exec. editor CBS News, 1964-67; instr. English evening divsn. CCNY, 1948-49; vis. lectr. English, guest fellow Silliman Coll., Yale U., 1975-76; lit. advisor White House Libr, 1977-81. Writer, prodr.: (film documentaries) Henry Moore: Man of Form, D-Day Plus 20 Years, Sandburg's Prairie Years, Degas Racing World (Duke Ellington score), Ben-Gurion on the Bible, Anthony Eden on Vietnam; author: Lincoln As They Saw Him, 1956, (novel) The Return, 1959, The Man Who Rode the Tiger: The Life and Times of Judge Samuel Seabury, 1963 (Gavel award ABA), Working for the Reader, 1970, (novel) Get These Men Out of the Hot Sun, 1972, The Fiery Trial: A Life of Lincoln, 1974, (novel) The Montauk Fault, 1981, (novel) Kings in the Counting House, 1983, Dangerous Dossiers: The Secret War Against America's Authors, 1988, Words Still Count With Me: A Chronicle of Literary Conversations, 1995; editor: Washington, D.C., in Lincoln's Time, 1958, Civilians Under Arms: Stars and Stripes, Civil War to Korea, 1996, The Letters of Carl Sandburg, 1968, America at Random, 1969, Spectator of America, 1971; (play) Mister Lincoln, 1980, Knight Errant, 1995; contbr. to the New Yorker, Art News, Am. Heritage, The Progressive. Mem. exec. bd. Newspaper Guild of N.Y., CIO, 1948-49. Served with counter-intelligence sect. 5th wing USAAF, 1942-43, MTO; Army corr., mng. editor Stars and Stripes, Oran-Casablanca and Sicily edits. 1943-45. Decorated six battle stars, Knight Order of Merit (Italy); recipient Human Rights award Newspaper Guild of N.Y., 1958, Broadcast Preceptor award San Francisco State Coll., 1970, Lincoln award Civil War Roundtable of N.Y., 1981, George Polk Career award L.I. U., 1993, 25 Yr. News Achievement award Soc. of Silurians, 1993, Lit. Lions award N.Y. Pub. Libr. Fellow Soc. Am. Historians (bd. dirs.); mem. Authors League (council 1962—, pres. fund 1976—), Dramatists Guild, Authors Guild (pres. 1971-75), Internat. P.E.N. (U.S. del. London). Jewish. Club: Century Assn. (N.Y.C.). Office: 203 E 72nd St New York NY 10021-4568

MITGANG, IRIS FELDMAN, lawyer, educator; b. Chgo., Sept. 2, 1937; d. Harry and Leanore (Nelson) Feldman; m. Robert Newton Mitgang, Sept. 9, 1956 (div. Dec. 1974); children: Alix Susan, Steven Ross, Jennifer Lynn. AB, U. Chgo., 1958; MA, U. Rochester, 1967; JD, U. Calif., Davis, 1976. Bar: Calif. 1976, U.S. Dist. Ct. (no. and ea. dists.) Calif.; cert. specialist family law. Ptnr. Dodge, Reyes, Brorby, Randall, Mitgang & Titmus, Walnut Creek, Calif., 1978-90; prin. Law Office Iris F. Mitgang, Walnut Creek, Calif., 1990—; instr. legal writing Sch. Law U. Calif., Davis, 1975-76; adj. prof. family law Sch. Law John F. Kennedy U., Walnut Creek, 1977-87, Sch. Law Golden Gate U., San Francisco, 1987; mem. pro tempore judges panel Contra Costa Superior Ct.; spkr. in field. Mem. editorial bd. Law Rev. U. Calif., Davis Sch. Law, 1976; contbr. various articles to profl. jours. Bd. dirs. Leadership Conf. Civil Rights, Washington, 1979-81, ACLU, Northern Calif.; founding mem. Rape Crisis Ctr. Contra Costa County. Recipient Woman of Yr. award Bus. and Profl. Women, 1979, Women's Leadership award State of Calif., 1980. Mem. State Bar Calif., Nat. Women's Polit. Caucus (nat. chair 1979-81, nat. adv. bd. chair 1981-85, vice chair 1977-79, politic. action chair 1977-79), Am. Acad. Family Mediators, Contra Costa Bar Assn. (co-chair fam. law mediation sect. 1992—), Calif. Women Lawyers, Alameda Contra Costa Trial Lawyers (bd. dirs. 1992-95, chair mentors program), Assn. Family and Conciliation Cts., Assn. Cert. Family Law Specialists, Calif. Dispute Resolution Coun., Soc. Profls. in Dispute Resolution. Democrat. Jewish. Office: Law Offices Iris F Mitgang 1850 Mount Diablo Blvd Ste 605 Walnut Creek CA 94596-4427

MITHOFF, RICHARD WARREN, lawyer; s. Richard Warren Sr. and Frances (Maas) M.; m. Virginia Lynn McTaggart; children: Michael Karl, Caroline Rebecca. BBA, U. Tex., 1968, JD, 1971. Bar: Tex., U.S. Supreme Ct. Law clk. U.S.Dist. (ea. dist.) Tex., Tyler, 1972-74; ptnr. Jamail, Kolius & Mithoff, Houston, 1974-83, Mithoff & Jacks, Houston, 1983—; guest speaker in U.S. and Can. Endowed Richard Warren Mithoff Professorship U. Tex. Fellow Houston Bar Found., Tex. Bar Found. (life), Am. Bd. Profl. Liability Attys.; mem. Am. Coll. Trial Lawyers, Internat. Soc. Barristers, Am. Bd. Trial Advocates, Houston Trial Lawyers Assn. (pres. 1986-87), Tex. Trial Lawyers Assn. (bd.dirs. 1982), Ass. Trial Lawyers Am., State Bar Tex. (com. pattern jury charges 1981—). Office: Mithoff & Jacks Penthouse 1 Allen Ctr Houston TX 77002

MITHUN, RAYMOND O., advertising agency executive, banker, real estate and insurance executive; b. Warren, Minn., Mar. 20, 1909; s. Louis and Alma (Anderson) M.; m. Doris Berg, Aug. 9, 1932; children—Lewis, John, Raymond, Jr. A.B., U. Minn., 1930. From printers devil to editor Buffalo Jour., 1922; bus. mgr., 1924; editor Minn. Daily, 1929; pub. Wright Co. Press, 1929-30; city editor Mankato (Minn.) Free Press, 1930; copywriter, radio dir., account exec. Batten, Barton, Durstine & Osborn, Inc., 1930-32; founder, chmn. Campbell-Mithun, Inc., Mpls., 1933; chmn. Mithun Enterprises; owner State Bank of Chanhassen, Minn. Admitted to Advtg. Hall Fame, 1989. Mem. Delta Upsilon, Sigma Delta Chi (Journalism award 1930). Clubs: Minneapolis, Minikahda (Mpls.); Tavern (Chgo.); Minnesota (St. Paul); El Dorado (Palm Desert), Thunderbird (Palm Desert); Woodhill Country (Wayzata, Minn.). Home: 630 Indian Mound St Wayzata MN 55391-1709 Office: 900 Wayzata Blvd E Wayzata MN 55391-1836

MITOVICH, JOHN, professional society administrator; b. Youngstown, Ohio, Feb. 8, 1927; s. John and Rose (Elieff) M.; m. Rebecca E. Webb, Aug. 1, 1953; children: Jon, Rosemary, Victoria, Janet, Martha, Matthew; m.

Mary Lou Brennan, Nov. 27, 1985; m. Nancy Lexow Reichard, July 14, 1990. B.S. in Journalism, Ohio U., 1951. Advt. and pub. relations specialist Gen. Electric Co., Schenectady, 1955-57, Pittsfield, Mass., 1957-58; pub. affairs specialist Gen. Electric Co., Lynn, Mass., 1958-62; mgr. community relations Gen. Electric Co., Johnson City, N.Y., 1962-64; cons. community and govt. relations Gen. Electric Co., N.Y.C., 1964-66; exec. v.p. Rockford (Ill.) C. of C., 1966-70; pres. Southwestern Area (Conn.) Assn. Commerce and Industry, 1970-90; pres., chief exec. officer Metropool Ridesharing Corp., 1980-85; vice chmn. Greater Stamford Conv. and Visitors Bur., 1987-90; pres. SACIA/West, Albuquerque, N.Mex., 1990—; lectr. econ. devel./western style U. Zagreb (Croatia) Sch. of Mgmt., 1991. Mem. bd. selectmen, North Reading, Mass., 1961-62, chmn. indsl. devel. commn., 1960-62; mem. Rockford Mayor's Urban Devel. Adv. Commn., 1966-68, Ill. Gov. Commn. on Urban Area Govt., 1969-70; founder-dir. Winnebago County (Ill.) Opportunities Industrialization Center, 1968-70, Met. Rockford Housing Devel. Corp., Forward Rockford, Inc., 1969-70; mem. Gov.'s Commn. Services and Expenditures, 1971; corp. chmn. N.Mex. Project Uplift, 1992; active N.Mex. Total Quality Mgmt. Coun. Task Force, 1992, Albuquerque Shared Vision Community Devel., 1993. Served with USMC, 1952-54. Recipient Gen. Electric Mgmt. award, 1958, Associated Industries Mass. award, 1958, Freedoms Found. disting. service award, 1965, Rockford Community Leadership award, 1970, Disting. Salesman's award Southwestern Conn. Sales and Mktg. Exec., 1974, Walter H. Wheeler Jr. Bus. Leadership award, 1990; Dwight B. Havens acad. scholar Acad. Orgn. Mgmt., 1976. Mem. Conn. Assn. C. of C. Execs. (v.p. 1979, pres. 1981-82), Greater Albuquerque C. of C. Republican. Methodist. Home: 6316 Wilmington Dr NE Albuquerque NM 87111-6424 *A good man isn't good for everything: knowing this is the best guide toward the pursuit of one's life goals.*

MITRA, SANJIT KUMAR, electrical and computer engineering educator; b. Calcutta, West Bengal, India, Nov. 26, 1935; came to U.S., 1958; MS in Tech., U. Calcutta, 1956; MS, U. Calif., Berkeley, 1960, PhD, 1962; D of Tech. (hon.), Tampere (Finland) U., 1987. Asst. engr. Indian Statis. Inst., Calcutta, 1956-58; from teaching asst. to assoc. Univ. Calif., Berkeley, 1958-62; asst. prof. Cornell U., Ithaca, N.Y., 1962-65; mem. tech. staff Bell Telephone Labs., Holmdel, N.J., 1965-67; prof. U. Calif., Davis, 1967-77; prof. elec. and computer engrng. U. Calif., Santa Barbara, 1977—, chmn. dept. elec. and computer engrng., 1979-82; dir. Ctr. for Info. Processing Rsch., 1993-96; cons. Lawrence Livermore (Calif.) Nat. Lab., 1974—; cons. editor Van Nostrand Reinhold Co., N.Y.C., 1977-88; mem. adv. bd. Coll. Engrng. Rice U., Houston, 1986-89; mem. adv. coun. Rsch. Inst. for Math. and Computing Sci., U. Groningen, The Netherlands, 1995—. Author: Analysis and Synthesis of Linear Active Networks, 1969, Digital and Analog Integrated Circuits, 1980; co-editor: Modern Filter Theory and Design, 1973, Two-Dimensional Digital Signal Processing, 1978, Miniaturized and Integrated Filters, 1989, Multidimensional Processing of Video Signals, 1992, Handbook for Digital Signal Processing, 1993. Named Disting. Fulbright Prof., Coun. for Internat. Exch. of Scholars, 1984, 86, 88, Disting. Sr. Scientist, Humboldt Found., 1989. Fellow AAAS, IEEE (Edn. award Crcts. and Systems Soc. 1988, disting. lectr. Crcts. and Systems Soc. 1991—, Tech. achievement award Signal Processing Soc. 1996), Internat. Soc. Optical Engring.; mem. Am. Soc. for Engrng. Edn. (F.E. Terman award 1973, AT&T Found. award 1985), European Assn. for Signal Processing. Achievements include patents for two-port newtorks for realizing transfer functions; nonreciprocal wave translating device; discrete cosine transform-based image coding and decoding method. Office: Univ Calif Dept Elec Computer Eng Santa Barbara CA 93106

MITRANO, JOSEPH CHARLES, school principal; b. Rochester, N.Y., Sept. 22, 1940; s. Charles V. and Anna Marie (Robinson) M. BA, St. John's Coll., 1963; MA, U. Detroit, 1967; STB, U. Toronto, Ont., Can., 1969; EdS. Cert. tchr., adminstr., Calif., ednl. specialist. Tchr. Cath. Cen. Sch., Detroit, 1965-70, counselor, 1970-75; dean St. John Fisher Coll., Rochester, 1976-84, tchr., 1980-84; counselor U. Toronto, 1985-86; prin. Bishop O'Dowd High Sch., Oakland, Calif., 1986—; bd. dirs. Elan Engrng., Novi, Mich., Fred M. Tinker, Inc., Fairport, N.Y. Mem. Assn. Secondary Sch. Prins., Nat. Assn. Sch. Pers. Adminstrs., Calif. Adminstrs. Assn., Basilian High Sch. Prins. (pres.), Oakland C. of C. Roman Catholic. Avocations: golf, traveling, antique cars. Office: Bishop O'Dowd High Sch 9500 Stearns Ave Oakland CA 94605-4720

MITSAKOS, CHARLES LEONIDAS, education educator, consultant; b. Lowell, Mass., Oct. 17, 1939; s. Leonidas A. and Vasiliki (Sampatakakis) M.; m. Stella Martakos, June 23, 1963; children: Charles L. Jr., Andria Estelle. BS in Edn., Lowell State Coll., 1961; EdM, Boston U., 1963, EdD, 1977. Tchr., team leader, social studies curriculum specialist Lexington (Mass.) Pub. Schs., 1961-67; social studies coord., cons. Chelmsford (Mass.) Pub. Schs., 1967-78; asst. supt. of schs. Andover (Mass.) Pub. Schs., 1978-83; supt. of schs. Winchester (Mass.) Pub. Schs., 1984-92; clin. faculty supr. Sch. Edn., Boston Coll., Chestnut Hill, Mass., 1992-93; prof. edn., chair dept. edn. Rivier Coll., Nashua, N.H., 1993—; ednl. cons. to schs. and sch. dists. in 15 states, U.S. V.I., U.S. Dept. Def. Dep. Schs. and Ministries of Edn., 1970—; dir. Mid. Sch. Staff Devel. Inst. for Social Desegregation Program, Fairfield county, S.C., 1972; mem. staff, lectr. in team tchg. and social studies edn. NSF Insts., Stanford U., Ind. U., SUNY, Geneseo, Xavier U., U. N.C., Boston U., 1968-75; sr. lectr. sch. adminstrn. and curriculum devel. Sch. Grad. Studies, Rivier Coll., Nashua, N.H., 1977-93, numerous others. Author, gen. editor: (multimedia program for elem. sch.) The Family of Man Social Studies Program, 1971-77; co-author: (textbooks) America! America!, 1977, revised 2d edit., 1987, Ginn Social Studies, 1987; author: (workbook) America! America! Workbook, 1982, (textbook) Earth's Geography and Environment, 1991; others. Mem. Profl. Stds. Bd. N.H. Dept. Edn., Fin. Com. and Steering Com. So. N.H. Sch. to Careers Partnership; past chmn. task force on teenagers and religious edn. Greek Orthodox Archdiocese of North and South Am.; former trustee U. Lowell; chairperson affirmative action com., chairperson com. to oversee U. Lowell Rsch. Found.; former mem. ad hoc budget com. Town of Winchester; former mem. bd. dirs., chairperson nominating com. and search com. for resident dirs. Andover Com. for A Better Chance; fund-raising chairperson, mem. edn. com., former trustee, newsletter editor local ch. Recipient Disting. Alumni award U. Lowell, Coll. of Edn., 1987. Democrat. Greek Orthodox. Avocations: writing travel articles, mosaic iconography, travel, reading. Office: Rivier Coll 420 Main St Nashua NH 03060-5043

MITSCHER, LESTER ALLEN, chemist, educator; b. Detroit, Aug. 20, 1931; s. Lester and Mary Athelda (Pounder) M.; m. Betty Jane McRoberts, May 29, 1953; children: Katrina, Kurt, Mark. B.S., Wayne U., 1953, Ph.D., 1958. Research scientist, group leader Lederle Labs., Pearl River, N.Y., 1958-67; prof. Ohio State U., Columbus, 1967-75, U. Kans., Lawrence, 1975—; chmn. dept. medicinal chemistry U. Kans., 1975-92; intersearch prof. Victorian Coll. of Pharmacy, Monash U., Melbourne, Australia, 1975—; cons. NIH, Am. Cancer Soc., Abbott Labs., Searle Labs. Author: (with D. Lednicer) The ORganic Chemistry of Drug Synthesis, Vol. 1, 1976, Vol. 2, 1980, Vol. 3, 1984, Vol. 4, 1990, The Chemistry of the Tetracycline Antibiotics, 1978; contbr. over 200 articles to profl. jours. Recipient Disting. Alumnus award Sch. Pharmacy, Wayne State U., 1980, Research Achievement award Acad. Pharm. Scis., 1980, Volweiler research award Am. Assn. Colls. Pharmacy, 1985, Higuchi-Simmons award U. Kans., 1986. Fellow AAAS; mem. Am. Soc. Pharmacognosy (pres. 1992-93), Am. Chem. Soc. (former chmn. councilor medicinal chemistry divsn., Bristol-Myers Smissman rsch. award 1989), Chem. Soc. London, Japanese Antibiotics Assn., Soc. Heterocyclic Chemistry, Internat. Union of Pure and Applied Chemistry (commr. medicinal chemistry divsn.), Internat. Orgn. for Chemistry in Developing Countries (steering com.). Presbyterian. Office: Dept Medicinal Chemistry U Kans Lawrence KS 66045-2506

MITSEFF, CARL, lawyer; b. Detroit, Nov. 16, 1928; s. Frank H. and Katherine (Schaffer) M.; m. Phyllis Schlitters, June 28, 1952; children: C. Randall, Bradley Scott, Julie, Emily, Faye. B.S., Wayne State U., 1952, LL.B., 1955. Bar: Mich. 1956. Practiced in Detroit, 1956—; staff atty. Burroughs Corp., 1955-60; mem. firm LeVasseur, Mitseff, Egan & Capp, 1960-80, Mitseff & Baril, 1980-85, Fitzgerald, Hodgman, Cox, Cawthoren & McMahon, 1986-90, Cox & Hodgman, 1990—; spl. asst. atty. gen. State of Mich.; lectr. in field. Mem. ABA, State Bar Mich., Internat. Assn. Ins. Counsel, Internat. Assn. Indsl. Accident Bds. and Commns., Detroit Athletic Club (bd. dirs.), Beavers (pres.), Lochmoor Club, Grosse Pointe Yacht Club, Pi Kappa Alpha, Delta Theta Phi. Home: 612 N Brys Dr Grosse Pointe MI 48236-1247 Office: 1000 First Federal Bldg Detroit MI 48226

MITSTIFER, DOROTHY IRWIN, honor society administrator; b. Gaines, Pa., Aug. 17, 1932; d. Leonard Robert and Laura Dorothy (Crane) Irwin; m. Robert Mitchell Mitsifer, June 17, 1956 (dec. Aug. 1984); children: Kurt Michael, Brett Robert. BS, Mansfield U., 1954; MEd, Pa. State U., 1972, PhD, 1976. Cert. home economist. Tchr. Tri-County High Sch., Canton, Pa., 1954-56, Loyalsock Twp. Sch. Dist., Williamsport, Pa., 1956-63; exec. dir. Kappa Omicron Phi, Williamsport, Pa., 1964-86, Kappa Omicron Phi, Omicron Nu, Haslett, Mich., 1986-90, Kappa Omicron Nu, East Lansing, Mich., 1990—; prof. continuing edn. Pa. State U., University Park, 1976-80; prof. Mansfield (Pa.) U., 1980-86, pres.'s intern, 1984-86. Editor Kappa Omicron Nu Forum, 1986—; contbr. articles to profl. jours. Pres., bd. dirs. Profl. Devel. Ctr. Adv. Bd., Vocat. Edn., Pa. State U., 1980-86. Mem. ASCD, Am. Home Econs. Assn., Mich. Home Econs. Assn. (exec. dir. 1986—), Am. Vocat. Assn., Am. Soc. Assn. Execs., Nat. Soc. Fund Raising Profls., Coll. Edn. Alumni Soc. Pa. State U. (pres. 1986-88, bd. dirs. 1980-90), Kappa Delta Pi. Avocations: sewing, camping, fishing. Home: 1425 Somerset Close St East Lansing MI 48823-2435 Office: Kappa Omicron Nu 4990 Northwind Dr Ste 140 East Lansing MI 48823-5031

MITTAL, MANMOHAN, electronic design automation engineer; b. Muzaffarnagar, India, Sept. 5, 1950; came to U.S., 1981; s. Keder Nath and Prakash (Wati) M.; m. Shashi Rani, Jan. 28, 1976; children: Vivek, Vibhav. BSEE, Inst. Tech. Banaras Hindu U., Varanasi, India, 1971; MASEE, U. Ottawa, Ont., Can., 1981; PhD in Elec. and Computer Engrng., Wash. State U., 1984. Electronics engr. IIMS Banaras Hindu U., 1971-73; design engr. Bharat Heavy Elecs. Ltd., Haridwar, India, 1973-79; grad. rsch./teaching asst. Wash. State U., Pullman and U. Ottawa, 1979-84; DA mgr. CAE design automation Silicon Systems, Inc., Tustin, Calif., 1984-88; mgr. std. cell design automation Vitesse Semiconductor Corp., Camarillo, Calif., 1988-94; sole proprietor, cons. 2M Soft Tech. Group, Thousand Oaks, Calif., 1994-96; dir. corp. design automation C-Cube Micro Systems, Milpitas, Calif., 1996—. Contbr. tech. papers to profl. jours. U. medal Inst. Tech., Banaras Hindu U., 1972; fellow U. Ottawa, 1979-81; grantee Wash. State U., 1981-84. Mem. IEEE (sr., sec. exec. com. Orange County chpt. 1985-88, mem. tech. program. com., custom integrated cirs. conf. 1988-94, bipolar circuits and tech. conf. 1985-90), N.Y. Acad. Scis., Assn. Computing Machines, Sigma Xi, Tau Beta Pi. Hindu. Achievements include patent for Incremental Hierarchical Netlist Extraction Tool. Avocations: traveling, badminton, tennis. Office: C-Cube Micro Systems 1778 McCarthy Blvd Milpitas CA 95035

MITTEL, JOHN J., economist, corporate executive; b. L.I., N.Y.; s. John and Mary (Leidolf) M.; 1 child, James C. B.B.A., CUNY. Researcher econs. dept. McGraw Hill & Co., N.Y.C.; mgr., asst. to pres. Indsl. Commodity Corp., J. Carvel Lange Inc. and J. Carvel Lange Internat., Inc., 1956-64, corp. sec., 1958-86, v.p., 1964-80, exec. v.p., 1980-86; pres. I.C. Investors Corp., 1972—, I.C. Pension Adv., Inc., 1977—; bd. dir. several corps.; plan adminstr., trustee Combined Indsl. Commodity Corp. and J. Carvel Lange Inc. Pension Plan, 1962-86, J. Carvel Lange Internat. Inc. Profit Sharing Trust, 1969-86, Combined Indsl. Commodity Corp. and J. Carvel Lange Inc. Employees Profit Sharing Plan, 1977-86. Mem. grad. adv. bd. Bernard M. Baruch Coll., CUNY, 1971-72. Mem. Conf. Bd., Am. Statis. Assn., Newcomen Soc. N.Am. Club: Union League (N.Y.C.). Co-author: How Good A Sales Profit Are You, 1961, The Role of the Economic Consulting Firm. Office: 10633 St Andrews Rd Boynton Beach FL 33436-4714

MITTELSTADT, CHARLES ANTHONY, advertising executive; b. Eau Claire, Wis., Mar. 19, 1918; s. Frederick William and Pearl (White) M.; m. Angelica Farber, Feb. 20, 1957; children—Nancy Lee, Charles Anthony II, Monica, Simone. B.S., U. Wis., 1942, postgrad., 1945-47; grad., Advanced Mgmt. Program, Harvard, 1960. Radio announcer sta. WIBA, Madison, Wis., 1945-47; account exec. Foote, Cone & Belding, Chgo., 1948-52, Campbell-Mithun, Chgo., 1953-54; mktg. dir. Tatham-Laird, Chgo., 1955-56; exec. v.p. The Marschalk Co., N.Y.C., 1957-64, also bd. dirs.; chmn. plans bd., mgr. Interpub. Group Cos., Inc., Frankfurt, Germany, 1964-66; pres., chief operating officer Erwin Wasey, Inc., Los Angeles, 1967-69; sr. v.p., mgr. Ctr. for Advt. Services Interpub. Group of Cos., Inc., 1969-92, cons., 1991—. Trustee, v.p. N.Y. Foundling Hosp., 1979—. Mem. Wis. Alumni Club, Harvard Alumni Club, N.Y. Athletic Club (N.Y.C.), Westchester Country Club (bd. govs., v.p. 1988-93), Am. Yacht Club. Home: 12 Griswold Rd Rye NY 10580-1802 *Be your own person, do your own thinking. Always give something back to those less fortunate.*

MITTELSTAEDT, GERARD E., library director; b. Sheboygan, Wis., Jan. 27, 1948; s. Arthur R. and Gelane M. (Merget) M.; m. Mona S. Althaus, May 18, 1985; 1 child, Jennifer S. BA in Geography, U. Tex., 1970, MLS, 1978. Reference libr. McAllen (Tex.) Meml. Libr., 1978, head audio/video svcs., 1979, asst. dir., 1979, dir., 1980—; mem. planning com. South Tex. Libr. System, Corpus Christi, 1980—; chmn., adv. Hidelgo County Libr. System, McAllen, 1985-86. Mem. Am. Libr. Assn, Tex. Libr. Assn., Valley Libr. Assn. (pres. 1987-88), Joshua Slocum Soc. (life), Beta Phi Mu. Roman Catholic. Avocation: sailing. Home: 2011 Daffodil Ave Mcallen TX 78501-6157 Office: 601 N Main St Mcallen TX 78501-4638

MITTEMEYER, BERNHARD THEODORE, university official, surgeon, retired army officer; b. Paramaribo, Suriname, Oct. 30, 1930; (parents Am. citizens).; s. John Frederick and Hannah (Roy) M.; children: Thomas Theodore, Jan Charles, Robert James, Sarah Ann. BS in Biology, Moravian Coll., 1952, LLD (hon.), 1982; MD, Temple U., 1956; student, Army Med. Field Svc. Sch., Ft. Sam Houston, Tex., 1957, Command and Gen. Staff Coll., Ft. Leavenworth, Kans., 1961, Army Sr. Svc. Coll., Carlisle, Pa., 1970; DSc (hon.), Wm. Jewell Coll., 1985. Diplomate Am. Bd. Urology, Am. Bd. Quality Assurance and Utilization Rev. Physicians. Intern Santa Barbara (Calif.) Cottage and County Hosps., 1956-57; commd. lt. U.S. Army, 1957; advanced through grades to lt. gen., 1981, ret., 1985; bn. surgeon, div. surgeon 101st Airborne Div., Fort Campbell, Ky., 1957-59; resident, gen. surgery Fitzsimons Army Med. Ctr., Denver, 1959-61; resident urol. surgery Tripler Army Med. Ctr., Honolulu, 1962-65; asst. chief urology svc. Walter Reed Army Med. Ctr., Washington, 1971-74, chief, 1974-76, chief dept. surgery and urology svc., 1976-77; clin. prof. surgery (urology), Dept. Surgery Uniformed Svc. U. of the Health Scis., Bethesda, Md., 1976—; comdr. U.S. Army, Med. Command U.S. Army Hosp. Eighth Army, Seoul, Republic of Korea, 1977-78, chief med. corps affairs, 1978-80; comdg. gen. Walter Reed Army Med. Ctr., Washington, 1980-81; surgeon gen. Dept. of Army, Washington, 1981-85, ret.; sr. v.p., corp. med. dir. Whittaker Health Svcs., Los Angeles, 1985-86; exec. v.p., provost Tex. Tech U Health Scis Ctr., Lubbock, 1986—, prof. surgery, 1986—, interim dean Sch. Medicine, 1988-90; vis. prof., guest lectr. in urology Georgetown U., U. Mo., U. Pitts., Korea U., Pa. State U., U. Mass., U. Va., N.C. Bowman Gray Sch. Medicine, Armed Forces Inst. Pathology, Walter Reed Army Inst. Rsch., 1975—; cons. in urology to U.S. Army Surgeon Gen., 1974-77; pres. selection bd. for grad. med. edn., U.S. Army Med. Dept., 1978-80; clin. and nonclin. presentations to med. congresses, seminars, univs.; mem. med. adv. com. to Spl. Com. on Post-Secondary Med., Dental and Allied Health Edn., 1987-88. Contbr. articles to profl. jours.; producer films and exhibits. Med. adv. com. to Climate for Econ. Vitality Task Force of Tex. Strategic Econ. Policy Commn., 1988; advisor to bd. regents Uniformed Svcs. U. of Health Scis., Bethesda, Md., 1980-81, mem. ex officio, 1981-85; bd. commrs. U.S. Soldiers' and Airmen's Home, Washington, 1981-85; bd. trustees Moravian Coll., 1982-86; bd. dirs. Lubbock Symphony Orch., Sci. Spectrum, Lubbock Conv. and Visitors Bur. Decorated D.S.M., Legion of Merit with oak leaf cluster, D.F.C, Meritorious Svc. medal, Bronze Star with V device for valor, Air medal with oak leaf cluster, Army Commendation medal, Vietnam Campaign Ribbon with three campaign stars, Comenius award Moravian Coll., 1978, Founders medal Assn. Mil. Surgeons, 1978, Alumni Achievement award in health policy, Temple U. Sch. Medicine, 1988. Fellow Am. Coll. Physician Execs. (mem. coun. 1989—, bd. dirs. 1986-88, v.p. bd. regents 1988), ACS (N. Tex. chpt.), Am. Coll. Quality Assurance and Utilization Rev. Physicians; mem. AMA (ho. dels. 1981-85), Tex. Med. Assn. (cons. coun. med. edn. 1987—), Lubbock-Crosby-Garza County Med. Soc., Am. Urol. Assn. (South Cen. sect.), Soc. Gov. Svc. Urologists, Soc. Univ. Urologists, Uniformed Svcs. U. Surg. Assocs., Am. Acad. Med. Dirs., Soc. Med. Cons. to Armed Forces, Assn. of U.S. Army, AF Assn., Lubbock C. of C., (Armed Svc. com. 1988—), Sci. Spectrum, Lubbock (bd. dirs. 1988—). Republican. Methodist. Home: PO Box 65285 Lubbock TX 79464-5285 Office: Tex Tech U Health Scis Ctr 3601 4th St Lubbock TX 79430-0001

MITTEN, DAVID GORDON, classical archaeologist; b. Youngstown, Ohio, Oct. 26, 1935; s. Joe Atlee and Helen Louise (Boyd) M.; children: Claudia Antonia Sabina, Eleanor Elizabeth. BA, Oberlin Coll., 1957; MA in Classical Archaeology, Harvard U., 1958, PhD in Classical Archaeology, 1962. Instr. dept. fine arts Harvard U., Cambridge, Mass., 1962-64, Francis Jones asst. prof. classics, 1964-68, assoc. prof., 1968-69, James Loeb prof. classical art and archaeology, 1969—, curator ancient art Harvard U. Art Mus., 1976—; assoc. dir. Harvard-Cornell Sardis Expdn., 1976—; Whitehead vis. prof. archaeology Am. Study of Classical Studies, Athens, Greece, 1990-91. Author: (with S.F. Doeringer) Master Bronzes from the Classical World, 1967, Classical Bronzes: Mus. Art, RISD, 1975, (with Arielle P. Kozloff) The Gods Delight: The Human Figure in Classical Bronze, Cleve. Mus. Art, 1988. Woodrow Wilson fellow Harvard U., 1958; Fulbright fellow Am. Sch. Classical Studies at Athens, 1959-60; Archaeol. Inst. Am. Olivia James fellow, 1969-70; John Simon Guggenheim Found. fellow, 1976-77. Mem. Archaeol. Inst. Am., Assn. Field Archaeology (co-founder), Am. Schs. Oriental Rsch., Brit. Sch. Archaeology (Athens, Greece), Am. Numismatic Soc. Office: Sackler Mus 316 Harvard Univ 485 Broadway Cambridge MA 02138-3802

MITTENDORF, ROBERT, physician, epidemiologist; b. Ironton, Ohio, Aug. 6, 1943; s. Robert William and Martha Jane (Whitley) M.; m. Marguerite Jean Herschel, Nov. 10, 1980; children: Jeffrey David, Robert William II, Inga. BS, Ohio State U., 1966; MD, U. Ky., 1974; MPH, Harvard U., 1987, D Pub. Health, 1991. Diplomate Am. Bd. Ob-Gyn. Attending physician St. Margaret's Hosp., Boston, 1977-87; chief of surgery Winthrop (Mass.) Hosp., 1986-88; project dir., collaborative breast cancer study Harvard U., Boston, 1989-91; dir. Office Clin. Rsch. Tufts Sch. Medicine, Boston, 1991-92; dir. health studies, dept. ob-gyn. U. Chgo., 1992—; mem. scientific adv. group anti-epileptic drugs in pregnancy, Research Triangle Park, N.C., 1993—; cons. Nat. Ctrs. for Disease Control and Prevention, Atlanta, 1994—; mem. bd. mgrs., U. Chgo. Health Plan, Chgo., 1994—; manuscript reviewer for Jour. of the AMA, Chgo., 1992—. Author: Control of Transmissible Diseases in Health Care, 1995; contbr. articles to profl. jours. Med. dir. Cambridge Econ. Opportunity Com., 1977-78. Capt. USAF, 1966-70. Mem. AMA, Soc. Perinatal Obs., Soc. Epidemiol. Rsch. Democrat. Achievements include devel. of a linear regression model that permits the more precise determination of the estimated date of confinement in pregnant women; discovery that strenuous phys. activity is associated with a reduced risk of breast cancer, using a multivariate logistic regression model. Through statis. meta-analysis, discovered that certain prophylactic antibiotics are highly efficacious in preventing the serious infections associated with total abdominal hysterectomy. Home: 5244 South Greenwood Ave Chicago IL 60615 Office: Chgo Lying-In Hosp MC2050 5841 S Maryland Ave Chicago IL 60637

MITTERMEIER, JANICE, commercial airport executive. Airport dir. John Wayne Airport, Costa Mesa, Calif. Office: John Wayne Airport Orange County 3151 Airway Ave Bldg K-101 Costa Mesa CA 92626-4607

MITTERMEYER, BERNHARD T., dean. Interim dean Tex. Tech. U. Health Sci. Ctr., Lubbock. Office: Tex Tech U Health Sci Ctr 3601 4th St Lubbock TX 79430*

MITTERMILLER, JAMES JOSEPH, lawyer; b. Washington, Apr. 13, 1953; s. Jack and Alice Marie (Froeba) M.; m. Elizabeth Gaillard Simons, June 23, 1979; children: Samuel Stoney, Paul Andrew, Laurie Alice, Claire Mary. Student, U. Heidelberg, 1973-74; BA, Claremont Men's Coll., 1975; JD, U. Calif. Berkeley, 1978. Bar: Calif., U.S. Dist. Ct. (so., ctrl. and ea. dists.) Calif., U.S. Ct. Appeals (9th cir.), U.S. Supreme Ct. Assoc. Sheppard, Mullin, Richter & Hampton, L.A., 1978-86, ptnr., 1986—; panelist Calif. Continuing Edn. of Bar, L.A. and San Diego, 1984—. Dir. Legal Aid Soc. of San Diego, 1990—. Recipient Wiley Manuel Pro Bono award Calif. State Bar, 1992. Mem. Assn. Bus. Trial Lawyers, Am. Inns of Ct., Claremont McKenna Coll. Alumni Assn. San Diego (bd. dirs.). Avocations: swimming, surfing. Office: Sheppard Mullin Richter & Hampton 501 W Broadway 19th Fl San Diego CA 92101

MITTLEBERG, ERIC MICHAEL, pharmaceutical administrator; b. N.Y.C., Nov. 7, 1951; s. Irving Ralph and Rose (Schneider) M.; m. Jane Susan Baumoehl, Dec. 25, 1977; children: Alyson, Lauren. BS in Pharmacy, St. Johns U., Jamaica, N.Y., 1974, MS in Ind. Pharmaceutics, 1978, PhD in Pharmaceutics, 1982. Registered pharmacist, N.Y. Assoc. scientist Hoffmann-LaRoche Inc., Nutley, N.J., 1974-78; dept. head process improvement Lederle Labs, Pearl River, N.Y., 1978-83; mgr. mfg. devel. Key Pharm., Miami, Fla., 1983-86; dir. prodn., tech. svcs. Schering Labs, Miami, 1986-89; sr. dir. pharm. devel./tech. svcs. worldwide R.W. Johnson Pharm. Rsch. Inst., Raritan, N.J., 1989—. Mem. Internat. Soc. Pharm. Engrs., Acad. Pharm. Sci., Am. Pharm. Assn. Office: RW Johnson Pharm Rsch Inst Rt 202 Box 300 Raritan NJ 08869

MITTLER, DIANA (DIANA MITTLER-BATTIPAGLIA), music educator and administrator, pianist; b. N.Y.C., Oct. 19, 1941; d. Franz and Regina (Schilling) Mittler; m. Victor Battipaglia, Sept. 5, 1965 (div. 1982). BS, Juilliard Sch., 1962, MS, 1963; DMA, Eastman Sch. Music, 1974. Choral dir. William Cowper Jr. High Sch. and Springfield Gardens Jr. High Sch., Queens, N.Y., 1963-68, coordinator of music Flushing High Sch., Queens, 1968-79; asst. prin. music Bayside High Sch., Queens, 1979-86; assoc. prof. music Lehman Col. CUNY, 1986-87, prof., 1987—, choral dir., 1986—; dir. ednl. projects New World Records, 1987—; ednl. cons. Flushing Coun. on Culture and the Arts; cons. Sta. WNET; assoc. condr. Queens Borough-Wide Chorus, 1964-70; pianist, founder Con Brio Chamber Ensemble, 1978; faculty So. Vt. Music Festival, 1979-83; soloist with N.Y. Philharmonic, 1956; solo and chamber music appearances; examiner N.Y.C. Bd. Edn. Bd. Exams., 1985—. Author: 57 Lessons for the High School Music Class, 1983, Franz Mittler: Austro-American Composer, Musician and Humourous Poet, 1993. Choral dir. and accompanist various charitable, religious, mil., civic holiday functions. N.Y. State Regents scholar, 1958-62; scholarships, Juilliard Sch. and Eastman Sch. Music. Contbr. articles to music publs.; performance Internat. Summer Acad. Mozarteum, Salzburg, Austria, 1995. Mem. Golden Key Soc., Am. Choral Dirs. Assn., Music Edn. Nat. Conf., Sonneck Soc. Democrat. Home: 10857 66th Ave Flushing NY 11375-2247 Office: Lehman Coll Music Dept Bedford Pk Blvd W Bronx NY 10468

MITZELFELD, JIM, lawyer, journalist; b. Royal Oak, Mich., Apr. 26, 1961; s. Thomas Henry and Audrey Mae (Howard) M.; m. Lisa Jeanne Grayson, Sept. 28, 1985. BA in Journalism, Mich. State U., 1984; JD, U. Mich., 1996. Intern newspaper reporter The Times, Hammond, Ind., 1981; editor-in-chief The State News, East Lansing, Mich., 1982-83; intern reporter Democrat & Chronicle, Rochester, N.Y., 1983; newspaper reporter The Oakland Press, Pontiac, Mich., 1984-85, The Flint (Mich.) Jour., 1985-86, UP Internat., Lansing, 1986, AP, Lansing, 1986-88, The Detroit News, Dearborn, Mich., 1988-90; state capitol reporter The Detroit News, Lansing, 1990-93; intern law clk. to Judge David W. McKeague U.S. Dist. Ct. for We. Dist. Mich., 1994; summer assoc. Butzel Long, Lansing, 1994; law clk. Holland & Hart, Denver, 1995, Miller, Confield, Lansing, Mich., 01995; law clk. to Judge David W. McKeague U.S. Dist. Ct. (we. dist.) Mich., 1996—. Polit. commentator Off the Record Pub. TV, 1986-93. Recipient Nat. Best of Gannett Runner-up award, 1991, Top Well Done prize Best of Gannett, 1993, 2d place prize Mich. Assn. Press Editl. Assn., 1994, Pulitzer prize for beat reporting, 1994; honored by Mich. State Senate for pub. svc., 1993. Mem. Soc. Profl. Journalists (Journalist of Yr. Detroit Chpt. 1994), Mich. State U. Alumni Assn., State News Alumni Assn. (pres., co-founder 1991-93). Episcopalian. Avocations: travel, golf, photography, videography, hockey. Home: 1905 Anderson Ave Ann Arbor MI 48104-4747 Office: U Mich 5395 Wild Oak Dr East Lansing MI 48823-7252

MITZNER, KENNETH MARTIN, electrical engineering consultant; b. Bklyn., May 7, 1938; s. Louis Bernard and Dora (Sandler) M.; m. Ruth Maria Osorio, Dec. 26, 1968; children: Camille Lorena, Esther Jeannette, Sharon Michelle. BS, MIT, 1958; MS, Calif. Inst. Tech., 1959, PhD, 1964. Mem. tech. staff Hughes Aircraft, Malibu, Calif., 1959-64; prin. engr. B-2 divsn. Northrop Corp., Pico Rivera, Calif., 1964-94; owner Mitzner Sci. and Tech., Torrance, Calif., 1995—; instr. U. Calif., Santa Barbara, 1964-65; lectr. in field. Author: (handbook) Demonstrations Against Abortion & Death Selection, 1970; contbr. articles to profl. jours. Pres. Mobilization for the Unnamed, Torrance, Calif., 1970—; bd. dirs. Ams. United for Life, 1971-94, Nat. Right to Life Com., 1980-81, Jewish Life Issues Com., Solana Beach, 1983—; sec. Calif. Pro Life Coun., Sacramento, 1972; mem. L.A. County Select Citizens Com. on Life Support Policies, L.A., 1983-85;. Named Patron of Life Calif. Pro Life Coun., 1976, Pres's award, 1979; Howard Hughes fellow, 1959-64; grantee Fullbright Found., Govt. Italy, 1961-62. Fellow IEEE; mem. U.S. Nat. Commn. Internat. Union Radio Sci. (del. to 20th gen. assembly), Electromagnetics Acad. Avocations: historic research, stamp collecting.

MIURA, AKIO, quality assurance professional; b. Tokyo, Oct. 7, 1936; s. Takeshi and Sakiko (Andoh) M.; m. Takako Nakatani, Apr. 14, 1968; 1 child, Masahiro. BS, Waseda U., Tokyo, 1959. Cert. quality auditor; registered lead auditor; lead assessor. Staff Mitsubishi Corp., Tokyo, 1959-75; mgr. indsl. machinery Mitsubishi Corp., 1975-78, asst. gen. mgr. indsl. machinery, 1984-90; exec. dir. Kinka Kikai Co., Gifu, Japan, 1978-84; sr. cons. N.C. Kist & Assocs., Inc., Naperville, Ill., 1990—; pres. Internat. Quality Systems, Inc., Tokyo, 1990—. Author: Guide for Preparation of Quality Manual, 1992, Practice of ISO 9000, 1994.; contbr. articles to profl. jours. Mem. ASME, Am. Soc. Qulaity Control (sr.), Internat. Quality Inst. (chmn.). Avocations: baseball, chinese boxing, karate, fencing, classical music. Home and Office: 3-24-14-703 Shimo meguro, Meguroku 153, Japan

MIURA, ROBERT MITSURU, mathematician, researcher, educator; b. Selma, Calif., Sept. 12, 1938; emigrated to Can., 1975; s. Richard Katsuki and Frances Yoneko (Yukutake) M.; m. Kathryn Bannai; children: Derek Katsuki, Brian Robert, Jared Bannai Nagae, Sean Takeo. BS, U. Calif.-Berkeley, 1960, MS, 1962; MA, Princeton U., 1964, PhD, 1966. Rsch. assoc. Princeton U. Plasma Physics Lab., 1965-67; assoc. rsch. scientist Courant Inst. Math. Sci., N.Y.C., 1967-68; asst. prof. math. NYU, 1968-71; assoc. prof. math. Vanderbilt U., 1971-75; assoc. prof. math. U. B.C., Vancouver, B.C., Can., 1975-78, prof., 1978—; chmn. joint com. on math. in life scis. Am. Math. Soc.-Soc. Indsl. and Applied Math., 1981-84; bd. dirs. Soc. for Math. Biology, 1995—. Editor: Backlund Transformations, 1976, Nonlinear Phenomena in Physics and Biology, 1981, Some Mathematical Questions in Biology-Neurobiology, 1982, Muscle Physiology, 1986, DNA Sequence Analysis, 1986, Plant Biology, 1986; assoc. editor Can. Applied Math. Quar., Japan Jour. Indsl. and Applied Math.; adb. bd. Jour. Math. Biology; co-editor-in-chief Methods and Applications of Analysis; contbr. articles to profl. jours. Mem. steering com. Ctr. Math. Rsch., U. Montreal, 1990-94. John Simon Guggenheim fellow, 1980-81; U. B.C. hon. Killam fellow, 1980-81. Fellow Royal Soc. Can.; mem. AAAS, Am. Math. Soc., Soc. Indsl. and Applied Math., Can. Applied Math. Soc., Can. Math. Soc., Soc. Math. Biology, Pacific Inst. Math. Sci. (interim exec. bd. 1996), Sigma Xi. Office: U BC Dept Math, 1984 Mathematics Rd, Vancouver, BC Canada V6T 1Z2

MIXON, ALAN, actor; b. Miami, Fla., Mar. 15, 1933; s. James E. and Matilda (Beers) M. Student, U. Miami, 1951-52. Appeared in: premiere prodn. play Sweet Bird of Youth, Miami, 1956, N.Y.C., 1956; appeared in: premiere prodn. play View from the Bridge, Chgo. and San Francisco, 1957, 59, Royal Hunt of the Sun, Broadway and Hollywood, 1966; New York prodns. include Suddenly Last Summer, 1958, Desire Under the Elms, 1963, Trojan Women, 1963-64, The Alchemist, 1964, Sign in Sidney Brustein's Window, 1964-65, The Child Buyer, 1964-65, The Devils, 1965-66, A Whitman Portrait, 1966, Black Comedy, 1966-67, Unknown Soldier and His Wife, 1967, Iphegenia in Aulis, 1967-68, Love Suicide at Schofield Barracks, 1972, Small Craft Warnings, 1972, Mourning Becomes Electra, 1972, Equus, 1974-75, Benito Cereno, 1976; London prodn. Whitman Portrait, 1969; TV appearances include Theatre in America. Served with AUS, 1953-54.

MIXON, DEBORAH LYNN BURTON, elementary school educator; b. Charleston, S.C., Mar. 26, 1956; d. Harold Boyd and Peggy Wynell (Seagraves) Burton; m. Steven Douglas Schmidt (div. Mar. 1982); 1 child, Julie Ann Schmidt; m. Timothy Lamar Mixon, Oct. 11, 1982; children: Phillip Lamar, Catherine Elizabeth. BS in Edn., U. Ga., 1994. Cert. early childhood educator, Ga. Office coord. Morrison's Cafeteria, Athens, Ga., 1974-76; cashier Winn-Dixie, Athens, 1976-78; data entry clk. Athens Tech. Data Ctr., 1978-79; adminstrv. sec. U. Ga., Athens, 1980-86; sec. to plant mgr. Certain Teed Corp., Athens, 1986-87; s. adminstrv. sec. U. Ga., Athens, 1987-93; tchr. 4th grade Hall County Sch. Sys., Gainesville, Ga., 1994—. Leader Cub Scouts den Boy Scouts Am., 1993-94; troop vol. Girl Scouts U.S., 1992—; vol. leader 4-H Clarke County, Athens, 1992-94. Presdl. scholar U. Ga., 1993-94. Mem. Assn. for Childhood Edn. Internat., Profl. Assn. Ga. Educators, Golden Key, Kappa Delta Epsilon (perfect scholar 1994). Avocations: hiking, camping, swimming, canoeing, reading. Home: 171 Scottwood Dr Athens GA 30607-1338

MIYAKE, AKIO, biologist, educator; b. Kyoto, Japan, June 29, 1931; s. Yoshikazu and Yukie (Yamazaki) M.; m. Sadako Harada, Mar. 15, 1965 (dec. June 1986); children: Akiko, Toshio; m. Terue Harumoto, Dec. 30, 1988; 1 child, Yuka. BS, Kyoto U., 1953, D of Science, 1959. Asst. Osaka (Japan) City U., 1953-63; visiting scholar Ind. U., Bloomington, 1959-61; lectr. Kyoto (Japan) U., 1963-70; group leader Max-Planck Inst. for Molecular Genetics, West Berlin, 1970-74; visiting scholar U. Pisa, Italy, 1975-77, U. Münster, West Germany, 1978-83; prof. U. Camerino, Italy, 1983—. Contbr. articles on sexual reprodn. in microorganisms to profl. jours. and books. Recipient Zool. Soc. of Japan Prize, 1981. Mem. Zool. Soc. Japan, Genetics Soc. of Japan, AAAS, Soc. Protozoologists. Avocations: origin and evolution of life, Italian opera music. Home: Corso Italia 150, I-62022 Castelraimondo Italy Office: U Camerino Dept Cell Biol, Via F Camerini 2, I-62032 Camerino Italy

MIYAKE, ISSEY, fashion designer; b. Hiroshima, Japan, Apr. 22, 1938. Student, Tama Art U., Tokyo, 1959-63, La Chambre Syndicale de la Couture Parisienne, Paris, 1965. Asst. designer Guy Laroche, Paris, 1966-68; asst. designer Hubert de Givenchy, Paris, 1968-69; designer Geoffrey Beene, N.Y.C., 1969-70; founder Miyake Design Studio, N.Y.C., 1970—, Issey Miyake, Inc., N.Y.C., 1971—. Exhbns. of work include: Seibu Mus. Art, Tokyo, 1977, Musee des Arts Decoratifs, Paris, 1978, MIT, Cambridge, 1982, San Francisco Mus. Modern Art, 1983, Touko Mus. of Contemporary Art, Tokyo, 1990; represented in permanent collections: Met. Mus. Art, N.Y.C., Victoria and Albert Mus., London. Author: Issey Miyake: East Meets West, 1978, Issey Miyake: Bodyworks, 1983. Office: Issey Miyake USA Corp 3 W 18th St Fl 7 New York NY 10011-4610*

MIYAMOTO, CURTIS TRENT, medical educator; b. Bristol, Pa., Nov. 26, 1957; s. Sadao and Amy E. (Omoto) M.; m. Maria Amparo Gomez, Sept. 24, 1983; children: Maria Victoria, David James, Robert Paul. BS, Muhlenberg Coll., 1979; MD, U. Navarra, Pamplona, Spain, 1986. Lic. physician, Pa.; cert. radiation oncologist. Sr. instr. Allegheny Univ. Hosps., Phila., 1991—, co-founder Brain Tumor Ctr., 1994—; bd. dirs. Richard Zaloga Found., Old Forge, Pa.; mem. radiation safety, credentials, surg. and invasive procedure rev., risk mgmt., quality improvement coms., instnl. rev. bd. Allegheny Univ. Hosps.; faculty Radiation Oncology Self Assessment Program. Author: (book chpt.) Management of Salivary Gland Lesions, 1992; co-author: (book chpt.) Radiobiology in Radiotherapy, 1988, Recent Results in Cancer Research-Systemic Radiotherapy with Monoclonal Antibodies, 1996; contbr. articles to profl. jours. including Am. Jour. Clin. Oncology, Internat. Jour. Radiation Oncology; mem. editl. bd. Radiation Oncology Investigations; article reviewer Am. Jour. Clin. Oncology. Mem. worship com. First Presbyn. Ch., Morristown, N.J., 1996; v.p. PTA, Glenolden, Pa., 1993. Outstanding scholar Hahnemann U., 1991. Fellow AMA (Physician's Recognition award 1994), Am. Cancer Soc.; mem. Interam. Coll. Physicians & Surgeons, Alpha Phi Omega (life), Sigma Xi. Republican. Presbyterian. Achievements include extensive work with biologic response modifiers. Home: 32 Parkdale Pl Marlton NJ 08053 Office: Allegheny Univ Hosps Ctr City Broad and Vine Sts Philadelphia PA 19102

MIYAMOTO, RICHARD TAKASHI, otolaryngologist; b. Zeeland, Mich., Feb. 2, 1944; s. Dave Norio and Haruko (Okano) M.; m. Cynthia VanderBurgh, June 17, 1967; children: Richard Christopher, Geoffrey Takashi. BS cum laude, Wheaton Coll., 1966; MD, U. Mich., 1970; MS in Otology, U.So. Calif., 1978. Diplomate Am. Bd. Otolaryngology. Intern Butterworth Hosp., Grand Rapids, Mich., 1970-71, resident in surgery, 1971-72; resident in otolaryngology Ind. U. Sch. Medicine, 1972-75; fellow in otology and neurotology St. Vincent Hosp. and Otologic Med. Group, L.A., 1977-78; asst. prof. Ind. U. Sch. Medicine, Indpls., 1978-83, assoc. prof., 1983-88; prof. 1988—; chmn. 1987, chief Otology and Neurotology dept. Otolaryngology, Head and Neck Surgery, Ind. U., 1982—, chmn. dept. Otolaryngology, 1987—, Arilla DeVault prof., 1991; chief Otolaryngology, Head and Neck Surgery Wishard Meml. Hosp., 1979—. Mem. editorial bd. Laryngoscope, Am. Jour. of Otology, Otolaryngology-Head and Neck Surgery, European archives of Oto-Rhino-Laryngology, Anales de Otorrinolaringologia Mexicana; contbr. articles to profl. jours. Mem. adv. coun. Nat. Inst. Deafness and other communication disorders, 1989—; mem. med. adv. bd. Alexander Graham Bell Assn. for the Deaf, The Ear Found. Served to maj. USAF, 1975-77. Named Arilla DeVault Disting. investigator Ind. U., 1983. Fellow Am. Acad. Otolaryngology (gov. 1982—), ACS, Am. Otological, Rhinological, and Laryngological Soc. (Thesis Disting. for Excellence award), Am. Neurotology Soc. Am. Auditory Soc. (mem. exec. com. 1985—); mem. Otosclerosis Study Group (coun. 1993—), Am. Otol. Soc. (coun. 1992—), Marines Meml. Assn., Wheaton Coll. Scholastic Honor Soc., Cosmos Club of Washington, Columbia Club of Ind., Royal Soc. Medicine London, Collegium Oto-Laryngologicum Amecitiae Sacrum; Alpha Omega Alpha. Avocation: tennis. Office: Indiana U Sch Med 702 Barnhill Dr Indianapolis IN 46202-5128*

MIYARES, BENJAMIN DAVID, editor, publisher, consultant; b. Tampa, Fla., July 23, 1940; s. Benigno and Mary Carolyn (Dominguez) M.; m. Martha Suzanne Urban, May 14, 1966; children—David, Jeffrey, Beth. B.A. in Journalism, St. Bonaventure U., Olean, N.Y., 1962. News dir. radio sta. WSET, Glens Falls, N.Y., 1962-63; with subs. Edgell Communications, Inc. (magazines for industry), N.Y.C., 1963-89; editor Food and Drug Packaging mag., 1968-89, editorial dir. company, 1975-89, corp. v.p., 1977-80, exec. editor, 1980-89; publisher Candy Marketer, 1985-87, Instructor, 1987; pres. BDM Enterprises, Mktg./Communications Cons., Bay Village, Ohio, 1989—; cons. in packaging field. Pres. council Nat. Packaging Week, 1975; editorial com. Am. Bus. Press, 1973-74. Served with AUS, 1963. Fellow Inst. Packaging Profls. (v.p. 1976-78, pres. 1978-79). Office: BDM Enterprises 31408 Narragansett Ln Cleveland OH 44140-1068

MIYASAKI, GEORGE JOJI, artist; b. Kalopa, Hawaii, Mar. 24, 1935. BFA, Calif. Coll. Arts and Crafts, 1957, MFA, 1958. Asst. prof. art Calif. Coll. Arts and Crafts, Oakland, 1958-64; mem. faculty dept. art U. Calif., Berkeley, 1964-94; prof. emeritus U. Calif. John Hay Whitney fellow, 1957-58; Tamarind printing fellow, 1961; Guggenheim fellow, 1963-64; Nat. Endowment for Arts fellow, 1980-81, 85-86. Mem. Nat. Acad. of Design. Home: 2844 Forest Ave Berkeley CA 94705-1309

MIYASAKI, SHUICHI, lawyer; b. Paauilo, Hawaii, Aug. 6, 1928; s. Torakichi and Teyo (Kimura) M.; m. Pearl Takeko Saiki, Sept. 11, 1954; children: Joy Michiko, Miles Tadashi, Jan Keiko, Ann Yoshie. BSCE, U. Hawaii-Honolulu, 1951; JD, U. Minn., 1957; LLM in Taxation, Georgetown U., 1959; grad. Army War Coll., 1973. Bar: Minn. 1957, Hawaii 1959, U.S. Supreme Ct. 1980. Examiner, U.S. Patent Office, 1957-59; dep. atty. gen. State of Hawaii, 1960-61; mem., dir., sec./treas. Okumura Takushi Funaki & Wee, Honolulu, 1961-90; pvt. practice, Honolulu, 1991—; atty. Hawaii Senate, 1961, chief counsel ways and means com., 1962, chief counsel judiciary com., 1967-70; civil engr. Japan Constrn. Agy., Tokyo, 1953-54; staff judge adv., col. USAR, Ft. DeRussy, Hawaii, 1968-79; local legal counsel Jaycees, 1962; lectr. Nat. Assn. Pub. Accts. Hawaii Chpt. Ann. Conv., 1990, 94, Mid Pacific Inst. Found., Honolulu, 1990, Econ. Study Club of Hawaii, 1990, Meiji Life Ins. Co. Japan, 1992, Cent. YMCA, 1992. Legis. chmn. armed services com. C. of C. of Hawaii, 1973; instl. rep. Aloha council Boy Scouts Am., 1963-78; exec. com., sec., dir. Legal Aid Soc. Hawaii, 1970-72; state v.p. Hawaii Jaycees, 1964-65; dir., legal counsel St. Louis Heights Community Assn., 1963, 65, 73, 91-96; dir., legal counsel Citizens Study Club for Naturalization of Citizens, 1963-68; advisory bd. Project Dana Honolulu, 1991-96, vice chair 91, 92; life mem. Res. Officers Assn. U.S. Served to 1st lt., AUS, 1951-54. Decorated Meritorious Service medal with oak leaf cluster. Mem. ABA, Hawaii Bar Assn., U.S. Patent Office Soc., Hawaii Estate Planning Council, Rotary, Central YMCA Club, Waikiki Athletic Club, Army Golf Assn., Elks, Phi Delta Phi. Office: 1001 Bishop St Honolulu HI 96813-3429 *Personal philosophy: Study hard, work hard, play hard, love hard, have time for nonsense, help others and be fair to all concerned.*

MIYATA, GEN, history of religion educator; b. Kyoto, Japan, Feb. 11, 1933; s. Zenichiro and Ine (Yoshida) M.; m. Hiroko Fujiwara, Feb. 3, 1968; children: Kenichi, Mamoru, Teizo. BA, Tokyo U., 1956, MA, 1958. Lectr. Tenri (Japan) U., 1964-70, assoc. prof., 1970-79, prof., 1979—, chairperson dept. religious studies, 1981-87, 89-91, 92-93, dean faculty letters, 1987-89, 91-92, dean faculty human studies, 1993—; vis. prof. Ind. U., Bloomington, 1980-81. Mem. Japanese Assn. for Am. Studies (councilor 1972—), Japanese Assn. for Religious Studies (dir. 1989—). Tenrikyo. Office: Tenri U, 1050 Somanouchi cho, Tenri Nara, Japan 632

MIYAZAKI, MASATAKA, language professional and educator, English; b. Ishikura, Mori-cho, Hokkaido, Aug. 24, 1936; m. Kimiko Wakasa, Mar 5, 1965; children: Kyosuke, Noriyuki, Fumika. BA, Hokkaido (Japan) Ednl. Coll., 1959; MA, Meiji Gakuin U., Tokyo, 1971. Elem. sch. tchr. Kameda Elem. Sch., Hakodate, Japan, 1959-63; jr. high tchr. English Fukabori Jr. H.S., Hakodate, Japan, 1963-68; tchr. H.S. English Showa-daiich H.S., Tokyo, Japan, 1968-69; lectr. English Hakodate (Japan) U., 1971-76, asst. prof. English, 1976-82, prof. English, 1982—. Author: (poems) The Spring Face, 1970, Mountain in Flame, 1981, Absent-minded Professor, 1995; translator: Faerie Queene, Vol. I, 1986, Vol. II, 1989. Mem. Hokkaido Poetry Assn., All Japan Kendo Assn. (Renshi). Home: 2-21-9 Hi yoshi-cho, Hakodate 042, Japan Office: Hakodate U, 51-1 Takaoka-cho, Hakodate 041, Japan

MIYAZAWA, AKIRA, advertising executive; b. Tokyo, Oct. 28, 1932; s. Koji and Kyoko M.; m. Atsuko Uda, Oct. 19, 1958; 1 child, Kentaro. LLB, Tokyo U., 1956; cert. in advanced mgmt. program, Harvard U., 1980. Bus. analyst Peoples Fin. Corp., Tokyo, 1956-64; v.p. McCann-Erickson Hakuhodo Inc., Tokyo, 1980-81, sr. v.p., 1981-82, exec. v.p., 1982-85, dir., 1985-96, advisor, 1996—. Avocations: golf, reading books. Office: McCann-Erickson Inc, Shin Aoyama Bldg E 1-1, Minami-Aoyama 1-chome, Minatoku, Tokyo 107, Japan

MIZE, JOE HENRY, industrial engineer, educator; b. Colorado City, Tex., June 14, 1934; s. Kelly Marcus and Birtie (Adams) M.; m. Betty Bentley, Mar. 16, 1966; 1 dau., Kelly Jean. B.S. in Indsl. Engring, Tex. Tech. Coll., 1958; M.S. (Research Found. grantee) in Indsl. Engring, Purdue U., 1963, Ph.D., 1964. Registered profl. engr., Ala., Okla. Indsl. engr. White Sands Missile Range, N.Mex., 1958-61; grad. research asst. Purdue U., Lafayette, Ind., 1961-64; asso. prof. engring. Auburn (Ala.) U., 1964-69; dir. Auburn (Ala.) U. (Computer Center), 1965-66; prof. engring. Ariz. State U., Tempe, 1969-72; prof., head Sch. Indsl. Engring. and Mgmt. Okla. State U., Stillwater, 1972-80; dir. Univ. Ctr. for Energy Research Okla. State U., 1980-83, Regents prof., 1982—; cons. to Air War Coll., 1968-69, U.S. Army, Ops. Analysis Standby Unit, U. N.C., 1965-69, various mfg. firms, 1964—; program adv. Office of Mgmt. and Budget, Exec. Office of the President, Washington, 1974-79; adv. to NSF, 1974-79, Nat. Center for Productivity and Quality of Work Life, 1973-78; chmn. tech. adv. council So. Growth Policies Bd., 1975-77; accrediting visitor Engrs. Council for Profl. Devel., 1973-80. Author: (with J.G. Cox) Essentials of Simulation (translated into Japanese 1970), 1968, Prosim V.: Instructor's Manual, 1971, Student's Manual, 1971, (with C.R. White and George H. Brooks) Operations Planning and Control, 1971, (with J.L. Kuester) Optimization Techniques with Fortran, 1973, (with W.C. Turner and K.E. Case) Introduction to Industrial and Systems Engineering, 3d edit., 1993 (named Book of Yr., Am. Inst. Indsl. Engrs. 1979), Guide to Systems Integration, 1991; contrbr. articles to profl. jours., more. Recipient Disting. Engring. Alumnus award Purdue U., 1978. Mem. Am. Inst. Indsl. Engrs. (exec. v.p. 1978-80, pres. 1981-82, H.G. Maynard Innovative Achievement award 1977, Gilbreth Indsl. Engring. award 1990), Am. Soc. for Engring. Edn. (sec. govt. rels. com. 1975-76), Nat. Soc. Profl. Engrs., Okla. Soc. Profl. Engrs. (Outstanding Engring. Achievement award 1977, Outstanding Engr. in Okla. 1981), Inst. Mgmt. Scis., Coun. Indsl. Engring. Acad. Dept. Heads (chmn. 1975-76), NAE, Nat. Rsch. Coun., Sigma Xi, Tau Beta Pi, Alpha Pi Mu. Office: Oklahoma State U Indsl Engring Dept Stillwater OK 74078

MIZE, LARRY, professional golfer. Profl. golfer, 1981—; PGA tour victories include: Memphis Classsic, 1983, Masters, 1987, Northern Telecom Open, 1993, Buick Open, 1993. mem. U.S. Ryder Cup Team, 1987. Office: care PGA 100 Avenue Of Champions Palm Beach Gardens FL 33418*

MIZEL, LARRY A., housing construction company executive; b. 1942; married. BA, U. Okla., 1964; JD, U. Denver, 1967. Chmn. bd., chmn. exec. com., dir. MDC Holdings Inc., 1972—, chmn. bd., pres., chief exec. officer, 1988—. Office: MDC Holdings Inc 3600 S Yosemite St Denver CO 80237-1812*

MIZEL, MARK STUART, orthopedic surgeon; b. N.Y.C., May 23, 1945; s. Harold Henry and Irene (Adelman) M. BSME, Columbia U., 1966, MSME, 1968; MD, Tufts U., 1977. Diplomate Am. Bd. Orthopedic Surgery. Intern, George Washington U. Hosp., 1977-78, resident in surgery, 1978-79; resident Mass. Gen. Hosp., Boston, 1979-82; fellow in foot and ankle surgery U. Calif., San Francisco, 1983; practice medicine specializing in orthopedic surgery Orthopedic Ctr. of Lake Worth, Fla., 1983-91; clin. assoc. prof. Orthopedics and Rehab. U. Miami, 1989-91; clin. asst. prof. orthopedic surgery, Tufts U., 1991-95; dir. Boston Foot & Ankle Ctr., 1991-95; asst. prof. orthopedic surgery Johns Hopkins, 1995—. Assoc. editor Foot & Ankle. Served as aviator USN, 1969-72; Vietnam. Fellow ACS, Am. Acad. Orthopedic Surgeons, Am. Orthopedic Foot and Ankle Soc. (membership com. 1988-90, orthotics and prosthetics com. 1990-91, chmn. regional rearview subcom., 1993-96). Office: Johns Hopkins Orthopedics Dept 601 N Caroline St Baltimore MD 21287

MIZELL, ANDREW HOOPER, III, concrete company executive; b. Franklin, Tenn., Sept. 26, 1926; s. Andrew Hooper, Jr. and Jennie McEwen (Fleming) M.; B.A., Vanderbilt U., 1950; m. Julia Yolanda Mattei, Dec. 20, 1947; children—Andrew Hooper, Julia Fleming. Supt., Wescon Constrn. Co., Nashville, 1950-52; accountant McIntyre & Asso., Nashville, 1952-55; credit mgr. Ingram Oil Co., Nashville, 1955-56, v.p. and dir., 1956-62; v.p., dir. Comml. Sign & Advt. Co., Nashville, 1957-59; v.p. and dir. Gen. Properties Co., New Orleans, 1957-62; v.p. and dir. Minn. Barge & Terminal Co., St. Paul, 1957-62; mgr. real estate and devel. Murphy Corp., El Dorado, Ark., 1962-63, mgr. retail sales, 1962-63; pres. and chmn. bd. Transit Ready Mix, Inc., Nashville, 1963—; pres., Conco, Inc., Apollo Concrete Products, Inc.; ptnr. Mizell Riggs Enterprises. Active United Givers Fund, 1965-66; chmn. Concrete div. Office Emergency Planning, 1965—; mem. Nat. UN Day Com., 1978. Served with USNR, 1944-46. Named Ark. Traveler, 1966, Ky. Col., 1969. Mem. Nat. Ready Mix Concrete Assn. (chmn. membership com. Tenn. sect. 1971—, chmn. marketing com. Tenn. chpt. 1973—), Assn. Gen. Contractors, Tenn. Bldg. Material Assn., Nat. Fedn. Ind. Businessmen, Portland Cement Assn., Nat. Area Bus. and Edn. Radio, Asso. Builders and Contractors, Spl. Indsl. Radio Service Industry, Tenn. Road Builders, Boat Owners Assn. U.S., Nashville C. of C., U.S. C. of C., Am. Concrete Inst. Clubs: Nashville Yacht, Nashville City, Belle Meade Country, The Honors Course, Commodore Yacht (past commodore). Home: 4340 Beekman Dr Nashville TN 37215-4504

MIZELL, JOY REGISTER, critical care nurse; b. Canal Point, Fla., Dec. 3, 1936; d. Noonan A. and Opal A. (Duncan) Register; children: Sandra, Randa, William Michael. Student, Cook County Coll., Gainesville, Tex., 1977, 81; BS in Nursing, Tex. Womans U., Denton, 1978. Nurse Mariners Hosp., Tavernier, Fla., 1980-81; founder, owner, operator The Silk Leaf, Lewisville, Tex., 1981-83; sales exec. Sea Pines Real Estate, Fernandina Beach, Fla., 1984-85; developer's rep. Excel-Edco Investments, Inc., Palataka, Fla.; pub. rels. officer Bank of Burke County, Waynesboro, Ga., 1987-88; nurse critical care unit/ICU Kennestone Hosp., Marietta, Ga., 1988-90; nurse ICU Nassau Gen. Hosp., Fernandina Beach, Fla., 1990—; contract field RN Vis. Nurse Assn., 1991-93; community educator Assoc. Home Health, West Palm Beach, Fla., 1993-95; owner Your Daily Care, West Palm Beach, Fla., 1995—. Mem. Nat. Assn. Geriatric Care Mgrs. (Fla. chpt.), Fla. Assisted Living Assn., Pres. Round Table for Women in Bus., Lewisville C. of C., Ambassador's Club (Lewisville), Fernandina Beach Builders Assn. (co-founder), Sardis (pres. 1986-87), Sardis Bus. Assn. (sec. 1987-88), Waynesboro Bus. Assn. (sec., bd. dirs.), Broadway Home Health Bd., Profl. Resource Network. Office: Your Daily Care 931 Village Blvd Ste 905-300 West Palm Beach FL 33409

MIZGALA, HENRY F., physician; b. Montreal, Nov. 28, 1932; s. Louis and Mary (Ropeleski) M.; m. Pauline Barbara Delaney, Oct. 26, 1957; children: Paul Stephen, Cynthia Louise, Liane Mary, Melanie Frances Mizgala Dressler, Nancy Elizabeth Mizgala Lewis. B.A. magna cum laude, Loyola Coll., Montreal, 1953; M.D., C.M., McGill U., 1957. Rotating intern, then resident in medicine St. Mary's Hosp., Montreal, 1957-59; asst. physician St. Mary's Hosp., 1963-66; resident in medicine Royal Victoria Hosp., Montreal, 1959-60; Dazian fellow cardiology Mt. Sinai Hosp., N.Y.C., 1960-61, USPHS fellow cardiology, 1961-62; resident in cardiology Montreal Gen. Hosp., 1962-63, assoc. physician, 1966-74; asst. physician, cons. cardiology Lachine (Que.) Gen. Hosp., 1964-80; cardiologist Montreal Heart Inst., also dir. CCU, 1974-80; cons. Centre Hosp. Baie des Chaleurs, Gaspe, Que., 1975-80; hon. cons. Montreal Heart Inst., 1980—; prof. medicine U. B.C., 1980—; cardiologist The Vancouver (B.C.) Hosp. and Health Scis. Ctr.; cons. B.C. Cancer Agy., Vancouver, 1981—; cons. staff Univ. Hosp., U. B.C. site, 1981-94; mem. faculty McGill U. Med. Sch., Montreal, 1968-74; asso. prof. medicine McGill U. Med. Sch., 1973-74; assoc. prof., then prof. Montreal U. Med. Sch., 1974-81; prof. medicine, head div. cardiology U. B.C., 1980-87. Mem. editl. bd. Can. Jour. Cardiol. 1988—, Jour. Am. Coll. Cardiology, 1992-95; contbr. numerous articles to med. jours. Fellow Royal Coll. Phys. and Surg. Can., Am. Coll. Cardiology, Am. Heart Assn. (council clin. cardiology); mem. Can. Med. Assn., Can. Cardiovascular Soc. (treas. 1974-90), Que. Med. Assn., B.C. Med. Assn., B.C. and Yukon Heart and Stroke Found. (bd. dirs., sr. bd. dirs.), Alpha Omega Alpha. Office: U BC Div Cardiology Dept Med, 865 W 10th Ave, Vancouver, BC Canada V5Z 1L7

MIZRAHI, ABRAHAM MORDECHAY, retired cosmetics and health care company executive, physician; b. Jerusalem, Apr. 16, 1929; came to U.S., 1952, naturalized, 1960; s. Solomon R. and Rachel (Haliwa) M.; m. Suzanne Eve Glasser, Mar. 15, 1956; children: Debra, Judith, Karen. B.S., Manchester Coll., 1955; M.D., Albert Einstein Coll. Medicine, 1960. Diplomate: Am. Bd. Pediatrics, Nat. Bd. Med. Examiners. Intern U. N.C., 1960-61; pediatric resident Columbia-Presbyn. Med. Center, N.Y.C., 1961-63; NIH fellow in neonatology Columbia-Presbyn. Med. Center, 1963-65; assoc. dir. Newborn Service Mt. Sinai Hosp., N.Y.C.; also dir. Newborn Service Elmhurst Med. Center, 1965-67; staff physician Geigy Pharm. Corp., N.Y.C., 1967-69; head cardio-pulmonary sect. Geigy Pharm. Corp., 1969-71; sr. v.p. corp. med. affairs USV Pharm. Corp., Tuckahoe, N.Y., 1971-76; v.p. health and safety Revlon, Inc., N.Y.C., 1976-89, sr. v.p. human resources, 1989-94; ret., 1994; assoc. in pediatrics Columbia U., 1963-67; cons. in neonatology Misericordia-Fordham Med. Ctr., 1967-89; clin. affiliate N.Y. Hosp.; clin. asst. prof. Cornell U. Med. Coll., 1982—. Contbr. articles to profl. jours. Trustee Westchester (N.Y.) Jewish Center. Mem. AMA, N.Y. State and County Med. Soc., Am., N.Y. acads. medicine, Am. Soc. Clin. Pharmacology and Therapeutics, Am. Pub. Health Assn., Am. Occupational Med. Assn. Home: 7 Jason Ln Mamaroneck NY 10543-2108 *The principles that have guided my life are old Biblical concepts. Firstly, that God had created Adam and Eve and all Men are, therefore, brothers and sisters. Secondly, God created Man and, therefore every human being has a spark of God in him. It, therefore, follows that killing diminshes God's presence on earth and saving of a human being increases His presence.*

MIZRAHI, ISAAC, fashion designer; b. Bklyn., Oct. 14, 1961; s. Zeke and Sarah M. Attended, Parsons Sch. Design, 1982. Design asst. Perry Ellis, 1982-84, Jeffrey Banks, 1984-85, Calvin Klein, 1985-87; founder Isaac Mizrahi, 1987—, added menswear line, 1990—. Designed costumes Twyla Tharp's ballet Brief Fling, Am. Ballet Theatre. Recipient Perry Ellis new fashion talent award Coun. Fashion Designers Am., 1989; named Best Womenswear Designer 1989 Coun. Fashion Designers Am., 1990. Office: 104 Wooster St New York NY 10012-3809*

MIZROCH, JOHN F., lawyer; b. Norfolk, Va., Sept. 28, 1948; s. Solomon B. and Muriel G. Mizroch; m. Martha Melissa Bankston; children: Zachary, Elliott, Brandon, Marissa. BA, U. Va., 1970, MA, 1972; JD, Coll. of William and Mary, 1975. Bar: Va. 1975, D.C. 1977, Colo. 1980, Tex. 1985. Asst. commonwealth atty. Commonwealth Atty. Office, Arlington, Va., 1975-76; fgn. service officer USIA, Washington, 1976-79; pvt. practice real estate devel., Winter Park, Colo., 1980-84; v.p., counsel VCMI, Dallas, 1984-86; gen. counsel W.O. Bankston, Enterprise, Dallas, 1986-87; dep. asst. sec. commerce Office of Trade Devel., Washington, 1987-89; advisor to minority Joint Econ. Com. of Congress, Washington, 1989-90; mng. dir., gen. coun. R.J.M. Internat., Washington, 1991-93; exec. dir. U.S. Environ. Tech. Export Coun., 1993—. Town councilman Winter Park Town Council, 1982-84. Mem. ABA. Home: 4825 V St NW Washington DC 20007-1510

MLAY, MARIAN, government official; b. Pitts., Sept. 11, 1935; d. John and Sonia M.; A.B., U. Pitts., 1957; postgrad. (Univ. fellow) Princeton U., 1969-70; J.D., Am. U., 1977. Mgmt. positions HEW, Washington, 1961-70, dep. dir. Chgo. region, 1971-72, dir. div. consol. funding, 1972-73, dep. dir. office policy devel. and planning USPHS, Washington, 1973-77; dir. program evaluation EPA, Washington, 1978-79, dep. dir. Office of Drinking Water, 1979-84, dir. Office of Ground Water Protection, 1984-91, dir. Oceans and Coastal Protection, 1991-95; sr. rschr. Nat. Acad. Pub. Adminstrn. 1995—. Bd. dirs. D.C. United Fund, 1979-80. Recipient Career Edn. award Nat. Inst. Public Affairs, 1969. Mem. ABA, D.C. Bar (steering com. energy, environment and natural resources sect.). Author articles in field. Home: 3747 1/2 Kanawha St NW Washington DC 20015-1838 Office: Nat Acad Pub Adminstrn 1120 G St NW Ste 850 Washington DC 20005-3801

MLOCEK, SISTER FRANCES ANGELINE, financial executive; b. River Rouge, Mich., Aug. 4, 1934; d. Michael and Suzanna (Bloch) M. BBA, U. Detroit, 1958; MBA, U. Mich., 1971. CPA, Mich. Bookkeeper Allen Park (Mich.) Furniture, 1949-52, Gerson's Jewelry, Detroit, 1952-53; jr. acct. Meyer Dickman, CPA, Algaze, Staub & Bowman, CPAs, Detroit, 1953-58; acct., internal auditor Sisters, Servants of Immaculate Heart of Mary Congregation, Monroe, Mich., 1959-66, asst. gen. treas., 1966-73, gen. treas., 1973-76; internal auditor for parishes Archdiocese of Detroit, 1976-78; asst. to exec. dir. Leadership Conf. of Women, Silver Spring, Md., 1978-83; dir. of fin. Nat. Conf. of Cath. Bishops/U.S. Cath. Conf., Washington, 1989-94; CFO Sisters Servants of the Immaculate Heart of Mary, Monroe, Mich., 1994—; trustee Sisters, Servants of Immaculate Heart of Mary Charitable Trust Fund, Monroe, 1988—. Author: (manual) Leadership Conference of Women Religious/Confernce of Major Superiors of Men, 1981. Treas. Zonta Club of Washington Found., Washington, 1983-88, pres., 1992-93; bd. dirs. Our Lady of Good Counsel High Sch., Wheaton, Md., 1983-89. Mem. AICPA, D.C. Inst. CPAs (mem. not-for-profit com. 1992-94, CFOs com. 1990-94. Democrat. Roman Catholic. Office: Sisters Servants Immaculate Heart Mary 610 W Elm Ave Monroe MI 48162-7909

MLSNA, TIMOTHY MARTIN, lawyer; b. Berwyn, Ill., Feb. 13, 1947; s. Theodore Joseph and Dorothy Clara (Kurth) M.; m. Kathryn Kimura, Oct. 4, 1975; children: Lauren Marie, Matthew Christopher, Michael Timothy. BS, MacMurray Coll., 1969; JD, Northwestern U., 1974. Bar: Ill. 1974, U.S. Dist. Ct. (no. dist.) Ill. 1974. Assoc. McDermott, Will & Emery, Chgo., 1974-80, ptnr., 1980-81; ptnr. Kirkland & Ellis, Chgo., 1981-95; pres. Timothy M. Mlsna & Assoc. Ltd., Chgo., 1995—. Trustee MacMurray Coll., Jacksonville, Ill., 1987—, The Associated Colls. of Ill., 1994—. Home: 28 Chatham Ln Oak Brook IL 60521-2349 Office: Timothy M Mlsna & Asosc Ltd 360 N Michigan Ave Chicago IL 60601

MLYNIEC, WALLACE JOHN, law educator, lawyer, consultant; b. Berwyn, Ill., July 10, 1945; s. Casimir Adele and Adeline Mary (Kaczka) M. BS, Northwestern U., 1967; JD, Georgetown U., 1970. Bar: D.C. 1971, Alaska 1971, U.S. Dist. Ct. D.C. 1971, U.S. Ct. Appeals (D.C. cir.) 1971, U.S. Supreme Ct. 1974. Exec. dir. ABA standards U.S. Cir. Jud. Conf. Project on ABA Standards, Washington, 1971-73; dir. Juvenile Justice Clinic, Georgetown U., Washington, 1973—, prof. law, 1973—; coord. clin. edn, 1986-89, assoc. dean, 1989—; cons. Nat. Adv. Com. on Juvenile Justice, Washington, 1979-80; cons. pvt. and pub. agys. on juvenile and criminal justice, 1974—; chmn. Juvenile Justice Adv. Group, D.C., 1980-82; mem. Nat. Resource Ctr. on Child Abuse and Neglect. Recipient Stuart Stillar Found. award, 1994; Meyer Found. grantee, 1980-82; Swedish Bicentennial fellow, 1985. Mem. Am. Assn. Law Schs. (mem. com. on polit. interference 1983-84, chair 1991, standing com. on clin. edn., William Pincus award 1996), ABA (mem. adv. com. on family ct. rules 1984), D.C. Bar Assn. (chmn. juvenile justice sect. 1973).

MNOOKIN, ROBERT HARRIS, lawyer, educator; b. Kansas City, Mo., Feb. 4, 1942; s. I.J. and Marion (Sittenfeld) M.; m. Dale Seigel, June 16, 1963; children: Jennifer Leigh, Allison Heather. A.B., Harvard U., 1964, LL.B., 1968. Bar: D.C. 1970, Calif. 1971. Fulbright scholar Econometric Inst., Netherland Sch. Econs., 1964-65; assoc. Howard, Prim, Smith, Rice & Downs, San Francisco, 1970-72; of counsel Howard, Prim, Smith, Rice & Downs, 1972-93; vis. prof. Stanford U. Sch. Law, 1980-81, prof. law, 1981-89, Adelbert H. Sweet prof. law, 1989-93; Samuel Williston prof. Harvard Law Sch., Cambridge, Mass., 1993—; dir. Harvard negotiation rsch. project Harvard U., Cambridge, 1993—, chair program on negotiation, 1993—; lectr. U. Calif., Berkeley, 1972, dir. childhood and govt. project, 1972-74, acting prof. law, 1973-75, prof. law, 1975-81; dir. Stanford Ctr. on Conflict and Negotiation, 1988-93; vis. fellow Wolfson Coll. and Centre for Socio-Legal Studies, Oxford, Eng., 1978; fellow Center for Advanced Studies in Behavioral Scis., 1981-82; vis. prof. Harvard Law Sch., 1990-91; arbitrator IBM-Fujitsu Arbitration, 1985—. Author: In the Interest of Children, 1985, Dividing the Child, 1992, Child, Family and State, 3d edit., 1995, Barriers to Conflict Resolution, 1995; contbr. articles to profl. jours. Mem. overseer's com. to visit Law Sch., Harvard U., 1972-78; trustee Berkeley Pub. Library, 1973-80, chmn., 1975-77, vice chmn., 1978-80. Fellow Am. Acad. Arts and Scis.; mem. ABA, Calif. Bar Assn. Home: 10 Follen St Cambridge MA 02138-3503 Office: Hauser 416 Harvard Law Sch Cambridge MA 02138

MO, LUKE WEI, physicist, educator; b. Shangtung, China, June 3, 1934; s. Si-leng and Shu-feng (Lo) M.; m. Doris Chang, Dec. 31, 1960; children: Curtis L., Alice. B.S. in Elec. Engring, Nat. Taiwan U., 1955; M.S. in Physics, Nat. Tsinghua U., Taiwan, 1959; Ph.D., Columbia U., 1963. Research asso. Columbia U., N.Y.C., 1963-64; research physicist Stanford (Calif.) Linear Accelerator, 1965-69; asst. prof. physics U. Chgo., 1969-76; prof. physics Va. Poly. Inst. and State U., Blacksburg, 1976—. Contbr. articles to profl. jours. Served with Taiwan Air Force, 1955-56. Recipient Alumni Research Excellence award Va. Poly. Inst. and State U., 1980, Guggenheim fellow, 1981, NSF grantee, 1969—. Fellow Am. Phys. Soc. Office: Dept Physics Va Poly Inst and State U Blacksburg VA 24061

MOAG, RODNEY F., language educator, country music singer; b. Warsaw, N.Y., Oct. 15, 1936; s. Hugh Alexander and Imogene (Hodges) M.; m. Raechel Ann Foley, Feb. 9, 1964 (div. Aug., 1984); children: Robin Gray, Hugh Daniel, Jeffry Lee. BS, Syracuse U., 1961; MA, U. Wis., 1966, PhD, 1973. Dir. college preparatory program for visually impaired U. Mo., Columbia, 1974; vis. Fulbright prof. U. South Pacific, Suava, Fiji Islands, 1975-78; vis. assoc. prof. U. Mich., Ann Arbor, 1978-80, adj. prof., 1981, vis. assoc. prof., 1982; sr. lectr. U. Tex., Austin, 1981, 83-87, 1988-90, assoc. prof., 1990—. Author: (texts) Fiji MIndi, 1977, Malayalam, 1986; country music artist: several records, one CD, 1995. Mng. dir. Amateur Radio Repeaters of Washtenaw, 1984-86; pres. Mich. Repeater Coun., 1985-88; v.p. Austin Amateur Radio Club, 1993-94; vol. programmer, KO-OP. Mem. Ctrl. Tex. Bluegrass Assn., Austin Amateur Radio Club, Austin Repeater Orgn., Tex. VHF FM Soc. Avocations: amateur radio, country and blue grass music. Home: 6909 Miranda Dr Austin TX 78752 Office: Univ Tex Lang Dept Austin TX 78712

MOAKLEY, JOHN JOSEPH, congressman; b. Apr. 27, 1927; m. Evelyn Duffy, 1957. LLB, Suffolk U., 1956. Bar: Mass. 1957. Pvt. practice Boston, 1957-72; mem. 93rd-104th Congresses from 9th Mass. dist., 1973—; ranking minority mem. com. on rules. Chmn. com. on rules Mass. Senate, 1964-70; mem. Boston City Coun., 1971-72, chmn. appropriations and fin. com. With USNR, 1943-46. Office: US Ho of Reps 235 Cannon HOB Washington DC 20515*

MOAK-MAZUR, CONNIE JO, investment consultant, marketing professional; b. Ft. Worth, Feb. 5, 1947; d. David Clark and Dorothy Carol (Jackson) Moak; m. Jay Mazur, May 31, 1987. BBA, N. Tex. State U., 1969. Cert. bus. edn. tchr. V.p. Lionel D. Edie & Co., N.Y.C., 1969-77; mgr. Peat, Marwick, Mitchell & Co., N.Y.C., 1977-80; v.p. Shaw Data, N.Y.C., 1980, Fred Alger Mgmt., N.Y.C., 1980-82; ptnr. Glickenhaus & Co., N.Y.C., 1982-93; mng. dir. Wasserstein Perella Capital, 1993-95; group v.p. Schroder Wertheim Investment Svcs., N.Y.C., 1993-95; spkr. in field. Contbr. articles to profl. jours. Mem. Fin. Women's Assn., Am. Pension Conf., Internat. Found. Employee Benefit Plans, Assn. Investment Mgmt. Sales Execs. (bd. dirs., pres.). Avocations: downhill skiing, jogging, horseback riding. Home: 150 E 69th St Apt 19C New York NY 10021-5704 Office: Schroder Wertheim Investment Svcs 787 7th Ave New York NY 10190

MOATES, G. PAUL, lawyer; b. Los Angeles, May 26, 1947; s. Guy Hart and Virginia Rose (Mayolett) M.; m. Paulette Anita Minkus, Mar. 21, 1970; 1 child, Amanda Frances. B.A., Amherst Coll., 1969; J.D., U. Chgo., 1975. Bar: Ill. 1975, D.C. 1976, U.S. Ct. Appeals (D.C. cir.) 1976, U.S. Supreme Ct. 1980, U.S. Ct. Appeals (6th cir.) 1984, U.S. Ct. Appeals (3d cir.) 1991, U.S. Ct. Appeals (7th cir.) 1993. Assoc. firm Sidley & Austin, Washington, 1975-82, ptnr., 1982—. Contbr. articles to profl. jours. Served with U.S. Army, 1970-73. Mem. ABA, Ill. Bar Assn., D.C. Bar Assn. Office: Sidley & Austin 1722 I St NW Washington DC 20006-3705

MOAWAD, ATEF, obstetrician, gynecologist, educator; b. Beni Suef, Egypt, Dec. 2, 1935; came to U.S., 1959; s. Hanna and Baheya (Hunein) M.; m. Ferial Fouad Abdel Malek, Aug. 22, 1966; children: John, Joseph, James. Student, Cairo U. Sch. Sci., 1951-52; MB, BCh, Cairo U. Sch. Medicine, 1957; MS in Pharmacology, Jefferson Med. Coll., 1963. Diplomate Am. Bd. Ob-Gyn; licentiate Med. Coun Can. Rotating intern Cairo U. Hosp., 1958-59, Elizabeth (N.J.) Gen. Hosp., 1959-60; resident in ob-gyn. Jefferson Med. Coll. Hosp., Phila., 1961-64; lect. dept. pharmacology U. Alta., Can., 1966; asst. prof. dept. ob-gyn. and pharmacology U. Alta., Can., 1967-70, assoc. prof., 1970-72; assoc. prof. dept. ob-gyn. and pharmacology U. Chgo., 1972-75, prof. dept. ob-gyn. and pediatrics, 1975—, co-dir. perinatal ctr., 1974-80; obstetrician-gynecologist, chief obstetrics, co-dir. perinatal ctr. The Chgo. Lying-in Hosp. U. Chgo., 1980—; vis. investigator dept. ob-gyn. U. Lund, Sweden, 1969. Co-author book chpts., jour. articles. Mem. perinatal adv. com. Chgo. March of Dimes, 1977—, health profl. adv. com., 1983—; mem. perinatal adv. bd. com. State of Ill., 1978—; mem. Chgo. Maternal Child Health Adv. Com., chmn., 1991—; mem. Mayor's Adv. Com. on Infant Mortality, 1991—. Fellow Jefferson Med. Coll., 1960-61, Case Western Reserve U., 1964-65; grantee Brush Found., 1966-67, Maternal Fetal Medicine Unites Network NIH, 1994; recipient award Phila. Obstet. Soc., 1964, Disting. Teaching award Am. Profs. Gynecology and Obstetrics, 1993. Fellow Am. Coll. Ob-Gyn. (Purdue-Frederick award 1978), Royal Coll. Surgeons (Can.); mem. Soc. for Gynecol Investigation, Pharmacol. Soc. Can., Am. Gynecol. and Obstet. Soc., Soc. Perinatal Obstetricians, N.Y. Acad. Scis., Chgo. Gynecol. Soc., Can. Med. Assn., Christian Med. Soc., Edmonton Obstetrics Soc. Office: U Chgo Dept Ob-Gyn 5841 S Maryland Ave Chicago IL 60637-1463

MOAZZAMI, SARA, civil engineering educator; b. Tehran, July 24, 1960; d. Morteza Moazzami and Ezzat Akbari. BS, George Washington U., 1981; MS, U. Calif., Berkeley, 1982, PhD, 1987. Rsch. asst. George Washington U., Washington, 1980-81; teaching asst. U. Calif., Berkeley, 1982-83, rsch. asst., 1983-87; prof. Univ. Conn., Stamford, 1987-91, Calif. Polytechnic State U., San Luis Obispo, 1991—; mem. 1989 Santa Cruz Earthquake Reconnaissance Team, Earthquake Engring. Rsch. Inst., Oakland, Calif., 1989; speaker internat. confs. in field. Author: (book) 3-D Inelastic Analysis of Reinforced Concrete Frame-Wall Structures, 1987. Recipient Genevieve McEnerney fellowship U. Calif., Berkeley, 1981-82, Martin Mahler prize in Materials Testing, George Washington U., 1981, Columbian Women Soc. scholarship, Washington, 1979-80. Mem. Am. Soc. Civil Engring. (scholarship 1980), Earthquake Engring. Rsch. Inst., Soc. Women Engrs. Avocations: biking, swimming, sewing, travel. Office: Calif Polytechnic State Univ Sch Engring San Luis Obispo CA 93407

MOBBS, MICHAEL HALL, lawyer; b. Lawrenceburg, Tenn., Dec. 25, 1948; s. Hershel Leon and Doris (Davis) M.; m. Ellene Winn, June 19, 1976; children: Michael Hall Jr., Clifton Stevenson, Ellene Glenn. BA summa cum laude, honors with exceptional distinction in Russian studies, Yale U., 1971; JD, U. Chgo., 1974. Bar: Ala. 1974, D.C. 1978, U.S. Supreme Ct. 1980. Assoc. Bradley, Arant, Rose & White, Birmingham, Ala., 1974-77; assoc. Stroock & Stroock & Lavan, Washington, 1977-81, ptnr., 1990-93; ptnr. Squire, Sanders & Dempsey, 1994—; rep of sec. def. to Strategic Arms Reduction Talks, Washington and Geneva, 1982-85; spl. counsel to head of del. and rep. of sec. def. to Negotiations on Nuclear and Space Arms, Washington and Geneva, 1985; asst. dir. of U.S. Arms Control and Disarmament Agy., Washington, 1985-87. Ford Fund scholar, 1967-71; Bates fellow, 1970; recipient Fellows' prize Jonathan Edwards Coll. Yale U., 1971. Mem. Ala. State Bar, ABA (mem. com. on central and eastern european law initiatives), Am. Soc. Internat. Law, D.C. Bar, Fed. Bar Assn., Phi Beta Kappa. Democrat. Clubs: Yale of N.Y.C.; City Tavern (Washington). Author: (with George G. Lorinczi) An Importer's Roadmap to U.S. Import Restrictions, 1984, CBMs For Stabilizing the Strategic Nuclear Competition, 1986, Remarks on Verification of Arms Control Agreements, 1988, (with William J. Vanden Heuvel) Overview of the Laws Governing Foreign Investment in the USSR, 1990, On the Road in Eastern Europe, 1991, Environmental Protection in the CIS and Eastern Europe: Emerging Trends May Affect Your Business, 1993. Home: 636 E Capitol St NE Washington DC 20003-1233 Office: Squire Sanders & Dempsey PO Box 407 1201 Pennsylvania Ave NW Washington DC 20044-0407

MOBERG, DAVID OSCAR, sociology educator; b. Montevideo, Minn., Feb. 13, 1922; s. Fred Ludwig and Anna E. (Sundberg) M.; m. Helen H. Heitzman, Mar. 16, 1946 (dec. Oct. 16, 1992); children: David Paul, Lynette, Jonathan, Philip; m. Marlys Taege, July 23, 1994. AA, Bethel Jr. Coll., 1942; AB, Seattle Pacific Coll., 1947; MA, U. Wash., 1949; PhD, U. Minn., 1952. Assoc. instr. U. Wash., Seattle, 1948-49; faculty Bethel Coll., St. Paul, 1949-68, prof. sociology, 1959-68, chmn. dept. social scis., 1952-68; prof. sociology Marquette U., Milw., 1968-91, prof. emeritus, 1991—, chmn. dept. sociology and anthropology, 1968-77; cons. Nat. Liberty Found., 1970-71, Fetzer Inst., 1995—; cons. Nat. Interfaith Coalition on Aging, 1973-75, mem. nat. adv. bd., 1980-89; guest rschr. Sociology of Religion Inst., Stockholm, summer 1978; adj. prof. San Francisco Theol. Sem., 1964-73, McCormick Theol. Sem., 1975-78, 81-82; vis. prof. U. So. Calif., 1979, Princeton Theol. Sem., 1979, So. Bapt. Theol. Sem., 1982, Soc. for Care of Handicapped in the Gaza Strip of Palestine, 1995; mem. adv. bd. Ecumenical Ministry with Mature Adults, 1983-92; resource scholar Christianity Today Inst., 1985—. Author: The Church as A Social Institution, 1962, 2d edit. 1984, (with Robert M. Gray) The Church and the Older Person, 1962, 2d edit., 1977, Inasmuch: Christian Social Responsibility in the 20th Century, 1965, White House Conference on Aging: Spiritual Well-Being Background and Issues, 1971, The Great Reversal: Evangelism and Social Concern, 1972, 2d edit. 1977, Wholistic Christianity, 1985; also articles, chpts. in symposia.; editor: International Directory of Religious Information Systems, 1971, Spiritual Well-Being: Sociological Perspectives, 1979, Rev. Religious Research, 1968-72, Jour. Am. Sci. Affiliation, 1962-64, Adris Newsletter, 1971-76; co-editor Research in the Social Scientific Study of Religion, 1986—; assoc. editor: Social Compass, 1968—; mem. editl. bd. Christian Univ. Press, 1979-84, Perspectives on Sci. and Christian Faith, 1988—; consulting editor Calif. Sociologist, 1982—. Fulbright lectr. U. Groningen, Netherlands, 1957-58, Fulbright lectr. Muenster U., West Germany, 1964-65. Fellow Am. Sci. Affiliation (editor jour. 1962-64, publs. com. 1984-91, social ethics com. 1985-88, program chair 1995-96), Gerontol. Soc. Am.; mem. Am. Sociol. Assn., Internat. Sociol. Assn. (sociology of religion rsch. com. 1972—), Wis. Sociol. Assn. (pres. 1969-71), Midwest Sociol. Assn. (Wis. bd. dirs. 1971-73), Assn. Devel. Religious Info. Sys. (coord. ADRIS 1971—, editor ADRIS newsletter 1971-76), Religious Rsch. Assn. (editor Rev. Religious Rsch. 1968-72, contbg. editor 1973-77, assoc. editor 1983—, bd. dirs. 1959-61, 68-72, pres. 1981-82, H. Paul Douglass lectr. 1986), Assn. for Sociology of Religion (exec. coun. 1971-73, pres. 1976-77), Soc. for Sci. Study Religion (exec. coun. 1971-74), Evangelicals for Social Action (planning com. 1973-75), Christian Sociol. Soc. (steering com. 1973-81, newsletter lit. reveiwer 1981-93), Family Rsch. Coun. (assoc. 1985-88, rsch. network 1989—), Psychologists Interested in Religious Issues (profl. affiliate 1984—), Midwest Coun. for Social Rsch. on Aging (fellow 1961-64, 87—), Am. Soc. on Aging, Forum on Religion and Aging, Fairview Elder Enterprises (bd. dirs. 1990—). Home: 7120 W Dove Ct Milwaukee WI 53223-2766 Office: Marquette U Dept Social & Cultural Sci Milwaukee WI 53201-1881 *As I try to live with eternity's values in view, my entire lifetime seems to grow ever briefer instead of lengthier.*

MOBERLY, DAVID LINDSEY, foundation executive; b. Irvine, Ky., Apr. 25, 1929; s. Earl and Blanche (Finney) M.; m. Peggy Compton, Dec. 30, 1951; children—Kent, Lynn. A.B., U. Ky., 1951; postgrad., Am. U., 1950; M.A., U. Ky., 1953; Ph.D., Kent State U., 1965. Tchr. Jefferson County Bd. Edn., Louisville, 1951-54; dean of boys Jefferson County Bd. Edn., 1954-55, asst. prin., 1955-57; ednl. adv. AID, U.S. State Dept., Tripoli, Benghazi, Libya, 1957-61; edn. program officer, research and survey team AID, U.S. State Dept., Nairobi, Kenya, 1961-62; instr., resident project coordinator in Tanzania Kent State U., 1962-65; supt. schs. Bd. Edn., Tallmadge, Ohio, 1966-67, Warren, Ohio, 1967-71, Cleve. Heights, 1971-74; supt. schs. Evanston (Ill.) Twp. High Sch., 1974-76, Seattle Sch. Dist. 1, 1976-81; pres. Seattle Found., 1981-84; nat. edn. mgr. Deloitte, Hoskins & Sells, 1984-89; asst. state supt. State of Wash., 1989-95; dep. supt. State of Washington, 1995-96; spl. participant documentary on problems in edn. ABC-TV, 1976. Area chmn. Ohio's Right-to-Read project, 1969-71; chmn. alumni com. for edn. com. Kent State U., 1968-71; mem. nat. adv. bd. Corp. for Pub. Broadcasting; U.S. del. to World Orgn. of Teaching Profession in, Rome, Italy, 1958; Mem. Seattle council Boy Scouts Am.; bd. dirs. Jr. Achievement; trustee Pacific Sci. Center Found., Seattle; mem. Pvt. Sector's Initiative Bd., Seattle. Mem. NEA, Am. Assn. Sch. Adminstrs., Wash. Assn. Sch. Adminstrs., Mcpl. League, Seattle C. of C., Kappa Delta Pi, Phi Delta Kappa. Club: Rotarian. Home: 3045 44th Ave W Seattle WA 98199-2401

MOBERLY, LINDEN EMERY, educational administrator; b. Laramie, Wyo., Jan. 4, 1923; s. Linden E. and Ruth (Gathercole) M. BS, Coll. Emporia, 1952; MS, Kans. State Tchrs. Coll., 1954; m. Viola F. Mosher, Apr. 29, 1949. Tchr. sci., Florence, Kans., 1952-54, Concordia, Kans., 1954-56, Grand Junction, Colo., 1957-60; asst. prin. Orchard Mesa Jr. High Sch., Grand Junction, 1960-66, prin., 1967-84; field cons. Nat. Assn. Secondary Sch. Prins., 1985—. Sgt. USMC, 1941-46. Recipient Outstanding Secondary Prin. award Colo. Assn. Sch. Execs., 1978. Mem. NEA, VFW, Nat. Assn. Secondary Prins. (bd. dir. 1979-83), Colo. Edn. Assn. (bd.dir. 1968-71), Colo. North Central Assn. Colls. and Secondary Schs., Colo. Assn. Secondary Sch. Prins. (bd. dir. 1974-77), Lions, Sons of the Revolution, Marine Corps League (life), VFW (life), Masons (award of Excellence 1990). Home: 2256 Kingston Rd Grand Junction CO 81503-1221

MOBERLY, ROBERT BLAKELY, lawyer, educator; b. Madison, Wis., Sept. 17, 1941; s. Russell Louis and Hildegarde (Reimer) M.; m. Lynne Webb; children—Laura, Richard, Reed. B.S., U. Wis., 1963, J.D., 1966. Bar: Wis. 1966, Tenn. 1977, Fla. 1984 (faculty affiliate). Law clk. Wis. Supreme Ct., 1966-67; arbitrator, trial examiner, mediator Wis. Employment Relations Commn., 1968-71; practice law Milw., 1971-73; prof. U. Tenn. Coll. Law, Knoxville, 1973-77, U. Fla., 1977—; vis. prof. U. Ill. Inst. for Labor Rels., 1973, U. Louvain, Belgium, 1975, Polish Acad. Scis., 1981; mem. arbitration panels, Fed. Mediation and Conciliation Svc., Am. Arbitration Assn., Nat. Mediation Bd.; prin. investigator U.S. Labor Dept., 1988; mem. com. on mediation and arbitration Fla. Supreme Ct., 1989—, chair arbitration subcom., standards of conduct subcom. Author: Public Employment Labor Relations, 1974, Arbitration and Conflict Resolution, 1979; contbr. articles to profl. jours. Mem. ABA, Fla. Bar Assn. (exec. council labor law sect. 1986-88), Nat. Acad. Arbitrators (chmn. S.E. region 1976-79), Indsl. Relations Rsch. Assn., Soc. Profls. in Dispute Resolution, Internat. Soc. Labor Law and Social Legislation (mem. exec. bd. 1989-92), Assn. Am. Law Schs. (chair labor law sect. 1989, chair-elect alternative dispute resolution sect. 1996). Office: U Fla Coll Law PO Box 117625 Gainesville FL 32611-2038

MOBIUS, MICHAEL, chemicals executive; b. 1950. With Stinnes AG, Germany, 1978-91; pres. Stinnes Corp., N.Y.C., 1991—. Office: Stinnes Corporation 120 White Plains Rd#6FL Tarrytown NY 10591-5522*

MOBLEY, JOHN HOMER, II, lawyer; b. Shreveport, La., Apr. 21, 1930; s. John Hinson and Beulah (Wilson) M.; m. Sue Lawton, Aug. 9, 1958; children: John Lawton, Anne Davant. AB, U. Ga., 1951, JD, 1953. Bar: Ga. 1952, U.S. Dist. Ct., D.C. Ptnr. Kelley & Mobley, Atlanta, 1956-63, Gambrell & Mobley, 1963-83; sr. ptnr., Sutherland, Asbill & Brennan, 1983—. Chmn. Cities in Schs. of Ga.; dir. Cities in Schs. Capt. JAGC, USAF, 1953-55. Mem. ABA, D.C. Bar, State Bar Ga., Atlanta Bar Assn., Am. Judicature Soc., Atlanta Lawyers Club, Phi Delta Phi. Clubs: Atlanta Athletic, Atlanta Country, Commerce, Piedmont Driving, Georgian (Atlanta), N.Y. Athletic, Metropolitan (Washington). Home: 4348 Sentinel Post Rd NW Atlanta GA 30327-3910 Office: Sutherland Asbill & Brennan 999 Peachtree St NE Atlanta GA 30309-3996

MOBLEY, KAREN RUTH, art gallery director; b. Cheyenne, Wyo., Aug. 26, 1961; d. David G. and Marlene G. (Franz) M. BFA, U. Wyo., 1983; MFA, U. Oka., 1987. Sales assoc. Morgan Gallery, Kansas City, Mo., 1984-85; grad. asst. U. Okla. Mus. Art, Norman, 1985-87; dir. Univ. Art Gallery N.Mex. State U., Las Cruces, 1988-93; exec. dir. Nicolaysen Art Mus., Casper, Wyo., 1993—; guest artist Okla. City Community Coll., 1986. Paintings exhibited in numerous exhbns. including Phoenix Triennial, 1990, New Am. Talent, Laguna Gloria Art Mus., Austin, Tex., 1992, Adair Margo Gallery, El Paso, 1992, 93, 94, Wyo. Arts Coun. Gallery and Casper Coll., 1995. Wyo. Arts Coun. Individual Artist grantee 1994; named Outstanding Young Women Am. Mem. Am. Assn. Mus., Mountain Plains Mus. Assn., N.Mex. Mus Assn., Coll. Art Assn., Phi Beta Kappa, Phi Kappa Phi. Home: PO Box 1574 Casper WY 82602-1574 Office: Nicolaysen Art Mus 400 E Collins Dr Casper WY 82601-2815

MOBLEY, MARK, music critic, feature writer; b. Pitts., May 19, 1964; s. Dozier Mell and Carolyn (Estridge) M. MusB in Percussion Performance, Fla. State U., Tallahassee, 1985; MusM, Peabody Conservatory, 1987. Music critic, feature writer The Virginian-Pilot, Norfolk, Va., 1987—. Host Defenestration 895 Sta.-WHRU-FM, 1991—. Nat. Arts Journalism program fellow, 1995-96. Office: The Virginian-Pilot 150 W Brambleton Ave Norfolk VA 23510-2018

MOBLEY, TONY ALLEN, university dean, recreation educator; b. Harrodsburg, Ky., May 19, 1938; s. Cecil and Beatrice (Bailey) M.; m. Betty Weaver, June 10, 1961; 1 child, Derek Lloyd. BS, Georgetown Coll., 1960; MS, Ind. U., 1962, D Recreation, 1965; MRE, So. Sem., Louisville, 1963. Chmn. dept. recreation and pks. Western Ill. U., Macomb, 1965-72, Pa. State U., University Park, 1972-76; prof., chmn. recreation and pks., dean Sch. Health, Phys. Edn. and Recreation Ind. U., Bloomington, 1976—; chair health adv. coun. White River Park Commn., State of Ind., 1979—; v.p Ind. Sports Corp., Indpls., 1983-89; bd. dirs. Nat. Inst. for Fitness and Sport, Indpls., 1984—; J.B. Nash scholar, lectr. Am. Assn. Leisure and Recreation, Reston, Va., 1985. Contbr. over 50 articles to profl. jours. Bd. dirs. Monroe County YMCA, Bloomington, 1984-88. Am. Coun. Edn. adminstrv. internship fellow, N.C. State U., 1970-71. Fellow Am. Acad. Pk. and Recreation Adminstrn. (pres. 1985-86); mem. Nat. Recreation and Pk. Assn. (pres. 1978-79, Nat. Disting. Profl. award 1981), Assn. Rsch., Adminstrn., Profl. Couns. and Socs. (pres. 1986-87, award 1987), Am. Alliance Health, Phys. Edn., Recreation and Dance (Coll. and Univ. Adminstrs. Coun. Honor award 1986), Soc. Pk. and Recreation Edn. (pres. 1974-75, award 1978), Ind. Pk. and Recreation Assn. (Outstanding Profl. award 1985). Avocations: golf, travel. Office: Ind U Sch Health Phys Edn & Rec Recreation Rm 111 Bloomington IN 47405

MOBLEY, WILLIAM HODGES, management educator; b. Akron, Ohio, Nov. 15, 1941. BA, Denison U., 1963; PhD, U. Md., 1971. Mgr. employee relations research PPG Industries, Pitts., 1971-73; prof. U. S.C., Columbia, 1973-80; head dept. of mgmt. Tex. A&M U., College Station, 1980-83, dean. coll. of bus. adminstrn., 1983-86, exec. dep. chancellor, 1986-88, pres., 1988-93; chancellor Tex. A&M U. Sys., College Station, 1993-94; prof. mgmt. Tex. A&M U., College Station, 1994—; cons. Indsl. Psychologist, College Sta., 1980—; bd. dirs. So. Region Inst. for Internat. Edn., Pool Energy Svc., Da

Vinci Sci. Co.; vis. fellow Cornell U., 1994, vis. prof. Hong Kong U. Sci. and Tech., 1995-96. Author: Employee Turnover, 1982. Bd. dirs. Amma Found., 1991—, Internat. Food and Agrl. Devel. and Econ. Coop., U.S. Agy. Internat. Devel., 1992-94; mem. tri-lateral task force on N.Am. Higher Edn. Coop., USIA, 1993-95; mem. Pres. Bush's Commn. on Minority Bus. Devel., 1990-92, U.S. com. of the Pacific Econ. Coop. Coun., 1995—. Fulbright scholar Found. for Scholarly Exchange, Republic China, 1978-79; recipient DAAD, Rep. Germany, 1984; Fellow NDEA U.S. Dept. of Edn., 1968-71. Fellow APA, Am. Psychol. Soc. Home: 431 Chimney Hill Dr College Station TX 77840-1833 Office: Grad Sch Bus Tex A&M Univ College Station TX 77843-4221

MOCCIA, MARY KATHRYN, social worker; b. Harrisburg, Pa.; d. John Joseph and Winifred Louise Trephan. BEd, U. Hawaii, 1978, MSW with distinction, 1980; postgrad., Fuller Theol. Sem., 1987. Diplomate clin. social work. Intern Koko Head Mental Health Clinic, Honolulu, 1978-79, Dept. Social Services and Housing, Honolulu, 1979-80; vol. worker, group coleader Waikiki Mental Health Ctr., Honolulu, 1979, social worker, 1980; workshop facilitator St. Louis-Chaminade Edn. Ctr. Dept. Insts. and Workshops, Honolulu, 1980-83; founding mem. Anorexia and Bulimia Ctr. Hawaii, Honolulu, 1983, pvt. practice psychotherapy and cons., 1983—; personal counselor Chaminade U. Honolulu, 1980-88; clin. social worker Queen's Med. Ctr., 1988—; practicum instr. U. Hawaii, 1992—; guest lectr. U. Hawaii Sch. Social Work, Honolulu, 1980-81; vol. telephone specialist Suicide and Crisis Ctr. and Info. and Referral Service, Honolulu, 1981-83; group leader obesity program Honolulu Med. Group, 1988—; mem. Hawaii Coun. Self Esteem, 1993; condr. various workshops on anorexia and bulimia. Guest appearances on local tv and radio programs. Mem. Manoa Valley Ch. Mem. NASW, Nat. Assn. Christians in Social Work, Acad. Cert. Social Workers, Registry Clin. Social Workers, Mortar Bd. (pres., nat. del. 1978), Phi Kappa Phi, Pi Lambda Theta, Alpha Tau Delta (pres. 1970). Avocations: traveling, dancing, swimming, lifting weights, Bible study. Office: Queens Med Ctr Dept Social Work 1301 Punchbowl St Honolulu HI 96813-2413

MOCH, ROBERT GASTON, lawyer; b. Montesano, Wash., June 20, 1914; s. Gaston and Fleeta Belle (Metcalf) M.; m. Barbara M. Kent, Sept. 2, 1940 (dec.); children: Marilynn A., Michael K., Robert M.; m. LaVerne I. Miller, May 29, 1968. BA magna cum laude, U. Wash., 1936; JD, Harvard Coll., 1941. Bar: Mass. 1941, Wash. 1945. Asst. crew coach U. Wash., 1936-39; head crew coach Mass. Inst. Tech., 1939-44; practiced in Boston, 1941-44, Seattle, 1945—; asso. Herrick, Smith, Donald, Farley & Ketchum, 1941-44, Eggerman, Rosling & Williams, 1945-50, Weter, Roberts & Shefelman, 1950-53; ptnr. Roberts & Shefelman, 1953-87; of counsel Foster, Pepper & Shefelman, 1988—; Del. Nat. Conf. on Law and Poverty, 1965, Nat. Defender Conf., 1969; chmn. King County Pub. Defender Adv. Com., 1970. Mem. U. Wash. Crew, 1933-36. Recipient Olympic Gold medal, 1936; named to Helms Rowing Hall of Fame, U. Wash. Hall of Fame. Mem. ABA, Wash. Bar Assn., Seattle-King County Bar Assn. (past trustee, com. chmn.), U. Wash. Alumni Assn. (pres. 1978-79, Disting. Svc. award 1986), Wash. Alumni Advs. (pres. 1985-87), Rainier Club, Rotary, Phi Beta Kappa, Beta Gamma Sigma, Alpha Kappa Psi, Phi Delta Phi, Phi Gamma Delta. Mem. Christian Ch. Home: 22509 SE 42nd Ter Issaquah WA 98029-7229 Office: Foster Pepper & Shefelman 1111 3rd Ave Ste 3400 Seattle WA 98101-3299

MOCHARY, MARY VERONICA, lawyer; b. Budapest, Hungary, Sept. 7, 1942; d. Alexander and Elizabeth (Aranyi) Kasser; m. Stephen E. Mochary, Sept. 25, 1965 (div. 1990); children: Alexandra Veronica, Matthew Neal. BA, Wellesley Coll., 1963; JD, U. Chgo., 1967. Bar: Ark. 1968, N.J. 1970. Ptnr. Fayetteville, Ark., 1968-70, Mochary & Mochary, Montclair, N.J., 1970-85, Cerny & Mochary, Montclair, 1980-84, Lane & Mittendorf, Woodbridge, N.J., 1984-85; legal advisor U.S. Dept. State, Washington, 1985-89, spl. negotiator real estate issues, 1989-92; ptnr. Wine & Assocs., Washington, 1990—; cons. Hughes, Hubbard & Read, Washington; pres. Technopulp, Inc., Montclair, 1982—, Iamco, Inc., Montclair, 1982—; ptnr. Kand M Co., Montclair, 1982—, Atlantic Highlands Real Estate, Montclair, 1982-89. Mayor Twp. of Montclair, 1980-84; mgr. Kasser Art Found., Montclair, 1982—; Rep. candidate U.S. Senate, State of N.J., 1984; co-chmn. re-election campaign Tom Kean for Gov., N.J., 1985; treas. Com. N.J. Rep. Women in 1985; mem. regional adv. bd. Anti-Defamation League of B'nai B'rith, Montclair Library Bd., 1980—, Montclair Twp. Council, 1980—; chmn. Rep. Task Force Women's Polit. Caucus N.J., Overseas Neighbors Internat., 1985; bd. dirs. Am. Hungarian Found., 1970—, Found. Ednl. Alternatives, Urban League, 1985—. Raoul Wallenberg Com. of U.S., 1985—, Nat. Mus. for Women in the Arts, Washington, 1994—; mem. Women's Internat. Forum, 1992—; founder, bd. dirs. WISH;. Recipient Disting. Service award Am. Hungarian Found., 1984. Mem. ABA, N.J. Bar Assn., Ark. Bar Assn., N.J. Conf. Mayors, N.J. Elected Women Ofcls., Suburban Essex Bus. and Profl. Women (named Woman of Yr. 1985), Wellesley Club (pres. N.J. chpt. 1983-84), Women's Internat. Forum, Adirondack League Club, Ocean Reef Club, Angler's Club (Key Largo, Fla.), Rappahannock County Garden Club. Avocations: skiing, travelling, politics, assisting charitable orgns. and conservation, gardening. Office: 26 Park St Montclair NJ 07042-3443 also: 2700 Virginia Ave NW Washington DC 20037-1908

MOCHEL, MYRON GEORGE, mechanical engineer, educator; b. Fremont, Ohio, Oct. 9, 1905; s. Gustave A. and Rose M. (Minich) M.; m. Eunice Katherine Steinicke, Aug. 30, 1930 (dec. Dec. 1982); children: Kenneth R., David G., Virginia June. BSME, Case Western Res. U., 1929; MSME, Yale U., 1930. Registered profl. engr. N.Y., Mass., Pa. Devel. engr. nitrogen div. Allied Chem. Corp., Hopewell, Va., 1930-31; devel. engr. R&D dept. Mobil Corp., Paulsboro, N.J., 1931-37; design and devel. engr. gearing div. Westinghouse Electric Corp., Pitts., 1937-43; rsch. assoc. underwater sound lab. Harvard U., Cambridge, Mass., 1943-45; supr. of tng. steam turbine div. Worthington Corp., Wellsville, N.Y., 1945-49; prof. mech. engr. Clarkson U., Potsdam, N.Y., 1949-71; prof. emeritus Clarkson U., Potsdam, 1971—; lect. U. Pitts., 1938-43, N.Y. State U. Adult Edn., Wellsville, 1946-49, Oswego, 1965, N.Y. State High Sch. Enrichment Program, Potsdam, 1962-71; cons. Designers for Industry, Cleve., 1953, rsch. engr. Morris Machine Works, Baldwinsville, N.Y., 1954, design engr. Racquette River Paper Co., Potsdam, 1955. Author: Fundamentals of Engineering Graphics, 1960, Pre-Engineering and Applied Science Fundamentals, 1962, Fortran Programming, Programs and Schematic Storage Maps, 1971; coauthor: (with Eunice S. Mochel) Funds For Fun, 1983, (with Donald H. Purcell) Beyond Expectations, 1985; contbr. articles to profl. jours. Officer, vol. St. Lawrence Valley Hospice, 1983; pres. Mayfield Tenants Assn., 1989-91. Mem. ASME, Am. Soc. Engring. Edn. (advt. mgr. Jour. Engring. Graphics 1963-66, sec. 1966-67, high schs. laision on engring. graphics 1962-65, awards com. chmn. 1965-66), Am. Assn. Ret. Persons (founder St. Lawrence County chpt., income tax counselor 1988-89, medicare/medicaid assistance program counselor 1988—, pres. 1989-90). Republican. Mem. Unitarian Universalist Ch. Home and Office: 9C Mayfield Apt # 1 Potsdam NY 13676-1322

MOCHRIE, DOTTIE, professional golfer; b. Saratoga Springs, N.Y., 1966. Student, Furman University. Top ranked player LPGA Tour, 1992. 3 time NCAA All-American; recipient Rolex Player of the Year Award, 1992; recipient Vare Trophy, 1992; leading money winner LPGA, 1992. Winner tournaments including Mazda Classic, 1989, Crestar Classic, 1990, Nabisco Dinah Shore, 1992, Sega Women's Championship, 1992, Welch's Classic, 1992, Sun-Times Challenge, 1992, LPGA Leading Money Winner, 1992, Wendy's Three-Star Challenge, 1992, PING/Welch's Championship, 1995, JC Penney/LPGA Skins Game, McCall's LPGA Classic. Address: care LPGA Ste B 2570 W International Speedway Blvd Daytona Beach FL 32114-7103*

MOCHRIE, RICHARD D., physiology educator; b. Lowell, Mass., Feb. 17, 1928; s. William Blair and Helen (Stephens) M.; m. Helene Mary Buchanan, Aug. 19, 1950; children—Barbara Jean Washer, Steven Howard, Lois Ann Blair. B.S., U. Conn., 1950, M.S., 1953; Ph.D., N.C. State U., 1958. Research technician U. Conn., 1950-53; grad. asst. N.C. State U., 1953-54, instr., 1954-58, asst. prof., 1958-61, assoc. prof., 1961-72, prof. lactational physiology and nutrition, 1972-89, prof. emeritus, 1989—, faculty rep. athletics, 1983-88; U.S. organizer U.S.-Autralian Forage Workshop, also coeditor procs. Author: Lactation Laboratory Outline, 1971; contbr. numerous articles to sci. jours.; Ruminant Nutrition and Metabolism to Ency. Biochemistry, 1967. Precinct com. chmn., county conv. del. Cary and Wake County (N.C.) Dem. Party, 1972—; mem. Cary Recreation Commn., 1989-92, chmn., 1964-70; mem. Wake County Parks and Recreation Commn., 1977, chmn., 1978-83; bd. dirs. Raleigh YMCA; master track and field ofcl.; v.p. N.C. U.S.A. Track & Field, pres., 1992-94. With AUS, 1946-47. Recipient Upjohn Co. citation for contbn. to quality milk mgmt., 1978; inducted into Chelmsford (Mass.) H.S. Hall of Fame, 1995. Mem. Nat. Mastitis Coun. (dir. 1973-86, v.p. 1975, pres. 1976, disting. svc. award 1978), Am. Dairy Sci. Assn. Found. (charter), Assn. Ofcl. Analytical Chemists (assoc. referee), Interstate Milk Shippers, N.C. Recreators Found. (chmn. 1981-89), Nat. Recreation and Park Assn. (citizen bd. mem. divsn. 1984-94, bd. dirs. 1984-90), Atlantic Coast Conf. (pres. 1986), N.C. Recreation and Park Soc. (bd. dirs. 1981-85, Citation award 1986), N.C. State U. Faculty Club (bd. dirs. 1990-92, pres. 1991-92), Cary Exch. (pres. 1963-64), Dairy Shrine, Gamma Sigma Delta (cert. of merit 1978), Sigma Chi, Pi Alpha Sigma, Sigma Xi. Democrat. Presbyterian (deacon 1959-61). Home: 505 S Dixon Ave Cary NC 27511-3254

MOCK, DAVID CLINTON, JR., internist; b. Redlands, Calif., May 6, 1922; s. David Clinton and Eithel (Benson) M.; m. Marcella Enriqueta Fellin, Nov. 13, 1952. A.B., U. So. Calif., 1944; M.D., M.H.D., Hahnemann Med. Coll., 1948. Intern Hahnemann Hosp., Phila., 1948-49; resident San Mateo (Calif.) County Hosp., 1949-51, 54, VA Hosp., Oklahoma City, 1954-55; research fellow in exptl. therapeutics U. Okla., Oklahoma City, 1956-57, L.N. Upjohn fellow, 1958, dir. exptl. therapeutics unit, 1959-62; dir., preceptorship program, 1968-76; assoc. prof. medicine U. Okla., Oklahoma City, 1963-72, prof., 1972-84, emeritus prof. medicine, 1984—, assoc. dean med. student affairs, 1970-76, assoc. dean postdoctoral edn., 1976-82, dir. continuing med. edn., 1980-83, dir. Transitional Yr. program, 1980-84, dir. History of Medicine program, 1982-84; assoc. mem. Faculty of Homeopathy Royal London Homeopathic Hosp., Eng.; pres., dir. Coachella Valley Fruit Co., Inc., Indio, Calif. Lt. comdr. USPHS, 1951-53; now capt. Res. Fellow ACP; mem. Am. Fedn. Clin. Research, N.Y. Acad. Scis. Unitarian. Home: 570 Alameda Blvd Coronado CA 92118-1617

MOCK, FRANK MACKENZIE, lawyer; b. South Bend, Ind., May 17, 1944; s. Frank Carlton and Julia (Baughmann) M.; m. Virginia Johns, Dec. 31, 1974 (div. Feb. 1991); children: Shannon, John, Bridget. BA, Duke U., 1966, JD, 1969. Bar: Fla. 1969. Assoc. Mahoney, Adams, Criser, Jacksonville, Fla., 1969-74, ptnr., 1977-92; gen. counsel Builders Investment Group, Valley Forge, Pa., 1974-77; ptnr. Baker & Hostetler, Orlando, Fla., 1992—. Mem. ABA, Duval County Bar Assn., Orange County Bar Assn., Dade County Bar Assn., Palm Beach County Bar Assn., Turnaround Mgmt. Assn. Republican. Episcopalian. Avocations: hiking, fishing, reading. Home: 2147 Santa Antilles Rd Orlando FL 32806-1533 Office: Baker & Hostetler 200 S Orange Ave Orlando FL 32801-3410

MOCK, HENRY BYRON, lawyer, writer, consultant; b. Greenville, Tex., Feb. 1, 1911; s. Henry Byron and Ellena (Edmonds) M.; m. Mary Morris, Nov. 11, 1949. A.B., U. Ariz., 1933; J.D., Georgetown U., 1939, George Washington U., 1940. Asst. sec. to Congresswoman Isabella Greenway of Ariz., 1934-35; office mgr., legal research asst., recreation div. WPA, Washington, 1935-38; asst. atty. WPA, 1938; legal adv. President's Adv. Com. on Edn., 1938-39; asst. solicitor Dept. Interior, 1939-41; chief counsel U.S. Grazing Service, Salt Lake City, 1941-42; adminstr. region IV U.S. Bur. Land Mgmt., Colo., Utah, 1947-54; area adminstr. U.S. Bur. Land Mgmt., Idaho, Ariz., Utah, Nev., 1954-55; exec. resource cos., 1955—; adj. prof. law U. Utah, 1979—. Contbr. profl. publs. Chmn. Dept. Interior storm relief com. Western U.S., 1949; mem. U.S. Pub. Land Law Rev. Commn., 1964-70, vice chmn., 1965-70; mem. Interior Oil Shale Com., 1964. Served pvt. to capt. with AUS, 1942-46, MTO. Mem. D.C., Va., Utah bar assns. Bar Supreme Ct. of U.S., Am., Fed. bar assn., U.S. C. of C., Bar of Ct. Mil. Appeals, Am. Inst. Mining and Metall. Engrs., Am. Soc. Range Mgmt., Am. Soc. Pub. Adminstrn. (past Utah pres.), Western Polit. Sci. Assn., Am. Forestry Assn., Pi Kappa Alpha. Clubs: Rotary (Salt Lake City), Alta (Salt Lake City). Home and Office: 900 Donner Way Apt 101 Salt Lake City UT 84108-2107

MOCK, LARRY JOHN, elementary education educator; b. Quincy, Ill., Jan. 13, 1950; s. Frank Paul and Elizabeth Katherine (Hugenberg) M. BS, Quincy U., 1972; MEd, Ga. State U., 1985, specialist in edn., 1989, postgrad., 1993—. Cert. tchr. grades 1-8, Ga. Tchr. grade 4 Cmty. Dist. #3, Clayton, Ill., 1972-74; tchr. adult edn. Atlanta (Ga.) Pub. Schs., 1975-91, tchr. grade 5, 1991-94, tchr. grade 3, 1994-95; asst. prin. Atlanta Pub. Schs. Author: Daily Living Lab Manual, 1978. Chairperson Ho. Dist. 68 Dekalb County Dem. Party, Atlanta, 1993-94; active Butler St. YMCA, Scottie Club of Greater Atlanta. Mem. NEA (Atlanta chpt.), ASCD, Am. Rsch. Assn., Am. Parkinson Disease Assn., Ga. Coun. for Social Studies, East Atlanta Cmty. Assn. (treas., sec., v.p. 1980-93), Capitol View PTA, Phi Kappa Phi (Alumnus chpt.). Avocations: traveling, gardening, family geneology, local history, Scotty Terrier dog shows. Home: 1213 Gracewood Ave SE Atlanta GA 30316-2665

MOCK, MELINDA SMITH, orthopedic nurse specialist, consultant; b. Austell, Ga., Nov. 15, 1947; d. Robert Jehu and Emily Dorris (Smith) Smith; m. David Thomas Mock, Oct. 20, 1969. AS in Nursing, DeKalb Coll., 1972. RN, Ga.; cert. orthopedic nurse specialist, orthopedic nurse. Nursing technician Ga. Baptist Hosp., Atlanta, 1967, staff nurse, 1979; asst. corr. Harcourt, Brace & World Pub. Co., Atlanta, 1968-69; receptionist-sec. Goodbody & Co., Atlanta, 1969-70; nursing asst. DeKalb Gen. Hosp., Decatur, Ga., 1970-71; staff nurse Doctor's Meml. Hosp., Atlanta, 1972-73; staff nurse Shallowford Cmty. Hosp., Atlanta, 1973, relief charge nurse, 1973, charge nurse, 1973-76, head nurse, 1976-79, orthopedic nurse specialist emergency room, 1979; rehab. specialist Internat. Rehab. Assocs., Inc., Norcross, Ga., 1981, sr. rehab. specialist, 1981, rehab. supr., 1981-82; cons., founder, propr. Healthcare Cost Cons., Alpharetta, Ga., 1982-83; cons., founder, pres. Healthcare Cost Cons., Inc., Alpharetta, 1983—; mem. legis. com. of adv. coun. Ga. Bd. Nursing, Atlanta, 1984-85; mem. adv. coun. Milton H.S. Coop. Bus. Edn., 1986-89; mem. Congressman Patrick Swindall Sr. Citizen Adv. Coun., 1988, Congressman Ben Jones Vets. Affairs Adv. Com., 1989-92, White House Conf. on Small Bus. (appointed by Newt Gingrich 1995), Nat. Fedn. Specialty Nursing Orgns. Task Force on Profl. Liability Ins., 1987-89, Dep. voter registrar Fulton County, Ga., 1983-87; Rep. treas. 23d house dist., mem. Fulton County Rep. Com., 1989—, nominating com., 1991, 92, 93, 95, 96, chmn. polit action com., 1993-95, asst. treas., 1994-95, sec., 1995—; treas. 41st House Dist. Rep. Party, 1993—; 1st vice chairwoman 6th Congl. Dist. Rep. Party, 1993—; mem. State Com. Ga. Rep. Party, 1993—; del. Fulton County Rep. Conv., 1991, 92, 94, 95, 96, del. Ga. 4th Congrl. Dist., 1991, 92, parliamentarian, 1992, credentials com., 1992, Ga. Rep. Conv., 1991, 92, 93, 95, 96, del. Ga. 6th Congrl. Dist. Rep. Party Convention, 1993, 95, 96; alt. del.-at-large Nat. Rep. Conv., 1996; mem. Chattahoochee Rep. Women, 1989—, chmn. campaign com., 1992-94, rec. sec., 1995—; chmn. nominating com. House Dist. 23, 1990; mem. steering com. to re-elect state rep. Tom Campbell, 1990; mem. campaign staff to re-elect state senator Sallie Newbill, 1990; health advisor campaign to elect Matt Towery for lt. gov., 1990, health adv. compaign to elect Bob Barr U.S. Senate, 1991-92; mem. election com. Mark Burkhalter for State Rep.; vol. campaign staff to re-elect Congressman Newt Gingrich, 1992, 94, 96; mem. campaign staff to elect Jim Hunt as state rep., 1996; vol. campaign to elect Tom Price to state senate, 1996. Recipient Nat. Disting. Service Registry award, 1987; named one of Outstanding Young Women Am., 1984. Mem. NAFE, Nat. Assn. Orthopedic Nurses (nat. policies com. 1981-82, chmn. govt. rels. com. 1987-90, nat. treas. 1991-95, nurse Washington intern 1987, legis. contbr. editor news 1989, chmn. legis. workshop, 1989, co-chmn. legis. workshop, 1990, guest editl. Orthopaedic Nursing Jour. 1988, spkr. 1990, 92, 93, 94, Ann. Congress, del. 1982, 91, 92, 93, 94, 96, Pres's. award 1992, chmn. budget and fin. com. 1991-95, nat. bylaws and policies com. 1995—, bylaws and policies com. Altanta chpt. 1994—, pres.-elect Atlanta chpt. 1996—), Orthopedic Nurses Assn. (nat. bd. dirs. 1977-79, nat. treas. 1979-81, Coun. Splty. Nursing Orgns. Ga. (nominating com. 1976-77), Ga. Med. Auditors Assn., Nat. Nurses in Bus. Assn., Assn. Rehab. Nurses (bd. dirs. Ga. chpt. 1980-81, del. people-to-people program to China 1981), Nat. Fed. Ind. Bus. (guardian 1988—, adv. coun. 1990—, healthcare task force chmn. 1992—, vice-chmn./fed. liaison Ga. adv. coun. 1995—), Am. Bd. Nursing Specialities (chmn. nominating com. 1993-94, 94-95, chmn. com. on specialty bd. rev. 1993-95), Ga. Jaycees (dist. 4C rep. Ga. Jaycee Legis. 1984, 85), Ga. seatbelt coalition, Orthopaedic Nurses Cert. Bd. (bd. dir. 1991—, pres. 1992-93, task force on advanced practice991-92), North Fulton C. of C. (vice chmn. health service effectiveness alliance 1984-85, chmn. 1985-86, co-chmn./editor periodical 1985, 3rd Quarter Workhorse award 1985), Alpharetta Jaycees (adminstrv. v.p. 1984-85, internal v.p. 1985-86), Alpharetta Jaycee Women (bd. dirs. 1983). Baptist. Avocations: reading, boating, cmty. svc. activities. Home: 424 Michael Dr Alpharetta GA 30201 Office: Healthcare Cost Cons Inc PO Box 466 St Alpharetta GA 30239

MOCK, RANDALL DON, lawyer; b. Oklahoma City, Aug. 9, 1943; s. John Haskell and M. Louise M.; m. Sally Merkle, June 4, 1966; children: Adam Peterson, Caroline Louise. BBA, U. Okla., 1965, JD, 1968; LLM in Taxation, NYU, 1970. Bar: Okla. 1968, U.S. Tax Ct. 1970, U.S. Supreme Ct. 1974; CPA. Dir. Mock, Schwabe, Waldo, Elder, Reeves and Bryant, Oklahoma City; sec., bd. dirs. Okla. Attys. Mut. Ins. Co. Editor: Oklahoma Law Review, Tax Law Review; co-author: Oklahoma Corporate Forms. Pres. Oklahoma City Estate Planning Coun., 1987-88, dir., 1980-88; pres. Oklahoma City Tax Lawyers Group, 1973; bd. dirs., mem. exec. com. Met. YMCA; trustee Westminster Sch. Fellow Am. Coll. Tax Counsel; mem. Okla. Bar Assn. (sect. taxation), Beacon Club (v.p., bd. dirs.), Order of Coif. Office: Mock Schwabe Waldo Elder Reeves & Bryant 15th Fl 1 Leadership Sq 211 N Robinson Ave Oklahoma City OK 73102-7157

MOCK, ROBERT CLAUDE, architect; b. Baden, Fed. Republic of Germany, May 3, 1928; came to U.S., 1938, naturalized, 1943; s. Ernest and Charlotte (Geismar) M.; m. Belle Carol Bach, Dec. 23, 1952 (div.); children: John Bach, Nicole Louise; m. Marjorie Reubenfeld, Dec. 20, 1964. BArch, Pratt Inst., 1950; MArch, Harvard U., 1953. Registered architect, N.Y., Conn., N.J., Nat. Council Archtl. Registration Bds. Architect George C. Marshall Space Center, Huntsville, Ala., 1950-51; archtl. critic Columbia Sch. Architecture, N.Y.C., 1953-54; dir. facility design Am. Airlines, N.Y.C., 1955-60; founder Robert C. Mock & Assocs. (architects and engrs.), N.Y.C., 1960—; Mem. Mayor's Panel of Architects, N.Y.C. Prin. works include: Shine Motor Inn, Queens, N.Y., 1961 (recipient 1st prize motel category Queens C. of C. 1961), temporary terminal bldg. Eastern Air Lines , La Guardia Airport, N.Y.C., 1961, cargo bldgs United Airlines and Trans World Airlines, Kennedy Airport, N.Y.C., Bridgeport (Conn.) Airport, 1961, Eastern Air Lines Med. Ctr., Kennedy Airport, 1962, ticket office Trans World Airlines Fifth Ave., N.Y.C., 1962, terminal bldgs. Eastern Air Lines and Trans World Airlines , La Guardia Airport, N.Y.C., 1963, 7 bldgs. Mfrs. Hanover Trust Co. , 1964-66, kitchen and commissary bldg. Lufthansa German Airlines, 1964, Ambassador Club, La Guardia Airport, 1964, Happyland Sch., N.Y.C., 1965, cargo bldgs. Alitalia and Lufthansa German Airlines, Kennedy Airport, 1965, FAA-Nat. Prototype Air Traffic Control Tower, 1966; Lufthansa German Airlines; Irish Internat. Airlines, El Al Israel Airlines, Varig Brazilian Airlines; passenger terminals Kennedy Airport, 1970; Swiss Air Cargo Terminal, Lufthansa German Airlines, cargo terminals El Al Israel airline cargo terminal, Kennedy Airport, 1972, passenger terminal Aerolineas Argentina, 1974, N.Am. hdqrs. Aerolineas Argentinas, N.Y.C., 1974, corp. hdqrs. Am. Airlines, 1977, N.Am. hdqrs. Varig Brazilian Airlines, N.Y.C., 1977, Norel-Ronel Indsl. Pk., Hollywood, Fla., 1979, N.Am. hdqrs. Irish Internat. Airlines , N.Y.C., 1979, corp. hdqrs. Bankers Trust Co., N.Y.C., 1980, cargo terminal Air India, cargo terminal Flying Tiger, Kennedy Airport, 1982, 2 flight kitchen bldgs. Ogden Food Corp., Kennedy Airport, 1984, 88 and LaGuardia Airport, 1987, Greenwich Assn. Retarded Citizens Sch., 1983, passenger terminal extension Varig Brazilian Airlines , 1985, 3 restaurants La Guardia Airport, 1987, residences Palm Beach, Fla., 1989-92, Bethesda, Md., 1993, Fenwick Island, Del., 1994, Potomac Falls, Md., 1995. Recipient United Way Vol. of Yr. award, 1984. Mem. Am. Arbitration Assn. Clubs: City, Harvard, Admirals Cove. Office: 185 Byram Shore Rd Greenwich CT 06830-6909

MOCK, THEODORE JAYE, accounting educator; b. Traverse City, Mich., May 28, 1941; s. Raymond Doris and Georgeann (Lardie) M.; m. Mary Jo Icenhower, Mar. 25, 1962; children—Christopher, Cameron. B.S. in Math., Ohio State U., 1963, M.B.A. in Fin., 1964; Ph.D. in Bus. Adminstrn., U. Calif.-Berkeley, 1969. Dir. AIS Research Ctr. UCLA, 1969-73; dir. Ctr. Acctg. Research, Arthur Andersen Alumni prof. acctg. U. So. Calif., 1982—; vis. prof. Norwegian Sch. Econs. and Bus., Bergen, 1988, Bond U., Gold Coast, Australia, 1990, 92, So. Cross U., Lismore, Australia, 1994; adj. prof. U. Limburg, The Netherlands, 1991—; hon. prof. Hong Kong City U., 1995—; bd. dirs. Maastricht (The Netherlands) Acctg. Rsch. Ctr., U. Limburg, 1991—. Author: (monographs) Risk Assessment, 1985, Internal Accounting Control (Am. Acctg. Assn. Wildman medal), 1983, Measurement and Accounting Information Criteria, 1976, Impact of Future Technology on Auditing, 1988, Auditing and Analytic Review, 1989; mem. editorial bd. Auditing: A Jour. of Practice and Theory, 1983-86, 88-93, editor, 1993—; mem. editorial bd. The Acctg. Rev., 1972-78. Recipient CPA Faculty Excellence award Calif. CPA Found. for Edn. and Rsch., 1983; Fulbright scholar U. Otago, Dunedin, New Zealand, 1988, U. Limburg, Maastricht, The Netherlands, 1993. Mem. Acctg., Orgns. and Soc. (editorial bd. 1978-93), Am. Acctg. Assn. (dir. rsch. 1982-84, acad. vice chmn. auditing sect. 1990-91, chair auditing sect. 1991-92). Office: U So Calif Sch of Acctg Los Angeles CA 90089-1421

MOCKO, GEORGE PAUL, minister; b. Little Falls, N.Y., Feb. 15, 1934; s. George and Anna (Swancara) M.; m. Elizabeth Carol Davidson, Sept. 2, 1956; children: David, Paul, Kristopher, Elissa. BA, Hartwick Coll., 1956; BD, Phila. Sem., 1959, STM, 1972; DD (hon.), Gettysburg Coll., 1978. Ordained to ministry Evang. Luth. Ch. in Am., 1959. Pastor Jacob's and Outwood Chs., Pine Grove, Pa., 1959-62; assoc. pastor St Mark's Ch., Wilmington, Del., 1962-65, sr. pastor, 1965-78; sr. pastor Ascension Evang. Luth. Ch., Towson, Md., 1978-91; bishop Del.-Md. Synod Evang. Luth Ch. in Am., Towson, 1991—. Author books; contbr. articles to profl. jours. Home: 501 Sussex Rd Baltimore MD 21286-7609 Office: Evang Luth Ch in Am 7604 York Rd Baltimore MD 21204-7508 *Colossians speaks of Christ as the one in whom "all things hold together". I know that Christ is the one who holds me together. Proclaiming and living his life, the church holds our society together.*

MODANO, MICHAEL, professional hockey player; b. Livonia, Mich., June 7, 1970. Right wing/center Minn. North Stars, 1988-93, Dallas Stars, 1993—; player World Hockey League East All-Star Game, 1988-89, NHL All-Rookie Game, 1989-90, NHL All-Star Game, 1993. *

MODDERMAN, MELVIN EARL, health administrator; b. Coopersville, Mich., Nov. 13, 1940; s. Ray J. and Alberta Ruth (Sietsema) M.; m. Ida Sue Evans, Sept. 6, 1969; children: Scott David, Christopher Braeden, Geoffrey Alan. BS, U. Mich., 1963; MHA, Baylor U., 1968; MBA, St. Mary's U., San Antonio, 1976; D in Bus. Adminstrn., George Washington U., 1982. With 36th med. battalion U.S. Army, Hanau, Fed. Republic Germany, 1963-66; project officer hosp. constrn. Office Surgeon Gen., Dept. Army, Washington, 1968-70; adminstr. 3d Surg. Hosp., U.S. Army, Vietnam, 1970-71; asst. prof. grad. program Baylor U. AHS, Ft. Sam Houston, Tex., 1971-75; policy analyst Office Surgeon Gen., Dept. Army, Washington, 1976-79, chief pers. policy, 1981-83, dep. dir. pers., 1983-84; prof. and program dir. grad. program Baylor U. AHS, Ft. Sam Houston, Tex., 1984-88; chmn. health care adminstrn. Acad. Health Scis., Ft. Sam Houston, 1988-90; dep. comdr. for adminstrn., chief exec. officer Ireland Army Community Hosp., Ft. Knox, Ky., 1990-92; adminstr. Lincoln Trail Hosp., Radcliff, Ky., 1992—; mem. geographic distbn. tech. subpanel Grad. Med. Edn. Nat. Adv. Com., 1979-81. Ruling edler First Presbyn. Ch., Elizabethtown, Ky., 1993—; chmn. com. Eagle Dist. Boy Scouts Am. Troop 497, 1988-90. Accrediting Commn. on Edn. for Health Svcs. Commn. fellow, 1985. Fellow Am. Coll. Healthcare Execs. (regent U.S. Army 1990-92); mem. Ky. Hosp. Assn., Louisville Metro Hosp. Coun. Home: 217 W French St Elizabethtown KY 42701-1901 Office: Lincoln Trail Hosp Adminstr's Office 3909 S Wilson Rd Elizabethtown KY 42701-8425

MODE, CHARLES J., mathematician, educator; b. Bismarck, N.D., Dec. 29, 1927; s. Charles and Fannie E. (Hansen) M.; m. Eleanore L. Perdelwitz; 1 dau., Martha Lisa. B.S. in Genetics, N.D. State U., 1952; M.S. in Genetics, Kans. State U., 1953; Ph.D. in Genetics, U. Calif., Davis and Berkeley, 1956; postgrad. in stats. (Univ. fellow), N.C. State U., 1956-57.

Asst. prof. math. Mont. State U., 1957-59, asso. prof., 1960-62, prof., 1963-66, mem. genetics group, 1957-66; asso. prof. math. stats. SUNY, Buffalo, 1966-70; prof. math. Drexel U., 1970—; cons. to industry. Author: Multi-type Branching Processes - Theory and Applications, 1971, Stochastic Processes in Demography and their Computer Implementation, 1985; contbr. numerous articles to profl. publs.; assoc. editor: Math. Bioscis, 1975—. Mem. Inst. Math. Stats., Biometric Soc., Am. Math. Soc., AAAS, Population Assn. Am., Sigma Xi, Phi Kappa Phi, Pi Mu Epsilon. Lutheran. Home: 502 Balsam Rd Cherry Hill NJ 08003-3202 Office: Drexel Univ Dept Math Philadelphia PA 19104

MODE, PAUL J., JR., lawyer; b. Columbus, Ohio, Feb. 23, 1938; s. Paul J. and Dorothy O. Mode; m. Elaine Rush, June 13, 1961; children: Rebecca D., David B. BME with distinction, Cornell U., 1961; LLB magna cum laude, Harvard U., 1967. Bar: D.C., U.S. Supreme Ct. Assoc. Wilmer, Cutler & Pickering, Washington, 1967-70, 73-74, ptnr., 1975—, mem. mgmt. com., 1983-86, chmn. mgmt. com., 1987—; chief counsel U.S. Senate Subcom. on Constl. Amendments, Washington, 1970-73; panelist Ctr. for Pub. Resources Panel of Disting. ADR Neutrals, 1989—. Author: (with others) Litigation, vol.12, No.4, 1986; mem. editorial bd. Harvard Law Rev., 1966-67, Alternatives to the High Cost of Litigation, 1991—; contbr. articles to profl. jours. Mem. issues staff Robert F. Kennedy Presdl. campaign, 1968. Lt. (j.g.) USN, 1961-64. Avocations: tennis, collecting antique maps. Home: 2750 Brandywine St NW Washington DC 20008-1040 Office: Wilmer Cutler & Pickering 2445 M St NW Washington DC 20037-1435

MODEL, PETER, molecular biologist; b. Frankfort, Germany, May 17, 1933; s. Leo and Jane (Ermel) M.; m. Pat Goldman, 1961 (div. 1981); 1 child Paul; m. Marjorie Russel, June 21, 1981; 1 child Sascha. BA, Stanford U., 1954; PhD, Columbia U., 1965. Rsch. assoc. Columbia U., N.Y.C., 1965-1967; fellow Rockefeller U., N.Y.C., 1967-69, mem. faculty, 1969—, prof., 1987—; bd. dirs. Biotechnica Inst., Cambridge, Mass., 1981-86. Mem. editorial bd. Jour. Virology, Virology; contbr. articles to profl. jours. Bd. dirs. United Help, N.Y., 1980, Self Help Community Svc., N.Y., 1980. 1st Lt. U.S. Army, 1954-56. Mem. Am. Soc. Virology, Am. Soc. Microbiology, Am. Soc. for Biochemistry and Molecular Biology. Democrat. Office: Rockefeller U Lab of Genetics 1230 York Ave New York NY 10021-6307

MODELAND, PHYLLIS J., author; b. Carthage, Mo., Dec. 22, 1938; d. Howard Levi and Pauline (Crawford) Anderson; m. Dennis L. Rossiter, Mar. 30, 1968 (dec. Apr. 1992); 1 child, Eric Shawn; m. Vernon L. Modeland, May 29, 1996. Head libr. Trs. Regional Libr. Br., Odessa, Mo., 1979-83; editor, gen. mgr. Ozark County Times Newspaper, Gainesville, Mo., 1989; freelance writer, tchr., editor, lectr., photographer. Author: On the Scent of Danger, 1989, Moxie, 1990, A Living History of the Ozarks, 1992; contbr. articles to profl. jours., periodicals, short story anthologies. Mem. Soc. Children's Book Writers, Authors Guild, Western Writers of Am., PEN Ctr. USA West, Women Writing the West, Rocky Mountain Fiction Writers, Heartland Writers Guild, Ozarks Writers League (v.p. 1990, Dan Saults award 1988, 93), Mo. Writers Guild (Best Column. 1989, Best Book 1991, Best Major Work 1992). Avocations: photography, hand spinning. Home: Box 1299 Flippin AR 72634

MODELL, ARTHUR B., professional football team executive; b. Bklyn., June 23, 1925; m. Patricia Breslin, July 25, 1969; stepchildren: John, David. Owner, pres. Cleve. Browns football team(now Baltimore Ravens), 1961—; pres. Nat. Football League, 1967-70. Office: Baltimore Ravens 11001 Owings Mills Blvd Owings Mills MD 21117*

MODELL, JEROME HERBERT, anesthesiologist, educator; b. St. Paul, Sept. 9, 1932; s. William and Frieda (Singer) M.; m. Shirley Graves, Nov. 25, 1977; children—Charles, Jack, Julie. B.A., U. Minn., 1954, B.S., 1957, M.D., 1957. Intern U.S. Naval Hosp., St. Albans, N.Y., 1957-58; resident U.S. Naval Hosp., 1958-60; practice medicine specializing in anesthesiology Gainesville, Fla., 1969—; attending staff U.S. Naval Hosp., St. Albans, 1960-61; chief anesthesiology U.S. Naval Hosp., Pensacola, Fla., 1961-63; asso. prof. dept. anesthesiology U. Miami (Fla.) Sch. Medicine, 1963-69; prof., chmn. dept. anesthesiology U. Fla. Coll. Medicine, Gainesville, 1969-92, sr. assoc. dean clin. affairs, 1990-95, exec. assoc. dean, 1996—; assoc. v.p. U. Fla. Health Sci. Ctr. Affiliations, 1992-96; assoc. v.p. U. Fla. Health Sci. Ctr. Affiliations, 1992-96. Author: The Pathophysiology and Treatment of Drowning and Near-Drowning, 1971, (with others) Introduction to Life Support, 1973; also numerous scientific articles. Served to lt. comdr. USN, 1957-63. Recipient NIH Research Career Devel. award. Mem. AMA, AAAS, Assn. U. Anesthetists, Am. Soc. Anesthesiologists, N.Y. Acad. Scis., Am. Coll. Chest Physicians. Home: PO Box 14347 Gainesville FL 32604-4347

MODELL, JOHN, historian, educator; b. N.Y.C., June 3, 1941; s. Walter and Merriam (Levant) M.; m. Judith Schachter, June 2, 1963; children: Jennifer, Matthew Thelonious. AB, Columbia U., 1962, MA, 1963, PhD, 1969; postgrad. (Social Sci. Research Council research tng. fellow), U. Pa., 1969-70. Research asst. Bur. Applied Social Research, Columbia U., 1962-65; lectr. Kingsborough Community Coll., 1965-66; dir. research Japanese Am. Research Project, UCLA, 1966-69; asst. prof. history U. Minn., 1969-72, assoc. prof., 1972-77, prof., 1977-83; prof. Carnegie Mellon U., 1983—, acting dean Coll. Humanities and Social Scis., 1985-87; Cardozo vis. prof. history Yale U., 1991; adj. prof. human devel. Brown U., 1996—; rsch. assoc. Phila. Social History Project, U. Pa., 1974-85; mem. adv., planning com. Ctr. for Coordination of Study of Social Indicators, Social Sci. Rsch. Coun., 1980-85; mem. com. child devel. rsch. and pub. policy NRC, 1981-86; mem. coun. Inter-Univ. Consortium for Polit. and Social Rsch., 1982-86; mem. MacArthur Found. Rsch. Network on Successful Pathways through Middle Childhood; mem. Network Program on Aging and Social Change, Nat. Inst. Aging. Author: The Economics and Politics of Racial Accommodation: The Japanese of Los Angeles 1900-1942, 1977, Into One's Own: From Youth to Adulthood in the United States, 1920-75, 1989, (with others) The Economic Basis of Ethnic Solidarity, 1981, Recent Social Trends in the United States 1960-90, 1991; editor, author: (with others) The Kikuchi Diary: Chronicle of an American Concentration Camp, 1973; editor: (with others) Theory, Method, and Practice in Social and Cultural History, 1992, Children in Time and Place: Developmental and Historical Insights, 1993; mem. editorial bd. Jour. Social History, 1985—, Historical Methods, 1985-87, Pub. Opinion Quar., 1987-91, Jour. of Research in Adolescence, 1990-93, The Historian, 1990-91. John Simon Guggenheim Meml. fellow, 1978-79. Home: 2048 Beechwood Blvd Pittsburgh PA 15217-1744 Office: Carnegie Mellon U Dept History Pittsburgh PA 15213

MODELL, MICHAEL STEVEN, lawyer, business executive; b. Bklyn., Mar. 11, 1953; s. William D. and Shelby Modell. BA in Internat. Svc., Govt. Pub. Adminstrsn., Am. U., 1974; JD, St. Johns U., Jamaica, N.Y., 1977. Bar: N.Y. 1978, Fla. 1978, U.S. Dist. Ct. (so. dist.) N.Y. 1979, U.S. Dist. Ct. (ea. dist.) N.Y. 1979. Pres. Henry Modell and Co., Inc. (Modell's Sporting Good), N.Y.C., 1988—; bd. dirs. Empire Blue Cross & Blue Shield, Nat. Retail Fedn. Foster parent Save the Children Found., N.Y.C., 1970—; big brother Big Brother Orgn., N.Y.C., 1970-80; v.p., trustee Crohns and Colitis Found. of Am., N.Y.C., 1968—. Mem. Young Pres.' Orgn., Real Estate Bd. of N.Y., Pi Sigma Alpha, Seawane Club (Hewlett), Friars Club (N.Y.C.). Office: Modells Sporting Goods 20th Fl 498 7th Ave New York NY 10018-6701

MODER, JOHN JOSEPH, academic administrator, priest; b. St. Louis, Apr. 9, 1948; s. Helen (Freihaut) M. BA in English and Philosophy, St. Mary's U., San Antonio, 1970; MA in Philosophy, Fordham U., 1972, PhD in Philosophy, 1977; M Div, U. St. Michael's, 1979. Joined Soc. of Mary, ordained priest Roman Cath. Ch., 1979. Mem. faculty Assumption High Sch., East St. Louis, Ill., 1973-75, Vianney High Sch., St. Louis, 1975-77; faculty mem. Irish Christian Bros. Sch., Mono Mills, Ont., Can., 1977-79; asst. prof. philosophy St. Mary's U., San Antonio, 1979-86, assoc. prof. philosophy, trustee, co-chmn. peace commn., 1986-88, pres., 1988—. Bd. advisors Communities-in-Schs., San Antonio, 1988—. Mem. Am. Cath. Philos. Assn., Am. Cancer Soc., Hispanic Assn. Colls., World Affairs Coun., Greater San Antonio C. of C., Rotary Club of San Antonio. Avocations: hiking, reading, travel, running. Office: St Mary's U Office of Pres 1 Camino Santa Maria St San Antonio TX 78228-8572

MODER, LISA MARIE, software engineer, manufacturing process engineer; b. Muchengladbach, Germany, Apr. 18, 1965; came to U.S., 1967; d. John Andrew and Sue Elaine (Anderson) Bondch; m. David Lincoln Moder, May 2, 1987; children: Daniel Lee, Sean Michael, Christopher James. BSEE Tech., Met. State Coll., 1990. Software engr. Erbtec Engring., Boulder, Colo., 1989—. Mem. IEEE. Democrat. Avocations: collecting, creating elec. gadgets, computer games. Home: 3355 Newland St Wheat Ridge CO 80033-6440 Office: Erbtec Engring 2760 29th St Ste 100 Boulder CO 80301-1230

MODERACKI, EDMUND ANTHONY, music educator, conductor; b. Hackensack, N.J., July 18, 1946; s. Edmund Joseph and Helen Theresa (Fisher) M. BA, Montclair State Coll., 1968, postgrad., 1970-71; MA, Hunter Coll., 1970, postgrad., 1970-72; postgrad., Newark State Coll., 1969-70, Seton Hall U., 1970, Rutgers U., 1976-78, Ctr. for Understanding Media, 1973. Tchr. music pub. schs. River Vale, N.J., 1968—; asst. condr. Ridgewood (N.J.) Symphony Orch., 1969—, trustee, pres., 1986-87, 94-95; asst. condr. Adelphi Chamber Orch., 1994-95; tuba soloist Rutherford Cmty. Band, Ridgewood Village Band, Waldwick Band, Ridgewood Concert Band, 1978—, Ridgewood Concert Band, 1983—; guest condr., 1985, 86, 88, 93; mgr. All Bergen High Sch. Band, 1994. Town historian River Vale; mem. steering com. Bergen County Teen Arts, 1991—. Recipient County Exec. Vol. award, 1991, Tchr. Recognition award Gov. of State of N.J., 1990; Bergen County PTA fellow, 1976. Mem. NEA, Music Educators Nat. Conf., N.J. Orch. Assn. (trustee 1981-85), N.J. Edn. Assn. (Del. assembly alt. 1983-93, mem. state membership com. 1986—), Music Educators Bergen County (bd. mem. at-large 1995—), River Vale Edn. Assn. (pres. 1981-83, 88-91), Brigade Am. Revolution (bd. dirs. at large 1991-95, info. officer 1989-95, adj. 1996—), Phi Mu Alpha Sinfonia, Kappa Delta Pi. Home: 531 Westwood Ave River Vale NJ 07675-5526 Office: Woodside Sch River Vale NJ 07675

MODEROW, JOSEPH ROBERT, package distribution company executive; b. Kenosha, Wis., 1948. Grad., Calif. State U., Fullerton, 1970; JD, Western State U., 1975. Bar: Calif. 1975, U.S. Dist. Ct. (cen. dist.) Calif. 1975, U.S. Supreme Ct. 1982. Now sr. v.p., sec., gen. counsel, dir. United Parcel Svc Am., Inc., Atlanta, Ga. Office: United Parcel Svc of Am Inc 55 Glenlake Pky NE Atlanta GA 30328-3474

MODERY, RICHARD GILLMAN, marketing and sales executive; b. Chgo., Sept. 20, 1941; s. Richard Gustave Modery and Betty Jane (Gillman) Perok; m. Kay Francis Whitby, July 31, 1966 (div. July 1977); children: Stacey Lynn, Marci Kay; m. Anne-Marie Lucette Arsenault, Feb. 27, 1979. Student, Joliet (Ill.) Jr. Coll., 1959-61, Aurora (Ill.) Coll., 1963-65, Davenport Bus. Coll., Grand Rapids, Mich., 1969-71, Northwestern U., Evanston, Ill., 1987. Mktg. products mgr. Rapistan, Inc., Grand Rapids, 1964-75; mgr. estimating, project mgmt., customer svc. E.W. Buschman Co., Cin., 1975-78; exec. v.p. Metzgar Conveyor Co., Grand Rapids, 1979-84; mng. dir. Metzco Internat (cen. and S.Am.), Grand Rapids, Mich., 1981-84, Transfer Technologies, Inc., Grand Rapids, 1984-87; gen. ptnr., pres., chief exec. officer Nat. Monument Co., Grand Rapids, 1986—; v.p. Translogic Corp., Denver, 1987-88; corp. officer, v.p. mktg., field ops. and sales S.I. Handling Systems, Inc., Easton, Pa., 1988-91; v.p. mktg., sales and engring. Integrated Material Handling Co., Tomkins Industries, Inc., Oshkosh, Wis., 1991-93; pres. Handling Concepts, Inc., Chgo., Can., 1993—. Patentee in field. Commr. City of East Grand Rapids, Mich. Traffic Commn., 1983-86. Served with USNG, 1963-69. Mem. Internat. Material Mgmt. Soc., Am. Mgmt. Assn., Material Handling Inst. Am., Material Handling Inst. (speaker nat. confs.), Am. Mktg. Assn., Conveyor Equipment Mfrs. Assn., Material Handling Equipment Distbrs. Assn., Masons (32 degree). Avocations: tropical fish, photography, travel, power walking, golf. Home: 2255 Palmer Cir Naperville IL 60564-5672 Office: Handling Concepts Inc 2255 Palmer Cir Naperville IL 60564-5672

MODESTINO, JAMES WILLIAM, electrical engineering educator; b. Boston, Apr. 27, 1940; s. William and Mary Elizabeth (Dooley) M.; m. Leone Marie MacDougall, Aug. 25, 1962; children: Michele Marie, Lee Ann. BS, Northeastern U., 1962; MS, U. Pa., 1966; MA, Princeton U., 1968, PhD, 1969. Mem. tech. staff Gen. Telephone Electronics Labs., Waltham, Mass., 1969-70; asst. prof. Northeastern U., Boston, 1970-72; prof. Rensselaer Poly. Inst., Troy, N.Y., 1972-93, inst. prof., 1993—, dir. Ctr. for Image Processing Rsch., co-dir. Internat. Ctr. for Multimedia Edn.; vis. prof. U. Calif., San Diego, 1981-82; vis. faculty fellow GE Corp. R&D Ctr., 1988-89; vis. prof. MIT, Cambridge, Mass., 1995-96; pres. Modcom Inc., Ballston Lake, N.Y., 1981—; v.p. ICUCOM Inc., Troy, N.Y., 1986—. Recipient Sperry Faculty award Sperry Corp., 1986. Fellow IEEE (S.O. Rice Prize Paper award 1984, mem. bd. of govs. Info. Theory Soc. 1988-92). Avocations: sailing, jogging, tennis, skiing. Office: Rensselaer Poly Inst 110 8th St Troy NY 12180-3522

MODIC, STANLEY JOHN, business editor, publisher; b. Fairport Harbor, Ohio, Dec. 29, 1936; s. Frank and Mary (Zakrajsek) M.; m. Albina DiMichele, May 27, 1961; children—Mark Francis, Laurel Marie. BS in Commerce, Ohio U., 1958. Reporter The Telegraph, Painesville, Ohio, 1960-63; city editor The Telegraph, 1964-65; asst. editor Steel Mag., Cleve., 1965-67; news editor Steel Mag., 1968-70; mng. editor Industry Week (formerly Steel Mag.), Cleve., 1970-72; exec. editor Industry Week (formerly Steel Mag.), 1972; editor Industry Week, 1972-86; sr. editor Industry Week (formerly Steel Mag.), 1986-89; editor-in-chief Purchasing World Mag., 1989-90; editor-in-chief Tooling and Prodn. Mag., 1990—, pub., editor in chief, 1991—. Mcpl. clk. Fairport Harbor, 1960-61; mem. Fairport Harbor Village Council, 1962-63, pres., 1962-63. Recipient G.D. Crane award Am. Bus. Press, 1991. Mem. Am. Soc. Bus. Press Editors, Am. Fedn. Musicians, Press Club (pres. Cleve. chpt. 1978-79), Am.-Slovenian Club, KC, Elks, Sigma Delta Chi (pres. Cleve. chpt. 1975-76). Clubs: K.C. (Cleve.), Press (Cleve.) (pres. 1978-79); Am.-Slovenian (Fairport Harbor). Home: 5842 Woodhill St Painesville OH 44077-5167 Office: 29100 Aurora Rd Cleveland OH 44139-1855

MODIGLIANI, FRANCO, economics and finance educator; b. Rome, June 18, 1918; came to U.S., 1939, naturalized, 1946; s. Enrico and Olga (Flaschel) M.; m. Serena Calabi, May 22, 1939; children: Andre, Sergio. D. Jurisprudence, U. Rome, 1939; D. Social Sci., New Sch. Social Rsch., 1944; LLD (hon.), U. Chgo., 1967; D. honoris causa, U. Louvain, Belgium, 1974, Istituto Universitario di Bergamo, 1979, Hartford U.; LHD (hon.), Bard Coll., 1985, Brandeis U., 1986, New Sch. Social Research, 1989; LLD, Mich. State U., 1989; D (hon.), U. Ill., 1990, U. Valencia, Spain, 1992. Instr. econs. and statistics N.J. Coll. Women, New Brunswick, 1942; instr., then asso. econs. and statistics Bard Coll., Columbia, 1942-44; lectr., asst. prof. math. econs. and econometrics New Sch. Social Rsch., 1943-44, 46-48; rsch. asso., chief statistician Inst. World Affairs, N.Y.C., 1945-48; rsch. cons. Cowles Commn. Rsch. in Econs. U. Chgo., 1949-54; asso. prof., then prof. econs. U. Ill., 1949-52; prof. econs. and indsl. adminstrn. Carnegie Inst. Tech., 1952-60; vis. prof. econs. Harvard U., 1957-58; prof. econs. Northwestern U., 1960-62; vis. prof. econs. MIT, 1960-61, prof. econs. and finance, 1962—, Inst. prof., 1970-88, Inst. prof. emeritus, 1988—; fellow polit. economy U. Chgo., 1948; Fulbright lectr. U. Rome, also, Palermo, Italy, 1955. Author: The Debate Over Stabilization Policy, 1986, Il Caso Italia, 1986, The Collected Papers of Franco Modigliani, 3 vols., 1980, 4th and 5th vols., 1989; co-author: National Incomes and International Trade, 1953, Planning Production, Inventories and Work Forces, 1960, The Role of Anticipations and Plans in Economic Behavior and Their Use in Economic Analysis and Forecasting, 1961, New Mortgage Designs for Stable Housing in an Inflationary Environment, 1975, (with Frank J. Fabozzi) Capital Markets: Institutions and Instruments, 1991, (with Frank J. Fabozzi) Mortgage and Mortgage-Backed Security Markets, 1992, (with Frank J. Fabozzi, Michael G. Ferri) Foundations of Financial Markets and Institutions, 1994. Recipient Nobel prize in econ. sci., 1985; Cavaliere Di Gran Croce Repubblica Italiana, 1985, Premio Coltura for Econs., Repubblica Italiana, 1988, Premio APE award, 1988, Graham and Dodd award, 1975, 80, James R. Killian Jr. Faculty Achievement award, 1985, Lord Found. prize, 1989, Italy Premio Columbus, 1989, Italy Premio Guido Dorso, 1989, Italy Premio Stivale D'oro, 1991, Italy Premio Campione D'Italia, 1992; named hon. citizen of Town of Modigliana, Italy, 1993. Fellow NAS, Am. Econ. Assn. (v.p. 1971, pres. 1976), Econometric Soc. (coun. 1960, v.p. 1961, pres. 1962), Am. Acad. Arts and Scis., Internat. Econ. Assn. (v.p. 1977-83, hon. pres. 1983—); mem. Am. Fin. Assn. (pres. 1981), Accademia Nazionale dei Lincei (Rome), Shadow Fin. Regulatory Com.

MODINE, MATTHEW AVERY, actor; b. Loma Linda, Calif., Mar. 22, 1959; m. Caridad Rivera, 1979; 2 children: Bowman, Ruby. Appeared in films Baby, Its You, 1983, Private School, 1983, Streamers, 1983 (Best Actor award, Venice Film Festival 1983), The Hotel New Hampshire, 1984, Mrs. Soffel, 1984, Birdy, 1984, Vision Quest, 1985, Full Metal Jacket, 1987, Orphans, 1987, Married to the Mob, 1988, Gross Anatomy, 1989, Memphis Belle, 1990, Pacific Heights, 1990, Wind, 1992, Equinox, 1993, And the Band Played On, HBO, 1993 (Emmy nominee for Lead Actor in a Special, 1994), Short Cuts, 1993, The Browning Version, 1994, Bye Bye, Love, 1995, Fluke, 1995; numerous TV commls.; dir. of short film, Smoking, 1994, Jacob, 1994. Office: William Morris Agy 151 El Camino Beverly Hills CA 90212*

MODLIN, GEORGE MATTHEWS, university chancellor emeritus; b. Elizabeth City, N.C., July 13, 1903; s. John William and Nannie E. (Matthews) M.; m. Virginia Pendleton Brinkley, June 2, 1928. A.B., Wake Forest (N.C.) U., 1924, LL.D., 1947; M.A., Princeton, 1925, Ph.D., 1932; Dr. Laws, Stetson U., 1962, Hampden-Sydney Coll., 1971, U. Richmond, 1971. Asst. in econs. Princeton U., 1927-28, instr., 1928-32, asst. prof., 1932-38; part- time lectr. econs. Rutgers U., 1936-38; prof. econs., dean Sch. Bus. Adminstrn. U. Richmond, Va., 1938-46, pres., 1946-71, chancellor, 1971-86, chancellor emeritus, 1986—; Mem. pub. panel War Labor Bd., 1943-45. Author: (with F.T. De Vyver) Development of Economic Society, 1936, rev., 1946, (with A.M. McIsaac) Social Control of Industry, 1938. Trustee Keesee Ednl. Fund, 1963—; trustee, v.p. Titmus Found., 1971—; trustee Va. Found. Ind. Colls., pres., 1956-58. Mem. Richmond C. of C. (pres. 1951), So. U. Conf. (pres. 1955), So. Assn. Bapt. Schs. and Colls. (pres. 1952), Assn. Va. Colls. (pres. 1952), Assn. Am. Colls. (pres. 1962), Phi Beta Kappa, Kappa Alpha, Beta Gamma Sigma, Omicron Delta Kappa. Clubs: Country of Virginia, Commonwealth; University (N.Y.C.). Office: Univ of Richmond Richmond VA 23173

MODLIN, HOWARD S., lawyer; b. N.Y.C., Apr. 10, 1931; s. Martin and Rose Modlin; m. Margot S., Oct. 18, 1956; children: James, Laura, Peter. AB, Union Coll., Schenectady, 1952; JD, Columbia U., 1955. Bar: N.Y. 1956, D.C. 1973. Assoc., Weisman, Celler, Spett & Modlin, P.C., N.Y.C., 1956-61, ptnr., 1961-76, mng. ptnr., 1976-95, pres., 1996—; sec., dir. Gen. DataComm Industries, Inc., Middlebury, Conn.; dir. Am.-Book-Stratford Press, Inc., N.Y.C., Fedders Corp., Liberty Corner, N.J., Trans-Lux Corp., Norwalk, Conn. Chmn. bd. dirs. Daus. of Jacob Geriatric Ctr., Bronx, N.Y. Mem. ABA, Assn. Bar City N.Y., D.C. Bar Assn. Office: Weisman Celler Spett & Modlin 445 Park Ave New York NY 10022-2606

MODUGNO, MARIA, publishing executive. V.p., editor-in-chief, children's division Little, Brown and Co. Inc., Boston. Office: Little Brown & Co Inc 34 Beacon St Boston MA 02108-1415

MOE, ALDEN JOHN, university dean; b. Cookston, Minn., Apr. 9, 1939; s. Melvin Truman and Martha Mathilde (Njus) M.; m. Margery Elizabeth Sharbono, Aug. 1959 (div. 1983); m. Elayne Ackerman, Jan. 2, 1984; children: Christine Marie, Perry Wayne. BS, U. Minn., 1963; MA, Clarke Coll., Dubuque, Iowa, 1967; PhD, U. Minn., 1971. Tchr. St. Anthony Village, Minn., 1963-66; instr. Clarke Coll., 1967-69, U. Minn., 1969-71; from asst. to assoc. prof. Purdue U., West Lafayette, Ind., 1971-82; prof. La. State U., Baton Rouge, 1982-85, assoc. dean, 1985-88; dean of edn. Lehigh U., Bethlehem, Pa., 1988—. Author: Vocabulary of First Grade Children, 1982, Ginn Word Book for Teachers, 1983, Occupational Literacy Education, 1986, Keystones for Reading, 1988, Analytical Reading Inventory, 5th edit., 1995. Mem. Internat. Reading Assn. (bd. dirs. 1980-83), Am. Ednl. Rsch. Assn., nat. Conf. Rsch. in English. Democrat. Avocations: flying, playing bridge, reading mysteries, collecting antiques. Home: 5606 Meadow Dr Orefield PA 18069-9027 Office: Lehigh U Dean of Edn Bethlehem PA 18015

MOE, ANDREW IRVING, veterinarian; b. Tacoma, Jan. 2, 1927; s. Ole Andrew and Ingeborg (Gordham) M.; BS in Biology, U. Puget Sound, 1949; BA, Wash. State U., 1953, DVM 1954; m. Dorothy Clara Becker, June 25, 1950; children: Sylvia Moe McGowan, Pamela Moe Barker, Joyce. Meat cutter Art Hansen, Tacoma, 1943-48; gen. practice as veterinarian Baronti Vet. Hosp., Eugene, Oreg., 1956-57; veterinarian, regulatory Calif. Animal Health br. Calif. Dept. Food and Agr. Resident veterinarian II, Modesto, Calif., 1957-64, acting veterinarian-in-charge Modesto Dist. Office (veterinarian III), 1976-77, ret., 1990—. Watersafety instr. ARC, 1958-61. Capt., Vet. Corps., 1954-56, 62; comdr. 417th Med. Svc. Flight Res. (AFRES), 1965-66, 71-73; lt. col. Biomed. Scis. Corps USAF, ret., 1982. Recipient Chief Veterinarian badge, 1975. Mem. VFW (life), AVMA, Calif. Vet. Med. Assn., No. San Joaquin Vet. Med. Assn. (pres. 1979), Calif. Acad. Vet. Medicine (charter), Res. Officers Assn. (life), Ret. Officers Assn. (life), Assn. Mil. Surgeons U.S. (life), U.S. Animal Health Assn., Sons of Norway, Shriners (bd. dirs., dir. Modesto Shrine 1995), Masons (Illustrious Master Modesto chpt. 1983, Allied Masonic degrees, pres. Modesto Masonic Luncheon Club 1991, Meritorious Svc. medal 1992), Internat. Order of the Rainbow for Girls, Theta Chi. Alpha Psi. Lutheran (del. 102d Synod 1961). Home: 161 Norwegian Ave Modesto CA 95350-3542 *Personal philosophy: Try to be comparatively good.*

MOE, CHESNEY RUDOLPH, physics educator; b. Ont., Can., Oct. 6, 1908; s. Oscar and Edith (Miller) M.; m. Berthe Newton, Aug. 24, 1935 (dec. Sept. 1950); 1 son, Ronald; m. Bernice Woolman, July 21, 1951 (dec. May 1993); 1 dau., Donna. A.B., Stanford, 1929, A.M., 1931; Ph.D., U. So. Calif., 1941. Registered profl. engr., Cal. Asst. in physics San Diego State U., 1929-30, instr., 1931-35, asst. prof., 1935-39, asso. prof., 1939-45, prof. physics, 1945—, chmn. dept. physics, 1948-51, 53-56, 61-64, asso. chmn. div. phys. scis., 1956-61; cons. in acoustics Tracor, San Diego, 1965-74, Jet Propulsion Lab., Pasadena, 1968-70; dir. Electronics Investment Corp., 1959-63. Served as comdr. USNR, 1942-46, 1951-54; capt. Res. ret. Fellow Acoustical Soc. Am. (contbr. to jour.); mem. Sigma Xi, Phi Delta Kappa, Sigma Pi Sigma, Kappa Sigma. Home: 750 State St # 206 San Diego CA 92101-6033

MOE, JAMES DOUGLAS, lawyer; b. St. Louis, Aug. 3, 1940; s. Odd Einar and Ruth Marion (Reed) M.; m. Janice Elynor Baker, Aug. 7, 1965; children: Ann Elynor, Molly Ruth, Daniel Odd. AB, Stanford U., 1962; LLB, U. Minn., 1965. Bar: Minn. 1965, U.S. Supreme Ct. 1986. Atty. Cargill, Inc., Mpls., 1965-86, v.p., asst. gen. counsel, 1986—, asst. sec., 1987--. Mem. Ind. Sch. Dist. 273 Bd. Edn., Edina, Minn., 1982-88; commr. Edina Baseball Assn., 1987-90, pres. 1990—. Mem. ABA, Minn. Bar Assn., Hennepin County Bar Assn., Minn. Corp. Counsel Assn. (bd. dirs. 1987-89), Phi Delta Phi. Republican. Congregationalist. Avocations: hunting, fishing, skiing, walking. Office: Cargill Inc 15615 Mcginty Rd Wayzata MN 55391-2364

MOE, ORVILLE LEROY, racetrack executive; b. Spokane, Wash., Nov. 26, 1936; s. Clarence Orville and Georgia Maria (Lombard) M.; m. Deonne Wesley Schultz, Jan. 11, 1953; children: Susan Marie, Terry Ann. Co-owner Moe's Sudden Svc. Fuel Co., Spokane, Wash., 1956-74; sec. Gold Res. Mining Corp., Spokane, 1973-89, Bonanza Gold Corp., Spokane, 1973-85; pres., founder Spokane Raceway Park, Inc., 1971—; regional v.p. Am. Hot Rod Assn., Kansas, Mo., 1968-84, mktg. dir., 1978-84; co-producer Internat. Car Show Assn., Spokane, 1969-90. Co-producer Spokane Auto Boat Speed Show, 1964—. Mem. Nat. Rep. Senatorial Com., 1984—; mem., trustee Rep. Presdl. Task Force, mem. 1992 Presdl. Trust Rep. Nat. Com. Mem. ISCA, Eagles, Am. Hot Rod Assn. (exec. v.p. Spokane, Wash. 1986—), Internat. Footprint Assn., Am. Auto Racing Assn. (regional v.p.). Republican. Avocations: auto racing, mining, collecting and rebuilding autos, fishing, ice hockey. Office: Spokane Raceway Park Inc 101 N Hayford Rd Spokane WA 99204-9510

MOE, RICHARD PALMER, lawyer; b. Duluth, Minn., Nov. 27, 1936; s. Russell James and Virginia Mary (Palmer) M.; m. Julia Neimeyer, Dec. 26, 1964; children—Eric Palmer, Andrew Neimeyer, Alexandra Julia. B.A., Williams Coll., 1959; LL.B., U. Minn., 1966. Bar: Minn. 1967, D.C. 1979, N.Y. 1991. Adminstrv. asst. to mayor City of Mpls., 1961-62; to lt. gov. State of Minn., 1963-66; fin. dir. Minn. Democratic Farmer-Labor Party, 1967-69, chmn., 1969-72; adminstrv. asst. to Sen. Walter F. Mondale of

Minn., Washington, 1972-76; chief of staff Vice Pres. Walter F. Mondale, 1977-81; counsel Davis Polk & Wardwell, Washington, 1981-85, ptnr., 1985-92; pres. Nat. Trust for Hist. Preservation, Washington, 1992—. Office: Nat Trust for Hist Preservation 1785 Massachusetts Ave NW Washington DC 20036-2117

MOE, RONALD CHESNEY, public administration researcher; b. San Diego, May 28, 1937; s. Chesney R. and L. Bernice (Weston) M.; m. Carolyn Carr, May 18, 1962 (div. Feb. 1974); children: Steven, Cynthia; m. Grace Tyler, Apr. 30, 1976. BA, Claremont Coll., 1959; MA, Columbia U., 1962, PhD in Pub. Law and Govt., 1968. Asst. prof. San Diego State U., 1967-70; sr. policy advisor Office of Econ. Opportunity, Exec. Office of the Pres., Washington, 1970-71, Cost of Living Coun., Exec. Office of the Pres., Washington, 1971-73; specialist govt. orgns. and mgmt. Congl. Rsch. Svc. Libr. of Congress, Washington, 1973—. Contbr. chpts. to books, articles to profl. jours. Mem. exec. bd. Congregational Chs. of Am., Milw., 1985-89. Capt. U.S. Army Res., 1961-63. Ctr. Study of Am. Govt. fellow Johns Hopkins U., Washington, 1993—; recipient ASPA Louis Brownlow award, 1988, 91, 95-96. Fellow Nat. Acad. Pub. Adminstrn.; mem. Acad. Polit. Sci., Cosmos Club (Washington), Phi Beta Kappa. Republican. Home: 4700 Connecticut Ave NW 407 Washington DC 20008 Office: Congl Rsch Svc Libr of Congress Washington DC 20540

MOE, STANLEY ALLEN, architect, consultant; b. Fargo, N.D., May 28, 1914; s. Ole Arnold and Freda Emily (Pape) M.; m. Doris Lucille Anderson, May 25, 1937; children: Willa Moe Crouse, Myra Moe Galther. BArch, U. Minn., 1936; D of Engring. (hon.), U. N.D., 1993. lic. architect several states; NCARB cert. Project architect several firms in Midwest, 1936-42; project architect U.S. Army Corps Engrs., Africa, 1942-43; ptnr. H.S. Starin, Architects & Engrs., Duluth, Minn., 1943-47; sr. ptnr. Moe & Larsen, Architects & Engrs., L.A., 1947-54; ptnr., gen. mgr., exec. v.p. Daniel, Mann, Johnson & Mendenhall, L.A., 1954-71, corp. v.p., 1972-79; prin. Stanley A. Moe, AIA, L.A., 1979—; dir. design of major mil. projects in Eritrea, Sudan, Egypt, Yemen for Allied Forces, 1942-43; chmn. control com. DMJM & Assocs., 1958-63; designer of prototype, tng. and operational facilities for Titan I Ballistic Missile program for USAF; project dir. Space Shuttle facilities Kennedy Space Ctr., 1973; project dir. for design of aircraft maintenance complex Iranian Aircraft Industries, 1978; project mgr. for design of major med. facility program Min. of Def. and Aviation, Saudi Arabia, 1975-76; project mgr. design of Boufarik Internat. Airport, Algeria, 1983. Pres. San. Fernando Valley Young Reps., 1952, Van Nuys (Calif.) Jaycees, 1950. Recipient Dsiting. Svc. award for cmty. svc. Van Nuys Jaycees, 1949, Sioux award U. N.D. Alumni Assn., 1985, Trustees Soc. award U. Minn., 1992. Mem. AIA (Calif. coun.), Delta Tau Delta. Republican. Presbyterian. Avocations: world travel, hunting, fishing, historic restoration. Home and Office: 447 S Plymouth Blvd Los Angeles CA 90020-4706

MOE, THOMAS O., lawyer; b. Des Moines, 1938. BA, U. Minn., 1960, LLB, 1963. Bar: Minn. 1963. Ptnr. Dorsey & Whitney P.L.L.P, Mpls., 1964-89; mng. ptnr. Dorsey & Whitney P.L.L.P., Mpls., 1989—. Mem. Order of Coif. Office: Dorsey & Whitney 220 S 6th St Minneapolis MN 55402-4502*

MOE, TOMMY (THOMAS SVEN MOE), skier, former Olympic athlete; b. Missoula, Mont., 1970. Gold medalist, men's Downhill alpine skiing Olympic Games, Lillehammer, Norway, 1994; Silver medalist, men's Super-G alpine skiing Olympic Games, 1994; skier Fedn. Ski World Cup Circuit. Office: US Skiing Assn PO Box 100 Park City UT 84060-0100*

MOECK, WALTER F., conductor, music director; b. Milw., Mar. 18, 1922; s. Walter Ernst and Verena Helen (Klein) M.; m. Barbara Conklin; children: Karen, Richard, Stephen. MusB in Trumpet, Eastman Sch. Music, 1947; studies with Pierre Monteux, L'Ecole Monteux, 1951-53; MA in Conducting, U. Iowa, 1955; D in Fine Arts & Music (hon.), London Inst. Applied Rsch., 1993. Instr. brass Univ. Ala., Tuscaloosa, 1947-54, condr. symphony, 1950-54; assoc. condr. Birmingham (Ala.) Symphony, 1948-60; condr. Southeastern Composers Symphony, Tuscaloosa, 1950-54; mus. dir. Birmingham Ballet Co., 1955-62; mus. dir., condr. Ala. Pops Symphony, Birmingham, 1955-73, L.A. Repertoire Orch., 1975-88, San Fernando Valley Theater of Performing Arts, L.A., 1977-88, Am. Philharmonia New Project, L.A., 1978—; instr. Birmingham Southern Coll., Samford U., Montevallo U., Indian Springs Sch., 1954-68; cons., judge various mus. orgns., L.A. and Birmingham, 1947—; tchr. writing various groups and individuals, L.A., 1968—; guest condr. New Orleans Philharm., 1980, Burbank (Calif.) Symphony Orch., 1972, Bakersfield (Calif.) Philharm., 1971, Phila. Symphony Orch., 1953; condr., musical dir. Fine Arts Orch. Scottsdale/Phoenix, Sun City Concert Band. Composer: Trumpet Etudes (2 vols.), 1980, various warm-up exercises for all brass instruments, 1980; contbr. articles to Brass Warm-Ups, 1974. Mayor, pres. Town of Hoover, Ala., 1966; pres. Ch. Coun., L.A., 1973-74; mem. Pres. George Bush's Presdl. Task Force, Nat. Rep. Senatorial Com., Nat. Rep. Congrl. Com., Nat. Rep. Com. With U.S. Army, 1943-46. Recipient Key to City of Birmingham, 1986, Merit medal Pres. Bush, 1990, Man of the Yr. award Internat. Biog. Centre of Cambridge, Eng., 1993; Walter Moeck Week proclaimed in his honor musicians of Birmingham, 1986. Fellow Internat. Inst. of Arts and Letters (life); mem. Calif. Symphony Assn. Republican. Roman Catholic. Avocations: golf, reading, hiking. Home: 14507 W Trading Post Dr Sun City West AZ 85375-5794 Office: Fine Arts Orch Scottsdale Coll 9000 E Chaparral Rd Scottsdale AZ 85250-2614

MOECKEL, BILL REID, retired university dean; b. Pekin, Ill., Sept. 2, 1925; s. Willis E. and Daisy M. M.; m. Pauline C. Fox, Sept. 1, 1946; children—Steven, Cindy, Nancy. B.S., U. Ill., 1948, M.S., 1949, Ph.D., 1953. Instr. mktg. U. Mo., 1949-51; asst. prof. Ga. State U., 1953-54; asso. dean Sch. Bus., Ohio State U., 1954-67; dir. USAF Sch. Logistics, 1958-65; dean Sch. Bus., Miami U., Oxford, Ohio, 1967-87. Served with AUS, 1943-46. Mem. Am. Assembly Collegiate Schs. Bus. (nat. pres. 1981-82), Air Force Inst. Tech. Assn. Grads, Beta Gamma Sigma (nat. pres. 1976-78), Alpha Delta Sigma, Omicron Delta Kappa, Alpha Kappa Psi, Pi Sigma Epsilon, Mu Kappa Tau, Beta Alpha Psi.

MOEHLMAN, MICHAEL SCOTT, lawyer; b. Columbus, Ohio, Apr. 11, 1938; s. Arthur Henry and Marguerite Caroline M.; m. Carol Jean Shafer, Sept. 28, 1963; 1 son, Matthew. B.A., Harvard U., 1960; LL.B., U. Tex., 1963. Bar: Tex. 1963. Ptnr. Baker & Botts, Houston, 1963—. Bd. dirs. St. Martin's Episcopal Children's Ctr. Mem. ABA (com. bank securities, com. bus. bankruptcy, com. savs. instns.) Tex. Bar Assn. (com. revision corp. law), Houston Bar Assn. (judicature com.), Am. Judicature Soc., Houston Bar Found. (chmn. bd. dirs.), Phi Delta Phi, Houston Club (chmn. fin. com., bd. dirs., pres.), Houston Racquet Club, Houston Yacht Club, Havard Club (Boston), St. Charles Bay Hunting Club. Episcopalian. Clubs: Houston (chmn. fin. com., bd. dirs.), Houston Racquet, Houston Yacht, Harvard (Boston), St. Charles Bay Hunting. Office: Baker & Botts 1 Shell Plz 30th Fl Houston TX 77002

MOELING, WALTER GOOS, IV, lawyer; b. Quantico, Va., Feb. 16, 1943; s. Walter Goos III and Dorothy (Tritle) M.; m. Nell Frances Askew, Aug. 27, 1965; children: Charles H., Christine E. BA, Duke U., 1965, JD, 1968. Bar: Ga. 1968. Assoc. Powell, Goldstein, Frazer & Murphy, Atlanta, 1968-75, ptnr., 1975—. Bd. dirs. So. Banking Law and Policy Conf., 1989—, Southeastern Conf. for Bank Dirs., 1996—, Children's Rehab. Ctr., Atlanta, 1982—, Gatchell Home, Atlanta, 1983—; bd. dirs. REACH, Inc., 1989—, chmn. bd. dirs., 1993. Mem. ABA (mem. banking com. 1986—), Ga. Bar Assn., Ga. Bankers Assn. (assoc., chairperson bank counsel sect. 1992-95), Cmty. Bankers Assn. (assoc.), Capital City Club, Willow Point Country Club. Democrat. Unitarian. Avocations: golf, fly-fishing. Office: Powell Goldstein Frazer & Murphy 191 Peachtree St NE Ste 16 Atlanta GA 30303-1741

MOELLEKEN, WOLFGANG WILFRIED, Germanic languages and literature educator; b. Jan. 14, 1934; s. August and Emmy (d'Oliva) M.; m. Melita Anne Hildebrandt, Dec. 27, 1958; children: Brent Roderick Wilfred, Alan Patrick Wilfred, Sonja Melita Clarice. Student, U. Cologne, 1955-57; BE, U. B.C., 1961; MA, U. Wash., 1962, PhD, 1965. Asst. prof. U. Calif., Riverside, 1964-67; assoc. prof. U. Va., 1967-68, SUNY, Stony Brook, 1968-69; prof. U. Calif., Davis, 1969-77; prof. Germanic langs. and lits., head dept. fgn. langs. and lits. Purdue U., 1977-79; prof. Germanic langs. SUNY, Albany, 1979—, chmn. dept., 1979-82, 88-92; vis. prof. Univ. Augsburg , Univ. Marburg; dir. Ctr. for German Speech Islands in Am.; corr. mem. Rsch. Ctr. on Multilingualism, Brussels. Author numerous books and monographs; editor: German Lang. and Lit. Monographs, 1976—; founding editor: Purdue U. Monographs in Romance Langs., Davis Medieval Texts and Studies; contbr. articles to profl. jours. Calif. Humanities Inst. grantee and fellow; Regents fellow; Am. Council Learned Socs. grantee; Am. Philos. Soc. grantee; SUNY Research Found. fellow; Austrian Govt. fellow; Deutsche Forschungsgemeinschaft research and teaching prof.; NEH grantee; Fulbright sr. research fellow. Mem. Belgian Rsch. Assn. (rsch. prof.). Office: SUNY Dept Germanic Langs Li Albany NY 12222

MOELLENBECK, ALBERT JOHN, JR., engineering executive; b. St. Louis, Aug. 4, 1934; s. Albert John and Josephine Marie (Fruth) M.; m. Charlotte Anne Zimmerman, Nov. 26, 1960; children: Albert, Mary, Cheryl, Joan. BSCE, U. Mo., Rolla, 1960; postgrad., Harvard U., 1979. Registered prof. engr., Calif., N.Y., N.J., N.Mex. Engring. technician Calif. Divsn. Hwys., Sacramento, 1956-59; sr. engr. Calif. Dept. Water Resources, Sacramento, 1960-66; constrn. mgmt. engr. nuclear energy divsn. GE, San Jose, Calif., 1967-70; project mgr. R. Parsons Co., Pasadena, Calif., 1971-73; CEO, pres. Nuclear Power Svcs., N.Y.C., 1973-87; CEO BioTech Industries, Wyckoff, N.J., 1988-92; prin. A.J. Moellenbeck P.A., 1992—; expert lectr. U. Calif., Berkeley, 1963-66; expert examiner Calif. P & V Stds., Sacramento, 1964-68; expert instr. San Jose State U., 1967-69. Chief editor: Professional Engineering Examination Handbook, 1968; contbr. tech. articles to jours. With USN, 1952-55. Mem. ASME (nuclear codes com. 1972—, award 1990), ASCE, Am. Nuclear Soc. Achievements include patent for upflow biol. reactor treatment system. Home: 36 Wilderness Gate Rd Santa Fe NM 87501-5986

MOELLER, ACHIM FERDINAND GERD, art dealer, curator, consultant, publisher; b. Heidelberg, Germany, July 21, 1942; came to U.S., 1967; s. Friedrich Hermann and Liselotte Gerda Emilie (Kehrer); m. Danièle Poli, Mar. 24, 1971 (div. 1978); children: Frèdèric, Bèatrice; m. Colette Jeannine Estiveau, Aug. 11, 1986; 1 child, Stephanie. Baccalauréat, Lycée Français, Sarrebruck, Germany, 1961; student econs., Wildenstein & Co., N.Y.C., 1966-67. Asst. mgr. Kunsthaus Lempertz, Cologne, Germany, 1964-66; dir., v.p. Marlborough-Gerson Gallery, N.Y.C., 1967-71; pres. Achim Moeller Ltd., London, 1971-84, Achim Moeller Fine Art Ltd, N.Y.C., 1983—; curator in chief John C. Whitehead Collection, Washington, N.Y.C., 1981—; expert Lyonel Feininger, N.Y.C., 1980—. Pub., editor, author: (exhbn. catalogs) Lyonel Feininger, 1969, 75, 85, 86, 90, (book catalogs) Kirchner-Heckel, 1975, Kandinsky, 1977, Ph. Guston, 1977, Julius Bissier, 1987, John C. Whitehead Collection, 1987, Feininger-Tobey, The Complete Correspondence, 1991, Feininger in Paris, 1892-1911, 1992. Mem. Pvt. Art Dealers Assn. U.S.A., French Nat. Syndicate of Art Dealers, Confedn. Internat. de Negociants en Oeuvres d'Art, Rotary Internat. (Paul Harris fellow), Am. Coun. of Germany, Nat. Arts Club. Avocations: violin, literature, chess, photography, contemporary art. Office: 167 E 73d St New York NY 10021

MOELLER, AUDREY CAROLYN, energy company executive, corporate secretary; b. Pitts., May 10, 1935; d. Nicholas William and Edith Tecla (Russman) M. Grad. high sch., Pitts. Legal sec. Equitable Resources Inc., Pitts., 1955-72, asst. corp. sec., 1972-80, corp. sec., 1980-86, v.p., corp. sec., 1986—; also corp. sec. Equitable Resources Inc. subs.; dir. EOT Capital Corp., EREC Capital Corp., ERI Investments, Inc. Com. mem. United Way Allegheny County, Pa., 1978, United Way Southwestern Pa., 1984. Mem. Loyal Christian Beneift Assn. (nat. coun. 1993), Am. Soc. Corp. Secs. (asst. sec., chmn. membership Pitts. chpt. 1995, treas. 1996), Pa. Assn. Notaries. Democrat. Roman Catholic. Avocations: choral singing, golf. Home: 1015 Edward Dr Pittsburgh PA 15227-3917 Office: Equitable Resources Inc 420 Blvd Of The Allies Pittsburgh PA 15219-1323

MOELLER, DADE WILLIAM, environmental engineer, educator; b. Grant, Fla., Feb. 27, 1927; s. Robert A. and Victoria (Bolton) M.; m. Betty Jean Radford, Oct. 7, 1949; children: Garland Radford, Mark Bolton, William Kehne, Matthew Palmer, Elisabeth Anne. BS in Civil Engring., Ga. Inst. Tech., 1947, MS in Environ. Engring., 1948; PhD in Nuclear Engring., N.C. State U., 1957. Commd. jr. asst. san. engr. USPHS, 1948, advanced through grades to san. engr. dir., 1961; research engr. Los Alamos Sci. Lab., 1949-52; staff asst. Radiol. Health Program, Washington, 1952-54; research asso. Oak Ridge Nat. Lab., 1956-57; chief radiol. health tng. Taft San. Engring. Center, Cin., 1957-61; officer charge Northeastern Radiol. Health Lab., Winchester, Mass., 1961-66; assoc. dir. Kresge Center Environ. Health, Harvard Sch. Pub. Health, 1966-83, prof. engring. in environmental health, head dept. environmental health scis., 1968-83, dir. Office of Continuing Edn., 1982-84, assoc. dean continuing edn., 1985-93; environ. cons., 1993—; pres. Dade Moeller & Assocs., Inc., 1993—; cons. radiol. health. Author: (textbook) Environmental Health, 1992; contbr. articles to profl. jours. Chmn. Am. Bd. Health Physics, 1967-70; mem. Nat. Coun. Radiation Protection and Measurements, 1968—; mem. com. 4 Internat. Commn. on Radiol. Protection, 1978-85; chmn. nat. air pollution manpower devel. adv. com. U.S. EPA, 1972-75; mem. adv. com. reactor safeguards U.S. NRC, 1973-88, chmn., 1976, chmn. adv. com. nuclear waste, 1988-93. Fellow Am. Pub. Health Assn., Am. Nuclear Soc.; mem. Am. Acad. Environ. Engrs., Nat. Acad. Engring, Health Physics Soc. (pres. 1971-72), AAAS. Home and Office: 147 River Island Rd New Bern NC 28562-3656

MOELLER, JAMES, state supreme court justice; b. Valley, Nebr., Nov. 14, 1933; s. Hans and Marie Grace (Shumaker) M.; m. Nancy Lee Kiely, Dec. 16, 1961; children: Amy Jo, Linda Anne. BA, Nebr. Wesleyan U., 1954; JD with high distinction, George Washington U., 1959. Bar: Ariz. 1959, U.S. Dist. Ct. Ariz. 1959, U.S. Ct. Appeals (9th cir.) 1961. Assoc. Lewis and Roca, Phoenix, 1959-64, ptnr., 1964-70; ptnr. Moeller Hover Jensen & Henry, Phoenix, 1970-77; judge Maricopa County Superior Ct., Phoenix, 1977-87; assoc. justice Ariz. Supreme Ct., Phoenix, 1987-92, vice chief justice, 1992-96. Editor-in-chief George Washington U. Law Rev., 1958-59. Bd. dirs. Found. for Blind Children, Scottsdale, Ariz., 1964-70, Ariz. Found. Prevention of Blindness, Phoenix, 1966-70; Rep. committeeman, Phoenix and Scottsdale, 1965-69. Served with U.S. Army, 1954-56. Mem. ABA, Am. Judicature Soc., Ariz. Bar Assn., Maricopa County Bar Assn. Methodist. Avocations: travel, puzzles, history. Office: Ariz Supreme Ct 432 Ariz Courts Bldg 1501 W Washington Phoenix AZ 85007

MOELLER, ROBERT JOHN, management consultant; b. Mpls., July 20, 1938; s. Ben G. and Catheryn D. M.; m. Sharon Lee Holmberg, Sept. 1, 1962; children: Mark Thomas (dec.), Maria Therese. BBA, U. Minn., 1962, MBA, 1965; grad. exec. mgmt. program, Columbia U., 1972; grad. exec. internat. mgmt., Mankato U., 1990. Asst. brand mgr. toiletries Procter & Gamble, Cin., 1965-68; group product mgr. No. div. Am. Can Co., Greenwich, Conn., 1968-71, dir. mktg. Dixie div., 1971-73; v.p. mktg. and sales Tonka Toy Co., Mpls., 1973-77; v.p. mktg. and sales Toro Co., Mpls., 1977-79, v.p. gen. mgr. outdoor appliance div., 1979-80, v.p. gen. mgr. irrigation div., 1980-84, exec. v.p. internat. and irrigation div., 1984-88; pres., chief oper. officer Mackay Envelope Corp., Mpls., 1988-90; sr. v.p. mktg. meat sector Cargill, Inc., 1991-94; pres. Moeller & Assoc., 1994—; bd. dirs. Vista Info. Solutions. Vice chair bd. trustees Voyageur Outward Bound Sch., 1993—; bd. dirs. State of Minn. Prison Industries, St. Paul, 1984—; commr. Chaska (Minn.) Planning Comm., 1988—; pres. Dist. 112 Ednl. Found., Chaska, 1987-92; pres. Chaska Civic Theatre, 1978-80; chmn. Jonathan Archtl. Rev. Commn., 1976-78. With USN, 1955-61. Avocations: skiing, sailing, tennis, music, golf.

MOELLERING, JOHN HENRY, aviation maintenance company executive; b. Ft. Wayne, Ind., Feb. 4, 1938; s. Robert Charles and Irene Pauline (Nolde) M.; m. Karla Louise Fritzsche, Dec. 21, 1963; children: John Henry, Matthew C., Ann Elizabeth. BS, U.S. Mil. Acad., 1959; MS, U. Calif., Berkeley, 1962; postgrad., Army Command and Gen. Staff Coll., 1971-72, Army War Coll., 1976-77. Registered profl. engr., La. Commd. 2d lt. U.S. Army, 1959, advanced through grades to lt. gen., 1985; aide de camp Combat Devel. Command, 1961-63; command and staff 24th Inf. Div., Fed. Republic Germany, 1964-67; ops. officer Engr. Group, Vietnam, 1967-68; instr. civil engring., asst. prof. history U.S. Mil. Acad., 1968-71; with Office Army Chief of Staff, Pentagon, 1972-73; White House staff, 1973-74; bn. comdr. 101st Airborne Div., 1974-76; dist. engr. Vicksburg, Miss., 1977-79; exec. to Army Chief of Staff, Pentagon, 1979-81; asst. div. comdr. 9th Inf. Div., Ft. Lewis, Wash., 1981-82; commandant West Point, N.Y., 1982-84; comdg. gen. Ft. Leonard Wood, Mo., 1984-85; asst. to chmn. Joint Chiefs of Staff, Pentagon, Washington, 1985-87; corp. v.p. Automatic Data Processing, Inc., San Ramon, Calif., 1987-90; pres., chief exec. officer Lear Siegler Mgmt. Svcs. Corp., Oklahoma City, 1990-93; exec. v.p., COO UNC Inc., Annapolis, Md., 1993—. Editor, contbr.: Evolution of Modern Warfare, 1969, Battalion Commanders Speak Out, 1977. Chmn. Class of '59 fund com. U.S. Mil. Acad., 1984-89; bd. dirs. Last Frontier coun. Boy Scouts Am.; bd. dirs. U. Okla. Sch. Continuing Edn. and Pub. Svc.; v.p.Oklahoma County unit Am. Cancer Soc.; mem. Def. Sci. Bd., The Pentagon. Decorated Def. DSM, Army DSM, Legion of Merit, Bronze Star; White House fellow, 1973-74. Mem. Econ. Club Okla., Oklahoma City C. of C. (bd. dirs.), Phi Kappa Phi. Home: 1526 Shipsview Rd Annapolis MD 21401-5740 Office: 175 Admiral Cochrane Dr Annapolis MD 21401-7367

MOELLERING, ROBERT CHARLES, JR., internist, educator; b. Lafayette, Ind., June 9, 1936; s. Robert Charles and Irene Pauline (Nolde) M.; children: Anne Elizabeth, Robert Charles, Catherine Irene; m. Mary Jane Ferraro, July 11, 1987. BA, Valparaiso U., 1958, DSc, 1980; MD cum laude, Harvard U., 1962. Diplomate: Am. Bd. Internal Medicine. Intern Mass. Gen. Hosp., Boston, 1962-63, resident, 1963-64, postdoctoral fellow in infectious diseases, 1967-70, resident, 1966-67, mem. infectious disease unit and asst. physician, 1970-76, assoc. physician, 1976-83, hon. physician, 1983—, cons. bacteriology, 1972-87; instr. medicine Harvard U. Med. Sch., Boston, 1970-72, asst. prof., 1972-76, assoc. prof., 1976-80, prof., 1980—; chmn. dept. medicine, physician-in-chief New Eng. Deaconess Hosp., 1981—; Shields Warren-Mallinckrodt prof. clin. rsch. Harvard U. Med. Sch., Boston, 1981-89; pres., CEO Deaconess Profl. Practice Group, 1995—; Shields Warren-Mallinckrodt prof. med. rsch. Harvard U. Med. Sch., Boston, 1989—; mem. subcom. on susceptibility testing Nat. Com. for CLin. Lab. Standards, 1976-88; mem. subcom. on antimicrobial agts. and chemotherapy, 1978-80; subcom. on antimicrobiol disc. diffusion susceptibility testing, 1980-88. Mem. editl. bd. Antimicrobial Agts. and Chemotherapy, 1977-81, editor, 1981-85, editor-in-chief, 1985-95; editor European Jour. Clin. Microbial Infectious Diseases, 1990—; consulting. editor Infectious Disease Clinics N.Am., 1986—; editor Les Infections, 1983; editl. bd. New Eng. Jour. Medicine, 1977-81, European Jour.Clin. Microbiology, 1981—, Jour. Infectious Diseases, 1981-85, 89-93, Infectious Disease Alert, 1981-92, Pharmacotherapy, 1982—, Antimicrobial Agts. Ann., 1984-87, Zentralblatt Fur Bacteriologie, Microbiologie and Hygience, 1984—, Jour. of Infection, 1986—, Innovations, 1986-90, Residents Forum in Internal Medicine, 1988-90, Diagnostic Microbiology and Infectious Disease, 1989-90, Internat. Jour. Antimicrobial Agts., 1990—, Infectious Diseases iin Clin. Practice, 1991-92. Served with USPHS, 1964-66. Grantee USPHS, NIH. Fellow ACP, Am. Acad. Microbiology, Infectious Diseases Soc. Am. (v.p. 1988-89, pres. elect 1989-90, pres. 1990-91, past pres. 1991-92); mem. Am. Soc. Microbiology, Am. Clin. and Climatol. Assn., Internat. Soc. Chemotherapy, Am. Soc. Clin. Investigation, Assn. Am. Physicians, European Soc. Clin. Microbiology, Am. Fedn. Clin. Rsch., Assn. Profs. Medicine, Roxbury Clin. Records Club, Mass. Med. Soc. (councilor), Brit. Soc. Antimicrobial Chemotherapy, Coun. Biology Editors, Alpha Omega Alpha, Phi Kappa Psi. Home: 49 Longfellow Rd Wellesley MA 02181-5220 Office: New Eng Deaconess Hosp Dept Medicine 110 Francis St Boston MA 02215-5501

MOELMANN, LAWRENCE R., lawyer; b. Oak Park, Ill., Oct. 13, 1947. AB magna cum laude, Princeton U., 1970; JD, U. Mich., 1973. Bar: Ill. 1973, U.S. Dist. Ct. (no. dist.) Ill. 1973, U.S. Ct. Appeals (7th cir.). Ptnr. Hinshaw & Culbertson, Chgo. Mem. ABA (fidelity and surety law com., tort and ins. practice sect. 1978—, vice-chair 1992—), Ill. State Bar Assn., Cook County Bar Assn., Defense Rsch. Inst. (chair fidelity and surety com. 1995—), Internat. Assn. Defense Counsel (fidelity and surety com., chair 1992-93), Nat. Bond Claims Assn., Surety Claims Inst. Address: Hinshaw & Culbertson 222 N La Salle St Ste 300 Chicago IL 60601-1005

MOELY, BARBARA E., psychology researcher, educator; b. Prairie du Sac, Wis., July 17, 1940; d. John Arthur and Loretta Ruth (Giese) M.; children: John Jacob Moely Wiener, David Andrew Moely Wiener. Student Carroll Coll., 1958-60; BA, U. Wis., 1962, MA, 1964; PhD, U. Minn., 1968. Asst. prof. U. Hawaii, Honolulu, 1967-71; rsch. psychologist UCLA, 1971-72; asst. prof. Tulane U., New Orleans, 1972-75, assoc. prof. psychology, 1975-85, prof., 1985—, dept. chmn., 1992—. Contbr. articles to profl. jours. Grantee U.S. Office Edn., Handicapped Pers. Preparation, 1977-80, Tulane U., 1973, 75, 77, 78, 83-84, Inst. for Mental Hygiene, City of New Orleans, 1983-84, Nat. Inst. Edn., 1983-84, La. Edn. Quality Support Fund, 1988, 89, 91, 92. Mem. AAUP (v.p. La. conf. 1992-93, sec. 1993—, pres. Tulane 1992-94), APA, Soc. Rsch. in Child Devel., Am. Ednl. Rsch. Assn., Southwestern Soc. for Rsch. in Human Devel. (pres. 1986-88), Phi Beta Kappa (pres. Alpha chapter La. 1981-82, sec. 1995—). Office: Tulane Univ Dept Psychology New Orleans LA 70118

MOEN, RODNEY CHARLES, state senator, retired naval officer; b. Whitehall, Wis., July 26, 1937; s. Edwin O. and Tena A. (Gunderson) M.; m. Catherine Jean Wolfe, 1959; children: Scott A., Jon C., Rodd M., Catherine J., Daniel M. Student Syracuse U., 1964-65; BA, U. So. Calif., 1972; postgrad. Ball State U., 1975-76. Contbg. editor Govt. Photography, 1970-74; gen. mgr. Western Wis. Communications Coop., Independence, Wis., 1976-83; mem. Wis. Senate, 1983—, mem. health, human svcs. and aging com., 1983—. Lt. USN, 1955-76, Vietnam. Democrat. Home: 2119 Dewey St Whitehall WI 54773-9591 Office: State Capitol PO Box 7882 Madison WI 53707-7882

MOENS, PETER B., biology researcher and educator; b. Sukabumi, Indonesia, May 15, 1931; s. Pieter B. and Anneke D. (Ritsema van Eck) M.; m. Marja Schroder, May 8, 1953; children: Richard, Theodore, Vivian, Cecilia, Francis. B.S. in Forestry, U. Toronto, 1959, M.A., 1961, Ph.D., 1963. Lectr. biology York U., Downsview, Ont., Can., 1963-64; asst. prof. York U., 1964-67, asso. prof., 1967-71, prof., 1971—, chmn. dept. biology, 1981-84. Editor: Genome; Chromosoma, 1988—. Fellow Royal Soc. Can.; mem. Genetics Soc. Am., Can. Soc. Cell Biology, Genetics Soc. Can. (pres. 1979), Am. Soc. Cell Biology. Office: York U, Dept Biology, Downsview, ON Canada M3J 1P3

MOENS, THOMAS ODIN, lawyer, computer consultant; b. Moline, Ill., Dec. 11, 1961; s. Arlen L. and Judith E. (Minick) M. AA, Black Hawk Coll., Moline, 1986; BS, U. Iowa, 1988, JD, 1992. Bar: Ill. 1992, Iowa 1993, U.S. Ct. Appeals (7th cir.) 1993, U.S. Dist. Ct. (ctrl. dist.) Ill. 1993. Entertainer, musician, Moline, 1982-89; mng. editor Transnat. Law and Contemporary Problems, Iowa City, 1990-92; assoc. Blackwood, Nowinski, Huntoon & Swanson, P.C., Moline, 1991—; computer applications cons. Ipse Dixit Pub., Moline, 1988—. Mem. ABA, Ill. State Bar Assn., Iowa State Bar Assn., Scott County Bar Assn., Rock Island County Bar Assn., Rock Island Jaycees (bd. dirs. 1994—), Ill. Quad Cities Rotary, Quad Cities Credit Assn., Quad City Bicycle Club, Iowa Trails Coun., Rails to Trails Conservancy, Cornbelt Running Club, Phi Theta Kappa. Avocations: bicycling, running, gardening, music. Office: Blackwood Nowinski Huntoon & Swanson 1000 36th Ave Ste 100 Moline IL 61265-7126

MOERDLER, CHARLES GERARD, lawyer; b. Paris, Nov. 15, 1934; came to the U.S., 1946, naturalized, 1952; s. Herman and Erna Anna (Brandwein) M.; m. Pearl G. Hecht, Dec. 26, 1955; children: Jeffrey Alan, Mark Laurence, Sharon Michele. BA, L.I.U., 1953; JD, Fordham U., 1956. Bar: N.Y. 1956, U.S. Supreme Ct. 1962. Asso. firm Cravath, Swaine & Moore, N.Y.C., 1956-65; spl. counsel coms. City of N.Y. and judiciary N.Y. State Assembly, 1960-61; commr. bldgs. City of N.Y., 1966-67; sr. ptnr., chmn. litigation dept. Stroock & Stroock & Lavan, N.Y.C., 1967—; bd. dirs., gen. counsel, dir. N.Y. Post Co., Inc., 1987-92; cons. housing, urban devel. and real estate to Mayor of N.Y.C., 1967-73; mem. com. on character and fitness of applicants for admission to Bar, Appellate div. 1st Dept., N.Y., 1977—; commr. N.Y. State Ins. Fund, 1978—, vice chmn., 1986-94, chmn., 1995—; mem. Mayor's Com. on Judiciary, 1994—. Mem. editorial bd. N.Y. Law Jour., 1985—; assoc. editor Fordham Law Rev., 1956. Asst. dir. Rockefeller nat. presdl. campaign com., 1964; adv. bd. Sch. Internat. Affairs Columbia U., 1977-80; bd. govts. L.I.U., 1966, trustee, 1985-91; chmn. Cmty. Planning

Bds. 8 and 14, Bronx County, 1977-78; nat. bd. govs. Am. Jewish Congress, 1966; bd. overseers Jewish Theol. Sem. Am., 1993-95; trustee St. Barnabas Hosp., Bronx, N.Y., 1985—. Recipient Walker Metcalf award L.I. U., 1966. Mem. Am. Bar Assn., N.Y. State Bar Assn., N.Y. County Lawyers Assn., Internat. Bar Assn., Assn. of Bar of City of N.Y., Free Sons of Israel, World Trade Ctr. Club, Metro. Club. Home: 7 Rivercrest Rd Bronx NY 10471-1236 Office: Stroock Stroock & Lavan 7 Hanover Sq New York NY 10004-2616

MOERDYK, CHARLES CONRAD, school system administrator; b. Kalamazoo, Sept. 4, 1948; s. Vernon Frank and Eileen Marie (Riverside) M.; m. Cheryl Ann Rudge, July 29, 1967 (div. 1984); children: Paulette Ann, Carie Ann; m. Cynthia Marie Peters, Sept. 1, 1984. BBA, Western Mich. U., 1970; M of Edn. Adminstrn., Northern Mich. U., 1990. CPA Mich. 1974. Acct. J.R. Rugg & Co., Grand Rapids, Mich., 1970-71; controller Newman Visual Edn. Inc., Grand Rapids, Mich., 1971-73; asst. auditor gen. State of Mich., Lansing, 1973-74; ptnr. Goodman deMink & Cerutti, Kalamazoo, 1974-79; cons. pvt. practice, Kalamazoo & Crystal Falls, Mich., 1980-85; interim dir. support svcs. Planned PArenthood Assn., Chgo., 1981-82; bus. mgr. Breitung Twp. Schs., Kingsford, Mich., 1985-89, Alma (Mich.) Pub. Schs., 1989—; adj. prof. Davenport Coll., Alma, 1991—; dir., treas. Gra Co Fed. Union, Alma, 1991-94. Mem. World Future Soc. Avocations: singing, aviation. Home: PO Box 305 Alma MI 48801-0305 Office: Alma Pub Schs 1500 Pine Ave Alma MI 48801-1275

MOESCHLER, JOHN BOYER, physician, educator; b. Omaha, Mar. 14, 1950; s. William Joseph and Norma Rose (Boyer) M.; children: Kate, Emily. BS, Creighton U., 1972; MD, U. Nebr., 1975. Bd. cert. Am. Bd. Pediatrics, Am. Bd. Med. Genetics. Intern Univ. Nebr. Med. Ctr., Omaha, 1975-76, resident, 1976-78; fellow Univ. Wash., Seattle, 1978-80; asst. prof., dept. pediatrics Univ. Nebr. Med. Ctr., Meyer Children's Rehab. Inst., Omaha, 1980-83; asst. prof., dept. pediatrics, sect. med. genetics W.Va. Univ. Med. Sch., Morgantown, 1983-85; asst. prof., dept. maternal and child health Dartmouth Med. Sch., Dartmouth-Hitchcock Med. Ctr., Hanover, N.H., 1985-88; assoc. prof., dept. maternal and child health Dartmouth Med. Sch., Dartmouth-Hitchcock Med. Ctr., Hanover, 1988—; dir. Clin. Genetics & Child Devel. Ctr. Dartmouth-Hitchcock Med. Ctr., Hanover, 1988—; med. dir., Clinic for Children with Neuromotor Disabilities Dept. Health & Human Svcs., Bur. Spl. Med. Svcs., N.H., 1985—; med. dir., Genetic Svcs. Program Dept. Health & Human Svcs., Bus. of Spl. Med. Svcs., N.H., 1988—; bd. dirs. Planned Parenthood of No. New England; attending physician Children's Orthopedic Hosp., Seattle, 1978-80; assoc. dir. Birth Defects Clinic, Children's Meml. Hosp., Omaha, 1982-83; cons. Nebr. State Svcs. for Crippled Children, 1980-83; dir. pediatric rehab. MCRI and Univ. Nebr. Hosp., Omaha, 1982-83; steering com. New England Regional Genetics Group, 1988—; presenter in field. Contbr. articles to Jour. Pediatrics, Am. Jour. Med. Genetics, Am. Jour. Disabled Child, Jour. Ment. Def. Rsch., Jour. Ultrasound Med., Dysmorphology and Clin. Genetics, Jour. Clin. Dysmorphology, Prenatal Diagnosis, Am. Jour. Diseases Children, Devel. Medicine and Child Neurology, Clin. Genetics, and others. Fellow Am. Acad. Pediatrics, Am. Acad. Cerebral Palsy & Devel. Medicine; mem. Soc. for Devel. Pediatrics, Am. Soc. Human Genetics (info. and edn. com. 1990—), Am. Assn. on Mental Retardation, N.H. State Med. Soc., Grafton County Med. Soc. Home: 9 Woodside Rd Durham NH 03824-2120 Office: Clin Genetics Dartmouth-Hitchcock Med Ctr Chils Development Ctr Hanover NH 03756

MOESE, MARK DOUGLAS, environmental consultant; b. Jersey City, Aug. 3, 1954; s. Harold Francis and Mary Frances (Wilk) M.; m. Elizabeth Renker Cozine, Apr. 20, 1991; children: Elizabeth Renker, Kevin Harold. BS, Fairleigh Dickinson U., 1976, MS, 1979; PhD, NYU, 1988. Rsch. asst. West Indies Lab., St. Croix, U.S.V.I., 1978-79, NYU Med. Ctr., Tuxedo, N.Y., 1980-86; staff scientist Hazen and Sawyer, P.C., N.Y.C., 1982-85; supr. risk assessment EBASCO Environ., Lyndhurst, N.J., 1986-94, Foster Wheeler Environ., Lyndhurst, 1994-96, Betterchem Corp., Campbell Hall, N.Y., 1996—; cons. Taiwan Power Co., Taipei, 1987, 89, Hub River Power Co., Fauji Corp., Karachi, Pakistan, 1991-92, Chinese Rsch. Acad. Environ. Scis., 1993; human and environ. risk assessments profl. Ebasco Environ., 1986-94, Foster Wheeler Environ., Lydnhurst, N.J., 1994-96, Betterchem Corp., 1996—; cons. to pharm. industry. Contbr. articles to profl. jours. Sigma Xi grantee-in-aid, 1978; grad. fellow NYU Med. Ctr., 1980-86. Mem. ASTM (voting mem., E-47 com., sediment toxicity subcom.), Soc. for Risk Analysis, Soc. Environ. Toxicology and Chemistry. Office: Betterchem Corp 702F Sarah Wells Trl Campbell Hall NY 10916

MOESER, ELLIOTT, principal. Prin. Nicolet High Sch., Glendale, Ill. Recipient Blue Ribbon Sch. award, 1990-91. Office: Nicolet High Sch 6701 N Jean Nicolet Rd Milwaukee WI 53217-3701

MOFFAT, DONALD, actor; b. Plymouth, Eng., Dec. 26, 1930; s. Walter George and Kathleen Mary (Smith) M.; m. Anne Murray Ellsperman, May 22, 1954 (div. Aug. 1968); children: Kathleen Wendy, Gabriel Robin; m. Gwen Arner, May 1969; children: Lynn Marie, Catherine Jean. Student, Royal Acad. Dramatic Art, 1952-54. Actor: (plays) including War and Peace, 1964, Man and Superman, 1964, The Hostage, 1964, Judith, 1964, The Wild Duck, 1965-66, You Can't Take It With You, 1965-66, Krapp's Last Tape, 1965, Right You Are, 1966, School for Scandal, 1966, Above Repertory, 1967, Cherry Orchard, 1967-68, Cock-a-Doodle Dandy, 1968-69, Hamlet, 1968-69, Chemin de Fer, 1969, Hadrian VII, 1970, Father's Day, 1970-71, Trial Catonsville Nine, 1971, Hotel Paradiso, 1971, The Tavern, 1973, Childs Play, 1973, Forget-Me-Not Lane, 1973, The Miser, 1974, The Kitchen, 1975, Heartbreak House, 1976, Misalliance, 1976, Waiting for Godot, 1977, Terra Nova, 1979, Painting Churches, 1983, Play Memory, 1983, Passion Play, 1984, The Iceman Cometh, 1985-86, Henry IV Part I, 1987, Titus Andronicus, 1989, Uncommon Ground, 1991, The Heiress, 1995; (television) Armistead Maupin's Tales of the City, 1993; (films) Rachel, Rachel, 1968, R.P.M, 1969, Great Northfield, Minnesota Raid, 1970, Showdown, 1972, Terminal Man, 1973, Eleanor and Franklin, 1977, On the Nickel, 1979, Strangers, 1979, Health, 1979, Promises in the Dark, 1979, Popeye, 1980, The Thing, 1983, The Right Stuff, 1983, Alamo Bay, 1985, Far North, 1988, Music Box, 1989, Class Action, 1990, Kaleidescope, 1990, Regarding Henry, 1991, Babe Ruth, 1991, Housesitter, 1991, A Clear and Present Danger, 1994; dir.: Akron (Ohio) Shakespeare Festival, 1961, McCarter Theatre, Princeton (N.J.) U., 1963, 66, Playhouse-in-the-Park, Cin., 1964, Assn. Producing Artists Repertory, 1966-67, 68-69, Father's Day N.Y., 1971; assoc. artistic dir.: Gt. Lakes Shakespeare Festival, 1963; mng. artist: L.A. Actors' Theatre, 1976-77. With Royal Arty., 1949-51. Office: care William Morris Agency c/o Scott Henderson 151 S El Camino Dr Beverly Hills CA 90212-2704*

MOFFAT, JOHN WILLIAM, physics educator; b. Copenhagen, Denmark, May 24, 1932; s. George William and Esther (Winther) M. PhD, Trinity Coll., Cambridge (Eng.) U., 1958; DSc, U. Winnipeg, 1989. Sr. research fellow Imperial Coll., London, Eng., 1957-58; scientist Research Inst. Advanced Studies, Balt., 1958-60; prin. scientist Research Inst. Advanced Studies, 1961-64; scientist CERN, Geneva, Switzerland, 1960-61; asso. prof. dept. physics U. Toronto, Ont., Can., 1964-67; prof. U. Toronto, 1967—. Contbr. articles to profl. jours. Dept. Sci. and Indsl. Research fellow, 1958-60; NRC Can. grantee, 1965. Fellow Cambridge Philos. Soc. (Eng.); mem. N.Y. Acad. Scis., Can. Astron. Soc., Internat. Union Astronomers. Office: Univ of Toronto, Dept Physics, Toronto, ON Canada

MOFFATT, HUGH MCCULLOCH, JR., hospital administrator, physical therapist; b. Steubenville, Ohio, Oct. 11, 1933; s. Hugh McCulloch and Agnes Elizabeth (Bickerstaff) M.; m. Ruth Anne Colvin, Aug. 16, 1958; children: David, Susan. AB, Asbury Coll., 1958; cert. in phys. therapy, Duke U., 1963. Lic. in phys. therapy and health care adminstrn. Commd. officer USPHS, 1964, advanced through grades to capt.; therapist USPHS, N.Y.C., 1964-66, Sitka, Alaska, 1970-72; therapist cons. USPHS, Atlanta, 1968-70; clinic adminstr. USPHS, Kayenta, Ariz., 1972-73; hosp. dir. USPHS, Sitka, 1973-78; therapist cons. Idaho Dept. Health, Boise, 1966-68; contract health officer USPHS, Anchorage, 1978-89, ret., 1989; phys. therapy cons. Ocean Beach Hosp., Ilwaco, Wash., 1989—, Harbors Home Health Svcs., Aberdeen, Wash., 1990—; therapist cons. Our Lady of Compassion Care Ctr., Anchorage, 1979—, Alaska Native Med. Ctr., Anchorage, 1988—. With U.S. Army, 1955-57. Mem. Am. Phys. Therapy Assn., Commd. Officers Assn. USPHS, Res. Officers Assn., Ret. Officers Assn., Am. Assn. Individual Investors, Am. Assn. Ret. Persons, Eagles. Avocations: automobile repairs, woodworking, camping, fishing, church choir.

MOFFATT, JOYCE ANNE, performing arts executive; b. Grand Rapids, Mich., Jan. 3, 1936; d. John Barnard and Ruth Lillian (Pellow) M. BA in Lit., U. Mich., 1957, MA in Theatre, 1960; HHD (hon.), Sch. Psychology, San Francisco, 1991. Stage mgr., lighting designer Off-Broadway plays, costume, lighting and set designer, stage mgr. stock cos., 1954-62; nat. subscription mgr. Theatre Guild/Am. Theatre Soc., N.Y.C., 1965-67; subscription mgr. Theatre, Inc.-Phoenix Theatre, N.Y.C., 1963-67; cons. N.Y.C. Ballet and N.Y.C. Opera, 1967-70; asst. house mgr. N.Y. State Theater, 1970-72; dir. ticket sales City Ctr. of Music and Drama, Inc., N.Y.C., 1970-72; prodn. mgr. San Antonio's Symphony/Opera, 1973-75; gen. mgr. San Antonio Symphony/Opera, 1975-76, 55th St. Dance Theater Found., Inc., N.Y.C., 1976-77, Ballet Theatre Found., Inc./Am. Ballet Theatre, N.Y.C., 1977-81; v.p. prodn. Radio City Music Hall Prodns., Inc., N.Y.C., 1981-83; artist-in-residence CCNY, 1981—; propr. mgmt. cons. firm for performing arts N.Y.C., 1983—; exec. dir. San Francisco Ballet Assn., 1987-93; mng. dir. Houston Ballet Assoc., 1993-95; gen. mgr. Chgo. Music and Dance Theater, Inc., 1995—; cons. Ford Found., N.Y. State Coun. on Arts, Kennedy Ctr. for Performing Arts.; mem. dance panels N.Y. State Coun. on Arts, 1979-81; mem. panels for Support to Prominent Orgns. and Dance, Calif. Arts Coun., 1988-92. Appointee San Francisco Cultural Affairs Task Force, 1991; chmn. bd. Tex. Inst. for Arts in Edn., 1994—; trustee of I.A.T.S.E. Local 16 Pension and Welfare Fund, 1991-94. Mem. Assn. Theatrical Press Agts. and Mgrs., Actors Equity Assn., United Scenic Artists Local 829, San Francisco Visitors and Conv. Bur. (bd. dirs.). Club: Argyle (San Antonio). Office: Chicago Music & Dance Theater Mezz Level 203 No LaSalle Chicago IL 60601

MOFFATT, KATY (KATHERINE LOUELLA MOFFATT), musician, vocalist, songwriter; b. Ft. Worth, Nov. 19, 1950; d. Lester Huger and Sue-Jo (Jarrott) M. Student, Sophie Newcomb Coll., 1968, St. John's Coll., 1969-70. Rec. artist Columbia Records, 1975-79, Permian/MCA Records, 1982-84, Enigma Records, L.A., 1985, Wrestler Records, L.A., 1987-88, Red Moon Records, Switzerland, 1988-93, Philo/Rounder Records, 1989-93, Round Tower Music, U.K., Ireland, Europe, 1993—, Watermelon Records, U.S., 1994—. Folksinger, Ft. Worth, 1967-68; musician, vocalist, songwriter, rec. artist: (films) Billy Jack, 1970, Hard Country, 1981, The Thing Called Love, 1993; prodn. asst. film, Sta. KIII-TV, Corpus Christi, 1970, audio engr., Sta. KRIS-TV, Corpus Christi, 1970; musician, vocalist in blues band, Corpus Christi, 1970; receptionist, bookkeeping asst., copywriter, announcer, Sta. KFWT, Ft. Worth, 1971, musician, vocalist, songwriter, Denver, 1971-72, on tour, 1973, 75—, Denver, 1974, on tour, 1976-79, European tour, 1977, Can. tour, 1984-85, on tour in Europe, U.S., Can. and Asia, 1985—; albums include Katy, 1976, Kissin' In The California Sun, Am. release, 1977, internat. release, 1978, A Town South of Bakersfield, 1985, Walkin' on the Moon, European release, 1988, U.S. release, 1989, Child Bride, 1990, (duet album with brother Hugh) Dance Me Outside, 1992, (Switzerland only) Indoor Fireworks, 1992, The Greatest Show On Earth A.K.A. The Evangeline Hotel, 1994, Hearts Gone Wild, 1994, Tulare Dust, 1995, (duet album with Kate Brislin) Sleepless Nights, 1996; singles include Take it as it Comes, 1981, Under Loved and Over Lonely, 1983; songs include The Magic Ring, 1971; Gerry's Song, 1973, Kansas City Morning, 1974, Take Me Back To Texas, 1975, (Waitin' For) The Real Thing, 1975, Didn't We Have Love, 1976, Kissin' in the California Sun, 1977, Walkin' on the Moon, 1989. Recipient Record World Album award, 1976; named one of 4 Top New Female Vocalists, Cashbox Singles Awards, 1976; nominee for Top New Female Vocalist, Acad. Country Music, 1985. Mem. AFTRA, SAG, NARAS, Am. Fedn. Musicians.

MOFFATT, MICHAEL ALAN, lawyer; b. Indpls., Feb. 22, 1964; s. James L. Kelso and Peggy A. Tackett; m. Nancy Norman, Sept. 23, 989; children: Patricia Margaret, Michael Alan. BA in Polit. Sci., Depauw U., 1986; JD, Ind. U., 1989. Bar: Ind. 1989, U.S. Dist. Ct. (so. and no. dists.) Ind. 1989, U.S. Ct. Appeals (7th cir.) 1991. Law clk., atty. White & Raub, Indpls., 1987-94; atty. Wooden McLaughlin & Sterner, Indpls., 1994-95, Barnes & Thornburg, Indpls., 1995—; lectr. litigation, paralegal program, Ind. U./Purdue U. Contbr. articles to legal jours. Cons. pediatric ethics com. Meth. Hosp., Indpls., 1990-92; co-chmn. Keep Am. Beautiful, Greencastle, Ind., 1986, bd. dirs., sec., 1990-94; mem. devel. control com. Geist Harbors Property Owerns' Assn., Indpls., 1993-94, cons., 1994. Mem. Fed. Bar Assn., Ind. Stae Bar Assn., Ind. Defense Lawyers Assn., Ind. Workers' Compensation Inst., Indpls. Bar Assn., Defense Rsch. Inst., Exch. Club. Avocations: golf, basketball, war gaming, softball. Office: Barnes & Thornburgg 1313 Merchants Bank Bldg 11 South Meridian St Indianapolis IN 46204-3556

MOFFET, HUGH LAMSON, pediatrician; b. Monmouth, Ill., Jan. 6, 1932; s. Victor Logue and Helen (Sipfle) M.; m. Donna Mae Pienschke, Sept. 20, 1984; children: Cynthia, Sandra, Douglas. AB, Harvard U., 1953; MD, Yale U., 1957. Instr. Bowman Gray Sch. Medicine, Winston-Salem, N.C., 1957-60; asst. prof. Northwestern U., Chgo., 1960-68, assoc. prof., 1968-71; assoc. prof. U. Wis., Madison, 1971-75, prof., 1975—; head div. infectious diseases Children's Meml. Hosp., Chgo., 1960-71. Author: (book) Clinical Microbiology, 1975, 2d rev. edit., 1980, Pediatric Infectious Diseases, 1975, 3d rev. edit., 1989. Capt. USAR, 1953-68.

MOFFETT, B. J., church administrator. Dir. of Benevolence Ch. of God. Office: Church of God PO Box 2430 Cleveland TN 37320-2430

MOFFETT, CHARLES SIMONTON, museum director, curator, writer; b. Washington, Sept. 19, 1945; s. Charles Simonton M. and Faith Atherton Locke Phelps; m. Jane Pettigrew Daniels, July 28, 1979; children: Kate Serena, Charles Locke. B.A., Middlebury Coll., 1967; M.A., NYU, 1970. Ford Found. fellow Nelson Gallery Art, Kansas City, Mo., 1969-70; expert Sotheby Parke Bernet, N.Y.C., 1970-71; guest asst. curator Met. Mus., N.Y.C., 1974-75, assoc. curator, 1976-81, curator European paintings, 1981-83; curator-in-charge Fine Arts Mus. San Francisco, 1983—, chief curator, summer 1987; sr. curator paintings Nat. Gallery Art, Washington, 1987-92; dir. The Phillips Collection, Washington, 1992—; organizer mus. exhbns., author catalogues; mem. spl. exhbns. panel Nat. Endowment for Arts, 1987; project dir. publs. grant from J. Paul Getty Trust to Fine Arts Mus. San Francisco, 1987; fellow conf. on econs. of arts, presenter Salzburg (Austria) Conf., 1993; grad. Mus. Mgmt. Inst., 1990, sr. mus. assoc., 1994—. Trustee San Francisco Day Sch., 1987, Middlebury Coll., 1987-90, Sterling and Francine Clark Art Inst., 1996—. Andrew Mellon fellow Met. Mus. Art, 1975; travel grantee Met. Mus. Art, 1980; recipient award for best exhbn. Soho News Arts Awards, 1978; co-recipient Prix Bernier for Manet 1832-1883, 1983, recipient Alumni Achievement award Middlebury Coll., 1985, Kaufman award Nat. Gallery Art, 1989. Episcopalian. Office: The Phillips Collection 1600 21st St NW Washington DC 20009-1003

MOFFETT, J. DENNY, lawyer; b. Atlanta, Sept. 20, 1947; s. James Denny Moffett Jr. and Dorothy (Mckenzie) McCall; m. Mary F. Ray, June 6, 1987; children: David, Jenny. BA, U. Okla., 1969; JD with honors, George Washington U., 1972, LLM in Taxation, 1974. Bar: Okla. 1972, U.S. Tax Ct. 1973. Legis. asst. U.S. Senate, Washington, 1973-74; ptnr. Conner & Winters, Tulsa, 1974-90, McKenzie, Moffett, Elias & Books, Tulsa, Oklahoma City, 1990—; adj. faculty U. Tulsa Law Sch., 1978; arbitrator Nat. Assn. Securities Dealers. Commr. Ark.-Okla. River Compact Commn., 1990-94; pres. Nicholas Club Tulsa, 1984; endowment com. Trinity Episcopal Ch., 1990—. 2d lt. U.S. Army, 1972-74; bd. dirs. Am. Cancer Soc., Tulsa, 1991-94. Mem. Am. Arbitration Assn., Tulsa Tax Club (pres. 1981, 94). Republican. Home: 2132 E 32d Pl Tulsa OK 74105 Office: McKenzie Moffett et al 1000 Philtower Bldg Tulsa OK 74103

MOFFETT, JAMES ROBERT, oil and gas company executive; b. Houma, La., Aug. 16, 1938; s. Robert E. and Mary G. (Pollack) M.; m. Louise C. Hohmann, June 5, 1960; children: Crystal Louise, James R. B.S., U. Tex., 1961; M.S., Tulane U., 1963. Cons. geologist oil and gas industry New Orleans, 1964-69; v.p. founding ptnr. McMoRan Exploration Co., New Orleans, 1969-74; pres., chief exec. officer McMoRan Oil & Gas Co., New Orleans, 1974-81, 81-85; chmn., chief exec. officer McMoRan Oil & Gas Co., from 1985; dir. McMoRan Oil & Gas Co., New Orleans, from 1974; vice-chmn. Freeport McMoRan Inc., New Orleans, 1981-85, chmn., chief exec. officer, 1985—, dir., 1981—. Mem. Nat. Petroleum Council, Washington, 1979, Commn. on the Future of South, 1986; bd. dirs. La. Energy Nat. PAC, Metairie, La., 1979, World Trade Ctr., New Orleans, Am. Cancer Soc. Greater New Orleans, Bus. Task Force Edn., Inc.; chmn. bd. La. Coun. Fiscal Reform; chmn. bus. coun. New Orleans and River Region, 1985-87. 2d lt. U.S. Army, 1961-68, capt. Res. ret. Recipient T award Ex Students Assn. U. Tex., 1960, Hornblower Yr. award Pub. Relations Soc. Am., 1986, Vol. Yr. award Urban League Greater New Orleans, 1987; Minnie Stevens Piper Found. scholar U. Tex., 1960, Jacques E. Yenni, S.J. award Loyola U. of New Orleans for Outstanding Community Svc., Jr. Achievement Bus. Hall of Fame award, 1987, Loyola U. of New Orleans' Integritas Vitae award, 1988; named One of Ten Outstanding Persons of 1985 Inst. for Human Understanding, New Orleans. Mem. All Am. Wildcatters, New Orleans Geol. Soc., Petroleum Club New Orleans, Greater New Orleans Mktg. Com. (exec. com. 1987), Geology Found U. Tex. (adv. council 1972-85), Devel. bd. U. Tex., La. Ind. producers Royalty Owners Assn.. South La. Mid-Continent Oil Gas Assn. (v.p.), Dinner Steering Com. (Disting. Citizen award 1983, 85 Boy Scouts Am. New Orleans div.), Green Wave Club. Republican. Office: Freeport-McMoRan Inc 1615 Poydras St New Orleans LA 70112-1254*

MOFFETT, JONATHAN PHILLIP, drummer, musical director, songwriter; b. New Orleans, Nov. 17, 1954; s. Eddie Vernon and Elnora (Dillon) M.; m. Rhonda Catherine Bartholomew, June 26, 1976; children: Tamara Renee, Julian Ryann. Grad. high sch., New Orleans. Drummer, vocalist Patti Austin, Los Angeles, 1982; drummer Cameo Tour, Atlanta, 1982, 83, 86, Lionel Richie, Los Angeles, 1983; drummer, mus. dir. Michael Jackson and the Jacksons' Victory Tour, Los Angeles, 1984; drummer Madonna, Los Angeles, 1985-87, Tina Marie, Los Angeles, 1986; drummer, mus. dir. Jermaine Jackson, Los Angeles, 1986-87; drummer The Jacksons Tour, Los Angeles, 1979, 81, 84, Elton John World Tour, 1988; recorded with Julian Lennon, Peter Cetera, Marilyn Martin, The Jacksons, Kenny Loggins, Chico DeBarge, Nia Peeples, Richard Marx, Jodi Watley; mem. Elton John World Tour, 1989, Madonna World Tour, 1990, George Michael Tour and Rock in Rio Festival. Designer (drum equipment sculpture) Victory Tour Set, 1984; appeared on TV and in videos with Marilyn Martin, Tony Terry, The Kane Gang, Isacc Hayes, Rick James, Cameo, Madonna's Virgin Tour video, Madonna's Ciao Italia Tour video, Elton John/Bernie Taupin's Two Rooms; appeared on TV shows for The O'Jays (Arsenio Hall Show), Jasmine Guy (Arsenio Hall Show), Linsey Buckingham (Arsenio Hall Show, Jay Leno-Tonight Show), Wilson Phillips (Arsenio Hall Show, Jay Leno-Tonight Show), Go West (Arsenio Hall Show), Brenda Russell (Arsenio Hall Show, Jay Leno-Tonight Show), Richard Marx/Randy Meisner (NBC's 70's Celebration Spl.), theme to CBS series Angel Street; producer, writer song All Dressed Up for film soundtrack Coming to America; Elton John Album, 1989, Madonna Album, 1989; recordings (albums) Madonna's Like A Prayer, 1989, Brian Eno, 1990, Richard Marks' Rush Street, 1991 and Paid Vacation, 1994, Or-N-More, 1991, 10-Inch Men, Anri, 1992, Anli, 1992 (# 1 Japanese Female Pop Artist), Barry Manilow's Anthology Collection, 1993, Sing Like Talking (Japanese pop fusion band); (singles) I'm Breathless; (commls.) Lexus Auto-The Drummer, Travel Lodge, Calif. Lottery KENO; tours include Madonna Blond Ambition, 1990, George Michael Cover to Cover Eng.-Japan-U.S.A., 1990-91, Janet Jackson (world), 1993-94, Patti Austin Playboy Jazz Festival, 1993; films include Madonna Truth or Dare, 1991; concerts include Rock in Rio festival with George Michael, 1991, Patti Austin (Playboy Jazz Festival), L.A., 1993, Sadao Watanabe (Japanese jazz saxophonist), Japan; videos include George Michael/Elton John's Don't Let the Sun Go Down on Me, 1991, Richard Marks' Keep Coming Back, 1991, (with Billy Cobham, Mariah Carey) Randy Jackson's instrnl. video, 1993; house band drummer Byron Allen Show. Mem. Musician's Union. Democrat. Roman Catholic. Avocations: drawing, painting.

MOFFETT, KATHARINE E., publisher; b. Oakland, Calif., Dec. 11, 1970; d. David Robinson and Susan Elise (Carlson) M. BA, Claremont McKenna Coll., 1993. Editor The Insider The Heritage Found., Washington, 1993-94, assoc. pub. Policy Rev., 1994—. Vol. the Jr. League, Washington. Republican. Presbyterian. Office: The Heritage Foundation Policy Review 214 Massachusetts Ave NE Washington DC 20002

MOFFETT, KENNETH LEE, superintendent schools; b. Mt. Vernon, Wash., May 6, 1935; s. Charles R. and Edith May (Barker) M.; m. Diane Muriel Buckley, July 30, 1966; children: Kendis Charlene, Patrick Charles. BA, Western Wash. State U., 1957; MA, Calif. State U., Los Angeles, 1958-60; EdD, U. So. Calif., 1972. Tchr. pub. schs., Inglewood, Calif., 1957-61, 63-65, asst. prin., 1965-69, prin., 1969-73; tchr. U.S. Dependent Sch., Pirmasens, Fed. Republic Germany, 1961-62, asst. prin., Erlangen, Fed. Republic Germany, 1962-63; asst. supt. Inglewood Sch. Dist., Calif., 1973-76; supt. Lennox Sch. Dist., Calif., 1976-86; supt. ABC Unified Sch. Dist., Cerritos, Calif., 1986—; mem. adv. bd. Ad Hoc Com. on Mental Health for Tchrs., Los Angeles, 1980-81; chmn. scholarship com. Bank of Am., 1979-84. Mem. adv. com. Los Angeles Area council Boy Scouts Am., 1981-83; mem. support group for U. So. Calif., 1978-84; bd. dirs. Centinela Valley Guidance Clinic, Inglewood, 1978-82. Recipient Service awards PTA, Inglewood, 1973, Lennox, 1982, Am. Assn. of Sch. Adminstrs. Nationl Supt. of the Year, 1994. Mem. Centinela Valley Adminstrs. Assn. (charter pres. 1979-80), Assn. Calif. Sch. Adminstrs. (region chmn. 1980-82, Service award 1982), Centinela Valley Supts. Group (chmn. 1980-84), Centinela Valley Trustees and Adminstrs. Assn. (sec.-treas. 1977-78). Republican. Methodist. Office: ABC Unified Sch Dist 16700 Norwalk Blvd Artesia CA 90703-1838

MOFFITT, CHARLES WILLIAM, insurance sales executive; b. Altoona, Pa., Mar. 24, 1932; s. Charles William and Beatrice Jeanette (Shellenberger) M.; m. Marianne Foley Potter, May 23, 1980; children: Michelle Ann Hunt, Charles William III, Deborah K.; stepchildren: Christopher Potter, Kimberly Bryan. B.A., Pa. State U., 1957. Examiner Pa. R.R., Buffalo, 1957-62; asst. to pres. White Cross Stores, Inc., Monroeville, Pa., 1962-65; sec. White Cross Stores, Inc., 1965-70, v.p. adminstrn., sec., 1970-72; dir. labor relations and legal affairs Revco D.S., Inc., Cleve., 1972-75; asst. v.p. personnel Revco D.S., Inc., 1974-75; pres. Fashion Wearhouse, Inc., Altoona, Pa., 1975-87; owner Omega Advt. Co.; pres. Olympus I, Inc., 1980-87; agt. Prin. Fin. Group, 1988-90, Variable Annuity Life Ins. Co., 1990—. Co-author: Mincemeat Cartoons, Altoona Mirror Newspaper. Bd. dirs. Bedford Springs Music Festival, 1984-87, Blair County Arts Found., 1987-91. Republican. Roman Catholic. Home and Office: 2033 Southpoint Dr Hummelstown PA 17036-8944

MOFFITT, DONALD EUGENE, transportation company executive; b. Terre Haute, Ind., May 22, 1932; s. James Robert and Margaret Mary (Long) M.; m. Billie Duffy, Feb. 21, 1989; 1 child, Jaime. BA, Ind. State U., 1954; postgrad., Ind. U., 1956; grad., Advanced Mgmt. Program, Harvard U., 1972. Acct. Foster Freight Lines, Indpls., 1955-56; with Consol. Freightways Inc., San Francisco, 1956-88, v.p. planning, 1961-69; v.p. fin., motor carrier subs. Consol. Freightways Corp. Del., 1969-75; v.p. fin., treas. parent co. Consol. Freightways Inc., San Francisco, 1975-81; exec. v.p. Consol. Freightways Inc., Palo Alto, Calif., 1981-86; vice chmn. parent co. bd. Consol. Freightways, Inc., Palo Alto, Calif., 1986-88; chmn., CEO Circle Express, Indpls., 1988-90; pres., CEO Consol. Freightways, Inc., Palo Alto, Calif., 1990—, chmn., CEO, 1995—, also bd. dirs.; chmn. bd. dirs. all subsidiaries Consolidated Freightways, Inc., 1990—. Bd. dirs. Bay Area Coun., Calif. Bus. Roundtable, Conf. Bd., Boy Scouts Am., ARC; bd. dirs., exec. com. Hwy. Users Fedn.; bd. trustees Automotive Safety Found.; bus. adv. coun. Northwestern U. Transp. Ctr. Mem. Nat. C. of C. (Washington) (bd. dirs.). Office: Consol Freightways Inc 3240 Hillview Ave Palo Alto CA 94304-1201

MOFFITT, GEORGE, JR., foreign service officer; b. N.Y.C., June 18, 1918; s. George and Margaret (Buchanan) M.; m. Lois Anderson, July 7, 1946; children: Katherine M., Margaret Louise. Student, U. Wis., 1950-51. With indsl. firm, 1937-39; fgn. service officer in Haiti, Iraq, Can., Belgium, Burma, Netherland Antilles, Cyprus,, Washington 1939—; counselor of embassy Brussels, 1966-71; polit. adviser to comdr.-in-chief Allied Forces, So. Europe, 1971—. Bd. dirs. Fulbright Found. for Belgium and Luxembouurg; vice chmn. Burlington Bicentennial Commn.; chmn. Cen. Conn. Adv. Coun. on Aging, 1979-80, Conn. Coalition on Aging, 1979-80; bd. dirs. Conn. Assn. for Human Svcs., 1980-81, Cen. Conn. Regional Planning Agy., 1985-87;

corporator Wheeler Clinic; mem. Conn. Gov.'s Commn. on Energy Assistance, 1987—, Bristol (Conn.) Bd. Pub. Welfare, 1988-92; hon. pres. Burlington Libr. Assn., mem., 1979-88. Home: 2 Chimney Crest Ln Bristol CT 06010-7969

MOFFITT, PHILLIP WILLIAM, magazine editor; b. Kingsport, Tenn., Sept. 11, 1946; s. Wallace and Claire Matilda (Allen) M. BS, U. Tenn., 1968, MS, 1971. Co-founder 13-30 Pub. (now Whittle Communications), Knoxville, Tenn., 1971, editor, 1971-79, pres., 1976—; editor-in-chief 13-30 Publs. Group, Knoxville, Tenn., 1979-86; editor, pres. Esquire Magazine, N.Y.C., 1979-84, editor-in-chief, pres., 1984-86; chmn. Light Source Computer Images, Inc., 1989—. Co-author: The Power to Heal, 1990, Medicine's Great Journey, 1992; contbr. columns to Esquire Mag., 1979-88. Bd. dirs. C.J. Jung Found. Mem. Mag. Pubs. Assn. (bd. dirs. 1984—). Home and Office: 1 Pelican Point Rd Belvedere Tiburon CA 94920-2456

MOGABGAB, WILLIAM JOSEPH, epidemiologist, educator; b. Durant, Okla., Nov. 2, 1921; s. Anees and Maude (Jopes) M.; m. Joy Roddy, Dec. 24, 1948 (div. July 1988); children: Robert (dec.), Ann, Kay, Edward R., Jean, Robert M. Berryman, William J.M. Berryman; m. Rose Warren Berryman, July 18, 1988. B.S., Tulane U., 1942, M.D., 1944. Diplomate Am. Bd. Internal Medicine, Am. Bd. Microbiology. Intern Charity Hosp. La., New Orleans, 1944-45, resident, 1946-49, vis. physician, 1949-51, sr. vis. physician, 1971-75; cons., 1976—; mem. faculty Tulane U. Sch. Medicine, 1948—, prof. medicine, 1962-92; cons. infectious diseases, epidemiology, internal medicine New Orleans Dept. Health, 1992—; vis. investigator, asst. physician Hosp. Rockefeller Inst. Med. Research, N.Y.C., 1951-52; chief infectious disease VA Hosp., Houston, 1952-53; asst. prof. medicine Baylor U. Coll. Medicine, 1952-53; head virology div. NAMRU 4, USNTC, Great Lakes, Ill., 1953-55; cons. infectious disease VA Hosp., New Orleans, 1956—; cons. FDA Orphan Products Devel. Grants Program, 1984—. Assoc. mem. commn. influenza Armed Forces Epidemiological Bd., 1959-71; mem. New Orleans Mayor's Health Adv. Com., 1983—. With UNS, 1945-46; comdr. USNR, ret. 1981. Fellow Nat. Found. Infantile Paralysis, 1951-52. Fellow ACP, Am. Acad. Microbiology, Infectious Disease Soc. Am., Am. Coll. Epidemiology; mem. Soc. Exptl. Biology and Medicine, So., Central socs. clin. research, Am. Fedn. Clin. Research, Am. Soc. Cell Biology, Am. Soc. Microbiology, Am. Soc. Clin. Investigation, Tissue Culture Assn., Am. Pub. Health Assn., Am. Soc. Internal Medicine, Am. Soc. Clin. Pharmacology and Therapeutics, So. Med. Soc., AMA, AAAS, Am. Soc. Internal Medicine, Southwestern Assn. Clin. Biology, Soc. Epideniol. Research, Am. Soc. Virology. Research, publns. agts. of and vaccines for respiratory infections, viruses, mycoplasma, new antibiotics. Home: 3 Fortress Rd New Orleans LA 70122-1336

MOGEL, LEONARD HENRY, author; b. Bklyn., Oct. 23, 1922; s. Isaac and Shirley (Goldman) M.; m. Ann Vera Levy, Oct. 23, 1949; children: Wendy Lynn, Jane Ellen. B.B.A., Coll. City N.Y., 1947. Salesman N.Y. Printing Co., N.Y.C., 1946-48; sales mgr. Pollak Printing Co., N.Y.C., 1948-52; advt. dir. Diners Club, Inc., N.Y.C., 1952-56; pub. Diners Club for Signature and Bravo mags., 1956-67; pres. Leonard Mogel Assos., Inc. (nat. advt. reps.), N.Y.C., 1952-67; prin. owner San Francisco Warriors Profl. Basketball Team, 1963-64; pres. Twenty First Century Communications Inc., N.Y.C., 1967-72; pub. Cheetah and Weight Watchers mags., 1967-75; dir. Regents Pub. Co. div. Simon & Schuster, 1960-67; advt. cons. Harvard Lampoon, 1968; pub. Nat. Lampoon, 1970-86, Liberty mag., 1971-73, Ingenue mag., 1973-75, Heavy Metal mag., 1977-86; adj. prof. NYU Sch. Continuing Edn., 1973-78; panelist Folio Mag. Pub. Conf., 1975-76; pres. Perfect World Entertainment, 1996. Exec. prodr.: (feature films) Heavy Metal, 1981; author: Everything You Need to Know to Make It in the Magazine Business, 1979, Making It in the Media Professions, 1988, Making It in Advertising, 1993, Making It in Public Relations, 1993, Making It in Broadcasting, 1994, Making It in Book Publishing, 1996. Sponsor Albert Einstein Med. Coll., Birch Wathen Sch., N.Y.C. Served with AUS, 1942-46, CBI.

MOGEL, WILLIAM ALLEN, lawyer, educator, author; b. N.Y.C., Mar. 7, 1942; s. Harry H. and Therese M.; m. Judith; children: Elisabeth, Andrew. B.A. cum laude, Hobart Coll., 1963; LL.B., U. Pa., 1966. Bar: D.C. 1967, Md. 1971. Ptnr., Morley Caskin, Washington, 1991—; adj. instr. Am. U., Washington, 1982—; active Washington Bd. Trade. Author: Transportation & Marketing of Natural Gas, 1985, 86, Natural Gas: Current Federal and State Developments, 1987; editor-in-chief: Energy Law Jour., 1980—; editor: Natural Gas Yearbook, 1988-92; co-editor: Energy Law & Transactions; contbr. articles to profl. jours. Trustee Hobart Coll., 1983-88. Served to capt. U.S. Army, 1966-69. Mem. Fed. Energy Bar Assn. Home: 8806 Transue Dr Bethesda MD 20817-6931 Office: Morley Caskin 1225 I St NW Washington DC 20005-3914

MOGELEVER, BERNARD, public relations executive; b. Newark, Oct. 15, 1940; s. Louis J. and Kate (Rosenblatt) M.; m. Diane Hinkley, Feb. 1966; children: Elisa, Jonathan G. BA, Rutgers U., New Brunswick, N.J., 1962. News & feature writer S.I. Advance, N.Y., 1965-66; pub. rels. writer The Nat. Found., N.Y.C., 1966-68; exec. A.A. Schechter Assocs., N.Y.C., 1968-73; sr. v.p. Harshe-Rotman & Druck, Inc., N.Y.C., 1973-82; exec. v.p. Ruder Finn & Rotman, N.Y.C., 1982-85; sr. v.p. Burson-Marsteller, 1985-91; pres. Mogelever Comm., Inc., N.Y.C., 1991—. Lt. USAF, 1962-65.

MOGERMAN, SUSAN, state agency administrator. CEO, dir. State of Ill. Historic Preservation Agy., Springfield. Office: State Ill-Hist Preservation Agy Old State Capitol Springfield IL 62701

MOGHISSI, KAMRAN S., obstetrician/gynecologist, educator; b. Tehran, Iran, Sept. 11, 1925; came to U.S., 1959, naturalized, 1965; s. Ahmad and Monireh (Rohani) M.; m. Ida Laura Tedeschi, Jan. 2, 1952; children: Diana J., Soraya R. ChB, MB, U. Geneva, 1951, MD, 1952. Diplomate Am. Bd. Ob-Gyn., Am. Bd. Reproductive Endocrinology. Intern, Univ. Hosp., Geneva, 1951-52, Horton Gen. Hosp., United Oxford Hosps., Banbury, Eng., 1952-53; resident in ob-gyn. Gloucestershire Royal Hosp., Eng., 1953-54, St. Helier Hosp., London, 1954-55, Leeds Regional Hosp. Bd., Yorkshire, Eng., 1955-56, Detroit Receiving Hosp., 1961, attending gynecologist, 1962; assoc. prof. ob-gyn. U. Shiraz Med. Sch., Iran, 1957-59; rsch. assoc. ob-gyn. and physiol. chemistry, Wayne State U., Detroit, 1959-61, asst. prof., 1962-66, assoc. prof., 1966-70, prof., 1970—, dir. div. reproductive endocrinology and infertility, 1970-94; vice chmn., 1983-88, chmn. dept. ob-gyn., 1988-91; sr. attending physician ob-gyn. Hutzel Hosp., Detroit, 1963, vice chief, 1978-82, 83-89, chief, 1982-83, 88-91, chief of staff, 1991-93, attending surgeon, chief ob-gyn. Harper-Grace Hosp., 1983-84, attending surgeon, emeritus, chief ob-gyn. emeritus, 1991—; obstetrician, gynecologist, chief, Detroit Med. Ctr., 1988-91; cons. and lectr. in field. Contbr. chpts. to books, articles to profl. jours. Developer exhibits in medicine, movies and teaching prodns.; mem. numerous editorial bds.; cons. in field. Fellow ACS, Am. Coll. Ob-Gyn. Am. Gynecol. and Obstetric Soc.; mem. AMA (ho. of dels. 1992—), AAAS, Am. Soc. Reprodn. Medicine (formerly Am. Fertility Soc., pres. 1990-91), Soc. Study Reprodn., Am. Soc. Andrology, Wayne County Med. Soc., Mich. Soc. Ob-Gyn, Central Assn. Ob-Gyn., N.Y. Acad. Scis., Soc. Reproductive Endocrinologists (charter mem., pres. 1990), Soc. Reproductive Surgeons (charter mem.), Soc. for Assisted Reproductive Tech. (charter mem.), Lochmoor Club (Grosse Pointe), Renaissance Club (Detroit). Home: 56 Moorland Dr Grosse Pointe Shores MI 48236-1112 Office: Hutzel Hosp 4707 St Antoine Blvd Detroit MI 48201-1427

MOGIL, BERNARD MARC, judge; b. N.Y.C., May 13, 1949; s. Roman and Musia (Mosiewicka) Mogilanski; m. Terry Gerbs, Nov. 21, 1975; 4 children. BA, CCNY, 1970; postgrad. in law, Ind. U., 1970-71; JD, N.Y. Law Sch., 1974. Bar: N.Y. 1975, Fla. 1974, U.S. Ct. Appeals (2nd cir.) 1975, U.S. Dist. Ct. (so. dist. and ea. dist.) N.Y. 1975, D.C. 1978. Asst. gen. counsel N.Y.C. Health Dept., 1975-76; assoc. Hayt, Hayt & Landau, Great Neck, N.Y., 1976-81; spl. asst. atty. gen. N.Y. Medicaid fraud prosecutor, N.Y.C., 1981-84; sole practice Garden City, N.Y., 1984-86; judge Nassau County Dist. Ct., Hempstead, N.Y., 1987-90, Nassau County Ct., Mineola, N.Y., 1991—; pilot Civil Air Patrol, Garden City, 1982-86; chief counsel Nassau County Conservative Party, 1982-86. Contbr. articles to profl. jours. Chief counsel, lt. col. Civil Air Patrol N.Y. Wing, Garden City, 1980-86; mgr. Little League Baseball, Syosset, N.Y., 1991-92, Great Neck, N.Y., 1993. Mem. N.Y. State Bar Assn., Fla. Bar Assn., D.C. Bar Assn., Nassau County Bar Assn., Flying Judges Assn. Ltd. (pres.). Conservative. Jewish. Avocations: music, private aircraft flying, linguistics, firearms. Home: 9 Willow Ln Great Neck NY 11023-1138 Office: County Ct Nassau County 262 Old Country Rd Mineola NY 11501-4255 *Justice? A concept grounded in moral righteousness, with the potential of sinking into the mire of afforable only to the mega-wealthy. America must seriously look at itself if it is to survive as a free people.*

MOGIL, H(ARVEY) MICHAEL, meteorologist, educator; b. N.Y.C., July 9, 1945; s. Nathan and Linda (Balansky) M.; m. Sheila Rose Schleiderer, Mar. 13, 1965 (div. 1987); children: Fredrika Sharon, Allyn Keith; m. Barbara G. Levine, Feb. 6, 1988. BS in Meteorology, Fla. State U., 1967, MS in Meteorology, 1969. Cert. cons. meteorologist. Cons. How the Weatherworks, Rockville, Md., 1979—; trainer NOAA, Washington, 1985-95; instr. U. Mo., Columbia, 1989-92, Loyola Coll., Balt., 1992—; tchr. 5th grade math. and sci. Sandy Springs Friends Sch., 1995-96; co-chair Project "Sky Awareness Week", Rockville, 1991—; adv. bd. Rockville Consortium for Sci., 1990—. Co-author: Weather Study Under a Newspaper Umbrella, 1989, The Amateur Meteorologist, 1993, Anytime Weather Everywhere, 1996; creator video tape tchr. guide Our Sea of Clouds, 1992, A Hurricane: Through the Eyes of Children, 1993; contbr. numerous articles to profl. jours. Mem. Nat. Sci. Tchrs. Assn. (reviewer 1983—), Nat. Earth Sci. Tchrs. Assn., Nat. Weather Assn. (chmn. tng. com. 1986-89, Mem. of the Yr. 1988), Am. Meteorol. Soc. Avocations: biking, reading, gardening, travel.

MOGK, JOHN EDWARD, law educator, association executive, consultant; b. Detroit, Feb. 10, 1939; s. Clifford Anthony and Evelyn Lenore (Paselk) M.; m. Lylas Heidi Good, Aug. 23, 1964; children: Marya, Tenley, Matthew. BBA, U. Mich., 1961, JD with distinction, 1964; diploma in comparative law, U. Stockholm, 1965. Bar: N.Y. 1966, Mich. 1970. Assoc. atty. Shearman & Sterling, N.Y.C., 1964-68; mem. faculty Wayne State U. Sch. Law, 1968—, dir. grad. studies, 1990—; chmn. MERRA Rsch. Corp., 1977-94, pres., 1974-94; cons. econ. and urban devel., arbitrator. Editor Michigan International Lawyer and Utilities Law Rev.; contbr. articles to profl. jours. Chmn. Mich. TOP Task Force, 1972; vice chmn. Mich. Constrn. Code Commn., 1973; mem. exec. com. Southeastern Mich. Coun. Govts., 1970; chmn. Detroit Sch. Boundary Commn., 1970, Downtown Detroit Vacant Bldg. Com., 1991-93; mem. Detroit Bd. Edn., 1970; mgr. Detroit Empowerment Zone Proposal, 1994; project exec. New Detroit Stadium, 1995. Named Outstanding Wayne State U. Assoc. Prof., 1971, Outstanding Wayne Law Sch. Prof., 1977, 83, 93, Outstanding Young Man in Detroit, 1972, One of Ten Outstanding Young Men in U.S., 1973, One of Four Outstanding Vols. in U.S., 1974; recipient Presdl. citation Wayne State U., 1977, State of Mich., 1988, 94; Am.-Scandinavian fellow, 1965; vis. fellow U. Warwick, Eng., 1985-86. Mem. ABA, Mich. Bar Assn., Assn. of Bar of City of N.Y. Home: 1000 Yorkshire Rd Grosse Pointe MI 48230-1432

MOGOL, ALAN JAY, lawyer; b. Balt., July 29, 1946; s. Jesse and Kitty (Stutman) m.; m. Ellen Epstein, June 19, 1969; children: Andrew Stephen, Jonathan David. BA with distinction, U. Va., 1968, JD, 1971. Bar: Md. 1972, U.S. Dist. Ct. Md. 1972, U.S. Ct. Appeals (4th cir.) 1972, U.S. Supreme Ct. 1978. Assoc. Ober, Kaler, Grimes & Shriver, Balt., 1971-77, ptnr., 1978—, chmn. bus. dept., 1980-81, 84-85, 1991—; lectr. on continuing edn. Md. Inst. Continuing Profl. Edn. for Lawyers, 1988-92, trustee, 1990-93; spkr. seminars Nat. Health Lawyers Assn., Washington, 1986-87, Rocky Mountain Mgmt., Denver, 1987, Med. Imaging Expo., 1995, Washington, 1995. Co-author: (book chpt.) in Structuring the Secured Loan Agreement, 1991; contbr. articles on ins. and equipment leasing to jours., newspapers. Bd. dirs. Transitional Living Coun., Balt., 1972-92; bd. trustees Md. Inst. of Continuing Profl. Edn. for Lawyers, 1990-93. Mem. ABA, Equipment Leasing Assn. Am. (lawyers com. 1986-89, program com. 1986-91, speaker seminars), Md. Bar Assn. (uniform comml. code com. 1988—, chmn. 1991-93, vice chmn. bus. sect. 1995—). Avocation: tennis. Office: Ober Kaler Grimes & Shriver 120 E Baltimore St Baltimore MD 21202-1674

MOGUEIS, ARTURO CAÑARES, farmer, Philippines provincial official; b. San Fernando, Masbate, The Philippines, May 12, 1927; s. Francisco Tizon and Eufromia Bartolata (Cañares) M.; m. Ursucena Cantonjos Ontog, Oct. 5, 1952; children: Francisco, Gracia, Lourdes, Carmela. AB, Ovilla Coll., Masbate, 1969. Farmer San Fernando, 1969—; tchr. pub. sch., Irosim, Sorsogon, The Philippines, 1948-49; clk. Gov.'s Office, Masbate, 1952-54; ins. supr. Philippine Am. Life, Masbate, 1955-63; pres. Farm Sys. Devel. Corp., Masbate, 1976-79; bd. dirs. Farm Sys. Devel. Corp., Manila, 1984-87; chmn. Provincial Agrl. and Fishery Coun., Masbate, 1987—; mcpl. councilor San Fernando, Masbate, 1995—; chmn. Diwata Heights Devel. Coop., Inc., San Fernando, 1992—, Ticao Island Dist. Fedn. Coops., San Fernando, 1992—. Pres. Victory Labor Union, San Fernando, 1950-52; councilor Mcpl. Govt., San Fernando, 1964-67, 72-75, mayor, 1968-71, sec., 1980-82; capt. Barrio Govt., San Fernando, 1983-86; chmn. Mcpl. Coop. Devel. Coun., San Fernando, 1992; founder, donor site Ipil H.S., San Fernando, 1978. Recipient civic award Citizens of San Fernando, Calif., 1969, Most Outstanding Mayor award and Outstanding Mayor of Yr. award Presdl. Arm on Cmty. Devel., Manila, 1970, Outstanding Mayor and Exemplary Leader award United Commentators, Manila, 1970, Scroll of Honor and Distinction citation Biog. Rschrs. Soc. The Philippines, 1970. Roman Catholic. Avocations: grafting fruit trees. Home: IPIL, Masbate San Fernando 5416, The Philippines Office: PAFC, Masbate, San Fernando 5416, The Philippines

MOGUL, LESLIE ANNE, business development and marketing consultant; b. Balt., Mar. 9, 1948; d. Harry and Elaine Mogul; m. William Kasper. AS, Miami Dade Jr. Coll., 1969; BA, Temple U., 1976. Accredited pub. rels. Account exec. Gray & Rogers, Inc., Phila., 1976-80; pres. Leslie Mogul, Inc., Phila., 1980-84; v.p. McKinney, Inc., Phila., 1984-87; assoc. dir. comm. Scripps Meml. Hosps., San Diego, 1987-93; dir. pub. rels. Scripps Health, San Diego, 1993, dir. customer rels. and mktg., 1994-95; dir. bus. devel. Harborview Med. Ctr. Hosp., San Diego, 1995—. Recipient over 25 awards local and nat. pub. rels. and comm. orgns. Mem. Pub. Rels. Soc. Am. (dir.-at-large 1993-94), Alumni Leadership Calif. Office: Harborview Med Ctr 1855 1st Ave San Diego CA 92101

MOGY, CATHERINE WADDELL, nurse anesthetist, critical care nurse; b. Florence, S.C., Mar. 13, 1964; d. Harold Dean and Sarah Margaret (Windham) Waddell; m. Richard A. Mogy, Sept. 13, 1986; children: Austin Waddell, Sarah Catherine. ADN, Florence-Darlington Tech Ctr., 1985; BSN, Med. U. S.C., Florence, 1989; cert., Richland Meml. Sch. Anesthesia, 1991. RN, S.C.; cert. advanced cardiac life supports, nurse anesthetist. Staff nurse McLeod Regional Med. Ctr., Florence, S.C., 1985-86; staff nurse ICU Bruce Hosp., Florence, 1986-89; nurse anesthetist Carolina's Hosp. System, 1991—. Recipient Francis Marion almuni scholarship. Mem. Am. Assn. Nurse Anesthetists, ANA, Sigma Theta Tau.

MOHAIDEEN, A. HASSAN, surgeon, healthcare executive; b. Ramanathapuram, India, Aug. 14, 1940; s. Abdul and Mariam (Pitchai) Kader; m. Zarina M. Meera, May 30, 1965 (dec. July 1986); children: Ahamed, Mariam, Najeeba, Azeema; m. Laurie J. Kucich, June 23, 1989; children: Yasmin Sara, Leila Jahan. MD, U. Madras, India, 1965; MBA, Wagner Coll., 1996. Diplomate Am. Bd. Surgery, Am. Bd. Quality Assurance and Utilization. Intern Govt. Stanley Hosp., Madras, 1965-66, Good Samaritan Hosp., West Islip, N.Y., 1967-68; resident in gen. and vascular surgery L.I. Coll. Hosp., Bklyn., 1968-73, asst. attending surgeon, 1973-76, assoc. attending surgeon, 1976-78, attending surgeon, 1978—, chief divsn. vascular surgery, 1980-93; sr v.p., 1995—; dir. vascular lab. L.I. Coll. Hosp., Bklyn., 1981-93; sr. v.p., managed care and exec. vice-chmn. dept. surgery The Bklyn.-Caledonian Hosp. Ctr. (affiliate of NYU), 1995—; sr. v.p. Bklyn.-Caledonian Hosp. Ctr. (affiliate of NYU), 1995—; asst. surgeon G.H.Q. Hosp., Ramnad, India, 1966-67; assoc. attending surgeon Meth. Hosp., Bklyn., 1982-90, attending surgeon, 1991; asst. attending surgeon Bklyn. Caledonian Med. Ctr., 1973-85, mem. courtesy staff, 1985-94, attending surgeon, 1994—; attending physician Victory Meml. Hosp., Bklyn., 1982-95; vis. physician Kings County Hosp. Ctr., Bklyn., 1973—; clin. instr. in surgery Downstate Med. Ctr., SUNY, Bklyn., 1973-78, clin. asst. prof. surgery, 1978—; mem. exec. com. of med. staff L.I. Coll. Hosp., Bklyn., 1979-93, treas. med. staff, 1982-85, pres., 1985-87, med. chmn. Guild Ball com., 1981, mem. quality assurance com. dept. surgery, 1988-94, chmn. credentials com., 1990-93, quality assurance and risk mgmt. com., 1990-93; bd. dirs. Aetna Health Plans of N.Y., AIDS adv. com., 1987—, stds. com., 1986-94, quality assurance com.; mem. credentials com. Prucare, 1988-92; sr. v.p. managed care Bklyn. Hosp., 1995—; mem. quality mgmt. com. Oxford Health Plans, 1995—; mem. quality improvement com. Chubb Health, N.Y., 1994—. Contbr. articles to med. jours. Fellow ACS (com. on Long Island dist. applicants, 1988—), Royal Coll. Physicians and Surgeons Can. (cert.), Internat. Coll. Surgeons; mem. AMA (Physician's Recognition award), AAAS, Am. Coll. Physician Execs., Med. Soc. of State of N.Y., N.Y. State Soc. of Surgeons, N.Y. Acad. of Scis., Med. Soc. of County of Kings (mediation com., 1979-85), Bklyn. Surg. Soc., Soc. for Non-Invasive Vascular Technicians, Kings Physicians I.P.A. (pres./med. dir., 1985-95), Bklyn. Physicians I.P.A. (v.p., 1985-96, pres.). Avocations: photography, computers, walking. Office: 705 86th St Brooklyn NY 11228-3219

MOHAMED, DONNA FAHIMAH, counselor; b. Chapel Hill, N.C., Oct. 19, 1959; d. Thomas Lloyd and Helen Eleanor (Helms) Pendergraft; m. Dilip Gandhi, Aug. 19, 1978; 1 child, Sundeep; m. Mustafa Hussein Al-Bar, Apr. 15, 1991; 1 child, Maidah Nasreen. BA in Religious Studies with high honors and distinction, U. N.C., 1994. Rehab. therapist John Umstead Hosp. Continuing Treatment, Butner, N.C., 1985-86; immigration paralegal Law Offices of Douglas Holmes, Durham, N.C., 1986-87; immigration specialist Law Offices of Manlin Chee, Greensboro, N.C., 1987-92; program dir., accredited counselor Immigration & Minority Assistance Network, Durham, 1992—; pro bono project rep. Lawyers Com. for Human Rights, Fredericksburg, Va., 1987-88; minority devel. counselor, Ibad Ar-Rahman Sch., Durham, 1990-91; immigration cons. to bd. dirs. Jamaat Ibad Ar-Rahman, Inc., Durham, 1990—; dir. cmty. counseling IMAN, Durham, 1991—; speaker N.Am. Coun. for Muslim Women, Chgo., 1994; panelist on cultural awareness, Dept. Edn. and Counseling, U. N.C., Chapel Hill, 1994; organizer, presenter ann. workshops Coll. Bound Program for Youth, Chapel Hill, 1992—. Recipient 1st prize ann. cooking contest Triangle Muslim Women's Group, 1992. Mem. Am. Muslim Coun., Am. Immigration Lawyers Assn. (pro bono affiliation), Muslim Women's Orgn. (pres. Chapel Hill, N.C. chpt. 1991-93), Muslim Student's Assn. (exec. dir. Chapel Hill chpt. 1992-93), Islamic Soc. N.Am., Social Scientists Am., Golden Key Nat. Honor Soc. Democrat. Office: Immigration and Minority Assistance Network PO Box 51458 Durham NC 27717-1458

MOHAMED, JOSEPH, real estate broker, developer, engineering contractor; b. Omar, W.Va., Mar. 19, 1928; s. Mose and Minnie Elizabeth (Martin) M.; m. Patricia Louise Olmstead, Apr. 11, 1947 (div. 1972); children: Joseph Jr., John W., James R., Leslie Louise; m. Shirley Ida Medeiros, June 22, 1979. AA in Bus. Adminstrn., Sacramento City Coll., 1950; BBA Personnel, Sacramento State U., 1952; postgrad. U. Pacific, U. Calif., Davis, Am. River Coll. Founder comml. trucking operation, Calif., 1949-52, Baja, Calif., Mex., 1953; founder Mexican Co. of Agr. and Livestock, Ltd., Ensenada, Baja, Calif., Mex., 1953-57; owner Quintair, Inc., Calif., 1954—; contractor, real estate developer, 1949—; owner Joseph's Landscape Svc., Sacramento, 1952-72, Joseph Mohamed Enterprises, 1972—; pest control adviser, Calif., 1970—. Mem. Rep. Nat. Com., Rep. Presdl. Task Force, Sacramento Regional Arts Coun., 1965—, Govs.' Emergency Drought Task Force, 1977, Civil Affairs Assn., Calif. Rental Assn., 1975—, Sacramento Apartment Assn., Calif. Apartment Assn., Nat. Apartment Assn.; dir. McClellan Aviation Museum Found., Sacramento County Sheriff's Mounted Posse, 1961—. Served with U.S. Army, 1946-48, USAR, 1949-78. Decorated Legion of Merit; recipient Master Aviator Badge. Mem. Sacramento U. Alumni Assn., Sacramento State Horseman's Assn., Calif. State Horseman's Assn., Sacramento Metro. C. of C., Navy League of U.S., Reserve Officer's Assn., Assn. of U.S. Army, Elk Grove C. of C., Sacramento Bd. of Realtors, Calif. Assn. Realtors, Nat. Assn. Realtors. Clubs: Comstock (Sacramento), Commonwealth (San Francisco). Lodges: Masons, Shriners, Elks.

MOHAN, D. MIKE, transportation company executive; b. Chico, Calif., Apr. 10, 1945; s. Alfred and Velda June (Clark) M.; m. Dixie Watson, June 21, 1969; children—Laurel, Patrick, Christopher. B.A., U. Calif.-Berkeley, 1967, M.B.A., 1968; A.M.P., Harvard U., 1983. With So. Pacific Transp. Co., 1968—; asst. to pres. So. Pacific Transp. Co., San Francisco, 1981-82; v.p.-maintenance So. Pacific Transp. Co., 1982-83, exec. v.p., 1983-88, also dir.; pres., chief oper. officer So. Pacific Transp. Co., San Francisco, Denver & Rio Grande Western R.R., 1988—; now with Kingsley Group; bd. dirs. Rio Grande Industries. Mem. Nat. Freight Traffic Assn., Assn. Am. R.R.s (bd. dirs.). Avocations: sports; hiking. Office: Kingsley Group 1 Post St Ste 2550 San Francisco CA 94104*

MOHAN, J. PATRICK, lawyer; b. Balt., Apr. 10, 1948; s. Joseph F. and Laura (Reed) M.; m. Linda Lee, Aug. 26, 1972; children—Brian, Michael, Bradley, Timothy, Kerry. B.S., Ohio State U., 1970; J.D., U. San Francisco, 1973; LL.M., Georgetown U., 1977. Bar: Calif. 1973, U.S. Dist. Ct. (no. dist.) Calif. 1973. U.S. Ct. Appeals (9th cir.) 1974, Ohio 1977, Ill. 1980. Atty., Chevron Oil Co., New Orleans, 1973-75; atty. U.S. SEC, Washington, 1975-77; assoc. atty. Moritz, McClure, Hughes & Kerscher, Columbus, Ohio, 1977-79; corp. counsel, asst. sec. A.E. Staley Mfg. Co., Decatur, Ill., 1979-85; asst. gen. counsel and asst. sec. Staley Continental, Inc., Rolling Meadows, Ill., 1985-87, v.p., gen. counsel, asst. sec., 1987-88; exec. v.p. adminstrn., gen. counsel, sec. Staley Mfg. Co., Decatur, Ill., 1988—. Home: 3010 E Fulton Ave Decatur IL 62521-4541 Office: A E Staley Mfg Co 2200 E Eldorado St Decatur IL 62521-1578

MOHAN, JOHN J., lawyer; b. St. Louis, May 22, 1945; s. John Joseph and Virginia Loretta (Durkin) M.; m. Elaine Bronwyn Lipe, May 29, 1982; children: Bryn Elizabeth, John Burke. BS Indsl. Engring., St. Louis U., Sch. Engring. and Earth Scis., 1967; JD, St. Louis U., 1971. Bar: Mo. 1971, Ill. 1971, U.S. Dist. Ct. (we. dist.) Mo. 1971, U.S. Dist. Ct. (ea. dist.) Mo. 1980, U.S. Dist. Ct. (so. dist.) Ill. 1981, U.S. Ct. Appeals (8th cir.) 1987. Asst. prosecuting atty. St. Louis County, 1971-72; asst. cir. atty. St. Louis Cir. Atty's. Office, 1972-74; spl. asst. state's atty. St. Clair County Atty's. Office, Belleville, Ill., 1974—; assoc. Lashley, Caruthers, Theis, Rava & Hamel, St. Louis, 1979-80; ptnr. Schreiber, Tueth & Mohan, Clayton, Mo., 1981-83, Danis, Reid, Murphy, Tobben, Schreiber & Mohan, Ladue, Mo., 1983-87, Hinshaw & Culbertson, St. Louis, 1987—. Mem. U. Mo. Law Sch. Found. Scholarship. Mem. ABA, Am. Arbitration Assn. (cert. mediator, arbitrator 1988—), U.S. Arbitration and Mediation Midwest (cert. mediator, arbitrator 1985—), Ill. State Bar Assn., Mo. Bar, Bar Assn. Metropolitan St. Louis, St. Clair County Bar, St. Louis County Bar, Defense Rsch. Inst., Mo. Orgn. Defense Lawyers, Maritime Law Assn., Phi Delta Phi. Home: 529 Big Horn Basin Ct Ballwin MO 63011-4818 Office: Hinshaw & Culbertson 1010 Market St Ste 350 Saint Louis MO 63101-2000

MOHANTY, BINAYAK PRASAD, hydrologist, environmental engineer; b. Bhubaneswar, Orissa, India, June 23, 1964; came to U.S., 1989; s. Harish Chandra and Indulata Mohanty; m. Deepanwita Mohanty, July 14, 1991. B in Engring., Orissa U. Agr. and Tech., 1985; M in Engring., Asian Inst. Tech., 1987; PhD, Iowa State U., 1992. Instr. Orissa U. Agr. and Tech., Bhubaneswar, India, 1985; rsch. assoc. Asian Inst. Tech., Bangkok, Thailand, 1987-88; rsch. asst., postdoctoral rschr. Iowa State U., Ames, 1989-93; rsch. scientist U.S. Salinity Lab. USDA-ARS, Riverside, Calif., 1993—. Assoc. editor: Paddy Field Engineering, 1988, 92; contbr. articles to profl. jours. Mem. Am. Geophys. Union, Am. Soc. Agrl. Engrs., Soil Sci. Soc. Am., Agronomy Soc. Am., Nat. Ground Water Assn., Soil and Water Conservation Soc., Alpha Epsilon, Gamma Sigma Delta. Achievements include multidimensional physical process based spatial analysis techniques, integration of GIS, MODFLOW, and crop water stress models, discovery of hysteresis in spatio-temporal variability of soil temperature, discovery of multimodal hydraulic conductivity functions in unsaturated soil, development and improvement of hydraulic conductivity measurement techniques. Office: US Salinity Lab 450 Big Springs Rd Riverside CA 92507

MOHIUDDIN, SYED MAQDOOM, cardiologist, educator; b. Hyderabad, India, Nov. 14, 1934; came to U.S., 1961, naturalized, 1976; s. Syed Nizamuddin and Amat-Ul-Butool Mahmoodi; m. Ayesha Sultana Mahmoodi, July 16, 1961; children: Sameena J., Syed R., Kulsoom S. M.B., B.S., Osmania U., 1960; M.S., Creighton U., Omaha, 1967; D.Sc., Laval U., Que., Can., 1970. Diplomate: Am. Bd. Internal Medcine (cardiovascular disease). Intern Altoona (Pa.) Gen. Hosp., 1961-62; resident in cardiology Creighton Meml. Hosp., also St. Joseph Hosp., Omaha, 1963-65; mem. staff Creighton Meml. Hosp., also St. Joseph Hosp., 1965—; prof. adjoint Laval

U. Med. Sch., 1970; practice medicine specializing in cardiology Omaha, 1970—; prof. Creighton U. Med. Sch., 1977—, assoc. dir. div. cardiology, 1983-96; prof. pharmacy practice Creighton U. Sch. Pharmacy, 1986—; dir divsn. cardiology, 1996—; cons. Omaha VA Hosp. Research fellow Med. Research Council Can., 1968; grantee Med. Research Council Can., 1970; grantee NIH, 1973. Fellow ACP, Am. Coll. Cardiology (gov. for Nebr. 1987-90), Am. Coll. Clin. Pharmacology, Am. Coll. Chest Physicians; mem. AAAS, Am. Heart Assn. (fellow coun. clin. cardiology, bd. dirs. 1973-75), Am. Fedn. Clin. Rsch., Nebr. Heart Assn. (chmn. rsch. com. 1974-76, dir. 1973—), Gt. Plains Heart Com. (Nebr. rep. 1976-84, pres. 1977-78), N.Y. Acad. Scis., Nebr. Cardiovascular Soc. (pres. 1980-81). Democrat. Islam. Home: 12531 Shamrock Rd Omaha NE 68154-3529 Office: 601 N 30th St Omaha NE 68131-2137

MOHLEJI, SATISH CHANDRA, electrical engineer; b. New Delhi, India, Aug. 16, 1940; came to U.S. 1970; s. Raghbir Singh and Kashmiro Devi (Sharma) M.; m. Manjula Sharma, Apr. 5, 1972; children: Anjali, Shalini, Nandita. BE with hons., U. Bombay, India, 1962; M.Engring., Tech. U. N.S., Can., 1967; PhD, U. Windsor, Can., 1970; MS in Mgmt. Sci., Am. U., Washington, 1988. Registered profl. engr., Ont., 1967-79. Asst. engr. World Wide Engrs. pvt. Ltd., New Delhi, 1962-63, Dodsal Pvt. Ltd., New Delhi, 1963-64; engr. trainee Richard Zimmerman, K.G., Stuttgart, Germany, 1964; engr. Std. Elec. Lorenz, Stuttgart, 1964-65, Lear Siegler, Inc., Grand Rapids, Mich., 1970-71; prin. engr. MITRE Corp., McLean, Va., 1971—. Contbr. articles to profl. jours. Mem. rsch. adv. panel Aviation Wk. and Space Tech. Pub., 1986-87. Fellow AIAA (assoc., chmn. aircraft ops. tech. com.); mem. IEEE (sr.) Internat. Fedn. Automatic Control (chmn. air traffic control automation tech. com.) RTCA (spl. com. SC-166 tech. working group, chmn. 1989-92). Avocations: photography, gardening. Home: 12324 Ox Hill Rd Fairfax VA 22033-2407 Office: The MITRE Corp 1820 Dolly Madison Blvd Mc Lean VA 22102-7500

MOHLER, BRIAN JEFFERY, diplomat; b. Niskayuna, N.Y., May 28, 1948; s. Donald and Rosemary (Brown) M. BA, Johns Hopkins U., 1970, MA, 1972. Economist Congl. Rsch. Svc. Libr. of Congress, Washington, 1973-74; staff asst. Bur. Econ. Affairs, Washington, 1974-76, economist, 1979-82; consul Am. Consulate Gen., Strasbourg, France, 1976-78; desk officer European community affairs Bur. European Affairs, Washington, 1982-84; petroleum attache Am. Embassy, Riyadh, Saudi Arabia, 1986-88, counselor for econ. affairs, 1988-90; dep. chief of mission Am. Embassy, Abu Dhabi, United Arab Emirates, 1990-93; desk officer Japanese affairs Bur. East Asian and Pacific Affairs, Washington, 1984-86, dep. dir. of econs. for Japanese affairs, 1993-95; counselor for econ. affairs Am. Embassy, Tokyo, 1995—. 2d lt. U.S. Army, 1972, capt. USAR, 1972-85. Recipient Superior Honor award Dept. of State, 1993, Meritorious Honor award, 1987. Mem. Am. Fgn. Svc. Assn., Confrerie de la Chaine des Rotisseurs, Sigma Nu. Roman Catholic.

MOHLER, GEORGIA ANN, geriatrics nurse practitioner; b. Iowa Falls, Iowa, Mar. 11, 1941; d. George Edward and Norma Dorothy (Wolf) M. Diploma, Meth.-Kahler, Rochester, Minn., 1962; BSN, U. Wash., 1971. RN, Wash.; cert. geriatric nurse practitioner. Relief charge nurse, team leader Swedish Hosp., Seattle, 1963-72; pub. health nurse Vis. Nurse Svc., Seattle, 1971-72; relief charge nurse and medicare coord. Restorative Care Ctr., Seattle, 1972-81; unit coord. Tacoma Luth. Home and Retirement Ctr., Tacoma, 1981-82; nurse practitioner Tacoma Luth. Home, 1983—, dir. home health agy. and nurse practitioner, 1993—. Contbr. to profl. jours. Mem. Pierce County Nurse Practitioner Group, Nat. Conf. Gerontol. Nurse Practitioners. Lutheran. Home: 909 N I St Apt 401 Tacoma WA 98403-2136

MOHLER, MARIE ELAINE, nurse educator; b. Norma, N.D., Mar. 2, 1946; d. Ervin and Katie M. (Nichol) Hansen; children: Zane, Tracy, KyLynn, Todd, Lynnette. Diploma in nursing, Trinity Hosp. Sch. Nursing, Minot, 1967; BSN, Mont. State U., 1969, M in Nursing, 1970; diploma nurse midwifery, SUNY, Bklyn., 1973. RN, N.D.; cert. nurse midwife Am. Coll. Nurse Midwifes. Staff nurse pediatrics Trinity Hosp., Minot, 1967; resident nurse girl's dormitory Mont. State U., Bozeman, 1967-68; staff nurse med.-surg. wards Bozeman (Mont.) Deaconess Hosp., 1969; relief nurse Student Health Ctr. Mont. State U., Bozeman, 1970; camp nurse Camp Pinemore Minoqua, Wis., 1971; part-time staff nurse labor & delivery-maternity-newborn Bannock Meml. Hosp., Pocatello, Idaho, 1972-75; cons. maternal-newborn, pediatric wards Bannock Meml. Hosp., Pocatello, 1972-75; staff nuse maternity-newborn ward John Moses Hosp., Minot, 1977; part time staff nurse maternal-newborn ward St. Joseph's Hosp., Minot, 1978-81; nurse assessor Luth. Social Svc. N.D. and Family Care Network, 1991-93; instr. Ariz. State U., Tempe, 1971-72, No. Ariz. U., Flagstaff, 1972, Idaho State U., Pocatello, 1972-75; asst. prof. Minot (N.D.) State Coll. divsn. Allied Health, 1975-76; instr. medicine U. Miss. Med. Ctr., Jackson, 1976-77; assoc. prof. Minot (N.D.) State U. Coll. Nursing, 1977—; pres. coun. coll. faculties N.D. U. Sys., 1993-94, chair faculty compensation com., 1993-94, 96—, others; mem. budget and salary com., constl. rev. com. Minot State U., 1993-94, others. Author of various videotapes and slide series. Recipient Minot C. of C. Disting. Prof. award, 1986; Burlington No. Found. Faculty Achievement award, 1987; grantee in field. Mem. Assn. Women's Health, Obstetric and Neonatal Nurses (chair legis. chpt.), Alpha Tau Delta. Office: Minot State Univ Coll Nursing 500 University Ave Minot ND 58701

MOHLER, MARY GAIL, magazine editor; b. Milaca, Minn., Dec. 15, 1948; d. Albert and Deane (Vedders) M.; m. Paul Rodes Trautman, June 5, 1976 (div. 1994); children: Elizabeth Deane, David Albert Rodes, Theodore DeForest Lloyd. B.A., U. Calif.-Davis, 1974; M.A. in Lit., SUNY-Stony Brook, 1976. Asst., then editor-reporter Family Circle Mag., N.Y.C., 1979-81; editorial coordinator Ladies' Home Jour., N.Y.C., 1981, assoc. articles editor, 1982, mng. editor, 1982-93, sr. editor, 1994—; editor in chief Ladies' Home Jour. Parent's Digest. Medieval philosophy fellow SUNY-Binghamton, 1978. Mem. MLA, Am. Soc. Mag. Editors, Phi Beta Kappa. Clubs: Medieval; Overseas Press. Office: Ladies Home Jour 125 Park Ave New York NY 10017-5529

MOHLER, RICHARD ALBERT, JR., academic administrator, theologian; b. Lakeland, Fla., Oct. 9, 1959; s. Richard Albert Sr. and Janet Rae (Johnson) M.; m. Mary Ann Kahler, July 16, 1983; children: Mary Katherine, Christopher Albert. BA magna cum laude, Samford U., 1980; MDiv, So. Bapt. Theol. Sem., Louisville, 1983, PhD, 1989; postgrad., St. Meinrad Sch. Theology, 1985, Oxford (Eng.) U., 1986. Ordained min. So. Bapt. Ch. Pastor Union Grove Bapt. Ch., Bedford, Ky., 1982-87; asst. to pres., coord. found. support, dir. capital funding So. Bapt. Theol. Sem., Louisville, 1983-89, pres., 1993—; editor The Christian Index, Atlanta, 1989-93; assoc. dir. The So. Sem. Found., 1983-89; lectr. in field. Assoc. editor Preaching, 1985-93, contbg. editor, 1993—; gen. editor: The Gods of the Age of the God of the Ages?, 1993; contbr. articles to profl. jours. Mem. Am. Acad. Religion, Soc. Biblical Lit., Evangelical Theol. Soc., So. Bapt. Hist. Soc., Bapt. Pub. Rels. Assn., So. Bapt. Press Assn., Evangelical Press Assn., Nat. Assn. Evangelicals, Ga. Bapt. Hist. Soc., Rotary Internat., Phi Kappa Phi, Omicron Delta Kappa. Named one of 50 young leaders under 40 years of age TIME Mag. Office: So Bapt Theol Sem 2825 Lexington Rd Louisville KY 40280

MOHLER, RONALD RUTT, electrical engineering educator; b. Ephrata, Pa., Apr. 11, 1931; s. David Wealand and Elizabeth (Rutt) M.; m. Nancy Alice Strickler, May 6, 1950; children: Curtis Gene, Pamela Louise, Susan Lynn, Anita Marie, John Scott, Andrew Thomas, Jennifer Lee, Lisa Nancy. B.S. (scholarship), Pa. State U., 1956; M.S., U. So. Calif., 1958; Ph.D., U. Mich., 1965. Designer, trainee Textile Machine Works, Rockwell Internat. Corp., Reading, Pa., 1949-56; staff mem. Hughes Aircraft Co., Culver City, Calif., 1956-58, Los Alamos Sci. Lab., 1958-65; asso. prof. elec. engring. U. N.Mex., Albuquerque, 1965-69; prof. elec. engring./aerospace, mech. and nuclear engring. U. Okla., 1969-72, prof., chmn. info. and computing scis., 1970-72; dir. Systems Research Center, 1969-72; adj. prof. elec. engring. and nuclear engring. U. N.Mex., Los Alamos Grad. Center, 1959-65; cons. Sandia Corp., Albuquerque, 1966-69, Aerojet-Gen. Corp., Sacramento, 1966; vis. assoc. prof. system sci. UCLA, 1968-69; cons. community health project OEO, Oklahoma City, 1970-71; prof. elec. and computer engring. Oreg. State U., Corvallis, 1972—; head dept. Oreg. State U., 1972-79, 90; pres. Pace Tech., Inc., 1982—; vis. prof. U. Rome, 1973, 75, Imperial Coll., London, 1978-79, U.S. Naval Postgrad. Sch., 1983-85, Australian Nat. U., 1988, Sydney U., 1995; cons. Optimization Software, L.A., 1973—, Bonneville Power Adminstrn., 1975—, Internat. Inst. Applied Systems Analysis, 1988—. Author: Optimal Control of Nuclear Reactors, 1970, Bilinear Control Processes, 1973, Nonlinear Systems: Dynamics and Control, vol. 1, 1991, Applications to Bilinear Control, vol. II, 1991, Disease Dynamics, 1993; editor: Theory and Application of Variable Structure Systems, 1972, Variable Structure Systems with Application to Biology and Economics, 1975, Recent Developments in Variable Structure Systems, Economics and Biology, 1979, Nonlinear Time Series and Signal Processing, 1988, assoc. editor Annals of Nuclear Energy, 1973—; contbr. jours. Chmn. St. Stephens Sch. Bd., Norman, 1970-72. Recipient NATO award, 1979; rsch. grantee NSF, 1966—, Sandia Labs., 1966-68, ONR, 1981-92, NASA, EPRI, BPA, 1990—; AEC fellow, 1961-65, Hughes fellow, 1956-58; Acad. Sci. exch. scientist to USSR and China, 1980, US-CIS (USSR) Commn. on Engring. Edn., 1991—. Fellow IEEE (life, local chmn. 1975); mem. Am. Soc. Engring. Edn., Control System Soc., Sigma Xi, Tau Beta Pi, Pi Tau Sigma. Democrat. Pioneer rsch. on bilinear systems and worldwide collaboration. Home: 2050 NW Dogwood Dr Corvallis OR 97330-1102

MOHLER, STANLEY ROSS, physician, educator; b. Amarillo, Tex., Sept. 30, 1927; s. Norton Harrison and Minnie Alice (Ross) M.; m. Ursula Luise Burkhardt, Jan. 24, 1953; children: Susan Luise, Stanley Ross, Mark Hallock. B.A., U. Tex., 1953, M.A., 1953, M.D., 1956. Diplomate: Am. Bd. Preventive Medicine. Intern USPHS Hosp., San Francisco, 1956-57; med. officer Center Aging Research, NIH, Bethesda, Md., 1957-61; dir. Civil Aeromed. Rsch. Inst., FAA, Oklahoma City, 1961-66; chief aeromed. applications div. Civil Aeromed. Rsch. Inst., FAA, Washington, 1966-78; prof., vice chmn. dept. community medicine, dir. aerospace medicine Wright State U. Sch. Medicine, Dayton, Ohio, 1978—; rsch. assoc. prof. preventive medicine and pub. health U. Okla. Med. Sch., 1961—; vice chmn. Am. Bd. Preventive Medicine, 1978—, sec.-treas., 1980—. Co-editor: Space Biology and Medicine (5 vol. series), 1995 (Life Scis. Book award Internat. Acad. Astronautics); contbr. articles to profl. jours. Bd. dirs. Sr. Citizens Assn. Oklahoma City, 1962—, Flying Physicians Assn., 1961—. Served with AUS, 1946-48. Recipient Gail Borden Rsch. award, Boothby award Aerospace Med. Assn., 1966, FAA Meritorious Svc. award, 1974; co-recipient Life Scis. Book award in space, biology and medicine Internat. Acad. Astronautics, 1995. Fellow Geriatrics Soc., Aerospace Med. Assn. (pres. 1983, Harry G. Moseley award 1974, Lyster award 1984), Am. Coll. Preventive Medicine, Gerontol. Soc.; mem. AMA, Aircraft Owners and Pilots Assn. (Sharples award 1984, Hubertus Strughold award 1991), Alpha Omega Alpha. Home: 6539 Reigate Rd Dayton OH 45459-3214 Office: Wright State U Sch Medicine PO Box 927 Dayton OH 45401-0927

MOHN, MELVIN PAUL, anatomist, educator; b. Cleve., June 19, 1926; s. Paul Melvin and Julia (Jacobik) M.; m. Audrey Faye Lonergan, June 28, 1952; children—Shorey Faye, Andrew Paul. A.B., Marietta Coll., 1950; Sc.M., Brown U., 1952, Ph.D. in Biology, 1955. Instr. SUNY Downstate Med. Ctr., Bklyn., 1955-59, asst. prof., 1959-63; asst. prof. anatomy U. Kans. Sch. Medicine, Kansas City, 1963-65, assoc. prof., 1965-72, prof., 1972-89, prof. emeritus, 1989—; cons. Nat. Med. Audiovisual Ctr., Atlanta, 1972; vis. lectr. U. Miami Sch. Medicine, Fla., 1966. Bd. dirs. U. Kans. Med. Ctr. Credit Union, 1968-77, Kansas City Youth Symphony, 1972-77; mem. U.S. Pony Club, 1964-71, Med. Arts Symphony, 1965-71, 90—, Spring Hill Chorale, 1990—. Served with USN, 1944-46, PTO. McCoy fellow, 1950, Arnold biology fellow, 1954. Fellow AAAS; mem. Am. Soc. Zoologists, Am. Assn. Anatomists, Am. Inst. Biol. Sci., Phi Beta Kappa, Sigma Xi, Beta Beta Beta. Republican. Methodist. Club: Lions, Rotary, Lodge: Masons. Home: Yankee Bit Farm 23595 W 223rd St Spring Hill KS 66083-4029 Office: U Kans Med Ctr Dept Anatomy 39th and Rainbow St Kansas City KS 66103

MOHNEY, RALPH WILSON, minister; b. Paris, Ky., May 20, 1918; s. Silas Phillip and Clarine (Wilson) M.; m. Nell Marie Webb, Dec. 31, 1948; children—Richard Bentley, Ralph Wilson. B.A., Transylvania Coll., 1940; B.D., Vanderbilt U., 1943; S.T.M., Boston U., 1945; postgrad., Harvard, Garrett Bibl. Inst.; D.D., Emory and Henry Coll., 1959. Ordained elder Meth. Ch., 1944; pastor Winter Street Congl. Ch., Bath, Me., 1943-45, Manker Meml. Meth. Ch., Chattanooga, 1945-50, Washington Pike Meth. Ch., Knoxville, 1950-56; supt. Kingsport dist. Holston Conf. Meth. Ch., 1956- 59; pres. Tenn. Wesleyan Coll., 1959-65; sr. minister Centenary Meth. Ch., 1965-66, First Centenary United Meth. Ch., Chattanooga, 1967-81, First Broad St. United Meth. Ch., Kingsport, Tenn., 1981-87; asst. dir. Growth Plus Ministries Gen. Bd. Discipleship, Chattanooga, 1988-92, Disting. evangelist in residence, 1991-96; staff mem. Large Ch. Initiative, 1988-89; Staley Disting. lectr. Columbia Coll., 1973, Emory and Henry Coll., 1975, Pfeiffer Coll., 1976, Union Coll., 1977; del. World Conf. Christian Youth, Oslo, Norway, 1947; adult counselor Meth. Youth Caravan to Poland., 1947; chmn. Holston Conf. Commn. on World Peace, 1952-56; leader Annual Lenten Pilgrimage to Holy Land, 1973-80; pres. Holston Council on Finance and Adminstrn., 1968-76, mem., 1976-84; mem. Gen. Council Finance and Adminstrn., 1976-84, mem. exec. com., 1976-80; chmn. Commn. on Christian Higher Edn., 1956-59; res. del. Gen. Conf. Meth. Ch., del. jurisdictional conf. Meth. Ch., 1960, 68; del. Meth. Ch. (Gen. Conf.), 1976; mem. Gen. Bd. Christian Social Concerns, 1960-72, World Council Meth. Ch., 1966-70; mem. steering com. United Meth. TV Presence and Ministry, 1979-81; mem. S.E. radio and film commn. Meth. Ch., 1968-76; dir. Holston Conf. Found., 1984-92; exchange minister Eng., 1984, New Zealand, 1987. Co-author: Parable Churches, 1989, Churches of Vision, 1990, Vision 2000: Planning for Ministry Into the Next Century, 1991. Bd. dirs. E. Tenn. State Coll. Wesley Found., 1955-59, U. Tenn. Wesley Found., 1956-62; pres. Athens United Fund, 1965, Affiliated Ind. Colls. Tenn., 1963-65, Chattanooga Meth. Ministers Assn., 1966-67, Chattanooga Clergyman's Assn., 1968. Mem. Pi Kappa Alpha, Pi Kappa Delta. Club: Kiwanis. Home: 1004 Northbridge Ln Chattanooga TN 37405-4214

MOHOLY, NOEL FRANCIS, clergyman; b. San Francisco, May 26, 1916; s. John Joseph and Eva Gertrude (Cippa) M.; grad. St. Anthony's Sem., Santa Barbara; STB, Faculte de Theologie, Universite Laval, Quebec, Que., Can., 1944, STL, 1945, STD, 1948; Joined Franciscan Friars, 1935; ordained priest Roman Catholic Ch., 1941; tchr. fundamental theology Old Mission Santa Barbara, 1942-43, sacred theology, 1947-58; tchr. langs. St. Anthony's Sem., 1943-44; Am. adminstr. (handling affairs of the cause in U.S.) Cause of Padre Junipero Serra, 1950-55, vice postulator, 1958—; retreat master San Damiano Retreat, Danville, Calif., 1964-67. Mem. Ann. Assay Commn. U.S. Mint, 1964. Occupied numerous pulpits, assisted in several Franciscan Retreat Houses; condr. series illustrated lectrs. on cause of canonization of Padre Junipero Serra to students of all Franciscan study houses in U.S., summer 1952, also speaker in field at various clubs of Serra Internat. in U.S., Europe and Far East, on NBC in documentary with Edwin Newman, Padre Serra, Founding Father, 1985, PBS on Firing Line with William F. Buckley: Junipero Serra—Saint or Sinner, 1989, CBS, ABC broadcasts and conducted own local TV series. Mem. Bldg. Com. for Restoration Hist. Towers and Facade of Old Mission Santa Barbara, 1950-53; exec. dir., treas. Old Mission Restoration Project, 1954-58; mem. Calif. Hist. Landmarks Adv. Com., 1962-71, Calif. Hist. Resources Commn., 1971-76, Calif. Bicentennial Celebration Commn., 1967-70; pres. Serra Bicentennial commn., 1983-86, dir. Old Spanish Days in Santa Barbara, Inc., 1950-58, Nat. and internat. authority on Saint Irenaeus, mariology, Calif. history (particularly history of Father Serra). Decorated Knight comdr. Order of Isabella la Catolica, 1965. Pres. Father Junipero Serra 250th Anniversary Assn., Inc., 1964—. Named hon. citizen Petra de Mallorca, 1969, Palma de Mallorca, 1976; recipient Cross of Merit Sovereign Mil. Order of Knights Malta, 1989. Mem. Mariol. Soc. Am., Native Sons Golden West, Associacion de los Amigos de Padre Serra, K.C., Calif. Missions Study Assn. Author: Our Last Chance, 1931; Saint Irenaeus; the Father of Mariology, 1952; The California Mission Story, 1975; The First Californian, 1976; co-author (with Don DeNevi) Junipero Serra, 1985; producer phonograph records Songs of the California Missions, 1951, Christmas at Mission Santa Barbara, 1953, St. Francis Peace Record, 1957; producer VCR The Founding Father of the West, 1976. Home: The Old Mission 2201 Laguna St Santa Barbara CA 93105-3611 Office: Serra Cause The Old Mission Santa Barbara CA 93105-3611

MOHR, ELLEN G., English language educator; b. Mt. Pleasant, Iowa, Dec. 5, 1942; d. F.W. and Martha Margaret (Desenberg) Grube; m. Jan A. Mohr, Aug. 18, 1972; children: Jon, Jennifer. BS in Edn., N.W. Mo. U., 1964, MA in English, 1970. English instr. George Washington Middle Sch., Ridgewood, N.J., 1968-69, Excelsior Springs (Mo.) High Sch., 1970-71, Greenfield Middle Sch., Cin., 1972-73; writing ctr. dir. Johnson County Community Coll., Overland Park, Kans., 1980—; staff devel. intern Johnson County Comm. Coll., Overland Park, Kans., 1994-95, faculty dir. Ctr. for Teaching and Learning, 1995—. Author: Midwest Writing Center Association Proceedings Book, Writing Lab., Newsletter. Recipient Faculty Recognition award Mich. Consortium for C.C.'s, 1991-92, Disting. Status award Johnson County C.C., 1994-96. Mem. Midwest Writing Ctr. Assn. (chair bd. dirs. 1986-91), Nat. Writing Ctr. Assn. (exec. bd. 1989-92, named peer tutor cons.), Kans. Assn. Tchrs. of English, Phi Delta Kappa. Home: 10826 King St Shawnee Mission KS 66210-1267

MOHR, JAY PRESTON, neurologist; b. Mar. 5, 1937; s. John G. and Marguerite F. Mohr; A.B., Haverford Coll., 1958; M.S., U. Va., 1963, M.D., 1963; m. Joan L. Seal, Mar. 10, 1962; children—Thea, Gregory. Intern, then asst. resident in medicine Mary Imogene Bassett Hosp., Cooperstown, N.Y., 1963-65; asst. resident in neurology N.Y. Neurol. Inst., Columbia-Presbyn. Med. Ctr., N.Y.C., 1965-66; fellow in neurology Mass. Gen. Hosp., Boston, 1966-69; instr. neurology Johns Hopkins U. Med. Sch., also U. Md. Med. Sch., 1969-71; assoc. neurologist Mass. Gen. Hosp., also asst. prof. Harvard U. Med. Sch., 1972-78; prof. neurology, chmn. dept. U. South Ala. Med. Sch., Mobile, 1978-83; Sciarra prof. clin. neurology Columbia U. Coll. Physicians and Surgeons, N.Y.C., 1983—; dir. cerebrovascular research N.Y. Neurol. Inst., N.Y.C., 1983—. Served as maj. M.C., U.S. Army, 1969-72. Diplomate Am. Bd. Neurology and Psychiatry. Fellow Am. Acad. Neurology; mem. Am. Neurol. Assn., Am. Heart Assn. (stroke council), Sigma Xi. Democrat. Quaker. Contbr. articles to med. jours. Home: PO Box 1014 Shelter Island Heights NY 11965-1014 Office: NY Neurol Inst 710 W 168th St New York NY 10032-2603 also: Presbyn Hosp Columbia-Presbyn Med Ctr New York NY 10032-3784

MOHR, JOHN LUTHER, biologist, environmental consultant; b. Reading, Pa., Dec. 1, 1911; s. Luther Seth and Anna Elizabeth (Davis) M.; m. Frances Edith Christensen, Nov. 23, 1939; children: Jeremy John, Christopher Charles. AB in Biology, Bucknell U., 1933; student, Oberlin Coll., 1933-34; PhD in Zoology, U. Calif., Berkeley, 1939. Research asso. Pacific Islands Research, Stanford, 1942-44; rsch. assoc. Allan Hancock Found., U. So. Calif., 1944-46, asst. prof., 1946-47, asst. prof. dept. biology, 1947-54, asso. prof., 1954-57, prof., 1957-77; chmn. dept., 1960-62, prof. emeritus, 1977—; vis. prof. summers U. Wash. Friday Harbor Labs., 1956, '57; marine borer and pollution surveys harbors So. Calif., 1948-51, arctic marine biol. research, 1952-71; chief marine zool. group U.S. Antarctic research ship Eltanin in Drake Passage, 1962, in South Pacific sector, 1965; research deontology in sci. and academia; researcher on parasitic protozoans of anurans, crustaceans, elephants; analysis of agy. and industry documents, ethics and derelictions of steward agy., sci. and tech. orgns. as they relate to offshore and coastal onshore oil activities, environ. effects of oil spill dispersants and offshore oil industry discharges and naturally occurring radioactive material NORMs. Active People for the Am. Way; mem. Biol. Stain Commn., 1948-80, trustee, 1971-80, emeritus trustee, 1981—, v.p., 1976-80. Recipient Guggenheim fellowship, 1957-58. Fellow AAAS (coun. 1964-73), So. Calif. Acad. Scis., Sigma Xi (exec. com. 1964-67, 68, 69, chpt.-at-large bd. 1968-69); mem. Am. Micros. Soc., Marine Biol. Assn. U.K. (life), Am. Soc. Parasitologists, Western Soc. Naturalists (pres. 1960-61), Soc. Protozoologists, Soc. Integrative and Comparative Biology, Ecol. Soc. Am., Planning and Conservation League, Calif. Native Plant Soc., Save San Francisco Bay Assn., Ecology Ctr. So. Calif., Assn. Forest Svc. Employees Environ. Ethics, Common Cause, Huxleyan, Sierra Club, Phi Sigma, Theta Upsilon Omega. Home: 3819 Chanson Dr Los Angeles CA 90043-1601

MOHR, JULIAN BOEHM, chemical company executive; b. Atlanta, Apr. 29, 1930; s. Samuel and Marian (Boehm) M.; BA, Washington and Lee U., 1952; m. Teena Stern, June 24, 1956 (div. Aug. 1970); children: Julie Lin, Greg Eugene; m. Sandra Simmons, Jan. 31, 1973 (div. Feb. 1983); children: Leslie, Julian Boehm, Mark; m. Mary Gary, Oct. 14, 1986. With Momar, Inc., Atlanta, 1952—, treas., 1956—, pres., 1965—; v.p. Momar (Can.) Ltd., Toronto, 1961—, treas. Momar Export, Inc., Atlanta, 1960, pres. 1965—; ptnr. pres. Julio, Ltd., real estate devel. and property mgmt.; gen. partner Dogwood Stables I; dir. Cansa divsn. Momar South Africa, Capetown, Momar Insl. Services Ltd., Stourport, Eng., Momar (London) Ltd., Momar Dhb Sdn, Kuala Lumpur, Malaysia; adv. dir. Caral S.A.R.L. divsn. Momar Inc., Vernon, France, Momar Australia, Sydney; bd. dirs. Action Expediting Inc., Atlanta. Pres. exec. bd. Atlanta Civic Ballet, Inc., 1964-69; adv. bd. Bus. Sch. Georgia State U., 1990—; bd. dirs. Dignity, 1994—, Shepherd Spinal Ctr. Hosp., 1996—. Jewish (trustee temple 1968—). Named Alumni of Yr. The Marist Sch., 1989. Mem. B'nai B'rith, Civitan of Atlanta, Toastmasters (pres. 1959), Commerce (charter), Standard Town and Country (governing bd. 1978-85, 89-90, pres. 1991-92). Mem. Beta Gamma Sigma. Home: PO Box 20224 Atlanta GA 30325-0224 Office: Ste 115 1830 Ellsworth Industrial Blvd NW Atlanta GA 30318-3746

MOHR, L. THOMAS, newspaper executive; b. Endicott, N.Y., Dec. 25, 1955; s. Lionel Charles and Anne (Tredwell) M.; m. Pageen Rogers, July 13, 1985; children: Mary Catherine, Jack. BA with honors, Queens U., Kingston, Ont., Can., 1979; MBA, U. Calif., Berkeley, 1987. Gen. mgr. Foster City (Calif.) Progress, 1981-82; classified advt. mgr. Peninsula Times Tribune, Palo Alto, Calif., 1982-85, mktg. mgr., 1985-86, advt. sales dir., 1986-87; dir. mktg. and advt. sales Bakersfield Californian, 1987-90; classified advt. dir. Star Tribune, Mpls., 1990-93, v.p., 1993—. Bd. dirs. March of Dimes, Mpls., 1994—. Mem. Newspaper Assn. Am. (bd. dirs. classified fedn. 1993—), New Media Fedn. (bd. dirs.). Republican. Roman Catholic. Avocations: running, tennis, golf, cross country skiing. Home: 3080 Quinwood Ln N Plymouth MN 55441-2807 Office: Star Tribune 425 Portland Ave Minneapolis MN 55488-0001

MOHR, LAWRENCE CHARLES, physician; b. S.I., N.Y., July 8, 1947; s. Lawrence Charles Sr. and Mary Estelle (Dawsey) M.; m. Linda Johnson, June 14, 1970; 1 child, Andrea Marie. AB, U. N.C., 1975, MD, 1979. Diplomate Am. Bd. Internal Medicine. Commd. 2d lt. U.S. Army, 1967, advanced through grades to col., 1989; med. intern Walter Reed Army Med. Ctr., Washington, 1979-80, resident in medicine, 1980-82, chief resident, 1982-83, attending physician, 1984-86, pulmonary fellow, 1986-87; command surgeon 9th Inf. Div., Ft. Lewis, Wash., 1983-84; med. cons. Madigan Army Med. Ctr., Tacoma, 1983-84; White House physician Washington, 1987-93; asst. prof. medicine Uniformed Svcs. U. of the Health Scis., Bethesda, Md., 1984-91; assoc. clin. prof. medicine George Washington U., Washington, 1990-94; prof. medicine Med. U. S.C., Charleston, 1994—, dir. environ. hazards assessment program, 1995—; assoc. prof. medicine Uniformed Svcs. U. of Health Scis., Bethesda, Md., 1991-94; mem. Working Group on Disability in U.S. Presidents, 1995—. Bd. dirs. Internat. Lung Found., Washington; mem. adv. bd. Nat. Mus. Health and Medicine, Washington. Decorated Silver Star, Bronze Star with 2 V devices and 3 oak leaf clusters, Purple Heart, Meritorious Svc. medal with oak leaf cluster, Air medal, Army Commendation medal with oak leaf cluster; recipient Erskine award Walter Reed Army Med. Ctr., 1982; named Outstanding Med. Resident, 1982. Fellow ACCP (order mil. med. merit); mem. AMA, Army and Navy Club, Phi Beta Kappa. Episcopalian. Avocations: mountain climbing, skiing. Home: Ste 11-R 310 Broad St Charleston SC 29401 Office: Med U S C Environ Hazards Assess Prgm 171 Ashley Ave Charleston SC 29425

MOHR, ROGER JOHN, advertising agency executive; b. Milw., Sept. 8, 1931; s. Reinhold and Clara (Meissner) M.; m. Pauline Spicuzza, Oct. 18, 1958; children: Gregory, Mary Margaret, Kristin, Thomas, Kathleen. B.S. in Speech, Marquette U., 1953; postgrad. radio and TV, Northwestern U., 1955-56. Staff announcer radio sta. WBKB, West Bend, Wis., 1952, WCAN, Milw., 1952-54; with Arthur Meyerhoff Assos., Inc., Chgo., 1956-80; pres. Arthur Meyerhoff Assos., Inc., 1965-80; pres. BBDO, Chgo., 1980-82, chmn., 1982-90, vice chmn. internat., 1991-93. Chmn. Lake Bluff (Ill.) Plan Commn., 1972-75; mem. Lake Forest (Ill.) Plan Commn., 1994—; bd. dirs. Chgo. City Ballet, 1982-84, Off the Street Club, 1976-78; mem. adv. coun. Marquette U. Sch. Comm., 1993—. Served with AUS, 1954-55. Mem. Am. Assn. Advt. Agys. (chmn. Chgo. coun. 1966-67, sec., treas., nat. bd. dirs. 1976-77), Evans Scholars Alumni Assn. (pres. 1964-65), Western Golf Assn. (bd. dirs. 1980—, v.p. 1994—), Knollwood Club (bd. govs. 1980-85, 89-92), Tavern Club (bd. govs., v.p. 1988-94). Home: 2000 Knollwood Rd Lake Forest IL 60045-1137

MOHR, SELBY, retired ophthalmologist; b. San Francisco, Mar. 11, 1918; s. Selby and Henrietta (Foorman) M.; AB, Stanford U., 1938, MD, 1942; m. Marian Buckley, June 10, 1950; children—Selby, John Vincent, Adrianne E., Gregory P. Asst. resident in ophthalmology U. Calif. Hosp., 1942-43; pvt. practice ophthalmology, San Francisco, 1947-88; mem. past pres. med. staff Marshall Hale Meml. Hosp.; mem. staff Mt. Zion Hosp., St Francis Meml. Hosp. Dir. Sweet Water Co., Mound Farms, Inc., Mound Farms Oil & Gas, Inc. Lt. (j.g.) USNR, 1943-46; PTO. Diplomate Am. Bd. Ophthalmology. Fellow Am. Acad. Ophthalmology; mem. AMA, Calif., San Francisco Med. Socs., Pan-Pacific Surg. Soc., Pan-Am. Assn. Ophthalmology. Home: 160 Sea Cliff Ave San Francisco CA 94121-1125

MOHRAZ, JUDY JOLLEY, college president; b. Houston, Oct. 1, 1943; d. John Chesler and Mae (Jackson) Jolley; m. Bijan Mohraz; children: Andrew, Jonathan. BA, Baylor U., 1966, MA, 1968; PhD, U. Ill., 1974. Lectr. history Ill. Wesleyan U., 1972-74; asst. prof. history So. Meth. U., Dallas, 1974-80, coord. women's studies, 1977-81, assoc. prof. history, 1980-94, asst. provost, 1983-88, assoc. provost for student academics, 1988-94; pres. Goucher Coll., Towson, Md., 1994—; cons. Ednl. Testing Svc., Princeton, N.J., 1984-93, Nat. Park Svcs., Seneca Falls, N.Y., 1992-93. Trustee The Lamplighter Sch., 1991-94, St. Mark's Sch. Tex., 1993-94; adv. bd. U. Tex. Southwestern Med. Sch., 1992-94; active Leadership Dallas, 1994. Recipient Disting. Alumni award Baylor U., 1993; named Woman of Merit, Omicron Delta Kappa, 1993. Home: Pres House 1021 Dulaney Valley Rd Baltimore MD 21204 Office: Goucher Coll Office of Pres 1021 Dulaney Valley Rd Baltimore MD 21204-2794

MOHRFELD, RICHARD GENTEL, heating oil distributing company executive; b. Camden, N.J., Dec. 30, 1945; s. Herbert Henry and Elizabeth Weldon (Gentel) M.; m. Ann Bacon, June 20, 1971 (div. 1975); m. Janice Lee Strickland, July 1, 1978; children: Kathryn Elizabeth, Christopher Hall. BSc in Geology, Dickinson Coll., 1971. Staff geologist Temple U., Phila., 1971-74; pres. Mohrfeld Inc., Collingswood, N.J., 1974—; bd. dirs. South Jersey Savs. & Loan Assn., Turnersville, N.J., 1984—. Bd. dirs. Boy Scouts Am., Camden County, N.J., 1985—; trustee, treas. Knight Park Trustees, Collingswood, 1986—; trustee Health Care Support Found., Inc., 1994—. Sgt. USAF, 1969-71. Mem. Air Conditioning Contractors Am. (pres. 1986-88), Fuel Mchts. Assn. N.J. (pres. 1992-94), Rotary (pres. Collingswood 1980-81). Episcopalian. Avocations: travel, photography. Home: 47 Treaty Elms Ln Haddonfield NJ 08033-3413 Office: 24 Lees Ave Collingswood NJ 08108-1926

MOHRMAN, KATHRYN, academic administrator. Pres. The Colo. Coll., Colo. Springs. Office: Colorado College Office of the President 14 E Cache La Poudre St Colorado Springs CO 80903-3294

MOHRMANN, LEONARD EDWARD, JR., chemist, chemical engineer; b. Winston Salem, N.C., June 14, 1940; s. Leonard E. and Helen (Bean) M.; m. Sue Ross, June 18, 1966; children: Leonard III, Vaden, Nelwyn Ann. BS in Chemistry, U. Tex., 1963; PhD in Chemistry, Fla. State U., 1971; BSChemE, Tex. A&M U., 1980. Tech. lab. coord. Tex. A&M U., College Station, 1971-81, rsch. assoc., 1981-82; chemist, chemical engr. Tex. Dept. Health, Austin, 1982-92, Tex. Water Commn., Austin, 1992-93, Fugro Environ., Inc. formerly Fugro McClelland, Houston, 1993-95, Tex. Dept. Health, Austin, 1995—. Contbr. articles to sci. jours. Active Mathcounts program Tex. Soc. Profl. Engrs., Austin, 1991-92, Jr. Achievement Program, Houston, 1994-95. Recipient Appreciation cert. Tex. Soc. Profl. Engrs., 1993. Achievements include development of Texas regulations for special waste disposal, medical waste handling and disposal, special waste program for municipal waste. Office: Tex Dept Health Bur Labs 1100 W 49th Austin TX 78756-3194

MOHS, FREDERIC EDWARD, surgeon, educator; b. Burlington, Wis., Mar. 1, 1910; s. Frederic Carl and Grace Edith (Tilton) M.; m. Mary Ellen Reynolds, June 18, 1934; children: Frederic Edward, Thomas James, Jane Ann. MD, U. Wis., 1934. Intern Multnomah County Hosp., Portland, Ore., 1934-35; Bowman Cancer Research Fellow U. Wis. Med. Sch., 1935-38, asso. in cancer research, instr. in surgery, 1939-42, asst. prof. chemosurgery, 1942-48, asso. prof. chemosurgery, 1948-69, clin. prof. surgery, 1969-85, emeritus prof. surgery, spl. cons., 1985—. Author: Chemosurgery: Microscopically Controlled Surgery for Skin Cancer; Contbr. articles, papers on treatment of cancer by means of Mohs micrographic surgery. Recipient Lila Gruber award for cancer rsch. Am. Acad. Dermatology, Internat. Facial Plastic Surgery award 3d Internat. Symposium on Plastic and Reconstructive Surgery of Head and Neck, Discovery award Dermatology Found., 1995. Fellow AMA; mem. AAAS, Am. Assn. Cancer Rsch., Dane County Med. Soc. (pres. 1959- 60), Am. Coll. Mohs Micrographic Surgery and Cutaneous Oncology (founder, 1st pres.). Home: 3616 Lake Mendota Dr Madison WI 53705-1475

MOIR, ALFRED KUMMER, art history educator; b. Mpls., Apr. 14, 1924; s. William Wilmerding and Blanche (Kummer) M. A.B., Harvard U., 1948, A.M., 1949, Ph.D., 1953. From instr. to assoc. prof. Newcomb Coll., Tulane U., 1952-62; mem. faculty U. Calif., Santa Barbara, 1962-91, prof. art history, 1964-91, prof. emeritus, 1991—, chmn. dept., 1963-69; dir. Edn. Abroad Program U. Calif., Italy, 1978-80; cons. for acquisitions Isaac Delgado Mus. Art, 1953-57; v.p. Friends La. State Mus., 1959-62, Friends New Orleans Pub. Libr., 1959-62; pres. So. Calif. Art Historians, 1964-66, 67-69; chmn. Tri-Counties Com. to Rescue Italian Art, 1967-68; art historian in residence Am. Acad. Rome, 1969-70, 80; cons. NEH, 1971-78; vis. prof. U. Minn., 1973; hon. curator of drawings U. Calif.-Santa Barbara Art Mus., 1985-94;. Author: (with others) Art in Italy, 1600-1700, 1965, The Italian Followers of Caravaggio, 2 vols, 1967, Caravaggio's Copyists, 1976, Caravaggio, 1982, Van Dyck, 1994; editor: (with others) Seventeenth Century Italian Drawings in the Collection of Janos Scholz, 1974, European Drawings in the Santa Barbara Museum of Art, 1976, Regional Styles of Drawing in Italy 1600-1700, 1977, Old Master Drawings from the Feitelson Collection, 1983, Old Master Drawings from the Collection of John and Alice Steiner, 1985, (with others) Van Dyck's Antwerp, 1991. Trustee Santa Barbara Free Sch., 1968-71; gov. Brooks Inst. Art Gallery, 1968-69. Served with AUS, 1943-46. Named hon. alumnus Tulane U., 1963, Outstanding Alumnus of 1993, The Blake Sch., Mpls., 1993. Mem. Coll. Art Assn., Medieval Acad. Am., Soc. Archtl. Historians, Renaissance Acad. Am., Soc. Fellows of Am. Acad. in Rome, Ateneo Veneto (fgn. mem.). Clubs: Harvard (La. pres. 1959-62, Boston), University Calif. at Santa Barbara Faculty (pres. 1968). Office: U Calif Dept Art History Santa Barbara CA 93106

MOISE, EDWIN EVARISTE, mathematician, educator; b. New Orleans, Dec. 22, 1918; s. Edwin Evariste and Annie Josephine (Boatner) M.; m. Mary Lorena Leake, May 28, 1942 (div. 1980); children: Edwin Evariste, Claire Mary. Student, La. State U., 1935-37; BA, Tulane U., 1940; PhD in Pure Math., U. Tex., 1947; MA (hon.), Harvard U., 1960. Instr. math. U. Mich., 1947-49, from asst. prof. to prof. math., 1951-60; James Bryant Conant prof. edn. and math. Harvard U., 1960-71; vis. prof. Centro de Investigación y de Estudios Avanzados, Instituto Politecnico Nacional, Mexico City, 1970-71; Disting. prof. Queens Coll., CUNY, 1971-80, 81-87, now emeritus; Hudson prof. Auburn U., 1980-81; Temp. mem. Inst. Advanced Study, Princeton, 1949-51, 56-57; mem. writing team Sch. Math. Study Group, summers 1958-60. Author: Elementary Geometry from an Advanced Standpoint, 1963, (with Floyd L. Downs, Jr.) Geometry, 1964, Number Systems of Elementary Mathematics, 1965, Calculus: Part I, 1966, Calculus: Part II, 1967, Geometric Topology in Dimensions 2 and 3, 1977, Introductory Problem Courses in Analysis and Topology, 1982. With USNR, 1942-46. Mem. Am. Math. Soc. (mng. editor bull. 1958-63, v.p. 1973-74), Math. Assn. Am. (v.p. 1965, pres. 1967-68), Phi Beta Kappa. Home: 77 Bleecker St Apt 323E New York NY 10012-1553

MOIZE, JERRY DEE, lawyer, government official; b. Greensboro, N.C., Dec. 19, 1934; s. Dwight Moody and Thelma (Ozment) M.; m. Margaret Ann Wooten, Aug. 13, 1976; 1 child, Jerry Dee Jr. AB cum laude, Elon (N.C.) Coll., 1957; JD, Tulane U., New Orleans, 1960; diploma, Army Command & Gen. Staff Sch., USAR, 1981. Bar: Colo. 1961, U.S. Dist. Ct. Colo. 1961, U.S. Ct. Mil. Appeals 1962, U.S. Supreme Ct. 1965, N.C. 1965. Legal clk. Air Def. Commd., Colorado Springs, Colo., 1960-61, assistance officer, 1962-63; chief legal assistance divsn. 2nd Army, Ft. Meade, Md., 1964-65; staff JAG, Indiantown Gap Mil. Reservation, 1965; law clk. to hon. Eugen Gordon U.S. Dist. Ct. (mid. dist.) N.C., Winston-Salem, 1965-66; dir. Legal Aid Soc. Forsyth County, Winston-Salem, 1966-69; exec. dir. Forsyth Bail Project, Winston-Salem, 1968-69, Lawyer Referral Svc. of Bar of 21st Jud. Dist., Winston-Salem, 1968-69; staff atty. office of gen. counsel FAA, Washington, 1969-70, acting chief admin. & legal resources, 1970-71; staff atty. office of gen. counsel Dept. Housing & Urban Devel., Washington, 1971; area counsel Jackson (Miss.) field office Dept. Housing & Urban Devel., 1971-83, chief counsel Jackson (Miss.) field office, 1983-94; chief counsel Office Gen. Counsel Miss., Jackson, 1994—; lectr. U. W.Va. Conf. on Poverty Law, 1968. Editor N.C. Legal Aid Reporter, 1968-69, N.C. Legal Aid Directory, 1968, Avlex Legal Index (2nd supplement), 1971; contbr articles to profl. jours., articles to splty. mags. Dem. candidate N.C. Ho. of Reps., Guilford County, 1964; mem. mil. com. Forsyth County N.C. Red Cross, 1967-68; pack leader Andrew Jackson coun. Boy Scouts Am., 1986-92; active Project Adv. Group U.S. Office Econ. Opportunity Legal Svcs. Program, 1968-69, Adv. Com. on Housing & Urban Devel., Miss., Law Rsch. Inst., 1980-81, Pilot Mountain Preservation & Park Com., Winston-Salem, 1968-70; mem. Race Com. Whitworth Hunt Races, 1973-76. Capt. AUS, 1960-65; ret. lt. col. USAR, 1966-87. Decorated Meritorous Svc. medal, Army Commendation medal with one oak leaf cluster, Army Res. Forces Achievement medal with three oak leaf clusters, Nat. Def. Svc. medal. Mem. Fed. Bar Assn., N.C. State Bar, Miss. Hist. Assn., Miss. Track Club, Iron Bridge Hunt Club (v.p. 1964-65), Whitworth Hunt Club (founder, master of foxhounds 1975-76), The Austin Hunt (joint master of foxhounds 1976-79), Caledonian Soc. Miss., Sons of Confederate Vets., Pi Gamma Mu. Republican. Episcopal. Avocations: riding to hounds, running, book collecting. Home: Ivanhoe 935 Bellevue Pl Jackson MS 39202 Office: Dept Housing & Urban Devel Miss State Office 9th Fl Fed Bldg 100 W Capitol Jackson MS 39269

MOJICA, AGNES, academic administrator. Chancellor Internat. Am. U. of PR, San German, P.R.; chair governing bd. Hispanic Assn. Colls. and Univs., 1995-96, co-chair leadership group. Mem. Consortium of Presidents and Chancellors for the Prevention of the Use and Abuse of Drugs and Alcohol. Mem. Assn. Industrialists of P.R., Western C. of C., Am. Assn. Higher Edn., Assn. Profl. Women, Club de Roma (P.R. chpt.), Altrusa, Rotary (hon.), Alpha Delta Kappa, Phi Delta Kappa. Office: Inter Am U Office of the Chancellor San German PR 00753

MOJICA, AURORA, trade association administrator; b. Mayaguez, P.R., Feb. 19, 1939; d. Luis Martinez and Anna Celida Montalvo; m. Aristides Mojica, Jan. 19, 1957 (div. July 1967); children: Ty, Marc Anthony, Raymond Francis, Sharai, Angeles. BS in Mgmt. and Labor Rel., Cornell U., 1979; postgrad., Boston U.; M in Tng. and Edn., 1996. Asst. dir. Attica Commn., N.Y.C., 1974, South Bklyn. Health Ctr., N.Y.C., 1975-79; sec. to the dept., dir. cmty. rels. (1st woman apptd.) Fire Dept. N.Y.C., 1979-81; dir. pub. cmty. rels. WYC Koff Heights Hosp., N.Y.C., 1981-84, Interfaith Adopt-A-Bldg., N.Y.C., 1984-86; dir. women health svcs. Woodhull Med. and Mental Health Ctr., N.Y.C., 1986-87; dir. individual and family grants program Fed. Emergency Mgmt. Agy., P.R., 1987-88; exec. dir. Nat. Image, Inc., Washington, 1988-90; pres. Wall St. chpt. Nat. Image, Inc.; regional tng. dir., safety rep. N.Y. State Dept. Transp., Long Island City, 1990-96; ind. cons., corp. trainer and developer, 1996—; cons. Agy. for Internat. Devel., Mex., Costa Rica and Peru, 1981; trainer Venezuela and P.R., Cornell U. P.R. Studies, N.Y., 1971—; trainer and bd. dirs. Neighborhood Reinvestment, N.Y.C., 1984-86; freelance corp. trainer/developer Marymount Manhattan Coll., Suffolk County Coll., various city, state and fed. govt. groups, nonprofit and profit corps. Bd. dirs. Dialogue on Diversity, Washington; founding mem. 100 Hispanic Women, Inc. Recipient Susan B. Anthony award for Pub. Svc., NOW, N.Y.C., 1981, Pub. Svc. award U.S. Dept. Labor, 1985, Gov. award for excellence, 1994, Women of Achievement award N.Y. State Dept. Transportation, 1994, Advisors Program for Women award Gov. N.Y., 1994; cert. of Recognition Sesame Street CTW, N.Y.C. 1983,; Named Hispanic Woman of the Yr. in Health Hispanic Woman's Network, Bklyn., 1987; Nat. Hispana Leadership Inst. fellow, 1990, 91. Roman Catholic.

MOJTABAI, ANN GRACE, author, educator; b. N.Y.C., June 8, 1937; d. Robert and Naomi (Friedman) Alpher; m. Fathollah Mojtabai, Apr. 27, 1960 (div. 1966); children: Chitra, Ramin. B.A. in Philosophy, Antioch Coll., 1958; M.A. in Philosophy, Columbia U., 1968, M.S. in L.S., 1970. Lectr. philosophy Hunter Coll., CUNY, 1966-68; librarian CCNY, 1970-76; fellow Radcliffe Inst. Ind. Study, Cambridge, Mass., 1976-78; Briggs-Copeland lectr. in English Harvard U., 1978-83; writer-in-residence U. Tulsa, 1983—, Yaddo Found., Saratoga, N.Y., 1975, 76. Author: Mundome, 1974, The 400 Eels of Sigmund Freud, 1976, A Stopping Place, 1979, Autumn, 1982, Blessed Assurance, 1986, Ordinary Time, 1989, Called Out, 1994. Recipient Richard and Hinda Rosenthal award Am. Acad. and Inst. Arts and Letters, 1983, Lillian Smith award So. Regional Council, 1986, Lit. Acad. award AAAL, 1993; Guggenheim fellow, 1981-82. Mem. PEN, Mark Twain Soc., Tex. Inst. Letters, Phi Beta Kappa. Home: 2102 S Hughes St Amarillo TX 79109-2212 Office: U Tulsa Dept English 600 S College Ave Tulsa OK 74104-3126

MOK, CARSON KWOK-CHI, structural engineer; b. Canton, China, Jan. 17, 1932; came to U.S., 1956, naturalized, 1962; s. King and Chi-Big (Lum) M.; B.S. in Civil Engring., Chu Hai U., Hong Kong, 1953; M.C.E., Cath. U. Am., 1968; m. Virginia Wai-Ching Cheng, Sept. 19, 1959. Structural designer Wong Cho Tong, Hong Kong, 1954-56; bridge designer Michael Baker Jr., Inc., College Park, Md., 1957-60; structural engr., chief design engr., asso. Milton A. Gurewitz Assos., Washington, 1961-65; partner Wright & Mok, Silver Spring, Md., 1966-75; owner Carson K.C. Mok, Cons. Engr., Silver Spring, 1976-81, pres., 1982—; facility engring. cons. Washington Met. Area Transit Authority, 1985-86; pres. Transp. Engring. and Mgmt. Assocs., P.C., Washington, 1986—; adj. asst. prof. Howard U., Washington, 1976-79, adj. assoc. prof., 1980-81; bd. dirs. U.S. Pan Asian Am. C. of C. Sec., N.Am. bd. trustees, China Grad. Sch. Theology, Wayne, Pa., 1972-74, pres., 1975-83, v.p., 1984-91; elder Chinese Bible Ch. Md., Rockville, 1978-80; chmn. Chinese Christian Ch. Greater Washington, 1958-61, 71, elder, 1972-76; dir. Evergreen Family Friendship Svc., Inc., A Pub. Benefit Corp., Palm Springs, Calif., 1993—. Recipient Outstanding Standard of Teaching award Howard U., 1980; registered profl. engr., Md., D.C. Mem. ASCE, ASTM, Constrn. Specification Inst., Nat. Assn. Corrosion Engrs., Concrete Reinforcing Steel Inst., Am. Concrete Inst., Am. Welding Soc., Prestressed Concrete Inst., Post-Tensioning Inst., Soc. Exptl. Mechanics., Internat. Assn. Bridge and Structural Engring., Pui Ching Mid. Sch. Alumni Assn. (pres. nation's capital chpt. 1991—) Contbr. articles to profl. jours. Home: 4405 Bestor Ct Rockville MD 20853-2137 Office: 9001 Ottawa Pl Silver Spring MD 20910-2257

MOKODEAN, MICHAEL JOHN, lawyer, accountant; b. Canton, Ohio, Dec. 24, 1925; s. Michael and Elizabeth (Stroia) M.; m. Jean Cristea, Apr. 17, 1950 (dec.); children: Michael Dan, Christine Ann; m. Josephine Woodward, Jan. 28, 1995. B.S. in Edn, Kent (Ohio) State U., 1948; J.D., William McKinley Sch. Law, Canton, 1955. Bar: Ohio 1955; C.P.A., Ohio. Agt. IRS, Canton, 1950-56; self-employed atty. C.P.A., Canton, 1957-69; tax accountant Elmer Fox & Co., Las Vegas, Nev., 1969; mgr. tax and ins. Diebold, Inc., Canton, 1969-74; sec., house counsel Diebold, Inc., 1974-78, v.p. legal, 1978-87, cons., 1987-89; part-time instr. tax accounting Walsh Coll., N. Canton, 1963-64, bd. advisers, 1976—; bd. advisers Stark Tech. Coll., Canton, 1972-76. Bd. advisers Doctors' Hosp., Massillon, Ohio, 1986—. With AUS, 1943-46. Mem. Brookside Country Club. Roman Catholic. Home: 2607 Charing Cross Rd NW Canton OH 44708-1575

MOKRASCH, LEWIS CARL, neurochemist, educator; b. St. Paul, May 9, 1930; s. Lewis and Anna (Dvorak) M.; m. Jane Carolyn Church, Apr. 20, 1974. B.S. magna cum laude, Coll. St. Thomas, 1952; Ph.D., U. Wis., 1955. Research assoc. dept. psychiatry and neurology La. State U. Med. Center, New Orleans, 1956-57; assoc. prof. dept. biochemistry La. State U. Med. Center, 1971-76, prof., 1976-92, prof. emeritus, 1992—, acting head dept., 1978-79; instr. medicine U. Kans. Med. Center, Kansas City, 1957-59, assoc. in medicine, dir. neurochemistry lab., 1959-62; asst. biochemist McLean Hosp., Belmont, Mass., 1960-64, assoc. biochemist, 1964-71; assoc. dept. biol. chemistry Harvard Med. Sch., Boston, 1964-67; asst. prof., 1967-71; adj. assoc. prof. biology Hellenic Coll., Brookline, Mass., 1969-71; staff scientist Neurosciences Research Programs, Brookline, 1970-71; vis. prof. neurology Duke U. Med. Center, 1981-82; lectr. in field. Author book written on myelin; contbr. articles to profl. jours.; book reviewer for jours. Sci. and FASEB. Pres. Belmont Preservation Soc., 1969; candidate Bd. Selectman, Belmont, 1969; active Met. Opera Guild, Piedmont Opera Guild, Winston Salem Piedmont Triad Symphony Guild, Reynolda Ho. Mus. Am. Art, Sr. Svcs. Program, Winston Salem. Grantee NIMH, 1973-74, Nat. Inst. Neurol. Disability and Blindness, 1957-90, Schlieder Found., 1971-72, 83-84, La. Bd. Regents, 1986-88. Fellow Am. Assn. Clin. Chemists; mem. AAUP, Am. Soc. Neurochemistry (local chmn. 1974), Am. Soc. Biol. Chemists, Soc. Neurosci. (pres. local chpt. 1974-75), Soc. Rsch. Adminstrs. (membership chmn. New Eng. sect.), Nat. Citizens Coalition Nursing Home Reform, Nat. Taxpayers Union, N.C. Taxpayers United, Nat. Alliance Sr. Citizens, Am. Assn. Individual Investors (founder, past pres. Piedmont chpt.),Peoples Med. Soc. Libertarian. Achievements include first demonstration of adaptive enzyme regulation in animals and allosteric control of fructose bisphosphatase, of incorporation of hydrouracil into transfer RNA, of thermogenic mechanism for arousing hibernators, of metabolic control in hibernation, of altered hydrophobic proteins in neurological disorders, of biosynthesis of hydrophobic proteins and mitochondrial proteins in brain in vitro, of altered transport processes in cells of neurological disease victims, of defective transport of acetylcholine precursors into cells of Alzheimer's victims and that such transport is modulatable; development of coestimation method for ketoses, aldoses, and pentoses; first isolation in pure form of receptor hydrophobic proteins from mammalian brain. Home: 1422 Reynolda Rd Winston Salem NC 27104-1016 *Before I entered Science, I regarded it as a Priesthood of individuals dedicated to the service of humanity, whose common goal was the enhancement of human life and the remedying of its ills. After 30 years in Science, I hold this thesis more strongly and have found many colleagues who agree with it. I am certain now that the failures and abuses of Science derive from the use of it for the goals of wealth, fame and power.*

MOLAND-BOOTH, KATHRYN JOHNETTA, computer scientist, software engineer; b. Tallahassee, Nov. 5, 1961; d. John and Kathryn Vastavia (Gadson) M.; m. Ronald Lynn Booth, May 7, 1994. BS in Sociology, Fla. A&M U., 1982; MS in Computer Sci., Southern U., 1987; PhD in Info. Systems, Nova U., 1996. Programmer, summer intern IBM, Lexington, 1985; mem. tech. staff Bell Communications Rsch., Piscataway, N.J., 1986; programmer Logos Corp., Mount Arlington, N.J., 1987-88, Telecommunications Inds., Vienna, Va., 1988; systems analyst Advanced Tech., Inc., Reston, Va., 1988; project leader Advanced Tech., Inc., Aiken, S.C., 1989-90; sr. systems analyst, project leader Westinghouse Savannah River Co., Aiken, S.C., 1990-94; devel. mgr. SCT Utility Systems, Inc., Columbia, S.C., 1994—; tech. mem. Occurrence Reporting Spl. Interest Group, Oak Ridge, Tenn., 1991-94. Bd. govs. Am. Biog. Inst. Rsch. Assn. Mem. IEEE (treas. 1991-92, vice chair 1992-93, chair 1993-94, mem. tech. coun. software enging.), NAFE, Nat. Mgmt. Assn., Project Mgmt. Inst., Assn. Computing Machinery. Avocations: bowling, tennis, reading. Home: 3315 Camak Dr Augusta GA 30909-9431 Office: SCT Utility Systems Inc 9 Science Ct Columbia SC 29203

MOLDEN, HERBERT GEORGE, publisher; b. Taunton, Mass., June 14, 1912; s. Ernest William and Edith (Parker) M.; m. Eleanor Caswell, Aug. 26, 1935; children: Marilyn (Mrs. Robert Erb), Parker C. Ph.B., Brown U., 1934. Head history dept. Storm King Sch., Cornwall on Hudson, N.Y., 1934-44; salesman, promotion mgr., exec. editor Macmillan Co., 1944-60; v.p. McCormick-Mathers Pub. Co., Inc., Wichita, Kans., 1960-61; with Am. Book Co., 1961-69, pres., 1968—; pres. Cambridge Book Co., 1970-78, H.G. Molden Co. Inc., Fairfield, Conn., 1978—; v.p., dir. N.Y. Times Media Co., 1971-76. Mem. Phi Beta Kappa.

MOLDENHAUER, JUDITH A., graphic design educator; b. Oak Park, Ill., Feb. 28, 1951; d. Raymond L. and Jean Marie (Carqueville) M. BFA, U. Ill., 1973; MA, Stanford U., 1974; MFA, U. Wis., 1977. Design supr. N.E. Mo. State U., Kirksville, Mo., 1977-79; asst. prof. design, design dept. Kans. City Art Inst., Mo., 1979-83; asst. prof. art, graphic design Sch. Art U. Mich., Ann Arbor, 1983-92; vis. lectr. Wayne State U., 1990-92, asst. prof. graphic design, 1992—, area coord. graphic design, 1992—; free-lance designer The Detroit Inst. Arts, Toledo (Ohio) Mus. Art, Burroughs Corp. (Unisys) Detroit, Detroit Focus Gallery; vis. designer N.S. Coll. Art and Design, 1986; juror Ohio Mus. Assn., 1986, Collaborator Presdl. Initiative "Health Start": prenatal and pre-conceptional booklets and ednl. modules designs, 1992—. Contbr. articles to profl. jours. Co-recipient grant Nat. Endowment for Arts, 1988; recipient Rackham grant U. Mich., Ann Arbor, 1987, award of distinction, merit award Am. Assn. Museums, 1985, 86, Excellence Design award Beckett Paper Co., 1991, Gold award for softcover books Printing & Publishing Competition, 1994. Mem. Am. Ctr. Design, Univ. and Coll. Designers Assn. (merit award 1979, gold award 1979), Coll. Art Assn. (chmn. panel 1991), Women's Caucus for Art (panel chmn. 1987), Amnesty Internat., Women in Design (excellence award Chgo. 1985, Sierra Club, Audubon Soc. Lutheran. Office: Wayne State U Dept Art and Art History 150 Art Bldg Detroit MI 48202

MOLDENHAUER, NANCY A., social worker. BSEd, Valparaiso U., 1976; MSW, U. Mich., 1984, cert. specialist in aging, 1984. Instr. Meiji Gakuin and Tokyo Med. and Dental U., 1977-81; corp. communication trainer Saito Internat., Inc., Tokyo, 1981-82; conf. coord. Ctr. for Japanese Studies U. Mich., Ann Arbor, 1982-84; gerontol. social worker Turner Geriatric Clinic U. Mich. Hosps., Ann Arbor, 1983-84; med. social worker Mo. Bapt. Med. Ctr., St Louis, 1985-88; geriatric social work specialist program on aging Jewish Hosp. Wash. U. Med. Ctr., St. Louis, 1988-92; dir. case mgmt. and corp. svcs. Aging Consult, St. Louis, 1993-95; adj. prof. Wash. U., St. Louis, 1991-95; trainee in aging NIH, 1983-84. Named OWL Woman of Worth, 1993. Mem. NASW, Acad. Cert. Social Workers, Gerontol. Soc. Am., Am. Soc. Aging, Nat. Coun. on Aging, Alzheimer's Assn., Older Women's League (local bd. dirs., pres. 1991-95, nat. bd. dirs., v.p. 1993—), Challenge Metro (bd. dirs., pres. 1986-90). Democrat. Unitarian. Avocations: gourmet cooking, restaurants, wine, fishing, foreign movies. Office: Open Mind Open Memory 6103 Larkspur Dr Alexandria VA 22310

MOLDENHAUER, WILLIAM CALVIN, soil scientist; b. New Underwood, S.D., Oct. 27, 1923; s. Calvin Fred and Ida (Killam) M.; m. Catherine Ann Maher, Nov. 26, 1947; children—Jean Ann, Patricia, Barbara, James, Thomas. B.S., S.D. State U., 1949; M.S., U. Wis., 1951, Ph.D., 1956. Soil surveyor S.D. State U., Brookings, 1948-54; soil scientist U.S. Dept. Agr., Big Spring, Tex., 1954-57; soi. scientist U.S. Dept. Agr., Ames, Iowa, 1957-72, Morris, Minn., 1972-75; rsch. leader Nat. Soil Erosion Rsch. Lab., Agrl. Rsch. Svc. U.S. Dept. Agr., West Lafayette, Ind., 1975-85; prof. dept. agronomy Purdue U., West Lafayette, 1975-85, prof. emeritus, 1985—. Contbr. articles to profl. jours. Served with U.S. Army, 1943-46. Fellow Am. Soc. Agronomy, Soil Sci. Soc., Soil Conservation Soc. Am. (pres. 1979), World Assn. Soil and Water Conservation (pres. 1983-85, exec. sec. 1985—). Home and Office: 317 Marvin Ave Volga SD 57071-2011

MOLE, MARIE L., stock broker, financial company executive; b. N.Y.C., June 9, 1957; d. Anthony M. and Maria L. (Pastor) Noya; m. Richard A. Mole, July 13, 1984; children: Erica, Richard. BA cum laude, Hunter Coll., 1977. Corp. syndicate asst. Lehman Bros., N.Y.C., 1977-79; sr. trader Westinghouse Pension Investment Corp., N.Y.C., 1979-84; options trader Union Bank of Switzerland, N.Y.C., 1984-85; PCS derivative product mgr., prin. Morgan Stanley & Co., N.Y.C., 1985—. Republican. Roman Catholic. Avocations: reading, writing articles, boating. Office: Morgan Stanley & Co Inc 1251 Ave of the Am 33d Fl New York NY 10020

MOLE, RICHARD JAY, accounting company executive; b. Berea, Ohio, Aug. 10, 1951; s. Wells Warren Jr. and Helen Irene (Buse) M.; m. Kathleen Ann Brennan, Oct. 28, 1978; children: Kevin Michael, Eileen Anne. BBA, U. Notre Dame, 1973; MBA, U. Pitts., 1974. CPA, Ohio, Pa.; CMA, CFM. Staff acct. James P. Ross, CPA, Elyria, Ohio, 1974-75; mgr. acctg. Dean J. Benshoff, PA, Mogadore, Ohio, 1975-77, John P. Hyland, CPA, Cleve., 1980; fin. adminstr. St. Joseph Ch. and Sts. Joseph and John Interparochial Sch., Strongsville, Ohio, 1977-80; v.p., contr. Citadel Alarm, Inc. div. Revco Drug Stores, Inc., Cleve., 1980-82; pres. Richard J. Mole, CPA, Inc., Andover, Ohio, 1982—. Chmn. bldg. com., v.p. Andover Pub. Libr., 1983—; mem. Ashtabula County Bd. Mental Retardation, Ashtabula, Ohio, 1987-89; chmn. fin. com. parish coun. Our Lady of Victory Cath. Ch., Andover, 1985-90; bd. dirs. Ashtabula County 503 Corp., 1986-92, pres.,

1990-92; bd. dirs. Ashtabula County Revolving Loan Fund, 1986-92, pres., 1990-92; treas. Civic Devel. Corp. Ashtabula County, 1994—; mem. Leadership Ashtabula County, 1989, grad. charter class; bd. dirs. Pymatuning Area Indsl. Devel. Corp., Andover, pres., 1986-88, 93-94; chmn. Andover Twp. Zoning Commn., 1989-94, mem., 1995, sec., 1996—; treas. Andover Civic Improvement Corp., 1992-96, pres., 1996—; treas. Andover Found., Inc., 1993—; coach, mgr. Pymatuning Area Youth Orgn., 1987-91, 95, pres., 1991-92. Recipient leadership award Civic Devel. Corp., Ashtabula, 1985, Quality of Living award Pymatuning Area Indsl. Devel. Corp., 1986, Best of County award Ashtabula County Growth Partnership, 1992, Leadership award State of Ohio, 1993. Fellow AICPA, Ohio Soc. CPAs, Pa. Inst. CPAs; mem. Nat. Assn. Accts., Rotary Internat. (bd. dirs. Andover 1984—, pres. 1985-86, 96—, treas. 1988-96, Paul Harris fellow 1993), Andover C. of C. (v.p. 1983-85, treas. 1985-87). Republican. Office: Richard J Mole CPA Inc 124 S Main St Andover OH 44003-1270

MOLEN, GERALD ROBERT, film producer; b. Great Falls, Mont., Jan. 6, 1935; s. Gerald Richard Molen and Edith Lorraine (Meyer) Burris; m. Patricia Jane Lindke, July 29, 1954; children: Steven Robert, Lorion Marie Molen Bunyea. Grad., Van Nuys (Calif.) High Sch., 1953. Transp. mgr. Universal City (Calif.) Studios, 1967-70; transp. coord. Ind. Producers, Hollywood, Calif., 1971-79; freelance prodn. mgr. Hollywood, 1980-91. Prodn. mgr.: (films) Postman Always Rings Twice, 1980, Tootsie, 1982, A Soldiers Story, 1983, The Color Purple, 1985; assoc. prodr.: (film) Batteries Not Included, 1986; exec. prodr.: (films) Bright Lights, Big City, 1987, A Far Off Place, 1993, The Flintstones, 1994, Little Rascals, 1994; prodr.: (films) Hook, 1991, Jurassic Park, 1992, Schindlers List, 1993 (Acad. award, Golden Globe award 1994); appeared in films: Rain Man, 1988 (also co-prodr.), Days of Thunder, 1990 (also exec. prodr.), Jurassic Park, 1992. Sgt. USMC, 1953-56. Mem. Dirs. Guild Am., SAG. Republican. Avocations: golf, travel, movies. Home: 17156 Ballinger St Northridge CA 91325-1928

MOLEN, JOHN KLAUMINZER, lawyer; b. Gary, Ind., June 13, 1952; s. Franklin B. and Jane Anne (Klauminzer) M.; m. Susan Wilson Blair, Aug. 10, 1985; children: Mary Wilson, Elisabeth Blair. AB with honors, U. N.C., 1974, MBA, 1978, JD with honors, 1978. Bar: Ala. 1978. Assoc. Bradley, Arant, Rose & White, Birmingham, Ala., 1978-84, ptnr., 1984—. Mem. Rotary Club Birmingham-Sunrise. Presbyterian. Avocations: sailing, swimming. Office: Bradley Arant Rose & White 2001 Park Pl Ste 1400 Birmingham AL 35203-2736

MOLER, EDWARD HAROLD, lawyer; b. Oklahoma City, May 26, 1923; s. Harold Stanley and Rosemary (Callahan) M.; m. Donna Blocksom Cram, Sept. 12, 1964; children: John Frederick, Shelley Elizabeth, Christopher Bryan. BA, U. Okla., 1947, LLB, 1948. Bar: Okla. 1948, U.S. Supreme Ct. 1951. Pvt. practice law Oklahoma City, 1948-52, 61—, asst. mcpl. counselor, 1952-59, mcpl. counselor, 1959-61; spl. justice Okla. Supreme Ct., 1977. Trustee Oklahoma City Mcpl. Improvement Authority, 1960-61; bd. dirs. Mummers Theatre, Inc., 1969—; bd. dirs. Greater Oklahoma City YMCA, 1981-91. 2d lt. USAAF, 1943-45. Mem. ABA, Okla. Bar Assn., Oklahoma County Bar Assn. (bd. dirs. 1963-67, pres. 1968), Rotary, Phi Delta Phi, Phi Gamma Delta (pres. local chpt. 1946, pres. Nu Omega Housing Assn. 1963-65). Home: 2540 NW Grand Blvd Oklahoma City OK 73116-4110 Office: City Pl Oklahoma City OK 73102

MOLER, ELIZABETH ANNE, federal agency administrator, lawyer; b. Salt Lake City, Jan. 24, 1949; d. Murray McClure and Eleanor Lorraine (Barry) M.; m. Thomas Blake Williams, Oct. 19, 1979; children: Blake Martin Williams, Eleanor Bliss Williams. BA, Am. U., 1971; postgrad., Johns Hopkins U., 1972; JD, George Wash. U., 1977. Bar: D.C. 1978. Chief legis. asst. Senator Floyd Haskell, Washington, 1973-75; law clk. Sharon, Pierson, Semmes, Crolius & Finley, Washington, 1975-76; profl. staff mem. com. on energy and natural resources U.S. Senate, Washington, 1976-77, counsel, 1977-86, sr. counsel, 1987-88; commr. FERC, Washington, 1988-93, chair, 1993—. Mem. ABA, D.C. Bar Assn. Democrat. Home: 1537 Forest Ln Mc Lean VA 22101-3317 Office: FERC Ste 11A 888 First St NE Ste 11A Washington DC 20426

MOLER, JAMES CLARK, marketing research executive; b. West Union, Ohio, Nov. 17, 1930; s. Joseph Adam and Kathryn Susan (Clark) M.; m. Barbara Lucille Painter, Sept. 14, 1953 (div. 1973); children: Kathy, James. BBA, U. Cin., 1953. Various positions Burgoyne, Inc., Cin., 1956-62, v.p. client svc., 1962-65, exec. v.p., 1965-69; pres. J.C. Moler and Assocs., Cin., 1969-71, B&B Rsch. Svcs., Inc., Cin., 1971—. Lt. USN, 1953-56. Mem. Am. Mktg. Assn., Mktg. Rsch. Assn. Avocations: woodworking, stamp collecting, tennis. Office: B&B Rsch Svcs Inc 8005 Plainfield Rd Cincinnati OH 45236-2500

MOLFENTER, DAVID P., electronics executive; b. 1945. CEO Magnavox Electronic Systems, Fort Wayne, Ind. Office: Magnavox Electronic Sys 1313 Production Rd Fort Wayne IN 46808

MOLGAT, GILDAS L., Canadian government official; b. Ste. Rose du Lac, Man., Can., Jan. 25, 1927; s. Louis and Adele (Abraham) M.; m. Allison Malcom, July 31, 1958; children: Anne Marie, Mathurin Paul. B.Comm. with honors, U. Man., 1947. Elected M.L.A. Man., 1953, re-elected, 1958, 59, 62, 1966, 69; leader Liberal Party in Man., 1961-68, leader opposition, 1961-68; summoned to Senate of Can., 1970—, dep. spkr., 1983-84, 89-91, spkr., 1994—; joint chmn., spl. joint com. Senate and House of Commons on constn. of Can., 1971, on Reform of the Senate of Can., 1982; apptd. dep. leader Opposition in Senate, 1991, dep. leader govt., 1993, chmn. com. of whole on Meech Lake Constnl. Accord, 1987-88, task force on Meech Lake Constnl. Accord and Yukon and N.W. Territories, 1987-88, chmn. submissions group, 1988; chmn. Man. Lib. Fed. campaign, 1972; govt. whip, 1973; elected pres. Liberal Party of Can., 1973. Founding chmn. St. Boniface Hosp. Rsch. Found., 1971. Served with Royal Winnipeg Rifles, 1946-66, hon. lt. col., 1966, hon. col., 1985. Mem. Royal United Svcs. Inst. Man. (hon. pres. 1990), Army, Navy and Air Force Vets. of Can. (Winnipeg Unit #1 hon. pres. 1992), Man. Army Cadet League (founding pres. 1971), Army Cadet League Can. (pres. 1977-79), Can. Corps Commissionaires, Royal Can. Legion, Société Franco-Manitobaine, St. Andrew's Soc. Roman Catholic. Office: Spkr Senate of Canada, Parliament Bldg Rm 389-S, Center Block, Ottawa, ON Canada K1A 0A4

MOLHO, EMANUEL, publisher; b. N.Y.C., Jan. 27, 1936; s. Isaac Emanuel and Alvira (Altchek) M.; m. Brenda Nadel, Sept. 25, 1965; children—Deborah Rochelle, Brian Emanuel. B.A., N.Y. U., 1957; M.B.A., Wharton Sch., U. Pa., 1960. Pres. French & European Publs., Inc., N.Y.C., 1961—, French & Spanish Book Corp., 1967—; pres. Librairie de France, Inc., 1961—. Recipient Orden de Merito Civil Spain, 1975. Mem. Am. Booksellers Assn., French-Am. C. of C. in U.S. (exec. com.), Paris Am. Club. Office: Librairie de France Rockefeller Center Promenade 610 5th Ave New York NY 10020-2497

MOLHOLM, KURT NELSON, federal agency administrator; b. Denver, June 24, 1937; s. Ervin Maurice and Helen Pauline (Nelson) M.; m. Sonja Dell Williams, Aug. 17, 1967; children: Kevin William, Paul Nelson. BS, U. Oreg., 1959; MS, George Washington U., 1974; grad., Indsl. Coll. Armed Forces, 1974. Computer specialist D.L.A. Adminstrv. Support Ctr., Alexandria, Va., 1963-65; with Hdqrs. Def. Logistics Agy., Alexandria, 1965-85, chief planning and policy office, 1975-76, chief ADP/T tech. div., 1984-85; adminstr. Def. Tech. Info. Ctr., Alexandria, 1985—; pres. Nat. Fedn. Abstracting and Info. Svcs., Phila., 1993-94, treas., 1990-93; del. Va. Govs. Conf. Librs. Info. Svcs., 1990, Fed. Libr. Pre-White House Conf. On Librs. Info. Sci., 1990; vice chmn. Fed. Libr. and Info. Ctr. Com., 1992-93; chmn. Commerce, Energy, NASA, NLM, Def. Info. Group, 1991-94; mem. NATO Agard Tech. Info. Panel, 1985-91, Internat. Coun. Sci. and Tech. Info., 1993—, Info. Infrastructure Task Force, 1993—. 1st lt. U.S. Army, 1960-63. Recipient Meritorious award William A. Jump Meml. Found., 1973. Methodist. Office: Ctr 8725 John J Kingman Rd Fort Belvoir VA 22060-6218

MOLHOLT, PAT, academic administrator, associate dean; b. Fond du Lac, Wis., Oct. 19, 1943; d. Elmore Harrison and Leona Ann (Reschke) Leu; divorced; children: Rebecca Marie, Stephanie Anne. BS, U. Wis., 1966, MLS, 1970; postgrad., Rensselaer Poly. Inst., 1985—. Library intern Milw. Pub. Library, 1966-67; astronomy librarian, dept. astronomy U. Wis., Madison, 1970-73; physics librarian U. Wis. Libraries, Madison, 1973-77; asst. prof., dir. U. Wyo. Sci. and Tech. Library, Laramie, 1977-78; assoc. dir. Rensselaer Poly. Inst. Libraries, Troy, N.Y., 1978-92, affirmative action advisor to pres., 1988-92; asst. v.p., assoc. dean scholarly resources Columbia U., N.Y.C., 1992—; co-dir. art and architecture thesaurus program J. Paul Getty Trust, Williamstown, Mass., 1983-86; rsch. analyst U.S. Dept. Edn., Washington, 1987-88; pres. Universal Serials and Book Exch., 1988-89; trustee Capital Dist. Libr. Coun., 1986-89; bd. visitors U. Pitts. Sch. Libr. and Info. Studies, 1993-95; mem. adv. bd. libr. sci. program Wayne State U., Detroit, 1992-95; mem. IBM Higher Edn. Custome Adv. Coun., 1995—; mem. Biomed. Libr. rev. com. Nat. Libr. of Medicine, 1995—. Contbr. articles to profl. jours. Mem. adv. bd. Sch. Info. and Pub. Policy, SUNY-Albany, 1989; mem. steering com. N.Y. Gov.'s Conf. on Libr. and Info. Svcs., 1989-90; active N.Y. State Regent's Vis. Com. on State Archives, 1991—. Fellow Spl. Librs. Assn. (pres. 1983-84, John Cotton Dana award 1989); mem. ALA, NSF (mem. adv. bd., divsn. networking comm. rsch. and infrastructure 1991-92), Sci. Libr. Assn., Am. Soc. Info. Sci. (chair tech. program com. mid-yr. meeting, 1994). Office: Columbia U Health Scis 701 W 168th St Rm 201 New York NY 10032-2704

MOLINA, MARIO JOSE, physical chemist, educator; b. Mexico City, Mexico, Mar. 19, 1943; came to U.S., 1968; s. Roberto Molina-Pasquel and Leonor Henríquez; m. Luisa Y. Tan, July 12, 1973; 1 child, Felipe. Bachillerato, Acad. Hispano Mexicana, Mexico City, 1959; Ingeniero Químico, U. Nacional Autónoma de México, 1965; postgrad., U. Freiburg, Fed. Republic Germany, 1966-67; Ph.D., U. Calif., Berkeley, 1972. Asst. prof. U. Nacional Autónoma de México, 1967-68; research assoc. U. Calif.-Berkeley, 1972-73; research assoc. U. Calif.-Irvine, 1973-75, asst. prof. phys. chemistry, 1975-79, assoc. prof., 1979-82; sr. rsch. scientist Jet Propulsion Lab., 1983-89; prof. dept. earth, atom and planet sci., dept. chemistry MIT, Cambridge, 1989—, Martin prof. atmospheric chemistry. Mem. Pres.'s Com. of Advisors on Sci. and Tech. Recipient Tyler Ecology award, 1983, Esselen award for chemistry in pub. interest, 1987, Max-Planck-Forschungs-Preis, Alexander von Humboldt-Stiftung, 1994, Nobel Prize in Chemistry, 1995. Mem. NAS, Am. Chem. Soc., Am. Phys. Soc., Am. Geophys. Union, Pres.'s Com. on Advisors on Sci. and Tech., Sigma Xi. Achievements include discovering the theory that fluorocarbons deplete ozone layer of stratosphere. Home: 8 Clematis Rd Lexington MA 02173-7117 Office: MIT Dept of EAPS 77 Massachusetts Ave # 54-1312 Cambridge MA 02139-4301 *We have to understand our environment to find out if we are tampering with it. One of our accomplishments has been to call attention to society's potential altering of the atmosphere.*

MOLINARI, SUSAN K., congresswoman; b. S.I., N.Y., Mar. 27, 1958; d. Guy V. and Marguerite (Wing) M.; m. Bill Paxon, 1994. BA, SUNY, Albany, 1980, MA, 1982. Former intern for State Senator Christopher Mega; former rsch. analyst N.Y. State Senate Fin. Com.; former fin. asst. Nat. Rep. Gov.'s Assn.; ethnic community liaison Rep. Nat. Com., 1983-84; minority leader N.Y.C. Council, 1986-90; mem. 101st-104th Congresses from 14th (now 13th) N.Y. dist., 1990—; mem. budget com., chmn. transp. and infrastructure subcom. on railroads. Roman Catholic. Office: US Ho of Reps 2435 Rayburn HOB Washington DC 20515*

MOLINDER, JOHN IRVING, engineering educator, consultant; b. Erie, Pa., June 14, 1941; s. Karl Oskar and Carin (Ecklund) M.; m. Janet Marie Ahlquist, June 16, 1962; children: Tim, Karen. BSEE, U. Nebr., 1963; MSEE, Air Force Inst. Tech., 1964; PhD EE, Calif. Inst. Tech., 1969. Registered profl. engr., Calif. Project officer Ballistic Systems Div., Norton AFB, Calif., 1964-67; sr. engr. Jet Propulsion Lab., Pasadena, Calif., 1969-70; prof. engring. Harvey Mudd Coll., Claremont, Calif., 1970—; part-time lectr. Calif. State U., Los Angeles, 1970-74; mem. tech. adv. panel Kinemetrics, Pasadena, 1985-86; part-time mem. tech. staff Jet Propulsion Lab., Pasadena, 1974—, rep. NASA Hdqrs., Washington, 1979-80; vis. prof. elec. engring. Calif. Inst. Tech., 1982-83. Contbr. articles to profl. jours. Served to capt. USAF, 1963-67. Mem. IEEE. Avocations: bicycling, reading, computers. Office: Harvey Mudd Coll Dept of Engring 301 E 12th St Claremont CA 91711-5901

MOLINE, JON NELSON, philosopher, educator, college president; b. Ft. Worth, May 12, 1937; s. Paul Ross and Elsie Virginia (Nelson) M.; m. Sandra Lois Reininger, Aug. 13, 1960; children—Kevin, Eric. A.B., Austin Coll., 1960; Ph.D., Duke U., 1964; LHD, Austin Coll., 1995. Asst. prof. U. Wis., Madison, 1964-69; assoc. prof. U. Wis., 1969-73, prof. philosophy, 1973-86, prof. environ. studies, 1974-86; faculty adviser U. Wis. (Nat. Humanities Faculty), 1976-82; v.p., dean St. Olaf Coll., Northfield, Minn., 1987-94; pres. Tex. Lutheran Coll., Seguin, 1994—; vis. asst. prof. U. Ill. at Chgo., 1969; vis. assoc. prof. U. Tex., Austin, 1971-72; fellow Nat. Humanities Center, 1979-80. Pres. Madison Symphony Orch., 1975-77; bd. dirs. Fund for Improvement Post-Secondary Edn., 1985-91; mem. Nat. Coun. on the Humanities, 1991—, vice-chair, 1993—. Vis. fellow Inst. for Research in Humanities, 1973, 75-76; Spencer Found. fellow, 1974; Rockefeller Found. humanities fellow, 1975-76. Office: Texas Lutheran College 1000 W Court St Seguin TX 78155-5978

MOLINE, SANDRA LOIS, librarian; b. San Antonio, Dec. 13, 1938; d. Udo F. and Olivia Marie (Link) Reininger; m. Jon Nelson Moline, Aug. 13, 1960; children: Kevin, Eric. BA in Chemistry, Austin Coll., 1960; postgrad., Duke U., 1962-64; MA in History of Sci., U. Wis., 1976, MLS, 1977. Tchr. chemistry and physics Durham (N.C.) High Sch., 1960-64; head physics libr. U. Wis., Madison, 1977-88; head reference svcs. Sci. and Engring. Libr. U. Minn., Mpls., 1988-94; libr. Reader's Svcs. Libr., Luth. Coll., Seguin, 1994—. Bd. dirs. Mid-Tex. Symphony, 1995—; trustee Seguin-Guadalupe County Pub. Libr., 1996—. Mem. Spl. Librs. Assn. (physics, astronomy, math, sci.-tech. divsns.), Librs. Assembly (sec., treas. 1980, pres. 1983), Madison Acad. Staff Assn. (steering com. 1980-83, pres. 1982). Home: 605 Fleming Dr Seguin TX 78155-3413

MOLINEAUX, CHARLES BORROMEO, lawyer, arbitrator, columnist, poet; b. N.Y.C., Sept. 27, 1930; s. Charles Borromeo and Marion Frances (Belter) M.; m. Patricia Leo Devereux, July 2, 1960; children: Charles, Stephen, Christopher, Patricia, Peter, Elizabeth. BS cum laude, Sch. Fgn. Service, Georgetown U., 1950; JD, St. John's U., N.Y.C., 1959. Bar: N.Y. 1959, Mass. 1981, D.C. 1988. Assoc., then ptnr. Nevius, Jarvis & Pilz and successor firms, N.Y.C., 1959-77; ptnr. Gadsby & Hannah, N.Y.C., 1978-80; v.p., gen. counsel Perini Corp., Framingham, Mass., 1980-87; pvt. practice, Washington, 1987—; mem. adj. faculty Internat. Law Inst., Washington, 1989—. Author numerous poems. Committeeman Republican Party, Nassau County, N.Y., 1965-71, Fairfax County, Va. Mem. exec. com., 1969. Served to 1st lt. U.S. Army, 1954-56. Fellow Am. Bar Found.; mem. ASCE, Am. Arbitration Assn. (mem. constrn. ADR task force 1994—), Chartered Inst. Arbitrators, Fedn. Internationale des Ingenieurs-Conseils (Assoc. Gen. Contractors del. constrn. contract com.), Del. Hist. Soc., London Ct. Internat. Arbitration, Fellowship Cath. Scholars. Roman Catholic. Home: 8321 Weller Ave Mc Lean VA 22102-1717 Office: 8100 Boone Blvd Vienna VA 22182-2642

MOLINO, PATRICIA MARY, communications executive; b. Jersey City, N.J., Nov. 20, 1946; d. Nicholas and Jean (Rocco) M.; m. Ronald J. Sullivan. BS, NYU, 1968, MA, 1987. Writer Am. Mus. Nat. History, N.Y.C., 1968-69; dir. pub. affairs Bot. Garden, N.Y.C., 1969; dir. pub. rels. Hunter Coll. CCNY, 1970-74; dir. communications Deutsch, Shea & Evans, N.Y.C., 1975; dir. pub. info. Meml. Sloan-Kettering Cancer Ctr., N.Y.C., 1976-84; pres. Patricia Molino Communications, N.Y.C., 1985-89; sr. v.p. healthcare Makovsky & Co., N.Y.C., 1989; pres. Molino Assocs., N.Y.C., 1989—. Bd. dirs. Family Dynamics, N.Y.C., 1986—. Mem. AAAS, Pub. Relations Soc. Am., N.Y. Acad. Scis. Avocation: real estate. Office: Molino Associates Inc 1775 Broadway Ste 401 New York NY 10019

MOLINOFF, PERRY BROWN, biologist, science administrator; b. Smithtown, N.Y., June 3, 1940; s. Henry Charles and Thelma (Brown) M.; m. Marlene Sirota, 1963; children: Jeffrey, Sharon. BS, Harvard U., 1962, MD, 1967. Intern U. Chgo. Hosp. & Clinics, 1967-68; research assoc. NIMH, Bethesda, Md., 1968-70; vis. fellow Univ. Coll., London, 1970-72; asst. prof. U. Colo. Health Sci., Denver, 1972-76; assoc. prof. U. Colo. Health Sci., 1976-80, prof., 1980-81; prof., chmn. U. Pa., Phila., 1981-94; v.p. C.N.S. Drug Discovery Bristol-Myers Squibb, Wallingford, Conn., 1995—. Editor: Basic Neurochemistry, 1989, Biology of Normal and Abnormal Brain Function, 1990, Goodman and Gilman: The Pharmacological Basis of Therapeutics, 1996; editl. adv. bd. Molecular Pharmacology, 1976—. Med. adv. bd. Dysautonomia Found., 1977—. Lt. comdr. USPHS, 1968-70. Mem. Soc. Neurosci. (membership com., treas.), Am. Heart Assn. (rsch. com.), John Morgan Soc. (sec.-treaas. 1988—), Pa. Heart Assn. Home: 10 Broad St Weston CT 06883 Office: Bristol-Myers Squibb 5 Research Pkwy PO Box 5100 Wallingford CT 06492-7600

MOLINSKY, BERT, tax consultant; b. Bronx, N.Y., Feb. 25, 1938; s. Joseph and Ida G. (Rosenberg) M.; m. Donna L. Thurman, June 26, 1964; children: Avery, Lucy, Lois, Sarah. Student, U. Ariz., 1956-61, Diablo Valley Coll., 1986-88, Calif. State U., Hayward, 1988-92. CFP; CLU; ChFC; Enrolled Agt. Field supt. INA Life, Phoenix, 1968-72; regional life mgr. Sentry Life Ins. Co., Oklahoma City, 1972-73, Mpls., 1973-75, San Francisco, 1975-78; mgr. Acacia Mutual Life, Oakland, Calif., 1978-80; gen. agt. Am. United Life, Concord, Calif., 1980-82; owner East Bay Triple Check Tax Svcs., Walnut Creek, Calif., 1982—, Triple Check Tax and Fin. Svc., Peoria, Ariz., 1993—; instr. Golden Gate U. CPD, San Francisco, 1983-93, Mt. Diablo Sch. Dist., Concord, 1986-93; faculty Coll. for Fin. Planning, Denver, 1983—; bd. dirs. Triple Check Licensee Coun. Contbr. articles to profl. jours. Nat. dir. U.S. Jaycees, Phoenix, 1967; pres. Bnai Brith Coun. of Lodges, San Francisco, 1986. With USNR, 1955-72. Named Jaycee of Yr. Ariz. Jaycees, 1967. Fellow Nat. Tax Practice Inst.; mem. Enrolled Agts., East Bay Assn Life Underwriters (pres. 1985-86), Nat. Assn. Enrolled Agts. Avocation: sports. Office: Plaza Del Rio Ctr 9401 W Thunderbird Rd # 140 Peoria AZ 85381 also: PO Box 100 Peoria AZ 85380-0100

MOLITOR, GRAHAM THOMAS TATE, lawyer; b. Seattle, Apr. 6, 1934; s. Robert Franklin and Louise Margaret (Graham) M.; m. Carlotta Jean Crate, July 30, 1960; children: Graham Thomas Tate, Anne Therese, Christopher Robert. BS, U. Wash., 1955; LLB, Am. U., 1963. Bar: D.C. 1963. Rsch. asst. U. Wash., Seattle, 1957; bailiff U.S. Criminal Ct. D.C., 1958-59; legis. counsel U.S. Ho. of Reps., Washington, 1961-63; dir. candidate rsch. Rockefeller for Pres. Com., 1963-64, 68; D.C. counsel, asst. dir. govt. rels. Nabisco, Inc., Washington, 1964-70; dir. govtl. rels. Gen. Mills, Inc., Washington, 1970-77; pres., CEO Pub. Policy Forecasting, Inc., Potomac, Md., 1977—; prin. ptnr. Pub. Policy Communicators, 1989-91; prin., ptnr. Pub. Policy Action Inst., Potomac; adv. bd. Creative Bus. Strategies, Inc.; adj. prof. Grad. Sch. Bus., Am. U., Washington, 1969-75, 79-85, Montgomer Coll., Rockville, Md., 1987-88; dir. rsch. White House Conf. on Indsl. World Ahead, 1971-72; mem. White House Adv. Com. on Social Indicators, 1975-76; chmn. Commn. on the Future of Montgomery County, 1986-88; guest lectr. numerous univs.; del. White House Confs. on Food, Nutrition and Health, 1969-71, White House Conf. on Youth, 1970; bd. dirs. First Global Conf. on the Future, Inc., Can., 1980—. Contbg. editor Food Tomorrow Newsletter, 1976-77; co-editor, chmn. editl. bd. Ency. of the Future, 1991—; mem. bd. editors Hudson Inst. Study of World Food Problems, 1975-77; mem. editl. bd. Bus. Tomorrow Newsletter, 1977-79; mem. bd. advisors New Mktg. Techs. Monitor, 1983-85; polit. editor: On the Horizon, 1993-95; contbr. articles to profl. jours. Mem. Food Adv. Bd., N.Y.C., 1980—. Served to 1st lt. U.S. Army, 1958-61. Recipient Disting. Service award Grocery Mfrs. Am., 1973-74, Disting. Service award Nat. Consumer Info. Center, 1974, Disting. Service award Am. Mgmt. Assn., 1975. Mem. Washington Bus.-Govt. Rels. Coun., Washington Indsl. Roundtable, E.D. Export Coun., World Future Soc. (gen. chmn. 2d Gen. Assembly 1975, v.p., dir. 1981-94, v.p., legal counsel 1994—, Disting. Svc. award 1975), Univ. Club, Phi Kappa Sigma, Phi Alpha Delta. Republican. Presbyterian. Home and Office: 9208 Wooden Bridge Rd Rockville MD 20854-2416

MOLITOR, KAREN ANN, lawyer; b. Chgo., Apr. 20, 1953; d. Edward William and Elizabeth M. (Schmolke) Swanson; m. Patrick John Molitor, Apr. 26, 1971; children: Elizabeth Ann, Patrick John Jr. BS with honors, U. Ark., 1986, JD, 1990. Bar: Conn. 1990, U.S. Dist. Ct. Conn. 1990, U.S. Ct. Appeals (2d cir.) 1994. Assoc. atty. Shipman & Goodwin, Hartford, Conn., 1990-93; asst. atty. gen. Conn. Atty. Gen.'s Office, Storrs, Conn., 1993-94; gen. coun. Conn. Performing Arts, Inc., Hartford, 1994—. Mem. ABA, Conn. Bar Assn., Nat. Assn. Coll. and Univ. Attys., Phi Beta Kappa. Roman Catholic. Avocations: bicycling, reading, physical fitness. Home: 28 Sunset Terr West Hartford CT 06107 Office: Meadows Music Theatre 61 Savitt Way Hartford CT 06120

MOLITOR, SISTER MARGARET ANNE, nun, former college president; b. Milford, Ohio, Sept. 19, 1920; d. George Jacob and Mary Amelia (Lockwood) M. B.A., Our Lady of Cin. Coll., 1942; M.Ed., Xavier U., 1950; LL.D.; M.A., Catholic U. Am., 1963, Ph.D., 1967. Joined Sisters of Mercy, 1943; tchr. elementary schs. Cin., 1946-50, secondary schs., Cin. and Piqua, Ohio, 1951-60; faculty Edgecliff Coll., Cin., 1962-73; pres. Edgecliff Coll., 1973-80; archivist Cin. Province Sisters of Mercy; research cons. various religious communities. Bd. dirs. Citizens Com. on Youth; trustee Chatfield Coll., Clermont Mercy Hosp., Mercy St. Theresa Retirement Ctr.; mem. Area Coun. Planning Task Force, Cin. Community Devel. Adv. Coun.; pres. Better Housing League of Greater Cin. Recipient Woman of Year award Cin. Enquirer, 1977, 200 Greater Cincinnatians Bicentennial award, 1988. Mem. Greater Cin. Consortium Colls. and Univs. (pres. 1980). Address: 2335 Grandview Ave Cincinnati OH 45206-2219

MOLITOR, PAUL LEO, professional baseball player; b. St. Paul, Aug. 22, 1956; m. Linda Kaplan; 1 child, Blaire. Student, U. Minn., 1975-77. With Milw. Brewers, 1978-92, Toronto Blue Jays, 1992-95, Minnesota Twins, Mpls., 1996—; mem. Am. League All-Star Team, 1980, 85, 88, 91-94. Named Am. League Rookie of Yr. Sporting News, 1978, Sporting News Coll. All-America Team, 1977; recipient Silver Slugger award, 1987, 88, 93, World Series MVP award, 1993, Midwest League MVP award. Office: Minnesota Twins 501 Chicago Ave S Minneapolis MN 55415*

MOLITORIS, BRUCE ALBERT, nephrologist, educator; b. Springfield, Ill., June 26, 1951; s. Edward and Joyce (Tomasko) M.; m. Karen Lynn Wichterman, June 16, 1973; children: Jason, Jared, Julie. BS, U. Ill., 1973, MS in Nutrition, 1975; MD, Wash. U., 1979. Resident Sch. Medicine U. Colo., Denver, 1979-81, nephrology fellow, 1981-84, asst. prof. medicine, 1984-88, assoc. prof. medicine, 1988-93, prof., 1993; dir. nephrology Ind. U. Med. Sch., Indpls., 1993—; vis. scientist U. Colo., MCDB, Boulder, 1989-90, Max Planck Inst., Federal Republic of Germany, 1984-85; NIH reviewer, 1991-94; dir. home dialysis Denver VA Ctr., 1984-93. Mem. editl. bd. Am. Jour. Physiology, 1989—, Am. Jour. Kidney Diseases, 1991, Am. Jour. Kidney Disease, 1996; assoc. editor Jour. Ivnestigative Medicine, 1994—; contbr. articles to profl. jours. Pres. Cherry Creek Village South Homeowners Assn., 1989-90; v.p. Our Father Luth. Ch., Denver, 1989-90; coach Cherry Creek Soccer Assn., Greenwood Village, 1988-91, Centennial little league Titans Basketball; bd. dirs. CSSA, 1993. Recipient Upjohn Achievement award, 1979, Liberty Hyde Bailey award, 1973. Mem. Am. Soc. Nephrology, Internat. Soc. Nephrology, N.Y. Acad. Sci., Am. Soc. Clin. Investigation, Am. Fedn. for Clin. Rsch. (nat. counselor 1991-94), Western Assn. Physicians. Avocations: bridge, fishing, antiques. Office: Indiana Univ Med Ctr Fesler Hall 115 1120 South Dr Indianapolis IN 46202-5135

MOLITORIS, JOLENE M., federal agency administrator. BA, Cath. U. Am.; MA, Case Western Res. U. From asst. liaison officer to exec. dir. Ohio Rail Transp. Authority, 1977-83; dep. dir. Ohio Dept. Transp., 1984-92; adminstr. Fed. Railroad Adminstrn., Washington, 1993—; former chair Region 1 Nat. Conf. State Rail Ofcls. Recipient Pres. award for outstanding achievement Maglev/High Speed Rail Assn., 1989, 92. Office: Fed Railroad Adminstrn 400 7th St SW Washington DC 20590-0001

MOLL, CLARENCE RUSSEL, academic administrator emeritus, consultant; b. Chalfont, Pa., Oct. 31, 1913; s. George A. and Anna A. (Schmidt) M.; m. Ruth E. Henderson, Nov. 19, 1941; children: Robert Henderson, Jonathan George. BS, Temple U., 1934, EdM, 1937; LHD, Pa. Mil. Coll., 1949; PhD, NYU, 1955; LLD, Temple U., 1963; ScD, Chungang U., Seoul, Korea, 1969; LLD, Swarthmore Coll., 1970, Gannon U., 1981; LittD, Delaware Valley Coll., 1976; Ped D, Widener U., 1981. Instr. physics and chemistry Conshohocken (Pa.) High Sch., 1935-37; instr. sci. Freehold (N.J.)

High Sch., 1937-38; instr. physics, chemistry Memorial High Sch., Haddonfield, N.J., 1938-42; instr. electronics and radar U.S. Navy, Phila., 1942-43; assoc. prof. physics and electrical engring. Pa. Mil. Coll., Chester, Pa., 1943-45; registrar, coordinator engring. program Pa. Mil. Coll., 1945-47, dean admissions, student personnel, prof. edn., 1947-56, v.p., dean personnel services, 1956-59, pres. coll., 1959-72; pres. Widener U. (formerly PMC Colls.), 1972-81, chancellor, 1981-88, pres. emeritus, 1988—; pres. RC Assocs., Inc., 1981—; instr. electronics Temple U., 1944-46; headmaster Pa. Mil. Prep. Sch., 1945-47; bd. dirs. Fedders Corp., Ironworkers Savs. Bank. Author: numerous mag. articles. History of Pennsylvania Military College. Chmn. Pa. Commn. Ind. Colls., 1969, Found. for Ind. Colls. Pa., 1970; chmn. Com. for Financing Higher Edn. in Pa., 1975; trustee Pa. Inst. Tech.; mem. commr. Am. Assn. Homes and Avcs. for Aging, Continuing Care Accrediting Commn., 1985-95. Recipient Horatio Alger award, 1962, Disting. Alumnus award Temple U., 1964, B'nai B'rith Citizen Service award, 1966, Distinguished Citizen award, 1971, Themis award Del. County Bar, 1976, Good Citizenship award Phila. Bar, 1976, Exec. of Yr. award Soc. Advancement Mgmt., 1978. Mem. Assn. Mil. Colls. and Schs. (pres. 1969), Pa. Assn. Colls. and Univs. (pres. 1970, Sheepskin award 1982), Am. Soc. Engring. Edn., Springhaven Club (Wallingford, Pa.), Racquet Club, University Club (Wilmington, Del.), Tau Beta Pi, Phi Delta Kappa, Alpha Sigma Lambda, Phi Kappa Phi. Lutheran. Home: 1960 Dog Kennel Rd Media PA 19063-1008 Office: Widener U Pres. Office Chester PA 19013

MOLL, CURTIS E., manufacturing executive; b. 1933. Diploma, Wesleyan Coll., 1961, So. Meth. U., 1963. Chmn., CEO MTD Products Inc. Office: MTD Products Inc PO Box 368022 Cleveland OH 44136

MOLL, JOHN LEWIS, electronics engineer; b. Wauseon, Ohio, Dec. 21, 1921; s. Samuel Andrew and Esther (Studer) M.; m. Isabel Mary Sieber, Oct. 28, 1944; children: Nicolas Josef, Benjamin Alex, Diana Carolyn. B.Sc., Ohio State U., 1943, Ph.D., 1952; Dr. h.c., Faculty Engring., Katholieke U. Leuven, (Belgium), 1983. Elec. engr. RCA Labs., Lancaster, Pa., 1943-45; mem. tech. staff Bell Telephone Labs., Murray Hill, N.J., 1952-58; mem. faculty Stanford U., 1958-69, prof. elec. engring., 1959-69; tech. dir. optoelectronics Fairchild Camera and Instrument Corp., 1969-74; dir. integrated circuits labs. Hewlett-Packard Labs., Palo Alto, Calif., 1974-80; dir. IC structures research, sr. scientist Hewlett-Packard Labs., 1980-87, dir. Superconductivity Lab., 1987-90, mem. tech. staff, 1990—. Author: Physics of Semi Conductors, 1964; co-author Computer Aided Design and VLSI Device Development, 1985, rev. edit., 1988; inventor (with Ebers) first analytical transistor model, 1953, still valid and useful for circuit design. Recipient Howard N. Potts medal Franklin Inst., 1967, Disting. Alumnus award Coll. Engring., Ohio State U., 1970, Benjamin C. Lamme medal Coll. Engring., Ohio State U., 1988, Vladimir Karapetoff award Eta Kappa Nu, 1995; Guggenheim fellow, 1964. Fellow IEEE (Ebers award 1971, Thomas A. Edison medal 1991), Am. Acad. Arts and Scis.; mem. Am. Phys. Soc., Nat. Acad. Engring., Nat. Acad. Scis., N.Y. Acad. Scis. Home: 4111 Old Trace Rd Palo Alto CA 94306-3728 Office: Hewlett Packard Labs PO Box 10350 3500 Deer Creek Rd Bldg 26M Palo Alto CA 94303-0867

MOLL, JOSEPH EUGENE, chemical engineer, chemical company executive; b. Evansville, Ind., Sept. 3, 1950; s. Jacob Eugene and Mary Ann (Zenthoefer) M., m. Karen Jean Pennington, Aug. 20. 1977; children: Laura, Angela, Jared. BS in Chem. Engring., Purdue U., 1972. Cert. ofcl. USS Swimming. Mem. mfg. mgmt. staff GE, Selkirk, Danville, N.Y., Ill, 1972-74; product devel. engr. GE, Pittsfield, Mass., 1974-75; tech. specialist Betz Labs., Kokomo, Ind., 1975-78; account mgr. Betz Labs., Evansville, Ind., 1978-88; account exec. Betz Indsl., Evansville, 1988-90, area mgr., 1990—; mem. Mayor's Tech. Adv. Com., Mt. Vernon, Ind., 1983—. Instr. ARC, Evansville, 1971-73; ofcl. Ill. High Sch. Assn., Danville, 1972-73; min. of the word St. Matthew's Ch., Mt. Vernon, Ind., 1980—; amb. Promise Keepers Men's Ministry, 1994—, Sunday sch. tchr., 1996—; asst. cubmaster Boy Scouts Am., 1993—. Mem. AICE (v.p. 1971-72), Tech. Assn. of Pulp and Paper Industry, Am. Water Works Assn., Purdue Alumni Assn. (life), John Purdue Coaches Club, Elks, Omega Chi Epsilon, Triangle Fraternity. Roman CAtholic. Avocations: golf, weight tng., swimming, bible study group. Home: 28 Parkridge Dr Mount Vernon IN 47620-9405 Office: Betz Labs 3751 Pennridge Dr Ste 116 Bridgeton MO 63044

MOLL, LLOYD HENRY, banker; b. Reading, Pa., June 26, 1925; s. Lewis J. and Katie (Rothermel) M.; m. Luise G. Keiper, Oct. 25, 1947; children: Lloyd E., Darryl M. BA, Albright Coll., Reading, 1952. Aircraft engine installer War Dept., 1942-47; tire inspector Firestone Tire & Rubber Co., Pottstown, Pa., 1947-48; asst. mgr. Household Fin. Corp., Reading, 1952-57; v.p. Meridian Asset Mgmt. Inc. and Meridian Trust Co. (formerly Am. Bank & Trust Co. of Pa.), Reading, 1957-94; v.p. sales and mktg. Investors Trust Co., Wyomissing, Pa., 1995—; co-founder, past dir. Estate Planning Council of Berks County. Served with AUS, 1945-47. Mem. Am. Inst. Banking. (dir., chmn. bank relations Berks County chpt., pres. 1972-73), Toastmasters (pres. Reading club 1992), Optimists (pres. Reading club 1978-79). Democrat. Home: 213 W 39th St Crestwood Reading PA 19606 Office: Investors Trust Co 2201 Ridgewood Rd #180 Wyomissing PA 19610-1190 *Although it has been known to fail me on occasion I try to live by my understanding of the "Golden Rule". When it does fail me I'm usually able to discount such failure by recounting in my mind the many times it has been a two-way street or by convincing myself that I didn't try hard enough in this particular instance. All too often it comes to me much later that the other fellow's interpretation of the "Golden Rule" was far superior to mine. When this happens I have added to my learning. When it does not happen, it forces me to try that much harder to avoid "PERFECTION".*

MOLLARD, JOHN DOUGLAS, engineering and geology executive; b. Regina, Sask., Can., Jan. 3, 1924; s. Robert Ashton and Nellie Louisa (McIntosh) M.; m. Mary Jean Lynn, Sept. 18, 1952; children: Catherine Lynn, Jacqueline Lee, Robert Clyde Patrick. BCE, U. Sask., 1945; MSCE, Purdue U., 1947; PhD, Cornell U., 1952; LLD (hon.), U. Regina, 1995. Registered profl. engr., profl. geologist Sask., Alta. and B.C., Can. Resident constrn. engr. Sask. Dept. Hwys and Transp., 1945; grad. asst. Purdue U., West Lafayette, Ind., 1946-47; rsch. engr. sch. civil engring. Cornell U., Ithaca, N.Y., 1950-52; air surveys engr., soil and water conservation and devel. Prairie Farm Rehab. Adminstrn., Govt. of Can., 1947-50; chief, airphoto analysis and engring. geology divsn. Prairie Farm Rehab. Adminstrn., Govt. of Can., Regina, 1953-56; pres. J.D. Mollard and Assocs. Ltd., Regina, 1956—; aerial resource mapping surveys tech. adv. Colombo plan, Govts. Ceylon and Pakistan, 1954-56; advisor Shaw Royal Commn. on Nfld. Agr.; Disting. lectr. series Ea. Can. Geotech. Soc., 1969; Cross Can. disting. lectr. Can. Geotech Soc., 1993; C.J. Mackenzie Disting. Grad. Meml. lectr. Coll. Engring. U. Sask., 1994; guest lectr., vis. lectr., instr. over 50 short courses on remote sensing interpretation aerial photos and satellite imagery numerous univs., cities and provinces in Can., also Cornell U., Ithaca, N.Y., Harvard U., Cambridge, Mass., U. Calif., Berkeley, U. Wis., Madison, U. Hawaii, 1952—. Author: Landforms and Surface Materials of Canada, 7 edits.; co-author: Airphoto Interpretation and the Canadian Landscape, 1986; contbr. over 100 articles to profl. pubs. Organizer, canvasser United Appeal campaigns; former bd. dirs. Regina Symphony Orch. Recipient Engring. Achievement award Assn. Profl. Engrs. Sask., 1984, Massey medal Royal Can. Geog. Soc., 1989. Fellow ASCE, Geol. Soc. Can., Geol. Soc. Am., Am. Soc. Photogrammetry and Remote Sensing (award for contbns. airphoto interpretation and remote sensing 1979), Internat. Explorers Club; mem. Engring. Inst. Can. (Keefer medal 1948), Assn. Cons. Engrs. Can., Can. Geotech. Soc. (1st R.M. Hardy Meml. Keynote lectr. 1987, Thomas Roy award with engring. geology divsn. 1989, R.F. Legget award 1992), Regina Geotech. Soc., Geol. Soc. Sask., Can. Soc. Petroleum Engrs., Regina YMCA (former dir.), Rotary (former dir. Regina club). Mem. United Ch. of Can. Avocations: jogging, reading, golf, tennis, nature study. Home: 2960 Retallack St, Regina, SK Canada S4S 1S9 Office: JD Mollard/Assoc 810 Avord Tower, 2002 Victoria Ave, Regina, SK Canada S4P 0R7

MOLLENAUER, LINN FREDERICK, physicist; b. Washington, Pa., Jan. 6, 1937. B of Engring. Physics, Cornell U., 1959; PhD in Physics, Stanford U., 1965. Asst. prof. physics U. Calif., Berkeley, 1965-72; rsch. staff mem. Bell Labs./Lucent Techs., Holmdel, N.J., 1972—. Co-editor: (with J.C. White) Tunable Lasers, 1987. Recipient Rank prize in Photonics, 1991, Ballantine medal Franklin Inst., 1986. Fellow AAAS, IEEE, Optical Soc. Am. (R.W. Wood prize 1982), Am. Phys. Soc.; mem. NAE. Office: AT&T Bell Labs Rm 4C-306 Crawfords Corner Rd Holmdel NJ 07733

MOLLER, HANS, artist; b. Wuppertal-Barmen, Germany, Mar. 20, 1905; came to U.S., 1936, naturalized, 1944; s. Ernst and Auguste (Heer) M.; m. Helen Rosenblum, Feb. 28, 1933. Student, Art Sch., Barmen, Germany, 1919-27, Berlin Acad., 1927-28. tchr. graphic design and painting Cooper Union, N.Y.C., 1944-56. One man shows include Bonestell Gallery, N.Y.C., 1942-43, Arts Club Chgo., 1945, U. Mich., 1945, Kleeman Galleries, N.Y.C., 1945, 47, 48, 49, 50, Pen and Palette Gallery, St. Louis, 1949, Grace Borgenicht Gallery, N.Y.C., 1951, 53, 54, 56, Fine Arts Assocs., 1957, Otto Gerson Gallery, 1960, Albert Landry Gallery, N.Y.C., 1962, Midtown Gallery (now Midtown Payson Galleries), 1964, 67, 70, 73, 76, 79, 81, 84, 87, Allentown Art Mus., Pa., 1969, 80, 93, Norfolk Mus., Va., 1970, Muhlenberg Coll., Allentown, 1977, Lehigh U., 1977, Madison (Conn.) Gallery, 1987, Hobe Sound (Fla.) Gallery, 1989, Baum Sch. Art, Allentown Art Mus., 1995, Torsteu Bröhan Gallery, Düsseldorf, Germany, 1995; exhibited in group shows at Colby Coll., F.A.R. Coll., Durand-Ruel Galleries, N.Y.C., Nierendorf Gallery, N.Y.C., Pa. Acad., Phila., Chgo. Art Inst., Whitney Mus. and Met. Mus., N.Y.C., Nat. Acad. N.Y., Bklyn. Mus., Corcoran Gallery, Washington, Va. Mus. Fine Arts, Richmond, Walker Art Center, Mpls., Worcester Mus., Mass., Phila. Print Club, Nat. Inst. Arts and Letters, N.Y.C., Maine Coast Artists, Rockport, 1991, Forty Years Maine Painting, 1952-92; included in, Mass. Pepsi Cola Show, N.Y.C., 1946; represented in permanent collections NAD, N.Y.C, Pa. Acad., Phila., The Michener Found., Mus. Modern Art, N.Y.C., Bklyn. Mus., Nat. Gallery Victoria, Australia, Staedtisches Mus., Wuppertal, Fed. Republic Germany, Walker Art Center, Mpls., Yellowstone Art Center, Billings, Mont., Phillips Meml. Gallery, Washington, Whitney Mus., N.Y.C., Detroit Inst. Art, Cummer Gallery, Jacksonville, Fla., N.Y. Pub. Library, Allentown Art Mus., Princeton U., Butler Inst. Am. Art, Youngstown, Ohio, Sunrise Found., Charleston, W.Va., Portland Mus. Art, Maine, Guggenheim Mus., N.Y.C., Nat. Mus. Am. Art, Washington, Va. Mus. Fine Art, Richmond, also univ. assns., pvt. collections, retrospective exhbn., 1926-56, 1956-62, Olsen Found. at U. Bridgeport, Bennington Coll., Dartmouth Coll., Trinity Coll., Mt. Holyoke Coll., Middlebury Coll., U. Vt., Portland Sch. Art, Bates Coll., U. Maine. Recipient first purchase prize Nat. Religious Art Exhbn., 1964, Edwin Palmer Meml. prize N.A.D., 1968, 80, Samuel Finley Breese Morse medal, 1969, Murry Kupferman prize Audubon Artists, 1973, Andrew Carnegie prize N.A.D., 1974, Hibbard Meml. award, 1975, purchase prize Childe Hassam Fund, 1966, 70, 76, 1st prize and merit medal Butler Inst. Am. Art, 1978, Edwin Palmer Meml. prize Nat. Acad. N.Y., 1980, 92, Andrew Carnegie prize, 1985. Mem. NAD, Audubon Artists Inc. (Gold medal and prize 1992). Home: 2207 W Allen St Allentown PA 18104-4327

MOLLER, JACQUELINE LOUISE, elementary education educator; b. Oneida, N.Y., June 21, 1942; d. Charles and Mary Louise (Dunne) M. BS, SUNY, Oswego, 1964. Cert. tchr., N.Y. Tchr. Oneida Sch. Dist., 1964—. Recipient 1st Pl. award WCNY TV, 1993, Outstanding award, 1995, Case award for innovative teaching with telecomm. N.Y. State Pub. TV, 1992, 94; Mid. State Tchrs. Ctr. grantee, 1992, 94, 95. Mem. Oneida Tchrs. Assn. (former sec. 1966-70), Parent-Tchr-Student Assn. (life, sec.), Delta Kappa Gamma (former pres., treas.). Avocations: golf, computers, public acess television participant, reading. Home: 588 Stoneleigh Rd Oneida NY 13421-1814 Office: Willard Prior Elem Sch East Ave Oneida NY 13421

MOLLER-GUNDERSON, MARK ROBERT, minister, administrator; b. Evanston, Ill., Feb. 1, 1950; s. Robert Leroy Gunderson and Marcia Louise (Scheuvnemann) G.; m. Mary Ann Moller, Sept. 1, 1973; children: David, Maria. BS, U. Ill., 1972; MDiv, Luth. Sch. Theology, 1976. Pastor Pilgrim Luth. Ch., Portland, Oreg., 1977-82, St. Matthew Luth. Ch., Madison, Wis., 1982-87; asst. to bishop Greater Milw. SYNOD, 1988-92; exec. dir. Evang. Luth. Ch. Am., Chgo., 1992—; chaplain Fire Dept., Portland, 1978-82, Milw., 1991-92, Park Ridge, Ill., 1994—. Chair Oreg. Fair Share, 1977-82, Citizen Action, 1978-84. Avocations: sailing, biking, triathlons, cross country skiing, running. Office: Evang Lutheran Ch in Am 8765 W Higgins Rd Chicago IL 60631-4101

MOLLER-GUNDERSON, MARY ANN, clergy member, church administrator. Exec. dir. Division for Congregational Ministries of the Evangelical Lutheran Church in America, Chicago, Ill. Office: Evang Luthern Ch in Am 8765 W Higgins Rd Chicago IL 60631-4101

MOLLIGAN, PETER NICHOLAS, lawyer; b. New Orleans, Mar. 8, 1938; s. Peter Nicholas and Violet Augusta (Scheeler) M.; children: Liza J., Jessica L., Rene N. BA, La. State U., 1960; JD, San Francisco Law Sch., 1970. Bar: Calif. 1970. Claims mgr. Govt. Employees Ins. Co., San Francisco, 1963-70; trial atty., pres., CEO Molligan, Cox & Moyer, San Francisco, 1970—; pro-tem judge San Francisco Supreme Ct., 1989—. Lt. (j.g.) USN, 1960-65. Fellow Am. Coll. Trial Lawyers; mem. Am. Bd. Trial Advocates, Nat. Bd. Trial Advocates, ATLA, Calif. Trial Lawyers Assn. Avocations: tennis, chess. Office: Molligan Cox & Moyer 703 Market St San Francisco CA 94103-2102

MOLLMAN, JOHN PETER, book publisher, consultant electronic publishing; b. Belleville, Ill., Feb. 8, 1931; s. Kenneth John and Maurine (Farrow) M.; m. Jane Michael Kendall, Aug. 22, 1953; children—Sarah Chase, Eric Cleburne. B.Arts, Washington U., St. Louis, 1952. Advt. specialist Gen. Electric Co., Schenectady and Boston, 1952-54; mgr. Enterprise Printing Co., Millstadt, Ill., 1956-66; gen. mgr. Monarch Pub. Co., N.Y.C., 1966-67; dir. prodn. Harper & Row Pubs., N.Y.C., 1967-74; pub. Harper's Mag. Press, N.Y.C., 1971-74; v.p. prodn. Random House Inc., N.Y.C., 1974-81; sr. v.p. World Book-Childcraft Inc., Chgo., 1981-88; pres. World Book Pub., 1988-91; pub. cons., 1991-92; dir. intellectual property devel. Multimedia Publishing Microsoft, 1992-96; cons. in electronic pub. Kirkland, Wash., 1996—. Chmn. graphics standards rsch. com. NEH; mem. vis. com. Washington U., pub. com. Art Inst. of Chgo. With U.S. Army, 1954-56. Mem. Assn. Am. Pubs., Siwanoy Club (Bronxville, N.Y.), Sigma Delta Chi, Omicron Delta Kappa. Unitarian. Home: 4511 103rd Ln NE Kirkland WA 98033-7639

MOLLO, JOHN, film costume designer, military historian; b. London, Mar. 18, 1931; s. Eugene Simonovitch and Ella Clara (Cockell) M.; m. Margaret Ann Mollo, Apr. 4, 1956 (div. 1966); m. Louise Alexandra Mary Mollo, Aug. 12, 1968; 1 child, Thomas Frederick George. Student, Farnham Sch. Art, 1947-49. Ptnr. Hist. Rsch. Unit, London, 1964-70, Mollo Publs., London, 1970-90, John Mollo Assocs., Hungerford, Eng., 1981—. Costume designer for films Star Wars, 1977 (Academy award best costume design 1977), Alien, 1978, The Empire Strikes Back, 1978, Outland, 1980, Gandhi, 1982 (Academy award best costume design 1982), The Lords of Discipline, 1982, Greystoke, 1983, King David, 1984, Revolution, 1985, Cry Freedom, 1986, White Hunter, Black Heart, 1989, Chaplin, 1991, Rudyard Kipling's Jungle Book, 1994, others; mil. adviser The Jewel in the Crown, 1981; hist. advisor The Charge of the Light Brigade, Barry Lyndon, others; author: Military Fashion, 1972, Uniforms of the American Revolution, 1975,. Acting capt., Inf. Brit. Army, 1950-56, Hong Kong and Eng. Recipient Acad. award for Star Wars, 1978, for Gandhi, 1982, also 2 nominations, 5 nominations Brit. Acad. Film and TV Arts. Mem. Soc. for Army Hist. Rsch., Acad. Motion Picture Arts and Scis. Avocations: painting, listening to music, collecting watercolors and militaria.

MOLLO-CHRISTENSEN, ERIK LEONARD, oceanographer; b. Bergen, Norway, Jan. 10, 1923; came to U.S., 1951, naturalized, 1955; s. Axel and Helga (Holmboe) Mollo-C.; m. Johanna D. Waller, Nov. 20, 1948; children—Jan E., Peter E., Anne. S.B. in Aero. Engring, Mass. Inst. Tech., 1948, S.M., 1949, Sc.D., 1954. With Norwegian Def. Research Establishment, 1949-51, sr. sci. officer, 1951; grad. student, then research assoc. Mass. Inst. Tech., 1951-55, prof. aeronautics, 1955-84, prof. meteorology, 1964-73, prof. oceanography, 1973-84; chief oceanography divsn. NASA/Goddard Space Flight Ctr., 1983-90, assoc. dir. earth scis., 1990-91, ret., 1991; cons. to industry, from 1955. Guggenheim fellow, 1957. Fellow Am. Phys. Soc.; mem. AIAA (Von Karman award 1970), Am. Meteorol. Soc., Am. Geophys. Union., Am. Acad. Arts and Scis. Home: 10 Barberry Rd Lexington MA 02173-8026

MOLLOHAN, ALAN B., congressman, lawyer; b. Fairmont, W.Va., May 14, 1943; s. Robert H. and Helen (Holt) M.; m. Barbara Whiting, Aug. 7, 1976; children: Alan, Robert, Andrew, Karl, Mary Kathryn. AB in Polit. Sci., Coll. William and Mary, 1966; JD, W.Va. U., 1970. Assoc. law firm, 1970-82; mem. 98th-104th Congresses from 1st W.Va. dist., 1983—; mem. appropriations com., budget com. Mem. ABA, W.Va. Bar, Moose, Elks. Baptist. Office: US Ho of Reps Office of Postmaster 2427 Rayburn Ho Office Bldg Washington DC 20515

MOLLOY, BRIAN JOSEPH, lawyer; b. Jersey City, July 19, 1953; s. Joseph G. and Agnes L. (Mullaney) M.; m. Christina M. Cencek, June 14, 1975; children: Brooke Leigh, Evan Joseph. BA, Kean Coll. of N.J., 1975; JD, Seton Hall U., 1978. Bar: N.J. 1978, U.S. Dist. Ct. N.J. 1978, U.S. Ct. Appeals (3d cir.) 1987, U.S. Supreme Ct. 1987. Ptnr. Wilentz, Goldman & Spitzer P.A., Woodbridge, N.J., 1978—. Mem. ABA, N.J. Bar Assn., Middlesex County Bar Assn. Home: 31 Hawthorne Dr Westfield NJ 07090-1947 Office: Wilentz Goldman & Spitzer PO Box 10 90 Woodbridge Ctr Dr Ste 900 Woodbridge NJ 07095-1146

MOLLOY, SYLVIA, Latin American literature educator, writer; b. Buenos Aires, Argentina, Aug. 29, 1938; came to U.S. 1967; d. Herbert Edward and Margarita Berta (Chasseing) M. Licence es Lettres, U. Paris, 1960, Diplome D'Etudes Superieures, 1961, Doctorat de U. Paris, 1967. Asst. prof. Spanish SUNY, Buffalo, 1967-69; asst. prof. Spanish Vassar Coll., Poughkeepsie, N.Y., 1969-70; asst. prof. Spanish Princeton U., Princeton, N.J., 1970-73, assoc. prof., 1973-81, Emory L. Ford prof., 1981-86; prof. Spanish Yale U., New Haven, 1986-90; ALbert Schweitzer prof. of Humanities NYU, 1990—. Author: La Diffusion de la Litterature Hispanoamericaine en France, 1972, Las Letras de Borges, 1979, En Breve Carcel, 1981, At Face Value: Autobiographical Writing in Spanish America, 1991; co-author Women's Writing in Latin America, 1991; author short stories and contbr. articles to profl. jours.; cons., editorial bd. Revista Iberoamericana, 1979-81, 1985—, Latin Am. Literary Rev., 1985—, Revista de Filologia, Buenos Aires, 1985—. fellow Am. Philos. Soc., 1970, NEH, 1976; Social Sci. Research Council grantee, 1983; Guggenheim Found. fellow, 1986-87. Mem. MLA, Asociacion Internacional de Hispanistas, Instituto Internacional de Literatura Iberoamericana.

MOLNAR, ANTHONY WILLIAM, publishing and training company executive; b. Weehawken, N.J., Sept. 30, 1938; s. Anthony George Molnar and Margaret J. (Bleidorn) Saunders; m. Barbara Ann Stootkoski, Sept. 24, 1960; children: Sandra Lynn, Susan Gail, Melissa Mary. AAS, Pace Coll., 1965, BBA, 1968, MBA, 1974; advanced mgmt. program, Harvard U., 1984. Sr. acctg. supr. Abex Corp., N.Y.C., 1959-68; asst. contr. GAB Bus. Services Inc., N.Y.C., 1968-77, v.p., treas., 1974-77; contr. Macmillan Pub. Co., N.Y.C., 1977-78; with John Wiley & Sons Inc., N.Y.C., 1978-88, sr. v.p., chief fin. officer, 1986-88; pres., chief exec. officer Wilson Learning Corp., 1987-88, Your Better Self, Inc., Bedminster, N.J., 1988-91; fin. dir. Nat. Consumer Ins. Co., 1991-94; contr. Stat-A-Matrix, Inc., Edison, N.J., 1994—. With USNR, 1957-59. Mem. Fin. Execs. Inst.

MOLNAR, DONALD JOSEPH, landscape architecture educator; b. Springfield, Ill., Dec. 24, 1938; s. Joseph and Mabel Irene (Woods) M.; m. Carol Jeanette Smith, Aug. 22, 1958; children: Elaina Deanne, Amy Lynn, Holly Suzanne. BFA in Landscape Architecture, U. Ill., 1960, MFA in Landscape Architecture, 1964. Landscape architect Simonds and Simonds, Pitts., 1961-63; landscape architect campus planning U. Ill., Urbana, 1963-72; asst. dir., planner capital programs U. Ill., Urbana and Chgo., 1971-81; assoc. prof. landscape architecture Purdue U., West Lafayette, Ind., 1981-85, dir. landscape architecture coop. program, 1983—, prof. landscape architecture, 1985—, chair landscape architecture program, 1987—, dir. internat. exch. landscape architecture, 1988—; cons. to architect, engrs., park agys., 1964—, MObile Homes Mfr. Assn., Chgo., 1966-76. Author: Anatomy of a Park, 2d edit., 1986; illustrator: Anatomy of a Park, 1971, Visual Approach to Park Design, 1980; developer software CompuPave, 1992. Mem., program coord. Champaign (Ill.) Devel. Coun., 1966-78. Named Hon. Parks Commr., Champaign Park Dist., 1981. Fellow Am. Soc. Landscape Architects (licensing com. Ill. chpt. 1968-70, registration com. Ind. chpt. 1982-85, pres. 1991-92, award 1982). Avocations: travel, computers. Office: Purdue U Landscape Architecture Prog 1165 Horticulture Bldg West Lafayette IN 47907-1165

MOLNAR, LEWIS K., health facility administrator. With Continental Ill. Bank, Chgo., 1961-62; ceo Shriner's Hosp. Crippled Children, Tampa, Fla., 1962—. Office: Shriner's Hosp Crippled Children 2900 N Rocky Point Dr Tampa FL 33607-1435*

MOLNAR, THOMAS, philosophy of religion educator, author; b. Budapest, Hungary, June 26, 1921; s. Alexander and Aurelie (Blon) M. M.A. in French Lit., Université de Bruxelles, 1948, M.A. in Philosophy, 1948; Ph.D., Columbia U., 1952; PhD honoris causa, U. Mendoza (Argentina), 1986. Prof. French and world lit. Bklyn. Coll., 1957—; prof. philosophy of religion U. Budapest, 1991—; adj. prof. European intellectual history L.I. U., 1967—; guest prof. polit. philosophy Potchefstroom U., South Africa, 1969; guest prof. philosophy Hillsdale Coll., Mich., 1973-74; vis. prof. Yale U., 1983; vis. prof. philosophy U. Dijon, France, 199p; prof. philosophy of religion U. Budapest, 1991—, permanent vis. prof. philosophy of religion dept. philosophy, 1991—. Author: Bernanos, His Political Thought and Prophecy, 1960, The Future of Education, 1961, The Decline of the Intellectual, 1962, The Two Faces of American Foreign Policy, 1962, Africa, A Political Travelogue, 1965, Utopia, The Pernennial Heresy, 1967, Sartre, Ideologue of Our Time, 1968, Ecumenism or New Reformation?, 1968, The Counter-Revolution, 1969, La Gauche vue d'en facem 1970, L'Animal politique, 1974, The European Dilemna, 1974, God and the Knowledge of Reality, 1974, Le Socialisme san visage, 1976, Authority and Its Enemies, 1976, Christian Humanism, A Critique of the Secular City and Its Ideology, 1978, Le Modèle dé figure, l'Amerique de Tocqueville à Carter, 1978, Theists and Atheists, A Typology of Non-Belief, 1980, Politics and the State: A Catholic View, 1982, Le Dieu Immanent, 1982, Tiers-Monde, Idéologie Rèalitè, 1982, L'Eclipse du Sacre, 1986, The Pagan Temptation, 1987, Twin Power: Politics and the Sacred, 1988, L'Europe entre Panethèses, 1990, Philosophical Grounds, 1991, The Church, Pilgrim of Centuries, 1991, L'Amèicanologie, Le triomphe du modèle planètaire?, 1991, Az Ideális éllam kritikája, 1991, L'Hègèmonie libèrale, 1992, The Emerging Atlantic Culture, 1994, Archetypes of Thought, 1995, Return to Philosophy, 1996, La modernite et ses antidotes, 1996; also numerous articles in Am. and European scholarly jours. Relm Found. grantee for travel and study in French-speaking Africa, 1963-64, for travel in S.Am., 1966, for writing Sartre, Ideologue of Our Time, 1967; Earhart Found. grantee, 1992. Home: 238 Heights Rd Ridgewood NJ 07450-2414

MOLNAU, CAROL, state legislator; b. Sept. 17, 1949; m. Steven F. Molnau; 3 children. Attended, U. Minn. Mem. Minn. Ho. of Reps., 1992—. Active Our Saviors Luth. Ch., 4-H, Chaska City Coun. Mem. Agrl. Com., Econ. Devel., Infrastructure & Regulation Fin.-Transportation Fin. Divsn., Fin. Inst. & Ins.: Internat. Trade & Economic Devel. Republican. Home: 495 Pioneer Trl Chaska MN 55318-1151 Office: 287 State Office Bldg Saint Paul MN 55155

MOLO, STEVEN FRANCIS, lawyer; b. Chgo., June 30, 1957; s. Steven and Alice (Babinski) M.; m. Mary Wood, Dec. 31, 1986; children: Alexander, Madeline, Julia. BS, U. Ill., 1979, JD, 1982. Bar: Ill. 1982. Asst. atty. gen. Office Atty. Gen., Chgo., 1982-86; assoc. Winston & Strawn, Chgo., 1986-89, ptnr., 1989—; adj. prof. Loyola U. Law Sch., Chgo., 1988-93,. Northwestern U. Law Sch., Chgo., 1989—; mem. faculty Nat. Inst. Trial Advocacy, Chgo., 1989—. Co-author: Corporate Internal Investigations, 1993, updated annually, 1993—; bd. editors Bus. Crimes Bull: Litigation and Compliance, 1994—; contbr. articles to legal jours. Counsel Ill. Jud. Inquiry Bd., 1986-90; spl. reapportionment counsel Cook County Judiciary, 1988-89, spl. reapportionment counsel to Rep. leadership Ill. Ho. of Reps. and Senate, 1991-92. Named one of World's Leading White Collar Crime Lawyers, Euromoney PLC, 1995. Mem. ABA, FBA, Ill. Bar Assn., Chgo. Bar Assn., Theodore Roosevelt Assn., Chgo. Athletic Assn., Econ. Club Chgo., Tavern Club, Chgo. Inn of Ct. (master of bench). Office: Winston & Strawn 35 W Wacker Dr Chicago IL 60601

MOLONEY, JAY, agent. Agent Creative Artists Agy. Office: Creative Artists Agy 9830 Wilshire Blvd Beverly Hills CA 90212-1804*

MOLONEY, THOMAS E., lawyer; b. Rockville Ctr., N.Y., Jan. 9, 1949. BS, U. Dayton, 1971; JD, U. Notre Dame, 1974. Bar: Ohio 1974. Ptnr. Baker & Hostetler, Columbus, Ohio. Office: Baker & Hostetler Capital Sq 65 E State St Ste 2100 Columbus OH 43215-4213

MOLONEY, THOMAS JOSEPH, lawyer; b. Bklyn., Oct. 14, 1952; s. Thomas J. and Grace (Nelson) M.; m. Molly K. Heines, Dec. 26, 1976. AB, Columbia U., 1973; JD cum laude, NYU, 1976. Bar: N.Y. 1977, U.S. Dist. Ct. (so. dist.) N.Y. 1977, U.S. Dist. Ct. (ea. dist.) N.Y. 1978, U.S. Ct. Appeals (2d cir.) 1981. Assoc. Cleary, Gottlieb, Steen & Hamilton, N.Y.C., 1976-84, ptnr., 1984—; bd. dirs. N.Y. Lawyers for Pub. Interest, N.Y.C., 1986-91; mediator U.S. Bankruptcy Ct. for So. Dist. N.Y., 1995. Asst. counsel Gov.'s Jud. Nominating Com., N.Y.C., 1981-85; chmn. bus. adv. coun. Washington Irving H.S., 1994—. Mem. ABA, Am. Bankruptcy Inst., Assn. of Bar of City of N.Y. (bankruptcy, corp. reorganization coms. 1983-86, chair com. legal assistance), Order of Coif. Avocations: chess, golf, dance, travel, wine. Office: Cleary Gottlieb Steen & Hamilton 1 Liberty Plz New York NY 10006-1404

MOLONEY, THOMAS WALTER, consulting firm executive; b. N.Y.C., Feb. 8, 1946; s. Thomas Walter and Anne (Heney) M. BA, Colgate U., 1967; MA, Columbia U., 1970, MPH, 1973, MBA, 1975. Program dir. Nat. Ctr. for Deaf-Blind, New Hyde Park, N.Y., 1971-72; spl. asst. to dir. and dean N.Y. Hosp., N.Y.C., 1973-74; asst. v.p. Robert Wood Johnson Found., 1975-80; sr. v.p. The Commonwealth Fund, N.Y.C., 1980-92; dir. pub. policy and health programs The Inst. for Future, 1992—; vis. lectr. Princeton (N.J.) U., 1975-80; bd. dirs. Grantmakers in Health, N.Y.C., 1984—, chmn. bd., 1984-88; mem. health adv. com. GAO, 1987—; mem. health adv. coun. Johns Hopkins U. Sch., Hygiene and Pub. Health, Balt., 1989-91; bd. dirs. Found. Health Svcs. Rsch., Washington, 1985-92; mem. bd. visitors Med. Sch., U. Calif. at Davis, 1988—; mem. vis. com. Grad. Sch. Mgmt. and Urban Policy New Sch. for Social Rsch., N.Y.C., 1988-92; mem. Nat. Bd. Examiners, 1986-90; mem. sr. adv. bd. global leadership program U. Mich. Grad. Sch. Bus., Ann Arbor, 1988—; mem. pres. com. The N.Y. Acad. Scis., 1987-90; policy scholar The Eisenhower Ctr. Columbia U., N.Y.C., 1992—, Inst. Health Policy Studies U. Calif., San Francisco, 1992—. Author books; editor: New Approaches to the Medicaid Crisis, 1983; contbr. articles to profl. jours. bd. dirs. New Eng. Med. Ctr., Boston, 1982-89. Policy scholar Inst. Health Policy Studies U. Calif., San Francisco, 1992—, Eisenhower Ctr. Columbia U., 1992—. Fellow AAAS; mem. Inst. Medicine, Nat. Acad. Scis., Nat. Acad. Social Ins., N.Y. Acad. Medicine, N.Y. Acad. Scis. (pres' com. 1987-90). Home: 72 Norwood Ave Montclair NJ 07043-1935 Office: Inst for the Future Fl 8 111 5th Ave New York NY 10003

MOLONY, MICHAEL JANSSENS, JR., lawyer; b. New Orleans, Sept. 2, 1922; s. Michael Janssens and Marie (Perret) M.; m. Jane Leslie Waguespack, Oct. 21, 1951; children: Michael Janssens III (dec.), Leslie, Megan, Kevin, Sara, Brian, Ian, Duncan. JD, Tulane U., 1950. Bar: La. 1950, D.C. 1979, U.S. Dist. Ct. (ea. and mid. dists.) La. 1951, U.S. Ct. Appeals (5th cir.) 1953, U.S. Supreme Ct. 1972, U.S. Dist. Ct. (we. dist.) La. 1978, U.S. Ct. Appeals (11th and D.C. cirs.) 1981. Ptnr. Molony & Baldwin, New Orleans, 1950; assoc. Jones, Flanders, Waechter & Walker, 1951-56; ptnr. Jones, Walker, Waechter, Poitevent, Carrere & Denegre, 1956-75, Milling, Benson, Woodward, Hillyer, Pierson & Miller, 1975-91, Chaffe, McCall, Phillips, Toler & Sarpy, 1991-92, Sessions & Fishman, 1993—; instr., lectr. Med. Sch. and Univ. Coll. Tulane U., 1953-59; mem. Eisenhower Legal Com., 1952. Bd. commrs. Port of New Orleans, 1976-81, pres., 1978; mem. bd. rev. Associated Br. Pilots, 1990—; bd. dirs. La. World Expn. Inc., 1974-84; bd. dirs., exec. com. New Orleans Tourist and Conv. Commn., 1971-74, 78, chmn.; family attractions com. 1973-75; chmn. La. Gov.'s Task Force on Space Industry, 1971-73; chmn. La. Gov.'s Citizens' Adv. Com. Met. New Orleans Transp. and Planning Program, 1971-77; mem. La. Gov.'s Task Force Natural Gas Requirements, 1971-72; mem. La. Gov.'s Proaction Commn. for Higher Edn., 1995; mem. Goals Found. Coun. and ex-officio mem. Goals Found., Met. New Orleans Goals Program, 1969-72, vice chmn. ad hoc planning com. Goals Met. New Orleans, 1969-73; vice chmn. Port of New Orleans Operation Impact, 1969-70, mem. Met. Area Com., New Orleans, 1970-84; trustee, Pub. Affairs Rsch. Coun. La., 1970-73, mem. exec. com. Bus./Higher Edn. Coun., U. New Orleans, 1980-94, bd. dirs., 1980—, v.p. 1986-88, pres., 1988-90, chmn. Task Force on Pub. Higher Edn. Funding, 1990-95, chmn. legis. com., 1995—, Task Force on Edn./Econ. Devel. Alliances, 1993-95; mem. Mayor's Coun. on Internat. Trade and Econ. Devel., 1978; mem. Mayor's Transition Task Force Econ. Devel., 1994; bd. dirs. mem. exec. com. La. Partnership for Tech. and Innovation, 1989—; bd. dirs. Acad. Sacred Heart, 1975-77, Internat. House, 1985-86, U. New Orleans Found., 1991—; mem. vis. com. Loyola Sch. Bus. Adminstrn., Loyola U., New Orleans, 1981—, trustee Loyola U., 1985-91, vice chmn. bd. trustees, 1990-91; mem. Dean's Coun. Tulane U. Law Sch., 1988—, vice chmn. building com., 1991-95; bd. dirs., mem. exec. com. Internat. Trade Mart, chmn. internat. bus. com., 1983-85; World Trade Ctr.-New Orleans (bd. dirs. 1983—, mem. Port Activity com. 1985-91, transp. com. 1991-95, legis. com. 1996—, govt. affairs com. 1996—); chmn. Task Force on Internat. Banking, 1982; mem. Mayor's Task Force on Drug Abuse, 1989-90. Capt. JAGDR, USAAF, 1942-46, PTO, Recipient Leadership award AIAA, 1971, Yenni award Loyola U., New Orleans, 1979, New Orleans Times Picayune Loving Cup, 1986, First Citizen of the Learning Soc. Dean's award UNO Met. Coll, 1992; also various civic contbn. awards; co-recipient Silver Anvil award Pub. Rels. Soc. Am., 1991. Mem. ABA (labor and employment law and litigation sects., com. equal opportunity law, chmn. regional com. liaison with equal opportunity commn., office of fed. contract compliance programs), D.C. Bar Assn., Fed. Bar Assn., La. Bar Assn. (past sec.-treas., bd. govs. 1957-60, editor jour. 1957-59, sec. spl. supreme ct. com. on drafting code jud. ethics), New Orleans Bar Assn. (dir. legal aid bur. 1954, chmn. standing com. legis. 1968, vice chmn. standing com. pub. rels. 1970-71), Am. Judicature Soc., La. Law Inst. (asst. sec.-treas. 1958-70), Am. Arbitration Assn. (bd. dirs., 1995—, chmn. reg. adv. coun., chmn. reg. adv. coun. employment law, mem. spl. panel large complex arbitration/mediation cases, Whitney North Seymour Sr. award 1991), So. Inst. Mgmt. (founder), AIM, U.S. C. of C. (urban and regional affairs com. 1970-73), La. C. of C. (bd. dirs. 1963-66), New Orleans Area C. of C. (v.p. met. dean affairs 1969, past chmn. labor rels. coun., bd. dirs. 1970-78, pres.-elect 1970, pres. 1971, dir., exec. com. 1972, ex officio mem., bd. dirs. 1979—), Bienville Club, City Club, English Turn Golf and Country Club, Pickwick Club, Plimsoll Club, Serra Club, So. Yacht Club, Sigma Chi (pres. alumni chpt. 1956). Roman Catholic. Home: 3039 Hudson Pl New Orleans LA 70131-5337 Office: Sessions & Fishman 201 Saint Charles Ave New Orleans LA 70170-1000

MOLPUS, DICK H., resource management company executive; b. Philadelphia, Miss., Sept. 7, 1949; s. Richard and Frances (Blount) M.; m. Sally Nash, May 27, 1971; children—Helen Nash, Richard Gregory. BBA, U. Miss., 1971. V.p. mfg. Molpus Co., Phila., 1971-80; exec. dir. Gov's Office Fed.-State Programs, Jackson, Miss., 1980-83; sec. of state State of Miss., Jackson, 1984-96; pres. Molpus Co. and Woodlands Resource Mgmt. Group, Phila., 1996—; dir. Citizens Bank and Trust Co. Vice pres. Miss. Agr. and Forestry Mus., 1979; campaign dir., chmn. bd. United Givers Fund, Neshoba County, Miss., 1979-80; bd. dirs. Miss. PTA, 1980—; founder Parents for Pub. Schs. orgn., 1989. Recipient Friends of Children award Miss. Assn. Elem. Sch. Adminstrs., 1984, Pub. Ofcl. of Yr. award Miss. chpt. Am. Soc. for Pub. Adminstrn., 1985. Mem. Miss. Forestry Assn. (bd. dirs. 1980-87), Nat. Assn. Secs. of State (pres. 1992), Nature Conservancy (bd. dirs. Miss. chpt.), Sigma Chi, Omicron Delta Kappa, Pi Sigma Alpha (Theta Beta chpt.). Avocations: hiking, tennis, running, reading. Office: PO Box 59 Philadelphia MS 39350

MOLSON, ERIC H., beverage company executive; b. Montreal, PQ, Can., Sept. 16, 1937; s. Thomas Henry Pentland and Celia Frances (Cantlie) M.; m. Jane Mitchell, Apr. 16, 1966; 3 children. AB, Princeton U., 1959. With The Molson Cos. Ltd., Montreal, chmn. bd., 1988—. Office: The Molson Cos Ltd, 1555 Notre Dame St E, Montreal, PQ Canada H2L 2R5

MOLTZ, JAMES EDWARD, brokerage company executive; b. Williamsport, Pa., July 25, 1932; s. George N. and Margaret L. (Abell) M.; m. Barbara Vance, Sept. 8, 1956; children: George Wilson, James Clay, John Thomas. BS, Williams Coll., 1954; MBA, Wharton Sch., U. Pa., 1956. Chartered fin. analyst. Fin. analyst Cyrus J. Lawrence Inc., N.Y.C., 1957-62, rsch. dir., 1962-64, gen. ptnr., 1964-71, mng. ptnr., 1971-73; chmn., pres. C.J. Lawrence/Deutsche Bank Securities Corp., N.Y.C., 1973-95; chief investment officer Deutsche Morgan Grenfell/C.J. Lawrence Inc., 1996—. Mem. fin. com. Williams Coll.; trustee Sterling and Francine Clark Art Inst., Darien (Conn.) Libr., Williamsport (Pa.) Found., Williamsport-Lycoming Found.; elder Noroton (Conn.) Presbyn. Ch.; trustee Woods Hole Oceanographic Inst. Mem. Fin. Analysts Fedn., N.Y. Soc. Security Analysts (former dir.), Rockefeller Ctr. Club, Union League Club (N.Y.C.), Wee Burn Country Club (dir.), Windsor Club (Vero Beach). Home: 29 Indian Spring Trl Darien CT 06820-2109 Office: Deutsche Morgan Grenfell/ CJ Lawrence Inc 1290 Avenue Of The Americas New York NY 10104

MOLTZ, MARSHALL JEROME, lawyer; b. Chgo., May 22, 1930; s. Nathan and Rose (Nathanson) M.; m. Rita G., Dec. 26, 1954; m. 2d, Mary Ann, Nov. 4, 1967; children: Alan J., Michelle S. Yastrow, Marilyn F. Moltz-Hohmann, Julie A., Steven E., Rachel N. BS, Northwestern U., 1951, JD, 1954. Bar: Ill. 1954, Mo. 1954. Assoc., John B. Moser, Chgo., 1957; assoc. Goldberg, Devoe, Shadur & Mikva, Chgo., 1957-58; assoc. Lester Plotkin, Chgo., 1958-59; sole practice, Chgo., 1959-65; ptnr. Moltz & Spagat, Chgo., 1966-67; sole practice, Chgo., 1967-68; ptnr. Moltz & Wexler, Chgo., 1968-80; sole practice Chgo. 1980—; pres. Mercury Title Co.; faculty mem. profl. liab. in real estate transactions ABA Regional Inst., 1993; mem. Blue Ribbon com. Cook County Recorder of Deeds; speaker real estate law; atty. Counseling Ctr. of Lake View Mental Health Orgn., Chgo. With M.I., U.S. Army, 1955-56; ETO. Recipient Louden Wigmore prize Northwestern U. Law Sch., 1954. Mem. ABA, Am. Coll. Real Estate Lawyers, Ill. State Bar Assn., Chgo. Bar Assn. (mem. real property law com. 1958—, chmn. Torrens sub-com. 1968-75, vice chmn. real property law com. 1974-75, chmn. real property law com. 1975-76, speaker and faculty mem. various seminars 1993-96, faculty mem. residential real estate seminar, 1995, 96), VFW, Phi Alpha Delta (law fraternity). Author course outlines Ill. Inst. Continuing Legal Edn., 1972, 73; editorial bd. Northwestern U. Law Rev., 1953-54. Home: 112 Harvard Ct Glenview IL 60025-5917 Office: 77 W Washington St Ste 1620 Chicago IL 60602-2903

MOLYNEAUX, DAVID GLENN, newspaper travel editor; b. Marion, Ind., Oct. 16, 1945; s. Glenn Ingersol and Barbara Wingate (Draudt) M.; m. Ann Louise Geery, Aug. 8, 1970; children: Miles David, Rebecca Susan. BS in Econs., Miami U., Oxford, Ohio, 1967. Reporter The Plain Dealer, Cleve., 1967-75, city editor, 1976-78, assoc. editor, 1979-80, editorial page editor, 1980-82, travel editor, 1982—. Editor: 75 Years-An Informal History of Shaker Heights, 1987. Trustee Shaker Heights Pub. Libr., 1987—. With U.S. Army, 1968-70. Mem. Cleve. Press Club. Office: Plain Dealer 1801 Superior Ave E Cleveland OH 44114-2107

MOLZ, FRED JOHN, III, hydrologist, educator; b. Mays Landing, N.J., Aug. 13, 1943; s. Fred John Jr. and Viola Violet (MacDonald) M.; m. Mary Lee Clark, Dec. 17, 1966; children: Fred John IV, Stephen Joseph. BS in Physics, Drexel U., 1966, MCE, 1968; PhD in Hydrology, Stanford U., 1970. Hydraulic engr. U.S. Geol. Survey, Menlo Park, Calif., 1970; asst. prof. Auburn (Ala.) U., 1970-74, alumni asst. prof., 1974-76, alumni assoc. prof., 1976-80, asst. dean research, 1979-84, dir. Eng. exptl. sta., 1981-84, prof., 1980-84, Feagin prof., 1984-89, Huff eminent scholar, 1990-95; westinghouse disting. sci. Clemson U., 1995—; cons. Battelle N.W., Richland, Wash., 1982-83, 84-85, Argonne (Ill.) Nat. Labs., 1983-85, Electric Power Rsch. Inst., Menlo Park, Calif., 1984-85, U.S. NRC, 1991—. Author: (with others) Numerical Methods in Hydrology, 1971, Modeling Wastewater Renovation, 1981; contbr. articles to profl. jours. Recipient Disting. Faculty award Auburn U. Alumni Assn., 1987; grantee EPA, 1983, 86, 90, U.S. Dept. Edn., 1991, NSF, 1992, 94. Mem. Am. Geophys. Union (Horton award 1992), Am. Soc. Agronomy, Nat. Ground Water Assn., Am. Inst. Hydrology. Avocations: reading, travel, investing. Home: 213 Amethyst Way Seneca SC 29672 Office: Clemson U Dept of Environ Sys Engring 342 Computer Ct Anderson SC 29625

MOLZ, OTIS, oil industry executive. Chmn. Farmland Industries Inc., Kansas City, Mo., 1993—. Office: Farmland Industries Inc PO Box 7305 Kansas City MO 64116*

MOLZ, REDMOND KATHLEEN, public administration educator; b. Balt., Mar. 5, 1928; d. Joseph T. and Regina (Barry) M. B.S., Johns Hopkins U., 1949, M.A., 1950; M.A.L.S., U. Mich., 1953; D.L.S., Columbia U., 1976. Librarian I and II Enoch Pratt Free Library, Balt., 1953-56; pub. relations officer Free Library of Phila., 1958-62; editor Wilson Library Bull. H.W. Wilson Co., Bronx, N.Y., 1962-68; chief planning staff Bur. Libraries and Learning Resources U.S. Office Edn., Washington, 1968-73; prof. library sci. Sch. Library Service Columbia U., N.Y.C., 1976-80, Melvil Dewey prof., 1980-93; prof. pub. affairs Sch. Internat. and Pub. Affairs, Columbia U., N.Y.C., 1993—; cons. U.S. Nat. Commn. Libraries and Info. Sci., Washington, 1974-75, U.S. Adv. Commn. Intergovtl. Relations, Washington, 1979-80. Author: Federal Policy and Library Support, 1976 (Ralph R. Shaw award 1977), National Planning for Library Service, 1935-75, 1984, Library Planning and Policy Making: The Legacy of the Public and Private Sector, 1990, The Federal Roles in Support of Public Library Services, 1990, The Federal Roles in Support of Academic and Research Libraries, 1991; coeditor: The Metropolitan Library (anthology), 1972; author TV script Portraits in Print, 1959. Recipient Leadership Tng. award Fund for Adult Edn., 1956-57; recipient Disting. Alumnus award Sch. Library Sci. U. Mich., 1969, George Virgil Fuller award Columbia U., 1975, Johns Hopkins U. scholar, 1949-50, Horace H. Rackham fellow U. Mich., 1952-53, Columbia U. scholar, 1974-76, Tangley Oaks fellow, 1975-76; Council Library Resources Inc. Officers' grantee, 1974. Mem. ALA (councilor 1972-74, 76-80, exec. bd. 1976-80, chmn. legis. com. 1985-86), Freedom to Read Found. (dir. 1972-79, pres. 1977-79). Office: Columbia U Sch Internat & Pub Affairs New York NY 10027

MOLZ, ROBERT JOSEPH, manufacturing company executive; b. Yonkers, N.Y., Mar. 15, 1937; s. Philip and Maria Hilda (Geist) M.; m. Diane Ruth Horowitz, July 31, 1960; children—Jennifer Ann, Erica Beth. B.S., CCNY, 1960, M.A., 1966; Ph.D., N.Y. Med. Coll., 1969. Tech. services supr. E.I. DuPont de Neumours Co. Inc., Wilmington, Del., 1971-73, product mgr., 1973-75, quality assurance mgr. clin. systems div., 1976, research and devel. mgr. clin. systems div., 1976-84, asst. dir. research and devel. div. agrl. chem. dept., 1984-86, dir. departmental plans div., med. products dept., 1986-88, dir. med. scis. programs, cen. R&D, 1988-91, dir. new bus. devel., Cen. R&D, 1991-92, exec. dir. rsch. support, 1992—. Mem. Am. Chem. Soc. Roman Catholic. Home: 306 Dove Dr Newark DE 19713-1212 Office: EI DuPont de Nemours Co Inc Cen R&D Market St Wilmington DE 19801

MOLZEN, DAYTON FRANK, consulting engineering executive; b. Newton, Kans., Jan. 6, 1926; s. Walter N. and Ionia Maude (Gordon) M.; m. Margaret Jean Hanna, Aug. 13, 1949; children: George Walter, Lucena Ann. B.S., Kans. State U., 1950. Project engr. Kans. Hwy. Commn., Garden City, 1950-51; design engr. Wilson & Co., Engrs., Albuquerque and Salina, Kans., 1953-60; civil engr., pres. D.F. Molzen and Assocs., Inc., Albuquerque, 1960-74; pres. Molzen-Corbin & Assos., Albuquerque, 1974—. Served with A.C. U.S. Army, 1942-45; Served with USAF, 1951-53. Fellow Am. Cons. Engrs. Coun. (nat. bd. dirs. 1982-85, exec. dir. N.Mex. 1985-93); mem. ASCE, Cons. Engrs. Coun. (past pres.), Am. Pub. Works Assn. Clubs: Masons, Shriners, Rotary, Appaloosa Horse (past pres. N.Mex., nat. dir.). Home: 3216 Calle De Estella NW Albuquerque NM 87104-3003 Office: 2701 Miles Rd SE Albuquerque NM 87106-3228

MOMMSEN, KATHARINA, retired German language and literature educator; b. Berlin, Sept. 18, 1925; came to U.S., 1974, naturalized, 1980; d. Hermann and Anna (Johannsen) Zimmer; m. Momme Mommsen, Dec. 23, 1948. Dr.phil., U. Tübingen, 1956; Dr. habil., Berlin Free U., 1962. Collaborator Acad. Scis., Berlin, 1949-61; assoc. prof. Free U., Berlin, 1962-70; prof. German Carleton U., Ottawa, Can., 1970-74; Albert Guerard prof. lit. Stanford U., 1974-94, ret., 1995; vis. prof. U. Giessen, Tech. U. Berlin, 1965, State U. N.Y., Buffalo, 1966, U. Calif., San Diego, 1973. Author over 150 publs. on 18th-20th century German and comparative lit.; editor: Germanic Studies in America. Mem. Internat. Assn. Germanic Langs. and Lit., Goethe Soc., Schiller Soc. Home: 980 Palo Alto Ave Palo Alto CA 94301-2223

MONA, DAVID L., public relations executive; b. Mpls., May 4, 1943. BA in Journalism and Mass Communication, U. Minn, 1965. Reporter, editor Sta. WCCO-TV, 1962-65; reporter Mpls. Tribune, 1965-69; mgr. media rels. Luth. Brotherhood, 1969-70; dir. corp. communications Internat. Multifoods, 1970-78; v.p. communications The Toro Co., 1978-81; pres. David L. Mona Assocs., from 1981; chief exec. officer Mona, Meyer, McGrath & Gavin (now Shandwick USA); now mng. dir. Office: Shandwick USA Ste 500 8400 Normandale Lake Blvd Bloomington MN 55437-3889*

MONACELLI, AMIETO, professional bowler. Top money leader, top average Pro Bowlers Assn., 1990. Office: c/o Pro Bowlers Assn 1720 Merriman Rd Akron OH 44313-5252*

MONACELLI, GIANFRANCO, publishing executive; b. Milan, July 19, 1939; came to U.S., 1965; s. Rodolfo and Isabella (Paolillo) M.; m. Eugenia Hyman, Dec. 20, 1965; children: Nurit, Fausto, Alexander. Dr., U. Turin, Italy, 1963, Acad. Santa Cecilia, Italy, 1964; BS, Mannes Coll., 1967; postgrad., Columbia U., 1969. Gen. mgr. Rizzoli Internat. Bookstore, N.Y.C., 1969-72, v.p., 1972-75; exec. v.p. Rizzoli Internat., Milan, 1975-78; pres., chief exec. officer Rizzoli Internat. Publs., Inc., N.Y.C., 1975-93, Rizzoli Internat. Bookstores, Inc., N.Y.C., 1975-92, Rizzoli Editore Corp., N.Y.C., 1975-89; sr. v.p. RCS Rizzoli Corp., N.Y.C., 1989-93; pres. USITAL Ltd., N.Y.C., 1993—, The Monacelli Press, Inc., N.Y.C., 1994—; vis. com. U. Miami, Coral Gables, Fla., 1988-89. Trustee Mannes Coll., N.Y.C., 1979-81; pres. Weathersfield Music Festival, Vert., 1993—. Mem. Century Assn., Am.-Italy Soc. (pres. 1993-94).

MONACHINO, FRANCIS LEONARD, music educator. MMus, Tulane U., 1967—. With Tulane U., New Orleans, 1967—, now Dawnman prof. performing arts. Office: Tulane U Grad Sch Dept of Music New Orleans LA 70118

MONACO, ANTHONY PETER, surgery educator, medical institute administrator; b. Phila., Mar. 12, 1932; s. Donoto Charles and Rose (Consalvi) M.; m. Mary Louise Oudens, June 4, 1960; children: Anthony Peter, Marck Churchill, Christopher Donnoto, Lisa Oudens. B.A. in Chemistry, U. Pa., 1952; M.D. magna cum laude, Harvard U., 1956. Diplomate Am. Bd. Surgery, Am. Bd. Thoracic Surgery. Prof. surgery Harvard Med. Sch., Boston, 1977-95, Peter Medawar prof. transplantation surgeyr, 1995—, mem. bd. acad. advisors, 1974-83; chief transplantation div. Sears Surg. Research Lab. Boston City Hosp., 1967-73; sci. dir. Cancer Research Inst., New Eng. Deaconess Hosp., Boston, 1980—; chief div. organ transplantation Cancer Research Inst., New Eng. Deaconess Hosp., 1975—; mem. surgery study sect. NIH, 1973-77, mem. clin. sci. study sect., 1983—; mem. adv. com. endstage renal disease Bur. Quality Assurance, HEW, 1975-76; mem. merit rev. bd. immunology VA, Washington, 1977-80. Author: Biology of Tissue Transplantation, 1964; editor: Transplantation Procedures, 1970, 81; jour. Transplantation, 1969—. Trustee New Eng. Organ Bank, Boston, 1970—, chmn., 1981—; bd. dirs. Kidney Found. Mass., 1978-81; mem. Harvard Med. Sch. Alumni Council, 1979-81. Recipient nat. scholar Harvard Med. Sch., 1952-56; recipient Henry Asbury Christian award Harvard Med. Sch., 1956, Lederle Med. Faculty award Harvard Med. Sch., 1968. Mem. Transplantation Soc. (charter, v.p. 1971-74, pres. 1985, internat. pres. 1986), Am. Soc. Transplant Surgeons (charter, treas. 1982-85, pres. 1985—), Am. Surg. Assn., Soc. Univ. Surgeons, ACS (pres. Mass. chpt. 1985). Club: Harvard (Boston). Home: 25 Farlow Rd Newton MA 02158-2407 Office: Harvard Med Sch-Surgery Boston MA 02218

MONACO, JOHN J., molecular genetics research educator. Prof. U. Cin. Sch. of Medicine. Recipient Eli Lilly and Co. Rsch. award in Microbiology and Immunology, Am. Soc. Microbiology, 1995. Office: U Cin Sch of Medicine Dept Molecular Genetics 231 Bethesda Ave Cincinnati OH 45267-0524

MONAGHAN, EILEEN, artist; b. Holyoke, Mass., Nov. 22, 1911; d. Thomas F. and Mary (Doona) Monaghan; m. Frederic Whitaker. Student, Mass. Coll. Art. Represented in collections NAD, Okla. Mus. Art, Hispanic Soc., High Mus. Art, Atlanta, Norfolk museums, U. Mass., Springfield (Mass.) Mus. Fine Art, Reading (Pa.) Art Mus., Charles and Emma Frye Art Mus., Seattle, Kans. State U., Wichita, St. Lawrence U., N.Y., NAD, also in numerous pvt. collections, ann. exhbns., nat. and regional watercolor shows; author: Eileen Monaghan Whitaker Paints San Diego, 1986. Recipient Wong award Calif. Watercolor Soc., Ranger Fund purchase Nat. Acad. Design, Allied Artists Am., DeYoung Mus. show award, Soc. Western Artists award, 1st award Springville (Utah) Mus., numerous others. Mem. NAD (academician, Obrig prize, Walter Biggs Meml. award), Am. Watercolor Soc. (Silver medal, Dolphin fellow), Watercolor West Soc. (hon.), San Diego Watercolor Soc. (hon.), Providence Watercolor Club (award), Phila. Watercolor Club. Address: 1579 Alta La Jolla Dr La Jolla CA 92037-7101

MONAGHAN, MATTHEW JOHN, lawyer; b. Portland, Maine, June 14, 1961; s. Thomas Francis and Anne Marie (Perry) M.; m. Karen Ellen Hopkins, Aug. 10, 1985; children: Erin, Casey. BA, Bowdoin Coll., 1984; JD, Lewis & Clark Coll., 1987. Bar: Maine 1987, U.S. Dist. Ct. Maine, 1987, U.S. Ct. Appeals (1st cir.) 1991, U.S. Supreme Ct., 1991. Assoc. Monaghan, Leahy, Hochadel & Libby, Portland, 1987-92, ptnr., 1992—. Bd. dirs., v.p. Am. Heart Assn., Maine affil., 1993—; deacon Woodfords Congregational Ch., Portland, 1994—. Mem. Maine State Bar Assn., (co-chmn. legal edn. and admission com. 1991-95), Maine Trial Lawyers, ABA. Office: Monaghan Leahy Hochadel & Libby 95 Exchange St Portland ME 04101

MONAGHAN, THOMAS JUSTIN, prosecutor. U.S. atty. Dept. Justice, Omaha, 1993—. Office: US Attys Office PO Box 1228 Omaha NE 68101-1228

MONAGHAN, THOMAS STEPHEN, restaurant chain executive; b. Ann Arbor, Mich., Mar. 25, 1937; m. Marjorie Zybach, Aug. 25, 1962; children—Mary, Susan, Margaret, Barbara. Student, Ferris State Coll., U. Mich.; Ph.D. (hon.), Cleary Coll., 1982, Madonna Coll., 1983, Eastern Mich. U., 1984, So. Fla. U., 1985. Ptnr. Dominick's Pizza, Ypsilanti, Mich., 1960-65; pres., chmn. bd. founder Domino's Pizza, Inc., Ann Arbor, Mich., 1960—; owner Detroit Tigers, 1983-92. Author: (autobiography) Pizza Tiger. Bd. dirs. Cleary Coll., Ypsilanti, Henry Ford Hosp., Detroit, Detroit Renaissance, U. Steubinville, Ohio, St. Joseph's Hosp. Devel. Bd., Ann Arbor. Served with USMC, 1956-59. Named Entrepreneur of Yr. Harvard U. Bus. Sch., 1984, Pizzaman of Yr. Nat. Assn. Pizza Owners, 1984; recipient Golden Plate award Am. Acad. Achievement, 1984, Golden Chain award Multi Unit Franchise Svc. Orgn., 1986, Horatio Alger award, 1986, Restaurant Bus. Leadership award, 1986, Pope John Paul II Family Fidelity award 1988, Pine Mission's Knights of Charity award, 1990, Semper Fidelis award USMC, 1990. Mem. Internat. Franchise Assn. (Entrepreneur of Yr. 1986), Nat. Restaurant Assn. (Silver Plate award 1985), Mich. Restaurant Assn., Ypsilanti C. of C., U. Mich. Pres.'s Club, Ann Arbor Pres.'s Assn., Missionary Vehicle Assn. (bd. dirs.), AIA (hon.), Mich. Soc. Architects (hon.). Club: Barton Hills Country (Ann Arbor). Lodge: K.C. Avocations: collecting Frank Lloyd Wright furniture and memorabilia, classic cars. Office: Domino's Pizza Inc 30 Frank Lloyd Wright Dr Ann Arbor MI 48105-9755*

MONAHAN, DAVID EMORY, lawyer; b. San Diego, Nov. 19, 1937; s. James Stanley and Lillian (Emory) M.; m. Patricia Ann Bailey, Apr. 18, 1959 (div. 1981); children: James, Michael, Leslie. BS, Calif. Maritime Acad., 1958; LLB, Loyola U., L.A., 1966. Bar: Calif. 1966. Assoc. Gray, Cary, Ware & Freidenrich, San Diego, 1966-72; ptnr. Gray, Cary, Ware & Freidenrich (formerly Gray, Cary, Ames & Frye), San Diego, 1972—. Mem. Am. Coll. Trial Lawyers, Am. Bd. Trial Advocates (pres. San Diego chpt.), Internat. Assn. Def. Counsel, Nat. Assn. R.R. Trial Counsel. Home: 5855 La Jolla Corona Dr La Jolla CA 92037-7406 Office: Gray Cary Ware & Freidenrich 1st Interstate Pla 401 B St San Diego CA 92101-4223

MONAHAN, EDWARD CHARLES, academic administrator, marine science educator; b. Bayonne, N.J., July 25, 1936; s. Edward C. and Helen G. (Lauenstein) M.; m. Elizabeth Ann Eberhard, Aug. 27, 1960; children: Nancy Elizabeth, Carol Frances, Eilis Marie. B of Engring. Physics, Cornell U., 1959; MA, U. Tex., 1961; PhD, MIT, 1966; DSc, Nat. U. Ireland, Dublin, 1984. Rsch. asst. Woods Hole (Mass.) Oceanographic Inst., 1964-65; asst. prof. physics No. Mich. U., Marquette, 1965-68; asst. prof. oceanography Hobart and William Smith Coll., Geneva, N.Y., 1968-69; asst. prof. dept. meteorology, oceanography U. Mich., Ann Arbor, 1969-71, assoc. prof. dept. atmosphere and ocean sci., 1971-75; dir. edn. and rsch. Sea Edn. Assn., Woods Hole, 1975-76; statutory lectr. phys. oceanography U. Coll., Galway, Ireland, 1976-86; prof. marine scis. U. Conn., Avery Point, 1986—; dir. Conn. Sea Grant Coll. Program, Avery Point, 1986—. Editor: Oceanic Whitecaps and Their Role in Air-Sea Exchange Processes, 1986, Climate and Health Implications of Bubble-Mediated Sea-Air Exchange, 1989; co-editor: (with B. Jähne) Air-Water Gas Transfer, 1995; contbr. numerous articles to profl. jours. Recipient more than 115 rsch. grants, 1966—. Fellow Royal Meteorol. Soc.; mem. AAUP, Am. Geophys. Union, Am. Meteorol. Soc. (profl.), Am. Soc. Limnology and Oceanography, Acoustical Soc. Am., Internat. Assn. Theoretical and Applied Limnology, Irish Meteorology Soc., Irish Marine Sci. Assn., European Geophys. Soc., The Oceanography Soc. (life). Avocation: recreational sculling.

MONAHAN, JOHN T., law educator, psychologist; b. N.Y.C., Nov. 1, 1946; s. John Joseph and Dorothy (King) M.; m. Linda Costa, Aug. 24, 1969; children: Katherine, John. BA, SUNY, 1968; PhD, Ind. U., 1972. Asst. prof. U. Calif., Irvine, 1972-80; prof. U. Va., Charlottesville, 1980-84, Doherty prof., 1985—; dir. mental health law MacArthur Found., Chgo., 1988—. Author: Predicting Violent Behavior, 1981 (Guttmacher award 1981), Social Science in Law, 1994. Recipient Disting. Contbn. Pub. Policy award APA, Washington, 1990. Mem. APA (Isaac Ray award 1996). Home: 939 Rosser Ln Charlottesville VA 22903-1645 Office: U Va Sch Law 580 Massie Rd Charlottesville VA 22903-1789

MONAHAN, RICHARD F., lawyer; b. Walla Walla, Wash., Feb. 20, 1940; s. Donald H. and Ina L. (Applegate) M.; m. Brenda A. Titus, May 4, 1944; children: Bridie Lynn Monahan Hood, E. Casey. BS, U. Idaho, 1962, JD, 1968. Bar: Wash. 1968, U.S. Dist. Ct. Wash. 1970, U.S. Ct. Appeals 1993. Assoc. Minnick & Hayner, Walla Walla, 1969-75, ptnr., 1975; ptnr. Roach & Monahan, Walla Walla, 1976—. Pres. Walla Walla YMCA, 1988-94, Walla Walla United Way, 1984. Mem. Walla Walla County Bar Assn. (pres. 1985), AQHA (dir. 1985—), Walla Walla C. of C. (pres. 1978). Avocations: quarter horse racing, golf. Home: 1015 Bryant Walla Walla WA 99362 Office: Roach and Monahan PO Box 1815 11 S Second Walla Walla WA 99362

MONAN, JAMES DONALD, college president; b. Blasdell, N.Y., Dec. 31, 1924; s. Edward Roland and Mary Gertrude (Ward) M. AB, Woodstock Coll., 1948, PhL, 1949, STL, 1956; PhD, U. Louvain, 1959; post-doctoral research, Munich, Oxford, Paris; LHD (hon.), Le Moyne Coll., 1973, St. Joseph's Coll., 1973, New Eng. Sch. Law, 1975, Northeastern U., 1975; LLD (hon.), Harvard U., 1982, Loyola U., Chgo., 1987, Nat. U. Ireland, 1991. Prof. philosophy Le Moyne Coll., Syracuse, N.Y., 1960-68; v.p., acad. dean Le Moyne Coll., 1968-72; pres. Boston Coll., Chestnut Hill, Mass., 1972—; cons. to N.Y. Jesuit Provincial for Higher Edn., 1966-72; dir. First Nat. Bank Boston, Bank of Boston Corp. Author: The Philosophy of Knowing, 1952, A Prelude to Metaphysics, 1967, Moral Knowledge and Its Methodology in Aristotle, 1968. Chmn. edn. div. Boston United Way, 1974; chmn. steering com. of coll. pres. under phase II of ct.-ordered desegregation Boston Pub. Sch. System, 1974-76, Coun. for Aid to Edn., 1985—, The Partnership, 1984—, Sr. Thea Bowman Black Cath. Ednl. Found., 1989—, Gov.'s Internat. Trade Adv. Bd., 1992—; bd. dirs. Nat. One to One, 1991—; co-chair Greater Boston One-to-One, 1992—; trustee Le Moyne Coll., 1961-69, Fordham U., 1969-75, Boston Coll., 1972—, Canisius Coll., 1976-82, Georgetown U., 1979-84, Sta WGBH, 1972—; exec. com. Boston Higher Edn. Ptnrship, 1988—; mem. com. to Review and Implement Apostolic Constitution Ex Corde Ecclesiae, 1991—. Mem. Assn. Jesuit Colls. and Univs. (dir., chmn. exec. com. 1983-86), Assn. Ind. Colls. and Univs. Mass. (exec. com. 1988-91, chmn. 1977-78), Nat. Assn. Ind. Colls. and Univs., Harvard Bd. Overseers (com. to visit grad. sch. bus. adminstrn., 1987-93), Nat. Collegiate Athletic Assn. (pres.'s commn. 1984-88), Metaphys. Soc. Am., Jesuit Philos. Assn., Soc. Phenomenology and Existential Philosophy, Soc. Ancient Greek Philosophy. Home: Boston Coll Chestnut Hill MA 02167

MONASEE, CHARLES ARTHUR, retired healthcare foundation executive; b. Gary, Ind., Apr. 29, 1924; s. Sam Hasell and Phyllis (Kresham) M.; m. Lyra Ann Halper, Jan. 28, 1950; children—Pam, Lisa. B.S., U. Chgo., 1944. With Am. Cmty. Stores, 1955-80, pres., 1968-80; pres. Am. Community Stores Corp., Omaha, 1971-80; exec. v.p. parent co. Cullum Companies, 1976-80; group pres. Riekes Group, ALCO Standard Corp., 1980-84; pres. Health Future Found., 1984-96. Pres., bd. dirs. United Way Midlands, 1977-78; bd. dirs. Omaha Symphony Assn., 1968-94, Boys Town, 1973-79, Creighton U., Omaha, 1976—, Ctr. Human Nutrition, 1987—; past chmn. bd. Joslyn Mus.; trustee Nebr. Meth. Hosp., 1974-86, Temple Israel, Omaha; nat. trustee NCCJ, 1986-89; bd. govs. Boys Clubs Omaha, 1975—; past mem. adv. coun. U. Nebr. Med. Ctr., 1978-88; pres. Omaha Jewish Cmty. Ctr., 1972-75; active SAC Hdqs. Consultation Com., 1976-92. Lt.col. USAF, 1943-55. Decorated Bronze Star. Mem. Air Force Assn., Plaza Club. Home: 9977 Spring St Omaha NE 68124-2654

MONAT, WILLIAM ROBERT, university official; b. Biwabik, Minn., Oct. 9, 1924; s. William Stephen and Milda Aleta (Sundby) M.; m. Josephine Ann Sclafani, Sept. 9, 1951; children: Lise Ann, Kathryn, Margaret, William Michael, Eric. A.A., Virginia (Minn.) Jr. Coll., 1947; B.A. magna cum laude, U. Minn., 1949, Ph.D., 1956; postgrad., Wayne U., 1949-50. Asst. prof. Wayne U., 1954-57; exec. asst. to Gov. Mich., 1957-60; asso. prof. Pa. State U., 1960-65, prof. polit. sci., 1965-69; asso. dir. Inst. Pub. Adminstrn., 1962-69; majority budget dir. Pa. Ho. of Reps., 1968-69; prof., chmn. dept. polit. sci. No. Ill. U., De Kalb, 1969-71, provost, 1976-78, Regency prof., 1986-92; Regency prof. emeritus, 1992—; pres. No. Ill. U., De Kalb, 1978-84; chancellor Ill. Bd. Regents, 1984-86; prof., dean faculties Baruch Coll., City U. N.Y., 1971-74, v.p. acad. affairs, 1974-76; cons. USPHS, 1958, Office of Sec. Dept. Labor, 1963-64, Bur. Labor Stads., 1966, Office of Gov. Pa., 1968; bd. dirs. 1st Nat. Bank DeKalb, Castle Bancgroup, Inc., Castle Mortgage Co., Castle Finance Co. Author: Labor Goes to War, 1965, The Public Library and its Community, 1967, Politics, Poverty and Education, 1968; Editor: Public Adminstration in Era of Change, 1962; Contbr. articles to profl. jours. Mem. Gov.'s Commn. on Sci. and Tech., 1983-87; trustee Grad. Sch. Polit. Mgmt., N.Y., 1986—. With AUS, 1943-46. Recipient Outstanding Achievement award U. Minn., 1981; decorated Bronze Star medal. Mem. Am. Polit. Sci. Assn., Am. Soc. Pub. Adminstrn., Phi Beta Kappa. Home: 1605 Mayflower Dr De Kalb IL 60115-1723

MONBERG, JAY PETER, management consultant; b. N.Y.C., Aug. 19, 1935; s. Carl-Johannes and Maria Anna Sophie (Haugwitz-Hardenberg-Reventlow) Hammerich-Monberg; B.B.A., Northwestern U., 1962, M.B.A., 1968. Corp. controller Furnas Elec. Co., Batavia, Ill., 1966-67; sr. v.p., dir. Logan Mfg. Co., Chgo., 1967-72; exec. v.p. Moser Industries, Inc., Naperville, Ill., after 1972; pres., chief exec. officer, dir. Wickman Machine Tools Inc., Elk Grove Village, Ill., also sector exec. John Brown Co., Ltd., London, 1977-80; internat. mgmt. cons., 1980—. Mem. dean's council Grad. Sch. Mgmt., Northwestern U., 1973—. Fellow Inst. Dirs. of U.K., , Inst. Mktg., British Inst. Mgmt.; mem. European Planning Fedn., Inst. of Mktg., Strategic Planning Soc., Internat. Soc. Planning and Strategic Mgmt., Am. Mgmt. Pres. Assn. Scandinavian-Am. Found., Rebild Nat. Park Soc. (v.p.), Dania Soc., Danish Nat. Com. (trustee), Sheffield Hist. Soc., Danish Am. Lang. Found. (pres.), Danish-Am. C. of C. (v.p., dir.), Chgo. Council on Fgn. Relations, Chgo. Com., Internat. Trade Club of Chgo. Clubs: Execs., Mid-Am., Internat., 100 Club of Cook County, Union League (Chgo.); The Am. Club (London, Eng.), The English Speaking Union (London). Home: 5201 S Torrey Pines Dr Unit 1249 Las Vegas NV 89118 also: 1 Passage du Cedre Saint Marceau, 45100 Orleans France Office: 100 Kenilworth Rd, Coventry CV4 7AH, England also: Lerchenborgvej 1 Vanlose, Copenhagen Denmark

MONCREIFF, ROBERT P., lawyer; b. Evanston, Ill., Mar. 26, 1930; s. W. Philip and Maxine E. M.; m. Elisabeth M.; children: Anne, Philip, Jane. BA, Yale U., 1952; MA, Oxford U., Eng., 1954; LLB, Harvard U., 1957. Bar: Mass. 1957. Assoc. Palmer & Dodge, Boston, 1957-62, ptnr., 1963-95, of counsel, 1995—. City councillor, Cambridge, Mass., 1970-74. Office: Palmer & Dodge 1 Beacon St Boston MA 02108-3106

MONCRIEF, WILLIAM ALVIN, JR., oil and gas producer; b. Little Rock, Mar. 27, 1920; d. William Alvin and Elizabeth (Bright) M.; m. Deborah Beggs, Jan. 30, 1947; children: William A. III, R.W., C.B., T.O. B.S. in Petroleum Engring., U. Tex., Austin, 1942. Registered profl. engr., Tex. Ptnr. Moncrief Oil, Ft. Worth, 1945—; dir. First Republic Bank, Dallas. Regent, U. Tex. system. Served to ensign USNR, 1944-45, PTO. Named Disting. Engring. Grad. U. Tex.-Austin, 1983. Republican. Episcopalian. Clubs: Shady Oaks of Ft. Worth (pres.); Eldorado (Indian Wells, Calif.); Brookhollow (Dallas). Office: Moncrief Oil Moncrief Bldg 9th And Commerce St Fort Worth TX 76102

MONCURE, JAMES ASHBY, historian; b. Abingdon, Va., June 4, 1926; s. Walter R.D. and Harriet Ashby (Ogburn) M.; m. Jennie Bruce Belk, June 15, 1952; 1 son, James Ashby. BA, U. Richmond, 1949; MA, Columbia U., 1954-74, PhD, 1960. Mem. faculty U. Richmond, 1954-74, prof. English history, 1967-74; dean U. Richmond (Univ. Coll.), 1968-74, dir. univ. summer sch. study abroad program, 1963-70; v.p. for acad. and student affairs Elon Coll., 1974-83, prof. history, 1974-87; Pres. Richmond Experiment Internat. Living, 1957-59, Duntreath Community Assn., 1959-61, Richmond Internat. Council, 1967-69. Editor white paper on activities of Va. Gen. Assembly, 1958, 60, 62 for Va. C. of C., Research Guide to European Historical Biography, 1991, 93, 8 vols. Bd. dirs. English Speaking Union, YMCA, Experiment Internat. Living, E.R. Patterson Edn. Found. Served with inf., M.C. AUS, 1944-46, 50-51. Decorated Bronze Star medal, Combat Inf. badge; Richmond Community ambassador to Eng., 1954. Mem. Experiment Nat. Alumni Assn. (bd. dirs.), Am. Hist. Assn., Archeol. Inst. Am., Conf. Brit. Studies, Va. Social Sci. Assn., Omicron Delta Kappa, Pi Sigma Alpha, Phi Alpha Theta, Cross Keys. Baptist (chmn. bd. deacons). Home: 3336 Seven Lks West End NC 27376

MONCURE, JOHN LEWIS, lawyer; b. Houston, Nov. 4, 1930; s. Walter Raleigh Daniel and Margaret (Atkins) M.; m. Norma Steed, Dec. 29, 1954 (dec. June 1982); children—John Carter, Michael Lewis, Douglas Lee, Stuart Richard, Mary Margaret; m. Margaret Edmonston, Nov. 12, 1983. B.B.A., U. Houston, 1953; J.D., U. Tex., 1956. Bar: Tex. 1956. Assoc. Butler, Binion, Rice, Cook & Knapp, Houston, 1956-68; ptnr. Prappas, Moncure & Eidman, Houston, 1969-86, John L. Moncure and Assocs., Houston, 1987—; lectr. bus. law U. Houston, 1958-59, 68-69. Mem. sch. bd. St. Thomas Episcopal Sch., Houston, 1965-78; mem. vestry St. Thomas Episc. Ch., 1975-78. Named Distinguished Alumni Coll. Bus., U. Houston, 1968. Fellow Am. Coll. Probate Counsel; mem. Am., Tex., Houston bar assns., Assn. Christian Schs. (trustee), Coll. Bus. Alumni Assn. U. Houston (pres., dir.), U. Houston Alumni Fedn. (treas., dir.), Sigma Alpha Epsilon. Democrat. Home: 1100 Richmond Ave Apt 10 Houston TX 77006-5447 Office: 1200 River Oaks Tower 3730 Kirby Dr Houston TX 77098-3927

MONDALE, JOAN ADAMS, wife of former vice president of U.S.; b. Eugene, Oreg., Aug. 8, 1930; d. John Maxwell and Eleanor Jane (Hall) Adams; m. Walter F. Mondale, Dec. 27, 1955; children—Theodore, Eleanor Jane, William Hall. BA, Macalester Coll., 1952. Asst. slide librarian Boston Mus. Fine Arts, 1952-53; asst. in edn. Mpls. Inst. of Arts, 1953-57; weekly tour guide Nat. Gallery of Art, Washington, 1965-74; hostess Washington Whirl-A-Round, 1975-76. Author: Politics in Art, 1972. Mem. bd. govs. Women's Nat. Dem. Club; hon. chmn. Fed. Coun. on Arts and Humanities, 1978-80; bd. dirs. Associated Coun. of Arts, 1973-75, Reading Is Fundamental, Am. Craft Coun., N.Y.C., 1981-88, J.F.K. Center Performing Arts, 1981-90, Walker Art Ctr., Mpls., 1987-93, Minn. Orch., Mpls., 1988-93, St. Paul Chamber Orch., 1988-90, Northern Clay Ctr., 1988-93, St. Paul, 1988-93, Nancy Hauser Dance Co., Mpls., 1989-93, Minn. Landmarks, 1991-93; trustee Macalester Coll., 1986—. Presbyterian. Office: Unit 45004 Box 200 APO AP 96337-5004

MONDALE, THEODORE ADAMS, state senator; b. Mpls., Oct. 12, 1957; s. Walter Frederick and Joan (Adams) M.; m. Pamela Burris, June 12, 1988; children: Louis F., Amanda J., Berit C. BA in History, U. Minn., 1985; JD, William Mitchell Coll. Law, 1988. Assoc., law firm Larkin, Hoffman Daly & Lindgren, 1988-91; state senator Minn. State Senate, St. Paul, 1990—; v.p. pub. programs United HealthCare; legal counsel United HealthCare Corp., Mpls. Press aide Carter for Pres. Com., 1976; surrogate speaker Carter Reelection Com., 1979-80, Mondale for Pres. Com., 1983-84; midwest dir. Dukakis for Pres. Com., 1988. Home: 3800 France Ave S Saint Louis Park MN 55416-4912 Office: Minn Senate 226 State St Saint Paul MN 55107-1611

MONDALE, WALTER FREDERICK, former vice president of United States, diplomat, lawyer; b. Ceylon, Minn., Jan. 5, 1928; s. Theodore Sigvaard and Claribel Hope (Cowan) M.; m. Joan Adams, Dec. 27, 1955;children: Theodore, Eleanor, William. BA cum laude, U. Minn., 1951, LLB, 1956. Bar: Minn. 1956. Law clk. Minn. Supreme Ct.; pvt. practice law, 1956-60; atty. gen. State of Minn., 1960-64; U.S. senator from Minn., 1964-77, v.p. of U.S., 1977-81; mem. Nat. Security Council, 1977-81; mem. firm Winston & Strawn, 1981-87; ptnr. Dorsey & Whitney, Mpls., 1987-93; U.S. amb. to Japan Tokyo, 1993—. Author: The Accountability of Power—Toward a Responsible Presidency, 1975; mem. Minn. Law Rev. Dem. nominee for Pres. U.S., 1984. With U.S. Army, 1951-53. Mem. Minn. Law Review. Presbyterian.

MONDAVI, ROBERT GERALD, winery executive; b. Virginia, Minn., June 18, 1913; s. Cesare and Rosa (Grassi) M.; m. Marjorie Declusin, 1940 (dec.); children: Robert, Timothy, Marcia; m. Margrit Biever, 1980. BA, Stanford U., 1936. Dir. Sunny St. Helena Wine Co., St. Helena, Calif., 1937-45; v.p., gen. mgr., Charles Krug Winery, St. Helena, 1943-66; pres. Robert Mondavi Winery, Oakville, Calif., 1966-91, chmn. bd., 1991—. Office: Robert Mondavi Winery PO Box 106 Oakville CA 94562-0106*

MONDAY, JON ELLIS, music publishing company executive; b. San Jose, Calif., Oct. 6, 1947; s. John Lang Monday and Marjorie (Meinecke) Licht; m. Anna Genia Hochman, Nov. 6, 1968; 1 child, Rachel. V.p., gen. mgr. Takoma Records, L.A., 1970-79; dir. mktg. Chrysalis Records, Inc., L.A., 1979-82; v.p. product devel. Romox, Inc., Campbell, Calif., 1982-85; v.p. mgmt. info. systems Epyx, Inc., Redwood City, Calif., 1985-89; pres., co-founder MusicWriter, Inc., Los Gatos, Calif., 1989—. Producer various records including Gospel Nights, 1979, Last Chance..., 1978, A Christmas Yet to Come, 1975; co-inventor NoteStation music distribution system. Mem. Vedanta Soc. (bd. dirs.). Office: MusicWriter Inc 170 Knowles Dr Ste 203 Los Gatos CA 95030-1833

MONDESI, RAUL, professional baseball player; b. San Cristobal, Dominican Republic, Mar. 12, 1971. Grad. H.S., Dominican Republic. Outfield L.A. Dodgers, 1993—. named N.L Rookie of The Yr., Baseball Writers' Assn. Am., 1994, N.L Rookie of Yr., The Sporting News, 1994; selected to N.L. All-Star Team, 1995. Office: LA Dodgers 1000 Elysian Park Ave Los Angeles CA 90012*

MONDLIN, MARVIN, retail executive, antiquarian book dealer; b. Bklyn., July 1, 1927; s. Samuel and Thelma (Schultz) M.; m. Phyllis Grossman, Oct. 23, 1962 (div. 1968); 1 child, Gerri; m. Irene Szmulewicz, Sept. 4, 1970. Student, Cornell U., 1945; student of Aesthetic Realism, with Eli Siegel, 1945-68; student, CCNY, 1948, Bklyn. Coll., 1969-71. Ptnr. Amory Books, N.Y.C., 1953-59; clk. Strand Book Store, N.Y.C., 1951, estate book buyer, 1959-71, 74-76, sr. exec. v.p., 1976—; bus. mgr. Definition Press, N.Y.C., 1957; cataloger U. Cath. de Louvain, Belgium, 1972. Proofreader, copy editor Dover Publs., N.Y.C., 1958; editor Yearbook of Internat. Assocs., 1974. Mem. Antiquarian Booksellers Assn. Am., Appraisers Assn. Am., Bibliog. Soc. Am., Bibliog. Soc. London, Am. Photog. Hist. Soc., European Soc. History of Photography. Avocations: photography, non-silver processes lab. work, natural history, horticulture, music. Home: 889 Broadway New York NY 10003-1212 Office: Strand Book Store 828 Broadway New York NY 10003-4805

MONE, PETER JOHN, lawyer; b. Brockton, Mass., Apr. 8, 1940; s. Edward Patrick and June E. (Kelliher) M.; m. Sharon Lee Bright, Oct. 9, 1965; children: Kathleen, Peter. AB, Bowdoin Coll., 1962; JD, U. Chgo., 1965. Ptnr., Baker & McKenzie, Chgo., 1968—. Mem. Winnetka Caucus, Ill., 1984-85. Served to capt. U.S. Army, 1966-67; Vietnam. Decorated Purple Heart, Bronze Star, Air medal. Fellow Am. Coll. Trial Lawyers, Internat. Acad. Trial Lawyers; mem. Soc. Trial Lawyers, Chgo. Trial Lawyers Club, Internat. Assn. Def. Counsel, Skokie Country Club. Democrat. Roman Catholic. Avocations: photography, golf, paddle tennis, softball. Home: 1035 Sunset Rd Winnetka IL 60093-3622 Office: Baker & McKenzie 1 Prudential Plz 130 E Randolph St Chicago IL 60601

MONE, ROBERT PAUL, lawyer; b. Columbus, Ohio, July 23, 1934; s. Henry P. and Ann E. (Freedlund) M.; m. Lucille L. Willman, May 3, 1960; children: Robert, Maria, Andrew, Richard. BA, U. Dayton, 1956; JD, U. Notre Dame, 1959. Bar: Ohio 1959. Law clk.to presiding judge U.S. Dist. Ct. (no. dist.) Ohio, Cleve., 1960-62; assoc. George, Greek, King, et al, Columbus, 1962-66, ptnr., 1966-79; ptnr. McConnaughey, Stradley, et al, Columbus, 1979-81, Thompson Hine & Flory LLP, Columbus, 1981—. Cpl. U.S. Army, 1959-60. Mem. ABA, Ohio State Bar Assn., Fed. Energy Bar Assn., Columbus Bar Assn., Nat. Generation and Transmission Coop. Lawyers Assn. (1st pres.), Rotary. s. Home: 2300 Tremont Rd Columbus OH 43221-3706 Office: Thompson Hine & Flory LLP 10 W Broad St Columbus OH 43215-3418

MONEO, JOSÉ RAFAEL, architecture educator; b. Tudela, Navarra, Spain, May 9, 1937; s. Rafael and Maria Teresa (Vallés); m. Belén Feduchi; children: Belén, Teresa, Clara Matilde. Degree in architecture, Madrid, 1961, DArch, 1963; DArch (hon.), Harvard U., 1986. Postgrad. fellow Spanish Acad., Rome, 1963-65; prof. architecture Barĉelona, Spain, 1971-80, Madrid, 1981-84; prof. architecture Sch. Design, Harvard U., Cambridge, Mass., 1985—, chmn. dept. architecture, 1985—. Prin. works include Bankinter, Madrid, Logronó Hall, Merida Roman Art Mus., Atocha Sta., Madrid, Seville (Spain) Airport, Auditorium of Barcelona, Auditorium of San Sebastian, Thyssen-Bornemesza Mus., Madrid, Wellesley Coll. Davis Mus., Miro Collection Mus., Mallorca, Diagonal Bldg., Barcelona. Recipient Arnold W. Brunner Mem. prize in Architecture, Am. Acad. Arts and Letters, 1994. Office: Harvard U Dept Architecture Cambridge MA 02138

MONEY, JOHN WILLIAM, psychologist; b. Morrinsville, N.Z., July 8, 1921; came to U.S., 1947, naturalized, 1962; s. Frank and Ruth (Read) M. MA with honors, Victoria U. Coll., N.Z., 1943; postgrad., U. Pitts., 1947; PhD, Harvard U., 1952; DHL (hon.), Hofstra U., 1992. Jr. lectr. philosophy and psychology U. Otago, N.Z., 1945-47; part-time vis. lectr. Bryn Mawr Coll., Pa., 1952-53; mem. faculty Johns Hopkins U., 1951—, prof. med. psychology, 1972-86, assoc. prof. pediatrics, 1959-86, prof. emeritus med. psychology and pediatrics, 1986—; psychologist Johns Hopkins Hosp., 1955—, founder psychohormonal research unit, 1951, founding mem. gender identity com., 1966—; vis. prof. pediat. Albert Einstein Coll. Medicine, 1969, Coll. Medicine U. Nebr., 1972; vis. prof. endocrinology Harvard U., 1970; vis. prof. ob-gyn. U. Conn., 1975; Rachford lectr. Children's Hosp., Cin., 1969; bd. dirs. Sex Info. and Edn. Coun. U.S., 1965-68, Neighborhood Family Planning Ctr., 1970-82; mem. task force homosexuality NIMH, 1967-69; mem. study sect. devel. and behavioral scis. NIH, 1970-74; mem. task force on nomenclature Am. Psychiat. Assn., 1977-79, 85-87; pres. Am. Found. Gender and Genital Medicine and Sci., 1978—; mem. bd. advisors Elysium Inst., 1980—; mem. adv. bd. Internat. Coun. Sec. Edn. and Parenthood, 1981—; mem. external com. for rev. of Inst. for Sex Rsch., Ind. U., 1980; mem. sci. adv. bd. Kinsey Inst. for Rsch. in Sex, Gender and Reprodn., 1982—; hon. chmn. internat. adv. bd. Nat. Inst. Rsch. in Sex Edn., Counseling and Therapy, 1991; Kan Tongpo vis. prof. dept. psychiatry U. Hong Kong, 1994. Mem. editl. bd. numerous jours.; field editor Medicine and Law: an Internat. Jour., 1982—. Recipient Hofheimer prize Am. Psychiat. Assn., 1956, Gold medal Children's Hosp., Phila., 1966, citation Am. Urol. Assn., 1975, Harry Benjamin medal of honor Erickson Ednl. Found., 1976, Outstanding Contbn. award Md. Psychol. Assn., 1976, Lindemann lectr. pediatrics Cornell U., 1983, Bernadine Disting. lectr. U. Mo., 1985, Maurice W. Laufer Meml. lectr. Bradley Hosp. and Brown U., 1986, Disting. Scholar award Harry Benjamin Internat. Gender Dysphoria Assn., 1987, Outstanding Rsch. Accomplishments award Nat. Inst. Child Health and Human Devel., 1987, Gloria Scientae award, 1991, Lifetime Outstanding Sci. Contbn. award Internat. Cmty. Profls. for Treatment of Sex Offenders, 1991, Richard J. Cross award Robert Wood Johnson Med. Sch., 1992, Career Achievement award N.Y. Soc. Forensic Scis., 1994, Coun. of Sex Edn. and Parenthood Internat. award, 1994; named Sexologist of Yr. Polish Acad. Sex. Sci., 1988; James McKeen Cattell fellow Am. Psychol. Soc., 1993; subject of book John Money: A Tribute (E. Coleman, editor), 1991. Fellow AAAS (life), Soc. Sci. Study Sex (charter, pres. 1974-76, award 1976, Past Pres. award 1987, Kinsey award western regional chpt. 1996), Harriet Lane Alumni Soc., Nat. Inst. Rsch. Sex Edn., Counseling and Therapy (hon.); mem. APA (master lectr. 1975, Disting. Sci. award 1985), Deutsche Gesellschaft für Sexualforschung, Internat. Orgn. Study Human Devel., Soc. Pediat. Psychology, Lawson Wilkins Pediat. Endocrine Soc. (founder), Am. Assn. Sex Educators, Counselors and Therapists (hon. mem., awards 1976, 85), European Soc. Pediat. Endocrinology (corr.), Internat. Acad. Sex Rsch. (charter, award 1991), Assn. Sexologists (life), Columbian Sexol. Soc. (hon.), Internat. Soc. Psychoneuroendocrinology, N.Y. Acad. Scis., Md. Soc. Med. Rsch., Internat. Coll. Pediats., Czechoslovak Sexology Soc. (hon., mem. internat. adv. bd. 1995), New Zealand Soc. on Sexology (hon., life), Sociedad Brasileira de Sexologia (hon.), Sociedad Andaluza de Sexologia (hon.), Can. Sex Rsch. Forum (hon.), Asian Fedn. for Sexology (hon.), Assn. de Especialistas en Sexologia (hon.). Home: 2104 E Madison St Baltimore MD 21205-2337 Office: Johns Hopkins Hosp Baltimore MD 21205 *It has always been my policy to combine research with clinical care, academic teaching and public education. I have combined a lifelong interest in world travel and in research by lecturing on all continents except Antarctica.*

MONEY, MAX LEE, nursing educator, medical, surgical nurse; b. Pineville, Ky., Apr. 17, 1949; s. Arthur Lee and Laura (Hendrickson) M. ASN, Lincoln Meml. U., 1991, BSN, 1993. RN, Ky., Tenn. Staff nurse ICU Pineville Cmty. Hosp., 1991-93, med.-surg. flr. supr., 1993-94, staff nurse med.-surg., 1994—; instr. sch. nursing Lincoln Meml. U., Harrogate, Tenn., 1994—; mem. profl. adv. bd. Comprehensive Home Health, Middlesboro, Ky., 1994; in-svc. educator Pineville Cmty. Hosp., 1994. Agent coll. fair Lincoln Meml. U., 1994, organizer breast cancer awareness seminar Schenck ctr., 1994; tchr. Sunday sch. Harmony Bapt. Ch., Pineville, 1994. Recipient Bronze Good Citizenship award Nat. Soc. of Sons of Am. Revolution, 1991, Nursing Leadership award Tenn. Nurses Assn., 1991. Mem. ANA, Nat. League Nursing (adv. 1992—), Ky. Nurses Assn. (pres. satellite 6B). Avocations: tea rose gardening, swimming, gospel music. Home: RR 1 Box 53 Pineville KY 40977-9706 Office: Lincoln Meml U Sch Nursing Schenck Health Scis Ctr Harrogate TN 37752

MONEY, RUTH ROWNTREE, child development specialist, consultant; b. Brownwood, Tex.; m. Lloyd Jean Money; children: Jeffrey, Meredith, Jeannette. BA in Biology, Rice U., 1944; MA in Devel. Psychology, Calif. State U., Long Beach, 1971; BA in Early Childhood Edn., U. D.C., 1979. Rsch. psychologist Early Edn. Project, Capitol Heights, Md., 1971-73; lectr. No. Va. C.C., Anandale, 1973-74; tchr. preschs. Calif. and Va., 1979-81; dir. various preschs., Washington and Va., 1981-85; instr. guided studies Pacific Oaks Coll., Pasadena, Calif., 1986-88; cons. infant programs Resources for Infant Educarers, L.A., 1986—; founder, dir. South Bay Infant Ctr., Redondo Beach, Calif., 1988-92; instr. child devel. Harbor Coll., L.A., 1992-93; bd. dirs. Resources for Infant Educarers, 1986—; pres. bd. dirs. South Bay Infant Ctr., Redondo Beach, 1988-94, treas., 1994—. Producer (ednl. videos) Caring for Infants, 1988—. Mem. League of Women Voters, 1956—, v.p., 1972-76. Mem. Nat. Assn. for Edn. of Young Children, Assn. for Childhood Edn. Internat. Avocations: traveling, hiking. Home: 904 21st St Hermosa Beach CA 90254-3105 Office: Resource Infant Educarers 1550 Murray Cir Los Angeles CA 90026-1644

MONEYPENNY, EDWARD WILLIAM, petroleum exploration and production executive; b. Long Branch, N.J., Jan. 28, 1942; s. Edward Henry and Eleanor Kathleen (O'Hagen) M.; BS in Acctg., St. Joseph's U., 1964;

MS in Acctg. Sci., U. Ill., 1967; m. Connie Wills, Feb. 19, 1966; children—Matthew, Jonathan, Christopher. Audit mgr. Coopers & Lybrand, Phila., 1970-76; mgr. corp. acctg. Sun Co., Inc., Radnor, Pa., 1976-78; v.p. fin. adminstrn. Sun Prodn. Co., Dallas, 1978-81; v.p. fin. and CFO Oryx Energy Co. (formerly Sun Exploration & Prodn. Co.), Dallas, 1981-91; sr. v.p. fin., CFO Oryx Energy Co, Dallas, 1992-94, exec. v.p. fin., bd. dir. and CFO, 1994—; mng. gen. ptnr. Sun Energy Ptnr. L.P. Bus. adv. coun. U. Ill. Sch. Bus., 1994—. 1st lt. U.S. Army, 1967-70. CPA, Tex. Mem. AICPA, Fin. Execs. Inst., Tex. Soc. CPAs. Home: 4712 Stonehollow Way Dallas TX 75287-7524 Office: Oryx Energy Co 13155 Noel Rd Dallas TX 75240-5090

MONFILS-CLARK, MAUD ELLEN, analyst; b. Amstelveen, The Netherlands, June 7, 1955; d. Wouter William Frederic and Jeane Albertina (Verbauwen) Monfils; m. Harry Carl Clark, Nov. 26, 1983 (div. 1993). BSBA, Calif. State U., L.A., 1990. Physicians assocs. mgr. L.A. County Health Dept., L.A., 1990-92, fin. mgr., 1992-93, health planning analyst, 1993-95; contract officer Gen. Relief Health Care Program, 1995—; active Comm. Strategy Group, L.A., 1994—, Workforce Devel., L.A., 1994—; mem. staff Stragetic Planning Leadership Team, L.A., 1994—, High Desert Hosp. Strategic Planning Com., L.A., 1994—. Co-recipient Nat. Assn. Counties award, 1994, Pub. Svc. Excellence award, 1994. Avocations: gardening, needlepoint, writing, reading.

MONG, ROBERT WILLIAM, JR., publisher; b. Fremont, Ohio, Jan. 22, 1949; s. Robert William and Betty (Dwyer) M.; m. Carla Beth Sweet, July 25, 1975 (div. 1979); m. Diane Elizabeth Reischel, Jan. 23, 1988; children: Eric Robert, Elizabeth Diana. BA, Haverford (Pa.) Coll., 1971. Reporter Cin. Post, 1973-75, Capital Times, Madison, Wis., 1975-77; city editor Madison Press Connection, 1977-79; asst. city editor Dallas Morning News, 1979-80, bus. editor, 1980-81, projects editor, 1981-83, asst. mng. editor, 1983-88, dep. mng. editor, 1988-90, mng. editor, 1990-96; pub. Owensboro Messenger-Inquirer, 1996—. Mem. Am. Soc. Newspaper Editors, Newspaper Assn. Am. Office: Messenger-Inquirer PO Box 1480 1401 Frederica St Owensboro KY 42302-1480

MONGAN, AGNES, museum curator, art historian, educator; b. Somerville, Mass., 1905. B.A., Bryn Mawr Coll., 1927; spl. student, Fogg Mus., Harvard U., 1928-29; A.M., Smith Coll., 1929, L.H.D. (hon.), 1941; Litt.D. (hon.), Wheaton Coll., 1954; L.H.D. (hon.), U. Mass., 1970; D.F.A. (hon.), LaSalle Coll., 1973, Colby Coll., 1973, U. Notre Dame, 1980, Boston Coll., 1985. Research asst. Fogg Mus., Harvard U., Cambridge, Mass., 1929-37; keeper of drawings Fogg Mus., Harvard U., 1937-47, curator of drawings, 1974-75, asst. dir., 1951-64, assoc. dir., 1964-68, acting dir., 1968-69, dir., 1969-71, cons., 1972—; Martin A. Ryerson lectr. fine arts Harvard U., 1960-75; vis. dir. Timken Art Gallery, San Diego, 1971-72; Kreeger-Wolf disting. vis. prof. Northwestern U., 1976; Bingham vis. prof. U. Louisville, 1976; Waggoner vis. prof. U. Tex., Austin, 1977, vis. prof. fine arts, 1981; Samuel H. Kress prof.-in-residence Nat. Gallery Art, Washington, 1977-78; vis. prof. fine arts U. Calif.-Santa Barbara, 1979; vis. dir. Met. Mus. and Arts Ctrs., Coral Gables, Fla., 1980; Brazilian Govt. lectr., 1954; Amy Sackler Meml. lectr. Mt. Holyoke Coll., 1966-67; vis. prof. fine arts U. Tex. Austin, 1981; Baldwin lectr. Oberlin Coll., 1966; lectr. throughout U.S., Can., Japan; organized numerous exhbns.; leader, lectr. yearly tours Europe to Friends of the Fogg groups. Former mem. editorial bd. Art Bull.; mem. adv. bd. Arte Veneta, Venice; editor: Heart of Spain (Georgiana Goddard King), 1941; One Hundred Master Drawings, 1949; contbr. to exhbn. and catalogue In Pursuit of Perfection: The Art of J.-A.-D.-Ingres, 1983; contbr. catalogue In Quest of Excellence, 1983; intro. to catalogue The Fine Line, 1985, exhbn. catalogue Ingres and Delacroix, Germany and Belgium, 1986; contbr. Silverpoint Drawings in the Fogg Art Museum, 1987, Some Brief Comments on Left-Handedness for Fogg Old Master Drawings Symposium, 1987; contbr. to books in field. Trustee, mem. corp. Inst. Contemporary Art, Boston, 1940-60; a founder, v.p. Pan-Am. Soc. New Eng., 1940-62; mem. U.S. Nat. Commn. for UNESCO, 1954-57, White House Com. for Edn. in Age of Sci., 1961; trustee Chaplebrook Found.; mem. vis. com. art dept. Wheaton Coll., 1961-68; mem. vis. com. to Art Mus., Smith Coll., to 1970; mem. council for arts MIT; mem. adv. bd. Skowhegan Sch. Painting and Sculpture, 1974—; mem. exec. com. Save Venice, Council for Villa I Tatti; mem. vis. com. dept. textiles Boston Mus. Fine Arts; bd. dirs. Brit. Inst.; mem. exec. com. Somerville Hist. Soc.; vice chmn. Com. for Restoration of Italian Art. Decorated Palms d'Academie (France), cavaliere ufficiale (Italy); recipient Julius Stratton award Friends of Switzerland, 1978, Signet Soc. Medal for Achievement in the Arts Harvard U., 1986, 350th Harvard medal for Extraordinary Service, 1986, Benemerenti medal Vatican, 1987; honored by Women's Caucus for the Arts, 1987; Benjamin Franklin fellow Royal Acad. Art; Inst. Internat. Edn. grantee, 1935; Fulbright scholar, 1950. Fellow Am. Acad. Arts and Scis.; mem. Coll. Art Assn. (bd. dirs. 1949-54), Am. Assn. Art Mus. Dirs. (assoc.), Academie de Montauban, Phi Beta Kappa (hon.). Office: Fogg Museum Harvard U Art Museums Cambridge MA 02138

MONGAN, JAMES JOHN, physician, hospital administrator; b. San Francisco, Ca., Apr. 10, 1942; s. Martin and Audrey Vera (Cunningham) M.; m. Jean Trotter Holmes, Apr. 22, 1972; children—John Holmes, Sarah Holmes. Student, U. Calif., Berkeley, 1959-62; BA, Stanford U., 1963, MD, 1967. Intern Kaiser Found. Hosp., San Francisco, 1967-68; med. officer USPHS, Denver, 1968-70; profl. staff mem. U.S. Senate Fin. Com., Washington, 1970-77; dep. asst. sec. for health HEW, Washington, 1977-79; assoc. dir. human resources Domestic Policy Staff, White House, 1979-81; asst. surgeon gen. USPHS, 1979-81; exec. dir. Truman Med. Center, U. Mo., Kansas City, 1981—; dean sch. medicine U. Mo., Kansas City, 1987-96; pres., COO Mass. Gen. Hosp., 1996—; prof. medicine Kansas City Sch. Medicine U. Mo.; prof. in healthcare adminstrn. Kansas City Sch. Bus. and Pub. Adminstrn. U. Mo.; mem. health adv. com. GAO. Commr. Dept. Vets. Affairs Commn. on Future Structure of Vets. Health Care, 1990-91; mem. Pew Health Profesions Commn., Kaiser commn. on Future of Medicaid, Joint Commn. Users Adv. Group; trustee Pembroke Hills Sch., Kansas City, Mo.; bd. dirs. Midwest Rsch. Ins., Kansas City, Mo. Med. officer USPHS, 1968-70, asst. surgeon gen., 1979-81; trustee Kaiser Family Found.; chmn. Commonwealth Fund Health Adv. Com. Mem. NAS (Inst. Medicine), Am. Hosp. Assn. (trustee 1988-91), Am. Assn. Teaching Hosps. (bd. dirs. coun. teaching hosps. 1984-90). Home: 831 Westover Rd Kansas City MO 64113-1121 Office: U Mo Kansas City Sch Med 2411 Holmes St Kansas City MO 64108-2741

MONGE, JAY PARRY, lawyer; b. N.Y.C., Mar. 15, 1943; s. Joseph Paul and Dorothy Emma (Oschmann) M.; m. Julia T. Burdick, 1966 (div. 1994); children: Justin Parry, Lindsay Newton; m. Elizabeth Ann Tracy, 1994. AB, Harvard U., 1966; LLB, U. Va., 1969. Bar: Ill. 1969, N.Y. 1981. Assoc. Mayer, Brown & Platt, Chgo., 1969-75, ptnr., 1976-79; ptnr. Mayer, Brown & Platt, N.Y.C., 1980—, mng. ptnr., 1981-94. Contbr. legal commentaries Ill. Inst. Continuing Legal Edn., 1974, 78, 81, 84, 87, 93, 96. Trustee Wagner Coll., 1996—. Mem. ABA, Assn. Bar City N.Y., Chgo. Club, Onwentsia Club, Sky Club. Office: Mayer Brown & Platt 1675 Broadway New York NY 10019

MONICAL, ROBERT DUANE, consulting structural engineer; b. Morgan County, Ind., Apr. 30, 1925; s. William Blaine and Mary Elizabeth (Lang) M.; m. Carol Arnetha Dean, Aug. 10, 1947 (dec. 1979); children: Mary Christine, Stuart Dean, Dwight Lee; m. Sharon Kelly Eastwood, July 13, 1980; 1 stepson, Jeffrey David Eastwood. B.S.C.E., Purdue U., 1948, M.S.C.E., 1949. Engr. N.Y.C. R.R., Cin., 1949-51, So. Rwy., Cin., 1951; design engr. Pierce & Gruber (Cons. Engrs.), Indpls., 1952-54; founder, partner Monical & Wolverton (Cons. Engrs.), Indpls., 1954-63; founder, partner Monical Assocs., Indpls., 1963—, pres., 1975—; v.p. Zurwelle-Whittaker, Inc. (Engrs. and Land Surveyors), Miami Beach, Fla., 1975-90; Mem. Ind. Adminstrv. Bldg. Council, 1969-75; chmn., 1973-75; mem. Meridian St. Preservation Commn., 1971-75, Ind. State Bd. of Registration for Profl. Engrs. and Land Surveyors, 1976-84, chmn., 1979, 83. Served with USNR, 1943-46, USAR, 1948-53. Mem. ASCE (Outstanding Civil Engr. award Ind. sect. 1987), Cons. Engrs. Ind. (pres. 1969, Cons. Recognition award 1986), Am. Cons. Engrs. Council (pres. 1978-79), Ind. Soc. Profl. Engrs. (Engr. of Yr. 1980), Nat. Soc. Profl. Engrs., Prestressed Concrete Inst., Am. Concrete Inst., Post-Tensioning Inst., Am. Inst. Steel Constrn., Am. Arbitration Assn., Indpls. Sci. and Engring. Found. (pres. 1992-93), Am. Legion, Lions, Masons, Shriners. Mem. Christian Ch. Home and Office: 14238 Skipper Ct Carmel IN 46033-8715

MONIS, ANTONIO, JR. (TONY MONIS), electric industry executive. P-res. Consolidated Electrical Distributors, Thousand Oaks, Calif. Office: Consolidated Electrical Distrs 31356 Via Colinas Thousand Oaks CA 91362-3915*

MONISMITH, CARL LEROY, civil engineering educator; b. Harrisburg, Pa., Oct. 23, 1926; s. Carl Samuel and Camilla Frances (Geidt) M. BSCE, U. Calif., Berkeley, 1950, MSCE, 1954. Registered Civil Engr., Calif. From instr. to prof. of civil engring. dept. civil engring. U. Calif., Berkeley, 1951—, chmn. dept. civil engring., 1974-79, Robert Horonjeff prof. civil engring., 1986—; cons. Chevron Rsch. Co., Richmond, Calif., 1957-93, U.S. Army CE Waterways Expt. Sta., Vicksburg, Miss., 1968—, B.A. Vallerga, Inc., Oakland, Calif., 1980—, ARE, Austin, Tex. and Scotts Valley, Calif., 1978-92; cons. Bechtel Corp., San Francisco, 1982-86. Contbr. numerous articles to profl. jours. Served to 2d lt. U.S. Army Corps Engrs., 1945-47. Recipient Rupert Myers medal U. NSW, 1976; named Henry M. Shaw Lectr. in Civil Engring., N.C. State U., 1993; sr. scholar Fulbright Found., U. NSW, 1971. Fellow ASCE (hon. mem., pres. San Francisco sect. 1979-80, ednl. activities com. 1989-91, State of Art award 1977, James Laurie prize 1988), AAAS, NAE; mem. ASTM, Assn. Asphalt Paving Technologies (hon., pres. 1968, W.J. Emmons award 1961, 65, 85), Transp. Rsch. Bd. (assoc., chmn. pavement design sect. 1973-79, K.B. Woods award 1972, 1st disting. lectureship 1992, Roy W. Crum award 1995), Am. Soc. Engring. Edn., Internat. Soc. for Asphalt Pavements (chmn. bd. dirs. 1988-90), Asphalt Inst. (roll of honor 1990), Sigma Xi, Tau Beta Pi, Xi Epsilon. Avocations: swimming, stamp collecting. Office: U Calif Dept Civil Engring 115 McLaughlin Hall Berkeley CA 94720

MONIZ, ERNEST JEFFREY, physics educator; b. Fall River, Mass., Dec. 22, 1944; s. Ernest Perry and Georgina (Pavao) M.; m. Naomi Hoki, June 9, 1973; 1 child, Katya. B.S., Boston Coll., 1966; Ph.D., Stanford U., 1971. Prof. physics MIT, Cambridge, Mass., 1973—; dir. Bates Linear Accelerator Ctr. MIT, Middleton, Mass., 1983-91, head physics dept., 1991-95; assoc. dir. for sci. Office of Sci. and Tech., Exec. Office of the Pres., MIT, 1995—; cons. Los Alamos Nat. Lab., 1975-95; assoc. dir. for sci. Office of Sci. and Technology Policy, Exec. Office of the Pres. Contbr. numerous articles to profl. jours. Office: Old Executive Office Blgd Washington DC 20502

MONK, ALBERT C., III, manufacturing executive; b. 1939. With A.C. Monk & Co., 1961—; pres., CEO Monk & Austin (named changed to Dimon International), Farmville, N.C., 1990—. Office: Dimon International 1200 W Marlboro Rd Farmville NC 27828-2304*

MONK, ALLAN JAMES, baritone; b. Mission City, B.C., Can., Aug. 19, 1942; m. Marlene Folk; 3 children. Student, Elgar Higgin and Boris Goldovsky. Operatic debut in Old Maid and the Thief San Francisco, 1967; joined touring co., later main co. San Francisco Opera; appeared with Tulsa Opera, Pitts. Opera, Edmonton Opera, Vancouver Opera, So. Alta. Opera, Chgo. Opera, Balt. Opera, Miami Opera, Colo. Opera, Mont real Opera, Hawaii Opera Theatre, Port'and Opera.;, 1976. Met. Opera debut as Schaunard in La Boheme, 1976, sang title role in Wozzeck, Wolfram in Tannheuser, Dr. Malatesta in Don Pasquale, Rodrigo in Don Carlo, Sharpless in Madame Butterfly, Herald in Lohengrin; sang with Can. Opera Co. as Abelard in Heloise and Abelard, Macbeth, Rigoletto, Belcore in L'Elisir D'Amoure, Jago in Otello, as Ford in Falstaff, four villains in Les Contes d'Hoffman; with Nat. Arts Ctr. Opera Festival, Ottawa, Ont., Can., title role in Don Giovanni, Almaviva in Le Nozze Di Figaro, gulielmo in Cossi Fan Tutti, Tomsky in Pique Dame, Marcello in La Boheme; Carnegie Hall debut as Vladislav in Dalibor, 1977; European debut as Wozzeck, 1980; solo recitalist; toured with Nat. Arts Ctr. Orch. in USSR, Poland, Italy, 1973; movie debut as Baron Douphol in La Traviata, 1983. Named Artist of Yr. Can. Music Council, 1983, laureat Order of Can., 1985. Office: 97 Woodpark Close SW, Calgary, AB Canada T2W 6HI

MONK, ART, football player; b. White Plains, N.Y., Dec. 5, 1957. Student, Syracuse U. With Washington Redskins, 1980-94, N.Y. Jets, 1994-95. Named to Pro Bowl team, 1984-86, Sporting News All-Pro team, 1984, 85. Set record for most consecutive games with a reception (178), 1994; holds record for most career receptions.

MONK, DEBRA, actress. Stage appearances include (Broadway) Company, Nick & Nora, Prelude to a Kiss, Pump Boys and Dinettes (also co-author), Redwood Curtain (Tony award featured actress in play 1993), Picnic (Tony nomination featured actress 1994), (off-Broadway) Death Defying Acts, 3 Hotels (Helen Hayes award leading actress 1994), Assassins, Man in His Underwear, The Innocent's Crusade, Molieère in Spite of Himself, Oil City Symphony (co-author, Drama Desk award Best Ensemble 1988); TV appearances include NYPD Blue, Women and Wallace, The Becky Bell Story, Law and Order, Redwood Curtain; film appearances include Mrs. Winterbourne, 1996, Substance of Fire, 1996, Prelude to a Kiss, for Love or Money, 1993, Fearless, 1993, Quiz Show, 1993, Jeffery, 1994, The Bridges of Madison County, 1994, Bed of Roses, 1996, Reckless, 1995. Office: Gage Group 315 W 57th St Apt 4H New York NY 10019-3147

MONK, DIANA CHARLA, artist, stable owner; b. Visalia, Calif., Feb. 25, 1927; d. Charles Edward and Viola Genevieve (Shea) Williams; m. James Alfred Monk, Aug. 11, 1951; children: Kiloran, Sydney, Geoffrey, Anne, Eric. Student, U. Pacific, 1946-47, Sacramento Coll., 1947-48, Calif. Coll. Fine Arts, San Francisco, 1948-51, Calif. Coll. Arts & Crafts, Oakland, 1972. Art tchr. Mt. Diablo Sch. Dist., Concord, Calif., 1958-63; pvt. art tchr. Lafayette, Calif., 1963-70; gallery dir. Jason Aver Gallery, San Francisco, 1970-72; owner, mgr. Monk & Lee Assocs., Lafayette, 1973-80; stable owner, mgr. Longacre Tng. Stables, Santa Rosa, Calif., 1989—. One-person shows include John F. Kennedy U., Orinda, Calif., Civic Arts Gallery, Walnut Creek, Calif., Vallery Art Gallery, Walnut Creek, Sea Ranch Gallery, Gualala, Calif., Jason Aver Gallery, San Francisco; exhibited in group shows at Oakland (Calif.) Art Mus., Crocker Nat. Art Gallery, Sacramento, Le Salon des Nations, Paris. Chair bd. dirs. Walnut Creek (Calif.) Civic Arts, 1972-74, advisor to dir., 1968-72; exhibit chmn. Valley Art Gallery, Walnut Creek, 1977-78; juror Women's Art Show, Walnut Creek, 1970, Oakland Calif. Art. Home and Office: Longacre Tng Stables 1702 Willowside Rd Santa Rosa CA 95401-3922

MONK, MEREDITH JANE, artistic director, composer, choreographer, film maker, director; b. N.Y.C., Nov. 20, 1942; d. Theodore G. and Audrey Lois (Zellman) M. BA, Sarah Lawrence Coll., 1964; ArtsD (hon.), Bard Coll., 1988, U. of the Arts, 1989. Artistic dir., founder House Found. for Arts, N.Y.C., 1968—. Prin. works include Vessel, 1971, Quarry, 1976, Turtle Dreams, 1983, Recent Ruins, 1979, The Games, 1983, Book of Days, 1988, Facing North, 1990, Atlas, 1991, Three Heavens and Hells, 1992, Volcano Songs, 1994, American Archeology, 1994. Guggenheim fellow, 1972, 86, Norton Stevens fellow, 1993-94; Recipient Obie award Village Voice, 1972, 76, 85, Creative Arts award Brendeis U., 1974, Deitches Kritiker Preis for best record, 1981, 86, Bessie award N.Y. Dance and Performance awards, 1985, Nat. Music Theatre award, 1986, Dance Mag. award, 1992, John D. and Catherine T. MacArthur award, 1995, 1st Sarah Lawrence Alumna Achievement award, 1995, Samuel Scripps award, 1996. Fellow MacDowell Colony (Sigma Phi Omega award 1987); mem. ASCAP. Office: House Found for Arts 131 Varick St New York NY 10013-1410

MONK, NANCY DINA, artist, educator; b. Mpls., Aug. 1, 1951; d. Dale Bertram and Jean Ellen (Groettum) M. BFA, Colo. State U., 1973; MFA, U. Minn., 1976. Instr. Pasadena (Calif.) City Coll., 1989-95. One-woman shows include U. Calif., Irvine, 1981, Koplin Gallery, L.A., 1982, L.A. Jr. Arts Ctr., L.A., 1984, Polytechnic Sch., Pasadena, 1990, Gosdick-Nelson Gallery, Alfred, N.Y., 1991, Robert Lehman Gallery, Bklyn., 1993, Claremont (Calif.) Grad. Sch. East Gallery, 1993, Jan Kesner Gallery, L.A., 1996; exhibited in group shows at Mpls. Inst. Arts, 1977, Corning (N.Y.) Glass Mus., 1979, L.A. Mcpl. Art Gallery, 1979, Mandell Gallery, L.A., 1980, Baxter Gallery, Pasadena, 1981, Spark Gallery, Denver, 1982, Reria Internat. de Ceramica Vidrio, Valencia, Spain, 1982, Limbo Gallery, Southampton, N.Y., 1985, Moderne Internat. Glaskunsi, Ebeltoft, Denmark, 1986, Heller Gallery, N.Y.C., 1987, Long Beach (Calif.) Art Mus., 1988, Gallery Functional Art, Santa Monica, Calif., 1989, Kavesh Gallery, Ketchum, Idaho, 1990, L.A. C. of C., 1992, Armory Ctr. for Arts, Pasadena, 1993, Hunsaker/Schlesinger, L.A., 1995, others. NEA grantee, 1986, 90, City of PAsadena Arts grantee, 1992.

MONK, RICHARD FRANCIS, air force officer, health care administrator; b. Washington, Feb. 9, 1947; s. Leslie G. and Doris Coleman (White) M.; m. Rhonda Lee Wise, Mar. 24, 1978; children: Ryan Michael, Robyn Lynn. BA in Chemistry, N.C. Wesleyan Coll., 1969; postgrad., Med. Coll. Va., 1969-72; MS, Trinity U., San Antonio, 1975. Assoc. adminstr. French Hosp., San Francisco, 1977-78; adminstr. Mono Gen. Hosp., Bridgeport, Calif., 1978-79, Polk Cmty. Hosp., Dallas, Oreg., 1979-80, San Cruval, Green Valley, Ariz., 1980; commd. officer USAF, 1981, advanced through grades to maj., 1991; CFO, March Regional Hosp., Riverside, Calif., 1981-85; asst. prof. Uniformed Svcs. U. Health Scis., Bethesda, Md., 1985-88; squadron comdr. 15th Med. Group, Honolulu, 1988-91; hosp. comdr. Homestead AFB, Homestead, Fla., 1992; assoc. adminstr. 355th Med. Group, Tucson, 1992-94; ops. officer 355th Med. Support Squadron, Tucson, 1994-95. 1st counselor LDS Ch., Tucson, 1994-95. Fellow Am. Coll. Health Care Execs.; mem. Internat. Brotherhood Magicians (v.p. ring 172). Libertarian. Avocations: magic, hiking, weight training. Home: 14239 Butlers Bridge San Antonio TX 78232-5490 Office: HQ Fifth US Army SGSO Attn AFKB-MD Fort Sam Houston TX 78234

MONK, RICHARD HUNLEY, JR., textile company executive; b. Anniston, Ala., Aug. 25, 1939; s. Richard Hunley and Marjorie Louise (Schneider) M.; m. H. Ann McDougald, June 24, 1961; children: Jennifer L. Borden, Richard H. III. AB, Emory U., 1961, LLB, 1963. Pvt. legal practice Atlanta, 1963-65; legal counsel WestPoint Pepperell, West Point, Ga., 1965-74, asst. sec., 1967-70, sec., 1970-83, v.p., 1973-90, gen. counsel, 1977-83, pres. internat. div., 1983-90; exec. v.p. Avondale Mills, Inc., Sylacauga, Ala., 1990, pres., COO, 1990-94, pres., 1990-95, bd. dirs., 1990-95, chief adminstrv. officer, sec., 1994-95; former mem. bd. dirs. First Nat. Bank and First Nat. Bankshares, West Point, Lantor Internat., Manchester, Eng., chmn. Arthur Sanderson & Sons Ltd., Uxbridge, Eng., 1985-90; sec. West Point-Pepperell Found., 1971-83, vice chmn., 1976-83. Bd. dirs. Chattahoochee-Lee Jr. Achievement, Lanett, Ala., 1978-82; commr. West Point Housing Authority, 1968-74; trustee Chattahoochee Valley Ednl. Found., 1969-86, v.p., 1980-81, pres., 1981-83; past pres. Chattahoochee Valley Hist. Soc.,West Point; mem. exec. bd. G.H. Lanier coun. Boy Scouts Am., 1981-88, fin. chmn., 1981-83, v.p., 1982-83, pres., 1983-85; Chmn. Sylacauga Remembers Committee(World War II 50th Anniversary Commemoration) 1992-95; mem. bd. visitors Presbyn. coll., Clinton, S.C., 1981-84, vice chmn. bd. visitors, 1982-83, chmn. bd. visitors, 1983-84; trustee Presbyn. Coll., 1987—; bd. dirs. Valley United Fund, West Point, 1967-73, 76-81, v.p., 1977-78, pres., 1978-79; Sylacauga City Sch. Fedn., 1992—, Coosa Valley Med. Ctr. Fedn., 1992—; chmn. Sylacauga Remembers com., 1992-95; fin. chmn. Troup County YMCA of Ga., 1983-90. Mem. ABA, Ga. Textile Mfrs. Assn. (bd. dirs. 1977-80, 81-83, 86-88, treas. 1983-84, v.p. 1984-85, pres. 1985-86), Am. Textile Mfrs. Inst., Soc. Internat. Bus. Fellows, State Bar Ga. (sec. antitrust sect. 1970-72, vice chmn. 1972-73, chmn. 1973-74, co-chmn. corp. counsel com. 1981-82, ex-officio dir. 1988—), Sylacauga C. of C. (bd. dirs. 1995—), Am. Yarn Spinners Assn. (2nd v.p. 1991-92, 1st. v.p. 1992-93, pres. 1993-94, bd. dirs. 1991-94), Coosa Valley Country Club (Sylacauga, Ala.).

MONMONIER, MARK, geographer, graphics educator; b. Balt., Feb. 2, 1943; s. John Carroll and Martha Elizabeth (Mason) M.; m. Margaret Janet Kollner, Sept. 4, 1965; 1 child, Jo Kerry. BA, Johns Hopkins U., 1964; MS, Pa. State U., 1967, PhD, 1969. Asst. prof. U. Rhode Island, Kingston, 1969-70, SUNY, Albany, 1970-73; assoc. prof Syracuse U., N.Y., 1973-79, prof., 1979—; cons. N.Y. State, Albany, 1974-93, Nat. Geog. Soc., 1987, Microsoft Corp., 1993—; rsch. geographer U.S. Geol. Survey, Reston, Va., 1979-84; dep. dir. N.Y. Ctr. for Geographic Info. and Analysis, 1989-90; Robinson vis. fellow George Mason U., 1985; Ida Beam Disting. vis. prof. U. Iowa, 1985; mem. adv. bd. GIS Law and Policy Inst. Author: Maps, Distortion and Meaning, 1977, Computer-assisted Cartography, 1982, Technological Transition in Cartography, 1985, Maps with the News, 1989, How to Lie with Maps, 1991, 2d edit. 1996, Mapping It Out, 1993, Drawing the Line, 1995; co-author: The Study of Population: Elements, Patterns, Processes, 1982, Map Appreciation, 1988; editor: The American Cartographer, Falls Church, Va., 1977-82; assoc. editor mapping Scis. and Remote Sensing, 1987—; contbg. editor Cartographica, 1984—. Statistician, Police Dept, Syracuse, 1978-80. Fellow John Simon Guggenheim Meml. Found., 1984; recipient Chancellor's citation for Disting. Acad. Achievement, 1993. Mem. Assn. Am. Geographers, Am. Cartographic Assn. (pres. 1983-84), Authors Guild, Can. Cartographic Assn., N.Am. Cartographic Info. Soc., Pa. Acad. Sci. (editl. bd. 1979—), Philip Lee Phillips Soc., Soc. for History of Technology, Sigma Xi, Pi Tau Sigma, Tau Beta Pi. Roman Catholic. Home: 302 Waldorf Pky Syracuse NY 13224-2240 Office: Syracuse U Dept Of Geography Syracuse NY 13244

MONNIG, DONNA SUE, librarian; b. Cin., Mar. 28, 1944; d. Richard Kirker and Rose June (Kinning) Stoms; m. William Bernard Monnig, July 8, 1967; children: Aaron William, Thomas Richard. BA, U. Cin., 1966; MA, Rosary Coll., 1970. Tchr. Finneytown (Ohio) H.S., 1966-69; head lit. dept. Pub. Libr. of Cin. and Hamilton County, 1970—, ref. libr., 1970-83, dept. head, 1983—, chair book selection policy com., 1993-94. Pres. Hope Cottage Guild, Covington, Ky., 1978; sec. Literacy Network of Greater Cin., 1990, mem. awards com., 1992-93. Mem. Ohioana Libr. Assn., Beta Phi Mu. Republican. Roman Catholic. Office: Pub Libr Cin & Hamilton Co Lit Dept 800 Vine St Cincinnati OH 45202-2009

MONRAD, ERNEST EJNER, trust company executive; b. Little Falls, N.Y., May 30, 1930; s. Karl J. and Augusta (Olsen) M.; m. Elizabeth Ann Haffenreffer, June 15, 1951; children: Ernest Scott, Elizabeth, Bruce H. AB in Econs, Harvard U., 1951; LLB, U. Va., 1956. Bar: Mass. 1956. Asso. firm Herrick & Smith, Boston, 1956-59; treas. H.P. Nichols, Inc., Boston, 1960-64; v.p. Alsace Corp., Boston, 1964-67; trustee Northeast Investors Trust, Boston, 1960-69, chmn. trustees, 1969—; v.p., bd. dirs., clk. Furman Lumber Co., Inc., Boston, 1971—; trustee, corporator Boston 5 Cent Savs. Bank, 1972—, mem. bd. investment, 1976—; trustee Century Shares Trust, 1976—, Ostrander High Income Res. fund, 1988-90; bd. dirs. New Am. High Income Fund, Inc. Trustee Simmons Coll., acting chmn., 1991-92; trustee Harvard Coll. Fund, chmn., 1987-89; pres. bd. trustees Fessenden Sch., West Newton, Mass., 1971-78; mem. com. on univ. resources Harvard U., 1978; corporator Mass. Gen. Hosp., Boston, 1980-90; bd. overseer Mus. Fine Arts, 1990—; commr. trust fund Town of Weston, Mass., 1975. 2d lt. U.S. Army, 1951-53. Mem. Boston Security Analysts Soc. (dir. 1973-75). Home: 91 Dean Rd Weston MA 02193-2709 Office: Northeast Investors Trust 50 Congress St Boston MA 02109-4002

MONROE, BROOKS, investment banker; b. Greenville, S.C., July 24, 1925; s. Clarence Jenningsand Edith Cabot (Johnson) M.; m. Hilda Marie Meredith, June 30, 1956. B.S. in Commerce, U. Va., 1948, J.D., 1951; grad., Inst. Investment Banking, U. Pa., 1959. Dir. pub. relations Scott, Horner & Co., Lynchburg, Va., 1951-53; sales mgr. Scott, Horner & Co., Richmond, Va., 1953-56; v.p., gen. sales mgr. Scott, Horner & Co., Lynchburg, 1956-59; sales mgr. nat. and underwriting Francis I. duPont & Co., N.Y.C., 1959-61; gen. partner Francis I. duPont & Co., 1961-66, Paine, Webber, Jackson & Curtis, N.Y.C., 1966-69; pres., chief exec. officer Brooks Monroe & Co., Inc., N.Y.C., 1969—; chmn. HHM Corp., Wilmington and Beverly Hills, Calif., 1969—, Bargeland Corp., Phila., 1970—, IGAS Corp., Pitts., 1975—; chmn. PPM Internat., Inc., Spartanburg; S.C.founder, chmn. Execs. Guardian Co., N.Y.C., 1971—; Tchr. U. Va., 1949-51; asso. mem. Am., N.Y. stock exchanges, 1961-72; mem. Pacific Stock Exchange, 1962-66, Chgo. Bd. Trade, 1962-66. Bd. dirs. McIntire Sch. Commerce U. Va. Served with USAAF, 1943-46, PTO. Mem. U. Va. Alumni Assn. (N.Y. pres. 1978-81), Sigma Chi, Delta Sigma Rho, Pi Delta Epsilon, Omicron Delta Kappa, Delta Theta Pi. Republican. Presbyterian. (trustee). Clubs: Boar's Head Sport, (Charlottesville, Va.), Farmington Country (Charlottesville); Bond, City Midday, Union League (N.Y.C.); Quogue (N.Y.) Field, Quogue Beach; Clan Munro (Scotland and U.S.). Home: Ednam Forest Charlottesville VA 22903 Office: PO Box 5246 2 Boars Head Pl Charlottesville VA 22905

MONROE, FREDERICK LEROY, chemist; b. Redmond, Oreg., Oct. 13, 1942; s. Herman Sylvan Monroe and Mary Roberta (Grant) Monroe Emery; B.S. in Chemistry, Oreg. State U., 1964; M.S. in Environ. Engring., Wash. State U., 1974. Control specialist Air Pollution Control Authority, Centralia, Wash., 1969-70; asst. chemist Wash. State U., 1970-74; environ. engr. Ore-Ida Foods, Inc., Idaho, 1974-77; cons., Idaho, 1977-78; applications engr. AFL Industries, Riviera Beach, Fla., 1979-80; mgr. chem. control PCA Internat., Matthews, N.C., 1980-85; quality assurance mgr. Stork Screens Am., Charlotte, N.C., 1985-93, environ. mgr., 1993—, grade IV N.C. wastewater treatment operator. Pres. Unity Ch., 1982-84. Served with USAF, 1964-68, maj. Res. ret.; served with N.G., 1973-78. Decorated Air Force Commendation medal; recipient Blue Thumb award Charlotte-Mecklenburg Utility Dist., 1993. Fellow Am. Inst. Chemists; mem. Am. Chem. Soc. Republican. Achievements include approved international shipment of hazardous wastes for recycling. Home: 2835 Hilliard Dr Charlotte NC 28205-2268 Office: Stork Screens Am Service Rd 3001 N Interstate 85 Charlotte NC 28269-4493

MONROE, HASKELL M., JR., university educator; b. Dallas, Mar. 18, 1931; s. Haskell M. and Myrtle Marie (Jackson) M.; m. Margaret Joan Phillips, June 15, 1957; children: Stephen, Melanie, Mark, John. B.A., Austin (Tex.) Coll., 1952, M.A., 1954; Ph.D., Rice U., Houston, 1961. From instr. to prof. Tex. A&M U., 1959-80; asst. dean Tex. A&M U. (Grad. Sch.), 1965-68, asst. v.p. acad. affairs, 1972-74, dean faculties, 1974-80, assoc. v.p. acad. affairs, 1977-80; pres. U. Tex., El Paso, 1980-87; chancellor U. Mo., Columbia, 1987-91; prof. history U. Mo., 1987—; instr. Schreiner Inst., Kerrville, Tex., summer 1959; vis. lectr. Emory U., summers 1967, 72; faculty lectr. Tex. A&M U., 1972; alumni lectr. Austin Coll., 1980; bd. dirs. Southwestern Bell Corp., Boone County Nat. Bank. Contbr. articles, revs.; editor: Papers of Jefferson Davis, 1964-69; adv. editor: Texana, 1964-71; bd. editorial advisers: Booker T. Washington Papers, 1965-85 . Bd. dirs. Brazos Valley Rehab. Center, 1975-77, Salvation Army, El Paso, 1984-87, Columbia, Mo., 1988—, Crime Stoppers of El Paso, United Way Columbia, 1988-94; trustee Bryan Hosp., 1976-79, chmn., 1979; bd. ch. visitors Austin Coll., 1977-78; deacon First Presbyn. Ch., Bryan, 1961-63, elder, 1965-67, 69-71, 73-74, clk. of session, 1973-74, chmn. pulpit nominating com., 1971-72; mem. presbytery's council Presbytery of Brazos, 1969-71, mem. resources for the 80s steering com., 1978-80; elder 1st Presbyn. Ch., El Paso, 1984-87, 1st Presbyn. Ch., Columbia, 1994—; mem. exec. bd. Great Rivers coun. Boy Scouts of Am., 1990—; mem. Pres. Coun. NCAA, 1986-87. Served with USNR, 1954-56. Recipient Citation of Appreciation, LULAC, 1982, also numerous achievement awards; grantee Social Sci. Rsch. Coun., Tex. A&M U., Huntington Libr. Mem. Am. Hist. Assn., Orgn. Am. Historians, So. Hist. Assn. Hist. Found. Presbyn. and Reformed Chs. (pres. 1970-72), Coll. Football Assn. (chmn. bd. 1989-90, bd. dirs.), Truman Scholarship Panel, So. Conf. Deans Faculties and Acad. V.P.s (pres. 1978), Rotary (El Paso, hon. Columbia, Mo.). Home: 3200 Westcreek Cir Columbia MO 65203-0904 Office: U Mo 306 Reynolds Ctr Columbia MO 65211

MONROE, JAMES WALTER, organization executive; b. Fairfax, S.D., Feb. 13, 1936; s. Sherman William and Frances (Burnett) M.; m. Dorothy Lou Gillette, Apr. 1, 1961; children—Steven James, David Walter, Melody Anne, Andrew Scott. Student, Huron (S.D.) Coll., 1954-56, U. Nebr., 1956-57; B.A., Nebr. Wesleyan U., 1960. Mgr. Belleville (Kans.) C. of C., 1960-61, Concordia (Kans.) C. of C., 1961-62; asst. chief Div. Nebr. Resources, 1962-65; dir. S.D. Indsl. Devel. Expansion Agy., 1965-67, Nebr. Dept. Econ. Devel., 1967-71; sec. Nebr. Resources Found., 1967-71; exec. dir. Omaha Econ. Devel. Council, 1971-76; pres. Kansas City (Mo.-Kans.) Area Devel. Council, 1976-90; pres., chief exec. officer New Orleans and the River Region C. of C., 1990—, Metrovision Found., Econ. Devel. Coun. Metro, New Orleans; mem. Am. Indsl. Devel. Council, 1965—, chmn. certification bd., 1981-82; sec. labor mgmt. council Greater Kansas City, 1979-90; mem. exec. com. Gov.'s Econ. Devel. Adv. Council, 1979-81. Bd. dirs. Am. Econ. Devel. Coun., 1992—. Served with AUS, 1957-59. Mem. Nat. Assn. Corporate Real Estate Execs. (pres. econ. devel. council 1986-88). Republican. Presbyterian. Home: Park VII 170 Walnut St Apt 3C New Orleans LA 70118-4866 Office: New Orleans & River Reg 301 Camp St New Orleans LA 70130-2825

MONROE, KENDYL KURTH, retired lawyer; b. Clayton, N.Mex., Sept. 6, 1936; s. Dottis Donald and Helen (Kurth) M.; m. Barbara Sayre, Sept. 12, 1956; children: Sidney, Dean, Loren. AB, Stanford U., 1958, LLB, 1960. Bar: N.Y. 1961, Calif. 1961. Assoc. Sullivan & Cromwell, N.Y.C., 1960-67, ptnr., 1968-94; chmn. TEB Charter Svcs., Inc., Teterboro N.J.; bd. dirs. Air Am. Inc., Santa Fe, No. Minerals Co., Keesville, N.Y., El Valle Escondido Ranch Ltd. Co., Seneca. Chmn. Lambs Theatre, N.Y.C., Pub. Health Rsch. Inst., N.Y.C.; bd. dirs. Greenwich Village Soc. Historic Preservation, N.Y.C., N.Y. Chamber Soloists, N.Y.C., Seamen's Ch. Inst., N.Y.C. Mem. Calif. State Bar Assn., Assn. Bar City N.Y., Met. Club (N.Y.C.). Home: Kenton Rte Seneca NM 88437

MONROE, L. A. J., oil well drilling company executive; b. Springhill, Ark., Nov. 8, 1919; s. Eugene and Alma Edna (Collins) M.; m. Elizabeth Kirkland Moore, Apr. 18, 1942; children: Jamison, Mark Kirkland. B.S., Tex. Christian U., 1942. With Nat. Supply Co., 1945-65; regional mgr. Nat. Supply Co. (Gulf Coast), 1960-62, gen. mgr. sales, domestic and Can. cos., 1962-65; with Dixilyn-Field Drilling Co., Houston, 1965-83; pres., chief exec. officer Dixilyn-Field Drilling Co., 1971-83, chmn. bd., 1978-83; ptnr. Monroe & Bruner, Inc., 1983-92, chmn., 1983-92; chmn. Monroe & Monroe, Inc., Houston, 1992—; dir. First City Bank of Highland Village. Trustee Tex. Christian U.; adminstrv. bd. Chapelwood United Meth. Ch., Houston. Served with U.S. Navy, 1942-45. Named Most Valuable Alumnus Tex. Christian U., 1974, named to Hall of Fame Tex. Christian U., 1991. Mem. Internat. Assn. Drilling Contractors, Nat. Ocean Industry Assn., Mid-Continent Oil and Gas Assn. Republican. Baptist. Clubs: River Oaks Country, Ramada, Petroleum (past dir.), Houston; Les Ambassador (London). Office: Monroe & Monroe Inc 415 Brown Saddle St Houston TX 77057-1411

MONROE, MELROSE, retired banker; b. Flowery Branch, Ga., Apr. 13, 1919; d. Willis Jeptha and Leila Adell Cash; m. Lynn Austin, June 14, 1942. AB in Edn., Ga. State U., 1968. Negotiator Trust Co. Bank, Atlanta, 1962-89, ret., 1989. Mem. Nat. Women's C. of C. (pres. 1987-88), Atlanta Women's C. of C. (dir. 1965-66, pres. Fidelis SS class 1962-63), Am. Legion Aux. (pres. 5th dist. 1986-87, Ga. state chaplain 1989-90, state historian 1991-92, state 2d v.p. 1992-93, 1st v.p. 1993-94, pres. 1994-95), Order of Ea. Star (worthy matron 1951-52). Democrat. Home and Office: 4263 Woodland Brook Dr NW Atlanta GA 30339-4722

MONROE, MURRAY SHIPLEY, lawyer; b. Cin., Sept. 25, 1925; s. James and Martha (Shipley) M.; m. Sally Longstreth, May 11, 1963; children: Tracy, Murray, Courtney, David. BE, Yale U., 1946, BS, 1947; LLB, U. Pa., 1950. Bar: Ohio 1950, U.S. Dist. Ct. (so. dist.) Ohio 1954, U.S. Dist. Ct. (mid. dist.) Tenn. 1981, US. Dist. Ct. (mid. dist.) N.C. 1974, U.S. Dist. Ct. (mid. dist.) Pa. 1986, U.S. Dist. Ct. (ea. dist.) Pa. 1960, U.S. Dist. Ct. (we. dist.) Mo. 1974, U.S. Dist. Ct. Mass. 1978, U.S. Dist. Ct. (ea. dist.) La. 1979, U.S. Dist. Ct. (no. dist.) Ill. 1980, U.S. Ct. Appeals (4th cir.) 1984, U.S. Ct. Appeals (6th cir.) 1969, U.S. Supreme Ct. 1977, U.S. Ct. Appeals (3d cir.) 1990. Assoc. Taft, Stettinus & Hollister, Cin., 1950-58, ptnr., 1958—; mem. lawyers com. Nat. Ctr. for State Cts., 1985—; faculty Ohio Legal Ctr. Inst., 1970-93. Contbr. articles to profl. jours. Trustee, treas. The Coll. Prep. Sch., 1972-76; trustee The Seven Hills Schs., 1982-88, chmn. bd., 1982-85. 2d lt. USNR, 1943-46. Recipient award Seven Hills Schs., 1985. Fellow Ohio Bar Found.; mem. ABA (speaker symposiums), Ohio Bar Assn. (coun. dels. 1977-82, bd. govs. antitrust sect. 1960-95, dir. emeritus 1995—, chmn. bd. govs. 1973-75, Merit award 1976, speaker symposiums), Bankers Club (Cin.), Cin. Country Club, Tau Beta Pi. Republican. Episcopalian. Avocations: sailing, tennis. Office: 425 Walnut St Ste 1800 Cincinnati OH 45202-3957

MONROE, ROBERT RAWSON, engineering construction executive; b. Oakland, Calif., Sept. 25, 1927; s. Robert Ansley and Muriel Estelle (Burnham) M.; m. Charlotte Boies Anderson, Oct. 16, 1951; children: Robert Anderson, Nancy Lynn Monroe Sims, Susan Leslie Monroe Gordon. BS in Naval Sci., U.S. Naval Acad., 1950; MA in Internat. Rels., Stanford U., 1962. Commd. ensign USN, 1950, advanced through grades to vice-admiral, 1977; dir. Navy Systems Analysis, 1972-73, comdr. South Atlantic Force, 1973-74; comdr. Operational Test and Evaluation Force USN, 1974-77; dir. Def. Nuclear Agy., 1977-80, dir. Navy Rsch., Devel., Test and Evaluation, 1980-83, ret., 1983; joined Bechtel Nat., Inc., San Francisco, 1984, mgr. def. and space, 1984-89, v.p., 1985, sr. v.p., ptnr., 1987, mgr. mktg. and govt. ops., 1989-91, mgr. spl. projects, 1992-93; mgr. govt. ops. Bechtel Nat., Inc., Washington, 1993—; mem. nat. security adv. bd. Los Alamos (N. Mex.) Nat. Lab., 1983-88; mem. tech. evaluation panel U.S. Dept. Energy, 1983-88; mem. engring. adv. com. Oak Ridge (Tenn.) Nat. Lab., 1986-89, Rensselaer Poly Inst., 1990-91; mem. bd. advisors Office Tech. Assessment, Washington, 1987-89, Nat. Contract Mgmt. Assn., 1986-91; mem. task forces Def. Sci. Bd., Washington, 1983-89; corp. mem. Charles Stark Draper Lab., Cambridge, Mass., 1983—; affiliate mem. Ctr. for Internat. Security and Arms Control, Stanford U., 1989-93; chmn. space transp. panel NASA's Tech. and Commercialization Adv. Com., 1995—. Decorated Def. D.S.M., USN D.S.M., Legion of Merit, Bronze Star medal with combat device, Joint Svcs. Commendation medal, USN Commendation medal with combat device; Legion of Honor (France). Mem. AIAA, Nat. Security Indsl. Assn., Soc. Am. Mil. Engrs., Am. Def. Preparedness Assn., U.S. Naval Inst. Avocations: tennis, golf, hiking, reading. Home: 2313 Sawdust Rd Vienna VA 22181-3044 Office: Bechtel Nat Inc 1015 15th St NW Ste 700 Washington DC 20005-2605

MONROE, RUSSELL RONALD, psychiatrist, educator; b. Des Moines, June 7, 1920; s. Ronald Russell and Mildred (Schmidt) M.; m. Lillian Constance Brooks, June 23, 1945; children—Constance Ellen Monroe Teevan, Nancy Brooks Monroe Amoss, Russell Ronald Jr. B.S., Yale U., 1942, M.D., 1944; cert. in psychoanalysis, Columbia U., 1950. Intern New Haven Hosp., 1944-45; resident Rockland State Hosp., Orangeburg, N.Y., 1947-50; from asst. to assoc. prof. psychiatry Tulane U. Sch. Med., New Orleans, 1950-60; prof. U. Md. Sch. Med., Balt., 1960—; chmn. dept. U. Md. Sch. Med., 1976-85; dir. Inst. Psychiatry and Human Behavior U. Md., 1976-85; vis. prof. Am. U., Beirut, Lebanon, 1966-67; mem. adv. commn. Nat. Inst. Law Enforcement and Criminal Justice, 1977-80. Author: Episodic Behavioral Disorders, 1970, Brain Dysfunction in Aggressive Criminals, 1978, Creative Brainstorms, 1992. Served to capt. AUS, 1945-47. Commonwealth fellow, 1966-67, NIMH fellow, 1966-67; grantee NIMH. Fellow Am. Psychiat. Assn., Am. Coll. Psychiatrists; mem. Am. Acad. Psychoanalysis (charter). Clubs: Hamilton St., So. Yacht. Home: 236 W Lafayette Ave Baltimore MD 21217-4210 Office: U Md Sch Medicine 645 W Redwood St Baltimore MD 21201-1542

MONROE, SIDNI MCCLUER, special education educator; b. Alexandria, Minn., Mar. 11, 1949; d. Frank and Catharine (Peterson) Shapiro; m. Larry K. Monroe, July 21, 1973; 1 child, Colin Yung Hwan. BA in Math., SUNY, Buffalo, 1971; postgrad., Pitts. State U., 1976-78; MA in Spl. Edn., Marshall U., 1984; postgrad., Columbia U., 1984-85. Cert. secondary math., learning and severely handicapped, gifted tchr., Calif. Insvc. tchr. trainer math. U.S. Peace Corps, 1971-75; tchr. spl. edn. Unified Sch. Dist. # 250, 1976-78, Joplin (Mo.) Regional Ctr., 1978-80; grad. teaching asst., cons. asst. Marshall U., Huntington, W.Va., 1982; program dir. Ohio Ctr. for Youth and Family Devel., Ironton, Ohio, 1982-84; office mgr. Ctr. for Study and Edn. of Gifted Columbia U., N.Y., 1984-85; dir. residential assessment, diagnostic edn. specialist State. Dept. Edn. Diagnostic Ctr., L.A., 1986-92; del. Citizen Amb. Program Early Childhood Spl. Edn. to Russia and Ea. Europe, 1992. Mem. Coun. Exceptional Children.

MONROE, THOMAS EDWARD, industrial corporation executive; b. Ironton, MO, Nov. 19, 1947; s. Donald Mansfield and Edwina Frances (Carr) M.; children: Thomas Edward II, Katherine Jenna. B.A., Drury Coll., 1969; postgrad., Washington U. Sch. Bus. Adminstrn., St. Louis, 1970. Acctg. mgr., asst. controller Am. Transit Corp., St. Louis, 1970-74; mgr. corp. devel., asst. treas. Chromalloy Am. Corp., St. Louis, 1974-77, v.p. fin., 1977-78, exec. v.p., 1978-82; dir. Chromalloy Fin. Corp., 1976-82, Am. Universal Ins. Co., 1978-82; chmn. Capital Assocs. Corp., 1982—, Fed. Air Ambulance, The Safe Deposit Co., CompuVault, Inc., James Flying Svc., Inc., Lindbergh Leasing, Inc. Mem. St. Louis Club, Algonquin Club. Presbyterian. Office: Capital Assocs Corp 515 S Lindbergh Blvd Saint Louis MO 63131-2731

MONROE, VERNON EARL, JR. (THE PEARL MONROE), former professional basketball player; b. Phila., Nov. 21, 1944; s. Vernon Earl and Rose (Smith) M. B.S. in Edn., Winston-Salem State U., 1967. Basketball player Balt. Bullets, 1967-71, N.Y. Knickerbockers, N.Y.C., 1971-80; capt. N.Y. Knickerbockers, 1976-79; pres. Electra Pretty Pearl Records, Pretty Pearl, Inc. Recipient Big Apple award Jr. Achievement N.Y., 1977, Global award Mt. Calvary Ch., 1977, Daily News Front Page award, 1986; named Rookie of Yr., NBA, 1969; named to Sporting News All-Am. 1st Team, 1966, NBA All-Rookie Team, 1968, NAIA Basketball Hall of Fame, 1975, Central Intercollegiate Athletic Assn. Hall of Fame, 1977; inductee Naismith Meml Basketball Hall of Fame, 1989. Mem. Groove Phi Groove. Republican. Reached 15,000 points, 1977; mem. NCAA Coll. Divsn. championship team, 1967, NBA championship team, 1973. Office: 1775 Broadway New York NY 10019-1903*

MONROE, WILLIAM LEWIS, human resources executive; b. Detroit, May 11, 1941; s. Lewis Stewart and Ada Jeanette (Williams) M.; m. Sharon Lynne Kahal, June 30, 1967; children: Andrea M. Dunk, William J. BA, Western Mich. U., 1963, MA, 1964. Rsch. analyst Chrysler Corp., Detroit, 1965-72, labor economist, 1972-77, mgr. retirement, savs. and unemployment benefit plans, 1977-81; dir. employee benefits W. R. Grace & Co., N.Y.C., 1981-87, v.p. human resources, 1987—, bd. trustee, v.p. coun. on employee benefits, 1989—, pres. coun. on employee benefits, 1995—; corp. bd. dirs. Internat. Found. Employee Benefits, 1986-88; mem. bus. rsch. adv. coun. to U.S. Dept. Labor/Bur. Labor Stats., 1987—; mem. Human Resources Policy Inst. Boston U., 1993-96. Co-chmn. closing com. PTSA Sch., Birmingham, Mich., 1977; chmn. personnel com. Wilton Presbyn. Ch., Wilton, Conn., 1982-86; officer, bd. dirs. Forest Hills Property Owners Assn. Birmingham, 1974-80; mem. exec. bd. Gulf Stream coun. Boy Scouts Am., 1993—. Served with USAR, 1965-71. Mem. Soc. for Human Resources & Mgmt., Boca Raton (Fla.) Resort and Club, Princeton Club N.Y.C. Republican. Presbyterian. Avocations: tennis, golf. Office: W R Grace & Co 1 Town Center Rd Boca Raton FL 33486-1010

MONROE, WILLIAM SMITH, mandolin player, singer; b. Rosine, Ky., Sept. 13, 1911; s. James Buchanan and Malissa (Vandiver) M.; m. Carolyn Brown, 1935 (div.); children: James, Melissa. Worked in oil refinery; mem. WSN Grand Ole Opry, 1939—. Played on, WLS Barn Dance, East Chicago, Ind., 1929-34, formed group, The Monroe Brothers, 1934-38, playing on radio stas. in. N.C. and S.C.; formed group, The Blue Grass Boys, 1938—, nationwide concert and festival appearances; recorded for, Victor Records, 1940-41, Columbia Records, 1945-49, Decca (now MCA), 1950—; songs recorded include My Little Georgia Rose; albums include In The Pines, 1988, Live at The Opry, 1989, The Country Music Hall of Fame, 1991, The Essential Bill Monroe and His Blusgrass Boys (1945-49),1992, Mule Skinner Blues, 1991, The Music of Bill Monroe 1936-1994, 1994. Elected to County Music Hall of Fame, 1970. Originated term bluegrass and defined its style. Office: care Buddy Lee Attractions 38 Music Sq E Ste 300 Nashville TN 37203-4304

MONROY, VICTOR M., polymers scientist; b. Tampico, Tamaulipas, Mexico, Aug. 8, 1953; s. Mario and Maria Luisa (Soto-Serdan) M.; m. Deborah Costley, Dec. 27, 1980; children: Mario Alexander, Stephanie Claire Anais, Sebastian John Philip. BS Chem. Engring., Inst. Tech. Cd. Madero, Mexico, 1975; PhD in Macromolecular Phys. Chem., Inst. Charles Sadron CNRS, Strasbourg, France, 1983. Deve. engr. Hules Mexicanos, S.A., Altamira, Tamps., Mexico, 1976-77; R&D engr. Industrias Negromex, S.A. de C.V., Mexico City, 1984-85, R&D supr., 1985-86, analytical instrumentation mgr., 1987, rsch. mgr., 1988-90; rsch. assoc. General Tire, Inc., Akron, Ohio, 1993, mgr., 1994; rsch. dir. Continental Gen. Tire, Inc., Akron, 1995—; vis. scientist, prof. The U. Akron, 1990-93; cons. General Tire, Inc., 1991-92, COPERBO, Cabo, Brazil, 1992-93. Author Kirk-Othmer Ency. of Chem. Tech., 1995; contbr. articles to profl. jours.; patentee in field. Nat. researcher Sistema Nacional de Investigadores, Mexico City, 1989; grantee Nat. Coun. Sci. and Tech., Mexico City, 1977, Edison Polymer Innovation Corp., Akron, 1990. Fellow Am. Inst. Chemists; mem. Indsl. Rsch. Inst., Dirs. of Indsl. Rsch./Analytical Groups, Am. Chem. Soc. Roman Catholic. Avocations: jogging, martial arts, soccer, reading, music. Office: Continental Gen Tire Inc 1800 Continental Blvd Charlotte NC 28273

MONSEES, JAMES EUGENE, engineering executive, consultant; b. Sedalia, Mo., Mar. 27, 1937; s. Olen Owen and Ruth Caroline (Weiffenbach) M.; m. Leda L. Hoehns, Oct. 8, 1961; children: Brenda G., Mark E. BSCE, U. Mo., 1960, MSCE, 1961; PhDCE, U. Ill., 1970. Registered profl. engr., Ill., Md., Washington, Ohio, Calif., Wash., Colo. Grad. asst. U. Mo., Columbia, 1958-61; project mgr. USAF Spl. Weapons Ctr., Albuquerque, 1961-64; engr. Exxon, Baton Rouge, 1964-66; rsch. assoc. U. Ill., Champaign, 1967-69; sr. v.p. A.A. Mathews, CRS Engrs., Arcadia, Calif. and Rockville, Md., 1969-80; dept. mgr. Battelle Meml. Inst., Columbus, Ohio, 1980-82; v.p.-engr. Lachel L. Hanson & Assocs., Golden, Colo., 1982-83; chief tunnel engr. Metro Rail Transit Couns., L.A., 1983-1990; project mgr. Collider/SSC The PB/MK Team, Dallas, 1990-94; sr. v.p., tech. dir., prin. profl. assoc. Parsons Brinckerhoff, N.Y.C.; mem. Seismic Lifeline Com., San Francisco, 1987—; mem. exec. com. Rapid Excavation/Tunnel Conf., Denver, 1989—. Author: (with others) Guidelines for Tunnel Lining Design, 1984, Mining Handbook, 1992, Tunnel Engineering, 1994, Tunnel Engineering Handbook, 1996. Mem. U.S. Nat. Com. for Rock Mechanics, Wash., D.C., 1983-86, 88-94, Internat. Soc. for Rock Mechanics, 1983—. 1st Lt. USAF, 1961-64. Recipient Mo. Honor award U. Mo., 1992. Fellow ASCE; mem. NAE, Am. Underground Space Assn. (bd. dirs. 1995—), The Moles, Underground Tech. Rsch. Coun. Republican. Avocations: shooting, biking, tennis, reading, dog training. Home: 834 Mill Creek Cir Lancaster TX 75146-2839 Office: Parsons Brinckerhoff Ste 200 7220 S Westmoreland Rd Dallas TX 75237-2984

MONSEES, TIMOTHY WILLIAM, lawyer; b. Kansas City, Mo., May 19, 1955; s. William Eugene and Barbara Jo (Simons) M.; m. Laura Franklin, July 19, 1980; children: W. Benjamin, Samuel R., Megan E. BS, U. Mo., 1977, JD, 1981. Bar: Mo. 1981, Tex. 1985, Kans. 1994. Ptnr. Myerson, Monsees & Morrow, P.C., Kansas City, until 1995, Monsees, Miller & DeFeo, P.C., Kansas City, 1995—. Mem. ATLA (sustaining), Mo. Bar Assn., Tex. Bar Assn., Kans. Bar Assn., Mo. Assn. Trial Lawyers, Kansas City Met. Bar Assn., Hillcrest Country Club, Order of Coif, Order of Barristers, Leadership Club, U. Mo. Jefferson Club, Delta Upsilon. Reorganized Ch. of Jesus Christ of LDS. Avocations: snow skiing, running, youth athletics, golfing, basketball.

MONSEN, ELAINE RANKER, nutritionist, educator, editor; b. Oakland, Calif., June 6, 1935; d. Emery R. and Irene Stewart (Thorley) Ranker; m. Raymond Joseph Monsen, Jr., Jan. 21, 1959; 1 dau., Maren Ranker. B.A., U. Utah, 1956; M.S. (Mead Johnson grad. scholar), U. Calif., Berkeley, 1959, Ph.D. (NSF fellow), 1961; postgrad. NSF sci. faculty fellow, Harvard U., 1968-69. Dietetic intern Mass. Gen. Hosp., Boston, 1956-57; asst. prof. nutrition, lectr. biochemistry Brigham Young U., Provo, Utah, 1960-63; mem. faculty U. Wash., 1963—, prof. nutrition and medicine, 1984—, prof. nutrition, adj. prof. medicine, 1976-84, chmn. div. human nutrition, dietetics and foods, 1977-82, dir. grad. nutritional scis. program, 1994—, mem. Council of Coll. Arts and Scis., 1974-78, mem. U. Wash. Press com., 1981—; chmn. Nutrition Studies Commn., 1969-83; vis. scholar Stanford U., 1971-72; mem. sci. adv. com. food fortification Pan-Am. Health Orgn., São Paulo, Brazil, 1972; tng. grant coordinator NIH, 1976—. Editor Jour. Am. Dietetic Assn., 1983—; mem. editorial bd. Coun. Biology Editors, 1992-96; author research papers on lipid metabolism, iron absorption. Bd. dirs. A Contemporary Theatre, Seattle, 1969-72; trustee, bd. dirs. Seattle Found., 1978-95, vice chmn., 1987-91, chmn., 1991-93; pres. Seattle bd. Santa Fe Chamber Music Festival, 1984-85; mem. Puget Sound Blood Ctr. Bd., 1996—. Grantee Nutrition Found., 1965-68, Agrl. Rsch. Svc., 1969—; recipient Disting. Alumnus award U. Utah, F. Fischer Meml. Nutrition Lectr. award, 1988, L.F. Cooper Meml. Lectr. award, 1991, L. Hatch Meml. Lectr. award, 1992. Mem. Am. Inst. Nutrition, Am. Soc. Clin. Nutrition (sec. 1987-90), Am. Dietetic Assn., Soc. Nutrition Edn., Am. Soc. Parenteral and Enteral Nutrition, Wash. Heart Assn. (nutrition council 1973-76), Phi Beta Kappa, Phi Kappa Phi. Office: U Wash 306 Raitt Hall Box 353410 Seattle WA 98195

MONSEN, RAYMOND JOSEPH, JR., economist, educator, art patron; b. Payson, Utah, Mar. 13, 1931; s. Raymond Joseph and Lucile (Monsen); m. Elaine Ranker, Jan. 21, 1959; 1 dau., Maren Ranker. B.S., U. Utah, 1953; M.A., Stanford U., 1954; Ph.D., U. Calif. at Berkeley, 1960. Asst. prof. econs. Brigham Young U., 1960-63; cons. to govt. and banking industry, 1962-63; assoc. prof. Coll. of Bus., U. Wash., Seattle, 1963-65; prof. U. Wash., 1966-86, prof. dept. mgmt., 1986, chmn. dept. bus., govt. and society, 1966, 73-81, prof. emeritus, 1986—; dir. research Coll. of Bus., U. Wash. (Grad. Sch. Bus.), 1964-68; Guggenheim fellow, dept. econs. Harvard U., 1968-69; vis. prof. Grad. Sch. Bus., Stanford U., 1971-73; vis. prof. U. Calif., Berkeley, Spring 1985. Author: Modern American Capitalism: Idealogies and Issues, 1963, (with Mark Cannon) American Power Groups and Their Ideoloies, 1965, Business and the Changing Environment, 1973, (with others) Management, Systems, and Society, 1976, (with K. Walters) Nationalized Companies: Capitalism Challenged, 1983; editor: (with B. Saxberg) The Business World, 1967; contbr. over 50 articles to profl. jours.; photographic and ceramic collections exhibited at Portland Crafts Ctr., 1968, U. Wash. Art Gallery, 1969, 79, 86, 94-95, San Francisco Art Mus., 1973, Seattle Art Mus., 1974, 76, Portland Art Mus., 1977, La Jolla (Calif.) Mus., 1989, San Francisco Friends of Photography, 1995, Pontiac Art Mus., Portland Art Mus., Maine, 1995-96, U. Calif. at San Diego Art Mus., 1996. Past pres. contemporary art coun. Seattle Art Mus., 1967, trustee, 1968-85; mem. vis. com. U. Pugent Sound Law Sch., 1981-88; mem. vis. com. Met. Mus. Art, N.Y.C., 1992—; founder-trustee Seattle Opera Assn., Henry Art Gallery Assn., U. Wash.; past trustee Salt Lake Art Ctr., Pacific N.W. Art Assn.; established Monsen Photography collection U. Wash. Art Mus., 1978. Mem. Am. Econs. Assn., Acad. of Mgmt., Seattle Tennis Club. Avocation: art patron.

MONSKY, JOHN BERTRAND, investment banking executive; b. Montgomery, Ala., May 17, 1930; s. Harry and Belle (Golding) M.; m. Joan Gilbert, June 8, 1952; children: Leslie Joy, John Richard, Harry Robert. B.A., Yale, 1952; M.B.A., Harvard, 1954. Sec. Devoe & Raynolds Co., Inc., Louisville, Ky., 1956-65; v.p., dir. Universal Marion Corp., Jacksonville, Fla., 1965-69, pres., chmn. bd., chief exec. officer, 1969-71, cons., 1971—; vice chmn. ServAmerica, Inc., Jacksonville, 1972-74, co-chmn. bd. dirs., 1974-80, chmn. bd. dirs., 1980—; pres., chmn. bd. dirs. First Fla. Capital Corp., 1985—; dir. Fla. Wire & Cable Co., Jacksonville, 1975-82. Past pres. bd. trustees Jacksonville Country Day Sch.; bd. dirs. Jacksonville Art Mus.; trustee Bolles Sch., Jacksonville, Jacksonville Symphony Assn. Served with USAF, 1954-56. Mem. Jacksonville Area C. of C. (com. of 100), Jackson County Citizen Involvement Clubs, Harvard Bus. Sch. Club of Ky. (exec. com. 1964-65), Phillips Acad. Andover Alumni Club of Ky. (pres. 1963-64), Epping Forest Cmty. Master Assn. (bd. dirs. 1994—), Yale Club N.E. Fla. (bd. dirs. 1987—), Yale Club of N.Y.C., Harvard Club (Jacksonville), Assn. Yale Alumni (del. 1996—), River Club, Ponte Vedra Club, Epping Forest Yacht Club. Home: Epping Forest 7015 Gaines Ct Jacksonville FL 32217-2672 Office: 300 B Wharfside Way Jacksonville FL 33207-8153

MONSMA, MARVIN EUGENE, library director; b. Prairie City, Iowa, May 14, 1933; s. John and Johanna Hester (Branderhorst) M.; m. Elaine Gross, Aug. 2, 1963; children: Kristy Lynne Monsma De Vos, Kimberly Sue Monsma Rottschafer, Michelle Eileen Monsma Haan. AB, Calvin Coll., 1957; AM in Secondary Edn., Mich. State U., 1961; AMLS in Librarianship, U. Mich., 1967. English tchr. Muskegon (Mich.) Christian Sch., 1957-60, Grand Rapids (Mich.) Christian H.S., 1960-63, Unity Christian H.S., Hudsonville, Mich., 1963-65; asst. libr. Calvin Coll. & Sem., Grand Rapids, 1965-67, head gen. svcs., 1967-68, asst. libr. dir., 1968-69, acting libr. dir., 1969-70, libr. dir., 1970—. Christian Reformed. Avocations: classical music, gardening, nature. Office: Calvin Coll and Sem Hekman Libr 3207 Burton St SE Grand Rapids MI 49546-4301

MONSON, ARCH, JR., fire alarm manufacturing company executive; b. Thorntown, Ind., Nov. 10, 1913; s. Arch and Mabel (Miller) M.; m. June Hammersmith, Jan. 10, 1959; children—Eminel, Arch III, Dwight, Jay. Grad. high sch. Pres. Monson-Pacific Inc., San Francisco, 1935—; pres. Monson Electric Co. div. Monson-Pacific Inc., San Francisco, 1935—; West coast mgr. Autocall div. Fed. Signal Corp., Blue Island, Ill., 1945—; owner, operator St. George Ranch, Geyserville, Calif., 1959—; dir. Ampex Corp., Redwood City, Calif., Signal Co. Inc., Beverly Hills, Calif. Chmn. Nat. Jamboree Boy Scouts Am., 1973, v.p. nat. exec. bd., 1973-74, pres., 1975-77; Trustee Pacific Med. Center, San Francisco, 1964—, mem. exec. com., 1969—; trustee Golden Gate U., YMCA of San Francisco, Salvation Army. Recipient Silver Beaver award Boy Scouts Am., 1968, Silver Antelope award, 1968, Silver Buffalo award, 1971. Mem. San Francisco Electric Club, Pacific Coast Elec. Assn., Nat. Elec. Contractors Assn., San Francisco Conv. and Visitors Bur., Internat. Assn. Fire Chiefs, Internat. Municipal Signal Assn. Republican. Presbyn. (elder). Clubs: Mason (Shriner, 33 deg.), Rotarian, Bohemian (pres. 1962, 63), Olympic, The Family. Home: 2825 Broadway San Francisco CA 94115-1060

MONSON, CAROL LYNN, osteopath, physician, psychotherapist; b. Blue Island, Ill., Nov. 3, 1946; d. Marcus Edward and Margaret Bertha (Andres) M.; m. Frank E. Warden, Feb. 28, 1981. B.S., No. Ill. U., 1968, M.S., 1969; D.O., Mich State Coll. Osteo. Medicine, 1979. Lic. physician, Mich., diplomate Am. Bd. Osteo., Am. Bd. Family Physicians, Am. Bd. Osteo. Gen. Practice, diplomate MSUCOM. Expeditor-psychotherapist H. Douglas Singer Zone Ctr., Rockford, Ill., 1969-71; psychotherapist Tri-County Mental Health, St. Johns, Mich., 1971-76; pvt. practice psychotherapy, East Lansing, Mich., 1976-80; intern Lansing Gen. Hosp., Mich., 1979-80, residency dir. family practice, 1988—; pvt. practice osteo. medicine, Lansing, 1980—; mem. staff Ingham Med. Hosp., Lansing Gen. Hosp. (now Mich. Capital Med. Ctr.), chmn. gen practice, 1987-89; field instr. Sch. Social Work, U. Mich., 1973-76; clin. instr. Central Mich. Dept. Psychology, 1974-75; clin. prof. Mich. State U., 1980-88, asst. prof., 1988—, tng. supr. family medicine residency, 1988—, residency dir. family medicine, 1994—; mem. adv. bd. Substance Abuse Clearinghouse, Lansing, 1983-85, Kelly Health Care, Lansing, 1983-85, Americor Health Svcs., Lansing, 1984-88, Lansing Home Care, 1988-94. Mem. Am. Osteo. Assn., Am. Acad. Family Practice, Internat. Transactional Analysis Assn., Mich. Assn. Physicians and Surgeons (program com. 1992—, governance coun., 1996—), Ingham County Osteo. Assn. (pres. 1993-95, 96—), Nat. Assn. Career Women (conv. com. 1984—), Lansing Assn. Career Women, Soc. Tchrs. of Family Medicine, Mich. Assn. Osteo Family Physicians (pres.-elect 1994, pres. 1995-96), Am. Coll. Family Physicians (residency insp. 1991—), Zonta (chmn. service com. Mid Mich. Capital Area chpt.). Avocations: gardening; orchid growing; antique collecting. Office: 2445 W Jolly Rd Ste 400 Okemos MI 48864

MONSON, DAVID CARL, school superintendent, farmer, state legislator; b. Langdon, N.D., July 30, 1950; s. Carl Arthur and Shirley Jean (Klai) M.; m. Mary Kathryn Greutman, July 8, 1972; children: Cordell Carl, Cale David, Jared Arthur. Cert. tchr., adminstr., N.D. Sci. tchr. Hankinson (N.D.) Pub. Sch., 1972-75; tchr. Nekoma (N.D.) Pub. Sch., 1975-76; tchr., prin. NeKoma (N.D.) Pub. Sch., 1976-79; tchr., supt. Nekoma (N.D.) Pub. Sch., 1979-80; tchr., prin. Milton (N.D.)-Osnabrock High Sch., 1981-84; supt. Adams (N.D.) Pub. Schs., 1984-88; ins. agt. N.Y. Life, Fargo, N.D., 1988-95; farmer Osnabrock, 1975—; state rep. N.D. State Legis., Bismarck, 1993—; supt. Edinburg (N.D.) Pub. Schs., 1995—; bd. dirs. No. Canola Growers, Langdon, N.D. Mem. sch. bd. dirs. Osnabrock Sch. Bd., 1989—; leader Bobcats 4-H Club, 1988—. Mem. N.D. Farm Bur., N.D. Coun. Sch. Adminstrs., Nat. Assn. Life Underwriting (Quality award 1992, 93, 94) Eagles, Knights of Pythias of N.D. and Sask. (grand sec. 1985-93, award 1990). Republican. Lutheran. Avocations: skiing, gardening, hunting, coin collecting.

MONSON, DAVID SMITH, accountant, former congressman; b. Salt Lake City, June 20, 1945; s. Smith Weston and Dorothy (Brammer) M.; m. Julianne Johnson, Feb. 4, 1971; children: David Johnson, Traci Lyn, Marianne, Kari, Smith Douglas. BS in Acctg., U. Utah, 1970. C.P.A., Utah. Acct. Elmer Fox and Co., Salt Lake City, 1970-72; auditor State of Utah, Salt Lake City, 1973-76; lt. gov. State of Utah, 1977-84; mem. 99th Congress, 1985-87; v.p. I Corp., 1987-91; bus. cons. and acct., 1992—; mem. exec. com. Nat. Conf. Lt. Govs., 1978-84 mem. State Bd. Regents, 1981-84. Bd. dirs. Utah Soc. to Prevent Blindness, 1976-83; chmn. Utah Cancer Crusade, 1979-80, chmn. Bd. Salt Lake County Am. Cancer Soc., 1980-81; govt. group chmn. United Way, 1979, assoc. campaign chmn., 1981, campaign chmn. 1982; treas. Utah Reps., 1975-76; trustee Ballet West, 1977-81, Travis Found., 1977-84, bd. dirs. Osmond Found., 1982-84, Utah Opportunities Industrialization Ctrs., Inc., 1988-91; sec. bd. dirs. Utah Sports Found., Inc., 1988-91. Recipient Outstanding Young Man Am. award, 1977, 81; named One of 3 Outstanding Young Men Utah Jaycees, 1980-81. Mem. Council State Govts. (v.p. Western conf. 1974-75). Republican. Mem. Ch. Jesus Christ Latter Day Saints. Home: 792 Northview Dr Salt Lake City UT 84103-4027 *Two principles have been the overriding factors in motivating the actions I have taken throughout my life—a strong desire to be the successful leader and provider of a stable family unit and a faith in and a desire to follow the teachings of a loving God.*

MONSON, DIANNE LYNN, literacy educator; b. Minot, N.D., Nov. 24, 1934; d. Albert Rachie and Iona Cordelia (Kirk) M. BS, U. Minn., 1956, MA, 1962, PhD, 1966. Tchr., Rochester Pub. Schs. (Minn.), 1956-59, U.S. Dept. Def., Schweinfurt, W.Ger., 1959-61, St. Louis Park Schs. (Minn.), 1961-62; instr. U. Minn., Mpls., 1962-66; prof. U. Wash., Seattle, 1966-82; prof. literacy edn. U. Minn., Mpls., 1982—, chmn. Curriculum and Instrn., 1986-89. Co-author: New Horizons in the Language Arts, 1972; Children and Books, 6th edit., 1981; Experiencing Children's Literature, 1984; (monograph) Research in Children's Literature, 1976; Language Arts: Teaching and Learning Effective Use of Language, 1988; Reading Together: Helping Children Get A Good Start With Reading, 1991; assoc. editor Dictionary of Literacy, 1995. Recipient Outstanding Educator award U. Minn. Alumni Assn., 1983, Alumni Faculty award, 1991, (associate editor) The Literacy Dictionary, 1995. Fellow Nat. Conf. Rsch. in English (pres. 1990-91); mem. Nat. Coun. Tchrs. of English (exec. com. 1979-81), Internat. Reading Assn. (dir. 1980-83, Arbuthnot award 1993), ALA, U.S. Bd. Books for Young People (pres. 1988-90). Lutheran. Home: 740 River Dr Saint Paul MN 55116-1069 Office: U Minn 350 Peik Hall Minneapolis MN 55455

MONSON, JAMES EDWARD, electrical engineer, educator; b. Oakland, Calif., June 20, 1932; s. George Edward and Frances Eleanor (Fouche) M.; m. Julie Elizabeth Conzelman, June 25, 1954; children—John, Jamie, Jennifer. BSEE, Stanford U., 1954, MSEE, 1955, PhD in Elec. Engring., 1961. Mem. tech. staff Bell Telephone Labs., Murray Hill, N.J., 1955-56; devel. engr. Hewlett-Packard Co., Palo Alto, Calif., 1956-61; Robert C. Sabini prof. engring. Harvey Mudd Coll., 1961—. Mem. governing bd. Claremont Unified Sch. Dist., 1966-71, pres., 1969-70; pres. Claremont Civic Assn., 1974-75; bd. dirs. Claremont YMCA, 1978-82. NSF fellow, 1954-55; Fulbright research grantee, 1975-76; Fulbright sr. lectr., 1980; Japan Soc. Promotion of Sci. fellow, 1984. Mem. AAUP, IEEE, Magnetics Soc. Japan, Phi Beta Kappa, Sigma Xi, Tau Beta Pi. Home: 353 W 11th St Claremont CA 91711-3806 Office: Harvey Mudd Coll 301 E 12th St Claremont CA 91711-5901

MONSON, JOHN RUDOLPH, lawyer; b. Chgo., Feb. 4, 1941; s. Rudolph Agaton and Ellen Louise (Loeffler) M.; m. Susan Lee Brown, May 22, 1965; children: Elizabeth Louisa, Christina Lee, Donald Rudolph. BA with honors, Northwestern U., 1963; JD with distinction, U. Mich., 1966. Bar: Ill. 1966, N.H. 1970, Mass. 1985. Atty. assoc. Chapman & Cutler, Chgo., 1966-68, Levenfeld, Kanter, Baskes & Lippitz, Chgo., 1968-70, Nighswander, Martin & Mitchell, Laconia, N.H., 1970-71; ptnr. Wiggin & Nourie, P.A., Manchester, N.H., 1972—; pres. Wiggin & Nourie, P.A., Manchester, 1991-94. Mem. N.H. Fish and Game Commn., Concord, 1980-94, chmn., 1983-93; sr. bd. dirs. Brown-Monson Found., 1991—; incorporator Cath. Med. Ctr., 1988-95, Optima Health, 1994—. Fellow Am. Coll. Trust and Estate Counsel. Republican. Avocations: skiing, hunting, running. Home: 24 Wellesley Dr Bedford NH 03110-4531 Office: Wiggin & Nourie PA 20 Market St Manchester NH 03101-1931

MONSON, THOMAS SPENCER, church official, publishing company executive; b. Salt Lake City, Aug. 21, 1927; s. George Spencer and Gladys (Condie) M.; m. Frances Beverly Johnson, Oct. 7, 1948; children—Thomas L., Ann Frances, Clark Spencer. BS with honors in mktg. U. Utah, 1948; MBA, Brigham Young U., 1974, LLD (hon.), 1981. With Deseret News Press, Salt Lake City, 1948-64; mgr. Deseret News Press, 1962-64; mem. Council Twelve Apostles, Ch. of Jesus Christ of Latter Day Saints, 1963-85, mem. first presidency, 1985—, bishop, 1950-55; pres. Canadian Mission, 1959-62; chmn. bd. Deseret News Pub. Co., 1977—; dir. Deseret Mgmt. Corp.; pres. Printing Industry Utah, 1958; bd. dirs. Printing Industry Am., 1958-64; mem. Utah exec. bd. U.S. West Communications. Mem. Utah Bd. Regents; mem. nat. exec. bd. Boy Scouts Am.; trustee Brigham Young U.. With USNR, 1945-46. Recipient Recognition award, 1964, Disting. Alumnus award U. Utah, 1966; Silver Beaver award Boy Scouts Am., 1971; Silver Buffalo award, 1978; Bronze Wolf award World Orgn. of the Scout Movement, 1993. Mem. Utah Assn. Sales Execs., U. Utah Alumni Assn. (dir.), Salt Lake Advt. Club, Alpha Kappa Psi. Club: Exchange (Salt Lake City). Office: LDS Ch 47 E South Temple Salt Lake City UT 84150 also: Deseret News Pub Co PO Box 1257 30 E 1st St Salt Lake City UT 84110

MONTAG, JOHN JOSEPH, II, librarian; b. Omaha, Jan. 8, 1948; s. John Joseph and Ruth Helen (Johnston) M.; m. Linda Kay Lubanski, Apr. 8, 1971; children: Nicole Elizabeth, Megan Kristine. BA, Midland Luth. Coll., 1970; postgrad., Wash. State U., 1970-74; MA, U. Iowa, 1976; postgrad., U. Nebr., 1982-84. English tchr. pub. schs., Nebr., Iowa, 1972-75; reference librarian Concordia Coll., Moorhead, Minn., 1976-81; asst. prof. library sci. U. Nebr., Lincoln, 1981-84; dir. Office of Info. State Library Iowa, Des Moines, 1984-86, state librarian, 1986-87; dir. Thomas Library Wittenberg U., 1987-95, Cochrane-Woods Libr. Nebr. Wesleyan U., Lincoln, 1995—; trustee Bibliog. Ctr. for Research, Denver, 1986-87; adv. bd. No. Lights Library Network, Detroit Lakes, Minn., 1980-81; chair Southwest Ohio Consortium Higher Edn. Libr. Coun., 1991-94. Contbr. articles to profl. jours. Univ. Found. library improvement grantee, U. Nebr., 1983; Challenge grantee NEH, 1992. Mem. ALA, Assn. Coll. and Research Libraries. Office: Cochrane Woods Libr Nebr Wesleyan U 5000 St Paul Ave Lincoln NE 68504

MONTAGU, ASHLEY, anthropologist, social biologist; b. London, June 28, 1905; came to U.S., 1927, 30; naturalized, 1940; s. Charles Ehrenberg and Mary (Plotnick) M.; m. Helen Marjorie Peakes, Sept. 18, 1931; children: Audrey, Barbara, Geoffrey. Spl./student, U. London, 1922-25; student, U. Florence, 1928-29; Ph.D., Columbia U., 1937; D.Sc. (hon.), Grinnell Coll., 1967, U. N.C., 1987; D.Litt. (hon.), Ursinus Coll., 1972. Research asso. Brit. Mus. Natural History, London, 1926-27; curator phys. anthropology Wellcome Hist. Med. Mus., 1929-30; asst. prof. anatomy N.Y. U., 1931-38; asso. prof. anatomy Hahnemann Med. Coll. and Hosp., Phila., 1938-49; chmn. dept. anthropology Rutgers U., 1949-55; vis. lectr. dept. social sci. Harvard, 1945; sr. lectr. VA Postgrad. Tng. Program Psychiatry and Neurology, 1946—; lectr. New Sch. Social Research, 1931-59; vis. prof. U. Del., 1955; Regents prof., U. Calif., Santa Barbara, 1962; lectr. Princeton U., 1978-83; dir. Inst. Natural Philosophy, 1979-81; fellow Stevenson Hall, Princeton U., 1978—; dir. rsch. N.J. Com. Phys. Devel. and Health, 1953-57; family affairs editor, anthrop. adv. NBC-TV, 1954; chmn. Anisfield-Wolf Award Com., 1954-95; co-chmn. Attach, 1992—; responsible for drafting statement on race for UNESCO, 1949-50, cons., 1949; a drafter NSF Bill, 1946-47, co-drafter constn. Am. Assn. Human Genetics, 1949; hon. corr. mem. anthrop. socs. Paris and Florence. Produced, financed, wrote and directed: film One World or None for, Nat. Commn. on Atomic Info. and Am. Fedn. Sci. Workers, 1946; Author: Coming into Being Among the Australian Aborigines, 1937, 2d edit., 1974, Man's Most Dangerous Myth: The Fallacy of Race, 1942, 5th edit., 1974, Edward Tyson, M.D., F.R.S., (1650-1708): and the rise of human and comparative anatomy in England, 1943, Introduction to Physical Anthropology, 1945, 3d edit., 1960, Adolescent Sterility, 1946, On Being Human, 1950, 2d edit., 1966, On Being Intelligent, 1951, Statement on Race, 1952, 3d edit., 1972, Darwin, Competition and Cooperation, 1952, The Natural Superiority of Women, 1953, 3d edit., 1992, The Direction of Human Development, 1955, 2d edit., 1970, Immortality, 1955, Biosocial Nature of Man, 1956, Anthropology And Human Nature, Man: His First Million Years, 1957, 1970, The Reproductive Development of the Female, 1957, 3d edit., 1979, Education and Human Relations, 1958, The Cultured Man, 1958, Human Heredity, 1959, 2d edit., 1963, Handbook of Anthropometry, 1960, Man in Process, 1961, Prenatal Influences, 1962, The Humanization of Man, 1962, Race, Science, and Humanity, 1963, The Dolphin in History, (with John Lilly 1963), Life Before Birth, 1964, 2d edit., 1978, The Science of Man, 1964, (with E. Steen) Anatomy and Physiology, 1959, 2d edit., 1983, (with C.L. Brace) Man's Evolution, 1965, The Idea of Race, 1965, (with C.L. Brace) The Human Revolution, 1965, 2nd edit., 1977, Up the Ivy, 1966, The American Way of Life, 1967, The Anatomy of Swearing, 1967, (with E. Darling) The Prevalance of Nonsense, 1967, Man Observed, 1968, Man, His First Two Million Years, 1957, 3d edit., 1962, Sex, Man, and Society, 1969, (with E. Darling) The Ignorance of Certainty, 1970, Immortality, Religion, and Morals, 1955, 2nd edit., 1971, Touching, 1971, 3d edit., 1986, (with M. Levitan) Textbook of Human Genetics, 1971, 2d edit., 1977, The Elephant Man, 1971, 3d edit., 1996, America As I See It, 1971, (with S.S. Snyder) Man and the Computer, 1972, The Endangered Environment, 1974, The Nature of Human Aggression, 1976, (with C.L. Brace) Human Evolution, 1977, (with Floyd Matson) The Human Connection, 1979, (with Floyd Matson) The Dehumanization of Man, 1983, Growing Young, 1981, What We Know About Race, 1985, Times Change...Do People?, 1985, The Peace of the World, 1986, Living and Loving, 1986, Humanity Speaking to Humankind, 1986, The World of Humanity, 1986, Coming into Being, 1988, the Story of People, 1988; editor Nat. Hist. Soc. Series, Classics of Anthropology; adv. editor Sci. Tech. and Humanities; anthropology editor Isis, 1936-56, publs. editor, 1937-45. Guardsman with Welsh Guards, 1919. Recipient 1st prize Morris Chaim prize Centennary 2d Dist. Dental Soc., 1936, Chgo. Forum Lit. contest, 1943, Rollo May award Saybrook Inst. Humanistic Studies, 1991, Verney award Pre-Perinatal Psychol. Assn. N.Am., 1993; recipient Disting Svc. award Assn. Childbirth at Home Internat., 1970, Am. Anthrop. Assn., 1984, Phi Beta Kappa, 1985, Inst. Human Behavior, 1986, Nat. Assn. Parents and Profls. Safe Alternatives in Childbirth, 1986, Am. Humanist of Yr. award, 1995, Assn. for Humananistic Psychol. Pathfinder award, 1995, Ashley Montagu Peace award Common Bond Inst. of U.S. and Harmony Inst. of Russia, 1995. Fellow AAAS; mem. Royal Soc. Medicine (affiliate), Internat. Soc. Study of Race Rels., Internat. Assn. Human Biologists, Am. Assn. Anatomists, Am. Soc. Study of Child Growth and Devel., Am. Assn. Maternal and Child Health, Am. Assn. Phys. Anthropologists (Charles Darwin Lifetime Achievement award 1994), Sigma Xi. (affilicate Royal Society of Medicine). Expert forensic problems witness on legal, sci. problems relating to race and anthrop. matters, 1930. Home: 321 Cherry Hill Rd Princeton NJ 08540-7617 *To be kind, to be, to do, and to depart gracefully.*

MONTAGU, JEAN IVAN, electro-optic company executive; b. Courberoie, France, July 9, 1933; came to U.S., 1952, naturalized 1958; s. Leonide Petrovich and Jenny (Spalenice) K.; m. Kyra Lockhart Gordon, Apr. 1, 1961; children—Sasha, Dominic. B.S. in Mech. Engring., MIT, 1955, M.S. in Mech. Engring., 1956. Asst. prof. Cath. U., Rio de Janeiro, Brazil, 1967-68; engr. Honeywell, Boston, 1958; v.p., founder Mechanics for Electronics, Salem, N.H., 1959-67; chmn., chief exec. officer Gen. Scanning, Inc., Watertown, Mass., 1968—; dir. Can. Corp. Mgmt., Toronto, 1981-86, Ctr. for Blood Research Lab., Boston, 1980-83; instr. Northeastern U., Boston, 1968. Inventor in thermodynamics and electromagnetics. Contbr. section to book, articles to profl. jours. Office: Gen Scanning Inc 500 Arsenal St Watertown MA 02172-2806

MONTAGUE, BRIAN JOHN, consulting company executive; b. Washington, Oct. 9, 1951; s. H.C. and Dorothy (Brand) M.; m. Kathryn Valente, Oct. 2, 1993. B.A., Bridgewater Coll., 1973; student, St. Mary's (Md.) Coll., 1975, George Washington U., 1980, Miss. State U., 1981. Toxicology technician Hazelton Labs., Vienna, Va., 1973-74; asst. mgr. Chesapeake Sea Farms, Ridge, Md., 1974-76; tng. instr., program coord. Natural Resources Dept., Annapolis, Md., 1976-77; fishery biologist Nat. Aquarium, U.S. Fish and Wildlife Svc., Washington, 1977-82, curator aquarium, 1982-88; pres. Aquatic Images, Annapolis, 1989—; lectr. local interest groups. Office: Aquatic Images 740 Red Cedar Rd Annapolis MD 21401-6000

MONTAGUE, DROGO K., urologist; b. Alpena, Mich., Dec. 11, 1942; s. Frank Wright and Susan Alice (Kidder) M.; m. Margaret Mary Barrett; children: Mark Andrew, Lisa Joy. Student, U. Mich., 1963, MD cum laude, 1968. Diplomate Am. Bd. Urology. Intern Cleve. Clinic Hosp., 1968-69, resident in gen. surgery, 1969-70, resident in urology, 1970-73; assoc. staff urologist Cleve. Clinic Found., 1973-75, staff urologist, 1975—, head sect. prosthetic surgery, 1981—, urology residence program dir., 1985—, dir. Ctr. for Sexual Function, 1987—; prof. surgery Ohio State U. Coll. Medicine, 1992—; trainee cardiovascular rsch. tng. program NIH, 1962-68; trustee Am. Bd. Urology, 1989-95, mem. examination com., 1975-80, examiner cert. exam., 1980-88, rep. to Am. Bd. Med. Specialties, 1989-95. Reviewer various publs. in field; contbr. numerous articles to profl. publs., chpts. to books; editor: Disorders of Male Sexual Function, 1988, Surgical Treatment of Erectile Dysfunction, 1993; author audiovisual tapes in field. James B. Angell scholar, 1961, 62, Nat. Found. scholar, 1963-68; recipient Russell and Mary Hugh Scott Edn. award, 1989, Iowa Rsch. award, 1967. Fellow ACS; mem. Am. Urolog. Assn. (chmn. sci. exhibits com. North Cen. sect. 1977, mem. residency edn. com. 1979-83, vice chmn. audio visual com. 1989-95, mem. various coms., editor Am. Urolog. Assn. Video Libr. 1995—), Am. Assn. Genitourinary Surgeons, Cleve. Urolog. Soc. (sec.-treas. 1978-80, v.p. 1980-81, pres. 1981-82, 94-95), Soc. for Study of Impotence (pres. 1995). Office: Cleve Clinic Found Dept Urology 9500 Euclid Ave Cleveland OH 44195-0001

MONTAGUE, EDGAR BURWELL, III (MONTY MONTAGUE), industrial designer; b. Charlotte, N.C., Aug. 6, 1958; s. Edgar B. Jr. and Mary Sue (Calhoun) M.; m. Nancy Oliver Stallworth, Feb. 25, 1984; children: Nancy Lea, Edgar Eubank. B Environ. Design cum laude, N.C. State U., 1980. Indsl. design Design/Joe Sonderman, Inc., Charlotte, 1980-85; design prin. Machen Montague, Inc., Charlotte, 1985-93, BOLT, Charlotte, 1994—. Holder 8 design and/or utility patents; work published in Product Design 1-6, Design for Humanity. Designer corp. identity program Habitat for Humanity, Charlotte, 1987 (logo design now used throughout world). Recipient ann. design award Internat. Design mag., 1988-93, ID-40 ID Mag., 1994. Mem. Indsl. Designer Soc. Am. (co-founder Carolina chpt., program chmn. 1981-83, vice chmn. 1984, 93, Kudo award for chpt. svc. 1982, Indsl. Design Excellence awards 1989-94). Avocations: travel, art, time with family. Office: BOLT 2221 Edge Lake Dr Ste 100 Charlotte NC 28217-4509

MONTALBAN, RICARDO, actor; b. Mexico City, Nov. 25, 1920; s. Jenaro and Ricarda M.; m. Georgiana Young; children: Mark, Victor, Laura, Anita. Appeared in Mexican motion pictures, 1942-46; appeared in numerous films in U.S. including, Fiesta, 1947, Kissing Bandit, 1949, Neptune's Daughter, 1949, Battleground, 1950, Sombrero, 1953, Latin Lovers, 1954, Sayonara, 1957, Let No Man Write My Epitaph, 1960, Cheyenne Autumn, 1964, The Money Trap, 1965, Madame X, 1966, Sweet Charity, 1968, Escape From the Planet of the Apes, 1971, Conquest of the Planet of the Apes, 1972, The Train Robbers, 1972, Joe Panther, 1976, Won Ton Ton, The Dog Who Saved Hollywood, 1976, Star Trek II: The Wrath of Khan, 1982, Cannonball Run II, 1984, The Naked Gun, 1988; TV films include The Pigeon, 1969, The Aquarians, 1970, Fireball Forward, 1972, The Mark of Zorro, 1974, McNaughton's Daughter, 1976, Fantasy Island, Return to Fantasy Island, 1978; TV advertisements Chrysler, 1973—; TV appearances include Columbo, Star Trek, Return to Fantasy Island; starred in: ltd. series McNaughton's Daughter, 1976; TV series Fantasy Island, 1978-84 (Recipient Emmy award 1978), The Colbys, 1986-87. Mem. Acad. Motion Picture Arts and Scis. Office: William Morris Agency 151 El Camino Beverly Hills CA 90212*

MONTANA, JOSEPH C., JR., former professional football player; b. New Eagle, Pa., June 11, 1956; s. Joseph C. Montana, Sr., and Theresa M.; m. 1st, Kim Monses, 1975 (div.); m. 2nd, Cass Castillo (div. 1983); m. 3rd, Jennifer Wallace, 1984; 2 children, Alexandra, Elizabeth. B.B.A. in Mktg., U. Notre Dame, 1978. Quarterback San Francisco 49ers, 1979-93; mem. Super Bowl Championship Team, 1982, 85, 90; named to Pro Bowl, 1981, 83, 84, 85, 87, 89, 90, 93; quarterback Kansas City Chiefs, 1993-95. Author (with Alan Steinberg): Cool Under Fire, 1989. Named MVP at Super Bowl, 1982, 85, MVP at NFL, 1989, Player of Yr., The Sporting News, 1989, Man of Yr., The Sporting News, 1989; named to Pro Bowl 1981, 83-85, 87, 89, 90, 93. Holds NFL career records for highest completion percentage (63.67), highest passer rating (93.5), NFL single-season record for highest passer rating (112.4), 1989, NFL record for most consecutive games with 300 or more yards passing (5), 1982, most consecutive passes completed (22), 1987. Office: care Internat Mgmt Group 1 Erieview Plz Ste 1300 Cleveland OH 44114

MONTANA, PATRICK JOSEPH, management educator; b. N.Y.C.; s. Joseph Paul and Constance (Frezza) M. B.S. cum laude, L.I. U., M.S. cum laude; Ph.D., N.Y. U., 1966; M.B.A., U. Cin., 1974. Asst. dean, asso. prof., dir. placement, chmn. mgmt. L.I. U., Bklyn., 1960-66; asso. prof. Drexel U., Phila., 1966-67; asst. dean N.Y. U. Grad. Sch. Bus. Adminstrn., N.Y.C., 1967-69; asst. v.p., dir. planning and human resources devel. Sperry & Hutchingson Co. (trading stamps and subsidiaries), N.Y.C., 1969-74; U.S. presdl. interchange exec., 1973; pres. Profl. Inst., Am. Mgmt. Assn., N.Y.C., 1974-76, Nat. Center Career Life Planning, 1975-80, 80—; prof. mgmt. Hofstra U. Sch. Bus.; corp. cons. New Choices mag.; adj. prof. mgmt. and mktg. Fordham U. Grad. Sch. Bus., N.Y.C., 1969-79; curriculum cons. U. P.R., 1968; guest lectr. Congress for Internat. Progress in Mgmt., 1965, IBM Corp. Mgmt. Sch., 1964-65, 76-77; mediator Pub. Employee Relations Bd., 1969; bd. dirs. Ednl. Systems and Publs., 1970-75. Author: The Marketing Executive of the Future, 1967, You Can Change Your Future, 1976, Managing Nonprofit Organizations, 1977, Marketing in Nonprofit Organizations, 1978, Career Life Planning for Americans, 1978, Overcoming Mid and Late Career Crises, 1978, Successful Teamwork—How Managers and Secretaries Achieve It, 1979, Managing Terrorism, 1982; Retirement Programs: How to Develop and Implement Them, 1985; Work Force Management in the Arabian Peninsula, 1986, Management, 1987, Preretirement Planning, 1988, Stepping Out, Starting Over, 1992, Managing Public and Nonprofit Organizations, 1994; contbr. numerous articles to profl. publs. Recipient achievement award Wall Street Jour., 1959-60, U.S. Sec. Labor's recognition award 1974, Disting. Alumnus award L.I. U.; fellow Ford Found., 1963-64. Mem. Am. Assembly Collegiate Schs. Bus. (accreditation com. 1970-72, standards com. 1973-75, govt. relations com. 1976-78), Am. Mktg. Assn. (awards com., continuing edn. com.), Beta Gamma Sigma, Eta Mu Pi. Office: Hofstra U Sch Bus Hempstead NY 11550

MONTANA, PATSY See ROSE, RUBYE BLEVINS

MONTCALM, NORMAN JOSEPH, lawyer; b. Trois-Rivieres, Que., Can., July 8, 1945; s. Aimé and Alida (Filion) M.; m. Marie Lanctôt, July 28, 1973; children: Julie, Valérie, Jean-François. BA, Collège des Trois-Riviéres, 1967; BCL, McGill U., 1971. Bar: Que. 1972. Legal counsel Hydro-Que., Montreal, 1972-79; v.p. legal affairs, sec. Civitas Corp., Montreal, 1979-83; legal counsel Imasco Ltd., Montreal, 1983-88, sec., legal counsel, 1988-89; ptnr. Legault Longtin Laurin Halpin, Montreal, 1992—. Mem. St. Justine Hosp. Found., Montreal, 1986—, Order of Que. Olympic Games, Montreal, 1988—. Mem. Can. Bar Assn., Que. and Montreal bar assns. (various coms.), Montreal C. of C. Roman Catholic. Home: 221 Carlyle, Mount Royal, PQ Canada H3R 1T1 Office: Legault Longtin Laurin Halpin, 630 Blvd René-Lévesque W # 1800, Montreal, PQ Canada H3B 1S6

MONTE, BONNIE J., performing company executive; b. Stamford, Ct., Nov. 27, 1954; d. Eugene N. and Ruth M. (Thompson) M. BA, Bethany Coll., 1976; diploma, Hartman Conservatory, Stamford, 1978. Assoc. artistic dir. Williamstown (Mass.) Theatre Festival, 1981-89; casting dir. Manhattan Theatre Club, N.Y.C., 1989-90; artistic dir. N.J. Shakespeare Festival, Madison, 1990—; mem. faculty Drew U., Madison, 1991—; guest artist, vis. asst. prof. U. Notre Dame, fall 1994. Grantee Lotte Crabtree Found., Boston, 1977. Democrat. Avocations: equerry, cycling, archery, writing, travel. Office: NJ Shakespeare Festival c/o Drew U 36 Madison Ave Madison NJ 07940-1434

MONTE, WILLIAM DAVID, education educator; b. San Diego, Aug. 17, 1958; s. Thomas Gilbert Monte and Lisa Ruth Veale; m. Amy Lisa Schuenemann, Jan. 9, 1982; children: Sarah Nicole, William David. BS in Ministry, Bethany Coll., Santa Cruz, Calif., 1981; MA in Theology, Fuller Theol. Sem., Pasadena, Calif., 1987; MA in Edn., Claremont (Calif.) Grad. Sch., 1991, postgrad., 1992—. Cert. multiple subjects, Calif. Tchr. Mira Mesa Christian Sch., San Deigo, 1982-83; tchr. ESL Armenean Social Svc. Ctr., L.A., 1988-89; substitute tchr. Baldwin Park (Calif.) Unified Sch. Dist., 1988-89; tchr. Upland (Calif.) Unified Sch. Dist., 1989-94; faculty assoc. office tchr. edn. Claremont Grad. Sch., 1994—; adj. faculty dept. edn. Whittier Coll., 1995—; founder, pres. ednl. cons. firm DIDASKEIN, San Dimas, Calif., 1986—. Contbr. articles to profl. jours. AB 1470 Tech. grantee State of Calif., 1990-91; Minority Student fellow Claremont Grad. Sch., 1992-93. Mem. Religious Edn. Assn., Computer Using Eductors, Assn. for Moral Edn., Assn. for Religion and Intellectual Life, Pi Lambda Theta. Avocations: computers/multimedia, tennis, photography, creative writing, model building. Home: 538 Andover Ave San Dimas CA 91773-3201 Office: Claremont Grad Sch 121 E 10th St Claremont CA 91711-3911

MONTECEL, MARIA ROBLEDO (CUCA ROBLEDO MONTECEL), educational association administrator; b. Laredo, Tex., Jan. 14, 1953; d. Ismael and Paula (Benavides) Robledo; m. Lucas Montecel, Aug. 18, 1979; children: Ismael Gavino, Xavier Mario. BSSW magna cum laude, Our Lady of Lake U., 1972; MEd, Antioch U., 1975; PhD in Urban Edn., U. Wis., 1985. Rsch. asst. D.C. Devel. Assocs., Inc., San Antonio, 1973-75; test designer Dissemination and Assessment Ctr. for Bilingual Edn. U. Tex., San Antonio, 1975-76; grad. rsch. asst. office rsch. Sch. Edn. U. Wis., Milw., 1980-81, program dir. Midwest NODAC dept. cultural founds. Sch. Edn., 1985; evaluator Ctr. for Mgmt. Innovation in Multicultural Edn. Intercultural Devel. Rsch. Assn., San Antonio, 1976-77, dir. bilingual edn. cost analysis project, 1977-78, dir. divsn. rsch., devel. and evalutation, 1978-80, rsch. specialist, 1982-85, dir. Ctr. for Prevention and Recovery Dropouts, 1985-88, 90-92, dir. tng. and tech. assistance, 1988-89, dir. valued youth program, 1988-90, dep. dir., 1992, exec. dir., 1992—; trustee Our Lady of Lake U. Mem. editorial bd. Tex. Rschr.; contbr. articles to profl. jours. Vol. advocate Alamo Area Rape Crisis Ctr.; mem. rsch. com. Hispanas Unidas; participant Leadership Tex. '85; invited mem. Tex. State Task Force Dropout Prevention; chmn. lifelong learning coun. San Antonio 2000; cons. edn. and immigrant students Mellon Found.; bd. dirs. Mex.-Am. Solidarity Found.; founding bd. dirs. CIVICUS World Alliance Citizen Participation; bd. dirs. community edn. leadership program Mott Found.; mem. nat. adv. coun. Race and Ethnic Studies Inst., Tex. A & M; mem. ednl. review bd. Tex. Ctr. Ednl. Rsch.; mem. nat. adv. bd. ERIC/CRESS, 1994. Recipient High Achievement Commendation, Antioch Coll., 1975, Peter F. Drucker award Coca-Cola Valued Youth Program; Women and Minority Rsch. fellow Nat. Inst. Edn., 1979, Title VII Doctoral fellow U. Wis., 1980-82. Mem. Am. Edn. Rsch. Assn., Nat. Assn. Bilingual Edn., Nat. Dropout Prevention Network (charter), Alphi Chi. Roman Catholic. Avocations: reading, writing, fishing, golf. Office: Intercultural Devel Rsch Assn 5835 Callaghan Rd Ste 350 San Antonio TX 78228-1125

MONTEIRO, GEORGE, English educator, writer; b. Cumberland, R.I., May 23, 1932; s. Francisco José and Augusta (Temudo) M.; m. Lois Ann Hodgins, Aug. 14, 1958 (div. 1992); children: Katherine, Stephen, Emily; m. Brenda Murphy, Mar. 25, 1995. AB, Brown U., 1954; AM, Columbia U., 1956; PhD, Brown U., 1964; DHL honoris caus, U. Mass., Dartmouth, 1993. Instr., asst. prof., then assoc. prof. Brown U., Providence, 1961-72, prof. English, 1972—; vis. prof. Providence Coll., 1967-68; Fulbright prof. Am. lit. U. Sao Paulo, 1969-71. Author: Henry James and John Hay: The Record of a Friendship, 1965, The Coffee Exchange: Poems, 1982, Robert Frost and the New England Renaissance, 1988, The Presence of Camões, 1996; editor: The Man Who Never Was: Essays on Fernando Pessoa, 1982, The Correspondence of Henry James and Henry Adams, 1877-1941, 1992; translator: In Crete with the Minotaur and Other Poems, 1980, Fernando Pessoa: Self Awareness and Thirty Other Poems, 1988, A Man Smiles at Death with Half a Face, 1991. Decorated Order of Prince Henry the Navigator, govt. of Portugal, 1989. Office: Brown U Dept English Providence RI 02912

MONTEIRO, LOIS ANN, medical science educator; b. Central Falls, R.I., Mar. 22, 1934; d. William Henry and Martha Mae (Leach) Hodgins; m. George Monteiro, Aug. 14, 1958 (div. Feb. 1992); children: Katherine, Stephen, Emily. RN, Roger Williams Hosp., Providence, 1954; BA, Brown U., k1958, PhD, 1970; MS, Boston U., 1960. Asst. prof. Boston U., 1960-65; asst. prof. Brown U., Providence, R.I., 1971-77, assoc. prof., 1978-82, prof., 1983—, chmn. dept., 1985—, assoc. dean medicine, 1991—; vis. prof. U. Va., 1990; bd. dirs. Harvard Cmty. Health Plan, 1990-95, Harvard Pilgrim Health Care Plan, New Eng., 1995—. Author: Montoring Health Status, 1976, Cardiac Rehabilitation, 1980; contbr. articles to profl. jours. Mem. Commn. State of R.I., Providence, 1989—. NSF grantee, 1969, Robert W. Johnson Found. grantee, Princeton, N.J., 1983, NIH grantee, 1987; Bunting Inst. fellow, Cambridge, Mass., 1981. Mem. Am. Sociol. Assn., R.I. State Nurses Assn. (pres. 1974-76), Women in Medicine/Assn. Am. Med. Colls. Democrat. Presbyterian. Avocation: collecting books on nursing history. Office: Brown U Dept Med Sci Box G-A413 Providence RI 02912

MONTEIRO, RICARDO J., lawyer; b. Caldas Da Rainha, Portugal, Apr. 16, 1967; s. Luis S. and Maria J. (Malaquias) M. BA in Psychology, L.I. U., 1989; JD cum laude, Widener U., 1992. Bar: N.J. 1992, U.S. Dist. Ct. N.J. 1992. Office mgr. Atlas Metal Finishing, Inc., Newark, 1987-90; mgr., atty. Globe Metal Finishing, Inc., Newark, 1990-92; assoc. Fausto Simoes, Esq., Newark, 1992-94; ptnr. Simoes and Monteiro, P.C., Newark, 1994—. Counsel Portuguese Am. Police Assn., Newark, 1992, C.A.F.I.C., Newark, 1993, Portuguese Americans United, Newark, 1994. Recipient Am. Jurisprudence award Lawyers Coop. Pub., 1991. Mem. ABA, ATLA, Assn. Regional Caldense (pres. 1994), Phi Kappa Phi, Phi Delta Phi. Avocations: skiing, golf. Home: PO Box 190 541 Bethany Rd Holmdel NJ 07733

MONTEITH, CLIFTON JAMES, artist; b. Detroit, July 8, 1944; s. James Elsworth and Shirley Alice (Bossardet) M.; m. Elizabeth Ann Sutherland, June 14, 1969 (div. Apr. 1985); 1 child, Matthew Fredrick; m. Nancy Louise Paepke, Sept. 29, 1986. BFA, Mich. State U., 1968, postgrad., 1973-74. Instr. painting, drawing and sculpture Mich., Conn., N.Y., 1968-84; twig furniture and sculpture designer and builder Lake Ann, Mich., 1985—; guest lectr. U. Mich. Sch. Art, Ann Arbor, 1987, instr. twig design and constrn. workshop, 1987, 90, 92; guest lectr. Calvin Coll., Grand Rapids, Mich., 1990, Parnham Coll., Dorset, Eng., 1993; lectr. So. Ohio Mus., Portsmouth, Ohio, 1993, Takumi-Jyuku wood working sch., Makigahora, Gifu, Japan, 1994, Far East Sch. Archs. and Engrs., Osaka, Japan, 1994, Osaka Designer's Coll., 1994, Artist's Forum, Internat. House of Japan, Tokyo, 1994, Dennos Mus., Traverse City, Mich., 1995; spkr. Organic Arch. Forum, Coll. Art Assn. Ann. Conf., N.Y.C., 1994. One man shows include Carl Hammer Gallery, Chgo., 1989, 91, Miami Univ. Mus., Oxford, Ohio, 1992; exhibited in group shows Carl Hammer Gallery, Chgo., 1988, 89, 90, 94, Design N.Y., N.Y.C., 1989, Joy Emery Gallery, Grosse Pointe Farms, Mich., 1989, 90, Artful Domain Gallery, Birmingham, Mich., 1990, Am. Primitive Gallery, N.Y.C., 1990, Judith Racht Gallery, Harbert, Mich., 1990, Perception Gallery, Grand Rapids, Mich., 1990, Columbus (Ohio) Cultural Arts Ctr., 1990, Muskegon (Mich.) C.C., 1990, Contemporary Arts Ctr., Cin., 1990, Columbia Coll. Art Gallery, Chgo., 1991, Joan Robey Gallery, Denver, 1991, Detroit Inst. Arts, 1991, The Westman Collection, Birmingham, 1991, Art Inst., Chgo., 1991, Ohio Designer Craftsman Traveling Exhbn., 1993, Gallery of Functional Art, Santa Monica, Calif., 1993; works included in publs. including Traverse the Mag., 1986, Detroit Monthly, 1988, Country Living, 1989, Chgo. Tribune, 1989, 91, La Architectura, Milan, 1989, N.Y. Times, 1990, Detroit News, 1990, Town and Country, 1990, Grand Rapids Press, 1990, Cin. Enquirer, 1990, Am. Craft, 1990, Antique Monthly, 1991, Making Rustic Furniture (Daniel Mack), 1992, U.S. News and World Report, 1992, Record Patriot, 1993, Rustic Traditions (Ralph Kylloe), 1993, The Japan Times, 1994, Record Eagle, 1995. Nat. Endowment of Arts fellow, 1992, Japan fellow U.S.-Japan Friendship Commn., 1994. Mem. Am. Craft Coun. Libr. Home: PO Box 9 20341 E Fowler Rd Lake Ann MI 49650

MONTEITH, LARRY KING, university chancellor; b. Bryson City, N.C., Aug. 17, 1933; s. Earl and Essie (King) M.; m. Nancy Alexander, Apr. 19, 1952; children: Larry, Carol, Steve. BSEE, N.C. State U., 1960; MSEE, Duke U., 1962, PhDEE, 1965. Registered profl. engr., N.C. Mem. tech. staff Bell Telephone Labs., Burlington, N.C., 1960-62; mem. tech. staff Resch. Triangle Inst., Raleigh, 1962-66, group leader rsch. sect., 1966-68; adj. asst. prof. elec. engring. N.C. State U., Raleigh, 1965-68, assoc. prof., 1968-72, prof., 1972—, head dept. elec. engring., 1974-78, dean of engring., 1978-89, interim chancellor, 1989-90, chancellor, 1990—; bd. dirs. Microelectronics Ctr. N.C., Rsch. Triangle Inst. Contbr. articles to profl. jours. Trustee Nat. Tech. Univ., Triangle Univ. Ctr. Advanced Studies, Inc.; corp. mem. Underwriters Labs., Inc.; bd. visitors Air U. With USN, 1952-55. Recipient Disting. Engring. Alumnus award Duke U., 1984, Outstanding Engring. Achievement award N.C. Soc. Engrs., 1990. Fellow IEEE, Am. Soc. for Engring. Edn.; mem. NSPE (edn. adv. group), Raleigh C. of C. (bd. dirs.), Rotary Internat. (Paul Harris fellow Rotary Found. 1991), Phi Beta Kappa, Sigma Xi, Sigma Iota Rho, Phi Kappa Phi, Eta Kappa Nu, Tau Beta Pi, Sigma Beta Delta. Home: 1903 Hillsborough St Raleigh NC 27607-7348 Office: NC State U Chancellor's Office Pullen Rd Raleigh NC 27695

MONTELEONE, PATRICIA, academic dean. Dean. assoc. v.p. St. Louis u. Sch. Medicine. Office: St Louis U Sch Medicine 1402 S Grand Blvd Saint Louis MO 63104

MONTELONGO, MICHAEL, career officer; b. N.Y.C.; m. Debra Tenison; 1 child, Amanda. BS in Nat. Security and Pub. Affairs, U.S. Military Acad.; MBA in Corp. Strategy and Fin., Harvard U., 1988; grad., Command and Gen. Staff Coll., 1992. Commd. 2d lt. U.S. Army, 1977, advanced through grades to lt. col., platoon leader, 1980, staff officer, 1982, ops. officer, company comdr., 1986; admissions officer U.S. Military Acad., West Point, N.Y., 1991, asst. prof. social scis. dept., 1991; rsch. analyst office economic and manpower analysis U.S. Army, 1991; adviser, spl. asst. Comdr.-in-Chief U.S. Southern Command, 1991; bat. exec. officer, bat. and brigade ops. officer U.S. Army, 1993; special asst. to U.S. Army chief of staff U.S. Army, Washington, 1994; senate legis. asst., 1995; sec. supervisory com. Ft. Bliss Fed. Credit Union, 1994; ch. music min., 1969—. Sec. Nat. Soc. Hispanic MBA, 1995; Mex.-Am. legal Def. and Ednl. Fund Advanced Legal Program, 1993, Leadership El Paso Program, 1993; trustee Unite El Paso, 1993. U.S. Army Advanced Civil Schooling fellow, 1986, Inter-Univ. Seminar on Armed Forces and Soc. fellow, 1990, Congl. Hispanic Caucus Inst. fellow, 1992, Army Congl. fellow, 1995. Home: 5589 Anne Peake Dr Fairfax VA 22032-3132 Office: 283 Senate Russell Bldg Washington DC 20510-4304

MONTEPIO, JUANITA-BUSTAMANTE, nursing administrator, medical/surgical nurse; b. Malabon-Rizal, The Philippines, May 30, 1943; came to U.S., 1967; d. Serafin-Ramos and Julita-Pendon (Pudadera) Bustamante; m. Reynaldo-Nava Montepio, May 30, 1988; children: Mira-Joyce, Sheila May. Student, U. Philippines, Quezon City and Iloilo City; grad. in nursing, St. Paul's Sch. Nursing, Iloilo City; B in Nursing, U. San Agustin, Iloilo City. RN, BLS. Head nurse nursery St. Paul's Hosp., Iloilo, 1965-66; head nurse surgery Sin Gian Clinic, Manila, 1966-67; staff nurse St. Therese Hosp., Wankegan, Ill., 1967-69; head nurse surgery Walther Meml. Hosp., Chgo., 1969-70, Toronto Gen. Hosp., Ontario, Can., 1970-77; staff nurse surgery San Gabriel Med. Ctr., L.A., 1977-82, staff nurse II surgery, 1982-88, staff nurse III oncology, 1988-92, coord. clin. care, 1992—; charge nurse med.-surg. obstetrics Valley Vista Hosp., L.A., 1977-82; mem. Quest Team-Ptnrs. Care-Team & Case Mgmt. Mem. La Carlota City Assn. Am. (bd. dirs. 1991—, pres. 1994—, Merit award 1993), Negrenses Am. Inc., Circulo Ilonggo (sec. 1972—, Merit award 1977). Republican. Roman Catholic. Avocations: traveling, reading, cooking, gardening, theatres. Home: 205 N Rimhurst Ave Covina CA 91724-2938 Office: San Gabriel Med Ctr 218 Sta Anita St San Gabriel CA 91776

MONTERO, FERNAN GONZALO, advertising executive; b. Buenos Aires, May 22, 1948; came to U.S., 1952; s. Adolfo and Donne (Strang) M.; m. Cheryl Bowman, Dec. 30, 1976. BBA, U. Wis., 1971; M. Journalism in Advt., Northwestern U., 1972. With Young & Rubicam Inc., 1972-82; pres. Young & Rubicam Argentina, Buenos Aires, 1982-85; dep. area mgr. Young & Rubicam Latin Am., Sao Paulo, Brazil, 1985-87; sr. v.p., dir. bus. devel. Young & Rubicam Inc., N.Y.C., 1987-91, chmn., CEO Latin Am., 1991-92; chmn., CEO Europe Young & Rubicam Inc., London, 1993—. Office: Young & Rubicam, Greater London House, Hampstead Rd London NW1, England

MONTES, FELIX MANUEL, educational researcher, technological consultant; b. Caripito, Monagas, Venezuela, Oct. 20, 1953; came to U.S., 1981; s. Henry Victor Adams and Elia Margarita Montes. Systems analyst, Ctrl. Occidental U., Barquisimeto, Venezuela, 1976; BS, U. Ariz., 1983, MS in Mgmt. Info., 1985; PhD in Ednl. Psychology, U. Ariz., 1990. Systems analyst Regional Computer Co., Barquisimeto, 1976-81; assoc. faculty Ctrl. Occidental Univ., Barquisimeto, 1977-81; grad. rsch. asst. U. Ariz., Tucson, 1988-89; immersion lang. tchr. U.S. State Dept., Marana, Ariz., 1989-90; project dir. U. Ariz., Tucson, 1990-91; ednl. rsch. in teaching Intercultural Devel. Rsch. Assn., San Antonio, Tex., 1991—; tech. cons. Tex. Assn. Bilingual Edn., San Antonio, 1993-94. Developer (software) Classroom Support System, 1984-90, Automatic Generation of Rsch. Info., 1991-94; contbr. articles to Newsletter Interculture Devel. Rsch. Assn., 1992—. Adv. Children Intercultural Devel. Rsch. Program, 1991—; spkr. to edn. profls. at univs. and confs. Recipient scholarship Univ. Ariz., 1984-90, fellowship Charles Stewart Mott Found., San Antonio, 1994-95, Recognition award City Commn. on Literacy, San Antonio, 1994. Mem. Internat. Soc. for Tech. in Edn., Am. Ednl. Rsch. Assn., Hispanic Assn. Colls. and Univs., S.W. Ednl. Rsch. Assn., Nat. Coun. on Measurement in Edn., La. Soc. Nat. Hispanica, Sigma Delta Pi, Phi Kappa Phi. Avocations: universal edn., space exploration, universal literacy, planet earth. Office: Intercultural Devel Rsch Assn 5835 Callaghan Rd Ste 350 San Antonio TX 78228-1125

MONTFORD, JAMES WEBSTER, JR., artist; b. New London, Conn., July 28, 1951; s. James Webster and Bessie (Taylor) M.; children: Dale, Daniel. BA in Fine Arts with honors, Brandeis U., 1974; MA, Columbia U., 1976; MFA, Md. Inst. Art, 1978; postgrad., Columbia U., 1992-94. Instr. art U. Conn., Avery Point, 1983-89; vis. artist Western Md. Coll., Westminster, 1977, Coppin St. Coll., Balt., 1978, U. Conn., 1982. Ehibited in group shows at Macy Gallery, N.Y.C., 1991, Hampden Gallery, Amherst, 1994—, others; represented in permanent collections at DeCordove Mus., 1992, others. Pollock-Krasner Found. grantee, 1993, Tiffay Found. grantee, 1993, NE Found. grantee, 1992; NEA fellow, 1994, Art Matters, Inc. fellow, 1995; recipient Individual Artist award Conn. Commn. on Arts, 1993. Home and Studio: 156 Broadway Norwich CT 06360-4404

MONTFORD, JOHN THOMAS, lawyer, state legislator; b. Ft. Worth, June 28, 1943; s. Thomas L. and Jewell F. (Coursey) M.; m. Pamela Jacobs, June 3, 1966 (div.); 1 child, Melinda; m. Debra Kay Mears, Dec. 24, 1975; children: Melonie, John Ross. BA, U. Tex.-Austin, 1965, JD, 1968; LLD (hon.), Lubbock (Tex.) Christian U., 1989. Bar: Tex. 1968. Pvt. practice law, Lubbock, Tex., 1971-78; criminal dist. atty. Lubbock County, Tex., 1979-82; state senator Dist. 28, Lubbock, 1983—. Trustee S. Park Hosp., Lubbock, 1981-82; bd. dirs., trustee Tex. Boys Ranch, Lubbock, 1982—; chmn. profl. div. United Way, Lubbock, 1980; energy com. So. Legis. Conf., 1983; senate appointee So. Growth Policies Bd., 1983; chmn. adv. coun. Lubbock Substance Abuse Prevention Partnership; mem. bd. govs. West Tex. Chpt. Multiple Sclerosis. Mem. dean's roundtable U. Tex. Sch. Law, 1988. Maj. USMC, 1968-71. Recipient Outstanding Young Man of Lubbock award Jaycees, 1973, Headliner of Yr. award Greater Lubbock Press Club, 1979, Man of Yr./Law Enforcement award Lubbock Optimist Club, 1979, Boss of Yr. award Legal Secs. Assn., 1980, Exec. of Yr., Lubbock Sales Exec. Assn., 1981; named Finest Freshman, Tex. Bus. Mag., 1983, Outstanding State Senator Tex. Youth Commn., 1988, Legislator of Yr. Tex. Pub. Health Assn., 1988, Legislator of Yr. Tex. Pub. Employees Assn. and State Employees, 1989, Outstanding Tex. Leader award John Ben Shepperd Pub. Leadership Forum, 1989, Best New Legislator award Tex. Monthly mag., 1983,, Disting. Alumni, L.D. Bell High Sch., 1984, Lubbock's Man of the Yr. League of Women Voters and Am. Diabetes Assn., 1987, Disting. Svc. award Tex. C. of C., 1989, Outstanding Legislator in State of Tex. Epsilon Sigma Phi, 1989, Legislator of Yr. award Tex. Soc. Profl. Surveyors, 1989, Legislator of Yr. award 71st Legislature, Tex. Mcpl. League, 1989, Tree of Life award Jewish Nat. Fund, 1989; named one of the Ten Best Legislators 71st Legislature, Dallas Morning News, Tex. Monthly, 1989, 72d Legislature, 1991, Tex. Monthly, 1989, 91, Outstanding Legislator Epsilon Sigma Phi, 1989, Legislator of Yr. 71st Legislature Tex. Soc. Profl. Syrveyors, 1989, Tex. Mcpl. League, 1989; recipient Outstanding Svc. award Tex. Electric Coops., 1989, Pub. Ofcl. award Tex. Pub. Power Assn., 1990, George Woods award in politics NAAACP, 1990, Legislative Leadership award 72d Legislator Tex. C. of C., 1992, One of the Seven Best Legislators 73d Legislature Dallas Morning News, 1993, One of the Ten Best Legislators 73d Legislature Tex. Monthly, 1993, Legislator of the Yr. Tex. Public Employees Assn., 1993, Bowie award Tex. State Guard Assn., 1993, award Lubbock Arts Festival, 1994, award Tex. Mental Health Assn., 1994, honor award Tex. Commn. on the Arts, 1994, and numerous others. Mem. State Bar Tex. (com. admissions), Tex. Criminal Def. Lawyers Assn., Tex. Dist. and County Attys. Assn. (legis. com.), Western States Water Council, Tex. Assn. Community Schs. (hon. life), Tex. Heart Inst. (nat. adv. coun. 1991), Order of Coif (hon.), Omicron Delta Kappa, Delta Theta Phi. Club: Jaycees (v.p. 1974), Met. Rotary, Lubbock Lions. Office: PO Box 1709 Lubbock TX 79408-1709

MONTGOMERY, ANNA FRANCES, elementary school educator; b. Spokane, Wash., Nov. 5, 1945; d. Carl Jacob and Edna Frances (Evans) Kuipers; m. William Lee Montgomery Jr., Oct. 7, 1989. AA, Mid. Ga. Coll., 1965; BS in Elem. Edn., Woman's Coll. of Ga., 1966; MEd, Ga. Coll., 1969, specialist in edn., 1973. Cert. elem. tchr., Ga. Classroom tchr. Muscogee County Sch. Dist., Columbus, Ga., 1966—, reading tchr. Title 1 tutorial program, summer 1975, instr. staff devel. program, 1977-80; social sci. lead tchr. Wesley Heights Elem. Sch., Columbus, 1992—; tennis and athletic instr. Camp Tegawitha, Tobyhanna, Pa., summer 1970; presenter workshop Chattahoochee Valley Coun. for Social Studies, 1977; mem. social studies textbook adoption com. Muscogee County Sch. Dist., 1977-78, 82-83, sick leave com., 1993-95; judge Columbus Regional Social Sci. Fair, 1977, 93-96. Treas. Wesley Heights PTA, 1983-86; vol. Med. Ctr. Aux., Columbus, 1975-79; pres. pastor's Bible study class St. Luke United Meth. Ch., 1993-94, 96, mem. Sarah cir., cir. #11, sec., 1969-71, 78-80, co-chmn., 1976-78; mem. Bessie Howard Ward Handbells Choir; devel. chmn. Ga. state divsn. Centennial/fellowships com. AAUW, 1974-76. Recipient Valley Forge Tchrs. medal Freedoms Found. at Valley Forge, 1975; named Very Important Lady award Girl Scouts Am., Columbus, 1976, Outstanding Young Woman Am., 1982. Mem. AAUW (chmn. centennial fellowship com. Columbus br. 1973-75), Ga. PTA (hon. life), Profl. Assn. Ga. Educators (bldg. rep. Muscogee County chpt. 1983—, sec. 1992-94, treas. 1994—), Nat. Coun. Social Studies (mem. hostess and registration coms. ann. meeting 1975), Ga. Coun. for Social Studies, Ga. Sci. Tchrs. Assn., Valley Area Sci. Tchrs. (corr. sec. 1996-97), Ga. Coll. Alumni Assn., Mid. Ga. Coll. Alumni Assn., Order of Amaranth (charity com. 1991-93, 95, assoc. conductress 1996), Scottish Rite Ladies Aux., Alpha Delta Kappa (Rho chpt., sec. 1975-76, pres.-elect 1976-78, pres. 1978-80), Delta Kappa Gamma (Beta Xi chpt., pres. 1980-82, chmn. pubs. and publicity 1976-78, chmn. profl. affairs 1978-80, nominations com. chair 1981-82, chmn. world fellowship and fund raising 1984-86, chmn. fin. 1990-92, chmn. membership 1994-96), Wesley Heights Elem. Sch. PTA. Avocations: reading, gardening, travel, fishing, playing clarinet and handbells. Home: 5134 Stone Gate Dr Columbus GA 31909-5573

MONTGOMERY, BETTY D., state official, former state legislator. BA, Bowling Green State U.; JD, U. Toledo, 1976. Former criminal clk. Lucas County Common Pleas Ct.; asst. pros. atty. Wood County, Ohio, pros. atty., 1980-88; pros. atty. City of Perrysburg, Ohio; mem. Ohio Senate, 1989-94; atty. gen. State of Ohio, Columbus, 1995—. Mem. Nat. Dist. Atty. Assn., Ohio Bar Assn., Toledo Bar Assn., Wood County Bar Assn. Address: 1164 Dawn Dr Reynoldsburg OH 43068-9999 Office: Attorney Generals Office State Offical Tower 30 E Broad St Columbus OH 43215-3428

MONTGOMERY, CHARLES BARRY, lawyer; b. Latrobe, Pa., Apr. 17, 1937. BA cum laude Muskingum Coll., 1959; JD U. Mich., 1962. Bar: Ill. 1962, U.S. Dist. Ct. (no. dist.) Ill., 1982, U.S. Supreme Ct. 1971. Atty. Jacobs & McKenna, 1962-67; founder, ptnr. Jacobs, Williams and Montgomery, Ltd., 1967-85; sr. ptnr. Williams and Montgomery, Ltd., Chgo., 1985—; instr. advocacy inst. U. Mich., Ann Arbor, 1985, advanced program Nat. Inst. Trial Advocacy, 1986, trial acad. Internat. Assn. Def. Counsel, 1987, law inst. program Def. Rsch. Inst; pub. speaker ins. litigation; contbr. articles to profl. jours. Fellow Internat. Acad. Trial Lawyers; mem. ABA (vice-chair medicine and law com. 1989-90), Am. Arbitration Assn., Chgo. Bar Assn., Def. Rsch. Inst., Ill. Assn. Def. Trial Counsel, Ill. Assn. Hosp. Attys., Ill. State Bar Assn., Internat. Assn. Def. Counsel, Nat. Assn. R.R. Trial Counsel, Soc. Trial Lawyers, Legal Club of Chgo., Trial Lawyers Club of Chgo. Office: Williams and Montgomery Ltd 20 N Wacker Dr Chicago IL 60606-2806

MONTGOMERY, CHARLES HARVEY, lawyer; b. Spartanburg, S.C., Jan. 28, 1949; s. Dan Hugh and Ann Louise (Gasque) M.; m. Renée Jean Gubernot, Mar. 27, 1971; children: Charles Scott, Marie Renée. BA, Duke U., 1971; JD, Vanderbilt U., 1974. Bar: N.C. 1974, U.S. Dist. Ct. (ea. dist.) N.C. 1974, U.S. Supreme Ct. 1979, U.S. Dist. Ct. (mid. dist.) N.C. 1991. Assoc. Jordan Morris & Hoke, Raleigh, N.C., 1974-75; atty. Wake County Legal Svcs., Raleigh, 1975-76; sole practice Raleigh, 1977; ptnr. Montgomery & Montgomery, Cary, N.C., 1978-79, Sanford Adams McCullough & Beard, Raleigh, 1979-86, Adams McCullough & Beard, Raleigh, 1986-89, Toms Reagan & Montgomery, Cary, 1989-92, Toms & Montgomery, Cary, 1992-93; sole practice Cary, 1993—; bd. dirs. Br. Bank and Trust, Cary. Councilman Town of Cary, 1977-81, 83-87; vice chair Wake County Dem. party, Raleigh, 1991-92; commr. Wake County, Raleigh, 1992. Mem. ABA, N.C. Bar Assn. (chair pub. info. com. 1994—, dir. family law coun. 1994—), Wake County Bar Assn., N.C. Trial Lawyers Assn. Methodist. Avocation: sailing. Office: Ste 315 PO Box 1325 1135 Kildare Farm Rd # 315 Cary NC 27512

MONTGOMERY, CHARLES HOWARD, retired bank executive; b. Bloomington, Ill., Mar. 23, 1930; s. Dewey H. and Madeline (Wonderlin) M.; m. Diane Dickerson Cohen, Aug. 30, 1978; children: Alison, Douglas. A.B., Ill. Wesleyan U., 1951; M.S., U. Ill., 1960. CPA, Ill. Auditor Lybrand Ross Bros. & Montgomery, Rockford, Ill., 1955-59; with Abbott Labs., North Chicago, Ill., 1959-67; controller Abbott Labs., 1965-67; v.p. finance Anchor Coupling Co., Libertyville, 1967-69; v.p., comptroller First Nat. Bank Chgo., 1969-73, sr. v.p., 1973-75, exec. v.p., 1976-88, comptroller, 1973-88; comptroller First Chgo. Corp.; ret.; past chmn. Inter-Assn. Com. Bank Acctg. Served with AUS, 1952-53. Mem. Fin. Execs. Inst., AICPA, Ill. Soc. CPAs, Tau Kappa Epsilon, Phi Kappa Phi, Univ. Club (Chgo.). Home: 5490 S South Shore Dr Chicago IL 60615-5920

MONTGOMERY, DAVID BRUCE, marketing educator; b. Fargo, N.D., Apr. 30, 1938; s. David William and Iva Bernice (Trask) M.; m. Toby Marie Franks, June 11, 1960; children: David Richard, Scott Bradford, Pamela Marie. BSEE, Stanford U., 1960, MBA, 1962, MS in Stats., 1964, PhD in Mgmt. Sci., 1966. Asst. prof. mgmt. MIT, 1966-69, assoc. prof., 1969-70; assoc. prof. mktg. and mgmt. sci. Stanford U., 1970-73, prof., 1973-78, Robert A. Magowan prof. mktg., 1978-92, Sebastian S. Kregge prof. mktg. strategy, 1992—; prin. The MAC Group Inc., 1969-91; mem. adv. bd. LEK Partnership, London; mem. sci. adv. bd. Univ. Connection, Bonn, Germany; acad. trustee Mktg. Sci. Inst., 1994—, exec. dir., 1995—. Author: (with Glen L. Urban) Management Science in Marketing, 1969, (with Massy and Morrison) Stochastic Models of Buying Behavior, 1970, (with Day et al) Planning: Cases in Computer and Model Assisted Marketing, 1973, (with others) Consumer Behavior: Theoretical Sources, 1973, (with G. J. Eskin) Data Analysis, 1975; editor 4 books; contbr. over 70 articles and tech. reports. Trustee Family Service Assn. of Mid Peninsula, 1972-73. Recipient citation for outstanding contbns. to use of computers in mgmt. edn. Hewlett Packard, 1977. Fellow Royal Statis. Soc.; mem. Inst. Mgmt. Scis., Am. Mktg. Assn., Econometric Soc., Am. Inst. Decision Scis., Tau Beta Pi. Republican. Congregational. Home: 960 Wing Pl Stanford CA 94305-1028 Office: Stanford U Grad Sch Bus Stanford CA 94305

MONTGOMERY, DAVID CAMPBELL, physicist, educator; b. Milan, Mo., Mar. 5, 1936; s. Merrill Edward and Ruth E. (Campbell) M.; m. Shirley Arlene Imig, July 20, 1957; children: Kathleen Montgomery Sutton, Elizabeth. Student, U. Mo., 1953-55; B.S., U. Wis., 1956; M.A., Princeton, 1958, Ph.D., 1959; D honoris causa, Eindhoven U. of Tech., The Netherlands, 1996. Research assoc. Princeton U., 1959-60; instr. U. Wis., 1961-62; asst. prof. U. Md., 1962-65; assoc. prof. U. Iowa, Iowa City, 1965-70; prof. U. Iowa, 1970-77; prof. physics Coll. William and Mary, Williamsburg, Va., 1977-84; prof. Dartmouth Coll., Hanover, N.H., 1984-88, Eleanor and A. Kelvin Smith prof. physics, 1988—; vis. prof., rschr. U. Colo., 1966, U. Alaska, 1968, U. Calif.-Berkeley, 1969-79, Bell Labs., 1971, U. Wis., 1989; lectr. Internat. Summer Sch. Theoretical Physics, Les Houches, France, 1972, U. Wis., Madison, 1973; vis. prof. Hunter campus CUNY, 1973-74, U. Nagoya, Japan, 1983, Columbia U., N.Y.C., 1985, Tech. U., Eindhoven, The Netherlands, spring 1992; vis. scientist Nat. Ctr. Atmospheric Rsch., Boulder, Colo., summers 1975, 76, 79, 87; cons. NASA Hdqs., Washington, 1977-82, JET Joint Undertaking, Culham, U.K., fall 1991; vis. rsch. prof. U.

Md., 1977-84; mem. vis. staff Los Alamos Sci. Lab., summers 1977, 78, 79, 80, 81, 86, 91, 92, 94; cons., collaborator, vis. staff mem. Los Alamos Sci. Lab.; former cons. Oak Ridge Nat. Lab., NASA; vis. rschr. Los Alamos Nat. Lab., 1987-88; J.M. Burgers prof. Eindhoven Tech. U., The Netherlands, 1995-96. Former assoc. editor: Physics of Fluids, Internat. Jour. Engrng. Sci.; contbr. more than 150 rsch. articles to profl. publs.; also monographs. Fellow Am. Phys. Soc.; mem. N.Y. Acad. Scis., Phi Beta Kappa, Sigma Xi, Pi Mu Epsilon, Phi Mu Alpha. Achievements include introduction of modern fluid turbulence methods into space and controlled fusion theory; developed maximum entropy, or "most probable" states, method of describing coherent structures achieved as a product of turbulent relaxation. Home: 46 River Rd Hanover NH 03755-6612 Office: Dartmouth College Physics Dept Hanover NH 03755

MONTGOMERY, DAVID PAUL, professional baseball team executive; b. Phila.; m. Lyn Sagendorph. BA in History, U. Pa., 1968; MBA, Wharton Sch., U. Pa., 1970. With Phila. Phillies, 1971—, successively mem. sales dept., dir. mktg., dir. sales, exec. v.p., COO. Office: Phila Phillies PO Box 7575 Philadelphia PA 19101-7575*

MONTGOMERY, DONALD JOSEPH, physicist, educator; b. Cin., June 11, 1917; s. Robert John and Stella (Steffen) M.; m. Mary Miller, July 27, 1951; children—Denis Broyles, Malcolm David, Steven Michael, Laurence Matthew. Chem.E., U. Cin., 1939, Ph.D., 1945; postgrad., Cornell U., 1941-42. Instr. elec. engrng. U. Cin., 1942-44; physicist Flight Propulsion Lab., NACA, Cleve., 1944-45; research asso. physics, asst. prof. Princeton, 1945-46; sci. liaison officer Office Naval Research, London, Eng., 1947-48; research fellow physics U. Manchester, Eng., 1947-48; chief spl. problems br. Interior Ballistics Lab., Ballistic Research Labs., Aberdeen Proving Ground, Md., 1948-50; head gen. physics sect. Textile Research Inst., Princeton, N.J., 1950-53; asso. prof. physics Mich. State U., East Lansing, 1953-56; prof. Mich. State U., 1956-61, research prof. physics, prof. engrng. research, 1961-66, prof. physics, chmn. dept. metallurgy, mechanics and material sci., 1966-71, research prof. engrng. sci., 1971-88, prof. emeritus, 1988; Cons. Chemstrand Research Center, Durham, N.C., 1956-88, Owens-Ill., 1966-88; spl. asst. to dir. Office Grants and Research Contracts, NASA, 1964-65; vis. research physicist Space Sci. Lab., U. Calif.-Berkeley, 1965-66; vis. scholar dept. polit. sci. U. Ill., 1984-87. Author: Cosmic Ray Physics, 1949; also chpts. in books, articles, revs. Recipient Distinguished Faculty award Mich. State U., 1961, Distinguished Alumnus award U. Cin., 1969; Fulbright lectr. in physics; Guggenheim fellow U. Grenoble, France, 1959-60; Fulbright researcher in engring., econs. U. Augsburg, Germany; asso. Internat. Inst. Empirical Socioecons., Leitershofen-Augsburg, 1974-75. Fellow Am. Phys. Soc.; mem. AAAS, Am. Nuclear Soc. (charter), Am. Assn. Physics Tchrs., Biophys. Soc., Am. Acad. Mechanics, Textile Rsch. Inst., Am. Soc. Engrng. Edn., Internat. Assn. Impact Assessment, Internat. Soc. Tech. Assessment, Am. Acad. Polit. & Social Sci., Policy Studies Assn., Acad. Polit. Sci., Coun. Applied Social Rsch., Fulbright Alumni Assn., Mich. Acad. Art, Letters & Sci., N.Y. Acad. Scis., Soc. Social Studies of Sci., Sigma Xi, Tau Beta Pi, Phi Kappa Phi, Omicron Delta Kappa. Achievements include development of practical formula for predicting charge transfer in static electrification of solids, of scheme for sociotechnical assessment of consequences of public policy measures as an aid to decision making; research on materials science. Home: 2391 Shawnee Trl Okemos MI 48864-2529 Office: Mich State U Coll Engrng East Lansing MI 48824-1226

MONTGOMERY, DONALD RUSSELL, labor consulting firm executive; b. Canora, Sask., June 8, 1920; s. Milton Templeton and Margaret Genva (Culbert) M.; m. Lu Eirene Huggard, May 20, 1954; children—Charmeine, Donald Kirk. Student, Turner Bus. Coll. With United Steelworkers of Am., 1940—; steelworkers area supr. Toronto-Barrie area, 1953-74; sec.-treas. Toronto and Lakeshore Labour Coun., 1953-64, pres., 1964-74; sec.-treas. Can. Labour Congress, 1974-84; cons. union adminstrn., indsl. rels., Ottawa and Toronto; pres., chief exec. officer MertoLabour Cons. Inc., Toronto, 1989—; founding mem. Labor Coun. Devel. Found.; former mem. Export Trade Devel. Bd., adv. com. Aviation Unions; bd. dirs. GSW Ltd. (formerly Gen. Steel Wares Ltd.); cons. in field to labor unions, govts. and employers. Contbr. numerous papers on unions, labor edn. to profl. jours. Mem. Assn. Comml. and Tech. Employees. Home: 19 Bay Point Rd, Toronto, ON Canada M6S 2E8 Office: MetroLabour Cons Inc, PO Box 98546, 873 Jane St, Toronto, ON Canada M6N 5N6

MONTGOMERY, EDWARD ALEMBERT, JR., not-for-profit developer; b. Pitts., July 2, 1934; s. Edward Alembert and Marian (Elder) M.; m. Susan Oliver, June 18, 1938; children—Martha Oliver, Margaret Elder. B.A., Trinity Coll., Conn., 1956; postgrad., Harvard Bus. Sch., Cambridge, 1959. Vice pres. in charge N.Y.C. div. Mellon, N.Y.C., 1970-74; v.p., mgr. Mellon, London, Eng., 1974-77; sr. v.p. Mellon Bank N.A., Pitts., 1977-85; chmn., chief exec. officer Mellon Bank East, Phila., 1985-88, ret., 1988; vice chmn. Mellon Bank Corp., Pitts., 1985-89, also bd. dirs.; v.p. resource devel. United Way Southeastern Pa., Phila., 1990—; bd. dirs. Fisher Sci. Internat. Inc. Trustee emeritas Trinity Coll., Hartford, 1978—; bd. dirs. Acad. Natural Scis., Phila., 1985—, Phila. OIC, 1985—; chmn. emeritas Am. Music Theater Festival; v.p. resource devel. United Way S.E. Pa. Sgt. U.S. Army, 1956-58. Mem. Pvt. Industry Coun. Phila. (bd. dirs.), Greater Phila. C. of C. Republican. Presbyterian. Avocations: golf; skiing; reading. Office: United Way Southeastern Pa 7 Benjamin Franklin Pky Philadelphia PA 19103-1208*

MONTGOMERY, ELIZABETH ANNE, English language educator; b. Santa Monica, Calif., Nov. 5, 1965; d. William Fairbairn and Janice Lynn (Winkler) M. BA in Lit., Claremont McKenna Coll., 1987, MA in Edn., 1995. Cert. tchr., Calif. Tchr. English Berlitz Internat., Beverly Hills, Calif., 1990; tchr. ESL Canoga Park (Calif.) H.S., 1990-91; tchr. English Inlingua Lang. Sch., Fribourg, Switzerland, 1991, Berlitz Internat., Berne, Switzerland, 1991; tchr. English-ESL Internat. Sch. Berne, 1991-92; writer Flintridge Cons., Pasadena, Calif., 1992-93; tchr. English Pomona (Calif.) H.S., 1993—; mem. Task Force on Proficiency Testing, Pomona, 1994-95. Watson fellow Thomas J. Watson Found., 1987-88. Mem. ASCD, NEA, Calif. Tchrs. Assn., Calif. Assn. for Bilingual Edn., Nat. Coun. Tchrs. English, Associated Pomona Tchrs. Office: Pomona H S 475 Bangor St Pomona CA 91767-2443

MONTGOMERY, GEORGE CRANWELL, lawyer, former ambassador; b. Chattanooga, Aug. 24, 1944; s. George Donaldson and Mary Elizabeth (Cranwell) M.; m. Carol Lanfear, 1 child, Erynn Elizabeth. BA, U. Va., 1966; JD, Vanderbilt U., 1975. Bar: U.S. Ct. Appeals (D.C. cir.) 1976. Mem. legis. staff Senator Howard Baker, Washington, 1975-80; spl. counsel Senate Majority Leader, Washington, 1980-85; U.S. amb. to Oman, 1985-89; ptnr. Baker, Donelson, Bearman and Caldwell, Washington, 1989—; bd. dirs. Vinnell Corp.; mem. bd. visitors Georgetown U. Sch. of Bus. Mem. Coun. on Fgn. Rels. With USN, 1966-72, capt. Res. Mem. ABA, D.C. Bar Assn., Sigma Chi. Office: Baker Donelson Bearman & Caldwell 801 Pennsylvania Ave NW Ste 800 Washington DC 20004-2615

MONTGOMERY, GILLESPIE V. (SONNY MONTGOMERY), congressman; b. Meridian, Miss., Aug. 5, 1920; s. Gillespie M. and Emily (Jones) M. B.S., Miss. State U. Mem. Miss. Senate, 1956-66, 90th-104th Congresses from 3rd Miss. Dist., 1967-96; chmn. vets. affairs com., 1981-94; mem. vets. affairs com., chmn. spl. com. on S.E. Asia 90th-102d Congresses, 1978-96; ranking minority mem., 1994-96; mem. armed services. com. 90th-103d Congresses, chmn. select com. on missing persons in southeast Asia, 1975-96; mem. vets. affairs com.; mem. Woodcock Commn., 1977. Pres. Miss. N.G. Assn., 1959; pres. Miss. Heart Assn., 1967-68. Served with AUS, World War II, Korea, ret. maj. gen. Miss N.G. Decorated Bronze Star medal, Combat Inf. Badge; recipient Miss. Magnolia award, 1966, Lifetime Achievement award Mil. Educators & Counselors Assn., 1992. Mem. VFW, Am. Legion 40 and 8, Congl. Prayer Breakfast Group (pres. 1970). Episcopalian. Lodges: Masons; Shriners; Scottish Rite. Office: US Ho Reps Office of Postmaster Washington DC 20510

MONTGOMERY, HENRY IRVING, financial planner; b. Decorah, Iowa, Dec. 18, 1924; s. Harry Biggs and Martha Grace (Wilkinson) M.; m. Barbara Louise Hook, Aug. 14, 1948; children: Barbara Ruth, Michael Henry, Kelly Ann, Andrew Stuart. Student U. Iowa, 1942-43, 47-48; B.B.A., Tulane U., 1952, postgrad., 1952; postgrad. U. Minn., 1976. Cert. fin. planner, Colo. Field agt. OSS, SSU, CIG, CIA, Central Europe, 1945-47; pres. Nehi Bottling Co., Decorah, Iowa, 1952-64; prin. Montgomery Assocs., Mktg. Cons., Trieste, Italy and Iowa, 1965-72; pres. Planners Fin. Svcs., Inc., Mpls., 1972-95, chmn., 1995—; prin. Montgomery Investment Mgmt., 1992—. Author: Race Toward Berlin, 1945. Served with U.S. Army, 1943-46; ETO. Mem. Inst. Cert. Fin. Planners (bd. dirs. 1977-82, pres. 1980-81, chmn. 1981-82, Cert. Fin. Planner of Yr. 1984, chmn. Fin. Products Standards Bd. 1984-88), Nat. Assn. Securities Dealers (mem. dist. 8 com. 1988-91, vice chmn. 1990), Internat. Assn. Fin. Planning (internat. dir. 1976-81), Mpls. Estate Planning Coun., Met. Tax Planning Group (pres. 1984-87), Twin City Fin. Planners (pres. 1976-78), Twin Cities Soc. of Inst. Cert. Fin. Planners, Am. Legion, Elks (Decorah), Beta Gamma Sigma. Avocations: Italian and German langs. Office: Planners Fin Svcs Inc 7710 Computer Ave Ste 100 Minneapolis MN 55435-5417

MONTGOMERY, HUBERT THERON, JR., physician, health care administrator; b. Birmingham, Ala., July 29, 1935; s. Hubert Theron and Edna M. (Morrison) M.; m. Sarah Diane Bryans, Sept. 19, 1969; children: Alfred Peter, Melanie Anne, Laurel Elaine, Amy Diane. AB, Birmingham So. Coll., 1957; MD, Tulane U., 1961. Diplomate Am. Bd. Surgery, Am. Bd. Plastic Surgery. Rotating intern St. Vincent Hosp., Birmingham, 1961-62; resident surgery Lloyd Noland Hosp., Fairfield, Ala., 1964-68; pvt. practice Montgomery, Ala., 1968-73, 75—; resident plastic surgery U. Tenn., Memphis, 1974-75; pres., chief exec. officer Med One Inc., Montgomery, 1983—; exec. v.p., chief exec. officer Central Ala. Preferred Provider, Inc., Montgomery, 1984—; sec.-treas. Montgomery Surg. Ctr., Inc., 1984-85; sect. chief plastic surgery Bapt. Med. Ctr., Montgomery, 1976-78, St. Margaret's Hosp., Montgomery, 1987—. Sec.-treas. Ala. Soc. Plastic Surgeons, 1990-92, pres. 1994-96; mem. Hitchcock Award Com., Montgomery, 1985. Maj. U.S. Army, 1963-69. Named New Bus. of Yr., Ala. Bus. Rev., Montgomery, 1985. Fellow ACS; mem. Capitol City Kiwanis (dir. 1987-88), Montgomery Country Club, Wynn Lakes Country Club, Newcomen Soc. N.Am. Baptist.

MONTGOMERY, JAMES EDWARD, JR., lawyer; b. Champaign, Ill., Feb. 8, 1953; s. James Edward Sr and Vivian M.; m. Linda C.; children: James III, Anne. AB Polit. Sci., Duke U., 1975; JD, So. Meth. U., 1978. Bar: Tex., 1978, Md., 1994; U.S. Dist. Ct. (ea. dist.) Tex. 1978, U.S. Dist. Ct. (we. dist.) Tex., 1985, U.S. Dist. Ct. (so. dist.) Tex. 1986, U.S. Dist. Ct. (no. dist.) Tex. 1987, U.S. Dist. Md., 1994; U.S. Ct. Appeals (5th cir.) 1979; U.S. Supreme Ct., 1993. Assoc. Strong, Pipkin, Nelson & Parker, Beaumont, Tex., 1978-81; owner Sibley & Montgomery, Beaumont, 1981-85; assoc. Law Offices of Gilbert Adams, Beaumont, 1985; prin. James E. Montgomery, Beaumont, 1985-88; ptnr. Montgomery & Kontiusczy, Beaumont, 1988-89; assoc. Sawtelle, Goode, Davidson & Troilo, San Antonio, Tex., 1989-91; shareholder Davidson & Troilo, San Antonio, 1991-94; pres. Montgomery & Assocs., San Antonio, 1994—. Editor: Fifth Cir. Reporter, 1983-86. Bd. dirs. Boys and Girls Clubs of San Antonio, 1995; dist. chmn. Boy Scouts, San Antonio, 1994. Mem. ABA, State Bar of Tex., San Antonio Bar Assn., Rotary (v.p. Alamo Hts. chpt. 1989), 5th Cir. Bar Assn. (bd. dirs. 1983-86), Jefferson County Bar Assn. (treas. 1986). Avocations: tennis, skiing, golf, reading. Office: Montgomery & Assocs P C Ste 620 613 NW Loop 410 San Antonio TX 78216

MONTGOMERY, JAMES FISCHER, savings and loan association executive; b. Topeka, Nov. 30, 1934; s. James Maurice and Frieda Ellen (Fischer) M.; m. Diane Dealey; children: Michael James, Jeffrey Allen, Andrew Steven, John Gregory. BA in Acctg., UCLA, 1957. With Price, Waterhouse & Co., C.P.A.'s, Los Angeles, 1957-60; controller Conejo Valley Devel. Co., Thousand Oaks, Calif., 1960; asst. to pres. Gt. Western Fin. Corp., Beverly Hills, Calif., 1960-64; pres. United Financial Corp of Calif., Los Angeles, 1964-75; chmn., c.e.o. Great Western Financial Corp., Chatsworth, Calif., 1975—; fin. v.p., treas. United Fin. Corp., Los Angeles, 1964-69, exec. v.p., 1969-74, pres., 1975; pres. Citizens Savs. & Loan Assn., Los Angeles, 1970-75. Served with AUS, 1958-60. Office: Great Western Fin Corp 9200 Oakdale Ave Chatsworth CA 91311-6519*

MONTGOMERY, JAMES MORTON, public relations, marketing executive, association executive; b. Birmingham, Ala., July 4, 1931; s. Hugh Nelson and Sidney Tazewell (Morton) M.; m. Helen Patton Martin, June 12, 1954 (div. Oct. 1987); children: Louis Martin, Caroline Montgomery Brown, Helen Montgomery DeBevoise, Fleta Montgomery Edwards; m. Helen Preston Tapp, Jan. 29, 1994. AB, U. Ala., 1953, MBA, 1958. Mktg. instr. U. Ala., Tuscaloosa, 1953-54, 56-57; dir. publs. Gulf States Paper Corp., Tuscaloosa, 1957-60, advt. dir., 1960-63, pub. rels. mgr., 1963-71, corp. communications mgr., 1971-76; v.p. pub. info. Am. Forest Inst., Washington, 1976-77; v.p. regions Am. Forest Inst., Atlanta, 1980-86; exec. v.p. So. Forest Inst., Atlanta, 1977-86; pres. Montgomery & Assocs., pub. rels. and mktg., Atlanta, 1986—; strategic ptnr. Golin/Harris (Shandwick) Pub. Rels., 1992—; comms. cons., Atlanta, 1973-86; guest, adj. lectr. various univs. in Ala. and Ga., 1965—; coord. Advt. Coun. Smokey Bear, N.Y.C., 1970-76. Mem. adv. bd. Metro Atlanta Salvation Army, 1993—; v.p. U. Ala. Nat. Alumni Assn., 1974-75; mem. State Rep. Exec. Com., Ala., 1962-70. 1st lt. USAF, 1954-56. Named to Ga. Pub. Rels. Hall of Fame, Order of the Phoenix. Fellow Pub. Rels. Soc. Am. (accredited chpt. pres. 1972, nat. assembly 1973-76, 80-81), Clan Montgomery Soc. Internat. (pres. 1993-95), Phoenix Soc. (trustee 1984-85), Burns Club Atlanta (pres. 1990-91), Kiwanis Internat. (pres. Tuscaloosa Club 1972-73), Atlanta Club, Soc. Profl. Journalists, Beta Gamma Sigma, Omicron Delta Kappa, Delta Tau Delta. Presbyterian.

MONTGOMERY, JEFFREY THOMAS, professional baseball player; b. Wellston, Ohio, Jan. 7, 1962. BS Computer Sci., Marshall Coll., 1984. With Cin. Reds, 1983-88, Kansas City Royals, 1988—; mem. Am. League All-Star Team, 1992-93, 96. Names Am. League Fireman of Yr., Sporting News, 1993. Office: Kansas City Royals PO Box 419969 Kansas City MO 64141-6969*

MONTGOMERY, JERRY LYNN, education educator; b. Owensville, Ind., Apr. 21, 1935; s. Philip Matthew and Lois Caroline (Anderson) M.; m. Murelyn Ann Rogers, Sept. 21, 1957 (div. Apr. 1976); stepchildren: Rebecca Williams Slominski, Matthew Williams; m. Gretchen Wendelroth Golzé, May 14, 1977; children: Robin Montgomery, Lori Abbott, Vicki Randolph. BS, Purdue U., 1957; MA, Ball State U., 1964, EdD, 1969. Vocat. agrl. Milton (Ind.) Pub. Schs., 1957-58, Carthage (Ind.) Pub. Schs., 1958-61; sci. tchr. Angola (Ind.) City Schs., 1961-66; edn. prof. Marietta (Ohio) Coll., 1969—; sci. educator Project Discovery, Athens, Ohio, 1994—; goal #4 com. Marietta (Ohio) City Schs., 1993—, grade 4 profiency test com. Ohio Dept. of Edn., Columbus, Ohio, 1994—; mem. young engrs. and scientists Marietta Telesis Group, Marietta, 1992—. Recipient Outstanding Educator Martha Holden Jennings Found., 1989. Mem. Assn. of Tchr. Educators (credentials com. 1991—), Nat. Sci. Tchrs. Assn., Sci. Edn. Coun. Ohio, Ohio Acad. of Sci., Phi Delta Kappa. Avocations: reading, canoeing, traveling, fishing, camping. Home: 105 Rathbone Ter Marietta OH 45750-1443 Office: Marietta Coll 215 5th St Marietta OH 45750-3029

MONTGOMERY, JOHN ATTERBURY, research chemist, consultant; b. Greenville, Miss., Mar. 29, 1924; s. Daniel Cameron and Ruth (Atterbury) M.; m. Jean Kirkman, July 19, 1947; children: John Jr., Elaine Porter, Kirkman, Ruth Adrianne. AB cum laude, Vanderbilt U., 1946, MS in Organic Chemistry, 1947; PhD in Organic Chemistry, U. N.C., Chapel Hill, 1951. Research chemist So. Research Inst., Birmingham, Ala., 1952-56; dir. organic chemistry So. Research Inst., 1956-74, v.p., 1974-81, sr. v.p., dir. Kettering Meyer Lab., 1981-90, disting. scientist rsch., 1990—; exec. v.p., dir. rsch., chief exec. officer Biocryst, 1990—; adj. prof. Birmingham So. Coll., 1957-62; adj. sr. scientist U. Ala., Birmingham, 1978—; bd. dirs. Am. Assn. Cancer Research, Assn. Am. Cancer Insts.; mem. Pres. Reagan's Cancer Panel. Author over 600 rsch. papers; editor profl. books; mem. editl. bd. numerous profl. jours. Recipient T.O. Soine Meml. award U. Minn., 1979. Fellow N.Y. Acad. Scis.; mem. Am. Chem. Soc. (councilor 1971-86, recipient Herty medal 1974, So. Chemist award 1980, Burger award 1986, Edward E. Smissman Bristol-Myers Squibb Award, 1995), Am. Assn. Cancer Research (Cain Meml. award 1982), Am. Soc. Pharmacology and Exptl. Therapeutics, Internat. Soc. Heterocyclic Chemistry (adv. bd. 1982-83), Sigma Xi, Alpha Chi Sigma. Republican. Episcopalian. Clubs: Country of Birmingham, The Club (Birmingham) Lodge: Rotary. Home: 3596 Springhill Rd Birmingham AL 35223-2032 Office: So Research Inst PO Box 55305 Birmingham AL 35255-5305 also: BioCryst Pharmaceuticals 2190 Parkway Lake Dr Birmingham AL 35244-2812

MONTGOMERY, JOHN DICKEY, political science educator; b. Evanston, Ill., Feb. 15, 1920; s. Charles William and Lora Kathryn (Dickey) M.; m. Jane Ireland, Dec. 19, 1954; children—Faith, Patience, John. A.B., Kalamazoo Coll., 1941, A.M., 1942, LL.D., 1962; A.M., Harvard, 1948, Ph.D., 1951. Dir. devel. research center African studies program Boston U., 1961-63; prof. pub. adminstrn. Harvard U., 1963-86, Ford Found. prof. internat. studies, 1986—, chmn. dept. govt., 1980-84; dir. Pacific Basin Rsch. Ctr. Soka U. Am., L.A., 1991—. Author: The Purge in Occupied Japan, 1953, Forced to be Free, 1957, The Politics of Foreign Aid, 1962, Foreign Aid in International Politics, 1967, Technology and Civic Life, 1974, Aftermath, Tarnished Outcomes of American Foreign Policy, 1986, Bureaucrats and People, 1988; co-editor: (with Dennis Rardinelli) Great Policies, Strategic Innovations in Asia and the Pacific Basin, 1995. Home: 36 Hyde Ave Newton MA 02158-2311 Office: Harvard U 79 Jfk St Cambridge MA 02138-5801

MONTGOMERY, JOHN E., government official; b. Chgo., Jan. 30, 1946; m. Susan Maree Smith, June 6, 1969; children: Marcus John, Matthew Glenn, Anne Maree, Berkley Diane, Joseph Young. BA in Physics cum laude with honors, Brigham Young U., 1970; M in Hosp. Adminstrn., U. Minn., 1972; PhD in Engrng. Sci., U. Calif., Berkeley, 1981; grad., Marine Corps Command and Staff Coll., 1982. Commd. ensign USN, 1972, advanced through grades to capt., 1989; asst. to adminstrv. officer Naval Hosp., San Diego, 1972-73; rsch. assoc. Naval Sch. Health Care Adminstrn., Bethesda, Md., 1973-74; ops. rsch. analyst sys. engrng. br., bur. medicine and surgery Dept. Navy, Washington, 1977-78; asst. dir. rsch. dept. Naval Sch. Health Scis., Bethesda, 1978-81; exec. officer 1st med. bn. 1st Force Svc. Support Group, Camp Pendleton, Calif., 1982-84; dir. for adminstrn. Naval Hosp., Camp Pendleton, Calif., 1984-85; spl. asst. to dir. Office of Civilian Health and Med. Program of Uniformed Svcs., Aurora, Colo., 1985-89; exec. officer Naval Hosp., Bremerton, Wash., 1989-91; head health care planning and devel. dept. Naval Hosp., San Diego, 1991-93; dir. managed care support office Office of Civilian Health and Med. Program of Uniformed Svcs., Aurora, Colo., 1993-94; dir Office of Civilan Health and Med. Program Uniformed Svcs., Aurora, Colo., 1994—; instr. Va. Commonwealth U., Washington, 1973-74, Ctrl. Mich. U., Washington, 1979-81; adj. asst. prof. George Washington U., Washington, 1978-81. Contbr. articles to profl. jours. Decorated Commendation medal; recipient Award for Excellence in Health Care Adminstrn., McGaw Found.; scholar McGaw Found. Mem. Am. Coll. Healthcare Execs. (affiliate), Inst. Ops. Rsch. and Mgmt. Scis. Avocations: running, reading, poetry, golfing. Office: Dept Def OCHAMPUS Aurora CO 80045

MONTGOMERY, JOHN RICHARD, pediatrician, educator; b. Burnsville, Miss., Oct. 24, 1934; s. Guy Austin and Harriet Pauline (Owens) M.; m. Dottye Ann Newell, June 26, 1965; children: John Newell, Michelle Elizabeth. BS, U. Ala., 1955, MD, 1958. Intern U. Miss., Jackson, 1958-59, resident in pediatrics, 1959-60; resident in pediatrics Baylor Coll. Medicine, Houston, 1960-61, 63-64, fellow in pediatric infectious diseases and immunology, 1964-66, asst. prof. pediatrics, 1966-70, assoc. prof. pediatrics, 1970-75, prof. pediats., 1975—, chief pediatric programs U. Ala. Sch. Medicine, Huntsville, 1975-95. Served with AUS, 1961-62; Korea. Mem. Soc. Pediatric Rsch., Am. Assn. Immunologists, Infectious Diseases Soc. Am., N.Y. Acad. Scis., Am. Acad. Pediatrics (pres. Ala. chpt. 1991-93), Sigma Xi, Phi Beta Kappa. Contbr. articles to profl. jours.; assisted in devel. of germ-free environ. bubble to protect patient with no natural immunity (patient later subject of movie The Boy in The Bubble).

MONTGOMERY, JOHN WARWICK, law educator, theologian; b. Warsaw, N.Y., Oct. 18, 1931; s. Maurice Warwick and Harriet (Smith) M.; m. Joyce Ann Bailer, Aug. 14, 1954; children: Elizabeth Ann, David Warwick, Catherine Ann; m. Lanalee de Kant, Aug. 26, 1988. A.B. with distinction in philosophy, Cornell U., 1952; B.L.S., U. Calif., Berkeley, 1954, M.A., 1958; B.D., Wittenberg U., 1958, M.S.T., 1960; Ph.D., U. Chgo., 1962; Docteur de l'Université, mention Théologie Protestante, U. Strasbourg, France, 1964; LLB, LaSalle Extension U., 1977; diplôme cum laude, Internat. Inst. Human Rights, Strasbourg, 1978; M. Phil. in Law, U. Essex, Eng., 1983. Bar: Va. 1978, Calif. 1979, D.C. 1985, Wash. 1990, U.S. Supreme Ct. 1981, Eng. 1984; lic. real estate broker Calif.; cert. law librarian; diplomate Med. Library Assn.; ordained to ministry Luth. Ch., 1958. Librarian, gen. reference service U. Calif. Library, Berkeley, 1954-55; instr. Bibl. Hebrew, Hellenistic Greek, Medieval Latin Wittenberg U., Springfield, Ohio, 1956-59; head librarian Swift Libr. div. and Philosophy, mem. federated theol. faculty U. Chgo., 1959-60; assoc. prof., chmn. dept. history Wilfred Laurier U. (formerly Waterloo Luth. U.), Ont., Can., 1960-64; prof., chmn. div. ch. history, history of Christian thought, dir. European Seminar program Trinity Evang. Div. Sch., Deerfield, Ill., 1964-74; prof. law and theology George Mason U. Sch. Law (formerly Internat. Sch. of Law), Arlington, Va., 1974-75; theol. cons. Christian Legal Soc., 1975-76; dir. studies Internat. Inst. Human Rights, Strasbourg, France, 1979-81; founding dean, prof. jurisprudence, dir. European program Simon Greenleaf U. Sch. Law, Anaheim, Calif., 1980-88; Disting. prof. theology and law, dir. European program Faith Evang. Luth. Sem., Tacoma, Wash., 1989-91; prin. lectr. in law Luton U., Eng., 1991-92, reader in law, 1992-93, prof. law and humanities, dir. Ctr. Human Rights, 1993—; vis. prof. Concordia Theol. Sem., Springfield, Ill., 1964-67, DePaul U., Chgo., 1967-70; hon. fellow Revelle Coll., U. Calif., San Diego, 1970; rector Freie Fakultaten Hamburg, Fed. Republic Germany, 1981-82; lectr. Rsch. Scientists Christian Fellowship Conf. St. Catherines Coll., Oxford U., 1985, Internat. Anti-Corruption Conf., Beijing, China, 1995; Pascal lectr. on Christianity and the Univ., U. Waterloo, Ont., Can., 1987; adj. prof. Puget Sound U. Sch. Law, Tacoma, 1990-91; numerous other invitational functions. Author: The Writing of Research Papers in Theology, 1959; A Union List of Serial Publications in Chicago Area Protestant Theological Libraries, 1960; A Seventeenth-Century View of European Libraries, 1962; Chytraeus on Sacrifice: A Reformation Treatise in Biblical Theology, 1962; The Shape of the Past: An Introduction to Philosophical Historiography, 1962, rev. edition, 1975; The Is God Dead Controversy, 1966; (with Thomas J.J. Altizer) The Altizer-Montgomery Dialogue, 1967; Crisis in Lutheran Theology, 2 vols., 1967, rev. edit., 1973; Es confiable el Christianismo?, 1968; Ecumenicity, Evangelicals, and Rome, 1969; Where is History Going?, 1969; History and Christianity, 1970; Damned Through the Church, 1970; The Suicide of Christian Theology, 1970; Computers, Cultural Change and the Christ, 1970; In Defense of Martin Luther, 1970; La Mort de Dieu, 1971; (with Joseph Fletcher) Situation Ethics: True or False?, 1972; The Quest for Noah's Ark, 1972, rev. edit., 1974; Verdammt durch die Kirche, 1973; Christianity for the Toughminded, 1973; Cross and Crucible, 2 vols., 1973; Principalities and Powers: The World of the Occult, 1973, rev. edit., 1975; How Do We Know There is a God?, 1973; Myth, Allegory and Gospel, 1974; God's Inerrant Word, 1974; Jurisprudence: A Book of Readings, 1974, 4th edit., 1992; The Law Above the Law, 1975; Cómo Sabemos Que Hay un Dios?, 1975; Demon Possession, 1975; The Shaping of America, 1976; Faith Founded on Fact, 1978; Law and Gospel: A Study for Integrating Faith and Practice, 1978, 3rd edit., 1994; Slaughter of the Innocents, 1981; The Marxist Approach to Human Rights: Analysis & Critique, 1984; Human Rights and Human Dignity, 1987, Wohin marschiert China?, 1991, Evidence for Faith: Deciding the God Question, 1991, Giant in Chains: China Today and Tomorrow, 1994, Law and Morality: Friends or Foes?, 1994, Jésus: La Raison Rejoint L'Histoire, 1995; editor: Lippincott's Evangelical Perspectives, 7 vols., 1970-72; International Scholars Directory, 1973, Simon Greenleaf Law Rev., 7 vols., 1981-88; contbg. editor: Christianity Today, 1965-84, New Oxford Review, 1993-95; films: Is Christianity Credible?, 1968; In Search of Noah's Ark, 1977; Defending the Biblical Gospel, 1985 (11 videocassette series); (TV series) Christianity on Trial, 1987-93; contbr. articles to acad., theol., legal encys. and jours., chpts. to books. Nat. Luth. Ednl. Conf. fellow, 1959-60; Can. Council postdoctoral sr. research fellow, 1963-64; Am. Assn. Theol. Schs. faculty fellow, 1967-68; recipient Angel award Nat. Religious Broadcasters, 1989, 90, 92. Fellow Trinity Coll. (Newburgh, Ind.), Royal Soc. Arts (Eng.), Victoria Inst. (London), Acad. Internat. des Gourmets et des Traditions Gastronomiques (Paris), Am. Sci. Affiliation (nat. philosophy sci. and history sci. commn. 1966-70); mem. Lawyers Christian Fellowship (hon. v.p. 1995—), Nat. Conf. U. Profs., Calif. bar Assn. (human rights commn. 1980-83), Internat. Bar Assn., ALA, World Assn. Law Profs., Mid. Temple and Lincoln's Inn (barrister mem.), Am. Soc. Internat. Law, Union Internat. des Avocats, Nat. Assn. Realtors, Tolkien Soc. Am., N.Y. C.S. Lewis Soc., Am. Hist. Assn., Soc. Reformation Rsch., Creation Rsch. Soc., Tyndale Fellowship (Eng.), Stair Soc. (Scotland), Presbyn. Hist. Soc. (North Ireland), Am.

Theol. Libr. Assn., Bibliog. Soc. U. Va., Evang. Theol. Soc., Internat. Wine and Food Soc., Soc. des Amis des Arts (Strasbourg), Chaine des Rôtisseurs (commandeur), Athenaeum (London), Wig and Pen (London), Players' Theatre Club (London), Sherlock Holmes Soc. London, Soc. Sherlock Holmes de France (hon.), Club des Casseroles Lasserre (Paris), Ordre des chevaliers du Saint-Sepulcre Byzantin (commandeur), Phi Beta Kappa, Phi Kappa Phi, Beta Phi Mu. Office: 4 Crane Ct # 9, Fleet St, London EC4A 2EJ, England also: 2 rue de Rome, 67000 Strasbourg France

MONTGOMERY, JON B., museum administrator. Supt. Appomattox Court House Nat. Hist. Park, Appomattox, Va. Office: Appomattox Court House Nat His Park PO Box 218 Appomattox VA 24522-0218

MONTGOMERY, KEITH NORRIS, SR., insurance executive, state legislator; b. Natchez, Miss., Sept. 22, 1951; s. Charles Norris Jr. and Miriam (Marron) M.; m. Joan Marie Bishop; children: Keith Jr., Mason, Brenton. BBA, U. Miss., 1974. Sales rep. Boyle-Midway, Monroe, La., 1975-77, Am. Nat. Ins., Jackson, Miss., 1977-79; owner Exec. Benefits, Clinton, Miss., 1979—; state rep. Miss. Ho. of Reps., Jackson, 1993—. City councilman City of Clinton, 1985-93. Master sgt. USAR, 1972—. Mem. Am. Legis. Exch. Coun., Miss. Econ. Coun., Jackson Assn. Health Underwriters (bd. dirs. 1992-94), Clinton C. of C. Republican. Methodist. Home: 104 Countrywood Cir Clinton MS 39056-5717 Office: PO Box 2204 Clinton MS 39060-2204

MONTGOMERY, LESLIE DAVID, biomedical engineer, cardiovascular physiologist; b. Otterbein, Ind., Sept. 4, 1939; s. Gerald Wesley and Doris Elnora (Sosbe) M.; m. Patricia Ann Trigg, Aug. 25, 1971; children: Gerald Wesley, Nathaniel Brendon, David Patrick. BA, Monmouth Coll., 1962; MS in Engring., Iowa State U., 1963; PhD in Engring., UCLA, 1972. Rsch. engr. N.Am./Rockwell, L.A., 1963-73; owner LDM Assocs., San Jose, Calif., 1973—; rsch. engr. SRI Internat., San Mateo, Calif., 1980-85; dir. rsch. Ctr. for Neurodiagnostic Study, Inc., 1987-91; sr. rsch. engr. Bionetics Corp., 1994-95, Lockheed Martin Engring. Svcs., 1995—; NRC postdoctoral fellow NASA-Ames, Calif., 1973-75; NRC sr. postdoctoral fellow Wright Patterson AFB, Ohio, 1986-88, NASA-Ames Rsch. Ctr., 1992-94. Contbr. articles to profl. jours.; author presentations on physiology and biomed. engring. Fellow Aerospace Med. Assn. (assoc.); mem. Biomed. Engring. Soc. Republican. Presbyterian. Avocations: woodwork, computer programming. Home and Office: 1764 Emory St San Jose CA 95126-1910

MONTGOMERY, MARTHA M., nursing educator; b. Kalkaska, Mich., Feb. 23, 1934; d. Alvah James Montgomery and Genevieve (Ragan) Shaffer. Dipl., Henry Ford Hosp., Detroit, 1955; BSN, Wayne State U., 1962, MSN, 1964. Cert. orthopedic nurse. Staff nurse, head nurse Henry Ford Hosp., Detroit, 1955-59; faculty, staff nurse Evang. Deaconess Hosp., Detroit, 1961-65; staff nurse, rsch. asst. Wayne State U., Detroit, 1963, 75-76; cmty. health nurse Vis. Nurse Assn., Detroit, 1988—; instr. nursing Henry Ford C.C., Dearborn, Mich., 1964—. Instrl. designer and formative evaluator (tv prodn.) Newer Media Approaches to Edn. for Nursing, 1968-71; co-author, editor, cons. in design (brochure) The Curriculum Master Plan, 1981. Grantee Helene Fuld Health Trust, 1990, 93. Mem. ANA, N.Am. Nursing Diagnosis Assn., Am. Fedn. Tchrs., Assn. Ednl. Comm. and Tech., Assn. for Devel. Computer-Based Instrl. Sys., Nat. Assn. Orthopedic Nurses, Sigma Theta Tau (Lambda chpt.). Avocations: hiking, backpacking, camping, travel, golf. Office: Henry Ford Cmty Coll 5101 Evergreen Rd Dearborn MI 48128-2407

MONTGOMERY, MICHAEL BRUCE, lawyer, consultant; b. Santa Barbara, Calif., Sept. 12, 1936; s. Clair Gruwell Montgomery and Florence Louise (Moran) Quigley; m. Carmen Luisa Montalvan, June 16, 1990; children by previous marriage: Michael, Megan. BS, UCLA, 1960; LLB, U. So. Calif., 1963. Bar: Calif. 1963, Hawaii 1985, Fla. 1985. Staff atty. div. hwys. State of Calif., Sacramento and L.A., 1965; assoc. Martin & Flandrick, San Marino, Calif., 1965-66; owner, pres. Michael B. Montgomery, L.C., Pasadena, Calif., 1966—; agy atty. Huntington (Calif.) Park Redevel. Agy., 1988-93, Walnut (Calif.) Improvement Agy., 1988-92; spl. counsel County of San Bernardino, Calif., 1988-89; city atty. Diamond Bar, Calif., 1993—; U.S. rep. Atlantic Tuna Commn., Madrid, 1985-94. Contbr. numerous articles to profl. jours. Chmn. Calif. Rep. Party, 1977-79; mayor City of South Pasadena, 1980-81; chmn. Calif. Electoral Coll., Sacramento, 1980; commr. Calif. Fair Polit. Practices Commn., 1985-89. Sgt. U.S. Army, 1954-57, ensign USNR, 1960. Mem. Calif. Bar Assn., Fla. Bar Assn., Hawaii Bar Assn., United Sport Fishermen Internat. (pres. 1987-92), Jonathan, Plaza. Office: 10501 Valley Blvd Ste 121 El Monte CA 91731-2403

MONTGOMERY, MICHAEL DAVIS, advanced technology consultant, hotelier; b. San Luis Obispo, Calif., June 4, 1936; s. Herold Ray and Elva Dee (Davis) M.; m. Rita Martin, Dec. 28, 1957 (div. Sept. 1975); children: Jeanne, Gwen, Michele. MSEE, Stanford U., 1959; PhD, U. N.Mex., 1967. Group leader Max Planck Inst. for Astrophysics, Munich, 1974-76; group leader advanced concepts Los Alamos (N.Mex.) Nat. Labs., 1976-83; program mgr. for simulation Maxwell Labs. Inc., San Diego, 1983-84, dep. for DNA programs, 1984-85, v.p. rsch. and devel., 1986-91, sr. v.p. applied tech., 1991-92; sr. cons., 1993—; owner Casa Del Mar Inn, Santa Barbara, Calif., 1991—. Assoc. editor Jour. Geophys. Research; contbr. articles to sci. jours. Served to lt. comdr. USN, 1959-62. Recipient Sr. Scientist award Alexander Von Humboldt Found., 1972. Mem. AAAS, Am. Phys. Soc., Phi Beta Kappa, Sigma Xi, Tau Beta Pi. Avocations: amateur radio. Home: 18 Bath St Santa Barbara CA 93101-3803 Office: Casa Del Mar Inn 18 Bath St Santa Barbara CA 93101-3803

MONTGOMERY, NANCY VINCENT, English as a second Language educator; b. Beardstown, Ill., Apr. 24, 1946; d. James Earl and Thelma Margaret (Wardell) Vincent; m. James Thomas Montgomery, Dec. 16, 1967; children: Allison, Jeff. BS, So. Ill. U., 1968; MEd, U. N. Tex., 1986, E. Tex. State U., 1992. Cert. tchr. elem. edn., ESL, mid-mgmt. adminstrn. Tchr. Granite City (Ill.) Pub. Schs., 1968-74, Met. Christian Sch., Dallas, 1975-79, Jakarta (Indonesia) Internat. Sch., 1980-82, Dallas Ind. Sch. Dist., 1982—; project leader Dallas Ind. Sch. Dist., 1988, leadership devel. acad., 1990, alternative cert. mentor, 1991—, staff devel. assoc., 1993; adj. instr. Dallas C.C. Dist., 1991—; del. to Citizen to Citizen Amb. Program to Russia for Reading Edn. Author: (literacy program) Language Acquisition, 1990, Intergenerational Literacy, 1993. Pres. coun. So. Ill. U., Carbondale. Named Finalist, Perot Found. Excellence in Teaching, 1988, 91, Outstanding Tchr., Kiwanis Club, 1993; grantee Am. Airlines, 1990, Jr. Svc. League, 1993; named Tchr. of Yr., 1994-95. Mem. Internat. Reading Assn. (Dallas coun. bldg. rep.), ASCD, Nat. Staff Devel. Coun., Tex. Jr. Coll. Tchrs. Assn., Tex. Assn. Improvement of Reading, Tex. State Reading Assn. Avocations: world traveling, studying tribal cultures, reading, physical fitness. Home: 9218 Middle Glen Dr Dallas TX 75243-6334

MONTGOMERY, PAULA KAY, school editor, publishing executive; b. Omaha, Sept. 23, 1946; d. Floyd Woodrow and Adelyn Ann (Peterson) M. BA in English, Fla. State U., 1967, MLS in Libr. Sci., 1968; PhD in Reading Edn., 1989. Sch. libr. Montgomery County Pub. Sch., Rockville, Md., 1969-72, libr. specialist, 1972-79; chief sch. libr. Md. State Dept. Edn., Balt., 1979-88; pub. Sch. Libr. Media Activities Monthly, Balt., 1984—; del. Gov.'s Conf. on Librs., Balt., 1990. Author: Teaching Library Media Skills, 1983, Thematic Approaches to Literature, 1991, Subject Approaches to Literature, 1991, Subject Approaches to Literature, 1991, Literary Forms Approach to Literature, 1995, The Bookmark Book, 1995; editor: (book series) Library Media Skills, 1982—. Mem. ALA, Nat. Assn. State Ednl. Media Profls. (pres. 1987), Assn. Edn. Communication and Tech. Lutheran. Office: 17 E Henrietta St Baltimore MD 21230-3910

MONTGOMERY, PHILIP O'BRYAN, JR., pathologist; b. Dallas, Aug. 16, 1921. BS, So. Meth. U., 1942; MD, Columbia U., 1945. Diplomate Am. Bd. Pathology, Am. Bd. Clin. Pathology and Forensic Pathology. Intern Mary Imogene Bassett Hosp., Cooperstown, N.Y., 1945-46; fellow in pathology Southwestern Med. Sch., Dallas, 1950-51, asst. prof. pathology, 1953-55, assoc. prof., 1955-61, prof., 1961—, assoc. dean, 1968-70, Ashbel Smith prof. pathology, 1991—; rsch. asst. pathology and cancer rsch. Cancer Rsch. Inst. New Eng. Deaconess Hosp., Boston, 1951-52; spl. asst. to chancellor U. Tex. System, 1971-75; exec. dir. Cancer Ctr. U. Tex. Health Sci. Ctr. Dallas, 1975-89; pathologist Parkland Meml. Hosp., Dallas, 1952—, Dallas City Zoo, 1955-68; med. examiner DallasCounty, 1955-58; cons. Navarro County Meml. Hosp., Corsicana, Tex., 1952-53, McKinney (Tex.) Vets. Hosp., 1952-65, Lisbons Vets. Hosp., Dallas, 1953—, St. Paul Hosp., Dallas, 1958—, Flow Meml. Hosp., Denton, Tex., 1958-65; pathologist Tex. Children's Hosp., Dallas, 1954-55. Contbr. numerous articles to profl. jours., sci. abstracts, jours. Bd. dirs. Planned Parenthood of Dallas, 1958-63, pres., 1958-60; trustee St. Mark's Sch. Tex., 1958—, v.p., chmn. exec. com. bd. trustee, 1966-68, v.p., 1968-69, pres. 1974-76; trustee Lamplighter Sch., 1967-70; chmn. Dallas Area Libr. Planning Coun., 1970-72, Goals for Dallas Health Task Force com., 1975-76, Fleet Adm. Nimitz Mus. commn., 1979-81; mem. adv. bd. Dallas Citizens coun., chmn. health com. 1988-89; bd. dirs. Met. YMCA, 1960-63, Dallas Coun. on World Affairs, 1962-65; pres., bd. dirs. Damon Runyon, Walter Winchell Cancer Fund, 1974-79; cord. Dallas Arts Dist., 1982-95. Fellow Am. Soc. Clin. Pathologists; mem. Am. Assn. Pathologists and Bacteriologists, Am. Assn. Cancer Rsch., Internat. Acad. Pathology, Am. Acad. Forensic Scis., Soc. Exptl. Biology and Medicine, Internat. Soc. Cell Biology, Biophys. Soc., Am. Soc. Cell Biology, Am. soc. Exptl. Pathology, Tissue Culture Assn., Internat. Fedn. Med. Electronics, Profl. Group Med. Electronics of Inst. Radio Engrs., AAAS, Optical Soc. Tex. (founding), Pan-Am. Med. Assn., AMA, So. Med. Assn., Tex. Med. Assn., AAUP. Office: 5323 Harry Hines Blvd Dallas TX 75235-7200

MONTGOMERY, REX, biochemist, educator; b. Halesowen, Eng., Sept. 4, 1923; came to U.S., 1948, naturalized, 1963; s. Fred and Jane (Holloway) M.; m. Barbara Winifred Price, Aug. 9, 1948 (dec.); children: Ian, David, Jennifer, Christopher. BSc, U. Birmingham, Eng., 1943, PhD, 1946, DSc, 1963. Rsch. assoc. U. Minn., 1951-55; mem. faculty U. Iowa, Iowa City, 1955—; prof. biochemistry U. Iowa, 1963—, assoc. dean U. Iowa Coll. Medicine, 1974-95, v.p. rsch., 1989-90; vis. prof. Nat. Australian U., 1969-70; mem. physiol. chemistry study sect. NIH, 1968-72; mem. drug devel. contract rev. com., 1975-87; chmn. com. biol. chemistry NAS, 1961-64; pesticide and fertilizer adv. bd. Iowa Dept. Agr., 1990-91; bd. dirs. Wallace Tech. Transfer Found., 1989-93; chmn. bd. dirs. Neurotron Inc., 1990-95; mem. rsch. com. Iowa Corn Promotion Bd., 1995—; cons. in field. Author: Chemical Production of Lactic Acid, 1949, Chemistry of Plant Gums and Mucilages, 1959, Quantitative Problems in Biochemical Sciences, 2d edit., 1976, Biochemistry: A Case-Orientated Approach, 6th edit., 1996; mem. editl. adv. bd. Carbohydrate Rsch., 1968-80; mem. editl. bd. Molecular Biotherapy, 1988-92; contbr. articles to profl. jours. Postdoctoral fellow Ohio State U., 1948-49; fellow Sugar Research Found., Dept. Agr., 1949-51. Home: 701 Oaknoll Dr Iowa City IA 52246-5168 Office: U Iowa Coll Medicine Dept Biochemistry Iowa City IA 52242

MONTGOMERY, ROBERT F., state legislator, retired surgeon, cattle rancher; b. Ogden, Utah, May 13, 1933; s. William Floyd and Adrianna (Van Zweden) M.; m. Jelean Skeen, June 24, 1953; children: Lance, Dana, Kristen, Keri, Tanya. AS, Weber State U., 1953; BS, Brigham Young U., 1957; MD, U. Utah, 1961. Pvt. practice Anaheim, Calif., 1966-88; senator Utah State Senate, 1992—; chief surgery Anaheim Gen. Hosp., 1970, Anaheim Meml. Hosp., 1972-74. Rep. chmn. Weber County, Utah, 1991-93; pres. Am. Cancer Soc., Salt Lake City, 1992-93. Sgt. U.S. Army, 1953-55, Korea. Mem. Rotary, Utah Elephant Club, Travelor's Century Club. Mormon. Avocations: traveling, reading, hunting, fishing, golfing. Home: 1825 Mountain Rd Ogden UT 84414-2903

MONTGOMERY, ROBERT HUMPHREY, JR., lawyer; b. Boston, Apr. 1, 1923; s. Robert Humphrey and Mary (Murray) M.; m. Henriette de Sieyes, 1952; children: Margaret, Anne (dec.), Samuel Bishop. AB, Harvard U., 1947; LLB, Columbia U., 1950. Bar: N.Y. 1953, D.C. 1978. Ptnr. Paul, Weiss, Rifkind, Wharton & Garrison, N.Y.C., 1950-93, of counsel, 1994—. Chmn. Alliance for the Arts, N.Y.C., 1985—; bd. dirs. Arts Connection, N.Y.C., 1985—; trustee Vassar Coll. Sgt. U.S. Army, 1943-46. Mem. Century Assn., Groucho Club (London). Democrat. Home: 31 E 79th St New York NY 10021-0101 Office: Paul Weiss Rifkind Wharton & Garrison 1285 Avenue Of The Americas New York NY 10019-6028

MONTGOMERY, ROBERT MOREL, JR., lawyer; b. Birmingham, Ala., June 9, 1930; s. Robert Morel and Ella Bernice (Smith) M.; m. Mary Lemerle McKenzie, Mar. 6, 1953; 1 child, Courtnay Elizabeth. B.S., U. Ala., 1952; LL.B., U. Fla., 1957. Bar: Fla. 1957; diplomate Acad. Fla. Trial Lawyers. With Howell & Kirby Attys at Law, Jacksonville, Fla., 1957-59; ptnr. Howell, Kirby, Montgomery, Sands & D'Aiuto, Jacksonville, Fla., 1959-66, Howell, Kirby, Montgomery, D'Aiuto, Dean & Hallowes, West Palm Beach, Fla., 1966-75, Montgomery, Lytal, Reiter, Denny & Searcy, West Palm Beach, Fla., 1976-85, Montgomery Searcy & Denny, West Palm Beach, Fla., 1986-89; sr. ptnr. Montgomery & Larmoyeux, West Palm Beach, Fla., 1989—; civil trial adv. Nat. Bd. Trial Advocacy. Chmn. Palm Beach Opera; vice chmn. Kravis Ctr., Palm Beach Cultural Coun. 1st lt. AUS, 1952-54. Mem. ABA, Fla. Bar Assn. (lectr. continuing edn.), Palm Beach County Bar Assn., Trial Lawyers Assn. Am., Inner Circle Advs. Home: 1800 S Ocean Blvd Palm Beach FL 33480-5104 Office: PO Box 3086 West Palm Beach FL 33402-3086

MONTGOMERY, ROBERT RAYNOR, pharmaceutical company executive; b. Sydney, Australia, July 6, 1943; s. Robert John and Gillian Eileen (Raynor) M.; children: Natasha, Karyn. Matriculation, St. Patrick Coll., Goulburn, Australia, 1962. Chartered acct. Sr. Peat Marwick Mitchell & Co., Sydney, 1967; supervising sr. Peat Marwick Mitchell & Co., London, 1967-68; supr. Peat Marwick Mitchell & Co., N.Y.C. and Rome, 1968-69; mgr. Peat Marwick Mitchell & Co., Athens, Greece, 1969-74; sr. mgr. Peat Marwick Mitchell & Co., Brussels, 1974-77; area contr. Alcon Labs., Inc., Brussels, 1977-78; dir. internat. fin. and adminstrn. Alcon Labs., Inc., Ft. Worth, 1978-81; v.p. corp. fin. Alcon Labs., Inc., 1981-82, v.p., chief fin. officer, dir., 1982-83, sr. v.p. fin. and adminstrn., 1983-89, exec. v.p., 1990—; bd. dirs. Visx, Ryder Internat., Arlon Labs., Inc. Commonwealth scholar U. NSW, Stanford Bus. Sch. Office: Alcon Labs Inc 6201 South Fwy Fort Worth TX 76134-2001

MONTGOMERY, ROBIN VERA, realtor; b. Boise, Idaho, July 21, 1928; d. Bruce Cameron and Grace Evangeline (Matthews) M.; m. Lewis Robert Goldberg, June 10, 1956 (div. June 1978); children: Timothy, Holly, Randall. BA in Journalism, U. Mich., 1957; BArch, U. Oreg., 1972. Architect Robin's Roost, Eugene & Florence, Oreg., 1972-82; realtor Exclusive Realtors, L.A., 1989—. Program chair Hadassah, Eugene, 1968; pres. Elec. Wires Underground, Eugene, 1967. With USN, 1949-53. Mem. Calif. Assn. Realtors, Theta Sigma Phi. Democrat. Avocations: hiking, films, writing, concerts. Home: 1334 S Carmelina Ave Apt 7 Los Angeles CA 90025-1962

MONTGOMERY, ROGER, dean; b. N.Y.C., May 28, 1925; s. Graham Livingston and Ann Katharine (Cook) M.; m. Mary Elizabeth Hoyt, Apr. 23, 1949 (dec. Feb. 1980); children: Richard W., Thomas V., John L., Peter G. Student, Oberlin Coll., 1942-44, 47, N.C. State U., 1953-55; MArch, Harvard U., 1957. Architect Zeller & Hunter, Springfield, Ohio, 1948-53; assoc. prof. architecture Washington U., St. Louis, 1957-64, prof. architecture, 1964-67; architect, planner Anselevicius & Montgomery, St. Louis, 1957-70; prof. U. Calif., Berkeley, 1967—, assoc. dean environ. design, 1976-79, 81-84, acting dean, 1988-89, dean, 1989—; emeritus prof., 1995—, emeritus dean, 1996—; pres. Calif. Council on Archtl. Edn., 1986, bd. dirs., 1983-87. Co-author: Architecture in State of Washington, 1980; co-editor: Housing in America, 1979, Housing Policy for the 1980's; contbr. articles to profl. jours. mem. Redevel. Commn., Berkeley, 1978-80, pres. 1980. Served with U.S. Army, 1945-47. Mem. AIA, Am. Planning Assn., Urban Land Inst., Planners Network. Office: U Calif 228 Wurster Hall Berkeley CA 94720-1850

MONTGOMERY, RONALD EUGENE, chemist, research and development director; b. Rural Valley, Pa., Feb. 17, 1937; s. Harry Noble amd Wilda Ruth (Bleakney) M.; m. Judith Ann Cyphert, June 3, 1961; children: Cheryl Joy, Sharon Lynn, Wendlene Kay, David Wesley. BS, Waynesburg Coll., 1959; MA, Duke U., 1961, PhD, 1963. Rsch. chemist FMC Corp., Middleport, N.Y., 1964-70, mgr. Organic Synthesis, 1970-76, mgr. Discovery, 1976-80; mgr. process rsch. & engring. FMC Corp., Princeton, N.J., 1980-82, dir. process rsch. & engring., 1982-88, dir. devel. chemistry, 1988-90, dir. rsch. & devel., 1990—. Mem. sch. bd. Royalton-Hartland Ctrl. Sch. Dist., Middleport, N.Y., 1972-76, Five-Mile Woods, Yardley, Pa., 1982—. Avocations: botany, geology, birding, canoeing, geneology. Office: FMC Corp Agrl Chem Group PO Box 8 Princeton NJ 08543

MONTGOMERY, ROSE ELLEN GIBSON, secondary education educator, organist; b. Barbourville, Ky.; d. Charles Butler and Mattie Cecilia (Corey) Gibson; m. William Goebel Montgomery; children: Pamela Janeese, Leilani Rose, William Goebel Jr. (dec.). BS, Hawaii Pacific U., 1965; MEd, Bowie (Md.) State U., 1970; postgrad., U. Philippines, 1970-73, U. Md., 1980-82; PhD, Am. Internat. U., 1995. Cert. tchr., Md. Tchr. Pearl Harbor Luth. Elem. Sch., Honolulu, 1965-67, Dept. Def. Schs., Luzon, The Philippines, 1973-92; tchr. Prince George's County Schs., Bowie, 1967-70, 73-92, Laurel, Md., 1992-96; ch. organist Pearl Harbor Meml. Ch., 1963-67, Clark Air Base Chapel, Luzon, 1970-73. Co-author: (handbook) World of Work, 1972; inventor 6-string guitar chord stamp for tchg. guitar. Active Girl Scouts U.S. and Boy Scouts Am., Honolulu; developer Meml. Garden, Bowie, 1973-74. Named Outstanding Organist, Pearl Harbor Christian Ch., 1966; recipient base comdr.'s award Clark Air Base, 1970-73, Outstanding Tchr. of Yr. award City of New Carrollton, Md., 1987, Md. Tchr. of Yr. for Prince George's County, 1993. Mem. NEA (life), Prince George's County Edn. Assn. (del.). Republican. Roman Catholic. Avocations: organ, guitar, story telling. Home: 2802 Stonybrook Dr Bowie MD 20715-2157 Office: Dwight David Eisenhower Mid Sch 13725 Briarwood Dr Laurel MD 20708-1301

MONTGOMERY, ROY DELBERT, retired gas utility company executive; b. Indpls., Apr. 24, 1926; s. Lloyd Sipes and Nona Mae (Brummett) M.; m. Barbara Ann Reno, Apr. 21, 1946; children: Stephanie, Rebecca, Jeffrey, Laura. Student, Purdue U., 1950-51; M.E., Internat. Corr. Schs., 1953; A.S. in Mgmt. and Adminstrn., Ind. U., 1973. Registered profl. engr. Ind. Engr. Citizens Gas & Coke Utility, Indpls., 1952-59, supt., 1959-60, dir., 1960-73, exec. dir., 1973-78, v.p., 1978-82, sr. v.p., 1982-86, cons., 1986-88. Contbr. articles to profl. jours. Vice pres. exploring Crossroads of Am. Coun. Boy Scouts Am., Ind., 1978; corp. rep. Jr. Achievement Ind., 1970-82; pres. Fairway Trace at Pendia I, 1994—, Fairway Trace Home Owners Assn., 1995—. Recipient Bronze Big Horn award Boy Scouts Am. Explorer Div., Ind., 1978. Mem. Am. Gas Assn. (merit award 1966), Ind. Gas Assn., Scientec Club Ind., Kiwanis. Republican. Avocations: oil painting, boating, golf, genealogy.

MONTGOMERY, RUTH SHICK, author; b. Sumner, Ill.; d. Ira Whitmer and Bertha (Judy) Shick; m. Robert H. Montgomery, Dec. 26, 1935 (dec. 1993). Student, Baylor U. and Purdue U.; LL.D., Baylor U., 1956, Ashland Coll., 1958. Former news reporter Waco (Tex.) News-Tribune; women's editor Louisville Herald-Post; feature writer St. Louis Post-Dispatch, Indpls. Star; news reporter Detroit Times, Detroit News, Chgo. Tribune; Washington corr. N.Y. Daily News, 1944-55; fgn. corr. S.Am., Europe, Far and Middle East, intermittently 1946-68; spl. Washington corr. Internat. News Service, 1956-58; syndicated columnist Capital Letter King Features, Hearst Headline Service, 1958-68. Author: Once There Was a Nun, 1962, Mrs. LBJ, 1964, A Gift of Prophecy, 1965, A Search for the Truth, 1966, Flowers at the White House, 1967, Here and Hereafter, 1968, Hail to the Chiefs, 1970, A World Beyond, 1971, Born to Heal, 1973, Companions Along The Way, 1974, The World Before, 1976, Strangers Among Us, 1979, Threshold to Tomorrow, 1983, Aliens Among Us, 1985; subject of book Ruth Montgomery: Herald of the New Age, 1986. Recipient Pall Mall Journalism award, 1947; Front Page award Indpls. Press Club, 1957; George Holmes Journalism award, 1957; best non-fiction award Ind. U., 1966; Most Valuable Alumna award Baylor U., 1967; inducted into Journalism Hall of Fame (Ind.), 1993. Mem. White House Corrs. Assn., State Dept. Corrs. Assn., Theta Sigma Phi (Woman of Year award 1966), Alpha Chi Omega, Kappa Kappa Kappa. Clubs: Nat. Press (pres. 1950-51, gov. 1951-54). Only woman selected to cover Pres. Roosevelt's funeral, 1945. Home: 3115 Gulf Shore Blvd N Penthouse 2 Naples FL 33940

MONTGOMERY, SETH DAVID, retired state supreme court chief justice; b. Santa Fe, Feb. 16, 1937; s. Andrew Kaye and Ruth (Champion) M.; m. Margaret Cook, Oct. 29, 1960; children: Andrew Seth, Charles Hope, David Lewis. AB, Princeton U., 1959; LLB, Stanford U., 1965. Bar: N.M. 1965. Ptnr. Montgomery & Andrews, P.A., Santa Fe, 1965-89, of counsel, 1994—; justice N.Mex. Supreme Ct., 1989-94, chief justice, 1994; adj. prof. law U. N.Mex. Sch. Law, Albuquerque, 1970-71; chmn. N.Mex. adv. coun. Legal Svcs. Corp., Santa Fe, 1976-89. Bd. visitors Stanford U. Sch. Law, 1967-70, 82-85, U. N.Mex. Sch. Law, 1982-89; pres., chmn. Santa Fe Opera, 1981-86; pres. Santa Fe Opera Found., 1986-89; chmn., vice chmn. Sch. Am. Rsch., Santa Fe, 1985-89; bd. dirs. New Vistas, Santa Fe, 1986-89, First Interstate Bank of Santa Fe, 1977-89, Old Cienega Village Mus., 1980-89. Lt. (j.g.) USN, 1959-62. Named Citizen of Yr., Santa Fe C. of C., 1986, Sunwest Bank of Santa Fe, 1994; recipient Disting. Cmty. Svc. award Anti-Defamation League, 1991, Western Area Outstanding Achievement award Nat. Multiple Sclerosis Soc., 1992, award for advancement of law N.Mex. Trial Lawyers, 1994, Award for Outstanding Judge Albuquerque Bar Assn., 1994. Fellow Am. Coll. Trial Lawyers, Am. Coll. Trust and Estate Counsel, Am. Bar Endowment, N.Mex. Bar Assn. (bd. bar commrs. 1986-89, sec., treas. 1988-89, Professionalism award 1993); mem. ABA, Am. Judicature Soc. Democrat.

MONTGOMERY, THEODORE ASHTON, physician; b. Los Angeles, Oct. 27, 1923; s. Wayne A. and Hazel (Osmer) M. MD, U. So. Calif., 1947; MPH cum laude, Harvard U., 1955. Diplomate: Am. Bd. Preventive Medicine, Am. Bd. Pediatrics. Intern Los Angeles County Gen. Hosp., 1946-48; intern Los Angeles Children's Hosp., 1948; resident Los Angeles Childrens' Hosp., 1950-51, St. Louis Childrens' Hosp., 1951-52; asst. in pediatrics Washington U., St. Louis, 1951-52; instr. pediatrics U. So. Calif., 1952-55; practice medicine specializing in pediatrics Los Angeles, 1952-54; lectr. pub. health U. Calif., Berkeley, 1960-83; cons. child health Calif. Dept. Pub. Health, 1954-60, chief maternal and perinatal health, 1960-61, acting chief bur. maternal and child health, 1961-63, asst. chief div. preventive med. services, 1963-66, chief, 1966-68, chief preventive medicine program, 1968-69, dep. dir. of Dept., 1969-73; chief div. disease control Alameda County Health Care Services Agy., 1973-74; cons. maternal and child health Calif. Dept. Health, Berkeley, 1974-78; chief maternal and child health br. No. Calif. Regional Office, Calif. Dept. Health Services, 1978-83; WHO fellow med. care adminstrn., Europe, 1966; co-chmn. Calif. Inter-agy. Council on Tb, 1966-72; vice chmn. Calif. Drug Research Adv. Panel, 1969-70;; White House Conf. Mental Retardation, 1963; Gov.'s chmn. Calif. Regional Hemodialysis Rev. Com., 1968-73; exec. sec. Gov.'s Population Study Commn., 1966; mem. com. on Tb, Calif. Lung Assn., 1973-74. Author: (with others) Standards and Recommendations for Public Prenatal Care, 1960, Guide to Hearing Testing of School Children, 1961; contbr. articles to med. jours. Bd. dirs. Calif. Interagy. Coun. on Family Planning, 1970-73; chmn. Calif. State Interdepartmental Com. on Food and Nutrition, 1977-79, pres. Clan Montgomery Soc. Internat., 1981-84, regional commr., 1985-91. With M.C. AUS, 1948-50. Fellow Am. Acad. Pediatrics (chmn. Calif. com. Indian health 1973-76, mem. nat. com. on Indian health 1963-79, vice chmn. 1977-79), Am. Pub. Health Assn. (chmn. task force on population policy 1971-72); mem. Alpha Epsilon Delta, Delta Omega. Home: 85 Wildwood Gdns Piedmont CA 94611-3831

MONTGOMERY, WALTER GEORGE, communications executive, consultant; b. Elmira, N.Y., Aug. 24, 1945; s. Elwood Herbert Montgomery and Eleanor Leila (Manchester) Spiegel; m. Pamela Sue Shaw, June 11, 1966 (div. Oct. 1976); children: Caleb Manchester, Kirsten Shaw; m. Marian Amy Gruber, Sept. 18, 1977; children: Abigail Lynn, Samuel Edwin, Rebecca Eleanor. AB, Syracuse U., 1967; MA, Brown U., 1976, PhD, 1979. Lectr. Keene (N.H.) State Coll., 1976-79, asst. prof., 1979; assoc. Kekst & Co., N.Y.C., 1979-82, ptnr., 1983; v.p. Am. Express Co., N.Y.C., 1983-85, sr. v.p., 1985-87; ptnr., vice chmn. Robinson, Lake, Lerer & Montgomery, N.Y.C., 1987—. With U.S. Army, 1970-72. Office: Robinson Lake Lerer & Montgomery Sawyer Miller Group 75 Rockefeller Plz New York NY 10019-6908*

MONTGOMERY, WILLIAM ADAM, lawyer; b. Chgo., May 22, 1933; s. John Rogerson and Helen (Fyke) M.; m. Jane Fauver, July 28, 1956 (div. Dec. 1967); children: Elizabeth, William, Virginia; m. Deborah Stephens, July 29, 1972; children: Alex, Katherine. AB, Williams Coll., 1955; LLB,

Harvard U., 1958. Bar: D.C. 1958, Ill. 1959, U.S. Ct. Appeals (7th cir.) 1959, U.S. Supreme Ct. 1977. Atty. civil div., appellate sect. Dept. Justice, Washington, 1958-60; assoc. Schiff Hardin & Waite, Chgo., 1960-68, ptnr., 1968-93; v.p., gen. counsel State Farm Ins. Cos., Bloomington, Ill., 1994—. Author: (39 corp. practice series) Tying Arrangements, 1984, also articles. Fellow Am. Coll. Trial Lawyers; mem. ABA (coun. antitrust sect. 1989-92), Ill. Bar Assn., Chgo. Bar Assn., Seventh Cir. Bar Assn. (pres. 1988-89), Legal Club Chgo., Law Club Chgo., Econ. Club Chgo. Avocations: skiing, woodturning. Office: State Farm Ins Cos 1 State Farm Plz Bloomington IL 61710-0001

MONTGOMERY, WILLIAM D., U.S. ambassador; b. Carthage, Mo., Nov. 8, 1945; m. Lynne Germaine Montgomery; 3 children. BA, Bucknell U.; MA, George Washington U.; student, Nat. War Coll., 1986-87. With Fgn. Svc., 1974; econ. officer Fgn. Svc., Belgrade, Yugoslovia, 1975-78; comml. then polit. officer Fgn. Svc., Moscow, 1979-81; line officer, secretariat staff then exec. asst. to under sec. polit. affairs Dept. State, 1981-84, exec. asst. to dep. sec., 1991-93; dep. chief mission Dar es Salaam, Tanzania, 1984-85, Sofia, Bulgaria, 1988-91; U.S. ambassador Bulgaria, 1993-96; spl. advisor to Pres. and sec. state for Bosnia peace implementation of the Bosnia peace plan, 1996—. Decorated Bronze Star; recipient Order of the Horseman of the Madara, Bulgaria, Commendation medal with V Device U.S. Army. Mem. Am. Fgn. Svc. Assn. Office: US Dept State Rm 6313 2201 C St NW Washington DC 20521

MONTGOMERY, WILLIAM J., finance company executive; b. 1930; married. BA, Dartmouth Coll., 1952. Sales rep. IBM Corp., 1954-59; div. mgr. Security Leasing Co., 1959-62; v.p. U.S. Leasing Corp., 1962-68; pres. Computer Property Corp., 1968-70, Singer Leasing Corp., 1970-74, Chase Manhattan Leasing Corp., 1974-79; chmn., chief exec. officer, dir. Xerox Credit Corp., Stamford, Conn., 1979-91; chmn., CEO Am. Fin. Group, Boston, 1991-93; ptnr. The Alta Group, Hanover, N.H., 1993—. Office: The Alta Group 11 Berrill Farms Ln Hanover NH 03755-3206

MONTGOMERY, WILLIAM WAYNE, surgeon; b. Proctor, Vt., Aug. 20, 1923; s. Charles Lynn and Ann (Jones) M. AB, Middlebury (Vt.) Coll., 1944; MD, U. Vt., 1947. Diplomate: Am. Bd. Otolaryngology. Intern Mary Fletcher Hosp., Burlington, Vt., 1947-48; gen. practice medicine W. Rutland, Vt., 1948-50; resident otolaryngology Mass. Eye and Ear Infirmary, 1952-55, mem. staff, 1956—, sr. surgeon in otolaryngology, 1966—; mem. staff Mass. Gen. Hosp., 1956—, surgeon otolaryngology, 1966-86; prof. Harvard Med. Sch., 1986-94, John W. Merriam prof. otology and laryngology, 1994—, med. dir. voice lab., 1993. Author: Surgery of the Upper Respiratory System, vol. I, II, The Mustache that Walks Like a Man, 1995; contbr. articles to med. jours. Served as batallion surgeon USMCR, 1950-52, Korea. Decorated Purple Heart, Bronze Star, Commendation medal; recipient Disting. Alumni award U. Vt. Med. Sch., 1968, Alumni Achievement award Middleburg Coll., 1985. Fellow ACS; mem. AMA, Am. Acad. Ophthalmology and Otolaryngology (instr. 1963-67), Am. Broncho-Esophagological Assn., Am. Laryngol. Assn. (James E. Newcomb award 1990), Am. Otologic Soc., Am. Laryngol., Rhinol. and Otol. Soc. (Cert. of merit 1990), Pan Am. Med. Assn., Mass. Med. Soc. (program chmn. 1966—), Suffolk Med. Soc., Am. Triological Soc. (Mosher award 1963, v.p. 1987), New Eng. Otolaryngol. Soc. (pres. 1977-78), Am. Soc. Head and Neck Surgery, Am. Acad. Facial Plastic and Reconstructive Surgery. Spl. research paranasal sinuses and laryngeal surgery. Home: 20 Hilltop Rd Chestnut Hill MA 02167-1846 Office: 243 Charles St Boston MA 02114-3002

MONTIJO, RALPH ELIAS, JR., engineering executive; b. Tucson, Oct. 26, 1947; m. Guillermina Paredes, Dec., 1947; children: Rafael (dec.), Suzanne, Felice. BSEE, U. Ariz., 1952; postgrad. in digital computer engring., U. Pa., 1953-57; postgrad. in mgmt., U. Calif., Los Angeles, 1958-60; DSc (hon.), London Inst. for Applied Rsch., 1993. Registered profl. engr., Tex. With RCA Corp., 1952-67; design and devel. engr. RCA Corp., Camden, N.J., 1952-55; mgr. West Coast EDP engring. RCA Corp., L.A., 1960-61, mgr. EDP systems engring., 1961-64; mgr. special systems and equipment planning, product planning divsn. RCA Corp., Cherry Hill, N.J., 1964-65; mgr. Calif. Dept. of Motor Vehicles program RCA Corp., Sacramento, 1965-66; mgr. spl. EDP programs RCA Corp., 1966-67; with Planning Rsch. Corp., 1967-72; dep. div. mgr. Eastern and European ops., computer systems div. Planning Rsch. Corp., Washington, 1968; dep. div. mgr. advanced systems planning, reservations systems, computer systems div. Planning Rsch. Corp., Moorestown, N.J., 1968-69; v.p., gen mgr. Internat. Reservations Corp. div. Planning Rsch. Corp., L.A., 1969-70, exec. v.p., 1970-71, pres., 1971-72, also bd. dirs.; v.p. Systems Sci. Devel. Corp. subs. Planning Rsch. Corp., L.A., 1972—; CEO Omniplan Corp., Culver City, Calif. and Houston, 1972—. Contbr. 37 articles to profl. jours.; patentee in field. Recipient Alumni Achievement award U. Ariz., 1985, Centennial medal U. Ariz., 1989. Mem. IEEE, NSPE, Am. Mgmt. Assn., Assn. Computing Machinery, U. Ariz. Alumni Assn. (pres. So. Calif. chpt. 1980-81, centennial medallion award 1989, alumni achievement award 1985, pres. Houston chpt. 1992-93, officer nat. bd. dirs.). Republican. Roman Catholic. Home: 2222 Gemini Ave Houston TX 77058-2049

MONTLE, PAUL JOSEPH, entrepreneur; b. Medford, Mass., Aug. 28, 1947; s. Joseph Frederick and Frances Elizabeth (Fogarty) M.; m. Elizabeth Anne Rusch, Mar. 3, 1973 (div. 1996); children: Alexis Elizabeth, Daphne Caroline. BA in Econs., Tufts U., 1969; postgrad., Boston U., 1969-70. Pres., chief exec. officer Killebrew, Montle Internat. Inc., Boston, 1971-73; v.p. Burgess & Leith, Boston, 1973-75, Hawthorne Securities Corp., 1975-76; founder, pres. First New Eng. Securities Corp., Boston, 1976-80, chmn., 1980-83; founder, pres. The Yankee Cos. Inc., Boston, 1977-88, chmn., chief exec. officer, 1988-89; founder, pres. Montle Internat., Boston, Houston, Hong Kong, London, 1987—, Am. Pacific Properties, Inc., Houston, 1990-92, Glenville Properties Inc., Houston, 1990—; chmn., CEO Teleconcepts, Inc., 1992-93, founder, chmn., CEO Lone Star Casino Corp, 1992—; founder, gen. ptnr. Travis Ptnrs. G.P., 1991—, Great So. Capital Ptnrs. G.P., 1994—; also bd. dirs., pres. Viral Testing Systems Corp., 1992-94, also bd. dirs., Motion Media Techs. Corp., 1991-92, also bd. dirs.; chmn., CEO 1st Response Med. Inc., 1993; trustee, treas. Derby Acad., Hingham, Mass., 1985-90; bd. dirs. South Shore Playhouse Assn., Cohasset, Mass., 1987-90; internat. bd. overseers Tufts U., 1993—. Mem. Houston Club, Woods Hole Golf Club, Houston Racquet Club. Avocations: sailing, golf, tennis. Office: Lone Star Casino Corp 1 Riverway Ste 2550 Houston TX 77056

MONTO, ARNOLD SIMON, epidemiology educator; b. Bklyn., Mar. 22, 1933; s. Jacob and Mildred (Kaplan) M.; m. Ellyne Gay Polsky, June 15, 1958; children: Sarah D. Monto Maniaci, Jane E., Richard L., Stephen A. BA in Zoology, Cornell U., Ithaca, N.Y., 1954; MD, Cornell U., N.Y.C., 1958. Diplomate Am. Coll. Epidemiology. Intern, asst. resident in medicine Vanderbilt U. Hosp., Nashville, 1958-60; USPHS postdoctoral fellow in infectious disease Stanford U. Med. Ctr., Palo Alto, Calif., 1960-62; mem. staff virus diseases sect. mid. Am. rsch. unit Nat. Inst. Allergy and Infectious Disease, Panama Canal Zone, 1962-65; from asst. prof. to prof. epidemiology U. Mich. Sch. Pub. Health, Ann Arbor, 1965—, chmn. dept. population planning and internat. health, 1993—, dir. Ctr. for Population Planning, 1993—; vis. scientist Clin. Rsch. Ctr., Northwick Park Hosp., Harrow, Eng., 1976; scholar-in-residence bd. on sci. and tech. for internat. devel. NAS and Inst. Medicine, Washington, 1983-84; vis. scientist div. communicable diseases WHO, Geneva, 1986-87; mem. pulmonary diseases adv. com. Nat. Heart, Lung and Blood Inst., Bethesda, Md., 1979-83; mem. nat. adv. coun. Nat. Inst. Allergy and Infectious Diseases, Bethesda, 1989-93,. Contbr. articles to med. jours. Recipient career devel. award NIH. Fellow Am. Coll. Epidemiology, Infectious Diseases Soc. Am.; mem. APHA (governing coun. 1978-80), Am. Epidemiol. Soc. Achievements include research on respiratory viral infections in the community; demonstration of effectiveness of influenza vaccine in severe disease in the elderly; prevention of spread of influenza virus and treatment of illness, occurrence, causes and treatment of common cold. Office: U Mich Sch Pub Health 109 S Observatory Ann Arbor MI 48109

MONTONE, LIBER JOSEPH, engineering consultant; b. Apr. 21, 1919; s. Vito and Philomena (Carnicelli) M.; m. Clara Elisabeth Edwards, June 1, 1945; 1 child, Gregory Edwards. MS, Temple U., 1961; PhD (hon.), 1994. Registered profl. engr., Pa. Quality control supr. Haskell Electronic and Tool Corp., Homer, N.Y., 1950-53; researcher IBM Airborne Computer Lab., Vestal, N.Y., 1954-56; devel. engr. Western Electric Co. and Bell Labs., Laureldale, Pa., 1956-61; sr. devel. engr. Western Electric Co. Inc., Reading, Pa., 1961-65, sr. staff engr. R&D, 1965-82; cons. Naples, Fla., Fenwick Island, Del., 1983—; biomed. engr., cancer rsch. projects pathology and clin. lab. St. Joseph's Hosp., Reading, 1961-80; tech. cons. Reading Hosp., 1961-78. Contbr. articles to profl. jours. including The Engr., Am. Assn. Clin. Scientists Symposium. Capt. USAAF, 1942-45, ETO. Recipient Outstanding Paper award Engring. Rsch. Ctr., Princeton, N.J., 1963. Mem. NSPE, Fla. Engring. Soc., Res. Officer's Assn. (life). Achievements include patents in field; invention (with others) diagnostic cystic fibrosis capillary conduction test method. Office: 4242 Vanderbilt Dr Naples FL 33963

MONTORIO, JOHN ANGELO, magazine editor; b. Montclair, N.J., June 26, 1948; s. John Daniel and Lorraine (DiVita) M.; m. Lois Ann Marco, May 15, 1977; children—John Nicholas, Nicholas Ross. B.A. cum laude in English, Seton Hall U., 1970; M.A. in English, U. Va., 1972. Sr. editor Gralla Pubs., N.Y.C., 1973-74; assoc. editor Lebhar-Friedman Pubs., N.Y.C., 1974-76; asst. editor Fairchild Pubs., N.Y.C., 1976-77; Sunday mag. editor Washington Star, 1977-81; asst. bus.-fin. editor, dep. home editor N.Y. Times, N.Y.C., 1981-83; Sunday mag. editor Newsday, L.I., N.Y., 1983—. Recipient pubs. award Newsday Inc., 1984. Democrat. Roman Catholic. Office: The NY Times Co 229 W 43rd St New York NY 10036-3913

MONTOYA THOMPSON, VELMA, federal agency administrator; b. L.A., Apr. 9, 1938; d. Jose Gutierrez and Consuelo (Cavazos) Montoya; m. Earl A. Thompson; 1 child, Bret L. Thompson. BA in Diplomacy and World Affairs, Occidental Coll., 1959; MA in Internat. Rels., Fletcher Sch. of Law and Diplomacy, 1960; MS in Econs., Stanford U., 1965; PhD in Econs., U. Calif., L.A., 1977. Asst. prof. Econs. Calif. State U., L.A., 1965-68; vis. assoc. prof. U. So. Calif., 1979; instr. U. Calif., L.A., 1981-82; staff economist The Rand Corp., Santa Monica, Calif., 1973-82; asst. dir. for strategy, White House Office of Policy Devel. Exec. Office of the Pres., 1982-83; expert economist, Office of Regulatory Analysis, Occupational Safety and Health Adminstrn. U.S. Dept. of Labor, 1983-85; dir. of Studies in Pub. Policy and Assoc. Prof. of Political Economy, Sch. of Bus. Mgmt. Chapman U., 1985-87; adj. prof., Sch. of Bus. Mgmt. Pepperdine Univ., 1987-88; pres. Hispanic-Am. Pub. Policy Inst., 1984-90; assoc. prof. of Fin., Sch. of Bus. Adminstrn. Calif. State Polytechnic Univ., Pomona, 1988-90; commr. Occupational Safety and Health Review Commn., 1990—; cons. Urban Inst., 1974, Mexican-Am. Study Project UCLA, 1966, Graduate and Profl. Fellowships to the Office of Post Secondary Education, U.S. Dept. of Edn.; editorial referee Contemporary Policy Issues, Economic Inquiry, Policy Analysis, The Journal of Economic Literature; discussion leader Am. Assembly on Rels. Between the U.S. and Mex.; pres. del. White House Conf. on Aging, 1981; reader of 1988 proposals for the U.S. Dept of Edn. for the Improvement and Reform of Schs. and Teaching; research participant U.S. Dept. of Edn. Delphi Assessment of Drug Policies for Use in Minority Neighborhoods, 1989; mem. hispanic adv. panel Nat. Commn. for Employment Policy, 1981-82; lectr. Brookings Inst. Seminars for U.S. Bus. Leaders; bd. adv. Close-Up Found., 1982-83; discussant Western Economic Assn. Meetings, 1985, 93; bd. adv. Nat. Rehab. Hosp., 1991-94; mem. nat. exec. adv. bd. Harvard Jour. of Hispanic Policy, 1993-95. Bd. regents U. Calif., 1994—; mem. adv. com. U.S. Senate Rep. Conf. Task Force on Hispanic Affairs, 1991—; mem. census adv. com. on Hispanic Population for 1990 Census, US. Dept. of Commerce, 1988-93, bd. advisors Nat. Rehab. Hosp., 1991-94, adv. com. U.S. Senate Rep. Conf. Task Force on Hispanic Affairs, 1991—, nat. exec. adv. bd. Harvard Jour. Hispanic Policy, 1993-95, bd. regents U. Calif., 1994—. Named One of the 100 U.S. Hispanic Influentials Hispanic Bus. Mag., 1982, 90, Woman of the Yr. Mex.-Am. Oportunity Found., 1983, The East L.A. Com. Union, 1979, Marshall scholar, Fulbright scholar; recipient Freedom Found. at Valley Forge Honor Econ. Edn. Excellence Cert., 1986, Univ. fellow Stanford Univ., Internat. Rels. fellow Calif. PTA, John Hay Whitney Opportunity fellow; Calif. State Univ. Found. Faculty Rsch. grantee. Mem. ASTM (com. on rsch. and tech. planning 1985-87), Am. Econ. Assn. (session chair ann. meetings 1995), Nat. Coun. of Hispanic Women, State Bar of Calif., Calif. State Bar Ct. (exec. com. 1987-89, disciplinary bd. 1986-89), Western Econ. Assn., Indsl. Rsch. Inst. for Pacific Nations (adv. bd. 1988-89), Salesian Boys and Girls Club (bd. dirs 1989—), Vets. in Com. Svc. (adv. com. 1989-94), Phi Beta Kappa, Omicron Delta Epsilon, Phi Alpha Theta. Home: 6970 Los Tilos Rd Los Angeles CA 90068

MONTRONE, PAUL MICHAEL, scientific instruments company executive; b. Scranton, Pa., May 8, 1941; s. Angelo H. and Beatrice M. (Giancini) M.; m. Sandra R. Gaudenzi, May 30, 1963; children: Michele Marie Cogan, Angelo Henry, Jerome Lawrence. B.S. in Accounting magna cum laude, U. Scranton, 1962; Ph.D. in Fin., Econs. and Ops. Research, Columbia U., 1965. Ops. analyst Office Sec. Def., Washington, 1965-67; exec. v.p., chief fin. officer Wheelabrator-Frye Inc., Hampton, N.H., 1970-83; exec. v.p. Signal Cos., Inc., La Jolla, Calif., 1983-85; pres. Engineered Products Group Signal Cos., Inc., Hampton, N.H., 1983-85; exec. v.p. fin. and adminstrn. AlliedSignal Inc., Morristown, N.J., 1985-86; pres. The Henley Group Inc., Hampton, N.H., 1986-92, bd. dirs.; chmn., CEO Wheelabrator Techs. Inc., Hampton, N.H., 1987-90; pres., co-owner The Gen. Chem. Group Inc., 1989-94, chmn. bd., 1994—; pres., CEO, bd. dirs. Fisher Sci. Internat., Inc., Hampton, 1991—; vice chmn. Abex Inc., Hampton, 1992-95; bd. dirs. Wheelabrator Techs.; adv. bd. ICI, Inc., Zeneca Inc., Sintokagio, Ltd. Mng. dir. Met. Opera Assn.; mem. dean's adv. coun. The Bus. Roundtable, Bus. Sch. Columbia U., N.Y.C. Capt. U.S. Army, 1965-67. Roman Catholic. Clubs: Brook, University (N.Y.C.); Bald Peak Colony (Melvin Village, N.H.); Lyford Cay (Nassau, Bahamas). Office: Fisher Sci Internat Inc Liberty Ln Hampton NH 03842-1808

MONTROSE, DONALD W., bishop; b. Denver, May 13, 1923. Student, St. John's Sem., Calif. Ordained priest Roman Cath. Ch., 1949. Aux. bishop Roman Cath. Ch., Los Angeles, 1983; bishop Diocese of Stockton, Calif., 1985—. Office: Diocese of Stockton PO Box 4237 1105 N Lincoln St Stockton CA 95203-2410*

MONTROSS, ERIC SCOTT, professional basketball player; s. Scott and Janice M.; m. Laura, Aug. 27, 1994. Student in Speech Comm., U. N.C. Ctr. Boston Celtics, 1994—. Named All-Am. Second team AP, All-ACC First team, All-Tournament teams ACC, NCAA East Region, NCAA Final Four, All-Rookie Second team, Schick, 1994-95. Avocations: reading, bass fishing, skeet shooting, travel, country music. Office: Celtics Ltd Partnership 151 Merrimac St Boston MA 02111

MONTS, ELIZABETH ROSE, insurance company executive; b. LaPorte, Ind., June 13, 1955; d. William David and Marguerite Elizabeth (Burge) Miller; m. James Edwin Monts, May 26, 1978 (div. Aug. 1982); 1 child, Katherine Elizabeth. AA with highest honors, Coll. of Mainland, 1984; BS magna cum laude, U. Houston, Clear Lake, 1989. CPA. Credit adjustment asst. Jaymar-Ruby, Inc., Michigan City, Ind., 1974-79; acctg. clk. Am. Indemnity Co., Galveston, Tex., 1979-80, staff acct., 1980-81, adminstrv. acct., 1981-85, asst. treas., 1985-86, asst. treas., asst. dept. mgr., 1986-87, sec., asst. dept. mgr., 1987-91, asst. v.p., asst. dept. mgr., 1991—. V.I.P. escort Rep. Nat. Conv., Houston, 1992. Mem. AICPA, Fedn. Ins. Women Tex. (regional dir. 1992-94), Tex. Soc. CPA's, Ins. Women Galveston County (pres. 1987-88, 90-91), Beta Gamma Sigma, Phi Kappa Phi, Alpha Chi. Republican. Methodist. Avocations: travel, gardening. Office: Am Indemnity Co PO Box 1259 Galveston TX 77553-1259

MONTY, CHARLES EMBERT, utility company executive; b. Plainfield, Conn., Mar. 9, 1927; s. Arthur Ovila and Mary Louise (Bromley) M.; children: Charles E., Mary, Janice, Nathan, Marcia. BSEE, Northeastern U., 1950; MBA, U. Maine, 1969. Registered profl. engr., Maine. Chmn. bd. dirs. Maine Yankee Atomic Power Co., 1988-92; chief oper. officer Cen. Maine Power Co., 1984-89; also bd. dirs.; energy cons., 1989—; mem. mgmt. com. New Eng. Power Pool, 1982-86. Mem. IEEE, Maine Assn. Engrs. Republican. Mem. United Chs. of Christ.

MONTY, GLORIA, television producer; b. Union City, N.J.; d. Joseph and Concetta M. (Mango) Montemuro; m. Robert Thomas O'Byrne, Jan. 8, 1952. BA, NYU; MA, Columbia U. Dir. New Sch. Social Rsch., N.Y.C., 1952-53; dir. Old Towne Theatres, Smithtown, N.Y., 1952-56, Abbey Theatre Workshop, N.Y.C., 1952-56; cons. ABC. Dir. numerous TV programs, including Secret Storm, 1956-72, Bright Promise, numerous episodes ABC Wide World Entertainment; exec. prodr. General Hospital, 1977-86, 90-92, The Hamptons, 1983-85; made-for-TV movies, including Confessions of a Married Man, 1982, The Imposter, 1984; exec. prodr. in devel. for primetime TV 20th Century Fox, 1987-90; head cons. daytime TV ABC, 1987-90; prin. Gloria Monty Prodns. for new ABC daytime drama devel.; developer (with Grosso-Jacobson) movie for NBC, 1992-93. Recipient Emmy awards, 1982, 84, Am. Soc. Lighting Dirs. award, 1979, Most Successful TV Show in History of TV award ABC, 1982, Spl. Editors award Soap Opera Digest, 1984, numerous others; named Woman of Yr., Paulist Choristers So. Calif., 1986. Mem. Women in Film, Dirs. Guild Am. (mem. exec. com.), Stuntman's Assn. (hon.), Thunderbird Country Club (Rancho Mirage, Calif.), Bel Air Country Club (Calif.).

MONTY, JEAN CLAUDE, telecommunications company executive; b. Montreal, Que., Can., June 26, 1947; s. Jean R. Monty; m. Jocelyne Belanger, May 17, 1969; children—Jean Sebastien, Pierre-Paul. BA, College Sainte-Marie, Montreal, 1967; MA in Econs., U. Western Ont., London, Ont. Can., 1969; MBA, U. Chgo., 1970. Vice pres. Merrill Lynch Can., Montreal, 1973-74; asst. v.p. Bell Can., Montreal, 1974-82; v.p. Bell Can., 1982-85, exec. v.p., from 1985, pres., 1989—, chief exec. officer, 1990-93; exec. v.p. BCE Inc., 1987-89; ceo Northern Telecom Ltd., 1993—; pres. Bell Can. Mgmt. Corp.; chmn. Bell Cellular; dir. Mut. Life Can., Rostland Corp., Bimcor, BN Ins., Internat. Bus. Council Can. Bd. dirs., v.p. Maison des Sciences et des Techniques, Montreal, 1985; bd. dirs. Fondation sur la Recherche des Maladies Mentales, Montreal, 1984-85, l'Institut de Cardiologie de Montreal. Home: 1437 Mt Royal Blvd, Outremont, PQ Canada H2V 2J5 Office: Bell Can, 1050 Beaver Hall Hill, Montreal, PQ Canada H2Z 1S4 Also: No Telecom Ltd, 2929 Maderson E, Mississauga, ON Canada L4W 4M7*

MONTZ, FLORENCE STOLTE, church official; b. Lowden, Iowa, June 7, 1924; d. Emil L. and Emma Marie (Meier) Stolte; m. C. R. Montz, June 15, 1947; children: Jennifer Montz Rechlin, Fredrick John. BS, RN, U. Iowa, 1947; LLD (hon.), Concordia Coll., Bronxville, N.Y., 1984; LHD (hon.), Concordia Coll., St. Paul, 1988. RN, Iowa. V.p., then pres. N.D. dist. Luth. Women's Missionary, Luth. Ch.-Mo. Synod, Bismarck, 1960-68, 1st v.p. internat., 1967-71, pres., 1971-75; editor Better Health mag. Luth. Ch.-Mo. Synod, Bismarck, 1983—, also bd. dirs.; Parish nurse instr. Trinity Hosp., Minot, S.D., 1995—. Mem. Assn. Lutheran Older Adults (pres. 1996—), Sigma Theta Tau. Home: PO Box 1293 Bismarck ND 58502-1293

MONYPENY, DAVID MURRAY, lawyer; b. Jackson, Tenn., Apr. 29, 1957; s. Kent Brooks Monypeny and Kathryn (Warner) Sadowski. BBA, U. Okla., 1980; JD, U. Memphis, 1983. Bar: Tenn. 1983; CPA. Atty. Glankler, Brown et al, Memphis, 1983-85; CPA Frazer, Thomas & Tate, Memphis, 1985-87; atty. Diamond, Finklestein, Monypeny, Memphis, 1987-88, Lawrence & Monypeny, Memphis, 1988-94, Monypeny, Simpson et al, Memphis, 1994—; atty., cons. Jerry Lee Lewis, Nesbit, Miss. Author: (video) Wiping Out Tax Debt You Can't Afford to Pay, 1993. Mem. Bellevue Ch., Memphis, 1983-96; campaign fin. chair Neil Small Chancellor, Memphis, 1990. Republican. Baptist. Avocations: music, video. Office: Monypeny Simpson Walker & Schatz 6256 Poplar Ave Memphis TN 38119

MOODY, CHERYL ANNE, social services administrator, social worker, educator; b. Winston-Salem, N.C., July 31, 1953; d. Fred Bertram and Mary Edna (Weekley) M. BSW with honors, Va. Commonwealth U., 1975; MSW, U. Mich., 1979. Social worker Family Svcs., Inc., Winston-Salem, 1974-77; sch. social work intern Huron Valley Jr. High Sch., Milford, Mich., 1977-78; children's social work intern Downriver Child Guidance Clinic, Allen Park, Mich., 1978-79; children's svcs. specialist Calhoun County Dept. Social Svcs., Battle Creek, Mich., 1979-81; children's psychiat. social worker Eastern Maine Med. Ctr., Bangor, 1981-82, sr. med. social worker, 1982-85; clin. social worker Ctr. for Family Svcs. in Palm Beach County, Inc., West Palm Beach, Fla., 1988-89, Jupiter, Fla., 1989-91; dir. children's programs Children's Home Soc. of Fla., West Palm Beach, 1985—; asst. prof. social work Fla. Atlantic U., Boca Raton, 1993—. Vol. group leader Lupus Found., Boca Raton, 1994—. Mem. NASW, Acad. Cert. Social Workers. Democrat. Methodist. Avocations: reading, knitting, drawing. Home: 6212 62nd Way West Palm Beach FL 33409-7130 Office: Children's Home Soc of Fla 3600 Broadway West Palm Beach FL 33407-4844

MOODY, EVELYN WILIE, consulting geologist; b. Waco, Tex.; d. William Braden and Enid Eva (Holt) Wilie; children: John D., Melissa L., Jennifer A. Student, Baylor U., 1934-35; BA with honors in Geology and Edn. U. Tex., 1938, MA with honors in geology, 1940. Cert. profl. geologist; cert. permanent tchr., Tex. Geologist Ark. Fuel Oil Co., Shreveport, La., New Orleans and Houston, 1942-45; teaching asst. Colo. Sch. Mines, Golden, 1946-47; exploration cons. geologist Gen. Crude Oil Co., Houston, 1975-77; ind. cons. geologist, Houston, 1977—; exploration cons. geologist Shell Oil Co., Houston, 1979-81; faculty dept. continuing edn. Rice U., Houston, 1978. Contbr. articles to profl. jours.; editor: The Manual for Independents, 1983, The Business of Being a Petroleum Independent (A Road Map for the Self Employed), 1987; co-author: How (to Try) To Find An Oil Field, 1981. Mem. Am. Assn. Petroleum Geologists (del. Houston chpt. 1986-89, 89-91, 91-94, 94—), Soc. Ind. Profl. Earth Scientists (hon. Houston chpt., sec. 1978-79, vice chmn. 1979-80, chpt. chmn. 1980-81, nat. dir. 1982-85, chpt. award for Outstanding Svc. 1986, editor SIPES Bull., 1983-85, treas. SIPES Found. 1984, pres. 1985, Nat. award for Outstanding Svc. 1988, SIPES Found. award 1994, hon. mem. in SIPES Houston chpt., 1994), Geol. Soc. Am., Watercolor Soc. Houston, Art Students League N.Y.C., Art Assn., Am. Inst. Profl. Geologists, Houston Geol. Soc. (chmn. libr. com. 1978—), Soc. Econ. Paleontologists and Mineralogists, Pi Beta Phi (nat. officer 1958-60, 66-68), Pi Lambda Theta. Republican. Presbyterian.

MOODY, FLORENCE ELIZABETH, education educator, retired college dean; b. Penn Yan, N.Y., Sept. 29, 1932; d. James William Southby and Rebecca (Worrall) M.; B.S., SUNY, Geneseo, 1954; M.S., Syracuse (N.Y.) U., 1961; Ed.D. (NDEA fellow), U. Rochester (N.Y.), 1969. Elem. sch. tchr., N.Y. State, 1954-64, 66-68; coord. profl. devel. Eastern Regional Inst. Edn., Syracuse, 1969-71; mem. faculty SUNY, Oswego, 1971-92, prof. elem. edn., 1978-92, assoc. dean profl. studies, 1980-85, dean, 1985-92; mem. N.Y. State Tchr. Edn. Cert. and Practice Bd., 1983-89; mem. Tchr. Edn. Conf. Bd., 1982-84. Nat. sec. Nat. Women's Party, 1974-76; bd. dirs. Oswego County Extension Service, 1974-76. Danforth asso., 1978—. Mem. Am. Assn. Colls. Tchr. Edn. (pres. N.Y. State chpt. 1983-84), Assn. Tchr. Educators, Assn. Supervision and Curriculum Devel., Am. Ednl. Research Assn., N.Y. State Assn. Tchr. Educators (sec., exec. bd. 1976-78), Kappa Delta Pi, Pi Lambda Theta, Phi Delta Kappa, Delta Kappa Gamma. Presbyterian. Club: Order Eastern Star. Home: 44 Franklin Ave Oswego NY 13126-1711

MOODY, FREDERICK JEROME, mechanical engineer, consultant thermal hydraulics; b. Aurora, Ill., Apr. 2, 1935; s. Frederick J. and Ruth K. (King) M.; m. Phyllis Arlene Ivemeyer, Aug. 27, 1955; children: David, John, Paul, Daniel. B.S. in Mech. Engring., U. Colo., 1958; M.S. in Mech. Engring., Stanford U., 1965, Ph.D. in Mech. Engring., 1971. Engr., GE, San Jose, Calif., 1958-78, prin. engr., 1978-81, cons. engr., 1981—; adj. prof. San Jose State U., 1971—; consulting engr. thermal-hydraulics GE, 1958—. Author: Introduction to Unsteady Thermofluid Mechanics, 1990; co-author: The Thermal-Hydraulics of a Boiling Water Nuclear Reactor, 1977, 2nd edit., 1993. Sunday Sch. tchr. Calvary Baptist Ch., Los Gatos, Calif., 1960—; chmn. bd. dirs. Med. Inst. Chaplains, San Jose, 1984. Fellow ASME (George Westinghouse Gold Medal 1980). Republican. Home: 2265 Sunrise Dr San Jose CA 95124-2640 Office: Gen Electric Co Mail Code 747 175 Curtner Ave San Jose CA 95125-1014

MOODY, GENE BYRON, engineering executive, small business owner; b. Calhoun, Ga., Aug. 29, 1933; s. Denzel Elwood and Mary Edna (Hughes) M.; m. Willie Earline Chauncey, Sept. 1, 1955; children: Byron Eugene, Iva Marie Levy. BSCE, U. Tenn., 1956. Registered profl. engr., Ala., Ark., Ga., La., Miss., Tex. V.p. S.I.P. Engring. Corp., Baton Rouge, 1968-70; project engr. S.I.P., Inc., Houston, 1970-73; dir. of engring. Jacus Assoc., Mpls., 1972-73; dir. of civil engring. Barnard & Burk, Baton Rouge, 1973-79; project mgr. Process Svcs., Baton Rouge, 1979-80, Salmon & Assoc., Baton Rouge, 1980-81; chief engr. Minton & Assoc., Lafayette, La., 1982; mgr. Assoc. Engr. Cons., Baton Rouge, 1982-86; owner Gene B. Moody, P.E.,

Baton Rouge, 1986—. Author: Good Homemakers, 1988, Deliverance Manual, 1989; contbr. articles to profl. jours. Deacon South Side Bapt. Ch., Baton Rouge, 1974; tchr. Hamilton Bible Camp, Hot Springs, Ark., 1981-91; trustee Manna Bapt. Ch., Baton Rouge, 1989-91. With U.S. Army, 1957. U. Chattanooga scholar, 1951, U. Tenn. scholar, 1953. Fellow ASCE; mem. Am. Soc. Safety Engrs., La. Soc. Profl. Surveyors, Soc. Automotive Engrs., Inst. Transp. Engrs., La. Engring. Soc., Transp. Res. Rsch. Bd. Mem. Christian Ch. (minister). Home and Office: 9852 Hillyard Ave Baton Rouge LA 70809-3109

MOODY, GRAHAM BLAIR, lawyer; b. Roswell, N. Mex., July 20, 1925; s. Graham Blair and Vinnie Charlotte (Burton) M.; m. Linda Alden Swanson, Apr. 11, 1970 (separated); children: Graham Blair III, Stuart, Katherine, Charlotte, Douglas, Margaret. BA, Yale U., 1947; MBA, Harvard U., 1947; LLB, U. Calif., Berkeley, 1955. Bar: Calif. 1956, U.S. Dist. Ct. (no. dist.) Calif. 1956, U.S. Ct. Appeals (9th cir.) 1956, U.S. Supreme Ct. 1963. Asst. to dist. mgr. producing dept. Standard Oil of Calif., L.A., 1948-52; head law clk. to chief justice U.S. Supreme Ct., Washington, 1955-56; assoc. McCutchen, Doyle, Brown & Enersen, San Francisco, 1956-64; ptnr. McCutchen, Doyle, Brown & Enersen, 1964-85, of counsel, 1985-86; ptnr. Moody & Moody, 1987-94. Vestryman St. Clement's Episc. Ch., then All Souls Episc. Ch., 1960-68, Ch. of Our Savior, 1988-90; bd. dirs., 1st pres. Eugene O'Neill Found., Tao House, Danville, Calif., 1975-76; bd. dirs. League to Save Lake Tahoe, 1978—, pres., 1980-82, 88-90, mem. exec. com., 1980-93; bd. dirs. Trauma Found., 1988—, Point Reyes Bird Obs., Stinson Beach, Calif., 1991—, mem. exec. com. vice chair, 1996—, Calif. Kidney Cancer Found., 1994—, Henry Ohloff House, San Francisco, 1994—, Friends of Redwoods, Mill Valley, Calif., 1991-92. Supply officer USN. Mem. ABA, Am. Law Inst. (life), Pacific-Union Club, Yale Club (past pres. local club).

MOODY, JAMES L., JR., retail food distribution company executive; b. Manchester, N.H., 1931; married. AB, Bates Coll., 1953. With Gen. Electric Co., 1955-59; with Hannaford Bros. Co., Scarborough, Maine, 1959—; treas. Hannaford Bros. Co., 1961-69, pres., 1969-84, chief exec. officer, 1973-92, chmn., 1992—, also bd. dirs.; dir. Penobscot Shoe Co., UNUM Corp., Sobey's Stores Ltd., Can., Hills Dept. Stores, Mass., Colonial Group of Funds, Mass. Served with U.S. Army, 1953-55. Office: Hannaford Bros Co PO Box 1000 Portland ME 04104*

MOODY, JAMES T(YNE), federal judge; b. LaCenter, Ky., June 16, 1938; s. Harold B. and Dorothy M. (Simmons) M.; m. Kay A. Gillett, Dec. 26, 1960; children: Patrick, Jeffrey, Timothy, Kathleen. BA, Ind. U., 1960, JD, 1963. Bar: Ind. 1963, U.S. Dist. Ct. (no. and so. dists.) Ind. 1963, U.S. Supreme Ct. 1972. Atty. Cities of Hobart and Lake Station, Ind., 1963-73; sole practice Hobart, 1963-73; judge Lake County (Ind.) Superior Ct., 1973-79; magistrate U.S. Dist. Ct. (no. dist.) Ind., Hammond, 1979-82, judge, 1982—; mem. faculty bus. law Ind. U., 1977-80. Republican. Office: US Dist Ct 128 Fed Bldg 507 State St Hammond IN 46320-1503

MOODY, LAMON LAMAR, JR., retired civil engineer; b. Bogalusa, La., Nov. 8, 1924; s. Lamar Lamon and Vida (Seal) M.; BS in Civil Engring., U. Southwestern La., 1951; m. Eve Thibodeaux, Sept. 22, 1954 (div. 1991); children: Lamon Lamar III, Jennifer Eve, Jeffrey Matthew. Engr., Tex. Co., N.Y.C., 1951-52; project engr. African Petroleum Terminals, West Africa, 1952-56; chief engr. Kaiser Aluminum & Chem. Corp., Baton Rouge, 1956-63; pres., owner Dyer & Moody, Inc., Cons. Engrs., Baker, La., 1963-94, also chmn. bd., dir.; ret., 1994. Chmn., Baker Planning Commn., 1961-63. Trustee La. Coun. on Econ. Edn., 1987-93. Served with USMCR, 1943-46. Decorated Purple Heart; registered profl. engr., La., Ark., Miss., Tex.; registered profl. land surveyor, La., Tex. Fellow ASCE, Am. Congress Surveying and Mapping (award for excellency 1972); mem. La. Engring. Soc. (dir., v.p. 1980-81, pres. 1982-83, Charles M. Kerr award for public relations 1971, A.B. Patterson medal 1981, Odom award for disting. svc. to engring. profession, 1986), Profl. Engrs. in Pvt. Practice (state chmn. 1969-70), La. Land Surveyors Assn. (pres. 1968-69, Land Surveyor of Yr. award 1975), Cons. Engrs. Coun., Pub. Affairs Rsch. Coun. of La. (exec. com., trustee 1983—), Good Roads and Transp. Assn. (bd. dirs. 1984—), Baker C. of C. (pres. 1977, Bus. Leader of Yr. award 1975), NSPE (nat. dir. 1982-83), Blue Key. Republican. Baptist. Clubs: Masons (32 deg., K.C.C.H. 1986), Kiwanis (dir. 1964-65). Home: 451 Ray Weiland Dr Baker LA 70714-3353 Office: 2845 Ray Weiland Dr Baker LA 70714-3247

MOODY, PATRICIA ANN, psychiatric nurse, artist; b. Oceana County, Mich., Dec. 16, 1939; d. Herbert Ernest and Dorothy Marie (Allen) Baesch; m. Robert Edward Murray, Sept. 3, 1960 (div. Jan. 1992); children: Deanna Lee Cañas, Adam James Murray, Tara Michelle Murray, Danielle Marie Murray; m. Frank Alan Moody, Sept. 26, 1992. BSN, U. Mich., 1961; MSN, Washington U., St. Louis, 1966; student, Acad. of Art, San Francisco, 1975-78. RN; lic. coast guard, ocean operator. Psychiat. staff nurse U. Mich., Ann Arbor, 1961-62, Langley-Porter Neuro-Psychiat. Inst., San Francisco, 1962-63; instr. nursing Barnes Hosp. Sch. Nursing, St. Louis, 1963; psychiat. nursing instr. Washington U., St. Louis, 1966-68; psychiat. nurse instr. St. Francis Sch. Nursing, San Francisco, 1970-71; psychiat. staff nurse Calif. Pacific Med. Ctr., San Francisco, 1991—; psychiat. staff nurse Charter Heights Behavioral Health Sys., Albuquerque; owner, cruise cons. Cruise Holidays Albuquerque. Oil and watercolors included in various group exhbns., 1982-93. V.p. Belles-Fundraising Orgn., St. Mary's Hosp., San Francisco, 1974; pres. PTO, Commodore Sloat Sch., 1982. Recipient Honor award Danforth Found., 1954, Freshman award Oreon Scott Found., 1958; merit scholar U. Mich., 1957. Mem. San Francisco Women Artists (Merit award for oil painting 1989), Artist's Equity (bd. dirs. No. Calif. chpt. 1987-89, pres. No. Calif. chpt. 1990), Met. Club. Republican. Lutheran. Avocations: cycling, hiking, sailing, photography, piano. Home: 219 Spring Creek Albuquerque NM 87122 Office: Cruise Holidays Albuquerque 11032 Montgomery Blvd NE Albuquerque NM 87111

MOODY, ROBERT ADAMS, neurosurgeon; b. bl. Swampscott, Mass., Oct. 1, 1934; s. George F. and Florence P. M.; m. Claudia; children: Robert Adams, II, Cathy, Paul, Lisa, Sherri. B.A., U. Chgo., 1955, B.S., 1956, M.D., 1960. Intern Royal Victoria Hosp., Montreal, Que., Can., 1960-61; resident in neurosurgery U. Vt. Affiliated Hosps., 1961-66; fellow Lahey Clinic, Boston, 1963-64; asst. prof. neurol. surgery U. Chgo. Med. Sch., 1966-71; sr. clin. instr., then asst. clin. prof. Tufts U. Med. Sch., 1972-74; prof. neurosurgery Abraham Lincoln Med. Sch., U. Ill., Chgo., 1975-81; chmn. div. neurosurgery Cook County Hosp., Chgo., 1974-81; assoc. chmn. dept. surgery Cook County Hosp., 1976-81; clin. prof. neurosurgery SUNY-Binghamton, 1983—; chmn. neurosurgery Guthrie Clinic, Sayre, Pa., 1981-95; ret., 1995. Contbr. articles med. jours. USPHS fellow, 1957-58. Mem. ACS, Am. Assn. Neurol. Surgeons, Pa. Neurosurg. Soc. (councillor 1986-87, pres.-elect 1988, pres. 1989), Mid-Atlantic Neurosurg. Soc., Ctrl. Neurosurg. Soc. (pres. 1978-79), Alumni Assn. Lahey Clinic Found., Sigma Xi. Office: Guthrie Clinic Guthrie Sq Sayre PA 18840

MOODY, ROBERT M., bishop; b. Balt., July 23, 1939; m. Lance Baty Martin; children: Leanne Moody Stoufer, Sharon Ruth Schechtel, Christian, Elizabeth. Grad., Rice Univ., 1962; postgrad. in law, U. Tex.; MDiv, Va. Theol. Seminary, 1966, DD, 1988. Rector St. James Ch., Riverton, Wyo., 1970-75, Grace Ch., Alexandria, Va., 1975-88; elected Bishop Coadjutor Diocese Okla., Oklahoma City, 1988-89, 4th diocesan bishop, 1989—. Office: 924 N Robinson Ave Oklahoma City OK 73102-5814

MOODY, ROLAND HERBERT, retired librarian; b. Manchester, N.H., July 17, 1916; s. Louis and Alice (Heath) M.; m. Ethel Corwin, Aug. 20, 1939; children—Jonathan Corwin, Ellen Jane. A.B., Dartmouth, 1938; B.S. in L.S, Columbia, 1941. Asst. res. desk Dartmouth Library, 1938-39; asst. reference and circulation librarian Middlebury (Vt.) Coll. Library, 1939-40; gen. asst. Harvard Coll. Library, 1941-43, keeper collections, 1946-48; circulation librarian Lamont Library, 1948-53; dir. Northeastern U. Library, 1953-83, dean libraries and learning resources, 1975-83. Served with inf. AUS, 1943-45, ETO. Decorated Bronze Star. Mem. Am., Mass. library assns., Am. Assn. U. Profs. Conglist. (deacon).

MOODY, STANLEY ALTON, entrepreneur, financial consultant; b. Portland, Maine, Oct. 16, 1939; s. Alton Elwood and Mary Gwendolyn (Young) M.; m. Jo-Ann Newton Vercoe, Dec. 15, 1975 (dec. Apr. 1992); children: Karen Elizabeth, Kirt Edward, Leslie Ann; m. Barbara Marie Katkus, June 28, 1992; 1 child, Jonathan Edwards. BSEE, U. Maine, 1962; postgrad., George Washington U., 1963-66; MA in Theol. Studies, Gordon-Conwell Theol. Sem., 1994; postgrad., Trinity Theological Sem., 1995—. Various positions Eastman Kodak Co., Kelsey-Hayes Co., Components, Inc., 1962-73; prin. Stan Moody Assoc., Augusta, Maine, 1973—; pres. Newton and Moody, Inc., Portland, Maine, 1980-84, Family Bookstores of New Eng., Portland, 1973—; dir. bus. cons. Maine Devel. Found., 1984-86. Author: Entrepreneurship in Maine, 1985, Telecommunications Design Strategy for Maine, 1986, No Turning Back, 1989, I Will Walk Again, 1993. Candidte for Gov. Maine, 1978; pastor North Manchester Meeting House, 1994—; chmn. Greater Portland C. of C. Energy Awareness Task Force, 1977; budget com. Town of Manchester, 1995—; chmn. Manchester Comm. awards Spirit of Am. Found., 1996. Mem. Safari Club Internat. Maine (v.p. 1993, pres. elect 1994), N. Am. Hunt Club (life). Republican. Avocations: hunting, fly fishing, writing. Home: PO Box 240 Manchester ME 04351-0240 Office: Stan Moody Assoc 7 N Chestnut St Augusta ME 04330-5040

MOODY, W. JARVIS, think-tank executive. Chmn., then chmn. Inst. for Defense Analyses, Alexandria, Va. Office: Inst Def Analyses 1801 N Beauregard St Alexandria VA 22311-1733*

MOODY, WILLARD JAMES, SR., lawyer; b. Franklin, Va., June 16, 1924; s. Willie James and Mary (Bryant) M.; m. Betty Glenn Covert, Aug. 2, 1948; children: Sharon Paige Moody Edwards, Willard J. Jr., Paul Glenn. AB, Old Dominion U., 1946; LLB, U. Richmond, 1952. Bar: Va. 1952. Pres. Moody, Strople & Kloeppel Ltd., Portsmouth, Va., 1952—; commr. Chancery, Portsmouth, 1960—, Accounts, 1960—. Del. Va. Ho. of Reps., Portsmouth, 1956-68; senator State of Va., 1968-83; chmn. Portsmouth Dems., 1983—. Recipient Friend of Edn. award Portsmouth Edn. Assn., 1981. Mem. ABA, Va. Bar Assn., Portsmouth-Norfolk County Bar Assn. (pres. 1960-61, lectr. seminars), Va. Trial Lawyers Assn. (pres. 1968-69), Hampton Roads C. of C. (bd. dirs. 1983-86), Portsmouth C. of C. (bd. dirs. 1960-61), Inner Circle Advs., VFW. Club: Cosmopolitan. Lodges: Moose, Elks. Home: 120 River Point Cres Portsmouth VA 23707-1028 Office: Moody Strople & Kloeppel Ltd 500 Crawford St Portsmouth VA 23704-3844

MOODY, WILMA LEE, paralegal; b. Quinton, Okla., May 12, 1949; d. Jesse Luke and Grace Pearl (Prater) Moody-Harris; m. Jerry D. Duvall, Jan. 31, 1964 (div.); children: Darren L., Deanna L.; m. Anderson Brown Morris II, Mar. 24, 1990. Student, Eastern Okla. State Coll., 1971; BS, Northeastern Okla. State U., 1975; Paralegal, U. Okla., 1979. CPCU; cert. BLS. Legal sec. A. James Gordon, Atty., McAlester, Okla., 1973; dep., minute clk. Pittsburg County Ct. Clk., McAlester, Okla., 1973-74; sec., bookkeeper Horne & Co., McAlester, Okla., 1974; legal sec. Bill Ervin, Atty., McAlester, Okla., 1975-77; bookkeeper, dep. & minute clk. Payne County Ct. Clk., Stillwater, Okla., 1977-79; instr. legal secs. Indian Meridian Vo Tech, Stillwater, Okla., 1977-79; sr. trial legal asst. Buck, Merritt & Hoyt, Oklahoma City, 1978-79; sec./legal asst., instr./legal sec. Okla. State Senate, Marvin York Vo Tech, Oklahoma City, 1980-82; legal asst. Warren L. Griffin, Atty., Midwest City, Okla., 1982-87, Lampkin, McAffrey & Tawwater and C.L. Frates and Co., Oklahoma City, 1987, 87—. Ch. missions N.W. Bapt. Ch., Oklahoma City, 1989-90, children's Sun. sch. dir., 1988-92; family support leader 1/160 Field Artillery, Pauls Valley, Okla., 1991—; adv. coun. Okla. Mil. Dept., Oklahoma City, 1993—. Mem. ABA, NAFE, State Filers Assn. (edn. com. 1993—, chair 1994—), Nat. Assn. Legal Secs. (dir. pub. rels. 1980), Nat. Assn. Legal Assts., Bus. Women's Assn. (Beta Sigma Phi chpt. pres.). Democrat. Baptist. Avocations: arts and crafts, designing, music. Office: C L Frates and Co 5005 N Lincoln Blvd Oklahoma City OK 73105-3324

MOOERS, CHRISTOPHER NORTHRUP KENNARD, physical oceanographer, educator; b. Hagerstown, Md., Nov. 11, 1935; s. Frank Burt and Helen (Miner) M.; m. Elizabeth Eva Fauntleroy, June 11, 1960; children: Blaine Hanson MacFee, Randall Walden Lincoln. BS, U.S. Naval Acad., 1957; MS, U. Conn., 1964; PhD, Oreg. State U., 1969. Postdoctoral fellow U. Liverpool (Eng.), 1969-70; asst. prof. U. Miami (Fla.), 1970-72, assoc. prof., 1972-76; assoc. prof. U. Del., Newark, 1976-78, prof., 1978-79; prof., chmn. dept. oceanography Naval Postgrad. Sch., Monterey, Calif., 1979-86; dir. Inst. Naval Oceanography, Stennis Space Ctr., Miss., 1986-89; sci. advisor to dir. Inst. for Naval Oceanography, 1989; rsch. prof. U. N.H., Durham, 1989-91; prof., chmn. div. applied marine physics U. Miami, Fla., 1991-93, dir. Ocean Pollution Rsch. Ctr., 1992—; coord. Coastal Ocean Scis. Program, 1991—. Editor Jour. Phys. Oceanography, 1991-96; mng. editor Coastal and Estuarine Studies, 1978—. Served with USN, 1957-64. NSF fellow, 1964-67; NATO fellow, 1969-70; Sr. Queen Elizabeth fellow, 1980. Mem. AAAS, The Oceanography Soc. (interim councilor 1987-88), Am. Geophys. Union (pres. ocean sci. sect. 1982-84), Eastern Pacific Oceanic Conf. (chmn. 1979-86), U.S. Nat. Com. Internat. Union Geodesy and Geophysics, 1992—, U. Nat. Oceanographic Lab. Sys./Fleet Improvement Com. (chair 1994-97), Am. Meteorol. Soc., Marine Tech. Soc., Sigma Xi. Achievements include pioneering direct observation of transient coastal ocean currents and fronts plus mesoscale and coastal ocean prediction rsch. Home: 2521 Inagua Ave Coconut Grove FL 33133-3811 Office: U Miami Div Applied Marine Physics RSMAS 4600 Rickenbacker Causeway Miami FL 33149-1098 *My central goal is to understand the ocean as a physical system by combining the interpretation of observations with dynamical theory and numerical models. Special emphasis has been on the dynamics of coastal oceans (continental shelf regions), now the scientific basis for practical mesoscale ocean prediction applied to marginal and semi-enclosed seas.*

MOOMAW, RONALD LEE, economics educator; b. Orkney Springs, Va., Aug. 1, 1943; s. Leo V. and Vivian (Fansler) M.; m. Juliana Pendleton, Dec. 27, 1971; children: Sara Christina, Kate Winston. BS with highest distinction, U. Va., 1964; PhD, Princeton (N.J.) U., 1976. Vis. asst. prof. U. Va., Charlottesville, 1968-72; asst. prof., assoc. prof. econs. Okla. State U., Stillwater, 1972-83, prof., 1983—, head dept., 1987-93; sr. rsch. assoc. Urban Inst., Washington, 1980-81; vis. assoc. prof. U. B.C., Vancouver, Can., 1983-84; prof. bus. adminstrn. CBA Assocs., 1994—; editorial bd. Internat. Reg. Sci. Rev., 1995—. Co-author: Profile of Oklahoma, 1977, Economics and Contemporary Issues, 1996; asst. editor Jour. of Econs., 1991—, Jour. of Regional Sci., 1994—; editl. bd. Internat. Regional Sci. Rev.; contbr. articles to profl. jours. Vestryman St. Andrew's Episcopal Ch., Stillwater, 1979-80, treas., 1990—; mem. budget com. Diocese of Okla., 1994—. Woodrow Wilson fellow, 1964, NSF fellow, 1964-66. Mem. Am. Econ. Assn., So. Econ. Assn. (bd. trustees 1989-91), Regional Sci. Assn., So. Regional Sci. Assn. (exec. com. 1985-87), Missouri Valley Econ. Assn. (v.p. 1993-95, pres.-elect 1995-96, pres. 1996—). Office: Coll Bus Okla State U Stillwater OK 74078

MOON, HARLEY WILLIAM, veterinarian; b. Tracy, Minn., Mar. 1, 1936; s. Harley Andrew Moon and Catherine Mary (Engesser) Lien; m. Irene Jeannette Casper, June 9, 1956; children: Michael J., Joseph E. Anne E. Teresa J. BS, U. Minn., 1958, DVM, 1960, PhD, 1965. Diplomate Am. Bd. Veterinary Pathologists. Instr. Coll. Vet. Medicine U. Minn., St. Paul, 1960-62, NIH postdoctoral fellow, 1963-65; vis. scientist Brookhaven Nat. Lab., Upton, N.Y., 1965-66; assoc. prof. Coll. Vet. Medicine U. Sask., Saskatoon, Can., 1966-68; rsch. vet. Nat. Animal Disease Ctr. Agrl. Rsch. Svc., USDA, Ames, Iowa, 1968-88, ctr. dir., 1988—; Franklyn Ramnsey chair in veterinary medicine & prof. Ames, Iowa; assoc. prof. Iowa State U., Ames, 1970-73, prof. 1973-74; cons. U. N.C., Chapel Hill, 1985-92, Pioneer Hy-Bred Internat., Johnson, Iowa, 1986-92. Contbr. articles reporting rsch. on animal diseases. Recipient Superior Svc. award USDA. Mem. NAS, Am. Coll. Vet. Pathologists, AVMA, Am. Soc. Microbiologists, AAAS, NAS, Sigma Xi, Phi Zeta. Avocation: farming. Home: 800 Shagbark Dr Nevada IA 50201-2702 Office: Iowa State University Veterinary Medicine Research Institute 1802 Elmwiid Dr Ames IA 50011*

MOON, HAROLD WARREN, JR., professional football player; b. L.A., Nov. 18, 1956; m. Felicia Hendricks; children: Joshua, Jeffrey, Chelsea, Blair. Degree in comm., U. Wash., 1978. With Edmonton Eskimos, 1978-84, Houston Oilers, 1984-94, Minnesota Vikings, 1994—. Named to Pro Bowl, 1988-93, Sporting News NFL All-Pro team, 1990. AFC Passing Leader, 1992; holds NFL single-season records for most passes attempted-665, 1991; most passes completed-404, 1991, sheares NFL single game record for most times sacked-12, 1985; shares NFL single season records for most games with 300 or more yards passing-9, 1990, most fumbles-18, 1990; Played in Grey Cup CFL Championship Game 1978-82. Address: Minnesota Vikings 9520 Viking Dr Eden Prairie MN 55344-3825

MOON, HENRY, dean. BA in Geography, Va. Poly. Inst. & State U., 1978; MS in Geography, U. Ala., 1984; PhD in Geography, U. Ky., 1986. Edn. advisor Toledo Indsl., Recreation and Employee Svcs. Coun., Inc.; acad. advisor The Buckeye Ctr.; prof. geography and planning U. Toledo, dean univ. coll.; cons., presenter and rschr. in field. Author: Environmental Geography Lab Manual, 1986, Environment Geography Lab Manual, 2d edit., 1990; co-author: A Workbook in Human Geography, 1987; contbr. chpts. to books and articles to profl. jours.; jour. article reviewer The Profl. Geographer, 1987—, The Ohio Jour. Sci., 1987—, The Social Sci. Jour., 1989—, Growth and Change, 1990—; software reviewer The Profl. Geographer, 1988—; manuscript reviewer John Wiley and Sons, 1992—, Routledge, 1993—, Prentice Hall, 1995—; book reviewer The Profl. Geography, 1993—; grant program reviewer Idaho Bd. Edn., 1993, Inst. for Studies and Transformations, Ahmedabad, India, 1993; chair program rev. team U. Toledo Dept. Elem. and Early Childhood Edn., 1994, U. Toledo Greek Program, 1995, U. Toledo Dept. Psychology, 1995, others. Advisor Area Growth Com., 1986-90, Ashland Ave. Revitalization Com., 1986—, Buckeye Basin Mgmt. Team, 1986—, City of Toledo, 1986—, Toledo Met. Area Coun. Govts., 1986—, Viva! Toledo, 1986-90, Collingwood Springs Redevel. Corp., 1987—, Com. of 100, 1987—, Heritage South Comml. Revitalization Assn., 1987—, Toledo-Lucas County Port Authority, 1987—, Archbold Area Schs., 1991—; sect. chair Toledo Met. Area Coun. of Govts. N.W. Ohio Strategic Plannign Conf./Gen. Assembly, 1989; chair Toledo Met. Area Coun. Govts. Com. One, 1989-91, Toledo Met. Area Coun. Govts. Citizen Adv. Com., 1990-92, N.W. Ohio Passenger Rail Task Force, 1993; mem. Toledo Express Airport Master Planning Com., 1991-92, Archbold Area Schs. Facilities Planning Team, 1994—, City of Toledo and Lucas County, Overall Econ. Devel. Planning Com., 1995—, City of Toledo Competitive Coun.; trustee Arrowhead Park Assn. Recipient Most Outstanding Paper award 62nd Annual Meeting of the Ala. Acad. Sci., 1984, GM Vol. Spirit award, 1995, Buick Vol. Spirit award, 1995; grantee U. Ala. Student Govt. Assn., 1984, Ala. Acad. Sci., 1984, Collingwood Springs Redevel. Corp., 1987, U. Toledo Office of Rsch., 1987, Toledo-Lucas County Port Authority, 1988, Toledo Met. Area Coun. Govts., 1988, U.S. Dept. Energy, 1991, 92, 94, Williams County Econ. Devel. Corp., 1994, Environ. Sys. Rsch. Inst., Inc., 1995, many others. Fellow Ohio Acad. Sci. (v.p. geography sect. 1990-92); mem. Assn. Am. Geographers, East Lakes Divsn. Assn. Am. Geographers (chair), Am. Land Resource Assn. (charter mem. 1985-87), Toledo Area C. of C. (advisor 1986—), Archbold Area C. of C. (advisor 1991—). Office: Office of the Dean U Toledo Univ Coll 401 Jefferson Ave Toledo OH 43604-1005

MOON, JOHN HENRY, SR., banker; b. Van Buren, Ark., Aug. 19, 1937; s. B.R. and Alma (Witte) M.; m. Agnes Rose Dickens, Aug. 16, 1958; children: John Henry, Randall Allen. AA, Delmar Coll., Corpus Christi, 1956; BBA cum laude, Tex. A&M Univ., Kingsville, 1958. Sr. acct. Tex. Eastern Transp. Co. and subs., 1958-63; exec. v.p., dir. Houston Research Inst., 1963-68; sr. v.p., asst. to chmn. bd., dir. Main Bank, 1968; vice chmn. bd., dir. N.E. Bank, 1969; CEO, chmn. bd., dir. Pasadena (Tex.) Nat. Bank, 1970-81; gen. ptnr. Moon and Assocs., Ltd., 1977—; chmn. bd., pres. Interservice Life Ins. Corp., Phoenix, Cmty. Bank, Houston, 1975-81, Interstate Bank, Houston, 1977-81; chmn. bd., pres. Cmty. Capital Corp., Pasadena, 1975—, Peoples Bank, Houston, 1983-93; chmn. bd. Cmty. Nat. Bank, Friendswood, Tex., 1981-93; chmn. bd. Peoples Nat. Bank, Pasadena, Tex., 1984-93; dir. San Jacinto River Authority, 1991-93; chmn., pres. Sam Houston Pky. Transp. Corp., 1991—; bd. dirs. Harris County Indsl. Devel. Corp., 1996—. Past bd. dirs. Pasadena Heart Assn., Salvation Army, Tex. Assn. Prevention of Blindness; past chmn. City of Pasadena Bd. Devel.; past chmn. adv. bd. Pasadena Civic Ctr.; past dir. S.E. Econ. Devel., Inc. Named Outstanding Young Man of Yr., Pasadena Jr. C. of C., 1973; named to Pasadena Hall of Fame, 1988. Mem. AICPA, Pasadena C. of C. (bd. dirs. Southeast Econ. Devel., Citizen of Yr. 1994), Tex. Soc. CPAs, Tex. Bankers Assn., Ind. Bankers Assn., Rotary. Home: 3914 Peru Cir Pasadena TX 77504-2320 Office: PO Box 910 Pasadena TX 77501-0910

MOONEY, DONALD JAMES, JR., lawyer; b. Albany, N.Y., Nov. 14, 1950; s. Donald James and Marguerite (Walsh) M.; m. Ann Marie Tracey, June 16, 1972 (div. 1993); children: Ryan, Maureen; m. Jennifer Mooney, July 17, 1993; children: Caroline, Nora Esther. BA, U. Notre Dame, 1972; JD, U. Cin., 1975. Bar: Ohio 1975, U.S. Supreme Ct. 1980, U.S. Ct. Appeals (6th cir.) 1976, U.S. Dist. Ct. (so. dist.) Ohio 1976. Staff atty. U.S. Ct. Appeals, 6th Cir., Cin., 1975-76; assoc., ptnr. Paxton and Seasongood, Cin., 1977-88; ptnr. Benesch, Friedlander, Coplan & Aronoff, Cin., 1988—. Chmn., mem. Cin. Planning Commn., 1983—; bd. dirs. Vol. Lawyers for the Poor Found., Cin., 1988—; mem. Cin. Human Rels. Commn., 1976-80; del. Dem. Nat. Convs., 1980, 84, 88. Mem. ABA, Fed. Bar Assn., Ohio Bar Assn., Cin. Bar Assn., Cincinnatus Assn. (treas. 1995-96). Democrat. Roman Catholic. Office: Benesch Friedlander Coplan & Aronoff 600 Vine St Cincinnati OH 45202-2400

MOONEY, EDWARD JOSEPH, JR., chemical company executive; b. Omar, W.Va., May 19, 1941; s. Edward Joseph Sr. and Johnny Mae (Kidd) M.; m. Mary Martha Muy, Aug. 22, 1964; children—Elizabeth Anne, Edward Joseph III. BS in Chem. Engring., U. Tex., 1964, JD, 1967; Sr. Exec. Program, MIT, 1979. Bar: Tex. 1967, Ill. 1973. Corp. counsel Howe-Baker Corp., Tyler, Tex., 1969-70; gen. counsel Nalco Chem. Co., Oak Brook, Ill., 1970-80, group gen. mgr., 1980-82, v.p., 1982-84, sr. v.p., 1985; group v.p. Nalco Chem. Co., Sugarland, Tex., from 1985; pres. Nalco Chem. Co., Naperville, Ill., 1990—. Mem. Ill. Bar Assn., State Bar Tex., Am. Patent Law Assn. Office: Nalco Chem Co 1 Nalco Ctr Naperville IL 60563-1252*

MOONEY, JAMES HUGH, newspaper editor; b. Pitts., Aug. 18, 1929; s. James H. and Kathryn A. (Hall) M.; m. Eileen Jane Casey, July 30, 1960; children: Mark Hall, Sean Francis, Annina Marie, James Matthew, Lorelei Jane, Paul Adam, Kathryn Celeste. B.A. in Journalism, Duquesne U., Pitts., 1957. With advt. dept., then editorial dept. Pitts. Post-Gazette, 1953-61; writer-editor Nat. Observer, 1961-77, Nat. Geographic, 1977-79; editor Found. News mag., Washington, 1979-81; press sec. Congressman Mickey Edwards of Okla., Washington, 1982; asst. nat. editor Washington Times, 1982-83; editor Status Report, 1983-92; dir. info. resources Ins. Inst. for Hwy. Safety, 1992-93; editor Western Pa. Medicine, Johnstown, 1993-95, Embassy Flash, Aspen Hill, Md., 1995—. Mem. editorial adv. bd. Nat. Study Ctr. Trauma and Emergency Med. Systems. Served with AUS, 1951-53. Mem. European Assn. Sci. Editors, Washington Automotive Press Assn., Nat. Press Club. Home: 13820 N Gate Dr Silver Spring MD 20906-2215

MOONEY, JAMES PIERCE, II, cable television executive; b. Fall River, Mass., May 28, 1943; s. James Pierce and Maria Anna (Antalek) Mooney Thompson; m. Louise Askew Rauscher, May 6, 1989; 1 child, James Pierce IV. J.D., NYU, 1968. Congl. liaison officer EEOC, Washington, 1969-71; staff dir. U.S. Rep. John Brademas, Washington, 1971-77; chief of staff Office of Majority Whip, U.S. Ho. of Reps., Washington, 1977-81; v.p. govt. relations Nat. Cable TV Assn., Washington, 1981, exec. v.p., 1981-84; pres., CEO N000, Washington, 1984-93. Recipient Cable Pioneers award for leadership, 1986; named Exec. of Yr. Cable TV Bus. mag., 1986.

MOONEY, JERRY D., medical services executive, diversified financial service executive. Pres., CEO ServiceMaster Diversified Health Svcs., Memphis. Office: ServiceMaster Diversified Health Svcs 5050 Poplar Ave Memphis TN 38157*

MOONEY, JOHN BRADFORD, JR., oceanographer, engineer, consultant; b. Portsmouth, N.H., Mar. 26, 1931; s. John Bradford and Margaret Theodora (Akers) M.; m. Martha Ann Huntley, Dec. 25, 1953 (dec. May 1990); children: Melinda Jean, Pamela Ann, Jennifer Joan; m. Jennie Marie Duca, Nov. 24, 1990. BS, U.S. Naval Acad., 1953; postgrad., George Washington U., 1970, 71, 76; grad. nat. and internat. security program, Harvard U., 1980. Commd. ens. USN, 1953, advanced through grades to rear adm., 1979; chief staff officer Submarine Devel. Group 1, 1971-73; commdr. Bathyscaphe Trieste II, 1964-66, Submarine Menhaden, 1966-68; comdg.

officer Naval Sta., Charleston, S.C., 1973-75; dep. dir. Deep Submergence Systems Div., Office Chief Naval Ops., Washington, 1975-77; comdr. Naval Tng. Ctr., Orlando, Fla., 1977-78; dir. Total Force Planning Div., Office Chief Naval Ops., Washington, 1978-81; oceanographer USN, 1981-83, chief naval rsch., 1983-87, ret., 1987; pres. Harbor Br. Oceanographic Instn., Inc., Ft. Pierce, Fla., 1989-92, marine bd., 1991-94; bd. dirs. Coltec Industries, 1992—; mem. marine programs adv. coun. U. R.I., Narragansett, 1989—; chmn. study panel on undersea vehicles and nat. needs NRC, 1993—, mem. adv. com. for postdoctoral and sr. rsch. associateship programs, 1995—; mem. panel to visit the former Soviet Union to evaluate undersea tech. for U.S. govt., 1993, chair, 1995. At controls of Trieste II when hull of Thresher was found on floor of Atlantic, 1964; coordinated deep search and recovery of hydrogen bomb lost off coast of Spain, 1966; condr. recovery operation from depth of 16,400 feet in Mid-Pacific, 1972. Decorated Legion of Merit with 1 gold star; recipient spl. citation Armed Forces Recreation Assn., 1975, Dist. Eagle Scout award, 1986. Fellow NAE, Marine Tech. Soc. (pres. 1991-93), Explorers Club; mem. U.S. Naval Inst., Nat. Geog. Soc., Smithsonian Assocs., Masons, Shriners, Order of DeMolay. Avocations: racquetball, sailing. Home and Office: 2111 Jeff Davis Hwy #1009S Arlington VA 22202

MOONEY, MARILYN, lawyer; b. Pitts., July 29, 1952; d. James Russell and Mary Elizabeth (Cartwright) M. BA summa cum laude, U. Pa., 1973, JD, 1976. Bar: Mass. 1977, D.C. 1985, Pa. 1990, U.S. Dist. Ct. D.C. 1985, U.S. Ct. Appeals (D.C. cir.) 1985, U.S. Supreme Ct. 1986. Atty. E. I. du Pont de Nemours & Co., Wilmington, Del., 1976-84, Washington, 1985; assoc. Fulbright & Jaworski L.L.P., Washington, 1985-90, ptnr., 1990—. Contbr. articles to profl. jours. Active Greater Washington Bd. Trade, D.C. Pub. Affairs Coun., 1992—. Mem. ABA, Fed. Regulation of Securities Com. (subcom. registration statements-1933 Act 1986—), Internat. Bar Assn. Office: Fulbright & Jaworski LLP 807 Pennsylvania Ave NW Washington DC 20004-2604

MOONEY, MICHAEL EDWARD, lawyer; b. Beloit, Wis., Jan. 21, 1945; s. William C. and Edith (Slothower) M. BA in Econs., St. Norbert Coll., 1966; JD, Boston Coll., 1969. Bar: Mass. 1969, Maine 1969, U.S. Tax Ct. 1975, U.S. Ct. Internat. Trade 1986. Assoc. Nutter, McClennen & Fish, LLP, Boston, 1969-77; sr. ptnr. Nutter, McClennen & Fish, Boston, 1978-89, mng. ptnr., 1989—; mem. exec. com. Fedn. Tax Inst. New England, 1987—, mem. artery bus. com., 1994—; spkr., lectr. numerous seminars. Co-editor: Considerations in Buying or Selling a Business, 1985; mem. bd. editors Accounting for Law Firms, 1988—. Bd. dirs. Lincoln and Therese Filene Found., Boston, Alliance Francaise of Boston, 1987—, Internat. Bus. Ctr. New Eng., 1986-89; clk. U.S.S. Constitution Bicentennial Salute, Inc. Fellow Am. Coll. Tax Counsel; mem. Boston Bar Assn. (chmn. tax highlights com. 1986-95, mem. fin. com. 1990-92), Boston Tax Forum, Boston Ptnrs. in Edn. (lawyers fund com.), Artery Bus. Com. Office: Nutter McClennen & Fish 1 International Pl Boston MA 02110-2600

MOONEY, MICHAEL JOSEPH, college president; b. Evansville, Ind., Dec. 15, 1942; s. Joseph Thomas and Marie Louise (DeJean) M.; m. Hannelore Karasek, Dec. 27, 1969; children: Susanne, Julia. AB summa cum laude, St. Meinrad Coll., 1964; STL magna cum laude, Univ. Innsbruck, Austria, 1968; M in Philosophy, Columbia U., 1973, PhD, 1982. Lectr. dept. religious studies, St. Mary's U., Halifax, N.S., Can., 1968-70, Union Theol. Sem., N.Y.C., 1972-74; project coord. Columbia U., N.Y.C., 1973-74, preceptor dept. religion, 1975-76, spl. asst. to exec. v.p. for acad. affairs, 1976-77, asst. provost, 1977-79, assoc. provost, 1979-82, dep. provost, 1982-89; pres. Lewis and Clark Coll., Portland, Oreg., 1989—; visitor Inst. for Advanced Study, Princeton, N.J., 1984; trustee Jour. Philosophy, 1982—; bd. dirs. Nat. Asssn. Ind. Colls. and Univs., 1995—; mem. Commn. on Internat. Edn., Am. Coun. on Edn., 1993-95;; bd. dirs. Reid Hall, Inc., N.Y.C. and Paris, 1977-89, v.p., 1983-89. Author: Vico in the Tradition of Rhetoric, 1985 (Gottschalk prize Am. Soc. 18th Century Studies 1985); editor: Renaissance Thought and Its Sources, 1979; co-editor: Toward a Theology of Christian Faith: Readings in Theology, 1968, Vico and Contemporary Thought, 1976, Small Comforts for Hard Times: Humanists on Public Policy, 1977. Bd. dirs. Roothbert Fund, 1980-92, Portland Opera Assn., 1992-93; trustee Scuola d'Italia, N.Y.C., 1986-90, World Affairs Coun., 1992—, Oreg. Ballet Theater, 1992—; mem. adv. com. Chamber Music N.W., 1990—. Recipient Rome prize Am. Acad. in Rome, 1989; Roothbert Fund fellow, 1972, Kent fellow Danforth Found., 1972, Woodrow Wilson fellow, 1972, Presdl. fellow Columbia U., 1972, F.J.E. Woodbridge Disting. fellow Columbia U., 1973; NEH grantee, 1984; Cavaliere Ufficiale, Order Merit, Republic of Italy, 1991. Fellow Italian Acad. for Advanced Studies in Am. (sr.); mem. Soc. for Values in Higher Edn., Am. Soc. for Eighteenth-Century Studies, Internat. Soc. for History of Rhetoric, Renaissance Soc. Am., Am. Acad. Religion, Am. Philos. Assn. Office: Lewis & Clark Coll Office of Pres 0615 SW Palatine Hill Rd Portland OR 97219-7879

MOONEY, RICHARD EMERSON, newswriter; b. Plainfield, N.J., Mar. 31, 1927; s. Wandell M. and Alice (Joy) M.; m. Elizabeth B. Coleman, Oct. 30, 1954; children: James C., Stephen E., John B. B.A., Yale U., 1947; postgrad. (Nieman fellow), Harvard U., 1955-56. Writer United Press, N.Y.C., 1948-51; econ. reporter United Press, Washington, 1951-56, N.Y. Times, Washington, 1957-63; European econ. correspondent N.Y. Times, Paris, 1963-67; econ. reporter N.Y. Times, N.Y.C., 1967; asst. to exec. editor N.Y. Times, 1968, asst. to mng. editor, 1969, dep. fgn. editor, 1970-72, asst. fin. editor, 1972-76, mem. editl. bd., 1982-95; contbg. editor, 1995—; v.p. Hartford Courant, 1976-81, exec. editor, 1976-81, dir., 1977-81. Author: (with Edwin L. Dale, Jr.) Inflation and Recession, 1959. Trustee Hartford Courant Found., 1977-81. Served with USNR, 1944-48. Mem. Yale Club (N.Y.). Home: 130 E 67th St New York NY 10021-6136 Office: NY Times 229 W 43rd St New York NY 10036-3913

MOONEY, SEAN, anchorman, television producer; b. Rochester, N.Y., May 21, 1959; s. Gene E. Mooney and Mary Elizabeth (Tracy) Parnell; m. Lauren Patricia Manning, Oct. 24, 1992; 1 child, Taylor Elizabeth. BFA, U. Ariz., 1981. Prodr., host Major League Baseball Prodns., N.Y.C., 1982-88; with Titan TV, Stamford, Conn., 1988-93; freelance reporter, 1993-94; news anchor, reporter Sta. WWOR-TV-United Paramount Network 9, Secaucus, N.J., 1994—. Active Child Reach, R.I., 1982—. Recipient Bronze medal Internat. Film & TV Assn., 1984, Moniter award, 1985, Emmy award NATAS, 1986, nominee Emmy award, 1996. Mem. Am. Fedn. TV & Radio Artists, Screen Actors Guild. Republican. Roman Catholic. Avocations: scuba diving, guitar, reading, fitness training. Office: WWOR TV-UPN 9 9 Broadcast Plz Secaucus NJ 07096

MOONEY, WILLIAM PIATT, actor; b. Bernie, Mo., May 2, 1936; s. Lowell E. and Louise S. M.; m. Valorie Shaw Goodall, Jan. 13, 1962; children: Sean Goodall, William Norvell. Student Am. theater wing, U. Colo. pres. William Mooney Assocs., cons. to industry for exec. presentations. Appeared in continuing role of Paul Martin on TV series All My Children, 1972—; one-man show Half Horse, Half Alligator & Damn Everything But the Circus; stage appearances: Brownsville Raid, We, A Man for All Seasons, Lolita; films: The Next Man, Network, A Flash of Green, Beer, Second Sight, C.A.T. Squad; author/star mus. play Banjo Reb and the Blue Ghost; co-author: ASAP-The Fastest Way to Create a Memorable Speech, 1992, Ready-to-Tell Tales, 1994, A Storyteller's Guide, 1995. Dir. jazz mus. Jam. Grammy nominee, 1995. Address: 8 Brookside Ct East Brunswick NJ 08816-2611

MOONIE, CLYDE WICKLIFFE, financial consultant; b. San Francisco, May 23, 1918; s. William B. and Vivienne (Selby) M.; m. Liana Maria Gabrielli, June 18, 1949; children: Gregory James, Barbara Marie. M.B.A., U. Chgo., 1941. C.P.A., Calif. C.P.A., N.Y. Mgr. Arthur Andersen & Co., C.P.A.s, 1941-58; adminstrv. mgr. Marcona Mining Co. S.A., 1958-62; controller Minerals & Chems. Philipp Corp., 1962-67; v.p., controller Engelhard Minerals & Chems. Corp, N.Y.C.; (merger Minerals & Chems. Philipp Corp. and Engelhard Industries, Inc.), 1967-73, sr. v.p., 1973-76, exec. v.p., 1976-80; exec. v.p. Phibro-Salomon Inc. (formerly Engelhard Minerals & Chems. Corp.), 1981-82; exec. dir. Fin. Acctg. Standards Adv. Council, 1983-86; fin. cons., 1982—; mem. panel arbitrators Am. Arbitration Assn. Served to capt. AUS, 1942-45. Recipient Forbes gold medal Calif. C.P.A. Soc., 1945. Mem. Am. Inst. C.P.A.s, Fin. Execs. Inst. Home and Office: Apt PH 4 Lafayette Ct Greenwich CT 06830

MOONVES, LESLIE, television company executive; b. N.Y.C., Oct. 6, 1949; s. Herman and Josephine (Schleifer) M.; m. Nancy Wiesenfeld, Dec. 17, 1978; children: Adam, Sara, Michael. BA, Bucknell U., 1971. Devel. exec. Catalina Prodns., Burbank, Calif., 1980-81; v.p. devel. Saul Ilson Prodns. Columbia Pictures TV, Burbank, 1981-82; v.p. movies and mini-series 20th Century Fox, L.A., 1982-85, Lorimar, Inc., Culver City, Calif., 1985-87; exec. v.p. creative affairs Lorimar-Telepictures, Culver City, 1987-90; pres. Lorimar TV, Burbank, 1990-93, Warner Bros. TV, Burbank, 1993-95, CBS Entertainment, Los Angeles, 1995—. Developer, producer TV series including Dallas, Dark Justice, Guns of Paradise, Knots Landing, Midnight Caller, Sisters, Family Matters, Full House, Perfect Strangers, Family Man, I'll Fly Away, Reasonable Doubts, Step by Step, Hangin' with Mr. Cooper, the Jackie Thomas Show, Crossroads, Homefront, Going to Extremes, Shaky Ground, It Had to Be You, Time Trax, Against the Grain, Lois & Clark: The Adventures of Superman, Cafe Americain, How'd They Do That, Living Single, Family Album, Getting By. Bd. dirs. L.A. Free Clinic. Mem. Acad. TV Arts and Scis. (exec. com.), Hollywood Radio & TV Soc. (bd. dirs. 1988-91, pres. 1991). Democrat. Jewish. Office: CBS Entertainment 7800 Beverly Blvd Los Angeles CA 90036*

MOOR, ANNE DELL, education director; b. Atlanta, Mar. 29, 1947; d. Kenneth Orman and Lida Louise (Springer) Dupree; m. Philip Ellsworth Moor, June 6, 1970; children: Andrew, Laura. BA, La Grange Coll., 1968. Cert. elem. edn. tchr., Tenn. Tchr. DeKalb County Bd. Edn., Atlanta, 1968-71, Briarcliff Bapt. Presch., Atlanta, 1972-73, Tates Sch., Knoxville, 1973-76; dir. after sch. care Cedar Springs Presbyn., Knoxville, 1993—. Discussion leader Bible Study Fellowship, Knoxville, 1980-93. Mem. Assn. for Childhood Edn. Internat., Tenn. Assn. for Young Children, Knoxville Area Assn. for Young Children. Presbyterian. Avocations: watercolor, hiking, needlework, vocal soloist. Office: Cedar Springs Presbyn Ch 9132 Kingston Pike Knoxville TN 37923-5227

MOOR, ROB, professional basketball team executive; b. Geneva, Switzerland; came to U.S., 1966; Degree, U. Calif., Irvine. Staff in distribution MGM Studios; staff in royalties, licensing and profits Twentieth Century Fox Studios; exec. v.p. Los Angeles Kings NHL; pres. Minn. Timberwolves, 1994—. Mem. Greater Minneapolis C. of C. (bd. dirs.). Office: Minn Timberwolves 600 First Ave N Minneapolis MN 55403

MOOR, ROY EDWARD, finance educator; b. Riverside, Calif., Oct. 11, 1924; s. Hugh Erin and Clara Viola Moor; m. Beverly A. Colbroth, Aug. 29, 1959; children—Cynthia Ann, Sheryl Lynn. B.A., UCLA, 1949; Ph.D., Harvard U., 1958. Vice pres., chief economist Fidelity Bank, Phila., 1965-68; vice pres., chief economist Drexel Firestone, Phila., 1968-71, Warburg Paribas Becker, N.Y.C., 1971-81; sr. v.p., chief economist First Chgo. Corp., 1981-86; prof. fin. Ill. Inst. Tech., Chgo., 1986—; dir. Nat. Bur. Econ. Research, Cambridge, Mass. Author: Federal Budget as an Economic Document, 1962. Fellow Nat. Assn. Bus. Economists (pres. 1973). Home: 1013 Woodrush Ct Westmont IL 60561-8823 Office: Ill Inst Tech 10 W 31st St Chicago IL 60616-3729

MOORADIAN, ARSHAG DERTAD, physician, educator; b. Aleppo, Syria, Aug. 20, 1953; came to U.S., 1981; s. Dertad and Araxie (Halajian) M.; m. Deborah Lynn Miles, June 25, 1985; children: Arshag Dertad Jr., Ariana Araxie. BS, Am. U., Beirut, 1976, MD, 1980. Diplomate Am. Bd. Internal Medicine. Asst. prof. medicine UCLA, 1985-88; assoc. prof. U. Ariz., Tucson, 1988-91; prof. St. Louis U., 1991. Contbr. articles to Jour. Endocrinology, Diabetes, Jour. Gerontology, Neurochemistry Rsch. VA grantee, 1985—. Mem. Am. Fedn. Clin. Rsch., Gerontol. Soc. Am., Endocrine Soc., Am. Diabetes Assn. (chmn. task force on micronutreints 1990-91). Mem. Armenian Orthodox Ch. Achievements include identification of a potential biomarker of aging; research on age-related changes in the blood-brain barrier, on age-related changes in thyroid hormone action, on diabetes related changes in the central nervous system. Office: Saint Louis U Med Sch 1402 S Grand Blvd Saint Louis MO 63104-1004

MOORE, ACEL, journalist; b. Phila., Oct. 5, 1940; s. Jerry A. and Hura Mae (Harrington) Acel M.; m. Carolyn Weaver, June 1964 (div. 1974); 1 child, Acel; m. Linda Wright Avery, Aug. 6, 1988. Student, Settlement Music Sch., 1958, Charles Morris Price Sch., 1966-67. Copyboy Phila. Inquirer, 1962-64, editorial clk., 1964-68, staff reporter, 1968-80, editorial writer/columnist, 1980-81, asso. editor, 1981—, also mem. edit. bd.; co-producer Black Perspective on the News (Nat. PBS weekly news program), 1972-78. Served with U.S. Army, 1959-62. Recipient Pulitzer prize, 1977, Robert F. Kennedy Journalism prize, 1977, Heywood Broun prize, 1977, Pa. Prison Soc. award, 1977, Humanitarian award House of Umoja, 1977, Community Service award Youth Devel. Center, 1976, Journalism award Phila. Party, 1977, Phila. Bar Assn. award, 1970, Ann. Paul Robeson award, 1977, Clarion award, 1977, Media award Mental Health Assn., 1977; Nieman fellow Harvard U., 1979-80. Mem. Nat. Assn. Black Journalists, Phila. Assn. Black Journalists (pres.), Am. Soc. Newspaper Editors, Sigma Delta Chi (Phila. chpt. Pub. Service awards 1972, 77, Reporting award 1977). Office: Phila Inquirer 400 N Broad St Philadelphia PA 19130-4015

MOORE, ALBERT CUNNINGHAM, lawyer, insurance company executive; b. Miami, Fla., May 31, 1931; s. Elias Richard and Virginia Adelaide (Thompson) M.; m. Anne Cambreleng Bonynge, aug. 24, 1957; children: Emily Robinson French, Barbara Raffield Walton, Catherine Anne Bonynge Wells. A.B., U. N.C., 1953; J.D., U. Va., 1959. Bar: N.Y. 1960. Atty. White & Case, N.Y.C., 1959-69; corporate sec. Studebaker-Worthington, Inc., N.Y.C., 1969-72; sr. v.p., gen. counsel Crum & Forster, 1973-87. Former trustee N.J. Shakespeare Festival; former bd. dirs. DeBordieu Property Owners Assn., Debordieu Arch. Rev. Bd. With USNR, 1953-56. Mem. ABA, Wilton Ctr. Tennis Club (N.H.), DeBordieu Club (S.C.), Phi Alpha Delta, Chi Phi. Home: 1318 Debordieu Blvd Georgetown SC 29440

MOORE, ALDERINE BERNICE JENNINGS (MRS. JAMES F. MOORE), association and organization administrator; Sacramento, Apr. 17, 1915; d. James Joseph and Elise (Thomas) Jennings; BA, U. Wash., 1941; m. James Francis Moore, Aug. 14, 1945. Sec. to div. Plant supr. Pacific Tel. & Tel. Co., Sacramento, 1937-39; exec. sec. Sacramento Community Chest Fund Raising Dr., 1941; sec. USAAF, Mather Field, Sacramento, 1942; statistician Calif. Western States Life Ins. Co., 1943; treas. Women's Aux. Stranger's Hosp., Rio de Janeiro, Brazil, 1964-65. Vice pres. Douglaston (N.Y.) Women's Club, 1955; mem. Douglaston Garden Club, 1951-55; pres. Nina Opland chpt. Women's Cancer Assn. U. Miami, 1960-61; corr. sec. Coral Gables (Fla.) Garden Club, 1960-62; pres. Miami Alumnae Club of Pi Beta Phi, 1961-62; mem. Putnam Hill chpt. D.A.R., Greenwich Conn., 1967-75, Palm Beach chpt., 1978—; mem. Woman's Club, Greenwich, Conn., 1967-75; mem. Women's Panhellenic Assn., Miami, 1961-62; internat. treas. Ikebana Internat., Tokyo, Japan, 1966-67, parliamentarian Tokyo chpt., 1966-67, N.Y. chpt., 1968-69; mem. Coll. Women Assn. Japan, 1965-66; mem. Tchrs. Assn. Sogetsu Sch. Japanese Flower Arranging, 1966—, Atlantis Golf Club. Served to 1st.lt. WAVES, 1943-45. Mem. Internat. Platform Assn., AAUW, Pi Beta Phi (local v.p. alumnae club .1969-71). Baptist. Club: Steamboat Investment (pres. 1972-73). Home: 316 Fairway Ct Lake Worth FL 33462

MOORE, ALFRED ANSON, corporate executive; b. Muttontown, N.Y., Oct. 1, 1925; s. Benjamin Moore and Alexandra (Emery) McKay; m. Sarah Carolyn Rush, July 1954 (div. 1973); m. Betty Ruth Teipel, July 19, 1974; children: Jeremiah, Alexandra. BA, Yale U., 1946; postgrad., Harvard U., 1946-47. Reporter, re-writer Bergen Evening Record, Hackensack, N.J., 1948-49; v.p. Emery Kunston, Cin., 1961-62; pres. Profl. Realty Service, Cin., 1967, Emery Realty, Cin., 1969; dir. Thomas Emery's Sons, Inc., Cin., 1949—; pres. Chelsea Moore Corp., N.Y. and Cin., 1953-91, chmn. bd., 1979—; trustee various personal trusts, Ohio, Maine, Pa., 1969—, ptnr. various real property devels., Ohio, S.C., Colo., 1964—; executor Estate of Alexandra E. McKay, Monticello, Fla., 1983-89; co-chmn. Emery Ctr. Corp., 1987—. Chmn. bd. Contemporary Arts Ctr., Cin., 1977-80, trustee, 1972—; chmn. Save the Terminal, Cin., 1972-73; trustee, sec. Community Improvement Corp., Cin., 1975—; trustee Am. Farm Sch., Thessaloniki, Greece, 1980-83, Seven Hills Sch., 1987-92, Nat. Dropout Prevention Fund., 1988-90; trustee, v.p. Miami Purchase Assn., Cin., 1962-67, 87-90. Lt. (j.g.) USNR, 1943-46, ETO, PTO. Named Benefactor, City Mgr., Cin., 1968. Mem. Soc. Colonial Wars, Camargo Club, Racquet Club, Mason. Republican. Avocations: squash, shooting, fishing. Office: Carew Tower 2300 Carew Tower 441 Vine St Cincinnati OH 45202-2913

MOORE, ANDREA S., state legislator; b. Libertyville, Ill., Sept. 2, 1944. Attended, Drake U. m. William Moore; 3 children. Mem. Ill. Ho. of Reps., 1993—; mem. com. on elections and state govt., mem. com. on aging, mem. cities and villages com., mem. environ. and energy com., mem. labor and commerce com. Republican. Home: 361 S Saint Marys Rd Libertyville IL 60048-9407 Office: Ill Ho of Reps State Capitol Springfield IL 62706 also: 2014-H Stratton Bldg Springfield IL 62706 also: 733 N Milwaukee Ave Libertyville IL 60048-1913*

MOORE, ANDREW GIVEN TOBIAS, II, investment banker, educator; b. New Orleans, Nov. 25, 1935; m. Ann Elizabeth Dawson, June 5, 1965; children—Cecily Elizabeth, Marianne Dawson. B.B.A., Tulane U., 1958, J.D., 1960. Bar: La. 1960, Del. 1963. Law clk. to chief justice Del. Dover, 1963; assoc. firm Killoran & Van Brunt, Wilmington, Del., 1964-70; partner Killoran & Van Brunt, 1971-76; partner firm Connolly, Bove & Lodge, Wilmington, 1976-82; justice Del. Supreme Ct., Wilmington, 1982-94; sr. mng. dir. Wasserstein Perella & Co., Inc., N.Y.C., 1994—; mem. Del. Bar Examiners, 1975-82; mem. Del. Gen. Corp. law com., 1969-83; chmn. joint com. Del. Bar Assn.-Del. Bankers Assn., 1978-79; chmn. Del. Jud. Proprieties Com., 1983-94, Del. Bench and Bar Conf., 1988-94; trustee Del. Bar Found., 1984-94; faculty Tulane Inst. European Legal Studies, Paris Inst., 1990—; adj. prof. law Georgetown U. Law Ctr., Widener U. Sch. Law, U. Iowa Coll. Law; guest lectr. law Tulane U., U. Toronto, Can., U. Tex., Villanova U., Washington U., St. Louis, U. Iowa, Geo. Mason U., DeVrije U. van Brussel, Cath. U. Louvain La Neuve; mem. pres.'s coun. Tulane U., 1990—; chmn. Tulane Corp. Law Inst., 1988—; Lehmann disting. vis. prof. law Washington U., St. Louis, 1994, 96; Mason Ladd disting. vis. prof. U. Iowa, 1995; disting. vis. prof. law St. Louis U., 1995. Trustee Del. Home and Hosp. for Chronically Ill, Smyrna, 1966-70, chmn., 1966-69; mem. New Castle County Hist. Rev. Bd., Wilmington, 1974-82; mem. Del. Cts. Planning Com., 1982-94; dean's coun. Tulane U. Law Sch., 1988—; bd. visitors Walter F. George Sch. Law, Mercer U., 1985-91, chmn., 1988-90. With JAGC, USAF, 1960-63. Mem. ABA, La. Bar Assn., Del. Bar Assn. (v.p. 1976-77, exec. com. 1982-83), Am. Judicature Soc. (bd. dirs. 1982-86), Order Barristers, Phi Delta Phi, Delta Theta Phi (hon.), Omicron Delta Kappa. Democrat. Presbyterian. Office: Wasserstein Perella & Co 31 W 52nd St New York NY 10019-6118

MOORE, ANDREW TAYLOR, JR., banker; b. Tarboro, N.C., June 17, 1940; s. Andrew Taylor and Mary Dare (Allsbrook) M. BA in History, Duke U., 1962; LLB, U.Va., Charlottesville, 1965. Asst. sec. Signet Banking Corp., Richmond, 1965-71, asst. v.p., corporate sec., 1971-75, v.p., corporate sec., 1975-82, sr. v.p., corporate sec., 1982-94. Bd. dirs. Theatre IV, Richmond, Va., 1981—, Va. State YMCA adv. coun., Lynchburg, 1988—, trustee 1994—; trustee Hist. Richmond Found., 1993—. With U.S. Army, 1967. Mem. Va. Hist. Soc. (pres. coun. 1995—), Commonwealth Club. Presbyterian. Avocations: jogging; gardening; travel. Home: 2011 Hanover Ave Richmond VA 23220-3539

MOORE, ANN S., magazine publisher; b. McLean, VA, 1950; d. Monty and Bea Sommovigo; m. Donovan Moore; 1 son, Brendan. MBA, Harvard U., 1978. With Time, Inc., New York, NY, 1978—; founding publisher Sports Illustrated For Kids, 1989-91; publisher People Weekly, 1991-94, pres., 1994—. Office: People Magazine Rockefeller Ct Time & Life Building New York NY 10020*

MOORE, ANNE FRANCES, museum director; b. Jan. 6, 1946; d. William Clifton and Frances Woods Moore; m. Michael P. Mezzatesta, Mar. 14, 1970 (div. 1987); children: Philip Moore, Alexander Woods, Marya Frances; m. Ernest Hutton, 1996. BA in Art History, Columbia U., 1969, MA, 1971, MEd in Fine Arts, 1971, MA in Art History, 1982. Tchr. Manassas (Va.) High Sch., 1971-72, Poly. Prep. Country Day Sch., Bklyn., 1972-74; edn. instr. Kimbell Art Mus., Ft. Worth, 1980-83, rsch. assoc., lectr., 1983; assoc. mus. educator, outreach dir. Dallas Mus. Art, 1986-88; curator of edn., lectr. dept. art Oberlin (Ohio) Coll., 1988-90, curator acad. programs, lectr. dept. art, 1991-92; acting dir. The Allen Meml. Art Mus. at Oberlin Coll., 1991-92, dir., 1992—. Bd. trustees Intermus. Conservation Assn. Mem. Assn. Art Mus. Dirs., Assn. Coll. and Univ. Mus. and Galleries, Am. Assn. Mus. (edn. com.), Ohio Mus. Assn., Coll. Art Assn. Office: Allen Memorial Art Museum Oberlin College Oberlin OH 44074

MOORE, ANTHONY R., lawyer; b. Cleve., Feb. 19, 1950. AB, Harvard U., 1972; JD, U. Va., 1975. Bar: Ohio 1975. Ptnr. Jones, Day, Reavis & Pogue, Cleve. Office: Jones Day Reavis & Pogue North Point 901 Lakeside Ave E Cleveland OH 44114-1116*

MOORE, ARTHUR JAMES, editor; b. San Antonio, May 7, 1922; s. Arthur James and Martha (MacDonald) M. B.A., Emory U., 1947. With N.Y. Daily News, 1947-50; editorial asst. Musical Am., 1950; editor, contbr. encys. other reference books Columbia U. Press, 1951-53; with Methodist Bd. of Global Ministries (formerly Bd. Missions), 1953-87; editor World Outlook, 1964-70; editor New World Outlook, 1970-87, dir. editorial dept. Edn. and Cultivation Div., 1980-87; cons. in field, 1987—; mem. press staff World Council Chs. assembly, Evanston, Ill., 1954, New Delhi, India, 1961; spl. corr. Religious News Service, Vatican Council, 1965, World Conf. Ch. and Soc., 1966. Mem. editorial bd. Christianity and Crisis, 1967-72, bd. dirs., 1971-82, contbg. editor, 1974-93; contbg. author: Religion and Peace, 1966, Ethics in the Present Tense, 1991; contbr. to various nat. mags. Served with USNR, 1942-45. Recipient Citation of Honor Associated Ch. Press, 1990; named to United Meth. Assn. of Communicators Hall of Fame, 1988. Mem. Alpha Tau Omega. Methodist. Home: 252 Henry St Brooklyn NY 11201-4651

MOORE, BARRY W., management consultant. Exec. v.p. Kurt Salmon Assocs. Inc., Atlanta. Office: Kurt Salmon Assocs Inc 1335 Peachtree St NE Atlanta GA 30309

MOORE, BEA, religious organization executive. Pres. The Woman's Home and Foreign Mission Society, Loudon, N.H.; nat. pres. The Woman's Home and Foreign Mission Society, Charlotte, N.C. Office: Woman's Home & Foreign Mission 845 Loudon Ridge Rd Loudon NH 03301-1712

MOORE, BENJAMIN, theatrical producer; b. Boston, Oct. 25, 1945; s. Charles Frederick and Adeline Reeves (Nichols) M.; m. Mary Bradford Paine, May 31, 1969 (div. Jan. 1982); children: Alexandra Paine, Brendan Adams; m. Barbara Ann Dirickson, June 25, 1983; children: Lillian, Richard Braden. BA, Dartmouth U., 1967; MFA, Yale U., 1970. Asst. mng. dir. Yale Repertory Theatre, New Haven, 1969-70; gen. mgr. Westport (Conn.) Country Playhouse, 1970; prodn. dir. Am. Conservatory Theatre, San Francisco, 1970-79, gen. mgr., 1979-81, mng. dir., 1981-85; mng. dir., bd. dirs. Seattle Repertory Theatre, 1985—. Active Seattle Arts Commn., 1986-90, chair, 1989. Mem. Wash. State Arts Alliance (bd. dirs. 1985—), League Resident Theatres (mem. exec. com. 1986—), Rainier Club. Office: Seattle Repertory Theatre 155 Mercer St Seattle WA 98109-4639

MOORE, BETTY JEAN, retired education educator; b. L.A., Apr. 4, 1927; d. Ralph Gard and Dora Mae (Shinn) Bowman; m. James H. Moore, Nov. 25, 1944 (div. 1968); children: Barbara, Suzanne, Sandra; m. George W. Nichols, Oct. 15, 1983. BA, Pasadena Coll., 1957; MA, U. Nev., 1963; PhD, U. Ill., 1973. Tchr. Calif. pub. schs., 1953-63, sec. tchr., 1963-68; asst. prof. Ea. Ill. U., Charleston, 1968-71; grad. teaching asst. U. Ill., Champaign, 1971-73; asst. prof. to assoc. prof. S.W. Tex. State U., San Marcos, 1973-83, prof. edn., 1983-89, ret., 1989, prof. emeritus, 1995—; sch. evaluator; cons. in field; reading clinic dir. S.W. Tex. State U., 1974-85; cons. Min. Edn., Rep. of Singapore, 1980. Contbr. articles to profl. jours.; author: Teaching Reading, 1984; producer/dir. 5 ednl. videos. Active fund raising various charitable orgns. Mem. Internat. Reading Assn. (chpt. pres. 1964-65), Nat. Council Tchrs. English, AAUP. Presbyterian. Avocations: reading, writing, swimming, cooking. Office: Southwest Tex State U C & I Dept San Marcos TX 78666

MOORE, BEVERLY COOPER, lawyer; b. Greensboro, N.C., Dec. 8, 1909; s. Adolphus Greene and Georgia (Cooper) M.; m. Irene Warren Mitchell, July 10, 1943; children: Beverly Cooper Jr., Irene Warren Moore Miller. AB, U. N.C., 1931; JD, Yale U., 1934. Bar: N.C. 1934, U.S. Dist. Ct. N.C. 1934, U.S. Ct. Appeals (4th cir.) 1954, U.S. Supreme Ct. 1945. Practice law Greensboro, 1934—; ptnr. Smith, Helms Mulliss & Moore (and predecessors), 1946-94, ptnr. emeritus, 1995—; mem. N.C. Gen. Assembly, 1941-42. Contbr. to legal publs. Trustee Consol. U. N.C., 1967-72; chmn. bd. trustees U. N.C.-Greensboro, 1972-75. Served with USAAF, 1942-45. Fellow Am. Bar Found.; mem. ABA (ho. of dels. 1962-68, 73-75, 76-80, bd. govs. 1970-73), N.C. Bar Assn. (pres. 1958-59), Greensboro Bar Assn. (pres. 1949-50), Assn. of Bar of City of N.Y., Internat. Bar sssn., Am. Coll. Trial Lawyers, Practising Law Inst. (trustee 1965-72), Am. Judicature Soc. (bd. dirs. 1964-67), Am. Law Inst., Fed. Jud. Conf., Am. Counsel Assn. (pres. 1970-71), Inst. Jud. Adminstrn., Nat. Center Adminstrv. Justice (dir. 1979-81, chmn. 1981-82), Southeastern Legal Found. (chmn. legal adv. bd. 1979-87), SAR, Phi Beta Kappa, Selden Soc. (London). Episcopalian. Clubs: Sedgefield Country, Greensboro City, Greensboro Country. Home: 906 Country Club Dr Greensboro NC 27408-5602 Office: P O Box 21927 Greensboro NC 27420

MOORE, BOB STAHLY, communications executive; b. Pasadena, Calif., July 3, 1936; s. Norman Hastings and Mary Augusta (Stahly) M. Student, U. Mo., 1954-58, MIT, 1958-62. News dir. WPEO, Peoria, Ill., 1958-60, KSST, Davenport, Iowa, 1960-62, WIRE, Indpls., 1962-64, WCFL, Chgo., 1964-67; White House corr. Metromedia, Inc., Washington, 1967-71; news dir. Gateway Communications, Altoona, Pa., 1972-74; Washington Bur. chief MBS, 1974-76; v.p. news MBS, Arlington, Va., 1976-78; White House corr. MBS, 1978-81; dir. communications Fed. Home Loan Bank Bd., Washington, 1981-85; spl. asst. to bd. govs. Fed. Res. System, Washington, 1985—. Active ARC. Served with USAF, 1961-63. Recipient profl. awards Ind. News Broadcasters, 1963, Ill. News Broadcasters, 1965, UPI, 1960, 63, 65, AP, 1956, 58, 61, 65, 67, Mo. News Broadcasters, 1956, 61. Mem. Radio and Television News Dirs. Assn. (Profl. award), White House Corrs. Assn., State Dept. Corrs. Assn., Radio-Television Corrs. Gallery (U.S. Capitol), Chgo. Council on Fgn. Relations, Pub. Relations Soc. Am., Nat., Washington, Chgo. press clubs, U.S. Jr., Mo., Ill. chambers commerce, Sigma Delta Chi. Presbyterian. Home: 817 Crescent Dr Alexandria VA 22302-2214 Office: 20th and Constitution NW Washington DC 20551

MOORE, BOBBIE FAY, geriatrics nurse practitioner, nurse administrator; b. Woodward, Okla., Jan. 21, 1943; d. Marion Byron and Lelah Catherine (Anderson) Carey; m. Donald Kent Strickland, Apr. 2, 1959 (div. June 1968); children: Donald, Michael; m. Myrl Lynn Moore, Apr. 15, 1988. ADN, N.Mex. State U., Carlsbad, 1983; geriatric nurse practitioner, U. Colo., Denver, 1985. Cert. geriatric nurse practitioner, Am. Nurses Credentialing Ctr., N.Mex. Charge nurse Landsun Homes, Carlsbad, 1971-76; office nurse Dr. C. Munkers, Marquette, Mich., 1976-78; staff and treatment rm. nurse Guadalupe Med. Ctr., Carlsbad, 1978-83; nursing supr., nurse practitioner Landsun Homes, Carlsbad, 1985—, lic. nursing home adminstr., 1990—; mem. nursing adv. bd. N.Mex. State U., 1985—. Tchr. Sunday sch. Meth. Ch., Carlsbad; treas. Continuing Edn. Commn., Carlsbad, 1988—; counselor Boy Scouts Am., Carlsbad, 1989—; youth spnosor 1st United Meth. Ch., Carlsbad, 1990—. Mem. N.Mex. Nurse Practitioner Coun. Avocations: reading, walking. Home: 103 E Riverside Dr Carlsbad NM 88220-5231

MOORE, BOBBY See RASHAD, AHMAD

MOORE, BRADFORD L., lawyer; b. Brownfield, Tex., Feb. 9, 1952; s. Billie Buell and Jimmy (Green) M.; m. Carmelita Chaffin, June 20, 1971; children: April V., Ashli F. BA, Tex. Tech U., 1974, JD, 1977. Bar: Tex. 1978, U.S. Dist. Ct. (no. dist.) Tex. 1978, U.S. Dist. Ct. (we. dist.) Tex. 1987, U.S. Supreme Ct. 1987. V.p. McGowan & McGowan PC, Brownfield, 1978-90; pvt. practice, Brownfield, 1990—. Pres. Brownfield Little Girls Basketball, 1987-90. Recipient award for outstanding representation of abused children Tex. Dept. Human Svcs., 1984. Mem. Brownfield Bar Assn. (social chmn. 1980—), Rotary (sgt.-at-arms Brownfield 1980-81), Kiwanis (pres. Brownfield 1984-86). Office: PO Box 352 Brownfield TX 79316-0352

MOORE, BRIAN, writer; b. Belfast, No. Ireland, Aug. 25, 1921; came to U.S., 1960; s. James Bernard and Eileen (McFadden) M.; m. Jean Denney, Oct. 1967; 1 son, Michael. Author: The Lonely Passion of Judith Hearne, 1955, The Feast of Lupercal, 1957, The Luck of Ginger Coffey, 1960, An Answer From Limbo, 1962, The Emperor of Ice-Cream, 1965, I Am Mary Dunne, 1968, Fergus, 1970, The Revolution Script, 1971, Catholics, 1972, The Great Victorian Collection, 1975, The Doctor's Wife, 1976, The Mangan Inheritance, 1979, The Temptation of Eileen Hughes, 1981, Cold Heaven, 1983, Black Robe, 1985, The Color of Blood, 1987, Lies of Silence, 1990, No Other Life, 1993, The Statement, 1995. Recipient Que. Lit. prize, 1958, U.S. Nat. Arts and Letters award, 1961, Fiction award Gov.-Gen. Can., 1961, 75, W.H. Smith award, 1973, James Tait Black Meml. award, 1975, Heinemann award Royal Soc. Lit., 1986, Sunday Express Book of Yr. award, 1987, Lifetime Achievement award L.A. Times, 1994; Guggenheim fellow, 1959; Can Coun. sr. fellow, 1962, 76; Scottish Arts Coun. Internat. fellow, 1983. Office: care Curtis Brown 10 Astor Pl New York NY 10003-6935

MOORE, BROOKE NOEL, philosophy educator; b. Palo Alto, Calif., Dec. 2, 1943; s. Ralph Joseph and Dorothy Louise (Noll) M.; m. Linda Ely; children: Sherry, Bill. BA, Antioch Coll., 1966; PhD, U. Cin., 1973. Asst. prof. Calif. State U., Chico, 1970-74, assoc. prof., 1974-79, prof., 1980—. Author: Philosophical Possibilities Beyond Death, 1981; co-author: Critical Thinking, 1987, 4th edit., 1995, The Power of Ideas, 1990, 3rd edit., 1995, The Cosmos, God and Philosophy, 1992, Moral Philosophy, 1993, The Power of Ideas: A Brief Edition, 1995, Making Your Case, 1995; mem. editl. bd. Tchg. Philosophy, 1972. Mem. Am. Philos. Assn. Office: Calif State U Chico Dept of Philosophy Chico CA 95929

MOORE, C. BRADLEY, chemistry educator; b. Boston, Dec. 7, 1939; s. Charles Walden and Dorothy (Lutz) M.; m. Penelope Williamson Percival, Aug. 27, 1960; children—Megan Bradley, Scott Woodward. B.A. magna cum laude, Harvard U., 1960; Ph.D., U. Calif., Berkeley, 1963. Predoctoral fellow NSF, 1960-63; asst. prof. chemistry U. Calif., Berkeley, 1963-68, assoc. prof., 1968-72, prof., 1972—, vice chmn. dept., 1971-75, chmn. dept. chemistry, 1982-86, dean Coll. Chemistry, 1988-94; professeur associé Faculté des Scis., Paris, 1970, 75; Miller Rsch. Prof. U. Calif., Berkeley, 1972-73, 87-88; vis. prof. Inst. for Molecular Sci., Okazaki, Japan, 1979, Fudan U., Shanghai, 1979, adv. prof., 1988—; vis. fellow Joint Inst. for Lab. Astrophysics, U. Colo., Boulder, 1981-82; faculty sr. scientist Lawrence Berkeley Nat. Lab.; mem. editl. bd. Jour. Chem. Physics, 1973-75, Chem. Physics Letters, 1980-85, Jour. Phys. Chemistry, 1981-87, Laser Chemistry, 1982—. Editor: Chemical and Biochemical Applications of Lasers; assoc. editor Annual Review of Physical Chemistry, 1985-90; contbr. articles to profl. jours. Trustee Sci. Svc., Inc., 1995—. Recipient Coblentz award, 1973, E.O. Lawrence Meml. award U.S. Dept. Energy, 1986, Lippincott award, 1987, 1st award Inter-Am. Photochem. Soc., 1988; nat. scholar Harvard U., 1958-60; fellow Alfred P. Sloan Found., 1968, Guggenheim Found., 1969, Humboldt Rsch. award for Sr. U.S. Scientists, 1994. Earle K. Prize, Am. Physical Soc. 1994. Fellow AAAS, Am. Acad. Arts and Scis., Am. Phys. Soc. (Plyler award 1994); mem. NAS (chmn. com. undergrad. sci. edn.), Am. Chem. Soc. (past chmn. divsn. phys. chemistry, Calif. sect. award 1977). Avocation: cycling. Home: 936 Oxford St Berkeley CA 94707-2435 Office: U Calif Dept Chemistry 211 Lewis Hall Berkeley CA 94720

MOORE, CALVIN C., mathematics educator, administrator; b. N.Y.C., Nov. 2, 1936; s. Robert A. and Ruth (Miller) M.; m. Doris Lienhard, Sept. 14, 1974. A.B. summa cum laude, Harvard U., 1958, M.A., 1959, Ph.D. in Math., 1960. Research instr. U. Chgo., 1960-61; asst. prof. U. Calif. at Berkeley, 1961-65, asso. prof., 1965-66, prof. math., 1966—, dean phys. scis., 1971-76, chair dept. math., 1996—; dir. Center Pure and Applied Math, 1977-80; dep. dir. Math. Scis. Research Inst., 1981-85; asst. v.p. acad. planning and personnel U. Calif. Systemwide Adminstrn., 1985-86, assoc. v.p. acad. affairs, 1986-94; mem. Inst. for Advanced Study, 1964-65; mem. at large NRC, 1971-73; mem. Math. Sci. Edn. Bd., 1991-93, mem. exec. com.; mem. Pres.'s Com. on Nat. Medal Sci., 1979-81; chiar task force on rewards and recognition in math. scis. Joint Policy Bd. for Math., 1993-95. Chmn. bd. govs.: Pacific Jour. Math., 1972-76; editor: Mathematische Zeitschrift, Ill. Jour. Math, Pacific Jour. Math.; exec. editor research announcements; mng. editor: Bull. Am. Math. Soc.; contbg. editor: Advances in Mathematics; contbr. articles to profl. jours. Fellow Am. Acad. Arts and Scis.; mem. Am. Math. Soc. (exec. com., council mem. at large, v.p., chmn. bd. trustees). Home: 1408 Eagle Point Ct Lafayette CA 94549-2328 Office: U Calif at Berkeley Dept Math Evans Hall Berkeley CA 94720

MOORE, CAROLE IRENE, librarian; b. Berkeley, Calif., Aug. 15, 1944. AB, Stanford U., 1966; MLS, Columbia U., 1967. Reference libr. Columbia U., N.Y.C., 1967-68; reference libr. U. Toronto, Can., 1968-80, head cataloguing, 1980-85, assoc. libr., 1985-86, chief libr., 1986—; mem. nat. adv. bd. Nat. Libr. Can., Ottawa, 1991-94; bd. dirs. Rsch. Librs. Group. 1994—, U. Toronto Press, 1994—. Recipient Disting. Alumni award Columbia U., 1989. Mem. ALA, Can. Libr. Assn., Can. Assn. Rsch. Librs. (pres. 1989-91). Avocation: gardening. Office: U Toronto Libr, 130 Saint George St, Toronto, ON Canada M5S 1A5

MOORE, CAROLYN LANNIN, video specialist; b. Hammond, Ind., Aug. 14, 1945; d. William Wren and Julia Audrey (Mathews) Lannin; m. F. David Moore, Oct. 21, 1967; children: Jillian Winter Moore Mirise, Douglas Mathew, Owen Glen. BA, Ind. U., 1967; MA, Purdue U., 1991. Stockholders corr. Sears Roebuck and Co., Chgo., 1967-68; caseworker Lake County Dept. of Pub. Welfare, Hammond, Ind., 1968-71; field dir. Campfire Girls Inc., Highland, Ind., 1975-77; project dir. Northwest Ind. Pub. Broadcasting, Highland, 1984-85, interim exec. dir., 1985-87; cons. Telecommunications and Grant Writing, Munster, Ind., 1981-85; prin. Carolyn Moore and Assocs.-Laughing Cat Prodns., Munster, Ind., 1987—; instr. Purdue U.-Calumet, Ind., 1989; instr. Valparaiso (Ind.) U., 1990-91; lectr. in field. Prodr. TV series Visclosky Viewpoint, 1985-87; video prodr. A Kid's Eye View of the Symphony, 1987; vol. on-air talent WIN Channel 56; co-host This Week in Munster. Mem. Munster Cable TV Commn., 1984—; bd. dirs. N.W. Ind. Literacy Coalition, Inc.; mem. Lake County Master Gardeners; vol. on-air-talent WYIN Ch. 56; bd. dirs. Ednl. Referral Ctr.. Mem. AAUW, NAFE, Alliance for Cmty. Media, Assn. Ind. Video and Filmakers Inc., Munster C. of C., Communicators N.W. Ind. (treas. 1996), N.W. Ind. World Trade Coun., Ind. U. Alumni Assn., Scherwood Ladies Golf Leagues, Wicker Park Ladies Golf League (pres.). Democrat. Catholic. Avocations: golf, reading, sailing. Home and Office: Carolyn Moore & Assocs Laughing Cat Prodns 9604 Cypress Ave Munster IN 46321-3418

MOORE, CHARLES AUGUST, JR., psychologist; b. Medford, Oreg., Feb. 22, 1944; s. Charles August and Bernadine (Newlun) M. BS, Lewis and Clark Coll., 1965; MA, U. Colo., 1967, PhD, 1972. Lic. psychologist, Calif., Oreg. Teaching asst. U. Colo., Boulder, 1965-66, 70-71, rsch. asst., counselor, practicum supr., 1966-67, 71-72; asst. psychologist State Home and Tng. Sch., Grand Junction, Colo., 1967; intern in psychology Camarillo (Calif.) State Hosp., 1968-69; psychology assoc., program psychologist Camarillo Drug Abuse Program (The Family), 1969-70; intern in psychology Oxnard (Calif.) Mental Health Ctr., 1969; clin. psychologist, dir. intern tng. Rural Clinics, Reno, 1972; clin. psychologist Kern County Mental Health Svcs., Bakersfield, Calif., 1972-74; clin., cons. psychologist San Diego County Mental Health Svcs., 1974-88; pvt. practice La Jolla (Calif.) Clinic, 1976-78; August Ctr., Chula Vista, Calif., 1978-85; staff psychologist Dept. Vet.'s Affairs Domiciliary, White City, Oreg., 1988—; guest lectr. Calif. State Coll., Bakersfield, 1973-74; mem. Health Systems Agy. Mental Health Task Force, 1979; mem. doctoral dissertation com. U.S. Internat. U., 1975-76; mem. mental health task force San Diego County Bd. Suprs., 1979. Contbr. articles to profl. jours. Mem. Univ. City Community Coun., San Diego, 1976-78; bd. dirs. Pub. Employees Assn., 1976-77. Recipient Experiment in Internat. Living European Study award Lewis and Clark Coll., 1962; USPHS fellow, 1967-68; U. Colo. Grad. Sch. Rsch. grantee, 1971; recipient Hands and Heart award Dept. Vets. Affairs, 1989-90, Domiciliary Spl. Contbn. and Outstanding Performance awards, 1990, 91. Mem. APA, Am. Psychology and Law Soc., Calif. Psychol. Assn., Western Psychol. Assn., San Diego County Psychol. Assn., Assn. County Clin. Psychologists San Diego, San Diego Psychology and Law Soc., San Diego Soc. Clin. Psychologists. Office: Dept VA Domiciliary Psychology Svc 8495 Crater Lake Hwy White City OR 97503-3011

MOORE, CHARLES HEWES, JR., industrial and engineered products executive; b. Coatesville, Pa., Aug. 12, 1929; s. Charles Hewes and Jane Richards (Scott) M.; m. Judith L. McClellan, June 23, 1971; children: Charles Hewes III, James, David, Susan, Kevin, Christopher, Margery, Brian, Amanda. BME, Cornell U., 1952. With Lenape Forge Co. div. Gulf & Western Industries, West Chester, Pa., 1952-73; pres. Lapp div. Interpace Corp., Le Roy, N.Y., 1973-77; pres., chief exec. officer Allied Thermal Corp. subs. Interpace, 1978-79; sr. v.p., dir. Interpace, 1979-80; exec. v.p., dir. Interpace Corp., Parsippany, N.J., 1980-81; pres., chief exec. officer, dir. Clevepak Corp., 1981-83, 84-86, chief exec. officer, vice chmn. bd., dir., 1983-84; mng. dir. Peers & Co., 1987-88; chief exec. officer Peers Mgmt. Resources, Inc., 1987-88; pres., chief exec. officer Ransburg Corp., Indpls., 1988-92; pres. ITW Finishing Systems and Products, Indpls., 1990-92; exec. v.p. Ill. Tool Works Inc., Glenview, 1991-92; vice-chmn. Advisory Capital Ptnrs., Inc., Greenwich, Conn., 1993-94; CEO, chmn. bd. dirs. Xpander Pak Inc., 1995—; athletic dir. Cornell U., 1994—; bd. dirs. Turner Corp., Elcotel, Inc. Mem. mgmt. policy coun., mem. adv. bd. Fundamental Mgmt.; chmn. audit com., pub. sector dir. U.S. Olympic Com. Recipient Gold medal in 400 meter hurdles, 1952 Olympics, Herbert Adams Meml. award for advancement of Am. sculpture, Nat. Sculpture Soc., 1985. Mem. Pine Valley Golf Club (N.J.), Royal and Ancient Golf Club St. Andrews (Scotland). Republican. Episcopalian. Office: Cornell U Teagle Hall Campus Rd Ithaca NY 14853-6501

MOORE, CHRISTOPHER HUGH, writer; b. Stoke-on-Trent, Eng., June 9, 1950; arrived in Can., 1954; s. M. Vincent and Kathleen A. (Lennox) M.; m. Louise A. Brophy, May 7, 1977; children: Elizabeth, Kate. BA with honors, U. B.C., Vancouver, 1971; MA, U. Ottawa, Ont., Can., 1977. Staff historian Nat. Historic Pks. Svc., Louisbourg, N.S., Can., 1972-75; sec. to bd. Heritage Can. Found., Ottawa, 1977-78; writer, historian Toronto, Ont., 1979—. Author: Louisbourg Portraits, 1982, The Loyalists, 1984, 94; co-author: Illustrated History of Canada, 1987, The Story of Canada, 1992. Recipient Gov. Gen.'s Lit. award Can., 1983, Sec. of State Prize Govt. Can., Ottawa, 1985, Mr. Christie's Prize Christie-Brown Ltd., Toronto, 1993. Mem. Writers' Union of Can. (chair contracts com. 1990-94, mem. nat. coun. 1995—), Can. Hist. Assn. Office: 396 Pacific Ave # 202, Toronto, ON Canada M6P 2R1

MOORE, CHRISTOPHER ROBERTSON KINLEY, petroleum geologist; b. Manchester, England, Sept. 28, 1954; came to U.S., 1989; s. James Robertson Kinley and Irene (Mason) M.; m. Marian Isabel Pope, Sept. 3, 1977; children: Andrew Christopher, Scott David. BA, U. Cambridge, 1975, MA, 1979. Geologist Brit. Petroleum Co., Scotland, England, Tunisia, 1975-80; sr. geologist Tricentrol Oil Corp., London, 1980-88; planning mgr. ARCO Brit. Ltd., London, 1988-89; from exploration planning advisor to dir. exploration ARCO Internat. Oil & Gas Co., Plano, Tex., 1989—. Fellow Geol. Soc. London; mem. Am. Assn. Petroleum Geologists, Soc. Petroleum Engrs., Geol. Soc. Am. Home: 2133 Country Club Dr Plano TX 75074 Office: Arco Internat Oil & Gas Co 2300 W Plano Pkwy Plano TX 75075

MOORE, DAN STERLING, insurance executive, sales trainer; b. Lincoln, Nebr., June 27, 1956; s. Jack Leroy and Carolyn Marie (Bachman) M.; m. Marla Janine Collister, June 2, 1979; children: Tyler David, Anna Rose. Student, Red Rocks Coll., 1977. Lic. ins. exec. Asst. mgr. European Health Spa, Englewood, Colo., 1975-78; sales mgr. Colo. Nat. Homes, Westminster, 1979-80; sales assoc. Dale Carnegie, Denver, 1981; sales mgr. Paramount Fabrics, Denver, 1981-84; sales assoc. Mighty Distbg., Arvada, Colo., 1984-87; dist. mgr. Nat. Assn. for Self Employed/United Group Assn., Englewood, Colo., 1987—; dist. mgr. Communicating for Agr. Assn., 1993—. Leader, trainer Alpine Rescue Team, Evergreen, Colo., 1971-74; minister Jehovah's Witnesses, 1972—. Avocations: golf, skiing, backpacking, scuba diving, tennis. Home: 892 Nob Hill Trl Franktown CO 80116-8716 Office: Nat Assn Self Employed/United Group 6551 S Revere Pky Ste 135 Englewood CO 80111-6410

MOORE, DAN TYLER, writer; b. Washington, Feb. 1, 1908; s. Dan T. and Luvean Jones (Butler) M.; m. Elizabeth Valley Oakes, Mar. 12, 1932; children: Luvean O. (Mrs. Owens), Elizabeth Oakes (Mrs. Thornton), Harriet (Mrs. Lester Ballard), Dan Tyler III. BS, Yale, 1931. Chief counter-intelligence OSS, Middle East, 1943-44; pres. Middle East Co., Cleve., 1946-48, China Co., Cleve., 1946-48; asst. to pres. Intercontinental Hotels Corp., Istanbul, Turkey, 1948-50; freelance writer Cleveland Heights, Ohio, 1950—. Author: The Terrible Game, 1957, Cloak and Cipher, 1962, Wolves, Widows and Orphans, 1966, Lecturing For Profit, 1967, (movie) Gymkata 1988; contbr. articles and stories to popular mags. Pres. Greater Cleve. Muscular Dystrophy Assn., 1952-65; mem. exec. com. Cuyahoga County Dem. Party, 1951-70, mem. state exec. com., 1962-65; commr. Ohio Fed. Jury, 1961-68; trustee, bd. dirs. Cleve. Mus. Natural History; bd. dirs. Near East Coll. Assn., Karamu Theatre, Cleve. Served with AUS, 1942-44. Mem. Internat. Platform Assn. (chmn. bd., dir. gen.). Clubs: Met. (Washington, D.C.); Yale (N.Y.C.); Union, Tavern, Skating and Rowfant (Cleve.). Home: 2564 Berkshire Rd Cleveland OH 44106-3365

MOORE, DANIEL CHARLES, physician; b. Cin., Sept. 9, 1918; s. Daniel Clark and May (Strebel) M.; m. Betty Maxine Tobias, Aug. 5, 1945 (div. 1988); children: Barbara, Nancy, Daniel, Susan. Grad., Amherst (Mass.) Coll., 1940; M.D., Northwestern U., 1944. Diplomate: Am. Bd. Anesthesiologists. Intern Wesley Meml. Hosp., Chgo., 1944; resident Wesley Meml. Hosp., 1945; dir. anesthesia Va. Mason Hosp., Seattle, 1947-72; anesthesiologist (Mason Clinic), 1947-72, sr. cons. in anesthesia, 1972-83; clin. prof. U. Wash. Sch. Medicine, 1963—. Author: Regional Block, 1953, Stellate Ganglion Block, 1954, Complications of Regional Anesthesia, 1955, Anesthetic Techniques for Obstetrical Anesthesia and Analgesia, 1964, also papers. Served as capt. M.C. AUS, 1945-47. Recipient Ralph M. Waters award Ill. Soc. Anesthesiologists, Carl Koller Gold medal European Soc. Regional Anaesthesia, 1995. Mem. Am. Soc. Anesthesiologists (1st v.p. 1953-54, 2d v.p. 1954-55, pres. 1958-59, distinguished service award 1976), AMA (sec. anesthesiology sect. 1956-58), Am. Acad. Anesthesiology, Am. Soc. Regional Anesthesia (adv. bd., Gaston Labat award 1977), Wash. Soc. Anesthesiologists (pres. 1949-50), Wash. Med. Soc., King County Med. Soc., Faculty Anaesthetists Royal Coll. Surgeons (hon.), Northwest Forum, Beta Theta Pi, Nu Sigma Nu. Home: Madison Park Pl # 103 2000 43rd Ave E Seattle WA 98112-2759 Office: PO Box 900 Seattle WA 98111-0900

MOORE, DANIEL EDMUND, psychologist, educator, retired educational administrator; b. Pitts., Dec. 31, 1926; s. John Daniel and Alma Helen (Goehring) M.; m. Rose Marie Blunkosky, Nov. 11, 1949; children: Catherine Chiodo, Claire Marie Moore Caveney, Mary Moore Brilmyer, Suzanne Moore Gray, Elizabeth Moore Sullivan. BSEd, Duquesne U., 1949, MEd, 1952; postgrad., California (Pa.) State Coll., 1954-56, U. Pitts., 1958-59, Mt. Mercy Coll., 1959-60, Cath. U. Am., 1966, W.Va. U., 1970-72. Lic. psychologist; cert. sch. psychologist. Tchr. math. Cecil Twp. Sch. Dist., McDonald, Pa., 1949-52, Pitts. Public Schs., 1952-53; with Mt. Lebanon Twp. (Pa.) Sch. Dist., 1953-88, psychologist, 1954-71, dir. pupil personnel svcs., 1988; psychol cons. Peters Twp. Sch. Dist., McMurray, Pa., 1961-88, Blackhawk Sch. Dist., Beaver, Pa., 1989—, Quaker Valley Sch. Dist., Sewickley, Pa., 1989-90; lectr., supr. Grad. and Undergrad. Sch. Edn. Duquesne U.; psychologist DePaul Inst., Pitts., 1992—; lectr. ednl. psychology Grad. Sch. Edn., Duquesne U., 1957-92, supr. student tchrs., 1989-92; ednl. cons. St. Francis Schs. Nursing, New Castle and Pitts., 1959-91; mem. test adv. bd. Ednl. Records Bur., 1976-86; hearing officer Right to Edn. Office, Dept. Edn., Harrisburg, Pa., 1975—; in-svc. adv. bd. Pa. Dept. Edn. Hearing Officers. Mem. Chartiers Valley Sch. Dist. Bd., 1963-94, pres., 1971, v.p., 1991; mem. Pkwy. West Tech. Sch. Bd. 1965-67; bd. dirs. secondary sch. rsch. program Ednl. Testing Svc., Princeton, 1971-85; bd. dirs. Robert E. Ward Home for Children, 1975-87, St. Agatha Parish Coun., 1988—, Pathfinder Sch., 1989, v.p., 1990-94, pres. sch. bd., 1991-92; vol. Bridgeville Area Food Bank, 1988—; chairperson Parish 100 Jubilee Ceremony, Goodwill Villa Bd., Goodwill Plaza, Inc., Goodwill Villa Bd. of Incorporators, 1992—; pres. bd. dirs. Goodwill Plaza, 1992—; jubilee chairperson St. Agatha's, Bridgeville, Pa. With USNR, 1945-48. Henry C. Frick grantee, 1970, 73; named Jaycee Educator of Yr. for South Hills Area, Ward Home Outstanding Community Leader, 1984. Mem. Am., Pa. psychol. assns., Coun. Exceptional Children (pres. 1957), Phi Delta Kappa (pres. chpt. 1974-75, chmn. lay awards com. 1979—, Svc. Key award 1985). Roman Catholic. Home: 213 Station St Bridgeville PA 15017-1806 Office: 428 Forbes Ave Pittsburgh PA 15219-1603

MOORE, DAVID AUSTIN, pharmaceutical company executive, consultant; b. Phoenix, May 8, 1935; s. Harry Theodore and Helen Ann (Newport) M.; m. Emily J. McConnell, Jan. 26, 1991; children by previous marriage: Austin Newport, Cornelia Christina, Christopher Robinson. Grad. h.s., Glendale, Ariz.; study opera and voice with Joseph Lazzarini, 1954, 55, 57-64; studied opera and voice, Italy, 1955-56; study with Clarence Loomis, 1958-60; D Naturopathy, Clayton Sch. Natural Healing, Birmingham, Ala., 1994. Pres., owner David A. Moore, Inc., Phoenix, 1969-71, Biol. Labs. Ltd., Phoenix, 1972-78; pres., co-owner Am. Trace Mineral Rsch. Corp., Phoenix, 1979-83; pres., owner Biol. Mineral Scis., Ltd., Phoenix, 1979-82; rsch. dir., pres., owner Nutritional Biols. Inc., Phoenix, 1979-83; nutritional dir.-owner Nutritional Biol. Rsch. Co., Phoenix, 1984-85; rsch. dir., product formulator, owner Nutrition and Med. Rsch., Scottsdale, Ariz., 1986—; biochem. cons. Nutripathic Formulas, Scottsdale, 1975-88; introduced di Calcium Phosphate free concept and 100 percent label disclosure, 1979-83. Pub. NMR Newsletter. Inventor first computerized comprehensive hair analysis interpretation, 1976. Recipient Plaque Am. Soc. Med. Techs., 1982, Mineralab Inc., 1976. Avocation: singing opera and Italian songs, teaching voice, coaching singers. Home and Office: PO Box 98 Barnesboro PA 15714-0098

MOORE, DAVID GRAHAM, sociologist, educator; b. Norwich, Conn., May 9, 1918; s. Royal Tolman and Alta Gladys (Jenkin) M.; children by previous marriage: Barbara E., Linda C. Turbyville; m. Margaret Louise Rider, Dec. 2, 1950; children: David G., Kathryn R. (Mrs. T.J. Miller). B.A., U. Ill., 1940, M.A., 1943; Ph.D., U. Chgo., 1954. Personnel research Western Electric Co., 1940-41; mem. personnel staff Sears, Roebuck and Co., 1941-43, 46-50; personnel dir. Am. Flange & Mfg. Co., 1943-46; asst. prof. sociology, indsl. relations U. Chgo., 1950-55, asso. prof. bus. adminstrn., sociology, dir. exec. program, 1955-56; prof. mgmt. Mich. State U., 1956-58, head dept. personnel and prodn. adminstrn., 1958-61, prof. mgmt., sociology, 1961-63; dean N.Y. State Sch. Indsl. and Labor Relations, Cornell U., 1963-71; sr. v.p. Conf. Bd., N.Y.C., 1971-73; exec. v.p. Conf. Bd., 1973-79; prof., chmn. dept. bus. adminstrn. U. North Fla., 1979-86, prof. bus. adminstrn., 1986-89, asst. to pres., 1983-84; vis. Ford Found. prof. behavioral scis. U. Wis., fall 1962. Co-author: Human Relations in Industry, 4th edit, 1964, SRA Employee Inventory, 1951, The Enterprising Man, 1964. Mem. Am. Sociol. Assn., Soc. Applied Anthropology, Acad. Mgmt., Indsl. Relations Research Assn. Home: 91 San Juan Dr Apt D-1 Ponte Vedra Beach FL 32082-1336 Office: U North Fla PO Box 17074 Jacksonville FL 32245-7074

MOORE, DAVID LEWIS, trade association executive; b. Arvin, Calif., Aug. 22, 1931; s. John Chessher and Bonnie (Carter) M.; m. Priscella Jane Martin, Aug. 1, 1953; children: John, Leslie, David, Elizabeth, Andrew. BS, U. So. Calif., 1954. Owner, operator White Wolf Potato Co., 1956-87; chmn. Western Growers Assn., Irvine, Calif., 1984-87, pres., chief exec. officer, 1987—; apptd. Fed. Res. Bd., 1992—; mem. Coun. on Calif. Competitiveness, 1992, Eximbank Adv. Com., 1990—, Agrl. Policy Adv. Com. for Trade, 1987—, Calif. Econ. Devel. Corp., 1987—, Calif. Fgn. Market Devel. Export Incentive Com., 1986-87, Kern County Water Resources Bd., 1978-87; pres. Arvin Co-op Gin, 1968-75, Arvin-Edison Water Storage Dist., 1971-87; vice chmn. Cal-Cot, 1971-76. Former vestryman St. Paul's Episc. Ch., Bakersfield, Calif.; trustee Bakersfield Coll. Found., 1986-87; founder presdl. assocs. U. So. Calif., L.A. Capt. USAF, 1954-56. Republican. Avocations: golf, tennis, travel. Home: 4507 Roxbury Rd Corona Del Mar CA 92625-3126 Office: Western Growers Assn 17620 Fitch Irvine CA 92714-6022

MOORE, DEMI (DEMI GUYNES), actress; b. Roswell, N.Mex., Nov. 11, 1962; d. Danny and Virginia Guynes; m. Bruce Willis, Nov. 21, 1987; 3 daughters: Rumer Glenn, Scout LaRue, Tallulah Belle. Studies with Zina Provendie. Actress: (feature films) Choices, 1981, Parasite, 1981, Young Doctors in Love, 1982, Blame it on Rio, 1984, No Small Affair, 1984, St.

Elmo's Fire, 1985, About Last Night..., 1986, Wisdom, 1986, One Crazy Summer, 1987, The Seventh Sign, 1988, We're No Angels, 1989, Ghost, 1990, Mortal Thoughts, 1991 (also co-producer), The Butcher's Wife, 1991, Nothing But Trouble, 1991, A Few Good Men, 1992, Indecent Proposal, 1993, Disclosure, 1994, The Scarlet Letter, 1995, Now and Then, 1995 (also prodr.), Undisclosed, 1996, Striptease, 1996, The Juror, 1996; (TV series) General Hospital, 1982-83; (TV movies) If These Walls Could Talk, 1996 (also exec. prodr.); (voice) The Hunchback of Notre Dame, 1996. Office: Creative Artists Agy Inc 9830 Wilshire Blvd Beverly Hills CA 90212-1804*

MOORE, DONALD FRANCIS, lawyer; b. N.Y.C., Dec. 14, 1937; s. John F. and Helen A. (McLoughlin) M.; m. Alice L. Kalmar; children: Christina M., Marianne, Karen L., Alison A. AB, Fordham U., 1959; JD, St. John's U., Bklyn., 1962. Bar: N.Y. 1962, D.C. 1970, U.S. Supreme Ct. 1993. Assoc. Paul, Weiss, Rifkind, Wharton & Garrison, N.Y.C., 1962-70, ptnr., 1970—. Editor in chief St. John's U. Law Rev., 1962. Served to 1st lt. U.S. Army, 1962-64. Mem. N.Y. State Bar Assn., Assn. of Bar of City of N.Y. Roman Catholic. Avocation: fishing. Home: 7 Wedgewood Ct Glen Head NY 11545-2229 Office: Paul Weiss Rifkind Wharton & Garrison 1285 Ave Of The Americas New York NY 10019-6064

MOORE, DORSEY JEROME, dentistry educator, maxillofacial prosthetist; b. Boonville, Mo., Feb. 8, 1935; s. Lloyd Elliott Moore and Mary Elizabeth (Day) Katemann; m. Mary Louise Foote, May 2, 1959; children: Elizabeth L., David J. DDS, U. Mo., Kansas City, 1959. Diplomate Am. Bd. Prosthodontics. Commd. ensign USN, 1955, advanced through grades to capt., 1973; gen. practice dentistry various naval stas., 1959-63; practice in prosthodontics USS Proteus AS-19, 1963-66; resident in prosthodontics and maxillofacial prosthetics Naval Dental Sch., Bethesda, Md., 1966-69, chief maxillofacial prosthetics div., 1969-70; sr. dental advisor Naval Adv. Group, Comdr. Naval Forces, Saigon, Vietnam, 1970-71; chief maxillofacial prosthetics div. Nat. Naval Dental Ctr., 1971-76; chief maxillofacial prosthetics br. Naval Regional Med. Ctr., Great Lakes, Ill., 1976-79, ret., 1979; vis. lectr. U. Mo. Sch. Dentistry, Kansas City, 1976-79, H.G.B. Robinson prof., chmn. dept. removable prosthodontics, 1979—; assoc. prof. U. Saigon Sch. Dentistry, 1970-71; advisor to Min. of Health, Saigon, 1970-71; profl. lectr. George Washington U., Washington, 1971-76; clin. assoc. prof. surgery U. Kans. Sch. Medicine, 1987—; cons. maxillofacial prosthetics NIH Treatment Ctr., 1973—, Nat. Cancer Inst., 1973—, VA Hosp., North Chicago, Ill., 1976—, ADA Couns. Dental Edn., Hosp. Dental Svc. and Commn. on Accredition, 1978—; vice chancellor Devel. Adv. Com., 1983—; examiner Mo. Specialty Bd. Prosthodontics, 1982—; internat. cir. course lectr. Am. Prosthetics Soc., Indonesia, 1974, Guatelmala, 1975, N.Z., 1976, S.Africa, 1981; nat. cons. U.S. Naval Dental Sch., Bethesda, 1991—. Author: Practical Oral Rehabilitation of the Edentulous Patient, 8th edit., 1995; mem. editorial bd. Cancer of the Head and Neck: A Comprehensive Review of the Literature, 1982—; contbr. over 40 articles and abstracts to profl. jours. Mem. adminstrv. ch. bd. Cen. Methodist Ch., 1981-88, pres. official ch. bd., 1983-85; bd. dirs. Ednl. Rsch. Found. Prosthodontics, 1982—, chmn. 1988—; bd. dirs. Penn Valley Fitness Trail Assn., 1982—. Decorated Legion of Merit with combat V, other awards; Navy Cross of Gallantry with palm (Republic of Vietnam). Fellow Am. Acad. Maxillofacial Prosthetics (bd. dirs. 1972-75, mem. exec. com. 1973-76, pres. 1978-79, mem. exec. coun. 1979-82), Am. Coll. Prosthodontics (charter), Acad. Denture Prosthetics, Internat. Coll. Dentist, Midwest Acad. Prosthodontics; mem. ADA. Avocations: jazz musician, string bassist. Office: U Mo-Kans City Sch Dentistry 650 E 25th St Kansas City MO 64108-2716

MOORE, DUDLEY STUART JOHN, actor, musician; b. Dagenham, Essex, Eng., Apr. 19, 1935; s. John and Ada Francis (Hughes) M.; m. Suzy Kendall, 1966 (div.); m. Tuesday Weld, 1975 (div.); 1 child: Patrick; m. Brogan Lane (Denise Brogan), Feb. 21, 1988 (div.); m. Nicole Rothschild, April 16, 1994. Student, Guildhall Sch. Music; BA, Oxford (Eng.) U., 1957, MusB, 1958. Author: Dud and Pete: The Dagenham Dialogues, 1971; stage debut with Oxford U. Drama Soc., 1955; other stage appearances include Beyond the Fringe, London, 1960-62, Broadway, 1962-64, Play It Again Sam, 1970, Good Evening, 1973-75; appeared with Vic Lewis, John Dankworth Jazz Band, 1959-60; composed incidental music Royal Ct. Theatre, 1958-60; appeared in own BBC-TV series with Peter Cook Not only...but also, 1964, 66, 70; Royal Command Performance, ITV, 1965, Goodbye Again, ITV, 1968; appeared on BBC-TV series It's Lulu, not to mention Dudley Moore, 1972, Dudley, 1993, Daddy's Girls, 1994—; toured U.S., 1975; appeared on various TV and radio shows with jazz piano trio; actor (films) The Wrong Box, 30 is a Dangerous Age, Cynthia, Alice in Wonderland, Those Daring Young Men in their Jaunty Jalopies, Bedazzled, The Bed Sitting Room, The Hound of the Baskervilles, Foul Play, 10, Wholly Moses, Arthur (Golden Globe award 1983, Acad. award nomination 1983), Six Weeks, Lovesick, Romantic Comedy, Unfaithfully Yours, Best Defense, Mickey & Maude (Golden Globe award 1985), Santa Claus The Movie, Like Father, Like Son, Arthur on the Rocks, (voice over) The Adventures of Milo and Otis, 1989, Crazy People, 1990, Blame it on the Bellboy, 1991, A Weekend in the Country; (TV) Daddy's Girls, 1995; also various TV shows.; composer (film music) 30 is a Dangerous Age, Cynthia, Inadmissible Evidence, The Staircase, Six Weeks; rec. artist (albums) The Other Side of Dudley Moore, Today, Genuine Dud, Derek and Clive - Live, Beyond the Fringe and All That Jazz, Dudley Moore Trio - Down Under, Bedazzled, Songs Without Words, 1992, others. Named Male Star of Yr. N.A.T.O., 1983; Organ scholar Oxford U., 1958. Mem. St. James's Club, Annabel's Club, Harry's Bar, Tramp Club. Office: care Mr Lou Pitt 8942 Wilshire Blvd Beverly Hills CA 90211-1934 also: Dennis Selinger I.C.M., Oxford House 76 Oxford St, W1R 1RB London England

MOORE, DUNCAN, healthcare executive; b. Nashville, June 23, 1941; married. B, Fla. State U., 1963; MHA, U. Iowa, 1965. Adminstrv. extern Washington Hosp. Ctr., 1964; adminstrv. resident Vanderbilt U. Hosp. & Clinic, Nashville, 1965-66, asst. dir, 1967, adminstrv. asst., 1966-67; asst. adminstr. Sparks Regional Med. Ctr., Ft. Smith, Ark., 1967-71; adminstr. Imperial Point Med. Ctr., Ft. Lauderdale, Fla., 1971-74; pres. Trinity Regional Hosp., Ft. Dodge, Iowa, 1974-80; corp. gen. mgr. Sisters of St. Francis Health Care, Peoria, Ill., 1980-82; adminstr. Phoebe Putney Meml. Hosp., Albany, Ga., 1982-88; pres., chief exec. officer Tallahassee (Fla.) Meml. Regional Med. Ctr., 1988—. Mem. Am. Coll. Healthcare Execs., SEHC (bd. dirs.), Ga. Hosp. Assn. (former chmn.), Iowa Hosp. Assn. (treas.). Office: Tallahassee Meml Regional Med Ctr Miccosukee Rd & Magnolia Dr Tallahassee FL 32308*

MOORE, DUNCAN THOMAS, optics educator; b. Biddeford, Maine, Dec. 7, 1946; s. Thomas Fogg Moore and Virginia Robinson Wing; m. Gunta Liders, July 1995. BA in Physics, U. Maine, 1969, DSc (hon.), 1995; MS in Optics, U. Rochester, 1970, PhD in Optics, 1974. Asst. prof. U. Rochester, N.Y., 1974-78, assoc. prof., 1978-86, prof., 1986—, Kingslake prof., 1993—, dean engring. and applied sci., 1995—; pres., founder Gradient Lens Corp., Rochester, 1980; dir. N.Y. State Ctr. Advanced Optical Tech., Rochester, 1987-94, Inst. Optics, Rochester, 1987-93; vis. scientist Nippon Schlumberger, Tokyo, 1983; Congl. fellow Am. Phys. Soc., Washington, 1993-94; sci. advisor to Sen. John D. Rockefeller IV, W. Va., 1993-94; bd. dirs. Amarel Precision Instruments, Inc. Contbr. numerous articles to profl. jours.; patentee in field. Chmn. Hubble Indpendent Rev. Panel, 1990-91; mem. adv. bd. high tech. Rochester C. of C., 1988—. Recipient Disting. Inventor of Yr. award Intellectural Property Law Assn., 1993, Grin Optics award Japanese Applied Physics Soc., 1993, Sci. and Tech. award Greater Rochester C. of C., 1992. Mem. Lasers and Electro-Optics Soc. of IEEE, NRC, Am. Ceramic Soc., Am. Soc. Precision Engring., Optical Soc. Am. (editor Applied Optics 1989-92, bd. dirs. 1987-90, 92-93, v.p. 1994, pres. 1996), Am. Assn. Engring. Soc., Materials Rsch. Soc., Internat. Soc. Optical Engring. (mem. bd. govs. SPIE 1986-88), Coun. Scientific Socs. (co-chair govt. affairs com. 1996—), Forum on Physics and Soc. (exec. com. 1996—). Home: 4 Claret Dr Fairport NY 14450-4610 Office: U Rochester Inst Optics 509 Wilmot Bldg Rochester NY 14627

MOORE, E. HARRIS, bishop. Bishop Western Mo. Ch. of God in Christ, Kansas City.

MOORE, EDWARD FORREST, computer scientist, mathematician, former educator; b. Balt., Nov. 23, 1925; s. James Bernard and Edith (Thorn) M.; m. Elinor Constance Martin, July 30, 1950; children—Nancy, Shirley, Martha. BS in Chemistry, Va. Poly. Inst., 1947; MS in Math., Brown U., 1949, PhD in Math., 1950. Asst. prof. math. U. Ill., 1950-51; mem. tech. staff Bell Tel. Labs., Murray Hill, N.J., 1951-61, 62-66; vis. prof. elec. engring. Mass. Inst. Tech., 1961-62; vis. lectr. applied math. Harvard, 1961-62; prof. computer scis., math. U. Wis.-Madison, 1966-85; now ret. Author: Sequential Machines, 1964. Membership chmn. Fair Housing Com. of Chathams, N.J., 1964; treas. Francis Wayland Found., 1970-73; bd. dirs. Madison Campus Ministry, 1970-75. Served with USNR, 1944-46. Mem. AAAS, Nat. Speleological Soc., Wis. Speleological Soc., Am. Math. Soc., Soc. Indsl. and Applied Math., Math. Assn. Am., Bat Conservation Internat., N.Y. Acad. Scis., State Hist. Soc. Wis., Sigma Xi, Phi Kappa Phi, Phi Lambda Upsilon. Baptist. Home: 4337 Keating Ter Madison WI 53711-1563

MOORE, ELLIS OGLESBY, retired public affairs consultant; b. N.Y.C., May 12, 1924; s. Francis Lee and Gertrude (Ellis) M.; m. Peggy Sorrells, June 21, 1944; children: Ellis Oglesby, Jane Elizabeth Avallone, Kathleen Arnett, John Francis, Michael William. Student, Washington and Lee U., 1941-43. Reporter Pine Bluff (Ark.) Coml., 1946-47, Memphis Comml. Appeal, 1947-52; writer, exec. press and publicity NBC, N.Y.C., 1952-63; pub. relations exec. Standard Oil Co. (N.J.), N.Y.C., 1963-66, Am. Broadcasting Cos. Inc., N.Y.C., 1966-85; v.p. pub. relations Am. Broadcasting Cos. Inc., 1972-79, v.p. corp. relations, 1979-82, v.p. pub. affairs, 1982-85; pub. affairs cons., 1985-90. Served with AUS, 1943-46. Recipient Nat. Headliners award, 1950. Home: 984 Esplanade Pelham NY 10803-2904

MOORE, EMMETT BURRIS, JR., physical chemist; b. Bozeman, Mont., June 14, 1929; s. Emmett Burris and Iris Marie (Brown) M.; m. Diane Elizabeth Girling, Oct. 1, 1960; children: Karen Elizabeth, Robin Diane. B.S. in Chemistry, Wash. State U., 1951; Ph.D. in Phys. Chemistry (Shell fellow), U. Minn., 1956. Teaching asst. U. Minn., Mpls., 1951-55; asst. prof. physics U. Minn., Duluth, 1957-59; mem. staff Boeing Sci. Research Labs., Seattle, 1959-73; lectr. chemistry Seattle U., 1973; dir. power plant siting Minn. Environ. Quality Bd., St. Paul, 1973-76; gen. mgr. Richland (Wash.) Divsn. Olympic Engring. Corp., 1976-78; staff scientist Pacific N.W. Nat. Lab., 1978—; mem. environ. engring. rev. panel EPA, 1989—; alt. mem. Hartford Adv. Bd., 1995—; adj. prof. environ. sci. Wash. State U., 1990—. Contbr. articles to profl. jours. Trustee Mid-Columbia Symphony Soc., 1978-85, v.p., 1980-81, pres., 1981-83; trustee Richland Light Opera Co., 1984-88, bus. mgr., 1984-88. Fellow AAAS; mem. Am. Phys. Soc., Am. Chem. Soc. (chmn. Pauling award com. 1971, sec. Puget Sound sect. 1971-73, mem. energy panel of com. on chemistry and pub. affairs 1983-86), Am. Assn. Physics Tchrs. (v.p. Wash. sect. 1965-66, pres. 1966-67), N.W. Sci. Assn., Phi Beta Kappa, Phi Kappa Phi, Phi Eta Sigma, Alpha Chi Sigma, Phi Lambda Upsilon, Sigma Alpha Epsilon (v.p. province 1972-73). Episcopalian (vestryman 1967-69, 76-79, 91, sr. warden 1969, del. diocesan conv. 1969-72). Home: 2323 Greenbrook Blvd Richland WA 99352-8427 Office: Wash State U 100 Sprout Rd Richland WA 99352

MOORE, ERNEST EUGENE, JR., surgeon, educator; b. Pitts., June 18, 1946; s. Ernest Eugene Sr. and Mary Ann (Burroughs) M.; m. Sarah Van Duzer, Sept. 2, 1978; children: Hunter Burroughs, Peter Kitrick. BS in Chemistry, Allegheny Coll., 1968; MD, U. Pitts., 1972. Surg. resident U. Vt., Burlington, 1972-76; chief of trauma Denver Gen. Hosp., 1976—, chief dept. surgery, 1984—; chief div. of emergency med. svcs. U. Colo., Denver, 1984—, prof. surgery, vice chmn. dept., 1985—; dir. rsch. Colo. Trauma Inst., Denver, 1984—. Editor: Critical Decisions in Trauma, 1987, Trauma, 1988, rev. edits., 1991, 96, Early Care of the Injured, 1989; assoc. editor Jour. Trauma, Am. Jour. Surgery, Surgery-Problem Solving Approach, 2d edit., 1994, others; patentee retrohepatic vena cava shunt. Fellow ACS (com. on trauma, vice chair 1990), Soc. Univ. Surgeons (pres. 1989), am. Assn. Surgery of Trauma (pres. 1993), Internat. Assn. Surgery of Trauma and Surg. Intensive Care (pres.-elect 1995), Pan Am. Trauma Assn. (pres. 1991), Southwestern Surg. Congress (v.p. 1996), Western Trauma Assn. (pres. 1989). Republican. Avocations: skiing, hockey, hunting, running, fishing, camping. Home: 2909 E 7th Avenue Pky Denver CO 80206-3839 Office: Denver Gen Hosp Dept Surgery Denver CO 80204

MOORE, F. RICHARD, music educator; b. Uniontown, Pa., Sept. 4, 1944; s. Franklin L. and Anna Jane (White) M.; children: Amanda, Dariel, Marick. BFA in Music Composition, BFA Music Performance, Carnegie-Mellon U., 1966; postgrad., U. Ill., 1966-67; MSEE, Stanford U., 1975, PhD, 1977. Acoustics researcher AT&T Bell Labs., Murray Hill, N.J., 1967-79; music prof. U. Calif.-San Diego, La Jolla, 1979—, dir. comuter audio research lab., 1979—, dir. ctr. for music experiment, 1982-92, chair dept. music, 1996—; percussionist Pitts. Symphony, 1964-66. Author: Programming in C with a Bit of UNIX, 1985, Elements of Computer Music, 1990; contbr. articles to profl. jours. Grantee for computer music research System Devel. Found., 1982-88, NEA, 1979—, Rockefeller Found., 1978, Ford Found., 1982. Mem. IEEE, Am. Engring. Soc., Acoustical Soc. Am. Avocations: aviation, amateur radio, skiing. Office: U Calif San Diego Dept Music La Jolla CA 92093-0037

MOORE, FAYE ANNETTE, social services professional; b. Glasgow, Mont., Feb. 21, 1938; d. Chester Oliver and Viola Adelaide (Skalet) Baker; m. Russell Dale Guthrie, July 1, 1961 (div. Nov. 1975); children: Tamia Lee, Owen Bradley; m. William Bateman Moore, Jan. 6, 1979. BA Sociology, Mont. State U., 1959; MA Social Work, U. Chgo., 1961; MBA, N. Mex. State U., 1984, PhD Ednl. Adminstrn., 1989. Social worker Ill. Childrens Home and Aid Soc., Chgo., 1961-63; social worker Divsn. Social Svcs., Fairbanks, Alaska, 1964-72, supr. social worker, 1972-74, staff mgr., 1974-75; regl. mgr. Divsn. Family and Youth Svcs., Anchorage, Alaska, 1976-80, regl. adminstr., 1991—; adminstr. Rsch. Ctr. N.Mex. State U. Coll. Bus., Las Cruces, 1984-86; instr. Golden Gate U., Holloman AFB/Alamogordo, N.Mex., 1989-91, Webster U., Ft. Bliss, El Paso, Tex., 1989-91; presenter confs. in field. Contbr. articles to profl. jours. Recipient Supervisory Employee of the Year Commissioner's award Dept. of Health and Social Svcs., 1993. Mem. NASW, Realtor Assn. N.Mex. (state dir. 1990-91, chmn. state edn. com. 1991), Las Cruces Assn. Realtors (v.p. 1991), Am. Bus. Comm. Assn., Beta Gamma Sigma, Phi Kappa Phi. Avocations: gardening, walking, knitting, sewing. Home: PO Box 244403 Anchorage AK 99524-4403 Office: Divsn Family and Youth Svcs 550 W 8th Ave Ste 304 Anchorage AK 99501-3572

MOORE, FLETCHER BROOKS, engineering company executive; b. Heiberger, Ala., June 15, 1926; s. Amzi Wallace and Mary Elizabeth (May) M.; m. Margaret Marian Foreman, Sept. 5, 1954; children—Larry Brooks, Ronald Howell. B.S. in Electronic Engring, Auburn U., 1948; M.S. in Electronic Engring, Ga. Inst. Tech., 1949. With U.S. Navy Mine Counter-Measures Sta., Panama City, Fla., 1949-52, Army Ballistic Missile Redstone Arsenal, Ala., 1952-60; with Marshall Space Flight Ctr., NASA, Huntsville, Ala., 1960-81; dir. Astrionics Lab. NASA Marshall Space Flight Ctr., 1968-81; chief missile system Teledyne Brown Engring., Huntsville, 1981-83; v.p. Control Dynamics Co., Huntsville, 1983-91; pres. Logicon Control Dynamics, Inc., Huntsville, 1991-94; divsn. dir. Control Dynamics, a Divsn. of bd. Systems, Huntsville, 1994—. Past chmn. alumni engring. coun. Auburn U.; mem. Auburn U. rsch. coun.; vice chairman. Ala. Indsl. Coun. on Engring. Edn.; mem. adminstrv. sci. adv. coun. U. Ala., Huntsville. Mem. AIAA, Inst. of Navigation, NASA Alumni League (past pres. Marshall Space Flight Ctr. chpt.). Home: 119 Sherwood Dr SE Huntsville AL 35802-2430

MOORE, GARY ALAN, academic administrator, educator; b. Indianola, Iowa, Jan. 23, 1946; s. Robert Lincoln and Ruby Marie Moore; B.S., Nebr. Wesleyan U., 1968; M.A. (grad. teaching asst. 1971-74), U. Nebr., Lincoln, 1973, Ph.D., 1974; m. Annemarie Neubecker; 1 son, Adrian David. Prof. bus. and econs. SUNY, Geneseo, 1985—, head Jones Sch. Bus., 1990—; mediator, factfinder N.Y. Public Employment Relations Bd., Albany, 1977—; mediator, arbitrator N.Y. Bd. Mediation, Albany, 1980—. Served with USAR, 1970. Grantee SUNY, N.Y. Com. Work Environment and Productivity. Mem. Am. Econ. Assn., Indsl. Relations Research Assn., Acad. Legal Stud. Bus., Blue Key, Omicron Delta Epsilon, Pi Gamma Mu. Author: (with R. Elkin) Labor and the Economy, 1983, (with A. Magaldi and J. Gray) Legal Environment of Business, 1987; contbr. research papers to profl. jours. Office: Sch Bus SUNY Geneseo NY 14454

MOORE, GEOFFREY HOYT, economist; b. Pequannock, N.J., Feb. 28, 1914; s. Edward H. and Marian (Leman) M.; m. Ella C. Goldschmid, July 12, 1938 (dec. June 2, 1975); children: Stephen, Peter, Kathleen, Pamela; m. Melita H. Riley, Sept. 28, 1975. BS, Rutgers U., 1933, MS, 1937; PhD, Harvard, 1947. Assoc. prof. econs. NYU, 1947-48; assoc. dir. Nat. Bur. Econs. Rsch., N.Y.C., 1948-64, dir. rsch., 1965-67, v.p. rsch., 1968, 73-75, dir. bus. cycle rsch., 1975-79; commr. labor stats. Dept. Labor, 1969-73; dir. Ctr. for Internat. Bus. Cycle Rsch., Columbia U., N.Y.C., 1979-96, EC Cycle Rsch. Inst., 1996—; instr. agrl. econs. Rutgers U., 1936-42; sr. rsch. fellow Hoover Instn., Stanford U., 1973-78; adj. scholar Am. Enterprise Inst., 1975-80; vis. lectr. Columbia U., 1953-54, sr. rsch. scholar, 1983—. Author: (with W. A. Wallis) A Significance Test for Time Series, 1941, Production of Industrial Materials in World Wars I and II, 1944, Statistical Indicators of Cyclical Revivals and Recessions, 1950, The Diffusion of Business Cycles, 1955, Measuring Recessions, 1958, Business Cycle Indicators, 1961, Tested Knowledge of Business Cycles, 1962, (with J. Shiskin) Indicators of Business Expansions and Contractions, 1966, (with P. Klein) The Quality of Consumer Instalment Credit, 1967, The Anatomy of Inflation, 1969, The Cyclical Behavior of Prices, 1971, How Full is Full Employment, 1973, Slowdowns, Recessions and Inflation, 1975, An Inflation Chronology, 1977, Business Cycles, Inflation and Forecasting, 1983, (with P. Klein) Monitoring Growth Cycles in Market-Oriented Countries, 1985, (with M. Moore) International Economic Indicators: A Sourcebook, 1985, The Service Industries and the Business Cycle, 1987, Leading Indicators for the 1990's, 1989, (with K. Lahiri) Leading Economic Indicators, 1991, (with E. Boehm and A. Banerji) Using Economic Indicators to Reduce Risk in Stock Market Investments, 1992. Mem. N.Y. State Coun. Econ. Advisers, 1973-74. Subject of book edited by Philip A. Klein, Analyzing Modern Business Cycles: Essays Honoring Geoffrey H. Moore, 1990. Fellow Am. Statis. Assn. (pres. 1968), Nat. Assn. Bus. Economists, Am. Econs. Assn. (disting. fellow); mem. Nat. Economists Club, Forecasters Club N.Y., Cosmos Club, Phi Beta Kappa, Alpha Zeta. Home: 1171 Valley Rd New Canaan CT 06840-2428

MOORE, GEORGE CRAWFORD JACKSON, lawyer. BA, U. Fla., 1963; PhB in Soviet Law, U. St. Andrews, Scotland, 1966; MA in English Law with honors, Cambridge U., Eng., 1968, LLM in Internat. Law, 1969. Bar: Eng. (Barrister, Inner Temple) 1970, Jamaica 1971, Fla. 1973, Turks & Caicos Islands 1974, Antigua and Barbuda, Brit. V.I., Grenada, Montserrat, St. Lucia 1977; U.S. Supreme Ct. 1976. Legis. asst. to U.S. sen. Washington, 1970-72; asst. pub. defender Palm Beach County, Fla., 1973; pvt. practice West Palm Beach, Fla., 1973—; chmn. Fla. Export Coun. of U.S. Dept. Commerce, 1991-92; chmn. Fla. Coun. Internat. Devel., 1983-84, chmn. emeritus, 1990—; chmn. Fla. Gov.'s Conf. on World Trade and Investment, 1989; founding pres. World Trade Coun. of Palm Beach County, 1981—. Editor spl. issues Fla. Bar Jour., 1982, 87, chmn. editorial bd., 1988-89; mem. editorial bd. The Internat. Lawyer jour. of ABA, 1979-84; contbr. articles to profl. jours. Chmn. Fla. Econ. Growth and Internat. Devel. Commn., 1989-90. Fellow Soc. Internat. Bus. Fellows; mem. ABA, Fla. Bar (chmn. internat. law sect. 1994—). Office: 105 S Narcissus Ave Ste 812 West Palm Beach FL 33401-5530

MOORE, GEORGE ELLIOTT, management consultant; b. Pilot, N.C., Nov. 20, 1935; s. Woodrow Wilson and Kate Nell Moore; m. Barbara Jean Spivey, Aug. 29, 1958; children: Sharon Lynne, Todd Elliott. BA, U. N.C., 1962. Exec. dir. Sci. and Humanities Symposium, Duke U., Durham, N.C., 1962-66; dir. fed. programs Roanoke (Va.) City Schs., 1966-68; dir. devel. Hollins (Va.) Coll., 1968-80; assoc. vice chancellor N.C. State U., Raleigh, 1980-83; exec. v.p., chief exec. officer N.C. Med. Soc., Raleigh, 1983-93; sr. cons. Mgmt. Concepts, Inc., Raleigh, 1994—; treas. Carolina Drs. Care, Inc., Raleigh, 1987-93, also bd. dirs.; bd. dirs. Med. Soc. Svcs., Inc., Raleigh, State Med. Jour. Advt. Bur., Inc., Chgo.; trustee, officer N.C. Med. Soc. Found., Inc., 1988-93. Contbg. author: Corporate Foundation Support for Public Institutions, 1985, Multiple Foundations: Advantages and Problems, 1986. Mem. adv. bd. Kate B. Reynolds Health Care Trust, Winston-Salem, N.C., 1983-93; committeeman N.C. Citizens for Bus. and Industry, Raleigh, 1984-94; bd. dirs. N.C. Forum for Rsch. and Econ. Edn., Raleigh, 1988-93; sec. bd. trustees Hollins Coll., 1968-80. Sgt. USMC, 1954-58. Recipient Grand award Alumni Programs, U.S. Steel Found., Pitts., 1978, Award for Excellence in Publs., Time Inc., N.Y.C., 1979, 80. Mem. Am. Soc. Assn. Execs., Am. Assn. Med. Soc. Execs., N.C. Inst. Medicine, Assn. Execs. N.C. (bd. dirs. 1983—), Capital City Club, Raleigh Country Club, Pine Valley Country Club. Avocations: golf, carpentry and restoration, reading.

MOORE, GEORGE EMERSON, JR., geologist, educator; b. Lebanon, Mo., Jan. 2, 1914; s. George Emerson and Dorothea Louisa (Niewohner) M.; m. Wilma Corrine Leonard, May 20, 1939; children: George E. III, Dana Corinne, Craig G. A.B., U. Mo., 1936, M.A., 1938; Ph.D., Harvard U., 1947. Instr. U. Mo., 1938-39; teaching asst. Harvard U., 1940-42, 1946-47; geologist A.P. Green Fire Brick Co., Mexico, Mo., 1942-46; instr. Ohio State U. at Columbus, 1947-48, asst. prof., 1948-57, assoc. prof., 1957-64, prof., 1964-84, prof. emeritus, 1984—; geologist U.S. Geol. Survey, 1952-83. Fellow Geol. Soc. Am.; mem. Phi Beta Kappa, Sigma Xi. Home: 58 Mulberry Dr Wakefield RI 02879-1416

MOORE, GEORGE EUGENE, surgeon; b. Minn., Feb. 22, 1920; s. Jesse and Elizabeth (MacRae) M.; m. Lorraine Hammell, Feb. 22, 1945; children—Allan, Laurie, Linda, Cathy, Donald. B.A., U. Minn., 1942, M.A., 1943, B.S., 1944, B.M., 1946, M.D., 1947, Ph.D. in Surgery, 1950. Intern surgery U. Minn. Hosps., 1946-47; med. fellow gen. surgery, 1947, dir. tumor clinic, 1951-53; sr. research fellow USHPS, 1947-48; faculty U. Minn. Med. Sch., 1948-53, cancer coordinator, 1951-53; chief surgery Roswell Park Meml. Inst., Buffalo, 1953-72; dir. Roswell Park Meml. Inst., 1953-67; dir. pub. health research N.Y. State Health Dept., Albany, 1967-73; clin. prof. surgery State U. N.Y. at Buffalo, 1962-73, also prof. research biology, 1955-69; dir. surg. oncology Denver Gen. Hosp., 1973—; prof. surgery U. Colo., 1973—. Author: Diagnosis and Localization of Brain Tumors, 1950, Cancerous Diseases, 1970; contbr. 660 articles to profl. jours. Recipient Outstanding Citizen award Buffalo Evening News, 1958, Outstanding Sci. Achievement award, 1959, Disting. Achievement award Modern Medicine mag., 1962, Chancellor's medal U. Buffalo, 1963, Charles Evans Hughes award pub. administrn. Albany, 1963, Bronfman prize Am. Pub. Health Assn., 1964, Tchr. of Yr. award Dept. Surgery, U. Colo., 1977, Disting. Svc. award U. Colo., 1990, Meritorious Svc. Regents award U. Colo., 1990. Mem. Soc. U. Surgs., Halsted Soc., Am. Surg. Assn., Colo. Oncology Found. (pres.). Home: 12048 S Blackhawk Dr Conifer CO 80433-7107 Office: Denver Gen Hosp 645 Bannock St PO Box 1806 Denver CO 80204
Individuals are miraculous temporal genetic patterns whose accomplishments will always transcend those of any committee, consensual group, or political assembly; society must provide special early educational opportunities for creative youngsters and those with genius. I hope to see the practical development of cell therapy for the infectious and cancerous diseases and genetic corrections of inherited disorders.

MOORE, GISELLE JOSEPHINE, nurse practitioner; b. Nassau, Bahamas; d. John Palmer and Valerie Irene (Merrells) M. BSN, Barry Coll., 1981; MSN, U. Fla., 1990. Advanced registered nurse practitioner, Fla. RN Shands Hosp., Gainesville, Fla., 1982-87; advanced registered nurse practitioner U. Fla./Shands, Gainesville, 1987—; . Fla., Gainesville. Editor: Women's Cancer: A Gynecological Oncology Perspective, 1992—; mem. editl. bd. Cancer Nursing Jour., 1993—. Cons. Am. Cancer Soc., Gainesville, 1993—. Mem. Soc. Gyn. Nurse (chmn. publs.), Oncology Nurse Soc., Am. Holistic Nurses Assn., Fla. Nurses Assn., Sigma Theta Tau. Republican. Ch. of England. Avocations: sailing, wine tasting, growing African violets. Home: 2317 NW 69th Ter Gainesville FL 32606-6393

MOORE, GORDON E., electronics company executive; b. San Francisco, Jan. 3, 1929; s. Walter Harold and Florence Almira (Williamson) M.; m. Betty I. Whittaker, Sept. 9, 1950; children: Kenneth, Steven. BS in Chemistry, U. Calif., 1950; PhD in Chemistry and Physics, Calif. Inst. Tech., 1954. Mem. tech. staff Shockley Semicondr. Lab., 1956-57; mgr. engring. Fairchild Camera & Instrument Corp., 1957-59, dir. research and devel., 1959-68; exec. v.p. Intel Corp., Santa Clara, Calif., 1968-75; pres., chief exec. officer Intel Corp., 1975-79, chmn., chief exec. officer, 1979-87, chmn., 1987—; bd. dirs. Varian Assocs. Inc., Transamerica Corp. Fellow IEEE; mem. Nat. Acad. Engring., Am. Phys. Soc. Office: Intel Corp 2200 Mission College Blvd Santa Clara CA 95052-8119

MOORE, HAL G., mathematician, educator; b. Vernal, Utah, Aug. 14, 1929; s. Lewis Henry and Nora (Gillman) M.; m. D'On Empey, July 20, 1956; children: David, Nora (Mrs. Bret C. Hess), Alison (Mrs. Samuel M. Smith). BS, U. Utah, 1952, MS, 1957; PhD, U. Calif., Santa Barbara, 1967. Tchr. Salt Lake City Public Schs., 1952-53; instr. math. Carbon Jr. Coll., also Carbon High Sch., Price, Utah, 1953-55, Purdue U., Lafayette, Ind., 1957-61; adminstrv. asst. dept. math Purdue U., 1960-61; from asst. prof. math. to assoc. prof. math. Brigham Young U., Provo, 1961-71, prof., 1971-95; prof. emeritus, 1995—; assoc. chmn. dept. Math. Brigham Young U., 1986-89. Author: Precalculus Mathematics, 2d edit, 1977, (with Adil Yaqub) Elementary Linear Algebra With Applications, 1980, College Algebra and Trigonometry, 1983, A First Course in Linear Algebra, 1992; contbr. articles to profl. jours. Mem. High Coun., Ch. of Jesus Christ of Latter Day Saints, 1985-91, MTC br. pres., 1991-94, Bishop, 1958-61, 78-82. NSF faculty fellow U. Calif., Santa Barbara, 1964-66. Mem. Am. Math Soc., Math Assn. Am. (bd. govs. 1989-92), Utah State Math. Coalition (planning dir. 1990, bd. dirs. 1991-92), Sigma Xi (dir. 1974-80, 82-85, com. chmn. 1982-90), Phi Kappa Phi. Home: 631 W 650 S Orem UT 84058-6027 Office: 631 W 650 South Orem UT 84058-6027 *Revelation used to reason can work together and bring human beings closer to the truth of their existence and place in the universe. But charity and love and dedication are as necessary to the success of the union as they are to all others.*

MOORE, HENDERSON ALFRED, JR., retired savings and loan executive; b. Hattiesburg, Miss., May 28, 1912; s. Henderson Alfred and Lucy Alice (Currie) M.; m. Mary Cleo Barnes, June 16, 1946 (dec. Dec. 1976); children: Betty Barnes Moore McKenzie, H.A., Lucy Currie Moore Pledger (dec.); m. 2d, Dot Marie R. Evans, Oct. 24, 1979. BA, U. Miss., 1934, LLB, 1936, JD, 1968. Bar: Miss. 1936. Mem. Moore and Jones, Hattiesburg, 1961-77, of counsel, 1977—; exec. v.p. Magnolia Fed. Bank for Savs. (formerly First Magnolia Fed. Savs. and Loan Assn., and formerly First Fed. Savs. and Loan Assn. of Hattiesburg), Hattiesburg, 1961-68, pres., 1968-77, chmn. bd., chief exec. officer, 1977-84, chmn. emeritus, 1984—; city pros. atty., 1938-41, 47-49; city judge, 1941-42, city atty., 1949-53. Mem. Forrest County Indsl. Bd., 1965-77; mem. Hattiesburg Redevel. Authority, 1981-87, vice chmn., 1984, chmn., 1985. Miss. Econ. Council, 1960-84. Lt. USN, 1942-46. Mem. Inst. Fin. Edn., Miss. Bar Found., ABA, South Central Bar Assn., Miss. State Bar, Newcomen Soc. N.Am., Miss. Econ. Council (dir. 1960-84), U.S. League of Savs. Assn. (dir. 1968-71, 74-77), Fed. Home Loan Bank (dir. 1973-74), Miss. Savs. and Loan League (past pres.), Southwestern Savs. and Loan Conf. (dir. 1965-67), Miss. Folklore Soc., Hattiesburg Civic Assn., Soc. War of 1812, SAR, Miss. Hist. Soc., Hattiesburg C. of C., U. So. Miss. Found., U. So. Miss. Alumni Assn. (Alumni Hall of Fame 1995), U. Miss. Alumni Assn., Pi Kappa Alpha, Phi Alpha Delta, Phi Kappa Phi, Hattiesburg Country Club, Elks. Home: 2312 Carriage Rd Hattiesburg MS 39402-2526 Office: 100 W Front St Hattiesburg MS 39401-3460

MOORE, HENRY ROGERS, consulting engineer, retired railroad executive; b. Chatham, Va., Jan. 15, 1916; s. Charles Anderson and Lillian (Moon) M.; m. Billie Henslee, Mar. 26, 1949; 1 child, Mary James Moore Quillen. BSCE with honors, Va. Poly. and State U., 1940. Various positions So. Ry., southeastern U.S., 1939-52, div. supt., 1952-56; asst. chief engr. Washington, and chief engr. MWS, So. Ry., Charlotte, N.C., 1956-64; gen. supt. transp. Atlanta, 1965-68, gen. mgr., 1968-82; cons. AMTRAK, 1983-86; exec. v.p., chief oper. officer AMTRAK, Washington, 1986-88; pres. R.R. Transp. Cons. Inc., Atlanta, 1982—. Mem. Atlanta Athletic Club. Methodist. Home and Office: PO Box 98208 Atlanta GA 30359-1908

MOORE, HERMAN JOSEPH, professional football player; b. Danville, Va., Oct. 20, 1969. BA in Rhetoric & Comm. Studies, U. Va., 1991. Wide receiver Detroit Lions, 1991—. Named to The Sporting News All-Am. 1st team, 1990; selected to Pro Bowl, 1994. Office: Detroit Lions 1200 Featherstone Rd Pontiac MI 48342

MOORE, J. SCOTT, materials engineer; b. Detroit, Sept. 27, 1952; s. James Brown and Marguerite Louise (Loyselle) M.; m. Soon Ki Lee, Apr. 15, 1987; 1 child, Ross Lee. BS, Rensselaer Poly. Inst., 1974, MS, 1977, PhD, 1981. From engr. to sr. contracts adminstrn. IBM, Yorkstown Heights, N.Y., 1982-95. Mem. IEEE, Sigma Xi. Avocations: Buddhism, vedanta, yoga, writing children's books. Home and Office: 25-107 Barker St Mount Kisco NY 10549

MOORE, JACKSON WATTS, corporate executive; b. Birmingham, Ala., Nov. 2, 1948; s. Joseph Watts and Shellye Louise (Jackson) M.; m. Elizabeth Wilson, June 12, 1971; children: Jackson Jr., Wilson, Shellye. BS, U. Ala., 1970; JD, Vanderbilt U., 1973. Assoc. Martin, Tate, Morrow and Marston, Memphis, 1973-77; mng. ptnr. Wildman, Harrold, Allen, Dixon and McDonnell, Memphis, 1977-89; pres., COO Union Planters Corp., Memphis, 1989—, also bd. dirs.; bd. dirs. Union Planters Nat. Bank, Mid-South Pub. Comms. Network, Memphis Devel. Found., PSB Bancshares, Clanton, Ala. Bd. dirs. Boy Scouts Am., Memphis Emmaus Comty.; chmn. bd. Vanderbilt Law Sch.; bd. trustees pres.'s cabinet U. Ala. Capt. U.S. Army, 1973. Mem. Memphis Country Club, Memphis Hunt and Polo Club. Republican. Methodist. Avocations: golf, tennis, reading. Home: 6486 May Creek Cv Memphis TN 38119-6529 Office: Union Planters Corp 7130 Goodlett Farms Pkwy Memphis TN 38018*

MOORE, JACQUELYN CORNELIA, labor union official, editor; b. Balt., Dec. 25, 1929; d. James C. and Harriette I. (Conaway) Thomas; m. Clarence Carbin Moore, Jan. 19, 1947 (dec. Feb. 1970); children: Clarence Joseph, Janet Elizabeth Moore Marshall. Mail clk. U.S. P.O., Phila., 1966-93; editor Local 509 Newsletter, Nat. Alliance of Postal and Fed. Employees, Washington, 1969-74, editorial newsletter chmn., 1969-74, sec. Dist. 5, 1972-74, nat. editor Nat. Alliance, 1974—, mem. exec. bd., 1974—, union photographer, 1974—, dir. 202 Housing for Elderly Corp. bds., Chattanooga, New Orleans, 1981—, Atlanta, 1988—, sec. supervisory com. Nat. Fed. Credit Union, 1977-82, 84-94, chair 1994—. Vol. D.C. Voting Rights Corp., Washington, 1979—; sustaining mem. Dem. Nat. Com., 1977—. Mem. Coalition of Labor Union Women, Nat. Bus. and Profl. Women's Club, Nat. Press Club. Roman Catholic. Home: 1102 R St NW Washington DC 20009-4364 Office: 1628 11th St NW Washington DC 20001-5011

MOORE, JAMES ALFRED, ski company executive, lawyer; b. Madisonville, Ky., Oct. 20, 1915; s. Virgil Yandell and Dorothy Ina (Price) M.; m. Lucile Carpenter, June 29, 1970; children by previous marriage: Marjorie M. Eickel, James Kelly, Kathleen M. Marozzi; m. Judith Gallen, June 10, 1995. A.B., U. Ky., 1936; LL.B., Harvard U., 1939. Bar: Pa. 1940, D.C. 1969, Va. 1978. Assoc. firm Pepper, Hamilton & Scheetz, Phila., 1940-51; partner Pepper, Hamilton & Scheetz, 1951-69; partner firm Pepper, Hamilton & Scheetz, Washington, 1969-77; pres. Camelback Ski Corp., Tannersville, Pa., 1963-86, chmn., bd. dirs., 1986-93, chmn. emeritus, 1993—. Contbr. articles to various law revs. Bd. dirs. Phila. Soc. for Crippled Children and Adults, 1959-69. Served from ensign to lt. comdr. USNR, 1942-45. Mem. Am. Bar Assn., Am. Law Inst. Republican. Methodist. Club: Merion Cricket (Haverford, Pa.). Home: PO Box 1241 Front Royal VA 22630-1241 Office: Camelback Ski Corp PO Box 168 Tannersville PA 18372-0168

MOORE, JAMES L., JR., beverage company executive; b. 1942. BA, Davidson Coll., 1964; MBA, Univ. N.C., 1968. Dist. mgr. Pepsi-Cola Co., 1972-74, mgr. market planning Pepsi-Cola Bottling group, 1974-75, v.p., area mgr. Houston, 1975-76; v.p., gen. mgr. Atlantic Soft Drink, Knoxville, Tenn., 1977-82, v.p. mktg., 1982-83, pres., chief exec. officer, 1983-87; pres., chief exec. officer Coca-Cola Bottling Co. Consolidated, 1987—, also dir. 1st lt. U.S. Army, 1972-76. Office: Coca-Cola Bottling Co 1900 Rexford Rd Charlotte NC 28211*

MOORE, JAMES MENDON, industrial engineering educator, consultant; b. Winchester, Mass., Apr. 25, 1925; s. Mendon Preston and Fannie Judith (Merrill) M.; m. Lenna Mary Maguire, June 10, 1950; children: Thomas P., Richard M., Terry R., Alan M. B.S., Rensselaer Poly. Inst., 1950; M.S., Cornell U., 1956; Ph.D., Stanford U., 1964. Instr. Cornell, Ithaca, N.Y., 1952-56; asst. prof. mech. engring. Clarkson Coll. Tech., Potsdam, N.Y., 1956-59; instr. Stanford U., 1959-60; prof., chmn. indsl. engring. dept. Northeastern U., Boston, 1961-73; head dept. indsl. engring. and ops. research Va. Poly. Inst. and State U., Blacksburg, 1973-75, prof., 1976-90; pres. Moore Productivity Software, Blacksburg, 1976—; Lucas vis. prof. engring. prodn. U. Birmingham, Eng., 1975-76; sr. Fulbright lectr. Tech. U. Finland, Helsinki, 1968-69; dir. rsch. Hefei U., China, 1988, County Bd. Suprs., 1990—; chmn. bd. Internat. Found. Prodn. Rsch., 1991-93. Author: Plant Layout and Design, 1962; Co-author: Computer Aided Layout: A User's Guide, 1978, Applications of Graph Theory Algorithms, 1979, An Engineer's Guide to Spreadsheets, Word Processors & Data Base Managers, 1986; co-editor: The Production System: An Efficient Integration of Resources; asso. editor: Internat. Jour. Prodn. Research, 1973-1983. Served with AUS, 1943-45. Decorated Bronze Star, Purple Heart. Fellow Am. Inst. Indsl. Engrs. (pres. chpt. 1963-64), Royal Soc. Home: 1607 Greenwood Dr Blacksburg VA 24060-5937

MOORE, JAMES R., lawyer; b. Longview, Wash., Sept. 14, 1944; s. James Carlton and Virginia (Rice) M.; m. Patricia Riley, Aug. 25, 1967 (div. 1978); 1 child, Katherine M.; m. Christine M. Monkman, July 14, 1979 (div. 1996); stepchildren: Amy McKenna, John McKenna; 1 foster child, Zia Sunseri. BA, Whitman Coll., 1966; JD, Duke U., 1969. Bar: Wash. 1970, U.S. Ct. Appeals (4th cir.) 1972, U.S. Supreme Ct. 1973, U.S. Ct. Appeals (9th cir.) 1974, D.C., 1995. Law clk. to Hon. J. Barnes U.S. Ct. Appeals (9th cir.), L.A., 1969-70; trial atty. pollution control, land/natural resources div. U.S. Dept. Justice, Washington, 1970-74; asst. U.S. atty. U.S. Atty.'s Office, Seattle, 1974-82; regional counsel U.S. EPA Region 10, Seattle, 1982-87; counsel Perkins Coie, Seattle, 1987-88, ptnr., 1989—; trainer, speaker on environ. litigation, negotiation and law. Contbr. articles to profl. jours. Bd. dirs. Environ. Law Inst., 1995—; chair audit com. Whitman Coll., 1994—. Mem. ABA (sect. natural resources 1987—), Wash. State Bar Assn. (environ. and land use sect. 1974—, spl. dist. coun. 1988-95). Democrat. Office: Perkins Coie 1201 3rd Ave Ste 4100 Seattle WA 98101-3000 also: 607 14th St NW Washington DC 20005-2007

MOORE, JAMES TERRENCE, II, industrial distribution company executive; b. Detroit, June 16, 1948; s. James Terrence Sr. and Marion Grace (Gleason) M.; m. Lizabeth Clair Kinsey; children: Ryan Barry, Bryce Ward, Kevan Patrick. BA, Olivet Coll., 1970. Salesman, adminstr. SKF Industries, Inc., Phila., 1970-73; asst. v.p. Detroit Ball Bearing Co., 1973-78; pres., COO Moore Bearing Co., Denver, 1978—, Am. Bearing & Power Transmissions, Charlotte, N.C., 1985—; former exec. v.p. Invetech, Detroit, also bd. dirs., now pres., COO; bd. dirs. Power Transmission Distbr. Assn.; past chmn. Young Execs. Bearing Specialist Assn., 1985. Mem. Rep. Senatorial Inner Circle, Washington, 1980—; bd. dirs. Manresa Jesuit Retreat House, Bloomfield Hills, Mich., 1986—; chmn. Catholic Services Appeal, Birmingham, Mich., 1986-87; rep. St. Regis Parish Council, Birmingham, Mich., 1986-87. Mem. Am. Mgmt. Assn., Profit Sharing Council Am. Roman Catholic. Clubs: Pine Lake Country; Detroit Athletic; Renaissance. Avocations: reading, hiking. Office: Invetech Co 1400 Howard St Detroit MI 48216-1917*

MOORE, JEAN MOORE, secondary education educator; b. Selma, Ala., Oct. 30, 1945; d. James Freeman and Millie Jane (Bean) Moore; m. Herman Moore, Jr., June 27, 1975; stepchildren: Kevin, Kelvin. Diploma, Selma U., 1965; BS in English and History, Ala. State U., 1967, MEd in Secondary Edn., 1973. Cert. secondary tchr., Ala. Tchr. Dallas County High Sch., Selma, 1967—. Asst. sec. matron's div. Ala. Women's Bapt. State Conv., 1985—. Named Tchr. of Yr., Dallas County High Sch., 1983, 85; Selma U. Bus. and Profl. Womens scholar, 1964. Mem. NEA, Nat. Council Tchrs. English, Ala. Edn. Assn., Academic and Curriculum Devel. Assn., Dallas County Profl. Tchrs. (sec. 1984-85), Elks (Elk of Yr. award, Selma 1983), Order Eastern Star. Democrat. Home: 2712 Prospect Ln Selma AL 36703-1432

MOORE, JEANNE, arts educator and administrator; b. L.A., Aug. 28, 1932; d. George E. and Ellen Kearny (Patrick) M. AA, Pasadena (Calif.) City Coll., 1952; BA with honors, UCLA, 1954; MM, U. So. Calif., 1965, DMA, 1970. Music tchr. Arvin (Calif.) H.S., 1955-60, Santa Maria (Calif.) H.S., 1960-65, Arroyo H.S., El Monte, Calif., 1965-66; asst. prof. edn. U. Victoria, B.C., Can., 1968-70; asst. prof. music edn. Bowling Green (Ohio) State Coll., 1970-71; prof. music West Chester (Pa.) State Coll., 1971-72; lectr. music San Jose (Calif.) State U., 1972-73; asst. prof. music Madison Coll., Harrisonburg, Va., 1974-76; coord. fine arts W.Va. Dept. Edn., Charleston, 1977—; choral dir. Santa Maria Choral Soc., 1963-64, Silver Lake Presbyn. Ch., L.A., 1966-67, Wesley United Meth. Ch., San Jose, 1972-74; contbr./cons. Nat. Study of Sch. Evaluation, Falls Church, Va., 1983-85, 89. Author, editor more than 40 books/monographs; editor, project coord.: (6 books, audio and video) West Virginia Music Test Item Bank, K-4, 1989, (2 books, slides and video) West Virginia Museum Resources for Teaching Art, 1991; co-author: Beyond the Classroom: Informing Others, 1987. Staff mem. Gov.'s Task Force on Arts Edn., W.Va., 1990-94. Nat. Endowment for Arts grantee, 1989-90, 91-92. Mem. Nat. Art Edn. Assn., Nat. Coun. State Suprs. Music (pres. 1984-86), Music Educators Nat. Conf., W.Va. Music Educators Assn. (bd. dirs. 1977—, Presdl. award 1990), W.Va. Art Edn. Assn. (bd. dirs. 1986—, Outstanding Adminstr. award 1991, 92, 93), Phi Delta Kappa, Pi Kappa Lambda, Mu Phi Epsilon. Episcopalian. Home: 102 Brammer Dr Charleston WV 25311-1738 Office: WVa Dept Edn 1900 Kanawha Blvd E Rm B-330 Charleston WV 25305-0002

MOORE, JEANNETTE AILEEN, animal nutrition educator; b. Bellflower, Calif., Jan. 6, 1957; d. Harry Joseph Jr. and Alba Aurora (Celaya) M.; m. Matthew Henry Poore, Oct. 2, 1982. BS in Animal Scis., Calif. State Polytechnic U., 1980; MS in Animal Scis., U. Ariz., 1983, PhD in Nutritional Scis., 1987. Grad. asst. U. Ariz., Tucson, 1981-83, grad. rsch. assoc., 1984-87, postdoctoral rsch. assoc., 1988-90; co-mgr. Triple Creek Ranch, Virgilina, Va., 1983-84; postdoctoral rsch. assoc. N.C. State U., Raleigh, 1990-92; vis. asst. prof. N.C. State U., Raleigh, 1992—, faculty advisor Animal Sci. Club, 1992—, advisor Acad. Quadrathlon Team, 1993-94, advisor Rodeo Club, 1994—. Author: (computer spreadsheet) Ruminant Animal Diet Evaluator, 1993; mem. editl. bd. Jour. Animal Sci., 1995—; contbr. articles to profl. jours. Supt. jr. ewe show, N.C. State Fair, Raleigh, 1992—; vol. N.C. Sci. and Math Partnership, Wake county, N.C., 1991—. Mem. Am. Soc. Animal Sci., Am. Dairy Sci. Assn., Am. Inst. Nutrition, Am. Coll. Nutrition, Nat. Assn. Colls. and Tchrs. Agr., Coun. Agrl. Sci. and Tech., Alpha Zeta. Avocations: horseback riding, aerobics, reading, travel. Office: NC State U Dept Animal Sci Box 7621 Raleigh NC 27695-7621

MOORE, JERRY, religious organization administrator. Exec. sec. Home Mission Bd. of the Nat. Baptist Convention, USA, Washington, D.C. Office: Home Mission Bd 1612 Buchanan St NW Washington DC 20011-4216

MOORE, JOAN ELIZABETH, human resources executive, lawyer; b. Valleyfield, Que., Can., Apr. 29, 1951. BS in Social Scis., Mich. State U., 1973; JD, Case Western Res. U., 1976. Bar: Ohio 1977. Pers. exec. Ford Motor Co., Dearborn, Mich., 1976-80; cons. James Lash & Co., Southfield, Mich., 1980-83; pres., owner The Arbor Cons. Group, Inc., Plymouth, Mich., 1983—; owner Integrated Pers. Systems Inc., Plymouth, 1986—. V.p., bd. dirs. Pvt. Industry Coun., Wayne County, Mich., 1985-87; grad. Leadership Detroit VII, 1986, active alumni bd.; mem. computer subcom. Mich. Tech. Coun., 1986—; bd. dirs. Am. Cancer Soc. Mem. ABA, Ohio Bar Assn., Soc. for Human Resources Mgmt. (cert. Sr. Profl. in Human Resources), Leadership Detroit Alumni, Ann Arbor Art Assn. (bd. dirs.), Children's Aid Soc. (pers. advisor), Human Resources Assn. Greater Detroit (pres.-elect 1995). Office: The Arbor Cons Group 711 W Ann Arbor Trl Plymouth MI 48170-1677

MOORE, JOANNE IWEITA, pharmacologist, educator; b. Greenville, Ohio, July 23, 1928; d. Clarence Jacob and Mary Edna (Klepinger) M. A.B., U. Cin., 1950; Ph.D., U. Mich., 1959. Rsch. asst. Christ Hosp. Inst. Med. Rsch., Cin., 1950-55; rsch. asst. U. Mich., Ann Arbor, 1955-57, teaching fellow, 1957-59; postdoctoral fellow in pharmacology Emory U., Atlanta, 1959-61; asst. prof. pharmacology U. Okla. Coll. Medicine, Oklahoma City, 1961-66, assoc. prof., 1966-71, acting chmn., 1969-71, prof., interim chmn., 1971-73, prof., chmn. dept., 1973—, David Ross Boyd prof., chair, 1993; mem. gen. rsch. support rev. com. NIH, 1975-79, mem. biomed. scis. study sect., 1986-90; mem. adv. bd. Fogarty Internat. Ctr., 1992-94. Contbr. articles to profl. jours. USPHS grantee, 1963-69, 72-74, 79-87. Mem. AAAS, Am. Soc. Pharmacology and Exptl. Therapeutics, Assn. Med. Sch. Pharmacology, Am. Heart Assn. (bd. dirs. Okla. affiliate 1973-88, pres. 1979-80, chmn. bd. 1983-85, bd. dirs. Oklahoma City div. 1988-91, pres. 1989-90), Sigma Xi. Office: U Okla Coll Medicine Dept Pharmacology 753 BMSB OUHSC Oklahoma City OK 73190

MOORE, JOHN ALEXANDER, biologist; b. Charles Town, W.Va., June 27, 1915; s. George Douglas and Louise Hammond (Blume) M.; m. Anna Betty Clark, 1938; 1 child. Student, Columbia Coll., Columbia U. Asst. zoology dept. Columbia U., N.Y.C., 1936-39, chair zoology dept., 1949-52, prof., 1954-68; tutor in biology Bklyn. Coll., 1939-41; instr. Queens Coll., 1941-43; asst. prof. zoology Barnard Coll., 1943-47, assoc. prof., 1947-50, prof., 1950-68, chair zoology dept., 1948-54, 60-66; rsch. assoc. Am. Mus. Natural History, 1942—; prof. biology U. Calif., Riverside, 1969-82, prof. emeritus, 1982—; mem. com. on human resources NRC, 1979-82, mem. coord. coun. for edn. 1991-95, mem. com. on undergrad. sci. edn., 1992—, Nat. Sci. Resources Ctr., 1994—; Walker Ames prof. U. Wash., 1966; mem. Biol. Scis. Curriculum Study, 1959-76; mem. Commn. on Sci. Edn., 1967-73, chair, 1971-73. Author: Principles of Zoology, 1957, Heredity and Development, 1963, 2d edit., 1972, A Guide Book to Washington, 1963, Biological Science: An Inquiry into Life, 1963, 3d edit., 1973, (with others) Interaction of Man and the Biosphere, 1970, 3d edit., 1979, Science for Society: A Bibliography, 1970, 2d edit., 1971, Readings in Heredity and Development, 1972, Science as a Way of Knowing - Evolutionary Biology, 1984, Science as a Way of Knowing - Human Ecology, 1985, Science as a Way of Knowing - Genetics, 1986, Science as a Way of Knowing - Developmental Biology, 1987, Science as a Way of Knowing - Form and Function, 1988, Science: A Way of Knowing - A Conceptual Framework for Biology, Part I, 1989, Part II, 1990, Part III, 1991, Science as a Way of Knowing: The Foundations of Modern Biology, 1993, Nature in the New World, 1989, Nature Portrayed-the Natural World of the Americas, 1989; editor: Physiology of the Amphibia, 1964, Ideas in Modern Biology, 1965, Ideas in Evolution and Behavior, 1970, Dobzhansky's Genetics of Natural Populations, 1981; supr.: Biological Science: An Inquiry into Life, 1963, 3d edit., 1973, Genes, Cells and Organisms-Great Books in Experimental Biology, 17 vols., 1988. Fulbright rsch. scholar, Australia, 1952-53; Guggenheim fellow, 1959. Mem NAS, AAAS (mem. project 2061 1985-89), Genetics Soc. Am., Am. Soc. Zoologists (pres. 1974), Am. Soc. Naturalists (pres. 1972), Soc. for Study Evolution (pres. 1963), Am. Acad. Arts and Scis. Avocations: photography, history of American science, history of illumination. Home: 11522 Tulane Ave Riverside CA 92507-6649 Office: U Calif Dept Biology Riverside CA 92521-0427

MOORE, JOHN CORDELL, retired lawyer; b. Winchester, Ill., July 20, 1912; s. John Clayton and Winifred (Peak) M.; m. Pauline Ruyle, July 29, 1939 (dec. 1979); m. Wilma K. Smith Jackson, Aug. 1981. A.B., Ill. Coll., 1936, LL.D., 1967; LL.B., Georgetown U., 1949, J.D., 1967; postgrad. in geology, Am. U., 1955-57. Bar: Tenn., U.S. Supreme Ct. Rep. Universal Credit Co., St. Louis, 1937-39; tchr. Capitol Page Sch.; also clk. to mem. Ho. of Reps., 1939-41; examiner Metals Res. Co., 1941-42; exec. dir. Fgn. Liquidation Commn. for S. and C. Am., Balboa, C.Z., 1946-47; with Office Alien Property, Dept. Justice, 1947-50; asst. dir. property mgmt. Interior Dept., 1950-52, dir. security for dept., 1952-61; adminstr. Oil Import Adminstrn., 1961-65, asst. sec. for mineral resources, 1965-69; now lawyer, also internat. energy cons.; U.S. rep. oil and energy com. OECD, Paris, 1965-69; former dir. Clark Oil, Milw. Served to comdr. USNR, 1942-46; capt. Res. Mem. NRA (life), VFW, Fed. Bar Assn., Tenn. Bar Assn., Am. Legion, Scott County (Winchester, Ill.) Hist. Soc. (life), Delta Theta Phi, Elks, Army-Navy Club, Nat. Lawyers Club (Washington), Jacksonville Country Club.

MOORE, JOHN DENNIS, publisher; b. Mexico, Mo., Mar. 2, 1931; s. Dennis Talmage and Vona Mae (Vance) M.; m. Lydia Benz Ahern, Aug. 15, 1959; children: Alison Ahern, Lydia Benz, John Talmage, Maude Ahern, Meredith Coleman. Student, Princeton U., 1948-51, U.S. Naval Acad., 1951-53; B.A., U. Mo., Columbia, 1953; postgrad., Harvard Law Sch., 1955-56. Coll. traveler The Dryden Press, Inc., N.Y.C., 1957-59; coll. traveler The Macmillan Co., N.Y.C., 1959-60; editor The Macmillan Co., 1960-67; assoc. exec. editor Columbia U. Press, N.Y.C., 1968-74; editor in chief Columbia U. Press, 1974-80, pres., bd. dirs., 1980—; bd. dirs., pres. Columbia U. Music Press; bd. dirs. Univ. Presses of Calif., Columbia and Princeton, Chichester, West Sussex, Eng., 1979—, chmn., 1981-83, 85-87, 96—; trustee Composer's Recordings, Inc., 1984—. Bd. dirs. Greenwich (Conn.) Health Assn., 1970-75; bd. dirs. assoc. The Family Ctr., Greenwich, 1975—; trustee Princeton Libr. in N.Y.c., 1984—; mem. vestry St. Barnabas Ch., Greenwich, 1995—. With U.S. Army, 1953-55. Mem. Assn. Am. Univ. Presses (chair internat. com. 1994-96, bd. dirs. 1996—). Episcopalian. Clubs: Publishers Lunch (N.Y.C.), Princeton (N.Y.C.), Faculty House Columbia U. (N.Y.C.), Century Assn. (N.Y.C.); Nassau (Princeton, N.J.), the Book Table (N.Y.C.). Office: Columbia U Press 562 W 113th St New York NY 10025-8000

MOORE, JOHN EDWIN, JR., college president; b. Aurora, Mo., Nov. 7, 1942; s. John Edwin and Emma Lou (Harback) M.; children: John E. III, Catherine Porter. BA cum laude, Yale U., 1964, MA in Teaching, 1965; EdD, Harvard U., 1971. Tchr. N.C. Advancement Sch., Winston-Salem, 1965-66; rsch. asst. Tech. Edn. Rsch. Ctr., Cambridge, Mass., 1969-70; adminstrv. asst., treas. Kirkwood Sch. Dist. R-VII, St. Louis, 1970-73, asst. supt., treas., 1973-74; adj. prof. U. Mo., St. Louis, 1973-74; v.p. Athens (Greece) Coll., 1974-75; asst. commr. edn. Dept. Elem. and Secondary Edn., Jefferson City, Mo., 1975-83; pres. Drury Coll., Springfield, Mo., 1983—; part-time instr. Far-East div. U. Md., 1967-68. Bd. dirs. United Way Ozarks, campaign chmn., 1988; bd. dirs. Mo. Colls. Fund, chmn., 1988-89; bd. dirs. Make-A-Wish Found. With U.S. Army, 1966-68. Recipient Vincent Conroy Meml. award Harvard Grad. Sch. Edn., 1971; named one of Outstanding Young Men Am., 1973. Mem. Springfield Area C. of C. (v.p. 1988, bd. dirs. Springfieldian of Yr. 1989), Nat. Assn. Intercollegiate Athletics (coun. pres.'s), Rotary (pres. Springfield chpt. 1988-89). Presbyterian (elder). Avocations: hunting, fishing, gardening, conservation. Home: 1234 N Benton Ave Springfield MO 65802-1902 Office: Drury Coll 900 N Benton Ave Springfield MO 65802-3712

MOORE, JOHN GEORGE, JR., medical educator; b. Berkeley, Calif., Sept. 17, 1917; s. John George and Mercedes (Sullivan) M.; m. Mary Louise Laffer, Feb. 8, 1946; children: Barbara Ann, Douglas Terence, Bruce MacDonald, Martha Christine. B.A., U. Calif., Berkeley, 1939; M.D., U. Calif., San Francisco, 1942. Diplomate: Am. Bd. Ob-Gyn (pres. 1974-78, chmn. 1978-82). Asst. prof. U. Iowa, 1950-51; asso. prof. UCLA, 1951-65, prof., chmn. dept. ob-gyn, 1968-88; prof., chmn. dept. ob-gyn Columbia U. Coll. Physicians and Surgeons, N.Y.C., 1965-68; chief of gynecology VA Hosp., Sepulveda, Calif., 1988-94. Contbr. articles to profl. jours. Served to maj. M.C. U.S. Army, 1942-46. Decorated Silver Star, Bronze Star, Purple Heart.; NIH grantee U. Copenhagen; Royal Postgrad. Sch. Medicine, London. Mem. ACS, ACOG, Soc. Gynecol. Investigation (pres. 1967), Assn. Profs. Gynecology and Obstetrics (pres. 1975), Western Assn. Gynecol. Oncologists (pres. 1976), Am. Gynecol. Soc., Pacific Coast Ob-Gyn. Soc., L.A. Ob-Gyn. Soc., Pepperdine U. Assocs. Home: Tamarron Unit 843 PO Box #3131 Durango CO 81302-3131

MOORE, JOHN HEBRON, history educator; b. Greenville, Miss., Feb. 26, 1920; s. John Pressley and Cora (Hebron) M.; m. Margaret Burr DesChamps, Dec. 20, 1955; 1 child, John Hebron Jr. BS in Aero-engring., Miss. State U., 1946; MA in History, U. Miss., Oxford, 1951; PhD, Emory U., 1955. Asst. prof. Delta State U., Cleveland, Miss., 1955-56; asst. prof. U. Miss., Oxford, 1956-57, assoc. prof., 1957-62, prof., 1962-70, chmn. history dept., 1966-69; prof. Fla. State U., Tallahassee, 1970-93, chmn. history dept., 1975-80; prof. emeritus, 1993—. Author: Agriculture in Antebellum Mississippi, 1958, Andrew Brown and Cypress Lumbering in the Old Southwest, 1967, The Emergence of the Cottom Kingdom in the Old Southwest: Mississippi, 1770-1860, 1988. With U.S. Army, 1941-43, USAAF, 1943-45, ETO, PTO. Mem. Agrl. History Soc. (pres. 1985), So. Hist. Assn., Miss. Hist. Soc. Presbyterian. Home: 2529 Blarney Dr Tallahassee FL 32308-3152

MOORE, JOHN HENRY, II, federal judge; b. Atlantic City, Aug. 5, 1929; s. Harry Cordery and Gertrude (Wasleski) M.; m. Joan Claire Kraft, Dec. 29, 1951; children—Deborah Joan, Katherine Louise. Student, Cornell U., 1947; BS, Syracuse U., 1952; JD, U. Fla., 1961. Bar: Fla. 1961. Assoc. Fisher & Phillips, Atlanta, 1961; ptnr. Flemming O'Bryan & Fleming, Fort Lauderdale, Fla., 1961-67, Turner, Shaw & Moore, Fort Lauderdale, Fla., 1967; judge 17th Jud. Circuit, Fort Lauderdale, Fla., 1967-77, U.S. Dist. Ct.

Appeals for 4th Cir., West Palm Beach, Fla., 1977-81; judge U.S. Dist. for Mid. Dist. Fla., Jacksonville, 1981-92, chief judge, 1992—; mem. Fla. Constitution Revision Com., 1977-78; chmn. Fla. Jud. Qualifications Commn., 1977-81. Bd. dirs. Community Service Council, Fort Lauderdale, 1970-75; pres. Broward County Assn. for Retarded Children, Fort Lauderdale, 1962; hon. bd. trustees Broward Community Coll., Fort Lauderdale, 1970. Served to comdr. USNR, 1948-71, Korea. Named hon. Alumnus Nova U., 1977; recipient cert. of good govt. Gov. of Fla., 1967. Mem. ABA, Fla. Bar Assn., Fed. Bar Assn., Jacksonville Bar Assn., Fla. Conf. Circuit Judges (chmn.-elect 1977), Fla. Blue Key (hon.), U.S. Navy League, Naval Res. Assn., Ret. Officers Assn. Republican. Presbyterian. Clubs: Timuquana Country, Jacksonville Quarterback, Seminole (Jacksonville). Lodge: Rotary. Avocations: golf, tennis, boating. Office: US Dist Ct PO Box 53137 Jacksonville FL 32201-3137*

MOORE, JOHN JOSEPH, lawyer; b. West New York, N.J., Jan. 24, 1933; s. George Thomas and Dorothy (Zimmer) M.; m. Carmela Macrini, Mar. 10, 1957; children: Christine, John Joseph. B.S., Jersey City State Coll., 1956; LL.B., N.Y. Law Sch., 1961; LL.M., NYU, 1970. Bar: N.Y. 1961. Since practiced in N.Y.C.; assoc. with firm Dwyer & Lawler, after 1961; then mem. firm Reid, Devlin, Grubbs & Moore (now Alio & McDonough); chmn. bd. Leber Inc., 1983-93; mem. Barry McTierman and Moore, 1970—; guest lectr. disclosure Fordham U.; tchr. social studies pub. schs., Union City, N.J.; Sponsor, coach local Biddy Basketball Team, 1972—. Author: Discovery and Inspection, 1969, Legal Significance, 1975; editor: Defendant, 1969-73, 1987-92. Trustee devel. fund Jersey City State Tchrs. Coll., 1973-81; trustee Jersey City State Coll., 1982, vice chmn. bd. trustees, 1983-87, chmn., 1989—; chmn. governing bds. Assn. State Colls. N.J., 1985-87; chair Civilian Rev. Complaint Bd., Teaneck, N.J., 1992—; mem. Bd. Higher Edn. State N.J., 1985-87, Coun. N.J. State Colls., 1984-85; mem. governing bds. Assn. State Colls. N.J., 1985-89. With AUS, 1956-58. Mem. ABA, Am. Arbitration Assn. (arbiter 1968—), N.Y. State Bar Assn., N.Y. County Bar Assn., Def. Assn. N.Y. (pres. 1973-74, chmn. bd. 1974-75), Assn. State Colls. N.Y. (gov. bd. 1985-93), Cath. Ins. Guild (pres. 1972-73, chmn. bd. 1973-74), Def. Rsch. Inst. (regional v.p. 1983-86), Downtown Athletic Club (N.Y.C.), Manhattan Club, Oritani Field Club (Hackensack, N.J.), Hackensack Golf Club. Roman Catholic (dir. mus. group). Home: 573 Standish Rd Teaneck NJ 07666-2605 Office: 25 Broadway New York NY 10004-1010

MOORE, JOHN LEO, JR., journalist, writer, editor; b. Providence, R.I., June 24, 1927; s. John Leo and Annabelle Cecilia (Eastwood) M.; m. Dorothy Dolores Drankwicz, 1952; children: John Leo III, Christopher, Meredith Margaret Moore Poffenberger. AB, Brown U., 1950. Reporter Pawtucket (R.I.) Times, 1950-66, Providence (R.I.) Jour.-Bulletin, 1966; correspondent Carpenter News Svc., Washington, 1966-69; assoc. editor Nat. Jour., Washington, 1969-74; asst. mng. editor Congl. Quarterly, Washington, 1974-78, asst. dir. books, 1978-90; freelance writer, editor Washington, 1990—; cons. World Bank Internat. Monetary Fund, Washington, 1990—. Editor: (Books) Guide to U.S. Elections, 2nd edit. 1985, 3rd rev. edit. 1994, CQ's Washington Guidebook, 1990, Congressional Ethics, 1992; author: Speaking of Washington, 1993. Committeeman Boy Scouts Am. Troop 15, Pawtucket, 1946-50, Troop 12, 1964-66; pres. Local 185 Newspaper Guild, Pawtucket, 1964-66; v.p. Community Assn., Severna Forest, Md., 1976-78. Named Eagle Scout, 1943; recipient salute Pawtucket C. of C., 1965, resolution of praise Pawtucket City Coun., 1966; cited for disting. reporting pub. affairs Am. Polit. Sci. Assn., 1961. Mem. Soc. Profl. Journalists. Roman Catholic. Avocations: photography, home improvement, lawn and garden work, reading, walking. Home and Office: 807 Cottonwood Dr Severna Park MD 21146-2813

MOORE, JOHN NEWTON, retired natural science educator; b. Columbus, Ohio, Apr. 2, 1920; s. Lawrence Newton and Grace C. (Jones) M.; m. Wilma Marie Proctor, Aug. 30, 1941; children—Douglas Warren, Donald Norman. A.B., Denison U., Granville, Ohio, 1941; M.S., Mich. State U., E. Lansing, 1943, Ed.D., 1952. Grad. asst. botany Mich. State U., 1941-43, instr. math., 1943-44, mem. faculty, 1946-82, prof. natural sci., 1970-82, prof. emeritus, 1982—; vis. prof. edn. Tenn. Temple Coll., summer 1974; bd. dirs. Creation Research Soc., 1963-86. Author: Questions and Answers on Creation/Evolution, 1976, How to Teach Origins, 1983; co-editor: Biology: A Search for Order in Complexity, rev. edit, 1974; mng. editor: Creation Research Soc. Quar, 1965-77; author chpts. in books. Served to lt. (j.g.) USNR, 1944-46. Fellow Creation Research Soc.; mem. Lambda Chi Alpha, Beta Beta Beta. Address: 119 Edward Ave Lehigh Acres FL 33936-5411

MOORE, JOHN NORTON, lawyer, diplomat, educator; b. N.Y.C., June 12, 1937; s. William Thomas and Lorena (Norton) M.; m. Barbara Schneider, Dec. 12, 1981; children: Victoria Norton, Elizabeth Norton. AB in Econs., Drew U., 1959; LLB with honors, Duke U., 1962; LLM, U. Ill., 1965; postgrad., Yale U., 1965-66. Bar: Fla. 1962, Ill. 1963, Va. 1969, D.C. 1972, U.S. Supreme Ct. 1972. Walter L. Brown prof. law, dir. Ctr. Oceans Law and Policy Ctr. for Nat. Security Law, U. Va., 1965-72, 76—; counselor on internat. law Dept. State, Washington, 1972-73; chmn. Nat. Security Coun. Task Force on Law of Sea and dep. spl. rep. of Pres. and amb. Law of Sea Conf., 1973-76; fellow Woodrow Wilson Internat. Ctr. for Scholars, Washington, 1976; adj. prof. Georgetown Law Ctr., 1978—; mem. Nat. Adv. Com. on Oceans and Atmosphere, 1984-85; mem. U.S. del. Conf. Security and Coop. in Europe, 1984; spl. counsel, dep. agt. for U.S. to World Ct.; former cons. to the Pres.'s Intelligence Oversight Bd., Arms Control and Disarmament Agy., U.S. Info. Agy.; chmn. bd. dirs. U.S. Inst. Peace; co-chmn. with the U.S. dep. atty. gen. Moscow Seminar on the Rule of Law, 1990; legal advisor during Gulf crisis for Kuwait's Amb. to U.S., including legal adviser to the Kuwait Rep. to UN Boundary Commn., 1991-94. Author: Law and the Indo-China War, 1972 (Phi Beta Kappa award); editor: Law and Civil War in the Modern World, 1976, Readings in International Law, 1979, The Arab-Israeli Conflict, 3 vols., 1976, 4th vol., 1991, Nat. Security Law, 1990, Crisis in the Gulf, 1992, Nat. Security Law Documents, 1995; contbr. articles on oceans policy, nat. security, internat. law, congl.-exec. rels. in fgn. policy and democracy-building to profl. jours. Sesquicentennial assoc. Ctr. Advanced Studies, U. Va., 1971-72; mem. adv. bd. on law of sea State Dept., 1977-80, mem. adv. bd. on internat. law, 1982; chmn. bd. dirs. U.S. Inst. Peace, 1986-89, 89-91; chmn. oceans policy com. Rep. Nat. Com.; mem. Consortium on Intelligence. Recipient Alumni award in arts Drew U., 1976; Compass Disting. Achievement award for significant contbns. to art and sci. of oceanography and marine tech., 1994; NIH fellow Yale U., 1965-66. Mem. ABA (past vice-chmn. sect. internat. law and past 5-term chmn. com. on law and nat. security), Am. Law Inst., Am. Oceanic Orgn. (exec. coun.), Marine Tech. Soc. (exec. coun.), Coun. Fgn. Rels., Order of Coif, Cosmos Club, N.Y. Yacht Club, Freedom House (bd. dirs.), Phi Beta Kappa. Republican. Episcopalian. Home: 824 Flordon Dr Charlottesville VA 22901-7810 Office: U Va Sch Law North Grounds Charlottesville VA 22901 *Life offers opportunity to pursue many worthwhile interests. In selecting among them it has seemed most useful to focus on those issues of sufficiently broad general significance as to justify the efforts of a lifetime. For me that has meant focus on enhancing the role of law, improving the functioning of government, controlling and reducing international conflict, and the policy choices of the ocean frontier.*

MOORE, JOHN RONALD, manufacturing executive; b. Pueblo, Colo., July 12, 1935; s. John E. and Anna (Yesberger) M.; m. Judith Russelyn Bauman, Sept. 5, 1959; children: Leland, Roni, Timothy, Elaine. BS, U. Colo., 1959; grad. advanced mgmt. program, Harvard Grad. Sch. Bus., 1981. Mgmt. trainee Montgomery Ward & Co., Denver, 1960-65; distbn. mgr. Midas Internat. Corp., Chgo., 1965-71; v.p., gen. mgr. Midas, Can., Toronto, Ont., 1972-75; pres. Auto Group Midas Internat. Corp., Chgo., 1976-82, pres., chief exec. officer, 1982—, also bd. dirs.; bd. dirs. Midas Australia Pty. Ltd., Melbourne. Served with U.S. Army, 1953-55. Mem. Ill. Mfr.'s Assn., Motor Equipment Mfrs. Assn. (pres.'s council 1982—), Internat. Franchising Assn., Econ. Club of Chgo., Comml. Club Chgo., Harvard Bus. Sch. Alumni Assn., U. Colo. Alumni Assn. Republican. Office: Midas Internat Corp 225 N Michigan Ave Chicago IL 60601-7601 *There is very little we accomplish in our lifetime that results from effort we alone expend. All of us should have the wisdom to express our appreciation to our families and associates who have helped us attain our goals and accomplishments—for failure to do so tarnishes our successes and breeds selfishness.*

MOORE, JOHN RUNYAN, agricultural and resource economics educator; b. Columbus, Ohio, Sept. 30, 1929; s. Lawrence Levi and Hazel Marie (Runyan) M.; m. Marjorie Ann Coy, June 14, 1953; children: Lee, Andrew. BSc in Agriculture, Ohio State U., 1951; MSc in Agrl. Econs., Cornell U., 1955; PhD in Agrl. Econs., U. Wis., Madison, 1959. County 4-H Club agt. Ohio Coop. Extension Svc., Stuebenville, 1951; grad. rsch. asst. Cornell U., Ithaca, N.Y., 1953-55, U. Wis., Madison, 1955-58; asst. prof. Mich. State U., East Lansing, 1958-62; mktg. specialist, econ. cons. Ford Found., New Delhi, 1968-70; assoc. prof. U. Md., College Park, 1962-68, prof. in world food situation and food mktg., 1968-95, prof. emeritus, 1995—; econ. cons. FTC, Washington, 1963-64, World Bank, India and Nigeria, 1971-74, U.S. AID, Indonesia, Malawi, Haiti, Liberia and Egypt, various dates, FAO, Beijing, 1990. Co-author: (book) Market Structure of Agriculture Industries, 1964, U.S. Investment In Latin American Food Processing, 1966, Indian Food Grain Market, 1972. Trustee S.E. Consortium for Internat. Devel., 1978-95. Lt. (j.g.) USNR, 1951-53. Recipient Internat. Honor award USDA, Washington, 1985, Cert. of Appreciation, 1986. Mem. Am. Agrl. Econ. Assn. (Thesis award 1960), Am. Econ. Assn., Internat. Agrl. Econ. Assn., Trees for the Future (trustee), Rotary. Avocations: photography, travel, gardening, golf.

MOORE, JOHN STERLING, JR., minister; b. Memphis, Aug. 25, 1918; s. John Sterling and Lorena (Bounds) M.; m. Martha Louise Paulette, July 6, 1944; children: Sterling Hale, John Marshall, Carolyn Paulette. Student, Auburn U., 1936-37; AB, Samford U., 1940; ThM, So. Bapt. Theol. Sem., 1944. Ordained to ministry So. Bapt. Conv., 1942. Pastor chs. Pamplin, Va., 1944-48, Amherst, Va., 1949-57; pastor Manly Meml. Bapt. Ch., Lexington, Va., 1957-84, pastor emeritus, 1984—; mem. Hist. Commn., So. Bapt. Conv., 1968-75; pres. Va. Bapt. Pastor's Conf., 1963. Author: History of Broad Run Baptist Church, 1762-1987, 1987; co-author: Meaningful Moments in Virginia Baptist Life, 1715-1972, 1973; editor Va. Bapt. Register, 1972—; contbr. articles to profl. jours. Chmn. Lexington Mayor's Com. on Race Rels., 1962-65; bd. dirs. Stonewall Jackson Hosp., 1967-72, pres., 1969-71; treas. Rockbridge Mental Health Clinic, 1971-84. Recipient Disting. Svc. award Hist. Commn., So. Bapt. Conv., 1988. Mem. Am. Soc. Ch. History, So. Bapt. Hist. Soc. (bd. dirs. 1972-91, pres. 1975-76, sec. 1977-85), Va. Bapt. Hist. Soc. (exec. com. 1963—, pres. 1984-85), Va. Hist. Soc., Masons. Home: 8709 Gayton Rd Richmond VA 23229-6331

MOORE, JOHN TRAVERS, poet, author; b. Wellston, Ohio, Aug. 24, 1908; s. Thomas Emmet and Mary (Tripp) M.; m. Margaret Rumberger, June 16, 1928. LL.B., U. Dayton, 1933, JD, 1985. Bar: Ohio 1933. Gen. practice Dayton, 1933-38; editor several youth and juvenile publs., 1938-42; mng. editor Plane Facts, USAAF publ., 1943-45. Author: A Child's Book of Psalms, 1946; (poetry) Near Centerville, 1950; Cincinnati Parks, 1953, Modern Crusaders, 1955, Poems, 1955; (poetry) God's Wonderful World, 1964, My Prayer, 1964; The Story of Silent Night, 1965; (poetry) When you Walk Out in Spring, 1965, Cinnamon Seed, 1967; Town and Countryside Poems, 1968; (poetry) There's Motion Everywhere, 1970; Poems: On Writing Poetry, 1971; (poetry) We Are Like Wine, 1972, All Along the Way, 1973, The First Moon Landing, 1979, Sappho's Poetry, 1979, Pepito's Journey, 1987, Ednl. Poster Poetry series, 1987, Pepito's World, 1988; (with Mrs. Moore) Sing-Along Sary, 1951, Little Saints, 1953, Big Saints, 1954, The Three Tripps, 1959, On Cherry Tree Hill, 1960; The Little Band and the Inaugural Parade, 1969; (poetry) Certainly, Carrie, Cut the Cake, 1971; Pepito's Speech at the United Nations, 1971, repub., 1985; televised trilogy Pepito's Speech, 1991; contbr. to numerous periodicals, anthologies. Recipient Golden Balloon award from child dels. to UN from 150 countries. Address: 104 1st Ave E Hendersonville NC 28792-5096 *Extended love and devotion is the greatest gift to mankind and I have enjoyed such for over a half century. In morality is strength to allow one to walk out head up without fear into the unknown. My career is dedicated to producing the constructive rather than the static or destructive in an art. Only man can leave a record on the earth and I realize that the continuous revival of my writings attests to my striving, as will my literary papers. I heartily subscribe to the joy of life.*

MOORE, JOHN W., academic administrator. Pres. Ind. State U., Terre Haute. Office: Indiana State U Office of President Terre Haute IN 47809

MOORE, JOHN W., lawyer; b. Atlanta, Apr. 26, 1947; s. John Wilbur Moore and Marjory ELizabeth (Davis) Johnston; m. Phyllis Arue Norris, Jan. 16, 1982; 1 child, Ashley Alillian. BA, Emory U., 1968, JD, 1974. Bar: Ga. 1974. Assoc. Troutman Sanders, Lockerman & Ashmore, Atlanta, 1974-79; ptnr. Troutman Sanders, Atlanta, 1982—; assoc. counsel Cousins Properties Inc., Atlanta, 1980-81. Bd. dirs. Am. Cancer Soc., Atlanta, 1984. With U.S. Army, 1969-71, Vietnam. Mem. State Bar Ga., Atlanta Bar Assn., Phi Beta Kappa. Republican. Presbyterian. Avocations: hiking, fishing, bicycling, golf. Office: Troutman Sanders 600 Peachtree St Ste 5200 Atlanta GA 30308-2216

MOORE, JOHN WARD, chemistry educator; b. Lancaster, Pa., July 17, 1939; s. Joseph D. and Lillian B. M.; m. Elizabeth Augustin, Aug. 26, 1961. AB, Franklin & Marshall Coll., 1961; PhD, Northwestern U., 1965. Asst. prof. Ind. U., Bloomington, 1965-71; assoc. prof. Eastern Mich. U., Ypsilanti, 1971-76, prof., 1976-89; prof. U. Wis., Madison, 1989—; cos. Ecology Ctr. of Ann Arbor, 1979-81; vis. prof. U. Wis., Madison, 1981-82; vis. assoc. prof. U. Nice, France, 1987—; dir. Project SERAPHIM, 1982—, Inst. for Chem. Edn., 1989—. Editor Jour. Chem. Edn.: Software, 1988—, Jour. Chem. Edn., 1996—; contbr. articles to profl. jours. Recipient Disting. Faculty award for rsch., publ. and svc. Ea. Mich. U., 1977, sci. faculty profl. devel. award NSF, 1979, Disting. Faculty award Mich. Assn. Governing Bds., 1982, Catalyst award Chem. Mfg. Assn., 1982, silver medal CASE Prof. Yr., 1986, George C. Pimentel award in chem. edn. Am. Chem. Soc., 1991, James Flack Norris award in chem. edn., 1991, Upjohn award for excellence in tchg., 1993, Underkofler award for excellence in tchg. Wis. Power & Light Co., 1995. Home: 3995 Shawn Trl Middleton WI 53562-3521 Office: U Wis Dept Chemistry Dept Chemistry 1101 University Ave Madison WI 53706-1396

MOORE, JOHN WILLIAM, university president; b. Bayonne, N.J., Aug. 1, 1939; s. Frederick A. and Marian R. (Faser) M.; m. Nancy Baumann, Aug. 10, 1968; children: Matthew, Sarah, David. BS in Social Sci. and Edn., Rutgers U., 1961; MS in Counseling and Student Pers. Svcs., Ind. U., 1963; EdD, Pa. State U., College Station, 1970. Asst. to dean Coll. Edn. Pa. State U., University Park, 1968-70; asst. to dean students U. Vt., Burlington, 1970-71, asst. prof. edn. adminstrn., 1973-76, asst. v.p. acad. affairs, 1973-76, assoc. v.p. acad. affairs, 1976-77; v.p. policy and planning Old Dominion U., Norfolk, Va., 1977-78, exec. v.p., 1982-85; pres. Calif. State U., Stanislaus, Turlock, 1985-92, Ind. State U., 1992—. Author: (with others) The Changing Composition of the Work Force: Implications for Future Research and Its Application, 1982, also articles, papers presented at profl. meetings. Pres. United Way, Modesto Calif., 1989; campaign chair United Way Wabash Valley, Terre Haute, Ind.; bd. dirs. Pvt. Industry Coun., Modesto, 1989, Union Hosp., Swope Mus., Am. Assn. Colls. and Univs.; bd. dirs., exec. com. Alliance for Growth and Progress, Terre Haute, Ind., 1992—, Terre Haute C. of C., Wabash Valley United Way, Bus. and Modernization Tech. Corp., Ind. Econ. Devel. Commn., PSI Energy. Recipient Disting. Svc. award Old Dominion U. Alumni Assn., 1985, Hispanic C. of C., 1982; recipient Community Svc. award Norfolk Commn. Edn., 1985, Leadership award United Way,1 986, Svc. award Pvt. Industry Coun., 1989; Alumni fellow Pa. State U., 1990. Mem. Am. Assn. State Colls. and Univs. (rep. Calif. chpt. 1988-92, bd. dirs. 1994—), Gould Med. Found. (bd. dirs. 1988-92, trustee 1988-92), Modesto Symphony Orch. Assn. (bd. dirs. 1990-92), Am. Coun. Edn., Commn. on Women in Higher Edn., Turlock C. of C. (bd. dirs. 1988-92), Rotary. Methodist. Avocations: fitness training, skiing, coaching youth sports. Office: Ind State U Condit House Terre Haute IN 47809

MOORE, JOHN WILSON, neurophysiologist, educator; b. Winston-Salem, N.C., Nov. 1, 1920; s. John Watson and Marjorie (MacAlpine) M.; m. Natalie Bayless, May 6, 1944 (div. 1977); children: John Reid, Marjorie Lee, Stephen Wilson; m. Ann E. Stuart, Apr. 2, 1978; 1 son, Jonathan Watson Stuart-Moore. B.S. in Physics, Davidson (N.C.) Coll., 1941; M.S., U. Va., 1942, Ph.D. in Physics, 1945. Asst. prof. physics Med. Coll. Va., 1946-50; biophysicist Naval Med. Research Inst., 1950-54, Lab. of Biophysics, Nat. Inst. Nervous Diseases and Blindness, NIH, 1954-61; mem. faculty Duke U., 1961—, prof. physiology and pharmacology, 1965-88, prof. neurobiology, 1988—; vis. prof. dept. neurobiology Harvard U. Med. Sch., 1978-79. Trustee, mem. exec. com. Marine Biol. Lab., Woods Hole, Mass. DuPont fellow, 1941-46; Nat. Neurol. Research Found. scientist, 1961-66. Mem. IEEE, AAAS, Am. Physiol. Soc., Biophys. Soc. (coun., Cole award 1981), Soc. Neurosci., Marine Biol. Lab. Corp., Soc. Gen. Physiologists, Phi Beta Kappa, Omicron Delta Kappa. Office: Duke Univ Dept Neurobiology PO Box 3209 Duke Univ Med Ctr Durham NC 27710-0001

MOORE, JULIA ALICE, federal government executive; b. Jersey City, N.J., Sept. 10, 1950; d. John Richard and Jean (Alexander) M.; m. Harry C. Blaney III, Feb. 14, 1976. BS in Fgn. Svc., Georgetown U., Washington, 1972. Analyst Washington Analysis Corp., Washington, 1972-73; assoc. dir. Joseph S. White & Assoc., Washington, 1973-75; dep. dir. Arms Control Assn., Washington, 1982-84; legis. & pub. affairs officer U.S. Dept. of State, Washington, 1975-86; v.p. communications World Wildlife Fund, Washington, 1986-90; sr. assoc. Ogilvy & Mather Pub. Affairs, Washington, 1990-91; exec. dir. Physicians for Social Responsibility, Washington, 1991-94; dir. legis. and pub. affairs NSF, Arlington, Va., 1994—. Author: OP-EDS. Mem. Coun. on Fgn. Rels. Named Rusk Fellow, Georgetown U., 1985. Mem. Nat. Press Club, Internat. Inst. for Strategic Studies, Arms Control Assn. Roman Catholic. Home: 4700 Connecticut Ave NW 601 Washington DC 20008-5629 Office: NSF 4201 Wilson Blvd Arlington VA 22230

MOORE, JULIANNE, actress. BA, Boston Univ. With The Guthrie Theater, 1988-89. Actress: (theatre) Serious Money, 1987, Bone-the-Fish, 1988, Ice Cream with Hot Fudge, 1990, Uncle Vanya, (TV soap operas) As the World Turns (Emmy award outstanding ingenue in daytime drama series 1988), The Edge of Night, (TV movies) Money, Power, Murder, 1989, Lovecraft, 1991, (feature films) The Hand That Rocks the Cradle, 1992, The Gun in Betty Lou's Handbag, 1992, Body of Evidence, 1993, Benny & Joon, 1993, The Fugitive, 1993, Short Cuts, 1993, Vanya on 42nd Street, 1994, Roommates, 1995, Nine Months, 1995, Safe, 1995, Assassins, 1995. Office: CAA 9830 Wilshire Blvd Beverly Hills CA 90212

MOORE, KAREN NELSON, judge; b. Washington, Nov. 19, 1948; d. Roger S. and Myrtle (Gill) Nelson; m. Kenneth Cameron Moore, June 22, 1974; children—Roger C., Kenneth N., Kristin K. A.B. magna cum laude, Radcliffe Coll., 1970, J.D. magna cum laude, Harvard U., 1973. Bar: D.C. 1973, Ohio, 1976, U.S. Ct. Appeals (D.C. cir.) 1974, U.S. Supreme Ct. 1980, U.S. Ct. Appeals (6th cir.) 1984. Law clk. Judge Malcolm Wilkey, U.S. Ct. Appeals (D.C. cir.), 1973-74; law clk. Assoc. Justice Harry A. Blackmun, U.S. Supreme Ct., Washington, 1974-75; assoc. Jones, Day, Reavis & Pogue, Cleve., 1975-77; asst. prof. Case Western Res. Law Sch., Cleve., 1977-80, assoc. prof., 1980-82, prof., 1982-95; judge U.S. Ct. Appeals (6th cir.), Cleve., 1995—; vis. prof. Harvard Law Sch., 1990-91. Mem. Harvard Law Rev., 1971-73. Contbr. articles to legal publs. Trustee Lakewood Hosp., Ohio, 1978-85, Radcliffe Coll., Cambridge, 1980-84. Fellow Am. Bar Found.; mem. Cleve. Bar Assn. (trustee 1979-82), ABA (standing com. jud. selection, tenure and compensation 1978-82), Am. Law Inst., Am. Assn. Law Schs. (chmn. civil procedure sect. 1985, academic freedom and tenure com. 1985-89, chmn. 1987-89), Harvard Alumni Assn. (bd. dirs. 1984-87), Phi Beta Kappa. Office: US Ct Appeals 6th Cir 256 US Courthouse 201 Superior Ave Cleveland OH 44114

MOORE, KATHLEEN, dancer; b. Chgo.. Student with Sonia Arova, Thor Sutowski, Ala. Sch. Fine Arts; student, Sch. Am. Ballet, Am. Ballet Theatre Sch. Joined ABT II, 1980; mem. corps de ballet Am. Ballet Theatre, N.Y.C., 1982-88, soloist, 1988-91, prin. dancer, 1991—. Repertoire includes Dark Elegies, Don Quixote (Kitri's Wedding), Fall River Legend, Fancy Free, Giselle, Rodeo, Romeo and Juliet, The Leaves Are Fading, Nine Sinatra Songs, Everlast, Enough Said, Gaite Parisienne, The Rite of Spring, Pillare of Fire, The Informer, Brief Fling, Duets, Sinfonietta, Sunset, Les Liasons Dangereuses, Manon, Undertow, others; created roles in Agnes de Mille's The Informer, Mark Morris' Drink to Me Only With Thine Eyes. Office: Am Ballet Theatre 890 Broadway New York NY 10003-1211

MOORE, KATHRYN MCDANIEL, education educator; d. Lawrence W. and Doris K. McDaniel; m. Dan Emery Moore, Aug. 20, 1966; children: Todd Lawrence, Jason Emery. BA and BS, Ohio State U., 1965, MA, 1966; PhD, U. Wis., 1972. Project asst. office of dean of students U. Wis., Madison, 1966-68, asst. to assoc. dean Coll. Letters and Sci., 1970-71; asst. prof., assoc. prof. edn. dept. Cornell U., 1971-77; assoc. prof. ctr. study of hogher edn. Pa. State U., 1977-84, prof., sr. rsch. assoc. ctr. study of higher edn., 1984-86, dir., prof. ctr. study of higher edn., 1986-88; prof. edn. policy and leadership dept. ednl. adminstrn. Mich. State U. Coll. Edn., East Lansing, 1988—, chmn., 1991—; speaker and reviewer in field. Mem. editl. bd. Rev. Higher Edn., 1991-94, Innovative Higher Edn., 1991—, Am. Ednl. Rsch. Jour., 1989-92, Jour. Higher Edn., 1995—; mem. adv. bd. Higher Edn. Abstracts, 1984—; contbr. to monographs, books and articles to profl. jours. Grantee in field; recipient Disting. Alumni award Ohio State U., 1987. Mem. Am. Ednl. Rsch. Assn., (various coms.), Am. Assn. Higher Edn., Nat. Ctr. Edn. Stastics (nat. adv. bd. 1977-81, other coms.), Assn. for Study of Higher Edn. (pres. 1983, various coms.), History of Edn. Soc. (nominations com., bd. dirs. 1981-83, Henry Barnard prize com. 1977-85, chair 1980-81), Ohio State Alumni Assn. (bd. dirs. 1990-95, chair 1995—), Ohio State U. Commn. on Women (alumni rep. 1991-92), Golden Key Soc. (hon. mem.), Phi Beta Kappa, Phi Kappa Phi. Office: Mich State U Ednl Adminstrn 418 Erickson Hall East Lansing MI 48824

MOORE, KENNETH CAMERON, lawyer; b. Chgo., Oct. 25, 1947; s. Kenneth Edwards and Margaret Elizabeth (Cameron) M.; m. Karen M. Nelson, June 22, 1974; children: Roger Cameron, Kenneth Nelson, Kristin Karen. BA summa cum laude, Hiram Coll., 1969; JD cum laude, Harvard U., 1973. Bar: Ohio 1973, U.S. Dist. Ct. Md. 1974, U.S. Ct. Appeals (4th cir.) 1974, D.C. 1975, U.S. Dist. Ct. (no. dist.) Ohio 1976, U.S. Ct. Appeals (6th cir.) 1977, U.S. Ct. Appeals (D.C. cir.) 1979, U.S. Supreme Ct. 1980. Law clk. to judge Harrison L. Winter, U.S. Ct. Appeals, 4th Cir., Balt., 1973-74; assoc. Squire, Sanders & Dempsey, Washington, 1974-75, Cleve., 1975-82, ptnr., 1982—, mem. fin. com., 1990—. Chmn. Ohio Fin. Com. for Jimmy Carter presdl. campaign, 1976; del. Dem. Nat. Conv., 1976; chief legal counsel Ohio Carter-Mondale Campaign, 1976; mem. Cleve. com., Cleve. Coun. World Affairs; mem. bd. advisors The Environ. Counselor; dir. environ. law Environ. Resource Inst. Served with AUS, 1970-76. Mem. ABA, Fed. Bar Assn., Ohio Bar Assn., Greater Cleve. Bar Assn., Cleve. City Club. Home: 15602 Edgewater Dr Cleveland OH 44107-1212 Office: Squire Sanders & Dempsey 4900 Society Ctr 127 Public Sq Cleveland OH 44114-1216

MOORE, KENNETH EDWIN, pharmacology educator; b. Edmonton, Alta., Can., Aug. 8, 1933; came to U.S., 1957, naturalized, 1966; s. Jack and Emily Elizabeth (Tarbox) M.; m. Barbara Anne Stafford, Sept. 19, 1953; children—Grant Kenneth, Sandra Anne, Lynn Susan. B.S., U. Alta., 1955, M.S., 1957; Ph.D., U. Mich., 1960. Instr. pharmacology Dartmouth Med. Sch., Hanover, N.H., 1960-61; asst. prof. Dartmouth Med. Sch., 1962-66; assoc. prof. pharmacology Mich. State U., East Lansing, 1966-70; prof. Mich. State U., 1970—, chmn. dept. pharmacology and toxicology, 1987—; vis. scholar Cambridge (Eng.) U., 1974; instr. Lansing Community Coll., 1975-81; cons. NIH, also pharm. industry. Author 1 book; contbr. articles to profl. jours. Fellow Am. Coll. Neuropsychopharmacology; mem. Am. Soc. Pharmacology and Exptl. Therapeutics (chmn. bd. publs. trustees 1992-96), Soc. Exptl. Biology and Medicine, Soc. Neurosci. Home: 4790 Arapaho Trl Okemos MI 48864-1402 Office: Dept Pharmacology Mich State U East Lansing MI 48824

MOORE, KENNETH GARRISON, federal agency administrator; b. Balt., June 19, 1947; s. George Donald and Alice Elizabeth (Colquitt) M.; m. Annette Louise Thomas, 1965 (div. Aug. 1972); children: Kenneth G. II, Harvey Andrew; m. Beverly Anne McGuyer, Sept. 29, 1973; children: Lori Dawn, Kari Elizabeth. Diploma, Furman U., 1965. With Office Sec. Def., Washington, 1973-74, Fed. Energy Adminstrn., Washington, 1974-76; with Dept. Energy, Washington, 1976-90, dir. planning and assessment, 1991; sr. faculty Fed. Exec. Inst., Charlottesville, Va. Chief petty officer USN, 1965-72; reservist Pentagon, Washington, 1972-91. Mem. Wendel Farques F &

AM & Sons. Baptist. Home: Dept of Energy Energy Efficiency & Renew Energy 10212 Aspen Willow Dr Fairfax VA 22032

MOORE, KENNETH JAMES, agronomy educator; b. Phoenix, June 6, 1957; s. George Taylor and Barbara Joyce (Amy) M.; m. Gina Marie McCarthy Aug. 11, 1979; children: Ellyn Elizabeth, David Taylor, Mark Daniel. BS in Agr., Ariz. State U., 1979; MS in Agronomy, Purdue U., 1981, PhD in Agronomy, 1983. Asst. prof. agronomy U. Ill., Urbana, 1983-87; assoc. prof. N.Mex. State U., Las Cruces, 1988-89; rsch. agronomist Agrl. Rsch. Svc., USDA, Lincoln, Nebr., 1989-93; prof. Iowa State U., Ames, 1993—; adj. assoc. prof. U. Nebr. Lincoln, 1989-93, prof., 1993—. Author: Crop Science Laboratory Manual, 1988; assoc. editor Agronomy Jour., 1989-93, tech. editor, 1994—; assoc. editor Crop Sci., 1994; contbr. chpts. to books. Bd. dirs. Lincoln Children's Mus., 1991-93; mem. mgmt. com. N.E. YMCA, Lincoln, 1991-93; mem. youth policy forum Lincoln YMCA, 1991-92. Recipient Point of Light award USDA, 1991. Fellow Am. Soc. Agronomy; mem. Crop Sci. Soc. Am. (divsn. chmn. 1990-92, Young Crop Scientist award 1993), Am. Forage and Grassland Coun. (Outstanding Young Scientist award 1982, merit award 1991), Am. Soc. Animal Sci., Am. Dairy Sci. Assn. Republican. Presbyterian. Avocations: swimming, fishing, music. Office: Iowa State U Agronomy Dept 1567 Agronomy Hall Ames IA 50011

MOORE, KEVIN JOHN, lawyer; b. N.Y.C., Aug. 13, 1956; s. John Seymour and Maxine (Brown) M.; m. Mary Alice Fitzpatrick, May 18, 1985. BA, Drew U., 1978; JD, NYU, 1981. Bar: N.J. 1981, U.S. Dist. Ct. N.J. 1981. Assoc. Jamieson, Moore, Peskin & Spicer, Princeton, N.J., 1981-86, ptnr., 1986—; teaching asst. polit. sci. dept. Drew U., Madison, N.J., 1974-78; mem. NYU Rev. of Law and Social, 1979-80. Contbr. articles to profl. law revs. Participant Fenwick for Senate Campaign, Princeton, 1981; mem., sec. Delaware Valley Regional Coun. of Hyacinth AIDS Found. Trustee scholar Drew U., Madison, 1974-78. Mem. ABA, N.J. Bar Assn. (hard use, real property, trust and probate sects.), Princeton Bar Assn. (pres. 1991-92). Avocations: reading, theatre, art. Home: 8 Hillside Ct Lambertville NJ 08530 Office: Jamieson Moore Peskin & Spicer 300 Alexander Park Princeton NJ 08543-5276

MOORE, KEVIN MICHAEL, federal judge; b. 1951. BA, Fla. State U.; JD, Fordham U. Bar: Fla. 1976. U.S. atty. no. dist. State of Fla., Tallahassee, 1987-89; dir. U.S. Marshals Svc., Arlington, Va., 1989-92; judge US. Dist. Ct. So. Dist. Fla., Miami, 1992—. Office: US Dist Ct Federal Justice Bldg 99 NE 4th St Rm 1168 Miami FL 33132-2139

MOORE, LARRY GLENN, school system administrator; b. Indpls., July 27, 1950; s. William R. and E. LaVon (Slinker) Birge; m. Doris J. Vaught; children: Ronin G., Clayton R., Jacob Y. BA, Hanover (Ind.) Coll., 1972; MA, Ball State U., 1976; EdS, Ind. U., 1979; EdD, U. Sarasota, 1996. Cert. secondary tchr. and administr., Ind. Tchr. math. Madison (Ind.) Consolidated Schs., 1972-79; asst. prin. Southwestern Schs., Hanover, Ind., 1979-81; prin. Trimble County High Sch., Bedford, Ky., 1981-83, Crothersville (Ind.) Jr.-Sr. High Sch., 1984-86, South Spencer (Ind.) H.S., 1986-90; supt. Cannelton (Ind.) City Schs., 1993—. Edn. chmn. Perry County Substance Abuse Com., Tell City, 1994—; bd. dirs. Perry County Health Dept., 1994—; mem. cmty. ctr. facility com. City of Cannelton, Ind., 1994—. With USMC, 1969-72. Mem. Ind. Assn. Pub. Sch. Supts., Ind. High Sch. Athletic Assn., Nat. Assn. Secondary Sch. Prins., Nat. Fedn. Interscholastic Officals Assn., North Ctrl. Assn. vis. com. chmn.), Am. Legion, Kiwanis (treas. Cannelton club 1993—), Mensa, Phi Delta Kappa. Avocations: travling, racquetball, reading. Office: Cannelton City Schs 109 S 3rd St Cannelton IN 47520-1504

MOORE, LAURENCE JOHN, business educator; b. Greeley, Colo., May 7, 1938; s. John Harold and Ruth Anderson M.; m. Nancy Kay Hibbert, Aug. 31, 1963; children: Rebecca Ann, John Andrew, Stefani Ruth. BA in Econs., Monmouth Coll., Ill., 1962; MS in Econs., Ariz. State U., 1965, DBA in Mgmt. Sci., 1970. Dist. mktg. rep. Standard Oil Co. (Ind.), Chgo., 1962-63; sr. analyst long range and capital planning, 1964-66; head quantitative studies Continental Ill. Bank, Chgo., 1966-67; mem. faculty dept. mgmt. sci. Coll. Bus. Va. Poly. Inst. and State U., Blacksburg, 1970—; prof. Coll. Bus. Va. Poly. Inst. and State U., 1977-85, C&P Disting. prof. bus., 1985—, head dept. Coll. Bus., 1976-83, dir. univ. fin. planning and analysis, 1983-84; dir. univ. planning Va. Poly. Inst. and State U., Blacksburg, 1988-89; cons. in field. Author: (with S.M. Lee, B.W. Taylor) Management Science, 1981, 4th edit., 1993, (with S.M. Lee) Introduction to Decision Sciences, 1975, (with E.R. Clayton) GERT Modeling and Simulation: Fundamentals and Applications, 1976. Served with U.S. Army, 1957-59. Recipient Disting. Service award SE region Am. Inst. Decision Scis., 1977. Fellow Am. Inst. Decision Scis. (pres. 1983-84, Disting. Svc. awrd 1986); mem. Inst. Mgmt. Sci. (Disting. Svc. award SE region), Inst. for Ops. Rsch. and Mgmt. Sci., Inst. Indsl. Engrs., Alpha Iota Delta, Beta Gamma Sigma, Omicron Delta Epsilon, Sigma Iota Epsilon. Presbyterian. Home: PO Box 11134 Blacksburg VA 24062-1134 Office: Va Poly Inst and State U Dept Mgmt Sci 1007 Pamplin Hall Blacksburg VA 24061-5102

MOORE, LAWRENCE JACK, lawyer; b. Brownwood, Tex., Jan. 24, 1926; s. Lawrence Houston and Lena Emily (Grantham) M.; m. Eloise Camille Dickinson, May 24, 1947; children: John L., James D., Jane E. Moore Horner. Student Howard Payne U., 1946-47, Tarleton State U., 1942-43; LLB, U. Tex., 1949. Bar: Tex. 1949, N.Y. 1980. Pvt. practice, 1949-57; city atty., Ballinger, Tex., 1950, 55-57; county atty. Runnels County, Tex., 1951-54; atty. Texaco Inc., 1957-70, assoc. gen. counsel, 1970-79; v.p., gen. counsel Caltex Petroleum Corp., Dallas, 1979-89; mem. Johnson & Gibbs, P.C., Dallas, Houston, Austin, Tex., Washington, 1989-91; pvt. practice, 1992—; adv. bd. Internat. and Comparative Law Ctr., Internat. Oil and Gas Ctr. of Southwestern Legal Found.; mem. devel. bd., U. Tex., Dallas, 1986-91; dir. Nat. Fgn. Trade Coun., N.Y., 1985-93. Served to cpl. AUS, 1944-46. Mem. ABA, State Bar Tex., University Club (N.Y.C.), Country Club of Darien (Conn.), Petroleum Club (Dallas), Horseshoe Bay Country Club, Barton Creek Country Club (Lakeside), Masons. Republican. Methodist. Office: PO Box 8510 Horseshoe Bay TX 78654-9210

MOORE, LINDA KATHLEEN, personnel agency executive; b. San Antonio, Tex., Feb. 18, 1944; d. Frank Edward and Louise Marie (Powell) Horton; m. Mack B. Taplin, May 25, 1963 (div. Feb. 1967); 1 child, Mack B.; m. William J. Moore, Mar. 8, 1967 (div. Nov. 1973). Student, Tex. A&I Coll., 1962-63. Co-owner S.R.O. Internat., Dallas, 1967-70; mgr. Exec. Girls Pers. & Modeling Svcs., Dallas, 1970-72, Gen. Employment Enterprises, Atlanta, 1972-88; owner, mgr. More Pers. Svcs., Inc., Atlanta, 1988-94, pres., chmn. bd., 1994—; Contbr. short story to Writer's Digest. Mem. NAFE, Nat. Fedn. Bus. and Profl. Women, Am. Soc. Profl. and Exec. Women, Women Bus. Owners, Nat. Assn. Women Cons., Nat. Assn. Personnel Svcs., Ga. Assn. Personnel Svcs., Women's Clubs, C. of C. (speaker's bur.), Better Bus. Bur. Office: More Pers Svcs Inc Ste A-1190 4501 Circle 75 Pkwy Atlanta GA 30339

MOORE, LOIS JEAN, health science facility administrator; married; 1 child. Grad., Prairie View (Tex.) Sch. Nursing, 1957; BS in Nursing, Tex. Woman's U., 1970; MS in Edn., Tex. So. U., 1974. Nurse Harris County (Tex.) Hosp. Dist., 1957—; pres., chief exec. officer Harris County Hosp.; adminstr. Jefferson Davis Hosp., Houston, 1977-88, exec. v.p., chief ops. officer, 1988—; Mem. adv. bd. Tex. Pub. Hosp. Assn. Contbr. articles to profl. jours. Mem. Mental Health Needs Council Houston and Harris County, Congressman Mickey Leland's Infant Mortality Task Force, Houston Crack-down Com., Gov.'s task force on health care policy, 1991; chairperson Tex. Assn. Pub. and Nonprofit Hosps., 1991, subcom. of Gov.'s task force to identify essential health care svc., 1992; bd. dirs. ARC, 1991—, Greater Houston Hosp. Coun., March of Dimes, United Way. Recipient Pacesetter award North-East C. of C., 1991; named Nurse of Yr. Houston Area League Nursing, 1976-77, Outstanding Black Achiever YMCA Century Club, 1974, Outstanding Women in Medicine YWCA, 1989. Mem. Am. Coll. Hosp. Adminstrs., Tex. Hosp. Assn. (chmn. pub. hosp. com.), Young Hosp. Adminstrs., Nat. Assn. Pub. Hosps. (bd. dirs., mem. exec. com. Tex. assn.), License Vocat. Nurses Assn., sigma Theta Tau. Home: 3837 Wichita St Houston TX 77004-6536 Office: Harris County Hosp Dist PO Box 66769 Houston TX 77266-6769

MOORE, MALCOLM ANDREW STEPHEN, cancer researcher; b. Edinburgh, Scotland, Jan. 18, 1944; came to U.S., 1974; m. Francine Zuckerman, May 30, 1989; children: Julian Alexander Stephen, Andrew Stephen. MB, U. Oxford, 1963, BA in Human Physiology 1st class honors, 1964, DPhil, 1967, MA, 1970. Prize fellow Magdalen Coll. U. Oxford, 1965-70; head lab. devel. biology Walter and Eliza Hall Inst. Med. Rsch., 1970-74; prof. biology Cornell U. Grad. Sch. Med. Sci., 1974—, head James Ewing Lab. Devel. Hematopoiesis, 1974—, Enid A Haupt chair cell biology, 1989—; attending biologist div. med. oncology Meml. Sloan-Kettering Cancer Ctr., 1987—. Contbr. over 350 articles to profl. jours. Mem. sci. adv. bd. Cancer Rsch. Inst., 1988, N.Y. Blood Ctr., 1989. Co-recipient Armand Hammer Cancer prize, 1987, William B. Coley award for disting. rsch. in immunology Cancer Rsch. Inst., 1995; recipient David Syme prize U. Melbourne, 1973, numerous others. Mem. Leukemia Soc. Am. (Trustee, Kenny award 1987), Am. Assn. Immunologists, Am. Assn. Cancer Rsch. (Rhoads Meml. award 1980), Am. Soc. Hematology (Henry Stratton lectr. 1990), Leukocyte Biol. Soc., Harvey Soc. Office: Meml Sloan-Kettering Cancer Ctr R717 1275 York Ave New York NY 10021-6007

MOORE, MALCOLM FREDERICK, manufacturing executive; b. Kankakee, Ill., Sept. 19, 1950; s. Robert Dunham and Josephine Frances (Jones) M.; m. Patricia Claudine Bennert, June 13, 1971; children: Michael Dunham, Emily Suzanne, Marjorie Nicoll. BSBA, Am. U., 1972; M of Mgmt., Northwestern U., 1982. Internat. mktg. mgr., product mgr. FMC Corp., Chgo., 1973-84, mktg. and engring. mgr., 1985-90; cons. Frank Lynn & Assoc., Chgo., 1984-85; v.p., gen. mgr. Lindberg unit of Gen. Signal, Watertown, Wis., 1990-93; pres. Abar Ipsen Industries, Inc., Bensalem, Pa., 1993-96, Centorr Vacuum Industries, Nashua, N.H., 1993-96, Linac Holdings, Inc., Rockford, Ill., 1994-96, Pangborn Corp., Hagerstown, Md., 1996—. Inventor material handling equipment. Mem. The Exec. Com. Episcopalian. Office: Pangborn Corp Pangborn Blvd Hagerstown MD 21741-0380

MOORE, MARC ANTHONY, university administrator, writer, retired military officer; b. Dallas, July 15, 1928; s. Edward Clark and Mary Cathrine (Spake) M.; m. Mary Joan Donahue, Sept. 5, 1953; children—Daniel, Mary Ellen, Virginia, Andria. B.A., So. Meth. U., 1951; M.A., George Washington U., 1970; grad., Amphibious Warfare Sch., 1960, Nat. War Coll., 1974; LHD (hon.), Philippine Women's U., 1987. Served as enlisted man U.S. Marine Corps, 1946-48, commd. 2d lt., 1951, advanced through grades to maj. gen., 1978; regtl. comdr. Camp Pendleton, Calif., 1971; regtl. exec. officer Vietnam, 1970; with Joint Chief Staff Ops., Washington, 1977-78; asst. dir. Marine Command and Staff Coll., 1972-73; dir. div. English and history U.S. Naval Acad., 1974-76; comdg. gen. 4th Marine Div., New Orleans, 1978-80; chief of staff U.S. Forces, Japan, from 1980, now ret.; former chancellor San Diego campus, v.p. for devel. Nat. U., 1990-91; teaching asst. dept. psychology George Washington U., 1974; instr. dept. behavioral sci. U.S. Naval Acad., 1975-76; adj. faculty Nat. U., 1983. Co-founder Leadership 2000; mem. coun. advisors Calif. State U., San Marcos, 1993-96; mem. bd. advisors Marine Mil. Acad., 1983-95; founder, bd. advisors Command Mus. and Warfare Leadership Ctr., Marine Recruit Depot, San Diego, 1984—. Decorated Legion of Merit, Bronze Star with oak leaf cluster, Air medal, D.S.H., Order Sacred Treasure (Japan); recipient Disting. Alumni award So. Meth. U., 1981, Superior Svc. medal, Dept. Def., Meritorious Svc. medal Dept. Def. Mem. Marine Corps Assn., Phi Delta Theta. Roman Catholic. Home: 3611 Lago Sereno Escondido CA 92029-7902

MOORE, MARGARET BEAR, American literature educator; b. Zhenjiang, China, Mar. 14, 1925; came to U.S., 1929; d. James Edwin Jr. and Margaret Irvine (White) Bear; m. Rayburn S. Moore, Aug. 30, 1947; children: Margaret Elizabeth Moore Kopcinski, Robert Rayburn. BA, Agnes Scott Coll., 1946; MA, U. Ga., 1973. Book rev. editor East Ark. Record, Helena, Ark., 1948-50; bibliographer Perkins Libr. Duke U., Durham, N.C., 1950-52; instr. in English Hendrix Coll., Conway, Ark., 1955-56, U. Ctrl. Ark., Conway, 1958-59; editor Inst. Cmty. & Area Devel. U. Ga., Athens, 1974-79; tchr. Latin Athens Acad., 1980-81; ind. scholar Athens, 1981—. Author (book revs.) Am. Lit., 1989, 94, Nathaniel Hawthorne Rev., 1992; contbr. articles to profl. jours. Tchr. Presbyn. Ch., Va., Ark., N.C. and Ga., 1945—; deacon, elder First Presbyn. Ch., Athens, 1974—. Mem. MLA, Am. Lit. Assn., Philol. Assn. Carolinas, Soc. for Study So. Lit., South Atlantic MLA, Nathaniel Hawthorne Soc. (exec. com. 1987-90), William Gilmore Simms Soc., Peabody Essex Mus., House of Seven Gables, Va. Hist. Soc., Mortar Bd., Phi Beta Kappa, Phi Kappa Phi. Avocations: reading, walking, travel. Home: 106 St James Dr Athens GA 30606-3926

MOORE, MARK HARRISON, criminal justice and public policy educator; b. Oak Park, Ill., Mar. 19, 1947; s. Charles Eugene and Jean (McFeely) M.; m. Martha Mansfield Church, June 15, 1968; children—Phoebe Sylvina, Tobias McFeely, Gaylen Williams. Student, Phillips Acad., 1962-65; B.A., Yale U., 1969; M.Public Policy, Harvard U., 1971, Ph.D., 1973. Teaching fellow, instr. public policy J.F. Kennedy Sch. Govt., Harvard U., Boston, 1971-73; asst. prof. J.F. Kennedy Sch. Govt., Harvard U., 1973-74, 75-76, assoc. prof., 1976-79, Guggenheim prof. criminal justice policy and mgmt., 1979—; spl. asst. to adminstr., chief planning officer Drug Enforcement Adminstrn., U.S. Dept. Justice, Washington, 1974-75; cons. U.S. Dept. Justice, 1975-76, 81. Author: Buy and Bust: The Effective Regulation of an Illicit Market in Heroin, 1977, Creating Public Value: Strategic Management in Government, 1995, (with others) Dangerous Offenders, 1985, From Children to Citizens: Vol. 1, The Mandate for Juvenile Justice, 1987, (with Malcolm K. Sparrow) Ethics in Government, 1990, (with Malcolm K. Sparrow and David Kennedy) Beyond 911: A New Era for Policing, 1991; editor: (with Joel Fleishman and Lance Leibman) Public Duties, 1980, (with Dean Gerstein) Alcohol and Public Policy, 1981. Mem. Assn. Schs. Public Policy and Mgmt., Phi Beta Kappa. Home: 331 Waverley St Belmont MA 02178-2418 Office: JF Kennedy Sch Govt Harvard U 79 Jfk St Cambridge MA 02138-5801

MOORE, MARY FRENCH (MUFFY MOORE), potter, community activist; b. N.Y.C., Feb. 25, 1938; d. John and Rhoda (Teagle) Walker French; m. Alan Baird Minier, Oct. 9, 1982; children: Jonathan Corbet, Jennifer Corbet, Michael Corbet. BA cum laude, Colo. U., 1964. Ceramics mfr., Wilson, Wyo., 1969-82, Cheyenne, Wyo., 1982—; commr. County of Teton (Wyo.), 1976-83, chmn. bd. commrs., 1981, 83, mem. dept. pub. assistance and social svc., 1976-82, mem. recreation bd., 1978-81, water quality adv. bd., 1976-82. Bd. dirs. Teton Sci. Sch., 1968-83, vice chmn., 1979-81, chmn., 1982; bd. dirs. Grand Teton Music Festival, 1963-68, Teton Energy Coun., 1978-83, Whitney Gallery of Western Art, Cody, Wyo., 1995—; mem. water quality adv. bd. Wyo. Dept. Environ. Quality, 1979-83; Dem. precinct committeewoman, 1978-81; mem. Wyo. Dem. Cen. Com., 1981-83; vice chmn. Laramie County Dem. Cen. Com., 1983-84, Wyo. Dem. nat. committeewoman, 1984-87; chmn. Wyo. Dem. Party, 1987-89; del. Dem. Nat. Conv., 1984, 88, mem. fairness commn. Dem. Nat. Com., 1985, vice-chairwoman western caucus, 1986-89; chmn. platform com. Wyo. Dem. Conv., 1982; mem. Wyo. Dept. Environ. Quality Land Quality Adv. Bd., 1983-86; mem. Gov.'s Steering Com. on Troubled Youth, 1982, dem. nat. com. Compliance Assistance Commn., 1986-87; exec. com. Assn. of State Dem. Chairs, 1989; mem. Wyo. Coun. on the Arts, 1989-95, chmn., 1994-95, Dem. Nat. Com. Jud. Coun., 1989—; legis. aide for Gov. Wyo., 1985, 86; project coord. Gov.'s Com. on Childrens' Svcs., 1985-86; bd. dirs. Wyo. Outdoor Coun., 1984-85; polit. dir., dep. mgr. Schuster for Congress, 1994-95. Recipient Woman of Yr. award Jackson Hole Bus. and Profl. Women, 1981, Dem. of Yr. Nellie Tayloe Ross award, Wyo. Dems., 1990. Mem. Alden Kindred of Am., Jackson Hole Art Assn. (bd. dirs., vice chmn. 1981, chmn. 1982), Assn. State Dem. Chairs, Soc. Mayflower Descendents, Pi Sigma Alpha. Home: 8907 Cowpoke Rd Cheyenne WY 82009-1234

MOORE, MARY TYLER, actress; b. Bklyn., Dec. 29, 1936; d. George and Marjorie Moore; m. Richard Meeker; 1 child, Richard (dec.); m. Grant Tinker, 1963 (div. 1981); m. Robert Levine, 1983. Chmn. bd. MTM Enterprises, Inc., Studio City, Calif. Appeared in TV series Richard Diamond, Private Eye, 1957-59, Dick Van Dyke Show, 1961-66, Mary Tyler Moore Show, 1970-77, Mary, 1978, Mary Tyler Moore Hour, 1979, Mary, 1985, Annie McGuire, 1988, miniseries Gore Vidal's Lincoln, 1988; in TV movies Love American Style, 1969, Run a Crooked Mile, 1969, First You Cry, 1978, Heartsounds, 1984, Finnegan Begin Again, 1984, The Last Best Year, 1990, Thanksgiving Day, 1990, Stolen Babies, 1993 (Emmy award, Outstanding Supporting Actress in a Miniseries or Special, 1993); films: X-15, 1961, Thoroughly Modern Millie, 1967, Don't Just Stand There, 1968, What's So Bad About Feeling Good?, 1968, Change of Habit, 1969, Ordinary People, 1980 (Acad. Award nominee for best actress 1981), Six Weeks, 1982, Just Between Friends, 1986; appeared on Broadway in Whose Life Is It Anyway?, 1980, Sweet Sue, 1987; in TV spl. How to Survive the Seventies, 1978, How To Raise a Drug Free Child. Recipient Emmy award Nat. Acad. TV Arts and Scis. 1964-65, 73-74, 76, Golden Globe award 1965, 81; named to TV Hall of Fame, 1985.

MOORE, MCPHERSON DORSETT, lawyer; b. Pine Bluff, Ark., Mar. 1, 1947; s. Arl Van and Jesse (Dorsett) M. BS, U. Miss., 1970; JD, U. Ark., 1974. Bar: Ark. 1974, Mo. 1975, U.S. Patent and Trademark Office 1977, U.S. Dist. Ct. (ea. dist.) Mo. 1977, U.S. Ct. Appeals (8th, 10th and Fed. cirs.). Design engr. Tenneco, Newport News, Va., 1970-71; assoc. Rogers, Eilers & Howell, St. Louis, 1974-80; ptnr. Rogers, Howell, Moore & Haferkamp, St. Louis, 1981-89; ptnr. Armstrong, Teasdale, Schlafly & Davis, St. Louis, 1989-95; ptnr. Polster, Lieder, Woodruff & Lucchesi, St. Louis, 1995—. Bd. dirs. Legal Services of Eastern Mo., 1984—. With USAR, 1970-76. Mem. ABA, Bar Assn. Met. St. Louis (chmn. young lawyers sect. 1981-82, sec. 1984-85, v.p. 1985-86, chmn. trial sect. 1986-87, pres. 1988-89), Ark. Bar Assn., St. Louis Bar Found. (sec. 1984-85, v.p. 1988-89, pres. 1989-90), The Mo. Bar (chmn. patent, trademark and copyright law com. 1992-94, co-chmn. 1994-95), St. Louis County Bar Assn., Women Lawyers Assn., Am. Intellectual Property Law Assn., Mound City Bar Assn., Phi Delta Theta Alumni (treas. St. Louis chpt. 1987-88, sec. 1988-89, v.p. 1989-90). Episcopalian. Club: Univ. (St. Louis). Home: 33 Deerfield Rd Saint Louis MO 63124-1412 Office: Polster Lieder Woodruff & Lucchesi 763 S New Ballas Rd Saint Louis MO 63141-8750

MOORE, MECHLIN DONGAN, business consultant; b. N.Y.C., May 21, 1930; s. Albere Ethier and Pamela (Robinson) M.; m. Elizabeth Ann Tonkin, Feb. 11, 1956 (dec. 1992); children: Lansing, Pamela; m. Valery Ann Shields, July 14, 1995. A.B., Harvard U., 1952. Reporter Washington Post, 1955-59; dir. build Am. better com. Nat. Assn. Real Estate Bds., D.C., 1960-64; dir. info. Urban Land Inst., D.C., 1964-66; exec. v.p. Central Assn. Seattle, 1966-70; asst. to pres. United Airlines, Inc., Chgo., 1971-72, sr. v.p. external affairs, 1972-74, group v.p. mktg., 1975-76, sr. v.p. pub. affairs, 1976-79; pres. Ins. Info. Inst., N.Y.C., 1979-91; pvt. practice Naples, Fla., 1991—; pres. Eagles Mere Water Co., 1993-96; bd. dirs. Internat. Inst. Coun., Automobile Protection Corp.; bd. electors Ins. Hall of Fame; bd. govs. Internat. Ins. Seminars. Contbg. author publs. Nat. Assn. Real Estate Bds.; assoc. editor Jour. Property Mgmt. Adv. bd. mem. Traffic Inst. Northwestern U.; past mem. St. George's Vestry, N.Y.C. 1st lt. U.S. Army, 1952-54. Recipient Disting. Service award Central Assn. Seattle, 1972. Mem. Univ. Club, Pelican Marsh Golf Club. Republican. Episcopalian. Home: 1273 Grand Isle Ct Naples FL 33963

MOORE, MICHAEL, film director. Films include Silver City, 1951, Stalag 17, 1953, Pony Express, 1953, Little Boy Lost, 1953, Jamaica Run, 1953, The Desperate Hours, 1955, Hot Dog...The Movie, 1984, Secret Admirer, 1985, Paper Hearts, 1993; actor, dir., prodr. Roger and Me, 1989; actor, dir. prodr., writer Canadian Bacon, 1994; TV movies include Convicted, 1986, Gypsy, 1993; dir., creator, host TV Nation, 1994— (Outstanding Informational Series Emmy award, 1995); dir. films include Paradise Hawaiian Style, 1965, An Eye for an Eye, 1966, The Fastest Guitar Alive, 1967, The Frontiersman, 1968, Buckskin, 1968; prodr., writer Clay Farmers, 1988. Office: ICM 8942 Wilshire Blvd Beverly Hills CA 90211-1934*

MOORE, MICHAEL T., lawyer; b. Mullins, S.C., Feb. 21, 1948; s. Claude Richard and Melinda Doris (Stone) M.; m. Leslie Jean Lott, Nov. 12, 1978; children: Michael T. Jr., Emmett Russell Lott. BA, U. Fla., 1970, JD, 1974. Assoc. Burlingham, Underwood & Lord, N.Y.C., 1974-77, Hassan, Mahassni, Burlington, Underwood & Lord, Jeddah, Saudi Arabia, 1977-79; ptnr. Holland & Knight, Miami, Fla., 1982—; bd. dirs. Holland & Knight, Miami, 1986—, exec. ptnr. Miami office, 1993—; bd. dirs. Marine Arbitration Bd., Inc., Miami, 1985—; pres. The Marine Coun., 1989-90. Editor-in-chief Southern District Digest, 1980-82; contbr. articles to profl. jours. Mem. Orange Bowl Com.; bd. dirs. United Way Greater Miami, 1994—, U.S. Sailing Ctr., YMCA; chmn. Alexis de Tocqueville Soc.; mem. Miami River Coordinating Com.; trustee St. Stephens Sch.; mem. Coral Gables (Fla.) Youth Adv. Bd. Mem. ABA, Maritime Law Assn. U.S., Fla. Bar Assn., Dade County Bar Assn. (bd. dirs. 1981—, Outstanding Young Lawyer award 1982). Republican. Home: 3515 Anderson Rd Miami FL 33134-7050 Office: Holland & Knight 701 Brickell Ave PO Box 15441 Miami FL 33101

MOORE, MICHAEL THOMAS, mining executive; b. Bklyn., Oct. 10, 1934; s. Michael Joseph and Lucille M. (Wild) M.; m. Beatrice Lorraine Quinto, Sept. 10, 1960; children: Teresa, Stephanie, Jennifer, Elisabeth. BS in Bus., Indiana U. of Pa., 1956; postgrad., U. Pitts., 1959-63, Am. U., 1963-64, NYU, 1964-66. Fin. analyst, supr. U.S. Steel Corp., Duquesne, Pa., 1956-63; plant controller Am.-Standard, Balt., 1963-64; sr. fin. analyst Celanese Corp., N.Y.C., 1964-66; asst. controller to controller Cleve.-Cliffs Inc., 1966-72, v.p. controller, 1972-75, sr. v.p., 1975-83, exec. v.p., CFO, 1983-86, pres., dir., 1986, pres., dir., CEO, 1987, pres., CEO, 1987—, chmn., CEO, 1988—; bd. dirs. KeyCorp, LTV Corp. Bd. dirs. Cleve. Tomorrow, 1989—; trustee Fairview Health Sys., Cleve., 1990—. With U.S. Army, 1957-58. Named Outstanding Alumnus Indiana U. of Pa., 1981, Mining Industry CEO of Yr., 1993. Mem. Am. Iron and Steel Inst. (bd. dirs. 1987—), Nat. Mining Assn. (bd. dirs. 1987—), Bus. Roundtable, Am. Iron Ore Assn. (bd. dirs. 1987—), Union Club, The Fifty Club, Westwood Country Club, Pepper Pike Club, Rolling Rock Club, Quail Creek Country Club, Laurel Valley Golf Club. Roman Catholic. Office: Cleveland Cliffs Inc 1100 Superior Ave E Cleveland OH 44114-2518

MOORE, MIKE, state attorney general; m. Tisha Moore; 1 child, Kyle. Grad., Jackson County Jr. Coll., 1972; BA, U. Miss., 1974, JD, 1976. Asst. dist. atty. State of Miss., 1977-78, dist. atty., 1979, atty. gen., 1988—. Mem. ABA, Miss. State Bar Assn. Office: Office of Atty Gen PO Box 220 Jackson MS 39205-0220*

MOORE, MILO ANDERSON, banker; b. Orange, N.J., Aug. 26, 1942; s. Milo H. and Helen (Wiley) M.; m. Judith J. Colosimo, May 4, 1968; children: Milo Robert, Matthew Wiley, Marykate Bartlett. BS, Ithaca Coll., 1964; MBA, Rutgers U., 1971. Traffic supt. N.Y. Tel. Co., N.Y.C., 1964-71; trust officer Midlantic Nat. Bank, Newark, 1971-76; v.p. Shearson Loeb Rhoades, N.Y.C., 1976-80; sr. v.p. Donaldson Lufkin & Jenrette, N.Y.C., 1980-85; sr. mng. dir. Bear, Stearns & Co., 1985-92; v.p. Chem. Pvt. Banking, Morristown, N.J., 1992—. Advisor Jr. Achievement, Bronx, N.Y., 1967-68; pres. Chatham Jaycees, N.J., 1974; big bros. Morris County Big Bros., Morristown, 1971-81; pres. Stanley Congl. Ch., Chatham, N.J., 1995—; trustee SAGE Inc., 1994—. Mem. Securities Industry Assn. (tax shelter com. 1982-85), Glenburnie Club (pres. 1989—), Canoe Brook Country Club (Summit, N.J.), Beta Gamma Sigma. Office: Chem Pvt Banking 67 Summit Ave Summit NJ 07901-3614

MOORE, NANCY NEWELL, English language educator; b. Deadwood, S.D., Apr. 11, 1939; d. Harold Richard and Laura Mae (Howe) Newell; m. John Howard Moore, Feb. 23, 1962 (div. Oct. 1980). BA, Lake Forest Coll., 1961; MA, Northwestern U., 1963; PhD, U. Ill., 1968. Instr. of English U. Ill., Champaign-Urbana, 1967-68; asst. prof. of English U. Wis., Stevens Point, 1968-72, assoc. prof., 1972-76, prof., 1976—, asst. to chancellor for women, 1972-74, dept. chmn., 1974-77, chmn. faculty senate, 1981-84. Contbr. articles to profl. jours. Recipient grant for Canadian Studies, Can. Govt., 1986. Mem. AAUW, NOW, Midwest MLA, Assn. for Can. Studies in U.S., Shakespeare Assn. Am., Women in Higher Edn., Phi Eta Sigma. Unitarian. Office: Univ Wisconsin Stevens Point WI 54481

MOORE, NICHOLAS G., finance company executive; m. Jo Anne Moore; children: Kelly, Garrett, Patrick, Katy. BS in Acctg., St. Mary's Coll.; JD, U. Calif., Berkeley. With Coopers & Lybrand, 1968—; prin. tax practice Coopers & Lybrand, San Jose, Calif., 1974-81; coun. Coopers & Lybrand, N.Y.C., 1984, exec. com., 1988, vice chmn. west region, 1991-92, client svc. vice chmn., 1992-94, chmn., CEO, 1994—. Bd. bus. coun. N.Y. State, bd. trustees coms. for econ. devel.; bd. dirs. Co-Operation Ireland; mem. Bus.-

Higher Edn. Forum, U.S. C. of C. Ctr. for Workfore Preparation, N.Y.C. Partnership; vice chmn. bus. com. Met. Mus. of Art; adv. coun. Weissman Ctr. for Internat. Bus. Baruch Coll.; bd. regents St. Mary's Coll., Calif. Mem. AICPA, Calif. Bar Assn., Calif. Soc. CPAs, N.Y. State Soc. CPAs. Office: 1301 Avenue of the Americas New York NY 10019*

MOORE, OLIVER SEMON, III, publishing executive, consultant; b. Jersey City, July 26, 1942; s. Oliver S. and Ann Loy (Spies) M.; m. Dina Downing DuBois, Feb. 23, 1961 (div. 1974); 1 child, Deborah; m. Christine Laine Meyers, May 12, 1990; 1 child, Kathryn Laine. BA, U. Va., 1964. Chief bur. Richmond (Va.) Times-Dispatch, 1964-66; corr. Time mag., N.Y.C., 1966-67, contbg. editor, 1967-68; assoc. editor Newsweek, N.Y.C., 1969-71; freelance writer, 1972-75; mng. editor Motor Boating and Sailing, N.Y.C., 1976-78, editor, 1980-82; exec. editor US Mag., N.Y. Times Co., 1978-80; dep. editor Town & Country Mag., N.Y.C., 1982-84; editor Sci. Digest Mag., N.Y.C., 1984-86; pub. dir. Yachting Mag., N.Y.C., 1986—; editorial dir. Outdoor Life, N.Y.C., 1993-95; v.p. The Outdoor Co., N.Y.C., 1994-95; editor-at-large Motor Boating & Sailing, 1995—; pres. Alamo Pub. Svcs., Inc., Detroit, 1995—. Author: (poems) Voices International, 1969; contbg. editor Sports Afield, 1996—. Recipient Merit award Art Dirs. Club, 1981, award of merit Soc. Publ. Designers, 1981, Excellence in Media award Nat. Arbor Day Found., 1985. Mem. Nat. Marine Mfrs. Assn., Am. Soc. Mag. Editors, Mag. Pubs. Assn., N.Y. Yacht Club, Grosse Pointe (Mich.) Club, Bayview (Mich.) Yacht Club, The Huntsman (Mich.). Republican. Episcopalian. Avocations: sailing, antique cars. Office: Alamo Pub Svcs Inc 3645 Crooks Rd Troy MI 48084-1642

MOORE, OMAR KHAYYAM, experimental sociologist; b. Helper, Utah, Feb. 11, 1920; s. John Gustav and Mary Jo (Crowley) M.; m. Ruth Garnand, Nov. 19, 1942; 1 child, Venn. BA, Doane Coll., 1942; MA, Washington U., St. Louis, 1946, PhD, 1949. Instr. Washington U., St. Louis, 1949-52; teaching assoc. Northwestern U., Evanston, Ill., 1950-51; rsch. asst., prof. sociology Tufts Coll., Medford, Mass., 1952-53; researcher Naval Rsch. Lab., Washington, 1953-54; asst. prof. sociology Yale U., New Haven, 1954-57, assoc. prof. sociology, 1957-63; prof. psychology Rutgers U., New Brunswick, N.J., 1963-65; prof. social psychology, sociology U. Pitts., 1965-71, prof. sociology, 1971-89, prof. emeritus, 1989—; scholar-in-residence Nat. Learning Ctr.'s Capital Children's Mus., Washington, 1989-90; pres. Responsive Environ. Found., Inc., Estes Park, Colo., 1962—; assessor of rsch. projects The Social Scis. and Humanities Rsch. Coun. Can., 1982—; adj. prof. U. Colo., Boulder, 1992—. Contbg. editor Educational Technology; contbr. numerous articles to profl. jours.; patentee in field; motion picture producer and director. Recipient Award The Nat. Soc. for Programmed Instruction, 1965, Award Doane Coll Builder Award, 1967, Ednl. Award Urban Youth Action, Inc., 1969, Award House of Culture, 1975, Cert. of Appreciation, 1986, Cert. of Appreciation D.C. Pub. Schs., 1987, da Vinci Award Inst. for the Achievement of Human Potential, 1988, Cert. of Appreciation Capital Children's Museum, 1988, award Jack & Jill of America Found., 1988, Cert. of Appreciation U.S. Dept. of Edn., 1988, Cert. of Appreciation D.C. Pub. Schs., 1990, Person of Yr. in Ednl. Tech. award Ednl. Tech. mag., 1990. Mem. AAAS, Am. Math. Soc., Am. Psychol. Assn., Internat. Sociol. Assn., Am. Sociol. Assn., Assn. for Symbolic Logic, Assn. for Anthrop. Study of Play, Philosophy Sci. Assn., Psychonomics Soc., Soc. for Applied Sociology, Soc. for Exact Philosophy, Math. Assn. Am. Republican. Avocation: mountaineering. Home and Office: 2341 Upper High Dr PO Box 1673 Estes Park CO 80517

MOORE, PAT HOWARD, engineering and construction company executive; b. Laredo, Tex., Sept. 16, 1930; s. Howard Warren and Odette Evelyn (Bunn) M.; m. Elsie Mae Crossman, Mar. 23, 1954; children: Linda Marie Ford, Margaret Ann, Andrew Patrick. BA, Rice U., 1952, BS in Civil Engring., 1953; postgrad., Tulane U., 1956-58. Registered profl. engr., Tex., La. Spl. investigator Army Counter Intelligence Corps., Houston, 1954-56; div. engr. McDermott Inc., Morgan City, La., 1956-58; pres., dir. Navasota Tel. Co., Tex., 1958-63; project mgr. Brown & Root, Inc., Houston, 1963-67, exec. v.p., chief fin. officer, dir., 1990-95; pres., dir. Fluor Ocean Svcs., Houston, 1968-80; sr. v.p. Raymond Internat., Inc., Houston, 1980-86; pres., dir. Martin Moore Inc., Bellaire, Tex., 1986-90; dir. Charter Builders, Inc., Dallas, 1988-90; mgmt. cons. Bellaire, 1996—; adv. dir. Tex. Commerce Bank, Houston; lectr. civil engring. Rice U., 1996—. Bd. govs. Rice U., 1984-88. With U.S. Army, 1954-56. Fellow ASCE. Lodge: Kiwanis (pres. 1960). Home: 5251 Birdwood Rd Houston TX 77096-2503 Office: PO Box 1156 Bellaire TX 77402-1156

MOORE, PATSY SITES, food services director; b. San Marcos, Tex., Mar. 29, 1939; d. Sam W. and Hilda (Wiede) Sites. BS in Home Econs. Edn., S.W. Tex. State U., 1970. Owner, operator Westoner Kindergarten & Nursery Sch., San Marcos, 1965-68; food svc. dir. San Marcos Consol. Ind. Sch. Dist., 1975—. Member steering com. Play Scape/Children's Park, San Marcos, 1992. Mem. Am. Sch. Food Svc. Assn., Tex. Sch. Food Svc. Assn., Ctrl. Tex. Sch. Food Svc. Dirs. Assn. (founder, past pres.), Order Eastern Star. Lutheran. Avocations: gardening, oil painting, lapadary. Home: 285 Hilliard Rd San Marcos TX 78666-8905 Office: San Marcos Consol Ind Sch Dist PO Box 1087 San Marcos TX 78667-1087

MOORE, PAUL, JR., bishop; b. Morristown, N.J., Nov. 15, 1919; s. Paul and Fanny Weber (Hanna) M.; m. Jenny McKean, Nov. 26, 1944 (dec.); children: Honor, Paul III, Adelia, Rosemary, George Mead, Marian Shaw, Daniel Sargent, Susanna McKean, Patience; m. Brenda Hughes Eagle, May 16, 1975. Grad., St. Paul's Sch., Concord, N.H., 1937; B.A., Yale U., 1941; S.T.B., Gen. Theol. Sem., N.Y.C., 1949, S.T.D. (hon.), 1960; D.D. (hon.), Va. Theol. Sem., 1964, Berkeley Divinity Sch., 1971; PhD (hon.), City Coll. N.Y. Ordained to ministry Protestant Episcopal Ch., 1949; mem. team ministry Grace Ch., Jersey City, 1949-57; dean Christ Ch. Cathedral, Indpls., 1957-64; suffragan bishop Washington, 1964-70; bishop coadjutor Diocese, N.Y., 1970-72; bishop Diocese, 1972-89; lectr. St. Augustine's Coll., Canterbury, Eng., 1960; chmn. commn. Delta ministry Nat. Coun. Chgs., 1964-67; mem. urban divsn., nat. exec. coun. Episcopal Ch., 1952-68; dep. to Gen. Conv., 1961, Anglican Congress, 1963; chmn. com. 100; legal def. fund NAACP. Author: The Church Reclaims the City, 2d edit, 1970, Take A Bishop Like Me, 1979. Trustee Bard Coll.; former trustee Gen. Theol. Sem., Trinity Sch., Bereeley Div. Sch. at Yale U., N.Y.C.; mem. Fund for Free Expression; mem. adv. coun. Gov.'s Com. on AIDS, 1983-87; chmn. The Timor Project, Project on Religion and Human Rights. Capt. USMCR, 1941-45, PTO. Decorated Navy Cross, Silver Star, Purple Heart.; recipient Margaret Sanger award Planned Parenthood, 1984, Frederick Douglas award North Star Fund, 1989, Freedom of Worship medal Franklin and Eleanor Roosevelt Inst., 1991; Yale Corp. sr. fellow, 1987-90. Mem. Century Club (N.Y.C.), Knickerbocker Club (N.Y.C.). Club: Century (N.Y.C.). Home and Office: 55 Bank St New York NY 10014-2146

MOORE, PEARL B., nurse; b. Pitts., Aug. 25, 1936; d. Hyman and Ethel (Antis) Friedman; diploma Liliane S. Kaufmann Sch. Nursing, 1956; BS in Nursing, U. Pitts., 1968, M. Nursing, 1974; 1 child, Cheryl. Staff nurse Allegheny Gen. Hosp., Pitts., 1957-60; instr. Liliane S. Kaufman Sch. Nursing, Pitts., 1960-70, asst. dir., 1970, dir., 1970-72; cancer nurse specialist Montefiore Hosp., Pitts., 1974-75; coordinator Brain Tumor Study Group, Pitts., 1975-83; adj. asst. prof. U. Pitts., 1983—. Fellow Am. Acad. Nursing; mem. Am. Nurses Assn., Oncology Nursing Soc. (exec. dir. 1983—, Disting. Svc. award 1995), Am. Soc. Clin. Onoclogy, Am. Soc. Assn. Execs., Nurses Alumnae U. Pitts., Sigma Theta Tau. Contbr. articles in field to profl. publs. Home: 4221 Winterburn Ave Pittsburgh PA 15207-1101 Office: 501 Holiday Dr Pittsburgh PA 15220-2749

MOORE, PENELOPE, librarian; b. Sylacauga, Ala., Apr. 16, 1937; d. Frank Durward and Dorothy (Roberts) M. BA, Birmingham-So., 1959; MA, U. Miss., Oxford, 1960; MLS, U. Ala., Tuscaloosa, 1973. English tchr. Sylacauga (Ala.) High Sch., 1960-62, Lee High Sch., Huntsville, Ala., 1962-68; office mgr. Bell and Lang Law Firm, Sylacauga, 1969-72; libr. Mountainview Elem. Sch., Sylacauga, 1973—. Bd. dirs. Sylacauga Arts Coun., 1980—, Isabel A. Comer Mus. and Arts Ctr., Aylacauga, 1982-88, A Plus, Montgomery, Ala., 1992—; founder Sylacauga Community Chorus, 1976; active Ala. Libr. Media Leadership Group. Recipient Outstanding Achievement award Sylacauga Arts Coun., 1989; named Sylacauga Woman of the Yr. by Sylacauga Exchange Club, 1983, Ala. State Tchr. of Yr., 1992, Outstanding Vol. by United Way of Sylacauga, 1993. Mem. Ala. Libr. Assn., Ala. Instrl. Media Assn., Libr. and Media Profl. Orgn. (Outstanding Svc. to Ala. Librs. 1992), S.E. Regional Vision for Edn., Alpha Delta Kappa. Republican. United Methodist. Home: PO Box 479 Sylacauga AL 35150-0479 Office: Mountainview Elem School 100 Fluker St Sylacauga AL 35150-2291

MOORE, PETER BARTLETT, biochemist, educator; b. Boston, Oct. 15, 1939; s. Francis Daniels and Laura Benton (Bartlett) M.; m. Margaret Sue Murphy, Jan. 30, 1966; children: Catherine, Philip. BS, Yale U., 1961, MA (hon.); PhD, Harvard U., 1966. Postdoctoral fellow U. Geneva, 1966-67, MRC Lab. of Molecular Biology, Cambridge, Eng., 1967-69; asst. prof., then assoc. prof. dept. molecular biophysics Yale U., New Haven, 1969-76, assoc. prof. dept. of chemistry, 1976-79, prof., 1979—, chmn. dept. chemistry, 1987-90. Contbr. numerous articles to profl. publs. Guggenheim Found. fellow, 1979-80. Fellow AAAS; mem. Am. Chem. Soc., Am. Soc. Biol. Chemists and Molecular Biologists, Biophys. Soc. Office: Yale U Dept of Chemistry 225 Prospect Ave New Haven CT 06512-1958

MOORE, PETER STEWART, editor; b. Bridgeport, Conn., Oct. 29, 1956; s. Richard Garfield and Dorothy (Habel) M.; m. Claire McCrea, May 30, 1987; children: Jake, Tyler. BA, Bates Coll., 1978. History writer Panarizon Pub., N.Y.C., 1979-80; asst. editor/writer NEXT Mag., N.Y.C., 1980-81; sr. editor Moviegoer Mag./Whittle Comm., Knoxville, 1982-86; articles editor Playboy Mag., Chgo., 1986-95; mng. editor Men's Health, Emmaus, Pa., 1995—. Office: Mens Health 33 E Minor St Emmaus PA 18098

MOORE, PHILIP WALSH, appraisal company executive; b. Burmont, Pa., Aug. 1, 1920; s. Louise J.F. and Florence (Walsh) M.; m. Katherine Shean, Dec. 26, 1967 (div.); children: Jourdan, Thomas, Philip, Edward; m. Marya Phaedra Cocalis; children: Stuart, Kristina. AB, Princeton U., 1942; MBA, NYU, 1950. Security analyst First Boston Corp., N.Y.C., 1946-48, v.p. gen. adminstrn., 1967-70; asst. to pres. Schroder Rockefeller and Co., N.Y.C., 1948-50; pres. First Research Co., Miami, Fla., 1950-67, chmn., chief exec. officer, 1971-84; pres. J&W Seligman Valuations Corp., N.Y.C., 1984—; founder, then bd. dirs. Flagship Banks (now Sun Trust Banks), Miami, 1964. Author: Florida Real Estate, 1960, Branch Banking Strategy, 1964, National Image of Economic South, 1976, Valuation Revisited, 1987; author, editor: Internat. Banking Services, 1981. Trustee Ransom Everglades Sch., Miami, 1956-82; mem. adminstrv. com. Lincoln Ctr. Performing Arts, N.Y.C., 1969-75; mem. devel. council U. Hosp., Jacksonville, Fla., 1985—. Served to lt. USN, 1942-46, ETO, PTO. Mem. Inst. Bus. Appraiser, Nat. Assn. Bus. Economists, Am. Soc. Appraisers, Investment Assn. N.Y.C. (pres. 1948-50), So. Assn. Sci. and Industry (trustee, chmn. 1955-72), Overseas Mgmt. Internat. (bd. dirs. 1972-80), Phi Beta Kappa. Republican. Roman Catholic. Clubs: Down Town (N.Y.C.); River (Jacksonville); Ponte Vedra (Fla.). Avocations: tennis, gardening, reading. Home: 78 San Juan Dr Ponte Vedra Beach FL 32082-1330

MOORE, POWELL ALLEN, former government official, consultant; b. Milledgeville, Ga., Jan. 5, 1938; s. Jere N. and Sarah (Allen) M.; m. Katherine Southward, Oct. 14, 1961; children: Frances Moore Preston, Powell Allen Jr. B.A. in Jounalism, U. Ga., 1959. Press sec. to Richard Russell, U.S. Senate, Washington, 1966-71; dep. dir. pub. info. Dept. Justice, Washington, 1971-72; dep. spl. asst. to Pres. for legis. affairs The White House, Washington, 1973-75, dep. asst. to Pres. for legis. affairs, 1981-82; cons. pub. affairs Washington, 1975-81; asst. sec. for congl. rels. Dept. State, Washington, 1982-83; v.p. legis. affairs Lockheed Corp., Washington, 1983-85, Ginn, Edington, Moore and Wade, Washington, 1985-90; pres. ASL Internat., Washington, 1990-93; sr. prin., mng. dir. Capitoline, MS&L, Washington, 1993—. Dir. press Com. to Re-elect the Pres., Washington, 1972; cons. Pres. Ford Com., 1976, Reagan-Bush Com., 1980. Served to capt., inf. U.S. Army, 1959-62. Mem. Belle Haven Country Club, Capitol Hill Club, Met. Club. Republican. Episcopalian.

MOORE, RAYBURN SABATZKY, American literature educator; b. Helena, Ark., May 26, 1920; s. Max Sabatzky and Sammie Lou (Rayburn) M.; m. Margaret Elizabeth Bear, Aug. 30, 1947; children: Margaret Elizabeth, Robert Rayburn. A.B., Vanderbilt U., 1942, M.A., 1947; Ph.D., Duke U., 1956. Script writer King Biscuit Time, Interstate Grocer Co., KFFA, 1947-50; Vice pres. Interstate Grocer Co., Helena, 1947-50; research and grad. asst. Duke U., 1952-54; asst. prof. English, Hendrix Coll., Conway, Ark., 1954-55; asso. prof. Hendrix Coll., 1955-58, prof., 1958-59; asso. prof. U. Ga., Athens, 1959-65; prof. U. Ga., 1965-90, prof. emeritus, 1990—, chmn. Am. studies program, 1968-90, chqnn. div. lang and lit., 1975-90; vis. scholar Duke U., 1958, 64. Author: Constance Fenimore Woolson, 1963, For the Major and Selected Short Stories of Constance Fenimore Woolson, 1967, Paul Hamilton Hayne, 1972, A Man of Letters in the Nineteenth-Century South: Selected Letters of Paul Hamilton Hayne, 1982; sr. editor: History of Southern Literature, 1985, Selected Letters of Henry James to Edmund Gosse (1882-1915): A Literary Friendship, 1988, The Correspondence of Henry James and the House of Macmillan, 1877-1914: All the Links in the Chain, 1993; mem. editorial bd. U. Ga. Press, 1972-74, Ga. Rev., 1974-82, chmn., 1980-82; contbr. articles, revs. to profl. jours. Mem. troop com. Boy Scouts Am., Athens, 1973-75; deacon, elder Presbyterian Ch., 1962—; mem. Lamar Meml. Lectures com. Mercer U., 1984-91. Served to capt. U.S. Army, 1942-46, PTO. Mem. MLA (exec. com. Gen. Topics VI 1972-75), Soc. Study So. Lit. (exec. com. 1968, 74-79, 85-88, 91-94, v.p. 1981-82, pres. 1983-84), South Atlantic Grad. English Coop. Group (exec. com. 1969-79, chmn. 1971-72), South Atlantic Modern Lang. Assn. (exec. com. 1975-77, nominating com. 1985-87), William Gilmore Simms Soc. (exec. com. 1993—, pres.-elect 1993-95, editl. adv. bd. Letters of Henry James complete edit. 1995—), Blue Key, Phi Beta Kappa, Sigma Chi. Office: U Ga Dept English Park Hall Athens GA 30602

MOORE, RAYMOND A., consultant, retired agriculture educator; b. Britton, S.D., Nov. 16, 1927; s. Arthur L. and Anna (Schuur) M.; m. Marlys Schiefelbein, Jun 17, 1951; children: Craig, Jay, Kent, Jeff. BA in Agrl. Edn. and Econs., S.D. State U., 1951, MS in Agronomy, 1958; PhD in Crop Physiology and Ecology, Purdue U., 1963. Instr. vocat. agriculture Bennett County H.S., Martin, S.D., 1951-56; instr., prof., adminstr. S.D. State U., Brookings, 1956-94, dir. emeritus agrl. expt. sta., 1994—; cons. Coop. States Rsch. Svcs. USDA, Washington, Producers Renewable Products, St. Paul. Contbr. chpts. to books, articles to profl. jours. With USN, 1945-47. Nat. Sci. Faculty fellow forage & pasture mgmt. CSRS/U.S. Dept. Agriculture, 1965; Citizens Ambassador Program People to People Internat. travel grantee, U.S. Dept. Agriculture travel grantee. Mem. Am. Soc. Agronomy, Kiwanis Internat., Sigma Xi, Gamma Sigma Delta. Avocations: hunting, fishing, gardening, farming. Home: 207 17th Ave Brookings SD 57006-2609 Office: SD State U PO Box 2207 Brookings SD 57007

MOORE, RICHARD, public relations executive; b. Marietta, Ohio. Grad., Ohio State U., 1980. Account exec. Haverhill Mass. Gazette, 1980-82, Northwest Pub. Power Assn., 1982-83; account exec. Miller Comm., 1983-85, account supr., 1985-87, gen. mgr., 1988; v.p., gen. mgr. Miller Comm., Mountain View, Calif., 1988; ptnr. Copithorne & Bellows, San Francisco, 1988—. Office: Copithorne & Bellows 100 1st St Ste 2600 San Francisco CA 94105-2637*

MOORE, RICHARD ALAN, landscape architect; b. St. Louis, Jan. 17, 1930; s. Ira Mack and Helen Adoline (Fakes) M.; m. Patricia Ruth Burke, Mar. 15, 1952 (div. 1967); children: Sheryl Louise, Richard Dennis, Sara Lynn, Sandra Lee. BS, U. Mo., 1951; MLA, U. Oreg., 1957. Registered landscape architect, Calif., Hawaii. Asst. prof., head dept. landscape architecture Calif. State Poly. Coll., Pomona, 1957-61; assoc. prof., head dept. landscape architecture N.C. State U., Raleigh, 1962-67; pvt. practice landscape architecture Pomona, Calif., 1957-61; dir. land devel. and planning Oceanic Properties Inc., Honolulu, 1967-69; pvt. practice Honolulu, 1969-70, 79—; dir. ops. Eckbo, Dean, Austin & Williams, Honolulu, 1970-71, v.p. ops., 1971-73; pres. EDAW, Inc., San Francisco, 1973-76, chmn. bd., 1976-78; prof. landscape architecture Tex. A&M U., Bryan, 1977-79. Prin. works include Whispering Pines Motor Lodge, N.C., 1964 (award of merit N.C. chpt. AIA 1964), North Shore Devel. Plan, Kauai, Hawaii, 1973, Comprehensive Zoning Ordinance, County of Kauai, 1973 (Am. Soc. Landscape Architects honor award 1973, HUD honor award 1974), Lihue Devel. Plan, Kauai, 1975, Koloa, Poipu, Kalaheo Devel. Plan, Kauai, 1978, Gen. Plan Update, Kauai, 1982, Mililani Town Devel. Plan, 1967-69 (Am. Soc. Landscape Architects merit award 1970), Lanai Land Mgmt. and Devel. Study, 1969 (Am. Soc. Landscape Architects merit award 1970), Wailea Master Devel. Plan, 1971, Kukuiula Devel. Plan, 1983, Lanai Project Dist. Master Plan, 1983-89, Maliu Ridge Devel. Plan, North Kohala, 1985, Mililani Mauka Devel. Plan, 1988, Devel. Plan, Lanai City Comml. Dist., 1990, Dandan Golf Course, Guam, 1991. 1st lt. U.S. Army, 1951-53, Korea. Fellow Am. Soc. Landscape Architects; mem. Masons. Avocations: sports, drawing, painting.

MOORE, RICHARD ALLAN, mathematics educator; b. Mansfield, Ohio, Jan. 11, 1924; s. Robert Allan and Ruth (Miller) M.; m. Ruth Marguerite Neuhoff, July 30, 1949; children—Peter Allan, Susan Rebecca Moore McJunkin, Sarah Marguerite. A.B., Washington U., St. Louis, 1948, M.A. in Math, 1950, Ph.D., 1953. Instr. math. U. Nebr., 1953-54, Yale, 1954-56; mem. faculty Carnegie-Mellon U., Pitts., 1956-87; prof. math. Carnegie-Mellon U., 1967-87, prof. emeritus, 1987—, assoc. head dept., 1965-71, 75-85, chmn. dept., 1971-75; vis. lectr. Pa. Dept. Pub. Instrn., 1968-70; cons. in field, 1967—. Author. Mem. sch. bd. Churchill Area Schs., 1963-71; sch. bd. Eastern Area Spl. Schs., 1964-69. Served with AUS, 1943-45. Recipient Ryan Teaching award, 1969. Mem. Am. Math. Soc., Math. Assn. Am., Math. Coun. Western Pa. (bd. dirs. 1962-70), Pa. Coun. Tchrs. Math. (bd. dirs. 1966-68), Sigma Xi, Phi Kappa Phi. Episcopalian. Research papers, textbook ordinary differential equations. Home: 165 Fieldcrest Dr Pittsburgh PA 15221-3742

MOORE, RICHARD EARL, communications creative director; b. Pontiac, Mich., Nov. 3, 1940; m. Noriko Negishi, Feb. 1, 1966. B.F.A., Art Ctr. Coll. Design, Los Angeles, 1968. Sr. designer Lippincott & Margulies, N.Y.C., 1969-71; prin. Richard Moore Assocs., N.Y.C., 1972-76; vice chmn., co-founder Muir Cornelius Moore, N.Y.C., 1976-90; prin. Richard Moore Assocs., N.Y.C., 1990—; juror frequent internat. advt. competitions; chmn. frequent internat. seminars on mktg. comm. Recipient numerous creative awards. Mem. Am. Inst. Graphic Art, Art Directors Club, Type Directors Club. Avocations: mountaineering; wilderness photography, scuba diving, skiing.

MOORE, RICHARD HARLAN, biology educator, university official; b. Houston, Sept. 16, 1945; s. Russell Lewis and Hazel Dean (Harlan) M.; m. Robin Morris, May 14, 1977; 1 child, Merlin R. Morris-Moore. BA in Gen Biology, Vanderbilt U., 1967; MA in Zoology, U. Tex., 1970, PhD in Marine Zoology, 1973. Staff scientist Environment Cons. Inc., Dallas, 1973-74; asst. prof. biology Coastal Carolina U., Conway, 1974-77, assoc., 1977-86, chmn. sci. div., 1978-79, dean Sch. Sci., 1979-87, prof., 1986—, asst. vice chancellor for rsch., 1987-93, asst. v.p., 1993—; rsch. assoc. Belle W. Baruch Inst. for Marine Biology and Coastal Rsch., Columbia, S.C., 1974—. Author: (with H.D. Hoese) Fishes of the Gulf of Mexico, 1971; contbr. articles to profl. jours. Leader Boy Scouts Am., Port Aransas, Tex., 1980-82; com. chmn. S.C. Crawfish Festival Assn., Pawleys Island, 1980—, chmn. bd. dirs., 1995—. Recipient NSF grants 1975, 77. Mem. Am. Soc. Ichthyologists and Herpetologists, Am. Fisheries Soc., Ecological Soc. Am., Southeastern and Gulf Estuarine Rsch. Socs., Southeastern Fishes Coun. Office: Coastal Carolina U PO Box 1954 Conway SC 29526-1954

MOORE, RICHARD KERR, electrical engineering educator; b. St. Louis, Nov. 13, 1923; s. Louis D. and Nina (Megown) M.; m. Wilma Lois Schallau, Dec. 10, 1944; children: John Richard, Daniel Charles. B.S., Washington U. at St. Louis, 1943; Ph.D., Cornell U., 1951. Test equipment engr. RCA, Camden, N.J., 1943-44; instr. and research engr. Washington U., St. Louis, 1947-49; research asso. Cornell U., 1949-51; research engr., sect. supr. Sandia Corp., Albuquerque, 1951-55; prof., chmn. elec. engring. dept. U. N.Mex., 1955-62; Black and Veatch prof. U. Kans., Lawrence, 1962-94; prof. emeritus, 1994—; dir. remote sensing lab. U. Kans., 1964-74, 84-93; pres. Cadre Corp., Lawrence, 1968-87; cons. cos., govt. agys. Author: Traveling Wave Engineering, 1960; co-author: (with Ulaby and Fung) Microwave Remote Sensing, Vol. I, 1981, Vol. II, 1982, Vol. III, 1986; contbr. to profl. jours. and handbooks. Served to lt. (j.g.) USNR, 1944-46. Recipient Achievement award Washington U. Engring. Alumni Assn., 1978, Outstanding Tech. Achievement award Geosci. and Remote Sensing Soc., 1982, Louise E. Byrd Grad. Educator award U. Kans., 1984, Irving Youngberg Rsch. award U. Kans., 1989. Fellow AAAS, IEEE (sect. chmn. 1960-61, Outstanding Tech. Achievement award coun. oceanic engring. 1978, Australia prize 1995); mem., NAE, AAUP, Am. Soc. Engring. Edn., Am. Geophys. Union, Internat. Sci. Radio Union (chmn. U.S. commn. F 1984-87, internat. vice chmn. commn. F 1990-93, chmn. 1993), Kiwanis, Sigma Xi, Tau Beta Pi. Presbyterian (past elder). Achievements include research in submarine communications, radar altimetry, radar as a remote sensor, radar oceanography; patent for polypanchromatic radar. Home: 1620 Indiana St Lawrence KS 66044-4046 Office: U Kans R S & Remote Sensing Lab 2291 Irving Rd Lawrence KS 66045-2969

MOORE, RICHARD LAWRENCE, structural engineer, consultant; b. Rocky Ford, Colo., Feb. 7, 1934; s. Lawrence and Margaret Kathryn (Bolling) M.; m. Donna St. Clair, Mar. 26, 1972 (div. 1983); 1 child, Andrew Trousdale; m. Margaret Ann Guthrie, May 4, 1984. BSCE, U. Colo., 1957; MS, Princeton U., 1963; PhD, Calif. Western U., Santa Ana, 1975. Registered profl. engr., Mass., Maine, Colo., Pa., Iowa, Nebr., N.Mex., Wyo., Ill., Ark., Mo., N.D., Mich., Okla., Mont. Structural engr. Cameron Engrs., Denver, 1964-66; v.p. Moore Internat., Jeddah, Saudi Arabia, 1967-78; asst. to pres. C.H. Guernsey Co., Oklahoma City, 1979-82; pres. R.L. Moore Co., Boston, 1983—; v.p., dir. Isolink Ing., Basel, Switzerland, 1990—; nat. chmn. Roof Cons. Inst., Raleigh, N.C., 1988-92; prof. Episcopal Sch. Theology, Denver, 1967-71. Patentee in field. Member Mound City (Mo.) Libr. Bd., 1963-64; pres. Dist. Rep. Party, Boston, 1988—; sr. warden St. John Chrysostom Epis. Ch., Denver, 1966-71. Danforth Found. scholar, 1962. Mem. ASCE, NSPE, Am. Concrete Inst., Nat. Forensic Ctr. Avocations: golf, travel, antique pocket watch collecting. Home and Office: RL Moore Co 534 E Broadway Boston MA 02127-4407

MOORE, RICHARD THOMAS, federal agency administrator; b. Milford, Mass., Aug. 7, 1943; s. Thomas James and Helen Eliza (Andrew) M.; m. Joanne Bednarz, May 26, 1979. BA in History, Clark U., 1966; MA in Student Pers., Colgate U., 1967; postgrad., Clark U., 1967-70, U. Mass., 1981-85. Cert. tchr. secondary level social studies. Assoc. dean students Assumption Coll., Worcester, Mass., 1967-69; asst. to pres. Bentley Coll., Waltham, Mass., 1969-77; mem. Mass. Ho. of Reps., Boston, 1977-94; assoc. dir. mitigation Fed. Emergency Mgmt. Agy., Washington, 1994—; pres. Mass. Selectmen's Assn., Boston, 1975-76; chmn. House Com. on Election Laws, Boston, 1992-94, House Com. on Taxation, Boston, 1983-85, House Com. on State Adminstrn., Boston, 1983. Chmn. Blackstone Nat. Heritage Corridor Commn., Uxbridge, Mass., 1988-90; presdl. elector Mass. Electoral Coll., Boston, 1992; chmn. Mass. Dem. Leadership Coun., Boston, 1990-93. Named Outstanding Legislator Mass. Town Clks. Assn., Boston, 1993, New Dem. of Yr. Mass. Dem. Leadership Coun., Boston, 1994. Mem. Am. Soc. Pub. Adminstrn. (mem. bd. Mass. chpt. 1981-85), Nat. Emergency Mgmt. Assn. Roman Catholic. Avocations: politics, collecting political items. Address: 700 7th St SW Apt 215 Washington DC 20024-2464

MOORE, ROB, professional football player; b. N.Y.C., Oct. 27, 1968. BS in Psychology, Syracuse U., 1990. With N.Y. Jets, 1990-94; wide receiver Ariz. Cardinals, Phoenix, 1994—. Named to Sporting News Coll. All-Am. Team, 1989, NFL Pro Bowl Team, 1994. Office: Ariz Cardinals 8701 S Hardy Phoenix AZ 85284

MOORE, ROBERT EDWARD, electronics executive; b. Winsted, Conn., July 29, 1923; s. Alfred Edward and Elizabeth (Clark) M.; m. Georgiana Muriel Moore, Dec. 22, 1946; children—Kathleen Moore Roberson, Brian Robert, John Craig. B.S. in Mech. Engring, U. Wis., 1948. Registered profl. engr., D.C. Chief insp. Rockwell-Standard Corp., Newark, Ohio, 1948-51; sec.-treas. A.E. Moore Co., Oshkosh, Wis., 1951-53; v.p. John I. Thompson & Co., Washington, 1953-65; founder, chmn., pres. Potomac Rsch., Inc. (merged with Electronic Data Systems Corp. 1979), Alexandria, Va., 1965-79, cons., 1979-81; chmn. Potomac Rsch. Internat., Fairfax, Va., 1981—. Served with U.S. Army, 1943-46. Mem. ASME. Episcopalian. Home: 11171 Crest Hill Rd Marshall VA 22115-2712 Office: Potomac Rsch Internat 11320 Random Hills Rd Fairfax VA 22030-6001

MOORE, ROBERT HENRY, insurance company executive; b. Madisonville, Ky., Sept. 16, 1940; s. William Lee Moore and Robbie (Pritchett) Ruby; m. Diana Churchill, Aug. 17, 1963 (div. 1978); children: Randall Lee, Robin Churchill; m. Patricia Mary George, Oct. 4, 1981; 1 child, Christopher Robert. BA, Davidson (N.C.) Coll., 1962; MA, U. N.C., 1964; PhD, U. Wis., 1972. Asst. dir. admissions Davidson Coll., 1963-64; teaching asst. U. Wis., Madison, 1965-68; staff and faculty U.S. Mil. Acad., West Point, N.Y., 1968-70; lectr., asst. prof. U. Md., College Park, 1970-76, assoc. prof., 1976; cons. U.S. Congress, Washington, 1976-77; emerging issues coordinator The Conf. Bd., N.Y.C., 1977-79; dir. govt. relations Benefacts, Inc., Washington, 1977-78; v.p. Alexander & Alexander, Inc., Washington, 1978-81; v.p. Alexander & Alexander Svcs. Inc., N.Y.C., Washington, 1981-85, sr. v.p. corp. rels., 1985-95, sr. v.p. (inactive), 1995—; chmn., pres. A & A Govt. and Industry Affairs Inc., Washington, 1990-94; del. Nat. Security Affairs Conf., Washington, 1978-82; mem. adv. bd. Career Opportunities Inst., U. Va., Charlottesville, 1982-86, Ctr. for New Am. Work Force, 1992—, co-chair rsch., 1995—; mem. corp. adv. bd. Queens Coll., CUNY, 1985—; mem. V.P.'s Forum, 1989-94; mem. coun. Conf. Bd. Corp. Comm. Execs., 1990-94; mem. Pub. Rels. Sem., 1993—. Co-author: (with others) School for Soldiers: West Point and the Profession of Arms, 1974 (NYT award 1974); contbr. articles to profl. jours.; contbr. interviews to nat. mags., newspapers, radio and TV. Mem. kitchen cabinet Points of Light Found., 1991-95; active Fairfax Unitarian Ch. With U.S. Army, 1968-70, capt. USAR, 1970-72. Ops. Crossroads Africa fellow, 1960; U. Md. rsch. grantee, 1972, 76; Inter-Univ. Seminar on Armed Forces and Society fellow. Fellow Internat. Ins. Soc., Soc. Risk Analysis; mem. Nat. Assn. Ins. Brokers (exec. com., bd. dirs. 1987, pres. 1985-96, chmn. past presidents adv. coun. 1989-93), Inst. Dirs. (London), U.S. C. of C. (civil justice action group 1985-87), The Tysons Club.

MOORE, ROBERT LOWELL, JR. (ROBIN MOORE), author; b. Boston, Oct. 31, 1925; s. Robert Lowell Sr. and Eleanor (Turner) M.; m. Joan Friedman, Sept. 15, 1952 (div. 1955); 1 child, Margo Joan; m. Mary Olga Troshkin, Feb. 17, 1973. AB, Harvard U., 1949. European corr. Boston Globe, 1947; ind. TV prodr. N.Y.C., 1949-52; dir. pub. rels. Sheraton Corp. Am., Boston, 1952- 54, dir. advt. and pub. rels., 1954-56, bd. dirs., 1954-62. Author: Pitchman, 1956, The Devil to Pay, 1961, The Green Berets, 1965, The Country Team, 1967, Fiedler, 1968, The French Connection, 1969, Court Martial, 1970, The Khaki Mafia, 1971, The Fifth Estate, 1974, Compulsion, 1982; (with Xaviera Hollander) The Happy Hooker, 1972, The Treasure Hunter, 1975, Dubai, 1976, Mafia Wife, 1977, The Banksters, 1977, Rhodesia, 1978, The Big Paddle, 1978, Search and Destroy, 1978, The Washington Connection, 1979; (with Milt Machlin) The Family Man, 1985, Force nine, 1987, The Man Who Made It Snow, 1990, The White Tribe, 1991, The Moscow Connection, 1994; screenwriter: The Green Berets, 1967, The French Connection, 1971, The Happy Hooker, 1973, Inchon, 1979, Hoffa, The Sparrowhood Curse, 1996. With USAAF, 1944-46, ETO. Decorated Air medal with two bronze oak leaf clusters. Mem. Met. Club (N.Y.C.). Developed pvt. TV closed circuit network for hotels. Home: 179 Nashawtuc Rd Concord MA 01742-1634

MOORE, ROBERT MADISON, food industry executive, lawyer; b. New Orleans, June 21, 1925; s. Clarence Greer and Anna Omega (Odendahl) M.; m. Evelyn Eileen Varva, Apr. 11, 1953; children: Eileen Alexandria Moore Wynne, John Greer. B.B.A., Tulane U., 1943; J.D., U. Va., 1952; LL.M. (Food Law Inst. fellow), NYU, 1953. Bar: La. 1956, Calif. 1972. Asst. to pres., gen. counsel Underwear Inst., N.Y.C., 1953-55; pvt. practice law New Orleans, 1955-56; asst. gen. atty., dir. Legal services, sec. and gen. atty. Standard Fruit & Steamship Co., New Orleans, 1957-72; v.p., gen. counsel Castle & Cooke Foods, 1972-81; v.p., gen. counsel Castle & Cooke, Inc., 1973-81, sr. v.p. law and govt., 1981-82; pres. Internat. Banana Assn., 1983—; dir. Ferson Optics of Del., Inc., 1958-69, Baltime Securities Corp., Pan American Devel. Found. Asst. atty. gen., La., 1958-63. Served with AUS, 1943-46. Mem. ABA, Calif. Bar Assn., La. Bar Assn., SAR (sec. 1960-61), Essex Club, Cosmos Club, Phi Delta Phi, Alpha Tau Omega. Democrat. Roman Catholic. Home: 3323 R St NW Washington DC 20007-2310 Office: 1929 39th St NW Washington DC 20007-2110

MOORE, ROBERT WILLIAM, professional organization executive; b. Claysburg, Pa., June 4, 1924; s. Frank B. and Sarah A. (Edelbute) M.; m. Helen Lingenfelter, July 17, 1948; children: Thomas R., Priscilla Jane. B.A., Pa. State U., 1948. With Price Waterhouse & Co., Pitts., 1948-62; mgr. Price Waterhouse & Co., 1955-62; asst. contr. Con-Gas Svc. Corp., Pitts., 1962-65, Consol. Natural Gas Svc. Co., Inc., Pitts., 1966-72; contr. Consol. Natural Gas Svc. Co., Inc., 1972-78, Consol. Natural Gas Co., Pitts., 1972-78; pres. Fin. Execs. Inst., Morristown, N.J., 1978-89, pres. emeritus, 1989—; mem. Fin. Acctg. Standards Adv. Coun., 1978-89. Bd. dirs. Central Blood Bank, Pitts., 1960-78, treas. corp., 1962-68, chmn. finance com., 1962-68, chmn. bd., 1969-72; mem. exec. bd. Pa. State U. Alumni Council, 1975-83; mem. exec. com. Campaign for Pa. State U., bd. vis.; pres. Pa. State Coll. Bus. Adminstrn. Soc., 1981-83. Served with AUS, 1943-45. Mem. Am., Pa. insts. C.P.A.s, Nat. Assn. Accountants, Fin. Execs. Inst., Pa. State U. Alumni Assn., Pa. Soc., Beta Alpha Psi (nat. forum), Delta Tau Delta. Episcopalian. Clubs: University (dir., pres. 1975-76), Valley Brook Country (dir. 1968-70, v.p. bd. 1970), Duquesne (Pitts.), University, St. Clair Country, Morris County Golf, Morristown (N.J.).

MOORE, ROBERT YATES, neuroscience educator; b. Harvey, Ill., Dec. 5, 1931; s. Raymon Irwin and Marie Louise (Fischer) M.; children: Elizabeth Allen, Matthew McCormick, Joshua Gilbert, Thomas Douglas. BA magna cum laude, Lawrence U., 1953; MD with honors, U. Chgo., 1957, PhD, 1962; MD (hon.), Lund (Sweden) U., 1974. Diplomate: Am. Bd. Psychiatry and Neurology. Intern Univ. Hosp., Ann Arbor, Mich., 1958-59; resident U. Chgo., 1959-64, asst. prof. neurology and anatomy, 1964-66, assoc. prof., 1966-70, prof., 1970-74; prof. neurosci. U. Calif., San Diego, 1974-79; prof., chmn. dept. neurology SUNY, Stony Brook, 1979-90; dir. Ctr. for Neurosci., prof. psychiatry, neurology and behavirol neurosci. U. Pitts., 1990—; cons. Contbr. numerous articles to profl. jours. Recipient numerous grants. Fellow Am. Acad. Neurology; mem. Am. Neurol. Assn., Soc. Neurosci., Internat. Brain Research Orgn., Am. Assn. Anatomists. Office: U Pitts Ctr for Neurosci Biomed Sci Tower W 1656 Pittsburgh PA 15261

MOORE, ROGER ALBERT, JR., archaeologist; b. Tampa, Fla., Dec. 18, 1946; s. Roger Albert Moore and Frieda E. (Heil) Hutchison; m. Susan Kay Waters, Sept. 8, 1978; children: Tabitha Rose, Roxie Ann. BA in Anthropology, Ohio State U., 1972; student, U. Tenn., 1974-75; MA in Anthropology, Ea. N.Mex. U., 1981. Lic. archael. surveyor, N.Mex., Colo., Utah, Wyo., Ariz. Crew chief, field foreman U. Tenn., Knoxville, 1973-74, excavator, lab. asst., 1974-75; excavator, lab. asst. Cahokia Mounds State Park, Collinsville, Ill., 1974; lithic analyst Ea. N.Mex. U., Portales, 1975-78; lab. dir. U. Colo., Cortez, 1978-79; field dir. ESCA-Tech, Inc., Ridgeway, Colo., 1980; lab. dir. Navajo Nat. Archaeology Dept., Farmington, N.Mex., 1980-82; supervisory archaeologist San Juan County Mus. Assn., Bloomfield, N.Mex., 1982-88; owner, prin. investigator Moore Anthropol. Rsch., Aztec, N.Mex., 1988—; instr. San Juan Coll., Farmington, 1983. Co-author: Old Dallas Historical Archaeology Project, 1987; contbr. articles to profl. jours. Vol. Portales (N.Mex) Food Coop., 1976-78, Salmon Ruin Mus., Bloomfield, 1982-88, Bonds for Books Plus Com., Aztec, 1994; mem. lithic dictionary com. N.Mex. Archaeol. Coun., 1989—; chmn. com. B.L.M. Cultural Adv. Group, Farmington, 1991—. With U.S. Army, 1967-69. Mem. Soc. Am. Archaeology (life), N.Mex. Archaeol. Coun., Archaeol. Soc. N.Mex. (cert., Archaeol. Achievement award 1994), Ariz. Archaeol. and Hist. Soc., Tenn. Anthropol. Assn. (life), San Juan County Mus. Assn. (bd. dirs. 1993-95), Nat.Trust for Hist. Preservation, Aztec C. of C. (bd. dirs. 1995—), Phi Kappa Phi. Republican. Presbyterian. Avocations: running, hiking, tennis, reading. Office: Moore Anthropol Rsch PO Box 1156 102 N Main Aztec NM 87410-1156

MOORE, ROGER GEORGE, actor; b. London, Oct. 14, 1927; s. George and Lily (Pope) M.; m. Luisa Mattioli, Apr. 11, 1968; children: Deborah, Geoffrey, Christian. Student, Royal Acad. Dramatic Arts, London, 1944-45. Theatrical performances London, 1944-54, N.Y.C., 1953—. Star: (TV series) The Alaskans, 1960-61, Ivanhoe, 1957-58, Maverick, 1961, The Saint, 1962-68, The Persuaders, 1971-72, The Muppet Show, 1981; actor: (films) including The Last Time I Saw Paris, 1954, Interrupted Melody, 1955, The King's Thief, 1955, Diane, 1956, The Miracle, 1959, Rape of the Sabines, 1961, Gold of the Seven Saints, 1961, Rachel Cade, 1961, No Man's Land, 1961, Crossplot, 1969, The Man Who Haunted Himself, 1970, Live and Let Die, 1973, Gold, 1974, The Man With The Golden Gun, 1974, Lucky Touch, 1975, Shout at the Devil, 1975, Street People, 1975, Sherlock Holmes in New York, 1976, The Spy Who Loved Me, 1977, The Wild Geese, 1977, Escape to Athena, 1978, Moonraker, 1978, North Sea Ransom, 1979, The Sea Wolves, 1981, Sunday Lovers, 1981, The Cannonball Run, 1981, For Your Eyes Only, 1981, Octopussy, 1982, The Naked Face, 1984, A View to a Kill, 1984, Bullseye, 1990, Bed and Breakfast, 1992, The Quest, 1996; author: James Bond Diary, 1973. Chmn. Stars Orgn. for Spastics, 1973-75, v.p., 1976-77. Served to capt. Brit. Army, 1945-48; goodwill ambassador UNICEF 1995—. Clubs: St. James's, Garrick (London). Address: Chalet Fenil, Grund BEI, Staad Switzerland*

MOORE, ROSEMARY KUULEI, headmaster; b. San Diego, Apr. 16, 1955; d. Edward James and Rina Larn (Young) M.; m. Lance Wesley Holter, June 16, 1994; children: Ian Everest Yannell, Jade River Holter, Sean Maru Yannell, Michael McKinley Yannell. Student, U. So. Calif., L.A., 1975, U. Hawaii, Kahului, 1980. Project coord. Hawaiian Sea Village, Amfac Property Corp., Kaanapali, 1979-80; shopping ctr. mgr. Whalers Village, Amfac Property Corp., Kaanapali, 1980-83; comm. mgr., adminstrv. dir. Amfac Property Corp., Kaanapali, 1983, property mgr., 1983-85; v.p. Kahikinui (Hawaii) Homes Project, 1990-93; chair, com. rels. dir. Haleakala Waldorf Sch., Kula, Hawaii, 1991-92; headmaster Haleakala Waldorf Sch., Kula, 1992—. Author: Lightworker, 1990, Mikey & Cocoa are Friends, 1992; contbr. articles to profl. jours. Coord. hwy. beautification Dept. Transp., Maui, 1992—; mem. steering com. Valley Isle Voters Assn., Maui, 1994. Mem. Nat. Wildlife Soc., Cousteau Soc. Avocations: writing, surfing, skin diving, hiking, camping. Office: Haleakala Waldorf Sch RR 2 Box Kula HI 96790

MOORE, ROY DEAN, judge; b. Chickasha, Okla., Jan. 15, 1940; s. Frank B. and Delia Pauline (Morgan) M.; m. Carolyn Kaye Wood, Aug. 10, 1962; children—Darla Kaye, Jared Dean, Amy Darise. B.A., Central State U., 1962, M. Teaching, 1966; J.D., Oklahoma City U., 1970; grad., Nat. Coll. State Trial Judges, 1972. Bar: Okla. 1970. Coach debate, instr. dramatics Kingfisher (Okla.) High Sch., 1962-67; instr. English and journalism, head dept. lang. arts. Jarman Jr. High Sch., Midwest City, Okla., 1967-70; pros. atty. City of Lawton, Okla., 1970; spl. dist. judge 5th Jud. Dist. Okla., 1971-72; pvt. practice law Lawton, 1973-90; dist. judge 5th Jud. Dist. Okla., 1990—. Pres. Swinney PTA, 1975-76; Editor: Problems in Teaching in the Secondary School, 1966. Pres. Comanche County Mental Health Assn., 1973-74, bd. dirs., 1972-76; co-chmn. Kingfisher County Reps. for Congressman James V. Smith, 1966; mem. state exec. com. Okla. Republican Com., 1973-74, chmn. auditing com., 1977-78; del. Rep. Nat. Conv., 1976; chmn. cts. com. Assn. South Central Okla. Govts. Crime Commn.; chmn. Comanche County Reps. for Reagan for Pres., 1973-83; mem. adv. bd. Jim Taliferro Mental Health Center, 1977-78; del. Nat. Mental Health Assn. Conv., 1975; bd. dirs. Lawton Campfire Girls; elder N.W. Ch. of Christ, 1977—; dir. Back to Bible Campaigns, 1976—. Mem. Am., Okla., Comanche County bar assns., Okla. Trial Lawyers Assn., Lawton Antique Auto Club, Ford Retractible Club Am., Alpha Psi Omega, Delta Theta Phi. Republican. Mem. Ch. of Christ (elder). Clubs: Fraternal Order of Police, Lion. Home: 2114 NW Atlanta Ave Lawton OK 73505-3923

MOORE, S. CLARK, judge; b. Norfolk, Va., Aug. 28, 1924; s. Samuel Clark and Mary Elizabeth (Pate) M. BA, San Diego State Coll., 1949; JD, U. So. Calif., L.A., 1957, LLM, 1960. Bar: Calif. 1957, U.S. Dist. Ct. (cen. dist.) Calif. 1957, U.S. Ct. Appeals (9th cir.) 1960. Dep. atty. gen. Calif. State Atty. Gen., L.A., 1957-72, asst. atty. gen., 1972-75, sr. asst. atty. gen., 1975-82, chief asst. atty. gen., 1982-83; judge Santa Anita Mcpl. Ct., 1984-94, Pomona Mcpl. Ct., Calif., 1995—; mem. Fed. cts. practice standards com., 1981-84, countywide criminal justice coord. com., 1989-90, courthouse security task force, 1989-90. With U.S. Army, 1943-46. Decorated European Theater medal, Asiatic Pacific medal, Am. Theater medal, Victory medal, Good Conduct medal, Philipine Liberation medal. Mem. L.A. Bar Assn. (former chmn. criminal justice sect., exec. com. bar delegation 1982-84), L.A. Mcpl. Cts. Judges Assn. (sec. 1989, vice chair 1988-89, chair 1989-90, exec. com. 1987-88, 90-91), Presiding Justices Assn. Republican. Office: Pomona Mcpl Ct 350 W Mission Pomona CA 91766-1607

MOORE, SALLY FALK, anthropology educator; b. N.Y.C., Jan. 18, 1924; d. Henry Charles and Mildred (Hymanson) Falk; m. Cresap Moore, July 14, 1951; children: Penelope, Nicola. B.A., Barnard Coll., 1943; LL.B., Columbia U., 1945, Ph.D., 1957. Asst. prof. U. So. Calif., Los Angeles, 1963-65, assoc. prof., 1965-70, prof., 1970-77; prof. UCLA, 1977-81; prof. anthropology Harvard U., Cambridge, Mass., 1981—, Victor Thomas prof. anthropology, 1991—, dean Grad. Sch. Arts and Scis., 1985-89. Author: Power and Property in Inca Peru, (Ansley Prize 1957), 1958, Law as Process, 1978, Social Facts and Fabrications, 1986, Moralizing States, 1993, Anthropology and Africa, 1994. Trustee Barnard Coll., Columbia U., 1991-92; master Dunster House, 1984-89. Rsch. grantee Social Sci. Rsch. Coun., 1968-69, NSF, 1972-75, 79-80, Wenner Gren Found., 1983; Guggenheim fellow, 1995-96. Fellow Am. Acad. Arts & Scis., Am. Anthrop. Assn., Royal Anthrop. Inst.; mem. Assn. Polit. and Legal Anthropology (pres. 1983), Am. Ethnological Soc. (pres. 1987-88), Assn. Africanist Anthropologists (pres.-elect 1995). Democrat. Office: Harvard U 348 William James Hall Cambridge MA 02138

MOORE, SCOTT, state official; b. York, Nebr., 1960; m. Danene Tushar, 1989. BA in Polit Sci., U. Nebr. Legis. aide Nebr. Legislature, 1981-86, mem., 1986-94, chair appropriations com.; sec. of state State of Nebr., 1995—; with Moore & Sons. Office: State Capitol # 2300 PO Box 94608 Lincoln NE 68509-4608 Address: 2025 B St Lincoln NE 68502 also: State Legislature State Capital Lincoln NE 68516*

MOORE, SEAN, pathologist, educator; b. Belfast, No. Ireland, Nov. 24, 1926; arrived in Can., 1951; s. James Bernard and Eileen (McFadden) M.; m. Cynthia Balch, Oct. 1957; children: John Brian, Martha Ailish, Patrick Balch. MB, BChir, Queen's U., Belfast, 1950. From asst. to assoc. pathologist Montreal Gen. Hosp., Que., Can., 1958-69; pathologist-in-chief Jewish Gen. Hosp., Montreal, 1969-71; chmn. dept. pathology McMaster U., Hamilton, Ont., Can., 1972-78, dir. labs. med. cen., 1972-84; pathologist-in-chief Royal Victoria Hosp., Montreal, 1984-94; chmn. dept. pathology, Strathcona prof. pathology McGill U., Montreal, 1984-94. Editor: Injury Mechanisms in Atherosclerosis, 1981; mng. editor: Experimental and Molecular Pathology; contbr. articles to profl. jours. Fellow Royal Coll. Physicians & Surgeons (Can.). Home: 522 Clarke Ave, Montreal, PQ Canada H3Y 3C9 Office: McGill U Dept Pathology, 3775 University St, Montreal, PQ Canada H3A 2B4

MOORE, SHARON HELEN SCOTT, gerontological nurse; b. L.I., N.Y., Nov. 7, 1947; d. James G. and Bernice Virginia (Conklin) Scott; m. Richard A. Moore Sr., July 5, 1966; children: Brian Keith, Richard A. Jr., Kevin Scott, Shannon Nicole. AAS, Fayetteville (N.C.) Tech. Inst., 1979; BSN, Med. U. S.S., 1993. Cert. gerontol. nursing. DON Elizabethtown (N.C.) Nursing Home; head nurse VA Med. Ctr., Fayetteville; coord. patient care Hospice Charleston, S.C.; DON, dir. human resources Sea Island Health Care Corp., Johns Island, S.C.; bd. dirs. Phoebe Taylor Family Clinic. Active St. James United Meth. Ch.; pres. family support group S.C. Army NG; vol. ARC, Fayetteville; bd. dirs. CYDC Big Brothers/Big Sisters. Indian Nurse scholar Nat. Soc. Colonial Dames Am., 1992. Mem. Nat. League Nursing, N.C. Nurses Assn. Office: Sea Island Comprehensive Health Care Corp PO Box 689 Johns Island SC 29457

MOORE, SHIRLEY THROCKMORTON (MRS. ELMER LEE MOORE), accountant; b. Des Moines, July 4, 1918; d. John Carder and Jessie (Wright) Throckmorton; student Iowa State Tchrs. Coll., summers 1937-38, Madison Coll., 1939-41; M.C.S., Benjamin Franklin U., 1944; CPA, Mc.; m. Elmer Lee Moore, Dec. 19, 1946; children: Fay, Lynn Dallas. Asst. bookkeeper Sibley Hosp., Washington, 1941-42, Alvord & Alvord, 1942-46, bookkeeper, 1946-49, chief accountant, 1950-64, fin. adviser to sr. ptnr., 1957-64; dir. Allen Oil Co., 1958-74; pvt. practice acctg., 1964—. Mem. sch. bd. Takoma Acad., Takoma Park, Md., 1970—; mem. hosp. bd. Washington Adventist Hosp., 1974-85; chmn. worthy student fund Takoma Park Seven Day Adventist Ch., 1987—; trustee Benson Found., 1963—; vol. Am. Women's Voluntary Svc., 1942-45. Recipient Disting. Grad. award Benjamin Franklin U., 1961. Mem. Am., D.C. (pub. rels. com. 1976—) insts. CPAs, Am. Women's Soc. CPAs, Am. Soc. Women Accts. (legislation chmn. 1960-62, nat. dir. 1952-53, nat. treas. 1953-54), Bus. and Profl. Women's Club (treas. D.C. 1967-68), Benjamin Franklin U. Alumni Assn. (Disting. Alumni award 1964, charter, past dir.), D.A.R., Md. Assn. CPAs (charter chmn. membership com. Montgomery Prince George County 1963-64, chmn. student rels. com. 1964-67, pres. 1968-69, mem. fed. tax com. 1971-73). Mem. Seventh Day Adventist Ch. Contbr. articles to profl. jours. Home and Office: 1007 Elm Ave Silver Spring MD 20912-5839

MOORE, SUSANNA, writer; b. Bryn Mawr, Pa., Dec. 9, 1948; d. Richard Dixon and Anne (Shields) M.; 1 child, Lulu Lenane Sylbert. Author: My Old Sweetheart, 1982 (Am. Book award nomination for best first novel 1983, Sue Kaufman prize for first fiction Am. Acad. Inst. Arts and Letters 1983), The Whiteness of Bones, 1989, Sleeping Beauties, 1993, In the Cut, 1995. Recipient Literary Lion award N.Y. Pub. Libr., 1993. Office: Wylie Aitken & Stone 250 W 57th St New York NY 10107

MOORE, THEODORE C., JR., oceanography educator; b. Kinston, N.C., Feb. 16, 1938. BS, U. N.C., 1960; PhD in Oceanography, U. Calif. San Diego, 1968. Rsch. assoc. oceanography Oreg. State U., 1968-69, asst. prof., 1969-75; assoc. prof. to prof. oceanography U. R.I., 1975—; prof. marine geology U. Mich., Ann Arbor, 1989—. Mem. AAAS, Am. Geophys. Union. Office: U Mich Ctr Great Lakes & Aquatic Scis 2200 Bonisteel Dr Ann Arbor MI 48109-2099*

MOORE, THOMAS CARROL, botanist, educator; b. Sanger, Tex., Sept. 22, 1936; s. Thomas M. and Willie Mae M.; m. Arvida Inmon DePriest, Sept. 1, 1956; children—Cynthia, Linda, Alan. B.A. in Biology, U. N. Tex., Denton, 1956; M.A. in Botany, U. Colo., 1958, Ph.D. (Outstanding Grad. Student in Biology award 1960, USPHS predoctoral fellow 1960-61), 1961. Instr. biology, then part-time instr. U. Colo., 1958-60; asst. prof. Ariz. State Coll., Flagstaff, 1961-63; mem. faculty Oreg. State U., Corvallis, 1963-93, prof. botany, 1971-93, prof. emeritus, 1993—, chmn. dept. botany and plant pathology, 1973-86, asst. to v.p. for rsch. and grad. studies, 1972-73; vis. prof. Colo. State Coll., 1963. Mem. editorial bd. Plant Physiology, 1981-86; editor in chief Jour. Plant Growth Regulation; contbr. articles to profl. jours. Recipient Mosser award outstanding undergrad. teaching Oreg. State U., 1966. Mem. Am. Soc. Plant Physiologists, Bot. Soc. Am., Am. Phytopathol. Soc., Internat. Plant Growth Substances Assn., Plant Growth Regulator Soc. Am., Sigma Xi. Democrat. Lodge: Elks. Home: 560 NW Merrie Dr Corvallis OR 97330-6524 Office: 2082 Cordley Hall Oreg State Univ Corvallis OR 97331

MOORE, THOMAS DAVID, academic administrator; b. Rochester, N.Y., July 26, 1937; s. Robert Franklin and Hilda (Kennedy) M.; m. Virginia Muller, June 13, 1959; children: Kathleen Mary, Michael David, Thomas David. BSS, St. John Fisher Coll., 1959; MS, SUNY, Brockport, 1962; EdD, Rutgers U., 1966. Tchr. Rochester City Schs., 1959-62; grad. asst. Rutgers U., New Brunswick, N.J., 1963-65; from asst. to full prof. Kent (Ohio) State U., 1965-93, asst. v.p. acad. affairs, 1976-83, v.p. faculty affairs and personnel, 1984-86, provost, v.p. acad. and student affairs, 1987-91; provost, v.p. acad. affairs Ctrl. Washington U., 1993—. Roman Catholic. Avocations: sports, film, public affairs, music.

MOORE, THOMAS E., biology educator, museum director; b. Champaign, Ill.; s. Gerald E. and Velma (Lewis) M.; m. E. Eleanor Sifferd, Feb. 4, 1951; children: Deborah S., Melinda S. BS, U. Ill., 1951, MS, 1952, PhD, 1956. Tech. asst. Ill. Natural History Survey, Urbana, 1950-56; instr. zoology U. Mich., Ann Arbor, 1956-59, asst. prof. zoology, 1959-63, assoc. prof. zoology, 1963-66, prof. biology, 1966—, curator insects, 1956—, dir. exhibit mus., 1988-93; vis. prof. Orgn. for Tropical Studies, San Jose, Costa Rica, 1970, 72; bd. dirs. Orgn. Tropical Studies, San Jose, 1968-79; mem. steering com. tropical biome U.S. Internat. Biol. Program, 1969-72; mem. conf. planning com. Nat. Inst. for Environment, 1991-92; mem. steering com. Univ. Colloquium on Environ. Rsch. and Edn., 1991-93. Co-editor: Lectures on Science Education, 1991-1992, 1993; Cricket Behavior and Neurobiology, 1989; author movie 17-Year Cicadas, 1975. County rep. Huron River Watershed Coun., Ann Arbor, 1987-95; mem. Mich. H.S. Accreditation Adv. Com., Ann Arbor, 1988-92; mem. U. Mich. Senate Adv. Com. on Univ. Affairs, 1993—, vice chair, 1995-96; bd. mem. U. Mich. Acad. Freedom Lecture Fund, 1995—, treas., 1995-96; cons. NSF Visual Tech. in Environ. Curricula, 1994—. Rsch. grantee NSF, 1963-66, 66-69, rsch. equipment grantee, 1984-86. Fellow AAAS, AAUP (pres. U. Mich. chpt. 1996—), Royal Entomol. Soc. London, Linnaen Soc. London; mem. Assn. Tropical Biology (pres. 1973-75), Sigma Xi (pres. U. Mich. chpt. 1994-96, coun. 1993—). Home: 4243 N Delhi Rd Ann Arbor MI 48103-9485 Office: Mus of Zoology U Mich Ann Arbor MI 48109-1079

MOORE, THOMAS GALE, economist, educator; b. Washington, Nov. 6, 1930; s. Charles Godwin and Beatrice (McLean) M.; m. Cassandra Chrones, Dec. 28, 1958; children: Charles G., Antonia L. B.A., Geroge Washington U., 1957; M.A., U. Chgo., 1959, Ph.D., 1961. Fgn. research analyst Chase Manhattan Bank, N.Y.C., 1960-61; asst. prof. econs. Carnegie Inst. Tech., 1961-65; assoc. prof., then prof. econs. Mich. State U., East Lansing, 1965-74; sr. staff economist Council Econ. Advisers, 1968-70; hon. research fellow Univ. Coll., London, 1973-74; adj. scholar Am. Enterprise Inst., 1971—, CATO Inst., 1982—; sr. fellow Hoover Inst. on War, Revolution and Peace-Stanford U., 1974—, dir. domestic studies program, 1974-85; mem. Council Econ. Advisers, Washington, 1985-89; mem. Nat. Critical Materials Council, 1985-89; mem. econ. adv. bd. Dept. Commerce, 1971-73; mem. adv. com. RANN, 1975-77, NSF, 1975-77; cons. Dept. Transp., 1973-74, 81-83; mem. adv. panel Synthetic Fuels Corp., 1982; mem. adv. bd. Reason Found., 1982—; dir. Stanford Savs. & Loan, 1979-82, chmn., 1982. Author: The Economics of American Theater, 1968, Freight Transportation Regulation, 1972, Trucking Regulation: Lessons from Europe, 1976, Uranium Enrichment and Public Policy, 1978; co-author: Public Claims on U.S. Output, 1973; contbr. articles to profl. jours. Served with USN, 1951-55, Korea. Fellow Earhart Found., 1958-59; fellow Walgreen Found., 1959-60, Hoover Instn., 1973-74. Mem. Am. Econ. Assn., Mont. Pelerin Soc., Chevy Chase Club. Home: 3766 La Donna Ave Palo Alto CA 94306-3150 Office: Stanford U Hoover Instn Stanford CA 94305

MOORE, THOMAS KAIL, chief judge; b. Idaho Falls, Idaho, Jan. 15, 1938; s. Burton L. and Clara E. (Kail) Moore; m. Judith Diane Gilman, July 30, 1966; children: David T., Jonathan G. AB in Phys. Scis., Harvard U., 1961; JD, Georgetown U., 1967. Bar: D.C., V.I., Va. Law clk. to Hon. John A. Danaher U.S. Ct. Appeals (D.C. Cir.), 1967-68; staff atty. Office Gen. Coun., Office Sec. Dept. Transp., Washington, 1968-69; assoc. Stanford, Reed & Gelenian, Washington, 1969-70; asst. U.S. Atty. U.S. Attys. Office, Washington, 1970-71; asst. U.S. Atty. U.S. Attys. Office (ea. dist.), Va., 1971-76, prin. asst. Alexandria office, 1974-76; asst. U.S. Atty. U.S. Attys. Office (V.I. dist.), 1976-78; pvt. practive St. Thomas, V.I., 1978-81; shareholder Hoffman & Moore, P.C., St. Thomas, 1981-87; ptnr. Grunert, Stout, Moore & Bruch, St. Thomas, 1987-92; chief judge U.S. Dist. Ct. (V.I. dist.), 1992—. Editor-in-chief Georgetown Law Journal, 1966-67. Scoutmaster Antilles Sch. Troop; trustee V.I. Montessori Sch. Capt. USAF, 1961-64, USAFR. Mem. ABA, V.I. Bar Assn. (judicial), V.I. C. of C., St. Thomas Yacht Club. Avocations: tennis, swimming, sailing. Office: Dist Ct of VI 5500 Veterans Dr Ste 310 Charlotte Amalie VI 00802-6424

MOORE, THOMAS LLOYD, librarian; b. Springfield, Ill., Oct. 4, 1942; s. Edward Joseph and Dorothy A. (Menezes) M.; m. Ann Mary Walsh, Aug. 29, 1971; children: Sean Christopher, Martin Thomas, Kathleen Adele. AA, Springfield Coll., 1963; BA, Cardinal Glennon Coll., St. Louis, 1968; MA in Library Sci., Rosary Coll., 1973. Tchr. Little Flower Grade Sch., Springfield, 1963-66; head of adult services Elk Grove Village (Ill.) Pub. Library, 1973-74; dir. Northlake (Ill.) Pub. Library Dist., 1974-75, Danville (Ill.) Pub. Library, 1975-78; adminstrv. librarian Palatine (Ill.) Pub. Library Dist., 1978-81; dir. Wake County Dept. of the Pub. Library, Raleigh, N.C., 1981—. Bd. dirs. Commit to a Healthier Raleigh, 1991-93, Planned Parenthood of the Capital & Coast, 1993—, sec., 1994—; bd. dirs. Pirates Cove Homeowners Assn., 1992, v.p., 1993-94, pres., 1995—; mem. Libr. Power Adv. Com., 1993—; mem. ASSIST Wake to Health Coalition, 1992-

94. Mem. ALA, N.C. Library Assn. Democrat. Roman Catholic. Office: Wake County Pub Libr 4020 Carya Dr Raleigh NC 27610-2913

MOORE, THOMAS PAUL, broadcast executive; b. Danville, Ill., Feb. 29, 1928; s. Lester Rufus and Mabel Ellen (Jackson) M.; m. Jean LaVonne Sather, Aug. 31, 1952; children: Randyl Ellen, Patricia Kay, Gregory Sather. BA, North Cen. Coll., Naperville, Ill., 1952; postgrad., Denver U., 1952-53. Newscaster Sta. KFEL-AM-FM-TV, Denver, 1952-54; sales rep. Sta. KGMC, Englewood, Colo., 1954-56; sales mgr. Sta. KDEN-AM-FM, Denver, 1956-62; pres. Stas. WBCO, WQEL, Bucyrus, Ohio, 1962—; bd. dirs. First Fed. Savings and Loan, Bucyrus, 1990—. Lay leader, mem. program council Ohio Sandusky Conf., United Methodist Ch., 1966-69 (pres. gen. laity bd. and laymen's found. 1968-72); mem. Gen Council on Ministries, 1980-84, N.W. Ohio Water Devel. Adv. Com., 1967-69, Sandusky River Basin Water Pollution Study Com., 1968-69; v.p., bd. mgrs. EUB Men, Evang. United Brethren Ch., 1958-68; pres. Rocky Mountain Conf., 1957-61; mem. gen. bd. Nat. Council Christian Chs. Am., 1968-72; charter pres. Bucyrus Bratwurst Festival, Inc., 1968; adv. bd. Bucyrus Salvation Army, 1964-68; mem. planning com. East Ohio Conf., 1972-76 (chmn. commn. on minimum salaries, 1968-72, lay leader, 1972-76); vice chmn. council ministries, mem. episcopal com., 1972-76, head. del. to gen. conf., Portland, Oreg., 1976, Balt., 1984; head del. to Jurisdictional Conf., Sioux Falls, 1976, Duluth, Minn., 1984; pres. United Meth. Communications, 1972-76, mem. gen. council fin. and adminstrn., 1976-80; mem. communications commn. Nat. Council Chs., 1972-76; mem. communications con. Ohio Council Chs.; mem. Episc. com., chmn. New Vision Task Group, both East Ohio Conf., North Cen. Jurisdiction, United Meth. Ch.; mem. exec. com. Council on Ministries, 1980-86; mem. World Meth. Council, 1986-91; trustee United Theol. Sem., 1972-80; trustee Ohio Northern U., 1986—, mem. exec. com., 1991—, chair student affairs com., 1991-95, chair, 1995—; mem. exec. com. East Ohio del. to United Meth. Gen. Conf. and Jurisdictional Conf., 1987-91; v.p. Community Improvement Corp., Bucyrus, 1989-91; mem. Overall Econ. Devel. Com. of Crawford County; chmn. Crawford County Traffic Safety Council, 1979-89; pres. Crawford County Econ. Devel. Adv. Coun., 1992-94; mem. Crawford County Devel. Bd., Inc.; mem. exec. com. of del. to 1988 Gen. Conf. United Meth. Ch., St. Louis; bd. dirs. Bucyrus Community Hosp., 1992-96, mem. fin. com., 1993-96, chair nominating com., 1993-96, campaign dir., chair fundraising com., 1993-96, v.p. bd. dirs., 1994-96; chmn. N. Ctrl. Ohio Health Sys., 1996—. Served with USN, 1946-48. Named a Civic Leader of Am., 1968. Mem. Nat. Assn. Broadcasters (legis. liaison 1984-91, mem. small market radio com.), Ohio Assn. Broadcasters (pres. 1982-85), North Ctrl. Ohio Broadcasters Assn. (pres. 1983-84, 96—, v.p. 1985-96), Bucyrus Area C. of C. (chmn. airport study com. 1967-68, bd. dirs. 1964-67, pres. 1989-91), Rotary (pres. Bucyrus chpt. 1992-93). Office: SAMOR Stas 403 E Rensselaer St Bucyrus OH 44820-2438

MOORE, THOMAS RONALD, lawyer; b. Duluth, Minn., Mar. 27, 1932; s. Ralph Henry and Estelle Marguerite (Hero) M.; m. Margaret C. King, Sept. 10, 1955; children: Willard S., Clarissa, Charles R.H. BA magna cum laude, Yale U., 1954; JD, Harvard U., 1957. Bar: N.Y. 1958, U.S. Supreme Ct. 1958. Instr. Internat. Program in Taxation Harvard Law Sch., 1956-57; assoc. Dewey Ballantine, N.Y.C.; ptnr. Breed, Abbott & Morgan, N.Y.C., Finley Kumble & Wagner, N.Y.C., Hawkins, Delafield & Wood, N.Y.C.; pvt. practice Law Offices of Thomas R. Moore, N.Y.C.; lectr. on law Cornell Law Sch., NYU, So. Fed. Tax Inst., N.Y.C., U. Hartford, Practising Law Inst., N.Y.C., Las Vegas, New Orleans; lectr. N.Y.C., San Antonio, Tampa, L.A., Moscow, Charlottesville, Va., Washington, Kansas City. Author: Plantagenet Descent, 31 Generations from William the Conqueror to Today, 1995; co-author: Estate Planning and the Close Corporation; editor-in-chief Gastronome; bd. editors: The Tax Lawyer; contbr. articles to profl jours., popular press and TV commentaries. Bd. dirs. exec. com. Citymeals on Wheels; pres. bd. dirs. Nat. Soc. to Prevent Blindness, 1973-81, chmn., 1981-83, now hon. pres.; sec.-treas., trustee A.D. Henderson Found., Del.; trustee, Fla.; bd. dirs. Phoenix Theatre Inc., Inst. Aegean Prehistory, Found. Future of Man, Am. and Internat. Friends of Victoria and Albert Mus., London; conservator N.Y. Pub. Libr.; trustee Found. for Renaissance of St. Petersburg (Russia), Malcolm Wiener Found., Lawrence W. Levine Found. Recipient Coat of Arms and created Knight of Order of St. John by Queen Elizabeth II, Order of Crown of Charlemagne, Order of Plantagenet, Order of Barons of Magna Charta; recipient Key to Kansas City by Mayor of Kansas City, Mo., 1989; Yale scholar of House, 1954; honoree Thomas R. Moore Disting. Pub. Servant award Nat. Soc. to Prevent Blindness. Mem. ABA, N.Y. State BAr Assn. (exec. com.), Assn. of Bar City of N.Y., Confrerie de la Chaine des Rotisseurs (nat. pres., dir., exec. com. world coun. Paris), Chevalier du Tastevin, Nat. Wine Coalition (bd. dirs. 1989—), Downtown Assn., Univ. Club, Church Club, Delta Sigma Rho. Republican. Episcopalian. Office: 730 5th Ave Ste 900 New York NY 10019-4105

MOORE, THOMAS SCOTT, lawyer; b. Portland, Oreg., Nov. 17, 1937; s. Harry Alburn and Geraldine Elizabeth (Scott) M.; m. Saundra L. Wagner, Sept. 7, 1957 (div. 1974); children: Cindy, Kristin, Thomas, Victoria, Wendy; m. Alice H. Zeisz, Nov. 5, 1976; 1 child, Alice G. BA, Willamette U., 1959, JD cum laude, 1962. Bar: Oregon 1962. Pvt. practice Portland, 1962—. Contbr. articles to law jours. Republican. Avocation: tennis. Office: 4512 SW Kelly Ave Portland OR 97201-4257

MOORE, THURSTON ROACH, lawyer; b. Memphis, Dec. 10, 1946; s. Richard Charlton Moore and Halcyon Hall (Roach) Lynn; m. Grace Branch, Nov. 8, 1969. BA with distinction, U. Va., 1968, JD, 1974. Bar: Va. 1974. Rsch. analyst Scudder, Stevens & Clark, N.Y.C., 1968-71; ptnr. Hunton & Williams, Richmond, Va., 1974—; bd. dirs. Exec. Info. Sys., Inc., Darien, Conn., Met. Advantage Corp., Richmond. Bd. dirs. Met. Bus. Found., Richmond, Mary Morton Parsons Found., Charlottesville, Va., The Nature Conservancy, Charlottesville, vice chmn. Va. chpt.; trustee Va. Aerospace Bus. Roundtable, Hampton, 1989—, Va. Ea. Shore Sustainable Devel. Corp., 1995—. Mem. ABA (bus. law sect., chmn. ptnrs. com., mem. fed. regulation security com.), Va. Bar Assn., Va. State Bar. Office: Hunton & Williams 951 E Byrd St Richmond VA 23219-4040

MOORE, TOM, film and theater director; b. Meridian, Miss., Aug. 6, 1943; s. Heustis T. and Maryanne (Moody) M. B.A., Purdue U., 1965; M.F.A., Yale U., 1968. Tchr. Am. Dramatic Inst., U. London, 1968; guest dir. SUNY-Buffalo, 1968, Brandeis U., Boston, 1968; artistic dir. Peterborough Players (N.H.), 1971; lectr. Seminar Am. Studies, Salzburg, Austria, 1974. Dir. Broadway plays: Grease (one of the longest-running shows in history of Broadway), 1972-80, Over Here, 1974-75, Once in a Lifetime, 1978, Division Street, 1980, Frankenstein, 1981, 'night Mother, 1983 (Pulitzer Prize) (dir. film by same name 1986), The Octette Bridge Club, 1985, A Little Hotel on the Side, Nat. Actors Theatre, 1992; off-Broadway play: Welcome to Andromeda, 1973; plays Am. Conservatory Theatre, San Francisco, 1977-81, Williamstown (Mass.) Theatre Festival, 1976, 79, 93, Mark Taper Forum, Los Angeles, 1980, 82, 83, 84, 86, 91, Tyrone Guthrie Theatre, Mpls., 1975, Arena Stage, Washington, 1975, Old Globe Theatre Festival, San Diego, 1982, 85, Ahmanson Theatre, Los Angeles, 1983, Am. Repertory Theatre, Cambridge, Mass., 1982, 84, La Jolla (Calif.) Playhouse, 1990; film Journey, 1972; co-dir. Fridays, ABC-TV; dir. thirtysomething, ABC-TV, LA Law, NBC-TV (Emmy nominee 1991), Almost Grown, CBS-TV, Wonder Years, ABC-TV (Humanitas prize for Square Dance episode, 1990), Cheers, NBC-TV, Northern Exposure, CBS-TV, Picket Fences, CBS-TV, Civil Wars, ABC-TV, Class of '96, Fox TV, Mad About You, NBC-TV; TV movies Maybe, Baby, and Fine Things, NBC, 1990; TV pilots The Flamingo Kid, 50 Minute Man. Recipient Tony award nomination 1974, 83, Golden Knight award Malta Film Festival, 1973, Cine Golden Eagle award, 1973, 6 Dramalogue awards, 1981-86. Fellow Am. Film Inst.

MOORE, TRESI LEA, lawyer; b. Brownwood, Tex., Dec. 3, 1961; d. Dean Moore and Patsy Ruth (Evans) Adams. BA in Fgn. Svc., BA in French, Baylor U., 1984, JD, 1987. Bar: Tex. 1987, U.S. Dist. Ct. (no. dist.) Tex. 1988, U.S. Ct. Appeals (5th cir.) 1989. Atty. Richard Jackson & Assocs., Dallas, 1987-91, Amis, Moore & Davis (and predecessor firm), Arlington, Tex., 1992—. Vol. Legal Svcs. of North Tex., Dallas, 1988—, Dallas Com. for Fgn. Visitors, 1989-92; bd. dirs. Plano Internat. Presch. Recipient Pro Bono Svc. award Legal Svcs. of North Tex., 1989, 90, 91. Mem. AAUW (pub. policy dir. Plano, Tex. br. 1992, 93-94, v.p. 1994-95), ABA, State Bar Tex. (mem. mentor program for lawyers com. 1994—, mem. local bar svcs. com. 1994—), Dallas Bar Assn., Tarrant County Bar Assn., Dallas Women Lawyers Assn. (bd. dirs. 1989-90, v.p. 1992, pres. 1993). Avocations: scuba diving, reading, bicycling, hiking, growing herbs. Office: Amis Moore & Davis 2301 E Lamar Blvd Ste 250 Arlington TX 76006-7416

MOORE, VERNON LEE, agricultural consultant, retired food products company executive; b. Creston, Iowa, Mar. 29, 1928; s. Newton and Eulalia Pearl (Lewis) M.; m. Lorene Shirley Moore, Jan. 29, 1949; children: Dianne, Nancy, Jack. BS in Agr., Iowa State U., 1951. Instr. vocat. agrl. Gowrie (Iowa) Sch. Dist., 1951-55; with Land O'Lakes, Inc., Mpls., 1955-88, sr. v.p., 1988, ret., 1988; pvt. practice agrl. cons., 1989—. Bd. dirs. exec. com. Agrl. Coop. Devel. Internat., Washington, 1972-89, Am. Inst. Coop., Washington, 1975-88, Minn. 4-H Found., Washington, 1980-91; bd. dirs. Vols. in OVerseas Coop. Devel., Washington, 1980-88, The Coop. Found., St. Paul, 1978-88; commr. Civil Svc. Commn., Columbia Hts., Minn., 1974—; mem. U. Minn. Adv. Com., St. Paul, 1984-91; various leadership positions Fridley United Meth. Ch., Minn., 1971—; Minn. dir. Chs. United in Global Mission Russian Farms Projects, 1992—. Recipient Internat. Coop. award Coop. Coordinating Group, 1987. Lodges: Rotary, Masons, Shriners. Avocations: photography, woodworking, gardening.

MOORE, WALTER BRUCE, career officer; b. Big Spring, Tex., Mar. 4, 1940; s. Walter C. and Mildred A. (Foytik) M.; m. Mary Ann Hennig, June 17, 1993; children: Robert, Leslie, Kelly, Richard. BS in Animal Husbandry, Tex. A&M U., 1962; MPA, Auburn U., 1974. Commd. 2d lt. U.S. Army, 1962, advanced through grades to maj. gen., 1991; student U.S. Army Inf. Sch., Ft. Benning, Ga., 1962; asst. S-3 Student Brigade, Ft. Benning, Ga., 1962; platoon leader Co. C, 1st Bn., 46th Inf. 1st Armored Div., Ft. Hood, Tex., 1962-63; student U.S. Army Primary Helicopter Sch. Ft. Wolters, Tex., 1963; rotary wing aviator 25th Aviation Bn, 25th Inf. Div., Hawaii, 1963-65; aviator 173d Aviation Co., Hawaii, 1965-66, Vietnam, 1966; asst. S-4 11th Combat Aviation Bn., Vietnam, 1966-67; student U.S. Army Aviation Sch., Ft. Stewart, Ga., 1967; gunnery instr., instr. pilot, flight commdr. U.S. Army Aviation Sch., Ft. Rucker, Ala., 1967-69; student U.S. Army Inf. Sch., Ft. Benning, 1969-70; flight standardization office 1st Aviation Brigade, Vietnam, 1970, comdr. 162d Aviation Co., 1970-71; pers. mgmt. officer Office Pers. Ops., Washington, 1971-73; stidemt U.S. Army Inf. Sch., Ft. Benning, 1973, Air Command and Staff Coll., Maxwell AFB, Ala., 1973-74; exec. officer, sec. gen. staff 9th Inf. Div., Ft. Lewis, Wash., 1974-77, cmdr. 2d Bn, 2d Inf., 1977-79, chief Bn. Tng. Mgmt. System, 1979; student U.S. Army War Coll., Carlisle Barracks, Pa., 1979-80; asst. chief of staff G-3, Berlin Brigade U.S. Command, Berlin, 1980-82; comdr. 3d Brigade 101st Airborne Div., Ft. Campbell, Ky., 1982-84, chief of staff, 1985-86; asst. div. comdr 3d Inf. Div. (Mech.) U.S. Army Europe, 1986-88; chief of staff XVIII Airborne Corps and Ft. Bragg, Ft. Bragg, N.C., 1988-89; asst. chief staff UN Command/Combined Forces Command, Korea, 1989-91. Decorated Legion of Merit with two oak leaf clusters, Def. Supr. Svc. medal, D.F.C. with oak leaf cluster, Bronze Star with oak leaf cluster, Meritorious Svc. medal with two oak leaf clusters, Air Medal with 35 oak leaf clusters, Army Commendation medal with V device and two oak leaf clusters, Expert Infantryman badge, Master Army Aviator badge, Sr. Parachutist badge, Air Assault badge, Ranger tab. Home: 23030 Whisper Cyn San Antonio TX 78258-3210

MOORE, WALTER PARKER, JR., civil engineering company executive; b. Houston, May 6, 1937; s. Walter Parker Sr. and Zoe Alma (McBride) M.; m. Mary Ann Dillingham, Aug. 19, 1959; children: Walter P. III, Melissa Moore Magee, Matthew Dillingham. BA in Civil Engring., Rice U., 1959, BS in Civil Engring., 1960; MS in Civil Engring., U. Ill., 1962, PhD in Civil Engring., 1964. Registered profl. engr., Ark., Ariz., Colo., Fla., Ga., Idaho, Ill., Ind., Kans., Maine, Md., Mich., Minn., Mo., Nev., N.H., N.Mex., N.Y., N.C., Okla., Oreg., Pa., R.I., Tex., Utah, Wash., Wis., Wyo. Rsch. asst. U. Ill., Urbana, 1960-64; design engr. Walter P. Moore & Assocs., Inc., Houston, 1966-70, sec., treas., 1970-75, exec. v.p., 1975-83, pres., chmn., 1983—, chmn., 1993—; engring. adv. coun. Rice U., 1970-74, adj. prof. architecture, 1975-82, archtl. adv. coun., 1988—; pres. Rice U. Alumni Assn., 1975; civil engring. vis. com. U. Tex. Austin, 1975-77; adv. com. effects of earthquake motions on reinforced concrete bldgs. U. Ill. Adv. Com., 1980; pres. Rice U. Engring. Alumni Assn., 1983, vis. lectr. Cornell U., 1986; mem. sesquicentennial com. State of Tex. Bus. and Fin. Com., 1986; vis. lectr. U. Ill., 1988, 89; engring. adv. coun. Tex. A&M U., 1990—; Thomas A. Bullock Endowed Chair Leadership and Innovation Coll. Arch., Dept. Civil Engring. Texas A&M U., 1994—, dir. Ctr. Bldg. Design and Constrn., dir. Ctr. Constrn. Edn. Group editor (monograph) Tall Building Systems and Concepts; mem. editorial adv. bd. Constrn. Bus. Rev., 1992—. Bd. dirs. Kiwanis Club Houston, 1974-76, Rice Design Alliance, 1976-79, Rice Ctr. for Community Design and Rsch., 1977-82, Harris County Heritage Soc., 1984-86, River Oaks Bank, 1983-91, Compass Bank, 1991-92; bd. dirs., v.p. The Forest Club, 1976-78; chmn. architects and engrs. United Way, 1985; mem. exec. com. River Oaks Bank, 1984-91. Capt. U.S. Army, 1964-66. Recipient Outstanding Civil Engring. Alumnus award U. Ill., 1992, Outstanding Engring. Alumnus award Rice U., 1993, Master Builder award Assoc. Gen. Contrs., Houston chpt., 1995. Fellow Am. Concrete Inst.; mem. AIA (hon. Houston chpt.), NAE, NSPE, ASCE (activities chmn. 1968-69, sec. structures group Tex. sect. 1976-77, vice-chmn. 1977-78, structural standards divsn., exec. com. 1989—, chmn. A7 com. 1988—, keynote speaker nat. conv. New Orleans 1986), Am. Cons. Engrs. Coun. (bd. dirs. CEC-T 1981-83, v.p. 1990-92), Internat. Assn. Bridge and Structural Engrs., Am. Concrete Inst. (mem. com. # 318, bd. direction 1989-91, Alfred E. Lindau award 1992), Soc. Am. Mil. Engrs., Coun. on Tall Bldgs. and Urban Habitat (mem. steering group 1971—, editor Com. 3 1975—, chmn. final plenary session Hong Kong Fourth World Congress, 1990, Hong Kong Forth World Congress, 1990, internat. and regional conference 1990—), Consulting Engrs. Coun. Tex. (bd. dirs. 1974-76, v.p. 1976-77, pres. 1977-78), Tex. Soc. Profl. Engrs. (Young Engr. of Yr. 1969-70, region IV Engr. of Yr., 1985), Post Tensioning Inst. (juror nat. awards 1983—), Structural Engrs. Assn. Tex. Episcopalian. Office: 2d Fl 3131 Eastside St Fl 2 Houston TX 77098-1919 also: Tex A&M U Dept Civil Engring CE/TTI Bldg Rm 710F College Station TX 77843-3136

MOORE, WARD WILFRED, medical educator; b. Cowden, Ill., Feb. 12, 1924; s. Cecil Leverett and Velma Leona (Frye) M.; m. Frances Laura Campbell, Jan. 29, 1949; children—Scott Thomas, Ann Gail, Brian Dean, Kevin Lee. A.B., U. Ill., 1948, M.S., 1951, Ph.D., 1952. Instr., rsch. assoc. U. Ill., 1952-54; asst. prof. Okla. State U., Stillwater, 1954-55, Ind. U., Bloomington, 1955-59; assoc. prof. Ind. U., 1959-66, prof. physiology, 1966-89, prof. physiology and biophysics emeritus, 1989—, acting chmn. dept. anatomy, 1971-73, assoc. dean basic med. scis., 1971-89, assoc. dean, dir. med. scis. program, 1976-89; vis. prof. Postgrad. Med. Center, Karachi, Pakistan, 1963-64; staff mem. Rockefeller Found., 1968-71; vis. prof., chmn. dept. physiology, faculty sci. Mahidol U., Bangkok, Thailand, 1968-71. Served with U.S. Army, 1943-46. Mem. Am. Physiol. Soc., Endocrine Soc., Am. Soc. Nephrology, Soc. Study Reproduction, Am. Assn. Anatomists, Soc. Exptl. Biology and Medicine, Am. Assn. Med. Colls., AAAS, Am. Inst. Biol. Scis., AAUP, Ind. Acad. Sci., Ind. Hist. Soc., Sigma Xi, Phi Sigma. Home: 3421 E Latimer Rd Bloomington IN 47401-4219 Office: Ind U Myers Hall # 203 Bloomington IN 47405

MOORE, WAYNE V., pediatrician, educator, endocrinologist; b. Wichita, Kans., May 3, 1942. BA, Friends U., 1964; PhD, U. Minn., 1969, MD, 1970. Diplomate Am. Bd. Pediatrics, Am. Bd. Pediatric Endocrine; lic. physician, Kans., Minn. Fellow in biochemistry U. Minn., Mpls., 1969-70, intern in pediatrics, 1970-71, resident in pediatrics, 1971-72; clin. assoc. NIH, Bethesda, Md., 1972-74; asst. prof. pediatrics U. Kans. Med. Ctr., Kansas City, 1974-78, assoc. prof., 1978-82, prof., 1982—; head. sect. pediatric endocrinology and metabolism U. Kans. Med. Ctr., 1974—, attending physician pediatric inpatient svc., 1976—, elected mem. grad. sch. faculty in biochemistry, 1977, departmental reviewer dept. diatetics and nutrition, 1974-75, acad. com. student promotions subcom., 1975—, physiology chmn. search com., 1975-76, ad-hoc com. for devel. tenure guidelines, 1976-77, faculty coord. for pediatric grand rounds, 1975-81, pediatric rsch. com., 1976-79, adminstrn. PKU and congenital hypothyroid follow-up clinic, 1976—, ad-hoc com. for rev. Nat. Intensive Care Unit, 1976-77, ENT chmn. search com., 1978, chmn. CRC adv. com., 1978-79, utilization rev. com., 1979-80, promotion and tenure com. dept. pediatrics, 1979-82, acting. chmn. pediatrics, 1981-83, instn. promotion and tenure com., 1984-86, dean search com., 1985, departmental awards com., 1986-87, dept. promotion and tenure com., 1987-88, chmn., 1988—, coll. promotion and tenure com., 1988-89, 89-91, telethon com., pediatric dept. rsch. com., 1988—; vis. prof. U. Okla-Tulsa, 1979, U. S.D., 1979, U. Minn., 1980, European Soc. for Pediatric Endocrinology, 1986; mem. Nat. Pituitary Agy., 1978-85, chmn. growth hormone subcom., 1984-89. Reviewer Jour. AMA, Endocrinology, Jour. Pediatrics, Diabetes, Jour. Clin. Endocrinology and Metabolism; contbr. over 150 articles and abstracts to profl. and sci. jours., chpt. to book. Am. Cancer Soc. scholar, 1970; grantee Nat. Pituitary Agy., 1975-85, State Dept. Child and Maternal Health, 1976—, NIH, 1980-85, 81-84, 87-90, Muscular Dystrophy Assn., 1980-82, Carey Endorsement, 1983—, Genetech, 1985—, Astrowe Found., 1986-87, 87-88, Juvenile Diabetes Found., 1986-88, Amoco Found., 1986—, Cosmopolitan Club, 1987—, Am. Heart Assn., 1987-89, 89-90, Ctr. for Disease Control., 1987-90, Mother Mary Ann Found., 1991—. Mem. Am. Acad. Pediatrics (v.p. Kans. chpt. 1988, pres. Kans. chpt. 1991), Am. Pediatric Soc., Am. Diabetes Assn. (grantee 1986-87), Endocrine Soc., Pediatric Endorcine Soc. (chmn. com. on future use of polypeptide hormones 1986-88), Human Growth Found., Soc. for Pediatric Rsch., Southwest Pediatric Soc., Kans. Med. Soc., Kans. Diabetes Assn., Greater Kansas City Diabetes Assn. (invited lectr. 1979—), Kansas City Endocrine Roundtable, Lawson Wilkins Pediatric Endocrine Soc., Sigma Xi, Alpha Omega Alpha. Achievements include research in mechanism of action growth hormones, early detection and treatment of chronic complications associated with diabetes, Islet transplantation, treatment of prediabetes with nicotinamide, role of intrathymic transplantation in development of tolerance, isolation and characterization of antigen presenting cells, early detection of vascular dysfunction in type 1 diabetes, treatment of short stature growth hormone, development of an implantable glucose sensor. Office: U Kans Pediatric Endocrine Dept 3901 Rainbow Blvd Kansas City KS 66160-0001

MOORE, WILLIAM B., lawyer; b. 1941. BA, Stanford U., 1963; JD, U. Ill., 1966. Bar: Ill. 1966. Atty. Trans Union Corp., 1966-73, sr. atty., 1973-79, sec., 1977-81, gen. counsel, 1979-81; corp. counsel IC Industries, 1982-86; sec., dept. gen. counsel Whitman Corp., 1987-90, v.p., sec., gen. counsel. Mem. Am. Soc. Corp. Secs. Inc (pres. Chgo. regional group 1979-80, dir. 1980-83). Office: Whitman Corp 3501 Algonquin Rd Rolling Meadows IL 60008-3149

MOORE, WILLIAM CULLEN, retired electronics company executive; b. Portland, Oreg., Nov. 17, 1912; s. William Cullen and Lillian (Rodé) M.; m. Helen Hays Edgar, Aug. 8, 1936; children: Shirley Carol, Ronald Cullen, Paul Alan, Katherine Leone. BA in Physics, Reed Coll., Portland, 1936; MA in Physics, Boston U., 1949. Electronics engr. United Airlines, Chgo., 1937-38; project leader Motorola, Inc., Chgo., 1938-47; sect. head govt. electronics group Motorola, Inc., Scottsdale, Ariz., 1958-78; ret.; project supr./instr. Upper Air Lab., Boston U., 1947-51; chief engr. Tracerlab, Inc., Boston, 1951-53; engring. mgr. Boonton (N.J.) Radio Corp., 1953-58; cons./facilitator (space) Motorola Mus. of Electronics, Schaumburg, Ill., 1987-90; investigator Apollo comms. NASA, Madrid, Spain, 1971. Contbr. articles to profl. jours. Mem. sch. bd. Lombard (Ill.) Sch. Dist., 1946-47, Mountain Lakes (N.J.) Sch. Dist., 1956-58; mem. allocations panels United Way, 1977-94. Fellow AIAA (assoc.; sect. chair 1963-64); mem. IEEE (sr.; sect. chair 1940—). Achievements include patents on coupling transformer; coded range signal responsive system (aviation); low level bridge discriminator; transponder for moving vehicle tracking system (space). Home: 9915 W Royal Oak Rd GH-1089 Sun City AZ 85351-3160

MOORE, WILLIAM GROVER, JR., consultant, former air freight executive, former air force officer; b. Waco, Tex., May 18; s. William Grover and Annie Elizabeth (Pickens) M.; student Kilgore (Tex.) Coll., 1937-39, Sacramento State Coll., 1951, George Washington U., 1962; grad. Air War Coll., Air U., 1957, Nat. War Coll., 1962; m. Marjorie Y. Gardella, Jan. 18, 1943; 1 dau., Allyson. Enlisted U.S. Army Air Force, 1940, commd. 2d lt., 1941, advanced through grades to gen., 1977; comdr. 777th Squadron, 15th AF, Italy, 1944-45, 3535th Maintenance and Supply Group, Mather AFB, Calif., 1951, 3d Bomb Group, Korea, 1952; chief bases and units div. Hdqrs. USAF, 1952-56; asst. dep. chief of staff ops. Hdqrs. USAF Europe, 1957-61; comdr. 314th Troop Carrier Wing, Sewart AFB, Tenn., 1962-63, 839th Air Div., 1963-65; asst. J3 U.S. Strike Command, 1965-66; comdr. 834th Air Div., Vietnam, 1966-67; dir. operational requirements Hdqrs, USAF, 1967-70; comdr. 22d AF, 1970-73, 13th AF, 1973; chief of staff Pacific Command, 1973-76; asst. vice chief of staff Hdqrs. USAF, 1976-77; comdr. in chief Mil. Air Lift Command, 1977-79; ret., 1979; pres., chief operating officer Emery Air Freight Corp., Wilton, Conn., 1981-83; bus. cons., 1983—; pres. Met. Nashville Airport Authority, 1984—. Decorated Def. D.S.M., Air Force D.S.M. with 2 oak leaf clusters, Legion of Merit with 4 oak leaf clusters, Silver Star, D.F.C. with oak leaf cluster, Air medal with 9 oak leaf clusters, AF Commendation medal with 10 oak leaf clusters (U.S.); Croix de Guerre with palm (France); Armed Forces Honor medal 1st class (Vietnam); Republic of China Cloud and Banner; Legion of Honor (Republic of Philippines); recipient L. Mendel Rivers award of excellence; Jimmy Doolittle fellow in aerospace edn., 1978; named to Minuteman Hall of Fame, 1979. Mem. Air Force Assn., Nat. Def. Transp. Assn., Am. Ordnance Assn. Home: 932 W Main St Franklin TN 37064-2730 Office: Nashville Internat Airport 1 Terminal Dr Ste 501 Nashville TN 37214-4110

MOORE, WILLIAM JASON, museum director; b. Asheboro, N.C., Aug. 4, 1938; s. Lonnie James and Pauline (Hamilton) M.; m. Jane Beane, Dec. 16, 1962; 1 son, William David. B.B.A., High Point Coll., 1960. Asst. to archeologist Town Creek Indian Mound, Mt. Gilead, N.C., 1959; dir. Greensboro Mus., (N.C.), 1963—; assessor Am. Assn. Mus., Washington, 1976—. Mem. N.C. Mus. Council (award 1976; pres. 1973-74), Am. Assn. Mus., Am. Assn. State and Local History. Episcopalian. Lodge: Rotary.

MOORE, WILLIAM JOHN MYLES, electrical engineer, researcher; b. Edinburgh, Scotland, May 3, 1924; arrived in Can., 1928; s. William Harold and Doris Kate (Paddon) M.; m. Ruth Elizabeth Duffy, Aug. 21, 1948; children: Roberta Louise, Marilyn Elizabeth. B in Applied Sci., U. B.C., Can., 1946; postgrad., NRC, Ottawa, Can., summer 1947; M in Engring., McGill U., 1948. Rsch. officer NRC Can., Ottawa, Ont., 1948-51, 55-88, sect. head power engring sect. elec. engring. div., 1988-90, ret., 1990; rsch. officer Can. Armament R&D Establishment, Valcartier, Que., 1951-52, head analysis sect., 1952-54, group leader analysis, control and simulation sects., 1954-55; cons. prof. Huazhong U. Sci. and Tech., Wuhan, Peoples Republic of China., 1988. Author: The Current Comparator, 1987; holder 10 patents. Fellow IEEE (chmn. Ottawa sect. 1966-67, chmn. Elec. and Electronic Measurement and Test Instrumentation Conf. and Instrumentation and Measurement Symposium 1969, pres. Group on Instrumentation and Measurement 1974, chmn. power systems instrumentation and measurement com. Power Engring. Soc. 1981-82, Morris E. Leeds award, 1987, Centennial medal 1984, A.G.L. McNaughton medal 1991), Assn. Prof. Engrs. Ont. Avocations: downhill skiing, personal computing. Home: 797 Dunloe Ave, Ottawa, ON Canada K1K 0K3

MOORE, WILLIAM LEROY, JR., career officer, physician; b. Savannah, Ga., June 1, 1934; s. William Leroy Sr. and Helen Louise (Robbins) M.; m. Anna Elizabeth Ballard, Mar. 15, 1958; children: William L., Christopher A., Mary Beth. Student, Ga. Inst. Tech., 1951-52; AB, Emory U., 1955; MD, Med. Coll. Ga., 1959; postgrad. mil. tng. courses, 1962-94. Diplomate Am. Bd. Internal Medicine, Am. Bd. Infectious Diseases. Commd. capt. U.S. Army, 1962, advanced through grades to maj. gen., 1991; intern Floyd Hosp., Rome, Ga., 1959-60; pvt. practice Rome, 1960-61; resident in internal medicine Brooke Gen. Hosp., Ft. Sam Houston, Tex., 1965-68; rsch. fellow in infectious diseases U. Tex. Southwestern Med. Sch., Dallas, 1968-70; resident in internal medicine Parkland Meml. Hosp., Dallas, 1968-70; gen. med. officer Martin Army Hosp., Ft. Benning, Ga., 1962, 5th Spl. Forces Group, Spl. Warfare Ctr., Ft. Bragg, N.C., 1962-63; gen. internist, group surgeon, commdg. officer 1st Spl. Forces Group, Spl. Action Force, Okinawa, Japan, 1963-65; asst. chief to chief infectious disease svc. Brooke Gen. Hosp., Ft. Sam Houston, Tex., 1970-74; chief internal medicine svc., chief dept. medicine, chief profl. svcs. Eisenhower Army Med. Ctr., Ft. Gordon, Ga., 1978-83; comdr. Frankfurt (Germany) Army Regional Med. Ct., 97th Gen. Hosp., 1983-86; project mgr. Office of Surgeon Gen., Washington, 1986-88; adj. faculty Nat. Def. U., Ft. Lesley J. McNair, Washington, 1986-88; vice comdr. Joint Mil. Med. Command, Randolph AFB, Tex., 1988-91; comdr. Brooke Army Med. Ctr., Ft. Sam Houston, Tex., 1988-91, U.S. Army Med. Dept. Ctr. & Sch., Ft. Sam Houston, Tex., 1991-94; state epidemiologist, dir. communicable & environ. disease Tenn. Dept.

Health, 1995—; clin. prof. medicine divsn. infectious diseases Vanderbilt U. Sch. Medicine, Nashville, 1994—; clin. assoc. in medicine U. Tex. Southwestern Med. Sch., 1969-70; clin. assoc. prof. Medicine, U. Tex. Med. Sch., 1970-74; chief. sect. of infectious diseases, Med. Coll. Ga., 1974-75, assoc. prof., 1974-78, clin. prof., 1978-83; prin. investigator infectious disease rsch. VA Hosp., Augusta, Ga., 1974-78, asst. chief med. svc., 1974-75, dir. clin. microbiology lab., 1974-78, epidemiologist, 1974-78; head intenal medicine infectious disease 97th gen. Hosp., Frankfurt, 1983-86, Walter Reed Army Med. Ctr., 1986-88; clin. prof. medicine U. Tex. Health Sci. Ctr., San Antonio, 1989-94; mem. ref. panel on Am. Hosp. Formulary Svc. of Am. Soc. Hosp. Pharmacists, 1974-78; faculty Advisor Lane-Walker AMSA Free Clinic, Augusta, 1975-78; mem. various coms. and bds., VA Hosp., Augusta, 1974-78. Contbr. articles to profl. jours. Mem. Army Comty. Coun. San Antonio, 1988-94; dir., bd. dirs. Army Med. Dept. Mus. Found. Inc., 1989-94; bd. dirs. San Antonio Area chpt. ARC, 1989. Decorated Army Commendation medal, Meritorious Svc. medal (3), Legion of Merit with three oak leaf clusters, Disting. Svc. medal Army Med. Dept. Regiment, 1994, Order of Mil. Med. Merit; recipient Scholastic Excellence award C.V. Mosby Co., 1959, Dirs. Commendation VA Hosp., Augusta, 1978, Surgeon Gen.'s A Profl. Designer fr Internal Med., 1982. Fellow ACP, Infectious Diseases Soc. Am.; mem. NAS (nat. rsch. coun. 1995-96), Assn. Mil. Surgeons U.S. (mem.-at-large exec. coun. Alamo chpt. 1989), Soc. Med. Cons. to Armed Forces (chmn. com. on cons. activities 1977-79), Am. Heart Assn. (bd. dirs. San Antonio divsn. 1988-89), San Antonio Rsch. Club (sec., pres. 1970-74), Tenn. Med. Assn., Nashville Acad. Medicine, Tenn. Pub. Health Assn., Coun.State and Territorial Epidemiologists. *Strict adherence to moral and ethical principles, willingness to work hard, use all of one's talents to benefit others and take advantage of all of the opportunities one finds to improve one's self while serving others are the elements of success in this life.*

MOORE, WILLIAM PAUL, educational psychologist, researcher; b. Kansas City, Mo., Jan. 5, 1958; s. William Stone and Lola (Kester) M.; m. Kelly Rae Howlett, Aug. 1, 1987; 1 child, William Samuel. BS in Secondary Edn., U. Kans., 1981, MA in Curriculum and Instrn., 1984, PhD in Ednl. Psychology, 1991. Cert. tchr., Kans., Mo. Social scis. instr. Parsons (Kans.) Unified Sch. Dist., 1981-82; social scis. instr., dept. chair Turner Unified Sch. Dist., Kansas City, 1984-86; asst. testing coord. U. Kans., Lawrence, 1988-89; program evaluation, ednl. rschr. Kansas City Pub. Schs., 1989-92; sr. rsch. coord. U. Kans., 1992-93, asst. prof., dir. rsch., 1993-95; mem. adv. bd. U. Kans. Med. Ctr., 1994; sr. mng. cons. Great Plains Rsch. and Evaluation, 1995—. Mem. editl. bd. Occupational Therapy Jour. Rsch., 1994—; contbr. articles to profl. jours. Bd. dirs. Child Abuse Prevention Coalition, Mission, Kans., 1994—, Lighthouse Pre-Sch., Kansas City, Mo., 1996—. Recipient faculty rsch. award U. Kans., 1994. Mem. ASCD, APA, Am. Pscyhol. Soc., Nat. Coun. on Measurement in Edn., Am. Ednl. Rsch. Assn. Democrat. Avocations: sailing, golfing, tennis. Home and Office: 913 N Mesa St Olathe KS 66061-5963

MOORE, WILLIAM THEODORE, JR., judge; b. Bainbridge, Ga., May 7, 1940; s. William T. and Mary (Talbert) M.; m. Jane Hodges, July 18, 1964; children: Sarah S., Mary T. William T III. AA, Ga. Military Coll., 1960; JD, U. Ga., 1964; Law (hon.), Ga. Military Coll., 1978. Bar: Ga. 1964, U.S. Dist. Ct. (so. dist.) Ga. 1964, U.S. Ct. Appeals (5th and 11th cirs.) 1979, U.S. Supreme Ct. 1980. U.S. atty. So. Dist. Ga. U.S. Dept. of Justice, Savannah, 1977-81; ptnr. Corish, Smith, Remler & Moore, Savannah, 1967-77, Sparkman, Harris & Moore, Savannah, 1981-87, Oliver Maner & Gray, Savannah, 1988-94; atty. Savannah-Chatham County Bd. Pub. Edn., 1975-77, mem. U.S. Atty. Gen's. Adv. com. D.C. 1978-81. Recipient Spl. Appreciation award Ga. Bur. of Investigation, 1980, U.S. Dept. Treasury Bur. of Alcohol, Tobacco & Firearms, D.C., 1980; Extraordinary Svc. award Savannah Chapt. Fed. Bar Assn., 1980. Fellow Am. Bd. Criminal Lawyers (pres. 1993); mem. Nat. Assn. Criminal Def. Lawyers, Nat. Assn. Former U.S. Attys. (bd. dirs. 1984—), Ga. Assn. Criminal Def. Lawyers (v.p. 1986—), Ga. Bar Assn. Democrat. Epsicopalian. Avocations: jogging, weight training. Office: US Dist Courthouse 125 Bull St PO Box 10245 Savannah GA 31412

MOORE, WILLIAM VINCENT, political science educator; b. Columbia, Mo., Apr. 13, 1944; s. Willis and Mabelle (Rogers) M.; m. Suzanne Shelton, July 14, 1967 (div. Feb. 1984); children: Mark, Laura. BA, So. Ill. U., 1966, MA, 1968; PhD, Tulane U., 1975. Instr. Fla. Meml. Coll., Miami, 1968-69, Xavier U., New Orleans, 1970-72; asst. prof. to assoc. prof. polit. sci. Coll. of Charleston, S.C., 1972-83, prof., 1983—, scholar-in-residence, 1976, dir. summer sessions, 1984-87, chmn. dept., 1987-93, dir., masters in pub. adminstrn. dept., 1993—; chmn. S.C. Interagy. Merit Coun., Columbia, 1987—. Author: Political Extremism in the U.S.A., 1983; co-author: Politics and Government in South Carolina, 1994; contbr. articles to profl. jours. Recipient Disting. Teaching award Coll. of Charleston, 1981; grantee U. N.C., 1980; rsch. fellow U. S.C., 1983; NEH seminar Harvard U., 1995. Mem. Am. Polit. Sci. Assn., So. Polit. Sci. Assn., S.C. Polit. Sci. Assn. (pres. 1983-84), Phi Kappa Phi (chpt. pres. 1982-84), Pi Sigma Alpha (chpt. pres. 1987-93). Avocations: tennis, racquetball. Home: 1555 N Pinebark Ln Charleston SC 29407-3513 Office: Coll of Charleston Polit Sci Dept Charleston SC 29424

MOORE, WILLIS HENRY ALLPHIN, history and geography educator; b. N.Y.C., Dec. 14, 1940; s. Carl Allphin and Mary Catherine (Moody) M.; children: Patrick Kakela, Michael Kirby, Catherine Malia. BA Letters, U. Okla., 1962; MEd in Adminstrn., U. Hawaii, 1971. Teaching asst. dept. history U. Hawaii, 1962-64; dir. edn. Bernice P. Bishop Mus., Honolulu, 1967-76; pres. Hawaii Geog. Soc., Honolulu, 1976-78, exec. sec., editor, 1978—; mem. Hawaii Com. for Humanities, 1976-78; producer, narrator film-lecture programs Nat. Audubon Soc. and travelogue forums; instr. in history, geography and polit. sci. Chaminade U. of Honolulu, 1986—; lectr. elderhostel U. Hawaii, Hawaii Pacific U.. Co-author/co-editor: Hawaii Parklands, Sociological History of Honolulu, Total Solar Eclipse over Hawaii, 1991; contbr. articles to Honolulu Advertiser, Pacific Daily News, Guam, Pacific Mag., Honolulu Star-Bull. Lay reader St. Andrew's Cathedral; active Nat. Mus. Am. Indian. Mem. Internat. Map Trade Assn., Am. Assn. State & Local History, Am. Mus. Assn., Pacific Sci. Assn., Hawaii Mus. Assn. (pres. 1972-74), Pacific Asia Travel Assn., Hawaii Pub. Radio, Am. Guild Organists, Soc. Prfs. Dispute Resolution, Sierra Club (chmn. Hawaii chpt. 1973-75), Hawaiian Hist. Soc., Nat. Soc. of Arts and Letters. Office: PO Box 1698 Honolulu HI 96806-1698

MOORE, YVETTE M., artist, illustrator; b. Radville, Sask., Can., July 23, 1954; d. Raymond Joseph and Rosalie Marie (Bourassa) Paulhus; m. Richard Kevin Moore, May 12, 1972; children: Tyler, Rynette, Chantelle, Sarah. Diploma of tech., Sask. Tech. Inst., Moose Jaw, Sask., Can., 1988. Clk. Radville (Sask., Can.) Credit Union Ltd., 1973-75; owner, mgr. Hannigan's, Radville, 1981-85; archtl. technologist Arnott, Kelley & O'Connor, Regina, Sask., Can., 1988-89; artist Yvette Moore Fine Art & Designs, Moose Jaw, Sask., 1988-93, pres., 1993—; pres. Cranberry Rose Gallery, Ltd., 1995—. Illustrator: A Prairie Alphabet, 1992, A Prairie Year, 1994. Bd. dirs. Moose Jaw Mcpl. Heritage, 1989-93, chmn., 1992-93. Recipient Merit cert. Art Dirs. Club, 1993. Mem. Can. Artists Representation, Sask. Writers Guild, Sask. Gymnastics Assn. (level III judge). Avocations: gardening, heritage restoration and preservation, decorations, reading, antiques. Home: 1101 Clifton Ave, Moose Jaw, SK Canada S6H 3L4

MOORE DE GOLIER, DANIELLE, political activist; b. Valhalla, N.Y., Dec. 6, 1947; d. Daniel Livingston and Lucy Ann (Collesano) Wilson; m. David Frederick DeGolier, Apr. 8, 1967 (div. 1984); children: Andrea Lynn, Jeffrey David; m. Charles Edward LaGreca, Feb. 14, 1986 (div. May 1993); m. Steven Tracey Moore, July 7, 1996. AA in Liberal Arts Human and Social Scis., Niagara County C.C., 1991. Founder, pres. Citizens Against Pollution Niagra County, 1980-82; founder, facilitator Love Addicts Anonymous Niagra Falls, 1982-88. Author: (children's book) A Lap for Leonard, 1977; columnist The Niagara Gazette, 1975-76, Nat. Women's Polit. Caucus, 1978. Lobbyist state/fed. upgrade adoption laws granting adopted adults access to med. info. via anonymous computer network, 1975; founder, pub. rels. dir. Peoples Animal Lovers Soc., 1975-76; pres. Niagara Area chpt., pub. rels. dir. Animal Birth Control Soc. Western N.Y., 1976; founder, pres. Citizens Against Pollution, Niagara County, 1980-82, Love Addicts Anonymous, Niagara Falls, 1982-89; lobbyist state/fed. stalkers act., Niagara Falls, 1991-93, fed. sponsorship to upgrade domestic violence laws, 1990-94. Statue erected in honor of her Citizens Against Pollution work, Lewistion, N.Y., 1982. Mem. NOW (pres. Niagara County chpt. 1993-94); People Animal Lovers Soc. (founder, pub. rels. dir. 1975-76), Animal Birth Control Soc. Western N.Y. (pres. Niagra County chpt., pub. rels. dir. 1975-77. Avocations: writing, animal, environmental and humanitarian work.

MOOREFIELD, JAMES LEE, retired insurance executive, lawyer; b. Beckley, W.Va., June 12, 1922; s. Terrence Clyde and Judith (Shepherd) M.; m. Joyce Ward, Dec. 9, 1944; children: Nancy Jo, James Stewart, David Lee. BS, Concord Coll., Athens, W.Va., 1947; LLB, U. Va., 1953. Bar: Mass. 1954, U.S. Supreme Ct. 1964. Tchr. high sch., coach Raleigh County (W.Va.) Bd. Edn., 1947-48; with Paul Revere Life Ins. Co., Worcester, Mass., 1953-80; v.p., gen. counsel Paul Revere Life Ins. Co., 1968-76, sec., 1970-74, sr. v.p., 1974-80; pres. Health Ins. Assn. Am., Washington, 1980-87; bd. dirs. Guaranty Bank & Trust Co., Conifer Group, Inc., Bank of New Eng., Worcester, John Alden Corp.; moderator Town of West Boylston, Mass., 1959-74, NHC; coordinator campaign of Elliot Richardson for lt. gov. and atty. gov., Mass., 1964—; mem. HHS Organ Transplant T.F., 1985-86, Pvt. Pub. Sector Adv. Com. on Catastrophic Ill., 1986; mem. Nat. ARC Adv. com. on AIDS, 1985-87; mem. Dunlop Group of Six, 1981-87. Contbr. legal, and ins. articles to profl. jours. Bd. dirs. Worcester chpt. ARC, chmn., 1974, 75; bd. dirs., treas. Worcester Meml. Hosp.; bd. dirs. Worcester City Missionary Soc., 1967-72; corporator Holden Dist. Hosp., 1967-72. Served with AUS, 1943-46, 50-52. Mem. ABA, Ins. Econ. Soc. (exec. com. 1968-80), Mass. Bar Assn., Worcester County Assns., Assn. Life Ins. Counsel. Republican. Congregationalist. Lodges: Masons, Rotary. Home: 41 Highpoint Cir S Apt 307 Naples FL 33940-8324

MOOREFIELD, JENNIFER MARY, legislative staff member; b. Danville, Va., Nov. 10, 1950; d. Folger Lester and Mildred (Cox) M. BA in Psychology, Averett Coll., 1972; A in Applied Sci., Danville C.C., 1986; postgrad., Longwood Coll., 1995—. Social worker Henry County Social Svcs., Collinsville, Va., 1972-75, sr. social worker, 1975-80; clk. inventory control Dan River, Inc., Danville, Va., 1981-83; staff asst. U.S. Congressman Dan Daniel, Danville, 1984-88; staff asst. U.S. Congressman L.F. Payne, Danville, 1988-91, casework supr., 1991—; office mgr. U.S. Congressman L.F. Payne, Danville, 1991—. Bd. recording sec. Danville Speech & Hearing Ctr., 1988; Sunday Sch. tchr. Emmanuel Wesleyan Ch., Danville, 1975—; dir. Wesleyan Kids for Missions, Danville, 1993—, Ch. Vacation Bible Sch., Danville, 1993. Mem. Luncheon Pilot Club of Danville, Inc. (recording sec. 1988-89, pres.- elect 1989-90, pres. 1990-91), Va. Dist.- Pilot Internat. (area fundraising leader 1990-91, dist. chaplain 1993-94). Avocations: reading, computers, music, photography, calligraphy. Home: 136 Brookview Rd Danville VA 24540-3408 Office: Office of Congressman LF Payne 700 Main St Ste 301 Danville VA 24541-1819

MOORE MOIF, FLORIAN HOWARD, electronics engineer; b. Shelby, Ohio, Aug. 23, 1929; s. Carl Leslie and Mona Pearl (Dearth) M.; m. Dorothy Elizabeth Morse, Dec. 19, 1950. AA, Harvard U., 1974. Cert. indsl. maint. electrician; tchg. cert. indsl. electricity, indsl. electronics. With Diebold Inc., Boston, 1955-56; mem. electronics R & D staff Radio Corp. Am., Burlington, Mass., 1956-59; mem. electronics/mech. R & D staff MIT, Cambridge, 1959-74; mem. electricity/electronics/electromech. R & D staff Charles Stark Draper Labs., Cambridge, 1974-76; tchr. indsl. electronics Ashland County Joint Vocat. Sch., Ashland, Ohio, 1976-78; buyer Autocall divsn. Fed. Signal Corp., Shelby, 1978-79; journeyman electrician Excel Wire & Cable divsn. United Tech., Tiffin, Ohio, 1980-86; tchr. indsl. electricity Madison Comprehensive H.S., Mansfield, Ohio, 1986-88; pres., CEO Florian H. Moore & Assocs., Shelby, 1988—. Vol. Ohio Geneal. Libr., Mansfield; foster parent Commonwealth of Mass., 1962-82 (38 children). With USAF, 1948-52. Mem. Ohio Geneal. Soc. (v.p. Richland-Shelby gen. chpt. 1993-95, 95—), Am. Contingent 10th Foot Royal Lincolnshire Regtl. Assn. (life), DAV (life), Order Internat. Fellowship (charter, U.S. rep. 1995), Masons (32d degree), Kappa Delta Pi (life). Avocations: history, snow skiing, sky diving, computer programming. Home and Office: 6234 State Route 61 N Shelby OH 44875-9575

MOORER, MICHAEL, professional boxer; b. Detroit, Mich., 1968; m. Bobbie; s. Michael, Jr. Champion World Boxing Assn., light heavyweight title, Pittburgh, Pa., 1990, World Boxing Assn. and Internat. Boxing Federation, heavyweight title, Las Vegas, Nev., 1994.

MOORER, THOMAS HINMAN, retired naval officer; b. Mt. Willing, Ala., Feb. 9, 1912; s. Richard Randolph and Hulda (Hill) M.; m. Carrie Ellen Foy, Nov. 28, 1935; children: Thomas Randolph, Mary Ellen, Richard Foy, Robert Hill. B.S., U.S. Naval Acad., 1933; grad., Naval War Coll., 1953; LL.D. (hon.), Sanford U., Auburn U., Troy U., The Citadel. Commd. ensign U.S. Navy, 1933, advanced through grades to adm., 1957; held several fleet commands at sea; chief naval ops., 1967-70, chmn. joint chiefs of staff, 1970-74, ret., 1974; dir. Blount Inc., Montgomery, Ala., 1974—; dir. U.S. Life Ins. Corp., Arlington, Va., CACI, Arlington; adviser Center Strategic and Internat. Studies, The Citadel. Co-author: U.S. Overseas Bases: Problems of Projecting American Military Power Abroad, 1977, Sea Power and Strategy in the Indian Ocean, 1981. Chmn. Naval Aviation Mus. Found., Inc. Decorated Def. Dept. D.S.M. with oak leaf cluster, Navy D.S.M. with 4 stars, Army D.S.M., Air Force D.S.M., Silver Star, Legion of Merit, D.F.C., Purple Heart, others; recipient Forrestal award, 1975; named to Nat. Aviation Hall of Fame, 1987, Naval Aviation Hall of Honor, 1988. Mem. U.S. Naval Acad. Alumni Assn., U.S. Naval Inst., Ret. Officers Assn., Assn. Naval Aviation (chmn. 1974—), Chevy Chase Club, Army-Navy Club. Republican. Baptist. Home: 6901 Lupine Ln Mc Lean VA 22101-1580 Office: 1800 K St NW Washington DC 20006-2202

MOORHEAD, CARLOS J., congressman; b. Long Beach, Calif., May 6, 1922; s. Carlos Arthur and Florence (Gravers) M.; m. Valery Joan Tyler, July 19, 1969; children: Theresa, Catharine, Steven, Teri, Paul. BA, UCLA, 1943; JD, U. So. Calif., 1949. Bar: Calif. 1949, U.S. Supreme Ct. 1973. Pvt. practice law Glendale, Calif., 1949-72; dir. Lawyers Reference Service, Glendale, 1950-66; mem. 93d-104th Congresses from 22d (now 27th) Dist. Calif., 1973-96; mem. judiciary com., chmn. subcom. on cts. and intellectual property, vice chmn. commerce com., mem. subcom. on energy & power, subcom. on telecomm. & fin.; dean Calif. Congl. Rep. Delegation; apptd. to Fed. Cts. Study Com. Pres. Glendale Hi-Twelve Club; mem. Verdugo Hills council Boy Scouts Am.; mem. Calif. Assembly, 1967-72; mem. Calif. Law Revision Commn., 1971-72; pres. 43d Dist. Republican Assembly, Glendale Young Republicans; mem. Los Angeles County Rep. Central Com., Calif. Rep. Central Com.; pres. Glendale La Crescenta Camp Fire Girls, Inc. Served to lt. col. AUS, 1942-46. Recipient Man of Yr. award USO, 1979. Mem. Calif. Bar Assn. L.A. County Bar Assn., Glendale Bar Assn. (past pres.), Glendale C. of C., Masons, Shriners, Lions, Moose, VFW. Presbyterian. Office: US House of Representatives 2346 Rayburn House Office Bldg Washington DC 20515

MOORHEAD, GERALD LEE, architect; b. Davenport, Iowa, Feb. 18, 1947; s. Wayne Lee and Marilou (George) M. BA, Rice U., 1969, BArch, 1971. Architect Middleton & Statton, El Paso, Tex., 1967, MA Floyd Assos., Houston, 1968, CRS Design Inc., Houston, 1969-70, Phillips & Peterson AIA, Houston, 1969-73; architect, v.p. Charles Tapley Assos., Houston, 1973-83; propr. Lloyd Jones Fillpot Assocs., 1986-87, Gerald Moorhead, Architect, 1983—. Photography exhibited in group shows Galveston Arts Coun., Tex., 1976, Jewish Community Center, Houston, 1977, Cronin Gallery, Houston, 1977; one-man photog. exhbns. include Autry House Gallery, Houston, 1979; contbg. editor Tex. Architect; regional corr. Archtl. Record; contbr. articles on architecture to profl. publs.; exhbn. curator: Houston Mus. Natural Science, 1990, Mus. Fine Arts, Houston, 1991, FotoFest, Houston, 1996. Treas. Houston Ctr. for Photography, 1985-87. Recipient Spl. award Houston AIA/Houston Home & Garden, 1979, Honor award Houston AIA, 1979, Young Architect award Houston AIA, 1985, Internat. prize Union Architects of Kazahkstan, 1991; named Architect Laureate of Kazahkstan, 1992. Fellow AIA; mem. Soc. Archtl. Historians, Nat. Trust for Hist. Preservation, Tex. Soc. Architects (1st Honor award 1976, Interiors award 1986, Flowers Journalism award 1995), Rice Design Alliance. Home: 1842 Marshall St Houston TX 77098-2639

MOORHEAD, JOHN B., lawyer; b. Riverside, Calif., Sept. 22, 1945. BA cum laude, U. Pacific, 1967; JD, U. Calif., 1970. Bar: Colo. 1970. Ptnr. Baker & Hostetler, Denver. Editor Hastings Law Jour. 1969-70. Mem. ABA, Colo. Bar Assn., Denver Bar Assn., Order of Coif, Blue Key, Thurston Soc. Office: Baker & Hostetler 303 E 17th Ave Ste 1100 Denver CO 80203-1264*

MOORHEAD, PAUL SIDNEY, geneticist; b. El Dorado, Ark., Apr. 18, 1924; s. Earle William and Ethel (Martin) M.; m. Betty Blanton Belk, June 8, 1949 (dec. 1989); children: Ann, Emily, Mary; m. Rebecca Otter, 1992. A.B., U. N.C., 1948, M.A. in Zoology, 1950; Ph.D., U. Tex., 1954. Research assoc. U. Tex. Med. Sch., Galveston, 1954-56, U. Pitts. Med. Sch., 1956-58; assoc. mem. Wistar Inst. Anatomy and Biology, Phila., 1959-69; assoc. prof. genetics and pediatrics U. Pa. Sch. Medicine, 1969-85, emeritus, 1985—; mem. rsch. staff Children's Hosp., Phila., 1974-85, mem. rsch. staff emeritus, 1985—. Contbr. numerous articles on genetics and cytology to sci. jours. Served to ensign USNR, 1942-46. Fellow AAAS; mem. Am. Soc. Human Genetics, AAUP, Environ. Mutagenesis Soc., Tissue Culture Assn. (pres. 1980-82), N.Y. Acad. Scis., Sigma Xi. Home and Office: PO Box 4 Claiborne MD 21624

MOORHEAD, SYLVESTER ANDREW, education educator retired; b. Denver, Feb. 23, 1920; s. Ray Rodney and Cora Margaret (Payne) M.; m. Katherine May Schlessman, July 21, 1945; children: Rodney A., Sylvia Kay, Kent A., Pamela Ann. B.A., U. No. Colo., 1942; Ph.D., Stanford U., 1950. Tchr. secondary sch. Redwood City, Calif., 1947-48, Sunnyvale, Calif., 1948-49; mem. faculty U. Miss., 1949—, prof. edn., 1955—, dean U. Sch. Edn., 1961-85, dean emeritus, 1985—. Contbr. articles profl. jours. Served with USAAF, 1942-45. Mem. NEA (life), Kappa Delta Pi, Phi Delta Kappa. Baptist. Lodge: Rotary. Home: 211 Vivian St Oxford MS 38655-2719

MOORHEAD, THOMAS BURCH, lawyer, pharmaceutical company executive; b. Evanston, Ill., May 3, 1934; s. John William and Jane (Hendrich) M.; m. Christie Barnard, Dec. 31, 1966 (div. June 1992); children: Merrell Hendrich, Hannah Christie, Rachel McGill. BA, Yale U, 1956; postgrad., The Hague Acad. Internat. Law, 1958; JD, U. Pa., 1959; LLM, NYU, 1964. Bar: N.Y. 1960, Conn. 1971. Assoc. Milbank, Tweed, Hadley & McCloy, N.Y.C., 1959-63; assoc. counsel, asst. sec. Hooker Chem. Corp., N.Y.C., 1963-68, dir. indsl. rels., 1968-69, v.p. indsl. rels., 1969-72; v.p. employee rels. Champion Internat. Corp., N.Y.C., 1972-74; v.p. adminstrn. Beker Industries Corp., Greenwich, Conn., 1974-76; v.p. corp. affairs Estée Lauder, Inc., N.Y.C., 1976-84, sr. v.p., 1984-87; v.p. human resources Carter-Wallace, Inc., N.Y.C., 1987—; bd. dirs., vice chmn. Transaction Billing Resources, Inc., 1991—; elected mem. Corp. Culinary Inst. of Am., 1993—. Mem. New Canaan (Conn.) Rep. Town Com., 1980-85; elected mem. New Canaan Town Coun., 1985—, vice chmn., 1989—; bd. dirs. Employment Policy Found., 1993—, Les Amis d'Escoffier Soc., 1990—, Les Amis d'Escoffier Found., 1990—, Yale U. Alumni Fund, 1987-92, Nat. Choral Coun., 1988-93, United Way Tri-State, Inc., 1986-89, United Way New Canaan, 1983-89, pres., 1986-87; mem. Conn. Oversight Commn., Metro-North Commuter R.R., 1985-89; U.S. del. ILO, 1985, 93, 94, 95, head U.S. employer del., 1994, 95. Mem. ABA, Assn. of Bar of City of N.Y., Am. Soc. Internat. Law, Met. Club, New Canaan Country Club, Gridiron Club of New Canaan (pres. 1990—), Yale Club. Home: 148 Ramhorne Rd New Canaan CT 06840-3007 Office: 1345 Avenue Of The Americas New York NY 10105

MOORMAN, JOHN A., librarian; b. Humboldt, Nebr., Sept. 15, 1947; m. Ileen Mary Geiger, Dec. 20, 1968; children: Johanna, Jessica, John A. AB, Guilford Coll., Greensboro, N.C., 1969; MSLS, U. N.C., 1972; postgrad., U. N.C., Greensboro, 1974-75, U. Ill., 1994—. Pub. svcs. and circulation libr. Guilford Coll., 1972-75; dir. Elbert Ivey Meml. Libr., Hickory, N.C., 1975-80, Brazoria County Libr. System, Angleton, Tex., 1980-86, Oak Lawn (Ill.) Pub. Libr., 1986-88; exec. dir. Cumberland Trail Libr. System, Flora, Ill., 1989-92; city libr. Decatur (Ill.) Pub. Libr., 1992—. Author: Managing Small Library Collections in Businesses and Community Organizations: Advice for Non-Librarians, 1989. Mem. Econ. Devel. Coord. Com.; mem. exec. com. bd. dirs. Downtown Decatur Coun.; grad. Decatur Leadership Inst., 1993. Mem. ALA, Ill. Libr. Assn. (chmn. pub. policy com. 1993), Nat. Soc. Fund Raising Execs., Decatur C. of C. (small bus. coun. seminar com.), Decatur Civil War Round Table, Decatur Rotary Club. Quaker. Avocations: travel, reading, woodworking, sports. Home: 315 Hackberry Pl Decatur IL 62521-5503 Office: Decatur Pub Libr 247 E North St Decatur IL 62523-1128

MOORMAN, ROBERT LAWSON, real estate appraiser; b. Waco, Tex., Sept. 2, 1951; s. George Robertson and Gladys Lee Billie (Scoggin) M.; m. Rebecca Ann Averitt, Sept. 9, 1983; children: Jason, Benjamin, Kate, William, Bethany. BBA, So. Meth. U., 1973; MS in Fin., Tex. A&M U., 1990. CRP; cert. real estate appraiser; registered investment adviser. Self-employed musician Austin, N.Mex., 1973-83; asst. v.p. Brenham (Tex.) Nat. Bank, 1983-85, First Nat. Bank, Navasota, Tex., 1985-87, First Savs. Assn., Brenham, 1987-89; asst. lectr. fin. Tex. A&M U., College Station, 1990-93; pres. RLM Fin. Group, Inc., Brenham, 1990—. Editor: (book) Goals for Washington County, 1984. Dir. Brenham Opportunity Ctr., 1983-85; mem. Downtown Parking Com., Brenham, 1985; chmn. Parks Adv. Bd., Brenham, 1988-93; pres. Washington County Coalition, Brenham, 1993. Recipient Bookman Peters Banking fellowship Tex. A&M Grad. Sch. Bus., 1989, 90. Mem. Nat. Assn. Ind. Fee Appraisers (IFAS 1993—), Brenham Rotary Club, Nat. Assn. of Realtors Appraisal Divsn. (GAA 1995—), Am. Soc. Appraisers, Appraisal Inst. (assoc.), Soc. of Tex. A&M Real Estate Profls., Inst. of CFP. Avocations: guitar, jogging, nutrition, home repair and remodeling. Office: The RLM Fin Group Inc 114 S Park St Brenham TX 77833-3645

MOORMAN, ROSE DRUNELL, county administrator, systems analyst; b. Miami, Fla., May 13, 1945; d. Willie and Claudia (Fluker) M. BA in Mathematics, Fisk U., 1967; MSE in Computer and Info. Scis., U. Pa., 1976. Computer programmer GE, Valley Forge, Pa., 1967-70; programmer/analyst Price Waterhouse Co., Phila., 1970-72; sr. programmer/analyst Inst. Environ. Medicine U. Pa., Phila., 1972-77; systems analyst Honeywell, Ft. Washington, Pa., 1977-78; dir. tech. svcs. Gill Assocs., Inc., Washington, 1978-83; owner, CEO Computer and Info. Mgmt., Inc., Miami, 1983-88; mgr. tech. support City of Miami, 1988-94, coord. diversity, 1994-95; exec. adminstr. to county commr. Metro-Dade County, 1996—; facilitator Women in Info. Processing, Washington, 1979-83; computer edn. adv. panel Dade County Pub. Schs., 1984-88. Editor: (newsletter) Bits and Bytes, 1979-82; co-editor: (newsletter) Ebenezer Speaks, 1992—. Active Ebenezer United Meth. Ch., Miami, 1954—, treas., chair fin. com., 1992—, Family Christian Assn., 1989-94; troop leader Girl Scouts Am., 1990—; pres. Loran Park Sch. PTA, Miami, 1991-93; treas., bd. dirs. Overtown Comty. Health Clinic, Miami, 1992—, New Miami Group, Inc., 1994—; mem. Dade Heritage Trust, Miami, 1994—; mem. Dade County Hist. Preservation Bd., 1996—. Recipient Leadership award ARC, 1957, 63, Bronze medallion for Community Svc. NCCJ, 1963, Svc. Excellence award Delta Sigma Theta, 1986. Meritorious Svc. award Fisk U., 1992. Mem. NAACP, Nat. Forum Black Pub. Adminstrs. (bd. dirs., 2d v.p. 1993—), Nat. Coun. Negro Women. Republican. Avocations: bridge, collecting cookbooks and kaleidoscopes, hunting, gardening, hist. preservation of structures and cultures. Home: 820 NW 172nd Ter Miami FL 33169-5305 Office: Metropolitan Dade County Ste 220 111 NW 1st St Miami FL 33128

MOORS, LEONARD JERALD, JR. (JERRY MOORS), musician; b. Santa Rosa, Calif., Oct. 10, 1939; s. Leonard Jerold and Vera Geraldine (Fitzgerald) M.; m. Suzanne Stoughton, June 1994; children: Leland, Megan, Lenny, Daniel, Lauren. Student, Eastman Sch. Music, 1957-59; BA, Sonoma State U., 1967; postgrad., U. Calif., Davis, 1967-69. Freelance arranger, band leader, and pianist Sonoma County, Calif., 1960-65, Santa Rosa, Calif., 1969-73; pianist Ray Anthony Band, 1973-74; pianist, arranger Johnny Russell Orch., Reno, 1975-78; orch. leader, conductor various hotels, Lake Tahoe, Nev., 1978-80; mus. dir., pianist Sonny King Show, Las Vegas, 1980-84; freelance pianist Reno, 1985-88; pianist, mus. advisor Eagle House, Eureka, Calif., 1989; pianist BenBow Inn, Calif., 1990; freelance pianist San Francisco Bay area, 1991—; pianist Contra Costa Ballet Ctr., Marin Ballet. Composed numerous mus. pieces including Sonatina for Brass Quintet, 1958, Quest, 1977, Ocean Suite, 1957. Recipient Delius Composition award U. Fla., 1977; named ShowCase Artist of Year For the Love of Jazz Soc., 1978.

Democrat. Hindu. Avocation: kite flying. Home: PO Box 45 Fields Landing CA 95537

MOOS, EUGENE, federal agency administrator. BS Argrl. Chemistry, Wash. State U. Adv. to House Majority leader Tom Foley; former Congl staff mem., dir. Wheat, Soybeans, Feed Grains subcom., House agrl. com., sr. staff profl. Ho. Reps.; pres. Gene Moos & Assocs. cons., Washington; under sec. agr. for farm and fgn. agrl. svcs. Dept. Agr., Washington, 1993; owner family farm, 1967—; adv. to U.S. Delegation Multilateral Trade Negotiations, Geneval 1st pres., founding mem. East West Trade Coun. Mem. Nat. Assn. Wheat Growers (internat. trade adv.), Nat. Assn. Wheat Growers (pres.). Office: Dept Agr Farm and Fgn Agrl Svcs 14th & Independence Ave SW Washington DC 20250*

MOOS, H. WARREN, physicist, astronomer, educator, administrator; b. N.Y.C., Mar. 26, 1936; s. Henry H. and Dorothy E. (Warren) M.; m. Doris Elaine McClure, July 13, 1957; children: Janet, Paul, Daniel, David. BS, Brown U., 1957; MA, U. Mich., 1959, PhD, 1962. Rsch. assoc. Stanford (Calif.) U., 1961-63; acting asst. prof. Johns Hopkins U., Balt., 1963-64, asst. prof., 1964-68, assoc. prof., 1968-71, prof., 1971—, dir. Ctr. for Astrophys. Scis., 1988-93, chmn. Physics & Astronomy, 1993—; cons. in field; mem. com. on planetary and lunar exploration NRC/Nat. Acad. Sci., Washington, 1982-86; mem. space and earth sci. adv. com. NASA, Washington, 1984-87; vis. fellow Joint Inst. for Lab. Astrophysics, 1972-73, 80-81. Editor: Optical Properties of Ions in Crystals, 1967; contbr. over 250 articles to profl. jours. Sloan Found. fellow, 1965-69. Fellow Am. Phys. Soc.; mem. Am. Astron. Soc., Internat. Astron. Union. Achievements include prin. investigatorof far ultraviolet spectroscopic explorer; co-investigator of Apollo 17 ultraviolet spectrometer, of Hopkins Ultraviolet Telescope, of Voyager ultraviolet spectrometer, of space telescope imaging spectograph; research on ultraviolet astronomy of fusion plasma diagnostics. Home: 804 Post Boy Ct Baltimore MD 21286 Office: Johns Hopkins U 34th & Charles Sts Baltimore MD 21218

MOOS, VERNA VIVIAN, special education educator; b. Jamestown, N.D., July 1, 1951; d. Philip and Violena (Schweitzer) M. BS in Edn., Valley City State U., 1973; MEd, U. So. Miss., 1983, EdS, 1988; AA, Minot State U., 1987; postgrad., East Tex. State U., U. Tex., N.D. State U., U. N.D., Kans. State U., McGill U. Supr. recreation Valley City (N.D.) Recreation Dept., 1969-73; tchr. Harvey (N.D.) Pub. Schs., 1973-75; tchr. spl. edn. Belfield (N.D.) Pub. Schs., 1975-77; edn. therapist N.D. Elks Assn., Dawson, 1976-77; tchr. spl. edn. Dickinson (N.D.) pub. Schs., 1977-87; ednl. technician ABLE, Inc., Dickinson, 1984-87; tchr. spl. edn. Pewitt Ind. Sch. Dist., Omaha and Naples, Tex., 1987—; tchr. adult edn. N.E. Tex. C.C., Mt. Pleasant, 1989—. Local and area dir. Tex. Spl. Olympics, Austin, 1988—; local, regional and state dir. N.D. Spl. Olympics, 1972-87; local coord. Very Spl. Arts Festival; mem. Am. Heart Assn., 1979-87, N.D. Heart Assn., 1979-87; mem. adminstrv. bd. First United Meth. Ch., Naples, Tex., 1994—. Named Dickinson Jaycees Outstanding Young Educator, 1979, Dickinson C. of C. Tchr. of Yr., 1985, Dallas area Coach of Yr., Tex. Spl. Olympics, 1993, Dir. of Yr., N.D. Spl. Olympics, 1985. Mem. NEA, Coun. Exceptional Children, Naples C. of C., Delta Kappa Gamma (scholar), Phi Delta Kappa, Kappa Delta Pi. Avocations: travel, reading, working, sports. Home: PO Box 788 Omaha TX 75571-0788 Office: Pewitt CISD PO Box 1106 Omaha TX 75571-1106

MOOSBURNER, NANCY, nutritionist; b. Houston, Tex., Apr. 6, 1943; d. Henry Fenno and Shirley Louise (McCandless) Laughton; m. Stephen Weinert, Nov. 1964 (div. Nov. 1974); children: Catherine, Jeffery; m. Otto Moosburner, Feb. 7, 1976; 1 child, Brian. BS, U. Nevada Reno, 1979, MS, 1982. Edn. specialist Nev. Dept. of Edn., Carson City, 1980-83, state dir., 1983-84; sch. nutrition program supr. Douglas Co. Sch. Dist., Minden, Nev., 1987-93; dir. sch. nutrition St. Helens (Oreg.) Sch. Dist., 1993-94; instr. Truckee Meadows C.C., Reno, Nev., 1982-83, Portland C.C., St. Helens, 1993-94; child nutrition program supr. Auburn (Wash.) Sch. Dist., 1994—; state pres Nev. Sch. Food Svc. Assn., Minden, 1992-93. Contbr. articles to profl. jours. Recipient Excellence in Food Svc. award U.S. Dept. Agri., 1989; named Outstanding Women of Am., 1977. Mem. Am. Dietetic Assn., Am. Sch. Food Svc. Assn. (dir. West region 1991-93, mem. exec. bd.), Soc. for Nutrition Edn., Am. Family and Consumer Svcs. Assn. (formerly Am. Home Econs. Assn.), Oreg. Sch. Food Svc. Assn. (pub. communication 1993-94). Democrat. Avocations: bee keeping, gardening, antiques, cooking, walking. Home: PO Box 2628 Longview WA 98632-8665

MOOSE, GEORGE E., government official; b. N.Y.C., June 23, 1944; s. Robert and Ellen Amanda Lane (Jones) M.; m. Judith Roberta Kaufmann, Jan. 3, 1981. BA, Grinnell Coll., 1966, LLD (hon.), 1990; postgrad., Syracuse U., 1967. Spl. asst. to under sec. for polit. affairs Dept. of State, Washington, 1977-78, dep. dir. for South Africa, 1978-79; internat. affairs fellow Coun. Fgn. Rels., N.Y.C., 1979-80; dep. polit. counselor U.S. Mission to UN Dept. of State, 1980-83; U.S. ambassador to Benin, 1983-86; dep. dir. mgmt. ops. Dept. of State, Washington, 1986-87, dir. mgt. ops., 1987-88; U.S. ambassador to Senegal, 1988-91; U.S. alt. rep. UN Security Coun., 1991-92; diplomat in residence, Howard U. Dept. of State, Washington, 1992-93; asst. sec. African Affairs Dept. of State, 1993—. Recipient Superior Honor award Dept. of State, Grenada, 1974, 79, Meritorious Honor award, Washington, 1975, Presdl. Performance award, 1989, 94. Mem. Am. Fgn. Service Assn. Office: Bureau African Affairs Dept Of State Washington DC 20520

MOOSE, RICHARD M., federal official; b. Little Rock, Feb. 27, 1932; m. Margaret Davis; 2 children. BA, Hendrix Coll.; MA, Columbia U. Joined Fgn. Svc., 1956; assigned Fgn. Svc., Mexico City, 1957-59, Yaounde, Cameroon, 1957-69; from exec. secretariat Dept. State to Congl. fellow Am. Polit. Sci. Assn., 1962-66; spl. asst. to Walt W. Rostow Nat. Security Coun., 1966-67; conducted study nat. security decision-making Ford Found., 1968-69; staff sec. Nat. Security Coun., 1969; sr. staff mem. Senate Com. on Fgn. Rels., 1969-74, staff dir. sub. com. on fgn. assistance, 1974-76; dep. under sec. mgmt. Dept. State, 1977, asst. sec. African Affairs, 1977-80; sr. advisor Lehman Bros., Kuhn Loeb, N.Y.C., 1981-83, London, 1983-85; mng. dir. Shearson Lehman, 1985-88; sr. v.p. internat. and govt. affairs Am. Express Co., 1988-93; under sec. for mgmt. Dept. State, Washington, 1993—. Editor 2 books; contbr. articles to N.Y. Times. Mem. Coun. Fgn. Rels. With U.S. Army, 1954-56. Office: Under Secy Mgmt Dept State 2201 C St NW Washington DC 20520-0001

MOOSSA, A. R., surgery educator; b. Port Louis, Mauritius, Oct. 10, 1939; s. Yacoob and Maude (Rochecoute) M.; m. Denise Willoughby, Dec. 28, 1973; children: Pierre, Noel, Claude, Valentine. BS, U. Liverpool, Eng., 1962, MD (hon.), 1965; postgrad., Johns Hopkins U., 1972-73, U. Chgo., 1973-74. Intern Liverpool Royal Infirmary, 1965-66; resident United Liverpool Hosps. and Alder Hey Children's Hosp., 1966-72; from asst. prof. surgery to assoc. prof. U. Chgo., 1975-77, prof., dir. surg. rsch., chief gen. surgery svc., vice chmn. dept., 1977-83; chmn. dept. surgery U. Calif.-San Diego Med. Ctr., 1983—; Litchfield lectr. U., Oxford, Eng., 1978; praelector in surgery U. Dundee, Scotland, 1979; Hampson Trust vis. prof. U. Liverpool, Eng., 1992, G.B. Ong. vis. prof. U. Hong Kong, 1993, Philip Sandblon vis. prof. U. Lund, Sweden. Editor: Tumors of the Pancreas, 1982, Essential Surgical Practice, 1983, 3d edit., 1995, Comprehensive Textbook of Oncology, 1985, 2d edit., 1991, Gastrointestinal Emergencies, 1985, Problems in General Surgery, 1989, Operative Colorectal Surgery, 1993. Fellow Royal Coll. Surgeons (Hunterian prof. 1977); mem. ACS, Am. Surg. Assn., Soc. Univ. Surgeons, Am. Soc. Clin. Oncology. Office: U Calif San Diego Med Ctr 200 W Arbor Dr San Diego CA 92103-1911

MOOSSY, JOHN, neuropathologist, neurologist, consultant; b. Shreveport, La., Aug. 24, 1925; s. John Yazbeck and Rose (Ferris) M.; m. Yvonne Reese, Mar. 15, 1951; children: John Jefferson, Joan Marie. MD, Tulane U., 1950. Intern Charity Hosp. of New Orleans, 1950-51, neurology resident, 1951-53; neuropathology fellow Columbia U. Coll. of Physicians and Surgeons, N.Y.C., 1953-54; assoc., lectr. in neuropathology Tulane U. Sch. Medicine, New Orleans, 1954-57; asst. to prof. in pathology, neurology La. State U., New Orleans, 1957-65; prof. pathology, grad. faculty U. Pitts., 1965-67; prof. pathology neuropathology Bowman Gray Sch. of Medicine, Winston-Salem, N.C., 1967-72; prof. pathology and neurology, dir. div. neuropathology U. Pitts., Winston-Salem, N.C., 1972-93; emeritus prof. U. Pitts., 1993—; dir. Cerebrovascular Disease Study, World Fedn. of Neurology, Antwerp, Belgium, 1960-61; cons. Armed Forces Inst. of Pathology, Washington, 1977—, mem. sci. adv. bd., Washington, 1984-86. Editor: Cerebral Vascular Disease Seventh Conference, 1970, Cerebrovascular Diseases 12th Research Conference, 1981; editor-in-chief Jour. Neuropathology and Exptl. Neurology, 1981-91; mem. editorial bd. Archives Neurology, 1982-92. Recipient Excellence in Teaching award U. Pitts. Sch. of Medicine, 1987-88; named Commencement Speaker U. Pitts. Sch. of Medicine, 1989. Mem. Am. Acad. Neurology (sec.-treas. 1963-655), Am. Neurol. Assn. (v.p. 1977-78), Am. Assn. Neuropathologists (pres. 1974-75, Neuropathology award 1992), Internat. Soc. Neuropathology, Coun. Biology Editors.

MOOTE, A. LLOYD, history educator; b. Hamilton, Ont., Can., Mar. 22, 1931; s. Stanley Alanson and Esther Grace (Wood) M.; m. Barbara Brown, Dec. 27, 1956 (div. 1982); children: Karen, Peter, Daphne, Robert; m. Dorothy Carter May, May 30, 1986. B.A., U. Toronto, 1954; M.A., U. Minn., Mpls., 1956, Ph.D., 1958. Teaching asst. U. Minn., Mpls., 1955-58; lectr. U. Toronto, 1958-61; asst. prof. U. Cin., 1961-62, U. So. Calif., L.A., 1962-65; assoc. prof. U. So. Calif., Los Angeles, 1965-71, prof. dept. history, 1971-92; prof emeritus U. So. Calif., 1993—; vis. prof. Queen's U., Kingston, Ont., 1965-66; chmn. gen. edn. program U. So. Calif., 1978-81; mem. Inst. Advanced Study, Princeton, 1988-89; affiliated prof. Rutgers U., 1994—. Author: The Seventeenth Century, 1970, The Revolt of the Judges, 1971, The World of Europe: The Seventeenth Century, 1973, 2d edit., 1979, Louis XIII: The Just, 1989, paperback edit., 1991; mem. editorial bd. French Hist. Studies, 1971-74; internat. adv. bd. European History Quar., 1983—. Recipient William Korean prize Soc. French Hist. Studies, 1962, creative scholarship award U. So. Calif. Assocs., 1973, faculty book award U. So. Calif. chpt. Phi Kappa Phi, 1990; younger scholar NEH, 1969; grantee Am. Philos. Soc., 1962, Haynes Found., 1973, Wellcome Inst. for History Medicine, 1993-94, Burroughs-Wellcome Fund, 1996; Guggenheim fellow, 1976, fellow U. Essex, Eng., 1993-94, Rutgers Ctr. for Hist. Analysis, 1995-97. Mem. Am. Hist. Assn., Past and Present Soc., Soc. French Hist. Studies (pres. 1984-85), Western Soc. for French History, Soc. for Study French History (U.K.), Sixteenth-Century Studies Conf. Home: 149 Meadowbrook Dr Princeton NJ 08540-3664

MOOTY, JOHN WILLIAM, lawyer; b. Adrian, Minn., Nov. 27, 1922; s. John Wilson and Genevieve (Brown) M.; m. Virginia Nelson, June 6, 1952 (dec. 1964); children: David N., Bruce W., Charles W.; m. Jane Nelson, Jan. 15, 1972. B.S.L., U. Minn., 1943, LL.B., 1944. Bar: Minn. 1944. Ptnr. Gray, Plant, Mooty & Bennett, Mpls., 1945—; chmn. bd. Internat. Dairy Queen, Inc.; bd. dirs. Bur. of Engraving, Inc., Riverway Co. and subs., Rio Verde Svcs., Inc., Ariz., Turnquist, Inc. Author: (with others) Minnesota Practice Methods, 1956. Chmn. Gov.'s Task Force on Edn., 1981; pres. Citizens League Mpls., 1970; acting chmn. Republican Party of Minn., 1958. Mem. ABA, Minn. Bar Assn., Hennepin County Bar Assn., U. Minn. Alumni Assn. (pres. 1982). Clubs: Interlachen (Mpls.), Lafayette (Mpls.), Minikahda (Mpls.), Mpls. (Mpls.). Home: 6601 Dovre Dr Minneapolis MN 55436-1711 Office: 3400 City Ctr 33 S 6th St Minneapolis MN 55402-3601

MORA, BENEDETTO P., elementary school administrator; b. Bklyn., Dec. 19, 1946; s. Louis and Beatrice Mora; m. Kathleen R. Gribbin, June 28, 1969; children: Michael, Brian. BS, U. Bridgeport, 1968; MA, Glassboro (N.J.) Coll., 1978. Cert. tchr., supr., prin., chief sch. adminstr. Elem. tchr. Mullica Twp. (N.J.) Sch., 1968-70; elem. tchr. Pleasantvile (N.J.) Schs., 1970-78, coord. of math., 1978-82, supr. of math., 1982-89, supr. of curriculum, instr., 1989-91, dir. curriculum, instr., 1991—; adj. prof. Jersey City State Coll., 1982; per diem cons. for K-8 math. Holt/Reinhart & Winston, 1981-87; workshop presenter Atl. County Dept. of Edn. Mem. Pleasantville/Absecon Coordination Team, 1988—; Pleasantville Edn. Found., 1987-92. Grantee N.J. Dept. Edn., 1980, 81, 87. Mem. ASCD, Pleasantville Adminstrn. Assn. (treas. 1989, pres. 1985-89), N.J. Prin. and Supr. Assn. (del. 1989), Nat. Assn. Elem. Sch. Prin., New Jersey Prins. and Suprs. Assn., Assn. Math. Tchrs. N.J. Office: Pleasantville Pub Schs 115 W Decatur Ave Pleasantville NJ 08232-3121

MORA, FEDERICO, neurosurgeon; b. Guatemala, Guatemala, Jan. 11, 1926; came to the U.S., 1945; s. Carlos Federico and Rosa (Castaneda) M.; m. Natalie Viriginia Ramin, June 30, 1951; children: Federico, Clara Luz, Ana Maria, Claudia Inéz, Juan Rafael. Student, Harvard Coll., 1945-46, MD, 1950. Diplomate Am. Bd. Neurol. Surgery. Pvt. practice neurol. surgery Guatemala and Albuquerque, 1958—; asst. prof. surgery and anatomy U. N.Mex. Sch. Medicine, Albuquerque, 1969-70. Capt. USAFR, 1954-56. Mem. Alpha Omega Alpha. Democrat. Avocations: scuba diving, nature studies. Home: 1809 Avenida Alturas NE Albuquerque NM 87110-4956 Office: Albuquerque Neurosurg Group 715 Grand Ave NE Ste 301 Albuquerque NM 87102-3668

MORA, FRANCISCO, artist, printmaker; b. Uruapan, Mexico, May 7, 1922; s. Jose Maria and Clotilde (Perez) M.; m. Elizabeth Catlett, Oct. 31, 1946; children: Francisco, Juan, David. Student, Escuela de Pintura y Escultura La Esmeralda, 1941-46. Tchr. drawing Sch. Pub. Edn. Mexico, 1949-54; art adviser Mexican Acad. Edn., 1956—. Exhibited one-man shows Nitra, Prague, Czechoslovakia, 1971, Cite International de l'universite, Paris, 1972, Saxon Princes Palace, Dresden, 1973, Green Room Nat. Fine Arts Museum, Mexico, 1974-75, New Visions Gallery, San Diego, 1981, Atlanta, 1988, Salon de la Plastica, Mexico City, 1983, Tougaloo, Miss., 1986, U. Ariz. Mus., 1987, Kenkeleba Gallery, N.Y.C., 1988, In Faust Gallery, Hamburg, 1989, Miss. Mus. Art W. Catlett, 1990, Montgomery (Ala.) Mus. Art, 1991, Polk Mus. Art, Lakeland, Fla., 1991-92, Mus. African Am. Art, Detroit, 1992, Malcol Brown Gallery, Shaker Heights, Ohio, 1993, Isobel Neal Gallery, Chgo., 1994, Jame Lewis Mus., Balt., 1994-95, Queens' Coll. Mus., N.Y.C., Third World Mus., L.A., 1996, I-Space; illustrator books, pamphlets, mags. Mem. Salon de la Plastica Mexicana (founding mem.), Mexican Acad. Edn. (founding mem.). Home: Apartado Postal 694, 62000 Cuernavaca Morelos, Mexico

MORA, JAMES ERNEST, professional football coach, professional sports team executive; b. Glendale, Calif., May 24, 1935; s. Mario Joseph and Helen Laverne (Thompson) M.; m. Connie Beatrice Saunders, Dec. 18, 1959; children—James L., Michael J., Stephen P. B.S., Occidental Coll., 1957; M.A., U. So. Calif., 1967. Asst. coach U. Washington, Seattle, WA, 1975-78, Seattle Seahawks, Seattle, WA, 1978-82, New England Patriots, Foxboro, MA, 1982-83; head coach Philadelphia Stars (name changed to Baltimore Stars), Baltimore, MD, 1983-86, New Orleans Saints, New Orleans, LA, 1986—; head coach, v.p. New Orleans Saints, L.A., 1994—. Served to capt. USMCR, 1957-60. Mem. Am. Football Coaches Assn. Republican. Lutheran. Avocations: working out; golf; skiing; reading; biking. Office: care New Orleans Saints 5800 Airline Highway Metairie LA 70003-5151*

MORACA-SAWICKI, ANNE MARIE, oncology nurse; b. Niagara Falls, N.Y., Sept. 28, 1952; d. Joseph R. and Joan (Forgione) Moraca; m. Richard L. Sawicki, Sept. 15, 1979. BSN, D'Youville Coll., 1974; MS in Nursing, SUNY at Buffalo, 1977. Asst. prof. nursing D'Youville Coll., Buffalo, 1977-81; clin. editor Springhouse (Pa.) Corp., 1981-82; charge nurse Mt. St. Mary's Hosp., Lewiston, N.Y., 1982-84; surg. coord., adminstrv. asst. Dr. Richard L. Sawicki, Niagara Falls, N.Y., 1983—; part-time faculty mem. Niagara County C.C., Sanborn, N.Y.; bd. dirs. adult day care program Health Assn. Niagara County Inc. Contbr.: Nurses Legal Handbook, 1985, Pharmacotherapeutics: A Nursing Process Approach, 1986, 4th edit., 1996; clin. editor, contbr. Nurses Ref. Libr. Series Vols. on Drugs, Definitions, Procedures and Practices; clin. reviewer Manual of Med./Sug. Nursiong, 1995, contbr., 1996; clin. reviewer Critical Care Handbook and IV Drug Handbook, 1995; clin. cons. Critical Care Plans, 1987, Taber's Cyclopedic Med. Dictionary, 16th edit., 1989. Recipient Cert. of Appreciation Niagara County C.C., 1988, 91, 92, Cmty. Svc. award Am. Cancer Soc., 1978, Miss Hope award, 1977, Am. Cancer Soc. Nursing Fellowship Grant, 1977; Grad. fellow SUNY, Buffalo, 1976-77. Mem. AAUP, N.Y. State Nurse's Assn., Health Assn. Niagara County (chairperson elect 1995, bd. dirs. adult day care program), Sigma Theta Tau. Home: 4658 Vrooman Dr Lewiston NY 14092-1049

MORACZEWSKI, ROBERT LEO, publisher; b. Saint Paul, Nebr., May 13, 1942; s. Leo and Florence May (Wadas) M.; m. Virginia Kay Rohman, July 26, 1960; children—Mark, Matthew, Monika, Michael. BS in Agrl. Journalism, U. Nebr., 1964. Assoc. editor Farmer Mag. Webb Co., St. Paul, 1964-72; mng. editor Farm Industry News Webb Co., St. Paul, 1972-74; editor Big Farmer Mag., Chgo., 1974-75; editorial dir. Webb Agrl. Services, St. Paul, 1976; editor The Farmer, The Dakota Farmer Webb Co., St. Paul, 1983-89; group pub. Webb Co., St. Paul, 1989-90; v.p., 1990—; exec. dir. Minn. Agri-Growth Coun. Contbr. articles to profl. jours. Recipient numerous media awards. Mem. Am. Agrl. Editors Assn., Nat. Agrl. Mktg. Assn., Investigative Reporters and Editors Assn. Roman Catholic. Home: 26589 Everton Cir N Wyoming MN 55092-9008 Office: Webb Div Intertec Pub 7900 Internat Dr Minneapolis MN 55425

MORAHAN, PAGE S., microbiologist, educator; b. Newport News, Jan. 7, 1940; d. Robert Bruce and Margaret (Coleman) S. BA, Agnes Scott Coll., Decatur, Ga., 1961; MA, Hunter Coll., N.Y.C., 1964; PhD, Marquette U., Milw., 1969. Asst. prof. microbiology Med. Coll. of Va., Richmond, 1971-74, assoc. prof., 1974-81, prof., 1981-82; prof. and chmn. dept. microbiology Med. Coll. Pa., Phila., 1982-93, assoc. dean faculty affairs, 1993-94, assoc. provost faculty affairs, 1994—; adv. com. NCI Cancer Ctr. Rev. Com., Washington, 1986-90, mem. manpower rev. com., 1977-81; mem. test com. Nat. Bd. Med. Examiners, 1990-94, Hubbard award com., 1994-95, bd. dirs., 1995—; mem. AAMC Women in Medicine Coord. com., 1994—; lectr. in field; conductor seminars in field. Editor Jour. of Reticuloendothelial Soc., 1982-88, Infection and Immunity, 1982-85; contbr. over 100 articles to profl. jours., chpts. to books. Sec., Spring Garden Historic Dist. Civic Assn., 1984-85, bd. dirs., 1985-86; mem.-at-large adminstrn. bd. First United Meth. Ch. of Germantown, 1990-95. Recipient rsch. career devel. award NIH, 1974-79, Lindback award, 1988; grantee NIMH, 1989-94, Nat. Inst. Arthritis and Infectious Disease, 1987-94, Nat. Cancer Inst., 1989-94; fellow Am. Coun. Edn., 1992-93; also others. Mem. AAAS, Am. Acad. Microbiology, Am. Assn. Immunologists, Am. Assn. for Cancer Rsch., Soc. for Exptl. Biology and Medicine, Soc. Virus Rsch., Reticuloendothelial Soc. (councilor 1981, chmn. membership com. 1984), Am. Soc. Microbiology (med. microbiology and immunology com. of pub. affairs bd. 1989-92), Assn. Med. Microbiology (pres. 1989, dir. 2d ednl. workshop 1988, adv. com. 3d, 4th, 5th ednl. workshops 1990, 92, 94), Phi Beta Kappa, Sigma Xi. Methodist. Office: Med Coll Pa/ Hahnemann U Office Facilty Affairs Broad & Vine St Mail Stop 979 Philadelphia PA 19102-1192

MORAIN, WILLIAM DOUGLAS, surgeon, educator; b. Jefferson, Iowa, June 17, 1942; s. Frederick Elwyn and Lois (Garver) M.; m. Dagmar Ristic, Sept. 6, 1969; children: Anne, Peter William. AA, Graceland Coll., 1962; BA, Grinnell Coll., 1964; MD, Harvard, 1968. Diplomate Am. Bd. Plastic Surgery (bd. dirs. 1992—, sec.-treas. 1994—). Intern, resident in surgery Peter Bent Brigham and Children's Hosp., Boston, 1968-71; resident, chief resident in plastic surgery Stanford Med. Ctr., Calif., 1973-76; prof. surgery Dartmouth Med. Sch., Hanover, N.H., 1987—; staff surgeon Dartmouth-Hitchcock Med. Ctr., Hanover, 1976—; chief plastic surgery VA Hosp., White River Junction, Vt., 1976—; pres. Plastic Surgery Ednl. Found., 1991. Author: The Cutaneous Arteries of the Human Body (Webster Soc. prize 1982), 1983. Assoc. editor: Advances in Plastic Surgery, 1983—; editor-in-chief Annals of Plastic Surgery, 1992—; Medical Heritage, 1985—; Dartmouth Medical Alumni Bulletin, 1984-93. Assoc. producer EF Teleplast, 1984-87. Producer videoteleconf. series, 1985. Contbr. articles to profl. jours. Bd. dirs. Bel Canto Chamber Singers, Hanover, 1984. Served to maj. U.S. Army, 1971-73. Recipient Disting. Service award Plastic Surgery Ednl. Found., 1985. Fellow ACS (v.p. N.H. chpt. 1985-87, pres. 1987-89); mem. Am. Soc. Plastic and Reconstructive Surgeons (bd. dirs. 1984-91, Presdl. Appreciation award 1981), Am. Assn. Plastic Surgeons, Northeastern Soc. Plastic Surgeons (pres. 1992), Soc. Head and Neck Surgeons, New Eng. Surg. Soc. Mem. United Ch. of Christ. Avocations: singing; antiquarian book collecting. Home: 6 Wheelock Wood Hanover NH 03755-1558 Office: Dartmouth-Hitchcock Med Ctr One Medical Center Dr Lebanon NH 03756

MORALES, ARMANDO, artist; b. Granada, Nicaragua, Jan. 15, 1927. Student, Sch. Fine Arts, Managua, Pratt Graphic Art Ctr., N.Y.C. instr. advanced painting Cooper Union, N.Y., 1972, 73. Exhibited art at Bienal Modern Art, Sao Paulo, Brazil, 1953, 55, 59, Carnegie Inst., Pitts., 1958, 64, 67, Arte Am y Espana, Madrid, Barcelona, Rome and Berlin, 1961, Guggenheim Inst., N.Y., 1960, The Emergent Decade, Cornell U., Guggenheim Mus., 1966. Recipient Ernst Wolf award V Bienal, Sao Paulo, Brazil, 1959, award Arte Am y Espana, Madrid, 1963, J.L. Hudson award Carnegie Inst., 1964. Office: c/o Claude Bernard Gallery 900 Park Ave 12th Fl New York NY 10021

MORALES, DAN, state attorney general. Grad. with honors, Trinity U., 1978; JD, Harvard U., 1981. Asst. dist. atty. Bexar County, 1983-85; former mem. Ho. of Reps. Tex.; atty. gen. State of Tex., Austin, 1991—. Bd. dirs. NCCJ, World Affairs Coun.; trustee So. Meth. U., Schreiner Coll., Kerrville; elder First Presbyn. Ch. Named one of Seven Best Legislators Dallas Morning News, Politician of Yr. San Antonio Express News; recipient Outstanding Svc. award Ind. Colls. and Univs., Outstanding Leadership award Texan's War on Drugs,. Mem. Tex. Lyceum Assn. Office: Office of Atty Gen PO Box 12548 Austin TX 78711-2548*

MORALES, HERMINIO BLANCO, Mexican government official; b. Chihuahua, Mex., July 25, 1950; married; 2 children. BA, Econ. Tech. Inst. Monterrey, Mex., 1971; student, U. Colo., 1971-72; MA, PhD, U. Chgo., 1978. Analyst U. Chgo., 1975-78; asst. sec. treas. Govt. Mex., 1978-80; prof. economy Rice U., Houston, Tex., 1980-85; advisor to presidency Govt. Mex., 1985-88, undersec. for fgn. trade Secretariat of Trade and Industry, 1988-90, head negotiator Free Trade Treaty, 1990-93, undersec. for trade negotiations, 1993-94, sec. of commerce and indsl. devel., 1995—. Office: Embassy of Mexico 1911 Pennsylvania Ave NW Washington DC 20006*

MORALES, JOHN RUEDA, corporate accounting executive; b. Chgo., Oct. 16, 1956; s. Juan Santa Maria and Elena (Rueda) M.; m. Carla Ann Cosentino, Apr. 19, 1980; 1 child, Samantha. BA, St. Xavier U., 1979. CPA, Ill. Mgmt. analyst Chgo. Water Reclamation Dist., 1980-85; sr. auditor Ernst & Young, Chgo., 1985-87; prin. auditor Am. Nat. Can Co., Chgo., 1987-90; supr. internal audit Square D Co., Palatine, Ill., 1990-93, contr. corp. acctg., 1993-95, sr. fin. analyst mktg. group, 1996—. Sponsor Chgo. Tng. Alliance, 1992, 93, 94, 95, 96. Mem. AICPA, Ill. Soc. CPAs, Inst. Internal Auditors. Avocations: golf, swimming, billiards, reading, travel. Office: Square D Co Executive Pla Palatine IL 60067

MORALES, PABLO, Olympic athlete, swimmer. Olympic swimmer Barcelona, Spain, 1992. Recipient 100m Butterfly Gold medal Olympics, Barcelona, 1992. World record holder for 100 meter butterfly 52.84 seconds, set June 23, 1986, Orlando, Fla. Office: US Olympic Com 1750 E Boulder St Colorado Springs CO 80909-5724*

MORALES-BORGES, RAUL HECTOR, physician; b. San Juan, P.R., Aug. 2, 1963; s. Raul and Sonia Margarita (Borges) M. BS, U. P.R., 1985; MD, San Juan Bautista Sch. Med., 1990. Diplomate P.R. Bd. Med. Examiners. Aux. sales rep. Borges Warehouse of Textiles, Gurabo, P.R., 1981-85; tutor Computer Lab. U. P.R., Cayey, 1984, asst. researcher Ecol. Lab., 1985; intern Henry Ford Hosp., Detroit, 1990-91, resident, 1991-93; fellow, medical oncology Providence Hosp./U. Mich., Mich., 1993—; chief fellow med. oncology, 1995; mem. prostate specific antigen clin. policy team Henry Ford Hosp., 1991-93, smoking cessation task force 1993; summer tutor Edn. Dept. P.R., Gurabo, 1986-87; mem. lung cancer working group Providence Hosp., 1993-95, leukemia/lymphoma working group, 1995, breast cancer working group 1995; presenter in field. Organizer Com. of Profl. Assn., San Juan, 1988-90, Com. of San Jose Marathon, 1985-91. Mem. AMA, ACP (assoc.), N.Y. Acad. Scis., Nat. Assn. Drs., Am. Soc. of Blood and Marrow Transplant, Soc. for Nutritional Oncology Adjuvant Therapy. Roman Catholic. Achievements include research in tumor infiltrating lymphocytes in tumor infiltrating lymphocytes in melanoma RCC, HLD-DR as a metastatic marker, adoptive immunoltherapy, phase II trial of VP-16 and mitotantrone for metastatic breast cancer. Home: PO Box 873 Gurabo PR 00778

MORAN, BARBARA BURNS, librarian, educator; b. Columbus, Miss., July 8, 1944; d. Robert Theron and Joan (Brown) Burns; m. Joseph J. Moran, Sept. 4, 1965; children: Joseph Michael, Brian Matthew. AB, Mount Holyoke Coll., S. Hadley, Mass., 1966; M.Librarianship, Emory U., Atlanta, 1973; PhD, SUNY, Buffalo, 1982. Head libr. The Park Sch. of Buffalo,

Snyder, N.Y., 1974-78; prof. Sch. Info. and Libr. Sci. U. N.C., Chapel Hill, 1981—, asst. dean, 1987-90; dean Sch. Info. and Libr. Sci., U. N.C., Chapel Hill, 1990—; participant various seminars; evaluator various edn. progs.; cons. in field. Author: Academic Libraries, 1984; co-author: (with Robert D. Stueart) Library Management, 4th edit., 1993; contbr. articles to profl. jours., chpts. to books; mem. editl. bd. Jour. Acad. Librarianship, 1992-94, Coll. and Rsch. Libraries, 1996—. Coun. Libr. Resources grantee, 1985, Univ. Rsch. Coun. grantee, 1983, 89, others. Mem. ALA, Assn. for Libr. and Info. Sci. Edn., Popular Culture Assn., N.C. Libr. Assn., Beta Phi Mu. Home: 1307 Leclair St Chapel Hill NC 27514-3034 Office: Univ NC Sch Info & Libr Sci Chapel Hill NC 27599-3360

MORAN, CHARLES A., securities executive; b. Chgo., Feb. 7, 1943; s. Charles W. and Rose B. (Sutcher) M.; m. Donna L. Orbach, Sept. 3, 1967; children: Scott Alan, Erin Lizabeth. AB, Princeton U., 1964; JD, U. Mich., 1967; postgrad. advanced mgmt., Harvard U., 1982. CFP. With Chase Manhattan Bank, N.Y.C., 1967-70; pension trust officer, adminstrv. officer, officer in charge new bus. devel., pension div. Mfrs. Hanover Trust Co., N.Y.C., 1970-87, sr. v.p., officer-in-charge employee benefit trust div., 1979-80; chmn. bd., pres. MH/Edie Investment Counsel (formerly Lionel D. Edie & Co.), N.Y.C., 1980-82, officer-in-charge corp. trust div., 1982-83, officer in charge-global securities group, 1983-87; pres. Govt. Securities Clearing Corp., N.Y.C., 1987-96, Strategic Financial Adv., N.Y.C., N.J., 1996—; bd. dirs. Mfrs. Hanover Trust Co. Calif., Mfrs. Hanover Data Svcs. Corp., Mortgage Backed Securities Clearance Corp., Nat. Securities Clearance Corp.; chmn. bd. dirs. Inform, Inc.; former lectr. bus. and econs. Bloomfield Coll.; former lectr. sociology and fin. employee benefits C.W. Post Coll., L.I. U.; cons. Urban Vol. Cons. Group, Inc.; mem. adv. coun. Dept. Labor; mem. adv. bd. BNA Pension Reporter; mem. Employees Retirement Income Security Act of 1974 Roundtable; mem. industry adv. com. Future Electronic Funds Payments Svcs. Fed. Res. Contbr. articles to profl. jours. Mem. AAUP, Am. Inst. Banking, Am. Pension Conf. (treas. 1976-79), N.Y. State Bankers Assn. (employees trust com.), Assn. PVt. Pension and Welfare Plans (dir., mem. exec. com.), ERISA Industry Com. (pres., dir., mem. exec. com., treas.), Am. Bankers Assn. (chmn. employee benefit trust com. 1977-82), Internat. Found. Pension and Welfare Plans, Bank Adminstrn. Inst. (mem. tech. commn.), N.Y. C. of C. (task force on pub. pensions), The Inst. of Cert. Fin. Planners, N.J. Soc. Inst. Cert. Fin. Planners, Princeton Club. Office: Strategic Fin Adv 55 Water St Fl 22D New York NY 10041

MORAN, DANIEL AUSTIN, mathematician; b. Chgo., Feb. 17, 1936; s. Austin Thomas and Violet Lillian (Johnson) M.; m. Karen Krull, Sept. 14, 1963; children: Alexander, Claudia. B.S. summa cum laude, St. Mary's of Tex., 1957; M.S., U. Ill., 1958, Ph.D., 1962. Research instr. U. Chgo., 1962-64; asst. prof. Mich. State U., 1964-68, assoc. prof., 1968-76, prof. math., 1976—; vis. scholar U. Cambridge, 1970-71, U. North Wales, 1978. Contbr. articles to profl. jours. Mem. Math. Assn. Am., Sigma Xi, Pi Mu Epsilon, Delta Epsilon Sigma, Kappa Mu Alpha. Roman Catholic. Home: 2633 Roseland Ave East Lansing MI 48823-3870 Office: Dept Math Michigan State Univ East Lansing MI 48824

MORAN, EDWARD KEVIN, lawyer, consultant; b. N.Y.C., Mar. 4, 1964; s. Edward Joseph and Margaret Anne (Hauff) M.; m. Janet Athanasidy, Dec. 9, 1990. BA, SUNY, Binghamton, 1986; JD, N.Y. Law Sch., 1989. Bar: Conn. 1989, N.Y. 1990, N.J. 1990. Summer assoc. N.Y.C. Police Dept. Legal Bur., 1987; mng. atty. Landau, Miller and Moran, N.Y.C., 1990—; cons. Bottom Line Group, N.Y.C., 1992—. Editor-in-chief N.Y. Law Sch. Jour. Internat. and Comparative Law, 1988-89. Mem. Conn. Bar Assn., N.Y. State Bar Assn., Assn. Trial Lawyers Am., N.Y. State Trial Lawyers Assn. Office: Landau Miller and Moran 233 Broadway New York NY 10279-0001

MORAN, FRANK SULLIVAN, accounting executive; b. Detroit, Oct. 11, 1918; s. Thomas and Lucy (Sullivan) M.; m. Georgene Stritch, Jan. 4, 1941; children: Frank Jr., Midge, George, Elaine Kelly. AB in Philosophy, U. Detroit, 1940. Ptnr. Plante & Moran, Southfield, Mich., 1950—, mng. ptnr., 1955-82, chmn., 1982—. Office: Plante & Moran CPAs 27400 Northwestern Hwy Southfield MI 48034-4724

MORAN, JAMES BYRON, federal judge; b. Evanston, Ill., June 20, 1930; s. James Edward and Kathryn (Horton) M.; children: John, Jennifer, Sarah, Polly; stepchildren: Katie, Cynthia, Laura, Michael. AB, U. Mich., 1952; LLB magna cum laude, Harvard U., 1957. Bar: Ill. 1958. Law clk. to judge U.S. Ct. of Appeals (2d cir.), 1957-58; assoc. Bell, Boyd, Lloyd, Haddad & Burns, Chgo, 1958-66, ptnr., 1966-79; judge U.S. Dist. Ct. (no. dist.) Ill., Chgo., 1979—. Dir. Com. on Ill. Govt., 1960-78, chmn., 1968-70; vice chmn., sec. Ill. Dangerous Drug Adv. Coun., 1967-74; dir. Gateway Found., 1969—; mem. Ill. Ho. of Reps., 1965-67; mem. Evanston City Council, 1971-75. Served with AUS, 1952-54. Mem. Chgo. Bar Assn., Chgo. Council Lawyers, Phi Beta Kappa. Clubs: Law, Legal. Home: 117 Kedzie St Evanston IL 60202-2509 Office: US Dist Ct 219 S Dearborn St Chicago IL 60604-1702

MORAN, JAMES J., JR., lawyer; s. James J. and Marilyn A. (Sullivan) M.; m. Mary Therese Stevens, Oct. 6, 1979; children: Sean M., James E., Matthew S. AB cum laude, Boston Coll., 1975, JD, 1978. Bar: Mass. 1978, U.S. Ct. Appeals (1st cir.) 1979, U.S. Dist Ct. Mass. 1979, U.S. Tax Ct. 1979, U.S. Supreme Ct. 1982; CPCU. Assoc. Haussermann, Davison & Shattuck, Boston, 1978-84; assoc. Morrison, Mahoney & Miller, Boston, 1984-87, ptnr., 1988—; mem. legal com. Commonwealth Automobile Reinsurers, 1988; mem. CLU/CPCU adv. com. Mass Divsn. Ins., 1988-89; v.p., gen. counsel Ind. Property-Casualty Insurers Mass. Inc., 1991—; counsel Profl. Ind.Ins. Agts. of Mass., Inc., 1985—; ins. broker, Mass.; New Eng. regional regulatory counsel Alliance of Am. Insurers, 1994—; speaker in field. Contbr. articles to profl. jours. Bd. dirs. (gubernatorial appointee) Mass. Pollution Liability Reinsurance Corp., 1988-90. Mem. ABA (Tort and Ins. practice sect.), Internat. Assn. Def. Coun., Mass. Bar Assn., CPCU Soc. (pres. Boston chpt. 1993-94), Fedn. Regulatory Coun., Ins. Libr. Assn. Boston (trustee 1983—, pres. 1989-90). Democrat. Roman Catholic. Office: Morrison Mahoney & Miller 250 Summer St Boston MA 02210-1134

MORAN, JAMES M., automotive sales executive; b. 1918; married. Owner Courtesy Motor Sales Inc. (formerly Hudson Motor Franchise Inc.), Chgo., 1947-68; chmn. JM Family Enterprises Inc., Deerfield Beach, Fla., 1969—. Office: JM Family Enterprises 100 NW 12th Ave Deerfield Beach FL 33442-1702*

MORAN, JAMES MICHAEL, JR., astronomer, educator; b. Plainfield, N.J., Jan. 3, 1943; s. James Michael and Martha (Algermissen) M.; m. Barbara Putney Smith, Nov. 30, 1974; children: Susan Harrison, Michael Putney. BS, U. Notre Dame, 1963; SM, MIT, 1965, PhD, 1968. Mem. staff MIT Lincoln Lab., Lexington, 1968-70; sr. radio astronomer Smithsonian Astrophys. Obs., Cambridge, Mass., 1970—; prof. practice of astronomy Harvard U., Cambridge, 1979-89, prof. astronomy, 1989—; trustee N.E. Radio Obs. Corp., Cambridge, 1983—. Contbr. numerous articles on radio astronomy to profl. publs. Co-recipient Rumford prize Am. Acad. Arts and Scis., 1971; recipient Sr. award Alexander von Humboldt Soc., 1993. Fellow AAAS; mem. IEEE (sr.), Am. Astron. Soc. (Pierce prize 1978), Explorers Club. Avocations: photography, flying, hiking. Achievements include development of technique of very long baseline interferometry. Home: 93 Anson Rd Concord MA 01742-5704 Office: Harvard-Smithsonian Center for Astrophysics 60 Garden St Cambridge MA 02138-1516

MORAN, JAMES P., psychotherapist; b. Jersey City, Aug. 8, 1946; s. Raymond A. and Catherine I. (Nolan) M. BA in Classical Langs., Seton Hall U., 1968; MA in Edn., 1971; MSW, Yeshiva U., 1987; MBA in Adminstrn., Grad. Theol. Found., Donaldson, Ind., 1991. Cert. social worker, N.J.; cert. addictions specialist Am. Acad. Health Care Providers/Addictive Disorders. Coord. counseling/edn. North Haven (Conn.) Alcohol Edn. and Program Svcs., 1972-76; pvt. practice psychotherapy Colonia, N.J., 1976—. Exec. com. Ctrl. Jersey Health Planning Coun., Princeton, N.J., 1983-89; mem. Middlesex County Health Planning Coun., Woodridge, N.J., 1983-89; bd. dirs. Middlesex County Mental Health Assn., Woodbridge, 1990-95; profl. adv. com. Raritan Bay Hospice, Perth Amboy, N.J., 1991—. Mem. NASW, APHA, Am. Orthopsychiat. Assn., Nat. Assn. Alcoholism and Drug Abuse Counselors, N.J. Pub. Health Assn., N.Y. Acad. Sci. Office: 15 Midwood Way Colonia NJ 07067

MORAN, JAMES PATRICK, JR., congressman, stockbroker; b. Buffalo, N.Y., May 16, 1945; s. James Patrick and Dorothy (Dwyer) M.; m. Mary Craig, Dec. 27, 1967 (div. 1974); children: Jimmy, Mary; m. Mary Howard; children: Michael, Patrick, Dorothy. BA in Econs., Coll. of Holy Cross, Worcester, Mass., 1967; postgrad., CUNY, 1967-68; MA in Pub. Adminstrn., U. Pitts., 1970. Budget analyst HEW, Washington, 1969-74; budget and fiscal policy specialist, Congl. rsch. Libr. of Congress, Washington, 1974-76; sr. staff appropriations com. U.S. Senate, Washington, 1976-79; city councilman Alexandria, Va., 1979-91, vice-mayor, 1982-84, mayor, 1985-91; investment broker A.G. Edwards & Sons, Alexandria, Va., 1979—; mem. 102nd-103rd Congresses from 8th Va. dist., Washington, D.C., 1991—; mem. govt. reform & oversight coms.; ranking minority mem. civil svcs. subcom.; mem. internat. rels. on internat. ops. & human rights coms. Councilman, City of Alexandria, 1979-82, vice-mayor, 1982-84, mayor, 1985—; chmn. No. Va. Transportation Bd., 1988—, United Way, 1977-79; vice chmn. Mental Health Retard and Substance Abuse Bd., 1976-78, vice chmn. D.E.O., 1976-78;dir., Met. Area Council Govts., dir. No. Va. Transp. Commn., 1985—. Recipient Outstanding Citizenship award YMCA, 1983. Mem. C. of C. (dir. 1985-86). Democrat. Roman Catholic. Home: 205 Uhler Ter Alexandria VA 22301-1551 Office: US Ho of Reps 405 Cannon HOB Washington DC 20515*

MORAN, JOAN JENSEN, physical education and health educator; b. Chgo., Sept. 25, 1952; d. Axel Fred and Mary J. (Maes) J.; m. Gregory Keith Moran. BS in Edn., Western Ill. U., 1974; MS in Edn., No. Ill. U., 1978. Cert. tchr., Ill. Tchr., coach East Coloma Sch., Rock Falls, Ill., 1974—; part-time recreation specialist Woodhaven Lakes, Sublette, Ill., 1975-79; cons. Ill. State Bd. Edn., Springfield, 1984—; instr. NDEITA, Ill., 1988—; facilitator Project Wild, Ill., 1990—. Instr. ARC, Rock Falls, 1978—, Am. Heart Assn., Rock Falls, 1978—; exec. bd. East Coloma Cmty. Club; fitness del. to Russia and Hungary, 1992; cons. Alcohol Awareness & Occupant Restraint Ill. State Bd. Edn., Substance Abuse Guidance Edn. Com., Rock Falls Drug Free Cmty. Grant com., Whiteside County CPR Coord. com. Recipient Western Ill. U. Alumni Achievement award, 1993, Western Ill. Master Tchr. award, 1993, Svc. award Ill. Assn. Health, Phys. Edn., Recreation and Dance, 1991, 92, Outstanding Young Woman award, 1986, Phys. Educator of Yr. award, 1988; named Mid. Sch. Phys. Edn. Tchr. of Yr. Midwest AAHPERD, 1993, Ill. Assn. Health, Phys. Edn., Recreation and Dance, 1992, Gov.'s Coun. Health and Phys. Edn. award, 1991, Am. Tchr. of Yr. award Walt Disney Co., 1993, Excel award ISBE, 1995. Mem. AAHPERD, NEA, Ill. Assn. Health, Phys. Edn., Recreation and Dance (v.p. teenage youth 1988-90, pres. 1994, past pres., conv. coord. 1995), No. Dist. Ill. Assn. Health, Phys. Edn., Recreation and Dance, Ill. Edn. Assn. (newsletter editor 1984-85, exec. bd. 1985-90, treas. 1985-90), East Coloma Edn. Assn. (pres., pub. rels., v.p. 1993-94, Environ. Edn. Assn. Ill. Democrat. Lutheran. Avocations: skiing, hiking, biking, reading, traveling. Home: 1903 E 41st St Sterling IL 61081-9449

MORAN, JOHN, religious organization administrator; b. Oct. 4, 1935; m. Retha Jane Patrick; children: John II, James, Helen. Missionary Nigeria, 1963-68; pastor, 1969-87; pres. The Missionary Ch., Fort Wayne, Ind., 1987—. Mem. Nat. Assn. Evang. (mem. exec. bd. 1987—, vice dist. supt. 1977-81, mem. Nat. Assn. Evang./Nat. Black Evang. Assn. com. on racial reconciliation 1995—). Office: Missionary Ch PO Box 9127 3811 Vanguard Dr Fort Wayne IN 46899-9127

MORAN, JOHN A., investment company executive; b. L.A., Mar. 22, 1932; s. Benjamin Edward and Louise (Chisholm) M.; m. Mary Darlene Whittaker, Aug. 14, 1954 (div. Oct. 1984); children—Kelli, Marisa, Elizabeth. B.S., U. Utah, 1954; postgrad., NYU, 1958-59, U. So. Calif., 1959-60. Assoc. Blyth & Co., Inc, N.Y.C. and Los Angeles, 1958-64; v.p. Blyth & Co., Inc, Los Angeles, 1964-67; v.p. Dyson-Kissner Corp., N.Y.C., 1967-74, exec. v.p., 1974-75, pres., 1975-84, chmn., 1984-90; chmn. exec. com. Dyson-Kissner-Moran, N.Y.C., 1990-94; bd. dirs. Bessemer Securities. Chmn. Rep. Nat. Fin. Com., 1993-95; mem. nat. adv. bd. U. Utah. Lt. USNR, 1955-58. Mem. Chief Execs. Orgn. Republican. Roman Catholic. Clubs: Metropolitan, Racquet and Tennis (N.Y.C.); Larchmont Yacht (N.Y.); Winged Foot Golf, (Mamaroneck, N.Y.).

MORAN, JOHN BERNARD, government official; b. Saginaw, Mich., Nov. 26, 1936; s. Leo Lewis and Marie Katherine (Langley) M.; m. Diann Marie Markey, May 20, 1963 (div.); m. Barbara Jane Livingston, Aug. 18, 1978; children—Leslie Marie, Leanne Rene, Jeffrey John. B.S. in Metall. Engring., Ill. Inst. Tech., 1959. Sr. automotive specialist Dow Chem. Co., Midland, Mich., 1962-71; program dir. research EPA, Research Triangle Park, N.C., 1971-75; dir. monitoring tech. div. EPA, Washington, 1975-76; dir. div. safety research Nat. Inst. for Occupational Safety and Health, Ctrs. for Disease Control, USPHS, HHS, Morgantown, W.Va., 1976-77, 83-88; dir. research and devel. safety products div. Am. Optical Corp., Southbridge, Mass., 1977-80; v.p., dir. ops. Geomet, Inc., Rockville, Md., 1980-83; program dir. Hartford Engring. Tech., Inc., Windsor, Conn., 1988; assoc. dir. health and safety laborers Associated Gen. Contractors, 1988-89; dir. safety and health Laborers Health and Safety Fund, 1989-95; spl. asst. to dep. asst. sec. Worker Health and Safety U.S. Dept. Energy, Washington, 1995; dir. policy OSHA, U.S. Dept. Labor, Washington, 1996—; mem. Nat. Mine Health Rsch. Adv. Com., Atlanta, 1980-84; govt. del. ILO, Geneva, 1985; mem. Nat. Adv. Com. on Constrn. Safety and Health, 1985-88, 92-95, Bur. Labor Stats. Rsch., 1991-95, hazardous material transp. info. com. NAS, 1991-93, Hazardous Materials Control Rsch. Inst.; chmn. lead sub-com. Bldg. Constrn. Trades Dept., 1991-95; adj. assoc. prof. mech. engring. W.Va. U., 1985-88; vis. ext. prof. U. Conn., Storrs, 1988-90; mem. Fed. Facilities Environ. Restoration Com., constrn. com. A 10 Am. Nat. Stds. Inst.; co-chair EPA-Labor Superfund Task Force, 1990-95; mem. nat. lead task force HUD, 1993-95; cons., expert witness. Patentee; contbr. articles to profl. jours, chpts. to books. Mem. Task Force on Hazardous Materials, Rockville, Md., 1983. chmn. Nat. Inst. Environ. Health Sci., 1990. Served to capt. USMC, 1959-65. Recipient Bronze medal for commendable service EPA, 1974, Commitment to Life award Nat. Safe Workplace Inst., 1988. Mem. Internat. Soc. Respiratory Protection (pres. 1985-87, bd. dirs. 1987-89), Am. Conf. Govtl. Indsl. Hygienists. Roman Catholic. Home: 1605 Savannah Hwy North SC 29112-9625

MORAN, JOHN HENRY, JR., retired electrical engineer, consultant; b. Phila., Sept. 22, 1923; s. John Henry and Mary Joseph (Sheehan) M.; m. Jane Miriam Daly, June 29, 1946; children—Terrence, Kathleen, Michael, Patrick. B.S.E.E., Case Western Res. U., 1947. Profl. engr., N.Y., Ohio. Devel. engr. Allis-Chalmers, West Allis, Wis., 1947-55; engr. Lapp Insulator, LeRoy, N.Y., 1955-63, chief elec. engr., 1963-86, mgr. bushing engring., 1977-86; prin. cons., 1986—. Author: High Voltage Bushings, 1989; co-author: Electrostatics and Its Applications, 1973; author tech. papers; patentee. Active Genesee Boy Scouts Am., 1936-88. Served with USN, 1942-46, U.S., ETO. Fellow IEEE (life); mem. Electrostatic Soc. Am. (founding, v.p. 1978-82). Republican. Roman Catholic. Home and Office: 9053 Roanoke Rd Stafford NY 14143-9524

MORAN, JOHN JOSEPH, retired food and beverage company executive; b. Scranton, Pa., Sept. 1, 1916; s. Edward Francis and Mary Ellen (Conlin) M.; divorced; children: Mary Anne Moran Greenall, Patricia, Cynthia (dec.). B.S., Rutgers U., 1942; grad., Advanced Mgmt. Program, Harvard, 1964. C.P.A., N.J. With Wiley, Block & White (C.P.A.'s), Paterson, N.J., 1937-42, Wright Aero. Corp., Paterson, 1933-37; br. chief War Assets Adminstrn., 1946-50; asst. controller J.P. Stevens & Co., 1950-59; controller Heublein Inc., 1959—, treas., 1968—, v.p., 1971-82, asst. to chmn., 1977-82, cons., 1982-86. Served to lt. comdr. USNR, 1942-46. Mem. Fin. Execs. Inst., Am. Inst. C.P.A.s, Harvard Advanced Mgmt. Assn. Catholic. Home: 3 Sawmill Xing Wethersfield CT 06109-1345 Office: 9 Potter Xing Wethersfield CT 06109-1327 *I've tried to run my life as follows: Do the best job possible; be honest, conscientious, and kind to people; try to help others, and stay healthy.*

MORAN, JOHN THOMAS, JR., lawyer; b. Oak Park, Ill., Mar. 15, 1943; s. John T. and Corinne Louise (Dire) M.; m. Catherine Casey Pyne, May 16, 1981; 1 child, Sean Michael Pyne-Moran. AB cum laude, U. Notre Dame, 1965; JD, Georgetown U., 1968. Bar: Ill. 1969, Colo. 1976, U.S. Supreme Ct. 1973. Chief appeals div. Pub. Defender Cook County, Ill., 1970-82; gen. counsel Pub. Defender Cook County, Chgo., 1984-86; chief litigation atty. Frank & Flaherty, Chgo., 1982; cons. ABA, Chgo., 1982-83; sole practice Chgo., 1986-93; founder Law Offices of John Thomas Moran:, 1993-95. Editor: Gideon Revisited, 1983. Bd. dirs. Lawyers for the Creative Arts, 1973—. Ford Found. grantee Internat. Common Law Colloquium, London, 1976, NEH grantee, Harvard Law Sch., 1977. Mem. Ill. State Bar Assn., Appellate Lawyers Assn., Nat. Legal Aid and Defenders Assn., Am. Soc. Internat. Law, Georgetown U. Law Ctr. Alumni Soc., Sorin Soc. U. Notre Dame. Avocation: sailing. Home: 930 Oakwood Ave Wilmette IL 60091-3320 Office: The Delaware Bldg 36 W Randolph St Ste 800 Chicago IL 60601-3516

MORAN, JULIETTE M., management consultant; b. N.Y.C., June 12, 1917; d. James Joseph and Louise M. B.S., Columbia U., 1938; M.S., NYU, 1948. Research asst. Columbia U., 1941; jr. engr. Signal Corps Lab., U.S. Army, 1942-43; with GAF Corp. (formerly Gen. Aniline & Film Corp.), 1943-82; successively jr. chemist process devel. dept., tech. asst. to N.Y. process devel. dept., tech. asst. to dir. Central Research Lab., tech. asst. to dir GAF Corp., 1953-55, supr. tech. service comml. devel. dept., 1955-59, sr. devel. specialist, 1959-60, mgr. planning, 1961, asst. to the pres., 1962-67, v.p., 1967-71, sr. v.p., 1971-74, exec. v.p., 1974-80, dir., 1974-83, vice chmn., 1980-82, cons., 1982—. Bd. dirs. N.Y. State Sci. and Tech. Found. Recipient Greater N.Y. Advt. award for excellence in communications N.Y. chpt. Assn. Indsl. Advertisers, 1972, Alumni Achievement award N.Y. U. Grad. Sch. Arts and Scis., 1977. Fellow AAAS, Am. Inst. Chemists; mem. Am. Chem. Soc., Comml. Devel. Assn. Home: 10 W 66th St New York NY 10023-6206

MORAN, M. MARCUS, JR., retail executive; b. Fitchburg, Mass., Apr. 19, 1943; s. M. Marcus Sr. and Claire Paulette (Aubuchon) M.; m. Tonia Francavilla, July 29, 1966; children: Marcus III, Coutney L., Justin M. BBA, Nichols Coll., 1966; MBA, Babson Coll., 1967. Prof. North Shore Community Coll., Beverly, Mass., 1967-70; pres., treas. W. E. Aubuchon Co., Inc., Westminster, Mass., 1970—, 1993—, also bd. dirs.; bd. dirs., chmn. investment com., vice-chmn. of bd. I-C Fed. Credit Union, Fitchburg, Mass., 1987—; past instr. acctg. and fin. Fitchburg State Coll., Boston U., North Shore Community Coll., Mt. Wachusett C.C. Author: Business Mathematics, 1969. Pres., bd. dirs. United Way, Fitchburg, 1984-88; trustee Fitchburg State Coll./FTC Found., 1978—; past trustee Nichols Coll., Notre Dame Acad., Worcester, Mass.; bd. dirs. Julie Country Day Sch., Leominster, Mass., 1980, Cushing Acad., Ashburnham, Mass., 1989—; chmn. bus. edn. fund, Monty Tech. Vocation Sch. Recipient Key to City-Life Saving, City of Fitchburg, 1965, Community Leadership award Fitchburg State Coll., 1991, Disting. Citizen award Boy Scouts Am., 1993. Mem. Fay Club (past dir., pres. 1970—), Beta Gamma, Zeta Alpha Phi. Republican. Roman Catholic. Avocation: education. Home: Round Meadow Pond Westminster MA 01473 Office: W E Aubuchon Co Inc 95 Aubuchon Dr Westminster MA 01473

MORAN, MARTIN JOSEPH, fundraising company executive; b. Bklyn., Nov. 3, 1930; s. Dominick and Mary (Lydon) M.; m. Mary Therese Schofield, June 5, 1954; children: Martin Joseph, John P., Maureen M., Thomas S., Robert P., William M., Maria M. BA, St. John's U., 1952. Profl. fundraising cons., 1956—; founder Martin J. Moran Co., Inc., N.Y.C., 1964, pres., 1964-74, chmn. bd., 1974—. Mem. Cardinal's Com. for Edn., N.Y.C., 1970-79, Cardinal's Com. for Laity Archdiocese N.Y., 1979—, Am. Revolution Bicentennial Commn., Oyster Bay, N.Y.; mem. Massapequa Park (N.Y.) Bd. Zoning Appeals, 1972-84, chmn., 1978-84; mem. Massapequa Park Ethics Commn., 1969-72; trustee Notre Dame Coll., S.I., 1969-72, La Salle Acad., N.Y.C., 1971-87; mem. pres.'s council Cath. U.P.R., Ponce, 1966-71. Served as aviator USNR, 1952-56. Decorated knight Order Holy Sepulchre, Pope Paul VI, 1968, Knight of Malta, Pope Paul VI, 1973; recipient Pietas medal St. John's U., N.Y., 1988; bd. councilors, sec., treas. Equestrian Order Holy Sepulchre of Jerusalem, 1990—, sec.-treas. 1990-93, pres., 1993—. Mem. Navy League, Navy Hist. Assn., St. John's U. Alumni Assn. (pres. 1987-94), Am. Assn. Fund Raising Counsel (bd. dirs. 1970—), Nassau County Hist. Soc., Friendly Sons of St. Patrick. Roman Catholic. Club: Madison Square Garden (N.Y.C.); Lost Tree Club (North Palm Beach, Fla.), Old Port Yacht Club. Lodge: KC. Home: 1300 Lakeshore Dr Massapequa Park NY 11762-1764 also: 677 Village Rd No Palm Beach FL 33408-3329 Office: Martin J Moran Co 1 Penn Plz New York NY 10119-0002

MORAN, PATRICIA GENEVIEVE, corporate executive; b. Evanston, Ill., July 26, 1945; d. James M.; children: Christine Coyle, Thomas Beddia, Donald Beddia. Attended, Marquette U. Pers. mgr. Sesco, 1983-84, dir. corp. transp., assoc. rels. dir., 1984-85, v.p. assoc. rels., 1985-88; group v.p. sales Southeast Toyota, Deerfield Beach, Fla., 1988-89, pres., 1989-94; v.p. H.R. JM Family Enterprises, Inc., Deerfield Beach, pres., 1989-94. Dir. Beacon Coun., Miami, Fla., 1992—, Broward Econ. Devel., Ft. Lauderdale, Fla., 1991—, Youth Automotive Tng. Ctr., Hollywood, Fla., 1985—. Named Top 50 Working Women by Working Woman's Mag. Mem. Ft. Lauderdale C. of C. (dir. 1991—), Tower Club, The Haven (adv. bd. 1994-95). Office: JM Family Enterprises 100 NW 12th Ave Deerfield Beach FL 33442-1702*

MORAN, PAUL JAMES, journalist, columnist; b. Buffalo, July 20, 1947; s. Paul James and Frances (Sciortino) M.; m. Kim Maldiner, Mar. 17, 1975 (div. July 1979); m. Colette Stass (separated); 1 child, Heather. Student, SUNY, Buffalo, 1965-67, Millard Fillmore Coll., 1971-73. Sports editor Tonawanda News, North Tonawanda, N.Y., 1972-75; writer/columnist Fort Lauderdale (Fla.) News/Sun Sentinel, 1975-85, N.Y. Newsday, Melville, 1985—; cons. Green Country Racing Assn., Tulsa, 1983-85. Contbr. articles to mags. and newspapers. Sgt. USAF, 1967-71. Recipient Eclipse award Thoroughbred Racing Assn., 1985, 90, Disting. Writing award Am. Soc. Newspaper Editors, 1990, Deadline Writing award Soc. Silurians, 1990, Deadline Reporting award L.I. Press Club, 1991, Disting. Sports Writing award N.Y. Newspaper Pubs. Assn., 1992, (with others) Journalism collection Best Newspaper Writing 1991. Mem. N.Y. Turf Writers' Assn. (pres. 1990-92, sec.-treas. 1992-94), Nat. Turf Writers' Assn. (bd. dirs. 1987-90). Republican. Avocations: photography, art collecting. Home: 270 Jericho Tpke Floral Park NY 11001-2107 Office: Newsday 235 Pinelawn Rd Melville NY 11747-4226

MORAN, PHILIP DAVID, lawyer; b. Lynn, Mass., June 3, 1937; s. J. Francis and Margaret M. (Shanahan) M.; m. Carole A. Regan, May 12, 1962; children: Maura F., Philip David. A.B., Holy Cross Coll., 1958; Ed.M., Salem State Coll., 1961; J.D., Suffolk U., 1968. Bar: Mass. 1968, U.S. Dist. Ct. Mass., 1972, U.S. Supreme Ct., 1988, U.S. Ct. Appeals (1st cir.), 1993. House counsel Viatron Computer Systems Corp., Burlington, Mass., 1968-71; ptnr. Kane & Moran, Lynn, Mass., 1972-78; pvt. practice law Salem, Mass., 1978—; asst. dist. atty. Essex County (Mass.), 1974-78. Bd. dirs. Nat. Right to Life Inc., 1977-83, 87—, treas., 1981-83; Contbg. author: Encyclopedia of Biomedical Policy, 1995. Bd. dir. Mass. Citizens for Life, 1973—, pres. 1979-80, chmn. 1991-93. mem. Salem Conservation Commn., 1980-89, chmn., 1982-89; mem. pres.'s coun. Holy Cross Coll., 1985—; mem. Nat. Inst. Trial Advocacy U. Colo., 1973; gen. chmn bicentenary com. Maynooth Coll., Boston, 1994-96. With U.S. Army, 1960-66. Recipient Ignatius O'Connor Pro Life award, 1994, Gold medal St. Patrick Maynooth Coll., Ireland, 1996. Mem. Mass. Bar Assn., Salem Bar Assn., Lynn Bar Assn., Am. Trial Lawyers Assn., Nat. Acad. Elder Law Attys., Murray Inn of Ct. Roman Catholic. Avocations: swimming, reading, gardening, boating. Home: 415 Lafayette St Salem MA 01970-5337 Office: 265 Essex St Salem MA 01970-3400

MORAN, RACHEL, lawyer, educator; b. Kansas City, Mo., June 27, 1956; d. Thomas Albert and Josephine (Portillo) M. AB, Stanford U., 1978; JD, Yale U., 1981. Bar: Calif. 1984. Assoc Heller, Ehrman, White & McAuliffe, San Francisco, 1982-83; prof. law U. Calif., Berkeley, 1984—; vis. prof. UCLA Sch. Law, 1988, Stanford (Calif.) U. Law Sch., 1989; ann. civil rights lectr. Creighton U. Sch. Law, Omaha, 1989; Pirsig lectr. William Mitchell Coll. St. Paul, 1989, others. mem. steering com. Nat. Resource Ctr., Berkeley, 1988-89; chair Chicano/Latino Policy Project, 1993-96. Contbr. numerous articles to profl. jours. Grantee Joseph and Polly Harris Trust

Inst. Govtl. Studies, Berkeley, 1987-89, Faculty Devel. U. Calif., Berkeley, 1985-86; recipient Disting. Tchg. award U. Calif. Mem. ABA, AAUP, Calif. Bar Assn., Phi Beta Kappa. Democrat. Unitarian. Avocations: jogging, aerobics, reading, listening to music. Office: U Calif Sch Law Boalt Hall Berkeley CA 94720

MORAN, ROBERT FRANCIS, JR., library director; b. Cleve., May 3, 1938; s. Robert Francis Sr. and Jeanette (Mulholland) M.; m. Judith Mary Pacer, Dec. 28, 1968; children: Mary Jeanette, Catherine, Margaret. BA, Cath. U. Am., Washington, 1961, MLS, 1965; MBA, U. Chgo., 1976. Head librarian St. Patrick's Sem., Menlo Park, Calif., 1965-69; coordinator and reference librarian U. Chgo., 1969-72; serials librarian U. Ill., Chgo., 1972-78, acquisitions librarian, 1977-80; dir. library services Ind. U. Northwest, Gary, 1980—, asst. vice chancellor tech., 1991—; v.p., sec., treas. Northwest Ind. Area Library Services Authority, Merrillville, 1982-91. Contbr. articles to profl jours. Mem. ALA, Libr. Adminstrn. and Mgmt. Assn. (com. chmn. 1981-86, sect. chmn. 1986-88, chmn. program com. 1988-91, chair nominating com. 1991-92, networked info. discussion group 1994—). Democrat. Roman Catholic. Office: Ind Univ NW Library 3400 Broadway Gary IN 46408-1101

MORAN, SHEILA KATHLEEN, theatrical producer; b. Norwalk, Conn.; d. Edmond Joseph and Alice Marie (Laux) M.; m. John Joseph Reynolds, Apr. 2, 1987 (dec. Apr. 1993). BA, Manhattanville Coll., Purchase, N.Y. Sportswriter, reporter AP, N.Y.C., 1969-71, N.Y. Post, N.Y.C., 1972-76, L.A. Times, 1976-80; actress, freelance writer L.A., 1981-90; producer Evensong Assocs., N.Y.C., 1990—. Vol. VA Hosp., L.A., 1987-90, Meml. Sloan Kettering Cancer Ctr., N.Y.C., 1990-93. Mem. AFTRA, Screen Actors Guild, Actors' Equity Assn., Producers Group, N.Y.C., Inner Circle, Coffee House, N.Y.C. Democrat. Roman Catholic.

MORAN, THOMAS FRANCIS, chemistry educator; b. Manchester, N.H., Dec. 11, 1936; s. Francis Leo and Mamie Marie (Morin) M.; m. Joan Elinor Belliveau, June 25, 1960; children: Dorothy, Michael, Linda, Mary. BA, St. Anselm's Coll., 1958; PhD, Notre Dame U., 1962. Teaching and rsch. fellow Notre Dame U., South Bend, Ind., 1958-62; USAEC postdoctoral fellow Brookhaven Nat. Lab., Upton, N.Y., 1962-64; staff scientist Brookhaven Nat. Lab., 1964-66; asst. prof. Ga. Inst. Tech., Atlanta, 1966-68; assoc. prof. Ga. Inst. Tech., 1968-72, prof. chemistry dept., 1972—. Contbr. articles to profl. jours. Danforth fellow Danforth Found. Mem. Am. Chem. Soc., Am. Physical Soc., Am. Soc. Mass Spectrometry, AAAS, Sigma Xi (award). Home: 2324 Annapolis Ct NE Atlanta GA 30345-3803 Office: Chemistry Dept Ga Inst Tech Atlanta GA 30332

MORAN, THOMAS HARRY, university administrator; b. Milw., Oct. 21, 1937; s. Harry Edward and Edna Agnes Moran; BS, U. Wis., 1964, MA, 1972, PhD, 1974; m. Barbara Ellen Saklad, June 10, 1969; children: David Thomas, Karen Ellen. Dir. capital budgeting Wis. Dept. Adminstrn., 1962-64; exec. dir. Wis. Higher Ednl. Aids Bd., 1964-69; spl. cons. tax policy Wis. Dept. Revenue, 1973-74; dep. dir. Wis. Manpower Coun., Office of Gov., 1974-76; v.p. bus. and fin., treas. U. Detroit, 1976-78; exec. assoc. v.p. health affairs U. So. Calif., L.A., 1979-87; v.p. bus. affairs, 1988—. USN fellow, 1957-59; U.S. Office Edn. rsch. fellow, 1973. Mem. Am. Assn. Higher Edn., Phi Kappa Phi. Office: U So Calif 200 Town & Gown University Park Los Angeles CA 90007

MORAN, TIMOTHY, newspaper editor; b. N.Y.C., Jan. 1, 1952; s. Cyril Peter and Joan Marie (Gilbride) M.; m. Donna Marie Pasqualino, July 17, 1988; children: Derek, Christopher. BA, L.I. U., 1976, postgrad., 1976-78. Mng. editor Today's Office, Garden City, N.Y., 1977-85, Engring. Tools, Hasbrouck Heights, N.J., 1987-88; mng. editor Elec. Engring. Times divsn. CMP Publs., Manhassett, N.Y., 1988-93, exec. editor, 1993—. Office: CMP Publs 600 Community Dr Manhasset NY 10300

MORAND, BLAISE E., bishop; b. Tecumseh, Ont., Can., Sept. 12, 1932. Ordained priest Roman Cath. Ch., 1958. Ordained coadjutor bishop Diocese of Prince Albert, Sask., Can., 1981, bishop, 1983—. Office: Diocese of Prince Albert, 1415 4th Ave W, Prince Albert, SK Canada S6V 5H1

MORAND, PETER, research agency executive; b. Montreal, Que., Can., Feb. 11, 1935; s. Frank and Rose Alice (Fortier) M.; m. Dawn McKell, Oct. 10, 1957; children: Clifford, Tanya. BSc with honors, Bishop's U., Lennoxville, Que., 1956, DCL (hon.), 1991; PhD, McGill U., Montreal, 1959. NATO postdoctoral fellow Imperial Coll., London, 1959-61; sr. rsch. chemist Ayerst Labs., Montreal, 1961-63; asst. prof. chemistry U. Ottawa, Can., 1963-67, acad. asst. vice rector, 1968-71, dean sci.and engring., 1976-81, prof. chemistry, dir. rsch. svcs., 1981-87, vice rector univ. R&D, 1987-90; pres. Natural Scis. and Engring. Rsch. Coun., Ottawa, 1990—; bd. dirs. Ottawa-Carleton Econ. Devel. Corp., Can., ESTCO Energy, Inc. Contbr. articles to profl. jours.; patentee in field. Trustee B.C. Applied Systems Inst., Vancouver, Can., 1990—. Natural Scis. and Engring. Rsch. Coun. grantee, 1964-90. Fellow Chem. Inst. Can.; mem. Soc. of Rsch. Adminstrs., Rideau Club, Cercle Univ. Office: 26 Central Ave, Ottawa, ON Canada K2P OM9

MORANG, DIANE JUDY, writer, television producer, business entrepreneur; b. Chgo., Apr. 28, 1942; d. Anthony Thomas Morang and Laura Ann Andrzejczak. Student, Stevens Finishing Sch., Chgo., 1956, Fox Bus. Coll., 1959-60, UCLA, 1967-69. Mem. staff Drury Ln. Theatre, Chgo., 1961-62; staff AM Show ABC-TV, Hollywood, Calif., 1970-71; exec. prodr., creator (TV series) Forts, Fights, and Trails, 1995; chair, mem. judging panel Regional Emmy awards, 1989, judge 2 categories, 1985. Author: How to Get into the Movies, 1978; author, creator: The Rainbow Keyboard, 1991; exec. producer, creator, Forts, Fights and Trails (TV Series), 1996. Bd. dirs., mem. scholarship com. Ariz. Bruins UCLA Alumni Assn. Mem. NATAS (mem. Emmy-award winning team 1971), Ariz. Authors Assn. (bd. dirs.). Roman Catholic.

MORANIS, RICK, actor; b. Toronto, Ont., Can., Apr. 18, 1954. Appeared in films Ghostbusters, 1984, Streets of Fire, 1984, The Wild Life, 1984, Brewster's Millions, 1985, Head Office, 1985, Club Paradise, 1986, Little Shop of Horrors, 1986, Spaceballs, 1987, Ghostbusters II, 1989, Honey, I Shrunk the Kids, 1989, Parenthood, 1989, My Blue Heaven, 1990, L.A. Story, 1991, Honey, I Blew Up the Kid, 1992, Splitting Heirs, 1993, The Flintstones, 1994, Little Giants, 1994, Big Bully, 1995; actor, co-writer, co-dir.: (films) Strange Brew, 1983; actor, writer: (TV) Second City TV, 1980-81, SCTV Network 90, 1981-82 (Emmy award 1982), (with Dave Thomas) A Funny Thing Happened on the Way to the Olympics, 1988; albums include (with Dave Thomas) Great White North, 1981, Strange Brew, 1983. Office: CAA 9830 Wilshire Blvd Beverly Hills CA 90212*

MORANT, RICARDO BERNARDINO, psychology educator; b. New Britain, Conn., Feb. 13, 1926; s. J. Ramon and Rosario (Ciscar) M.; m. G. Francisca Giner, Dec. 26, 1955; children—Ramon, Francisca, Dolores, Ricardo. A.B., Harvard, 1948; postgrad., Wesleyan Coll., Middletown, Conn., 1948-49; M.A., Clark U., 1950, Ph.D., 1952. Faculty Brandeis U., Waltham, Mass., 1952—; prof. psychology Brandeis U., 1965—, Fierman prof. psychology, 1968—, chmn. dept., 1962-73, chmn. Sch. Social Scis., 1982-86, chmn. Latin Am. Studies, 1984-91; Prin. investigator NIMH, Spencer Found., Rothman Found. 1960—; spl. research space perception, body orientation. Bd. dirs. Council for Pub. Schs., 1970-73; mem. steering com. Sensory Aid Eval. and Devel. Ctr., MIT, 1963-67; chmn. bd. trustees Hiatt Ednl. Programs, 1982—. Served with USNR, 1946-48. Fellow Am. Psychol. Assn.; mem. Eastern, New Eng., Mass psychol. assn., Psychonomic Soc. Home: 35 Cliff Rd Wellesley MA 02181-3001 Office: Brandeis Univ Waltham MA 02154

MORARDINI, MICHAEL ROBERT, professional baseball player; b. Kittanning, Pa., Apr. 22, 1966. Student, U. Ind. Second baseman Phila. Phillies Nat. League Baseball Team, 1990—. Mem. U.S. Olympic Baseball Team, 1988, Phila. Phillies Nat. League Champaions, 1993; named to Nat. League All-Star Team, 1995. Office: Phila Phillies PO Box 7575 Philadelphia PA 19101

MORARI, MANFRED, chemical engineer, educator; b. Graz, Austria, May 13, 1951; came to U.S., 1975; s. Manfred and Hilde (Florian) M.; m. Marina Korchynsky, May 12, 1984. Diploma Chem. Engring., Eidgenoessische Technische Hochschule, Zurich, Switzerland, 1974; PhD in Chem. Engring., U. Minn., 1977. Asst. prof. U. Wis., Madison, 1977-81, assoc. prof., 1981-83; prof. chem. engring. Calif. Inst. Tech., Pasadena, 1983—, McCollum-Corcoran prof., 1991—, exec. officer, 1990-93, prof. control and dynamical sys., 1993—; exec. officer, 1993—; Gulf vis. prof. chem. engring. Carnegie Mellon U., 1987. Contbr. articles to profl. jours. Recipient D.P. Eckman award Am. Automatic Control Coun., 1980. Mem. IEEE (George S. Axelby Outstanding Paper award 1990), NAE, AIChE (A. P. Colburn award 1984, Profl. Progress award 1995), Am. Soc. for Engring. Edn. (Curtis W. McGraw rsch. award 1989), Am. Chem. Soc. Home: 2735 Ardmore Rd San Marino CA 91108-1768 Office: Calif Inst Tech Chem Engring 210-41 Pasadena CA 91125

MORATH, INGE, photographer; b. Graz, Austria, May 27, 1923; d. Edgar Eugen and Mathilde (Wiesler) M.; m. Arthur Miller, Feb. 1962; 1 child, Rebecca Augusta. BA, U. Berlin; DFA (hon.), U. Hartford, 1984. Formerly translator and editor ISB Feature Sect., Salzburg and Vienna, Austria; later editor lit. monthly Der Optmist, Vienna and Austrian editor Heute Mag.; former free-lance writer for mags. and Red White Red Radio Network; with Magnum Photos, Paris and N.Y.C., 1952—; mem. Magnum Photos, 1953—; tchr. photography course Cooper Union, 2 years; lectr. at various univs. including U. Miami, U. Mich. Exhibited photographs one-woman shows Wuehrle Gallery, Vienna, 1956, Leitz Gallery, N.Y.C., 1958, N.Y. Overseas Press Club, 1959, Chgo. Art Inst., 1964, Oliver Woolcott Meml. Library, Litchfield, Conn., 1969, Art Mus., Andover, Mass., 1971, U. Miami, 1972, U. Mich., 1973, Carlton Gallery, N.Y.C., 1976, Neikrug Galleries, N.Y.C., 1976, 79, Grand Rapids (Mich.) Art Mus., 1979, Mus. Modern Art, Vienna, 1980, Kunsthaus, Zurich, Switzerland, 1980, Burden Gallery Aperture Inc., N.Y.C., 1987, Moscow Ctr. Photojournalists, 1988, Sala del Canal, Madrid, 1988, Cathedral, Norwich, Eng., 1989, Am. Cultural Ctr., Brussels, 1989, Kolbe Mus., Berlin, 1991, Mus. Rupertinum, Salzburg, 1991; retrospective Neue Galerie, Linz, Austria, Amerika House, Berlin, 1993, Hradčin, Prague, 1993, Royal Photographic Soc., Bath, Eng., 1994, Mus. Contemporary Art, Madrid, 1995, Book Fair, Frankfurt, 1995, Leica Gallery, N.Y.C., 1996; numerous group shows include Photokina, Cologne, Ger., World's Fair, Montreal, Que., Can.; represented in permanent collections Met. Mus. Art, Boston Mus. Art, Art Inst. Chgo., Bibliothèque Nationale, Paris, Kunsthaus, Zurich, Prague (Czechoslovakia) Art Mus., Rupertinum Mus., Salzburg, Austria; photographer for books Guerreà la Tristesse (Dominique Aubier), 1956, Venice Observed (Mary McCarthy), 1956, (with Yul Brynner) Bring Forth the Children (Yul Brynner), 1960, From Persia to Iran (Edouard Sablier), 1961, Tunisia (Claude Roy, Paul Sebag), 1961, Le Masque (drawings by Saul Steinberg), 1967, In Russia (Arthur Miller), 1969, East West Exercises (Ruth Bluestone Simon), 1973, Boris Pasternak: My Sister Life (O. Carlisle, translator), 1976, In the Country (Arthur Miller), 1977, Chinese Encounters (Arthur Miller), 1979, Salesman in Beijing (Arthur Miller), 1984, Images of Vienna (Barbara Frischmuth, Pavel Kohout, Andre Heller, Arthur Miller), 1981, Inge Morath: Portraits, 1987, In Our Time, 1990, Russian Journal (E. Yevtushenko, A. Voznesensky, O. Andreyev Carlisle), 1991, Inge Morath: Fotografien 1952-92, Inge Morath: Spain in the 50s, 1994, The Danube, 1995; editor, co-photographer books Paris/Magnum, Aperture Inc., biography Grosse Photographen unserer Zeit, 1975; contbr. numerous photographs to European, U.S., S. Am., Japanese mags., and to numerous anthologies including Life series on photography and photographic yearbooks. Recipient Great Austrian State Prize for photography, 1991, various citations for shows. Mem. Am. Soc. Mag. Photographers. Home: Tophet Rd PO Box 232 Roxbury CT 06783 Office: Magnum Photos 151 W 25th St New York NY 10001-7204

MORATH, MAX EDWARD, entertainer, composer, writer; b. Colorado Springs, Colo., Oct. 1, 1926; s. Frederic Palmer and Gladys Hester Nancy (Ramsell) M.; m. Norma Loy Tackitt, Oct. 23, 1953 (div. 1992); children: Kathryn, Christine, Frederic; m. Diane Fay Skomars, May 24, 1993. BA in English, Colo. Coll., 1948; postgrad., Stanford NBC-Radio-TV Inst., Palo Alto, Calif., 1951; MA in Am. Studies, Columbia U., 1996. Touring nationally in concerts and theater The Ragtime Man, 1996-97; recordings on Epic, RCA, Vanguard, SoloArt, Omega, Premier. Mem. Broadcast Music, Inc., Am. Fedn. Musicians, AFTRA, Screen Actors Guild, Actors Equity Assn.

MORAVCSIK, JULIUS MATTHEW, philosophy educator; b. Budapest, Hungary, Apr. 26, 1931; came to U.S., 1949; s. Julius and Edith (Fleissig) M.; m. Marguerite Germain Truninger, Sept. 14, 1954; children: Adrian Clay, Peter Matthew. BA, Harvard U., 1953, PhD, 1959. Asst. prof. U. Mich., Ann Arbor, 1960-66, assoc. prof., 1966-68; prof. Stanford (Calif.) U., 1968—. Author: Understanding Language, 1975, Thought and Language, 1990, Plato and Platonism, 1992. Recipient Sr. Humanist prize Humboldt Found., 1983; fellow Ctr. Advanced Studies Behavioral Scis., 1986-87, Inst. Advanced Studies, 1988. Mem. Am. Philos. Assn. (pres. Pacific divsn. 1987-88), Am. Soc. Aesthetics (trustee 1988-92), Soc. Ancient Greek Philosophy (pres. 1989-91). Avocations: golf, tennis. Office: Stanford U Dept Of Philosophy Stanford CA 94305

MORAVEC, CHRISTINE D. SCHOMIS, medical educator; b. L.A., Apr. 26, 1957. BA, John Carroll U., 1978, MS, 1984; PhD, Cleve. State U., 1988. Tchr. Trinity H.S., Garfield Heights, Ohio, 1978-80; grad. teaching asst. dept. biology John Carroll U., Cleve., 1982-84; rsch. assoc. dept. cardiovascular biology Cleve. Clinic Found., 1990-93, project scientist dept. cardiovascular biology, 1990-93, asst. staff dept. cardiovascular biology, 1993-94; asst. prof. dept. physiology & biophys. Case Western Res. U. Sch. Medicine, Cleve., 1993—; adj. asst. prof. Cleve. State U., 1994—; asst. staff Ctr. Anesthesiology Rsch. Cleve. Clinic Found., 1994—. Contbr. articles to profl. jours. Grad. fellow Cleve. Clinic Found., 1984-88, Postdoctoral fellow, 1988-89, recipient Tarazi fellow, 1989. Mem. Am. Physiol. Soc., Am. Heart Assn. (basic sci. coun. 1990—), Ohio Physiol. Soc., Electron Microscopy Soc. Northeastern Ohio, Cardiac Muscle Soc. Office: Cleve Clin Found Ctr Anesthesiology Found 9500 Euclid Ave FF40 Cleveland OH 44195

MORAWETZ, CATHLEEN SYNGE, mathematician; b. Toronto, May 5, 1923; came to U.S., 1945, naturalized, 1950; d. John Lighton and Elizabeth Eleanor Mabel (Allen) Synge; m. Herbert Morawetz, Oct. 27, 1945; children: Pegeen Morawetz Rubinstein, John Synge, Lida Morawetz Jeck, Nancy. BA, U. Toronto, 1945; SM, MIT, 1946; PhD, NYU, 1951; hon. degree, Eastern Mich. U., 1980, Smith Coll., 1982, Brown U., 1982, Princeton U., 1986, Duke U., 1988, N.J. Inst. Tech., 1988, U. Waterloo, 1993. Research assoc. Courant Inst., NYU, 1952-57, asst. prof. math., 1957-60, assoc. prof., 1960-65, prof., 1965—, assoc. dir., 1978-84, dir., 1984-88. Editor Jour. Math. Analysis and Applications, Comms. in PDE; author articles in applications of partial differential equations, especially transonic flow and scattering theory. Trustee Princeton U., 1973-78, Sloan Found., 1980—. Guggenheim fellow, 1967, 79; Office Naval Rsch. grantee, until 1990. Fellow AAAS; mem. NAS, Am. Math. Soc. (term trustee 1975-85, pres. 1995—), Am. Acad. Arts and Scis., Soc. Indsl. and Applied Math. Office: 251 Mercer St New York NY 10012-1110

MORAWETZ, HERBERT, chemistry educator; b. Prague, Czechoslovakia, Oct. 16, 1915; came to U.S., 1945, naturalized, 1951; s. Richard and Frida (Glaser) M.; m. Cathleen Synge, Oct. 28, 1945; children: Pegeen Morawetz Rubinstein, John S., Lida Morawetz Jeck, Nancy B. B.A. Sci., U. Toronto, 1943, M.A. Sci., 1944; Ph.D., Poly Inst. Bklyn., 1951. With Bakelite Co., 1945-49; mem. faculty Poly. U. (formerly Poly. Inst. Bklyn.), 1951-81, prof. polymer chemistry, dir. Inst. Polymer Research, 1971-81; Inst. prof., 1981-86, Inst. prof. emeritus, 1986—; mem. materials research adv. com. NSF, 1977-80. Author: Macromolecules in Solution, 1965, rev. edit., 1975; Polymers: The Origins and Growth of a Science, 1985; mem. editorial bd. Jour. Polymer Sci., 1969-89; contbr. articles to profl. jours. Recipient Heyrovsky medal Czechoslovakia Acad. Sci., 1990; Case Centenary scholar, 1980; Whitby Meml. lectr. U. Akron, 1984. Fellow AAAS; mem. Am. Chem. Soc. (award in polymer chemistry 1986, assoc. editor Macromolecules 1991—). Home: 246 W 12th St New York NY 10014-1912 Office: 333 Jay St Brooklyn NY 11201-2907

MORBY, JACQUELINE, venture capitalist; b. Sacramento, June 19, 1937; d. Junior Jennings and Bertha (Backer) Collins; m. Jeffrey L. Morby, June 21, 1959; children: Andrew Jennings, Michelle Lorraine. BA in Psychology, Stanford U., 1959; M in Mgmt., Simmons Grad. Mgmt. Sch., Boston, 1978. Assoc. TA Assocs., Boston, 1978-81, gen. ptnr., 1982-89, mng. dir., 1989—; bd. dirs. Ontrack Computer Sys., Mpls., Rockville, Md., Axent Tech., Inc., Rockville, Pivotpoint, Inc., Waltham, Mass., R&D Sys., Inc., Colorado Springs, Colo., Ansys, Inc., Houston, Pa., Pacific Mutual Life Ins., Co., Newport Beach, Calif. Trustee Chatham Coll.; mem. Mass. Gov.'s Coun. on Growth and Tech. Mem. Nat. Venture Capital Orgn. Avocations: theatre, reading, art, skiing, travel. Office: TA Assocs 125 High St Boston MA 02110-2704

MORBY, JEFFREY LEWIS, banker, investment banker; b. Reno, Aug. 4, 1937; s. Andrew E. and Velda (Warren) M.; m. Jacqueline Collins, June 21, 1959; children: Andrew J., Michelle L. BS in Engring., Stanford U., 1959; MBA, Harvard U., 1961. Gen. mgr. Argentina/Brazil divs. Bank of Boston, Buenos Aires, Sao Paulo, 1969-75; sr. v.p. Latin Am. Bank of Boston, Boston, 1975-78, sr. v.p. loan rev. div., 1978-80, sr. v.p. N.E. div., 1980-81, sr. v.p. strategic planning, 1981-83, group exec. v.p. investment banking, 1983-84; vice chair, bd. dirs. Crocker Nat. Corp., San Francisco, 1984-86; vice chair, dir. Am. Express Bank, Ltd., N.Y.C., 1986-88; vice chmn. Mellon Bank Corp., Pitts., 1990—; chmn. Mellon Bank Europe, 1993—; bd. dirs. Boston Co., Boston Safe Deposit and Trust Co. Founder, pres. Bank of Boston Found., Buenos Aires, 1982; founder Argentine Sch. Exports, Buenos Aires, 1982; bd. dirs. New Eng. Coun., Boston, 1984, Pitts. Office Promotion, 1990, Pitts. Cultural Trust, Duquesne U. Recipient Congressman's medal U.S. Congress, 1954; Howard Hughes fellow Hughes Aircraft Co., 1959-61. Mem. Internat. Fin. (del. 1991), Internat. Monetary Conf. (alt. del. 1990-96), Bankers Roundtable, Duquesne Club, Laurel Valley Club, Allegheny Club. Avocations: sports, reading, travel. Office: Mellon Bank Corp 1 Mellon Bank Ctr Pittsburgh PA 15258-0001

MORCOTT, SOUTHWOOD J., automotive parts manufacturing company executive; b. 1939; married. Student, Davidson Coll.; MBA, U. Mich. Pres. Dana Corp., Toledo, 1963—; sales engineer, plant mgr. Dana Corp., Tyston, Ind., 1963-75; pres. Dana World Trade Corp., 1969; v.p. ops. Hayes Dana Ltd. Dana Corp., 1975-77, exec. v.p., gen. mgr., 1977-78, pres. Hayes-Dana Ltd., 1978-80, group v.p. Dana svc. parts group, 1980-84, pres. N.Am. ops., 1984-86, pres., chief operating officer, 1986—, chief exec. officer, 1989—, also chmn., dir., 1990—. Office: Dana Corp 4500 Dorr St Toledo OH 43615*

MORDECAI, BENJAMIN, theatrical producer, drama educator; b. N.Y.C., Dec. 10, 1944; s. Allen Lewis Mordecai and Florence Doris (Goldman) Holl; m. Sherry Lynn Morley, July 20, 1974; 1 child, Rachel Elizabeth. BA, Buena Vista Coll., 1967; MA, Eastern Mich. U., 1968; postgrad., Ind. U., 1968-70. Founder, producing dir. Ind. Repertory Theatre, Indpls., 1971-82; mng. dir. Yale Repertory Theatre, New Haven, 1982-93; assoc. dean Yale Sch. Drama, New Haven, 1992—; mng. ptnr. Benjamin Mordecai and Assocs., New York, 1992—; cons. Found. for the Extension and Devel. of the Am. Profl. Theatre, N.Y.C., 1974; adj. prof. Yale Sch. of Drama, 1982—; ind. cons., New Haven, 1984—. Dir: (plays) Fables Here and Then, 1972, Dracula, 1973, Bird in the Hand, 1975; assoc. prodr.; (plays) Fences, 1987 (Tony award 1987), Joe Turner's Come & Gone, 1988 (N.Y. Drama Critics Circle award 1988), A Walk in the Woods, 1988; gen. mgr.; (play) A Walk in the Woods (USSR), 1989; exec. prodr.: (play) The Piano Lesson, 1990 (N.Y. Drama Critics Circle award 1990, Drama Desk award 1990), Two Trains Running, 1992, Angels in America (N.Y. Drama Critics award 1993, Tony award 1993, 94); prodr.: Redwood Curtain, 1993, Twilight: Los Angeles, 1992, 94; assoc.prodr.: The Kentucky Cycle, 1993; prodr.: Gate of Heaven (U.S. Holocaust Mus.), 1995, August Wilson's Seven Guitars, 1996. Recipient Disting. Svc. award Indpls. Jaycees, Indpls., 1979, spl. commendation City-County Coun., Inpls., 1982, Robert Whitehead award, 1993; named Outstanding Young Alumnus, Buena Vista Coll., 1987. Mem. League of Resident Theatres (exec. com. 1981-91), Assn. Arts Adminstrn. Educators (sec.-treas. 1984-88), Am. Theatre Exchange Initative (bd. dirs. 1987—, pres. 1994—), Writers Theatre (bd. advisors 1983—), Stage Dirs. and Choreographers Found. (bd. dirs. 1990—), League Am. Theatres & Prodrs., Nat. Theatre Conf.

MORDEN, JOHN REID, Canadian government corporation administrator; b. Hamilton, Ont., Can., June 17, 1941; s. Warren Wilbert and Isabelle Gemmell (Reid) M.; m. Margaret Elizabeth Keens, June 27, 1964; children: Michael, Geoffrey. BA, Dalhousie U., Halifax, N.S., Can., 1962. Min., dep., permanent rep. Can. Mission UN, N.Y.C., 1980-82; counsellor Can. Embassy, Tokyo, 1975-78; dir. gen. Dept. External Affairs, Ottawa, Ont., 1982-84, asst. dep. min. trade policy, 1985-86; asst. dep. min. native claims Dept. Indian and No. Affairs, Ottawa, 1984-85; asst. sec. to cabinet Privy Coun. Office, Ottawa, 1986-87; dir. Can. Security Intelligence Svc., Ottawa, 1987-91; dep. min. of fgn. affairs, 1991-94; pres., CEO Atomic Energy Can. Ltd., Ottawa, 1994—; mem. internat. adv. bd. York U. Sch. Bus.; alt. gov. European Bank for Reconstrn. and Devel., 1991-94; bd. dirs. Can. Energy Coun., Red Cross Fractionation Corp. Mem. Can. Nuclear Assn., Nuclear Project Mgrs., Order St. Lazarus of Jerusalem, Rideau Club, Five Lakes Club. Avocations: reading, music, ballet,. Office: Atomic Energy Can Ltd, 244 Slater St, Ottawa, ON Canada K1A 0G2

MORDO, JEAN HENRI, financial executive; b. Cairo, Arab Republic of Egypt, Feb. 2, 1945; came to U.S., 1970; s. Henri and Aimee (Arditi) M. m. Nicole Setton, 1966 (div. 1984); children: Candice, Nathaniel; m. Barbara Van Buren, Mar. 31, 1985; 1 child, Janelle. MS in Engring., Ecole Poly., Paris, 1966, MS in Stats., 1969; MBA, Stanford U., 1972. Cons. McKinsey & Co., N.Y.C., 1972-78; dir. planning Otis Elevator Co., West Palm Beach, Fla., 1978-80, dir. fin., 1980-82; v.p. fin. planning Otis Elevator Co., Farmington, Conn., 1982-84, v.p., contr., 1982-85, v.p. fin., 1985-89, 1989—, pres. Latin Am. ops., 1989-92; sr. v.p. fin. Pratt and Whitney, Hartford, Conn., 1992—. Home: 50 Woodford Hills Dr Avon CT 06001-3923 Office: Pratt & Whitney 400 Main St #101-06 East Hartford CT 06118-1873

MORDY, JAMES CALVIN, lawyer; b. Ashland, Kans., Jan. 3, 1927; s. Thomas Robson and Ruth (Floyd) M.; m. Marjory Ellen Nelson, Nov. 17, 1951; children: Jean Claire Mordy Jongeling, Rebecca Jane Mordy King, James Nelson. AB in Chemistry, U. Kans., 1947; JD, U. Mich., 1950; postgrad., George Washington U., 1950-51. Bar: Kans. 1950, Mo. 1950; cert. in bus. bankruptcy law Am. Bankruptcy Bd. Cert. Assoc. Morrison, Hecker, Buck, Cozad & Rogers, Kansas City, Mo., 1950-59; ptnr. Morrison & Hecker, Kansas City, 1959—. Contbg. author: Missouri Bar Insurance Handbook, 1968, Missouri Bar Bankruptcy Handbook, 1991, 2d edit., 1995; contbr. articles to profl. jours. Chmn. bd. Broadway United Meth. Ch., Kansas City, 1964-70, chmn. bd. trustees, chmn. fin. com., 1988-90, 94; bd. dirs., exec. com. Della C. Lamb Neighborhood House, Kansas City, 1973-80; coun. mem. St. Paul Ch. Theology, Kansas City, 1986-95; del. 17th World Meth. Conf., Rio, 1996. Comdr. USNR, 1945-46, 51-53. Summerfield scholar, 1943-47; Am. Coll. Bankruptcy fellow; recipient Shepherd of the Lamb award, 1996, Della C. Lamb Neighborhood House award, 1980. Fellow Am. Bar Found. (life); mem. ABA, Am. Judicature Soc., Am. Bankruptcy Inst., Mo. Bar Assn., Kans. Bar Assn., Kansas City Met. Bar Assn., Lawyers Assn. Kansas City, Workout Profls. Assn. Kansas City, Univ. Club (v.p., bd. dirs. 1983, 86), Barristers Soc., Phi Beta Kappa, Delta Tau Delta (pres. Kansas City alumni chpt. 1965-72, pres. U. Kans. House Corp. 1966-72), Alpha Chi Sigma, Phi Alpha Delta. Avocations: travel, geography (maps), history, music, theology. Home: 8741 Ensley Ln Leawood KS 66206-1615 Office: Morrison & Hecker 2600 Grand Blvd Kansas City MO 64108-4606

MORE, DOUGLAS MCLOCHLAN, lawyer; b. N.Y.C., Apr. 21, 1926; s. Morgan Berkeley and Lucinda (Bateson) M.; m. Pamela Bennett Marr, Aug. 6, 1954; children—Robin Maclachlan More Eddy, Alison Marr More Davies. Grad., Phillips Exeter Acad., 1943; B.A., Harvard U., 1947; LL.B., Columbia U., 1950. Bar: N.Y. State bar 1950, Conn. bar 1981, Fla. bar 1983. With N.Y. Trust Co., 1950-51; asso. firm Bigham, Englar, Jones & Houston, N.Y.C., 1951-53; fin. analyst Johns-Manville Corp., 1953-54; assoc. firm Kissam & Halpin, N.Y.C., 1954-59; assoc. counsel Hooker Chem. Corp., 1959-63, gen. counsel, 1963-72, v.p., 1967-72; v.p. law Airco, Inc., 1972-75; gen. counsel Beker Industries Corp., 1975-81, v.p., 1975-78, sr. v.p., 1978-81; ptnr. firm More Phillips & Duncan, P.C., Greenwich, Conn., 1981-88, of counsel, 1988—. Served to lt. (j.g.) USNR, 1943-46. Mem. ABA, Conn. Bar Assn., Greenwich Bar Assn., Phi Delta Phi, Phoenix S-K Club,

Hasty Pudding Inst. 1770 (Harvard). Home and Office: 27 Skylark Rd Greenwich CT 06830-4624

MOREHART, DONALD HADLEY, food products executive; b. Little Rock, Nov. 6, 1938; s. Homer H. and Golda (Welton) M.; m. Maribeth Hornsby, July 8, 1961; children: Barry, Linley. BA, DePaul U.; BBA, U. of Ark., 1960. Various positions Anderson Clayton Foods, Dallas, 1960-77; v.p. refined oil Central Soya Co. Inc., Ft. Wayne, Ind., 1977—; chmn. adv. com. Inst. Shortening & Edible Oils, Washington, 1985—. Bd. dirs. Ft. Wayne Edn. Found., Metro YMCA; mem. Leadership Ft. Wayne, 1988. Republican. Methodist. Office: Central Soya Co Inc PO Box 2507 Fort Wayne IN 46801-2507

MOREHEAD, CHARLES RICHARD, insurance company executive; b. Independence, Mo., Jan. 25, 1947; s. Robert E. and Ruth Elizabeth (Taylor) M.; m. Donna Joyce Shores, Feb. 17, 1968 children: Grant, Blaine. BSBA, U. Mo., 1971. CPA, Fla. Mem. staff Peat, Marwick, Mitchell & Co., Kansas City, Mo., 1972-75; audit mgr. Peat, Marwick, Mitchell & Co., Jacksonville, Fla., 1976-83, audit ptnr., 1983-86; treas. Standard Havens, Inc., Kansas City, 1975-76; treas., CFO Am. Heritage Life Ins. Co., Jacksonville, Fla., 1986-94, exec. v.p., CFO, 1994—, also bd. dirs. Mem. AICPA, Fla. Soc. CPA's. Home: 4050 Chicora Wood Pl Jacksonville FL 32224 Office: Am Heritage Life Ins Co 1776 Am Heritage Life Dr Jacksonville FL 32224

MOREHEAD, JAMES CADDALL, JR., architect, educator; b. Bradenton, Fla., Oct. 29, 1913; s. James Caddall and Jeannette Dandridge (White) M.; m. Martha Petty Netting, Aug. 27, 1940; children: James Caddall, III, Naomi Willson, Kenneth Fielding. B.A., Princeton U., 1935; B.Arch., Carnegie Mellon U., 1939. Instr. math. Carnegie Mellon U., 1936-40; architecture, 1938-40; instr. architecture Rice U., 1940-42, 46, asst. prof., 1946-48, assoc. prof., 1948-51, prof., 1951-79, prof. emeritus, 1979—, head dept., 1953-61; registrar, 1964-79; asso. Wilson, Morris & Crain, Houston, 1951-55; past partner Morehead and Ransom (Architects); pvt. practice of architecture, 1960—; dir. of permits City of Piney Point Village, Tex., 1954-81, 86—. Author: (with J.C. Morehead, Sr.) Handbook of Perspective Drawing, 1952, Perspective and Projective Geometries, A Comparison, 1955, Elementary Structures, 2 vols, Intermediate Structures, ACSA Learning Packages, 1974, 75, A Walking Tour of Rice U., 1984, 2d edit., 1990. Dir. San Jacinto Girl Scouts, 1954-61; Mem. Study Commn. on Archtl. Edn. in South, So. Regional Edn. Bd., 1953, chmn. planning and zoning commn., Piney Point Village, Tex., 1954-81. Served as lt. col. F.A. AUS, 1942-46. Decorated Bronze Star with oak leaf cluster; recipient Alpha Rho Chi Medal in Architecture Carnegie Inst. Tech., 1939; Award of Merit Houston chpt. AIA, 1953. Fellow AIA (treas. Houston chpt. 1950-51); mem. Houston Philos. Soc. Scarab. Home: 354 Piney Point Rd Houston TX 77024-6506

MOREHOUSE, LAWRENCE GLEN, veterinarian, educational administrator; b. Manchester, Kans., July 21, 1925; s. Edwy O. and Ethel (Glenn) M.; m. GeorgiaAnn Lewis, Oct. 6, 1956; children: Timothy, Glenn Ellen. BS in Biol. Sci., Kans. State U., 1952, DVM, 1952; MS in Animal Pathology, Purdue U., 1956, PhD, 1960. Veterinarian County Vet. Hosp., St. Louis, 1952-53; supr. Brucellosis labs. Purdue U., Lafayette, Ind., 1953-60; staff veterinarian lab. svcs. USDA, Washington, 1960-61; discipline leader in pathology and toxicology, animal health div. USDA Nat. Animal Disease Lab., Ames, Iowa, 1962-64; prof., chmn. dept. veterinary pathology Coll. Vet. Medicine U. Mo., Columbia, 1964-67, 84-86; dir. Vet. Med. Diagnostic Lab., 1968-88; prof. emeritus Coll. Vet. Medicine U. Mo., Columbia, 1986—; cons. USDA, to comdg. gen. U.S. Army R & D Command, Am. Inst. Biol. Scis., NAS, Miss. State U., St. Louis Zoo Residency Tng. Program, Miss. Vet. Med. Assn., Okla. State U., Pa. Dept. Agr., Ohio Dept. Agr. Co-editor: Mycotoxic Fungi, Mycotoxins, Mycotoxicoses: An Encyclopedic Handbook , 3 vols., 1977; contbr. numerous articles on diseases of animals to profl. jours. With USN, 1943-46, U.S. Army, 1952-56. Recipient Outstanding Svc. award U.S. Dept Agr., 1959, Merit Cert., 1963, 64, Disting. Svc. award Coll. Vet. Medicine U. Mo., 1987. Fellow Royal Soc. Health London; mem. Am. Assn. Vet. Lab. Diagnosticians (E.P. Pope award 1976, chmn. lab. accreditation bd. 1972-79, 87-90), World Assn. Vet. Lab. Diagnosticians (bd. dirs. 1983—), N.Y. Acad. Sci., U. S. Animal Health Assn., Am. Assn. Lab. Animal Sci., Mo. Soc. Microbiology, Am. Assn. Avian Pathologists, N.Am. Conf. Rsch. Workers in Animal Diseases. Presbyterian. Home: 916 Danforth Dr Columbia MO 65201-6164 Office: U Mo Vet Med Diagnostic Lab PO Box 6023 Columbia MO 65201

MOREHOUSE, RICHARD EDWARD, psychology educator; b. LaCrosse, Wis., May 21, 1941; s. Ervin Lenard and Anna Martha (Weiland) M.; m. Rita Spangler, Aug. 20, 1966; 1 child, Lyda Ann. BS, U. Wis., 1971, MST, 1973; PhD, The Union Inst., 1979. Teaching asst. U. Wis., LaCrosse, 1971-72; ednl. cons. Coop. Ednl. Svcs. Agy., LaCrosse, 1972-80; dir. coop. edn. Viterbo Coll., LaCrosse, 1980-85, from asst. to prof. psychology, 1985—; dept. chmn. Viterbo Coll., LaCrosse, 1986-93; vis. prof. U. Turku, Finland, summer 1990; vis. scholar Tex. Wesleyan U., Ft. Worth, 1993-94. Co-author: Student Study Guide for Human Development Across the Lifespan, 1991, 94, Beginning Qualatative Research, 1994; co-editor: Analytic Teaching, 1991—. Gifted Edn. grantee Elem. and Secondary Edn. Act, 1976-79, Tchr. Tng., Cmty. Awareness grantee Wis. Humanities, 1982, Coll., Cmty. Symposium grantee, 1983. Mem. N.Am. Assn. for Cmty. Inquiry (founder, 1st pres. 1994), Am. Psychol. Soc. (charter mem.). Democrat. Unitarian. Home: 1131 Charles St La Crosse WI 54603-2508 Office: Viterbo Coll 815 9th St S La Crosse WI 54601-4777

MOREIRA, MARCIO MARTINS, advertising executive; b. Sao Paulo, Brazil, Nov. 20, 1947; came to U.S. 1980; naturalized, 1990; s. Guido Martins and Maria Rosa (Macrine) M.; children from previous marriage: Joaquim Pedro Rezende Martins Moreira; m. Maria Auxiliadora Godinho, Oct. 18, 1981; children: Eliana Maria Godinho Martins Moreira. Ed., U. Sao Paulo, Brazil, 1970. TV producer-copywriter McCann-Erickson, Sao Paulo, Brazil, 1967-71; creative dir. McCann-Erickson, Sao Paulo, 1974-77; group creative dir. McCann-Erickson, London, Lisbon and Frankfurt, 1971-74; executive creative dir. McCann-Erickson, Latin America, 1977-80; internat. creative dir. McCann-Erickson, N.Y.C., 1980-88; vice chmn., chief creative officer McCann Erickson Worldwide, N.Y.C., 1988—; vice chmn., regional dir. Asia-Pacific McCann-Erickson Worldwide, N.Y.C., 1995—; lectr. various univs. Author: Terraplenagem, 1968 Liquidacao, 1979; lyricist, 1968—; contbr. articles to profl. jours. U.S. judge, pres. jury Cannes Film Festival, 1989; chmn. bd. judges The New York Festivals. Recipient 5 Clio awards, 1976-89, Gold Lion, Silver Lion, Bronze Lion awards, Cannes, France, H.K. McCann award, Brazil, 1977, Paul Foley award Interpub. Group of Cos., 1983, Terence Cardinal Cooke medal for Disting. Svc. in Health Care, N.Y. Med. Coll., 1994. Mem. Brazilian-Am. C. of C. (bd. dir.). Republican. Roman Catholic. Avocations: cinema, songwriting, cars, speedwalking. Office: McCann-Erickson Worldwide 750 3rd Ave New York NY 10017-2703

MORELAN, PAULA KAY, choreographer; b. Lafayette, Ind., Nov. 24, 1949; d. Dickie Booth and Marian Maxine (Fetterhoff) M.; m. Kerim Sayan, Aug. 10, 1974. Student U. Utah, 1968-69; BFA, Tex. Christian U., 1972; postgrad., El Centro Coll., 1969-70. Tchr., Rosello Sch. Ballet, Dallas, 1972-74; mgr., tchr. Ballet Arts Ctr., Dallas, 1974-76; owner, tchr. Ballet Classique, Garland, Tex., 1976-87, Garland Ballet Acad., 1977-87; asst. to Mythra Rosello, Tex. Civic Ballet, Dallas, 1972-74; assoc. artistic dir. Dance Repertory Theatre Dallas, 1974-75; artistic dir. Dance Repertory Theatre Dallas, 1975-76, Garland (Tex.) Ballet Assn., 1977-90, Classical Ballet Acad., Performing Arts Sch., 1987-90; resident choreographer Garland Civic Theatre, 1988—.

MORELAND, ALVIN FRANKLIN, veterinarian; b. Morven, Ga., Sept. 5, 1931; s. Robert Hamilton and Laura Eloise (Edenfield) M.; m. Mary Ellen Hardee, Feb. 12, 1955; children: Ellen, Frank, Clyde. BS in Edn., Ga. Tchrs. Coll., 1951; MSEd, U. Ga., 1952, DVM, 1960. Diplomate Am. Coll. Lab. Animal Medicine. Asst. prof. U. Va. Sch. Medicine, Charlottesville, 1962-63; asst. prof. to prof. U. Fla. Coll. Vet. Medicine, Gainesville, 1963-95, prof. emeritus, 1995—; cons. vet. NASA, Kennedy Space Ctr., Fla., Bionetics Corp., 1983—. Contbr. articles to profl. jours. Served to lt. USNR, 1952-56. Mem. AVMA, Am. Assn. Lab. Animal Sci., Fla. Vet. Med. Assn. (Gold Star award 1976), Alachua Vet. Med. Assn., Internat. Assn. Aquatic Animal Medicine. Methodist.

MORELAND, DONALD EDWIN, plant physiologist; b. Enfield, Conn., Oct. 12, 1919; s. Albert Sinclair and Ruth (Cowan) M.; m. Verdie Brown Stallings, Nov. 6, 1954; 1 child, Donna Faye; stepchildren: Frank C., Paul Ziglar. BS in Forestry, N.C. State U., 1949, MS in Plant Physiology, 1950, PhD in Plant Physiology, 1953. Plant physiologist SUNY Coll. Forestry, Syracuse, 1952-53; plant physiologist USDA-Agrl. Rsch. Svc., Raleigh, N.C., 1953-71, rsch. leader, 1972-78, sr. exec., 1979—; asst. prof. to prof. N.C. State U., Raleigh, 1953—; mem. toxicology study sect. NIH, USPHS, Bethesda, Md., 1963-67. Editor: Biochemical Responses Induced by Herbicides, 1982; mem. editorial bd. Pesticide Biochemistry and Physiology, 1971—, Pesticide Sci., 1987—; contbr. articles to profl. jours. 1st lt. U.S. Army, 1941-46. AEC predoctoral fellow, 1950-52. Fellow AAAS, Weed Sci. Soc. Am. (outstanding rsch. award 1973); mem. Am. Chem. Soc., Plant Growth Regulator Soc. Am., Am. Soc. Plant Physiologists, So. Weed Sci. Soc., Sigma Xi. Avocations: woodworking, surf fishing, square dancing. Home: 1508 Pineview Dr Raleigh NC 27606-2562 Office: USDA-Agrl Rsch Svc NC State U Crop Sci Dept 4123 Williams Hall Raleigh NC 27695

MORELLA, CONSTANCE ALBANESE, congresswoman; b. Somerville, Mass., Feb. 12, 1931; d. Salvatore and Mary Christine (Fallette) Albanese; m. Anthony C. Morella, Aug. 21, 1954; children: Paul, Mark, Laura; guardians of: Christine, Catherine, Louise, Rachel, Paul, Ursula. AA, Boston U., 1950, AB, 1954; MA, Am. U., 1967, D of Pub. Svc. (hon.), 1988; D of Pub. Svc. (hon.), Norwich U. and Dickinson Coll., 1989. Tchr. Montgomery County (Md.) Pub. Schs., 1956-60; instr. Am. U., 1968-70; prof. Montgomery Coll., Rockville, Md., 1970-86; mem. Md. Ho. Dels., Annapolis, 1979-86, 100th-103rd Congresses from 8th Md. dist., 1987—; adv. bd. Am. Univ., Washington; trustee Capitol Coll. Laurel, Md. Trustee Capitol Coll, Laurel, Md., 1977—; chair Sci. Com. Tech. Subcom., Basic Rsch. Subcom., coun. mem. Montgomery County United Way; adv. coun. Montgomery County Hospice Soc.; hon. bd. mem. Nat. Kidney Found; active Human Rights Caucus, co-chair Congressional Women's Caucus, Black Caucus; chair Gov. Reform and Oversight Com. Avocations: theatre, tennis, reading. Office: US Ho of Reps 106 Cannon House Office Bldg Washington DC 20515 also: 51 Monroe St Rockville MD 20850-2417*

MORELLO, JOSEPH ALBERT, musician, educator; b. Springfield, Mass., July 17, 1928; s. Joseph Charles and Lilia (LaPalme) M.; m. Jean Ann Mehnert. Grad. high sch., Springfield. Ind. drummer Springfield, 1945-49; drummer Gil Melé, Stan Kenton, Tal Farlow, Johnny Smith, N.Y.C., 1953-55, Dave Brubeck Quartet, touring worldwide, 1955-68; clinician Selmer Ludwig Drum Co., Elkhart, Ind., 1957-92; leader Joe Morello Quartet, 1979—; clinician DW Drums, Oxnard, Calif., 1993—; rec. artist Digital Music Products Inc., 1993—. Rec. artist Savoy, Capitol, Norgran, Blue Note, Columbia, RCA labels; innovator finger control in jazz drumming; author: Joe Morello Drum Method, The Natural Approach to Technique, 1993, Joe Morello Drum Method 2, 1994, also New Directions in Rhythm, Rudimental Jazz, Off the Record, Master Studies; releases include (with Joe Morello Quartet) Going Places, 1993, Morello's Standard Time, 1994. Recipient New Star award Downbeat mag., 1955, Melody Maker mag. award, 1963-67, Jazz mag. award, 1964-67, Thomas A. Edison lifetime achievement award, 1990, record, CD and tape release RCA Bluebird Label, 1989, CD Joe Morello Quartet Going Places release DMP Label, 1990; poll winner Downbeat mag., 1963-65, Playboy mag., 1963-67; named to Hall of Fame, Modern Drummer mag., 1988, Percussive Arts Soc. Hall of Fame, 1993. Avocation: photography.

MORENA, JOHN JOSEPH, manufacturing engineer, executive; b. Rockaway Beach, N.Y., Dec. 6, 1937; s. John Michael and Theresa (Verdoni) M.; children from a previous marriage: John Joseph, Stephen Scott, Todd Theodore; m. Diane Pizo, Feb. 9, 1990. Student, NYU, 1956-65, SUNY, 1956-65, Fla. Atlantic U., Boca Raton, Fla., 1988-91. Cert. mfg. engr. With AIL, Melville, N.Y., 1962-66, Maxson Electronics, Great River, N.Y., 1966-70, Airtron/Litton Inc., Morris Plains, N.J., 1970-72, Microlab/FXR, Livingston, N.J., 1972-74; v.p. Fibes Drums Inc., Farmingdale, N.Y., 1974-77; pres. Meam Inc., Farmingdale, 1977-79, GSU Inc., Farmingdale, 1976-80, Am. Composites Edn. Inc., Stuart, Fla., 1980—; tech. dir. Am. Composites Mfg. Learning Ctr., Stuart, Fla., 1983—; primary tech. advanced materials advisor Superconducting Super Collider, Dallas, 1988-94; exec. dir. Am. Maglev Star Orgn., Stuart, 1991—. Author: Advanced Composite Mold Making, 1988, World Composites Encyclopedia, 1992, Advanced Composites World Reference Dictionary, 1995; contbr. articles to profl. jours.; patentee in field. Avocations: instrumental music, painting, boating, sports, writing. Home: 4540 NE Sandpebble Trce Apt 104 Stuart FL 34996-1486 Office: Am Composites Edn Inc Am Composites Bldg 425 California Ave Stuart FL 34994-2917

MORENCY, PAULA J., lawyer; b. Oak Park, Ill., Mar. 13, 1955. AB magna cum laude, Princeton U., 1977; JD, U. Va., 1980. Bar: Ill. 1980, U.S. Dist. Ct. (no. dist.) Ill. 1980, U.S. Ct. Appeals (7th cir.) 1981, U.S. Ct. Appeals (5th cir.) 1990. Assoc. Mayer, Brown & Platt, Chgo., 1980-86, ptnr., 1987-94; ptnr. Schiff Hardin & Waite, Chgo., 1994—. Contbr. author: Federal Litigation Guide Vol. 3, 1985. Mem. ABA, Chgo. Coun. of Lawyers (bd. govs. 1989-93). Office: Schiff Hardin & Waite 7200 Sears Tower Chicago IL 60606

MORENO, CHRISTINE MARGARET, lawyer; b. Miami, Fla., Sept. 7, 1960; d. Arthur and Christine Moreno. BS magna cum laude, Barry U., 1981; JD cum laude, U. Miami, Coral Gables, Fla., 1984. Bar: Fla. 1984, D.C. 1985, U.S. Dist. Ct. (so. dist.) Fla. 1985, U.S. Dist. Ct. (mid. dist.) Fla. 1987, U.S. Tax Ct. 1987, U.S. Supreme Ct. 1988, U.S. Ct. Appeals (11th cir.) 1988; CPA, Fla. Law intern U.S. Securities Exch. Commn., Miami, Fla., 1984; assoc. atty. Ruden, Barnett, McCloskey, Ft. Lauderdale, Fla., 1984-85, Koppen, Watkins, Ptnrs. & Assocs., Miami, 1985-89; mayor City of North Miami, 1989-91; owner, atty., CPA Law Offices of Christine M. Moreno, North Miami, Stuart, Fla., 1989—; commr. Jensen Beach (Fla.) Cmty. Redevelopment Agy., 1994—; bd. dirs. North Miami Energy Adv. Bd.; life time dir. Mayor's Econ. Task Force, North Miami, 1989—. Co-author: (book) Senior Citizens Handbook, 1990; mem. staff U. Miami Law Review, 1982-84. Bd. dirs. Nat. League of Cities, Washington, 1990-91; v.p. polit. action Miami Dade Cmty. Coll. Alumni, 1991—. Mem. Am. Inst. CPAs, North Dade Bar Assn. (bd. dirs.), Fla. Inst. CPAs, North Miami Jaycees (Jaycee of yr. 1993), Rep. Party Dade County (com. woman 1990-94), Phi Alpha Delta Internat. Law Fraternity (Miami alumni chpt. justice 1985—). Avocation: public service. Office: 13122 W Dixie Hwy Miami FL 33161 also: 630 SE Monterey Rd Stuart FL 34994

MORENO, FEDERICO ANTONIO, federal judge; b. Caracas, Venezuela, Apr. 10, 1952; came to U.S., 1963; s. Francisco Jose and Rejane Genevieve (Nogues) M.; m. M. Cristina M. Morales-Gomez, May 31, 1977; children: Cristi, Ricky, Victoria. AB cum laude, U. Notre Dame, 1974; JD, U. Miami, 1974. Bar: Fla. 1978, U.S. Dist. Ct. (so. dist.) 1978, (mid. dist.) 1986, U.S. Ct. Appeals (5th cir.) 1979, (11th cir.) 1981, U.S. Supreme Ct. 1981. Ptnr. Thornton, Rothman & Moreno, Miami, 1982-86; judge Dade County Cir. Ct., Miami, 1986-90; dist. judge U.S. Dist. Ct. (so. dist.) Fla., Miami, 1990—. Recipient People Helping People award United Way, 1980, Pro Bono award Pub. Interest Law Bank, 1985. Mem. ABA, Fed. Bar Assn., Fla. Bar Assn., Dade County Bar Assn., Trial Lawyer's Assn. Roman Catholic. Office: US Courthouse 301 N Miami Ave Miami FL 33128-7702*

MORENO, G(ILBERTO) MARIO, federal agency administrator; b. Uvalde, Tex., Jan. 3, 1947; m. Susana Gomez; children: Christina Collins, Amielle. BA in Econs., Tex. A&M U.; MA in Urban and Regional Planning, St. Mary's U., San Antonio, JD. Planning dir., asst. city mgr. City of Brownsville, Tex., 1972-78; exec. dir. AYUDA, Inc., Washington, 1982-84; regional counsel Mex. Am. Legal Def. and Edn. Fund, Washington, 1985-94; asst. sec. for intergovtl. and interagy. affairs U.S. Dept. Edn., Washington, 1994—. John L. Loeb fellow Harvard U. Grad. Sch. Design, 1978-79. Office: US Dept Edn Office Intergovtl/Interagy 600 Independence Ave SW Washington DC 20202-0404

MORENO, GLEN RICHARD, banker; b. San Jose, Calif., July 24, 1943; s. John and Ellen (Oberg) M.; m. Cheryl Lynne Eschbach, Mar. 26, 1966. B.A. with distinction, Stanford U., 1965; J.D., Harvard U., 1969. Group exec. Citicorp, N.Y.C., 1969-87; dir. Fidelity Internat. Ltd., Bermuda, 1987—; chmn. Indonesian Capital Fund Ltd.; dir. ED&F Man Group PLC; bd. dirs. India Fund., Rea Bros. PLC. Bd. govs. Ditchley Found., Oxford, Eng., 1983—. Mem. Bucks Club. Home: "Neala" RR 1 Box 73 Madison VA 22727-9729 also: 3 Whitehall Ct Flat 124A, London SW1A 2EL, England Office: Fidelity Investments, 25 Lovat Ln, London EC3, England

MORENO, MANUEL D., bishop; Educator U. of Calif., L.A., St. John's Sem., Camarillo, Calif. Ordained priest Roman Cath. church, 1961. Ordained aux. bishop of Los Angeles, titular bishop of Tanagra, 1977; installed as bishop of Tucson, 1982—. Office: PO Box 31 192 S Stone Ave Tucson AZ 85702

MORENO, RICHARD DALE, lawyer; b. Lake Charles, La., Feb. 1, 1951; s. Fred Mercica and Elsie Mae (Savant) M.; m. Mary Mellanie Denton, Aug. 11, 1972; 1 child, Victoria. BSEE, La. Tech. U., 1972; JD, La. State U., 1991. Bar: La. 1991, U.S. Dist. Ct. La. 1991, U.S. Ct. Appeals (5th cir.) 1991. Engr. Hughes Aircraft Co., Canoga Park, Calif., 1974-78, Standard Sys., Inc., Sulphur, La., 1978-88; law clk. Alvin J. Rubin, Cir. Judge U.S. Ct. Appeals, 5th Cir., Baton Rouge, 1991; law clk. Henry A. Politz, Chief Judge U.S. Ct. Appeals, 5th Cir., Shreveport, 1991-92; assoc. Kantrow, Spaht, Weaver and Blitzer, Baton Rouge, 1992—; mem. lease law rev. com. La. Law Inst., Baton Rouge, 1991—. Contbr. articles to profl. jours.; editor/revisor: Louisiana Landlord and Tenant Law, 1993-95. Mem. ABA, La. State Bar Assn. Office: Kantrow Spaht Weaver & Blitzer PO Box 2997 (70821) 445 North Blvd #300 Baton Rouge LA 70802

MORENO, RITA, actress; b. Humacao, P.R., Dec. 11, 1931; m. Leonard I. Gordon, June 18, 1965; 1 child, Fernanda Luisa. Spanish dancer since childhood, night club entertainer; appeared on Broadway in The Sign in Sidney Brustein's Window, 1964-65, Gantry, 1969-70, The Last of the Red Hot Lovers, 1970-71, The National Health, 1974, The Ritz, 1975, Wally's Cafe, 1981, The Odd Couple, 1985; (off Broadway) After Play, 1995; motion picture debut, 1950, and appeared in numerous films including West Side Story, Carnal Knowledge, The King and I, Singing in the Rain, The Four Seasons, I Like it Like That, 1994, Angus, 1995, Wharf Rat, 1995. Recipient Acad. Award for best supporting actress, 1962; Grammy award for best rec., 1973; Antoinette Perry award for best supporting actress Broadway play, 1975; Emmy award, 1977, 78. In Guinness Book of World Records as only person to win Acad., Grammy, Tony and Emmy awards. Address: care Agency for Performing Arts 9000 W Sunset Blvd Los Angeles CA 90069-5801

MOREST, DONALD KENT, neuroscience educator; b. Kansas City, Mo., Oct. 4, 1934; s. F. Stanley and Clara Josephine (Riley) M.; m. Rosemary Richtmyer, July 13, 1963; children: Lydia, Claude. BA, U. Chgo., 1955; MD, Yale U., 1960. Sr. asst. surgeon USPHS, Bethesda, Md., 1960-63; asst. prof. U. Chgo., Ill., 1963-65; asst. to assoc. prof. Harvard Med. Sch., Boston, 1965-77; prof., dir. Ctr. for Neurol. Scis. U. Conn. Health Ctr., Farmington, 1977—; cons. NIH, Bethesda, 1975—. Contbr. articles to profl. jours. and books. Recipient Loeser award U. Conn. Health Ctr., Farmington, 1982; Career Devel. awardee NIH, 1971; named Javits neurosci. investigator NIH, 1984, Claude Pepper awardee, 1990. Mem. Am. Assn. Anatomists (C.Judson Herrick award 1966), Soc. for Neurosci., Assn. for Rsch. in Otolarynology, Conn. Acad. Sci. & Engrng. (elected), Cajal Club (pres. 1980). Avocations: flute, badminton. Home: 18 Shady Ln West Simsbury CT 06092-2232

MORET, MARC, chemicals executive; b. Ménières, Switzerland, Nov. 15, 1923; married; 3 children. D Pub. Econs., U. Fribourg and Sorbonne, Paris, 1948. With practical indsl. tng. and assignments Swissair, Sulzer Bros., Nestlé S.A.; gen. mgr. Guigoz Internat.; from head of agro sales, to head agro and nutrition divsns. Sandoz Ltd., 1968, head finance dept., 1976, bd. dirs., 1977—, vice chmn. bd. dirs., 1980-85, pres., CEO, 1981-94, chmn. bd. dirs., 1985—. Office: Sandoz Ltd, Lichtstrasse 35, CH 4002 Basel Switzerland also: Sandoz Inc 608 5th Ave New York NY 10020-2303

MORETON, THOMAS HUGH, minister; b. Shanghai, China, Dec. 2, 1917; came to U.S., 1946; s. Hugh and Tsuru M; m. Olive Mae Rives, Apr. 1, 1947 (dec. Apr. 1986); children: Ann Rives Moreton Smith, Andrew Hugh, Margaret Evelyn Moreton Hamar; m. Selma Littig, June 7, 1986. LLB, 1939, BD, 1942, PhD, 1946; ThD, Trinity Sem., 1948; LittD, 1949. Ordained to ministry Bapt. Ch., Glasgow, Scotland, 1942. Min. various chs., also tchr. Seaford Coll. Eng., 1945-46; tchr. coll. and sem. level. div. courses various schs., Atlanta, Oklahoma City, 1946-51; founder Tokyo Gospel Mission, Inc., House of Hope, Inc., Tokyo, 1951—; also World Gospel Fellowship, Inc., Norman, Okla., 1967—; pastor chs., Moore, Okla., Shawnee, Okla., Ada., Okla., Del City, Okla., Tahlequah, Okla. and Oklahoma City, 1968—; preacher numerous fgn. countries; internat. tour dir., radio broadcaster. Contbr. articles to religious jours. Charter mem. Am.-Japan Com. for Assisting Japanese-Am. Orphans. Chaplain AUS, 1952-63. Recipient various awards Japanese govt. Fellow Royal Geog. Soc., Philos. Soc.; mem. Royal Soc. Lit., Am.-Japan Soc., Israel-Japan Soc.

MORETTI, AUGUST JOSEPH, lawyer; b. Elmira, N.Y., Aug. 18, 1950; s. John Anthony and Dorothy M. (De Blasio) M.; m. Audrey B. Kavka, Nov. 8, 1981; children: David Anthony, Matthew Alexander. BA magna cum laude, Princeton U., 1972; JD cum laude, Harvard U., 1975. Assoc. Heller, Ehrman, White and McAuliffe, San Francisco, 1976-82, ptnr., 1982—; lectr. bus. adminstrn. U. Calif. Berkeley, 1977-79. Bd. dirs. Ann Martin Children's Ctr.; mem. adv. panel U. Calif. Berkeley Entrepreneur Program. Mem. ABA. Office: Heller Ehrman White & McAuliffe 525 University Ave Palo Alto CA 94301-1903

MOREY, CARL REGINALD, musicologist, academic administrator; b. Toronto, Ont., Can., July 14, 1934; s. Reginald Donald and Julia Beatrice (Mabey) M.; m. Lorna Ann Dalton, June 2, 1960 (dec.); 1 child, Rachel Adriana. Mus.B., U. Toronto, 1957; Mus.M., Ind. U., 1961, Ph.D., 1965. Asst. prof. Wayne State U., Detroit, 1962-63; assoc. prof. U. Windsor, Ont., Can., 1964-70; prof. music U. Toronto, 1970—, dean faculty of music, 1984-90, Jean A. Chalmers prof., dir. Inst. for Can. Music, 1991—. Avocation: swimming. Home: 540 Palmerston Blvd, Toronto, ON Canada M6G 2P5 Office: U Toronto, Faculty of Music, Toronto, ON Canada M5S 1A1

MOREY, CHARLES LEONARD, III, theatrical director; b. Oakland, Calif., June 23, 1947; s. Charles Leonard Jr. and Mozelle Kathleen (Milliken) M.; m. Mary Carolyn Donnet, June 10, 1973 (div. 1975); m. Joyce Miriam Schilke, May 29, 1982; 1 child, William. AB, Dartmouth Coll., 1969; MFA, Columbia U., 1971. Artistic dir. Peterborough (N.H.) Players, 1977-88, Pioneer Theatre Co., Salt Lake City, 1984—; adj. asst. prof. theatre U. Utah, Salt Lake City, 1984—. Actor: N.Y. Shakespeare Festival, Playwrights Horizons, New Dramatists, ARK Theatre Co., Ensemble Studio Theatre, Cubiculo, Folger Theatre, Syracuse Repertory Theatre, Theatre by Sea, others; over 150 plays acted in or directed; guest dir. Ensemble Studio Theatre, ArK Theatre, Am. Stage Festival, McCarter Theatre, Pioneer Theatre Co., PCPA Theatrefest, The Repertory Theater of St. Louis, Meadow Brook Theatre; author new adaptations Alexander Dumas' The Three Musketeers, Bram Stoker's Dracula, Charles Dickens' A Tale of Two Cities, Victor Hugo's The Hunchback of Notre Dame; TV appearances include: Young Maverick, Edge of Night, World Apart, Our Town. Trustee Utah Arts Endowment, Inc. Mem. Soc. Stage Dirs. and Choreographers, AEA, SAG, AFTRA, Salt Lake City C. of C. (Honors in the Arts award 1991), Utah Assn. Gifted Children (Community Svc. award 1991), Peterborough Players (Edith Bond Stearns award 1990). Democrat. Episcopalian. Office: Pioneer Theatre Co U Utah Salt Lake City UT 84112

MOREY, JAMES NEWMAN, advertising executive; b. N.Y.C., Nov. 13, 1933; s. Ira and Mary Ernestine (Newman) M.; m. Frances Mae Rogers, Aug. 23, 1958 (div. 1978); children: Allison, David Newman, John Rogers; m. Marsha Ann Rogler, Nov. 8, 1980; 1 son, Stephen Rogler. B.A., Ohio U., 1955; M.A., Columbia U., 1956; postgrad., Duke U., 1958-59. Advt. copywriter Maxon Inc., 1957; copywriter, TV producer, creative dir. Howard

Marks, Inc., Cleve., 1960-61; copywriter Marshalk div. Interpublic, Cleve., 1961; creative dir. Wyse Advt., Cleve., 1962-63; sr. copywriter Hutchins Advt. Co., Rochester, N.Y., 1964-66, creative dir., exec. v.p., 1967-68, pres., 1969-70; pres. Hutchins-Darcy, Inc., Rochester, N.Y., 1971-76; pres., chief operating officer Hutchins/Young & Rubicam, Rochester, N.Y., 1977-79, pres., chief exec. officer, 1980-91, chmn., 1991-95; cons. in field, 1996—; exec. v.p., mem. exec. com. Cato Johnson USA div. Young & Rubicam Inc., Rochester, 1991-93. Advt. cons. Monroe County Rep. Party, Rochester, N.Y., 1967-72; adv. bd. Human Rels. Commn., Rochester, 1968-73; pres. Friends of Child Welfare, 1966-67; mem. coun. Empire State Coll. SUNY, Saratoga Springs, 1972-82; coord. Upstate N.Y. for Media-Advt. Partnership for Drug Free Am., 1987-88; adv. bd. Comms. Magnet Program Franklin H.S., 1988-91; bd. edn. Wyo. Cen. Sch., 1993-95; leader shared decision-making planning com. Wyo. Ctrl. Sch., 1993-94; baseball coach Warsaw Kiwanis Little League, 1993-95; trustee Wyo. Free Libr., 1994-95, pres., 1995—; coord. pub. rels. com. Wyo. Playground Com., 1996—. Mem. Am. Assn. Advt. Agys. (treas. N.Y. State coun. 1985-86, chmn. 1987-88, bd. govs. 1988-91), Rochester Advt. Coun. (dir. 1979-80, Lantern award for pub. svc. 1988, City of Rochester Volunteerism award 1991), Sigma Chi, Omicron Delta Kappa. Republican. Episcopalian. Home: 1061 Tower Rd Wyoming NY 14591-9557 Office: Hutchins/Young Rubicam Inc 400 Midtown Tower Rochester NY 14604-2001

MOREY, PHILIP STOCKTON, JR., mathematics educator; b. Houston, July 11, 1937; s. Philip Stockton and Helen Holmes (Wolcott) M.; m. Jeri Lynn Snyder, Sept. 5, 1964; children: William Philip, Christopher Jerome. BA, U. Tex., 1959, Ma, 1961, PhD, 1967. Asst. prof. math. U. Nebr., Omaha, 1967-68; assoc. prof. Tex. A&I U., Kingsville, 1968-76; prof. Tex. A&M U., Kingsville, 1976—; lectr. U. Tokyo, 1976, U. Hokkaido, 1977, 88. Contbr. articles to Tensor N.S., Internat. Jour. Engring. Sci, Tex. Jour. Sci. Recipient Researcher of Yr. awrd Tex. A&I Alumni Assn., 1985. Mem. Tex. Acad. Sci. (chmn. math. sect. 1982, '85), Am. Math. Soc., Tensor Soc., (Japan). Achievements include research in extensor analysis, tensor analysis, differential geometry, mathematical physics. Home: 1514 Lackey St Kingsville TX 78363-3199 Office: Tex A&M Univ Dept Math Kingsville TX 78362

MOREY, ROBERT HARDY, communications executive; b. Milw., Sept. 5, 1956; s. Lloyd W. and Ruby C. (McElhaney) M. AA, Ricks Coll., 1978; BA, Brigham Young U., 1983. Program dir. Sta. KABE-FM, Orem, Utah, 1982-83, sales mgr., 1983; nat. mgr. ops. Tiffany Prodns. Internat., Salt Lake City, 1983-84; account exec. Osmond Media Corp., Orem, 1984; corp. sec., bd. dirs. Positive Communications, Inc., Orem, 1984—, chief exec. officer, 1987—; gen. mgr. Sta. KSRR, Orem, 1985—; pres. K-Star Satellite Network, Orem, 1986—, Broadcast Media Svcs., Orem, 1989-93; gen. mgr. Sta. KMGR, Salt Lake City, 1993; ops. mgr. KQMB-FM, Salt Lake City, 1994-95, gen. mgr., 1995—; guest lectr. various colls. and univs., 1981—. Chmn. Rep. voting dist., Orem, 1984. Recipient Community Service award Utah Valley Community Coll., 1983; named one of Outstanding Young Men in Am. U.S. Jaycees, 1983. Avocations: reading, collecting stamps. Home: PO Box 828 Orem UT 84059-0828 Office: Sta KSRR Ventura Media Ctr 1240 E 800 N Orem UT 84057-4318

MORFORD, JAMES WARREN, international health care executive; b. Duluth, Minn., Feb. 22, 1945; s. James Andrew and Christine (Warner) M.; m. Pamela Ann Carlson, July 20, 1974; children: James Warren II, Melissa Lynn. AA, U. Minn., 1965; BS, U. Ariz., 1969. Asst. account exec. Tathum, Laird and Kudner Advt., Chgo., 1969; salesman Guest Pac Corp., Mt. Vernon, N.Y., 1970; v.p. Student Service Directory, Mt. Vernon, 1970-71; dir. mktg. Doctors Diagnostic Labs., Mpls., 1971-76, pres., 1976-78; pres., CEO Lab. Cons. Internat., Mpls., 1977-80; COO Morford Clin., Ltd., Mpls., 1980-88; pres. Morford Properties, Inc., Mpls. and Tucson, 1980—; COO Foothills Women's Ctr., Tucson, 1988-95; chmn., CEO Pan Am. Health Ltd., Tucson, 1995—; pres., chmn., bd. dirs. Sistemas de Salud Panamericanos, S.A., Centro Panamericano de Diagnostico pro Imagenes, S.A., Mexico City, 1991—. Mem. Med. Group Mgmt. Assn., Ariz. Med.Group Mgmt. Assn., Minn. Med. Group Mgmt. Assn., Aircraft Owners and Pilots Assn., Chi Phi. Republican. Methodist. Avocations: flying (pilot with advanced ratings). Home: 5081 N Camino Sumo Tucson AZ 85718-6053 Office: PanAm Health Sys 5081 N Camino Real Tucson AZ 85718-6053

MORFORD, LYNN ELLEN, state official; b. Peoria, Ill., June 17, 1953; d. Raymond Scott Jr. and Georgiana (Woodhall) M. BA, Millikin U., 1975; MA, Sangamon State U., Springfield, Ill., 1984. News reporter Stas. WJBC-WBNQ, Bloomington, Ill., 1975-76, Sta. WSOY-AM-FM, Decatur, Ill., 1976-78, Stas. WXCL-WZRO-FM, Peoria, 1978, Sta. KACY-AM-FM, Ventura, Calif., 1978, Sta. WKAN, Kankakee, Ill., 1979-82; freelance news reporter Sta. WMAQ, Chgo., 1982; news dir. Stas. WXCL-WKQA-FM, Peoria, 1983; press sec. Ill. Ho. of Reps. Rep. Press Office, Springfield, 1984-85; chief Press Office, Ill. Dept. Commerce and Community Affairs, Springfield, 1986-95, comms. mgr., 1995—; mem. adv. bd. Ill. AP, 1983; radio news contest judge Okla. AP, 1983; bd. dirs. Ill. News Broadcasters Assn., 1980-84. Chmn. pub. rels., mem. adv. bd. Leadership Ill., 1992—, spring conf. chair, 1994; chmn. pub. rels. Springfield St. Patrick's Day Parade Com., 1991—; chmn. pub. rels. film fund raiser Vachel Lindsay Assn., Springfield, 1989; mem. Springfield Jr. League, 1990-91; mem. Samaritans St. John's Hosp., Springfield, 1995—, Ill. River Econ. Devel. Action Team, 1996—, Orlene Moore Scholarship Com., 1996—, Student of Yr. Selection Com., 1996—; pres., bd. trustees Sherman Pub. Libr. Dist., 1995—. Recipient Best Contbr. award Ill. AP, 1983; Robert Howard scholar Sangamon State U., 1983; named to Hon. Order of Ky. Cols., 1992. Methodist. Avocations: golf, competitive sewing and baking (state fair champion), vocal music, gardening, decorating. Home: 2 Willow Hill Dr Sherman IL 62684-9769 Office: Ill Dept Commerce and Community Affairs 620 E Adams St Springfield IL 62701-1615

MORFORD-BURG, JOANN, state senator, investment company executive; b. Miller, S.D., Nov. 26, 1956; d. Darrell Keith Morford and Eleanor May (Fawcett) Morford-Steptoe; m. Quinten Leo Burg, Nov. 12, 1983. BS in Agrl.-Bus., Comml. Econs., S.D. State U., 1979; cert. in personal fin. planning, Am. Coll., 1992. Agrl. loan officer 1st Bank System, Presho, S.D., 1980-82, Wessington Springs, S.D., 1982-86; agrl. loan officer Am. State Bank, Wessington Springs, 1986; registered investment rep. SBM Fin. Svcs. Inc., Wessington Springs, 1986—; mem. S.D. State Senate, Wessington Springs, 1990—, majority whip, 1993-94, minority whip, 1994—; mem. senate appropriations com. 1993—; chair senate ops. and audit com. 1993, 94; mem. ops. and audit com., 1995—; active Nat. Conf. State Legislators' Assembly of Fed. Issues Environ. Com., 1995—. Mem. Midwestern-Can. task force Midwest Conf., 1990-94; mem. transp. com., commerce com., taxation com. S.D. State Senate, Pierre, 1990-92; treas. twp. bd. Wessington Springs, 1990-92; mem. Wessington Springs Sch. Improvement Coun. Mem. Future Farmers Am. (adv. bd. Wessington Springs chpt.), S.D. State U. 4-H Alumni Assn., Nat. Life Underwriters Assn. (Huron chpt.), Order Ea. Star (various offices 1980—). Democrat. Methodist. Home and Office: 38678 SD Highway 34 Wessington Springs SD 57382-5806

MORGA BELLIZZI, CELESTE, editor; b. N.Y.C., Mar. 8, 1921; d. Louis and Emma (Macari) Morga; m. John J. Bellizzi, Sept. 1, 1942; children: John J., Robert F. Student, Columbia U., 1940-41, SUNY, Albany, 1970. Cert. med. lab. technician. Medical lab. technician USMC Hosp., N.Y.C., 1942, Woman's Hosp., N.Y.C., 1942-52; spl. investigator N.Y. State Atty. Gen.'s Office, Albany, 1958-65; editor Internat. Drug Report publ., The Narc Officer publ. Internat. Narcotic Enforcement Officers Assn., Albany, 1965—. Dir. Albany Inst. History and Art, 1988-90, N.Y. State Press Women, Albany, 1987; advisor UN Non-govtl. Orgns. Drug Com., N.Y.C., 1980-90, White House Conf. Drug Free Am., Washington, 1987; mem. com. Bethlehem Drug Prevention Program, Delmar, N.Y., 1987-90, Action Commn. Narc Edn., Delmar, 1984-90; v.p. Women's Rep. Party Albany, 1972. Recipient Pres.'s award INEOA, 1982, Disting. Svc. award Houston Police Dept., 1981. Mem. Nat. Fedn. Press Women, Nat. Press Club, Univ. Club, Albany Country Club, Aberdeen Country Club. Avocations: painting, golf, tennis. Office: Internat Narcotic Enforcement Officers Assn 112 State St Albany NY 12207-2005

MORGAN, ALAN D., state education official. State supt. education State of N.Mex. Office: N Mex Edn Dept Edn Bldg 300 Don Gaspar Ave Santa Fe NM 87501-2786

MORGAN, ALAN VIVIAN, geologist, educator; b. Barry, Glamorgan, Wales, Jan. 29, 1943; emigrated to Can., 1964, naturalized, 1977; s. George Vivian Williams and Sylvia Nesta (Atkinson) M.; m. Marion Anne Medhurst, June 14, 1966; children: Siân Kristina, Alexis John. B.Sc. with honors in Geology and Geography, U. Leicester, Eng., 1964; M.Sc. in Geography, U. Alta., Calgary, Can., 1966; Ph.D. in Geology, U. Birmingham, Eng., 1970. Postdoctoral fellow U. Western Ont. and U. Waterloo, Ont., Can., 1970-71; asst. prof. earth scis. and man-environ. studies U. Waterloo, 1971-78, assoc. prof. earth scis., 1978-85, prof., 1985—; assoc. dir. Quaternary Scis. Inst. U. Waterloo, Ont., Can., 1992—; mem. Brit. Schs. Exploring Soc. Ctrl. Iceland Expdn., 1960; rep. Can. Geosci. Coun., 1977-83, exec. dir., 1988-94, 96—; mem. con. on global change Royal Soc. Can., 1988-91, mem. com. on pub. wareness of sci., 1989-94; coord. global change Geol. Survey Can.a, 1990-92. Author 6 field guides; editor newsletter OYEZ, 1990-94; contbr. articles to numerous profl. publs.; dir., prodr. documentary film The Heimaey Eruption, 1974. Recipient award for MS thesis Can. Assn. Petroleum Geologists, 1967, Bancroft award Royal Soc. Can., 1994—, John H. Moss award Nat. Assn. Geology Tchrs., 1995; Charles Lapworth scholar, 1970; Nat. Scis. and Engring. Rsch. Coun. Can. grantee, 1971—. Fellow Geol. Assn. Can. (sec.-treas. 1975-83), Geol. Soc. Am.; mem. Am. Quaternary Assn. (pres. 1990-92), Can. Quaternary Assn. (pres. 1987-89), Brit. Quaternary Research Assn., Internat. Union Quaternary Research (sec. gen. XII congress 1983-87). Office: U Waterloo, Dept Earth Scis, Waterloo, ON Canada N2L 3G1

MORGAN, ALFRED VANCE, management consulting company executive: b. Liberal, Kans., Apr. 13, 1936; s. Forrest Francis and Gertrude Irene (Henning) M.; m. Peggy Ann Riley, June 29, 1960; children: Trudie Marie, Vance Riley, Allen Forrest, Bradley Augustus, Kelly James. BBA, U. Kans., 1958; MBA, U. So. Calif., 1966; postgrad., Am. Inst. Banking, 1965, internat. bus. machines degree, 1964. Asst. mgr. Fruehauf Trailer Co., L.A., Calif., 1960-61; asst. mktg. dir. Security Pacific Nat. Bank, 1961-65; mktg. exec. Doyle, Dane, Bernbach Advt., 1965-66; cons. Harbridge House, Inc., Boston, 1966-71; pres. Morgan Bus. Assocs., Inc., Santa Barbara and Boston, 1971; instr. bus. L.A. City Coll., 1971-72; instr. mgmt. Santa Barbara City Coll., 1973. Contbr. articles to profl. publs. With AUS, 1958-60. Mem. Am. Mktg. Assn. L.A., Am. Soc. Profl. Cons., U. So. Calif. Grad. Sch. Bus. Alumni Assn. Office: 1676 E Valley Rd Santa Barbara CA 93108

MORGAN, ANDREW WESLEY, artist, educator; b. Cleve., July 29, 1922; s. John B. and Bertha (Amersbach) M.; m. Dahlia Kaplow, May 18, 1973; children from previous marriage—Alexander, Vincent, Nicholas. B.A., Kenyon Coll., 1948; M.F.A., U. N.C., 1952; postgrad., N.Y.U., 1955-57; L.H.D. (hon.), Tarkio Coll. Head art dept. Greenwich (Conn.) Country Day Sch., 1952-59; chmn. dept. art, dir. gallery U. Miss., 1959-60; pres. Kansas City (Mo.) Art Inst., 1960-70; prof., chmn. art dept. U. Miami, Fla., 1970-87; Commr. Municipal Art Commn., Kansas City, 1965-70; co-chmn. Mid-Am. Urban Design Conf., 1966. One-man shows include Stanford (Conn.) Mus., 1958, Pietrantonio Gallery, N.Y.C., 1960, Lowe Mus., 1980, Viscaya Mus., Miami, Fla., 1984, Leedy-Voulkos Art Ctr., Kansas City, Mo., 1990, Polk Mus., Lakeland, Fla., 1991, New World Sch. for Arts Gallery, Miami, 1992, U. Miami, 1993, Art Mus. No. Ariz. U., 1993-94; one-person show Ctr. for Visual Comm., Coral Gables, Fla., 1995; groups shows include Boston Arts Festival, 1960, Mid-South Annual, Memphis, 1961, Roko Gallery, N.Y.C., 1960, U. Miss., 1959, N.E. Ann. (Jury award oil prize), Silver Mine, Conn., 1958, Ctr. for Contemporary Art, 1989, Six Miami Painters, 1st Ave. Gallery, 1993, Fla. Landscape, 1994. Active Com. Econ. Devel., Kans., 1965-70; bd. dirs. Kansas City Regional Coun. Higher Edn.; pres. bd. dirs. Union Ind. Colls. Art, 1967-70; mem. visual arts bd. Nat. Found. for Arts, Miami, 1988; adv. bd. Vt. Studio Ctr., Johnson, 1989. With AUS, 1942-46. Mem. Nat. Assn. Schs. Art (dir.), Coll. Art. Assn. Home: 10331 SW 59th Ave Miami FL 33156-4114

MORGAN, ANNETTE N., state legislator; b. Kennett, Mo., Aug. 31, 1938; m. William P. Morgan, 1961; children: John, Katherine. BA, U. Mo., MA. Tchr. adult edn.; mem. Mo. Ho. of Reps. Mem. Adult Edn. Assn. Democrat. Presbyterian. Home: 221 W 48th St #1601 Kansas City MO 64112 Office: Mo Ho of Reps State Capitol Building Jefferson City MO 65101-1556

MORGAN, ARLENE NOTORO, newspaper editor, reporter, recruiter; b. Phila., July 27, 1945; d. James Vincent and Mary Rose (Actis-Grande) Notoro; m. David J. Morgan, Mar. 3, 1948; children: Elizabeth, Lauren. BS in Journalism, Temple U., 1967. Reporter Delaware County Daily Times, Chester, Pa., 1967-69; reporter Philadelphia Inquirer, 1969—, dep. metro. editor, 1990-91, sr. editor, 1991—. Bd. dirs. Friends Hosp., Phila., 1978—. Recipient Community Service award Phila. chpt. VFW, 1983, Rafters Charities, Phila., 1982, Phila. Newspapers Inc. Employee Recognition award, 1987. Mem. Soc. Profl. Journalists. Roman Catholic. Avocations: ballet, travel, opera and art appreciation, advocate to the mentally ill. Office: Phila Inquirer 400 N Broad St Philadelphia PA 19130-4015

MORGAN, BEVERLY CARVER, physician, educator; b. N.Y.C., May 29, 1927; d. Jay and Florence (Newkamp) Carver; children—Nancy, Thomas E. III, John E. M.D. cum laude (Mosby Scholar), Duke U., 1955. Diplomate Am. Bd. Pediatrics (oral examiner 1984-90, mem. written examination com. 1990—), Nat. Bd. Med. Examiners. Intern, asst. resident Stanford U. Hosp., San Francisco, 1955-56; clin. fellow pediatrics, trainee pediatric cardiology Babies Hosp.-Columbia Presbyn. Med. Center, N.Y.C., 1956-59; research fellow cardiovascular diagnostic lab. Columbia-Presbyn. Med. Center, N.Y.C., 1959-60; instr. pediatrics Coll. Physicians and Surgeons, Columbia U., 1960; dir. heart sta. Robert B. Green Meml. Hosp., San Antonio, 1960-62; lectr. pediatrics U. Tex., 1960-62; spl. research fellow in pediatric cardiology Sch. Medicine, U. Wash., Seattle, 1962-64; from instr. to prof. pediatrics Sch. Medicine, U. Wash., 1962-73, chmn. dept. pediatrics, 1973-80; mem. staff U. Wash. Hosp., chief of staff, 1975-77; mem. staff Harborview Med. Ctr.; mem. staff Children's Orthopedic Hosp. and Med. Ctr., dir. dept. medicine, 1974-80; prof., chmn. dept. pediatrics U. Calif., Irvine, 1980-88, prof. pediat. and pediat. cardiology, 1980—; pediatrician in chief Children's Hosp. Orange County, 1988; mem. pulmonary acad. awards panel Nat. Heart and Lung Inst., 1972-75; mem. grad. med. edn. nat. advisory com. to sec. HEW, 1977-80; mem. Coun. on Pediatric Practice; chmn. Task Force on Opportunities for Women in Pediatrics, 1982; mem. nursing rev. com. NIH, 1987-88. Contbr. articles to profl. jours.; mem. editorial bd. Clin. Pediatrics, Am. Jour. Diseases of Children, Jour. of Orange County Pediatric Soc., Jour. Am. Acad. Pediatrics, Los Angeles Pediatric Soc. Recipient Women of Achievement award Matrix Table, Seattle, 1974; Distinguished Alumnus award Duke U. Med. Sch., 1974; Ann. award Nat. Bd. Med. Coll. Pa., 1977; USPHS career devel. awardee, 1966-71. Mem. Am. Acad. Pediat. (chmn. com. on pediat. manpower 1984-86), Am. Coll. Cardiology, Soc. for Pediat. Rsch., Am. Fedn. Clin. Rsch., Am. Pediat. Soc., Assn. Med. Sch. Pediat. Dept. Chmn. (sec.-treas. 1981-87), Western Soc. for Pediat. Rsch., Alpha Omega Alpha. Home: 601 Lido Park Dr Newport Beach CA 92663-4411 Office: U Calif Irvine Med Ctr Dept Pediatrics 101 City Blvd W Orange CA 92668-2901

MORGAN, BEVERLY HAMMERSLEY, middle school educator, artist; b. Wichita Falls, Tex.; d. Vernon C. and Melba Marie (Whited) Hammersley; m. Robert Lewis Morgan, Sept. 21, 1957 (div. 1972); children: Janet Claire, Robert David. BA, So. Meth. U.; MA, U. Ala., 1980; AA certification, 1982; postgrad., U. Tex., 1991—. Cert. art tchr., Tex., Ala., elem. tchr., Ala. Art tchr. Ft. Worth Pub. Schs., 1955-60; 6th grade tchr. Huntsville (Ala.) Pub. Schs., 1960-61; English tchr. Lincoln County Schs., Fayetteville, Tenn., 1961-62; 6th grade tchr. Huntsville Pub. Schs., 1962-68, art tchr., 1972—. One man shows include U. Ala., 1980, Huntsville Art League, 1981. Mem. Huntsville-Madison County Art Tchrs., Huntsville Art League, Huntsville Mus. Art, Huntsville Tchrs. Assn., Internat. Platform Assn. Republican. Avocations: bridge, travel, collector of Hammersley English bone china. Home: 12027 Chicamauga Trl SE Huntsville AL 35803-1544

MORGAN, BRUCE RAY, international consultant; b. Los Angeles, Oct. 28, 1932; s. Francis Raymond and Rose Hall (Black) M.; m. Bette Jeanne Moore, Oct. 7, 1957; children: Michael John, Brian Leo, Jeanne Ann. A.A., Sacramento Jr. Coll., 1952; B.S., U. Calif.-Berkeley, 1954, LL.B., 1957. Bar: Calif. 1957. Judge adv. USAF, Saudi Arabia and Morocco, 1958-61; atty. firm Thelen, Marrin, Johnson & Bridges, San Francisco, 1961-67; dep. dir. Peace Corps, Nepal, 1967-68, dir, 1968-70; exec. dir. Center Research and Edn., Denver, 1971-75; dir. U.S. representation to Saudi Arabia-U.S. Joint Commn. on Econ. Coop., Riyadh, 1975-76; pres. Bruce Morgan Assocs., Inc., Washington, 1976—. Editor: Calif. State Bar Jour. Legis. Rev, 1957. Served with USAF, 1958-61. Mem. U.S., Calif. bars. Office: Bruce Morgan Assocs 1010 N Glebe Rd Ste 500 Arlington VA 22201-4749

MORGAN, CAROL MIRÓ, marketing executive; b. Ancon, Republic of Panama, Jan. 31, 1942; d. Morton A. and Dora (Rebolledo) Blum; m. Edward J. Morgan, July 24, 1963 (div. Jan. 1972); children: Edward M., John G.; m. Doran J. Levy, Oct. 3, 1986. BS, Spring Hill Coll., 1962, Met. State U., 1986; MA, Kans. State U., 1966. Cert. tchr., La. Instr. Ohio State U., Columbus, 1966-67; staff writer Palm Beach (Fla.) Daily News, 1967-70; tchr. Isidore Newman Sch., New Orleans, 1972-77; dir. pub. rels. Hennepin County Med. Ctr., Mpls., 1977-79; mgr. pub. rels. Peavey Co., Mpls., 1979-81; owner, pres. Carol Morgan Assocs., Inc., Mpls., 1981-92, Strategic Directions Group, Inc., St. Paul, 1992—. Home: 1029 Lombard Ave Saint Paul MN 55105-3256 Office: Strategic Directions Group Inc 46 E 4th St Ste 1100 Saint Paul MN 55101

MORGAN, CAROLYN F., lawyer; b. Gadsden, Ala., Nov. 23, 1945; d. Sephes Jonah and Garnet Sylvia (Watson) M.; m. Galen Kennah, Dec. 16, 1967 (div. Nov. 1979); children: Jason, Jennifer; m. David Cummings, May 6, 1995. BS, Jacksonville State U., 1970; JD, Cumberland Sch. of Law, 1983. Bar: Ala., U.S. Dist. Ct. (no. dist.) Ala., U.S. Ct. Appeals (11th cir.), U.S. Supreme Ct. Social worker II State of Ala., Gadsden, Birmingham, 1969-80; asst. city atty. City of Gadsen, 1983-84; asst. dist. atty. State of Ala., Anniston, 1984-90; corp. counsel BE & K, Inc., Birmingham, 1990-95; asst. gen. counsel BE&K Inc, Birmingham, 1995—. Office: BE&K Inc 2000 Internat Park Dr Birmingham AL 35243

MORGAN, CHARLES DONALD, JR., manufacturing executive; b. Ft. Smith, Ark., Feb. 4, 1943; s. Charles Donald Sr. and Betty (Speer) M; m. Jane Dills Morgan, Aug. 20, 1966; children: Caroline Speer, Charles Robert. ME, U. Ark., 1966. Systems engr. IBM, Little Rock, Ark., 1966-71; v.p. Acxiom Corp. (formerly CCX Network, Inc.), Conway, Ark., 1972-75; pres. CCX, Conway, Ark., 1976-82, chief exec. officer, 1983—, also chmn. bd. dirs.; bd. dirs. First State Bank & Trust, Conway. Trustee Hendrix Coll., Conway, 1985—; chmn. bd. dirs. Jobs for Ark. Future, 1986-87, mem. commn. 1988—; mem. Southern Growth Policies Bd., N.C., 1986, Ark. Bus. Council, 1987—. Mem. Third Class Mailers Assn., Pub. Chief Exec. Officers Council. Episcopalian. Avocation: auto racing. Office: Acxiom Corp 301 Industrial Blvd Conway AR 72032-7168*

MORGAN, DAVID ERNEST, computer and communications research executive; b. Terre Haute, Ind., Mar. 22, 1942; s. George Ernest and Barbara Marguerite (Lutz) M.; m. Judith Johanna Clement, July 2, 1966; children: Heidi Elizabeth, Gwendolen Anne. BS in Math, Rose Poly. Inst., 1964; MS in Math., U. Mich., 1965; PhD in Computer Sci., U. Waterloo, Ont., Can., 1971. Reporter, photographer WTHI Radio and TV, Terre Haute, 1961-64; mem. tech. staff Bell Telephone Labs., Holmdel, N.J., 1964-70; prof. computer sci. U. Waterloo, 1970-80, dir. networks rsch. lab., 1972-80; v.p. Telecom Network Tech., Toronto, Ont., 1975-80; mgr. arch. and tech. Digital Equipment Corp., Maynard, Mass., 1977-78, 80-84; dir. computer and networks lab. Indsl. Tech. Inst., Ann Arbor, Mich., 1984-86; v.p. rsch. Motorola Inc., Schaumburg, Ill., 1986—; pres. Mordata Ltd., Waterloo, 1973-86; dir., exec. com. Corp. of Open Systems, McLean, Va., 1986-94; vice chmn., adv. bd. Microelectronics and Computer Corp., Austin, Tex., 1992-93; mem. Ill. Gov.'s Task Force Comm., 1992-93; bd. dirs. Computer-Based Patient Record Inst., Chgo., 1992—; speaker numerous confs. and seminars; vis. rsch. scientist MIT Media Labs, 1995—. Contbr. articles to profl. jours.; patentee/inventor in field. Weston-Wabash scholarship Westin-Wabash Found., 1960; fellowship IBM, 1970, grad. study fellowship Bell Labs., 1965. Mem. IEEE, SME, Am. Nat. Stds. Inst. (mem. X3 com. 1984-87, TI com. 1988—), Tau Beta Pi. Avocations: vocal music, photography, travel. Office: 3436 Kennecott Dr Arlington Heights IL 60004

MORGAN, DAVID FORBES, minister; b. Toronto, Ont., Can., Aug. 3, 1930; came to U.S., 1954; s. Forbes Alexander and Ruth (Bamford) M.; m. Delores Mae Storhaug, Sept. 7, 1956; children—Roxanne Ruth, David Forbes II. BA, Rocky Mt. Coll.; ThB, Coll. of the Rockies, MDiv; postgrad. Bishop's Sch. Theology; LittD (hon.), Temple Coll., 1956, D.C. Nat. Coll. Ordained priest. Pres., Coll. of the Rockies, Denver, 1960-73; founder and rector Prior Order of Christ Centered Ministries, Denver, 1973—; canon pastor St. John's Cathedral, Denver, 1982—; bd. dir. Alpha Inc., Denver, 1981—. Author: Christ Centered Ministries, A Response to God's Call, 1973; Songs with A Message, 1956. Clubs: Oxford, Denver Botanic Garden. Home: 740 Clarkson St Denver CO 80218-3204 Office: St Johns Cathedral 1313 Clarkson St Denver CO 80218-1806

MORGAN, DENNIS RICHARD, lawyer; b. Lexington, Va., Jan. 3, 1942; s. Benjamin Richard and Gladys Belle (Brown) M. BA, Washington and Lee U., 1964; JD, U. Va., 1967; LLM in Labor Law, NYU, 1971. Bar: Ohio 1967, Va. 1967, U.S. Ct. Appeals (4th cir.) 1968, U.S. Ct. Appeals (6th cir.) 1971, U.S. Supreme Ct. 1972. Law clk. to chief judge U.S. Dist. Ct. Ea. Dist. Va., 1967-68; mem. Marshman, Snyder & Seeley (now Marshman, Snyder & Corrigan), Cleve., 1971-72; dir. labor rels. Ohio Dept. Adminstrv. Svcs., 1972-75; asst. city atty. Columbus, Ohio, 1975-77; dir. Ohio Legis. Reference Bur., 1979-81; assoc. Clemans, Nelson & Assocs., Columbus, 1981; pvt. practice, Columbus, 1978-92; lectr. in field; guest lectr. Cen. Mich. U., 1975; judge moot ct. Ohio State U. Sch. Law, 1981, 83, grad. div., 1973, 74, 76, Baldwin-Wallace Coll., 1973; legal counsel Dist. IV Communications Workers Am., 1982-88; pers. dir. Pub. Utilities Commn. Ohio, 1989-91; asst. atty gen. State of Ohio, 1991—. Vice-chmn. Franklin County Dem. Party, 1976-82, dem. com. person Ward 58, Columbus, 1973-95; chmn. rules com. Ohio State Dem. Conv., 1974; co-founder, trustee Greater West Side Dem. Club; negotiator Franklin County United Way, 1977-81; regional chmn. ann. alumni fund-raising program U. Va. Sch. Law; commr. Greater Hilltop Area Commn., 1989—; pres. Woodbrook Village Condominium Assn., 1985—. Robert E. Lee Rsch. scholar, summer, 1965; recipient Am. Jurisprudence award, 1967. Capt. U.S. Army, 1968-70. Mem. Indsl. Rels. Rsch. Assn., ABA, Fed. Bar Assn., Am. Judicature Soc., Pi Sigma Alpha. Roman Catholic. Clubs: Shamrock, Columbus Metroplitan (charter). Home: 1261 Woodbrook Ln # G Columbus OH 43223-3243

MORGAN, DONNA JEAN, psychotherapist; b. Edgerton, Wis., Nov. 16, 1955; d. Donald Edward and Pearl Elizabeth (Robinson) Garey. BA, U. Wis., Whitewater, 1983, MS, 1985. Cert. psychotherapist, Wis.; cert. mental health alcohol and drug counselor; nat. cert. alcohol and drug abuse counselor; lic. marriage and family therapist, Wis.; lic. ind. social worker; lic. clin. social worker; nat. cert. counselor. Pvt. practice Janesville, Wis., New Focus, Waukesha and Mukwonago, Wis.; clin. supr. Stoughton (Wis.) Hosp.; prin. Morgan and Assocs., Janesville, Wis. Mem. underaged drinking violation alternative program Rock County, 1986—; co-chmn. task force on child sexual abuse, 1989-91; mem. Rock County Multi-disciplinary Team on Child Abuse, 1990—; mem. spkrs. bur. Rock County C.A.R.E. House, 1990—. Mem. APA, Am. Counseling Assn., Am. Profl. Soc. on the Abuse of Children, Wis. Profl. Soc. on the Abuse of Children (bd. dirs. 1994—), Rock County Mental Health Providers, Am. Assn. Mental Health Counselors, Wis. Assn. Mental Health Counselors, South Ctrl. Wis. Action Coalition, Am. Assn. Marriage and Family Therapy (clin. mem.), Am. Assn. Christian Counselors. Office: 321 E Milwaukee St Janesville WI 53545 also: 2717 N Grandview Blvd Ste 20 Waukesha WI 53188 also: 211 N Rochester St Mukwonago WI 53149

MORGAN, E. A., church administrator. Chaplain Ch. of the Living God Exec. Bd. Office: Church of the Living God 735 S Oakland Dr Decatur IL 62522

MORGAN, EDMUND SEARS, history educator; b. Mpls., Jan. 17, 1916; s. Edmund Morris and Elsie Sears (Smith) M.; m. Helen Theresa Mayer, June 7, 1939; children: Penelope, Pamela.; m. Marie Caskey, June 22, 1983. A.B.,

Harvard U., 1937, Ph.D., 1942. Instrument maker Radiation Lab., Mass. Inst. Tech., 1942-45; instr. U. Chgo., 1945-46; asst. prof. Brown U., 1946-49, asso. prof., 1949-51, prof., 1951-55, acting dean grad. sch., 1951-52; prof. Yale U., 1955-65, Sterling prof., 1965-86, prof. emeritus, 1986—; Research fellow Huntington Library, 1952-53; Johnson research prof. U. Wis., 1968-69. Author: The Puritan Family, 1944, Virginians at Home, 1953, (with Helen M. Morgan) The Stamp Act Crisis, 1953, The Birth of the Republic, 1956, The Puritan Dilemma, 1958, The Gentle Puritan, 1962, Visible Saints, 1963, Roger Williams, 1967, So What About History, 1969, American Slavery American Freedom, 1975, The Challenge of the American Revolution, 1976, The Meaning of Independence, 1976, The Genius of George Washington, 1980, Inventing the People, 1988; Mem. editorial bd.: N.E. Quar; Contbr. articles and revs. to hist. jours. Trustee Smith Coll., 1984-89. Mem. Organ. Am. Historianss (pres. 1971-72), Colonial Soc. Mass., Mass. Hist. Soc., Am. Antiquarian Soc., Am. Philos. Soc., Am. Acad. Arts and Scis., Conn. Acad. Arts and Scis., Brit. Acad., Royal Hist. Soc.

MORGAN, ELIZABETH, plastic and reconstructive surgeon; b. Washington, July 9, 1947; d. William James and Antonia (Bell) M.; children: 1 dau., Ellen. BA magna cum laude, Harvard U., 1967; postgrad. (fellow), Oxford U., Somerville Coll., 1967, 70; MD, Yale U., 1971; law student, Georgetown U., 1986-87; PhD in Psychology, U. Canterbury, Christchurch, New Zealand, 1995. Diplomate Am. Bd. Surgery, Am. Bd. Plastic Surgery. Intern Yale-New Haven Hosp., 1971-72, resident, 1972-73, 76-77; resident Tufts-New Eng. Med. Center, Boston, 1973-76, Harvard-Cambridge (Mass.) Hosp., 1977-78; columnist Cosmopolitan mag., 1973-80; practice medicine specializing in plastic and reconstructive surgery Washington, 1978-86, McLean, Va., 1978-86. Author: The Making of a Woman Surgeon, 1980, Solo Practice, 1982, Custody, A True Story, 1986, The Complete Book of Cosmetic Surgery for Men, Women and Teens, 1988, To Save My Child, 1996. Trustee Kent (Conn.) Sch. Fellow ACS, Am. Soc. Plastic and Reconstructive Surgeons; mem. Internat. Soc. for Study Dissociation., New Zealand Psychol. Soc. Episcopalian.

MORGAN, EVAN, chemist; b. Spokane, Wash., Feb. 26, 1930; s. Evan and Emma Anne (Klobucher) M.; m. Johnnie Lu Dickson, Feb. 14, 1959; 1 child, James. BS, Gonzaga U., 1952; MS, U. Wash., 1954, PhD, 1956. Staff chemist IBM Corp., Poughkeepsie, N.Y., 1956-60; group supr. Olin Mathieson Co., New Haven, 1960-64; assoc. prof. chemistry High Point (N.C.) Coll., 1964-65; sr. rsch. chemist Reynolds Metals Co., Richmond, Va., 1965-72; chemist Babcock & Wilcox, Lynchburg, Va., 1975-95, Lynchburg Tree Steward, Lynchburg, 1995—, 1995—. Mem. Am. Chem. Soc. Home: 5128 Wedgewood Rd Lynchburg VA 24503-4208

MORGAN, FLORENCE MURDINA, nurse; b. Northern Manchester, Jamaica, Mar. 1, 1936; came to U.S., 1967; d. James William and Juanita Agatha (Lorraine) M. RN, Wanstead Hosp., Hermon Hill London, 1962; State Cert. Midwife, Rochford Hosp., Essex, Eng., 1963; Queens Nurse, Queens Inst. Dist. Nursing, Eng., 1965; BSN cum laude, CUNY, 1989, MSN, 1992. Cert. Childbirth Educator. Staff nurse Toronto Gen. Hosp., 1964-65; jr. supr., queens nurse/midwife Surrey County Coun., Kingston-on-Thames, Eng., 1965-66; staff midwife St. Luke's Hosp., Guildford, Surrey, 1966-67; staff nurse No. Westchester Hosp., Mt. Kisco, N.Y., 1967-70, Vis. Nurse Svc., N.Y.C., 1970-71; pvt. duty med. surg. nurse N.Y.C., 1971-76; staff nurse divsn. substance abuse Beth Israel Med. Ctr., N.Y.C., 1976—; Tb coord., tchr. health, tb. prevention, AIDS prevention Beth Israel Med. Ctr., N.Y.C., 1993—; vol. nursing Spalding Hosp., Jamaica, 1955-57. Vol. Luth. Ch., N.Y.C., 1967-76; vol. 1199 Polit. Action., N.Y.C., 1989-95. Mem. N.Y. Acad. Scis., Hunter-Bellevue Alumni Assn., Sigma Theta Tau. Democrat. Avocations: swimming, tennis, arts and crafts, dance, unpublished poems. Home: 445 E 14th St Apt 3D New York NY 10009

MORGAN, FRANK, mathematics educator. BS, MIT, 1974; PhD, Princeton U., 1977; ScD (hon.), Cedar Crest Coll., 1995. Moore instr. to assoc. prof., Green prof. MIT, Cambridge, 1977-87, also chmn. undergrad. math. dept.; prof. and chmn. dept. math. Williams Coll., Williamstown, Mass., 1987—; vis. prof. Rice U., Houston, 1982-83, Stanford U., 1986-87; mem. Inst. Advanced Study, Princeton, N.J., 1990-91. Author: Geometric Measure Theory, 1988, Riemannian Geometry, 1993, Calculus Lite, 1995. Recipient Haimo award for disting. coll. or univ. tchg. of math. Math. Assn. Am., 1993. Office: Williams College Dept of Mathematics Williamstown MA 01267

MORGAN, FRANK BROWN WEBB, JR., high tech executive, consultant; b. San Antonio, Aug. 26, 1935; s. Frank Brown Webb and Annie Kathleen (Harman) M.; m. Janice Dorine Schlittenhardt, Aug. 19, 1961; children: Roxanne, John Harman. BA in English, U. Kans., 1961. Bur. chief, reporter UPI, Santa Fe, 1961-64; staff corr. Wall St. Jour., Dallas, L.A., 1964-67; bur. chief, reporter Newsweek mag., L.A., Boston, 1967-73; founder, pres. Morgan Assocs., Boston, 1973-74; pub., owner Pittsfield/Farmington, N.H. Press, Pittsfield, 1973-74; v.p. The Boston Co., 1974-76, 1st Nat. Stores, Boston, 1976-78; founding editor INC. mag., Boston, 1978-79; pres. Miller Communications Inc., Boston, 1979-91; bd. dirs. Boston Computer Soc.; editor The Common, Metro-Boston, 1973-76. Bd. dirs. Fund for Arts in Newton, Mass., 1982, The Copley Soc. Boston. With U.S. Army, 1957-59. Recipient Hancock Ins. Co. bus. writing award Newsweek mag., 1971. Mem. Mass. Hist. Soc., Donald Ross Soc., St. Botolph Club (bd. dirs. 1975—), The Athenaeum, Kohala and Mauna Kea Golf Club. Avocations: golf, travel, reading, sports. Home and Office: PO Box 1169 Kapaau HI 96753

MORGAN, FRANK EDWARD, II, lawyer; b. Burlington, Vt., May 16, 1952; s. Robert Griggs and Ruth (Jepson) M. First Class Cert. Merit, U. Edinburgh, Scotland, 1973; AB with honors, Brown U., 1974; LLM, Cambridge U., Eng., 1976; JD, U. Va., 1978. Bar: Mass. 1978, N.Y. 1990. Assoc. Gaston & Snow, Boston, 1978-82; v.p., gen. counsel Madison Fund, Inc. and Adobe Resources Corp., N.Y.C., 1982-87; ptnr. Gaston & Snow, N.Y.C., 1987-91, Mayer, Brown & Platt, N.Y.C., 1991-96, Dewey Ballantine, N.Y.C., 1996—. Mem. ABA, N.Y. State Bar Assn., Am. Soc. Internat. Law. Republican. Congregationalist. Home: 400 E 70th St New York NY 10021-5387 Office: Dewey Ballantino 1301 Ave of the Americas New York NY 10019-6092

MORGAN, (GEORGE) FREDERICK, poet, editor; b. N.Y.C., Apr. 25, 1922; s. John Williams and Marion Haviland (Burt) M.; m. Constance Canfield, Dec. 20, 1942 (div. Aug. 1957); children: Gaylen, Veronica, George F.; m. Rose Fillmore, Aug. 14, 1957 (div. Aug. 1969); m. Paula Deitz, Nov. 30, 1969. A.B. magna cum laude, Princeton U., 1943. Founder The Hudson Rev., N.Y.C., 1947, editor, pres., 1947—; chmn. adv. council dept. Romance langs. and lits. Princeton U., N.J., 1973-91. Author: A Book of Change, 1972, Poems of the Two Worlds, 1977, The Tarot of Cornelius Agrippa, 1978, Death Mother and Other Poems, 1979, The River, 1980, Refractions, 1981, Northbook, 1982, Eleven Poems, 1983, The Fountain and Other Fables, 1985, Poems: New and Selected, 1987, Poems for Paula, 1995. Served with U.S. Army, 1943-45. Decorated chevalier de l'Ordre des Arts et des Lettres, Govt. of France, 1984. Clubs: Knickerbocker (N.Y.C.) (gov. 1981-89), University (N.Y.C.), Somerset (Boston). Office: The Hudson Review 684 Park Ave New York NY 10021-5043

MORGAN, GAYLIN F., public realtions executive; b. Cedar Falls, Iowa, Nov. 3, 1938. BS in Journ., Bus., Iowa State U., 1962. Creative dir. Reiman Assocs., 1965-75; pres. Morgan & Myers, Jefferson, Wis., 1976—. Office: Morgan & Myers 146 E Milwaukee St Jefferson WI 53549-1696

MORGAN, GLEN D., superintendent. Supt. Ind. Sch. Dist. #1, Lewiston, Idaho. Recipient State Finalist for Nat. Supt. of Yr. award, 1993. Office: Ind Sch Dist # 1 3317 12th St Lewiston ID 83501-5308

MORGAN, HENRY COKE, JR., judge; b. Norfolk, Va., Feb. 8, 1935; s. Henry Coke and Dorothy Lea (Pebworth) M.; m. Margaret John McGrail, Aug. 18, 1965; 1 stepchild, A. Robertson Hanckel Jr.; children: Catherine Morgan Stockwell, Coke Morgan Stewart. BS, Washington and Lee U., 1957, JD, 1960. Bar: Va. 1960, U.S. Dist. Ct. (ea. dist.) Va. 1961, U.S. Ct. Appeals (4th cir.) 1964. Asst. city atty. City of Norfolk (Va.), 1960-63; ptnr., chief exec. officer Pender & Coward, Virginia Beach, Va., 1963-92; vice chmn., gen. counsel Princess Anne Bank, 1986-92; judge U.S. Dist. Ct. (ea. dist.) Va. 1992—. Served with U.S. Army, 1958-59. Episcopalian. Office: US Dist Ct Walter E. Hoffman U.S. Courthouse 600 Granby St Norfolk VA 23510-1915

MORGAN, HOWARD EDWIN, physiologist; b. Bloomington, Ill., Oct. 8, 1927; s. Lyle V. and Ethel E. (Bailey) M. Student, Ill. Wesleyan U., 1944-45; MD, Johns Hopkins U., 1949. Intern Vanderbilt U., Nashville, 1949-51; resident in ob-gyn. Vanderbilt U., 1951-53, instr., 1953-55, instr. physiology, 1957-59, asst. prof. physiology, 1959-62, assoc. prof., 1962-65, prof. physiology, 1965-67; Evan Pugh prof., chmn. physiology Pa. State U., Hershey, 1967-87; sr. v.p. rsch. Geisinger Clinic, Danville, Pa., 1987—; v.p. rsch. Am. Heart Assn., 1977-79; mem. Nat. Heart, Lung and Blood Adv. Coun., 1979-83. Editor: Physiol. Revs, 1973-79, Am. Jour. Physiology: Cell Physiology, 1981-84. With U.S. Army, 1955-57. Recipient award of Merit Am. Heart Assn., 1979, Carl Wiggers award, 1984; Howard Hughes scholar, 1982. Mem. Am. Physiol. Soc. (pres., Daggs award 1992), Am. Heart Assn. (pres., Disting. Achievement award 1988, Gold Heart award 1994), Am. Soc. Biol. Chemists, Biochem. Soc., Biophys. Soc., Internat. Soc. Heart Rsch. (pres., Peter Harris award 1995), Inst. Medicine of NAS. Office: Geisinger Clinic Weis Ctr for Rsch 100 N Academy St Danville PA 17822

MORGAN, HUGH JACKSON, JR., bank executive; b. Nashville, Aug. 10, 1928; s. Hugh Jackson and Robert Ray (Porter) M.; m. Ann Moulton Ward, Aug. 28, 1954; children—Ann, Grace, Caroline, Hugh. A.B., Princeton U., N.J., 1950; LL.B., Vanderbilt U., Nashville, 1956; A.M.P., Harvard Bus. Sch., 1976. Bar: Tenn. 1956. Practice law Miller & Martin, Chattanooga, 1956-60; atty. So. Natural Gas Co., Birmingham, Ala., 1961-65, gen. atty., 1966-70, v.p., 1971-78, pres., 1982-84, chmn. bd., 1984-87; v.p. Sonat Inc., Birmingham, Ala., 1973-78, sr. v.p., 1979-84, exec. v.p., 1984, vice chmn. bd., 1984-87; vice chmn. Nat. Bank of Commerce, Birmingham, Ala., 1987-90; chmn. Nat. Bank Commerce, Birmingham, Ala., 1990—, also bd. dirs.; bd. dirs. AlaTenn Resources, Inc., Ala.-Tenn. Nat. Gas Co., Blue Cross-Blue Shield Ala. Chmn. Birmingham Airport Authority, 1986—; trustee Episcopal High Sch., Alexandria, Va., Children's Hosp. Ala., Birmingham, 1974—. Served to lt. (j.g.) USN, 1950-53. Recipient Bennett Douglas Bell Meml. prize Vanderbilt Law Sch., 1956. Mem. Order of the Coif. Clubs: Mountain Brook (pres. 1972), Redstone, (Birmingham); Belle Meade (Nashville); Linville Golf (N.C.). Lodge: Rotary. Home: 3121 Brookwood Rd Birmingham AL 35223-2016 Office: Nat Bank of Commerce 1927 1st Ave N Birmingham AL 35203-4009

MORGAN, JACK M., lawyer; b. Portales, N.Mex., Jan. 15, 1924; s. George Albert and Mary Rosana (Baker) M.; BBA, U. Tex., 1948; LLB, 1950; m. Peggy Flynn Cummings, 1947; children: Marilyn, Rebecca, Claudia, Jack. Admitted to N.Mex. bar, 1950; sole practice law, Farmington, N.Mex., 1956—; mem. N.Mex. State Senate, 1973-88 . Served with USN, 1942-46. Mem. Am. Bar Assn., N.Mex. Bar Assn., S.W. Regional Energy Council (past chmn.), Kiwanis, Elks. Republican. Office: PO Box 2151 Farmington NM 87499-2151

MORGAN, JACQUI, illustrator, painter, educator; b. N.Y.C., Feb. 22, 1939; d. Henry and Emily (Cook) Morganstern; m. Onnig Kalfayan, Apr. 23, 1967 (div. 1972); m. Tomás Gonda, Jan. 1983 (dec. 1988). B.F.A. with honors, Pratt Inst., Bklyn., 1960; M.A., Hunter Coll., CCNY, 1978. Textile designer M. Lowenstein & Sons, N.Y.C., 1961-62, Fruit of the Loom, N.Y.C., 1962; stylist-design dir. Au Courant, Inc., N.Y.C., 1966—; assoc. prof. Pratt Inst., Bklyn., 1977—; guest lectr. U. Que., Syracuse U., Warsaw TV & Radio, Poland, NYU, Parsons Sch. Design, N.Y.C., Sch. Visual Arts, N.Y.C., Va. Commonwealth U., others; mem. profl. juries; curator Tomás Gonda retrospective exhbn.; condr. workshops. One-person shows include Soc. Illustrators, N.Y.C., 1977, Art Dirs. Club, N.Y.C., 1978, Gallerie Nowe Miasto, Warsaw, 1978, Gallerie Baumeister, Munich, W.Ger., 1978, Hansen-Feuerman Gallery, N.Y.C., 1980; group shows include Mus. Contemporary Crafts, N.Y.C., 1975, Smithsonian Instn., Washington, 1976, Mus. Warsaw, 1976, 78, Mus. Tokyo, 1979, Nat. Watercolor Soc., 1989, Salmagundi Club, 1990, New Eng. Watercolor Soc. Open, 1990, Miss. Watercolor Grand nat., 1990, Illustration West 29, 1990, Adirondack Nat., 1990, Die Verlassenen Schuhe, 1994; represented in permanent collections: Smithsonian Instn., Mus. Warsaw; author-illustrator: Watercolor for Illustration; produced three of seven instrnl. watercolor videos; series of prints pub., 1995; series of plates publ, 1995; contbr. articles to profl. jours. Recipient more than 150 awards from various orgns. including Soc. Illustrators, Fed. Design Coun., Comm. Arts Mag., Am. Inst. Graphic Arts, N.Y. Art Dirs. Club, Print Design Ann. Mem. Graphic Artists Guild (dir. 1975-79), Soc. Illustrators, Women Artists of the West, Pa. Watercolor Soc. Studio: 692 Greenwich St New York NY 10014-2876 *Finally, I understand that it's the pleasure of the process and the internal knowledge of improvement that gives the greatest satisfaction.*

MORGAN, JAMES C., electronics executive; b. 1938. BSME, Cornell U., MBA. With Textron Inc., 1963-72, West Ven Mgmt., San Francisco, 1972-76; chmn. bd., pres., CEO Applied Materials, Inc., Santa Clara, Calif., 1976-87, chmn. bd., CEO, 1987—. Office: Applied Materials Inc 3050 Bowers Ave Santa Clara CA 95054-3201*

MORGAN, JAMES DURWARD, computer company executive; b. N.Y.C., Sept. 10, 1936; s. Durward Field and Harriet (Airey) M.; m. Ruth Ann Dobson, Jan. 14, 1967; children: Jennifer, Andrew. BEE, Yale U., 1961, MEE, 1962. Systems engr. Calspan Corp., Buffalo, 1962-68; v.p. Comptek Rsch. Inc., Buffalo, 1968-83, 90—, also bd. dirs.; v.p. Barrister Info. Systems Corp., Buffalo, 1983-90; also bd. dirs. Barrister Info. Systems Corp., 1983—. Mem. adv. coun. Erie C.C., Amherst, N.Y., 1985—, past chmn.; bd. dirs. Yale Alumni Bd., Buffalo, 1987—. Served with USN, 1959-61. Mem. IEEE, ACM (past chmn. local chpt.). Home: 34 Ironwood Ct East Amherst NY 14051-1628 Office: Comptek Rsch Inc 2732 Transit Rd Buffalo NY 14224-2523

MORGAN, JAMES EARL, librarian, administrator; b. Wheeling, W.Va., June 30, 1941; s. James H. L. and Ethel Irene (Goodwin) M.; m. Carman H. Head, Dec. 23, 1966; 1 child, Scott Andrew. B.S. in Edn., Ariz. State Coll., 1965; M.S.L.S., Fla. State U., 1966. Reference asst. social scis. Fla. State U., Tallahassee, 1965-66; head pub. services Ga. Coll., Milledgeville, 1967-69; dir. pub. services U. Tex. Med. Br., Galveston, 1969-73; dir. libraries U. Conn. Health Ctr., Farmington, 1973-76, Oreg. Health Sci. U., Portland, 1976—. Contbr. articles to profl. jours. Grantee Nat. Library Medicine, 1974-76, 78-81. Mem. ALA (life), Med. Libr. Assn. (chmn. Pacific N.W. chpt. 1981), Oreg. Health Scis. Librs. Assn., Pacific N.W. Libr. Assn., Spl. Libr. Assn., Oreg. Libr. Assn., Portland Area Spl. Librarians Assn., Assn. Coll. and Rsch. Librs., Am. Med. Informatics Assn., Nat. Rural Health Assn. Democrat. Office: Oreg Health Scis Univ Library Biomedical Info Comm Ctr 3181 SW Sam Jackson Park Rd Portland OR 97201-3098

MORGAN, JAMES EVAN, lawyer; b. Poughkeepsie, N.Y., Nov. 8, 1959; s. Evan and Johnnie Lu Morgan; m. Catherine Barr Altman, Sept. 21, 1991. BA, Lynchburg Coll., 1984; JD, N.Y. Law Sch., 1989. Bar: N.Y. 1993. Talk show host Sta. WLGM-AM Radio, Lynchburg, Va., 1982-86; legal editor Matthew Bender & Co., Inc., N.Y.C., 1989-91; ptnr. Morgan Cons., Chgo., 1992—; investigator Chgo. Bd. Options Exch., 1993—. Editor: Bender's Federal Tax Service, 1989-91, Modern Estate Planning, 1989-91; pub., editor: Minerva, 1990. Mem. ABA (bus. law sect., com. on fed. regulation of securities, market regulation subcom. 1994—), Coun. on Fgn. Rels. Avocations: playing violin and viola, composing music. Office: Chgo Bd Options Exch 400 S LaSalle St Chicago IL 60605

MORGAN, JAMES NEWTON, research economist, educator; b. Corydon, Ind., Mar. 1, 1918; s. John Jacob Brooke and Rose Ann (Davis) M.; m. Gladys Lucille Hassler, May 12, 1945; children—Kenneth, Timothy, Salim, Janet. BA, Northwestern U., 1939; PhD, Harvard U., 1947. Asst. prof. econs. Brown U., Providence, 1947-49; Carnegie research fellow U. Mich., Ann Arbor, 1949-51; asst. prof. econ., asst. program dir. Inst. for Social Research, U. Mich., Ann Arbor; asst. prof. econs., asst. program dir. Inst. Social Research Ctr. for Advanced Study in Behavior Sci., Palo Alto, Calif., 1955-56; prof. econs., program dir. Inst. Social Research U. Mich., Ann Arbor, 1956-88, prof. emeritus, 1988—; bd. dirs. Consumers Union, Mt. Vernon, N.Y., 1955-82; com. on sci. and pub. policy NAS, 1983-86, report rev. com., 1987-91; com. on basic rsch. in behavior and social sci. NRC, Washington, panel on census requirements, 1992-95. Fellow Am. Statis. Assn., Am. Acad. Arts and Scis., Gerontol. Soc. Am., Wissenschaftskolleg zu Berlin; mem. Nat. Acad. Scis., Am. Econ. Assn. Methodist. Avocations: swimming; gardening. Home: 1217 Bydding Rd Ann Arbor MI 48103-3103 Office: Inst Social Research Thompson St Ann Arbor MI 48104

MORGAN, JAMES PHILIP, pharmacologist, cardiologist, educator; b. Cin., Jan. 13, 1948; s. James Weldon and Dorcas Adele (Meyer) M.; m. Kathleen Greive, Dec. 22, 1973; children: James Patrick, Jonathan Michael. BS, U. Cin., 1970, PhD, 1974, MD, 1976. Diplomate Am. Bd. Internal Medicine and Subspecialty Cardiovascular Disease. Fellow in internal medicine Mayo Clinic, Rochester, Minn., 1976-79, fellow in cardiovascular disease, 1979-83; asst. in medicine, Beth Israel Hosp., Boston, 1983—; instr. pharmacology U. Cin., 1975-76; asst. prof. pharmacology, instr. medicine, Mayo Clinic, 1981-83; asst. prof. medicine, Harvard U., Boston, 1983, assoc. prof., 1988—; affiliate faculty, dept. pharmacology, Harvard Med. Sch., 1994—; chief and prgram dir. cardiovascular divsn. Beth Israel Hosp., 1994—. Contbr. articles to profl. jours. Recipient Young Investigators award Am. Coll. Cardiology, 1982; Balfour award Mayo Clinic, 1983, Advanced Cardiac Life Support Spl Recognition award Mayo Clinic, 1983, Research Career Devel. award NIH, 1985-90. Mem. AMA, Am. Heart Assn., Biophys. Soc. Am. Soc. Pharmacology and Exptl. Therapeutics, Masons. Avocation: philatelics. Office: Beth Israel Hosp Cardiovascular Div 330 Brookline Ave Boston MA 02215-5400

MORGAN, JANE HALE, retired library director; b. Dines, Wyo., May 11, 1926; d. Arthur Hale and Billie (Wood) Hale; m. Joseph Charles Morgan, Aug. 12, 1955; children: Joseph Hale, Jane Frances, Ann Michele. BA, Howard U., 1947; MA, U. Denver, 1954. Mem. staff Detroit Pub. Library, 1954-87, exec. asst. dir., 1973-75, dep. dir., 1975-78, dir., 1978-87; mem. Mich. Libr. Consortium Bd.; exec. bd. Southeastern Mich. Regional Film Libr.; vis. prof. Wayne State U., 1989—. Trustee New Detroit, Inc., Delta Dental Plan of Mich., Delta Dental Plan of Ohio; v.p. United Southwestern Mich.; pres. Univ.-Cultural Center Assn.; bd. dirs. Rehab. Inst., YWCA, Met. Affairs Corp., Literacy Vols. Am., Detroit, Mich. Ctr. for the Book, Interfaith Coun.; bd. dirs., v.p. United Community Svcs. Met. Detroit; chmn. Detroiters for Adult Reading Excellence; chmn. adv. coun. libr. sci. U. Mich., mem. adv. coun. libr. sci. Wayne State U.; dir. Met. Detroit Youth Found.; chmn. Mich. LSCA adv. coun.; mem. UWA Literacy Com., Attys. Grievance Com., Women's Commn., Mich. Civil Svc. Rev. Com.; vice chair Mich. Coun. for Humanities; mem. Commn. for the Greening of Detroit; adv. com. Headstart; mem. Detroit Women's Com., Detroit Women's Forum, Detroit Exec. Svc. Corps. Recipient Anthony Wayne award Wayne State U., 1981, Summit award Greater Detroit C. of C.; named Detroit Howardite of Year, 1983. Mem. ALA, Mich. Library Assn., Women's Nat. Book Assn., Assn. Mcpl. Profl. Women, NAACP, LWV, Women's Economic Club, Alpha Kappa Alpha. Democrat. Episcopalian.

MORGAN, JEFF, research engineer; b. Salt Lake City, Sept. 3, 1954; s. David Nyle and Dene Huber (Olsen) M.; m. Linda Mae Marquez, May 28, 1982 (div.). BS, U. Calif., San Diego, 1976; MS, U. Hawaii, 1978, PhD, 1982. Rsch. assoc. U. Hawaii, Honolulu, 1982-85; sr. rsch. assoc. Stanford U., Palo Alto, Calif., 1985-91; rsch. engr. U. Wash., Seattle, 1991—. Mem. Am. Astron. Soc. Office: U Wash Dept Astronomy FM-20 Seattle WA 98195

MORGAN, JOAN, financial planner; b. Key West, Fla., Dec. 4, 1953; d. Henry Sturgis Morgan and Fanny Gray Little Pratt. BA, Barnard Coll., 1975; MBA, Columbia U., 1977; postgrad., Adelphi U., 1983. Cert. fin. planner. Assoc., syndicate dept. Morgan Stanley & Co., N.Y.C., 1977-80; fin. planner, asst. v.p. Bankers Trust, N.Y.C., 1983-86; prin. Joan Morgan Adminstrv. Svcs., N.Y.C., 1986-93; fin. planner Am. Express Fin. Advisors, Inc., Washington, 1993-95. Bd. dirs. The Madeira Sch., McLean, Va., 1993—; mem. adv. bd. dirs. DearKnows, Ltd., N.Y.C., 1985—. Mem. Inst. Cert. Fin. Planners, Internat. Assn. Fin. Planners, Nat. Assn. Women Bus. Owners, Columbia Bus. Sch. Club of Washington (pres. 1991-92). Republican. Episcopalian. Avocations: skiing, sailing, tennis. Home: 5044 Millwood Ln NW Washington DC 20016

MORGAN, JOHN BRUCE, hospital care consultant; b. Youngstown, Ohio, Oct. 25, 1919; s. John Benjamin and Ida May (Lane) M.; m. Marian Frampton, July 11, 1969; children: John B., Carolyn, Leonard, Suzanne (dec.). B.S., Miami U., 1941; M.B.A., Harvard U., 1946. Field rep. Gen. Motors Acceptance Corp., Youngstown, 1941; pres. Asso. Hosp. Service, Inc., Youngstown, 1947-74; pres. Hosp. Care Corp. (Blue Cross), Cin., 1974-83, cons., 1983—; pres. Health Maintenance Plan, Cin., 1974-83, Health Care Mutual, Cin., 1974-83; chmn. bd. govs., chmn. exec. com. Blue Cross Assn., Chgo., 1981-82; chmn. bd. Community Life Ins. Co., Worthington, Ohio, 1979-83; mem. joint exec. com. Blue Cross-Blue Shield Assns., mem. joint bds., Chgo.; mem. bus. adv. com. Miami U., Oxford, Ohio. Gen. chmn. United Fund campaign, Youngstown, 1965; pres. Cancer Soc., 1965; chmn. bd. trustees Ch. of the Palms, 1996. Served with AUS, 1942-46. Mem. Am.Hosp. Assn. (Justin Ford Kimball award 1983), Ohio Hosp. Assn., Ohio C. of C. (bd. dirs.), Youngstown Area C. of C. (pres. 1966-67), Delray Beach, Fla. C. of C., Youngstown Country Club, Delray Dunes Golf and Country Club (bd. dirs., v.p.), Rotary (bd. dirs. Delray Beach club, pres. 1992, Paul Harris fellow), Masons, Elks, Sigma Alpha Epsilon, Delta Sigma Pi. Mem. United Ch. of Christ. Home: 9 Slash Pine Dr Boynton Beach FL 33436-5524 Office: 1351 William Howard Taft Rd Cincinnati OH 45206-1721

MORGAN, JOHN DAVIS, government and business consultant; b. Newark, Feb. 14, 1921; s. John Davis and Caroline Frommel (Schaller) M.; m. Leta Maude Bretzinger, June 27, 1953; children: John Davis III, Bret Zinger. B.S., Pa. State U., 1942, M.S., 1947, Ph.D., 1948, E.M., 1950; grad. extension course, Indsl. Coll. of Armed Forces, Washington, 1953. Asst. for materials and stockpile policies Nat. Security Resources Bd., Washington, 1948-51; dir. materials rev. div. DPA, Washington, 1951-53; materials expert ODM, Washington, 1953-56; mem. staff President's Cabinet Com. on Mineral Policy, 1953-54; cons. bus. and def. problems in metals, minerals and fuels Washington, 1956-71; mem. nat. def. exec. res. for ODM, 1956-58, OCDM, 1958-61, Office Emergency Planning, 1961-71, Emergency Minerals Adminstrn., 1972-95; mem. spl. stockpile advisory com. to ODM, 1957-58; com. on scope and conduct of materials research NAS, 1959-60, then, mem. com. on mineral sci. and tech., 1966-70; mem. Interagy. Adv. Com. on Mining and Mineral Research, 1977-95; head dept. sci. and math. Daytona Beach C.C., Fla., 1961-71; asst. dir. mineral position analysis U.S. Bur. Mines, Dept. Interior, Washington, 1971-74, acting dir. bur., 1973-74, 77-78, assoc. dir. mineral and materials supply/demand analysis, 1974-79, chief staff officer, 1979-95, Interior Dept. liaison to Coun. Internat. Econ. Policy Staff, 1973-77, to Econ. Policy Bd. Staff, 1974-77, to Dept. Def. Materials Steering Group, 1975-95, to FPA-FEMA Stockpile Com., 1975-88, to Winter Energy Emergency Planning Group of Dept. of Energy, 1977-95; alt. Interior rep. Trade Policy Rev. Group, 1975-81; chmn. minerals rev. com. Non-Fuel Minerals Policy Study, 1978; chmn. materials supply task force NSC Stockpile Study, 1983-87; liaison to Dept. Def. Stockpile Com., 1988-95; mem. Def. Logistics Agy. Market Impact Com., 1988-95; mem. Def. Dept. Adv. Com. Operation and Modernization of Stockpile, 1993-95; U.S. rep. UN Sci. Conf. on Resources, 1949; lectr. numerous univs. including Nat. Def. U., War Coll., Indsl. Coll., Def. Intelligence Coll., 1949—; hon. prof. Indsl. Coll., 1983—; invited spkr. nat. meetings sci. and engring. socs., 1949—. Author: Domestic Mining Industry of the U.S. in World War II, 1949; corr.: Mining Ann. Rev., London, 1958-95; contbr. articles to profl. jours. Served from 2d lt. to maj. Corps Engrs. AUS, 1942-46. Decorated Bronze Star; recipient Distinguished Service gold medal Interior Dept., 1976; named Meritorious Exec. Sr. Exec. Service, 1983. Fellow Soc. Am. Mil. Engrs.; mem. Soc. Research Soc. Am., Soc. Mining Engrs. (Disting. mem.), AIME (nat. Krumb lectr. 1973, Legion of Honor 1989), Mining and Metall. Soc. Am., Am. Def. Preparedness Assn., Sigma Xi, Tau Beta Pi, Sigma Tau, Pi Mu Epsilon, Phi Lambda Upsilon, Phi Kappa Phi, Phi Eta Sigma, Sigma Gamma Epsilon. Club: Cosmos (Washington). Home: 5013 Worthington Dr Bethesda MD 20816-2748

MORGAN, JOHN DERALD, electrical engineer; b. Hays, Kans., Mar. 15, 1939; s. John Baber and Avis Ruth (Wolf) M.; m. Elizabeth June McKneely, June 23, 1962; children: Laura Elizabeth, Kimberly Ann, Rebecca Ruth,

John Derald. BSEE, La. Tech. U., 1962; MS, U. Mo., Rolla, 1965, Degree in Elec. Engring. (hon.), 1987; PhD, Ariz. State U., 1968. Registered profl. engr., forensic engr., Mo., N.Mex. Elec. engr. Tex. Eastman div. Eastman Kodak Co., 1962-63; instr. U. Mo., Rolla, 1963-65, Ariz. State U., 1965-68; asso. prof. elec. engring. U. Mo., Rolla, 1968-72; Alcoa Found. prof. elec. engring. U. Mo., 1972-75, chmn. elec. engring., 1978-85, assoc. dir. Ctr. Internat. Programs, 1970-78, Emerson Electric prof., 1975-85; dean engring. N.Mex. State U., 1985—; cons. to industry. Author: Power Apparatus Testing Techniques, 1969, Computer Monitoring and Control of Electric Utility Systems, 1972, Control and Distribution of Megawatts Through Man-Machine Interaction, 1973, Electromechanical and Electromagnetic Machines and Devices, 1986; also articles. Pres. bd. trustees First Meth. Ch., Rolla, 1971-73; pres. adminstrv. bd. First United Meth. Ch. Rolla, 1978-79; v.p., mem. bd. adminstrn. People to People, 1976; bd. dirs., cubmaster Ozarks dist. Boy Scouts Am., 1968-79, asst. dist. commr., 1971-73, cubmaster Yucca coun., 1986-90, coun. commr., 1989-90, asst. scout master, 1990—, dist. com. Sushine Dist.; dist. chmn. Meramec dist., 1978-80; bd. dirs. Mo. Partners of the Americas. Recipient Scouters Key award and Scouter Tng. award Ozarks coun., Boy Scouts Am., 1971, Dist. award of merit 1977, Silver Beaver award, 1982, Cub Leader award, Webelos Leader award, Sunshine Dist. Yucca coun.; T.H. Harris scholar, 1959-61; John H. Horton scholar, 1961-62. Fellow IEEE (chmn. internat. practices subcom. 1972-79, sec. PSE com., vice chmn., chmn. 1979-85, chmn. ednl. resources subcom. 1973-78, selected award of Merit St. Louis sect., Educators award St. Louis sect., honor award St. Louis sect., Centennial award 1984), Nat. Acad. Forensic Engrs., ASTM; mem. NSPE (bd. govs., nat. dir., vice chmn., S.W. chmn. Profl. Engrs. in Edn.. v.p.), N.Mex. Soc. Profl. Engrs. (N.Mex. Engr. of Yr. 1993), Am. Soc. Engring. Edn., Sigma Xi, Tau Beta Pi, Eta Kappa Nu, Omicron Delta Kappa, Phi Kappa Phi, Kappa Sigma (faculty and alumni advisor), Epsilon Gamma (grand master, grand procurator, PSI exec. of yr. 1993). Home: 2425 Janet Ann Ln Las Cruces NM 88005-5119 Office: NMex State U Main Campus Coll Engring PO Box 30001 Las Cruces NM 88003-8001

MORGAN, JOHN STEPHEN, state legislator, materials science researcher; b. Washington, Dec. 23, 1963; s. James Donald and Virginia Louise (Hendrickson) M. BS, Loyola Coll., Balt., 1984; MS in Engring., Johns Hopkins U., 1988, PhD, 1990. Rsch. assoc. Johns Hopkins U., Balt., 1986-90; sr. engr. Johns Hopkins U., Laurel, Md., 1990—; mem. Md. Ho. of Dels., Annapolis, 1991—; mem. joint com. on legis. ethics Md. Gen. Assembly, Annapolis, 1995—; ranking minority mem. Commerce and Govt. Matters Com., Md. Ho. of Dels., 1995—. Chmn. adv. com. Bd. Edn. Howard County, Md., 1989-90. Recipient Charles Miller award Howard County Rep. Party, 1988. Mem. Am. Phys. Soc. (Congl. Sci. fellow 1994-95), Materials Rsch. Soc., Kiwanis. Lutheran. Home: 7920 Ashford Blvd Laurel MD 20707-5874 Office: Md Gen Assembly Lowe House Office Bldg Annapolis MD 21401

MORGAN, KATHRYN LAWSON, historian, educator; 1 child, Susan Morgan Crooks. M.A., Howard U., 1952, U. Pa., 1967; Ph.D., U. Pa., 1970. Asst. prof. U. Del., Newark, 1970-71; lectr. Swarthmore Coll., Pa., spring 1970, prof. history and folklore, 1972—; vis. assoc. prof. Bryn Mawr Coll., 1972-75, Haverford Coll., 1972-74, U. Calif.-Berkeley, winter 1975; cons. Research for Better Schs., Phila., 1968-69, Black History Mus., Phila., 1966-76, Smithsonian Instn., 1974-76, Ednl. Film Service, 1977. Author: Children of Strangers; Stories of a Black Family, 1980, Books Across the Seas, Selected for Youth, 1981; contbr. articles to profl. jours., mags. Danforth Found. fellow, 1968-70; Smithsonian Instn.-Am. Philos. Soc. grantee, 1983. Avocations: traveling; storytelling; theatre; music. Office: Swarthmore Coll Dept Hist Swarthmore PA 19081

MORGAN, LARRY RONALD, minister; b. Springhill, La., Mar. 12, 1936; s. Woodrow Wilson Morgan and Alma Elizabeth (Dunn) Burch; m. Elizabeth Dianne Baker, May 24, 1958; children: Elizabeth Denise Morgan Davis, Dennis Kevin. ADiv, Bapt. Missionary Assn. Theol. Sem., Jacksonville, Tex., 1990. Ordained to ministry Bapt. Ch., 1971. Clk., carrier U.S. P.O., Springhill, La., 1956-71; assoc. pastor Webb Chapel Bapt. Ch., Dallas, 1971-72, pastor, 1972—; clk., trustee Bapt. Missionary Assn. Sem., Jacksonville, 1983-86; chmn. bd. trustees Bapt. Progress, Dallas, 1984-87. Pres. PTA Browning Elem. Sch., Springhill, 1969-70. With USAR, 1959-66. Mem. Bapt. Missionary Assn. Am. (v.p. hdqrs. Little Rock 1985-86, pres. 1986-88), Dallas County Bapt. Assn. (moderator 1982-84). Home: 14517 Heartside Dr Dallas TX 75234-2152

MORGAN, LAWRENCE ALLISON, headmaster, educational administrator; b. Norman, Okla., June 12, 1935; s. Lawrence Nelson and Catherine (Edwards) Morgan; m. Nancy Catherine Somogyi, July 3, 1960; children: Michael Lawrence, Katherine Elizabeth, Thomas Leverett. AB, Harvard U., 1957; MA, Washington U.-St. Louis, 1969, Webster U., 1977. Faculty, Thomas Jefferson Sch., St. Louis, 1957-66, trustee, 1959—, dir. admissions, 1966-80, v.p., bd. trustees, 1966-80, headmaster, pres., 1980—; trustee Riverways Sch., 1986-87. Bd. dirs. Jefferson Twp., Dem. Club, 1971-72. Episcopalian. Clubs: Harvard Club (St. Louis, Boston, N.Y.C.). Avocations: travel; photography; camping; cycling; hiking. Home: 9112 Pardee Spur Saint Louis MO 63126-2718 Office: Thomas Jefferson Sch 4100 S Lindbergh Blvd Saint Louis MO 63127-1643

MORGAN, LEON ALFORD, retired utility executive; b. Washington, Dec. 29, 1934; s. Albert Lewis and Alice Viets (Alford) M.; children: David Richard, Sherry Alice; m. Jacqueline Jamieson, Feb. 14, 1993. BSEE, Worcester (Mass.) Poly. Inst., 1957. Registered profl. engr., Conn. With United Illuminating Co., New Haven, 1957-94; gen. ops. mgr., then v.p. ops. United Illuminating Co., 1973-76, exec. v.p., 1976-83, sr. v.p. fin., 1984-94. Republican. Episcopalian. Home: 43 Forest Brook Rd Guilford CT 06437-2245

MORGAN, LEWIS RENDER, federal judge; b. LaGrange, Ga., July 14, 1913; s. William Ellington and Bettie (Render) M.; m. Sue Phillips, July 29, 1944; children: Parks Healy, Sue Ann. Student, U. Mich., 1930-32; LLB, U. Ga., 1935; LLB (hon.), Atlanta Law Sch., 1963, La Grange Coll., 1977. Bar: Ga. 1935. Mem. Wyatt & Morgan, LaGrange, 1935-61; judge U.S. Dist. Ct. (no. dist.) Ga., 1961-68, chief judge, 1965-68; judge U.S. Cir. Ct. Appeals (5th and 11th cirs.), Newnan, Ga., 1968—, now sr. justice; Mem. budget com. U.S. Courts, 1967—; Mem. Gen. Assembly Ga., 1937-39; exec. sec. A. Sidney Camp (congressman), 1939-42; Mem. visitors com. U. Ga. Law Sch., 1970-73; mem. spl. div. U.S. Ct. Appeals for D.C., 1978—; mem. Temporary Emergency Ct. Appeals, 1979—. Mem. Chi Psi, Phi Delta Phi. Presbyn. Home: Cameron Mill Rd La Grange GA 30240 Office: US Ct Appeals 11th Cir PO Box 759 Newnan GA 30264-0759*

MORGAN, LINDA J., federal agency administrator; m. Michael E. Karam; 1 child, Meredith Lyn. AB in Hispanic Studies, Vassar Coll., 1973; JD, Georgetown U., 1976; postgrad., Harvard U., 1991. Assoc. Welch & Morgan, Washington; staff counsel U.S. Senate Com. on Commerce, Sci. and Transp., 1978-86, gen. counsel; mem. Interstate Commerce Commn., Washington, 1994—, chmn., 1995—. Mem. D.C. Bar Assn., Women's Bar Assn., Women's Transp. Seminar. Office: Comm on Commerce Science & Trans 508 Dirksen Senate Bldg Washington DC 20510*

MORGAN, LONA SCAGGS, speech professional educator; b. Chillicothe, Ohio, Oct. 2, 1949; d. Drewey P. and Ruth A. (McCloskey) Scaggs; m. Terry A. Morgan, Dec. 23, 1972; 1 child, Zachary Drew Morgan. BS in Hearing and Speech Sci., Ohio U., 1971; MEd in Adminstrn., Supervision, U. South Fla., 1983. Cert. speech and hearing sci., ednl. adminstrn. Speech pathologist Ross County Soc. for Crippled Children and Adults, Chillicothe, 1971; speech pathologist Zanesville (Ohio) City Schs., 1971-72, Hernando County Schs., Brooksville, Fla., 1973-74, Pasco County Sch. Dist., New Port Richey, Fla., 1974—; speech pathologist, speech mentor Pasco County Sch. Dist., 1994—. Recipient Pasco Pub. Schs. Found. grant, 1993. Mem. Fla. Speech and Hearing Assn., West Paco Jr. Woman's Club, Phi Delta Kappa. Methodist. Avocations: reading, travel, country-western line dancing. Home: 7011 Tanglewood Dr New Port Richey FL 34654-5721 Office: Pasco County School Board Calusa Elem School 5720 Orchid Lake Dr New Port Richey FL 34654

MORGAN, LORRIE (LORETTA LYNN MORGAN), country singer; b. Nashville, June 27, 1959; d. George Morgan; divorced; m. Keith Whitley (dec. 1989); children: Morgan, Jesse. Rec. artist RCA, 1989—. Albums: Leave the Light On, 1989, Something in Red, 1991, Tell Me I'm Dreaming, 1992, Watch Me, 1992, Trainwreck of Emotion, 1993, Greatest Hits, 1995; (with Sammy Kershaw) War Paint, 1994; #1 Song: I Didn't Know My Own Strength; #1 gold single: Something in Red, 1991; TV movies include: Proudheart, 1993, ABC Movie of the Week - The Enemy Within, 1995. Office: care Susan Nadler Mgmt 1313 16th Ave S Nashville TN 37212

MORGAN, LOU ANN, physical education educator; b. Andrews, N.C., Apr. 26, 1949; d. Jerry Myditt and Alice Josephine (O'Dell) Long; m. Frederick Wayne Morgan, July 9, 1972; children: Mandi Marie, Chad William. BS, Mars Hill Coll., 1971. Tchr. Farmer (N.C.) Elem. Sch., 1971-74, Flat Rock (N.C.) Jr. High Sch., 1974-81; craft dir. Camp Windy Wood, Tuxedo, N.C., 1981-84; tchr. weekday early edn. 1st Bapt. Ch., Hendersonville, N.C., 1983-84; phys. edn. specialist Dana (N.C.) Elem. Sch., 1984—. Co-author: (video) Outdoor Education ... Success for Everyon, 1993. Mem. scholarship com. 1st Bapt. Ch., Hendersonville, 1993—, mem. weekday early edn. com., 1985-86, mem. recreation/activities com., 1993-94. Named Outstanding Spring Vol. Henderson County Parks and Recreation, 1992; recipient Gov.'s Award for Fitness N.C. Gov.'s Coun. on Phys. Fitness and Health, 1994. Mem. AAHPERD, N.C. Assn. Health, Phys. Edn., Recreation and Dance (phys. edn. Western regional rep. 1994-95, Phys. Edn. Leadership Tng. steering com. 1989, 93, presider, presenter 1991, 94, Norm Leafe State Phys. Edn. Tchr. of Yr. 1990). Republican. Baptist. Avocations: painting, gardening, biking, fitness. Home: 447 Sunset Dr Hendersonville NC 28791 Office: Dana Elem Sch PO Box 37 Dana NC 28724-0037

MORGAN, LUCY W., journalist; b. Memphis, Oct. 11, 1940; d. Thomas Allin and Lucile (Sanders) Keen; m. Alton F. Ware, June 26, 1958 (div. Sept. 1967); children—Mary Kathleen, Andrew Allin; m. Richard Alan Morgan, Aug. 9, 1968; children—Lynn Elwell, Kent Morgan. A.A., Pasco Hernando Community Coll., New Port Richey, Fla., 1975; student, U. South Fla., 1976-80. Reporter Ocala Star Banner, Fla., 1965-68; reporter St. Petersburg Times, Fla., 1967-86, capitol bur. chief, 1986—; assoc. editor and bd. dirs. Times Pub. Co. Recipient Paul Hansel award Fla. Soc. Newspaper Editors, 1981, First in Pub. Service award Fla. Soc. Newspaper Editors, 1982, First Place award in pub. service Fla. Press Club, 1982, Pulitzer award for investigative reporting Columbia U., 1985, First Place award in investigative reporting Sigma Delta Chi, 1985; named to Kappa Tau Alpha Hall of Fame, 1992. Home: 1727 Brookside Blvd Tallahassee FL 32301-6769 Office: St Petersburg Times 336 E College Ave Tallahassee FL 32301-1551

MORGAN, MARABEL, author; b. Crestline, Ohio, June 25, 1937; d. Howard and Delsa (Smith) Hawk; m. Charles O. Morgan, Jr., June 25, 1964; children—Laura Lynn, Michelle Rene. Ed., Ohio State U. Pres. Total Woman, Inc., Miami, Fla., 1970—; pub. speaker. Author: The Total Woman, 1973, Total Joy, 1976, The Total Woman Cookbook, 1980, The Electric Woman, 1985. Office: care Total Woman Inc 1300 NW 167th St Miami FL 33169-5738

MORGAN, MARILYN, federal judge; b. 1947; 1 child, Terrence M. Adamson. BA, Emory U., 1969, JD, 1976. Bar: Ga. 1976, Calif. 1977. Ptnr. Morgan & Towery, San Jose, Calif., 1979-88; bankruptcy judge U.S. Bankruptcy Ct. (no. dist.) Calif., 1988—; mem. bankruptcy adv. com. U.S. Dist. Ct., 1984-88; law rep. 9th Cir. Jud. Conf., 1987-88. Mem. adv. bd. Downtown YMCA, 1984-88; dir. The Women's Fund, 1987-88. Mem. Santa Clara County Bar Assn. (chmn. debtor and creditor and insolvency com. 1979, 81, treas. 1982, pres. 1985-86), Santa Clara County Bar Assn. Law Found. (trustee 1982, 86-88, pres. 1985, law related edn. trustee 1986-88), Nat. Assn. Bankruptcy Trustees (founding mem., v.p., sec. 1981-88), Rotary Club San Jose (bd. dirs. 1992—), Nat. Assn. Bankruptcy Trustees (founder). Office: US Bankruptcy Ct 280 S 1st St Rm 3035 San Jose CA 95113-3010*

MORGAN, MELANIE KARYN, lawyer; b. Kans. City, Mo., July 29, 1962; married; 2 children. BA in Philosophy, Coll. of William and Mary, 1984, JD, 1987. Bar: Tex. 1987. Assoc. atty. Geary, Stahl & Spencer, Dallas, 1987-89; atty. PepsiCo, Inc.-Frito-Lay, Inc., Dallas, 1989-91, sr. atty., 1991-94, of counsel, 1994—. Mem. ABA, Dallas Bar Assn., Dallas Assn. Young Lawyers, Collin County Bar Assn., Promotion Mktg. Assn. of Am. (legal com.).

MORGAN, MONROE, retired savings and loan executive; b. Long Beach, Calif., Sept. 4, 1921; s. Karle Barett and Ethel (Monroe) M.; m. Ann Betts, Sept. 30, 1949; children: Sarah Nell, Daniel, Margaret Jane. BA, Pomona Coll., 1942. Cert. vol. counselor Health Ins. Counseling and Advocacy Program, Calif. Acctg. exec. Coast Fed. Savs. and Loan Assn., Los Angeles, 1945-50; sec., treas. Am. Savs. and Loan Assn., Whittier, Calif., 1952-56; sr. v.p. Gt. Western Fin. Corp., Beverly Hills, Calif., 1956-87; also officer subs. savs. and loan assns.; trustee Depositors Investment Trust, 1984-85; mem. investment mgmt. com. Internat. Found. Employees Plans, 1970-76; chmn. Thrift Industry Acctg. Com., 1976-78. Active Los Angeles County Art Mus.; chmn. Ethnic Arts Coun., 1977-80; dir. non-profit food distbn. orgn. Love Is Feeding Everyone, 1986-90, treas., 1981-94; bd. dirs. Amberjack, Ltd., Bloomington, Ill., 1985; mem. alumni coun. Pomona Coll., 1989-92, chmn. edn. com., 1992-94. Maj. USMCR, 1942-45, 50-51. Mem. Savs. and Loan Instns. (bd. govs. 1957-62), Fin. Mgrs. Soc. for Savs. Instns., Calif. Savs. and Loan League, Savs. Assns. Fin. Execs. (pres. 1968-75), Fin. Analysts Fedn. Home: 922 San Vicente Blvd Santa Monica CA 90402-2004

MORGAN, NEIL, author, newspaper editor, lecturer, columnist; b. Smithfield, N.C., Feb. 27, 1924; s. Samuel Lewis and Isabelle (Robeson) M.; m. Caryl Lawrence, 1945 (div. 1954); m. Katharine Starkey, 1955 (div. 1962); m. Judith Blakely, 1964; 1 child, Jill. AB, Wake Forest Coll., 1943. Columnist San Diego Daily Jour., 1946-50; columnist San Diego Evening Tribune, 1950-92, assoc. editor, 1977-81, editor, 1981-92; assoc. editor, sr. columnist San Diego Union-Tribune, 1992—; syndicated columnist Morgan Jour., Copley News Service, 1958—; lectr.; cons. on Calif. affairs Bank of Am., Sunset mag. Author: My San Diego, 1951, It Began With a Roar, 1953, Know Your Doctor, 1954, Crosstown, 1955, My San Diego 1960, 1959, Westward Tilt, 1963, Neil Morgan's San Diego, 1964, The Pacific States, 1967, The California Syndrome, 1969, (with Robert Witty) Marines of Margarita, 1970, The Unconventional City, 1972, (with Tom Blair) Yesterday's San Diego, 1976, This Great Land, 1983, Above San Diego, 1990, (with Judith Morgan) Dr. Seuss & Mr. Geisel, 1995; conbr. non-fiction articles to Nat. Geog., Esquire, Redbook, Reader's Digest, Holiday, Harper's, Travel and Leisure, Ency. Brittanica. Served to lt. USNR, 1943-46. Recipient Ernie Pyle Meml. award, 1957, Bill Corum Meml. award, 1961, Disting. Svc. citation Wake Forest U., 1966, grand award for travel writing Pacific Area Travel Assn., 1972, 78, Fourth Estate award San Diego State U., 1988, The Morgan award Leadership Edn. Awareness Devel. San Diego, 1993; co-recipient Ellen and Roger Revelle award, 1986; named Outstanding Young Man of Yr. San Diego, 1959. Mem. Authors Guild, Am. Soc. Newspaper Editors, Soc. Profl. Journalists, Explorers Club, Soc. of Am. Travel Writers, Bohemian Club, Phi Beta Kappa, Omicron Delta Kappa. Home: 7930 Prospect Pl La Jolla CA 92037-3721 Office: PO Box 191 San Diego CA 92112-4106

MORGAN, PETER F., English educator, philosophy educator; b. Stafford, Eng., Sept. 1, 1930; s. Frederick John and Kathleen (May) M.; m. Eleanor Thompson, 1958 (div. 1983); children: Peter, Martin, Alison, Katy. BA, U. Birmingham, U.K., 1951; MA, U. London, 1955, PhD, 1957. Lectr. Victoria Coll., B.C., 1959-60; lectr. U. Toronto, 1960-64, asst. prof., 1964-68, assoc. prof., 1968-74, prof., 1974—; chmn. panel symposium on visual rhetoric Scarborough Coll., 1991, mem. panel on futurism, 1991. Author: Literary Critics and Reviewers in Early Nineteenth-Century Britain, 1983, Poetic and Pictorial Elements, 1992; editor: The Letters of Thomas Hood, 1973, Jeffrey's Criticism, 1983; co-editor Victorian Periodicals Rev., 1973-78, also adv. editor, 1979—, Ultimate Reality and Meaning, 1989—; cons. editor Jour. Mental Imagery, 1986—; contbr. articles to profl. jours. Mem. Soc. Study of Ultimate Reality and Meaning (pres. 1992—). Office: Int'l Society Study Human Ideas, University of Toronto, Toronto, ON Canada M5S 1A1

MORGAN, RAYMOND F., plastic surgeon; b. Pitts., Apr. 24, 1948; s. Edwin J. and Alberta (Hirt) M.; m. Sue Ann Malone, Oct. 3, 1951; children: Ryan Frederic, Alexander Evan, Elizabeth Anne. BS, U. Pitts., 1969, MEd, 1972, DMD, 1972; MD, W.Va. U., 1976. Diplomate Am. Bd. Plastic Surgery, Am. Bd. Hand Surgery. Intern Johns Hopkins U. Hosp., Balt., 1976-77, resident surgery, 1977-80, resident plastic surgery, 1980-82; resident hand surgery Union Meml. Hosp., Balt.; staff U. Va. Health Scis. Ctr., Charlottesville, M.T. Edgerton prof., chmn. dept. plastic surgery, 1988—. Mem. ACS, Soc. Univ. Surgeons, So. Surg. Assn., Am. Soc. for Surgery of the Hand, Am. Assn. Plastic Surgeons. Office: U of Va Dept of Plastic Surgery Charlottesville VA 22908

MORGAN, RAYMOND VICTOR, JR., university administrator, mathematics educator; b. Brownwood, Tex., May 10, 1942; s. Raymond Victor and Lovey Lucile (Tate) M.; m. Mary Jane Folks, Aug. 13, 1967; children: Jason Wesley, Jeremy Victor. BA, Howard Payne U., 1965; MA, Vanderbilt U., 1966; PhD, U. Mo., 1969. Asst. prof. So. Meth. U., Dallas, 1969-75; assoc. prof. Sul Ross State U., Alpine, Tex., 1975-82, math. dept. chmn., 1976-85, prof., 1982—, dean of scis., 1979-86, exec. asst. pres., 1985-90, pres., 1990—; bd. dirs. Tex. Internat. Edn. Consortium; bd. dirs. Southwestern Livestock Exposition, 1993—. Author textbook: Agricultural Mathematics, 1978; author articles. Founder, regional commr. Alpine Soccer League, 1984; v.p., coach Alpine Baseball League, 1983; pres. Alpine PTA, 1982-83; founder, pres. So. Meth. U. Faculty Club, 1973-75; mem. exec. com. Tex. Assn. Coll. and Univ. Student Personnel Adminstrs., 1990-92. NSF grantee, 1979. Mem. Am. Assn. Higher Edn., Tex. Assn. Coll. Tchrs. (chpt. v.p. 1978-79), Math. Assn. Am. (chmn. Tex. sect. 1985-86). Republican. Mem. Ch. of Christ. Clubs: Lions (pres. 1979-80, Lion of Yr. 1980, 83), Alpine Country. Avocations: motorcycling, golf, shooting. Home: PO Box 1341 Alpine TX 79831-1341 Office: Sul Ross State U E Highway 90 PO Box C114 Alpine TX 79831-0114

MORGAN, RHELDA ELNOLA, secondary school educator; b. St. Louis, June 10, 1947; d. Harry and Lillie Bertha (Citizen) Marbry; m. Edward Lee Morgan; 1 child, Tawanna Ka-Rhelda. BA in Edn., Harris-Stowe Coll., 1968; MA in Teaching, Webster U., 1981; postgrad., St. Louis U., 1989—. Primary tchr. Brunswick Elem. Sch., Gary, Ind., 1969-72, Walbridge Sch., St. Louis, 1972-84; lang. arts tchr. Ford Mid. Sch., St. Louis, 1984-87; lang. arts tchr., lang. dept. chairperson Marquette Visual & Performing Arts Mid. Sch., St. Louis, 1987-88; English tchr. Cen. Visual & Performing Arts High Sch., St. Louis, 1988-89, social studies tchr., 1989-90, English/fgn. lang. dept. chairperson, 1989-93; counselor Hugh O'Brian Youth Seminar, St. Louis, 1992, 93; English tchr. Soldan Internat. High Sch., St. Louis, 1993—; cons. for scholarship pageant edn. dept. Ch. of God in Christ, Jurisdiction 1, St. Louis, 1988-89; mem. adj. faculty Harris-Stowe State Coll., 1994—; mem. edn. adv. com. Principia Coll., 1993—; supervising tchr. for apprentices and practice tchrs. Recipient Trophy for 14 Yrs. as Aux. Treas. Mem. Nat. Coun. Tchrs. English, Popular Culture/Am. Culture, Ladies Aux. VFW (treas. 2910, 1972-86). Pentecostal. Avocations: reading, crocheting.

MORGAN, RICHARD ERNEST, political scientist, educator; b. Centre County, Pa., May 17, 1937; s. James Ernest and Helen Estelle (Hogge) M. A.B., Bowdoin Coll., Brunswick, Maine, 1959; A.M., Columbia U., 1961, Ph.D., 1967. Instr. in govt. Columbia U., 1962-63, 65-67, asst. prof. govt., 1967-68; asso. prof. govt. Bowdoin Coll., 1969-75, William Nelson Cromwell prof. constl. law and govt., 1975—; fellow in law and govt. Harvard U. Law Sch., 1968-69; research dir. Twentieth Century Fund Project on Polit. Surveillance in Am., 1975-79. Author: The Politics of Religious Conflict, 1968, The Supreme Court and Religion, 1972, (with others) American Politics: Directions of Change, Dynamics of Choice, 1979, Domestic Intelligence: Monitoring Dissent in America, 1980, Disabling America: The Rights Industry in Our Time, 1984, People, Power and Politics, 1994; contbr. articles to profl. publs.; editor: (with James E. Connor) The American Political System: Introductory Readings, 1971. Chmn. Spl. Commn. on Legis. Compensation, State of Maine, 1973-74; chmn. Maine adv. com. U.S. Commn. on Civil Rights, 1985-87. Served to 1st lt. U.S. Army, 1963-65. Mem. Am. Polit. Sci. Assn., New. Eng. Polit. Sci. Assn. (pres. 1988-89). Republican. Episcopalian. Home: RR 2 South Harpswell ME 04079-9802 Office: Bowdoin Coll Brunswick ME 04011

MORGAN, RICHARD GREER, lawyer; b. Houston, Dec. 23, 1943; s. John Benjamin (stepfather) and Audrey Valley (Brickwede) Haus; children: Richard Greer, Jonathan Roberts. AB in History, Princeton U., 1966; JD, U. Tex., 1969. Bar: Tex. 1969, D.C. 1970, Minn. 1976, U.S. Ct. Appeals (D.C. cir.) 1970, U.S. Ct. Appeals (5th and 9th cirs., temporary emergency ct. appeals) 1976. Atty., advisor to commr. Lawrence J. O'Connor, Jr. Fed. Power Commn., Washington, 1969-71; assoc. Morgan, Lewis & Bockius, Washington, 1971-75; ptnr. O'Connor & Hannan, Washington, 1975-89, Lane & Mittendorf, Washington, 1989—; bd. dirs. Hexagon, Inc.; instr. law seminars; lectr. in field. Author: Gas Lease and Royalty Issues, Natural Gas Yearbook, 1989, 90, 91, 92; contbr. articles on energy law to profl. jours. Bd. dirs. Florence Crittenton Home, U. Tex. Law Sch. Found. Mem. ABA, Fed. Bar Assn. (bd. dirs.), Fed. Energy Bar Assn., D.C. Bar Assn., Princeton Alumni Council, Princeton Club Washington (exec. com., pres.-elect). Home: 2772 Unicorn Ln NW Washington DC 20015-2234 Office: 919 18th St NW Fl 8 Washington DC 20006-5503

MORGAN, ROBERT ARTHUR, accountant; b. Decatur, Ill., Oct. 23, 1918; s. Robert Howard and Katherine (Massey) M.; m. Julia Ann Franklin, June 28, 1941; children: Robert A., Susan Ruth. BS, U. Ill., 1941. Acct. Pure Oil Co., 1941; acct. Caterpillar Tractor Co., Peoria, Ill., 1945-56, controller, 1956-78; mem. Fin. Acct. Standards Bd., Stamford, Conn., 1978-82; cons. Morton, Ill., 1982—. Contbr. articles to acctg. periodicals. Past mem. fin. acctg. standards adv. coun. Fin. Acctg. Found.; pres. bd. edn. Morton Twp. High Sch., 1960-68. Civilian auditor AUS, 1942-44. Mem. Nat. Assn. Accts. (nat. dir., nat. v.p. 1965-66, chmn. mng. practices 1974-75), Machinery and Allied Products Inst. (fin. coun. II 1956-78), Fin. Execs. Inst. (mem. com. corp. reporting 1977-78), Internat. Fedn. Accts. (chmn. com. fin. and mgmt. acctg. 1983).

MORGAN, ROBERT B., insurance company executive; b. 1934. AB, Eastern Ky. U., 1954. Tchr. Ind. Sch. System, 1954-56; casualty underwriter Ins. Co. of N.Am., Phila., 1960-66; asst. casualty mgr. Cin. Ins. Co., Inc., 1966-69, asst. v.p., 1969-71, v.p., gen. mgr., 1972-75, exec. v.p., gen. mgr., 1975, pres., 1976, pres., chief exec. officer, 1986—; pres. Cin. Fin. Corp., 1981, pres., chief exec. officer, 1991—. Capt. AUS, 1956-58. Office: Cin Fin Corp PO Box 145496 6200 S Gilmore Rd Cincinnati OH 45250*

MORGAN, ROBERT DALE, federal judge; b. Peoria, Ill., May 27, 1912; s. Harry Dale and Eleanor (Ellis) M.; m. Betty Louise Harbers, Oct. 14, 1939; children—Thomas Dale, James Robert. A.B., Bradley U., 1934; J.D., U. Chgo., 1937. Bar: Ill. 1937. Practice in Peoria, 1937-42, 46-67, Chgo., 1946-50; partner firm Morgan, Pendarvis & Morgan, Peoria, 1946-57, Davis, Morgan & Witherell, Peoria, 1957-67; U.S. judge So. Dist Ill. (became Central Dist. 1979), Peoria, 1967—, sr. status U.S. judge, 1982. Contbr. articles to law revs. Mayor, Peoria, 1953-57; Bd. dirs. YMCA, Peoria, 1940-72, pres., 1947-53; Trustee Bradley U. Served from 1st lt. to maj. AUS, 1942-46. Mem. ABA, Am. Judicature Soc., Ill. Bar Assn., Peoria County Bar Assn. Presbyterian. Clubs: Creve Couer (Peoria), Rotary (Peoria) (pres. 1962-63), Country (Peoria). Office: US Dist Ct 228 Fed Bldg 100 NE Monroe St Peoria IL 61602-1003

MORGAN, ROBERT MARION, educational research educator; b. Ponca City, Okla., Feb. 5, 1930; s. Perry Harrison and Velma Beatrice (Stowe) M.; m. Constance Louise Claus, Jan. 3, 1963; children—Stephen, Melayne. B.S., Okla. State U., 1955, M.S., 1956; Ph.D., Ohio State U., 1958; LL.D., Dongah U., Pusan, Korea. Asst. prof. U. N.M., 1958-62; pres. Gen. Programmed Teaching Corp., Palo Alto, Calif., 1961-64; v.p. Ranchers Corp., Albuquerque, 1962-64; dir. ednl. systems Litton Industries, College Park, Md., 1964-66; dep. dir. div. vocational research U.S. Office Edn., Washington, 1966-68; prof., head dept. ednl. research Fla. State U., Tallahassee, 1968-74; dir. Center for Ednl. Tech., 1968-75, Learning Systems Inst., 1975—; Lectr. Catholic U. Am., 1966-68, Seoul (Korea) Nat. U., 1970-71; cons. AID, Republic of Brazil, Korea, Italian Air Force, Navy Dept., U.S. Naval Acad.; Chmn. Fla. Research and Devel. Council, 1969—; mem. sch. bd. U. Sch., Tallahassee, 1969-74. Author: Programmed Instruction—A Concept of Learning, 1963, An Educational Systems Analysis for the Republic of Korea, 1970; also articles. Bd. dirs. U.S. Coalition for Edn. for

All, 1992—; trustee Aerospace Ednl. Found. With AUS, 1949-52. Fellow Royal Soc. Arts; mem. Am. Ednl. Research Assn., Am. Psychol. Assn., Nat. Soc. for Programmed Instrn., Am. Mgmt. Assn., Sigma Xi. Republican. Presbyterian. Lodge: Rotary. Home: 3322 Remington Run Tallahassee FL 32312-1462 Office: Fla State Univ 205 Dodd Hall Tallahassee FL 32306

MORGAN, ROBERT P., music theorist, educator; b. Nashville, July 28, 1934; s. Hugh J. and Robert (Porter) M.; m. Carole Ann Montgomery, June 12, 1965. BA, Princeton U., 1956, MFA, 1960, PhD, 1969; MA, U. Calif., 1958. Instr. U. Houston, 1963-67; asst. prof. Temple U., Phila., 1967-70, assoc. prof., 1970-75, prof., 1975-79; prof. U. Chgo., 1979-89, Yale U., New Haven, 1989—; vis. prof. U. Pa., Phila., 1976-78, Yale U., 1987; adv. bd. Fromm Music Found., Chgo., 1984-89. Author: Twentieth Century Music, 1991; mem. editorial bd. Critical Inquiry, 1980—, Studies in the Criticism and Theory of Music, 1981—, Composers of the Twentieth Century; composer orch., chamber ensemble, voice and piano works; articles in field. Grantee German Govt., 1960-62; Woodrow Wilson fellow, 1956-57, NEH sr. fellow, 1983-84. Mem. Am. Musicol. Soc. (council mem. 1982-85), Soc. for Music Theory (bd. dirs. 1985—), Coll. Music Soc., Yale Club (N.Y.C.). Democrat. Avocations: tennis, skiing. Office: Yale Univ Dept Of Music New Haven CT 06520-8310

MORGAN, ROBERT PETER, engineering educator; b. Bklyn., Feb. 26, 1934; s. Jack and Minna (Cohen) M.; m. Nancy Beverly Hutchins, Dec. 20, 1958; children: Thomas Albert, Jonathan Andrew. B.Ch.E., Cooper Union, 1956; S.M., MIT, 1959, Nucl.E., 1961; Ph.D., Rensselaer Poly. Inst., 1965. Asst. dir. MIT Practice Sch., Oak Ridge, 1958-59; instr. chem. engring. Rensselaer Poly. Inst., 1960-64; asst. prof. nuclear and chem. engring. U. Mo., 1964-68; assoc. prof. engring. Washington U., St. Louis, 1968-74, prof. tech. and human affairs, 1974-87, Elvera and William Stuckenberg prof. tech. and human affairs, 1987—, dir. Ctr. for Tech. Assessment and Policy, 1968—, chmn. dept. tech. and human affairs, 1976-83; sci. and pub. policy fellow Brookings Instn., 1982-83; council mem. Vols. in Tech. Assistance; chmn. adv. subcom. NASA Tech. Transfer Program, 1978-80; mem. nat. adv. bd. program on ethics and values in sci. and tech. NSF, 1977-79; mem. com. on research grants NRC, 1983-86; Sigma Xi nat. lectr., 1981-83; vis. sr. analyst Office of Tech. Assessment of U.S. Congress, 1989-90. Author: The Role of U.S. Universities in Science and Technology for Development, 1979, Renewable Resource Utilization for Development, 1981; Science and Technology for International Development: An Assessment of U.S. Policies and Programs, 1984; contbr. numerous articles to profl. publs.; mem. editorial bd. Telecommunications Policy, 1976-80, Sci., Tech. and Human Values, 1977-79, 81-88 . Recipient Disting. Faculty award Washington U., 1989; AEC fellow, 1959-60. Fellow AAAS (com. on sci., engring. and pub. policy 1977-80, program com. 1992—); mem. AAUP, Fedn. Am. Scientists, Am. Soc. Engring. Edn. (Chester F. Carlson award 1978), Tau Beta Pi. Office: Washington U Campus Box 1106 Saint Louis MO 63130

MORGAN, ROBIN EVONNE, poet, author, journalist, activist, editor; b. Lake Worth, Fla., Jan. 29, 1941; 1 child, Blake Ariel. Grad. with honors, The Wetter Sch., 1956; student, pvt. tutors, 1956-59, Columbia U.; DHL (hon.), U. Conn., 1992. Free-lance book editor, 1961-69; editor Grove Press, 1967-70; editor, columnist World column Ms. Mag., N.Y.C., 1974-87, editor in chief, 1989-93, internat. cons. editor, 1993—; vis. chair and guest prof. women's studies New Coll., Sarasota, Fla., 1973; disting. vis. scholar, lectr. Ctr. Critical Analysis of Contemporary Culture, Rutgers U., 1987; invited spl. cons. UN com. UN Conv. to End All Forms Discrimination Against Women, Sao Paulo and Brasilia, Brazil, 1987; mem. adv. bd. ISIS (internat. network women's internat. cross-cultural exch.); spl. advisor gen. assembly conf. on Gender UN Internat. Sch., 1985-86; free-lance journalist, lectr. cons., editor, 1969—; invited speaker numerous confs., orgns., acad. meetings, U.S. and abroad. Author, compiler, editor: Sisterhood Is Powerful: An Anthology of Writings from the Women's Liberation Movement, 1970, Swedish edit., 1972, Sisterhood Is Global: The International Women's Movement Anthology, 1984, U.K. edit., 1985, Spanish edit., 1994; author: (nonfiction) Going Too Far: The Personal Chronicle of a Feminist, 1978, German edit., 1978, The Anatomy of Freedom: Feminism, Physics and Global Politics, 1982, 2d edit., 1994, fgn. edits. U.K., 1984, Germany, 1985, Argentina, 1986, Brazil, 1992, The Demon Lover: On the Sexuality of Terrorism, 1989, U.K. edit., 1989, Japanese edit., 1992, The Word of a Woman: Feminist Dispatches 1968-91, 1992, 2d edit., 1994, U.K. edit., 1992, Chinese edit., 1996, A Woman's Creed, English, Arabic, French, Russian, Spanish, Portuguese, Chinese and Persian edits., 1995, (fiction) Dry Your Smile: A Novel, 1987, U.K. edit., 1988, The Mer-Child: A New Legend, 1991, German edit., 1995 (poetry) Monster: Poems, 1972, Lady of the Beasts: Poems, 1976, Death Benefits: Poems, 1981, Depth Perception: New Poems and a Masque, 1982, Upstairs in the Garden: Selected and New Poems, 1968-88, 1990, (plays) In Another Country, 1960, The Duel, 1979; co-editor: The Woman: Anthology, 1969; contbr. numerous articles, essays, book revs., poems to various publs.; presenter poetry readings, univs., poetry ctrs., radio, TV, others, 1970—. Mem. 1st women's liberation caucus CORE, 1965, Student Nonviolent Coordinating Com., 1966; organizer 1st feminist demonstration against Miss Am. Pageant, 1968; founder, pres. The Sisterhood Fund, 1970; founder, pres. N.Y. Women's Law Ctr., 1970; founder N.Y. Women's Ctr., 1969; co-founder, bd. dirs. Feminist Women's Health Network, Nat. Battered Women's Refuge Network, Nat. Network Rape Crisis Ctrs.; bd. dirs. Women's Fgn. Policy Coun.; adv. trustee Nat. Women's Inst. for Freedom of Press; founding mem. Nat. Mus. Women in Arts; co-founder Sisterhood is Global Inst. (internat. think-tank), 1984, officer, 1989—, co-organizer, U.S. mem. official visit Coalition of Philippines Women's Movement, 1988; chair N.Y. state com. Hands Across Am. Com. for Justice and Empowerment, 1988; mem. adv. bd. Global Fund for Women. Recipient Front Page award for disting. journalism, Wonder Woman award for internat. peace and understanding, 1982, Feminist of Yr. award Fund for Feminist majority, 1990; writer-in-residence grantee Yaddo, 1980; grantee Nat. Endowment for Arts, 1979-80, Ford Found., 1982, 83, 84. Mem. Feminist Writers' Guild, Media Women, N.Am. Feminist Coalition, Pan Arab Feminist Solidarity Assn. (hon.), Israeli Feminists Against Occupation (hon.). Office: Ms Mag 230 Park Ave New York NY 10169-0005

MORGAN, RUTH PROUSE, academic administrator, educator; b. Berkeley, Calif., Mar. 30, 1934; d. Ervin Joseph and Thelma Ruth (Prcesang) Prouse; m. Vernon Edward Morgan, June 3, 1956; children: Glenn Edward, Renée Ruth. BA summa cum laude, U. Tex., 1956; MA, La. State U., 1961, PhD, 1966. Asst. prof. Am. govt., politics and theory So. Meth. U., Dallas, 1966-70, assoc. prof., 1970-74, prof., 1974-95; prof. emeritus, 1995—; asst. provost So. Meth. U., Dallas, 1978-82, assoc. provost, 1982-86, provost ad interim, 1986-87, provost, 1987-93, provost emerita, 1993—; pres. RPM Assocs., 1993—; v.p. ABATECH, Inc., 1995—; Tex. state polit. analyst ABC, N.Y.C., 1972-84. Author: The President and Civil Rights, 1970; mem. editorial bd. Jour. of Politics, 1975-82, Presdl. Studies Quar., 1980—; contbr. articles to profl. jours. Active Internat. Women's Forum, 1987—; trustee Hockaday Sch., 1988-94; trustee The Kilby Awards Found., 1993-95; bd. dirs. United Way, Met. Dallas, 1993—; mem. adv. com. U.S. Army Command and Gen. Staff. Coll., 1994—; chmn. adv. com. Archives of Women of the Southwest, 1995—. Mem. Am. Polit. Sci. Assn., So. Polit. Sci. Assn. (mem. exec. coun. 1979-84), Southwestern Polit. Sci. Assn. (pres. 1982-83, mem. exec. coun. 1981-84), The Dallas Forum of Internat. Women's Forum (pres. 1996-98), Charter 100 Club (pres. 1991-92), Dallas Summit Club (pres. 1992-93), Phi Beta Kappa, Pi Sigma Alpha, Phi Kappa Phi, Theta Sigma Phi. Avocations: photography, travel.

MORGAN, SAMUEL P(OPE), physicist, applied mathematician; b. San Diego, July 14, 1923; s. Samuel Pope and Beatrice Marie (Summers) M.; m. Mary Caroline Annin, Jan. 23, 1948; children: Caroline Gail, Lesley Anne, Alison Lee, Diane Elizabeth. B.S., Calif. Inst. Tech., 1943, M.S., 1944, Ph.D. in Physics, 1947. Mem. tech. staff AT&T Bell Labs., Murray Hill, N.J., 1947-59; head dept. math. physics AT&T Bell Labs., 1959-67, dir. computing tech., 1969-70, dir. computing sci. research center, 1967-82, disting. mem. tech. staff, 1982—. Research, publs. on electromagnetic theory, applied math., queueing theory; patentee in field. Fellow IEEE; mem. AAAS, Am. Phys. Soc., Sigma Xi. Home: 9 Raleigh Ct Morristown NJ 07960-2535 Office: AT&T Bell Labs New Providence NJ 07974

MORGAN, SCOTT ELLINGWOOD, publisher, lawyer; b. Kansas City, Kans., June 29, 1957; s. Ray Ellingwood and Mary Grace (Burkhardt) M.; m. Kathleen O'Leary, Oct. 8, 1983; children: Kelly, Calvin, Grace. BS in Journalism, U. Kans., 1979, JD, 1983. Bar: Kans. Mem. staff Senator Nancy Kassebaum, Washington, 1979-80; staff atty. U.S. Customs, Washington, 1983; staff counsel U.S. Senate Judiciary Com., Washington, 1983-86; rep. Fed. Election Com., Washington, 1986-87; chief counsel Bob Dole for Pres., Washington, 1987-88, Office of Gov., Topeka, Kans., 1988-91; atty. Schleicher, Latz, P.C., Kansas City, 1991-92; pres. Morgan Quitno Press, Lawrence, 1989—. Editor: State Rankings, 1990—, Health Care State Rankings, 1993—, Crime State Rankings, 1994—, City Crime Rankings, 1995—. Nominee U.S. Congress 2nd Dist. Kans., 1990; Rep. chmn. 2nd Dist. Kans., 1991. Congregationalist. Office: Morgan Quitno Press PO Box 1656 Lawrence KS 66044

MORGAN, STEPHEN CHARLES, academic administrator; b. Upland, Calif., June 2, 1946; s. Thomas Andrew and Ruth Elizabeth (Miller) M.; m. Ann Marie McMurray, Sept. 6, 1969; 1 child, Kesley Suzanne. BA, U. La Verne, 1968; MS, U. So. Calif., 1971; EdD, U. No. Colo., 1979. Devel. officer U. La Verne, Calif., 1968-71, asst. to pres., 1971-73, dir. devel., 1973-75, v.p. devel., 1975-76, pres., 1985—; dir. devel. U. So. Calif., L.A., 1976-79; exec. dir. Ind. Colls. No. Calif., San Francisco, 1979-85; dir. Ind. Colls. So. Calif., L.A., 1985—. Bd. dirs. Mt. Baldy United Way, Ontario, Calif., 1988—, McKinley Children's Ctr., San Dimas, Calif., 1989—; chair nat. com. on higher edn. Ch. of Brethren, Elgin, Ill., 1988-90; dir. Pomona Valley Hosp. Med. Ctr., Inter Valley Health Plan, 1992—. Mem. Assn. Ind. Calif. Colls. and Univs. (exec. com. 1989—, vice chair 1996—), L.A. County Fair Assn., Western Coll. Assn. (exec. com. 1992—, pres. 1996—), Pi Gamma Mu. Avocations: orchid culture, fly fishing, golf. Home: 2518 N Mountain Ave Claremont CA 91711-1579 Office: U of LaVerne Office of Pres 1950 3rd St La Verne CA 91750-4401

MORGAN, STEVEN MICHAEL, lawyer; b. Cleve., May 19, 1954; s. Harry David and Lilyan (Schwartz) M.; m. Cynthia Lough, Aug. 17, 1983; children: Alyssa Patrice, Rachel Elizabeth. BA, Northwestern U., 1976; JD, Vanderbilt U., 1979. Bar: Pa. 1979, Tex. 1986. Atty. Aluminum Co. of Am., Pitts., 1979-84; environ. counsel Tex. Instruments, Dallas, 1984-87; chmn. environ. health & safety sect. Arter Hadden & Witts, Dallas; now ptnr. Akin, Gump, Strauss, Hauer & Feld, Dallas; lectr. U. Tex., Arlington, 1988—, Tex. A&M U., Coll. Sta., 1988—. Mem. ABA (natural resources sect.), State Bar of Texas (environ. sect.), Dallas Bar Assn. (environ. law sect.), Air Pollution Control Assn., Richardson C. of C. (chmn. environ. com., recipient leadership award 1988-89). Avocations: wine collecting, travel, sports. Office: Akin Gump Strauss et al 4100 First City Center 1700 Pacific Ave Dallas TX 75201-7322

MORGAN, SYLVIA DENISE (MRS. HAROLD MORGAN), school administrator; b. Rome, Ga., Sept. 1, 1952; d. Herman Hamilton and Garnette Lucille (Strickland) Haynes; m. Harold Morgan, Feb. 22, 1980; 1 child, Amber. BS in English, Knoxville Coll., 1974; MEd, Ga. State U., 1977; EdS, Jacksonville State U., 1989. Tchr. Ga. Sch. for the Deaf, Cave Spring, 1974-80, reading lab. coord., 1980-82, curriculum dir., 1982-90, vocat. supr., 1990-94, case mgmt./mgr. coord., 1994—. Mem. NAACP, Nat. Edn. Assn., Ga. Assn. Educators, Ga. Educators for the Hearing Impaired, Alpha Kappa Alpha. Avocations: speaking, writing. Home: 8 Tasso Cir Rome GA 30161-5776

MORGAN, THOMAS BRUCE, author, editor, public affairs executive; b. Springfield, Ill., July 24, 1926; s. David Edward and Mabel Ariel (Wolfe) M.; m. Joan T. Zuckerman, Oct. 3, 1950 (div. 1972); children: Katherine Tarlow, Nicholas David; m. Mary Clark Rockefeller, May 4, 1974 (div. 1988); stepchildren: Geoffrey, Michael, Sabrina Strawbridge; m. Hadassah Teitz Brooks, Aug. 19, 1990; stepchildren: Shoshana Goldhill, Benjamin Brooks. BA, Carleton Coll., 1949. Assoc. editor Esquire Mag., N.Y.C., 1949-53; sr. editor Look Mag., N.Y.C., 1953-58; freelance writer N.Y.C., 1958-69; press sec. Mayor John V. Lindsay, N.Y.C., 1969-73; sr. editor New York Mag., 1974-75; editor The Village Voice, N.Y.C., 1975-76; publisher Politicks mag., N.Y.C., 1976-79; novelist, freelance writer, 1979-89; pres. WNYC Comm. Group, N.Y.C., 1990-94; pres., CEO UN Assn. of U.S.A., N.Y.C., 1994-95; freelance writer, 1996—; press sec. Stevenson for Pres., 1960, McCarthy for Pres., 1968. Author: Friends and Fellow Students, 1956, Self-Creations, 1965, (novel) This Blessed Shore, 1966, Among the Anti-Americans, 1967, (novel) Snyder's Walk, 1987; screenwriter documentary feature film Albert Schweitzer, 1957 (Acad. award); contbr. numerous articles to nat. mags. Trustee Carleton Coll., Northfield, Minn., 1975-79, 80—. With AC, U.S. Army, 1945. Mem. PEN, Authors Guild, Century Assn. Democrat. Jewish. Home and Office: 1155 Park Ave New York NY 10128

MORGAN, THOMAS OLIVER, bishop; b. Jan. 20, 1941; s. Charles Edwin and Amy Amelia (Hoyes) M.; m. Lillian Marie Textor, 1963; three children. BA, U. Sask., Can., 1962; BD, King's Coll., London, 1965; DD (hon.), Coll. of Emmanuel and St. Chad, Sask., 1986. Curate Ch. of the Saviour, Blackburn, Lancashire, Eng., 1966-69; rector Ch. of the Good Shepherd, Porcupine Plain, Sask., Can., 1969-73; rector Ch. of the Saviour, Kinistino, 1973-77, Shellbrook, 1977-83; Archdeacon Sask., 1983-85; bishop Diocese of Sask., Prince Albert, 1985-93, Diocese of Saskatoon, Sask., 1993—. Office: Diocese of Saskatoon, PO Box 1965, Saskatoon, SK Canada S7K 3S5

MORGAN, THOMAS ROWLAND, retired marine corps officer; b. Allentown, Pa., Jan. 6, 1930; s. Harry Campbell and Olwen (Pierce) M.; m. Barbara A. Croze, June 29, 1957; children—Lynn A., Susan E., Beth E. B.A. in History, Colgate U., 1952; student, Marine Corps Command and Staff Coll., 1965-66; M.A. in Edn., U. Va., 1973. Commd. 2d lt. USMC, 1952, advanced through grades to gen., 1986; naval aviator Naval Air Sta., Pensacola, Fla., 1953-54; asst. maintenance officer 3d Marine Aircraft Wing, El Toro, Calif., 1954-55; personnel officer Marine Aircraft Group Western Pacific, 1954-55; dep. comdr. Fleet Marine Force, aide to comdg. gen. 1st Marine Aircraft Wing, Pacific, 1955; asst. ops. officer Marine Aircraft Group, Kaneohe Bay, Hawaii, 1956-57; squadron pilot, ground tng. officer Marine Attack Squadron, Hawaii, 1957-59; flight instr. Naval Air Sta., Olathe, Kans., 1959; personnel officer, aircraft maintenance officer Marine Fighter Squadron, Beaufort, S.C., 1959-61; exec. officer Hdqrs. and Maintenance Squadron, Atsugi, Japan, 1961-62; fleet liaison officer Marine Corps Air Sta., Yuma, Ariz., 1962-65; comdr. Marine Fighter Attack Squadron, Beaufort, 1966-67; group ops. officer, officer-in-charge DaNang DASC, Vietnam, 1968-69; exec. officer Marine Corps Air Sta., Quantico, Va., 1969-71; exec. officer Naval ROTC unit U. Va., 1971-73; chief war plans br. J-5 U.S. European Command Hdqrs., Stuttgart, Fed. Republic Germany, 1973-76; asst. to dep. chief of staff requirements and programs Hdqrs. U.S. Marine Corps, Washington, 1976-77; asst. div. comdr. 3d Marine Div., Okinawa, Japan, 1977-78; asst. chief of staff C-5 Combined Forces Command, Seoul, 1978-80; dep. comdr. FMF Pacific, Camp Smith, Hawaii, 1980-81; dep. chief of staff for requirements and programs Hdqrs Marine Corps, Washington, 1981-85, dep. chief staff for plans, policies and ops., acting Chief of Staff, 1985-86, asst. commandant, 1986-88, ret. Decorated D.S.M., Def. Superior Service medal, Legion of Merit, Bronze Star medal, Meritorious Service medal, Air medal; Order of Nat. Security medal, Cheonsu medal (Korea). Mem. Am. Legion. Avocations: golf, skiing, water sports.

MORGAN, TIMI SUE, lawyer; b. Parsons, Kans., June 16, 1953; d. James Daniel and Iris Mae (Wilson) Baumgardner; m. Rex Michael Morgan, Oct. 28, 1983; children: Tessa Anne, Camma Elizabeth. BS, U. Kans., 1974; JD, So. Meth. U., 1977. Bar: Tex. 1977, U.S. Dist. Ct. (no. dist.) Tex. 1978, U.S. Ct. Appeals (5th cir.) 1979, U.S. Tax Ct. 1980; cert. tax law specialist. Assoc. Gardere & Wynne, Dallas, 1977-79; assoc. Akin, Gump, Strauss, Hauer & Feld, Dallas, 1979-83, ptnr., 1984-86; of counsel Stinson, Mag & Fizzell, Dallas, 1986-88; sole practice Dallas, 1988—; adj. lectr. law So. Meth. U., 1989-90, '92—. Bd. dirs. Dallas Urban League Inc., 1987-91. Mem. ABA (mem. taxation sect.), State Bar Tex. (mem. taxation sect.), Dallas Bar Assn., So. Meth. U. Law Alumni Coun. (sec. 1985-86), Order of Coif, Beta Gamma Sigma. Republican. Episcopalian. Home: 3719 Euclid Ave Dallas TX 75205

MORGAN, TODD MICHAEL, investment advisor; b. St. Paul, June 28, 1947; s. Alfred Blair and Evelyn (Sachs) M.; m. Cheri Rappaport, Sept. 3, 1969; children: Tammy, Joshua. BS, U. Minn., 1969. V.p. Piper Jaffray & Hopwood, Mpls., 1969-77; ptnr. Goldman Sachs & Co., N.Y.C., 1977-91; ltd. ptnr. Goldman, Saches & Co., 1991—. Bd. advisors N.Y. Hosp., N.Y.C., 1989-91; vice chmn. Coalition to Free Soviet Jews, 1989-91; bd. govs., mem. fin. com. Cedars Sinai Hosp., L.A., 1991; bd. dirs. Big Bros. Greater L.A.; chmn. major gifts L.A. United Jewish Appeal, 1995—. Office: Goldman Sachs & Co 333 S Grand Ave Los Angeles CA 90071-1504*

MORGAN, VIRGINIA, magistrate judge; b. 1946. BS, Univ. of Mich., 1968; JD, Univ. of Toledo, 1975. Bar: Mich. 1975, Federal 1975, U.S. Ct. Appeals (6th cir.) 1979. Tchr. Dept. of Interior, Bur. of Indian Affairs, 1968-70, San Diego Unified Schs., 1970-72, Oregon, Ohio, 1972-74; asst. prosecutor Washtenaw County Prosecutor's Office, 1976-79; asst. U.S. atty. Detroit, 1979-85; magistrate judge U.S. Dist. Ct. (Mich. ea. dist.), 6th circuit, Detroit, 1985—. Recipient Spl. Achievement award Dept. of Justice, Disting. Alumni award U. Toledo, 1993. Fellow Mich. State Bar Found.; mem. Nat. Assn. Women Judges, Mich. Bar Assn., Fed. Magistrate Judges Assn. (pres. 1995—), Fed. Bar Assn. (chpt. pres.-elect 1995—). Office: US Courthouse 231 W Lafayette Blvd Detroit MI 48226-2719

MORGAN, WALTER EDWARD, management consultant; b. Hempstead, N.Y., Nov. 19, 1940; s. Edward A. and Anne (Wright) M.; m. Lorraine Roberson, June 1, 1962; children: Walter Edward Jr., Gary L., Cheryl E. BA magna cum laude in polit. sci., Morgan State Coll., 1962; MA magna cum laude in govt. and politics, U. Md., 1969; postgrad., U. So. Calif., 1974-78, George Washington U., 1979-88; PhD in Bus. Mgmt., LaSalle U., 1993. Adminstrv. specialist Social Security Adminstrn., Balt., 1966-68; dir. tng. Skills Upgrading, Inc., Balt., 1968-69; sr. assoc. Al Nellum & Assocs., Washington, 1969-71; v.p. Pagan & Morgan Assocs., Balt., 1971-74; pres., chief exec. officer Morgan Mgmt. Systems, Inc., Columbia, Md., 1974—. Vice pres. United Way Cen. Md., Balt., 1974; commr. Howard County Compensation Commn., Md., 1986; mem. Judicial Nominating Com., Howard, Md., 1983. 1st lt. U.S. Army, 1962-66. Mem. NAACP, Inst. Mgmt. Consultants, Pi Alpha Alpha, Alpha Kappa Mu. Office: Morgan Mgmt Systems Inc 5401 White Mane Columbia MD 21045-2407

MORGAN, WAYNE PHILIP, art and popular culture exhibition producer; b. Dunnville, Ont., Can., Apr. 1, 1942. Cert., Sch. Art, Regina Coll., 1963; BA, U. Sask., Can., 1966; student, Emma Lake Artists Workshop, Sask., 1964-68, McGill U., Montreal, 1968, Art and Mass Culture Banff Ctr. for Arts, 1991. Community resident artist Weyburn (Sask.) Arts Council, 1967-70; dir., curator Dunlop Art Gallery, Regina (Sask.) Public Library, 1970-84; head curatorial services div. Winnipeg Art Gallery, Man., Can., 1984-85; ind. exhbn. prodr. specializing in popular culture, 1985—; mem. explorations jury Can. Coun., 1977-79; mem. secretariat Regina Arts Commn., 1979—; chmn. visual arts subcom. Ottawa-Carleton Adv. Com. for Arts. Mem. Western Can. Art Assn. (founding mem.), Sask. Mus. Assn. (bd. dirs. 1978-80, pres. 1982-84), Sask. Craft Coun. (founding mem.), Can. Mus. Assn. (bd. dirs. 1984-86, chmn. profl. devel. stds. com. 1985-86), Can. Ephemera Soc., Am. Ephemera Soc., Popular Culture Assn., Am. Culture Assn., Am. Game Collectors Assn., N.Y. State Hist. Assn. Home: 75 Markham St Unit 2, Toronto, ON Canada M6J 2G4

MORGAN, WILLIAM BRUCE, naval architect; b. Fairfield, Iowa, Dec. 20, 1926; s. Orville Burns and Mary Verle (Balderson) M.; m. Mary Maxine Gillam, June 21, 1950; children: Margaret Ann, Ann Elise. BS in Marine Engring., U.S. Mcht. Marine Acad., 1950; MS in Hydraulic Engring., U. Iowa, 1951; DEng in Naval Architecture, U. Calif., 1961. Hydraulic engr. David Taylor Model Basin, Bethesda, Md., 1951-52, naval architect, 1952-58, naval architect supr., 1958-62; head propeller br. David Taylor Model Basin, Bethesda, 1962-70; head hydromechanics div. David Taylor Naval Ship Research & Devel. Ctr. (formerly David Taylor Model Basin), Bethesda, Md., 1970-79; head hydromechanics directorate David Taylor Model Basin, Bethesda, Md., 1979—; chmn. exec. com. Am. Towing Tank Conf., 1983-86; mem. exec. com. Internat. Towing Tank Conf., 1984-90. Co-inventor ventilated propeller, supercavitating propeller with air ventilation; contbr. articles to profl. jours. Recipient Navy Superior Civilian USN, 1974, Meritorious Exec. award Office of Pres., 1987, William Froude medal Royal Instn. Naval Architects, 1989, Capt. Robert Dexter Conrad award USN, 1993. Fellow Soc. Naval Architects and Marine Engrs. (hon. life; exec. com. 1985—, Davidson medal 1986), ASME (chmn. fluids engring. div. 1981-82); mem. NAE, Schiffbautechnische Gesellschaft, Am. Soc. Naval Engrs. (Gold Medal award 1993), Chinese Soc. Naval Architects and Marine Engrs. (hon.), Sigma Xi. Mem. Ch. of the Brethen. Home: 110 Upton St Rockville MD 20850-1836 Office: David Taylor Model Bas Bethesda MD 20084-5000

MORGAN, WILLIAM J., accounting firm executive; b. Bklyn., Jan. 12, 1947; s. William J. and Emma T. (Kraft) M.; m. Patricia A. Maltz, Mar. 23, 1968; children: Michele, Jennifer. BS St. John's U., 1968. CPA, N.Y., Conn., N.J. Ptnr. in charge Metro. N.Y. Area, manufacturing, retailing and distbn. practice, audit staff KPMG Peat Marwick, N.Y.C., 1968-72, audit supr., 1972-74, audit mgr., 1974-77, ptnr.-in-charge pvt. bus. adv. service, N.Y.C., 1977-79, exec. office, ptnr.-in-charge recruiting, 1979-82, ptnr. comml. health care practice, Short Hills, 1982-91; ptnr.-in-charge N.J. audit practice, 1989-91, mng. ptnr. Fairfield/Westchester counties practice, 1991-94; mem. Bus. Unit Planning Task Force, 1987-90, mem. compensation com., 1990-91, bd. dirs., 1991-95, chmn. profit distbn. com., 1991-95, mem. future direction com., 1991-93, pension task force, 1991-92; mem. acctg. adv. bd. Grad. Sch. Bus. Fordham U., 1979-82, mem. standardization com. Nat. Retail Mchts. Assn., 1979; bd. dirs.N.Y. chpt. small bus. fund drive ARC, 1978; trustee Tri County Scholarship Fund, 1984-91; chmn. Blackberry Hill Property Owners Assoc., 1986-87; v.p., exec. com., adv. bd. Fairfield coun. Boy Scouts Am., 1993-95; chmn. Fairfield County Info. Exchange, 1992-94; bd. dirs. S.W. Area Commerce and Industry Assn., 1994—, Inroads Fairfield and Westchester County chpt., 1992-95; mem. Bus. Execs. for Nat. Security, Ambs. Roundtable. Mem. Am. Inst. CPA's (small bus. devel. com. 1979-81, acctg. lit. awards com. 1983-86), N.J. Soc. CPA's (chmn. acctg. and auditing stds. com. 1988-90, trustee 1990-92, mem. pub. rels. task force, 1987, subcom. health care acctg. 1983-86), N.Y. State Soc. CPA's (retail acctg. com. 1975-78, com. on edn. in coll. and univs. 1978-82), Nat. Assn. Accts. (dir. manuscripts 1975-77, v.p. N.Y. chpt. 1977-81, pres. N.Y. chpt. 1981-82, nat. publs. com. 1982-83, com. acad. relations 1983-84, nat. dir. 1983-86, Disting. Service award 1975), Health Care Fin. Mgmt. Assn. (N.J. chpt. chmn. auditing com. 1982-83, legis. task force com. 1985-86, chmn. joint ventures com., 1987-88). Club: Fairmount Country (bd. govs., treas. 1987-90), Woodway Country, Conn. Golf, Landmark Club. Roman Catholic. Home: 14 Talmadge Hill Rd Darien CT 06820 Office: KPMG Peat Marwick 3001 Summer St Stamford CT 06905-4317

MORGAN, WILLIAM LIONEL, JR., physician, educator; b. Honolulu, Nov. 18, 1927; s. William Lionel and Lucy Salisbury (Grimes) M.; m. Joan Brunjes, Apr. 10, 1954; children: Nancy Salisbury, Linda Pittman. B.A. cum laude, Yale U., 1948; M.D. magna cum laude, Harvard U., 1952. Diplomate: Am. Bd. Internal Medicine. (mem. bd. 1973-80, mem. residency review com. 1975-80, chmn. residency rev. com. 1979-80). Intern Mass. Gen. Hosp., Boston, 1952-53; resident in medicine Mass. Gen. Hosp., 1953-54, 56-57, fellow in cardiology, 1957-58; asso. physician div. cardiovascular disease Henry Ford Hosp., Detroit, 1958-62; asso. prof. medicine U. Rochester (N.Y.) Sch. Medicine and Dentistry, 1962-65, prof., 1966-89, prof. medicine emeritus, 1989—, asso. chmn. dept. medicine, 1966-89. Author: (with G.L. Engel) The Clinical Approach to the Patient, 1969. Served with USPHS, 1954-56. Mem. ACP (Master), Am. Clin. and Climatol. Assn., Phi Beta Kappa, Alpha Omega Alpha. Home: 160 Collingsworth Dr Rochester NY 14625-2024 Office: Dept Medicine Strong Meml Hosp 601 Elmwood Ave Rochester NY 14642

MORGAN, WILLIAM NEWTON, architect, educator; b. Jacksonville, Fla., Dec. 14, 1930; s. Thomas and Kathleen (Fiske) M.; m. Bernice E. Leimback, July 31, 1954; children: William Newton, Dylan Thomas. AB magna cum laude, Harvard Coll., 1952, MArch Grad. Sch. of Design, 1958. Pres. William Morgan Architects, P.A., Jacksonville, Fla., 1961—; critic various archtl. schs.; lectr. in field. Prin. works include Fla. State Mus., Jacksonville Police Meml. Bldg., Pyramid Condominium, Ocean City, Fed. Cts. and Offices, Ft. Lauderdale, Fla., Westinghouse World Hdqs., Orlando, Fla., Neiman-Marcus store, Ft. Lauderdale, 1st Dist. Ct. Appeal, Tallahassee, Fla., Conf. Ctr., Tallahassee, U.S. Embassy, Khartoum, Sudan, U.S. Courthouse, Tallahassee; author; Prehistoric Architecture in the Eastern

United States, 1980, Prehistoric Architecture in Micronesia, 1988, Ancient Architecture of the Southwest, 1994. Subject of The Architecture of William Morgan (Paul Spreiregen) 1987; Fulbright grantee, 1958-59; grantee Graham Found. Advanced Studies Arts; Lehman fellow Harvard U., 1957, Wheelwright fellow, fellow NEA, 1991; Sam Gibbons Eminent scholar Fla. A&M U. and U. South Fla. Fellow AIA (past chmn. com. design). Office: William Morgan Architects 220 E Forsyth St Jacksonville FL 32202-3320

MORGAN, WILLIAM RICHARD, mechanical engineer; b. Cambridge, Ohio, Mar. 27, 1922; s. Wilbur Alfred and Treva Beatrice (Minto) M.; m. Marjorie Eleanor Stevens, Feb. 17, 1946; children: Carol M. Morgan Dingledy, William R., Jr. BSME, The Ohio State U., 1944; MSME, Purdue U., 1950, PhD in Mech. Engring., 1951. Lic. profl. engr., Ohio. Power plant design engr. Curtiss Wright Corp., Columbus, Ohio, 1946-47; instr., rsch. fellow Purdue U., West Lafayette, Ind., 1947-51; supr. exptl. mech. engring. GE, Cin., 1951-55, mgr. controls analysis, devel. Aircraft Gas Turbine Divsn., 1955-59, mgr. XV5A vertical take-off and landing aircraft program, 1959-65, mgr. acoustic engring. Flight Propulsion Divsn., 1965-69, mgr. quiet engine program Flight Propulsion Divsn., 1969-71; pres. Cin. Rsch. Corp., 1971-73; v.p., COO SDRC Internat., Cin., 1973-79; engring. and mgmt. cons. Cin., 1979—. Author of papers presented at Brookhaven Nat. Lab., AEC Heat Transfer Symposium, 1954, ASME Fall Meeting, Thermal Conductivity of Insulation Material for Use in Nuclear Reactors, 1957, Am. Inst. Aero. Engrs. Ten-Ton V/STOL Lift Fan Transport, 1961, Dynamics Loads Symposium, XV5A Dynamic Load Characteristics, 1963, Joint Meeting of AGARD-Nato on Aircraft Engine Noise and Sonic Boom, 1969, ASME Meeting, Analytical Prediction of Fan/Compressor Noise, 1969. Lt. j.g. USNR, WWII. Westinghouse Rsch. fellow. Mem. ASME, Masonic Lodge, Scottish Rite Lodge. Achievements include patents in Humidity Detection and Indicating Instrument, Stall Prevention/Acoustic Tip Treatment, Acoustic Treatment, Inlet Noise Reduction Configuration. Home and Office: 312 Ardon Ln Cincinnati OH 45215-4102

MORGAN-LAWLER, BARBARA, educator; b. Talladega, Ala., Sept. 29, 1949; d. Otherl James and Lizzie (Garrett) Morgan; m. James Lawler III, Dec. 13, 1969; 1 child, Erikka Janeen. BA, Talladega Coll., 1971; MS, Jacksonville State U., 1971; AA, U. Montevallo, 1984. Cert. tchr., Ala. Tchr. communications Gadsden (Ala.) State Community Coll.; tchr. speech/theater Talladega Coll.; broadcast journalist, disc jockey Sta. WEYY Radio, Talladega; tchr. English lit. advanced placement Talladega City Bd. Edn.; bd. advisers Talladega Coll. Contbr. articles to Curriculum Guide in Research and Writing. Recipient Chi Honors Se Miner, Outstanding Advanced Placement award, 1988. Mem. NEA, Ala. Edn. Assn., Ala. Speech and Theatre Assn., Nat. Coun. Tchrs. English, ACTE, Internat. Thespian Soc. (Outstanding Theatre Dir.), AASSP, Talladega Coll. Local Alumni Assn., Zeta Phi Beta. Home: 929 College St Talladega AL 35160-4801 Office: Talladega HS 1177 McMillan St Talladega AL 35160

MORGANROTH, FRED, lawyer; b. Detroit, Mar. 26, 1938; s. Ben and Grace (Greenfield) M.; m. Janice Marilyn Cohn, June 23, 1963; children: Greg, Candi, Erik. BA, Wayne State U., 1959, JD with distinction, 1961. Bar: Mich. 1961, U.S. Dist. Ct. (ea. dist.) Mich. 1961, U.S. Ct. Claims 1967, U.S. Supreme Ct. 1966; trained matrimonial arbitrator. Ptnr. Greenbaum, Greenbaum & Morganroth, Detroit, 1963-68, Lebenbom, Handler, Brody & Morganroth, Detroit, 1968-70, Lebenbom, Morganroth & Stern, Southfield, Mich., 1971-78; sole practice Southfield, 1979-83; ptnr. Morganroth & Morganroth P.C., Southfield, 1983-94, Morganroth, Morganroth, Alexander & Nye, P.C., Birmingham, Mich., 1994—. Mem. ABA (family law sect. 1987—), Mich. Bar Assn. (hearing panelist grievance bd. 1975—, Oakland County family law com. 1988—, vice chmn. 1992-93, chair 1993—), State Bar Mich. (mem. family law coun. of family law sect. 1990—, treas. 1993-94, chmn.-elect 1994-95, chmn. 1995-96), Detroit Bar Assn., Oakland Bar Assn. (cir. ct. mediator 1984—), Am. Arbitration Assn. (Oakland County family law com. 1985—, vice chmn. 1992-93, chmn. 1993-94, trained matrimonial arbitrator), Detroit Tennis Club (Farmington, Mich., pres. 1978-82), Charlivaux Country Club. Jewish. Avocations: comml. pilot, tennis. Home: 30920 Woodcrest Ct Franklin MI 48025-1435 Office: 300 Park St Ste 410 Birmingham MI 48009

MORGANTE, JOHN-PAUL, state government training administrator; b. Yonkers, N.Y., June 26, 1962; s. Enzo and Teresa (DellaToffola) M.; m. Ellen Rothberger, May 26, 1984; children: Camden Anne, Bethany Nicole, Hailee Marie. BA, U. So. Calif., L.A., 1984. Ordained to ministry Christian Ch., 1987; cert. profl. in human resources. Adminstrv. dir. MCM Internat., Lomita, Calif., 1984-91; exec. dir. Champions for Christ, Austin, Tex., 1991-93; pres. Annimar Assocs., Austin, 1994; tng. specialist Bur. Nutrition Svcs., Tex. Dept. Health, Austin, 1994—. Mem. ctrl. com. Orange County (Calif.) Reps., 1988-89; intern U.S. Rep. Robert Badham, Washington, 1983, campaign worker, 1984,; intern Assemblyman Curt Pringle, Garden Grove, Calif., 1988; campaign worker U.S. Senator Chic Hecht, 1982, U.S. Rep. Robert Dornan, 1984, Reagan/Bush, 1984, Jerry Keel, 1996; del. Tex. Rep. Conv., 1996. Recipient Rep. Presdl. Legion of Merit, Presdl. Commemorative Honor Roll, 1991, Staff Mem. of the Yr., 1987. Mem. ASTD, Soc. for Human Resource Mgmt., Am. Soc. Assn. Execs., Internat. Soc. Meeting Planners. Avocations: golf, travel. Office: Tex Dept Health Bur Nutrition Svcs 1100 W 49th St Austin TX 78756

MORGEN, LYNN, public relations executive. Grad., CCNY. Former rep. Gruntal & Co., First Manhattan Co.; assoc. ECOM Cons., 1978-79, v.p. investor rels., 1979-82; ptnr. Morgen-Walke Assocs., 1982—. Office: Morgen-Walke Assocs Inc 380 Lexington Ave Ste 5100 New York NY 10168-0002*

MORGENROTH, EARL EUGENE, entrepreneur; b. Sidney, Mont., May 7, 1936; s. Frank and Leona (Ellison) M.; m. Noella Nichols, Aug. 2, 1958; children: Dolores Roxanna, David Jonathan, Denise Christine. BS, U. Mont., 1961. From salesman to gen. mgr. Sta. KGVO-AM Radio, Missoula, Mont., 1958-65; sales mgr. Stas. KGVO-TV, KTVM-TV and KCFW-TV, Missoula, Butte, Kalispell, Mont., 1965-66, gen. mgr., 1966-68; gen. mgr. Sta. KCOY-TV, Santa Maria, Calif., 1968-69; v.p., gen. mgr. Western Broadcasting Co., Missoula, 1966-69, gen. mgr., pres., 1969-81; gen. mgr., pres. numerous cos., Mont., Calif. Idaho, P.R., Ga., 1966-84; pres., chmn. Western Broadcasting Co., Missoula, 1981-84, Western Communications, Inc., Reno, 1984-90; prin. Western Investments, Reno, 1984—; chmn. Western Fin., Inc., Morgenroth Music Ctrs., Inc., Mont., Mont. Band Instruments, Inc.; chmn. E & B Music Inc., Times Square, Inc. Mem. Mont. Bank Bd., Helena; commencement spkr. U. Mont., 1988; bd. dirs. U. Mont. Found., 1985-95. With. U.S. Army, 1954-57. Named Boss of Yr. Santa Maria Valley J.C.s, 1968. Mem. U. Mont. Century Club (pres.), Missoula C. of C. (pres.), Rocky Mountain Broadcasters Assn. (pres.), Craighead Wildlife-Wildlands Inst. (bd. dirs.), Boone and Crockett Club (bd. dirs., v.p. comm.), Grizzly Riders Internat. (bd. dirs., v.p.), Bldg. A Scholastic Heritage (bd. dirs.). Republican. Methodist. Home: 3525 Brighton Way Reno NV 89509-3871

MORGENS, WARREN KENDALL, lawyer; b. Oklahoma City, May 25, 1940; s. Alvin Gustav and Helen Alene (McFarland) M. Student, Westminster Coll., Fulton, Mo., 1958-60; BSBA, Washington U., St. Louis, 1962, JD, 1964. Bar: Mo., 1964, D.C., 1981. Atty. gen. counsel's office SEC, Washington, 1968-69; asst. atty. gen. State of Mo., St. Louis, 1969-72; ptnr. Park, Craft & Morgens, Kansas City, Mo., 1973-76; pvt. practice law Kansas City, 1976-81; mng. atty. Hoskins. King, McGannon & Hahn, Washington, 1981-85; spl. ptnr. Barnett & Alagia, Washington, 1985-89; of counsel Anderson, Hibey, Nauheim & Blair, Washington, 1989-93; pvt. practice Washington, 1993—; bd. dirs. George Washington Nat. Bank, Alexandria, Va., George Washington Banking Corp. Patron Nat. Symphony, Washington, 1966-68, 81-85, Washington Performing Arts Soc., 1989—, Kansas City Philharmonic, 1974-80, Supreme Ct. Hist. Soc., Washington, 1982—, The Williamsburg (Va.) Found., 1982—. Named one of Outstanding Young Men Am., 1977. Mem. Mo. Bar Assn., D.C. Bar Assn., Univ. Club (St. Louis). Republican. Presbyterian. Avocations: hiking, sailing, fishing, golf. Home and Office: 1805 Crystal Dr #201 Arlington VA 22202-4403

MORGENSEN, JERRY LYNN, construction company executive; b. Lubbock, Tex., July 9, 1942; s. J.J. and Zelline (Butler) M.; m. Linda Dee Austin, Apr. 17, 1965; children: Angela, Nicole. BCE, Tex. Tech U., 1965. Area engr. E.I. Dupont Co., Orange, Tex., 1965-67; div. engr. E.I. Dupont Co., La Place, La., 1967-73; project mgr. Hensel Phelps Constrn. Co., Greeley, Colo., 1973-78, area mgr., 1978-80, v.p., 1980-85, pres., 1985—. Office: Hensel Phelps Constrn Co 420 Sixth Ave PO Box O Greeley CO 80632

MORGENSTEIN, WILLIAM, shoe company executive; b. Bklyn., Jan. 11, 1933; s. Samuel and Jeanne Marie (Mittentag) M.; m. Sylvia Dove, June 8, 1952; children: Lee Brian, David Barry. BS in Fin., U. Ala., 1955. Salesman Greenwald Shoe Co., Birmingham, Ala., 1954-56; sr. buyer Melville Shoe Corp., N.Y.C., 1958-67; pres. Kitty Kelly Shoe Co., N.Y.C., 1967-70; exec. v.p. A.S. Beck Shoes, N.Y.C., 1970-71, Sandia Internat., Englewood Cliffs, N.J., 1971-75; pres., chief exec. officer Marquesa Internat. Corp., Englewood, N.J., 1975-95; sales exec. Signature Group divsn. Montgomery Ward, 1995—; internat. cons. footwear exporting, 1965—. Served with U.S. Army, 1956-58. Mem. Footwear Distbrs. and Retailers Am. (vice chmn., bd. dirs., exec. com.), Internat. Footwear Assn. (chmn. 1989—, vice chmn. 1986—, exec. com. 1986—), 210 Assn. (Pres.' Circle 1987), Toastmasters (past pres. Teaneck, N.J. chpt.). Republican. Jewish. Avocations: history, golf.

MORGENSTERN, DAN MICHAEL, jazz historian, educator, editor; b. Munich, Germany, Oct. 24, 1929; came to U.S., 1947; s. Soma and Ingeborg Henrietta (von Klenau) M.; m. Elsa Schocket, Mar. 31, 1974; children: Adam Oran, Joshua Louis. Student, Brandeis U., 1953-56. Editorial asst. N.Y. Post, 1957-58; N.Y. corr. Jazz Jour., London, 1958-61; assoc. editor, then editor in chief Metronome mag., 1961; editor Jazz mag., 1962-64; assoc. editor Down Beat mag., 1964-67, editor, 1967-73; lectr. jazz history Peabody Instn., Balt., 1978-80; vis. prof., sr. research fellow in Am. Music, Bklyn. Coll., 1979; dir. Inst. Jazz Studies, Rutgers U., 1976—; bd. dirs. Jazz Inst. Chgo., N.Y. Jazz Mus. Producer ann. 10-concert series Jazz in the Garden, Museum Modern Art, N.Y.C., 1961-66; co-producer concert series Jazz on Broadway, 1963, Just Jazz; 10 program TV series, Public Broadcasting Service, 1971; author: The Jazz Story: An Outline History, 1973, Jazz People, 1976; translator, editor: (Joachim E. Berendt) The New Jazz Book, 1962, rev. edit., 1975; co-editor Ann. Rev. Jazz Studies, 1982—. Served with U.S. Army, 1951-53. Recipient Deems Taylor award ASCAP, 1977, Grammy award for best album notes 1973, 74, 76, 81, 91. Mem. NARAS (gov. 1971—, trustee 1976-79, 81-84, 85-89, 91—, v.p. 1979-83, 1st v.p. 1983-85), Nat. Endowment for Arts (chmn. jazz adv. panel 1971-73, cons. music programs 1973-80), Music Critics Assn., PEN, Authors Guild. Home: 365 W End Ave Apt 603 New York NY 10024-6563 Office: Rutgers U Inst Jazz Studies Newark NJ 07102

MORGENSTERN, LEON, surgeon; b. Pitts., July 14, 1919; s. Max Samuel and Sarah (Master) M.; m. Laurie Mattlin, Nov. 27, 1967; 1 son, David Ethan. Student, CCNY, 1936-37; B.A. magna cum laude, Bklyn. Coll., 1940; M.D., N.Y. U., 1943. Diplomate: Am. Bd. Surgery. Intern Queens Gen. Hosp., Jamaica, N.Y., 1943-44; fellow, asst. resident in pathology Queens Gen. Hosp., 1947-48, resident in surgery, 1948-52; practice medicine, specializing in surgery Los Angeles, 1953-59, 60—, Bronx, N.Y., 1959-60; dir. surgery Cedars of Lebanon Hosp., Los Angeles, 1960-73; dir. surgery Cedars-Sinai Med. Center, Los Angeles, 1973-88, emeritus dir. surgery, 1989—; dir. Bioethics Program Cedars-Sinai Med. Ctr., L.A., 1995—; clin. prof. surgery UCLA Sch. Medicine, 1973-85, prof. in residence, 1985—; dir. bioethics program Cedars-Sinai Med. Ctr., 1995—; asst. prof. surgery Albert Einstein Coll. Medicine, N.Y.C., 1959-60. Assoc. editor Mount Sinai Jour. Medicine, 1984-88; contbr. articles to profl. pubs. Served to capt. M.C. U.S. Army, 1944-46. Mem. Soc. for Surgery Alimentary Tract, Soc. Am. Gastrointestinal Endoscopic Surgeons (hon.), Am. Gastroent. Assn., L.A. Surg. Soc. (pres. 1977), ACS (sec.-treas. 1976-77, pres. 1978, bd. dirs. So. Calif. chpt. 1976-78, gov.-at-large), Internat. Soc. Surgery, Western Surg. Assn., Pacific Coast Surg. Assn., AMA, Calif. Med. Assn., Los Angeles County Med. Assn., Am. Surg. Assn., others. Home: 5694 Calpine Dr Malibu CA 90265-3812

MORGENSTERN, MATTHEW, computer scientist; b. N.Y.C.. BSEE, Columbia U., 1968, MSEE and Computer Sci., 1970; MS in Computer Sci. and Mgmt., MIT, 1975, PhD in Computer Sci., 1976. Asst. prof. computer sci. Rutgers U., New Brunswick, N.J., 1976-82; research computer scientist Info. Scis. Inst., U. So. Calif., Los Angeles, 1982-84; sr. computer scientist SRI Internat., Menlo Park, Calif., 1984-90; dir. R & D programs advt. info. tech. divsn. Xerox, Cambridge, Mass., 1990-92; prin. scientist Xerox Design Rsch. Inst./Cornell U., Ithaca, N.Y., 1992—; cons. Hewlett-Packard Corp., Palo Alto, Calif., 1990. Co-author: Database Security VIII, 1994; contbr. articles to profl. jours. Mem. IEEE, Am. Assn. Artificial Intelligence, Assn. Computing Machinery, Sigma Xi, Tau Beta Pi, Eta Kappa Nu. Office: Xerox Design Research Inst Cornell Univ 502 Theory Center Ithaca NY 14853

MORGENSTERN, SHELDON JON, symphony orchestra conductor; b. Cleve., July 1, 1939; s. Irwin Arthur and Harriet Sue Morgenstern; m. Patricia Lou Bradshaw; 1 child, Sali Sharpe Hagan. BMus, Northwestern U., 1961; MMus, New Eng. Conservatory, 1966; DMA (hon.), Greensboro (N.C.) Coll., 1986. Mem. conducting staff New Eng. Conservatory, 1966-67; music dir. Greensboro Symphony Orch., 1967-74; prin. guest conductor Betica Philharmonic, Seville, Spain, 1978-82, Polish Radio Orch., Warsaw, Poland, 1990—; music dir. Ea. Music Festival, Greensboro, 1962—; music advisor Miss. Symphony Orch., 1985-86; bd. mem. Istanbul (Turkey) Internat. Festival, 1975—, Company for Televised Theatre; mus. cons. U.S. Dept. Interior for Wolf Trap Farm Park, 1972; mem. adv. bd. Avery Fisher Award, 1978—. Recipient O'Henry award City of Greensboro, 1980, Long Leaf Pine award State N.C., 1989, Nat. Alumni award Northwestern U., 1990. Home: Ferme Veudagne, Ch des Trois Noyers, 01210 Ferney-Voltaire France Office: Ea Music Festival PO Box 22026 Greensboro NC 27420-2026

MORGENTALER, ABRAHAM, urologist, researcher; b. Montreal, Quebec, Can., May 14, 1956; came to U.S., 1974; s. Henry Morgentaler and Chawa Rosenfarb; m. Susan Deborah Edbril, June 12, 1982; children: Maya Edbril, Hannah Edbril. AB, Harvard U., 1978, MD, 1982. Diplomate Am. Bd. Urology. Intern Harvard Surg. Svc.-N.E. Deaconess Hosp., Boston, 1982-83; resident Harvard Program in Urology, Boston, 1984-88; instr. surgery Harvard Med. Sch., Boston, 1988-92, asst. prof. surgery (urology), 1993—; staff urologist, dir. male infertility program and impotency Beth Israel Hosp., Boston, 1988—; dir. andrology lab. Beth Israel Hosp., 1990—. Author: The Male Body, 1993. Mem. AMA, Am. Urologic Assn., Am. Fertility Soc., Am. Soc. Andrology, Boston Fertility Soc., Am. Assn. Clin. Urologists. Achievements include detection of protein abnormalities in infertile sperm, detection of temperature dependent protein expression in rat testis, use of investigational stents for treatment of benign prostatic hypertrophy. Office: Beth Israel Hosp 330 Brookline Ave Boston MA 02215-5400

MORGENTHAU, ROBERT MORRIS, lawyer; b. N.Y.C., July 31, 1919; s. Henry Jr. and Elinor (Fatman) M.; m. Martha Pattridge (dec.); children: Joan, Anne, Elinor, Robert P., Barbara; m. Lucinda Franks, Nov. 19, 1977; children: Joshua, Amy. Grad., Deerfield (Mass.) Acad., 1937; BA, Amherst Coll., 1941, LLD (hon.), 1966; LLB, Yale U., 1948; LLD (hon.), N.Y. Law Sch., 1968, Syracuse Law Sch., 1976, Albany Law Sch., 1982, Colgate U., 1988. Bar: N.Y. 1949. Assoc. firm Patterson Belknap & Webb, N.Y.C., 1948-53; ptnr. Patterson Belknap & Webb, 1954-61; U.S. atty. So. Dist. N.Y., 1961-62, 62-70; dist. atty. New York County, 1975—; former pres. N.Y. State Dist. Attys. Assn.; lectr. London Sch. Econs., 1993. Pres. Police Athletic League; Dem. candidate for Gov. of N.Y., 1962; bd. dirs. P.R. Legal Def. and Edn. Fund; trustee Baron de Hirsch Fund, Federated Jewish Philanthropies, Temple Emanu-El, N.Y.C.; co-chair N.Y. Holocaust Meml. Commn.; chmn. Gov.'s Adv. Com. on Sentencing, 1979; counsel N.Y. State LAw Enforcement Coun.; mem. N.Y. exec. com. State of Israel Bonds. Lt. comdr. USN, 1941-45. Recipient Emory Buckner award Fed. Bar Coun., 1983, Yale Citation of Merit, 1982, Fordham-Stein prize, 1988, Thomas Jefferson award in law U. Va., 1991, Brandeis medal U. Louisville, 1995, Omanut award Yeshiva U., 1995, Trumpeter award Nat. Consumers League, 1995. Fellow Am. Bar Found.; mem. ABA, N.Y. State Bar Assn., Assn. of the Bar of the City of N.Y., N.Y. County Lawyers Assn. (Disting. Pub. Svc. award 1993), Phi Beta Kappa. Office: Office Dist Atty One Hogan Pl New York NY 10013

MORGNANESI, LANNY M., journalist; b. Trenton, N.J., Sept. 21, 1951; s. Orlando John and Kathryn Theresa (Mercurio) M.; m. Lucille Heu, Nov. 27, 1987; 1 child, Dante Michael. BA in Liberal Arts, Millersville U., 1973; MA in Journalism, U. Mo., 1975. Reporter Bucke County Courier Times, Levittown, Pa., 1975-80, editl. page writer, 1980, assoc. editor, 1980-84; copy editor, advisor New China News Agy., Beijing, 1984-85; asst. city editor The Fla. Times-Union, Jacksonville, Fla., 1986-90, zoned editions editor, 1990-92, city editor, 1992-93; exec. editor The Intelligencer/Record, Doylestown, Pa., 1993—; exec. prodr., host cable TV show The Intelligencer Monthly, Suburban Cmty. TV, Doylestown, 1994—. Bd. dirs. Ctrl. Bucks Family YMCA, Doylestown, 1993—. Mem. Am. Soc. Newspaper Editors, Pa. Soc. Newspaper Editors, Pa. Newspaper Pubs. Assn. Office: The Intelligencer/Record 333 N Broad St Doylestown PA 18901

MORGNER, AURELIUS, economist, educator; b. N.Y.C., May 23, 1917; s. Oscar A. and Anna G. (Hoffmeister) M. B.S. in Bus. Adminstrn., U. Mo., 1938, M.A. in Econs., 1940; Ph.D., U. Minn., 1955. Investigator Dept. Labor, 1941; project dir. Employment Stblzn. Research Inst., 1941-42; instr. bus. adminstrn. U. Minn., 1942-46; lectr. Northwestern U., 1946-47; assoc. prof. Tex. A&M U., 1947-56, prof., 1956-58; vis. prof. U. São Paulo, Brazil, 1958-60; dir. grad. social studies U. São Paulo, 1959-60; prof. econs. U. So. Calif., L.A., 1960—; chmn. dept. U. So. Calif., 1962-69; prof. internat. econs. Sch. Internat. Relations, 1960—; Pub. panel mem. Chgo. Regional War Labor Bd., 1943-45; pub. rep. minimum wage com. Dept. Labor, 1942,43; cons. Govt. Eucador, 1965-68, Govt. Guyana, 1968, state Nev., 1970, Philippines, 1971-72, Yemen Arab Republic, 1974-75; U.S. State Dept. vis. lectr., Brazil, summer 1966. Co-author: Local Labor Markets, 1948, Problems in Economic Analysis, 1948, Problems in the Theory of Price, 1954 (trans. Spanish 1965, Portuguese 1967). Ford faculty fellow Columbia U., 1954-55. Mem. So. Calif. Econ. Assn. (pres. 1965-66), Am. Econs. Assn., Western Econ. Assn., Am. Arbitration Assn., Internat. Studies Assn. Office: U So Calif Dept Econs Los Angeles CA 90089

MORI, ALLEN ANTHONY, university dean, consultant, researcher; b. Hazleton, Pa., Nov. 1, 1947; s. Primo Philip and Carmella (DeNoia) M.; m. Barbara Epoca, June 26, 1971; 1 child, Kirsten Lynn. BA, Franklin and Marshall Coll., Lancaster, Pa., 1969; MEd, Bloomsburg U. Pa., 1971; PhD, U. Pitts., 1975. Spl. edn. tchr. White Haven (Pa.) State Sch. and Hosp., 1969-70, Hazleton Area Sch. Dist., 1970-71, Pitts. Pub. Schs., 1971-74; supr. student tchrs. U. Pitts., 1974-75; prof. spl. edn. U. Nev., Las Vegas, 1975-84; dean coll. edn. Marshall U., Huntington, W.Va., 1984-87; dean sch. edn. Calif. State U., L.A., 1987—; hearing officer pub. law 94-142 Nev. Dept. Edn., Carson City, 1978—; mem. Nev. Gov.'s Com. on Mental Health and Mental Retardation, 1983-84; cons. Ministry Edn., Manitoba, Can., 1980-82; pres. Tchr. Edn. Coun. State Colls. and Univs., 1993-94. Author: Families of Children with Special Needs, 1983; co-author: Teaching the Severely Retarded, 1980, Handbook of Preschool, Special Education, 1980, Adapted Physical Education, 1983, A Vocational Training Continuum for the Mentally and Physically Disabled, 1985, Teaching Secondary Students with Mild Learning and Behavior Problems, 1986, 93; contbr. numerous articles, book revs. and monographs to profl. jours. Bd. dirs. Assn. Retarded Citizens San Gabriel Valley, ElMonte, 1989-94. Recipient grants U.S. Dept. Edn., 1976-91, Nev. Dept. Edn., W.Va. Dept. Edn., Calif. State U. Chancellor's Office. Mem. Assn. Tchr. Educators, Coun. for Exceptional Children (div. on Career Devel. exec. com. 1981-83), Nat. Soc. for Study of Edn., Kiwanis, Phi Beta Delta, Phi Delta Kappa, Pi Lambda Theta. Avocations: jogging, travel. Office: Calif State U 5151 State University Dr Los Angeles CA 90032-4221

MORI, HANAE, fashion designer; b. Muikaichi, Shimane, Japan, 1926; m. Ken Mori, May 1947; children: Akira, Kei. BA in Lit., Tokyo Women's Christian Coll., 1947. Pres., founder, designer Hanae Mori Group, N.Y.C., 1951—; uniform designer Japan Airlines, Tokyo, 1967, 70, 73; costume designer Monaco Ballet, 1976, Paris Opera Ballet, 1986, (opera) Madame Butterfly at La Scala, Milan, 1985. Author: Designing for Tomorrow, 1978, A Glass Butterfly, 1984, Hanae Mori 1960-1989, 1989. Adviser Ministry of Cultural Affairs, Tokyo; mem. overseas bd. Boston Symphony Orch.; mem. various cultural coms., Tokyo. Recipient Neiman Marcus award, 1973, Purple Ribbon, Govt. of Japan, 1988, La Croix Chevalier des Arts et Lettres, Govt. of France, 1984, Legion of Honor, 1989. Mem. Chambre Syndicale de Haute Couture Parisienne. Avocations: opera, theater. Office: Hanae Mori New York Inc 27 E 79th St New York NY 10021-0101

MORI, JUN, lawyer; b. San Francisco, Dec. 13, 1929; s. Isamu Arthur and Hide (Nakae) M.; m. May Tsutsumoto, Apr. 25, 1954; children: Jean Kikuko, Richard Isamu, Ken Arthur. B.A., UCLA, 1955; LL.B., Waseda U., Tokyo, Japan, 1951; J.D., U. So. Calif., 1958. Bar: Calif. 1959, U.S. Supreme Ct. 1971, D.C. 1979. Dep. commr. of corp. State of Calif., 1959-60; sr. ptnr. firm Mori & Ota, Los Angeles, 1960-84, Kelly Drye & Warren, L.A., N.Y.C., Washington and Tokyo, 1984—; dir. Yamaha Internat. Corp., Buena Park, Calif.; legal adviser Sumitomo Bank of Calif., Los Angeles, 1962—. Chmn. Los Angeles-Nagoya Sister City Affiliation, 1966-67; trustee UCLA Found.; mem. com. on Pacific Basin studies UCLA; pres. Bd. Harbor Commrs., City of Los Angeles, 1980-82, 86-88, 89; mem. adv. bd. Office Internat. Trade, Calif. Dept. Econ. and Bus. Devel.; mem. President's Export Coun., 1976-80. Mem. Am. Bar Assn., Am. Judicature Soc., Japanese Am. Jr. C. of C. (pres. 1962-63), Japan Am. Soc. So. Calif., Los Angeles World Affairs Council. Home: 2219 Cheswic Ln Los Angeles CA 90027-1134 Office: Kelley Drye & Warren 515 S Flower St Los Angeles CA 90071-2201 also: 101 Park Ave New York NY 10178*

MORI, JUNICHI, veterinary medicine educator; b. Tokyo, Feb. 24, 1932; s. Yuichi and Mitsuko (Sugiura) M.; m. Sachiko Komori, Oct. 5, 1961; children: Shunsuke, Atsuko. DVM, Tokyo U., 1955, PhD, 1972. Rsch. scientist Nat. Inst. Animal Industry Nat. Agrl. Experiment Sta. Ministry Agrl., Chiba and Shimane, Japan, 1955-75; head lab. of animal reproduction Nat. Inst. Animal Industry Ministry Agrl., Tsukuba and Chiba, Japan, 1975-82; assoc. prof. U. Osaka Prefecture, Sakai, Osaka, Japan, 1982-84, prof., 1984-95; prof. emeritus U. Osaka Prefecture, Sakai, Japan, 1995—, dean Coll. Agr., 1992-94; prof. Kitasato U., Towada, Japan, 1995—. Author 17 books on animal reproduction, 2 animal sci. dictionaries; contbr. numerous articles to profl. jours. Mem. Japanese Soc. Animal Reproduction (bd. dirs. 1988—, Acad. award 1970), Japanes Soc. Vet. Sci. (councilor 1982—), Japanese Soc. Reproductive Immunology (bd. dirs. 1988—), Japanese Soc. Fertility and Sterility (councilor 1984—), Soc. for Study of Reproduction, N.Y. Acad. Scis. Home: 3-18-4 Kohinata, Bunkyo-ku, Tokyo 112, Japan Office: Kitasato U, 35-1 Higasi 25 bancho, Towada shi 034, Japan

MORIAL, MARC HAYDEL, mayor; b. New Orleans, Jan. 3, 1958; s. Ernest and Sybil M.; divorced; 1 child, Kemah. Bar: La. Legis. intern U.S. Sen. Russell Long, Washington, 1979; dir. U. Pa. Office of Supportive Svcs., Phila., 1979-80; summer assoc. U.S. Atty. U.S. Dist. Ct. (so. dist.) N.Y., 1982; legis. asst. U.S. Rep. George T. Leland, Washington, 1983; atty. Barham & Churchill, New Orleans, 1983-85; pvt. practice New Orleans, 1985—; mem. La. Senate, Baton Rouge, 1991-93, mem. revenue and fiscal affairs com., commerce com., labor and indsl. rels. com., select com. crime & drugs, intergovtl. rels. com., Pres. Clinton's action com. on crime & drugs, senate select com. on econ. devel.; mayor City of New Orleans, 1993—; adj. prof. law, polit. sci. Xavier U. La., New Orleans, 1988-90. Del. Nat. Rainbow Coalition Conv., 1986, La. State Dem. Conv., 1986, Dem. Nat. Conv., Atlanta, 1988; cooperating atty. NAACP Legal Def. Fund, mem. nat., New Orleans br.; gen. counsel La. Assn. Minority and Women Owned Businesses, Inc., La. Voter Registration/Edn. Crusade; cooperating atty. Minority Bus. Enterprise Legal Def. and Edn. Fund; divestment coord., legal advisor New Orleans Anti-Apartheid Coalition, 1983—; bd. dirs. La. ACLU, La. Spl. Olympics, Milne Boys Home; mem. project steering com. Voting Rights Law Reporter; mem. Young Leadership Coun., Friend of New Orleans Ctr. for Creative Arts. Recipient Chmns. award Congl. Black Caucus, 1989, Outstanding Svc. award Lutcher (La.) H.S., 1990, La. NAACP Cmty. Svc. award, 1988; named Legis. Rookie of Yr. Baton Rouge Bus. Report, 1992, All Rookie Team by polit. columnist John Maginnis, 1993, Legis. Newcome of Yr., 1992. Mem. ABA (standing com. on world order under law 1982-83), Nat. Bar Assn., La. State Bar Assn. (Pro Bono Pub. award 1988), La. Assn. Criminal Def. Attys., Nat. Conf. Black Lawyers, Amnesty Internat. USA, Transafrica, Louis A. Martinet Legal Soc. New Orleans, La. Trial Lawyers Assn. (pres. adv. coun.), Nat. Black Law

Students Assn. (nat. bd. dirs. 1981-83), Alpha Phi Alpha. Office: Office of the Mayor 1300 Perdido St New Orleans LA 70112-2114*

MORIARTY, CATHY, actress; b. Bronx, N.Y., Nov. 29, 1960; d. John and Catherine M. Actress: (films) Raging Bull, 1980 (Academy award nomination best supporting actress 1980), Neighbors, 1981, White of the Eye, 1987, Kindergarten Cop, 1990, Soapdish, 1991, The Mambo Kings, 1992, The Gun in Betty Lou's Handbag, 1992, Matinee, 1993, Another Stakeout, 1993, Another Midnight Run, 1993, Pontiac Moon, 1994, Forget Paris, 1995, Casper, 1995, A Brother's Kiss, 1995, Bless This House, 1995, (TV series) Tales from the Crypt (CableACE award), Hugo Pool, 1996. Office: ICM 8942 Wilshire Blvd Beverly Hills CA 90211

MORIARTY, DONALD WILLIAM, JR., banker; b. Amarillo, Tex., Sept. 15, 1939; s. Donald William and Lorraine Julia (Walck) M.; m. Rita Ann Giller, Nov. 28, 1964; children: Mary Kathleen, Jennifer Ann, Anne Marie, Kerry Lee, Erin Teresa. Student, St. Benedict's Coll., 1957-59, 60-61; B.Sc., Washington U., 1962; M.Sc., St. Louis U., 1965, Ph.D., 1970. Cost acct. Emerson Electric, St. Louis, 1959-63; grad. fellow in econs. St. Louis U., 1963-65, instr., 1965-68; asst. prof. U. Mo., St. Louis, 1968-70; with Fed. Res. Bank of St. Louis, 1968-83, v.p., 1971-74, sr. v.p., controller, 1974-77, 1st v.p., 1977-83; sr. v.p. Gen. Bancshares Corp., 1983-86; exec. v.p. Commerce Bancshares, Inc., 1986-87; bank cons., 1987-89; pres., CEO, bd. dirs. Duchesne Bank, St. Peters, Mo., 1989—; bd. dirs. Mid-Am. Payments Exchange, Duchesne Bank; vis. instr. Webster Coll., 1975-82; adviser City of Des Peres (Mo.), chmn. fin. com., 1976-78, chmn. mgmt. com., 1978-81, mem. personnel commn., 1978-81, mem. planning and zoning com., 1981-83. Trustee, vice chmn. St. Joseph Hosp., 1982-93; mem. adv. bd. St. Joseph Acad., 1982-86; mem. pres.'s coun. St. Louis U., 1983—; bd. dirs. ea. Mo. region NCCJ, 1987-93; dist. chmn. Boy Scouts Am., 1991-93, vice chmn. 1994—. Recipient Alumni Merit award St. Louis U., 1979. Mem. Am. Econ. Assn., Am. Fin. Assn., Am. Mgmt. Assn., St. Peters C. of C., St. Charles C. of C., Beta Gamma Sigma, Alpha Kappa Psi. Club: Media.

MORIARTY, GEORGE MARSHALL, lawyer; b. Youngstown, Ohio, Sept. 16, 1942; s. George Albert Moriarty and Caroline (Jones) Bass; m. Elizabeth Bradley Moore, Sept. 11, 1965 (div. 1986); children: Bradley Marshall, Caroline Walden, Sarah Cameron. BA magna cum laude, Harvard U., 1964, LLB magna cum laude, 1968. Bar: Mass. 1969, U.S. Dist. Ct. Mass. 1973, U.S. Ct. Appeals (1st cir.) 1976, U.S. Ct. Appeals (D.C. cir.) 1984, U.S. Claims Ct. 1983, U.S. Supreme Ct. 1976. Law clk. to Hon. Bailey Aldrich U.S. Ct. Appeals (1st cir.), Boston, 1968-69; law clk. to Hon. Warren Burger, Hon. Hugo Black, Hon. Potter Stewart, Hon. Byron White U.S. Supreme Ct., Washington, 1969-70; spl. asst. to Hon. Elliot L. Richardson, Dept. Health, Edn. & Welfare, Washington, 1970-71, exec. asst., 1971-72; assoc. Ropes & Gray, Boston, 1972-77, ptnr., 1977—. Trustee Boston Athenaeum, Brigham & Women's Hosp., Ptnrs. Health Care Sys. Inc.; warden Trinity Ch. in City of Boston, vestryman. Mem. ABA, Am. Law Inst., Boston Bar Assn., Somerset Club, Tavern Club, Met. Club. Office: Ropes & Gray 1 Internat Pl Boston MA 02110

MORIARTY, JOHN, opera administrator, artistic director; b. Fall River, Mass., Sept. 30, 1930; s. John J. and Fabiola Marie (Ripeau) M. MusB summa cum laude, New Eng. Conservatory, 1952; D.M. New England Conservatory, 1992. Artistic adminstr. Opera Soc. of Washington, 1960-62, Santa Fe Opera, N.Mex., 1962-65; dir. Wolf Trap Co., Vienna, Va., 1972-77; chmn. opera dept. Boston Conservatory , 1973-89; chmn. opera dept. New Eng. Conservatory, 1989—; prin. condr. Central City Opera, Denver, 1978—, artistic dir., 1982—; panelist Nat. Inst. Music Theater, 1985, 86, 87, Conn. Arts Council, 1982, 84; adjudicator various contests including Met. Opera auditions, 1965—. Author: Diction, 1975. Trustee Boston Concert Opera. Recipient Frank Huntington Beebe award, Boston, 1954, Disting. Alumni award New Eng. Conservatory Alumni Assn., 1982, Gold Chair award Cen. City Opera House Assn., 1988. Mem. Nat. Opera Assn., Sigma Alpha Iota, Delta Omicron, Pi Kappa Lambda. Office: New Eng Conservatory 290 Huntington Ave Boston MA 02115-5018 also: Cen City Opera House Assn 621 17th St Ste 1601 Denver CO 80293-1601

MORIARTY, MICHAEL, actor; b. Detroit, Apr. 5, 1941; s. George and Eleanor (Paul) M.; m. Françoise Martinet, June 1966 (div.); 1 son, Matthew; m. Anne Hamilton Martin. B.A., Dartmouth Coll., 1963; postgrad. (Fulbright fellow), London Acad. Music and Dramatic Arts; D.F.A. (hon.), Fairleigh Dickinson U. Profl. debut with N.Y. Shakespeare Festival as Octavius Caesar in Antony and Cleopatra, Delacorte Theatre, N.Y.C., 1963, also Florizel in The Winter's Tale, 1963; stage appearances include Love's Labour Lost, 1965, Troilus and Cressida, 1965, Major Barbara, 1966, Henry IV, 1968, The House of Atreus, 1968, The Resistible Rise of Arturo Ui, 1968, Mourning Becomes Electra, 1969, The Alchemist, 1970, In the Jungle of Cities, 1970, Peanut Butter and Jelly, 1970, The Night Thoreau Spent in Jail, 1971, The Trial of the Catonsville Nine, 1971, Find Your Way Home, 1974 (Tony award for best actor 1974), King Richard III, 1974, Long Day's Journey into Night, 1983, Caine Mutiny-Court Martial, Richard III, My Fair Lady, 1994; films include Glory Boy, 1971, Hickey & Boggs, 1972, Bang the Drum Slowly, 1973, The Last Detail, 1974, Report to the Commissioner, 1975, Shoot It, 1976, Who'll Stop the Rain, 1978, Too Far to Go, 1979 (San Sebastian Internat. Film Festival award), Reborn, 1982, Q, 1982, The Stuff, 1985, Pale Rider, 1985, Troll, 1986, The Hanoi Hilton, 1987, It's Alive III: Island of the Alive, 1987, Return to Salem's Lot, 1987, Full Fathom Five, 1990; TV appearances include The Glass Menagerie, 1973 (Emmy award for best supporting actor in drama 1974), Holocaust, 1978 (Emmy award), The Deadliest Season, 1979, The Equalizer (Emmy nomination for best guest lead performance 1989), NBC Movie of the Week Born Too Soon, 1992; TV series: Law & Order, 1990-94 (Emmy nominations for best lead actor 1991, 92, 94); HBO movie Tailspin; writer: Flight to the Fatherland; writer, star: Ballad of Dexter Creed; composer score: The 15th Time; albums include Reaching Out, 1990, The Michael Moriarty Jazz Trio, 1991. Recipient Outstanding Creative Versatility award Yeshiva U., Emmy nomination lead actor Law and Order, 1993, Golden Globe nomination lead actor, 1993. Office: The Agency 1800 Avenue of the Stars Ste 400 Los Angeles CA 90067*

MORICE, JAMES L., public relations executive; b. St. Louis, Mo., Aug. 30, 1948. BA in History, Ind. U., 1970; MS in Journalism, U. Mo., 1973. Gen. assignment and labor reporter St. Louis-Globe Democrat, 1973-77; investigative reporter Milw. Sentinel, 1977-78; counselor Fleishman-Hillard, 1978-82, v.p., sr. ptnr., 1982-84, exec. v.p., sr. ptnr., 1984—. Office: Fleishman-Hillard Inc 200 N Broadway Saint Louis MO 63102-2730

MORICE, JOSEPH RICHARD, history educator; b. Phila., Apr. 2, 1923; s. Joseph and Anna (Seary) M.; m. Josephine Tumminello, May 31, 1958; children—Ann Marie, Jacqueline. B.A., LaSalle Coll., 1947; M.A., Fordham U., 1951; M.Litt., U. Pitts., 1953, Ph.D., 1962. Mem. faculty Duquesne U., Pitts., 1948-89; prof. history Duquesne U., 1963-89, chmn. dept., 1965-69, dir. debate, 1955-89, emeritus prof. history, 1990—; mng. editor Duquesne Rev., 1956-73. Vol. Pub. Acct. Office, 1991-94. With AUS, 1943-45. Mem. Orgn. Am. Historians, Cath. Host. Soc. W. Pa., Phi Kappa Phi, Phi Alpha Theta. Home: 1632 Worcester Dr Pittsburgh PA 15243-1534

MORIKAWA, DENNIS J., lawyer; b. Feb. 14, 1946. BA, Dennison U., 1968; JD, Syracuse U., 1974. Bar: Pa. 1974, U.S. Supreme Ct. 1983. Ptnr. Morgan, Lewis & Bockius, Phila. Mem. ABA (mgmt. co-chair occupational safety and health law com. 1989-92). Office: Morgan Lewis & Bockius 2000 One Logan Sq Philadelphia PA 19103

MORILLO, VIRGINIA LYNN, hotel executive; b. Silver Spring, Md., Nov. 20, 1967; d. Petronio E. and Wendy A. Morillo. Student, Strayer Coll., 1990-93. Asst. contr. Sheraton Nat. Hotel, Arlington, Va., 1989—. Mem. Nat. Soc. Pub. Accts. Avocations: reading, environmental issues, swimming, scuba diving, travelling. Office: Sheraton National Hotel 900 S Orme St Arlington VA 22204-4520

MORIMOTO, CARL NOBORU, computer system engineer, crystallographer; b. Hiroshima, Japan, Mar. 31, 1942; came to U.S., 1957, naturalized, 1965; s. Toshiyuki and Teruko (Hirano) M.; m. Helen Kiyomi Yoshizaki, June 28, 1969; children: Matthew Ken, Justin Ray. BA, U. Hawaii, 1965; PhD, U. Wash., 1970. Research assoc. dept. chemistry Mich. State U., East Lansing, 1970-72; postdoctoral fellow dept. biochemistry and biophysics Tex. A&M U., College Station, 1972-75; sr. sci. programmer Syntex Analytical Instruments Inc., Cupertino, Calif., 1975-78; prin. programmer analyst, software engring. mgr. Control Data Corp., Sunnyvale, Calif., 1978-83; mem. profl. staff GE Aerospace, San Jose, Calif., 1983-93; prin. engr. GE Nuclear Energy, San Jose, 1993—. Mem. Am. Crystallographic Assn., Assn. Computing Machinery, Am. Chem. Soc., Sigma Xi. Am. Baptist. Home: 4003 Hamilton Park Dr San Jose CA 95130-1223

MORIN, CARLTON PAUL, private investments executive; b. Ashland, Maine, July 10, 1932; s. Leo Joseph and Leona (Nadeau) M.; children: Catherine Lee, Cynthia Ann, Bruce Carlton. AB, U. Maine, 1954; LLB, Seton Hall U., 1964. Tax acct. Internat. Nickel Co., Inc., N.Y.C., 1956-62; tax mgr. Abex Corp., N.Y.C., 1962-67; asst. to contr. Todd Shipyards Corp., N.Y.C., 1967-68; asst. treas. Interlake, Inc., Chgo., 1968-75, Congoleum Corp., Milw., 1975-77; treas. Congoleum Corp., 1977-79, v.p., treas., 1979-80, v.p. treasury and adminstrn., 1980-83, v.p. corp. devel., 1983-86; pvt. practice pvt. investor Portsmouth, 1986-92; chmn. Piscataqua Savs. Bank, 1991-92; bd. dirs. Kinderworks Corp., Casco Bay Gear and Apparel. With USMC, 1954-56. Office: PO Box 6676 Portsmouth NH 03802-6676

MORIN, JAMES C., editorial cartoonist; b. Washington; s. Charles Henry and Elizabeth (Donnelly) M.; m. Danielle Flood; children: Elizabeth, Spencer. BFA, Syracuse U., 1975. Editorial cartoonist Beaumont (Tex.) Eeterprise, 1976-77, Richmnd (Va.) Times Dispatch, 1977-78, The Miami (Fla.) Herald, 1978—. Author, cartoonist: (books) Famous Cats, 1982, Jim Morin's Field Guide to Birds, 1985, Line of Fire, 1991. Pulitzer Prize finalist, Columbia U., 1978,'90. Mem. Assn. of Am. Editorial Cartoonists, Overseas Press Club, Nat. Cartoonists Soc., Soc. of Profl. Journalists (Green Eyeshade award). Avocations: oil painting, acoustic guitar playing. Office: The Miami Herald 1 Herald Plz Miami FL 33132-1609

MORIN, PIERRE JEAN, retired management consultant; b. Quebec City, Que., Can., Aug. 5, 1931; s. Augustin Norbert and Yvonne (Gaudry) M.; m. Colette Poulin, Apr. 3, 1954; children: Anne, Gilles, Louis. B.S., Concordia U., Montreal, 1964; M.S., Laval U., Que., 1970, D.Sc., 1973. Quality control technician Dow Brevery, Montreal, Que., 1952-56; research assoc. Royal Victoria Hosp., Montreal, 1957-67; coordinator of research Que. Heart Inst., 1967-73; dir. research labs. Laval Hosp., Que., 1973-80, lectr. dept. medicine, 1973-77; dir. gen. Community Service Ctr., 1980-88; mgmt. cons., 1988-91, ret., 1991; cons. Que. Minister of Environ., 1975-84. Contbr. articles to profl. jours. and news media. Bd. dirs. St. Mary's Hosp., Three Rivers, Que. Schering Travelling fellow, 1971. Mem. AAAS. Roman Catholic. Home: 336 Rg Castor, Leclercville, PQ Canada G0S 2K0 *Well assumed failure may be a must towards later success.*

MORIN, WILLIAM JAMES, management consultant; b. Kankakee, Ill., Aug. 5, 1939; s. Carl Wesley and Viola Grace (Seaberlie) M.; children: Mark, Timothy, Jason. BS, So. Ill. U., 1961, MS, 1963. Pres. Drake, Beam, Morin, N.Y.C., 1977-79, chmn., chief exec. officer, 1979-95; pres., CEO WTM Assocs., 1995—. Author: Successful Termination, Outplacement Techniques, Parting Company, Silent Sabotoge, 1995. Mem. Assn. Outplacement Cons. Firms (standards com.).

MORIN, YVES-CHARLES, linguistics educator, researcher; b. St. Germain, Yvelines, France, Nov. 7, 1944; arrived in Can. 1972; s. Georges and Denise (Montaudouin) M.; 1 child, Yannig. Lic., U. Paris, 1967; Diploma in Engring., Ecole Centrale, 1967; M.A. in Linguistics, U. Mich., 1970, Ph.D. in Computer Sci., 1971. Engr. Mil. Radar Estab., Pontoise, France, 1971-72; asst. prof. U. Montreal, Montreal, Que., Can., 1972-76, assoc. prof., 1967-82, prof., 1982—, mem. exec. com. Faculty of Arts and Scis., 1984-86; invited prof. Bourguiba Inst., Tunis, Tunisia, 1977; mem. cons. bd. Humanities and Social Scis. Research Council of Canada, Ottawa, 1980-83; vis. scholar Centre d'Etudes Metriques de Nantes (France), 1994. Contbr. articles to profl. jours. Served to lt. Logistics-Radar, 1971-72; France. Harkness fellow Commonwealth Fund, 1967. Mem. Linguistic Soc. Am., Can. Linguistic Soc., Can. Jour. Linguistics, Société Asiatique, Sigma Xi, Phi Kappa Phi. Office: Univ Montreal, Dept Linguistics, CP 6128, Montreal, PQ Canada H3C 3J7

MORING, JOHN FREDERICK, lawyer; b. Farmville, Va., Oct. 30, 1935; s. Scott O'Ferrall and Margaret Macon (Mitchell) M.; m. Margaret Ann Clarke, Mar. 30, 1959; children: Martha, Elizabeth, Scott, Lee. BS, Va. Poly. Inst., 1957; JD, George Washington U., 1961. Bar: Va. 1961, D.C. 1962, U.S. Supreme Ct. 1964. Assoc. Morgan, Lewis & Bockius, Washington, 1961-68, ptnr., 1969-78; ptnr. Jones, Day, Reavis & Pogue, Washington, 1978-79, Crowell & Moring, Washington and London, 1979—; sec. Associated Gas Distbrs., Inc., 1977—. Local gas utility columnist Nat. Gas Jour., 1989—; mem. editl. bd. Natural Gas Contracts, 1994—. Pres. Sterling Citizens Assn., Alexandria, Va., 1971-77; Rep. candidate 23d Dist./Va. Gen. Assembly, Alexandria, 1973; chmn. Alexandria Rep. Com. on Candidate Recruitment, 1974; bd. govs. St. Stephen's and St. Agnes Sch., Alexandria, 1989-95; pres. St. Stephen's Found., Inc., 1990-93; sr. warden Immanuel Ch. of the Hill, Alexandria, 1988, 89; trustee Ch. Schs. of Diocese of Va., 1996—. 2d lt. U.S. Army, 1958. Mem. ABA (natural resources law sect. 1982-86, coun.), Fed. Energy Bar Assn. (sec. 1963-66, pres. 1982-83), Belle Haven Country Club. Episcopalian. Avocations: golf, fishing, canoeing. Home: 509 Canterbury Ln Alexandria VA 22314-4747 Office: Crowell & Moring 1001 Pennsylvania Ave NW Washington DC 20004-2505 also: 2010 Main St Irvine CA 92714-7203 also: 180 Fleet St, London ECAA2 HD, England

MORIS, LAMBERTO GIULIANO, architect; b. Siena, Tuscany, Italy, Mar. 29, 1944; came to U.S., 1972; s. Gualtiero Luigi and Giovanna (Avanzati) M.; m. Tracy P. Schilling, 1970 (div. 1985); children: Giacomo, Stefano; m. Beverly Chiang, Mar. 28, 1986; 1 child, Christopher. MA in Arch., U. Florence, Italy, 1970. Assoc. Marquis Assocs., San Francisco, 1972-78, prin., 1978-85; prin. Simon Martin-Vegue Winkelstein Moris, San Francisco, 1985—; tchr. San Francisco City Coll.; juror DuPont Antron Design Awards, 1989; mem. adv. com. Acad. of Art-Coll., San Francisco, 1991—. Mem. San Francisco Opera Guild. Fellow AIA (mem. Coll. Fellows, mem. interior arch. sect., juror Honor Award for interiors 1996); mem. Italingua Inst. (bd. dirs.), Oakland Met. C. of C., The Engrs. Club, Il Cenacolo Club. Roman Catholic. Avocations: coin collecting, skiing, travel. Office: Simon Martin-Vegue Winkelstein Moris 501 2nd St Ste 701 San Francisco CA 94107-1431

MORISATO, SUSAN CAY, actuary; b. Chgo., Feb. 11, 1955; d. George and Jessie (Fujita) M.; m. Thomas Michael Remec, Mar. 6, 1981. BS, U. Ill., 1975, MS, 1977. Actuarial student Aetna Life & Casualty, Hartford, Conn., 1977-79; actuarial asst. Bankers Life & Casualty, Chgo., 1979-80, asst. actuary, 1980-83, assoc. actuary, 1983-85, health product actuary, 1985-86, v.p., 1986-95; sr. v.p., 1996—; participant individual forum Health Ins. Assn. Am., 1983; spkr. health forum Life Ins. Mgmt. Rsch. Assn., 1992, long-term care conf. Sharing the Burden, 1994. Mem. adv. panel on long term care financing Brookings' Inst. Fellow Soc. Actuaries (conf. spkr. 1988, 94, workshop leader 1990, 93, news editor health sect. news 1988-90); mem. Am. Acad. Actuaries, Health Ins. Assn. Am. (long term care task force 1988—, chair 1993-95, conf. spkr. 1990, tech. adv. com. 1991-93, mem. health care reform strategy com. 1993-95, mem. supplemental ins. com. 1996, mem. legis. policy com. 1996—), Nat. Assn. Ins. Commrs. (ad hoc actuarial working group for long term care nonforfeiture benefits 1992), Chgo. Actuarial Assn. (sec. 1983-85, program com. 1987-89), Phi Beta Kappa, Kappa Delta Pi, Phi Kappa Phi. Office: Bankers Life & Casualty Co 222 Merchandise Mart Plz Chicago IL 60654-1001

MORISHIGE, FUKUMI, surgeon; b. Fukuoka, Japan, Oct. 24, 1925; s. Fukumatsu and Teruko M.; m. Fumie Osada, Apr. 18, 1954; children: Kyoko, Hisakazu, Noritsugu. MD, Kurume U., 1952, DMS, 1962; PhD, Fukuoka U., 1983. Intern Kurume U., 1951-52; asst. Kurume (Japan) U., Dept. Pathology, 1952-55, Kyoto (Japan) U. Inst. Chest Disease, 1955-58; v.p. Tachiarai Hosp., Fukuoka, Japan, 1959-67, Torikai Hosp., Fukuoka, Japan, 1968-80; chmn. Tachiarai Hosp., Fukuoka, Japan, 1980-84; dir. Nakamura Hosp., Fukuoka, Japan, 1984-86, supreme advisor, 1987—; dir. Morishige Cancer Clinic, Chiba, Japan, 1992—; resident fellow Linus Pauling Inst. of Sci. and Medicine, Palo Alto, Calif., 1976—; chemistry advisor Nissan Chem. Industries Ltd., Tokyo, 1983—. Author: Nutrition of Nucleic Acid, 1983, Brain Blood Circulation, 1986; contbr. articles to profl. jours. Fellow Linus Pauling Inst. Sci. and Medicine; mem. Japan Soc. Magnetic Resonance (founder, bd. dirs. 1978—, exec. sec. 1979—), Internat. Assn. for Vitamin & Nutritional Oncology (exec. com. 1983—), Japanese Cancer Assn., Japanese Assn. for Thoracic Surgery, Japan Surg. Soc. Democrat. Buddhist. Home and Office: Miyakono 2-10-13, Ooami-Shirasato-Machi, Sambu Chiba 299-32, Japan Office: Sta Pla Hotel 1401, 2-1-1 Hakata-Eki-Mae, Hakata Fukuoka, Japan

MORISHITA, AKIHIKO, trading company executive; b. Osaka, Japan, Oct. 14, 1941; came to U.S., 1981; s. Sueyoshi and Toshiko Morishita; m. Fumiko Okamura; children: Shizuko, Kumiko, Okamura. BA in Econs., Wakayama U., Wakayama, Japan, 1965. Mgr. Hanwa & Co. Ltd., Osaka, 1965-80; cons. oil dept. Pacific Southwest Trading Co., San Diego, 1981-82; exec., v.p. Pacific Marine Bunkering, Inc., L.A., 1982—. Mem. L.A. Oilmen's Club, Woodland Hills Country Club. Home: 4610 Don Pio Dr Woodland Hills CA 91364-4205

MORISON, JOHN HOPKINS, casting manufacturing company executive; b. Milw., June 29, 1913; s. George Abbot and Amelia (Elmore) M. m. Olga de Souza Dantas, July 29, 1944; children: Maria de Souza Dantas, John Hopkins III. AB, Harvard U., 1935; LLD, New Eng. Coll., 1973. Various positions Bucyrus-Erie Co., South Milwaukee, Wis., U.S. and Latin Am., 1935-49; pres., dir. Hitchiner Mfg. Co., Inc., Milford, N.H., 1949-93, chmn. bd., 1973-93, chmn. emeritus, 1994—; pres., treas. Upland Farm Inc., Peterborough, N.H.; chmn. RiverMead Retirement Community, Peterborough, N.H., 1991—; bd. dirs. Markem Corp., Keene, N.H. Munters Corp. USA, Ft. Myers, Fla. Commr. N.H. Commn. on Arts, 1967-77; mem. regional exec. com. Boy Scouts Am., Framingham, Mass., 1970-76; mem. exec. com., pres., N.H. Coun. on World Affairs, 1955-76; trustee Canterbury Shaker Village, 1982-96; trustee Land Use Found. N.H., 1970-75, World Peace Found., 1962-90, Currier Gallery Art; pres. bd. dirs. Matthew Thornton Health Plan, 1972-82; bd. dirs. Forum on N.H.'s Future, 1979-81; pres., distbg. dir. N.H. Charitable Fund, 1968-79; mem. corp. MacDowell Colony; v.p. bd. govs. N.H. Public TV, 1979-89. Lt. (j.g.) USNR, 1943-46. Recipient Lifetime Achievement award N.H. Bus. and Industry Assn., 1993, N.H. High Tech. Coun., 1996, Granite State award U. N.H., 1994. Mem. Somerset Club. Unitarian. Home: RR 1 Box 326 Lyndeborough NH 03082-9734

MORISSETTE, ALANIS, musician. Recipient Grammy award for Album of Yr., Best Female Rock Vocal Performance, Best Rock Song, Best Rock Album, 1996. Office: Maverick Music Co 8000 Beverly Blvd Los Angeles CA 90048*

MORITA, KAZUTOSHI, psychology educator, consultant; b. Tokyo, Nov. 25, 1937; s. Kyoichi and Tomiko Morita; m. Yoshie Nakahashi, Oct. 10, 1968; children: Toshio, Hideyo. BA in Psychology, U. Tokyo, 1961. Lectr. Sanno Jr. Coll., Tokyo, 1968-71, asst. prof., 1972-79, mgr. Inst. Orgnl. Behavior, 1973-77, asst. v.p., 1978-79; asst. prof. indsl. and orgnl. psychology and behavioral sci. Sangyo Noritsu U., Ishehara, Japan, 1980-83; prof. Sanno U. Sch. Mgmt. and Informatics, Kanagawa, Japan, 1984—, mgr. adminstrv. dept., 1988—; vis. scholar U. Mich., Ann Arbor, 1971, Harvard U., Cambridge, Mass., 1972; com. mem. human resource devel. project Ministry Internat. Trade and Industry, 1973-76; com. mem. long range plan for edn. Ministry Edn., 1975-77; vice chmn. Conf. Commerce Activities Adjustment, Fujisawa, Japan, 1988—. Author, editor: Cases of Organizational Development in Japan, 1978, Formats for Human Resource Management, 1990; author: Behavioral Sciences in Business, 1984. Recipient Ueno Godo prize 18th All Japan Mgmt. Conf., 1966. Mem. Japanese Assn. Indsl. and Orgnl. Psychology (editorial com. 1986—). Home: 14-3 Matsukazedai, Chigasaki Kanagawa 253, Japan Office: Sanno U, 1573 Kamikasuya, Isehara Kanagawa 259-11, Japan

MORITA, (NORIYUKI) PAT, actor, comedian; b. Isleton, Calif., 1932; m. Yuki Morita, 1970; children: Tia, Aly. Grad. high sch., Fairfield, Calif. Ind. nightclub comedian, actor Los Angeles, 1964—. Regular mem. cast: (TV series) Sanford and Son, 1974-75, (as Arnold) Happy Days, 1975-76, 82-83; starring roles: (TV series) Mr. T and Tina, 1976, Blansky's Beauties, 1977, Ohara, 1987; TV films include The Vegas Strip War, Amos, Return to Manzanar, Greyhounds; feature films: Thoroughly Modern Millie, 1967, Midway, 1976, When Time Ran Out, 1980, Savannah Smiles, 1982, Jimmy the Kid, 1983, The Karate Kid, 1984 (Acad. award nomination 1985), The Karate Kid Part II, 1986, Collision Course, 1987, The Karate Kid Part III, 1989, Do or Die, 1991, Honeymoon in Vegas, 1992, Even Cowgirls Get the Blues, 1994, The Next Karate Kid, 1994, American Ninja 5, 1995. Recipient Lifetime Achievement award Assn. Asian/Pacific Am. Artists, 1987. *

MORITA, RICHARD YUKIO, microbiology and oceanography educator; b. Pasadena, Calif., Mar. 27, 1923; s. Jiro and Reiko (Yamamoto) M.; m. Toshiko Nishihara, May 29, 1926; children—Sally Jean, Ellen Jane, Peter Wayne. B.S., U. Nebr., 1947; M.S., U. So. Calif., 1949; Ph.D., U. Calif., 1954. Microbiologist Mid-Pacific Expdn., 1950, Danish Galathea Deep-Sea Expdn., 1952, Trans-Pacific Expdn.; Postdoctoral fellow U. Calif., Scripps Inst. Oceanography, 1954-55; asst. prof. U. Houston, 1955-58; asst. prof., assoc. prof. U. Neb., 1958-62; prof. microbiology and oceanography Oreg. State U., Corvallis, 1962—; prog. dir. biochemistry NSF, 1968-69; Disting. vis. prof. Kyoto Univ.; cons. NIH, 1968-70; researcher in field. Contbr. articles to sci. lit. Patentee in field. Served with U.S. Army, 1944-46. Grantee NSF, 1962—, NIH, 1960-68, NASA, 1967-72, Office Naval Research, 1966-70, Dept. Interior, 1968-72, NOAA, 1975-82, Bur. Land Mgmt., 1982, EPA, 1986—; recipient awards including King Fredericus IX Medal and Ribbon, 1954, Sr. Queen Elizabeth II Fellowship, 1973-74, Hotpack lectr. and award Can. Soc. Fellow Japan Soc. for Promotion Sci.; mem. Am. Soc. Microbiology (Fisher award). Office: Oreg State U Dept Microbiology Corvallis OR 97331

MORITA, TOSHIYASU, technical institute administrator; b. Tokyo, Feb. 8, 1967; s. Hiroshi and Fusako (Ishikawa) M. Grad. high sch., 1985. Programmer Origin Systems, Inc., Austin, Tex., 1987; engr. Cyclops Electronics, Boerne, 1988-90; programmer Taito R&D, Bothell, Wash., 1990; mgr. new tech. Lucas Arts Entertainment, San Rafael, Calif., 1990-93; tech. dir. Sega Tech. Inst., Redwood City, Calif., 1993-94, Sega of Am., Redwood City, 1994-96, Sega Soft, Redwood City, 1996—. Mem. IEEE Computer Soc. (affiliate), Mensa.

MORITSUGU, KENNETH PAUL, physician, government official; b. Honolulu, Mar. 5, 1945; s. Richard Yutaka and Hisayo Joan (Nishikawa) M.; children: Erika Lizabeth, Vikki Lianne. Student, Chaminade Coll. Honolulu, 1963-65; BA in Classical Langs. with honors, U. Hawaii, 1967; MD, George Washington U., 1971; MPH, U. Calif., Berkeley, 1975; DSc (hon.), Coll. Osteopathic Medicine, U. New Eng., 1988, Midwestern U., 1993; D Pub. Svc. (hon.), U. North Tex., 1994. Diplomate Am. Bd. Preventive Medicine (fellow); cert. correctional health profl. Intern USPHS Hosp., San Francisco, 1971-72, resident, 1972-75; commd. USPHS, 1968, advanced through grades to med. dir., 1979; promoted to rank of rear adm., asst. surgeon gen., 1988; staff med. officer USPHS Hosp., San Francisco, 1972-73; regional cons. med. manpower planning and devel. HEW, San Francisco, 1976-78; chief internat. edn. programs br. HEW, Washington, 1978; dep. dir. div. medicine HEW, 1978; dir. Bur. Health Professions, div. medicine HHS, Rockville, Md., 1978-83, dir. Nat. Health Service Corps, 1983-87, dep. dir. Bur. Health Professions, 1987; med. dir. Fed. Bur. Prisons Dept. Justice, Washington, 1987—. Decorated D.S.M.; recipient Commendation medal, Meritorious Svc. medal, Outstanding Svc. medal, Surgeon Gen.'s medallion, Surgeon Gen.'s medal, Dirs. award for Exceptional Svcs., U.S. Marshal's Svcs., John D. Chase award for outstanding physician adminstrn., AMSUS, Nathan Davies award AMA, others. Fellow Am. Coll. Preventive Medicine, Royal Soc. Health, Royal Soc. Medicine; mem. APHA, Assn. Tchrs. Preventive Medicine, Assn. Mil. Surgeons U.S., Res. Officers Assn., Mensa, Am. Guild Organists. Home: 726 Sonata Way Silver Spring MD 20901-5063 Office: US Dept Justice Fed Bur Prisons 320 1st St NW Ste 1000 Washington DC 20534-0002

MORITZ, CHARLES FREDRIC, book editor; b. Cleve., Jan. 23, 1917; s. Frederic and Alberta (Hartwig) M. B.A., Ohio State U., 1942; student, Harvard U., 1946-47, Columbia U., 1947-48; B.S. in L.S, Middlebury (Vt.) Coll., 1948, M.A., 1950. Asst. librarian rare book room and reference dept. Yale Library, 1948-50; mem. staff N.Y. Pub. Library, 1950-52; asst. prof. Grad. Sch. Library Service, Rutgers U., 1955-58; editor of Current Biography, 1958-92. Cons. editor Current Biography, 1993—; contbr. book revs. for Booklist, 1952-55; also articles. Served with AUS, 1942-45. Mem. ALA, Bibliog. Soc. Am. Democrat. Lutheran. Home: 3210 Arlington Ave 3-E Bronx NY 10463 Office: Current Biography 950 University Ave Bronx NY 10452-4224

MORITZ, DONALD BROOKS, mechanical engineer, consultant; b. Mpls., June 17, 1927; s. Donald B. and Frances W. (Whalen) M.; m. Joan Claire Betzenderfer, June 17, 1950; children: Craig, Pamela, Brian. B.S. in Mech. Engring., U. Minn., 1950; postgrad., Western Res. U., 1956-58. Registered profl. engr., Ill. Minn., Ohio. V.p., gen. mgr. Waco Scaffold Shoring Co., Addison, Ill., 1950-72; group v.p. Bliss and Laughlin Industries, Oak Brook, Ill., 1972-83; sr. v.p. AXIA Inc. (formerly Bliss and Laughlin Industries, Oak Brook, 1983-84, exec. v.p., chief operating officer, 1984-88; cons. Exec. Svc. Corps Chgo., 1988—; pres. Image-A-Nation, Unltd., 1988—; bd. dirs. Am. Photographic Acad. Patentee in field. Served with USN, 1945-46. Mem. ASME, Scaffold and Shoring Inst. (founder, past pres.), Mensa, Meadow Club. Office: Moritz and Assocs PO Box 305 Clarendon Hills IL 60514-0305

MORITZ, EDWARD, historian, educator; b. Columbia, S.C., Jan. 24, 1920; s. Edward and Edith (Jumper) M.; m. Betty Gene Reid, Apr. 8, 1946; children—Stephen Edward, John Reid, Richard Douglas, Sarah Anne. B.A., Miami U., Oxford, Ohio, 1949; M.A. (Taft scholar), U. Cin., 1950; Ph.D. (Knapp scholar), U. Wis., 1953. Instr. U. Wis., Madison, 1953-55; mem. faculty Kalamazoo (Mich.) Coll., 1955—, prof. history, 1963—, chmn. dept., 1965-88, prof. emeritus, 1988—; vis. prof. Oxford, Eng., 1971-72. Author: Winston Churchill, Parliamentary Career, 1908-12. Served with USAAF, 1942-46. Kellog fellow, 1971. Mem. Am. Hist. Assn., Conf. Brit. Studies, AAUP, Phi Beta Kappa, Phi Eta Sigma. Home: 420 Edgemoor Ave Kalamazoo MI 49001-4207 *This quote of the Earl of Montrose has influenced me over the years: He either fears his fate too much, or trusts it not at all; who will not put it to the touch--to win or lose it at all.*

MORITZ, MICHAEL EVERETT, lawyer; b. Marion, Ohio, Mar. 30, 1933; s. Charles Raymond and Elisabeth Bovie (Morgan) M.; m. Lou Ann Yardley, Sept. 12, 1959; children: Ann Gibson, Jeffrey Connor, Molly Elisabeth, Catharine Morgan. BS, Ohio State U., 1958, JD summa cum laude, 1961. Bar: Ohio 1961, U.S. Tax Ct. 1970. Assoc. Dunbar, Kienzle & Murphey, Columbus, Ohio, 1961-65, ptnr., 1966-72; ptnr. Moritz, McClure, Hughes & Kerscher, Columbus, 1972-80, Baker & Hostetler, Columbus, 1980—; adj. prof. Capital U. Law Sch., Columbus, 1969-70; lectr. Ohio Legal Ctr. Inst., Columbus, 1967; bd. dirs. Cardinal Health, Inc., Columbus; chmn. legal div. United Appeal Franklin County, Columbus, 1964; pres. Capital City Young Rep. Club, Columbus, 1966; mem. Franklin County Rep. Exec. Com., Columbus, 1966—; mem. bd. dirs. The Ohio State U. Found., Ohio State U. Coll. Bus. Pacesetters Club; trustee Kenyon Festival Theatre, 1981-86, Players Theatre Columbus, 1986-88; commr. Ohio Elections Commn., 1993—. With USN, 1954-56. Recipient Disting. Svc. award Columbus Jaycees, 1966. Mem. ABA, Ohio Bar Assn., Columbus Bar Assn., Am. Judicature Soc., Ohio State U. Faculty Club, Order of Coif, Phi Gamma Delta, Beta Gamma Sigma. Clubs: Muirfield Village Golf Club, Scioto Country, Capital, Columbus, Ohio State U. President's, Wedgewood Golf & Country Club, Jefferson Golf and Country Club, The Club at Seabrook Island. Office: Baker & Hostetler 65 E State St Columbus OH 43215-4213

MORITZ, MILTON EDWARD, security consultant; b. Reading, Pa., Sept. 5, 1931; s. Edward Raymond and Anna May M.; m. Elizabeth Ann Walls, June 6, 1952; children: Betsy Ann Moritz Koppenhaver, Stephen Edward, Sandra E. Student, U. Md., 1950-51, Fla. State U., 1959-60. Enlisted U.S. Army, 1949, chief warrant officer 3, 1968, spl. agt. M.I.; ret., 1970; safety and security dir. Harrisburg (Pa.) Hosp., 1970-72; security mgr. Sprint, Carlisle, Pa., 1972-94; prin. Moritz Assocs., Harrisburg, 1994—; lectr., instr. Harrisburg Area Community Coll.; mem. Indsl. Security Adv. Coun. Pres. Greater Harrisburg Crime Clinic, 1974. Decorated Bronze Star with oak leaf cluster. Mem. Am. Soc. Indsl. Security (past pres., chmn. bd. dirs.), Assn. Former Intelligence Officers, Internat. Narcotic Enforcement Officers Assn., Pa. Crime Prevention Assn. (bd. dirs.). Republican. Lutheran. Home and Office: 7723 Avondale Ter Harrisburg PA 17112-3805

MORITZ, TIMOTHY BOVIE, psychiatrist; b. Portsmouth, Ohio, July 26, 1936; s. Charles Raymond and Elisabeth Bovie (Morgan) M.; m. Joyce Elizabeth Rasmussen, Oct. 13, 1962 (div. Sept. 1969); children: Elizabeth Wynne, Laura Morgan; m. Antoinette Tanasichuk, Oct. 31, 1981; children: David Michael, Stephanie Lysbeth. BA, Ohio State U., 1959; MD, Cornell U., 1963. Diplomate Am. Bd. Psychiatry and Neurology. Intern in medicine N.Y. Hosp., N.Y.C., 1963-64, resident in psychiatry, 1964-67; spl. asst. to dir. NIMH, Bethesda, Md., 1967-69; dir. Community Mental Health Ctr., Rockland County, N.Y., 1970-74, Ohio Dept. Mental Health, Columbus, Ohio, 1975-81; med. dir. psychiatry Miami Valley Hosp., Dayton, Ohio, 1981-82; med. dir. N.E. Ga. Community Mental Health Ctr., Athens, Ga., 1982-83, Charter Vista Hosp., Fayetteville, Ark., 1983-87; clin. dir. adult psychiatry Charter Hosp., Las Vegas, Nev., 1987-94; pvt. practice psychiatry Las Vegas, Nev., 1987—; prof. Wright State U., Dayton, Ohio, 1981-82; asst. prof. Cornell U., N.Y.C., 1970-73; cons. NIMH, Rockville, Md., 1973-83. Author: (chpt.) Rehabilitation Medicine and Psychiatry, 1976; mem. editorial bd. Directions in Psychiatry, 1981—. Dir. dept. mental health and mental retardation Gov.'s Cabinet, State of Ohio, Columbus, 1975-81. Recipient Svc. award Ohio Senate, 1981, Svc. Achievement award Ohio Gov., 1981. Fellow Am. Psychiat. Assn. (Disting. Svc. award 1981); mem. AMA, Nev. Assn. Psychiat. Physicians, Nev. State Med. Assn., Clark County Med. Soc., Cornell U. Med. Coll. Alumni Assn. Office: Timothy B Moritz MD 3815 S Jones Blvd # 7 Las Vegas NV 89103-2289

MORLAND, JOHN KENNETH, sociology and anthropology educator; b. Huntsville, Ala., July 4, 1916; s. Howard Cannon and Ethel Mae (Cowan) M.; m. Margaret Louise Ward, Feb. 26, 1949; children: Carol, Katherine, Evelyn. B.S., Birmingham So. Coll., 1938; B.D., Yale U., 1943; Ph.D., U. N.C., 1950. Instr. Yale in China Middle Sch., Changsha, Hunan, 1943-46; exec. sec. Yale in China Assn., New Haven, 1946-47; asst. prof. Coll. William and Mary, Williamsburg, Pa., 1949-53; Charles A. Dana prof., chmn. dept. sociology and anthropology Randolph Macon Woman's Coll., Lynchburg, Va., 1953-87; rsch. analyst City of Lynchburg, 1989-94; cons. U.S. Dept. Edn., Dept. Commerce, NEH, So. Regional Coun. NSF, Ednl. and Rsch. Found., Lynchburg, Va. Author: Social Problems in the United States, 1975, Millways of Kent, 1958, (with John Williams) Race, Color and the Young Child, 1976, (with Jack Balswick) Social Problems: A Christian Understanding and Response, 1990; contbr., editor: The Not So Solid South, 1971. Pres. bd. nat. ministries Am. Bapt. Chs., USA, 1973-79. Named Eminent Laureate of Va., 1981; recipient Disting. Alumnus award Birmingham-So. Coll., 1985, Nat. Conf. Christians and Jews Humanitarian award, 1994; Fulbright scholar Chinese U., Hong Kong, 1966-67; grantee NSF, Taiwan, 1975, U.S. Dept. Edn., 1972. Fellow Am. Anthropol. Assn.; mem. Am. Sociol. Assn., So. Sociol. Soc., Va. Social Sci. Assn. (pres. 1963), AAUP (pres. 1962). Home: 1619 Dogwood Ln Lynchburg VA 24503-1923 Office: Randolph Macon Womans Coll PO Box 477 Lynchburg VA 24505-0477

MORLAND, RICHARD BOYD, retired educator; b. Huntsville, Ala., June 27, 1919; s. Howard Cannon and Ethel May (Cowan) M.; A.B., Birmingham-So. Coll., 1940; M.Ed., Springfield Coll., 1947; Ph.D. (So. Fellowships Fund fellow 1957-58), N.Y. U. 1958; m. Jessie May Parrish, Mar. 17, 1949; 1 child, Laura. Phys. dir. YMCA, Frankfort, Ky., 1940-41; dir. athletics, head basketball coach Fla. So. Coll., 1947-50; lectr. in edn., N.Y. U., 1950-51; chmn. dept. phy. edn., Stetson U., Deland, Fla., 1952-60, head basketball coach, 1952-57, assoc. prof., 1958-63, prof. philosophy of edn., 1963-89, J. Ollie Edmunds prof., 1982-85, sr. active prof., 1989-90, chmn. grad. coun., 1962-69, chmn. dept. edn., 1969-75. Contbr. articles to profl. jours. Lt. USNR, 1941-45. Decorated 11 battle stars, USS Lexington. Named to Stetson U. Sports Hall of Fame; recipient McEniry award for Excellence in teaching, 1983; Richard B. Morland Distinguished Alumni award named in his honor; Bronze bust by Harry Messersmith dedicated, 1992. Mem. Philosophy of Edn. Soc. (pres. region 1963-64), Fla. Coun. Deans and Dirs. Tchr. Edn. (pres. 1974-75), Am. Ednl. Rsch. Assn., Am. Edn. Studies Assn., Soc. Profs. Edn., Fla. Founds. Edn. and Policy Studies Soc. (exec. bd. 1987-90), Univ. Profs. for Acad. Order, DeLand Country Club, Omicron Delta Kappa, Phi Alpha Theta, Kappa Delta Pi, Phi Delta Kappa (pres. region 1977-78, editorial bd. Phi Delta Kappan 1978-83, named Regional Educator of Yr. 1991), panel gallup poll on edn., 1995, Kappa Alpha. Democrat. Methodist. Home: 524 N Mcdonald Ave Deland FL 32724-3643

MORLEY, GEORGE WILLIAM, gynecologist; b. Toledo, June 6, 1923; s. Francis Wayland and Florence (Sneider) M.; m. Constance J. Morley, July 27, 1946 (dec. 1960); children: Beverly, Kathryn, George W. Jr.; m. Marcheta F. Morley, June 14, 1963. BS, U. Mich, 1944, MD, 1949, MS, 1955; cert. in Gynecologic Oncology, Am. Bd. Ob-Gyn., 1974. Diplomate Am. Bd. Ob-Gyn. Intern U. Mich. Hosp., 1949-50, asst. resident, 1950-51, resident, 1951-52, jr. clin. instr., 1952-53, sr. clin. instr., 1953-54; mem. faculty Sch. Medicine U. Mich., Ann Arbor, 1956—, dir. gynecology svc., 1973-85, dir. gynecologic oncology svc., 1964-86, 94-95, Norman F. Miller prof. dept. ob.-gyn., 1987—, assoc. chmn., 1987-91; Chmn. Mich. Jud. Commn., Lansing, 1988-92. Contbr. to med. publs. George W. Morley professorship established U. Mich., 1995. Fellow, ACS (bd. govs. 1986-91), Am. Coll. Ob.-Gyn. (pres. 1987); mem. Rotary. Republican. Presbyterian. Avocations: golf, music. Home: 1120 Chestnut St Ann Arbor MI 48104-2826 Office: U Mich Med Ctr 1500 E Medical Center Dr Ann Arbor MI 48109-0999

MORLEY, HARRY THOMAS, JR., real estate executive; b. St. Louis, Aug. 13, 1930; s. Harry Thomas and Celeste Elizabeth (Davies) M.; m. Nelda Lee Mulholland, Sept. 3, 1960; children: Lisa, Mark, Marci. BA, U. Mo., 1955; MA, U. Denver, 1959. Dir. men's student activities Iowa State Tchrs. Coll., 1955-57; dir. student housing U. Denver, 1957-60; pvt. practice psychol. consulting St. Louis, 1960-63; dir. adminstrn. County of St. Louis, Mo., 1963-70; regional dir. HUD, Kansas City, Mo., 1970-71; asst. sec. adminstrn. HUD, 1971-73; pres. St. Louis Regional Commerce and Growth Assn., 1973-78, Taylor, Morley, Inc., St. Louis, 1978—; teaching cons.-lectr. Washington U., St. Louis, 1962-70. Bd. dirs., mem. exec. com. St. Louis Coll. Pharmacy; past chmn. Better Bus. Bur.; chmn. Mo. Indsl. Devel. Bd., Mo. State Hwy. Commn.; bd. dirs. St. Luke's Hosps., St. Johns Hosp., Downtown St. Louis, Inc., Laclede's Landing Redevel. Corp. Served with USN, 1951-53. Mem. Am. C. of C. Execs., Nat. Assn. Homebuilders, St. Louis Homebuilders Assn. (pres.), St. Louis Advt. Club, Mo. Athletic Club, St. Louis Club, Noonday Club, Castle Oak Country Club, Round Table Club, Sunset Country Club. Republican. Methodist. Home: 14238 Forest Crest Dr Chesterfield MO 63017-2818 Office: 1224 Fern Ridge Pky Saint Louis MO 63141-4451

MORLEY, JOHN EDWARD, physician; b. Eshowe, Zululand, South Africa, June 13, 1946; came to U.S., 1977; s. Peter and Vera Rose (Phipson) M.; m. Patricia Morley, Apr. 4, 1970; children: Robert, Susan, Jacqueline. MB, BCh, U. Witwatersrand, Johannesburg, South Africa, 1972. Diplomate Am. Bd. Internal Medicine, subspecialty cert. endocrinology and geriatrics. Asst. prof. Mpls. VA Med. Ctr. and U. Minn., 1979-81; assoc. prof. U. Minn., Mpls., 1981-84; prof. UCLA San Fernando Valley, 1985-89; dir. GRECC Sepulveda (Calif.) VA Med. Ctr., 1985-89; Dammert prof. gerontology, dir. div. geriatric medicine St. Louis U. Med. Ctr., 1989—; dir. geriatric rsch., edn. and clin. ctr. St. Louis VA Med. Ctr., 1989—; mem. adv. panel of geriatrics and endocrinology U.S. Pharmacopeial Conv., Inc., Rockville, Md., 1990—. Author: (with others) Nutritional Modulation of Neuronal Function, 1988, Neuropeptides and Stress, 1988, Geriatric Nutrition, 1990, 2d edit., 1995, Medical Care in the Nursing Home, 1991, Endocrinology and Metabolism in the Elderly, 1992, Memory Function and Aging Related Disorders, 1992, Aging and Musculoskeletal Disorders, 1993, Aging, Immunity and Infection, 1994, Sleep Disorders and Insomnia in the Elderly, 1993, Quality Improvement in Geriatric Care, 1995, Focus on Nutrition, 1995, Applying Health Services Research to Long-Term Care, 1996, As We Age, 1996; mem. editl. bd. Peptides, 1983—, Internat. Jour. Obesity, 1986-89, Jour. Nutritional Medicine, 1990—, Clinics in Applied Nutrition, 1990-92; editor geriatrics sect. Yearbook of Endocrinology, 1987—, Nursing Home Medicine, 1992—, Clin. Geriatrics, 1992—, others. Mem. adv. bd. Alzheimer's Assn., St. Louis, 1990-92; mem. adv. com. for physicians Mo. Divsn. Aging, Jefferson City, 1990—; bd. dirs. Mo. Assn. Long Term Care Physicians, 1991—, Long Term Care Ombudsman Program, St. Louis, 1992, Fund for Psychineuroimmunology, 1990—, Hamilton Hts. Health Resource Ctr., 1992—. Recipeint Mead Johnson award Am. Inst. Nutrition, 1985. Mem. ACP (geriatrics subcom. 1991-92), Am. Soc. Clin. Investigation, Endocrine Soc., Am. Fedn. Clin. Rsch., Am. Acad. Behavioral Sci., Am. Geriatrics Soc. (assoc. editor jour. 1989-93, pres. Mo.-Kans. affiliate 1996—), Am. Fedn. Clin. Rsch., Gerontology Soc. Am., Am. Diabetes Assn., Am. Soc. Pharmacy and Therapeutics, Soc. for Neurosci., La Asociacion de Gerontologica y Geriatrica, A.C. (hon.), Assn. Dirs. Geriatric Acad. Programs. Office: Saint Louis U Sch Medicine 1402 S Grand Blvd Rm M238 Saint Louis MO 63104-1004

MORLEY, LAWRENCE WHITAKER, geophysicist, remote sensing consultant; b. Toronto, Feb. 19, 1920; s. George Whitaker and Mary Olive (Boyd) M.; divorced; children; Lawrence, Patricia, Chris, David; m. Beverly Anne Beckworth; step-children: Sandra Wellman, Stephen Burdett, Richard Burdett. BA, U. Toronto, 1946, MA, 1949, PhD, 1952; DSc (hon.), York U., Toronto, 1974. Dir. geophysics div. Geol. Survey Can., Ottawa, 1952-71; dir. gen. Can. Centre for Remote Sensing, Ottawa, 1971-80; exec. dir. Inst. for Space and Terrestrial Sci., Toronto, 1982-91; pres. Teledetection Internat., 1991—. Lt. Can. Navy, 1941-45. Fellow Royal Soc. Can.; mem. Can. Soc. Remote Sensing (founding pres. 1971-74), Am. Geophys. Union, Am. Soc. Photogrammetry and Remote Sensing, Soc. Exploration Geophysicists, Can. Geophys. Union, Can. Geomatics Inst. Home and Office: 767 2d Ave W, Owen Sound, ON Canada N4K 4M2

MORLEY, LLOYD ALBERT, mining engineering educator; b. Provo, Utah, Oct. 28, 1940; s. John Jr. and Dorothea (Nielsen) M.; m. Jo Ann Bryant, Feb. 22, 1975; 1 child, Paul Loring. BS in Mining Engring., U. Utah, 1968, PhD in Mining Engring., 1972. Teaching asst., rsch. assoc. U. Utah, Salt Lake City, 1968-71; asst. prof. mining engring. Pa. State U., University Park, 1971-75, assoc. prof., 1975-80, prof., 1980-85; prof., head dept. mineral engring. U. Ala., Tuscaloosa, 1985-93, endowed chair mining engring., 1993—; cons. Jim Walter Resources, Inc., Brookwood, Ala., 1987—, Pitts. and Midway Coal Mining Co., Englewood, Colo., 1990—, Drummond Co., Inc., Birmingham, Ala., 1991—; engr. in tng., Utah. Author: Mine Power Systems, 1990; contbr. articles to profl. jours. Staff sgt. USNG, 1958-66. Recipient Wilson Outstanding Teaching award Pa. State U., 1980; Outstanding Rsch. Report awards U.S. Bur. Mines, 1983-84, grantee, 1971-87. Fellow IEEE (bd. dirs. 1991-92, 94, v.p. publs. 1994); mem. Industry Applications Soc. IEEE (Mining Best Paper awards 1984, 88, 90, pres. 1988, Disting. lectr. 1991, Disting. Svc. award 1995), Soc. for Mining, Metallury and Exploration AIME, Masons. Republican. Episcopalian. Avocations: high-fidelity systems, classic sports cars, rose growing, music. Office: U Ala Dept Mineral Engring PO Box 870207 Tuscaloosa AL 35487-0207

MORLEY, MICHAEL B., public relations executive; b. Madras, India, Nov. 18, 1935; s. Gordon and Violet M.; m. Ingrid Hellman, Aug. 20, 1957; children: Andrew, Helen, Ann. Attended, Eastbourne Coll. Dir. Harris & Hunter Pub. Rels., 1960-67; mng. dir. Daniel J. Edelman, 1967; pres. Edelman Internat., 1970; dep. chmn. Edelman Worldwide, 1992—; pres. Edelman N.Y., 1994—. Comms. Advt. and Mktg. Edn. Found. fellow, 1981; decorated Knight of First Class, Order of Lion, Rep. Finland, 1978. Mem. Internat. Pub. Rels. Assn., Internat. Pub. Rels., Brit. C. of C., Japan Soc., Bus. Coun. Internat. Understanding, Inc., Korea Soc. Home: 1 Devon Pl Cresskill NJ 07626-1608 Office: Edelman Pub Rels Worldwide 1500 Broadway New York NY 10036-4015*

MORLEY, ROGER HUBERT, company executive, consultant; b. Cleve., June 21, 1931; s. Hubert Patrick and Ayleen Marie (Mosier) M. BS in Indsl. Engring., Ohio U., 1953; MBA, Harvard U., 1957. Contr. Stromberg-Carlson, Rochester, N.Y., 1957-60; v.p., gen. mgr. GATX, Chgo., 1960-67, Burndy Corp., Norwalk, Conn., 1967-68; exec. v.p., CFO, Gould Inc., Chgo., 1968-74; pres., vice chmn. Am. Express, N.Y.C., 1974-81; co-mng. dir. R&R Inventions, Eng., 1986—; bd. dirs. Lorraine Investments SA, Luxembourg, Bank of Am.-Ill., Biogen, Inc., Cambridge, Mass., Artal SA, Luxembourg, Iris India Fund, Luxembourg; assoc. lectr. U. Rochester, 1958-60; mem. U.S. adv. bd. European Inst. Bus. Adminstrn., 1975-81. Bd. dirs., mem. exec. com. Lincoln Ctr. for Performing Arts, 1974-81, chmn. consol. corp. fund drive, 1975-81; bd. dirs. Vis. Nurse Svc. N.Y., 1974-81, Sunny Bank Anglo-Am. Hosp., Cannes, France, 1985-87; trustee Darwin Trust Edinburgh, Scotland, 1991—; trustee, chmn. fin. com. Barnard Coll., 1976-80; v.p. Schiller Internat. U., Heidelburg, Germany, 1982—; mem. Com. de Jumelage, Ville de Grasse, 1983-87. Capt. USAF, 1953-55. Mem. Nat. Assn. Securities Dealers (gov.-at-large), Grasse Country Club (France), Links (N.Y.C.), Harvard Club N.Y.C., Univ. Club (Chgo.). Republican. Avocations: golf, tennis, travel, reading. Home and Office: L'Horizon, Clos Barnier Sperácèdes, 06530 Alpes-Maritimes France

MORLOCK, CARL GRISMORE, physician, medical educator; b. Crediton, Ont., Can., Sept. 11, 1906; came to U.S., 1934, naturalized, 1939; s. Charles Edward and Emma (Grismore) M.; m. Katherine Ruth Mercer, Sept. 18, 1937; children: Anne Louise, William Edward. B.A., U. Western Ont., 1929, M.D., 1932; fellow internal medicine, Mayo Found., Grad. Sch. U. Minn., 1934-37; M.S. in Medicine, U. Minn., 1937. Intern Victoria Hosp., London, Ont., 1932-33; resident Victoria Hosp., 1933-34; practice medicine specializing in internal medicine and gastroenterology Rochester, Minn., 1934—; assoc.prof. internal medicine Mayo Found., 1949-62, prof. clin. medicine, 1962-72; prof. medicine Mayo Med. Sch., 1972—. Contbr. articles on gastrointestinal subjects to med. jours. Fellow ACP; mem. Am., Minn. med. assns., Osler Med. Soc., Am. Gastroent. Assn., Gideons Internat. Sigma Xi, Alpha Omega Alpha. Baptist. Home: 211 2nd St NW Apt 1303 Rochester MN 55901-2897 Office: Mayo Clinic 200 1st St SW Rochester MN 55905-0001

MORLOK, EDWARD KARL, engineering educator, consultant; b. Phila., Nov. 3, 1940; s. Edward Karl and Anna Marie (Kurtz) M.; m. Ottilia Angela Husz, Dec. 14, 1968 (div. July 1983); 1 child, Jessica Angela; m. Patricia Campbell Conboy, Mar. 23, 1991. BE, Yale U., 1962; PhD, Northwestern U., 1967; MA (hon.), U. Pa., 1973. Civil engr., transp. U.S. Dept. Commerce, Washington, 1966-67; from asst. prof. civil engring. to assoc. prof. Northwestern U., Evanston, Ill., 1967-73, asst. dir. rsch., transp. ctr., 1969-73; 1907 Found. assoc. prof. U. Pa., Phila., 1973-75, chmn., transp. grad. group, 1983-86, 91—, UPS found. prof. transp., 1975—, chair systems grad. program, 1988-91; cons. nat. transp. policy study commn., Washington, 1978-79. Author: Analysis Transportation Technology and Network Structure, 1969, Introduction to Transportation Engineering and Planning, 1978; assoc. editor Transp. Rsch. Jour., 1975—; consulting editor series in transp. for McGraw-Hill Publ. Co., 1980—; contbr. more than 60 articles to profl. jours. Mem. Nat. Assembly Engring. panel on innovation in transp., Washington, 1979-80, panel on hazardous material transp., Washington, 1980-81. Recipient U.S. Sr. Scientist award Alexander von Humboldt Found., 1980-81; rsch. grantee Commonwealth of Pa., Consol. Rail Corp., U.S. Dept. Transp., NASA, NSF. Mem. Inst. Ops. Rsch. and Mgmt., Transp. Rsch. Forum (v.p. 1974-75, pres. 1975-76, bd. disting. mems. 1983—), Transp. Rsch. Bd. (rev. com. of coun. of univ. transp. ctrs. 1985-88, coun. mem. 1988-90, chair freight transp. planning and mktg. com. 1994—). Lutheran. Office: U Pa Dept Systems Engring 220 S 33rd St Philadelphia PA 19104-6315

MORNES, AMBER J. BISHOP, computer software trainer; b. Ft. Rucker, Ala., Oct. 20, 1970; d. David Floyd and Holly Brooke (Decker) Bishop; m. David Michael Mornes, May 22, 1993. BA in Psychology, U. Colo., Boulder, 1992. Asst. dir. admissions Rocky Mountain Coll. Art and Design, Denver, 1992-94, placement and alumni svcs. coord., 1995-96; computer software instr. New Horizons Computer Learning Ctr., Aurora, Colo., 1996—. Vol. Colo. Art Educator Assn., 1993—. Mem. APA (student affiliate), Nat. Art Edn. Assn., Colo. Art Edn. Assn. Home: 2500 S York St Apt 11 Denver CO 80210-5245 Office: New Horizons Computer Learn Learning Ctr 2851 S Parker Rd Ste 1300 Aurora CO 80014

MORNING, JOHN, graphic designer; b. Cleve., Jan. 8, 1932; s. John Frew and Juanita Kathryn (Brannan) M.; m. Carole Ann Coleman, Jan. 24, 1964 (div. July 1984); children: Ann Juanita, John Floyd. BFA, Pratt Inst., 1955. Art dir. McCann-Erickson, Inc., N.Y.C., 1958-60; pvt. practice design N.Y.C., 1960—; bd. dirs. Dime Savings Bank N.Y. Bd. dirs. Repertory Theater Lincoln Ctr., 1970-73, N.Y. Landmarks Conservancy, Charles E. Culpepper Found., 1990—, Henry St. Settlement, chmn., 1979-86, Bklyn. Acad. Music, 1993, Lincoln Ctr. Inst., 1993; trustee Wilberforce U., com. on edn. Mus. Modern Art; chmn. bd. trustees Pratt Inst., Bklyn., 1988-92; bd. dirs. Mus. for African Art, N.Y.C., co-chair, 1991-94; vice chmn. N.Y.C. Cultural Affairs Adv. Commn., 1994—. With U.S. Army, 1956-58. Recipient Alumni medal Pratt Inst., 1972, Presdl. Recognition award Pres. of U.S., 1984, Lillian D. Wald Humanitarian award, 1992. Mem. Am. Inst. Graphic Arts, Am. Acad. Dramatic Arts (trustee 1988-95), Assn. Governing Bds. Colls. and Univs. (bd. dirs.). Republican.

MOROLES, JESUS BAUTISTA, sculptor; b. Corpus Christi, Tex., Sept. 22, 1950. AA, El Centro Coll., Dallas, 1975; BFA, No. Tex. State U., 1978. bd. dirs. Internat. Sculpture Ctr., Washington; instr. Nat. Mus. Am. Art Symposium, 1992. One-person shows include Davis-McClain Gallery, Houston, 1982, 84, 86, 88, 90, 92, Janus Gallery, Santa Fe, 1984, 85, 86, 89, 90, 92, Marilyn Butler Gallery, Scottsdale, Ariz., 1986, 89, Richard Green Gallery, L.A., 1989, 91, N.Y., 1989, Santa Monica, Calif., 1990, Chgo. Internat. Art Exposition, Klein Art Works, Chgo., 1991, Mus. S.E. Tex., Beaumont, 1992, Wirtz Gallery, San Francisco, 1990, Escultura, 1991, Expositum, Polanco, Mex., 1991, Adams-Middleton Gallery, Dallas, 1992, Carl Schlosberg Fine Art, Sherman Oaks, Calif., 1992; commd. Tex. Commerce Bank, Dallas, 1983, Riata Devel., Houston, 1984, Siena Sq., Boulder, Colo., 1985, Nat. Health Ins. Co., Dallas, 1986, IBM, Raleigh, N.C., 1986; represented in permanent collections Albuquerque Mus., Mus. Fine Arts, Santa Fe, Old Jail Art Ctr., Albany, Tex., U. Houston, Mint Mus., Charlotte, N.C., Dallas Mus. Art, Nat. Mus. Am. Art, Smithsonian, Washington. Visual Art fellow Southeastern Ctr. Contemporary Art, Winston-Salem, N.C., 1982; Pres. Citation award U. No. Tex., 1992; Matching grnatee Nat. Endowment Arts, Birmingham Botanical Gardens, 1984.

MOROWITZ, HAROLD JOSEPH, biophysicist, educator; b. Poughkeepsie, N.Y., Dec. 4, 1927; s. Philip Frank and Anna (Levine) M.; m. Lucille Rita Stein, Jan. 30, 1949; children: Joanna Lynn, Eli David, Joshua Alan, Zachary Adam, Noah Daniel. BS, Yale U., 1947, MS, 1950, PhD, 1951. Physicist Nat. Bur. Stds., 1951-53, Nat. Heart Inst., Bethesda, Md., 1953-55; mem. faculty Yale U., 1955-88, assoc. prof. biophysics, 1960-68, prof. molecular biophysics and biochemistry, 1968-88, master Pierson Coll., 1981-86; mem. faculty George Mason U., Fairfax, Va., 1988—, Robinson prof. biology and natural philosophy, 1988—; dir. Krasnow Inst. for Advanced Study, 1993—; chmn. com. on models for biomed. rsch. NRC, 1983-85, mem. bd. on basic biology, 1986-92. Author: Life and the Physical Sciences, 1964, (with Waterman) Theoretical and Mathematical Biology, 1965, Energy Flow in Biology, 1968, Entropy for Biologists, 1970, (with Lucille Morowitz) Life On The Planet Earth, 1974, Ego Niches, 1977, Foundations of Bioenergetics, 1978, The Wine of Life, 1979, Mayonnaise and the Origin of Life, 1985, Cosmic Joy and Local Pain, 1987, The Thermodynamics of Pizza, 1991, Beginnings of Cellular Life, 1992, (with James Trefil) The Facts of Life, 1992, Entropy and the Magic Flute, 1993; editor Complexity, 1994—; contbr. articles to profl. jours. Mem. sci. adv. bd. Santa Fe Inst., 1991—. Mem. Biophys. Soc. (mem. exec. com. 1965), Nat. Ctr. for Rsch. Resources (mem. coun. 1987-92). Office: George Mason U Krasnow Inst Advanced Study Fairfax VA 22030

MORPHEW, DOROTHY RICHARDS-BASSETT, artist, real estate broker; b. Cambridge, Mass., Aug. 4, 1918; d. George and Evangeline Booth (Richards) Richards; grad. Boston Art Inst., 1949; children—Jon Eric, Marc Alan, Dana Kimball. Draftsman, United Shoe Machinery Co., 1937-42; blueprinter, advt. artist A.C. Lawrence Leather Co., Peabody, Mass., 1949-51; propr. Studio Shop and Studio Potters, Beverly, Mass., 1951-53; tchr. ceramics and art, Kingston, N.H., 1953—; real estate broker, pres. 1965-81;

two-man exhbn. Topsfield (Mass.) Library, 1960; owner, operator Ceramic Shop, West Stewartstown, N.H. Served with USNR, 1942-44. Recipient Profl. award New Eng. Ceramic Show, 1975; also numerous certificates in ceramics. Home: 557 Palomino Trl Englewood FL 34223-3951 Studio: 57 Algonac Rd Cape Neddick ME 03909

MORPHY, JAMES CALVIN, lawyer; b. Pitts., Jan. 16, 1954; s. Robert Samson and Autumn (Phillips) M.; m. Priscilla Winslow Plimpton, July 11, 1981; children: Calvin, Katherine, Victoria. BA, Harvard U., 1976, JD, 1979. Bar: N.Y. 1980. Assoc. Sullivan & Cromwell, N.Y.C., 1979-86, ptnr., 1986—, mng. ptnr. gen. practice group, 1992—, mng. ptnr. M&A group, 1995—. Contbg. author N.Y. Lawyers' Guide to Bus. Orgns. Mem. ABA (com. on fed. securities law 1992—), Assn. Bar of City of N.Y. Office: Sullivan & Cromwell 125 Broad St New York NY 10004-2400

MORRA, BERNADETTE, newspaper editor, journalist; b. Toronto, Ont., Can., Jan. 22, 1961; d. John Anthony and Josephine Lucia (Slobodzian) Morra; m. James Molloy, June 20, 1993. BA, U. Toronto, 1983. Fashion writer Toronto Star, 1988-94, fashion editor, 1994—; pub. speaker fashion various TV and radio shows, Toronto chpt. Fashion Group Internat., 1988—; judge various student and profl. design competitions. Contbr. articles to profl. jours. Recipient Merit award Art Dirs. Club Toronto, 1990. Mem. Southern Ont. Newspaper Guild. Office: Toronto Star Newspapers Ltd, 1 Yonge St, Toronto, ON Canada M5E 1E6

MORREL, WILLIAM GRIFFIN, JR., banker; b. Lynchburg, Va., Aug 25, 1933; s. William Griffin and Virginia Louise (Baldwin) M.; m. Sandra Virginia Coats, Jan. 31, 1959; children: William Griffin, John Coats, Elisabeth White, Jere Coleman. BS, Yale U., 1955; postgrad. Rutgers U., 1965-67. With Md. Nat. Bank, Balt., 1955-84, asst. v.p., 1959, v.p., 1964, sr. v.p., 1975-84, mgmt. com. 1979-84, chmn. three lending coms., others; pres., bd. dirs. Md. Nat. Overseas Investment Corp.; chmn. bd. London Interstate Bank Ltd.; chmn. bd. dirs. Md. Internat. Bank; sr. v.p., chief operating officer Abu Dhabi Internat. Bank, Inc., 1984-86, pres., chief exec. officer Heritage Internat. Bank, 1986-89; dir., pres., CEO Madison Fin. Group, 1989—; chief exec. officer, chmn. The Valley Fin. Group, Balt., 1989—; pres., chief exec. officer Summit Bancorp, Balt., 1990-92; consul of the Netherlands at Balt., 1978-84. Mem. Balt. Consular Corps, 1978-84; chmn. Md. World Trade Efforts Commn., 1983-84; mem. Md. Trade Policy Council, 1985-88; vice chmn. Dist. Export Council, 1983—. Contbr. articles to profl. jours. Sr. fellow Ctr. for Internat. Banking Studies, Darden Grad. Bus. Sch. U. Va., 1978-91. Served with U.S. Army, 1956-58. Mem. Bankers Assn. for Fgn. Trade (bd. dirs. 1975-78), Robert Morris Assocs. (nat. bd. dirs. 1984-88), Internat. Lending Council (bd. dirs., chmn., 1978-80), Md. Hist. Soc. (trustee), Balt. Council Fgn. Relations (trustee), Econ. Devel. Council. Republican. Presbyterian. Clubs: Yale, Farmington Country, Elkridge, Md. Club. Home: 6 Beechdale Rd Baltimore MD 21210-2207 Office: The Madison Fin Group Inc PO Box 16265 Baltimore MD 21210-0265

MORRELL, ARTHUR ANTHONY, lawyer, state legislator; b. New Orleans, Mar. 22, 1943; s. Reynard and Mildred (Gray) M.; m. Cynthia Hedge; children: Todd, Matthew, Jean-Paul, Nicholas. BA, So. U., 1970, JD, 1978. Bar: La. 1978, all state and fed. cts. In-flight exec. rep. Ea. Airlines, New Orleans, 1968-72; ticket agt. Ea. Airlines, Chgo., 1972-75; passenger svc. agt. Ea. Airlines, New Orleans, 1968-70; fed. voters examiner Civil Svcs. Dept., New Orleans, 1975-77; pres., owner ACTMP Enterprises, New Orleans, 1982—; pvt. practice, New Orleans, 1982—; owner, breeder La. Horsemen, New Orleans, 1985—; mem. La. Ho. of Reps., New Orleans, 1984—. Mem. Very Spl. Arts; bd. dirs Total Cmty. Action. With Spl. Forces, U.S. Army, 1963-66. Mem. ABA, La. Trial Lawyers Assn., Assn. for Effective Govt., Am. Legion (Post 395), Delta Theta Pi. Democrat. Roman Catholic. Office: Ste 107-10 3200 Saint Bernard Ave New Orleans LA 70119-1929

MORRELL, FRANK, neurologist, educator; b. N.Y.C., June 4, 1926; s. Benjamin R. and Rose (Langson) M.; m. Lenore Korkes, Mar. 24, 1957 (div.); children: Seth, Paul, Michael, Suzanna; m. Leyla deToledo, May 25, 1978. AB, Columbia U., 1948, MD, 1951; MS, McGill U., Montreal, Can., 1955. Diplomate Am. Bd. Psychiatry and Neurology. Intern in medicine Montefiore Hosp., Bronx, N.Y., 1951-52, resident in neurology, 1953-54; fellow EEG Nat. Hosp., London, 1952-53; fellow Montreal Neurol. Inst., 1954-55; from asst. prof. to assoc. prof. neurology U. Minn., Mpls., 1955-61; prof., chmn. dept. neurology Stanford (Calif.) U., 1961-69; vis. prof. N.Y. Med. Coll., 1969-72; prof. Rush Med. Coll., Chgo., 1972—; William Lennox lectr. Western Inst. of Epilepsy, Colo., 1980; Hans Berger lectr. Med. Coll. Va., 1987; assoc. neurosci. rsch. program MIT, Boston, 1965-76; cons. in field. Contbr. numerous articles to profl. jours. Served as cpl. USAF, 1944-45. Fellow Royal Soc. Medicine, Am. Acad. Neurology; mem. Am. Electroencephalographic Soc. (pres.), Am. Epilepsy Soc., Soc. for Neurosci. Jewish. Office: Rush Presbyn-St Luke's Med Ctr 1653 W Congress Pky Chicago IL 60612-3833

MORRELL, GENE PAUL, liquid terminal company executive; b. Ardmore, Okla., Oct. 4, 1932; s. Paul T. and Etta L. (Weaver) M.; m. Jan A. Foster, Aug. 20, 1954; children: Jeffrey T., Kelly Ann, Rob Redman. BS in Geology, U. Okla., 1954, LLB, 1962. Bar: Okla. 1962, D.C. 1973. Geologist Gilmer Oil Co., Ardmore, Okla., 1957-59, atty.-geologist, 1962-63; sole practice, Ardmore, 1963-69; ofcl. Dept. Interior, Washington, 1969-72; v.p. Lone Star Gas Co., Washington, 1972-76; sr. v.p. United Energy Resources, Inc., Houston, 1976-86; vice chmn. Petro United Terminals, Inc., Houston, 1986—. Contbr. articles to profl. jours. Commr. City of Ardmore, 1967-69, vice-mayor, 1968. Mem. ABA, Okla. Bar Assn., D.C. Bar Assn., Am. Assn. Petroleum Geologists, Coun. Fgn. Rels., Phi Alpha Delta, Sigma Alpha Epsilon. Episcopalian. Clubs: City Tavern (Washington), Ramada-Tejas, Houston Artillery, Galveston Country, The Yacht Club (Galveston).

MORRELL, JAMES WILSON, consulting company executive; b. Kalamazoo, Feb. 13, 1931; s. Wilson and Evelyn Jewel (Anderson) M.; m. Marylyn J. Eck, June 21, 1952; children—Martha Jo Morrell-Trinkaus, David James. BA, Kalamazoo Coll., 1953. Foodservice mgr. for Kalamazoo Coll. Saga Corp., Kalamazoo, 1955-57, dist. mgr. edn. div., 1958-61; regional v.p. edn. div. Saga Corp., Kalamazoo, Mich., 1962-66, v.p. adminstrn., 1966-68, exec. v.p. adminstrn., 1968-70, pres. SCOPE, 1970-71; pres. Saga Enterprise, 1972-78, exec. v.p., chief oper. officer, 1978-82, exec. v.p., mem. Office of Pres., 1983-85, vice chmn., 1985-86; owner J.W. Morrell & Assocs., Atherton, Calif., 1986—; pres., CEO Telesensory Corp., Mountain View, Calif., 1992—; bd. dirs. Muffins-Muffins, Telesensory Corp., Schwab Trust Co., Fabri-Kal Corp, Foster Farms Corp. Chmn. Resource Ctr. for Women, Palo Alto, Calif., 1976-77, March of Dimes, San Mateo County, Calif., 1983-85; co-chmn. modernization project Stanford U. Hosp., 1985; bd. dirs. Foodservice Ctr., NYU, 1980-86 ; chmn. World Bus. Forum, San Francisco, 1981-82 ; bd. dirs., trustee Kalamazoo Coll., 1985—, vice chmn., 1990—; bd. dirs. World Bus. Coun., 1990—. With U.S. Army, 1953-55. Mem. Sharon Heights Country Club, Menlo Park Circus club. Republican. Presbyterian. Avocations: golf, photography, opera. Home and Office: 2 Mesa Ct Menlo Park CA 94027-6418 also: Telesensory PO Box 7455 Mountain View CA 94039-7455*

MORRELL, JANINE MARJORIE DACUS, secondary education educator; b. San Antonio, Nov. 24, 1957; d. Dayle McClain and Marjorie Lucille (Voskuhl) Dacus; m. Dave Charles Morrell, Oct. 11, 1981; children: Morgan Marjorie, Alexandra Janine, Taylor Lynn. BS in Secondary Edn., U. Tex., 1980. Cert. social studies tchr., Tex. Tchr. world history Clear Creek H.S., League City, Tex., 1983-84, tchr. world geography , including honors class, 1984-90; tchr. U.S. history and world geography Clear View Alternative H.S., League City, 1991—. Mem. Houston 100 Club, 1994; participant Houston Rodeo Chili Cook-off, 1992—. Tchr. of Yr. finalist Clear Lake Rotary Club, Houston, 1994. Mem. Tex. Fedn. Tchrs. Avocations: country and western dancing, waterskiing, reading, gardening. Home: 15330 McConn St Webster TX 77598-2008 Office: Clear View Alternative HS 400 S Kansas Ave League City TX 77573-4070

MORRELL, WAYNE BEAM, JR., artist; b. Clementon, N.J., Dec. 24, 1923; s. Wayne Beam and Martha L. (Plack) M.; student Drexel Inst., Phila. Sch. Indsl. Art.; grad. Famous Artist Sch., Westport, Conn.; m. Lillian Eunice Major, July 14, 1952 (dec. 1994); children: David Wayne (dec.), Lisa Anne. Exhibited one-man show Washington County Art Mus., Hagerstown, Md., 1973, Drexel U., 1992; exhibited nat. group shows including NAD, Conn. Acad. Fine Arts, Butler Inst. Am. Art, Am. Artists Profl. League, Knickerbocker Artists, N.Y.C., Newman Gallery, Phila., Houston, Palm Beach, Fla., Carmel, Calif., Guild Boston Artists, Wadsworth Atheneum, Addison Gallery Am. Art, Mus. Fine Arts, Columbus, Ga., New Britain Mus., Smithsonian Inst., Expn. Intercontinental, Monaco, France, Gateway Art Gallery, Palm Beach, Fla., Bleich Galleries, Carmel, Calif., Mus., Bombay, India, 1967, City Hall, Hong Kong, 1975-76; indsl. exhibitor, designer John Oldham Studios, 1955-58, art dir., 1958-61; designer Paris and Brussells Worlds Fairs, other maj. exhibits; designer cover Reader's Digest, 1967, Yankee mag., 1980. Served with AUS, 1949-52. Recipient Louis Seley purchase award; Gold medal Rockport Art Assn., 1969; Gold medal Jordan Marsh, Boston; award Council Am. Art Socs., 1971; Canelli Gold Medal award Academic Artists Assn., 1974; others. Mem. Allied Artists Am. (Jane Peterson award 1969, 74), Am. Artists Profl. League, Am. Vet. Soc. Artists, Springfield Acad. Artists (past council), Rockport Art Assn. (William Mariboe award, Harriet Mattson award, award for Winter Marshes 1980, Meyerowitz Meml. award 1989, William Meyerwith award 1989), North Shore Art Assn., Americana Gallery, Golden Web, Santa Fe, Montcrest Gallery, Chattanooga (Tenn.) 210 Gallery, Grand Central Art Galleries, Newman Galleries Phila. and Bryn Mawr, Pa., Dassin Gallery, L.A., Salmagundi Club (Louis Seley Purchase award 1969, Gwynne Lennon prize 1971, Phillip J. Ross award 1971, 1st hon. mention 1971). Home and Office: 1 Squam Hollow Rockport MA 01966-2164

MORRILL, RICHARD LELAND, geographer, educator; b. L.A., Feb. 15, 1934; s. Robert W. and Lillian M. (Riffo) M.; m. Joanne L. Cooper, 1965; children: Lee, Andrew, Jean. B.A., Dartmouth Coll., 1955; M.A., U. Wash., 1957, Ph.D., 1959. Asst. prof. geography Northwestern U., 1959-60; NSF research fellow U. Lund, Sweden, 1960-61; asst. prof. U. Wash., Seattle, 1961-65; asso. prof. U. Wash., 1965-69, prof., 1969—, chmn. dept. geography, 1974-83, asso. dir. environ. studies, 1974—; chmn. urban planning PhD program, 1992—; vis. asso. prof. U. Chgo., dir. Chgo. Regional Hosp. Study, 1966-67; cons. population, regional and urban planning. Author: Geography of Poverty, 1970, Spatial Organization of Society, 1973, Political Redistricting and Geographic Theory, 1981, Spatial Diffusion, 1987. Mem. King County Boundary Rev. Bd. Guggenheim fellow, 1983-84. Mem. Assn. Am. Geographers (Meritorious Contbn. award 1970, mem. coun. 1970-73, sec. 1979-81, pres. 1981-82), Regional Sci. Assn., Wash. Regional Sch. Assn. (pres. 1993-94), Population Assn. Am., Lambda Alpha. Office: Dept Geography U Wash Seattle WA 98195

MORRILL, RICHARD LESLIE, university administrator; b. Weymouth, Mass., June 4, 1939; s. Duncan Russel and Violet Erma (Gibson) M.; m. Martha Leahy, June 24, 1964; children: Katie, Amy. A.B. in History magna cum laude, Brown U., 1961; B.D. in Religious Thought, Yale U., 1964; Ph.D. in Religion, Duke U., 1968. Instr. Wells Coll., Aurora, N.Y., 1967-68; asst. prof. Chatham Coll., Pitts., 1968-74, assoc. prof., 1974-77, assoc. provost and asst. to pres., 1973-77; assoc. provost Pa. State U., University Park, 1977-79; pres. Salem Coll. and Acad., Winston-Salem, N.C., 1979-82, Centre Coll., Danville, Ky., 1982-88, U. Richmond, Va., 1988—; bd. dirs. Ctrl. Fidelity Banks, Inc.; v.p. So. Univ. Conf., 1993—; chmn. Assoc. Colls. of the South, 1993-94; v.p. So. Univ. Conf., 1993—; mem. governing coun. Wye Faculty Seminar, 1994—; mem. presdl. adv. com. KPMG Peat Marwick, 1989—; cons. edn. divsn. Lilly Endowment, 1990—. Author: Teaching Values in College, 1980; contbr. articles to profl. jours. Bd. dirs., mem. program com. Teagle Found., 1989—; mem. nat. bd. visitors Ind. U. Ctr. on Philanthropy, 1991—; mem. commn. on leadership devel. Am. Coun. on Edn., 1992-94; trustee Williamsburg Investment Trust, 1993—; mem. Richmond Symphony Coun., 1995—; mem. Va. Coun. for Internat. Edn., 1995-96; bd. dirs. Assn. Am. Colls. and Univs., 1996—. Woodrow Wilson fellow, 1961-62; James B. Duke fellow Duke U., 1964-67. Mem. Soc. for Values in Higher Edn. (dir. 1981-84), Am. Acad. Religion, Am. Soc. for Christian Ethics, Am. Assn. Higher Edn., So. Assn. Colls. and Schs. (commr. 1985—), Coll. Athletic Conf. (chmn. 1985-87), Council Ind. Ky. Colls. and Univs. (sec. 1984-86, v.p. 1986-88, exec. com. 1984-86), Assn. Presbyn. Colls. and Univs. (exec. com. 1984-86), Phi Beta Kappa. Club: University. Lodge: Rotary. Home: 7000 River Rd Richmond VA 23229-8532 Office: U Richmond Pres Office Richmond VA 23173-1903

MORRILL, THOMAS CLYDE, insurance company executive; b. Chgo., July 1, 1909; s. Walter and Lena Elpha (Haney) M.; m. Hazel Janet Thompson, Oct. 18, 1930; children: Dorothy Mae (Mrs. Gerald L. Kelly), Charles T. Student, Cen. Coll. Arts and Scis., Chgo., 1928-29, Northwestern U., 1929-30. With Alfred M. Best Co., Inc., 1929-45, assoc. editor, 1940-45; with N.Y. State Ins. Dept., 1945-50, dep. supt. ins., 1947-50; with State Farm Mut. Automobile Ins. Co., Bloomington, Ill., 1950-77, v.p., 1952-77; chmn. bd. State Farm Fire and Casualty Co., Bloomington, 1970-86, State Farm Gen. Ins. Co., Bloomington, 1970-91; cons. State Farm Ins. Cos., Bloomington, 1991—; founder, chmn., dir. Ins. Inst. for Highway Safety. Chmn. exec. subcom. Nat. Hwy. Safety Adv. Com., 1971-73; chmn. tech. com. on transp. White House Conf. on Aging, 1971; mem. Pres.'s Task Force on Hwy. Safety. Clubs: Union League (Chgo.); Union Hills Country, Lakes (Sun City, Ariz.).

MORRILL, WILLIAM ASHLEY, research executive; b. Bronxville, N.Y., Apr. 23, 1930; s. Ashley B. and Katharine A. (Anderson) M.; m. Lois Birrell, Dec. 27, 1953 (div. 1978); children: Margaret, Carolyn, Elizabeth, Janet; m. Nancy Porter, Aug. 26, 1978. B.A., Wesleyan U., 1952; M.P.A., Syracuse U., 1953. Mgmt. analyst, acting chief plans and policy Directorate of Manpower and Orgn., USAF, 1953-62; asst. div. chief AEC unit Bur. of Budget, Washington, 1962-65, Mil. Divsn. Bur. Budget, 1965-67; dep. dir. Nat. Security Programs div. Office of Mgmt. and Budget, 1967-71; dep. county exec. Fairfax County, Va., 1971-72; asst. dir. Office Mgmt. and Budget, Washington, 1972-73; asst. sec. for planning/evaluation HEW, 1973-77; mem. Energy Policy and Planning Office, White House, 1977; sr. fellow Mathematica Policy Research, Princeton, N.J., 1977-79, sr. v.p., 1979-80, pres., 1980-86; pres. Mathtech, Inc., 1985-95, chmn., 1985-96; sr. fellow, 1996—; mem. com. on child devel. rsch. and pub. policy NRC, 1978-87, chmn., 1983-87, com. on nat. stats., 1989-92, mem. Commn. on Behavioral and Social Scis. and Edn., 1990—. Chmn. No. Va. Planning Dist. Commn., 1965-70, , 1986-89, William A. Jump Meml. Found. Recipient Meritorious award William A. Jump Meml. Found., 1966, Citizen of Yr. award for Fairfax County, Washington Star, 1970, Disting. Alumni award Maxwell Sch., Syracuse U., 1974, Disting. Svc. award Nat. Conf. on Social Welfare, 1976. Mem. Assn. Pub. Policy Analysis & Mgmt. (pres. 1982-83, mem. policy coun.), Nat. Acad. Pub. Adminstrn. (trustee 1984-93, vice-chmn. 1991-93), Coun. for Excellence in Govt. (bd. trustees 1983—, chmn. 1986-89). Home: PO Box 38 New Hope PA 18938-0038 Office: Mathtech Inc 202 Carnegie Ctr Ste 111 Princeton NJ 08540-6233

MORRIN, PETER PATRICK, museum director; b. St. Louis, Oct. 31, 1945; s. Kevin Charles and Helen Louise (Clanton) M.; m. Carolyn Brooks, Oct. 5, 1974; children: Matthew, Rebecca. AB, Harvard U., 1968; MFA, Princeton U., 1972. Asst. prof., dir. art gallery Vassar Coll., Poughkeepsie, N.Y., 1974-78; curator 20th century art High Mus. Art, Atlanta, 1979-86; dir. J.B. Speed Art Mus., Louisville, 1986—; panelist Nat. Endowment Arts. Contbr. articles to profl. publs. Served with USAR, 1968-74. Office: JB Speed Art Mus PO Box 2600 Louisville KY 40201-2600

MORRIN, THOMAS HARVEY, engineering research company executive; b. Woodland, Calif., Nov. 24, 1914; s. Thomas E. and Florence J. (Hill) M.; m. Frances M. Von Ahn, Feb. 1, 1941; children: Thomas H., Diane, Linda, Denise. BS, U. Calif., 1937; grad., U.S. Navy Grad. Sch., Annapolis, Md., 1941. Student engr. Westinghouse Electric Mfg. Co., Emeryville, Calif., 1937; elec. engr. Pacific Gas & Electric Co., 1938-41; head microwave engring. div. Raytheon Mfg. Co., Waltham, Mass., 1947-48; chmn. elec. engring. dept. Stanford Research Inst., 1948-52, dir. engring., research, 1952-60, gen. mgr. engring., 1960-64, vice pres. engring., sci., 1964-68; pres. University City Sci. Inst., Phila., 1968-69; pres., chmn. bd. Morrin Assos., Inc., Wenatchee, Wash., 1968-72. Trustee Am. Acad. Transp. Served as officer USNR, 1938-58, comdr. USN, 1945-48. Decorated Bronze Star; recipient Bank Am. award for automation of banking during 1950's, 1992. Fellow IEEE, AAAS; mem. Sci. Research Soc. Am., U.S. Naval Inst., Navy League, Marine Meml. Club (San Francisco). Address: 654 23rd Ave San Francisco CA 94121-3709 *In my 82nd year I feel privileged in having lived through the greatest advances made in the world: from the horse and buggy to people traveling 17,000 miles per hour in an earth orbit and sending probes throughout the solar system; from the pony express to world-wide instantaneous communications; from the one-room school to world-wide web. Although it has been a wonderful ride, as I expressed to my wife many years ago, our advances in technology have exceeded society's ability to match it with moral and cultural values. There is always such a time lag but in due time it always adjusts.*

MORRIN, VIRGINIA WHITE, retired college educator; b. Escondido, Calif., May 16, 1913; d. Harry Parmalee and Ethel Norine (Nutting) Rising; BS, Oreg. State Coll., 1952; MEd, Oreg. State U., 1957; m. Raymond Bennett White, 1933 (dec. 1953); children: Katherine Anne, Marjorie Virginia, William Raymond; m. 2d, Laurence Morrin, 1959 (dec. 1972). Social caseworker Los Angeles County, Los Angeles, 1934-40, 61-64; acctg. clk. War Dept., Ft. MacArthur, Calif., 1940-42; prin. clk. USAAF, Las Vegas, Nev., 1942-44; high sch. tchr., North Bend-Coos Bay, Oreg., 1952-56, Mojave, Calif., 1957-60; instr. electric bus. machines Antelope Valley Coll., Lancaster, Calif., 1961-73; ret., 1974. Treas., Humane Soc. Antelope Valley, Inc., 1968—. Mem. Nat. Aero. Assn., Calif. State Sheriffs' Assn. (charter assoc.), Oreg. State U. Alumni Assn. (life). Address: 3153 Milton Dr Mojave CA 93501-1329

MORRIONE, MELCHIOR S., management consultant, accountant; b. Bklyn., Dec. 31, 1937; s. Charles and Dionisia (Eletto) M.; m. Joan Finnerty, June 22, 1968; children—Karyn Morrione Frick, Nicole Morrione. BBA magna cum laude, St. John's U., 1959. CPA, N.J., N.Y. Tax ptnr. Arthur Andersen & Co., N.Y.C., 1959-91; mng. dir. MSM Consulting, LLC, Woodcliff Lake, N.J., 1992—; lectr. in field. Contbr. articles to profl. jours.; mem. editorial bd. Internat. Tax Jour. Served with U.S. Army, 1960-61. Mem. AICPAs, N.Y. State Soc. CPAs, N.J. Soc. CPAs, Internat. Fiscal Assn., Internat. Tax Assn. Republican. Roman Catholic. Clubs: Ridgewood Country (N.J.). Avocations: golf, tennis. Office: MSM Consulting LLC 11 Ginny Dr Woodcliff Lake NJ 07675

MORRIONE, PAOLO, polypropylene company executive. Pres., CEO Himont Inc.(acquired by Montell North America Inc.), Wilmington, Del. Office: Montell North America Inc Box 15439 2801 Centerville Rd Wilmington DE 19850*

MORRIS, ALBERT JEROME, pest control company executive; b. N.Y.C., Jan. 3, 1919; s. Peter and Minnie (Miller) M.; Barbara McLeod, Feb 6, 1943; children: Peter A., Lee Ellen Morris Guenther, Lisa Ann Morris Rasche. BS in Electronics, U. Calif., Berkeley, 1941; MS in Electronics, Stanford U., 1948, Degree of Engr., 1950. Registered profl. engr., Calif. Sr. v.p., co-founder Levinthal Elec. Products, Palo Alto, Calif., 1953-60; pres., dir. Radiation at Stanford, Palo Alto, 1960-63; pres., chief exec. officer Energy Systems Inc., Palo Alto, 1963-66, Genesys Systems Inc., Palo Alto, 1967-84; pres., chief exec. officer Biosys, Palo Alto, 1983-88, chmn. bd., 1989; also chmn. bd. TurboEnergy Systems, Phoenix, 1989-90; chmn. bd., chief exec. officer Neural Systems Corp., Palo Alto, 1991—; cons. to schs. of engring., Stanford U. and 18 other major univs.; chmn. San Francisco coun. Western Electronics Mfrs. Assn., 1965; chmn. bd. Western Electronics Show and Conv., Calif., 1961. Author over 50 papers on ship stabilization, high power electronics, med. electronics and continuing edn. Recipient Best Paper award IEEE/ASEE Frontiers in Edn. Conf., 1978. Fellow IEEE, Sigma Chi Iota; mem. AAAS. Avocation: tennis.

MORRIS, ANN HASELTINE JONES, social welfare administrator; b. Springfield, Mo., Feb. 3, 1941; d. Mansur King and Adelaide (Haseltine) Jones; m. Ronald D. Morris, Nov. 29, 1963 (div. 1990); children: David, Christopher. BA in Edn. and Art, Drury Coll., 1963. Art instr. Ash Grove (Mo.)/Bois D'Arc Pub. Sch. Dist., 1963-64; instr. Drury Coll., Springfield, 1966-67; tchr. Springfield R-12 Sch. Dist., 1974-86; exec. dir. S.W. Ctr. for Ind. Living, Springfield, 1986—; adv. com. Springfield R-12 Spl. Edn., 1993—; tech. cons. and alternative dispute resolution mediator Ams. with Disabilities Act EEOC, Dept. of Justice Network, 1993—. Bd. dirs. Ozark Greenways, 1991-93, Springfield Deaf Relay, 1988-90; adv. task force Allied Health Program Devel. S.W. Bapt Univ., 1988; mem. Drury Coll. Women's Aux., 1984—, conservator of the peace, handicap parking enforcement action team, 1991—; bd. treas. Mo. Parent Act, 1989-91, Diversity Network of the Ozarks, 1990—; svc. coord. Youthnet, 1990—; community adv. bd. Rehab. Svcs., St. John's Regional Health Care Ctr., 1988-91; mem. Springfield Homeless Network, 1989—, others; apptd. to Mo. Gov.'s Coun. on Disability; pres. Statewide Ind. Living Coun. Mem. NOW (sec. 1991), P.E.O., Mo. Assn. of Ctrs. for Ind. Living (v.p. 1990—), Mo. Assn. for Social Welfare (bd. treas. 1989-95), Nat. Assn. of Ind. Living Ctrs. (AIDS task force 1993—), Assn. of Programs for Rural Ind. Living, Nat. Soc. of Fund Raising Execs., Mo. Rehab. Assn., C. of C. (healthcare divsn.), Zeta Tau Alpha. Home: 1748 E Arlington Rd Springfield MO 65804-7742

MORRIS, ARLENE MYERS, marketing professional; b. Washington, Pa., Dec. 29, 1951; d. Frank Hayes Myers and Lula Irene (Slusser) Kolcan; m. John L. Sullivan, Feb. 17, 1971 (div. July 1982); m. David Wellons Morris, July 27, 1984. BA, Carlow Coll., 1974; postgrad., Western New England Coll., 1981-82. Sales rep. Syntex Labs., Inc., Palo Alto, Calif., 1974-77; profl. sales rep. McNeil Pharm., Spring House, Pa., 1977-78, mental health rep., 1978-80, asst. product dir., 1981-82, dist. mgr., 1982-85, new product dir., 1985-87, exec. dir. new bus. devel., 1987-89, v.p. bus. devel., 1989-93; v.p. bus. devel. Scios Nova IMC, Mountain View, Calif., 1993—. Mem. Found. of Ind. Colls., Phila., 1989. Mem. Pharm. Advt. Coun., Am. Diabetes Assn., Am. Acad. Sci., Healthcare Bus. Womens Assn., Lic. Execs. Soc. Home: 11701 Winding Way Los Altos CA 94024-6331 Office: Scios Nova 2450 Bayshore Pky Mountain View CA 94043-1107

MORRIS, C. ROBERT, law educator; b. Denver, June 29, 1928; s. Clarence and Lillian (Eppstein) M.; m. Sandra Mueller, Sept. 1, 1970. BA, St. John's Coll., Annapolis, Md., 1948; JD, Yale U., 1951. Bar: Tex. 1951, Minn. 1974. Asst. prof. law Rutgers U., Camden, N.J., 1954-57; assoc. prof. law Rutgers U., 1957-60, prof. law, 1960-64; prof. law Univ. Minn., Mpls., 1964—. 1st lt. USAF, 1951-53. Office: U Minn Sch Law 229 19th Ave S Minneapolis MN 55455-0444

MORRIS, (WILLIAM) CARLOSS, lawyer, insurance company executive; b. Galveston, Tex., June 7, 1915; s. William Carloss and Willie (Stewart) M.; m. Doris Poole, Dec. 2, 1939; children: Marietta (Mrs. Morgan Maxfield), William Carloss III, Malcolm Stewart, Melinda Louise (Mrs. Glen Ginter). BA with distinction, Rice Inst., 1936; JD with highest honors, U. Tex., 1939. Bar: Tex. 1938. With Stewart Title Guaranty Co., Houston, 1939—, pres., 1951-75, chmn. bd. dirs., chief exec. officer, 1975-91; chmn. bd. dirs., co-chief exec. officer Stewart Info. Services Inc., 1975—; bd. dirs. Morris, Lendais, Hollrah and Snowden, Houston. Chmn. Interdisciplinary Commn. on Housing and Urban Growth, 1974-77; chmn. Star Hope Mission, 1951-90, hon., 1991—; pres. Tex. Safety Assn., 1950-51; bd. dirs. Goodwill Industries; bd. dirs., mem. exec. com. Billy Graham Evangelistic Assn.; chmn. Baylor Coll. Medicine, 1968, trustee, 1952—; trustee, deacon 1st Bapt. Ch., Houston, chmn. bd. deacons, 1987-89; trustee Baylor U., 1952-72, past vice chmn. bd. dirs.; trustee Oldham Little Ch. Found., B.M. Woltman Found. Inducted into Tex. Bus. Hall of Fame, 1995. Fellow Am. Bar Found., State Bar Tex. Found.; mem. ABA (past chmn. younger lawyers sect.), Tex. Bar Assn., Tex. Young Lawyers Assn. (past pres.), Chancellors, Order of Coif, Phi Delta Phi, Alpha Tau Omega. Clubs: River Oaks Country, University. Lodge: Kiwanis. Office: 1980 Post Oak Blvd Ste 800 Houston TX 77056-3807

MORRIS, CHARLES ELLIOT, neurologist; b. Denver, Mar. 30, 1929; s. Jacob M. and Lillian Y. M.; m. Naomi Carolyn Minner, June 28, 1951; children: Jonathan E., David C. B.A., U. Denver, 1950, M.A. in Biochemistry, 1951; M.D., U. Colo., 1955. Diplomate: Am. Bd. Psychiatry and Neurology. Intern Los Angeles County Gen. Hosp., 1955-56; resident in neurology, teaching fellow neurology Harvard U. Med. Sch.-Boston City Hosp., 1956-59; mem. faculty U. N.C. Med. Sch., Chapel Hill, 1961-77; prof. neurology and medicine U. N.C. Med. Sch., 1976-77; attending neurologist Guam Meml. Hosp., Tamuning, also neurologist in charge Nat. Inst. Neurol.

and Communicative Disorders and Stroke Rsch. Ctr., Agana, 1970-71; prof. neurology, 1976—, chmn. dept. Finch U. Health Scis. Chgo. Med. Sch., acting chief neurology svc. VA Med. Ctr., North Chgo., 1976-91; prof. dept. cell biology and anatomy, 1991-94; prof. neurosci., 1994—; vis. lectr. dept. neurology Rush Med. Coll., 1994—. Contbr. articles to profl. jours., chpts. to books. Served to lt. comdr. M.C., USNR, 1959-61. Mem. Am. Acad. Neurology, Assn. Rsch. in Nervous and Mental Diseases, AMA, AAAS, Am. Epilepsy Soc., So. Soc. Clin. Investigation, Ill. Med. Soc., Lake County Med. Soc., Sigma Xi, Alpha Omega Alpha, Phi Lambda Upsilon. Office: FUHS/Chgo Med Sch Dept Neurology 3333 Green Bay Rd North Chicago IL 60064-3037

MORRIS, CLAYTON LESLIE, priest; b. Eugene, Oreg., June 23, 1946; s. Joseph William Morris and Betty Fern (Rasmussen) Morris Darby; m. Mary Susan Pacquer, Dec. 30, 1968; children: Andrea Christine, Jonathan William. B Music, Willamette U., 1968; MA in Theology, Grad. Theol. Union, 1971, PhD in Theology, 1986; MDiv, Ch. Div. Sch., 1971. Ordained priest Episcopal Ch., 1971. Assoc. priest St. Andrew's Ch., Saratoga, Calif., 1971-74; rector St. Mark's Ch., King City, Calif., 1974-79; organist, choirmaster St. Paul's Ch., Oakland, Calif., 1979-80; teaching fellow, instr. Ch. Div. Sch., Berkeley, 1979-86; dir. music All Souls Ch., Berkeley, Calif., 1980-86; assoc. rector St. Mark's Ch., Palo Alto, Calif., 1986-91; staff officer liturgy and music Episc. Ch. Ctr., N.Y., 1991—. Mem. N.Am. Acad. Liturgy, Assn. Anglican Musicians, Assn. Diocesan Liturgy and Music Commns., Consultation on Common Texts, Associated Parishes Coun. Office: Episcopal Church Ctr 815 2nd Ave New York NY 10017-4503

MORRIS, DANIEL KEARNS, journalist; b. Youngstown, Ohio, Jan. 14, 1954; s. John Mackey and Nancy Todd (Kearns) M.; m. Lisa Rachel Herrick, Aug. 25, 1984; children: Sarah Herrick, Nicholas Herrick. Student, Boston U., 1972-73; AB, U. Mich., 1978. VISTA vol. Winnebago (Nebr.) Indian Reservation, 1977-78; editor Pierian Press, Ann Arbor, Mich., 1979-81; pub., editor Alternative Rev. of Lit. and Politics mag., Ann Arbor, 1981-82; press sec. Richard Fellman for U.S. Congress campaign, Omaha, 1982; producer, editor Nat. Pub. Radio, Washington, 1983-88; producer CBS News, Washington, 1988-91, ABC News Nightline, Washington, 1991—. Field organizer McGovern for President, Washington, 1972. Recipient Robert F. Kennedy Journalism award RFK Found., 1988, News and Documentary Emmy award 1994. Home: 6208 31st St NW Washington DC 20015-1518 Office: ABC News 1717 Desales St NW Washington DC 20036-4401

MORRIS, DAVID, retired electrical engineer; b. N.Y.C., July 18, 1924; s. Morris Elia and Esther (Kohn) M.; m. Minnie Kramer, Feb. 2, 1957. BEE, CCNY, 1947, MEE, 1954. Elec. engr. Magnetic Amplifiers Inc., L.I., N.Y., 1951-53; chief engr. Square Root Mfg. Corp., Yonkers, N.Y., 1953-56; sect. head Poly. R&D, Bklyn., 1956-58; chief engr. Brach div. Gen. Bronze Corp., Newark, N.J., 1958-62; unit head Kearfott div. Singer Corp., Little Falls, N.J., 1962-70; group leader Monroe div. Litton Industries, Orange, N.J., 1970-72; sr. mem. tech. staff Lepel High Frequency Labs., Maspeth, N.Y., 1972-80, I.T.T. Avionics, Nutley, N.J., 1980-89; ret., 1989. Contbr. articles to profl. jours.; 7 patents in field. Mem. IEEE (life). Achievements include development of off line transistor switching regulator; radiation hardened hybrid electro-magnetic device for protection of semiconductor circuits; multi-winding power inductor; design of magnetic amplifiers for servo mechanisms used in the Ballistic Missile early warning system; power systems for N.Y. Fire Dept., T.F.X. fighter aircraft, AH64 Apaache helicopter. Avocations: experimental physics, classical music, chess. Home: 806 Maple Hill Dr Woodbridge NJ 07095

MORRIS, DESMOND, author; m. Ramona Morris; 1 son. Author: Biology of Art, 1962, Apes and Monkeys, 1965, Big Cats, 1965, Mammals: A Guide to the Living Species, 1966, The Naked Ape, 1968, The Human Zoo, 1969, Patterns of Reproductive Behavior, 1971, Intimate Behavior, 1971, Manwatching: A Field Guide to Human Behavior, 1977, The Soccer Tribe, 1981, The Book of Ages, 1983, The Art of Ancient Cyprus, 1985, Bodywatching: A Field Guide to the Human Species, 1985, The Illustrated Naked Ape, 1986, Catwatching, 1986, Dogwatching, 1986, The Secret Surrealist, 1987, Catlore, 1987, The Animals Roadshow, 1988, The Human Nestbuilders, 1988, Horsewatching, 1988, The Animal Contract, 1990, Animalwatching, 1990, Babywatching, 1991, Christmas Watching, 1992, The World of Animals, 1993, The Human Animal, 1994, Body Talk, A World Guide to Gestures, 1994, The Naked Ape Trilogy, 1994, Illustrated Cat Watching, 1994, Illustrated Babywatching, 1995; co-author: (with Ramona Morris) Men and Snakes, 1965, Men and Apes, 1966, Men and Pandas, 1966, The Giant Panda, 1981, Gestures: Their Origins and Distribution, 1979; autobiography Animal Days, 1979; editor: Primate Ethology, 1969, (fiction) Inrock, 1983. Address: care Jonathan Cape, 20 Vauxhall Bridge Rd, London SWIV 2SA, England

MORRIS, DEWEY BLANTON, lawyer; b. Richmond, Va., Sept. 15, 1938; s. Thomas Cecil and Mary Katherine (Rowlett) M.; m. Nancy Edmunds, Aug. 27, 1960; children: Sally Pendleton, Katherine Archer. BA, U. Va., 1960, LLB, 1965. Bar: Md. 1965, Va. 1968, D.C. 1991, U.S. Dist. Ct. Md. 1965, U.S. Dist. Ct. (ea. dist.) Va. 1968, U.S. Ct. Appeals (4th cir.) 1966. Assoc. Piper & Marbury, Balt., 1965-67; ptnr. Hunton & Williams, Richmond, 1967—. Served to 1st lt., USMC, 1960-62. Mem. ABA (bus. law sect.), Va. Bar Assn. (bus. law sect.), Richmond Bar Assn., Raven Soc., Commonwealth Club, Country Club Va. (Richmond), Army & Navy Club (Washington), Kiwanis, Phi Alpha Delta, Omicron Delta Kappa. Presbyterian. Clubs: Commonwealth, Country Club Va. (Richmond). Lodge: Kiwanis. Avocations: golf, tennis, skiing, photography. Home: 302 Locke Ln S Richmond VA 23226-1714 Office: Hunton & Williams Riverfront Plaza East Tower 951 E Byrd St Richmond VA 23219-4040

MORRIS, DIANE MARIE, special education consultant, travel consultant; b. Joliet, Ill., June 17, 1953; d. Milton W. and Anna Mae (Jungles) M. Assoc., Joliet Jr. Coll., 1973; BS in Spl. Edn., Ill. State U., 1975, MS in Spl. Edn., 1980. Cert. in spl. edn., learning disabilities, behavior disorders, educable mentally handicapped, regular edn.; approval in spl. early childhood; cert. in travel cons.; supervisory endorsement for learning disabled, behavior disorders, educable mentally handicapped. Summer sch. aide Laraway Sch., Joliet, 1970, 71; bookstore employee Joliet Jr. Coll., 1972-73; spl. edn. aide Joliet Pub. Grade Schs., 1975-76, tchr. spl. edn., 1976-82, supportive learning specialist, 1982—; travel cons. Wanderlich Travel, Joliet, 1982—; mem. inst. adv. com. Will County Regional Supt.'s Office, Joliet, 1983-89, master tchr. selection com., 1987; mem. adv. bd. Emily Howe Fisk Found.-Altrusa Club, Joliet, 1992—; participant learning disabled rsch. studies, 1980, 87. Mem., holder several offices Joliet Bus. and Profl. Women, 1982—; sec. Joliet Altrusa Club, 1991—; del. to China, Citizens Amb. Program, Spokane (Wash.) chpt., 1984. Recipient Disting. Svc. Scroll, Joliet PTA Coun., 1982. Mem. Coun. for Exceptional Children (cons. leadership tng. inst. 1994), Ill. Coun. for Exceptional Children (regional dir. 1989-96, asst. editor newsletter, Clarissa Hug Tchr. of Yr. 1994), Will County Coun. for Exceptional Children (pres. 1983, Program award 1993-94, Disting. Svc. award 1984), Delta Kappa Gamma, Alpha Delta Kappa, Kappa Delta Pi. Avocations: travel, biking, reading. Home: 16255 W Diane Way Manhattan IL 60442-9775 Office: Joliet Pub Grade Schs 420 N Raynor Ave Joliet IL 60435-6065

MORRIS, DONALD ARTHUR ADAMS, college president; b. Detroit, Aug. 31, 1934; s. Robert Park and Margaret Lymburn (Adams) M.; m. Zella Mae Stormer, June 21, 1958; children: Dwight Joseph, Julie Adams. B.A., Wayne State U., 1961; M.P.A., U. Mich., 1966, Ph.D., 1970; LLD (hon.), Olivet Coll., 1987. Copy boy Detroit Times, 1952-55, reporter, 1955-57, edn. writer, 1957-60; adminstrv. asst. Wayne State U., Detroit, 1960-62; mng. editor news service U. Mich., 1962-64, mgr. spl. programs, 1964-68; mgr. Met. Detroit Devel. Program, 1968-71; v.p. for devel. Hobart and William Smith Colls., Geneva, N.Y., 1971-76; exec. v.p. Hobart and William Smith Colls., 1976-77; pres., prof. polit. sci. Olivet (Mich.) Coll., Mich., 1977-92; pres. emeritus Olivet Coll., Mich., 1992—, cons., 1992-93; trustee Mich. Intercollegiate Athletic Assn., 1977-92, Assn. Ind. Colls. and Univs. Mich., 1977-92, chair, 1984-85; cons. evaluator North Ctrl. Assn. Colls. and Schs., 1986-92; mem. Mich. Jud. Tenure Commn., 1991-94; mem. Newspaper Guild of Detroit, 1952-60, exec. bd., 1958-60. Contbr. articles to profl. jours. Trustee Olivet Coll., 1977-92, Mich. Coll. Found., 1977-92, exec. com., 1989-92; mem. Mich. Higher Edn. Assistance and Student Loan Authorities, 1986—, chair, 1989-94; bd. dirs. Planned Parenthood of Finger Lakes, N.Y., 1973-77, pres., 1975-77; bd. dirs., treas. Genesee Regional Family Planning Program N.Y., 1975-77; trustee Coun. Higher Edn., United Ch. of Christ, 1977-92, mem. exec. com., 1982-92, chair, 1986-88; trustee Glen Lake Cmty. Libr. Bd., 1993—, pres., 1994—; mem. Sleeping Bear Noontiders, 1993—, sec., 1995—, South Manitou Meml. Soc., 1980—. Mem. Am. Assn. for Higher Edn., Sigma Delta Chi, Omicron Delta Kappa, Alpha Lambda Epsilon, Kappa Sigma Alpha, Gamma Iota Sigma, Alpha Mu Gamma, Phi Mu Alpha Sinfonia, Rotary (local pres. 1987-88, Paul Harris fellow). Congregationalist. Home: 8330 S Dunns Farm Rd Maple City MI 49664-9614 also: 6551 E Dorado Blvd Tucson AZ 85715-4705

MORRIS, DOROTHEA LOUISE, nurse midwife; b. Emporia, Kans., Oct. 30, 1944; d. Clarence Earl and Dorothy Ann (Draper) Richardson; m. David B. DeKalb, May 1, 1966 (div. Dec. 1981); children: Michele E. DeKalb, Cheryl L. Lines, David B. DeKalb Jr.; m. James Henry Morris, July 4, 1984. Diploma, Beth-El Sch. Nursing, Colorado Springs, Colo., 1966; BSN, Alaska Meth. U., 1975; MPA, Troy State U., 1988; MSN, U. N.Mex., 1990. RN Colo., N. Mex. Commd. 2d lt. USAF, 1977, advanced through grades to lt. col.; staff nurse Meml. Hosp., Colorado Springs, 1966-67; staff nurse, supr. Albany (Oreg.) Gen. Hosp., 1969; staff nurse, obstetrics Harrisonville (Mo.) Hosp., 1970, USAF Hosp., Anchorage, 1970-75; staff nurse, instr. BOCES, Verona, N.Y., 1976-77; staff nurse, instr. ADN program Mohawk Valley C.C., Utica, N.Y., 1976-77; staff nurse obstetrics Chanute AFB, Rantoul, Ill., 1977-79; nurse-midwife Homestead AFB (Fla.) Hosp., 1980-85, Weisbaden (Germany) Regional Med. Ctr., 1985-88; nurse-midwife, instr. Midwifery Sch., Andrews AFB, Md., 1990—; asst. dir. Air Force Nurse-Midwifery Program, Andrews AFB, 1991—; pres. CNM Svc. Dirs., Inc., 1995-97. Lt. col. USAF, 1977—. Mem. Am. Coll. Nurse Midwives (cert.), Nurses Assn. Obstetrics and Gynecology, NANP in Reproductive Health, Uniformed Nurse Practitioner Assn., Order Ea. Star. Baptist. Avocations: painting, knitting, crocheting. Home: 4024-2 Ashwood Cir Andrews AFB MD 20762 Office: SGHOM Malcolm Grow 89 MDOS/SGOGM Andrews AFB Washington MD 20762

MORRIS, EARLE ELIAS, JR., state official, business executive; b. Greenville, S.C., July 14, 1928; s. Earle Elias and Bernice (Carey) M.; m. Jane L. Boroughs, Apr. 12, 1958; children: Lynda Lewis, Carey Mauldin, Elizabeth McDaniel, Earle Elias III; m. Carol Telford, Oct. 4, 1972; 1 son, David Earle. BS, Clemson Coll., 1949, LLD; D.Pub. Svc. (hon.), U. S.C., 1980, S.C. State Coll., 1990; Dr. Med. Sci., U. S.C.; LLD (hon.), The Citadel, Cen. Wesleyan Coll.; HHD (hon.), Lander Coll., Francis Marion Coll., 1984. Pres., chmn. bd. Morris & Co., Inc. (wholesale grocers), Pickens, S.C.; v.p., dir. Pickens Bank, 1956-69, Bankers Trust S.C., Pickens, 1968-75; pres. Gen. Ins. Agy., Pickens, 1970—; sec. Carolina Investors, Inc., chmn., 1993—; ptnr. Morris Realty Co., Pickens; mem. S.C. Ho. of Reps., 1950-54, S.C. Senate, 1954-70; lt. gov. State of S.C., 1971-75, comptr. gen., 1976—; chmn. bd. Santee Cooper Fisheries (Far East) Ltd., Hong Kong, Tai Pan Technologies, Ltd., Hong Kong; dir. Brunswick Worsted Mills, S.C. Devel. Corp., Pickens Savs. & Loan Assn. Pres. Clemson U. Found., 1984-85. Served to brig. gen. S.C. N.G., maj. gen. S.C. S.G. Recipient Algernon Sydney Sullivan award, 1980, Donald L. Scantlebury award, 1985, Nations Most Valuable Pub. Ofcl. award, 1993, Pub. Svc. award Am. Legion, 1993; named Disting. Alumnus, Clemson Coll. Mem. Nat. Assn. State Comptrollers (pres. 1982), Nat. Assn. State Auditors, Comptrollers and Treasurers (pres. 1988-89), S.C. Nat. Guard Assn. (pres. 1980-81), S.C. Jr. C. of C., S.C. Rehab. Assn. (v.p.), Govtl. Acctg. Standards Adv. Coun. (chmn. 1989-96), Fin. Acctg. Found. (trustee 1985-88, 96—), Blue Key, Sigma Alpha Epsilon, Phi Kappa Phi. Presbyterian (elder, former deacon, synod trustee). Clubs: Palmetto, Faculty (Columbia); Poinsett (Greenville). Lodges: Masons, Shriners, Lions. Home: 159 Lake Murray Ter Lexington SC 29072-9103 Office: Office of Comptr Gen State of SC Columbia SC 29211 *In my personal, public and professional life I have tried to follow the Biblical admonition of "loving mercy, doing justly, and walking humbly."*

MORRIS, EDWIN ALEXANDER, retired apparel manufacturing company executive; b. Concord, N.C., Aug. 13, 1903; s. William Lee M. and Martha Margaret (Ervin) M.; m. Mary Ella Cannon, Nov. 1, 1933; children: Joseph E., Mary Lou (dec.). BS in Commerce, Washington and Lee U., 1926. Joined Blue Bell, Inc., Greensboro, N.C., 1937; pres., chief exec. officer Blue Bell, Inc., 1948-66, chmn. bd., chief exec. officer, 1966-74, chmn. bd., 1974-81, dir., 1940-81. Bd. dirs. emeritus N.C. Citizens Assn.; trustee emeritus Wesley Long Hosp., Greensboro, 1958-83; bd. dirs. Nat. Taxpayers Union, Washington, Washington and Lee U. Planning and Devel. Com., The Jesse Helms Ctr. Found., Wingate Coll., N.C., 1989-91, Students for Am., Raleigh, N.C., 1990-94, The John Locke Found., Raleigh, 1992-94, N.C. Taxpayers United, Raleigh; bd. overseers Duke Comprehensive Cancer Ctr., Durham, 1985—. Presbyterian. Clubs: Greensboro Country, Greensboro City. Office: 400 W Market St Ste 408 Greensboro NC 27401-2241

MORRIS, EDWIN THADDEUS, construction consultant; b. N.Y.C., Jan. 13, 1912; s. Edwin T. and Helen (Hughes) M.; m. Winifred Walsh, Apr. 23, 1938; children—Edwin Thaddeus, Joan M., David M., Patrick J. Student, Manhattan Coll., 1928-30. Field engr. Madigan Hyland Cons. Engrs., 1936-37; supt. Raymond Concrete Pile Co., 1937-43; project mgr., gen. supt., officer subsidary Raymond Internat. Companies, 1946-58; v.p. Raymond Internat., Inc. (and subsidiaries), 1958-60, sr. v.p. overseas heavy constrn. div., 1960-66; pres., dir. Balt. Contractors, Inc., 1966-76; pres. Edwin T. Morris Constrn. Consultants, Inc., Towson, Md., 1976—. Served to lt., C.E. USNR, 1943-46. Mem. Engring. Soc. of Balt. Clubs: Explorers (N.Y.C.), Moles (N.Y.C.). Home: 7927 Ruxway Rd Towson MD 21204-3515

MORRIS, ELIZABETH TREAT, physical therapist; b. Hartford, Conn., Feb. 20, 1936; d. Charles Wells and Marion Louise (Case) Treat; BS in Phys. Therapy, U. Conn., 1960; m. David Breck Morris, July 10, 1961; children: Russell Charles, Jeffrey David. Phys. therapist Crippled Children's Clinic No. Va., Arlington, 1960-62, Shriners Hosp. Crippled Children, Salt Lake City, 1967-69, Holy Cross Hosp., Salt Lake City, 1970-74; pvt. practice phys. therapy, Salt Lake City, 1975—. Mem. nominating com. YWCA, Salt Lake City. Mem. Am. Phys. Therapy Assn., Am. Congress Rehab. Medicine, Am. Alliance for Health Phys. Edn. Recreation & Dance, Nat. Speakers Assn., Utah Speakers Assn., Salt Lake Area C. of C., Friendship Force Utah, U.S. Figure Skating Assn., Toastmasters Internat., Internat. Assn. for the Study Pain, Internat. Platform Assn., World Confederation Phys. Therapy, Medart Internat. Home: 4177 Mathews Way Salt Lake City UT 84124-4021 Office: PO Box 526186 Salt Lake City UT 84152-6186

MORRIS, ERROL M., filmmaker; b. Hewlett, N.Y., Feb. 5, 1948; s. Abner and Cinnabelle (Burzinsky) M.; m. Julia Bynum Sheehan; 1 child, Nathaniel Hamilton. BA, U. Wis., 1969; student, Princeton U., U. Calif., Berkeley. Pres. Fourth Floor Prodns., Inc., Cambridge, Mass. Dir., producer Gates of Heaven, 1978, The Thin Blue Line, 1987, A Brief History of Time, 1991. Guggenheim fellow, 1990, MacArthur fellow, 1990-94. Office: Fourth Floor Prodns 678 Massachusetts Ave Cambridge MA 02139-3355

MORRIS, EUGENE JEROME, lawyer; b. N.Y.C., Oct. 14, 1910; s. Max and Regina (Cohn) M.; m. Terry Lesser, Mar. 28, 1934 (dec. Sept. 1993); 1 child, Richard S.; m. Blanche Bier Finke, June 22, 1994. B.S.S., CCNY, 1931; LL.B., St. John's U., 1934. Bar: N.Y. 1935. Practiced N.Y.C., 1935—; sr. and founding partner firm Demov, Morris & Hammerling, 1946-87; v.p., sr. counsel Ea. region Am. Title Ins. Co., N.Y.C., 1990-93; of counsel Spector & Feldman, 1991—; adj. prof. land use regulation NYU Grad. Sch. Pub. Arminstrn., 1978-81; adj. prof. legal issues in real estate, Real Estate Inst. NYU, 1988—; spl. master Supreme Ct. State of N.Y., 1979—; arbitrator Civil Ct. N.Y., 1994—. Editor weekly column N.Y. Law Jour., 1965-87, It's the Law, Real Estate Forum, 1982-87; editor-in-chief N.Y. Practice Guide: Real Estate, 4 vols., 1986, Real Estate Development, 4 vols., 1987; contbr. articles to profl. jours. Mem. N.Y. State Tax Revision Commn., 1977-80, N.Y.C. Rent Guidelines Bd., 1983-85. Served with AUS, 1943-45. Recipient Justice award N.Y. sect. Am. Jewish Congress, 1996. Mem. ABA (chmn. spl. com. housing and urban devel. 1970-73, coun. sect. real property, probate and trust law 1971-74, assoc. editor Real Property, Probate and Trust Jour. 1979-86, editor Real Property, Probate and Property mag., articles editor 1986-94), Am. Judges Assn., Assn. Bar City N.Y. (chmn. com. housing and urban devel. 1971-74, com. on lectures and continuing edn. 1980-83, coun. on jud. adminstrn. 1989-92), N.Y. State Bar Assn. (exec. com. 1980—, chmn. com. meetings and lectures 1982-92, CLE com. 1984-90, ho. of dels. 1986-95), Citizens Union, Lambda Alpha (bd. dirs. 1990—, pres. N.Y. chpt. 1990-93, sec. 1993-95, treas. 1996—). Home: 200 Central Park S New York NY 10019-1415 *After 60 years of marriage and 62 years of practicing law, I feel I am ready for retirement. However, like the old fire horse when the bell rings I run; thus I am still teaching real estate law as an Adjunct Professor at the New York Universitsy Real Estate Institute, am counsel to my firm and stay active in bar associations, civic groups and fraternities.*

MORRIS, FLORENCE HENDERSON, auditor; b. Mobile, Ala., Sept. 8, 1964; d. Thomas Gordan Henderson and Joanne Elizabeth (Pfleger) Martin; m. Fred S. Morris, July 28, 1995. BS in Fin., U. Ala., 1986. Payment and receipt rep. SouthTrust Bank of Mobile, 1988-89; internal bank auditor SouthTrust Corp., Birmingham, 1989-90, compliance audit officer, 1990-92; prin. compliance auditor, asst. v.p. SouthTrust Corp. and SouthTrust Bank of Ga., Atlanta, 1992-95; compliance audit supr., v.p. SouthTrust Corp., Birmingham, 1995—. Mem. Inst. Internal Auditors, Bankers Adminstrn. Inst. (cert. bank compliance officer), Am. Bankers Assn., Ala. Fin. Assn., U. Ala. Alumna, Delta Sigma Pi. Office: SouthTrust Corp Audit Dept PO Box 2554 Birmingham AL 35290

MORRIS, FRANK CHARLES, JR., lawyer, educator; b. Pitts., May 11, 1948; s. Frank Charles and Mary Louise (Veverka) M.; m. Kathleen Williams; children: Frank Charles III, Alexander Greg. BS with distinction, Northwestern U., 1970; JD, U. Va., 1973. Bar: Pa. 1973, U.S. Ct. Appeals (4th and 7th cirs.) 1974, D.C. 1975, U.S. Ct. Appeals (1st, 2d and 9th cirs.) 1975, U.S. Ct. Appeals (10th cir.) 1976, U.S. Supreme Ct. 1976, U.S. Ct. Appeals (5th and D.C. cirs.) 1977, U.S. Dist. Ct. D.C. 1977, U.S. Dist. Ct. (ea. dist.) Wis. 1980, U.S. Dist. Ct. (ea. dist.) Pa., 1993, U.S. Ct. Appeals (11th cir.) 1981, U.S. Dist. Ct. Md. 1985, U.S. Ct. Appeals (6th and 8th cirs.) 1987, U.S. Ct. Appeals (3rd cir.) 1991. Rsch. asst. Bernard Dunau, Washington, 1972-73; appellate ct. br. atty. NLRB, Washington, 1973-76; assoc. McGuiness & Williams, Washington, 1976-78; assoc. Epstein Becker & Green, P.C., Washington, 1978-80, ptnr. 1981-88, sr. ptnr. 1988—; mem. adj. faculty Law Sch., Cath. U. Am., Washington, 1979-80, adj. prof. Law, 1984—, Law Sch., George Washington U., Washington; mem. faculty Sch. Indsl. and Labor Rels. EEO study program Cornell U., N.Y.C., 1979—, Inst. for Applied Mgmt. and Law, Newport Beach, Calif., 1982—, ALI-ABA course Employment Discrimination and Civil Rights Actions, 1988—, Trial Evidence, Civil Practice, and Effective Litigation Techniques in Fed. and State Cts.; co-chair ALI-ABA Fed. Jud. Ctr., Video Law Review, Ams. with Disabilities Act, 1992; co-chair video law rev. ALI-ABA, 1991, How To Present and Challenge Experts in Employment Cases, 1994; co-chair Current Devels. in Employment Law, 1994—; lectr. in field. Author: Current Trends in the Use (and Misuse) of Statistics in Employment Discrimination Litigation, 1977, 2d edit., 1978. Contbg. editor EEO Today, 1979-80; editor-in-chief The Equal Employer newsletter, 1981-86; edit. adv. bd. ADA Policy & Law, 1992—, Corp. Counsel's Guide to ADA, 1993—. Dir. Northwestern U. Alumni Admissions Coun., Washington Area Coun., 1978-81. Recipient Sustained Superior Performance award NLRB Gen. Counsel, 1974, cert. commendation for outstanding performance NLRB Gen. Counsel, 1975; named to Outstanding Young Men Am., U.S. Jaycees, 1982; commendation for collective bargaining Social Security Adminstrn. Commr., 1988. Mem. ABA (labor and employment law, adminstrv. and litigation sects.), Pa. Bar Assn., D.C. Bar Assn. (administrv. law, labor relations and litigation divs.), Fed. Bar Assn., Northwestern U. Alumni Club (bd. govs. 1975—), D.C. Rd. Runners Club, John Evans Club of Northwestern U. Roman Catholic.

MORRIS, FRANK EUGENE, banker; b. Detroit, Dec. 30, 1923; s. Frank and Beatrice (Perkins) M.; m. Geraldine Elizabeth Coltharp, Dec. 22, 1944; children—Susan, Lisa, Betsy. B.A., Wayne U., 1948; M.A., U. Mich., 1949, Ph.D. in Econs, 1955. Research dir. Investment Bankers Assn., Washington, 1955-61; asst. to sec. debt mgmt. Treasury Dept., 1961-63; v.p. Loomis Sayles and Co., Boston, 1963-68; pres. Fed. Res. Bank Boston, 1968-88; Peter Drucker prof. mgmt. Boston Coll., 1989-94; tchg. fellow U. Mich., 1949-51; bd. dirs. Thermo Electron Corp., Thermo Remediation Corp.; trustee SEI Mut. Funds. Served to 1st lt. USAAF, 1943-45.

MORRIS, G. RONALD, automotive executive; b. East St. Louis, Ill., Aug. 30, 1936; s. George H. and Mildred C. M.; m. Margaret Heino, June 20, 1959; children: David, Michele, James. B.S. in Metall. Engring, U. Ill., 1959. Metall. engr. Delco-Remy div. Gen. Motors Corp., 1959-60; factory metallurgist Dubuque Tractor Works, John Deere Co., Iowa, 1960-66; with Fed.-Mogul Corp., 1966-79, v.p., group mgr. ball and roller bearing group, 1979; pres. Tenneco Automotive div. Tenneco, Inc., Deerfield, Ill., 1979-82; pres., chief exec. officer PT Components, Inc., Indpls., 1982-88; vice-chmn. Rexnord Corp., Indpls., 1988-89; chmn., pres., chief exec. officer CTP Holdings Inc., 1986-88; chmn. Integrated Technologies, Inc., Indpls., 1990-92, also bd. dirs.; pres., chief exec. officer Western Industries, Inc., Milw., 1991—, also bd. dirs.; bd. dirs. Mulligan & Assocs., Chgo., Milnot Holding Corp., St. Louis, NN Ball & Roller, Inc., Erwin, Tenn.; corp. bd. dirs. Milw. Sch. of Engring. Mem. Pres.'s Coun., U. Ill.; corp. bd. dirs. Milw. Sch. of Engring. Mem. ASM, SAE, Meridian Hills Country Club (Indpls.), Exmoor Country Club (Highland Park, Ill.), Marshwood Country Club (Savannah, Ga.), Blue Mound Golf and Country Club (Wauwatosa, Wis.), Elks, Masons. Republican. Presbyterian. Office: Western Industries Inc 1215 N 62nd St Milwaukee WI 53213-2915

MORRIS, GARRETT, actor, singer; b. New Orleans, Feb. 1, 1937. Student, Tanglewood, Juilliard Sch. Music, Manhattan Sch. Music.; BA, Dillard U. Debut as singer and music arranger with Harry Belafonte folk singers; Broadway stage appearances include What The Wine Sellers Buy; Broadway stage appearances include Hallelujah Baby, Showboat, Porgy and Bess, I'm Solomon, Ain't Supposed to Die A Natural Death, The Great White Hope; other stage appearance in I'm Not Rappaport, 1990; appeared in films Where's Poppa?, 1970, The Anderson Tapes, 1971, Cooley High, 1975, Car Wash, 1976, How to Beat the High Cost of Living, 1980, The Census Taker, 1984, The Stuff, 1985, Critical Condition, 1987, The Underachievers, 1988, Dance to Win, 1989, Husbands, Wives, Money, and Murder, 1989 ; television series: Roll Out!, 1973-74, NBC's Saturday Night Live, 1975-80, It's Your Move, 1984-85, Hunter, 1986-90, Roc, 1990-91, Martin, 1992—; TV film The Invisible Woman, 1983, Maid For Each Other, 1992; author: play The Secret Place, 1969, Daddy Picou and Marie Le Veau, 1981. Mem. AFTRA, SAG, Equity. Office: Stone Manners Talent Agy 8091 Selma Ave Los Angeles CA 90046-2571*

MORRIS, GERALD DOUGLAS, newspaper editor; b. Boston, May 7, 1937; s. George Christopher and Lucy Bell (MacPhee) M.; m. Elaine Louise Owen, Nov. 13, 1964 (div. 1976); children: Laura Louise, Douglas Owen; m. Mary Elizabeth Simpson Stevens, Apr. 15, 1977; children: Jeffrey David Stevens Morris, Wendy Elizabeth Stevens Morris. Student, Boston U., 1959. Reporter Patriot Ledger, Quincy, Mass., 1961-66; copy editor Boston Globe, 1966—, travel editor, 1989—; syndicated columnist Globe-Trotting, 1970—. Author: Boston Globe Guide to Boston, 1989, New England under Sail, 1993. Chmn. Canton (Mass.) Cable Adv. Bd., 1990-92. With U.S. Army, 1959-61. Mem. Soc. Am. Travel Writers, Skal Club Boston, Lions (pres. Canton 1969-70, 80-81). Avocations: photography, travel. Home: 78 Cheney St Orange MA 01364-1603 Office: Globe Newspaper Co 135 Morrissey Blvd Boston MA 02125-3310

MORRIS, GRANT HAROLD, law educator; b. Syracuse, N.Y., Dec. 10, 1940; s. Benjamin and Caroline Grace (Judelson) M.; m. Phyllis Silberstein, July 4, 1967; children: Joshua, Sara. A.B., Syracuse U. (N.Y.), 1962, J.D., 1964; LL.M., Harvard U., 1971. Bar: N.Y. 1964. Atty. N.Y. Mental Hygiene Law Recodification Project, Inst. Public Adminstrn., N.Y.C., 1964-66; mem. faculty Wayne State U. Law Sch., 1967-73, prof. law, 1970-73, dean acad. affairs, 1971-73; prof. law U. San Diego Law Sch., 1973—, Univ. prof., 1996-97, acting dean, 1977-78, 88-89, assoc. dean grad. legal edn., 1978-81; prof. law in psychiatry Wayne State U. Med. Sch., 1970-73; adj. prof. U. Calif. San Diego Med. Sch., 1974-84, clinical prof., 1984—; legal counsel Mich. Legis. Com. to Revise Mental Health Statutes, 1970-73; organizer law and psychiatry sect. Assn. Am. Law Schs., 1973, chmn., 1973-74; patients advocate, San Diego County, 1977-78; cons. Criminal Code Commn., Ariz. Legis., 1974; reporter task force on guidelines governing roles of mental health profls. in criminal process Am. Bar Assn. standing com. on assn. standards for criminal justice, 1981-84; cert. rev. hearing officer San Diego Superior Ct., 1984-90, ct. commr./judge pro tem, 1990-92, mental health hearing officer, 1992—; hearing officer San Diego Housing Commn., 1988-92; mem. exec. com. sect. law and mental disability Assn. Am. Law Schs., 1990—. Author: The Insanity Defense: A Blueprint for Legislative Reform, 1975; co-author: Mental Disorder in the Criminal Process: Stan Stress and the Vietnam/Sports Conspiracy, 1993; editor, contbr.: The Mentally Ill and the Right to Treatment, 1970. Mem. Phi Alpha Delta (faculty adv. 1970-73, 75-92). Home: 8515 Nottingham Pl La Jolla CA 92037-2125 Office: U San Diego Law Sch 5998 Alcala Park San Diego CA 92110-2492

MORRIS, HENRY ALLEN, JR., publisher; b. Moncks Corner, S.C., Feb. 9, 1940; s. Henry Allen Sr. and Edith Luther (Wall) M.; divorced; 1 child, Anthony Duane Allen. A in Acctg., Palmer Jr. Coll., Charleston, S.C., 1959; BA in English cum laude, Belmont Abbey Coll., N.C., 1974. Office mgr. Gas Engine and Electric Co., Charleston, 1959; cargo coord. S.C. State Ports Authority, Charleston, 1959-70; headmaster St. Stephen Acad., S.C., 1973-77; gen. mgr. The Berkeley Democrat, Moncks Corner, 1977-86, owner, 1989—; pub., editor Berkeley Ind., Moncks Corner, 1987—; pres. Berkeley Pub. Inc., Moncks Corner, 1987—. Author: (short story) The Easter Gift, 1973. Bd. dirs. Council of Govts. Regional Forum, Charleston, 1987, Winthrop Coll., 1983, Moncks Corner Downtown, Inc., 1986-87; mem. Moncks Corner City Council, 1983-88; mayor pro tem, 1986-88; commr. S.C. Vocat. Rehab. Agy.; treas. bd. dirs. Berkeley County YMCA. Recipient Pres. award Berkeley Arts Council, 1985, Charleston Jaycees, 1971, Friend of Edn. award Berkeley County Sch. System, 1991; named Handicapped Man of Yr., Moncks Corner's Mayor's Com., 1990. Mem. Low County Soc. Profl. Journalists (pres.), S.C. Mcpl. Assn. (lesis. com.), Trident United Way (mem. exec. bd. 1983-91), Trident C. of C. (bd. dirs.), Charleston Opera Club (founder), Rotary (past pres.). Episcopalian. Avocations: reading, painting, collecting art. Home: 117 Merrimack Dr Moncks Corner SC 29461-3580

MORRIS, HENRY MADISON, JR., education educator; b. Dallas, Oct. 6, 1918; s. Henry Madison and Ida (Hunter) M.; m. Mary Louise Beach, Jan. 24, 1940; children: Henry Madison III, Kathleen Louise, John David, Andrew Hunter, Mary Ruth, Rebecca Jean. BS with distinction, Rice Inst., 1939; MS, U. Minn., 1948, PhD, 1950; LLD, Bob Jones U., 1966; LittD, Liberty U., 1989. Registered profl. engr., Tex. Jr. engr. Tex. Hwy. Dept., 1938-39; from jr. engr. to asst. engr. Internat. Boundary Commn., El Paso, 1939-42; instr. civil engring. Rice Inst., 1942-46; from instr. to asst. prof. U. Minn., Mpls., also research project leader St. Anthony Falls Hydraulics Lab., 1946-51; prof., head dept. civil engring. Southwestern La. Inst., Lafayette, 1951-57, Va. Poly. Inst., Blacksburg, 1957-70; v.p. acad. affairs Christian Heritage Coll., San Diego, 1970-78, pres., 1978-80; dir. Inst. for Creation Rsch., 1970-80, pres., 1980-96, pres. emeritus, 1996—. Author: (with Richard Stephens) Report on Rio Grande Water Conservation Investigation, 1942, That You Might Believe, 1946, 2d edit., 1978, (with Curtis Larson) Hydraulics of Flow in Culverts, 1948, The Bible and Modern Science, 1951, rev. edit., 1968, (with John C. Whitcomb) The Genesis Flood, 1961, Applied Hydraulics in Engineering, 1963, The Twilight of Evolution, 1964, Science, Scripture and Salvation, 1965, 2d edit., 1971, Studies in The Bible and Science, 1966, Evoluation and the Modern Christian, 1967, Biblical Cosmology and Modern Science, 1970, The Bible has the Answer, 1971, Science and Creation: A Handbook for Teachers, 1971, (with J. M. Wiggert) Applied Hydraulics, 1972, A Biblical Manual on Science and Creation, 1972, The Remarkable Birth of Planet Earth, 1973, Many Infallible Proofs, 1974, 2d edit., 1996, Scientific Creationism, 1974, 2d edit., 1985, Troubled Waters of Evolution, 1975, The Genesis Record, 1976, Education for the Real World, 1977, 3d edit., 1991, The Scientific Case for Creation, 1977, The Beginning of the World, 1977, 2d edit., 1991, Sampling the Psalms, 1978, 2d edit., 1991, King of Creation, 1980, Men of Science, Men of God, 1982, 2d edit. 1988, Evolution in Turmoil, 1982, The Revelation Record, 1983, History of Modern Creationism, 1984, 2d edit., 1993, The Biblical Basis for Modern Science, 1984, Creation and the Modern Christian, 1985, Science and the Bible, 1986, Days of Praise, 1986, The God Who is Real, 1988, The Remarkable Record of Job, 1988 (with Martin Clark) The Bible Has the Answer, 2d edit., 1987; (with Gary E. Parker) What is Creation Science, 1982, 2d edit., 1988, The Long War Against God, 1989, (with John D. Morris), Science, Scripture and the Young Earth, 1989, The Bible Science and Creation, 1991, Creation and the Second Coming, 1991, Biblical Creationism, 1993, The Defender's Bible, 1995, The Creation Trilogy, 1996;. Fellow AAAS, ASCE, Am. Sci. Affiliation; mem. Am. Soc. Engring. Edn. (sec.-editor civil engring. divsn. 1967-70), Trans-Nat. Assn. Christian Schs. (pres. 1983-95), Creation Rsch. Soc. (pres. 1967-73), Am. Geophys. Union, Geol. Soc. Am., Am. Assn. Petroleum Geologists, Geochem. Soc., Gideons (pres. La. 1954-56), Phi Beta Kappa, Sigma Xi, Chi Epsilon, Tau Beta Pi. Baptist. Home: 6733 El Banquero Pl San Diego CA 92119-1129 *The Bible is the inerrant word of God and thus should be believed and obeyed in all things.*

MORRIS, HENRY MADISON, JR., engineering executive, civil engineer; b. Dallas, Oct. 6, 1918; m. Mary L. Beach, 1940; children: Henry, Kathleen, John, Andrew, Mary, Rebecca. BS, Rice Inst., 1939; MS, U. Minn., 1948, PhD in Civil Engring., 1950; LLD, Bob Jones U., 1966; DLitt, Liberty U., 1989. Mem. State Hwy. Dept., Tex., 1938-39; jr. engr. to asst. engr. Internat. Boundary Commn., 1939-42; instr. civil engring. Rice Inst., 1942-46; instr. to asst. prof., project supr. St. Anthony Falls Hydraulic Lab., U. Minn., 1946-51; prof. civil engring., dept. head Southwestern La. Inst., 1951-56; prof. applied sci. U. So. Ill., 1957; prof. civil engring., dept. head Va. Poly. Inst. & State U., 1957-70; v.p. acad. affairs Christina Heritage Coll., 1970-78; dir. Inst. Creation Rsch., San Diego, 1970-80, pres., 1980—; pres. Nat. Assn. Christian Schs., 1984—. Fellow AAAS, ASCE; mem. Am. Geophys. Union, Geol. Soc. Am., Am. Assn. Petroleum Geology, Sigma Xi. Office: Institute for Creation Research PO Box 2667 El Cajon CA 92021-0667*

MORRIS, HERBERT, lawyer, educator; b. N.Y.C., July 28, 1928; s. Peter and Minnie (Miller) M.; m. Virginia Ann Grenier, Apr.3, 1956 (div. Nov. 1977); children: Jacob Jeremy, Benjamin John.; m. Margery Ruth Maslon, June 8, 1980. A.B., UCLA, 1951; LL.B., Yale, 1954; D. Phil., Oxford (Eng.) U., 1956. Bar: Calif. 1958. Mem. faculty UCLA, 1956—, prof. philosophy and law, 1962—, dean div. humanities, 1983-92, interim provost Coll. Letters and Sci., 1992-93; rsch. clin. assoc. So. Calif. Psychoanalytic Inst., 1977-89; retired, 1994. Editor: Freedom and Responsibility, 1961, The Masked Citadel, 1968, Guilt and Shame, 1971, On Guilt and Innocence, 1976. Home: 233 S Medio Dr Los Angeles CA 90049-3911 Office: UCLA Sch Law 405 Hilgard Ave Los Angeles CA 90024-1301

MORRIS, JAMES ALOYSIUS, economist, educator; b. Lawrence, Mass., May 25, 1918; s. George Thomas and Elizabeth (Reardon) M.; m. Marjorie Leila Frampton, May 30, 1942 (dec. Jan. 1993); children: Stephen Frampton, Elizabeth Harvey; m. Frances Harvey Chalk, Sept. 24, 1994. B.A. with high honors, Northeastern U., 1942, LL.D., 1968; A.M., Harvard U., 1947, Ph.D., 1951; Litt.D., Coll. Charleston, 1970; L.H.D., Lander Coll., 1971, Francis Marion Coll., 1982. Adj. prof. U. S.C., Columbia, 1947-51; assoc. prof. U. S.C., 1951-56, prof. econs., dir. grad. studies, dir. Econ. Rsch. Bur., 1956-61, dean Sch. Bus. Adminstrn., 1961-66, v.p. advanced studies and research, dean Grad. Sch., 1966-68, chmn. faculty com. on admissions and athletics, Disting. prof., 1972-77; econ. cons., 1977—; commr. S.C. Commn. on Higher Edn., 1968-72, Edn. Commn. of the States, 1968-72, So. Regional Edn. Bd.; past chmn. bd. dirs., exec. com. S.C. Blue Cross-Blue Shield; past vice chmn. Gov.'s Productivity Coun.; past chmn. Charlotte br. Fed. Res. Bank, Rep. Nat. Bank; labor arbitrator Fed. Mediation Svcs., Am. Arbitration Assn., 1948—; vis. rsch. prof. Nuffield Coll., Oxford U., 1953-54; cons. to dir. ICA, 1955; spl. econ. adviser to dir. USOM, Turkey, 1956-57; past chmn. S.C. Regional Export Expansion Coun.; past mem. Nat. Export Expansion Coun.; past mem. Gov.'s Task Force on the Economy, Gov.'s Adv. Group on Health Planning; past chmn. Gov.'s Adv. Group on Mental Health Planning; past chmn. bd. S.C. Bd. Econ. Advisers, S.C. Law Inst.; adv. bd. dirs. Earth Sci. Rsch. Inst., Heathwood Hall Episc. Sch.; pres. Carolina Econ. Assocs. Inc., 1979—. Author: Woolen and Worsted Manufacturing in the Southern Piedmont, 1952; contbr. articles and revs. to profl. jours. Bd. dirs. United Comty. Svcs., S.C. Coun. Econs. Edn., 1988—; pres. emeritus U. S.C. Ednl. Found.; past chmn. bd. dirs. Nat. Lab. Higher Edn.; past mem. corp. Northeastern U.; trustee Episc. Divsn. Upper S.C., 1988—; bd. trustees Richland Meml. Hosp., 1995—; mem. adv. bd. Still Hopes Episcopal Home. Lt. col. U.S. Army, 1940-41, 42-46. Mem. Am. Econ. Assn., So. Econ. Assn., Nat. Assn. Bus. Economists, Am. Arbitration Assn., Forum Club, Forest Lake Country Club, Palmetto Club, Rotary. Episcopalian. Home: 1829 Senate St Columbia SC 29201-3837 Office: U SC Columbia SC 29208

MORRIS, JAMES MALACHY, lawyer; b. Champaign, Ill., June 5, 1952; s. Walter Michael and Ellen Frances (Solon) M.; m. Mary Delilah Baker, Oct. 17, 1987; children: James Malachy Jr., Elliot Rice Baker, Walter Michael. Student, Oxford U. (Eng.), 1972; BA, Brown U., 1974; JD, U. Pa., 1977. Bar: N.Y. 1978, U.S. Dist. Ct. (so. and ea. dists.) N.Y. 1978, Ill. 1980, U.S. Tax Ct. 1982, U.S. Supreme Ct. 1983; admitted to Barristers Chambers, Manchester, Eng., 1987. Assoc. Reid & Priest, N.Y.C., 1977-80; sr. law clk. Supreme Ct. Ill., Springfield, 1980-81; assoc. Carter, Ledyard & Milburn, N.Y.C., 1981-83; sole practice N.Y.C., 1983-87; counsel FCA, Washington, 1987—; acting sec., gen. counsel FCS Ins. Corp., McLean, Va., 1990—; cons. Internat. Awards Found., Zurich, 1981—, Pritzker Architecture Prize Found., N.Y.C., 1981—, Herbert Oppenheimer, Nathan & VanDyck, London, 1985—. Contbr. articles to profl. jours. Mem. ABA, Ill. Bar Assn., N.Y. State Bar Assn., N.Y. County Lawyers Assn., Assn. Bar City N.Y., Brit. Inst. Internat. and Comparative Law, Lansdowne Club (London), Decatur (Ill.) Club. Office: PO Box 1407 Mc Lean VA 22101-1407

MORRIS, JAMES MATTHEW, history educator; b. Reed City, Mich., July 13, 1935; s. Fred Michael and Florence C. (Weiland) M.; m. Nancy Christina Becker, Aug. 23, 1958; children: Patrick J., Anne C., Michael J., John E., Joseph A., Mary Jane. BA, Aquinas Coll., 1957; MA, Central Mich. U., 1962; Phd, U. of Cin., 1969. High sch. tchr. Mich., 1957-1962; instr.history Coll. Steubenville, Ohio, 1962-64; asst. prof. Providence Coll., R.I., 1967-71; prof. Christopher Newport U., Newport News, Va., 1971—, dept. chair, 1994—; host radio series Sta. WGH-FM, Hampton, Va., 1978-83; prodr., host Crossroads TV series Centex TV Network, Williamsburg, Va., 1982-83; orientation speaker Nat. Com. on U.S.-China Rels., Coll. William and Mary, Williamsburg, 1987-92. Author: Our Maritime Heritage, 1979, History of the U.S. Navy, 1984, History of the U.S. Army, 1986, America's Armed Forces: A History, 1991; sr. editor: America's Maritime Legacy, 1979. Recipent edn. award U.S. Dept. Edn., Washington, 1985, disting. prof. award, Alpha Chi, Zeta Chpt., Newport News, Va., 1985. Mem. U.S. Naval Inst., N.Am. Soc. for Oceanic Historians, Soc. for Mil. History. Roman Catholic. Home: 303 Woodroof Rd Newport News VA 23606-2211 Office: Christopher Newport U 50 Shoe Ln Newport News VA 23606-2998

MORRIS, JAMES PEPPLER, bass; b. Balt., Jan. 10, 1947; s. James Deal and Geraldine (Peppler) M.; m. Joanne Frances Vitali, Nov. 15, 1971; 1 dau., Heather Frances; remarried Susan Louise Quittmeyer, Jan. 3, 1987. Student, U. Md., 1965-66, Peabody Conservatory, 1966-68, Acad. Vocal Arts, 1968-70. Recorded with Angel Records div. EMI and Deutche Grammophone, Sony, Phillips. Debut at Met. Opera, N.Y.C., 1971, singer, 1970—, opera and concert singer throughtou U.S., Can., S.Am., Europe, Australia, Japan, 1970—; recs. include Wotan in the New Ring Cycles. Recipient Grammy award for rec. of Wagner's Ring Cycle. Mem. Actors Equity (Can.), Am. Guild Mus. Artists. Office: care Colbert Artists Mgmt Inc 111 W 57th St New York NY 10019-2211

MORRIS, JAMES THOMAS, utilities executive; b. Terre Haute, Ind., Apr. 18, 1943; s. Howard James and Kathlyne (Eastes) M.; m. Jacqueline Harrell, Apr. 2, 1965; children: John Timothy, Jeffrey Todd, Jennifer Lynn. AB, Ind. U., 1965; MBA, Butler U., 1970, DBA (hon.), 1982; DBA (hon.), Vincennes U., 1978, Ind. State U., 1985, U. So. Ind., 1987, Franklin Coll., 1987, Rose-Hulman Inst. Tech., 1990, Martin U., 1992. Trainee Am. Fletcher Nat. Bank, Indpls., 1966-67; adminstrv. asst., chief of staff Mayor Richard G. Lugar, Indpls., 1967-73; v.p. Lilly Endowment, Inc., Indpls., 1973-84, pres., 1984-89; pres. Indpls. Water Co. and IWC Resources, 1989—; chmn. IWC Resources, 1991—; mem. U.S. del. NATO Com. on Challenges of Modern Soc., 1970-71. Chmn. bd. trustees Marion County Health and Hosp. Corp., 1976-83; chmn., trustee Ind. State U., 1971-79; bd. dirs. Indpls. Conv. and Visitors Assn., United Way of Greater Indpls., 1980—, Goodwill Industries Ind., Greater Indpls. Progress com., YMCA of Greater Indpls., Boy Scouts Am.; mem. exec. bd. U.S. Olympic Com., 1985-92; trustee, vice chmn. U.S. Olympic Found., 1987-93, Butler U., Christian Theol. Sem.; mem. U.S. Olympic Oversight Commn., 1988; elder Second Presbyn. Ch.; trustee NCAA Found., 1990, Freedoms Found., 1990; apptd. dir. by Pres. Bush Environ. of The Americas Bd., 1991. Named Outstanding Young Man in Indpls., 1972, one of five Outstanding Young Hoosiers, 1973; recipient Disting. Eagle Scout award, 1985, Disting. Alumni award Butler U., 1986, Disting. Service award Ind. U., 1987, Disting. Alumni Svc. award Ind. U., 1991, Horatio Alger award 1992, Whitney Young award Indpls. Urban League. Mem. Indpls. C. of C. (bd. dirs. 1985-89), Meridian Clubs. Republican. Office: Indianapolis Water Co 1220 Waterway Blvd Indianapolis IN 46202-2157

MORRIS, JANE ELIZABETH, home economics educator; b. Marietta, Ohio, Nov. 28, 1940; d. Harold Watson and LaRue (Graham) M. Student, U. Ky., 1960; BS, Marietta Coll., 1962, postgrad., 1963; MA, Kent State U., 1970, postgrad., 1985-87; postgrad., Coll. Mt. St. Joseph, 1984-86, John Carroll U., 1986, Ashland Coll., 1987. Cert. high sch. tchr., Ohio. Tchr. home econs. Chagrin Falls (Ohio) Mid. and High Sch., 1963-95; head cheerleading advisor Chagrin Falls H.S., 1970-80, freshman class advisor, 1981-82, head fine and practical arts dept., 1982-84, sophomore class advisor, 1982-85, 87-89, mem. prin.'s cabinet, 1987-88, tchr., adminstr. adv. coun., 1990-93. Vice chmn. The Elec. Women's Round Table, Inc., Cleve., 1968, chmn., 1969-71; treas. Trees Condominium Assn., 1981-83, pres., 1991-94; active Chagrin Falls chpt. Am. Heart Assn., Am. Cancer Soc., Geauga County Humane Soc. Mem. NEA, Career Edn. Assn., Ohio Edn. Assn., N.E. Ohio Edn. Assn., Chagrin Falls Edn. Assn. (bldg. rep. 1986-95, negotiating team 1990, negotiating com. 1993, commendation State of Ohio rep. assembly 1995), Alpha Xi Delta. Methodist. Avocations: swimming, interior design, sewing, gourmet cooking.

MORRIS, JASON, Olympic athlete. Mem. Olympic team Seoul, Korea, 1988; judo Barcelona, Spain, 1992. Recipient 172 lbs. Class Pan Am. Games champ, 1987, 91, 172 lbs. Class Judo Silver medal Olympics, Barcelona, 1992. Office: US Olympic Com 575 Swaggertown Rd Schenectady NY 12302-9628*

MORRIS, JERRY DEAN, academic administrator; b. Gassville, Ark., May 11, 1935; s. James Henry and Maud Idella (Taylor) M.; m. Marilyn Jo Pitman, June 11, 1955; children: Joseph, Neil, Laura, Kara. BS, U. Ark., 1960, MEd, 1964, EdD, 1971. Cert. sch. adminstr., Ark. High sch. tchr. Cotter (Ark.) Pub. Schs., 1959-60, high sch. prin., 1960-63; jr. high prin. Mountain Home (Ark.) Pub. Schs., 1963-66, high sch. prin., 1966-67, asst. supt., 1967-69; editor Ark. Sch. Bds. Newsletter, U. Ark., Fayetteville, 1969-70; dir. placement services East Tex. State U., Commerce, 1970-71, dean admissions & records, 1971-73, dean grad. sch., 1973-81, v.p. acad. affairs, 1982-86, pres., 1987—; cons. Ark. Basic Edn., 1970, U. Cen. Ark., Conway, 1972, coordinating bd. Tex. Colls. & Univs., Austin, 1981. Pres. Commerce C. of C., 1975; bd. dirs. Commerce Lions Club, 1977; chmn. Commerce United Way, 1978; mem. Commerce Indsl. Devel. Assn., 1974—. Named an Outstanding Young Man in Edn., Ark. Jaycees, 1966, Outstanding Young Man in Am., 1967. Mem. Tex. Assn. Coll. Tchrs., Assn. Tex. Grad. Schs. (pres. 1978-79), Coun. of So. Grad. Schs. (bd. dirs. 1976-79), Coun. of Grad. Schs. in U.S., Coun. of Pub. U. Pres. and Chancellors (exec. com. 1989-90), Assn. of Tex. Colls. and Univs. (exec. com. 1989-90), Phi Delta Kappa. Methodist. Avocations: jogging, gardening, reading, singing, travel. Home: ET Sta PO Box 3001 Commerce TX 75429-3001 Office: East Tex State U ET Station Commerce TX 75429

MORRIS, JOHN, composer, conductor, arranger; b. Elizabeth, N.J., Oct. 18, 1926; s. Thomas Arthur and Helen (Sherratt) M.; m. Francesca Bosetti; children: Evan Bosetti, Bronwen Helen. Student, Julliard Sch. Music, 1946-48, U. Wash., 1947, New Sch. Social Research, 1946-49. Composer mus. scores for (films) The Producers, The Twelve Chairs, The Gamblers, Blazing Saddles (nominated Acad. award 1976), The Bank Shot, Young Frankenstein, Sherlock Holmes Smarter Brother, Silent Movie, The Last Remake of Beau Geste, The In-Laws, The World's Greatest Lover, In God We Trust, High Anxiety, The Elephant Man (nominated Acad. award 1981), Table for Five, History of the World Part I, Yellowbeard, The Doctor and the Devils, Clue, To Be or Not To Be, Woman in Red, Johnny Dangerously, Haunted Honeymoon, Dirty Dancing, Spaceballs, Ironweed, The Wash, Stella, Life Stinks, (Broadway stage plays) My Mother, My Father and Me, Doll's House, Camino Real, (mus.) A Time for Singing, (off-Broadway) Take One Step, Young Andy Jackson, 15 scores for N.Y. Shakespeare Festival, Am. Shakespeare Festival, Stratford, Conn., (TV shows) Fresno, Katherine Anne Porter, Ghost Dancing, The Firm, The Mating Season, Splendor in the Grass, The Electric Grandmother, The Scarlet Letter, The Adams Chronicles, Georgia O'Keeffe, The Franken Project, The Tap Dance Kid (Emmy award 1986), Make Believe Marriage, ABC After Sch. Spl. Theme, Making Things Grow Theme, The French Chef Theme, The Desperate Hours, The Skirts of Happy Chance, Infancy and Childhood, The Fig Tree, The Little Match Girl, Our Sons, The Last to Go, The Last Best Year, The Sunset Gang, Coach Theme, Favorite Son, Journey Into Genius, When Lions Roar, Scarlett Mini Series, several documentary films; mus. supr., conductor, arranger numerous TV spls., Broadway and off-Broadway shows and recordings including Anne Bancroft Spl. #1 (Emmy award), 'S Lemmon 'S Gershwin 'S Wonderful (Emmy award), Hallmark Christmas Spls., (Broadway) Mack and Mabel, Much Ado About Nothing, Bells Are Ringing, (off-Broadway) Hair, (records) Wildcat, All-American, Bells Are Ringing, First Impressions, Bye-Bye Birdie, Kwamina, Baker Street, Rodgers and Hart, George Gershwin vols. I and II, Jerome Kern, Lyrics of Ira Gershwin, Cole Porter, others. Mem. ASCAP, Acad. Motion Picture Arts and Scis., Am. Fedn. Musicians. Avocations: computers, humorous poetry, cooking. Office: Alan Stein 270 Madison Ave New York NY 10016-0601

MORRIS, JOHN E., lawyer; b. N.Y.C., Sept. 30, 1916; s. John and Honora C. (Long) M.; m. Patricia E. Grojean. A.B., CCNY; A.M., Columbia U.; J.D., Harvard U. Bar: N.Y. 1942, U.S. Dist. Ct. (so. and ea. dists.) N.Y. Trial lawyer Clarke & Reilly, 1946-50; ptnr. Morris & Duffy, N.Y.C., 1950—. Served to lt. USCG, 1942-46; ETO. Mem. ABA, N.Y. State Bar Assn., N.Y. County Lawyers Assn. (mem. judiciary com.), Harvard Law Sch. Assn., Airplane Owners & Pilots Assn., Internat. Assn. Ins. Counsel, USCG Combat Vets. Assn., Harvard Club, N.Y. Athletic Club (N.Y.C.), Great Dane Club Am. (bd. dirs.). Roman Catholic. Office: 170 Broadway Fl 7 New York NY 10038-4154

MORRIS, JOHN LUNDEN, global logistics and communications executive; b. Wilmington, Del., Feb. 26, 1943; s. Arthur Lunden and Carolyn Wilson (Bickell) M.; m. Sally Carolyn Wheeler, Mar. 9, 1967; children: Christopher Wheeler, Kevin Arthur. BA, U. Del., 1965; postgrad., Rutgers U., 1968-71. Ocean container specialist E.I. DuPont de Nemours & Co., Inc., N.Y.C., 1968-72; mgr. pricing U.S. gulf Seatrain Lines, Inc., Weehauken, N.J., 1972-73; dir. pricing Europe Seatrain Lines, Inc., Rotterdam, Holland, 1973-75; dir. market planning, advt. Seatrain Lines, Inc., Weehauken, 1975-76; dir. pricing Seatrain Agys., Inc., N.Y.C., 1976-80; dir. mktg. Prudential Lines, Inc., N.Y.C., 1980-85; dir. mktg. and rsch. Trans Atlantic Associated Freight Confs., N.Y.C., 1985-87; exec. dir. U.S. Atlantic and Gulf Venezuela Conf., Jersey City, 1987-91; chief exec. officer Inter-Am. Freight Conf., Jersey City, 1987-94; pres. INTRANSCO, Internat. Transp. Solutions, Inc., Montclair, N.J., 1994—; agt. Trade Compass, MCI Telecomm. Inc., 1995—, Microsoft; dir. global comms. sys. Mediterranean Shipping Co., N.Y.C., 1996—; mem. electronic systems adv. com. U.S. Customs Svc., Washington, 1988—; study com. Fed. Maritime Commn., Washington, 1987, 89-91, expert witness, Fed. Cts., Boston, N.Y.C.; spkr., presenter N.Y./N.J. Port Authority, World Trade Inst., Brazilian-Am. C. of C., Montclair C. of C. Mem. Twp. Transp. Adv. Com., Montclair, 1982-85; chmn. Upper Montclair troop 7 Boy Scouts Am., 1982-88; trustee Montclair Hist. Soc., 1996—. Mem. Assn. Banyan Users Internat. (dir.), Christian Bus. Men's Club (N.Y.C.), Transp. Rsch. Forum, Assn. for Corp. Computing Tech. Profl., Internat. Trade Users Assn. Presbyterian. Avocations: bicycling, golf, touring, art and architectural history. Office: INTRANSCO Internat Transp Solutions PO Box 862 Upper Montclair NJ 07043-0862 also: Mediterranean Shipping Co 420 Fifth Ave New York NY 10018-2702

MORRIS, JOHN SELWYN, philosophy educator, college president emeritus; b. Tonypandy, Wales, July 2, 1925; came to U.S., 1954, naturalized, 1993; s. Jenkin and Hannah M. (Williams) M.; m. Enid Elry Walters, Apr. 10, 1954; 1 child, Paul John. B.A., Univ. Coll. South Wales and Monmouthshire, 1951; M.A., Cambridge (Eng.) U., 1953; student, Union Theol. Sem., 1957-60; M.A., Colgate U., 1961; Ph.D., Columbia U., 1961; LL.D. (hon.), Hartwick Coll., 1979; LHD (hon.), Elmyra Coll., 1990; DLitt, Skidmore Coll., 1991. Ordained to ministry Presbyterian Ch., 1954; minister Vernon (N.Y.) and Vernon Center Presbyn. chs., 1954-57; instr. Colgate U., Hamilton, N.Y., 1960-63; asst. prof. Colgate U., 1963-66, assoc. prof., 1966-70, prof. philosophy and religion, 1970-79, dir. div. humanities, 1970-72, dir. div. univ. studies, 1972-73, provost, dean of faculty, 1973-79, acting pres., 1977; prof. philosophy Union Coll., Schenectady, 1979-90, pres., chancellor Union U., 1979-90, pres. emeritus, rsch. prof. philosophy, 1990—; Leverhulme vis. fellow U. Exeter, Eng., 1968-69; chmn. Commn. Ind. Colls. and Univs., 1984-86; bd. dirs. Trustco N.Y. Bd. dirs. Schenectady Found.; trustee Skidmore Coll. With RAF, 1943-47. Recipient Disting. Svc. award Colgate U. Alumni Corp., 1978, Schenectady Patroon award, 1989. Mem. AAUP, Am. Philos. Assn., Am. Acad. Religion, Royal Inst. Philosophy, Soc. for Study Theology, Nat. Welsh Am. Found. (bd. advisors). Office: Union Coll Humanities Ctr Schenectady NY 12308

MORRIS, JOHN WOODLAND, II, businessman, former army officer; b. Princess Anne, Md., Sept. 10, 1921; s. John Earl and Allice (Cropper) M.; m. Geraldine Moore King, May 12, 1947; children: Susan K., John Woodland III. BS, U.S. Mil. Acad., 1943; MS, U. Iowa, 1947; postgrad., Army War Coll., 1961-62, U. Pitts., 1966. Commd. 2d lt. U.S. Army, 1943, advanced through grades to lt. gen., 1971; dep. dist. engr. Savannah, Ga., 1952-54; resident engr. Goose Bay, Labrador, 1955-57; staff officer Office Chief Engrs., 1957-60; comdg. officer 8th Engr. Bn., Korea, 1960-61; dist. engr. Tulsa, 1962-65; dep. comdt. U.S. Mil. Acad., 1965-67; dep. chief legis. liaison Office Sec. Army, Washington, 1967-69; comdg. gen. 18th Engr. Brigade, Vietnam, 1969-70; div. engr. Missouri River Div., Omaha, 1970-72; dir. civil works Office C.E., Washington, 1972-75; dep. chief engr. U.S. Army, 1975-76, chief engr., 1976-80; ret., 1980; exec. dir. Royal Volker Stevin, 1980-84; pres. J.W. Morris Ltd., 1981—; prof. U. Md., 1983-86; chmn. bd., chief exec. officer PRC Engring., 1986-88, cons.; cons., engr. advisor Zorc, Rissetto, Weaver & Rosen, 1988-92; engr. advisor Seltzer & Rosen, 1992—; bd. dirs. Air Water Tech., Morganti Constrn. Co. Mem. Indian Nations coun. Boy Scouts Am., 1962-65; chmn. Water Resources Congress, 1988-90; trustee U.S. Mil. Acad. Assn. Grads, 1986—; advisor dean engring. and math. U. Vt., 1990—. Decorated Legion of Merit with three oak leaf clusters, Army D.S.M., Def. D.S.M.; recipient Merit award Am. Cons. Engrs. Council; Palladium medal Audubon Soc. Fellow ASCE; mem. AIA (hon.), Internat. Navigation Congress (v.p.), U.S. Soc. Mil. Engrs. (pres.), Nat. Acad. Engrs., U.S. Com. on Large Dams (past chmn. environ. effect com., named Constrn. Man of Yr. 1977, Navigation Hall of Fame 1990, Golden Beaver award for engring. 1995). Episcopalian. Home: 1329 N Lynnbrook Dr Arlington VA 22201-4918 Office: 3800 N Fairfax Dr Ste 5 Arlington VA 22203

MORRIS, JORDEN WALTER, dancer, educator; b. Banff, Alta., Can., Aug. 19, 1967; s. Walter Edgard Morris and Penny Ann (Stenton) Tillenius. Student, U. Winnipeg, 1993. Tchr./coach Royal Winnipeg Ballet, Can., 1985, 88—, mem. corps de ballet, 1987-89, soloist, 1989-92, prin. dancer, 1992—; asst. choregrapher Les Ballet Jazz De Montreal, Que., 1979; guest artist Banff (Alta.) Centre Sch. Fine Arts, 1984. Repertoire includes lead roles in Rodeo, Giselle, Romeo and Juliet, Four Last Songs, Lilac Garden, The Nutcracker, Swan Lake, Symphony in D, Stoolgame, Myth, Pas des Déeses, Dark Elegies, La Princesse et le Soldat; gala performer Canadian AIDS Benefit, Toronto, Ont., 1990. Recipient Alan Hooper scholarship Banff Centre Fine Arts, 1981, Larry MCkinnon scholarship Royal Winnipeg Ballet, 1984. Mem. Canadian Actors Equity Assn. (adv. com. 1990, union dep. 1995-96). Avocations: carpentry, guitars, mountain climbing, horse ranching. Home: 3H-440 Assiniboine Ave, 11-C 778 McMillan Ave, WPO, MB Canada R3M 0V3 Office: Royal Winnipeg Ballet, 380 Graham Ave, Winnipeg, MB Canada R3C 4K2

MORRIS, JUSTIN ROY, food scientist, consultant, enologist, research director; b. Nashville, Ark., Feb. 20, 1937; s. Roy Morris; m. Ruby Lee

Blackwood, Sept. 5, 1956; children: Linda Lee, Michael Justin. BS, U. Ark., 1957, MS, 1961; PhD, Rutgers U., 1964. Rsch. asst. Rutgers U., New Brunswick, N.J., 1957-61, instr., 1961-64; extension horticulturist U. Ark., Fayetteville, 1964-67, from asst. to assoc. prof., 1967-75, prof., 1975-85; univ. prof., 1985—; dir. New Inst. Food Sci. and Engring. Ctr. for Food Processing and Engring., 1995—; cons. viticulture sci. program Fla. A&M U., Tallahassee, 1979-81; cons. viticulture and enology program Grayson City Coll., Denison, Tex., 1987—; cons. J. M. Smucker Co., Orrville, Ohio, 1982-91. Co-author: Small Fruit Crop Management, 1990, Quality and Preservation of Fruits, 1991, Modern Fruit Science Text Book, 1995; assoc. editor: Am. Jour. Enology and Viticulture, 1985; contbr. more than 300 articles to sci. jours. Recipient rsch. award Nat. Food Processors Assn., 1982, Faculty Disting. Svc. award for rsch. and pub. svcs. U. Ark., 1993, Disting. Achievement award ASEV/ES, 1995. Fellow Am. Soc. for Hort. Sci. (assoc. editor 1985, Gourley award 1979, Outstanding Rsch. award 1983); mem. Ozark Food Processors Assn. (exec. v.p. 1988—), Coun. for Agrl. Sci. and Tech. (bd. dirs. 1987-93, chmn. nat. concerns 1987-91, pres.-elect 1993, pres. 1994, 95), Inst. Food Technologists (co-organizer fruit and vegetable divsn. 1987—), Gamma Sigma Delta. Achievements include development of mechanical cane fruit harvester, of mechanical strawberry harvester, of modified grape harvester for wine grapes, of mechanical shoot positioner for grapes; development of systems for the production, harvesting, handling, utilization, and marketing of grape juice and wine. Office: U Ark Dept Food Sci 272 Young Ave Fayetteville AR 72704-5585

MORRIS, KENNETH BAKER, mergers, acquisition and real estate executive; b. Bklyn., Feb. 12, 1922; s. Clarence E. and Mabel (Baker) M.; m. Dorothy E. Kohler, Sept. 3, 1960; children: Laura Susan, Sandra Lee. Student bus. adminstrn., Manhattan Coll., 1940-43, B.C.E., 1949; postgrad., Inst. Design, 1959-62, U. Nebr., 1970. Registered profl. engr., N.Y., N.J., Conn., Pa., Mass., Ga., Can. licensed profl. planner, also real estate broker. Asst. to pres., chief engr. Kretzer Constrn. Corp., N.Y.C., 1956-58; cons. engr. Kenneth B. Morris (P.E.), N.Y.C., Augusta, Ga., 1958-61; dir. plant and properties N.Y. U., 1961-66, bus. mgr., 1966-68; v.p. Cooper Union U., N.Y.C., 1968-74; v.p. charge gen. svcs. East River Savs. Bank, N.Y.C., 1974-79; sr. ptnr. cons. Morris Real Estate Co., N.Y.C., 1979—; adj. prof. Pace U., NYU, Fordham U.; Pres., bd. dirs. Grammercy Greenwich Corp., N.Y.C.; bd. dirs. Washington Sq. S.E.; adv. com. Poly. Inst. N.Y.; devel. and fin. adv. com. Cabrini Med. Center. Contbr. articles to mags. and newspapers. Mem. adv. bd., chmn. edn. com. Salvation Army. Served with USAAF, 1943-45. Mem. N.Y. Savs. Bank Assn. (chmn. security com.), Nat. Assn. Real Estate Execs., N.Y. State Real Estate Bd. (city planning com., edn. com., internat. real estate com., taxes and assessments com.), N.Y. State Soc. Real Estate Appraisers, A.I.M., N.Y.C. East Side C. of C. (past pres. and chmn. bd.), Am. Soc. Appraisers (sr. mem.), N.Y. State C. of C. (edn. com.), Lion (1st v.p. club), Am. Arbitration Assn. (nat. panel arbitrators, arbitrator for Am. Stock Exch., City Real Estate Bd.), Nat. Inst. Social Scis., Highlands Country Club.

MORRIS, KENNETH DONALD, lawyer; b. Montclair, N.J., Apr. 5, 1946; s. Thomas Almerin and Katherine Louise (Jacobs) M.; m. Susan Sauer, May 1, 1976; children: Ian, Jennifer. BA, Ohio Wesleyan U., 1968; MBA, George Washington U., 1971, JD, 1972. Bar: Pa. 1973, N.J. 1975, D.C. 1989. Atty. Westinghouse Electric, Pitts., 1972-74, Tenneco Chems., Inc., N.J., 1974-76; asst. corp. counsel Ronson Corp., Bound Brook, N.J., 1976-78; assoc. Walder, Sondak, Berkley & Brogan, Newark, 1978-81; sec., gen. counsel, mem. mgmt. com. NOR-AM Chem. Co. subs. Schering AG, Wilmington, Del., 1981-94, environ. com., 1987—, mem. fiduciary com., 1988—; sec., gen. counsel AgrEvo USA Co., Wilmington, 1994—. Incorporator, pres. Charter Oaks Assn.; mem. Gov.'s Internat. Trade Coun., Del. Wolcott Found. scholar, 1969. Mem. ABA (antitrust sect., tort and ins. sect., corp. counsel com., banking and bus. law sect., multinational corps. subcom.), Am. Arbitration Assn. (panel arbitrators), Del. Bar Assn., Am. Corp. Counsel Assn. (dir. Delvacca chpt.), Def. Rsch. Inst. (corp. counsel com.), George Washington U. Sch. Govt. and Bus. Adminstrn. Alumni Assn. (Phila. chpt.), George Washington U. Nat. Law Ctr. Alumni Assn., European-Am. Gen. Counsel Assn., Fed. Bar Assn. (corp. counsel com.), Nat. Agrl. Chem. Assn. (vice chmn. law com.). Republican. Presbyterian. Avocations: classical music, running, sailing, tennis. Office: AgrEvo USA Co 2711 Centerville Rd Wilmington DE 19808-1643

MORRIS, LEIGH EDWARD, hospital executive officer; b. Hartford City, Ind., Dec. 26, 1934; s. Fredus Orlando and Martha (Malott) M.; m. Marcia Renee Meredith, Oct. 7, 1967; children: Meredith Anne, Curtis Paul. BS in Commerce, Internat. Coll., 1954; BSBA, Ball State U., 1958; M in Health Adminstrn., U. Minn., 1972. Mem. labor relations staff Borg-Warner Corp., Muncie, Ind., 1961-64; various positions then personnel mgr. Internat. Harvester Co., Ft. Wayne, Ind., 1964-70; pres. Huntington (Ind.) Meml. Hosp., 1972-78, La Porte (Ind.) Hosp., 1978—; bd. dirs. First of Am. Bank of Ind., Am. Hosp. Svcs., Inc.; chmn., bd. dirs. Am. Hosp. Pub. Co.; chmn. La Porte Devel. Corp., 1980-81. Chmn. La Porte chpt. ARC, 1984-86. With U.S. Army, 1958-60. Recipient Disting. Alumni award Ball State U., Muncie, Ind., 1968, James A. Hamilton award U. Minn., Mpls., 1972. Fellow Am. Coll. Healthcare Adminstrn., Health Care Fin. Mgmt. Assn.; mem. APHA, Am. Hosp. Assn. (trustee, regional chmn. 1985-89), Soc. for Healthcare Planning and Mktg. (bd. dirs.), Ind. Hosp. Assn. (chmn. 1980-81), La Porte C. of C. (chmn. 1981-82), Constantian Soc., Masons. Republican. Presbyterian. Avocations: classic cars, civic affairs. Home: 1519 Indiana Ave La Porte IN 46350-5105 Office: La Porte Hosp Inc PO Box 250 La Porte IN 46352-0250

MORRIS, LINDA, television writer, producer. Writer Dorothy, 1979, Welcome Back Kotter, 1979, Private Benjamin, 1981-82, Just Our Luck, 1983-84, Alice, 1979-85, Our Time, 1985, Roomies, 1987, I Married Dora, 1988, Hooperman, 1989, Doogie Howser, M.D., 1989-91; co-exec. prodr. Frasier, 1992 (Emmy award for Outstanding Comedy Series 1995). Office: Broder Kurland Webb Uffner 9242 Beverly Blvd Ste 200 Beverly Hills CA 90210*

MORRIS, LOIS LAWSON, education educator; b. Antoine, Ark., Nov. 27, 1914; d. Oscar Moran and Dona Alice (Ward) Lawson; m. William D. Morris, July 2, 1932 (dec.); 1 child, Lavonne Morris Howell. B.A., Henderson U., 1948; M.S., U. Ark., 1951, M.A., 1966; postgrad. U. Colo., 1954, Am. U., 1958, U. N.C., 1968. History tchr. Delight High Sch., Ark., 1942-47; counselor Huntsville Vocat. Sch., 1947-48; guidance dir. Russellville Pub. Sch. System, Ark., 1948-55; asst. prof. edn. U. Ark., Fayetteville, 1955-82, prof. emeritus, 1982—; ednl. cons. Ark. Pub. Schs., 1965-78. Mem. Commn. on Needs for Women, 1976-78, Hist. Preservation Alliance Ark.; pres. Washington County Hist. Soc., 1983-85; pres. Pope County Hist. Assn.; mem. Ark. Symphony Guild; charter mem. Nat. Mus. in Arts; bd. dirs. Potts Inn Mus. Found. Named Ark. Coll. Tchr. of Year, 1972; recipient Plaque for outstanding svcs. to Washington County Hist. Soc., 1984. Contbr. articles to jours. Mem. LWV, AAUW, Ark. Coun. Social Studies (sec.-treas.), Washington County Hist. Soc. (exec. bd. 1977-80), NEA, Nat. Coun. Social Studies, Ark. Edn. Assn., Ark. Hist. Assn., Pope County Hist. Assn. (pres. 1991-92), The So. Hist. Assn., U. Ark. Alumni Assn., Sierra Club, Nature Conservancy, So. Hist. Assn., Ark. River Valley Arts Assn., Phi Delta Kappa, Kappa Delta Pi, Phi Alpha Theta. Democrat. Episcopalian. Address: 1601 W 3rd St Russellville AR 72801-4725 *I appreciate good teachers - the historian who taught research skills and forced me to write crisp, clear sentences; the botanist who unlocked plant life and pointed to tiny flowers growing in the grass; and the young artist who urged simplification through the use of light and big brushes. These teachings continue through retirement years.*

MORRIS, MAC GLENN, advertising bureau executive; b. Bessemer City, N.C., Jan. 24, 1922; s. Manly T. and Erin C. (Cline) M.; m. Janelle Connevey, July 27, 1946; children—Robert S., Janelle C., Patricia A., John Logan. A.B., Davidson Coll., 1942. Space salesman Progressive Farmer mag., N.Y.C., 1946-52; exec. v.p., advt. dir. This Week mag., 1952-68; pres. Newspaper One, N.Y.C., 1968-71; sr. v.p. nat. sales Newspaper Advt. Bur., N.Y.C., 1972-87; proprietor MGM Assocs., Princeton, N.J., 1987—; bd. dirs. Princeton Bank & Trust Co. divsn. Chem. Bank N.J., N.A., now owned by P.N.C. Bank, N.Y.C. Served to 1st lt., pilot USMCR, World War II. Decorated D.F.C. (2), Air medal (7). Mem. Newcomen Soc. in N. Am., Pi Kappa Phi. Presbyn. (deacon). Club: Springdale Golf (Princeton, N.J.) (bd. govs.). Home and Office: 417 Herrontown Rd Princeton NJ 08540-2932 *I am always an optimist at my work, with friends, and with my family.*

MORRIS, MALCOLM STEWART, title company executive, lawyer; b. Houston, May 8, 1946; s. William Carloss and Doris Eletta (Poole) M.; m. Rebecca Ann Simmons, June 14, 1969; children: Matthew William, Andrew James. BBA, So. Meth. U., 1968; JD, U. Tex., 1970, MBA, 1972. Bar: Tex. 1970. Legis. aid State of Tex., Sen. Charles Wilson, Austin, 1969-70; examiner Stewart Title Austin Inc., 1970-71; trainee Bank of the S.W., Houston, 1973-74; bus. mgr. Richard Hogue Evangelism, Inc., Houston, 1974-75; v.p. ops. Stewart Title Guaranty Co., Houston, 1975-87, sr. exec. v.p., asst. chmn., 1987-91, pres., CEO, 1991—; ptnr. Morris, Lendais, Hollrah, et al., Houston; mem. bd. Stewart Title Ins. Co., N.Y.C. Deacon 1st Bapt. Ch., Houston, 1982—. Fellow Am. Bar Found., Houston Bar Assn.; mem. Phi Delta Phi. Baptist. Office: Stewart Title Guaranty Co 1980 Post Oak Blvd Ste 800 Houston TX 77056

MORRIS, MARJORIE HALE, retail executive, artist, writer, photgrapher, appraiser; b. Chattanooga, Aug. 4, 1940; d. Laurie Everett and Marjorie (Hunt) H.; 2 children. Student El Camino Jr. Coll., 1958-60. Stewardess Am. Airlines, 1960-62, mem. staff nat. advt. and publicity, 1961-62; mgr. Viking Ski Shop, Pacific Palisades, Calif., 1963-64; Pepsi Cola Corp. rep. to Republican Nat. Conv., 1964; co-owner, mgr. Ready Room Restaurant, L.A., 1967; architects adv., restaurant devel. and design, Honolulu, Dallas, Atlanta, L.A., 1967-73; mgr., buyer Great Things, Honolulu, 1972-74; mgr. Braille Inst. Thrift Shop, L.A., 1975-78, dir. 1978—, devel. officer, 1980-86; account exec. Alexanders Moving & Storage, Atlas Van Lines, 1981-86, interstate truckdriver, 1986-87; U.S. promotional cons. Kids Only Market, Granville Island, Vancouver, B.C., Can., 1985; owner Marjorie Morris, appraisers; freelance writer and photographer, 1974—; designer floats Pacific Palisades Parade, 1965, TransPace Race Com., Honolulu, 1972. Team mother Pacific Palisades Little League, 1974-76. Mem. Beverly Hills C. of C. (Outstanding Svc. to Cmty. awards 1976, 77). Originator, dir. Christmas Tree Project, Beverly Hills; cover editor Calif. Yacht Club Mag., 1976; founder, editor Waterlines, newsletter of Flotilla 12-7, USCG Aux., 1979. Mem. Am. Soc. Appraisers (panel speaker nat. conv. 1983). Address: PO Box 2651 Mckinleyville CA 95519

MORRIS, MARK WILLIAM, choreographer; b. Seattle, Wash., Aug. 29, 1956; s. William and Maxine (Crittenden) M. Studied with, Verla Flowers and Perry Brunson. Artistic dir. Mark Morris Dance Group, N.Y.C., 1980—, Théâtre Royal de la Monnaie, Brussels, 1988—; choreographer White Oaks Dance Project, 1990; performed with Lar Lubovitch Dance Co., Hannah Kahn Dance Co., Laura Dean Dancers and Musicians, Eliot Feld Ballet, Koleda Balkan Dance Ensemble. Choreographer for Mark Morris Dance Group: Mythologies, 1986, L'Allegro, il Penseroso ed il Moderato, 1988, Dido and Aeneas, 1989, The Nutcracker, 1991, Lucky Charms, 1994, Rondo, 1994, The Office, 1994, others; choreographer: Mort Subite, Boston Ballet, 1986, Esteemed Guests, Joffrey Ballet, 1986, Drink to Me Only With Thine Eyes, Am. Ballet Theatre, 1988, Ein Herz, Paris Opera Ballet, 1990, Nixon in China, Houston Grand Opera, 1987, Orfée et Euridice, Seattle Opera, 1988, The Death of Klinghoffer, Théâtre de la Monnaie, 1991; (television) Great Performances/Dance in America: The Hard Nut, 1992; dir: Die Fledermaus, Seattle Opera, 1988. Recipient N.Y. Dance and Performance award, 1984, 90; Guggenheim fellow, 1986. Office: Mark Morris Dance Group 225 Lafayette St Rm 504 New York NY 10012-4015*

MORRIS, MAX F., lawyer; b. Yuba City, Calif., Dec. 24, 1943. BAE, U. Fla., 1965, JD, 1968. Bar: Fla. 1968. Law clk. to judge U.S. Ct. Appeals (5th cir.), 1968-70; ptnr. Baker & Hostetler, Orlando, Fla. Mem. ABA, Am. Resort Devel. Assn. (bd. dirs.), Orange County Bar Assn., Fla. Bar (mem. real property, corp. and bus. law sect.). Office: Baker & Hostetler SunBank Ctr 200 S Orange Ave Ste 2300 Orlando FL 32801-3440*

MORRIS, MICHAEL J., book publishing executive. With Mike Morris Ltd., London, England, 1963-73; chmn. ICBP, London, England, 1973-83, Joshua Morris Pub. Inc., Wilton, Conn. Office: Joshua Morris Pub Inc 355 Riverside Ave Westport CT 06880-4810

MORRIS, MURL DALE, retired secondary education educator, business executive; b. Pocahontas, Ark., Aug. 8, 1952; s. Murl Daniel and Willa Dean (Hawkins) M.; m. Deborah Therese Gorecki, June 26, 1971; children: Heather E., Holly A. BS/BSE in Pub. Broadcasting/Journalism, U. ctrl. Ark., 1975; MS, Kans. State U., 1977; MS in Tchg., U. Ill., 1980; EdS, Ball State U., 1985; PhD, U. Miss., 1991. Cert. phys. edn. tchr., mid-mgmt. adminstr., Tex.; cert. gen. sci. and phys. edn. tchr., Ark. With U.S. Postal Svc., Hot Springs, Ark., 1985-86; football/track coach and sci. tchr. Lakeside Pub. Schs., Hot Springs, 1986-87; asst. h.s. prin. Warren (Ark.) Pub. Schs., 1987-89; asst. jr./sr. high prin. Corning (Ark.) Pub. Schs., 1989-90; dissertation rschr. U. Miss., Oxford, 1990-91; asst. jr. high prin. Ashdown (Ark.) Pub. Schs., 1991-92; adj. reading prof. Brookhaven Coll., Farmers Branch, Tex., 1992-93; part-time instr. Ft. Worth (Tex.) Ind. Sch. Dist., 1993-94; headmaster St. Andrews Episcopal Sch., Grand Prairie, Tex., 1994-95; owner Morris Transport, Inc., Keller, Tex., 1995—; adj. prof. Am. U. of Hawaii. Capt. U.S. Army, 1976-84. Decorated Army Commendatin medal, Meritorious Svc. medal; U. Ill. grad. assistantship, 1978-79; U. Miss. doctoral fellow, 1988-91. Mem. Am. Legion, Hon. Order Ky. Cols., Kappa Delta Pi, Phi Delta Kappa, Pi Kappa Alpha. Republican. LDS. Avocations: camping, hiking, outdoor family-related activities. Home: PO Box 602 713 Clover Ct Keller TX 76244-0602

MORRIS, NORVAL, criminologist, educator; b. Auckland, New Zealand, Oct. 1, 1923; s. Louis and Vera (Burke) M.; m. Elaine Richardson, Mar. 18, 1947; children: Gareth, Malcolm, Christoper. LLB, U. Melbourne, Australia, 1946, LLM, 1947; PhD in Criminology (Hutchinson Silver medal 1950), London Sch. Econs., 1949. Bar: called to Australian bar 1953. Asst. lectr. London Sch. Econs., 1949-50; sr. lectr. law U. Melbourne, 1950-58, prof. criminology, 1955-58; Ezra Ripley Thayer teaching fellow Harvard Law Sch., 1955-56, vis. prof., 1961-62; Boynthon prof., dean faculty law U. Adelaide, Australia, 1958-62; dir. UN Inst. Prevention Crime and Treatment of Offenders, Tokyo, Japan, 1962-64; Julius Kreeger prof. law and criminology U. Chgo., 1964—, dean Law Sch.,, 1975-79; chmn. Commn. Inquiry Capital Punishment in Ceylon, 1958-59; mem. Social Sci. Rsch. Coun. Australia, 1958-59; Australian del. confs. div. human rights and sect. social def. UN, 1955-66; mem. standing adv. com. experts prevention crime and treatment offenders. Author: The Habitual Criminal, 1951, Report of the Commission of Inquiry on Capital Punishment, 1959, (with W. Morison and R. Sharwood) Cases in Torts, 1962, (with Colon Howard) Studies in Criminal Law, 1964, (with G. Hawkins) The Honest Politicians Guide to Crime Control, 1970, The Future of Imprisonment, 1974, Letter to the President on Crime Control, 1977, Madness and the Criminal Law, 1983, Between Prison and Probation, 1990, The Brothel Boy and Other Parables of the Law, 1992, In Oxford History of the Prison, 1995. Served with Australian Army, World War II, PTO. Decorated Japanese Order Sacred Treasure 3d Class. Fellow Am. Acad. Arts and Scis. Home: 1207 E 50th St Chicago IL 60615-2908 Office: U Chgo Law Sch 1111 E 60th St Chicago IL 60637-2702

MORRIS, OWEN GLENN, engineering corporation executive; b. Shawnee, Okla., Feb. 3, 1927; s. Vestus and Myrtle (Lindsey) M.; m. Joyce Gast; children: Deborah Moree, Janine Inez. B.S. in Mech. Engring, U. Okla., 1947, M.Aero. Engring., 1948; postgrad., U. Va., 1952-53, Va. Poly. Inst., 1955-56, Coll. William and Mary, 1957-58. Aero., research scientist NASA, Langley Field, Va., 1948-61; mgr. mission engring. NASA (Apollo), Houston, 1961-64; mgr. reliability and quality assurance NASA (Apollo), 1964-66, chief project engr. lunar module, 1966-69, mgr. lunar module, 1969-72; mgr. NASA (Apollo Spacecraft Program), 1972-73; dep. mgr. NASA (Space Shuttle Orbiter), 1973-80; mgr. systems integration NASA (Space Shuttle), 1974-80; pres. Eagle Engring., 1980-86; pres., chief exec. officer Eagle Aerospace, Houston, 1987-90, chmn., chief exec. officer, 1990-93, chmn. bd., 1992—. Mem. Tex. Water Control Improvement Dist. Bd., 1969-76. Served with USNR, 1943-46. Recipient U.S. Medal of Freedom, 1972, NASA Distinguished Service medal, 1973, NASA Exceptional Service medal, 1969. Asso. fellow Am. Inst. Aeros. and Astronautics; mem. Am. Asrronautical Soc., Am. Aviation Hist. Soc., Acad. Model Aeros., Tau Beta Pi, Tau Omega. Presbyterian (elder 1964—). Club: Rotary. Home: 14914 Timberland Ct Houston TX 77062-2922 Office: Eagle Aerospace 910 Gemini St Houston TX 77058-2704

MORRIS, PATRICIA SMITH, media specialist, author, educator; b. Franklin, N.J., Jan. 31, 1940; d. Joseph P. and Pauline C. (Lasinski) Smith; m. Carl W. Morris; children: Margaret, Sarah, Maureen. BA, Paterson State Coll.; MLS, Rutgers U. Media specialist Hanover Park (N.J.) Regional H.S. Bd. Edn. Author: Stepping into Research!, 1990; 6 Vols. of Young Adult Reading Activities Library, 1993. Exec. co-dir. N.J. Connection. Recipient N.J. Gov's. Tchr. Recognition award, 1989, Pres. award EMA, 1995; named Outstanding Ednl. Media Specialist of N.J., 1990. Mem. ALA, NEA, Am. Assn. Sch. Librs., N.J. Edn. Assn., Morris County Sch. Media Assn. (past pres.), Ednl. Media Assn. N.J. (exec. bd.). Office: Whippany Park HS Whippany Rd Whippany NJ 07981

MORRIS, PHILIP JOHN, aerospace engineering educator; b. Llandudno, Wales, Apr. 21, 1946; came to U.S., 1973; s. William Garnet and Dora (Butterworth) M.; m. Brenda Mary English, Aug. 24, 1968; children: Nicola Carol, Karen Elizabeth, Anthony Richard. BSc with honors, Southampton (Eng.) U., 1967, MSc, 1969, PhD, 1972. Rsch. assoc. U. Toronto, Ont., 1971-73; rsch. engr. Lockheed-Ga. Co., Marietta, 1973-77; asst. prof. Pa. State U., University Park, 1977-80; assoc. prof. Pa. State U., 1980-86, prof., dir. computational fluid dynamic studies, 1986—, Boeing prof. aerospace engring., 1992—; cons., Lockheed Ga. Co., 1977-88. Contbr. to tech. publs. Mem. AIAA (aeroacoustics tech. com. 1981-84, 89-95, chmn. 1993-95). Avocations: soccer, running. Office: Pa State U 233 Hammond Bldg # P University Park PA 16802-1401

MORRIS, RALPH WILLIAM, chronopharmacologist; b. Cleveland Heights, Ohio, July 30, 1928; s. Earl Douglas and Viola Minnie (Mau) M.; m. Carmen R. Mueller; children: Christopher Lynn, Kirk Stephen, Timothy Allen and Todd Andrew (twins), Melissa Mary. BA, Ohio U., Athens, 1950, MS, 1953; PhD, U. Iowa, 1955; postgrad., Seabury-Western Theol. Sem., 1979-81, McHenry County Coll., 1986-88. Research fellow in pharmacology, then teaching fellow U. Iowa, 1952-55; instr. dept. pharmacology Coll. Medicine, 1955-56; asst. prof. dept. pharmacognosy and pharmacology Coll. Pharmacy, 1956-62, assoc. prof., 1962-69; prof. pharmacology Med. Center, U. Ill., 1969—; adj. prof. edn. Coll. Edn. U. Ill. at Chgo., 1976-85; vis. scientist San Jose State U., Calif., 1982-83; mem. adv. com. 1st aid and safety Midwest chpt. ARC, 1972-83; cons. in drug edn. to Dangerous Drug Commn., Ill. Dept. Pub. Aid, Chgo., Ill. Dept. Profl. Regulataions, Ill. Dept. Corrections and suburban sch. dists. Referee and contbr. articles to profl. and sci. jours., lay mags., radio and TV appearances. Trustee Palatine (Ill.) Pub. Libr., 1967-72, pres., 1969-70; trustee N. Suburban Libr. System, 1968-72, pres. 1970-72, mem. long-range planning com., 1975-81; chmn. Ill. Libr. Trustees, 1970-72, intellectual freedom com.; mem. Title XX Ill. Citizens Adv. Coun., 1981-83; trusteee McHenry (Ill.) Pub. Libr. Dist., 1987-89, pres., 1987-89; trustee St. Gregory's Abbey, Three Rivers, Mich., 1989—; bd. dirs. United Campus Ministry U. Ill. at Chgo., 1983-87. Recipient Golden Apple Teaching award U. Ill. Coll. Pharmacy, 1966; cert. of merit Town of Palatine, 1972. Mem. AAAS, Am. Assn. Coll. Pharmacists, Am. Pharm. Assn., Ill. Pharm. Assn., Internat. Soc. Chronobiology, European Soc. Chronbiology, Am. Soc. Pharmacology and Exptl. Therapeutics, Am. Library Trustee Assn., Ill. Library Trustee Assn. (v.p. 1970-72, dir. 1969-72), Sigma Xi, Rho Chi, Gamma Alpha. Episcopalian. Home: 584 Shoreline Dr Barrington IL 60010-3883 Office: U Ill MC 865 833 S Wood St Chicago IL 60612-7229

MORRIS, REBECCA ROBINSON, lawyer; b. McKinney, Tex., July 27, 1945; d. Leland Howell and Grace Laverne (Stinson) Robinson; m. Jesse Eugene Morris, July 18, 1964; children: Jesse III, Susan, John. BBA in Acctg., So. Meth. U., 1974, JD, 1978. Bar: Tex. 1979, U.S. Dist. Ct. (no. dist.) Tex. Acct. Electronic Data Systems Corp., Dallas, 1975; assoc. atty. Dresser Industries, Inc., Dallas, 1978-81, staff atty., 1981-83, corp. atty., 1983-86, asst. sec., 1984-90, sr. atty. corp. adminstrn., 1986-87, corp. counsel, 1987—, sec., 1990—, v.p., 1994—. Trustee Plano (Tex.) Ind. Sch. Dist., 1979-91, 93-94, pres., 1980-85, sec., 1986-91; bd. dirs. Plano Futures Found., Inc., 1992—, pres., 1992-93. Mem. ABA, AICPA, Tex. State Bar, Dallas Bar Assn., Tex. Soc. CPAs, Am. Soc. Corp. Secs. (mem. securities law com. 1988—, proxy system com. 1990-93, exec. steering com. 1993-94, budget com. 1993—, chmn. 1995—, bd. dirs. 1991-94, chmn. mem. com. Dallas chpt. 1986, treas. 1987, v.p. 1988, pres. 1989), Am. Corp. Counsel Assn. (corp. and securities law com. 1991—), SMU Law Rev. Corp. Counsel Symposium (bd. advisors 1996—). Methodist. Home: 1718 14th Pl Plano TX 75074-6404 Office: Dresser Industries Inc 2001 Ross Ave Box 718 Dallas TX 75221-0718

MORRIS, RICHARD WARD, author; b. Milw., June 16, 1939; s. Alvin Harry and Dorothy Lydia (Wissmueller) M. BS, U. Nev., 1962, PhD, 1968; MS, U. N.Mex., 1964. Exec. dir. COSMEP, Inc., San Francisco, 1968-95. Author: Poetry Is a Kind of Writing, 1975, Light, 1979, The End of the World, 1980, The Fate of the Universe, 1982, Evolution and Human Nature, 1983, Dismantling the Universe, 1983, Time's Arrows, 1985, The Nature of Reality, 1987, The Edges of Science, 1990, Assyrians, 1991, (with others) The Word and Beyond, 1982, Cosmic Questions, 1993.

MORRIS, ROBERT, lawyer, writer; b. Jersey City, Sept. 30, 1915; s. John Henry and Sarah (Williams) M.; m. Joan Russell Byles, Dec. 27, 1951; children: Robert, Paul E., Roger, Joan Byles Barry, William E., John Henry II, Geoffrey. AB, St. Peters Coll., Jersey City, 1936; JD, Fordham U., 1939; LLD, St. Francis Coll., Bklyn., 1954, U. Plano, 1976; LHD, Fujen U., Taipei, Taiwan, 1971. Bar: N.Y. 1939, Tex. 1962, U.S. Supreme Ct. 1952. Newspaper reporter, 1934-36; tchr. Greek, Latin and govt. St. Peters Prep. Sch., Jersey City, 1936-39; with firm Hines, Rearick, Dorr & Hammond, N.Y.C., 1939-40; asst. counsel N.Y. State Investigating Com., 1940-41; sec. to Congressman F. R. Coudert, Jr., 1946-50; sec.-treas. Monrovia Port Mgmt. Co., Africa, 1947-49; with firm Hochwald, Morris & Richmond, N.Y.C., 1946-52; spl. counsel U.S. Senate Internal Security Subcom., 1951-53, chief counsel, 1953, 56-58; judge Mcpl. Ct., N.Y.C., 1954-56; counsel to U.S. senators Hickenlooper and Lodge on U.S. Senate Fgn. Relations Com., 1950; adviser U.S. Senate Rules Com., 1955; pres. U. Dallas, 1960-62; pres. U. Plano, Tex., 1964-71, 73-77, chancellor, 1971-72; observer Zimbabwean parliamentary elections, 1979. Author: No Wonder We Are Losing, 1958, Disarmament, Weapon of Conquest, 1963, What Is Developmental Education?, 1967, Self-Destruct, 1979, Our Globe Under Siege, 1982, vol. II, 1985, vol. III, 1988, also nat. column; contbr. articles to profls. Candidate for Rep. nomination to U.S. Senate from N.J., 1958, 60, 84, from Tex., 1964, 70; chmn. Nat. Com. to Restore Internal Security, 1979—; bd. dirs. Insts. for Achievement Human Potential, 1977-89, bd. govs., 1989—; bd. dirs. Univ. Profs. for Acad. Order, 1988-91, U.S. Coun. World Freedom, 1981-91, Am.'s Future, 1985—, chmn. bd. and pres., 1995—. Lt. comdr. USNR, 1941-46, comdr. ret. Mem. ABA (internat. law sect.), Mil. Order World Wars (comdr. Monmouth chpt. 1984—), Am. Zimbabwean Assn. (chmn. 1978-87), Univ. Club (N.Y.C.), Mantoloking Yacht Club, Shanghai-Tiffin Club, Circumnavigators, Army-Navy Club (Washington), Admirals Club. Home: 1237 Ocean Ave Mantoloking NJ 08738-1613 Office: PO Box 234 Mantoloking NJ 08738-0234

MORRIS, ROBERT C., historian, archivist, educator; b. Alexandria, Va., Aug. 6, 1942; s. Chester O. and Mary Louise (Eisele) M.; m. Darlene K. Kerstetter, Sept. 19, 1964. BA, U. N.Mex., 1964; AM, U. Chgo., 1965, PhD, 1976. Instr. U. Md., College Park, 1968-69; instr. Rutgers U., Newark, 1970-71, vis. prof. history, 1983, 85-87; manuscripts curator N.J. Hist. Soc., Newark, 1972-74, library dir., 1974-79; head spl. collections, assoc. prof. history and edn. Tchrs. Coll., Columbia U., N.Y.C., 1979-82; spl. collections adminstr. Schomburg Ctr. Research in Black Culture, N.Y.C., 1982-87, mem. selection com. Scholars-in-Residence program, 1987—; dir. Nat. Archives N.E. Region, 1987—; mem. N.J. Hist. Records Adv. Bd., Trenton, 1976-79, 88—; mem. com. on scholarly programs, higher edn. and libraries, N.J. Hist. Commn., Trenton, 1976-87; mem. N.J. planning com. White House Conf. on Libraries, 1979; cons. exec. com. Hist. Soc. U.S. Dist. Ct. for Dist. N.J., N.Y. Fed. Exec. Bd., Fed. Exec. Bd. Met. No. N.J.; cons. CARE, Inc., N.Y.C., 1985-88. Author: Reading, 'Riting, and Reconstruction: The Education of Freedmen in the South 1861-1870, 1981 (nominated for Pulitzer prize in history), Freedmen's Schools and Textbooks: Black Education in the South, 1861-1870, 1980, "Educational Recontruction" in the Facts of

Reconstruction: Essays in Honor of John Hope Franklin, 1991; contbr. numerous articles to profl. publs. Mem. Mid-Atlantic Regional Archives Conf. (chmn. 1985-87), Orgn. Am. Historians, Am. Hist. Assn., Assn. for Study of Afro Life and History, Soc. Am. Archivists, Archivists Round Table Met. N.Y., Phi Beta Kappa. Democrat. Presbyterian. Avocations: archaeology, art, theater, tennis, biking. Office: Nat Archives NE Region 201 Varick St New York NY 10014-4811

MORRIS, ROBERT CHARLES, lawyer; b. Utica, N.Y., Sept. 21, 1940; s. Robert Edward and Dorothy Leona (Raefle) M.; m. Susan McGauley, Aug. 15, 1964; children: Kimberly, Gregory, Margaret. BA, Colgate U., 1963; JD, Albany Law Sch., 1966. Bar: N.Y. 1967, U.S. Dist. Ct. 1967. Asst. county atty., 1971-77; city atty. Glens Falls, N.Y., 1978-85; atty. FitzGerald Morris Baker Firth, Glens Falls, 1985—. Past pres. Warren County Am. Cancer Soc; past pres. trustees First Presbyn. Ch., Glens Falls; past pres. Glens Falls Hist. Mus.; regional devel. bd. Glens Falls Nat. Bank; trustee Lakeside Chapel Cleverdale; past com. man Warren County Rep. Com.; past pres. Warren County Young Reps. Office: FitzGerald Morris et al One Broad St Plz Glens Falls NY 12801

MORRIS, ROBERT CHRISTIAN, education educator; b. Anderson, Ind., Mar. 1, 1948; s. Robert Childs and Velma Jane (Vogley) M.; m. Linda Marie Butkus, Jan. 14, 1989. AB, Duke U., 1970; MS, Ind. State U., 1971, PhD, 1977. Cert. tchr.; lic. prin., supt. Profl. football player Houston Oilers, 1970; tchr. social studies Roanoke (Va.) Schs., 1970-71, 74-76; profl. football player New Orleans Saints, 1971-73; asst. prof. edn. Auburn (Ala.) U., 1976-81; assoc. prof. edn. U. S.C., Columbia, 1981-84, No. Ill. U., DeKalb, 1984-87; prof., head dept. edn., leadership, tech. and rsch. Ga. So. U., Statesboro, 1987-91; dean. sch. edn. U. Indpls., 1991-93; prof. edn. West Ga. Coll., Carrollton, 1993—; cons. Mt. Morris (Ill.) Pub. Schs., Dixon Pub. Sch., 1986; cons., evaluator bi-lingual programs Dixon (Ill.) Pub. Schs. Author: A Resource Guide for Working with Youth-At-Risk, 1992, (pamphlet) A Field Practicum for Tchrs. of Gifted Children, 1982—; editor: Vantil on Education, 1978, Youth at Risk: A Resource Guide, 1991, Solving the Problems of Youth-At-Risk, 1992, Using What We Know About At-Risk Youth: Lessons From the Field, 1994; contbr. over 100 articles to profl. jours. Sponsor Sigma Nu Auburn U., 1977-81, Phi Kappa Sigma No. Ill. U., 1984-88, Alpha Tau Omega West Ga. Coll., 1993—; regional co-dir. Auburn Spl. Olympics, Auburn, 1977-81; games dir. S.C. Spl. Olympics, Columbia, 1982-84. Mem. ASCD, VFW, Am. Assn. Colls. for Tchrs. Edn., Am. Ednl. Rsch. Assn., John Dewey Soc. (exec. sec.-treas. 1982—), Profs. of Curriculum, Soc. Profs. of Edn., Phi Delta Kappa (former v.p. local chpt.), Phi Kappa Sigma (sponsor/advisor local chpt.), Kappa Delta Pi (sec.-treas.), Civitan. Avocations: weightlifting, travel, painting. Home: 628-E Cedar Villas Cedar St Carrollton GA 30117 Office: West Ga Coll Dept Ednl Leadership Carrollton GA 30118

MORRIS, ROBERT G(EMMILL), retired foreign service officer; b. Des Moines, July 20, 1929; s. Robert William and Iva May (Gemmill) M.; m. Beverly Schupfer, July 3, 1955; children: Robert William II, John Schupfer, Richard Edward. BS, Iowa State U., 1951; postgrad., Charles Francis U., Graz, 1951-52; MS, Calif. Inst. Tech., 1954; PhD, Iowa State U., 1957. Asst. prof. S.D. Sch. Mines and Tech., Rapid City, 1958-59, assoc. prof., 1959-62, prof., head dept. physics, 1962-68; phys. sci. officer Office of Naval Research, Washington, 1968-73, dir. electronics program, 1973-74; U.S. fgn. service officer U.S. Dept. State, Washington, 1974-78; counselor for sci. and technol. affairs U.S. Mission to OECD, Paris, 1978-82, U.S. Embassy, Bonn, Fed. Republic Germany, 1982-85; dep. asst. sec. of state for sci. and tech. affairs Washington, 1985-87; fgn. svc. officer U.S. Embassy, Buenos Aires, 1987-90, Madrid, 1990-92. Contbr. articles to profl. jours. Fulbright scholar, Austria, 1951; Swiss govt. fellow, Zurich, 1957. Fellow APS; mem. IEEE, Am. Fgn. Service Assn.

MORRIS, ROBERT JULIAN, JR., art gallery owner; b. Decatur, Ill., Jan. 12, 1932; s. Robert J. and M. Letitia (Ross) M.; m. J. Jean Nelson Morris, June 6, 1952; children: R. Thomas, Debora L., Charles A., Sandra J. BS in Chemistry, U. Ill., 1954; MS in Chemistry, Marshall U., 1961. Analytical chemist Union Carbide Chemicals, South Charleston, W.Va., 1954-61; sr. research chemist U.S. Gypsum Co., Des Plaines, Ill., 1961-63; research mgr. MacAndrews and Forbes Co., Camden, N.J., 1963-66; tech. dir. Nat. Can Corp., Chgo., 1966-73; v.p. corp. engring. Coachmen Industries Inc., Middlebury, Ind., 1973-74; pres. Coachmen Homes Corp., 1974-76; chmn. bd., chief exec. officer Medallion Plastics Inc., Elkhart, Ind., 1976-93; owner Robert Morris Gallery, Goshen, Ind., 1993—. Contbr. articles to profl. jours. Bd. dirs. Career Ctr., Elkhart, 1983-89, Ind. Voc. Tech. Coll., Plastics R&D Ctr. Ball State U., 1987-94. Mem. Rotary. Republican. Methodist. Avocations: fine art black and white photographic silver prints, camping. Home: 113 E Madison St Goshen IN 46526 Office: Robert Morris Gallery 113 E Madison Goshen IN 46526

MORRIS, ROBERT LEE, gallery administrator, jewelry designer; b. Nurnberg, Federal Republic Germany, July 7, 1947; came to U.S., 1947; s. Jack Bret and Sara Ellen (Holloway) M. BA, Beloit Coll., 1969. Owner, pres. Robert Lee Morris, N.Y.C., 1977—, Artwear, 1977-94. Trustee Beloit (Wis.) Coll., 1989—. Recipient Coty award N.Y.C., 1981, Coun. Fashion Designers Am. award, 1985, M Spl. award Internat. Gold, N.Y.C., 1986, Disting. Svc. award Beloit Coll. Alumni Assn., 1988, Woodmark award, 1992, FAAB award, 1992, Coun. Fashion Designers Am. award, 1994. Office: Robert Lee Morris Co 161 6th Ave Fl 14 New York NY 10013-1205*

MORRIS, ROBERT LOUIS, management consultant; b. Phila., Aug. 24, 1932; s. Joseph Aloysius and Philomena Mary Ellen (Clauser) M.; BS, Drexel U., 1955; MS, U. Pa., 1957; postgrad. U. Cin., 1965-66, U. Chgo., 1969-71; m. Elizabeth Marie Smyth, Sept. 10, 1955; children—Robert L., Thomas J., Lawrence F., Elizabeth M., Mary Ellen, Richard B. Group leader Procter & Gamble Co., Miami Valley Labs., 1958-68; dir. computing services research and devel. div. Kraft, Inc., Glenview, Ill., 1968-71; dir. research and process devel. Continental Baking Co., Rye, N.Y. and St. Louis, 1971-77, v.p. tech. affairs, 1978-92; tech. dir. food and chem. products ITT Inc., N.Y.C., 1977-78; pres., Managing Tech., Inc., Williamsburg, Va., 1992—. Bd. dirs. Fundacion Chile, Santiago, 1978-79, 83-85; mem. Greenwich Rep. Town Meeting, 1977. Served with AUS, 1957. NSF fellow, 1955-56; Wilson S. Yerger fellow, 1956-57. Fellow Am. Inst. Chem. Engrs.; mem. Assn. Rsch. Dirs., Indsl. Rsch. Inst. (bd. dirs. 1988-91), Am. Chem. Soc., Am. Assn. Cereal Chemists, Inst. Food Techs. Roman Catholic. Clubs: Ford's Colony Golf. Patentee in field. Office: Managing Tech Inc PO Box 679 Lightfoot VA 23090-0679

MORRIS, ROBERT RENLY, minister, clinical pastoral education supervisor; b. Jacksonville, Fla., Feb. 15, 1938; s. Joseph Renly and Sybil (Stephens) M.; m. Lenda Smith, Dec. 7, 1963; children: Christopher Renly, Jennifer Kelly. BA, U. Fla., 1959; MDiv, Columbia Theol. Sem., Atlanta, 1962, ThM, 1967, D Ministry, 1990. Ordained to ministry Presbyn. Ch. (U.S.A.), 1962. Min. to students Ga. State Coll., Atlanta, 1959-60; asst. min. Trinity Presbyn. Ch., Atlanta, 1960-62; min. Clanton (Ala.) Presbyn. Ch., 1963-65, Kelly Presbyn. Ch., McDonough, Ga., 1965-67; pastoral counselor Ga. Assn. for Pastoral Care, Atlanta, 1966-68; coord. pastoral svcs. Winter Haven (Fla.) Hosp. and Community Health Ctr., 1969-79; min. Presbytery of Greater Atlanta, mem. div. pastoral care, 1984-86; dir. clin. pastoral edn. Emory Ct. for Pastoral Svcs., Atlanta, 1979—; adj. faculty Candler Sch. Theology, 1979-88. Contbr. book chpts., articles to profl. jours. Mem. AIDS Task Force, Atlanta, 1988-95, Task Force on Chem. Dependency, 1988. Mem. Am. Assn. Pastoral Counselors, Coll. Chaplains, Am. Assn. Marriage and Family Therapists (clin.), Assn. for Clin. Pastoral Edn. (cert. supr., gen. assembly nominating com. 1984, chmn. 1985, coord. ann. conf. 1986, long range planning com. of C com., standards com. S.E. region 1990-93), Beta Theta Pi. Democrat. Avocations: antique key collecting, canoeing, fishing, sailing. Home: 542 Cross Creek Pt Stone Mountain GA 30087-5328 Office: Emory U Hosp Dept Pastoral Svcs 1364 Clifton Rd NE Atlanta GA 30322-1059

MORRIS, RUSSELL D., federal agency administrator; b. Columbus, Ohio, May 14, 1941; s. Russell F. and Helen Katherine (Rothwell) M.; m. Rebecca Ruth Rainer, Sept. 18, 1965; 1 child. BSc, Ohio State U., 1963, MBA, 1964, PhD, 1973. Officer Huntington Nat. Bank, Columbus, Ohio, 1964-68; grad. asst. Ohio State U., 1968-70; analyst Fed. Res. Bd., 1970-73, 1973-80; gen. mgr. U.S. Postal Svc., 1973-80, asst. commr., 1980-88, dep. commr., 1988-91; commr. fin. mgmt. svc. Dept. the Treasury, Washington, 1991—. Contbr. articles to profl. jours. Recipient Outstanding Achievement award Assn. Govt. Accts., 1979-80, Govt. Mgmt. Excellence award Pres. Coun. on Mgmt. Improvement, 1988. Mem. Phi Alpha Kappa, Phi Kappa Tau. Unitarian. Avocations: golf, tennis, blue grass banjo, Old testament research. Office: Dept of the Treasury Financial Mngmnt Service 401 14th St NW Washington DC 20227-0001

MORRIS, RUSTY LEE, architectural consulting firm executive; b. Glenwood Springs, Colo., Nov. 28, 1940; d. Raymond M. and Raylene Pearl Marie (Hendirck) Morris; m. Robert W. Sosa, Nov. 20, 1995; children: Thomas John, Michael Joseph (dec.), Michelle Renee Bentley. Student, York Christian Coll., 1974-75, U. Nebr., 1975-76, Mesa State Coll., 1992-95; grad., Colo. Christian U., 1996, postgrad., 1996—. Specialist comm. security Martin-Marietta Corp., Larson AFB, 1962-63; communications security specialist classified def. project Boeing Aerospace Div., Larson AFB, Wash., 1963-64; with F.W. Sickles div. Gen. Instrument Corp., Chicopee, Mass., 1965-68; adminstr. judicial affairs J. Arthur Hickerson, Judge, Springfield, Mass., 1969-71; researcher Mont. United Indian Assn., Helena, 1970-72; adminstrv. asst. Vanderbilt U. Hosp., Nashville, 1980-82; paid bus. supr. Sears Svc. Ctr., Grand Junction, Colo., 1987-89; founder, chief exec. officer Vast Spl. Svcs., Grand Junction, 1988—; courier U.S. Census Bur., Grand Junction, 1990; spl. program coord. Colo. Dept. Parks and Recreation, Ridgway, 1990-91; acad. athletic program founder, coord. Mesa State Coll., 1992-93, math. and sci. rep., student govt., 1992—, athletic coun., 1993—, student health ctr. com., 1993—, faculty search com., 1993; founder, CEO Rolling Spokes Assn.; world cons. on archtl. contracts for structural and/or outdoor recreational facilities. Author: Abuse of Women with Disabilities, 1996. Vol. Easter Seals Soc., 1964-67, vol. instr. Adult Literacy Program, 1984-87; vol. T.V. host Muscular Dystrophy Assn. Am., 1975-94; bd. dirs. Independent Living Ctr., 1985-87, Handicap Awareness Week, 1989; trails com. Colo. State Parks and Outdoor Recreation, 1988—; condr. seminars Ams. With Disabilites Act, 1989—; cons. Bur. Reclamation, 1988—, Bur. Land Mgmt., 1989—; staff trainer Breckenridge Outdoor Recreation Ctr., 1989-90; emergency svcs. officer Colo. Civil Air Patrol, Thunder Mountain Squadron, 1989—; bd. dirs. Handicap Awareness, 1989; dir. com. Colo. State Trails Commn., 1989-90; mem. Dem. Nat. Com., 1991—; dist. com. Grand Junction Sch. Dist., 1992—; mem. Restore the Com., Avalon, 1993—; bd. dirs., presenter No. Colo. chpt. Colo. Orgn. of Victim Assistance; with victim assistance Mesa County Sheriff's Dept., 1993—. Recipient Hometown Hero award, 1993. Mem. AAUW, Internat. Platform Assn., Handicap Scholarship Assn. (bd. dirs. 1994, award 1993), Nat. Orgn. Victim Assistance (presenter 1988—), Nat. Coun. Alcoholism and Drug Abuse (vol. 1987—), Mother's Against Drunk Driver's (bd. dirs. Mesa County chpt., v.p. 1985—), Concerns of Policy Survivors, Club 20 of Western Colo. (mem. com. status), Great Outdoor Colo., Grand Junction C. of C., Grand Junction Symphony, Mus. Western Colo., Mesa State Coll. Geology Club, Toastmasters (Able Toastmaster, winner speech contests 1985-87). Home and Office: Vast Spl Svcs 612 N 15th St Grand Junction CO 81501-4422

MORRIS, SETH IRWIN, architect; b. Madisonville, Tex., Sept. 1, 1914; s. Seth Irwin and Carrie (Holleman) M.; m. Suzanne Kibler, Dec. 29, 1945; children: Mark Peter, Maria, David Kibler, Laura Houston, John Hampson. B.A., Rice Inst., 1935. Practice architecture Houston, 1935-87; ptnr. Wilson & Morris, 1938-87, Wilson, Morris & Crain, 1946-87, Wilson, Morris, Crain & Anderson, 1954-87; ptnr. S.I. Morris Assocs., 1972-87, cons., 1988—; ptnr. Morris/Aubry Architects, 1980-85, Morris Architects, 1986-87; cons. Jackson & Ryan, 1989—. Prin. works include Harris County Domed Stadium (Astrodome), 1965, Houston Pub. Library, 1975,, S.W. Home Office Texaco Inc., 1975, Prudential Ins. Co., 1977, One Houston Center, 1977, Brown and Root, Inc. hdqrs, 1978, Alfred C. Glassell, Jr. Sch. Art, 1979, 1st City Bank Tower, 1981, Wortham Theater Ctr., 1985. Chmn. bd. trustees Houston Mus. Fine Arts, 1961-63, 67-68, pres., 1967-68; chmn. bd. trustees Contemporary Arts Mus., 1988-89; bd. govs. Rice U., Houston.; bd. dirs. ARC Harris County. Served to comdr. USNR, 1942-46. Decorated Legion of Merit; Order Cloud and Banner China; recipient numerous archtl. honor awards Tex. Soc. Architects, numerous archtl. honor awards Houston chpt. AIA; nat. awards AIA, Gold medal Assn. Rice U. Alumni, 1991; named Disting. Alumnus Rice U., 1981. Fellow AIA; mem. Tex. Soc. Architects (Llewellen Pitts award 1992), Assn. Gen. Contractors (master builder awrd 1994), Houston C. of C. (dir. 1964-86). Presbyterian (elder). Home: 2 Waverly Ct Houston TX 77005-1842 Office: 2370 Rice Blvd Ste 210 Houston TX 77005-2644

MORRIS, STEPHEN ALLEN, elementary school educator; b. Garden Grove, Calif., Mar. 2, 1957; s. Eddie Melvin and Lesta Joy (Birdsall) M.; m. MariLynn Edith; stepchildren: Tyler, Trevor. BS in Phys. Edn., Calif. State U., Fullerton, 1987. Cert. tchr., Calif. Elem. tchr. Riverside (Calif.) Unified Sch. Dist., 1990—; lectr. Calif. Elem. Edn. Assn., Torrance, 1994—, The Edn. Ctr., Torrance, 1994—; cons. Inland Area Math. Project, Riverside, 1992—. Author: Everything You Wanted to Know About Division...In a Day!, 1993. Mem. Benjamin Franklin Elem. Sch. Site Coun., Riverside, 1992. Mem. ASCD, Nat. Coun. Tchrs. Math., Calif. Math. Coun. Baptist. Avocations: running, cycling, silkscreening. Home: 7245 Ayers Rock Rd Riverside CA 92508-6043 Office: Ben Franklin Elem Sch 19661 Orange Terrace Pky Riverside CA 92508-3256

MORRIS, STEPHEN BURRITT, marketing information executive; b. Morristown, N.J., Aug. 13, 1943; s. Grinnell and Cornelia Rogers (Kellogg) M.; m. Victoria Ann French, Feb. 18, 1967; children: Christopher Jackson, Robin Taylor. BA, Yale U., 1965; MBA, Harvard U., 1969. With product mgmt. Gen. Foods Corp., White Plains, N.Y., 1969-83, gen. mgr. Maxwell House Coffee div., 1983-85; v.p. Gen. Foods Corp., 1983-87, pres. Maxwell House div., 1986-87; founder, dir. Spectra Mktg. Systems Inc., Chgo., 1987-90; pres., CEO Vid Code Inc., Waltham, Mass., 1990-92; pres. The Arbitron Co., N.Y.C., 1992—; bd. dirs. John B. Stetson Co., 1991—. Trustee N.Y. Theatre Workshop, 1995—. Served to 2d lt. USMCR, 1965-66. Avocations: tennis; skiing; gardening. Home: 300 Mt Holly Rd Katonah NY 10536 Office: The Arbitron Co 142 W 57th St New York NY 10019-3300

MORRIS, STEPHEN JAMES MICHAEL, lawyer; b. Los Angeles, Aug. 22, 1934; s. Thomas Ambrose and Kathryn Adele Brown M.; m. Ann Austin Moseley, Aug. 31, 1956 (div.); children: Brook Barrett, Clea Alden; m. Anne Sturdy Abbott, June 30, 1990. B.A., Pomona Coll., 1956; LL.B., U. Calif. at Berkeley, 1961. Bar: Calif. 1962. Since practiced in Los Angeles; law clk. for Judge Albert Lee Stephens, U.S. Ct. Appeals 9th Circuit, 1961, Judge Albert Lee Stephens Jr., U.S. Dist. Ct., Central Dist. Calif., 1962; asso. firm Walker, Wright, Tyler & Ward (attys.), Los Angeles, 1962-66; founding partner Dietsch, Gates, Morris & Merrell (and predecessor firm), Los Angeles, 1966-78; ptnr. Hahn Cazier & Smaltz, Los Angeles, 1978-87, Morgan, Lewis & Bockius, 1987-95; of counsel Musick, Peeler & Garrett, 1995—. Bd. dirs. Pasadena Symphony Assn., 1985—, sec., 1988-90, pres., 1990-94; bd. dirs. Assn. Calif. Symphony Orchs., 1994—, sec., 1995—. 1st lt. Armored Corps AUS, 1956-58. Mem. ABA, State Bar Calif. (del. 1973-76), Los Angeles County Bar Assn. (exec. com. bus. and corp. law sect. 1973-75), Calif. Club (dir. 1992—), Valley Hunt Club (dir. 1977-83, treas. 1979-81, v.p. 1981-82, pres. 1982-83), Chancery Club, Sigma Tau, Phi Alpha Delta. Home: 270 S Arroyo Blvd Pasadena CA 91105-1507 Office: Musick Peeler & Garrett 1 Wilshire Blvd Ste 2000 Los Angeles CA 90017-3383

MORRIS, STEVLAND See WONDER, STEVIE

MORRIS, STEWART, JR., title insurance company executive; b. Houston, Oct. 14, 1948; s. Stewart Sr. and Joella (Mitchel) M. BA, Rice U., 1971; MBA, U. Tex., 1973. V.p. Stewart Title Co., Houston, 1975-87, sr. exec. v.p., asst. to pres., 1987-91, pres., 1991—; bd. dirs. Southern Nat. Bank, Houston. Bd. dirs. Houston chpt. Cystic Fibrosis Found., 1985—. Mem. Am. Land Title Assn., Am. Driving Soc. (bd. dirs. 1984—), Houston Area Carriage Assn. (pres. 1995—), Carriage Assn. Am. (pres. 1995—). Office: 1980 Post Oak Blvd # 800 Houston TX 77056-3807

MORRIS, THOMAS BATEMAN, JR., lawyer; b. Columbus, Ohio, Aug. 11, 1936; s. Thomas Bateman and Margaret (O'Shaughnessy) M.; m. Ann Peirce, Feb. 23, 1963; children: Lauren, Thomas III, Richard. AB, Princeton U., 1958; JD, Harvard U., 1962. Bar: Pa. 1962. Ptnr. Dechert Price & Rhoads, Phila., 1962—, chmn., 1990—; bd. dirs. PNC Bank N.A., Phila., Berwind Corp., Phila., Asten, Inc., Charleston, S.C., Envirite Corp., Plymouth Meeting, Pa., Peirce-Phelps, Inc., Phila., Harmac Med. Products, Inc., Buffalo. Co-chmn. Greater Phila. Internat. Network, 1978—; trustee Princeton U., 1975-80; bd. trustees Thomas Jefferson U., 1989—. Hon. Consul King of Belgium, Phila., 1974-89. Mem. ABA, Pa. Bar Assn., Phila. Bar Assn. (chmn. city tax policy com.), Internat. Bar Assn. (chmn. com. on structure and ethics of law practice), Phila. Club, Phila. Cricket Club, Princeton Club, Sunnybrook Golf Club, Pine Valley Golf Club. Home: 8320 Seminole St Philadelphia PA 19118-3932 Office: Dechert Price & Rhoads Bell Atlantic Tower 1717 Arch St Philadelphia PA 19103-2713

MORRIS, THOMAS QUINLAN, hospital administrator, physician; b. Yonkers, N.Y., Jan. 3, 1933; s. William Thomas and Mary Berenice (Quinlan) M.; m. Jacqueline Ingram, Sept. 12, 1959; children: Thomas, Amy, MaryAnne. BS, U. Notre Dame, 1954; MD, Columbia U., 1958. Diplomate Am. Bd. Internal Medicine. From instr. to assoc. prof. clin. medicine Coll. Physicians and Surgeons, Columbia U., N.Y.C., 1964-79, prof., 1979—, acting chmn. dept. medicine, 1978-82, assoc. dean academic affairs, 1979-82, vice dean faculty of medicine, 1982-84, vice chmn. dept. medicine, 1993-94, sr. assoc. v.p. for health scis., vice dean faculty medicine, 1994—; acting dir. Med. Services, Presbyn. Hosp., N.Y.C., 1978-82, pres., 1985-90; v.p. for programs N.Y. Acad. Medicine, 1990-94, advisor 1994—. Med. editor Complete Home Medical Guide, 1985. Trustee Mary Imogene Bassett Hosp., Cooperstown, N.Y., 1980—, chmn. 1994—; trustee Am. Univ. of Beirut, N.Y.C., 1985—. Served to capt. USAF, 1962-64. Fellow ACP; mem. Greater N.Y. Hosp. Assn. (bd. govs. 1985-90), League of Voluntary Hosps. and Homes (chmn. bd. dirs. 1985-89). Clubs: The Century, Harvey Soc. (N.Y.C.). Office: Coll Physicians and Surgeons 630 W 168th St New York NY 10032-3702 also: New York Acad Medicine 2 E 103rd St New York NY 10029-5207

MORRIS, THOMAS ROBBINS, political science educator; b. Roanoke, Va., July 28, 1944; s. Robert Vaughan and Ethel (Robbins) M.; children from previous marriage: Sheila Dawn, Tabbitha Lyn, Sharon Robbins, Rosalyn Vaughan. B.A. in History, Va. Mil. Inst., 1966; M.A., U. Va., 1969, Ph.D. in Govt., 1973; postgrad. Princeton Theol. Sem., 1966-67. Asst. prof. U. Richmond, Va., 1971-78, assoc. prof. polit. sci., 1978-87, prof., 1987—, chair dept., 1981-84; polit. analyst WTVR-Channel 6 TV, Richmond, 1981—; vis. scholar U. Utah, 1986-87. Author: The Virginia Supreme Court: An Institutional and Political Analysis, 1975, Virginia Government and Politics: Readings and Comments, 2d edit., 1984. Bd. dirs. Housing Opportunities Made Equal, Richmond, Va., 1982—. Liberal arts fellow Harvard Law Sch., Cambridge, Mass., 1976-77, NEH fellow U. Wis.-Madison, 1979-80; named Disting. Educator, U. Richmond, Va., 1982. Mem. Am. Polit. Sci. Assn., Omicron Delta Kappa. Methodist. Office: Dept Polit Sci U Richmond Richmond VA 23173

MORRIS, THOMAS WILLIAM, symphony orchestra administrator; b. Rochester, N.Y., Feb. 7, 1944; s. William H. and Eleanor E. M.; m. Jane Allison, Aug. 7, 1965; children: Elisa L., Charles A., William H. A.B., Princeton U., 1965; M.B.A., Wharton Sch. U. Pa., 1969. Adminstrv. asst., Ford Found. fellow for adminstrv. interns in arts Cin. Symphony, 1965-67; payroll clk. bus. office Boston Symphony Orch., 1969-71, asst. mgr. bus. affairs, 1971-73, mgr., 1973-78, gen. mgr., 1978-86, v.p. spl. projects and planning, 1986; pres. Thomas W. Morris and Co., Inc., Boston, 1986-87; exec. dir. Cleve. Orch., 1987—; chmn. policy com. Maj. Orch. Mgrs., 1977-79; chmn. orch. panel Nat. Endowment for Arts, 1979—. Chmn. Cleve. Cultural Coalition, 1992-95; mem. Cleve. Bicentennial Commn., 1993—. Mem. Am. Symphony Orch. League (dir. 1977-79). Office: Cleve Orch Severance Hall Cleveland OH 44106

MORRIS, WILLIAM CHARLES, investor; b. St. Louis, Apr. 15, 1938; s. Barney Lockhart and Kathryn (Evers) M.; m. Susan VanAvery Follett, Aug. 26, 1961; children: Edward F., David L., Kenneth V. SB in Chem. Engring., MIT, 1960; MBA, Harvard Bus. Sch., 1963. Assoc. Mobil Chem. Co., N.Y.C., 1963-66, Lehman Bros., N.Y.C., 1967-72; mng. dir. Lehman Bros. Kuhn Loeb Inc. (and predecessor), N.Y.C., 1973-84; sr. advisor Shearson Lehman Bros., N.Y.C., 1985-87; chmn. Carbo Ceramics Inc., Dallas, 1987—; chmn., pres. J&W Seligman & Co., Inc., N.Y.C., 1988—; chmn. Tri-Continental Corp., N.Y.C., 1988—, The Seligman Group of Investment Cos., N.Y.C., 1988—; bd. dirs. Kerr McGee Corp., Oklahoma City, 1977—. Trustee Sarah Lawrence Coll., 1991—; adv. dir. Metro. Opera Assn., N.Y., 1995—. Served as ensign USCGR, 1961. Home: 5 Hampshire Cir Bronxville NY 10708-5803 Office: J & W Seligman & Co Inc 100 Park Ave Fl 8 New York NY 10017-5516

MORRIS, WILLIAM JOSEPH, paleontologist, educator; b. Balt., Oct. 14, 1923; s. Benjamin Moss and Aida (Ruble) M.; m. Ann Bates, Aug. 11, 1945; children—Lynn Ann (Mrs. Thomas W. Nadal), Carol Florence. B.A., Syracuse U., 1947; M.A., Princeton, 1948, Ph.D., 1950. Asst. prof. to asso. prof. geology Tex. A. and M. U., 1950-55; asso. prof. to prof. geology Occidental Coll., 1955—; also research asso. in vertebrate paleontology Los Angeles County Mus. Natural History, 1957—; Mem. Nat. Geog. Soc. expdn. to Baja, Calif., 1968-73. Contbr. articles profl. jours. Served with AUS, 1942-45. Recipient Arnold Guyot award Nat. Geog. Soc., 1968. Fellow Geol. Soc. Am., So. Calif. Acad. Scis. (pres. 1969-70, dir. 1958-70); mem. AAAS, Soc. Vertebrate Paleontologists, Soc. Study Evolution, Sigma Xi. Club: Explorers (N.Y.C.). Home: 707 S 3rd Ave Battle Ground WA 98604-3213 *I maintain that a commitment to intellectual and personal integrity is necessary for spiritual well-being. My rules are not complex. Honesty and an undeviating sense of responsibility to those who have offered opportunities and placed their trust in me are a part of my life. Intelligence appears necessary in order to contribute significantly to our society, but often lacking in those with adequate mental status is perseverance. One must be firm in belief and determination, and have a mature skepticism that can lead to invention.*

MORRIS, WILLIAM OTIS, JR., lawyer, educator, author; b. Fairmont, W.Va., Dec. 2, 1922; s. William Otis and Flora Helois (Preston) M.; m. Hazel Irene Kolbus, May 28, 1948; children: Barbara Ann, Melinda Lou. Student, Fairmont State Coll., 1940-41; AB, Coll. William and Mary, 1944; LLB, U. Ill., 1946, JD, 1968; D of Honorable Causes, Nicolaus Copernicus U., Torun, Poland, 1992; DHC, Nicholas Copernicus U., Torun, Poland, 1992. Bar: Va. 1945, Ill. 1946, U.S. Supreme Ct. 1949. Prof. bus. law U. Ill., 1947-55; assoc. prof. law Stetson U., 1955-58; prof. law W.Va. U., Morgantown, 1958-94, prof. emeritus, 1994—; vis. U. Vienna, Austria, Nat. U., Singapore, Nat. U., Seoul, Korea, U. Sydney, Australia, East China Inst. of Law and Politics, U. Thessaloniki, Greece. Author: Dental Litigation, 1972, 2d edit., 1977, The Law of Domestic Relations in West Virginia, 1975, Veterinarian in Litigation, 1976, Revocation of Professional License, 1985, Handbook of Dental Law, 1994, The Dentist's Legal Advisor, 1994; mem. bd. editors Jour. Law and Ethics in Dentistry, Med. Malpractice Prevention, Clin. Jour.; contbr. articles to profl. jours. Decorated Merit medal (Poland); recipient Spl. award Nat. U. Seoul, Old Guard Medallion Coll. William and Mary, 1994, Lifetime Achievement award Loyola U. Coll. Dentistry, 1994. Fellow Cleve. Clinic Med. Inst.; mem. Va. Bar, Ill. Bar, Am. Trial Lawyers Assn., W.Va. Trial Lawyers Assn., Order of Coif, Order of White Jackets. Republican. Lutheran. Home: 644 Bellaire Dr Morgantown WV 26505-2421 Office: WVa U 117 Law Ctr Morgantown WV 26506

MORRIS, WILLIAM SHIVERS, III, newspaper executive; b. Augusta, Ga., Oct. 3, 1934; s. William Shivers Jr. and Florence (Hill) M.; m. Mary Sue Ellis, Jan. 18, 1958; children: William Shivers IV, John Tyler, Susie Blackmar. A.B. in Journalism, U. Ga., 1956. Asst. to pres., pub. Southeastern Newspapers and Augusta Newspapers, 1956-60; v.p., dir. Savannah Newspapers, Inc. and Savannah News-Press, Inc., Ga., 1960-63; v.p., dir. Southeastern Newspapers Corp., 1963-65, chmn. bd., chief exec. officer; chmn. bd., chief exec. officer Banner-Herald Pub. Co., Athens, Ga., 1965, Morris Communications Corp., Augusta, Southwestern Newspapers Corp., N. Am. Publs., Inc., Fla. Pub. Co., Jacksonville; chmn. bd., chief exec. officer, pub. Augusta Chronicle, Athens Star, and Augusta Herald, Ga., 1966-94, Augusta Chronicle and Athens Star, Ga., 1966—; pub. Juneau Empire; dir. Ga. Power Co., Atlanta, So. Co., Atlanta, Associated Press. Trustee Augusta Coll. Found.; bd. regents Univ. System Ga., 1967-73.

Served to capt. USAF, 1956-58. Hon. mem. Golden Quill Soc., 1960. Mem. Am. Newspaper Pubs. Assn., Southeastern Newspaper Pubs. Assn. (dir. 1966—), So. Newspaper Pubs. Assn., Internat. Press Inst. Presbyterian (elder). Clubs: Pinnacle (Augusta) (pres.); University (N.Y.C.); Oglethorpe (Savannah); Commerce (Atlanta). also: Morris Communications Corp PO Box 936 Augusta GA 30903-0936 also: Amarillo Globe-News Div PO Box 2091 Amarillo TX 79166-0001*

MORRIS, WILLIE, author, editor; b. Jackson, Miss., Nov. 29, 1934; s. Henry Rae and Marion (Weaks) M.; m. Celia Ann Buchan, Aug. 30, 1958 (divorced 1969); 1 child, David Rae; m. JoAnne Shirley Prichard, Sept. 14, 1991. BA, U. Tex., 1956; BA (Rhodes scholar 1956), New Coll., Oxford (Eng.) U., 1959, M.A., 1960; Ph.D. (hon.), Grinnell Coll., 1967, Gettysburg Coll., 1968. Assoc. editor Tex. Observer, Austin, 1960; editor in chief Tex. Observer, 1960-62; assoc. editor Harper's mag., 1963-65, exec. editor, 1965-67, editor in chief, 1967-71; v.p. Harper's Mag., Inc., 1967-71; writer-in-residence U. Miss., 1980-91; hon. fellow Silliman Coll., Yale. Author: The South Today, 100 Years After Appomattox, 1965, (autobiography) North Toward Home (Carr P. Collins nonfiction award, Houghton-Mifflin lit. award 1967), Yazoo: Integration in a Deep Southern Town, 1971, (children's fiction) Good Old Boy, 1971, (novel) The Last of the Southern Girls, 1973, (memoir) James Jones: A Friendship, 1978, (essays) Terrains of the Heart and Other Essays, 1981, (nonfiction) The Courting of Marcus Dupree, 1983 (Christopher medal), (essays) Always Stand in Against the Curve, 1983, Homecomings, 1989 (Miss. Disting. Book award), (chidren's fiction) Good Old Boy and the Witch of Yazoo, 1989, Faulkner's Mississippi, 1990, (stories) After All, It's Only a Game, 1992, (autobiography) New York Days, 1993 (Gov.'s artistic achievement award 1994, Best Book of 1993 Miss. award Miss. Inst. Arts and Letters), My Dog Skip, 1995, Introductory Essay Official Games and Souvenir Program for 1996 Centennial Olympics. Mem. P.E.N. Club, Soc. Rhodes Scholars, ACLU, Phi Beta Kappa, Phi Eta Sigma, Sigma Delta Chi, Delta Tau Delta.

MORRIS, WRIGHT, novelist, critic; b. Central City, Nebr., Jan. 6, 1910; s. William H. and Grace (Osborn) M.; m. Mary E. Finfrock, 1934 (div. 1961); m. Josephine Kantor, 1961. Student, Pomona Coll., 1930-33; hon. degrees, Westminster Coll, U. Nebr., Pomona Coll. Prof. San Francisco State U., 1962-75. Author: My Uncle Dudley, 1942, The Man Who Was There, 1945, The Inhabitants, 1946, The Home Place, 1948, The World in the Attic, 1949, Man and Boy, 1951, The Works of Love, 1952, The Deep Sleep, 1953, The Huge Season, 1954, The Field of Vision, 1956 (Nat. Book award 1957), Love Among the Cannibals, 1957, The Territory Ahead, 1958, Ceremony in Lone Tree, 1960, The Mississippi River Reader, 1961, What a Way to Go, 1962, Cause for Wonder, 1963, One Day, 1965, In Orbit, 1967, A Bill of Rites, a Bill of Wrongs, a Bill of Goods, 1968, God's Country and My People, 1968, Wright Morris: A Reader, 1970, Fire Sermon, 1971, War Games, 1971, Love Affair: A Venetian Journal, 1972, Here is Einbaum, 1973, A Life, 1973, About Fiction, 1975, Real Losses, Imaginary Gains, 1976, The Fork River Space Project, 1977, Earthly Delights, Unearthly Adornments: The American Writer as Image Maker, 1978, Plains Song, 1980 (Am. Book award 1981), Will's Boy, 1981, Photographs and Words, 1982, Solo: An American Dreamer in Europe, 1933-34, 1983, A Cloak of Light, 1985, Collected Stories, 1986, Time Pieces: Word and Image, 1989, Writing My Life: An Autobiography, 1992, Three Easy Pieces, 1993, Two for the Road, 1994. Recipient Robert Kirsch award for body of work, 1981, Life Achievement award Nat. Endowment for Arts, 1986; Guggenheim fellow, 1942, 46, 54. Mem. Nat. Inst. Arts and Letters, Am. Acad. Arts and Scis. (Whiting award 1982). Office: care Harper & Collins Pubs 10 E 53rd St New York NY 10022-5244

MORRISETT, LLOYD N., foundation executive; b. Oklahoma City, Nov. 2, 1929; s. Lloyd N. and Jessie Ruth (Watson) M.; m. Mary Frances Pierre, June 10, 1952; children: Sarah, Julie. BA, Oberlin Coll., 1951, LHD (hon.), 1971; postgrad., U. Calif., 1951-53; PhD, Yale U., 1956; hon. degree, Northwestern U., 1975, RAND Grad. Sch., 1995. Instr. U. Calif., 1956-57, asst. prof., 1957-58; staff mem. Social Sci. Research Council, 1958-59; exec. asst. Carnegie Corp. of N.Y., 1959-61, exec. assoc., 1961-63, exec. assoc. and asst. to pres., 1963-65, v.p., 1965-69; v.p. Carnegie Found. for Advancement Teaching, 1965-69; pres. Markle Found., 1969—; trustee Sys. Devel. Found., 1970-88; trustee N.Y. Rand Inst., 1969-75, chmn. bd., 1972-75; trustee Riverside Rsch. Inst., 1971-74, Rsch. Triangle Inst., 1970-79, Ednl. Testing Svc., 1983-87; trustee Oberlin Coll., 1972-88, chmn. bd., 1975-81; trustee Rand Corp., 1973-83, 85-95, chmn. bd., 1986-95; chmn. bd. trustees Children's TV Workshop, 1970—; bd. dirs. The Multi Media Corp., 1990—, Classroom, Inc., 1992—, Infonautics Corp.; mem. adv. bd. Walt Whitman Ctr., Rutgers U., 1993—; mem. bd. overseers Darmouth Sch. Medicine, 1995—; mem. steering com. NRC, 1994—. Mem. Council on Fgn. Relations, 1968—; mem. N.Y. State Commn. on Quality, Cost and Financing Elementary and Secondary Edn., 1969-72; bd. dirs. System Devel. Corp., 1966-70; mem. vis. com. Office for Info. Tech., Harvard, 1974-80; mem. Am. Council on Germany, 1975-79, The Cleve. Conf., 1972—; bd. dirs. Haskins Labs., 1976—; mem. MultiMedia Corp., 1990—; mem. Classroom, Inc., 1992—; adv. bd. mem. Rutgers U.-W. Whitman Ctr, 1993—; mem. Infonautics Corp., 1994; Steering Com. mem. Nat. Rsch. Coun., 1994—; bd overseers mem. Dartmouth Sch. of Medicine, 1995—. Fellow NSF, 1956. Fellow Am. Psychol. Assn., AAAS; mem. N.Y. Acad. Scis. (bd. govs. 1989—), Sigma Xi. Home: 12 Castle Rd Irvington NY 10533-2017 Office: The Markle Found 75 Rockefeller Plz Ste 1800 New York NY 10019

MORRISEY, MARENA GRANT, art museum administrator; b. Newport News, Va., May 28, 1945. BFA in Interior Design, Va. Commonwealth U., 1967, MA Art History, 1970. With Orlando (Fla.) Mus. Art, 1970—, exec. dir., 1976—; former v.p., chmn. mus. svcs. com., mem. ad hoc com. on collections sharing and long range planning com., past chmn. exhbns. and edn. com. Am. Fedn. Arts; former mem. nat. adv. coun. George Washington U. Clearinghouse on Mus. Edn.; former mem. accreditation com. Nat. Found. for Interior Design Edn. Rsch. Former mem. strategic planning adv. coun. Orange County Sch. Dist.; former mem. advt. rev. bd. BBB; former mem. Orlando Pub. Art Adv. Bd., Orlando Leadership Coun., Orlando Hist. Bldg. Commn.; former chmn. art selection com. Orlando Internat. Airport; former mem. bd. dirs. Sta. WMFE-TV. Named Orlando's Outstanding Woman of Yr. in Field of Art; recipient Fla. State of Arts award. Mem. Am. Assn. Mus. (former mem. governing bd., accreditation commn., profl. stds. and practices com., internat. com. on mus.), Assn. Art Mus. Dirs., Southeastern Mus. Conf. (past pres.), Fla. Art Mus. Dirs. Assn. (past pres.), Fla. Assn. Mus. (former bd. dirs.), Greater Orlando C. of C. (past mem. steering com. Leadership Orlando, former mem. Project 2000), Jr. League Orland-Winter Park, Rotary Club Orlando (program com. Orlando, membership com., chmn. found. com., Paul Harris fellow). Office: Orlando Museum of Art 2416 N Mills Ave Orlando FL 32803-1426

MORRISH, ALLAN HENRY, electrical engineering educator; b. Winnipeg, Man., Can., Apr. 18, 1924; s. Stanley and Agnes (Payne) M.; children: John Stanley, Allan Richard. B.Sc. with Honors, U. Man., 1943; M.A., U. Toronto, 1946; Ph.D., U. Chgo., 1949. Mem. faculty U. B.C., Vancouver, Can., 1949-52; research asst. Radiation Lab., McGill U., Montreal, Que., Can., 1952-53; with dept. elec. engring. U. Minn., Mpls., 1953-64; prof. dept. elec. engring. U. Minn., 1959-64; prof. U. Man., Winnipeg, 1964—; head dept. physics U. Man., 1966-87, disting. prof., 1984—; vis. prof. Monash U., Clayton, Victoria, Australia, 1971-72, U. Calif., Davis, 1978, Ariz. State U., Tempe, 1984, U. Wash., Seattle, 1984, Tex. A&M U., College Station, 1989, Iowa State U., Ames, 1991; cons. Honeywell, Inc., Hopkins, Minn., 1956-57, 59-63. Author: The Physical Principles of Magnetism, 1965, Canted Antiferromagnetism: Hematite, 1994; also articles. NRC Can. postdoctoral fellow U. Bristol, Eng., 1950-51; Guggenheim fellow U. Oxford, Eng., 1957-58. Fellow Royal Soc. Can., Inst. of Physics (Eng.); mem. Am. Phys. Soc., Can. Assn. Physicists (pres. 1974-75, medal for achievement in physics 1977), Sigma Xi. Research on magnetic materials using superconducting solenoids. Home: 71 Agassiz Dr, Winnipeg, MB Canada R3T 2K9

MORRISH, THOMAS JAY, golf course architect; b. Grand Junction, Colo., July 6, 1936; s. Wilbur Merle and Margaret Beula (Cronk) M.; m. Louise Ann Dunn, Apr. 2, 1965; children: Carter J., Kimberly L. Coder. AA, Mesa Coll., Grand Junction, 1956; BS in Landscape and Nursery Mgmt., Colo. State U., 1964. Golf course arch. Robert Trent Jones, Montclair, N.J., 1964-67, George Fazio, Jupiter, Fla., 1967-69, Desmond Muirhead, Newport Beach, Calif., 1969-72, Jack Nicklaus, North Palm Beach, Fla., 1972-83; prin. Jay Morrish & Assocs. Ltd., Flower Mound, Tex., 1983—. Prin. golf course designs include: Troon Golf & Country Club, Scottsdale, Ariz., Las Colinas Sports Club, Irving, Tex., Mira Vista, Ft. Worth, Foothills Golf Course, Phoenix, Forest Highlands, Flagstaff, Ariz. (One of 100 Top Golf Courses in World, Golf mag., Golf Digest), Bentwater on Lake Conroe, Houston, Shadow Glen Golf Club, Olathe, Kans. (Best New Private Course, Golf Digest 1989), Troon North Golf & Country Club, Scottsdale (One of 100 Top Courses in U.S., Golf mag.), Harbor Club on Lake Oconee, Greensboro, Ga., Loch Lomond, Scotland, The Country Club of St. Albans, Mo., Broken Top, Bend, Oreg., numerous others. Edn. grantee State of Colo., 1961-64; Trans-Miss. golf scholar, 1962-64. Mem. Am. Soc. Golf Course Archs., Nat. Golf Found., Safari Club Internat., Dallas Safari Club. Republican. Avocation: hunting. Office: 3700 Forums Dr Ste 207 Flower Mound TX 75028-1840

MORRISON, ANGUS CURRAN, aviation executive; b. Toronto, Ont., Can., Apr. 22, 1919; s. Gordon Fraser and Mabel Ethel (Chalcraft) M.; m. Carlotta Townsend Munoz, Mar. 1, 1947; children—Sandra, James, Christian, Mark. Student, Upper Can. Coll., Bishop's Coll. Sch. Pres. Atlas Aviation, Ltd., Ottawa, Ont., 1946-51; sec. Air Industries and Transport Assn. Can., Ottawa, 1951-62; pres., chief exec. officer Air Transport Assn. Can., 1962-85; ret., 1985—; v.p., dir. Munoz Corp., Montclair, N.J., 1969-73. Councillor Town of Almonte, Ont., 1960-65. Served with Royal Can. Armoured Corps, 1939-46. Recipient Diplome Paul Tissandier Fedn. Aeronautique Internationale, 1977, Casi C.D. Howe award, 1987, Companion of Order of Flight, 1989; named to Can.'s Aviation Hall of Fame, 1989. Assoc. fellow Can. Aeronautics and Space Inst.; mem. Internat. N.W. Aviation Coun., Chartered Inst. Transport. Anglican. Clubs: Rideau, Wings. Home: Burnside, PO Box 609, Almonte, ON Canada K0A 1A0

MORRISON, ASHTON BYROM, pathologist, medical school official; b. Northern Ireland, Oct. 13, 1922; came to U.S., 1955; s. Samuel and Henrietta (Good) M.; m. Claire Morris, M.D.; 1 dau., Mary Claire. MB, Queen's U, Belfast, No. Ireland, 1946; PhD, Queens U., Belfast, No. Ireland, 1950, MD (hon.), 1988; MD, Duke U., 1946. Intern Royal Victoria Hosp., Belfast, 1947; asst. lectr. Queens U., 1947-52; registrar dept. exptl. medicine Cambridge U., 1952-55, dir. med. studies Corpus Christi Coll., 1954-55; assoc. Duke U., N.C., 1955-58; asst. prof. pathology U. Pa. Sch. Medicine, 1958-61; assoc. prof. U. Rochester Sch. Medicine, 1961-65; prof. pathology, chmn. dept. Rutgers U. Med. Sch., 1965-80; v.p. acad. affairs Eastern Va. Med. Authority, 1980-83; dean Eastern Va. Med. Sch., 1980-83; prof. pathology Robert Wood Johnson Med. Sch.-U. Medicine and Dentistry N.J., Camden, 1983-93; assoc. dean in charge Robert Wood Johnson Med Sch.-U. Medicine and Dentistry N.J., Camden, 1983-89, prof. pathology emeritus, 1994—; prof. pathology Ea. Va. Med. Sch., 1994—; 22nd Scott Heron lectr. Royal Victoria Hosp., Belfast, No. Ireland, 1978. Recipient Disting. Alumnus award Duke U. Med. Sch., 1987. Mem. Am. Assn. Investigative Pathologists (emeritus), Am. Physiol. Soc. (emeritus), Soc. Exptl. Biology and Medicine (emeritus), Am. Soc. Nephrology (emeritus). Home: 615 Shirley Ave Norfolk VA 23517-2023 Office: Eastern Va Med Sch 358 Mowbray Arch Ste 108 Norfolk VA 23507

MORRISON, BRUCE ANDREW, congressman; b. N.Y.C., Oct. 8, 1944; s. George and Dorothea A. (Meyer) M.; m. Nancy A. Wanat, Sept. 22, 1991; 1 child, Drew. S.B., MIT, 1965; M.S., U. Ill., 1970; J.D., Yale U., 1973; Litt.D. (hon.), Quinnipac Coll. Staff atty. New Haven Legal Assistance Assn., 1973-74, mng. atty., 1974-76, exec. dir., 1976-81; mem. 98th-101st Congresses from 3d Conn. dist., 1983-90; mem. Dem.-at-Large whip, mem. banking com., judiciary com., D.C. Com., select com. on children, youth and families, vet. affairs, chmn. L.I. Sound Caucus, chmn. Third World Debt Caucus; chmn. judiciary subcom. on immigration, refugees, and internat. law U.S. Ho. of Reps.; co-chmn. ad hoc com. on Irish affairs; mem. U.S. commn. on immigration reform; chair Irish Ams. for Clinton-Gore. Bd. dirs. U. Limerick (Ireland) Found. Mem. ABA, Conn. Bar Assn., New Haven County Bar Assn., Am. Immigration Lawyers Assn. Lutheran. Office: Federal Housing Finance Bd 1777 F St NW Washington DC 20006

MORRISON, CATHERINE JOAN, economics educator; b. Champaign, Ill., June 17, 1953; d. Stanley Roy and Phyllis May (Parkinson) M.; m. Ernst R. Berndt, Jan. 4, 1985 (div. Apr. 1993); 1 stepchild, Jeffrey David. BA with honors in Econs., U. B.C., Vancouver, 1977, MA in Econs., 1978, PhD in Econs., 1982. Instr. NYU, N.Y.C., 1981-82; asst. prof. econs. Tufts U., Medford, Mass., 1982-88, assoc. prof., 1988-94, prof., 1994-95; chair dept. econs. Tufts U., Medford, 1994-95; prof. econs. U. Calif., Davis, 1995—; cons. Datametrics, Ltd., Calgary, 1978-81, Bur. Census, Ctr. Econ. Studies, 1984-87, Analysis Group, Belmont, Mass., 1989-90, Jack Faucett Assocs., 1993; rsch. economist divsn. productivity and tech. Bur. Labor Stats., Internat. Affairs and Activities, 1981, Nat. Bur. Econ. Rsch., 1983-86; rsch. assoc. N.B.E.R., 1986-92; participant Nat. Bur. Econ. Rsch. Summer Inst., 1982—; guest prof. U. Mannheim, Germany, 1985; vis. scholar Uppsala (Sweden) U., 1986, 88, 89; assoc. Conf. on Rsch. in Income and Wealth, 1988—; vis. prof. Bilkent U., Ankara, Turkey, 1989; resident scholar Fed. Res. Bd., 1992; mem. vis. com. to evaluate grad. program Northeastern U., 1993. Mem. bd. advisors Jour. Productivity Analysis; mem. editl. bd. Atlantic Econ. Rev.; referee NSF, Internat. Econ. Rev., Quar. Jour. Econs., Rev. Econ. Studies, Econometrica, Am. Econ. Rev., Internat. Jour. Econs., Rand Jour. Econs., Rev. Econs. and Stats., Jour. Bus. and Econ. Stats., Econ. Jour., Economica, Jour. Econometrics, Jour. Polit. Economy, Scandanavian Jour., So. Econ. Jour., Jour. Devel. Econs., Jour. Productivity Analysis, Jour. Macroecons., Internat. Tax and Pub. Fin.; contbr. articles to profl. jours. Can. Coun. fellow/U. B.C. Programme in Natural Resource Econs., 1977-78, 78-79, Can. Coun. doctoral fellow, 1979-80, 80-81; grantee NSF, 1983, 86, 87, 88, Mellon Found., Tufts U., 1984, Resources for the Future Small Grants Program, 1985, Tufts U., 1989, Bur. Labor Stats., 1994-95. Avocation: teddy bear artist. Office: U Calif Davis Dept Agrl Econs Davis CA 95616

MORRISON, CLINTON, banker; b. Mpls., Mar. 26, 1915; s. Angus Washburn and Helen (Truesdale) M.; m. Mary K. Morrison. B.A., Yale U., 1937; M.B.A., Harvard U., 1939. With Shell Oil Co., N.Y.C., St. Louis, 1939-41; with Vassar Co., Chgo., 1946-48, Holding Co., Mpls., 1948, First Nat. Bank, Mpls., 1955-80; former vice chmn. bd., chmn. trust com. First Nat. Bank; former dir. Gt. No. Ins. Co., Minn. Title Fin. Corp., Munsingwear, Inc.; Dep. regional dir. Far East Fgn. Operations Adminstrn. for U.S. Govt., 1953- 55; mem. Internat. Pvt. Investment Adv. Council to AID, Dept. State, 1967-68, Nat. Adv. Council on Minority Bus. Enterprise, 1968-72. Life trustee Mpls. Art Inst., Mpls. Coll. Art and Design; former trustee Lakewood Cemetery Assn. Served to maj. Q.M.C. AUS, 1942-46. Mem. U.S. C. of C. (chmn. 1975-76), Bankers Assn. (exec. com. trust div. 1969-72), Twin Cities Soc. Security Analysts, Mpls. Econ. Roundtable. Home: 2400 Cedar Point Dr Wayzata MN 55391-2618 Office: 601 2d Ave S Ste 4940 Minneapolis MN 55402-4303

MORRISON, DARREL GENE, landscape architecture educator; b. Orient, Iowa, June 20, 1937; s. Raymond Delbert and Rosy Christina (Mensing) M.; m. Dawna Lee Hauptman, June 29, 1963 (div. Sept. 1987); children: Jon David, Scott Darrel. B.S.L.A., Iowa State U., 1959; M.S.L.A., U. Wis., 1969. Landscape architect Md. Nat. Capital Park and Plan Commn., Silver Spring, 1962-64, T.D. Donovan & Assocs., Silver Spring, Md., 1964-66, City Washington, 1966-67; research asst. U. Wis., Madison, 1967-69, mem. faculty, 1969-83; John Bascom prof. U. Wis., 1978; dean environ. design U. Ga., Athens, 1983-92, prof. environ. design, 1992-96; faculty Sch. Natural Resources and Environment U. Mich., Ann Arbor, 1996—. Co-editor: Landscape Jour., 1981-88. Served with U.S. Army, 1960-62. Recipient Disting. Tchg. award U. Wis., 1976, Bracken medal Pa. State U., 1996; named Outstanding Educator Coun. Educators in Landscape Architecture, 1977, 94. Fellow Am. Soc. Landscape Architects (v.p. 1987-89). Office: Sch Natural Resources and Environment Dana Bldg Univ Michigan Ann Arbor MI

MORRISON, DAVID, science administrator; b. Danville, Ill., June 26, 1940; s. Donald Harlan Morrison and Alice Lee (Douglass) Guin; m. Nancy Dunlap, June 19, 1966 (div. 1977); m. Janet L. Irick, Aug. 23, 1981. BA, U. Ill., 1962; PhD, Harvard U., 1969. Prof. astronomy U. Hawaii, Honolulu, 1969-88, vice chancellor rsch., 1983-85, dir. IRTF telescope, 1985-88; dep. assoc. adminstr. NASA OFfice Space Sci., Washington, 1981; chief space sci. div. NASA Ames Rsch. Ctr., Moffett Field, Calif., 1988—; pres. Astron. Soc. of the Pacific, San Francisco, 1982-84; chmn. Divsn. for Planetary Scis., Washington, 1980-81; councillor Am. Astron. Soc., Washington, 1982-85; pres. Internat. Astron. Union Commn. on Planets, 1991-94. Author: Exploration of the Universe, 1987, 91, The Planetary System, 1988, Cosmic Catastrophes, 1989, Exploring Planetary Worlds, 1993; editor: Satellites of Jupiter, 1982; contbr. articles to profl. jour. Fellow AAAS, 1982, Com. for Sci. Investigation of Claims of Paranormal, 1983, Calif. Acad. Sci. Mem. Cosmos Club. Achievements include advanced research for Voyager and Galileo planetary exploration missions. Home: 14660 Fieldstone Saratoga CA 95070 Office: NASA Ames Rsch Ctr # N245-1 Moffett Field CA 94035

MORRISON, DAVID CAMPBELL, immunology educator; b. Stoneham, Mass., Sept. 1, 1941; s. Walter Howard and Grace Falkner (May) M.; m. Pamela Wentworth, May 9, 1981; children: Michael Lawrence, Jenilee Angelica. BS magna cum laude, U. Mass., 1963; PhD, Yale U., 1969. Assoc. NIH, Bethesda, Md., 1969-71; assoc. Research Inst. Scripps Clinic, La Jolla, Calif., 1971-74, asst. prof., 1974-78, assoc. prof., 1978-80; assoc. prof. Emory U., Atlanta, 1980-81, prof., 1981-85; prof. Kans. U., Kansas City, 1985—; chmn. dept. microbiology Med. Ctr. Kans. U., Kansas City, 1985-91; assoc. dir. Cancer Ctr. Kans. U., Kansas City, 1991-95; cons. EPA, Washington, 1976-80, NIH bacteriology and mycology study sect., Bethesda, 1986-90; mem. NIAID allergy immunology and transplant rsch. com. NIH, 1995—; vis. scientist Max Planck Inst., Freiburg, Fed. Republic Germany, 1975. Editor Immunology Letters, 1991-95, Infection and Immunity, 1992-94, Jour. Endotoxin Rsch., 1993—. Recipient Rsch. Career Devel. award NIH, 1975, Merit award, 1990, Disting. Prof. of Cancer Rsch. Kansas Masons, 1994—. Fellow Infectious Disease Soc. Am.; mem. Am. Assn. Immunologists, Am. Soc. Exptl. Pathology, Am. Soc. Microbiology, Reticuloendothelical Soc., Am. Soc. Biochemistry and Molecular Biology, Internat. Endotorin Soc. (pres.-elect). Avocations: gardening, banjo. Home: 6235 Mission Dr Mission Hills KS 66208-1252 Office: U Kans Med Ctr Cancer Ctr Kansas City KS 66160

MORRISON, DAVID FRED, freight company executive; b. Columbus, Ohio, Aug. 15, 1953; s. Fred Liew and Sophie Ann (Snider) M.; 1 child, Ian. BA, Stanford U., 1975; MBA, U. So. Calif., 1978. Sr. corp. planning analyst Tiger Internat., L.A., 1978-80, mgr. new bus. devel., 1980-81; dir. planning and controls Hall's Motor Transit Co., Mechanicsburg, Pa., 1981-82; mng. dir., gen. mgr. Consol. Freightways Export-Import Svc., San Francisco, 1984-86; asst. treas. McKesson Corp., San Francisco, 1987-90, treas., 1990-91; dir. strategic planning Consol. Freightways, Inc., Palo Alto, Calif., 1982-84, 86-87, v.p., treas., 1991—. Bd. dirs. Am. Sports Inst., Mill Valley, Calif., 1992—. Fellow State of Calif., 1977, Commerce Assocs., 1977. Mem. Nat. Assn. Corp. Treas., Fin. Execs. Inst. (silver medal 1978), Turnaround Mgmt. Assn. Avocations: tennis, rugby, nordic skiing. Office: Consol Freightways Inc 3240 Hillview Ave Palo Alto CA 94304-1201

MORRISON, DAVID LEE, librarian, educator; b. New London, Conn., Aug. 28, 1948; s. Samuel and Beatrice (Kinslinger) M. BA in Classics with highest honors, U. Calif., Santa Barbara, 1979; MLS, U. Ariz., 1986. Documents libr. Marriott Libr., U. Utah, Salt Lake City, 1987—, instr. libr. literacy course, 1990—; workshop presenter in field; guest lectr. U. Ariz. Grad. Libr. Sch., fall 1988-94; participant confs. in field. Fay and Lawrence Clark Powell scholar U. Ariz., 1983. Mem. ALA (govt. docs. round table info. tech. com. 1987-89), Utah Libr. Assn. (GODORT bylaws com. 1987-88, 91-92, chmn. nominating com. 1987-88, continuing edn. com. 1987-89, vice chmn., chmn.-elect 192-93, chmn. GODORT 1993-94), Patent and Trademark Depository Libr. Assn. (fin. com. 1988-96, sec.-treas. 1989-90, 92-96), Patent Documentation Soc. Home: 859 So Blair St Salt Lake City UT 84111 Office: U Utah Documents Div Marriott Libr Salt Lake City UT 84112

MORRISON, DEBORAH JEAN, lawyer; b. Johnstown, Pa., Feb. 18, 1955; d. Ralph Wesley and Norma Jean (Kinsey) Morrison; m. Ricardo Daniel Kamenetzky, Sept. 6, 1978 (div. Nov. 1991); children: Elena Raquel, Julia Rebecca. BA in Polit. Sci., Chatham Coll., 1977; postgrad., U. Miami, Fla., 1977-78; JD, U. Pitts., 1981. Bar: Pa. 1981, Ill. 1985. Legal asst. Klein Y Mairal, Buenos Aires, Argentina, 1978-79; legal intern Neighborhood Legal Svcs., Aliquippa, Pa., 1980-81; law clk. Pa. Superior Ct., Pitts., 1981-84; atty. John Deere Credit Co., Moline, Ill., 1985-89; sr. atty. Deere & Co., Moline, Ill., 1989—. Mem. ABA, Pa. Bar Assn., Phi Beta Kappa, Order of the Coif. Democrat. Mem. United Methodist. Office: Deere & Co John Deere Rd Moline IL 61265

MORRISON, DONALD FRANKLIN, statistician, educator; b. Stoneham, Mass., Feb. 10, 1931; s. Daniel Norman and Agnes Beatrice (Packard) M.; m. Phyllis Ann Hazen, Aug. 19, 1967; children: Norman Hazen, Stephen Donald. B.S. in Bus. Adminstrn, Boston U., 1953, A.M., 1954; M.S., U. N.C., 1957; Ph.D., Va. Poly. Inst. and State U., 1960; M.A. (hon.), U. Pa., 1971. Mem. staff Lincoln Lab., M.I.T., 1956; cons. math. statistician NIMH, Bethesda, Md., 1956-63; mem. tech. staff Bell Labs., Holmdel, N.J., 1967; mem. faculty, dept. stats. Wharton Sch., U. Pa., 1963—, prof. stats., 1973—, chmn. dept., 1978-85. Author: Multivariate Statistical Methods, 3d edit., 1990, Applied Linear Statistical Methods, 1983; editor: The American Statistician, 1972-75; assoc. editor: Biometrics, 1972-74; contbr. articles to profl. jours. Served with USPHS, 1956-58. NSF grantee, 1966. Fellow Am. Statis. Assn., Inst. Math. Stats.; mem. AAAS, Internat. Statis. Inst., Biometric Soc., Royal Statis. Soc., Psychometric Soc., B&M R.R. Hist. Soc., Nat. R.R. Hist. Soc. Democrat. Home: 118 E Brookhaven Rd Wallingford PA 19086-6327 Office: U Pa Wharton Sch Philadelphia PA 19104-6302

MORRISON, DONALD GRAHAM, business educator, consultant; b. Detroit, Feb. 26, 1939; s. Roderick and Ethelyne (Murray) M.; m. Sherie Leaver, Sept. 12, 1964; children—Heather Margaret, Tracey Michelle. B.S.M.E., MIT, 1961; Ph.D. in Ops. Research, Stanford U., 1965. Instr. Stanford U., Calif., 1965-66, vis. prof., 1982; mem. faculty Columbia U., N.Y.C., 1966-87, prof., 1973-87, Armand G. Erpf prof. bus., 1985-87; William E. Leonard prof. Anderson Grad. Sch. Mgmt., UCLA, 1987—; vis. prof. U. Calif., Berkeley, 1970-71; cons. in field, UCLA faculty athletic rep. to NCAA. Editor in chief Mgmt. Sci., 1983-90; founding editor Mktg. Sci., 1980-82. Elder Hitchcock Presbyn. Ch., Scarsdale, N.Y., 1978-84, Westwood Presbyn. Ch., L.A., 1991-94, 95—; treas. Scarsdale Jr. H.S. PTA, 1977-78; acad. trustee Mktg. Sci. Inst., 1986-92; mem. Decision, Risk and Mgmt. Sci. rev. bd. NSF, 1989-91. Mem. Inst. Mgmt. Sci. (pres. 1990-92), Ops. Rsch. Soc. Am., Am. Statis. Assn. Presbyterian. Avocations: golf; jogging; bridge. Office: UCLA Anderson Grad Sch Mgmt 110 Westwood Plz Los Angeles CA 90095-1481

MORRISON, DONALD WILLIAM, lawyer; b. Portland, Oreg., Mar. 31, 1926; s. Robert Angus and Laura Calista (Hodgson) M.; m. Elizabeth Margaret Perry, July 25, 1953; children: Elizabeth Laura, Carol Margaret. B.S.E.E., U. Wash., 1946; LL.B., Stanford U., 1950. Bar: Oreg. 1950, Calif. 1950, N.Y. 1967, Ill. 1968, Ohio 1974. Assoc. Pendergrass, Spackman, Bullivant & Wright, Portland, 1950-57; ptnr. Pendergrass, Spackman, Bullivant & Wright, 1957-60; gen. atty. Pacific N.W. Bell, Portland, 1960-66; atty. AT&T, N.Y.C., 1966-68; counsel Ill. Bell Telephone Co., Chgo., 1968-74; v.p., gen. counsel Ohio Bell Telephone Co., Cleve., 1974-91; of counsel Arter & Hadden, Cleve., 1991—. Trustee Citizens League Rsch. Inst., Health Trustees Inst., Cleve.; vice chair, mem. exec. com. Cleve. Coun. on World Affairs; mem. adv. com. Cleve. Play House; adv. com. Cleve. Bot. Garden; mem. vis. com. Cleve. State U. Law Sch. With USN, 1943-50. Recipient various bar and civic appreciation awards. Mem. ABA, Ohio State Bar Assn., Bar Assn. Greater Cleve., Oreg. State Bar Assn., Calif. Bar Assn., The Country Club, Rowfant Club. Office: Arter & Hadden 1100 Huntington Bldg Cleveland OH 44115

MORRISON, FRANCIS SECREST, physician; b. Chgo., July 29, 1931; s. Clifton B. and Marie B. (LaPierre) M.; m. Dorothy Daniels, Nov. 29, 1957; children: Francis, Thomas, Kenneth. Student, U. Ill., Chgo., 1949-51; B.S. with honors, Miss. State U., 1954; M.D., U. Miss., 1959. Diplomate: Am. Bd. Internal Medicine. Intern Hosp. of U. Pa., Phila., 1959-60; resident in internal medicine Hosp. of U. Pa., 1960-62; trainee in hematology Blood Research Lab., Tufts-New Eng. Med. Center, Boston, 1962-64; research fellow Blood Research Lab., Tufts-New Eng. Med. Center, 1964-65; vis.

investigator St. Mary's Hosp., London, 1966; attending physician, dir. div. hematology and oncology Univ. Hosp., Jackson, Miss., 1969-80; dir. div. hematology Univ. Hosp., 1980-92, dir. blood transfusion service, 1974-92, chief of staff, 1986; cons. in hematology Miss. Meth. Rehab. Ctr., Jackson, 1976; asst. prof. medicine U. Miss., Jackson, 1969-70, dir. div. hematology, 1969-92, assoc. prof., 1970-76, prof., 1976-95, prof. emeritus medicine, 1995—, med. dir. MetraHealth Gov. Programs, 1995—; mem. faculty U. Miss. Grad. Sch. Medicine, 1971-80; profl. adv. Jackson Community Blood Bank, Inc., 1973-75; dir. regional cancer program, also regional blood program Miss. Regional Med. Program, 1971-75; exec. dir. Miss. Regional Blood Ctr., 1975-79; mem. adv. bd. Jackson-Hinds Comprehensive Health Ctr., 1973-78; rsch. cons. Alcorn A. and M. Coll., 1973-74; med. dir. Travelers Medicare Miss. 1994-95; guest lectr. various health orgns. and TV programs; mem., chmn. hemophilia adv. bd. Miss. Bd. Health, 1974-90; chmn. task force on regionalization Am. Blood Commn., 1978-80; mem. Miss. Gov.'s Council on Aging, 1976-88; bd. dirs. Lake Lorman Corp., 1983-87, pres., 1987-88; commr. Lake Lorman Utility Dist., 1983-90, sec., treas., 1984-89, pres., 1989-91. Contbr. numerous articles on hematology and oncology to med. jours. Pres. parish coun. St. Peter's Cathedral, Jackson, 1972-74; chmn. Natchez-Jackson Diocesan Com. Community Svcs., 1972-76l bd. dirs. Miss. Opera Assn., 1973-78, Miss. Found. for Med. Care, 1993—; pres. bd. St. Joseph High Sch., 1974-75; bd. dirs. Med. Alumni of U. Miss., 1987—, mem. exec. com., 1990—, pres., 1992, mem. dean's med. alumni adv. com., 1987—. Served to comdr. M.C., USN. Fellow ACP; mem. Am. Assn. Blood Banks (sci. workshop com. 1975-78, Component Therapy com. 1987-90, sci. program com. 1988-90, extracorporeal therapy com. 1989-93, S. Cen. dist. adv. group 1985-93), Internat. Soc. Blood Transfusion, Am., Internat. socs. hematology, Jackson Acad. Medicine (pres. 1976), Am. Coll. Nuclear Medicine (alt. del. Miss. 1975), Am. Assn. Cancer Edn. (exec. com. 1978-81), Am. Assn. Cancer Rsch., N.Y. Acad. Scis., Miss. Acad. Scis., World Fedn. Hemophilia, Internat. Soc. Thrombosis and Haemostasis, Cen. Med. Soc., So. Med. Assn., So. Assn. Oncology (founding mem. 1988), Miss. Med Assn. (com. on blood transfusion 1976-77, ho. of dels. 1985-94, fin. com. 1985-90), Am. Soc. Nuclear Medicine, Am. Soc. Clin. Oncology, S.W. Oncology Group (prin. investigator), Soc. Cryobiology, Am. Cancer Soc. (dir. 1971-82, pres. Miss. div. 1977, chmn. exec. com. 1978, nat. del. 1981-82), South Central Assn. Blood Banks (hon. life, bd. dirs. 1974-89, program chmn. 1975, v.p. 1977-79, pres. 1987-88, pres. found. 1992-94), So. Blood Club (pres. 1977), Council Community Blood Centers (trustee 1975-79), Am. Soc. for Apheresis (bd. dirs. 1987-93, sec. treas, 1987-88, v.p. 1988-89, pres. 1990, program com., fin. com., internat. affairs com. 1990—, chmn. 1992—), World Apheresis Assn (bd. dirs. 1990—, pres.-elect 1993, pres. 1994), Internat. Platform Assn., Chain des Rotisseurs (founding Jackson Bailli, 1994, conseiller l'ordre mondial), Sigma Xi, Phi Kappa Phi, Omicron Delta Kappa. Home: 173 Lakeshore Dr Jackson MS 39213-9473 Office: Metrahealth 775 Woodlands Pky Ridgeland MS 39157-5212

MORRISON, FRED BEVERLY, real estate consultant; b. Gt. Neck, N.Y., May 21, 1927; s. Fred B. and Beverly (Fitzgerald) M.; m. Janet Thornton Johnson, May 22, 1948; children—Jane, Susan, Martha, James, Ann, David. BA, Columbia U., 1948, LLB, 1951. Bar: D.C. 1952. Asst. gen. counsel ARC, Washington, 1951-54; nat. exec. sec., voluntary home mortgage program Housing and Home Fin. Agy., Washington, 1954-57; investment v.p. mortgages Met. Life Ins. Co., N.Y.C., 1957-67; pres. Lomas & Nettleton Co., Dallas, 1967-76; pres., CEO Western Mortgage Corp., L.A., 1976-78; exec. v.p. real estate industries div. Crocker Nat. Bank, L.A., 1978-84; pres. Pearce, Urstadt, Mayer & Greer, N.Y.C., 1984-89; real estate cons., 1989—; bd. dirs. Guardian Life Ins. Co., MetLife Internat. Real Estate Equity Shares; chmn. Fed. Nat. Mortgage Assn. Adv. Com., 1981. Mem. Mortgage Bankers Assn. Am. (gov. 1979-84). Club: Union League (N.Y.C.). Home: 947 Post Rd Wakefield RI 02879-7521

MORRISON, FRED LAMONT, law educator; b. Salina, Kans., Dec. 12, 1939; s. Earl F. and Madge Louise (Glass) M.; m. Charlotte Foot, Dec. 27, 1971; children: Charles, Theodore, George, David. AB, U. Kans., 1961; BA, Oxford (Eng.) U., 1963, MA, 1968; PhD, Princeton U., 1967; JD, U. Chgo., 1967. Bar: Minn. 1973. Asst. prof. law U. Iowa, Iowa City, 1967-69; assoc. prof. law U. Minn., Mpls., 1969-73, prof. law, 1973-90, prof., 1990—, acting dean, 1994-95, Oppenheimer Wolff and Donnelly prof., 1990—; counselor on internat. law U.S. State Dept., Washington, 1982-83; of counsel Popham, Haik, Schnobrich & Kaufman, Mpls., 1983—. mem. adv. com. on internat. law U.S. Dept. State, Washington, 1987-89; mem. internat. adv. bd. Inst. on Internat. Law, Kiel, Fed. Republic of Germany, 1989—. Home: 1412 W 47th St Minneapolis MN 55409-2204 Office: U Minn Law Sch 229 19th Ave S Minneapolis MN 55455-0444

MORRISON, GARY BRENT, hospital administrator; b. Anamosa, Iowa, Aug. 30, 1952; s. Kenneth Dale and Norma Elizabeth (Higgens) M.; children: Daniel, Lindsay. BA Polit. Sci., U. Mich., Dearborn, 1975; M Health Svc. Adminstrn., U. Mich., 1978. With Univ. Hosp. Univ. Mich., Ann Arbor, 1975-78, Robert Packer Hosp., Sayre, Pa., 1978-88; assoc. adminstr. St. Mary's Hosp., Rochester, Minn., 1988-90, adminstr., 1990-93; exec. v.p., COO Scott & White Meml. Hosp., Temple, Tex., 1993—. Dir. Tex. State Tech. Coll.; mem. Airport Adv. Bd.; bd. dirs. Better Bus. Bur., Temple Free Clinic, Temple Edn. Found. Mem. Am. Coll. Healthcare Execs. (diplomate), Tex. Assn. Pub. and Not-for-Profit Hosps. (bd. dirs.). Office: Scott & White Meml Hosp 2401 S 31st St Temple TX 76508-0001

MORRISON, GEORGE HAROLD, chemist, educator; b. N.Y.C., Aug. 24, 1921; s. Joseph and Beatrice (Morel) M.; m. Annie Foldes, Oct. 19, 1952; children—Stephen, Katherine, Alfred. B.A., Bklyn. Coll., 1942; Ph.D., Princeton, 1948. Instr. chemistry Rutgers U., 1948-50; research chemist AEC, 1949-51; head inorganic and analytical chemistry Gen. Tel. & Electronic Labs., 1951-61; prof. chemistry Cornell U., 1961—; chmn. com. analytical chemistry NAS-NRC, 1965-77; Internat. Francqui chair U. Antwerp, Belgium, 1989. Editor Analytical Chemistry, 1980-91; contbr. articles to profl. jours. Served with AUS, 1943-46. Recipient Benedetti-Pichler award Am. Microchem. Soc., 1977, Ea. Analytical Symposium Jubilee award, 1986, Pitts. Analytical Chemistry award Soc. for Analytical Chemists of Pitts., 1990; NSF sr. fellow U. Calif., San Diego, 1967-68, Guggenheim fellow, U. Paris, Orsay, 1974-75, NIH sr. fellow Harvard Med. Sch., 1982-83. Mem. Am. Chem. Soc. (award analytical chemistry 1971), Soc. Applied Spectroscopy (award 1975), Sigma Xi. Office: Cornell Univ Baker Lab Chemistry Ithaca NY 14853

MORRISON, GILBERT CAFFALL, psychiatrist; b. Beaumont, Tex., Feb. 28, 1931; s. Frank William and Ardis Emma (Caffall) M.; m. Betty Joyce Neville, June 28, 1952; children: Kay Morrison Mammen, Keith Neville, Kimberly Sue Morrison Pelz, Christopher Gilbert. Student, Southwestern U., 1948-50; B.S., Tulane U., 1952, M.D., 1957; Ph.D., So. Calif. Psychoanalytic Inst., 1978. Intern Touro Infirmary, New Orleans, 1957-58; resident in psychiatry Cin. Gen. Hosp. U. Cin., 1958-60; fellow in child psychiatry Children's Psychiat. Center, U. Cin., 1960-62, asst. prof. child psychiatry, 1964-68; with So. Calif. Psychoanalytic Inst., 1968-73; clin. prof. psychiatry and child psychiatry dept. psychiatry and human behavior U. Calif., Irvine, 1968—; practice medicine specializing in psychiatry, child psychiatry, psychoanalysis and family psychiatry Newport Beach, Irvine, Calif., 1973—; supervising and tng. psychoanalyst So. Calif. Psychoanalytic Inst., Los Angeles, 1978. Author, editor: Emergencies in Child Psychiatry, 1975. Served to lt. comdr. M.C. USNR, 1962-64. Fellow Am. Psychiat. Assn. (life), Am. Orthopsychiat. Assn., Am. Acad. Child Psychiatry, Am. Psychoanalytic Assn.; mem. Orange County Coun. Child Psychiatry (pres. 1975-76). Home: 22382 Valdemosa Mission Viejo CA 92692-1194 Office: 7700 Irvine Center Dr Ste 210 Irvine CA 92718-2924

MORRISON, GORDON MACKAY, JR., investment company executive; b. Boston, Jan. 18, 1930; s. Gordon Mackay and Alice (Blodgett) M.; m. Barbara J. Lee, June 15, 1954; children: Lee, Leighton, Faith. AB, Harvard U., 1952, MBA, 1954. Regional mgr. Bankers Leasing Corp., Boston, 1965-68; portfolio mgr. Loomis, Sayles and Co., Boston, 1969-71; sr. v.p. Ft. Hill Investors Mgmt., Boston, 1972-75; chmn. bd. Bradford Gordon, Inc., Boston, 1976—; trustee East Boston Savs. Bank, 1962-91, Meridian Mut. Holding Co., 1991—. Bd. dirs. The New Eng. Hosp., 1961—. Republican. Congl. Club: Harvard. Lodge: Masons. Home: 32 Old Orchard Rd Sherborn MA 01770-1037 Office: Bradford Gordon Inc 50 Congress St Boston MA 02109-4002

MORRISON, HARRY, chemistry educator, university dean; b. Bklyn., Apr. 25, 1937; s. Edward and Pauline (Sommers) M.; m. Harriet Thurman, Aug. 23, 1958; children: Howard, David, Daniel. BA, Brandeis U., 1957; PhD, Harvard U., 1961. NATO-NSF postdoctoral fellow Swiss Fed. Inst., Zurich, 1961-62; rsch. assoc. U. Wis., Madison, 1962-63; asst. prof. chemistry Purdue U., West Lafayette, Ind., 1963-69, assoc. prof., 1969-76, prof., 1976—, dept. head, 1987-92, dean Sch. Sci., 1992—; acad. adv. com. Indsl. Rsch. Inst., 1993-96; bd. dirs. Lilly Industries. Contbr. numerous articles to profl. jours. Bd. fellows Brandeis U. Mem. Am. Chem. Soc., Am. Soc. Photobiology, Internat. Photochem. Soc., Coun. for Chem. Rsch. (chmn. 1995), Phi Beta Kappa, Sigma Xi. Office: Purdue U Sci Adminstrn Sci Adminstrn Math Bldg West Lafayette IN 47907-1390

MORRISON, HELENA GRACE, guidance counselor; b. Neillsville, Wis., Aug. 20, 1957; d. Harold Allen and Nettie Stella (Schafer) Freedlund; m. William James Morrison, Sept. 11, 1981; 1 child, Meghan Marie. BS, U. Wis., Stevens Point, 1980; MEd, Nat. Louis U., Evanston, Ill., 1990; cert., Western Ky. U., 1994, postgrad. Cert. guidance counselor; cert. tchr. Tchr. grades 2 through 3 Pittsville (Wis.) Elem. Sch., 1980-82; tchr. grade 2 Vernon Parish Schs., Leesville, La., 1987-88; tchr. grade 3 Dept. Def. Dependant Schs., Vogelweh, Germany, 1989-92; student svcs. specialist, tchr. gifted edn. LaRue County Schs., Hodgenville, Ky., 1993—, gifted coord., 1995—; leader grade 3 team Vogelweh Elem. Sch., 1990-92; editor Hodgenville Elem. Sch. Yearbook, editor HES News, 1993—. Statistician Kaiserslantern Softball, Vogelweh, 1991; coach girls softball LaRue County Softball, Hodgenville, 1994. Mem. ASCD, Nat. Geog. Soc., Ky. Assn. for Gifted Edn., Ky. Counseling Assn. Avocations: softball, bicycling, sewing, reading. Home: 3220 Dangerfield Rd Hodgenville KY 42748-9223 Office: Hodgenville Elem Sch 208 College St Hodgenville KY 42748-1404

MORRISON, HOWARD IRWIN, computer services executive; b. Bklyn., Aug. 16, 1929; s. Philip Oscar and Anne Sylvia (Eisler) M.; m. Barbara May Kraut, Aug. 8, 1936 (dec. 1967); children: Peter, Scott, Dina; m. Joyce Elaine White, June 18, 1977. BA in Govt., George Washington U., 1951. Dir. computer divsn. CEIR Inc., Arlington, Va., 1956-61; pres. Computer Concepts, Silver Spring, Md., 1961-64; sr. v.p. Computer Applications Inc., N.Y.C., 1964-70; exec. v.p. Auerbach Pubrs., Inc., Phila., 1971-76; chmn. Delphi Sys. Inc., Burlington, Mass., 1976-80; pres. Arthur D. Little Sys., Burlington, Mass., 1976-80, Morrison Assocs., Sudbury, Mass., 1981-82; sr. v.p. Datacom Sys., Inc., N.Y.C., 1982-83; pres. PC Telemart Inc., Fairfax, Va., 1983-84; sr. v.p. Centel Info. Sys., Reston, Va., 1984-88; sr. v.p. comml. sales C3, Inc., Herndon, Va., 1989-90; prin. Morrison Assocs. Inc., Herndon, 1990-93; sr. v.p. Sistex, Inc., Rockville, Md., 1992-96; pres. Sistex, Inc., Rockville, 1996—; sr. v.p. CAS Inc., Rockville, Md., 1994-96; pres. Sistex Inc., Rockville, Md., 1996—. Author: A Computer Executives View of USSR, 1972. With USN, 1948-53. Democrat. Jewish. Home: 118 Monroe St Rockville MD 20850

MORRISON, JAMES FREDERICK, consultant; b. Evanston, Ill., Aug. 12, 1933; s. Paul Leslie and Carolyn Lola (Rosemeier) M.; m. Myra Val Wokoun, June 22, 1957; children: Myra Hollie Morrison Nielsen, Cynthia Leslie Morrison Karlsson. BA, Northwestern U., 1955, MBA, 1958. CPA, Wis. Accounting mgr. Froedtert Malt Corp., Milw., 1958-61; asst. controller, asst. v.p. Northwestern Nat. Ins. Co., Milw., 1961-65; controller Eutectic Welding Alloys Corp., Flushing, N.Y., 1965-68; internal auditor Sterling Drug, N.Y.C., 1968-69; controller Internat. Flavors and Fragrances, N.Y.C., 1970-76; mng. dir., v.p. Europe Internat. Flavors and Fragrances, London, 1977-80; v.p. new bus. group U.S. Internat. Flavors and Fragrances, N.Y.C., 1981-84; v.p. export and communications U.S. Internat. Flavors and Fragrances, Hazlet, N.J., 1984-96; cons., 1996—. Co-chmn. Milw. Festival of Arts, 1964-65; mem. Manhasset (N.Y.) Bd. Edn., 1970-75, v.p., 1975; bd. dirs. United Way Monmouth County, 1991—, chmn. priorities com., 1992, 93, strategic planning com., 1995—. 1st lt. USAF, 1955-57. Mem. AICPA, Fin. Execs. Inst. (pres. L.I. chpt. 1975-76), Internat. Trade Facilitation Coun. (vice-chmn. 1991—), Wis. Soc. CPA's, Internat. Commerce Club N.J., Systems and Procedures Assn. (pres. Milw. chpt. 1965), Eastern Sr. Golf Assn. (treas. 1994—), Beta Gamma Sigma. Presbyterian. Avocation: golf. Home: 14 Circle Dr Rumson NJ 07760-1112 Office: Internat Flavor & Fragrances 600 State Hwy 36 Hazlet NJ 07730

MORRISON, JAMES IAN, research institute executive; b. Irvine, Scotland, Dec. 22, 1952; came to U.S., 1985; s. James Morrison and Janet Miller (McCondach) Munro; m. Nora Cadham, Dec. 6, 1980; children: David, Caitlin. BPhil, U. Newcastle-upon-Tyne, Eng., 1976; MA, U. Edinburgh, Scotland, 1974; PhD, U. B.C., Can., 1985. Isntr. B.C. Inst. Tech., Vancouver, 1980-85; rsch. assoc. U. B.C., Vancouver, 1980-85; rsch. fellow Inst. for the Future, Menlo Park, Calif., 1985-86, dir. health care rsch. program, 1986—, pres., 1990—; bd. dirs. Interim Svcs., Ft. Lauderdale, Fla.; mem. corp. adv. bd. Bristol-Myers Squibb, Princeton, N.J., 1992—; mem. UNIS Press Adv. Bd, 1990—. Co-author: Looking Ahead at American Health Care, 1988, Directing the Clinical Laboratory, 1990, System in Crisis: The Case for Health Care Reform, 1991, Reforming the System: Containing Health Care Costs in an Era of Universal Coverage, 1992, Future Tense: The Business Realities of the Next Ten Years, 1994, The Second Curve: Managing the Velocity of Change, 1996; contbr. articles to profl. jours. Mem. environ. scanning com. United Way of Am., 1990—. Social Sci. Rsch. Coun. scholar U. Newcastle-upon-Tyne, 1974-76. Avocation: golf. Office: Inst for the Future 2744 Sand Hill Rd Menlo Park CA 94025-7020

MORRISON, JAMES R., retired banker; b. Duluth, Minn., May 1, 1924; s. Earl Angus and Jessie (McLean) M.; m. Clarice Mae Wolf, June 5, 1949; children—Kenneth, Alan, Jane, Richard. M.B.A., U. Chgo., 1976. Br. mgr. Parkersburg State Bank, Iowa, 1947-49; asst. cashier Bank of Sparta, Wis., 1949-50; cashier Tobacco Exchange Bank, Edgerton, Wis., 1950-53; sr. v.p. Fed. Res. Bank Chgo., 1953-89, ret.; bd. dirs. Bank of Tokyo-Mitsubishi Chgo.; chmn. subcom. on credits and discounts Fed. Res. Sys., Chgo., 1984-86; mem. Mt. Prospect Fin. Commn., 1989—. Served with U.S. Army, 1943-46, ETO.

MORRISON, JAMES WILLIAM, JR., lobbyist, government relations consultant; b. Bluefield, W.Va., Jan. 14, 1936; s. James William and Winnie Ella (Hendricks) M.; B.A., W.Va. State Coll., 1957; M.P.A., U. Dayton (Ohio), 1970; m. Marva Elizabeth Tillman, Aug. 8, 1957 (div.); children: Traquita Renee, James William, III. Inventory mgr. Dayton Air Force Depot/Def. Electronics Supply Center, 1959-63; mgmt. specialist Air Force Logistics Command, Dayton, 1963-72; exec. asst. to dir. mgmt. systems NASA, Washington, 1972-74; sr. mgmt. asso. Exec. Office of Pres., Office Mgmt. and Budget, 1974-79; asst. dir. econ. and govt. U.S. Office Personnel Mgmt., 1979, dir. congl. rels., 1979-81, assoc. dir. compensation, 1981-87; sr. mgr. CNA Ins. Co., 1987-88; pres. Morrison Assocs., 1988—; vis. lectr. pub. exec. project State U. N.Y., Albany, 1974-76. Mem. adv. com. Dayton Bd. Edn., 1971. Served to 1st lt. U.S. Army, 1957-59. Recipient Sustained Superior Performance award Def. Supply Agy., 1963; Exceptional Service award Exec. Office Pres., Office Mgmt. and Budget, 1977; Disting. Service award U.S. CSC, 1978; Presdl. cert. of Appreciation, 1979; award for meritorious service Office of Personnel Mgmt., 1980; Presdl. rank award meritorious exec., 1983; award for disting. service Office Personnel Mgmt., 1984; Presdl. Rank award-Disting. Exec., 1985. Mem. Alpha Phi Alpha, Pi Delta Phi, Pi Alpha Alpha. Democrat. Presbyterian. Contbr. articles to profl. jours. Home: 11311 Morning Gate Dr North Bethesda MD 20852 Office: 1000 Potomac St NW Ste 401 Washington DC 20007-3501

MORRISON, JEANETTE HELEN **See LEIGH, JANET**

MORRISON, JOEL LYNN, cartographer, geographer; b. Johnsville, Ohio, July 19, 1940; s. James Everett Morrison and Janet Maxine Rogers Rumpf; m. Carolyn Lee Coffman McVey, June 23, 1962 (div. May 1972); Ashley Scott, Anja Lynne; m. Beverly Sargent, Dec. 14, 1974; stepchildren: Anne Marie Hudson, Jane Elizabeth Hudson. BA cum laude, Miami U., Oxford, Ohio, 1962; MS, U. Wis., 1964, PhD, 1968. From instr. to prof. U. Wis., Madison, 1968-83, chmn. dept. geography, 1977-80; sr. sci. advisor for geography Nat. Mapping div. U.S. Geol. Survey, Reston, Va., 1983-86, asst. div. chief for rsch., 1986-95; geography divsn. chief U.S. Bur. Census, Washington, 1995—; adj. prof. U. Md., College Park, 1983-87; fellow Newberry Libr., 1974; adv. editor Rand McNally Corp., 1971—; chmn. U.S. Bd. on Geog. Names, 1995—; mem. bd. direction Internat. Union Surveying and Mapping, 1985-87, Nat. Ctr. for Geog. Info. and Analysis, 1990-94; mem. U.S. nat. com. for internat. geog. union NAS, NRC, 1985-92; pres. Am. Congress on Surveying and Mapping, 1981-82, pres. Internat. Cartographic Assn., 1984-87; speaker and presenter in field. Sr. author: Elements of Cartography, 6th edit., 1995; chief editl. cons. Atlas of North America, 1985; editor-in-chief Mapping Scis. and Remote Sensing, 1984—; sr. cons. Goode's World Atlas, 19th edit., Rand McNally Co., Chgo., 1995; contbr. chpts. to books, numerous articles to profl. jours. NDEA Title IV fellow, 1962-65. Mem. URISA, Assn. Am. Geographers, Am. Congress on Surveying and Mapping, Am. Soc. for Photogrammetry and Remote Sensing, AM/FM Internat., Cosmos Club, Phi Beta Kappa, Omicron Delta Kappa, Phi Eta Sigma, Pi Mu Epsilon. Home: 2022 Turtle Pond Dr Reston VA 22091 Office: US Bur Census Washington DC 20233-7400

MORRISON, JOHN HADDOW, JR., engineering company executive; b. Bozeman, Mont., Aug. 24, 1933; s. John Haddow Sr. and Rosalie (Lehrkind) M.; m. Shirley Easbey, Sept. 11, 1954; children: Robert, Richard. BS, Mont. State U., 1955. Registered profl. engr., Mont., Nev., Utah, Ariz., Oreg., Calif.; registered land surveyor, Mont. Project engr. Morrison-Maierle, Inc., Helena, Mont., 1957-64, chief airport design, 1967-73, chief exec. officer, 1973-88, chmn., 1988—, also bd. dirs. Bd. dirs. Mont. State U. Found., Inc., 1983—, chmn. 1992-94; sec.-treas. Helena YMCA, 1977-80. With U.S. Army 1955-57. Mem. ASCE, NSPE (pres. Helena chpt. 1968-69, Outstanding Young Engr., Helena chpt. 1965), Cons. Engrs. Council Mont. (past sec., past v.p., pres. 1986-87). Methodist. Lodges: Optimists (pres. 1976); Masons. Avocations: golf, photography. Home: 201 N Hannaford St Helena MT 59601-4725 Office: Morrison Maierle Inc 910 Helena Ave PO Box 6147 Helena MT 59604

MORRISON, JOHN HORTON, lawyer; b. St. Paul, Sept. 15, 1933. BBA, U. N.Mex., 1955; BA, U. Oxford, 1957, MA, 1961; JD, Harvard U., 1962. Bar: Ill. 1962, U.S. Supreme Ct. 1966. Assoc., Kirkland & Ellis, Chgo., 1962-67, ptnr., 1968—. Named Officer Most Excellent Order Brit. Empire, 1994; Rhodes scholar. Mem. ABA, Ill. Bar Assn., Internat. Bar Assn., Chgo. Bar Assn. Home: 2717 Lincoln St Evanston IL 60201-2042 Office: Kirkland & Ellis 200 E Randolph St Chicago IL 60601-6436

MORRISON, JOHN LEWIS, former food company executive, investor; b. Mpls., Apr. 6, 1945; s. John Washburn and Charlotte (Lewis) M.; m. Christine Anderson, June 23, 1967; children—Kelly, John. B.A., Yale U., 1967; M.B.A., Harvard U., 1971. V.p. Kidder, Peabody & Co., Inc., N.Y.C., 1971-76; asst. treas. Pillsbury Co., Mpls., 1976-79; gen. mgr. Pillsbury-Mex., Mex. City, Mex., 1979-81; group v.p. Pillsbury Internat., Mpls., 1981-84; pres. Pillsbury Internat. Group, Mpls., 1984-87; exec. v.p., chmn. consumer food group Pillsbury Internat. Group; mng. dir. Goldner Hawn Johnson & Morrison Inc., Mpls., 1989—; Bd. dirs. Diamond Brands Internat., Human Capital Corp. Bd. dirs. 1978-79, Abbott-Northwestern Hosp., Mpls., 1978—, Mpls. Inst. Arts, 1985—. Recipient All-Am. award in Hockey, NCAA, 1967; particpant U.S. Olympic Hockey Team, Grenoble, France, 1968; Mallory award Yale U., New Haven, 1967. Republican. Presbyterian. Clubs: Woodhill Country (bd. dirs. 1984—), Mpls. (bd. dirs. 1987—), Links (N.Y.C.), Mill Reef (Antigua). Avocation: sports. Office: By Holding Inc 7171 France Ave S Minneapolis MN 55435-4304*

MORRISON, JOHN MARTIN, lawyer; b. McCook, Nebr., June 18, 1961; s. Frank Brennor and Sharon Romain (McDonald) M.; m. Catherine Helen Wright, Aug. 17, 1991; 1 child, Allison Kay. BA, Whitman Coll., 1983; JD, U. Denver, 1986. Bar: Mont. 1987, U.S. Dist. Ct. Mont. 1988, U.S. Ct. Appeals (9th cir.) 1989, U.S. Supreme Ct., 1996. Legis. asst., legal counsel U.S. Senate, Washington, 1987-88; ptnr. Morrison Law Offices, Helena, Mont., 1988-93, Meloy & Morrison, Helena, 1994—. Contbr. articles to profl. jours. Alt. del. Dem. Nat. Conv., N.Y.C., 1980; del. Dem. Nat. Platform Com., 1992. Recipient Lewis F. Powell/ACTL/Bur. of Nat. Affairs Advocacy awards, 1986. Mem. ATLA, Mont. Bar Assn., Mont. Trial Lawyers Assn. (pres.-elect, bd. dirs. 1991—), Western Trial Lawyers Assn. (bd. govs. 1990-95), Trial Lawyers Pub. Justice (chair 1989-90). Avocations: skiing, fly fishing, mountain climbing, river rafting, running. Office: Meloy & Morrison 80 S Warren St Helena MT 59601-5700

MORRISON, KARL FREDERICK, history educator; b. Birmingham, Ala., Nov. 3, 1936; s. Karl and Gladys (McConatha) M.; m. Anne Blunt, Aug. 29, 1964; children: Andrew, Sarah. BA, U. Miss., 1956; MA, Cornell U., 1957, PhD, 1961. Acting instr. history Stanford U., 1960-61; instr. U. Minn., 1961-62, asst. prof., 1962-64; asst. prof. Harvard U., 1964-65; assoc. prof. U. Chgo., 1965-68, prof., 1968-84, chmn. dept. history, 1970-76; Ahmanson-Murphy disting. prof. Medieval and Renaissance history U. Kans., Lawrence, 1984-88; Lessing prof. history and poetics Rutgers U., New Brunswick, N.J., 1988—; vis. asst. prof. Columbia U., N.Y.C., summer 1963; vis. prof. Princeton U., 1992; mem. faculty selection com. U. Cyprus, 1991—; vis. mem. Inst. for Advanced Study, 1966-67, 76-77; v.p. Midwest Medieval Conf., 1975-76, pres., 1976-77. Author: The Two Kingdoms, 1964, Rome and the City of God, 1964, Carolingian Coinage, 1967, Tradition and Authority in the Western Church, 1969, Europe's Middle Ages, 1970, The Mimetic Tradition of Reform in the West, 1982, I am You: The Hermeneutics of Empathy in Western Literature, Theology and Art, 1988, History as a Visual Art in the Twelfth-Century Renaissance, 1990, Understanding Conversion, 1992, Conversion and Text, 1992; contbr. articles to Speculum, other jours. in field. Bd. trustees Princeton Cmty. Housing Inc., 1994—. Recipient award in humanities McKnight Found., 1963; Guggenheim fellow, 1987. Fellow Medieval Acad. Am. (counsellor 1972-75, orator of fellows 1996—, Haskins medal 1994); mem. Am. Hist. Assn., Medieval Assn. Midwest (pres. 1977-78), Medieval Assn. Mid-Am. (pres. 1988-89), Internat. Mus. Surg. Scis. and Hall of Fame (bd. dirs. 1982-84). Office: Rutgers U Dept History 5059 New Brunswick NJ 08903

MORRISON, KENNETH DOUGLAS, author, columnist; b. Mpls., Apr. 1, 1918; s. Kenneth Mortimore and Florence Myrtle (Sutton) M.; m. Helen Curtis, Feb. 25, 1943; children: Kenneth D., Sally, Steven C., Mary. A.B., Carleton Coll., 1940; grad. study, U. Miami, 1940-41, U. Minn., 1941. Free lance writer Mpls., 1941; editor publs. Minn. Dept. Conservation, 1942-47; Minn. rep. to Nat. Audubon Soc., 1947-49, dir. pub relations, editor Audubon mag., 1949-56, v.p., 1955-56; dir. Mountain Lake Sanctuary and Singing Tower Am. Found., 1956-80, dir. environ. concerns, 1980-82, fellow, 1982-83; syndicated nature-conservation newspaper columnist 4 papers, 1985—; Audubon tour lectr., 1958-63; interviewer naturalists Wildlife Unltd., TV sta. WOR-TV, N.Y.C., 1951- 52; Mem. Minn. Bird Commn., 1951-54; trustee emeritus Fla. Nature Conservancy; trustee Fla. Conservation Found.; v.p., trustee Conservation 70's; mem. Gov. Fla. Natural Resources Com., State Parks Adv. Council, 1971-79. Author: Favorite Birds of America, 1951, Favorite Animals of America, 1951, Mountain Lake Almanac, 1984; Compiler: (with Mrs. M. E. Herz) Where to Find Birds In Minnesota, 1950. Bd. dirs. Defenders Wildlife; adv. bd. Webber Coll., 1969—. Recipient Gov. Fla. Wildlife Conservation award, 1960, Gulf Oil Conservation award, 1982, Feinstone Environ. award SUNY, 1987, Carleton Coll. Disting. Achievement award, 1990. Mem. Wilson Ornithol. Soc., Wilderness Soc., Cornell U. Ornithol. Lab., Fla. Audubon Soc. (pres., Award of Merit 1964, Cruickshank Conservation award 1993), Hawk Mountain Sanctuary Assn. (bd. sponsors), Nature Conservancy, Sierra Club, Friends of Earth, Pi Delta Epsilon. Methodist. Home: 1351 Hollister Rd Babson Park FL 33827-9684 *We ought to keep in mind that we are mammals and that we need to renew regularly our contact with the basic, simple life of soil, sun, water, animals and trees.*

MORRISON, MABLE JOHNSON, business technology educator; b. Carthage, Miss., July 13, 1930; d. Horace Lawrence and Mable Barnette Johnson; children: Lisa Susan Stone, Rayburn Holmes Bates Jr. BS in Commerce, U. Miss., 1952; MEd, Miss. State U., 1976. Cert. tchr. bus. edn., mktg. Bus. tchr. Clinton (Miss.) Pub. Schs., 1952-53; sec. Jackson (Miss.) Pub. Schs., 1954-64, tchr. bus., 1964-69, tchr., coord. mktg., 1971-78; instr. bus. Jones County Jr. Coll., Ellisvile, Miss., 1978-84; instr. bus. tech. Miss. Gulf Coast C.C., Gautier, 1984-92. Mem. Am. Vocational Assn., Delta Kappa Gamma, Phi Beta Lambda (adviser, Outstanding Adviser 1991). Episcopalian. Avocations: gardening, volunteer work. Home: 3100 Phil Davis Rd Ocean Springs MS 39564-9076

MORRISON, MANLEY GLENN, real estate investor, former army officer; b. Weston, W.Va., July 29, 1915; s. Henry Frank and Alice (Riffle) M.; m. Ida Lerlene Johnson, Dec. 12, 1942 (dec. 1982); children: Manley James (dec.), Richard Glenn, Sandra Lynn.; m. Samma Annette Muffley, July 30, 1983. B.S., U. Md., 1958; M.A., Am. U., 1960; postgrad., U. Pitts., 1961, Ind. U., 1968; grad., Command and Gen. Staff Coll., Ft. Leavenworth, Kans., 1956, Army War Coll., Carlisle Barracks, Pa., 1960, DeVry Inst. Tech., 1974; D.H.L., Mass. Coll. Optometry, 1973. Table waiter Mills Cafeteria, Columbus, Ohio, 1935-36; mgr. Speer's Cafe, Twin Falls, Idaho, 1937-38; exec. chef steward U.P. R.R., Sun Valley, Idaho, 1939-42; commd. 2d lt. U.S. Army, 1942, advanced through grades to brig. gen., 1969; chief statis. analysis Hdqrs. EUCOM and USAREUR, Berlin, Nurnberg, Heidelberg, 1948-52; chief Manpower Div., Office Surgeon Gen., Washington, 1952-55; comptroller Walter Reed Army Med. Center, Washington, 1956-59; dir. adminstrn. and asst. exec. officer Office Surgeon Gen., Washington, 1960-62; chief of systems analysis Office of Mgmt., dep. chief of staff for logistics Dept. Army Gen. Staff, Washington, 1962-64; exec. officer, dir. personnel and adminstrn. Office of Surgeon, Hdqrs. U.S. Army Europe, Heidelberg, 1964-67; exec. officer Office of Comptroller, Office Army Surgeon Gen., Washington, 1967-69; chief of Army Med. Service Corps, Washington, 1969-73; ret., 1973, self-employed as real estate investor, 1973—. Community Scout leader, Heidelberg, 1948-52; bd. dirs. Teen Clubs, Am. Youth Assocs., Heidelberg, 1967; chmn. Residents' Coun. Freedom Pla., Peoria, Ariz. Decorated D.S.M., Legion of Merit, Bronze Star, Commendation medal with oak leaf cluster. Mem. Assn. Mil. Surgeons U.S., Alumni Assn. Army War Coll., Fed. Health Care Execs. Inst. Alumni Assn., Baylor U. Alumni Assn., Phi Kappa Phi, Pi Sigma Alpha. Republican. Club: Union Hills Country (Sun City, Ariz.) (bd. dirs. 1985-86, pres.). Lodge: Masons. Home: 13373 N Plaza Del Rio Blvd #7764 Peoria AZ 85381-4874 *I have sincerely tried to assess each problem and challenge in a positive manner. Once the decision has been made and an objective plan established, I have attempted to achieve the objectives while avoiding what I consider the most Common Mistakes of Man: (1) the delusion that individual advancement is made by crushing others, (2) the tendency to worry about things that cannot be changed or corrected, (3) insisting that a thing is impossible because we cannot accomplish it, (4) neglecting development and refinement of the mind and not acquiring the habit of reading and studying, (5) refusing to set aside trivial preference, (6) attempting to compel other persons to believe and live as we do, (7) attempting to quantify in mathematical terms the depth of human experience.*

MORRISON, MARCY, state legislator; b. Watertown, N.Y., Aug. 9, 1935; m. Howard Morrison; children: Liane, Brenda. BA, Queens Coll., 1957; student, Colo. Coll., U. Colo. Mem. Colo. Ho. of Reps., awd, 1992—; mem. judiciary, health, environ., welfare and instns. coms. Mem. Manitou Springs (Colo.) Sch. Bd., 1973-83, pres., 1980-82, County Park Bd., 1976-83, State Bd. Health, 1985-93, pres., 1988-90, Mountain Scar Commn., 1989, Future Pub. Health, 1989-90, Health Policy Commn., 1990-92; commr. El Paso County, 1985-92, chmn., 1987-89; active Citizens Goals, United Way. Named Outstanding Sch. Bd. Mem., Pikes Peak Tchrs. Assn., 1978, Woman of Spirit, Penrose-St. Francis Hosp. Sys., 1991. Mem. LWV, Health Assn. Pikes Peake Area, Women's Edn. Assn., El Paso Mental Health Assn. Republican. Jewish. Home: 302 Sutherland Pl Manitou Springs CO 80829-2722 Office: Colo Ho of Reps State Capitol Denver CO 80203*

MORRISON, MARTHA KAYE, photolithography engineer; b. San Jose, Calif., Oct. 5, 1955; d. Myrle K. and Arthena R. Morrison; 1 child, Katherine A. AA, West Valley Coll., Saratoga, Calif., 1978. Prodn. worker Signetics Co., Sunnyvale, Calif., 1973-75, equipment engr., 1976-78, 79-80, prodn. supr., 1978-79; expediter Monolithic Memories, Sunnyvale, 1975-76; photolithography engr. KTI Chems., 1980-81; founder, chief engr., CEO Optalign, Inc., Livermore, Forest Ranch, Calif., 1981—; participant West Valley Coll. Tennis Team # 1 Singles and Doubles, 1976-78; regional profl. ranking NCTA Opens Singles/Doubles, 1982-85, 93, 94, 95, rankings 15-20 singles/#2-#8 doubles; instr. tennis Chico Racquet Club, 1994, Butte Creek Country Club, 1995—; participant exhbn. tennis match with Rosie Cosals and Billie Jean King, 1994. Dir. benefit Boys & Girls Club of Chico. Named Champion Chico Open Finalist Woodridge Open, 1994, 1993 #2 NCTA Women's Open Doubles, Doubles #3, 1994, Tracy Open, 1996. Mem. USPTA (cert.), Tennis Profl. Chico Racquet Club, Butte Creek Country Club. Office: PO Box 718 Forest Ranch CA 95942-0718

MORRISON, MARTIN EARL, computer systems analyst; b. Oakland, Calif., Mar. 28, 1947; s. Raymond Earl and June (Cabral) M. AB with distinction, U. Calif., Berkeley, 1967, MA, 1969, postgrad., 1969-73. Certified (life) nat. tournament dir.; cert. jr./community coll. tchr. (life), Calif. Instr. classics and English composition U. Calif. at Berkeley, 1967-73; instr. legal argument Boalt Hall Law Sch., 1972; with exec. office CF Air Freight, Inc., 1979-83, asst. to traffic mgr. for spl. projects, 1982-83, computer systems mgr., 1982-83; computer systems analyst Qantel Bus. Computers, 1983-86, sr. computer systems analyst, 1986-92; sr. tech. writer Shared Med. Systems, 1992—. Author: Writing Argument, 1972, USCF Yearbooks, 1974-76, Official Rules of Chess, 1975, 77, Chess Competitor's Handbook, 1980, Latin Works for Transparent Language Computer Program, 1992-93; editor: Chess Voice, 1968-73, Keeping Ancient Rome Alive, 1987-89; chess editor: Oakland Tribune, 1965-66; columnist Via Lorenzo, 1987-88, Metric Today, 1985—; pub., bus. mgr. Chess Life & Rev., 1977-78. Asst. concertmaster Berkeley Community Chorus and Orch., 1980-83; concertmaster Oakland Philharm., 1987-90, bd. dirs., corp. sec., 1988-90; 1st violin Albany Trio, 1987—; vol. staff Chabot Sci. Ctr., 1981-84, chmn. computer system mgmt. staff; sec., treas. AstroSoft, 1983-87. Schola Gregoriana San Francisco, 1989—, Schola Cantemus, 1992—. Fellow U.S. Metric Assn. (chmn. consumer edn. com. 1984—, Spl. Citation 1986, cert. advanced metrication specialist 1987); mem. Am. Philol. Assn., Am. Classical League, Eastbay Astron. Soc. (bd. dirs. 1981-84, v.p. 1983-84), Internat. Assn. Chess Press (v.p. 1973-77), Chess Journalists Assn. (pres. 1972-75), World Chess Fedn. (internat. life arbiter, mem. rules com. 1973-78, chmn. 1976-78), U.S. Chess Fedn. (bd. dels. 1968-78, 1st v.p. Pacific Region 1972-73, nat. sec. 1972-75, tech. dir. 1973-76, exec. dir. 1976-78, Spl. Svc. award 1985, Disting. Svc. award 1995), Calif. Alumni Assn. (life, scholarship com., chmn. 1987-93, Disting. Chmn. award 1990), San Lorenzo Garden Homes Assn. (v.p./sec. 1985-86, pres. 1986-92), Phi Beta Kappa. Home: 136 Loma Verde Dr San Lorenzo CA 94580-1782

MORRISON, MICHAEL GORDON, university president, clergyman, history educator; b. Green Bay, Wis., Mar. 9, 1937; s. Gordon John and Gertrude (Crilly) M. A.B., St. Louis U., 1960, M.A., 1965, Ph.L., 1965, S.T.L., 1969; Ph.D., U. Wis., 1971. Ordained priest Roman Catholic Ch., 1968. Joined S.J., 1955; asst. v.p. acad. affairs Marquette U., Milw., 1974-77; v.p. acad. affairs Creighton U., Omaha, 1977-81, acting pres., 1981, pres., 1981—, dir.; mem. governing bd. Creighton Prep. Sch., 1993—. Bd. dirs. Health Future Found., 1983—, Xavier U., 1992—, Omaha 100 Inc., 1991—; mem. cons. com. SAC, 1988—; mem. adv. bd. Salvation Army, 1992—; trustee Duchesne Acad. of Sacred Heart, 1995—. Recipient Human Rights award Anti-Defamation League, 1982, Humanitarian award Nat. Conf. Christians and Jews, 1989. Mem. Assn. Jesuit Colls. and Univs. (bd. dirs.), Assn. Ind. Colls. and Univs. Nebr. (bd. dirs. 1981—), Nat. Assn. Ind. Colls. and Univs. (bd. dirs. 1993—),Greater Omaha C. of C. (bd. dirs. 1993—), Alpha Sigma Nu, Beta Alpha Psi. Office: Creighton U 2500 California St Omaha NE 68178-0001

MORRISON, PATRICE B., lawyer; b. St. Louis, July 8, 1948; d. Frank J. and Loretta (S.) Burgert; m. William Brian Morrison, Aug. 12, 1969; 1 child, W. Brett. AB, U. Miami, 1971, MA, 1972; JD, Am. U., 1975; LLM in Taxation, Georgetown U., 1978. Bar: Fla. 1975, D.C. 1977, N.Y. 1983. Atty. U.S. Dept. Treas., Washington, 1975-79; atty., ptnr. Nixon Hargrave Devans & Doyle, LLP, Palm Beach County, Fla., 1980-89, Nixon, Hargrave, Devans & Doyle, LLP, Rochester, N.Y., 1989—; bd. dirs. Cloverwood Devel., Inc. Author: (jour.) The Practical Lawyer, 1986, 91. Bd. dirs. Alzheimer's Assn., Rochester, 1990-95, Nat. Women's Hall of Fame, 1990-92; mem. Rochester Women's Network; mem. exec. com. Estate Planning Coun. Rochester, 1992-95. Mem. Am. Immigration Lawyers Assn. Republican. Office: Nixon Hargrave Devans & Doyle LLP PO Box 1051 Clinton Sq Rochester NY 14603

MORRISON, PERRY DAVID, librarian, educator; b. Mpls., Nov. 30, 1919; s. Arthur D. and Vera Mae (Perry) M.; m. Catherine Jean Gushwa, Apr. 22, 1946 (dec. Oct. 1991). A.A., Pasadena City Coll., 1940; A.B., Whittier Coll., 1942, M.A., 1947; B.L.S., U. Calif., Berkeley, 1949, D.L.S., 1961. Asst. Huntington Library, San Marino, Calif., 1947-48; asst. univ. librarian, head social sci. librarian U. Oreg., Eugene, 1949-63; prof. Sch. Librarianship U. Oreg., 1967-82, prof. emeritus, 1982—, dean Sch. Librarianship, 1970-73, coordinator library research, univ. library, 1978-82, part-time reference librarian, 1982-89, acting asst. univ. librarian, 1979-80; coll. librarian, dir. library sci. program Sacramento State Coll., 1963-65; assoc. prof. U. Wash. Sch. Librarianship, 1965-67; cons. Monash U. Library, Australia, 1975-76, Central Oreg. Community Coll., 1977, Victoria State Coll., Toorak, Melbourne St. Coll., Kevin Grove St. Coll., Australia, 1980, Portland Community Coll., 1981, Treaty Oak Ednl. Dist., Oreg., 1983; dir. various Office Edn. Insts., 1968-75; mem. grant award appraisal panels Office Edn., Washington, 1972-74. Author: Career of the Academic Librarian, 1969; contbr. numerous articles, revs. to profl. jours.; editorial bd. Serials Libr., 1978-92, Social and Behavioral Scis. Libr., 1978-92; issue editor: Libr. Trends. 1981; compiler: A Journey Through Time: The Oregon Library Association, 1940-90. Mem. adv. bd. Lane County Law Libr., 1986-92; treas. Residents Assn. Cascade Manor, Eugene, Oreg., 1993-95; active Learning in Retirement Program com. U. Oreg., 1993-95. Capt. U.S. Army, 1942-46. Mem. ALA (life), Spl. Librs. Assn. (hon. life, pres. Oreg. chpt. 1974-75), Oreg. Libr. Assn. (hon. life, pres. 1961-62), Pacific N.W. Libr. Assn. (editor and bus. mgr. jour. 1967-71), Assn. Coll. and Rsch. Librs. Assn. (coms.), Lane County Assn. Oreg. Pub. Employees Retirement System (pres. 1985-86), U. Oreg. Ret. Profs. Assn., Faculty Club U. Oreg. (treas. 1981-82). Democrat. Mem. United Ch. of Christ. Home: 65 W 30th Ave Apt 416 Eugene OR 97405-3373 Office: Library U Oreg Eugene OR 97403

MORRISON, PORTIA OWEN, lawyer; b. Charlotte, N.C., Apr. 1, 1944; d. Robert Hall Jr. and Josephine Currier (Hutchison) M.; m. Alan Peter Richmond, June 19, 1976; 1 child, Anne Morrison. BA in English, Agnes Scott Coll., 1966; MA, U. Wis., 1967; JD, U. Chgo., 1978. Bar: Ill. 1978. Ptnr. Rudnick & Wolfe, Chgo., 1978—, also chmn. real estate dept., mem. governing policy com.; lectr. in field. Mem. ABA, Am. Coll. Real Estate Lawyers, Chgo. Bar Assn. (real property com., subcom. real property fin., alliance for women), Pension Real Estate Assn., Chgo. Fin. Exch., Chgo. Real Estate Women. Office: Rudnick & Wolfe 203 N La Salle St Ste 1800 Chicago IL 60601-1210

MORRISON, RAYMOND EARL, JR., engineering executive; b. Latham, N.Y., Dec. 3, 1941; s. Raymond Earl, Sr., and Mary Ellen (Doran) M.; m. Christine Marie Owocki, Oct. 22, 1982; children—Arianne, Michael, Janine. A.A.S., Hudson Valley Community Coll., 1967; B.S., SUNY-Oswego, 1964; M.S., Syracuse U., 1970; Ph.D., U. Mo., 1975. Tng. mgr. Los Alamos Nat. Lab., N.Mex., 1975-80, sr. budget, fiscal analyst, 1980-83; exec. dir. High Tech. Adv. Council, Atlanta, 1983-87; exec. dir. Assn. Media Based Continuing Edn. for Engrs. Inc., Atlanta, 1987-89; cabinet mem. Indsl./Tech. Edn. State of Ark., 1989-91; editor The Evolution of Engring. Tech. in the Field of Engring. Edn., 1990-92; cons. Morrison & Assocs., Los Alamos, 1970-75, State Dept. Edn., Atlanta, 1983-84, William T. Grant Found., 1991; internal cons. U. Calif., Los Alamos, 1980-83, Los Alamos Tech. Assn., 1979-81. Contbr. articles to profl. jours. Mem. bd. reviewers Los Alamos Schs. Credit Union, 1979-81; mem. exec. com. Private Industry Council, Santa Fe, N.M., 1980-82. Recipient Outstanding Contbn. to Engring. Tech. Edn. in State of Ga., 1987, Cert. of Recognition Ark. Assn. for Continuing and Adult Edn., 1991. Mem. Nat. Soc. Profl. Engrs., Soc. Automotive Engrs. (sec. 1968-69), Am. Soc. Engring. Edn. (dir. 1979-82, S.I.G. chmn. 1980), Am. Psychol. Assn., AAAS, Soc. Mfg. Engrs., Rotary Internat. Home: 3051 Woodlake Ct Marietta GA 30062-5451 Office: Lockheed Martin Aeronautical Systems D/90-21 Z/0311 86 S Cobb Dr Marietta GA 30063

MORRISON, ROBERT LEE, physical scientist; b. Omaha, Nov. 22, 1932; s. Robert Alton and Lulu Irene (Ross) M.; m. Sharon Faith Galliher, Feb. 19, 1966; children: Dennis, Karyn, Cheryl, Tamara, Traci. BA, U. Pacific, Stockton, Calif., 1957, MS, 1960. Chief chemist Gallo Winery, Modesto, Calif., 1957-66; rsch. scientist Lawrence Livermore Nat. Lab., Livermore, Calif., 1966-69, sr. rsch. scientist, 1973-93; pres. Poolinator, Inc., Gardena, Calif., 1970-72; owner R.L. Morrison Techs., Modesto, 1993—; cons., speaker, presenter in field. Contbr. numerous articles to profl. jours.; patentee in field. Recipinet Excellence in Nuclear Weapons award U.S. Dept. Energy, 1990, others. Mem. Am. Chem. Soc. Avocations: flying, skiing, scuba diving, photography. Home: 1117 Springcreek Dr Modesto CA 95355-4820

MORRISON, ROBERT LEWIN, lawyer; b. Waukegan, Ill., Feb. 26, 1947; s. Robert L. Morrison; m. Nancy Gaye; children: Robert, Patrick. BS in Econs., DePauw U., 1969; JD, U. Mich., 1972. Bar: Calif., 1972. Joined Pillsbury, Madison & Sutro, L.A., 1972, ptnr., 1977—; faculty lender liability litigation PLI, 1989; speaker, lectr. in field. Assoc. editor U. Mich. Law Rev. Mem. State Bar Calif., L.A. County Bar, L.A. Jr. C. of C., Fin. Lawyers Conf., Phi Beta Kappa, Omicron Delta Epsilon (hon.), Order of Coif. Office: Pillsbury Madison & Sutro Citicorp Plz 725 S Figueroa St Ste 1200 Los Angeles CA 90017-5443

MORRISON, ROBERT TOWNSEND, nephrologist; b. Boston, Dec. 26, 1951; s. Robert Stier and Marie Day (Townsend) M.; m. Margaret Lou Dougherty, July 10, 1976; children: Sarah Marie, Samuel Thomas. BS, Rensselaer Poly. Inst., 1976; student, Columbia U., 1981; MD, Albany Med. Coll., 1985. Assoc. Herbert F. Gold and Assocs., Brookline, Mass., 1976; ins. claims adjuster GAB Adjustment Corp., Boston, 1976-78; lab. technician Rockefeller U., N.Y.C., 1980-81; resident in internal medicine USAF Med. Ctr., Wright-Patterson AFB, Ohio, 1985-88; fellow in nephrology Wilford Hall USAF Med. Ctr., Lackland AFB, Tex., 1988-90; chief nephrology svc. 13th Air Force Med. Ctr., Republic of Philippines, 1990-91, David Grant USAF Med. ctr., Travis AFB, Calif., 1991-94; med. dir., CEO, chief nephrology GMH Dialysis Ctr., Xenia, Ohio, 1994—; nephrologist, internist Med. Svc. Assocs., Xenio, Ohio, 1994—; asst. clin. prof. medicine U. Calif. at Davis, Sacramento, 1991-94, Wright State U. Sch. Medicine, Dayton, Ohio, 1995—; nephrology cons. Pacific Air Command, USAF, Clark AB, The Philippines, 1990-91; instr. Uniformed Svcs. U. Health Scis., 1988-90. Author jour. articles and abstracts. Co-chair combined fed. campaign United Way of Solano County, 1993-94; chmn. drives ARC, Albany, N.Y., 1982-83; chmn. Hunger Task Force of Riverside Ch., 1979-81. Maj. USAF, 1985-94, Res., 1994—. Mem. ACP, Nat. Kidney Found., Soc. Air Force Physicians, Am. Soc. Nephrology, Greene County Med. Soc. (bd. dirs.), Ohio Med. Assn., Sigma Chi (pres. chpt. 1975-76). Democrat. Avocations: running, camping, hiking, movies, theater. Home: 126 W North College St Yellow Springs OH 45387-1563 Office: Med Svc Assocs 1182 N Monroe Dr Xenia OH 45385

MORRISON, ROGER BARRON, geologist; b. Madison, Wis., Mar. 26, 1914; s. Frank Barron and Elsie Rhea (Bullard) M.; BA, Cornell U., 1933, MS, 1934; postgrad. U. Calif., Berkeley, 1934-35, Stanford U., 1935-38; PhD, U. Nev., 1964; m. Harriet Louise Williams, Apr. 7, 1941 (deceased Feb. 1991); children: John Christopher, Peter Hallock and Craig Brewster (twins). Registered profl. geologist, Wyo. Geologist U.S. Geol. Survey, 1939-76; vis. adj. prof. dept. geoscis. U. Ariz., 1976-81, Mackay Sch. Mines, U. Nev., Reno, 1984-86; cons. geologist; pres. Morrison and Assocs., Ltd., 1978—; prin. investigator 2 Landsat-1 and 2 Skylab earth resources investigation projects NASA, 1972-75. Fellow Geol. Soc. Am.; mem. AAAS, Internat. Union Quaternary Rsch. (mem. Holocene and paleopedology commns., chmn. work group on pedostratigraphy), Am. Soc. Photogrammetry, Am. Soc. Agronomy, Soil Sci. Soc. Am., Internat. Soil Sci. Soc., Am. Quaternary Assn., Am. Water Resources Assn., Colo. Sci. Soc., Sigma Xi, Colorado Mountain Club. Author 3 books, co-author one book, co-editor 2 books; editor: Quaternary Nonglacial Geology, Conterminous U.S., Geol. Soc. Am. Centennial Series, vol. K-2, 1991; mem. editorial bd. Catena, 1973-88; contbr. over 150 articles to profl. jours. Research includes Quaternary geology and geomorphology, hydrogeology, environ. geology, neotectonics, remote sensing of Earth resources, paleoclimatology, pedostratigraphy. Office: 13150 W 9th Ave Golden CO 80401

MORRISON, SAMUEL FERRIS, secondary school educator; b. Glasgow, Scotland, Oct. 7, 1941; came to U.S., 1949; s. Thomas Green and Susan (McCaskill) M.; m. Kathryn Emily Schnaible, Aug. 14, 1971; 1 child, Ian James. BA, U. Wyo., 1968, MEd, 1985. Tchr. social studies Platte County Sch. Dist. 1, Wheatland, Wyo., 1968—, athletic dir., 1987—. With U.S. Army, 1963-65. Mem. NEA, Wyo. Edn. Assn., Platte County Edn. Assn. (pres. 1972-73). Democrat. Presbyterian. Avocations: golf, woodworking, photography. Home: 200 Front Rd Wheatland WY 82201-9158 Office: Wheatland Jr High Sch 13 And S Oak St Wheatland WY 82201

MORRISON, SCOTT DAVID, computer company engineer, telecommunications company engineering supervisor; b.Duluth, Minn., May 8, 1952; s. Robert Henry and Shirley Elaine (Tester) M.; m. Jana Louise Bergeron, May 29, 1976; children: Robert Scott, Matthew John. Cert. in welding, Duluth Area Inst. Tech., 1971; student U. Wis.-Superior, 1976-77, BA Concordia Coll., 1988, St. Paul, Minn., MBA St. Thomas University, St. Paul, Minn., 1991. Cert. in quality tech., Am. Soc. Quality Control and St. Paul Tech. Vocat. Inst., 1985; lic. vocat. instr., Minn., 1984. Assoc. in Mfg. Mgmt., North Hennepin Community Coll., 1985; cert. welder Litton Ship Systems, Pascagoula, Miss., 1971-72, Barko Hydraulics, Superior, Wis., 1972-76; welder and cert. level II non-destructive examination inspector Am. Hoist and Derrick Co., Mpls., 1978-80; quality supr. Colight Inc., Mpls., 1980, Tol-O-Matic, Inc., Mpls., 1980-82; quality assurance engr. ADC Telecommunications, Mpls., 1982-84, design assuranceengr., 1985-86, product assurance engr. engr. in devel. test procedures for telecommunications equipment Brit. Telcom Test Labs., Ipswich, West Midlands, Eng.,1986, 1986-1987, sr. product assurance engr., quality improvement facilitator, 1987-88, product engring supr. 1988-90, supervisor design assurance, quality assurance, component engring., 1990-92; dir. quality and reg. affairs Waters Instruments, Inc., 1992-96, sr. quality engr., corp. ops. Compaq Computer Corp., Houston, Texas, 1996—; Judge, U.S. Amateur Boxing Fedn., Mpls., 1978-87, 95—; examiner Minn. Quality award Minn. Coun. for Quality, 1993, 95; mem. quality coun. Am. Electronics Assn., 1994-95; mem. bd. dirs. Rochester Quality Coun., 1994-95; examiner Malcolm Baldridge Nat. Quality award Nat. Inst. Standards and Technology, 1994-95, sr. examiner, 1996—; adj. instr. Riverland Technical Coll., Rochester, Minn., 1995; lic. profl. boxing judge Tex. Dept. Licensing and Regulation, 1996—; cert. lead auditor British Standards Instn., 1996. Adjunct Instr. Anna Maria College, Graduate Program in Total Quality Mgmt., Falmouth, Cape Cod, Mass., 1996—; Recipient Technical Excellence award ADC Telecomms., 1987, 88. Mem. ASTM, Am. Soc. Quality Control (cert. quality engr. cert. quality auditor, quality mgr., chmn. host and attendance subcom. 1986-87), Am. Welding Soc., Soc. Mfg. Engrs., Internat. Platform Assn. Roman Catholic. also: Compaq Computer Corp 20555 SH 249 Houston TX 77070

MORRISON, SHELLEY, actress; b. N.Y.C., Oct. 26, 1936; d. Maurice Nissim and Hortense (Alcouloumre) Mitrani; m. Walter R. Dominguez, Aug. 11, 1973. Student, L.A. City Coll., 1954-56. Actress: (films) Interns, 1962, The Greatest Story Ever Told, 1964, Castle of Evil, 1965, Divorce, American Style, 1965, How to Save a Marriage, 1966, Funny Girl, 1967, Three Guns for Texas, 1969, Man & Boy, 1971, Blume in Love, 1972, McKenna's Gold, 1967, Breezy, 1973, People Toys, 1973, Rabbit Test, 1975, Max Dugan Returns, 1982, Troop Beverly Hills, 1988, (TV movies) Three's a Crowd, 1969, Once an Eagle, 1974, The Night That Panicked America, 1975, Kids Don't Tell, 1984, Cries From the Heart, 1994, (TV series) Laredo, 1965-67, The Flying Nun, 1966-70, First and Ten, 1987, I'm Home, 1990, The Fanelli Boys, 1990, Love, Lies and Murder, 1990, Playhouse 90, Dr. Kildare, The Fugitive, Gunsmoke, Marcus Welby, and many others, 1960-70, Man of the People, Sisters, 1991, 92, Murder She Wrote, 1992, Johnny Bago, 1993, Columbo, 1993, L.A. Law, 1994, Live Shot, 1995, Courthouse, numerous others, (stage prodns.) Pal Joey, 1956, Bus Stop, 1956, Only in America, 1960, Orpheus Descending, 1960, Spring's Awakening, 1962, over 65 other prodns., 1956-1970; prodr., writer live shots, 1975—. Condr. seminars (with husband Walter Dominquez) about Native Americans to keep traditions and ceremonies flourishing. Honored (with husband Walter Dominguez) for work with homeless City of L.A., 1985, for work during L.A. riots, 1992. Mem. SAG, AFTRA, Actors Equity Assn. Democrat.

MORRISON, SHIRLEY MARIE, nursing educator; b. Stuttgart, Ark., June 13, 1927; d. Jack Vade Wimberly and Mabel Claire (Dennison) George; m. Dana Jennings Morrison, Mar. 12, 1951 (dec. Dec. 1995); children: Stephen Leslie, Dana Randall, William Lee, Martha Ann Morrison Carson. Diploma, Bapt. Hosp. Sch. Nursing, Nashville, 1949; BSN, Calif. U., Fullerton, 1977; MSN, Calif. U., L.A., 1980; EdD, Nova Southeastern U., 1987. RN, Tex., Calif.; cert. pub. health nurse, Calif.; cert. secondary tchr., Calif. Staff nurse perinatal svcs. Martin Luther Hosp., Anaheim, Calif., 1960-77, relief 11-7 house supr., 1960-77; dir. vocat. nursing program Inst. Med. Studies, 1978-81; mem. faculty BSN program Abilene (Tex.) Intercollegiate Sch. Nursing, 1981-92, dir. ADN program, 1992—; prof. adv. bd. Nurse Care, Inc., Abilene, 1988—. Mem. adv. bd. parent edn. program Abilene Ind. Sch. Dist., 1985—; active Mar. Dimes, Abilene, 1990—, Ednl. Coalition for Bob Hunter, Abilene, 1994; bd. dirs. Hospice Big Country, Abilene, 1987—. Grantee NIH, 1992. Mem. Nat. Orgn. Assn. Degree Nurses (mem. program com. 10th anniversary nat. conv.), Tex. Orgn. Assoc. Degree Nurses, So. Nursing Rsch. Soc. (rsch. presenter), Health Edn. Resource Network Abilene (founding mem., pres. elect, pres. 1995-96). Democrat. Methodist. Avocations: traveling, reading. Home: PO Box 2583 Abilene TX 79604 Office: Abilene Intercollegiate Sch Nursing 2149 Hickory St Abilene TX 79601-2339

MORRISON, STEPHEN GEORGE, lawyer; b. Pasadena, Calif., Aug. 10, 1941; s. Ira George and Virginia Lee (Zimmer) M.; m. Gail Louise Moore, June 10, 1972; 1 child, Gregory Stephen. BBA, U. Mich., 1971; JD, U. S.C., 1975. Ptnr. Nelson, Mullins, Riley & Scarborough, Columbia, S.C., 1975—; adj. prof. U. S.C., Columbia, 1973-75, 82—; pres. Defense Rsch. Inst., 1995; presenter in field. Author/editor: Products Liaibility Pretrial Notebook, 1989, South Carolina Appellate Practice Handbook, 1986. Bd. dirs. S.C. Com. Humanities, Columbia, 1986—, S.C. Gov. Sch. Arts, Columbia, 1988-95; pres., bd. dirs. Richland County Pub. Defender Assn., Columbia, 1991-95. Fellow S.C. Bar Found.; mem. Internat. Assn. Defense Coun., Lawyers for Civil. Justice (bd. dirs. 1995—). Democrat. Episcopalian. Avocations: fishing, country music, chamber music, physics, history. Home: 2626 Stratford Rd Columbia SC 29204 Office: Nelson Mullins Riley & Morrison 1330 Lady St 3d Fl Columbia SC 29201

MORRISON, TONI (CHLOE ANTHONY MORRISON), novelist; b. Lorain, Ohio, Feb. 18, 1931; d. George and Ella Ramah (Willis) Wofford; m. Harold Morrison, 1958 (div. 1964); children: Harold Ford, Slade Kevin. B.A., Howard U., 1953; M.A., Cornell U., 1955. Tchr. English and humanities Tex. So. U., 1955-57, Howard U., 1957-64; editor Random House, N.Y.C., 1965—; assoc. prof. English SUNY, Purchase, NY, 1971-72; Schweitzer Prof. of the Humanities SUNY, Albany, NY, 1984-89; Robert F. Goheen Prof. of the Humanities Princeton Univ., Princeton, NJ, 1989—; Visiting prof., Yale Univ., 1976-77, Bard Coll., 1986-88. Author: The Bluest Eye, 1969, Sula, 1973 (National Book award nomination 1975, Ohioana Book award 1975), Song of Solomon, 1977 (National Book Critics Circle award 1977, American Acad. and Inst. of Arts and Letters award 1977), Tar Baby, 1981, (play) Dreaming Emmett, 1986, Beloved, 1987 (Pulitzer Prize for fiction 1988, Robert F. Kennedy Book award 1988, Melcher Book award Unitarian Universalist Assn. 1988, National Book award nomination 1987, National Book Critics Circle award nomination 1987), Jazz, 1992, Playing in the Dark: Whiteness and the Literary Imagination, 1992, Nobel Prize Speech, 1994; editor: The Black Book, 1974, Race-ing Justice, En-Gendering Power: Essays on Anita Hill, Clarence Thomas, and the Construction of Social Reality, 1992; lyricist: Honey and Rue, 1992. Recipient New York State Governor's Art award, 1986; Washington College Literary award, 1987; Elizabeth Cady Stanton award National Organization for Women; Nobel prize in Literature Nobel Foundation, 1993. Mem. Author's Guild (council). Office: Princeton U Dept Creative Writing 185 Nassau St Princeton NJ 08544-2003 also: care Suzanne Gluck Internat Creative Mgmt 40 W 57th St New York NY 10019-4001*

MORRISON, TROY LEE, religious organization administrator; b. Oct. 3, 1931; m. Frances A. Gunter, Aug. 10, 1952; children: Marsha Buttram, J. Mark. BS, Jacksonville State U., 1954; BD, So. Bapt. Theol. Sem., 1962, MDiv, 1973, DMin, 1977. Rural diversified farmer, 1931-49; technician Reigal Textile Corp., 1950-51; salesman Belk-Hudson Clothing, 1951-52, Am. Bankers Ins., 1952-54; asst. prin., tchr. Alexandria H.S., Anniston, Ala.,

1954-55; co-owner, internal coord. Gunter-Morrison Bldg. Supply Co., Piedmont, Ala., 1957-58; pastor Bethlehem Bapt. Ch., Springfield, Ky., 1959-62, First Bapt. Ch., Carrollton, Ky., 1962-64, Southside Bapt. Ch., Gadsden, Ala., 1964-66, Farmdale Bapt. Ch., Louisville, 1966-68, 12th St. Bapt. Ch., Gadsden, 1968-85; cluster coord., dir. ch.-min. rels., dir. chaplaincy Ala. Bapt. State Conv., Montgomery, 1985-90, exec. sec.-treas., 1990—. Contbr. articles to profl. jours. Bd. dirs. Cmty. Svcs., Gadsden, Bapt. Meml. Hosp., Gadsden, Bapt. Hosp. Found., Gadsden, Ala. Retarded Citizens, Gadsden, Babe Ruth Baseball Found., Gadsden, Croyle's Big Oak Ranch for Homeless Boys, Gadsden; mem. Zoning Bd. Adjustment, Gadsden; pres. Human Rels. Bi-Racial Coun., Gadsden; mem. Coosa Valley Youth Svcs. for Delinquent Youth, Anniston, Ala.; mem. profl. consultation com. Children's Hosp., Birmingham, Ala.; mem. doctoral com. Sch. Nursing, U. Ala. Birmingham. Recipient Am. Legion Patriotism award; named Ala. Col., State. of Ala. Mem. Lions Club (Piedmont), Piedmont C. of C., Rotary Club (Carrollton), Kiwanis Club, Civitan Club (bd. dirs., sec.-treas., pres.), Gadsden C. of C., Kappa Phi Kappa, Sigma Tau Delta, Scabbard and Blade. Avocations: fishing, golf, bowling, watching college and professional sport events. Home: 2234 Sagewood Dr Montgomery AL 36117

MORRISON, VAN, musician, songwriter; b. Belfast, Ireland, Aug. 31, 1945; s. George and Violet Morrison; 1 child, Shana. Founder, lead singer rock group Them, 1964-67, albums include Them, 1965, Them Again, 1966, Them featuring Van Morrison, 1972; solo career, 1967—; albums include Blowin' Your Mind, 1967, Astral Weeks, 1968, Moondance, 1968, Best of Van Morrison, 1970, His Band and Street Choir, 1970, Tupelo Honey, 1971, St. Dominic's Preview, 1972, Hard Nose the Highway, 1973, It's Too Late To Stop Now, 1974, TB Sheets, 1974, Veedon Fleece, 1974, This Is Where I Came In, 1977, A Period of Transition, 1977, Wavelength, 1978, Into the Music, 1979, Common One, 1980, Beautiful Vision, 1982, Inarticulate Speech of the Heart, 1983, Live at the Grand Opera House Belfast, 1984, A Sense of Wonder, 1985, No Guru, No Method, No Teacher, 1986, Poetic Champions Compose, 1987, (with The Chieftains) Irish Heartbeat, 1988, Live for Ireland, 1988, Avalon Sunset, 1989, Enlightenment, 1990, The Best of Van Morrison, 1990, Hymns to the Silence, 1991, Bang Masters, 1991, The Best of Van Morrison, 1993, Too Long in Exile, 1993, A Night in San Francisco, 1994, Days Like This, 1995; composer numerous hit singles including Gloria, 1965, Brown Eyed Girl, 1967, Moondance, 1968, Domino, 1970, Wild Night, 1971.

MORRISON, WALTON STEPHEN, lawyer; b. Big Spring, Tex., June 16, 1907; s. Matthew Harmon and Ethel (Jackson) M.; m. Mary Lyon Bell, Dec. 19, 1932. Student Tex. A&M U., 1926-28; J.D., U. Tex., 1932. Bar: Tex. 1932. Asso., Morrison & Morrison, Big Spring, 1932-36, ptnr., 1939, 46; atty. County of Howard, 1937-39, judge, 1941-42, 47-48; atty. City of Big Spring, 1949-58; sole practice, Big Spring, 1953—; lectr. Am. Inst. Banking. Served with USAF, 1942-46. Fellow Tex. Bar Found., Am. Coll. Probate Counsel; mem. Tex. City Attys. Assn. (pres. 1955-56), Am. Judicature Soc., Tex. Bar Assn., ABA. Baptist. Clubs: Rotary (pres. 1949), Masons, Shriner. Home: 1501 E 11th Pl Big Spring TX 79720-4903 Office: PO Box 792 113 E 2nd St Big Spring TX 79720-2502

MORRISON, WILLIAM DAVID, lawyer; b. Phila., Aug. 19, 1940; s. Maxey Neal and Mary Fuller (Chase) M.; m. Barbara Heath, Aug. 25, 1962 (div.); children: David Conrow, Stephen Munro, John Pomeroy; m. Sandra Elizabeth Butter, Mar. 16, 1983; children: Charles, Nicholas, Sophie Natasha. BA, Princeton U., 1962; LLB, Yale U., 1965. Bar: N.Y. 1966, Calif. 1975. Assoc. Winthrop, Stimson, Putnam & Robert, N.Y.C., 1965-74; ptnr. Erickson & Morrison, and predecessor firms, Los Angeles, 1974-78, LeBoeuf, Lamb, Leiby & Macrae, N.Y.C., 1978-88, Bryan Cave, St. Louis, 1988—; lectr. on Saudi Arabian law. Active Internat. Inst. for Strategic Studies. Mem. ABA, Assn. Bar City of N.Y., Calif. Bar Assn., Internat. Bar Assn., The Pilgrims, Brooks, Marks Club, Whites, Annabel's, RAC Club (London), Princeton Club (N.Y.C.). Author chpt. in Saudi Arabia: Keys to Business Success, 1981; contbr. articles to profl jours. Home: 34 Norland Sq. London England Office: Bryan Cave, 29 Queen Anne's Gate, London SW1H 9BU, England

MORRISON, WILLIAM FOWLER, JR., health care consultant; b. Wilmington, N.C., June 26, 1928; s. William Fowler and Gladys (Polvogt) M.; m. Patricia Biggs; children: William Stephen, Janet Elizabeth, Nancy Elise. A.B. in Biology, Johns Hopkins, 1949; hosp. adminstrv. residency, Rex Hosp., Raleigh, N.C., 1949-51. Asst. dir. Ch. Home and Hosp., Balt., 1953-55; dir. Ch. Home and Hosp., 1955-65; dir. coll. hosps. Med. Coll. Va., 1965-69; pres. New Hanover Regional Med. Ctr., Wilmington, N.C., 1969-90; mem. faculty Sch. Hosp. Adminstrn., Med. Coll. Va., 1965-90; cons. in field. Author articles. Bd. dirs. Blue Cross Va., 1968-69, Va. Hosp. Assn., 1968-69, Md., D.C., Del. Hosp. Assn., 1964-65, N.C. Hosp. Assn., 1975-77, 79-82, Health Scis. Found., 1975-90; mem. N.C. State Health Coordinating Coun., 1979-86. Served with USAF, 1951-53. Mem. Am. Coll. Health Care Execs. (life), Sigma Phi Epsilon. Lutheran. Home: 8740 Bald Eagle Ln Wilmington NC 28405-9317

MORRISS, FRANK, film editor. Editors: (TV movies) Duel, 1971, The Law, 1974, The Execution of Pvt. Slovik, 1974, (films) Charley Varrick, 1973, Ode to Billy Joe, 1976, First Love, 1977, I Wanna Hold Your Hand, 1978, Youngblood, 1978, Hometown, U.S.A., 1979, Inside Moves, 1980, Whose Life Is It, Anyway?, 1981, The Earthling, 1981, (with Edward Abroms) Blue Thunder, 1983 (Academy award nomination best film editing 1983), (with Donn Cambern) Romancing the Stone, 1984 (Academy award nomination best film editing 1984), American Flyer, 1985, Short Circuit, 1986, Hot to Trot, 1988, (with Dallas Puett) Disorganized Crime, 1989, (with Puett) Bird on a Wire, 1990, Short Time, 1990, (with Tony Lombardo) The Hard Way, 1991, Point of No Return, 1993, Another Stakeout, 1993. Office: care Motion Picture Editors 7715 W Sunset Blvd Ste 220 Los Angeles CA 90046-3912

MORRISS, FRANK HOWARD, JR., pediatrics educator; b. Birmingham, Ala., Apr. 20, 1940; s. Frank Howard Sr. and Rochelle (Snow) M.; m. Mary J. Hagan, June 29, 1968; children: John Hagan, Matthew Snow. BA, U. Va., 1962; MD, Duke U., 1966. Diplomate Am. Bd. Pediatrics, Am. Bd. Perinatal and Neonatal Medicine. Intern Duke U. Med. Ctr., Durham, N.C., 1966-67, resident in pediatrics, 1967-68, fellow in neonatology, 1970-71; fellow in neonatology U. Colo., Denver, 1971-73; asst. prof. to prof. U. Tex. Med. Sch., Houston, 1973-86; prof. U. Iowa Coll. Medicine, Iowa City, 1987—, chmn. dept., 1987—. Editor: Role of Human Milk in Infant Nutrition and Health, 1986; contbr. numerous articles to profl. jours, chpts. to books. Lt. comdr. USN, 1968-70. NIH grantee, 77-87, 90—. Mem. Am. Pediatric Soc., Soc. Pediatric Rsch., Am. Acad. Pediatrics, Soc. Gynecol. Investigation, Midwest Soc. Pediatric Rsch., Assn. Med. Sch. Pediatric Dept. Chmn. Methodist. Avocation: tennis. Office: U Iowa Hosps & Clinics Dept Pediatrics Iowa City IA 52242

MORRISSETTE, BRUCE ARCHER, Romance languages educator; b. Richmond, Va., Apr. 26, 1911; s. James Archer and Mary (Bell) M.; m. Dorothy Behrens, Oct. 12, 1940; 1 child, James. B.A., U. Richmond, 1931, Litt.D., 1975; Docteur d'Université, Clermont-Ferrand, France, 1933; Ph.D., Johns Hopkins U., 1938. Jr. instr. French Johns Hopkins U., 1934-38; from asst. prof. to prof. Romance langs. Washington U., St. Louis, 1938-62; vis. prof. U. Wis., 1962; prof. French lit. U. Chgo., 1962—, mem. bd. publs., 1963-66, chmn. dept. Romance langs. and lits., 1967-70, 73-76, Bernard E. and Ellen C. Sunny Disting. Service prof., 1974—; vis. prof. U. Ill. at Urbana, 1967-68, U. Calif. at Los Angeles, 1969; Fulbright lectr. U. Western Australia, 1969; lectr. colls., univs. Author: L'Esthétique symboliste, 1933, Life and Works of Mlle Desjardins, 1947, The Great Rimbaud Forgery, 1956, La Bataille Rimbaud, 1959, Les Romans de Robbe-Grillet, 1963, Alain Robbe-Grillet, 1966, The Novels of Robbe-Grillet, 1975, Intertextual Assemblage from Topology to the Golden Triangle, 1979, Novel and Film: Essays in Two Genres, 1985; also numerous articles; assoc. editor: French Rev. and Symposium, 1963-69, Modern Philology, 1974-79, Critical Inquiry, 1976—. Mem. Christian Gauss Prize Award Com., 1967-69. Decorated chevalier Ordre des Palmes Academiques, France, 1962; chevalier Ordre du Mérite National France, 1980. Mem. Modern Lang. Assn. Am. (exec. council 1962-66), AAUP, Am. Assn. Tchrs. French, Soc. des Professeurs Francais, Assn. Internat. des Etudes Francaises, Soc. des Rosettes et Rubans de France. Address: PO Box 167 Harbert MI 49115-0167

MORRISSEY, CHARLES THOMAS, historian, educator; b. Newton, Mass., Nov. 11, 1933; s. Leonard Eugene and Margaret (McCarthy) M. AB, Dartmouth Coll., 1956; MA, U. Calif., Berkeley, 1957. Instr. Dartmouth Coll., Hanover, N.H., 1961-62; oral historian Harry S. Truman Library, Independence, Mo., 1962-64; chief John F. Kennedy Libr. Oral History Project, Washington, 1965-66; dir. Vt. Hist. Soc., Montpelier, 1966-71, 73-75, Ford Found. Oral History Project, 1971-73; adj. prof. history U. Vt., Burlington, 1969-73, 75-85; vis. summer instr. in oral history Portland State U., 1979-82, 84—, Vt. Coll., Montpelier, 1985—; oral history cons. Oral History Inst., Montpelier, 1975—; dir. Oral History and Archives Office, Baylor Coll. Medicine, Houston, 1985—; bd. advisors Who's Who in the East; lectr. in field. Author: Vermont: A Bicentennial History, 1981, (with others) Vermont, 1985; editor: Oral History Assn. Newsletter, 1968-71, Vermont History, 1966-71, 73-76, Internat. Jour. Oral History, 1985-89; contbg. editor: Vermont Life mag., 1969-81, editor, 1982-83; also articles; radio commentator Sta. WDEV, Waterbury, Vt., 1982—. Recipient Harvey Kantor award New England Assn. Oral Historians, 1980. Fellow Ctr. for Research on Vt.; mem. Soc. Am. Archivists, Acad. Cert. Archivists, Oral History Assn. (pres. 1971-72), Am. Assn. for History of Medicine, Nat. Coun. on Public History (coun. 1980-82), Sharpshooters Club (North Fayston, Vt.), Cosmos Club (Washington).

MORRISSEY, DOLORES JOSEPHINE, insurance executive; b. N.Y.C., July 22; d. Joseph Lawrence and Madeleine Catherine (Curran) M. B.S., NYU, 1963, M.B.A., 1968. Sr. v.p., treas. Bowery Savs. Bank, N.Y.C., 1958-87; exec. v.p. Mut. of Am., N.Y.C., 1987-94, Mut. of Am. Capital Mgmt., N.Y.C., 1994—; bd. dirs. Mut. of Am., N.Y.C., 1972-85; pres. Mut. of Am. Investment Corp., 1989—; pres., CEO Mut. of Am. Instnl. Fund; mem. adv. commn. N.Y. State Comptroller Investment Adv. Com., N.Y.C., 1979-87. Dir. Yorkville Christian-Jewish Coun., N.Y.C., 1978—; past pres. Soroptimist Internat. of N.Y., N.Y.C. Mem. Money Marketeers of NYU, NYU Bus. Forum, Women's Bond Club, Women's Econ. Round Table, Alpha Kappa Delta. Roman Catholic. Avocations: travelling; photography; opera. Home: 180 East End Ave New York NY 10128-7763 Office: Mutual of America 320 Park Ave New York NY 10022

MORRISSEY, EDMOND JOSEPH, classical philologist; b. N.Y.C., June 5, 1943; s. William J. and Anne K. (Gaffney) M.; m. Patricia M. Hanlon, Oct. 11, 1987; children: William, Edmond, Patrick, Kathleen, Jennifer, Lisa, Paula. A.B. summa cum laude, Boston Coll., 1965; B.A., U. Oxford, 1967, M.A., 1971; M.A., Harvard U., 1969, Ph.D., 1974. Seminarian Pope John XXIII Nat. Sem., Weston, Mass., 1974-77; collaborator prof. Sterling Dow Harvard U., Cambridge, Mass., 1977-95; cons. in pub. and photoreprodn. Author: Studies in Inscriptions Listing the Agonistic Festivals, 1974, A Quinquagesimal History of the Church of St. Bernadette, 1987; contbr. articles to profl. jours. Pres., chmn. adminstrn. fin., St. Bernadette's Ch., Archdiocese of Boston, 1980—; founding dir. Theol. Lectures Series, Randolph, Mass., 1978—, Randolph Hist. Commn., 1988—; staff vol. Cardinal Medeiros Program for Handicapped, 1980-82; treas., bd. dirs. Randolph Community Food Pantry, 1994—. Marshall scholar, 1965-67; Wilson scholar, 1965—; Gen. Motors scholar, 1962-65; Ford Found. fellow, 1967-69; Harvard U. fellow, 1969-71. Mem. Am. Inst. Archaeology, Am. Philol. Assn., Alumni Assn. Harvard, Oxford U. Alumni Assn., Boston Coll. Alumni Assn. Democrat. Roman Catholic. Home: 4 Bennington St Randolph MA 02368-2106

MORRISSEY, FRANCIS DANIEL, lawyer; b. Chgo., June 28, 1930; m. Corinne Seither, 1989; children: Francis, Mary. A.B., St. Mary of the Lake U., 1952; J.D., Loyola U., Chgo., 1958. Bar: Ill. 1958, U.S. Dist. Ct. (no. dist.) Ill. 1958, U.S. Ct. Appeals (7th cir.) 1963, U.S. Ct. Appeals (D.C. cir.) 1978, U.S. Ct. Appeals (2d cir.) 1969, U.S. Ct. Appeals (5th cir.) 1972, U.S. Supreme Ct. 1962. Assoc. Baker & McKenzie, Chgo., 1958-62, ptnr., 1962—. Contbr. articles to legal jours. Recipient Francis J. Rooney St. Thomas More Loyola U., 1977, Medal of Excellence Loyola U. Chgo., 1988. Fellow Am. Coll. Trial Lawyers, Am. Bar Found.; mem. Nat. Conf. Bar Examiners (past chmn., pres.), Bd. Law Examiners Ill. (past pres.), Chgo. Bar Assn. (bd. mgrs.), Ill. Appelaate Lawyers Assn. (past pres.), Ill. Trial Lawyers Assn. Office: Baker & McKenzie 1 Prudential Plz 130 E Randolph St Chicago IL 60601

MORRISSEY, JOHN CARROLL, lawyer; b. N.Y.C., Sept. 2, 1914; s. Edward Joseph and Estelle (Caine) M.; m. Eileen Colligan, Oct. 14, 1950; children: Jonathan Edward, Ellen (Mrs. James A. Jenkins), Katherine, John, Patricia, Richard, Brian, Peter. BA magna cum laude, Yale U., 1937, LLB, 1940; JSD, N.Y. U., 1951; grad., Command and Gen. Staff Sch., 1944. Bar: N.Y. State 1940, D.C. 1953, Calif. 1954, U.S. Supreme Ct. 1944. Asso. firm Dorsey and Adams, 1940-41, Dorsey, Adams and Walker, 1946-50; counsel Office of Sec. of Def., Dept. Def., Washington, 1950-52; acting gen. counsel def. Electric Power Adminstrn., 1952-53; atty. Pacific Gas and Electric Co., San Francisco, 1953-70; assoc. gen. counsel Pacific Gas and Electric Co., 1970-74, v.p., gen. counsel, 1975-80; individual practice law San Francisco, 1980—; dir. Gas Lines, Inc. Bd. dirs. Legal Aid Soc., San Francisco; chmn. Golden Gate dist. Boy Scouts Am., 1973-75; commr. Human Rights Commn. of San Francisco, 1976-89, chmn., 1980-82; chmn. Cath. Social Svc. of San Francisco, 1966-68; adv. com. Archdiocesan Legal Affairs, 1981—; regent Archdiocesan Sch. of Theology, St. Patrick's Sem., 1994; dir. Presidio Preservation Assn., 1995—. Col. F.A. U.S. Army, 1941-46. Decorated Bronze star, Army Commendation medal. Mem. NAS, AAAS, ABA, Calif. State Bar Assn., Fed. Power Bar Assn., N.Y. Acad. Scis., Calif. Conf. Pub. Utility Counsel, Pacific Coast Electric Assn., Pacific Coast Gas Assn., Econ. Round Table of San Francisco, World Affairs Council, San Francisco C. of C., Calif. State C. of C., Harold Brunn Soc. Med. Rsch., Electric Club, Serra Club, Commonwealth Club, Yale Club of San Francisco (pres. 1989-90), Pacific-Union Club, Sometimes Tuesday Club, Sovereign Mil. Order Malta, Phi Beta Kappa. Roman Catholic. Home: 2030 Jackson St San Francisco CA 94109-2840 Office: PO Box 77000 123 Mission St Rm 1709 San Francisco CA 94177

MORRISSEY, THOMAS JEROME, investment banker; b. Racine, Wis.; s. Patrick William and Lillian (Mitchell) M.; PhB, U. Wis., 1940; postgrad. U. Ill., 1942, U.S. Naval Acad., 1942; m. Clovene Marie Nogel, Feb. 21, 1957. Merchandising trainee Vick Chem. div. Richardson-Merrill, Inc., N.Y.C., 1940-41, sales promotion asst., 1941-42, mgr. mil. sales, 1942; pvt. practice mktg. and fin. cons., N.Y.C., 1952-54; dir. mktg. rsch. Pharmacraft Labs. div. Seagrams Distillers, Inc., N.Y.C., 1946-48, mgr. sales promotion, 1948-49, gen. sales mgr., 1949-52; asst. to pres. Turner-Smith Drug Co., N.Y.C., 1954-55, sales mgr., Smithtown, L.I., N.Y., 1955-57; mgr. advt. and sales Denver Chem. Mfg. Co., Stamford, Conn., 1957-58, N.Y.C., 1958-59; v.p., dir. mktg., account exec. Ralph Allum Advt. Agy., N.Y.C., 1959-67; v.p. Community Sci., Inc., 1959-67; account exec. Walston & Co., Inc., N.Y.C., 1967-74, Harris, Upham & Co., Inc., 1974-76; sr. account exec., v.p. Smith Barney Harris Upham & Co., 1976—. Lt. USNR, 1942-46. Decorated Silver Star; knighted Knight of Grace Soverign Orthodox Order of St. John of Jerusalem, Knights Hospitaller. Mem. The Marketeers (pres. 1963-67), Astoria Park Tennis Assn. (pres. 1967-70), Ea. Lawn Tennis Assn. (del. 1967-69), Met. Badminton Assn. (del. 1968- 4), Vet. Corps of Artillery of State of N.Y. (commd. major 1989) Mil. Order of Foreign Wars (bd. govs.), St. George's Soc., New Eng. Soc., Sigma Chi. Clubs: Dutch Treat (chmn. 1960-61), Army and Navy (pres.), Cen. Badminton (pres. 1971-83), Badminton Club of City of N.Y. (sec. 1985-95), West Side Tennis (Forest Hills), Princeton U. Club, St. George's Soc., New England Soc. Rsch. in field. Home: 865 United Nations Plz New York NY 10017-1803 Office: c/o Smith Barney Inc 40 W 57th St Fl 19 New York NY 10019-4001

MORRONE, FRANK, electronic manufacturing executive; b. Marano Marchesato, Cosenza, Italy, May 13, 1949; s. Luigi and Emma (Molinaro) M.; m. Katherine Ann Kuehn, Feb. 1, 1975; children: Louis H., Cecilia E., Joseph V. BSEE, U. Wis., 1972; M in Mgmt., Northwestern U., 1993. Project engr. 3M Co., St. Paul, 1972-73; product engr., mgr. Eaton Corp., Kenosha, Wis., 1973-79; chief elec. engr. Tree Machine Tool, Racine, Wis., 1979-80; v.p. engring. MacPower divsn. Manu-Tronics, Inc., Kenosha, 1980-84, exec. v.p., 1984—, bd. dirs., sec., 1988—. Mem. exec. bd. southeast coun. Boy Scouts Am., Racine, 1987—; bd. dirs. Kenosha Libr., 1987—. Mem. IEEE. Office: Manu-Tronics Inc 8701 100th St Kenosha WI 53142

MORROW, ANDREW NESBIT, interior designer, business owner; b. Fremont, Nebr., Feb. 22, 1929; s. Hamilton N. and May (Oberg) M.; m. Margaret M. Stoltinberg; children: Megan Beth, Molly Jean, Andrew C. BFA, U. Nebr., 1950. Interior designer Hardy Furniture, Lincoln, Nebr., 1950-61, Morrow Interiors, Lincoln, 1961—; bd. visitors Found. for Interior Design Edn. and Rsch., 1976-84; mem. standards com. Found. for Interior Design Edn. and Research, N.Y.C. Exhibitor Fremont Art Gallery, 1986, Haymarket Art Gallery, 1984. Pres. First Luth. Ch., Lincoln, 1987-90; bd. dirs. Lincoln Symphony, 1988-91, Nebr. Republicans for Choice, 1992, Luth. Family Svcs. of Nebr., 1994, Luth. Family Svc. Nebr. Found., 1995—; treas. NCID, 1992—. Fellow Am. Soc. Interior Designers (bd. dirs. Nebr.-Iowa chpt. 1974-78, pres. 1986-88); mem. Interior Design Educators Council (hon.). Republican. Avocations: gardening, horseback riding, cross-country skiing. Home: 1531 Kingston Rd Lincoln NE 68506-1524 Office: Morrow Interiors Inc 1010 K St Lincoln NE 68508-2851

MORROW, BARRY NELSON, screenwriter, producer; b. Austin, Minn., June 12, 1948; s. Robert Clayton and Rose Nell (Nelson) M.; m. Beverly Lee McKenzie, Mar. 3, 1969; children: Clayton McKenzie, ZoeAnna Rachel. BA, St. Olaf Coll., 1970; DHL (hon.), U. La Verne, Calif., 1990. Media specialist U. Iowa, Iowa City, 1974-81; freelance screenwriter Los Angeles, 1981-90; pres. Morrow-Heus Prodns., 1990—. Storywriter (TV film) Bill, 1981 (Emmy award 1982); screenwriter: (TV films) Bill: On His Own, 1983, Conspiracy of Love, 1987, Silent Victory, 1988, The Karen Carpenter Story, 1989, (feature film) Rain Man, 1988 (co-recipient Acad. award Best Original Screenplay 1989); screenwriter, exec. prodr.: Christmas on Division Street, 1991; exec. prodr.: Switched at Birth, 1991 (Emmy nomination), Gospa, 1995; screenwriter, prodr. Race the Sun, 1996; monologist: Bill for Short, 1992. Recipient Pres.'s award Am. Acad. for Cerebral Palsy and Devel. Medicine, 1978, Outstanding Contbn. award Mid-Am. Congress on Aging, 1983, SI award NASW, 1991, Pope John XXIII award Viterbo Coll., 1992. Mem. Writers Guild Am. West, Acad. TV Arts and Scis., Acad. Motion Picture Arts and Scis.

MORROW, CHARLES TABOR, aerospace consulting engineer; b. Gloucester, Mass., May 3, 1917; s. Charles Harvey and Melissa Luella (Tabor) M.; m. Julia Buxton Brown, June 4, 1949; children: Hope Elizabeth, Anne Barbara. AB, Harvard U., 1937, SM, 1938, SD, 1946. Sr. project engr. Sperry Gyroscope Co., Great Neck, N.Y., 1946-51; research physicist Hughes Aircraft Co., L.A., 1951-55; mgr. sci. and engring. relations Ramo Wooldridge Co., L.A., 1955-60; mgr. tech. relations Aerospace Corp., L.A., 1960-67; staff scientist LTV Research Ctr., Anaheim, Calif. and Dallas, 1967-76; cons. in field., Dallas and Encinitas (Calif.), 1977—. Author: Shock and Vibration Engineering, 1963; also numerous articles to profl. jours. Pres. Covey Aux. San Diego Mus. Natural History, 1983-85. Fellow Acoustical Soc. Am., Inst. Environ. Scis. (Vigness award 1971), AIAA (assoc.); mem. IEEE (life), Inst. Noise Control Engring. (founding), Am. Soc. Engring. Edn., Sigma Xi. Avocations: music, photography, natural history, travelling. Home and Office: 1345 Cherrytree Ct Encinitas CA 92024-4011

MORROW, CHERYLLE ANN, accountant, bankruptcy, consultant; b. Sydney, Australia, July 3, 1950; came to U.S., 1973; d. Norman H. and Esther A. E. (Jarrett) Wilson. Student, U. Hawaii, 1975; diploma Granville Tech. Coll., Sydney, 1967. Acct., asst. treas. Bus. Investment, Ltd., Honolulu, 1975-77; owner Lanikai Musical Instruments, Honolulu, 1980-86, Cherylle A. Morrow Profl. Svcs., Honolulu, 1981—; fin. managerial cons. E.A. Buck Co., Inc., Honolulu, 1981-84; contr., asst. trustee THC Fin. Corp., Honolulu, 1977-84, bankruptcy trustee, 1984-92; v.p., sec., treas. Innervation, Inc., 1989—; panel mem. Chpt. 7 Trustees dist. Hawaii U.S. Depart. Justice, 1988-91; co-chair Small Bus. Hawaii Legislative Action Com., 1990-92. Mem. Small Bus. Hawaii PAC, Lanikai Community Assn., Arts Coun. Hawaii; vol., mem. Therapeutic Horsemanship for Handicapped, program chair, 1990-92, vice chair, 1990—; vol., mem. Small Bus. Adminstrn. Women in Bus. Com. 1987—, vice and program chair, 1990—; vol. tax preparer IRS VITA, 1990—. Mem. AARP (vol. tax preparer TCE 1991—), NAFE, Australian-Am. C. of C. (bd. dir. 1985-92, corp. sec. 1986-92, v.p. 1988-92), Pacific Islands Assn. Women (corp. sec./treas. 1988-90), Pacific Islands Assn. (asst. treas. 1988—). Avocations: reading, music, dancing, sailing, gardening. Office: Innervation, Inc 145 Hekili St Ste 300 Kailua HI 96734-2804

MORROW, DAVID AUSTIN, III, veterinary medical educator; b. Arch Spring, Pa., Jan. 14, 1935; s. David Austin and Mary Harnish (Burket) M.; m. Sarah Linda MacDonough, Aug. 28, 1965; children: David Austin IV, Laurie Elizabeth, Melanie MacDonough. BS, Pa. State U., 1956; DVM, Cornell U., 1960, PhD, 1967. Postdoctoral fellow Cornell U., Ithaca, N.Y., 1965-68; assoc. prof. Mich. State U., East Lansing, 1968-81, prof. Coll. Vet. Medicine, 1981-90, prof. emeritus, 1990—; vet. cons., 1990—; vis. scientist Colo. State U., Ft. Collins, 1975-76. Editor: Current Therapy in Theriogenology, 1980, 2d edit., 1986. Elder Presbyn. Ch.; trustee Pa. State U., 1987—, chmn. bd. trustees phys. plant com., 1994—, mem. presdl. selection com., 1995. Recipient Norden Disting. Teaching award Mich. State U., 1975, Outstanding Teaching award, 1979, 80, 84, 85, 86, Dairy Sci. Disting. Alumnus award Pa. State U., 1992, Hon. Lion Ambassador award Pa. State U., 1993, Hon. Alumnus award Mich. State U. Coll. Veterinary Medicine, 1993. Mem. AVMA (Borden award 1980, Am. Feed Mfg. award 1992), Am. Coll. Theriogenologists (charter diplomate), Pa. State U. Coll. Agr. Alumni Soc. (pres.-elect 1985-86, pres. 1987-89, past pres. 1989-91), Pa. State U. Alumni Coun. (exec. bd. 1983-95, pres.-elect 1989-91, pres. 1991-93, past pres. 1993-95), Phi Zeta (pres. 1977-79), Phi Kappa Phi (exec. bd.), Golden Key (hon.). Republican. Avocations: skiing; gardening. Home and Office: 1060 Haymaker Rd State College PA 16801-6900

MORROW, E. ELAINE, geriatrics nurse, home health nurse; b. Big Spring, Tex., July 12, 1943; d. Charles Gordon and Loyce Bell (Childress) Hickman; m. Kenneth Wayne Morrow, July 26, 1960; children: Kerrie Ann Morrow Hutchings, Terrie Jan Purvis (dec.). LVN, Howard County Jr. Coll., 1968; diploma, Meth. Hosp. Sch. Nursing, Lubbock, Tex., 1973. TN, Tex.; BCLS instr. Pub. health nurse Pub. Health Dept., Big Spring, Tex., 1973-75; night supr. Hall Bennett Hosp., Big Spring, 1975-79; instr. Dallas/Ft. Worth Med. Ctr., Grand Prairie, Tex., 1979-81, admission/UR nurse, 1985-88; edn. instr. Dallas/Ft. Worth Med. Ctr., Grand Prairie, 1988-90; primary home care nurse North Ctl. Tex. Home Health, Ft. Worth, 1982-85; clin. supr., asst. dir. Dallas/Ft. Worth Home Health, Grand Prairie, 1990-93; dir., adminstr. N.E. Home Health Agy., Bedford, Tex., 1993-96; case mgr. Total Home Health Svcs., Austin, Tex., 1996—; affiliate faculty Am. Heart Assn., 1989-92; developer first aid course for child care workers. Mem. Nat. Assn. for Home Health, Home Health Nurses' Assn., Nat. Assn. Bus. Women, Nat. League Nursing (advocate), Beta Sigma Phi. Avocations: reading, ceramics, bowling, camping, yard work.

MORROW, ELIZABETH, business owner, sculptress, museum association administrator, educator; b. Sibley, Mo., Feb. 28, 1947; d. Elman A. and Lorine (Hostetter) Morrow; married, 1970 (div. 1979); children: Jan Pawel, Lorentz Arthur. Student, William Jewell Coll., 1958-59, Colo. Coll., 1959-60, U. Okla., 1960-62; BFA, U. Kans., 1964, MFA, 1967; postgrad., U. Minn., 1965, U. Kans., 1968. Pres. E. Morrow Co., Kansas City, Mo., 1966-67; head dept. art U. Hawaii, Honolulu, 1968-69, Tarkio (Mo.) Coll., 1970-74; exec. dir. Pensacola (Fla.) Mus. Art, 1974-76; pres., owner Blair-Murrah Exhbns., Sibley, Mo., 1980—; pres. bd. trustees, chief exec. officer Blair-Murrah, Inc., 1991—; sec.-treas. Coun. for Cultural Resources, 1995—. Del. White House Conf. on Small Bus., 1986. Lew Wentz scholar U. Okla., 1960-62. Mem. AAUW, Internat. Coun. of Mus., Internat. Coun. Exhbn. Exch., Internat. Soc. Appraisers, Am. Assn. Mus., Nat. Orgn. of Women Bus. Owners, Nat. Assn. Mus. Exhibitions, Ft. Osage Hist. Soc., Friends Art, Internat. Com. Fine Arts, Internat. Com. Conservation, Internat. Sculpture Ctr., DAR, Delta Phi Delta. Republican. Avocations: historical and cultural activities, antique cars, midwest farm auctions. Home: Vintage Hill Orch Sibley MO 64088 Office: Blair-Murrah Vintage Hill Orch Sibley MO 64088 also: 7 rue Muzy, PO Box Nr 554, 1211 Geneva 6 Switzerland

MORROW, GEORGE LESTER, retired oil and gas executive; b. New Haven, Apr. 27, 1922; s. Lester W.W. and Esther (Morrow) M.; m. Mary L. Evenburg, Dec. 28, 1946; children: Susan Morrow Donaldson, William, John, Thomas. B.S., Rutgers U., 1943; M.B.A., U. Chgo., 1954. Registered profl. engr., Ill. With Peoples Gas Light and Coke Co., Chgo., 1947-77; v.p.

ops. Peoples Gas Light and Coke Co., 1966-71, pres., 1971-77; also dir.; pres. Natural Gas Pipeline Co. Am., 1977-83; vice chmn., dir. Midcon Corp., 1983-87. Capt. AUS, 1943-46. Mem. Am. Gas Assn., Sarasota Yacht Club, Lake Zurich Golf Club. Presbyterian.

MORROW, GRANT, III, medical research director, physician; b. Pitts., Mar. 18, 1933; married, 1960; 2 children. BA, Haverford Coll., 1955; MD, U. Pa., 1959. Intern U. Colo., 1959-60; resident in pediatrics U. Pa., 1960-62, fellow neonatology, asst. instr., 1962-63, instr., 1963-66, assoc., 1966-68; asst. prof., 1968-70, assoc. prof., 1970-72; assoc. prof. U. Ariz., 1972-74, prof., 1974-78, assoc. chmn. dept., 1976-78; med. dir. Columbus (Ohio) Children's Hosp., 1978-94; prof. neonatology and metabolism, chmn. dept. Ohio State U., 1978-94; med. dir., dir. divsn. biochem. disorders Children's Hosp. Rsch. Found., Columbus, 1994—. Mem. Am. Pediatric Soc., Am. Soc. Clin. Nutrition, Soc. Pediatric Rsch. Achievements include research on children suffering inborn errors of metabolism, mainly amino and organic acids, patients on total parental nutrition. Office: Children's Hosp Rsch Found 700 Childrens Dr Columbus OH 43205-2696

MORROW, JAMES FRANKLIN, lawyer; b. Shenandoah, Iowa, Oct. 23, 1944; s. Warren Ralph and Margaret Glee (Palm) M. BS, Kans. State U., 1967; JD, U. Ariz., 1973. Bar: Ariz. 1973, U.S. Dist. Ct. Ariz. 1973. Ptnr. Bilby, Shoenhair, Warnock & Dolph, Tucson, 1973-83, Streich Lang, P.A., Tucson, 1984—. Mng. editor U. Ariz. Law Rev., 1972-73. Past chmn. bd. trustees Palo Verde Mental Health Svcs.; past pres. U. Ariz. Alumni Assn.; past chmn. bd. Palo Verde Hosp., Ariz. Tech. Devel. Corp.; past pres. bd. Cath. Cmty. Svcs.; chmn. bd. dirs. U. Ariz. Found. Capt. U.S. Army, 1967-70. Mem. Am. Coll. Real Estate Lawyers, Am. Coll. Mortgage Attys., State Bar Ariz. (cert. real estate specialist, adv. com. real estate specialists, past chmn. real estate property sect.), Pima County Bar Assn., Calif. Bar Assn. Democrat. Roman Catholic. Avocation: golf. Office: Streich Lang PA Ste 1700 One South Church Ave Tucson AZ 85701

MORROW, JOHN E., lawyer; b. Los Angeles, Mar. 17, 1943; s. Charles Henry and Lillian (Harmon) M.; m. Sue C. Taylor, June 28, 1989. BS, U. Southern Calif., 1965; JD, U. Chgo., 1968; postgrad. U. Munich (Germany), 1969. Bar: Calif. 1969, Ill. 1971. Law clk. to judge U.S. Dist. Ct. (cen. dist.) Calif., 1969-70; ptnr. Baker & McKenzie, Chgo., 1970-73, 75-76, 83—, Zurich, Switzerland, 1974-75, Hong Kong, 1976-82. Mem. ABA (subcom. on internat. bus. law com. of corp. sect.). Office: Baker & McKenzie 1 Prudential Plz 130 E Randolph St Fl 36 Chicago IL 60601

MORROW, PAUL EDWARD, toxicology educator; b. Fairmont, W.Va., Dec. 27, 1922; s. Paul Reed and Imogene (Tench) M.; m. Anne Kelly, June 14, 1947; children—Robert Randolph, William David. BS in Chemistry, U. Ga., 1942, MS in Chemistry, 1947; PhD in Pharmacology, U. Rochester, N.Y., 1951. Diplomate Am. Bd. Indsl. Hygiene. Indsl. hygienist Tenn. Eastman Corp., Kingsport, 1942-43; instr. pharmacology and toxicology U. Rochester, 1952-56, asst. prof. radiation biology and pharmacology, 1956-60, assoc. prof. radiation biology and pharmacology, 1960-66, prof. radiation biology and pharmacology, 1967-85, assoc. prof. pharmacology and toxicology, 1967-69, prof. pharmacology and toxicology, 1969-85, emeritus prof. toxicology, 1985—, acting chmn. dept. radiation biology and biophysics, 1975-77; NIH-USPHS fellow U. Göttingen, Germany, 1959-60, U. Zurich, Switzerland, 1960-61; mem. Internat. Commn. for Radiol. Protection Com., 1967-77; space sci. bd. Nat. Acad. Scis., 1967; adv. com. NRC, 1968, toxicology info. program com., 1979-82; mem. Nat. Coun. for Radiation Protection, 1977-87. Contbg. author: Inhalation Carcinogenesis, 1970, Environmental Factors in Respiratory Disease, 1972, Respiratory Defense Mechanisms, 1978, Pulmonary Diseases and Disorders, 1978; editor: Assessment of Airborne Particles, 1972, Polluted Rain, 1980, Occupational and Industrial Medicine: Concepts and Methods, 1984, Aerosols in Medicine, 1985, 93, others; contbr. numerous articles to profl. jours. Advisor particulate matter control criteria Nat. Air Pollution Control Adminstrn., Nat. Acad. Scis. Health Effects of Fossil Fuel Combustion Products, 1968-69; cons. Comitato Nazionale Per L'Energia Nucleare, Casaccia Center, Rome, Italy, 1968-69; mem. temporary staff Med. Research Council, Carshalton, Eng., 1968-69; chmn. com. air pollution Rochester Com. Sci. Info., 1972—; chmn. com. environ. health planning Genesee Region Health Planning Council, 1970-74. Served with USNR, 1943-45. Recipient Aerosol Rsch. award Internat. Soc. Aerosols Med., 1988, Founders award Chem. Industry Inst. Toxicology, 1989, Mercer award Am. Assn. Aerosol Rsch. and Internat. Soc. of Aerosols in Medicine, 1995. Fellow AAAS, N.Y. Acad. Scis., Acad. Toxicology Scis.; mem. Am. Indsl. Hygiene Assn., Am. Inst. Biol. Scis., Radiation Research Soc., Am. Coll. Toxicology, Health Physics Soc., Soc. Toxicology (Inhalation Toxicology Speciality Sect. Achievement award 1985), Am. Thoracic Soc., Am. Assn. Aerosol Research, Gesellschaft für Aerosolforschung, Soc. of Leukocyte Biology, Internat. Soc. Aerosols in Med., Am. Acad. Hygiene. Home: 200 Laney Rd Rochester NY 14620-3018 Office: U Rochester Dept Biophysics Box EHSC Rochester NY 14642

MORROW, RALPH ERNEST, historian, educator; b. Marshall County, Ind., Sept. 16, 1920; s. Ralph E. and Myrtle (Parrish) M.; m. Vera Cummings, June 4, 1949; children: Jason Drew, Leslie Ellen. B.S., Manchester (Ind.) Coll., 1943; A.M., Ind. U., 1948, Ph.D., 1953. Instr. Ind. U., 1948-50, Mich. State U., 1953-55; mem. faculty Washington U., St. Louis, 1955—, prof. history, 1963—, chmn. dept., 1960-65, from 1967, dean Grad. Sch., 1967-79, dean Faculty Arts and Scis., 1979-84, provost, 1984-86, prof. emeritus, historian of the univ., 1986—; cons. on call Danforth Found. Author: Northern Methodism and Reconstruction, 1956. Served to lt. (j.g.) USNR, 1943-46, PTO. Guggenheim fellow, 1959-60. Mem. Am. Hist. Assn. (chmn. com. coll. and univ. tchg. 1967-70), Orgn. Am. Historians. Presbyterian. Office: Washington Univ 1 Brookings Dr # 1133 Saint Louis MO 63130-4862

MORROW, RICHARD MARTIN, retired oil company executive; b. Wheeling, W.Va., Feb. 27, 1926; married. B.M.E., Ohio State U., 1948. With Amoco Corp., 1948-91; v.p. Amoco Prodn. Co., 1964-66; exec. v.p. Amoco Internat. Oil Co., 1966-70; exec. v.p. Amoco Chem. Corp., 1970-74, pres., 1974-78; pres. Amoco Corp., 1978-83, chmn. chief exec. officer, 1983-91; ret., 1991; bd. dirs. Potlatch Corp., Marsh & McLennan Cos., Inc., Seagull Energy Corp. Trustee U. Chgo. and Rush-Presbyn. St. Luke's Med. Ctr. Office: Amoco Corp 200 E Randolph St Ste 7909 Chicago IL 60601-6436

MORROW, RICHARD TOWSON, lawyer; b. Glendale, Calif., Aug. 3, 1926; s. Ray Leslie and Marion Elizabeth (Towson) M.; m. Virginia Alice Kaspar, June 28, 1947; children: Kathleen Ann, Randall Ray, Nancy Lynn. Student, Occidental Coll., 1944-45; BA, UCLA, 1947; LLB, U. So. Calif., 1950. Assoc. Musick & Burrell, Los Angeles, 1950-53; lawyer Walt Disney Prodns. (now Walt Disney Co.), Burbank, Calif., 1953-64; v.p. Walt Disney Prodns., Burbank, Calif., 1964-69, v.p., gen. counsel, 1969-85, dir., 1971-84; ptnr. Hufstedler, Kaus & Beardsley, Los Angeles, 1985-90, of counsel, 1990-91; ret., 1991; trustee Roy Disney Family Found., Burbank. Former pres., bd. dirs. Glendale YMCA, Calif.; former mem. adv. bd. Glendale Salvation Army; former trustee Glendale Cmty. Found., 1991-94. Served to lt. (j.g.) USNR, 1944-46. Mem. ABA (chmn. corp. law dept. com. 1982-84, coun. bus. law sect. 1984-88), Calif. Bar Assn., L.A. County Bar Assn. (corp. law dept. sect. chair 1973-74, trustee 1969-85, 1st recipient Outstanding Corp. Counsel award 1984), Glendale Bar Assn., Am. Law Inst., Calif. Club, Chancery Club (L.A.), Lakeside Golf Club (North Hollywood, Calif.), Alisal Men's Golf Club (Solvang). Republican. Presbyterian. Avocation: golf. Home: 665 Hillside Dr Solvang CA 93463-2157

MORROW, ROB, actor; b. New Rochelle, N.Y., Sept. 21, 1962; s. Murray and Diane Francis (Markowitz) M. mem. Ensemble Studio Theatre. Stage appearances include Escape from Riverdale, 1984, The Return of Pinnochio, 1988, The Chosen, 1987-88, The Substance of Fire, 1990; TV series Tattingers, 1988, Northern Exposure, 1990-94 (Lead Actor in TV Drama Emmy award nominee 1991, 92, 93, Lead Actor in TV Drama Golden Globe nominee 1991, 92, 93), Mother, 1996; films: Private Resort, 1985, Quiz Show, 1994, Last Dance, 1995. Mem. Naked Angels (co-founder). Jewish. *

MORROW, SCOTT DOUGLAS, choreographer, educator; b. N.Y.C., Jan. 29, 1954; s. Alfred Lionel and Lorraine (Power) M. Grad., High Sch. Performing Arts, N.Y.C., 1972; BFA in Dance, SUNY, Purchase, 1976; MA in Choreography, UCLA, 1986. Prin. instr. Phil Black Dance Studio, N.Y.C., 1969-77; dir. dance div. No. Ill. U., DeKalb, 1976-78; artistic dir., resident choreographer No. Ill. Repertory Dance co., 1976-78; artistic dir. Scott Morrow Dance Theatre Co. and Sch., L.A., 1978-85; prin. instr. Mary Tyler Moore Los Angeles Dance Ctr., 1979-80; resident dance master South Coast Repertory Acting Conservatory, Calif., 1979-82; vis. prof. Wright State U., Ohio, 1981; ballet master, resident choreographer Empire State Ballet, Buffalo, 1984-85; asst. prof. U. Kans., Lawrence, 1985-88; resident choreographer Kans. U. Dance Co., Lawrence, 1985-88; choreographer Morrow Dance Theatre-in-Residence, U. Kans., 1985-88, 92d St. Dancer Ctr., YMHA and YWHA, N.Y.C., 1989; assoc. dir., dir. edn. pub. sch. dance programs K-12, Bronx Dance Theatre Performing Arts Ctr., N.Y.C., 1990-93; mem. faculty Internat. Summer Sch. Royal Acad. Dancing, N.Y.C., 1991, 92; dance specialist State Edn. Dept. Summer Inst. on Assessment in Arts, N.Y., 1992; founder, dir. Inst. Advancement Edn. Dance, N.Y.C., 1992—; mem. faculty Calif. State U. Sys. Summer Inst. for Tchg. and Learning, 1994; advisor Performing Arts Medicine Ctr., Kessler Inst. Rehab., N.J., 1995—; Walter H. Annenberg disting. vis. artist-scholar The Renaissance Sch., N.Y.C., 1995—; cons. presenting and commissioning program Nat. Endowment for Arts, 1993—; peer rev. panel Fund for Innovation in Edn. U.S. Edn. Dept., 1993—; co-chmn. dance edn. com. World Dance Allliance: Americas Ctr., 1993—. Choreographer: (mus. theater) Broadway Musical Classics on International Tour, (film musicals) Chestnuts, Rainbows Edn., (teleseries) Adventures of Hans Christen Andersen, (indsl. show) Le Parfum Salvador Dali; world premieres presented at numerous festivals including Morningside Dance Festival, N.Y.C., Mid Am. Dance Festival, L.A. Dance Kaleidoscope Festival, Middfest Internat., Ohio, Smithsonian Instn's Duke Ellington Festival, Washington, Marche Internat. de Disque et de l'Edition Musicale, Cannes, France; creator over 40 ballets. Nat. Festival for the Performing Arts Choreographers fellow, 1989; named Choreographer of the Yr., Kaymore Found. for Arts, 1984, Master Educator and Disting. Fellow, Am. Bd. Master Educators, 1987; Alvin Ailey scholar, Sch. Am. Ballet scholar, Harkness House for Ballet Arts scholar, Walter H. Annenberg Disting. Vis. Artist-Scholar, The Renaissance Sch., Long Island City, N.Y., 1995—; recipient Grand Prize for Choreography, Ann. Internat. Artistic Impression Competition, 1991, citation U.S. Edn. Dept., 1993, contbns. to growth and advancement of performing arts award, U.S. Art1 Coun. Co-op, 1993; grantee numerous founds., corps., univs. Office: Lorraine Prodns 2269 Ocean Ave Brooklyn NY 11229-3103

MORROW, SUSAN H., interior designer; b. Bklyn., Aug. 27, 1943; d. Murray and Roslyn (Benjamin-Polsky) Chalkin; m. Robert Morrow (div.); children: Christopher, Andrew. BFA, Syracuse U., 1964; MA, NYU, 1965; cert. Post Coll. With Bagatelle Assocs., Roslyn, N.Y., 1972-74, The Wallpaper Place, Roslyn, 1974-75, Trio Designs, Huntington, N.Y., 1975-80, SHS Designs, Inc., North Hills, N.Y., 1980—; designer Designs For ..., Manhasset, N.Y., 1981—, ptnr., 1982—; pres. Wallpapers and ..., 1985—; designer Cinderella Project, Bklyn. Union Gas Urban Renewal, 1979, Human Resources, Ind. Living Project, 1982—; designer Designs For..., Roslyn, N.Y.; designer and converter Class Reunion, 1987. Designer Showcase Mansions; contbr. articles to mags. Co-chairperson budget adv. com. Roslyn Schs.; v.p. Norgate Civic Assn., Roslyn. Named Woman of Yr., Hadassah, 1974. Mem. Am. Soc. Interior Designers, 110 Assn. Profl. Women, Assn. Environ. Designers, Mensa, Internat. Platform Assn., LWV (v.p.). Home: PO Box H Sea Cliff NY 11579-0707 Office: Designs For 24 Skillman St Roslyn NY 11576-1183

MORROW, WALTER EDWIN, JR., electrical engineer, university laboratory administrator; b. Springfield, Mass., July 24, 1928; s. Walter Edwin and Mary Elizabeth (Ganley) M.; m. Janice Lila Lombard, Feb. 25, 1951; children—Clifford E., Gregory A., Carolyn F. S.B., M.I.T., 1949, S.M., 1951. Mem. staff Lincoln Lab., MIT, Lexington, Mass., 1951-55, group leader, 1956-65; head div. communications MIT Lincoln Lab., 1966-68, asst. dir., 1968-71, asso. dir., 1972-77, dir., 1977—. Contbr. articles to profl. publs. Recipient award for outstanding achievement Pres. M.I.T., 1963, Edwin Howard Armstrong Achievement award IEEE Communications Soc., 1976. Fellow IEEE, Nat. Acad. Engring. Achievements include patent for synchronous satellite, electric power plant using electrolytic cell-fuel cell combination. Office: MIT Lincoln Lab 244 Wood St PO Box 73 Lexington MA 02173

MORROW, WILLIAM CLARENCE, lawyer, mediator, investor; b. Austin, Tex., Aug. 9, 1935; s. Theodore Faulkner and Gladys Lee (Ames) M.; 1 stepchild, Shana Lynn Barbee; m. Sandra Jean Scott, Jan. 19, 1959 (div. Feb. 1971); m. Sheila Beth Pfost, June 29, 1973. children: Scott Fitzgerald Morrow, Elizabeth Ann Rettig. BA, Baylor U., 1957; JD, So. Meth. U., 1962. Bar: Tex., 1962. Trial atty. SEC, Ft. Worth, 1963-65; former ptnr. Cotton, Bledsoe, Tighe, Morrow & Dawson, Lynch, Chappell, Alsup & Midland; exec. v.p. Magnatex Corp., Midland, 1980-86; v.p., gen. counsel and sec. Elcor Corp., Midland, 1986-88. Mem. Midland City Coun., 1992-95, mayor pro tem, 1994-95; former vice chmn. Tex. Rehab. Commn.; pres. Found. Mental Health and Mental Retardation Permian Basin; pres. United Way of Midland, 1985, Indsl. Found. Midland, 1987; trustee Midland Community Theatre, 1980—, chmn. 1995—; elder 1st Presbyn. Ch., Midland. Mem. Tex. Bar Assn., Midland County Bar Assn., Midland C. of C. (past v.p.), Petroleum Club of Midland (past bd. dirs.), Phi Delta Phi. Home: 3110 Gulf Ave Midland TX 79705-8205 Office: 2500 N Big Spring Midland TX 79705

MORROW, WINSTON VAUGHAN, financial executive; b. Grand Rapids, Mich., Mar. 22, 1924; s. Winston V. and Selma (von Egloffstein) M.; m. Margaret Ellen Staples, June 25, 1948 (div.); children: Thomas Christopher, Mark Staples; m. Edith Burrows Ulrich, Mar. 2, 1990. AB cum laude, Williams Coll., 1947; JD, Harvard U., 1950. Bar: R.I. 1950. Assoc. atty. Edwards & Angell, Providence, 1950-57; exec. v.p., asst. treas., gen. counsel, bd. dirs. Avis, Inc. and subs., 1957-61; v.p., gen. mgr. Rent A Car div. Avis, Inc., 1962-64, pres., bd. dirs., 1964-75; chmn., chief exec. officer, bd. dirs. Avis, Inc. and Avis Rent A Car System, Inc., 1965-77; chmn., pres., bd. dirs. Teleflorists Inc. and subs., 1978-80; pres. Westwood Equities Corp., L.A., 1981-95, CEO, 1984-95, also bd. dirs.; chmn., pres., chief exec. officer Ticor Title Ins. Co., 1982-91, also bd. dirs.; chmn. TRTS Data Svcs. Inc., 1985-91; bd. dirs. AECOM Tech. Corp., L.A., 1990—; dir. William & Scott, Inc., 1994-96; mem. Pres.'s Industry and Govt. Spl. Travel Task Force, 1968, travel adv. bd. U.S. Travel Svcs., 1968-76, L.A. City-wide Airport Adv. Com., 1983-85; co-chmn. L.A. Transp. Coalition, 1985-91. Mem. juvenile delinquency task force Nat. Coun. Crime and Delinquency, 1985-86, L.A. Mayor's Bus. Coun., 1983-86, Housing Roundtable, Washington, 1983-85; chmn., pres. Spring St. Found., 1991—; bd. dirs. Police Found., Washington, 1983-91; trustee Com. for Econ. Devel., Washington, 1987-91. Decorated Stella Della Solidarieta Italy, Gold Tourism medal Austria). Mem. Fed. Bar Assn., R.I. Bar Assn., Car and Truck Rental Leasing Assn. (nat. pres. 1961-63), Am. Land Title Assn. (bd. govs. 1989-90), L.A. Area C. of C. (bd. dirs. 1983-90), The Huntington (fellow), Williams Club, L.A. Tennis Club, Phi Beta Kappa, Kappa Alpha. Home: 4056 Farmouth Dr Los Angeles CA 90027-1314 also: Meadowview Farm Cushing Corners Rd Freedom NH 03836-0221

MORSCH, THOMAS HARVEY, lawyer; b. Oak Park, Ill., Sept. 5, 1931; s. Harvey William and Gwenodyne (Maun) M.; m. Jacquelyn Casey, Dec. 27, 1954; children: Thomas H. Jr., Margaret, Mary Susan, James, Kathryn, Julia. BA, Notre Dame U., 1953; B.S.L., Northwestern U., 1953, J.D., 1955. Bar: Ill. 1955, D.C. 1955. Assoc. Crowell & Leibman, Chgo., 1955-62; ptnr. Leibman, Williams, Bennett, Baird & Minow, Chgo., Ill., 1962-72, Sidley & Austin, Chgo., 1972—; bd. dirs. Chgo. Lawyers Com. for Civil Rights Under Law, chmn., 1982-83; bd. dirs. Pub. Interest Law Initiative, pres., 1993-95; No. Dist. Ill. Civil Justice Reform Com., 1991-95; mem. vis. com. Northwestern U. Law Sch., 1989-90. Pres. Republican Workshops of Ill., 1970; gen. counsel Ill. Com. to Re-elect the Pres., 1972; mem. LaGrange Plan Commn., Ill., 1972-80, LaGrange Fire and Police Commn., 1968-72; trustee LaGrange Meml. Hosp., 1983-89; adv. bd. Catholic Charities of Chgo., 1985—. Fellow Am. Coll. Trial Lawyers; mem. ABA, Ill. State Bar Assn., Chgo. Bar Assn. (bd. mgrs. 1979-81), D.C. Bar Assn., Northwestern Law Sch. Alumni Assn. (pres 1988-89), Chgo. Bar Found. (bd. dirs., pres. 1995—). Roman Catholic. Clubs: Legal, Univ. (Chgo.), Mid Day (Chgo.); LaGrange Country, Palisades Park Country (Mich.), Point O'Woods Country (Mich.). Home: 301 S Edgewood Ave La Grange IL 60525-2153 Office: Sidley & Austin 1 First Nat Plz Chicago IL 60603

MORSE, EDMOND NORTHROP, investment management executive; b. Balt., Dec. 31, 1922; s. Edmond Harris and Ethel (Dannenberg) M.; m. Sidney Harvey Phillips, June 5, 1948; children: Edmond H., David F., Judith B., Anne S., John B. BA, Brown U., 1944; M.B.A., Harvard, 1947. With Smith, Barney & Co. (investment bankers), N.Y.C., 1947-81; gen. partner Smith, Barney & Co. (investment bankers), 1961-64, v.p., dir., 1964-68, sr. v.p., dir., 1968-70, exec. v.p., dir., 1970-76; exec. v.p., dir. Smith Barney, Harris Upham, 1976-81; exec. v.p. First Manhattan Co., 1981-89; gen. ptnr. Morse Equity Ptnrs., Darien, Conn., 1989—; dir. First Century Ptnrs.; dir., vice chmn. Lockwood Mathews Mansion Mus., Norwalk, Conn. Bd. dirs. Easter Seal Rehab. Ctr., Stamford, Conn. 1st lt. USMCR, 1943-46. Mem. Wee Burn Country Club. Home: Ridge Acres Darien CT 06820 Office: 36 Old Kings Hwy S Darien CT 06820-4523

MORSE, EDWARD J., automotive executive; b. 1949. Pres. Morse Ops., Ft. Lauderdale, 1970—, Ed Morse Chevrolet, Inc., Ft. Lauderdale, Fla., 1979—. Office: Morse Operations Inc 6363 NW 6th Way Ste 400 Fort Lauderdale FL 33309-6119*

MORSE, EDWARD LEWIS, periodical publishing executive; b. N.Y.C., Jan. 5, 1942; s. Jonah Benjamin and Rebecca (Freiberg) M.; m. Linda Kasle Jones, Aug. 15, 1965; children: Michael Ari, Molly Rachel. BA, Johns Hopkins U., Balt., 1963; MA, Johns Hopkins U., Washington, 1966; PhD, Princeton U., 1969. Asst. prof. internat. politics Woodrow Wilson Sch. Princeton (N.J.) U., 1969-75; sr. rsch. fellow Coun. on Fgn. Rels., N.Y.C., 1975-78; exec. asst. to undersec. econ. affairs U.S. Dept. State, Washington, 1978-79, dep. asst. sec. for internat. energy policy, 1979-81; dir. internat. affairs Phillips Petroleum Co., Bartlesville, Okla., 1981-84; mng. dir. Petroleum Fin. Co., Ltd., Washington, 1984—; pres., publisher Petroleum Intelligence Weekly, N.Y.C., 1988—. Author: Foreign Policy and Interdependence in Gaullist France, 1973, Modernization and the Transformation of International Relations, 1976; contbr. articles to various publs. Home: 2 E End Ave New York NY 10021-1192 Office: Petroleum Intelligence Wkly 575 Broadway New York NY 10012-3230

MORSE, HELVISE GLESSNER, physical and life sciences educator; b. Frederick, Md., Sept. 17, 1925; d. George Edward and Rosa May (Durphy) Glessner; m. Melvin Laurance Morse, Jan. 25, 1949; children: Margaret Louise, Laurance Clinton. BA, Hood Coll., 1946; MS, U. Ky., 1949, U. Colo., Denver, 1963; PhD, U. Colo., Denver, 1966. Supr. cytogenetics lab. Children's Hosp., Denver, 1978-79; postdoctoral fellow U. Colo. Med. Ctr., Denver, 1966-67, rsch. assoc., 1968-73, rsch. cytogeneticist, 1974-78, asst. prof. biochemistry, biophysics and genetics, 1979-88, assoc. prof., 1988—; dir. Core cytogenetics lab. U. Colo. Cancer Ctr., Denver, 1988—; Eleanor Roosevelt Inst. Cancer Rsch. fellow U. Colo., Denver, 1979—; mem. cytogenetics subcom. Nat. Children's Cancer Study Group, U.S.A. and Can., 1980-87. Contbr. articles on gene mapping, cytogenetics and Leukemia research to profl. publs., 1970—. Active So. Poverty Law Ctr. Mem. NAACP, Mortar Bd., Sigma Xi. Democrat. Avocations: photography of wild flowers, attending local symphony orchestra concerts and opera. Home: 254 S Jasmine St Denver CO 80224-1033 Office: Univ Colo Health Scis Ctr Dept Biochem/Biophys/Genet 4200 E 9th Ave Denver CO 80220-3706

MORSE, JACK HATTON, utilities consultant; b. San Diego, June 4, 1923; s. John Henderson and Alberta (Peterson) M.; m. Kathleen Clark (div.); children: David Eugene, Steven Allen; m. Jean Larson. BA, San Diego State U., 1956, M in Bus. Sci., 1971. Exec. San Diego Gas & Electric, 1947-89; cons. Pub. contbr. Sea Power mag., 1987-89. Pres. Cystic Fibrosis Found., San Diego, 1980-83, Project Handclasp, 1991—, Oceans Found., 1992-94. Comdr. USNR, 1943-46, 52-54. Recipient Dr. Frederick Patterson award United Negro Coll. Fund, San Diego, 1989. Mem. IEEE, Pacific Coast Elec. Assn., Pacific Coast Gas Assn. (Silver medal 1981), Navy League U.S. (nat. pres., chmn. adv. com. 1987-89, Disting. Svc. award 1979, 88, 89), La Jolla Beach and Tennis Club, Masons. Republican. Mem. LDS Ch. Avocation: traveling. Home and Office: 6125 Terryhill Dr La Jolla CA 92037-6837

MORSE, JAMES L., state supreme court justice; b. N.Y.C., Sept. 11, 1940; m. Gretchen B, June 19, 1965; children: Rebecca Penfield, Rachel Lasell. AB, Dartmouth Coll., 1962; JD magna cum laude, Boston U., 1969. Bar: Vt. 1970, U.S. Dist Ct. Vt. 1970, U.S. Ct. Appeals (2d cir.) 1970, U.S. Supreme Ct. 1973. Law clk. to Judge Sterry R. Waterman U.S. Ct. Appeals (2nd cir.), 1969-70; pvt. practice Burlington, Vt., 1970-73, 75-76; asst. atty. gen. State of Vt., Montpelier, 1973-75, defender gen., 1976-81; judge Vt. Superior Ct., Montpelier, 1981-88; justice Vt. Supreme Ct., Montpelier, 1988—. Editor in chief Boston U. Law Rev., 1967-69. Lt. USNR, 1963-66. Mem. Vt. Bar Assn. Office: Vt Supreme Ct 109 State St Montpelier VT 05609-0001*

MORSE, JOHN HARLEIGH, lawyer; b. Estherville, Iowa, Sept. 22, 1910; s. James W. and Winifred E. (Williams) M.; m. Marie A. Forrest, Nov. 11, 1936 (div. June 1962); children: James W. II, Bruce F.; m. Ann U. Stanton, May 23, 1964. B.A., State U. Iowa, 1930; M.B.A., Harvard U., 1932; JD, Yale U., 1935. Bar: N.Y. 1936. Since practiced in N.Y.C.; with firm Carter, Ledyard & Milburn, 1935; with firm Cravath, Swaine & Moore, 1936-76, ptnr., 1946-76; vice chair Nat. Forge Co., 1977-91. Pres. Forest Property Owners Assn., 1992-94. Mem. ABA (chmn. labor relations law sect. 1961-62), Forest Country Club, Phi Beta Kappa, Phi Gamma Delta. Home and Office: 16301 Fairway Woods Dr Fort Myers FL 33908-5333

MORSE, JOHN M., book publishing executive. Exec. editor, v.p. Merriam-Webster Inc., Springfield, Mass. Office: Merriam Webster Inc 47 Federal St Springfield MA 01105-3805

MORSE, JOHN MOORE, architect, planner; b. Brookline, Mass., Aug. 23, 1911; s. Arthur Moore and Helen (Stearns) M.; m. Emily Hall (dec. 1988); children: David Hall, Catherine Morse Wikkerink; m. Helen Taverniti, Aug. 5, 1989. AB, Harvard U., 1934, MArch, 1940. Registered architect, Wash. Tchr. Loomis Sch., Windsor, Conn., 1934-36; ptnr. Bassetti & Morse, Seattle, 1947-62; prin. John Morse & Assocs., Seattle, 1962-78; ptnr. Morse Stafford Ptnrship., Seattle, 1978-85; prin. John Morse Architect & Planner, Seattle, 1985—. Mem. King County (Wash.) Planning Commn., 1965-70, Design Rev. Bd., Mill Creek, Wash., 1987-89; chmn. Seattle Urban Design Bd., 1966; bd. dirs. Cornish Coll. Arts, Seattle, 1974-80. Fellow AIA (pres. Seattle chpt. 1969, various local and nat. awards). Democrat. Office: 7027 32nd NE Seattle WA 98115

MORSE, KAREN WILLIAMS, academic administrator; b. Monroe, Mich., May 8, 1940; m. Joseph G. Morse; children: Robert G., Geoffrey E. BS, Denison U., 1962; MS, U. Mich., 1964, PhD, 1967; DSc (hon.), Denison U., 1990. Rsch. chemist Ballistic Rsch. Lab., Aberdeen Proving Ground, Md., 1966-68; lectr. chemistry dept. Utah State U., Logan, 1968-69, from asst. to assoc. prof. chemistry, 1969-83, prof. chemistry dept., 1983-93, dept. head Coll. Sci., 1981-88, dean Coll. Sci., 1988-89, univ. provost, 1989-93; pres. Western Wash. U., Bellingham, 1993—; mem., chair Grad. Record Exam in chemistry com., Princeton, N.J., 1980-89, Gov.'s Sci. Coun., Salt Lake City, 1986-93, Gov.'s Coun. on Fusion, 1989-91, ACS Com. on Profl. Tng., 1984-92; cons. 1993; nat. ChemLinks adv. com. NSF, 1995; bd. advisor's orgn. com. 2008 summer Olympic Games, Seattle, 1995; faculty Am. Assn. State Colls. and Univs. Pres.'s Acad., Aug. 1995; chair Coun. of Pres., 1995—. Contbr. articles to profl. jours.; patentee in field. Mem. Cache County Sch. Dist. Found., Cache Valley, Logan, 1988-93; swim coach, soccer coach; trustee First United Presbyn. Ch., Logan, 1979-81, 82-85; adv. bd. Sci. Discovery Ctr., Logan, 1993; mem. bd. dirs. United Way, Whatcom County, 1993—; exec. com. Fourth Corners Econ. Devel. Bd., 1993—; mem. policies and procedures com. AASCU, 1993—. Recipient Disting. Alumni in Residence award U. Mich., 1989. Fellow AAAS; mem. Am. Chem. Soc. (Utah award Salt Lake City and Cen. dists. 1988), Bus. and Profl. Women Club (pres. 1984-85), Philanthropic Edn. Orgn., Phi Beta Kappa, Sigma Xi, Phi Beta Kappa Assocs., Phi Kappa Phi, Beta Gamma Sigma. Avocations: skiing, biking, photography. Office: Western Washington Univ Office of Pres Bellingham WA 98225-5996

MORSE, LEON WILLIAM, traffic, physical distribution and transportation management executive, consultant; b. N.Y.C., Nov. 13, 1912; s. Benjamin and Leah (Shapiro) M.; m. Goldie Kohn, Mar. 30, 1941; children:

Jeffrey W., Saul J. BS, NYU, 1935; grad. Acad. Advanced Traffic, 1937, 1954; DBA, Columbia Pacific U., 1979. Registered practitioner STB, Fed. Maritime Commn. Individual bus., traffic mgmt. cons., Phila., 1950-58; gen. traffic mgr. W.H. Rorer, Inc., Ft. Washington, Pa., 1958-78; adj. prof. econs. of transp., logistics Pa. State U., Ogontz campus, 1960-82; owner Morse Assocs.; course leader seminars in freight traffic mgmt., phys. distbn. mgmt., transp. contract negotiations and freight claims for univs. in the U.S.; bd. dirs. Sr. Security Assocs., Inc.; Bd. trustees Temple B'rith Shalom. Author: Practical Handbook of Industrial Traffic Management, 1980, 87, (manuals) Job of the Traffic Manager, Effective Traffic Management, Fundamentals of Traffic Management, Transportation Contract Negotiations and Freight Claims. Capt. transp. corps, AUS, World War II. Recipient Del. Valley Traffic Mgr. of Yr. award, 1963. Mem. Traffic and Transp. Club of Phila., Traffic Club of Phila., Traffic Club of Norristown, Am. Soc. Internat. Execs. (past pres., bd. dirs., sec., cert.), Assn. Transp. Practitioners, Am. Soc. Transp. and Logistics (emeritus), Council Logistics Mgmt., Transp. Research Forum, Health & Personal Care Distribution Conf. (pres. 1973-75, chmn. bd. 1975-77), Sr. Security Assn., Inc. (bd. dirs.), Delta Nu Alpha Transp. Fraternity, Mason, Shriner.

MORSE, LOWELL WESLEY, banking and real estate executive; b. West Palm Beach, Fla., May 1, 1937; s. Alton and Blanche (Yelverton) M.; B.S., U. Santa Clara, 1968; grad. Def. Lang. Inst., Monterey, Calif., 1959; m. Vera Giacalone, June 22, 1958; children: Lowell Wesley, Stephen D., Michael S. Russian linguist U.S. Army Security Agy., 1957-60; asst. city mgr. City of Pacific Grove (Calif.), 1961-66; city mgr. Town of Los Altos Hills (Calif.), 1967-69; chmn. Morse & Assos., Inc., Portland, Oreg., 1972—; founder, dir. Comerica Bank Calif., San Jose, 1979—; chmn. Cypress Ventures Inc., Portland, The Bagel Basket, Inc.; bd. trustees Regent U. Served with U.S. Army, 1957-60. Home: 21042 SW Wyndham Hill Ct Tualatin OR 97062-7711 Office: 5335 Meadows Rd Ste 365 Lake Oswego OR 97035-3114

MORSE, MARVIN HENRY, judge; b. Mt. Vernon, N.Y., July 19, 1929; s. Frank Irving and Lillian (Seeger) M.; m. Betty Anne Hess, Dec. 27, 1953; children: Martin Albert, Michael Howard, Lee Anne. AB, Colgate U., 1949; LLB, Yale U., 1952. Bar: N.Y. 1952, Ky. 1956, Md. 1964, U.S. Supreme Ct. 1960, U.S. Ct. Appeals (6th cir.), U.S. Dist. Ct. (we. dist.) Ky., U.S. Ct. Mil. Appeals, U.S. Ct. Claims, U.S. Ct. Appeals (D.C. cir.), U.S. Ct. Appeals (fed. cir.), U.S. Dist. Ct. (no. dist.) Tex., U.S. Dist. Ct. Hawaii. Pvt. practice Louisville, 1956-62; asst. counsel Office of Gen. Counsel Dept. Navy, Washington, 1962-65, Office of Gen. Counsel Office Sec. Def., Washington, 1965-68; asst. gen. counsel GSA, Washington, 1968-70, U.S. Postal Svc., Washington, 1970-73; adminstrv. law judge Fed. Energy Regulatory Commn., Washington, 1973-75, Postal Rate Commn., Washington, 1975-77, CAB, Washington, 1977-80; dir. adminstrv. law judges Office Pers. Mgmt., Washington, 1980-82; chief adminstrv. law judge SBA, Washington, 1982-87, asst. adminstr. office of hearings and appeals, 1986-87; adminstrv. law judge Exec. Office of Immigration Rev. Dept. Justice, Washington, 1987—; mem. Adminstrv. Conf. of U.S., 1980-84, govt. mem., 1985-86, 87-95, liaison mem.; faculty and faculty coord. The Nat. Jud. Coll., 1977, 79-80. Author: (with S. Groner) ABA Handbook chpt. on adminstrv. law, 1981. Trustee Washington area chpt. Am. Digestive Disease Soc., 1976-87. With JAGC, USAF, 1952-56, to col. USAFR, ret. 1979. Decorated USAF Legion of Merit; recipient Disting. Svc. award Am. Digestive Disease Soc., 1980. Mem. ABA (exec. com. 1977-82, 84-87, chmn. 1980-81, conf. adminstrv. law judges, del. ho. of dels. 1984-87, lawyers in govt. com. 1985-86, jud. selection, tenure and compensation com. 1987-93), Fed. Bar Assn. (nat. coun. 1976—, chmn. career svc. sect. 1983-86, chmn. judiciary sect. 1986-88, sect. coord. 1988-90, sec. 1991-92, del. to ABA ho. of dels. 1992-93, v.p. 1993-94, pres.-elect 1994-95, pres. 1995—), Am. Law Inst., Fed. Adminstrv. Law Judges Conf. (exec. com. 1975-77, 82—), Nat. Assn. Adminstrv. Law Judges (hon.), Fed. Am. Inn of Ct. (coun. 1990-92, pres. 1992-94). Home: 8027 Cindy Ln Bethesda MD 20817-6912 Office: US Dept Justice 5107 Leesburg Pike Falls Church VA 22041-3234

MORSE, PETER HODGES, ophthalmologist, educator; b. Chgo., Mar. 1, 1935; s. Emerson Glover and Carol Elizabeth (Rolph) M. AB, Harvard U., 1957; MD, U. Chgo., 1963. Diplomate: Am. Bd. Ophthalmology. Intern U. Chgo. Hosp., 1963-64; resident Wilmer Inst. Johns Hopkins Hosp., Balt., 1966-69; fellow, retina service Mass. Eye and Ear Infirmary, Boston, 1969-70; asst. prof. ophthalmology, chief retina service U. Pa., 1971-75, assoc. prof., 1975; assoc. prof. U. Chgo., 1975-77; prof. ophthalmology, 1979-93, sec. dept. ophthalmology, 1976-77, chief retina service, prof., 1979-93; clin. prof. ophthalmology U. S.D. Sch. Medicine, Sioux Falls, 1993—; prof. La. State U., 1978; chmn. dept. ophthalmology, chief retina service Ochsner Clinic and Found. Hosp., New Orleans, 1977-78; clin. prof. Tulane U., 1978. Author: Vitreoretinal Disease: A Manual for Diagnosis and Treatment, 1979, 2d edit., 1989, Practical Management of Diabetic Retinopathy, 1985; co-editor: Disorders of the Vitreous, Retina, and Choroid; bd. editors Perspectives in Ophthalmology, 1976—, Retina, 1980—; contbr. articles to profl. jours. Served with USNR, 1964-66. Fellow ACS, Coll. Ophthalmologists Eng., Am. Acad. Ophthalmology, Royal Soc. Health (Eng.), Royal Coll. Ophthalmologists (Eng.); mem. AMA, La. Med. Soc., Orleans Parrish Med. Soc., New Orleans Acad. Ophthalmology, La. Ophthalmol. and Otolaryngol. Soc., Miss. Ophthalmol. and Otolaryngol. Soc., Assn. Rsch. Vision and Ophthalmology, Retina Soc., Soc. Heed Fellows, Ophthalmol. Soc. U.K., Pan Am. Assn. Ophthalmology, Oxford Ophthalmol. Congress, All-India Ophthalmol. Soc., Soc. Eye Surgeons, Vitreoretinal Soc. (India), Sigma Xi. Republican. Episcopalian. Home: 1307 S Holly Dr Sioux Falls SD 57105-0221 Office: Central Plains Clinic Ltd Dept Ophthalmology 1100 E 21st St Sioux Falls SD 57105-1020

MORSE, RICHARD, social scientist; b. Boston, Oct. 12, 1922; s. Stearns and Helen Ward (Field) M.; m. Romola Thomas Chowdhry, June 23, 1949; children: Ashok Daniel, Martha Sunita Kelly. A.B., Dartmouth Coll., 1946; postgrad., Banaras Hindu U., Aligarh Muslim U., Gokhale Inst. Politics and Econs., India, 1947, Columbia, 1950; A.M., ABD, Harvard, 1958. Edn. officer ECA, Burma, 1950-53; asst. rep. Ford Found., Burma, 1954-56; sr. internat. economist Stanford Research Inst., Menlo Park, Calif., 1958-64, 66-69; cons. Ford Found., India, 1964-66; indsl. devel. cons. Andover, Mass., 1969-74; rsch. assoc., sr. fellow, co-coord. Participatory Devel. Group East West Ctr., Honolulu, 1974-94; sr. fellow emeritus East West Ctr., Honolulu, 1994—; study dir. Nat. Acad. Sci. and Nat. Acad. Engring. Internat. Panel on Internat. Industrialization Inst., 1972-73; chmn. bd. govs. Inst. Current World Affairs, 1972-74, trustee, 1988-91; bd. dirs. Inst. World Affairs, 1988-91, mem. adv. coun., 1992—; co-founder, dir. Hawaii Entrepreneurship Tng. and Devel. Inst., 1977—; mem. adv. com. Immigrant Ctr. Enterprise Project, Honolulu, 1992—. Co-author (with Eugene Staley): Modern Small Industry for Developing Countries, 1965, Village Voices in Rural Development and Energy Planning, 1987; co-editor: Grassroot Horizons: Connecting Participatory Development Initiatives East and West, 1995. Served with AUS, 1942-45. Fellow Inst. Current World Affairs, 1946-49; recipient certificate of honor Hawaii Ho. of Reps., 1994. Mem. Am. Econ. Assn., Am. Agrl. Econs. Assn., Am. Assn. Asian Studies, Economists Allied for Arms Reduction, Nitrogen Fixing Tree Assn., UN Assn. (exec. bd. Hawaii divsn.). Home: 1621 Halekoa Dr Honolulu HI 96821-1126 Office: 1777 E West Rd Honolulu HI 96822-2323

MORSE, RICHARD JAY, human resources and organizational development consultant, manufacturers' representative company executive; b. Detroit, Aug. 2, 1933; s. Maurice and Belle Rosalyn (Jacobson) M. BA, U. Va., 1955; MA in Clin. Psychology, Calif. State U., L.A., 1967. Area pers. adminstr. Gen. Tel. Co. of Calif., Santa Monica, 1957-67; sr. v.p. human resources The Bekins Co., Glendale, Calif., 1967-83; pvt. cons. human resources and orgn. devel. Cambria, 1983—. Contbr. articles to profl. jours. Fund raiser various orgns., So. Calif., 1970—. Mem. Internat. Soc. Performance Improvement (founding mem. 1958—). Republican. Jewish. Avocations: travel, tennis, walking, swimming. Home and Office: 6410 Cambria Pines Rd Cambria CA 93428-2009

MORSE, RICHARD MCGEE, historian; b. Summit, N.J., June 26, 1922; s. William Otis and Marie (Zimmerman) M.; m. Emerante de Pradines, Dec. 30, 1954; children—Marise, Richard. Grad., Hotchkiss Sch., 1939; B.A. magna cum laude, Princeton U., 1943; M.A., Columbia U., 1947, Ph.D., 1952; M.A. (hon.), Yale U., 1963. Successively lectr., instr., asst. prof. history Columbia, 1949-58; dir. Inst. Caribbean Studies, U. P.R., 1958-61; vis. lectr. history Harvard U., 1960; prof. history, chmn. dept. SUNY-L.I., 1961-62; assoc. prof. history Yale U., 1962-63, prof., 1963-78, chmn. Council Latin Am. Studies, 1963-64, 65-70; William H. Bonsall prof. history Stanford U., Calif., 1978-84; sec. Latin Am. Program, Wilson Ctr., Washington, 1984-89; advisor U. Nuevo León Mex., 1958-60; L.Am. cons. to Ford Found., 1958-64, 73-75; vis. prof. El Colegio de Mex., 1981; sec. Interam. Found. Arts, 1963-68; disting. lectr. U. Guyana, 1975; Charles Phelps Taft Meml. lectr. history U. Cin., 1978; disting. Fulbright lectr. U. Rio de Janeiro, 1983; mem. selection com. Guggenheim Found., 1969-88, chmn. 1978-88; vis. scholar Getty Ctr., 1994. Author: From Community to Metropolis, A Biography of São Paulo, Brazil, 1958, The Bandeirantes, 1965, (with others) The Founding of New Societies, 1964, La Investigación urbana latino americana, 1971, Las Ciudades Latinoamericanas, 1973, Lima en 1900, 1973; play The Narrowest Street, 1945; El Espejo de Próspero, 1982, New World Soundings, 1989; also numerous articles; co-editor: Columbia Volumes on Contemporary Civilization, 1954-55; bd. editors Hispanic Am. Hist. Rev, 1960-65, 74-79; adv. editor Caribbean Studies, 1961-89, Jour. Urban History, 1973-90, Cuadernos Americanos, 1986—, Wilson Quarterly, 1989-92. Served to lt. USNR, 1943-46, PTO. Recipient Nat. Theatre Conf. prize play award, 1945, Conf. Latin Am. History prize essay award, 1962; Woodrow Wilson fellow, 1946-47; State Dept. fellow, 1947-48; Guggenheim fellow, 1964-65; Social Sci. Research Council fellow, 1964-65; fellow Center Advanced Studies Behavioral Scis., 1970-71; Stanford Humanities Ctr. fellow, 1983-84, Inst. Advanced Studies U. São Paulo, 1987; recipient medal of merit Getulio Vargas Found., 1975, medal of honor U. São Paulo, 1988, Casa Rui Barbosa medal, 1992, Brazilian Order Cruzeiro do Sul, 1993. Mem. Conf. Latin Am. History (chmn. 1969), Phi Beta Kappa. Home: 4412 Volta Pl NW Washington DC 20007-2019

MORSE, ROBERT ALAN, actor; b. Newton, Mass., May 18, 1931; s. Charles and May (Silver) M.; children: Andrea, Robin, Hillary; m. Elizabeth Roberts, 1989; 1 child, Allyn. Motion pictures include The Cardinal, 1963, The Loved One, 1965, How to Succeed in Business without Really Trying, 1967, Oh Dad, Poor Dad, Mama's Hung You In The Closet And I'm Feelin' So Sad, 1967, Where Were You When the Lights Went Out?, 1968, The Boatniks, 1970, Hunk, 1987, The Emperor's New Clothes, 1987; actor in many plays including The Matchmaker, 1955, Say Darling, 1957, Take Me Along, 1959, How to Succeed in Business without Really Trying, 1960 (Tony award 1961), Sugar, 1972, So Long 174th St., Tru, 1990 (Tony award best actor, 1990, Drama League N.Y. Distinguished Performance award, 1990, Emmy award Outstanding Leading Actor in a Miniseries or Special, 1993), Show Boat, 1993; star TV series That's Life, 1968-69, miniseries Wild Palms, 1993. With USN, 1950-54. Office: Bauman Hiller & Assocs 5757 Wilshire Blvd Ste 512 Los Angeles CA 90036*

MORSE, ROBERT WARREN, research administrator; b. Boston, May 25, 1921; s. Walter L. and Ethel (Prince) M.; m. Alice Muriel Cooper, Jan. 25, 1943; children: Robert Warren, Pamela Morse Moschetti, James Prince. B.S., Bowdoin Coll., 1943, D.Sc. (hon.), 1966; Sc.M., Brown U., 1947, Ph.D., 1949. Mem. faculty Brown U., 1946-64, prof. physics, 1958-64, chmn. dept., 1960-62, dean coll., 1962-64; asst. sec. of navy, research and devel. Washington, 1964-66; pres. Case Inst. Tech., 1966-67, Case Western Res. U., Cleve., 1967-71; dir. research Woods Hole (Mass.) Oceanographic Instn., 1971-73, sr. scientist, 1973-83, scientist emeritus, 1983—, asso. dir., dean grad. studies, 1973-79; dir. PPG Industries, Research Corp. Tech.; Howard Found. fellow Royal Soc. Mond Lab., Cambridge (Eng.) U., 1954-55; mem. com. undersea warfare Nat. Acad. Scis., 1957-64, chmn., 1962-64; vis. lectr. U. Oslo, 1962; chmn. interagy. com. oceanography Fed. Council Sci. and Tech., 1964-66; chmn. bd. on human resources Nat. Acad. Scis., 1970-74, chmn. ocean affairs bd., 1971-76; vis. scientist Scripps Instn. Oceanography, La Jolla, Calif., 1982. Author articles on ultrasonics, superconductivity, properties metals, underwater acoustics. Overseer Bowdoin Coll., 1971-87. Served to lt. (s.g.) USNR, 1943-46. Recipient Navy Distinguished Pub. Service medal, 1966. Fellow Am. Phys. Soc. (chmn. divsn. solid state physics 1963-64), Acoustical Soc. Am. (pres. 1965-66), Am. Acad. Arts and Scis.; mem. Woods Hole Golf Club, Sigma Xi. Home: Box 574 North Falmouth MA 02556-2308

MORSE, SAUL JULIAN, lawyer; b. N.Y.C., Jan. 17, 1948; s. Leon William and Goldie (Kohn) M.; m. Anne Bruce Morgan, Aug. 21, 1982; children: John Samuel, Elizabeth Miriam. BA, U. Ill., 1969, JD, 1972. Bar: Ill. 1973, U.S. Dist. Ct. (so. dist.) Ill. 1976, U.S. Ct. Appeals (7th cir.) 1983, U.S. Supreme Ct. 1979, U.S. Tax Ct. 1982. Law clk. State of Ill. EPA, 1971-72; law clk. Ill. Commerce Commn., 1972, hearing examiner, 1972-73; trial atty. ICC, 1973-75; asst. minority legal counsel Ill. Senate, 1975, minority legal counsel, 1975-77; mem. Ill. Human Rights Commn., 1985-91; dir. Ill. Comprehensive Health Ins. Plan, treas., chair grievance com.; gen. counsel Ill. Legis. Space Needs Commn., 1978-92; sole practice, Springfield, Ill., 1977-79; ptnr. Gramlich & Morse, Springfield, Ill., 1980-85; prin. Saul J. Morse and Assocs., 1985-87; ptnr. Morse, Giganti and Appleton, 1987-92; v.p., gen. counsel Ill. State Medical Soc., 1992—; lectr. in continuing med. edn. 1986-90; counsel symposia; bd. dirs. Springfield Ctr. for Ind. Living, 1984-89, Ill. Comprehensive Health Ins. Plan Bd., United Cerebral Palsy Land of Lincoln, United Way Sangamon County, mem., bd. dirs. Springfield Jewish Fedn., 1992-95; mem. task force on transp. Republican Nat. Com., 1979-80, Springfield Jewish Community Rels. Coun., 1976-79, 82; mem. spl. com. on zoning and land use planning Sangamon County Bd., 1978. Named Disabled Adv. of Yr., Ill. Dept. Rehab. Svcs., 1985; recipient Chmn.'s Spl. award Ill. State Med. Soc., 1987, Susan S. Suter award as outstanding disabled citizen of Ill., 1990. Mem. Nat. Health Lawyers Assn., Am. Soc. Law and Medicine, ABA (vice chmn. medicine and law com. 1988-90, tort and ins. practice sect., forum com. on health law), Ill. State Bar Assn. (spl. com. on reform of legis. process 1976-82, spl. com. on the disabled lawyer 1978-82, young lawyers sect. com. on role of govt. atty. 1977-80, chmn. 1982, sect. council adminstrv. law, vice chmn. 1981-82), Sangamon County Bar Assn., Am. Soc. Med. Assn. Counsel, Phi Delta Phi. Home: 1701 S Illini Rd Springfield IL 62704-3301 Office: Ill State Med Soc 600 S 2nd St Ste 200 Springfield IL 62704-2542

MORSE, SUSAN E., film editor. Editor: (films) Manhattan, 1979, Stardust Memories, 1980, Arthur, 1981, A Midsummer Night's Sex Comedy, 1982, Zelig, 1983, Broadway Danny Rose, 1984, The Purple Rose of Cairo, 1985, Hannah and Her Sisters, 1986 (Academy award nomination best film editing 1986), September, 1987, Radio Days, 1987, Another Woman, 1988, New York Stories ("Oedipus Wrecks"), 1989, Crimes and Misdemeanors, 1989, Alice, 1990, Shadows and Fog, 1992, Husbands and Wives, 1992, Manhattan Murder Mystery, 1993, Bullets Over Broadway, 1994.

MORSE, TRUE DELBERT, business and agricultural consultant, former undersecretary of agriculture; b. Carthage, Mo., Jan. 21, 1896; s. Delbert Lewis and Olive (Lawrence) M.; m. Mary Louise Hopkins, Nov. 20, 1927; 1 son, James Buckner. B.S. in Agr, U. Mo., 1924; LL.B., LaSalle Extension U., 1932. Bar: Mo. 1932. Exec. sec. Mo. Fed. Co-op. Livestock Shipping Assn., Columbia, 1920; part-time extension asst. in livestock marketing U. Mo., 1922-24, extension specialist agrl. econs., 1924-25; farm mgr., appraiser and head research Doane Agrl. Service, Inc., St. Louis, 1925-43, pres., 1943-52, chmn. bd., 1952-53; editor (originator) Doane Agrl. Digest, St. Louis, 1938-53; head farm mgr. and rural appraiser schs. Am. Soc. Farm Mgrs. and Rural Appraisers, 1945-46; faculty mem. Sch. Banking, U. Wis.; dir. Mut. Savs. Life Ins. Co.; under sec. agr., also pres. CCC, Washington, 1953-61; bus. and agrl. cons., asst. to pres. Alton Box Board Co., 1961-72; pres. U.S. Commodity Credit Corp., 1953-61; dir., spl. cons. Pet Inc., 1962-71; spl. cons. Farm Jour., Inc., 1961-70; chmn. bd. Man Exec., Inc., 1972—; mem. Pres.'s Adv. Bd. Econ. Growth and Stability, Presdl. Task Force for Rural Devel.; mem. Pres. Nixon's task force for Rural Devel., 1969-70; head U.S. delegations Internat. Wheat Agreement and Internat. Sugar Agreement; trustee, sec. Nat. Council Community Improvement; dir. Found. Am. Agr.; trustee, exec. dir. Agrl. Inst.; chmn. nat. com. rural devel. program, dir. Council Chs. Nat. Capital area. Author appraisal and farm loan handbooks and univ. bulls.; Contbr. farming pubs. Trustee Nat. Benevolent Assn. Christian Chs.; b. dirs. Nat. City Christian Ch. Corp., Christian Bd. Pubns.; adv. council Nat. Capital area council Boy Scouts Am.; mem. bd. Community Planning and Research Council. Named Churchman of Yr. Washington Area, 1958; recipient Animal Agr. award Am. Meat Inst., 1960. Mem. Am. Soc. Farm Mgrs. and Rural Appraisers (pres. 1941), Am. Farm Econs. Assn. (past v.p.), Alpha Gamma Rho, Alpha Zeta, Alpha Pi Zeta, Gamma Sigma Delta. Republican. Mem. Disciples Christ Ch. (pres. St. Louis Christian Missionary Soc. 1935-40, v.p. Mo. Christian Chs. 1943, pres. local ch., 1941-43, trustee Mo. Bible Coll., an organizer Sun City ch). Clubs: Rotary, Lakes. Address: 10330 W Thunderbird Blvd El Dorado B-314 Sun City AZ 85351

MORSE, WILLIAM SENTENNE, investment company executive; b. Hartford, Conn., May 3, 1946; s. Nathaniel Berwin and Alice Claire (Kilpatrick) M.; m. Carolyn Bliss Wheeler, May 17, 1975; children: Christopher William, Leigh Elizabeth. BA in Econs., Middlebury Coll., 1968. Registered investment advisor. Credit analyst Conn. Bank and Trust, Hartford, 1969-70, investment analyst, 1971-72, asst. treas., 1972-75, asst. v.p., 1976-79, v.p., 1980-85, sr. v.p., 1986-90; pres. Morse Investment Mgmt. Co., Hartford, 1991—; trustee, investment com. Stowe-Day Found., Hartford, 1992—. Sponsor, advisor Jr. Achievement, Hartford, 1976-81; coun. mem. Capitol Region Coun. on Govt., Hartford, 1982-85. Mem. Asn. Investment Mgmt. and Rsch., Country Club Farmington (dir. and treas. 1992—, trustee employee pension plan 1993—). Avocations: reading, golfing, skiing, camping. Office: Morse Investment Mgmt Co 15 Lewis St Hartford CT 06103-2506

MORSS, LESTER ROBERT, chemist; b. Boston, Apr. 6, 1940; s. Sumner M. and Sylvia F. (Woolf) M.; m. Helaine Sue Gubin, June 19, 1966; children: Sydney, Benjamin, Rebecca, Alisa. BA, Harvard U., 1961; PhD, U. Calif., Berkeley, 1969. Postdoctoral rsch. assoc. Purdue U., West Lafayette, Ind., 1969-71; from asst. prof. to assoc. prof. Rutgers U., New Brunswick, N.J., 1971-80; chemist, sr. chemist Argonne (Ill.) Nat. Lab., 1980—; vis. prof. U. Liège, Belgium, 1978-79, U. Paris, Orsay, 1993. Author, co-editor: The Chemistry of the Actinide Elements, 1986, Syntheses of Lanthanide and Actinide Compounds, 1991; editor procs. Rare Earth Rsch. Conf., 1986—. Lt. USN, 1961-65, Atlantic and Mediterranean. Recipient Sr. Scientist award Alexander von Humboldt Found., 1992. Fellow AAAS; mem. Am. Chem. Soc. (sec. div. nuclear chemistry and tech. 1990-92), Am. Nuclear Soc., Sigma Xi (pres. Argonne chpt. 1988-89). Jewish. Home: 1680 Verdun Dr Winfield IL 60190-1716 Office: Argonne Nat Lab Chem Dv Bldg 200 Argonne IL 60439

MORT, GARY STEVEN, physical education educator; b. San Francisco, Jan. 2, 1959; s. Robert Joseph and Antoinette Patricia (Dominguez) M.; m. Rochelle Ann Dias, Aug. 02, 1980; children: Aaron Nicholas, Courtney Faith. BS Phys. Edn., San Jose State, 1983; MS Ednl. Adminstrn., Nat. Univ., Fresno, Calif., 1989. Cert. tchr. phys. edn., Calif. Tchr. phys. edn. Alum Rock Unified, San Jose, Calif., 1984-85, Clovis (Calif.) Unified Schs., 1985—, 1993—. Found. grantee Clovis Found., 1993-94; named Coach of the Yr., North Yosemite League, Fresno area, 1990. Mem. AAHPERD (presenter nat. conv. 1992, 93, 95), Calif. Assn. Health, Phys. Edn., Recreation and Dance), U.S. Water Polo (dist. sec. 1974—), Calif. Consortium of Ind. Study. Avocations: golf, rock climbing, skiing, running and hiking. Home: 8564 Chickadee Ln Clovis CA 93611-9461 Office: Gateway High Sch Enterprise High Sch 1550 Herndon Ave Clovis CA 93611-0569

MORTENSEN, ARVID LEGRANDE, lawyer; b. Bremerton, Wash., July 11, 1941; s. George Andrew and Mary Louise (Myers) M.; m. Elaine Marie Mains, Aug. 2, 1968; children: Marie Louise, Anne Catherine, Joseph Duncan. BS in English and Psychology, Brigham Young U., 1965, MBA in Mktg. and Fin., 1967; JD cum laude, Ind. U., 1980. Bar: Ind. 1980, U.S. Supreme Ct. 1983, Mo. 1985, D.C. 1985; CLU, 1971; Accredited Estate Planner, 1995. Agt. Conn. Mut. Life Ins. Co., Salt Lake City, 1967-68, agt. and br. mgr., Idaho Falls, Idaho, 1968-74; with Rsch. and Rev. Svc. Am., Inc./Newkirk Assocs., Inc., Indpls., 1974-83, sr. editor, 1975-79, mgr. advanced products and seminars, 1979-80, sr. mktg. exec., 1980-83; tax and fin. planner, Indpls., 1980-85, St. Louis and Chesterfield, Mo., 1985-90, Tampa Bay, Fla., 1990-91, Orange County, Calif., 1991—. mem. sr. mgmt. com., v.p. Allied Fidelity Corp., 1983-85, Allied Fidelity Ins. Co., 1983-85, Tex. Fire and Casualty Ins. Co., 1983-85; v.p., bd. dirs. Gen. Am. Ins. Co., St. Louis, 1985-86; v.p. Gen. Am. Life Ins. Co., St. Louis, 1985-90; pvt. practice law, Indpls., 1980-85, St. Louis, Chesterfield and Bridgeton, Mo., 1985-90, Tampa Bay, 1990-91, Orange County, 1991—; active with Ch. Jesus Christ of Latter-day Saints, Denver, Idaho Falls, Idaho, Indpls., St. Louis, Chesterfield, Tampa Bay Area and Orange County, Calif., Profl. Assn. Diving Instrs. cert. Divemaster, 1989—; lic. amateur radio operator FCC, 1994—. Mem. Assn. Advanced Life Underwriting, Mo. Bar Assn., Bar Assn. Met. St. Louis, D.C. Bar Assn., Ind. Bar Assn., Am. Soc. CLU's, Nat. Assn. Life Underwriters, Orange County.. Author: Employee Stock Ownership Plans, 1975, Fundamentals of Corporate Qualified Retirement Plans, 1975, 78, 80, Buy-Sell Agreements, 1988, The Key Executive Sale, 1989, (with Norman H. Tarver) The IRA Manual, 1975-87 edits., (with Norman H. Tarver) The Keogh Manual, 1975, 77, 78, 80 edits., (with Norman H. Tarver) The Section 403 (b) Manual, 1975, 77, 78, 80, 84, 85, 87 edits., sole author 1991,93 , 94, edit., (with Leo C. Hodges) The Life Insurance Trust Handbook, 1980; contbr. articles to profl. jours.; editor-in-chief various tax and fin. planning courses; bd. editors Ind. Law Rev., 1977-78. Office: 620 Newport Center Dr Ste 1100 Newport Beach CA 92660-8011 Also: PO Box 6362 Laguna Niguel CA 92607-6362

MORTENSEN, AUDREY R., church administrator. Lay leader, former chair steering com. Commn. for Women Evang. Luth. Ch. in Am., Chgo., Ill. Office: 350 J Q Hammons Pkwy Springfield MO 65806

MORTENSEN, EUGENE PHILLIPS, hospital administrator; b. N.Y.C., Mar. 28, 1941; s. Eugene Phillips and Mary (Hogarty) M.; m. Ellen Louise McDavitt, Aug. 8, 1964; children: Jeffrey Phillips, Jennifer-Kristine McDavitt. BA, Seton Hall U., 1963; MS in Mgmt., Frostburg State U., 1974; M in Profl. Studies, Cornell U., 1976. Commd. 2d lt. U.S. Army, 1963, advanced through grades to col., 1984; ret., 1994; med. budget advisor Office Army Surgeon Gen., Cholon, Vietnam, 1968-69; chief materials mgmt. br. and test and standards Office of Compt., Office Surgeon Gen., Washington, 1969-71; chief systems div. and health care system br. U.S. Army Health Svcs. Data Systems Agy., Ft. Detrick, Md., 1971-74, resigned, 1974; asst. adminstr. for gen. svcs. St. Joseph's Hosp. and Med. Ctr., Paterson, N.J., 1976-79, for clin. svcs., 1979-83, v.p. clin. svcs., 1983-89, exec. v.p., chief operating officer, 1989-92; sr. v.p. for operation, chief oper. officer Jersey City Med. Ctr., 1992—; chief op. officer Liberty Home Care Agency, 1994—. Mem. editorial bd. Perinatal Newsletter, 1984-92. Coach Upper Saddle River (N.J.) Soccer Assn., 1986—; webelos den leader cub scouts, Boy Scouts Am., Upper Saddle River, 1986-90, asst. scoutmaster, 1990—; trustee N.J. Vis. Health Svcs., Totawa, 1988-92; trustee, mem. adv. bd. Passaic Valley Hospice, Totawa, 1986-92; bd. trustees Hudson County Occupational Ctr., 1993—. Decorated Bronze Star. Fellow Am. Coll. Healthcare Execs. (coun. regents); mem. Am. Hosp. Assn., N.J. Hosp. Assn. (coun. on govt. rels. 1992-94), Paterson C. of C. (bd. dirs. 1989-92). Republican. Roman Catholic. Home: 8 Iron Latch Ct U Saddle Riv NJ 07458-2005 Office: Jersey City Med Ctr 50 Baldwin Ave Jersey City NJ 07304-3154

MORTENSEN, GORDON LOUIS, artist, printmaker; b. Arnegard, N.D., Apr. 27, 1938; s. Gunner and Otillia Ernestine (Reiner) M.; m. Phoebe Hollis Hansen, Apr. 10, 1965 (div. 1968); m. Linda Johanna Sisson, Dec. 7, 1969. B.F.A., Mpls. Coll. Art and Design, 1964; postgrad., U. Minn., 1969-72. One-man shows include Minn. Mus., St. Paul, 1967, Concept Art Gallery Pitts., 1981, 83, 85, 87, 89, 91, 93, C.G. Rein Galleries, Mpls., 1978, 80, 85, 89, 91, 93, others; exhibited in group shows Miami U., Oxford, Ohio (1st place award 1977), Phila. Print Club (George Bunker award 1977), 12th Nat. Silvermine Guild Print Exhbn., New Canaan, Conn., 1976, 78, 80, 83, 86, 94 (Hearsch Mag. award 1978, Purchase award 1983, 86), 4th Miami Internat. Print Biennial (4th place award 1980), Rockford Internat., 1981, 85 (Juror's award 1981), Boston Printmakers Nat. Exhbn., 1977, 79, 80, 81, 83 (Purchase award 1977, 79, 83), others; represented permanent collections, Achenbach Found. Graphic Arts at Palace Legion of Honor, San Francisco, Bklyn. Mus., Phila. Mus. Art, Libr. of Congress, Minn. Mus. Art, Met. Mus. and Art Ctr., Miami, Fla., Mus. Am. Art, Washington, Art Inst. Chgo., Mus. Art at Carnegie-Mellon Inst., Pitts., Walker Art Ctr., Mpls., Dulin Gallery Art, Knoxville, Tenn., numerous corp. collections; profiled in numerous art jours. Served with USMC, 1957-60. Mem. Boston Printmakers, Phila. Print Club, Artists Equity, Albany Print Club. Home and Office: 4153 Crest Rd Pebble Beach CA 93953-3052

MORTENSEN, JAMES E., management consultant; b. Brayton, Iowa, Mar. 15, 1925; s. Axel C. and Mabel (Ide) M.; m. Genevieve Edsall, Nov. 8, 1946; 1 son, Arthur C. Student, U. Denver, 1946-48, Columbia Exec. Program, 1965. Gen. mgr. dog food div. Cargill, Inc., Mpls., 1949-56; exec. v.p. Battle Creek Dog Food Co., Mich., 1956-57; dir., vice chmn. bd., chief fin. officer pres. affiliates Young & Rubicam, Inc., N.Y.C., 1957-81; now ind. cons.; pres. Asbury Terrace, Inc., 1965-69; mem. adv. bd. NPD Group Inc., Port Washington, N.Y.; editor Digital Jour. Trustee Caramoor Ctr. Music and Art, Katonah, N.Y., Mus. of Fine Arts, St. Petersburg, Fla. Decorated Bronze Star, Purple Heart. Mem. Am. Radio Relay League (bd. dirs.), Internat. Digital Radio Assn. Republican (pres. Irvington, N.Y. 1961-62). Home: PO Box 328 Indian Rocks Beach FL 34635-0328

MORTENSEN, PETER, banker; b. Ellwood City, Pa., Dec. 4, 1935; s. Norman Peter and Mary Letitia (Brown) M.; m. Collette; children: Linda V. Haning, Kelly J. Hebble, Nancy Sarah Patton, Karen Sue Harris. B.A., Coll. of Wooster, Ohio, 1956. With First Nat. Bank of Pa., Hermitage, Pa., 1959—; pres., chief exec. officer F.N.B. Corp., Hermitage, Pa., 1973—, chmn., 1987—. Mem. United Church of Christ. Avocation: hunting.

MORTENSEN, RICHARD EDGAR, engineering educator; b. Denver, Sept. 29, 1935; s. Edgar Steele and Frieda Amalie (Boecker) M.; m. Sarah Jean Raulston, Oct. 12, 1974 (div. 1978). BSEE, MIT, 1958, MSEE, 1958; PhD, U. Calif., Berkeley, 1966. Co-op. engr. GE Co., Schenectady, N.Y., 1955-57; mem. tech. staff Space Tech. Labs., L.A., 1958-61; rsch. asst. U. Calif., Berkeley, 1961-65; prof. engring. UCLA, 1965-91, prof. emeritus, 1991—; cons. TRW, Inc., Redondo Beach, Calif., 1966-70, Aerojet-Gen. Corp., Azusa, Calif., 1970-72, Applied Sci. Analytics, Inc., Canoga Park, Calif., 1980-82; guest lectr. Indian Inst. Sci., Bangalore, India, 1991. Author: Random Signals and Systems, 1987; contbr. to profl. publs. Team mem. Beyond War, Topanga, Calif., 1986-89; alcoholism counselor. Grantee NSF, 1987-90. Mem. IEEE, Soc. Indsl. and Applied Math., Sigma Xi, Tau Beta Pi, Eta Kappa Nu. Avocations: hiking, yoga. Office: Dept Elec Engring 405 Hilgard Ave Los Angeles CA 90024-1301

MORTENSEN, ROBERT HENRY, landscape architect; b. Jackson, Mich., June 9, 1939; s. Henry and Charlotte Marie (Brown) M.; divorced; children: Phillip, Paul, Susan, Julia; m. Meta Jane Hearne Blakely, Nov. 1975; stepchildren: Laura, Kathryn. B Landscape Architecture, Ohio State U., 1961; M Landscape Architecture, U. Mich., 1965. Registered landscape architect, Ohio, Fla., Va., Md., Ohio. Landscape architect various firms, Louisville, 1960, 61-63; with Ohio Div. Parks, Columbus, 1960-61; landscape architect various firms, Toledo, 1963, 65-67; pvt. practice Ann Arbor, Mich., 1963-65; ptnr. firms Toledo, 1967-78; pres. Harvey Jones and Assocs., Clearwater, Fla., 1979-81; owner Mortensen Assocs., Toledo and Falls Church, Va., 1979-85; prin. Mortensen, Lewis & Scully, Inc., Vienna, Va., 1985-93; owner Mortensen Assocs., Vienna, Va., 1993—; assoc. prof. U. Mich. Grad. Sch., 1973; vis. lectr. Ohio State U., 1965—, Bowling Green (Ohio) State U., 1969—, U. Mich., 1971, Purdue U., 1971, Mich. State U., 1973—; mem. archtl. environ. rev. com. Ohio Arts Coun., 1974-78; adj. prof. Dept. Landscape Architecture, U. Md., 1992—. Editor: Handbook of Professional Practice, 1972, Marketing Landscape Architectural Services to the Federal Government, 1974. Mem. Ohio Bd. Unreclaimed Strip Mined Lands, 1973-76; mem. Lucas County facilities rev. com. Health Planning Assn. N.W. Ohio, 1972-76, chmn. maternal and child health subcom., 1972-74; bd. dirs. No. Va. Cmty. Appearance Alliance, 1988—, chair, 1991, pres., 1994. Recipient Disting. Svc. award Health Planning Assn. N.W. Ohio, 1973, Disting. Alumni award U. Mich. Sch. Natural Resources, 1985, Disting. Alumnus award Ohio State U. Coll. Engring., 1985. Fellow Am. Soc. Landscape Architects (trustee 1977-82, v.p. 1982-83, pres.-elect 1983-84, nat. pres. 1984-85, del. to Internat. Fedn. Landscape Architects 1987-92, del. Internat. Landscape Alliance 1994—); mem. Ohio Soc. Landscape Architects (pres. 1969-74), Toledo C. of C. (chmn. sts. and hwys. transit com. 1972-73), Greater Merrifield Bus. and Profl. Assn. (bd. dirs. 1993—), Washington Golf and Country Club, Sigma Phi Epsilon. Home: 6843 Churchill Rd Mc Lean VA 22101-2822 Office: Mortensen Assocs 2787 Hartland Rd Falls Church VA 22043-3529 *One of the best continuing educational experiences for a practising professional is to teach students what you have learned. They respond in a critical and ever-so-fresh "so what" atmosphere, and demand more of you sometimes than you demand of yourself. Thus, there is learning on both sides of the lectern.*

MORTENSEN, WILLIAM S., banking executive; b. 1932. Chmn. bd., pres., CEO 1st Fed. Bank Calif., Santa Monica, 1955—, now CEO. Office: 1st Fed Bank Calif 401 Wilshire Blvd Santa Monica CA 90401-1416*

MORTENSEN-SAY, MARLYS (MRS. JOHN THEODORE SAY), school system administrator; b. Yankton, S.D., Mar. 11, 1924; d. Melvin A. and Edith L. (Fargo) Mortensen; BA, U. Colo., 1949, MEd, 1953; adminstrv. specialist U. Nebr., 1973; m. John Theodore Say, June 21, 1951; children: Mary Louise, James Kenneth, John Melvin, Margaret Ann. Tchr. Huron (S.D.) Jr. High Sch., 1944-48, Lamar (Colo.) Jr. High Sch., 1950-52, Norfolk Pub. Sch., 1962-63; sch. supt. Madison County, Madison, Nebr., 1963—. Mem. NEA (life), AAUW, Am. Assn. Sch. Adminstrs., Dept. Rural Edn., Nebr. Assn. County Supts., N.E. Nebr. County Supts. Assn., Assn. Sch. Bus. Ofcls., Nat. Orgn. Legal Problems in Edn., Assn. Supervision and Curriculum Devel., Nebr. Edn. Assn., Nebr. Sch. Adminstrs. Assn. Republican. Methodist. Home: 4805 S 13th St Norfolk NE 68701-6627 Office: Courthouse Madison NE 68748

MORTENSON, M. A., JR., construction executive. Chmn., pres., ceo M. A. Mortenson Co., Mpls., 1960—. Office: M A Mortenson Co 700 Meadow Ln N Ste 710 Minneapolis MN 55422-4817*

MORTENSON, THOMAS THEODORE, medical products executive, management consultant; b. Hallock, Minn., Dec. 18, 1934; s. Theodore William and Esther (Hanson) M.; m. Alice L. Girdvain, June 27, 1958; children: Kim M. Mortenson Zimmerman, Laura Dee Mortenson Paulides. BSBA, U. N.D., 1956, postgrad., 1957-58. Sales rep. Johnson & Johnson, Detroit, 1960-66; tng. and product dir. Johnson & Johnson, New Brunswick, N.J., 1967-72; dir. mktg. devel. C.R. Bard, Murray Hill, N.J., 1973-75; gen. mgr. MacBick, Murray Hill, 1976-78; dir. mktg. Bard Med. Systems, Murray Hill, 1979-81, dir. sales, 1982; dir. sales and mktg. Bac-Data Med. Info. Systems, Totowa, N.J., 1983-84; v.p. mktg. and sales United Med. Corp., Haddenfield, N.J., 1985-86; exec. v.p. Daltex Med. Scis., West Orange, N.J., 1987-92; assoc. ConMed Corp., Utica, N.Y., 1993—; guest lectr. Am. Mgmt. Assn., 1971, Mktg. Scis. Inc., N.Y.C., 1978, Internat. Novel Drug Delivery Techs., Tustin, Calif., 1987. With U.S. Army, 1957-58. Mem. Am. Mgmt. Assn. (instr. 1971), Berkeley Swim Club (Berkeley Heights, N.J.) (pres. 1979-82, bd. dirs. 1974-84). Avocations: woodworking, golf, volleyball, auto restoration. Home: 44 Ironwood Rd New Hartford NY 13413-3906 Office: 310 Broad St Utica NY 13501

MORTHAM, SANDRA BARRINGER, state official; b. Erie, Pa., Jan. 4, 1951; d. Norman Lyell and Ruth (Harer) Barringer; m. Allen Mortham, Aug. 21, 1950; children: Allen Jr., Jeffrey. AS, St. Petersburg Jr. Coll., 1971; BA, Eckerd Coll. Cons. Capital Formation Counselors, Inc., Bellair Bluffs, Fla., 1972—; commr. City of Largo, Fla., 1982-86, vice mayor, 1985-86; mem. Fla. Ho. of Reps., 1986-94, Rep. leader pro tempore, 1990-92, minority leader, 1992-94; Sec. of State State of Fla., 1995—. Bd. dirs. Performing Arts Ctr. & Theatre, Clearwater, Fla.; exec. com. Pinellas County Rep. Com., Rep. Nat. Com. Named Citizen of Yr., 1990; recipient Tax Watch Competitive Govt. award, 1994, Bus. and Profl. Women "Break the Glass Ceiling" award, 1995, Fla. League of Cities Quality Floridian award, 1995, also numerous outstanding legislator awards, achievement among women awards from civic and profl. orgns. Mem. Am. Legis. Exch. Coun., Nat. Rep. Legislators Assn., Largo C. of C. (bd. dirs. 1987—, pres.), Largo Jr. Woman's Club (pres., Woman of Yr. award 1979), Suncoast Community Woman's Club (pres., Outstanding Svc. award 1981, Woman of Yr. award 1986), Suncoast Tiger Bay, Greater Largo Rep., Bellair Rep. Woman's, Clearwater Rep. Woman's. Presbyterian. Home: 6675 Weeping Willow Dr Tallahassee FL 32311 Office: Secretary of State The Capitol, PL-02 Tallahassee FL 32399-0250

MORTIMER, HENRY TILFORD, JR., financial assurance executive; b. N.Y.C., Aug. 12, 1942; s. Henry Tilford and Marie Elise (Duggan); m. Susan E. Lewis, Dec. 28, 1989; children: Henry Tilford III, Caroline Elise; stepchildren: Richard Bierbaum, Caroline Bierbaum. BA, Harvard U., 1964, MBA, 1969. First v.p. Blyth Eastman Dillon, Paris, 1969-79; pres. Blyth Eastman Dillon Internat., 1972-79; sr. v.p. E.F. Hutton & Co. Inc., N.Y.C., 1979-85; pres. Am. Internat. Adv. Group, N.Y.C., 1985—; mng. dir. Fin. Security Assurance Co., N.Y.C., 1985—; bd. dirs. Tipiak, S.A., Nantes, France, Danskin, Inc. 1st lt. U.S. Army, 1965-67. Republican. Episcopalian. Home: 102 Boulder Trail Bronxville NY 10708 Office: Fin Security Assurance 350 Park Ave New York NY 10022-6022

MORTIMER, PETER MICHAEL, lawyer; b. Detroit, May 20, 1943; s. Robert J. and Harriet C. (Evenson) M.; m. Sharon M. Olson, Aug. 20, 1966; children: Katherine, Trever, Peter. AB magna cum laude, Cornell U., 1965; JD cum laude, Harvard U., 1968. Bar: D.C. 1968, N.Y. 1970. Atty. Office Legal Adviser, U.S. Dept. State, Washington, 1968; assoc. Milbank, Tweed, Hadley & McCloy, N.Y.C., 1969-76, ptnr., 1977—, mem. compensation com., 1992—, co-practice group leader banking & instnl. investment group, 1995—; resident ptnr. Milbank, Tweed, Hadley & McCloy, Hong Kong, 1977-79, London, 1983-88. Fellow Frick Collection, N.Y.C., 1981—, Pierpont Morgan Libr., N.Y.C., 1980—, mem. coun., 1981-83. Decorated Order of Francisco de Miranda 1st class (Venezuela). Mem. D.C. Bar, Assn. Bar City N.Y., Century Assn., Down Town Assn., Grolier Club (admissions com. 1991—), Short Hills Club, Baltusrol Golf Club, Phi Beta Kappa. Address: 57 Jefferson Ave Short Hills NJ 07078 Office: Milbank Tweed Hadley & McCloy 1 Chase Manhattan Plz New York NY 10005-1401

MORTIMER, RORY DIXON, lawyer; b. Flint, Mich., Jan. 6, 1950; s. Kenneth N. and Phyllis (Rouleau) M.; m. Patricia Ann Amstadt, Sept. 18, 1971; children: Melissa Marie, Ryan Douglas. BA, Mich. State U., 1972; JD, Detroit Coll. Law, 1978. Bar: S.C. 1978, Mich. 1979, U.S. Ct. Appeals (4th cir.) U.S. Tax Ct., U.S. Supreme Ct. 1979. Trust officer C&S Nat. Bank, Charleston, S.C., 1978-79; pvt. practice law Summerville, S.C., 1979-80; ptnr. Chellis & Mortimer, Summerville, 1980-85, Chellis, Mortimer & Frampton, Summerville, 1985-95; sr. ptnr. Mortimer, Leiendecker & Rose, Summerville, 1995—; gen. counsel Commr. of Pub. Wks., Summerville, 1982—. Atty., Dorchester County Human Devel. Bd., 1987—. Mem. ATLA, S.C. Bar Assn., S.C. Trial Lawyers Assn., Mich. Bar Assn., Am. Soc. CLUs and ChFC (pres. 1989). Republican. Roman Catholic. Avocations: golf, tennis. Home: 105 Old Postern Rd Summerville SC 29483-3770 Office: Mortimer Leiendecker & Rose 1810 Trolley Rd Summerville SC 29485-8282

MORTIMER, WENDELL REED, JR., superior court judge; b. Alhambra, Calif., Apr. 7, 1937; s. Wendell Reed and Blanche (Wilson) M.; m. Cecilia Vick, Aug. 11, 1962; children: Michelle Dawn, Kimberly Grace. AB, Occidental Coll., 1958; JD, U. So. Calif., L.A., 1965. Bar: Calif. 1966. Trial atty. legal divsn. Legal div. State of Calif., L.A., 1965-73; assoc. Thelen, Marrin, Johnson & Bridges, L.A., 1973-76, ptnr., 1976-93; pvt. practice San Marino, Calif., 1994-95; judge L.A. Superior Ct., 1995—. With U.S. Army, 1960-62. Mem. ABA, Los Angeles County Bar Assn., Pasadena Bar Assn., Calif. Judges Assn., Am. Judicature Soc., Am. Judges Assn., Legion Lex. Home: 1420 San Marino Ave San Marino CA 91108-2042

MORTIMER, WILLIAM JAMES, newspaper publisher; b. Provo, Utah, June 26, 1932; s. William Earl and Margaret (Johnson) M.; m. Paula Ann Deline, Sept. 17, 1956; children: Jeffrey, David, Gregory, Bradley, Judy, William James II, Jennifer. BS, Utah State U, 1954; MS, Columbia U., 1957. Reporter Deseret News, Salt Lake City, 1957-59, pres., pub., 1985—; sales mgr. Deseret News Press, Salt Lake City, 1959-63; gen. mgr. Deseret News Press, 1979-80, Deseret Book Co., Salt Lake City, 1966-79; sr. account exec. Wheelwright Lithographing, Salt Lake City, 1963-66; dir. LDS Ch. Printing Svcs., Salt Lake City, 1980-85; v.p., dir. Newspaper Agy. Corp., Salt Lake City, 1985—; pres. Printing Industries of Utah, 1964-65, Utah Retail Mchts. Assn., Salt Lake City, 1977-79. Author: How Beautiful Upon the Mountains, 1963. Campaign chmn. Salt Lake Area United Way, 1987; hon. col. Utah N.G.; chmn. Utah Partnership Ednl. and Econ. Devel.; mem. exec. com. Salt Lake Conv. and Visitors Bur.; chmn. bd. Pioneer State Theatre, 1990-93; pres. Utah Arts Endowment; bd. dirs. Utah Symphony. 1st lt. U.S. Army, 1954-56, Korea. Named Disting. Citizen of Yr., Salt Lake City, 1995. Mem. Utah-Idaho-Spokane AP Assn. (pres. 1993-94), Utah Press Assn. (pres. 1994-95), Salt Lake Area C. of C. (chmn. bd. 1988-89), Alta Club. Mem. LDS Ch. Avocations: music, reading, family activities. Home: 8763 Kings Hill Dr Salt Lake City UT 84121-6135 Office: Deseret News Pub Co PO Box 1257 Salt Lake City UT 84110-1257

MORTLOCK, ROBERT PAUL, microbiologist, educator; b. Bronxville, N.Y., May 12, 1931; s. Donald Robert and Florance Mary (Bellaby) M.; m. Florita Mary Welling, Sept., 1954; children—Florita M., Jeffrey R., Douglas P. B.S., Rensselaer Poly. Inst., N.Y., 1953; Ph.D., U. Ill., Urbana, 1958. Asst. prof. microbiology U. Mass., Amherst, 1963-68, assoc. prof. microbiology, 1968-73, prof. microbiology, 1973-78; prof. microbiology Cornell U., Ithaca, N.Y., 1978—. Editor: Microorganisms as Model Systems for Studying Evolution, 1984, The Evolution of Metabolic Function, 1992. Served to 1st lt. U.S. Army, 1959-61. Fellow Am. Acad. Microbiology; mem. AAAS, Am. Soc. Microbiology, Northeastern Microbiologists, Physiology, Ecology and Taxonomy (pres. 1984-91). Office: Cornell U Sect Microbiology Wing Hall Ithaca NY 14852

MORTOLA, EDWARD JOSEPH, academic administrator emeritus; b. N.Y.C., Feb. 5, 1917; s. John and Letitia (Pellarano) M.; m. Doris Slater, May 3, 1941; children: Doreen Mortola LeMoult, Elaine Mortola Clark. B.A., Fordham U., 1938, M.A., 1941, Ph.D., 1946, L.H.D. (hon.), 1964; postgrad., Columbia U., 1946; L.H.D. (hon.), Medaille Coll., 1980; LL.D. (hon.), Bryant Coll., 1965, Syracuse U., 1967, N.Y. Law Sch., 1968; Litt.D. (hon.), Manhattan Coll., 1967, Coll. St. Rose, 1971; LL.D. (hon.), Western State U., 1985; L.H.D. (hon.), Pace U., 1987. Grad. fellow, sch. edn. Fordham U., 1938-39, asst. registrar, 1939-41, asst. registrar, city hall div., lectr. grad. faculty, sch. edn., 1946-47; instr. math. Cooper Union and Townsend Harris High Sch., N.Y.C., 1941-42; mem. faculty St. Peter's Coll., Jersey City, part time 1946-47; with Pace U., N.Y.C., 1947—; asst. dean Pace U., 1947-49, dean, 1949-50, provost, 1950-54, v.p., 1954-60, pres., 1960-84, chancellor, 1984-90, chancellor emeritus, 1990—; mem. Community Planning Bd. 1, Borough Manhattan, 1954-66, chmn., 1956-58; mem., chmn. legis. com. Assn. Colls. and Univs. State N.Y., v.p., 1965-66, pres., 1967-68; mem. adv. council on higher edn. State Edn. Dept.; trustee, past pres. Com. on Ind. Colls. and Univs.; mem. Middle States Assn. Colls. and Schs., N.Y. Gov.'s Commn. on Quality, Cost and Finance of N.Y. State Elementary and Secondary Edn., 1969-71, Westchester Planning Commn., 1966-73, Westchester County Assn., N.Y.C. Council on Econ. Edn., Commn. on Ind. Colls. and Univs. State N.Y., chmn., 1961-63; mem. council Fordham U.; mem. Mayor's Com. on Long-Term Fin. of N.Y.C.; former mem. adv. bd. Elizabeth Seton Coll.; past dir. and sec. Greater N.Y. Council Fgn. Students; chmn. bd. govs. Fordham U. Alumni Fedn., 1958-60; formerly trustee Rosemont Coll., St. Joseph's Sem., Yonkers, N.Y.; co-chmn. N.Y. State Edn. Dept. Task Force on Teaching Profession, 1987-88; chmn. Lincoln Ctr. Inst., 1987; bd. dirs. Lincoln Ctr., 1987—; hon. dir. N.Y.C. Partnership, 1987—. Bd. govs. New Rochelle Hosp.; hon. bd. govs. White Plains Hosp.; Downtown-Lower Manhattan Assn., Econ. Devel. Council; former trustee Instructional TV. Served with USNR, 1942-46; lt. comdr. Res. Decorated cavaliere, commendatore dell'Ordine Al Merito Republic of Italy., Knight of Malta; recipient Ann. Achievement award in edn. Fordham Coll., 1960, William O'Brien award Cardinal Newman Found., 1964, Ednl. and Youth Advancement award Westchester chpt. Am. Com. Italian-Immigration, 1969, James E. Allen Jr. Meml. award Disting. Svc. to Edn. Bd. Regents N.Y. State, 1977, Leadership in Edn. award Assn. Colls. and Univs. State of N.Y., 1986, Outstanding Achievement award 100 Yr. Assn. of N.Y., 1983, Big Bros. of N.Y. Achievement award, 1987, Distinguished Alumni award Fordham U. Sch. Edn. Alumni Assn., 1970, Outstanding Achievement award One Hundred Yr. Assn., 1983, Achievement award in edn. Big Bros. N.Y., 1987, Starr award Good Counsel Acad., 1991; named Man of Yr. B'nai B'rith Youth Services, 1975. Mem. N.Y. Acad. Pub. Edn. (pres. 1962-64, dir.), N.Y. C. of C. (chmn. edn. com. 1966-68, mem. exec. com.), Nat. Office Mgmt. Assn., NEA, N.Y. Adult Edn. Coun., Knights of Malta. Clubs: Metropolitan (N.Y.C.), Univ. (N.Y.C.); Larchmont Yacht Club, Old Port Yacht Club.

MORTON, BRIAN, writer, editor, educator; b. N.Y.C., July 8, 1955; s. Richard Paul and Tasha (Brisman) M. BA, Sarah Lawrence Coll., 1978. Tchr. grad. dept. English NYU, N.Y.C., 1992—; tchr. 92d St. Y, N.Y.C., 1992-94, The New Sch. for Social Rsch., N.Y.C., 1995—; exec. dir., rev. editor Dissent Mag., N.Y.C., 1994—. Author: The Dylanist, 1991; contbr. articles to profl. publs. including Dissent, The Nation, The New Leader, Lingua Franca; book rev. editor Dissent Mag., 1988—. Office: Dissent Ste 1700 521 5th Ave New York NY 10175

MORTON, CAROLINE JULIA, marketing executive; b. N.Y.C.; BS in Edn., U. Pa.; MBA, N.Y. U.; grad. cert. in profl. writing and effective communication, CCNY. Vice pres. mktg. mgmt. V-TEC Corp., Hopewell, Va.; pres. CMR Co., Hopewell; past cons. Advt. Women of N.Y. Mem. AAWU, Am. Mktg. Assn. (past dir.), Advt. Women of N.Y., Fedn. Profl. Bus. Women, Am. Mgmt. Assn., Women in Communications. Contbr. articles to profl. jours. Address: 5705 Courthouse Rd Prince George VA 23875-3216

MORTON, DAVID RAY, sales and marketing executive; b. Rockford, Ill., Dec. 7, 1948; s. Raymond Thomas and Nathalie Ilene (Hendricks) M.; m. Carol Lynn Pott, Apr. 1, 1972; children: Rebecca Lynn, Eric David. BS in Forestry, U. Ill., 1971; MBA, Ohio State U., 1983. Field svc. rep. So. Forest Products Assn., New Orleans, 1972-73; sales rep. chem. divsn. Ga. Pacific Corp., Columbus, Ohio, 1973-76; lumber broker Fireside Forest Industries, Columbus, 1976-77; sr. tech. sales & svc. rep. chem. divsn. Ga. Pacific Corp., Columbus, 1977-84; dir. mktg. Monitronix Corp., Columbus, 1984-85; dir. mktg. & sales Freeman Mfg. & Supply Co., Cleve., 1985-88; nat. sales and mktg. mgr. Hexcel Corp.-Resins Group, L.A., 1988-95; sales mgr. Hapco, Inc., Hanover, Mass., 1995-96, v.p. sales, 1996—. Del.-at-large Rep. Platform Planning Com., Avon Lake, Ohio, 1992. Sgt. maj. U.S. Army N.G., 1971—. Mem. Soc. Mfg. Engrs. (treas. 1982-84), Am. Foundrymen's Soc. (publ. chmn. 1992—), Ohio State Alumni Assn., U. Ill. Alumni Assn., Polyurethane Mfrs. Assn. (del. 1990—), Ohio N.G. Enlisted Assn., Enlisted Assn. N.G. U.S., Phi Kappa Sigma. Avocations: sailing, handball, tennis, woodworking. Home: 296 Chestnut Ct Avon Lake OH 44012-2141

MORTON, DONALD CHARLES, astronomer; b. Kapuskasing, Ont., Can., June 12, 1933; s. Charles Orr and Irene Mary (Wightman) M.; m. Winifred May Austin, Dec. 12, 1970; children: Keith James, Christine Elizabeth. BA, U. Toronto, 1956; PhD, Princeton U., 1959. Astronomer U.S. Naval Rsch. Lab., Washington, 1959-61; from rsch. assoc. to sr. rsch. astronomer with rank of prof. Princeton (N.J.) U., 1961-76; dir. Anglo-Australian Obs., Epping and Coonabarabran, Australia, 1976-86; dir. gen. Herzberg Inst. Atstrophysics, NRC of Can., Ottawa, Ont., 1986—. Contbr. numerous articles to profl. jours. Fellow Australian Acad. Sci.; mem. Internat. Astron. Union, Royal Astron. Soc. (assoc. 1980), Astron. Soc. Australia (pres. 1981-83, hon. mem. 1986), Royal Astron. Soc. Can., Am. Astron. Soc. (councilor 1970-73), Can. Astron. Soc. Australian Inst. Physics (Pawsey Meml. lectr. 1985), Can. Assn. Physicists, U.K. Alpine Club, Am. Alpine Club, Alpine Can. Club. Avocations: mountaineering, rock climbing, ice climbing, marathon running. Office: Herzberg Inst Astrophysics, NRC Can 5071 W Saanich Rd, Victoria, BC Canada V8X 4M6

MORTON, DONALD JOHN, librarian; b. Bklyn., Jan. 11, 1931; s. Ellwood Stokes and Gladys (Hassler) M.; m. Ann Mayo Tilden, Aug. 16, 1958; children—Saundra Kay, Donald John, Mary Ann. BS, U. Del., 1952; MS, La. State U., 1954; PhD, U. Calif. at Berkeley, 1958; MS in Libr. Sci., Simmons Coll., 1969, Dr. Arts in Library Sci, 1976. Asst. prof. botany N.M. State U., Las Cruces, 1957-58; asst. prof. plant pathology N.D. State U., Fargo, 1959-61; plant pathologist Agr. Dept., Tifton, Ga., 1961-65; asso. prof. plant pathology U. Del., Newark, 1965-68; librarian Northeastern U., Boston, 1968-70; head librarian, asst. prof. history of medicine U. Mass. Med. Sch., Worcester, 1970-74; dir. libr., assoc. prof. libr. sci. U. Mass. Med. Sch., 1974-94, libr. cons., 1994—; tchr. med. librarianship Worcester State Coll., 1974-94; libr. cons., 1994—; cons. in field; mem. adv. com. med. librarianship Simmons Coll., 1972-94; mem. task force com. New Eng. Regional Libr. Svc., 1971-94; mem. cooperating staff Worcester Found. Exptl. Biology, 1972-94; chmn. Coun. Developing Med. Librs., 1974; pres. North Atlantic Health Scis. Librs., 1974-75, Worcester Area Coop. Librs., 1974-75. Contbr. articles to profl. jours. Mem. Oliver Wendell Holmes endowment com. Boston Med. Libr., 1973-74, U. Mass. Bicentennial Com., 1973-75. Mem. Am. Assn. Univ. Adminstrs., Simmons Coll. Libr. Sch. Alumni Assn. (pres. 1975-76), Worcester Art Mus., Worcester Hist. Soc., Northboro Hist. Soc., Am. Soc. Info. Sci., ALA, Mass. Libr. Assn., Med. Libr. Assn. (chmn. New Eng. group 1974-75), Mycol. Soc. Am., Spl. Librs. Assn., New Eng. Coll. Librarians, Sigma Xi, Phi Kappa Phi, Phi Sigma, Delta Tau Delta. Home: 314 High St Hampton NH 03842-4004

MORTON, EDWARD JAMES, insurance company executive; b. Ft. Wayne, Ind., Nov. 8, 1926; s. Clifford Leroy and Clara Marie (Merklein) M.; m. Jean Ann McClernon, Apr. 30, 1949; children: Marcia Lynn, Anne; m. Matthild Schneider, Sept. 19, 1986; 1 child, Katharine. BA, Yale U., 1949. With John Hancock Mut. Life Ins. Co., Boston, 1949—, v.p., then sr. v.p., 1967-74, exec. v.p., 1974-82, pres., chief operating officer, 1982-86, chmn., chief exec. officer, 1987-92, also bd. dirs.; bd. dirs. John Hancock Mutual Life Ins. Co. Trustee Gettysburg Coll.; bd. dirs. Eisenhower World Affairs Inst., 1993;mem. vis. com. dept. Ancient Egyptian, Nubian and Near Eastern Art, Mus. Fine Arts, Boston; hon. life overseer Children's Hosp.; chmn. Boston Geog. Savs. Bond Campaign, 1991. Fellow Soc. Actuaries; mem. Nat. Assn. Security Dealers (prin.), Actuaries Club Boston, Comml. Club of Boston, Algonquin Club of Boston, Phi Beta Kappa. Office: John Hancock Mut Life Ins Co PO Box 111 Boston MA 02117-0111

MORTON, ERIC, liberal arts educator; b. Detroit, Feb. 24, 1934; s. Lee Jack and Theresa Magdalen (Leonard) M.; children: Tracey Lynn, Theresa Dallas. AA, Merritt Coll., 1992; BA, U. Calif., Berkeley, 1992; M of Profl. Studies, Cornell U., 1994; grad., SUNY, Binghamton, 1994—. Internat. organizer Am. Fedn. of State, County, Mcpl. Employees, Calif., 1970-73; field rep. State Senator Nicholas Petris, Oakland, Calif., 1973-75; mktg. adminstr. Safegate Aviation Systems, Oakland, 1975-80; asst. to dir. recreational sports U. Calif., 1980-92; grad. tchg. asst. Africana Studies and Rsch. Ctr., Cornell U., 1992-94; rschr., tchr. SUNY, Binghamton, 1994—; mem., multicultural core group Cornell U., 1992-94. Compiler (book) Mississippi Black Paper, 1965; contbr. articles to profl. jours. Active polit. campaigns; project mgr. Ctr. for Ind. Living, Berkeley, 1975-77. With U.S. Army, 1951-54. Recipient Award Met. Trans. Commn., 1973. Avocations: photography, reading. Home: 2019 Stuart St Berkeley CA 94703-2237

MORTON, FREDERIC, author; b. Vienna, Austria, Oct. 5, 1924; s. Frank and Rose (Ungvary) M.; m. Marcia Colman, Mar. 28, 1957; 1 dau., Rebecca. B.S., Coll. City N.Y., 1947; M.A., New Sch. Social Research, 1949. Author: The Hound, 1947, The Darkness Below, 1949, Asphalt and Desire, 1952, The Witching Ship, 1960, The Schatten Affair, 1965, Snow Gods, 1969, An Unknown Woman, 1976, The Forever Street, 1984, Crosstown Sabbath, 1987, (biography) The Rothschilds, 1962 (nominated for Nat. Book award), A Nervous Splendor-Vienna 1888/9, 1979 (nominated for Nat. Book award), Thunder at Twilight-Vienna 1913/14, 1989; books translated into 14 langs.; actor (documentary made in English and German) Crosstown Sabbath, 1995 (broadcast in Austria, Germany, Switzerland, U.S.); contbr. to publs. including Martha Foley's Best Am. Short Stories and other anthologies, N.Y. Times, Harper's mag., Atlantic mag., Nation, Playboy, Esquire, N.Y. Mag., Hudson Rev., others; columnist Village Voice, Conde-Nast Traveler. Recipient Author of Year award Nat. Anti-Defamation League, B'nai B'rith; Hon. Professorship award Republic of Austria, 1980, Tom Osborne Disting. lectureship U. Nebr., 1989; Dodd, Mead Intercollegiate Lit. fellow, 1947; Yaddo residence fellow, 1948, 50; Breadloaf Writers' Conf. fellow, 1947; Columbia U. fellow, 1953; recipient Golden Merit award City of Vienna, 1986. Mem. Author's Guild (exec. council), P.E.N. Home: 110 Riverside Dr New York NY 10024-3715 Office: The Lantz Office 888 7th Ave New York NY 10106 *As a writer I'm trying to tell the truth interestingly.*

MORTON, HERBERT CHARLES, editor, economist; b. Mpls., July 19, 1921. B.A., U. Minn., 1942, M.A., 1950, Ph.D., 1964. Info. specialist War Assets Adminstrn., 1946-47; staff writer, telegraph news editor St. Paul Pioneer Press & Dispatch, 1947-53; rsch. editor, asst. prof. Amos Tuck Sch., Dartmouth Coll., 1953-56; dir. publs. Brookings Instn., Washington, 1956-

68; dir. Office Publs. U.S. Bur. Labor Stats., 1968-70, assoc. commr., 1971-75; dir. pub. affairs Resources for Future, Washington, 1975-80; sr. fellow Resources for Future, 1981-82; cons. Russell Sage Found., 1980-84; dir. Office Scholarly Communication, Am. Coun. Learned Socs., 1984-87; cons. Ford Found., 1964-65, Internat. Inst. Applied Systems Analysis, 1978, Nat. Commn. on Unemployment Stats., 1978, Nat. Enquiry into Scholarly Communication, 1978-79, vis. lectr. Amos Tuck Sch., 1966, Am. U., 1970. Author: Public Contracts and Private Wages, 1965, The Story of Webster's Third, 1994; co-author: An Introduction to Economic Reasoning, 1956, 5th edit., 1979, Scholarly Communication: The Report of the National Enquiry, 1979, Energy Today and Tomorrow, 1983, The ACLS Survey of Scholars, 1989; editor: Brookings Papers on Public Policy, 1965; co-editor: The American Business Corporation, 1972, Writings on Scholarly Communication, 1988; cons. editor Scholarly Publishing, 1984-92; mem. editl. bd. Book Research Quarterly, 1985-94; contbr. articles to profl. jours. Trustee Joint Coun. Econ. Edn., 1960-68; bd. dirs. Am. U. Press Svcs. Inc., 1966-68. Served with Signal Corps AUS, 1942-46. NEH fellow, 1989. Mem. Soc. Scholarly Pub. (bd. dirs. 1988-92), Dictionary Soc. N.Am., Am. Dialect Soc. Home: 7106 Laverock Ln Bethesda MD 20817-4734

MORTON, JAMES CARNES, JR., public relations executive; b. Duncan, Okla., May 8, 1945; s. James Carnes and Syble Lyda (Looney) M.; m. Susan Phillips, May 25, 1968; children: James III, Terrissa Anne, Scott Thomas. BA, Westminster Coll., 1967; JD, U. Mo., 1972. Bar: Mo. 1972. Tax acct. Arthur Andersen Co., St. Louis, 1972-74; tax atty. Gen. Dynamics Corp., St. Louis, 1974-76; asst. gen. counsel Michelin Tire Corp., Greenville, S.C., 1976-86; gen. counsel Michelin Tire Corp. and Michelin Tires (Can.) Ltd., Greenville, S.C., 1990-92; dir. pub. rels. and govt. affairs Michelin Tire Corp., Greenville, S.C., 1986-92; exec. dir. external rels. Michelin N.Am., Greenville, S.C., 1992-96; v.p. pub. rels. and govt. rels. Michelin N.Am., Inc., 1996—. Bd. dirs. Greenville Symphony Orch., 1986-89, United Way Greenville, 1987-88, Greenville YMCA, 1988-89; mem. S.C. State Reorgn. Commn., 1987—; mem. bd. visitors and fin. com. Christ Church Episcopal Sch., Greenville, 1991—. Capt. U.S. Army, 1967-72, Vietnam. Mem. ABA, S.C. Bar, Rubber Mfrs. Assn. (bd. dirs. 1995—, govt. affairs com., tire mgmt. com., tire industry safety coun.), Mo. Bar Assn. (nonresident), S.C. C. of C. (bd. dirs., pres. 1993-94, bd. dirs. Edn. Resource Found., chmn. 1994-95, exec. com. 1981-84, 86-95, Svc. Recognition award 1982), Greater Greenville C. of C. (chmn. govt. affairs com. 1990, bd. dirs. 1990-93), Greenville Country Club, Greenville City Club, Commerce Club, Faculty House Club (U.S.C.). Presbyterian. Avocations: tennis, golf. Office: Michelin NAm PO Box 19001 Greenville SC 29602-9001

MORTON, JAMES DAVIS, lawyer; b. Pitts., Jan. 30, 1928; s. Roy S. and Magdeline M. (Meeder) M.; m. Ann Medved, Sept. 7, 1957; children: Timothy, Ann, Gary. BS in Bus. Administrn., U. Pitts., 1951, Dr. of Laws, 1954. Bar: Pa. 1955, Fla. 1979. Assoc. Brown, Critchlow, Flick, Peckham & Miller, Pitts., 1954-55; shareholder Buchanan Ingersoll, P.C. (and predecessor firms), Pitts., 1955—; dir. Indsl. Sci. Corp., Pitts. Dir. Civic Light Opera, Pitts., 1985—; del. Pa. Constl. Conv., Harrisburg, 1967-68. Fellow Am. Coll. Trial Lawyers; mem. Acad. Trial Lawyers Allegheny County (past pres.), U.S. Dist. Ct. West. Dist. Pa. (com. mem. civil justice adv. group), Edgewood Country Club (past pres.). Republican. Episcopalian. Office: Buchanan Ingersoll PC 20th Fl 301 Grant St 1 Oxford Centre Pittsburgh PA 15219-1410

MORTON, JAMES IRWIN, hospital administrator; b. Chulumani, Sud Yungas, Bolivia, Feb. 28, 1935; came to U.S., 1952; s. Harrison Cecil and Flossie Mae (Irwin); m. Beverly Jean Nash, June 9, 1957; c1 child, Linda Kathleen. BA, Andrews U., 1957; MHA, U. Mich., 1959. Commd. 2nd lt. USAF, 1959, advanced through grades to col., 1988.; adminstr. Whitfield (Miss.) Med. Surg. Hosp., 1988—; pres. coun. Jackson-Vicksburg Hosp., 1992-93; cons. to surgeon gen. USAF, Washington, 1980-88. Charter mem. The Miss. Chorus, 1989—, bd. dirs., treas., 1990-93. Decorated Legion of Merit. Fellow Am. Coll. Healthcare Execs. (pres. Miss. affiliates 1991-92, Miss. Regent 1994-99). Avocations: singing, computers, photography, reading. Office: Whitfield Med Surg Hosp Whitfield MS 39193

MORTON, JEFFREY BRUCE, aerospace engineering educator; b. Chgo., Apr. 25, 1941; s. Max E. and Tillie (Forman) M.; m. Judy Gail Moss, June 14, 1964; children: Jonathan, Amy, Michael. BS, Mass. Inst. Tech., 1963; PhD, Johns Hopkins U., 1967. Sr. scientist U. Va., Charlottesville, 1967-68, asst. prof., 1968-72, assoc. prof., 1972-80, prof., 1980—; lectr. U. Va., 1967-68; pres. M.J. Systems Inc., Charlottesville, 1976—. Contbr. articles to profl. jours. Assoc. Fellow AIAA; mem. Am. Soc. Engring. Edn. (southeast sect. rsch. award 1981), Am. Physical Soc., Sigma Xi. Office: U Va Dept Mech Aerospace Engring Charlottesville VA 22901

MORTON, LAUREL ANNE, elementary education educator; b. Cin., July 27, 1954; d. James William and Rosemary (Danner) M. BA in Social Sci., Calif. State U.-Stanislaus, Turlock, 1978; teaching credential, Calif. State Polytech U., Pomona, 1986; MA in Edn., Calif. State Poly. U., Pomona, 1992. Cert. tchr., Calif., Colo. Sr. loan clk. Shearson Am. Express Mortgage Corp., Newport Beach, Calif., 1978-82; adminstrv. asst. Investco Corp., Santa Barbara, Calif., 1982-83; supr. loan servicing dept. County Savs. Bank, Santa Barbara, 1983-84; comm. asst. Fuller Theol. Sem., Pasadena, Calif., 1984-85; elem. tchr. Howard Sch., Ontario, Calif., 1986-91; tchr. Bon View Elem. Sch., Ontario, 1992—, 4th grade team leader, 1993-94, track leader, 1995-96. Mem. Nat. Honor Soc., Phi Kappa Phi, Zeta Tau Alpha. Avocations: tennis, theater, dancing, travel, museums or venues of educational interest. Home: 1919 Stonehouse Rd Sierra Madre CA 91024-1409 Office: Bon View Elem Sch 2121 S Bon View Ontario CA 91761-4408

MORTON, LELAND CLURE, judge; b. Knoxville, Tenn., Feb. 20, 1916; s. George W. and Birdie (Myers) M.; m. Marjorie J. Hernandez, Sept. 13, 1945 (dec. 1993). BA, U. Tenn., 1934, JD, 1936. Bar: Tenn. 1937. Pvt. practice law, Knoxville, 1937-41, 46-70; spl. agt. FBI, Washington, 1941-42, Cen. and S.Am., 1942-46; judge U.S. Dist. Ct. (mid. dist.) Tenn., Nashville, 1970-77, chief judge, 1977-84, sr. judge, 1984—; instr., U. Tenn.; co-founder Vol. State Bank, Knoxville, 1964. Counselor East Tenn. council Boy Scouts Am., 1937-40; bd. dirs. Cerebral Palsy Found., Boys Club, Boys of Tenn. Mem. Tenn. Bar Assn., Nashville Bar Assn., S.R., Phi Kappa Phi. Republican. Methodist. Office: US Dist Ct 228 US Courthouse 9 E Broadway Cookeville TN 38501*

MORTON, MALVIN, social welfare administrator, consultant; b. Temeha, Tex., June 24, 1906; d. Charles Newton and Bessie Howell (Warner) M. MA in Social Svcs., U. Pitts., 1945. Caseworker Fed. Emergency Relief Adminstrn., Ft. Worth, 1933-35; program dir. YWCA, Greensboro, N.C., 1935-40; dir. teenage girls program YWCA, Indpls., 1940-43; social work cons. Community Chest Welfare Fedn., Pitts., 1945-47; pub. rels. dir. United Charities, Chgo., 1947-52; exec. dir. Chgo. Fedn. of Settlements & Neighborhood Ctrs., Chgo., 1952-61; publs. dir. Am. Pub. Welfare Assn., Chgo., 1961-71; dir. communications Florence Crittendon Assn. of Am., Chgo., 1971-74, ret., 1974; founder, bd. dirs. Contact Chgo.; attendance internat. social welfare confs., Munich, Athens, Washington, Copenhagen, Helsinki. Editor Pub. Welfare, 1952-61. Patron Olive Branch Mission, Chgo., 1963—; founder, adviser Citizenship Coun. Greater Chgo., 1956—; exec. dir. Chgo. Mayor's Civic Com. for Jane Addams Centennial, 1960; bd. dirs. Friends of Lit., 1978—, pres. 1990-92. Recipient honors Am. Assn. S.W. with Groups, 1993, U. Pitts. Sch. Social Work, 1993, Tex. Wesleyan U., 1993. Mem. NASW (life), Am. Med. Writers Assn. (life, Chgo. chpt.), Lyric Opera Chgo., Goodman Theater Chgo., Art Inst. Chgo. Democrat. Methodist. Home: Bethany Home 4950 N Ashland Ave # 478 Chicago IL 60640-3417

MORTON, MARILYN MILLER, genealogy and history educator, lecturer, researcher, travel executive, director; b. Water Valley, Miss., Dec. 2, 1929; d. Julius Brunner and Irma Faye (Magee) Miller; m. Perry Wilkes Morton Jr., July 2, 1958; children: Dent Miller Morton, Nancy Marilyn Morton Driggers, E. Perian Morton Ethridge. BA in English, Miss. U. for Women, 1952; MS in History, Miss. State U., 1955. Cert. secondary tchr. Tchr. English, speech and history Starkville (Miss.) H.S., 1952-58; part-time instr. Miss. State U., 1953-55; mem. spl. collection staff Samford U. Libr., Birmingham, Ala., 1984-92; lectr. genealogy and history, instr. Inst. Genealogy & Hist. Rsch., Samford U., Birmingham, 1985-93, assoc. dir., 1985-88, exec. dir., 1988-93; founding dir. SU British and Irish Inst. Genealogy & Hist. Rsch. Samford U., Birmingham and British Isles, 1986-93; owner, dir. Marilyn Miller Morton Brit-Ire-U.S. Genealogy, Birmingham, also British Isles, 1994—; instr. genealogy classes Samford U. Metro Coll., 1989-94; lectr. nat. conf. Fedn. of Geneal. Socs. Contbr. articles and book revs. to profl. jours. Active Birmingham chpt. Salvation Army Aux., 1982—. Inducted into Miss. U. for Women Hall of Fame, 1952. Fellow Irish Geneal. Rsch. Soc. London; mem. Internat. Soc. Brit. Genealogy and Family History, Nat. Geneal. Soc. (mem. nat. program com. 1988—, lectr. nat. mtgs.), Assn. Profl. Genealogists, Soc. Genealogists London, Antiquarian Soc. Birmingham (sec., 2d v.p. 1982-84), DAR (regent Cheaha chpt. 1977-78), Daus. Am. Colonists (regent Edward Waters chpt. 1978-79), Nat. League of Am. Penwomen, Phi Kappa Phi (charter mem. Samford U. chpt. 1972). Avocations: reading, travel, walking, public speaking, chess. Home and Office: 3508 Clayton Pl Birmingham AL 35216-3810

MORTON, MARSHALL NAY, financial executive; b. Chgo., Oct. 3, 1945; s. Frederick Samuel and Margaret Elizabeth (Burke) M.; m. Caroline Sanders, Sept. 13, 1969; children—Marshall Burke, Margaret Elizabeth. BA, U. Va., 1970, MBA, 1972. Fin. analyst West Point Pepperell Inc., Ga., 1972-73, budget dir., 1973-74, fin. mgr., 1974-75, asst. treas., 1975-81, treas., 1981-86, v.p., controller, 1986—, sr. v.p., CFO, Media Gen., Inc., Richmond, Va., 1989—. Pres., Valley United Fund, West Point, 1982, Am. Cancer Soc., West Point chpt., 1985-87; v.p. fin. Lanier Council Boys Scouts Am., 1986-87; former bd. dirs. Commonwealth Girl Scout Coun. of Va., also pres.; pres. The Robert E. Lee Coun. Boys Scouts Am. Served with USN, 1966-68, Vietnam. Episcopalian. Mem. Richmond Metro C. of C. (former bd. dirs.), Union League Club (N.Y.C.), Country Club of Va., The Commonwealth Club. Avocations: tennis, sailing. Office: Media Gen Inc 333 E Grace St Richmond VA 23293-1000

MORTON, STEPHEN DANA, chemist; b. Madison, Wis., Sept. 7, 1932; s. Walter Albert and Rosalie (Amlie) M.; B.S., U. Wis., 1954, Ph.D., 1962. Asst. prof. chemistry Otterbein Coll., Westerville, Ohio, 1962-66; postdoctoral fellow water chemistry, pollution control U. Wis., Madison, 1966-67; water pollution research chemist WARF Inst., Madison, 1967-73; head environ. quality dept., 1973-76; mgr. quality assurance Raltech Sci. Services, 1977-82; pres. SDM Cons., 1982—. Served to 1st lt. Chem. Corps, AUS, 1954-56. Mem. AAAS, Am. Chem. Soc., Am. Water Works Assn., Am. Soc. Limnology and Oceanography, Water Environ. Fedn. Author: Water Pollution—Causes and Cures, 1976. Home: 1126 Sherman Ave Madison WI 53703-1620

MORTON, WILLIAM GILBERT, JR., stock exchange executive; b. Syracuse, N.Y., Mar. 13, 1937; s. William Gilbert and Barbara (Link) M.; m. Margaret Halleron, Nov. 26, 1982; children: Andrew Baker, William Gilbert III, Sarah Ellsworth, Kate Spencer. BA, Dartmouth Coll., 1959; MBA, NYU, 1965. Asst. v.p. Discount Corp. N.Y., 1960-67; co-mgr. trading, sr. v.p., dir. Mitchell Hutchins Inc., 1967-79; mng. stock exch. floors, sr. v.p., dir. Dean Witter Reynolds Inc., 1979-85; chmn., chief exec. officer Boston Stock Exch. Inc., 1985—; chmn. allocation com. N.Y. Stock Exch., floor ofcl., 1976-81, various working coms., 1970-85; bd. dirs. Tandy Corp., Ft. Worth, Investment Funds, Morgan Stanley Asset Mgmt. Inc., N.Y. Bd. dirs. Vt. Acad., Saxton's River, Bostonian Soc., Nat. Football Found. and Coll. Hall of Fame, N.Y.; trustee search com. Dartmouth Alumni Coun., 1988-91. With USMC, 1959-65. Mem. Boston Econ. Club, Mass. Bus. Roundtable, Algonquin Club (Boston), Racquet and Tennis Club N.Y.C., Stratton Mt. Country Club (Vt.), Colo. Arlberg Club (Winter Park), Brae Burn Country Club (Newton), Ekwanok Country Club (Vt.), Royal Poinciana Club, Theta Delta Chi. Republican. Presbyterian. Office: Boston Stock Exch 1 Boston Pl Boston MA 02108-4400

MORTVEDT, JOHN JACOB, soil scientist; b. Dell Rapids, S.D., Jan. 25, 1932; s. Ernest R. and Clara (Halvorson) M.; m. Marlene L. Fodness, Jan. 23, 1955; children: Sheryl Mortvedt Jarratt, Lori Mortvedt Klopf, Julie Mortvedt Stride. BS, S.D. State U., 1953, MS, 1959; PhD, U. Wis., 1962. Soil chemist TVA, Muscle Shoals, Ala., 1962-87, sr. scientist, 1987-92, regional mgr. field programs dept., 1992-93; ext. soils specialist Colo. State U., Ft. Collins, 1994-95. Editor: Micronutrients in Agriculture, 1972, 2d edit., 1991; contbr. articles to profl. jours. 1st lt. U.S. Army, 1953-57. Fellow AAAS, Soil Sci. Soc. Am. (pres. 1988-89, editor-in-chief 1982-87, Profl. Svc. award 1991), Am. Soc. Agronomy (exec. com. 1987-90); mem. Internat. Soil Sci. Soc., Colombian Soil Sci. Soc. (hon.), Exch. Club (pres. Florence, Ala. chpt. 1987-88), Toastmasters (pres. Florence chpt. 1964-65), Phi Kappa Phi. Avocations: photography, golf. Office: Colo State U Dept Soil and Crop Scis Fort Collins CO 80523

MORUD, ROLLIE D., school system administrator. Supt. Dickinson (N.D.) Pub. Schs. Recipient Nat. Superintendent of the Yr. awd., North Dakota, Am. Assn. of School Administrators, 1993. Office: Dickinson Pub Schs 444 4th St W Dickinson ND 58601-4951

MORWAY, RICHARD A., newspaper publishing executive; m. Vincenza Morway; children: Andrea, Cynthia. BBA, Cleve. State U.; MBA, Lake Erie Coll., 1994. From gen. acctg. clk. to asst. treas./asst. contr. Plain Dealer Pub. Co., Cleve., 1969-92, treas., 1992—; sec., treas. Plain Dealer Charities, Inc.; treas. Delcom, Inc. Mem. fin. support rev. com. Greater Cleve. Growth Assn.; active Blue Cross/Blue Shield Adv. Coun.; bd. dirs. Project Learn. Mem. Internat. Newspaper Fin. Execs. Office: Plain Dealer Pub Co 1801 Superior Ave E Cleveland OH 44114-2107

MOSAVI, REZA KHONSARI, laser physicist; b. Tehran, Iran, Sept. 23, 1944; came to U.S., 1964; s. Fazlolah Khonsari and Ghodsi (Khonsari) M.; m. Margaret Carol Booze, July 13, 1968; children: Leila, Sara. BS in Physics, Miami U., Oxford, Ohio, 1968; MS in Physics, U. Mass., 1970; PhD in Nuclear Engring., U. Cin., 1974. Rsch. scientist Battelle Columbus (Ohio) Labs., 1973-75; mgr. laser tech. sect. Atomic Energy Orgn. Iran, Tehran, 1975-84; cons., Cin., 1984-85; mgr. laser ops. Chromalloy Rsch. & Tech., Orangeburg, N.Y., 1985-94; cons. in laser material processing Howmet Advanced Refurbishment and Coatings, North Haven, Conn., 1994—; mem. nat. rev. and selection com. for allocation rsch. funds in engring. Iranian Ministry Sci. and Higher Edn., Tehran, 1983-84. Contbr. articles to profl. jours.; patentee in field. 1st lt. Iranian Army, 1975-77. Mem. Soc. Mfg. Engrs., Optical Soc. Am., Laser Inst. Am. Moslem. Avocations: reading, travel. Home: 115 Perry Rd Hamden CT 06514

MOSBACHER, MARTIN BRUCE, public relations executive; b. N.Y.C., Nov. 4, 1951; s. Walter and Grete (Wolffs) M.; m. Andrea Dow, Jan. 25, 1981; children: Sarah Mariel, Rachel Helene. BA in Polit. Sci., CCNY, 1972, MS in Urban Planning, 1975. Spl. asst. to speaker N.Y. State Assembly, Albany, 1976-78; mgr. pub. rels. Sea-Land Corp., Menlo Park, N.J., 1979-83; dir. pub. rels. Commodity Exch., Inc., N.Y.C., 1983-86; prin. NYCOM Assocs., N.Y.C., 1986-88; chmn. Trimedia Inc., N.Y.C., 1988—. Del. Dem. Nat. Conv., Miami, Fla., 1972. Mem. Internat. Assn. Bus. Communicators, Futures Industry Assn., Pub. Rels. Soc. Am. Office: Trimedia Inc 425 Madison Ave Fl 600 New York NY 10017-1110

MOSCA, ANTHONY JOHN, substance abuse professional; b. Cambridge, Mass., June 28, 1944; s. Anthony Mosca and Margaret Mary Kelleher; m. Sheryl Lyn Everett, July 12, 1986. BA in Psychology, U. N.H., 1978; MA in Psychology, Assumption Coll., Worcester, Mass., 1984; postgrad., Rivier Coll., Nashua, N.H., 1990. Lic. mental health counselor, Mass.; cert. addictions specialist, Am. Acad. Health Care Providers in the Addictive Disorders. Psychiat. counselor, milieu coord. New England Meml. Hosp., Stoneham, Mass., 1979-80; alcoholism counselor Nor Cap Lodge, Foxboro, Mass., 1980-82; alcohol and drug counselor Bournwood Hosp., Brookline, Mass., 1982-83; coord. of vocat. evaluation unit Project Hire, Norwood, Mass., 1983-85; rehab. counselor Driving Under the Influence program, Tewksbury, Mass., 1985-86; clin. dir./substance abuse counselor New Beginnings Counseling, Inc., Lowell, Mass., 1986-88; substance abuse specialist Human Resource Inst., Lowell, Mass., 1986-94; coord. Structured Outpatient Addictions Program Behavioral Health Consortium No. Mass., Lawrence, 1994—; pvt. practice A.S.M. Counseling, Dracut, Mass., 1988—; guest speaker Sharsheen Vocat. Tech. High Sch., Billerica, Mass., 1986. Campaign cons., Seabrook, N.H., 1975; handicap access advocate, Lowell, Dracut, 1990—; guest speaker disabled students group., Middlesex C.C., Lowell, 1993, Ctr. Ind. Living, Lawrence, 1995. Recipient letter of commendation from Nancy Reagan. Mem. Internat. Assn. of Addictions and Offender Counselors, Am. Counseling Assn., Am. Acad. of Health Care Providers in the Addictive Disorders, Am. Mental Health Counselors Assn., Mass. Mental Health Counselors Assn. Avocations: keeping current on material regarding the addictions field, fantasy football leagues. Home: 59 Mill St Unit 106 Dracut MA 01826-3248 Office: Behavioral Health Consortium No Mass 30 General St Lawrence MA 01841-2961

MOSCARINO, GEORGE J., lawyer; b. Cleve., May 30, 1934. AB, Ohio U., 1955; JD, Case Western Res. U., 1958. Bar: Ohio 1958. Asst. atty. gen. U.S. Attys. Office, Cleve., 1960; asst. pros. atty. U.S. Attys. Office, Cuyahoga County, Ohio, 1961-70; ptnr. Jones, Day, Reavis & Pogue, Cleve. Fellow Am. Coll. Trial Lawyers; mem. ABA (mem. grand jury com. 1983-86, spl. advisor gran jury com. 1986—, mem. sect. coun. 1984-88, mem. criminal justice sect.). Office: Jones Day Reavis & Pogue North Point 901 Lakeside Ave E Cleveland OH 44114-1116*

MOSCATO, ANTHONY CHARLES, federal official; b. N.Y.C., Sept. 4, 1945; s. Charles Joseph and Anne (Antreassian) M.; m. Deborah Louise (Stackawitz), Feb. 10, 1973; children: Charles Joseph, Emily Clair. BA, Columbia U., 1967; JD, George Washington U., 1970. Trial atty. tax div. U.S. Dept. Justice, Washington, 1976-77, spl. asst. to asst. atty. gen. justice mgmt. div., 1977-79, dir. property mgmt. and procurement staff justice mgmt. div., 1979-81, dir. evaluation staff justice mgmt.div., 1981-84, dir. fin. staff justice mgmt. div., 1984, counselor to asst. atty. gen. justice mgmt. div., 1984-87, dep. asst. atty gen., adminstrn. justice mgmt. div., 1987-89, acting insp. gen. Office of Insp. Gen., 1989-90, dep. asst. atty. gen., adminstrn., justice mgmt. div., 1990-92, dir. exec. office U.S. attys., 1992-94; dir. exec. office Immigration Rev., 1994—. Recipient Atty. Gen.'s award for Disting. Svc., 1988, Atty. Gen's. Medallion, 1990, Presdl. Meritorious Exec. Rank award, 1991, Edmund Randolph award, 1993. Office: Exec Office Immigration Review 5107 Leesburg Pike Ste 2400 Falls Church VA 22041

MOSCHELLA, SAMUEL L., dermatology educator; b. East Boston, Mass., Apr. 22, 1921. BS, Tufts U., 1943, MD cum laude, 1946. Diplomate Am. Bd. Dermatology. Intern in medicine Boston City Hosp., 1946-47; resident in dermatology U.S. Naval Hosp., Phila., 1948, St. Albans, 1951; postgrad. in skin and cancer Bellevue Hosp., N.Y.C., 1952-53; chief dermatology U.S. Naval Hosp., Phila., 1953-54, chief dermatology, asst. chief medicine, Guantanamo Bay, Cuba, 1948-51, chief dermatology, Chelsea, Mass., 1956-62, chmn. dept. dermatology, Phila., 1962-67; chmn. dept. dermatology Lahey Clinic Med. Ctr., Burlington, Mass., 1969-82; clin. prof. dermatology Harvard U. Med. Sch., Boston, 1980-91, prof. emeritus, 1991—; cons. U.S. Pub. Health Leprasorium, Carville, La., 1968—, U.S. Naval Hosp., Phila., 1967-72, Bethesda, Md., 1976—; guest lectr. U. Pa. Grad. Sch., 1962-67, Harvard Sch. Tropical Medicine, 1975—. Author/editor: (with otherw) Dermatology, 3d edit., 1992; contbr. articles to profl. jours.; also papers, book chpts. Fellow ACP; mem. AMA, Am. Acad. Dermatology, Am. Dermatol. Assn., Am. Soc. Dermapathology, Internat. Leprosy Assn., Internat. Soc. Dermatology, New Eng. Dermatologic Soc., Mass. Acad. Dermatology, Boston Dermatology Soc., Mass. Med. Soc., soc. Investigative Dermatology. Home: 887 Commonwealth Ave Newton MA 02159-1036 Office: Lahey Clinic Med Ctr 41 Mall Rd Box 541 Burlington MA 01805

MOSCHNER, ALBIN F., electronics executive; m. Mary Ann; children: Jessica, Christopher, Erica, Matthew. BEEE, CUNY, 1974; MEEE, Syracuse U., 1979. Various pos. IBM, Rochester, Minn., 1974-88, ETA Systems, 1988-89, Tricord Systems, 1989-91; v.p. ops. Zenith, Glenview, Ill., 1991-93, pres. and COO, 1993—, CEO, 1995—; mem. bd. dirs. Zenith, 1992—, Polaroid Corp., Pella Corp., Lake Forest (Ill.) Bank & Trust, 1995—. Mem. bd. trustees WTTW, Chgo.; mem. adv. bd. Ill. Kellogg Grad. Sch. Mem. IEEE, Econ. Club of Chgo., Fgn. Rels. Coun. of Chgo. Office: Zenith Electronics Corp 1000 Milwaukee Ave Glenview IL 60025-2423

MOSCONA, ARON ARTHUR, biology educator, scientist; b. Israel, July 4, 1922; came to U.S., 1955, naturalized, 1965; s. David DeAbravanel and Lola (Krochmaal) M.; m. Malka Kempinsky, July 6, 1954; 1 child, Anne. M.Sc., Hebrew U., Jerusalem, 1947, Ph.D., 1950. Postgrad. fellow Strangeways Research Lab., Cambridge, Eng., 1950-52; vis. investigator Rockefeller Inst., N.Y.C., 1955-57; prof. biology U. Chgo., 1958—, Louis Block prof. biol. scis., 1972-92, Louis Block prof. emeritus, 1992—; chmn. Com. on Devel. Biology, 1969-76; vis. prof. Stanford U., 1959, U. Montreal, 1960, U. Palermo, Italy, 1966, Hebrew U., Jerusalem, 1972, Tel-Aviv (Israel) U., 1977, 79, Kyoto U., Japan, 1980. Author: (with A. Monroy) Introductory Concepts in Developmental Biology, 1979; founder, editor: Current Topics in Developmental Biology, 1965; past mem. editorial bd. Jour. Molecular Neurosci., New Biologist, Mechanisms of Aging and Development, Cell Differentiation, Cancer Research, Devel. Neurosci., Experimental Cell Research; contbr. 260 articles to profl. jours. Recipient Claude Bernard medal in exptl. medicine, 1962, Alcon prize in visual sci., 1990, Gold medal Azabu Univ., Japan, 1991. Fellow AAAS, Am. Acad. Arts and Scis., Lombardo Inst. (Milan), N.Y. Acad. Scis.; mem. NAS, Internat. Soc. Devel. Biology (pres. 1977-81), Am. Soc. Devel. Biology, Internat. Soc. Cell Biology, Am. Soc. Zoology, Sigma Xi.

MOSCOWITZ, ALBERT JOSEPH, chemist, educator; b. Manchester, N.H., Aug. 20, 1929; s. Mark and Sarah (Kavesh) M. B.S., City Coll. N.Y., 1950; M.A., Harvard, 1954, Ph.D., 1957. NRC-Am. Chem. Soc.-Petroleum Research Fund postdoctoral fellow Harvard, 1957-58, Washington, 1958-59; mem. faculty U. Minn., 1959—, prof. chemistry, 1965—; vis. prof. U. Copenhagen, Denmark, 1961-62, 67-68, 76; Seydel-Woolley vis. prof. Ga. Inst. Tech., 1966; cons. to industry, 1960—. Chmn. nat. screening com. Fulbright-Hays awards for, Scandinavia and Iceland, 1966; vice chmn. Gordon Conf. in Theoretical Chemistry, 1968, chmn., 1970. Adv. editorial bd.: Chem. Physics Letters, 1967-80; assoc. editor: Jour. Chem. Physics, 1970-73; Contbr. profl. jours. Fulbright lectr., 1961; Sloan fellow, 1962-66. Fellow AAAS, Am. Phys. Soc., N.Y. Acad. Scis.; mem. Am. Chem. Soc., Faraday Soc., Royal Soc. Chemistry (Eng.), Royal Danish Acad. Scis. and Letters (fgn. mem.), Harvard Club Minn., Skylight Club, Sigma Xi, Phi Beta Kappa. Home: The Towers 19 S 1st St Minneapolis MN 55401-1839 Office: U Minn Dept Chem Minneapolis MN 55455

MOSEBAR, DONALD HOWARD, professional football player; b. Yakima, Wash., Sept. 11, 1961. Student, U. So. Calif. Center L.A. Raiders, 1983—. Named NFL All-Pro team center, The Sporting News, 1991, Played in Super Bowl XVIII, 1983. Played in Pro Bowl, 1990-91. Office: L.A. Raiders 332 Center St El Segundo CA 90245-4047

MOSELEY, CARLOS DUPRE, former music executive, musician; b. Laurens, S.C., Sept. 21, 1914; s. Carlos Roland and Helen Allston (DuPre) M. BA magna cum laude, Duke, 1935; postgrad., Phila. Conservatory Music, 1941-44; student piano with Harold Morris, Olga Samaroff, Sophia Rosoff; LHD (hon.), Wofford Coll., 1966, Duke U., 1985; MusD (hon.), Converse Coll., 1971; DFA (hon.), U. S.C., 1989; LHD (hon.), The Juilliard Sch., 1995. Head fgn. information research div. OWI, N.Y.C., 1944-45; chief music sect. State Dept., Washington, 1946-48; music officer Office Mil. Govt. for Bavaria, Munich, Germany, 1948-49; chief fine arts and exhibits sect. reorientation br. Army Dept., N.Y.C., 1949-50; dir. Sch. Music, prof. music U. Okla., 1950-55; dir. press and pub. relations N.Y. Philharmonic Symphony Soc., N.Y.C., 1955-59; assoc. mng. dir. N.Y. Philharmonic Symphony Soc., 1959-61, mng. dir., 1961-70, pres., 1970-78, vice chmn., 1978-83, chmn., 1983-85, chmn. emeritus, 1985—; U.S. del. to UNESCO Music Conf., Paris, 1948; U.S. del Internat. Music Coun., Paris, 1953; mem. music panel Nat. Endowment for Arts, 1967-69, N.Y. State Coun. on Arts, 1973-77, Nat. Coun. on Arts, 1985-91. Soloist, N.Y. Philharmonic Orch., N.Y.C. Symphony, Berkshire Music Center Orch., San Diego Symphony, Portuguese Nat. Symphony, Lisbon, Vt. Symphony, others. Trustee Fan Fox and Leslie R. Samuels Found., Eleanor Naylor Dana Charitable Trust, Charles A. Dana Found.; mem. Lincoln Ctr. coun. Lincoln Ctr. for Performing Arts, 1961-78; chmn. performing arts adv. com. Asia Soc., 1970-91; mem. Met. Opera Assn. Winner MacDowell Nat. Young Artists Competition, 1939; recipient N.Y.C. Mayor's medal of honor for arts and culture, 1978, Disting. Svc. citation U. Okla., 1989, Order of the Palmetto, State of S.C., Nat. citation Nat. Fedn. Music Clubs, 1991, Lifetime Achievement award S.C. Gov.'s Sch. of the Arts, 1995. Mem. Met. Opera Assn., Century

Assn. (N.Y.C.), Piedmont Club (S.C.), Phi Beta Kappa, Mu Phi Epsilon, Pi Kappa Lambda, Phi Eta Sigma. Office: care Dana Charitable Trust 375 Park Ave New York NY 10152

MOSELEY, CHRIS ROSSER, marketing executive; b. Balt., Apr. 13, 1950; d. Thomas Earl and Fern Elaine (Coleman) Rosser; m. Thomas Kenneth Moseley. BA with honors, The Coll. of Wooster, 1972. Asst. dir. advt. and promotion Sta. WBAL-TV, Balt., 1972-74; dir. pub. rels. Mintz & Hoke Advt. Inc., Hartford, Conn., 1974-75; promotion mgr. Sta. WFSB-TV, Hartford, 1975-77; audience promotion mgr. Sta. WTVJ-TV, Miami, Fla., 1977-78; pres. CMA Mktg. Cons., Hyde Park, N.Y., 1979-82; promotion mgr. Ind. Network News-Sta. WPIX-TV, N.Y.C., 1982-84; sr. v.p., mgmt. supr. Christopher Thomas Muller Jordan Weiss, N.Y.C., 1984-89, Earle Palmer Brown/N.Y., N.Y.C., 1989-90; sr. v.p. mktg. and comm. Discovery Comms., Inc., Bethesda, Md., 1990—. Recipient Best Bus.-to-Bus. award Art Direction mag., 1984, award of achievement in media rels. and edn. Nat. Resources Coun. Am., 1991, Best Editorial Excellence award Mag. Age, 1992, Best Overall Mktg. Campaign award MIP/MIPCOM, 1994, 1st Place Print award: Media Promotion, London Internat. Advt. awards, 1993, Gold award Broadcast Designers, 1993, Mktg. 100 award Ad Age, 1995, Cable Marketer of Yr. award Ad Age, 1995. Mem. CTAM (chair, Mark award 1995), NCTA (conv. com. 1995), WIC, AWNY, PROMAX Internat. (chair elect), CTPAA. Democrat. Avocations: horticulture, travel. Home: PO Box 418 Riderwood MD 21139-0418 Office: Discovery Networks Discovery Comms Inc 7700 Wisconsin Ave Bethesda MD 20814-3578

MOSELEY, FREDERICK STRONG, III, investment banker; b. N.Y.C., May 4, 1928; s. Frederick S. Jr. and Jane Hamilton (Brady) M.; m. Elizabeth Hall Perkins, June 12, 1952; children: Frederick Strong IV, Elizabeth Howland Edwards, Cassandra Hamilton Berry. Ed., Harvard U., 1951. With F.S. Moseley & Co., Boston, 1955—; gen. partner F.S. Moseley & Co., 1959-69, mng. partner, 1970-73; pres., chief exec. officer, dir. F.S. Moseley, Estabrook Inc., 1973-75; chmn., chief exec. officer Moseley, Hallgarten & Estabrook Holding Corp., 1976-79; chmn., co-chief exec. officer Moseley, Hallgarten, Estabrook & Weeden Holding Corp., 1979-82, chmn., 1982-88; sr. v.p. Gruntal and Co., Inc., Boston, 1988-90; mng. dir. Seaward Mgmt. Corp., Boston, 1990—; gov., mem. exec. com. Assn. Stock Exchange Firms, 1966-71; gov. Am. Stock Exchange, 1970-72; mem. regional firms adv. com. N.Y. Stock Exchange, 1973-76; bd. dirs. Fifty Assocs., Boston. Mem. corp. Mass. Gen. Hosp.; trustee Human Soc. of Commonwealth Mass., Brookwood Sch.; mem. corp. Trustees of Reservations; trustee, v.p. Mass. Soc. for Promoting Agr. 1st lt. AUS, 1953-55. Mem. Securities Industry Assn. (dir., governing council 1972), Asso. Harvard Alumni (dir. 1977-78, v.p. 1980). Clubs: Somerset (Boston), Myopia Hunt (Hamilton, Mass.), Midocean (Bermuda), Augusta Nat. (Ga.), Tarratine (Islesboro, Maine). Office: Seaward Mgmt Corp 10 Post Office Sq Boston MA 02109-4603

MOSELEY, FURMAN C., timber company executive; b. 1935. With Simpson Paper Co., 1960—, formerly exec. v.p., now chmn. bd., also dir.; pres. Simpson Investment Co., Seattle. Served USMC, 1956-59. Office: Simpson Paper Co 8140 Ward Pky Kansas City MO 64114-2006*

MOSELEY, JAMES FRANCIS, lawyer; b. Charleston, S.C., Dec. 6, 1936; s. John Olin and Kathryn (Moran) M.; m. Anne McGehee, June 10, 1961; children: James Francis Jr., John McGehee. AB, The Citadel, 1958; JD, U. Fla., 1961. Bar: Fla. 1961, U.S. Supreme Ct. 1970. Pres. Moseley, Warren, Prichard & Parrish, Jacksonville, Fla., 1963—; chmn. jud. nominating com. 4th Jud. Cir., 1978-80. Assoc. editor: American Maritime Cases; contbr. articles on admiralty, transp. and ins. law to legal jours. Pres. Jacksonville United Way, 1979; chmn. bd. dirs. United Way Fla., 1992-93, S.E. regional coun. United Way, 1992-96; trustee Jacksonville Cmty. Found.; chmn. bd. trustees Jacksonville Pub. Libr.; trustee Libr. Found., sec., 1987-91; trustee CMI Am. Found.; chmn. Jacksonville Human Svcs. Coun., 1989-91; chmn. bd. trustees United Way N.E. Fla., 1995—; bd. govs. United Way Am., 1996—. Fellow Am. Coll. Trial Lawyers, Am. Bar Found.; mem. Jacksonville Bar Assn. (pres. 1975), Fla. Coun. Bar Pres. (chmn. 1979), Maritime Law Assn. U.S. (exec. com. 1978-81, chmn. navigation com. 1981-88, v.p. 1992-96, pres. 1996—), Comm. Maritime Internat. (titulary), Com. on Collision (Lisbon Rules), Fed. Ins. Corp. Counsel (chmn. maritime law sect.), Internat. Assn. Def. Counsel (chmn. maritime com. 1989-91), Am. Inns of Ct. (master of bench), Assn. of Citadel Men (bd. mem. 1989-93, exec. com. 1994, Man Yr. award 1992), Citadel Inn of Ct. (sr. bencher), Deerwood Club, River Club, Downtown Athletic Club (N.Y.C.), India House (N.Y.C.), Army Navy Club (Washington), St. John's Dinner Club (pres. 1988). Home: 7780 Hollyridge Rd Jacksonville FL 32256-7134 Office: Moseley Warren Prichard & Parrish 1887 Bldg 501 W Bay St Jacksonville FL 32202

MOSELEY, JOHN TRAVIS, university administrator, research physicist; b. New Orleans, Feb. 26, 1942; s. Fred Baker and Lily Gay (Lord) M.; m. Belva McCall Hudson, Aug. 11 1964 (div. June 1979); m. Susan Diane Callow, Aug. 6, 1979; children: Melanie Lord, John Mark, Stephanie Marie, Shannon Eleanor. BS in Physics, Ga. Inst. Tech., 1964, MS in Physics, 1966, PhD in Physics, 1969. Asst. prof. physics U. West Fla., Pensacola, 1968-69; sr. physicist SRI Internat., Menlo Park, Calif., 1969-75, program mgr., 1976-79; vis. prof. U. Paris, 1975-76; assoc. prof. U. Oreg., Eugene, 1979-81, dir. chem. physics inst., 1980-84, prof. physics, 1984—, head physics dept., 1984-85, v.p. rsch., 1985-94, v.p. acad. affairs, provost, 1994—; mem. exec. com., coun. on acad. affairs NASULGC, 1994—, chair, 1996—; bd. dirs. Oreg. Resource and Tech., Portland; mem. com. on Atomic and Molecular Sci., 1983-85. Contbr. numerous articles to profl. jours. Mem. So. Willamette Rsch. Corridor, Eugene, 1985—, Lane Econ. Devel. Com., Eugene, 1988—; bd. dirs. Eugene/Springfield Metro Partnership, 1985—, Oreg. Bach Festival, Eguene, 1987-94, Eugene Arts Found., 1995—. Recipient Doctoral Thesis award Sigma Xi, 1969; Fulbright fellow, 1975; numerous rsch. grants, 1969—. Fellow Am. Physical Soc.; mem. Am. Chem. Soc., Am. Assn. for Advancement Sci., Am. Assn. Univ. Prof. Avocations: skiing, backpacking. Home: 2140 Essex Ln Eugene OR 97403-1851 Office: U Oreg Office of VP Acad Affairs and Provost Eugene OR 97403-1258

MOSELEY, KAREN FRANCES F., school system administrator, educator; b. Oneonta, N.Y., Sept. 18, 1944; d. Albert Francis and Dorothy (Brown) Flanigan; m. David Michael McLaud, Sept. 8, 1962 (div. Dec. 1966); m. Harry R. Lasalle, Dec. 24, 1976 (dec. Feb. 1990); 1 child, Christopher Michael; m. Kel Moseley, Jan. 22, 1994. BA, SUNY, Oneonta, 1969, MS, 1970. Cert. secondary edn. tchr., Fla., Mass., N.Y. Tchr. Hanover (Mass.) Pub. Schs., 1970-80; lobbyist Mass. Fed. Nursing Homes, Boston, 1980-84; tchr., dept. chair Palm Beach County Schs., Jupiter, Fla., 1985-95; chair of accredidation Jupiter H.S., 1990-91; Fulbright tchr., Denmark, 1994-95. Author: How to Teach About King, 1978, 10 Year Study, 1991. Del. Dem. Conv., Mass., 1976-84; campaign mgr. Kennedy for Senate, N.Y., 1966, Tsongas for Senate, Boston, 1978; dir. Plymouth County Dems., Marshfield, Mass., 1978-84; Sch. Accountability Com., 1991-95; polit. cons. Paul Tsongas U.S. Senate, Boston, 1978-84, Michael Dukakis for Gov., Boston, 1978-84. Mem. Nat. Honor Soc. Polit. Scientists, Classroom Tchrs. Assn., Mass. Coun. Social Studies (bd. dirs. Boston chpt. 1970-80), Mass. Tchrs. Assn. (chair human rels. com. Boston chpt. 1976-80), Plymouth County Social Studies (bd. dirs. 1970-80), Mass. Hosp. Assn. (bd. dirs. Boston chpt. 1980-84), Nat. Coun. for Social Studies, Fla. Sch. Supt. Assn. Roman Catholic. Avocations: reading, fishing, traveling, art collector, boating. Home: 369 River Edge Rd Jupiter FL 33477-9350 Office: Jupiter HS 500 Military Trl Jupiter FL 33458-5799

MOSELEY, MARK DEWAYNE, retired professional football player; b. Lanesville, Tex., Mar. 12, 1948; m. Sharon Allison; children: Megan Allison, Lindsay, Mark DeWayne, Michelle, Ellen. Student, Tex. A&M U., Stephen F. Austin Coll. Kicker Phila. Eagles, NFL, 1970, Houston Oilers, NFL, 1971-72, Washington Redskins, NFL, 1974-86; player NFL Pro Bowl, 1980, 83, NFL Championship Game, 1983, 84, Cleve. Browns, 1986-87; retired, 1987. Named Most Valuable Player of NFL, 1982 (the only placekicker in history of NFL to be named MVP). Address: PO Box 3 Haymarket VA 22069-0003

MOSELEY, SHERYL BUCK, nursing administrator; b. Greenville, N.C., Nov. 27, 1955; d. James Earl and Hilda Hatton (Johnston) Buck; m. William Earl Moseley, June 17, 1978. BSN, East Carolina U., 1978, MSN, 1993. Staff nurse rehab. Pitt County Meml. Hosp., Greenville, 1978-80, permanent charge nurse, 1980-81, head nurse rehab., 1981-87, nursing adminstr., 1988—. Co-coord. 514th MP Co. Family Support Group, Greenville, 1991, coord., 1992. Mem. ANA, Assn. Rehab. Nurses (cert.), N.C. Assn. Rehab. Nurses (sec. 1980-81, pres. 1985-86, bd. dirs. 1986-88), N.C. Nurses Assn., Nat. League for Nursing, N.C. Orgn. Nurse Execs., Am. Orgn. Nurse Execs., Sigma Theta Tau (Beta Nu chpt.). Mem. Free Will Baptist Ch. Avocations: cross stitching, sewing, reading, fishing. Address: Rte 5 Box 511B Greenville NC 27834 Office: Pitt County Meml Hosp PO Box 6028 2100 Stantonsburg Rd Greenville NC 27835-6028

MOSELEY-BRAUN, CAROL, senator; b. Chgo., Aug. 16, 1947; d. Joseph J. and Edna A. (Davie) Moseley; m. Michael Braun, 1973 (div. 1986); 1 child, Matthew. BA, U. Ill., Chgo., 1969; JD, U. Chgo., 1972. Asst. U.S. atty. U.S. Dist. Ct. (no. dist.) Ill., 1973-77; mem. Ill. Ho. of Reps., 1979-88; recorder of deeds Cook County, Ill., 1988-92; U.S. senator from Ill. Washington, 1993—; mem. fin. com., subcom. on social security and family policy, subcom. on medicare, long-term care and health ins., mem. com. on banking, housing and urban affairs, subcom. on HUD oversight and structure, subcom. on internat. fin. and monetary policy, subcom. on fin. instns. and regulatory relief. Office: US Senate 320 Hart Senate Bldg Washington DC 20510

MOSELY, LINDA HAYS, surgeon; b. New Orleans, Feb. 20, 1941; d. Charles Hodge Mosely and Florence (Morley) Mosely Williams. Student Emory U., 1959-61; BS, La. State U., 1963, MD, 1967. Diplomate Am. Bd. Surgery, Am. Bd. Plastic Surgery; lic. physician, Va., D.C., La. Rotating intern Charity Hosp., New Orleans, 1967-68, med. resident, 1968-69, gen. surgery resident, 1970-72; surgery resident Mt. Sinai Hosp., N.Y.C., 1969-70; hand surgery fellow Dr. Harold Kleinert, Louisville, 1972, 74; clin. surg. fellow U. Louisville Med. Ctr., 1972, gen. surgery resident, 1973; rsch. fellow Yale Med. Ctr., New Haven, 1975, plastic surgery resident, 1975-77; tutor specialist Middlemore Hosp., Auckland, N.Z., 1977-78; practice aesthetic surgery Clinica Planas, Barcelona, Spain, 1978-79; cons. plastic surgery John Fitzgerald Kennedy Hosp., Monrovia, Liberia, 1979; clin. and rsch. fellow Toronto Gen. Hosp., Ont., Can., 1979-80; pvt. practice medicine specializing in hand and plastic surgery, Alexandria, Va., 1980—. Mem. People to People Citizen Amb. Program-Soviet Union-Orthopedic Del., 1991. Contbr. articles to med. jours. Mem. ACS, Am. Soc. for Plastic and Reconstructive Surgeons, Am. Soc. for Surgery of Hand, Met. Washington D.C. Soc. for Surgery of Hand, D.C. Met. Plastic Surgery Soc., Med. Soc. Va., Alexandria Med. Soc., Tysons Corner, Va., Georgetown Club, Washington. Home: 5318 Echols Ave Alexandria VA 22311-1309 Office: 2500 N Van Dorn St Apt 128 Alexandria VA 22302-1601

MOSEMANN, LLOYD KENNETH, II, government official; b. Lancaster, Pa., May 16, 1936; s. Lloyd Kreider and Beatrice Elizabeth (Frey) M.; m. Arlene K. White, Sept. 6, 1957; children—Gigi Renee Mosemann Falke, Lloyd Kenneth III, Douglas Lamar, Holly Joy. A.B. in Social Sci., U. Chgo., 1957, A.M. in Internat. Relations, 1959. Gen. supply officer Navy Electronics Supply Office, Great Lakes, Ill., 1958-62; inventory mgmt. specialist Def. Electronics Supply Ctr., Dayton, Ohio, 1962-63; head integrated-retail supply and support br. Naval Supply Systems Command, Washington, 1963-69; dep. chief logistics support analysis office Def. Logistics Agy., Alexandria, Va., 1969-71; dep. for supply and maintenance Office Sec. of Air Force, Washington, 1971-74; dep. asst. sec. for logistics and communications Dept. Air Force, Washington, 1974-91, dep. asst. sec. for comm., computers and logistics, 1991-93, dep. asst. sec. for comm., computers and support systems, 1993—; mem. Air Force Exec. resources Bd., 1981—. Decorated D.S. M.; recipient Meritorious Svc. medal Sec. Air Force, 1977, Exceptional Civilian Svc. medal sec. Air Force, 1979, 81, 82, 87, Meritorious Sr. Exec. award Pres. of U.S., 1982, 87, Def. Meritorious Civilian Svc. medal, 1985. Mem. Soc. Logistics Engrs. (bd. advisers 1983—, Founders medal 1983), Am. Def. Preparedness Assn. (bd. dirs. 1974-83). Home: 2918 Melanie Ln Oakton VA 22124-1811 Office: Dept Air Force Safaqk Washington DC 20330

MOSENA, DAVID R., transportation executive. M in City Planning, U. Tenn. Dir. rsch. Am. Planning Assn., Chgo.; mem. staff City of Chgo., 1984-89, planning commr., 1989-91, chief of staff, 1991-92, aviation commr., 1992-96; pres. CTA, 1996—. Chmn. bd. dirs. U. Chgo. Lab. Schs. Office: CTA Merchandise Mart Plz PO Box 3555 Chicago IL 60654*

MOSER, ALMA P., engineering educator; b. Auburn, Wyo., Aug. 9, 1935; married, 1957; 4 children. BS, Utah State U., 1961, MS, 1963; PhD in Civil Engring., U. Colo., 1967. Assoc. engr. Thiokol Chem. Corp., 1961; from instr. to assoc. prof. mech. engring. Utah State U., Logan, 1961-76, prof. mech. engring., head dept., dir. piping sys. inst., 1976—; rsch. assoc. Johns-Manville Corp., 1972-75. Mem. ASME, Am. Water Works Assn., Sigma Xi. Achievements include research in engineering elasticity; viscoelasticity; crack propagation and fracture analysis; soil-structure interaction mechanics. Office: Utah State U Dept Mech Engring Logan UT 84322-0001*

MOSER, DEBRA KAY, medical educator. BS in Nursing magna cum laude, Humboldt State U., Arcata, Calif., 1977; M Nursing, UCLA, 1988, D Nursing Sci., 1992. RN, Calif., Ohio; cert. pub. health nurse, Calif. Staff nurse, relief supr. med.-surg. fl. Mad River Cmty. Hosp., Arcata, 1977-78, staff/charge nurse intensive care/cardiac care unit, 1978-86; clin. nursing instr. Humboldt State U., Arcata, 1985-86; staff/charge nurse surg. ICU Santa Monica (Calif.) Hosp., 1987-88; spl. reader UCLA Sch. Nursing, 1990-91, rsch. assoc., 1986-91, clin. rsch. nurse, 1988-92, project dir., 1991-92, asst. prof., 1992-94; asst. prof. dept. adult health and illness Ohio State U. Coll. Nursing, Columbus, 1994—; interviewer and study sponsor Modifiers of Myocardial Infraction Onset Study, Ohio State U., 1994—; mem. working group on ednl. strategies to Prevent Prehosp. Delay in Patients at High Risk for Acute Myocardial Infraction, Nat. Heart Attack Alert Program, NIH, Nat. Heart, Lung and Blood Inst., 1993-95; abstract grader sci. sessions program Am. Heart Assn., 66th Sci. Sessions, 1993; grad. advisor Sigma Theta Tau-Gamma Tau chpt., 1993-94; mem. med. adv. com. Westside YMCA Cardiac Rehab. Program, 1993-94; mem. Task Force on Women, Behavior and Cardiovascular Disease NIH, Nat. Heart, Lung and Blood Inst., 1991. Reviewer Am. Jour. Critical Care, 1992—, Heart and Lung, 1991—, Progress in Cardiovascular Nursing, 1993—, Heart Failure: Evaluation and Care of Patients With Left-Ventricular Systolic Function, 1993, Intensive Coronary Care, 5th edit., 1994, Rsch. in Nursing & Health, 1995—, Jour. Am. Coll. Cardiology, 1995; mem. editl. bd. Am. Jour. Critical Care, 1994—, Jour. Cardiovascular Nursing, 1995—; ad hoc reviewer Western Jour. Nursing Rsch., 1991; contbr. articles to profl. jours., chpts. to books. Recipient scholarship UCLA, 1988-90, scholarship Kaiser Permanente Affiliate Schs., 1990, Ednl. Achievement award LA-AACN, 1990, Alumni rsch. award UCLA, 1990, rsch. abstract award AACN-IVAC, 1993; grantee Sigma Theta Tau-Gamma Tau chpt., 1989-90, AACCN, 1989-90, 92-93, NIH, Nat. Ctr. Nursing Rsch., 1990-92, UCLA Program in Psychneuroimmunology, 1992-93, UCLA Sch. Nursing, 1993, UCLA Acad. Senate, 1993-94, AACCN/Sigma Theta Tau Internat., 1994-95, NIH, Nat. Inst. Nursing Rsch., 1991-96, Sigma Theta Tau Epsilon chpt., 1995, Ohio State U., 1995, Nat. Am. Heart Assn., 1995—. Mem. AACCN, Am. Heart Assn. Coun. Cardiovascular Nursing (New Investigator award 1995, Heart Failure Rsch. prize 1995), Sigma Theta Tau (rsch. com. 1990-94, excellence in rsch. award Gamma Tau chpt. 1993). Home: 6871 Meadow Oak Dr Columbus OH 43235 Office: Ohio State U Coll. Nursing Dept Adult Health & Illness 1585 Neil Ave Columbus OH 43210

MOSER, DONALD BRUCE, magazine editor; b. Cleve., Oct. 19, 1932; s. Donald Lyman and Kathryn (McHugh) M.; m. Penny Lee Ward, Dec. 20, 1975. BA, Ohio U., 1957; postgrad., Stanford U., 1957-58, U. Sydney, 1959-60. With Life mag., 1961-72, West Coast bur. chief, 1964-65, Far East bur. chief, 1966-69, asst. mng. editor, 1970-72; free-lance writer, 1972-77; exec. editor Smithsonian mag., Washington, 1977-80; editor Smithsonian mag., 1981—, editor-in-chief. Author: The Peninsula, 1962, The Snake River Country, 1974, A Heart to the Hawks, 1975, Central American Jungles, 1976, China-Burma-India, 1978; contbr. articles to numerous mags., jours. Served with U.S. Army, 1953-55. Stegner fellow, 1957-58; Fulbright scholar, 1959-60. Mem. Phi Beta Kappa. Office: Smithsonian Mag Arts & Indsl Bldg 900 Jefferson Dr SW Washington DC 20560-0003

MOSER, HAROLD DEAN, historian; b. Kannapolis, N.C., Oct. 31, 1938; s. Walter Glenn and Angie Elizabeth (Allen) M.; m. Carolyn Irene French, Mar. 28, 1964; children: Andrew Paul, Anna Elizabeth. A.A., Wingate Coll., 1959; B.A. cum laude, Wake Forest U., 1961, M.A. Univ. fellow, 1963; Ph.D. Ford fellow, U. Wis., 1977. Tchr. Robert B. Glenn High Sch., Winston-Salem, N.C., 1961-62; instr. history Chowan Coll., Murfreesboro, N.C., 1963-65; teaching asst dept. history U. Wis., Madison, 1967-69; Nat. Hist. Publ. Commn. fellow The Papers of Daniel Webster (Dartmouth Coll.), Hanover, N.H., 1971-72, asst. editor, 1972-73, assoc. editor, 1973-76, co-editor, 1976-77, editor corr. series, 1978-79; editor dir. The Papers of Andrew Jackson, 1979—; adv. bd. The Papers of Albert Gallatin, Baruch Coll., CCNY, 1987—; rsch. prof. history U. Tenn., Knoxville, 1987—. Contbr. articles to profl. jours. Mem. Am. Hist. Assn., So. Hist. Assn., Orgn. Am. Historians, Soc. Historians of Early Am. Republic, Assn. for Documentary Editing, Tenn. Hist. Soc., Phi Alpha Theta, Eta Sigma Phi, Phi Theta Kappa. Democrat. Episcopalian. Home: 9605 Tallahassee Ln Knoxville TN 37923-2737 Office: U Tenn Hoskins Library Knoxville TN 37996

MOSER, HUGO WOLFGANG, physician; b. Switzerland, Oct. 4, 1924; came to U.S., 1940, naturalized, 1943; s. Hugo L. and Maria (Werner) M.; m. Ann Boody, Dec. 28, 1963; children—Tracey, Peter, Karen, Lauren. M.D., Columbia U., 1948; A.M. in Med. Sci, Harvard U., 1956. Intern Columbia-Presbyn. Med. Center, N.Y.C., 1948-50; asst. in medicine Peter Bent Brigham Hosp., Boston, 1950-52; research fellow dept. biol. chemistry Harvard U., 1955-57; asst. resident, resident in neurology Mass. Gen. Hosp., 1957-59, asst. neurologist, 1960-67, assoc. neurologist, 1967-69, neurologist, 1969-76; teaching fellow neuropathology Harvard Med. Sch., 1959-60, instr. neurology, 1960-64, assoc. in neurology, 1964-67, asst. prof., 1967-69, asso. prof., 1969-72, prof., 1972-76; dir. research and tng. Walter E. Fernald State Sch., 1963-68, asst. supt., 1968-73, acting supt., 1973-74, supt., 1974-76; dir. Center for Research on Mental Retardation and Related Aspects of Human Devel., dir. univ. affiliated facilities for mentally retarded, 1965-74; co-dir. Eunice Kennedy Shriver Center for Mental Retardation, Inc., 1969-74; pres. John F. Kennedy Inst., Balt., 1976-88; prof. neurology and pediatrics Johns Hopkins U., 1976—. Author: (with others) Mental Retardation: An Atlas of Diseases with Associated Physical Abnormalities, 1972; Contbr. (with others) articles to med. jours. Served with AUS, 1943-44; to capt. U.S. Army, 1952-54. Recipient Hower award Child Neurology Soc., 1994. Mem. Am. Acad. Neurology, Am. Assn. Mental Deficiency, Am. Assn. Neuropathologists, Am. Neurol. Assn., Internat. Soc. Neurochemistry, Am. Pediatrics Soc., Sigma Xi, Alpha Omega Alpha. Home: 100 Beechdale Rd Baltimore MD 21210-2209 Office: Kennedy Inst Inc 707 N Broadway Baltimore MD 21205-1832

MOSER, KENNETH MILES, physician, educator; b. Balt., Apr. 12, 1929; s. Simon and Helene Joyce M.; m. Sara Falk, June 17, 1951; children—Gregory, Kathleen, Margot, Diana. B.A., Haverford Coll., 1950; M.D., Johns Hopkins U., 1954. Diplomate: Am. Bd. Internal Medicine. Intern, resident in medicine D.C. Gen. Hosp., Georgetown Hosp., 1954-59; chief pulmonary and infectious disease service Nat. Naval Med. Center, Bethesda, Md., 1959-61; dir. pulmonary div. Georgetown U. Med. Center, Washington, 1961-68; prof. medicine, dir. pulmonary and critical care med. div. U. Calif., San Diego Sch. Medicine, 1968—; dir. Specialized Ctr. Rsch. U. Calif.-San Diego/Nat. Heart Lund and Blood Inst., 1978—. Author 10 books in field of pulmonary medicine and thrombosis.; Contbr. articles to med. jours. Bd. dirs. Am. Lung Assn. of San Diego and Imperial Counties, 1969-76, Am. Lung Assn. of Calif., 1976-80; mem. manpower com. Nat. Heart, Lung and Blood Inst., bd. dirs. 1978—. Served with U.S. Navy, 1959-61. Fellow ACP, AAAS, Am. Coll. Chest Physicians; mem. Am. Thoracic Soc. (exec. bd., pres. 1985-86), Am. Heart Assn. Coun. on Thrombosis, Am. Physiol. Soc. Office: U Calif San Diego Med Ctr 200 W Arbor Dr San Diego CA 92103 *Participating in academic medicine and research is like being a member of a relay team engaged in a race of infinite length. Two forces keep one running through the often difficult terrain: the goal of improving health; and the privilege of passing the baton to many others who will seek that same goal.*

MOSER, LARRY EDWARD, marketing professional; b. Chgo., Oct. 29, 1952; s. Paul Edward and Catherine Molly (Sittner) M.; m. Michelle Ann Lorden, Sept. 21, 1974 (div. Jan. 1984); children: Jennifer, Jacqueline. BS in Mktg., No. Ill. U., 1974, MBA, 1976. CLU, CPCU. Statis. analyst Addressograph-Multigraph, Mt. Prospect, Ill., 1974-75; grad. asst., mktg. instr. No. Ill. U., DeKalb, 1975-76, 77; mktg. asst. Allstate Ins. Co., Northbrook, Ill., 1977-78; project coord. Allstate Ins. Co., Northbrook, 1978-80; agt. Allstate Ins. Co., West Dundee, 1980; mktg. project mgr. to sr. mktg. mgr. Allstate Ins. Co., Northbrook, 1981—; prin. coord. Allstate WYO flood ins. program Allstate Ins. Co., 1994—, mem. nat. flood ins. program mktg. com., 1995—; chmn. Allstate Share (United Way) Campaign, Northbrook, 1982-83, Allstate Helping Hands Com., Northbrook, 1985-86, Allstate Family Day Sports, Northbrook, 1991-94; pres. Allstate Men's Softball League, 1984—. Active Twinbrook YMCA parent/child prog., Schaumburg, Ill., 1983-90; commr. Schaumburg Athletic Assn. Girls Softball, 1990-92. Recipient Am. Mktg. Assn. Scholastic Achievement award No. Ill. Univ., DeKalb, 1974, James E. Bell Superior Promise & Scholarship in Mktg. Mgmt. No. Ill. Univ. Dept. Mktg., DeKalb, 1976, William J. Hendrickson award for Outstanding Contbn. From An Alumni, DeKalb, 1988. Mem. Am. Soc. CLU, Pi Sigma Epsilon (pres. 1975-76), Phi Kappa Sigma, Beta Gamma Sigma, Omicron Delta Kappa. Christian Catholic. Avocations: travel, golf, tennis, camping, softball. Home: 812 Krause Ave Streamwood IL 60107-3045 Office: Allstate Ins Co 2775 Sanders Rd Ste D10 Northbrook IL 60062-6110

MOSER, M(ARTIN) PETER, lawyer; b. Balt., Jan. 16, 1928; s. Herman and Henrietta (Lehmayer) M.; m. Elizabeth Kohn, June 14, 1949; children—Mike, Moriah, Jeremy. A.B., The Citadel, Charleston, S.C., 1947; LL.B., Harvard U., 1950. Bar: Md. 1950, U.S. Supreme Ct., U.S. Ct. Appeals (4th cir.), U.S. Dist. Ct. Md. Asst. states atty. City of Balt., 1951, 53-54; assoc. Blades Rosenfeld, Balt., 1950, 53-54; ptnr. Frank, Bernstein, Conaway & Goldman and predecessor firms, Balt., 1955-90, co-chmn. firm, 1983-86; counsel, 1991-92; of counsel Piper & Marbury, 1992—; instr. U. Balt. Law Sch., 1954-56, 86, U. Md. Law Sch., 1986-87. Contbr. articles to profl. jours. Del., chmn. local govt. com. Md. Constl. Conv., 1967-68; mem. Balt. City Planning Commn., 1961-66, Balt. Regional Planning Council, 1963-66, Md. Commn. to Study Narcotics Laws, 1965-67, Mayor's Task Force on EEO, 1966-67, Met. Transit Authority Adv. Council, 1962, Com. to Revise Balt. City Planning Laws, 1962, Com. to Revise Balt. City Charter Provision on Conflicts of Interest, 1969-70; mem. Citizens Adv. Com. on Dist. Ct., chmn., 1971, Dist. Adv. Bd. for Pub. Defender System for Dist. 1, 1973-85; mem. Atty. Grievance Commn. of Md., 1975-78, chmn. 82-86; chmn. Md. State Ethics Commn., 1987-89; bd. dirs. Sinai Hosp., 1983—, Ct. of Appeals Comm. to Study the Model Rules, 1983-86. Served with JAGC, U.S. Army, 1951-53. Fellow Am. Bar Found., Md. Bar Found.; mem. ABA (ho. of dels. 1978—, treas. 1993-96, bd. govs. 1984-87, 92—, ethics com. 1981-84, 87-90, chmn. 1981-82, 87-90, scope and cor. com. 1987-92, chmn. 1990-91), Md. State Bar Assn. (pres. 1979-80), Balt. Bar Assn. (pres. 1971-72), Fed. Bar Assn., Am. Law Inst., Wednesday Law Club, Lawyers' Round Table Club, Hamilton St. Club. Democrat. Jewish. Office: Piper & Marbury 36 S Charles St Fl 8 Baltimore MD 21201-3020

MOSER, MARVIN, physician, educator, author; b. Newark, Jan. 24, 1924; s. Sol and Sophia (Markowitz) M.; m. Joy Diane Lipez, July 1, 1954; children: Jill, Stephen, John. A.B., Cornell U., 1943; M.D., Downstate Coll. Medicine, N.Y.C., 1947. Diplomate: Am. Bd. Internal Medicine, subbd. cardiovascular disease. Intern univ. div. Kings County Hosp., N.Y.C., 1947-48; resident in medicine Kings County Hosp., 1948-49, Montefiore Hosp., N.Y.C., 1949-50; Nat. Heart Assn. fellow Mt. Sinai Hosp., N.Y.C., 1950-51; charge vascular service Walter Reed Army Hosp. Med. Centre, Washington, 1951-53; practice medicine specializing in cardiology White Plains, N.Y., 1953-95; assoc. physician cardiology Montefiore Hosp., 1953-75, in charge hypertension sect., 1960-71; attending physician cardiology White Plains Hosp., 1968-95, chief cardiology, 1969-78; adj. physician in cardiology Grasslands Hosp., Valhalla, N.Y., 1953-60; attending physician in medicine in charge Hypertension Clinic, Westchester County Med. Center, Valhalla, 1974-84; asst. clin. prof. medicine Albert Einstein Coll. Medicine, 1965-75; clin. prof. medicine N.Y. Med. Coll., 1974-84, Yale U. Sch. Medicine, 1984—; sr. med. cons. nat. high blood pressure program NIH, 1975—, mem. nat. high blood pressure coordinating com., 1976—; chmn. Joint Nat. Com.

Hypertension, 1975-76, vice-chmn., 1979, mem., 1984-88, 92; mem. exec. com. Nat. Citizens for Treatment High Blood Pressure, 1976-78, vice chmn., 1978-88; mem. N.Y. State Adv. Com. on Hypertension, 1977-84; chmn. Nat. Conf. on High Blood Pressure Control, 1979; mem. select panel on hypertension in Am. Congl. Subcom. on Aging, 1978-79; cons. cardiology N.Y. State Dept. Health, Gen. Hosp., Saranac Lake, N.Y., 1980-90; med. dir. Westchester County Hypertension Program, N.Y., 1979-88. Author: (with A.M. Master, M. Moser, H. Jaffee) Cardiac Emergencies and Heart Failure, 2d edit., 1955, (with A. Goldman) Hypertensive Vascular Disease, 1967, Hypertension, A Practical Approach, 1975, Lower Your Blood Pressure and Live Longer, 198; co-editor, contbr. Yale University School of Medicine Heart Book, 1992, Week by Week to a Strong Heart, 1992, Heart Healthy Cooking for all Seasons, 1996; assoc. editor Angiology, 1976-85; bd. editors Primary Cardiology, 1975-78, assoc. editor-in-chief, 1978-96. Chmn. Narcotics Guidance Coun., Scarsdale, 1968-72; trustee Scarsdale Bd. Edn., 1970-73, Trudeau Inst., 1992—, Third Ave. Value Fund, 1994—. Served U.S. Army, 1941-46; capt. M.C. USAF, 1951-53. Nat. Heart Inst. grantee, 1958-62; recipient Achievement award for contbns. to hypertension control Nat. High Blood Pressure Edn. Program, 1985. Fellow ACP, Am. Coll. Cardiology; mem. Am. Heart Assn. (fellow coun. clin. cardiology, coun. high blood pressure rsch. 1974—, coun. geriatric cardiology 1988—, v.p. 1994-96, pres. 1996—, chmn. N.Y. State com. on hypertension 1974-75), N.Y. Cardiol. Soc., Century Country Club. Home and Office: 13 Murray Hill Rd Scarsdale NY 10583-2829

MOSER, ROBERT HARLAN, physician, educator, writer; b. Trenton, N.J., June 16, 1923; s. Simon and Helena (Silvers) M.; m. Linda Mae Salsinger, Mar. 18, 1989; children from previous marriage: Steven Michael, Jonathan Evan. BS, Loyola U., Balt., 1944; MD, Georgetown U., 1948. Diplomate Am. Bd. Internal Medicine. Commd. 1st lt. U.S. Army, 1948, advanced through grades to col., 1966, intern D.C. Gen. Hosp., 1948-49, fellow pulmonary disease D.C. Gen. Hosp., 1949-50; bn. surgeon U.S. Army, Korea, 1950-51; asst. resident Georgetown U. Hosp., 1951-52; chief resident Georgetown U. Hosp. U.S. Army, 1952-53; chief med. service U.S. Army Hosp. U.S. Army, Salzburg, Austria, 1953-55, Wurzburg, Fed. Republic Germany, 1955-56; resident in cardiology Brooke Gen. Hosp. U.S. Army, 1956-57, asst. chief dept. medicine Brooke Gen. Hosp., 1957-59, chief Brooke Gen. Hosp., 1967-68, fellow hematology U. Utah Coll. Medicine, 1959-60, asst. chief U.S. Army Tripler Gen. Hosp., 1960-64, chief William Beaumont Gen. Hosp., 1965-67, chief Walter Reed Gen. Hosp., 1968-69, ret., 1969; chief of staff Maui (Hawaii) Meml. Hosp., 1969-73, chief dept. medicine, 1975-77; exec. v.p. Am. Coll. Physicians, Phila., 1977-86; v.p. med. affairs The NutraSweet Co., Deerfield, Ill., 1986-91; assoc. prof. medicine Baylor U., 1958-59; clin. prof. medicine Hawaii U., 1969-77, Washington U., 1970-77, Abraham Lincoln Sch. Medicine, 1974-75; adj. prof. medicine U. Pa., 1977-86, Northwestern U., 1987-91; adj. prof. Uniformed Svcs. U. Health Scis., 1979—; clin. prof. medicine U. N.Mex. Coll. Medicine, 1992—; flight contr. Project Mercury, 1959-62; cons. mem. med. evaluation team Project Gemini, 1962-66; cons. Project Apollo, 1967-73, Tripler Gen. Hosp., 1970-77, Walter Reed Army Med. Ctr., 1974-86; sr. med. cons. Canyon Cons. Corp.; mem. cardiovasc. and renal adv. com. FDA, 1978-82; chmn. life scis. adv. com. NASA, 1984-87, mem. NASA adv. coun., 1983-88, chmn. gen. med. panel Hosp. Satellite Network, 1984-86; mem. adv. com. NASA Space Sta., 1988-93; mem. Dept. Def. Com. on Grad. Med. Edn., 1986-87; mem. Life Scis. Strategic Planning Study Group, 1986-88; mem. space studies bd. NRC, 1988-93, space exploration initiation study, 1990, NASA Space Sta. Commn., 1992-93, mem. com. adv. tech. human sapp. space, 1996—. Author: Diseases of Medical Progress, 1955, rev. edit., 1969, House Officer Training, 1970; co-author: Adventures in Medical Writing, 1970, Decade of Decision, 1992; editor, chief div. sci. publs. Jour. AMA, Chgo., 1973-75; contbg. editor Med. Opinion and Rev., 1966-75; chmn. editorial bd. Diagnosis mag., 1986-89; mem. editorial bd. Hawaii Med. Jour., Family Physicians, Archives of Internal Medicine, 1967-73, Western Jour. Medicine, 1975-87, Chest, 1975-80, Med. Times, 1977-84, Quality Rev. Bull., 1979-91, The Pharos, 1991—, Emergency Med., 1993—, Travel Medicine, 1994—; contbr. over 200 articles to med. sci. jours and med. books. Master ACP (exec. v.p. 1977-86); fellow Am. Coll. Cardiology, Royal Coll. Physicians and Surgeons Can. (hon.), Am. Clin. and Climatol. Assn.; mem. AMA (adv. panel registry of adverse drug reactions 1960-67, coun. on drugs 1967-73),), Am. Med. Writers Assn., Am. Therapeutic Soc., Am. Osler Soc., Inst. Med., Nat. Assn. Phys. Broadcasters, Chgo. Soc. Internal Medicine, Coll. Physicians Phila., Soc. Med. Cons. to Armed Forces, Alpha Sigma Nu, Alpha Omega Alpha. Democrat. Jewish. Avocations: hiking, backpacking, white water rafting. Home and Office: Canones Rd # 616 Chama NM 87520

MOSER, ROBERT LAWRENCE, pathologist, health facility administrator; b. Passaic, N.J., Mar. 22, 1952; s. Robert George and Marjorie Ann (Frankenberger) M.; m. Rosemarie Scolaro, June 16, 1978; children: Rachel Ann, Alexander Robert. BA in Biology magna cum laude, Lafayette Coll., 1974; MD in Microbiology and Internal Medicine with honors, Hahnemann Med. Coll., 1978. Diplomate Am. Bd. Pathology, Am. Bd. Anatomic Pathology, Am. Bd. Clin. Pathology. Intern, fellow dept. Pathology The Johns Hopkins Hosp., Balt., 1978-79, resident, fellow dept. Pathology, 1979-81, chief resident, fellow dept. Pathology, 1981-82, resident, fellow dept. Lab. Medicine, 1982-84; cons. pathologist Perry Point (Md.) VA Med. Ctr., 1983-84; pathologist Helene Fuld Med. Ctr., Trenton, N.J., 1984-88; med. dir. St Francis Med. Ctr., Trenton, 1988-95; dir. clin. info. systems Franciscan Health Systems, 1995—; pres. Pathology Assocs., Lawrenceville, N.J., 1981—; dir. clin. info. sys. Franciscan Health Sys. Contbr. articles to profl. jours. Fellow Coll. Am. Pathologists, Coll. Physicians of Phila.; mem. Am. Med. Informatics Assn., Med. Soc. N.J., Mercer County Med. Soc., Ctrl. Jersey Ind. Physician Assn. (v.p. 1994), Phi Beta Kappa. Avocations: golf, gardening, skiing.

MOSER, ROYCE, JR., physician, medical educator; b. Versailles, Mo., Aug. 21, 1935; s. Royce and Russie Frances (Stringer) M.; m. Lois Anne Hunter, June 14, 1958; children: Beth Anne Moser McLean, Donald Royce. BA, Harvard U., 1957, MD, 1961; MPH, Harvard Sch. Pub. Health, Boston, 1965. Diplomate Am. Bd. Preventive Medicine (trustee), Am. Bd. Family Practice. Commd. officer USAF, 1962, advanced through grades to col., 1974; resident in aerospace medicine USAF Sch. Aerospace Medicine, Brooks AFB, Tex., 1965-67; chief aerospace medicine Aerospace Def. Command, Colorado Springs, Colo., 1967-70; comdr. 35th USAF Dispensary Phan Rang, Vietnam, 1970-71; chief aerospace medicine br. USAF Sch. Aerospace Medicine, Brooks AFB, 1971-77; comdr. USAF Hosp., Tyndall AFB, Fla., 1977-79; chief clin. scis. div. USAF Sch. Aerospace Medicine, Brooks AFB, 1979-81, chief edn. div., 1981-83, sch. comdr., 1983-85; ret., 1985; prof. dept. family and preventive medicine U. Utah Sch. Medicine, Salt Lake City, 1985—, vice chmn. dept., 1985-95; dir. Rocky Mountain Ctr. for Occupl. and Environ. Health, Salt Lake City, 1987—; cons. in occupational, environ. and aerospace medicine, Salt Lake City, 1985—; presenter nat. and internat. med. meetings. Author: Effective Management of Occupational and Environmental Health and Safety Programs, 1992; contbr. book chpts. and articles to profl. jours. Mem., past pres. 1st Bapt. Ch. Found., Salt Lake City, 1987-89; mem., chmn. numerous univ. coms., Salt Lake City, 1985—; bd. dirs. Hanford Environ. Health Found., 1990-92; mem. preventive medicine residency rev. com. Accreditation Coun. Grad. Med. Edn., 1991—; mem. ednl. adv. bd. USAF Human Sys. Ctr., 1991—; chmn. long-range planning comm. Am. Bd. Preventive Medicine, 1992-95. Decorated Legion of Merit (2). Fellow Aerospace Med. Assn. (pres. 1989-90, chair fellows group 1994—, Harry G. Mosely award 1988), Am. Coll. Preventive Medicine (regent 1981-82), Am. Coll. Occupl. and Environ. Medicine (v.p. med. affairs 1995—, Robert A. Kehoe award 1996), Am. Acad. Family Physicians; mem. Internat. Acad. Aviation and Space Medicine (selector 1989-94, chancellor 1994—), Soc. of USAF Flight Surgeons (pres. 1978-79, George E. Schafer award 1982), Phi Beta Kappa. Avocations: photography, fishing. Home: 664 Aloha Rd Salt Lake City UT 84103-3329 Office: Dept Family & Preventive Med 50 N Medical Dr Salt Lake City UT 84132-0001

MOSER, WILLIAM OSCAR JULES, mathematics educator; b. Winnipeg, Can., Sept. 5, 1927; s. Robert and Laura (Fenson) M.; m. Beryl Rita Pearlman, Sept. 2, 1953; children—Marla, Lionel, Paula. B.Sc., U. Man., 1949; M.A., U. Minn., 1951; Ph.D., U. Toronto, 1957. Lectr. U. Sask., 1955-57, asst. prof., 1957-59; asso. prof. U. Man., 1959-64; asso. prof. McGill U., 1964-66, prof., 1966—. Author: (with H.S.M. Coxeter) Generators and Relations for Discrete Groups, 1957, 4th edit., 1980; also research papers.; Editor: Can. Math. Bull. 1962-70, Can. Jour. Math., 1982-85. NRC fellow, 1951-53; Can. Council leave fellow, 1971. Mem. Am. Math. Soc., Can. Math. Soc. (pres. 1975-77), Math. Assn. Am. Office: McGill U Dept Math, 805 Sherbrooke St W, Montreal, PQ Canada H3A 2K6

MOSES, ABE JOSEPH, international financial consultant; b. Springfield, Mass., July 15, 1931; s. Mohammed Mustapha and Fatima (Merriam) M.; m. Donna C. Moses (dec.); children: James Douglas, John C., Peter J. BA, Amherst Coll., 1955; MA in Internat. Affairs, Johns Hopkins U., 1957. Legis. aide Sen. J.F. Kennedy, 1955-57; fgn. service officer Dept. State, 1960-65; v.p., gen. mgr. Libyan Desert Oil Co., Texfel Petroleum Corp., Tripoli, Libya, 1965-67; v.p. adminstrn., fin. Occidental Petroleum Corp., Libya, 1967-70; v.p. fin., dir. Northrop Corp., 1970-74; chmn. Transworld Trade Ltd., Washington, 1971—; v.p., mng. dir. world adv. group Chase Manhattan Bank, 1974-80; pres. Grolier Internat., Inc., Danbury, Conn., 1980-82; chief exec. officer, dir. Galadari Bros., Dubai, United Arab Emirates, 1982-86; internat. bus. and fin. cons. Traxol, Dubai, 1986—; fin. cons. Govt. Costa Rica, 1986-89; chmn. Aviation Sys. Corp., Arlington, Va., 1974, Dillon Internat., Akron, Ohio, 1986—; mng. dir. Sheraton Suites Akron, Cuyahoga Falls, Ohio, 1990—; owner's rep. Monarch Sheraton Hotel, Springfield, Mass., 1993-95; bd. dirs., v.p. Morgan Freeport Co., Hudson, Ohio; bd. dirs. Seeds of Peace, Washington. Pres., bd. dirs. Riverside Comty. Urban Redevel. Corp.; mem. exec. com., bd. dirs. Near East Found., N.Y.C., 1978—; pres. Riverfront Ctr. Assn., Cuyahoga Falls, 1992-95. Capt. USAF, 1957-60. Ford Found. fellow Johns Hopkins U., 1955, Barr Found. fellow, 1955-57. Mem. Mid. East Inst. Democrat. Home: 15 Bagburn Rd Monroe CT 06468-1432 Office: Riverside CURC 1989 Front St Cuyahoga Falls OH 44221-3811

MOSES, ALFRED HENRY, lawyer; b. Balt., July 24, 1929; s. Leslie William and Helene Amelia (Lobe) M.; m. Carol Whitehill, Nov. 24, 1955; Barbara, Jennifer, David, Amalie. BA, Dartmouth, 1951; postgrad., Woodrow Wilson Sch., Princeton U., 1951-52; JD, Georgetown U., 1956. Bar: D.C. 1956. Assoc. Covington & Burling, Washington, 1956-65, ptnr., 1965-94; spl. advisor, spl. counsel Pres. Jimmy Carter, Washington, 1980-81; amb. to Romania U.S. Embassy, Bucharest, 1994—; legal advisor minority rights Dem. Nat. Com., Washington, 1969, DC Commision on Urban Renewal, 1972; lectr. Am. Law Inst., ABA , New Orleans, 1970, Am. Inst. CPAs, ABA, Washington, 1969, Georgetown U. Law Ctr., 1971, Tax Exec. Inst., Washington, 1967-68, Tulane Tax Inst., New Orleans, 1971; commr. Pub. Housing, Fairfax County, Va., 1971-72. Contbr. articles, commentaries to internat. jours. and press. Co-chmn. legal div. United Givers Fund, Washington, 1975-76; mem. Coun. Fgn. Rels., N.Y.C., 1977—; bd. dirs. Paralysis Cure Rsch. Found., 1978-81; trustee Phelps Stokes Fund, N.Y.C., 1978-84; pres. Nat. Children's Island, Washington, 1975-76; pres. Golda Meir Assn., 1986-88, nat. chmn., 1988-93; trustee Jewish Publ. Soc., 1989-94, Haifa U., 1988-90; pres. Am. Jewish Com., 1991-94; mem. bd. regents Georgetown U., 1986-92. Mem. ABA, D.C. Bar Assn., Met. Club. Democrat. Jewish. Home: PO Box 7566 Washington DC 20044 Office: Am Embassy, Bucharest Romania

MOSES, CHARLES E., superintendent. Supt. Milford (Del.) Sch. Dist. Recipient State Finalist for Nat. Supt. of Yr. award, 1993. Office: Milford Sch Dist 906 Lakeview Ave Milford DE 19963-1732

MOSES, DANIEL DAVID, civil engineer; b. Courtois, Mo., May 28, 1949; s. Jewell Artie and Genevieve Alice (Wilson) M.; married, 1970 (div. 1984); 1 child, Daniel David Jr.; m. Delores Clara Leslie, June 29, 1985; 1 child, Christopher Daniel. AAS, Mineral Area Coll., Flat River, Mo., 1969. Registered profl. engr., Mo., Ill. Highway designer Mo. Highway and Transp. Dept., Kirkwood, 1969-79; civil engr. Harland Bartholomew & Assoc., St. Louis, 1979-83; sr. project engr. Booker Assoc., Inc., St. Louis, 1983-94, v.p., Ill. divsn. mgr., sr. project engr., 1994—. Bd. dirs. Nat. Kidney Found., St. Louis, 1994—; active Belleville (Ill.) Econ. Progress, 1993—. Mem. NSPE, Am. Pub. Works Assn., Soc. Am. Mil. Engrs. (1st v.p., pres. 1990-95, bd. dirs. 1995—). Presbyterian. Avocation: playing steel guitar. Home: 1349 Summerpoint Ln Fenton MO 63026 Office: Booker Assoc Inc 6701 N Illinois Fairview Heights IL 62208

MOSES, EDWARD CROSBY, artist; b. Long Beach, Calif.; s. Alfonsus Lemuel and Olivia (Branco) M.; m. Avilda Peters, Aug. 11, 1959; children: Cedd, Andrew. BA, U. Calif., Long Beach, 1954, MA, 1956. lectr. painting, drawing UCLA, 1961, 75-76, U. Calif., Irvine, 1968-72, Bakersfield Coll., Calif., 1977; guest lectr. Oberlin Coll., Wichita Art Mus., Cranbrook Inst. Numerous one-man shows, 1958—, latest include Andre Emmerich Gallery, N.Y.C., 1974-75, L.A. County Mus. Art, 1976, Tex. Gallery, Houston, 1979, High Mus. Art, Atlanta, 1980, Janus Gallery, L.A., 1982, Dorothy Rosenthal Gallery, Chgo., 1982—, L.A. Louver Gallery, Venice, 1985—, Louver Gallery, N.Y.C., 1989-93, Galerie Georges Lavrov, Paris; exhibited numerous group shows, 1958—, latest include Corcoran Gallery Art, Washington, 1979, High Mus., 1980, San Francisco Mus., 1980, San Francisco Art Inst., 1981, Mus. Modern Art, Paris, 1982, L.A. Mcpl. Gallery, 1982, Mus. Contemporary Art, L.A., 1983, 86, Nat. Gallery Art, Washington, 1984, Nat. Gallery of Modern Art, 1988, Smithsonian Instn., 1986, Galerie Koltontorvet, Copenhagen, Mus. Contemporary Art, L.A., 1986, Whitney Mus., 1991; represented in permanent collections U. Calif. Art Mus., Berkeley, Seattle Art Mus., San Francisco Art Mus., Mus. Modern Art, N.Y.C., San Francisco Art Inst., Chgo. Art Inst., Hirshhorn Mus., Phila., Akron Art Inst., Ohio, Harvard U., Cambridge, Mass., Yale U., New Haven, Walker Art Mus., Mpls., Corcoran Gallery Art, Whitney Mus. Am. Art, N.Y.C., Mus. Modern Art., N.Y.C., Los Angeles County Mus. Art, Nat. Mus. Am. Art at Smithsonian Inst., Washington, Phila. Mus. Art. Served with USN, 1944-46. Recipient Tamarind fellowship in lithography, 1968, Art in Pub. Places award Calif. Arts Coun., 1987; NEA grantee, 1976; Guggenheim fellow, 1980.

MOSES, EDWIN, former track and field athlete; b. Dayton, Ohio, 1955; m. Myrella Moses. Student, Morehouse Coll. Olympian hurdler; Worlds Top Ranked Intermediate Hurdler, 1976—. Chmn. USOC Substance Abuse Com., 1989—. Holder world record 400 meter hurdle; Olympic gold medalist, 1976, 84; 1st U.S. athlete to be voted delegate to Internat. Amateur Athletic Fedn.; named Sportsman of the Yr. U.S. Olympic Com. Office: Hurdler US Olympic Com 1750 E Boulder St Colorado Springs CO 80909-5724*

MOSES, FRANKLIN MAXWELL, retired chemical marketing executive; b. Kansas, Ohio, Oct. 17, 1918; s. Otto Franklin and Edith Mary (Diller) M.; m. Elizabeth Fleming, Feb. 27, 1948; children: Steven F., Gregory F., Christopher R. (dec.), Elizabeth Ann. B.S., Ohio State U., 1941; postgrad., U. Pitts., 1941-42. Indsl. engr. U.S. Steel Corp., Pitts., 1941-42; pilot Pan Am. World Airways, San Francisco, 1946-53; exec. v.p. Wilson & Geo Meyer & Co., South San Francisco, Calif., 1954-84; pvt. practice mktg. cons. Portola Valley, CA, 1984-94; ret., 1994; dir. Portola Ranch Assn., WGM Hydro, San Francisco. Served to capt. USMCR, 1942-46. Decorated with two Distinguished Flying Crosses, seven Air Medals. Mem. Calif. Acad. Scis., Marine Corps Aviation Soc., Assn. Naval Aviation, Tailhook Assn., Calif. Hist. Soc., Am. Inst. Wine and Food, Ohio State U. Alumni Assn. (life), St. Francis Yacht Club (San Francisco), California Club (L.A.), Portola Valley Polo Club, Los Altos Hunt Club, World Trade Club, Family Club, Shack Riders, Frontier Boys, Marines Meml. Club (San Francisco). Republican. Episcopalian. Home: 4 Coal Mine Vw Portola Valley CA 94028 *To be responsible - responsible to family, friends, country, work-place and to one's self. Offering the best you can all of the time.*

MOSES, HAMILTON, III, neurology educator, hospital executive, management consultant; b. Chgo., Apr. 29, 1950; s. Hamilton Jr. and Betty Anne (Theurer) M.; m. Elizabeth Lawrence Hormel, 1977 (dec. 1988); m. Alexandra McCullough Gibson, 1992. BA in Psychology, U. Pa., 1972; MD, Rush Med. Coll., Chgo., 1975. Intern in medicine Johns Hopkins Hosp., Balt., 1976-77, resident in neurology, 1977-79, chief resident, 1979-80, assoc. prof. neurology, 1986-94, vice chmn. neurology and neurosurgery, 1980-86, v.p., 1988-94, dir. Parkinson's Ctr., 1984-94; dir. neurol. inst., prof. neurology and neurosurgery and mgmt. U. Va., Charlottesville, 1994—; sr. advisor Boston Cons. Group, 1995—; sr. advisor The Boston Cons. Group, 1996; founder several tech. bus. Editor, major author: Principles of Medicine, 1985-96; editor newsletter Johns Hopkins Health, 1988—; contbr. numerous articles to med. jours. Mem. com. on med. ministries Episcopal Diocese Md., Balt., 1987; bd. dirs. Valleys Planning Ct. Mem. Am. Acad. Neurology (sec. 1989-91), Am. Neurol. Assn., Md. Neurol. Soc. (pres. 1984-86), Movement Disorders Soc., Md. Club, Green Spring Valley Hunt Club (Garrison, Md.). Republican. Avocations: landscape photography, sailing.

MOSES, IRVING BYRON, architect; b. Chgo., Aug. 5, 1925; s. Morris and Dorothy (Berns) M.; m. Toby June Kornfeld, June 29, 1947; children: Barbara Moses Tarr, Jack Robert, Carol Lynn. BS in Architecture Design, U. Ill., 1950. Time, motion and material research Small Homes Council of Ill., 1947-48; archtl. designer Holsman, Holsman, Klekamp & Taylor, Chgo., 1950-51; architect, ptnr. Comm, Comm & Moses, AIA, Chgo., 1951-62; prin. I. Moses Assocs., AIA, Chgo., 1962-78, Moses Assocs., AIA, Chgo., 1978—; cons. architect A. Epstein & Sons, Chgo., 1974-75, Globe Engring. Co., Chgo., 1975-77, Slip & Fall Litigation, 1980—; judge, arbitrator, Am. Arbitration Assn., 1976—. Author: Chicago School Architecture, 1982, Doors, 1984. Chmn. Appearance Review Commn., Highland Park, Ill., 1976-86; commr. Zoning Bd. Appeals, Highland Park, 1987—. Served with USN, 1943-46. Mem. AIA (chmn. membership commn. 1984-86, Bldg. award, 1965, 70, 75, 85), Am. Registered Architects, Ill. Soc. Architects. Club: Cliffdwellers (Chgo.). Avocations: art, running. Home: 145 Blackhawk Rd Highland Park IL 60035-5266 Office: Moses Assocs AIA 225 W Ohio St Chicago IL 60610-4119

MOSES, JEFFREY MICHAEL, customer services executive; b. Nov. 16, 1945; s. George John and Mildred (Kronz) M.; m. Barbrae Danowsky, Apr. 24, 1976; children: Apryl Richelle, Heather Lorien. AA, Eckel's Coll., Phila. Sales supr. Internat. Tariff Svcs., Inc., Washington, 1970-71; transp. analyst to mgr. of tariff pub. Charles Donley & Assocs., Pitts., 1973-81; transp. mgr. Texas Aromatics, Houston, 1981-83; dir. customer svcs. ChemCoast, Inc., LaPorte, Tex., 1983-91, v.p., 1991-96; pres. Compliance Packaging & Svcs., 1996—; mem. adv. bd. Tex. Workers' Compensation Ins. Fund. Mem. Internat. Hazardous Materials Inst. (chmn. bd. 1993, 94, cert. master transp. specialist), Am. Assn. Inspection and Lab. Cos. (chmn.).

MOSES, JOEL, computer scientist, educator; b. Petach Tikvah, Israel, Nov. 25, 1941; came to U.S., 1954, naturalized, 1960; s. Bernhard and Golda (Losner) M.; m. Margaret A. Garvey, Dec. 27, 1970; children: Jesse, David. B.A., Columbia U., 1962, M.A., 1963; Ph.D., M.I.T., 1967. Asst. prof. dept. elec. engring. and computer sci. M.I.T., 1967-71, assoc. prof., 1971-77, prof., 1977—, assoc. dir. Lab for Computer Sci., 1974-78, assoc. head computer sci. and engring., dept. elec. engring. and computer sci., 1978-81, head dept., 1981-89, D.C. Jackson prof., 1989—, dean Sch. Engring., 1991-95, provost, 1995—; vis. prof. Harvard Grad. Sch. Bus. Adminstrn., 1989-90; bd. dirs. Analog Devices, Inc., Coltec Industries Inc. Editor: The Computer Age: A Twenty Year View, 1979. Recipient Achievement award MIT Lab. for Computer Sci., 1985. Fellow IEEE, AAAS, Am. Acad. Arts and Scis.; mem. NAE, Assn. for Computing Machinery, Am. Soc. Engring. Edn. (Centennial Cert.). Office: MIT Dept Electrical Engring 3-208 Cambridge MA 02139

MOSES, LINCOLN E., statistician, educator; b. Kansas City, Mo., Dec. 21, 1921; s. Edward Walter and Virginia (Holmes) M.; m. Jean Runnels, Dec. 26, 1942; children—Katherine, James O'D., William C., Margaret, Elizabeth; m. Mary Louise Coale, 1968. A.B., Stanford, 1941, Ph.D., 1950. Asst. prof. edn. Columbia Tchrs. Coll., 1950-52; faculty Stanford U., 1952—, prof. stats., 1959—, exec. head dept., 1964-68; assoc. dean Stanford U. (Sch. Humanities and Scis.), 1965-68, 85-86, dean grad. studies, 1969-75; faculty Stanford U. (Med. Sch.), 1952—; adminstr. Energy Info. Adminstrn., Dept. of Energy, 1978-80; L.L. Thurstone disting. fellow U. N.C., 1968-69; com. mem. Am. Friends Svc. Com., intermittently 1954—, chmn. No. Calif. chpt., 1972-76, 84-88. Guggenheim fellow, 1960-61; fellow Ctr. for Advanced Study in Behavioral Scis., 1975. Fellow Am. Acad. Arts and Scis., Inst. Math. Statistics (council 1969-72); mem. Inst. of Medicine of Nat. Acad. Scis., Am. Statis. Assn. (council 1966-67), Biometric Soc. (pres. Western N. Am. region 1969), Internat. Statis. Inst. Office: Stanford U Dept Stats Stanford CA 94305

MOSES, MIKE, commissioner. Commr. Tex. Dept. Edn., Austin. Office: Office of Commr Tex Dept Edn 1701 N Congress Ave Austin TX 78701-1494*

MOSES, RAPHAEL JACOB, lawyer; b. Girard, Ala., Nov. 6, 1913; s. William Moultrie and Anna (Green) M.; m. Marian Eva Beck, Aug. 22, 1938 (dec. Feb. 1976); 1 child, Marcia (Mrs. William S. Johnson); m. Fletcher Lee Westgaard, Jan. 20, 1979. A.B., U. Colo., 1935, J.D., 1937. Bar: Colo. 1938. Practiced in Alamosa, 1938-62, Boulder, 1962—; pres. Moses, Wittemyer, Harrison & Woodruff (P.C.), from 1970, now of counsel; spl. asst. atty. gen. Rio Grande Compact, 1957-58; mem. Colo. Water Conservation Bd., 1952-58, chmn., counsel, 1958-76, cons., 1976-77; research asso., faculty law U. Colo., 1962-66, vis. lectr., 1966-76, resident counsel, 1964-66, regent, 1973-74; grad. faculty Colo. State U., 1963-67; mem. Western States Water Council, 1965-77, chmn., 1966-70. Trustee Rocky Mountain Mineral Law Inst., 1964-66; bd. dirs. U. Colo. Found., 1977—, chmn., 1977-79, mem. chancellor's adv. coun., 1981—; bd. dirs. Colo. Open Lands, 1983-91, U. Colo. Improvement Corp., 1980-90, Colo. Endowment for Humanities, 1986-89; mem. adv. bd. Natural Resources Ctr., U. Colo. Sch. Law, 1983-92, chmn., 1986-88. Served to lt. (s.g.) USNR, 1942-45. Recipient William E. Knous award U. Colo. Sch. Law, 1971, Norlin award U. Colo., 1972; Raphael J. Moses Disting. Natural Resources professorship established U. Colo., 1994. Fellow Am. Bar Found. (life), Colo. Bar Found. (trustee 1977-90), Am. Coll. Trial Lawyers; mem. ABA (chmn. water rights com. sect. natural resources 1959-60), Colo. Bar Assn. (pres. 1959-60, Award of Merit 1972), San Luis Valley Bar Assn. (pres. 1942), Am. Counsel Assn., Order of Coif (hon.). Presbyterian (elder). Clubs: Univ. (Denver); Boulder Country; Garden of the Gods (Colorado Springs). Home: 7060 Roaring Fork Trl Boulder CO 80301-3635

MOSES, ROBERT DAVIS, retired diversified industry executive; b. Hartford, Conn., Jan. 4, 1919; s. Eli Morris and Ida (Lublin) M.; m. Greta Westerfeld, Aug. 22, 1942; m. Renee J. Wolfson, Nov. 28, 1992; children: Linda Joan (Mrs. Paul Litwin) Dana Elaine, Elliot Davis. B.S. in Mech. Engring, Mich. State U., 1940; M.B.A., U. Hartford, 1975. Structure design engr. McDonnell Aircraft Corp., 1940-44; chief structures Piasecki Helicopter, Springfield, Pa., 1946-50; with Kaman Aerospace Corp., Bloomfield, Conn., 1950-72; exec. v.p. Kaman Aerospace Corp., 1969-72; v.p. Kaman Corp., Bloomfield, 1972-84; pres. Airkaman Inc., Airkaman Jacksonville Inc., Airkaman Omaha Inc., Danelin Enterprise Inc.; dir. Gerber Systems Tech., Inc.; ret. Mem. Conn. Gov.'s Select Com. on Airport Noise Abatement; trustee Ward Sch., U. Hartford.; pres. Friendship Forces Conn.; state ombudsman Nat. Guard and Res. Forces. Served with AUS, 1944-46. Mem. Am. Helicopter Soc., Mfg. Assn. Conn. (dir.), Greater Hartford C. of C. (dir. policies com., aviation com., energy com.), Conn. C. of C. (dir.), Mich. State U. Alumni Assn. (pres. Conn. 1964).

MOSES, ROBERT EDWARD, lawyer; b. Syracuse, N.Y., Feb. 23, 1936; s. Robert Henry and Kathryn Anne (Schoeneck) M.; m. Virginia Joan Speno, July 23, 1970; children: Robert, Kathryn, Hope, Frank. Student, U. Fribourg, Switzerland, 1957; BS, Georgetown U., 1958, JD, 1960. Bar: N.Y. 1961, U.S. Ct. Appeals (2d cir.) 1966, U.S. Supreme Ct. 1967. Assoc. Bond, Schoeneck & King, Syracuse, 1960-70, mem., 1970-74, ptnr., 1974—. Bd. dirs. George Jr. Republic Assn., Inc., Freeville, N.Y., 1976-88; bd. govs. Georgetown U., Washington, 1983-89; bd. regents LeMoyne Coll., Syracuse, 1985—; mem. adv. bd., spl. counsel Nat. Sports Acad., Lake Placid, N.Y., 1990-93. Lt. (j.g.) USCG, 1961-66. Mem. ABA, N.Y. State Bar Assn. (chmn. young lawyers sect. 1971-72, mem. exec. com. 1971-72, ho. of dels. 1972-75), Onondaga County Bar Assn., Onondaga County Bar Found. (bd. dirs. 1978—, pres. 1988-89), Am. Judicature Soc., Am. Arbitration Assn. (panel arbitrators 1969—), N.Y. State Econ. Devel. Coun. (mem. state legis. com. 1983—, chmn. 1983), Ft. Orange Club, Skaneateles Country Club. Republican. Roman Catholic. Home: West Lake Rd Otisco Lake Marietta NY 13110 Office: Bond Schoeneck & King LLP Fl 18 1 Lincoln Ctr Syracuse NY 13202-1355

MOSES, RONALD ELLIOT, retired toiletries products executive; b. Chelsea, Mass., Dec. 29, 1930; s. Isadore Philip and Ida (Finstein) M.; m. Eleanor Antoinette Vitale, June 22, 1952; children: Judith Jeanne, Thomas Charles. AB, Harvard U., 1952; MS in Chemistry, Northeastern U., Boston, 1959. Chemist Gen. Foods Corp., Woburn, Mass., 1954-60; sr. chemist Gillette Safety Razor Co., Boston, 1960-65, project chemist toiletries div., 1965-70, sr. mgr. rsch. toiletries div., 1970-73, dir. product devel. toiletries div., 1973-78, dir. product devel. personal care div., 1978-83, v.p. R&D personal care div., 1983-87; v.p. R&D personal care group Gillette North Atlantic, Boston, 1987-90, dir. R&D shaving and personal care group, 1990-91, v.p. R & D Toiletries Techs. Lab., 1991-93. Co-patentee gelatin fining and preparation, shaving product composition, hair conditioning composition. Lt. (j.g.) USN, 1952. Fellow Am. Inst. Chemists; mem. Am. Chem. Soc., Soc. Cosmetic Chemists, Winthrop Golf Club. Jewish. Avocations: classical music, reading, golf, model ships, computer programming. Home: 1039 Shirley St Winthrop MA 02152-1442

MOSES-FOLEY, JUDITH ANN, special education educator; b. Steubenville, Ohio, Sept. 1, 1936; d. Joseph and Katherine Ann (Pavich) Moses; m. John P. Foley, 1958 (div. 1986); children: Katherine Ann Foley, John Joseph Foley, Sean Michael Foley, Judith Kristina Foley; m. John H. Murphy, 1986 (dec. 1992). BS in Edn., Ohio U., 1958; MA in Ednl. Adminstrn., Fresno Pacific U., 1981; postgrad., Brigham Young U., 1982-84, U. San Francisco, 1985-86; student, U. N.Mex., 1993-94. Cert. in ednl. adminstrn., lang. arts, phys. edn., spl. edn., bilingual/TESOL, and as transition resource specialist, N.Mex. Adminstr., tchr., coach Madera (Calif.) Unified Schs., 1958-81; chair dept. phys. edn. Dos Palos (Calif.) H.S., 1963-64; prin. Chowchilla (Calif.) Elem. Schs., 1981-85; instr. phys. edn. Merced (Calif.) C.C., 1981-85; instr. polit. sci. and bus. adminstrn. West Hills C.C., Lemore, Calif., 1985-86; instr. phys. edn. Mohave C.C., Kingman, Ariz., 1989-90; transition resource specialist Silver Consol. Sch., Silver City, N.Mex., 1993—; adj. prof. early childhood edn. Western N.Mex. U., Silver City; spl. edn. resource specialist Silver H.S., Silver City, 1990—, coach U.S. acad. decathlon, 1991—; grant writer Circle of Life, 1994-95, 96—; coord., grant writer R.E.: Learning; mem. North Ctrl. Accreditation Steering Com., 1992-95; v.p. Divsn. of Transition and Curriculum Devel., State of N.Mex. Pres. Bobby Sox Softball League, Madera, 1975-78; head coach track and field Jr. Olympics, Madera County, 1970-81; coord. Gathering of War Birds Airshow, Madera, 1976-79. Recipient Master Tchr. award Calif. State U., Fresno, 1978-79; recipient scholarships and grants. Mem. ASCD. Avocations: flying, jewelry design, painting, water skiing, fishing. Home: PO Box 2 Buckhorn NM 88025-0002 Office: Silver Consol Schs 3200 N Silver St Silver City NM 88061-7283

MOSETTIG, MICHAEL DAVID, television producer, writer; b. Washington, July 21, 1942; s. Erich and Ann (Nelson) M.; m. Anne L. Groer. Student, Ind. U., 1960-61; BA in Polit. Sci., George Washington U., 1964; MA in European History, Georgetown U., 1968. Reporter Leslie E. Carpenter News Bur., Washington, 1961-65, Newhouse Nat. News Svc., Washington, 1965-69, UPI, London and Brussels, 1969-70; editor, reporter Nat. Jour., Washington, 1970-71; producer NBC News, Washington and N.Y.C., 1971-79; assoc. Grad. Sch. Journalism Columbia U., N.Y.C., 1979-83; producer MacNeil/Lehrer News Hour, 1983-85, sr. producer fgn. affairs and def., 1985—; mem. Internat. Inst. for Strategic Studies, London, Coun. Fgn. Rels., N.Y. Author: DeGaulle and His Anglo-Saxon Allies, 1968, (with Ronald Müller) Revitalizing America, 1980. With USCGR, 1966-68, USNR, 1968-78. Herman Lowe Meml. scholar Washington chpt. Sigma Delta Chi; Joan Barone award Radio-TV Corrs. Assn. Mem. Overseas Writers, Cosmos Club. Home: 3340 Northampton St NW Washington DC 20015-1653

MOSHER, GEORGE ALLAN, distribution company executive; b. Detroit, June 21, 1939; s. Carroll Leonard and Susan (Harris) M.; m. Julie Zaber, Dec. 31, 1966; children: Karen, Holly, Robert. AB, Harvard U., 1961, MBA, 1963. With sales promotion dept. Look mag., 1963-65; pres. Bus. & Instl. Furniture Co., Milw., 1965-75, Nat. Bus. Furniture Co., Milw., 1975—; chmn. Bus. Mailers, 1976; pres. Alfax Mfg. Co., N.Y.C., 1984—, Office Furniture Ctr., Boston, 1986—, Dallas Midwest, 1990—. Bd. dirs. Milw. Pub. Affairs Coun., 1975-84, v.p., 1982-83; bd. dirs. Future Milw., 1979-82, Vol. Ctr., 1988-91, Communique, 1986-90, Nat. Hospitality Supply, 1990—, Milw. Bus. Forum, 1975—, Capital Commerce Bancorp, 1994—, Conner Safety Products, 1995—. Mem. Wis. Direct Mktg. (founder, pres. 1987-88. Marketer of Yr. award 1991), Univ. Club, River Tennis Club (treas. 1983-86), Harvard Bus. Sch. Club (pres. 1973), Rotary, Harvard Club (Milw., N.Y.C.). Home: 4706 N Wilshire Rd Milwaukee WI 53211-1262 Office: 735 N Water St Milwaukee WI 53202-4910

MOSHER, GILES EDMUND, JR., banker; b. Boston, Jan. 1, 1933; s. Giles Edmund and Mary (Downs) M.; m. Thelma Ann Doyle, Sept. 22, 1956; children: Mary Beth, Susan, Michelle, Giles Edmund III, Alison, Caitlyn. BSBA, Boston Coll., 1955; postgrad., Northwestern U. Sch. Fin. Pub. Rels., 1963, Stonier Sch. Banking Rutgers U., 1965; hon. degree, Suffolk U., 1990. Mgr. credit dept. Newton-Waltham Bank & Trust Co., 1955-60, asst. treas., 1960-62, asst. v.p., 1962-64, v.p., 1964-65, sr. v.p., 1965-68, exec. v.p., 1968-69, pres., 1970-79; pres., chmn. bd. BayBank Middlesex, Burlington, Mass., 1979-91; pres., CEO BayBank, Burlington, Mass., 1991—; mem. BayBank Fin. and Leasing Corp.; bd. dirs. Boston Mut. Life Ins. Co., Mass. Bus. Devel. Corp.; mem. fin. and adminstrn. adv. com. Archdiocese of Boston. Trustee Newton-Wellesley Hosp.; trustee, mem. adminstrn. and fin. com., corp. com., exec. com. St. Elizabeth's Hosp., Brighton, Mass.; bd. dirs. Boston Coll., 1973; treas. Equestrian Order Holy Sepulchre of Jerusalem; mem. pres.'s coun. Bentley Coll.; mem. mil. affairs coun. Hanscom AFB; mem. corp. Woods Hole Oceanographic Instn. Named Man of Year City of Newton, 1960; recipient Bronze medallion Boys Clubs Am., 1964; Named One of Ten Outstanding Young Men of Greater Boston Jr. C. of C., 1964, One of Four Outstanding Young Men of Mass., 1965, One of Five Outstanding Young Men of New Eng., 1966; recipient Brandeis U. Disting. Community Service award, 1975, Disting. Citizen's award Minuteman Council Boy Scouts Am., 1980. Mem. Newton Taxpayers Assn. (dir.), Newton Bankers Assn. (pres.), Am. Banking Assn. (bd. govs. Boston chpt.), Newton C. of C., Boston Coll. Alumni Assn. (pres. 1970), Am. Assn. Sovereign Militia Order of Malta, Clover Club of Boston, Comml. Club of Boston, Brae Burn Country Club (West Newton, Mass.; chmn. fin. com.), Alpha Gamma Sigma. Home: 227 Windsor Rd Newton MA 02168-1119 Office: 7 New Eng Exec Park Burlington MA 01803

MOSHER, LAWRENCE FORSYTH, journalist; b. L.A., July 12, 1929; s. Jack Marsh and Alice (Forsyth) M.; m. Constance Bauerlein, 1963 (div. 1980); children: Kirsten Louise, Honor Forsyth. BA, Stanford U., 1952; B Fgn. Trade, Am. Grad. Sch. Internat. Mgmt., 1956. Reporter Bergen Record, Hackensack, N.J., 1958-59, N.Y. World-Telegram & Sun, N.Y.C., 1959-62; staff writer, then Beirut bur. chief Copley News Svc., San Diego, 1962-67; staff corr. The Nat. Observer, Silver Spring, Md., 1967-77; staff writer, then contbg. editor Nat. Jour., Washington, 1979-88; editor The Water Reporter, Washington, 1984-90; resident journalist Environ. Health Ctr., Washington, 1988-89; mng. editor Middle East Insight, Washington, 1989-90; editor High Country News, Paonia, Colo., 1990-91; Rocky Mountain corr. The Economist, 1991—; news dir. Sta. KVNF pub. radio Paonia, Colo., 1992-93; mem. Delta County planning commn., 1995—; writer-in-residence Fgn. Svc. Sch. Georgetown U., Washington, 1977-79, Ctr. for Contemporary Arab Studies. Contbr. chpts. to America's Wild and Scenic Rivers, 1983, Bordering on Trouble: Resources and Politics in Latin America, 1986, World Resources, 1987-89. Lt. (j.g.) USNR, 1952-54, Korea. Named Communicator of Yr., Nat. Wildlife Fedn., 1982. Mem. Nat. Press Club, Potomac Rowing Club. Democrat. Avocations: choral music, sailing, sculling, horseback riding, skiing. Home and Office: 323 4200 Dr Crawford CO 81415-9763

MOSHER, SALLY EKENBERG, lawyer; b. N.Y.C., July 26, 1934; d. Leslie Joseph and Frances Josephine (McArdle) Ekenberg; m. James Kimberly Mosher, Aug. 13, 1960 (dec. Aug. 1982). MusB, Manhattanville Coll., 1956; postgrad., Hofstra U., 1958-60, U. So. Calif., 1971-73; JD, U. So. Calif., 1981. Bar: Calif., 1982. Musician, pianist, tchr., 1957-74; music critic Pasadena Star-News, 1967-72; mgr. Contrasts Concerts, Pasadena Art Mus., 1971-72; rep. Occidental Life Ins. Co., Pasadena, 1975-78; v.p. James K. Mosher Co., Pasadena, 1961-82, pres., 1982—; pres. Oakhill Enterprises, Pasadena, 1984—; assoc. White-Howell, Inc., Pasadena, 1984—; real estate broker, 1984—; harpsichordist, lectr., 1994—. Contbr. articles to various publs. Bd. dirs. Jr. League Pasadena, 1966-67, Encounters Concerts, Pasadena, 1966-72, U. So. Calif. Friends of Music, L.A., 1973-76, Calif. Music Theatre, 1988-90, Pasadena Hist. Soc., 1989-91, I Cantori, 1989-91; bd. dirs. Pasadena Arts Coun., 1986-92, pres., 1989-92, chair adv. bd., 1992-93; v.p., bd. dirs. Pasadena Chamber Orch., 1986-88, pres., 1987-88; mem. Calif. 200 Coun. for Bicentennial of U.S. Constn., 1987-90; mem. Endowment Adv. Commn., Pasadena, 1988-90; bd. dirs. Foothill Area Cmty. Svcs., 1990-95, treas., 1991, vice chair, 1992-94, chair, 1994-95. Manhattanville Coll. hon. scholar, 1952-56. Mem. ABA, Calif. Bar Assn., Assocs. of Calif. Inst. Tech., Athenaeum, Kappa Gamma Pi, Mu Phi Epsilon, Phi Alpha Delta. Republican. Home: 1260 Rancheros Rd Pasadena CA 91103-2759 Office: 711 E Walnut St Ste 407 Pasadena CA 91101-4403

MOSHER, WENDY JEAN, retail chain official; b. New Bedford, Mass., Feb. 10, 1966; d. Robert Milton and Judith Louise (Rayno) M. Student, Butera Sch. Art, Boston, 1984-85. Cashier Sears, Roebuck & Co., North Dartmouth, Mass., 1984-88; sales mgr. trainee Sears, Roebuck & Co., Dedham, Mass., 1988-90, mgr. automotive svc., 1990-91; mgr. automotive ctr. Sears, Roebuck & Co., Concord, N.H., 1991-93, Sears, Roebuck and Co., Nashua, N.H., 1993—. Mem. NAFE, Merchant's Assn. N.H. (bd. dirs.). Home: 21 Lakeside Ave Lakeville MA 02347-2416 Office: Sears Roebuck and Co 310 Daniel Webster Hwy Ste 102 Nashua NH 03060-5731

MOSHIER, DAVID IRWIN, church administrator, communications consultant; b. Roanoke, Va., Sept. 14, 1954; s. Emery Irwin (dec.) and Evelyn Mae (Kunkel) M.; m. Bonnie Sharon Dailey, Feb. 13, 1982. Student, George Washington U., 1972-74, 76-79, 82, No. Va. C.C., Alexandria, 1981, United Wesleyan Coll., 1987; STD, Am. Bible Inst., 1991. Ordained to ministry Am. Evang. Christian Chs., 1992, Reformed Presbyn. Ch., 1995. Rsch. asst. mktg. dept. Clarendon Bank & Trust, Arlington, 1974; collection agt., installment loan dept. Clarendon Bank & Trust, Arlington, Va., 1974-75; loan collection officer George Washington U., Washington, 1975-77, sr. loan collection officer, 1977-79; student loan collection coord. Hahnemann Med. Coll. and Hosp., Phila., 1979-80; prin. account clk. George Washington U., Washington, 1980-83; pastor The Wesleyan Ch., Waldorf, Md., 1983-86; asst. pastor Floor Meml. Wesleyan Ch., Arlington, 1986-89; pastor First Wesleyan Ch., Alexandria, Va., 1989-91; dir. govt. rels. Am. Evang. Christian Chs., Alexandria, 1992-93, moderator Mid-Atlantic region, 1992-95, nat. exec. dir., 1993; pastor Fredericksburg (Va.) Area Reformed Presbyn. Mission, 1995—; bd. dirs. TransAmericas Transp. Info. Svcs., Inc., Falls Church, Va.; sec. ext. and evangelism Capital Dist. Wesleyan Ch., Great Falls, Va., 1986-88; spl. asst. Office Army Chief of Chaplains, Arlington, 1987-90; alumni coun. Flint Hill Sch., Oakton, Va., 1991—; supply pastor Cmty. Ch./Am. Rescue Workers, Capitol Heights, Md., 1992; ch. resls. cons. WABS Radio, Arlington, 1992-94; mem. adv. bd. Covered Bridge Ministries, Morristown, Ind., 1993—, others. Contbr. articles to profl. jours. Officer of election Electoral Bd., Alexandria, 1991-92, Arlington, 1992-93. Recipient Letter of Commendation, USMC Dir., C4 Systems, Washington, 1987, Cert. of Commendation, Army Chief of Chaplains, Washington, 1988, 89, 90, Cert. of Civil Svc., Desert Shield-Storm/Hqrs. U.S. Army, Washington, 1992. Mem. George Washington U. Gen. Alumni Assn. Republican. Home: Apt 102 4429 S 31st St Arlington VA 22206-2119 Office: Westminster Chapel PO Box 1449 Spotsylvania VA 22553-1449

MOSHIER, MARY BALUK, patent lawyer; b. Pitts., Aug. 20, 1905; d. Andrew and Johanna (Hlebasko) Baluk; m. Ross Warren Moshier; children: Thomas, Stephen. BA, U. Ark., 1929; postgrad., U. Chgo., 1945-46; JD, No. Ky. U., 1962. Bar: U.S. Patent Office 1944, Ohio 1962. Tchr. Gary (Ind.) Pub. Schs., 1930-35; tech. libr. Monsanto Co., Dayton, Ohio, 1936-41, patent chemist, 1942-45, asst. agt., atty., 1949-66; patent adviser U.S. Office of Naval Rsch., San Francisco, 1948-49; patents cons., pvt. practice, 1969—. Co-author: Anydrous Aluminum Chloride in Organic Chemistry, 1941. Mem. AAAS, AAUW, NOW, Lawyers Club of Sun City, Nat. Assn. Ret. Fed. Employees, U.S. Chess Fedn., Phi Alpha Delta Legal Frat. Internat. Democrat. Episcopalian. Avocations: reading, bridge, chess, gardening. Home and Office: 17300 N 88th Ave Apt 238 Peoria AZ 85382-3505

MOSHMAN, JACK, statistical consultant; b. Richmond Hill, N.Y., Aug. 12, 1924; s. Morris and Sadye (Posner) M.; m. Annette Gordon, Aug. 10, 1947; children: Gordon, Marc, Sherri, Ira. BA, NYU, 1946; MA, Columbia U., 1947; PhD, U. Tenn., 1953. Instr. Queens Coll., Flushing, N.Y., 1946-47, U. Tenn., Knoxville, 1947-53; statistician U.S. AEC, Oak Ridge, Tenn., 1948-50; sr. statistician Oak Ridge Nat. Labs., Oak Ridge, 1950-54; mem. tech. staff Bell Tel. Labs., Murray Hill, N.J., 1954-57; v.p. C-E-I-R Inc., Washington, 1957-66; mng. dir. EBS Mgmt. Cons., Washington, 1966-68; sr. v.p. Leasco Systems & Rsch., Bethesda, Md., 1968-69; pres. Moshman Assocs. Inc., Bethesda, Md., 1970—; adj. prof. Rutgers U., 1963-66; professorial lectr. George Washington U., 1959-62; chmn. Inst. for Safety Analysis, Rockville, Md., 1975-89. Editor: Faith, Hope & Parity, 1967; author Ency. sect. Computers & Politics, 1985, 90, 93; contbr. articles to profl. jours. Trustee Babbage Found., St. Paul, 1983-87. With U.S. Army, 1943-46, ETO. Fellow Am. Statis. Assn. (coun. 1956, 58); mem. Am. Fedn. Info. Processing Soc. Am. (bd. dirs., pres. 1986-87), Assn. for Computing Machinery (sec. 1956-64, v.p 1964), Inst. for Math. Stats., Inst. for Mgmt. Scis., Ops. Rsch. Soc. Am., Biometrics Soc. Avocation: psephology. Office: Moshman Assocs Inc 4340 East West Hwy Bethesda MD 20814

MOSICH, ANELIS NICK, accountant, author, educator, consultant; b. Yugoslavia, Aug. 30, 1928; came to U.S., 1939, naturalized, 1951; s. Dinko and Josephine (Ursich) M.; m. Dorothy V. Rasich, June 15, 1958; children: Lori, Lisa, Jeffrey. BS, UCLA, 1951, MBA, 1953, PhD (fellow), 1963. CPA, Calif. Mem. faculty UCLA, 1955-63, Calif. State U., Northridge, 1963-64; examiner for Calif. State Bd. Accountancy, 1964-70; prof. acctg. U. So. Calif., Los Angeles, 1964-74; William C. Hallett prof. acctg. U. So. Calif., 1974-81, Ernst & Young prof., 1981-90, chmn. acctg. dept., 1970-74, 77-78, prof. emeritus, 1993; cons. various bus. orgns., 1953—; expert witness; bd. dirs. Western Waste Industries; guest speaker various profl. and bus. groups in Calif., Oreg., N.Y., Tex., Fla., and Hawaii, 1963-93. Author: Intermediate Accounting, rev. 6th edit., 1989, Financial Accounting, 1970, 75, Accounting: A Basis for Business Decision, 1972, Modern Advanced Accounting, 4th edit., 1988, The CPA Examination: Text, Problems and Solutions, 1978; editor: Education column Calif. CPA Quar., 1965-66; contbg. editor: Education and Professional Training column Jour. Accountancy, 1971-77; contbr. numerous articles to jours. and acctg. Mem. productivity commn. City of L.A., 1993-94. With U.S. Army, 1953-55. Recipient Dean's award Sch. Bus. Adminstrn., U. So. Calif., 1973, 78, Fred B. Olds Support Group award U. So. Calif., 1994. Mem. AICPA, Calif. Soc. CPAs. Office: U So Calif Sch Acctg University Park Los Angeles CA 90089-1421

MOSIER, ARVIN RAY, chemist, researcher; b. Olney Springs, Colo., June 11, 1945; s. Isaac James Ellen Rena (Ross) M.; m. Susan Minnick, Dec. 30, 1965; children: Andrew, Katherine. BS, Colo. State U., 1967, MS, 1967-68, PhD, 1974. Chemist agr. research services USDA, Ft. Collins, 1967—; Contbr. papers and book chpt. to profl. publ. Mem. AAAS, Am. Soc. Agronomy, Soil Sci. Soc. Am., Internat. Soil Sci. Soc., Council Agrl. Sci. Tech., Phi Kappa Phi, Sigma XI, Gamma Sigma Delta. Republican. Methodist. Club: Aresnal Competitive Soccer. Avocations: tennis, soccer. Home: 903 Hilldale Dr Fort Collins CO 80526-4345 Office: USDA Agrl Rsch Svc PO Box E Fort Collins CO 80522-0470

MOSIER, HARRY DAVID, JR., physician, educator; b. Topeka, May 22, 1925; s. Harry David and Josephine Morrow (Johnson) M.; m. Nadine Oclea Merialtt, Aug. 24, 1949; children: Carolyn Josephine Mosier Polhlmeyer, William David, Daniel Thomas, Christine Elizabeth Mosier Mahoney; m. Marjorie Knight Armstrong, Sept. 26, 1963. B.S. magna cum laude, U. Notre Dame, 1948; M.D., Johns Hopkins U., 1952. Diplomate Am. Bd. Pediatrics, Am. Bd. Pediatric Endocrinology. Intern Johns Hopkins Hosp., Balt., 1952-53; resident in pediatrics Los Angeles Children's Hosp., 1953-54, resident pediatric pathology, 1954-55; fellow pediatric endocrinology Johns Hopkins U., 1955-57; asst. prof. pediatrics UCLA, 1957-61, assoc. prof., 1961-63; dir. research Ill. State Pediatric Inst., Chgo., 1963-67; assoc. prof. U. Ill., 1963-67; prof. pediatrics, head div. pediatric endocrinology U. Calif.-Irvine, 1967—; staff Children's Hosp. Med. Center, Long Beach, Calif., 1970—, U. Calif. Irvine Med. Center, Orange, 1979—; dist. cons. Medical Bd. Calif., 1995—. Contbr. articles to med. jours. With AUS, 1943-46, col. U.S. Army Med. Corps, 1990-91, Persian Gulf War. USAR Med. Corps. 1952-62, 83-93 (ret.). Office: U Calif Dept Pediatrics Irvine CA 92616

MOSIER, MARY C. (CATHY MOSIER), business owner; b. Dayton, Ohio, June 3, 1954; d. Herman Ullery and Cecilia Agnes (Mc Cluskey) Chrowl; m. Ronald Eugene Swank Jr., Jun. 7, 1975 (div. Oct. 1982); children: Angela, Ronald III, Samantha; m. David Michael Neufeld, Aug. 18, 1983 (div. 1991); children: Michael Brent Neufeld, Andrew Jonathan Neufeld; m. Steven Lynn Mosier, Nov. 6, 1992. Mgmt. asst. Air Force Maintenance, Supply and Munitions Mgmt. Engring. Team, Wright-Patterson AFB, Ohio, 1977-82, Air Force Svc. Info. and News Ctr., Kelly AFB, Tex., 1982-88; owner Cat's Crafts, San Antonio, 1988—; pres. Perfect Presentations, San Antonio, 1993—; stock fund mgr., resource advisor 76th Logistics Group, Kelly AFB, 1988—. Leader Webelos and Bear Dens Boy Scouts, 1994—. Recipient Dan Berkant award Air Force Assn., 1985. Mem. NAFE, Fed. Mgrs. Assn., Nat. Assn. Military Comptrollers. Republican. Avocations: crafts, reading, sports. Home and Office: Perfect Presentations 9830 Autumn Silver San Antonio TX 78250-5877

MOSK, RICHARD MITCHELL, lawyer; b. L.A., May 18, 1939; s. Stanley and Edna M.; m. Sandra Lee Budnitz, Mar. 21, 1964; children: Julie, Matthew. AB with great distinction, Stanford U., 1960; JD cum laude, Harvard U., 1963. Bar: Calif. 1964, U.S. Supreme Ct. 1970, U.S. Ct. Mil. Appeals 1970, U.S. Dist. Ct. (no., so., ea., and cen. dists.) Calif 1964, U.S. Ct. Appeals (9th dist.) 1964. Mem. staff Pres.'s Commn. on Assassination Pres. Kennedy, 1964; research clk. Calif. Supreme Ct., 1964-65; ptnr. Mitchell, Silberberg & Knupp, L.A., 1965-87; prin. Sanders, Barnet, Goldman, Simons & Mosk, P.C., L.A., 1987—; spl. dep. Fed. Pub. Defender, L.A., 1975-76; instr. U. So. Calif. Law Sch., 1978; arbitrator Iran-U.S. Claims Tribunal, 1981-84, substitute arbitrator, 1984—; mem. Los Angeles County Jud. Procedures Commn., 1973-82, chmn., 1978; bd. dirs. Internat. Arbitration Commn.; mem. adv. coun. Asia/Pacific Ctr. for Resolution International Trade Disputes, 1986—; chmn. Motion Picture Assn. Classification and Rating Adminstrn., 1994—. Contbr. articles to profl. jours. Mem. L.A. City-County Inquiry on Brush Fires, 1970; bd. dirs. Calif. Mus. Sci. and Industry, 1979-82, Vista Del Mar Child Ctr., 1979-82; trustee L.A. County Law Libr., 1985-86; bd. govs. Town Hall Calif., 1986-91; mem. Christopher Commn. on L.A. Police Dept., 1991; mem. Stanford U. Athletic Bd., 1991-95. With USNR, 1964-75. Hon. Woodrow Wilson fellow, 1960; recipient Roscoe Pound prize, 1961. Fellow Am. Bar Found.; mem. ABA (coun. internat. law sect. 1986-90), FBA (pres. L.A. chpt. 1972), L.A. County Bar Assn., Beverly Hills Bar Assn., L.A. Assn. Bus. Trial Lawyers, Internat. Bar Assn., Am. Arbitration Assn. (comml. panel, large complex case panel, Asia/Pacific panel), Hong Kong Internat. Arbitration Ctr. (mem. panel 1986—), Am. Film Mktg. Assn. (arbitration panel), L.A. Ctr. Internat. Comml. Arbitration, B.C. Internat. Arbitration Ctr. (mem. panel), World Intellectual Property Orgn. (mem. arbitration panel), Ctr. Pub. Resources (mem. arbitration panel), Phi Beta Kappa. Office: Sanders Barnet Goldman Simons & Mosk 1901 Avenue Of The Stars Los Angeles CA 90067-6078

MOSK, STANLEY, state supreme court justice; b. San Antonio, Sept. 4, 1912; s. Paul and Minna (Perl) M.; m. Edna Mitchell, Sept. 27, 1937 (dec.); 1 child, Richard Mitchell; m. Susan Hines, Aug. 27, 1982 (div.); m. Kaygey Kash, Jan. 15, 1995. Student, U. Tex., 1931; PhB, U. Chgo., 1933; postgrad., U. Chgo. Law Sch., 1934; JD, Southwestern U., 1935, postgrad., 1987; postgrad., The Hague Acad. Internat. Law, 1970, U. Pacific, 1970; LLD, U. San Diego, 1971, U. Santa Clara, 1976, Calif. Western U., 1984, Whittier Coll. Law, 1993, Pepperdine U., 1995, Western State U., San Diego, 1995. Bar: Calif. 1935, U.S. Supreme Ct. 1956. Practiced in Los Angeles, until 1939; exec. sec. to gov. Calif., 1939-42; judge Superior Ct. Los Angeles County, 1943-58; pro tem justice Dist. Ct. Appeal, Calif., 1954; atty. gen. Calif., also head state dept., justice, 1959-64; justice Supreme Ct. Calif., 1964—; mem. Jud. Coun. Calif., 1973-75, Internat. Commn. Jurists. Chmn. San Francisco Internat. Film Festival, 1967; mem. Dem. Nat. Com, Calif., 1960-64; mem. bd. regents U. Calif., 1940; pres. Vista Del Mar Child Care Svc., 1954-58; bd. dirs. San Francisco Law Sch., 1971-73, San Francisco Regional Cancer Found., 1980-83. With AUS, WWII. Recipient Disting. Alumnus award U. Chgo., 1958, 93. Mem. ABA, Nat. Assn. Attys. Gen. (exec. bd. 1964), Western Assn. Attys. Gen. (pres. 1963), L.A. Bar Assn., San Francisco Bar Assn., Am. Legion, Manuscript Soc., Calif. Hist. Soc., Am. Judicature Soc., Inst. Jud. Adminstrn., U. Chgo. Alumni Assn. No. Calif. (pres. 1957-58, 67), Order of Coif, B'nai B'rith, Hillcrest Country Club (L.A.), Commonwealth Club, Golden Gateway Tennis Club (San Francisco), Beverly Hills Tennis Club. Office: Supreme Ct Calif 303 2nd St San Francisco CA 94107-1366

MOSK, SUSAN HINES, lawyer; b. Pitts., Dec. 14, 1946; d. William James and Catherine Elizabeth (Cook) Hines; m. Stanley Mosk, Aug. 27, 1982 (div. Jan. 1995). B in Music Edn., Fla. State U., 1968, M in Music Edn., 1970; JD, U. Calif., San Francisco, 1990. Bar: Calif. 1990, U.S. Dist. Ct. (no. dist.) Calif. 1990, U.S. Ct. Appeals (9th cir.) 1990. Assoc. Payne, Thompson & Walker, San Francisco, 1990-94; of counsel Knecht, Haley, Lawrence & Smith, San Francisco, 1994-95; prin. Law Offices of Susan H. Mosk, San Francisco, 1995—; commr. Jud. Nominees Evaluation Commn., 1992-96. Author/editor: Rainmaking Guide to Corporate Counsel, 1993. Mem. steering com. Women's Leadership Coun. for U.S. Senator Diane Feinstein, 1992—; chair No. Calif. Women's Cabinet for Kathleen Brown Gubernatorial Campaign, San Francisco, 1994; co-chair fin. Willie L. Brown Mayoral Campaign, 1995. Mem. State Bar of Calif., Calif. Women Lawyers (bd. govs. 1992-94, 1st v.p. 1993-94), Queen's Bench. Democrat. Avocations: music, skiing, traveling, reading. Office: Law Offices of Susan H Mosk 185 Post Ste 300 San Francisco CA 94108

MOSKAL, ROBERT M., bishop; b. Carnegie, Pa., Oct. 24, 1937; s. William and Jean (Popivchak) M. BA, St. Basil Coll. Sem., Stamford, Conn., 1959; lic. sacred theology, Cath. U. Am., 1963; student, Phila. Mus. Acad. and Conservatory of Mus., 1963-66. Ordained priest Ukrainian Cath. Ch. 1963. Founder, pastor St. Anne's Ukrainian Cath. Ch., Warrington, Pa., 1963-72; sec. Archbishop's Chancery, Phila., 1963-67; apptd. vice-chancellor Archeparchy of Phila., 1967-74; pastor Annunciation Ukrainian Cath. Ch., Melrose Park, Phila., 1972-74; named monsignor, 1974; chancellor archdiocese, pastor Ukrainian Cath. Cathedral of the Immaculate Conception, Phila., 1974-84; apptd. bishop, 1981; Ordained titular bishop of Agathopolis and aux. bishop Ukrainian-Rite Archeparcy of Phila., 1981-83; first bishop Diocese of St. Josaphat, Parma, Ohio, 1983—; pro-synodal judge Archdiocean Tribunal, Phila., 1965-67; founder Ukrainian Cath. Hour: God is with Us, Sta. WIBF-FM, Phila, 1972-77, Christ Among Us, Sat. WTEL, 1975—; mem. Ukrainian Cath. Ch. Liturgical Subcommn., 1980; host to His Holiness Pope John Paul II. Bd. dirs. Ascension Manor, Inc., Phila., 1964-84, sec.-treas., 1964-78, exec. v.p., 1977-84. Office: PO Box 347180 5720 State Rd Parma OH 44134-7180

MOSKIN, JOHN ROBERT, editor, writer; b. N.Y.C., May 9, 1923; s. Morris and Irma (Rosenfeld) M.; m. Doris Marianne Bloch, Oct. 7, 1948 (div. 1978); children: Mark Douglas, David Scott, Nancy Irma; m. Lynn Carole Goldberg, Apr. 10, 1986. Grad., Horace Mann Sch., 1940; B.S., Harvard U., 1944; M.A., Columbia U., 1947. Reporter Boston Post, 1941-42, Newark News, 1947-48; asst. to gen. mgr. N.Y. Star, 1948-49; editor Westport (Conn.) Town Crier, 1949; med. editor Look mag., N.Y.C., 1950-51; articles editor Look mag., 1951-53, sr. editor, 1956-66, fgn. editor, 1966-71; mng. editor Woman's Home Companion, 1953-56; sr. editor Collier's, 1956; editor at large Saturday Rev., 1972-75; sr. editor World Press Rev., 1976-87, contbg. editor, 1987-93; editorial dir. Aspen Inst. Humanistic Studies, 1977-83; editorial dir. Commonwealth Fund, 1984-87, sr. editorial advisor, 1987-93. Author: (with others) The Decline of the American Male, 1958, Morality in America, 1966, Turncoat, 1968, The U.S. Marine Corps Story, 1977, 82, 87, 92, Among Lions, 1982, (with Julia Vitullo-Martin) The Executive's Book of Quotations, 1994, Mr. Truman's War, 1996; mem. editorial adv. com. Dimensions mag, 1970-71, Present Tense, 1973-90. Trustee Scarsdale Adult Sch., 1965-72, chmn., 1969-70; mem. Dana Reed Prize com. Harvard, 1947—; mem. com. Class of 1944, 1943—; mem. communications screening com. Council Internat. Exchange of Scholars, 1974-77, President's Coun. Heritage Coll., 1995—; bd. dirs. SIECUS, 1972-80, Jerusalem Found., 1977—, Marine Corps Hist. Found., 1979-82, 89-95, Faculty for Continuing Med. Edn., 1983-86. Served with AUS, 1943-46.

Recipient Benjamin Franklin gold medal for pub. service Woman's Home Companion, 1955, Page One award Newspaper Guild N.Y., 1965, Sidney Hillman Found. award, 1965; National Headliners award, 1967; Overseas Press Club award, 1969; citation for excellence, 1971; Disting. Service award Marine Corps Combat Corrs. Assn., 1978; Nat. Jewish Book award, 1983. Mem. Am. Hist. Assn., Authors Guild, Fgn. Editors Group (chmn. 1970-71), Nat. Press Club (Washington), Overseas Press Club (gov. 1975-79), Century Club, Harvard Club (N.Y.C.), Lotos Club, (bd. dirs. 1988-90, 94—pres. 1991-94), Sigma Delta Chi (mem. nat. freedom of info. com. 1964, 71). Home: 945 5th Ave New York NY 10021-2655 also: 157 Jerusalem Rd Tyringham MA 01264

MOSKIN, MORTON, lawyer; b. N.Y.C., Mar. 28, 1927; s. Barnett and Sonia (Burr) M.; m. Rita Lee Goldberg, June 15, 1952; children: Tina, Ilene, Jonathan. B.A., Pa. State Coll., 1947; LL.B., Cornell U., 1950. Assoc. White & Case, N.Y.C., 1950-61, ptnr., 1962-94, cons., 1995—; chmn. exec. com. Mallinckroot Group (formerly IMCERA, previously Internat. Minerals & Chem. Corp.), St. Louis, 1988-91, chmn. corp. governance com., 1993—, also bd. dirs.; sec. BT Mortgage Investors, Garden City, N.J., 1975-82. Bd. dirs. Fedn. Employment and Guidance Svcs.; bd. dirs., pres. Henry M. Blackmer Found., N.Y.C., Achievement Found., to 1994, Stamford, Conn.; bd. dirs. Jewish Cmty. Svcs. L.I., 1974-93, pres., 1984-87. Fellow Am. Bar Found.; mem. ABA, N.Y. State Bar Assn., N.Y. County Lawyers Assn. (dir. 1981-86), Norfolk (Conn.) Country Club, Cornell Club N.Y. Home: 1160 Park Ave Apt 15B New York NY 10128-1212 Office: White & Case 1155 Avenue Of The Americas New York NY 10036-2711

MOSKOS, CHARLES C., sociology educator; b. Chgo., May 20, 1934; s. Charles and Rita (Shukas) M.; m. Ilca Hohn, July 3, 1966; children—Andrew, Peter. B.A. cum laude, Princeton, 1956; M.A., UCLA, 1961, Ph.D., 1963; L.H.D. (hon.), Norwich U., 1992. Asst. prof. U. Mich., Ann Arbor, 1964-66; assoc. prof. sociology Northwestern U., Evanston, Ill., 1966-70, prof., 1970—; fellow Progressive Policy Inst., 1992—; mem. Presdl. Commn. on Women in the Mil., 1992. Author: The Sociology of Political Independence, 1967, The American Enlisted Man, 1970, Public Opinion and the Military Establishment, 1971, Peace Soldiers, 1976, Fuerzas Armadas y Societdad, 1984, The Military--More Than Just A Job?, 1988, A Call to Civil Service, 1988, Greek Americans, 1989, Soldiers and Sociology, 1989, New Directions in Greek American Studies, 1991, The New Conscientious Objection, 1993, All That We Can Be, 1996, Reporting War When There Is No War, 1996. Mem. bd. advisors Dem. Leadership Coun., 1989—; chmn. Theodore Saloutos Meml. Fund; mem. Archdiocesean Commn. Third Millenium, 1982-88. Served with AUS, 1956-58. Decorated D.S.M., Fondation pour les Etudes de Def. Nat. (France), S.M.K. (The Netherlands); named to Marshall rsch. chair ARI, 1987-88, 95-96; Ford. Found. faculty fellow, 1969-70; fellow Wilson Ctr., 1980-81, guest scholar, 1991; fellow Rockefeller Found. Humanities, 1983-84, Guggenheim fellow, 1992-93, fellow Annenberg Washington Program, 1995; grantee 20th Century Fund, 1983-87, 92-94, Ford Found., 1989-90. Mem. Praesidium Russia Assn. Armed Forces and Soc., Am. Sociol. Assn., Internat. Sociol. Assn. (pres. rsch. com. on armed forces and conflict resolution 1982-86), Am. Polit. Sci. Assn., Inter-Univ. Seminar on Armed Forces and Soc. (chmn. 1987—). Greek Orthodox. Home: 2440 Asbury Ave Evanston IL 60201-2307

MOSKOWITZ, ARNOLD X., economist, strategist, educator; b. N.Y.C., Jan. 27, 1944; s. Morris and Millie (Kozichovsky) M.; m. Sandra Moskowitz; children: Dara, Alex, Nicole. BS in Elec. Engring., CCNY, 1966; MS in Indsl. Mgmt., Poly. Inst. N.Y., 1970; MPhil, NYU, 1979, PhD in Econs. and Fin., 1985. Analyst Grumman Corp., N.Y.C., 1968-70; assoc. economist Dean Witter Reynolds Inc., N.Y.C., 1970-74, first v.p., economist, 1975-82, sr. v.p., economist, 1983-89; sr. v.p., dir. investment strategy County NatWest U.S.A., N.Y.C., 1989-90; chmn. Moskowitz Capital Cons. Inc., N.Y.C., 1990—; lectr. New Sch. Social Research, 1978—; adj. assoc. prof. fin. Pace U., N.Y.C., 1980-82; pres. Money Marketers NYU, 1988-89. Contbr. articles to profl. jours.; chpts. to books, including Security Selection and Active Portfolio Management; contbr. to Ency. of Economics, How to Beat Wall Street. Mem. Am. Econ. Assn., Nat. Econ. Club, Nat. Assn. Bus. Economists, Atlantic Soc., Beta Gamma Sigma. Jewish. Office: Moskowitz Capital Cons Inc 135 W 50th St Ste 1830 New York NY 10020-1201 *Our guidelines for success starts with our principles to provide the highest level of service to our customers and treat our employees as partners in the business. Our goal is to maintain the highest level of integrity in dealing with clients and workers in order to maximize our performances.*

MOSKOWITZ, HERBERT, management educator; b. Paterson, NJ, May 26, 1935; s. David and Ruth (Abrams) M.; m. Heather Mary Lesgnier, Feb. 25, 1968; children: Tobias, Rebecca, Jonas. BS in Mech. Engring., Newark Coll. Engring., 1956; MBA, U.S. Internat. U., 1964; PhD, UCLA, 1970. Rsch. engr. GE, 1956-60; systems design engr. Gen. Dynamics Convair, San Diego, 1960-65; asst. prof. Purdue U., West Lafayette, Ind., 1970-75, assoc. prof., 1975-79, prof., 1979-85, Disting. prof., 1985-87, James B. Henderson Disting. prof., 1987-91, Lewis B. Cullman Dist. prof. mfg. mgmt., 1991—, dir. ctr. mgmt. mfg. enterprises; cons. AT&T, Inland Steel Co., Abbott Labs., others; adv. panelist NSF, 1990—. Author: Management Science and Statistics Texts, 1975-90; assoc. editor Decision Scis. Jour., 1984-90, Jour. Behavioral Decision Making, 1986-90; contbr. articles to jours. in field. Bd. dirs. Sons of Abraham Synagogue, Lafayette, Ind., 1970—; mem. Lafayette Klezmorem, 1973—. Capt. USAF, 1956-60. Recipient Disting. Doctoral Student award UCLA Alumni Assn., 1969-70; Fulbright Rsch. scholar, 1985-86. Fellow Decision Scis. Inst. (sec. 1985-87, v.p. 1978-80); mem. Ops. Rsch. Soc. Am./Inst. Mgmt. Sci. (liaison officer 1977—, panel mem., advisor NSF and Fulbright Scholar program 1993—), Tau Beta Pi, Pi Tau Sigma. Jewish. Avocations: Jewish music, tennis. Home: 1430 N Salisbury St West Lafayette IN 47906-2420 Office: Purdue U Krannert Grad Sch Mgmt Ctr Mgmt Mfg ENterprises West Lafayette IN 47907-1310

MOSKOWITZ, JAY, public health sciences educator; b. N.Y.C., Jan. 9, 1943; s. Murray and Helene Moskowitz; m. Joanne Cathy Schindelheim, Dec. 27, 1970; children: Michael Bradley, Andrew Cory. B.S., Queens Coll., 1964; postgrad., CUNY, 1965; Ph.D., Brown U., 1969. Research assoc. in pharmacology NIH, 1969-71, grants assoc. div. research grants, 1971-72, acting chief spl. programs br., div. lung diseases, 1972-74; assoc. dir. program planning and evaluation Nat. Heart, Lung and Blood Inst., 1979-80, assoc. dir. sci. program ops., 1980-86, dir. office of program planning and evaluation, 1976-86; assoc. dir. for program planning and evaluation NIH, 1986-88, dir. Office Program Planning and Evaluation, Office of Dir., 1986-88, assoc. dir. for sci. policy and legislation, 1988-93; acting dir. Nat. Inst. on Deafness and Other Communication Disorders, 1988-90; dep. dir. for sci. policy & tech. transfer, prin. dep. dir. NIH, 1993; dep. dir. Nat. Inst. on Deafness and Other Communication Disorders, 1993-95; sr. assoc. dean for rsch. devel., prof. pub. health scis. Wake Forest U. Bowman Gray Sch. Medicine, Winston-Salem, N.C., 1995—. Contbr. articles to profl. jours. Served to lt. comdr. USPHS. Recipient Meritorious award William A. Jump Meml. Found., 1977, Dir.'s award NIH, 1978, Superior Svc. award USPHS, 1980, performance awards Sr. Exec. Svc., Presdl. Meritorious Exec. Rank award 1989, Disting. Svc. award HHS, 1991, Disting. Svc. award Nat. Inst. on Deafness and Other Comm. Disorders, 1994. Mem. Soc. Exptl. Biology and Medicine, AAAS. Jewish. Home: 7908 Lasley Forest Rd Lewisville NC 27023 Office: Wake Forest U Bowman Gray Sch Medicine Office Rsch Devel Winston Salem NC 27104

MOSKOWITZ, JOEL STEVEN, lawyer; b. N.Y.C., Jan. 14, 1947; s. Jack I. and Myra (Shor) M.; children: David, Michael, Ellen. BA, UCLA, 1967, JD, 1970. Bar: Calif. 197l, U.S. Ct. Appeals (9th cir.) 197l, U.S. Ct. Appeals (D.C. cir.) 1975, U.S. Supreme Ct. 1975, U.S. Ct. Appeals (2d cir.) 1979. Dep. atty. gen. Calif. Dept. Justice, Sacramento, 1970-83; dep. dir. Calif. Dept. Health Svcs., Sacramento, 1983-85; of counsel Gibson, Dunn & Crutcher, L.A., 1985-88, ptnr., 1988—. Author: Environmental Liability in Real Property Transactions, 1995; contbr. articles to legal publs. Mem. Phi Beta Kappa. Office: Moskowitz Wood Nyznyk LLP Ste 1800 2049 Century Pk E Los Angeles CA 90067

MOSKOWITZ, MICHAEL ARTHUR, neuroscientist, neurologist; b. N.Y.C., May 26, 1942; s. Irving Lawrence and Clara (Dranoff) M.; m. Mary Henderson, May 18, 1991; 1 child, Jenna Rachel. AB, Johns Hopkins U., 1964; MD, Tufts U., 1968. Diplomate Am. Bd. Psychiaty and Neurology, Am. Bd. Internal Medicine. Intern Yale U. Dept. Medicine, 1968-69, resident, 1969-71; resident in neurology Peter Bent Brigham Children Hosp., 1971-74; asst. prof. Med. Sch., Harvard U., Boston, 1975-79, assoc. prof., 1979-92, prof., 1992—; established investigator Am. Heart Assn., 1980-85; assoc. neurophysiologist and neurologist Mass. Gen. Hosp., Boston, 1981—; H.J. Barnett lectr. Canadian Heart Assn., Queens U., Kingston, Ont., 1993—, Witter lectr. U. Calif., San Francisco, 1994—, Barraquer-LaFora lectr. Spanish Neurol. Soc., Barcelona, Spain, 1994—, Decade of the Brain lectr. Am. Acad. Neurology, 1995, Briggs lecture dept. pharmacology U. Tex., San Antonio, 1995. Editl. bd. Stroke, Acta Neurol. Scandinavica Cephalalgia, Jour. Cerebral Blood Flow & Metabolism, Cerebrovascular Disease; contbr. articles to profl. jours. MIT postdoctoral fellow, 1974-76, Alfred Sloan Found. fellow, 1978-80; recipient Enrico Greppi award Italian Neurology Soc., 1986, 88, Tchr.-Investigator award Nat. Inst. Neurol. Disease and Stroke, 1975-80, Zülch prize Max-Planck Soc./Inst., 1996; rsch. grantee Bristol-Myers Squibb, 1993—, MGH Interdepartmental Stroke Ctr. Mem. Am. Heart Assn. (nat. rsch. com. 1991—, exec. com. stroke coun. 1991—), Am. Neurol. Assn., Am. Acad. Neurology, Am. Pain Soc., Soc. Neurosci., Internat. Soc. for Cerebral Blood Flow and Metabolism (bd. dirs.). Achievements include research in neuroscientific, neurology literature including stroke and migraine. Office: Mass Gen Hosp Charleston Navy Yard 149 13th St Charlestown MA 02129

MOSKOWITZ, ROLAND WALLACE, internist; b. Shamokin, Pa., Nov. 3, 1929. MD, Temple U., 1953. Intern Temple U. Hosp., Phila., 1953-54; fellow in internal medicine Mayo Clinic, Rochester, Minn., 1954-55, 57-60; mem. staff U. Hosps. Cleve.; prof. medicine Case Western Res. U. Sch. Medicine, Cleve. Mem. ACR, Alpha Omega Alpha. Office: U Hosps Cleve Divsn Rheum Diseases 11100 Euclid Ave Cleveland OH 44106

MOSKOWITZ, SAM (SAM MARTIN), author, editor, publisher; b. Newark, June 30, 1920; s. Harry and Rose (Gerber) M.; m. Christine Elizabeth Haycock, July 6, 1958. Partner Taurasi & Moskowitz (lit. agts.), N.Y.C., 1941-42; sales mgr. Hazel Specialty Co., Newark, 1944-52; mng. editor Gernsback Publishers, N.Y.C., 1952-54, Frosted Food Field, 1954-55; editor, asso. pub. Quick Frozen Foods, N.Y.C., 1955-72; editor, co-pub. Quick Frozen Foods, 1974-80; asso. pub. Quick Frozen Foods Internat., 1980-85; pub. Private Label, 1981-85; editor Beverage Industry, 1972-74; instr. creative writing City Coll. N.Y., 1953-55; spl. cons. frozen foods, sci. fiction; sci. fiction historian and anthologist. Author: 60 books on sci. fiction, including The Immortal Storm, 1954, Explorers of the Infinite, 1963, Seekers of Tomorrow, 1966, Science Fiction by Gaslight, 1968, Under the Moons of Mars, 1970, The Man Who Called Himself Poe, 1969, The Crystal Man, 1973, Out of the Storm, 1975, Strange Horizons, 1976, Far Future Calling, 1979, Science Fiction in Old San Francisco, 1980, A Merritt: Reflections in the Moon Pool, 1985, H.P. Lovecraft and Nils H. Frome, 1989, After All These Years (autobiography), 1991, The Haunted Pampero, 1992, Terrors of the Sea, 1994; editor Hyperion Press Science Fiction Classics, 1974. Served with AUS, 1942-43. Guest of honor 13th World Sci. Fiction conv., Cleve., 1955; recipient Big Heart award Pitts. World Sci. Fiction conv., 1960; Author's award for sci. fiction N.J. Assn. English Tchrs., 1966; Sci. Fiction Hall of Fame award, 1974; named Lit. Luminary of N.J. N.J. Inst. Tech., 1977; named to N.J. Lit. Hall of Fame, 1979. Mem. Eastern Frosted Foods Assn. (dir. 1962-72), Eastern Sci. Fiction Assn. (pres. 1945-50, 80-87), Sci. Fiction Writers Assn., Mystery Writers Am., Fantasy Amatuer Press Assn., First Fandom. Home: 361 Roseville Ave Newark NJ 07107-1721 *Attracted to science fiction in my youth by its suggested answers to provocative mysteries of time and space, I have devoted much of my life to revealing and illuminating its fascinating development, which has reflected mankind's most far-reaching aspirations and sometimes replaced, in modern tense, the voices of the ancient prophets.*

MOSKOWITZ, STANLEY ALAN, financial executive; b. N.Y.C., June 8, 1956; s. Sol and Kate (Mermelstein) M.; m. Eve Kronenberger, Sept. 20, 1981; children: Alana, Kate. BA, Queens Coll., 1978; MBA in Fin., St. John's U., 1980. Sr. credit analyst Mfrs. Hanover Leasing Corp., N.Y.C., 1979-81; gen. ptnr. Exec. Leasing Co., N.Y.C., 1981-83; pres. Execulease Corp., Elmont, N.Y., 1983—; bd. dirs. UFA/Fedn. of Greenwich, Conn., 1995—. Mem. Ea. Assn. Equipment Lessors (chmn. pub. rels. 1985-90, bd. dirs. 1988-92, Meretorious Svc. award 1986-87, chmn. ethics com. 1991-92), Omicron Delta Epsilon. Republican. Jewish. Avocations: reading, cycling. Office: Execulease Corp 1975 Linden Blvd Floral Park NY 11003-4004

MOSLER, JOHN, retired financial planner; b. N.Y.C., Sept. 24, 1922; s. Edwin H. and Irma M.; children: Bruce Elliot, John Edwin, Michele Andree. Student, Philips Exeter Acad., 1938-41, Princeton U., 1941-43; L.H.D., Fordham U., 1965; D.C.S., Duquesne U., 1968. With Mosler Safe Co., 1945-67, exec. v.p., 1948-61, pres., 1961-66, chmn., 1966-67; pres., dir. Mosler Lock Co., 1953-67, Mosler de Mexico S.A., 1953-67; exec. v.p., dir. Mosler Research Products, Inc., 1956-67; dir. 1st Caribbean Mainland Capital Co., Inc., 1962-68, chmn. bd., 1963-68, pres., 1966-68; v.p., dir. Am. Standard Inc., 1967-68; chmn. bd., dir., chief exec. officer Holmes Protection, Inc., 1968-73, Holmes Protection Services Corp., 1968-73; chmn. bd. Hidromex, S.A. de C.V., Mex., 1968—, Mosler N.V., Europe, 1973—; chmn. bd. Internat. Controls Corp., 1973-87, resigned, 1987; past chmn. bd. Royal Bus. Funds Inc.; pres. Mosler Investments. Mem. Mayor's Com. on Judiciary; pres. Am.-Romanian Flood Relief Com.; past dir. Jr. Achievement N.Y.; spl. U.S. amb. to Mauritius, to Zambia's Indpendence ceremony; vice chmn. N.Y. Rep. County Com.; chmn. John Mosler Found.; trustee, dir. Nat. Urban League; trustee Appeal of Conscience Found., Linden Hall Sch. for Girls, Lititz, Pa.; hon. trustee, past pres. N.Y. Urban League; founder Harlem Prep. Sch. With CIC, AUS, 1943-46. Decorated knight comdr. Ordo Supremus Militaris A. Lilio Regni Navarrae; Sovereign Order Hospitallers St. John of Jerusalem, Knights of Malta; comdt. L'Ordre Senegal; recipient Man of Conscience award Appeal of Conscience Found., 1969. Mem. Young Pres.'s Orgn. (past pres.), U.S. C. of C., N.Y. World Bus. Coun., Bankers of Mex. Club (Mex.), Princeton U. (N.Y.), Confrerie des Chevaliers du Tastevin, Manhattan, Real Nautico de Barcelona (Spain), Sag Harbor Yacht, Univ. Club, Wall St. Club.

MOSLEY, ELAINE CHRISTIAN SAVAGE, principal, chief education officer, consultant; b. St. Louis, Mo., Mar. 4, 1941; d. John W. Savage and Mabel (Mahone) Christian; m. Melvin Ronell Mosley, Aug. 7, 1966; children: Dawn Edith, Melanie Denise, Dana Jean, John Melvin. BS, Lincoln U., 1964, MEd, 1973; EdD, Okla. State U., 1982. Tchr. St. Louis Pub. Sch. System, 1964-70, Immaculate Conception Sch., Jefferson City, 1970-73; counselor Bartlesville (Okla.) Sch. System, 1973-75, elem. prin., 1975-83; elem. prin. Bartlesville Pub. Sch. System, 1983-85, Oak Park (Ill.) Pub. Sch. System, 1985-87; founder, prin., chief edn. officer Corp. Community Schs. of Am., Chgo., 1987—; adj. instr. Langston U. Urban Ctr., Tulsa, Okla., 1983; edn. cons. pub. speaking, workshops, seminars, nat., 1985—; bd. regents Rogers State Coll., Okla., 1978-85; adv. bd. First Nat. Bank, Okla., 1982-85; nat. edn. adv. bd. Channel One, Whittle Communications, 1989-91. Freelance writer in field. Active Westside Assn. Community Action, Chgo., mem. nat. adv. bd. Marwen Found., mem. early childhood adv. bd. North Ctrl. Regional Ednl. Lab. Named Citizen of the Day for contbns. to edn. Bartlesville Area C. of C., 1976; numerous other awards, citations. Mem. League of Black Women (Black Rose award for Edn. 1990), Assn. Supervision and Curriculum Devel., Nat. Assn. Edn. Young Children, Nat. Black Child Devel. Inst., Delta Sigma Theta (West Suburban chpt.), Jack & Jill of Am., Inc. (West Suburban chpt.). Democrat. Baptist. Avocations: writing, poetry reading (oral), singing, traveling, cooking. Home: 5666 Cascade Dr Lisle IL 60532-2047 Office: Corp Community Schs of Am 751 S Sacramento Blvd Chicago IL 60612-3365

MOSLEY, SASHA MORNAY LYNN, software consultant service company executive; b. Denver, Aug. 9, 1948; s. Robert Lee Mosley; children: Damon Lynn, Bijon Lynn. BA in Biology, Huston-Tillotson Coll., Austin, Tex., 1970; MEd in Adminstrn., McNeese State U., Lake Charles, La., 1976; postgrad., U. Houston, 1979; PhD, U. Colo., Denver, 1992. Cert. tchr., Tex. Tchr. biology Port Arthur (Tex.) Ind. Sch. Dist., 1970-80; tchr. math. Denver Pub. Schs., 1982; cons. Colo. Dept. Edn., Denver, 1982-83; dir. fin. aid Nat. Coll., Aurora, Colo., 1984-86; asst. dir. Mansfield Bus. Coll., Denver, 1986; tchr. computers Ea. Ind. Sch. Dist., San Antonio, 1987-88; tchr. sci. San Antonio Ind. Sch. Sys., 1988-89, tchr. biology, 1989—; owner, CEO, XuXa Software Inc., Denver, 1992—; assoc. prof. math. C.C. of Denver, 1983—; prof. stats. U. Denver, 1990-91; math. cons. Region 20 Edn. Ctr., San Antonio, 1989-92; acad. dean Denver Bus. Coll., summer 1994. Author, editor: Computer Programming Simplified, 1987, Computer Software Games, 1990; created computer program Creating your Future. Bd. dirs. Sacred Heart Cath. Schs., Port Arthur, 1975. With U.S. Army, 1970-72. Recipient appreciation award Pikes Peak C.C., Colorado Springs, Colo., 1983, Bd. Coop. Edn., Pueblo, Colo., 1983. Mem. NSF, Am. Fedn. Tchrs., Minority C. of C. (bd. dirs. 1985), KC, Phi Delta Kappa. Democrat. Avocations: software design, creating computer games, jazz.

MOSLEY, ZACK TERRELL, cartoonist; b. Hickory, Okla., Dec. 12, 1906; s. Zack Taylor and Irah Corinna (Aycock) M.; m. Betty Adcock, May 31, 1945; 1 dau., Jill M. Grad., Shawnee (Okla.) High Sch., 1925; student, Chgo. Acad. Fine Arts, 1926-27, Chgo. Art Inst., 1927-28. Worked in restaurants in Chgo. while studying art, began flying lessons, 1932; flown over U.S., parts of Can., Mex. and S.Am., Alaska, Europe.; col. Civil Air Patrol on active duty with coastal anti-sub patrol units.; now ret. col. CAP. Created: Smilin' Jack, 1933; selling it to, Chgo. Tribune and N.Y. News Syndicate (nationally syndicated), discontinued, 1973, free lance writer and artist; Author: Brave Coward Zack, 1976, The Hot Rock Glide, 1979, De-Icers Galore, 1980. Awarded Air Medal by Air Forces for Anti-submarine patrol flying during, World War II; named to Civil Air Patrol Hall Fame, 1976. Mem. Aviation Writers Assn., Aircraft Owners and Pilots Assn. (Sharples trophy for promoting gen. aviation), Nat. Cartoonists Soc., Quiet Birdmen. Episcopalian. Club: Elk.

MOSORA, FLORENTINA IOANA, physics educator; b. Cluj, Romania, Jan. 7, 1940; arrived in Belgium, 1968; d. Oprea and Cornelia (Stanescu) M.; m. Stephan Stan, Jan. 22, 1977; 1 child, Guy Bart. B in Biol. Sci. with highest distinction, U. Bucharest, Romania, 1961, B in Phys. Sci. with highest distinction, 1967, PhD in Biophysics cum laude, 1971. Cert. biologist and physicist. Rsch. fellow U. Bucharest, 1967-71; rsch. fellow U. Liege, Belgium, 1971-74, maitre de conferences, 1974-75; head rsch. fellow Inst. Physics, U. Liege, Belgium, 1975-79, lectr., 1979-88, prof., 1988—. Author: Elements of General Physics and Biophysics, vol. 1, 1974, vol. 2, 1975, Introduction to the Mechanics of Physiologic Fluids, 1984-85, Mechanics of Microcirculation, 1990: Editor: Biomechanical Transport Processes, 1991. Mem. European Med. Rsch. Coun. Devel. of Resch. in Nutrition and Stable Isotopes, 1991—. Decorated officer Ordre of Leopold II, (Belgium), 1981, comdr. Ordre de la Couronne (Belgium, 1992; recipient Agathon de Potter prize Royal Acad. Belgium, 1982. Mem. Stareso Oceanographic Rsch. Calvi (sci. coun. 1987—), Isotopes Stables (v.p. 1987—), Inst. Recherches Marines et Interactions Air-Mer (pres. 1989—), Hemo Liege (founder), Belgian Soc. Biophysics, Internat. Soc. Rsch. Circulation and Environ. Diseases, N.Y. Acad. Scis. Roman Catholic. Avocations: swimming, gymnastics. Home: Residence Verdi, Av Blonden 7, 4000 Liege Belgium Office: U Liege, Inst Physics B5, 4000 Liege Belgium

MOSQUEIRA, CHARLOTTE MARIANNE, dietitian; b. L.A., July 26, 1937; d. Leo and Magdalene Tollefson; children: Mark, Michael. BS, St. Olaf Coll., 1959; postgrad. U. Oreg. Med. Sch., 1959-60; MA, Central Mich. U., 1980. Registered dietitian. Dir. food svc. Holy Cross Hosp., Salt Lake City, 1973-77; dir. dietetics Riverside Meth. Hosp., Columbus, Ohio, 1977-79; dir. nutrition and food svc. Fresno (Calif.) Community Hosp. and Med. Ctr., 1980-91; mem. faculty Dept. Enology and Food Sci., Calif. State U., Fresno, 1984-93; dir. nutritional svc. Emanuel Med. Ctr., Turlock, Calif., 1991—. Mem. Am. Dietetic Assn., Calif. Dietetic Assn. Lutheran.

MOSS, AMBLER HOLMES, JR., academic administrator, lawyer, former ambassador; b. Balt., Sept. 1, 1937; s. Ambler Holmes and Dorothea Dandridge (Williams) M.; m. Serena Welles, May 6, 1972; children: Ambler H., Benjamin Sumner, Serena Montserrat, Nicholas George Oliver. B.A., Yale U., 1960; J.D., George Washington U., 1970. Bar: D.C., Fla. Joined Fgn. Service Dept. State, 1964; vice consul Barcelona, 1964-66; adviser U.S. del. to OAS, 1966-69; Spanish desk officer, 1968-70; assoc. firm Coudert Bros., Washington, 1971-73; resident atty. Coudert Bros., Brussels, Belgium, 1973-76; mem. U.S. Negotiating Team for Panama Canal treaties, 1977; dep. asst. Sec. of State, Washington, 1977-78; ambassador to Panama, 1978-82; of counsel Greenberg, Traurig, Askew, Hoffman, Lipoff, Quentel, Wolff P.A., 1982-87, 95—; prof., dir. N.S. Ctr. and former dean Grad. Sch. Internat. Studies U. Miami, Fla. Served with USN, 1960-64. Mem. ABA, Am. Soc. Internat. Law, Inter-Am. Bar Assn., Am. Fgn. Svc. Assn., Coun. Fgn. Rels., Am. Legion, Inter-Am. Dialogue (Washington), Navy League, Greater Miami C. of C. (gov. 1983-86), Royal Inst. Internat. Affairs (London), Internat. Inst. Strategic Studies (London), Army and Navy Club, Order of the Coif. Address: 5711 San Vicente St Coral Gables FL 33146-2724

MOSS, ARTHUR HENSHEY, lawyer; b. Reading, Pa., July 26, 1930; s. John Arthur and Christine Bracken (Henshey) M.; m. E. Leslie Fritz, Feb. 1982; 1 child by previous marriage, John Arthur. AB, Williams Coll., 1952; JD, U. Pa., 1955. Bar: Pa. 1956. Assoc. Montgomery, McCracken, Walker & Rhoads, Phila., 1960-69, ptnr., 1969—. Editor U. Pa. Law Review, 1953-55; chmn. Radnor-Haverford-Marple Sewer Authority, 1968-83: pres. Wayne Civic Assn., 1964-65; steward, deacon Wayne Presbyn. Ch., 1963-66, ruling elder, 1966-72, 79-84, 89-95, clk. of session, 1973-74, 78-89, trustee, 1987-93; commr. Gen. Assembly Presbyn. Ch. (U.S.A.), 1983; dir. John Bartram Assn., 1987—, treas. 1989—; trustee Presbytery of Phila., 1984, 94—, treas., 1996—. Lt. USN, 1955-60. Mem. ABA, Pa. Bar Assn., Phila. Bar Assn., Radnor Hist. Soc. (dir., sec. 1978-90), The Athenaeum of Phila., Broadacres Trouting Assn., Merion Golf Club, The Union League of Phila., Edgemere Club. Editor: U. Pa. Law Rev., 1954-55. Contbr. articles to profl. jours. Home: 200 Walnut Ave Wayne PA 19087-3423 Office: Montgomery McCracken Walker & Rhoads 123 S Broad St Philadelphia PA 19109-1321

MOSS, ARTHUR JAY, physician; b. White Plains, N.Y., June 21, 1931; s. Abraham Loeb and Ida (Bank) M.; m. Joy Folkman, June 23, 1957; children: Katherine, Deborah, David. BA, Yale U., 1953; MD, Harvard U., 1957. Resident Mass. Gen. Hosp., 1957-58, 60-61; fellow in cardiology med. ctr. U. Rochester, N.Y., 1961-65, from asst. to assoc. prof. sch. medicine and dentistry, 1966-71, clin. assoc. prof., 1971-82, clin. prof., 1982-91, prof. medicine, 1991—, dir. heart rsch. follow-up program med. ctr., 1971—; mem. cardiology adv. com. Nat. Heart, Lung, and Blood Inst., NIH, 1980-82, chmn., 1982-84. Author: Antiarrhythmic Agents, 1973; editor: Clinical Aspects of Life-threatening Arrhythmias, 1984, QT Prolongation and Ventricular Arrhythmias, 1992, Noninvasive Electrocardiology, 1995; editor-in-chief Ann. Noninvasive Electrocardiology, 1996—; editl. bd. Am. Jour. Cardiology, 1988—. Lt. USNR, 1958-60. Mem. Alpha Omega Alpha. Home: 581 Claybourne Rd Rochester NY 14618-1224 Office: Univ Rochester Med Ctr PO Box 653 Rochester NY 14642-8653

MOSS, BEN FRANK, III, art educator, painter; b. Phila., Feb. 28, 1936; s. B. Frank Jr. and Helen Charlotte (Figge) M.; m. Jean Marilyn Russel, Aug. 26, 1960; children: Jennifer Kathleen, Benjamin Franklin IV. BA, Whitworth Coll., 1959; postgrad., Princeton Theol. Seminary, 1959-60; MFA, Boston U., 1963; MA (hon.), Dartmouth Coll., 1993; studied with Walter Murch, Karl Fortess and Herman Keys. Instr. Gonzaga U., Spokane, Wash., 1964-65; assoc. prof., dir. MFA and vis. artist program Fort Wright Coll., Spokane, 1965-72; acting dean, co-founder Spokane Studio Sch., 1972-74; prof. painting and drawing Sch. Art and Art History U. Iowa, Iowa City, 1975-88; George Frederick Jewett prof. art. Dartmouth Coll., Hanover, N.H., 1988—; George Frederick Jewett prof. art., chmn. studio art dept. Vt. Studio Ctr., Johnson, 1990; chmn. studio art dept. Dartmouth Coll., Hanover, 1988-94; area head painting U. Iowa, 1985; artist-in-residence Queens Coll., U. Melbourne, Australia, 1993-94; vis. artist, lectr. in field. Represented in permanent collections Kraushaar Galleries, N.Y.C., Susan Conway Galleries, Washington, Gallery 68, Belfast, Maine; one-man shows include Susan Conway Galleries, 1990, Dartmouth Coll., 1989, 94, Kraushaar Galleries, 1981, 83, 87, Swarthmore Coll., Pa., 1984, Stony Brook (N.Y.) Sch., 1982, Saint-Gaudens, Picture Gallery, Cornish, N.H., 1981, Kans. State U., 1980, Francine Seders Gallery, Seattle, 1979, 82, Hudson D. Walker Gallery, Fine Arts Work Ctr., Provincetown, Mass., 1978, Arnot Art Mus., Elmira, N.Y., 1977, Kirkland Coll., Clinton, N.Y., 1977, Juniper Tree Gallery, Spokane, 1975, Middlebury (Vt.) Coll., 1971, Seligman Gallery, Seattle, 1967, 69, Cheney Cowels Meml. Mus., Spokane, 1967, Loomis Chaffee Sch., 1995, Tasis England Am. Sch., 1994, Queens Coll., U. Melbourne, 1994; exhibited in group shows at Susan Conway

Galleries, 1993, Chase Gallery City Hall, Spokane, 1993, Colby-Sawyer Coll., New London, N.H., 1992, Idaho State U., Pocatello, 1972, Francine Seders Gallery, 1972, Kraushaar Galleries, 1978—, Susan Conway Galleries, 1989—, Middlebury Coll. Mus. Art, Babcock Galleries, N.Y.C., Albany Inst. History and Art, Owensboro (Ky.) Mus. Fine Art, Westmoreland Mus. Art, Greenburg, Pa., Md. Inst. & Coll. Art, 1993-94, Gallery 68, 1992, Vt. Studio Ctr. Visiting Critics, Vergennes, 1992, 79th Ann. Maier Mus. Art, Randolph, Macon Women's Coll., Lynchburg, Va., 1990, Del. Ctr. Contemporary Arts, Wilmington, 1988, U. Iowa, 1976, 78, 80, 82, 84, 86, 88, Bladen Meml. Mus., Fort Dodge, Iowa, 1987, Phila. Mus. Art, 1986, Union League Club, N.Y.C., 1986, Blackfish Gallery, Portland, 1986, Columbia (S.C.) Mus. Art, 1985, Columbus Mus. Art, 1982-86, Paine Art Ctr., Oshkosh, Wis., 1985, Burpee Art Ctr., Rockford, Ill., 1985, Ill. State U., Normal, 1985, Wilkes Coll., Wilkes-Barre, Pa., 1985, Albright-Knox Mus., Buffalo, N.Y., 1984, Ark. Art Ctr., Little Rock, 1984, Millersville (Pa.) U., 1983, Fairfield (Conn.) U., 1983, Marion Koogler McKay Inst., San Antonio, 1983, Boston City Hall Gallery, 1983, Cedar Rapids (Iowa) Mus. Art, 1982, Montclair (N.J.) Jr. League, 1981, Iowa Arts Coun., Des Moines, 1980-81, Phillips Exeter Acad., 1994, Nat. Acad. Design, 1995, Boston U., 1995, numerous others. Sr. Faculty fellow Dartmouth Coll., 1993, MacDowell Colony, 1992, Devel. grant U. Iowa, 1980, 86; Summer fellowship U. Iowa, 1979, Rsch. and Travel grantee Ford Found., 1979-80, Yaddo Found., 1965, 72, Travel grantee U. Iowa Found., 1986; recipient Disting. Alumni award Boston U., 1988. Mem. NAD (academician mem.), Coll. Art Assn. Independent. Presbyterian. Avocations: music, poetry, travel, tennis. Office: Dartmouth Coll Hb 6081 Studio Art Hanover NH 03755

MOSS, BERNARD, virologist, researcher; b. N.Y.C., July 26, 1937; s. Jack and Goldie (Altman) M.; m. Toby Frima Lieberman, Dec. 25, 1960; children: Robert, Jennifer, David. BA, NYU, 1957, MD, 1961; PhD, MIT, 1967. Diplomate Am. Bd. Med. Examiners. Intern Children's Hosp., Boston, 1961-62; investigator, sect. head NIH, Bethesda, Md., 1966—, lab. chief, 1984—; mem. adv. bd. Virus Res., 1984—, Current Opinion Biotech., 1989—. Assoc. editor Virology Jour., 1976-92, editor., 1992—; mem. editorial bd. Jour. of Virology, 1972—, Antimicrobial Agts. and Chemotherapy, 1973-79, Jour. Biol. Chemistry, 1982-87; AIDS rsch. Human Retroviruses, 1989—; contbr. more than 400 articles to profl. jours. Mem. adv. com. Am. Cancer Soc., N.Y.C., 1983-86; bd. dirs. Found. Advanced Edn. in Scis., Bethesda, 1985-91; mem. NIH AIDS vaccine selection com., 1989—. Served as med. dir. USPHS, 1966—. Named one of 100 Most Innovative Scientists of 1986, Sci. Digest; recipient Solomon A. Berson Alumni Achievement award Sch. Medicine, NYU, Meritorious Svc. medal USPHS, Disting. Svc. medal USPHS, Dickson prize in medicine, Invitrogen award for eukaryotic gene expression, ICN Internat. prize in Virology. Mem. AAAS, Am. Soc. for Biochemistry and Molecular Biology, Am. Soc. Microbiology, Am. Soc. Virology (pres. 1995), Nat. Acad. Sci., Phi Beta Kappa, Sigma Xi, Alpha Omega Alpha.

MOSS, BILL RALPH, lawyer, publisher; b. Amarillo, Tex., Sept. 27, 1950; s. Ralph Voniver and Virginia May (Atkins) M.; m. Marsha Kelman, Mar. 2, 1985; 1 child, Brandon Price. BS with spl. honors, West Tex. State U., 1972, MA, 1974; JD, Baylor U., 1976; cert. regulatory studies program, Mich. State U., 1981. Bar: Tex. 1976, U.S. Dist. Ct. (no. dist.) 1976, U.S. Tax Ct. 1979, U.S. Ct. Appeals (5th cir.) 1983. Briefing atty. Ct. Appeals 7th Supreme Jud. Dist. Tex., Amarillo, 1976-77; assoc. Culton, Morgan, Britain & White, Amarillo, 1977-80; hearings examiner Pub. Utility Commn. Tex., Austin, 1981-83; asst. gen. counsel State Bar Tex., Austin, 1983-87; founder, owner Price & Co. Publs., Austin, 1987—; instr., lectr. West Tex. State U., Canyon, Ea. N.Mex. U., Portales, 1977-80. Active All Saint's Episcopal Ch. Mem. ABA, Tex. Bar Assn. (speaker profl. devel. programs 1983—), Nat. Orgn. Bar Counsel, Internat. Platform Assn., Alpha Chi, Lambda Chi Alpha, Omicron Delta Epsilon, Phi Alpha Delta, Sigma Tau Delta, Pi Gamma Mu. Home and Office: 2719 Mountain Laurel Ln Austin TX 78703-1142 Office: PO Box 164002 506 Explorer Dr Austin TX 78716

MOSS, CHARLES, advertising agency executive; b. Bklyn., Sept. 7, 1938; s. Samuel and Celia (Liebes) Moskowitz; m. Margo Jean Schekman, July 3, 1963 (div.); 1 child, Robert Evan; m. Susan Dukes Calhoun, Mar. 18, 1977; children: Mary Calhoun, Samuel Calhoun. BA cum laude, Ithaca Coll., 1961. Copywriter Doyle, Dane, Bernbach, N.Y.C., 1962-65; group copy supr. J. Tinker & Partners, N.Y.C., 1965-66; creative dir. Wells, Rich, Greene, Inc., N.Y.C., 1968-74; pres., chief operating officer Wells, Rich, Greene, Inc., 1971-76, vice chmn., corp. creative dir., 1976—, also bd. dirs.; now chmn. Moss/Dragoti (ptnr. co. Wells, Rich, Greene/BDDP), N.Y.C. Author (with Stan Dragoti); film Dirty Little Billy, 1971. Mem. adv. bd. NYU Sch. Continuing Edn.; mem. creative rev. bd. Com. for Drug Free Am. Served with AUS, 1962-68. Recipient Gold Key Copy Club, 1968, 1st prize Clio award, 1968, 1st prize Art Dirs. Club, 1968; Andy award N.Y. Advt. Club, 1968, spl. Tony award, Golden Apple award for I Love New York advt. campaign 1978, Clio Classic Hall of Fame award 1983, 86. Mem. Writers Guild Am., Screen Authors Guild, Vertical Club. Avocations: tennis, jogging. Office: Moss Dragoti 9 W 57th St New York NY 10019-2600

MOSS, CHARLES NORMAN, physician; b. L.A., June 13, 1914; s. Charles Francis and Lena (Rye) M.; A.B., Stanford U., 1940; M.D., Harvard U., 1944; cert. U. Vienna, 1947; M.P.H., U. Calif.-Berkeley, 1955; Dr.P.H., UCLA, 1970; m. Margaret Louise Stakias; children—Charles Eric, Gail Linda, and Lori Anne. Surg. intern Peter Bent Brigham Hosp., Boston, 1944-45, asst. in surgery, 1947; commd. 1st lt. USAF, M.C., USAAF, 1945, advanced through grades to lt. col., USAF, 1956; Long course for flight surgeon USAF Sch. Aviation Medicine, Randolph AFB, Tex., 1948-49, preventive medicine div. Office USAF Surgeon Gen., Washington, 1955-59; air observer, med., 1954, became sr. flight surgeon 1956; later med. dir., Los Angeles div. North Am. Rockwell Corp., Los Angeles; chief med. adv. unit Los Angeles County, now ret. Decorated Army Commendation medal (U.S.); Chinese Breast Order of Yun Hui. Recipient Physicians Recognition award AMA, 1969, 72, 76, 79, 82. Diplomate in aerospace medicine and occupational medicine Am. Bd. Preventive Medicine. Fellow Am. Pub. Health Assn., AAAS, Am. Coll. Preventive Medicine, Royal Soc. Health, Am. Acad. Occupational Medicine, Western Occupational Med. Assn., Am. Assn. Occupational Medicine; mem. AMA, Mil. Surgeons U.S., Soc. Air Force Flight Surgeons, Am. Conf. Govt. Hygienests, Calif. Acad. Preventive Medicine, (dir.), Aerospace Med. Assn., Calif., Los Angeles County med. assns., Assn. Oldetime Barbell and Strongmen. Research and publs. in field. Home: 7714 Cowan Ave Los Angeles CA 90045-1135 *Personal philosophy: "Seek ye the truth, for the truth shall make ye free."*

MOSS, CRUSE WATSON, automobile company executive; b. Kent, Ohio, Apr. 7, 1926; s. Cruse Watson and Lucile (Shafer) M.; m. Virginia Ann Patton, Dec. 22, 1949; children: Stephen, Carol Susan, Michael. BS in Indsl. Engring., Ohio U., 1948, LLD (hon.), 1985. Pres. Kaiser Jeep Automotive div., also exec. v.p. Kaiser Jeep Corp., 1960-70; group v.p. Am. Motors Corp., 1970; pres., dir. AM Gen. Corp., Detroit, 1970-79; chmn., chief exec. officer, dir. White Motor Corp., Farmington Hills, Mich., 1979-81; chmn. bd., chief exec. officer Gen. Automotive Corp., Ann Arbor, Mich., 1981—; chmn. bd. dirs., chief exec. officer The Flxible Corp., Delaware, Ohio; bd. dirs. The Burnham Fund Inc., N.Y.C. Mem. founders soc. Detroit Inst. Arts; dir. The Burnham Fund, Inc., N.Y.C. With USNR, 1944-46. Mem. Soc. Automotive Engrs., Confrerie des Chevaliers du Tastevin, Chief Execs. Orgn., Beta Theta Pi, Tau Beta Pi. Presbyterian. Clubs: Circumnavigators, Barton Hills Country, Detroit Athletic, Travis Pointe Country. Office: Gen Automotive Corp 2015 Washtenaw Ave Ann Arbor MI 48104

MOSS, DOUGLAS G., professional hockey team executive. CEO, pres. Buffalo Sabres. Office: Buffalo Sabres Meml Auditorium 140 Main St Buffalo NY 14202*

MOSS, ERIC OWEN, architect; b. L.A., July 25, 1943. BA, UCLA, 1965; MArch with honors, U. Calif., Berkeley, 1968, Harvard U., 1972. Prof. design So. Calif. Inst. Architecture, 1974—; prin. Eric Owen Moss Archs., Culver City, Calif., 1975—; Eliot Noyes chair Harvard U., Cambridge, Mass., 1990; Eero Saarinen chair Yale U., New Haven, 1991; lectr. Hirshhorn Mus. Symposium, Washington, 1990, Nat. AIA Conv., 1990, Mus. Contemporary Art, L.A., 1991, N.Y. Archtl. League, 1991, Archtl. Assn. Ireland, Dublin, Archtl. Assn., London, 1991, Royal Coll. Art, London, 1991, Smithsonian Inst., Washington, 1992, U. Calif., Berkeley, 1992, Osterreichiaches Mus. fur Angewandte Kunst, Vienna, Austria, 1992, UCLA, 1992, Royal Danish Acad. Fine Arts, Copenhagen, 1993, U. Lund, Sweden, 1993, Mus. Finnish Architecture, Helsinki, 1993, Royal Acad. Arts, London, 1993, U. Pa., Phila., 1994, others; tchr. U. Tex., Austin, 1983, Wash. U., St. Louis, 1984, U. Ill., Chgo., 1985, Tulane U., New Orleans, 1985, U. Minn., Mpls., 1985, Columbia U., N.Y.C., 1986, Rice U., Houston, 1988; participant various confs. Exhbns. of work include World Biennial of Architecture, Sofia, Bulgaria, 1989, Salle des Tirages du Credit Foncier de France, Paris, 1990, Bartlett Sch. Architecture and Urban Design, London, 1991, Gallery of Functional Art, Santa Monica, Calif., 1992, GA Gallery, Tokyo, 1992, Mus. fur Gestaltung Zurich, Switzerland, 1993, Santa Monica (Calif.) Mus. Art, 1993, Fonds Regional D'Art Contemporain du Centre, 1993, Aspen (Colo.) Art Mus., 1993, Centro de Arte y Comunicacion, Buenos Aires, 1993, Contemporary Arts Ctr., Cin., 1993, Philippe Uzzan Galerie, Paris, 1993, Contemporary Arts Ctr., Tours, France, 1993, Internat. Exhbn. Contemporary Architecture, Havana, Cuba, 1994, others. Recipient Progressive Architecture Design award, 1978, 92, Winning Interior Archtl. Record award, 1984, Interiors Design award, 1991. Fellow AIA (L.A. awards 1977, 79, 83, 88, 90, Calif. Coun. awards 1981, 86, 88, L.A. Honor awards 1991, Nat. Honor awards 88, 89, Calif. Coun. Urban Design/Adaptive Re-Use awards 1991, Nat. Interior Design awards 1992, 94, L.A. Design awards 1992, 93). Subject of monographs and numerous articles in mags. and jours. Office: 8557 Higuera St Culver City CA 90232-2535

MOSS, FRANK EDWARD, physics educator and researcher; b. Paris, Ill., Feb. 10, 1934; married 1962; 1 child. BEE, U. Va., 1956, MNE, 1961, PhD in Physics, 1964. Rsch. engr. electronics U. Va., 1956-61, sr. scientist cryog engring., 1967-71; assoc. prof. U. Mo., St. Louis, 1971-76, prof. physics, 1976—; NSF fellow U. Rome, 1965-66, vis. rschr., 1966-67. Mem. AAAS, Fedn. Am. Scientists, Am. Phys. Soc., Sigma Xi. Office: U Missouri Dept Physics Astronomy Saint Louis MO 63121*

MOSS, GARY CURTIS, lawyer; b. Taylorville, Ill., Feb. 17, 1944; s. William Clary and Sophronia Irene (McClellan) M.; m. Judith K. Jones, April 14, 1945; children—Gary Curtis, Kristin Suzanne. B.A., U. Ill.-Champaign, 1966; J.D., U. Iowa-Iowa City, 1969. Bar: Iowa 1969, Calif. 1970, U.S. Dist. Ct. (cen. dist.) Calif. 1972, Nev. 1991, U.S. Ct. Appeals (9th cir.) 1974, U.S. Dist. Ct. (so. and no. dists.) Calif. 1981, U.S. Dist Ct. Nev. 1991. Assoc., O'Melveny & Myers, Los Angeles, 1969-75; assoc. Seyfarth, Shaw, Fairweather & Geraldson, Los Angeles, 1975-78, ptnr., 1978-87; judge pro tem West Los Angeles Mcpl. Ct., 1981-83, Pasadena Mcpl. Ct., 1983—. Mem. ABA, State Bar Calif. (hearing referee, arbitrator mandatory fee arbitrations), State Bar Iowa, Los Angeles County Bar Assn. Republican. Club: Athletic (Los Angeles). Home: 3055 Westwind Rd Las Vegas NV 89102-6858 also: 3980 Howard Hughes Pky Ste 170 Las Vegas NV 89109-0906*

MOSS, GERALD S., dean, medical educator; b. Cleve., Mar. 4, 1935; s. Harry and Lillian (Alter) M.; m. Wilma Jaback, Sept. 1, 1957; children: William Alan, Robert Daniel, Sharon Lynn. BA, Ohio State U., 1956, MD cum laude, 1960. Diplomate Am. Bd. Surgery (apptd. assoc. examiner com. 1989); lic. Ill. Intern Mass. Gen. Hosp., Boston, 1960-61, resident, 1961-65; from asst. prof. to assoc. prof. dept. surgery Coll. Medicine U. Ill., Chgo., 1968-72, prof., 1973-77, 89—, head dept. surgery, 1989, dean, 1989—; prof. dept. surgery Pritzker Sch. Medicine U. Chgo., 1977-89; prof. dept. surgery U. Ill., Coll. of Medicine, 1989—; tutor in surgery Manchester (Eng.) Royal Infirmary, 1964; asst. chief surgical svcs. VA West Side Hosp., Chgo., 1968-70; attending surgeon dept. surgery Cook County Hosp., Chgo. 1970-72, chmn. 1972-77; dir. surgical rsch. Hektoen Inst. for Med. Rsch., Cook County Hosp., 1972-77, Micheal Reese Hosp. and Med. Ctr., Chgo., 1977-89, chmn. dept. surgery, 1977-89, chief svc. 1989, trustee, 1981, and numerou coms.; appointed to Nat. Rsch. Coun., NAS, 1966-68, Ad Hoc Subcom., NAE, 1970, Ad Hoc Study Sect., 1970, del. to Third Joint U.S-USSR Symposium, 1983, Blood Diseases and Resources Adv. Com., 1984-88, Planning Com. for discussing key blood problems, Nat. Heart and Lung Inst., 1987, chmn. Plasma and Plasma Products Com., 1979, bd. dirs., 1983, v.p., 1985, Ad Hoc Transition Com., Am. Blood Commn., 1989, Panel on Rsch. Opportunities, Office Naval Rsch. Program, 1987, exec. com., coord. com., Nat. Blood Edn. Program, 1988, Tech. Adv. Task Force Am. Hosp. Assn., 1988, chmn. review panel contract proposals, NIH, 1975, program project site visit, 1976, chmn. site-visit review group, 1977, adv. com. Blood Resources Work group, 1978, Planning Com. for Consensus, 1987, Small Bus. Innovation Rsch., 1988, Med. Rsch. Scv. Merit Review Bd. VA, 1978-81, Liaison Com. Graduate Med. Edn. AMA, 1979, and numerous other coms. for various med. organizations; cons. Nat. Heart and Lung Inst., Transfusion Medicine Acad. Awardees Program; vis. prof. Montefiore Med. Ctr. Bronx, N.Y., 1986, Ohio State U., 1988, U. N.Mex., Albuquerque, 1989, Seton Med. Ctr., Austin, Tex., 1990, U. Ill. Coll. Medicine, Peoria, 1991; guest lectr., participant numerous meetings, symposiums; cons. in field. Contbr. numerous articles to profl. jours., chpts. to books.. With U.S. Army, 1965-68, Vietnam. Teaching fellow Harvard Med. Sch., 1962; receipient Stitt Lectr. award Assn. Mil. Surgeons U.S.A., 1981; grantee U.S. Navy, 1969-84, U.S. Army, 1971-74, 75-78, NIH, 1969, 83-84, Dept. Pub. Health, 1973, HEW, 1974-77, UpJohn, 1974, Northfield Labs. 1985-89. Fellow ACS (pre and postoperative care com. 1975-83, rep. Am. blood comm. 1977—, mem. various coms., speaker various symposiums), Am. Soc. Surgery Trauma; mem. Am. Surgical Assn. (rep. Nat. Soc. Med. Rsch. 1984-88), Am. Trauma Soc., Am. Physicians Fellowship (rep. Israel Med. Assn.), Assn. Acad. Surgery (chmn. membership selection com. 1973-75, pres. elect 1974-75, pres. 1975-76, exec. coun. 1977-79), Soc. Univ. Surgeons (rep. Nat. Soc. Med. Rsch. 1973-77, com. Surgical Edn. 1979-81), Ctrl. Surgical Soc. (rep. Nat. Soc. Med. Rsch. 1973-77), Shock Soc. (chmn. planning com. 1986, chmn. program com. 1986, pres. elect 1986-87, pres. 1987-88), Soc. for Surgery Alimentary Tract (mem. com. west north ctrl. region 1978-82), Internat. Soc. Blood Transfusion, SurgicalBiology Club II, Nat. Soc. for Med. Rsch., Collegium Internationale Chirugiae Digestivae, Societe Internationale de Chirugie, Sigma XI, Alpha Omega Alpha (faculty advisor 1972-73). Office: U Ill Coll Medicine 1853 W Polk St # C 784 Chicago IL 60612-4316

MOSS, GUY B., lawyer; b. N.Y.C., Aug. 22, 1944; s. Tobias and Florence (Press) M.; m. Joyce Ann Green, Dec. 25, 1969; children: Jason, David. BA, Yale U., 1966; JD, Harvard Law Sch., 1969. Bar: Mass. 1969, U.S. Dist. Ct. Mass. 1970, U.S. Ct. Appeals (1st cir.) 1973, U.S. Supreme Ct. 1973. Instr. Suffolk U. Law Sch., Boston, 1969-70; law clk. Mass. Superior Ct., Boston, 1970-71; assoc. Lappin, Rosen, et al., Boston, 1972-73, Friedman & Atherton, Boston, 1973-74; ptnr. Widett, Slater & Goldman, Boston, 1974-90, Bingham, Dana & Gould, Boston, 1990—. Author: (audio cassettes) MCLE Legal Update, 1988-94, Enforcing Security Interests in Personal Property, 1992. Mem. ABA, Mass. Bar Assn., Boston Bar Assn., Comml. Law League Am., Am. Bankruptcy Inst. Home: 229 Franklin St Newton MA 02158-2324 Office: Bingham Dana & Gould 150 Federal St Boston MA 02110-1745

MOSS, JAMES TAYLOR, hospital administrator; b. New Iberia, La., July 19, 1947; married. B, U. Southwestern La., 1973; MHA, U. Ala., 1975. Adminstrv. resident Baptist Med. Ctr., Montgomery, Ala., 1974-75; dir. profl. svcs. Lake Charles (La.) Meml. Hosp., 1975-81; assoc. adminstr. Jackson-Madison County (Tenn.) Gen. Hosp., 1981-85, exec. v.p., chief oper. officer, 1985-86, pres., 1986—. Mem. Tenn. Hosp. Assn. Home: 163 Windemere Cir Jackson TN 38305-3948 Office: Jackson-Madison County Gen Hosp 708 W Forest Ave Jackson TN 38301-3901*

MOSS, JOE FRANCIS, sculptor, painter; b. Kincheloe, W.Va., Jan. 26, 1933; s. Thomas R. and Audra (Frazier) M.; m. Jean Elizabeth Marcrum, July 1, 1952 (dec.); children: Joe Marcum, Jon Eric, Jay Keith; m. Daphne Brauner, 1992. BA in Art, W.Va. U., 1955, MA in Art, 1960. Tchr. art Morgantown (W.Va.) High Sch., 1956-60; assoc. prof. art W.Va. U., Morgantown, 1960-70; prof. art U. Del., Newark, 1970—. One-man shows of sculpture Washington Gallery Modern Art, 1967, Russell Mus., Great Falls, Mont., 1973, Sculpture Now Gallery, N.Y.C., 1975, CUNY Grad. Center, 1975, J.B. Speed Mus., Louisville, 1977, Madison Sq. Park, N.Y.C., 1980, Marian Locks Gallery and Marian Locks East, Phila., 1981, Fine Arts Gallery U.M.B.C., Balt., 1986; 20-yr. retrospective Edison Fine Arts Gallery, Ft. Myers, Fla., 1985; exhibited in numerous group shows including, Mus. Modern Art, N.Y.C., 1966, Fischbach Gallery, N.Y.C., 1966, Fellows of the Center Exhbn., M.I.T., 1978, Sculpture Now, N.Y.C., 1979, Laumeier Sculpture Park, St. Louis, 1979, Neuberger Mus., Purchase, N.Y., 1981, Kunsthalle, Hamburg, Fed. Republic Germany, 1985, Robert Moses Plaza, N.Y.C., 1985-86, MIT, 1986 Lights Orot, Yeshiva U., N.Y.C., 1988-89, St. Mary's Coll., South Bend, Inc., 1989—, Hist. and Fine Arts Mus., Anchorage, 1987, Montreal, Can. 1988; traveling exhibits include Multiple Interaction, MIT, also Phila., N.Y.C., L.A., Sculpture 75 Exhbn., Phila., 1975, invitational exhibit, U. Tenn., Chattanooga, 1971; represented in permanent collections Arts and Humanities Council Huntington (W.Va.) Galleries, Polaroid Corp., Cambridge, Mass., Martin Fine Villa, Miami, Fla., Cedarcrest Coll., Allentown, Pa., Johnson Mus., Ithaca, N.Y., Urban Am., Washington, Bloomsburg (Pa.) State Coll., St. Louis Art Mus., Del. Art Mus., others, also pvt. collections; one-man shows of paintings Pa. State U., 1965, Pitts. Playhouse Gallery, 1965, W.Va. U., 1965; exhibited in group shows, Fifty Artists Fifty States, Burpee Mus., Rockford, Ill., 1965, Am. Fedn. Art, 1966-68, Bocour Collection, Keene (N.H.) State Coll., 1974, others, interviews, WTOP-TV, Washington, 1967, Voice of Am, 1967; speaker Internat. Sculpture Conf. Kans. U., Lawrence, 1974; feature CNN including Sci. Week in Rev. Grantee W.Va. U., 1963, 67, 68, U. Del. Research Found., 1971, 72, Dimer Found., 1976-77; vis. research fellow Ctr. for Advanced Visual Studies MIT, Cambridge, 1973, Nat. Endowment for Arts fellow, 1980-81, Del. State Arts Council fellow, 1980-81; recipient 1st prize Nat. Show Huntington Galleries Mus., 1963, Environmental Sculpture award Three Rivers Exhbn., 1968, sculpture award Appalachian Corridors Exhibit, 1968. Home: 801 Valley Rd Newark DE 19711-2585

MOSS, JOHN EMERSON, banker, former congressman; b. Carbon County, Utah, Apr. 13, 1915; s. John Emerson and Della Orta (Mower) M.; m. Jean Kueny, Sept. 15, 1935; children: Jennifer, Allison. In retail bus., 1938-43, real estate broker, 1945-85; mem. 83d-95th congresses 3d Dist. Calif., mem. govt. ops., interstate and fgn. commerce coms., chmn. select com. on govt. info., 1955-68; also chmn. oversight and investigation subcom.; dep. majority whip 2d session 87th-91st congresses; mem. 93d-94th congresses Democratic Policy and Steering Com.; chmn. bd. 1st Comml. Bank, Sacramento, 1979-85; chmn. Capitol Hist. Preservation Soc., 1985-92; Mem. Calif. Assembly, 9th Dist., 1948-52. Served with USNR, 1943-45. Mem. DAV, Laguna Hgts. Coop. Corp. (bd. dirs., v.p. 1993, pres. 1994—), C. of C., Commonwealth of Calif. Club.

MOSS, KATE, model; b. Croydon, England, Jan. 16, 1974. With Storm Agy., England, Women Model Mgmt., N.Y.; model Calvin Klein Jeans. Office: Women Model Mgt 107 Greene St Fl 2 New York NY 10012-3803

MOSS, LAWRENCE KENNETH, composer, educator; b. L.A., Nov. 18, 1927; s. Oscar and Sadye (Jacobs) M.; m. Graydon Hindley, Mar. 29, 1958; children: Pamela Ann, Claramarie, Jonathan, Ruth. Student, Pomona Coll., 1945-47; AB, UCLA, 1949; AM, Eastman Sch. Music, 1950; PhD, U. So. Calif., 1957. Prin. studies with Leon Kirchner, 1951-53; asst. prof. music theory Yale U., 1960-65, asso. prof. music theory, 1965-69; prof. music composition U. Md., 1969—. Composer: String Quartet, 1958, Sonata for Violin and Piano, 1959; 1 act comic opera The Brute, 1960; Four Scenes for Piano, 1961; Fromm commn., Scenes for Small Orchestra, 1961; women's chorus and piano In Spring, 1962; brass quintet Music for Five, 1963; soprano and piano Three Rilke Songs, 1963; chamber ensemble Remembrances, 1964; 2 act opera The Queen and the Rebels, 1965, rev. for chamber ensemble, 1989; piano for 4 hands Omaggio, 1966; flute, clarinet, doublebass Windows; flute, clarinet, viola, piano Patterns, 1967; wood-winds brass, percussion Exchanges, 1968; (New Haven Symphony commn.) soprano and orch. Ariel; 2 violins and viola Elegy, 1970; violin, piano, percussion Timepiece, 1970; (U. Chgo. Symphony commn.) orch. Paths, 1970; woodwind quintet and tape Auditions, 1971; alto saxophone and tape Evocation and Song, 1972; Fantasy for Piano, 1973; chorus and tape Exercise, 1973; soprano, oboe, tape, slides, lights Unseen Leaves, 1975; String Quartet, 1975; oboe, percussion Toot-Sweet, 1976; trombone, piano B.P., A Melodrama, 1976; Symphonies for Brass Quintet and Chamber Orchestra, 1977; piano and tape Omaggio II, 1977; oboe, harpsichord Little Suite, 1978; soprano, flute, clarinet, violin, percussion, dancer, slides, tape Nightscape, 1978; piano Ballad, 1979; piano, tape Hands Across the C, 1979; brass quintet Flight, 1979; tuba and bass-baritone Tubaria, 1979; dancer, tape, slides and lights Dreamscape, 1980; Flute choir Chanson, 1980; (Kindler Found. Commn.) string quartet String Quartet No. 3, 1980; cello solo Espressivo, 1981; clarinet, tape, dancer Images, 1981; soprano, flute, guitar Somewhere Inside Me, 1981; conductor soprano, flute, clarinet, viola, harp, piano, Loves, 1982 (NEA Consortium commn.); conductor, flute, clarinet, percussion, violin, cello, piano Music of Changes, 1986; tape, slides, lights, dancers, Rites, 1983; soprano, tape, Darkharbor, 1983; flute, percussion Aprèsludes, 1983; soprano, flute, piano At Night, 1984; dancer, tape Song to the Floor, 1984; piano A Musical Trip, 1984; piano, tenor Portals, 1984; movie Installation ... Lament, 1984; tape, dance That Gong-Tormented Sea, 1985; tenor, flute, clarinet, cello, percussion, violin, viola Voyages, 1985, Videotape Ephemeral Art, 1985; singer, tape, dancer Lesbia's Sparrow, 1985; dancer, percussion Incidental Music, 1986; flute, clarinet, violin, cello, percussion, piano Music of Changes, 1986; baritone, piano Drumtaps, 1986; clarinet solo Nature Studies, 1987; viola, tape Violaria, 1988; clarinet, mime/dancer, tape Blackbird, 1987; woodwind quintet Various Birds, 1987; chorus and piano Grand Is the Seen, 1988; 2 flutes, trumpet, harp, percussion, string quintet Clouds, 1989; soprano, tape Summer Night on the Youghiheny River, 1989, baritone, harp Lovesongs, 1990, soprano, violin, clarinet piano 4-hands Songs of the Earth and Air, Piano 4-hands Hommage, 1991, flute, clarinet, double bass, Through A Window..., 1992, Quartet for flute, cello, percussion and piano, chorus and piano, alto saxophone and tape Saxpressivo, The Gate, 1992; soprano, piano 2 songs to poems by Emily Dickinson, 1993; tenor, harp, oboe 10 Miracles, 1993; alto saxophone, piano 6 Short Pieces, 1993; China for tape alone, 1994; full orch., oboe and baritone soloists From Dawn to Dawn, 1995; band Chinese Lullaby, 1995. Served with AUS, 1954-56. Fulbright scholar Vienna, 1953-54; Guggenheim fellow Florence, 1959-60, 68-69; Morse fellow Yale U., to Rome, 1964-65; Nat. Endowment Humanities grantee, 1975, 77, 80; U. Md. Disting. Scholar/Tchr. award, 1982-83; composer-in-residence Rockefeller Cultural Ctr., Bellagio, Italy, 1986. Mem. ASCAP. Home: 220 Mowbray Rd Silver Spring MD 20904-1221 Office: U Md Dept Music College Park MD 20740

MOSS, LESLIE OTHA, justice administrator; b. Detroit, Mar. 8, 1952; s. Lonnie and Emma (Robinson) M. BA, U. Mich., 1982, postgrad., 1990—. Technician oper. rm. Sinai Hosp., Detroit, 1972-75; nurses' technician Detroit Osteo. Hosp., 1976-83; supr. Southfield (Mich.) Placement Ctr., 1983-85; rsch. asst. Wayne County Commr.'s Office, Detroit, 1985-86; fin. aid counselor Wayne State U., 1986-87; probation officer Dept. Corrections State of Mich., 1988—; exec. asst. Human Rights Dept., City of Detroit; rsch. asst. Law Dept. City of Detroit, 1990; asst. pers. mgr. Detroit Osteo. Hosp., 1991-93, Highland Pk. C.C., 1991-93; mental health worker Mich. Health Ctr.-Adult Mental Health and New Ctr. Hosp., Detroit, 1992-94; legal technician Ptnrs. Against Crime, Detroit, 1994; social work technician, 1994; sgt. of arms Detroit Police Res., 1987—; intern, assoc. prodr. local TV sta., Detroit, 1993; mem. bd. advisors, mem. bd. govs. Am. Biog. Rsch. Inst., dep. gov., 1994; exec. cons. in field., 1993—; asst. pers. mgr., 1993—. Bd. advisors Am. Biog. Inst., 1994; active re-election com. Mayor Coleman A. Young, Detroit, 1989-93; patient care counselor; adv. various causes, including industrialized Am., higher edn., automotive quality. Recipient Twentieth Century Achievement award Biog. Centre, 1994, Spl. Recognition award Detroit Pub. Sch. Sys., 1992, Internat. Man of Yr. award, 1992-93; award for mass media svc. participation Barden Cable Vision, Detorit, 1991, Man of the Yr. award, 1996, Disting. Alumni award Mumford H.S. Detroit, 1996; named Most Admired Man of Decade, 1994, Disting. Alumnus, Detroit Pub. Schs. Mich., 1995, Most Admired Man of the Yr., State of Mich., 1995. Mem. NAFE, NAACP (advisor 1989), Internat. Order of Merit, Assn. Pre-Med Students (cons. 1988—), Assn. Psychologists, Am. Biog. Rsch. Inst. Assn. (mem. bd. govs. 1993, dep. gov.), Internat. Platform Assn., U. Mich. Alumni Assn., Golden Key (life), Kappa Alpha Psi. Home & Office: 2020 Witherell St Ste 735 Detroit MI 48226-1618 Address: 1581 Kendall Detroit MI 48238

MOSS, MADISON SCOTT, editor; b. Charlotte, N.C., May 23, 1948; s. James Madison and Nellie Lee (Jenkins) M. BA in English, U. N.C., 1970. Editl. aide NASW, Inc., Washington, 1974, promotions specialist, 1974-79, assoc. editor, 1979-80, editor, 1980-90, mng. editor, 1990—. Creator numerous videos. Campaign coord. Eugene McCarthy for Pres., Rutherford

County, N.C., 1968. Recipient award for Pub. Excellence Comms. Concepts, 1993, 94, 95, Bronze award newspaper gen. excellence Soc. Nat. Assn. Publs., 1996. Mem. ACLU, U. N.C. Gen. Alumni Assn., Am. Found. AIDS Rsch. Democrat. Avocations: video producing, studying digital multimedia technology, reading. Office: NASW Inc 750 1st St NE # 700 Washington DC 20002

MOSS, MELVIN LIONEL, anatomist, educator; b. N.Y.C., Jan. 3, 1923; s. Maurice and Ethel (Lander) M.; m. Letty Salentijn, Apr. 1970; children (by previous marriage)—Noel Morrow, James Andrew. A.B., N.Y. U., 1942; D.D.S., Columbia, 1946, Ph.D., 1954. Mem. faculty Columbia, 1954—, prof., 1967-93; prof. emeritus, 1993; also dean Columbia (Sch. Dental and Oral Surgery.). Recipient Lederle Med. Faculty award, 1954-56. Fellow AAAS, Royal Anthrop. Soc. Gt. Britain; mem. Am. Assn. Anatomists, Am. Assn. Phys. Anthropologists, Internat. Assn. Dental Research (craniofacial biology award), Am. Soc. Zoologists, Sigma Xi, Omicron Kappa Upsilon. Research, numerous publs. on skeletal growth and application of computer-assisted methods of numerical and graphic analysis of growth. Home: 560 Riverside Dr New York NY 10027-3202

MOSS, MYRA ELLEN (MYRA MOSS ROLLE), philosophy educator; b. L.A., Mar. 22, 1937; m. Andrew Frank Rolle, Nov. 5, 1983. BA, Pomona Coll., 1958; PhD, The Johns Hopkins U., 1965. Asst. prof. Santa Clara (Calif.) U., 1968-74; prof. Claremont McKenna Coll., 1975—, chmn. Dept. of Philosophy, 1992-95; assoc. dir. Gould Ctr. for Humanities, Claremont, Calif., 1993-94; adv. coun. Milton S. Eisenhower Libr./Johns Hopkins U., 1994-96. Author: Benedetto Croce Reconsidered, 1987; translator Benedetto Croce's Essays on Literature & Literary Criticism, 1990; assoc. editor Special Issues; Symposia Journal of Value Inquiry, 1991, 92, 93 (Honorable Mention, Phoenix award). Dir. Flintridge (Calif.) Riding Club, 1991. Mem. Am. Philos. Assn., Am. and Internat. Soc. for Value Inquiry, Soc. for Aesthetics, Phi Beta Kappa (hon.). Avocations: gardening, horseback riding. Office: Claremont McKenna Coll 890 Columbia Ave Claremont CA 91711-3901

MOSS, RAYMOND LLOYD, lawyer; b. N.Y.C., Apr. 9, 1959. BA in Polit. Sci. cum laude, Bucknell U., 1981; JD, Hofstra U., 1984. Bar: Conn., N.Y., N.J., Ga., U.S. Supreme Ct. Atty. Dreyfus Corp., N.Y.C., 1984-85; corp. atty. Kramer, Levin, Nessen, Kamin & Frankel, N.Y.C., 1985-88; ptnr. Glass, McCullough, Sherill & Harold, Atlanta, 1988-92, Holland & Knight (and predecessor firms), Atlanta, 1993—; arbitrator Am. Arbitration Assns., Nat. Assn. Securities Dealers. Author column Conscience, 1983-84. Mem. ABA, N.Y. State Bar Assn., Assn. of Bar of City of N.Y., Ga. State Bar Assn., Phi Eta Sigma. Avocations: tai chi chuan, tennis, golf. Office: Holland & Knight 1360 Peachtree St Atlanta GA 30309

MOSS, RICHARD B., pediatrician; b. N.Y.C., Oct. 30, 1949. MD, SUNY, Downstate, 1975. Intern Children's Meml. Hosp., Chgo., 1975-76, resident, 1976-77; fellow Stanford (Calif.) U. Med. Sch., 1977-79, 80-81; now pediatrician Lucile Salter Packard Children's Hosp., Palo Alto, Calif.; prof. pediats. Stanford U. Med. Sch. Office: Stanford U Sch Med Ctr Dept Pediats Stanford CA 94305-5119

MOSS, RICHARD L., physiology educator; b. Fond du Lac, Wis., Nov. 2, 1947; s. Robert C. and Lenore H. Moss; m. Susan L. Rusch, Aug. 17, 1968; 1 child, James P. BS in Biology, U. Wis., Oshkosh, 1969; PhD in Physiology and Biophysics, U. Vt., 1975. Rsch. assoc. Boston Biomed. Rsch. Inst., 1975-79; asst. prof. physiology U. Wis., Madison, 1979-83, assoc. prof., 1983-87, prof., 1987—, chair dept., 1988—; dir. U. Wis. Cardiovascular Rsch. Ctr., 1995—; mem. cellular pharmacology and physiology rsch. study com. Am. Heart Assn., Dallas, 1990-93, Established Investigator, 1981-86; mem. physiology study sect. NIH, 1994—. Mem. editl. bd. Biophys. Jour., 1985-92, Jour. Gen. Physiology, 1987-91, Am. Jour. Physiology: Cellular, 1990-96, Physiol. Revs., 1985-91, Jour. Physiology (London), 1995—; contbr. articles to Biophys. Jour., Circulation Rsch., Nature, Jour. Physiology. NRSA fellow NIH, 1976-78. Achievements include research on regulation of heart and skeletal muscle contraction by selective extraction and/or exchange of regulatory protein from permeabilized muscle preparations, implicating role of thick filament proteins (i.e. light chain-2 and C-protein) in regulation of tension and kinetics of contraction. Office: U Wis Med Sch 1300 University Ave Madison WI 53706-1510

MOSS, ROBERT DREXLER, lawyer; b. Cleve., June 12, 1909; s. Morris and Rosa (Goldman) M.; m. Ruth K. Rivitz, Dec. 28, 1939; children: Kenneth H., Suzanne R. A.B., Case Western Res. U., 1931, LL.B., 1933, J.D., 1969. Bar: Ohio bar 1933, U.S. Supreme Ct 1960. Practice in Barberton, Ohio and Summit County, Ohio, 1937-95; ret., 1995; past chmn. Ohio Legal Services Fund. Pres. Barberton chpt. ARC, 1966-67;life mem. adv. bd. Salvation Army, Barberton Corps . Served to maj. USAAF, 1942-46. Decorated Bronze Star; recipient Outstanding Law Alumnus award Case Western Res. U., 1976, Sir Thomas More award Bishop Gilbert Sheldon, Vicar of Akron, Bishop for so. region of Cleve. diocese, 1990. Fellow Am. Bar Found. (life mem.); mem. ABA, Ohio State Bar Assn. (pres. 1968-69, Ohio Bar medal 1978), Akron Bar Assn. (pres. 1956-57), Ohio State Bar Assn. Found. (life), Summit County Legal Aid Soc. (pres. 1955). Jewish (past pres. temple). Clubs: Rotary (Barberton), Elks (Barberton), Masons (Akron) (32 deg.), Shriners (Akron), Akron City (Akron), Rosemont Country (Akron) (past pres.); Play House (Cleve.). Home: 1006 Bunker Dr Apt 301 Akron OH 44333-3079

MOSS, ROGER WILLIAM, JR., historian, writer, administrator; b. Zanesville, Ohio, Jan. 31, 1940; s. Roger William and Dorothy Elizabeth (Martin) M.; m. Gail Caskey Winkler, 1981; children by previous marriage: Elizabeth McQuiston, Victoria Stiles. BS in Edn., Ohio U., 1963, MA, 1964; postgrad., Attingham, Eng., summer 1966; PhD, U. Del., 1972. Curator of rare books Ohio U., 1962-64; lectr., dept. history U. Del., 1966-68, U. Md., 1967-68; exec. dir. Athenaeum of Phila., 1968—; adj. assoc. prof. architecture U. Pa., Phila., 1981—. Publs. include Morgan Collection, 1965, Master Builders, 1972, Century of Color, 1981, Biographical Dictionary of Philadelphia Architects, 1985, Philadelphia, 1986, Victorian Interior Decoration, 1986, Victorian Exterior Decoration, 1987 , Lighting for Historic Buildings, 1988 (Joel Polsky prize 1989), The American Country House, 1990; gen. editor Athenaeum Libr. of Nineteenth-Century Am. series, 1975—; editor: Paint in America, 1994; contbr. to profl. jours. Bd. dirs. Conservation Ctr. for Art and Hist. Artifacts, 1984-96, chmn., 1993-95, Woodlands Cemetery Co., 1990—, Rsch. Librs. Group, 1993-96; exec. com., Phila. Area Consortium Spl. Coll., Librs., 1988-93; sec. Christopher Ludwick Found., 1969—; bd. dirs., sec., treas. Victorian Soc. in Am., 1969-88; assoc. Nat. Preservation Inst., 1982-93; bd. dirs. Hist. House Assn. Am., 1978-83, Com. for Preservation of Archtl. Records, 1978-80, Phila. Area Cultural Consortium, 1977-82, also treas., Mus. Council Phila., 1976-78; sec. Hopkinson House Council, 1982-93, Clivden Council, Nat. Trust for Hist. Preservation, 1974-81, 84-86, Harriton House, 1969-81, Friends of Laurel Hill, 1978-83, Franklin Inn Club, 1976-79. NEH grantee, 1983-85. Fellow Royal Soc. Arts; mem. Soc. Archtl. Historians, Soc. Preservation New Eng. Antiquities, Hist. Soc. Pa., Libr. Co., Rushlight Club. Office: Athenaeum of Phila 219 S 6th St Philadelphia PA 19106-3719

MOSS, STEPHEN B., lawyer; b. Jacksonville, Fla., July 14, 1943; s. Rudy and Betty (Sobel) M.; m. Rhoda Goodman, Nov. 24, 1984; children: Kurt, Shannon. BA, Tulane U., 1964; JD, Samford U., 1968. Bar: Fla. 1968, U.S. Dist. Ct. (so. dist.) Fla., U.S. Tax Ct. From assoc. to ptnr. Heiman & Crary, Miami, Fla., 1971-74; pvt. practice law So. Miami, Fla., 1974-75; ptnr. Glass, Schultz, Weinstein & Moss P.A., Coral Gables, Fla., 1975-78, Ft. Lauderdale, Fla., 1978-80; ptnr. Holland & Knight, Ft. Lauderdale, 1980—; gen. counsel Greater Ft. Lauderdale C. of C., 1991-92. Capt. U.S. Army, 1968-70, Vietnam. Named Outstanding Kiwanian, Miami, 1974; Olympic torchbearer, 1996. Fellow ABA, Fla. Bar Found.; mem. Fla. Bar Assn., Greater Ft. Lauderdale C. of C. (chmn. bd. dirs., bd. govs. 1995, Chmn.'s award 1991), Tower Club, Tower Forum (pres. 1993-94). Democrat. Jewish. Avocations: running, softball, hiking, family activities. Office: Holland & Knight Fl 13 1 E Broward Blvd Fort Lauderdale FL 33301-1804

MOSS, STEPHEN EDWARD, lawyer; b. Washington, Nov. 22, 1940; s. Morris and Jean (Sober) M.; m. Abigail Deady, Dec. 19, 1964; children: Aubrey, Hilary. BBA, Baldwin-Wallace Coll., 1962; JD with honors, George Washington U., 1965, LLM, 1968. Bar: D.C. 1966, Md. 1971. Assoc. Cole & Groner, Washington, 1965-70; pvt. practice law Bethesda, Md., 1971-80; pres. Stephen E. Moss, P.A., Bethesda, 1981-89, Moss, Strickler & Weaver, Bethesda, 1990-94, Moss, Strickler & Sachitano, P.A., Bethesda, 1995—; lectr. in family law and trial practice. Fellow Am. Acad. Matrimonial Lawyers (cert.); mem. Montgomery County Bar Assn. (chmn. family law sect. 1981). Office: Moss Strickler & Sachitano PA 4550 Montgomery Ave Ste 700 Bethesda MD 20814

MOSS, SUSAN, nurse, retail store owner; b. Youngstown, Ohio, Aug. 17, 1940; d. Jarlath G. and Sara G. (Curley) Carney; divorced; children: John P., Jerri Ann Moss Williams. Lic. nurse, Choffin Sch., 1973; AS in Am. Bus. Mgmt., Youngstown State U., 1992. Surg. scrub nurse St. Elizabeth Hosp., Youngstown, 1972-78; office mgr. Moss Equipment Co., North Jackson, Ohio, 1978-83; pvt. duty nurse Salem, Ohio, 1979—; night nurse supr. Gateways for Better Living, Youngstown, 1982-84; owner Laura's Bride and Formal Wear, Salem, 1987—; CEO Strawberry Sunshine Svcs. Co., Salem, 1994—; cons. Edith R. Nolf, Inc., Salem. Author: (novelette) Turlaleen. Water therapy aide Easter Seal Soc., Youngstown, 1970-75, bd. trustees, 1973-75; mem. Hear, Now, Denver, 1989. Mem. LPN Assn. Ohio, Bus. and Profl. Women, Youngstown State U. Alumni Club, Short Hills Lit. Soc., Beta Sigma Phi (v.p., Silver Circle award 1986, Order of the Rose 1987). Democrat. Roman Catholic. Avocations: writing, painting, music, public speaking, traveling. Office: Laura's Bride & Formal Wear 1271 E Pidgeon Rd Salem OH 44460-4364

MOSS, THOMAS HENRY, science association administrator; b. Cleve., June 27, 1939; s. Joseph Harold and Elsa Margaret (Lemkau) M.; m. Kathleen Goddard, May 31, 1965; children: Ellen, Joseph, Cheryl, David. AB, Harvard U., 1961; PhD, Cornell U., 1965. Cons. analyst govtl. sci. policy U.S. Govt. Office Mgmt. and Budget, Washington, 1963-67; research physicist IBM Corp., Yorktown, N.Y., 1967-74, 75-76; staff dir., sci. advisor Office of Congressman George E. Brown, Washington, 1976-79; staff dir. subcom. sci., research and tech. Ho. of Reps., Washington, 1979-82; prof. physics, dean grad. studies and research Case Western Res. U., Cleve., 1982-96; exec. dir. Govt.-Univ.-Industry Roundtable, 1996—; with Nat. Acad. Scis, Washington; adj. prof. physics Columbia U., N.Y.C., 1966-76; mem. nat rev. com. Office of Nuclear Waste Isolation, Columbus, 1983—; bd. dirs. Univ. Tech. Inc., Cleve.; bd. dirs. Ctr. Great Lakes, Chgo., 1985—; v.p. Edison Poymer Innovation Corp., Independence, Ohio, 1986-90. Editor: The Three Mile Island Nuclear Accident-Lessons, 1981; asst. editor Environ. Profl. mag.; cons. editor Sci, Tech. and Human Values Environ. mag.; contbr. articles to profl. jours. Treas. Lake Bancroft Cmty. Assn., Falls Church, Va., 1980; mem. adv. bd. Small Bus. SBIR Program, Cleve., 1983-85; mem., v.p. Shaker Heights (Ohio) Bd. Edn., 1989-96; chmn. N.E. Region Ohio Systemic Statewide Initiative in Sci. and Math. Edn., 1992-95. ASME fellow, 1995-96, NSF fellow Nobel Instn., 1966-67. Fellow Am. Phys. Soc. (chmn. forum on physics and soc. 1990-91), Nat. Coun. Univ. Rsch. Adminstrs. (Nat. Innovation Program award 1987), Scientists Inst. Pub. Info. (Disting. Svc. award Harlem Prep. Sch. 1971); mem. AAAS (chmn. com. on sci., engrng. and pub. policy 1989-91). Avocations: gardening, camping. Office: NAS Rm 340 2101 Constitution Ave Washington DC 22312

MOSS, WILLIAM JOHN, lawyer; b. Duluth, Minn., Aug. 31, 1921; s. John Hugh and Mary (Quinn) M.; m. Kathryn Casale, June 14, 1947; children: Mary Moss Appleton, Katy Moss Warner, Elizabeth Bradley, Amy Moss Brown, John, Gerard, Hugh, Patricia Moss Sheng, Susan Moss Homola, Barbara Moss Bartol. A.B., Harvard U., 1947, LL.B., 1949. Bar: N.Y. 1950. Assoc. firm Cadwalader, Wickersham & Taft, N.Y.C., 1949-58, ptnr., 1959—. Served to maj. AUS, 1942-45. Republican. Roman Catholic. Home: RR 9D Garrison NY 10524 Office: Cadwalader Wickersham & Taft 100 Maiden Ln New York NY 10038-4892

MOSSAWIR, HARVE H., JR., lawyer; b. Morton, Miss., Aug. 9, 1942; s. Harve H. and Madeline (Price) M.; children: Anna Christine, Karen Elyse; m. Judy S. Bardugo, Aug. 5, 1985; 1 child, Leigh Sarah. BA with honors, U. Ala., 1964; MA in Econs., U. Manchester, 1965; JD with honors, U. Chgo., 1968. Bar: Calif. 1970. Asst. prof. U. Ala. Law Sch., Tuscaloosa, 1968-69; assoc. Irell & Manella, L.A., 1969-74, ptnr., 1974-94, of counsel, 1994—. Mem. bd. editors U. Chgo. Law Rev., 1966-68; contbr. articles to profl. jours. Fulbright scholar, 1964-65, Floyd Russell Mecham scholar, 1965-68. Mem. Calif. Bar Assn. Republican. Office: Irell & Manella 1800 Avenue Of The Stars Los Angeles CA 90067-4211

MOSSBERG, BARBARA CLARKE, educational writer and speaker; b. Hollywood, Calif., Aug. 9, 1948; d. Gerard Theodore and Antonina Rose (Rumore) Clarke; m. Christer Lennart Mossberg, June 21, 1974; children: Nicolino Clarke Mossberg, Sophia Antonina Clarke Mossberg. BA, UCLA, 1970; MA, Ind. U., 1972, PhD, 1976. From asst. to assoc. prof. U. Oreg., Eugene, 1976-88, assoc. and acting dean Grad. Sch., 1984-85, dir. Am. studies, 1984-86; exec. dir. VIA Internat., Washington, 1988-93; assoc. provost and dir. external rels. Hobart and William Smith Colls., Geneva, N.Y., 1993-94; sr. fellow Am. Coun. Edn., Washington, 1993—; prof., bicentennial chair U. Helsinki, Finland, 1982-83, sr. Fulbright Disting. lectr., 1990-91; Mellon fellow, moderator, resource fellow Aspen Inst., 1984, 88, 89; U.S. scholar in residence U.S. Info. Agy., Washington, 1986-88; dir. Am. studies summer inst. Swedish Ministry of Edn. and Culture, Uppsala U., 1986, 87, 88; dir. M. R. Smith coun. scholars Am. Coun. on Edn., Washington, 1994; cons. in field. Author: Emily Dickinson, 1983 (Choice award 1983); contbr. articles to profl. jours. U.S. rep. The Lahti (Finland) Internat. Writer's Reunion, 1983, Can. Couchiching Conf., 1994; spkr. Oreg. Commn. for the Humanities, Oreg., 1983-86; adv. bd. mem., moderator The Next Stage, Washington, 1993. Rsch. grantee U. Oreg., 1979, Nat. Endowment for the Humanities, Sweden, 1980, Am. Coun. Learned Socs., U. Manchester, 1985; Disting. Inst. scholar Mt. Vernon Inst., Washington, 1994, others. Mem. Emily Dickinson Soc. (founding mem., bd. mem., v.p. and program chair 1988-90), Soc. for Values in Higher Edn., Soc. Women Geographers, Women's Fgn. Policy Group, The Writer's Ctr. Avocations: poetry, photography, architecture, art, travel. Office: Am Coun on Edn One Dupont Circle NW Washington DC 20036

MOSS BOWER, PHYLIS DAWN, medical researcher; b. Waco, Tex., Oct. 27, 1959; d. Phillip Carroll and Teloiv Anita (Marrs) Eddins; m. W. Taylor Moss, Mar. 22, 1980 (div. Aug. 1990); children: Amber Nikkole Moss, Beau Christian Moss; m. Kevin Eugene Bower, May 27, 1992. Student, Tex. Tech. U., 1977-78, 4-C Bus. Coll., 1989-90. Tumor registry Scott & White Hosp., Waco, 1988-92; clin. rsch. in oncology LaGrange (Ill.) Hosp., 1992-93; clin. rsch. asst. pharm. Christie Clinic, Champaign, Ill., 1993—; spirit of Scott & White com. mem. Scott & White Hosp., Temple, Tex., 1992. Leader Girl Scouts USA, Waco, 1983; com. mem. Children's Miracle Network, Temple, 1988-92; breast cancer prevention team Nat. Surg. Adjuvant Bowel and Breast Protocol, LaGrange, 1992-93. Mem. Nat. Tumor Registrars Assn., Tex. Tumor Registrars Assn. (fin. com. mem. 1988-92, membership com. 1989-90), Soc. Clin. Rsch. Assn. (fin. com. mem. 1992—). Methodist. Avocations: calligraphy, embroidery, bowling, cooking, crafts. Home: RR 1 Box 71 Villa Grove IL 61956-9714 Office: Christie Clinic 101 W University Ave Champaign IL 61820-3909

MOSSBRUCKER, TOM, dancer; b. Tacoma. Scholarship student, The Joffrey Ballet Sch., 1975-77. Dancer Joffrey II Dancers, N.Y.C., 1978-80, The Joffrey Ballet, N.Y.C., 1980—. Office: The Joffrey Ballet 130 W 56th St New York NY 10019-3818

MOSSE, GEORGE LACHMANN, history educator, author; b. Berlin, Sept. 20, 1918; came to U.S., 1939, naturalized, 1945; s. Hans Lachmann-Mosse and Felicia M. Student, Cambridge (Eng.) U., 1937-39; B.S., Haverford Coll., 1941; Ph.D., Harvard U., 1946; D.Litt., Carthage Coll., 1973; D.H.L., Hebrew Union Coll., 1987; laurea honoris causa, U. Camerino, Italy, 1995. From instr. to assoc. prof. State U. Iowa, 1944-55; from assoc. prof. to prof. U. Wis., 1955-89, Bascom prof. history, 1964-83, Bascom-Weinstein prof. Jewish studies, 1983-89, prof. emeritus, 1989—; fellow Inst. for Advanced Studies Hebrew U., 1987; vis. prof. Stanford U., 1963-64, Hebrew U., 1969-70, 72, 74, 76, 78, Koebner prof., 1979-86, emeritus, 1986—, U. Munich, 1982-83, École des Hautes, Études, Paris, 1986; fellow Inst. Contemporary Jewry, Hebrew U., 1974—; vis. prof. Jewish Tehol. Sem. Am., 1977; sr. fellow Australian Nat. U., 1972, 79; Kaplan vis. prof. Jewish studies U. Cape Town (South Africa), 1980; vis. prof. U. Amsterdam, 1988, U. Tel Aviv, 1989, Pembroke Coll., Cambridge U., 1990, 91, 94, Cornell U., 1989, 92, A.D. White prof.-at-large, 1993—, U. San Marino, 1992, Shapiro Sr. scholar-in-residence U.S. Holocaust Meml. Mus., 1994-95. Author: The Struggle for Sovereignty in England, 1950, The Holy Pretence, 1957, The Reformation, 1953, 2d edit., 1963, The Crisis of German Ideology, 1964, The Culture of Western Europe, 1961, 3d edit., 1988, Nazi Culture, 1966, (with H. Koenigsberger) Europe in the Sixteenth Century, 1968, 2d edit., 1989, Germans and Jews, 1970, The Nationalisation of the Masses, Political Symbols and Mass Movements in Germany, 1975, Nazism, 1978, Towards the Final Solution: A History of European Racism, 1978, Masses and Men, Nationalist and Fascist Perceptions of Reality, 1980, German Jews Beyond Judaism, 1985, Nationalism and Sexuality: Respectability and Abnormal Sexuality in Modern Europe, 1985, Fallen Soldiers: Reshaping the Memory of the World Wars, 1990, Ebrei in Gerhania Fra Assimilazione i antisemitismo, 1991, Ich Bleibe Emigrant: Gespräche, 1991, Confronting the Nation: Jewish and Western Nationalism, 1993; editor: Police Forces in History, 1975, International Facism, 1979; co-editor: Europe in Review, 1957, Jour. Contemporary History, 1966—, (with Bella Vago) Jews and Non-Jews in Eastern Europe, 1975 (with Jehuda Reinharz) The Impact of Western Nationalisms, 1992; contbr. New Cambridge Modern History. Bd. dirs. Wiener Library, London, 1974-92, Leo Baeck Inst., N.Y.C., 1978—; bd. overseers Tauber Inst., Brandeis U., 1980—. Recipient Premio Storia Aqui, 1975, Premio Prezzolini, Florence, 1985, Goethe Medallie, Goethe Inst., 1988. Mem. AAUP (chmn. Iowa conf. 1954-55), Am. Soc. Reformation Research (pres. 1962), Am. Soc. Ch. History (council 1969-73), Am. Hist. Assn., Am. Acad. Arts and Scis., Phi Beta Kappa, Phi Eta Sigma (hon.). Home: 36 Glenway St Madison WI 53705-5206

MOSSE, PETER JOHN CHARLES, financial services executive; b. Mtarfa, Malta, Sept. 8, 1947; came to U.S., 1977; s. John Herbert Charles and Barbara Haworth (Holden) M.; m. Christine Marielle St. Preux, Oct. 17, 1994. BA, Oxford U., 1969; MBA, U. Pa., 1971; MA, Oxford U., 1989. Bank officer N.M. Rothschild & Sons Ltd., London, 1971-76; spl. projects officer banking Bumiputra Mcht. Bankers Berhad, Kuala Lumpur, Malaysia, 1976-77; v.p., treas., sec. NMR Metals Incorp., N.Y.C., 1977-79, exec. v.p., 1979-83; sr. v.p. Rothschild, Inc., N.Y.C., 1983-90; v.p., CFO, The Arista Group Inc., N.Y.C., 1991-93; U.S. rep. Travelex Fin. Svcs. Ltd., London, 1994-95; ptnr. Creelman Fine Arts, N.Y.C., 1995—. Mem. Pilgrims of the U.S., St. George's Soc. N.Y. (life), Oxford U. Alumni Soc. (exec. com. 1994—), The Gold Inst. (co. rep., bd. dirs. 1985-90), The Silver Inst. (co. rep., bd. dirs. 1989-90), The Copper Club, Commodity Exch., Inc. (co. rep. 1979-90). Episcopalian. Avocations: international travel, railroads. Home and Office: 353 E 72nd St Apt 33D New York NY 10021-4622

MOSSEL, PATRICIA FLEISCHER, opera executive; b. N.Y.C., Nov. 19, 1933; d. Burnet Thomas and Martha Camille (Leigh) Kraut; m. Allan A Fleischer, Dec. 30,. 1956 (div. 1987); children: Hillary Lee, Jason Allan; m. John W. Mossel, Sept. 4, 1993. BA, U. Rochester, 1955; MA, Yale U., 1956. Cert. fund raising exec. Tchr. Colby Coll., New London, N.H., 1956-57; editor Far Eastern Pub.-Yale U., New Haven, 1957-60; dir. devel. San Francisco Opera, 1979-84; dir. devel., mktg. and pub. relations The Wash. Opera, 1984-95, exec. dir., 1995—; mem. bd. San Francisco Symphony and Opera; bd. chmn., exec. dir. Mt. Diablo Rehabilitation Ctr.; co-founder Medi-Physics, Inc.; cons. D.C. Humanities Council, 1989—. Editor: Western Lit. on China, 1959. Mem. adv. council Fund Raising Sch., Indpls.; v.p. Nat. Soc. Fund Raising Exec. Found. bd. dirs., Washington, 1985-87. Mem. Nat. Soc. Fund Raising Execs. (named Fund Raising Exec. of Yr. 1986), Assocs. of Yale Alumni (del. 1988-91), Yale Club, Phi Beta Kappa. Republican. Presbyterian. Avocations: painting, writing, piano. Office: Washington Opera/Eisenhower Theater 2209 Kennedy Ctr Washington DC 20566-0012

MOSSINGHOFF, GERALD JOSEPH, lawyer, engineer; b. St. Louis, Sept. 30, 1935; m. Jeanne Carole Jack, Dec. 29, 1958; children: Pamela Ann Jennings, Gregory Joseph, Melissa M. Ronayne. BSEE, St. Louis U., 1957; JD with honors, George Washington U., 1961. Bar: Mo. 1961, D.C. 1965, Va. 1981. Project engr. Sachs Electric Corp., 1954-57; dir. congl. liaison NASA, Washington, 1967-73, dep. gen. counsel, 1976-81; asst. Sec. Commerce, commr. patents and trademarks U.S. Patent Office, 1981-85; pres. Pharm. Rsch. and Mfrs. Am., Washington, 1985—; adj. prof. Am. U., Washington Coll. Law, 1984—; amb. Paris Conv. Diplomatic Conf. Recipient Exceptional Svc. medal NASA, 1971, Disting. Svc. medal, 1980, Outstanding Leadership medal, 1981; granted presdl. rank of meritorious exec., 1980; Disting. Pub. Svc. award Sec. of Commerce, 1983. Fellow Am. Acad. Pub. Adminstrn.; mem. Reagan Alumni Assn. (bd. dirs.), Internat. Fedn. Pharm. Mfrs. Assn. (bd. dirs.), Cosmos Club, Knights of Malta, Order of Coif, Eta Kappa Nu, Pi Mu Epsilon. Home: Apt PH 28 1530 N Key Blvd Arlington VA 22209-1532 Office: Pharm Rsch and Mfrs Am 1100 15th St NW Washington DC 20005-1707

MOSSMAN, THOMAS MELLISH, JR., television manager; b. Honolulu, Nov. 20, 1938; s. Thomas Mellish and Marian (Ledwith) M.; children: Thomas Mellish III, James Michael; m. Jan Carla MacAlister, Dec. 31, 1989. Student, U. Hawaii, 1954-57; BA, U. Denver, 1958, MA, 1965. Producer-dir. KRMA-TV, Denver, 1960-64, KCET-TV, L.A., 1964-72; pres. Mosaic Films, L.A., 1972-73; prodn. and operations dir. KLCS-TV, L.A., 1973-78, station mgr., 1978-87; dept. dir. Archdiocese of L.A., 1987—; instr. Calif. State U., Northridge, 1981—; chairperson, founder L.A. Community TV, 1987-95. Chmn. exec. bd. Regional Ednl. TV Adv. Coun., 1989-93; chmn., founding mem. Alliance for Distance Edn. in Calif., 1991-95; pres. Cath. TV Network, 1993—. Mem. NATAS, Dirs. Guild Am., Alliance for Community Media. Episcopalian. Office: Archdiocese Los Angeles 1530 W 9th St Los Angeles CA 90015-1111

MOSSO, DAVID, accountant; b. Pasadena, Calif., Aug. 13, 1926; s. Joseph Ernest and Marian (Ure) M.; m. Lee McVoy Pierce, June 11, 1955; children: Janet, Andrew, Jocelyn. B.B.A. magna cum laude, Washburn U., 1950, D in Commerce (hon.), 1982; M.A. in Econs, U. Minn., 1951. CPA, Va. With Santa Fe Ry., 1942-44; instr. econs. and acctg. Washburn U., 1954-55; with U.S. Treasury Dept., 1955-77, commr. accounts, 1971-73, dep. asst. sec. treasury, 1973-75, asst. sec., 1975-77; with Fin. Acctg. Stds. Bd., 1978-96; bd. mem. Fin. Acctg. Standards Bd., 1978-85, vice chmn., 1986-87; asst. dir. rsch. Fin. Acctg. Stds. Bd., 1988-96; adj. prof. acctg. Fordham U., 1996—. Contbr. articles to profl. jours. Mem. Comptr. Gen.'s Acctg. Stds. Adv. Coun., 1987-96; mem. charter revision commn. City of Stamford, 1986-87, Internat. Adv. Group on Fed. Reporting, 1984-86; alt. trustee Nat. Gallery Art, 1975-77; dir. Stamford Emergency Med. Svc., 1993-94. 1st lt. AUS, 1944-46, 51-53. Recipient Alexander Hamilton award Treasury Dept., 1977. Mem. AICPA (Elijah Watt Sells award 1962), Va. Soc. CPAs (Gold medal 1962), Assn. Govt Accts. (fed. fin. mgmt. standards bd. 1971-77, dir. Washington chpt. 1972-73, Disting. Leadership award 1977, Elmer Staats award 1990), Treasury Hist. Assn. (pres. 1978), TauDelta Pi, Pi Gamma Mu, Phi Kappa Phi. Home: 111 Saddle Hill Rd Stamford CT 06903-2307 Office: 401 Merritt 7 Norwalk CT 06851-1000

MOSSOP, GRANT DILWORTH, geological institute director; b. Calgary, Alta., Can., Apr. 15, 1948; s. Cyril S. and Freida E. (Dilworth) M.; m. Ruth Shaver, May 24, 1969; children: Jenny, Jonathan, David. BSc in Geology, U. Calgary, 1970, MSc in Geology, 1971; PhD, DIC in Geology, Imperial Coll., U. London, 1973. Postdoctoral fellow U. Calgary, Alta., Can., 1974; asst. rsch. officer Alta. Rsch. Coun., Edmonton, 1975-77, assoc. rsch. officer, 1977-80, head geol. survey dept., 1980-84, sr. rsch. officer, 1985-91; dir. Geol. Survey of Can., Calgary, 1991—; acad. visitor dept. earth sci. Oxford (Eng.) U., 1984-85. Project mgr., editor Geol. Atlas of Western Canada Sedimentary Basin. Fellow Geol. Assn. Can. (pres. 1986-87); mem. Can. Soc. Petroleum Geologists. Home: 68 Colleen Cres SW, Calgary, AB Canada T2V 2R3 Office: Geol Survey Can, 3303-33d St NW, Calgary, AB Canada T2L 2A7

MOSS-SALENTIJN, LETTY (ALEIDA MOSS-SALENTIJN), anatomist; b. Amsterdam, The Netherlands, Apr. 14, 1943; came to U.S., 1968; d. Ewoud and Johanna Maria (Schoonhoven) Salentijn; m. Melvin Lionel Moss, Apr. 17, 1970. DDS, State U., Utrecht, The Netherlands, 1967, PhD, 1976. Asst. prof. histology, State U., Utrecht, 1967-68; asst. prof. Columbia U., 1968-74, assoc. prof., 1974-86, prof., 1986—, dir. dental radiology, 1980-86, dir. grad. program dental sci., 1986—, dir. postdoctoral affairs, 1987-90, asst.

dean postdoctoral programs, 1990-94, assoc. dean acad. affairs, 1995—. Author: Orofacial Histology & Embryology, 1972; Dental and Oral Tissues, 1980, 2d edit., 1984, 3d edit. 1990; contbr. chpts. to books, articles to profl. jours. Fellow Royal Microscopical Soc.; mem. Am. Assn. Anatomists, Internat. Assn. Dental Rsch., Am. Soc. Biomechanics, Sigma Xi. (chpt. sec. 1980-87, pres. 1987-89), Omicron Kappa Upsilon (pres. local chpt. 1987). Avocation: stained glass art. Home: 560 Riverside Dr Apt 20K New York NY 10027-3242 Office: Columbia U Assoc Dean Academic Affairs 630 W 168th St New York NY 10032-3702

MOST, JACK LAWRENCE, lawyer, consultant; b. N.Y.C., Sept. 24, 1935; s. Meyer Milton and Henrietta (Meyer) M.; children: Jeffrey, Peter; m. Irma Freedman Robbins, Aug. 8, 1968; children: Ann, Jane. BA cum laude, Syracuse U., 1956; JD, Columbia U., 1960. Bar: N.Y. 1960, U.S. Dist. Ct. (so. and ea. dists.) N.Y. 1963. Assoc. Hale, Grant, Meyerson and O'Brien, N.Y.C., 1960-66; dep. assoc. dir. OEO, Exec. Office of The Pres., Washington, 1965-67; asst. to gen. counsel C.I.T. Fin. Corp., N.Y.C., 1968-70; corp. counsel PepsiCo, Inc., Purchase, N.Y., 1970-71; v.p. legal affairs Revlon, Inc., N.Y.C., 1971-76; asst. gen. counsel Norton Simon, Inc., N.Y.C., 1976-79; ptnr. Rogers Hoge and Hills, N.Y.C., 1979-86; ptnr. Finkelstein Bruckman Wohl Most & Rothman LLP, N.Y.C., 1986—, mng. ptnr., 1990-93; corp. sec. Requa, Inc., Flowery Beauty Products, Inc., 1987—. Contbr. articles to profl. jour. and mags. Bd. dirs. Haym Salomon Home for the Aged, 1978-91, pres., 1981-82; bd. dirs. The Jaffa Inst. for Advancement of Edn., 1994-95, Jewish Fellowship of Hemlock Farms, 1995—; bd. dirs., pres. Haym Salomon Geriatric Found., 1992—; dmem. bd. advisors Touro Coll. Health Scis., 1989-90. Mem. ABA (fed. regulation of securities com., food, drug and cosmetic law com., trademark and unfair competition com.), N.Y. State Bar Assn. (food, drug and cosmetics sect.), Am. Soc. Pharmacy Law, YRH Owners Corp. (bd. dirs., pres. 1989-92), Lords Valley Country Club (bd. govs. 1984-90, 1st v.p. 1987-88, 2d v.p. 1988-90), Zeta Beta Tau, Omicron (trustee Syracuse chpt. 1988-91). Jewish. Home: 429 E 52nd St New York NY 10022-6430 Office: Finkelstein Bruckman Wohl Most & Rothman 575 Lexington Ave New York NY 10022-6102

MOST, NATHAN, securities exchange executive; b. L.A., Mar. 22, 1914; s. Bernard and Bertha (Saltzman) M.; m. Evelyn Rosenthal, July 10, 1964; children—Stephen, John, Robert, Barbara. BA, UCLA, 1935. Exec. v.p. Getz Bros. & Co., San Francisco, 1945-60; pres. Carad Corp., Palo Alto, Calif., 1961-64; exec. v.p. James S. Baker Co., San Francisco, 1964-65, Pacific Vegetable Oil Corp., San Francisco, 1965-70, Am. Import Co., San Francisco, 1970-74; pres. Pacific Commodities Exchange, San Francisco, 1974-76; spl. asst. to chmn. Commodity Futures Trading Commn., Washington, May-Dec. 1976; pres. Amex Commodities Exch., N.Y.C., 1977-80; v.p. new products devel. Am. Stock Exch., 1980-91, sr. v.p., 1991-96; pres., chmn. bd. Foreign Fund, Inc., Wilmington, Del., 1996—; pres. Amex Commodities Corp., Inc., N.Y.C., 1982—; v.p. Calif. Council Internat. Trade, 1966-67; pres. Commodity Club San Francisco, 1970—; bd. dirs. San Francisco-Pacific Commodity Exch., 1970—, San Francisco World Trade Assn., 1970—, World Affairs Council No. Calif., 1953-65; pres. San Francisco World Trade Assn., 1956-58. Councilman Atherton, Calif., 1959-64. Mem. Export Mgmt. Assn. No. Calif. (pres. 1972—), San Francisco Commodity Club (dir.). Home: 415 Pinehill Rd Hillsborough CA 94010-6614

MOSTELLER, FREDERICK, mathematical statistician, educator; b. Clarksburg, W.Va., Dec. 24, 1916; s. William Roy and Helen (Kelley) M.; m. Virginia Gilroy, May 17, 1941; children: William, Gale. ScB, Carnegie Inst. Tech. (now Carnegie-Mellon U.), 1938, MSc, 1939, DSc (hon.), 1974; AM, Princeton U., 1942, PhD, 1946; DSc (hon.), U. Chgo., 1973, Wesleyan U., 1983; D. of Social Scis. (hon.), Yale U., 1981; LLD (hon.), Harvard U., 1991. Instr. math. Princeton U., 1942-44; research assoc. Office Pub. Opinion Research, 1942-44; spl. cons. research br. War Dept., 1942-43; research mathematician Statis. Research Group, Princeton, applied math. panel Nat. Devel. and Research Council, 1944-46; mem. faculty Harvard U., 1946—, prof. math. stats., 1951-87, Roger I. Lee prof., 1978-87, prof. emeritus, 1987—, chmn. dept. stats., 1957-69, 75-77, chmn. dept. biostats., 1977-81, chmn. dept. health policy and mgmt., 1981-87; dir. Tech. Assessment Group, 1987—; dir. Ctr. for Evaluation Am. Acad. Arts and Scis., 1994—; vice chmn. Pres.'s Commn. on Fed. Stats., 1970-71; mem. Nat. Adv. Council Equality of Ednl. Opportunity, 1973-78, Nat. Sci. Bd. Commn. on Pre-coll. Edn. in Math., Sci. and Tech., 1982-83; Fund for Advancement of Edn. fellow, 1954-55; nat. tchr. NBC's Continental Class-room TV course in probability and stats., 1960-61; fellow Center Advanced Study Behavioral Sciences, 1962-63, bd. dirs., 1980-86; Guggenheim fellow, 1969-70; Miller research prof. U. Calif. at Berkeley, 1974-75; Hitchcock Found. lectr. U. Calif., 1985. Co-author: Gauging Public Opinion (editor Hadley Cantril), 1944, Sampling Inspection, 1948, The Pre-election Polls, 1948, 49, Stochastic Models for Learning, 1955, Probability with Statistical Applications, 1961, Inference and Disputed Authorship, The Federalist, 1964, The National Halothane Study, 1969, Statistics: A Guide to the Unknown, 3d edit., 1988, On Equality of Educational Opportunity, 1972, Sturdy Statistics, 1973, Statistics By Example, 1973, Cost, Risks and Benefits of Surgery, 1977, Data Analysis and Regression, 1977, Statistics and Public Policy, 1977, Data for Decisions, 1982, Understanding Robust and Exploratory Data Analysis, 1983, Biostatistics in Clinical Medicine, 1983, 3d edit., 1994, Beginning Statistics with Data Analysis, 1983, Exploring Data Tables, Trends and Shapes, 1985, Medical Uses of Statistics, 1986, 2d edit., 1992, Quality of Life and Technology Assessment, 1989, Fundamentals of Exploratory Analysis of Variance, 1992, Meta-analysis for Explanation, 1992, Doing More Good Than Harm, 1993, Medicine Worth Paying For, 1995; author articles in field. Trustee Russell Sage Found.; mem. bd. Nat. Opinion Research Center, 1962-66. Recipient Outstanding Statistician award Chgo. chpt. Am. Statis. Assn., 1971, Boston chpt., 1989, Myrdal prize Evaluation Research Soc., 1978, Paul F. Lazarsfeld prize Council Applied Social Research, 1979, R.A. Fisher award Com. of Pres.'s of Statis. Socs., 1987, Medallion of Ctrs. for Disease Control, 1988. Fellow AAAS (chmn. sect. U 1973, dir. 1974-78, pres. 1980, chmn. bd. 1981), Inst. Math. Statistics (pres. 1974-75), Am. Statis. Assn. (v.p. 1962-64, pres. 1967, Samuel S. Wilks medal 1986), Social Sci. Research Council (chmn. bd. dirs. 1966-68), Math. Social Sci. Bd. (acad. governing bd. 1962-67), Am. Acad. Arts and Scis. (council 1986-88), Royal Statis. Soc. (hon.); mem. Am. Philos. Soc. (council 1986-88), Internat. Statis. Inst. (v.p. 1986-88, pres.-elect 1989, pres. 1991-93), Math. Assn. Am., Psychometric Soc. (pres. 1957-58), Inst. Medicine of Nat. Acad. Scis. (council 1978), Nat. Acad. Scis., Biometric Soc. Office: 1 Oxford St Cambridge MA 02138-2901

MOSTELLER, ROBERT P., law educator; b. 1948. BA, U. N.C., 1970; MA, Harvard U., 1975; JD, Yale U., 1975. Bar: N.C. 1975, D.C. 1976. Law clk. to Hon. Braxton Craven U.S. Ct. Appeals (4th cir.), Asheville, N.C., 1975-76; atty., chmn. trial div., tng. dir. D.C. Pub. Defender Svc., 1976-83; assoc. prof. Duke U., 1983-87, prof., 1987—, sr. assoc. dean, 1989-91. Mem. Phi Beta Kappa (pres. 1969-70). Office: Sch Law Duke U Durham NC 27708

MOSTELLO, ROBERT ANTHONY, chemical engineer; b. Newark, Dec. 20, 1937; s. Anthony Joseph and Josephine Maria (Guarino) M.; m. Raquel Luisa Martinez, May 22, 1965; children: Elizabeth, Laura, Carolyn, Maria. BSChE, Newark Coll. Engring., 1958; M of Chem. Engring., Stevens Inst. Tech., 1967, PhD in Chem. Engring., 1971. Chem. process engr. Air Reduction Co., Jersey City, 1960-62; sr. chem. engr. Am. Cryogenics Inc., O'Fallon, Ill., 1962-64, Air Reduction Co., Jersey City, 1964-65; chief chem. engr. Procedyne Corp., New Brunswick, N.J., 1969-73; sr. engr. Allied Chem. Corp., Morris Twp., N.J., 1973-76; staff engr. Exxon Chem. Co., Florham Park, N.J., 1976-82; asst. to v.p. ops. Jacobs Engring. Group, Mountainside, N.J., 1982; prin. engr. assoc. BOC Process Plants, Murray Hill, N.J., 1983—. Author: (encys.) Encyclopedia of Chemical Process and Design, 1990, Inorganic Chemicals Handbook, 1993, (jour.) Can. Inst. Chem. Engring. Jour., (pub. report) Electric Power Res. Inst. Mem., sec. Welfare Bd., Somerville, N.J., 1987-90. Mem. AIChE (bd. dirs. and editor local chpt. 1974-75). Achievements include 8 patents in field of industrial gases production. Avocations: hiking, gardening, travel, reading. Office: BOC Process Plants 100 Mountain Ave New Providence NJ 07974

MOSTERT, PAUL STALLINGS, mathematician, educator; b. Morrilton, Ark., Nov. 27, 1927; s. Johannes F.T. and Lucy (Stallings) M.; m. Barbara Bond: children: Paul Theodore, Richard Stallings, Kathleen, Kristina. A.B., Rhodes Coll, 1950; M.S., U. Chgo., 1951; Ph.D., Purdue U., 1953. Mem. faculty Tulane U., 1953-70, prof. math., 1962-70, chmn. dept., 1968-70; prof. math. U. Kans., 1970-91, prof. emeritus math., 1991—, chmn. dept., 1970-73; vis. prof. U. Tubingen, Germany, 1962-63; vis. prof. math. U. Ky., 1984-85; mem. Inst. Advanced Study, Princeton, 1967-68; chmn. Rhodes Coll. Sci. Initiative Task Force, 1989-90; pres. Equix, Inc., 1984-85, Pennfield Biomechanics Corp., Inc., 1985-89, Equix Biomechanics, 1989—. Co-author: Splitting in Topological Groups, 1963, 3d edit., 1993, Elements of Compact Semigroups, 1966, The Cohomology Ring of Finite and Compact Abelian Groups, 1974; editor: Proc. Conf. Transformation Groups at New Orleans, 1969, Questiones Mathematicae; co-founder, exec. editor: Semigroup Forum, 1970-85, mng. editor, 1967-85, editor, 1985-88. Mem. Ky. Statewide Exptl. Program to Stimulate Competetive Rsch. Com., 1994—. With USNR, 1945-46. NSF sr. postdoctoral fellow, 1967-68. Mem. AAAS, Am. Math. Soc. (mem. at large coun. 1972-75, chmn. com. on acad. freedom, tenure and employment security 1973-76), Assn. Mems. of Inst. for Advanced Studies, Soc. Indsl. and Applied Math., Internat. Soc. for Optical Engring., Internat. Soc. for Neural Networks, Thoroughbred Owners and Breeders Assn. Office: Equix Biomechanics Ste 203 870 Corporate Dr Lexington KY 40503-5416

MOSTILLO, RALPH, medical association executive; b. Newark, Apr. 11, 1944; s. Joseph and Antoinette (Cipriano) M. BA in Chemistry magna cum laude, Rutgers U., Newark, 1972; MA in Biochemistry, Princeton U., 1974, PhD in Biochemistry, 1978. NIH rsch. fellow Princeton (N.J.) U., 1972-78; sr. scientist drug regulatory affairs Hoffmann-La Roche, Inc., Nutley, N.J., 1979-85; founder, chmn., chief exec. officer Am. Cancer Assn., Nutley, 1986—. Assoc. editor U.S. Pharmacopoeia XX-Nat. Formulary XV, 1980-85. With USN, 1962-66, Vietnam. Mem. Am. Chem. Soc., Am. Mgmt. Assn., Am. Mktg. Assn., N.Y. Acad. Scis., Am. Legion, Vietnam Vets. of Am., Phi Beta Kappa. Achievements include research on molecular transport systems in E. coli as general models for drug delivery into cells. Home: PO Box 505 Nutley NJ 07110-0505 Office: Am Cancer Assn PO Box 87 Nutley NJ 07110-0087

MOSTOFF, ALLAN SAMUEL, lawyer, consultant; b. N.Y.C., Oct. 19, 1932; s. Morris and Ida (Goldman) M.; m. Alice Tamara Popelowsky, July 31, 1955; children: Peter Alexander, Nina Valerie. BS, Cornell U., 1953; MBA, N.Y.U., 1954; LLB, N.Y. Law Sch., 1957. Bar: N.Y. 1957, D.C. 1964. Assoc. Olwine Connelly Chase O'Donnell & Weyher, N.Y.C., 1958-61; atty. SEC, Washington, 1962-66, asst. dir. 1966-69, assoc. dir. 1969-72, dir. div. investment mgmt. regulation, 1972-76; ptnr. Dechert Price & Rhoads, Washington, 1976—; adj. prof. Georgetown U. Law Ctr., 1972-82; mem. Fin. Acctg. Standards Adv. Bd., 1983-87; mem. adv. bd. Investment Lawyer. Mem. ABA (chmn. internat. devel. sub-com., com. on devels. in investment svcs.), Assn. of Bar of City of N.Y., Fed. Bar Assn. (chmn. exec. coun. securities regulation com. 1990-92), Am. Law Inst. Home: 6417 Waterway Dr Falls Church VA 22044-1325 Office: Dechert Price & Rhoads 1500 K St NW Washington DC 20005-1209

MOSTOVOY, MARC SANDERS, conductor, music director; b. Phila., July 1, 1942; s. Ira and Floretta (Schiff)M. MusB, Temple U., 1963; postgrad. musicology U. Pa., 1964-66; pvt. study in U.S.A., France, 1950-66; MusD (hon.), Combs Coll. of Music, 1980; diploma, Academie of Musique, Nice, France. Conductor, music dir. Concerto Soloists of Phila., 1964—; also dir., 1964—; cultural advisor to gov., Commonwealth of Pa., Harrisburg, 1971-77; music dir. Mozart on the Square, Phila., 1980-91, also dir., 1980-91; music advisor Walnut St. Theater, Phila., 1970—; editor various music compositions. Mem. adv. com. arts and cultural council Greater Phila. C. of C., 1984-88; mem. program adv. com. Nat. Mus. Am. Jewish History, 1985-86; bd. dirs. Citizens for the Arts in Pa., 1984-86. Condr. numerous nat. and internat. concert tours with Concerto Soloists Chamber Orch. of Phila.; artistic dir. Laurel Festival of the Arts, Jim Thorpe, Pa., 1990-95; mem. music adv. panel Pa. Coun. on the Arts, 1991-92. Recipient Orpheus Club award, 1958; Gov.'s citation, Commonwealth of Pa., 1976; Mayor's citation City of Phila., 1984; Temple U. scholar, 1960-63. Mem. Mus. Fund Soc. of Phila., Greater Phila. C. of C. Jewish. Office: Concerto Soloists Chamber Orch 338 S 15th St Philadelphia PA 19102-4906

MOSTOW, GEORGE DANIEL, mathematics educator; b. Boston, July 4, 1923; s. Isaac J. and Ida (Rotman) M.; m. Evelyn Davidoff, Sept. 1, 1947; children: Mark Alan, David Jechiel, Carol Held, Jonathan Carl. B.A., Harvard U., 1943, M.A., 1946, Ph.D., 1948; DSc (hon.), U. Ill., Chgo., 1989. Instr. math. Princeton U., 1947-48; mem. Inst. Advanced Study, 1947-49, 56-57, 75, trustee, 1982-92; asst. prof. Syracuse U., 1949-52; asst. prof. math. Johns Hopkins U., 1952-53, assoc. prof., 1954-56, prof., 1957-61; prof. math. Yale U., 1961-66, James E. English prof. math., 1966-81, Henry Ford II prof. math., 1981—, chmn., 1971-74; vis. prof. Conselho Nat. des Pesquisas, Inst. de Matematica, Rio de Janeiro, Brazil, 1953-54, 91, U. Paris, 1966-67, Hebrew U., Jerusalem, 1967, Tata Inst. Fundamental Rsch., Bombay, 1970, Inst. des Hautes Etudes Scientifiques, Bures-Sur-Yvette, 1966, 71, 75, Japan Soc. for Promotion of Sci., 1985, Eidgenossische Technische Hochschule, Switzerland, 1986; chmn. U.S. Nat. Com. for Math , 1971-73, 83-85, Office Math. Scis., NRC, 1975-78; mem. sci. adv. coun. Math. Scis. Rsch. Inst., Berkeley, Calif., 1988-91, Weizmann Inst., Israel, Tel Aviv U.; mem. vis. com. dept. math. Harvard U., 1975-81, MIT, 1981-94; Ritt lectr. Columbia U., 1982, Bergman lectr. Stanford U., 1983, Sachar lectr. Tel Aviv U., 1985, Karcher lectr. U. Okla., 1986, Markert lectr. Pa. State U., 1993. Assoc. editor Annals of Math, 1957-64, Trans. Am. Math. Soc, 1958-65, Am. Scientist, 1970-82, Geometrica Dedicata, 1985-90, Jour. D'Analyse, 1994—; editor Am. Jour. Math, 1965-69; assoc. editor, 1969-79; author rsch. articles. Fulbright rsch. scholar, Utrecht U., The Netherlands; Guggenheim fellow, 1957-58. Mem. AAAS, NAS (chmn. sect. math. 1982-84), Am. Math. Soc. (pres. 1987-88, Steele prize for paper of lasting importance 1993), Internat. Math. Union (chmn. U.S. del. to gen. assembly Warsaw 1982, exec. com. 1983-86), Phi Beta Kappa, Sigma Xi. Home: 25 Beechwood Rd Woodbridge CT 06525-1309 Office: Yale Univ Dept Mathematics New Haven CT 06520

MOSZKOWSKI, LENA IGGERS, secondary school educator; b. Hamburg, Mar. 8, 1930; d. Alfred G. and Lizzie (Minden) M.; m. Steven Alexander, Aug. 29, 1952 (div. Oct. 1977); children: Benjamin Charles, Richard David (dec.), Ronald Bertram. BS, U. Richmond, 1948; MS, U. Chgo., 1953; postgrad., UCLA, 1958. Tchr. Lab. asst. U. Chgo. Ben May Cancer Research Lab., Chgo., 1951-53; biology, sci. tchrs. Bishop Conaty High Sch., Los Angeles, 1967-68; chemistry, sci. tchr. St. Paul High Sch., Santa Fe Springs, Calif., 1968-69; chemistry, human ecology tchr. Marlborough Sch., Los Angeles, 1969-71; tchr. biology and sci. ecology L.A. Unified Sch. Dist., 1971—. Author: Termite Taxonomy Cryptotermes Haviland and C. Krybi, Madagascar, 1955, Ecology and Man, 1971, Parallels in Human and Biological Ecology, 1977, American Public Education, An Inside Journey, 1991-92. Founder, adminstr., com. mem. UCLA Student (and Practical Assistance Cooperative Furniture), Los Angeles, 1963-67; active participant UCLA Earth Day Program, Los Angeles, 1970. Recipient Va. Sci. Talent Search Winner Va. Acad. of Sci., 1946; Push Vol. Tchr. award John C. Fremont High Sch., Los Angeles, 1978. Mem. Calif. Tchrs. Assn., United Tchrs. L.A., Sierra Club. Democrat. Jewish. Avocations: civil rights, workers rights, redirecting public education, photography, animals. Home: 3301 Shelburne Rd Baltimore MD 21208-5626

MOTAYED, ASOK K., engineering company executive. MS, Rutgers U., 1974. Pres. Sheladia Assoc., Inc., Rockville, Md., 1979—. Office: Sheladia Assoc Inc 15825 Shady Grove Rd Rockville MD 20850-4008

MOTE, CLAYTON DANIEL, JR., mechanical engineer, educator, administrator; b. San Francisco, Feb. 5, 1937; s. Clayton Daniel and Eugenia (Isnardi) M.; m. Patricia Jane Lewis, Aug. 18, 1962; children: Melissa Michelle, Adam Jonathan. BSc, U. Calif., Berkeley, 1959, MS, 1960, PhD, 1963. Registered profl. engr., Calif. Asst. specialist U. Calif. Forest Products Labs., 1961-62; asst. mech. engr., 1962-63; lectr. mech. engring. U. Calif., Berkeley, 1962-63, asst. prof., 1967-69, asst. research engr., 1968-69, assoc. prof., assoc. research engr., 1969-73, prof., 1973—, vice chmn. mech. engring. dept., 1976-80, 83-86, chmn. mech. engring. dept., 1987-91, vice chancellor univ. rels., FANUC chair mech. systems, 1991—; research fellow U. Birmingham, Eng., 1963-64; asst. prof. Carnegie Inst. Tech., 1964-67; vis. prof. Norwegian Inst. Wood Tech., 1972-73, vis. sr. scientist, 1976, 78, 80, 84, 85; cons. in engring. design and analysis; sr. scientist Alexander Von Humboldt Found., Fed. Republic Germany, 1988, Japan Soc. for Promotion of Sci., 1991; mem. adv. bd. for mech. engring. Ga. Inst. Tech., Carnegie Mellon U.; pres. U. Calif. Berkeley Found.; trustee Behring-Hofmann Ednl. Inst. Mem. editl. bd. Soma Jour. Sound and Vibration, Machine Vibration; contbr. articles to profl. jours.; patentee in field. NSF fellow, 1963-64; recipient Disting. Teaching award, U. Calif., 1971, Pi Tau Sigma Excellence in Teaching award, U. Calif., 1975, Humboldt Prize, Fed. Republic Germany, 1988, Frederick W. Taylor Rsch. medal. Soc. Mfg. Engrs., 1991, Hetenyi award Soc. Exptl. Mechanics, 1992. Fellow NAE, AAAS, ASME (Blackall award 1975, v.p. environ. and transp. 1986-90, nat. chmn. noise control and acoustics 1980-84, chmn. San Francisco sect. 1978-79, Disting. Svc. award 1991, Charles Russ Richards award 1994, Rayleigh lectr. 1994), Internat. Acad. Wood Sci., Acoustical Soc. Am.; mem. ASTM (com. on snow skiing F-27 1984-87, chmn. new projects subcom.), Am. Acad. Mechanics, Am. Soc. Biomechanics, Orthopaedic Rsch. Soc., Internat. Soc. Skiing Safety (v.p., sec. 1977-85, bd. dirs. 1977—, chmn. sci. com. 1985—), Sigma Xi, Pi Tau Sigma, Tau Beta Pi. Office: U Calif 2440 Bancroft Way Berkeley CA 94704-1603

MOTHERSHEAD, J. LELAND, III, dean; b. Boston, Jan. 10, 1939; s. John L. Jr. and Elizabeth Rankin (Crossett) M.; m. Therese Petkelis, June 23, 1963; 1 child, John Leland VI. BA, Carleton Coll., 1960; MA in Tchg., Brown U., 1963. Tchr. Tabor Acad., Marion, Mass., 1962-63, Chadwick Sch., Rolling Hills, Calif., 1963-66; tchr., adminstr. Flintridge (Calif.) Prep. Sch., 1966-75, head lower sch., 1972-74, dir. student affairs, 1974-75; tchr. Southwestern Acad., San Marino, Calif., 1979-83, dean, 1983—. Mem. Western Assn. Schs. and Colls. (evaluation team 1994), Rotary (pres. San Marino Club 1994—). Avocation: building historic wooden ship models. Home: 1145 Oak Grove Ave San Marino CA 91108-1028 Office: Southwestern Acad 2800 Monterey Rd San Marino CA 91108-1780

MOTHERWAY, JOSEPH EDWARD, mechanical engineer, educator; b. Providence, Jan. 28, 1930; s. Edward John and Josephine Dorothea (Conway) M.; m. Sally Alicia Doherty, June 11, 1955; children: Carmel A., Suzanne M., Joseph Edward, Mavis E., Melita A., Megan L., William D., Edward J., Mara A. Sc.B., Brown U., 1955; M.S., U. Conn., 1961; postgrad., Columbia U., 1965-67; Ph.D., U. Conn., 1970. Mech. engr. Standard Oil (N.J.), Bayway, 1955-56; design engr. Electric Boat div. Gen. Dynamic Corp., Groton, Conn., 1956-58; design group leader Electric Boat div. Gen. Dynamic Corp., 1958-59; sr. project engr. Remington Rand Univac Lab., South Norwalk, Conn., 1959-60; chief engr. C.H.I. div. Textron, Inc., Warwick, R.I., 1960-64; lectr. Brown U., Providence, 1962-64; asst. prof. mech. engring. U. Bridgeport, Conn., 1964-65; assoc. prof. U. Bridgeport, 1965-70, Bullard prof. engring. design, 1970-82, head dept. mech. engring., 1971-75; prof. mech. engring. U. Mass., 1982—; pres. Alpha Engring. Co., 1975-96; Cons. U.S. Navy, 1965-69, Dorr-Oliver Inc., Consol. Controls Corp., Energy Research Corp., Malcolm Pirnie Engrs. Assoc. editor: Jour. Mech. Design, 1978-80; contbr. articles to profl. jours. Served with USMC, 1949-53. Recipient Engring. Service award Brown Engring. Assn., 1962; NSF Sci. Faculty fellow, 1968-69. Mem. ASME, Soc. Exptl. Mechanics, Am. Soc. Engring. Edn., Brown Engring. Assn. (pres. 1968-69), Sigma Xi, Tau Beta Pi. Home: 360 Earle Dr North Kingstown RI 02852-6245 Office: Dept Mech Engring U Mass Amherst MA 01003 *died, Feb. 8, 1996.*

MOTLEY, CONSTANCE BAKER (MRS. JOEL WILSON MOTLEY), federal judge, former city official; b. New Haven, Sept. 14, 1921; d. Willoughby Alva and Rachel (Huggins) Baker; m. Joel Wilson Motley, Aug. 18, 1946; 1 son, Joel Wilson, III. AB, NYU, 1943; LLB, Columbia U., 1946. Bar: N.Y. bar 1948. Mem. Legal Def. and Ednl. Fund, NAACP, 1945-65; mem. N.Y. State Senate, 1964-65; pres. Manhattan Borough, 1965-66; U.S. dist. judge So. Dist. N.Y., 1966-82, chief judge, 1982-86, sr. judge, 1986—. Mem. N.Y. State Adv. Council Employment and Unemployment Ins., 1958-64. Mem. Assn. Bar City N.Y. Office: US Dist Ct US Courthouse 500 Pearl St New York NY 10007-1501

MOTLEY, JOHN PAUL, psychiatrist, consultant; b. Carbondale, Pa., July 5, 1927; s. Joseph Adrian and Lillian (McCormick) M.; BS, Georgetown U., 1951; MD, Hahnemann Med. Coll., Phila., 1955; children: Marianne, Patricia, Kathleen, John Paul, Elizabeth, Joseph A. III, Grace, Michael. Intern, Hahnemann Med. Coll. Hosp., Phila., 1955-56; resident in psychiatry Inst. of Living, Hartford, Conn., 1956-59; practice medicine specializing in psychiatry, Point Pleasant, N.J., 1961—; mem. staff Jersey Shore Med. Ctr., 1961-72, chief of psychiatry, 1970-72; mem. staff Point Pleasant Hosp., 1961—, chief of psychiatry, 1961—; cons. in forensic psychiatry to various cts. and agys. Served with U.S. Army, 1944-46, ETO. Diplomate Am. Bd. Psychiatry and Neurology. Fellow Am. Psychiat. Assn.; mem. AMA, Royal Coll. Psychiatry, Am. Coll. Psychiatry, N.J. Psychiat. Assn. (past pres.). Clubs: Springlake Golf. Republican. Roman Catholic. Office: 3822 River Rd Point Pleasant Beach NJ 08742-2067

MOTSINGER, JOHN KINGS, lawyer; b. Winston-Salem, N.C., Aug. 13, 1947; s. Madison Eugene and Margaret Mary (Kings) M.; m. Elisabeth Sykes, June 18, 1989; children: Christian Sykes, Lissa Sykes, John, Jr. BA, Washington & Lee U., 1970; MS, Georgetown U., 1972; JD, Wake Forest U., 1983. Bar: N.C. 1983, U.S. Dist. Ct. (mid. dist.) N.C. 1984. Consumer affairs assoc. U.S Postal Svc., Washington, 1972-73; pres., gen. mgr. Sta. WIPS-Radio, Ticonderoga, N.Y., 1973-79; staff atty. United Guaranty Corp., Greensboro, N.C., 1983-86, Republic Mortgage Ins. Co., Winston-Salem, 1986-91; v.p. law RMIC Corp., Winston-Salem, 1988-91; exec. dir. Carolina Concilation Svcs. Corp., 1992—. Pres.-elect Unitarian-Universalist Fellowship of Winston-Salem, 1993-94. Mem. ABA, N.C. Bar Assn. (corp. counsel sect. councilor 1989-93), N.C. State Bar, Acad. of Family Mediators. Democrat. Unitarian-Universalist. Avocations: jogging, music, reading. Home: 204 W Cascade Ave Winston Salem NC 27127-2029 Office: Carolina Conciliation Svcs Corp 1001 S Marshall St Ste 65 Winston Salem NC 27101-5858

MOTT, STEWART RAWLINGS, business executive, political activist; b. Flint, Mich., Dec. 4, 1937; s. Charles Stewart and Ruth (Rawlings) M.; m. Kappy Wells, Oct. 13, 1979; 1 child, Samuel Apple Axle. Grad., Deerfield (Mass.) Acad., 1955; B.S. in Bus. Adminstrn, Columbia, 1961, B.A. in Comparative Lit, 1961, postgrad. English lit., 1961-62. Exec. trainee various cos., 1956-63; English instr. Eastern Mich. U., 1963-64; corp. dir. U.S. Sugar Corp., Clewiston, Fla., 1965—; investor various diversified cos., 1968—. Founder Flint Community Planned Parenthood, 1963; pres., founder Spectemur Agendo (merged with S.R. Mott Charitable Trust 1989), N.Y.C. and Flint, 1965—; bd. dirs. Fund For Peace, N.Y.C., 1967—, S.R. Mott Charitable Trust, 1968—, Nat. Com. for Effective Congress, N.Y.C., 1968—, Planned Parenthood Fedn. Am., 1964-81, Am. Commn. on U.S.-Soviet Rels., 1977-92, Citizens Research Found., 1977—, Ams. for Dem. Action, 1978-90, Friends of Family Planning, 1979-84, Voters for Choice, 1979-89; bd. dirs., founder Fund Constl. Govt., 1974—; bd. dirs. Population Action Council, 1978-82; maj. donor McCarthy, McGovern, Anderson campaigns. Mem. Phi Beta Kappa. *At age 18 I realized that two problems confront planet earth that dwarf and aggravate all conventional problems: namely the threat of nuclear war and the continuing worldwide population explosion. Coming to grips with these realities, I decided to dedicate my life to help find solutions to these two problems through public service in philanthropy and politics.*

MOTT, VINCENT VALMON, publisher, author; b. Washington, La., Sept. 18, 1916; s. Lucius and Marie (LeDoux) M.; m. Margaret McDonald, June 19, 1948; children: Vincent Valmon, Helene Virginia, John Michael. AB, Xavier U., 1938; MA, Fordham U., 1947, PhD, 1956. Instr. social sci. U. Scranton, Pa., 1947-51; instr. econs. Seton Hall U., South Orange, N.J., 1952-53; asst. prof. Seton Hall U., 1954-58, asso. prof., 1958-66, prof. mktg., 1966—; adj. asso. prof. sociology St. Peters Coll., Jersey City, 1955-60; Pres. Florham Park Press, Florham Park, N.J., 1957—; pres., prin. stockholder V.V.R.&D., Inc. Author: The American Consumer, 1972, (with N. Chirovsky) Philosophy in Economic Thought, 1972, Philosophical Foundations of Economic Doctrines, 1978, The Creole, 1991, Academia Revisited, 1994; editor: Jour. Bus., Seton Hall U., 1963-64. Mem. bd. advisers Scranton Inst. Indsl. Relations, 1949-50. Served with AUS, 1940-45. Home and Office: 12 Leslie Ave Florham Park NJ 07932-2165

MOTTALE, MOIS, oil industry executive. With Fallek Chemical Internat., Milan, Italy, 1974-80; pres., ceo. Aectra Refining and Marketing, Houston, 1980—. Office: Aectra Refining & Marketing 3 Riverway Ste 2000 Houston TX 77056-1909*

MOTTET, NORMAN KARLE, pathologist, educator; b. Renton, Wash., Jan. 8, 1924; s. Louis John and Amalia (Lentzner) M.; M. Nancy Noble, June 21, 1952; children: Gretchen, Kurt, Mark. BS summa cum laude, Wash. State U., 1947; MD, Yale U., 1952. Diplomate: Am. bd. Pathology. Postdoctoral fellow Strangeways Research Lab., Cambridge, Eng., 1952-53, vis. scientist, 1969-70; rotating intern, then intern in pathology Yale Med. Ctr., 1953-55, resident in pathology, 1955-56, mem. faculty med. Sch., 1951-52, 55-59; pathologist, dir. labs. Griffin Hosp., Derby, Conn., 1955-59; mem. faculty U. Wash. Med. Sch., Seattle, 1959—, prof. pathology, 1966—; dir. hosp. pathology Univ. Hosp. U. Wash. Med. Sch., Seattle, 1959-74; mem. extramural program council Fred Hutchinson Carcer Research Ctr., 1975. Contbr. articles to med. jours.; mem. editorial bds. Served with AUS, 1942-45. James Hudson Brown fellow, 1949-50; fellow nat. Found. Infantile Paralysis, 1952-53; recipient Keese prize Yale U., 1952; trainee pathology USPHS, 1954-55; spl. rsch. fellow USPHS, 1969-70. Fellow Am. Soc. Clin. Pathology; mem. AAAS, Am. Soc. Pathology, Tetatology Soc., Internat. Soc. Trace Element Research, Internat. Com. Occupational Health, Internat. Com. Trace Metals, Sigma Xi, Alpha Omega Alpha. Home: E 360 Old Olson Rd Shelton WA 98584 Office: U Wash Sch Medicine Dept Path Seattle WA 98195

MOTTO, JEROME ARTHUR, psychiatry educator; b. Kansas City, Mo., Oct. 16, 1921. MD, U. Calif., San Francisco, 1951. Diplomate Am. Bd. Neurology and Psychiatry. Intern San Francisco Gen. Hosp., 1951-52; resident Johns Hopkins Hosp., Balt., 1952-55; sr. resident U. Calif., San Francisco, 1955-56, from asst. prof. to prof. emeritus., 1956—. Contbr. articles to profl. jours. With AUS, 1942-46; ETO. Fellow Am. Psychiatric Assn. (life).

MOTTOLA, GARY F., lawyer; b. Englewood, N.J., May 2, 1947; s. Ross F. and Marie (Richards) M.; m. Irene Mottola, Apr. 19, 1981; 1 child, Alexandra. AB, Harvard U., 1969; JD, U. Calif., Berkeley, 1972. Bar: N.Y. 1973, N.J. 1977. Ptnr. Simpson Thacher & Bartlett, N.Y.C.; prof. law Vt. Law Sch. Office: Simpson Thacher & Bartlett 425 Lexington Ave New York NY 10017-3903*

MOTTRAM-DOSS, RENÉE, corporate executive; b. Erie, Pa., Apr. 7, 1939; d. Robert Harlan and Anita Gray; m. Arden Doss Jr., Mar. 7, 1986; children from previous marriage: Lisa Marie Mottram, Jeffrey Scott Mottram. Student, Barry U., 1968-70, Vt. State Coll., 1975-76. Various positions D.W.G. Corp., Royal Crown Cola, Arby's, Victor Posner Affiliated Cos., Miami Beach, Fla., 1972-90, sr. v.p., 1989—; chmn. Renar Devel. Co., St. Lucie West, Fla., 1990—. Bd. dirs. Coconut Grove Playhouse, Miami, Barry U., Miami. Recipient Twin award YWCA, 1984; named Outstanding Woman of Yr. Dade County Fla., 1983. Office: Renar Development Co. 7500 Reserve Blvd Port Saint Lucie FL 34986-3237*

MOTULSKY, ARNO GUNTHER, geneticist, physician, educator; b. Fischhausen, Germany, July 5, 1923; came to U.S., 1941; s. Herman and Rena (Sass) Molton; m. Gretel C. Stern, Mar. 22, 1945; children: Judy, Harvey, Arlene. Student, Cen. YMCA Coll., Chgo., 1941-43, Yale U., 1943-44; BS, U. Ill., 1945, MD, 1947, DSc (hon.), 1982, MD (hon.), 1991. Diplomate Am. Bd. Internal Medicine, Am. Bd. Med. Genetics. Intern, fellow, resident Michael Reese Hosp., Chgo., 1947-51; staff mem. charge clin. investigation dept. hematology Army Med. Service Grad. Sch., Walter Reed Army Med. Ctr., Washington, 1952-53; research assoc. internal medicine George Washington U. Sch. Medicine, 1952-53; from instr. to assoc. prof. dept. medicine U. Wash. Sch. Medicine, Seattle, 1953-61, prof. medicine, prof. genetics, 1961—; head div. med. genetics, dir. genetics clinic Univ. Hosp., Seattle, 1959-89; dir. Ctr. for Inherited Diseases, Seattle, 1972-90; attending physician Univ. Hosp., Seattle; cons. Pres.'s Commn. for Study of Ethical Problems in Medicine and Biomed. and Behavioral Research, 1979-83; cons. various coms. NRC, NIH, WHO, others. Editor Am. Jour. Human Genetics, 1969-75, Human Genetics, 1969—. Commonwealth Fund fellow in human genetics Univ. Coll., London, 1957-58; John and Mary Markle scholar in med. sci., 1957-62; fellow Ctr. Advanced Study in Behavioral Scis., Stanford U., 1976-77, Inst. Advanced Study, Berlin, 1984. Fellow ACP, AAAS; mem. NAS, Internat. Soc. Hematology, Am. Fedn. Clin. Research, Genetics Soc. Am., Western Soc. Clin. Research, Am. Soc. Human Genetics, Am. Soc. Clin. Investigation, Am. Assn. Physicians, Inst. of Medicine, Am. Acad. Arts and Scis. Home: 4347 53rd Ave NE Seattle WA 98105-4938 Office: U Wash Divsn Med Genetics Box 356423 Seattle WA 98195-6423

MOTZ, DIANA GRIBBON, federal judge; b. Washington, July 15, 1943; d. Daniel McNamara and Jane (Retzler) Gribbon; m. John Frederick Motz, Sept. 20, 1968; children: Catherine Jane, Daniel Gribbon. BA, Vassar Coll., 1965; LLB, U. Va., 1968. Bar: U.S. Dist. Ct. Md. 1969, U.S. Ct. Appeals (4th cir.) 1969, U.S. Supreme Ct. 1980. Assoc. Piper & Marbury, Balt., 1968-71; asst. atty. gen. State of Md., Balt., 1972-81, chief of litigation, 1981-86; ptnr. Frank, Bernstein, Conaway & Goldman, Balt., 1986-91; judge Md. Ct. of Special Appeals, Md., 1991-94, U.S. Ct. Appeals (4th Cir.), 1994—. Mem. ABA, Md. Bar Assn., Balt. City Bar Assn. (exec. com. 1988), Am. Law Inst., Am. Bar Found., Md. Bar Found., Lawyers Round Table, Fed. Cts. Study Com., Wranglers Law Club. Roman Catholic. Office: 101 W Lombard St Ste 920 Baltimore MD 21201-2626

MOTZ, JOHN FREDERICK, federal judge; b. Balt., Dec. 30, 1942; s. John Eldered and Catherine (Grauel) M.; m. Diana Jane Gribbon, Sept. 20, 1968; children: Catherine Jane, Daniel Gribbon. AB, Wesleyan U., Conn., 1964; LLB, U. Va., 1967. Bar: Md. 1967, U.S. Ct. Appeals (4th cir.) 1968, U.S. Dist. Ct. Md. 1968. Law clk. to Hon. Harrison L. Winter U.S. Ct. Appeals (4th cir.), 1967-68; assoc. Venable, Baetjer & Howard, Balt., 1968-69; asst. U.S. atty. U.S. Atty.'s Office, Balt., 1969-71; assoc. Venable, Baetjer & Howard, Balt., 1971-75, ptnr., 1976-81; U.S. atty. U.S. Atty.'s Office, Balt., 1981-85; judge U.S. Dist. Ct. Md., Balt., 1985—. Trustees Friends Sch., Balt., 1970-77, 1981-88, Sheppard Pratt Hosp., 1987—. Mem. ABA, Md. State Bar Assn., Am. Bar Found., Am. Law Inst., Am. Coll. Trial Lawyers. Republican. Mem. Soc. of Friends. Office: US Dist Ct 101 W Lombard St Rm 510 Baltimore MD 21201-2607

MOTZ, KENNETH LEE, former farm organization official; b. Grand Junction, Colo., Mar. 6, 1922; s. Harold I. and Acquila (Ulmer) M.; m. Margaret Florence Mitchell, Oct. 9, 1948; children: Gwendolyn Ann, Stephen Mitchell. AA, Mesa Jr. Coll., 1942; BSBA, Denver U., 1947. Bookkeeper Farmers Union Mktg. Assn., Denver, 1942-43; asst. sec. Nat. Farmers Union, Denver, 1947-50, 59-66, sec.-treas., 1966-72, 85-86, treas., asst. sec., 1972-85, retired, 1987; treas. Green Thumb, Inc., 1980-85, sec.-treas., 1985-86, retired, 1987; ins. acct. Nat. Farmers Union Ins. Cos., Denver, 1952-59. sec. uniform pension com. Nat. Farmers Union, 1959-93; Dem. precinct committeeman, 1960-68; elder Calvary Presbyn. Ch. Maj. USMCR, ret. 1982. Mem. Masons, Delta Sigma Pi. Presbyterian. Home: 11186 E Baltic Dr Aurora CO 80014-1070

MOTZ, MARVIN D., academic administrator, retired educator; b. Alamosa, Colo., Jan. 28, 1932; s. Edward Arthur and Naomi Ivy (Kenton) M.; m. Mary Myra Hill, Jan. 18, 1958; children: Natalie Ann, Stephanie Lynn, Thomas Scott, Susan Marie. BA in Bus. Adminstrn. & Secondary Edn., Adams State Coll., 1958, EdM in Secondary Edn. and Counseling, 1959; EdD in Psychology, Counseling & Guidance, U. No. Colo., 1969. Asst. dir. pub. rels. Adams State Coll., Alamosa, 1959-66, asst. prof. psychology, 1966-69, assoc. prof. psychology, 1969-72, prof. psychology, 1972-95, interim pres., 1980-81, 94-95; dir. Humor Acad., Alamosa, 1985-95. Trustee San Luis Valley Med. Ctr., Alamosa, 1987-95. Recipient Centennial Tchr. award State Bd. Trustees, 1990. Presbyterian. Avocations: sports, fishing, magic. Office: Humor Acad 91 Sierra Alamosa CO 81101

MOUCH, FRANK MESSMAN, college president, priest. BA, Pontifical Coll.; MEd, U. Fla.; STL, Angelicum U., Rome. Ordained priest Roman Cath. Ch., 1958. Pres. Cardinal Mooney High Sch., Sarasota, Fla., 1966-68; suptd. edn. Diocese of St. Petersburg, Fla., 1968-74; trustee St. Leo (Fla.) Coll., 1970-74, pres., 1987—; rector Pontifical Coll. Josephinum, 1974-84; dir. planning, devel., communications and bldg. Diocese of Venice, Fla., 1984-86; bd. dirs. Fla. Cath., 1985-87; trustee St. Vincent de Paul Sem., Boynton Beach, Fla., 1985-87, Acad. of Holy Names of Fla., 1992—; chaplain Cath. students U. Fla., 1964-66; asst. chancellor Diocese of St. Augustine, Fla., 1963-64; pastor Holy Redeemer Ch., Jacksonville, Fla., St. Martha Ch., Sarasota, others. Mem. Pontifical Coll. Alumni Assn. (Outstanding Alumni of Yr. 1987). Office: St Leo Coll Office of Pres 33701 State Rd 52W Saint Leo FL 33574-9999

MOUCHLY-WEISS, HARRIET, business executive; b. N.Y.C., Aug. 12, 1942; d. Robert and Anita (Shawmut) Berg; m. Charles Weiss, Sept. 13, 1975; children: Noa, Yoav. BA, Muhlenberg Coll., 1960; MA in Clin. Psychology, Hebrew U., 1964; 1993—. Clin. psychologist Hadassah Hosp., Israel, 1962-65; chmn. Ruder & Finn, Israel, 1968-80; sr. v.p. Ruder Finn & Rotman, N.Y.C., 1980-86; pres. GCI Internat., N.Y.C., 1986-92; mng. ptnr. Strategy XXI Group, Ltd., N.Y.C., 1993—. Bd. dirs. N.Y. State Gov.'s World Trade Coun., Com. for Econ. Growth Israel; bd. dirs. U. Haifa, Capital Circle, Com. for Econ. Growth of Israel, Israel Policy Forum; trustee Internat. Ctr. for Peace in the Mid East; State of the World Forum advisor; mem. Friends of the UN, The Chinese Found. of Culture and Arts for Children. Recipient cert. of appreciation, HUD. Mem. Women in Comms., Pub. Rels. Soc. Am., Itnernat. Pub. Rels. Assn., Com. of 200 (N.E. chair), Friends of UN. Avocations: art, art history, politics. Office: Strategy XXI Group Ltd 515 Madison Ave Fl 34 New York NY 10022-5403

MOUL, MAXINE BURNETT, state official; b. Oakland, Nebr., Jan. 26, 1947; d. Einer and Eva (Jacobson) Burnett; m. Francis Moul, Apr. 20, 1972; 1 child, Jeff. BS in Journalism, U. Nebr., 1969; DHL (hon.), Peru State Coll., 1993. Sunday feature writer, photographer Sioux City Iowa Jour., 1969-71; reporter, photographer, editor Maverick Media, Inc., Syracuse, Nebr., 1971-73, editor, pub., 1974-83, pres., 1983-90; grant writer, asst. coord. Nebr. Regional Med. Program, Lincoln, 1973-74; lt. gov. State of Nebr., Lincoln, 1991-93; dir. Dept. Econ. Devel., Lincoln, 1993—. Mem. Dem. Nat. Com., Washington, 1988-92, Nebr. Dem. State Ctrl. Com., Lincoln, 1974-88; del. Dem. Nat. Conf., 1972, 88, 92; mem. exec. com. Nebr. Dem. Party, Lincoln, 1988-93. Recipient Margaret Sanger award Planned Parenthood, Lincoln, 1991, Champion of Small Bus. award Nebr. Bus. Devel. Ctr., Omaha, 1991, Toll fellowship Coun. State Govts., Lexington, Ky., 1992. Mem. Bus. and Profl. Womem, Nebr. Mgmt. Assn. (Silver Knight award 1992), Nat. Conf. Lt. Govs. (bd. dirs. 1991-93), Nebr. Press Women, Women Execs. in State Govt., Cmty. Devel. Soc., U. Nebr.-Lincoln Journalism Alumni. Democrat. Avocations: reading, gardening. Office: State of Nebr PO Box 94666 Lincoln NE 68509-4666

MOUL, ROBERT GEMMILL, II, lawyer; b. Washington, July 7, 1961; s. Robert Gemmill and Mary Ann (Sargent) M.; m. Susan Marie Beck, Apr. 30, 1994. BA in History, George Washington U., 1983; JD, George Mason U., 1987. Bar: Va. 1988, U.S. Ct. Appeals (4th cir.) 1993, U.S. Dist. Ct. (ea. dist.) Va. 1994. Intern D.C. Corp. Counsel, Washington, 1982; law clk. Dunaway, McCarthy & Dye, Washington, 1983-85, Holland & Knight, Washington, 1985-86; gen. counsel Piedmont Photo Svcs., Charlotte, N.C., 1988-93; pvt. practice Vienna, Va., 1988-93; assoc. Lotfi & Assocs., P.C., Washington, 1993—; legal corr. NBC News, 1994. Spokesman Arlington (Va.) St. People Assistance Network, 1994. Pro Bono Publico, Alexandria and Arlington Bar Assns., 1993. Mem. ABA, Assn. Trial Lawyers Am., Va. Trial Lawyers Assn. Avocations: tennis, running, chess. Office: Lotfi & Assocs PC Ste 230 1101 30th St Washington DC 20007-3708

MOUL, WILLIAM CHARLES, lawyer; b. Columbus, Ohio, Jan. 12, 1940; s. Charles Emerson and Lillian Ann (Mackenbach) M.; m. Margine Ann Tessendorf, June 10, 1962; children—Gregory, Geoffrey. B.A., Miami U., Oxford, Ohio, 1961; J.D., Ohio State U., 1964. Bar: Ohio 1964, U.S. dist. Ct. (so. dist.) Ohio 1965, U.S. Ct. Appeals (2d cir.) 1982, U.S. Ct. Appeals (6th cir.) 1984, U.S. Ct. Appeals (3d cir.) 1985. Assoc., ptnr. George, Greek, King, McMahon & McConnaughey, Columbus, Ohio, 1964-79; ptnr. McConnaughey, Stradley, Mone & Moul, Columbus, 1979-81; ptnr.-in-charge Thompson, Hine & Flory, Columbus, 1981—. Chmn. Upper Arlington Civil Service Commn., Ohio, 1981-86. Mem. ABA,Ohio State Bar Assn. (labor sect. bd. 1983—), Columbus Bar Assn. (chmn. ethics com. 1980-82), Lawyers Club Columbus (pres. 1976-77), Athletic Club, Scioto Country Club, Wedgewood Country Club, Masons. Lutheran. Home: 2512 Danvers Ct Columbus OH 43220-2822 Office: Thompson Hine & Flory 10 W Broad St Ste 700 Columbus OH 43215-3419

MOULD, DIANE RENEE, pharmacologist; b. Englewood, N.J., Oct. 6, 1960; d. Spencer Herbert and Beverly Ann (Fortunato) M. BS in Chem. Biology, Stevens Inst. Tech., 1983; PhD of Pharmaceutics, Ohio State U., 1989. Rsch. asst. Stevens Inst. Tech., Hoboken, N.J., 1979-83; sci. rsch. assoc. Lederle Labs., Pearle River, N.Y., 1983-84; tchg. asst. Coll. Pharmacy Ohio State U., Columbus, 1984-90; clin. rsch. investigator Hoffmann-La Roche, Nutley, N.J., 1990—; cons. Projection Rsch., Clifton, N.J., 1992—, Knorr Co., Smoke Rise Kinnelon, N.J., 1983-90. Contbr. articles to profl. jours. Fellow Am. Found. Pharm. Edn., 1986-89. Fellow Phi Kappa Phi (award 1985); mem. Am. Assn. Pharm. Sci., Am. Soc. Clin. Pharmacology and Therapeutics, Drug Info. Assn. Avocations: painting, music, weight lifting, photography, parachuting.

MOULDER, WILLIAM H., chief of police; b. Kansas City, Mo., Feb. 19, 1938; s. Roscoe B. and Charleen M. (Flye) M.; m. Louise M. Pollaro, Aug. 2, 1957; children: Deborah, Ralph, Robert. BA, U. Mo., Kansas City, 1971, MA, 1976. Cert. police officer, Mo., Iowa. From police officer to maj. Kansas City (Mo.) Police Dept., 1959-84; chief of police City of Des Moines, 1984—. Mem. Internat. Assn. Chiefs of Police, Police Exec. Rsch. Forum, Iowa Police Exec. Forum. Avocations: racquetball, travel. Office: Office of Police Chief 25 E 1st St Des Moines IA 50309-4800

MOULDS, JOHN F., federal judge; m. Elizabeth Fry, Aug. 29, 1964; children: Donald B., Gerald B. Student, Stanford U., 1955-58; BA with honors, Calif. State U., Sacramento, 1960; JD, U. Calif, Berkeley, 1963. Bar: U.S. Supreme Ct., U.S. Dist. Ct. (no. dist.) Calif., U.S. Dist. Ct. (ea. dist.) Calif. 1968, U.S. Ct. Claims 1982, U.S. Ct. Appeals (9th cir.) 1967, Calif. Rsch. analyst Calif. State Senate Fact-Finding Com. on Edn., 1960-61; adminstrv. asst. Senator Albert S. Rodda, Calif., 1961-63; staff atty. Calif. Rural Legal Assistance, Marysville, 1966-68; dir. atty. Marysville field office and Sacramento legis. adv. office Calif. Rural Legal Assistance, 1968-69; staff atty. Sacramento Legal Aid, 1968-69; ptnr. Blackmon, Isenberg & Moulds, 1969-85, Isenberg, Moulds & Hemmer, 1985; magistrate judge U.S. Dist. Ct. (ea. dist.) Calif., 1985—, chief magistrate jduge, 1988—; moot ct. and trial practice judge U. Calif. Davis Law Sch., 1975—, U. of Pacific McGeorge Coll. Law, 1985—; part-time U.S. magistrate judge U.S. Dist. Ct. (ea. dist.) Calif., 1983-85; mem. 9th Cir. Capital Case Com., 1992—, U.S. Jud. Conf. Com. on the Magistrate Judge Sys., 1992—, Adv. Com. to the Magistrate Judges' Divsn. Adminstv. Office of U.S. Jud. Conf., 1989—. Author: (with others) Review of California Code Legislation, 1965, Welfare Recipients' Handbook, 1967; editor: Ninth Circuit Capital Punishment Handbook, 1991. Atty. Sacramento Singlemen's Self-Help Ctr., 1969-74; active Sacramento Human Relations Commn., 1969-75, chair, 1974-75; active community support orgn. U. Calif. at Davis Law Sch., 1971—; mem., atty. Sacramento Community Coalition for Media Change, 1972-75; bd. dirs. Sacramento Country Day Sch., 1982-90, Sacramento Pub. Libr. Found., 1985-87; active various polit. orgns. and campaigns, 1960-82. Mem. ABA, Fed. Bar Assn., Nat. Coun. Magistrates (cir. dir. 1986-88, treas. 1988-89, 2d v.p. 1989-90, 1st v.p. 1990-91), Fed. Magistrate Judges Assn. (pres.-elect 1991, pres. 1992-93), Calif. State-Fed. Jud. Coun. Conf. (panelist capital habeas corpus litigation 1992), Fed. Jud. Ctr. Training Conf. for U.S. Magistrate Judges (panel leader 1993), Milton L. Schwartz Inns of Ct. Office: 5054 US Courthouse 650 Capitol Mall Sacramento CA 95814-4708

MOULE, WILLIAM NELSON, electrical engineer; b. Highland Park, Mich., Sept. 13, 1924; s. Hollis Creager and Kate De Ette (Hill) M.; m. Barbara Ann Bagley, June 27, 1953; children: Janice Louise, Robert Hollis (dec.), Linda Anne, Nancy Lynn Moule Moles. BSEE, Mich. State U., 1949; MSEE, U. Pa., 1957. Reg. profl. engr., N.J. Design engr. Radio Corp. of Am., Camden, N.J., 1949-59; sr. design engr. Radio Corp. of Am., Moorestown, N.J., 1959-67; sr. engr. Emerson Elec. Co., St. Louis, 1967-70, Emerson Elec. Rantec Divsn., Calabasas, Calif., 1970; sr. staff engr. Raytheon Co., Santa Barbara, Calif., 1970-73, ITT Gilfillan, Van Nuys, Calif., 1973, Jet Propulsion Lab., Pasadena, Calif., 1973-79; sr. rsch devel. engr. Lockheed Advanced Devel. Co., Burbank, Calif., 1979—. Patentee numerous inventions, 1956—. Dir. nat. alumni bd. Mich. State U., East Lansing, 1984-87; pres. Big Ten Club of So. Calif., L.A., 1992. Staff sgt. USAF, 1943-46. Mem. IEEE (sr., L.A. chpt. sec., treas. Antennas and Propagation soc. 1987-89, vice chmn. 1989-90, chmn. 1990-91), 305th Bombardment Group Meml. Assn. (life). Democrat. Presbyn. Avocations: travel, photography, genealogy. Home: 5831 Fitzpatrick Rd Calabasas CA 91302 Office: Lockheed Martin Skunk Works 1011 Lockheed Wy Palmdale CA 93599

MOULTHROP, EDWARD ALLEN, architect, artist; b. Rochester, N.Y., May 22, 1916; s. Ray Josiah and Jetta (McDonald) M.; m. Mae Elizabeth Crotser, Jan 31, 1942; children: Mark, Philip, Samuel, Timothy. B.Arch., Western Res. U., 1939; M.F.A., Princeton, 1941. Asst. prof. architecture Ga. Inst. Tech., 1943-46, asst. prof. physics, 1944-46; chief designer Robert and Co. Asso. Architects and Engrs., Atlanta, 1948-72; prin. Edward Allen Moulthrop (architect and cons.), Atlanta, 1972—; 1st chmn. Ga. Art Commn., 1954-65. Exhibited in, Watercolor U.S.A., 1962, USIA traveling show to Russia, crafts, 1970, Wichita Nat. Decorative Arts and Ceramics Exhbn., 1972, Ga. artists exhibit, High Mus. Art, Atlanta, 1971, 72, 74, Vatican Mus., Italy, 1978; represented in permanent collections, Mus. Modern Art, N.Y.C., Boston Mus. Fine Arts, Met. Mus. Art, N.Y.C. (Recipient Nat. Design award Am. Inst. Steel Constrn. 1959, 67, 1st Purchase award for crafts Atlanta Arts Festival 1963, 64, 67, 72, 74, 77, 78, Craftsman U.S.A. award of merit 1966, Judges Choice award Western Colo. Center for Arts 1973, purchase award 1975, prize Marietta Coll. Crafts Nat. 1974, 76, Craftwork prize Am. Crafts Council 1976, 78, Ga. Gov.'s Award in Arts 1981), USIA traveling show to Europe, crafts, 1990-93, The Art of Woodturning, 1993—, Permanent Collection of the White House, 1993. Fellow AIA (pres. Ga. chpt. 1953), Am. Craft Coun.; mem. Ga. Engring. Soc. (pres. 1958, spl. hon. mem. 1969), Am. Craftsmens Coun. (Ga. rep. 1973-75), Ga. Designer Craftsmen (pres. 1975-76). Home and Office: 4260 Carmain Dr NE Atlanta GA 30342-3504

MOULTHROP, REBECCA LEE STILPHEN, elementary education educator; b. Lubbock, Tex., Mar. 5, 1944; d. Lee Edward and Geraldine (Lansford) Stilphen; m. John Stephen Martin Moulthrop, June 1967 (div. 1968); 1 child, Paul Martin. BS in edn., U. New Mex., 1966; MS in reading edn., Calif. State U., Fullerton, 1971; postgrad., U. LaVerne. Elem. tchr. Arnold Heights Elem. Sch., Moreno Valley, Calif., 1966-67, Hawthorn Elem. Sch., El Monte, Calif., 1968-69; chap. 1 reading specialist Posey Elem. Sch., Lubbock, 1971-72; elem. tchr. Arnold Heights Elem. Sch., Moreno Valley, 1972-74, Sunnymead Elem. Sch., Moreno Valley, 1974-80, Moreno Elem. Sch., Moreno Valley, 1980-88; chap. 1 program coord. Edgemont Elem. Sch., Moreno Valley, 1988-91; elem. tchr. Sunnymeadows Elem. Sch., Moreno Valley, 1991—; assertive discipline cons. Moreno Valley (Calif.) Unified Sch. Dist., 1979-85, mentor/tchr., 1985-89, adminstrn. designee/trainee, 1988-95; effective tchg./supervision coach Riverside (Calif.) County Sch. Office, 1984-87. Mem. NEA, Calif. Reading Assn., Internat. Reading Assn., Reading Edn. Guild, Delta Kappa Gamma, Phi Delta Kappa. Avocations: traveling, dancing, painting. Home: 12542 Peachleaf St Moreno Valley CA 92553 Office: Moreno Valley Unif Sch Dist 13911 Perris Blvd Moreno Valley CA 92553

MOULTON, DAVID AUBIN, library director; b. Portsmouth, N.H., Nov. 20, 1952; s. Howard Turner and Dorothy Margaret (McLaughlin) M. BA in History, U. New Hampshire, 1974; MLS, Simmons Coll., 1976. Asst. libr. Strayer Coll., Washington, 1976-83; dir. LRC Strayer Coll., Arlington, Va., 1983-86; dir. lbirs. Strayer Coll., Washington, 1987—; chair library networking com. Consortium for Continuing Higher Edn. in No. Va., 1987. Mem. covenants com. Parc East Condominium, Alexandria, Va, 1987-90. Mem. ALA, Dist. of Columbia Libr. Assn., Va. Libr. Assn., Phi Delta Kappa. Avocation: collecting childrens and boy's books, 1820-1940. Office: Strayer Coll 1025 15th St NW Washington DC 20005-2603

MOULTON, EDWARD QUENTIN, civil engineer, educator; b. Kalamazoo, Nov. 16, 1926; s. Burt Frederick and Esther (Fairchild) M.; m. Joy Wade, Jan. 2, 1954; children: Jennifer Fairchild, Charles Wade, David Frederick II, Alison Joy. BS, Mich. State U., 1947; MS, La. State U., 1948; PhD, U. Calif., Berkeley, 1956; DSc (hon.), Wittenberg U., 1980; LLD (hon.), Xavier U., 1983, Wilmington Coll., 1983. Registered profl. engr., Ohio. Instr. civil engring Mich. State U., 1947; hydraulic engring. fellow La. State U., 1947-48; engr. U.S. Waterways Expt. Sta., Vicksburg, Miss., 1948; rsch. fellow U. Wis., 1948-49; asst. prof. civil engring. Auburn U., 1949-50; lectr. civil engring. U. Calif., Berkeley, 1950-54; asst. prof. civil engring. Ohio State U., 1954-58, assoc. prof., 1958-64; asst. dean Ohio State U. (Grad. Sch.), 1958-62, assoc. dean Grad. Sch., Coll. Arts and Scis., chmn. geodetic sci., 1962-64, dean off-campus edn., asso. dean faculties for personnel budget, prof. engring. mechanics, 1964-66; dir. Coll. Sci. and Engring. Dayton campus Miami U.-Ohio State U., 1963-66; pres. U. S.D., 1966-68; exec. asst. to pres. Ohio State U., 1968-69, sec. trustees, 1968-79, prof. civil engring., 1968-79, v.p. adminstrv. ops., 1969-70, exec. v.p. adminstrv. ops., 1970-71, exec. v.p., 1971-73, v.p. bus. and adminstrn., 1973-79, v.p., sec. emeritus, 1984—; chancellor Ohio Bd. Regents, 1979-83, chancellor emeritus, 1984—; exec. v.p. Cranston Securities Co., 1983-84; pres. Lake Erie Coll., 1985-86; pres., gen. mgr. Columbus Symphony Orchestra, 1986-88; cons. civil engring. 1954—. Author articles, reports, bulls. on environ. engring. and edn. Trustee Blue Cross Ctrl. Ohio, 1971-77, 80-82, Columbus Symphony Orch., 1980-85, Riverside Meth. Hosp., 1979-95, chmn. fin. and assets com., 1983-94, treas., 1988-94, vice-chmn., 1994-95; nat. adv. coun. for small bus. to U.S. Sec. Treasury, 1975-76; steering com. Devel. Com. Greater Columbus, 1970-1980, chmn., 1978-79; nat. adv. coun. SBA, 1973-76; bd. dirs. Columbus Safety Coun., 1970-79, Greater Columbus Arts Coun., 1970-78, Mid-Ohio Health Planning Commn., 1973-74, Am. Univs. for Rsch. in Astronomy, 1972-79, Ohio Transp. Rsch. Ctr., 1979-83, U.S. Health Corp., 1995—; chmn. Grant/Riverside Meth. Hosps., 1995—; vice-chmn. Ohio Higher Edn. facilities Commn., 1979-83; active Ohio Sch. and Coll. Bd. Registration, 1979-83, Ohio Ednl. TV Commn., 1979-83, Midwest Edn. Commn., 1979-85; chmn. Columbus Symphony Grand Ball, 1983; chmn. judging Internat. Sci. and Engring. Fair, 1984. With USN, 1945-46. Fellow ASCE; mem. Ohio Hist. Soc. (bd. dirs. 1979-83), State Higher Edn. Exec. Officers (exec. com. 1981-83), Ohio Commodore, Scioto Country Club, Faculty Club (Columbus), Sigma Xi, Tau Beta Pi, Pi Mu Epsilon, Chi Epsilon, Delta Omega, Romophos, Sigma Alpha Epsilon. Congregationalist. Home: 1303 London Dr Columbus OH 43221-1541

MOULTON, HUGH GEOFFREY, lawyer, business executive; b. Boston, Sept. 18, 1933; s. Robert Selden and Florence (Bracq) M.; m. Catherine Anne Clark, Mar. 24, 1956; children: H. Geoffrey, Cynthia C. Moulton Bassett. B.A., Amherst Coll., 1955; LL.B., Yale U., 1958; postgrad. Advanced Mgmt. Program, Harvard U., 1984. Bar: Pa. 1959. Assoc. Montgomery, McCracken, Walker-Rhoads, Phila., 1958-66, ptnr., 1967-69; v.p., counsel Dolly Madison Industries, Inc., Phila., 1969-70; sec. Alco Std. Corp., Valley Forge, Pa., 1970-72, v.p. law, 1973-79, v.p., sec., gen. counsel, 1979-83, sr. v.p., gen. counsel, 1983-92, exec. v.p., chief adminstrv. officer, gen. counsel, 1992-94, exec. v.p., 1994—. Pres. Wissahickon Valley Watershed Assn., Ambler, Pa., 1975-78, treas., 1978—; mem. Pa. Coun. for Econ. Edn., bd. dirs., 1985-95; trustee Beaver Coll., 1991—. Mem. ABA, Pa. Bar Assn., Phila. Bar Assn., Am. Corp. Counsel Assn. (bd. dirs. Delaware Valley chpt. 1984-88, pres. 1986-87), Nature Conservancy (trustee Pa. chpt. 1991—, chmn. 1993—), Sunnybrook Golf Club (Plymouth Meeting, Pa.). Home: 300 Williams Rd Fort Washington PA 19034-2015 Office: Alco Standard Corp PO Box 834 Valley Forge PA 19482-0834

MOULTON, PHILLIPS PRENTICE, religion and philosophy educator; b. Cleve., Dec. 24, 1909; s. E. Phillips and Myrtle (Skeel) M.; m. Mary Cochran, June 14, 1947; children: Katharine, Lawrence. A.B., Ohio Wesleyan U., 1931; postgrad., Marburg U., Germany, 1931-32, Princeton Theol. Sem., 1941-42; B.D., Yale U., 1942, Ph.D., 1949. Religious work sec. Cleve. YMCA, 1937-40; nat. dir. univ. work Fed. Council Chs., 1944-47; coordinator religious activities Chgo. U., 1948-51; lectr. religion in higher edn. Union Theol. Sem., N.Y., 1951-54; chmn. dept. philosophy, coordinator gen.

edn. program Simpson Coll., Iowa, 1954-58; pres. Wesley Coll., prof. religion U. N.D., 1958-65, chmn. dept., 1963-65; prof. philosophy Adrian (Mich.) Coll., 1965-76; lectr. and cons. on small coll. athletics. Leader World Student Christian Fedn. Conf., 1951; Danforth lectr. religion and higher edn. Boston U., Northwestern U., summers 1953, 54; dir. Nat. Meth. Gt. Books Project, 1957; T.W. Brown fellow postdoctoral research Haverford Coll., 1965, 67-68; vis. scholar Union Theol. Sem., N.Y.C., 1971-72, Center for Study Higher Edn., U. Mich., 1976-78, Mil. Study Group, 1984-92. Author: Experiment in General Education, 1957, Violence—Or Aggressive Nonviolent Resistance, 1971, The Living Witness of John Woolman, 1973, Enhancing the Values of Intercollegiate Athletics at Small Colleges, 1978, Ammunition for Peacemakers, 1986 (winner Pilgrim Press manuscript contest); editor: Community Resources in Cleveland, Ohio, 1937, The Journal and Major Essays of John Woolman, 1971 (Am. Assn. State and Local History award of merit). Pres. Midwest Faculty Christian Fellowship, 1957-58; U.S. del. Ecumenical Youth and Internat. YMCA Conf., 1939; chmn. Nat. Danforth Campus Workshop, 1957; speaker 14th Internat. Philosophy Congress, Vienna, 1968. Am. Philos. Soc. research grantee, 1968; Inst. Internat. Edn. fellow, 1931-32; Hough fellow in sociology, 1936-37; Taylor Theol. fellow, 1931-32; Univ. scholar Yale, 1944-45. Mem. Am. Acad. Religion (pres. Midwest region 1961-62), Civilian-Based Def. Assn. (bd. dirs. 1986-92), Phi Beta Kappa, Delta Sigma Rho, Omicron Delta Kappa, Beta Theta Pi. Methodist, Quaker. Home: 17208 Friends House Rd Sandy Spring MD 20860-1200 *At age 16 I discovered the most important thing in life - a strong Christian faith. This has given me motivation, stability, and direction. It has stimulated me to question generally-accepted values, to distinguish the significant from the trivial, the enduring from the temporal. I believe the Christian interpretation of life provides the perspective needed to make one's efforts worthwhile.*

MOULTON, WILBUR WRIGHT, JR., lawyer; b. Pensacola, Fla., Dec. 3, 1935; s. Wilbur Wright and Evelyn (Nobles) M.; m. Ann Arnow, Nov. 10, 1978; 1 child, Kelly Arnow. BA, Duke U., 1957; LLB, U. Va., 1959; LLM in Taxation, NYU, 1964. Bar: Fla. 1959; cert. tax lawyer, Fla. Assoc. Beggs & Lane, Pensacola, 1964-69; gen. counsel The Moulton Trust, Pensacola, 1970-74; pvt. practice, Pensacola, 1974-83; ptnr. Carlton, Fields, Ward, Emmanuel, Smith & Cutler, P.A., Pensacola, 1983—, also bd. dirs. Pres. Pensacola Heritage Found., 1971-72, Lakeview Ctr., Inc., Pensacola, 1975-77, dir. emeritus, 1984; chmn. bd. Lakeview Found., Inc., Pensacola. Lt. USNR, 1960-64. Mem. ABA, Fla. Bar Assn., Estate Planning Coun. N.W. Fla. (pres. 1978), Escambia-Santa Rosa Bar Assn. (pres. 1988-89), Rotary, Pensacola Country Club. Democrat. Episcopalian. Avocations: reading, running, traveling. Office: Carlton Fields Ward Emmanuel Smith & Cutler PA 25 W Cedar St Pensacola FL 32501-5951

MOULTRIE, FRED, geneticist; b. Albertville, Ala., Apr. 18, 1923; s. Walter Louis and Minnie Alma (Bodine) M.; m. Frances Grace Aldridge, May 28, 1947; children: Marilyn R. Moultrie Phillips, Elizabeth Anne Moultrie Becker, Janet Carol Moultrie Gauger. BS, Auburn U., 1948, MS, 1949; PhD in Genetics, Kan State U., 1953. Asso. prof. Auburn U., 1951-55, prof., 1955-56; geneticist Arbor Acres Farm, Inc., Glastonbury, Conn., 1956-59; research coordinator Arbor Acres Farm, Inc., 1959-62, v.p., dir. research, 1962-64, exec. v.p., 1964-72, pres. domestic div., 1972-73; pres. Corbett Breeders, Westover, Md., 1973-81; v.p., dir. research Corbett Enterprises, Inc., 1973-81, Kennebec Internat., 1981-84; geneticist Perdue Farms, Salisbury, Md., 1984-88; genetics cons., 1988—. Served with USCGR, 1942-46. Mem. World's Poultry Sci. Assn., Am. Poultry Sci. Assn., Poultry Breeders Am. (pres. 1967-68), Sigma Xi, Phi Kappa Phi, Alpha Zeta, Gamma Sigma Delta. Club: Masons. Home and Office: 4360 Coulbourn Mill Rd Salisbury MD 21804

MOUNT, KARL A., manufacturing executive; b. Trenton, N.J., Feb. 15, 1945. BS in Commerce, Rider Coll., 1967. Sr. auditor S. D. Leidesdorf and Co., N.Y.C., 1967-75; contr. Alpha Metals Inc., Jersey City, N.J., 1975-83, v.p. fin., 1983-84, exec. v.p., 1984-87, pres., 1987-90; v.p. fin. Cookson Am. Inc., Providence, 1990-92; cons. J.F. Krahnert Assn., Edison, N.J., 1993-95; CFO Micro Ctrl., Inc., Old Bridge, N.J., 1995—. Office: 8998 Rte 18 N PO Box 1009 Old Bridge NJ 08857

MOUNT, THOMAS H(ENDERSON), independent film producer; b. Durham, N.C., May 26, 1948; s. Lillard H. and Bonnie M. Student, Bard Coll., 1968-70; MFA in Film, Art, Calif. Inst. Arts, 1973. Prodn. exec. Universal Studios, Universal City, Calif., 1975-79, pres. for prodn., 1976-84, ind. film producer, 1984—; ind. film producer Burbank, Calif., 1984—. Prodr.: (films) Roman Polanski's Pirates, 1985, Can't Buy Me Love, 1987, Frantic, 1987, Bull Durham, 1988, Stealing Home, 1988, Tequila Sunrise, 1988, Frankenstein Unbound, 1989, The Indian Runner, 1990, Death and the Maiden, 1994, Night Falls on Manhattan, 1995, (TV) Open Admissions, 1986, Son of the Morning Star, 1987, Death and the Miaden, 1991. Trustee Bard Coll., 1979-94.

MOUNT, WILLIE LANDRY, mayor; b. Lake Charles, La., Aug. 25, 1949; d. Lee Robert and Willia Veatrice (McCullor) Landry; m. Benjamin Wakefield Mount, Aug. 19, 1976. BS, McNeese State U., 1971. Geophys. asst. Lousiana Land and Exploration, Lake Charles, La., 1971-76; pharm. rep. Lederle, Lake Charles, 1976-80; realtor Mary Kay Hopkins, Lake Charles, 1976-87; co-owner Paper Place, Lake Charles, 1991-95; mayor City of Lake Charles, 1993—; mem. met. planning orgn. policy bd. IMCAL, Lake Charles, 1993—; Gov. Violent Crime & Homicide Task Force, Baton Rouge, 1993-95. Guest condr. Lake Charles Symphony, 1992; v.p. dist. D. La. Mcpl. Assn., Baton Rouge, 1995-96; pres. Jr. League of Lake Charles; mem. adv. bd. S.W. La. Literacy Coalition; active First United Meth. Ch., La. Meth. Conf., McNeese State U. Found., United Way, Children's Miracle Network; exec. com. Coun. for a Better La. Recipient Spiritual Aims award Kiwanis Club, 1991, Cmty. Svc. award, 1995; Dorthea Combre award NAACP, 1994; named Woman of Yr., Quota Club, 1991, Citizen of Yr., Women's com. S.W. La., 1992, Woman of Yr., Pub. Ofcl. of Yr. Msgr. Cramers KC. Mem. LWV, S.W. La. Mayor's Assn. (chmn. 1993-94). Home: 205 Shell Beach Dr Lake Charles LA 70601-5933 Office: Office of Mayor PO Box 900 Lake Charles LA 70602-0900

MOUNTAIN, CLIFTON FLETCHER, surgeon, educator; b. Toledo, Apr. 15, 1924; s. Ira Fletcher and Mary (Stone) M.; m. Marilyn Isabelle Tapper, Feb. 28, 1945; children: Karen Lockerby, Clifton Fletcher, Jeffrey Richardson. AB, Harvard U., 1947; MD, Boston U., 1954. Diplomate Am. Bd. Surgery. Dir. dept. statis. rsch. Boston U., 1947-50; cons. rsch. analyst Mass. Dept. Pub. Health, 1951-53; intern U. Chgo. Clinics, 1954, resident, 1955-58, instr. surgery, 1958-59; sr. fellow thoracic surgery Houston, 1959; mem. staff M.D. Anderson Hosp. and Tumor Rsch. Inst.; asst. prof. thoracic surgery U. Tex., 1960-63, assoc. prof surgery, 1973-76, prof., 1976-94, prof. emeritus, 1995—, prof. surgery Sch. Medicine, 1987—, chief sect. thoracic surgery, 1970-79, chmn. thoracic oncology, 1979-84, chmn. dept. thoracic surgery, 1980-85, chmn. program in biomath. and computer sci., 1962-64, Mike Hogg vis. lectr. in S.Am., 1967; mem. sci. mission on cancer USSR, 1970-78, and Japan, 1976-84; mem. com. health, rsch. and edn. facilities Houston Cmty. Coun., 1964-78; cons. Am. Joint Com. on Cancer Staging and End Result Reporting, 1964-74, Tex. Heart Inst., 1994—; mem. Am. Joint Com. on Cancer, 1974-86, chmn. lung and esophagus task force; mem. working party on lung cancer and chmn. com. on surgery Nat. Clin. Trials Lung Cancer Study Group, NIH, 1971-76; mem. plans and scope com. cancer therapy Nat. Cancer Inst., 1972-75, mem. lung cancer study group, 1977-89, chmn. steering com., 1973-75, mem. bd. sci. counselors divsn. cancer treatment, 1972-75; hon. cons. Shanghai Chest Hosp. and Lung Cancer Ctr., Nat. Cancer Inst. of Brazil; sr. cons. Houston Thorax Inst., 1994—. Editor The New Physician, 1955-59; mem. editorial bd. Yearbook of Cancer, 1960-88, Internat. Trends in Gen. Thoracic Surgery, 1984-91; contbr. articles to profl. jours., chpts. to textbooks. Chmn. profl. adv. com. Harris County Mental Health Assn.; bd. dirs. Harris County chpt. Am. Cancer Soc. Lt. USNR, 1942-46. Recipient award Soviet Acad. Sci., 1977, Garcia Meml. medal Philippine Coll. Surgeons, 1982, Disting. Alumni award Boston U., 1988, Disting. Achievement U. Tex. M.D. Anderson Cancer Ctr., 1990, Disting. Svc. award Internat. Assn. for the Study of Lung Cancer, 1991, Disting. Alumnus award Boston U. Sch. of Medicine, 1992. Fellow ACS, Am. Coll. Chest Physicians (chmn. com. cancer 1967-75), Am. Assn. Thoracic Surgery, Inst. Environ. Scis., N.Y. Acad. Sci., Assn. Thoracic and Cardiovascular Surgeons of Asia (hon.), Hellenic Cancer Soc. (hon.), Chilean Soc. Respiratory Diseases (hon., hon. pres. 1982); mem. AAAS, Am. Assn. Cancer Rsch., AMA, So. Med. Assn., Am. Thoracic Soc., Soc. Thoracic Surgeons, Soc. Biomed. Computing, Am. Fedn. Clin. Rsch., Internat. Assn. Study Lung Cancer (pres. 1976-78), Am. Radium Soc., Pan-Am. Med. Assn., Houston Surg. Soc., Soc. Surg. Oncology, James Ewing Soc., Sigma Xi. Achievements include conception and development of program for application of mathematics and computers to the life sciences, of resource for experimental designs, applied statistics and computational support; first clinical use of physiologic adhesives in thoracic surgery; demonstration of clinical behavior of undifferentiated small cell lung cancer; first laser resection of lung tissue at thoracotomy; development of international system for staging of lung cancer. Home: 1701 Hermann Dr # 2804 Houston TX 77004 Office: 6624 Fannin St Ste 200 Houston TX 77030-2314

MOUNTCASTLE, KATHARINE BABCOCK, foundation executive; b. Phila., Feb. 2, 1931; d. Charles H. and Mary (Reynolds) Babcock; m. Kenneth Franklin Mountcastle, Sept. 1, 1951; children: Mary Babcock, Laura Lewis, Kenneth Franklin, Katharine Reynolds. B.A., Sweet Briar (Va.) Coll., 1952. Dir., Internat. Social Service, N.Y.C., 1960-68; dir. Mary R. Babcock Found., Winston-Salem, N.C., 1954—; pres. Mary R. Babcock Found., Winston-Salem, 1980-85; trustee Z. Smith Reynolds Found., Winston-Salem, 1964—; pres. Z. Smith Reynolds Found., 1975-79; dir. NARAL Found., 1983-89. Trustee Sapelo Island Rsch. found., Ga.; bd. dirs. Fairfield County Comty. Found., People for the Am. Way, 1982-84. Presbyterian. Address: 37 Oenoke Ln New Canaan CT 06840-4516

MOUNTCASTLE, KENNETH FRANKLIN, JR., stockbroker; b. Winston-Salem, N.C., Oct. 8, 1928; s. Kenneth Franklin and May M.; BS in Commerce, U. N.C., Chapel Hill, 1950; m. Mary Katharine Babcock, Sept. 1, 1951; children: Mary Babcock, Laura Lewis, Kenneth Franklin, Katharine Reynolds. With Mountcastle Knitting Co., Lexington, N.C., 1952-55, Reynolds & Co., N.Y.C., 1955-71; with Reynolds Securities Inc. (co. name changed to Dean Witter Reynolds 1978), N.Y.C., 1971—, sr. v.p., 1974—. Trustee, New Canaan (Conn.) Country Sch., 1962-68, Ethel Walker Sch., Simsbury, Conn., 1973-85; trustee Coro Found., 1980—, nat. chmn., 1986-89; bd. dirs., past pres. Mary Reynolds Babcock Found., Winston-Salem, N.C.; bd. visitors U. N.C., Chapel Hill; bd. dirs. Inform, N.Y.C., Fresh Air Fund, N.Y.C., The Giraffe Project Friends of Thirteen, Bus. Execs. for Nat. Security. Served with U.S. Army, 1950-52. Mem. Country Club of New Canaan, Wee Burn Country Club (Darien, Conn.), Old Town Club (Winston-Salem, N.C.), Racquet and Tennis Club, City Midday Club, Ocean Forest Golf Club (Sea Island, Ga.), Pine Valley Golf Club, Bond Club, Stock Exch. Luncheon Club. Home: 37 Oenoke Ln New Canaan CT 06840-4516 Office: Dean Witter Reynolds 2 World Trade Ctr Fl 17 New York NY 10048-0203

MOUNTCASTLE, VERNON BENJAMIN, neurophysiologist; b. Shelbyville, Ky., July 15, 1918; s. Vernon Mountcastle and Anne-Francis Marguerite (Waugh) M.; m. Nancy Clayton Pierpont, Sept. 6, 1945; children: Vernon Benjamin III, Anne Clayton, George Earle Pierpont. BS in Chemistry, Roanoke Coll., Salem, Va., 1938, DSc (hon.), 1968; MD, Johns Hopkins U., 1942; DSc (hon.), U. Pa., 1976, U. Minn., 1995; MD (hon.), U. Zurich, 1983, U. Siena, 1984, U. Santiago, Spain, 1990. House officer surgery Johns Hopkins Hosp., 1942-43; mem. faculty Johns Hopkins Sch. Medicine, 1946—, prof. physiology, 1959, dir. dept., 1964-80, Univ. prof. neurosci., 1980-92, prof. emeritus, 1992—; dir. Neurosci. Research Program, Rockefeller U., 1981-84; dir. Bard Labs. Neurophysiology Johns Hopkins U., Balt., 1981-91; pres. Neurosci. Research Found., 1981-85; spl. research physiology brain; chmn. physiology study sect., mem. physiology tng. com. NIH, 1958-61; adv. council Nat. Eye Inst., 1971-74; mem. sci. adv. bd. USAF, 1969-71; vis. com. dept. psychology Mass. Inst. Tech., 1966-75; bd. biology and medicine NSF, 1970-73; mem. commn. on neurophysiology Internat. Union Physiol. Sci. Editor-in-chief: Jour. Neurophysiology, 1961-64; assoc. editor: Bull. Johns Hopkins Hosp, 1954-62; editorial bd.: Physiol. Revs, 1957-59, Exptl. Brain Research, 1966-85; editor, contbr.: Med. Physiology, 12th edit, 1968, 13th edit., 1974, 14th edit., 1980, (with G.M. Edelman) The Mindful Brain, 1978; author articles in field. Served to lt. (s.g.) M.C. USNR, 1943-46. Recipient Lashley prize Am. Philos. Soc., 1974, F.O. Schmitt prize and medal MIT, 1975, Sherrington prize and gold medal Royal Acad. Medicine, London, 1977, Horowitz prize Columbia U., 1978, Fyssen Internat. prize, Paris, 1983, Lasker award, 1983, Helmholtz prize, 1982, Nat. Medal Sci., 1986, McGovern prize and medal AAAS, 1990, award in neurosci. Fidia Fedn., 1990, Australia prize, 1993. Mem. NAS (chmn. sect. on physiology 1971-74), AAAS, Am. Physiol. Soc., Am. Acad. Arts and Scis., Harvey Cushing Soc., Am. Neurol. Assn. (hon., Bennett lectr. 1978), Soc. Neurosci. (pres. 1970-72, Gerard prize 1980), Am. Philos. Soc. (councillor 1979-82), Nat. Inst. Medicine, Physiol. Soc. (London, hon.), Acad. Scis. (France, fgn.), Royal Soc. London (fgn.), Phi Beta Kappa, Alpha Omega Alpha, Phi Chi, Sigma Xi. Home: 15601 Carroll Rd Monkton MD 21111-2009

MOUNTCASTLE, WILLIAM WALLACE, JR., philosophy and religion educator; b. Hanover, N.H., July 10, 1925; s. William Wallace and Grace Elizabeth (Zottarelli) M.; m. Ila M. Warner (div.); children: Christine, Susan, Gregory, Eric; m. Barbara Kaye Griffin, Oct. 19, 1979; 1 child, Cathleena; stepdaughter, Dasha. BA, Whittier Coll., 1951; STB, Boston U., 1954, PhD, 1958. Ordained to ministry United Meth. Ch. Asst. prof. philosophy and religion High Point (N.C.) Coll., 1958-60; mem. So. Calif. Ann. Conf. United Meth. Ch., 1954-60; assoc. prof., head dept. philosophy Nebr. Wesleyan U., Lincoln, 1960-63, prof., head dept. philosophy, 1963-67; mem. Neb. Ann. Conf. United Meth. Ch., 1960—; prof. philosophy Fla. So. Coll., Lakeland, 1967-69; assoc. prof. philosophy and religion U. W. Fla., Pensacola, 1969-79, prof. philosophy and religion, 1979-84, M.L. Tipton prof. philosophy and religion, 1980—. Author: Religion in Planetary Perspective, 1979, Science Fantasy Voices and Visions of Cosmic Religion, 1996; contbr. articles to profl. jours. Fighter pilot USAAF, 1942-48, PTO. Mem. NEA/United Faculty Fla., Am. Assn. Religion, Am. Philos. Assn.,. Democrat. Home: 4549 Sabine Dr Gulf Breeze FL 32561-9253 Office: U West Fla Dept Phil-Religious Studies Pensacola FL 32514

MOUNTZ, LOUISE CARSON SMITH, retired librarian; b. Fond Du Lac, Wis., Oct. 20, 1911; d. Roy Carson and Charlotte Louise (Scheurs) Smith; m. George Edward Mountz, May 4, 1935 (dec. Oct. 3 1951); children: Peter Carson, Pamela Teeters Mountz McDonald. Student, Western Coll., 1929-31; AB, The Ohio State U., 1933; MA, Ball State U., 1962; postgrad., Manchester Coll., 1954, Ind. U., 1960-61. Cert. tchr., Ind. Tchr. Monroeville (Ind.) High Sch., 1953-54, Riverdale High Sch., St. Joe, Ind., 1954-55; libr. High Sch., Avilla, Ind., 1955-58; head libr. Penn High Sch., Mishawaka, Ind., 1958-67, Northwood Jr. High Sch., Ft. Wayne, Ind., 1967-69, McIntosh Jr. High Sch., Auburn, Ind., 1969-74; dir. Media Ctr. DeKalb Jr. High Sch., Auburn, Ind., 1974-78; ret., 1978; cons. media ctr. planning Penn-Harris-Madison Sch. Corp., Mishawaka, 1966-67. Author: Biographies for Junior High Schools and Correlated Audio-Visual Materials, 1970; contbr. articles to profl. jours. Bd. dirs. DeKalb County chpt. ARC, 1938-42, 51-53, DeKalb County Heart Assn., 1946-52, DeKalb County Cmty. Concert Assn., 1946-58, Am. Field Svc. Mishawaka chpt., 1960-67; active Ft. Wayne Philharmonic Orch. Assn., Ft. Wayne Art Mus., Ft. Wayne Hist. Soc., DeKalb County Hist. Soc., Garrett Hist. Soc., DeKalb County Genealogy Soc., Preservation of DeKalb County Heritage Assn., DeKalb Meml. Hosp. Women's Guild, also life mem. Mem. AAUW, ALA, NEA, World Confedn. Orgns. Teaching Professions, Nat. Coun. Tchrs. English, Ind. Sch. Librarians Assn. (dir. 1963-67), Internat. Assn. Sch. Librarianship, Ind. Assn. Ednl. Communication and Tech., Assn. Ind. Media Educators, Nat. Ret. Tchrs. Assns., Nat. Trust Hist. Preservation, Hist. Landmarks Found. Ind., Delta Kappa Gamma (charter mem., Beta Beta chpt.), Kappa Kappa Kappa (pr. officer 1941-45, pres. Alpha Chi chpt. 1938-40, Garrett Assoc. chpt. 1971-73), Delta Delta Delta (house pres.). Methodist. Lodge: Order Ea. Star. Clubs: Greenhurst Country, Ft. Wayne Women's, Athena Lit. (hon. mem.), Ladies Lit. of Auburn. Home: 19 Castle Ct Auburn IN 46706-1439

MOUNTZ, WADE, retired health service management executive; b. Winona, Ohio, Nov. 19, 1924; s. Lowell J. and Ethel M. (Coppock) M.; m. Betty G. Wilson, June 3, 1946; children: David John, Timothy Wilson. BA, Baldwin-Wallace Coll., 1948; MHA, U. Minn., 1951; LHD (hon.), Ky. Wesleyan Coll., 1991. With Norton Meml. Infirmary, Louisville, 1951-69; adminstr. Norton Meml. Infirmary, 1958-69; pres. Norton-Children's Hosps., Inc., Louisville, 1969-81, NKC, Inc., Louisville, 1981-85; vice chmn. NKC, Inc., 1985-87, pres. emeritus, 1987—. Vice chmn. Comprehensive Health Planning Council Ky., 1968-73, chmn., 1973-79; bd. dirs. Louisville chpt. ARC, 1961-74; trustee Blue Cross Hosp. Plan, 1959-72; trustee Am. Hosp. Assn., 1971-76, chmn. bd., 1975. Served with A.C., USNR, 1943-45. Recipient Disting. Service award Ky. Hosp. Assn.; Disting. Layman award Ky. Med. Assn. Fellow Am. Coll. Hosp. Healthcare Execs. (gold medal), Masons. Home: 9 Muirfield Pl Louisville KY 40222-5074 Office: 4350 Brownsboro Rd Ste 110 Louisville KY 40207-1681

MOURA, JOSÉ MANUEL FONSECA, electrical engineering and computer science educator; b. Beira, Mozambique, Portugal, Jan. 9, 1946; s. José Saraiva and Maria José (Fonseca) M.; m. Maria Tereza Fernandes, 1969 (div. 1981); 1 child, Barbara Fernandes; m. Maria Manuela Veloso, 1982; children: André Veloso, Pedro Veloso. Engenheiro Electrotecnico, Instituto Superior Tecnico, Lisbon, 1969; M.S. in Elec. Engring., MIT, 1973, Sc. D. in Elec. Engring. and Computer Sci., 1975. Prof. auxiliar Instituto Superior Técnico, Lisbon, 1975-78, prof. aggregado, 1978, prof. catedrático, 1979-86; prof. Carnegie Mellon U., Pitts., 1986—; vis. assoc. prof. elec. engring. and computer sci. MIT, Cambridge, 1984-86; vis. scholar U. So. Calif., Los Angeles, summers 1978, 79, 80, 81. Editor: (with others) Nonlinear Stochastic Problems, 1983, Acoustic Signal Processing for Ocean Exploration, 1993. Contbr. articles to profl. jours.; editor-in-chief IEEE Trans. on Signal Processing, 1995—. Fellow IEEE; mem. NAS Portugal (corr. mem.), Am. Math. Soc., Soc. Indsl. and Applied Math., Ordem dos Engenheiros. Home: 6645 Woodwell St Pittsburgh PA 15217-1320 Office: Carnegie-Mellon U Dept Elec & Computer Engring 5000 Forbes Ave Pittsburgh PA 15213-3816

MOURA-RELVAS, JOAQUIM M.M.A., electrical engineer, educator; b. Aveiro, Portugal, May 9, 1926; s. Joaquim Moura and Maria Emilia Albuquerque (Branco de Melo) Relvas; m. Maria Alice Barata Portugal, May 9, 1953; children: Jose Pedro, Joao Paulo, Luis Filipe, Joaquim Jose, Francisco Manuel, Maria Isabel. Degree in Elec. Engr., U. Porto, Portugal, 1951. Asst. engr. CTT (State Telecomms.), Lisbon, Portugal, 1951-53; design engr. UEP (Elec. Power Co.), Porto, 1953-73; prof. U. Coimbra, Portugal, 1973-81; chief engr. EDP (Electricidade de Portugal), Lisbon, 1981-88; prof. Poly. Inst. of Gaya, Vila Nova de Gaia, Portugal, 1988—. Author: Introduction to Digital Electronics, 1971, Introduction to Microcomputers, 1981, Digital Electronics, 1986. Mem. AAAS, N.Y. Acad. Scis., Ordem dos Engenheiros, Planetary Soc. Avocations: swimming, walking, photography, home movies, historical books. Home: Av da Republica 1815, Vila Nova de Gaia 4430, Portugal Office: ISP Gaya, R Antonio R da Rocha 341, Vila Nova de Gaia 4430, Portugal

MOUREK, JOSEPH EDWARD, musician; b. Chgo., Jan. 5, 1910; s. Anton Peter and Anna (Prucha) M.; m. Jean Katherine Masek, Sept. 1, 1934. Pupil, Bruno Jaenicke, Pellegrino Lecce, Thorwold Otterstrom. Tchr. Interlochen (Mich.) Music Acad., 1929-31. French hornist, Chgo. Symphony Orch., 1929—, other appearances with opera, mus. comedies, also on radio, TV and films; rec. artist for, RCA, Columbia, Mercury, Angel, London, Decca records. Served with AUS, World War II. Recipient certificate of merit Mayor Daley of Chgo., 1971, Chgo. certificate of merit, 1971; named Chicagoan of Year Chgo. Press Club, 1971. Home: 6934 29th St Berwyn IL 60402-2942 Office: Orch Hall 220 S Michigan Ave Chicago IL 60604-2508

MOURNING, ALONZO, professional basketball player; b. Chesapeake, Va., Feb. 8, 1970. Student, Georgetown U. Center Charlotte Hornets, 1992—; now with Miami Heat; player All-Star Game, 1994. Named to NBA All-Rookie First Team, 1993, Dream Team II, 1994. Office: Miami Heat Miami Arena Miami FL 33136-4102*

MOURTON, J. GARY, communications executive; b. Mena, Ark., Jan. 22, 1947; s. Malvin G. and Helen J. (Eckhardt) M.; m. J. Gayle Lay, June 29, 1968; children: Jennifer, Lindsay, Kimberly, Natalie. B.S.B.A., U. Ark., 1969. C.P.A., Okla. Audit mgr. Arthur Andersen & Co., Tulsa, 1969-80; fin. officer T/SF Comm. Corp. (formerly Swab-Fox Cos. and Midwest Energy Corp.), Tulsa, 1980—. Mem. Am. Inst. C.P.A.s, Okla. Soc. C.P.A.s, Fin. Execs. Inst. Republican. Office: T/SF Comm Corp 2407 E Skelly Dr Tulsa OK 74105-6006

MOVIUS, WHITNEY BURTON See WHITNEY, ALISON BURTON

MOVSHOVITZ, HOWARD PAUL, film critic, educator; b. Trenton, N.J., Dec. 30, 1944; s. Abraham H. and Helen (Peskin) M.; m. Janis Hallowell, Dec. 23, 1989; 1 child, Zoe. BA, U. Pa., 1966; PhD, U. Colo., 1977. Film critic Colo. Pub. Radio, Denver, 1976—; asst. prof. U. Colo., Denver, 1978-90; film critic The Denver Post, 1987—; asst. adj. prof. U. Colo., Denver, 1978—; reporter Nat. Pub. Radio, Washington, 1986—. Mem. ACLU (bd. dirs. 1986-87). Office: Denver Post 1560 Broadway Denver CO 80202-5133

MOW, DOUGLAS FARRIS, former naval officer, consultant; b. Carbondale, Colo., Nov. 10, 1928; s. James Leroy and Marie (Gerkin) M.; m. Rosalie Stearns Johnson, June 16, 1951; children: Douglas Farris, Deborah, Laura, Nancy. B.S., U.S. Naval Acad., 1951; M.S. in Physics, U.S. Naval Postgrad. Sch., 1958; student, Armed Forces Staff Coll., 1964-65. Commd. ensign USN, 1951, advanced through grades to rear adm., 1977; night attack pilot San Diego, 1953-56; served with research and devel. div. (Def. Nuclear Agy.), Albuquerque, 1958-60; nuclear weapons employment officer (Carrier Air Wing 11), Naval Air Sta. Miramar, San Diego, 1960-62; pilot, ops. officer (Light Attack Squadron), Naval Air Sta. Lemoore, Calif., 1962-64; assigned to atomic energy div. (Office Chief of Naval Ops.), Washington, 1965-66; comdg. officer squadron Vietnam War, 1967-68; staff comdr. (7th Fleet), 1969; comdr. (Carrier Airwing 19), 1970-71, (Light Attack Wing One), Jacksonville, Fla., 1971-73; exec. asst./naval aide to Sec. Navy Washington, 1973-77; VSTOL program coordinator, 1977-80; comdr. (Tactical Wings Atlantic), Virginia Beach, Va., 1980-81; cons., 1982—. Decorated D.S.M., Silver Star, D.F.C. with 2 oak leaf clusters, Legion of Merit with 2 oak leaf clusters, Bronze Star with 2 oak leaf clusters, Air medal with 4 oak leaf clusters, Navy Commendation medal with 2 oak leaf clusters. Mem. U.S. Naval Inst. Republican. Episcopalian.

MOW, ROBERT HENRY, JR., lawyer; b. Cape Girardeau, Mo., Dec. 10, 1938; s. Robert H., Sr. and Ann Elise (Beck) M.; m. Jody K. Boggs, Aug. 29, 1987; children: Robert M., Brynn A., W.Brett, Rebecca M., W. Kirk, Allison M. Student, Westminster Coll., 1956-57; A.B. with distinction, U. of Mo., 1960; LL.B. magna cum laude, So. Meth. U., 1963. Bar: Tex. 1963, U.S. Dist. Ct. (no. dist.) Tex. 1965, U.S. Dist. Ct. (so. dist.) Tex. 1969, U.S. Dist Ct. (ea. dist.) Tex. 1976, U.S. Dist. Ct. (we. dist.) Tex. 1976, U.S. Ct. Claims 1973, U.S. Ct. Appeals (5th cir. 1972, U.S. Ct. Appeals (11th cir.) 1981, U.S. Ct. Appeals (Fed. cir.), 1994, U.S. Supreme Ct. 1978. Assoc., Carrington, Johnson & Stephens, Dallas, 1963-69; ptnr. Carrington, Coleman, Sloman, & Blumenthal, Dallas, 1970-85; Hughes & Luce, L.L.P., Dallas, 1985—. Editor-in-chief Southwestern Law Jour., 1962-63. Served to 1st lt. U.S. Army, 1963-65. Fellow Am. Coll. of Trial Lawyers, mem. Dallas Jr. Bar Assn. (pres. 1968), Dallas Assn. of Def. Counsel (chmn. 1976-77), Tex. Assn. of Def. Counsel (v.p. 1981-82), Am. Bd. of Trial Advocates (pres. Dallas chpt. 1983-84). Republican. Baptist. Office: Hughes & Luce LLP 1717 Main St Ste 2800 Dallas TX 75201-7342

MOW, VAN C., engineering educator, researcher; b. Chengdu, China, Jan. 10, 1939. B. Aero. Engring., Rensselaer Poly. Inst., 1962, Ph.D., 1966. Mem. tech. staff Bell Telephone Labs., Whippany, N.J., 1968-69; assoc. prof. mechanics Rensselaer Poly. Inst., Troy, N.Y., 1969-76, prof. mechanics and biomed. engring., 1976-82, John A. Clark and Edward T. Crossan prof. engring., 1982-86; prof. mechanical engring. and orthopedic bioengring. Columbia U., N.Y.C., 1986—; dir. Orthopedic Research Lab., Columbia-Presbyn. Med. Ctr., N.Y.C., 1986—; vis. mem. Courant Inst. Math. Sci., NYU, 1967-68; vis. prof. Harvard U., Boston, 1976-77; chmn. orthopaedics and musculoskeletal study sect. NIH, Bethesda, Md., 1982-84; hon. prof. Chengdu U. Sci. Tech., 1981, Shanghai Jiao Tong U., 1987; mem. grants rev. bd. Orthopaedic Rsch. Edn. Found., 1992-96; bd. dirs. Hoar Rsch. Found., 1993—; cons. in field. Assoc. editor Jour. Biomechanics, 1981—, Jour. Biomech. Engring., 1979-86; chmn. editorial adv. bd. Jour. Orthopedic

Rsch., 1983-90; adv. editor Clin. Orthopedic Rel. Rsch., 1993—; contbr. numerous articles to profl. jours. Founder Gordon Research Conf. on Bioengring. and Orthopedic Sci., 1980. NATO sr. fellow, 1978; recipient William H. Wiley Disting. Faculty award Rensselaer Poly. Inst., 1981; Japan Soc. for Promotion Sci. Fellow, 1986, Fogarty Sr. Internat. fellow, 1987; Alza disting. lectr. Biomed. Engring. Soc., 1987; H.R. Lissner award ASME, 1987, Kappa Delta award AAOS, 1980, Giovani Borelli award, 1991. Fellow ASME (chmn. biomechanics divsn. 1984-85, Melville medal 1982), Am. Inst. Med. Biol. Engring.; mem. NAE, Orthopaedic Rsch. Soc. (pres. 1982-83), Am. Soc. Biomechanics (founding), Internat. Soc. Biorheology, U.S. Nat. Com. on Biomechanics (sec.-treas. 1985-90, chmn. 1991-94). Office: Columbia-Presbyn Med Ctr BB-1412 630 W 168th St New York NY 10032-3702

MOW, WILLIAM, apparel executive; b. 1936. PhD, Purdue U., 1967. With Honeywell Inc., Boston, 1963-65; program mgr. Litton Industries, L.A., 1967-69; founder, pres., chmn. bd. MacroData Corp., L.A., 1969-76; sci. advisor Cutler Hammer, L.A., 1976-77; with Bugle Boy Industries, Inc., Simi Valley, Calif., 1977—, now chmn., CEO. Office: Bugle Boy 2900 N Madera Rd Simi Valley CA 93065-6236*

MOWAT, FARLEY MCGILL, writer; b. Belleville, Ont., Can., May 12, 1921; s. Angus McGill and Helen (Thomson) M.; m. Frances Elizabeth Thornhill, Dec. 21, 1947; children: Robert Alexander, David Peter; m. Claire Angel Wheeler, 1965. BA, U. Toronto, 1949, LLD, 1973; DLitt (hon.), Laurentian U., 1970; LLD, U. Lethbridge, Alta., 1973, U. P.E.I., 1979; DLitt, U. Victoria, B.C., 1982, Lakehead U., Thunder Bay, Ont., 1986; LHD (hon.), McMaster U., Hamilton, Ont., 1994; LLD (hon.), Queen's Univ., Kingston, Ont., 1995; DLitt (hon.), U. Coll. of Cape Breton, Sydney, Nova Scotia, 1996. Arctic exploration, sci. work, 1947-48, writer, 1950—. Author: People of the Deer, 1952, The Regiment, 1955, Lost in the Barrens, 1956, The Dog Who Wouldn't Be, 1957, Coppermine Journey, 1958, The Grey Seas Under, 1958, The Desperate People, 1959, Ordeal By Ice, 1960, Owls in the Family, 1961, The Serpent's Coil, 1961, The Black Joke, 1962, Never Cry Wolf, 1963, Westviking, 1965, The Curse of the Viking Grave, 1966, Canada North, 1967, The Polar Passion, 1967 (with John de Visser) This Rock Within the Sea, 1968, The Boat Who Wouldn't Float, 1969, The Siberians, 1971, A Whale for the Killing, 1972, Tundra, 1973, (with David Blackwood) Wake of the Great Sealers, 1973, The Snow Walker, 1975, Canada North Now, 1976, And No Birds Sang, 1979, The World of Farley Mowat, 1980, Sea of Slaughter, 1984, My Discovery of America, 1985, Woman in the Mist, 1987, The New Founde Land, 1989, Rescue the Earth, 1990, My Father's Son, 1992, Born Naked, 1993, Aftermath, 1995; author documentary script The New North (Gemini award 1989); film Sea of Slaughter (Conservation Film of Yr. award 1990, ACE award finalist 1990, award of Excellence Atlantic Film Festival 1990). Served to capt. inf. Canadian Army, 1939-45. Recipient Pres. Medal Univ. Western Ont., 1952, Anisfield Wolfe award, 1954, Gov. Gen.'s medal, 1957, Book of Yr. Medal Can. Library Assn., 1958, Hans Christian Anderson Internat. award, 1958, 65, Can. Women's Clubs award, 1958, Boys Clubs Am. award, 1962, Nat. Assn. Ind. Schs. award, 1963, Can. Centennial medal, 1967, Stephen Leacock medal for humor, 1970, Leacock Medal for Humour, 1970, Vicky Metcalf award, 1970, Mark Twain award, 1971, Book of Yr. award, 1976, Curran award, 1977, Queen Elizabeth II Jubilee medal, 1978, Knight of Mark Twain, 1980, Can. Author's award, 1981, 85, Can. Author of Year award, 1988, Can. Book of Yr. award, 1988, Torgi Can. Talking Book of Yr. award, 1989, Can. Achievers award Toshiba Can., 1990, Take Back the Nation award Coun. Cans., 1991, Authors award, Author of Yr. Found. for Advancement of Can. Letters, 1993; decorated officer Order of Can., 1981, L'Etoile de la Mer, 1972. Office: care Writers Union Can, 24 Ryerson Ave, Toronto, ON Canada M4T 2P3

MOWATT, E. ANN, women's voluntary leader. BA in History, Dalhousie U., Halifax, Nova Scotia, 1982; BL, 1985. Barrister, solicitor Patterson Palmer Hunt Murphy, 1986—; ptnr. Palmer, O'Connell, Leger, Roderick, Glennie, 1991. Bd. dirs. Saint John N.B., Can., 1987-93, also mem. exec., fin., social action, and camp coms., pres., 1991; bd. dirs. YWCA of Can., 1989—, also chair constn. task force, mem.-at-large, treas., v.p., now pres., 1995—; bd. dirs. Coalition of Nat. Vol. Orgns., 1994—; pres. Saint John chpt. Multiple Sclerosis Soc. Can., 1987-88, bd. dirs. Atlantic divsn., 1988—, mem. nat. bd. dirs., 1992-95, pres. Atlantic divsn., 1993—. Mem. Can. Bar Assn. (mem. N.B. coun. 1986-89), Law Soc. N.B. (mem. legal aid com. 1989-92). Avocations: reading, films, camping, canoeing, theatre. Home: 1054 Mollins Dr Apt 3, Saint John, NB Canada E2M 4L8 Office: 80 Gerard St E, Toronto, ON Canada also Office: PO Box 1324, PO Box 1425, Saint John, NB Canada E2L 4H8

MOWATT, WAYNE L., state agency administrator. Commr. State Edn. Dept., Augusta, Maine, 1995—. Office: State Edn Dept Office of the Commr State House Sta 23 Augusta ME 04333

MOWDAY, RICHARD THOMAS, management educator; b. Oakland, Calif., Sept. 4, 1947; s. Richard Walter and Jessie Elizabeth (Steet) M.; m. Mary Nelson; children: Graham Thomas, Garrett Nelson. BS in Manpower Adminstrn., San Jose State U., 1970; MS in Adminstrn., U. Calif., Irvine, 1972, PhD in Adminstrn., 1975. Asst. prof. U. Nebr., Lincoln, 1975-77; asst. prof. U. Oreg., Eugene, 1977-81, assoc. prof., 1981-86, prof. mgmt., 1986—, Holden Affilate prof. mgmt., 1988, Gerald B. Bashaw disting. prof. mgmt., 1990, assoc. dean, 1994—; vis. scholar Tuck Sch. Mgmt. Dartmouth Coll., Hanover, N.H., 1983-84; Hanson vis. prof. U. Washington, 1991—. Co-author: Employee-Organization Linkages, 1982, Managing Effective Organizations, 1985; co-editor: Research in Organizations, 1979; editor Acad. Mgmt. Jour., 1988-90, cons. editor, 1984-87; internat. cons. editor Jour. Occupational Psychology, 1983-91; editl. rev. bd. Jour. Vocat. Behavior, Jour. Mgmt., Adminstrv.. Sci. Quar., Jour. Mgmt. Inquiry. Fellow APA, Acad. of Mgmt. (div. chmn. 1984-85, bd. govs., v.p., program chmn., pres. Best Rsch. Paper award, orgnl. behavior div. 1986), Am. Psychol. Soc.; mem. Western Acd. Mgmt., Soc. Orgnl. Behavior. Congregationalist. Avocations: cross country skiing, bicycling, running. Home: 5225 Miramar St Eugene OR 97405-4842 Office: U Oregon Coll Bus Adminstrn Eugene OR 97403

MOWE, GREGORY ROBERT, lawyer; b. Aberdeen, Wash., Feb. 23, 1946; s. Robert Eden and Jeannette Effie (Deyoung) M.; m. Rebecca Louise Nobles, June 14, 1969; children: Emily, Tom. BA, U. Oreg., 1968, MA, 1969; JD magna cum laude, Harvard Law Sch., 1974. Bar: Oreg. 1974, U.S. Dist. Ct. Oreg. 1974, U.S. Ct. Appeals (9th cir.) 1974. Assoc. atty. Stoel Rives Boley Jones & Grey, Portland, Oreg., 1974-79; ptnr. Stoel Rivis Boley Jones & Grey, Portland, 1979—. Pres. bd. dirs. Planned Parenthood of Columbia/Willamette, Portland, 1989-90. 1st lt. U.S. Army, 1969-71, Vietnam. Mem. ABA, Phi Beta Kappa. Office: Stoel Rives Boley Jones & Grey 900 SW 5th Ave Ste 2300 Portland OR 97204-1232

MOWER, ERIC ANDREW, communications and marketing executive; b. N.Y.C., Oct. 10, 1944; s. Jack Henry Mower and Doris (Bernfeld) Schecter; m. Judith Ann Cotey, May 28, 1967; 1 child, Hillary Beth. BA, Syracuse (N.Y.) U., 1966, MA, 1968. Prin. Eric Mower and Assocs., Syracuse, 1968—. Pres. Health Sci. Ctr. Found., SUNY, Syracuse, 1983-88; pres., bd. dirs. Syracuse Symphony Orch., 1988-90; chmn. Ctrl. N.Y. chpt. Nat. Kidney Found., 1987-88, Ctrl. N.Y. Regional Market Task Force, 1988-90, Partnership for Arts; bd. dirs. Met. Devel. Assn., Everson Mus., Nat. Advt. Rev. Bd.; past mem. bd. dirs. Syracuse Stage, Jr. Achievement, Ctrl. N.Y. coun. Boy Scouts Am., Sta. WCNY-TV-FM; trustee Syracuse U. Mem. Am. Assn. Advt. Agys. (chmn. N.Y. state coun. 1986, chmn. bd. govs. ea. region 1988-89, nat. bd. govs. 1990—, sec.-treas. 1993-94, dir.-at-large), Greater Syracuse C. of C. (chmn. bd. dirs. 1992-93), Univ. Club (N.Y.C.), Friars Club, Century Club. Office: Eric Mower and Assocs Inc 500 Plum St Syracuse NY 13204-1401 also: Eric Mower and Assocs 360 Delaware Ave Buffalo NY 14202-1610 also: Eric Mower and Assocs 350 Linden Oaks Dr Rochester NY 14625

MOWERY, ANNA RENSHAW, state legislator; b. Decatur, Tex., Jan. 4, 1931; d. Lafayette William and Early Virginia (Bobo) Renshaw; m. Wesley Harold Mowery, June 2, 1951; children: Jeanette Mowery Hefferman, Mark William, Timothy Dean, Marianne Mowery Fichera. BA, Baylor U., 1951; MA, Ctrl. State U,, 1967. Tchr. Ft. Hood (Tex.) Pub. Schs., 1951-52; petroleum landman Ft. Worth, 1979-82; dist. dir. U.S. Congl. Dist. 6 Joe Barton, Ft. Worth, 1985-86; polit. cons., pres. Trinity Assocs., Ft. Worth, 1987-88; state rep. Tex. House Reps., Ft. Worth, 1988—. Chmn. Tarrant County (Tex.) Rep. Party, 1975-77; mem. Tex. Rep. Exec. Com., Ft. Worth, 1980-84, Greater Ft. Worth Literacy Coun., 1990—; mem. adv. bd. Sr. Citizen Svcs./Tarrant County, Ft. Worth, 1988—. Recipient 4-H Clubs Am. Alumni award, 1990; nominee Newsmaker of Yr., Ft. Worth Press Club, 1974, 76. Mem. Southwest Rep. Club, Tex. Women's Alliance, Ft. Worth Rep. Women (v.p. 1991-92), Women's Policy Forum. Baptist. Home: 4108 Hildring Dr W Fort Worth TX 76109-4722 District Office: Ste 534 Twr II 4100 International Plz Fort Worth TX 76109-4820 Office: Tex House of Reps State Capitol Austin TX 78768-2910

MOWRY, ROBERT DEAN, art museum curator, educator; b. Quinter, Kans., Sept. 27, 1945; s. Eugene Adrian and Pearl Helen (Kreft) M. BA with honors, U. Kans., 1967, MA with honors, 1974, MPhil. with honors, 1975. Curatorial asst. and translator Nat. Palace Mus., Taipei, Taiwan, 1975-77; asst. curator Oriental art Fogg Art Mus., Harvard U., Cambridge, Mass., 1977-80; curator Mr. and Mrs. John D. Rockefeller 3d collection Asia Soc., N.Y.C., 1980-86; curator Asian Art Harvard U. Art Mus., Cambridge, 1986-92; curator Chinese art and head dept. Asian art Harvard U. Art Mus., 1992—; lectr. dept. fine arts Harvard U., Cambridge, 1987-94; sr. lectr. Chinese and Korean art dept. fine arts Harvard U., 1994—; contbg. editor Art and Auction, N.Y.C., 1982-86; lectr. grad. program Cooper-Hewitt Mus., N.Y.C., 1983-86, Inst. Asian Studies, N.Y.C., 1982—. Author: Handbook of the Mr. and Mrs. John D. Rockefeller 3d Collection, 1981, The Chinese Scholar's Studio: Artistic Life in the Late Ming Period, 1987, China's Renaissance in Bronze: The Robert H. Clague Collection of Later Chinese Bronzes 1100-1900, 1993, Ancient China, Modern Clay: Chinese Influences on Five Ceramic Artists, 1994, Hare's Fur, Tortoise Shell and Partridge Feathers: Chinese Brown and Black Glazed Ceramics, 400-1400, 1996; contbr. articles to profl. jours. Vol. U.S. Peace Corps, Seoul Nat. U., Republic of Korea, 1967-69. Hackney scholar Freer Gallery Art, Washington, 1975-76; fellow U. Kans., Lawrence, 1971-75, J.D. Rockefeller 3d Fund, N.Y.C., 1976-77, Samuel Kress Found., N.Y.C., 1975. Mem. Coll. Art Assn. Am., Assn. for Asian Studies, Am. Com. for South Asian Art, Am. Assn. Mus., Nat. Trust for Hist. Preservation. Avocations: movies, reading, theatre, dance, opera, concerts. Office: Harvard U Art Mus Asian Dept 485 Broadway Cambridge MA 02138-3802

MOWRY, ROBERT WILBUR, pathologist, educator; b. Griffin, Ga., Jan. 10, 1923; s. Roy Burnell and Mary Frances (Swilling) M.; m. Margaret Neilson Black, June 11, 1949; children: Janet Lee, Robert Gordon, Barbara Ann. B.S., Birmingham So. Coll., 1944; M.D., Johns Hopkins U., 1946. Rotating intern U. Ala. Med. Coll., 1946-47, resident pathology, 1947-48; sr. asst. surgeon USPHS-NIH, Bethesda, Md., 1948-52; fellow pathology Boston City Hosp., 1949-50; asst. prof. pathology Washington U., St. Louis, 1952-53; asst. prof. pathology U. Ala. Med. Ctr., Birmingham, 1953-54, assoc. prof. pathology, 1954-57; prof. U. Ala. Med. Center, Birmingham, 1958-89, prof. emeritus, 1989—, prof. health svcs. adminstrn., 1976-84, dir. Anat. Pathology Lab., 1960-64, dir. grad. programs in pathology, 1964-72; sr. scientist U. Ala. Inst. Dental Research, 1967-72, dir. autopsy services, 1975-79; vis. scholar dept. pathology U. Cambridge, Eng., 1972-73; cons. FDA, 1975-81. Author: (with J.F.A. McManus) Staining Methods: Histologic and Histochemical, 1960; mem. editorial bd. Jour. Histochemistry and Cytochemistry, 1960-75, Stain Tech., 1965-90, AMA Archives of Pathology, 1967-76, Biotechnics and Histochemistry, 1991—. Served with USPHS, 1948-52. Mem. Am. Soc. Investigative Pathology, Internat. Acad. Pathology, Biol. Stain Commn. (v.p. 1974-76, pres. 1976-81, trustee 1966—), Soc. for Glycobiology, Am. Assn. Univ. Profs. Pathology, Phi Beta Kappa, Sigma Xi, Delta Sigma Phi, Alpha Kappa Kappa. Presbyterian. Achievements include perfection of staining methods for complex carbohydrates (Alcian blue and colloidal iron) and insulin (Alcian blue-aldehyde fuchsin); showed the utility of these in diagnostic histopathology. Home: 4165 Sharpsburg Dr Birmingham AL 35213-3234

MOXLEY, JACQULYN CATHERINE, elementary education educator; b. Phila., Sept. 9, 1955; d. Paul Allen and Virginia Catherine (Carpenter) Killeen; m. Ronald Whelchel Moxley, May 29, 1976; children: Robert, Steven, Cathleen. BA, Glenville (W.Va.) State Coll., 1976; MA, W.Va. Coll. Grad. Studies, 1985; grad., W.Va. Tchrs. Acad., 1992. Tchr. Fair Haven Christian Sch., Charleston, W.Va., 1976-77, Mill Creek Elem. Sch., Pecks Mills, W.Va., 1977-79, Spruce Grade Sch., Sharples, W.Va., 1979-93, Sharples Elem.-Mid. Sch., 1993—; cons. on social studies curriculum goals Logan County Bd. Edn., Logan, W.Va., 1993, mem. curriculum study group early childhood com., 1995; sec. faculty senate Spruce Grade Sch., 1990-93, mem. curriculum team, 1991-93, mem. sch. improvement coun., 1992-93; sec. faculty senate and curriculum team Sharples Elem. Sch., 1993-95, mem. sch. improvement coun., 1993-95. Advisor Washington Dist. Redskins Majorettes, Ramage, W.Va., 1993. Recipient Tchr. of Yr. award Spruce Grade Sch., 1992, Sharples Elem.-Mid. Sch., 1994. Democrat. Methodist. Avocations: sewing, crafts. Home: PO Box 51 Sharples WV 25183-0051 Office: Sharples Elem-Mid Sch Drawer B Sharples WV 25183

MOXLEY, JOHN HOWARD, III, physician; b. Elizabeth, N.J., Jan. 10, 1935; s. John Howard, Jr. and Cleopatra (Mundy) M.; m. Doris Banchik; children: John Howard IV, Brook, Mark. BA, Williams Coll., 1957; MD, U. Colo., 1961; DSc (hon.), Sch. Medicine Hannemann U. Bar: Diplomate Am. Bd. Internal Medicine. Intern Peter Bent Brigham Hosp., Boston, 1961-62, resident in internal medicine, 1962-66; with Nat. Cancer Inst., USPHS, 1963-65; asst. to dean, instr. medicine Harvard Med. Sch., Boston, 1966-69; dean Sch. Medicine, U. Md., 1969-73; vice chancellor health scis., dean Med. Sch., U. Calif.-San Diego, 1973-79; asst. sec. for health affairs Dept. Def., Washington, 1979-81; sr. v.p. Am. Med. Internat., Beverly Hills, Calif., 1981-87; pres. MetaMed. Inc., Playa Del Rey, Calif., 1987-89; mgr. dir. Korn/Ferry Internat., L.A., 1989—; cons. FDA, NIH; dir. Nat. Fund for Med. Edn., 1986—, chmn., 1993—; dir. Henry M. Jackson Found. for Adv. Mil. Medicine. Contbr. articles to profl. jours. Dir. Polyclinic Health Svcs. Games of XXIII Olympiad. Recipient gold and silver award U. Colo. Med. Sch., 1974, commr.'s citation for outstanding svc. to over-the-counter drug study FDA, 1977, spl. achievement citation Am. Hosp. Assn., 1983, Sec. of Def. medal for disting. pub. svc., 1981. Fellow ACP, Am. Coll. Physicians Execs. (Disting.); mem. Inst. Medicine NAS, AMA (chmn. coun. sci. affairs 1985), Calif. Med. Assn. (chmn. sci. bd. 1978-83, councilor), San Diego C. of C., Soc. Med. Adminstrs., Am. Hosp. Assn. (trustee 1979-81), Alpha Omega Alpha. Rotary. Office: Korn/Ferry Internat 1800 Century Park E Ste 900 Los Angeles CA 90067-1512

MOY, PEARL MEI-HUNG, antiques dealer; b. Hong Kong, Aug. 2, 1965; came to U.S., 1969; d. Wai Yu Moy and Ping Han Chan. Sales assoc. Polo-Ralph Lauren, Beachwood, Ohio, 1979-83, Stamford, Conn., 1983-85; assoc. product mgr.-men's divsn. Polo-Ralph Lauren, N.Y.C., 1985-92; antiques dealer Phelps-Bancroft Ltd., Tolland, Mass., 1993—. Fund raiser Boys and Girls Club, N.Y.C., 1991; cons. Beautification Com., N.Y.C., 1991; fund raiser Nat. Rep. Party, Washington, 1993, N.Y.C., 1992. Mem. Union League Club, Met. Club. Avocations: sailing, traveling, museums, skiing, reading.

MOY, RICHARD HENRY, academic dean, educator; b. Chgo., Feb. 2, 1931; s. Henry B. and Gladys (Pope) M.; m. Caryl L. Towsley, Aug. 21, 1954; children: Philip B., Eric R. BA in Pre-Medicine with gen. honors, U. Chgo., 1953, BS in Pre-Medicine, 1954, MD in Pathology with honors, 1957. Diplomate Am. Bd. Internal Medicine. Intern U. Chgo. Hosps. and Clinics, 1957-58, resident, 1960-63; clin. assoc. Nat. Cancer Inst. NIH, Bethesda, Md., 1958-60; instr. dept. internal medicine U. Chgo., 1962-63, rsch. assoc., asst. prof., 1964-68, assoc. prof., 1968-70; prof. internal medicine, dean Sch. Medicine So. Ill. U., Springfield, 1970-93, dean emeritus, 1974-93, 1993—; mem. health care program com. Health Care Svc. Corp., 1978-79, 82—, exec. com., 1979-80, 82-83, 84-86, 88—, fin. com., 1981-82, bd. orgn. and nominating com., 1984—, ad hoc com. for long range planning, 1982-83, bd. dirs., 1971—; mem. ad hoc rev. group for start-up assistance grants HEW, 1976; del. People-to-People Med. Edn. Trip to Africa, 1982; mem. med. determination bd. Ill. Dept. Pub. Health, 1980-85, adv. com. family practice residency, 1978, health svc. corps task force, 1980-93; mem. task force on future of mental health in Ill., 1986-87; panelist, lectr., cons. S.C. Commn. on Higher Edn., 1990, other orgns. Contbr. articles to profl. jours. Mem. adv. bd. Ill. Emergency Svcs. and Disaster Agy., 1984-93, Ill. Geriatric Edn. Ctr., 1989-93; chair emergency med. care com. Gov.'s Task Force on Earthquake Preparedness, 1989-90; bd. dirs. Am. Heart Assn. Ill., 1982-84; mem. planning com. St. John's Hosp., 1976-93, Meml. Med. Ctr., 1980-93; mem. VA med. assistance rev. com., 1974-78; chmn. citizens' task force to pass tax referendum Springfield Pub. Sch. Dist. 186, 1984; mem. site visit team Marshall U., 1974, 82, Duke U., 1978, Creighton U., 1980, UCLA, 1981, U. Okla., 1985, Temple U., 1988, Vanderbilt U. Sch. Medicine, 1992; chmn. site visit team U. Calif. Sch. Medicine, 1975, East Tenn. U., 1990, Med. Coll. Pa., 1991, Mich. State U., 1992, Loma Linda U. Med. Sch., 1994. Recipient Disting. Svc. award Med. Alumni Assn. U. Chgo., 1979, Recognition award Soc. Tchrs. of Family Medicine, 1981, Pub. Svc. award So. Ill. U. Carbondale Alumni Assn., 1984, Golden Achievement award Nat. Sch. Pub. Rels. Assn., 1985, Gold Medallion for Humanitarian Svc., Am. Lung Assn., 1993; named rector for medicine and sci. Lincoln Acad. Ill., 1991. Fellow ACP; mem. Assn. Am. Med. Colls. (various coms. and offices), AMA (sect. med. schs. 1977-93), Am. Bd. Med. Spltys. (rep. Assn. Med. Colls. 1986-91), Ill. Coun. Med. Deans (pres. 1978-79), Ill. Hosp. Assn. (ad hoc study group funding med. edn.), Ill. State Med. Soc., Nat. Bd. Med. Examiners (chair composite com. for U.S. med. licensing examination 1990-92, comprehensive part I and part II coms. 1986-92, John F. Hubbard award com. 1987, mem. ednl. adv. com. Nat. Fund for Med. Edn. 1988-90, chmn. 1988), Sangamon County Med. Soc., Springfield Med. Club, Cen. Ill. Consortium for Health Manpower Edn. (pres. 1976-77), Ill. State Acad. Sci. (hon.), Alpha Omega Alpha, Sigma Xi. Presbyterian. Avocations: med. history, fishing, reading. Office: So Ill U Sch Medicine 801 N Rutledge PO Box 19230 Springfield IL 62794-9230

MOYA, OLGA LYDIA, law educator; b. Weslaco, Tex., Dec. 27, 1959; d. Leonel V. and Genoveva (Tamez) M.; m. James Troutman Byrd, Aug. 24, 1985; children: Leanessa Geneva Byrd, Taylor Moya Byrd. BA, U. Tex., 1981, JD, 1984. Bar: Tex. 1984. Legis. atty. Tex. Ho. of Reps., Austin, 1985; atty. Tex. Dept. Agr., Austin, 1985-90; asst. regional counsel U.S. EPA, Dallas, 1990-91; asst. prof. law South Tex. Coll. of Law, Houston, 1992-95, assoc. prof. law, 1995—. Bd. dirs. Hermann Children's Hosp., Houston, 1993—; mem. Leadership Tex., Austin, 1991—; bd. dirs. Tex. Clean Water Coun., Austin, 1992, Mex.-Am. Legis. Policy Coun., 1986-90; U.S. del. to UN Conf. on the Environment for Latin Am. and the Caribbean, San Juan, 1995. Recipient Vol. of Yr. award George H. Hermann Soc., 1995, Hispanic Law Prof. of Yr. Hispanic Nat. Bar Assn., 1995. Mem. ABA (environ. law sect.), Hispanic Bar Assn. (bd. dirs. 1992—, Excellence award 1995), Mex.-Am. Bar Assn. Office: South Tex Coll of Law 1303 San Jacinto St Houston TX 77002

MOYA, PATRICK ROBERT, lawyer; b. Belen, N.Mex., Nov. 7, 1944; s. Adelicio E. and Eva (Sanchez) M.; m. Sara Dreier, May 30, 1966; children: Jeremy Brill, Joshua Dreier. AB, Princeton U., 1966; JD, Stanford U., 1969. Bar: Calif. 1970, Ariz. 1970, D.C. 1970, U.S. Dist. Ct. (no. dist.) Calif. 1970, U.S. Ct. Claims 1970, U.S. Tax Ct. 1970, U.S. Ct. Appeals (D.C. cir.) 1970, U.S. Supreme Ct. 1973. Assoc. Lewis and Roca, Phoenix, 1969-73, ptnr., 1973-83; sr. ptnr. Moya, Bailey, Bowers & Jones, P.C., Phoenix, 1983-84; ptnr., mem. nat. exec. com. Gaston & Snow, Phoenix, 1985-91; ptnr., Ariz. legal practice coord. Quarles & Brady, Phoenix, 1991—; instr. sch. of law Ariz. State U., 1972; bd. dir. Bobby McGee's U.S.A., Inc., 1982-86. Mem. Paradise Valley Bd. Adjustment, 1976-80, chmn., 1978-80; mem. Paradise Valley Town Coun., 1980-82; bd. dirs. Phoenix Men's Arts Coun., 1973-81, pres., 1979-80; bd. dirs. The Silent Witness, Inc., 1979-84, pres., 1981-83; bd. dirs. Enterprise Network, Inc., 1989-94, pres., 1991-92; bd. dirs. Phoenix Little Theatre, 1973-75, Interfaith Counseling Svc., 1973-75; precinct committeeman Phoenix Rep. Com., 1975-77; dep. voter registrar Maricopa County, 1975-76; mem. exec. bd. dirs. Gov.'s Strategic Partnership for Econ. Devel.; pres. GSPED, Inc.; mem. of Steering Com. for Sonora Ariz. Joint Econ. Plan; mem. Gov.'s Adv. Com., Ariz. and Mex., Ariz. Corp. Commn. Stock Exch. Adv. Coun., Ariz. Town Hall. Mem. ABA, Nat. Hispanic Bar Assn., Los Abogados Hispanic Lawyers Assn., Nat. Assn. Bond Lawyers, Ariz. Bar Assn., Maricopa County Bar Assn., Paradise Valley Country Club, Univ. Club. Office: Quarles & Brady 1 E Camelback Rd Ste 400 Phoenix AZ 85012-1649

MOYA, ROSEMARY MERCEDES, mental health administrator; b. Santa Fe, Aug. 11, 1957; d. Willie and Mercedes Sadie Ramona (Rivera) Padilla; m. Raymond Anthony Moya, Aug. 9, 1980; children: Joslyn Monique, Alyssa Nichole. BS in Edn., U. N.Mex., 1979, MPA, 1990. Adminstrv. asst. Hubbard Broadcasting, Albuquerque, 1980; staff asst. N.Mex. Mcpl. League, Santa Fe, 1980-81; staff asst. Div. Mental Health/Dept. of Health, Santa Fe, 1981-82, pers. adminstr., 1982-84, planner, 1981-88, health program mgr., 1988-91, chief community programs bur., 1991—. Parent vol. St. Francis Cath. Sch., 1990—; vol. Am. Cancer Soc., 1993, Easter Seals, Santa Fe, 1991; sec. liturgy com. Santa Maria de la Paz Cath. Com., 1991-94, chair liturgy com., 1994—, mem. bldg. com., 1991-94, mem. art selection com., 1992-94. N.Mex. Mcpl. League scholar, 1987-90; named Woman of Yr., Girls Club, Santa Fe, 1987. Mem. NAFE, Nat. Orgn. for Victim Assistance, Pi Alpha Alpha, Phi Kappa Phi. Democrat. Roman Catholic. Avocations: volleyball, skiing, tennis, camping, reading. Office: Dept Health/Div Mental Hlth 1190 S Saint Francis Dr Santa Fe NM 87505-4182

MOYARS-JOHNSON, MARY ANNIS, university official; b. Lafayette, Ind., July 19, 1938; d. Edward Raymond and Veronica Marie (Quigg) Moyars; m. Raymond Leon Molter, Aug. 1, 1959 (div. 1970); children: Marilyn Eileen Molter Davis, William Raymond, Ann Marie; m. Thomas Elmer Johnson, May 25, 1973 (div. 1989); children: Thomas Edward, John Alan, Barbara Suzanne. BS, Purdue U., 1960; MA, Purdue U., West Lafayette, Ind., 1991, postgrad., 1985—. Grader great issues Purdue U., West Lafayette, 1960-63, writer ednl. films, 1962-65, publicity dir. convocations and lectures, 1969-74, devel. officer Sch. Humanities, 1979-88, asst. to dir. Optoelectronics Rsch. Ctr., 1989-90, mgr. indsl. rels. Sch. Elec. Engring., 1990—; tchr. English and math. Benton Community Schs., Fowler, Ind., 1966-69; pub. rels. dir. Sycamore Girl Scout Coun., Lafayette, Ind., 1974-78; dir. pub. info. Ind. Senate, Majority Caucus, Indpls., 1977-78; sr. script writer Walters & Steinberg, Lafayette, 1988-89. Author: Colonial Potpourri, 1975; co-author: Historic Colonial French Dress, 1982; contbr. articles to profl. jours. Bd. govs. Tippecanoe County Hist. Assn., Lafayette, 1981—. Mem. Women in Communications, Inc. (v.p. program, Pres. award 1983), Ctr. for French Colonial Rsch. (dir. 1986-89, editor 1988-89), Am. Hist. Assn., Germanna Found., Palatines to Am., Ind. History Assn., Ind. Hist. Soc., Minitrista Coun. for Great Lakes Native Am. Studies, French Colonial Hist. Soc. Roman Catholic. Avocations: history, genealogy, embroidery. Home: 924 Elm Dr West Lafayette IN 47906-2246 Office: Sch Electrical Engring Purdue U West Lafayette IN 47907

MOYE, CHARLES ALLEN, JR., federal judge; b. Atlanta, July 13, 1918; s. Charles Allen and Annie Luther (Williamson) M.; m. Sarah Ellen Johnston, Mar. 9, 1945; children: Henry Allen, Lucy Ellen. A.B., Emory U., 1939, J.D., 1943. Bar: Ga. 1943. Since practiced in Atlanta; partner firm Gambrell, Russell, Moye & Killorin (and predecessors), 1955-70; chief judge U.S. Dist. Ct. (no. dist.) Ga., 1979-87, judge, 1970-87, sr. judge, 1988—. Chmn. DeKalb County Republican Exec. Com., 1952-56; chmn. Rep. Exec. Com. 5th Congl. Dist. Ga., 1956-64; mem. Ga. Rep. Central Com., 1952-64; Rep. candidate for Congress, 1954; del. Rep. Nat. Conv., 1956, 60, 64; chmn. Rep. Exec. Com. 4th Congl. Dist., 1964, Rep. presdl. elector, 1964. Mem. ABA, Fed. Bar Assn., Atlanta Bar Assn., State Bar Ga., Lawyers Club Atlanta, Am. Judicature Soc., Am. Bar Found., Am. Law Inst., Atlanta Athletic Club, Delta Tau Delta. Congregationalist. Home: 1317 Council Bluff Dr NE Atlanta GA 30345-4131 Office: US Dist Ct 2342 US Courthouse 75 Spring St SW Atlanta GA 30303-3309*

MOYE, JOHN EDWARD, lawyer; b. Deadwood, S.D., Aug. 15, 1944; s. Francis Joseph and Margaret C. (Roberts) M.; children: Kelly M., Mary S., Megan J. BBA, U. Notre Dame, 1965; JD with distinction, Cornell U., 1968. Bar: N.Y. 1968, Colo. 1971. Prof. law U. Denver, 1972-78, assoc. dean Coll. Law, 1974-78; prof. law So. Meth. U., Dallas, 1973; ptnr. Moye, Giles, O'Keefe, Vermeire & Gorrell, Denver, 1976—; lectr. Harcourt Brace Jovanovich, Chgo., 1972-95, Profl. Edn. Group, Minnetonka, Minn., 1982-95, West Profl. Tng. Program, 1995—; chmn. Bd. Law Examiners, Denver, 1988-92. Chmn. Denver Urban Renewal Authority, 1988-93, Colo. Hist. Found., Denver, 1987—; pres. Downtown Denver, Inc., 1986-88; mem. Consumer Credit Commn., 1985—; mem. bd. Stapleton Devel. Corp.,

1995—; Denver Botanic Gardens, 1996—. Named Prof. of Yr., U. Denver, 1972-74, 76-78, Outstanding Faculty Mem., 1975. Fellow Am. Bar Found.; mem. ABA, Colo. Bar Assn. (chmn. corp., banking and bus. sect. 1982-84, Young Lawyer of Yr. award 1980), N.Y. State Bar Assn., Denver Bar Assn. (Young Lawyer of Yr. award 1980), Law Club (pres. 1982-84). Republican. Roman Catholic. Office: 1225 17th St Denver CO 80202-5534

MOYER, ALAN DEAN, retired newspaper editor; b. Galva, Iowa, Sept. 4, 1928; s. Clifford Lee and Harriet (Jacques) M.; m. Patricia Helen Krecker, July 15, 1950; children: Virginia, Stanley, Glenn. BS in Journalism, U. Iowa, 1950. Reporter, copy editor Wis. State Jour., Madison, 1950-53; reporter, photographer Bartlesville (Okla.) Examiner-Enterprise, 1953; telegraph editor Abilene (Tex.) Reporter-News, 1954-55; makeup editor Cleve. Plain Dealer, 1955-63; mng. editor Wichita (Kans.) Eagle, 1963-70; exec. editor Wichita Eagle and Beacon, 1970-73; mng. editor Phoenix Gazette, 1973-82, Ariz. Republic, 1982-89; ret., 1989; pres., dir. Wichita Profl. Baseball, Inc., 1969-75; mem. jury Pulitzer Prizes, 1973-74, 85, 86, 88. Mem. AP Mng. Editors Assn. (dir. 1973-78), Am. Soc. Newspaper Editors, Wichita Area C. of C. (dir. 1970-72), Sigma Delta Chi. Office: Phoenix Newspaper Inc 120 E Van Buren St Phoenix AZ 85004-2227

MOYER, CHERYL LYNN, non-profit administrator; b. St. Petersburg, Fla., Apr. 4, 1953; d. Joseph Paul Safko and Doris Marie (Wolf) Sniegocki; m. John Arthur Weber (div. 1982); m. Ross Allen Moyer, June 21, 1983; children: Deborah, Martin, Brian, Spencer. BS, Lock Haven U., 1986; MPA, Pa. State U., 1987. Office mgr. Piper Aircraft Corp., Lock Haven, Pa., 1974-76; radio rep. Sta. WTGC Radio, Lewisburg, Pa., 1976-77; sales rep. Sears, Lycoming Mall, Pa., 1977-83; ptnr., dir. The Trading Post, Williamsport, Pa., 1983-85; mgr., founder Lock Haven U. Day Care, 1985-86; field mgr. Pa. Pub. Interest Coalition, State Coll., Pa., 1987-88; exec. dir. Pa. Assn. Families, Harrisburg, Pa., 1988-91; unit dir.-residential Resources for Human Devel., Phila., 1989-93; mgr. ob-gyn. clinic Meth. Hosp., Phila., 1993-94, bus. analyst, 1994; owner Family Fin. Svcs., 1994-95; chair bd. dirs., fin. dir. Matchmaker Internat. Midlantic; Nat. reg. lobbyist. Grantee Family Planning Svcs., 1994. Mem. Nat. Assn. Dual Diagnosis, Pa. State Alumni Assn., Interfaith Assn., Mensa. Home: 79 Tallowood Dr Medford NJ 08055

MOYER, F. STANTON, financial executive, advisor; b. Phila., June 7, 1929; s. Edward T. and Beatrice (Stanton) M.; m. Ann P. Stovell, May 16, 1953; 1 child, Alice E. B.S. in Econs., U. Pa., 1951. Registered rep. Smith, Barney & Co., Phila., 1951-54, Kidder, Peabody & Co., Phila., 1954-60; mgr. corp. dept. Blyth Eastman Dillon & Co., Inc. (formerly Eastman Dillon, Union Securities & Co.), Phila., 1960-65; instl. sales mgr. Blyth Eastman Dillon & Co., Inc. (formerly Eastman Dillon, Union Securities & Co.), 1965-67, gen. partner, 1967-71, 1st v.p., 1971-74, sr. v.p., 1974-80; v.p., resident officer Kidder, Peabody & Co. Inc., Phila., 1980-86; chmn. Pa. Mcht. Group Ltd., Radnor, 1987-88; exec. v.p. Rorer Asset Mgmt., Phila., 1990-92; chmn. Mercer Capital Mgmt., 1992-93, Global Mgmt. Group, Inc., 1993-95; mng. dir. Avonwood Capital Corp., 1995—. Trustee U. Pa., 1978-83, Hosp. of U. Pa., 1978-87; bd. dirs. Atwater Kent Mus., Phila., 1983—. Mem. Racquet Club (Phila.), St. Anthony Club (Phila.), Merion Cricket Club (Haverford, Pa.), Gulph Mills Golf Club (King of Prussia, Pa.), Edgartown (Mass.) Golf Club, Delta Psi. Republican. Episcopalian. Home: 445 Caversham Rd Bryn Mawr PA 19010-2901

MOYER, JOHN HENRY, III, physician, educator; b. Hershey, Pa., Apr. 1, 1917; s. John Henry and Anna Mae (Gruber) M.; m. Mary Elizabeth Hughes; children: John Henry IV, Michael, Carl, Anna Mary, Nancy Elizabeth, Mary Louise, Matthew Timothy. BS, Lebanon Valley Coll., 1939, DSc (hon.), 1968; MD, U. Pa., 1943. Diplomate Am. Bd. Internal Medicine, Nat. Bd. Med. Examiners; lic. physician Mass., Pa., Tex. Intern Pa. Hosp., Phila., 1943; resident in Tb and contagious diseases Belmont Hosp., Worcester, Mass., 1944-45; asst. instr. Tb and contagious diseases U. Vt., 1944-45; chief resident in medicine Brooke Gen. Hosp., San Antonio, 1947; fellow in pharmacology and medicine Sch. Medicine, U. Pa., Phila., 1948-50; attending physician, then. sr. attending physician Jefferson Davis Hosp., Houston, 1950-57, Meth. Hosp., Houston, 1950-57; from asst. prof. to prof. internal medicine and pharmacology Coll. Medicine, Baylor U., Houston, 1950-56, prof., 1956-57; prof., chmn. dept. medicine Hahnemann Med. Coll. and Hosp., Phila., 1957-74, exec. v.p. acad. affairs, 1971-73; sr. v.p., dir. profl. and ednl. affairs Conemaugh Valley Meml. Hosp., Johnstown, Pa., 1974-88; emeritus dir. profl. and ednl. affairs Conemaugh Valley Meml. Hosp., Johnstown, 1988—; prof. Temple U., 1977—; dir. regional affairs Sch. Medicine Temple U., 1977-88; clin. prof. Coll. Medicine Pa. State U., Hershey, 1976—; adj. prof. natural scis. U. Pitts., Johnstown, 1982-88; adj. prof. physician asst. sci. St. Francis Coll., 1983-88, sr. cons. physician asst. program adv. com., 1985-88; vis. prof., lectr. various ednl. instns.; mem. Pa. State Bd. Med. Edn. and Licensure, 1977-86, sec. to bd., 1982-86; mem. task force on profl. edn., mem. hypertension info. and edn. adv. com. U.S. HEW, 1972-75; chmn. high blood pressure control adv. bd. to sec. health State of Pa., 1980-86; cons. numerous profl. orgns. Editorial cons. Am. Jour. Cardiology, 1960-72; editor-in-chief Cyclopedia of Medicine, Surgery and Specialties, 1963-65; mem. editorial adv. bd. Internal Medicine News, 1969-92; editor 16 multi-authored textbooks; contbr. more than 600 articles to profl. jours. Mem. bd. trustees Pa. Heart Assn., 1959-65, v.p. bd. trustees, 1965; mem. bd. govs. Heart Assn. Southeastern Pa., 1958-64, 67-72; bd. dirs. Houston Heart Assn., 1952-57; mem., then emeritus fellow med. adv. bd. coun. for high blood pressure Am. Heart Assn., 1954—, chmn., 1964-65, mem., then emeritus fellow cen. adv. bd. coun. on circulation; deacon, Salem United Ch. of Christ. Maj. U.S. Army, 1945-48. Recipient Susan and Theodora R. Cummings Humanitarian award, 1962, 65, 66, Presdl. citation Cultural Exchg. Program, U.S. State Dept., 1964, Honors Achievement award Angiology Rsch. Found., 1965; named Alumni of Yr., Lebanon Valley Coll., Annville, Pa., 1967. Fellow ACP (Laureate award for Western Pa. 1986), Am. Coll. Cardiology (trustee 1961-68), N.Y. Acad. Scis. (emeritus), Am. Coll. Chest Physicians (emeritus); mem. AMA (emeritus, mem. ho. dels. 1966-72, cons. coun. on drugs 1968-72, mem. sect. coun. on clin. pharmacology and therapeutics), AAAS (emeritus), Am. Soc. Clin. Pharmacology and Therapeutics (emeritus dir., hon. dir.), Am. Fedn. Clin. Rsch. (emeritus), Am. Soc. Pharmacology and Exptl. Therapeutics (emeritus), Assn. Am. Med. Colls., Am. Acad. Med. Dirs., Am. Soc. Internal Medicine, Pa. Soc. Internal Medicine (pres. 1992-94, Pressman award for lifetime of contbns. and commitment to internal medicine 1996), Sems. and Symposia (pres.), Assn. Hosp. Med. Edn., Assn. Former Chmn. Medicine, U.S. Pharmacopaeia Convention (pres. 1970-75, bd. trustees 1970-80), Sigma Xi, many others. Republican. Achievements include extensive research in cardiovascular diseases. Address: 1090 Miller Rd Palmyra PA 17078-9602

MOYER, KENNETH EVAN, psychologist, educator; b. Chippewa Falls, Wis., Nov. 19, 1919; s. John Evan and Margaret (Lashway) M.; m. Doris Virginia Johnson, May 29, 1943; children: Robert Stephen, Cathy Lita. A.B. with honors, Park Coll., 1943; M.A., Washington U., St. Louis, 1948, Ph.D., 1951. Mem. faculty Carnegie-Mellon U., Pitts., 1949—; prof. psychology Carnegie-Mellon U., 1961—; cons. on higher edn. Gov. Norway, 1954; mem. research adv. com. Pa. Commonwealth Mental Health Found., 1956—. Author: The Physiology of Hostility, 1971, You and Your Child: A Primer for Parents, 1974, The Psychobiology of Aggression, 1976, Physiology of Aggression and Implications for Control, 1976, A Reader's Guide to Aggressive Behavior, 1977, Neuroanatomy, 1980, Bibliography of Aggressive Behavior: A Reader's Guide to the Literature, Vol. II, Violence and Aggression, 1987. Recipient Carnegie Found. award for excellence in teaching, 1954. Fellow AAAS, Am. Psychol. Assn.; mem. Psychonomic Soc., So. Soc. Philosophy and Psychology, Pitts. Psychol. Assn. (past dir.), Sigma Xi, Theta Kappa Theta. Research, publs. endocrinology emotion, startle response avoidance behavior, physiology aggression; demonstrated young children have capacity for prolonged attention spans if proper toys are used, that adrenal glands are not essential for effects electroconvulsive shock on behavior; devel. physiol. theory aggressive behavior. Home: 1211 Ridgewood Dr Lillian AL 36549-5303

MOYER, STEVEN E., lawyer; b. Mineola, N.Y., Aug. 30, 1944; s. Jack D. and Naomi R. (Epstein) M.; m. Joan Deborah Krausen, Aug. 13, 1972; children: Alexander, David. BA with honors, UCLA, 1966; JD, 1969; postgrad., London Sch. Econs., 1969-70. Sr. trial atty. L.A. County Pub. Defender, 1970-84; pvt. practice L.A., 1985; assoc., ptnr. Haight, Brown & Bonesteel, Santa Monica, Calif., 1986—; law educator Univ. West L.A. Sch. Law, 1993; arbitrator L.A. Superior Ct., 1993—. Mem. ABA, Calif. Bar Assn., L.A. County Bar Assn. (judicial qualifications com. 1994), Santa Monica Bar Assn., So. Calif. Defense Counsel, Phi Beta Kappa. Democrat. Jewish. Avocations: bicycling, skiing, drawing and painting, music. Office: Haight Brown & Bonesteel 1620 26th St Ste 400 N Santa Monica CA 90404-4041

MOYER, THOMAS J., state supreme court chief justice; b. Sandusky, Ohio, Apr. 18, 1939; s. Clarence and Idamae (Hessler) M.; m. Mary Francis Moyer, Dec. 15, 1984; 1 child, Drew; stepchildren: Anne, Jack, Alaine, Elizabeth. BA, Ohio State U., 1961, JD, 1964. Asst. atty. gen. State of Ohio, Columbus, 1964-66; pvt. practice law Columbus, 1966-69; dep. asst. Office Gov. State of Ohio, Columbus, 1969-71, exec. asst., 1975-79; assoc. Crabbe, Brown, Jones, Potts & Schmidt, Columbus, 1972-75; judge U.S. Ct. Appeals (10th cir.), Columbus, 1979-86; chief justice Ohio Supreme Ct., Columbus, 1987—. Sec. bd. trustees Franklin U., Columbus, 1986-87; trustee Univ. Club, Columbus, 1986; mem. nat. council adv. com. Ohio State U. Coll. Law, Columbus. Recipient Award of Merit, Ohio Legal Ctr. Inst.; named Outstanding Young Man of Columbus, Columbus Jaycees, 1969. Mem. Ohio State Bar Assn. (exec. com., council dels.), Columbus Bar Assn. (pres. 1980-81), Critchon Club, Columbus Maennerchor Club. Republican. Avocations: sailing, tennis. Office: Ohio Supreme Ct 30 E Broad St Fl 3 Columbus OH 43215-3414

MOYERS, BILL D., journalist; b. Hugo, Okla., June 5, 1934; s. John Henry and Ruby (Johnson) M.; m. Judith Davidson, Dec. 18, 1954; children: William Cope, Suzanne, John. BJ with honors, U. Tex., 1956; grad. student, U. Edinburgh, Scotland, 1956-57; MTh with honors, Southwestern Baptist Theol. Sem., 1959; DFA (hon.), Am. Film Inst. Personal asst. to Senator Lyndon B. Johnson, 1960; assoc. dir. Peace Corps, 1961-62, dept. dir., 1963; spl. asst. to Pres. Johnson, 1963-67, press sec., 1965-67; pub. Newsday, Garden City, N.Y., 1967-70; editor-in-chief Bill Moyers Jour. (weekly pub. affairs program on pub. TV), 1971-76, 78-81; chief corr. CBS Reports, CBS-TV, 1976-78; sr. news analyst CBS News, CBS-TV, 1981-86; exec. editor Pub. Affairs TV, Inc., 1987—; news analyst NBC News, 1995—. Author: Listening to America, 1971, Report from Philadelphia, 1987, The Secret Government, 1988, Joseph Cmapbell and the Power of Myth, 1988, A World of Ideas, 1989, 2d edit., 1990, Healing and the Mind, 1993. Recipient over 30 Emmy awards, Ralph Lowell medal for contbn. to pub. TV, George Peabody award, 1976, 80, 85-86, 88-90, Silver Baton award DuPont-Columbia U., 1979, 86, 88, Gold baton award, 1991, George Polk award, 1981, 86, career achievement award Internat. Documentary Assn., Eric Barnouw award Orgn. Am. Historians, medal of excellence N.Y. State Bd. Regents, James Madison award Nat. Broadcasting Editl. Assn., Lowell Mellett award, award NEA, spl. recognition Assn. for Continuing Higher Edn., Communicator of Decade award Religious Comm. Congress, Elmer Holmes Bibst award NYU, Religious Liberty award Am. Jewish Com., 1995; elected to TV Hall of Fame, 1995. Fellow Am. Acad. Arts and Scis. Office: Pub Affairs TV Inc 356 W 58th St New York NY 10019-1804

MOYERS, JUDITH DAVIDSON, television producer; b. Dallas, May 12, 1935; d. Henry Joseph and Eula E. (Dendy) Davidson; m. Bill D. Moyers; children: William Cope, Suzanne, John. BS, U. Tex., 1956; LittD (hon.), L.I. U., 1989, SUNY, 1990. Pres., exec. prodr. Pub. Affairs T.V., N.Y.C., 1987—; Bd. dirs. Paine Webber Mut. Funds, Ogden Corp. Exec. prodr. numerous T.V. documentaries (Emmy 1980, 93); contbr. articles to profl. jours., newspapers, mags. Trustee SUNY, 1976-90; commr. U.S. Commn. UNESCO, Washington, 1977-80, White House commn. Internat. Yr. of Child, Washington, 1978-80; mem. jud. selection com. State N.Y., 1992-93; dir. Pub. Agenda Found. Mem. Century Club. Mem. Congregational Ch. Office: Pub Affairs TV Inc 356 W 58th St New York NY 10019-1804

MOYERS, LOWELL DUANE, pipeline company executive; b. Globe, Ariz., June 10, 1930; s. Thomas Jefferson and Alta Beulah (Taylor) M.; m. Phyllis Jean Haviland, Oct. 29, 1951; children: Jennifer, Catherine, Nina. AA, Compton (Calif.) Jr. Coll., 1958, Fullerton Jr. Coll., 1958; student, Fullerton State Coll., 1965-66. Laborer Pacific Pipeline Constrn. Co., Montebello, Calif., 1947-48, timekeeper, 1948-51, foreman, 1953-60, supt., estimater, 1960-69, gen. supt., 1969-73; v.p. Victor Valley Pipeline Co., Victorville, Calif., 1973-77; mgr. Macco Constructors, Apple Valley, Calif., 1977-80; founder, pres., chmn. Ariz. Pipeline Co., Apple Valley, 1980—. Inventor constrn. equipment. Cpl. U.S. Army, 1951-53, Germany. Named among Men of Achievement in Pipeline Industry, Universal News, Inc., 1992. Mem. Pacific Coast Gas Assn., We. Pipe Liners Assn., Apple Valley Country Cub, The Lakes Country Club, Silverlakes Country Club. Republican. Avocations: golf, fishing, traditional New Orleans jazz. Office: Ariz Pipeline Co 17372 Lilac St Hesperia CA 92345-5162

MOYLAN, JOHN L., secondary school principal. Prin. DeMatha Cath. High Sch., Hyattsville, Md. Recipient Blue Ribbon Sch. award U.S. Dept. Edn., 1983-84, 90-91, Disting. Prin. award Archdiocese of Washington, 1991, Sch. Adminstr. award Md. Music Educators Assn., 1992, Disting. Ednl. Leadership award Washington Post, 1993. Office: DeMatha Cath High Sch 4313 Madison St Hyattsville MD 20781-1692

MOYLE, PETER BRIGGS, fisheries and biology educator; b. Mpls., May 29, 1942; s. John Briggs and Evelyn (Wood) M.; m. Marilyn Arneson, June 11, 1966; children—Petrea Ruth, John Noah. B.A., U. Minn., 1964; M.S., Cornell U., 1966; Ph.D., U. Minn., 1969. Asst. prof. Calif. State U. Fresno, 1969-72; from asst. prof. to prof. U. Calif., Davis, 1972—, chmn. dept. wildlife and fisheries, 1982-87; head, Delta Native Fishes Recovery Team, 1993-95. Author: Inland Fishes of California, 1976; Fishes: An Introduction to Ichthyology, 3d edit., 1996; Distribution and Ecology of Stream Fishes of Sacramento San Joaquin Drainage, 1982, Fish: An Enthusiast's Guide, 1993. Fellow Calif. Acad. Sci.; mem. Am. Fisheries Soc. (life, award of excellence West div. 1991, Outstanding Educator award 1995), Ecol. Soc. Am., Am. Soc. Ichthyologists and Herptologists, Soc. Conservation Biology., Natural Heritage Inst. (v.p. 1994—). Home: 612 Eisenhower St Davis CA 95616-3031 Office: Dept Wildlife & Fisheries U Calif Davis Davis CA 95616

MOYNAHAN, JOHN DANIEL, JR., insurance executive; b. Chgo., Dec. 10, 1935; s. John Daniel and Helen (Hurley) M.; m. Virginia Thomas, Oct. 10, 1959; children: Laura, Mark, Tricia, Kate. B.A. cum laude, U. Notre Dame, 1957. With Met. Life Ins. Co., N.Y.C., 1957—; regional v.p. Met. Life Ins. Co., from 1971, with nat. div. group nat. accounts, 1979-80, sr. v.p. group life and health ops., 1980-86, exec. v.p., 1986—. Office: Met Life Ins Co 1 Madison Ave New York NY 10010-3603

MOYNAHAN, JULIAN LANE, English language educator, author; b. Cambridge, Mass., May 21, 1925; s. Joseph Leo and Mary (Shea) M.; m. Elizabeth Rose Reilly, Aug. 6, 1945; children: Catherine (dec.), Brigid, Mary Ellen. A.B., Harvard U., 1946, A.M., 1951, Ph.D., 1957. Catalogure, rare books asst. Boston Pub. Library, 1948-49, 51; teaching fellow Harvard U., 1951-53; instr. English Amherst Coll., 1953-55; instr., asst. prof. English Princeton, 1955-63; Fulbright lectr. Am. and English lit. Univ. Coll., Dublin, 1963-64; assoc. prof. English Rutgers U., 1964-66, prof., 1966-93, disting. prof., 1976-93, prof. emeritus, 1993—; vis. prof. U. Wyo., summer 1965, Harvard U., summer 1967, Bread Loaf Sch., 1969; NEH vis. prof. Manhattanville Coll., 1972; Gauss lectr. Princeton U., 1975; vis. scholar English dept. U. Utah, spring 1980. Author: Sisters and Brothers, 1960, The Deed of Life, A Critical Study of D.H. Lawrence, 1963, Pairing Off, 1969, Vladimir Nabokov, 1971, Garden State, 1973, Where the Land and Water Meet, 1979, Anglo-Irish: The Literary Imagination in a Hyphenated Culture, 1994; editor: (D.H. Lawrence) Sons and Lovers: Text, Criticism, Backgrounds, 1968, 77, The Viking Portable Thomas Hardy, 1977; contbr. revs. and criticism to N.Y. Times Book Rev., New Republic, T.L.S., Washington Post Book World, N.Y. Rev. Books, London Observer; contbr., mem. editl. bd. The Recorder, Jour. Am. Irish Hist. Soc., 1994—. Bicentennial preceptorship Princeton, 1960-63, grants-in-aid Am. Council Learned Socs., Am. Philos. Soc.; mem. Pulitzer Prize Fiction Jury, 1981, chmn., 1987. Served with AUS, 1943-44. 7500 creative writing award Nat. Found. Arts, 1966; Ingram-Merrill award, 1967; NEH fellow, 1975; Guggenheim fellow, 1983-84. Mem. MLA, AAUP, PEN, Harvard Club of Princeton. Democrat. Home: 3439 Lawrenceville Rd Princeton NJ 08540-4717 also: 405 W 23rd St Apt 9B New York NY 10011-1412

MOYNE, JOHN ABEL, computer scientist, linguist, educator; b. Yezd, Iran, July 6, 1920; s. Abul Kasim and Sogra (Afshar) M.; came to U.S., 1956, naturalized, 1965; BA, Georgetown U., 1959, MA, 1960; PhD, Harvard U., 1970; m. Claudia Wienert, July 4, 1963; children: David, Nicholas, Parvin. With Brit. Govt., Iran and India, 1943-52, market research officer, Tehran, 1952; linguist U.S. Govt., Cyprus, 1953-56; rsch. assoc. Georgetown U., Washington, 1960-63; mgr. applied linguistics dept. IBM Corp., Cambridge, Mass., 1963-71; prof., chmn. computer sci. dept. Queens Coll., CUNY, Flushing, 1971-81, chmn. div. math. and natural scis., 1978-81, chmn. univ. faculty for Ph.D. in Computer Sci., 1978-82, exec. officer Grad. Sch. Ph.D. Program in Linguistics, 1983-88; prof. linguistics and computer sci. CUNY, 1971-91, prof. emeritus linguistics and computer sci., 1991—. Grantee, EURATOM, AEC, NSF, City U. N.Y. Mem. Linguistic Soc. Am., Assn. Computational Linguistics, Brit. Inst. Engring. Technology. Democrat. Episcopalian. Author: Hafiz of Shiraz, 1946; Life in India, 1949; Open Secret, 1984; Understanding Language: Man or Machine, 1985; Unseen Rain, 1986, Rumi: These Branching Moments, 1988; This Longing: Poetry, Teaching Stories, and Letters of Rumi, 1988, LISP: A First Language for Computing, 1991, Say I Am You, 1994; contbr. articles to profl. jours., chpts. to books. Home: 40 Prospect Ave Sea Cliff NY 11579-1029 Office: CUNY PhD Program Linguistics Grad Ctr 33 W 42nd St New York NY 10036-8003

MOYNE, YVES MARIE, water treatment executive; b. Jallieu, Isere, France, May 23, 1955; came to U.S., 1994; Baccaureat, Lycee Nationalise, Bourgoin Jallieu, 1973; PhD, Hautes Etudes Commerciales, Paris, 1980; M in Econs., U. La Sorbonne, Paris, 1980. Sr. KPMG Peat Marwick, Paris, 1980-83; fin. controller Lyonnaise Des Eaux, Paris, 1983-86, mgr. orgn., 1986-88; group dir. for Hong Kong, Macau and China Lyonnaise Des Eaux, Hong Kong, 1988-91; exec. dir. The Macau Water Supply Co., 1988-91; v.p., fin. and adminstr. Degremont, Rueil, France, 1991-94; chmn., pres., CEO of INFILCO Degremont, Inc., Richmond, Va., 1994—; v.p. JOUD, Crolles, France, 1994; prof. U. Paris IV, Creteil, 1981; lectr. pub. utility mgmt., S.E. Asia, and China; adv. to French Govt. for Fgn. Trade, 1995—. Author survey: For a Better Knowledge of The Consumers' Habits, 1978. Bd. dirs. Greater Richmond Tech. Coun., 1996—. With French Air Force, 1976-77, Istres, France. Mem. French Am. C. of C. (bd. dirs. 1996—). Avocations: architecture, skiing. Office: INFILCO Degremont Inc 2924 Emerywood Pky Richmond VA 23294-3746

MOYNIHAN, DANIEL PATRICK, senator, educator; b. Tulsa, Mar. 16, 1927; s. John Henry and Margaret Ann (Phipps) M.; m. Elizabeth Therese Brennan, May 29, 1955; children: Timothy Patrick, Maura Russell, John McCloskey. Student, CCNY, 1943; BA cum laude, Tufts U., 1948; MA, Fletcher Sch. Law and Diplomacy, 1949, PhD, 1961, LLD (hon.), 1968; Fulbright fellow, London (Eng.) Sch. Econs. and Polit. Sci., 1950-51; AM (hon.), Harvard U., 1966; LLD (hon.), Cath. U. Am., 1968, New Sch. Social Rsch., 1968, U. Notre Dame, 1969, Fordham U., 1970, St. Bonaventure U., 1972, Boston Coll., 1976, Yeshiva U., 1978, Rensselaer Polytech. Inst., 1983, Syracuse U. Sch. Law, 1984, Columbia U., 1987, U. Rochester, 1994; D in Pub. Adminstrn. (hon.), Hamilton Coll., 1968; DSI (hon.), Defense Intelligence Coll., 1984; numerous other hon. degrees. With Internat. Rescue Com., 1954; successively asst. to sec., asst. sec., acting sec. to gov. State of N.Y., 1955-58, mem. tenure commn., 1959-60, dir. Syracuse U. govt. rsch. project, 1959-61, spl. asst. to sec. labor, 1961-62, exec. asst. to sec., 1962-63, asst. sec. labor, 1963-65; dir. Joint Ctr. for Urban Studies MIT and Harvard U., 1966-69; prof. edn. and urban politics Kennedy Sch. Govt., Harvard U., 1966-73, sr. mem., 1966-77, prof. govt., 1973-77; asst. for urban affairs to Pres. U.S., 1969-70; counsellor to Pres. U.S., mem. Cabinet, 1969-70, cons. to Pres. U.S., 1971-73; mem. U.S. del. 26th Gen. Assembly, UN, 1971, Pres.'s Sci. Adv. Com., 1971-73; ambassador to India New Delhi, 1973-75; U.S. permanent rep. to UN, N.Y.C., 1975-76; U.S. senator from N.Y., 1977—, chmn. senate fin. com., 1993—, mem. senate fgn. rels. com., rules com. , environ., and pub. works com., joint com. on taxation, libr.; vice chmn. Pres.'s Temp. Commn. on Pennsylvania Avenue, 1964-73; chmn. adv. com. traffic safety dept. HEW; fellow Ctr. Advanced Studies, Wesleyan U., 1965-66; hon. fellow London Sch. Econs. and Polit. Sci., 1970—; sec. pub. affairs com. N.Y. State Dem. Com., 1958-60; alt. del. Dem. Nat. Conv., 1960, 76. Author: Maximum Feasible Misunderstanding, 1969, The Politics of a Guaranteed Income, 1973, Coping: On the Practice of Government, 1974, A Dangerous Place, 1978, Counting Our Blessings, 1980, Loyalties, 1984, Family and Nation, 1986, Came the Revolution: Argument in the Reagan Era, 1988, On the Law of Nations, 1990, Pandaemonium: Ethnicity in International Politics, 1993; co-author: Beyond the Melting Pot, 1963; editor: The Defenses of Freedom, 1966, On Understanding Poverty, 1969, Ethnicity: Theory and Experience, 1975, others; editorial bd. Pub. Interest; contbr. articles to profl. jours. Vice chmn. Woodrow Wilson Internat. Ctr. for Scholars, 1971-76; chmn. bd. trustees Joseph H. Hirshhorn Mus. and Sculpture Garden, 1971-85; mem. bd. regents Smithsonian Instn., 1987—. With USN, 1944-47. Recipient Meritorious Svc. award U.S. Dept. Labor, 1965, Centennial medal Syracuse U., 1969, Internat. League for Human Rights award, 1975, John LaFarge award for Interracial Justice, 1980, Medallion SUNY Albany, 1984, Henry medal Smithsonian Instn., 1985, SEAL Medallion, CIA, 1986, Meml. Sloan-Kettering Cancer Ctr. medal, 1986, Britannica award, 1986, Notre Dame U. Laetare medal, 1992, Thomas Jefferson award AIA, 1993. Mem. AAAS (vice chmn. 1971, dir. 1972-73), Am. Philos. Soc. (Hubert Humphrey award 1983, Thomas Jefferson medal 1993), Nat. Acad. Pub. Adminstrn., Am. Acad. Arts and Scis. (chmn. seminar on poverty), Century Club, Harvard Club. Office: US Senate 464 Russell Senate Bldg Washington DC 20510-3201

MOYNIHAN, GARY PETER, industrial engineering educator; b. Little Falls, N.Y., Mar. 5, 1956; s. Peter H. and Frances S. (Ferjanec) M.; m. Eleanor T. McCusker, Mar. 10, 1984; children: Andrew Ross, Keith Patrick. BS in Chemistry, Rensselaer Polytech. Inst., 1978, MBA in Opsl. Mgmt., 1980; PhD in Indsl. Engring., U. Ctrl. Fla., 1990. Prodn. supr. Am. Cyanamid, Bound Brook, N.J., 1978-79, Nat. Micronetics, Kingston, N.Y., 1980-81; assoc. mfg. engr. Martin Marietta Aerospace, Orlando, Fla., 1981-82, indsl. engr., 1982-85, sr. indsl. engr., 1985-87, group indsl. engr., 1987-90; asst. prof. indsl. engring. U. Ala., Tuscaloosa, 1990-96, assoc. prof., 1996—; cons. in field. Contbr. articles to profl. jours. Regents scholarship N.Y. State Bd. of Regents, 1974-78; rsch. fellow NASA, 1992-93; rsch. grant BellSouth Telecomm., 1994—; recipient Outstanding Tchg. award AMOCO Found., 1993-94. Mem. IEEE, Inst. of Indsl. Engrs. (sr. mem., chpt. dir. 1991-95, v.p. fin. and adminstrn. Aerospace & Def. Soc. 1994—). Achievements include design and development of information systems applications for the aerospace and foundry industries; rsch. in the measurement and prediction of on-line information system failure costs. Office: U Ala Dept Indsl Engring Tuscaloosa AL 35487

MOYNIHAN, MICHAEL J., artistic and producing director, writer; b. New Berlin, Wis., July 23, 1946; s. John F. and Irene A. (Gautier) M.; children: Margaret, Emily. Co-founder Friends Mime Theatre, Milw., 1973-91; artistic/producing dir. Milw. Pub. Theatre, 1991—; dir. Digital Theatrics, Milw., 1992—. Prodr. (play) Into the Water, 1993, The Snow Queen, 1991, Amber in Wasteland, 1992, (multi-media) Mondo Lingo, 1992 (Wis. Arts Bd. award 1992). Asst. exec. dir. MATA. Mem. Walkers Point Artists Assn., Dave-Click MUG, MKE ANRCHY, Ltd. Office: Milw Pub Theatre PO Box 07147 Milwaukee WI 53207-0147

MOYNIHAN, WILLIAM J., museum executive; b. Little Falls, N.Y., Apr. 8, 1942; s. Bernard J. and Mary A. (Flynn) M.; m. Irene A. Sheilds, July 2, 1966; children: Patricia, Erin, Sean. BA, SUNY, Binghamton, 1964; MA, Colgate U., 1966; PhD, Syracuse U., 1973. From asst. to assoc. prof. Colgate U., Hamilton, N.Y., 1973-77, from asst. to assoc. dean faculty, 1977-80, dean students, 1980-83, dean coll., 1983-88; v.p.m dir. Am. Mus. Natural History, N.Y.C., 1988-95; pres., CEO Milw. Pub. Mus., 1995—; bd. dirs. N.Y. State Mus.; adv. com. arts and culture Congressman J. Nadler, N.Y.C., 1993-95. Adv. editor Curator jour., 1991-95. Mem. Am. Mus. Assn., Am. Assn. Museums (mem. ethics com., bd. dirs.), Wis. Acad. of Scis., Arts and Letters (councillor-at-large 1995—), Univ. Club. Home: 203 W Coventry Ct Glendale WI 53217 Office: Milw Pub Mus 800 W Wells St Milwaukee WI 53233

MOYSE, HERMANN, JR., banker; b. Baton Rouge, Aug. 3, 1921; s. Hermann and Rosalie (Gottlieb) M.; m. Marie Louise Levy, June 4, 1942;

children—Lewis Arthur, Hermann III, Marie Rosalie. B.A., La. State U., 1942. With City Nat. Bank of Baton Rouge, 1946—, v.p., 1962-70, exec. v.p., 1970-72, pres., 1972-81, chmn., 1981-94, chmn. emeritus, 1995—, also dir.; pres., dir. Bistineau-Webster Oil Co.; sec., dir. Baton Rouge Realty Co., Ltd., Lottie Land & Devel. Co., Inc., Melrose Devel. Corp.; chmn. bd. First Commerce Corp., 1992—; bd. dirs. Pan Am. Life Ins. Co., Bank of Zachary, 1971-93. Pres. Capital Area United Givers Fund, 1966-67; mem. exec. com. Pub. Affairs Rsch. Coun., 1968-70; exec. com. Perkins Radiation Ctr.; bd. dirs. La. State U. Found. Maj. F.A. AUS, 1942-46. Decorated Bronze Star. Mem. Am. Bankers Assn. (governing coun. 1975-77), La. Bankers Assn. (pres. 1967-68, Baton Rouge Country Club, City Club of Baton Rouge. Office: City Nat Bank PO Box 1231 Baton Rouge LA 70821-1231

MOYSE, HERMANN, III, banker; b. Baton Rouge, Dec. 28, 1948; s. Hermann Jr. and Marie Louise (Levy) M.; m. Janet Lee Doise; children: Allison Leze, David Hermann, Aaron Lewis. BA, Coll. of Emporia, 1970; MSW, La. State U., 1973. Asst. dir. Capital Area Health Planning Agy., 1973-74; research assoc. La. State U., Baton Rouge, 1974-78; trainee to v.p. City Nat. Bank, Baton Rouge, 1978—, sr. v.p., 1985-94, also bd. dirs., chmn., 1994—; sec.-treas. Melrose Devel. Corp., Baton Rouge, 1986-87. Mem. Istrouma Council Boy Scouts Am.; mem. Capital Area United Way Agy. Svcs. Div., Baton Rouge, 1979-86, 88-91, vice chmn. 1981, bd. dirs., 1987—, chmn., 1989-90; v.p. Arts Coun. Greater Baton Rouge, 1990—; 1st v.p. La. Arts & Sci. Ctr., Baton Rouge, 1985—, pres., 1988; mem. Community Funds for Arts, 1989-90; mem. Arts & Humanities Coun., 1990—, v.p., 1991—, treas., 1992; mem. Community Funds for the Arts, 1989—, vice chmn., 1992; pres. Cath. Community Life Office, Baton Rouge, 1981, Baton Rouge Speech and Hearing Found., 1986, pres. 1983, treas., 1981; mem. St. Joseph's Acad. Adv. Bd., v.p., 1986-88, pres., 1987-88; bd. dirs. St. James Place; treas. Baton Rouge Crisis Intervention Ctr., 1984-85, v.p., 1987, pres., 1987; sec. St. Joseph's Children's Home, 1980; bd. dirs. Crime Stoppers, Inc., 1986—, v.p., 1989, pres. 1991—; pres. Mid City Devel. Alliance, 1991—; mem. adv. bd. Tau Ctr., 1990-93; trustee Episc. High Sch., 1990-92; treas. La. Delta Svc. Corps. Inc., 1995—; bd. trustees Gen. Health Sys., Inc, 1994; mem. Baton Rouge Crimestoppers; chmn. First Commerce Cmty. Devel. Corp., 1993—. Mem. La. Bankers Assn. (fed. affairs com. 1990—), La. Coun. Econ. Edn. (trustee 1987, regional v.p. 1990—, Community Vol. Activist award 1988), NCCJ (chpt. bd. dirs. 1988, treas. 1995), City Club, Baton Rouge Country Club. Democrat. Jewish. Office: City Nat Bank PO Box 1231 Baton Rouge LA 70821-1231

MOZIAN, GERARD PAUL, real estate company executive, business consultant; b. N.Y.C., Jan. 16, 1945; s. Gerard and Virginia (Chadik) M.; m. Mary Susan McKelvey, July 26, 1969. BMechE, Manhattan Coll., 1966; MBA, U. Pitts., 1967. Fin. adminstr. Philco-Ford Corp., Tehran, Iran, 1969-71; fin. analyst Gen. Waterworks Corp., Phila., 1971-73; regional contr. Gen. Waterworks Corp., Miami, Fla., 1973-75; v.p. fin. Gen. Devel. Utilities, Miami, 1975-78, sr. v.p. fin. and adminstrn., 1978-81, exec. v.p. ops., 1981-82, pres., 1982-87; sr. v.p. planning and fin. Gen. Devel. Corp., Miami, 1983-87; sr. v.p., chief fin. officer Gen. Devel. Corp., 1988-89; pres. Sugarmill Woods Inc., 1990-92; exec. v.p., CFO Montenay Internat. Corp., MIami, 1992—. Home: 7521 SW 113th St Miami FL 33156-4548 Office: 3225 Aviation Ave Miami FL 33133-4741

MOZLEY, PAUL DAVID, obstetrics and gynecology educator; b. Decatur, Ala., Oct. 27, 1928; s. James Howard and Ruth Dianne (Brindely) M.; m. Mary Dale Goss, Aug. 30, 1983; children from previous marriage: Susan Ruth, Paul David Jr., Sally Robin. BA, U. Ala., 1950; MD, Med. Coll. Ala., 1955. Diplomate Am. Bd. Ob-Gyn, Am. Bd. Psychiatry and Neurology. Commd. lt. USN, 1955; advanced through grades to capt., 1970, resident ob-gyn, Corona (Calif.) and San Diego Naval Hosp., 1956-59; resident in psychiatry Bethesda, Md., 1964-66, Phila. Naval Hosp., 1969-70; staff gynecologist U.S. Naval Hosp., Yokosuku, Japan, 1959-62; chief gynecologist U.S. Naval Hosp., Memphis, 1962-64; dir. med. services U.S. Naval Hosp., Naples, Italy, 1966-68, comdg. officer, 1969; chmn. neuropsychiatry Naval Regional Med. Ctr., Portsmouth, Va., 1970-75; ret., 1975; assoc. prof. psychiatry Eastern Va. Med. Sch., Norfolk, 1975-77, prof., interim chmn. dept., 1977-78, vice chmn. psychiatry, 1978-79; prof., dir. undergrad. edn. Dept. Ob-Gyn Sch. Medicine, East Carolina U., Greenville, 1979-84; prof. ob-gyn, chmn. dept., Coll. Community Health Scis. U. Ala., Tuscaloosa, 1984—, prof. ob-gyn, assoc. chmn. dept., Sch. Medicine, 1984—; dir. psychiat. services Norfolk Gen. Hosp., 1975-79; chmn. dept. ob-gyn DCH Regional Med. Ctr., Tuscaloosa, 1986—; cons. med. liability law legal firms., Ala., Tenn., 1980—. Contbr. numerous articles to profl. jours. Mem. Regional Parental Adv. Council, Montgomery, Ala., 1986-87; sponsor Tuscaloosa Symphony Assn. Recipient Meritorious Service medal Pres. U.S., 1975, Surgeon Gen.'s Merit award, 1975, Attending of Yr. award Residents in Psychiatry, 1979, Clin. Sci. Course award Dept. Ob-Gyn grad. class, 1982, Eastern Va. Sch. Medicine; named one of Outstanding Young Men in Am., Jaycees, 1964. Fellow ACS, Am. Coll. Ob-Gyn (chmn. various programs 1974, 76, 77, Chmn.'s award clin. research 1969), Am. Psychiat. Assn. (Continuing Med. Edn. Standards award 1977); mem. AMA (Physician's Recognition award 1986), Am. Soc. Psychosomatic Ob-Gyn (founding mem., pres. 1979-80, chmn. nominating com. 1981, permanent steering com. 1982), Va. Ob-Gyn Soc., Assn. Acad. Psychiatry, Va. Med. Soc., N.C. Neuropsychiat. Assn., Pitt County Med. Soc., Med. Assn. Ala., Ala. Psychiat. Assn., LWV, Alpha Epsilon Delta. Democrat. Mem. Ch. of Christ. Club: Torch (Portsmouth). Avocations: cabinetry, goldsmithing. Home: 21 Beech Hls Tuscaloosa AL 35404-4959 Office: The Univ of Ala Dept of Ob-Gyn PO Box 870376 Tuscaloosa AL 35487-0376

MPINGA, DEREK AMOS, mathematics educator; b. Kadoma, Zimbabwe, Aug. 8, 1943; married. AS, North Greenville Coll., 1970; BS in Math. and Physics, Carson Newman Coll., 1972; MA in Math., Tex. Christian U., 1975; MRE, Southwestern Theol. Seminary, 1976, EdD in Edn. Adminstrn., 1979. From instr. to asst. to prin. adminstrv. affairs Sanyati (Zimbabwe) High Sch., 1966-69; from field edn. adjunct to grad. teaching asst. Southwestern Theol. Seminary, Ft. Worth, 1976-79; prof. edn., adminstrn., acad. dean Bapt. Theol. Seminary Zimbabwe, Gweru, 1979-83; prof. edn., adminstrn., acad. dean, vice prin. Nairobi (Kenya) Grad. Sch. Theology, 1983-85; instr. math. and physics Americus (Ga.) High Sch., 1985-87; asst. prof. math. Tarrant County Jr. Coll. N.E., Ft. Worth, 1987-92; prof. math. North Lake Coll., Irving, Tex., 1992—; dir., Inst. of Science Technol. Engrng. and Math., 1993—; adj. tchr. math. Tarrant County Jr. Coll. , Ft. Worth, 1977-79, Nashville High Sch., 1982-83; mem. accrediting coun. theol. edn. in Africa and Madagascar, 1982-89; exec. dir. Leadership Devel. Assocs., Arlington, Tex. Dir. youth ministries Calvary Bapt. Ch., 1962-66, Sanyati Bapt. Ch., 1966-69; founding mem. Bapt. Youth Ministry Zimbabwe, 1963-83; chmn. bd. dirs. Bapt. Book Stores, 1980-83; sec. gen. Bapt. Conv. Zimbabwe, 1980-83; mem. world hunger and relief com. Bapt. World Alliance, 1980-90, founding mem. Internat. Conf. Theol. Educators, 1982—, All Africa Bapt. Fellowship, v.p., 1982-86; Africa adv. bd. Living Bibles Internat., 1981-84; deacon First Bapt. Ch., Arlington, 1991-94. Mem. Math. Assn. Am., Am. Math. Assn. Two Year Colls. (devel. math. com. 1989—, equal opportunity in math. com. 1989—, nominating com. 1993—, student math. league 1993—, del. Tex.-N.Mex. region 1993—), So. Assn. Colls. and Schs. (reaffirmation team 1992-93), Tex. Math. Assn. Two Year Colls. (chair devel. math. com. 1989-92), Tex. Jr. Coll. Assn., Tex. Faculty Assn., Phi Theta Kappa, Sigma Pi Sigma, Kappa Mu Epsilon. Home: 4905 Sagebrush Ct Arlington TX 76017-1027

MRAZ, ALANA L., elementary school principal. Prin. Rockland Sch., Libertyville, Ill. Recipient Elem. Sch. Recognition award U.S. Dept. Edn., 1989-90. Office: Rockland Sch 160 W Rockland Rd Libertyville IL 60048-2710

MRAZEK, DAVID ALLEN, pediatric psychiatrist; b. Ft. Riley, Kans., Oct. 1, 1947; s. Rudolph George and Hazel Ruth (Schayes) M.; m. Patricia Jean, Sept. 2, 1978; children: Nicola, Matthew, Michael, Alissa. AB in Genetics, Cornell U., 1969; MD, Bowman Gray Sch. Medicine, 1973. Lic. psychiatrist, child psychiatrist, N.C., Ohio, Colo., D.C., Va., Md.; med. lic. N.C., Ohio, D.C., Va., Md. Lectr. child psychiatry Inst. of Psychiatry, London, 1977-79; dir. pediatric psychiatry Nat. Jewish Ctr. for Immunology and Respiratory Medicine, Denver, 1979-91; chmn. psychiatry Childrens Nat. Med. Ctr., Washington, 1991—; acting chair psychiatry George Washington U. Sch. medicine, 1996—; dir. neuroscience Children's Rsch. Inst., 1995—; asst. prof. psychiatry U. Colo. Sch. Medicien, 1979-83, assoc. profl psychiatry and pediatrics, 1984-89, prof. 1990-91; prof. psychiatry and pediatrics George Washington U. Sch. Medicine, 1991—, acting chmn. psychiatry and behavioral scis., 1996—. Contbr. articles and book chpts. on child devel. and asthma to profl. pubis. Recipient Rsch. Scientist Devel. awards NIMH, 1983-88, 88-91. Fellow Am. Acad. Child Psychiatry, Royal Soc. Medicine, Am. Psychiat. Assn. (Blanche F. Ittleson award 1996), Royal Coll. Psychiatrists; mem. Am. Coll. Psychiatrists, Group for the Advancement of Psychiatry, Colo. Child and Adolescent Psychiatry Sco. (pres. 1994. Office: Childrens Nat Med Ctr Psychiatry Dept 111 Michigan Ave NW Washington DC 20010-2970

MRKONIC, GEORGE RALPH, JR., retail executive; b. Lawrence, Kans., July 13, 1952; s. George Ralph and Ruth (Clayton) M.; m. Barbara Machmer, June 22, 1974; children: Matthew George, John William, Kelsey Margaret. BA and MA in Econs., Stanford U., 1975; MBA, Harvard U., 1978. Fin. analyst WR Grace/Retail Group, N.Y.C., 1978-79, group mgr., 1979-80, dir. fin. planning, 1980-81, v.p., chief fin. officer, 1981; v.p., chief fin. officer Herman's Sporting Goods Inc., Carteret, N.J., 1981-85, sr. v.p., chief fin. officer, 1985-87; exec. v.p., dep. chief exec. officer Herman's Sporting Goods Inc., Carteret, 1986-87, pres., chief exec. officer, 1987; pres. Eyelab, Inc, River Edge, N.J., 1987-90; exec. v.p. splty. retailing K Mart Corp., Troy, Mich., 1990-94; pres. and vice chmn. Borders Group, Inc., Ann Arbor, Mich., 1994—; bd. dirs. Borders Group, Inc., Champion Enterprises, Comshare.

MRKVICKA, EDWARD FRANCIS, JR., financial writer, publisher, consultant; b. Aurora, Ill., Oct. 17, 1944; s. Edward Francis Sr. and Ruth Caroline (Phillips) M.; m. Madelyn Helen Rimnac, July 1, 1972; children: Edward Francis III, Kelly Helen. Cert. comml. pilot, U. Ill., 1965; diploma, Dept. Def., 1967, Bank Mktg. Assn., 1972; grad. cert., Bank Mktg. Assn., 1973. Mktg. officer Downers Grove (Ill.) Nat. Bank, 1964-72; asst. v.p. and mktg. officer Bank of Westmont, Ill., 1972-73; v.p. and cashier 1st State Bank Hanover Park, Ill., 1973-76; pres. 1st Nat. Bank Marengo, Ill., 1976-81, Reliance Enterprises, Inc., Fin. News Syndicate, Omni, Fin. Group, Eagle Publishing, Marengo, 1981—; pub. Money Insider newsletter; adv. coun. Am. Monetary Found., Fullerton, Calif., 1987; mem. panel of experts Boardroom Reports, 1990—. Pub.: (newletter) Money Insider; author: Battle Your Bank-And Win!, 1984, Moving Up, 1985; (with others) The Complete Book of Personal Finance, 1987, The Bank Book, 1989, 91, 94, 1,037 Ways to make or Save Up to $100,000 This Year Alone, 1991, The Rational Investor, 1992, Your Bank if Riping You Off, 1996; contbr. numerous articles to profl. jours. and newspapers. Bd. dirs. DuPage County Lung Assn., Downers Grove, Ill., 1970; mem. bd. Western Suburbs Combined Com. Appeal, Downers Grove, 1971; bd. dirs. McHenry County Easter Seals Clinic, Woodstock, Ill., 1979; v.p., treas. Marengo/Union Chamber, 1980; Am. rep. Cans. for Constitutional Money, 1990—. Sgt. USAF, 1965-69. Mem. Nat. Writers Union. Republican. Avocations: bowling, fishing. Office: Reliance Enterprises Inc PO Box 413 Marengo IL 60152-0413

MROZEK, DONALD L., lawyer; b. Chgo., Mar. 17, 1947. BSE, Northwestern U., 1969; JD with honor, DePaul U., 1973. Bar: Ill. 1973, U.S. Dist. Ct. (no. dist.) Ill. 1973, U.S. Dist. Ct. (no. dist. trial bar) Ill. 1973, U.S. Ct. Appeals (7th cir.) 1982, U.S. Supreme Ct. 1981. Ptnr. Hinshaw & Culbertson, Chgo. Mem. ABA, Ill. State Bar, Chgo. Bar Assn., Internat. Assn. Defense Counsel, Defense Rsch. Inst., Trial Lawyers Club Chgo. Office: Hinshaw Culbertson 222 N La Salle St Ste 300 Chicago IL 60601-1005*

MRÓZEK, KRZYSZTOF ANTONI, research scientist; b. Sopot, Poland, Aug. 2, 1959; came to the U.S., 1991; s. Jan Karol and Stefania (Borowska) M.; m. Ewa Bieguszewska, Dec. 30, 1983; 1 child, Małgonata. MD, Med. Acad., Gdańsk, Poland, 1983, PhD, 1990. Rsch. assoc. dept. biology and genetics Med. Acad., Gdańsk, 1982-90, asst. prof. dept. biology and genetics, 1990-94; rsch. assoc. dept. medicine Cytogenetics Rsch. Lab., Roswell Pk. Cancer Inst., Buffalo, N.Y., 1991-93; sr. rsch. assoc. divsn. medicine Cytogenetics Rsch. Lab., Roswell Pk. Cancer Inst., Buffalo, 1994—; lectr. in field. Contbr. chpts. to books, articles to profl. jours. Recipient Med. Scis. Faculty award Polish Acad. Scis., 1994. Mem. AAAS, Am. Assn. Cancer Rsch., Polish Genetics Soc., N.Y. Acad. Scis. Office: Roswell Park Cancer Inst Cytogenetics Rsch Lab Elm and Carlton Sts Buffalo NY 14263-0001

MRUK, CHARLES KARZIMER, agronomist; b. Providence, Sept. 23, 1926; s. Charles and Anna (Pisarek) M. BS in Agr., U. R.I., 1951, MS in Agronomy, 1957. Soil scientist soil conservation svc. Dept. Agr., Sunbury, Pa., 1951; insp. Charles A. McGuire Co., Providence, 1952; claims insp. R.R. Perishable Inspection Agy., Boston, 1953-55; asst. in agronomy U. R.I., 1955-57; agronomist Hercules Inc., 1957-79, tech. salesman, 1957-79; sr. tech. sales rep. BFC Chems., Inc., 1981-82; are devel. supr. Ea. States, 1982-84, ret., 1984; cons. turf maintenance Olympic Stadium and Grounds, Mexico City, 1968, Fenway Park, Boston, 1963-70; bd. mem. L. Troll/G.C.S.A.N.E. Turf Rsch. Fund; advisor Mass. TurfGrass Conf. and Trade Show, Chicopee. author and editor articles on turf culture and fertilizers, 1960-81. Mem. Rep. Ward Com., Providence, 1963-76. With USN, 1944-46. U.S. Golf Assn. Green Sect. grantee, 1955-57. Mem. Am. Soc. Agronomy, New Eng. Sports Turf Mgrs. Assn. (life), R.I. Golf Course Supts. Assn., Mass. Turf and Lawn Grass Coun. (dir., mem. planning com., chmn. fin. com., 1987, pres., 1987-89), VFW, Am. Registry Cert. Profls. in Agronomy (cert. agronomist), Sigma Xi, Alpha Zeta. Mem. Polish National Ch. Home: 75 Burdick Dr Cranston RI 02920-1517

MTEWA, MEKKI, foundation administrator; b. Sungo, Mangochi, Malawi, Apr. 13, 1946; m. Sekina Batuli; 1 child, Natasha. BA, Chapman Coll., 1974; MA in Polit. Sci., Calif. State U., Fullerton, 1975; postgrad., Miami U., Oxford, Ohio, 1975-76; diploma in exec. law and leadership studies, LaSalle Extension U., Chgo., 1977; PhD in Pub. Adminstrn. and Pub. Policy, Claremont Grad. Sch., 1979; postdoctoral in legal studies, Vrije U., Brussels, 1985-86. Regional adminstrv. sec. Agrl. Devel. and Mktg. Corp., Limbe, Malawi, 1964-66; adminstrv. sec. United Transport (Malawi) Ltd., Blantyre, 1966-67; legal asst. Lilley, Wills & Co., Limbe, 1968-70; exec. dir., founder Assn. for Advancement Policy, Research and Devel. in the Third World, 1981—; exec. v.p., dep. dir. POS Inst., Washington, 1982—; chmn., chief exec. officer Internat. Devel. Found. Inc., 1984—; chmn. Malawi Inst. Internat. Affairs, 1987—; sec.-gen. AFORD Alliance for Democracy, 1993; research asst. Calif. State U., Fullerton, 1974-75, adj. prof., spring 1978-79; research asst. Polit. Sci. Dept. Miami U., Oxford, Ohio, 1975-76; adj. asst. prof. polit. sci. and mgmt. U. D.C., 1982-85; asst. prof. polit. sci. Howard U., Washington, 1979-85; cons. in field; lectr. in field. Author: Public Policy and Development Politics: The Politics of Technical Expertise in Africa, 1980, The Consultant Connexion: Evaluation of the Federal Consulting Service, 1981, Malawi Democratic Theory and Public Policy: A Preface, 1986; editor: Science Technology and Development: Options and Policies, 1982, Perspectives in International Development, 1986, Contemporary Issues in African Administration and Development Politics, 1987, International Development and Alternative Futures: The Coming Challenges, 1988, Internat. Science and Technology: Theory, Philosophy and Policy, 1990; contbr. articles to profl. jours., chpts. to books; mem. adv. bd. CHANGE: The Internat. Tech. newspaper; guest editor Jour. Ea. African Research and Devel.; various TV and radio appearances; subject of articles. Dep. br. sec. Malawi Congress party, 1965-66; com. chair S.W. Scholarship Fund, S.S. Neighborhood Assembly, Washington; chair election com. Rosemary Coop. Housing project; sec.-gen. Alliance for Democracy in Malawi, 1993; parliamentary candidate Mangochi Centre Constituency in Malawi, 1994. Grantee Sci. and Tech. in So. Africa Devel. Coordination Conf., 1982, Peace Corps Coll. project, 1982; fellow Midwestern U. Consortium, Miami U., Alpha Assn. Phi Beta Kappa Alumni in So. Calif.; recipient Seminar award Fgn. Student Council. Mem. Internat. Services Assn. (bd. dirs.), Sci. Soc. Chile (bd. dirs.), Lions, Phi Sigma Alpha. Avocation: travel. Office: Internat Devel Found Ste 304 1730 K St NW Washington DC 20006-3868

MUCCI, GARY LOUIS, lawyer; b. Buffalo, Nov. 12, 1946; s. Guy Charles and Sally Rose (Battaglia) M.; m. Carolyn Belle Taylor, May 4, 1991. BA cum laude, St. John Fisher Coll., 1968; JD, Cath. U., 1972. Bar: N.Y. 1972. Law clk. to Hon. John T. Curtin U.S. Dist. Ct., Buffalo, 1972-74; assoc. atty. Donovan Leisure Newton & Irvine, N.Y.C., 1974-75; assoc. atty. Saperston & Day P.C., Buffalo, 1975-80, sr. ptnr., 1980—. Chmn. bd. Buffalo Philharm. Orch., 1985-86; pres. Hospice Buffalo, 1986-87; mem. N.Y. State Coun. on the Arts, 1987; chmn. Citizens Com. on Cultural Aid, Buffalo, 1992—; trustee St. John Fisher Coll. Recipient Brotherhood award NCCJ, Buffalo, 1983; named Man of Yr. William Paca Soc., 1984. Mem. Erie County Bar Assn., N.Y. State Bar Assn. Home: 27 Tudor Pl Buffalo NY 14222-1615 Office: Saperston & Day PC 3 Fountain Plz Ste 1100 Buffalo NY 14203-1414

MUCHIN, ALLAN B., lawyer; b. Manitowoc, Wis., Jan. 10, 1936; s. Jacob and Dorothy (Biberfeld) M.; m. Elaine Cort, Jan. 28, 1960; children: Andrea Muchin Leon, Karen, Margery Muchin Goldblatt. BBA, U. Wis., Manitowoc, 1958, JD, 1961. Gen. counsel IRS, Chgo., 1961-65; assoc. Altman, Kurlander & Weiss, Chgo., 1965-68, ptnr., 1968-74; co-mng. ptnr. Katten Muchin & Zavis, Chgo., 1974—, chmn. bd., 1995—; bd. dirs. Adrco, Inc., Chgo., Chgo. Bulls, Chgo. White Sox, Sportmart, Inc., Wheeling, Ill., Globe Glass & Mirror, Chgo., Alberto-Culver Co. Trustee Ravinia Music Festival, Highland Park, Ill., 1992—, Lyric Opera Chgo., 1993—; mem. adv. com. Loyola Family Bus. Ctr., Chgo., 1991—; co-com. chmn. Am. Com. for Weizmann Inst. of Sci., Chgo., 1991—. Mem. Econ. Club Chgo., Econ. Devel. Commn. (com. mem.), Comml. Club Chgo. Avocations: travel, tennis, reading. Office: Katten Muchin & Zavis 525 W Monroe St Ste 1600 Chicago IL 60661-3629

MUCHMORE, CHARLES J., lawyer; b. Delaware, Ohio, Jan. 5, 1950. BA cum laude, N.Mex. Highlands U., 1972; JD, U. N.Mex., 1976. Bar: Ariz. 1976. Ptnr. Muchmore & Wallwork, P.C., Phoenix; judge pro tem Maricopa County Superior Ct., 1986—. Fellow Ariz. Bar Found. (founder); mem. ABA (litigation sect., natural resourcess sect., energy and environ. law sect., tort and ins. practice sect.), Maricopa County Bar Assn., State Bar Ariz. (trial practice sect.), Ariz. Assn. Def. Coun., Def. Rsch. Inst., Internat. Assn. Def. Counsel (toxic and hazardous substances litigation com.), Am. Bd. Trial Advocates, Phi Kappa Phi. Office: Muchmore & Wallwork PC 2700 N Central Ave Ste 1225 Phoenix AZ 85004-1165*

MUCHMORE, DON MONCRIEF, museum, foundation, educational, financial fund raising and public opinion consulting firm administrator, banker; b. Wichita, Kans., Dec. 26, 1922; s. Floyd Stephen and Ivy Fay (Campbell) M.; m. Virginia Gunn, June 18, 1949 (div. Dec. 1978); children—Melinda, Marcia. B.A., Occidental Coll., Los Angeles, 1945; postgrad., U. So. Calif. Law Sch., 1945; postgrad. polit. sci., UCLA. Intern Nat. Inst. Pub. Affairs, Washington, 1944; exec. asst. to congressman Washington, 1946-48; teaching asst. UCLA, 1949-50; mem. faculty San Diego State U., 1950-51; asst. prof., adminstr. Calif. State U., Long Beach, 1951-56; pres., chief exec. officer The Campbell Found., L.A., 1956—; spl. asst. to supt. pub. instrn. Calif. Dept. Edn., Sacramento, 1956-57; exec. mus. dir. Calif. Mus. Sci. and Industry, L.A., 1957-62, 82-88; exec. v.p., chief exec. officer Calif. Mus. Found., L.A., 1957-62, 82-89; dep. dir. (on loan from mus.) Calif. Dept. Fin., Sacramento, 1960; exec. vice chancellor Calif. State Colls. and Univs. System, Long Beach, 1962-64; first exec. asst. to chmn. and chief exec. officer Calif. Fed. Savs. and Loan Assn., L.A., 1964-66; sr. v.p. Calif. Fed. Savs. and Loan Assn, L.A., 1966-82; pres., CEO PE Conservation Svcs., Inc., 1990-94; chmn. bd. dirs., CEO Opinion Rsch. of Calif., Opinion Surveyors, The State Poll and Mkt. Surveys, Inc., Long Beach, 1948-71, syndicated by L.A. Times, 1961-70, also M-R Assocs. campaigns; cons. in pub. opinion mus. mgmt. and fund raising, 1948-71; chmn., CEO, cons. DMM & Assocs., Long Beach, 1961—; sec., treas. EVENUP for the Homeless, 1994—, Am. Mus., 1994—; mem. Inst. Mus. Svcs., 1983-88. Contbr. chpts. to books. Participant in pub. opinion work Dem. and Rep. campaigns, 1954-72; mem., chmn. 4 presdl. commns., 1970-82, Just Say No Internat., 1989-91, Reading is Fundamental, 1989—, The Buckley Sch., 1989-90; cons. overseas traveling sci. exhibit, planning mus., 1984—, sr. adminstr., advisor, cons. to PCS (South Ctrl. L.A.) Sr. Citizens, 1995—; cons. Long Beach Com. Improvement League, 1995—; lead cons. New Solution to Homeless, 1993—; prin. officer Peruvians Cultural Exhibit, 1988—; prin. cons. cultural exhibit Wonders of World, 1992—, Queensway Bay, Long Beach, 1992—; bd. dirs. Bus. Tele Network, 1995—. Recipient Highest Mus. Edn. award Sigma Alpha Epsilon, 1992, Citizen of Yr. award and numerous other awards from nat., state and local groups; named Pollster of Yr. Washington Post, 1962; Elks Nat. scholar. Mem. Am. Assn. Mus., Calif. Mus. Assn. (pres. 1960, bd. dirs. 1982-88), Assn. Sci. and Tech. Ctrs. (bd. dirs. 1982-88), Am. Assn. Pub. Opinion Rsch., Am. Polit. Sci. Assn., AAAS. Home: 4225 N Virginia Vis Long Beach CA 90807-3122 Office: The Campbell Found DMM & Associates 4225 N Virginia Vis Long Beach CA 90807-3122

MUCHMORE, ROBERT BOYER, engineering consultant executive; b. Augusta, Kans., July 8, 1917; s. Ray Boyer and Charlotte (McPherron) M.; m. Betty Vaughan, Jan. 29, 1944; children: Andrew Vaughan, Douglas Boyer. BS, U. Calif., Berkeley, 1939; degree in Elec. Engrng., Stanford U., 1942. Project engr. Sperry Gyroscope Co., Garden City, N.Y., 1942-46; sr. mem. tech. staff Hughes Aircraft, Culver City, Calif., 1946-54; v.p., chief scientist TRW Systems, Redondo Beach, Calif., 1954-73; cons. TRW Systems, Sonoma, Calif., 1973—; lectr. in engrng. UCLA, 1954-58. Author: Essentials of Microwaves, 1952. Fellow IEEE; mem. AAAS, Assn. Computing Machinery, Sierra Club. Home: 4311 Grove St Sonoma CA 95476-6046

MUCHMORE, WILLIAM BREULEUX, zoologist, educator; b. Cin., July 7, 1920; s. Oliver Charles and Ruby (Breuleux) M.; m. Marjorie Murrin, Aug. 15, 1943; children—Susan Jane, Patricia Ann. B.A., Oberlin Coll., 1942; Ph.D. in Zoology, Washington U., St. Louis, 1950. Instr. biology U. Rochester, N.Y., 1950-52; asst. prof. U. Rochester, 1952-58, assoc. prof., 1958-70, prof., 1970-85, prof. emeritus, 1985—, asst. chmn. dept. biology, 1964-66, assoc. chmn., 1974-78; vis. prof. U. Hull, Eng., 1963-64; research assoc. Fla. State Collection Arthopods, 1974—. Contbr. articles to profl. jours. Served with U.S. Army, 1943-46. NSF grantee, 1958-69, 73-76; Fulbright travel grantee, 1963-64; Office Naval Research grantee, 1979-81. Fellow Rochester Acad. Sci., Nat. Speleological Soc.; mem. Am. Arachnological Soc., Am. Micro. Soc., Brit. Arachnological Soc., Centre Internat. de Documentation Arachnologique. Office: Dept Biology Univ of Rochester Rochester NY 14627

MUCHNICK, RICHARD STUART, ophthalmologist; b. Bklyn., June 21, 1942; s. Max and Rae (Kozinsky) M.; BA with honors. Cornell U., 1963, MD, 1967; m. Felice Dee Greenberg, Oct. 29, 1978; 1 child, Amanda Michelle. Intern in medicine N.Y. Hosp., N.Y.C., 1967-68, now assoc. attending ophthalmologist, chief Pediatric Ophthalmology Clinic; resident in ophthalmology, 1970-73; practice medicine, specializing in ophthalmology, notably strabismus and ophthalmic plastic surgery N.Y.C., 1974—; attending surgeon, chief Ocular Motility Clinic, Manhattan Eye, Ear and Throat Hosp., N.Y.C.; clin. assoc. prof. ophthalmology Cornell U., N.Y.C., 1984—. Served with USPHS, 1968-70. Recipient Coryell Prize Surgery Cornell U. Med. Coll., 1967. Diplomate Am. Bd. Ophthalmology, Nat. Bd. Med. Examiners. Fellow A.C.S., Am. Acad. Ophthalmology; mem. Am. Soc. Ophthalmic Plastic and Reconstructive Surgery, Am. Assn. Pediatric Ophthalmology and Strabismus, Internat. Strabismological Assn., N.Y. Soc. Clin. Ophthalmology, AMA, N.Y. Acad. Medicine, Manhattan Ophthal. Soc., N.Y. Soc. Pediatric Ophthalmology and Strabismus, Alpha Omega Alpha, Alpha Epsilon Delta. Clubs: Lotos, 7th Regt. Tennis. Clin. researcher strabismus, ophthalmic plastic surgery, 1973—. Office: 69 E 71st St New York NY 10021-4213

MUCK, STACEY LYNN, lawyer; b. Toledo, Feb. 25, 1966; d. Thomas Jude and Rebecca Jean (Heilman) M. BA, Fla. So. Coll., 1988; JD, Thomas M. Cooley Law Sch., Lansing, Mich., 1992. Bar: Fla. 1992, U.S. Dist. Ct. (mid. dist.) Fla. 1993, U.S. Ct. Appeals (11th cir.) 1993. Asst. state atty. 6th Jud. Cir. Office of State Atty., Clearwater, Fla., 1992—. Avocations: golf, tennis, snow skiing. Home: 12138 Jeffery Ln Dade City FL 33525-5922 Office: Office State Atty 6th Jud Cir 7530 Little Rd Rm 210 New Port Richey FL 34654-5522

MUCKENFUSS, CANTWELL FAULKNER, III, lawyer; b. Montgomery, Ala., Apr. 25, 1945; s. Cantwell F. and Dorothy (Dauphine) M.; m. A. Angela Lancaster, June 25, 1978; children: Alice Paran Lancaster, Cantwell F. IV. BA, Vanderbilt U., 1967; JD, Yale U., 1971. Bar: N.Y. 1973, D.C.

1976. Law clk. to presiding justice U.S. Ct. Appeals (6th cir.), 1971-72; atty., project developer Bedford Stuyvesant D and S Corp., Bklyn., 1972-73; spl. asst. to the dir. FDIC, Washington, 1974-77, counsel to the chmn., 1977-78; sr. dep. comptroller for policy Office of the Comptroller of the Currency, Washington, 1978-81; ptnr. Gibson, Dunn & Crutcher, Washington, 1981—; mem. editorial adv. bd. Issues in Bank Regulation, Rolling Meadows, Ill., 1977-91; mem. bd. advisors Rev. Fin. Regulation, N.Y.C., 1985—; bd. dis. Fair Tax Edn. Fund, Washington, 1987-90. Served with USNG, 1968-70, USAR, 1970-74. Recipient Spl. Achievement award U.S. Dept. Treasury, 1979, Presdl. Rank award U.S. Govt., 1980. Mem. ABA, Fed. Bar Assn. Democrat. Episcopalian. Clubs: Kenwood Country (Bethesda, Md.); Yale (N.Y.C.). Office: Gibson Dunn & Crutcher 1050 Connecticut Ave NW Ste 900 Washington DC 20036-5303*

MUCKENHOUPT, BENJAMIN, retired mathematics educator; b. Newton, Mass., Dec. 22, 1933; s. Carl Frederick and Sarah Joanna (Boell) M.; m. Mary Kathryn Heath, Aug. 29, 1964; children: Margaret, Carl Edward. A.B., Harvard U., 1954; M.S., U. Chgo., 1955, Ph.D., 1958. Instr. DePaul U., Chgo., 1958-59; asst. prof. math. DePaul U., 1959-60; faculty Rutgers U., New Brunswick, N.J., 1960-91; prof. math. Rutgers U., 1970-91; vis. assoc. prof. Mt. Holyoke Coll., 1963-65; visitor Inst. Advanced Study, Princeton, N.J., 1968-69, 75-76; vis. prof. SUNY-Albany, 1970-71. Contbr. articles to profl. jours. NSF rsch. grantee, 1965-88; Rutgers Rsch. Coun. fellow, 1968-69. Mem. Am. Math. Soc., Math. Assn. Am., Phi Beta Kappa, Sigma Xi. Home: 196 Woodfern Rd Neshanic Station NJ 08853-4054

MUCKERMAN, NORMAN JAMES, priest, writer; b. Webster Groves, Mo., Feb. 1, 1917; s. Oliver Christopher and Edna Gertrude (Hartman) M. B.A., Immaculate Conception Coll., 1940, M. in Religious Edn., 1942. Ordained priest Roman Catholic Ch., 1942. Missionary Redemptorist Missions, Amazonas, Para, Brazil, 1943-53; procurator missions Redemptorist Missions, St. Louis, 1953-58; pastor, adminstr. St. Alphonsus Ch., Chgo., 1958-67, St. Gerard, Kirkwood, Mo., 1967-71; mktg. mgr. circulation Liguori Pubs., Liguori, Mo., 1971-76; editor Liguorian Mag., Liguori, Mo., 1977-89. Author: How to Face Death Without Fear, 1976, Redemptorists on the Amazon, 1992; contbg. editor Liguorian, 1989-95. Recipient Nota Dez award Caixa Fed. Do Para, Brazil, 1958. Mem. Cath. Press Assn. (cons. 1971-95, bd. dirs. 1976-85, pres. 1981-84, St. Francis De Sales award 1985), St. Louis Press Club. Avocations: golf; travel; reading.

MUCKLER, JOHN, professional hockey coach, professional team executive; b. Midland, Ont., Can.; married; 5 children. Profl. hockey player, Ea. Hockey League, Baltimore, also Long Island Ducks; coach, gen. mgr. Long Island Ducks; 1st pres. N.Y. Jr. Met. League; coach, gen. dir. player pers., mgr. New York Rangers affiliate team, Am. Hockey League, Providence, R.I.; formerly head coach Minnesota North Stars; with Edmonton Oilers, 1981—, formerly co-coach; head coach Edmonton Oilers, 1989-1991; head coach Buffalo Sabres, 1991—, gen. mgr., 1994—. Office: Buffalo Sabres Meml Auditorium 140 Main St Buffalo NY 14202-4110*

MUDD, ANNE CHESTNEY, small business owner, mathematics educator, real estate agent; b. Macon, Ga., June 30, 1944; d. Bard Sherman Chestney and Betty (Bartow) Houston; children: Charles Lee Jr., Richard Chestney, Robert Jason. BA, U. Louisville, 1966, MA, 1976; postgrad., John Marshall Law Sch., 1995—. Math statistician U.S. Bur. Census, Jeffersonville, Ind., 1966-70; instr. math. U. Louisville, 1975-77, Coll. DuPage, Glen Ellyn, Ill., 1978-85, 92; tchr. math and substitute tchr. Lyons Twp. High Sch., La Grange, Ill., 1986-91; realtor First United Realtors, Western Springs, Ill., 1989-92; owner, mgr. retail bus., 1992—; math tutor Louisville 1969-77, Western Springs, Ill. 1977—. editor: Mathematics Textbook, 1991-92. Mem. steering com. Village Western Springs, 1986-87; bd. dirs. Children's Theater Western Springs, 1987-91; mem. Lyons Twp. H.S. Com. Student Discipline. Mem. NAFE, LWV (pres. 1983-85, bd. dirs.), Western Springs Hist. Soc. Avocations: local govt., theater, gardening. Home: 3958 Hampton Ave Western Springs IL 60558-1011

MUDD, JOHN PHILIP, lawyer; b. Washington, Aug. 22, 1932; s. Thomas Paul and Frances Mary (Finotti) M.; m. Barbara Eve Sweeney, Aug. 10, 1957; children: Laura, Ellen, Philip, Clare, David. BSS, Georgetown U., 1954; JD, Georgetown Law Center, 1956. Bar: Md. 1956, D.C. 1963, Fla. 1964, Calif. 1973. Pvt. practice Upper Marlboro, Md., 1956-66; v.p., sec., gen. counsel Deltona Corp., Miami, Fla., 1966-72; sec., gen. counsel Nat. Community Builders, San Diego, 1972-73; gen. counsel Continental Advisers (adviser to Continental Mortgage Investors), 1973-75, sr. v.p., gen. counsel, 1975-80; sr. v.p., gen. counsel Am. Hosp. Mgmt. Corp., Miami, 1980-89; legal coord. Amerifirst Bank, Miami, 1989-92; v.p., legal counsel Cartaret Savs. Bank, Morristown, N.J., 1991-93, cons., 1991-92; gen. counsel Golden Glades Hosp., Miami, 1992-93, Bank of N.Am., Miami, 1994—; gen. counsel Golden Glades Hosp., Miami, 1992-93; cons. FSLIC, 1988-89, J.E. Robert Cos., Alexandria, Va., 1988-89, Real Estate Recovery, Inc., Boca Raton, Fla., 1991-92, Bank N.Am., Ft. Lauderdale, Fla., 1992; dir. Unitower Mortgage Corp., Miami, Fla.; dir. Unitower Mortgage Corp., Miami; pres. Marquette Realty Corp., Miami. Former mem. Land Devel. Adv. Com. N.Y. State; chmn. student interview com. Georgetown U.; bd. dirs. Lasalle High Sch., Miami; corp. counsel Com. of Dade County, Fla.; trustee Golden Glades Gen. Hosp., Miami, Fla., 1992—, gen. counsel, 1991—, Bank of North Am., Miami, 1992—. Mem. Fla. Bar Assn., Calif. Bar Assn., Md. Bar Assn., D.C. Bar Assn., Fla. State Bar (exec. com. on corp. counsel com.). Democrat. Roman Catholic. Home: 411 Alhambra Cir Miami FL 33134-4901 Office: Bank of North Am Golden Glades Med Plz 8701 SW 137th Ave Ste 301 Miami FL 33183-4078

MUDD, ROGER HARRISON, news broadcaster, educator; b. Washington, Feb. 9, 1928; s. Kostka and Irma Iris (Harrison) M.; m. Emma Jeanne Spears, Oct. 28, 1957; children: Daniel H., Maria M., Jonathan, Matthew M. AB, Washington and Lee U., 1950; MA, U. N.C., 1953. Tchr. Darlington Sch., Rome, Ga., 1951-52; reporter Richmond News Leader, Va., 1953; news dir. Sta. WRNL, Richmond, 1953-56; reporter radio and TV Sta. WTOP, Washington, 1956-61; corr. CBS, 1961-80; chief Washington corr. NBC, 1980-87; Congl. corr. MacNeil/Lehrer News Hour, 1987-92, spl. corr., 1993—; prof. journalism Princeton U., 1992-94, Washington & Lee U., 1995-96. Host The History Channel, 1995—. Trustee Randolph-Macon Women's Coll., Lynchburg, Va., 1971-78, Robert F. Kennedy Journalism Awards Com., 1971-78, Blue Ridge Sch., Dyke, Va., 1978-84; bd. dirs. Fund for Investigative Journalism, PEN/Faulkner, 1985-92, Va. Found. for Humanities, Va. Hist. Soc., 1988-94, RIAS Berlin Commn., 1996—; mem. adv. com. Mt. Vernon Ladies Assn. With AUS, 1945-47. Mem. Radio-TV Corr. Assn. (chmn. exec. com. 1969-70).

MUDD, SIDNEY PETER, former beverage company executive; b. St. Louis, Jan. 21, 1917; s. Urban Sidney and Hallie Newell (Perry) M.; m. Ada Marie Herbermann, Oct. 22, 1942; children: Sidney Peter, Ada Marie, Peter, Michael, Mary, Elizabeth, Catherine. A.B. magna cum laude, St. Louis U., 1938; L.H.D., Coll. New Rochelle, N.Y., 1974; LHD, Iona Coll., 1985. Distr. Joyce Seven-Up, Chgo., 1938; sales mgr. Joyce Seven-Up, 1939; coordinator N.Y. ops. Joyce Seven-Up, New Rochelle, 1941; v.p. charge ops. Joyce Seven-Up, 1949-51; exec. v.p. N.Y. Seven-Up Bottling Co., Inc., New Rochelle, 1951-63; pres. N.Y. Seven-Up Bottling Co., Inc., 1963-73, dir., 1952-84, chmn. bd., 1973-84; pres. Joyce Beverages, Inc. (Joyce Advt.), 1973-84; past chmn. bd. Joyce Beverages/N.Y., N.J., Conn., Ill., Wis.; past dir. Joyce Beverages Inc., Joyce Advt., Joyce Beverages/N.Y., N.J., Conn., Chgo., Washington, Wis., Ill., Joyce Assocs.; dir., vice-chmn. Westchester Fed. Savs. Bank; bd. dirs. Marine Midland Bank Regional Bd., chmn. 1987-88. Past pres., bd. trustees St. Joseph's Hosp., N.Y.C., St. Francis Hosp.; chmn. Westchester County Assn.; past bd. lay advisers St. Agnes Hosp., White Plains; past chmn. bd. trustees Coll. of New Rochelle; past bd. dirs. U.S. Cath. Hist. Soc.; former trustee St. Louis U.; bd. dirs., v.p. John M. and Mary A. Joyce Found.; chmn. N.Y. Industry-Labor Com. for Resource Recovery; bd. dirs. Am. Alliance Resource Recovery Interests; pres. New Rochelle Devel. Council; bd. dirs. Keep Am. Beautiful, Inc.; chmn. Westchester 2000, 1984-85. Served with USNR. Decorated Knight of Malta, knight Equestrian Order of Holy Sepulchre; recipient St. Louis U. Alumni award, 1967, Dr. Martin Luther King Jr. award New Rochelle Community Action Agy., 1978, New Rochelle K.C. Civic award, 1978, Outstanding Citizen award New Rochelle YMCA, 1979, Disting. Service award Westchester region NCCJ, 1980, Medallion award Westchester Community Coll. Found., 1981; honoring resolution N.Y. State Senate, 1982; honoring resolution N.Y. State Assembly, 1982; honoring proclamation County of Westchester, City of Yonkers, City of White Plains, 1982; ARC award of excellence, 1983, Man of Yr. award Beverage Industry, 1974, Disting. Service award Sr. Personnel Employment Council, 1986, Disting. Achievement award Mental Health Assn., 1987, Disting. Citizen award New Rochelle Hosp. Med. Ctr., 1990; named to St. Louis U. Sports Hall of Fame, 1976, Beverage World Hall of Fame, 1984. Mem. Nat. Soft Drink Assn. (dir., pres. 1974-76, Disting. Achievement award 1980), N.Y. State Soft Drink Assn. (pres. 1966-67, Disting. Service award 1985, 86), Theta Kappa Phi, Crown and Anchor Soc. (St. Louis U.). Clubs: Winged Foot Golf (Westchester) (founder, past v.p., dir.); Sales and Mktg. Execs. *A happy life, a successful life is a life lived in love; love of God; love of self, love of others. To love and be loved is life's greatest reward on earth.*

MUDGE, LEWIS SEYMOUR, theologian, educator, university dean; b. Phila., Oct. 22, 1929; s. Lewis Seymour and Anne Evelyn (Bolton) M.; m. Jean Bruce McClure, June 15, 1957; children: Robert Seymour, William McClure, Anne Evelyn. B.A., Princeton, 1951, M. Div., 1955, Ph.D. (Kent fellow), 1961; B.A. with honors in Theology, Oxford (Eng.) U., 1954, M.A. (Rhodes scholar), 1958. Ordained to ministry Presbyn. Ch., 1955. Presbyn. univ. pastor Princeton, 1955-56; sec. dept. theology World Alliance Ref. Chs., Geneva, 1957-62; minister to coll. Amherst Coll., 1962-68, asst. prof. philosophy and religion, 1962-64, assoc. prof., 1964-70, prof. philosophy and religion, 1970-76, chmn. dept. philosophy and religion, 1968-69, 75-76; dean faculty, prof. theology McCormick Theol. Sem., Chgo., 1976-87, San Francisco Theol. Sem., 1987—; prof. Grad. Theol. Union, Berkeley, Calif., 1987-95; dir. Ctr. for Hermeneutical Studies, Grad. Theol. Union/U. Calif., Berkeley, 1990—; Stuart prof. theology Grad. Theol. Union, Berkeley, Calif., 1995—; mem. commn. on faith and order Nat. Council Chs., 1965-70; sec. spl. com. on confession faith United Presbyn Ch., 1965-67, chmn. spl. com. on theology of the call, 1968-71; chmn. theol. commn. U.S. Consultation on Ch. Union, 1977-89; co-chmn. Internat. Ref.-Roman Cath. Dialogue Commn., 1983-90; observer Extraordinary Synod Bishops, 1985. Author: One Church: Catholic and Reformed, 1963, Is God Alive?, 1963, Why is the Church in the World?, 1967, The Crumbling Walls, 1970, The Sense of a People: Toward a Church for the Human Future, 1992; also numerous articles and revs.; editor: Essays on Biblical Interpretation (Paul Ricoeur), 1980, (with James Poling) Formation and Reflection: the Promise of Practical Theology, 1987. Pres. Westminster Found. in New Eng., 1963-67; chmn. bd. Nat. Vocation Agy., 1972-75; mem. com. selection Rhodes Scholars, Wis., 1983-85, Iowa, 1986. Mem. Phi Beta Kappa. Democrat. Home: 2444 Hillside Ave Berkeley CA 94704 Office: San Francisco Theol Sem 2 Kensington Rd San Anselmo CA 94960-2905

MUDRY, MICHAEL, pension and benefit consultant; b. Lucina, Czechoslovakia, Dec. 5, 1926; (parents Am. citizens); s. John Zaleta and Helen (Molchan) M.; m. Kendall Archer, June 17, 1960; children: F. Goodrich Archer, Benjamin Kendall. BA, U. Conn., 1951. Sr. v.p. Hay/Huggins Co. Inc., Phila., 1956-93; self-employed pension and benefit cons. Wayne, Pa., 1994—; actuary Ch. Pensions Conf. Contbr. articles to profl. jours. Bd. mem., actuary Am. Coun. on Gift Annuities, Dallas, 1978—. Served with U.S. Army, 1945-46. Fellow Soc. Actuaries, Conf. Cons. Actuaries; mem. Am. Acad. Actuaries, Internat. Actuarial Assn., Internat. Assn. Cons. Actuaries. Democrat. Home: 749 Mancill Rd Wayne PA 19087-2004

MUECKE, CHARLES ANDREW (CARL MUECKE), federal judge; b. N.Y.C., Feb. 20, 1918; s. Charles and Wally (Roeder) M.; m. Claire E. Vasse; children by previous marriage: Carl Marshall, Alfred Jackson, Catherine Calvert. B.A., Coll. William and Mary, 1941; LL.B., U. Ariz., 1953. Bar: Ariz. 1953. Rep. AFL, 1947-50; reporter Ariz. Times, Phoenix, 1947-48; since practiced in Phoenix; with firm Parker & Muecke, 1953-59, Muecke, Dushoff & Sacks, 1960-61; U.S. atty. Dist. Ariz., 1961-64, U.S. dist. judge, 1964—, now sr. judge.; mem. 9th cir. Jud. Coun. com. review local dist. Ct. Rules. Mem. Phoenix Planning Commn., 1955-61, chmn., 1960; chmn. Maricopa County Dem. Party, 1961-62; trustee U. San Diego Coll. Law. Maj. USMC, 1942-45, USMCR, 1945-60. Mem. Fed. Bar Assn., Ariz. Bar Assn., Maricopa Bar Assn., Am. Trial Lawyers Assn., Dist. Judges Assn. Ninth Circuit, Phi Beta Kappa, Phi Alpha Delta, Omicron Delta Kappa. Office: US Dist Ct US Courthouse & Fed Bldg 230 N 1st Ave Ste 7015 Phoenix AZ 85025-0007

MUEDEKING, GEORGE HERBERT, editor; b. Arcadia, Wis., Aug. 19, 1915; s. George Fredrick and Rosalie Carolina (Brodt) M.; m. Harriet Laura Rollwagen, June 26, 1941; children—Miriam Harriet (Mrs. W. Ron Heyer), George David. B.A., Capital U., 1936, D.D. (hon.), 1955; M.A., Ind. U., 1938; B.D., Evang. Lutheran Theol. Sem., 1941; Ph.D., U. Calif., Berkeley, 1961. Ordained to ministry Luth. Ch., 1941; pastor Luth. Ch. of Holy Trinity, Long Beach, Calif., 1941-47, First Luth. Ch., Fullerton, Calif., 1947-51, Christ Luth. Ch., El Cerrito, Calif., 1951-59; instr. Pacific Luth. Theol. Sem., Berkeley, 1953-55, asst. prof., 1956-59, asso. prof., 1960-64, prof., 1965-66; editor Luth. Standard, Mpls., 1967-78, roving editor, 1978-80; lectr. Australian Luth. Tchrs. Coll., 1981-82; sr. mentor Calif. Luth. U., 1984, 87; resident faculty Luth. Bible Inst. Calif., 1993; v.p. Calif. dist. Am. Luth. Ch.; mem. com. on interpretation Am. sect. World Coun. Chs.; pres. Luth Editors Assn.; bd. dirs. Assn. ch. Press, Luths. for Life. Author: Emotional Problems and the Bible, 1956; editor FOCL-Point, 1991—; contbr. articles to religious publs. Mem. Assn. for Profl. Edn. for Ministry, Nat. Council on Family Relations, Minn. Press Club, Am. Acad. Religion and Mental Health, Am. Acad. Polit. and Social Sci., Phi Beta Kappa. Republican. Home and Office: 4414 Springwood Dr Napa CA 94558-1724

MUEHLBAUER, JAMES HERMAN, manufacturing executive; b. Evansville, Ind., Nov. 13, 1940; s. Herman Joseph and Anna Louise (Overfield) M.; m. Mary Kay Koch, June 26, 1965; children: Stacey, Brad, Glen, Beth, Katy. BSME, Purdue U., 1963, MS Indsl. Adminstrn., 1964. Registered profl. engr., Ind. Engr. George Koch Sons, Inc., Evansville, 1966-67; chief estimator George Koch Sons, Inc., 1968-72, chief engr., 1973-74, v.p., 1975-81, dir., 1978—, exec. v.p., 1982—; v.p., bd. dirs. Brake Supply Co., Evansville, Gibbs Die Casting Corp., Hendersonville, Ky., Uniseal, Inc., Evansville; bd. dirs. Citizens Nat. Bank, Evansville, Page-Koch (Europe) Ltd., Lichfield, Eng., Red Spot Paint & Varnish Co., Inc., Evansville. Co-author: Tool & Manufacturing Engineering Handbook, 1976; patentee in paint finishing equipment. Bd. dirs., past pres. Evansville Indsl. Found., 1980—; bd. dirs., past pres., past campaign chmn. United Way S.W. Ind., Evansville, 1983—; bd. dirs., past vice-chmn. Univ. So. Ind. Found., Evansville, 1988—, Deaconess Hosp., Evansville, 1986—, treas., 1991—. Named Engr. of Yr. S.W. chpt. Ind. Soc. Profl. Engrs., 1983; recipient Tech. Achievement award Tri-State Coun. for Sci. and Engring., Evansville, 1984, Purdue U. Alumni Citizenship award, 1991. Mem. Soc. Mfg. Engrs. (past nat. chmn. finishing and coating tech. divsn.), ASME, NSPE, Evansville Country Club, Evansville Petroleum Club, Evansville Kennel Club. Republican. Roman Catholic. Home: 2300 E Gum St Evansville IN 47714-2338 Office: George Koch Sons Inc 10 S 11th Ave Evansville IN 47744-0001

MUEHLEISEN, GENE SYLVESTER, retired law enforcement officer, state official; b. San Diego, Dec. 28, 1915; s. Adolph and Vesta C. (Gates) M.; m. Elsie Jane Conover, Sept. 14, 1940; 1 son, John Robert. Student, San Diego State Coll., 1935-39, San Diego Jr. Coll., 1957. U.S. park ranger Yosemite Nat. Park, summers 1936-39, 79-84; with San Diego Police Dept., 1940-60, dir. tng., 1957-59, comdg. officer patrol div., capt., 1958-60; exec. dir. Commn. on Peace Officer Standards and Tng., Calif. Dept. Justice, Sacramento, 1960-65, 67-76; assoc. dir. Pres.'s Commn. on Law Enforcement and Adminstrn. of Justice, Nat. Crime Commn., 1965-67; chmn. police sci. adv. com. San Diego Jr. Coll., 1957-60, police sci. faculty, 1957-60; staff instr. San Diego Police Acad., 1954-60; guest instr. police adminstrn. Sacramento State Coll., 1964; grad. FBI Nat. Acad. 51st Session, 1953, pres. of class, guest faculty, 1963-66; cons. Ford Found. Internat. Assn. Chiefs of Police Project, 1964-67; cons. U.S. Nat. Park Svc., 1965-84, spl. asst. to regional dir. Western region, 1977-79; adviser Royal Can. Mounted Police, 1961—; guest lectr., 1960—. Mem. tng. com. Internat. Assn. Chiefs of Police, 1963—; mem. adv. com. on police tng. Ford Found., 1964—; U.S. rep. Interpol Symposium on Police Edn. and Tng., Paris, 1965; chmn. Atty. Gen.'s Com. on Law Enforcement Standards, 1957-59; vice chmn. Calif. Commn. Peace Officer Standards and Tng., 1959-60; chmn. police services task force Calif. Council Criminal Justice, 1968-78 ; mem. Atty. Gen.'s Commn. Police-Community Relations, 1971—; mem. adv. com. FBI, 1972—; mem. Gov.'s Pub. Safety Planning Council, 1974—; Pres. San Diego Police Officers Assn., San Diego Police and Fire Retirement System; bd. dirs. San Diego Hist. Soc. Served to capt. USNR, World War II. The Gene Muehleisen Nature Area, Valley Oak Park, Sacramento dedicated, 1992. Mem. Nat. Conf. Police Assns. (com. chmn.), Calif. Peace Officers Assn. (com. chmn.), Peace Officers Research Assn. Calif. (pres. 1959-60, com. chmn.), Am. Soc. Pub. Adminstrn. (dir. San Diego County chpt.), Nat. Assn. State Dirs. Law Enforcement Tng. (pres. 1972-73), Am. Corrections Assn., Calif. Assn. Adminstrn. of Justice Educators, Park Rangers Assn. of Calif., Internat. Police Assn. (life, v.p. region 29 USA), Internat. Assn. Chiefs of Police (life), Calif. Parks and Recreation Soc. (Citizen of Yr. 1992), Sacramento Tree Found. (tech. adv. com. 1983—). Clubs: Kiwanis, San Diego Ski (pres.). Home and Office: 4221 Corona Way Sacramento CA 95864-5301

MUEHLNER, SUANNE WILSON, library director; b. Rochester, Minn., June 29, 1943; d. George T. and Rhoda (Westin) Wilson. Student Smith Coll., 1961-63; A.B., U. Calif.-Berkeley, 1965; M.L.S., Simmons Coll., 1968; M.B.A., Northeastern U., Boston, 1979. Librarian, Technische Univ. Berlin, Germany, 1970-71; earth and planetary scis. librarian MIT Libraries, Cambridge, 1968-70, 1971-73; personnel librarian, 1973-74, asst. dir. personnel services, 1974-76, asst. dir. pub. services, 1976-81; dir. libraries Colby Coll., Waterville, Maine, 1981—. Mem. ALA, New Eng. Assn. Coll. and Research Librarians (sec.-treas. 1983-85, pres. 1986-87), Maine Libr. Assn. (chmn. intellectual freedom com. 1984-88, OCLC Users Coun., 1988-95), Nelinet (bd. dirs. 1985-91, chair 1989-91). Office: Colby Coll Miller Libr Waterville ME 04901

MUELLER, BETTY JEANNE, social work educator; b. Wichita, Kans., July 7, 1925; d. Bert C. and Clara A. (Pelton) Judkins; children—Michael J., Madelynn J. MSSW, U. Wis., Madison, 1964, PhD, 1969. Asst. prof. U. Wis., Madison, 1969-72; vis. asso. prof. Bryn Mawr (Pa.) Coll., 1971-72; asso. prof., dir. social work Cornell U., Ithaca, N.Y., 1972-78, 92-94, prof. human services studies, 1978—; nat. cons. Head Start, Follow Through, Appalachian Regional Commn., N.Y. State Office Planning Services, N.Y. State Dept. Social Services, N.Y. State Div. Mental Hygiene, Nat. Congress PTA, ILO. Author: (with H. Morgan) Social Services in Early Education, 1974, (with R. Reinoehl) Computers in Human Service Education, 1989, Determinants of Human Behavior, 1995; contbr. articles to profl. jours. Grantee HEW, 1974-76, 79-80, State of N.Y., 1975—, Israeli Jewish Agy., 1985-87, Israeli Nat. Council for Research, 1986-87; Fulbright Research award, 1990. Mem. Leadership Am., Chi Omega. Democrat. Unitarian. Home: 412 Highland Rd Ithaca NY 14850 Office: Cornell U Human Services Studies N139MVR Hall Ithaca NY 14853

MUELLER, CARL GUSTAV, JR., lawyer; b. Houston, June 30, 1929; s. Carl G. and Louise (Young) M.; m. Joanne Youngblood, Aug. 2, 1950; children—Carl Clinton, Craig Steven, Robert Loyd. BBA, U. Tex., 1951, JD, 1953. Cert. in estate planning and probate law, comml. real estate law, residential real estate law, farm and ranch real estate law, Tex. Mem., tchr. Hines Baker Bible Class; former chmn. adminstrv. bd., former chmn.bd. trustees St. Luke's Meth. Ch.; dir., sec. Retina Rsch. Found.; bd. dirs. Student Aid Found. Fellow Am. Coll. Trust and Estate Counsel; mem. Tex. Bar Assn., Houston Bar Assn., Am. Coll. Real Estate Lawyers, Tex. Acad. Probate and Trust Lawyers, Tex. Acad. Real Estate Lawyers, Houston Estate and Fin. Forum (past pres.), Houston Real Estate Lawyers Counsel. Avocations: fishing, hunting, walking, travel. Office: 17 S Briar Hollow Ln Ste 204 Houston TX 77027-2810

MUELLER, CARL RICHARD, theater arts educator, author; b. St. Louis, Oct. 7, 1931; s. Anton John and Bonita Blanche (Lacy) M. BS, Northwestern U., 1954; MA, UCLA, 1960, PhD, 1967; cert., Freie U., Berlin, 1961. Prof. theater dept. Sch. Theater, Film and Television UCLA, 1967—; dramaturg New Theatre, Inc., L.A., 1975—; cons. U. Calif. Press., 1972—. Translator plays published include Buechner: Complete Plays and Prose, 1963, Brecht: The Visions of Simone Machard, 1965, Brecht: The Measures Taken, 1977, Hauptmann: The Weavers, 1965, Hebbel: Maria Magdalena, 1962, Strindberg: A Dream Play and The Ghost Sonata, 1966, Schnitzler: La Ronde and Game of Love, 1964, Hofmannsthal: Electra, 1964, Wedekind: The Marquis of Keith, 1964, Wedekind: The Lulu Plays, 1967, Zuckmayer: The Captain of Koepenick, 1972; translator plays produced include Anon: The Puppet Play of Dr. Johannes Faustus, Hauptmann: The Beaver Coat, Schnitzler: Dr. Bernhardi, Schnitzler: Anatol, Sternheim: The Underpants, Brecht: Mother Courage, Brecht: Caucasian Chalk Circle, Brecht: The Trial of Joan of Arc, Brecht: In the Jungle of Cities, Brecht: Man is Man, Brecht: He Who Says Yes, Brecht: He Who Says No, Brecht: The Exception and the Rule, Brecht: Round Heads, Peaked Heads, Brecht: Schweyk in the Second World War, Kleist: The Broken Jug, 1992, Lessing: Nathan the Wise, 1993, Toller, The Blind Goddess, 1993, Sophokles, Elektra, 1994, Zweig, Volpone, 1995, Sternheim, The Snob, 1996, Sophokles, Electra, 1996; gen. editor Visual Resources, Inc., 1976—; theater editor Mankind mag., 1975-82; editor New Theater/Teatro Nuevo, 1985-87; author catalogue and slides A Visual History of European Theater Arts, 1978, A Visual History of European Experimental Theater, 1983, Greek and Roman Classical Theatre Structures and Performance Iconography, 1991, Medieval Theater and Performance Iconography, 1991, The Theater of Meyerhold, 1992, Stanislavsky and the Moscow Art Theater, 1992, The Commedia dell'Arte, 1992, Russian Scene and Costume Design, vols. 1 and 2, 1993, The Baroque Stage, 1993, 18th and 19th Cen. European Theater Structures, Performance Ionography and Costume Designes, 1994, Renaissance Theater Structures, Performance Iconography and Costume Designs, 1994, The Genius of the Russian Theatre 1900-1990, 1995, 20th Century World Theater, From Appia to Dali, 1900-50, vol. 1, 1996, 20th Century World Theater, From Mother Courage to Hair, 1951-68, vol. 2, 1996, 20th Century World Theater, From Svoboda to Hockney, 1968-91, vol. 3, 1996, The Genius of the Russian Theater, From Meyerhold to the Present, 1996; dir.: (plays) Spring's Awakening, Endangered Species, Hedda Gabler, My Body, Frankly Yours, Hamlet, Macbeth. Served with U.S. Army, 1954-56. Recipient Samuel Goldwyn Creative Writing award Goldwyn Found., 1959; Fulbright exchange grantee Berlin, 1960-61. Mem. Internat. Arthur Schnitzler Research Assn., UCLA Center for Medieval and Renaissance Studies (mem. adv. com. 1980-83). Democrat. Office: UCLA Dept Theater Sch Theater Film and TV 102 E Melnitz Box 951622 Los Angeles CA 90095-1622 *Communication has always been the primary goal of my life. The challenge of passing on to generations of new students the life sustaining ideas of human culture is formidable; the joy of searching out new ideas and methods of thought and action is a privilege of which far too few of us take proper advantage.*

MUELLER, CHARLES BARBER, surgeon, educator; b. Carlinville, Ill., Jan. 22, 1917; s. Gustav Henry and Myrtle May (Barber) M.; m. Jean Mahaffey, Sept. 7, 1940; children: Frances Ann, John Barber, Richard Carl, William Gustav. A.B., U. Ill., 1938; M.D., Washington U., St. Louis, 1942; LHD (honoris causa), Blackburn Coll., 1987. Intern, then resident in surgery Barnes Hosp., St. Louis, 1942-43, 46-51; asst. prof. Washington U. Med. Sch., 1951-56; prof. surgery, chmn. dept. State U. N.Y. Med. Sch., Syracuse, 1956-67; prof. surgery McMaster U. Med. Sch., Hamilton, Ont., Can., 1967—; chmn. dept. McMaster U. Med. Sch., 1967-72. Contbr. articles to med. jours. Served with USNR, 1943-46. Decorated Purple Heart with 2 oak leaf clusters, Bronze Star; Jackson Johnson fellow, 1938-42; Rockefeller postwar asst., 1946-49; Markle scholar, 1949-54; recipient Alumni Achievement award Washington U., 1987. Mem. ACS (v.p. 1987-88, Disting. Svc. award 1984), Am. Surg. Assn., Ctrl. Surg. Assn., Soc. Univ. Surgeons, Assn. Acad. Surgery, Royal Coll. Physicians and Surgeons (Duncan Graham Disting. Svc. award 1992), Phi Beta Kappa, Sigma Xi, Alpha Omega Alpha, Phi Kappa Phi. Home: 139 Dalewood Crescent, Hamilton, ON Canada L8S 4B8 Office: McMaster U, 1200 Main St W, Hamilton, ON Canada L8N 3Z5

MUELLER, CHARLES FREDERICK, radiologist, educator; b. Dayton, Ohio, May 26, 1936; s. Susan Elizabeth (Wine) W.; m. Kathe Louise Lutterbei, May 28, 1966; children: Charles Jeffrey, Theodore Martin, Kathryn Suzanne. BA in English, U. Cin., 1958, MD, 1962. Diplomate Am. Bd. Radiology, Am. Bd. Nuclear Medicine. Asst. prof. radiology U. N.Mex., Albuquerque, 1968-72, asso. prof. radiology, 1972-74; assoc. prof. radiology Ohio State U., Columbus, 1974-79, acting chmn. dept. radiology, 1975, prof.

radiology, 1979—, prof. radiology, dir. post grad. program radiology, 1980—; bd. dirs. Univ. Radiologists, Inc., Columbus, v.p., 1980-86; pres., founder Ambulatory Imaging, Inc., Columbus, 1985—; founder Am. Soc. Emergency Radiology, 1988, pres., 1993-94. Author: Emergency Radiology, 1982; contbr. articles to profl. jours. Com. chmn. Boy Scouts of Am., Columbus, 1980-84. Served to capt. USAF, 1966-68. Research grantee Ohio State U. 1975, Gen. Electric Co., 1986-88. Fellow Am. Coll. Radiologists; mem. Assn. Univ. Radiologists, Am. Roentgen Ray Soc., Radiol. Soc. N.Am., AMA, N.Mex. Soc. Radiologists (pres. 1973-74), Ohio State Radiol. Soc. (pres. 1986-87). Republican. Presbyterian. Lodges: Commandery #6, Consistory. Avocations: flying, fly fishing, hiking. Office: Ohio State Univ Hosps Dept Radiology 410 W 10th Ave Columbus OH 43210-1240

MUELLER, CHARLES WILLIAM, electric utility executive; b. Belleville, Ill., Nov. 29, 1938; s. Charles A. and Clara R. (Jorn) M.; m. Janet Therese Vernier, July 9, 1960; children: Charles R., Michael G., Craig J. BSEE, St. Louis U., 1961, MBA, 1966. Registered profl. engr., Mo., Ill. Engr. Union Electric Co., St. Louis, 1961-75, supervisory engr., 1975-77, asst. dir. corp. planning, 1977-78, treas., 1978-83, v.p. fin., 1983-88, sr. v.p. adminstrv. svcs., 1988-93; pres., CEO, 1994—; bd. dirs. Union Colliery Co., St. Louis Electric Energy Inc., Regional Commerce and Growth Assn., Edison Electric Inst.; dir. The Boatmen's Nat. Bank of St. Louis, Assn. of Edison Illuminating Cos., St. Louis Children's Hosp., St. Louis Sci. Ctr., Civic Progress, The Mcpl. Theatre Assn. Trustee Webster U. Mem. IEEE, Mo. Athletic Club, Oak Hill Tennis Club, St. Clair Country Club, The Bogey Club, Saint Louis Club. Avocations: tennis, boating, travel. Office: Union Electric Co 1901 Chouteau Ave Saint Louis MO 63103-3003*

MUELLER, EDWARD ALBERT, retired transportation engineer executive; b. Madison, Wis., May 12, 1923; s. Edward F. and Lulu (Wittl) M.; m. Margaret Wetzel, Sept. 12, 1953; children: Lynn, Karen. Student, U. Wis., 1941-43; B.C.E., Notre Dame U., 1947; cert. in traffic, Yale U., 1953; postgrad., Fla. State U., 1955-62; M.C.E., Catholic U. Am., 1967. Registered profl. engr., Fla. Project engr. Carl C. Crane, Inc., 1947-50; engr. Ammann & Whitney, Inc., Milw., 1950-52; asst. dir., dir. traffic and planning div. Fla. State Rd. Dept., Tallahassee, 1955-63; engr. traffic and ops. Hwy. Research Bd., Washington, 1963-70; sec. Fla. Dept. Transp., Tallahassee, 1970-72; exec. dir. Jacksonville (Fla.) Transp. Authority, 1972-80; mgr. transp. div. Reynolds, Smith & Hills, 1980-83; v.p. Morales and Shumer Engrs., Inc., 1983-95; occasional lectr. U. Fla., 1971-76, U. N.Fla., 1974-76. Author: Steamboating on the St. Johns, 1979, Ocklawaha River Steamboats, 1983, St. Johns River River Steamboats, 1986, Perilous Journeys, 1990, Upper Mississippi River Ratting Steamboats, 1995; contbr. engring. articles to profl. jours. Mem. Fla. Com. of 100, 1970-72; bd. dirs. Luth. Social Svcs., Jacksonville, 1982-94, v.p., 1981-91; regional v.p. Fla.-Ga. dist. Luth. Laymen's League, 1982-92; curator Jacksonville MAritime Mus., 1990—, mem. exec. com., 1989-95, pres., 1993-95, exec. dir., 1995—. Recipient Disting. Service award Coll. Engring., U. Fla., 1975; named one of top 10 pub. works ofcls. in U.S., 1978. Mem. Southeastern Assn. State Hwy. Ofcls. (pres., v.p. 1971-72), Engrs. in Govt. (chmn., vice chmn. sec.), Fla. Engring. Soc. (pres. Northeast chpt. 1982-83, engr. of yr. Tallahassee chpt. 1972, Jacksonville chpt. 1974, award for outstanding tech. achievement 1976, outstanding svc. to engring. profession 1989), Inst. Transp. Engrs. (pres. 1977, disting. svc. award Fla. sect. 1976), Fla. Transit Assn. (pres. 1974, 75), Fla. Engring. Found. (sec. 1986-95). Lutheran. Home: 4734 Empire Ave Jacksonville FL 32207-2136

MUELLER, FREDERICK, principal. Prin. La Salle Acad., Providence. Recipient Blue Ribbon award U.S. Dept. Edn., 1990-91. Office: La Salle Acad 612 Academy Ave Providence RI 02908-2725

MUELLER, GERD DIETER, financial and administrative executive; b. Hannover, Germany, Nov. 12, 1936. Student, U. Munich, 1957-59; LLB, U. Cologne, Germany, 1961; LLM, Nordrhein-Westfalen, Duesseldorf, Germany, 1965. Mgr. fin. Bayer AG Leverkusen, Germany, 1965-72; sr. v.p. fin. svcs. Rhinechem Corp., N.Y.C., 1972-74; treas. Mobay Chem. Corp., Pitts., 1974-77; v.p. and treas. Mobay Corp., Pitts., 1977-83; exec. v.p. fin. Miles, Inc., Elkhart, Ind., 1983-86; exec. v.p. adminstrn. and fin. Mobay Corp., Pitts., 1986-88; exec. v.p., CFO Bayer U.S.A. Inc., Pitts., 1988-91; exec. v.p., chief adminstrv. and fin. officer Bayer Corp., Pitts., 1992—; pres. CDS Internat., N.Y.C. Mem. NAM. Officer: Bayer Corporation 1 Mellon Ctr 500 Grant St Pittsburgh PA 15219-2507

MUELLER, GERHARD G(OTTLOB), accounting educator; b. Eineborn, Germany, Dec. 4, 1930; came to U.S., 1952, naturalized, 1957; s. Gottlob Karl and Elisabeth Charlotte (Hossack) M.; m. Coralie George, June 7, 1958; children: Kent, Elisabeth, Jeffrey. AA, Coll. of Sequoias, 1954; BS with honors, U. Calif.-Berkeley, 1956, MBA, 1957, PhD, 1962; D Econs. (hon.), Swedish Sch. Econs. and Bus. Adminstrn., 1994. CPA, Wash. Staff accountant FMC Corp., San Jose, Calif., 1957-58; faculty dept. accounting U. Wash., Seattle, 1960—, assoc. prof., 1963-67, prof., 1967—, chmn. dept., 1969-78, dir. grad. prof. acctg. program, 1979-90, sr. assoc. dean, 1990-95, acting dean, 1994, Hughes M. Blake prof. internat. bus. mgmt., 1992-95, Julius A. Roller prof. acctg., 1995—; dir. Seattle Menu Specialists, Inc., U. Wash. Acctg. Devel. Fund, Overlake Hosp. Med. Ctr., Bellevue, chmn. bd. trustees, 1991-93; cons. internat. tax matters U.S. Treasury Dept., 1963-68; cons. Internat. Acctg. Rsch., 1964—; vis. prof. Cranfield Sch. Mgmt., Eng., 1973-74, U. Zurich, Switzerland, 1973-74; lectr. in field. Author: International Accounting, 1967; co-author: Introductory Financial Accounting, 3d edit., 1991, A Brief Introduction to Managerial and Social Uses of Accounting, 1975, International Accounting, 1978, 2nd edit., 1992, Accounting: An International Perspective, 1987, 3rd edit., 1994; editor: Readings in International Accounting, 1969, Accounting-A Book of Readings, 2d edit., 1976, A New Introduction to Accounting, 1971, A Bibliography of Internat. Accounting, 3d edit., 1973, Essentials of Multinational Accounting—An Anthology, 1979, Frontiers of International Accounting, 1986, AACSB Curriculum Internationalization Resource Guide, 1988; contbr. numerous articles to profl. jours. Expert legal witness, IRS, 1991-93. Recipient U. Wash. Disting. Teaching award, 1983, Disting. Service award, 1984; Price Waterhouse internat. accounting research fellow, 1962-64; Ford Found. fellow, 1958-59. Fellow Acad. Internat. Bus.; mem. AICPAs (internat. practice exec. com. 1972-75, exec. coun. 1987-89), Am. Acctg. Assn. (pres. 1988-89, acad. v.p. 1970-71, chmn. adv. bd. internat. acctg. sect. 1977-79, Wildman medal 1986, Nat. Outstanding Educator 1981, Disting. Internat. Lectr. in Black Africa 1987, Outstanding Internat. Acctg. Educator 1991), Fin. Execs. Inst., Wash. Soc. CPAs (pres. 1988-89, Outstanding Educator award 1985, Pub. Svc. award 1995), Acctg. Edn. Change Commn. (chmn. 1994—), Beta Alpha Psi (Acad. Acct. of Yr. 1987), Beta Gamma Sigma (Disting. scholar 1978-79), Alpha Gamma Sigma. Home: 9660 NE 34th St Bellevue WA 98004-1827 Office: U Washington Bus 353200 Seattle WA 98195-3200 *It has always been important to me to associate with people and tangible and intangible things of the highest quality. I make it a practice to set clear goals and then pursue them actively. A broad world view on all aspects of life engenders more success and happiness than special interest perspectives. I welcome change in professional matters, but seek constancy in personal and family affairs. Fate has played a role in my successes. I believe in God, Protestant ethics, and the merits of classical academic scholarship.*

MUELLER, JAMES BERNHARD, anesthesiologist, pain managememt consultant; b. Milw., Sept. 5, 1952; s. Bernhard Oscar and Perl Elizabeth (Benda) M.; m. Reba Marie Tisdale, Dec. 18, 1982; children: James Preston, Catherine Elizabeth. BS in Chemistry, Coll. Charleston, 1978; MD, Med. U. S.C., 1983. Diplomate Am. Bd. Anesthesiology, Am. Bd. Pain Medicine; added qualifications in pain mgmt. Commd. lt. USN, 1983, advanced through grades to lt. comdr., 1990; intern Naval Hosp., Portsmouth, Va., 1983-84, resident, 1986-87; fellow Naval Hosp./Med. Coll. Va., Richmond, 1986-87; staff anesthesiologist Naval Hosp., Richmond, 1987-89; resigned USN, 1991; staff anesthesiologist Julius Snyder and Assocs., Norfolk, Va., 1989-92; pvt. practice anesthesiology and pain mgmt. Irving, Tex., 1992-93, Dallas, 1993—; asst. prof. clin. anesthesiology Med. Coll. Hampton Rds., Norfolk, 1988-92, Med. Coll. Va., Richmond, 1989-92; lectr. Nurse Anesthesia Faculty Assocs., Richmond, 1989-92; med. cons. Janssen Pharmaceutica, N.J., 1989—. Contbr. book chpts. Mem. Operation Smile, The Philippines, 1988, Norfolk, 1989. Mem. Am. Soc. Anesthesiologists, Internat. Assn. for Study Pain, Soc. for Regional Anesthesia, Internat. Anesthesial Rsch. Assn., Va. Soc. Anesthesiologists (bd. dirs. 1990-92), Tex. Soc. Anesthesiologists, Tex. Med. Assn., Dallas County Med. Soc. Episcopalian. Home: 1454 Cottonwood Valley Ct Irving TX 75038 Office: 7777 Forest Ln B 143 Dallas TX 75230

MUELLER, JEAN MARGARET, nursing consultant; b. Huntington, N.Y., June 3, 1951. Diploma in Nursing, Pilgrim State Hosp., 1973; BSN, SUNY, Stony Brook, 1979; M in Profl. Studies, New Sch. for Social Rsch., 1986. RN, N.Y. Nurses aide Huntington Hosp., N.Y., 1971, LPN, 1972, RN, charge ICU/CCU, MICU/SICU, telemetry, 1973-77; charge nurse, MICU North Shore U. Hosp, Manhasset, N.Y., 1977-78; private duty cases, Holter monitor scanning, 1978-84; dir. nursing svcs., assoc. dir. nursing svcs. Nesconset (N.Y.) Nursing Ctr., 1984-86; nursing edn. instr. St. Charles Hosp., Port Jefferson, N.Y.; labor and delivery nurse SUNY, Stony Brook; teaching and rsch. nurse II Diabetes Ctr., SUNY, Stony Brook; tchg. hosp. insvc. educator I SUNY, Stony Brook, 1990-94; hosp. nursing svcs. cons. Office Health Sys. Mgmt., N.Y. State Dept. Health, Hauppauge, N.Y., 1994—; mem. adj. faculty Sch. of Nursing SUNY, Stony Brook, 1992—, St. Joseph's Coll., 1994; rsch. com. dept. family medicine with E. Stark, E.A.P.; hosp. nursing svcs. cons. office health sys. mgmt. N.Y. State Dept. Health, 1994—; lectr. Med., Emotional and Psychol. Indicators of Family Violence. Contbr. articles to profl. jours. Active Mothers Against Drunk Driving; mem. Suffolk County Family Violence Task Force. Recipient President's award for leadership tng. programs SUNY, 1993, for spl. needs of elderly tng. programs and humanistic approach to health care tng. programs, 1994. Mem. Nat. Nurses Assn., Sigma Theta Tau. Home: 234 Hallock Rd Stony Brook NY 11790-3026

MUELLER, JOHN C., lawyer; b. L.A., Sept. 19, 1952. AB, Stanford U., 1974; JD, U. So. Calif., 1977. Bar: Calif. 1977. Ptnr. Baker & Hostetler, L.A. Mem. ABA, L.A. County Bar Assn., State Calif. Bar. Office: Baker & Hostetler 600 Wilshire Blvd Los Angeles CA 90017-3212*

MUELLER, JOHN ERNEST, political science educator, dance critic and historian; b. St. Paul, June 21, 1937; s. Ernst A. and Elsie E. (Schleh) M.; m. Judy A. Reader, Sept. 6, 1960; children—Karl, Karen, Susan. A.B., U. Chgo., 1960; M.A., UCLA, 1963, Ph.D., 1965. Asst. prof. polit. sci. U. Rochester, N.Y., 1965-69, assoc. prof., 1969-72, prof., 1972—, prof. film studies, 1983—, founder, dir. Dance Film Archive, 1973—; lectr. on dance in U.S., Europe, Australia, 1973—; OP-ED columnist Wall St. Jour., 1984—, L.A., Times, 1988—, N.Y. Times, 1990—; mem. dance panel NEA, 1983-85; columnist Dance Mag., 1974-82; dance critic Rochester Dem. and Chronicle, 1974-82; mem. adv. bd. Dance in Am., PBS, 1975. Author: War, Presidents and Public Opinion, 1973 (book selected as one of Fifty Books That Significantly Shaped Public Opinion Rsch. 1946-95 Am. Assn. Pub. Opinion Rsch. 1995), Dance Film Directory, 1979, Astaire Dancing: The Musical Films, 1985 (de la Torre Bueno prize 1983), Retreat From Doomsday: The Obsolescence of Major War, 1989, Policy and Opinion in the Gulf War, 1994, Quiet Cataclysm: Reflections on the Recent Transformation of World Politics, 1995; co-author: Trends in Public Opinion: A Compendium of Survey Data, 1989; editor: Approaches to Measurement, 1969; co-editor: Jour. Policy Analysis and Mgmt., 1985-89; mem. editl. bd. Pub. Opinion Quar., 1988-91; producer 12 dance films/recorded commentator on 2d soundtrack of laser disc edit. Swing Time, 1986. Grantee NSF, 1967-70, 74-75, NEH, 1972-73, 74-75, 77-78, 79-81; Guggenheim fellow, 1988. Mem. Am. Acad. Arts and Scis., Am. Polit. Sci. Assn., Dance Critics Assn. (bd. dirs. 1983-85), Am. Assn. for Public Policy and Mgmt. (editorial bd. 1985-89). Home: 246 Roslyn St Rochester NY 14619-1812 Office: U Rochester Polit Sci Dept Rochester NY 14627

MUELLER, LOIS M., psychologist; b. Milw., Nov. 30, 1943; d. Herman Gregor and Ora Emma (Dettmann) M.; BS, U. Wis.-Milw., 1965; MA, U. Tex., 1966, PhD, 1969. Cert. family mediator. Postdoctoral intern VA Hosp., Wood, Wis., 1969-71; counselor, asst. prof. So. Ill. U. Counseling Center and dept. psychology, Carbondale, 1971-72, coordinator personal counseling, asst. prof., 1972-74, counselor, asst. prof., 1974-76; individual practice clin. psychology, Carbondale, 1972-76, Clearwater, Fla., 1977-90, Port Richey, Fla., 1990—; family mediator, 1995—; mem. profl. adv. com. Mental Health Assn. Pinellas County, 1978, Alt. Human Services, 1979-80; cons. Face Learning Center, Hotline Crisis Phone Service, 1977-87; advice columnist Clearwater Sun newspaper, 1983-90; pub. speaker local TV and radio stas., 1978, 79; talk show host WPLP Radio Sta., Clearwater, 1980-83, WTKN Radio Sta., Tampa Bay, 1988-89, WPSO Radio Sta., New Port Richey, 1991. Campaign worker for Sen. George McGovern presdl. race, 1972. Lic. psychologist, Ill., Fla. Mem. Am., Fla., Ill., Pinellas (founder, pres. 1978) psychol. assns., Am. Soc. Clin. Hypnosis, Fla. Soc. Clin. Hypnosis, Assn. Women in Psychology, West Pasco C. of C., Calusa Bus. & Profl. Women. Contbr. articles to profl. jours. Office: 9501 Us Highway 19 Ste 212 Port Richey FL 34668-4641

MUELLER, MARK CHRISTOPHER, lawyer; b. Dallas, June 19, 1945; s. Herman August and Hazel Deane (Hatzenbuehler) M.; m. Linda Jane Reed. BA in Econs., So. Meth. U., 1967, MBA in Acctg., 1969, JD, 1971. Bar: Tex. 1971, U.S. Dist. Ct. (no. dist.) Tex. 1974, U.S. Tax Ct. 1974; CPA, Tex. Acct. Arthur Young & Co., Dallas, 1967-68, A.E. Krutilek, Dallas, 1968-71; pvt. practice law, Dallas, 1971—; assoc. L. Vance Stanton, Dallas, 1971-72; instr. legal writing and rsch. So. Meth. U., Dallas, 1970-71, instr. legal acctg., 1975. Leading articles editor Southwestern Law Jour., 1970-71. Mem. NRA, Tex. Bar Assn., Tex. State Rifle Assn., Tex. Soc. CPA's, Dallas Bar Assn., Sons of Am. Revolution, Sons Republic Tex., Sons of Union Vets. of Civil War, Sons Confederate Vets., Mil. Order Stars and Bars, Order of Coif, Dallas Hist. Soc., Dallas County Pioneer Assn., Beta Alpha Psi, Phi Delta Phi, Sigma Chi. Club: Rock Creek Barbeque. Lodges: Masons, Shriners, Grotto, 32d degree KCCH Scottish Rite. Home: 7310 Brennans Dr Dallas TX 75214-2804 Office: Ste 410 9401 Lyndon B Johnson Fwy Dallas TX 75243-4540

MUELLER, MARNIE WAGSTAFF, insurance company executive, economist; b. Ft. Worth, Feb. 2, 1937; d. Robert McAlpine and Texas (Orms) W.; m. Robert Ernest Mueller; children: Sarah, Paul, Emily. BA in Econs., Wellesley Coll., 1959; MA in Econs., Yale U., 1961, PhD in Econs., 1965. CLU. Instr. Washington U., St. Louis, 1963-65; asst. prof. Wesleyan U., Middletown, Conn., 1972-77, vis. prof., 1994-95; various positions in rsch., planning and mktg. to sr. vp. corp. resources Conn. Mut. Life Ins. Co., Hartford, 1977-93. Fellow Ford Found., 1963-64, 75-76, sr. fellow Am. Leadership. Mem. Am. Econs. Assn. Episcopalian. Home: 102 N Beacon St Hartford CT 06105-2513

MUELLER, NANCY SCHNEIDER, retired biology educator; b. Wooster, Ohio, Mar. 8, 1933; d. Gilbert Daniel and Winifred (Porter) Schneider; m. Helmut Charles Mueller, Jan. 27, 1959; 1 child, Karl Gilbert. AB in Biology, Coll. of Wooster, 1955; MS in Zoology, U. Wis., 1957, PhD in Zoology, 1962. Instr. zoology U. Wis., Madison, 1966; asst. prof. poultry sci. and zoology N.C. State U., Raleigh, 1968-71; vis. prof. biology N.C. Ctrl. U., Durham, 1971-73, assoc. prof., 1973-79, prof., 1979-93; ret., 1993; vis. scientist U. Vienna, Austria, 1975. Contbr. articles, abstracts to profl. publs. Mem. Am. Soc. Zoologists, Am. Ornithologists Union, Cooper Ornithol. Soc., Wilson Ornithol. Soc., Wis. Acad. Sci., Arts and Letters, N.C. Acad. Sci., LWV (bd. dirs. 1988—, natural resources com. 1988—), Sigma Xi. Avocations: bird migration, conservation and environmental issues. Home: 409 Moonridge Rd Chapel Hill NC 27516-9385

MUELLER, PAUL HENRY, retired banker; b. N.Y.C., June 24, 1917; s. Paul Herbert and Helen (Cantwell) M.; m. Jean Bonnel Vreeland, Sept. 10, 1949; 1 child, Donald Vreeland. BS, NYU, 1940; AB, Princeton U., 1941; LittD (hon.), Heriot-Watt U., Edinburgh, Scotland, 1981; LHD (hon.), Bloomfield Coll., 1991. Page Citibank N.A., 1934; on leave, 1939-46, asst. cashier, 1947-52, asst. v.p., 1952-58, v.p., 1958-65, sr. v.p., 1965-74, chmn. credit policy com., 1974-82; chmn. Saab-Scania Am. Inc., 1982-90, Atlas Copco N.Am. Inc., 1975-93; dir. Atlas Copco AB, Stockholm, 1982-91, Skandinaviska Enskilda Banken Corp., 1983-93, Ericson N.Am., Inc., 1986-91; entered U.S. Fgn. Svc., served in Panama, Cairo, Washington, 1941-43; asst. adminstrv. sec. UN Montary and Fin. Conf., Bretton Woods, N.H., 1944; divisional asst. Dept. State, 1946; sec. West Indian Conf., 2d session, St. Thomas, V.I., 1946; vis. lectr. U. Va., 1980—; founding chmn., sr. fellow Ctr. Internat. Banking Studies, 1977-91. Contbg. author: Offshore Lending by U.S. Commercial Banks, 1975, 81, Bank Credit, 1981, Classics in Commercial Bank Lending, 1981, Vol. II, 1985, Loan Portfolio Management, 1988, Credit Culture, 1994, Credit Risk Management, 1995; author: (with Leif H. Olsen) Credit and the Business Cycle, 1979, Learning from Lending, 1979, Credit Doctrine for Lending Officers, 1976, 81, 96, Credit Endpapers, 1982, Perspective on Credit Risk, 1988; contbr. articles to profl. jours. Trustee Bloomfield Coll., N.J., 1983-91, vice chmn., 1987-88, chmn., 1988-91, trustee emeritus; treas. Marcus Wallenberg Found. (U.S.), 1984—. Served from 2d lt. to capt. USMCR, 1944-45. Decorated Royal Order Polar Star (Sweden); recipient Alumni award Grad. Sch. Credit and Fin. Mgmt., Dartmouth Coll., Disting. Svc. award Robert Morris Assocs., award for journalistic excellence, 1991. Mem. Bankers Assn. Fgn. Trade (hon., v.p. 1976), Pilgrims, SAR, Swedish-Am. C. of C. U.S. (chmn. 1989-90, hon. dir.), Royal Econ. Soc. (U.K.), Univ. Club (N.Y.C.), Beta Gamma Sigma. Republican. Presbyterian. Home: 75 Rotary Dr Summit NJ 07901-3131

MUELLER, PEGGY JEAN, dance educator, choreographer, rancher; b. Austin, Tex., June 14, 1952; d. Rudolph George Jr. and Margaret Jean (Locke) M.; m. John Yerby Tarlton, June 24, 1972 (div. June 1983). BS in Home Econs., Child Devel., U. Tex., Austin, 1974. Dance tchr. Shirley McPhail Sch. Dance, Austin, 1972-75; dance tchr. Jean Tarlton Sch. Dance, Alpine, Tex., 1975-77, College Station, Tex., 1977-80; dance tchr. Sul Ross State U., Alpine, 1975-77, Tex. A&M U., College Station, 1977-80, A&M Consol. Community Edn., Coll. Station, 1977-78, Jean Mueller Sch. Dance, Austin, 1980—, U. Tex., Austin, 1980—; dancer, contest judge Gt. Tex. Dance-Off, Austin, 1985-86; mem. equestrian com. Austin-Travis County Livestock Show and Rodeo, 1980-92, chmn. trail ride, 1986—; trail boss, pres. Austin Founders Trail Ride, 1986—; trail boss Bandera Longhorn Cattle Drive and Trail Ride, 1990, 91; choreographer, head cheerleader Austin Texans Pro Football Team, 1981; dance tchr. Austin Ballroom Dancers, 1988; dancer, agt. George Strait/Bud Light Comml. Auditions, 1990; head contest judge Am.'s Ultimate Dance Contest, Austin, 1994; contest judge Two-Stepping Across Am., Austin, 1994; speaker in field. Dancer Oklahoma, Austin, 1969, Kiss Me Kate, Austin, 1970; choreographer, lead role Cabaret, Alpine, 1976. Active Women's Symphony League Austin, 1972—, Settlement Club, Austin, 1987—; recreation chmn. St. Martin's Evang. Luth. Ch., Austin, 1972—; hon. trail boss St. Jude Children's Rsch. Hosp. Trail Ride, Austin and Kyle, Tex., 1991. Recipient Outstanding Trail Rider of Yr. award Wild Horse Trail Ride, Okla., 1984; named Tex. First Lady Trail Boss, Gov. Mark White, Mayor Frank Cooksey, Austin City Coun., 1986, Judge Bill Aleshire, Travis County Commrs., 1989, Outstanding Intramural Sports Team Mgr.-Player, Tex. A&M U., 1978-79. Mem. Tex Assn. Tchrs. of Dancing, Inc., U.S. Twirling and Gymnastics Assn., Univ. Tex. Ex-Students Assn., Tex. Execs. in Home Econs., Am. Vet. Med. Assn. Aux. (v.p. 1978-79, pres. 1979-80), Am. Horse Shows Assn., Internat. Arabian Horse Assn., Austin Women's Tennis Assn. (v.p. 1985-86, pres. 1986-90, spl. events chmn. 1990-92, advisor 1990—, winner 2d ann. Harriet Crosson Outstanding Player & Community Svc. award), Women's Team Tennis of Austin Assn. (pres.-elect 1992-93, pres. 1993-94), Capital Area Tennis Assn. (membership com. 1991, 92), Houston Salt Grass Trail Ride Assn., San Antonio Alamo Trail Ride Assn., Ft. Worth Chisholm Trail Ride Assn., U. Tex. Longhorn Alumni Band, Austin C. of C., Am. Bus. Women's Assn., Austin Alumnae Panhellenic Assn. (1st v.p. 1989-90, rush forum chmn. 1990, pres. 1990-91, parliamentarian 1991-92), Omicron Nu (v.p. 1973-74), Jr. Austin Woman's Club (historian 1990-91), Austin Country Club (team tennis captain 1994—), Zeta Tau Alpha (Austin Alumnae Chpt., alumnae photographer, social advisor 1982-87, treas. 1987-89, publicity chmn. 1989, Easter Seals fundraiser, Honor Cup winner 1990, pres. 1991-92, internat. convention official del. 1988, 92, nominating chmn. 1992-93, mem. yearbook com. 1992-94, 2d v.p. 1993-94). Republican. Clubs: Cen. Tex. Arabian Horse, Capitol Area Quarter Horse Assn., Jr. Austin Woman's, Austin Country. Avocations: theatre, piano, drums, sports, travel. Home: PO Box 14762 Austin TX 78761-4762 Office: Jean Mueller Sch Dance PO Box 14762 Austin TX 78761-4762

MUELLER, PETER STERLING, psychiatrist, educator; b. N.Y.C., Dec. 28, 1930; s. Reginald Sterling and Edith Louise (Welleck) M.; m. Ruth Antonia Shipman, Aug. 9, 1958; children: Anne Louise, Peter Sterling, Paul Shipman, Elizabeth Ruth. A.B., Princeton U., 1952; M.D., U. Rochester, 1956. Am. Cancer Soc. student fellow Francis Delafield Hosp., N.Y.C., summer 1955; intern Bellevue Hosp., Columbia U., N.Y.C., 1956-57; asst. resident in psychiatry Henry Phipps Psychiat. Clinic, Johns Hopkins Hosp., Balt., 1963-66; asst. prof. psychiatry Sch. Medicine, Yale U., New Haven, 1966-72; asso. prof. psychiatry Coll. Medicine and Dentistry of N.J., Rutgers Med. Sch., Piscataway, 1972-76; clin. prof. psychiatry Coll. Medicine and Dentistry of N.J., Rutgers Med. Sch., 1976-82; cons. for Rehab. Unit and Center for Indsl. Human Resources, Community Mental Health Center, 1973—; mem. courtesy staff dept. psychiatry Princeton Med. Center, 1976—; cons. in psychotherapy Conn. Valley Hosp., Middletown, 1966-72; cons. in psychiatry Carrier Clinic, Belle Mead, N.J., 1973—, VA Hosp., Lyons, N.J., 1975-78. Contbr. writings in field to profl. publs. U.S. and Brit., papers to profl. confs. on the use patents in U.S. and fgn. countries for direct dopamine agonists in the treatment of tobacco addiction. Served with USPHS, 1957-63. Recipient Exemplary Psychiatrist award Nat. Alliance for the Mentally Ill, 1994. Mem. Am. Psychosomatic Soc., Am. Psychiat. Assn., AAAS, Amyotrophic Lateral Sclerosis Found. (adv. bd.), Sigma Xi. Episcopalian. Home: 182 Snowden Ln Princeton NJ 08540-3915 Office: 601 Ewing St Princeton NJ 08540-2757 *For some, a hyperactive learning disorder is a curse that hobbles them throughout life; but for others, including myself, this disorder has become a somewhat uncomfortable and bewildering spur for lifelong compulsive puzzle-solving. This bittersweet mandate has produced the original, serendipitous, and occasionally disconcerting ideas which have marked my life.*

MUELLER, RICHARD WALTER, foreign service officer; b. Washington, Dec. 1, 1944; s. Walter Julius and Eleanor (Maack) M.; m. Claire McCormick, Mar. 15, 1975; children: Jonathan R., Eric R. AB, Coll. William and Mary, 1966. Joined Fgn. Svc., Dept. State, 1966; assigned Am. Embassy, Canberra, Australia, 1967-68; polit. officer Am. Embassy, Saigon, Vietnam, 1969-71; staff officer Office Sec. State, Washington, 1971-74; econ. officer U.S. Liaison Office, Beijing, Peoples Republic China, 1976-78; dep. dir. Office East-West Trade Dept. State, Washington, 1978-81, dep. dir. Office Chinese Affairs, 1981-83; chief econ. sect. Am. Consulate Gen., Hong Kong, 1983-86; dep. exec. sec. Office Sec. of State Dept. State, Washington, 1986-89, dep. asst. sec. Office Legis. Affairs, 1989-92; consul gen. Am. Consulate Gen., Hong Kong, 1993—. Office: Am Consulate General, 26 Garden Rd, Hong Kong Hong Kong

MUELLER, ROBERT KIRK, management consulting company executive; b. St. Louis, July 25, 1913; s. Edward Robert Otto and Lucille M. (Flaugher) M.; m. Jane Elizabeth Konesko, Dec. 27, 1939; children: Lucy Alison, Patricia Kirk, James Arno. BS, Washington U., St. Louis, 1934; MS, U. Mich., 1935; grad., Advanced Mgmt. Program, Harvard U., 1950. Chemist Sinclair Refining Co., East Chicago, Ind., 1935; with Monsanto Co., 1935-68, gen. mgr. plastic div., 1952-61, v.p., dir., exec. com. co., 1963-68; prodn. supt. Shawinigan Resins Corp., Springfield, 1938-40, pres., dir., 1952-61, chmn. bd., dir., 1961-63; supt. Longhorn Ordnance Works, 1942-44, plant mgr., 1944-46; indsl. research, cons., corp. exec. Arthur D. Little, Inc., 1968-88, v.p., 1973-77, chmn. bd., 1977-89; bd. dirs. Decision Resources, Inc., Waltham, Mass., Interneuron Pharms. Inc., Lexington, Mass., Arthur D. Little, Ltd., London, Bus. Ethics Found., Brookline, Mass.; chmn. faculty, lectr. Salzburg (Austria) Seminar in Am. Studies, 1970, bd. dirs., mem. exec. com., 1972-85. Author: Effective Management Through Probability Controls, 1950, Risk, Survival, and Power, 1970, The Innovation Ethnic, 1971, Board Life, Realities of Being a Corporate Director, 1974, Buzzwords: A Guide to the Language of Leadership, 1974, Metadevelopment, Beyond the Bottom Line, 1977, New Directions for Directors, Behind the Bylaws, 1977, Career Conflict, Management's Inelegant Dysfunction, 1978, Board Compass, What a Director Needs to Know in a Changing World, 1979, The Incompleat Board, The Unfolding of Corporate Governance, 1981, Behind the Boardroom Door, 1984, Corporate Networking: Building Channels of Information and Influence, 1986, Directors and Officers Guide to Advisory Boards, 1990, Boardworthiness: From a President's and Director's Perspective, 1992, Building a Power Partnership: The CEO and the Board of Directors, 1993, Anchoring Points for Corporate Directors: Obeying the Unenforceable, 1996. Trustee Cheswick Ctr., 1968—, Colby Sawyer Coll., N.H., 1972-91, Am. Austrian Found., 1988-94. Recipient Disting. Alumnus Achievement award Washington U., 1963. Fellow AAAS, N.Y. Acad. Scis.,

Inst. Dirs. (London), Internat. Acad. Mgmt.; mem. AIChE, Am. Chem. Soc., Am. Mgmt. Assn. (life, mem. internat. coun.), Soc. Chem. Industry, Nat. Assn. Corp. Dirs. (bd. dirs.), Algonquin Club (Boston). Office: Arthur D Little Inc 25 Acorn Park Cambridge MA 02140-2301

MUELLER, ROBERT LOUIS, business executive; b. Denver, Aug. 25, 1927; s. George Winchester and Ruth Mabel (Cole) M.; m. Sue McCoy, July 3, 1949; children: Robert, Richard, Edward, Mark; m. Susan Galbraith, June 23, 1985. BSMechE, Yale U., 1948. Chief computer Western Geophys. Co., Mont., Wyo., Colo., Tex., 1949-50; dist. mgr. Armco Steel Corp., Colo., Ohio, N.Y., 1950-63, L.B. Foster Co., N.Y.C., 1963-66; v.p. Wheeling Pitts. Steel Co., W.Va. and Pa., 1966-75; chmn., pres., chief exec. officer Connors Steel Co., Ala., 1975-82; pres., chief exec. officer Judson Steel Co., Calif., 1982-87; pres., COO Proler Internat., Houston, 1987-94, also bd. dirs., cons., 1994—. Co-author: Handbook of Drainage and Construction Products, 1954. With USN, 1945-46. Mem. ASCE, Assn. Iron and Steel Engrs., Duquesne Club (Pitts.), Houston City Club, Sedona Racquet Club.

MUELLER, RONALD RAYMOND, public relations executive; b. Sioux City, Iowa, Apr. 1, 1947; s. Clare Robert and Betty Louise (Abker). BS, U.S. Naval Acad., 1969; MA, U. Okla., 1982. Commd. ensign USN, Annapolis, Md., 1969; pub. affairs officer Dept. of Def., Washington, 1969-77; counselor Carl Byoir and Assocs., Boston, 1977-78; v.p. Carl Byoir and Assocs., Washington, 1978-82; sr. v.p. Fraser/Assocs., Washington, 1982-83; pres. Mueller/Assocs., Balt., 1983-84, Earle Palmer Brown Pub. Relations, Washington, 1984-87; exec. v.p., mng. dir. Ketchum Pub. Relations, Washington, 1987-91; exec. v.p. Burson-Marsteller, Chgo., 1991-92, Washington, 1992-96; CEO Cohn & Wolfe, Washington, 1996—; assoc. prof., lectr. George Washington U., 1978—; bd. dirs. Washington Sch. Psychiatry. Pres. Norfolk (Va.) Jaycees, 1970; bd. dirs. ChildSavers, 1992—. Capt. USNR, 1989—. Mem. Pub. Relations Soc. Am. (pres. Washington chpt. 1983), Pub. Relations Counselors Acad. Republican. Presbyterian. Office: Cohn & Wolfe 1801 K St NW Ste 1001-K Washington DC 20006

MUELLER, STEPHAN, geophysicist, educator; b. Marktredwitz, Ger., July 30, 1930; s. Hermann Friedrich and Johanna Antonie Fanny (Leuze) M.; m. Doris Luise Pfleiderer, July 31, 1959; children: Johannes Christoph, Tobias Ulrich. Dipl.-Phys., Inst. Tech. Stuttgart, 1957; M.Sc. in Elec. Engring., Columbia U., 1959; Dr.rer.nat., U. Stuttgart, 1962. Lectr. geophysics U. Stuttgart, 1962-64; vis. prof. S.W. Center Advanced Studies, Richardson, Tex., 1964-65; prof. geophysics U. Karlsruhe, 1964-71, dean Faculty Natural Scis., 1968-69; vis. prof. U. Tex., Dallas, 1969-70; prof. Swiss Fed. Inst. Tech., 1971—, U. Zurich, 1977—; dean Sch. Natural Scis., Swiss Fed. Inst. Tech., 1978-80; dir. Swiss Earthquake Service, 1971—; pres. Swiss Geophys. Commn., 1972-93, hon. pres. 1994; pres. European Seismol. Commn., 1972-76, Internat. Commn. Controlled Source Seismology, 1975-83; chmn. governing council Internat. Seismol. Centre, 1975-85; chmn. European-Mediterranean Seismol. Centre, 1976-82; chmn. Swiss Specialist Group of Geophysics, 1993—. German Acad. Interchange scholar, 1954-55. Fellow Royal Astron. Soc. (hon. fgn. assoc.), Am. Geophys. Union, Geol. Soc. London (hon.); mem. Internat. Assn. Seismology and Physics of Earth's Interior (pres. 1987-91), European Geophys. Soc. (pres. 1978-80, hon. mem.), European Union Geoscis. (Alfred Wegener medal 1993), German Geophys. Soc., Soc. Exploration Geophysicists, European Assn. Geoscientists and Engrs., Seismol. Soc. Am., Seismol. Soc. Japan, Acoustical Soc. Am., Swiss Geophys. Soc. (pres. 1977-80), Swiss Acad. Scis., Academia Europaea (founding mem.), German Acad. Leopoldina Researchers in Natural Scis., Internat. Assn. Geodesy (hon. assoc.), Swiss Fed. Comm. Geology, Sigma Xi. Co-editor Pure and Applied Geophysics, 1974-83; editor-in-chief Annales Geophysicae, 1982-87; editorial bd. Jour. Geophysics, 1969-87, Tectonophysics, 1971-77, 84—, Bolletino di Geofisica Teorica ed Applicata, 1978—, Jour. Geodynamics, 1983—, Tectonics, 1988—; Recipient Medaille de l'Ordre Grand-Ducal Luxembourgois de la Couronne de Chene, 1994, Gustav Steinmann medal, 1995. Office: ETH, Geophysics, CH-8093 Zurich Switzerland

MUELLER, ULRICH, literature educator; b. Goeppingen, Germany, Dec. 19, 1940; arrived in Austria, 1976; s. Rudolf and Julie (Bayer) M.; m. Ursula Speiser, Oct. 6, 1967; children: Michaela, Felix. PhD, U. Tuebingen, Fed. Republic Germany, 1967; PhD Habil., U. Stuttgart, Fed. Republic Germany, 1971. Asst. U. Tuebingen, 1967-68; asst. U. Stuttgart, 1968-71, lectr., 1972-76; prof. medieval lit. U. Salzburg (Austria), 1976—. Author books on medieval and modern lit. and music; contbr. articles and essays to profl. publs. Recipient Grimm prize, 1984. Mem. Oswald-von-Wolkenstein-Gesellschaft (pres.), Gesellschaft für Interkulturelle Germanistik (pres.). Avocations: photography, performing arts. Home: Niederalm 247, A-5081 Anif Austria Office: U Salzburg, Akademiestrasse 20, A-5020 Salzburg Austria

MUELLER, WERNER HEINRICH, organic chemist, technology development administrator; b. Aldersbach, Germany, Apr. 7, 1939; came to U.S., 1984; s. August and Rosina (Schned) M.; m. Janice Williams, Aug. 14, 1968; children: Carolyn, Alexander. BS, Tech. U. Munich, 1963, MS in Organic Chemistry, 1965, PhD in Organic Chemistry, 1967; postgrad., Temple U., 1967-68. Rsch. specialist Monsanto Co., Pensacola, Fla., 1968-72; group leader spl. chemistry Hoechst AG, Frankfurt, Germany, 1972-80, asst. to mem. bd., 1980-83; rsch. specialist div. electronic products Hoechst AG, Wiesbaden, Germany, 1983-84; asst. ops. mgr. Knapsack Works Hoechst AG, 1984-85; mgr. indsl. chemistry Am. Hoechst Corp., Coventry, R.I., 1985-88; assoc. dir. R&D adv. tech. group Hoechst Celanese, Corpus Christi, Tex., 1988-89, tech. dir. chems. group, 1989-93; dir. tech. devel. spl. chems. group Hoechst Celanese, Charlotte, N.C., 1993—; mem. indsl. vis. com. dept. chemistry and biochem. U. Tex., Austin, 1990-93. Contbr. articles to profl. jours. Mem. AAAS, Am. Chem. Soc., N.Y. Acad. Scis., Indsl. Rsch. Inst., Inc., Coun. for Chem. Rsch. Roman Catholic. Achievements include 75 patents in field of specialty chemicals, polymers, nylon intermediates, pharmaceuticals and agricultural chemicals. Office: Hoechst Celanese Corp Bldg 5200 77 Center Dr Charlotte NC 28217

MUELLER, WILLARD FRITZ, economics educator; b. Ortonville, Minn., Jan. 23, 1925; s. Fritz and Adele C. (Thormaehlen) M.; m. Shirley I. Liesch, June 26, 1948; children: Keith, Scott, Kay. B.S., U. Wis., 1950, M.S., 1951; Ph.D., Vanderbilt U., 1955. Asst. prof. U. Calif., Davis, 1954-57; prof. U. Wis., 1957-61; chief economist small bus. com. U.S. Ho. of Reps., 1961; chief economist, dir. bur. econs. FTC, 1961-68; exec. dir. President's Cabinet Com. Price Stability, 1968-69; faculty mem. U. Wis., Madison, 1969—, William F. Vilas rsch. prof. agrl. econs. emeritus, 1969—. Bd. editors Rev. Ind. Orgn., Antitrust Law and Econ. Rev., Antitrust Bull., Jour. Reprints for Antitrust Law and Economy. Served with USN, 1943-46. Recipient Distinguished Service award FTC, 1969. Fellow Am. Agrl. Econs. Assn.; mem. AAAS, Am. Econ. Assn., Am. Agr. Assn., Assn. Evolutionary Econs. (pres. 1974-75), Indsl. Orgn. Soc. (pres. 1989-90). Unitarian. Home: 121 Bascom Pl Madison WI 53705-3975 Office: U Wis 427 Lorch St Madison WI 53706-1513

MUELLER, WILLIAM MARTIN, former academic administrator, metallurgical engineering educator; b. Denver, Jan. 14, 1917; s. Charles Franklin M. and Nydia (Hough) Mueller; m. Kathryn C. Connor, Nov. 3, 1942; children: Kathryn Irene Ingram, Joann Elaine Goss. Met.E., Colo. Sch. Mines, 1940, M.S., 1949, D.Sc., 1952. Registered profl. engr., Colo. Metallurgist ALCOA, New Kensington, Pa., 1940-45; engr. Gates Rubber Co., 1945-47; instr. Colo. Sch. Mines, Golden, 1947-52; prof. metall. engring., dept. head Colo. Sch. Mines, 1974-79, v.p., 1979-83; staff metallurgist Dow Chem. Co., Rocky Flats, Colo., 1952-57; div. head Denver Research Inst., 1957-65; dir. edn. Am. Soc. Metals, Metals Park, Ohio, 1965-74; cons. Western Forge Corp., Colorado Springs, Colo., 1975-83; invited lectr. Beijing U., 1980; del. leader for People to People to China, 1984, to S.E. Asia, 1986, to USSR, 1990, to Russia, 1993. Author: (with Blackledge and Libowitz) Metal Hydrides, 1968, (with McCall) Microstructural Analysis, 1973; editor: Energetics in Metallurgical Phenomena, 4 vols., 1965-68, (with McCall) Metallographic Specimen Preparation, 1974; sr. editor: Advances in X-Ray Analysis, 1960-66. Recipient Waltman award Colo. Sch. Mines, 1940, Disting. Achievement award, 1972, Halliburton award, 1983. Fellow Am. Soc. Metals (life, trustee 1964-65); mem. ASTM (dir. 1980-83), AIME (life, com. chmn. 1980-83), Am. Soc. Engring. Edn., Mining and Metall. Soc. Am. Home: 14430 W Ellsworth Ave Golden CO 80401-5322 Office: Colo Sch Mines Hill Hall Golden CO 80401

MUELLER-HEUBACH, EBERHARD AUGUST, medical educator, obstetrician-gynecologist; b. Berlin, Feb. 24, 1942; U.S., 1968; s. Heinrich G. and Elisabeth (Heubach) Mueller; m. Cornelia R. Uffmann, Feb. 6, 1968; 1 child, Oliver Maximilian. Abitur, Lichtenbergschule, Darmstadt, W.Ger., 1961; M.D., U. Cologne (W.Ger.), 1966. Diplomate Am. Bd. Ob-Gyn.. Intern U. Cologne, 1967-68, Middlesex Gen. Hosp., New Brunswick, N.J., 1968-69; rsch. fellow Columbia U., N.Y.C., 1969-71; resident and chief resident Sloane Hosp. for Women, N.Y.C., 1971-75; asst. prof. U. Pitts. Sch. Medicine/Magee-Women's Hosp., 1975-81, assoc. prof., 1981-89; prof., chmn. dept. Ob-Gyn., Bowman Gray Sch. Medicine, Wake Forest U., Winston-Salem, N.C., 1989—. Reviewer Am. Jour. Ob-Gyn, 1978—, Obstetrics and Gynecology, 1979—; contbr. chpts. to books, articles to profl. jours. Fellow Am. Coll. Obstetricians and Gynecologists (Hoechst award 1972); mem. Tri-State Perinatal Orgn. (v.p. 1981), Pa. Perinatal Assn. (pres.-elect 1982-84, pres. 1984-86), Soc. Gynecologic Investigation, Soc. Perinatal Obstetricians, Am. Fedn. Clin. Rsch., Pitts. Ob-Gyn. Soc. (v.p. 1985-86, pres. 1986-87), Am. Gynecol. and Obstet. Soc., Perinatal Rsch. Soc., Coun. Univ. Chairs Obstetrics and Gynecology (sec.-treas. 1995—). Research on animal studies in fetal and maternal physiology; diabetes mellitus in pregnancy, high risk obstetrics. Office: Bowman Gray Sch Med Dept Ob-Gyn Medical Center Blvd Winston Salem NC 27157

MUELLNER, WILLIAM CHARLES, computer scientist, physicist; b. Chgo., Jan. 7, 1944; s. Frank Joseph and Catherine (Mika) M.; m. Marilyn Joy Bocan, Dec. 20, 1969; children: Kimberly Ann, Kevin Alan. BS in Physics, DePaul U., 1966; MS in Physics, Purdue U., 1968; PhD, U. Ill., 1973. Prof. Morton Coll., Cicero, Ill., 1969-76; engring. group leader Motorola Corp., Schaumburg, Ill., 1977-78; engring. mgr., sr. scientist Perkin-Elmer Corp., Oak Brook, Ill., 1978-80; prof., dept. chmn. computer sci. Elmhurst (Ill.) Coll., 1980—; cons. Perkin-Elmer Corp., Oak Brook, 1980-86. Author: Advanced C Language Programming, 1992; contbr. articles to Physics Rev. B., Solid State Communications. Mem. Am. Soc. Engring. Edn., Am. Phys. Soc., Assn. for Computing Machinery, Phi Kappa Phi. Achievements include 4 patents in field. Office: Elmhurst College 190 Prospect Ave Elmhurst IL 60126-3271

MUESING ELLWOOD, EDITH ELIZABETH, writer, researcher, publisher, editor; b. N.Y.C., Sept. 18, 1947; d. Carl Earl and Elsbeth (Bushbeck) Muesing; m. William Adonis Ellwood, Sept. 15, 1980; children: Jeanie, Colin, Caroline. BA, Fordham U., 1969; MA, NYU, 1971. Adminstrv. asst. The English Speaking Union, N.Y.C., 1979; freelance writer, researcher The Acad. Rsch. Group, Rutherford, N.J., 1975-78, 80-82; pres. Colin-Press, Bklyn., 1984-88; editor Ellwood Editing Svc., 1990-93; writer, editor Bushkill, Pa., 1993—. Author: U.S. Democracy: Myth vs. Reality, 1985, The Alternative to Technological Culture, 1986; contbr. haiku poems and sketches to mags., newsletters and anthologies, 1979—; contbr. articles to jours., mags., tabloids and newsletters; mem. panel experts Freelance Writers Report, monthly issue. Active Nat. Trust for Hist. Preservation, Washington, 1980—, South St. Seaport Mus., N.Y.C., 1974-83, 90-93; founding mem. Nat. Mus. Women in Arts, Washington, 1985-88; mem. Environ. Def. Fund, 1973-95—, Nature Conservancy, 1986-93, Nat. Chronic Pain Outreach Assn., 1991—; contbg. mem. Dem. Nat. Com., 1991—; founding patron Katharine Houghton Hepburn Fund, 1992, Planned Parenthood, 1989—. Mem. Nat. Writers Assn., Internat. Women's Writing Guild, Women in Scholarly Pub. (editor column in newsletter 1990), Am. Acad. Poets (contbr.), Interstitial Cystitis Assn., Nat. Writers Union, Nat. Trust Historic Preservation. Democrat. Roman Catholic. Avocations: water colors, sketching, music, guitar, collecting country furnishing antiques. Home and Office: 792 Saw Creek Est Bushkill PA 18324-9455

MUETH, JOSEPH EDWARD, lawyer; b. St. Louis, Aug. 8, 1935; s. Joseph and Marie Clare (Reher) M.; m. Ellen Agnes O'Heron, Dec. 24, 1973; children: Erin R., Patricia A. B.Chem. Engring., U. Dayton, 1957; LL.B., Georgetown U., 1960, LL.M., 1961. Bar: Calif. 1964. Practice law L.A.; ptnr. Wills, Green & Mueth, L.A., 1974-83; pvt. practice law Calif., 1983-94; of counsel Sheldon & Mak, Pasadena, Calif., 1994—; adj. prof. law U. Calif. Hastings Coll. Law, San Francisco, 1972-75; lectr. Claremont Grad. Sch., 1982—. Author: Copyrights Patents and Trademarks, 1974. Chmn. bd. Rio Hondo council Camp Fire Girls Inc., 1967-72. Mem. AAAS, Am., Los Angeles County bar assns., State Bar Calif., N.Y. Acad. Scis., L.A. Athletic Club.

MUFFOLETTO, BARRY CHARLES, engineering executive; b. Buffalo, N.Y., Oct. 19, 1950; s. Vincent Hugo and Lucille Elva (Sorge) M.; m. Michelle Louise Pariso, June 16, 1978; children: Daniel, Mark. AS in Elec. Tech., Erie Cmty. Coll., Buffalo, N.Y., 1975; BET in Elec. Engring., SUNY, 1983. Prodn. supr. Wilson Greatbatch Ltd., Clarence, N.Y., 1975-76; asst. prodn. mgr., 1976-77, project engr., 1977-79, process control engr., 1979-81, mgr. Welding Tech., 1981-82, dir. Battery Engring., 1982-94, dir. Capacitor Products, 1994—. Mem. IEEE, Am. Welding Soc., Am. Powder Metallurgy Inst., Am. Soc. Metals. Republican. Avocations: golf, fishing. Office: Wilson Greatbatch Ltd 10000 Wehrle Dr Clarence NY 14031

MUFFOLETTO, MARY LU, retired school program director, consultant, editor; b. Chgo., May 25, 1932; d. Anthony Joseph and Lucile (Di Giacomo) M. B in Philosophy, DePaul U., 1959; ME, U. Ill., 1967. Tchr. elem. edn. Community Cons., Palatine, Ill., 1959-65; tchr. gifted children Sch. Dist. 15, Palatine, 1965-67, curriculum supr., 1967-75; dir. gifted edn. program Sch. Dist. 15, Palatine, Ill., 1972-95; coord. state and fed. programs Sch. Dist. 15, Palatine, 1975-95; asst. prin. Sch. Dist. 15, Palatine, Ill., 1975-95, retired, 1995; assoc. prof. Nat. Coll. Edn., Evanston, Ill., 1979-95; editor Tchg. Ink, Inc., 1995—; chairperson State Bd. of Edn. Adv. Com. on Gifted Edn., Springfield, Ill., 1977-85; pres. No. Ill. Planning Commn. for Gifted, 1978-80. Editor: (tchr. activity books) Teaching Ink, 1995—. Mem. Nat. Coun. for Social Studies, Assn. for Curriculum and Supervision, Coun. for Exceptional Children, U. Ill. Alumni Assn. (pres. Champaign chpt. 1982-85, Loyalty award), Kiwanis, Phi Delta Kappa (sec. 1985-87). Home: 21302 W Brandon Rd Kildeer IL 60047-8618

MUFSON, MAURICE ALBERT, physician, educator; b. N.Y.C., July 7, 1932; s. Max and Faye M.; m. Diane Cecile Weiss, Apr. 1, 1962; children: Michael Jeffrey, Karen Andrea, Pamela Beth. A.B., Bucknell U., 1953; M.D., NYU, 1957. Intern Bellevue Hosp., N.Y.C., 1957-58; resident Bellevue Hosp., 1958-59; chief resident Cook County Hosp., Chgo., 1965-66; sr. surgeon USPHS Lab. Infectious Diseases, NIH, 1961-65; asst. prof. medicine U. Ill., 1965-69, assoc. prof., 1969-73, prof., 1973-76; prof., chmn. dept medicine Marshall U., 1976—; vis. scientist Karolinska Inst., 1984-85. Contbr. articles to profl. jours. Served with U.S. Navy, 1959-61. WHO grantee, 1967; recipient Meet-the-Scholar award Marshall U., 1986, REsearcher of Yr. award Sigmz Xi, Marshall U., 1989; co-recipient Louis Weinstein award Jour. Clin. Infectious Diseases, 1994. Fellow ACP (traveling scholar 1987, Laureate award W.Va. chpt.), Infectious Diseases Soc. Am.; mem. AMA, Soc. Exptl. Biology and Medicine, Ctrl. Soc. Clin. Rsch., So. Soc. Clin. Investigation, W.Va. State Med. Assn., Assn. Profs. Medicine (counselor 1992-95, pres.-elect 1995-96, pres. 1996-97), Alpha Omega Alpha. Office: Marshall U Sch Medicine Dept Medicine Huntington WV 25701

MUFTIC, FELICIA ANNE BOILLOT, consumer relations professional; b. Muskogee, Okla., Feb. 27, 1938; d. Lowell Francois and Geneva Margaret (Halstead) Boillot; m. Michael Muftic, Sept. 6, 1961; children: Tanya Muftic-Streicher, Theodore B., Mariana C. BA, Northwestern U., 1960. Exec. dir. Metro Dist. Atty.'s Consumer Office, Denver, 1973-79; talk show host KNUS, Denver, 1981-83; clk., recorder City and County of Denver, Colo., 1984-91; spl. projects dir. Consumer Credit Counseling, Denver, 1991-95; cons. consumer affairs pvt. practice, Denver, 1995—; pres. Muftic and Associates, Denver, 1980-83; commr. Uniform Consumer Credit Code, Colo., 1991—. Author: Colorado Consumer Handbook, 1982. Candidate for mayor, Denver, 1979. Named Media person of Yr., NASW, Colo., 1982; recipient Outstanding Contbrn. in Consumer Affairs award Denver (Colo.) Fed. Exec. Bd., 1982. Mem. Am. Arbitration Assn. (chmn. regional dispute settlement bd. 1993—), Inst. Internat. Edn. (bd. mem. 1980—), Rotary Internat. Democrat. Avocation: showing horses in dressage. Home and office: 3671 S Pontiac Way Denver CO 80237-1326

MUGGERIDGE, DEREK BRIAN, dean, engineering consultant; b. Godalming, Surrey, U.K., Oct. 10, 1943; arrived in Can., 1956; s. Donald William and Vera Elvina (Jackson) M.; m. Hanny Meta Buurman, Dec. 4, 1965; children: Karen Julie, Michael Brent. BS in Aero. Engring., Calif. State Polytech. U., 1965; MASc in Aerospace Engring., U. Toronto, 1966, PhD in Aerospace Engring., 1970. Spl. lectr. U. Toronto, Ont., Can., 1971; indsl. post-doctoral fellow Fleet Mfg. Co., Fort Erie, Ont., 1970-72; from asst. prof. to prof. Meml. U. of Nfld., St. John's, 1972-93, univ. rsch. prof., 1990-93; dir. Ocean Engring. Rsch. Ctr., 1982-93; dean Okanagan U. Coll., Kelowna, B.C., Can., 1993—; pres. Offshore Design Assocs. Ltd., Portugal Cove, Nfld., 1980—; sec., ptnr. Nfld. Ocean Cons., St. John's, 1981-93; ptnr. LNF Joint Venture Ltd., St. John's, 1984-90; vis. prof. U. Victoria, B.C., 1988-89. Co-author: Ice Interaction with Offshore Structures, 1988; contbr. articles to profl. jours.; contbr. conf. articles, reports. U. Toronto Grad. fellow, 1965, Nat. Rsch. Coun. Can. Grad. fellow U. Toronto, 1966-70. Mem. Assn. Profl. Engrs. & Geoscis. of Province of B.C. and Marine Engrs. Avocations: windsurfing, sailing, skiing. Home: 16438 Carr's Landing Rd, Winfield, BC Canada V4V 1C3 Office: Okanagan Univ Coll, 3333 College Way, Kelowna, BC Canada V1V 1V7

MUGNAINI, ENRICO, biobehavioral sciences and psychology educator, researcher, consultant; b. Colle Val d'Elsa, Italy, Dec. 10, 1937; came to U.S., 1969.; children: Karin E., Emiliano N.G. MD summa cum laude, U. Pisa, Italy, 1962. Microscopy lab. rsch. fellow Dept. Anatomy U. Oslo Med. Sch., 1963, asst. prof., head of electron microscopy lab., 1964-66, assoc. prof., 1967-69; prof. biobehavioral scis. and psychology, head lab. of neuromorphology U. Conn., Storrs, 1969-95; dir. inst. for neurosci. Northwestern U., Chgo., 1996—; vis. prof. Dept. Anatomy Harvard U., Boston, 1969-70; traveling lectr. Grass Found., spring 1986, fall 1990. Mng. editor USA Anatomy and Embryology Jour., 1989—; contbr. more than 100 articles to books and jours. Recipient Decennial Camillo Golgi award Acad. Nat. dei Lincei, 1981, Sen. Javits Neurosci. Rsch. Investigator award NIH, 1985-92. Mem. AAAS, Am. Assn. Anatomists, Am. Soc. Cell Biology, Internat. Brain Rsch. Orgn., Internat. Soc. Developmental Neurosci., N.Y. Acad. Scis., Norwegian Nat. Acad. Scis. and Letters, Soc. Neurosci., Cajal Club (pres. 1987-88). Office: U Northwestern Inst Neurosci 5-474 Searle Bldg 320 E Superior St Chicago IL 60611-3010

MUGRIDGE, DAVID RAYMOND, lawyer; b. Detroit, Aug. 6, 1949; s. Harry Raymond and Elizabeth Lou (Aldrich) M.; m. Sandra Lee Jackson, June 25, 1988; children: James Raymond, Sarah Lorraine. BA, U. of Ams., Puebla, Mex., 1970; MA, Santa Clara U., 1973; JD, San Joaquin Coll. of Law, 1985. Bar: Calif. 1986, U.S. Dist. Ct. (ea. dist.) Calif. 1986, U.S. Ct. Appeals (9th cir.) 1987. Staff atty. to presiding justice 5th Dist. Ct. Appeals, Fresno, Calif., 1985-87; assoc. Law Office of Nuttall, Berman, Magill, Fresno, 1987-88; pvt. practice Fresno, 1988—; tchr. civil litigation Fresno City Coll., 1988—; tchr. Spanish for legal profession, Fresno, 1994; arbitrator Fresno County Bar Assn., 1988-94; judge pro-tem Fresno County Juvenile Ct., 1992, 93, 94, 95, Fresno Mcpl. Ct., 1994, 95. Mem. ABA, Calif. Attys. for Criminal Justice, Nat. Assn. Criminal Def. Lawyers, Calif. Trial Lawyers Assn. Republican. Roman Catholic. Avocations: fishing, travel, photography, hiking. Home: 2100 Tulare St Ste 505 Fresno CA 93721 Office: 1111 Fulton St Mall # 304 Fresno CA 93721

MÜHLANGER, ERICH, ski manufacturing company executive; b. Liezen, Austria, Aug. 26, 1941; came to U.S., 1971, naturalized, 1975; s. Alois and Maria (Stückelschweiger) M.; m. Gilda V. Oliver, July 13, 1973; 1 child, Erich. Assoc. Engring., Murau Berufsschule Spl. Trade, Austria, 1959; student Inst. Tech. and Engring., Weiler Im Allgau, Germany, 1963-65. Salesman, Olin Ski Co. (Olin-Authier), Switzerland, 1965-67, mem. mktg. dept., 1967-69, svc. and mfg., 1969-71, quality control insp., Middletown, Conn., 1971-77, supr., 1977-78, gen. foreman, 1978-83, process control mgr., 1983-88; dir. mfg. Entech Corp., 1988-89; prodn. mgr. Metallizing div. Risden Corp., Thomaston, Conn., 1989-94, quality process engr., 1994— ; pres. Bus. Consolidating Svcs. Internat., Rocky Hill, Conn., 1989—, quality control technician, 1990—; quality process request divsn., fragrance divsn., 1993—; pres. Consulting Svcs. Internat. Charter mem. Presdl. Task Force, trustee; preferred mem. of U.S. Senatorial Club. Served to cpl. Austrian Air Force, 1959-60. Mem. Screenprinting Assn. Am., Am. Mgmt. Assn., Am. Soc. for Qualtiy Control, Mgmt. Club. Roman Catholic. Home: 13 Clemens Ct Rocky Hill CT 06067-3218 Office: 60 Electric Ave Thomaston CT 06787-1617 also: Bus Consolidating Svcs Internat Rocky Hill CT 06067

MUHLBACH, ROBERT ARTHUR, lawyer; b. Los Angeles, Apr. 13, 1946; s. Richard and Jeanette (Marcus) M.; m. Kerry Eldene Mahoney, July 26, 1986. BSME, U. Calif., Berkeley, 1967; JD, U. Calif., San Francisco, 1976; MME, Calif. State U., 1969; M in Pub. Adminstrn., U. So. Calif., 1976. Bar: Calif. 1976. Pub. defender County of Los Angeles, 1977-79; assoc. Kirtland & Packard, Los Angeles, 1979-85, ptnr., 1986—. Chmn. Santa Monica Airport Commn., Calif., 1984-87. Served to capt. USAF, 1969-73. Mem. ABA, AIAA, Internat. Assn. Def. Counsel, Am. Bd. Trial Advs. Office: Kirtland & Packard Ste 2600 1900 Avenue Of The Stars Los Angeles CA 90067-4507

MUHLBERGER, RICHARD CHARLES, former museum administrator, writer; b. Englewood, N.J., Jan. 20, 1938; s. George Albert and Margaret Bertha (Heins) M. A.A., Calif. Concordia Coll., 1958; B.A., Wayne State U., 1964; M.A. in Art History, Johns Hopkins U., 1967. Curator mus. edn. Worcester Art Mus., Mass., 1966-72; chmn. edn. Detroit Inst. Arts, 1972-75; dir. Mus. Fine Arts and George Walter Vincent Smith Art Mus., Springfield, Mass., 1976-87; vice dir. for edn. Met. Mus. Art, N.Y.C., 1987-89; dir. Knoxville (Tenn.) Mus. Art, 1990-91; mem. adv. panel NEH, 1976-78, Mass. Council on Arts and Humanities, 1979-81; mem. policy panel, mus. program Nat. Endowment Arts, 1981-83. Author: The Bible in Art, The New Testament, 1990, The Bible in Art, The Old Testament, 1990, The Christmas Story, 1990, What Makes a Raphael a Raphael, 1993, What Make a Bruegel a Bruegel, 1993, What Makes a Rembrandt a Rembrandt, 1993, What Makes a Monet a Monet, 1993, What Makes a Degas a Degas, 1993, What Make a Van Gogh a Van Gogh, 1993, What Makes a Leonardo a Leonardo, 1994, What Makes a Goya a Goya, 1994, What Makes a Cassatt a Cassatt, 1994, What Make a Picasso a Picasso, 1994;. Woodrow Wilson fellow, 1965-66; recipient Outstanding Young Man award Greater Worcester Jaycees, 1970. Mem. Am. Assn. Museums (chmn. com. on edn. 1974-76, councilor 1988-91), New Eng. Mus. Assn. (pres. 1985-87). Home: 41 Smithfield Ct Springfield MA 01108-3129

MUHLENBRUCH, CARL W., civil engineer; b. Decatur, Ill., Nov. 21, 1915; s. Carl William and Clara (Theobald) M.; m. Agnes M. Kringel, Nov. 22, 1939; children: Phyllis Elaine (Mrs. Richard B. Wallace), Joan Carol (Mrs. Frederick W. Wenk). BCE, U. Ill., 1937, CE, 1945; MCE, Carnegie Inst. Tech., 1943; LLD, Concordia U., River Forest, Ill., 1995. Research engineer Aluminum Research Labs., Pitts., 1937-39; cons. engring., 1939-50; mem. faculty Carnegie Inst. Tech., 1939-48; assoc. prof. civil engring. Northwestern U., 1948-54; pres. TEC-SEARCH, Inc. (formerly Ednl. and Tech. Consultants Inc.), 1954-67, chmn. bd., 1967—; Pres. Profl. Centers Bldg. Corp., 1961-77. Author: Experimental Mechanics and Properties of Materials; Contbr. articles engring. publs. Treas., bd. dirs. Concordia Coll. Found.; dir. Mo. Lutheran Synod, 1965-77, vice chmn. 1977-79. Recipient Stanford E. Thompson award, 1945. Mem. Am. Econ. Devel. Coun. (cert. econ. developer), Am. Soc. Engring. Edn. (editor Ednl. Aids in Engring.), NSPE, ASCE, Sigma Xi, Tau Beta Phi, Omicron Delta Kappa. Club: University (Evanston). Lodge: Rotary (dist. gov. 1980-81, dir. service projects Ghana and the Bahamas). Home and Office: Tec-Search Inc 4071 Fairway Dr Wilmette IL 60091-1005

MUILENBURG, ROBERT HENRY, hospital administrator; b. Orange City, Iowa, Apr. 29, 1941; s. Henry W. and Anna (Vander Zwaag) M.; m. Judith Ann Gebauer, Jan. 1, 1959; children: Ronald, Eric, Matthew. B.A., U. Iowa, 1964, M.A., 1966. Adminstrv. asst. Ill. Masonic Med. Ctr., Chgo., Ill., 1966-67; asst. adminstr. Ill. Masonic Med. Ctr., Chgo., Ill, 1967-68; assoc. adminstr. Ill. Masonic Med. Ctr., Chgo., Ill., 1968-71; assoc. adminstr. U. Utah Hosp., Salt Lake City, 1971-75, adminstr., 1975-78; adminstr. U. Wash. Med. Ctr., Seattle, 1978-84; clin. assoc. prof. health services adminstrn. and planning U. Wash., Seattle, 1978—; exec. dir. U. Wash. Med. Ctr., 1984—. USPHS trainee, 1966. Fellow Am. Coll. Hosp. Adminstrs.; mem. Am. Hosp. Assn. (del. 1984-88, chmn. metro. hosp. sect. 1987, bd.

dirs. 1992-94), Wash. State Hosp. Assn. (bd. dirs. 1982-84, 89-94), Seattle Area Hosp. Coun. (pres. 1983), Univ. Health System Consortium (bd. dirs. 1994—), Seattle C. of C. (bd. dirs. 1994—). Home: 10019 49th Ave NE Seattle WA 98125-8131 Office: U Wash Med Ctr RC-35 1959 NE Pacific St Seattle WA 98195-0004

MUIR, HELEN, journalist, author; b. Yonkers, N.Y., Feb. 9, 1911; d. Emmet A. and Helen T. (Flaherty) Lennehan; student public schs.; m. William Whalley Muir, Jan. 23, 1936; children: Mary Muir Burrell, William Torbert. With Yonkers Herald Statesman, 1929-30, 31-33, N.Y. Evening Post, 1930-31, N.Y. Evening Jour., 1933-34, Carl Byoir & Assos., N.Y.C., and Miami, Fla., 1934-35; syndicated columnist Universal Svc., Miami, 1935-38; columnist Miami Herald, 1941-42; children's book editor, 1949-56; women's editor Miami Daily News, 1943-44; freelance mag. writer, numerous nat. mags., 1944—; drama critic Miami News, 1960-65. Trustee Coconut Grove Libr. Assn., Friends U. Miami Libr., Friends Miami-Dade Pub. Libr.; vis. com. U. Miami Librs.; bd. dirs. Miami-Dade County Pub. Libr. System; past chmn., mem. State Libr. Adv. Coun., 1979-91, past chmn. Recipient award Delta Kappa Gamma, 1960; Fla. Libr. Assn. Trustees and Friends award, 1973, Coun. Fla. Librs. award, 1990; trustee citation ALA, 1984, Spirit of Excellence award, 1988; named to Fla. Women's Hall of Fame, 1984, Miami Centennial '96 Women's Hall of Fame. Mem. Women in Communications (Cmty. Headliner award 1973), Soc. Women Geographers (Meritorious Svc. award 1996), Author's Guild. Clubs: Florida Women's Press (award 1963); Cosmopolitan (N.Y.C.); Biscayne Bay Yacht. Author: Miami, U.S.A., 1953, 3d rev. edit., 1990, Biltmore: Beacon for Miami, 1987, 2d rev. edit., 1993, Frost In Florida: A Memoir, 1995. Home: 3855 Stewart Ave Miami FL 33133-6734

MUIR, J. DAPRAY, lawyer; b. Washington, Nov. 9, 1936; s. Brockett and Helen Cassin (Dapray) M.; m. Louise Rutherfurd Pierrepont, July 16, 1966. A.B., Williams Coll., 1958; J.D., U. Va., 1964. Bar: Md., Va., D.C. 1964, U.S. Supreme Ct. 1967. Asst. legal advisor for econ. and bus. affairs U.S. Dept. State, 1971-73; pvt. practice law, 1974—; mem. U.S. del. to Joint U.S./USSR Comml. Commn., 1972; chmn. D.C. Securities Adv. Com., 1981-84, mem. 1985-88. Bd. editors Va. Law Rev, 1963-64; contbr. articles to profl. jours. Mem. bd. dirs. Internat. Fedn. of Insts. for Advanced Study, 1992—. Lt. (j.g.) USNR, 1958-61. Mem. D.C. Bar (chmn. internat. law div. 1977-78, chmn. environ., energy and natural resources div. 1982-83, Met. Club (Washington), Chevy Chase (Md.) Club. Home: 3104 Q St NW Washington DC 20007-3027 Office: Ste 200 1025 Connecticut Ave NW Washington DC 20036-5405

MUIR, JOHN SCOTT, lawyer; b. San Francisco, June 20, 1930; s. James Hamilton and Edna Elizabeth (Scott) M.; m. Betty Ann Robustelli, Dec. 30, 1966; children: Kenneth Charles, Janet Elaine, Jeffrey Scott. AB, U. Calif., Berkeley, 1952, MA, 1955; JD, Golden Gate U., 1971. Bar: Calif. 1973, U.S. Dist. Ct. (no. dist.) Calif. 1973, U.S. Dist. Ct. Ariz. 1974, U.S. Supreme Ct. 1979. Tchr. Danville (Calif.) Elem. Sch. Dist., 1952-57; cons. Calif. Tchrs. Assn., Burlingame, 1957-88; pvt. practice Castro Valley, Calif., 1988-93, Sun City West, Ariz., 1993—; lectr. corp. law Francis Yee Bar Rev. Course, San Francisco, 1974-75, lectr. sch. law Calif. State U., Hayward, 1980. Author: Law and the Teacher, 1967, Teachers' Guide to Educational Expenses, 1966, Juvenile Court School Law, 1986, Bilingual Education Law, 1986. Active Dem. Nat. Com., Sun City West program chmn. 1995. Named Commodore Spinnaker Yacht Club, 1973. Mem. Sun City West Model Railroad Club (program chmn.), Sun City Scots. Avocations: magic, sailing, political activities.

MUIR, MALCOLM, federal judge; b. Englewood, N.J., Oct. 20, 1914; s. John Merton and Sarah Elizabeth (Stabler) M.; m. Alma M. Brohard, Sept. 6, 1940 (dec. 1985); children: Malcolm, Thomas, Ann Muir Weinberg, Barbara (dec.), David Clay. B.A., Lehigh U., 1935; LL.B., Harvard U., 1938. Sole practice Williamsport, Pa., 1938-42, 45-49; mem. firm Williamsport, 1949-70; judge U.S. Dist. Ct. (mid. dist.) Pa., 1970—. Active charitable orgns., Williamsport, 1939-70. Mem. ABA, Pa. Bar Assn. (pres.-elect 1970). Avocation: reading. Office: US Dist Ct PO Box 608 Williamsport PA 17703-0608

MUIR, RUTH BROOKS, counselor, substance abuse service coordinator; b. Washington, Nov. 27, 1924; d. Charles and Adelaide Chenery (Masters) B.; m. Robert Mathew Muir, Nov. 26, 1947 (dec. Feb. 20, 1996); children: Robert Brooks, Martha Louise, Heather Sue. BA in Art, Rollins Coll., Winter Park, Fla., 1947; MA in Rehab. Counseling, U. Iowa, 1979. Cert. substance abuse counselor, Iowa. Program advisor Iowa Meml. Union, Iowa City, 1959-66; counselor, coord. Mid Eastern Coun. on Chem. Abuse, Iowa City, 1976-81; patient rep. Univ. Hosp., Iowa City, 1982-85; rsch. project interviewer dept. psychiatry, U. Iowa Coll. Medicine, 1985-88. Art exhibited at Iowa City Sr. Ctr., 1987, 92, Iowa City Art Ctr., 1989, U. Iowa Hosp., 1991, Great Midwestern Ice Cream Co., 1991, Summit St. Gallery, 1995; creator, coord. therapeutic series Taking Control, Iowa City Sr. Ctr., 1986-87. Vol. coord. art exhibits Sr. Ctr., Iowa City, 1992-94; treas. bd. dirs. Crisis Ctr., Iowa City, 1975-77; sec. coun. elders Sr. Citizens Ctr., Iowa City, 1976-78; pres. Unitarian-Universalist Iowa City Women's Fedn., 1985; friend of U. of Iowa Mus. Art; mem. Johnson County Arts Coun., Opera Supers, Iowa City Unitarian U.N. Envoy; fgn. rels. coun., bd. dirs. annual changing family conf. U. Iowa, 1986-92; non-govtl. rep. Earth Summit Global Forum, 1992. Mem. AAUW (state cultural rep. 1990-92, Young Leader in Iowa 1996), Iowa City Unitarian Soc. (mem. adult program com. 1993-94, mem. unitarian care com. 1993-96), Pi Beta Phi (pres. alumnae club 1995—), U. Iowa Print and Drawing Study Club. Home and Office: 6 Glendale Ct Iowa City IA 52245-4430

MUIR, WARREN ROGER, chemist, toxic substances specialist; b. N.Y., 1945; s. Ernest Roger and Phyllis (Stirn) M.; m. Jo-Ann McNally; children: Amy, Douglas, Michael, Gregory, Daniel. AB in Chemistry cum laude, Amherst Coll., 1967; MS in Chemistry, Northwestern U., Evanston, Ill., 1968, PhD in Chemistry, 1971; postgrad. in epidemiology, Johns Hopkins U., 1975-77. Sr. staff mem. environ. health Council on Environ. Quality, EPA, Washington, 1971-78; dir. Office of Toxic Substances, EPA, 1978-81; pres. Hampshire Rsch. Assocs., Inc., 1981—, Hampshire Rsch. Inst., 1987—; assoc. environ. health scis. Johns Hopkins U., 1981—; rsch. prof. biology Am. U., 1985; sr. fellow INFORM, 1982-95; mem. Nat. Conf. Lawyers and Scientists, 1987-89. Contbr. articles on environ. quality to profl. jours. Mem., chair several Nat. Rsch. Coun. coms.; locl coord. Children's Friendship Project for No. Ireland, 1993—, bd. dirs. 1995—. Recipient NSF Acad. award, 1966, Howard Waters Doughty prize Amherst Coll., 1967, Forris Jewett Moore fellow, 1967; knighted assoc. officer brother Most Venerable Order of St. John, 1992; co-recipient Adminstrs.' award U.S. EPA, 1992. Mem. AAAS, Am. Chem. Soc. (Student award Conn. Valley sect. 1967), Soc. Risk Analysis, Soc. Epideiol. Rsch., Sigma Xi. Home: 9426 Forest Haven Dr Alexandria VA 22309-3151

MUIR, WILLIAM KER, JR., political science educator; b. Detroit, Oct. 30, 1931; s. William Ker and Florence Taylor (Bodman) M.; m. Paulette Irene Wauters, Jan. 16, 1960; children: Kerry Macaire, Harriet Bodman. B.A., Yale U., 1954, Ph.D., 1965; J.D., U. Mich., 1958. Bar: N.Y. 1960, Conn. 1965. Instr. U. Mich. Law Sch., 1958-59; assoc. firm Davis Polk & Wardwell, N.Y.C., 1959-60; lectr. in polit. sci. Yale U., 1960-64, 65-67; from assoc. to ptnr. Tyler Cooper Grant Bowerman & Keefe, New Haven, 1964-68; prof. polit. sci. U. Calif.-Berkeley, 1968—, dept. chmn., 1980-83; speechwriter v.p. U.S., 1983-85; columnist Oakland (Calif.) Tribune, 1992-93; writer Gov. of Calif., Sacramento, 1994; sr. cons. Calif. State Assembly, Sacramento, 1975-76; cons. Oakland (Calif.) Police Dept., 1970-72; vis. prof. polit. sci. Harvard U., summers 1976, 79. Author: Prayer in the Public Schools, 1967, later republished as Law and Attitude Change, 1974, Police: Streetcorner Politicians, 1977, Legislature: California's School for Politics, 1982, The Bully Pulpit: The Presidential Leadership of Ronald Reagan, 1993. Mem. Berkeley (Calif.) Police Rev. Commn., 1981-83; chmn. New Haven Civil Liberties Coun., 1965-68; Rep. candidate Calif. State Assembly, 1996. Recipient Hadley B. Cantril Meml. award, 1979, Disting. teaching award U. Calif., Berkeley, 1974, Phi Beta Kappa No. Calif. Assoc. Excellence In Teaching award, 1994. Mem. Am. Polit. Sci. Assn. (Edward S. Corwin award 1966). Republican. Presbyterian. Home: 59 Parkside Dr Berkeley CA 94705-2409 Office: Dept Polit Sci U Calif Berkeley CA 94720

MUIR, WILLIAM LLOYD, III, academic administrator; b. Norton, Kans., Mar. 20, 1948; s. John Thomas and Rosalie June (Benton) M. BBA, Kans. State U., 1977. Asst. sec. of state State of Kans., Topeka, 1971-72, fin. adminstr. atty. gen. office, 1972-79, comptroller, gov.'s office, 1979-87; dir. econ. devel. Kans. State U., Manhattan, 1987-91, asst. to v.p., 1991—; Faculty rep., senator, Kans. State U. student govt. assn., 1992—. Bd. dirs. United Way of Riley County, 1989—, chair, 1992; mem. task force City of Manhattan/Riley County Blank Page Econ. Devel., 1989-91; trustee Kans. State U. Found., 1993—; mem. Leadership Kans., 1989. Named to Outstanding Young Men in Am., 1983, 84, 85. Mem. Friends of Cedar Crest Assn., Inc., Nat. Geog. Soc., Sierra Club, Masons, Alpha Tau Omega (nat. officer), Alpha Kappa Psi. Episcopalian. Avocations: travel, volunteer work, advising. Home: 2040 Shirley Ln Manhattan KS 66502-2059 Office: Kansas State U 122 Anderson Hall Manhattan KS 66506-0100

MUIRHEAD, VINCENT URIEL, aerospace engineer; b. Dresden, Kans., Feb. 6, 1919; s. John Hadsell and Lily Irene (McKinney) M.; m. Bobby Jo Thompson, Nov. 5, 1943; children: Rosalind, Jean, Juleigh. B.S., U.S. Naval Acad., 1941; B.S. in Aero. Engring, U.S. Naval Postgrad. Sch., 1948; Aero. Engr., Calif. Inst. Tech., 1949; postgrad., U. Ariz., 1962, 64, Okla. State U., 1963. Midshipman U.S. Navy, 1937, commd. ensign, 1941, advanced through grades to comdr., 1951; nav. officer U.S.S. White Plains, 1945-46; comdr. Fleet Aircraft Service Squad, 1951-52; with Bur. Aeros., Ft. Worth, 1953-54; comdr. Helicopter Utility Squadron I, Pacific Fleet, 1955-56; chief staff officer Comdr. Fleet Air, Philippines, 1956-58; exec. officer Naval Air Tng. Center, Memphis, 1958-61; ret., 1961; asst. prof. U. Kans., Lawrence, 1961-63; assoc. prof. aerospace engring. U. Kans., 1964-76, prof., 1976-89, prof. emeritus, 1989—, chmn. dept., 1976-88; cons. Black & Veatch (cons. engrs.), Kansas City, Mo., 1964—. Author: Introduction to Aerospace, 1972, 5th edit., 1994, Thunderstorms, Tornadoes and Building Damage, 1975. Decorated Air medal. Fellow AIAA (assoc.); mem. Am. Acad. Mechanics, Am. Soc. Engring. Edn., Tau Beta Pi, Sigma Gamma Tau. Mem. Ch. of Christ (elder). Research on aircraft, tornado vortices, shock tubes and waves. Home: 503 Park Hill Ter Lawrence KS 66046-4841 Office: Dept Aerospace Engring Univ Kans Lawrence KS 66045

MUJICA, MARY BERNADETTE, mechanical engineer; b. Red Bank, N.J., Feb. 2, 1963; d. Patrick Peter and Linda Jean (Mohler) McCall; m. Frank Elias Mujica, Apr. 16, 1988; children: Keith Alan, Shannon Yvette, Angela Andrea, Kasey Alan. BSME summa cum laude, Bucknell U., 1985. Asst. to corp. maintenance mgr. Air Products & Chems., Allentown, Pa., 1985-86; plant maintenance engr. Air Products & Chems., Pasadena, Tex., 1986-87; prodn./quality engr. Air Products & Chems., Pasadena, 1987-88; chem. plant engr., project engr. Shell Oil/Chem., Deer Park, Tex., 1988-90, chem. plant and refinery effluent engr., 1990-92, safety/process safety mgmt. engr., 1992-93, asst. maintenance mgr., reliability engr., 1993—. Asst. leader Jr. Achievement, Allentown, 1985-86; industry sponsor Soc. Women Engrs., Allentown, 1985-86; mem. fin. com. Heritage Park Bapt. Ch., Webster, Tex., 1990-92; firefighter, mem. rescue squad Shell Emergency Response, 1990-94. Kodak scholar, 1982-85. Mem. Tau Beta Pi (sec. 1984). Avocations: cycling, rollerblading. Home: 1001 Glenshannon Ave Friendswood TX 77546-5339 Office: Shell Oil Co PO Box 100 Deer Park TX 77536-0100

MUJICA, MAURO E., architect; b. Antofagasta, Chile, Apr. 20, 1941; came to U.S., 1965, naturalized, 1970; s. Mauro Raul and Graciela (Parodi-Blayfus) M.; m. Barbara Louise Kaminar, Dec. 26, 1966; children: Lillian Louise, Mariana Ximena, Mauro Eduardo Ignacio III. BArch, MArch, Columbia U., 1971. Head designer Columbia U. Office Archtl. Planning, N.Y.C., 1966-71; project mgr. Walker, Sander, Ford & Kerr, Architects, Princeton, N.J., 1971-72; prin. Mauro E. Mujica, Architect, N.Y.C., 1972-74; dir. internat. div. Greenhorne & O'Mara, Inc., Riverdale, Md., 1974-78; ptnr. Mujica & Reddy Architects, Washington, 1978-80; prin. Mauro E. Mujica, Architect, Washington, 1980-81; ptnr. Mujica & Berlin Investment Bankers, Washington, 1982-85, Mujica Keppie Henderson Internat., Washington and Glasgow, Scotland, 1981-83, Mujica-Seifert Architects, Washington and London, 1983-87; pres., chief exec. officer The Pace Group, Washington, 1987-91; ptnr. PACE/WALSHE Internat., London and Washington. Chmn. bd. and CEO U.S. English Found., Washington, 1993—; hon. mem. Emmanuel Coll. Cambridge U., Eng., 1995; mem. adv. bd. U.S.-U.K. Fulbright Commn. Prin. works include: Tennis Clubhouse, Columbia U., Nat. Hosp., Puerto Barrios, Guatemala, Plaza Hotel interiors, La Paz, Bolivia. Fellow Inst. Dirs. (London); mem. AIA, Columbia U. Archtl. Alumni Assn, Capitol Hill Club, Bethesda Country Club. Republican.

MUJUMDAR, VILAS SITARAM, structural engineer, management executive; b. Indore, India, June 26, 1941; s. Sitaram and Kamala (Kulkarni) M.; m. Ingrid M. Dietrich, Mar. 1, 1969. BScin Civil Engring., Vikram U., India, 1961; MS, U. Roorkee, India, 1962; MBA, U. Santa Clara, Calif., 1980. Registered profl. engr., U.S., Can., U.K.; registered structural engr., Calif. Design engr. U.S.D. & Co., India, 1962-65, Donovan H. Lee & Ptnrs., London, 1965-66; asst. chief engr. Francon & Spancrete Ltd., Montreal, Can., 1966-68; gen. mgr., dir. engring. Modular Constructors, Woburn, Mass., 1968-70; sr. project engr., tech. mgr. LeMessurier Assocs., Cambridge, Mass., 1970-74; v.p. Precast Systems Cons., Woburn, Mass., 1974-77; prin. structural engr. Ecodyne Corp., Santa Rosa, Calif., 1977-79; v.p. Foster Engring., Inc., San Francisco, 1979-81, 3D/Internat. Inc., Houston, 1981-85; pres. VSM Assocs., Santa Rosa, Calif., 1986-88; v.p. BSHA, Inc., San Diego, 1988-90; pres. McNamara, Salvia, Mujumdar, Inc., San Diego, 1990-92; chief of office of regulation svcs. Div. State Architect Dept. Gen. Svcs., Calif., 1992—; tchr. concrete course Calif. State U., Long Beach; mem. steering com. U.S. - Japan Seismic Rsch. Author: Concrete Design Manual, Structural Engineer Review Course; inventor pre-cast concrete bldg. systems; contbr. articles to profl. jours. Merit scholar Govt. India, 1957-62, Gold medal; recipient numerous awards. Fellow ASCE, Inst. Structural Engrs., Am. Concrete Inst.; mem. Prestressed Concrete Inst. (chmn. several Earthquake Engring. coms.), Structural Engrs. Assn. Calif. (chmn. seismology com. 1992-93), Beta Gamma Sigma (hon. bus. soc.). Home: 2120 Parrish Dr Santa Rosa CA 95404-2323 Office: 1300 I St Ste 800 Sacramento CA 95814

MUKASEY, MICHAEL B., federal judge; b. 1941. AB, Columbia U., 1963; LLB, Yale U., 1967. Assoc. Webster Sheffield Fleishchmann Hithcock & Brookfield, 1967-72, Patterson, Belknap, Webb & Tyler, 1976-88; asst. U.S. atty. U.S. Dist. Ct. (so. dist.) N.Y., 1972-76, dist. judge, 1988—. Contbr. articles to profl. jours. Mem. Assn. of Bar of City of N.Y. (fed. cts. com. 1979-82, communications law com. 1983-86). Office: US Dist Ct US Courthouse 500 Pearl St New York NY 10007-1312

MUKAWA, AKIO, pathology educator; b. Kanazawa, Ishikawa, Japan, June 10, 1928; s. Tatsuchiyo and Moto (Ohtsuka) M.; m. Hiroko Matsuo, May 5, 1968; children: Chisui, Yasutake. MD, U. Kanazawa, Japan, 1954, PhD, 1959. Diplomate Am. Bd. Pathology. Resident pathology Queens Hosp. Ctr., N.Y.C., 1959-63; lectr. pathology U. Kanazawa Med. Sch., 1963-67; neuropathology fellow Albert Einstein Coll. Medicine, N.Y.C., 1966-67; dir. pathology Nat. Hosp. Kanazawa, 1967-72; prof. pathology Kanazawa Med. U., Uchinada, Japan, 1972-96; cons. Mukawa Inst. Pathology, Uchinada, 1996—. Author: Autopsy Technique, 1988. Mem. Japanese Path. Soc. (trustee 1971—), Am. Soc. Clin. Pathologists (fgn. fellow 1989—). Avocation: gardening. Home and Office: Taiseidai 55 Uchinada, Ishikawa 920-02, Japan

MUKERJEE, PASUPATI, chemistry educator; b. Calcutta, India, Feb. 13, 1932; s. Nani Gopal and Probhabati (Ghosal) M.; m. Lalita Sarkar, Feb. 29, 1964. B.Sc., Calcutta U., 1949, M.Sc., 1951; Ph.D., U. So. Calif., 1957. Lectr., vis. asst. prof. U. So. Calif., 1956-57; research assoc. Brookhaven Nat. Lab., L.I., 1957-59; reader in phys. chemistry Indian Assn. Cultivation of Sci., Calcutta, 1959-64; guest scientist U. Utrecht, Holland, 1964; sr. scientist chemistry dept. U. So. Calif., 1964-66; vis. assoc. prof. U. Wis., Madison, 1966-67, prof. Sch. Pharmacy,, 1967-94, emeritus prof., 1994—; vis. prof. Indian Inst. Tech., Kharagpur, 1971-72; mem. commn. on colloid and surface chemistry Internat. Union Pure and Applied Chemistry. Contbr. articles to profl. jours.; editorial bd. Jour. Colloid and Interface Sci., 1978-80, Asian Jour. Pharm. Scis., 1978-85, Colloids and Surfaces, 1980-86. Grantee USPHS, NSF, Nat. Bur. Standards, Petroleum Research Fund. Fellow AAAS, Acad. Pharm. Scis., Am. Inst. Chemistry; mem. Am. Chem. Soc. (editorial bd. Langmuir 1985-86), Am. Pharm. Assn., Acad. Pharm. Scis., Rho Chi. Home: 5526 Varsity Hl Madison WI 53705-4652 Office: 425 N Charter St Madison WI 53706-1508

MUKHERJEE, AMIYA K, metallurgy and materials science educator. PhD, Oxford (Eng.) U., 1962. Prof. U. Calif., Davis. Recipient Alexander von Humboldt award, 1988, Albert Easton White Disting. Tchr. award, 1992, Pfeil medal and prize Inst. Materials, 1993, U. Calif. prize and citation, 1993. Office: U Calif Davis Dept Chem Engring & Material Sci Davis CA 95616

MUKHERJEE, KALINATH, materials science and engineering educator, researcher; b. Calcutta, India, Feb. 19, 1932; naturalized U.S. citizen, 1966; s. Ramkrisna and Saraju Mukherjee; m. Patricia Stapleton, Aug. 20, 1959; children: Joia S., Maia S., Janam S. BS in Engring., Calcutta U., 1956; MS in Engring., U. Ill., Urbana, 1959, PhD, 1963. Metallurgist Indian Iron and Steel Co., 1956-57; rsch. asst. U. Ill., Urbana, 1957-63, rsch. assoc., instr., 1963-64; asst. prof. SUNY, Stony Brook, 1964-67; assoc. prof. Poly. Inst. Bklyn., 1967-72, prof., 1972-80; head dept. metallurgy Poly. Inst. N.Y., 1974-80; prof. Mich. State U., East Lansing, 1980—, chmn. dept., 1985—. Co-editor: Lasers in Metallurgy, 1982, Laser Processing of Materials, 1985, Laser Materials Processing III, 1989, Laser Materials Processing IV, 1994; eidtor: Metall./Materials Sci. Edn. yearbook, 1974—; contbr. numerous articles to profl. jours. Recipient Alumnus award Bengal Engring. Coll., India, 1989. Fellow AAAS, Am. Soc. Metals (Edn. award N.Y. chpt. 1976); mem. AIME, Am. Phys. Soc., Am. Soc. Engring. Edn., Metal Soc. N.Y., Minerals, Metals and Materials Soc. (bd. dirs. 1991-94, dir. structural materials divsn. 1991-94), Sigma Xi, Alpha Sigma Nu. Democrat. Office: Mich State U Dept Materials Sci & Mechs East Lansing MI 48824

MUKOYAMA, JAMES HIDEFUMI, JR., securities executive; b. Chgo., Aug. 3, 1944; s. Hidefumi James and Miye (Maruyama) M.; m. Kyung Ja Woo, June 20, 1971; children: Sumi Martha, Jae Thomas. BA in English, U. Ill., 1965, MA in Social Studies, 1966; honor grad. U.S. Army Inf. Sch., 1966; grad. U.S. Army Command and Gen. Staff Coll., 1979, U.S. Army War Coll., 1984. Registered prin., sr. registered options prin. Nat. Assn. Securities Dealers. Commd. 2nd. lt. U.S. Army, 1965-70; with USAR, 1970—, brig. gen., 1987-90, maj. gen., 1990-95; asst. dept. mgr. Mitsui & Co. (USA), Inc., Chgo., 1971-74; mem. Chgo. Bd. Options Exchange, 1974-75; v.p. 1st Omaha Securities, Chgo., 1975-76, Heartland Securities, Chgo., 1976-90; allied mem. N.Y. Stock Exchange, 1982-84; v.p. Lefta Advt., Chgo., 1976-90; v.p. Fleet Brokerage, Chgo., 1990-95, exec. v.p. and chief op officer Regal Discount Securities, 1995—. Mem. exec. bd. Hillside Free Meth. Ch., Evanston, Ill., 1982-93; dir. chgo. coun. Boy Scouts of America, 1993—; trustee Nat. Japanese Am. Meml. Found., 1995—. Decorated Silver Star, Legion of Merit, Purple Heart, 3 Bronze Stars; Vietnamese Army Cross of Gallantry; Japanese Army Parachutist badge; recipient cert. of merit Korean Army, others. Mem. U. Ill. Alumni Assn. (life), Assn. U.S. Army, U.S. Army War Coll. Alumni Assn. (life), Vets. of Fgn. Wars (life), Army Res. Assn. (pres., founder 1992—), Mil. Order Purple Heart (life), Am. Legion (life), Res. Officers Assn. (life), Sr. Army Res. Comdrs. Assn. (life). Home: 4009 Tracey Ct Glenview IL 60025-2468 Office: 209 W Jackson Blvd Fl 4 Chicago IL 60606-6907

MULARZ, THEODORE LEONARD, architect; b. Chgo., Nov. 6, 1933; s. Stanley A. and Frances (Baycar) M.; m. Ruth L. Larson, Nov. 9, 1963; children: Anne Catherine, Mark Andrew. BArch, U. Ill., 1959. Registered arch. Colo., Calif., Oreg. Prin. Theodore L. Mularz, AIA Architects, Aspen, 1963-77; v.p. Benedict-Mularz Assocs. Inc., 1978-81; prin. Theodore L. Mularz & Assocs., Aspen, 1981-90; pvt. practice, Ashland, Oreg., 1990—. Designer numerous archtl. projects including comml., indsl., religious, recreational, residential and historic restoration. Vice-chmn. Pitkin County Bd. Appeals, 1972-90, City of Aspen Bd. Appeals, 1985-90; City of Aspen Planning/Building Dept. adv. com., 1988-89; planning dir. search. com. City of Aspen, Pitkin County, 1989; mem. Colo. Bd. Examiners of Archs., 1975-85, pres., 1976-80, v.p., 1978; bd. dirs. Rogue Valley Symphony, Ashland, 1990-92, treas., 1991-92, chmn. fin. com., 1991-92. Served with USCGR, 1953-55. Fellow AIA (chair Southern Oreg. program com. 1994-95); mem. Nat. Coun. Archtl. Registration Bds. (profl. conduct com. 1977-78, procedures and documents com. 1978-82, chmn. edn. com. 1982-83, chmn. procedures and documents com. 1983-84, dir. 1982-84, pres. 1985-86, internat. rels. com. 1984-89, exec. com. 1984-87, mem. interprofl. coun. on registration 1984-85, pres., 1985, internat. oral exam. com. 1984-89), Colo. Soc. Architects (Cmty. Svc. award 1975), Aspen Archs. Collaborative (chmn. 1973-74), Aspen C. of C. (past dir., past pres., past v.p.), Aspen Hist. Soc. (com. chmn. 1963-64), Rotary (bull. editor Ashland Lithia Springs 1994-95). Roman Catholic. Home: 793 Elkader St Ashland OR 97520-3307 Office: 585 A St Ste 2 Ashland OR 97520-2069

MULASE, MOTOHICO, mathematics educator; b. Kanazawa, Japan, Oct. 11, 1954; came to U.S., 1982; s. Ken-Ichi and Mieko (Yamamoto) M.; m. Sayuri Kamiya, Sept. 10, 1982; children: Kimihico Chris, Paul Norihico, Yurika. BS, U. Tokyo, 1978; MS, Kyoto U., 1980, DSc, 1985. Rsch. assoc. Nagoya (Japan) U., 1980-85; JMS fellow Harvard U., Cambridge, Mass., 1982-83; vis. asst. prof. SUNY, Stony Brook, 1984-85; Hedrick asst. prof. UCLA, 1985-88; asst. prof. Temple U., Phila., 1988-89; assoc. prof. U. Calif., Davis, 1989-91, prof., 1991—, vice chair dept. math., 1995—; mem. Math. Scis. Rsch. Inst., Berkeley, Calif., 1982-84, Inst. for Advanced Study, Princeton, N.J., 1988-89; vis. prof. Max-Planck Inst. for Math., Bonn, Germany, 1991-92, Kyoto U., 1993, 94, Humboldt U., Berlin, Germany, 1995, 96. Contbr. articles to profl. jours. Treas. Port of Sacramento Japanese Sch., 1990-91. Mem. Math. Soc. Japan, Am. Math. Soc. (com. on internat. affairs 1993-96). Avocation: music. Office: U Calif Dept Math Davis CA 95616

MULCAHY, CHARLES CHAMBERS, lawyer, educator; b. Milw., Oct. 5, 1937; s. Thomas Lawrence and Mary (Chambers) M.; m. Judith Ann Schweiger, June 29, 1963; children: Mary Mulcahy Muth, Meg Mulcahy Ekmark, Beth. BS, Marquette U., 1959, JD, 1962. Bar: Wis. 1962, Fla. 1987. Atty., pres. Mulcahy & Wherry, Milw., 1966-91; atty. Whyte Hirschboeck Dudek S.C., Milw., 1991—; adj. prof. Marquette U. Law Sch., Milw., 1975-90; hon. consul Belgium, Milw., 1985—; pres. Pub. Policy Forum, 1992-94; bd. dirs. Wis. Mfrs. and Commerce, 1988-95; mem. Wis. Coun. on Mcpl. Collective Bargaining, 1993—; bd. dirs. Med. Coll. Wis., 1980—, Greater Milw. Com., 1976—. Author: Public Employer Managers Manual, 1968; co-editor: Public Employment Law , 1974, 2nd edit., 1979, 3rd. edit., 1988. County supr. Milw. County, 1964-76; pres. Milw. Tennis Classic, 1975—; chmn. War Meml. Corp., 1976-84; pres. Wis. World Trade Ctr., 1987-91 (Meritorious Svc. award 1991). With USAF, 1962-68. Recipient County Achievement award Nat. Assn. Counties, 1976; named Father of Yr. Children's Outing Assn., 1984; named to Marquette U. Athletic Hall of Fame, 1988. Mem. Milw. County Hist. Soc. (pres. 1980-81), Marquette Law Alumni Assn. (pres. 1971-72). Republican. Roman Catholic. Avocations: tennis, history, reading, travel. Home: 1820 E Fox Ln Fox Point WI 53217-2858 Office: Whyte Hirschboeck Dudek SC 111 E Wisconsin Ave Ste 2100 Milwaukee WI 53202-4809

MULCAHY, JOHN J., bishop; b. Dorchester, Mass., June 26, 1922. Student, St. John's Sem., Mass. Ordained priest, Roman Catholic Ch. 1947. Rector Pope John XXIII Sem. for Delayed Vocations, 1969-73; ordained titular bishop of Penafiel and aux. bishop Diocese of Boston, 1975—. Office: Archdiocese Boston 58 Blaney St Swampscott MA 01907-2559

MULCAHY, ROBERT EDWARD, management consultant; b. Cambridge, Mass., Mar. 2, 1932; s. George Frances and Hazel (Douglas) M.; m. Ethel Walworth, Nov. 14, 1953; children: Linda, Scott, Steven, Susan. B.S., Lowell Textile Inst., 1953. With Allied Chem. Corp., Morristown, N.J., 1953—; from engr. to mktg. mgr. Nat. Aniline div. Allied Corp., 1953-63, from dir. indsl. mktg. to v.p.-mktg. Fibers div., 1963-69, asst. to group v.p., corporate office, 1969, v.p. and gen. mgr.-consumer group Fabricated Products div., 1969-71, pres. Fibers div., 1971-74, group v.p., 1974-75, pres., dir., 1975-79, asst. to chmn. and dir., 1979-80; sr. assoc. The Corp. Dir., Inc., N.Y.C., 1981-83; pres. Counselors to Mgmt. Inc., 1984—.

MULCAHY, ROBERT WILLIAM, lawyer; b. Milw., Jan. 11, 1951; s. T. Larry and Mary Margaret (Chambers) M.; m. Mary M. Andrews, Aug. 3,

1974; children: Molly, Kathleen, Margaret, Michael. BS, Marquette U., 1973, JD, 1976. Staff atty. NLRB, Milw., 1976-79; ptnr. Mulcahy & Wherry, S.C., Milw., 1979-90, Michael, Best & Friedrich, Milw., 1990—; bd. dirs. WERC Coun. on Mcpl. Collective Bargaining, 1990-93. Co-author: Comparable Worth: A Negotiator's Guide, Public Sector Labor Relations in Wisconsin, Strike Prevention and Control Handbook. Bd. dirs. Milw. Repertory Theater, 1993—, Charles Allis/Villa Terrace, 1991—; mem. St. Monica Parish Coun., 1988—; mem. Whitefish Bay Police Commn.; divsn. chmn. United Performing Arts Fund, 1993-94. Mem. ABA, State Bar Wis. (chair labor sect. 1986-87), Milw. Bar Assn. (co-chair labor sect. 1988-95), Nat. Assn. Counties, Nat. Pub. Employers Labor Rels. Assn., Wis. Counties Assn., Indsl. Rels. Rsch. Assn., Mgmt. Resources Assn., Milw. Area Mcpl. Employers Assn. Office: Michael Best & Friedrich 100 E Wisconsin Ave Milwaukee WI 53202-4107

MULCKHUYSE, JACOB JOHN, energy conservation and environmental consultant; b. Utrecht, The Netherlands, July 21, 1922; came to U.S., 1982; s. Lambertus D. and Aagje (Van Geyn) M.; m. Cornelia Jacoba Wentink, Jan. 17, 1953; children: Jacobien, Hans, Dieuwke, Linda, Marlies. MSc, U. Amsterdam (the Netherlands), 1952, PhD, 1960. Dir. Chemisch-Farmaceutische Fabriek Hamu, the Netherlands, 1951-57; tech. asst. mgr. Polak & Schwarz (now IFF), the Netherlands, 1957-60; asst. tech. mgr. Albatros Superphosphate Fabrieken, the Netherlands, 1960-61; tech. mgr. for overseas subsidiaries Verenigde Kunstmestfabrieken, the Netherlands, 1961-64, gen. mgr. process engring. dept., 1964-70; dept. head process engring. dept. Unie van Kunstmestfabrieken, the Netherlands, 1970-82; sr. chem. engr. World Bank, Washington, 1982-83, sr. cons. chem. engr., 1983-87; ind. cons. environ. engring. World Bank and several cons. firms, 1987—. Author: (with Heath and Venkataraman) The Potential for Energy Efficiency in the Fertilizer Industry, 1985, (with Gamba and Caplin) Industrial Energy Rationalization in Developing Countries and Constraints in Energy Conservation, 1990, Process Safety Analysis: Incentive for the Identification of Inherent Process Hazards, 1992, Energy Efficiency and Conservation in the Developing World, 1992; editor: Environmental Balance of the Netherlands, 1972. Mem. AICE, Royal Dutch Chem. Soc., Fertilizer Soc. (pres. 1969-70), Internat. Inst. for Energy Conservation (bd. dirs. 1990-93), Rotary. Avocations: philosophy, tennis, advising developing countries. Home: Watersedge 5 Broken Island Rd Palmyra VA 22963-2064

MULDAUR, DIANA CHARLTON, actress; b. N.Y.C., Aug. 19, 1938; d. Charles Edward Arrowsmith and Alice Patricia (Jones) M.; m. James Mitchell Vickery, July 26, 1969 (dec. 1979); m. Robert J. Dozier, Oct. 11, 1981. B.A., Sweet Briar Coll., 1960. Actress appearing in: Off-Broadway theatrical prodns., summer stock, Broadway plays including A Very Rich Woman, 1963-68; guest appearances on TV in maj. dramatic shows; appeared on: TV series Survivors, 1970-71, McCloud, 1971-73, Tony Randall Show, 1976, Black Beauty, 1978; star: TV series Born Free, 1974, Hizzoner, 1979, Fitz & Bones, 1980, Star Trek: The Next Generation, 1988-89; NBC miniseries and TV series A Year in the Life, 1986; TV movie Murder in Three Acts, The Return of Sam McCloud, 1989; TV series L.A. Law, 1989-91; motion picture credits include McQ, The Lawyer, The Other, One More Train to Rob, Mati, etc. Bd. dirs. Los Angeles chpt. Asthma and Allergy Found. Am.; bd. advisors Nat. Ctr. Film and Video Preservation, John F. Kennedy Ctr. Performing Arts, 1986. Recipient 13th Ann. Commendation award Am. Women in Radio and TV, 1988, Disting. Alumnae award Sweet Briar Coll., 1988. Mem. Acad. Motion Picture Arts and Scis., Screen Actors Guild (dir. 1978), Acad. TV Arts and Scis. (exec. bd., dir., pres. 1983-85), Conservation Soc. Martha's Vineyard Island. Office: The Artists Group Ltd 1930 Century Park W Ste 403 Los Angeles CA 90067-6803

MULDER, DAVID S., cardiovascular surgeon; b. Eston, Sask., Can., July 28, 1938; s. Peter and Laura (Lovie) M.; m. Norma D. Johnston, Aug. 19, 1961; children—Scott D., Lizabeth J., John C. M.D., U. Sask., 1962; M.Sc., McGill U., 1964. Intern, resident in surgery Montreal Gen. Hosp., McGill U., 1963-67; resident in cardiac surgery U. Iowa, 1967-69; surgeon-in-chief Montreal Gen. Hosp., 1977—; prof. surgery McGill U., 1979—; chmn. dept. surgery, 1993—. Contbr. articles to med. jours. Fellow Royal Coll. Surgeons Can., ACS; mem. Soc. Univ. Surgeons, Am. Assn. Surgery of Trauma, Am. Assn. Thoracic Surgery, Soc. Thoracic Surgeons. Conservative. Home: 76 Sunnyside Ave, Westmount, PQ Canada H34 1C2 Office: Montreal Gen Hosp, Room D-6-136, Montreal, PQ Canada H3G 1A4

MULDER, DONALD GERRIT, surgeon, educator; b. Hospers, Iowa, 1924. M.D., Johns Hopkins U., 1952. Diplomate Am. Bd. Surgery, Am. Bd. Thoracic Surgery (chmn. 1983-85). Intern Johns Hopkins Hosp., Balt., 1952-53, resident, 1953-55; resident Calif. Med. Ctr., Los Angeles, 1955-57; instr. surgery U. Calif, Los Angeles, 1957-58, asst. prof., 1958-64, assoc. prof., 1964-69, prof., 1969—. Fellow ACS; mem. AMA. Office: Univ Calif Sch Medicine Los Angeles CA 90024

MULDER, DONALD WILLIAM, physician, educator; b. Rehobath, N.Mex., June 30, 1917; s. Jacob D. and Gertrude (Hofstra) M.; m. Gertrude Ellens, Feb. 22, 1943. B.A., Calvin Coll., 1940; M.D., Marquette U., 1943; M.S., U. Mich., 1946. Intern Butterworth Hosp., Grand Rapids, Mich., 1943-44; resident U. Hosp., Ann Arbor, Mich., 1944-46, Denver, 1947-49; asst. prof. medicine in neurology U. Colo., 1949-50; prof. neurology Mayo Found. Faculty, 1964—, Mayo Med. Sch., 1973—; cons. neurology Mayo Clinic, Rochester, Minn., 1950—; gov. Mayo Clinic, 1962-69, chmn. dept. neurology, 1966-71, pres. staff, 1971—, Andersen prof. neurology, 1977-83, prof. emeritus, 1983—; sci. advisor ALS. Contbr. articles on neuromuscular disease to sci. jours. Ret. capt. USNR. Recipient Disting. Alumni award Calvin Coll., 1992. Fellow A.C.P., Am. Acad. Neurology; mem. Am. Neurol. Assn. (hon.). Home: 331 75th St NW Rochester MN 55901-8868 Office: 200 1st St SW Rochester MN 55905-0001

MULDER, EDWIN GEORGE, minister, church official; b. Raymond, Minn., Mar. 25, 1929; s. Gerrit and Etta (Dresselhuis) M.; m. Luella Rozeboom, June 14, 1952; children: Timothy, Mary, Mark, Elizabeth. BA, Cen. Coll., Pella, Iowa, 1951, DD (hon.), 1979; BD, Western Theol. Sem., Holland, Mich., 1954. Ordained to ministry Ref. Ch. in Am., 1954. Pastor Reformed Ch. in Am., 1954-83, v.p. particular N.J. Synod, 1975-76, pres. particular N.J. Synod, 1976-77, v.p., then pres. Gen. Synod, 1978-80, gen. sec., 1983-94; chmn. bd. dirs. Relgion in Am. Life, 1995—; chair U.S. Ch. Leaders, 1989-94; mem. exec. com. World Alliance Reformed Chs., 1990—, Nat. Coun. Chs., 1991; mem. cen. com. World Coun. Chs., 1991-94. Trustee Cen. Coll., 1968-94. Office: Ref Ch in Am 475 Riverside Dr New York NY 10115-0122

MULDOON, BRIAN, lawyer; b. Phila., Oct. 7, 1947; s. Joseph Patrick and Isabella K. (O'Flynn) M.; m. Andrea K. Bloom, Apr. 1, 1984; 1 child, Lily Bloom. BA, Lafayette Coll., 1969; postgrad., U. Pa., 1969; JD, Temple U., 1978. Bar: Colo. 1978, U.S. Dist. Ct. Colo. 1978, U.S. Ct. Appeals (10th cir.) 1978. Law clk. to justice Colo. Supreme Ct., Denver, 1978-79; assoc. Holland & Hart, Denver, 1979-84, ptnr., 1984—; mem. Colo. Grievance Hearing Bd., 1983—. Contbg. author: Bloom, Lender Liability, Practice and Prevention, 1989. Mem. ABA, Assn. Trial Lawyers Am., Colo. Bar Assn., Colo. Trial Lawyers Assn., Denver Bar Assn. (chmn. subcom. on alternative dispute resolution 1985). Avocations: basketball, cycling, mountain climbing. Home: 337 Emerson St Denver CO 80218-3705 Office: Holland & Hart 555 17th St Ste 2900 Denver CO 80202-3929

MULDOON, FRANCIS CREIGHTON, Canadian federal judge; b. Winnipeg, Manitoba, Canada, Aug. 3, 1930; s. William John and Laura Grace (Meredith) M.; m. M. Lucille Shirtliff, Aug. 6, 1955; 2 children. BA, U. Manitoba, 1952, LLB, 1956. Cert. barrister, solicitor, notary pub. Lawyer Monnin, Grafton, Deniset & Co., Winnipeg, Man., 1956-70; chmn. Manitoba Law Reform Commn., Winnipeg, 1970-77; v.p. Law Reform Commn. Can., Ottawa, 1977-78, pres., 1978-83; judge Fed. Ct. Can., Ottawa, 1983—, Ct. Martial Appeal Ct., Ottawa, 1983—; Bencher Law Soc. Manitoba, Winnipeg, 1968-71. Contbr. articles to profl. jours. President Children Aid Soc. Winnipeg, 1969-70, Manitoba Medico-Legal Soc., Winnipeg, 1973-77. Lt. Can. Army, 1952-60. Disting. Svc. Manitoba Bar Assn., 1987; hon. mem. Bar U.S. Ct. Milit. Appeals, 1991. Mem. Med. Legal Soc. Ottawa-Carleton (co-founder), St. Paul's Coll. (hon.). Roman Catholic. Avocations: reading, bicycling, public speaking. Office: Fed Ct Can, Kent & Wellington Sts, Ottawa, ON Canada K1A 0H9

MULDOON, PAUL, creative writing educator, poet; b. Portadown, No. Ireland, 1951; came to U.S., 1987; BA in English Lang. and Lit., Queen's U., Belfast, No. Ireland, 1973. Prodr. arts programs radio BBC No. Ireland, 1973-78, sr. prodr. arts programs radio, 1978-85, TV prodr., 1985-86; Judith E. Wilson vis. fellow Cambridge U., 1986-87; creative writing fellow U. East Anglia, 1987; writer-in-residence 92d St. Y, N.Y.C., 198; Roberta Holloway lectr. U. Calif., Berkeley, 1989; lectr. Princeton (N.J.) U., 1990—, dir. creative writing program, 1993—; part-time tchr. writing divsn. Sch. of Arts, Columbia U., 1987-88; part-time tchr. creative writing program Princeton U., 1987-88; vis. prof. U. Mass., Amherst, 1989-90. Author: (poetry) Knowing My Place, 1971, New Weather, 1973, Spirit of Dawn, 1975, Mules, 1977, Immram, 1980, Why Brownlee Left, 1980, Out of Siberia, 1982, Quoof, 1983, Selected Poems 1968-83, 1986, Meeting the British, 1987, Madoc: A Mystery, 1990, Incantata, 1994, The Prince of the Quotidian, 1994, The Annals of Chile, 1994, others, (opera libretto) Shining Brow, 1993, (TV play) Monkeys, 1989, (translation from Irish) The Astrakhan Cloak, 1993, (children's book) The O-O's Party, 1981; editor: (poetry) The Scrake of Dawn, 1979, The Faber Book of Contemporary Irish Poetry, 1986, The Essential Byron, 1989; contbr. to anthologies. Recipient Eric Gregory award, 1972, Sir Geoffrey Faber Meml. award, 1980, 91, T.S. Eliot prize, 1994; John Simon Guggenheim Meml. fellow, 1990. Fellow Royal Soc. Lit.; mem. Aosdana. Office: Princeton Univ Creative Writing Program Princeton NJ 08544

MULDOON, ROBERT JOSEPH, JR., lawyer; b. Somerville, Mass., Nov. 16, 1936; s. Robert Joseph and Catherine Eileen (Hurley) M.; m. Barbara Joyce Mooney, Aug. 24, 1968; children: Andrew Robert, Catherine Lane, Timothy John. A.B., Boston Coll., 1960, MA, 1961, LL.B., 1965. Bar: Mass. 1965, U.S. Tax Ct 1966, U.S. Supreme Ct 1970. Law clk. Supreme Jud. Ct. Mass., 1965-66; assoc. Withington, Cross, Park & Groden, Boston, 1966-71; ptnr. Withington, Cross, Park & Groden, 1972-82, Sherin and Lodgen, LLP, Boston, 1982—; mem. Bd. Bar Examiners Mass.; chmn. Nat. Conf. Bar Examiners, 1985-86; prs. Mass. Continuing Legal Edn., Inc., 1992-94. Trustee Boston Coll. H.S., 1990—, chmn. bd. trustees, 1995—. Fellow Am. Coll. Trial Lawyers; mem. ABA, Am. Law Inst., Boston Bar Assn., Curtis Club. Office: Sherin and Lodgen LLP 100 Summer St Boston MA 02110-2104

MULFORD, DAVID CAMPBELL, finance company executive; b. Rockford, Ill., June 27, 1937; s. Robert Lewis Mulford and Theodora Henie Countryman; m. Jeannie Louise Simmons, Oct. 19, 1985; children: Robert Ian, Edward Maitland. BA in Econs. cum laude, Lawrence U., 1959; postgrad., U. Cape Town, South Africa, 1960; MA in Polit. Sci., Boston U., 1962; PhD, Oxford U., 1966; LLD (hon.), Lawrence U., 1984. White House fellow Dept. Treas., Washington, 1965-66, under asst. sec. internat. affairs, 1984-89; dir. White Weld & Co., N.Y.C. and London, 1966-74; sr. investment advisor Saudi Arabian Monetary Agy., Riyadh, 1974-84; asst. sec. internat. affairs Dept. of Treas., 1984-89; under sec. treasury internat. affairs U.S. Treas. Dept., Washington, 1989-92; vice chmn. CS First Boston, N.Y.C., 1992-93; chmn., CEO CS First Boston, London, 1993—. Author: Northern Rhodesia General Election, 1962, Zambia: The Politics of Independence, 1967. Trustee Lawrence U., 1986—. Decorated Legion d'Honneur, 1990; recipient Order of May Merit Pres. Argentina, 1993, Officers Cross of the Medal of Merit Pres. Poland, 1995; Rotary Internat. fellow Oxford U., U. Cape Town, 1961-62, Woodrow Wilson fellow Boston U., Oxford U., 1962, Ford Found. fellow St. Anthony's Coll., Oxford, 1963-65; named Disting. Alumni Boston U., 1992; Disting. scholar Ctr. Strategic and Internat. Studies, Washington, 1993—. Mem. Coun. Fgn. Rels., White House Fellows Assn., Metropolian Club (Washington). Republican. Home: 301 S St Asaph St Alexandria VA 22314-3745 Office: CS First Boston Ltd, 1 Cabot Square, London E14 4QJ, England

MULGREW, KATHERINE KIERNAN, actress; b. Dubuque, Iowa, Apr. 29, 1955; d. Thomas James and Joan Virginia (Kiernan) M.; m. Robert Harry Egan; children: Ian Thomas, Alexander James. Student, Northwestern U., U. Iowa; AA, NYU, 1976; studies with Stella Adler; trained at, Tyrone Guthrie Theater, Mpls. Formerly waitress and model. Played role of Emily in, Am. Shakespeare Festival's prodn. of Our Town; other stage appearances include Othello, Hartman Theatre, Stamford, Conn., Three Sisters, N.Y.C. Center, The Plow and the Stars, Irish Rebel Theatre, Orpheus Descending, Circle in the Square, Another Part of the Forest, Major Barbara, The Ballad of Soapy Smith and The Misanthrope, Seattle Repertory Theatre, Cat on a Hot Tin Roof, Syracuse Stage, Measure for Measure and Hedda Gabler, Mark Taper Forum, White Liars & Black Comedy, Roundabout Theatre Company; in films Lovespell, Remo Williams: The Adventure Begins, Lovespell, A Stranger is Watching, 1982, Throw Momma from the Train, 1987; former regular on daytime TV serial Ryan's Hope; appeared in TV mini-series The Word, Manions of America; in TV film Jennifer: A Woman's Story; star TV series Kate Loves a Mystery (formerly Mrs. Columbo), 1979, Heart Beat, Star Trek: Voyager, 1995—; TV spl. A Time for Miracles, 1980, Carly Mills; guest appearances on TV series Cheers, St. Elsewhere; actress TV shows Mother Seaton, Roses Are For the Rich, Roots: The Gift. Address: Special Artists Agency 335 n Maple Dr Ste 360 Beverly Hills CA 90210*

MULHERN, JOHN DAVID, former academic dean, educator; b. Milton, Mass., Dec. 11, 1928; s. John Henry and Mary Cecilia (Lehan) M.; m. Margaret Jane Gilligan, Jan. 24, 1959; children: Helen E., Mary T., John L., Thomas P., Margaret J. A.B., Boston Coll., 1950; M.Ed., State Coll., Bridgewater, Mass., 1955; Ph.D., U. Wis., 1960. Asst. prof. U. Wis., Madison, 1960-61, Boston Coll., Chestnut Hill, Mass., 1961-62, Okla. State U., Stillwater, 1962-63; dir. student teaching Marquette U., Milw., 1963-67; assoc. dean profl. studies SUNY Coll., Buffalo, 1967-76; dean Coll. Edn. Eastern Mich. U., Ypsilanti, 1976-80; dean Coll. Edn. U. S.C., Columbia, 1980-87, prof. ednl. adminstrn. and policies, 1987-93; prof. ednl. adminstrn. U. Tex.-Pan. Am., Edinburg, 1993-95; team leader Asian Devel. Bank Lower Secondary Edn. Project, Jakarta, Indonesia, 1995—; evaluation bd. mem. Nat. Council Accreditation Tchr. Edn., Washington, 1972-77. Author (with others) Educational Psychology workbook, 1967; contbr. articles to profl. jours. Served with USAF, 1950-54. Mem. Internat. Coun. Edn. Tchrs., Am. Assn. Coll. Tchrs. Edn., Am. Ednl. Rsch. Assn., Assn. Tchrs. Educators. Roman Catholic. Office: c/o EDC 1250 24th St NW Ste 300 Washington DC 20037-1124

MULHOLLAN, DANIEL PATRICK, library director; b. Louisville, July 12, 1944; s. Daniel Paul and Martha Nell (McClain) M.; m. Julianne Finlayson, June 3, 1967; children: Willa Joanna Mulhollan Neale, Erin Finlayson, Julianne Gertrude. BA with honors, Coll. of St. Thomas, St. Paul, 1966; PhD, Georgetown U., 1969. Sr. specialist Am. nat. govt., chief govt. divsn. Congrl. Rsch. Svc., Libr. of Congress, Washington, 1991, dir., 1994—; acting dep. libr. Libr. of Congress, Washington, 1992-94; cons. Greorgetown U., Washington, 1990-92; bd. visitors Sch. Libr. and Info. Scis., U. Pitts., 1995. Contbr. essay to book and articles to profl. jours. GE scholar, 1962; NDEA fellow, 1966. Mem. ALA, Am. Polit. Sci. Assn., Midwest Polit. Sci. Assn. Roman Catholic. Office: Library of Congress Congressional Rsch Svc 1st & Independence Ave SE Washington DC 20540

MULHOLLAN, PAIGE ELLIOTT, academic administrator emeritus; b. Ft. Smith, Ark., Dec. 10, 1934; s. Paige Elwood and Ruth Dickinson (Berry) M.; m. Mary Bess Flack, July 8, 1956; children: Paige E. Jr., Kelly V. BBA, U. Ark., 1956, MA in History, 1962; PhD in History, U. Tex., 1966. From asst. to assoc. prof. history U. Ark., Fayetteville, 1963-70; assoc. dean arts and scis. Kans. State U., Manhattan, 1970-73; dean arts and scis. U. Okla., Norman, 1973-78; provost, v.p. acad. affairs Ariz. State U., Tempe, 1978-81, exec. v.p., 1981-85; pres. Wright State U., Dayton, Ohio, 1985-94; ret., 1994; cons. examiner North Ctrl. Assn., Chgo., 1972-94; chair Interuniv. Coun. Ohio, 1993-94. Mem. Okla. Humanities Com., 1974-77, chmn., 1975-77; bd. dirs. Pub. Sta. WPTD-TV, Dayton Art Inst., Miami Valley Rsch. Found.; mem. adv. com. Air Force ROTC, 1989-93. 1st lt. U.S. Army, 1956-57. Mem. nat. Assn. State Univs. and Land Grant Colls. (commn. on arts and scis. 1973-78, chmn. 1974-76), Am. Assn. State Colls. and Univs. (bd. dirs. 1991-92), Coun. Colls. Arts and Scis. (bd. dirs. 1976-78, sec.-treas. 1977-78), Dayton Area C. of C., Ohio Coll. Assn. (pres. 1989). Avocations: jogging, sailing, birdwatching. Home: 24 Big Woods Dr Hilton Head Island SC 29926

MULHOLLAND, JOHN HENRY, physician, educator; b. Charlottesville, Va., May 24, 1932; s. Henry B. and Elizabeth (Brown) M.; m. Anne P.C., Sept. 1, 1956; children: Anne Randol, David Bearden, Jeffrey Bolton. BA, U. Va., 1955; MD, Johns Hopkins U., 1959. Diplomate Am. Bd. Internal Medicine; lic. physician, N.C., Md. Asst. prof. medicine Johns Hopkins U., Balt., 1966—; co-dir. nurse clin. assoc. program Union Meml. Hosp., Balt., 1972-90, gen. med. attending, 1968—, infections disease cons., 1968—; asst. prof. medicine U. Md., Balt., 1976-85, clin. assoc. prof. medicine, 1985—; assoc. med. dir. BCBSM, 1993-96, Doctors Health Sys., Md., 1995—. Author: Bugs and Drugs-Antibiotic Guidelines, 1970; contbr. numerous articles to profl. jours. Fellow ACP (chmn. arrangements com. 1975—, nat. chmn. group ins. programs subcom. 1986-87, membership policy com. 1986-87, postgrad. courses suybcom. 1990, gov. Md. region 1984-88); mem. AMA, Am. Clin. and Climatological Assn. (v.p. 1990), Md. Soc. Internal Medicine (mem. coun. 1976-78, 82-86), Md. Hosp. Edn. Inst. (mem. steering com. quality assurance/risk mgmt. project 1980—, mem. quality assurance/risk mgmt. tech. adv. com. 1985—), Balt. City Med. Soc. (nominating com. 1984—, chmn. liaison com. 1991—), Infectious Disease Soc. Am. Home: 1317 Walnut Hill Ln Baltimore MD 21204

MULHOLLAND, KENNETH LEO, JR., health care facility administrator; b. Chgo., July 16, 1943; s. Kenneth Leo Sr. and Virginia May (Groble) M.; m. Betty Lou Bledsoe, Feb. 18, 1978; children: Arthur G. Pope (dec.), Michelle Rae Pope Nobles. BS, Loyola U., 1969; M in Mgmt., Northwestern U., 1974. RN. Nurse VA Med. Ctr., Chgo., 1970-72, health care adminstr. tng., 1972-74; assoc. dir. tng. VA Med. Ctr., Lexington, Ky., 1976-77; assoc. dir. VA Med. Ctr., Muskogee, Okla., 1977-79; assoc. dir. VA Med. Ctr., Knoxville, Iowa, 1979-81, acting dir., 1981; assoc. dir. VA Med. Ctr., Richmond, Va., 1981-83; dir. VA Med. Ctr., Bronx, N.Y., 1983-85, Memphis, 1985—. Pres. Memphis Area Fed. Exec. Assn., 1988—; bd. dirs. Memphis chpt. ARC, 1985—, Health Sys. Agy., Memphis, 1985-87; mem. citizen's adv. bd. St. Joseph's Hosp., 1993—; mem. dean's adv. bd. Grad. Sch. Bus., Christian Brothers U., 1996—. Recipient Presdl. Rank award for meritorious executive, 1989. Mem. Memphis Area Fed. Exec. Assn. Lodge: Rotary. Home: 2024 Thorncroft Dr Germantown TN 38138-4017 Office: VA Med Ctr 1030 Jefferson Ave Memphis TN 38104-2127

MULHOLLAND, ROBERT EDGE, broadcasting company executive; b. Hartford, Conn., Sept. 27, 1933; s. Hugh Andrew and Gertrude (Edge) M.; 1 child, Todd Andrew. B.S. in Journalism, Northwestern U., 1955, M.S., 1956. News writer, producer Sta. WGN, Chgo., 1958-61; news writer NBC, Chgo., 1961-64; producer Huntley-Brinkley News, NBC, Washington, 1964-67; dir. news Sta. KNBC, Los Angeles, 1967-71; exec. producer NBC Nightly News, N.Y.C., 1971-74; exec. v.p. NBC News, N.Y.C., 1974-77; pres. NBC TV Network, 1977-81; pres., chief operating officer NBC, 1981-84, broadcast cons., 1984-86, dir. TV info. office, 1986-88; prof. journalism Northwestern U., Evanston, Ill., 1988-93. Served with AUS, 1956-58. Mem. TV Acad. Arts and Scis. Presbyterian.

MULHOLLAND, S. GRANT, urologist; b. Springfield, Ohio, Sept. 1, 1936; s. Stanford Wallace and Florence Kathryn (Grant) M.; m. Ruth Fritz, Aug. 21, 1961; children: David, Michael, Mark, John. BS, Dickinson Coll., Carlisle, Pa., 1958; MD, Temple U., 1962; MS, U. Va., 1966. Intern Reading (Pa.) Hosp., 1962-63; resident in surgery Tampa (Fla.) Gen. Hosp., 1963-64; resident in urology U. Va., Charlottesville, 1964-68; urologist U.S. Naval Hosp., St. Albans, N.Y., 1968-70; epidemiologist Grad. Hosp. of U. Pa., Phila., 1971-74, asst. urologist, 1970-77; chief urologist Phila. Gen. Hosp., 1972-77; asst. surgeon Children's Hosp. Phila., 1974-77; urologist Hosp. U. Pa., Phila., 1974-77; chmn. dept. urology Thomas Jefferson U. Hosp., Phila., 1977—; cons. VA Ctr., Phila., 1974-77; cons. urologist Lankenau Hosp., Bryn Mawr Hosp., VA Hosp., Wilmington, Del., 1977—. Author: Urinary Tract Infection, 1990, Bladder Infections, 1991, (with others) Prostate Cancer, 1992. Lt. comdr. USN, 1968-70. Grantee NIH, Jefferson U., 1989. Fellow ACS; mem. Am. Urol. Assn. (pres. 1988-89), Phila. Urol. Assn. (pres. 1988-89), Internat. Soc. Urology, AMA, Phila. Country Club (Gladwyne, Pa.). Republican. Avocations: golf, fishing, skiing. Home: 1050 Sentry Ln Gladwyne PA 19035-1009 Office: Jefferson Med Coll 1025 Walnut St # 1112 Philadelphia PA 19107-5001

MULHOLLAND, TERENCE JOHN (TERRY MULHOLLAND), professional baseball player; b. Uniontown, Pa., Mar. 9, 1963. Student, Marietta Coll. Pitcher San Francisco Giants, 1984-89, Phila. Phillies, 1989-94, N.Y. Yankees, 1994—; mem. Nat. League All-Star Team, 1993. Pitched no-hit victory, Aug. 15, 1990.

MULICH, STEVE FRANCIS, safety engineer; b. Kansas City, Mo., Apr. 23, 1934; s. Stephen Francis and Mary Margret (Mish) M.; m. m. Apr. 5, 1974 (div.); children: Michael Francis, Mischelle Marie, Merko Mathew, Cherie Regina, Michael Klaus, Gary John, Josette Marie. BS in Gen. Sci., U. Notre Dame, 1956. Phys. chemist high altitude combustion Army Rocket and Guided Missile Agy., Huntsville, Ala., 1957-59; ballistics facility mgr. Aerojet Gen. Corp., Sacramento, 1960-65; chief engr. minute man penetration aids MB Assoc., Bollinger Canyon, Calif., 1966-72; lab mgr. hazardous materials and ballistics Martin Marietta, Waterton, Colo., 1966-75; plant mgr. smog sampler collectors mfg. Gen. Tex. Corp., Santa Clara, Calif., 1976-77; chief engr. auto airbag plant mgr. Talley Industries, Mesa, Ariz., 1978-84; prin. engr., engring. unit mgr. high energy test labs. FMC Corp., Mpls., 1984-95; v.p. ops. NEI Corp., Rock Island, Ill., 1995—. Author: Solid Rocket Technology, 1967; inventor stun gun, combustion augemented plasma gun, semiconductor initiator. With U.S. Army, 1957-59. Recipient Acad. Achievement award Bausch & Lomb, Kenosha, Wis., 1952. Mem. IEEE, AIAA (assoc.), Am. Def. Preparedness Assn., Navy League. Avocations: skiing, sailing, climbing, camping, hiking. Home: 1325 104th Pl NE Minneapolis MN 55434-3620 Office: NEI Corp Rock Island IL 61204

MULKEY, CHARLES ERIC, environmental engineer; b. Sweetwater, Tenn., Jan. 27, 1955; s. Charles Franklin and Margaret Elizabeth (Autry) M. BA in Natural Scis., Johns Hopkins U., 1976; MS in Environ. Engring., U. Del., 1978. Registered profl. engr., Tenn.; cert. hazardous materials mgr.; diplomate Am. Acad. Environ. Engrs. Environ. engr. II TVA Water Quality Dept., Chattanooga, 1978-79, environ. engr. III, 1979-81, environ. engr. IV, 1981-87; environ. engr. IV TVA Watts Bar Nuclear Plant, Spring City, Tenn., 1987-88; sr. environ. engr. Watts Bar Nuclear Plant TVA Water Quality Dept., Spring City, Tenn., 1988-90; sr. environ. engr. PAI Corp., Oak Ridge, Tenn., 1990, Oak Ridge Nat. Lab., 1990—. Author tech. reports in field; contbr. articles to profl. jours. Publicity chmn. Chattanooga Engrs. Week, 1983-87. Maj. USAFR, 1994—. Recipient Davis fellowship U. Del., Newark, 1976-77, state scholarship, State of Md., Annapolis, 1972-76. Fellow ASCE; mem. NSPE (Nat. Publicity award 1984), Tenn. Soc. Profl. Engrs. (state dir. 1990-91, pres. Chattanooga chpt. 1989-90, v.p. 1988-89, sec. 1987-88, treas. 1986-87, young engrs. chmn. 1984-86), Water Environ. Fedn., Am. Acad. Hazardous Materials Mgrs., Res. Officers Assn. (life), Chattanooga Engrs. Club, U.S. Triathlon Fedn., U.S. Masters Swimming. Republican. Presbyterian. Avocations: triathlons, masters swimming. Office: Oak Ridge Nat Lab MS 6049 Bldg 2001 Oak Ridge TN 37831-6049

MULKEY, JACK CLARENDON, library director; b. Shreveport, La., Oct. 31, 1939; s. Jack Youmans and Hilda Lillian (Beatty) M.; m. Mary Lynn Shepherd, Jan. 30, 1971; 1 child, Mary Clarendon. B.A., Centenary Coll., 1961; postgrad. (Rotary scholar), U. Dijon, France, 1961-62, Duke U. Law Sch., 1962-63; M.S., La. State U., 1969. Jr. exec. Lykes Bros. S.S. Co., 1964-66; asst. dir. admissions Centenary Coll. of La., 1966-67; head reference services and acquisitions Shreveport Pub. Library, 1968-71; dir. Green Gold Library System of N.W. La., 1971-73; mgmt. cons. Miss. Library Commn., 1973-74, asst. dir., 1974-76, dir., 1976-78; dir. Jackson Met. Library System, 1978-85; assoc. dir. Ark. State Library, 1986—; adj. prof. U. So. Miss. Grad. Sch. Library Sci., 1979—; treas., bd. dirs. Southeastern Library Network (SOLINET), 1985-86; cons. in field; mem. White House Conf. Taskforce on Libraries and Info. Services, 1980—. Chmn. Miss. Govs. Conf. on Libraries, 1979; chmn. Miss. delegation White House Conf. on Libraries, 1979; hon. del. White House Conf. on Librs., 1991. Served with USAF, 1963-64. Mem. ALA (chmn. state libr. agy. sect. 1995-97), Southeastern Libr. Assn., Miss. Libr. Assn. (pres. 1981-82), Ark. Libr. Assn. (exec. bd. dirs. 1994-96), Chief Officers of State Libr. Agys., Phi Alpha Delta, Beta Phi Mu, Omicron Delta Kappa, Phi Kappa Phi. Episcopalian. Home: 1805 Martha Dr Little Rock AR 72212-3840 Office: 1 Capitol Mall Little Rock AR 72201

MULKEY, SHARON RENEE, gerontology nurse; b. Miles City, Mont., Apr. 14, 1954; d. Otto and Elvera Marie (Haglof) Neuhardt; m. Monty W. Mulkey, Oct. 9, 1976; children: Levi, Candice, Shane. BS in Nursing, Mont. State U., 1976. RN, Calif. Staff nurse, charge nurse VA Hosp., Miles City, Mont., 1976-77; staff nurse obstetrics labor and delivery Munster (Ind.) Cmty. Hosp., 1982-83; nurse mgr. Thousand Oaks Health Care, 1986-88; unit mgr. rehab. Semi Valley (Calif.) Adventist Hosp., 1988-89, DON TCU, 1989-91; DON Pleasant Valley Hosp. Extended Care Vacility and Neuro Ctr., 1991-93; dir. nurses Victoria Care Ctr., Ventura, Calif., 1993—; clin. supr. Procare Home Health, Oxnard, Calif., 1996—. Mem. ANA, Nat. Gerontol. Nursing Assn., Internat. Platform Assn., Alpha Tau Delta (pres. 1973-75), Phi Kappa Phi. Home: 3461 Pembridge St Thousand Oaks CA 91360-4565

MULL, JOCELYN BETHE, school administrator; b. Nassau, N.Y., Oct. 21, 1968; divorced; 1 child, Eron Michael. BA, SUNY, Buffalo, 1981, MA, 1989. Dir. edn. Ctr. for Positive Thought, Mus. African Am. Arts and Antiquities, Buffalo, 1978-83; tchr. English, Buffalo Bd. Edn., 1980—, cons. tchr. inclusion project, 1991-93, fed. magnet curriculum specialist Futures Acad., 1993—; case mgr. spl. edn., gifted and comprehensive programs Crenshaw H.S., L.A.; case mgr. spl. edn. and GATE coord. Crenshaw H.S. Author: (poetry) Goti, Paja, Mguu-The Knee, A Thigh and The Leg, 1980, Strength in the Water, 1995. Rec. coord., publicist Lighthouse Interdenominational Choir, 1988-94; project coord. Performing Artists Collective, Western N.Y. United Against Drugs, Buffalo, 1993—; mem. Mayor's Arts and Adv. Coun. Against Drugs and Violence, 1995. Recipient Educator of Excellence award PUSH Excel, Operation PUSH, 1981, N.Y. State English Coun., 1994, Creative Arts award, 1980, citation Martin Luther King Jr. Arts and Scis. award, 1986—, Outstanding Commemorative Youth award for performing arts and cmty. svc., 1980. Mem. ASCD, NEA (spl. edn. com.), Buffalo Tchrs. Fedn. (multicultural com.), AAUW, Phi Delta Kappa. Avocations: composing, singing, writing poetry. Office: Crenshaw High School 5010 11th Ave Los Angeles CA 90043

MULL, MARTIN, comedian, singer; b. Chgo., 1943; m. Sandra Baker. Grad., R.I. Sch. Design. Nightclub singer and comedian: recorded albums including Sex and Violins; appeared in TV series Soundstage, Domestic Life, Mary Hartman, Mary Hartman, 1976-77, His & Hers, 1990, Roseanne, (TV movies) The Day My Parents Ran Away, 1993, How the West Was Fun, 1994; star TV series Fernwood Tonight, 1977; guest on TV talk shows; appeared in movies FM, 1977, My Bodyguard, 1980, Serial, 1980, Take This Job and Shove It, 1981, Mr. Mom, Private School, 1983, Lots of Luck, Clue, 1987, O.C. amd Stiggs, 1987, Home is Where The Heart Is, 1987, Rented Lips, 1988, Cutting Class, 1989, Ski Patrol, 1990, Far Out Man, 1990, Think Big, 1990, Ted & Venus, 1991, Mrs. Doubtfire, 1994; writer cable TV documentary The History of White People in America, also co-author book, 1986; co-writer, host video The History of White People in America: Volume II, 1987; other TV work includes writer, prod., star Candid Camera Christmas Special, 1987, Portrait of a White Marriage. Office: care Agy Performing Arts 9000 W Sunset Blvd Ste 1200 West Hollywood CA 90069-5812

MULLAHEY, RAMONA KAM YUEN, land use planner, educator; b. Hilo, Hawaii, Nov. 1, 1945. BA, U. Hawaii, 1967, M Urban and Regional Planning, 1976. Sole proprietor Honolulu, 1976-87; prin. Mullahey & Mullahey, Honolulu, 1987—; nat. speaker on K-12 design edn. to variety internat., nat., regional orgns.; lectr. urban and regional planning U. Hawaii. Author: (book and video) Maintaining A Sense of Place Community Workbook, 1987, Community as a Learning Resource, 1994; editor newsletter Am. Planning Assn. Resources, 1990—. Mem. Rental Housing Trust Fund Commn., Hawaii, 1993—. Recipient Pub. Edn. award Am. Planning Assn., Hawaii chpt., 1993; Nat. Endowment for Arts grantee, Washington, 1986, 92, 94, local grantee; named 1 of 12 Nat. Women Leaders in K-12 Design Edn., The Urban Network. Mem. ASCD, Nat. Trust Historic Preservation (Nat. Preservation Honor award 1988), Am. Planning Assn. (pres. Hawaii chpt. 1992-93, immediate past pres. 1993—, Disting. Leadership award Hawaii Chpt. 1994), Orgn. Am. Leaders (pres. 1990-91), C. of C. of Hawaii (edn. coun.). Avocation: photography. Home and Office: PO Box 1348 Honolulu HI 96807-1348

MULLALEY, ROBERT CHARLES, manufacturing company executive; b. Marion, Iowa, Dec. 31, 1926; s. Harold C. and Blanche A. (McGuire) M.; m. Josephine E. Fiala, Apr. 23, 1949; children: Maureen, Kathleen, Mary, Daniel, Michael, Susan. BA, U. Iowa, 1949, JD, 1951. Bar: Iowa 1951, Tex. 1976. With Collins Radio Co., Richardson, Tex., 1951-75; v.p. adminstrn. Collins Radio Co., 1970-71, sr. v.p., 1971-75; also adv. dir.; v.p. Avantek, Inc., Santa Clara, Calif., 1976-82; bd. dirs. Celeritek, Inc. Author: History of the Mullaleys: A Twelve Hundred Year Journey from County Galway to Iowa, 1993. With USNR, 1945-46. Mem. Tex. Bar Assn., Phi Kappa Theta. Home: 710 Rose Ln Los Altos CA 94024-4146

MULLAN, DONALD WILLIAM, bishop; b. Galt, Ont., Apr. 26, 1937; s. William James and Lillian Maude (Sachs) M.; m. Cathy Templeman. P-residing bishop Christ Cath. Ch. Internat.; pastor Cathedral of St. Luke, Niagara Falls, Ont. Editor (mag.) The St. Luke Mag. Trustee Bd. Edn., Preston, Ont., 1962-68, Waterloo County, Ont., 1969-70, Wellington County, Ont., 1971-72. Mem. Order of Noble Companions of the Swan (prelate), Moose.

MULLAN, FITZHUGH, public health physician; b. Tampa, Fla., July 22, 1942; s. Hugh and Mariquita (Macmanus) M.; m. Judith Wentworth, June 9, 1968; children: Meghan Elizabeth, Jason Michael, Caitlin Patricia. BA, Harvard U., 1964; MD, U. Chgo., 1968; DSc, U. Osteo. Medicine, 1993; LHD, Coll. Osteo. Medicine Pacific, 1993. Intern Jacobi Hosp., Bronx, 1968-70; resident Lincoln Hosp., Bronx, 1970-72; physician Nat. Health Svc. Corp., Santa Fe, N.Mex., 1972-75; dir. Nat. Health Svc. Corps, Rockville, Md., 1977-81; scholar-in-residence Inst. Medicine, Washington, 1981-82; sr. med. officer NIH, Bethesda, Md., 1982-84; sec. for health and environment State of N.Mex., Santa Fe, 1984-85; assoc. prof. Johns Hopkins Sch. Hygiene and Pub. Health, Balt., 1986-88; dir. pub. health history project Office of Surgeon Gen., Rockville, 1988-90; dir. bur. health professions USPHS, Rockville, 1990-96; contbr. editor Health Affairs, Bethesda, 1996—. Author: White Coat, Clenched Fist: The Political Education of an American Physician, 1976, Vital Signs: A Young Doctor's Struggle With Cancer, 1983, Plagues and Politics: The Story of the United States Public Health Service, 1989; contbr. articles to profl. jours. Fellow Am. Acad. Pediatrics; mem. AMA, Am. Pub. Health Assn., Am. Assn. for History of Medicine, Inst. of Medicine of the Nat. Acad. of Sci. Office: Health Affairs Ste 600 7500 Old Georgetown Rd Bethesda MD 20814

MULLAN, JOHN FRANCIS (SEAN MULLAN), neurosurgeon, educator; b. County Derry, Northern Ireland, May 17, 1925; came to U.S., 1955; naturalized, 1962; s. John and Mary Catharine Ann (Gilmartin) M.; m. Vivian C. Dunn, June 3, 1959; children: Joan Claire, John Charles, Brian Francis. MB, BCh, BAO, Queen's U., Belfast, Northern Ireland, 1947, DSc (hon.), 1976; postgrad., McGill U., 1953-55. Diplomate Am. Bd. Neurol. Surgery. Trainee gen. surgery Royal Victoria Hosp., Belfast, 1947-50, trainee in neurosurgery, 1951-53; trainee gen. surgery Guy's Hosp. and Middlesex Hosp., London, 1950-51, Montreal Neurosurg. Inst., Que., Can., 1955; asst. prof. neurol. surgery U. Chgo., 1955-61, assoc. prof., 1961-63, prof., 1963—, John Harper Seeley prof., chmn. dept., 1967—, dir. Brain Rsch. Inst., 1970-84. Author: Neurosurgery for Students, 1961; contbr. over 150 articles to profl. jours.; mem. editorial bd. Jour. Neurosurgery, 1974-84, Archives of Neurology, 1976-87. Recipient Olivecrona medal Karolinska Inst., 1976, Wilder Penfield medal Can. Neurosurg. Soc., 1979, Jamieson medal Australian and New Zealand Neurosurg. Soc., 1980. Fellow ACS, Royal Coll. Surgeons; mem. Soc. Neurol. Surgeons (past pres.), Acad. Neurol. Surgery, Am. Assn. Neurol. Surgeons, Am. Neurol. Assn., Cen. Neurosurg. Soc., Chgo. Neurol. Soc., World Fedn. of Neurosurg. Socs. (sec. 1989-93, hon. pres. 1993—). Roman Catholic. Conductor of research on vascular diseases of the brain, pain, head injury. Avocations: walnut tree farming, gardening. Office: U Chgo Med Ctr 5841 S Maryland Ave Chicago IL 60637-1463

MULLANAX, MILTON GREG, lawyer; b. Galveston, Tex., Mar. 16, 1962; s. Milton Gayle and Sharon Kay (Sanders) M.; m. Susan Lynn Griebe, Apr. 19, 1986; 1 child, Adrienne Irene. BA in History, U. Tex., Arlington, 1987; JD, U. Pacific, 1991. Bar: Calif., 1991, Nev., 1992, Tex., 1993, Colo., 1993, Minn., 1994, D.C., 1993; U.S. Dist. Ct. (ea. dist.) Calif. 1991, U.S. Dist. Ct. Nev., 1993. Congrl. intern U.S. Rep. Richard K. Armey, Arlington, Tex., 1985; senate aide U.S. Sen. Phil Gramm, Dallas, 1985-86; legis. aide State Rep. Kent Grusendorf, Austin, Tex., 1987; law clk. Criminal Divsn. U.S. Atty., Sacramento, 1989-90; legal researcher Nev. Atty. Gen., Carson City, 1991-92, dep. atty. gen., 1992-94; pvt. practice Coppell, Tex., 1995—. Vol. Reagan/Bush 1984, Dallas/Ft. Worth, 1984, Rep. Nat. Conv., Dallas, 1984, Armey for Congress, Arlington, 1984, Vol. Lawyers of Washoe County, Reno, Nev., 1993-94. Mem. ABA, ATLA, Tarrant County Bar Assn. Avocations: sports, politics, reading, shortwave radio. Office: 600 S Denton Tap Rd Coppell TX 75019-4533

MULLANE, DENIS FRANCIS, insurance executive; b. Astoria, N.Y., Aug. 28, 1930; s. Patrick F. and Margaret (O'Neill) M.; m. Kathryn Mullman, June 28, 1952; children: Gerard, Kevin, Denise. BS in Mil. Engring, U.S. Mil. Acad., 1952; LHD (hon.), U. Conn., 1988, St. Joseph's Coll., 1990; LLD (hon.), U. Hartford, 1993, Trinity Coll., Hartford, Conn., 1995; MS in Fin. Svcs., The Am. Coll., Bryn Mawr, Pa., 1995. CLU. With Conn. Mut. Life Ins. Co., Hartford, 1956—, v.p., 1969-72, sr. v.p., 1972-74, exec. v.p., 1974-76, pres., 1977—, chief exec. officer, 1983-85, chmn., chief exec. officer, 1985-90; chief exec. officer, pres. Conn. Mut. Life Ins. Co., 1990-93; prin. Mulane Enterprises, Hartford, Conn., 1994—; with Mullane Enterprises, West Hartford, Conn., 1994—; bd. dirs. Conn. natural Gas Co.; chmn. The Am. Coll., Bryn Maur, Pa., 1993-96. Dir. U.S. Chamber, 1991-95. 1st lt. C.E., U.S. Army, 1952-56. Recipient John Newton Russell award, 1987, Knight of St. Gregory award. Mem. Am. Soc. Corp. Execs., Nat. Assn. Life Underwriters, Assn. Grads. U.S. Mil. Acad. (pres. 1989-93). Republican. Roman Catholic. Office: Mullane Enterprises 29 S Main St West Hartford CT 06107-2420

MULLANE, DONALD A., banker; b. Los Angeles, May 24, 1938; s. William Paul and Petra Hilda (DeVilla Fuerte) M.; m. Dorothy Ann Sarosy, July 2, 1960; children—Deborah, Donna, David, Donald, Douglas. Student, U. So. Calif., Los Angeles; participant Stanford exec. program, Stanford U.; cert., Am. Inst. Banking. Asst. cashier Bank of Am., So. Calif., 1958-69, asst. v.p., 1969-72, v.p., 1972-81, sr. v.p., 1981-85; exec. v.p. Bank of Am., Los Angeles and San Francisco, 1985—; chmn. bd. Bank of Am. State Bank; chmn. social policy com. Bank Am. Foun., Skid Row Housing Corp., 1991. Bd. dirs. Las Familas, L.A., 1985—, AP Giannini Found., 1986, Maryvale Inc., L.A. Sports Coun., St. Vincents Hosp.; bd. dirs. Calif. Cmty. Reinvestment Corp., chmn., 1990—; chmn. Jr. Achievement So. Calif., L.A., 1985-90; co-chmn. Cmty. Reinvestment Inst.; chmn. bd. Pacific Coast Sch. Banking, U. Wash., 1989—; bd. councilors Sch. of Pub. Adminstrn., U. So. Calif.; chmn. L.A. Cmty. Reinvestment Com. Recipient Disting. Achievement award Am. Heart Assn., L.A., 1985, Social Responsibility award Mex. Am. Legal Def. and Edn. Fund, 1992, Humanitarian award The H.E.L.P. Group,1 994, Corp. Leadership award Vis. Nurses Assn., 1994; named Outstanding Mgr., Bank of Am., 1979, 80, Outstanding Corp. Vol. Greater L.A. United Way, 1994, Minority Advocate of Yr. San Francisco Black C. of C., 1995; honoree Nat. Ctr. for Am. Indians, 1991, corp. honoree Latino Issues Forum, 1993, Asian Pacific Am. Legal Ctr., 1994. Mem. Retail Bank Am. (chmn. retail banking conf. 1986), L.A. C. of C., Calif. Bankers Assn. (bd. dirs. 1986—, pres. 1990-91), Hacienda Golf Club (La Habra, Calif.), City Club on Bunker Hill, Bankers Club San Francisco. Office: Bank of America 555 S Flower St Los Angeles CA 90071-2300

MULLANE, JOHN FRANCIS, pharmaceutical company executive; b. N.Y.C., Mar. 10, 1937; s. John Gerard and Rita Ann (Hoben) M.; m. Ruth Ann Cecka, Nov. 17, 1962; children—Rosemarie, Michael, Kathleen, Therese, Thomas. M.D., SUNY, 1963, Ph.D., 1968; J.D., Fordham U., 1977. Bar: N.Y. 1978, D.C. 1979. Assoc. med. dir. Ayerst Labs. div. Am. Home Products Corp., N.Y.C., 1973-75, dir. clin. research, 1975-76, v.p. clin., 1977, v.p. sci., 1978-82, sr. v.p., 1982, exec. v.p., 1983-88; pres. Mullane Health Care Cons., N.Y.C., 1989—; dir. drug devel. DuPont Med. Products, Wilmington, Del., 1990; sr. v.p. DuPont-Merck, Wilmington, 1991-94; exec. v.p. Amylin Pharms., 1994—. Contbr. articles to profl. jours. Served to lt. col. U.S. Army, 1970-73. Recipient Upjohn Achievement award, 1970; N.Y. Heart Assn. Crawford-Maynard fellow, 1966-68. Fellow Am. Coll. Clin. Pharmacology; mem. ABA, Am. Soc. Clin. Pharmacology and Therapeutics, Am. Assn. Study of Liver Diseases, Pelham Country Club, Lomas Sante Fe Country Club, Tara Golf and Country Club. Roman Catholic. Avocation: golf. Home: 1137 Via Mil Cumbres Solana Beach CA 92075 Office: Amylin Pharms 9373 Towne Centre Dr San Diego CA 92121-3027

MULLANEY, JOANN BARNES, nursing educator; b. Newport, R.I., Dec. 7, 1943; d. Elliott Calvert and Betty (Dawson) Barnes; m. Charles Patrick Mullaney, June 3, 1967 (div. 1973); 1 child, Mark Andrew. Diploma in Nursing, Newport Hosp. Sch. Nursing, 1965; BSN, Salve Regina Coll., Newport, 1976; BSN/MS in Psychiat. Mental Health Nursing, Boston Coll., 1977; PhD in Edn., U. Conn., 1983. RN, R.I.; clin. specialist, ANCC. Instr. Salve Regina U., Newport, 1979-83, asst. prof., 1983-85, sr. level coord., 1983-94, assoc. prof. nursing, 1985-95, prof., 1995—; psychiat. clin. specialist in pvt. practice The Center, Middletown, R.I., 1990—, utilization reviewer, Providence, 1990-92, ednl. cons., 1990—. Contbr. to book: Psychiatric Care Planning, 1989 (ASN Book of Yr. 1988). Mem. Atty.-Gen.'s Task Force on Domestic Violence, Providence, 1994; mem. Health Care Reform Coalition, Providence, 1993—, Nat./R.I. Action Not Gridlock Coun., 1993—; mem. R.I. House and Senate Women's Health Issues Commn., 1995. Recipient Air Force Nurse Educator award, 1988; grantee HEW, 1976, NIMH, 1977, 91-94, Lilly Co., 1994; M.A.C.N. scholar, 1995. Mem. ANA, AAUW, AAUP, NEON, ENRS, SERPA, RISNA (pres.-elect 1992-93, pres. 1993-95, pres. ex-officio 1995—), Mass. Assn. Coll. Nursing Rsch., Sigma Theta Tau (Delta Upsilon chpt.), Phi Lambda Theta. Home: 242 Gibbs Ave Newport RI 02840-2829

MULLANEY, JOSEPH E., lawyer; b. Fall River, Mass., Mar. 22, 1933; s. Joseph E. and Beatrice (Hancock) M.; m. Rosemary Woodman, June 22, 1957; children—Joseph E. III, Brian, Sean, Evan. A.B. magna cum laude, Coll. Holy Cross, Worcester, Mass., 1955; LL.B. magna cum laude, Harvard U., 1958. Bar: Ohio bar, D.C. bar, Mass. bar. Ptnr. Jones, Day, Cockley & Reavis, Cleve., 1960-70; gen. counsel Office Spl. Rep. Trade Negotiations, Exec. Office Pres., Washington, 1970-71, Cost of Living Council, 1971-72; assoc. gen. counsel Gillette Co., Boston, 1972-77, sr. v.p., gen. counsel, 1977-90, vice chmn. bd., 1990—; dir. Park St. Corp., Greater Boston Legal Services Corp.; mem., dir. Boston Mcpl. Research Bur. Bd. dirs. New Eng. Legal Found. Office: Gillette Co Prudential Towers Bldg Boston MA 02199

MULLARE, T(HOMAS) KENWOOD, JR., lawyer; b. Milton, Mass., Jan. 19, 1939; s. Thomas Kenwood and Catherine Marie (Leonard) M.; m. Joan Marie O'Donnell, May 27, 1967; children: Jennifer M., Tracy K., Jill M., Joyce M. AB, Holy Cross Coll., 1961; LLB, Boston Coll., 1964. Bar: Mass. 1964. Atty. New Eng. Electric System, 1964-70; v.p., gen. counsel, sec. AVX Corp., N.Y.C., 1970-73; v.p., gen. counsel, clk. Tyco Labs., Inc., Exeter, N.H., 1973-78; v.p., gen. counsel, sec. SCA Svcs., Inc., Boston, 1978-84; spl. counsel Houghton, Mifflin Co., Boston, 1984-85, v.p., dir. bus. software divsn., 1985-90; pres. North River Capital Co., Inc., Norwell, Mass., 1990—; also bd. dirs. Broadcast Info. Tech., Amherst, N.H.; bd. dirs. North River Capital Co., Inc., Norwell. Mem. regional adv. bd. Commonwalth of Mass. Dept. Mental Retardation; bd. dirs. Barque Hill Assn., Norwell, 1980-84, pres., 1981-83; pres. Ch. Hillers, Norwell, 1983-84; bd. dirs., chmn. South Shore Assn. for Retarded Citizens, Weymouth, Mass., 1993—. Mem. ABA, Mass. Bar Assn., Boston Bar Assn. Home: 31 Barque Hill Dr Norwell MA 02061-2815 Office: 175 Derby St PO Box 409 Hingham MA 02043

MULLARKEY, MARY J., state supreme court justice; b. New London, Wis., Sept. 28, 1943; d. John Clifford and Isabelle A. (Steffes) M.; m. Thomas E. Korson, July 24, 1971; 1 child, Andrew Steffes Korson. BA, St. Norbert Coll., 1965; LLB, Harvard U., 1968; LLD (hon.), St. Norbert Coll., 1989. Bar: Wis. 1968, Colo. 1974. Atty.-advisor U.S. Dept. Interior, Washington, 1968-73; asst. regional atty. EEOC, Denver, 1973-75; 1st atty. gen. Colo. Dept. Law, Denver, 1975-79, solicitor gen., 1979-82; legal advisor to Gov. Lamm State of Colo., Denver, 1982-85; ptnr. Mullarkey & Seymour, Denver, 1985-87; justice Colo. Supreme Ct., Denver, 1987—. Recipient Alumni award St. Norbert Coll., De Pere, Wis., 1980, Alma Mater award, 1993. Fellow ABA Found., Colo. Bar Found.; mem. ABA, Colo. Bar Assn., Colo. Women's Bar Assn. (recognition award 1986), Denver Bar Assn., Thompson G. Marsh Inn of Ct. (pres. 1993-94). Office: Supreme Ct Colo 2 E 14th Ave Denver CO 80203-2115

MULLE, GEORGE ERNEST, petroleum geologist; b. Collingswood, N.J., Dec. 21, 1919; s. George Melvin and Eleanor (Matilda) (Clevenger) M.; m. Molly Elizabeth Jones, Nov. 17, 1950; children: Alan Russell, David George, William Ernest. Student Rutgers U., 1942-44; A.B. in Earth Scis., U. Pa., 1948. Cert. petroleum geologist, Tex. Geologist, Tide Water Oil Co., Houston and Corpus Christi, 1948-51; dist. geologist La Gloria Oil & Gas Co., Corpus Christi, Tex., 1952-60; ptnr. Santa Rosa Gas Co., 1960-62; pvt. practice geology, Corpus Christi, 1962-73, 75-80, 83—; v.p. Corpus Christi Mgmt. Co., 1973-75; exploration mgr. So. Tex., Mormac Energy Corp., 1980-82. Pres. Palm Harbor Property Owners Assn., Rockport, Tex., 1984, 90, 91, 92, Bahia Log Libr., Corpus Christi, 1980, Santa Fe Log Libr., Corpus Christi, 1981; sec.-treas. The Villas of Harbor Oaks Owners Assn., 1985-88, v.p., 1992-94; del. People-to-People Petroleum Tech., People's Republic China, 1983. Served with USN, 1944-46. Mem. Corpus Christi Geol. Soc. (author book 1967), Soc. Ind. Profl. Earth Scientists (chmn. Corpus Christi chpt. 1995). Republican. Baptist. Avocation: photography. Home: 121 Ocean Dr Rockport TX 78382-9405

MULLEN, DANIEL ROBERT, finance executive; b. Swedesboro, N.J., Apr. 17, 1941; s. Harold Legrand and Gladys (DeVault) M.; m. Elizabeth A. Willers, Dec. 17, 1977; children: William H., Jonathan O. BS in Fin., Ariz. State U., 1966, postgrad., 1966-67. Appraiser Ariz. Dept. Revenue, 1966-68; financial analyst Amerco, Inc., Phoenix, 1968-70; treas., CFO Amerco, Inc., 1970-82; pres., dir. Continental Leasing Co., 1980—; v.p. Southwest Pipe and Supply Co., 1982; treas. Talley Industries, Inc., 1982—; v.p. Talley Industries, Inc., Phoenix, 1993—. Del. Ariz. Presdl. Dem. Conv., 1972; bd. dirs. Big Sisters of Ariz., 1975, Found. for Blind Children, 1984-90, Phoenix Little Theatre, 1985-91, Kachina Country Day Sch., 1988-94, New Way Sch., 1994—. With U.S. Army, 1959-62. Ariz. Soc. CPAs grantee, 1964-65. Mem. Fin. Execs. Inst. Home: 3627 E Medlock Dr Phoenix AZ 85018-1505 Office: 2702 N 44th St Phoenix AZ 85008-1583

MULLEN, EDWARD JOHN, JR., Spanish language educator; b. Hackensack, N.J., July 12, 1942; s. Edward J. and Elsie (Powell) M.; m. Helen Cloe Braley, Apr. 2, 1971; children: Kathleen, Julie Ann. B.A., W.Va. Wesleyan Coll., 1964; M.A., Northwestern U., 1965, Ph.D., 1968. Asst. prof. modern langs. Purdue U., West Lafayette, Ind., 1967-71; assoc. prof. Spanish U. Mo., Columbia, 1971-78, prof. Spanish, 1978—. Author: La Revista Contemporáneos, 1972, Carlos Pellicer, 1977, Langston Hughes in the Hispanic World and Haiti, 1977, The Life and Poems of a Cuban Slave: Juan Francisco Manzano 1797-1854, 1981, Critical Essays on Langston Hughes, 1986, Sendas Literarias: Hispanomerica, 1988, El cuento hispánico, 1994; co-editor Afro-Hispanic Rev., 1987—. Recipient Diploma de Honor Instituto de Cultura Hispánica, 1964; Woodrow Wilson fellow, 1964-65; Northwestern U. fellow, 1965-67; summer research grantee U. Mo., 1972, 76; grantee Am. Council Learned Socs., 1979. Mem. MLA, Am. Assn. Tchrs. Spanish and Portuguese, Assn. of Depts. Fgn. Langs. (pres. 1989-91). Home: 207 Edgewood Ave Columbia MO 65203-3413 Office: U Mo Dept Romance Langs 143 Arts and Sci Bldg Columbia MO 65211

MULLEN, EDWARD K., paper company executive. CEO Newark Group, Cranford, N.J. Office: Newark Group 20 Jackson Dr Cranford NJ 07016-3609*

MULLEN, EILEEN ANNE, staff training and development executive; b. Phila., Feb. 14, 1943; d. Joseph Gregory and Helen Rita (Kane) M. BS in English, St. Joseph U., 1967; MA in English, Villanova U., 1978. Cert. tchr., Pa. Tchr., St. Anastasia Sch., Newtown Square, 1960-67, West Cath. Girls High Sch., 1967-74; mgr. staff tng. and devel. ASTM, Phila., 1974—; instr. lit., speech and communications Widener U. Weekend Coll., Chester, Pa. and Wilmington, Del. Author: Speech Command, 1995; contbg. author articles on communications tng. programs; contbr. articles to profl. publs. Mem. ASTD (pres. Phila./Delaware Valley chpt. 1980-81, award for outstanding leadership as pres. 1981), Am. Soc. Assn. Execs. (Delaware Valley chpt.). Democrat. Roman Catholic. Office: ASTM 100 Barr Harbor Dr West Conshohocken PA 19428

MULLEN, FRANK ALBERT, university official, clergyman; b. Lafayette, Ind., Apr. 7, 1931; s. Albert Edwin and Bernice Elizabeth (Weidlich) M.; m. Ruth Charlotte Ackerman, May 28, 1960 (dec. Oct. 1969). BA, Wabash Coll., Crawfordsville, Ind., 1953; MDiv, Yale U., 1956; DD (hon.), Berkeley Div. Sch., New Haven, 1988. Ordained to ministry Christian Ch. (Disciples of Christ), 1956. Exec. dir. YMCA of Wilmington, Del., 1956-60, YMCA of Greater N.Y., N.Y.C., 1960-74; pastor St. Marks United Ch. of Christ, Ridgewood, N.Y., 1973—; assoc. dir. Campaign for Yale, Yale U., N.Y.C., 1975-79; min. Cmty. Ch. of Elmhurst, 1974—; dir. devel. Bapt. Med. Ctr., N.Y.C., 1980-83; dir. devel. Div. Sch. Yale U., New Haven, 1984—; dir. planned giving Guideposts, Inc., Carmel, N.Y., 1983-84. Trustee Park Avenue Christian Ch., N.Y.C., 1970—. Recipient Liberty Bell award Queens County Bar Assn., 1969, Alumni award of merit Wabash Coll., 1970; Wright fellow Yale U., 1955, fellow Trumbull Coll., 1985—. Mem. Assn. Theol. Schs., Coun. for Advancement in Secondary Edn., Wellness Assn., Travelers' Century Club. Home: 178-33 Croydon Rd Jamaica Estates NY 11432-2203 Office: Yale U 409 Prospect St New Haven CT 06511-2167 *Live for others. It is the only true way to find happiness.*

MULLEN, GRAHAM C., federal judge; b. 1940. BA, Duke U., 1962, JD, 1969. Bar: N.C. 1969. Ptnr. Mullen, Holland, Cooper, Morrow, Wilder & Sumner, 1969-90; judge U.S. Dist. Ct. (we. dist.) N.C., Charlotte, 1990—. Lt. USN, 1962-66. Mem. N.C. Bar Assn. (bd. govs. 1983-88), Mecklenburg County Bar Assn. Office: US Courthouse 401 W Trade St Charlotte NC 28202-1619

MULLEN, J. THOMAS, lawyer; b. Evanston, Ill., Aug. 27, 1940. BSE, Princeton U., 1963; JD cum laude, U. Mich., 1967. Bar: Ill. 1967. Ptnr. Mayer, Brown & Platt, Chgo. Bd. dirs. Legal Assistance Found. Chgo., 1979-85. Mem. ABA, Ill. State Bar Assn., Chgo. Bar Assn., Chgo. Coun. Lawyers. Office: Mayer Brown & Platt 190 S La Salle St Chicago IL 60603-3410*

MULLEN, JAMES GENTRY, physics educator; b. St. Louis, Sept. 17, 1933; s. James and Lillian A. (Nelms) M.; children by previous marriage: Anne Lynette, Barbara Gaye, James Gentry, Laura Marie; m. Sara Jane; children: Carol Melissa, Erin Joy, Elizabeth Nancy Jane, Kevin Alexander. B.S., U. Mo., 1955; M.S., U. Ill., 1957, Ph.D., 1960. Asst. physicist Argonne Nat. Lab., 1960-63, assoc. physicist, 1963-64; mem. faculty Purdue U., 1964—, asst. prof., 1964-66, assoc. prof., 1966-75, prof. physics, 1975—; pres. Word Technologies, Inc., West Lafayette, Ind., 1981-85; mem. organizing com., program chmn. Internat. Conf. for Applications of Mössbauer Effect, 1993. Contbr. to profl. jours. Fundamenteel Onderzoek Materie fellow, 1979-80. Mem. Am. Phys. Soc., Am. Assn. Physics Tchrs., AAUP, Sigma Xi, Phi Kappa Phi, Tau Beta Pi. Home: 3212 Elkhart St West Lafayette IN 47906-1151 Office: Purdue U Dept Physics West Lafayette IN 47907

MULLEN, JOSEPH PATRICK, professional hockey player; b. N.Y.C., Feb. 26, 1957. Student, Boston Coll. With St. Louis Blues, 1979-86, Calgary Flames, 1986-90; right wing Pitts. Penguins, 1990—; player NCAA All-Am. East Game, 1977-78, 78-79, NHL All-Star Game, 1989, 90, 94, Stanley Cup Championship Game, 1989, 91, 92. Recipient Ken McKenzie trophy, 1979-80, Lady Byng Meml. trophy, 1986-87, 88-89; named MVP, 1974-75. Office: Pitts Penguins Civic Arena Gate 9 Pittsburgh PA 15219*

MULLEN, PETER P., lawyer; b. N.Y.C., Apr. 8, 1928. A.B., Georgetown U., 1948; LL.B., Columbia U., 1951. Bar: N.Y. 1951. Assoc. firm Dewey Ballantine Bushby Palmer & Wood, N.Y.C., 1951-61; partner firm Skadden Arps Slate Meagher & Flom, N.Y.C., 1961—, exec. ptnr., 1982-94. Bd. dirs. Lawrence Hosp., Bronxville, N.Y., 1984-89, Project Orbis, Georgetown U., Washington, 1982—, chmn., 1985-92; mem. Bd. Edn. Bronxville, N.Y., 1976-81, pres., 1979-81, chmn. Gregorian U. Found., 1989—. Mem. Am. Bar

Assn., N.Y. State Bar Assn. (com. securities regulation 1980-83), Assn. Bar City N.Y. (com. corp. law 1964-67, com. admissions 1965-68, com. securities regulation 1970-73). Office: Skadden Arps Slate et al 919 Third Ave New York NY 10022-3903*

MULLEN, REGINA MARIE, lawyer; b. Cambridge, Mass., Apr. 22, 1948; d. Robert G. and Elizabeth R. (McHugh) M. BA, Newton Coll. Sacred Heart, 1970; JD, U. Va., 1973. Bar: Pa., Del., U.S. Dist. Ct. Del., U.S. Ct. Appeals (3d cir.), U.S. Supreme Ct. Dep. atty. gen. State Del. Dept. Justice, Wilmington, 1973-79, state solicitor, 1979-83, chief fin. unit, 1983-88; v.p., counsel MBNA Am. Bank, N.A., Newark, Del., 1988-91, 1st v.p., sr. v.p., counsel, 1991—; Mem. bd. Bar Examiners, State Del., 1979-89; bd. dirs. Del. Cmty. Investment Corp., Wilmington, 1994-96, Wilmington Music Festival, 1992—; mem. bd. profl. responsibility State of Del., 1996—. Bd. dirs. Wilmington Music Festival, 1992—; mem. fin. com. Chesapeake Bay Girl Scout coun. Wilmington, 1985-94, bd. dirs., 1988-94, v.p., 1990-94, mem. fund devel. com., 1994—, chair personnel com., 1996—; bd. dirs. Comty. Legal Aid Soc., 1994—, treas., 1995—. Mem. ABA, Del. State Bar Assn. (chair adminstrv. law sect. 1983-85). Democrat. Roman Catholic. Office: 400 Christiana Rd Newark DE 19713-4217

MULLEN, ROBERT CHARLES, school system administrator; b. Muskogee, Okla., Nov. 13, 1944; s. Charles W. and Kathryn B. (Hunt) M.; m. Celesta Rose Schmidt, June 25, 1966; children: Charles, Robert, Michael, Kevin. BS, Minot (N.D.) State U., 1966, MS, 1967; EdD, U. No. Colo., Greeley, 1981. Speech pathologist Benton-Tama-Iowa-Poweshiek Dept. Spl. Edn., Toledo, Iowa, 1967-68, hearing clinician, 1968-69, coord. speech and hearing, 1969-73; dir. ACCA Speech and Hearing Ctr., Fairbanks, Alaska, 1973-75; asst. dir. Alaska Treatment Ctr., Anchorage, 1975-76, exec. dir., 1976-79; dir. Reno County Edn. Coop. USD #610, Hutchinson, Kans., 1981-85, Rio Blanco Bd. Endl. Svcs., Rangely, Colo., 1985-89; supt. Rangely Pub. Schs. RE-4, 1989—; v.p. bd. dirs. Horizon Inc., Steamboat, Colo.; pres. Vocat. Edn. Adv. Bd., Colo. No. Community Coll., Rangely, 1988. Co-author: Exceptional Individuals: An Introduction, 1993. Commr. Mayor's Health Commn., Anchorage, 1976-79; Alaska rep. Nat. Conf. on Aging, WAshington; bd. mem. Spl. Edn. Adv. Bd., U. No. Colo., 1988; state com. mem. Colo. Parent/Profl. Partnership, Denver, 1988-90; mem. planning com. White house Conf. on Handicapped. U.s. Office Edn. grantee, Greeley, Colo., 1980, 81. Mem. Am. Assn. Sch. Adminstrs., Coun. Exceptional Children, Colo. Assn. Sch. Execs. Roman Catholic. Avocations: fishing, swimming, writing, geneology. Office: Rangely Pub Schs 402 W Main St Rangely CO 81648-2408

MULLEN, RON, insurance company executive; b. Tex., Aug. 8, 1939; s. Durward Lacy and Blanche V. (Coulson) M.; m. Carole King, Dec. 29, 1959; children: Lacy Lynne Holcomb, Misty Kay. Student, Abilene Christian Coll., 1957-58, San Antonio Coll., 1958-59; BBA, S.W. Tex. State U., 1965. C.L.U., Chartered Fin. Cons. City council mem. City of Austin, 1977-83, mayor, 1983-85; mgr. Prin. Fin. Group, Austin, 1965—; pres., prin. Fin. Group, Ron Mullen & Assocs. Inc., Austin, 1966—; chmn. TML Ins. Trust Fund Com., 1983—; mem. Gov.'s Task Force on State Employees Health Ins. Benefits, Austin, 1984. Chmn. Austin Transp. Study Com., Austin, 1983—, Greater Austin-San Antonio Corridor Coun., 1984—, Social Policy Adv. Com., Austin, 1979-80, March of Dimes campaign, Austin, 1974-75; co-chmn. Consumers United for Rail Equity, Austin, 1983—; v.p. Austin Symphony Orch., 1974-75; mem. exec. com. Capital Area Planning Coun., Austin, 1976—, exec. bd. Tex. Mcpl. League, Austin, 1983—, Gov.'s Task Force on Indigent Health Care, Austin, 1984, Tex. Adv. Commn. on Intergovtl. Rels., Austin, 1981—; chmn. Infant Parent Tng. Ctr., 1985-96; bd. dirs., chmn. South MoPac Transp. Com., 1986-87; life mem. Austin Jaycees, bd. dirs., 1974-75; vice-chmn. mental health Mental Retardation Bd.; vice chmn. South Tex. Audio Reader Svc. Recipient Road Hand award Tex. Dept. Hwys. and Transp., 1985, award for regional statesmanship Greater Austin-San Antonio Corridor Commn.; named Boss of Yr., Treaty Oaks chpt. Am. Bus. Women's Assn., 1978, Nat. Mgr. of Yr., Bankers Life Ins. Co., 1977, 82, 84-85, Alumnus of Yr. Austin Jaycees, 1988-90. Mem. Austin Coll. Life Underwriters (pres.), Tex. Assn. Life Underwriters (v.p. 1995-96), Austin Assn. Life Underwriters (pres. 1974-75), Austin Gen. Agts. and Mgrs. Assn. (pres. 1978-80), Sales and Mktg. Execs. of Austin (pres. 1972-73), Downtown Rotary (pres.). Baptist. Home: 6902 Mesa Dr # B Austin TX 78731-2822

MULLEN, WILLIAM JOSEPH, III, military analyst, retired army officer; b. Plattsburg, N.Y., Dec. 26, 1937; s. William Joseph Jr. and Georgia (Cook) M.; m. Norma Sturgeon, Aug. 6, 1962; 1 child, William Joseph IV. BS, U.S. Mil. Acad., West Point, N.Y., 1959; MS in Internat. Affairs, George Washington U., 1971. Commd. 2d lt. U.S. Army, 1959, advanced through grades to brig. gen., 1987; various assignments in U.S., Vietnam, Korea, Panama, Germany, Saudi Arabia, 1959-92; mem. staff, faculty U.S. Mil. Acad., West Point, 1967-70; comdr. 1st Brigade, 1st Inf. Div., Ft. Riley, Kans., 1983-86; asst. div. comdr. 5th Inf. Div., Ft. Polk, La., 1986-87; comdg. gen. U.S. Army Combined Arms Tng. Activity, Ft. Leavenworth, Kans., 1987-89, 1st Inf. Div. (Forward), Germany, 1989-91; dep. dir. ops. J3 Forces Command, Ft. McPherson, Ga., 1991-92; dir. mil. tng. sys. BDM Fed., Inc., Monterey, Calif., 1992—. Co-author: Changing an Army, An Oral History of Gen. W.E. DePuy, 1979; contbr. articles, book revs. to Mil. Rev. Decorated D.S.C., D.S.M. Mem. Assn. U.S. Army, Soc. of 1st Div. (chpt. officer 1968, assoc. 1989-93, trustee found. 1989-93, bd. dirs.), Legion of Valor. Avocations: sports, reading. ***When in doubt, I have always found direction from the guidance explicit in the 1st Infantry Division's motto, "Duty first!".***

MULLENDORE, WALTER EDWARD, economist; b. Harrah, Okla., Apr. 22, 1940; s. Newton and Ida Minnie (Lohmann) M.; m. Edra Janell Havenstrite, July 4, 1963; children—Matthew Edward, Karen Kay, Mark Andrew. BS, Okla. State U., 1961, MS, 1963; PhD in Econs, Iowa State U., 1968. Grad. asst. Okla. State U., 1961-63; instr. Iowa State U., 1965-67; mem. faculty dept. econs. U. Tex., Arlington, 1968—, prof., 1975—, dean Coll. of Bus., 1980-93. Contbr. articles to profl. jours. Served with U.S. Army, 1963-65. Mem. Mo. Valley Econ. Assn. (v.p. 1980-81, pres. 1982-83), Atlantic Econ. Soc., Regional Sci. Assn., Western Regional Sci. Assn., Gt. S.W. Rotary (pres. 1989-90), Omicron Delta Epsilon. Methodist. Home: 8003 John T White Rd Fort Worth TX 76120-3611 Office: U Tex Coll Bus Box 19479-UTA Arlington TX 76019

MULLENIX, KATHY ANN, relocation company administrator; b. Goodland, Ind., Mar. 8, 1955; d. Boyd Dale and Edith Marie Hoaks; 1 child, Joseph F. Hamburg IV. Diploma, South Newton Jr./Sr. H.S., Goodland, Ind., 1973. Asst. to pres. Planes Moving, Cin., 1981-88; sales mgr. Tru-Pak Moving, Greenville, S.C., 1988-89; account exec. Armstrong Relocation, Atlanta, 1989—. Den leader Cub Scouts, Blue Ash, Ohio, 1982-86; coach's asst. Soccer Assn., Mason, Ohio, 1985-88; treas. PTA Mason Mid. Sch., 1988; tutor Gwinnette Co. Adult Literacy, Lawrenceville, Ga., 1994. Mem. NAFE. Avocations: reading, dance, oil painting, horseback riding, camping. Office: Armstrong Relocation 6950 Business Ct Atlanta GA 30340-1429

MULLENIX, LINDA SUSAN, lawyer, educator; b. N.Y.C., Oct. 16, 1950; d. Andrew Michael and Roslyn Marasco; children: Robert Bartholomew, John Theodore, William Joseph. B.A., CCNY, 1971; M. Philosophy, Columbia U., 1974, Ph.D. (Pres.'s fellow), 1977; J.D., Georgetown U., 1980. Bar: D.C. 1981, Tex. 1991, U.S. Dist Ct. D.C. 1981, U.S. Supreme Ct. 1986. U.S. Ct. Appeals (D.C. cir.) 1981, U.S. Ct. Appeals (5th cir.) 1995. Assoc. prof., lectr. George Washington U., Washington, 1977-80; asst. prof. Am. U., Washington, 1979; clin. prof. Loyola U. Law Sch., Los Angeles, 1981-82, vis. asst. prof., 1982-83; vis. asst. prof. Catholic U. Law Sch., Washington, 1983-84, asst. prof., 1984-86, assoc. prof., 1986-90, prof., 1990; Jud. Fellow U.S. Supreme Ct. and Fed. Jud. Ctr., 1989-90; Bernard J. Ward Centennial prof. U. Tex., 1991—; Vinson & Elkins chair, U. Tex., 1993; vis. prof. Harvard Law Sch., 1994-95, Mich. Law Sch., 1996; assoc. Pierson, Ball & Dowd, Washington, 1980-81; adj. instr. Fordham U., N.Y.C., 1975-76, adj. asst. prof. 1977; adj. asst. prof. CCNY, 1977; adj. instr., adj. asst. prof. Cooper Union Advancement Sci., Art, N.Y.C., 1977; instr. N.Y. Inst. Tech., N.Y.C., 1976, U. Md. European div., Ramstein, Germany, 1974. Author: Mass Tort Litigation: Cases and Materials, 1996, Moore's Fed. Practice and Procedure, 1991; editor bibliographies Polit. Theory, A Jour. Polit. Philosophy, 1972-74, The Tax Lawyer Jour., 1978-80; contbg. editor Preview of U.S. Supreme Ct. Cases, Pub. Edn. Div. ABA, 1988—; reporter ABA Task Force on Class Actions, 1995—, co-reporter Report and Plan of Civil Justice Reform Act Adv. Group, S.D., Tex. 1991; assoc. reporter ALI, Restatement of the Law Governing Lawyers; contbr. articles to profl. publs. Alt. del. Va. Democratic State Conv., 1980. Fellow NDEA, 1971-74, Georgetown U. Law Sch., 1978; N.Y. State Regents scholar, 1967-71. Mem. ABA, Am. Law Inst., D.C. Bar Assn. (com. on ethics, CLE and the Model Rules 1987), Am. Assn. Law Schs. (exec. com. sect. on civil proc. 1987-88, exec. com. sec. on conflicts of law 1991-92, chair prof. devel. com. 1991-93), Phi Beta Kappa, Phi Alpha Delta. Home: 722 Crystal Creek Dr Austin TX 78746-4730 Office: U Tex Sch Law 727 E 26th St Austin TX 78705-3224

MULLENS, WILLIAM REESE, retired insurance company executive; b. Franklin, Tenn., Sept. 12, 1921; s. William Pope and Elizabeth (Reese) M.; m. Katherine Ann Jones, Nov. 24, 1945; children: Jo Ann Mullens Sanditz, Carol Ann Mullens Slegers. B.A., Vanderbilt U., 1942. With Bus. Men's Assurance Co., Kansas City, Mo., 1947-75; exec. v.p., dir. Bus. Men's Assurance Co., 1969-75; pres., dir. J.C. Penney Life Ins. Co., 1975-82; pres. Gt. Am. Res. Ins. Co., 1975-84, dir., 1975-89; dir. Nat. Fidelity Life Ins. Co., 1986-89. Served to lt. comdr. USNR, 1943-46. Fellow Soc. Actuaries; mem. Phi Beta Kappa, Alpha Tau Omega. Presbyterian. Home: 2502 N Broken Circle Rd Flagstaff AZ 86004

MULLER, CHARLOTTE FELDMAN, economist, educator; b. N.Y.C., Feb. 19, 1921; d. Louis and Lillian (Drogin) Feldman; m. Jonas N. Muller, 1942 (dec.); m. Carl Schoenberg, 1970; children: Jeremy Lewis Muller, Sara Linda Muller. A.B., Vassar Coll., 1941; A.M., Columbia U., 1942, Ph.D. in Econs., 1946. Instr. econs. Bklyn. Coll., 1943; lectr. Barnard Coll., 1943-46; asst. prof. Occidental Coll., 1947; asst. study dir. Survey Rsch. Ctr., U. Mich., 1948; rsch. assoc. U. Calif., Berkeley, 1948-50; lectr. Yale U. Sch. Pub. Health, 1952-53; asst. prof. Columbia U. Sch. Pub. Health, 1957-67; assoc. dir. Ctr. for Social Rsch. CUNY, 1967-86, prof. econs., 1978-91, prof. emerita, 1991—, prof. sociology, 1982-91, prof. urban studies Ctr. for Social Rsch., 1967-78; v.p. CUNY Acad. for Humanities and Scis., 1985-88; prof. health econs. Mt. Sinai Sch. Medicine, 1986-91, prof. emerita, 1991—, dir. div. health econs., 1988-91, prof. dept. geriatrics, 1990-91, assoc. dir. Internat. Longevity Ctr.,, 1991—; cons. Health Care Financing Adminstrn., U.S. VA; disting. alumna speaker Vassar Centennial, 1971. Author: Health Care and Gender, 1990; mem. editorial bd. Am. Jour. Pub. Health, 1980-84, Women and Health, Rsch. on Aging; contbr. numerous articles on health econs. to profl. publs. Mem. N.Y.C. Mayor's Com. on Prescription Drug Abuse, 1970-73; bd. dirs. Alan Guttmacher Inst., 1972-81, CUNY Rsch. Found., 1985-91; vice chmn. Med. and Health Rsch. Assn., N.Y.C.; mem. health care tech. study sect. Nat. Ctr. Health Svcs. Rsch., 1976-79; mem. commn. on nat. policy Am. Jewish Congress, 1980-91. Ford/Rockefeller Founds. grantee, 1972-73, 75-76; Russell Sage Found. grantee, 1985-90. Mem. APHA, NOW, Am. Econ. Assn. Jewish. Office: Mt Sinai Sch Medicine Box 1070 1 Gustave L Levy Pl New York NY 10029-6504

MULLER, DIETRICH ALFRED HELMUT, physicist, educator; b. Leipzig, Germany, Sept. 14, 1936; came to U.S., 1968; s. Herbert and Johanna (Potzger) M.; m. Renate Runkel, Mar. 23, 1968; children: Georg, Michael, Agnes. Student, U. Leipzig, German Dem. Republic; diploma in physics, U. Bonn, Fed. Republic Germany, 1961, PhD in Physics, 1964. Rsch. assoc. U. Bonn., 1965-68; rsch. assoc. U. Chgo., 1968-70, asst. prof., 1970-77, assoc. prof., 1977-84, prof. physics, 1985—, dir. Enrico Fermi Inst., 1986-92; prin. investigator on rsch. in high energy astrophysics using baloons and spacecraft, NASA; rsch. in exptl. physics and particle physics. Contbr. numerous articles to profl. jours. Fellow Am. Phys. Soc.; mem. AAAS, Am. Astron. Soc. Office: U Chgo Enrico Fermi Inst 933 E 56th St Chicago IL 60637-1460

MULLER, DONALD BRUCE, chemical executive; b. Long Beach, Calif., Sept. 19, 1947; s. Howard Eugene and Deloris June (Holthus) M.; m. Mary Louise Morris, Sept. 11, 1971; children: Bret David, Carolyn Adele, Susan Christine. BSChemE, Va. Poly. Inst., 1970. Mktg. research rep. DuPont Co., Wilmington, Del., 1970-73; mktg. rep. DuPont Co., various locations, 1973-79; v.p., gen. mgr. Mid-State Plastics, Seagrove, N.C., 1979-84; v.p., gen. mgr. Morganite, Inc., Dunn, N.C., 1984-85, CEO, 1985—, also bd. dirs.; bd. dirs. Morganite-U.K., Morriston, Wales and Wandsworth, Eng. Mem. Am. Mgmt. Assn., Soc. of Plastic Engrs. Republican. Episcopalian. Avocations: tennis, antique refinishing. Home: 3018 Eton Rd Raleigh NC 27608-1112 Office: Morganite Inc 1 Morganite Dr Dunn NC 28334-3635

MULLER, EDWARD ROBERT, lawyer; b. Phila., Mar. 26, 1952; s. Rudolph E. and Elizabeth (Steiner) M.; m. Patricia Eileen Bauer, Sept. 27, 1980; children: Margaret Anne, John Frederick. AB summa cum laude, Dartmouth Coll., 1973; JD, Yale U., 1976. Assoc. Leva, Hawes, Symington, Martin & Oppenheimer, Washington, 1977-83; dir. legal affairs Life Scis. group Whittaker Corp., Arlington, Va., 1983-84; v.p. Whittaker Health Svcs., Arlington, Va., 1984-85; v.p., gen. counsel, sec. Whittaker Corp., L.A., 1985-93, chief adminstrv. officer, 1988-92, CFO, 1992-93, bd. dirs., 1993—; v.p., gen. counsel, sec. BioWhittaker, Inc., Walkersville, Md., 1991-93; pres., CEO, bd. dirs. Mission Energy Co., Irvine, Calif., 1993—; mem. Brookings Task Force on Civil Justice Reform, 1988-89. Trustee Exceptional Children's Found., L.A., 1988-94, treas., 1988-93; bd. dirs. Oasis Resdl., Inc., 1995—; co-chair Internat. Energy Devel. Coun., Washington, 1993—; bd. govs. Jr. Achievement, 1995—. Office: Mission Energy Co 18101 Von Karman Ave Ste 1700 Irvine CA 92715-1046

MULLER, ERNEST H., geology educator; b. Tabriz, Iran, Mar. 4, 1923; (parents U.S. citizens); s. Hugo Arthur and Laura Barnett (McComb) M.; m. Wanda Custis, Apr. 7, 1951; children: Ruth Anne, David Stewart, Katherine Lee. BA, Wooster Coll., 1947; MS, U. Ill., 1949, PhD, 1952. Geologist U.S. Geol. Survey, Washington, 1947-54; asst. prof. geology Cornell U., Ithaca, N.Y., 1954-59; assoc. prof. Syracuse U., N.Y., 1959-63, prof., 1963-89, interim chmn. dept. geology, 1970-71, 79-81, prof. emeritus, 1989—; seasonal geologist N.Y. Geol. Survey, 1956-76; geologist Am. Geog. Soc., Chile, 1959; rsch. assoc. Natural History Mus., Rejkjavik, Iceland, 1968-69; vis. prof. Alaska Pacific U., Anchorage, 1979; Erskine vis. prof. U. Canterbury, Christchurch, New Zealand, 1974; mem. Bering Glacier (Alaska) Rsch. Group, 1988—, N.Y. Pleistocene Stratigraphy. Author: Geology of Chautauqua County, New York, 1964, Seaway Trail Rocks and Landscapes, 1987. 1st lt. USAAF, 1943-46. Fellow Geol. Soc. Am. (geomorphology panel 1962-64, 66-68, 75-77), AAAS; mem. Am. Quaternary Assn. (counselor 1982-86), Glaciological Soc., Nat. Assn. Geology Tchrs., Sigma Xi. Home: 874 Livingston Ave Syracuse NY 13210-2936 Office: Syracuse U 204 Heroy Geology Lab Syracuse NY 13244-1070

MULLER, FRANK B., advertising executive; b. Copenhagen, Nov. 25, 1926; came to U.S., 1927; s. Herman B. and Johanne M. (Ammentorp) M.; m. Judith Hunter, Apr. 14, 1956; children: Mark W., Hunter J., Chip. Student, Harvard U., 1944; BNS in Naval Sci., Tufts Coll., 1946; BS in Mech. Engring., Tufts U., 1948. Account supr. advt. dept. GE, 1948-55; exec. v.p. Muller Jordan Weiss Inc., N.Y.C., 1955-90; pres. MultiMedia Unltd., Inc., N.Y.C., 1990—. Lt. (j.g.) USNR, 1944-47. Mem. ASME. Republican. Congregationalist. Clubs: N.Y. Yacht (N.Y.C.); Saugatuck Harbor Yacht (Westport, Conn.) (bd. govs. 1965-75, 79-80, commodore 1970-71). Home: 46 Marion Rd Westport CT 06880-2923 Office: MultiMedia Unltd Inc 46 Marion Rd Westport CT 06880

MULLER, FREDERICA DANIELA, psychology educator; d. Leopold and Elena; m. Dr. L. Muller; children: Daniela, Adrian. Grad., Med. Inst. Radiology, Romania, 1962, PsyD in Clin. Psychology, 1965, M in Internat. Law and Bus., 1966; specialization courses in Psychodrama, Moreno Inst., Vienna, 1969; grad., Inst. Rsch. in Aging, Rome, 1970, Miami Inst. Psychology, 1987. Diplomate Am. Bd. Forensic Medicine, Am. Bd. Forensic Examiners; lic. psychologist, Pa.; lic. psychotherapist, Fla.; cert. family mediator, Fla. Supreme Ct. continuing edn. units provider psych. Prof. Sch. Continuing Edn. Barry U., North Miami, Fla.; instr. advanced courses in psychology, psychodrama, med. ethics, social manners; guest speaker Colloque Internat., Bucharest, Romania, 1989-93; guest lectr. U. Arboga, Sweden 1968-72; founder Internat. Studies for Biopsychosocial Issues, 1991; cons. dept. of marriage, family and child devel. systemic studies, Nova U., 1992; founder Euro Am. Coun. Co., 1980; with Santé Internat., Switzerland, 1982-85; dir. Ctr. Biopsychosocial Medicine, 1995. Conducted rsch. on stress and aging with Dr. Anna Aslan, world renowned author; developed 45 minute stress reduction program for use in the work place. Author: The Management of Occupational Stress and Its Linkage to Social Pressures; contbr. articles to profl. jours. Mem. APA, Medicins du Monde (hon.), Am. Soc. Group Psychotherapy and Psychodrama, Soc. Psychol., Studies Social of Issues, World Fedn. for Mental Health.

MULLER, GEORGE T., automotive executive; b. 1949. CPA. Acct. Arthur Andersen & Co., 1972-78; with Auto Parts Distbn., 1978-79; with Subaru of Am., Inc., Cherry Hill, N.J., 1979—, pres., COO. Office: Subaru of Am Inc 2235 Route 70 W Cherry Hill NJ 08002-3308 Office: PO Box 6000 Cherry Hill NJ 08034-6000*

MULLER, HENRY JAMES, journalist, magazine editor; b. Garmisch-Partenkirchen, Germany, Feb. 10, 1947; came to U.S., 1953; s. Henri Jacques and Helga (Mensch) M.; m. Maggie McComas, June 19, 1968. BA, Stanford U., 1968. Tchr. U.S. Peace Corps, Ethiopia, 1968-70; chief Vancouver (B.C., Can.) bur. Time mag., 1971-73; European econ. corr. Time mag., Brussels, 1973-77; chief Paris bur. Time mag., 1977-81; world editor Time mag., N.Y.C., 1982-85, chief of corrs., 1986-87, mng. editor, 1987-93; editorial dir. Time Inc., 1993—; faculty mem. profl. pub. course Stanford (Calif.) U., 1989—. Trustee Stanford U., 1991—, Carnegie Corp., 1992—, Overseas Press Club, 1993—. Recipient David Brower Environ. Journalism award Sierra Club, 1990, Gerald Loeb award for disting. bus. and fin. journalism, 1992. Mem. Am. Soc. Mag. Editors (bd. dirs. 1991-95), Coun. of Fgn. Rels. Avocations: hiking, reading, skiing. Office: Time Inc Time & Life Bldg Rockefeller Ctr New York NY 10020

MULLER, HENRY JOHN, real estate developer; b. N.Y.C., July 27, 1919; s. Henry and Anne (Wulf) M.; m. Cecelia M. Ziffer, May 19, 1943; children: Richard, Robert, Ceil Anne, Roger. BS, Bklyn. Poly. Inst., 1949. Engr. GE Co., Bloomfield, N.J., 1948-49, Prudential Ins. Co., Newark, 1949-56; dep. dir. Harvard U., 1956-64; sr. v.p. 1st Nat. City Bank, N.Y.C., 1964-71; chmn. Citicorp. Realty, N.Y.C., 1971-72; sr. v.p. Allied Maintenance Corp., N.Y.C., 1972-74; exec. v.p. Moorings Devel. Co., Vero Beach, Fla., 1974-77; pres. Muller & Assocs. Inc., Vero Beach, 1977-89, Criterion Svcs. Corp., Vero Beach, 1988—. With AUS, 1941-46. Mem. Tau Beta Pi, Lambda Chi Alpha. Home: 5954 River Run Dr Sebastian FL 32958-4709 Office: Criterion Svcs Corp 9025 U S Hwy 1 Sebastian FL 32958

MULLER, H(ENRY) NICHOLAS, III, foundation executive; b. Pitts., Nov. 18, 1938; s. Henry N. Jr. and Harriet (Kerschner) M.; m. Nancy Clagett, June 20, 1959 (div. 1985); children: Charles T., Brook W.; m. Carol A. Cook, Jan. 4, 1986. BA, Dartmouth Coll., 1960; PhD, U. Rochester, 1968. Instr. Dartmouth Coll., Hanover, N.H., 1964; lectr. Mt. Allison U., Sackville, N.B., Can., 1964-66; asst. prof. history U. Vt., Burlington, 1966-69; assoc. prof. history, 1970-73; prof. history U. Vt., Burlington, 1974-78, asst. dean Coll. Arts and Scis., 1969-70, assoc. dean Coll. Arts and Scis., 1970-73, dir. Living/Learning Ctr., 1973-78; pres. Colby-Sawayer Coll., New London, N.H., 1978-85; dir. State His. Soc. Wis., Madison, 1985-96; pres., CEO Frank Lloyd Wright Found., Scottsdale & Spring Green, Ariz./Wis., 1996—; chmn. State Hist. Records Adv. Bd., 1985—, Wis. Burial Sites Bd., 1988-96, Wis. Submerged Cultural Resources, Standex Internat. Corp., Salem, N.H., Nat. Trust for Hist. Preservation, Taliesin Archs., Scottsdale; mem. Gov. Coun. on Tourism, 1987-96. Co-author: An Anxious Democracy, 1982; co-editor: Science, Technology and Culture, 1974, In a State of Nature, 1982; sr. editor Vt. Life mag., 1975-87; editor Vt. History, 1977-85. Chmn. Bicentennial Com., Burlington, 1976, Vt. Coun. Hist. Preservation, 1975-78; fin. chmn. Vt. Bicentennial Commn., 1970-77; mem. Wis. Sesquicentennial Commn., 1995—; mem. N.H. Postsecondary Edn. Commn., 1983-85; trustee Vt. Hist. Soc., 1972-85, v.p., 1975-82; bd. dirs. USS Wisconsin, 1989-93, Wis. Preservation Fund Inc., 1989—; trustee, vice chmn., sec. Taliesin Preservation Commn., 1990—. Fellow Ctr. for Rsch. on Vt.; mem. Nat. Coun. on Pub. History (bd. dirs. 1988-90), Am. Assn. State and Local History (councillor 1988-91), Vt. Archeol. Soc. (pres. 1971-74), Madison Club. Office: Frank Lloyd Wright Found Taliesin-West Scottsdale AZ 85261-4430 also: Frank Lloyd Wright Found Taliesin Spring Green WI 53588

MULLER, JENNIFER, choreographer, dancer; b. Yonkers, N.Y., Oct. 16, 1944; d. Don Medford and Lynette (Heldman) Muller. BS, Juilliard Sch. Music, 1967. instr. in dance H.S. Performing Arts, 1967-72, Sarah Lawrence Coll., 1968-72, The Juilliard Sch., 1969-70, Nederlands Dans Theater, 1971-76, Utah rep., 1973-74; commns.: Alvin Ailey Am. Dance Theatre, N.Y.C., 1977, 85, Festival d'Avignon, France, 1980, Lyon Opera Ballet, France, 1984, Aterballetto, 1988, Ballet Stagium, 1991, Dansgroep Krisztina de Chatel, 1992, Tanz-Forum Staatsoper Koln, Sachsische Staatopera-Dresden, ARTSCAPE-Balt., 1991, 95, Aterballetto, Italy, 1993, Les Ballet Jazz de Montreal, 1994, Ballet du Nord, France, 1995, Bat Dor Dance Co., Israel, Nederlands Dans Theatre III, Ballet Contemporaneo, Argentina; cons. Met. Mus. Art, 1971-72. Mem. Pearl Lang Dance Co., N.Y.C, 1959-63, prin. dance, Jose Limon Dance Co., N.Y.C., 1963-71, assoc. dir., choreographer, prin. dancer, Louis Falco Dance Co., N.Y.C., 1968-74; founder, dir. choreographer: Jennifer Muller/The Works, N.Y.C., 1974—; choreographic works include: Nostalgia, 1971, Rust, 1971, Cantata, 1972, Tub, 1973, An American Beauty Rose, 1974, Biography, 1974, Speeds, 1974, Winter Pieces, 1974, Clown, 1974, Four Chairs, 1974, Wyeth, 1974, White, 1975, Strangers, 1975, Beach, 1976, Crossword, 1977, Predicaments for Five, 1977, Mondriaan, 1977, Lovers, 1978, Solo, 1979, Conversations, 1979, Chant, 1980, Terrain, 1981, Shed, 1982, Kite, 1983, Souls, 1984, The Enigma, 1986, Fields, 1986, Couches, 1986, Life/Times, 1986, Darkness and Light, 1986, Interrupted River, 1987, Occasional Encounters, 1988, City, 1988, The Flight of a Predatory Bird, 1989, Refracted Light, 1990, RIGHTeous About Passing (on the LEFT), 1990, Woman with Visitors at 3am, 1991, Regards, 1991, arm in arm in arm..., 1991, Thesaurus, 1991, Glass Houses, 1991, 2-1=1/Attic, 1992, Momentary Gathering, 1992, The Waiting Room, 1993, The Politician/Peeling the Onion, 1993, Orbs, Spheres and Other Circular Bodies, 1993, HUMAN/NATURE-A Response to the Longhouse Gardens, 1993, Pierrot, 1993, Desire-That DNA Urge, 1994, Point of View (A Case of Persimmons and Picasso), 1994, The Spotted Owl, 1995, Some Days are Like That, 1995; choreographer for theatrical prodns.: Frimbo, 1980, The Death of von Richthofen..., 1982, Fame, The Musical, 1988, Up Against It, 1989, The Seven Deadly Sins, 1990, Signature, 1990, Esther, 1993. Recipient Best Performance award Berlin Festival, 1977, Acad. award Juilliard Sch. Music, 1967, Carbonell award, 1989; grantee Nat. Endowment for Arts, 1971-77, 80-85, 86-87, 87-88, Creative Artists Pub. Svc., 1976-77, N.Y. State Coun. on Arts, 1976-77, 78-79, 85-93, N.Y.C. Dept. Cultural Affairs, 1978-79, 94. Mem. Am. Guild Mus. Artists, Soc. Stage Dirs. and Choreographers. Home and Office: The Muller/Works Found Inc 131 W 24th St New York NY 10011-1942

MULLER, JEROME KENNETH, photographer, art director, editor; b. Amityville, N.Y., July 18, 1934; s. Alphons and Helen (Haberl) M.; m. Nora Marie Nestor, Dec. 21, 1974. BS, Marquette U., 1961; postgrad., Calif. State U., Fullerton, 1985-86; MA, Nat. U., San Diego, 1988; postgrad., Newport Psychoanalytic Inst., 1988-90. Comml. and editorial photographer N.Y.C., 1952-55; mng. editor Country Beautiful mag., Milw., 1961-62, Reprodns. Rev. mag., N.Y.C., 1967-68; editor, art dir. Orange County (Calif.) Illustrated, Newport Beach, 1962-67, art editor, 1970-79, exec. editor, art dir., 1968-69; owner, CEO Creative Svcs. Advt. Agy., Newport Beach, 1969-79; founder, CEO Mus. Graphics, Costa Mesa, Calif., 1978—; tchr. photography Lindenhurst (N.Y.) High Sch., 1952-54; tchr. comic art U. Calif., Irvine, 1979; guest curator 50th Anniversary Exhbn. Mickey Mouse, 1928-78, The Bowers Mus., Santa Ana, Calif., 1978; organized Moving Image Exhbn. Mus. Sci. and Industry, Chgo., Cooper-Hewitt Mus., N.Y.C., William Rockhill Nelson Gallery, Kansas City, 1981; collector original works outstanding Am. cartoonists at major mus. One-man shows include Souk Gallery, Newport Beach, 1970, Gallery 2, Santa Ana, Calif., 1972, Cannery Gallery, Newport Beach, 1974, Mus. Graphics Gallery, 1993, White Gallery-Portland State U., 1996; author: Rex Brandt, 1972; contbr. photographs and articles to mags. Served with USAF, 1956-57. Recipient two silver medals 20th Ann. Exhbn. Advt. and Editorial Art in West, 1965. Mem. APA, Newport Harbor Art Mus., Mus. Modern Art (N.Y.C.), Met. Mus. Art, Art Mus. Assn. Am., Laguna Beach Mus. Art, L.A. Press Club, Newport Beach Tennis Club, Alpha Sigma Nu. Home: 2438 Bowdoin Pl Costa Mesa CA 92626-6304 Office: PO Box 10743 Costa Mesa CA 92627-0234

MULLER, JOHN BARTLETT, university president; b. Port Jefferson, N.Y., Nov. 8, 1940; s. Frederick Henry and Estelle May (Reeve) M.; m. Barbara Ann Schmidt, May 30, 1964 (dec. 1972); m. Lynn Anne Spongberg, Oct. 10, 1987. AB in Polit. Sci., U. Rochester, 1962; postgrad. in apologetics, Westminster Sem., Phila., 1962-63; MS in Psychology, Purdue U., 1968, PhD in Psychology, 1975. Asst. prof. psychology Roberts Wesleyan Coll., Rochester, N.Y., 1964-66, acting chmn. div. behavioral sci., dir. instl. research, 1967-70; vis. asst. prof. psychology Wabash Coll., Crawfordsville, Ind., 1970-71; research assoc. Ind. U.-Purdue U., Indpls., 1971-72; prof. psychology, v.p. for acad. affairs Hillsdale (Mich.) Coll., 1972-85; pres. BMW Assocs., Osseo, Mich., 1984-85, Bellevue (Nebr.) U., 1985—; bd. dirs. Nebr. Ind. Coll. Found., Omaha, Assn. Ind. Colls. Nebr., Lincoln; bd. advisors Norwest Bank of Bellevue, Applied Information Mgmt. Inst. Contbr. articles to profl. jours. and textbooks. Bd. dirs. Midlands Community Hosp., 1989—, Boys Club of Omaha. Nat. Inst. Mental Health fellowship Purdue U., 1963, Nat. Tchg. fellowship Fed. Govt., 1967, Townsend fellowship U. Rochester, 1962. Mem. APA, Bellevue C. of C. (bd. dirs. 1989-95), Phi Beta Kappa, Phi Kappa Phi. Republican. Home: 404 Ridgewood Dr Bellevue NE 68005-4745 Office: Bellevue U Office of the Pres 1000 Galvin Rd S Bellevue NE 68005-3058

MULLER, LYLE DEAN, religious organization administrator; b. Owatonna, Minn., Mar. 9, 1935; s. Robert John and Esther Ida (Eaker) M.; m. Marlene K. Kliemek, Sept. 7, 1957; children: Mark, Susan. BA, Valparaiso U., 1956; MDiv, Concordia Sem., 1961. Ordained to ministry Luth. Ch.- Mo. Synod. Pastor Emmanuel Luth. Ch., Ft. Wayne, Ind., 1961-63, Trinity Luth. Ch., Danville, Ill., 1963-69, St. Luke Luth. Ch., Itasca, Ill., 1969-79; exec. evangelism and missions no. Ill. Dist. Luth. Ch.-Mo. Synod, Hillsdale, 1979-90; exec. dir. evangelism svcs. Luth. Ch.-Mo. Synod, St. Louis, 1990—. Author: (manuals) Good News Day, 1982, Witness Workshop, 1983, Ministry to Inactives, 1987, Assimilation, 1988. Office: Luth Ch Mo Synod 1333 S Kirkwood Rd Saint Louis MO 63122-7226

MULLER, MARCEL W(ETTSTEIN), electrical engineering educator; b. Vienna, Austria, Nov. 1, 1922; came to U.S., 1940; s. Georg and Josephine (David) M.; m. Esther Ruth Hagler, Feb. 2, 1947; children: Susan, George, Janet. BSEE, Columbia U., 1949, AM in Physics, 1952; PhD, Stanford U., 1957. Sr. scientist Varian Assocs., Palo Alto, Calif., 1952-66; prof. elec. engring. Washington U., St. Louis, 1966-91, prof. emeritus, rsch. prof., 1991—; vis. lectr. U. Zurich, Switzerland, 1962-63; vis. prof. U. Colo., Boulder, summer 1969; vis. scientist Max Planck Inst., Stuttgart, Fed. Republic of Germany, 1976-77; cons. Hewlett-Packard Labs., Palo Alto, 1985-89, SRI Internat., Menlo Park, Calif., 1986—. Sgt. U.S. Army, 1943-46. Recipient Humboldt prize Alexander von Humboldt Soc., 1976; Fulbright grantee, 1977, grantee NSF, 1967—. Fellow IEEE, Am. Physical Soc. Achievements include development of Maser quantum noise theory; developments in micromagnetism; contributions to magnetic information storage; invention Magneprint security system. Home: 4954 Lindell Blvd Saint Louis MO 63108-1500 Office: Washington Univ Campus Box 1127 1 Brookings Dr Saint Louis MO 63130-4862

MULLER, MERVIN EDGAR, information systems educator, consultant; b. Hollywood, Calif., June 1, 1928; s. Emanuel and Bertha (Zimmerman) M.; m. Barbara McAdam, July 13, 1963; children: Jeffrey McAdam, Stephen McAdam, Todd McAdam. AB, UCLA, 1949, MA, 1951, PhD, 1954. Instr. in math. Cornell U., 1954-56; rsch. assoc. in math. Princeton U., 1956-59; sr. statistician, dept. mgr. IBM, N.Y.C., White Plains, 1956-64; sr. scientist statis. and elec. engring. Princeton U., 1968-69; prof. computer sci. and stats. U. Wis., 1964-71; prof. computer sci. George Mason U., 1985; dept. dir. World Bank, Washington, 1971-81, sr. advisor, 1981-85; Robert M. Critchfield prof. computer info. sci. Ohio State U., 1985—, dept. chair, 1985-94; chair sci. and tech. info. bd. NRC, NAS; bd. dirs. Advanced Info. Tech. Ctr., Columbus, Ohio. Contbr. numerous articles to profl. jours. Bd. trustees First Unitarian Ch., Bethesda, Md., 1975-79. Rsch. grantee AT&T, Columbus, Ohio, 1987. Fellow Am. Statis. Assn.; mem. Internat. Statis. Inst. (steering com. Internat. Rsch. Ctr., 1987-89), Internat. Assn. for Statis. Computing (sci. sec. 1979-83, pres. 1977-79). Avocations: reading, jogging, walking. Home: 4171 Clairmont Rd Columbus OH 43220-4501 Office: Ohio State U Dept Computer Info Sci 2015 Neil Ave Columbus OH 43210-1210

MULLER, NICHOLAS GUTHRIE, lawyer, business executive; b. Porterville, Calif., Nov. 27, 1942; s. Francis J. and Jane Ellen (Guthrie) M.; m. Sally Anne Diggles, June 10, 1964; children: Thomas, Amy. A.B. in English, U. Notre Dame, 1964; J.D., U. Calif., Berkeley, 1967. Bar: Colo. 1968; Lic. real estate broker, Colo. Summer intern Solicitor's Office, Dept. Interior, Washington, 1966; assoc. Gorsuch, Kirgis, Campbell, Walker & Grover, Denver, 1967-69; legal counsel Gates Aviation Corp., Denver, 1970-71; corp. sec., gen. counsel Gates Learjet Corp., Denver, 1971-72; legal counsel Samsonite Corp., Denver, 1972-75, gen. counsel, 1975-85, v.p., 1978-85; gen. counsel Gates Corp. and Gates Rubber Co., 1985-87; mem. mgmt. com., gen. counsel Colo. Power Ptnrs., Denver, 1987—; exec. dir. Colo. Ind. Energy Assn., Denver. Formerly bd. dirs. Presbyn./St. Luke's Med. Ctr.; bd. dirs. Mt. Med. Affiliates, Leadership Denver. Mem. ABA, Colo. Bar Assn. (bd. dirs., bd. govs.), Denver Bar Assn., Am. Corp. Counsel (dir. nat. assn. and Colo. chpt.), U.S. C. of C., Denver C. of C., Notre Dame Club of Denver, Rotary. Home: 25931 Village Cir Golden CO 80401-7228 Office: Colorado Power Ptnrs Ste 950 475 17th St Denver CO 80202

MULLER, PATRICIA ANN, nursing administrator, educator; b. N.Y.C., July 22, 1943; d. Joseph H. and Rosanne (Bautz) Felter; m. David G. Smith, Mar. 19, 1988; children: Frank M. Muller III, Kimberly M. Muller. BSN, Georgetown U., 1965; MA, U. Tulsa, 1978, EdD, 1983. RN. Staff devel. coord. St. Francis Hosp., Tulsa, 1978-79, asst. dir. for nursing svc., nursing edn., 1979-82, dir. dept. edn., 1982—; presenter various confs. and convs., 1978—. Contbr. articles to profl. jours. Mem. Leadership Tulsa, 1991. Mem. ANA, Nat. League for Nursing, Am. Soc. for Nursing Svc. Adminstrs., Am. Soc. for Health Manpower Edn. and Tng., Okla. Nurses Assn., Okla. Orgn. of Nurse Execs. (pres. 1992-93), Sigma Theta Tau. Office: St Francis Hosp 6161 S Yale Ave Tulsa OK 74136-1902

MULLER, PETER, lawyer, entertainment company executive, retail company executive, consultant; b. Teplitz-Sanov, Czechoslovakia, Mar. 4, 1947; came to U.S., 1949; s. Alexander and Elizabeth Rudolpha (Weingarten) M.; m. Irene Smolarski, Nov. 18, 1971 (div. 1973); children: Chloe, Aurora; m. Esther Unterman Meisler, Jan. 4, 1987 (div. 1995). BA, NYU, 1968, JD cum laude. Entertainment editor Ambience mag., N.Y.C., 1978-79, Women's Life mag., N.Y.C., 1980-81; sole practice N.Y.C., 1984—; chief exec. officer Producers Releasing Corp., N.Y. and Nev., 1987-88, pres. entertainment div., 1987-88; pres., founder Muller Entertainment Group, N.Y.C. and Calif., 1988—; pres., chief oper. officer ACA Joe, Inc., San Francisco and N.Y.C.; also bd. dirs. ACA Joe Inc., San Francisco and N.Y.C.; expert tech. adv. svc. for attys., Pa., 1987—; lectr. entertainment and comm. bus. to various orgns.; adj. prof. NYU. Author: Show Business Law, 1991, The Music Business: A Legal Perspective, 1994. Mem. Vol. Lawyers for the Arts, N.Y.C., 1987—. Mem. ABA (forum on entertainment and sports industries, forum on copyright, trademark and patent law), N.Y. State Bar Assn., NYU Alumni Assn. (bd. dirs. 1987—, v.p. bd. dirs., coun.), NYU Alumni Coun., Assn. of Am. Mgmt. Assn. (pres.). Avocations: sports, swimming, car enthusiast, writing, travel.

MULLER, RALPH W., hospital administrator; b. 1945. With FCC, Washington, 1967, Harvard U., Boston, 1967-68, 69-70, Orgn. Social and Tech. Info., Cambridge, Mass., 1969-70, Suffolk U., Boston, 1969-72, Commonwealth of Mass., Boston, 1972-74, U. Chgo., 1974-80; pres. U. Chgo. Hosp., 1980—. Office: U Chicago Hosps 5841 S Maryland Ave Chicago IL 60637-1463*

MULLER, RICHARD AUGUST, physicist, author; b. N.Y.C., Jan. 6, 1944; s. August Joseph and Catherine (Harabin) M.; m. Rosemary Findley, Sept. 3, 1966; children: Betsy, Melinda. AB, Columbia U., N.Y.C., 1964; PhD, U. Calif., Berkeley, 1969; LHD, Am. U. Switzerland, Leysin, 1989. Rsch. physicist U. Calif., Berkeley, 1969-78, assoc. prof. physics, 1978-80, prof. physics, sr. faculty scientist, 1980—; Jason cons. U.S. Dept. Def., Washington, 1974—; mem. arms control com. U.S. Nat. Acad. Scis., Washington, 1984-87; mem. adv. bd. Inst. Theoretical Physics, Santa Barbara, Calif., 1982-86; fellow Com. for Sci. Investigation Claims of Paranormal. Author: Nemesis, 1988, The Three Big Bangs, 1996. Recipient Founder's prize Tex. Instruments Found., 1977, Alan T. Waterman award NSF, 1978; MacArthur Found. fellow, 1982. Fellow AAAS, Am. Phys. Soc.; mem. Am. Geophys. Union, Fedn. Am. Scientists (trustee), Bohemian Club. Avocations: skiing, backpacking. Home: 2831 Garber St Berkeley CA 94705-1314 Office: Lawrence Berkeley Lab 50-232 Lbl Berkeley CA 94720 *Learning is the second greatest joy in life.*

MULLER, RICHARD STEPHEN, electrical engineer, educator; b. Weehawken, N.J., May 5, 1933; s. Irving Ernest and Marie Victoria Muller; m. Joyce E. Regal, June 29, 1957; children: Paul Stephen, Thomas Richard. ME, Stevens Inst. Tech., Hoboken, N.J., 1955; MSEE, Calif. Inst. Tech., 1957, PhD in Elect. Engring. and Physics, 1962. Engr.-in-tng., 1955. Test engr. Wright Aero/Curtiss Wright, Woodridge, N.J., 1953-54; mem. tech. staff Hughes Aircraft Co., Culver City, Calif., 1955-61; instr. U. So. Calif., L.A., 1960-61; asst. prof., then assoc. prof. U. Calif., Berkeley, 1962-72, prof., 1973—; guest prof. Swiss Fed. Inst. Tech., 1993; dir. Berkeley Sensor and Actuator Ctr., 1985—. Co-author: Device Electronics for Integrated Circuits, 1977, 2d rev. edit., 1986, Microsensors, 1990; contbr. more than 200 articles to profl. jours. Pres. Kensington (Calif.) Mcpl. Adv. Coun. Fellow Hughes Aircraft Co., 1955-57, NSF, 1959-62, NATO postdoctoral fellow, 1968-69, Fulbright fellow, 1982-83, Alexander von Humboldt prize, 1993, Tech. U. Berlin, 1994; Berkeley citation, 1994, Stevens Renaissance award, 1995. Fellow IEEE; mem. IEEE Press Bd., NAE, Nat. Materials (adv. bd. 1994—), Electron Devices Soc. (adv. com. 1984—), Internat. Sensor and Actuator Meeting (chmn. steering com.). Achievements include 18 U.S. and foreign patents; construction of first operating micromotor. Office: U Calif Dept EECS 401 Cory Hall Berkeley CA 94720-1770

MÜLLER, ROBBY, cinematographer; b. The Netherlands, Apr. 4, 1940. Cinematographer: (films) Summer in the City, 1970, The Goalie's Anxiety at the Penalty Kick, 1972, The Scarlet Letter, 1973, Alice in the Cities, 1974, The Wrong Move, 1975, Kings of the Road, 1976, The American Friend, 1977, Mysteries, 1979, Saint Jack, 1979, They All Laughed, 1981, The Glass Cell, 1981, Paris, Texas, 1984, Repo Man, 1984, Body Rock, 1984, Class Enemy, 1984, To Live and Die in L.A., 1985, The Longshot, 1986, Down By Law, 1986, Barfly, 1987, The Believers, 1987, Il Piccolo Diavolo, 1988, Mystery Train, 1989, Until the End of the World, 1991, Korczak, 1991, Mad Dog and Glory, 1993, (TV movies) Finnegan Begin Again, 1985. Office: Smith Gosnell Nicholson & Assocs PO Box 1166 1515 Palisades Dr Pacific Palisades CA 90272

MULLER, ROBERT JOSEPH, gynecologist; b. New Orleans, Dec. 5, 1946; s. Robert Harry and Camille (Eckert) M.; m. Susan Philipsen, Aug. 22, 1974; children: Ryan, Matt. BS, St. Louis U., 1968; BS, MSc, Emory U., 1976; MD, La. State U., New Orleans, 1981. Intern Charity Hosp., New Orleans, 1981-82; resident La. State U. Affiliate Hosp., 1982-85; resident staff physician La. State U. Med. Ctr., New Orleans, 1981-85; pvt. practice Camellia Women's Ctr., Slidell, La., 1985—; staff physician Tulane Med. Ctr., New Orleans, 1986—; med. dir. Northshore Regional Med. Ctr., Slidell, 1987—, New Orleans Police Dept., 1981-95, S.W. La. Search and Rescue, Covington, La., 1986—, St. Tammany Parish Sheriff Dept., Covington, 1989—, commdr., 1990—, Camellia City Classic, Slidell, 1989—, Crawfishman Triathalon, Mandeville, La., 1988—, Res-Q-Med Laser Team, 1984—. Contbr. articles to profl. jours. Recipient Commendation Medal New Orleans Police Dept., 1986, 87, 89, Medal Valor St. Tammany Parish Sheriff Office, Covington, 1990, Cert. Valor S.E. La. Search and Rescue, Mandeville, 1990; named one of Outstanding Young Men of Am., 1984. Mem. Am. Coll. Ob-Gyn., La. State Med. Soc., Profl. Assn. Diving Instrs. (divemaster 1991, asst. instr. 1995), So. Offshore Racing Assn. (med. dir. 1982—), Offshore Profl. Racing Tour (med. dir. staff 1990—), Am. Power Boat Assn. (med. staff 1984-89). Roman Catholic. Avocations: scuba diving, boating, shooting. Home: 128 Golden Pheasant Dr Slidell LA 70461-3007 Office: Camellia Womens Ctr 105 Smart Pl Slidell LA 70458-2039

MULLER, SCOTT WILLIAM, lawyer; b. Stamford, Conn., Feb. 15, 1950; s. Robert Sielke and Patricia (Harris) M.; m. Caroline Severance Adams, June 24, 1972; children: Christopher Adams, Robin McPherson, Peter Severance. BA, Princeton U., 1971; JD, Georgetown U., 1975. Bar: N.Y. 1976, U.S. Dist. Ct. (so. dist.) N.Y. 1977, U.S. Ct. Appeals (2d. cir.) 1978, U.S. Supreme Ct. 1978, U.S. Tax Ct. 1984, D.C. 1986. Law clk. to presiding justice U.S. Ct. Appeals (3d cir.), Phila., 1975-76; assoc. Davis, Polk & Wardwell, Washington, 1976-78, 82-84, ptnr., 1985—; asst. atty. criminal div. U.S. Atty.'s Office, N.Y.C., 1978-82. Served with NG, 1971-72. Mem. ABA, N.Y. State Bar Assn., Fed. Bar Assn., Assn. of Bar of City of N.Y. Republican. Episcopalian. Office: Davis Polk & Wardwell 1300 I St NW Washington DC 20005-3314*

MULLER, SIGFRID AUGUSTINE, dermatologist, educator; b. Panama City, Panama, Feb. 20, 1930; came to U.S., 1932, naturalized, 1967; s. Louis and Marciana (Espino) M.; m. Jane Barbara Zierden, Dec. 28, 1964; children—Sigfrid Augustine, Stephen, Scott, Maria. A.B., Pepperdine U., 1949; M.D., St. Louis U., 1953; M.S., Mayo Grad. Sch. Medicine, 1958. Intern Gorgas Hosp., C.Z., 1953-54; resident Indpls. Hosp., 1954-55, Mayo Grad. Sch. Medicine, 1955-58; practice medicine specializing dermatology Rochester, Minn., 1961—; cons. dermatology Mayo Clinic, 1961—; asst. prof. dermatology U. Panama, 1958-60; prof. dermatology Mayo Clinic, 1972-95, Robert H. Kieckhefer prof. dermatology, 1983-95, chmn. dept., 1983-94, dir. dermatology residency tng., 1983-94, dir. dermatopathology lab., 1983-94; prof. emeritus dermatology Mayo Med. Sch., 1995; chief dermatology, prof. med. U. Nev. Sch. Med., 1995—; dir. task force for genetics Nat. Program for Genetics, 1969; bd. dirs., treas. Found. for Internat. Dermatol. Edn., 1976-85, pres., 1985—. Contbr. articles to profl. jours. Asst. chief editor: Archives of Dermatology, 1974—, Medicins Cutanea, 1968—, Internat. Bull. Psoriasis, 1973—. Recipient Pres.'s award Pepperdine U., 1973, condecoracion Order of Vasco Nunez de Balboa, Panama, 1994. Fellow ACP; mem. AAAS, AMA, Am. Dermatol. Assn., Am. Acad. Dermatology, Soc. Investigative Dermatology, Am. Soc. Dermatopathology, Am. Fedn. Clin. Rsch., Minn. Dermatol. Soc. (pres. 1972-73), Soc. Dermatol. Genetics (pres. 1972-73), Noah Worcester Dermatol. Soc. (pres. 1972-73), Internat. Soc. Dermatology (v.p., sec.-gen. 1979-89, pres. 1989-94, hon. pres. 1994—), Found. for Internat. Dermatol. Edn. (sec./treas. 1975-84, pres. 1985—). Office: Ste E 630 South Rancho Dr Las Vegas NV 89106 *I have never felt like a foreigner in this wonderful land of opportunity. Rather, I perceived at an early age that achievement is within almost everyone's abilities. Ultimately, my success will not be determined by honors or recognition but by love: love of God, love of family, and love of my fellow man.*

MULLER, WILLARD C(HESTER), writer; b. Havre, Mont., May 7, 1916; s. Chester Rudolph and Clara (Hansen) M.; m. Carolyn Elfrid Bue, Jan. 27, 1945; children: Marolyn Jean, Barbara Anne, Nancy Eleanor. BA, Stanford U., 1941; MPA, Maxwell Grad. Sch. Govt. Adminstrn., 1943; student, Nat. War Coll., 1961-62. Newspaper reporter, short story writer Bremerton (Wash.) Daily Searchlight, 1934-36; White House corr. Bremerton Daily Searchlight and Port Angeles Evening News, Washington, 1941; mgmt. analyst USDA, 1942, 46-47; mem. staff for food, agr. and forestry U.S. Dept. Army and U.S. High Commr. for Germany, Munich and Frankfurt, Fed. Republic Germany, 1948-50; dist. adminstr., Am. consul U.S. Trust Territory of Pacific Islands, Truk, Caroline Islands, 1951-55; dep. dir. ICA, U.S. Ops. Mission to Nepal, Kathmandu, 1956-58; dir. U.S. Ops. to Somali Republic, 1958-61, Office East and Southern African Affairs, AID, Dept. State, Washington, 1962-65, AID, Kampala, Uganda, 1965-70; assoc. dir. for land reform AID, Saigon, Republic of Vietnam, 1970-73; ret. AID, 1973, cons., 1974-81; free lance writer, 1973—. Author various short stories; contbr. artciles to profl. jours. Chmn. steering com. 4-state program dialogue on peace Pacific NW dist. Am. Luth. Ch., Seattle, 1983-85; mem. Clallam br. Wash. State Centennial Commn., 1986-89; mem. Food Bank Bd., Port Angeles, Wash., 1986-90. Lt. USNR, 1943-45, PTO. Mem. Am. Soc. Pub. Adminstrn., Am. Forestry Assn., Am. Fgn. Service Assn., Pacific N.W. Morgan Horse Assn. Lodge: Kiwanis. Avocations: horseback riding, backpacking, world travel. Home: 3624 S Mount Angeles Rd Port Angeles WA 98362-8910 Office: 3624 S Mount Angeles Rd Port Angeles WA 98362-8910

MULLER, WILLIAM HENRY, JR., surgeon, educator; b. Dillon, S.C., Aug. 19, 1919; s. William Henry and Octavia Elizabeth (Bethea) M.; m. Hildwin Clare Headly, Mar. 23, 1946; children: William Henry III, Marietta John Lewis. BS, The Citadel, 1940, DS (hon.), 1972; MD, Duke U., 1943; DHL (hon.), Med. U. S.C., 1977. Diplomate Am. Bd. Thoracic Surgery, Am. Bd. Surgery (rep. conf. com. grad. tng. in surgery). Intern Johns Hopkins Hosp., Balt., 1944, asst. surgery, asst. resident, 1944-46, resident gen. surgery, instr. surgery, 1948-49, resident cardiovascular surgery, 1949; practice gen. surgery Dillon, 1947-48; asst. prof. surgery UCLA, 1949-53, assoc. prof. Sch. Medicine, 1953-54; attending specialist thoracic surgery Wadsworth VA Hosp., Los Angeles; chief sect. cardiovascular surgery Los Angeles County-Harbor Gen. Hosp., Torrance, Calif.; cons. surgery St. Johns's, Santa Monica Hosps., 1949-54; cons. cardiovascular surgery U.S. Naval Hosp., San Diego, 1953-54; Stephen H. Watts prof. surgery, chmn. dept. U. Va. Sch. Medicine, 1954-82, v.p. health affairs, 1976-88, univ. prof. surgery and health policy, 1988-90, S. Hurt Watts prof. surgery emeritus, 1990—, v.p. for health affairs emeritus; surgeon-in-chief U. Va. Hosp., 1954-82; chmn. S.E. Surg. Congress; mem. Pres.'s Panel on Heart Disease, 1972; past chmn. surgery study sect. NIH; mem. exec. com., div. med. scis. NRC. Mem. editorial bd.: Am. Jour Surgery, Annals of Surgery, Am. Surgeon; contbr. articles to med jours. Trustee, mem. exec. com. Duke U. Served as capt. M.C. AUS, 1946-47. Named One of 10 Outstanding Young Men of Yr. U.S. Jr. C. of C., Calif. Jr. C. of C., 1952; recipient Disting. Alumni award (1st award) Duke U. Med. Ctr., 1969; Thomas Jefferson award U. Va., 1982; McCallie Sch. Alumni Achievement award, 1986; Paul Harris fellow Nat. Rotary Found., 1988. Fellow ACS (past chmn., forum com. fundamental surg. problems, regent 1971—, chmn. bd. regents 1976-78, pres.-elect 1979); mem. Internat. Soc. Surgery, Internat. Cardiovascular Soc. (past v.p.), AMA, Am. Surg. Assn. (pres. 1974-75), So. Surg. Assn. (pres. 1975), Pacific Coast Surg. Assn., Am. Assn. Thoracic Surgery, Soc. Univ. Surgeons (past pres.), Soc. Surgery Alimentary Tract, Assn. Acad. Surgeons, James IV Assn. Surgeons (v.p. U.S.), Med. Soc. Va., Albemarle County Med. Soc., Soc. Vascular Surgery (past pres.), Am. Heart Assn. (chmn. surgery research study com., mem. central research com.), Va. Surg. Soc, Halsted Soc., Johns Hopkins Soc. Scholars, Raven Soc., Sigma Xi, Alpha Omega Alpha, Phi Chi. Office: U Va Health Sci Ctr PO Box 470 Charlottesville VA 22902-0470

MÜLLER-EBERHARD, HANS JOACHIM, medical research scientist, administrator; b. Magdeburg, Germany, May 5, 1927; came to U.S., 1959, naturalized, 1973; s. G. Adolf and Emma (Jenrich) Müller-E.; m. Irma Gigli, June 29, 1985. M.D., U. Göttingen, Fed. Republic Germany, 1953; M.D.Sc., U. Uppsala, Sweden, 1961; D. Medicinae h.c., Ruhr U., Bochum, W.Ger., 1982. Asst. physician dept. medicine U. Göttingen, 1953-54; asst., also asst. physician hosp. Rockefeller Inst., 1954-57; fellow Swedish Med. Research Council, 1957-59; asst. prof., then assoc. prof., also hosp. physician Rockefeller U., 1959-63; mem. dept. exptl. pathology Scripps Clinic and Research Found., La Jolla, Calif., 1963-74, chmn. dept. molecular immunology, 1974-82, chmn. dept. immunology, 1982-85, head div. molecular immunology, 1985-87; assoc. dir. Scripps Clinic and Research Found. (Research Inst.), 1978-86; dir. Bernhard Nocht Inst. for Tropical Medicine, Hamburg, Fed. Republic Germany, 1988-95; Cecil H. and Ida M. Green investigator med. rsch., 1972-86; lectr. immunochemistry U. Uppsala, 1961—; Harvey lectr., 1970; adj. prof. pathology U. Calif. Med. Sch., La Jolla, 1968-94; prof. U. Hamburg, 1990—; prof. internal medicine, prof. molecular medicine, dir. inst. molecular medicine for the prevention of human diseases U. Tex. Med. Sch., Houston, 1995—. Co-editor: Textbook of Immunopathology, 1976, Springer Seminars in Immunopathology, 1978-87; author numerous sci. articles; adv. editor: Jour. Exptl. Medicine, 1963—; mem. jour. editorial bds. Recipient Squibb award Infectious Diseases Soc. Am., 1970; T. Duckett Jones Meml. award Helen Hay Whitney Found., 1971; Distinguished Achievement award Modern Medicine mag., 1974; Karl Landsteiner Meml. award Am. Assn. Blood Banks, 1974; ann. Internat. award Gairdner Found., Can., 1974; Mayo H. Soley award Western Soc. Clin. Research, 1975; Emil von Behring prize Philipps U., Marburg, Ger., 1977; Caballero de la Orden de San Carlos (Colombia), 1984, Robert Koch Medal in Gold, 1987, Rous-Whipple award Am. Assn. Pathologists, 1988, Philip Levine award Am. Soc. of Clin. Pathologists, 1988. Fellow AAAS; mem. NAS, Am. Soc. Exptl. Pathology (Parke, Davis award 1966), Assn. Am. Physicians, Western Assn. Physicians, Am. Soc. Clin. Investigation, Am. Assn. Immunologists, Am. Acad. Allergy, Am. Soc. Biochemistry and Molecular Biology, German Soc. Immunology (hon.), Sigma Xi. Office: Inst Molecular Medicine 2121 W Holcombe Blvd Houston TX 77030

MULLIGAN, ELINOR PATTERSON, lawyer; b. Bay City, Mich., Apr. 20, 1929; d. Frank Clark and Agnes (Murphy) P.; m. John C. O'Connor, Oct. 28, 1950; children: Christine Fulena, Valerie Clark, Amy O'Connor, Christopher Criffan O'Connor; m. William G. Mulligan, Dec. 6, 1975. BA, U. Mich. 1950; JD, Seton Hall U., 1970. Bar: N.J., 1970. Assoc. Springfield and Newark, 1970-72; pvt. practice, Hackettstown, N.J., 1972; ptnr. Mulligan & Jacobson, N.Y.C., 1973-91, Mulligan & Mulligan, Hackettstown, 1976—; atty. Hackettstown Planning Bd., 1973-86, Blairstown Bd. Adjustment, 1973-95; sec. Warren County Ethics Com., 1976-78, sec. Dist. X and XIII Fee Arbitration Com., 1979-87, mem. and chair., 1987-91, mem. dist. ethics com. XIII, 1992—; mem. spl. com. on atty. disciplinary structure N.J. Supreme Ct., 1981—. lectr. Nat. Assn. Women Judges, 1979. Contbr. articles to profl. jours. Named Vol. of Yr. Attys. Vols. in Parole Program, 1978. Fellow Am. Acad. Matrimonial Lawyers (pres. N.J. chpt. 1995—); mem. ABA, Warren County Bar Assn. (pres. 1987-88), N.J. State Bar Assn., N.J. Women Lawyers Assn. (v.p. 1985—), Am. Mensa Soc., Kappa Alpha Theta, Union League Club (N.Y.C.), Baltusrol Golf Club (Springfield, N.J.)., Panther Valley Golf and Country Club (Allamuchy, N.J.). Republican. Home: 12 Goldfinch Way Hackettstown NJ 07840-3007 Office: 480 Hwy 517 PO Box 211 Hackettstown NJ 07840-0211

MULLIGAN, ERLINDA RITA, medical, surgical nurse; b. Gallup, N.Mex., June 11, 1954; d. Reginaldo Fred and Maggie (Apodaca) Gallegos; m. Michael Joseph Mulligan,; children: Raymond Fredrick, Margaret Rose, Erin Pablo, Kimberly Edel. ADN, U. N.Mex., Gallup, 1988. RN, N.Mex.; cert. med.-surg. nurse Am. Nurses Credentialing Ctr. Nurse Rehoboth McKinley Christian Hosp., Gallup, 1988-89, nurse I, 1989-90, nurse II, rep. med.-surg. and pediat. units, 1990-91, nurse III, 1991-92, nurse IV, 1992-95, surg./med. specialist, 1994-95. Active St. Francis Ch., Gallpu, 1954—, mem. choir, 1991-94; active St. Francis Sch. PTO, Gallup, 1982-92; mem. Right to Life Com. of N.Mex., 1992-94, sec. Gallup chpt., 1993-94. Roman Catholic. Avocations: reading, exercising, sewing, gardening, parenting. Home: 205 E Logan Ave Gallup NM 87301-6133

MULLIGAN, HUGH AUGUSTINE, journalist; b. N.Y.C., Mar. 23, 1925; s. John Joseph and Jeanette (Wilton) M.; m. Brigid Mary Murphy, Jan. 14, 1948. B.A. summa cum laude, Marlboro Coll., 1948, L.H.D. (hon.), 1973; M.A. in English Lit, Harvard U., 1951; M.S. in Journalism, Boston U., 1951. With AP, 1952—; feature writer AP, N.Y.C., 1956-65; fgn. corr. AP, Vietnam, 1965-68; fgn. corr. Biafra, Middle East, Paris Peace Talks, 1968-69, Cambodia, Laos, 1971, No. Ireland, Nigeria, Mid. East, China, Russia, Persian Gulf, Iceland, 1971-75, The Sahel, Angola, Ulster, Svalbard, Iran, 1975-77; as fgn. corr. covered wars in Vietnam, Middle East, Oman, Biafra-Nigeria, Cambodia, Upper Volta-Mali, No. Ireland, Vietnam, Middle East, Biafra-Nigeria, Oman, Upper Volta-Mali, No. Irel; as spl corr. covered papal journeys (Pope John Paul II) Mex., Poland, Ireland, U.S., Africa, Cen. Am., Brit. Isles, Can., 1979-87; columnist Mulligan's Stew, 1977-86. Author: The Torch is Passed, 1963, No Place to Die, The Agony of Vietnam, 1967, (with Sid Moody, John Barbour) Lightning Out of Israel, 1967, anthologies How I Got That Story, 1967, Reporting, Writing from Front Row Seats, 1971, Best Sports Stories, 1980, 82, The Family Book of Humor, The Best of Irish Wit an Wisdom, 1987, The Annotated Night Before Christmas, 1991, (with Sid Moody) The 50th Anniversary: Pearl Harbor, 1991; editor: anthologies The World in 1964, 1965; now A.P. sr. feature writer and roving reporter. Served with U.S. Army, 1944-46. Recipient Gold medal Am. Newspaper Pubs. Assn., 1951, award for feature writing Nat. Headliners, 1963, award for fgn. coverage, 1967, award for internat. reporting Overseas Press Club, 1967, award for fgn. corr. Sigma Delta Chi, 1970, Mng. Editor's award for top reportial performance AP, 1972, 78, Disting. Alumni award Boston U. Sch. Pub. Communication, 1983, Yankee Quill award Acad. New Eng. Journalists, 1993; Eugene Pulliam lectureship Ball State U., 1985. Mem. Overseas Press Club, Silurians Club. Roman Catholic. Home: 50 Crest Rd Ridgefield CT 06877-2115 Office: 50 Rockefeller Plz New York NY 10020-1605 *"Life is* *too short to read good books—read the best." This advice from a high school English teacher has given a golden glow to my leisure hours that TV's dreadful dross can never outsparkle.*

MULLIGAN, JAMES FRANCIS, retired business executive, lawyer; b. Attleboro, Mass., Aug. 27, 1925; s. Henry D. and Eleanor R. (Carey) M.; m. Mary Alice Mangels, Aug. 28, 1948; 1 child, Christopher. AB, Tufts U., 1947; JD, Columbia U., 1950. Bar: N.Y. 1950, Pa. 1968, U.S. Supreme Ct. 1986. Gen. atty. Erie-Lackawanna R.R., Cleve. and N.Y.C., 1950-61; gen. counsel Monroe Internat. div. Litton Industries, Orange, N.J., 1961-67; v.p., sec., gen. counsel Lukens Steel Co., Coatesville, Pa., 1967-83; v.p. law and corp. affairs, sec. Lukens, Inc., Coatesville, Pa., 1983-88; ret. Lukens, Inc., Coatesville, 1988. Pres. United Way Chester County, West Chester, Pa., 1980-81. Lt. (j.g.) USNR, 1943-46. Mem. Radley Run Country Club, Springhaven Country Club, Mariner Sands Country Club. Avocations: running, golf. Home: PO Box 213 Pocopson PA 19366-0213 Home (winter): 5623 SE Foxcross Pl Stuart FL 34997-8044

MULLIGAN, JAMES KENNETH, government official; b. Pawtucket, R.I., Aug. 31, 1911; s. James Alexander and Margaret (Fitzsimmons) M.; m. Louise Wring Lane, June 3, 1932; children—Kathryn Lane, Martha Louise, Jean Margaret. Ph.B., U. Chgo., 1934, M.A., 1937. Personnel adminstr. Chgo. Park Dist., 1938-40; dir. youth personnel Chgo. Nat. Youth Adminstrn., 1941-42; manpower analyst HEW, 1942-43; chief wage classification New Eng., Atlantic and Mediterranean area Dept. Navy, Boston, 1946-56; with U.S. CSC, Washington, 1956-71; exec. vice chmn. inter-agy. adv. group U.S. CSC, 1957-58; dir. Bur. Tng., 1959-71; cons. AID, State Dept., Nat. Civil Service League, WHO, 1971-79, Fed. Energy Adminstrn., UN, 1974-76; chmn. task force Presdl. Commn. on Exec., Legis. and Jud. Salaries, July-Dec. 1976; adj. instr. Boston U., 1955, Dept. Agr. Grad. Sch., 1958. Chmn. Personnel Bd. Wakefield, Mass., 1954-56; mem. adv. bd. Washington Tech. Inst., 1969-70, George Washington U., 1970—; mem. governing bd. Washington Interns in Edn., 1966-68. Served to lt. USNR, 1944-46. Recipient Commr.'s award CSC, 1968, founder's award Federal Exec. Inst., 1993. Address: 4615 Hunt Ave Chevy Chase MD 20815-5424

MULLIGAN, JOSEPH FRANCIS, physics educator; b. N.Y.C., Dec. 12, 1920; s. Joseph Lawrence and Mary (Collins) M.; m. Eleanor L. Wells 1984. Student, Fordham Coll., 1938-39, 41-43; A.B., Boston Coll., 1945, M.A., 1946; Ph.D. in Physics, Cath. U. Am., 1951. Instr. physics St. Peter's Coll., Jersey City, 1946-47; faculty Fordham U., 1955-68, assoc. prof. physics, 1963-68, chmn. dept., 1956-64, dean Grad. Sch. Arts and Scis., dean liberal arts faculty, 1964-67; prof. physics U. Md., Baltimore County, 1968-89, prof. emeritus, 1989—, dean for grad. studies and rsch., 1968-82; Mem. adv. com. grad. fellowship program NDEA, 1960-63. Author: Practical Physics: The Production and Conservation of Energy, 1980, Introductory College Physics, 2d edit., 1990, translated into 3-vol. Italian edit., Fisica, 1993; editor: Heinrich Rudolf Hertz (1857-1894); A Collection of Articles and Addresses, 1994; contbr. articles to profl. jours. NSF fellow U. Calif. at La Jolla, 1961-62. Mem. Am. Phys. Soc., Am. Assn. Physics Tchrs., History of Sci. Soc., AAAS, Sigma Xi. Home: 228 Canal Park Dr Salisbury MD 21804-7249 Office: U Md 5401 Wilkens Ave Baltimore MD 21228-5329

MULLIGAN, LOUISE ELEANORE, English literature educator; b. Carson, N.D., July 2, 1910; d. Thomas Edwin and Bessie Pearl (Gutcher) Griffith; m. Patrick Joseph Mulligan, Nov. 18, 1930; children: Sheila, Patrick, James, Elizabeth, Mary. BA, Bridgewater State U., 1962; MA, Boston Coll., 1968; PhD, U. Mass., 1975. Tchr. Braintree (Mass.) High Sch., 1962-67; prof. North Adams (Mass.) State Coll., 1967-80; adj. prof. Sacred Heart U., Bridgeport, Conn., 1981-82, Fla. So. Coll., Arcadia, Fla., 1990-93, Adult & Community Edn., Port Charlotte, Fla., 1993—; pres. Mass. League Sch. Publs., 1927-28, Mass. Speech League, 1966-67; bd. dirs. New England Assn. Tchrs. English, 1970-71. Author: America Sings, 1961. Recipient Citizenship award Charlotte Local Edn. Found., 1993. Mem. AAUW (program chair 1990-92, edn. chair 1989-90, pub. policy chair 1992-93), Univ. Club Charlotte County (pres. 1990-91, program chair 1993). Democrat. Roman Catholic. Avocations: golf, bridge, travel. Home: 953 Long Pond Rd Plymouth MA 02360-2635 Office: Fla So Coll 8789 SW County Road 761 Arcadia FL 33821-7038

MULLIGAN, MARTIN FREDERICK, clothing executive, professional tennis player; b. Sydney, Australia, Oct. 18, 1940; s. Frederick William and Marie Louise (Tome) M.; m. Rossella Rita Labella, Sept. 19, 1969 (div. Mar. 1980); children: Monica, Martin Thomas. Winner Tennis Singles Championships of Australia, 1952, 53, 55, 56, 57, 58; mem. Davis Cup team Australia, 1959, 60; winner Australian Hard Court Singles and Doubles tournaments, 1960, 64; finalist Wimbledon Singles tournaments, 1962; winner Italian Open Singles tournaments, 1963, 65, 67, German Open Singles tournament, 1963; winner singles and doubles titles Monte Carlo Championships, 1964; coach Italian Davis Cup team, 1966-76; winner, Davis Cup tournament, 1976; winner Spanish Open tournament, 1966, 67, Swedish Open tournament, 1966, 67, Austrian Open tournament, 1966, 67, Champion Cup tournament, 1966, 67; promotional cons. Alpina Australian Mfg. Co., 1973-74; cons. and internat. promotion mgr. Diadora Co., 1973-78; internat. promotion mgr. FILA U.S.A. Inc. subs. FILA-Italy Sportswear, Hunt Valley, Md., 1979-90, v.p. internat. promotion and pub. rels., 1979—; co-promotor, tournament dir. Italian Open Tennis Championships, 1972, 73; negotiator contracts between FILA and various sports profls. and celebrities. Ranked Number 3 in World in Tennis, 1967, ranked 5 times in world's top 10 tennis players. Avocation: stamp collecting. Office: FILA USA Inc 11350 Mccormick Rd Hunt Valley MD 21031-1016

MULLIGAN, MICHAEL DENNIS, lawyer; b. St. Louis, Mar. 9, 1947; s. Leo Virgil and Elizabeth (Leyse) M.; m. Theresa Baker, Aug. 7, 1971; children—Brennan, Colin. B.A. in Biology, Amherst Coll., 1968; J.D., Columbia U., 1971. Bar: Mo. 1971, U.S. Dist. Ct. (ea. dist.) Mo. 1972, U.S. Ct. Appeals (8th cir.) 1982, U.S. Tax Ct. 1985. Law clk. to judge U.S. Dist. Ct. (ea. dist.) Mo., 1971-72; assoc. Lewis & Rice, St. Louis, 1972-80, ptnr., 1980—. Served as cpl. USMC, 1968-70. Fellow Am. Coll. Probate Counsel; mem. ABA (mem. real property, probate and trust, and taxation sects.), Mo. Bar Assn. (mem. probate and trust, taxation sects.). Contbr. numerous articles to profl. jours. Mem. editorial bd. Estate Planning Mag., 1985—. Office: Lewis Rice & Fingersh 500 N Broadway Ste 2000 Saint Louis MO 63102-2130

MULLIGAN, RICHARD M., actor, writer; b. Bronx, N.Y., Nov. 13, 1932; s. Robert Edward and Ann-Elizabeth (Gingell) M.; m. Lenore Mulligan, June 25, 1978 (div.); 1 son, James. Regular on TV series The Hero, 1966-67, Diana, 1973-74, Soap, 1977-80 (Emmy award 1980), Reggie, 1983, Empty Nest, NBC, 1988-95 (Emmy award 1989); numerous other TV appearances include Kate McShane, Charlie's Angels, Medical Story, Dog & Cat, Doctor's Hospital, Knowledge, Little House on the Prairie, Love Boat, Switch, Kingston, Mike Douglas Show, Merv Griffin Show, Dinah Shore Show, Hollywood Squares; TV movies include Jealousy, Malibu, Harvey, The Pueblo Incident, Having Babies III; films include One Potato, Two Potato, 1964, The Group, 1966, Little Big Man, 1970, A Change in the Wind, 1972, The Big Bus, 1976, S.O.B, 1981, Trail of the Pink Panther, 1982, Summertime, 1983, Mickey and Maude, 1984, Meatballs II, 1984, Teachers, 1984, The Heavenly Kid, 1985, A Fine Mess, 1986, Quicksilver, 1986, (voice) Oliver and Company, 1988; Broadway debut in All the Way Home, 1960; other Broadway plays include Special Occasions; other stage appearances include Mating Dance (Theatre World award), The Crucible, Luv, Other People, Pound on Demand, Nobody Loves an Albatross, Hogan's Goat (Theatre World award), Beyond the Horizon, Glass Menagerie, The Great God Brown; playwright: Never Too Late. Mem. Actors Equity Assn., AFTRA, Screen Actor's Guild. *Que sais-je? (Montaigne).*

MULLIGAN, ROBERT PATRICK, film director, producer; b. N.Y.C., Aug. 23, 1925; s. Robert Edward and Elizabeth (Gingell) M. Grad., Fordham U. Dir.: TV prodns. including Philco Playhouse, Suspense, Playhouse 90; film prodr./dir.: films The Jimmy Piersall Story, Come September, The Spiral Road, To Kill a Mockingbird, Love with the Proper Stranger, Inside Daisy Clover, Summer of '42, Bloodbrothers, Same Time Next Year, The Other, Kiss Me Goodbye, Nickel Ride, Stalking Moon, Baby the Rain Must Fall, Pursuit of Happiness, Up the Down Staircase, Clara's Heart, The Man in the Moon. Office: United Talent Agy 9560 Wilshire Blvd Fl 5 Beverly Hills CA 90212-2401

MULLIGAN, ROBERT WILLIAM, university official, clergyman; b. Chgo., Oct. 11, 1916; s. John Sexton and Esther Mary (Cordesman) M. A.B., Loyola U., 1937; M.A., U. Detroit, 1946; Ph.D., Louvain U., Belgium, 1953; LL.D., U. Cin., 1976. Ordained priest Roman Cath. Ch., 1949; chmn. dept. philosophy Loyola U., 1953-59, trustee, 1958-71, v.p., dean faculties, 1959-69; provost Xavier U., Cin., 1971-72; pres. Xavier U., 1972-82; sec. St. Louis U., 1982-89; acad. v.p. St. Joseph's U., Phila., 1989—; cons. Grolier Soc., 1959-65; mem. vis. faculty Oxford U., Eng., 1970-71. Mem. adv. com. Bd. Higher Edn., Luth. Ch. Mo. Synod, 1966-67; chmn. bd. Greater Cin. Consortium Colls. and Univs., 1973; bd. dirs. Cin. chpt. ARC, Campion Hall, Oxford U., 1976—. Decorated chevalier Legion of Honor France; recipient Blue Key award, 1959; key City Cin., 1972. Mem. Am. Ednl. Assn., Am. Philos. Assn., Am. Cath. Philos. Assn. (chmn. Midwest chpt. 1956), Ill. Philos. Assn., No. Ill. Philos. Assn., Metaphys. Soc., Phi Sigma Tau (nat. pres. 1962—). Home: Loyola U Jesuit Residence 6525 N Sheridan Rd Chicago IL 60626-5385

MULLIKIN, HARRY COPELAND, mathematics educator; b. Flintville, Tenn., July 10, 1940; s. Houston Yost and Daisy (Copeland) M.; m. Gary W. Parker. Student, U. Paris, France, 1960-61; B.A., U. of the South, Sewanee, Tenn., 1963; M.A., U. Wis., Madison, 1964, Ph.D., 1968. Asst. prof. math. Pomona Coll., Claremont, Calif., 1968-74, assoc. prof. math., 1974-82, prof. math., 1982—, chmn. dept. math., 1979-85, William Polk Russell prof. math., 1984—, acting assoc. dean of students, 1982. Bd. dirs. Calif. br. Humane Soc. U.S., Long Beach, 1974-78; bd. dirs. Golden State Humane Soc., Garden Grove, Calif., 1974-82, sec., 1978-82. Woodrow Wilson fellow, 1963-64; recipient Disting. Prof. award Pomona Coll., 1972, 76, 80, 90. Mem. Am. Math. Soc., Math. Soc. Am., Assn. Computing Machinery, So. Calif. Phi Beta Kappa Alumni Assn. (treas. 1990-94), Phi Beta Kappa (chpt. pres. 1973-74, sec.-treas. 1979-80, 82-83). Democrat. Episcopalian. Home: 4433 N Glen Way Claremont CA 91711-2122 Office: Dept Math Pomona Coll Claremont CA 91711

MULLIKIN, THOMAS WILSON, mathematics educator; b. Flintville, Tenn., Jan. 9, 1928; s. Houston Yost and Daisy (Copeland) M.; m. Mildred Virginia Sugg, June 14, 1952; children—Sarah Virginia, Thomas Wilson, James Copeland. Student, U. South, 1946-47; A.B., U. Tenn., 1950; postgrad., Iowa State U., 1952-53; A.M., Harvard, 1954, Ph.D., 1958. Mathematician Rand Corp., Santa Monica, Calif., 1957-64; prof. math. Purdue U., 1964-93, interim v.p., dean grad. sch., 1991-93, dean grad. sch., prof. math emeritus, 1993—. Served with USNR, 1950-52. Mem. Am. Math. Soc., Soc. for Indsl. and Applied Math., AAAS, Sigma Xi. Home: Cape Carteret 104 Club Ct Swansboro NC 28584-9736

MULLIKIN, VERNON EUGENE, aerospace executive; b. Windsor, Ill., July 16, 1935; s. Charles Austin and Oma Leah (Gilbreath) M.; m. Mary Lou Walker (div.); children: Michael, Mark; m. Joan Marie Boes, Aug. 1, 1986. BS in Aero. Engring., U. Ill., 1957; MBA, So. Ill. U., Edwardsville, 1977. Aero. engr. Northrup Aircraft Co., Hawthorne, Calif., 1957-60; group engr. Douglas Missile & Space Systems, Santa Monica, Calif., 1960-63; chief engr. McDonnell Douglas Astronautics Co., St. Louis, 1963-87; program dir. Convair div. Gen. Dynamics Corp., San Diego, 1987-92; sr. sci. engr. Hughes Missile Systems Co., Tucson, 1992—. Mem. AIAA (cert. recognition 1987), Phi Eta Sigma, Sigma Gamma Tau, Tau Beta Pi, Beta Gamma Sigma. Office: GM Hughes Missile Systems PO Box 11337 Mail Zone 847-B3 Tucson AZ 85734

MULLIN, CHRIS(TOPHER) PAUL, professional basketball player; b. N.Y.C., July 30, 1963. Student, St. John's U., 1981-85. Basketball player Golden State Warriors, 1985—; mem. U.S. Olympic Team (received Gold medal), 1984, 92. Recipient Wooden award, 1985; named to Sporting News All-Am. First Team, 1985, NBA All-Star team, 1989-93, NBA First Team, 1992.. Office: Golden State Warriors Oakland Coliseum Arena 7000 Coliseum Way Oakland CA 94621-1945*

MULLIN, GERARD EMMANUEL, physician, educator, researcher; b. Pequannock, N.J., Nov. 5, 1959; s. Gerard Vincent Jr. and Frances Rita (Magnanti) M. BS in Biology and Chemistry, William Patterson Coll., 1981; MD, U. Medicine and Dentistry N.J., 1985; MS in Nutrition, U. Bridgeport, 1994. Diplomate Am. Bd. Internal Medicine, Am. Bd. Gastroenterology, Am. Bd. Med. Examiners. Intern Mt. Sinai Hosp., N.Y.C., 1985-86, resident, 1986-88; fellow in gastroenterology Johns Hopkins Hosp., Balt., 1988-91; fellow NIH, Bethesda, Md., 1989-91; instr., scientist Cornell U. Med. Coll., N.Y., 1991-93, asst. prof., 1993—. Cotbr. articles to med. and sci. jours. Bd. dirs. Our Lady of Fatima Chapel. Grantee Nat. Found. Ileitis and Colitis, 1990, 92-94, North Shore U. Hosp., 1991. Fellow ACP; mem. AMA, Crohn's and Colitis Found. Am. (Young Investigator of Yr. 1991, 93, grantee 1991, 93), N.J. Med. Sch. Alumni Assn. (bd. dirs.), Fieri No. N.J. (bd. dirs.), Alpha Omega Alpha, Phi Beta Sigma. Roman Catholic. Achievements include discovery that suppressor cell function is elevated in AIDS, lymphomas are increased in inflamatory bowel disease, helicobacter pylori gastritis causes increased gastric acid secretion and hypergastrinemia, intestinal T cells are activated and make IL2 in Crohn's disease but not ulcerative colitis, Crohn's Disease mucoser has a T-helper-1 profile of lymphokline gene expression, inflamatory bowel disease intestine has increased oxygen free radical production and decreased antioxidant content, inflammatory bowel disease has increased levels of chemokines, interleukin-10 and interleukin-13 heliobacter pylori has increased nitric oxide synthase gene expression, increased Rantes RNA levels and increased production of tumor necrosis factor and interleukin-6. Also discovered that intestines of patients with colon cancer and adenomatolls polyps have increased iron content and elevated oxyten free radical production. Office: Cornell U Med Coll N Shore U Hosp 300 Cmty Dr Manhasset NY 11030

MULLIN, J(ACK) SHAN, lawyer; b. Bellingham, Wash., Mar. 9, 1934; s. Jack D. and Naomi (Smith) M.; m. Lora Jane Fraser, Aug. 9, 1957; children: Barbara, Stephen, John, Anne. BS in Bus., U. Wash., 1956, JD, 1958. Bar: Wash. 1958, U.S. Supreme Ct. 1963. Assoc. Perkins Coie, Seattle, 1958-66, ptnr., 1967—; speaker various nat. and internat. sems. Co-author Legal Compliance Manual chpts. on internat. transactions, rev. edit., 1994. Co-founder Leadership Tomorrow, Seattle, 1982-83, bd. chmn., 1991; pres. Mcpl. League Seattle-King County, Seattle, 1976-78; trustee Law Sch. Found. U. Wash., Seattle, 1983-86, 90—, The Seattle Found., 1983-92; bd. dirs., exec. com. United Way King County, 1978-90, chmn. bd. dirs. 1987-88; co-founder, vice chmn. Seattle Alliance for Edn., 1990—; bd. dirs. United for Wash., Seattle, 1985-94; pres., bd. mgrs. The Archibald Found., 1991—; mem. bd. dirs. ARC (King County chpt. 1994—), mem. bd. dirs. Fred Hutchinson Cancer Rsch. Ctr., 1994—; chmn. bd. dirs. United Way King County Endowment Fund, 1996—. Capt. USAR, 1958-65. Mem. ABA (internat. law and corp. banking and bus. law sects.), Wash. State Bar Assn. (chmn. young lawyers sect. 1963-64, internat. law, corp. banking and bus. law, tax, and intellectual and indsl. property sects.), Seattle-King County Bar Assn. (internat. law sect.), Internat. Bar Assn. (bus. law sect.), Seattle Internat. Tax Roundtable, Greater Seattle C. of C. (gen. counsel 1980-82), Rainier Club, Seattle Tennis Club, Broadmoor Golf Club, Rotary, Beta Gamma Sigma, Phi Gamma Delta, Phi Delta Phi. Office: Perkins Coie 1201 3rd Ave Fl 40 Seattle WA 98101-3000

MULLIN, LENORE MARIE RESTIFO, computer scientist, researcher; b. Albany, N.Y., Dec. 18, 1947; d. Salvatore Joseph and Mary Madeline (Gadomski) Restifo; widowed; children: Lisa Marie, Craig Benjamin, Sara Townsend. BS, SUNY, New Paltz, 1974; MS, Syracuse U., 1978, PhD, 1988. Sci. programmer IBM, Fishkill, N.Y., 1974-76; rsch. programmer IBM, Yorktown Heights, N.Y., 1976-78, mem. rsch. tech. staff, 1978-81, 82-84; vis. lectr. math. and computer sic. Vassar Coll., Poughkeepsie, N.Y., 1981-82; grad. asst. Syracuse (N.Y.) U., 1984-85, rsch. asst. elec. and computer engring., 1985-86; rsch. assoc., prin. investiagtor Computer Applications in Software Engring. Ctr., Syracuse, 1986-89; sr. rschr. Computer Sci. Rsch. Inst. of Montreal, 1989-90; vis. prof. dept. computer scis. and elec. engring. U. Vt., Burlington, 1990-92; assoc. prof. dept. computer scis. U. Mo., Rolla, 1992-95, SUNY, Albany, 1995—. Leader LaLeche League, 1970—. Presdl. Faculty fellow NSF, 1993. Mem. IEEE, Soc. Indsl. and Applied Mechanics, Assn. for Computing Machines. Avocations: glass art, skiing, biking, physics. Office: SUNY Albany NY 12222

MULLIN, LEO FRANCIS, utility executive; b. Concord, Mass., Jan. 26, 1943; s. Leo F. and Alice L. (Fearns) M.; m. Leah J. Malmberg, Sept. 10, 1966; children: Jessica, Matthew. AB, Harvard U., 1964, MS, 1965, MBA, 1967. Assoc. McKinsey & Co., Washington, 1967-73, prin., 1973-76; sr. v.p. strategic planning Consol. Rail Corp., Phila., 1976-78; sr. v.p. 1st Chgo. Corp., 1981-84, exec. v.p., 1984-91; chmn. Am. Nat. Bank and Trust Co. Chgo. subs. 1st Chgo., Chgo., 1991-93; pres., COO 1st Chgo. Corp., Chgo., 1993-95; vice chmn. Unicom/Commonwealth Edison, Chgo., 1995—. Vice chmn. Chgo. Urban League, 1993—; chmn. bd. trustees Field Mus. Natural History, 1994—; bd. dirs. Chgo. chpt. Juvenile Diabetes Found., 1985—, Met. Planning Coun., 1983—, Children's Meml. Hosp., Chgo., 1989—, Chgo. Coun. Fgn. Rels., 1994—; mem. Chgo. Econ. Devel. Commn., 1992-95; trustee Northwestern U., 1992—. Mem. Chgo. Club, Harvard Club of Chgo., Econ. Club of Chgo. Office: Commonwealth Edison Co PO Box 767 Chicago IL 60690-0767

MULLIN, MICHAEL MAHLON, Biology and oceanography educator; b. Galveston, Tex., Nov. 17, 1937; m. Constance Hammond; children: Stephen J., Keith A., Laura A. AB, Shimer Coll., 1957, Harvard U., 1959; MA, Harvard U., 1960, PhD in Biology, 1964. Asst. prof., asst. rsch. biologist Inst. Marine Resources U. Calif., San Diego, 1965-71, assoc. prof. oceanography, assoc. rsch. biologist, 1971-77, chmn. grad. dept., 1977-80; assoc. dir., 1980-87; prof. oceanography Scripps Inst., 1977—; dir. marine life rsch. group Inst. Marine Resources, U. Calif., San Siego, 1987—, assoc. dean, 1993—. Mem. Ocean Sci. Bd., Nat. Rsch. Coun., 1979-81; sr. Queen;s fellow marine sci., Australia, 1981-82. Mem. Am. Soc. Limnology & Oceanography. Office: Univ CA San Diego Scripps Inst Oceanography Marine Life Rsch Group La Jolla CA 92093-0227*

MULLIN, PATRICK ALAN, lawyer; b. Newark, N.J., Jan. 13, 1950; s. Gerard Vincent and Frances Regina (Magnanti) M. BA, William Paterson Coll., 1972, MEd, 1974; JD, NYU, 1979, LLM in Taxation, 1985; postgrad., Harvard U., 1979. Bar: N.J. 1979, D.C. 1980, N.Y. 1990. Law clk. to Hon. Dickinson R. DeBevoise, U.S. Dist. Ct. N.J., Trenton, 1979-80; assoc. Charles Morgan Assocs., Washington, 1980-81, Michael A Querques, Orange, N.J., 1985-88; pvt. practice, Hackensack, N.J., 1988—. Joseph Solomon scholar for study of internat. law U. Bologna, Italy, 1978. Mem. ABA, N.J. Bar Assn., Berger County Bar Assn. Democrat. Roman Catholic. Avocations: jogging, martial artist, tennis. Office: Ct Plz N 25 Main St Ste 200 Hackensack NJ 07601-7015

MULLINAX, OTTO B., retired lawyer; b. Clearwater, Tex., June 28, 1912; s. Claxton Napoleon and Essie Ruth (Shelby) M.; m. Ernestine Maxey, July 20, 1941; 1 child, Michael Lewis. B.A., U. Tex., 1937, LL.B., 1937. Bar: Tex. 1937, U.S. Ct. Mil. Appeals 1957, U.S. Supreme Ct. 1958. Assoc. firm Mandell & Combs, Houston, 1938-40; sr. ptnr. Mullinax, Wells, Morris & Mauzy (named changed to Mullinax, Wells, Baab & Cloutman, 1980); ret., 1995. Author: Some Mullinax Roots: South Carolina to Texas, 1982, Thus Spake Idion, 1983, Sam Adams: Freedom Fighter, 1991, Gods, Prophets and Slaves, 1994, The Historical Jesus: A Socialist Revolutionary of the Common Table and Communal Code. Pres. Dallas UN Assn., 1971-72; bd. dirs. Ams. for Dem. Action, 1952-71; active 1st Unitarian Ch. Dallas, 1990; bd. dirs. The Hist. Jesus, 1996. Fellow Am. Law-Sci. Acad.; mem. Dallas Trial Lawyers Assn. (pres. 1956), Tex. Trial Lawyers Assn. (dir.), Nat. Assn. Compensation Claimants Attys. (assoc. editor jour. 1952-65). Home: 11806 Cheswick St Dallas TX 75218-1803 *The history of the ancient Mediterranian world, which I have studied since my retirement, is the best of all the histories I've tried to master. Those Moses books, the most ancient written histories of this planet are vastly mind expanding.*

MULLINEAUX, DONAL RAY, geologist; b. Weed, Calif., Feb. 16, 1925; s. Lester Ray and Mary Lorene (Drew) M.; m. Diana Suzanne Charais, Nov. 21, 1951; children: Peter, Lauren, Keith. Student, U. Wash., 1942, BS in Math, 1947, BS in Geology, 1949, MS in Geology, 1950, PhD in Geology, 1961. Drilling insp. U.S. Army C.E., 1948; geologist U.S. Geol. Survey, 1950-86; contracting geologist, 1987-90; scientist emeritus U.S. Geol. Survey, 1990—. Author articles on volcanic activity and hazards, Mt. St. Helens, other Cascade Range volcanoes, stratigraphy and engring. geology of Puget Sound lowland, Wash. With USNR, 1943-54, active duty, 1943-46, 51-53. Rsch. fellow Engring. Expt. Sta. U. Wash., 1949-50. Fellow Geol. Soc. Am. (E.B. Burwell Jr. award 1983); mem. Colo. Sci. Soc. Unitarian. Home: 14155 W 54th Ave Arvada CO 80002-1513 Office: PO Box 25046 Denver CO 80225-0046

MULLINIX, EDWARD WINGATE, lawyer; b. Balt., Feb. 25, 1924; s. Howard Earl and Elsie (Wingate) M.; m. Virginia Lee McGinnes, July 28, 1944; children: Marcia Lee Ladd, Edward Wingate. Student, St. John's Coll., 1941-43; JD summa cum laude, U. Pa., 1949. Bar: Pa. 1950, U.S. Supreme Ct. 1955. Assoc. Schnader, Harrison, Segal & Lewis, Phila., 1950-55, ptnr., 1956-92, now sr. coun.; mem. adv. bds. Antitrust Bull., 1970-81, BNA Antitrust and Trade Regulation Report, 1981-94; mem. Civil Justice Reform Act of 1990 adv. group U.S. Dist. Ct. (ea. dist.) Pa., 1991—; co-chmn. Joint U.S. Dist. Ct./Phila. Bar Assn. Alternative Dispute Resolution Com., 1990—; cons. on revision of local civil rules U.S. Dist. Ct. (ea. dist.) Pa., 1995—; mem. adv. com. U. Pa. Law Sch. Ctr. on Professionalism, 1988-92; judge pro tem Ct. Common Pleas of Phila. County Day Forward program; faculty participant Pa. Bar Inst., Phila. Bar Edn. Ctr., others. Trustee Sta. KYW-TV Project Homeless Fund, 1985-86. Served with USMCR, 1943-44; to lt. (j.g.) USNR, 1944-46. Fellow Am. Bar Found. (life), Am. Coll. Trial Lawyers (emeritus, mem. complex litigation com. 1980-91, vice-chmn. com. 1981-83); mem. ABA (spl. com. complex and multidist. litigation 1969-73, co-chmn. com. 1971-73, coun. litigation sect. 1976-80), Phila. Bar Assn., Juristic Soc., Hist. Soc. U.S. Dist. Ct. (ea. dist.) Pa. (bd. dirs. 1984—, pres. 1991-94), Hist. Soc. U.S. Ct. Appeals for Third Cir. (bd. dirs. 1991-94), Order of Coif, Union League (Phila.), Socialegal Club (Phila.), Aronimink Golf Club (Newtown Sq., Pa.). Republican. Presbyterian. Home: 251 Chamounix Rd Saint Davids PA 19087-3605 Office: 1600 Market St Ste 3600 Philadelphia PA 19103-4252

MULLINS, BETTY JOHNSON, realtor; b. Killen, Ala., Dec. 29, 1925; d. James E. and Vernie (Muse) Johnson; m. Charles Harvey Mullins, Nov. 18, 1944; children: Charles Harvey Jr., Susan. BS, U. North Ala., 1945. Tchr. Biloxi (Miss.) City Schs., 1945-46, Elizabeth City County Schs., Buckroe Beach, Va., 1946-47, Sheffield (Ala.) City Schs., 1949-58; with family automobile bus., 1958-86; real estate assoc. Neese Real Estate, Inc., Florence, Ala., 1986—. Pres. Project Courtview, Florence, 1980, Heritage Found., Florence, 1994—, Concert Guild, Florence, 1994; mem. Tenn. Valley Art Guild, Tuscumbia, Tenn. Valley Art Ctr., Tuscumbia, Friends of Kennedy Douglas Art Ctr., Florence; v.p. Salvation Army Aux., 1991-92; mem., past pres. United Meth. Women, First Meth. Ch., Florence, mem. adminstrv. bds.; bd. dirs. Friends of Libr., Florence, 1993—, Downtown Florence Unltd., Florence Main St., Bd. Rape Response; mem., past pres. Lauderdale-Colbert-Franklin Foster Grandparent Adv. Bd., Russellville, Ala., Ret. Sr. Vol. Program Adv. Bd.; pres. cabinet U. North Ala., mem. found. bd., 1994, 95, 96; trustee United Way, Shoals, 1992—; family built and maintains garden at First Meth. Ch., Florence in memory of Charles Mullins, Jr. Recipient Shoals Area Citizen of Yr., 1984, Shoals Area Top Prodr. Muscle Shoals Area Bd. Realtors, 1991, 92, 93, 94, Cmty. Svc. award U. North Ala., 1994; named Woman of Yr. Bus. and Profl. Women, 1980. Mem. LWV, Shoals-AAUW (pres. 1990-91), Nat. Bd. Realtors, U. North Ala. Alumni Assn. (past pres., bd. dirs., Alumni of Yr. award 1985, Cmty. Svc. award 1994, Found. Bd. 1994, 95, 96), Internat. Fertilizer Devel. Ctr. Century Club (past pres. Muscle Shoals, Ala. chpt.), Shoals C. of C. (past bd. dirs.), Tenn. Valley Hist. Assn., U. North Ala. Sportsman Club, Muscle Shoals Bd. Realtors, Ala. Bd. Realtors. Republican. Methodist. Avocation: family. Home and Office: PO Box 70 Florence AL 35631-0070

MULLINS, CHARLES BROWN, physician, academic administrator; b. Rochester, Ind., July 29, 1934; s. Charles E. and Mary Ruth B. (Bamberger) M.; B.A., N. Tex. State U., 1954; M.D., U. Tex., 1958; m. Stella Churchill, Dec. 27, 1955; children—Holly, David. Intern U. Colo. Med. Center, Denver, 1958-59; resident medicine Parkland Meml. Hosp., Dallas, 1962-64; USPHS rsch. fellow U. Tex. Southwestern Med. Sch., Dallas, 1964-65; chief resident medicine Parkland Meml. Hosp., 1965-66; USPHS spl. rsch. fellow cardiology br. Nat. Heart Inst., Bethesda, Md., 1967-68; practice medicine specializing in cardiology, Dallas, 1966—; mem. sr. attending staff Parkland Meml. Hosp., dir. med. affairs, 1977-79; mem. cons. staff Presbyn. Hosp., VA Hosp.; asst. prof. medicine U. Tex. Southwestern Med. Sch., Dallas, 1968-71, asso. prof., 1971-75, dir. clin. cardiology, 1971-77, prof., 1975-79, clin. prof. medicine, 1979-81, prof., 1981—; prof. medicine U. Tex. Health Sci. Center, Dallas, 1979-81; exec. vice-chancellor health affairs U. Tex. System, 1981—; chief exec. officer Dallas County Hosp. Dist., 1979-81. Served with M.C., USAF, 1959-62. Diplomate Am. Bd. Internal Medicine. Fellow ACP, Am. Coll. Cardiology (Tex. gov. 1974-77, chmn. bd. govs. 1976), Am. Heart Assn. Council on Clin. Cardiology; mem. Am. Fedn. Clin. Rsch., Assn. Acad. Health Ctrs., Assn. Univ. Cardiologists, Laennec Soc., AMA, Alpha Omega Alpha. Contbr. articles on cardiology to med. jours. Office: 601 Colorado St Austin TX 78701-2904

MULLINS, JAMES LEE, library director; b. Perry, Iowa, Nov. 29, 1949; s. Kenneth Wiley and Lorene (Gift) M.; m. Kathleen Stiso, May 10, 1986; 1 stepchild, Michael Stiso. BA, U. Iowa, 1972, MA, 1973; PhD, Ind. U., 1984. Instr. Ga. So. U., Statesboro, 1973-74; assoc. law librarian Ind. U., Bloomington, 1974-78; dir. library Ind. U., South Bend, 1978-96; dir. Falvey Meml. Libr., Villanova U., 1996—. Contbr. articles to profl. publs. Mem. exec. com. South Bend Art Ctr., 1984-89; mem. Mayor's Task Force Redevel., South Bend, 1986; pres. Fischoff Nat. Chamber Music Assn., 1989-91, Gov. Conf. on Libr. Planning Com., 1989-91, Mich. Freenet bd., 1993—; pres. Ind. Coop. Libr. Svcs. Authority, 1993-94. Mem. ALA, Ind. Library Assn., Assn. Coll. and Research Libraries, Ind. Lib. Endowment Bd. (pres. 1988-91). Lodge: Rotary. Avocations: reading, gardening, cross-country skiing, historic preservation. Office: Falvey Meml Libr Villanova Univ 800 Lancaster Ave Villanova PA 19085-1699

MULLINS, RICHARD AUSTIN, chemical engineer; b. Seelyville, Ind., Apr. 22, 1918; s. Fred A. and Ethel (Zenor) M.; B.S. in Chem. Engring., Rose Poly. Inst., 1940; postgrad. Yale, 1942-43; m. Margaret Ann Dellacca, Nov. 27, 1946 (dec. Nov. 1982); children—Scott Alan, Mark Earl. Chemist, Ayrshire Collieries Corp., Brazil, Ind., 1940-49; chief chemist Fairview Collieries Corp., Danville, Ill., 1949-54; preparations mgr. Enos Coal Mining Co., Oakland City, Ind., 1954-72, Enoco Collieries, Inc., Bruceville, Ind., 1954-62; mining engr. Kings Station Coal Corp.; mgr. analytical procedures Old Ben Coal Corp., 1973-84; ret., 1984. Am. Mining Congress cons. to Am. Standards Assn. and Internat. Orgn. for Standards, 1960-74; mem. indsl. cons. com. Ind. Geol. Survey, 1958-72; mem. organizing com. 5th Internat. Coal Preparation Congress, Pittsburgh, 1966. Mem. exec. bd. Buffalo Trace council Boy Scouts Am., also mem. speakers bur. Bd. dirs. Princeton Boys Club. Served with AUS, 1942-46; ETO. Decorated Medaille de la France Liberee (France); recipient Eagle Scout award, Boy Scouts Am., 1935, Silver Beaver award, 1962, Wood Badge Beads award, 1960; Outstanding Community Svc. award Princeton Civitan Club, 1964; Engr. of Year award S.W. chpt. Ind. Soc. Profl. Engrs., 1965; Prince of Princeton award Princeton C. of C., 1981, Sagamore of the Wabash award Ind. gov. R.D. Orr, 1984. Registered profl. engr., Ind., Ill. Mem. AIME (life mem.), ASTM (sr. mem., R.A. Glenn award 1985), Am. Chem. Soc., Nat. Soc. Profl. Engrs. (life mem.), Ind., Ill. mining insts., Ind. Coal Soc. (pres. 1958-59), Am. Mining Congress (chmn. com. coal preparation 1964-68), Am. Legion (life, past county comdr.), VFW (life), 40 & 8 (life), Ind. Soc. Profl. Land Surveyors, Rose Tech. Alumni Assn. (pres. 1976-77, Honor Alumnus 1980), Order of Ring, Sigma Nu. Methodist (lay speaker). Mason, Elk. Contbr. articles to profl. jours. Home: RR 4 Box 310 Princeton IN 47670-9412

MULLINS, RUTH GLADYS, nurse; b. Westville, N.S., Can., Aug. 25, 1943; d. William G. and Gladys H.; came to U.S., 1949, naturalized, 1955; student Tex. Womans U., 1961-64; BS in Nursing, Calif. State U.-Long Beach, 1966; MNursing, UCLA, 1973; m. Leonard E. Mullins, Aug. 27, 1963; children: Deborah R., Catherine M., Leonard III. Pub. health nurse, L.A. County Health Dept., 1967-68; nurse Meml. Hosp. Med. Center, Long Beach, 1968-72; dir. pediatric nurse practitioner program Calif. State U., Long Beach, 1973—, asst. prof., 1975-80, assoc. prof., 1980-85, prof., 1985—; health svc. credential coord. Sch. Nursing Calif. State U., Long Beach, Calif., chmn., 1979-81, coord. grad. programs, 1985-92; mem. Calif. Maternal, Child and Adolescent Health Bd., 1977-84; vice chair Long Beach/Orange County Health Consortium, 1984-85, chair 1985-86. Tng. grantee HHS, Divsn. Nursing Calif. Dept. Health; cert. pediatric nurse practitioner. Fellow Nat. Assn. Pediatric Nurse Assocs. and Practitioners (exec. bd., pres. 1990-91), Nat. Fedn. Nursing Specialty Orgns. (sec. 1991-93); mem. Am. Pub. Health Assn., Nat. Alliance Nurse Practitioners (governing body 1990-92), Assn. Faculties Pediatric Nurse Practitioner Programs, L.A. and Orange County Assn. Pediatric Nurse Practitioners and Assocs., Am. Assn. U. Faculty, Ambulatory Pediatric Assn. Democrat. Methodist. Author: (with B. Nelms) Growth and Development: A Primary Health Care Approach; contbg. author: Quick Reference to Pediatric Nursing, 1984; asst. editor Jour. Pediatric Health Care. Home: 6382 Heil Ave Huntington Beach CA 92647-4232 Office: Calif State U Dept Nursing 1250 N Bellflower Blvd Long Beach CA 90840-0006

MULLIS, KARY BANKS, biochemist; b. Lenoir, N.C., Dec. 28, 1944; s. Cecil Banks Mullis and Bernice Alberta (Barker) Fredericks; children: Christopher, Jeremy, Louise. BS in Chemistry, Ga. Inst. Tech, 1966; PhD in Biochemistry, U. Calif., Berkeley, 1973; DSc (hon.), U. S.C., 1994. Lectr. biochemistry U. Calif., Berkeley, 1972; postdoctoral fellow U. Calif., San Francisco, 1977-79, U. Kans. Med. Sch., Kansas City, 1973-76; scientist Cetus Corp., Emeryville, Calif., 1979-86; dir. molecular biology Xytronyx, Inc., San Diego, 1986-88; cons. Specialty Labs, Inc., Amersham, Inc., Chiron Inc. and various others, Calif., 1988—; chmn. StarGene, Inc., San Rafael, Calif.; v.p. Histotec, Inc., Cedar Rapids, Iowa; Disting. vis. prof. U. S.C. Coll. of Sci. and Math. Contbr. articles to profl. jours.; patentee in field. Recipient Preis Biochemische Analytik award German Soc. Clin. Chem., 1990, Allan award Am. Soc. of Human Genetics, 1990, award Gairdner Found. Internat., 1991, Nat. Biotech. award, 1991, Robert Koch award, 1992, Chiron Corp. Biotechnology Rsch. award Am. Soc. Microbiology, 1992, Japan prize Sci. and Tech. Found. Japan, 1993, Nobel Prize in Chemistry, Nobel Foundation, 1993; named Calif. Scientist of Yr., 1992, Scientist of Yr., R&D Mag., 1991. Mem. Am. Chem. Soc., Am. Acad. Achievement, Inst. Further Study (dir. 1983—). Achievements include invention of Polymerase Chain Reaction (PCR). Office: 6767 Neptune Pl Apt 5 La Jolla CA 92037-5924

MULLIS, MADELINE GAIL HERMAN, music educator, choir director; b. Lenoir, N.C., Oct. 26, 1936; d. William Richard and Madeline Edythe (Harris) Herman; m. Thad McCoy Mullis Jr., Dec. 18, 1960 (div. Oct. 1978); children: Thad McCoy III, Myra Lynn, Martin Harper. MusB, U. N.C., Greensboro, 1958; MA, Appalachian State U., 1963; level I Orff cert., Memphis State U. Cert. elem., secondary instrumental and choir music tchr. N.C. Jr. choir dir. St. Stephens Luth. Ch., Lenoir, 1969-80, sr. choir dir., 1960—, handbell choir dir., 1970—, deacon, 1980-82, 84-86; 88-90; Sunday sch. tchr. St. Stephens Luth. Ch., Lenoir, 1983-86; tchr. classroom music, chorus, band Caldwell County Schs., Lenoir, 1958-65, 77—, chair St. Stephens Worship and Music, Lenoir, 1988-93; del. N.C. Synod Conv., Hickory, N.C., 1990; pres. Agape Women's Circle, Lenoir, 1991-92. Chairperson Sesquicentennial Children's Chorus, Caldwell County, 1991; coord. 1st Caldwell County Children's Choral Festival, 1993. Recipient 24 Superior Ratings at Jr. H.S. Choral Festivals. Mem. NEA, N.C. Ctr. for Advancement of Tchg. (hon.), Assn. Luth. Musicians, N.C. Assn. Educators, Music Educators Nat. Conf., N.C. Music Educators Assn., Am. Orff-Schulwerk Assn., Cmty. Music Club (pres. 1993-95), Caldwell County Hist. Soc., Alpha Delta Kappa (hon.). Republican. Home: 119 Ellison Pl NE Lenoir NC 28645-3716 Office: 1406 Harper Ave NW Lenoir NC 28645-5059 also: Happy Valley Sch PO Box 130 Patterson NC 28661

MULLMAN, MICHAEL S., lawyer; b. N.Y.C., Sept. 17, 1946; s. Herbert and Harriet (Weissman) M.; m. Ellen Mullman, 1975; children: Jeremy, Cassie. BA in Polit. Sci. cum laude, Union Coll., Schenectady, N.Y., 1968; JD, Columbia U., 1971. Bar: N.Y. 1972, U.S. Ct. Appeals (2d cir.), U.S. Dist. Ct., 1975. Atty. Paskus, Gordon & Hyman, N.Y.C., 1976-80; ptnr. Schonwald, Schaffzin & Mullman, N.Y.C., 1980-89, Tenzer Greenblatt LLP, N.Y.C., 1989—. Bd. editors Columbia Jour. Law and Soc. Problems, articles edition, 1970-71. Vice chmn. Lincoln Towers Comm. Assn., N.Y.C., 1987—; v.p. 205 West End Ave. Owners Corp., N.Y.C., 1987—. Nott scholar Union Coll., 1967, Harlan Fiske Stone scholar Sch. Law Columbia U., 1971. Mem. Bar Assn. N.Y.C., Phi Beta Kappa. Avocations: tennis, skiing, reading, gardening. Office: Tenzer Greenblatt LLP 405 Lexington Ave New York NY 10174

MULLONEY, PETER BLACK, steel, oil and gas executive; b. Boston, Oct. 24, 1932; s. Daniel Clifford and Mabel (Black) M.; m. Marie Weprich. BA, Yale U., 1954. V.p. mktg. U.S. Steel Corp., Pitts., 1978-81; v.p., asst. to chmn. USX Corp., Pitts., 1981—; bd. dirs. Pitts. Vintage Grand Prix. Mem. adv. bd., sec. Salvation Army, Pitts.; vice chmn. World Affairs Coun. Pitts.; mem. bd. trustees La Roche Coll. Mem. Am. Iron and Steel Inst. (active com. on internat. trade, Washington, chmn. com. 1983-85), Internat. Iron and Steel Inst. (active com. on econ. studies, Brussels, chmn. com. 1983-85). Roman Catholic. Clubs: Duquesne (Pitts.), Harvard-Yale-Princeton, Pitts., Army and Navy (Washington), Pitts. Athletic Assn. Avocations: reading, walking. Home: 213 Grandview Ave Pittsburgh PA 15211-1525 Office: USX Corp 600 Grant St Pittsburgh PA 15219-2702

MULREANY, ROBERT HENRY, retired lawyer; b. Bklyn., Aug. 5, 1915; s. John Robert and Elfriede (Hartman) M.; m. Dorothy E. Muens, Sept. 7, 1940; children: Doreen Elizabeth Mulreany O'Brien, Carol Ann Mulreany Henwood. LLB, NYU, 1940. Bar: N.Y. 1940. Law clk. DeForest, Cullom & Elder, N.Y.C., 1933-39; mng. clk., atty. Neil P. Cullom, N.Y.C., 1939-42; since practiced in N.Y.C.; mem. DeForest & Elder, 1942-47, ptnr., 1947-49; ptnr. DeForest, Elder & Mulreany, 1949-69, sr. ptnr., 1954-69; ptnr. DeForest & Duer, 1969-87, of counsel, 1988-91; pres. Provident Loan Soc. N.Y., 1955-89, trustee, 1989—. Mem. adv. coun. Sch. Social Work, Columbia, 1960-64; mayor, Westfield, N.J., 1965-68; pres. Bd. Edn. Westfield, 1959-62; chmn. N.Y.C. Adv. Com. Pub. Welfare, 1963-67; chmn. bd. trustees Comty. Svc. Soc. of N.Y., 1959-72; trustee Overlook Hosp., 1970-78, chmn., 1976-78; trustee John A. Hartford Found.; trustee Smith Richardson Found., 1975—, Found. Ctr., Inc., 1975—; former trustee Westfield YMCA, Westfield Found., Tuskegee Inst.; trustee, pres. Overlook Hosp. Found., 1978-84, trustee, 1993—; trustee Smith Richardson Found. Lt. (j.g.) USNR, 1944-46. Mem. ABA, Bar Assn. City N.Y. Presbyterian. Clubs: Downtown Assn. (N.Y.C.), Echo Lake Country (Westfield, N.J.), Bay Head Yacht (N.J.). Home: 11 Euclid Ave Apt 4B Summit NJ 07901-2166

MULRONEY, (MARTIN) BRIAN, former prime minister of Canada; b. Mar. 20, 1939; s. Benedict and Irene (O'Shea) M.; m. Mila Pivnicki, 1973; 4 children. BA, St. Francis Xavier U., LLD, 1979; LLL, U. Laval, Que.; LLD, Meml. U. Nfld., Nfld., 1980, U. W.I., 1993, Tel Aviv U., 1994, Ctrl. Conn. State U., 1994, Barry U., 1995. Ptnr. Ogilvy Renault, Montreal, 1965-76; exec. v.p. Iron Ore Co. Can., Montreal, 1977-83, Iron Ore Co. of Can., Montreal, Que., 1976-77; mem. Parliament Can. from Ctrl. N.S., Ottawa, Ont., 1983-84; mem. Parliament Can. from Manicouagan, 1984-88, mem. Parliament Can. from Charlevoix, 1988-93, leader of Her Majesty's Loyal Opposition, 1983-84; prime minister Can., 1984-93; royal commr. Cliche Commn. investigating violence in Que. constrn. industry, 1974; sr. ptnr. Ogilvy Renault, Montreal, 1993—; chmn. internat. adv. bd. Barrick Gold Corp., Chem. Bank N.Y.; mem. internat. adv. coun. Power Corp. Can.; mem. adv. bd. The China Internat. Trust and Investment Corp.; mem. Bombadier/Aerospace Group N.Am.; trustee Freedom Forum; mem. internat. adv. coun. Inst. Internat. Studies; bd. dirs. Archer Daniels Midland Co., Barrick Gold Corp., Chem. Bank N.Y., Horsham Corp., Petrofina, S.A., Power Corp. Author: Where I Stand, 1983. Office: Ogilvy Renault, 1981 McGill College Ave Ste 1100, Montreal, PQ Canada H3A 3C1

MULRONEY, JOHN PATRICK, chemical company executive; b. Phila., 1935; married. BS, U. Pa., 1957, MS, 1959. With Rohm and Haas Co., Phila., 1958—; group leader engring. dept. Rohm & Haas Co., Phila., 1962-64, dept. head, 1964-67, asst. dir. rsch., 1967-71, pres., chief oper. officer, 1986—; asst. gen. mgr. Rohm and Haas Italy, Milan, 1971-73, gen. mgr., 1973-75; bus. mgr. AG Chem., Europe, 1975-77, regional dir. Europe, 1977-78; v.p. polymers, resins, monomers Indsl. Chem., 1978-80, v.p. tech., 1980-82, v.p. corp. bus., from 1982, also bd. dirs., 1982—; bd. dirs. Aluminum Co., Am. Teradyne Inc. Mem. Am. Inst. Chem. Engrs., Am. Chem. Soc. Office: Rohm and Haas Co 100 Independence Mall West Philadelphia PA 19106

MULRONEY, MICHAEL, lawyer, law educator, graduate program director; b. Chgo., Feb. 26, 1932; s. Alphonsus James and Genevieve (Moran) M.; m. Ellen Goen Mulroney, Dec. 28, 1959; children: Sean, Conor, Dermot, Kieran, Moira. BSC in Econ., State U. Iowa, 1954; JD, Harvard Law Sch., 1959. Bar: Iowa 1959, D.C. 1960, U.S. Supreme Ct., U.S. Ct. Appeals (2nd, 3rd, 4th, 5th, 6th, 7th, 8th, 9th and D.C. cirs.), U.S. Tax Ct., U.S. Dist. Ct. D.C., D.C. Ct. Appeals, D.C. Superior Ct. Atty. adv. U.S. Tax Ct., Washington, 1959-61; appellate atty. Tax Div. U.S. Dept. Justice, Washington, 1961-65; assoc. Lee, Toomey & Kent, Washington, 1965-68, ptnr., 1969-87, counsel, 1987-88; prof., dir. Grad. Tax Program Villanova (Pa.) Law Sch., 1988—; adjunct prof. Grad. Tax Program Georgetown Law Sch., Washington, 1986—. Author: Federal Tax Examinations Manual, 1988, Foreign Taxation, 1992; mng. editor: The Tax Lawyer, 1989—; contbr. articles to profl. jours. With U.S. Army, 1954-56. Fellow Am. Coll. of Tax Counsel; mem. ABA (taxation sect., chmn. tax lawyer com., mem. ct. procedure com., stds. of practice com., tchg. taxation com.; legal edn. and admissions to the bar sect.), D.C. Bar (tax sect.), Fed. Bar Assn. (tax sect.), Iowa Bar Assn. (tax sect.), J. Edgar Murdock Am. Inn. of Ct. (founding master), Internat. Fiscal Assn. (U.S. br. coun. mem.), Internat. Fiscal Rsch. Inst. (mem. coun. experts), Wash. Tax Lawyers' Study Group, Phila. Tax Conf. (mem. exec. coun.), Am. Assn. Law Schs. (tax sect.). Roman Catholic. Avocation: sports car racing. Office: Villanova Law Sch Villanova PA 19085

MULROW, PATRICK JOSEPH, medical educator; s. Patrick J. and Delia (O'Keefe) M.; m. Jacquelyn Pinover, Aug. 8, 1953; children: Deborah, Nancy, Robert, Catherine. AB, Colgate U., 1947; MD, Cornell U., 1951; MSc (hon.), Yale U., 1969. Intern N.Y. Hosp., 1951-52, resident, 1952-54; instr. physiology Med. Coll. Cornell U., 1954-55; research fellow Stanford U., 1955-57; instr. medicine Yale U., 1957-60, asst. prof., 1960-66, assoc. prof., 1966-69, prof. medicine, 1969-75; chmn. dept. medicine Med. Coll. Ohio, Toledo, 1975-95, prof. medicine, 1975—; chmn. ednl. com. Council for high blood pressure rsch. Am. Heart Assn., 1968-70, mem. exec. com., 1986—, vice-chmn. of coun., 1990-92, chmn. 1992-94, past chmn., 1995—; mem. study sect. NIH, 1970-74. Editorial bd. Jour. Clin. Endocrinology and Metabolism, 1966-70, 75-79, Endocrine Rsch., 1974—, Jour. Exptl. Biology and Medicine, Hypertension, 1994—; contbr. articles to profl. jours. With USNR, 1944-46. Mem. ACP, Am. Soc. Clin. Investigation, Assn. Am. Physicians, Am. Physiol. Soc., Endocrine Soc., Am. Fedn. Clin. Rsch., Am. Clin. and Climatol. Assn., Am. Heart Assn. (nat. rsch. com., chmn. cardiovasc. regulation rsch. study com. 1986-91), Assn. Profs. Medicine, Assn. Program Dirs. in Internal Medicine, Cen. Soc. Clin. Rsch. (pres. 1988-89), Internat. Soc. Hypertension, World Hypertension League (sec.-gen. 1995—), Inter-Am. Soc. Hypertension, Sigma Xi (pres. Yale chpt. 1965-66), Alpha Omega Alpha. Home: 9526 Carnoustie Rd Perrysburg OH 43551-3501 Office: Med Coll of Ohio Dept of Medicine PO Box 10008 Toledo OH 43699-0008

MULROY, RICHARD E., JR., lawyer. Sr. v.p., gen. counsel Mutual Life Ins. Co. of N.Y. Office: Mutual Life Ins Co of NY 1740 Broadway New York NY 10019-4315

MULRYAN, HENRY TRIST, mineral company executive, consultant; b. Palo Alto, Calif., Jan. 6, 1927; s. Henry and Marian Abigail (Trist) M.; m. Lenore Hoag, Aug. 25, 1948; children: James W., Carol. Student, Yale U., 1945-46; AB in Econs., Stanford U., 1948; postgrad., Am. Grad. Sch. Internat. Bus., 1949, Columbia U., 1983. V.p. mktg. Sierra Talc Co., South Pasadena, Calif., 1955-65; v.p. mktg. United Sierra, Trenton, N.J., 1965-67, v.p., gen. mgr., 1967-70, pres., 1970-77; v.p. Cyprus Mines Corp., Los Angeles, 1978-80; sr. v.p. ops. Cyprus indsl. minerals div. Amoco Minerals Co., Englewood, Colo., 1980-85; pres. Cyprus Indls. Minerals Co., Englewood, 1985-87; v.p. Cyprus Minerals Co., Englewood, 1985-87, sr. v.p. mktg., corp. adminstr., 1987-89; pres. Mineral Econs. Internat., 1989—. Served with U.S. Army, 1944-46. Clubs: Jonathan (Los Angeles). Lodge: Rotary (pres. South Pasadena club 1964-65) (bd. dirs. Princeton, N.J. club 1969-75). Office: 15237 W Sunset Blvd # 72 Pacific Palisades CA 90272-3690

MULTHAUP, MERREL KEYES, artist; b. Cedar Rapids, Iowa, Sept. 27, 1922; d. Stephen Dows and Edna Gertrude (Gard) Keyes; m. Robert Hansen Multhaup, Apr. 7, 1944; children: Eric Stephen, Robert Bruce. Student fine art, State U. of Iowa, 1942-43; student color theory, Rice U., 1971. Mem. teaching faculty Summit (N.J.) Art Assn., 1956-60; art instr. studio classes Springfield, N.J., 1954-55, Bloomfield (N.J.) Art Group, 1955-56, Westport, Conn., 1962-63; mem. teaching faculty Hunterdon Art Ctr., Clinton, N.J., 1985-92. One woman exhbns. include Coriell Gallery, 1995; exhibited in group shows at Nat. Assn. Women Artists, N.Y.C., 1957-93 (awards in figure painting), Hartford (Conn.) Athanaeum Mus., 1961 (1st prize), Highgate Gallery, N.Y.C., Waverly Gallery, N.Y.C., Leicester Gallery, London, Silvermine Gallery, Conn., Pendut Gallery, Tex., Benedict Gallery, Sidney Rothman Gallery, N.J., Stamford (Conn.) Mus., Bridgeport (Conn.) Mus., Montclair (N.J.) Mus., Newark Mus., Coriell Gallery, Albuquerque; included in traveling exhibit Nat. Assn. Women Artists, 1996-98. Bd. dirs., exhbn. chmn. Summit Art Assn., 1950-60, Silvermine Guild of Art, New Canaan, Conn., 1960-64; bd. dirs. Artist's Equity of N.J., 1977-84, chmn. state-wide event, 1983, 86; artist's adv. coun. Hunterdon Art Ctr., Clinton, 1988-92. Recipient awards in juried exhbns. in Iowa, Pa., N.J., Conn., N.Y.C. Mem. Nat. Mus. for Women in Arts (charter mem.), Nat. Assn. Women Artists Inc. (awards for figure painting 1957, 80, 89), Albuquerque United Artists. Avocations: entertaining, sewing, singing, playing the piano and reading, dancing. Home and Studio: 1321 Stagecoach Rd SE Albuquerque NM 87123-4320

MULVA, JAMES JOSEPH, oil company executive; b. Oshkosh, Wis., June 19, 1946; m. Miriam Mulva; 2 children. BBA in Fin., U. Tex., 1968, MBA in Fin., 1969. Mgmt. trainee, treas. Phillips Petroleum Co., Bartlesville, Okla., 1973; asst. treas. Phillips Petroleum Co., London, 1974; mgr. fgn. exch. and investment Phillips Petroleum Co., Bartlesville, 1976; v.p., treas. Europe/Africa div. Phillips Petroleum Co., London, 1980; mgr. corp. and planning Phillips Petroleum Co., Bartlesville, 1984, asst. treas., 1985, treas., 1986, v.p., treas., 1988-90, chief fin. officer, 1990-1995. With USN, 1969-73. Roman Catholic. Office: Phillips Petroleum Co 1250 Adams Bldg Bartlesville OK 74004*

MULVAGH, CHARLENE FRANCES, special education educator; b. Springfield, Mass., Nov. 16, 1949; d. Eugene Joseph and Frances Catherine McCarthy; m. Peter Joseph Mulvagh, Feb. 9, 1990; children: Aaron Joseph, Edward Daniel. BA, Cardinal Cushing Coll., 1972; MEd, Am. Internat. Coll., 1990. Tchr. spl. edn. Windsor (Conn.) Pub. Schs., 1972-76, Lower Merion (Pa.) Pub. Schs., 1977-83, Springfield (Mass.) Pub. Schs., 1984-87, Windsor Locks (Conn.) Pub. Schs., 1987-88, Windsor Pub. Schs., 1988—; parent advocate South Windsor Pub. Schs., 1991-94, Chicoppee Pub. Schs., Chico, Mass., 1993-94, South Hadley (Mass.) Pub. Schs., 1991-94. Mem. Kappa Gamma Pi. Democrat. Roman Catholic. Avocations: skiing, music. Home: 134 Pine Grove Dr South Hadley MA 01075-2199 Office: Windsor Bd Edn Windsor CT 06095

MULVANEY, JAMES FRANCIS, lawyer; b. Chgo., Nov. 2, 1922; m. Mary Ruth Rinderer, 1945; 7 children. BS, Loyola U., Chgo., 1942, JD, 1948. Atty. Chgo., 1948-55, San Diego, Calif., 1956-62; exec. v.p. U.S. Nat. Bank, 1963-72, pres., CEO, 1972-73; pres. San Diego Baseball Co., 1955-68; v.p., gen. counsel San Diego Padres Nat. League, 1968-73; ptnr. Mulvaney, Kahan & Barry, San Diego, 1974—; bd. dirs., chmn., CEO Calif. Higher Edn. Loan Authority Fin., 1983—. Bd. vis. U. San Diego Sch. Law, 1971-88; chmn. United Way Internat., 1991-94, mem. exec. com., United Way Am., 1987-93, various officers; co-chmn. San Diego Organizing Project, 1983—; bd. dirs. World SHARE, Inc., 1986-92, Old Globe Theatre London, Del Mar Charities, 1985-95; numerous other civic activities. Officer USN, WWII; lt. comdr. USNR, Korea. Recipient Mr. San Diego award, 1991, First Annual Spirit of Charity award Cath. Community Svcs., 1984, Brotherhood award Nat. Conf. Christians and Jews, Inc., 1983, Citizen of Yr. award Jr. C. of C. and The City Club, 1983, numerous others. Mem. San Diego County Bar Found. (treas., Outstanding Svc. award 1988), ABA, Calif. State Bar Assn., Ill. State Bar Assn., San Diego C. of C., San Diego Coun. on World Affairs, The City Club of San Diego, Navy League. Office: Mulvaney Kahan & Barry 401 W A St Fl 17 San Diego CA 92101-7901

MULVANEY, MARY JEAN, physical education educator; b. Omaha, Jan. 6, 1927; d. Marion Fowler and Blanche Gibons (McKee) M. BS, U. Nebr., 1948; MS, Wellesley Coll., 1951; LHD (hon.), U. Nebr., 1986. Instr. Kans. State U., Manhattan, 1948-50; instr. U. Nebr., Lincoln, 1951-57, asst. prof., 1957-62; asst. prof. U. Kans., Lawrence, 1962-66; assoc. prof. U. Chgo., 1966-76, prof., 1976-90, prof. emeritus, 1990—, chmn. women's divsn., 1966-76, chmn. dept. phys. edn. and athletics, 1976-90; mem. vis. com. on athletics MIT, 1978-81, Wellesley Coll., 1978-79. Recipient Honor award Nebr. Assn. Health, Phys. Edn. and Recreation, 1962. Mem. AAHPERD, Nat. Collegiate Athletic Assn. (mem. coun. 1983-87), Collegiate Coun. Women Athletic Adminstrs., Midwest Assn. Intercollegiate Athletics for Women (chmn. 1979-81), Nat. Assn. Collegiate Dirs. of Athletics (mem. exec. com. 1976-80, Hall of Fame 1990), Ill. Assn. Intercollegiate Athletics for Women (chmn. 1978-80), Univ. Athletic Assn. (sec. 1986-90, mem. exec. com. 1986-90, mem. dels. com., chmn. athletic adminstr.'s com. 1986-88), Mortar Bd., Alpha Chi Omega. Home: 12 Skyline Dr Ogden Dunes IN 46368-1017

MULVEE, ROBERT EDWARD, bishop; b. Boston, Feb. 15, 1930; s. John F. and Jennie T. (Bath) M. BA, U. Sem. Ottawa, 1953, PhB, 1953; MRE, Am. Coll., Louvain, Belgium, 1957; D Canon Law, Lateran U., Rome, 1964; DD (hon.), Rivier Coll., Nashua, N.H., 1979. Ordained priest Roman Catholic Ch., 1957; asst. chancellor of diocese, 1964-72, named monsignor, 1966, elevated to domestic prelate, 1970, named chancellor, 1972; aux. bishop Roman Catholic Diocese of Manchester, N.H., 1977-85; bishop of Wilmington, 1985-95; coadjutor bishop Roman Cath. Diocese of Providence, 1995—. Trustee Nat. Shrine Immaculate Conception, Washington D.C, 1987. Mem. Nat. Conf. Cath. Bishops (campaign for human devel. com. 1985, joint com. Orthodox and Roman Cath. Bishops 1986, chmn. bd. bishops Am. Coll. of Louvain, Belgium, 1986, Cath. Relief Services bd., 1987); Nat. Conf. Cath. Bishops/ U.S. Cath. Conf. (adminstrv. com. and bd. dirs. 1986, com. on personnel and adminstrv. services 1987). Office: One Cathedral Sq Providence RI 02903-3695

MULVEY, HELEN FRANCES, emeritus history educator; b. Providence, Feb. 22, 1913; d. William James and Anna (Nelson) M. A.B., Pembroke Coll., 1933; A.M., Columbia U., 1934; A.M., Radcliffe Coll., 1942; Ph.D., Harvard U., 1949. Instr. history Russell Sage Coll., Troy, N.Y., 1944-46; asst. prof. to prof. history, Conn. Coll., New London, 1946-83, prof. emeritus, 1983—, Brigida Pacchiana Ardenghi chair, 1975-78; vis. prof. Brit. history, U. Wis., Madison, 1971-72; vis. lectr. Yale U., 1974-83; lectr. Irish history, Pfizer Adult Edn., Groton, Conn., 1983-84; vis. scholar Phi Beta Kappa, Washington, 1982-83. Author articles, essays Irish and Brit. history; co-editor bibliog. vol. in A New History of Ireland, 9 vols. Anne Crosby Emery fellow, Brown U., 1933. Mem. Am. Hist. Assn., Am. Conf. for Irish Studies, North Am. Conf. on Brit. Studies, AAUP (chpt. pres. 1962-64), Phi Beta Kappa. Clubs: Harvard. Office: Conn Coll PO Box 5508 New London CT 06320

MULVIHILL, DAVID BRIAN, lawyer; b. Pitts., Jan. 21, 1956; s. Mead J. Jr. and Margaret (O'Brien) M.; m. Elizabeth Miles, May 21, 1988; stepchildren: Jennifer A. Miles, Heath A. Miles. BA, U. Pitts., 1977; JD, Duquesne U., 1981. Bar: U.S. Dist. Ct. (we. dist.) Pa. 1981, U.S. Ct. Appeals (3d cir.) 1985. Assoc. Mansmann, Cindrich & Titus, Pitts., 1981-86; ptnr. Cindrich & Titus, Pitts., 1986-94, Titus & McConomy, Pitts., 1994—. Bd. dirs. Make-A-Wish Found. Am., 1992—; bd. dirs. Make-A-Wish Found. Western Pa., 1986-93, v.p., 1989-90, pres. 1990-92. Recipient Jefferson medal Am. Inst. for Pub. Svc., 1991, Outstanding Citizen award Pitts. Post-Gazette, 1991. Mem. ABA, Pa. Bar Assn., Allegheny County Bar Assn., Acad. Trial Lawyers of Allegheny County, Nat. Order of Barristers. Avocations: reading, tennis, classic cars. Office: Titus & McConomy 4 Gateway Ctr Pittsburgh PA 15222

MULVIHILL, JAMES EDWARD, periodontist; b. Cleve., Sept. 24, 1940; s. John F. and Teresa J. (Carlos) M.; m. May Jane Forino, 1963; children—Karen, Kristen, Jason. B.A., Coll. of Holy Cross, 1962; D.M.D., Harvard U., 1966. Asst. dean for student affairs, coordinator Harvard-VA continuing edn. program Harvard Sch. Dental Medicine, Boston, 1970-71; dean clin. campus L.I. Jewish-Hillside Med. Ctr., Queens Hosp. Ctr. Affiliation, Jewish Inst. for Geriatric Care, Health Scis. Ctr. SUNY-Stony Brook, 1971-80; v.p. for edn. and research L.I. Jewish-Hillside Med. Ctr., New Hyde Park, N.Y., 1975-80; v.p., provost for health affairs, exec. dir. Health Ctr., prof. periodontics U. Conn., Farmington, 1980-92; attending periodontist John Dempsey Hosp., U. Conn. Health Ctr., Farmington, 1982-92; pres. John Dempsey Fin. Corp., Farmington, 1988-92; sr. v.p. for health policy The Travelers Corp., Hartford, Conn., 1992-94; chmn. bd. The Travelers Health Co., Hartford, 1992-93; sr. fellow in health policy Assn. of Acad. Health Ctrs., 1994; pres., CEO Managed Health, Inc., 1994, Comty. Health Plan of Queens/Nassau, New Hyde Park, N.Y., 1994-95, Forsyth Dental Ctr., Boston, 1995—; cons. in field. Author: (with others) Guide to Foreign Medical Schools, 1975, Editorial Instructions for Dental Authors, 1979-80, 1979, Human Subjects Research: The Operational Handbook for IRB's, 1982, 2d edit., 1984, Japanese edit., 1987; also articles, chpt. in book. Bd. dirs. and chair Nat. Fund for Med. Edn. Recipient Disting. Alumnus award Harvard Sch. Dental Medicine, 1982, Disting. alumnus award Holy Cross Coll., 1991. Fellow ADA, AAAS; mem. Am. Acad. Peridontology, Am. Assn. Dental Schs., Conn. State Dental Assn., Harvard Dental Alumni Assn., Harvard Odontological Soc., Internat. Assn. for Dental Rsch., Alpha Sigma Nu, Sigma Psi. Avocations: golf; gardening. Home: 2 Muls Hill St Andrews Dr Farmington CT 06032 Office: Forsyth Dental Center 140 The Fenway Boston MA 02115

MULVIHILL, ROGER DENIS, lawyer; b. Pitts., June 28, 1936; s. Dennis and Mary (Scheib) M.; m. Mary Brennan, Sept. 25, 1971; children: Christopher, Kerry, Suzanne. BS, Georgetown U., 1958; LLB, Yale U., 1961; LLM, NYU, 1965. Bar: N.Y. 1963. Ptnr. Olwine, Connelly, Chase, O'Donnell and Weyher, N.Y.C., 1969-91, Dechert Price & Rhoads, N.Y.C., 1991—; counsel Planning Bd. Bronxville, Westchester, N.Y., 1984-91. Author: (with others) Handbook for Raising Capital, 1987; contbr. numerous articles to profl. jours. Active Land Use Commn., Bronxville, N.Y.; dir. Religion in Am. Life, N.Y.C., 1986—. With U.S. Army, 1961-63. Mem. ABA, N.Y. State Bar Assn., Assn. of Bar of City of N.Y., Yale Club, Meadow Club, Bronxville Field Club. Roman Catholic. Avocations: tennis, skiing. Office: Dechert Price & Rhoads 477 Madison Ave New York NY 10022-5802*

MULVIHILL, TERENCE JOSEPH, investment banking executive; b. Omaha, Feb. 4, 1931; children: Mary Louise, Patricia, Kathleen (dec.), Joan, Carol, Nancy. BS in Econs., Georgetown U., 1952. Sec., treas. Mulvihill Co., Streator, Ill., 1955-64; instl. salesman Goldman, Sachs & Co., Chgo., 1964-71, v.p., 1971-80, asst. regional mgr., 1972-74, regional sales mgr., 1974-92, ptnr., 1980-92, COO, 1988-92, limited ptnr., 1992—; dir. Gen. Rental Fin. Co. Pres. St. Francis Xavier Sch. Bd., Wilmette, Ill., 1971, Regina Dominican H.S. Parents Assn., 1973; bd. dirs. Glenkirk Assn. for Retarded, Glenview, Ill., 1980-82, St. Joseph's Carondelet Child Ctr., Chgo., 1980-86; trustee Univ. of Chgo. Coun. Grad. Sch. of Bus., 1980—, Regina Dominican H.S. Charitable Trust, Wilmette, 1992, Marmion Military Acad., 1990—, Children's Meml. Hosp., Chgo., 1992—; mem. adv. com. Treas.'s Office of City of Chgo., 1990—; mem. Govs. Task Force Human Svcs. Reform, 1992—; governing mem. Orchestral Assn. Chgo. Symphony Orch., 1992—. 1st lt. U.S Army, 1952-54. Mem. Chgo. Coun. Fgn. Rels., Met. Club, Carlton Club, Bond Club of Chgo. (dir. 1981-82). Office: Goldman Sachs & Co 4900 Sears Tower Chicago IL 60606

MULVOY, MARK, journalist; b. 1942. BA, Boston Coll., 1964. Began career as sports writer Boston Globe, 1964-65; former reporter, writer, sr. editor Sports Illustrated mag.; now editor Sports Illustrated mag., N.Y.C. Office: Sports Illustrated 1271 Avenue Of The Americas New York NY 10020

MULVOY, THOMAS F., JR., newspaper editor, journalist; b. Boston, Feb. 4, 1943; s. Thomas Francis and Julia Frances (Harrington) M.; m. Anastasia Vakina Coulianos, June 1, 1985; children: Stephen Tasos, Michael Thomas, Nicholas Ramirez. AB in Philosophy, Boston Coll., 1964. News dir. Sta. WPLM AM/FM, Plymouth, Mass., 1965-66; copy editor The Boston Globe, 1967-74, asst. sports editor, 1974-76, news editor, 1976-79, asst. mng. editor, 1979-83, dep. mng. editor, 1983-86, mng. editor, 1986—. Stanford U. fellow, 1983. Roman Catholic. Avocations: reading, writing, golfing, walking. Office: The Boston Globe PO Box 2378 Boston MA 02107-2378

MUMAW, JAMES WEBSTER, lawyer; b. Youngstown, Ohio, Apr. 11, 1920; s. Daniel W. and Helen (James) M.; m. Lois M. Baird, May 28, 1948; children: Thomas, Daniel, William. A.B., Coll. of Wooster, 1941; J.D., U. Cin., 1948. Bar: Ohio 1949. Since practiced in Youngstown; partner Luckhart, Mumaw, Morrison & Zellers and predecessor firm, 1959-66; mem. firm Luckhart, Mumaw, Zellers & Robinson, 1966—; Dir. Ohio Bar Title Ins. Co., 1955-91, Western Res. Bank of Ohio, 1963-95. Mem. Youngstown City Bd. Edn., 1972-75; pres. Christ Mission Kindergarten Assn., Goodwill Industries, 1967-69; trustee Ohio Land Title Assn., 1975-78, v.p., 1981, pres., 1982-83, Penn Ohio Coll., 1989—. Served with AUS, 1943-46. Mem. Ohio State Bar Found. (life), ABA, Ohio State Bar (exec. com. 1978-81), Mahoning County Bar Assn. (pres. 1963-64), Am. Judicature Soc., Phi Alpha Delta. Presbyterian (elder, trustee). Club: Kiwanian. Home: 845 Wildwood Dr Youngstown OH 44512 Office: Legal Arts Center Youngstown OH 44503

MUMFORD, CHRISTOPHER GREENE, corporate financial executive; b. Washington, Oct. 21, 1945; s. Milton C. and Dorothea L. (Greene) M.; B.A., Stanford U., 1968, M.B.A., 1975. Cons., Internat. Tech. Resources Inc., 1974; asst. v.p. Wells Fargo Bank, San Francisco, 1975-78; v.p., treas. Arcata Corp., San Francisco, 1978-82, v.p. fin., 1982-87, exec. v.p., 1987-94. gen. ptnr. Scarff, Sears & Assocs., San Francisco, 1986-95, mng. dir. Questor Ptnrs. Fund, L.P., San Francisco, 1995—; v.p. bd. dirs. Triangle Pacific Corp., Dallas, 1986-88, Norton Enterprises Inc., Salt Lake City, 1988-90; bd. dirs. Community Home Med. Enterprises, Inc., Grass Valley, Calif., Crown Pacific Ltd., Portland, Oreg., Union Security Mortgage, Inc., Santa Ana, Calif., 1993-94. Office: 601 California St Ste 1450 San Francisco CA 94108-2823

MUMFORD, DAVID BRYANT, mathematics educator; b. Worth, Sussex, Eng., June 11, 1937; came to U.S., 1940; s. William Bryant and Grace (Schiott) M.; m. Erika Jentsch, June 27, 1959 (dec. July 30, 1988); children: Stephen, Peter, Jeremy, Suchitra; m. Jenifer Moore, Dec. 29, 1989. B.A., Harvard U., 1957, Ph.D., 1961; D.Sc. (hon.), U. Warwick, 1983. Jr. fellow Harvard U., 1958-61, asso. prof., 1962-66, prof. math., 1966-77, Higgins prof., 1977—, chmn. dept. math, 1981-84; v.p. Internat. Math. Union, 1991-94, pres., 1995—. Author: Geometric Invariant Theory, 1965, Abelian Varieties, 1970, Introduction to Algebraic Geometry, 1976. Recipient Fields medal Internat. Congress Mathematicians, 1974; MacArthur Found. fellow, 1987-92. Fellow Tata Inst. (hon.); mem. Accad. Nazionale dei Lincei, Nat. Acad. Scis., Am. Acad. Arts and Scis. Home: 26 Gray St Cambridge MA 02138-1510 Office: Harvard U 1 Oxford St Cambridge MA 02138-2901

MUMFORD, GEORGE SALTONSTALL, JR., former university dean, astronomy educator; b. Milton, Mass., Nov. 13, 1928; s. George S. and Alice (Herrick) M.; m. Nancy Carey, Dec. 22, 1949; children: Barbara, Elizabeth, Robert, George. A.B., Harvard U., 1950; M.A., Ind. U., 1952; Ph.D., U. Va., 1955. Mem. faculty Randolph-Macon Woman's Coll., 1952-53; mem. faculty Tufts U., Medford, Mass., 1955—; prof. astronomy Tufts U., 1968—, dean Coll. Liberal Arts, 1969-79, dean research and instl. programs, dean Grad. Sch. Arts and Scis., 1979-84; acting dir. Dudley Wright Ctr. for Innovation in Sci. Teaching, 1991-92; vis. astronomer Kitt Peak Nat. Obs., Tucson, 1962-82; cons. NSF, 1967-68; vis. astronomer Cerro Tololo Inter-Am. Obs., La Serena, Chile, 1969-72; dir. Wyman-Gordon Inc., Worcester, Mass. Corp; bd. dirs. Coun. of Grad. Schs. in U.S., 1979-83; mem. space sci. rev. panel NAS, 1989-95; mem. planetarium adv. com. Mus. Sci., Boston. Mem. AAAS, Am. Astron. Soc., Astron. Soc. Pacific, Am. Phys. Soc., Internat. Astron. Union, Am. Assn. Physics Tchrs., Royal Astron. Soc. Can., Royal Astron. Soc., N.E. Assn. Grad. Schs. (pres. 1981-82), Sigma Xi. Research in photometric studies of cataclysmic variables and related objects, early Am. astronomy, software for astronomy education. Home: Pegan Ln Dover MA 02030 Office: Tufts U Dept Physics And Astro Medford MA 02155

MUMFORD, MANLY WHITMAN, lawyer; b. Evanston, Ill., Feb. 25, 1925; s. Manly Stearns and Helen (Whitman) M.; m. Luigi Thorne Horne, July 1, 1961; children—Shaw, Dodge. A.B., Harvard U., 1947; J.D., Northwestern U, Chgo., 1950. Bar: Ill. 1950, U.S. Supreme Ct. 1969. Assoc. Chapman and Cutler, Chgo., 1950-62, ptnr., 1963-90. Contbr. articles to profl. jours. Served with USNR, 1942-46. Mem. Nat. Assn. Bond Lawyers (Bernard P. Friel medal 1987). Democrat. Clubs: Cliff Dwellers, University, Chgo. Literary. Avocation: computers. Home: 399 W Fullerton Pky Chicago IL 60614-2810 Office: 22 W Monroe St Ste 1503 Chicago IL 60603-2505

MUMFORD, STEPHEN DOUGLAS, population growth control research scientist; b. Louisville, Aug. 28, 1942; s. Adrian Leroy and Mildred Margaret (Cardwell) M.; m. Judy Sheng-Ju Lee, Dec. 26, 1966; children: Christopher Lee, Sonia Lea. BS in Agr., U. Ky., 1966; MPH in Internat. Health/Population Study, U. Tex., Houston, 1971, DrPH in Health Svcs. Adminstrn., 1975. Indsl. hygienist Ky. State Dept. Health, Frankfort, 1966-67; rsch. asst. dept. ob.-gyn. Baylor Coll. Medicine, Houston, 1973-75; rsch. statis. aide population studies U. Tex., Houston, 1971-75, rsch. asst. dept. reproductive biology/endocrinology, 1971-76; dir. rsch., sr. vasectomy counselor Planned Parenthood of Houston, 1972-76; adminstr. Nat. Swine Flu Immunization Program/Houston/Harris County, Tex., 1976-77; from sect. leader design/analysis divsn. to scientist Internat. Fertility Rsch. Program, Research Triangle Park, N.C., 1977-83; pres. Ctr. for Rsch. on Population and Security, Research Triangle Park, N.C., 1984—; bd. dirs. The Churchman Assocs., Inc., St. Petersburg, Fla. Author: The Pope and the New Apocalypse: The Holy War Against Family Planning, 1986, American Democracy and the Vatican: Population Growth and National Security, 1984, Population Growth Control: The Next Move is America's, 1977, The Decision-Making Process that Leads to Vasectomy: A Guide for Promoters, 1977, Vasectomy Counseling, 1977, The Life and Death of NSSM 200: How the Destruction of Political Will Doomed a U.S. Population Policy, 1994; contbr. numerous articles to profl. jours., chpts. to books; contbr. editor The Churchman, 1991—. Mem. Alan Guttmacher Inst., Assn. for Vol. Sterilization, Environ. Def. Fund, Fund for Feminist Majority, Nat. Abortion Rights Action League, Population Action Coun., Population Ref. Bur., Religious Coalition for Abortion Rights. Capt. U.S. Army, 1966-70. Recipient Cert. of Appreciation for Outstanding Contbns. to Advancing the Cause of Reproductive Rights, Feminist Caucus of Am. Humanist Assn., 1986, Humanist Disting. Svc. award, 1981, Margaret Mead Leadership prize in population and ecology, 1981, Award for Outstanding Single Project in Area of Human Rels., U.S. Jaycees, 1974-75, Award for Outstanding Chmn. of a Single Project in Area of Human Rels., 1974-75. Mem. Am. Humanist Assn., Am. Pub. Health Assn. (population sect.), Ams. for Immigration Control, Ams. for Religious Liberty, Fedn. for Am. Immigration Reform, Internat. Epidemiol. Assn., Nat. Coun. Internat. Health, Negative Population Growth, Res. Officers assn. of U.S., Soc. for Epidemiologic Rsch., World Future Soc., World Population Soc., Zero Population Growth, NOW. Avocations: gardening, fruit growing, woodworking, fishing, running. Home: 322 Azalea Dr Chapel Hill NC 27514-9120 Office: Ctr Rsch Population PO Box 13067 Research Triangle Park NC 27709-3067

MUMFORD, WILLIAM PORTER, II, lawyer; b. Kewanee, Ill., July 13, 1920; s. Harold E. and Mary K. (Harry) M.; m. Jean N. Hagemann, Nov. 22, 1951; children—William Porter III, James F., Michael E. B.S. in Accounting, U. Ill., 1943, J.D., 1949. Bar: Ill. bar 1949, Oreg. bar 1955; C.P.A., Ill., Oreg. Jr. accountant Price Waterhouse & Co., Chgo., 1949-51; practiced in Chgo., 1951-54, Grants Pass, Ore., 1955-57, Eugene, Oreg., 1957—; mem. firm McAdams & Kirby, 1951-55; sr. accountant B.K. Herndon & Co., 1955-57; partner Thompson, Mumford, Anderson & Fisher, 1957-86, ret., 1986. Eugene campaign mgr. Hatfield for Gov., 1960-62; Chmn. bd. trustees Oreg. State Library. Served to capt., inf. AUS, 1943-46. Mem. Am. Legion, Pi Kappa Alpha, Phi Alpha Delta. Republican. Club: Elk. Home: 1960 Alder St Eugene OR 97405-2938

MUMMA, ALBERT G., retired naval officer, manufacturing company executive, management consultant; b. Findlay, Ohio, June 2, 1906; grad. U.S. Naval Acad., 1926; D.Eng. (hon.) N.J. Inst. Tech.; m. Carmen Braley, 1927; children—Albert G. Jr., John S., David B. Commd. ensign USN, 1926, advanced through grades to rear adm.; head tech. intelligence div. Naval Forces Europe, World War II; comdr. David Taylor Model Basin, Mare Island Naval Shipyard, also chief Bur. Ships, U.S. Navy, 1955-59; builder nuclear high speed submarines, U.S.S. Enterprise, Long Beach, Bainbridge and Polaris submarines; ret., 1959; v.p., group exec. Worthington Corp., 1964, exec. v.p., dir. in charge all domestic ops., 1967, pres., chief operating officer, 1967, chmn. bd., 1967-71; chmn. Am. Shipbldg. Commn., 1971-73. Trustee emeritus Drew U., Madison, N.J. Recipient Adm. Jerry Land Gold medal; awarded Knight Grand Officer of Orange Nassau by the Queen of the Netherlands. Fellow Soc. Naval Architects and Marine Engrs. (hon.; past pres.); mem. Am. Soc. Naval Engrs. (hon.; past pres.), Nat. Acad. Scis. (past mem. research council; past chmn. numerous coms.), Nat. Acad. Engring. (life). Clubs: Army and Navy, Army and Navy Country (Washington), Baltusrol Golf (Springfield, N.J.); Mountain Lake (Lake Wales, Fla.). Home: 69 Mountain Lk Lake Wales FL 33859 summer: 1400 Waverly Rd # 25 Gladwyne PA 19035-1254

MUMMA, ALBERT GIRARD, JR., architect; b. Long Beach, Calif., July 2, 1928; s. Albert Girard and Carmen (Braley) M.; m. Janeal Thomas Woolf, Dec. 24, 1973; children: Eugenia M. Villagra, Albert Girard III, Peter Brenaman. B.Arch., U. Va., 1951. Designer McLeod & Ferrara, Architects, Washington, 1951-56; assoc. Deigert & Yerkes, Architects, 1956-62; prin. Mumma & Assocs., Washington, 1962—; archtl. designer hotel div. Marriott Corp., 1980-82. Prin. archtl. works include Nat. Arboretum Hdqrs. Bldg, 1961, Finnmark Sq., Silver Spring, Md., 1964, Inverness townhouses, Potomac, Md., 1971, Post Office and Fed. Bldg., Elkins, W.Va., 1971, U.S. Trade Fairs in Spain, Finland, Japan, El Salvador, Poland 1963-72, Fallswood housing project, Falls Church, Va., 1972, Bristow Village townhouses, Annandale, Va., 1972-73, Marriott Hotel, Dayton, Ohio, 1982, Plaza Venetia, Biscayne Bay, Miami, Fla., 1983, Houston Med. Ctr. Hotel, Newark Airport Hotel, 1984, pvt. residences, subdivision and townhouse projects, Washington, Md., Va., Pa., 1962—. Served with USMC, 1945-47. Recipient Design award Washington Bd. Trade, 1964; winner Newark Airport Hotel Competition, 1981. Mem. AIA (medal 1951), Rappahannock River Yacht Club.

MUMMA, GORDON, composer, educator, author; b. Framingham, Mass., Mar. 30, 1935; s. Colgan Thomas and Adamae (McCoy) M.; children: Christopher, Jonathan. Student, U. Mich., 1952-53. Guest lectr. Brandeis U., 1966, 67; composer, musician Merce Cunningham Dance Co., 1966-74, Sonic Arts Union, from 1966; guest lectr. U. Ill., 1969-70, Ferienkurse für Neue Musik, Darmstadt, Fed. Republic Germany, 1974; mem. faculty Cursos Latinoamericanos de Música Contemporánea, Montevideo, 1975, Buenos Aires, 1977, Dominican Republic, 1981; prof. music U. Calif., Santa Cruz, 1975-94; prof. emeritus U. Calif., 1994—; Darius Milhaud prof. Mills Coll., 1981; co-founder ONCE Festivals of Contemporary Music, Ann Arbor, Mich., 1961-66, Cybersonics, Ann Arbor, 1963; electronic designer Pepsi Pavilion, Expo 70, Osaka, Japan; tech. dir. Intermedia Inst., N.Y.C., 1970; founder Tao Chem. Co., performance-arts prodn. co., N.Y.C., 1976; vis. prof. U. Calif.-San Diego, 1985, 87; vis. disting. composer Mills Coll., 1989. Commd. works, recs. and performances include music for Venezia Space Theatre, Venice, Italy, 1963, Megaton for William Burroughs, Ann Arbor, 1964, Mesa, St. Paul de Vence, France, 1966, Hornpipe, Boston, 1967, Beam, Tokyo, 1969, Cybersonic Cantilevers, Syracuse, 1973, Some Voltage Drop, Paris, 1974, Passenger Pigeon, Albany, N.Y., 1976, (with David Cotter, Jann McCauley, Tom Robbins), Ear Heart, Portland, Oreg., 1977, (with Jann McCauley, Henk Pander, Peter West), Echo, Portland, 1978, Pontpoint, 1980, (with William Winant) Than Particle, 1985, (with Tandy Beal Dance Co.), Orait, 1988, (with Abel-Steinberg-Winant Trio) Ménages à Deux, 1990; author: (with James Klosty) Merce Cunningham, 1975, (with Jon Appleton) Development and Practice of Electronic Music, 1975. N.Y. State Council on Arts grantee; Nat. Endowment Arts grantee, 1977-78; Oreg. Arts Council grantee, 1977-78. Mem. Broadcast Music Inc., Internat. Horn Soc., Soc. Ethnomusicology. Office: Univ Calif Dept Music Santa Cruz CA 95064

MUMMA, MICHAEL JON, physicist; b. Lancaster, Pa., Dec. 3, 1941; s. John Henry and Violet Lyndell (Baxter) M.; m. Sage Bailey Tower, Aug. 20, 1966; children: Peter Robb, Amy Elizabeth. A.B. in Physics with honors, Franklin and Marshall Coll., 1963; Ph.D. in Physics, U. Pitts., 1970. Grad. research asst. U. Pitts., 1963-70; astrophysicist NASA Goddard Space Flight Center, Greenbelt, Md., 1970-76; head br. Infrared and Radio Astronomy NASA Goddard Space Flight Center, 1976-84, assoc. chief Lab. Extraterrestrial Physics, 1984-85, head Planetary Systems br., 1985-90, chief scientist Lab. Extraterrestrial Physics, 1990—; adj. research assoc. in physics Pa. State U., 1978-81, prof. physics, 1981-88; mem. numerous working groups and adv. coms. NASA, Nat. Bur. Standards, NSF, Nat. Acad. Scis., 1973—; lectr. in field. Contbr. numerous articles to profl. publs., 1970—; editor: The Study of Comets, Vols. 1, 2, 1976, Vibrational-Rotational Spectroscopy for Planetary Atmospheres, vols. 1, 2, 1982, Astrophysics from the Moon, 1990. Recipient NASA medal for Exceptional Sci. Achievement, 1986; Kershner award for physics, 1962; Coll. Trustee's scholar Franklin and Marshall Coll., 1963. Fellow Am. Phys. Soc., Washington Acad. Sci.; mem. AAAS, Am. Astron. Soc., Am. Geophys. Union, Internat. Astron. Union, Sigma Pi Sigma. Achievements include discovery of natural lasers in atmospheres of Mars, Venus, and Jupiter; first detection of water vapor, formaldehyde and methanol in comets; first definitive measurements of deuterium and hydrogen on Mars and Venus; first absolute wind measurements on Venus and Mars; invention of tunable diode laser heterodyne spectrometer and other advanced instruments; development of Doppler-limited infrared spectroscopy for laboratory and astrophysical applications, of absolute calibration procedures in vacuum ultraviolet, of molecular branching ratio technique for intensity calibration in vacuum ultraviolet; measurement of many absolute cross sections in vacuum ultraviolet; research on atomic and molecular physics and chemistry, on comets, on planetary atmospheres, on infrared astronomy, on high-resolution spectroscopy, and in the field of dissociative excitation of molecules. Office: Code 690 Goddard Space Flight Ctr Greenbelt MD 20771

MUMMERT, WANDA JEAN, family nurse practitioner, consultant; b. McAlester, Okla., Oct. 10, 1930; d. Carl A. and Verna W. Fawcett; m. Martin G. Mummert, Aug. 27, 1948 (dec. Feb. 1994); children: Jean A., J. Anna, Mary A. AAS in Nursing, Eastern Okla. State Coll., 1974; cert. FNP, Okla. U. Coll. Nursing, 1979. RNC, ANCC; RN, Tex., Okla. Staff nurse, nead nurse, relief house supr. McAlester (Okla.) Gen. Hosp., 1974-76; substitute tchr., practical nurse Kiamichi Area Vocat. Tech., McAlester, 1975-77; staff nurse, supr. Okla. Dept. Health, Atoka, 1977-78; FNP McAlester, 1979-94; patient care coord. Hospice of McAlester Okla., Inc., 1991-94; FNP East Tex. Med. Ctr., Hughes Springs, 1994—; mem. adv. bd. Head Start, Shawnee, Okla., 1989-90, Hospice of McAlester Okla., Inc., 1991-92. Precinct election ofcl. Pittsburg County Election Bd., McAlester, 1954-94; vol. nurse, disaster nurse ARC, McAlester, 1974-94; presenter Gov.'s Task Force on Health Care, McAlester, 1989; squadron med. officer, pilot, CAP, McAlester, 1974-75. Mem. ANA, Okla. Nurses Assn. (dist. v.p., pres. 1974—), Assn. Okla. Nurse Practitioners, Am. Acad. Nurse Practitioners, Internat. Flying Nurses Assn. (conv. co-chmn. 1980-93), Tex. Nurse Practitioners. Avocations: reading, fishing, traveling. Home: PO Box 477-A Hughes Springs TX 75656 Office: E Tex Med Ctr Rural Health Ctr 2nd and Ward Hughes Springs TX 75656

MUMZHIU, ALEXANDER, optical and imaging processing engineer, researcher; b. St. Petersburg, Russia, June 6, 1937; came to U.S., 1979; s. Mikhail and Henrietta (Rosenblum) M.; m. Natalya Takjas, Sept. 22, 1967; children: Jennifer, Daniel. Enginizing diploma, Leningrad Tech. Inst., 1959. Engr. Petzochemical Inst., St. Petersburg, Russia, 1959-65; sr. engr. optical dept. Mendeleev Inst. Metrology, St. Petersburg, Russia, 1965-79; prin. engr. Mid-West Instr., Troy, Mich., 1980-83; electro-optical engr. Perceptron Co., Farm Hills, Mich., 1983-84; cons. Arthur D. Little Co., Washington, 1984-85; sr. rsch. scientist Hunterlab., Reston, Va., 1985—. Contbr. articles to profl. jours. Recipient awards Moscow Indsl. Show. Mem. IEEE, OSA. Achievements include development of fundamental principles of imaging colorimetry; 2 U.S. patents for fiber optic sensor of rotation; design of first scanning spectrophometer, automatic lensmeter, thermoelectric flowmeter. Office: Hunterlab Inc 11491 Sunset Hills Rd Reston VA 22090-5207

MUNCH, DOUGLAS FRANCIS, pharmaceutical and health industry consultant; b. Bronx, N.Y., Mar. 15, 1947; s. Robert Joseph and Isabel (Fiordelisi) M.; m. Janice Ann Davis, Apr. 3, 1976; children: Sarah Christine, Eric Christopher. BSChemE, Villanova U., 1969; MS, U. Calif., Santa Barbara, 1974; PhD, Johns Hopkins U., 1978. Project engr. Grumman Aerospace Corp., Bethpage, N.Y., 1969-73; postdoctoral fellow U. South Ala., 1978-80; program mgr. Travenol Labs., Round Lake, Ill., 1980-82; dir. Kimberly Clark Corp., Atlanta, 1982-86; pres. Biomed. Products Group Inc., Roswell, Ga., 1986-87; cons., pres. D.F. Munch & Assocs., Roswell, 1986-88; pres., dir. Sphinx Pharmaceuticals, Inc., Durham, N.C., 1988-89; v.p., dir. Orthopharm Corp.-Advanced Care Products, Johnson & Johnson, Raritan, N.J., 1989-92; pres. D.F. Munch, Ltd., Basking Ridge, N.J., 1992—. Author: Cardiovascular Pharmacology, 1981; contbr. articles to profl. jours. Pres. Hollyberry Civic Assn., Roswell, 1980-87, Roswell Neighborhood Network, 1987, Basking Ridge (N.J.) Little League, 1992—; elder Basking Ridge Presbyn. Ch., 1992-95. Recipient Apollo Achievement award NASA, 1969; Profl. Achievement award Villanova U., 1987; NIH fellow, 1974-78. Fellow Royal Soc. Medicine; mem. Am. Physiol. Soc., Biomed. Engring. Soc., Johns Hopkins Med. and Surg. Assn. Avocations: woodworking, music, camping, cycling, swimming. Home: 41 Fieldstone Dr Basking Ridge NJ 07920-1605

MUNCK, ALLAN ULF, physiologist, educator; b. Buenos Aires, Argentina, July 4, 1925; came to U.S., 1945, naturalized, 1959; s. Carl and Elisabeth (Schmidt) M.; m. Claire Brosi, Oct. 5, 1957; children—Alexander Charles, Ingrid Claire, Kirsten Tanya. B.S. in Chem. Engring, Mass. Inst. Tech., 1948, M.S., 1949, Ph.D. in Biophysics, 1956. Chem. engr. Ducilo, Buenos Aires, 1949-50; mem. staff Huntington Lab. Mass. Gen. Hosp., Boston, 1956-57, Worcester Found. Exptl. Biology, Shrewsbury, Mass., 1957-59; mem. faculty Dartmouth Coll. Med. Sch., 1957—; prof. physiology Dartmouth Med. Sch., 1967—. Assoc. editor: Jour. Steroid Biochemistry; editorial bd.: Jour. Biol. Chemistry. Served with Argentine Army, 1949. Mem. Physiol. Soc., Endocrine Soc., Am. Soc. Biochemistry and Molecular Biology. Home: PO Box 114 Norwich VT 05055-0114 Office: Dartmouth Med Sch Dept Physiology Lebanon NH 03756

MUNCY, ESTLE PERSHING, physician; b. Tazewell, Tenn., Apr. 9, 1918; s. William Loyd and Flora Media (Monday) M.; m. Dorothy Davis, Dec. 31, 1946 (div. Apr. 1980); children: Robert H., Teresa A., Dorothy J., Estle II, James; m. Jean Marie Hayter, Mar. 19, 1985. AB, Lincoln Meml. U., 1939; MD, U. Tenn., 1943. Resident Dallas Meth. Hosp., 1948; tchg. resident Tufts Med. Sch., Boston, 1949-50; physician Jefferson City, Tenn., 1950-96. Author: The Muncys in the New World, 1988, People and Places in Jefferson County, Tennessee, 1994. Alderman Jefferson City, 1974-77; chmn. Jefferson City Planning Commn., 1976-79. Capt. M.C., U.S. Army, 1944-46. Nen, Tenn. Heart Assn. (pres. 1966-67), Hamblem County Med. Soc. (pres. 1960-61), Jefferson County Hist. Soc. (pres. 1993-94, historian 1995—). Republican. Baptist. Avocations: photography, gardening. Home: 1428 Russell Ave Jefferson City TN 37760-2529

MUND, GERALDINE, bankruptcy judge; b. L.A., July 7, 1943; d. Charles J. and Pearl (London) M. BA, Brandeis U., 1965; MS, Smith Coll., 1967; JD, Loyola U., 1977. Bar: Calif. 1977. Bankruptcy judge U.S. Cen. Dist. Calif., 1984—. Past pres. Temple Israel, Hollywood, Calif. Mem. ABA, L.A. County Bar Assn. Office: Roybal Bldg 255 E Temple St Los Angeles CA 90012-3334

MUND, RICHARD GORDON, foundation executive; b. Balt., Feb. 11, 1942; s. Allan Winfield and Irma Louetta (Kaufman) M.; m. Joan Ann Dennis, June 24, 1967; children: Mary Jean, John Winfield, Elizabeth Anne. Student, Johns Hopkins U., 1960-63; BA, Ill. Wesleyan U., 1965; M.A., U. Denver, 1967, Ph.D., 1970. Asst. dir. admissions Marshall U., Huntington, W.Va., 1970, dir. fin. aid, 1971, v.p. student affairs, 1971-77; coll. rels. coord. Mobil Oil Corp., N.Y.C., 1977-79; asst. sec. Mobil Found., Inc., N.Y.C., 1979, sec., exec. dir., 1980—; mem. contbns. coun. Conf. Bd.,

N.Y.C., 1980—, chmn., 1985. Trustee Huntington (W.Va.) Galleries, 1975-77, Coun. for Advancement and Support of Edn., 1987-89, Fairfax County Pub. Schs. Edn. Found., 1991—, Soc. of Yeager Scholars, Marshall U., 1995—; adv. coun. mem. ARC, BBB, Nat. Ctr. Non-Profit Bds., United Way Am. Mem. Kappa Delta Pi, Kappa Alpha Order, Phi Delta Kappa. Office: Mobil Found Inc 3325 Gallows Rd Fairfax VA 22037

MUNDEL, MARVIN EVERETT, industrial engineer; b. N.Y.C., Apr. 20, 1916; s. Maxwell Herbert and Aimee (Baer) M. B.S.M.E., NYU, 1936; M.S. in Indsl. Engring., State U. Iowa, Iowa City, 1938, Ph.D. in Indsl. Engring, 1939. Registered profl. engr., Ind., Wis. Prof. Purdue U., West Lafayette, Ind., 1942-52; dir. U.S. Army Mgmt. Tng., Rock Island, Ill., 1952-53; staff officer U.S. Bur. Budget, Washington, 1963-65; prin. M.E. Mundel & Assocs., Silver Spring, Md., 1953-63, 65—. Author texts: Motion and Time Study, 7th edit., 1994, (with David L. Danner) Improving Productivity and Effectiveness, 1983. Recipient Gold medal Asian Productivity Orgn., Tokyo, 1980; named Engr. of Yr., Washington Council Engrs., 1980. Fellow Inst. Indsl. Engrs. (pres. 1979-80, Frank and Lillian Gilbreth award 1982), World Acad. Productivity Sci. Home and Office: 821 Loxford Ter Silver Spring MD 20901-1131

MUNDELL, DAVID EDWARD, leasing company executive; b. Montreal, Que., Can., Dec. 27, 1931; s. Charles D.T. and Elise Warden (Dunton) M.; m. Willa Price McReynolds, July 25, 1969; children: David Edward (dec.), Elise Mundell. BSc, Royal Mil. Coll. Can., 1953; B Engring., McGill U., 1954; MBA, Harvard, 1957. With DuPont of Can., 1957-59; pres. Can.-Dominion Leasing Corp., Ltd., Toronto, 1959-65; exec. v.p. U.S. Leasing Corp., 1965-68; pres. U.S. Leasing Internat. Inc., San Francisco, 1976-89, CEO, 1976-90; Chmn. Orix U.S.A., San Francisco; chmn. Orix USA Corp. N.Y., San Francisco; bd. dirs. Blazer Homes Inc., Commodity Corp. N.J., San Francisco Varian Assocs., Inc., Palo Alto. Mem. Pacific-Union Club, Toronto Golf Club. Office: Orix USA 1 Bush St Ste 250 San Francisco CA 94104-4425*

MUNDELL, ROBERT ALEXANDER, economics educator; b. Kingston, Ont., Can., Oct. 24, 1932; s. William C. and Lila (Knifton) M.; m. Barbara Sheff, Oct. 14, 1957 (div. 1972); children: Paul Alexander, William Andrew, Robin Leslie. BA, U. B.C., Can., 1953; postgrad., U. Wash., 1953-54, London Sch. Econs. and Polit. Sci., 1955-56; PhD, MIT, 1956; postgrad., U. Chgo., 1956-57; Hon. Doctorate, Renmin U. China, 1985, U. Paris, 1992. Instr. econs. U. B.C., Vancouver, Can., 1957-58; acting asst. prof. econs. Stanford U., Calif., 1958-59; vis. prof. econs. Sch. Advanced Internat. Studies, Johns Hopkins U. Ctr., Bologna, Italy, 1959-61; sr. economist research dept. IMF, Washington, 1961-63; vis. prof. econs. McGill U., Montreal, Que., Can., 1973-74; Rockefeller vis. research prof. internat. econs. Brookings Instn., Washington, 1964-65; prof. Grad. Inst. Internat. Studies, Geneva, summers 1965—; Ford Found. vis. research prof. econs. U. Chgo., 1965-66, prof., 1966-71; prof. econs., chmn. dept. U. Waterloo, Ont., Can., 1972-74; prof. econs. Columbia U., N.Y.C., 1974—; economist Can. Royal Commn. on Price Spreads on Food Products, summer 1957; mem. joint fiscal mission to Peru OAS and Inter-Am. Devel. Bank, summer 1964; cons. FRS, IBRD, 1966—, U.S. Treasury Dept., 1969-74, EEC, 1970-73, UN, Govt. Panama; organizer, participant internat. confs., lectr. numerous univs. and profl. orgn. meetings. Author: The International Monetary System--Conflict and Reform, 1965, Man and Economics, 1968, International Economics, 1968, Monetary Theory--Interest, Inflation and Growth in the World Economy, 1971; contbr. sects. to books, encys., U.S. Congl. Hearings, numerous articles to profl. jours.; co-editor, contbr.: Monetary Problems of the International Economy, 1969, Trade, Balance of Payments and Growth, 1971; co-editor: The New International Monetary System, 1977; editor: Jour. Polit. Economy, 1966-70, Global Disequilibrium in the World Economy, 1989, 92, Building the New Europe, 1991, Debt, Deficit and Economic Importance, 1990. Recipient Jacques Rueff Prize medal, 1983; NSF rsch. grantee, 1967-70; Guggenheim fellow, 1970-71; Marshall lectr. Cambridge U., 1974. Mem. Can. Polit. Sci. Assn. (exec. coun. 1963-64), Can. Econ. Assn., Am. Econ. Assn. Office: Dept Econs Columbia U 1031 Internat Affairs 118th St & Amsterdam Ave New York NY 10027

MUNDEN, ROBIN GHEZZI, lawyer; b. Rome, May 22, 1947; (parents Am. citizens); s. Kenneth White and Lia (Ghezzi) M.; m. Gail J. Schoch, June 2, 1973. BA in Polit. Sci., U. Denver, 1970; JD cum laude, Northwestern U., 1973. Bar: Ill. 1973, U.S. Dist. Ct. (no. dist.) Ill. 1973. Litigation assoc. McDermott, Will & Emery, Chgo., 1973-79; gen. counsel King-Seeley Thermos Co., Prospect Heights, Ill., 1979-82; v.p., gen. counsel, sec. Household Mfg. Inc., Prospect Heights, Ill., 1982-89; ptnr. Trizna, Lepri & Munden, Chgo., 1990-93; v.p., gen. counsel DSC Logistics, Inc., Des Plaines, Ill., 1993—. Mem. editorial bd. Northwestern Univ. Law Review, 1971-73. Mem. Sheffield Neighbors, Chgo. Mem. ABA, Ill. Bar Assn., Chgo. Bar Assn., Burnham Pk. Yacht Club (Chgo.), Royal Ocean Racing Club (U.K.). Democrat. Avocation: sailing. Home: 2140 N Bissell St Chicago IL 60614-4202 Office: DSC Logistics Inc 1750 S Wolf Rd Des Plaines IL 60018-1924

MUNDHEIM, ROBERT HARRY, law educator; b. Hamburg, Germany, Feb. 24, 1933; m. Guna Smitchens; children: Susan, Peter. BA, Harvard U., 1954, LLB, 1957; MA (hon.), U. Pa., 1971. Bar: N.Y. 1958, Pa. 1979. Assoc. Shearman & Sterling, N.Y.C., 1958-61; spl. counsel to SEC, Washington, 1962-63; vis. prof. Duke Law Sch., Durham, N.C., 1964; prof. law U. Pa., Phila., 1965—, Univ. prof. law and fin., 1980-93, dean, 1982-89, Bernard G. Segal prof. law, 1987-89; co-chmn. Fried, Frank, Harris, Shriver & Jacobson, N.Y.C., 1990-92; v.p., gen. counsel Salomon Inc.; gen. counsel U.S. Dept. Treasury, Washington, 1977-80; dir. Ctr. for Study of Fin. Instns., U. Pa.; dir. Corestates Bank N.A., 1980-92, Commerce Clearing House, 1980-96, Appleseed Found., The Kitchen; gen. counsel Chrysler Loan Guarantee Bd., 1980; exec. v.p., gen. counsel Salomon, Inc., 1992—; mng. dir., mem. exec. com. Salomon Bros. Inc., N.Y.C., 1992—. Served with USAF, 1961-62. Recipient Alexander Hamilton award U.S. Dept. Treasury, 1980, Harold P. Seligson award Practicing Law Inst., 1988, Francis J. Rawle award, ABA-ALI, 1992. Mem. Am. Law Inst. (council, mem. exec. com.), Nat. Assn. Securities Dealers (gov.-at-large, vice-chmn.), San Diego Securities Regulation Inst. (chmn.). Author: Outside Director of the Publicly Held Corporation, 1976; American Attitudes Toward Foreign Direct Investment in the United States, 1979; Conflict of Interest and the Former Government Employee: Re-thinking the Revolving Door, 1981. Office: Salomon Brothers Inc 7 World Trade Ctr New York NY 10048-1102

MUNDINGER, DONALD CHARLES, college president retired; b. Chgo., Sept. 2, 1929; s. George Edward and Bertha (Trelkenberg) M.; m. June Myrtle Grubbe, June 17, 1951; children: Debra Sue, Donald William, Mary Ruth (dec.). Student, U. Ill., 1947-48; BA, Concordia Coll., River Forest, Ill., 1951, LLD (hon.), 1982; MA, Northwestern U., 1952; PhD, Washington U., St. Louis, 1956; DH (hon.), MacMurray Coll., Jacksonville, Ill., 1984, Ritsumeikan U., Kyoto, Japan, 1992; LLD (hon.), Ill. Coll., Jacksonville, 1993; postdoctoral study, Cambridge U. (Eng.), 1967-68. Asst. prof. polit. sci., chmn. dept. Augustana Coll., Sioux Falls, S.D., 1956-58; asst. prof. govt. Valparaiso (Ind.) U., 1958-61, assoc. prof., 1961-65, prof., 1965-73; dean Valparaiso (Ind.) U. (Coll. Arts and Scis.), 1965-67; dir. Overseas Center, Cambridge, Eng., 1967-68; v.p. acad. affairs Overseas Center, 1968-73; pres. Ill. Coll., Jacksonville, 1973-93; chmn. Fedn. Ind. Ill. Colls. and Univs., 1975-78; chmn. non-public adv. com. Ill. Bd. Higher Edn., 1988-91; postdoctoral fellow Center Study Higher Edn., U. Mich., 1964-65; chmn. bd. Council Ind. Colls., 1988-90. Contbr. articles to profl. jours. Mem. Ill. State Bar Assn. (com. on fed. judicial and related appointments 1983-89), Nat. Assn. Ind. Colls. and Univs. (commn. on new initiatives, 1988-90), Pi Sigma Alpha, Phi Eta Sigma. Home: 3803 Pheasant Walk Dr Valparaiso IN 46383-2205

MUNDLAK, YAIR, agriculture and economics educator; b. Pinsk, Poland, June 6, 1927; arrived in Israel, 1927; s. Lipa and Batia (Bodankin) M.; m. Yaffa Mundlak; children: Tal, Yaelle, Guy. BS in Agrl. Econs. with highest honors, U. Calif., Davis, 1953; MS in Stats., U. Calif., Berkeley, 1956, PhD in Agrl. Econs., 1957. Prof. agrl. econs. Hebrew U., Jerusalem, 1956-85, head dept. agrl. econs., 1965-73, dir. research Ctr. for Agrl. Econs. Research, 1968-85, dean faculty agriculture, 1972-74; vis. prof. econs. U. Chgo., 1966-67, 78-85, F.H. Prince prof. econs., 1978—; vis. prof. agrl. econs. U. Calif., Berkeley, 1961-63; vis. prof. econs. Harvard U., Cambridge, Mass., 1974-76; research fellow Internat. Food Policy Research Inst., Washington, 1976—; vis. fellow CORE, Louvain, Belgium, 1973; vis. rsch. fellow World Bank, 1990-91; cons. Ministry Agriculture, Devel. Research Ctr. The World Bank, Washington, 1972; mem. research coms. Nat. Council for Research and Devel., 1964-74. Co-author: (with Ben-Shahar, Berglas and Sadan) The West Bank and Gaza Strip—Economic Structure and Development Prospects, 1971; editor: Research in Agricultural Economics, 1976, (with F. Singer) Arid Zone Management, 1977; contbr. articles to profl. jours.; assoc. editor Jour. Econometrics, 1973-77. Pres. bd. trustees Israel Found., 1977-88. Recipient Bareli prize, 1965, Rothschild prize, 1972, Quality of Research Discovery award Am. Agrl. Econ. Assn., 1980, 82; Ford Found. research fellowship, 1966-67. Fellow Econometric Soc.; mem. Phi Beta Kappa. Office: Univ of Chgo Dept Econs 1127 E 59th St Chicago IL 60637 also: Faculty Agriculture, PO Box 12, Rehovot 76100, Israel*

MUNDORF, NANCY KNOX, early childhood educator; b. Columbus, Ohio, Jan. 19, 1947; d. John William and Cecilia Catherine (Callaghan) Knox; m. Michael John Mundorf, June 15, 1968; children: Colleen Ann, Mark John. BS in Home Econs., Ohio State U., 1968; MS, U. Nebr., 1982. Tchr. presch. Greenhills (Ohio) Coop. NurserySch., 1978-79; home economist Am Distbr., Omaha, 1979-83; parent educator Urban Program Boys Town, Omaha, 1983-85; health educator Omaha Children's Mus., U. Nebr. Med. Ctr., Omaha, 1986; ext. agt. U. Nebr., Omaha, 1986-88; gender equity specialist Lehigh County C.C., Schnecksville, Pa., 1988-90; ext. agt. Pa. State U., Reading, 1990-91; supervising tchr. Lipman Sch. U. Memphis, 1992-95; mem. adv. com. Omaha Pub. Sch. Supt.'s Vocat. Edn. Adv. Commn., 1986-88; rsch. in China. Mem. Tenn.Assn. Edn. of Young Children (co-chmn. ann. conf. program com. 1994-95), Nebr. Home Econs. Assn. (bd. dirs. 1981-86), Nat. Assn. for Edn. of Young Children, Am. Home Econs. Assn., Assn. Childhood Edn. Internat., Mid-South Ednl. Rsch. Assn., AAUW, Assn. Ext. 4-H Agts. Avocations: reading, needlework, music, travel. Office: c/o P & G Guangzhou Ltd P O Box 599 Cincinnati OH 45201 Office: PG Guangzhou Ltd 1 Pin He Rd, Guangzhou Econ & Tech Devel Dist, Guangzhou China

MUNDT, BARRY MAYNARD, management consultant; b. San Francisco, June 28, 1936; s. Kenneth Francis and Janet (Doughty) M.; m. Sally Hanscom, June 13, 1960; children: Kevin Warren, Trevor Stevens, Stacey Corbin. BS in Indsl. Engring., Stanford U., 1959; MBA, U. Santa Clara, 1964. Registered indsl. engr., Calif. Statistician Aerojet-Gen., Sacramento, 1957-58; reliability engr. Lockheed Missiles, Sunnyvale, Calif., 1959-61; mgmt. engr. C-E-I-R, Inc., Los Altos, Calif., 1961-65; sr. cons. Peat, Marwick, Livingston & Co., Los Angeles, 1965-68; mgr., prin. Peat, Marwick, Mitchell & Co., Atlanta, 1968-84; ptnr.-in-charge, ops. mgmt. cons. KPMG Peat Marwick Main & Co., N.Y.C., 1984-88; internat. mgmt. cons. ptnr. KPMG Internat., N.Y.C. and Amsterdam, The Netherlands, 1988-92; mgmt. cons., ptnr. KPMG Peat Marwick U.S., Montvale, N.J., 1992-95; prin. The Strategy Facilitation Group, Darien, Conn., 1995—. Author-editor: Managing Public Resources, 1982; co-author Il Manager Pubblico (Italy), 1986; contbr. articles to profl. jours. Mem. adv. campaign Atlanta Symphony Orch., 1974-82, Atlanta Arts Alliance, 1976-81; del. to assembly United Way of Met. Atlanta, 1974-84; bd. chmn., mem. Brandon Hall Sch., Atlanta, 1980—. Fellow Inst. Indsl. Engrs. (treas. 1976-81, prse. 1982-83, asst. treas. 1985-92). Episcopalian. Avocations: golf; residential remodeling. Home and Office: 26 Searles Rd Darien CT 06820-6222

MUNDT, RAY B., diversified industry executive; b. Appleton, Wis., Aug. 10, 1928; s. Benjamin J. and Jessie V. (Toft) M.; m. Ruth C. Stanchik, June 15, 1953; children: R. Scott, William C., Robert J., Mary Ruth. BS, U. Wis., Stevens Point, 1953; postgrad., Harvard U., 1969, Syracuse U. Salesman to v.p., gen. sales mgr. Kimberly-Clark Corp., Neenah, Wis., 1953-70; pres. Unisource Corp. (subsidiary Alco Standard Corp.), Valley Forge, Pa., 1970-73; exec. v.p. Alco Standard Corp., Valley Forge, 1973-74; chief operating officer Alco Standard Corp., 1973-80, pres., 1974-87, CEF, 1980-93, chmn., 1986-1996, also bd. dirs.; retired. Served with USNR, 1945-49. Clubs: Union League, Phila. Country, Harvard Bus. Sch. of Phila. Lodge: Masons. *

MUNDY, CARL EPTING, JR., commandant of the marine corps; b. Atlanta, July 16, 1935; s. Carl. Epting Sr. and Anne Louise (Dunn) M.; m. Linda Stringfield Sloan, Nov. 28, 1957; children: Elizabeth Anne, Carl Epting III, Timothy Sloan. BS, Auburn U., 1957; MS, Naval War Coll., 1977. 2d lt. USMC, 1957, advanced through grades to gen.; apptd. comdt. USMC, Washington, 1991—. Decorated Legion of Merit, Bronze Star, Purple Heart, Navy Commendation medal. Mem. Phi Kappa Tau. *

MUNDY, JAMES FRANCIS, lawyer; b. Wilkes Barre, Pa., Jan. 22, 1943; s. James F. and Mary Elizabeth (Lenahan) M.; m. Rose Ellen Zelonis, Mar. 15, 1969 (div. Jan. 1990); children: Leo, Timothy, Krystn. BS in Acctg., Kings Coll., 1965; JD, Cath. U., 1968. Bar: Pa., U.S. Dist. Ct. (ea. and mid. dists.) Pa. 1970, U.S. Ct. Appeals (3d. cir.), U.S. Supreme Ct. 1982; diplomate Am. Bd. Trial Advocates 1991. Assoc. Richter, Syken, Ross, Binder and O'Neill, Phila., 1970-72, Raynes, McCarty and Binder, Phila., 1972-76; ptnr. Raynes, McCarty, Binder and Mundy, Phila., 1976—; apptd. chair Atty. Disciplinary Bd., Pa., 1984-90; apptd. chair Pa. Appellate Ct. Nominating Commn., 1987-94; apptd. Trial Ct. Nominating Commn., Phila. County, 1987-94; apptd. Mandatory Legal Edn. Bd., 1992—. Co-author: The New Financial Responsibility Law, 1986. Mem. com. to benefit the children St. Christopher's Hosp. for Children, Phila., 1982-92; finance chair bd. trustees Coll. Misericordia, Dallas, 1983-90; co-chair statewide med. malpractice com. Pa. Senate, 1984-87; bd. trustees Kings Coll., Wilkes Barre, 1990—. Recipient Equal Justice award Cmty. Legal Svcs., 1990. Fellow Am. Coll. Trial Lawyers; mem. Pa. Bar Assn. (v.p. 1994-95, pres.-elect 1995—), Pa. Trial Lawyers Assn. (past pres. 1983-84, Milton Rasenberg Meml. award 1982), Phila. Trial Lawyers Assn. (past pres. 1979-80, Justice Michael Mussmano Meml. award 1987). Home: 174 Dam View Rd Media PA 19063 Office: Raynes McCarty Binder Ross & Mundy 20th Flr 1845 Walnut St Philadelphia PA 19103

MUNDY, JOHN HINE, history educator; b. London, Dec. 29, 1917; s. John and Clytie; m. Charlotte Fisher Williams, Sept. 3, 1942; children—Martha W., John W. B.A., Columbia, 1940, M.A., 1941, Ph.D., 1950. Mem. faculty Columbia U., N.Y.C., 1947-88, prof. history, 1962-88, prof. emeritus, 1988—, chmn. dept., 1967-70; vis. prof. Brown U., Providence, 1990-91; mem. Inst. Advanced Study, Princeton, 1963-64, 70-71. Author: Liberty and Political Power in Toulouse, 1954, The Medieval Town, 1958, Europe in the High Middle Ages, 1150-1309, 2d edit., 1990, The Repression of Catharism at Toulouse, the Royal Diploma of 1279, 1985, Men and Women at Toulouse in the Age of the Cathars, 1990, also articles. Served with AUS, 1943-46. Fulbright fellow, 1958-59; Am. Council Learned Socs. fellow, 1958-59; Guggenheim fellow, 1965, 77-78; Nat. Endowment Humanities fellow, 1970-71. Fellow Medieval Acad. Am. (2d v.p. 1986, 1st v.p. 1987, pres. 1988), Am. Acad. Arts and Scis. Home: 29 Claremont Ave New York NY 10027-6822

MUNECHIKA, KEN KENJI, research center administrator; b. Waimea, Kauai, Hawaii, June 18, 1935; s. Masako (Yasutake) Kitamura; m. Grace Shizue Wakayama, June 10, 1958; children: Curtis K., Stacy M., Kenny K. BS, U. Hawaii, 1958; MS, U. So. Calif., 1976, PhD, 1979. Commd. 2d lt. USAF, 1958, advanced through grades to col., 1980, ret., 1989; exec. dir. State of Hawaii, Honolulu, 1992-93; dir. Ames Rsch. Ctr. NASA, Mountain View, Calif., 1994-96; dir. Moffett Fed. Airfield NASA, Calif., 1996—. Mem. AIAA, Air Force Assn. Baptist. Avocations: golf, jogging, fishing. Home: 318 Casitas Bulevar Los Gatos CA 95030-1120 Office: NASA Moffett Fed Airfield Mail Stop 19-20 Moffett Field CA 94035

MUNERA, GERARD EMMANUEL, manufacturing company executive; b. Algiers, Algeria, Dec. 2, 1935; s. Gabriel and Laure (Labrousse) M.; m. Paule A. Ramos, July 28, 1959; children: Catherine, Philippe, Emmanuelle, Jean-Marie. M in Math., M in Physics, M in Chemistry, Ecole Polytechnique, Paris, 1956; CE, Ecole des Ponts et Chaussees, Paris, 1959. Chief county engr. Dept. Rds. and Bridges, South Algiers, 1959-62; cons. French Ministry Fgn. Affairs, Argentina, 1962-66; sr. v.p. fin. Camea Group Pechiney Ugine Kuhlmann, Buenos Aires, 1966-70, chmn. bd., chief exec. officer, 1976-77; exec. v.p. Howmet Aluminum Corp., Greenwich, Conn., 1976-77, pres., chief operating officer, 1977-79, pres., chief exec. officer, 1980-83; corporate v.p. nuclear fuels Pechiney, Brussels, 1983-85; vice chmn., chief exec. officer Union Minière, Brussels, 1985-89; head corp. planning and devel. RTZ, London, 1989-90; pres., CEO Minorco USA, Englewood, Colo., 1990-94, also bd. dirs.; chmn. and CEO Latin Am. Gold, Inc., N.Y.C., 1994-96, Synergex Inc., 1996—; bd. dirs. Arcadia Inc., Scaltech Inc., Latin Am. Gold Inc., NeVaun Resources Incchmn. CEO latin Am. Gold, Inc., 1994-96—, Synergex Inc., Latin Am., Gold Inc., Nevous Resources, Inc.. Patentee low-income housing system. Served with French Air Force, 1956-57. Decorated Legion of Honor. Roman Catholic. Office: Latin Am Gold Inc 55 Railroad Ave Greenwich CT 06830

MUNFORD, FREDERICK LOUIS, pharmacist, consultant; b. Cumberland, Va., Sept. 20, 1944; s. Frederick Stanley M.: 1 child from previous marriage, Sharri Khan; m. Thedosia Lynn Green, Oct. 25, 1975; children: Frederick Louis II, Corey. BS in Pharmacy, Howard U., 1967, MS in Human Nutrition, 1991, also postgrad. Pharmacist, asst. mgr. Peoples Drug Stores, Inc., Washington, 1967-71, mgr., pharmacist, 1971-76; staff pharmacist dept. pharmacy svcs. Howard Univ. Hosp., Washington, 1976-92; clin. pharmacist, nutrition cons. St. Elizabeth Hosp., Washington, 1992-93; staff pharmacist, nutrition cons. So. Md. Hosp., Clinton, Md., 1993—; pres. FLM Cons. Enterprises, Clinton, 1993—; adj. asst. prof. dept. pharmacy practice Coll. Pharmacy and Pharmacal Svcs. Howard U., Washington, 1982—. Assoc. min. Salem Bapt. Ch., Washington, 1992—; administr. B.M. Wiley Scholarship Fund for High Sch. Students, Cumberland, Va.; active NAACP. Mem. Am. Soc. Hosp. Pharmacists, Am. Soc. Cons. Pharmacists, Am. Pharm. Assn., D.C. Soc. Hosp. Pharmacy, Washington Pharm. Assn. (pres. 1987-88), Howard U. Pharmacy Alumni Assn. (pres. 1986-89, mem. Chauncey I. Cooper Grad. Scholarship Fund). Avocations: chess, jogging, skiing, racquetball. Office: FLM Cons Enterprises 8805 Junaluska Ter Clinton MD 20735-4312

MUNGAN, NECMETTIN, petroleum consultant; b. Mardin, Turkey, Mar. 1, 1934; came to U.S., 1953, came to Can., 1966; s. Kerim and Saide M.; m. Gunilla Ersman, May 19, 1962; children—Carl Edward, Christina Deniz, Nils Kerim, Tanya Katerina. BS Petroleum Engring., U. Tex., 1956, BA Math., 1957, MS Petroleum Engring., 1958, PhD Petroleum Engring., 1961. Head rsch. Sinclair Research, Tulsa, 1961-66; chief research officer Petroleum Recovery Inst., Calgary, Alta., Can., 1966-78; pres. Mungan Petroleum Cons., Ltd., Calgary, 1978-86; chief tech. advisor AEC Oil and Gas Co., Calgary, 1986-94; cons. Mungan Petroleum Cons. Ltd., Calgary, 1995—. Contbr. numerous articles to profl. publs. Named hon. citizen State of Tex., 1956, hon. prof. chem. and petroleum engring. U. Calgary, 1993; hon. prof. U. Buenos Aires, 1995, U. Campeche, Mex., 1995; recipient Excellence in Presentation of Tech. Paper award Am. Inst. Chem. Engrs., 1966; disting. lectr. emeritus, 1995—. Mem. Soc. Petroleum Engrs. (Uren Award, 1990), AIME (C.K. Ferguson award 1966, Disting. lectr 1969-70, Disting. Svc. award 1992), Petroleum Soc., Assn. Profl. Engrs., Geologists and Geophysicists Alta., Sigma Xi, Tau Beta Pi, Sigma Gamma Epsilon, Pi Epsilon Tau, Kappa Mu Epsilon. Office: Mungan Petroleum Cons Ltd, 1039 Durham Ave S W, Calgary, AB Canada T2T 0P8

MUNGER, BENSON SCOTT, professional society administrator; b. St. Johns, Mich., Jan. 21, 1942; s. Kenneth L. and Doris (Benson) M.; m. Bette Louise Johnson, June 15, 1963; children: Heidi Lynn, Chad Benson. BA, Mich. State U., 1965, PhD, 1969. Tchr. Grand Ledge Pub. Schs., Mich., 1965-66; mem. staff Southwest Regional Lab, Los Angeles, 1969-70; dir. negotiations Mich. Edn. Assn., East Lansing, 1970-75; vis. asst.prof. Indsl. Relations Ctr., U. Minn., Mpls., 1975-76; dep. exec. dir. Am. Coll. Emergency Physicians, 1976-80; exec. dir. Am. Bd. Emergency Medicine, East Lansing, Mich., 1980—, chmn. com. bd. execs., 1991—; commr. City of Johns, 1983—; bd. dirs. Old Kent Bank, St. Johns; cons. in field; chmn. com. bd. reps. and execs. Am. Bd. Med. Specialties, 1995—. Contbr. articles in field. Mich. State U. fellow, 1966-69. Mem. Am. Soc. Assn. Execs., Am. Assn. Med. Soc. Execs. Office: Am Bd Emergency Med 3000 Coolidge Rd East Lansing MI 48823-6319

MUNGER, BRYCE L., physician, educator; b. Everett, Wash., May 20, 1933; s. Leon C. and Lina (Eaton) M.; m. Donna Grace Bingham, July 20, 1957; children: Ailene, D'Arcy, Gareth Torrey, Bryce Kirtley. Student, U. Wash., 1951-54; M.D. magna cum laude, Wash. U., 1958. Intern in pathology Johns Hopkins U., 1958-59; asst. prof. anatomy Washington U., St. Louis, 1961-65; asso. prof. U. Chgo., 1965-66; prof. Milton S. Hershey Med. Center, Pa. State U., 1966-91, chmn. dept. anatomy, 1966-87; prof., head dept. anatomy U. Tasmania, Hobart, 1992—. Bd. dirs. Pa. Spl. Olympics Inc. Served with MC USAF, 1959-61. Mem. AAAS, Am. Assn. Anatomists, Am. Soc. Cell Biology, Phi Beta Kappa, Sigma Xi, Alpha Omega Alpha. Office: U Tasmania, Dept Anatomy, Hobart Tasmania 7001, Australia

MUNGER, EDWIN STANTON, political geography educator; b. LaGrange, Ill., Nov. 19, 1921; s. Royal Freeman and Mia (Stanton) M.; m. Ann Boyer, May 2, 1970; 1 child, Elizabeth Stanton Gibson. B.Sc., U. Chgo., 1948, M.Sc., 1949, Ph.D., 1951. Fulbright fellow Makerere U., 1949-50; research fellow U. Chgo.; field assoc. Am. Univs. Field Staff, 1950-60; faculty Calif. Inst. Tech., Pasadena, 1961—; prof. polit. geography Calif. Inst. Tech., 1960—; research fellow Stellenbosch U., 1955-56; vis. prof. U. Warsaw, 1973. Author books including Afrikaner and African Nationalsim, 1968, The Afrikaners, 1979, Touched by Africa: An Autobiography, 1983, Cultures, Chess and Art: A Collector's Odyssey Across Seven Continents, Vol. 1 Sub Saharan Africa, 1996; editor books including Munger Africana Library Notes, 1969-82; contbr. chpts. to books and numerous articles to profl. jours. Evaluator Peace Corps, Uganda, 1966, Botswana, 1967; chmn. State Dept. Evaluation Team South Africa, 1971; trustee African-Am. Inst., 1956-62; acting pres. Pasadena Playhouse, 1966; chmn. bd. trustees Crane Rogers Found., 1979-82, fellow, 1950-54; mem. exec. com. NAACP, Pasadena, 1979—, nat. del., 1984, 85; trustee Leakey Found., 1968—, pres., 1971-84; pres. Cape of Good Hope Found., 1985—; pres. Internat. Vis. Coun., L.A., 1991-93, bd. dirs., 1979-93. Recipient Alumni Citation award for pub. svc. U. Chgo., 1993. Fellow South African Royal Soc., Royal Soc. Arts, African Studies Assn. (founding bd. dirs. 1963-66); mem. PEN USA West (v.p.), Coun. Fgn. Rels., Cosmos Club, Athenaeum Club, Twilight Club. Office: Calif Inst Tech Div Humanities and Social Scis 1201 E California Blvd Pasadena CA 91125-0001

MUNGER, ELMER LEWIS, civil engineer, educator; b. Manhattan, Kans., Jan. 4, 1915; s. Harold Hawley and Jane (Green) M.; m. Vivian Marie Bloomfield, Dec. 28, 1939; children: John Thomas, Harold Hawley II, Jane Marie. B.S., Kans. State U., 1936, M.S., 1938; Ph.D., Iowa State U., 1957. Registered profl. engr., Nebr., Kans., Iowa, Vt.; registered pvt. land surveyor Republic of The Philippines. Rodman St. Louis-Southwestern Ry., Ark., Mo., 1937-38; engr. U.S. Engr. Dept., Ohio, Nebr., 1938-46; missionary engr. Philippine Episcopal Ch., 1946-48; engr. Wilson & Co., Salina, Kans., 1948; tchr. Iowa State U., 1948-51, 54-58; engr. C.E., U.S. Army, Alaska, 1951-54; from tchr. to dean Norwich U., Northfield, Vt., 1958-69; prof. gen. engring. U. P.R., Mayagüez, 1969-75; prof. civil engring. Mich. Tech. U., 1975-80; ret.; mem. spl. com. on engring. Inter-Am. Devel. Bank, U. W.I., 1971. Author: (with Clarence J. Douglas) Construction Management, 1970. Fellow ASCE; mem. Soc. Am. Mil. Engrs. (mil. engr. mem.), NSPE, Vt. Soc. Profl. Engrs., Am. Soc. Engring. Edn., Phi Kappa Phi, Sigma Tau, Tau Beta Pi, Chi Epsilon. Episcopalian. Clubs: Masons, Shriners. Home: 21260 Brinson Ave Apt 311 Port Charlotte FL 33952-5005

MUNGER, HAROLD CHARLES, architect; b. Toledo, July 25, 1929; s. Harold Henry and Lela Marie (Hoffman) M.; m. Patricia Ann Billeter, Oct. 2, 1954; children: Hal Peter, Peter Charles, David James. B.Arch., U. Notre Dame, 1951; cert., Davis Bus. Coll., 1947, U. Toledo, 1949, 50, Toledo Mus. Art, 1954, Leica Sch., 1982. Registered architect, Ohio, Mich., Ind., cert. Nat. Council Arctl. Registration Bds. Draftsman atomic energy br. Giffels & Vallet, Architects and Engrs., Detroit, 1951-52; chief designer, assoc. Britsch and Munger, Architects, Toledo, 1952-55; chief architect, ptnr. Munger, Munger and Assocs., Architects, Toledo, 1955-70, owner, proprieter, 1970-83; pres. Munger, Munger and Assocs., Inc., Toledo, 1983—; mem. nat. exam. evaluation com. Nat. Council Archtl. Registration Bds., Washington, 1983; presenter Ohio Assn. Sch. Officials, 1985; charter mem. Historic Dist. Design Rev. Bd., City of Perrysburg, Ohio, 1982—; mem. mayors com. planning, City of Perrysburg, mem. downtown task force, 1985; mem. archtl. jury Nat. Sch. Bds. Assn., 1961—; mem. pres.'s council

Toledo Mus. Art, 1985—; mem. archtl. ann. awards jury Ind. Masonry Inst., 1988. Author: Housing Physically Disabled Elderly, 1964; co-author: Lucas County Bldg. Code, 1955-56; assoc. editor: Ohio Architect, 1955-58, Architectural Graphics Standard, 8th edit., 1986—. Dist. officer, merit badge counselor, committeeman Toledo Area Boy Scouts Am., 1953—; mem. Vocat. Tech. High Sch. Bldg. Trades Adv. Com., Toledo, 1956-79, Perrysburg 1st City Charter Commn., 1960-62; co-chmn. Chase Park Urban Renewal Adv. awards Com., Toledo, 1962-65; pres. St. Rose Bd. of Edn., Perrysburg, 1966-69; trustee Way Pub. Library, 1960-80, Historic Perrysburg, Inc., 1977-81. Recipient Pub. and Comml. award Toledo Area Concrete Assn., 1965, Indsl. award Toledo Area Concrete Assn., 1973, Boss of Yr. award Per Ro Ma chpt. Am. Bus. Women's Assn., 1977, Bus. Assoc. of Yr. award, 1985, St. George award Cath. Com. on Scouting, Diocese of Toledo, 1978, Masonry Honor award Masonry Inst. Northwestern Ohio, 1981, 85 (2 awards), 86, 87, 89 (2 awards), 92, 95; Excellence in Masonry Design award Ohio Masonry Coun., 1986, 88, Man of Yr. award U. Notre Dame Alumni Club of Toledo, 1987, Best Project award Internat. Union Bricklayers, 1989, Toledo Design Forum award of excellence in architecture, 1991. Fellow AIA (nat. committeeman design, inquiry, housing, architecture for edn. 1965—, pres., past. bd. dirs., Devoted Service award 1963, Architect of Yr. award Toledo chpt. 1991); mem. Constrn. Specifications Inst. (charter mem. cert. of recognition), AIA Architects Soc. Ohio (pres., past dir. Silver Gavel award, 1969, honor award 1981, 86, 88, Gold medal award 1987 Ohio chpt., 25-Yr. Bldg. award of excellence 1991, AIA Ohio Gold Medal Firm of Yr., 1995), Toledo Club, Rotary (charter, cert. of recognition). Home: 425 W Front St Perrysburg OH 43551-1433 Office: Munger Munger & Assocs 225 N Michigan St Toledo OH 43624-1613 *Principles: less is more. Ideas: Judged by what we do. Goals: Self-respect and self-reliance.*

MUNGER, PAUL DAVID, educational administrator; b. Selma, Ala., Oct. 12, 1945; s. Paul Francis and Arlene Lorraine (McFillen) M.; m. Paula Jean Dominici, May 30, 1969; children: Kimberley Beth, Christopher David. AB in Philosophy, Kenyon Coll., 1967; MA in Govt., Ind. U., 1969. Commd. 2d lt. USAF, 1969, advanced through grades to capt., resigned, 1972; asst. dir. faculty devel. Ind. U., Bloomington, 1974-77; from asst. dean to dean continuing studies Am. U., Washington, 1980-83, asst. provost acad. devel., 1983-84; dir. Commn. on Future Acad. Leadership, Washington, 1984-86; v.p. Acad. Strategies, Washington, 1986-88; pres. Strategic Edn. Svcs. Inc., Sterling, Va., 1988—. Bd. advisors Madeira Sch., McLean, Va., 1993—; treas. Bus.-Higher Edn. Fedn., Washington, 1992—; asst. scoutmaster Boy Scouts Am., 1991-93, scoutmaster, 1994—. Mem. Am. Soc. Tng. & Devel. (chmn. strategic planning com. 1993—), Assn. Continuing Higher Edn., Am. Soc. Curriculum Devel. Office: Strategic Edn Svcs Inc 624 W Church Rd Sterling VA 20164-4608

MUNGER, PAUL R., civil engineering educator; b. Hannibal, Mo., Jan. 14, 1932; s. Paul Oettle and Anne Lucille (Williams) M.; m. Frieda Ann Mette, Nov. 26, 1954; children: Amelia Ann Munger Fortmeyer, Paul David, Mark James, Martha Jane Munger Cox. BSCE, Mo. Sch. Mines and Metallurgy, 1958, MSCE, 1961; PhD in Engring. Sci., U. Ark., 1972. Registered profl. engr., Mo., Ill., Ark. Minn. Instr. civil engring Mo. Sch. Mines and Metallurgy, Rolla, 1958-61, asst. prof., 1961-65; assoc. prof. U. Mo., Rolla, 1965-73, prof., 1973—; dir. Inst. River Studies, U. Mo., Rolla, 1976-93; exec. dir. Internat. Inst. River and Lake Systems, U. Mo., Rolla, 1984-93. Mem. NSPE, Mo. Soc. Profl. Engrs., Am. Soc. Engring. Edn., ASCE, Nat. Coun. Engring. Examiners (pres. 1983-84), Mo. Bd. Architects, Profl. Engrs. and Land Surveyors (chmn. 1978-84, 95—). Office: U Mo 111 Civil Engring Rolla MO 65401

MUNGER, SHARON, market research firm executive; M. Robert Munger; 3 children: Shawn, Shane, Blair. Grad. Vanderbilt U. Sec., data processor, acct. exec. M/A/R/C, Inc., Irving, Tex., from 1973; now pres., chief operating officer Irving, Tex. Office: M-A-R-C Inc 7850 N Belt Line Rd Irving TX 75063-6064*

MUNHALL, EDGAR, curator, art history educator; b. Pitts., Mar. 14, 1933; s. Walter and Anna (Burns) M.; life ptnr. Richard Barsam. BA, Yale U., 1955, PhD, 1959; MA, NYU, 1957. Instr. art history Yale U., New Haven, 1959-64, asst. prof., 1964-65; curator The Frick Collection, N.Y.C., 1965—; adj. prof. Columbia U., 1979, 81—. Decorated chevalier Ordre des Arts et des Lettres. Office: The Frick Collection 1 E 70th St New York NY 10021-4907

MUNIAIN, JAVIER P., theoretical physicist, reseacher; b. Madrid, Spain, Apr. 4, 1966; came to U.S., 1989.; s. Luis Perez De Muniain y Leal and Crescencia Mohedano Hernandez. BSc, U. Complutense of Madrid, 1990; M. in Physics, U. Calif., Riverside, 1992, PhD in Theoretical Physics, 1996. Rsch., teaching asst. U. Calif., Riverside, 1992-95. Author: Gauge Fields, Knots and Gravity, 1994; contbr. articles to profl. jours. Mem. Am. Phys. Soc., Riverside Wine Tasing Soc. (co-founder 1994). Avocations: classic car restoration, playing and studying chess, surfing, antiques, designing fashion clothing. Home: C/Alcala 236, Madrid Spain 28027 Office: U Calif Physics Dept Riverside CA 92521

MUNISTERI, JOSEPH GEORGE, construction executive; b. Rome, Sept. 24, 1930; s. Peter P. and Inez Gertrude (Ziniti) M.; m. Theresa Grasso, June 7, 1952; children: Joanne, Robert, Laura, Stephen, James, Richard. BE, Yale U., 1952. With Bechtel Corp., San Francisco, 1952-59; with The Lummus Co., N.Y.C., London and Houston, 1959-67, gen. mgr., 1964-67; sr. v.p. sales Brown & Root, Inc., Houston, 1967-75, group v.p. power div., 1975-80, group v.p. corp. devel., 1980-81, also bd. dirs.; pres. Enserch Engrs. & Constructors, Inc., Houston, 1981-85; exec. v.p. Ford, Bacon & Davis, Inc., Dallas, 1985-87; chmn., pres., CEO Comstock Group, Inc., Danbury, Conn., 1987-88; pres. Joseph G. Munisteri Co., Houston, 1989—; former chmn. bd. Pine-O-Pine. Former mem. Bd. dirs. Atomic Indsl. Forum; Bd. dirs. Am. Nuclear Energy Council. Mem. Atomic Indsl. Forum, Am. Inst. Chem. Engrs., Am. Nuclear Soc., Atomic Indsl. Forum, ASTM, Council Engring. Law, ASCE, Assn. Iron and Steel Engring., Assoc. Builders and Contractors (dir.). Clubs: Yale of N.Y, Yale S.E.T, Houston. Office: 4265 San Felipe #1100 Houston TX 77027

MUNITZ, BARRY, university administrator, English literature educator, business consultant; b. Bklyn., July 26, 1941; s. Raymond J. and Vivian L. (LeVoff) M.; m. Anne Tomfohrde, Dec. 15, 1987. BA, Bklyn. Coll., 1963; MA, Princeton U., 1965, PhD, 1968; cert., U. Leiden, Netherlands, 1962. Asst. prof. lit. and drama U. Calif., Berkeley, 1966-68; staff assoc. Carnegie Commn. Higher Edn., 1968-70; mem. presdl. staff, then assoc. provost U. Ill. System, 1970-72, acad. v.p., 1972-76; v.p., dean faculties Central campus U. Houston, 1976-77, chancellor, 1977-82, chmn. coordinating bd. faculty workload, 1976-80; chmn. Tex. Long Range Planning, 1980-82; pres., COO Federated Devel. Co., 1982-91; vice chmn. Maxxam Inc., L.A., 1982-91; chancellor Calif. State U. System, Long Beach, Calif., 1991—; prof. English lit. Calif. State U., L.A., 1991—; bd. dirs. Sta. KCET-TV, Am. Coun. on Edn., Nat. Bus. Higher Edn. Forum, SunAmerica Inc.; cons. in presdl. evaluation and univ. goverance. Author: The Assessment of Institutional Leadership, 1977, also articles, monographs. Mem. task force NSF. Recipient Disting. Alumnus award Bklyn. Coll., 1979, U. Houston Alumni Pres.'s medal, 1981; Woodrow Wilson fellow, 1963. Mem. Young Pres. Orgn., Heritage Club, Phi Beta Kappa. Office: Calif State U System Office of Chancellor 400 Golden Shore St Long Beach CA 90802-4209

MUÑIZ, TEODORO, medical association administrator; b. San Sebastian, P.R., Apr. 1, 1935; married; 1 child. BS, U. P.R., 1965; MS, Recinto Siencia Medica, 1970. Regional dir. Met. region Dept. Health; undersec. Dept. Health and Dept. Transp.; dir. mktg. and ops. Charter Med. Group, exec. dir. hosp. ops.; pres. P.R. Hosp. Assn., Rio Piedras, 1995—; pres. Junta Examinadora y Administrativa Hospitales. Office: PR Hosp Assn Ste 104 Villa Nevarez Profl Ctr San Juan PR 00927

MUNK, PETER, mining executive; b. Budapest, Hungary, Nov. 8, 1927; arrived in Can., 1948; s. Louis L. and Katherine (Adler) M.; m. Linda Gutterson; children: Anthony, Nina; m. Melanie Jane Bosanquet, 1973; children: Natalie, Cheyne, Marc David. BASc in Elec. Engring., U. Toronto, Ont., Can., 1953, LLD, 1995; LLD, Upsala Coll., N.J., 1991, U. Toronto, Que., Can., 1995, Bishops Coll., Quebec, 1995. Chmn., chief exec. officer So. Pacific Hotel Corp., Sydney, Australia, 1969-81; chmn. Barrick Resources, Toronto, 1981-83, Am. Barrick Resources Corp. (now Barrick Gold Corp.), Toronto, 1983—, The Horsham Corp., Toronto, 1987—; chmn., bd. dirs. Clark Oil & Refining Corp., St. Louis, Trizec Corp. Ltd.; bd. dirs. World Gold Coun., Geneva, Hollinger Inc., Toronto. Trustee Toronto Hosp.; bd. dirs. U. Toronto Found. Decorated officer Order of Can. Office: Barrick Gold Corp, 27th Fl S Tower, 200 Bay St, Toronto, ON Canada M5J 2J3

MUNK, PETER, oil industry executive; b. 1950. Self-employed Toronto, Ont., Can., 1964-86; officer Horsham Corp., Toronto, 1986—, AOC Holding, Inc., St. Louis, 1988—, Clark Oil & Refining Corp., St. Louis, 1992—. Office: Clark Oil & Refining Corp 8182 Maryland Ave Saint Louis MO 63105-3786*

MUNK, WALTER HEINRICH, geophysics educator; b. Vienna, Austria, Oct. 19, 1917; came to U.S., 1933; m. Edith Kendall Horton, June 20, 1953; children: Edith, Kendall. BS, Calif. Inst. Tech., 1939, MS, 1940; PhD in Oceanography, U. Calif., 1947; PhD (hon.), U. Bergen, Norway, 1975, Cambridge (Eng.) U., 1986, U. Crete, 1996. Asst. prof. geophysics Scripps Inst. Oceanography, U. Calif., San Diego, 1947-54, prof., 1954—; dir. Inst. Geophysics and Planetary Physics, U. Calif., La Jolla, 1960-82; prof. geophysics, dir. heard island expt. Scripps Inst., U. Calif. Author: (with Mac Donald) The Rotation of the Earth: A Geophysical Discussion, 1960, (with Worcester & Wunsch) Ocean Acoustic Tomography, 1995; contbr. over 200 articles to profl. jours. Recipient Albatross award Am. Misc. Soc., 1959, gold medal Royal Astron. Soc., 1968, Nat. Medal Sci., 1985, award Marine Tech. Soc., 1969, Capt. Robert Dexter Conrad award Dept. Navy, 1978, G. Unger VVetlesen prize Columbia U., 1993, Presdl. award N.Y. Acad. Scis., 1993; named Calif. Scientist of Yr., Calif. Mus. Sci. and Industry, 1969; fellow Guggenheim Found., 1948, 55, 62, Overseas Found., 1962, 81-82, Fulbright Found., 1981-82, sr. Queen's fellow, 1978. Fellow Am. Geophys. Union (Maurice Ewing medal 1976, William Bowie medal 1989), AAAS, Am. Meteorol. Soc. (Sverdrup Gold medal 1966), Acoustical Soc. Am., Marine Tech. Soc. (Compass award 1991); mem. Nat. Acad. Scis. (Agassiz medal 1976, chmn. ocean studies bd. 1985-88), Am. Philos. Soc., Royal Soc. London (fgn. mem.), Russian Acad. of Sci., Deutsche Akademie der Naturforscher Leopoldina, Am. Acad. Arts and Scis. (Arthur L. Day medal 1965), Am. Geol. Soc., NY Acad. of Scis. (Presidl. Awd., 1994). Office: U Calif San Diego Scripps Inst Oceanography 0225 La Jolla CA 92093

MUNN, CECIL EDWIN, lawyer; b. Enid, Okla., Aug. 8, 1923; s. Cecil Edwin and Margaret (Kittrell) M.; m. Carolyn Taylor Culver, May 8, 1948; children: Franklin Culver, Charlotte Munn Forswall. BA, U. Okla., 1945; JD cum laude, Harvard U., 1947. Bar: Okla. 1947, Tex. 1955. Practice in Enid, 1947-54, Ft. Worth, 1954—; partner firm Cantey & Hanger, Ft. Worth, 1960-91, of counsel, 1992—; with Champlin Petroleum Co., 1954-60, v.p., atty., 1958-60, dir., 1962-75. Fellow Am. Coll. Trial Lawyers, Am. Bar Found.; mem. ABA (chmn. natural resources law sect. 1970-71), Southwestern Legal Found. (past dir.), Tex. Bar Found., Phi Delta Theta, Phi Delta Phi. Presbyterian. Home: 42 Valley Ridge Rd Fort Worth TX 76107-3108 Office: 2100 Burnett Plz 801 Cherry St Fort Worth TX 76102-6803 *Some things in life are better decided wrong than left undecided. It is amazing how much one can accomplish if unconcerned with who gets the credit.*

MUNN, JANET TERESA, lawyer; b. De Funiak, Fla., Nov. 7, 1952; d. Willard Ernest and Olive Pauline (Wilkinson) M.; m. Michael E. Fass, Sept. 27, 1975. BA in Anthropology, Fla. State U., 1975, MA in Social Scis., 1977; JD with high honors, Nova U., 1985. Bar: Fla. 1985, U.S. Dist. Ct. (so. dist.) Fla. 1986, U.S. Dist. Ct. (mid. dist.) Fla. 1988, U.S. Ct. Appeals (11th cir.) 1989, U.S. Supreme Ct. 1990. Jud. clerk for Judge Jose A. Gonzalez Jr. U.S. Dist. Ct. (so. dist.) Fla., Ft. Lauderdale, 1985-87; litigation assoc. Steel Hector & Davis, Miami, Fla., 1987-91, litigation ptnr., 1992—. Editor: Southern District Digest, 1987-88. Leo S. Goodwin fellow Nova U., 1983-84. Mem. ABA (co-chmn. intellectual properties litigation com. litigation sect. 1991-92, chmn. trade regulation/intellectual property com. gen. practice sect. 1990-91, vice chmn. 1989-90), Fed. Bar Assn., Fla. Bar (Pro Bono award 1988), Dade County Bar Assn., Phi Kappa Phi. Office: 200 S Biscayne Blvd Ste 4000 Miami FL 33131-2310

MUNN, WILLIAM CHARLES, II, psychiatrist; b. Flint, Mich., Aug. 9, 1938; s. Elton Albert and Rita May (Coykendall) M.; student Flint Jr. Coll., 1958-59, U. Detroit, 1959-61; M.D., Wayne State U., 1965; children by previous marriage—Jude Michael, Rachel Marie, Alexander Winston. Intern David Grant USAF Med. Center, Travis AFB, Calif., 1965-66; resident in psychiatry Letterman Army Hosp., San Francisco, 1967-70; practice medicine, specializing in psychiatry, Fairfield, Calif., 1972—; chief in-patient psychiatry David Grant Med. Center, 1970-71, chmn. dept. mental health, 1971-72; psychiat. cons. Fairfield-Suisun Unified Sch. Dist., 1971—, Fairfield Hosp. and Clinic, 1971, N. Bay Med. Ctr.(formerly Intercommunity Hosp.), Fairfield, 1971—, Casey Family Program, 1980—, Solano County Coroner's Office, 1981; asst. clin. prof. psychiatry U. Calif., San Francisco, 1976—; cons. Vaca Valley Hosp., Vacaville, Calif., 1988—, VA Hosp., San Francisco, 1976, David Grant USAF Hosp., 1976. Served to maj., M.C., USAF, 1964-72, flight surgeon, chief public health, chief phys. exam. center McGuire AFB, N.J., 1966-67. Diplomate Am. Bd. Psychiatry and Neurology (examiner). Mem. Am. Psychiat. Assn., No. Calif. Psychiat. Soc., E. Bay Psychiat. Assn. Office: 1245 Travis Blvd Ste E Fairfield CA 94533-4842

MUNNELL, ALICIA HAYDOCK, economist; b. N.Y.C., Dec. 6, 1942; d. Walter Howe Haydock and Alicia (Wildman) Haydock Roux; m. Thomas Clark Munnell (div.); children: Thomas Clark Jr., Hamilton Haydock; m. Henry Scanlon Healy, Feb. 2, 1980. BA in Econs., Wellesley, 1964; MA in Econs., Boston U., 1966; PhD in Econs., Harvard U., 1973. Staff asst. bus. rsch. div. New Eng. Tel. Co., Boston, 1964-65; teaching fellow econs. dept. Boston U., 1965-66; rsch. asst. for dir. econ. studies program Brookings Instn., Washington, 1966-68; teaching fellow Harvard U., Cambridge, Mass., 1971-73; asst. prof. econs. Wellesley Coll., Mass., 1974; economist Fed. Res. Bank Boston, 1973-76, asst. v.p., economist, 1976-78, v.p., economist, 1979-84, sr. v.p., dir. rsch., 1984-93; asst. sec. for econ. policy Dept. Treasury, Washington, 1993-95; mem. Coun. of Econ. Advisors, 1995—; mem. Gov.'s Task Force on Unemployment Compensation, Mass., 1975; mem. spl. funding adv. com. for Mass. pensions, 1976; mem. Mass. Retirement Law Commn., 1976-82; staff dir. joint com. on pub. pensions Nat. Planning Assn., 1978; mem. adv. com. for urban inst. HUD grant on state-local pensions, 1978-81; mem. pension rsch. council Wharton Sch. Fin. and Commerce, U. Pa., 1979—; mem. adv. group Nat. Commn. for Employment Policy, 1980-81; mem. adv. bd. Nat. Aging Policy Ctr. in Income Maintenance, Brandeis U., 1980-84; participant pvt. sector retirement security and U.S. tax policy roundtable discussions Govt. Rsch. Corp., 1984; mem. supervisory panel Forum Inst. of Villers Found., 1984; mem. Medicare working group, div. of health policy rsch. and edn. Harvard U., 1984-87; mem. Commn. on Coll. Retirement, 1984-86; mem. com. to plan major study of nat. long term care policies Inst. Medicine, Nat. Acad. Scis., 1984-87; mem. steering com. Am. Assn. Ret. Persons, 1987—; mem. adv. council Am. Enterprise Inst., 1987—; com. mem. Inst. Medicine, Nat. Acad. Scis. Human Rights Com., 1987—; co-founder, pres. Nat. Acad. Social Ins., 1986—; bd. dirs. Pension Rights Ctr.; mem. program rev. com. Brigham and Women's Hosp., 1988—; mem. Commn. to Rev. Mass. Anti-Takeover Laws, 1988-89, econs. vis. com. MIT, 1989—. Author: The Impact of Social Security on Personal Saving, 1974, Future of Social Security, 1977 (various awards), Pensions for Public Employees, 1979, The Economics of Private Pensions, 1982; co-author: Options for Fiscal Structure Reform in Massachusetts, 1975; editor: Lessons from the Income Maintenance Experiments, 1987, Is There a Shortfall in Public Capital Investment?, 1991, (conf. proc.) Retirement and Public Policy, 1991, Pensions and the Economy: Sources, Uses, and Limitations of Data, 1992, co-editor: Pensions and the Economy: Sources, Uses, and Limitations of Data; contbr. articles to profl. jours., chpts. to books. Mem. Inst. Medicine of NAS, Nat. Acad. Pub. Adminstrn. Office: Council of Econ Advisers Old EOB Exec Office of the Pres Washington DC 20502

MUÑOZ, CARLOS RAMÓN, bank executive; b. N.Y.C., Dec. 8, 1935; s. Alejandro and Gladys Helena (Judah) M.; m. Wilhelmina Elaine North, June 8, 1957 (div. 1993); children: Carla Christine, Kyle Alexander. BA, Columbia U., 1957, MA, 1961. Insp., ofcl. asst. Citibank, N.A., N.Y.C., 1959-64, asst. mgr., then mgr. in Dominican Republic and P.R., 1965-70, asst. v.p., N.Y.C., 1971-72, v.p., dept. head, 1972-78, sr. v.p., regional mgr. and dir. Citicorp. USA, San Francisco, 1978-81, sr. v.p., mem. Credit Policy Com., 1982-95; exec. v.p., chief credit officer Dime Savings Bank, N.Y.C., 1995—. Bd. dirs. Episcopal Mission Soc., N.Y.C., 1974—, chmn. exec. com., 1990-93, v.p., 1995—; bd. dirs. Inner City Scholarship Fund, 1984-95, Corp. for Relief Widows and Orphans of Protestant Episcopal Clergymen in State N.Y., 1974-79; trustee Episcopal Diocese of N.Y., 1994—. Served as 1st lt. USAR, 1958-64. Recipient Productivity award State Senator Diane Watson, Los Angeles, 1981; named Fairfield County Alumnus of Yr., 1989-90. Mem. Columbia Coll. Alumni Assn. (bd. dirs. 1983—, treas. 1988-92, v.p. 1992-93, 1st v.p. 1994-96, pres. 1996—), Univ. Club (N.Y.C.). Republican.

MUNOZ, GEORGE, federal agency administrator. BBA with high honors, U. Tex., 1974; M in Pub. Policy, Harvard U., 1978, JD, 1978; LLM, DePaul U., 1984. CPA. Assoc. Gary, Thomasson, Hall & Marks, Corpus Christi, Tex., 1978-80; assoc., ptnr. Mayer, Brown & Platt, Chgo., 1980-89; mng. ptnr. GM&A Internat. Attys. & Bus. Counselors, p.c., Chgo., 1989-93; CFO, asst. sec. mgmt. U.S. Dept. Treasury, Washington, 1993—. Pres. Chgo. Bd. Edn., 1984-86; trustee Chgo. Symphony Orch., Northwestern Meml. Hosp., DePaul U., Chgo. Coun. on Fgn. Rels., Ill. Internat. Port Authority, Chgo. Econ. Devel. Commn. Office: Dept of Treasury Management 15th & Pennsylvania Ave NW Washington DC 20220*

MUNOZ, JOHN JOAQUIN, research microbiologist; b. Guatemala City, Guatemala, Dec. 23, 1918; came to U.S., 1938, naturalized, 1954; s. Juan Muñoz and Carmen Valdés; m. Margaret Allen, June 21, 1947; children: William Allen, Maureen Carmen, John Richard, Michael Raymond. Grad., Escuela Preparatoria, Guatemala City, 1938; B.S., La. State U., 1942; M.S., U. Ky., 1945; Ph.D., U. Wis., 1947. Asst. prof. U. Ill. Med. Sch., 1947-51; rsch. assoc. Merck-Sharp & Dohme Rsch. Labs., 1951-57; prof. bacteriology, dir. Stella Duncan Meml. Fund rsch. U. Mont., 1957-61, staff affiliate, 1968—; rsch. microbiologist Inst. Allergy and Infectious Diseases, NIH, Rocky Mountain Lab., 1961—, head allergy-immunology sect., 1968-79, head pertussis sect., 1979-82, acting head immunopathology sect., 1985-88, scientist emeritus, 1989—; spl. assignment Pasteur Inst., Paris, 1966-67, Walter and Eliza Hall Inst. Med. Rsch., Melbourne, Australia, 1982-83. Author: (with R.K. Bergman) Bordetella pertussis—immunological and other biological activities, 1977; Contbr. articles to profl. jours. Fellow Am. Acad. Microbiology (emeritus); mem. Am. Soc. Microbiology, Am. Assn. Immunologists, Soc. Exptl. Biology and Medicine, Reticuloendothelial Soc., Internat. Endotoxin Soc., Sigma Xi, Phi Sigma. Home: 199 Meadowlark Ln Hamilton MT 59840-9111 Office: NIH Rocky Mountain Lab 903 S 4th St Hamilton MT 59840-2932

MUÑOZ, MARGARET ELLEN, reading specialist; b. Jacksonville, Ill., Jan. 30, 1947; d. George William and Lois Lottie (Ankrom) Greene; m. Juan James Muñoz, Mar. 31, 1972; children: Aaron Joseph, Lauri Elizabeth. BA, Culver-Stockton Coll., 1969; MA, Western Ill. U., 1971. Cert. tchr. reading K-12 and English 7-12, Mo. Tchr. lang. arts 10-12 Quincy (Ill.) Sr. H.S., 1970-72; tchr. lang. arts 7-12 Sch. Dist. R-S, New Raymer, Colo., 1972-73; tchr. lang. arts 9-12 Kansas City (Mo.) Sch. Dist., 1973-78; tchr. lang. arts 10-12 Ft. Osage Sch. Dist., Independence, Mo., 1978-80; Tchr. Title I Reading 7-8 Independence Pub. Schs., 1980-81, 89—, tchr. ESL and Am. Indian K-12, 1985-89; chairperson Profl. Devel.-Palmer, Independence, 1993—; sponsor Sharing Stories With Children, Independence, 1993—; presenter reading strategies Ottawa U., Overland Park, Kans., 1994; mem. Dist. Profl. Devel., Independence, 1994—; presenter Chpt. I State Conf., 1994; mem. adv. bd. KCRPDC, 1995-96. Active Blue Ridge Blvd. United Meth. Ch., Kansas City, 1982—; officer Mothers' Coun., Boy Scouts Am., Kansas City, 1993—. Mem. ASCD, Mo. Nat. Edn. Assn., Independence/Ft. Osage Internat. Reading Assn. (com. chair 1984—), PTA (life). Avocations: reading, sewing, walking, time with family. Office: Palmer Jr HS 218 N Pleasant St Independence MO 64050-2655

MUNOZ, MICHAEL ANTHONY, professional football player; b. Ontario, Calif., Aug. 19, 1958; m. Dede Munoz; children: Michael Anthony, Michelle. BS in Pub. Adminstrn., U. So. Calif., 1980. Offensive tackle Cin. Bengals, 1980-93; with Tampa Bay Buccaneers, 1993-94. Appeared in films: The Border Line, 1980, The Right Stuff, 1983. Player Pro Bowl, 1981, 83-91; NFL All-Star team, The Sporting News, 1981, player NFL Championship Game, 1982; named Lineman of Yr., 1981, NFL Alumni, NFLPA and Cin. Bengals, Best Offensive Lineman, NFL, 1986; recipient Sports award Seagrams Seven Crown, 1982; named to 1985 All NFL Team.

MUÑOZ DONES CARRASCAL, ELOISA, hospital administrator, pediatrician, consultant, educator; b. San Lorenzo, P.R., Oct. 25, 1922; d. Pedro and Maria (Dones) Muñoz; m. José D. Carrascal, Dec. 7, 1962; children: Lilia, Maria. BA in Edn. cum laude, BS in Chemistry cum laude, U. P.R., Rio Piedras, 1943; MD, Tulane U., 1948. Diplomate Am. Bd. Pediatrics. Intern Arecibo Charity Dist. Hosp., 1948-49; resident in pediatrics San Juan (P.R.) City Hosp., 1949-51, chief newborn svc., attending pediatrician, 1951—, dir. neonatal-perinatal medicine, 1965—, dir. fellowship tng. program, 1972—; from instr. to assoc. prof. clin. pediatrics sch. medicine U. P.R., 1951-89, prof., 1989—; courtesy pediatrician neonatologist Tchrs. Hosp., Hato Rey, P.R., 1951-76, Ashford Presbyn. Drs. Hosp., Santurce, P.R., 1951-76, San Jorge H. H. Pavia Fernandez, Santurce, 1951-76; cons. pediatrician neonatologist Tchrs. H. Auxilio Mutuo H., Hato Rey, 1976—, Drs. H. San Jorge H. Ashford, San Juan, 1976—; mem. exec. com. San Juan City Hosp., 1976—, pres. med. faculty, 1976-77, 87-89, mem. instl. rev. bd., mem. ednl. rev. bd., mem. various coms.; lectr. in field. Contbr. articles to profl. jours. U.S. del. Care Orgn. Latin Am., 1962-63. Recipient Bronze medal Brazilian Acad. Human Scis., 1975, Hon. Cert. Internat. Yr. Women, City Mayor Lodo Carlos Romero Barceló, 1975, Hon. Cert. Disting. Svc. to Cmty., Julio Sellés Solá Elem. Sch., 1976, Pioneer Pediatrician award P.R. Pediat. Sect. Convention, 1993, Pioneer in Neonatology award P.R. Pediat. Sect. Convention, 1995, Pioneer Pidiat. Critical Care award Pediat. Critical Care Assn., 1996; grantee NIH, 1962. Fellow Am. Acad. Pediatrics (neonatal perinatal sect., mem. com. fetus and newborn P.R. chpt. 1956—, sec.-treas. 1962-64, mem. com. history perinatal sect. 1992—, Plaque in Recognition Disting. Pediatrician and Tchr. 1985), Pan Am. Pediatrics; mem. Am. Med. Women Assn., P.R. Med. Assn. (pediat. sect., mem. chamber of dels. 1962-63, Bronze plaque 1967, 91, Gold Pin 1980), P.R. Med. Women Assn. (sec.-treas. 1957-60, pres. 1960-64), Pan Am. Med. Women Assn. (pres. P.R. chpt. 1960-64, P.R. del. VIII Congress Manizales Colombia 1962), Pan Am. Med. Women Alliance (vis. lectr. 1962), Tulane Med. Alumni, London Royal Soc. Health, Colegio de Químicos, Soc. Dominicana de Pediatría (hon., vis. lectr. 1971), Dominican Rep. Soc. (hon.). Avocation: poetry. Home: Duke C 12 Esq Tulane Santa Ana Rio Piedras San Juan PR 00927 Office: Las Americas Profl Ctr Domenech 400 Ste 309 Hato Rey San Juan PR 00918

MUÑOZ-SOLÁ, HAYDEÉ SOCORRO, library administrator; b. Caguas, P.R., Dec. 27, 1943; d. Gilberto Muñoz and Carmen Haydeé (Solá) de Muñoz; m. Juan M. Masini-Soler, Jan. 8, 1966 (div. 1979); children: Juan Martín Masini-Muñoz, Haydeé Milagros Masini-Muñoz. BA in Psychology, U. P.R., Río Piedras, 1965, MLS, 1970; D in Libr. Sci., Columbia U., 1985. Asst. libr. U. P.R., Río Piedras, 1964-67; dir. libr. Interam. U., Aguadilla, P.R., 1974-75; head svcs. to pub. U. P.R., Aguadilla, 1975-76; cataloguer Cath. U., Ponce, P.R., 1976-79; catalogue U. P.R., Río Piedras, 1982-84, head libr. and info. sci. libr., 1984-85, prof. grad. libr. sch., 1986, dir. libr. sys., 1986-93; coord. external resources libr. sys. U. P.R.; dir. P.R. Newspaper Project, Río Piedras, 1986-90; mem. Adv. Com. on Pub. Librs., San Juan, 1987-93; proposal reviewer NEH, 1990—; chmn. Puerto Rican Del. to Nat. White House Conf. on Libr. and Info. Svcs., 1991. Author: La Información y la Documentación Educativa/Informe Sobre la Situación Actual en Puerto Rico, 1991, Memorias: Segunda Pre-Conferencia de Casa Blanca Sobre Bibliotecas y Servicios de Información en Puerto Rico, 1991; contbr. articles to profl. jours. Mem. Ponce Sport Club, 1976-83, ARC, Ponce, 1978. Recipient plaque White House Pre-Conf. on Libr. and Info. Scis., 1990; French Alps Study Tour scholar Assn. Caribbean Univ. Rsch. and Instl. Librs., 1989, Germany Study Tour scholar Fgn. Rels. Office, Germany, 1991. Mem. ALA, Am. Mgmt. Assn., Grad. Sch. Libr. and Info. Sci. Alumni Assn. (pres. 1988-90), Seminar for Acquisitions L.Am. Libr. Materials, Iberoamerican Nat. Librs. Assn. (pres. 1992-93), Puerto Rican Librs. Soc. (coord. So. area 1974, Lauro award 1989), Assn. Caribbean U. Rsch.

and Instnl. Librs. (Parchment award 1988), Asoc. para las Comunicaciones y Tecnologia Educativa, Mid. States Assn. Colls. and Schs. (collaborator), Am. Women Assn., Phi Delta Kappa (chair P.R. com. 1988-90, Kappan of Yr. 1990), Eta Gamma Delta. Roman Catholic. Avocations: reading, crewel work, embroidery, knitting, movies. Office: U of PR Library System PO Box 23302 University Sta San Juan PR 00931-3302

MUNRO, ALICE, author; b. Wingham, Ont., Can., July 10, 1931; d. Robert Eric and Anne Clarke (Chamney) Laidlaw; m. James Armstrong Munro, 1951 (div. 1976); children: Sheila, Jenny, Andrea; m. Gerald Fremlin, 1976. BA, U. Western Ont., 1952, DLitt (hon.), 1976. Author: (short stories) Dance of the Happy Shades, 1968 (Gov.-Gen.'s Lit. award 1969), A Place for Everything, 1970, Lives of Girls and Women, 1971 (Can. Booksellers award, 1972), (short stories) Something I've Been Meaning To Tell You, 1974, Who Do You Think You Are?, 1979 (pub. in U.S. as Beggar Maid: Stories of Flo and Rose, 1984, Gov.-Gen.'s Lit. award 1978), The Moons of Jupiter, 1982, The Progress of Love, 1986 (Gov. Gens. Lit. award 1987), Friend of My Youth, 1990, (short stories) Open Secrets, 1994, A Wilderness Station, 1994; TV scripts: A Trip to the Coast, 1973, Thanks For The Ride, 1973, How I Met My Husband, 1974, 1847: The Irish, 1978. Recipient Can.-Australia Lit. Prize 1994, Marian Engel award, 1986. Home: PO Box 1133, Clinton, ON Canada N0M 1L0 Office: care Alfred A Knopf Inc 201 E 50th St New York NY 10022-7703

MUNRO, BARBARA HAZARD, nursing educator, college dean, researcher; b. Wakefield, R.I., Nov. 28, 1938; d. Robert J. and Honore (Egan) Hazard; m. Bruce Munro, June 1, 1961; children: Karen Aimee, Craig Michael, Stephanie Anne. BS, MS, U. R.I., Kingston; PhD, U. Conn. RN, Conn. Asst. prof. U. of R.I. Coll. of Nursing, Kingston; assoc. prof., chmn. program in nursing rsch. Yale U., New Haven, Conn.; assoc. prof., asst. dir. Ctr. for Nursing Rsch. U. Pa., Phila.; dean, prof. Boston Coll. Sch. Nursing, 1990—; presenter and workshop leader various nursing confs. and seminars in U.S. Contbr. articles and rsch. to profl. pubs. Trustee St. Elizabeth's Med. Ctr. Boston, 1994—. Recipient Nat. Rsch. Svc. award. Fellow Am. Acad. Nursing; mem. ANA, Nat. League for Nursing, Sigma Theta Tau, Pi Lambda Theta, Phi Kappa Phi.

MUNRO, CRISTINA STIRLING, artistic director; b. London, May 22, 1940; came to U.S., 1977; m. Richard Munro (div. 1986); children: Alexandra, Nicholas. Attended various artistic schs., London. Mem. ballet corps Sadlers Wells Opera Ballet, London, 1960-62, Het Nederlands Ballet, The Hague, Holland, 1962-63; soloist London Festival Ballet, 1963-72; prin. soloist Eliot Feld Ballet, N.Y.C., 1972-75; prin. dancer, artistic dir. Old Dominion U., Norfolk, Va., 1975; artistic dir. Louisville Ballet Co., 1975-79; ballet mistress Houston Ballet, 1979-85; dir. Munro Ballet Studies, Corpus Christi, Tex., 1985—; artistic dir. Corpus Christi Ballet, 1985—; guest artist and choreographer numerous cos. in U.S. Recipient Giovanni Martini award Louisville, 1978. Mem. Imperial Soc. Tchrs. of Dance, Royal Acad. Dancing, Brit. Actors Equity Assn., Am. Guild Mus. Artists. Office: Munro Ballet Studios/ Corpus Christi Ballet 5610 Everhart Rd Corpus Christi TX 78411-4905

MUNRO, DONALD JACQUES, philosopher, educator; b. New Brunswick, N.J., Mar. 5, 1931; s. Thomas B. and Lucile (Nadler) M.; m. Ann Maples Patterson, Mar. 3, 1956; 1 child, Sarah de la Roche. A.B., Harvard U., 1953; Ph.D. (Ford Found. fellow), Columbia U., 1964. Asst. prof. philosophy U. Mich., 1964-68, asso. prof., 1968-73, prof. philosophy, 1973—, prof. philosophy and Asian langs., 1990—, chmn. dept. Asian langs. and cultures, 1993-95; vis. research philosopher Center for Chinese Studies, U. Calif., Berkeley, 1969-70; asso. Center for Chinese Studies, U. Mich., 1964—; chmn. com. on studies of Chinese civilization Am. Council Learned Socs., 1979-81; mem. Com. on Scholarly Communication with People's Republic China, 1978-82, China Council of Asia Soc., 1977-80, Com. on Advanced Study in China, 1978-82, Nat. Com. on U.S.-China Rels., Nat. Faculty of Humanities, Arts and Scis., 1986—; Evans-Wentz lectr. Stanford U., 1970; Fritz lectr. U. Wash., 1980; Gilbert Ryle lectr. Trent U., Ont., 1983; John Dewey lectr. U. Vermont, 1989; vis. rsch.scholar Chinese Acad. Social Scis. Inst. Philosophy, Beijing, 1983, dept. philosophy Beijing U., 1990. Author: The Concept of Man in Early China, 1969, the Concept of Man in Contemporary China, 1977;, editor: Individualism and Holism, 1985, Images of Human Nature: A Sung Portrait, 1988. Mem. exec. com. Coll. Literature, Sci. and The Arts U. Mich., 1986-89. Served to lt. (j.g.) USNR, 1953-57. Recipient letter of commendation Chief Naval Ops.; Disting. Svc. award U. Mich., 1968, Excellence in Edn. award, 1992; Rice Humanities award, 1993-94; Nat. Humanities faculty fellow, 1971-72; John Simon Guggenheim Found. fellow, 1978-79; grantee Social Sci. Rsch. Coun., 1965-66, Am. Coun. Learned Socs., 1982-83, China com. grantee NAS, 1990. Mem. Assn. for Asian Studies (China and Inner Asia Council 1970-72), Soc. for Asian and Comparative Philosophy. Club: Ann Arbor Racquet. Home: 14 Ridgeway St Ann Arbor MI 48104-1739 Office: Dept Philosophy U Mich Ann Arbor MI 48104 *I believe that much knowledge is interrelated and that academic disciplinary boundaries are transitory conveniences. The human significance of any research task I undertake should be obvious to those inside and outside my professional group (a goal I seek but do not always achieve).*

MUNRO, J. RICHARD, publishing company executive; b. 1931; married. B.A., Colgate U., 1957; postgrad., Columbia U., NYU; Litt. D. (hon.), Richmond U., 1983. With Time Inc. (now Time Warner Inc.), 1957—; pres. Pioneer Press Inc., subs. Time, 1969; pub. Sports Illus., 1969-71; v.p. Time Inc., 1971-75, group v.p. for video, 1975-79, exec. v.p., 1979-80, pres., 1980-86; chief exec. officer Time Inc. (name changed to Time Warner Inc.), 1980-90, chmn., 1986-90, chmn. exec. com., 1990—, also bd. dirs.; dir. IBM Corp. Mem. Pres.' Council on Phys. Fitness and Sport; trustee Experiment in Internat. Living, Brattleboro, Vt., Northfield Mount Hermon Sch., Colgate U.; bd. dirs. Urban League of Southwestern Fairfield County (Conn.), Jr. Achievement, United Negro Coll. Fund; bd. dirs., chmn. edn. com. N.Y.C. Partnership. Served with USMCR., Korea. Decorated Purple Heart with 2 clusters. Clubs: Country of New Canaan (Conn.), River, Winter of New Canaan. Office: Time Warner Inc 75 Rockefeller Plz New York NY 10019-6908*

MUNRO, JOHN HENRY ALEXANDER, economics educator, writer; b. Vancouver, B.C., Can., Mar. 14, 1938; s. Hector Gordon and Blanche (Almond) M.; m. Jeanette Roberta James, May 25, 1968; children: Robert Ryder, Valerie Marlene. B.A. with honors, U. B.C., Vancouver, 1960; M.A. in History, Yale U., 1961, Ph.D. in History, 1965. Instr. in history U. B.C., 1964-65, asst. prof. history and econs., 1965-68; assoc. prof. econs. U. Toronto, 1968-73, prof., 1973—; assoc. dir. Centre for Medieval Studies, U. Toronto, 1975-78; cons. on coinage to pub. U. Toronto Press, 1973—. Author: Wool, Cloth, and Gold, 1973, Bullion Flows and Monetary Policies in England and the Low Countries, 1350-1500, 1992, Textiles, Towns and Trade: Essays in the Economic History of Late-Medieval England and the Low Countries, 1994; contbr. articles to profl. jours., essays to books; mem. editorial bd. Textile History, 1980—; Medieval area editor Oxford Ency. of Econ. History, 1996—. Can. Coun. leave fellow, Belgium, 1970-71, Social Scis. and Humanities Rsch. Coun. Can. fellow, Engl. and Holland, 1979-80, Belgium, 1986-87, Eng. and Belgium, 1992-96, 96—, Connaught Rsch. fellow, 1993-94. Mem. Can. Econ. Assn., Econ. History Assn. (U.S.), Econ. History Soc. (U.K.), Medieval Acad. Am. (councillor 1990-93). Presbyterian. Home: 9 Woodmere Ct, Islington, ON Canada M9A 3J1 Office: Dept Econs U Toronto, 150 Saint George St, Toronto, ON Canada M5S 1A1

MUNRO, MEREDITH VANCE, lawyer; b. Natick, Mass., Aug. 4, 1938; s. George Lawrence and Florence Estella (Murphy) M.; m. Gail Wittekind, June 10, 1960 (div. 1974); children: Susan Heidi, Elizabeth Holly, Meredith Heather. AB, Princeton U., 1960; JD, Harvard U., 1963. Bar: Mass. 1963. Assoc. atty. Gaston Snow & Ely Bartlett, Boston, 1963-71, ptnr., 1971—; bd. dirs. Heath Cons. Inc., Stoughton, Mass., 1974—. Trustee The Tabor Acad., Marion, Mass., 1975—. Mem. Mass. Bar Assn., Boston Bar Assn. Avocations: antiques, gardening, cooking. Home: 5 Patricia Rd Framingham MA 01701-3931

MUNRO, MICHAEL DONALD, food and beverage industry executive; b. Kindley AFB, Bermuda, May 6, 1953; (parents Am. citizens); s. Donald M. and Marilyn Barbara (Ravenelle) M. AAS in Criminology, U. Md., 1978; BA in Sociology, SUNY, Plattsburg, 1981; MA in Mgmt., Embry-Riddle U., 1986. Commd. 2d lt. USAF, 1976, advanced through grades to capt., 1985; chief security adminstr. Plattsburg AFB, N.Y., 1979-81; ICBM launch officer Grands Forks AFB, Grand Forks AFB, N.D., 1981-83; ICBM flight comdr. Grands Forks AFB, N.D., 1984-86; satellite officer Colorado Springs, Colo., 1986-87; chief satellite officer U.S. Space Command, Colorado Springs, 1987; chief U.S. Space Def. Ops. Ctr., Colorado Springs, 1988-91; ret., 1991, profl. voice talent, broadcaster, 1991—; gen. mgr. Entertainment Concepts, Colorado Springs, 1991-94; mgr. corp. ops. The Gambler Nightclubs and Restaurants, 1994-95; food and beverage exec. The Westin Hotel, Denver, 1995-96; beverage dir. Sheraton/CAPSTAR Hotels, 1996—; cons. 1980 Winter Olympics, Lake Placid, N.Y., 1979-80; dir. Grand Forks City Govt., 1986. Contbr. articles to profl. jours. Mem. Pike's Peak Rodeo Com., Colorado Springs, 1987. Recipient Scholastic Achievement award Boeing Aerospace, 1988; named Outstanding Young Man Grand Forks County, 1985. Mem. Profl. Rodeo Cowboys Assn. (judge 1987-88, announcer, broadcaster 1988—), Assn. Govt. Execs., Crewmembers Assn. (pres. 1985-86), Grand Forks C. of C., Wild Horse Futurity Assn. (bd. dirs. 1992-94). Republican. Roman Catholic. Avocations: profl. rodeo, hunting, fishing, horseback riding. Home: PO Box 49266 Colorado Springs CO 80949

MUNRO, RALPH DAVIES, state government official; b. Bainbridge Island, Wash., June 25, 1943; s. George Alexander and Elizabeth (Troll) M.; m. Karen Hansen, Feb. 17, 1973; 1 son, George Alexander. BA in History and Edn. (scholar), Western Wash. U. Successively indsl. engr. Boeing Co.; sales mgr. Continental Host, Inc.; asst. dep. dir. ACTION Agy.; spl. asst. to gov. of Wash.; gen. mgr. Tillicum Enterprises & Food Services Co.; dir. Found. for Handicapped; pres. Northwest Highlands Tree Farm; now sec. of state State of Wash. Chmn. community service com. Seattle Rotary Club 4; founder 1st pres. Rotary Youth Job Employment Center, Seattle. Named Man of Yr. Assn. Retarded Citizens, Seattle, 1970. Mem. Nat. Assn. Secs. State (pres.), Nat. Assn. Retarded Children, Wash. Historic Mus. (dir.), Wash. Trust Historic Preservation (founder), Nature Conservancy. Republican. Lutheran. Office: Sec of State Legislative Bldg PO Box 40220 Olympia WA 98504-0220

MUNROE, GEORGE BARBER, former metals company executive; b. Joliet, Ill., Jan. 5, 1922; s. George Muller and Ruth (Barber) M.; m. Elinor Bunin, May 30, 1968; children by previous marriage: George Taylor, Ralph W. Taylor. AB, Dartmouth Coll., 1943; LLB, Harvard U., 1949; BA (Rhodes scholar), Christ Church, Oxford (Eng.) U., 1951, MA, 1956; DHL (hon.), No. Ariz. U., 1981; LLD (hon.), Dartmouth Coll., 1993. Bar: N.Y. 1949. Assoc. Cravath, Swaine & Moore, N.Y.C., 1949; atty. Office Gen. Counsel U.S. High Commn. Germany, Frankfurt and Bonn, 1951-53; justice U.S. Ct. Restitution Appeals Allied High Commn. Germany, Nuremberg, 1953-54; assoc. Debevoise, Plimpton & McLean, N.Y.C., 1954-58; with Phelps Dodge Corp., 1958-90, v.p., 1962-66; also bd. dirs., 1966-94; pres. Phelps Dodge Corp., 1966-75, 80-82, chief exec. officer, 1969-87, chmn. bd., 1975-87, chmn. fin. com., cons., 1987-90; bd. dirs. N.Y. Times Co., Santa Fe Pacific Gold Corp. Trustee, chmn. fin. com. Met. Mus. Art; bd. dirs. Acad. Polit. Sci. Lt. (j.g.) USNR, 1943-46. Mem. Mining and Metall. Soc. Am., Coun. Fgn. Rels., Century Assn., River Club, Univ. Club (N.Y.C.), Bridgehampton Club. Office: Phelps Dodge Corp 866 Third Ave 26th Fl New York NY 10022 :

MUNROE, PAT, retired newsman; b. Quincy, Fla., Nov. 3, 1916; s. Mark Welch and Mary Frances (Gray) M.; m. Mary Johnson Norris, Dec. 6, 1952; children: Anne Logan, Katherine Gray. B.S. in Indsl. Mgmt., Ga. Inst. Tech., 1939; M.S., Columbia Sch. Journalism, 1941. Reporter Atlanta Jour., 1939-40, Washington Post, 1946-47; former propr. Munroe News Bur., Washington, rep. book pubs. and newspapers, 1947-83; covered maj. polit. convs., presdl. campaigns, 1948—, (Vice Pres. Nixon's trip to Russia), 1959; chmn. standing com. corrs. U.S. Senate-House Press Galleries, 1955-56; bd. govs. Nat. Press Club, 1955-56. Bd. govs. Nat. Cathedral Sch., Washington; trustee Webb Sch., Bell Buckle, Tenn.; former trustee James Monroe Meml. Found., Fredericksburg, Va. Served to lt. comdr. USNR, 1941-45. Recipient Raymond Clapper Meml. award and cert. Columbia Sch. Journalism, 1957. Mem. White House Corrs. Assn., Chevy Chase Club, Univ. Club (N.Y.C.), Met. Club, Nat. Press Club, Sigma Delta Chi (pres. Washington 1964-65). Republican. Episcopalian. Home: 9025 Bronson Dr Potomac MD 20854-4607

MUNSAT, STANLEY MORRIS, philosopher, educator; b. Rutland, Vt., Apr. 12, 1939; s. Leo and Ethel (Geron) M.; m. Rosemary S.; children—Steven, Tobin. A.B., Cornell U., 1960; M.A., U. Mich., 1962, Ph.D., 1965. Asst. prof. U. Calgary, Alta., Can., 1963-66; asst. prof. philosophy U. Calif., Irvine, 1966-68; asso. prof. U. Calif., 1968-71, prof., 1971-72; prof. philosophy U. N.C., Chapel Hill, 1972—. Author: The Concept of Memory, 1967; Editor: The Analytic Synthetic Distinction, 1971; gen. editor: (with A.I. Melden) Wadsworth Basic Problems in Philosophy Series; contbr. articles to profl. jours. Mem. Am. Philos. Assn. Home: 837 Shadylawn Rd Chapel Hill NC 27514-2007 Office: Univ NC Dept Philosophy Chapel Hill NC 27514

MUNSAT, THEODORE L., neurologist, researcher; b. Rutland, Vt., Aug. 6, 1930; s. Leo and Ethel (Garon) M.; m. Carla Anne Hoffman, May 31, 1959; children: Amy, Peter. BS in Chemistry, U. Mich., 1952; MD, U. Vt., 1956; DSc (hon.), U. Marseille, France, 1987. Diplomate Am. Bd. Neurology and Psychiatry (examiner). Rsch. asst. pharmacology Cornell U. Med. Coll., 1955-56; intern Mt. Sinai Hosp., N.Y.C., 1957-58; resident in neurology Neurol. Inst., N.Y.C., Columbia Presbyn. Med. Ctr., 1958-60; chief resident in neurology UCLA Ctr. Health Scis., 1960-61, asst. prof. medicine, neurology dept., 1963-70, dir. Myasthenia Gravis Clinic, 1963-70, dir. UCLA Ctr. Health Scis., 1970-76; assoc. prof. neurology U. So. Calif. Sch. Medicine, 1970-73, prof., 1973—, dir. Muscle Disorder Clinic, 1970-76; prof., chmn. dept. neurology Tufts U. Sch. Medicine, 1976-83, prof. pharmacology, 1989—; dir. Neuromuscular Rsch. Unit Tufts-New Eng. Med. Ctr., 1976—; attending physician in neurology Wadsworth VA Hosp., 1963-70; staff neurologist L.A. County/U. So. Calif. Med. Ctr., 1970-76; neurologist in chief New Eng. Med. Ctr., 1976-83, co-dir. Muscular Dystrophy Clinic, 1976—, neuromuscular pathology lab., 1976—; program chmn. Congress Asian and Oceanic Neurologic Socs., 1983; 10th Carrell-Krusen lectr. Tex. Scottish Rite Hosp., Southwestern Med. Sch., Dallas, 1988, 1st Ann. Baird Med. Sci. Ctr. lectr. SUNY at Buffalo, 1988; cons. U.S. Naval Hosp., San Diego, Fresno County Gen. Hosp., Calif., State Calif. Vocat. Rehab. Svcs., Crippled Children Svcs., NIH, Serano Corp., Johns Hopkins Applied Physics Lab., others; adv. bd. Nat. Com. for Rsch. in Neurol. Diseases, Blindness and Stroke.; nat. adv. coun. Am. Fedn. for Aging Rsch. Contbr. numerous articles to profl. pubs.; mem. editorial bd. Muscle and Nerve, Jour. Neurol. Rehabilitation, Bull. L.A. Neurol. Socs.; reviewer New Eng. Jour. Medicine, Neurology, Muscle and Nerve, Science. Trustee Easter Seal Rsch. Found.; bd. dirs., vice chmn. Nat. Coalition for Rsch. in Neurologic Diseases; bd. dirs. Nat. Found. for Rsch. in Neurologic Disorders. Lt. comdr. M.C., USN, 1961-63. Recipient Teaching Excellence award Tufts U. Sch. Medicine, 1982. Mem. Am. Acad. Neurology (pres. 1987-89, councillor, exec. com., chmn. continuing edn. com.), Am. Neurologic Assn., Soc. Neurosci., AAAS, Assn. Am. Colls., Am. Pub. Health Assn., Assn. Rsch. in Nervous and Mental Diseases, Soc. Clin. Neurologists, Muscular Dystrophy Assn. Am. Inc. (chmn. med. adv. bd. L.A. County chpt.), Pan Am. Med. Assn., L.A. Soc. Neurology and Psychiatry, Mass. Neurologic Assn., Boston Soc. Neurology and Psychiatry, Greater Boston Post-Polio Assn. (hon. dir.), Societe Francaise de Neurologie, Phi Lambda Upsilon. Office: Tufts-New Eng Med Ctr Dept Neurology 750 Washington St Boston MA 02111-1533

MUNSCH, MARTHA HARTLE, lawyer; b. Meyersdale, Pa., Oct. 31, 1948. BA, U. Pitts., 1970; JD, Yale U., 1973. Bar: Pa. 1973. Ptnr. Reed Smith Shaw & McClay, Pitts.; asst. prof. law U. Pitts., 1976-78. Office: Reed Smith Shaw & McClay James H Reed Bldg 435 6th Ave Pittsburgh PA 15219-1886*

MUNSELL, ELSIE LOUISE, lawyer; b. N.Y.C., Feb. 15, 1939; d. Elmer Stanley and Eleanor Harriet (Dickinson) M.; m. George P. Williams, July 14, 1979. AB, Marietta Coll., 1960; JD, Marshall-Wythe Coll. William and Mary, 1972. Bar: Va. 1972, U.S. Dist. Ct. (ea. dist.) Va. 1974, U.S. Ct. Appeals (4th cir.) 1976, U.S. Supreme Ct. 1980. Tchr. Norview High Sch., Norfolk, Va., 1964-69; asst. Commonwealth atty. Commonwealth Atty.'s Office, Alexandria, Va., 1972-73; asst. U.S. atty. Alexandria, 1974-79; U.S. magistrate U.S. Dist. Ct. (ea. dist.) Va., Alexandria, 1979-81; U.S. atty. Dept. Justice, Alexandria, 1981-86; sr. trial atty. Office of Gen. Counsel, Dept. Navy, Washington, 1986-89, asst. gen. counsel installations and environ. law, 1989-91; dep. asst. environ. and safety Sec. Navy, 1991—. Active Va. Commn. on Status of Women, 1966-74; bd. vistors Coll. William and Mary, 1972-76; active Atty. Gen.'s Adv. Com. U.S. Attys., 1981-83; bd. dirs. Carpenter's Shelter, Inc., 1990-93. Mem. Environ. Law Inst. (assoc.), Sr. Execs. Assn. Episcopalian. Office: Dept Navy 1000 Navy Pentagon Washington DC 20350-1000

MUNSEY, VIRDELL EVERARD, JR., utility executive; b. Washington, Sept. 25, 1933; s. Virdell Everard and Mildred Lovenia (Wood) M.; m. Bernice Ann Wilson, Sept. 20, 1956; children: Wanda Louise, Allan Coll, Andrew Everard, Carolyn Jane. B.A. magna cum laude, Yale U., 1955; M.P.A., Harvard U., 1967. Reporter Washington Post, 1957-63; legis. asst. Rep. Henry S. Reuss, Washington, 1963-68; info. dir. United Democrats for Humphrey, Washington, 1968; asst. dir. public affairs Dem. Nat. Com., 1968; with Nat. Planning Assn., Washington, 1969-77; exec. v.p. Nat. Planning Assn., 1974-76; dep. asst. sec. for public affairs Dept. Treasury, Washington, 1977-81; cons. World Bank, 1981; with Va. Electric and Power Co., 1981-86, mgr. corp. communications, 1982-83, exec. dir. pub. policy, 1983-86, v.p. pub. policy, 1986; v.p. pub. policy Dominion Resources Inc., 1986—; mem. Va. Coal and Energy Commn., 1983-95. Chmn. Arlington County Dem. Party, 1967-69; mem. Arlington County Bd., 1972-75, chmn., 1973; vice chmn. No. Va. Transp. Commn., 1973, chmn., 1974; bd. dirs. Washington Met. Area Transit Authority, 1975; mem. transp. planning bd. Met. Washington Coun. Govts., 1973-75; treas. Competitive Power Policy Forum, 1990—. Served with U.S. Army, 1955-57. Am. Polit. Sci. Assn. fellow, 1966-67. Mem. United Ch. Christ. Office: 901 E Byrd St Richmond VA 23219-4069

MUNSON, ANNETTE MARLENE, pediatrics nurse; b. Columbia, Mo., Feb. 21, 1964; d. James Derril and E. Ethelene (Bennett) M. BSN, U. Pa., 1986, BS in Econs. and Mgmt., 1986; postgrad., U. Rochester, 1995—. Cert. pediatric nurse, ANCC, ACLS, Pedriatic Advance Life Support Instr., BCLS Instr., NALS. Commd. 2d lt. U.S. Army, 1986, advanced through grades to capt., 1990; staff nurse in pediatrics Walter Reed Army Med. Ctr., Washington, 1987-89, staff nurse in surg. ICU, 1989-90; staff nurse neonatal ICU William Beaumont Army Med. Ctr., Ft. Bliss, Tex., 1991-92; maternal/child nursing instr. Practical Nurse Course, Ft. Bliss, Tex., 1992-95; asst. head nurse Pediatrics William Beaumont Army Med. Ctr., Ft. Bliss, Tex., 1995; instr. coord. infant/child CPR, Safety Class William Beaumont Army Med. Ctr., 1991-93; coord. med. svcs. Area 19 El Paso Spl. Olympics, 1991-95; with 865th Gen. Hosp., Rochester, N.Y., 1995—. Mem AACN, ANA (coun. on maternal-child health nursing), Tex. Nurses Assn. Avocations: Skiing, running, volleyball, softball, playing cello.

MUNSON, ERIC BRUCE, hospital administrator; b. Elmhurst, Ill., Mar. 11, 1943; married. B, Wabash Coll., 1965; MHA, U. Chgo., 1967. Asst. to adminstr. Swedish Covenant Hosp., Chgo., 1966-67; asst. dir. U. Chgo. Hosps., 1970-73; assoc. adminstr. U. Hosp., Denver, 1973-77, adminstr., 1977-80; exec. dir. U. N.C. Hosp., Chapel Hill, 1980—. Home: 119 Black Oak Pl Chapel Hill NC 27514-6502 Office: Univ N C Hosps 101 Manning Dr Chapel Hill NC 27514-4220*

MUNSON, HAROLD LEWIS, education educator; b. Windham, N.Y., Aug. 2, 1923; s. Esmond Lewis and Gladys (Disbrow) M.; m. Evelyn Claire Moore, Sept. 8, 1946; children: Michael Lewis, Jeffrey Charles. A.B., Hobart Coll., 1947; M.A., SUNY, Albany, 1948; Ed.D., NYU, 1961. Tchr. social studies, counselor Cairo (N.Y.) Central Sch., 1948-50; dir. guidance Williamson (N.Y.) Central Sch., 1950-54; supr. guidance N.Y. State Edn. Dept., Albany, 1954-59; prof. edn., chmn. Center for Counseling, Family and Worklife Studies, U. Rochester, N.Y., 1959-85; prof. emeritus Center for Counseling, Family and Worklife Studies, U. Rochester, 1985—; prof. edn. Overseas Program, Boston U., 1985-87; pres. Munson Assocs., 1988—; vocat. cons. Social Security Adminstrn., HEW, 1962-79. Author: (with H.W. Houghton) Organizing Orientation Activities, 1956, My Educational Plans, 1959, 70, Guidance Activities for Teachers of English, Social Studies, Science, Mathematics and Foreign Languages, 1965, (with Gilbert Gockley) Career Insights and Self Awareness Games, 1973; contbg. author: Ency. of Careers, 1967, Elementary School Guidance: Concepts, Dimensions and Practice, 1970, The Foundations of Developmental Guidance, 1971, Career Education for Deaf Students: An Inservice Leader's Guide, 1975. Served with USNR, 1944-46. Mem. Am. Counseling Assn., Nat. Career Devel. Assn., Am. Sch. Counselor Assn., Phi Delta Kappa. Home: 745 Thayer Rd Fairport NY 14450-9514 Office: U Rochester Warner Grad Sch Edn and Human Devel Rochester NY 14627 *Success is whatever you want it to be. By defining it in such personal terms, everyone should be able to experience some degree of success. For me, it has been being able to feel a measure of personal fulfillment through my accomplishments in helping others to define and examine their own existence.*

MUNSON, HOWARD G., federal judge; b. Claremont, N.H., July 26, 1924; s. Walter N. and Helena (O'Halloran) M.; m. Ruth Jaynes, Sept. 17, 1949; children: Walter N., Richard J., Pamela A. B.S. in Economics, U. Pa., 1948; LL.B., Syracuse U., 1952. Bar: N.Y. With Employers' Assurance Corp., Ltd., White Plains, N.Y., 1949-50; mem. firm Hiscock, Lee, Rogers, Henley & Barclay, Syracuse, N.Y., 1952-76; judge U.S. Dist. Ct. No. Dist. N.Y., Syracuse, 1976—. Mem., pres. Syracuse Bd. Edn.; bd. dirs. Sta. WCNY-TV; chmn. ethics com. Onondaga County Legislature. Served with U.S. Army, 1943-45, ETO. Decorated Bronze Star, Purple Heart. Mem. Am. Coll. Trial Lawyers, Nat. Assn. R.R. Trial Counsel, Am. Arbitration Assn., Justinian Soc., Alpha Tau Omega, Phi Delta Phi. Office: US Dist Ct 349 US Courthouse P O Box 7376 Syracuse NY 13261-7376

MUNSON, JAMES CALFEE, lawyer; b. Asheville, N.C., May 17, 1944; s. James B. and Margaret (Calfee) M.; children: Garrett Calfee, Ingrid Grove, James Birger, Elizabeth Tippet; m. Melinda Tippet, Sept. 14, 1985. BA, Yale U., 1966; JD, U. Wis., 1969. Bar: Wis. 1970, Ill. 1971. Law clk. to presiding justice U.S. Dist. Ct., Milw., 1969-70; assoc. Kirkland & Ellis, Chgo., 1970-75, ptnr., 1975—. Bd. dirs. Ronald Knox Montessori Sch., Wilmette, Ill., 1975-78, Trevian Youth Soccer Club, Wilmette, 1984-88. Mem. ABA, Tavern Club, Indian Hill Club. Office: Kirkland & Ellis 200 E Randolph St Chicago IL 60601-6436

MUNSON, JOHN BACKUS, computer systems consultant, retired engineering company executive; b. Chgo., May 1, 1933; s. Mark Frame and Catherine Louise (Cherry) M.; m. Anne Lorraine Cooper, July 6, 1957; children: David B., Sharon A. BA, Knox Coll., 1955. With Unisys Corp., McLean, Va., 1957-93, v.p. corp. software engring., 1977-81, v.p. tech. ops., 1981-84, v.p., gen. mgr. space transp. systems, 1984-89, 89-93; v.p., gen. mgr. Space Systems div., 1989-94, retired, 1994; mem. sci. adv. bd. USAF, 1981-86, mem. USN panel on F14D issues, 1987-88. Recipient Exceptional Civilian Service award USAF, 1986, Superior Pub. Svc. award USN, 1988, cert. of appreciation NATO, 1984. Mem. bd. advisors U. Houston, Clear Lake, 1988-93, chmn. 1990-92; bd. dirs. Bay Area YMCA, 1988-93, chmn. 1992, Clear Lake Am. Heart Assn., 1989-93; co-chmn. Bay Area United Way, 1988—, chmn., 1992; Disting. visitor IEEE Computer Soc., 1981-94. Capt. U.S. Army, 1955-57. Named to Nat. Mgmt. Assn. Hall of Fame, 1994. Fellow IEEE (editor Trans. on Software Engring. 1982-84, bd. dirs. tech com. software engring. 1982—); mem. AIA, Am. Astronautical Soc. (bd. dirs. Southwest sect. 1989-94), Aerospace Industries Assn. (space com. 1989-94), U.S. Army Assn., Nat. Security Indsl. Assn., Armed Forces Communication Electronics Assn. (pres. Houston chpt. 1987-90), S.W. Regional Coun. Corp. CEOs. Home: 1018 Westcreek Ln Westlake Vlg CA 91362-5462 Office: 1018 Westcreek Ln Westlake Village CA 91362

MUNSON, JOHN CHRISTIAN, acoustician; b. Clinton, Iowa, Oct. 9, 1926; s. Arthur J. and Frances (Christian) M.; m. Elaine Hendershot, Sept. 2, 1950; children: John Christian, Holly Elizabeth. BS, Iowa State Coll., 1949; MS, U. Md., 1952, PhD, 1962; Navy Dept. scholar, MIT, 1956. Electronic scientist Naval Ordnance Lab., Washington, 1949-66; tech. dir. navy portion Practice Nine, Naval Air Systems Command, 1967; supt. acoustics divsn. Naval Rsch. Lab., 1968-85; v.p. Engring. & Sci. Assocs., 1983-94; chmn. bd. dirs., 1994; ret.; asst. extension prof. elec. engring. U.

Md., 1964-66; mem. Underwater Sound Adv. Group, 1969-75, U.S. Sonar Team, 1971-85, Mobile Sonar Tech. Com., 1972-85; cons., 1985—. Editor U.S. Navy Jour. Underwater Acoustics, 1983-91; patentee in field. Mem. exec. bd. D.C. Bapt. Conv., 1973—, chmn. fin. com., 1973; trustee Midwestern Bapt. Theol. Sem., 1970-80; trustee Bapt. Sr. Adult Ministries of Washington Met. Area, 1976-91, 92—, CEO, 1991-92; mem. Gen. Bd. Am. Bapt. Chs. U.S.A., 1994—; dir., pres. Allied Silver Spring Interfaith Svcs. to Srs. Today, 1994—; bd. mgrs. Am. Bapt. Hist. Soc., 1996—. Fellow IEEE, Signal Processing Soc. (mem. adminstrv. com. 1974-76, chmn. underwater acoustics com. 1973-76), Acoustical Soc. Am.; mem. Sigma Xi. Home: 119 Marine Ter Silver Spring MD 20905-5925 *I have a positive joy for life, and I am an incurable optimist: my basic attitude is that things will work out for the best—but only if we do our very best. Each of us has a responsibility to grow to our maximum capacity and to be of reasonable service to mankind. The proper balance among family, job, service to God, service to others, and attention to yourself is essential. Whatever you are doing, do it from the right motivation and with enthusiasm.*

MUNSON, LAWRENCE SHIPLEY, management consultant; b. N.Y.C., Jan. 10, 1920; s. Lawrence J. and Anna (Lee) M.; m. Gretchen Thannhauser, May 24, 1947; children: Catherine Anne, Shipley John. A.B., Harvard U., 1942, JD, 1948. Bar: N.Y. 1948. Assoc. Willkie, Owen, Farr, Gallagher & Walton, N.Y.C., 1948-51; assoc., then partner McKinsey & Co., Inc., N.Y.C., 1953-67; pres. Loral Corp., Scarsdale, N.Y., 1967-69; v.p. Allegheny Power System, Inc., N.Y.C., 1969-72; v.p., mng. prin. Louis Allen Assocs., Inc., 1972—. Author: How To Conduct Training Seminars, 1984, 2d edit., 1992. Chmn. bd. Planned Parenthood N.Y.C., 1966-70; mem. bd. Planned Parenthood Manhattan and Bronx, 1960-66, Planned Parenthood World Population, 1967-70; bd. dirs. Greater N.Y. Fund, 1966-88, chmn. mgmt. assistance com., 1970-75; pres. East Hampton Village Preservation Soc., 1982-87, trustee, 1982—, chmn., 1993—; bd. dirs. United Way N.Y.C., 1988-89. Served to maj. USAAF, 1942-46; with USAF, 1951-53. Mem. Am. Soc. Tng. and Devel. (pres. N.Y. met. chpt. 1988-89, chmn. bd. dirs. 1990-93), Maidstone Club (East Hampton), Harvard Club (N.Y.C.). Home: 25 Dayton Ln East Hampton NY 11937-2415

MUNSON, LUCILLE MARGUERITE (MRS. ARTHUR E. MUNSON), real estate broker; b. Norwood, Ohio, Mar. 26, 1914; d. Frank and Fairy (Wicks) Wirick; R.N., Lafayette (Ind.) Home Hosp., 1937; A.B., San Diego State U., 1963, student Purdue U., Kans. Wesleyan U.; m. Arthur E. Munson, Dec. 24, 1937; children—Barbara Munson Papke, Judith Munson Andrews, Edmund Arthur. Staff and pvt. nurse Lafayette Home Hosp., 1937-41; indsl. nurse Lakey Foundry & Machine Co., Muskegon, Mich., 1950-51, Continental Motors Corp., Muskegon, 1951-52; nurse Girl Scout Camp, Grand Haven, Mich., 1948-49; owner Munson Realty, San Diego, 1964—. Mem. San Diego County Grand Jury, 1975-76, 80-81, Calif. Grand Jurors Assn. (charter). Office: 2999 Mission Blvd Ste 102 San Diego CA 92109-8070

MUNSON, NANCY KAY, lawyer; b. Huntington, N.Y., June 22, 1936; d. Howard H. and Edna M. (Keenan) Munson. Student, Hofstra U., 1959-62; JD, Bklyn. Law Sch., 1965. Bar: N.Y. 1966, U.S. Supreme Ct. 1970, U.S. Ct. Appeals (2d cir.) 1971, U.S. Dist. Ct. (ea. and so. dists.) N.Y. 1968. Law clk. to E. Merritt Weidner Huntington, 1959-66, sole practice, 1966—; mem. legal adv. bd. Chgo. Title Ins. Co., Riverhead, N.Y., 1981—; bd. dirs., legal officer Thomas Munson Found. Trustee Huntington Fire Dept. Death Benefit Fund; pres., trustee, chmn. bd. Bklyn. Home Aged Men Found.; bd. dirs. Elderly Day Svcs. on the Sound. Mem. ABA, N.Y. State Bar Assn., Suffolk County Bar Assn., Bklyn. Bar Assn., NRA, DAR, Soroptimists (past pres.). Republican. Christian Scientist. Office: 197 New York Ave Huntington NY 11743-2711

MUNSON, PAUL LEWIS, pharmacologist; b. Washta, Iowa, Aug. 21, 1910; s. Lewis Sylvester and Alice E. (Orser) M.; m. Aileen Geisinger, Mar. 7, 1931 (div. 1948); 1 dau., Abigail (Mrs. Mark Krumel); m. Mary Ellen Jones, Aug. 15, 1948 (div. 1971); children: Ethan Vincent, Catherine Laura; m. Yu Chen, Feb. 27, 1987; 1 stepchild, Ming An Chen. B.A., Antioch Coll., 1933; M.A., U. Wis., 1937; Ph.D., U. Chgo., 1942; M.A. (hon.), Harvard, 1955. Fellow, asst. biochemistry U. Chgo., 1939-42; research biochemist William S. Merrell Co., Cin., 1942-43; research biochemist, head endocrinology research Armour Labs., Chgo., 1943-48; research asst., then research asso. Yale Sch. Medicine, 1948-50; asst. prof., asso. prof. pharmacology, then prof. Harvard Sch. Dental Medicine, 1950-65; prof. pharmacology, chmn. dept. U. N.C. Sch. Medicine, 1965-77, Sarah Graham Kenan prof., 1970—; Mem. U.S. Pharmacopeia Panel on Corticotropin, 1951-55; mem. pharmacology test com. Nat. Bd. Med. Examiners, 1966-71; mem. gen. medicine B study section NIH, 1966-70, chmn., 1969-70, mem. pharmacology-toxicology rev. com., 1972-76. Author numerous articles on hormones; co-editor: Vitamins and Hormones, 1968-82; editl. bd. Endocrinology, 1957-63, Jour. Pharmacology and Exptl. Therapeutics, 1959-65, Jour. Dental Rsch., 1962-64, Biochem. Medicine, 1967-84, Am. Jour. Chinese Medicine, 1973-79, Pharmacol. Revs., 1967-70, editor-in-chief, 1977-81; editor-in-chief: Principles of Pharmacology, 1981-94. Fellow AAAS, Am. Acad. Arts and Scis.; mem. Am. Soc. Pharmacology and Exptl. Therapeutics (council 1970-73, sec.-treas. 1971-72), Am. Soc. Biol. Chemists, Endocrine Soc. (council 1963-65, Fred Conrad Koch award 1976), Am. Soc. Bone and Mineral Research (William F. Neuman award 1982), Am. Chem. Soc., Biometrics Soc., Internat. Assn. Dental Research (councillor 1957-59), AAUP, ACLU (mem. internat. confs. on calcium regulating hormones, Elsevier Sci. Pubs. award 1989), Assn. Med. Sch. Pharmacology (council 1971-73, sec. 1972-73, pres. 1974-76), Am. Thyroid Assn. (nominating com. 1973), Sigma Xi. Dem. Socialist. Unitarian. Home and Office: 1520 Taylor Ave Parkville MD 21234-5241

MUNSON, RICHARD HOWARD, horticulturist; b. Toledo, Dec. 20, 1948; s. Stanley Warren and Margaret Rose (Winter) M.; m. Joy Ellen Smith, July 8, 1972; children: Sarah Joy, David Remington. BS, Ohio State U., 1971; MS, Cornell U., 1973, PhD, 1981. Plant propagator The Holden Arboretum, Mentor, Ohio, 1973-76; asst. prof. Agrl. Tech. Inst., Wooster, Ohio, 1976-78, Tex. Tech U., Lubbock, 1981-84; dir. botanic garden Smith Coll., Northampton, Mass., 1984-95; exec. dir. The Holden Arboretum, Kirtland, Ohio, 1995—; v.p. Childs Park Found., Northampton, Mass., 1985-95. Lt. col. USAR. Mem. Internat. Plant Propagators Soc., Am. Soc. for Hort. Sci., Am. Assn. Bot. Gardens and Arboreta (com. chmn. 1987-92), Am. Assn. Nurserymen, Internat. Soc. Arboriculture, Sigma Xi, Pi Alpha Xi, Gamma Sigma Delta. Republican. Methodist. Avocations: fishing, golf, woodworking, gardening. Office: Holden Arboretum 9500 Sperry Rd Kirtland OH 44094

MUNSON, RICHARD JAY, congressional policy analyst; b. Hollywood, Calif., Aug. 10, 1950; s. Jay S. and Grace P. (Palmer) M.; m. Diane MacEachern; children: Daniel, Dana. BA, U. Calif., Santa Barbara, 1971; MA, U. Mich., 1973. Instr. U. Mich., Ann Arbor, 1973-75; coord. Environ. Action Found., Washington, 1975-77; exec. dir. Solar Lobby, Washington, 1977-83, N.E.-Midwest Inst., Washington, 1986—. Author: The Power Makers, 1985, Cousteau, 1988, The Cardinals of Capitol Hill, 1993. Recipient Award for Exceptional Pub. Svc., U.S. Dept. Energy, 1978. Office: NE Midwest Inst 218 D St SE Washington DC 20003-1900

MUNSON, WILLIAM LESLIE, insurance company executive; b. Chgo., Apr. 28, 1941; s. David Curtiss and Leona Ruth (Anderson) M.; m. Marian Lee Blanton, July 16, 1966; children: Katherine, Sandra, Deborah. Student, U. Md., 1959-62; BBA cum laude, Coll. of Ins., 1968. CPCU, 1967. Asst. mgr. N.Y. Fire Ins. Rating Orgn., N.Y.C., 1959-69; br. mgr. CNA Ins. Co., N.Y.C., 1969-75; pres., dir. Commerce & Industry Ins. Co., N.Y.C., 1975-83; pres. Commerce & Industry of Can., 1980-83; sr. v.p., chief underwriting officer Am. Internat. Underwriters, 1983-87; exec. v.p. Home Ins. Co., 1987-93; pres., chief exec. officer Home Indemnity Ins. Co., 1987-93, also bd. dirs.; chmn. City Internat. Ins. Co. Ltd., 1991-93; pres., COO Merc. and Gen. Reins. Co. Am., 1993—; chmn., pres., CEO Toa-Re-Ins. Co. Am., 1993—; trustee Coll. of Ins., 1985—; bd. dirs. Nat. Coun. Compensation Ins., 1989-92, ISO Comml. Risk Svcs., 1993; mem. comml. lines com. Ins. Svcs. Office, 1989-92; trustee Am. Inst. for Charter Property Casualty Underwriters, 1996—. Pres. Wyckoff (N.J.) Bd. Edn., 1979-82; chmn. bd. lay leaders Grace United Meth. Ch., Wyckoff, 1989-92. Mem. Soc. CPCUs (bd. dirs. N.Y. chpt.), Conf. Spl. Risk Underwriters, Reinsurance Assn. Am. (bd. dirs.), Brokers Reinsurance Markets Assn. (bd. dirs.). Republican. Club: John St. (N.Y.C.). Home: 762 Albemarle St Wyckoff NJ 07481-1005 Office: Merc and Gen Reins 177 Madison Ave Morristown NJ 07960-6016

MUNSTER, ANDREW MICHAEL, medical educator, surgeon; b. Budapest, Hungary, Dec. 10, 1935; came to U.S., 1965; s. Leopold S. and Marianne (Barcza) M.; m. Joy O'Sullivan, Dec. 7, 1963; children: Andrea, Tara, Alexandra. MD, U. Sydney (Australia), 1959. Diplomate Am. Bd. Surgery. Research fellow Harvard U. Med. Sch., Boston, 1966-67; asst. prof. surgery U. Tex.-San Antonio, 1968-71, assoc. prof. surgery Med. U. S.C., Charleston, 1971-76; assoc. prof. Johns Hopkins U., Balt., 1976-85, prof. surgery, 1985—; dir. burn ctr. Balt. City Hosp., 1976—; v.p. Chesapeake Physicians, Balt., 1978-84. Author: Surgical Anatomy, 1971; Surgical Immunology, 1976; Burn Care for House Officers, 1980; contbr. numerous articles to med. jours. Pres., Chesapeake Ednl. Research Trust, Balt., 1980-84, Charleston Symphony, 1974-75, Charleston TriCounty Arts Council, 1975-76. Served to lt. col. U.S. Army, 1968-71. Recipient John Hunter prize U. Sydney, 1959; named Hunterian prof. Royal Coll. Surgeons, 1974. Fellow Royal Coll. Surgeons of Eng., Royal Coll. Surgeons of Edinburgh (Scotland), Am. Assn. Surgeons of Trauma, Colombian Coll. Surgeons (hon.); mem. Am. Burn Assn. (sec. 1990-93, 1st v.p. 1993-94, pres.-elect 1994-95, pres. 1995), Soc. Surg. Assn., Soc. Univ. Surgeons, Am. Surg. Assn. Office: Balt Reg Burn Ctr 4940 Eastern Ave Baltimore MD 21224-2735

MUNTZ, ERIC PHILLIP, aerospace engineering and radiology educator, consultant; b. Hamilton, Ont., Can., May 18, 1934; came to U.S., 1961, naturalized, 1985; s. Eric Percival and Marjorie Louise (Weller) M.; m. Janice Margaret Furey, Oct. 21, 1964; children: Sabrina Weller, Eric Phillip. B.A.Sc., U. Toronto, 1956, M.A.Sc., 1957, Ph.D., 1961. Halfback Toronto Argonauts, 1957-60; group leader Gen. Electric, Valley Forge, Pa., 1961-69; assoc. prof. aerospace engring. and radiology U. So. Calif., Los Angeles, 1969-71, prof., 1971-87, chmn. aerospace engring., 1987—; cons. to aerospace and med. device cos., 1967—; mem. rev. of physics (plasma and fluids) panel NRC, Washington, 1983-85. Contbr. numerous articles in gas dynamics and med. diagnostics to profl. publs., 1961—; patentee med. imaging, isotope separation, nondestructive testing, net shape mfg., transient energy release micromachine. Mem. Citizens Environ. Avc. Coun., Pasadena, Calif., 1972-76. Pilot RCAF, 1955-60. U.S. Air Force grantee, 1961-74, 82—; NSF grantee, 1970-76, 87—; FDA grantee, 1980-86. Fellow AIAA (aerospace Contbn. to Soc. award 1987), Am. Phys. Soc.; mem. NAE. Episcopalian. Home: 1560 E California Blvd Pasadena CA 91106-4104 Office: U So Calif Univ Pk Los Angeles CA 90089-1191

MUNTZ, ERNEST GORDON, historian, educator; b. Buffalo, Nov. 15, 1923; s. J. Palmer and Laura Estelle (Wedekindt) M.; m. Marjorie Corinne Wilson, June 29, 1948; children—Carolyn Odell, Deborah Lynn, Howard Gordon. A.B., Wheaton (Ill.) Coll., 1948; Ph.D., U. Rochester, N.Y., 1960. Asst. prof. social sci. Blue Mountain (Miss.) Coll., 1954-56; from asst. prof. to prof. history Union U., Jackson, Tenn., 1956-61; assoc. faculty U. Cin., 1961-91, prof. history, 1969-91, prof. emeritus, 1991—; dean Raymond Walters Coll., Cin., 1969-90, dean emeritus, 1991—; cons.-evaluator North Central Assn. Colls. and Schs., 1974-91, mem. Commn. on Instns. of Higher Edn., 1983-87. Served as officer USAAF, 1943-46. So. Fellowships Fund fellow, 1955. Mem. Am. Hist. Assn., Am. Assn. Community and Jr. Colls. (bd. dirs. coun. 2 yr. colls. of 4 yr. instns. 1988-90), Cincinnatus Assn., Phi Alpha Theta, Pi Gamma Mu. Presbyterian. Clubs: Cin. Literary, University. Home: 7950 Indian Hill Rd Cincinnati OH 45243-3906

MUNTZING, L(EWIS) MANNING, lawyer; b. Harrisonburg, Va., June 24, 1934; s. H. Gus and Virginia (Manning) M.; m. Nancy Snyder, June 20, 1959; children: Catherine Muntzing Boyden, Elizabeth Muntzing McKaig, Nancy Muntzing Seward, Kimberly Stuart. AB, U. N.C., 1956; postgrad., Woodrow Wilson Sch. Public and Internat. Affairs, Princeton U., 1956-57; LLB, Harvard U., 1960. Bar: D.C. 1960, Md. 1960, W.Va. 1960. Atty. Chesapeake & Potomac Telephone Cos., Washington, 1960-71; dir. of regulation Atomic Energy Commn., Washington, 1971-75; pvt. practice Washington, 1975-79; ptnr. Doub & Muntzing, Chartered, Washington, 1979-88, Doub, Muntzing & Glasgow, Washington, 1988-91, Newman & Holtzinger, Washington, 1991-94; spl. counsel Morgan, Lewis & Bockius, Washington, 1994—; vice-chmn. Adtechs Corp., 1995—; co-chmn. Pacific Basin Nuclear Cooperation Com., 1985-89. Editor: International Instruments for Nuclear Technology Transfer, 1978; mem. editorial adv. bd. Progress in Nuclear Energy Internat. Rev. Jour., 1976—. Trustee Bridgewater Coll., 1984—; mem. vis. com. MIT Nuclear Engring. Dept., 1985-90. Recipient Arthur S. Fleming Disting. Service award Atomic Energy Commn., 1974, Disting. Service award U.S. Atomic Energy Commn., 1974. Mem. NAS (coun. on internat. coop. in magnetic fusion 1983-84), ABA, FBA (chmn. atomic energy com. 1975-76, coun. on sci. tech. and the law sesct. 1976-78), Coun. of Sci. Soc. Pres. (exec. com. 1984-88, chmn. 1987, legal advisor 1988—), Am. Nuclear Soc. (pres. 1982-83, v.p. 1981-82, bd. dirs. 1977-80), Am. Assn. of Engring. Socs. (sec./treas. 1985), Am. Stds. of Testing Materials (chmn. rsch. and tech. planning com.), Internat. Nuclear Socs. Coun. (vice chmn. 1991-92, chmn. 1993-94), D.C. Bar Assn., Md. Bar Assn., W.Va. Bar Assn., Internat. Nuclear Law Assn. (vice chmn. 1995-97), Russian Order of St. John, Knights of Malta, Phi Beta Kappa. Republican. Presbyterian. Clubs: Harvard of Washington, Internat., Capitol Hill, Princeton. Home: 10805 Pleasant Hill Dr Rockville MD 20854-1512 Office: Morgan Lewis & Bockius 1800 M St NW Washington DC 20036-5802

MUNYER, EDWARD A., zoologist, museum adminstrator; b. Chgo., May 8, 1936; s. G. and M. (Carlson) M.; m. Marianna J. Munyer, Dec. 12, 1981; children: Robert, William, Richard, Laura, Cheryl. BS, Ill. State U., 1958, MS, 1962. Biology tchr. MDR High Sch., Minonk, Ill., 1961-63; instr. Ill. State U., Normal, 1963-64; curator zoology Ill. State Mus., Springfield, 1964-67, asst. dir., 1981—; assoc. prof. Vincennes (Ind.) U., 1967-70; dir. Vincennes U. Mus., 1968-70; assoc. curator Fla. Mus. Natural History, Gainesville, 1970-81; mem. Mus. Accreditation Vis. Com. Roster, 1976—. Contbr. articles to profl. jours. Mem. Am. Assn. Mus. (bd. dirs. 1990-95), Midwest Mus. Conf. (pres. 1990-92), Ill. Assn. Mus. (bd. dirs. 1981-86), Wilson Ornithol. Soc. (life). Office: Ill State Mus Spring & Edward Sts Springfield IL 62706

MUNZER, CYNTHIA BROWN, mezzo-soprano; b. Clarksburg, W.Va., Sept. 30, 1948; d. Ralph Emerson and Doris Marguerite (Dixon) Brown; 1 dau., Christina Marie. Student, U. Kans., 1965-69. Adj. prof. voice U. So. Calif., 1994—. Debut, Oxford (Eng.) Opera, 1969, Met. Opera debut, N.Y.C., 1973; performed 1973-96 with: Met. Opera, Phila. Opera, Wolftrap Festival, Washington Opera, Goldovsky Opera, Washington Civic Opera, St. Petersburg Opera, Dallas Opera, Metropolin. Opera-Japan, Boston Concert Opera, Dayton Opera, Chgo. Opera Theatre, Mich. Opera, Kansas City Opera, New Orleans Opera, Houston Grand Opera, Ft. Worth Opera, Florentine Opera-Milw., Minn. Opera, Central City Opera, Aspen Festival, Opera Colo., Boston Festival Orch., Ontario Opera, Salt Lake City Opera, Nev. Opera, Cleve. Opera, Opera Pacific, Des Moines Opera, Ky. Opera, Mobile Opera, Internat. Artist Series in Kuala Lumpur, Penang, Jakarta; Hong Kong Philharmonic, Shanghai Symphony, Singapore Symphony, Philippine Philharmonic, N.Y.C. Ballet, Am. Symphony, Nat. Symphony, Charleston Symphony, Phila. Orch., New Haven Symphony, Houston Symphony, Ft. Wayne Symphony, El Paso Symphony, San Antonio Symphony, Amarillo Symphony, Wichita Symphony, Milw. Symphony, Minn. Orch., Denver Symphony, Phoenix Symphony, Oreg. Bach. Festival, San Francisco Symphony, L.A. Philharm., Louisville Symphony, Rochester Philharmonic, Binghamton Symphony, Rhode Island Symphony, Carmel Bach Festival, Anchorage Symphony, L'Opera de Montreal, Colo. Opera Festival, New York Mozart Bicentennial Festival, Brattleboro Festival, Knoxville Opera, Gold Coast Opera, Hawaii Opera, Augusta Opera, Berkshire Opera, Madison Opera, Chattanooga Symphony. Recipient Frederick K. Weyerhaeuser award, Gramma Fisher Found. award, Goeran Gentele award, Sullivan Found. award, Geraldine Farrar award. Office: PO Box 77332 Los Angeles CA 90007-0332

MUNZER, STEPHEN IRA, lawyer; b. N.Y.C., Mar. 15, 1939; s. Harry and Edith (Isacowitz) M.; m. Patricia Eve Munzer, Aug. 10, 1965; children: John, Margaret. AB, Brown U., 1960; JD, Cornell U., 1963. Bar: N.Y. 1964, U.S. Supreme Ct. 1974, U.S. Dist. Ct. (so. and ea. dists.) N.Y., U.S. Ct. Appeals (3rd cir.). Formerly ptnr. Pincus Munzer Bizar & D'Alessandro, 1978-83; atty. and real estate investor Stephen I. Munzer & Assocs. P.C., 1984—; pres. Simcor Mgmt. Corp., N.Y.C., 1984—. Served to lt., USNR, 1965-75. Mem. Assn. of Bar of City of N.Y., N.Y. State Bar Assn., City Athletic Club, Washington Club. Jewish. Avocations: golf, skiing. Home: 850 Park Ave New York NY 10021-1845 also: 170 Shearer Rd Washington CT 06793-1013 Office: 777 3rd Ave New York NY 10017

MUNZER, STEPHEN R., law educator; b. 1944. BA, U. Kans., 1966; BPhil, Oxford U., Eng., 1969; JD, Yale U., 1972. Assoc. Covington & Burling, Washington, 1972-73; staff atty. Columbia U., N.Y.C., 1973-74; asst. prof. philosophy Rutgers U., New Brunswick, N.J., 1974-77; assoc. prof. U. Minn., Mpls., 1977-80, prof., 1980-81; prof. UCLA, 1982—. NEH fellow, 1991. Office: UCLA Sch Law 405 Hilgard Ave Los Angeles CA 90095-1476

MURAD, FERID, physician; b. Whiting, Ind., Sept. 14, 1936; s. John and Josephine (Bowman) M.; m. Carol Ann Leopold, June 21, 1958; children: Christine, Marianne, Carrie, Julie, Joseph. BA, DePauw U., 1958; MD, Case Western Res. U., 1965, PhD, 1965. Diplomate Nat. Bd. Med. Examiners. Intern and resident Mass. Gen. Hosp., Boston, 1965-67; clin. assoc. NIH, Bethesda, Md., 1967-70; from assoc. prof. to prof. U. Va., Charlottesville, 1970-81, dir. clin. research ctr., 1971-81, dir. clin. pharmacology, 1973-81; prof. Stanford (Calif.) U., 1981-88, assoc. chmn. dept. medicine, 1984-88; chief of medicine VA Med. Ctr., Palo Alto, Calif., 1981-88; v.p. pharm. div. Abbott Labs., 1988-92, CEO, pres. molecular geriatrics, 1993-95. Co-editor The Pharmacological Basis of Therapeutics, 7th edit., 1985; patentee in field; contbr articles to profl. jours. Recipient numerous awards for accomplishments in field. Mem. Am. Fedn. Clin. Research, Am. Soc. for Pharmacology and Exptl. Therapeutics, Endocrine Soc., NIH Alumni Assn. (mem. task force Evaluation of Research Needs in Endocrinology and Metabolic Diseases 1978-79, ad hoc mem. Molecular Cytology study sect. 1979, Pathology study sect. 1979, Endocrinology Tng. Grant study sect. 1980, Pharmacology study sect. 1980, 84), Am. Cancer Soc. (ad hoc rev. and site vis. 1979, sci. councillor NIDDK 1990-94, chmn. 1993-94), Am. Soc. Biol. Chemi st s, Am. Soc. Clin. Investigation, Assn. Am. Physicians, Western Assn. Physicians, NSF (ad hoc rev. 1982). Home: 1421 Lake Rd Lake Forest IL 60045-1425

MURAD, JOHN LOUIS, clinical microbiology educator; b. Tyler, Tex., Dec. 15, 1932; s. Louis George and Ruby (Sawyer) M.; m. Sameera Hamra; children: John Nichols, Philip Louis, David Clay, Richard Andrew. BA, Austin Coll., 1956; MS, North Tex. State U., 1958; PhD, Tex. A&M U., 1965. Instr. biology Stephen F. Austin State U., Nacogdoches, 1959-61, Tex. A&M U., College Station, 1961-65; mem. faculty La. Tech. U., Ruston, 1965-88, asso. prof. zoology, 1967-70, prof., 1970-88, dir. rsch. and grad. studies, Coll. Life Scis., 1971-88, ret., 1988; prof. med. lab. scis. U. Tex. Southwestern Med. Ctr., Dallas, 1991—; safety mgmt. cons. Author: Laboratory Exercises in Zoology, 1967, The Laboratory in Biology, 1968, Zoology, 1971, Workbook in Zoology, 1975, Explorations in Zoology, 1980, 2d edit., 1984, Adventures in Zoology, 1989; contbr. articles to profl. jours. Served with M.C. AUS, 1953-55, Korea. U. Tex. Med. Br. rsch. fellow Galveston, 1958-59; NSF travel grantee, 1972; NATO regional sci. participant Germany, 1972; Sci. Info. Exch. fellow Gt. Britain, 1974. Mem. ASCP, AAAS, ASTM, AAUP, Am. Inst. Biol. Scis., Am. Soc. Microbiology, Southwestern Soc. Microbiology, La. Acad. Sci., Tex. Acad. Sci., N.Y. Acad. Sci., Helminthol. Soc. Washington, Soc. Nematologists, European Soc. Nematology, Masons, Shriners, Kiwanis, Sigma Xi. Presbyterian (elder). Home: 5724 Melshire Dr Dallas TX 75230-2116

MURADIAN, VAZGEN, composer, viola d'amore player; b. Ashtarak, Armenia, Oct. 17, 1921; came to U.S., 1950, naturalized, 1956; s. Grigor and Arusiak (Vardanian) M.; m. Arpi Kirkyasharian, Aug. 29, 1964; children: Vardges, Armen. Grad., Benedetto Marcello State Conservatory Music, Venice, 1948; studied composition with Gabriele Bianchi; studied violin with, Luigi Ferro. Tchr. violin, solfeggio and theory of music Collegio Armeno, Venice, Italy, 1945-50; pvt. tchr. viola d'amore. Composer numerous works including 36 symphonies, 64 concertos for all classical instruments and concertos for lesser known instruments, 12 suites for orch., 4 moto perpetuos for violin and orch., 7 sonatas for solo violin, 7 sonatas for violin and piano, 2 sonatas for piano, sonata for viola d'amore, 2 quartets, 2 trios for violin, violoncello and piano, 56 songs with orch. and 8 songs for chorus and orch. on works of Shakespeare, Goethe, Dante, Hugo, others; author articles in field; debut, N.Y. Lincoln Center, 1972; violist with various U.S. orchs. including New Orleans Philharmonic, Wagner Opera Co.; appeared as viola d'amore soloist, U.S. and abroad, compositions performed throughout Europe and Am. Recipient Tekeyan prize, 1962. Mem. ASCAP, Viola D'Amore Soc. Achievements include being the only composer of music who wrote concerti for all classical instruments and many for lesser known instruments, so far 64 concerti for 35 different instruments. All major compositions written in classical sonata form. All melodies and themes are his own originals. Home: 269 W 72nd St New York NY 10023-2713

MURAI, RENE VICENTE, lawyer; b. Havana, Cuba, Mar. 11, 1945; came to the U.S., 1960; s. Andres and Silvia (Muñiz) M.; m. Luisa Botifoll, June 12, 1970; 1 child, Elisa. BA, Brown U., 1966; JD cum laude, Columbia U., 1969. Bar: Fla. 1970, N.Y. 1972, U.S. Supreme Ct. 1977. Atty. Reginald Heber Smith Fellow Legal Svcs. Greater Miami, Fla., 1969-71; assoc. Willkie, Farr & Gallagher, N.Y.C., 1971-73; ptnr. Paul, Landy & Beiley, Miami, 1973-79; shareholder Murai, Wald, Biondo & Moreno, Miami, 1979—; bd. dirs. PanAm. Bank, Miami; dir. Cuban Am. Bar Assn., 1982-96, pres., 1985; vice chmn., lectr. Internat. Conf. for Lawyers of the Ams., 1982, chmn. and lectr., 1984; mem. panel grievance com. Fla. Bar, 1983-86. Mng. editor Columbia Law Review, 1967-69. Dir., sec. The Archtl. Club of Miami, 1978-86; dir. Dade Heritage Trust, 1979-82, Facts About Cuban Exiles, Inc., 1982—, pres., 1989; dir. Legal Svcs. of Greater Miami, Inc., 1980-90, pres., 1986-88; dir. ARC, 1984-90, exec. com., 1988-90; mem. code enforcement bd. City of Coral Gables, 1982-86, 87, bd. adjustment, 1987-89, mem. city mgr. selection com., 1987, mem. charter rev. commn., 1990; bd. trustees U. Miami, 1994-96; dir. Mercy Hosp. Found., 1985-91, United Way, 1989-95, dir., 1986-89, chmn. voluntary sector trust; dir. Dade Cmty. Found., 1988-93, chair grants com., 1991-93; mem. task force leadership Dade Ptnrs. for Safe Neighborhoods, 1994—; mem. citizen's bd. U. Miami, 1982—, pres. 1994-95. Mem. ABA, Cuban-Am. Bar Assn., Dade County Bar Assn. (dir. 1987-88), Fla. Bar Found. (adminstrn. of justice com. 1989—, dir. 1991—, chmn. audit and fin. com. 1993—), Greater Miami C. of C., Spain-U.S. C. of C. Democrat. Roman Catholic. Avocation: sports. Home: 3833 Alhambra Ct Coral Gables FL 33134 Office: Murai Wald Biondo & Moreno PA 25 SE 2nd Ave #900 Miami FL 33131

MURANAKA, HIDEO, artist, educator; b. Mitaka, Tokyo, Japan, Feb. 4, 1946; s. Nobukichi and Hisae M. BFA, Tokyo Nat. U. of Fine Arts, 1970, MFA, 1972. Calif. Community Coll.- Instr. Cred. Drawing accepted for The Pacific Coast States Collection from the v.p. house, Washington, 1980, Nat. Mus. Art, Bklyn. Mus., Achenbach Found., Calif. Palace of Legion of Hon., Yergeau-Musee Internat. d'Art (Can.). Mem. Democratic Nat. Comm., Wash., 1985—. Recipient second prize Iternat. Art Exhbn. Museo Hosio, Italy, 1984, V.J.'s Artist award Palm Springs Desert Mus., 1995; named to Hist. Preservation Am. Hall of Fame. Mem. Oakland Mus. Assn., The Fine Arts Mus. San Francisco, Lepidopterist's Soc. Avocations: collecting butterflies, music. Home: 2254 Leavenworth St San Francisco CA 94133-2212

MURANE, WILLIAM EDWARD, lawyer; b. Denver, Mar. 4, 1933; s. Edward E. and Theodora (Wilson) M.; m. Rosemarie Palmerone, Mar. 26, 1960; children: Edward Wheelock, Peter Davenport, Alexander Phelps. AB, Dartmouth Coll., 1954; LLB, Stanford U., 1957. Bar: Wyo. 1957, Colo. 1958, Calif. 1958, D.C. 1978, U.S. Supreme Ct. 1977. Assoc. then ptnr. Holland & Hart, Denver, 1961-69; dep. gen. counsel U.S. Dept. Commerce, Washington, 1969-71; gen. counsel FDIC, Washington, 1971-72; ptnr. Holland & Hart, Denver, 1972—, chmn. litigation dept., 1986-90; pub. mem. Adminstrv. Conf. of the U.S., Washington, 1978-81. Bd. dirs. Ctr. for Law and Rsch., Denver, 1973-76, Acad. in the Wilderness, Denver, 1986—, Colo. Symphony Assn., 1994—; mem. bd. visitors Stanford U. Law Sch. Capt. USAF, 1958-61. Fellow Am. Coll. Trial Lawyers; mem. ABA (ho of dels. 1991—), U. Club, Cactus Club. Republican. Avocations: fishing, classical music. Office: Holland & Hart 555 17th St Ste 3200 Denver CO 80202-3929

MURASE, JIRO, lawyer; b. N.Y.C., May 16, 1928. B.B.A., CCNY, 1955; J.D., Georgetown U., 1958, LL.D. (hon.), 1982. Bar: D.C. 1958, N.Y. 1959. Sr. ptnr. Marks & Murase L.L.P., N.Y.C., 1971—; legal counsel Consulate Gen. of Japan; mem. Pres.'s Adv. Com. Trade Negotiations, 1980-82; mem. Trilateral Commn., 1985—; apptd. mem. World Trade Coun., 1984-94; adv. com. internat. investment, tech. and devel. Dept. State, 1975. Editorial bd.: Law and Policy in Internat. Bus. Trustee Asia Found., 1979-83, Japan Ctr. Internat. Exchange, Japanese Ednl. Inst. N.Y.; bd. dirs. Japan Soc., Japanese C. of C. in N.Y., Inc.; bd. regents Georgetown U.; adv. coun. Pace U., Internat. House Japan; pres. Japanese-Am. Assn. N.Y., Inc., 1996—. Recipient N.Y. Gov.'s citation for contbns. to internat. trade, 1982; named to Second Order of Sacred Treasure (Japan), 1989. Mem. ABA, Assn. of Bar of City of N.Y., N.Y. State Bar Assn., N.Y. County Lawyers Assn., Maritime Law Assn., Consular Law Soc., Fed. Bar Council, Am. Soc. Internat. Law, World Assn. Lawyers, Japanese-Am. Soc. Legal Studies, Am. Arbitration Assn., Lic. Execs. Soc., U.S. C. of C. Clubs: Nippon (dir.); Ardsley Country; N.Y. Athletic; Mid-Ocean (Bermuda). Office: Marks & Murase LLP 399 Park Ave New York NY 10022-4689

MURASHIGE, ALLEN, defense analysis executive; b. Lihue, Hawaii, Mar. 20, 1946; s. Fred A. and Evelyn Y.T. M.; m. Rae Ann Sears, June 7, 1981; children: Lance, Danielle. BS in Aero. Engring., U. Washington, 1968; MS in Statistics/Ops. Rsch., U. Denver, 1973; postgrad. Program for Execs. in Nat. Security, Harvard U., 1989; postgrad., Fed. Exec. Inst., 1993. Aero. engr. Air Force Western Test Range, Vandenberg AFB, Calif., 1968-70; aero. engr. Space & Missile Test Ctr., Vandenberg AFB, 1970-73, ops. analyst, 1973-77; ops. analyst Hdqrs. USAF in Europe, Ramstein AFB, Germany, 1977-84; chief current ops. div. Hdqrs. USAF in Europe, Ramstein AFB, 1985-87; sci., tech. advisor Air Force Studies and Analysis, Washington, 1987-95; U.S. rep. and com. chmn. NATO Adv. Group for Aero Rsch. & Devel., Paris, 1987—; mem. NATO Sci. and Tech. Coordinating Commn., 1994—; chief scientist air force modelling, simulation and analysis, 1995—; mem. Joint Tech. Coord. Group Sr. Adv. Bd., 1989—; mem. Dept. of Def. Simulation Validation Sr. Steering Com., 1990—, Joint Test & Evaluation Tech. Adv. Bd., 1993—; bd. dirs. Air Force Incentive Awards Bd., Pentagon, Washington, 1987—; rep. Dept. of Def. C3I Test and Evaluation Steering Com., Pentagon, 1989-91, Dept. of Def. Modeling and Simulation Policy Group, 1990-92; sr. civilian rep. Air Force Sci. Adv. Bd., 1992-94. Author tech. reports in field. Fellow Grad. Study in Ops. Rsch., 1972. Mem. AIAA, Mil. Ops. Rsch. Soc., Air Force Assn., Am. Def. Preparedness Assn., Internat. Platform Assn., Porsche Club of Am. Avocations: pvt. pilot, tennis, skiing. Office: USAF Modelling Simulation & Analysis Pentagon Washington DC 20330

MURASUGI, KUNIO, mathematician, educator; b. Tokyo, Mar. 25, 1929; s. Kiyoshi and Torae (Nakatani) M.; m. Yasue Kuwahara, Oct. 30, 1955; children—Chieko, Kumiko, Sachiho. B.Sc., Tokyo U. Edn., 1952, D.Sc., 1961. Research asso. Princeton (N.J.) U., 1962-64; asst. prof. U. Toronto, Ont., Can., 1964-66; asso. prof. U. Toronto, 1966-69, prof. dept. math., 1969-94; prof. emeritus, 1994—. Editor: Can. Jour. Math, 1969-71; assoc. editor: Jour. Knot Theory and its Ramification, 1992—; contbr. articles to profl. jours. Fellow Royal Soc. Can.; mem. Am. Math. Soc., Japanese Math. Soc. (Fall prize 1993). Anglican. Home: 611 Cummer Ave, Willowdale, ON Canada M2K 2M5 Office: 100 Saint George St, Toronto, ON Canada M5S 1A1

MURATA, JUNICHI, electronics company executive; b. 1935. With parent co. of Murata Automated Sys., Inc., 1957—; now CEO, pres. Murata Automated Sys., Inc., Charlotte, N.C. Office: Murata Automated Systems Inc 2120 S Interstate 85 Service Rd Charlotte NC 28208-2709*

MURATA, MITSUNORI, pediatrics educator; b. Mitsuhama, Ehime, Japan, Jan. 5, 1935; s. Gonzo Sunouchi and Kikue Murata; m. Misako Ishihara, Jan. 26, 1965; children: Tatsunobu, Yasuhiro, Hiroo. MD, Chiba (Japan) U., 1960, PhD, 1965. Med. diplomate. Intern Nat. Konodai Hosp., Chiba, Japan, 1960-61; asst. dept. pediatrics Chiba U., 1961-68; assoc. prof. dept. pediatrics Tokyo Women's Med. Coll. Daini Hosp., 1968-71, prof., 1971—, dir. dept. pediatrics, 1989—, dir., 1994—. Author, editor: Standards of Bone Maturation in Japanese, 1993; contbr. articles to profl. jours. Mem. Japan Pediatric Soc. (dir., sec.-gen. 1992—), Japan Endocrine Soc., Japanese Soc. Child Health. Home: 1-20-22 Sugano, Ichikawa Chiba, Japan 272 Office: Tokyo Womens Med Coll Daini Hosp, 2-1-10 Nishiogu, Arakawa Tokyo, Japan 116

MURATA, TADAO, engineering and computer science educator; b. Takayama, Gifu, Japan, June 26, 1938; came to U.S., 1962; s. Yonosuke and Ryu (Aomame) M.; m. Nellie Kit-Ha Shin, 1964; children: Patricia Emi, Theresa Terumi. B.S.E.E., Tokai U., 1962; M.S.E.E., U. Ill., 1964, Ph.D. in Elec. Engring., 1966. Research asst. U. Ill., Urbana, 1962-66; asst. prof. U. Ill. at Chgo., 1966-68, assoc. prof., 1970-76, prof., 1977—; assoc. prof. Tokai U., Tokyo, Japan, 1968-70; vis. prof. U. Calif., Berkeley, 1976-77; cons. Nat. Bur. Stds., Gaithersburg, Md., 9184-85; panel mem. NAS, Washington, 1981-82, 83-85; vis. scientist Nat. Ctr. For Sci. Rsch., France, 1981; guest rschr. Gesellschaft für Mathematik und Datenvearbeitung, Germany, 1979; Hitachi-Endowed prof. Osaka (Japan) U., 1993-94. Editor IEEE Trans. on Software Engring., 1986-92; assoc. editor Jour. of Cirs., Sysems and Computers, 1990—; contbr. articles to sci. and engring. jours. Recipient Sr. Univ. Scholar award U. Ill., 1990; dNSF grantee, 1978—, U.S.-Spain coop. research grantee, 1985-87. Fellow IEEE (mem. IEEE Computer Soc., Donald G. Fink Prize award 1991); mem. Assn. Computing Machinery, Info. Processing Soc. Japan, European Assn. for Theoretical Computer Sci., Upsilon Pi Epsilon (hon.). Avocations: golf; travel. Office: U Ill Dept Elec Engring & Comp Sci 851 S Morgan St Chicago IL 60607-7042

MURATORE, PETER FREDERICK, securities executive; b. Bklyn., Mar. 18, 1932; s. Fred John and Rose Mary (Muscatello) M.; m. Patricia Margaret Feerick, Jan. 21, 1956; children: John, Robert, Catherine. B.S. in Social Sci., Georgetown U., 1953. Owner, operator St. George Men's Shop, Bklyn., 1955-65; exec. v.p. E.F. Hutton & Co., Inc.., N.Y.C., 1965-88; dir. E.F. Hutton & Co., Inc., N.Y.C.; mem. exec. com. N.Y. dist. S.I.A.; guest lectr. Wharton Grad. Sch. Bus. U. Pa., Phila., 1979-82; ofcl. Am. Stock Exchange, N.Y.C., 1981-87; sr. exec. v.p. Shearson Lehman Hutton, N.Y.C., 1988-89; pres. Quest For Value Distributive, N.Y.C., 1989—; chmn., Hutton Equipment Mgmt. Co., Hutton Asset Recovery Fund; dir. New Energy Co. Ind., Hutton Aircraft Mgmt., Inc., Employees Pension Service Corp., New Energy Co., Ind. Bd. advisors Fin. Services Rev., 1982. Served to lt. j.g. USNR, 1953-55. Founder Bklyn. Prep. N.Y.C., 1964. Mem. Securities Industry Assn. (chmn. mktg. com. 1979-81). Roman Catholic. Home: Post House Rd Morristown NJ 07960 Office: Quest For Value Distributive Oppenheimer Tower World Fin Ctr New York NY 10281

MURATORE, ROBERT PETER, advertising executive; b. Bklyn., Oct. 31, 1957; s. Peter Fredrick and Patricia Margret (Feerick) M. BS, Lehigh U., 1979. Analyst client svc. IMS Am. Ltd., Wayne, N.J., 1979-81; sales analyst E.R. Squibb and Sons, Lawrenceville, N.J., 1981, supr. sales analysis, 1982; account exec. Thomas G. Ferguson Assocs., Inc., Parsippany, N.J., 1982-83, account supr., 1983-85, v.p., 1984-88, account group supr., 1985-87, mgmt. supr., 1987-90, sr. v.p., 1988-92, pres. Ferguson 2000 divsn., 1993-95, pres. Ferguson dir. divsn., 1995; pres., COO Kallir, Philips, Ross, Inc., N.Y.C., 1995—. Mem. Am. Profl. Platform Tennis Assn., Morris Country Golf Club, Delta Chi. Avocations: skiing, tennis, golf, platform tennis. Office: Thomas G Ferguson Assocs 30 Lanidex Plz W Parsippany NJ 07054-2717

MURAYAMA, MAKIO, biochemist; b. San Francisco, Aug. 10, 1912; s. Hakuyo and Namiye (Miyasaka) M.; children: Gibbs Soga, Alice Myra. B.A., U. Calif., Berkeley, 1938, M.A., 1940; Ph.D. (NIH fellow), U. Mich., 1953; ScD honoris causa, Open Internat. U., Sri Lanka, 1994. Rsch. biochemist Children's Hosp. of Mich., Detroit, 1943, 45-48, Bellevue Hosp., N.Y.C., 1943-45; Research biochemist Harper Hosp., Detroit, 1949-54; research fellow in chemistry Calif. Inst. Tech., Pasadena, 1954-56; research asso. in biochemistry Grad. Sch. Medicine, U. Pa., Phila., 1956-58; spl. research fellow Nat. Cancer Inst. at Cavendish Lab., Cambridge, Eng., 1958; sr. research biochemist NIH, Bethesda, Md., 1958-93. Author: (with Robert M. Nalbandian) Sickle Cell Hemoglobin, 1973; discovered DIPA (decompression-inducible platelet aggregation), 1975; discovered DIPA causes vascular occlusion in both acute mountain sickness and diver's syndrome. Fellow Am. Inst. Chemists; mem. AAAS, Am. Chem. Soc., Am. Soc. Biol. Chemists, Assn. Clin. Scientists, Undersea and Hyperbaric Med. Soc., Aerospace Med. Assn., Internat. Platform Assn., West African Soc. Pharmacology (hon.), N.Y. Acad. Sci., Sigma Xi. Achievements include patent for automatic amperometric titration apparatus; development of molecular mechanism of human red cell sickling and prevention of sickle cell crisis by oral prophylactic carbamide; discovery of decompression inducible platelet aggregation by means of simulation of decompression-inducible platelet aggretation of diving in frogs and mice that diver's disease and acute mountain sickness could be alleviated by piracetam and thymol, antiplatelet agents. Home: 5010 Benton Ave Bethesda MD 20814-2804

MURCH, WALTER SCOTT, director, writer, film editor, sound designer; b. N.Y.C., July 12, 1943; s. Walter Tandy and Katherine (Scott) M.; m. Muriel Ann Slater, Aug. 6, 1965; children: Walter, Beatrice, Carrie, Connie. BA, Johns Hopkins U., 1965. Ind. film editor, sound designer, 1969—. Sound recorder, supr. re-rec., film editor: (films) The Rainpeople, 1969, THX-1138, 1971, The Godfather, 1971, American Graffiti, 1973, The Conversation, 1974 (Best Sound award Brit. Acad. 1974, Best Editing award Brit. Acad. 1974, Acad. award nomination 1974), The Godfather Part II, 1974, Julia, 1977 (Acad. award nomination 1977), Apocalypse Now, 1979 (Acad. award 1979, Brit. Acad. award nomination), Dragonslayer, 1981, The Right Stuff, 1984, (writer, dir.) Return to Oz, 1985, Captain Eo, 1986, The Unbearable Lightness of Being, 1988, Ghost (Acad. award nomination), 1990, The Godfather Part III (Acad. award nomination), 1990, The Godfather Trilogy, 1991, House of Cards, 1993, Romeo is Bleeding, 1994, I Love Trouble, 1994, Crumb, 1995, First Knight, 1995, The English Patient, 1996; writer Black Stallion, THX 1138, Return to Oz, 1985. Mem. Writers Guild Am., Dirs. Guild Am., Acad. Motion Picture Arts and Scis. Home: 77 Bolinas Rd Bolinas CA 94924

MURCHAKE, JOHN, publishing executive; b. Washington, July 30, 1922; s. John Sr. and Mary Ann (Keretzman) M.; m. Mary Evelyn Graninger, June 15, 1946 (dec. Sept. 1989); children: Evelyn Ann, Stephen John. BA, George Washington U., 1961, MA, 1964. CPA, Md. Office mgr. Army Times Pub. Co., Washington, 1940-43, 46-47; subscription mgr. Kiplinger Washington Editors Inc., Washington, 1947-82; pres., CEO Co-Op New Issue Svc., Stuart, Fla., 1966—; pres. Jonev Orchids, Stuart, Fla., 1980—, J.M. and Assocs., Stuart, Fla., 1982—; pres., CEO Nat. Postal Forum, Washington, 1990-93; also bd. dirs.; mem. adv. bd. Smithsonian Postal History Mus., 1993—; chmn. founder Met. Washington Postal Customer Coun., 1972-74, Treasure Coast Fla. Postal Customers Coun., 1994; industry chmn. Mailers Tech. Adv. Com., 1978-80. Editor, founder: (newsletter) The Postal Counselor, 1974, Information, 1981, Port St. Lucie Orchid, 1993-94. Pres. Martin County Orchid Soc., Stuart, 1985-86. 1st lt. USAF, 1943-46, ETO. Decorated Air medal with 4 clusters; recipient of 2 Disting. Service awards U.S. Postal Service, Washington, 1980. Mem. Dir. Mktg. Assn. (pres., founder 1979, Profl. of Yr. 1980, Disting. Svc. award 1980, chmn. Max Sackheim awards com. Fla. chpt. 1987), Fulfillment Mgmt. Assn. (Lee C. Williams award 1980, pres., founder Washington chpt. 1977-78, founder Fla. chpt. 1987, Hall of Fame award 1989). Republican. Methodist. Avocations: stamp collecting, raising orchids, public speaking. Home: 974 NW Pine Lake Dr Stuart FL 34994-9427 Office: JM & Assocs PO Box 83 Stuart FL 34995-0083

MURCHIE, EDWARD MICHAEL, accountant; b. N.Y.C., Apr. 21, 1947; s. Edward Thomas and Dorothy (Busk) M.; m. Karen M. Raftery, Aug. 26, 1967; children: David, Maureen, Carolyn. B.S., Fordham U., Bronx, N.Y., 1968. C.P.A., N.Y. Staff acct. Price Waterhouse, N.Y.C., 1968-75; asst. controller Eltra Corp., N.Y.C., 1975-78; v.p. fin. Eltra Corp., Morristown, N.J., 1981, Converse Rubber, Wilmington, Mass., 1979-80, Allied Corp: Allied Electronic Components Co., Morristown, 1982-84; sr. v.p., chief fin. officer Emery Air Freight Corp., Wilton, Conn., 1984-87; sr. v.p., chief fin. officer Fairchild Industries, Inc., Chantilly, Va., 1987-88, pres., chief operating officer, 1989; pres., COO Vernitron Corp., N.Y.C., 1989-95; pres. Caledonia Capital Corp., Great Falls, Va., 1995—. Chmn., South Brunswick Rank Levelling Bd., N.J., 1977-78; bd. dirs. Norwalk/Wilton chpt. ARC, 1985. Mem. AICPA. Republican. Roman Catholic. Office: Caledonia Capital Corp PO Box 653 Great Falls VA 22066-0653

MURCHISON, BRADLEY DUNCAN, lawyer; b. Washington, Jan. 5, 1957; s. David Claudius and June Margaret (Guilfoyle) M.; m. Anita Lynne Cadieu, Oct. 14, 1957; children: Grace Guilfoyle, Meredith Lynne. AB in Polit. Sci., U. N.C., 1979; JD, George Washington U., 1982. Bar: N.C. 1983, U.S. Dist. Ct. (we. dist.) N.C. 1983, U.S. Tax Ct. 1983. Assoc. Thigpen and Hines, P.A., Charlotte, N.C., 1982-85; assoc. Moore & Van Allen, Charlotte, 1985-87, ptnr., 1988; assoc. gen. counsel Collins & Aikman Corp., Charlotte, 1988-89; asst. gen. counsel Collins & Aikman Products Co., Charlotte, 1989—. Active Lincoln Forum, N.C., 1995. Mem. N.C. Bar Assn., Am. Corp. Counsel Assn., Mecklenburg County Bar Assn. Republican. Roman Catholic. Avocations: fishing, hunting. Office: Collins & Aikman Products C 701 Mccullough Dr Charlotte NC 28262-3318

MURCHISON, DAVID CLAUDIUS, lawyer; b. N.Y.C., Aug. 19, 1923; s. Claudius Temple and Constance (Waterman) M.; m. June Margaret Guilfoyle, Dec. 19, 1946; children—David Roderick, Brian, Courtney, Bradley, Stacy. A.A., George Washington U., 1947, J.D. with honors, 1949. Bar: D.C. 1949, Supreme Ct. 1955. Assoc. Dorr, Hand & Dawson, N.Y.C., 1949-50; founding ptnr. Howrey & Simon, Washington, 1956-90; of counsel Howrey, Simon, Baker & Murchison, Washington, 1990—; legal asst. under sec. army, 1949-51; counsel motor vehicle, textile, aircraft, ordinance and shipbldg. divsns. Nat. Prodn. Authority, 1951-52; assoc. gen. counsel Small Def. Plants Adminstrn., 1952-53; legal adv. and asst. to chmn. FTC, 1953-55. Chmn. So. Africa Wildlife Trust. With AUS, 1943-45. Mem. ABA (chmn. com. internat. restrictive bus. practices sect. antitrust law 1954-55, sect. adminstrv. law, sect. litigation), FBA, D.C. Bar Assn., N.Y. State Bar Assn., Africa Safari Club Washington, Met. Club, Chevy Chase Club, Talbor Country Club, Order of Coif. Republican. Office: 1299 Pennsylvania Ave NW Washington DC 20004-2402

MURCHISON, DAVID RODERICK, lawyer; b. Washington, May 28, 1948; s. David Claudius and June Margaret (Guilfoyle) M.; m. Kathy Ann Kohn, Mar. 15, 1981; children: David Christopher, Benjamin Michael. BA cum laude, Princeton U., 1970; JD, Georgetown U., 1975. Bar: D.C. 1975, Fla. 1993. Legal asst. to vice chmn. CAB, Washington, 1975-76, enforcement atty., 1976-77; sr. atty. Air Transport Assn., Washington, 1977-80, asst. v.p., sec., 1981-85; sr. assoc. Zuckert, Scoutt and Rasenberger, Washington, 1980-81; v.p., asst. gen. counsel Piedmont Aviation, Inc., Winston-Salem, N.C., 1985-88; v.p., gen. counsel, sec. Braniff, Inc., Dallas, 1988-89; chief exec. officer Braniff, Inc., Orlando, 1990-94; fed. adminstrv. law judge Office of Hearings and Appeals, Charleston, W.Va., 1994—; lectr. continuing legal edn. program Wake Forest U., Winston-Salem, 1988. Contbr. articles to legal jours. Lt. USNR, 1970-72. Mem. ABA, Met. Club Washington. Republican. Roman Catholic. Home: 510 Linden Rd Charleston WV 25314 Office: Office Hearings and Appeals 2 Monongalia St Charleston WV 25302-2349

MURDOCH, BERNARD CONSTANTINE, psychology educator; b. Greensboro, N.C., Dec. 5, 1917; s. Homer Odell and Hilma Caroline (Lang) M.; m. Martha Grace Hood, June 29, 1946; children: Norma, Constance, Joyce, Diana. B.S., Appalachian State Tchrs. Coll., 1938; Ed.M., U. of Cincinnati, 1939; Ph.D., Duke, 1942; postgrad., N.Y. U., 1942-43. Licensed applied psychologist, Ga. Math. critic tchr. Appalachian State Tchrs. Coll. demonstration sch., 1938; math. and sci. tchr. Lexington (N.C.) High Sch., 1939-40; sci. tchr. Harding High Sch., Charlotte, N.C., 1945-46; also dir. Guidance and Testing Bur., Vets. Info. Center, Charlotte; prof. edn. and psychology Presbyn. Coll., Clinton, S.C., 1946-48; acad. dean Presbyn. Coll., 1947-48; also extension prof. edn. U. S.C., 1946-48; mem. research staff Am. Council on Edn., Office of Naval Rsch., Washington, 1948-50; dean Muskingum Coll., New Concord, Ohio, 1950-54; prof., head psychology dept. Wesleyan Coll., Macon, Ga., 1954-82, prof. emeritus, 1982—; chmn. dept. behavioral scis. Wesleyan Coll., 1973-82, also dir. testing.; pres. Fore(In)Sight Found. Inc., 1991—. Author: Consistency of Test Responses, 1942, Love and Problems of Living, 1992; co-author: The Production of Doctorates in the Sciences, 1936-48; contbr. to sci., ednl. and religious publs. Served to capt. USAAF, 1942-45. Fellow AAAS; mem. Am. Psychol. Assn. (life), Southeastern Psychol. Assn., Ga. Psychol. Assn. (dir., pres. 1969-70), Ga. Mental Health Assn. (dir.), NEA, Ga. Mental Health Council (psychology rep. 1973-74), Ga. State Bd. Examiners Psychologists (pres. 1974-75), Am. Ednl. Research Assn., Phi Kappa Phi (past pres.), Phi Delta Kappa, Kappa Delta Pi, Pi Gamma Mu. Presbyn. Club: Mason. Home: 1241 Adams St Macon GA 31201-1568 *Opportunities vary widely, and the necessary perception to capitalize on such also is a distinct variable. Those of us who have achieved a measure of "success" in vocational or other ways must feel very humble as we recognize our good fortune. We have not only had opportunities come before us, but we were able to perceive them in such a way as to accomplish whatever recognition has been ours. Millions have not been so fortunate.*

MURDOCH, DAVID ARMOR, lawyer; b. Pitts., May 30, 1942; s. Armor M. and N. Edna (Jones) M.; m. Joan Wilkie, Mar. 9, 1974; children: Christina, Timothy, Deborah. AB magna cum laude, Harvard U., 1964, LLB, 1967. Bar: Pa. 1967, U.S. Dist. Ct. (we. dist.) Pa. 1967, U.S. Ct. Mil. Appeals 1968, U.S. Supreme Ct. 1990, U.S. Ct. Appeals (3d cir.) 1991. Assoc. Kirkpatrick & Lockhart, Pitts., 1971-78, ptnr., 1978—. Co-author: Business Workouts Manual. Vice pres., bd. dirs. Avonworth Sch. Dist., 1977-83; chmn. bd. dirs. Pitts. Expt., 1980-82, mem. 1988-93, chmn., 1989-90; mem. Pa. Housing Fin. Agy., 1981-88, vice chmn., 1983-87; alt. del. Rep. Nat. Conv., 1980; elder The Presbyn. Ch. of Sewickley, 1986-92; past pres. Harvard Law Sch. Assn. W. Pa.; bd. advisors Geneva Coll., 1993-94, trustee, 1994—; trustee Sewickley Pub. Libr., 1994—, World Learning, Inc., 1995—; dir. Allegheny County Libr. Assn., 1994—; chair Czech Working Group, Presbyn. Ch. USA, 1995—. Capt. U.S. Army, 1968-71. Fellow Am. Coll. Bankruptcy, Am. Bar Found.; mem. ABA (mem. bus. bankruptcy com., chmn. subcom. on bankruptcy coms., trust indentures and claims trading 1991—), Pa. Bar Assn., Allegheny County Bar Assn., Am. Law Inst., Am. Coun. on Germany (coord. Pitts. chpt. 1995—), Nat. Soc. SAR, World Affairs Coun. Pitts., St. Andrews Soc. Pitts., Clan Donald USA, Duquesne Club, Harvard-Yale-Princeton Club, Edgeworth Club. Republican. Office: Kirkpatrick & Lockhart 1500 Oliver Bldg Pittsburgh PA 15222-2404

MURDOCH, (JEAN) IRIS, author; b. Dublin, Ireland, July 15, 1919; d. Wills John Hughes and Irene Alice (Richardson) M.; m. John Oliver Bayley, 1956. Student, Froebel Ednl. Inst., London, Badminton Sch., Bristol, Eng., Somerville Coll., Oxford, Eng. Read Literae Humaniores (1st class) Somerville Coll., 1938-42; asst. prin. Treasury, 1942-44; adminstrv. officer UNRRA, London, Belgium, Austria, 1944-46; Sarah Smithson studentship philosophy Newnham Coll., Cambridge (Eng.) U., 1947-48; fellow, univ. lectr. philosophy St. Anne's Coll., Oxford U., 1948-63, hon. fellow, 1963; lectr. Royal Coll. Arts, London, 1963-67. Author: Sartre Romantic Rationalist, 1953, Under the Net, 1954, The Flight From the Enchanter, 1955, The Sandcastle, 1957, The Bell, 1958, A Severed Head, 1961, (writer stage prodn. with J.B. Priestley), 1964, An Unofficial Rose, 1962, The Unicorn, 1963, The Italian Girl, 1964, play, 1967; The Red and The Green, 1965, The Time of the Angels, 1966, The Nice and the Good, 1968, Bruno's Dream, 1969, A Fairly Honourable Defeat, 1970, The Sovereignty of Good, 1970, An Accidental Man, 1971, The Black Prince, 1973 (James Tait Black Meml. prize), The Sacred and Profane Love Machine, 1974, A Word Child, 1975, Henry and Cato, 1976, The Fire and the Sun, 1977, The Sea, The Sea, 1978 (Booker prize), Nuns and Soldiers, 1980, The Philosopher's Pupil, 1983, The Good Apprentice, 1985, Acastos, Two Platonic Dialogues, 1986, The Book and the Brotherhood, 1987, The Message to the Planet, 1989, Metaphysics as a Guide to Morals, The Green Knight, 1993, Jackson's Dilemma, 1995; plays The Servants and the Snow, 1970, The Three Arrows, 1972, The Black Prince, 1989; contbr. papers to profl. meetings. Recipient Black Meml. prize, 1974, Whitbread Lit. award, 1974, Booker prize, 198's; decorated Dame Comdr. Order Brit. Empire. Hon. mem. AAAL, Am. Acad. Arts and Scis.; mem. Irish Acad.

MURDOCH, LAWRENCE CORLIES, JR., retired banker, economist; b. Phila., June 3, 1926; s. Lawrence C. and Barbara (Boyd) M.; children: Lawrence C. III, Anne G.; m. 2d Eleanor M. Egan, June 16, 1970. B.S. Wharton Sch., U. Pa. in Econs., 1948; M.B.A., Wharton Sch., U. Pa., 1956. With Fed. Res. Bank Phila., 1954-92; ret., 1992; bd. dirs. Cliveden Inc., 1981. Contbr. articles to consumer and monetary publs.; producer documentary films; spokesman (radio and TV). Lt. (j.g.) USN, 1948-54. Mem. Soc. Cin. (pres. 1990—), Little Egg Harbor Yacht Club (Beach Haven, N.J.), Beta Gamma Sigma, Zeta Psi. Home: 115 Hilltop Rd Philadelphia PA 19118-3737

MURDOCH, (KEITH) RUPERT, publisher; b. Melbourne, Australia, Mar. 11, 1931; came to U.S., 1974, naturalized, 1985; s. Keith and Elisabeth Joy (Greene) M.; m. Anna Maria Torv, Apr. 28, 1967; children: Prudence, Elisabeth, Lachlan, James. M.A., Worcester Coll., Oxford, Eng., 1953. Chmn. News Am. Pub. Inc. (pub. London Times), 1974—, News Internat., Ltd. Group, London; mng. dir. News Ltd. Group & Associated Cos., Australia; chmn. 20th Century Fox Prodns., 1985—, William Collins PLC, Glasgow, 1989—; owner, pub. numerous newspapers, mags. and TV stas. in U.S.A., Australia, U.K., Asia, 1983—; Chmn., CEO, News Corp. Ltd., Sydney, Australia, 1991—. Office: The News Corp Limited, 2 Holt St, Surry Hills Sydney NSW 2010, Australia*

MURDOCK, CHARLES WILLIAM, lawyer, educator; b. Chgo., Feb. 10, 1935; s. Charles C. and Lucille Marie (Tracy) M.; m. Mary Margaret Hennessy, May 25, 1963; children: Kathleen, Michael, Kevin, Sean. BSChemE, Ill. Inst. Tech., 1956; JD cum laude, Loyola U., Chgo., 1963. Bar: Ill. 1963, Ind. 1971. Asst. prof. law DePaul U., 1968-69; assoc. prof. law U. Notre Dame, 1969-75; prof., dean Law Sch. Loyola U., Chgo., 1975-83, 86—; dep. atty. gen. State of Ill., Chgo., 1983-86; of counsel Chadwell & Kayser, Ltd., 1986-89; vis. prof. U. Calif., 1974; cons. Pay Bd., summer 1972, SEC, summer 1973; co-founder Loyola U. Family Bus. Program; arbitrator Chgo. Bd. Options Exch., Nat. Assn. Securities Dealers, N.Y. Stock Exch., Am. Arbitration Assn.; co-founder, mem. exec. com. Loyola Family Bus. Ctr., 1990—. Author: Business Organizations, vols. 1 and 2, 1996; editor: Illinois Business Corporation Act Annotated, vols. 1 and 2, 1975; tech. editor The Business Lawyer, 1989-90. Chmn. St. Joseph County (Ind.) Air Pollution Control Bd., 1971; bd. dirs. Nat. Center for Law and the Handicapped, 1973-75, Minority Venture Capital Inc., 1973-75. Capt. USMCR. Mem. ABA, Ill. Bar Assn. (cert. of award for continuing legal edn.), Chgo. Bar Assn. (cert. of award for continuing legal edn., bd. mgrs. 1976-78), Ill. Inst. Continuing Legal Edn. (adv. com). Roman Catholic. Home: 2126 Thornwood Ave Wilmette IL 60091 Office: Loyola U Sch Law 1 E Pearson St Chicago IL 60611-2055

MURDOCK, DAVID H., diversified company executive; b. Kansas City, Apr. 10, 1923; m. Maria Ferrer, Apr., 1992. LLD (hon.), Pepperdine U., 1978; LHD (hon.), U. Nebr., 1984, Hawaii Loa Coll., 1989. Sole proprietor, chmn., chief exec. officer Pacific Holding Co., L.A.; chmn., chief exec. officer Dole Food Co. (formerly Castle & Cooke, Inc.), L.A., 1985—, also bd. dirs. Trustee Asia Soc., N.Y.C., L.A.; founder, bd. dirs. Found. for Advanced Brain Studies, L.A.; bd. visitors UCLA Grad. Sch. Mgmt.;bd. govs. Performing Arts Coun. of Music Ctr., L.A.; bd. govs. East-West Ctr., L.A.; patron Met. Opera, N.Y.C. With USAAC, 1943-45. Mem. Regency Club (founder, pres.) Bel-Air Bay Country Club, Sherwood Country Club (founder, pres.), Met. Club (N.Y.C.). Office: Dole Food Co Inc 31355 Oak Crest Dr Westlake Village CA 91362 also: Pacific Holding Co 10900 Wilshire Blvd Ste 1600 Los Angeles CA 90024-6536*

MURDOCK, MARY-ELIZABETH, history educator; b. Boston, Jan. 4, 1930; d. Lester Joseph and Elizabeth Rowe (Collingwood) M. A.B., Tufts U., 1952; A.M., Boston U., 1958; Ph.D., Brown U., 1962; S.M., Simmons Coll., 1970; cert. mgmt. inst. women in higher edn., Wellesley Coll., 1985; cert. master gardener, U. Mass., 1988. Tchr. Nat. Cathedral Sch., Washington, 1954-57; assoc. prof. Trenton State Coll, N.J., 1962-66, U. R.I., Kingston, 1966-69; archivist, dir. Sophia Smith collection Smith Coll., Northampton, Mass., 1970-84, lectr. history, 1973-86, instr. Southeast Asian ESL program, 1986-88; guest lectr. colls. and univs., 1986—; cons. N.Y.C. YWCA, 1974-75, HEN, 1976-86, Greenfield Cmty. Coll., Mass., 1983-86, Ednl. Testing Svc., Princeton, N.J., 1985—; faculty cons. Nat. Evaluation Sys., Amherst, Mass., 1984-92; bd. reviewers Hist. Jour. Mass., 1985-88; adv. bd. Ctr. Am. Studies, Concord, Mass., 1985-88; indexer Liberty Party newspaper (1845-48). Author articles, monographs, analytical catalogs. Mem.

Am. Studies Assn., New Eng. Am. Studies Assn., Orgn. Am. Historians (state membership chmn. 1980-88), Am. Assn. State and Local History, Hist. Deerfield Inc., Hist. Northampton, Nat. Trust for Hist. Preservation, Northampton Hist. Commn. (officer), Phi Alpha Theta. Avocations: choral singing, piano, painting, photography, gardening.

MURDOCK, MICKEY LANE, insurance company executive; b. Enterprise, Ala., Aug. 3, 1942. BS, U. Ala., Tuscaloosa, 1964. CPA, Ala. Acct. Hill & Flurry, CPAs, Montgomery, Ala., 1968-70; sr. v.p., CFO Nat. Security Group, Elba, Ala., 1970—; officer, dir. Nat. Security Ins. Co., Elba, 1975—, Nat. Security Fire & Casualty, Elba, 1975—, NASCO, Elba, 1975—, NATSCO, 1985—. Chair Water and Electric Bd., Elba, 1988-94, Indsl. Devel. Bd., Elba, 1990-95. Capt. USAF, 1964-68. Mem. Rotary (past pres., treas., dir.).

MURDOCK, PAMELA ERVILLA, wholesale travel company executive, retail travel company executive; b. Los Angeles, Dec. 3, 1940; d. John James and Chloe Conger (Keefe) M.; children: Cheryl, Kim. BA, U. Colo., 1962. Pres., Dolphin Travel, Denver, 1972-87; owner, pres. Mile Hi Tours, Denver, 1973—, MH Internat., 1987—, Mile-Hi Advt. Agy., 1986— . Bd. dirs. Rocky Mountain chpt. Juvenile Diabetes Found. Internat. Named Wholesaler of Yr., Las Vegas Conv. and Visitors Authority, 1984. Mem. NAFE, Am. Soc. Travel Agts., Colo. Assn. Commerce and Industry, Nat. Fedn. Independent Businessmen. Republican. Home: 5565 E Vassar Ave Denver CO 80222-6239 Office: Mile Hi Tours Inc 2160 S Clermont Denver CO 80222-5000

MURDOCK, ROBERT MCCLELLAN, military officer; b. Montclair, N.J., Sept. 27, 1947; s. George Rutherford and Mary (Newell) M.; m. Ann Marie Wingo, Aug. 20, 1977; 1 child, Kristen. BA, Davis and Elkins Coll., 1969; MA, Ctrl. Mich. U., 1979; postgrad., Armed Forces Staff Coll., 1983, U.S. Army War Coll., 1988. Lic. command pilot, USAF. Aide, chief of staff The Pentagon, Washington, 1980-82; ops. officer 22 Airlift Squadron, Travis AFB, Calif., 1984, comdr., 1985-87; dep. inspector gen. Hdqs. European Command, Stuttgart, Germany, 1988-90; vice comdr. 436 Airlift Wing, Dover AFB, Del., 1990-92; nat. def. fellow The Atlantic Coun., Washington, 1992-93; comdr. Air Force Inspection Agy., Kirtland AFB, N.Mex., 1993-96; dep. U.S. Mil. Rep. to NATO Brussels, Belgium, 1996—. Decorated D.F.C., Air medal. Mem. Air Force Assn., The Airlift and Tanker Assn., Order of Daedalians. Methodist. Avocations: skiing, golf, travel. Address: US Mil/Del PSC 80 Box 200 APO AE 09724 Office: Air Force Inspection Agy 9700 G Ave SE Kirtland AFB NM 87117

MURDOCK, ROBERT MEAD, art consultant, curator; b. N.Y.C., Dec. 18, 1941; s. Robert Davidson and Elizabeth Brundage (Mead) M.; m. Ellen Rebecca Olson, Apr. 22, 1967 (div.); children: Alison Mead, Anne Davidson; m. Deborah C. Ryan, Apr. 28, 1995. B.A., Trinity Coll., Conn., 1963; M.A., Yale U., 1965; student, Mus. Mgmt. Inst., U. Calif., Berkeley, 1980. Ford Found. intern Walker Art Center, Mpls., 1965-67; curator Albright-Knox Art Gallery, Buffalo, 1967-70; curator contemporary art Dallas Mus. Fine Arts, 1970-78; dir. Grand Rapids (Mich.) Art Mus., 1978-83; chief curator Walker Art Ctr., Mpls., 1983-85; program dir. IBM Gallery of Sci. and Art, N.Y.C., 1985-87, 90-93; dir. exhbns. Am. Fedn. Arts, N.Y.C., 1987-88; panelist, cons. Nat. Endowment for Arts, 1974-90. Author: (with others) Tyler Graphics: The Extended Image, 1987, A Gallery of Modern Art, 1994, Paris Modern, The Swedish Ballet 1920-1925, 1995; contbr. articles on David Novros, William Conlon, 1985, Bill Freeland, 1989, Nassos Daphnis, 1990; exhbn. catalogues Early 20th Century Art from Midwestern Muesums, 1981, Berlin/Hanover: The 1920's, 1977. Nat. Endowment for Arts fellow, 1973. Home: 202 1st Ave #14 New York NY 10009-3726

MURDOCK, STUART LAIRD, banker, investment adviser; b. Hackensack, N.J., July 18, 1926; s. Charles Watson and Mary-Evelyn (Mehrhof) M.; m. Lois Maura Anderson, Aug. 12, 1950; 1 dau., Susan Lynn. AB, Yale U., 1949; MBA, STanford U., 1951. Security analyst Bank of N.Y., 1952-53; portfolio mgr. Brown Bros. Harriman & Co., N.Y.C., 1954-56; trust investment officer United Mo. Bank Kansas City N/A, 1957-62, v.p., 1963-66, sr. v.p., sr. trust investment officer, 1967-70, exec. v.p., sr. trust investment officer, 1971-94. Retired marshal City of Countryside, Kans., 1968-93; past mem. fin. adv. com. to bd. trustees Pub. Sch. Retirement Sys. Kansas City; trustee Kans. Pub. Employees Retirement Sys.; adv. dir., past pres. Friends of the Zoo; bd. dirs. Youth Symphony of Kansas City. With U.S. Army, 1945-46. Mem. Kansas City Soc. Fin. Analysts (past pres.), Inst. Chartered Fin. Analysts, Fin. Analysts Fedn., C. of C., Yale Club (past pres.), Saddle and Sirloin Club (past pres.), Mercury Club, Desert Caballeros, Shriners. Home: 4613 W 113th Ter Leawood KS 66211-1728 Office: care United Mo Bank Kans 7109 W 80th Overland Park KS 66204

MURDOCK, WILLIAM JOHN, librarian; b. N.Y.C., Nov. 19, 1942; s. William and Catherine T. (Ryan) M.; m. Barbara Tyra, Nov. 24, 1968. BS, Manhattan Coll., 1964; MLS, Pratt Inst., 1966; MA, NYU, 1972. Librarian N.Y. Pub. Libr., N.Y.C., 1964-67; serials librarian Manhattan Coll., Riverdale, N.Y., 1967-70; asst. prof. CUNY-Lehman Coll., Bronx, 1970-77, chief circulation libr., 1970-77; dir. librs. Pace U., Pleasantville, N.Y., 1977-94, univ. libr., 1994—; chmn. Coun. of Librarians, N.Y.C., 1988-89. Contbr. articles to profl. jours. Candidate for bd. trustees Mt. Kisco, N.Y., 1991; mem. Republican. Nat. Com., 1989—; mem. Cath. Big Bros., Westchester, 1983—. Mem. ALA, N.Y. Libr. Assn., Westchester Libr. Assn. (treas. 1981-83), Westchester Assn. Libr. Dirs. (sec. 1986-87), AAUP, Assn. Coll. and Rsch. Librarians, Am. Legion. Avocations: travel, baseball, skydiving, auto cross racing. Office: Pace U 861 Bedford Rd Pleasantville NY 10570-2700

MURDY, WAYNE WILLIAM, mining company executive, financial officer; b. Los Angeles, July 4, 1944; s. Lee Robert and Louise Marie (Kleinemas) M.; m. Diana Yvonne DeCruse, Nov. 23, 1968; children: Dawn Marie, Christopher John, Joseph William, Elizabeth Anne. A.A., El Camino Coll., 1966; B.S., Calif. State U., Long Beach, 1968. C.P.A., Calif. With Atlantic Richfield Co., Los Angeles, 1969-78; gen. auditor Getty Oil Co., Los Angeles, 1978-81; group v.p. Texaco Trading & Transp. Inc., Denver, 1981-87; sr. v.p., chief fin. officer Apache Corp., Denver, 1987-92, Newmont Mining Corp. and Newmont Gold Co., Denver, 1993—. Mem. Am. Inst. C.P.A.s. Roman Catholic. Clubs: University (Denver); Village (Cherry Hills Village, Colo.). Office: Newmont Mining Corp 1 Norwest Ctr 1700 Lincoln St Denver CO 80203-4501

MUREN, DENNIS E., visual effects director; b. Glendale, Calif., Nov. 1, 1946; s. Elmer Ernest and Charline Louise (Clayton) M.; m. Zara Pinfold, Aug. 29, 1981; children: Gregory, Gwendolen. AA, Pasadena (Calif.) City Coll., 1966; student, Calif. State U., L.A. Freelance spl. effects expert, 1968-75; camera operator Cascade of Calif., Hollywood, 1975-76; visual effects dir. photography Indsl. Light & Magic, San Rafael, Calif., 1976-80, visual effects dir., 1980—; guest speaker Berlin Film Festival, UCLA, Film Dept., U. Calif. Berkeley Film Series, Liverpool (Eng.) U. Film Program, Mill Valley Film Festival Program, Siggraph '86, Siggraph '87, Am. Film Inst., Portland Creative Conf. '89. Cameraman, photographer various films including Star Wars, 1977, Close Encounters of the Third Kind, 1977, Battlestar Galactica, 1978, The Empire Strikes Back, 1980 (Oscar award); visual effects supr. films include Dragonslayer, 1981 (Oscar nomination), ET: The Extraterrestrial, 1982 (Oscar award), Return of the Jedi, 1983 (Oscar award, Brit. Acad. of Film and TV award), Indiana Jones and the Temple of Doom, 1984 (Oscar award, Brit. Acad. of Film and TV award), Young Sherlock Holmes, 1985 (Oscar nomination), Captain Eo, 1986, Star Tours, 1986, Innerspace, 1987 (Oscar award), Empire of the Sun, 1987, Willow, 1988 (Oscar nomination), Ghostbusters II, 1989, The Abyss, 1989 (Oscar award), Terminator 2, 1991 (Oscar award, Brit. Film and TV award), Jurassic Park, 1993 (Oscar award, Brit. Film and TV award), Casper, 1995; visual effects supr. (TV program) Caravan of Courage (Emmy award). Academy Scientific/Technical Award for the development of a Motion Picture Figure Mover for animation photography, 1981. Mem. Am. Soc. Cinematographers, Acad. Motion Picture Arts and Scis.

MURIAN, RICHARD MILLER, book company executive; b. East St. Louis, Ill., Sept. 17, 1937; s. Richard Miller Jr. and Margaret Keyes (Gregory) M.; m. Judith Lee, Aug. 11, 1961 (dec. Apr. 1992); 1 child, Jennifer Ann. BA, U. Calif., Davis, 1969; MLS, U. Calif., Berkeley, 1972; MA, Calif. State U., Sacramento, 1975; MDiv, Trinity Evang., 1977. Cert. history instr., libr. sci. instr., Calif. History reader Calif. State U., Sacramento, 1965-66; history reader U. Calif., Davis, 1966-68, philosophy researcher, 1968-69; bibliographer Argus Books, Sacramento, 1970-71; rsch. dir. Nat. Judical Coll., Reno, 1971-72; libr. Calif. State U., Sacramento, 1972-76; tv talk show host Richard Murian Show, L.A., 1979-80; pres. Alcuin Books, Ltd., Phoenix, 1981—; bd. mem. Guild of Ariz. Antiquarian Books; pres. East Valley Assn. Evangs., Mesa, Ariz., 1984-86; cons. Ariz. Hist. Soc., 1993—. Contbr. articles to profl. jours. Active U. Calif. Riverside Libr., 1981-83, KAET (PBS), 1988—, Ariz. State U., 1989—, Am. Assn. Mus., Ariz. Preservation Found., Grand Canyon Nature Assn.; cons. Ariz. Hist. Soc. Recipient Sidney B. Mitchell fellowship U. Calif., Berkeley, 1971. Mem. Am. Assn. Museums, Ariz. Preservation Found., Grand Canyon Nature Assn., Internat. Platform Assn., Phi Kappa Phi. Democrat. Presbyterian. Avocations: fgn. films, jazz. Office: Alcuin Books Ltd 115 W Camelback Rd Phoenix AZ 85013-2519

MURILLO-ROHDE, ILDAURA MARIA, marriage and family therapist, consultant, educator, dean; b. Garachine, Panama; came to U.S., 1945; d. Amalio Murillo and Ana E. (Diaz) de Murillo; m. Erling Rohde, Sept. 19, 1959. BS, Columbia U., 1951, MA, 1953, MEd, 1969; PhD, NYU, 1971; hon. diploma, Escuela Nat. de Enfermeria, Guatemala, 1964; diploma naturopatia, Centro Estudios Naturista, Barcelona, Spain, 1992. RN; lic. marriage and family therapist, N.J.; cert. mental health-psychiat. nursing, ANA; lic. sex. therapist, N.J. Instr., supr. Bellevue Psychiat. Hosp., N.Y.C., 1950-54; asst. dir., dir. psychiat. div. Wayne County Gen. Hosp., Eloise, Mich., 1954-56; chief nurse psychiat. div. Elmhurst Gen. Hosp., Queens, N.Y., 1956-58, Met. Hosp. Med. Ctr., N.Y.C., 1961-63; psychiat. cons. to govt. of Guatemala WHO, UN, Guatemala, 1963-64; assoc. prof., chmn. psychiat. dept. N.Y. Med. Coll. Grad. Sch. Nursing, N.Y.C., 1964-69; dir. mental health-psychiatry, asst. prof. NYU, N.Y.C., 1970-72; assoc. prof. Hostos Coll., CUNY, N.Y.C., 1972-76; assoc. dean. acad. affairs U. Wash., Seattle, 1976-81; prof., dean Coll. of Nursing SUNY, Downstate Med. Ctr., Bklyn., 1981-85; dean and prof. emeritus SUNY, Bklyn., 1985—; bd. dirs. Puerto Rican Family Inst., N.Y.C., 1983—; dir. Latin Am. Oncological Nurses Fuld Fellowships, 1989-90; psychiat. cons. Sch. Nursing, U. Antioquia, Medellin, Colombia, 1972-73, WHO; psychiat./rsch. cons. for master program Sch. Nursing, U. Panama, Project Hope, 1986. Editor: National Directory of Hispanic Nurses, 1981, 2d edit., 1986, 3d edit., 1994; contbr. numerous articles to profl. nat. and internat. jours., chpts. to books in field. Mem. Wash. State adv. com. U.S. Commn. on Civil Rights, Seattle, 1971-81; nat. adv. com. White House Conf. on Families, Washington, 1979-81; pres. King County Health Planning Council, Seattle, 1979-81; exec. com. Puget Sound Health Systems Agy., Seattle, 1979-81. Univ. Honors scholar NYU, 1972; named Citizen of the Day, Radio Sta. KIXI and N.W. Airlines, Seattle, 1979, Disting. lectr. Sigma Theta Tau, 1988-89, Woman of Yr., N.Y. Gotham Club Bus. and Profl. Women, 1989; recipient 1st Nat. Intercultural Nursing award Coun. of Intercultural Nursing, ANA, New Orleans, 1984, Women's Honors in Pub. Svc. award Minority Fellowship Programs and Cabinet Human Rights, ANA, 1986, Disting. Alumna award Divsn. Nursing, NYU Alumni Assn., 1989, 1st Nat. Dr. Hildegard Peplau award Las Vegas conv. ANA, 1992, Practice award Tchrs. Coll., Columbia U. Nursing Edn. Alumni, 1994; designated Living Legend for leadership in practice, edn. and rsch. Am. Acad. Nursing, 1994. Fellow Am. Assn. Marriage and Family Therapy; mem. ANA (affirmative action task force 1974-84, commn. human rights, cabinet human rights, rep. ANA at ICN Cong. Tokyo 1977, spokesperson Nat. Health Ins., conceived and designed Coun. Intercultural Nursing), Am. Orthopsychiat. Assn. (bd. dirs. 1976-79, treas. 1986-89), N.Y. Ass. Marriage and Family Therapy (pres. 1973-76), Nat. Assn. Hispanic Nurses (founder, 1st pres. 1976-80), Internat. Fedn. Bus. and Profl. Women (UN rep. to UNICEF London 1987—, del. to World UN Summit for Children N.Y.C. 1990, UN N.Y. Com. for Internat. Yr. of Family 1994), Am. Rsch. Inst. (dep. govt. 1987), NYU Club, Gotham Bus. and Profl. Women's Club. Democrat. Avocations: travel, reading, music, stamp collecting, skiing. Home: 300 W 108th St Apt 12A New York NY 10025-2704 Office: SUNY Bklyn Coll Nursing Box 22 450 Clarkson Ave Brooklyn NY 11203-2012

MURIS, TIMOTHY JOSEPH, law educator; b. Massillon, Ohio, Nov. 18, 1949; s. George William and Louise (Hood) M.; m. Susan Sexton, Aug. 10, 1974; children—Matthew Allen, Paul Austin. B.A., San. Diego State U., 1971; J.D., UCLA, 1974. Bar: Calif. 1974, U.S. Supreme Ct. 1983. Asst. to dir. policy planning and evaluation FTC, Washington, 1974-76, dir. Bur. Consumer Protection, 1981-83, dir. Bur. Competition, 1983-85; exec. assoc. dir. Office Mgmt. and Budget, Washington, 1985-88, cons., 1988-89; law and econs. fellow U. Chgo. Law Sch., 1979-80; asst. prof. antitrust and consumer law U. Miami Law Sch. and Law Econs. Ctr., Fla., 1976-79, assoc. prof., 1979-81, prof., 1981-83; Found. prof. law George Mason U., Va., 1988—; dep. counsel Presdl. Task Force on Regulatory Relief, Washington, 1981; cons. Coun. on Wage and Price Stability, Washington, 1981; mem. Nat. Issues Forum, Brookings Inst., 1986-88; mem. adv. bd. Anti-Trust and Trade Regulation Report, 1990—. Editor: The Federal Trade Commission Since 1970: Regulation and Bureaucratic Behavior, 1981. Mem. Reagan-Bush transition team for FTC, Washington, 1980; sr. advisor Bush-Quayle transition team, 1988-89. Am. Bar Found. affiliated scholar, 1979. Mem. ABA (antitrust law spl. com. to study role of FTC 1988-89), Calif. Bar Assn., Order of Coif. Office: George Mason U Sch Law 3401 Fairfax Dr Arlington VA 22201-4411

MURKISON, EUGENE COX, business educator; b. Donalsonville, Ga., July 2, 1936; s. Jeff and Ollie Mae (Shores) M.; m. Marilyn Louise Adams, July 3, 1965; children: James, David, Jennifer. Grad., U.S. Army JFK Spl. Warfare Sc., 1967, U.S. Naval War Coll., 1972, U.S. Army Command/Staff Coll., 1974; BSA, U. Ga., 1959; MBA, U. Rochester, 1970; PhD, U. Mo., 1986. Surveyor USDA, Donalsonville, Ga., 1956-59; commd. 2d lt. U.S. Army, 1959, advanced through grades to lt. col., 1974; inf. bn. leader U.S. Army, Vietnam, 1967-68; mechanized comdr. (G-3), ops. officer Brigade Exec. Officer, Korea, Europe and U.S., 1968-70; prof. leadership & psychology West Point, N.Y., 1970-73; ops. officer (J-3) Office of Chmn. Joint Chiefs of Staff, Washington, 1974-77; prof. mil. sci. and leadership Kemper Mil. Coll., 1977-81; ret. U.S. Army, 1981; instr. U. Mo., Columbia, 1981-84; asst. prof. Ga. So. U., Stateboro, 1984-89, assoc. prof., 1989-94, prof., 1995—; vis. prof. mgmt. and bus. U. Tirgoviste, Romania, 1994, 95, 96; vis. prof. human resource mgmt. Tech. U. Romania, Cluj-Napoca, 1995, 96. Contbr. of numerous articles to profl. jours. V.p. Optimist Club, 1993-94, dir., 1993, v.p., 1994-95; trustee Pittman Pk. Meth. Ch., Statesboro, 1992—, chmn., trustee, 1995—. Recipient Bronze Star medal with oak leaf cluster, Devel. award Ga. So. U., 1990, Teaching award U. Mo., 1983, Albert Burke Rsch. award, 1992; grantee IREX, 1994, SOROS, 1995. Mem. Am. Statis. Assn., Inst. Mgmt. Sci., So. Mgmt. Assn., Inst. for Info. and Mgmt. Sci., Internat. Acad. Bus. (program chair 1994, 95), Acad. Mgmt., Bus. History Conf., Newcomen Soc., Blue Key, Scabbard & Blade, Beta Gamma Sigma, Alpha Zeta. Republican. Avocations: bus. history, mil history, tomato prodn., hiking, boating. Office: Ga So U Coll Bus Adminstrn Statesboro GA 30460-8152

MURKOWSKI, FRANK HUGHES, senator; b. Seattle, Mar. 28, 1933; s. Frank Michael and Helen (Hughes) M.; m. Nancy R. Gore, Aug. 28, 1954; children: Carol Victoria Murkowski Sturgulewski, Lisa Ann Murkowski Martell, Frank Michael, Eileen Marie Murkowski Van Wyhe, Mary Catherine Murkowski Judson, Brian Patrick. Student, Santa Clara U., 1952-53; BA in Econs, Seattle U., 1955. With Pacific Nat. Bank of Seattle, 1957-58, Nat. Bank of Alaska, Anchorage, 1959-67; asst. v.p., mgr. Nat. Bank of Alaska (Wrangell br.), 1963-66; v.p. charge bus. devel. Nat. Bank of Alaska, Anchorage, 1966-67; commr. dept. econ. devel. State of Alaska, Juneau, 1967-70; pres. Alaska Nat. Bank, Fairbanks, 1971-80; mem. U.S. Senate from Alaska, Washington, D.C., 1981—; chmn. Com. on Energy and Natural Resources; mem. Com. on Fin., Vets Affairs Com., Indian Affairs Com., Japan-US Friendship Com.; Rep. nominee for U.S. Congress from Alaska, 1970. Former v.p. B.C. and Alaska Bd. Trade. Served with U.S. Coast Guard, 1955-57. Mem. AAA, AMVETS, NRA, Am. Legion, Polish Legion Am. Vets., Ducks Unltd., Res. Officer's Assn., Alaska Geog. Soc., Alaska World Affairs Coun., Fairbanks Hist. Preservation Found., Coalition Am. Vets., Alaska Native Brotherhood, Naval Athletic Assn., Am. Bankers Assn., Alaska Bankers Assn. (pres. 1973), Young Pres.'s Orgn., Alaska C. of C. (pres. 1977), Anchorage C. of C. (bd. dirs. 1966), B.C. C. of C., Fairbanks C. of C. (bd. dirs. 1973-78), Pioneers of Alaska, Internat. Alaska Nippon Kai, Capital Hill Club, Shilla Club, Army Athletic Club, Congl. Staff Club, Diamond Athletic Club, Washington Athletic Club, Elks, Lions. Office: US Senate 706 Hart Senate Bldg Washington DC 20510

MURNAGHAN, FRANCIS DOMINIC, JR., federal judge; b. Baltimore, Md., June 20, 1920; m. Diana Edwards; children: Sheila H., George A., Janet E. B.A., Johns Hopkins U., 1941; LL.B., Harvard U., 1948. Bar: Md. 1949. Asso. firm Barnes Dechert Price Smith & Clark, Phila., 1948-50; staff atty. Office of Gen. Counsel, U.S. High Commr. for Ger., 1950-52; asst. atty. gen. State of Md., 1952-54; asso. firm Venable Baetjer & Howard, Balt., 1952-57; partner Venable Baetjer & Howard, 1957-79; judge U.S. Ct. Appeals for 4th Circuit Balt., 1979—. Chmn. Balt. Charter Rev. Commn., 1963-64; trustee Walters Art Gallery, 1961, v.p. 1961-63, pres. 1963-80, chmn. 1980-85, chmn. emeritus, 1985—; pres. Balt. Sch. Bd., 1967-70; trustee Johns Hopkins U., 1976—. Lt. USNR, 1942-46. Mem. ABA, Am. Coll. Trial Lawyers. Office: US Ct Appeals 4th Cir 101 W Lombard St Baltimore MD 21201-2626

MURNICK, DANIEL ELY, physicist, educator; b. N.Y.C., May 5, 1941; s. Jacob Michael and Lena (Tishman) M.; m. Janet Barbara George, Oct. 26, 1969; children: Jonathan, Carolyn. AB in Physics and Math., Hofstra U., 1962; PhD, MIT, 1966. Physics instr. MIT, Cambridge, 1966-67; mem. tech. staff Bell Labs, Murray Hill, N.J., 1967-88; prof. physics Rutgers U., Newark, 1988—, chmn. dept. physics, 1988-95; cons. High Voltage Engring., Burlington, Mass., 1965-67, Diagnostics and Devices, Morristown, N.J., 1985—, Am. Standard, Piscataway, 1990—, Alimenterics Inc., Morris Plains, N.J., 1992—; mem. sci. adv. bd. Surgilase, Warwick, R.I., 1984-94. Contbr. more than 100 articles to profl. jours.; inventor method and apparatus for stable isotope analysis and for localized surface glazing. Recipient Humboldt award, Rep. of Germany, 1984. Fellow Am. Phys. Soc.; mem. IEEE, Am. Assn. Physics Tchrs., Sigma Xi. Office: Rutgers U Dept Physics 101 Warren St Newark NJ 07102-1811

MURO, ROY ALFRED, independent media service corporation executive; b. N.Y.C., Sept. 22, 1942; s. Angelo Dominick and Virginia (Guangi) M.; m. Lorraine D. Friedman, July 5, 1966; children: Bradley, Jessica. BS, Bklyn. Coll., 1964; MBA, N.Y. Grad. Sch. Bus., 1966. CPA, N.Y. Sr. acct. Price Waterhouse & Co., N.Y.C., 1966-71; comptr. Vitt Media Internat. Inc., N.Y.C., 1971-82, chmn., COO, 1982-91, chmn., 1991-94, CEO, 1991—; lectr. in field. Mem. AICPA, N.Y. State Soc. CPA's, Advt. Agy. Fin. Mgmt. Group, Nat. Agrimktg. Assn., Internat. Radio and TV Soc., N.Y. Credit and Fin. Mgmt. Assn. (lectr.),Am. Travel Mktg. Execs. Home: 8 Irene Ct East Brunswick NJ 08816-2223*

MUROFF, LAWRENCE ROSS, nuclear medicine physician; b. Phila., Dec. 26, 1942; s. John M. and Carolyn (Kramer) M.; m. Carol R. Savoy, July 12, 1969; children: Michael Bruce, Julie Anne. AB cum laude, Dartmouth Coll., 1964, B of Med. Sci., 1965; MD cum laude, Harvard U., 1967. Diplomate Am. Bd. Radiology, Am. Bd. Nuclear Medicine. Intern Boston City Hosp., Harvard, 1968; resident in radiology Columbia Presbyn. Med. Ctr., N.Y.C., 1970-73, chief resident, 1973; instr. dept. radiology, asst. radiologist Columbia U. Med. Ctr., N.Y.C., 1973-74; dir. dept. nuclear medicine, computed tomography and magnetic resonance imaging Univ. Community Hosp., Tampa, Fla., 1974-94; H. Lee Moffitt Cancer Hosp., 1994—; pres. Imaging Cons. Inc., Tampa, 1994—; clin. asst. prof. radiology U. South Fla., 1974-78, clin. assoc. prof., 1978-82, clin. prof., 1982—; clin. prof. U. Fla., 1988—. Contbr. articles to profl. jours. Pres. Ednl. Symposia, Inc., 1975—. Lt. comdr. USPHS, 1968-70. Fellow Am. Coll. Nuclear Medicine (disting. fellow., Fla. del.), Am. Coll. Nuclear Physicians (regents 1976-78, pres.-elect 1978, pres. 1979, fellow 1980), Am. Coll. Radiology (councilor 1979-80, 91—, chancellor 1981-87, chmn. commn. on nuclear medicine 1981-87, fellow 1981); mem. Am. Assn. Acad. Chief Residents Radiology (chmn. 1973), AMA, Boylston Soc., Fla. Assn. Nuclear Physician (pres. 1976), Fla. Med. Assn., Hillsborough County Med. Assn., Radiol. Soc. N.Am., Soc. Nuclear Medicine (coun. 1975-90, trustee 1980-84, 86-89, pres. Southeastern chpt. 1983, vice chmn. correlative imaging coun. 1983), Fla. Radiol. Soc. (exec. com. 1976-91, treas. 1984, sec. 1985, v.p. 1986, pres. elect 1987, pres. 1988-89, gold medal 1995), West Coast Radiol. Soc., Soc. Mag. resonance Imaging (bd. dirs. 1988-91, chmn. ednl. program 1989, chmn. membership com. 1989-93), Clinical Magnetic Resonance Soc. (pres. elect 1995—), Phi Beta Kappa, Alpha Omega Alpha. Office: 1527 S Dale Mabry Hwy Tampa FL 33629-5808

MUROTAKE, THOMAS HISASHI, emergency medicine technologist; b. Denison, Iowa, July 30, 1955; s. Thomas Hisashi and Nancy May (Morrow) M. EMT. Store mgr. Radio Shack, Van Nuys, Calif., 1980-81; EMT Snyder Ambulance, Van Nuys, Calif., 1981; sales mgr. Radio Shack, Canoga Park, Calif., 1981-82; teletype operator Credit Reports Inc., West L.A., 1982-83; self-employed EMT Event Med. Svcs., Los Alamitos, Calif., 1989—; platoon sgt. emergency treatment NCO Coc, 240th Support Bn. Calif. Army Nat. Guard, Long Beach, 1989-95; pub. affairs NCO 40th Inf. Divsn. Calif. Army Nat. Guard, Los Alamitos, Calif., 1995—; corp. support svcs. mgr. Informative Rsch., Garden Grove, Calif., 1983-93; notary public State of Calif., 1990—, Murotake Mobile Notary Svc., 1994-95, A Time to Sign, 1995—, MAGNet, 1995—. Author: Recollections, 1991, Collected Works, 1991. Vol. EMT Maryland City (Md.) Vol. Fire Dept., 1978-80, asst. publicity chmn. 1979-80, SOS Free Med. Clinic, 1993-95. With U.S. Army, 1973-80. Recipient Calif. Commendation medal State of Calif. Mil. Dept., 1991, 95, Achievement medal U.S. Army, 1994, Humanitarian Svc. medal U.S. Army, 1995, Counter-Drug Task Force ribbon State of Calif. Mil. Dept., 1995, State Svc. ribbon, 1995; named Non-Commd. Office of Yr. 240th Support Bn., 1991. Mem. Nat. Notary Assn., Am. Legion. Republican. Episcopalian. Avocation: writing. Home: 6881 Homer St Apt 45 Westminster CA 92683-3741

MURPHEY, ARTHUR GAGE, JR., law educator; b. Macon, Miss., June 16, 1927; s. Arthur Gage and Elizabeth (Crutcher) M.; m. Linda Chaney, May 17, 1975; children by previous marriage—Mason Alexander, Arthur Nesbit; 1 stepchild, Leslie Jo (Mrs. Thomas) Pafford. Student, Vanderbilt U., 1947-48; AB, U. N.C., 1951; JD, U. Miss., 1953; postgrad., London Sch. Econs., U. London, 1953-54; LLM, Yale U., 1962. Assoc. Satterfield, Ewing Williams and Shell, Jackson, Miss., 1953; asst. prof. U. Ga., Athens, 1956-58, Emory U., Atlanta, 1958-61; asst. prof. U. Akron, 1962-63, assoc. prof., 1963-67; prof. U. Ark., Little Rock, 1967—, asst. dean Sch. Law, 1970-73; vis. lectr. Case Western Res. U., Cleve., 1966; vis. prof. U. Miss., 1977. Faculty editor: Jour. Public Law, 1958-61; faculty adv.: Ga. Bar Jour., 1958-61; contbr. articles to profl. jours. Served with USAAF, 1945-47. Fulbright scholar, 1953-54; Stirling fellow, 1961-62; Ford Found. grantee, 1964. Mem. ABA, Ark. Bar. Assn, Phi Delta Phi, Beta Theta Pi, Phi Beta Kappa. Mem. Anglican Ch. Home: 1918 Old Forge Dr Little Rock AR 72227-5515 Office: U Ark Sch Law 1201 Mcalmont St Little Rock AR 72202-5142

MURPHEY, MARGARET JANICE, marriage and family therapist; b. Taft, Calif., July 24, 1939; d. Glen Roosevelt Wurster and Lucile Mildred (Holt) Lopez; m. Russell Warren Murphey, June 20, 1959; children: Lucinda Kalbfleisch, Rochelle Murphey, Janice Sorenson. BA in Social Sci., Calif. State U., Chico, 1986, MA in Psychology, 1989; postgrad., La Salle U. Sec. Folson State Prison, Calif., 1963-66; tchr. Desert Sands Unified Schs., Indio, Calif., 1969-72; claims determiner Employment Development Dept., Redding, Calif., 1976-78; sec. Shasta County Pers., Redding, 1978-79; welfare worker Shasta County Welfare Office, Redding, 1979-85; therapy intern Counseling Ctr. Calif. State U., Chico, 1989-90; therapist Family Svc. Assn., Chico, 1987-90, Butte County Drug and Alcohol Abuse Ctr., Chico, 1989-90; mental halth counselor Cibecue (Ariz.) Indian Health Clinic, 1990—; mem. Kinisba Child Abuse Com., 1994—. Vol. Pacheco Sch., Redding, 1972-76; Sunday sch. tchr., dir. vacation Bible sch. Nazarene Ch., Sacramento, Indio and Redding, 1958-85. Recipient Sch. Bell award Pacheco Sch. Mem. APA, Am. Counseling Assn., Psi Chi. Avocations: study of American Indian history, sewing, crafts, travel, canoeing. Home: PO Box 1114 Show Low AZ 85901-1114 Office: Cibecue Health Ctr Apache Behavioral Health PO Box 1089 Whiteriver AZ 85941-1089

MURPHEY, MICHAEL MARTIN, country western singer, songwriter; b. Tex., Mar. 14, 1945; married; children: Ryan, Brennan, Laura Lynn. Attended, UCLA. Profl. musician, 1962—; with Lewis & Clark Expedition, 1966-70. Songwriter for Monkees, Kenny Rogers, Nitty Gritty Dirt Band; pop hit Wildfire, 1975, What's Forever For, Carolina in the Pines, Love

Affairs, Still Taking Chances; founder Westfest Annual celebration; albums: Geronimo's Cadillac, 1971, Blue Sky Night Thunder, 1981, The Best of Michael Martin Murphey, 1981, The Heart Never Lies, 1986, Tonight We Ride, 1986, Americana, 1987, River of Time, 1988, Land of Enchantment, 1989, Best of County Michael Martin Murphey, 1990, Cowboy Songs, 1990, Cowboy Christmas: Cowboy Songs II, 1991, Cowboy Songs III, 1993, Americas Horses Sagebrush Symphony. Named Best New Artist, County Music Assn., Acad. County Music; recipient Grammy nomination for a Face in the Crowd, Nat. Am. Video award for She Wants, award Cowboy Hall of Fame (3), 1990-92, 95, 96. Office: PO Box Fff Taos NM 87571-2550

MURPHEY, MURRAY GRIFFIN, history educator; b. Colorado Springs, Colo., Feb. 22, 1928; s. Bradford James and Margaret Winifred (Griffin) M.; children—Kathleen Rachel, Christopher Bradford, Jessica Lenoir. A.B., Harvard U., 1949; Ph.D., Yale U., 1954. Asst. prof. U. Pa., Phila., 1956-61, assoc. prof., 1961-66, prof., 1966—, chmn. dept. Am. civilization, 1969-81, 87-94. Author: Development of Peirce's Philosophy, 1961, Our Knowledge of the Historical Past, 1973, (with E. Flower) A History of Philosophy in America, 1977, Philosophical Foundations of Historical Knowledge, 1994. Democrat. Home: 200 Rhyle Ln Bala Cynwyd PA 19004-2324 Office: U Pa 323A 3401 Walnut St Philadelphia PA 19104-3337

MURPHEY, RHOADS, history educator; b. Phila., Aug. 13, 1919; s. William Rhoads and Emily (Hawkins) M.; m. Katherine Elizabeth Quinn, Nov. 26, 1942 (dec. July 1950); children: Katherine Ann, Rhoads; m. Eleanor Taylor Albertson, Jan. 12, 1952; children: David, Ellen. A.B., Harvard U., 1941, M.A., 1942, Ph.D., 1950. Asst. prof. geography Ohio State U., 1950-51; from asst. prof. geography to prof. U. Wash., also Far Eastern Inst., 1952-64; prof. Asian studies and history U. Mich., Ann Arbor, 1964—; dir. Center Chinese Studies U. Mich., 1969-76, dir. Asian studies, 1975—, dir. South and S.E. Asian studies, 1987-90. Author: Shanghai-Key to Modern China, 1953, An Introduction to Geography, 4th edit., 1978 (with others) A New China Policy, 1965, The Scope of Geography, 1969, 1973, 3d rev. edit., 1982, The Treaty Ports and China's Modernization, 1970, China Meets the West, 1975 (with others) The Mozartian Historian, 1976, The Outsiders, 1977, The Fading of the Maoist Vision, 1980, (with others) Civilizations of the World, 1990, 3d edit,, 1996, A History of Asia, 1992, 2d edit., 1996, East Asia: A New History, 1996; co-editor (with others) Approaches to Modern Chinese nese History, 1967; asst. editor, the editor Jour. Asian Studies, 1959-65; regional editor Asia: (with others) Ency. Brit., 1953-61; editor Mich. Papers in Chinese Studies, 1967-77, Assn. Asian Studies Monographs, 1992—; contbr. articles to profl. jours. Social Sci. Research Council fellow, 1948-50; Ford Found. fellow, 1955-56; Guggenheim fellow, 1966-67; Nat. Endowment Humanities fellow, 1972-73, JSPS fellow, 1978-79. Mem. Assn. Am. Geographers (council 1963-66, Honors award 1980), Assn. Asian Studies (dir., exec. sec. 1976-83, v.p. 1985, pres. 1987-88). Home: 2012 Washtenaw Ave Ann Arbor MI 48104-3639

MURPHEY, ROBERT STAFFORD, pharmaceutical company executive; b. Littleton, N.C., Oct. 29, 1921; married; 2 children. B.S., U. Richmond, 1942; M.S., U. Va., 1947, Ph.D. in Organic Chemistry, 1949. Research chemist in medicinal chemistry A.H. Robins & Co. Inc., Richmond, Va., 1948-53, dir. chemistry research, 1953-55, assoc. dir., 1955-57, dir. research, 1957-60, dir. internat. research, 1960-66, dir. sci. devel., 1966-82, asst. v.p., 1967-73, dir. sci. devel., v.p., 1973-82, v.p. sci. affairs and corp. devel., 1982-83, sr. v.p. sci. affairs and corp. devel., 1983-87, sr. v.p., dir. new bus. devel., 1983-90; sr. v.p., dir. bus. devel. E.C. Robins Internat., Inc., Glen Allen, Va., 1990—. Mem. AAAS, Am. Chem. Soc. Office: E C Robins Internat Inc 11064 Staples Mill Rd Glen Allen VA 23060-2404

MURPHREE, HENRY BERNARD SCOTT, psychiatry and pharmacology educator, consultant; b. Decatur, Ala., Aug. 11, 1927; s. Henry Bernard and Nancy Mae (Burrus) M.; m. Dorothy Elaine Simmons, Nov. 14, 1953 (dec.); children: Julie Elizabeth, Susan Louise, Jefferson Van; m. Dorothy Elizabeth Olson, Sept. 23, 1993. Student, MIT, 1944-45; BA, Yale U., 1950; MD, Emory U., 1959. Intern internal medicine, fellow clin. pharmacology, instr. Emory U., 1959-61; resident psychiatry Med. Sch. Rutgers U., 1972-76, mem. grad. faculty psychology, 1972—; rsch. asst. Johns Hopkins U., Balt., 1950; asst. chief neuropharmacology Bur. Rsch., Princeton, N.J., 1961-68; from assoc prof. to prof. Univ. of Medicine and Dentistry Robert Wood Johnson Med. Sch., Piscataway, N.J., 1968—, assoc. dean acad. affairs Univ. Medicine and Dentistry, 1977-81, chmn. psychiatry Univ. Medicine and Dentistry, 1977-91; cons. medicinal chemistry and pharmacology FMC Chem. R&D Ctr., Princeton, N.J., 1962-68, Hoffman-LaRoche, Nutley and Verona, N.J., 1968-77. Contbr. articles to profl. jours. Founding mem. Somerset Coun. Alcoholism, Somerville, N.J., 1974-77; mem. Sci. Adv. Com., State of N.J., 1981—; bd. trustees Carrier Found., Belle Mead, N.J., 1981-95, vice chmn. bd., chmn. exec. com., 1989-95. Lt. MSC USN, 1951-55. Mem. Am. Soc. for Pharmacology and Exptl. Therapeutics, Am. Psychiat. Assn., Soc. Biol. Psychiatry, Am. Coll. Neuropsychopharmacology, Sigma Xi, Alpha Omega Alpha. Avocations: music, electronics. Home: 757 Route 518 Skillman NJ 08558-2513 Office: U Med & Dentistry NJ Robert Wood Johnson Med Sch 675 Hoes Ln Piscataway NJ 08854-5635 *Early on, in this sorry world, I pondered the concept of the "perfectibility of humankind". I concluded the best approach is education and devoted my career to teaching and consultation, a variant of teaching.*

MURPHREE, KENNETH DEWEY, elementary school educator; b. Memphis, July 28, 1953; s. Dewey and Garneita (Bryant) M.; m. Beverly Ann Hurt, Sept. 7, 1974. AE, N.W. Miss. Jr. Coll., Senatobia, 1973; BSE, Delta State U., 1975, ME, 1976, Ednl. Specialist degree in adminstrn. and supervision, 1992. Grad. asst. dept. elem. edn. Delta State U., 1975-76; elem. tchr. Helena (Ark.) West - Helena Pub. Schs., 1976-81; prin. Woodruff Elem. Sch., West Helena, 1981-93, Westside Elem. Sch., West Helena, 1993—. Mem. NAESP, ASCD, Ark. Assn. Ednl. Adminstrs., Ark. Assn. Elem. Sch. Prins., East Ark. Schoolmasters Assn., Lions (pres., past pres., 1st v.p., bd. dirs. tail twister West Helena), Phi Theta Kappa (past pres. Theta Sigma chpt.), Kappa Delta Pi, Phi Delta Kappa. Office: Westside Elem Sch 339 S Ashlar St West Helena AR 72390-3401

MURPHY, ALVIN LEO, educational administrator; b. New Orleans, July 19, 1934; s. James J. and Marie Adele (Perret) M.; m. Celeste Marie Ferry, Nov. 24, 1956; children: Angelle, Alice, Emily, Claire. BS in Secondary Edn., Loyola U., New Orleans, 1956; MEd, Loyola U., 1967. Tchr. De La Salle High Sch., New Orleans, 1958-67; asst. prin. De La Salle High Sch., 1967-72; asst. supt. Archdiocese of New Orleans, 1972-74, assoc. supt., 1974-83; prin. Archbishop Chapelle High Sch., Metairie, La., 1983-89; pres. Archbishop Chapelle High Sch., 1989—. Contbr. articles to profl. jours. Mem. Kenner Bus. Assn., 1989—, Metairie chpt. Am. Heart Assn., 1990—. 1st lt. U.S. Army, 1956-58. Recipient Blue Ribbon Sch. Excellence award U.S. Dept. Edn., 1987, 91, 95, One to Watch in '79 award New Orleans Mag., 1979, Presdl. award Nat. Cath. Ednl. Assn., 1984, St. Louis medal Archdiocese of New Orleans, 1983; named Outstanding Educator La., La. Libr. ASsn., 1994. Mem. Nat. Cath. Edn. Assn. (Nat. Outstanding Contbn. award 1980, reg. assoc. 1988—), Cath. Secondary Prin. Assn. (treas. 1985-87), Nat. Chief Adminstrs. of Cath. Edn., Am. Mgmt. Assn., Nat. Assn. Secondary Sch. Prins. Roman Catholic. Avocations: reading, sports, computers, photography. Office: Archbishop Chapelle High 8800 Veterans Memorial Blvd Metairie LA 70003-5235

MURPHY, ANDREW J., managing news editor. Now mng. editor, news editor Columbus (Ohio) Dispatch. Office: Columbus Dispatch 34 S 3rd St Columbus OH 43215-4201

MURPHY, ANN BURKE, systems analyst; b. Portland, Maine, Dec. 7, 1938; d. James Hudner and Mary Theresa (Monahan) Burke; m. John B. Murphy, Aug. 20, 1960 (div. Jan. 3, 1979); children: Kim Murphy Francis, Suzanne Murphy Farrell. BA in Math., U. Maine, 1960. Rsch. analyst United Tech. Corp., East Hartford, Conn., 1960-61, Travelers Ins. Co., Hartford, Conn., 1961-69; tennis profl., cons. East Hartford, 1969-82; adv. sys. analyst Phoenix Home Life, Hartford, 1982—; ofcl. linesperson Aetna Ins. Co. World Cup Tennis Tournament, Hartford, 1973-76; dir. Hartford Ins. Group City Tennis Open, 1978-80. Mem. New Eng. chpt. U.S. Tennis Assn. (bd. dirs. 1987-89, ranked #1 1972-93, hall of fame 1993, friendship cup capt.), Phi Beta Kappa, Phi Kappa Phi. Democrat. Roman Catholic. Home: 124 Bradley St East Hartford CT 06118-2357 Office: Phoenix Home Life Ins 1 American Row Hartford CT 06103-2833

MURPHY, ANN PLESHETTE, magazine editor-in-chief. Editor-in-chief Parents mag., N.Y.C. Office: Parents Magazine 685 3rd Ave New York NY 10017-4024*

MURPHY, ARTHUR JOHN, JR., lawyer; b. Aug. 13, 1950; s. Arthur John, Sr. and Joan Marie (von Albade) M.; m. Joanne Therese Blak, Dec. 18, 1976; children—Arthur John III, Matthew Newsom, Ryan. B.A., U. San Diego, 1972, J.D., 1975. Bar: Calif. 1975. Atty., SEC, Washington, 1975-78; assoc. Bronson, Bronson & McKinnon, San Francisco, 1979-82, ptnr., 1983—; lectr.; arbitrator Nat. Assn. Securities Dealers, 1982—. Contbr. securities law articles to profl. jours. Recipient Franklin award for Outstanding Grad., U. San Diego, 1972. Mem. ABA, Calif. Bar Assn. (exec. com. bus. law sect. 1986-90, chmn. 1989-90), San Francisco Bar Assn. Roman Catholic. Club: Olympic, Bankers Club of San Francisco. Home: 1116 Butterfield Rd San Anselmo CA 94960-1157 Office: Bronson Bronson & McKinnon 505 Montgomery St San Francisco CA 94111-2552

MURPHY, ARTHUR THOMAS, systems engineer; b. Hartford, Conn., Feb. 15, 1929; s. Arthur T. and Mary (Beakey) M.; m. Jane M. Gamble, Aug. 16, 1952; children: Thomas, Patricia, Mary, John, Sheila, Jane, Joseph. BEE, Syracuse U., 1951; MS, Carnegie-Mellon U., 1952, PhD, 1957. Registered profl. engr., Kans. Instr. Carnegie-Mellon U., Pitts., 1952-56; asst., assoc. prof., head. elec. engring. Wichita State U., Kans., 1956-61; vis. assoc. prof. mech. engring. MIT, Cambridge, Mass., 1961-62; prof., dean engring. Widener U., Chester, Pa., 1962-71, v.p., acad. dean, 1971-75; Brown prof., head mech. engring. dept. Carnegie-Mellon U., Pitts., 1975-79; prof. industry, mgr. computer and automated systems, sr. research fellow Du Pont de Nemours Co., Camp Hill, Pa., 1979-87; Du Pont fellow Du Pont de Nemours Co., Wilmington, Del., 1987—; vis. rsch. fellow Sony Corp. Rsch. Ctr., Yokohama, Japan, 1991-92, Internat. Superconductivity Tech. Ctr., Tokyo, 1993; vis. prof. control engring. U. Manchester, Eng., 1968-69; cons. Boeing Co., Wichita and Morton, Pa., 1957-68; bd. dirs. Rumford Pub. Co., Chgo., 1975-90; lectr. Pa. State U., 1983-87; Dupont rep. Chem. Rsch. Coun. Author: Introduction to System Dynamics, 1967; contbr. articles to profl. jours.; editor: Pergamon Press, 1966-75; patentee thick film filter connector, ceramic land grid array, superconducting active antenna array. Former mem. adv. coun. Tex. A&M U., Swarthmore Coll. DuPont fellow, 1987—; recipient DuPont Spl Accomplishment award, 1988, Mktg. Excellence award DuPont Co., 1990. Fellow AAAS, IEEE (exec. com., treas. computer packaging); mem. ASME (exec. com. control divsn.), Am. Soc. Engring. Edn. (chmn. grad. studies, instrumentation, awards com., DuPont rep., Western Electric Fund award 1966), Sigma Xi, Tau Beta Pi, Eta Kappa Nu, Sigma Pi Sigma, Pi Mu Epsilon, Phi Kappa Phi. Avocations: hiking, photography. Home: 388 Spring Mill Rd Chadds Ford PA 19317 Office: Du Pont Co Exptl Sta PO Box 80357 Wilmington DE 19880-0357

MURPHY, ARTHUR WILLIAM, lawyer, educator; b. Boston, Jan. 25, 1922; s. Arthur W. and Rose (Spillane) M.; m. Jane Marks, Dec. 21, 1948 (dec. Sept. 1951); 1 dau., Lois; m. Jean C. Marks, Sept. 30, 1954; children—Rachel, Paul. A.B. cum laude, Harvard, 1943; LL.B., Columbia, 1948. Bar: N.Y. State bar 1949. Asso. in law Columbia Sch. Law, N.Y.C., 1948-49; asso. dir. Legislative Drafting Research Fund, 1956, prof. law, 1963—; trial atty. U.S. Dept. Justice, 1950-52; asso. firm Hughes, Hubbard, Blair & Reed, N.Y.C., 1953-56, 57-58; partner firm Baer, Marks, Friedman & Berliner, N.Y.C., 1959-63; mem. safety and licensing panel AEC, 1962-73; mem. spl. commn. on weather modification NSF, 1964-66; mem. Presdl. Commn. on Catastrophic Nuclear Accidents, 1988-90. Author: Financial Protection against Atomic Hazards, 1957, (with others) Cases on Gratuitous Transfers, 1968, 3d edit., 1985, The Nuclear Power Controversy, 1976. Served with AUS, 1943-46. Decorated Purple Heart. Mem. ABA, Assn. of Bar of City of N.Y. (spl. com. on sci. and law). Office: Columbia Sch of Law 435 W 116th St New York NY 10027-7201

MURPHY, AUSTIN DE LA SALLE, economist, educator, banker; b. N.Y.C., Nov. 20, 1917; s. Daniel Joseph and Marie Cornelia (Austin) M.; m. Mary Patricia Halpin, June 12, 1948 (dec. May 1974); children: Austin Joseph, Owen Gerard; m. Lee Chilton Romero, Dec. 14, 1974; stepchildren: Thomas Romero, Robert Romero. AB, St. Francis Coll., Bklyn., 1938; AM (Hayden fellow 1938-40), Fordham U., 1940, PhD, 1949. Instr. econs. Fordham U., 1938-41; Instr. econs. Georgetown U., 1941-42; asst. statistician, statis. controls Bd. Econ. Warfare, 1942; sr. econs. research editor N.Y. State Dept. Labor, 1947-50; lectr. econs. Fordham U. Sch. Edn., 1946-55; instr. N.Y. U. Sch. Commerce, 1949-51; dean sch. bus. adminstrn. Seton Hall U., South Orange, N.J., 1950-55; Albert O'Neill prof. Am. enterprise, dean sch. bus. adminstrn. Canisius Coll., Buffalo, 1955-62; dir. edn. dept. NAM, 1962-63; exec. v.p. Savs. Banks Assn. N.Y. State, 1963-70; chmn., pres. River Bank Am. (formerly East River Savs. Bank), 1970-89, vice chmn., dir., 1990—; charter trustee Savs. Bank Rockland County, 1965-70; dir. Bank of Charleston (S.C.), 1989-91; chmn. bd., trustee Savs. Bank Life Ins. Fund, 1983-87; chmn. dist. I, mem. adv. coun. Conf. State Bank Suprs., 1986-93; bd. dirs. MSB Fund, Inc. Author: (with Fleming Frasca, and Mannion) Social Studies Review Book, 1946, Leading Problems of New Jersey Manufacturing Industries, (with Bullock and Doerflinger), 1953, Reasons for Relocation, 1955, Forecast of Industrial Expansion in Buffalo and the Niagara Frontier, 1956, Metropolitan Buffalo Perspective, 1958; editor Handbook of New York Labor Statistics, 1950. Mem. Livingston (N.J.) Charter Commn., 1954-55; mem. capital expenditures com., City of Buffalo, 1957-63; trustee Fordham U., 1973-79, N.Y. Med. Coll., 1978-81; bd. dirs. N.Y. council Boy Scouts Am., 1974—, Jr. Achievement of Buffalo, 1958-63, Invest-in-Am. 1st lt. U.S. Army, 1942-46. Named Knight of Malta, 1971. Mem. NAM (chmn. ednl. aids com. 1958-63), Am. Fin. Assn., Def. Transp. Assn. (life), Nat. Assn. Mut. Savs. Banks (bd. dirs., treas. 1976-81), Friendly Sons. St. Patrick (1st v.p.), DownTown Lower Manhattan Assn. (dir., vice chmn. 1982-93), World Trade Club, Larchmont Yacht Club, KC, Alpha Kappa Psi, Pi Gamma Mu. Home: 1060 Bayhead Dr Mamaroneck NY 10543-4701 Office: River Bank Am 145 Huguenot St New Rochelle NY 10801-5216 *Through the various happy events and the difficult and sorrowful, loss of loved ones as well as the vagaries of business life, I have found that an ongoing prayerful relationship to God brings a certain detachment and peace that overcomes life's passing problems.*

MURPHY, BARRY AMES, lawyer; b. Summit, N.J., Mar. 3, 1938; s. Robert Joseph and Florence C. (Ames) M.; m. Leslie Lynn Smith, June 9, 1962; children—Karen Irene, Sean Patrick, Conor Brendan, Ilana Taraleigh. B.A. in English, Stanford U., 1960; M.B.A., Harvard U., 1963; J.D., U. So. Calif., 1972. Bar: Calif. bar 1973, U.S. Supreme Ct 1976, U.S. Tax Ct 1976. Fin. analyst Office of Sec. Def., 1963-65; pres. Tech. Industries Inc., Los Angeles, 1966-72; invididual practice law San Mateo, Calif., 1972-74; corp. counsel Falstaff Brewing Co., San Francisco, 1974-77; sr. partner firm Levine & Murphy, San Francisco, 1978-81; v.p. Microvertics, Mountain View, Calif., 1981-86; pres. Murphy Law Corp., San Anselmo, 1987—. Mem. Am., Calif. bar assns., Calif. Trial Lawyers. Address: 28 Fern Ln San Anselmo CA 94960-1807

MURPHY, BENJAMIN EDWARD, actor; b. Jonesboro, Ark., Mar. 6, 1942; s. Patrick Henry and Nadine (Steele) M. Student, Loras Coll., 1960-61, Loyola U., New Orleans, 1961-62, U. Americas, 1962-63, 64-65; B.A. in Polit. Sci, U. Ill., 1964; student, Pasadena Playhouse, 1965-67; B.A. in Theatre Arts, U. So. Cal., 1968. Appeared in: TV series Name of the Game, NBC, 1968-70, Alias Smith and Jones, ABC, 1971-73, Griff, 1973-74, Gemini Man, NBC, 1976, The Chisholms, CBS, 1979-80, The Winds of War, 1983, Lottery, 1983-84, Berrenger's, NBC, 1985, The Dirty Dozen, Fox Network, 1988.

MURPHY, BETTY JANE SOUTHARD (MRS. CORNELIUS F. MURPHY), lawyer; b. East Orange, N.J.; d. Floyd Theodore and Thelma (Casto) Southard; m. Cornelius F. Murphy, May 1, 1965; children: Ann Southard, Cornelius Francis Jr. AB, Ohio State U.; student, Alliance Française and U. Sorbonne, Paris; JD, Am. U.; LLD (hon.), Eastern Mich. U., 1975, Capital U., 1976, U. Puget Sound, 1986; LHD, Tusculum coll., 1987. Bar: D.C. 1958. Corr., free lance journalist Europe and Asia, UPI, Washington; pub. relations counsellor Capital Properties, Inc. of Columbus (Ohio), Washington; practiced in Washington, 1959-74; mem. firm McInnis, Wilson, Munson & Woods (and predecessor firm); dep. asst. sec., adminstr. Wage and Hour Divsn. Wage and Hour div. Dept. Labor, 1974-75; chmn. and mem. NLRB, 1975-79; ptnr. firm Baker & Hostetler, 1980—; adj. prof. law Am. U., 1972-80; mem. adv. com. on rights and responsibilities of women to Sec. HEW; mem. panel conciliators Internat. Ctr. Settlement Investment Disputes, 1974-85; mem. Adminstrv. Conf. U.S., 1976-80, Pub. Svc. Adv. Bd., 1976-79; mem. human resouces com. Nat. Ctr. for Productivity and Quality of Working Life, 1976-80; mem. Presdl. Commn. on Exec. Exch., 1981-85. Trustee Mary Baldwin Coll., 1977-85, Am. U., 1980—, George Mason U. Found., Inc., 1990—, George Mason U. Edn. Found., 1993—; nat. bd. dirs. Med. Coll. Pa., bd. corporators, 1976-85; bd. dirs. Ctr. for Women in Medicine, 1980-86; bd. govs. St. Agnes Sch., 1981-87; mem. exec. com. Commn. on Bicentennial of U.S. Constn., chmn. internat. adv. com., 1985-92; vice chmn. James Madison Meml. Fellowship Found., 1989-96; bd. dirs. Meridian Internat. Ctr., 1992-96, Friends of Congl. Law Libr., 1992—, Friends of Dept. of Labor. Recipient Ohio Gov.'s award, 1980, fellow award, 1981, Outstanding Pub. Service award U.S. Info. Service, 1987; named Disting. Fellow John Sherman Myers Soc., 1986. Mem. ABA (adminstrv. law sect., chmn. labor law com. 1980-83, chmn. internat. and comparative law adminstrv. law sect. 1983-88, chmn. customs, tariff and trade com. 1988-90, employment law sect. 1990, chmn. internat. com. dispute resolution sect. 1995—), FBA, Inter-Am. Bar Assn. (editor newsletter, Silver medal 1967, co-chmn. labor law com. 1975-83), Bar Assn. D.C., World Peace Through Law Ctr., Am. Arbitration Assn. (bd. dirs. 1985—, mem. editl. bd. 1992, mem. exec. com. 1995—, mem. internat. arbitration com. 1995—), Rep. Nat. Lawyers Assn. (nat. v.p. 1990-95, nat. vice chmn. 1996—), Supreme Ct. Hist. Soc., Am. U. Alumni Assn. (bd. dirs.), Mortar Bd., Kappa Beta Pi. Republican. Office: Baker & Hostetler 1050 Connecticut Ave NW Washington DC 20036-5303

MURPHY, BEVERLEY ELAINE PEARSON, scientist, administrator, physician, educator; b. Toronto, Ont., Can., Mar. 15, 1929; d. Ernest Wallace and Edith (Johnson) Pearson; m. David Raymond Murphy, June 15, 1958; children: Madeleine, Catherine. B.A., U. Toronto, 1952, M.D., 1956; M.Sc., McGill U., Can., 1960, Ph.D., 1964. Cert. Med. Biochemistry, Endocrinology. Rotating interne Toronto Gen. Hosp., 1956-57; rsch. fellow Royal Victoria Hosp., Montreal, Que., Can., 1957-59, resident in medicine, 1959-61; rsch. fellow Queen Mary Vets. Hosp., Montreal, 1961-64, dir. endocrinology lab., 1964-78, cons. in endocrinology, 1970-73; asst., assoc. obstetrician & gynecologist Montreal Gen. Hosp., 1972-79; dir. reproductive physiology unit Montreal Gen. Hosp. Rsch. Inst., 1972—; sr. physician, sr. obstetrician and gynecologist Montreal Gen. Hosp., 1979—; med. scientist Royal Victoria Hosp., Montreal, 1981—; lectr., asst., assoc. prof. medicine McGill U., Montreal, 1964-74, prof., 1975—, prof. obstetrics and gynecology, 1979—, assoc. mem. dept. physiology, 1981—, prof. psychiatry, 1985—; lectr. in U.S., Fed. Republic of Germany, Eng., France, Mex., India, Italy, Switzerland, New Zealand, Can.; organizer Satellite Symposium, Internat. Congress Endocrinology, McGill U., 1982, Symposium on Psychoendocrinology, McGill U., 1989; reviewer grant applications for Med. Rsch. Coun. Can., Fonds de la recherche en Santé du Qué, March of Dimes, Ont. Mental Health Found., Can. Heart Found., Can. Liver Found., NSF, B.C. Health Scis; career investigator Med. Rsch. Coun. Can., 1968-94. Mem. editorial bd. Jour. Clin. Endocrinology Metabolism, 1975-79, Jour. Steroid Biochemistry, 1976-94, Jour. Immunoassay, 1979—; contbr. articles, abstracts to profl. jours.; patentee in field. Fellow Royal Soc. Can.; mem. ACP, Am. Soc. Clin. Investigation, Endocrine Soc., Can. Assn. Med. Biochemists, Can. Soc. Clin. Investigation, Can. Soc. Endocrinology and Metabolism (sec.-treas. 1984-89), Can. Investigators in Reproduction, Can. Biochem. Soc., Montreal Physiol. Soc. (pres. 1972-73, 73-74), Que. Assn. Lab. Physicians, Soc. Obstetricians and Gynecologists Can., Syndicat Professionel des Médecins Endocrinologues du Québec, Assn. Women in Sci. Avocations: art, music, jogging, skiing. Office: Montreal Gen Hosp, 1650 Cedar Ave, Montreal, PQ Canada H3G 1A4

MURPHY, BOB, professional golfer; b. Bklyn., Feb. 14, 1943; m. Gail Murphy. Profl. golfer, 1967—, Sr. PGA Tour, 1993—. Named Rookie of Yr., PGA Tour, 1968; winner in Phila. Classic, 1968, Thunderbird Classic, 1968, Greater Hartford Open, 1970, Jackie Gleason-Inverray Classic, 1975, Can. Open, 1986; PGA Sr. Tour wins include Bruno's Meml. Classic, 1993, GTE North Classic, 1993, Raley's Sr. Gold Rush, 1994, Hyatt Regency Maui Kaanapali Classic, 1994, IntelliNet Challenge, 1995, Paine Webber Invitational, 1995, nationwide Championship, 1995, VFW Sr. Championship, 1995. Office: care Eddie Elias Enterprise PO Box 5118 1720 Merriman Rd Akron OH 44334-0118*

MURPHY, CARYLE MARIE, foreign correspondent; b. Hartford, Conn., Nov. 16, 1946; d. Thomas Joseph and Muriel Kathryn (McCarthy) M. BA cum laude, Trinity Coll., 1968; M in Internat. Pub. Policy, Johns Hopkins U., 1987. Tchr. English, history St. Cecilia Tchr. Tng. Coll., Nyeri, Kenya, 1968-71; reporter Brockton (Mass.) Enterprise, 1972-73; freelance corr. Washington Post, Newsweek, Sunday Times of London, et al, Luanda, Angola, 1974-76; reporter Fairfax County Washington Post, 1976-77, fgn. corr. in South Africa, 1977-82, reporter immigration issues, 1982-85, bur. chief Alexandria, Va., 1985-89; fgn. corr. Mid. East Washington Post, Cairo, 1989-94. Vol. ARC, Washington, 1984, Whitman-Walker Found., Washington, 1988-89. Recipient Courage in Journalism award Internat. Women's Media Found., 1990, George Polk award L.I. U., 1991, Edward Weintal Journalism award Sch. Fgn. Svc., Georgetown U., 1991, Pulitzer Prize for internat. reporting, 1991; Edward R. Murrow fellow Coun. on Fgn. Rels., N.Y., 1994-95. Roman Catholic. Avocations: fgn. langs., hiking. Office: Washington Post Fgn Desk 1150 15th St NW Washington DC 20071-0001*

MURPHY, CHARLES HAYWOOD, JR., retired petroleum company executive; b. El Dorado, Ark., Mar. 6, 1920; s. Charles Haywood and Bertie (Wilson) M.; m. Johnie Walker, Oct. 14, 1939; children: Michael Walker, Martha, Charles Haywood, III, Robert Madison. Ed. pub. schs., Ark.; LLD (hon.), U. Ark., 1966. Ind. oil producer, 1939-50; ret. chmn., also bd. dirs. Murphy Oil Corp., El Dorado, Ark., 1972—; chmn. exec. com. 1st Comml. Corp., Little Rock. Bd. govs. Oschner Med. Found.; bd. adminstrs. Tulane U.; mem. nat. adv. bd. Smithsonian Instn.; past mem. Ark. Bd. Higher Edn. Served as infantryman World War II. Recipient citation for outstanding individual service in natural resource mgmt. Nat. Wildlife Fedn. Mem. Am. Petroleum Inst. (past exec. com., hon. bd. dirs.), Nat. Petroleum Council (past chmn.), 25 Yr. Club Petroleum Industry (past pres.).

MURPHY, CHARLES JOSEPH, investment banker; b. N.Y.C., Sept. 18, 1947; s. Charles Joseph and Mary V. (Vaughan) M.; m. Karen Lyn Canevari, Aug. 18, 1973; 4 children. BEE, Manhattan Coll., 1969; MBA, NYU, 1974, APC, 1975. Chartered fin. analyst; cert. advance profl. Avionics engr. Sikorsky Aircraft, Stratford, Conn., 1969-70; engr., rate analyst Am. Electric Power Co., N.Y.C., 1970-76; equity analyst First Boston Corp., N.Y.C., 1976-78, v.p. capital markets, 1982-84, mng. dir. utilities and telecommunications fin., 1984-87, head investment banking group, 1988-92, head investment banking dept., 1992-94; co-head worldwide investment banking, 1994-95; head global equities First Boston Corp., N.Y.C., 1995—; mem. CS First Boston operating com., 1993—, exec. bd., 1995—, co-chmn. investment banking operating com., 1994-95. Mem. N.Y. Soc. Security Analysts (sr.). Roman Catholic. Avocations: jogging; racquet sports; winter sports. Office: CS First Boston Corp Pk Ave Plz 55 E 52nd St New York NY 10055-0002

MURPHY, CHRISTOPHER JOSEPH, III, financial executive; b. Washington, Apr. 24, 1946; s. Christopher Joseph Murphy Jr. and Jean Murphy Vos; m. Carmen Morris Carmichael, Feb. 1, 1969; children: Christopher IV, Sean, Kelly, Kevin, Conor, Dillon. BA, U. Notre Dame, 1968; JD, U. Va., 1971; MBA with distinction, Harvard U., 1973. Bar: Va. 1971, U.S. Dist. Ct. D.C. 1971. Officer, pres. 1st Source Corp., South Bend, Ind., 1977—; bd. dirs. Weldun Internat., Bridgman, Mich., 1981-89, Meml. Health Systems, South Bend, 1981-90, chmn., 1990-92, Omega Health Group, Inc., South Bend, 1984-90, Comair Inc., Cin., 1989—, Discover Re Insurance Inc., 1991-95, Trust Corp. Mortgage Inc., 1991—, Quality Dining, 1994—, Titan Holdings, 1995—; adv. council Notre Dame Coll. Arts and Letters, 1981—, chmn., 1985-89; bd. dirs. South Bend C. of C., 1984-95; bd. dirs. Meml. Hosp., South Bend, 1980-86, South Bend Symphony, 1981-83, chmn. Med. Edn. Found., South Bend, 1982—; chmn. United Way Campaign, St. Joseph County, Ind., 1980. Mem. ABA, Young Pres.'s Orgn. (internat. bd. dirs. 1993-95, exec. com.), Ind. Bar Assn., Va. Bar Assn., St. Joseph County Bar

Assn., Nat. Assn. Bus. Economists (chpt. pres. 1980), Robert Morris Assocs., Nat. Assn. Publically Traded Cos. (bd. dirs. 1983—, chmn. 1986-87, 1990-95), Nat. Assn. Security Dealers (corp. adv. bd. 1988-92), Am. Bankers Assn. (chmn. payment systems policy bd. 1984-85). Roman Catholic. Office: 1st Source Corp 100 N Michigan St PO Box 1602 South Bend IN 46634

MURPHY, DANIEL HAYES, II, lawyer; b. Hartford, Conn., Jan. 8, 1941; s. Robert Henry and Jane Granville (Cook) M.; m. Deann Ellison, June 30, 1962; children—Edward Ellison, Jessica Jane. B.A., Yale U., 1962; LL.B., Columbia U., 1965. Bar: N.Y. 1965, U.S. Dist. Ct. (so. and ea. dists.) N.Y. 1967, U.S. Ct. Appeals (2d cir.) 1968, Conn. 1978, Calif. 1984, Fla. 1986. Assoc. White & Case, N.Y.C., 1965-70; asst. U.S. atty. So. Dist. N.Y., N.Y.C., 1970-74; pvt. practice law N.Y.C., 1974-76, 85—; assoc. Mendes & Mount, N.Y.C., 1977-81, jr. ptnr., 1981-85; spl. master Supreme Ct. N.Y. County, 1981—. Chmn. planning commn., Groton Long Point, Conn., 1977-84. Mem. ABA, N.Y. State Bar Assn., N.Y. County Lawyers Assn., Assn. Bar City N.Y., Yale Club N.Y.C., Ocean Reef Key Largo, Fla. Roman Catholic. Office: PO Box 874 Pelham NY 10803

MURPHY, DEBORAH LYNN WAITES, noise control engineer; b. Melbourne, Fla., Aug. 28, 1961; d. Frank B. Jr. and Jerleen Joy (Johnson) Waites; m. David Glenn Murphy, May 4, 1985 (div. 1995). BS in Ocean Engring., Fla. Atlantic U., 1981; MS in Engring., Calif. State U., 1989. Lic. engr.-in-tng., Fla. Assoc. engr., scientist McDonnell Astronautics, Huntington Beach, Calif., 1981-83, engr., scientist, 1983-85; engr., scientist Douglas Aircraft Co., Long Beach, Calif., 1985-87, engr., scientist specialist, 1987-89; mgr. noise abatement Sarasota (Fla.) Manatee Airport Authority, 1990-93, mgr. environ. affairs, 1993—; mem. subcom. aircraft noise Nat. Rsch. Coun., Transp. Rsch. Bd., Washington, 1991—. Contbr. to periodicals and procs. including Tech. Idea Exch., Procs. of NOISE-CON 90 and 94. Mem. Acoustical Soc. Am. (vice chmn. Orange County chpt. 1989, sec. Orange County chpt. 1985-88), Inst. Noise Control Engring. Home: 6316 Lincoln Rd Bradenton FL 34203-9703 Office: Sarasota Manatee Airport Au 6000 Airport Circle Sarasota FL 34243

MURPHY, DENNIS F., retail executive; b. Jersey City, Mar. 21, 1937; m. Catherine T. McCann; children: Linda C., Michael D., Matthew C. BS, St. Peter's Coll., 1958. Corp. sec., dir. ins. Merc. Stores Co. Inc., Fairfield, Ohio, 1965—. Office: Merc Stores Co Inc 9450 Seward Rd Fairfield OH 45014-5412

MURPHY, DIANA E., federal judge; b. Faribault, Minn., Jan. 4, 1934; d. Albert W. and Adleyne (Heiker) Kuske; m. Joseph Murphy, July 24, 1958; children: Michael, John E. BA magna cum laude, U. Minn., 1954, JD magna cum laude, 1974; postgrad., Johannes Gutenberg U., Mainz, Germany, 1954-55, U. Minn., 1955-58. Bar: Minn. 1974, U.S. Supreme Ct. 1980. Assoc. Lindquist & Vennum, 1974-76; mcpl. judge Hennepin County, 1976-78, Minn. State dist. judge, 1978-80; judge U.S. Dist. Ct. for Minn., Mpls., 1980-94, chief judge, 1992-94; judge U.S. Ct. of Appeals (8th cir.), Minneapolis, 1994—. Bd. editors: Minn. Law Rev., Georgetown U. Jour. on Cts., Health Scis. and the Law, 1989-92. Bd. dirs. Spring Hill conf. Ctr., 1978-84, Mpls. United Way, 1985—, treas., 1990-94, vice chair, 1996—; bd. dirs. Bush Found., 1982—, chmn. bd. dirs., 1986-91; bd. dirs. Amicus, 1976-80, also organizer, 1st chmn. adv. coun.; mem. Mpls. Charter Commn., 1973-76, chmn., 1974-76; bd. dirs. Ops. De Novo, 1971-76, chmn. bd. dirs., 1974-75; mem. Minn. Constl. Study Commn., chmn. bill of rights com., 1971-73; regent St. Johns U., 1978-87, 88—, vice chmn. bd., 1985-87, chmn. bd. 1995—; mem. Minn. Bicentennial Commn., 1987-88; trustee Twin Cities Pub. TV, 1985-94, chmn. bd., 1990-92; trustee U. Minn. Found., 1990—, treas., 1992—; bd. dirs. Sci. Mus. Minn., 1988-94, vice chmn., 1991-94; trustee U. St. Thomas, 1991—; dir. Nat. Assn. Pub. Interest Law Fellowships for Equal Justice, 1992-95. Fulbright scholar; recipient Amicus Founders' award, Outstanding Achievement award U. Minn., Outstanding Achievement award YWCA. Fellow Am. Bar Found.; mem. ABA (ethics and profl. responsibility judges adv. com. 1981-88, standing com. on jud. selection, tenure and compensation 1991-94, standing com. on fed. jud. improvements 1994—), Minn. Bar Assn. (bd. govs. 1977-81), Hennepin County Bar Assn. (gov. coun. 1976-81), Am. Law Inst., Am. Judicature Soc. (bd. dirs. 1982-93, v.p. 1985-88, treas. 1988-89, chmn. bd. 1989-91), Nat. Assn. Women Judges, Minn. Women Lawyers (Myra Bradwell award), U. Minn. Alumni Assn. (bd. dirs. 1975-83, nat. pres. 1981-82), Fed. Judges Assn. (bd. dirs. 1982—, v.p. 1984-89, pres. 1989-91), Hist. Soc. for 8th Cir. (bd. dirs. 1988-91), Fed. Jud. Ctr. (bd. dirs. 1990-94, 8th cir. jud. coun. 1992-94, U.S. jud. conf. com. on ct. adminstrn. and case mgmt. 1994—), Order of Coif, Phi Beta Kappa. Office: US Dist Ct 684 US Courthouse 110 S 4th St Minneapolis MN 55401

MURPHY, DONALD JAMES, lawyer; b. Milw., July 7, 1958; s. George Earl and HArriet Jean (Amundson) M.; m. Sue Elizabeth Hamann, July 30, 1983 (div. Feb. 1987); m. Lori Jean Wood Murphy, June 10, 1991; children: Riley Marie, Rogan Patrick. BBA, U. Wis., Whitewater, 1981; JD, Pepperdine U., 1984. Bar: Calif. 1984, Wis. 1985, U.S. Dist. Ct. (we. dist.) Wis. 1986, U.S. Ct. Appeals (7th cir.) 1989. Assoc. McLean & Irvin, L.A., 1985; ptnr. Pressentin & Murphy, Monona, Wis., 1985-92; sr. ptnr. Pressentin, Murphy & Roberts, Monona, Wis., 1992—; owner, broker Murphy Assocs., Madison, Wis., 1993—. Bd. dirs. East YMCA, Madison, 1990-94. Mem. ATLA, Wis. Trial Lawyers Assn., Wis. Bar Assn., Calif. Bar Assn., Wis. Realtors Assn., Optomists Club. Office: Pressentin Murphy & Roberts 100 River Pl Ste 240 Monona WI 53716-4027

MURPHY, DONN BRIAN, theater educator; b. San Antonio, July 21, 1930; s. Arthur Morton and Claire Frances (McCarthy) M. BA, Benedictine Coll., 1954; MFA, Catholic U., 1956; PhD, U. Wis., 1964. Prof. Georgetown U., Washington, 1954—; exec. dir. Nat. Theatre Corp., Washington, 1985—; tech. theater liaison The White House, Washington, 1961-65. Author: A Director's Guide to Good Theatre, 1968, Stage for a Nation, 1985, Helen Hayes: A Bio-Bibliography, 1993; (plays) Creation of the World, 1970, Something of a Sorceress, 1971, Tyger/Tyger, 1977; (with others) Eleanor: First Lady of the World, 1984. Cpl. U.S. Army, 1950-52. Recipient Outstanding Svc. award Am. Theatre Assn., 1984, Forrest Roberts award No. Mich. U., 1977; Ford Found. fellow, 1963; inducted Coll. Fellows of Am. Theatre, 1994. Democrat. Roman Catholic. Avocations: travel, motorcycling. Home: 2401 N Kenmore St Arlington VA 22207-4938

MURPHY, DONNA JEANNE, actress; b. Corona, N.Y., Mar. 7, 1959. Student, NYU Sch. of the Arts. Stage appearances include: (regional theater) Miss Julie, Pal Joey, (off-Broadway) Song of Singapore, Hey Love: The Songs of Mary Rodgers, Privates on Parade, Showing Off, Birds of Paradise, Little Shop of Horrors, A...My Name Is Alice,, Twelve Dreams, Hello Again, 1995, (Broadway) The King and I, 1996 (Best Leading Actress Tony award 1996), Passion (Leading Actress in Mus. Tony award 1994), The Mystery of Edwin Drood, They're Playing Our Song, The Human Comedy; appeared in film Jade, 1995; TV appearances include Law & Order, All My Children, Another World, Murder One, 1995-96, HBO Lifestories, 1996. Office: Silver Massetti & Assocs 145 W 45th St Fl 1204 New York NY 10036-4008

MURPHY, EDDIE, comedian, actor; b. Bklyn., Apr. 3, 1961; s. Vernon and Lillian Murphy Lynch; m. Nicole Mitchell, March 18, 1993; children: Bria, Myles. Student pub. schs., Bklyn. Began performing Richard M. Dixon's White House, L.I., N.Y.; performed at various N.Y.C. clubs, including The Comic Strip; with Saturday Night Live, N.Y.C., 1980-84; host 35th Ann. Emmy Awards, 1983. Starring roles in motion pictures include 48 Hours, 1982, Trading Places, 1983, Best Defense, 1984, Beverly Hills Cop, 1984, The Golden Child, 1986, Beverly Hills Cop II, 1987, Eddie Murphy Raw, 1987, Coming to America, 1988, Harlem Nights,1989, Another 48 Hours, 1990, Boomerang, 1992, The Distinguished Gentleman, 1992, Beverly Hills Cop III, 1994, The Vampire of Brooklyn, 1995, The Nutty Professor, 1996; oneman HBO spl., 1983; albums include Eddie Murphy, 1982, Eddie Murphy Comedian, 1983, How Could it Be, 1984, So Happy, 1989, Distinguished Gentleman, 1992, Love's Alright, 1993. Office: Eddie Murphy Prodns Inc 5555 Melrose Ave Los Angeles CA 90038-3149 also: Eddie Murphy Prodns Inc Carnegie Hall Tower 152 W 57th St New York NY 10019-3310*

MURPHY, EDMUND MICHAEL, federal agency administrator, demographer; b. Steubenville, Ohio, Apr. 7, 1936; s. Edmund Bernard and Catherine Margaret (Allen) M.; m. Mary Elizabeth Jeske, Dec. 15, 1962; 1 child, Maureen Cecilia. BA, Miami U., Oxford, Ohio, 1959; MA, U. Chgo., 1963, PhD, 1965. Asst. prof. U. Chgo., 1965-68, U. Pa., Phila., 1968-70; statistician Statistics Can., Ottawa, Ont., 1970-73; dir. rsch. Manpower and Immigration Dept. Can., Ottawa, 1973-77; dir. gen. Dept. Health and Welfare Can., Ottawa, 1977-78, asst. dep. min. policy and planning, 1978-82, asst. dep. min. social svcs. programs, 1982-86, asst. dep. min., sec. rev. of demography and its implications for social and econ. policy, 1986-92; sr. demographer Statistics Canada, Ottawa, 1992-94; pres., CEO Global Demographics Inc., Ottawa, 1994-96; cons., 1996—. Contbr. numerous articles to profl. jours. With Carleton Condominium Corp. # 43, Ottawa, 1983-93, pres., 1994-96. With U.S. Army, 1960-62. NSF fellow, 1962-65. Mem. Population Assn. Am., Population Assn. Can. Roman Catholic. Home: Chemin de la Dole, Les Grands Champs, 1274 Signy Vaud Switzerland Office: Global Demographics, 350 Sparks St Ste 1103, Ottawa, ON Canada K1R 7S8

MURPHY, EDWARD FRANCIS, sales executive; b. Chgo., July 30, 1947; s. Edward F. and Marjorie (Mooney) M.; m. Kay A. Worcester, Apr. 17, 1970; 1 child, Dean D. BA in Mktg., No. Ill. U., 1976. Dist. mgr. Midas Internat. Corp., Chgo., 1977-85; sales mgr. Raybestos, McHenry, Ill., 1985-89, Wagner Brakes, St. Louis, 1989—. Author: Vietnam Medal of Honor Heroes, 1987, Heroes of World War II, 1990, Korea's Heroes, 1990, Dak To, 1993, Semper Fi, 1996; hist. cons. (book) Above and Beyond, 1985. Sgt. U.S. Army, 1965-68. Recipient Dist. Svc. award Congl. Medal of Honor Soc., 1989. Mem. Medal of Honor Hist. Soc. (founder, pres. 1975—). Republican. Avocations: writing, flying. Home: 2659 E Kael St Mesa AZ 85213

MURPHY, EDWARD J., school system administrator. Dist. supt. Suffolk County (BOCES III), Dix Hills, N.Y. Recipient Nat. Superintendent of the Yr. awd., New York, Am. Assn. of School Administrators, 1992. Office: Suffolk County 507 Deer Park Ave Dix Hills NY 11746-5207

MURPHY, EDWARD PATRICK, JR., gas utility company executive; b. Syracuse, N.Y., Apr. 28, 1943; s. Edward Patrick and Rosemary Margaret (McCloskey) M.; m. Barbara Lynne Stibitz; children: E. Patrick III, Kevin C., Meghan L. BA in Acctg./Law, Clarkson U., 1965; exec. program, Columbia U., 1984. Mgmt. trainee The Bklyn. Union Gas Co., 1965, various staff and operating positions, 1966-75, budget dir., 1976-81, auditor, 1982-88, asst. v.p., 1988-89, v.p., 1990—. Vice chmn. bd. Bklyn. chpt. ARC, 1986-91, chmn., 1991-94; mem. aduit com. ARC of Greater N.Y., 1987—, chmn., 1994—. Mem. Am. Gas Assn. (mem. internal auditing com. 1982-88, vice chmn. 1985-86, chmn. 1986-87; mem. budgeting and fin. forecasting com. 1974-81, vice chmn. 1977-78, chmn. 1978-79; Outstanding Svc. award 1987). Avocations: golf, cooking, fishing. Office: Bklyn Union Gas Co One MetroTech Ctr Brooklyn NY 11201-3851

MURPHY, ELLIS, association management executive; b. Lincoln, Nebr.; s. Ellis F. and Virgie (Olson) M.; m. Judy Neel, 1975; children by previous marriage: Sharon, Michael, Edward, Randall; stepchildren: Mary, Janet, Susan. BS in Agr, Purdue U., 1947; MBA, Northwestern U., 1957; postgrad., Ill. Inst. Tech., 1969-81, U. Wash., 1950-51, Mexico City Coll., 1947, U. Chgo., 1964. Assoc. editor Pacific Builder & Engr., Seattle, 1948-51; tech. editor Portland Cement Assn., 1953-55; dir. public relations Chgo. chpt. AIA, 1955-56; account exec. Carrier & Jobson, Inc., Chgo., 1956-57; pres. Ellis Murphy, Inc., Chgo., 1957-73, Murphy, Tashjian & Assocs., Chgo., 1973-78; v.p. Lurie/Murphy Assocs., Inc., Chgo., 1979-83; pres. Murphy & Murphy Inc., Chgo., 1984—; cons. mktg. communication to various bus. firms, 1970—; instr. (part-time) mktg. Ill. Inst. Tech., Chgo., 1977-79; instr. (part-time) assn. mgmt. DePaul U., Chgo., 1985—; cons. to various trade assns., 1970—. Mem. Bd. Edn. Thornton Fractional Dist., Ill., 1961-67; trustee First Meth. Ch., Lansing, Ill., 1959-65; chmn. dirs. funds Purdue Club, Chgo. Major USMCR, 1943-46, 50-52. Mem. Public Relations Soc. Am. (citation 1963), Am. Mktg. Assn., Am. Soc. Assn. Execs., Chgo. Soc. Assn. Execs. (Disting. Service award 1986), Knights Templar, St. Bernard Commndery (past comdr.), Sigma Delta Chi. Club: Plaza. Home: 3100 N Sheridan Rd Chicago IL 60657-4954 Office: Murphy & Murphy Inc 325 W Huron #403 Chicago IL 60610

MURPHY, EUGENE F., aerospace, communications and electronics executive; b. Flushing, N.Y., Feb. 24, 1936; s. Eugene P. and Delia M.; m. Mary Margaret Cullen, Feb. 20, 1960. BA, Queens Coll., 1956; JD, Fordham U., 1959; LLM, Georgetown U., 1964. Bar: N.Y. With RCA Global Communications Inc., N.Y.C., 1964-81, v.p. and gen. counsel, 1969-71, exec. v.p. ops., 1972-75, pres., chief operating officer, 1975-76, pres., chief exec. officer, 1976-81; chmn., chief exec. officer RCA Communications Inc., N.Y.C., 1981-86; sr. v.p. communications and info. svcs. GE, N.Y.C., 1986-91; pres., chief exec. officer GE Aerospace, King of Prussia, Pa., 1992-93; pres., CEO GE Aircraft Engines, Cin., 1993—; bd. dirs. Lockheed Martin Corp.; mem. Pres. Reagan's Nat. Sec. Telecommunications Adv. Com.; bd. govs. Aerospace Industries Assn. Bd. Served with USMCR, 1959-60. Mem. Armed Forces Comm. and Electronics Assn. (past nat. chmn.). Clubs: Marco Polo, Plandome Country, Plandome Field and Marine. Office: GE Aircraft Engines Maildrop 101 1 Neumann Way Cincinnati OH 45215-1915

MURPHY, EUGENE FRANCIS, consultant, retired government official; b. Syracuse, N.Y., May 31, 1913; s. Eugene Francis and Mary Grace (Thompson) M.; m. Helene M. Murphy, Dec. 31, 1955; children: Anne F., Thomas E. M.E., Cornell U., 1935; M.M.E., Syracuse U., 1937; Ph.D., Ill. Inst. Tech., 1948. Teaching asst. Syracuse U., 1935-36; engr. Ingersoll-Rand Co., Painted Post, N.Y., 1936-39; instr. Ill. Inst. Tech., 1939-41; from instr. to asst. prof. U. Calif., Berkeley, 1941-48; staff engr. Nat. Acad. Scis., Washington, 1945-48; adv. fellow Mellon Inst., Pitts., 1947-48; with VA, N.Y.C., 1948-83; chief research and devel. div. Prosthetic and Sensory Aids Service, 1948-73; dir. Research Center for Prosthetics, 1973-78; dir. Office of Tech. Transfer, 1978-83, sci. advisor, 1983-85; mem. coun. Alliance for Engring. in Medicine and Biology, 1970-90; mem. adv. com. U. Wis., 1978-82, Case Western Res. U., 1981, Am. Found. for Blind, 1981-83; cons. disability and rehab. rsch., 1983—. Contbg. author: Human Limbs and their Substitutes, 1954, Orthopaedic Appliances Atlas, vol. 1, 1952, vol. 2, 1960, Human Factors in Technology, 1963, Biomedical Engineering Systems, 1970, Critical Revs. in Bioengring, 1971, CRC Handbook of Materials, Vol. III, 1975, Atlas of Orthotics, 1975, 2d edit., 1985, Therapeutic Medical Devices: Application and Design, 1982, McGraw-Hill Ency. Sci. and Tech. Yearbook, 1985; contbr. to Wiley Encyclopedia of Medical Devices and Instrumentation, 1988; editor Bull. Prosthetics Research, 1978-82; contbr. articles to profl. jours. Recipient Silver medal Paris, France, 1961; Meritorious Service award VA, 1971; Disting. Career award VA, 1983; Biomedical Engring. Leadership award Alliance for Engring. in Medicine and Biology, 1983; citation Outstanding Handicapped Fed. Employee, 1971; Profl. Achievement award Ill. Inst. Technology, 1983; Fulbright lectr. Soc. and Home for Cripples, Denmark, 1957-58. Fellow AAAS, ASME, Rehab. Engring. Soc. N.Am. (now RESNA), Internat. Soc. for Prosthetics and Orthotics, N.Y. Acad. Medicine; mem. NAE, ASTM, Soc. for Urology and Engring. (hon.), N.Y. Acad. Scis., Acoustical Soc. Am., Optical Soc. Am., Sigma Xi, Tau Beta Pi, Phi Kappa Phi. Home: 111 Savage Farm Dr Ithaca NY 14850-6500

MURPHY, EVELYN FRANCES, healthcare administrator, former lieutenant governor; b. Panama Canal Zone, Panama Canal Zone, May 14, 1940; d. Clement Bernard and Dorothy Eloise (Jackson) M. AB, Duke U., 1961, PhD, 1965; MA, Columbia U., 1963; hon. degrees, Regis Coll., 1978, Curry Coll., Northeastern U., Simmons Coll., Wheaton Coll., Anna Maria Coll., Bridgewater State Coll., Salem State Coll., Emmanuel Coll.; hon. degree, Suffolk U. Pres. Ancon Assocs., Boston, 1971-72; ptnr. Llewelyn-Davies, Weeks, Forrester-Walker & Bor, London, 1973-74; sec. environ. affairs Commonwealth of Mass., Boston, 1975-79, sec. econ. affairs, 1983-86, lt. gov., 1987-91; mng. dir. Brown Rudnick Freed and Gesmer, Boston, 1991-93; exec. v.p. Blue Cross/Blue Shield of Mass., Boston, 1994—; also bd. dirs. Blue Cross Blue Shield Mass., Boston; vis. pub. policy scholar Radcliffe Coll., 1991; vice chmn./chmn. Nat. Adv. Com. on Oceans and Atmosphere (Presdl. apptd.), 1979-80; bd. dirs. Shawmut Bank of Conn., Fleet Bank of Mass., Fleet Bank of Conn., Fleet Bank R.I. Recipient Disting. Svc. award Nat. Sierra Club, 1978, Nat. Govs. Assn. 1978, Outstanding Citizen award Mass. Audubon Soc., 1978; Harvard U. fellow, 1979-80. Mem. Women Execs. in State Govt. (chair 1987). Democrat. Avocation: jogging. Office: Blue Cross Blue Shield Mass 100 Summer St Boston MA 02110-2104

MURPHY, EWELL EDWARD, JR., lawyer; b. Washington, Feb. 21, 1928; s. Ewell Edward and Lou (Phillips) M.; m. Patricia Bredell Purnell, June 26, 1954 (dec. 1964); children: Michaela, Megan Patricia, Harlan Ewell. B.A., U. Tex., 1946, LL.B., 1948; D.Phil., Oxford U., Eng., 1951. Bar: Tex. 1948. Assoc. Baker & Botts, Houston, 1954-63, ptnr., 1964-93, head internat. dept., 1972-89; pres. Houston World Trade Assn., 1972-74; trustee Southwestern Legal Found., 1978—; chmn. Houston Com. on Fgn. Rels., 1984-85, Inst. Transnat. Arbitration, 1985-89, Internat. and Comparative Law Ctr., 1986-87; mem. J. William Fulbright Fgn. Scholarship Bd., 1991-96, vice chmn., 1992-93, chmn., 1993-95; vis. prof. U. Tex. Law Sch., 1993—; Disting. lectr., U. Houston Law Ctr., 1996—. Contbr. articles to profl. jours. Served to lt. USAF, 1952-54. Recipient Carl H. Fulda award U. Tex. Internat. Law Jour., 1980; Rhodes scholar, 1948-51. Mem. ABA (chmn. sect. internat. law 1970-71), Houston Bar Assn. (chmn. internat. law com. 1963-64, 70-71), Houston C. of C. (chmn. internat. bus. com. 1964, 65), Philos. Soc. Tex., Internat. Law Inst. (bd. dirs. 1994—). Home: 17 W Oak Dr Houston TX 77056-2117 Office: Baker & Botts 3000 One Shell Plz Houston TX 77002-4995

MURPHY, FRANCES LOUISE, II, newspaper publisher; b. Balt.; d. Carl James and L. Vashti (Turley) M.; m. James E. Wood (div.); children: Frances Murphy Wood Draper, James E. Jr., Susan Wood Barnes. BA, U. Wis., 1944; BS, Coppin State Coll., Balt., 1958; MEd, Johns Hopkins U., 1963. City editor Balt. Afro-Am., 1956-57; dir. News Bur., Morgan State Coll., Balt., 1964-71; chmn. bd. dirs. Afro-Am. Newspapers, Balt., 1971-74; assoc. prof. journalism SUNY, Buffalo, 1975-85, Howard U., Washington, 1985-91; editor Washington Afro-Am., 1951-56, pub., 1987—; bd. dirs. Afro-Am. Newspapers, Balt., 1985-87; mem. adv. bd. Partnership Inst., Washington, 1985-91; treas. African Am. Civil War Meml. Freedom Found., African Am. Leadership Summit. Trustee State Colls. Md., 1971-76; bd. dirs. Delta Rsch. and Ednl. Found., 1993-95; nat. bd. dirs. NACCP, 1971-76. Named One of 100 Most Influential Black Ams., Ebony mag., 1973, 74, Disting. Marylander, Gov. State of Md., 1975; recipient Ida B. Wells award Congl. Black Caucus, 1989, Public Svc. award African Methodist Episcopal Ch., 1991, Invaluable Svc. award Martin L. King Jr. Found., 1992, Black Women of Courage award Nat. Fedn. Black Women Bus. Owners, 1993, Black Awareness Ach. award Holy Redeemer Catholic Ch., 1993, Bus. of the Yr. award Bus. and Profl. Women's League, 1993, Oustanding Svc. award Capital Press Club, 1993, Black Conscious Commitment trophy Unity Nation, 1993, Dedicated Cmty. Svc. award Ward I Cmty. and D.C. Pub. Schs., 1994, Women of Strength award Nat. Black Media Coalition, 1994, 95, Outstanding Woman of Yr. award Alpha Gamma chpt. Iota Phi Lambda, 1994, Art Carter Excellence award Capital Press Club, 1994, Excellence in Comm. award Washington Inter-Alumni Coun. United Negro Coll. Fund, 1994, 95, Disting. Cmty. Svc. award The Questers, Inc., 1995, Outstanding Journalist award Masons, 1995, Outstanding Achievement award Beta Zeta chpt. Zeta Phi Beta, 1996, award in recognition of outstanding contbns. made to youth The Soc., 1996, Disting. Black Women award BISA, 1996. Mem. Nat. Newspaper Pubs. Assn. (editl. com. 1987—, Merit award 1987, 89-93), Soc. Profl. Journalists (Disting. Svc. in local journalism award Washington chpt. 1994), Links, Capital Press Club (exec. bd. 1987—, Outstanding Svc. award 1993, Art Carter award of excellence 1994), Delta Sigma Theta (Frances L. Murphy II Comm. award Fed. City Alumnae chpt. 1993, Fortitude Image award Prince George's County chpt. 1994), Kiwanis Club (first woman hon., 1995). Democrat. Episcopalian. Avocation: bridge. Home: 5709 1st St NW Washington DC 20011-2319 Office: Washington Afro-Am 1612 14th St NW Washington DC 20009-4307

MURPHY, FRANCIS, English language educator; b. Springfield, Mass., Mar. 13, 1932; s. Frank Edward and Sarah (O'Connor) M. B.A., Am. Internat. Coll., 1953; M.A., U. Conn., 1955; Ph.D., Harvard U., 1960; LittD (hon.), Am. Internat. Coll., 1986. Mem. faculty English lang. and lit. Smith Coll., 1959—, assoc. prof., 1966-69, prof., 1970—; vis. curator Springfield Mus. Fine Arts, 1975-76, Hudson River Mus., 1983-84. Editor: The Diary of Edward Taylor, 1964, Major Am. Poets, 1967, Form and Structure in Poetry, 1964, Edwin Arlington Robinson, 1970, Walt Whitman, 1969, The Uncollected Essays of Yvor Winters, 1973, The Complete Poems of Walt Whitman, 1975, Of Plymouth Plantation (William Bradford), 1981; author: Willard Leroy Metcalf, 1976, (with Dean Flower) A Catalogue of American Paintings, Water Colors and Drawings (to 1923) in the G.W.V. Smith Museum, 1976, The Landscape Within: J. Francis Murphy, 1982, The Book of Nature: American Painters and the Natural Sublime, 1983; co-editor: Norton Anthology of American Literature, 1979—, Mass. Rev., 1966-67.

MURPHY, FRANCIS SEWARD, journalist; b. Portland, Oreg., Sept. 9, 1914; s. Francis H. and Blanche (Livesay) M.; BA, Reed Coll., 1936; m. Clare Eastham Cooke, Sept. 20, 1974. With The Oregonian, Portland, 1936-79, TV editor, Behind the Mike columnist, 1952-79. Archeol. explorer Mayan ruins, Yucatan, Mex., 1950—, mem. Am. Quintana Roo Expdn., 1965, 66, 68. With AUS, 1942-46. Author: Dragon Mask Temples in Central Yucatan, 1988. Mem. Royal Asiatic Soc., City Club (bd. govs. 1950, 64-66), Explorers Club, Am. Club of Hong Kong, Oreg. Hist. Soc. Democrat. Congregationalist. Home: 4213 NE 32nd Ave Portland OR 97211-7149

MURPHY, GEORGE, special effects expert. Computer graphics artist/supervisor Industrial Light & Magic, San Rafael, CA. Films include: Hook, 1991, Death Becomes Her, 1992, Jurassic Park, 1993, Forrest Gump, 1994 (Acad. award best visual effects, Brit. Acad. Film and TV award for best visual effects 1994), Mission Impossible, 1995, Congo, 1995. Mem. Acad. Motion Picture Arts and Scis. (visual effects br.). Office: care ILM PO Box 2459 3160 Kerner Blvd San Rafael CA 94912

MURPHY, GEORGE AUSTIN, justice; b. Bklyn., Mar. 16, 1923; s. Frank V. and Catherine L. (Milroy) M.; m. Teresa Marie Short, July 3, 1952; children: Michael, Timothy, Terence, Mary, James, Maureen, Christopher, Marjorie, Paul. LLB, St. John's U., N.Y.C., 1949; BS, Fordham U., 1951. Bar: N.Y. 1949, U.S. Dist. Ct. (so. and ea. dists.) N.Y. 1951, U.S. Supreme Ct. 1956. Sole practice, Freeport, N.Y., 1949-52, Seaford, N.Y., 1956-69; mem. Kelly, McDonald, Deeley & Murphy, Freeport, 1953-55, Sullivan, Rowley & Murphy, 1970-78; justice N.Y. State Supreme Ct. 10th Jud. Dist., Mineola, 1979—. Councilman, Town of Hempstead (N.Y.), 1963-71; mem. N.Y. State Senate, 1971-72, N.Y. State Assembly, 1973-78. Served to lt. U.S. Army, 1943-46, ETO, CBI; maj. Res. ret. Mem. Nassau County Bar Assn., Nassau Lawyers Assn., Catholic Lawyers Assn., Am. Legion. Roman Catholic. Lodges: K.C., Elks. Office: Supreme Court Supreme Court Building Mineola NY 11501

MURPHY, GEORGE EARL, psychiatrist, educator; b. Portland, Oreg., Oct. 17, 1922; s. George Earl and Mary Ella (Wilcox) M.; m. Amanda Daniel, Mar. 24, 1976; children: Paul Douglas, Bruce Kevin. Student, U. Wash., 1940-42, U. Portland, 1946-47; BS, Oreg. State U., 1949; MD, Washington U., St. Louis, 1952. Diplomate Am. Bd. Psychiatry and Neurology. Intern Alameda County Hosp., Oakland, Calif., 1952-53, asst. resident in medicine, 1953-54; fellow in psychosomatic medicine Washington U., St. Louis, 1954-55; asst. resident in psychiatry Mass. Gen. Hosp., Boston, 1955-56, Washington U., St. Louis, 1956-57; instr. sch. of medicine Washington U., 1957-59, asst. prof. sch. of medicine, 1959-66, assoc. prof. sch. of medicine, 1966-69, prof. sch. of medicine, 1969-90, prof. emeritus psychiatry, 1990—; dir. psychiatry clinic Washington U., 1976-90, psychiat. student health, 1978-83, coursemaster human sexuality, 1978-90. Author: Suicide in Alcoholism, 1992; contbr. articles to profl. jours. Recipient Rsch. award for Advances in Suicide Prevention, Am. Suicide Found., 1994; Louis I. Dublin award for rsch. in suicide Am. Assn. Suicidology, 1995; NIMH grantee, 1963-83, 85-88. Fellow Am. Psychiat. Assn. (life); mem. Internat. Assn. for Suicide Prevention, Am. Psychopathological assn., Sigma Xi. Avocation: archaeology of the bronze age. Office: Washington U Sch Medicine Dept Psychiatry 4940 Childrens Pl Saint Louis MO 63110-1002

MURPHY, GEORGE WILLIAM, insurance executive; b. Yonkers, N.Y., Sept. 27, 1941; s. George William and Virginia Rose (Byrne) M.; m. Catherine Anne Scully, Sept. 26, 1964; children: Peggy Anne, Timothy Patrick. BBA in Acctg., St. John's U., Jamaica, N.Y., 1964. CPA, N.Y. Sr. acct. Price Waterhouse, N.Y.C., 1965-69; treas. SwissRe Corp., N.Y.C.,

1969; sr. v.p., treas. SwissRe Advisers, Inc., N.Y.C., 1969-89; treas. NARe Life Mgmt. Co., Inc., 1971-90, SwissRe Life Ins. Co., 1979-90, SR Geothermal, Inc., N.Y.C., 1981-90, Swiss-Am Reassurance Co., SwissRe Mgmt. Co., Swiss Reinsurance Co., Inc., N.Am. Reassurance Co., N.Am. Reinsurance Corp., 1981, Surety Support Svcs., Inc., Downers Grove, Ill., 1984; v.p. N.Am. Splty Ins. Co., Manchester, N.H., 1985; treas. SwissRe Svcs., Inc., Elmsford, N.Y., 1987, Western Atlantic Reinsurance Corp., Western Atlantic Mgmt. Corp., N.Y.C., 1988; exec. v.p., treas., COO SwissRe Holding(N.A.) Inc., N.Y.C., 1989-94; pres. SwissRe Leasing Inc., 1990, GT Holding Corp., 1990; treas. Alpine Life Ins. Co., Westport, Conn., 1991. Mem. AICPA, N.Y. State Soc. CPAs, Fin. Execs. Inst., Am.-Swiss Assn. (bd. dirs. 1991—). Roman Catholic. Avocation: jogging. Office: Lee-Nolan Assocs 1001 Franklin Ave Garden City NY 11530-2901

MURPHY, GERALD, government official; b. Washington, Aug. 25, 1938; s. Jeremiah T. and Jean (Curley) M.; m. Kathryn Beckman, Sept. 24, 1988; children by previous marriage: William Michael, Janet Marie, Kathleen Anne. B.C.S. with honors, Benjamin Franklin U., Washington, 1960, M.C.S., 1963. C.P.A., D.C. Dep. div. dir. Dept. Treasury, Washington, 1970-71, div. dir., 1971-74, asst. commr., 1974-75, dep. commr., 1975-79, dep. fiscal asst. sec., 1979-86; fiscal asst. sec. Dept. Treasury, 1986—; lectr. in acctg. Southeastern U., Washington, 1965-70, Dept. Agr. Grad. Sch., Washington, 1970-76; mem. Govt. Acctg. Standards Adv. Council, 1984-89; mem. Fed. Acctg. Standards Adv. Bd., 1991—. Served with U.S. Army, 1956. Recipient Meritorious Svc. award Dept. Treasury, 1972, Treasury Honor award, 1983, Pres.'s Rank award, 1992, Disting. Alumni award Benjamin Franklin U., Washington, 1976. Mem. Am. Inst. C.P.A.s, Assn. Govt. Accts. (nat. pres. 1977-78, Robert W. King award 1983), Sr. Execs. Assn., Fed. Exec. Inst. Alumni Assn. Roman Catholic. Office: Dept Treasury 15th & Pennsylvania Ave NW Washington DC 20220

MURPHY, GERALD PATRICK, urologist, educator; b. Harve, Mont., July 16, 1934; s. Francis J. and Margaret H. (Dolan) M.; m. Mary Bridget Cunningham, June 20, 1959; children: Anne Marie, Margaret, George, Maureen, Bridget, Gerald. B.Sc. summa cum laude, Seattle U., 1955; M.D., U. Wash., 1959; D.Sc., St. Thomas Inst., 1971, St. John's U., Jamaica, N.Y., 1979; LL.D., Niagara U., 1973; Litt.D., St. Bonaventure U., 1977; LLD (hon.), Daemon Coll., 1984, St. Thomas Inst., 1985. Diplomate Am. Bd. Urology. Buswell research fellow dept. urology U. Rochester, N.Y., 1959; intern in surgery Johns Hopkins Hosp., Balt., 1959-60; jr. asst. resident in urology Brady Urol. Inst., 1960-61, fellow in urology, 1964-65, sr. asst. resident in urology, 1964-65, chief resident, 1966-67, asst. prof. urology, 1968; asst. resident in surgery and urology Balt. City Hosp., 1961-62; research assoc., chief dept. surg. physiology Walter Reed Army Inst. Research, Washington, 1962-64; assoc. dir. clin. affairs Roswell Park Meml. Inst., Buffalo, 1968-70, chief dept urology, 1968-71, inst. dir., 1970-85, chief dept. exptl. surgery, 1968-85; assoc. prof. urology SUNY-Buffalo, 1968-70, prof., 1971-88, research prof. exptl. pathology Grad. Sch., 1972-88, 1st William J. Staubitz vis. prof. urology, 1982; group v.p. med. afairs Am. Cancer Soc., Atlanta, 1988—; prof. biology Niagara U., 1968-88; mem. adv. council N.Y. State Coll. Vet. Medicine, 1975-81, from 1982; exec. dir. Health Research Council of N.Y. State, 1975-87; sec.-gen. Internat. Union against Cancer, from 1974; mem. bd. sci. affairs Delta Regional Primate Research Ctr. (Tulane U.), 1979-81; also mem. various other profl. adv. bds.; cons. in field; trustee Damon Runyon-Walter Winchell Cancer Fund, 1979-88, v.p., bd. dirs., 1983; dir. nat. prostatic cancer project Nat. Cancer Inst., 1972-87; vis. prof. surgery U. Stellenbosch, Bellville, Cape Province, South Africa, 1967-68; dir.-at- large Am. Cancer Soc., 1972-88, pres., 1983, mem. exec. com. N.Y. State div, 1975-77, from 1978, pres. N.Y. State div, 1974-75, bd. dirs. N.Y. State div, 1978-88; mem. adv. council Gen. Motors Cancer Research Found., 1982—; mem. staff Ga. Bapt. Hosp., Atlanta; prof. urology Emory U., Atlanta; dir. rsch. Pac. Northwest Cancer Foundation, Seattle; moderator Tumor Progression and Heterogeneity, 39th Ann. Gordon Conf. on Cancer, New London, N.H., 1985; mem. CALSPAN/UB Research Ctr., Buffalo, 1986; John Kline Meml. lectr. U. Soc. Calif. Med. Ctr., 1991. Mem. editorial bd. Yearbook of Cancer, 1968—, Jour. Medicine, Clin. and Exptl., 1970—, Urol. Survey, 1972-89, Internat. Jour. Cancer, 1975-86, Cancer Bull. of M.D. Anderson Hosp., 1977-89, Current Surgery, 1978-84, Onkologie, 1978—, Oncology Times, 1980-90, Anticancer Research, 1980—, Neoplasia, 1983—, Current Opinion in Urology, 1991, Jour. Psychosocial Oncology, 1991—; editor in chief Jour. Surg. Oncology, 1979—, Seminars in Surgical Oncology, 1977—, The Prostate, 1979—, Ca-A Cancer Jour. for Clinicians, 1990—; mem. editorial adv. bd. Cancer, 1971—, Jour. Exptl. and Clin. Cancer Research, 1982—; cons. editor Urology, 1972—; editor Jour. Med. Primatology, 1973—, Oncology, 1975—; assoc. editor N.Y. State Jour. Medicine, 1973-85, Cancer jour., 1990—; corr. editor: Afican Jour. Medicine and Med. Sci., 1976; mem. internat. editorial rev. bd. King Faisal Specialist Hosp. Med. Jour., 1981-85; mem. internat. editorial adv. bd. Arab Jour. Medicine, 1982-85; mem. sci. rev. com. Florence Jour. Surgery, 1983—. V.p., bd. dirs. James Ewing Found., 1981-85. Served with M.C. U.S. Army, 1962-64. Recipient Schwentker award Johns Hopkins Hosp., 1962; recipient Heath Meml. award U. Tex. Cancer Ctr., M.D. Anderson Hosp. and Tumor Inst., 1978, cert. of appreciation for notable service in helping to save lives from cancer N.Y. State div. Am. Cancer Soc., 1982, Pro Pontifice et Ecclesia papal medal, 1982, silver medal Scientia Vincere Tenebras European Orgn. for Research and Treatment of Cancer, Brussels, 1982, Pub. Service award Alumni Assn. SUNY, 1984, Buffalonian of Yr. award, 1985, Disting. Alumnus award U. Wash. Sch. Med., 1985, Bronze Medal Nat. Hungarian Cancer Congress Com., 14th Internat. Cancer Congress, 1986, award in recognition contbns. to UB community for instn. new biotech. program CALSPAN/UB Research Ctr., 1986, Outstanding Alumnus award Seattle U., 1991, Isaac R. Lindley award Peruvian Cancer Soc., 1991. Mem. ACS (sr. mem. Commn. on Cancer 1978—), Am. Urol. Assn. (registry genitourinary pathology 1975-85), Am. Cancer Soc. N.Y. State divsn. (hon. life), Assn. Am. Cancer Insts. (pres. 1979-80, chmn. bd. dirs. 1980-81), N.Y. State Cancer Program Assn. (pres. 1982-83), Soc. Surg. Oncology (pres. 1982-83, chmn. exec. council 1983-84, Lucy Wortham James Basic Rsch. award 1991), Johns Hopkins Med. and Surg. Assn., Am. Soc. Nephrology, Internat. Soc. Nephrology, Soc. Univ. Urologists, Buffalo Urol. Soc. (ann. award for outstanding contbns. to urology 1983), Soc. Univ. Surgeons, Am. Fedn. Clin. Research, N.Y. Acad. Scis., Buffalo Acad. Medicine, Am. Assn. Cancer Research, AMA, Assn. Genito-Urinary Surgeons, N.Y. State Soc. Surgeons, N.E. Soc. Clin. Oncology, Am. Surg. Assn., Am. Soc. Clin. Oncology, Am. Radium Soc., Buffalo Urol. Soc. (hon. life), Alpha Omega Alpha (hon.). Home: 1134 23rd Ave E Seattle WA 98112-3521 Office: Pac. Northwest Cancer Foundation 120 Northgate Plaza Ste 205 Seattle WA 98125*

MURPHY, GLORIA WALTER, novelist, screenwriter; b. Hartford, Conn., Feb. 22, 1940; d. Frank and Elizabeth (Lemkin) Walter; m. Joseph S. Murphy; children: William Gitelman, Laurie Gitelman, Daniel Gitelman, Julie Gitelman, Caitlin Fleck. Student, No. Essex Community Coll., Haverhill, Mass., 1979-81, Boston U., 1981-82. Columnist Pandora's Box The Peabody (Mass.) Times, 1975; columnist Murphy's Law The Methuen (Mass.) News, 1979. Author: Nightshade, 1986, Bloodties, 1987, Nightmare, 1987, The Playroom, 1987, Cry of the Mouse, 1991, Down Will Come Baby, 1991, A Whisper in the Attic, 1992, A Shadow on the Stair, 1993, Simon Says, 1994 (CBS-TV movie Summer of Fear based on this novel 1996), A Stranger in the House, 1995. Mem. Mystery Writers Am., Authors Guild. Address: PO Box 670 Ringwood NJ 07456-0670

MURPHY, GORDON JOHN, engineering educator; b. Milw., Feb. 16, 1927; s. Gordon M. and Cecelia A. (Knerr) M.; m. Dorothy F. Brautigam, June 26, 1948; children—Lynne, Craig. B.S., Milw. Sch. Engring., 1949; M.S., U. Wis., 1952; Ph.D., U. Minn., 1956. Asst. prof. elec. engring. Milw. Sch. Engring., 1949-51; systems engr. A C Spark Plug div. Gen. Motors Corp., 1951-52, cons., 1959-62; instr. U. Minn., 1952-56, asst. prof. elec. engring., 1956-57; faculty Northwestern U., Evanston, Ill., 1957—; prof. Northwestern U., 1960—, head dept. elec. engring., 1960-69, dir. Lab. for Design of Electronic Systems, 1987—; cons. numerous corps., 1959—; founder, 1st chmn. Mpls. chpt. Inst. Radio Engrs. Profl. Group on Automatic Control, 1956-57, Chgo. chpt., 1959-61. Author: Basic Automatic Control Theory, 1957, 2d edit., 1966, Control Engineering, 1959; contbr. articles, papers to profl. jours.; patentee TV, electronic timers, periodontal instruments and motion control systems. Mem. indsl. adv. com. Milw. Sch. Engring., 1971—. Served with USNR, 1945-46. Recipient ECE Centennial medal U. Wis., Outstanding Alumnus award Milw. Sch. Engring. Alumni Assn.; named One of Chgo.'s Ten Outstanding Young Men Chgo. Jr. C. of C. Fellow IEEE (for edn. and rsch. in automatic control); mem. feedback control systems com. 1960-68, discrete systems com. 1962-68, adminstrv. com. profl. group on automatic control 1966-69, chmn. membership and nominating coms. 1966-67); mem. Am. Automatic Control Coun. (edn. com. 1967-69), Engr.'s Coun. for Profl. Devel. (guidance com. 1967-69), Nat. Electronic Conf. (bd. dirs. 1983-85), Am. Electronics Assn. (exec. com. M.W. coun. 1990-93), Sigma Xi, Eta Kappa Nu, Tau Beta Pi. Home: 638 Garden Ct Glenview IL 60025-4105 Office: Northwestern U Elec Engring Dept Evanston IL 60208

MURPHY, GORDON LAURENCE, insurance company executive; b. Stamford, Conn., Feb. 2, 1935; s. Dennis Joseph Sr. and Carolyn Gertrude (Fessenden) M.; m. Rosemary Elizabeth Engel; 1 child, Erin Maureen. BA with honors, Williams Coll., 1963; postgrad., Northwestern U., 1964. Group sales Conn. Gen. Life Ins. Co., Bloomfield, 1964-68, group adminstr., 1968-71, asst. sec. group underwriting, 1971-75, sec. corp. controllers, 1975-78; 2d v.p. field ops. Aetna Ins. Co., Hartford, Conn., 1978-82; sr. v.p. agy. div. INA/Aetna-CIGNA P&C Group, Phila., 1982-84; pres. Life Ins. Co. of N.A., Phila., 1984-92; chmn. bd. dirs. INA Life Ins. Co. N.Y., 1992—. Served to sgt. U.S. Army, 1954-59. Avocations: hiking, reading, duplicate bridge, white-water rafting, hunting. Home: PO Box 668 Wolfeboro NH 03894-0668

MURPHY, GREGORY GERARD, lawyer; b. Helena, Mont., Feb. 3, 1954; s. Michael Anthony and Elizabeth (Cooney) M.; m. Katherine Joan Koch, Dec. 30, 1977; children: Megan, Brian, Allison. BA, U. Mont., 1976; JD, U. Notre Dame, 1979. Bar: Oreg. 1979, U.S. Dist. Ct. Oreg. 1979, U.S. Ct. Appeals (9th cir.) 1979, Mont. 1980, U.S. Dist. Ct. Mont. 1980. Clk. to judge U.S. Ct. Appeals (9th cir.), Portland, 1979-80; assoc. Moulton, Bellingham, Longo & Mather P.C., Billings, Mont., 1980-84; shareholder Moulton, Bellingham, Longo & Mather, P.C., Billings, Mont., 1984—; trustee Mont. dist. U.S. Bankruptcy Ct., 1982-85; examiner Mont. Bd. Bar Examiners, 1990-95, chmn. 1995—; trustee Nat. Conf. Bar Examiners, 1990—, mem. multistate bar exam. com., 1986-94, chmn. 1994—. Assoc. editor Notre Dame Law Rev., 1978-79. Bd. dirs. Billings Symphony Soc., 1982-91, French hornist, 1981—. Thomas and Alberta White scholar U. Notre Dame, 1978-79. Mem. Mont. Bar Assn., Oreg. Bar Assn., Am. Law Inst., Yellowstone County Bar Assn., Rotary. Roman Catholic. Avocations: french horn, golf, camping. Home: 5533 Gene Sarazen Dr Billings MT 59106 Office: Moulton Bellingham et al PO Box 2559 Billings MT 59103-2559

MURPHY, GRETA WERWATH, retired college official; b. Milw., Aug. 24, 1910; d. Oscar and Johanna (Seelhorst) Werwath; m. John Heery Murphy, Sept. 18, 1941. Ed. Ohio State U., 1943-45; PhD in Comms. (hon.) Milw. Sch. Engring., 1993 . With Milw. Sch. Engring., 1928—, head admissions dept., 1931-42, dir. pub. rels, 1945-66, v.p. pub. rels. and devel., 1966-77, v.p., cons., 1978—, regent emeritus, 1985—. Mem. Milw. County Planning Commn., 1966—, vice chmn., 1974-75, chmn., 1976-77. Fellow Pub. Rels. Soc. Am. (founder, past pres. Wis. chpt.); mem. Am. Coll. Pub. Rels. Assn. (past dir., sec., trustee), Women's Advt. Club (pres.). Club: Womans of Wis. Home: 1032 Malaga Ave Miami FL 33134-6319 also: 5562 Cedar Bch S Belgium WI 53004-9646

MURPHY, HAROLD LOYD, federal judge; b. Haralson County, Ga., Mar. 31, 1927; s. James Loyd and Georgia Gladys (McBrayer) M.; m. Jacqueline Marie Ferri, Dec. 20, 1958; children: Mark Harold, Paul Bailey. Student, West Ga. Coll., 1944-45, U. Miss., 1945-46; LL.B., U. Ga., 1949. Bar: Ga. 1949. Pvt. practice Buchanan, Ga., from 1949; ptnr. Howe & Murphy, Buchanan and Tallapoosa, Ga., 1958-71; judge Superior Cts., Tallapoosa Circuit, 1971-77; U.S. dist. judge No. Dist. of Ga., Rome, 1977—; rep. Gen. Assembly of Ga., 1951-61; asst. solicitor gen. Tallapoosa Jud. Circuit, 1956; mem. Jud. Qualifications Commn., State of Ga., 1977. With USNR, 1945-46. Fellow Am. Bar Found.; mem. ABA, Ga. Bar Assn., Dist. Judges Assn. for 11th Cir. Bar Assn., Am. Judicature Soc., Tallapoosa Cir. Bar Assn., Old War Horse Lawyers Club, Am. Inns Ct. (past pres. Joseph Henry Lumpkin sect.), Fed. Judges Assn. (exec. com.). Methodist. Home: 321 Georgia Highway 120 Tallapoosa GA 30176-3114 Office: US Dist Ct PO Box 53 Rome GA 30162-0053

MURPHY, HELEN, recording industry executive; b. Glasgow, Scotland, Oct. 2, 1962; came to U.S., 1990; d. Francis and Kathleen (Gallagher) M.; m. Michael Christopher Luksha, Apr. 1, 1989. BA in Econs. with honors, U. Guelph, Can., 1982; MBA, U. Western Ontario, Can., 1984. CFA. Asst. mgr. securities rsch. Confederation Life, Toronto, Can., 1984-86; sr. analyst entertainment & merchandising Prudential Bache Securities, Toronto, Can., 1986-89; v.p. rsch. Richardson Greenshields Can., Toronto, 1989-90; v.p. investor rels. Polygram Records Inc., N.Y.C., 1990-91, v.p., treas., 1991-92, sr. v.p. corp. fin., treas., 1992-95; sr. v.p. investor rels. PolyGram Internat. Ltd., N.Y.C., 1995—; sr. v.p. mergers and acquisitions PolyGram Holding, Inc., N.Y.C., 1995—; lectr. U. Guelph, 1982-90. Fellow Nat. Investor Rels. Inst., N.Y. Soc. Security Analysts, N.Y. Treas. Group. Office: Polygram Records Inc 825 8th Ave New York NY 10019-7416

MURPHY, JAMES E., public relations and marketing executive. Degree in Journalism, U. Ill. Sr. corp. comms. officer Owens-Corning Fiberglas, Beatrice, Merrill Lynch; exec. v.p. Burson-Marsteller, vice chmn., 1990; chmn., CEO Burson-Marsteller, N.Y., 1991-93; pres. Murphy & Co., 1993—; mng. dir. worldwide mktg. and comm. Andersen Cons., 1993—. Mem. bd. advisors Medill Sch. Journalism, Northwestern U.; mem. adv. bd. Coll. Bus. and Commerce, U. Ill., also mem. devel. bd. Coll. Comm. Mem. Inst. Pub. Rels. Rsch. (trustee), Sky Club, Union League Club, Belle Haven Club, Woodway Country Club, Palmetto Golf Club, Preston Mountain Club. Office: Andersen Cons c/o Andersen Cons. 1345 Ave of Americas New York NY 10105

MURPHY, JAMES LEE, college dean, economics educator; b. Detroit, Feb. 14, 1939; s. Philip E. and Julie T. M.; m. Linda J. Masson, July 31, 1965; children—Janel K., John R. B.S., Spring Hill Coll., 1961; M.S., Purdue U., 1963, Ph.D., 1964. Asst. prof. econs. U. N.C., Chapel Hill, 1964-67, assoc. prof., 1967-72, prof., 1972—, chmn. dept., 1975-85, dir. summer session, 1987-88, dean summer sch., 1988—; vis. prof. Thammasat U., Bangkok, Thailand, 1968-69, Econs. Inst., U. Colo., Boulder, 1979, U. New South Wales, Sydney, Australia, 1980, overseas program U. Utah, 1974; cons. in field, 1968—. Author: Introductory Econometrics, 1973, Introductory Statistical Analysis, 1975, 2d edit., 1980, Spanish lang. edit., 1987, Statistical Analysis for Business and Economics, 1985, Statistical Analysis, 1993. NDEA fellow, 1961-64; NSF grantee, 1969-71. Mem. Am. Econ. Assn., So. Econ. Assn., Assn. Univ. Summer Sessions, N.Am. Assn. Summer Sessions. Republican. Roman Catholic. Office: U NC Dept Econs Gardner Hall Campus Box 3305 Chapel Hill NC 27599-3305

MURPHY, JAMES PAUL, lawyer; b. Jackson, Tenn., Apr. 29, 1944; s. Paul Joseph and Marjorie Mary (Smyth) M.; m. Marcia Mae Gaughan, Sept. 5, 1975. B.A., U. Notre Dame, 1966; J.D., U. Mich., 1969. Bar: Ohio 1969, D.C. 1984, Md. 1984, U.S. Dist. Ct. (no. dist.) Ohio 1970, U.S. Ct. Appeals (6th cir.) 1972, U.S. Supreme Ct. 1976, U.S. Dist. Ct. Md., 1984, U.S. Dist. Ct. D.C., 1984, U.S. Dist. Ct. of Appeals (4th cir., D.C. cir.) 1984. Vol. VISTA, 1969-70; assoc. Squire, Sanders & Dempsey, Cleve., 1970-79, ptnr., 1979—. Mem. ABA (litigation, antitrust sects.), Cleve. Bar Assn. (fed. ct. com.), Md. Bar Assn., D.C. Bar Assn., Ohio State Bar Assn. (antitrust sect.). Clubs: Westwood Country (Rocky River, Ohio), City (Washington). Home: 4512 Wetherill Rd Bethesda MD 20816-1837 Office: Squire Sanders & Dempsey PO Box 407 1201 Pennsylvania Ave NW Washington DC 20004-2401

MURPHY, JANET GORMAN, college president; b. Holyoke, Mass., Jan. 10, 1937; d. Edwin Daniel and Catherine Gertrude (Hennessey) Gorman. B.A., U. Mass., 1958, postgrad. 1960-61, Ed.D., 1974, LL.D. (hon.) 1984; M.Ed., Boston U., 1961. Tchr. English and history John J. Lynch Jr. High Sch., Holyoke, 1958-60; tchr. English, Chestnut Jr. High Sch., Springfield, Mass., 1961-63; instr. English and journalism Our Lady of Elms Coll., Chicopee, 1963-64; mem. staff Mass. State Coll., Lyndonville, Vt., 1977-83; pres. Mo. Western State Coll., St. Joseph, 1983—. Mem. campaign staff Robert F Kennedy Presdl. Campaign, 1967. Recipient John Gunther Tchr. award NEA, 1961, award Women's Opportunity Com., Boston Fed. Exec. Bd., 1963, Phi Delta Kappa Educator of Yr. award NAACP, 1992; named one of 10 Outstanding Young Leaders of Greater Boston Area, Boston Jr. C. of C., 1973. Office: Mo Western State Coll Office of the President 4525 Downs Dr Saint Joseph MO 64507-2246

MURPHY, JENNY LEWIS, special education educator; b. Trenton, Mo., Sept. 6, 1947; d. Homer Lewis and Betty Jo (Jennings) Kidd; mm. Larry D. Murphy, July 2, 1971; children: Daniel Joe, Jaclyn Kate. BS in Elem. Edn., Cen. Mo. State U., 1969. Cert. elem. tchr., severe devel. delayed edn., Mo. Tchr. severely handicapped Mo. State Sch., Chillicothe, 1981-84; dir., tchr. Grundy County Learning Ctr., Trenton, 1984-86; tchr., dir. spl. svcs. Livingston County R-III schs., Chula, Mo., 1986—; curriculum developer for ind. living State Schs. Mo. Mem. com. Trenton Handicap Bd., 1984-86; v.p. adv. bd. Ret. Sr. Vol. Program, Trenton, 1984-86. Mem. Coun. for Exceptional Children (children-mental retardation divsn. 1986—, profl. devel. com. 1991-94), Mo. Tchrs. Assn., N.E. Mo. Local Adminstrs. Spl. Edn., Classroom Tchrs. Assn. (v.p. 1988-89, sec. 1994-95. Democrat. Methodist. Home: RR 3 Box 82 Trenton MO 64683-9517 Office: Livingston County R-III Sch PO Box 40 Chula MO 64635-0040

MURPHY, JILL, public relations executive; b. Fla., May 2, 1962. BA in Journalism, Ohio Wesleyan U., 1985. With Rand Pub. Rels., 1985-89; v.p. Shandwick N.Am., N.Y.C., 1990—. Office: Shandwick NAm Inc 666 3rd Ave New York NY 10017-4011*

MURPHY, JOHN ARTHUR, tobacco, food and brewing company executive; b. N.Y.C., Dec. 15, 1929; s. John A. and Mary J. (Touhy) M.; m. Carole Ann Paul, June 28, 1952; children: John A., Kevin P., Timothy M., Kellyann, Robert B., Kathleen. B.S., Villanova U., 1951; J.D., Columbia U., 1954. Bar: N.Y. 1954. Since practiced in N.Y.C.; ptnr. firm Conboy Hewitt O'Brien & Boardman, 1954-62; asst. gen. counsel Philip Morris Co. Inc., N.Y.C., 1962-66, v.p., 1967-76, exec. v.p., 1976-78, group exec. v.p., 1978-84, pres., 1984-91, vice chmn., 1991-92, also bd. dirs.; asst. to pres. Philip Morris Internat., 1966-67, exec. v.p., 1967-71; pres., chief exec. officer Miller Brewing Co., Milw., 1971-78, chmn. bd., chief exec. officer, 1978-84. Trustee North Shore Univ. Hosp., Marquette U., 1973-91; mem. exec. com. Keep Am. Beautiful, Inc.; mem. bd. consultors Sch. Law Villanova U.; mem. bus. com. Met. Mus. Art. Decorated Knight of Malta. Mem. ABA, N.Y. State Bar Assn. Office: Philip Morris Cos Inc 100 Park Ave New York NY 10017-5516

MURPHY, JOHN CARTER, economics educator; b. Ft. Worth, July 17, 1921; s. Joe Preston and Rachel Elsie (Carter) M.; m. Dorothy Elise Haldi, May 1, 1949; children: Douglas C., Barbara E. Student, Tex. Christian U., 1939-41; BA, North Tex. State U., 1943, BS, 1946; AM, U. Chgo., 1949, PhD, 1955; postgrad., U. Copenhagen, 1952-53. Instr. Ill. Inst. Tech., 1947-50; instr. to assoc. prof. Washington U., St. Louis, 1950-62; vis. prof. So. Meth. U., Dallas, 1961, prof., 1962-90, prof. emeritus, 1990—, dir. grad. studies in econs., 1963-68, chmn. dept., 1968-71, faculty summer program in Oxford, 1982-91, dir., 1991, pres. faculty senate, 1988-89, co-dir. Insts. on Internat. Fin., 1982-87; vis. prof. Bologna (Italy) Ctr., Sch. Advanced Internat. Studies, Johns Hopkins U., 1961-62; UN tech. assistance expert, Egypt, 1964; vis. prof., spl. field staff Rockefeller Found., Thammasat U., Bangkok, 1966-67; sr. staff economist Coun. Econ. Advisers, 1971-72, U.S. dels. econ. policy com. and working party III OECD, 1971-72, U.S. del. 8th meeting Joint U.S.-Japan Econ. Com., 1971; cons. Washington U. Internat. Econs. Rsch. Project, 1950-53, U.S. Treasury, 1972, Fed. Res. Bank Dallas, 1994—; referee NSF; witness and referee congl. coms.; lectr. USIA Program, Germany, 1961-62, 84, Philippines, South Viet Nam, Thailand, 1972, France, Belgium, 1984; lectr. Southwestern and Midwestern Grad. Sch. Banking; adj. scholar Am. Enterprise Inst. for Pub. Policy Rsch., 1976—. Author: The International Monetary System: Beyond the First Stage of Reform, 1979; (with R.R. Rubottom) Spain and the U.S.: Since World War II, 1984; editor: Money in the International Order, 1964; contbr. articles to profl. books and jours. Chmn. rsch. com. on internat. conflict and peace Washington U., 1959-61; lectr. mgmt. tng. programs Southwestern Bell Telephone Co., 1961-66, St. Louis Coun. on Econ. Edn., 1958-61; mem. regional selection com. H.S. Truman Fellowships, 1976-89; pres. Dallas Economists, 1981, Town and Gown of Dallas, 1980-81; mem. Dallas Com. on Fgn. Rels. Lt. USNR, 1943-46. Decorated Silver Star; Fulbright scholar to Denmark, 1952-53; Ford Found. Faculty Research fellow, 1957-58; U.S.-Spanish Joint Com. for Cultural Affairs fellow, 1981; Sr. Fulbright lectr. Italy, 1961-62. Mem. Am. Econ. Assn., So. Econ. Assn. (bd. editors Jour. 1969-71), Midwest Econ. Assn., Am. Fin. Assn., Soc. Internat. Devel., Peace Rsch. Soc., Southwestern Social Sci. Assn. (pres. econs. sect. 1971-72), AAUP (chpt. pres. 1964-65). Home: 10530 Somerton Dr Dallas TX 75229-5323 Office: So Meth Univ Dept Econs Dallas TX 75275

MURPHY, JOHN CONDRON, JR., lawyer; b. Mpls., May 26, 1945; s. John Condron and Elaine Anne (Wentink) M.; m. Marie Antoinette Calcara, Aug. 17, 1968; children: Justin Peter, Jonathan Patrick. AB cum laude, Georgetown U., Washington, 1967; JD cum laude, U. Pa., 1972. Bar: Calif. 1972, D.C. 1978. Assoc. O'Melveny & Myers, L.A., 1972-75; spl. counsel U.S Securities & Exch. Commn., Washington, 1975-77; assoc. Cleary, Gottlieb, Steen & Hamilton, Washington, 1977-81, ptnr., 1982-84, 87—; gen. counsel Fed. Deposit Ins. Corp., Washington, 1984-87. Mem. bd. editors Banking Expansion Reporter, 1988—. editorial adv. bd. Bank Atty., 1988—; contbr. articles to profl. jours. Lt. j.g. USN, 1968-69. Mem. ABA (subcom. chmn. banking law com., chmn. acquisitions and dispositions subcom. 1992-95), Fed. Bar Assn. (chmn. banking law com. 1992-94), Columbia Country Club (Chevy Chase, Md.). Republican. Roman Catholic. Home: 6 Newlands St Chevy Chase MD 20815-4202 Office: Cleary Gottlieb et al 1752 N St NW Washington DC 20036-2806

MURPHY, JOHN CULLEN, illustrator; b. N.Y.C., May 3, 1919; s. Robert Francis and Jane (Finn) M.; m. Katherine Joan Byrne, July 14, 1951; children: John Cullen, Mary Cullene, Katherine Siobhan, Joan Byrne, Robert Finn, Brendan Woods, Cait Naughton, Mairead Walsh. Student, Phoenix Art Inst., Chgo. Art Inst., Art Students League, N.Y.C. Illustrator: numerous mags. including Colliers, 1946-51; illustrator: comic strip King Features Syndicate, 1950-69, Prince Valiant, King Features Syndicate, 1970—; Illustrator numerous books. Co-founder of The Wild Geese (an Irish-Am. Cultural Assn.). Maj. U.S. Army, 1941-46. Decorated Bronze star. Recipient 6 Best Story Strip Artist awards Nat. Cartoonists Soc., 1988. Mem. Nat. Cartoonists Soc. (pres., Best Story Strip Cartoonist award (6), Segar award 1983), Soc. Illustrators, Artists and Writers Assn. Roman Catholic. Club: Dutch Treat. Office: care King Features Syndicate Inc 235 E 45th St New York NY 10017-3305

MURPHY, JOHN JOSEPH, manufacturing company executive; b. Olean, N.Y., Nov. 24, 1931; s. John Joseph and Mary M.; m. Louise John; children: Kathleen A. Murphy Bell, Karen L. Murphy Rochelli, Patricia L. Murphy Smith, Michael J. AAS in Mech. Engring., Rochester Inst. Tech., 1952; MBA, So. Meth. U. Engr. Clark div. Dresser Industries, Olean, 1952-67; gen. mgr. roots blower div. Dresser Industries, Connersville, Ind., 1967-69; pres. crane, hoist and tower div. Dresser Industries, Muskegon, Mich., 1969-70; pres. machinery group Dresser Industries, Houston, 1970-75; sr. v.p. ops. Dresser Industries, Dallas, 1980, exec. v.p., 1982, pres., 1982-92, CEO, 1983-95; chmn. bd., 1983—; bd. dirs. PepsiCo, Inc., NationsBank Corp., Kerr-McGee Corp.; mem. Bus. Roundtable, Bus. Coun.; bd. dirs. U.S.-Russia Bus. Coun.; chmn. Citizens Democracy Corps. Trustee St. Bonaventure (N.Y.) U., So. Meth. U. With U.S. Army, 1954-56. Office: Dresser Industries Inc PO Box 718 2001 Ross Ave Dallas TX 75201-2911

MURPHY, JOHN JOSEPH, city official, retail executive; b. St. John's, Nfld., Can., Sept. 24, 1922; s. John and Gertrude (Wadden) M. Student, St. Bonaventure's Coll., 1929-40. Pres. Halley and Co. Ltd., St. Johns, Nfld., 1956—; Pres. John J. Murphy Ltd., St. Johns, Nfld., 1966—; mayor City of St. John's, 1981-90, 93—; chmn. bd. Cabot Celebrations (1997) Corp., 1992-93; worked in advt. and ins. investigation, 1943; freelance broadcaster, 1948; adv. bd. Royal trust. Former pres., senator Jaycees; pres. Nfld. Bd. of Trade, Nfld. Cancer Soc.; campaign chmn., life mem. Can. Cancer Soc.; chmn. new bldg. fund Can. Nat. Inst. for Blind; mem. Royal Commn. on Edn., 1968-71; campaign chmn. new bldg. fund Salvation Army, St. John Ambulance; bd. regents Meml. U. Nfld. Recipient Order of Can., 1985, Can. medal. 1992, Order of St. John, 1994. Mem. Royal Nfld. Yacht Club.

Avocations: sailing, archives. Home: 36 Smithville Crescent, Saint John's NF, NF Canada A1B 2V2 Office: City of St John's, PO Box 908, Saint John's, NF Canada A1C 5M2

MURPHY, JOHN NOLAN, mining executive, researcher, electrical engineer; b. Pitts., July 14, 1939; s. Maurice J. and Elizabeth (McVey) M.; m. Catherine V. Schneider, Nov. 24, 1962; 1 child, Michael J. BSEE, U. Pitts., 1961; MBA, Duquesne U., 1967. With U.S. Bur. Mines, Pitts., 1961—, rsch. supr., 1971-78, rsch. dir., 1978—. Contbr. numerous articles to profl. jours. Asst. scoutmaster Boy Scouts Am., Bethel Park, Pa., 1987—. Recipient Brian Morgans Meml. Lecture award U.K., 1983, Disting. Svc. award, Gold medal Dept. Interior, 1985. Mem. IEEE (sr.), Soc. Mining, Metallurgy and Exptl. Engring. (past chmn., bd. dirs. Pitts. chpt.), Nat. Mine Rescue Assn. (pres. 1990-91, bd. dirs. 1991—), Pitts. Coal Mine Inst. Am. (bd. dirs. 1989—). Avocation: golf. Office: Pitts Rsch Ctr Cochrans Mill Rd PO Box 18070 Pittsburgh PA 15236-0070

MURPHY, JOSEPH EDWARD, JR., broadcast executive; b. Mpls., Mar. 13, 1930; s. Joseph Edward Murphy and Ann Hynes; m. Diana Kuske, July 24, 1958; children: Michael, John. BA, Princeton U., 1952; postgrad., U. Minn., 1956-60. Chartered fin. analyst. Teaching asst. dept. history U. Minn., Mpls., 1957-59; dir. investment rsch. and fin. analysis, corp. sec. Woodward-Elwood & Co., Mpls., 1961-67; lectr. fin. grad. bus. sch. U. Minn., Mpls., 1968; v.p. Northwestern Nat. Bank, Mpls., 1967-83; chmn. Midwest Communications, Inc., Mpls., 1990-92; ret.; dir. Midwest Communications, Inc., 1956-89, vice chmn., 1985-89, sec.; bd. dirs., v.p. Northwest Advisers, Inc., 1982-83. Author: Adventure Beyond the Clouds: How We Climbed China's Highest Mountain and Survived, 1986 (Friends Am. Writers award 1986), With Interest: How to Profit From Interest Rate Fluctuations, 1987, Stock Market Probability, 1988, revised edit., 1994, South to the Pole by Ski, 1990, The Random Character of Interest Rates, 1990. Vice chmn., rep. 5th cong. dist. Minn. Coun. on Quality Edn., 1971-77; trustee, vice chmn. fin. com. Mpls. Soc. Fine Arts, 1977-78; bd. dirs., chmn. fin. com., mem. exec. bd. Childrens Theater Co., 1975-80; trustee, chmn. various coms. Macalester Coll., St. Paul, 1973-87. 2d lt. U.S. Army, 1952-55. Mem. Explorers Club, Am. Alpine Club (life, v.p. and bd. dirs. 1975-81), Himalayan Club (life), Mpls. Club. Avocations: mountaineering, exploration. Home: 2116 W Lake Isles Blvd Minneapolis MN 55405-2425

MURPHY, JOSEPH SAMSON, political science educator; b. Newark, Nov. 15, 1933; m. Susan Crile, 1984; children from previous marriage: Lisa, Susanne, Peter. Student, U. Colo., 1951-53; AB, Olivet Coll., Mich., 1955; Graham Kenan fellow, Woodrow Wilson fellow, U. N.C., 1955-56; MA, Brandeis U., 1959, PhD, 1961, DHL (hon.), 1988; LLD (hon.), U. Wis., 1989. Tchg. fellow, instr., asst. prof. Brandeis U., 1957-65; dir. V.I. Peace Corps Tng. Ctr., St. Croix, 1965-66; asst. Office Sec. HEW, Washington, 1966-67; assoc. dir. Job Corps, OEO, Washington, 1967-68; dir. U.S. Peace Corps, Ethiopia, 1968-70; vice chancellor for higher edn. State of N.J., 1970-71; pres. Queens Coll., prof. polit. sci. Grad. Faculty, CUNY, 1971-77; pres. Bennington (Vt.) Coll., 1977-82; chancellor CUNY, 1982-90; prof. CUNY Grad. Sch., N.Y.C., 1990—; cons. Constl. Commn., Addis Ababa, Ethiopia, 1993; bd. dirs. Yivo Inst. for Jewish Rsch., 1993—, UNESCO Global Project, 1992—; election observer The African Inst., Ethiopia, 1992. Author: The Theory of Universals in Eighteenth Century British Empiricism, 1961, Political Theory: A Conceptual Analysis, 1968; contbr. articles to profl. jours. Recipient Merit award U.S. Fgn. Service, 1965. Mem. AAAS, AAUP, Am. Philos. Assn., Am. Polit. Sci. Assn. Office: CUNY 450 W 41st St New York NY 10036-6807

MURPHY, JUDITH CHISHOLM, trust company executive; b. Chippewa Falls, Wis., Jan. 26, 1942; d. John David and Bernice A. (Hartman) Chisholm. BA, Manhattanville Coll., 1964; postgrad., New Sch. for Social Research, 1965-68, Nat. Grad. Trust Sch., 1975. Asst. portfolio mgr. Chase Manhattan Bank, N.A., N.Y.C., 1964-68; trust investment officer Marshall & Ilsley Bank, Milw., 1968-72; asst. v.p. Marshall & Ilsley Bank, 1972-74, v.p., 1974-75; v.p., treas. Marshall & Ilsley Invesmtent Mgmt. Corp., Milw., 1975-94; v.p. Marshall & Ilsley Trust Co., Phoenix, 1982—, Marshall & Ilsley Trust Co. Fla., Naples, 1985—; v.p., dir. instnl. sales Marshall & Ilsley Trust Co., Milw., 1994—; coun. mem. Am. Bankers Assn., Washington, 1984-86; govt. relations com. Wis. Bankers Assn., Madison, 1982-88. Contbr. articles to Trusts & Estates Mag., 1980, ABA Banking Jour., 1981, Maricopa Lawyer, 1983. Chmn. Milw. City Plan Commn., 1986—; commr. Milw. County Commn. on Handicapped, 1988-90; bd. dirs. Cardinal Stritch Coll., Milw., 1980-89, Children's Hosp. Wis., Milw., 1989—. Recipient Outstanding Achievement award YWCA Greater Milw., 1985, Sacajawea award Profl. Dimensions, Milw., 1988, Pro Urbe award Mt. Mary Coll., 1988, Vol. award Milw. Found., 1992; named Disting. Woman in Banking, Comml. West Mag., 1988. Mem. Milw. Analysts Soc. (sec. 1974-77, bd. dirs. 1977-80), Fin. Women Internat. (bd. dirs., v.p. 1976-80), Am. Inst. Banking (instr. 1975-78), TEMPO (charter), Profl. Dimensions (hon.), University Club, Woman's Club Wis., Rotary. Democrat. Roman Catholic. Home: 1139 N Edison St Milwaukee WI 53202-3147 Office: Marshall & Ilsley Trust Co 1000 N Water St Milwaukee WI 53202-3197

MURPHY, JULIET ANNE, lawyer; b. Kingston, Jamaica, West Indies, Apr. 22, 1963; came to U.S., 1978; d. Ramon Kirkett and Ouida Vivienne (Bair) M. BA, U. Fla., 1984, JD, 1987. Assoc. Rumberger, Kirk, Etal, Miami, Fla., 1987-89, Law Offices of David Mankin, Ft. Lauderdale, Fla., 1989-93, Law Offices of Peter Stassun, Ft. Lauderdale, 1993—; chair judicial selection Fla. chpt. Nat. Bar Assn., Stuart, 1993—; mem. judicial nominating com. The Fla. Bar, Tallahassee, 1992—, vice chair, 1994—; lemon law arbitrator Atty. Gen. Office. Mem. Nat. Assn. Negro Bus. and Profl. Women (pres. 1994—). Office: Law Offices Peter Stassun 600 S Andrews Ave Ste 200 Fort Lauderdale FL 33301-2802

MURPHY, KATHRYN MARGUERITE, archivist; b. Brockton, Mass.; d. Thomas Francis and Helena (Fortier) M. AB in History, George Washington U., 1935, MA, 1939; MLS, Cath. U., 1950; postgrad. Am. U., 1961. With Nat. Archives and Records Svc., Washington, 1940-89, ret., supervisory archivist Ctrl. Rsch. br., 1958-62, archivist, 1962—, mem. fed. women's com. Nat. Archives, 1974, rep. to fed. women's com. GSA, 1975; docent, 1989—; lectr. colls., socs. in U.S., 1950—; lectr. Am. ethnic history, 1978-79; free lance author and lectr. in field. Founder, pres. Nat. Archives lodge Am. Fedn. Govt. Employees, 1965—, del. conv., 1976, 78, 80, recipient award for outstanding achievement in archives, 1980. Recipient commendation Okla. Civil War Centennial Commn., 1965; named hon. citizen Oklahoma City, Mayor, 1963. Mem. ALA, Soc. Am. Archivists (joint com. hosp. librs. 1965-70), Nat. League Am. Pen Women (corr. sec. Washington 1975-78, pres. chpt. 1978-80), Bus. and Profl. Womens' Club Washington, Phi Alpha Theta (hon.). Contbr. articles on Am. ethnic history to profl. publs. Home: 1500 Massachusetts Ave NW Washington DC 20005-1821

MURPHY, KENNETH RAY, non-governmental organization executive; b. Lebanon, Ohio, Sept. 8, 1946; s. Raymond C. and Gloria J. (Machemehl) M.; m. Jennifer Pope, Aug. 15, 1969; children: Nicholas R., Samuel W. BA, Mich. State U., 1968; MA, Johns Hopkins U., 1971. Exec. dir. Environ. Resources Inc., Washington, 1970-72; reporter Bur. Nat. Affairs, Washington, 1973-75; editor Environ. Study Conf., U.S. Congress, Washington, 1975-79, staff dir., 1979-84; exec. Environ. and Energy Study Inst., Washington, 1984—. Mem. Sycamore Island Club. Office: Environ and Energy Study Inst 122 C St NW Ste 700 Washington DC 20001-2109

MURPHY, LAWRENCE THOMAS, professional hockey player; b. Scarborough, Ont., Can., Mar. 8, 1961. With L.A. Kings, 1980-83, Washington Capitals, 1983-89, Minn. North Stars, 1989-90; defenseman Pitts. Penguins, 1990—; player Cup All-Star Game, 1979-80, Stanley Cup Championships, 1991, 92, NHL All-Star Game, 1994. Recipient Max Kaminsky trophy, 1979-80. Holds NHL single-season record of 60 assists by rookie defenseman, 1980-81, record of 76 points by rookie defenseman, 1980-81. Office: Pitts Penguins Civic Arena Gate # 9 Pittsburgh PA 15219*

MURPHY, LESTER F(ULLER), lawyer; b. East Chicago, Ind., Nov. 28, 1936; s. Lester Fuller Sr. and Angelique (Molloy) M.; divorced; children: John Justin, Angelique, Lester Fuller III, Christopher, Colleen, Bridget, Erika, Shannon. AB, U. Notre Dame, 1959, JD, 1960. Bar: Ind. 1960, U.S. Dist. Ct. (no. and so. dists.) Ind. 1960, U.S. Ct. Appeals (7th cir.) 1961, U.S. Supreme Ct. 1963, Ill. 1976, U.S. Dist. Ct. (no. dist.) Ill. 1983, U.S. Ct. Appeals (8th cir.) 1985, Fla. 1987, U.S. Dist. Ct. (mid. dist.) Fla. 1989. Assoc. Riley, Reed, Murphy & McAtee, East Chgo., Ind., 1960-64, ptnr., 1964-65; ptnr. Murphy, McAtee & Murphy, East Chgo., 1965-68, Murphy, McAtee, Murphy & Costanza, East Chgo., 1968-87, Burke, Murphy, Costanza & Cuppy, East Chgo., 1988-90; adj. prof. Stetson Law Sch., St. Petersburg, Fla.; mem. faculty NITA. Author: Indiana Medical Malpractice, 1988 (with annual supplements); contbr. articles to profl. jours. Mem. ABA, Ind. Bar Assn., Fla. Bar Assn., Clearwater Bar Assn. (lectr.), Ind. Bar Found., Ind. CLE Found. (lectr.), Fla. Acad. Trial Lawyers, Nat. Bd. Trial Advocacy (cert.), Innisbrook Club (Tarpon Springs). Roman Catholic. Office: Burke Murphy Costanza & Cuppy 33920 Us Hwy N Ste 280 Palm Harbor FL 34684

MURPHY, LEWIS CURTIS, lawyer, former mayor; b. N.Y.C., Nov. 2, 1933; s. Henry Waldo and Elizabeth Wilcox (Curtis) M.; m. Carol Carney, Mar. 10, 1957; children—Grey, Timothy, Elizabeth. B.S. in Bus. Adminstrn, U. Ariz., 1955, LL.B., 1961. Bar: Ariz. bar 1961. Individual practice law Tucson, 1961-66; trust officer So. Ariz. Bank & Trust Co., 1966-70; atty. City of Tucson, 1970-71; mayor, 1971-87, ret.; mem. law firm Schroeder & Murphy, Tucson, 1978-88; trustee U.S. Conf. Mayors, 1978-87, chmn. transp. com., 1984-87; mem. pub. safety steering com. Nat. League Cities, 1973-87, mem. transp. steering com., 1973-87; v.p. Ctrl. Ariz. Project Assn., 1978-87; bd. dirs. Ariz. Bank, Community Food Bank. Mem. adv. bd. Ariz. Cancer Ctr., 1988—; bd. dirs. United Way Greater Tucson, 1988—. Served with USAF, 1955-58. Mem. Ariz. Bar Assn., Pima County Bar Assn., Ariz. Acad. Republican. Presbyterian.

MURPHY, MARGARET HACKETT, federal bankruptcy judge; b. Salisbury, N.C., 1948. BA, Queens Coll., Charlotte, N.C., 1970; JD, U. N.C., Chapel Hill, 1973. Bar: Ga. 1973, U.S. Bankruptcy Ct. Assoc. Smith, Cohen, Ringel, Kohler and Martin, Atlanta, 1973-79; ptnr. Smith, Gambrell & Russell (formerly Smith, Cohen, Ringel, Kohler and Martin), Atlanta, 1980-87; U.S. bankruptcy judge U.S. Dist. Ct. (no. dist.) Ga., Atlanta, 1987—. Office: 1290 US Courthouse 75 Spring St SW Atlanta GA 30303-3367

MURPHY, MARTIN JOSEPH, JR., cancer research center executive; b. Colorado Springs, Dec. 29, 1942; s. Martin Joseph Sr. and Gertrude F. (Heffting) M.; m. Ann A. Flesher, May 29, 1965; children: Siobhan, Deirdre, Martin Joseph III, Sean, Brendan. BS, Regis Coll., 1964; MS, N.Y.U., 1967, PhD, 1969. Vis. fellow Inst. de Pathologie Cellulaire, Paris, 1969-71, Christie Hosp., Manchester, Eng., 1971-72; visiting fellow John Curtin Sch. of Med. Rsch., Canberra, Australia, 1972-74; asst. prof. Sch. Medicine Cornell U., N.Y.C.; dir. Bob Hipple Lab for Cancer Rsch., N.Y.C., 1977-85; dir. hematology tng. program Sloan-Kettering Inst. for Cancer Rsch., N.Y.C., 1978-79; prof. Sch. of Medicine Wright State U., Dayton, 1984—; pres., CEO Hipple Cancer Rsch. Ctr., Dayton, 1985—; chmn. bd. dirs. AlphaMed Press, Inc., Dayton; bd. dirs. Dayton Clin. Oncology Program. Editor: In Vitro Aspects of Erythropoieis, 1978, Blood Cell Growth Factors: Their Biology and Clinical Applications, 1990, Blood Cell Growth Factors: Their Utility in Hematology and Oncology, 1991; editor-in-chief Internat. Jour. Cell Cloning, 1982-93, Stem Cells, 1993—; exec. editor The Oncologist; contbr. articles to profl. jours. NIH postdoctoral fellow, 1969-70, Damon Runyon fellow, 1970-71, Spl. fellow Leukemia Soc. Am., 1971, Pro Am. award Dayton Exec. Club. Mem. Assn. of Am. Cancer Inst., Am. Soc. Hematology, Am. Soc. Oncology, Am. Assn. for Cancer Rsch., Internat. Soc. for Exptl. Hematology, Dayton Area Cancer Assn. (trustee). Avocation: photography. Office: Hipple Cancer Rsch Ctr 4100 South Kettering Blvd Dayton OH 45439-2092*

MURPHY, MARY C., state legislator. BA, Coll. St. Scholastica; postgrad. U. Minn., Macalester Coll., U. Wis.-Superior, Am. U., Indiana U. H.s. tchr.; mem. Minn. Ho. of Reps., 1976—, mem. com. chair judiciary fin. com., tourism consumer affairs, labor-mgmt. relations coms.; active del. Duluth Central Labor Body AFL-CIO; mem., lector St. Raphael's Parish; dir. State Democratic Farmer-Labor Party, 1972-74, chmn. 8th Dist. credentials com., 1974—, chmn. St. Louis County Legis. Delegation, 1985-86. Mem. Duluth Fedn. Tchrs. (1st v.p. 1976-77, various coms.), Minn. Fedn. Tchrs. (legis. com. 1972-75), Am. Fedn. Tchrs. (del. nat. convs.), Minn. Hist. Soc., Alpha Delta Kappa. Office: State Office Bldg Saint Paul MN 55155-1201

MURPHY, MARY KATHLEEN, nursing educator; b. Elkins, W.Va., Jan. 27, 1953; d. Wyatt W. and Emma Loretta (Bohan) M.; children: Bridget Allyn, Kelley M. Poling. Diploma, Upshur County Sch. Nursing, Buckhannon, W.Va., 1982; ADN, Davis and Elkins Coll., 1984, BSN magna cum laude, 1986; MSN, W.Va. U. Cert. correctional health profl., substitute vocat. tchr. practical nursing, W.Va. Nurse, asst head nurse in ob-gyn. Meml. Gen. Hosp., Elkins, W.Va.; staff nurse, resource pool in ob-gyn. W.Va. U., Morgantown; DON Correctional Med. Systems, Huttonsville, W.Va.; instr. in nursing Davis and Elkins Coll.; nurse mgr. Elkins Mountain Sch. Randolph County Bd. Edn. Reviewer nursing texts Lippincott-Raven Pub. Mem. ANA, W.Va. Nursing Assn. (reviewer approval unit com. edn.), Inst. Noetic Scis., So. States Correctional Assn., Alpha Chi, Sigma Theta Tau.

MURPHY, MARY MARGUERITE, artist; b. S.I., N.Y., Mar. 29, 1958; d. Vincent Joseph and Teresa Marie (O'Connell) M.; m. James Thomas Primosch, Apr. 5, 1986. Student, Tyler Sch. Art, 1989-91; BA cum laude, Barnard Coll., 1981; MFA in Painting, Tyler Sch. Art, 1991; student, Skowhegan Sch. Painting/Sculp., 1990. tchg. fellow Tyler Sch. Art, Phila., 1989-91, instr., 1995; instr. Fleisher Art Meml., Phila., 1992—; vis. artist Ohio State U., Columbus, 1993; reader Ednl. Testing Svc., Princeton, N.J., 1994; tchg. artist Inst. for Arts in Edn., Phila., 1994; vis. artist lectr. Ohio State U., Columbus, 1993, Tyler Sch. Art, Phila., 1994; panel mem. Coll. New Rochelle, N.Y., 1985; panel moderator Beaver Coll., Glenside, Pa., 1995. One person shows include S.P.A.C.E.S., Cleve., 1994, Fleisher Art Meml., Phila., 1995, Larry Becker Contemporary Art, Phila., 1995; exhibited in group shows 80 Washington Sq. East Galleries, N.Y.C., 1985, Va. Ctr. for Creative Arts, Sweet Briar, Va., 1986, The Drawing Ctr., N.Y.C., 1989, Larry Becker Gallery, Phila., 1991, 95, Temple Univ. Gallery, Phila., 1991, State Theatre Ctr. for the Arts, Easton, Pa., 1991, Momenta Art Alternatives, Phila, 1991, Beaver Coll., Glenside,Pa., 1992, White Columns, N.Y.C., 1992, Moore Coll. of Art and Design, Phila., Pa., 1992, 1708 E Main St. Gallery, Richmond, Va., 1993, Ohio State U., Columbus, 1993, 55 Mercer St., N.Y.C., 1994, Vox Populi, Phila., 1994, 558 Broome St., N.Y.C., 1994, Tyler Sch. Art, Phila., 1994; works included in publs. Richmond Times Dispatch, Phila. City Paper, New Art Examiner, The Phila. Inquirer, The Plain Dealer; contbr. to The New Art Examiner. Mem. alumni bd. Tyler Sch. Art, Elkins Park, Pa., 1994—. Resident Va. Ctr. for Creative Arts, 1985, 86; fellow Skowhegan Sch. Painting and Sculpture, 1990, Nat. Endowment for Arts fellow in painting, 1993-94; Fleisher Challenge grantee Phila. Mus. Art, 1994. Mem. Coll. Art Assn. Roman Catholic. Home: # 220 231 N 3d St Philadelphia PA 19106

MURPHY, MICHAEL EMMETT, food company executive; b. Winchester, Mass., Oct. 16, 1936; s. Michael Cornelius and Bridie (Curran) M.; m. Adele Anne Kasupski, Sept. 12, 1959; children: Leslie Maura, Glenn Stephen, Christopher McNeil. B.S. in Bus. Adminstrn, Boston Coll., 1958; M.B.A., Harvard, 1962. Financial analyst Maxwell House div. Gen. Foods Corp., White Plains, N.Y., 1962-64; cost mgr. Maxwell House div. Gen. Foods Corp., San Leandro, Calif., 1964-65; controller Maxwell House div. Gen. Foods Corp., Jacksonville, Fla., 1965-67; controller Maxwell House div. Gen. Foods Corp., Hoboken, N.J., 1967-68, mgr. fin. planning and analysis, 1968-69; mgr. planning Hanes Corp., Winston-Salem, N.C., 1969-70, corp. controller, 1970—; v.p. adminstrn. Hanes Corp. (Hanes Knitwear), Winston-Salem, N.C., 1972-74; v.p. fin. Ryder System Inc., Miami, Fla., 1974-75, exec. v.p., 1975-79; exec. v.p., dir. Sara Lee Corp., Chgo., 1979-93, vice chmn., 1993—; bd. dirs. GATX Corp. Mgmt. adviser Jr. Achievement, 1965-66; mem. exec. com. Hudson County Tax Rsch. Coun., 1967-68; trustee Boston Coll., 1980-88; chmn. Civic Fedn. Chgo., 1984-86; bd. dirs. Jobs for Youth, Chgo., 1983-86, Lyric Opera, 1986—; bd. dirs. Northwestern Meml. Hosp., Chgo., Big Shoulders Fund, Chgo. Ctrl. Area Com., 1995—, Chgo. Cultural Ctr. Found., 1995—; prin. Chgo. United, 1995—. Mem. NAM (bd. dirs. 1989—, dir. Big Shoulders Fund 1995—), Fin. Execs. Inst., Hoboken C. of C., Winson-Salem C. of C., Miami C. of C., Internat. Platform Assn., UN Assn., Ouimet Scholar Alumni Group, Beta Gamma Sigma. Roman Catholic. Home: 1242 N Lake Shore Dr Chicago IL 60610-2361 Office: Sara Lee Corp 3 First National Plz Chicago IL 60602

MURPHY, MICHAEL R., federal judge; b. Denver, Aug. 6, 1947; s. Roland and Mary Cecilia (Maloney) M.; m. Maureen Elizabeth Donnelly, Aug. 22, 1970; children: Amy Christina, Michael Donnelly. BA in History, Creighton U., 1969; JD, U. Wyo., 1972. Bar: Wyo. 1972, U.S. Ct. Appeals (10th cir.) 1972, Utah 1973, U.S. Dist. Ct. Utah 1974, U.S. Dist. Ct. Wyo. 1976, U.S. Ct. Appeals (5th cir.) 1976, U.S. Tax Ct. 1980, U.S. Ct. Appeals (9th cir.) 1981, U.S. Ct. Appeals (fed. cir.) 1984. Law clk. to chief judge U.S. Ct. Appeals (10th cir.), Salt Lake City, 1972-73; with Jones, Waldo, Holbrook & McDonough, Salt Lake City, 1973-86; judge 3d Dist. Ct., Salt Lake City, 1986-95, pres. judge, 1990-95; judge U.S. Ct. Appeals (10th cir.), Salt Lake City, 1995—; mem. adv. com. on rules of civil procedure Utah Supreme Ct., Salt Lake City, 1985—, mem. bd. dist. ct. judges, 1989-90; mem. Utah State Sentencing Commn., Utah Adv. Com. on Child Support Guidelines, Utah Child Sexual Abuse Task Force. Recipient Freedom of Info. award Soc. Profl. Journalists, 1995, Utah Minority Bar Assn. award, 1995; named Judge of Yr., Utah State Bar, 1992. Mem. ABA, Wyo. Bar Assn., Utah Bar Assn. (chmn. alternative dispute resolution com. 1985-88), Salt Lake County Bar Assn., Sutherland Inn of Ct. II (past pres.). Roman Catholic. Office: 1823 Stout St Denver CO 80257*

MURPHY, MICHELE SUSAN, non-profit agency executive; b. Cleve., Aug. 11, 1949; d. Edward Jerry and Violet Agnes (Lozick) M. BS in Journalism, Ohio U., 1971; M Non-Profit Orgns., Case Western Res. U., 1993. Press rep. Cuyahoga Community Coll. West, Parma, Ohio, 1971-75; pub. info. specialist Cuyahoga Community Coll., Cleve., 1975-76, news bur. mgr., 1976-77, asst. dir. info. svcs., 1977-78, cons., 1979; coord. U.S. Senate Campaign, Cleve., 1981-82; communications liaison Cuyahoga County Bd. Elections, Cleve., 1982-94; exec. dir. Crime Stoppers of Cuyahoga County, Inc., Cleve., 1994; founder, exec. dir. Conflict Resolution Ctr. of the West Shore, Inc.; cons. in mktg. The City Club, Cleve., 1991. Mem. Leadership Cleve., Greater Cleve. Growth Assn., 1986; editor Rep. News, Cuyahoga County Rep. Orgn., 1983-84. Recipient Appreciation award Greater Cleve. Crime Prevention Com., 1992, Ohio State Chiefs of Police Assn., 1990, Vol. Achievement award CIVAC, Cleve., 1987, Cert. of Appreciation Community Rels. Bd., City of Cleve., 1987, Sports Promotion award Nat. Jr. Coll. Athletic Assn., 1973, 74, 75. Mem. Ohio Mediation Assn., Acad. Family Mediators, Cuyahoga County Police Chiefs Assn. (hon., named Citizen of Yr. 1995). Office: CRC West Shore Inc 24700 Center Ridge #6 Westlake OH 44145

MURPHY, N. B. (NAP MURPHY), state congressman, automobile dealer; b. Rural Rte. Crossett, Ark., Sept. 16, 1921; s. Charles Ed and Isadee M.; m. Maxine James, Dec. 20, 1949; children: James N., Stephen E., Ila Sue Murphy Campbell. Grad., Crossett (Ark.) High Sch., 1941. With acctg. and traffic dept. AD&N Railroad, 1941-48; owner gas svc. station, 1948-53; owner Murphy Ford Co., Hamburg, Ark., 1953—; mem. Ark. Ho. of Reps., 1959—; pres. M&M Svcs. Corp., Murphy Farms. Mem. Nat. Automobile Assn., Masons (32nd degree). Democrat. Avocations: playing the fiddle, composing songs. Home and Office: S Main St PO Box 271 Hamburg AR 71646-0271

MURPHY, NEWTON JEROME, steel company executive, holding company executive; b. Spencer, Iowa, Nov. 22, 1928; s. Newton Hawley and Marian Rebecca (Livingston) M.; m. Shirley Anne Howard; children: Kathleen, Sarah (dec.), Michael Howard, Laura. BA, U. Iowa, 1952. Trainee Studebaker Corp., South Bend, Ind., 1952-53; car distbr. Studebaker Corp., Buffalo, 1953-54; trainee, sales rep. U.S. Steel Corp., Pitts., 1954-60; asst. to mgr. sales U.S. Steel Corp., Balt., 1960-65; v.p., gen. mgr. Feralloy Corp., Balt., 1965-68; v.p., gen. mgr. Feralloy Corp., Chgo., 1968-71, pres., chief exec. officer, dir., 1971—; pres., chief exec. officer Salzgitter Indsl. Corp., Chgo., 1975—, also bd. dirs.; pres., ceo Chicago Cold Rolling, Chesterton, IN; chmn. owners com. Feralloy West Co., Chgo., 1984—; chmn. owners com. Feralloy Processing Co., Chgo., 1987—; bd. dirs. Salzgitter Machinery Inc., Chgo. Served with USN, 1946-48, PTO. Mem. Steel Service Ctr. Inst., Chgo. Execs. Club. Republican. Congregationalist. Club: Northshore Country (Glenview, Ill.). Avocations: golf, tennis. Office: Chicago Cold Rolling 751 E Porter Ave Ste 1 Chesterton IN 46304*

MURPHY, PATRICK JOSEPH, state representative; b. Dubuque, Iowa, Aug. 24, 1959; s. Lawrence John and Eileen (Heitz) M.; m. Therese Ann Gulick, Dec. 27, 1980; children: Jacob, John, Joey, Natalie. BA, Loras Coll., 1980. Transporter, security and safety officer, mental health technician Mercy Health Ctr., Dubuque, Iowa, 1975-88; documentation specialist software systems Cycare Systems Inc., Dubuque, 1988-90; state representative State of Iowa, Des Moines, 1989—. Adv. com. Iowa Birth Defects, 1995. Recipient Robert Tyson award Cmty. Action Assn., 1993, Pub. Svc. award Coalition for Family and Children's Svcs., 1994; Henry Toll fellow, 1996. Mem. NAACP, YMCA, Dubuque Mental Health Assn. (bd. dirs., Legis. of Yr.), Loras Club, FDR Club. Democrat. Roman Catholic. Avocations: weightlifting, jogging. Home: 1770 Hale St Dubuque IA 52001-6049 Office: Ho of Reps Des Moines IA 50319

MURPHY, PATRICK VINCENT, foundation executive; b. Bklyn, May 15, 1920; s. Patrick A. and Ellen (Jones) M.; m. Martha Elizabeth Cameron, June 2, 1945; children—Betty (Mrs. Thomas Kelley), Eileen (Mrs. Bernard Karam), Patrick, Anne T. (Mrs. Drew Zabriskie), Kevin, Gerard, Paul, Mark. B.A., St. John's U., 1954; M.P.A., City Coll. N.Y., 1960; LL.D. (hon.), U. Louisville. Patrolman N.Y. Police Dept., N.Y.C., 1945; dep. insp. N.Y. Police Dept., 1963; chief of police Syracuse, N.Y., 1963; deputy chief inspector N.Y. Police Dept., 1964; apptd. asst. dir. Office of Law Enforcement Assistance U.S. Dept. Justice, Washington, 1965-67; apptd. pub. safety dir. District of Columbia, 1967—; apptd. Adminstr. Law Enforcement Assistance Adminstrn. U.S. Dept. Justice, Washington, 1968-69; sr. staff Urban Inst., 1969—; apptd. commnr. Detroit Police Dept., 1970; commnr. N.Y. Police Dept., 1970-73; pres. Police Found., Washington, 1973—; dep. asst. sec. aviation & intl. affairs Dept. Transportation, Washington; dean police sci. City U. N.Y.; adv. Nat. Crime Commn. Cons. Nat. Adv. Commn. on Cvil Disorders; mem. Nat. Conf. on Crime and Delinquency. Served with USNR, World War II. Mem. Internat. Assn. Chiefs of Police, NCCJ, Beta Gamma Sigma. Office: Dept Transp Aviation & Internat Affairs 400 7th St SW Washington DC 20590-0001*

MURPHY, PHILIP FRANCIS, bishop; b. Cumberland, Md., Mar. 25, 1933; s. Philip A.M. and Kathleen (Huth) M. Ed. St. Mary Sem., Balt., N.Am. Coll., Rome. Ordained priest Roman Catholic Ch., 1958; asst. pastor St. Bernardine Ch., Balt., 1959-61; asst. vice rector N.Am. Coll., Rome, 1961-65; sec. to Cardinal Archbishop, Balt., 1965-74, chancellor, 1975; ordained titular bishop of Tacarata and aux. of Balt., 1976—. Office: Archdiocese of Balt 320 Cathedral St Baltimore MD 21201-4421

MURPHY, RANDALL KENT, consultant; b. Laramie, Wyo., Nov. 8, 1943; s. Robert Joseph and Sally (McConnell) M.; student U. Wyo., 1961-65; MBA, So. Meth. U., 1983; m. Cynthia Laura Hillhouse, Dec. 29, 1978; children: Caroline, Scott, Emily. Dir. mktg. Wycoa, Inc., Denver, 1967-70; dir. Communications Resource Inst., Dallas, 1971-72; account exec. Xerox Learning Systems, Dallas, 1973-74; regional mgr. Systema Corp., Dallas, 1975; pres. Performance Assocs.; pres., dir. Acclivus Corp., Dallas, 1976—; founder, chmn. Acclivus Inst., 1982—. Active, Dallas Mus. Fine Arts, Dallas Hist. Soc., Dallas Symphony Assn.; vice chmn. bd. trustees The Winston Sch., 1994—; mem. adv. bd. The Women's Ctr. of Dallas, 1995—. Served with AUS, 1966. Mem. Am. Soc. Tng. and Devel., Sales and Mktg. Execs. Internat., Inst. Mgmt. Scis., Soc. Applied Learning Tech., Nat. Soc. Performance and Instrn., , Assn. Mgmt. Cons., Am. Assn. Higher Edn., World Future Soc., Soc. for Intercultural Edn., Tng. and Rsch., Internat. Fedn. Tng. and Devel. Orgns., Inst. Noetic Scis., Nat. Peace Inst., Amnesty Internat. The Acad. Pol. Sci., The Nature Conservancy, Children's Arts & Ideas Found., So. Meth. U. Alumni Assn. U. Wyo. Alumni Assn. Roman Catholic. Author: Performance Management of the Selling Process, 1979; Coaching and Counseling for Performance, 1980; Managing Development and Performance, 1982; Acclivus Performance Planning System, 1983; (with others) BASE for Sales Performance, 1983, Acclivus Coaching, 1984, Acclivus Sales Negotiation, 1985; BASE for Effective Presentations, 1987, BASE for Strategic Sales Presentations, 1988, The New BASE for Sales Excellence, 1988, Major Account Planning and Strategy, 1989, Strategic Management of the Selling Process, 1989, Building on the BASE, 1992, Negotiation Mastery, 1995; co-inventor The Randy-Band, multi-purpose apparel accessory, 1968. Home: 6540 Crestpoint Dr Dallas TX 75240-8615

MURPHY, REG, publishing executive; b. 1934. Reporter Macon (Ga.) Telegraph and News, 1953-60; polit. editor, editorial page editor Atlanta Constitution, 1961-74; pub., editor San Francisco Examiner, 1975-81; pub., pres. Balt. Sun, 1981-90, chmn., 1990-92; exec. v.p. Nat. Geographic Soc., Washington, 1993—. Office: Nat Geographic Soc 1145 17th St NW Washington DC 20036-4701

MURPHY, RICHARD WILLIAM, retired foreign service officer, Middle East specialist, consultant; b. Boston, July 29, 1929; s. John Deneen Murphy and Jane (Diehl) Bonner; m. Anne Herrick Cook, Aug. 25, 1955; children: Katherine Anne, Elizabeth Drew, Richard McGill. Grad., Phillips Exeter Acad., 1947; AB, Harvard U., 1951, Cambridge (Eng.) U., 1953; postgrad. Arabic studies, U.S. Fgn. Service Inst., Beirut, 1959-60; LLD (hon.), New Eng. Coll., 1989, Balt. Hebrew U., 1992. Vice consul U.S. Consulate Gen., Salisbury, So. Rhodesia, 1955-58; consul Aleppo, Syria, 1960-63; polit. officer Am. Embassy, Jidda, Saudi Arabia, 1963-66, Amman, Jordan, 1966-68; pers. officer U.S. State Dept., Washington, 1968-69, dir. Office Arabian Peninsula Affairs, 1969-71, asst. sec. state for Near Ea. and South Asian affairs, 1983-89; U.S. amb. to Mauritania, 1971-74, Syria, 1974-78, The Philippines, 1978-81, Saudi Arabia, 1981-83; sr. fellow for Middle East Coun. Fgn. Rels., N.Y.C., 1989—; cons. Richard Murphy Assocs., N.Y.C., 1993—; chmn. Fgn. Students Svc. Coun., Washington, 1989-93, Mid. East Inst., Washington, 1993—, Chatham House Found., 1993—; mem. bd. advisors Naval War Coll., 1991-94; bd. dirs. MAXUS Energy, 1990-95, Harvard Med. Internat., 1995—. Trustee Am. U. of Beirut, 1995—. Served with U.S. Army, 1953-55. Recipient Superior Honor award, U.S. Dept. State, 1969, Pres.'s Disting. Svc. award, 1986, 88, 89. Mem. Coun. Fgn. Rels., Fgn. Svc. Assn., Inst. of Diplomacy (Non-proliferation Coun.), Kissinger Assocs. Republican. Episcopalian. Avocations: tennis, scuba diving. Home: 16 Sutton Pl # 9A New York NY 10022-3057

MURPHY, ROBERT BLAIR, management consulting company executive; b. Phila., Jan. 19, 1931; s. William Beverly and Helen Marie (Brennan) M.; B.S., Yale, 1953; children: Stephen, Emily, Julia, David, Catherine. Indsl. engr. DuPont Corp., Aiken, S.C., 1953-55; mgr. sales can div. Reynolds Metals Co., Richmond, Va., 1955-69; gen. mgr. corrugated div. Continental Can Co., N.Y.C., 1969-73; v.p. and gen. mgr. beverage div. Am. Can Co., Greenwich, Conn., 1973-75; asso. Heidrick & Struggles, Inc., N.Y.C., 1976-78, v.p., 1978; v.p., mng. dir. Stamford office Spencer Stuart & Assocs., 1978-84, ptnr., 1982-84; co-founder Sullivan-Murphy Assocs., 1984—. Clubs: Riverside Yacht (Greenwich); Yale (N.Y.C.); Merion Cricket (Haverford, Pa.). Home: 11 Indian Mill Rd Cos Cob CT 06807-1315 Office: 6 Landmark Sq Stamford CT 06901-2704

MURPHY, ROBERT BRADY LAWRENCE, lawyer; b. Madison, Wis., Dec. 5, 1905; s. Lawrence B. Murphy and Elizabeth M. Brady; m. Arabel Zenobia Alcott, Oct. 11, 1947. AB, U. Wis., 1929, AM, 1930, LLB, 1932, LLD (hon.), 1994. Bar: Wis. 1932. Mem. Murphy & Desmond, S.C. and predecessors, Madison, 1932—; lectr. U. Wis. Law Sch.; mem. Supreme Ct. Wis. Bd. Bar Examiners, 1981-86. Mem. Madison Police and Fire Commn., 1947-52; curator State Hist. Soc. Wis., 1948-90, pres., 1958-61; bd. dirs. Wis. History Found., 1958—, pres., 1960-90; bd. advisors Nat. Trust Hist. Preservation, 1967-73; bd. dirs. or advisor several founds.; bd. visitors U. Wis. Law Sch., 1975-81. Lt. USNR, 1943-46. Fellow Am. Bar Found.; mem. ABA, State Bar Wis., Am. Law Inst., Selden Soc. (Eng.), Bascom Hill Soc. (Wis.), Phi Beta Kappa Assocs., Phi Kappa Phi, Chi Phi, Phi Delta Phi. Republican. Roman Catholic. Clubs: Madison, Blackhawk Country. Home: 3423 Valley Creek Cir Middleton WI 53562-1991 Office: Murphy & Desmond S C 2 E Mifflin St Madison WI 53703-2868

MURPHY, ROBERT C(HARLES), judge; b. Balt., Oct. 9, 1926; married; 3 children. JD, U. Md., 1951, LLD (hon.), 1973; LLD (hon.), U. Balt., 1981, Washington Coll., 1993. Bar: Md. 1952, D.C. 1952, U.S. Supreme Ct. 1957. Law clk. to Hon. William P. Cole Jr., assoc. judge U.S. Ct. Customs and Patent Appeals, Washington, 1951-53; gen. counsel U. Md., 1955-57; spl. asst. atty. gen. Balt., 1957-62, asst. atty. gen., then dep. atty. gen., 1962-66, atty. gen., 1966-67; chief judge Md. Ct. Spl. Appeals, Annapolis, 1967-72, Md. Ct. Appeals, Annapolis, 1972—; adminstrv. head Md. Jud. Br., 1972—; chmn. Constl. Commn. on Jud. Disabilities, 1971-73; hon. mem. Coun. State Govts., mem. governing bd., mem. exec. com., 1985; chmn. bd. dirs. Nat. Ctr. State Cts., Williamsburg, Va., 1986-87; pres. J. Dudley Digges Am. Inn of Ct. With USN, 1944-46. Recipient Disting. Alumnus award U. Md., 1974, U. Md. Law Sch., 1987. Fellow Md. Bar Found.; mem. ABA, U. Md. Alumni Assn.-Internat. (chmn., trustee), Conf. Chief Justices (pres. 1986), Md. State Bar Assn., Order of Coif. Office: Ct Appeals Md 361 Rowe Blvd Fl 4 Annapolis MD 21401-1672

MURPHY, ROBERT EARL, scientist, government agency administrator; b. Yakima, Wash., Sept. 24, 1941; s. William Barry and Caroline Norbeth (Boyd) M.; m. Nancy Jane Hybner, June 26, 1965; children: Kimberly Elizabeth, Mark Hybner. B.S. in Math, Worcester (Mass.) Poly. Inst., 1963; M.A. in Astronomy, Georgetown U., 1966; Ph.D., Case Western Res. U., 1969. Astronomer U.S. Army Map Service, 1965-66; asst. prof. astronomy Inst. Astronomy, U. Hawaii, 1969-73; exec. dir. Md. Acad. Scis., Balt., 1973-76; pres. Scientia Inc., Balt., 1976—; chief planetary atmospheres programs and program scientist Galileo project NASA, Washington, 1977-81; head earth resources br., project scientist heat capacity mapping mission Goddard Space Flight Center, Greenbelt, Md., 1981-84; chief land processes br. NASA Hdqrs., Washington, 1984-89, chief biochemistry, geophysics bur., 1989-92, sr. sci. advisor internat. programs, 1993—. Author curriculum materials, articles in field. Mem. AAAS, Am. Astron. Soc., Am. Geophys. Union. Republican. Baptist. Office: NASA Hdqrs Earth Sci Divsn Code YS Washington DC 20546

MURPHY, ROBIN ROBERSON, computer science educator; b. Mobile, Ala., Aug. 25, 1957; d. Fred Blakely and Ada Lee (Wills) Roberson; m. Kevin Eddy Murphy, Aug., 27, 1982; children: Kathleen Freebern, Allan Roberson. B in Mech. Engring., Ga. Inst. Tech., 1980, MS in Computer Sci., 1989, PhD in Computer Sci., 1992. Project engr. Dow Chem. USA, Plaquemine, La., 1980-84; software project engr. Turbitrol Co., Atlanta, 1984-86; asst. prof. dept. math. and comp. sci. Colo. Sch. Mines, Golden, 1992—, assoc. dir. Ctr. Robotics and Intelligent Systems, 1994-95; mem. NSF vis. com. on computer sci. curriculum U. Va., Charlottesville, 1992-95. Author: (with others) The Handbook of Brain Theory and Neural Networks, 1995; contbr. articles to profl. jours. Rsch. grantee NSF, 1994—, Advanced Rsch. Projects Agy., 1994—, NASA, 1994—. Mem. AAAI, IEEE, AIAA, Assn. Computing Machinery. Office: Colo Sch Mines Dept Math and Computer Sci Golden CO 80401-1887

MURPHY, ROSEMARY, actress; b. Munich, Germany; came to U.S., 1939; d. Robert D. and Mildred (Taylor) M. Ed. in, Paris, France and Kansas City, Mo. Broadway appearances include Look Homeward Angel, 1958, Night of the Iguana, World premier at Spoleto (Italy) Festival of Two Worlds, 1959, Period of Adjustment, 1961, King Lear, 1963, Any Wednesday, 1964-66, Delicate Balance, 1966, Weekend, 1968, Butterflies are Free, 1970, Lady Macbeth, Stratford, Conn., 1973, Ladies of the Alamo, 1977, John Gabriel Borkman, 1980, Learned Ladies, 1982, Coastal Disturbances, 1987, The Devil's Disciple, 1988; motion picture appearances include To Kill a Mockingbird, 1962, Any Wednesday, 1966, Ben, 1972, Walking Tall, 1972, You'll Like My Mother, 1972, Forty Carats, 1973, Julia, 1976, September, 1987, For the Boys, 1991, And The Band Played On, 1993, The Tuskegee Airmen, 1995; TV appearance Eleanor and Franklin, 1975 (Emmy award for best supporting actress 1976), George Washington, 1983 (Tony award nominations 1961, 64, 67, award Motion Picture Arts Club 1966), E-Z Streets, 1996. Recipient Variety Poll award, 1961, 67. Address: 220 E 73rd St New York NY 10021-4319

MURPHY, SANDRA ROBISON, lawyer; b. Detroit, July 28, 1949; m. Richard Robin. BA, Northwestern U., 1971; JD, Loyola U., Chgo., 1976. Bar: U.S. Dist. Ct. (no. dist.) Ill. 1976. Assoc. Notz, Craven, Mead, Maloney & Price, Chgo., 1976-78; ptnr. McDermott, Will & Emery, Chgo., 1978—. Mem. ABA (family law sect.), Ill. Bar Assn. (chair sect. family law coun. 1987-88), Chgo. Bar Assn. (chair matrimonial law com. 1985-86), Am. Acad. Matrimonial Lawyers (sec. 1990-91, v.p. 1991-92, pres. Ill. chpt. 1992-93, pres.-elect 1994-95, pres. 1995—), Legal Club Chgo.

MURPHY, SHARON MARGARET, university official, educator; b. Milw., Aug. 2, 1940; d. Adolph Leonard and Margaret Ann (Hirtz) Feyen; m. James Emmett Murphy, June 28, 1969 (dec. May 1983); children: Shannon Lynn, Erin Ann. BA, Marquette U., 1965; MA, U. Iowa, 1970, PhD, 1973. Cert. K-14 tchr., Iowa. Tchr. elem. and secondary schs., Wis., 1959-69; dir. publs. Kirkwood C.C., Cedar Rapids, Iowa, 1969-71; instr. journalism U. Iowa, Iowa City, 1971-73; asst. prof. U. Wis., Milw., 1973-79; assoc. prof. So. Ill. U., Carbondale, 1979-84; dean/prof. Marquette U., Milw., 1984-94; provost, v.p. acad. affairs, prof. Bradley U., Peoria, Ill., 1994—; pub. rels. dir., editor Worldwide mag., Milw., 1965-68; reporter Milw. Sentinel, 1967; Fulbright sr. lectr. U. Nigeria, Nsukka, 1977-78. Author: Other Voices: Black, Chicano & American Indian Press, 1971; (with Wigal) Screen Experience: An Approach to Film, 1968, (with Murphy) Let My People Know: American Indian Journalism, 1981, (with Schilpp) Great Women of the Press, 1983; editor: (book, with others) International Perspectives on News, 1982. Bd. dirs. Dow Jones Newspaper Fund, N.Y., 1986-95, Peoria Symphony; v.p. women's fund Peoria Cmty. Found.; mem. Peoria Riverfront Commn. Recipient Medal of Merit, Journalism Edn. Assn., 1976, Amoco Award for Teaching Excellence, 1977, Outstanding Achievement award Greater Milw. YWCA, 1989; named Knight of Golden Quill, Milw. Press Club, 1977; Nat. headliner Women in Communication, Inc., 1985. Mem. Assn. Edn. in Journalism and Mass Comm. (pres. 1986-87), Internat. Comm. Assn., Tempo, Newspaper Assn. Am. Found. (trustee 1993-96), Peoria C. of C. (bd. dirs.), Soc. Profl. Journalists, Nat. Press Club. Democrat. Roman Catholic. Office: Bradley U Office of Provost Peoria IL 61625

MURPHY, TERENCE MARTIN, biology educator; b. Seattle, July 1, 1942; s. Norman Walter and Dorothy Louise (Smith) M.; m Judith Baron, July 12, 1969; 1 child, Shannon Elaine. BS, Calif. Inst. Tech., 1964; PhD, U. Calif. San Diego, La Jolla, 1968. Sr. fellow dept. biochemistry U. Wash., Seattle, 1969-70; asst. prof. botany U. Calif., Davis, 1971-76, assoc. prof., 1976-82, prof. biology, 1982—, chmn. dept. botany, 1986-90. Author: Plant Molecular Development, 1988; N.Am. exec. editor, N.Am. office, Physiologia Plantarum, 1988—; contbr. articles to profl. jours. Mem. AAAS, Am. Soc. Plant Physiologists, Am. Soc. Photobiology, Scandinavian Soc. Plant Physiology. Home: 725 N Campus Way Davis CA 95616-3518 Office: U Calif Sect Plant Biology Davis CA 95616

MURPHY, TERENCE ROCHE, lawyer; b. Laurium, Mich., Oct. 20, 1937; s. M. Leonard and Alice Lenore (Roche) M.; m. Suzanne Kathryn Dupré, Oct. 14, 1967 (div. Apr. 1980); children: Braden Mathias, Fiona Elizabeth Dupré ; m. Patricia Ann Sherman, May 21, 1983. A.B., Harvard Coll., 1959; J.D. cum laude, U. Mich., 1966. Bar: D.C. 1967, U.S. Supreme Ct. 1971. Trial atty. Dept. Justice, Washington, 1966-68; assoc. Wald, Harkrader & Ross, Washington, 1968-72, ptnr., 1972-83; ptnr. McDermott, Will & Emery, Washington, 1983-84, Adams, Duque & Hazeltine, Washington, 1984-86; founding ptnr. Murphy & Weber (formerly Murphy & Malone), 1986—; bd. dirs. internat. corps., bus. assns.; author, lectr. on internat. trade, antitrust and administrv. law; founding chmn. Brit.-Am. Bus. Coun., 1989-90, legal counsel, 1993—; officer, bd. dirs. Frankfurt Trade Fair (U.S. Subsidiary), Industry Coalition of Tech. Transfer. Co-editor: Coping With U.S. Export Controls, ann. edits., 1986, 87, 88; bd. advisor Internat. Fin. Law Rev., 1984—, Eurowatch, 1991—, The European Inst., 1993—; contbr. numerous articles to European and Am. legal publs. Mem. com. visitors U. Mich. Law Sch., 1975—; trustee Lawyer's Com. for Civil Rights Under Law, 1975-89. Lt. USN, 1959-63. Decorated U.S. Navy Commendation medal Cuban Missle Crisis, 1962, Hon. Officer Order Brit. Empire, 1993. Fellow Royal Soc. of Arts; mem. ABA (coun. adminstrv. law sect. 1980-83, co-chmn. com. on internat. and comparative adminstrv. law 1994—), Am. Law Inst., Am. Assn. Exporters and Importers (bd. dirs.), Internat. Bar Assn. (sec. antitrust and monopolies com. 1981-83), Am. Soc. Internat. Law, Brit.-Am. Bus. Assn. (Washington, founding dir. 1987—, chmn. 1989—, legal advisor 1992—), Royal Inst. Internat. Affairs (London), Am. Coun. on Germany, Deutsch-Amerikanische Juristen-Vereinigung (Bonn), Met. Club (Washington), Harvard Club (N.Y.C.). Home: 2710 Cathedral Ave NW Washington DC 20008-4120 Office: Murphy & Weber 818 Connecticut Ave NW Washington DC 20006-2702

MURPHY, THOMAS ALLEN, government research administrator, scientist; b. Kewanee, Ill., Aug. 26, 1937; m. Arlene Louise (Lippert) M.; m. Ellen Diane McParland, Aug. 26, 1962; children: Alison Louise, Patrick Thomas, Andrew Gavin. AB, Knox Coll., 1959; cert., Glasgow U., 1960; MS, Yale U., 1962, PhD, 1964. Rsch. assoc. Cornell U., Ithaca, N.Y., 1966-67; biologist Fed. Water Pollution Control Adminstrn., Edison, N.J., 1967-70; rsch. program mgr. EPA, Washington, 1970-75, dep. asst. adminstr., 1975-79; rsch. lab. dir. EPA, Corvallis, Oreg., 1979—; mem. del. Nat. Acad. Sci., Malaysia, 1987, Romania, 1990; mem. pres.'s reorgn. project, Exec. Office of the Pres., Washington, 1978. Capt. U.S. Army, 1964-66, Vietnam. Recipient Meritorious Exec. award Pres. of U.S., 1987. Home: 31465 Bellfountain Rd Corvallis OR 97333-9566 Office: EPA 200 SW 35th St Corvallis OR 97333-4902*

MURPHY, THOMAS AQUINAS, former automobile manufacturing company executive; b. Hornell, N.Y., Dec. 10, 1915; s. John Joseph and Alma (O'Grady) M.; m. Catherine Rita Maquire, June 7, 1941; children: Catherine, Maureen, Thomas Aquinas. B.S., U. Ill., 1938. With Gen. Motors Corp., 1938-88; asst. treas. Gen. Motors Corp., N.Y.C., 1959; comptroller Gen. Motors Corp., Detroit, 1967; treas. Gen. Motors Corp., 1968, v.p. in charge car and truck group, 1970-72, vice chmn., 1972-74, chmn., chief exec. officer, 1974-80, dir., 1980-88. Bd. dirs. U. Ill. Found. Served with USNR, 1943-46. Mem. Fin. Execs. Inst., Bus. Coun., Bloomfield Hills (Mich.) Country Club, Delray Dunes (Fla.) Golf Club, Ocean Club (Fla.). Office: 3044 W Grand Blvd Detroit MI 48202-3091

MURPHY, THOMAS BAILEY, state legislator; b. Bremen, GA, Mar. 10, 1924; s. W.H. and Leita (Jones) M.; m. Agnes Bennett, July 22, 1946; children: Michael L., Martha L., Marjorie Lynn, Mary June. Grad., N.Ga. Coll., 1943; LL.B., U. Ga., 1949. Bar: Ga. bar 1949. Since practiced in Bremen as partner firm Murphy & Murphy; mem. Ga. Ho. of Reps., 1961—, adminstrv. floor leader for gov., 1969-70, speaker pro tem, 1971-74, speaker, 1974—. Mem. Ga. Bar Assn., Am. Legion, VFW, Gridiron Secret Soc.; hon. life mem. Ga. Peace Officers Assn.; hon. mem. Ga. Fraternal Order Police, Ga. Sheriffs Assn. Democrat. Baptist. Club: Moose. Office: Ho of Reps State Capitol SW Rm 332 Atlanta GA 30334-1160

MURPHY, THOMAS J., JR., mayor; m. Mona McMahon. BS in Biology and Chemistry, John Carroll U., 1967; MS in Urban Affairs/Planning summa cum laude, Hunter Coll., 1973. Vol. Peace Corps, Paraguay, 1970-72; exec. dir. Perry Hilltop Citizen's Coun., 1973-76; chem. sales rep. Alcoa, 1967-70; exec. dir. North Side Civic Devel. Coun., 1976-78; state rep. 20th Legis. Dist., 1979-94; mayor City of Pitts., 1994—. Democrat. Office: Office of the Mayor 512 City County Bldg 414 Grant St Pittsburgh PA 15219-2404

MURPHY, THOMAS JOHN, publishing executive; b. Lockport, N.Y., Mar. 29, 1931; s. Matthew J. and Mary Frances (Tracy) M.; m. Maryann Elizabeth Stadnicki, Dec. 29, 1956; children: Kevin, Janine, Peter, Thomas. B.S., SUNY-Brockport, 1952; postgrad., Boston U., 1955-57, Northwestern U., 1976. Sales rep., asst. dir. advt., mgr. sales services, dir. tng., asst. dir. mktg., dir. mktg. McGraw-Hill Co., St. Louis, N.Y.C., 1954-73; v.p., gen. mgr. sch. dept. Holt, Rinehart & Winston pub. CBS, Inc., N.Y.C., 1973-78; sr. v.p. CBS Sch. Pub., 1978-80, pres., 1980-82; v.p. AICPA, 1982-88; ptnr. Profl. Pub. Svcs. Co., Westport, Conn., 1988—; pres. World Book Pubs., 1991. Contbr. articles to profl. jours. Bd. dirs. Brockport Found., 1977-83, Rec. for the Blind, 1980-89, Inter-Faith Housing Assn., 1991-94. Named to Heritage Hall of Fame, SUNY. Democrat. Roman Catholic. Home and Office: 4 Ivanhoe Ln Westport CT 06880-5038

MURPHY, THOMAS JOSEPH, archbishop; b. Chgo., Oct. 3, 1932; s. Barthomew Thomas and Nellie M. AB, St. Mary of the Lake Sem., 1954, STB, 1956, MA, 1957, STL, 1958, STD, 1960. Ordained priest Roman Cath. Ch., 1958. Various positions with Archdiocese of Chgo.; bishop of Great Falls-Billings Mont., 1978-87; coadjutor archbishop of Seattle, 1987-91, archbishop of Seattle, 1991—. Office: Archdiocese of Seattle 910 Marion St Seattle WA 98104-1274*

MURPHY, THOMAS JOSEPH, strategic communications consultant; b. Jersey City, Sept. 26, 1945; m. Carol Elizabeth Murphy, Sept. 10, 1988. BS in Econs., Siena Coll., 1967; postgrad., SUNY, Albany, 1968-71. Sr. budget analyst N.Y. State Ways & Means Com., Albany, 1972-76; dir. program devel. N.Y. State Assembly, Albany, 1977-79, dir. ops., 1980-82; ptnr. Policy Econs. Group, Washington, 1983-86; owner Thomas J. Murphy Assocs., Albany, 1987-91; ptnr. Decision Strategies Group, Albany, 1991—; chmn. Dormitory Authority of N.Y. State, 1995—, mem. N.Y. State Facilities Devel. Corp., 1995, N.Y. State Med. Care Facilities Agy., 1995; co-exec. dir. Med. Waste Policy Com., 1988-89; mem. rev. panel Office of Tech. Assessment, Washington, 1990. Exec. dir. Rep. Assembly Campaign Com., Albany, 1982. Roman Catholic. Home: 1 Fox Run Latham NY 12110-5035 Office: Decision Strategies Group 99 Washington Ave Albany NY 12210

MURPHY, THOMAS MILES, pediatrician; b. Sioux City, Iowa, Dec. 5, 1945; s. Charles Thomas and Madeline Elizabeth (McGovern) M.; m. Priscilla Rollin Coit, Oct. 4, 1969; 1 child, Nicholas Charles. AB in Math., Harvard Coll., 1969; MD, U. Rochester, 1973. Diplomate Am. Bd. Med. Examiners, Am. Bd. Internal Medicine, Am. Bd. Pediatrics, subbd. pulmonology; lic. physician, Va., D.C., Md., Ill., N.C. Intern internal medicine Georgetown U. Med. Divsn., D.C. Gen. Hosp., Washington, 1973-74; resident internal medicine Georgetown U. Med. Ctr., Washington, 1974-76, fellow pediatric pulmonary medicine, 1976-78; asst. prof. pediatrics Georgetown U. Sch. Medicine, Washington, 1979-80, asst. prof. clin. pediatrics, 1980-85; asst. prof. clin. pediatrics U. Chgo., 1985-87, asst. prof. pediatrics and medicine, 1990-93; asst. prof. pediatrics U. Chgo. Pritzker Sch. Medicine, 1987-90, chief sect. pulmonary medicine dept. pediatrics, 1992-93; chief divsn. pediatric pulmonary diseases Duke U., Durham, N.C., 1993—; assoc. dir. Pediatric Pulmonary and Cystic Fibrosis Ctr., Georgetown U., 1978-80; asst. prof. child health and devel. George Washington U. Sch. Medicine and Health Scis., Washington, 1980-85; assoc. chmn. dept. pulmonary medicine, co-dir. Cystic Fibrosis Ctr. for Care, Teaching and Rsch., Children's Hosp. Nat. Med. Ctr., Washington, 1980-85; dir. pediatric pulmonary fellowship tng. program U. Chgo., 1990-93, dir. Cystic Fibrosis Ctr., 1991-93, assoc. chief sect. allergy, immunology and pulmonology, dept. pediatrics, 1991-92. Contbr. articles to profl. jours., chpts. to books; cons. referee editor New Eng. Jour. Medicine, 1989—, Am. Rev. Respiratory Disease, 1989—, Am. Jour. Physiology: Lung Cellular and Molecular Physiology, 1990—, Pediatric Rsch., 1991—, Jour. Applied Physiology, 1991—, Pediatric Pulmonology, 1993—; contbg. editor The Hudson Monitor. Mem. ctr. com. Cystic Fibrosis Found., 1992—; chmn. childhood lung disease com. D.C. Lung Assn., 1980-83, lung disease com., 1984; mem. adv. coun. D.C. Sudden Infant Death Syndrome, 1981-83, chmn. med. adv. com., 1982-83. Recipient Community Svc. award So. Md. Lung Assn., 1980, Media award Am. Acad. Pediatrics, 1980, Svc. award homicide br. Met. Police Dept. D.C., 1983, Svc. award Met. D.C. chpt. Cystic Fibrosis Foun., Washington, 1985; rsch. grantee Am. Lung Assn., N.Y.C., 1992, NIH, Bethesda, Md., 1993. Mem. AAAS, Soc. Pediatric Rsch., Am. Physiol. Soc., N.Y. Acad. Scis., Am. Thoracic Soc. (program com. assembly on respiratory structure and function 1993—). Avocations: youth soccer, jazz. Office: Duke U Med Ctr PO Box 2994 Durham NC 27715-2994

MURPHY, THOMAS PATRICK, lawyer; b. Syracuse, N.Y., Feb. 12, 1952; s. George Edward and Sara Eileen (Murphy) M.; m. Susan Hollis Francher, Oct. 19, 1974 (div. Oct. 1992); m. Lise M. Adkins, Aug. 6, 1994; children: Casey Marie, Matthew Thomas. BS, Clarkson U., 1974; JD, Vermont Law Sch., 1978. Bar: N.Y. 1978, D.C. 1981, Md. 1988, Va. 1989. Asst. U.S. atty. U.S. Atty.'s Office, Washington, 1982-85; assoc. Highsaw & Mahoney, Washington, 1985-87, McGuire, Woods, Battle & Boothe, Washington, 1987-90; ptnr. Reed Smith Shaw & McClay, McLean, Va., 1990—. Contbr. articles to profl. jours. Chmn. bd. profl. responsibility D.C. Ct. Appeals. With USN, 1978-82, USNR, 1978-90. Recipient Spl. Achievement Award U.S. Dept. Justice, 1984. Mem. ABA, Fed. Bar Assn., N.Y. State Bar Assn., D.C. Bar Assn. (chmn. pro se litigants com.), Md. Bar Assn., Asst. U.S. Attys., Bd. Profl. Responsibility D.C. Ct. Appeals (hearing com.). Office: Reed Smith Shaw & McClay 8251 Greensboro Dr Ste 1100 Mc Lean VA 22102-3809

MURPHY, WALTER FRANCIS, political science educator, author; b. Charleston, S.C., Nov. 21, 1929; s. Walter Francis and Ruth (Gaffney) M.; m. Mary Therese Dolan, June 28, 1952; children: Kelly Ann, Holly Ann. AB magna cum laude, U. Notre Dame, 1950; AM, George Washington U., 1954; PhD, U. Chgo., 1957; DLitt (hon.), Coll. Charleston, 1989. Fellow govtl. studies Brookings Instn., 1957-58; faculty Princeton, 1958-95, prof. politics, 1965-95; McCosh Faculty fellow Ford Research prof. govtl. affairs, 1965-66, chmn. dept. politics, 1966-69, McCormick prof. jurisprudence, 1968-95; prof. emeritus, 1995—; Fulbright lectr., 1981, 88, 89; adv. com. on jud. conduct N.J. Supreme Ct., 1982-95. Author: Congress and the Court, 1962, Elements of Judicial Strategy, 1964, Wiretapping on Trial, 1965, (with C.H. Pritchett) Courts, Judges and Politics, 4th edit., 1987, (with M. Danielson) American Democracy, 1969, (with J. Tanenhaus) Comparative Constitutional Law, 1977, The Vicar of Christ, 1979, (with D. Lockard) Basic Cases in Constitutional Law, 3d edit., 1991, The Roman Enigma, 1981, (with J. Fleming and S.A. Barber) American Constitutional Interpretation, 2d edit., 1995, Upon This Rock, 1987; book rev. editor: World Politics, 1972-78; contbr. numerous articles to profl. jours. Mem. N.J. adv. com. U.S. Commn. Civil Rights, 1961-68, vice chmn., 1964-68; mem. N.J. Civil Rights Commn., 1968-70. Served to capt. USMC, 1950-55; col. Res., ret. Decorated D.S.C., Purple Heart; recipient Merriam-Cobb-Hughes award Am. Acad. Pub. Affairs, 1963, Chgo. Found. for Lit. award, 1980; Guggenheim fellow, 1973-74; Nat. Endowment for Humanities fellow, 1978-79. Fellow Am. Acad. Arts and Scis., Italian Acad. Advanced Study in Am.; mem. Am. Polit. Sci. Assn. (editorial bd. rev. 1966-72, Birkhead award 1958, sec. 1982-83, v.p. 1987-88, Lifetime Achievement award 1995), Pi Gamma Mu. Home: 1533 Eagle Ridge Dr NE Albuquerque NM 87122-9999

MURPHY, WALTER YOUNG, academic administrator, clergyman; b. Chester, S.C., Jan. 10, 1930; s. Samuel Fred and Iva (Simpson) M.; m. Marianne Perdue, Aug. 12, 1952; children—Mary Clarice, Julianne. AB, Emory U., 1950; MDiv, Candler Sch. Theology, 1953; LLD (hon.), Bethune Cookman Coll., 1975; DD (hon.), LaGrange Coll., Ga., 1980. Ordained to ministry, United Meth. Ch. Dir. religious life Oxford Coll., Emory U., Oxford, Ga., 1959-62; minister St. James United Meth. Ch., Athens, Ga., 1962-66; exec. v.p. Fla. So. Coll., Lakeland, 1972-76; pres. Andrew Coll., Cuthbert, Ga., 1976-80, La Grange (Ga.) Coll., 1980—; bd. dirs. Nations Bank, La Grange. Author: La Grange College: Georgia's Oldest Independent School, 1985. Bd. dirs. United Way, Lakeland, Fla., 1970-76, La Grange, 1980—, Ty Cobb Found., 1986—; pres. Chattahoocee coun. Boy Scouts Am., 1988-89; mem. Ga. State Scholarship Commn., 1986-94; trustee West Ga. Med. Ctr., 1990-93; mem. adv. com. Franklin D. Roosevelt Little White House Meml. Mem. La Grange C. of C., Rotary (gov. dist. 6900 1991-92), Nat. Assn. Schs., Colls. and Univs. of United Meth. Ch. (pres. 1990-91), The Commerce Club (Atlanta), Phi Beta Kappa, Omicron Delta Kappa, Sigma Chi. Democrat. Methodist. Home: 1102 Vernon St La Grange GA 30240-2940 Office: La Grange Coll 601 Broad St La Grange GA 30240-2955

MURPHY, WARREN BURTON, writer, screenwriter; b. Jersey City, Sept. 13, 1933; s. Joseph and Eleanore (Muller) M.; m. Dawn E. Walters, June 25, 1955 (div. 1974); children: Deirdre Lee, Megan Patricia, Warren Brian, Ardath Frances; m. Molly Cochran, Feb. 14, 1984; 1 child: Devin Miles. Reporter Hudson Dispatch, Union City, N.J., 1950-52, 1956-58, Jersey Jour., Jersey City, 1958-60; editor Kearny (N.J.) Observer, 1960-62; sec. to mayor Jersey City, 1962-71; novelist, screenwriter, 1972—; commr. N.J. Meadowlands, 1978-81; founding dir. Am. Crime Writers League. Author of more than 100 books including (novels) Razoni and Jackson series, 1974-76, Digger series, 1977-79, Trace series, 1983-87 (Mystery Writers of Am. Edgar award 1984); (with Richard Ben Sapir) The Destroyer series, 1971—, Dead End Street, 1973, One Night Stand, 1973, City in Heat, 1973, Down and Dirty, 1974, Lynch Town, 1974, On the Dead Run, 1975,

Leonardo's Law, 1978, Atlantic City, 1979, The Assassin's Handbook, 1982, The Red Moon, (Gold Medal award West Coast Review of Books) 1984, The Ceiling of Hell (Shamus award Pvt. Eye Writers of Am. 1985) 1984, Remo Williams and the Secret of the Sinanju, 1985, Murder in Manhattan, 1986, The Sure Thing, 1988, The Hand of Lazarus, 1988, The Temple Dogs, 1988, The Forever King, 1992; (with Molly Cochran) Grandmaster, (Mystery Writers of Am. Edgar award 1985) 1984, High Priest, 1987; author screenplay The Eiger Sanction, 1976, (story) Lethal Weapon II, 1989; creator TV series Murphy's Law. Served to sgt. USAF, 1952-56. Recipient Citizenship award Freedoms Found., Valley Forge, Pa., 1955, Pub. Rels. award Nat. League of Cities, 1963. Mem. Private Eye Writers of Am., Mystery Writers of Am., Writers Guild of Am., Mensa. Republican. Methodist. Avocations: chess, math., opera. Home and Office: 2094 Cedar Ln Bethlehem PA 18015-5409

MURPHY, WILLIAM ALEXANDER, JR., diagnostic radiologist, educator; b. Pitts., Apr. 26, 1945; s. William Alexander and LaRue (Eshbaugh); m. Judy Marie Lang, June 18, 1977; children: Abigail Norris, William Lawrence, Joseph Ryan. BS, U. Pitts., 1967; MD, Pa. State U., 1971. Diplomate Am. Bd. Radiology. Medicine intern Barnes Hosp., St. Louis, 1971-72, staff radiologist, 1975-93; radiology resident Washington U., St. Louis, 1972-75, prof. radiology, 1983-93; sect. chief Mallinckrodt Inst. Radiology, St. Louis, 1975-93; cons. Office Med. Examiner City and County St. Louis, 1977—; radiologist, prof. radiology, head divsn. diagnostic imaging, chmn. diagnostic radiology, John S. Dunn Sr. chair MD Anderson Cancer Ctr. U. Tex., 1993—. Contbr. numerous articles to profl. jours. and books. Fellow Am. Acad. Forensic Scis., Am. Coll. Radiology; mem. Radiol. Soc. N.Am., Am. Roentgen Ray Soc., Am. Soc. Bone and Mineral Research, Internat. Skeletal Soc., Assn. Univ. Radiologists. Methodist. Home: 4808 Bellview St Bellaire TX 77401-5306 Office: U Texas Anderson Cancer Ctr Div Dx Imaging 057 1515 Holcombe Blvd Houston TX 77030-4009

MURPHY, WILLIAM MICHAEL, literature educator, biographer; b. N.Y.C., Aug. 6, 1916; s. Timothy Francis and Florence Catherine (McDonald) M.; m. E. Harriet Doane, Sept. 2, 1939; children: David Timothy Michael, Susan Doane, Christopher Ten Broeck. B.A. magna cum laude, Harvard U., 1938, M.A., 1941, Ph.D., 1947. Instr. English Harvard U., 1938-40, 42-43, sec. univ. com. ednl. relations, 1940-42; asst. prof. English Union Coll., Schenectady, 1946-48, assoc. prof., 1948-60, prof., 1960-78, Thomas Lamont prof. ancient and modern lit., 1978-83, rsch. prof., 1983-94, prof. emeritus, 1995—; mem. adv. bd. Cornell Yeats Series, Ithaca, N.Y., 1978—; resident fellow Rockefeller Found. Study and Conf. Ctr., Bellagio, Italy, 1991. Author: David Worcester (1907-1947): A Memorial, 1953, The Yeats Family and the Pollexfens of Sligo, 1971, Prodigal Father: The Life of John Butler Yeats (1839-1922), 1978, Family Secrets: William Butler Yeats and His Relatives, 1995. Mem. N.Y. State com. U.S. Commn. on Civil Rights, 1962-74. Served to lt. USNR, 1943-46. Recipient Meritorious Service award United Negro Coll. Fund, 1967; fellow Am. Council Learned Soc., 1968; grantee Am. Philos. Soc., 1968, 75. Mem. MLA, AAUP, Am. Com. on Irish Studies, Can. Assn. Irish Studies, N.S. Bird Soc., Phi Beta Kappa (pres. Alpha chpt. 1954-56). Clubs: Harvard of Eastern N.Y. (pres. 1960-62); Fortnightly (Schenectady) (pres. 1966-67). Office: Humanities Bldg Union Coll Schenectady NY 12308

MURPHY, WILLIAM ROBERT, lawyer; b. New Haven, Oct. 6, 1927; s. Michael David and Loretta Dorothy (Murphy) M.; m. Virginia Anne Selfors, July 23, 1960; children: David M., Christopher W. B.A., Yale U., 1950, LL.B., 1953. Bar: Conn. 1953, U.S. Dist. Ct. Conn. 1957, U.S. Ct. Appeals (2d cir.) 1966, U.S Supreme Ct. 1956, U.S. Ct. Appeals (Fed. cir.) 1986. Assoc. Tyler Cooper & Alcorn, New Haven, 1957-60, ptnr., 1960—. Exec. editor: Yale Law Jour., 1952-53. Sec. John Brown Cook Found., 1971—; mem. Woodbridge Bd. Edn., Conn., 1969-75, Woodbridge Planning and Zoning Commn., 1967-69.Served to lt (j.g.) USNR, 1945-46, 53-56. James Cooper fellow Conn. Bar Found. Fellow Am. Coll. Trial Lawyers, Am. Bar Found.; mem. ABA, Conn. Bar Assn., New Haven County Bar Assn., Quinnipiack Club, Mory's Assn. Home: 15 Ledge Rd Woodbridge CT 06525-1801 Office: Tyler Cooper & Alcorn 205 Church St New Haven CT 06510-1805

MURPHY-BARSTOW, HOLLY ANN, financial consultant; b. St. Joseph, Mo., Jan. 16, 1960; d. Roy Edward and Kathryn Louise (Bachle) Murphy; m. Bruce William Barstow, Oct. 1, 1983; children: Brett Murphy, Taylor Lin. Student, U. Mo., 1978-79; BS, N.W. Mo. State U., 1981. Acct. exec. S.C. Johnson, Omaha, Nebr., 1982-83; dir. mktg. YMCA, Omaha, Nebr., 1983-85; fin. cons. Merrill Lynch, Omaha, Nebr., 1985-89, Smith Barney, Omaha, Nebr., 1989—; instr. fin. seminar Creighton U., Omaha, 1993—, Dana Coll., Blair, Nebr., 1993—; fin. corres. KMTV-3, KETV-7, WOWT-6, Omaha, 1993—. Pres. Am. Lung Assn. Nebr., Omaha, 1992-96; vice chair bd. trustees First Presbyn. Ch., Omaha, 1989-93; membership chair bd. mgrs. West YMCA, Omaha, 1991—; mem Columbian Sch. PTA; campaign chair Toys for Tots, 1994—; founding mem. Omaha Women's Fund. Named one of Ten Outstanding Young Omahans, Omaha Jaycees, 1994. Mem. Omaha Panhellenic Assn., Leadership Omaha (grad.), River City Roundup (trail boss 1989), Sigma Sigma Sigma. Avocations: reading, sewing, travel, golf. Office: Smith Barney 9394 W Dodge Rd # 250 Omaha NE 68114-3319

MURPHY-LIND, KAREN MARIE, health educator, dermatology nurse; b. Boston, Oct. 7, 1953; d. William Joseph and Mary Catherine (Mulcahy) Murphy; m. Gary W. Lind, Feb. 28, 1976; 1 child, Nicholas. RN, AS, Laboure Coll., Dorchester, Mass., 1993. Health edn./cmty. outreach coord. Mass. Gen. Hosp., Bunker Hill Health Ctr., Charlestown, 1993—, dermatology nurse, 1993—, Dept. Pub. Health breast cancer initiative outreach worker, 1992—, advisor cmty. adv. bd., 1992—. Mem. Health Charlestown Coalition, 1993—; bd. dirs. Am. Cancer Soc. Cen. Boston Breast, 1995—, co-chair cancer control core team, 1995—. Recipient Lifesaver pub. edn. award Am. Cancer Soc., Metro North, Mass., 1994, Make A Difference award, 1995. Mem. Am. Cancer Soc. (Ctrl. Boston bd. dirs. 1995—, co-chair Boston breast cancer control team 1995—), Mass. Nurses Assn., Dermatology Nurses Assn., Soc. Pub. Health Edn., Am. Assn. Office Nurses. Avocation: gourmet cooking. Home: 387 Central Ave Milton MA 02186-2803 Office: MGH Bunker Hill Health Ctr 73 High St Charlestown MA 02129-3037

MURR, JAMES COLEMAN, federal government official; b. Lake Charles, La., Oct. 29, 1944; m. Connie Paige Chadwell, Sept. 21, 1968; children: Christopher David, Richard Reno. BA, Tex. Tech U., 1966; MPA, Am. U., 1974. With Sears, Roebuck & Co., Tex., 1971-72, Dept. Labor, Washington, 1972-74, U.S. Customs Svc., Treasury, Washington, 1975-76; legis. analyst Office Mgmt. and Budget, Washington, 1977-81, br. chief, 1982-89, assoc. dir. administrn., 1990-93, asst. dir. legis. reference, 1994—. Capt. USAF, 1967-70. Roman Catholic. *

MURRA, JOHN VICTOR, anthropologist, educator; b. Odessa, Ukraine, Aug. 24, 1916; came to U.S., 1934, naturalized, 1950; B.A., U. Chgo., 1936, M.A., 1942, Ph.D., 1956; hon. doctorate, U. Barcelona, 1993. Instr. U. Chgo., 1943-47; asst. prof. U. P.R., 1947-49; from asst. prof. to prof. Vassar Coll., 1950-61; vis. prof. Yale, 1961-63; prin. investigator study Andes, NSF, 1963-66; vis. prof. U. San Marcos, Lima, Peru, 1958, 65-66; hon. prof. U. San Marcos, 1966; prof. anthropology Cornell U., 1968—; Lewis H. Morgan lectr. U. Rochester, 1969; area specialist UN Secretariat, 1951; founding mem. Inst. de Estudios Peruanos, Inst. Nacional de Antropologia e Historia of Ecuador; past mem. bd. Am. Com. Africa; mem. Inst. for Advanced Study, Princeton, 1974-75; directeur d'études associé Ecole des Hautes Etudes, Paris, 1975-76. Author: The Economic Organization of the Inka State, 1980. Served with Spanish Republican Army, 1937-39. Decorated Gran Cruz of Order of Sun (Perú); Guggenheim fellow, 1984-85. Mem. Am. Soc. Ethnohistory (pres. 1970-71), Am. Ethnol. Soc. (pres. 1972-73), Inst. Andean Research (pres. 1977—). Home: 515 Dryden Rd Ithaca NY 14850-4835

MURRAH, DAVID J., archivist, historian; b. Shattuck, Okla., Sept. 13, 1941; s. G. Leroy and M. Leila (Montgomery) M.; m. Sherry Edwards, Mar. 2, 1962 (div. 1966); 1 child, Jerel; m. Ann Lynskey, Dec. 29, 1973; children: Donna, Elaine, Gene. BA, Hardin-Simmons U., 1964; MA, Tex. Tech. U., 1970, PhD, 1979. Pub. sch. tchr. Springtown (Tex.) I.S.D., 1966-67, Morton (Tex.) I.S.D., 1967-71; asst. archivist S.W. Collection Tex. Tech U., Lubbock, 1971-76, asst. dir. S.W. Collection, 1976-77, dir. S.W. Collection, 1977-83, assoc. dir. librs., dir. S.W. Collection, 1983—; bd. dirs. Centercorp, Inc., Lubbock, 1990—. Author: C.C. Slaughter: Rancher, Banker, Baptist, 1981, Pitchfork Land and Cattle Co., 1983, Oil, Taxes and Cats, 1994; co-author: Lubbock & The South Plains, 1989, 2d edit., 1995. Bd. dirs. Broadway Festivals, Inc., Lubbock, 1990—. Recipient Disting. Svc. award Soc. Southwest Archivists, 1988. Mem. Soc. Am. Archivists, Tex. State Hist. Assn., West Tex. Hist. Assn. (pres. 1991-92). Democrat. Baptist. Office: Southwest Collection Tex Tech U PO Box 41041 Lubbock TX 79409-1041

MURRAY, ABBY DARLINGTON BOYD, psychiatric clinical specialist, educator; b. Johnstown, Pa., Mar. 1, 1928; d. Frank Reynolds and Marion Gasson (Allen) Boyd; m. Joseph Christopher Murray, Sept. 16, 1950; children: Anne, Joseph Jr., Mary, John, James. BSN, Georgetown U., 1950; MS Edn. in Guidance and Counseling, L.I. Univ., Brookville, N.Y., 1976; MEd Psychiat. Clin. Specialist, Columbia U., 1977; postgrad., Ctr. for Family Learning, New Rochelle, N.Y., 1981-82. Sch. nurse Huntington (N.Y.) Pub. Schs.; with VA Med. Ctr., Northport, Va., 1973-76; prof. U. Md., Balt., 1978-79, L.I. Univ., Brookville, 1979-81; psychiat. clin. specialist VA Med. Ctr., Brooklyn, Va., 1984-87, East Orange, N.J., 1987-89; nurse educator Ft. Monmouth, N.J., 1989—; family therapist Family & Cmty. Counseling Agy., Red Bank, N.J., 1989—; program planner, Ft. Monmouth. Republican. Roman Catholic. Avocation: tennis. Home: 91 Tanyard Ln Huntington NY 11743 also: 116 Manor Dr Red Bank NJ 07701

MURRAY, ALAN STEWART, publishing executive; b. Akron, Ohio, Nov. 16, 1954; s. John and Catherine (Case) M.; m. Lori Esposito, Sept. 8, 1984; children: Lucy Ann, Amanda. BA in English, U. N.C.; MS in Econs., London Sch. Econs. Editor bus. and econs. Chattanooga Times, 1977-79; reporter Congrl. Quarterly, Washington, 1980-81, 82-83, Nihon Keizai Shimbun, Tokyo, 1981-82; reporter econs. Wall Street Jour., Washington, 1983-92, dep. bur. chief, 1992-93, bur. chief, 1993—. Co-author: Showdown At Gucci Gulch, 1987 (Carey McWilliams award 1988); panelist Sta. PBS, Washington in Rev.; commentary Sta. NBC, News at Sunrise. Bd. dirs., exec. com. Small Enterprise Assistance Fund, Washington, 1992—. Recipient Overseas Press Club award, 1991, Gerald Loeb award, 1992, Excellence in Bus./Fin. Journalsim award John Hancock Fin. Svcs., 1992; John Motley Morehead scholar; Luce fellow, Tokyo, 1981-82. Mem. U. N.C. Gen. Alumnus Assn. (bd. dirs. 1993—, Disting. Young Alumnus award), Gridiron Club, Phi Beta Kappa. Office: Wall St Jour 1025 Connecticut Ave NW Washington DC 20036

MURRAY, ALBERT L., writer, educator; b. Nokomis, Ala., May 12, 1916; s. John Lee and Sudie (Graham) Young; m. Mozelle Menefee, May 31, 1941; 1 child, Michele. B.S. in Edn., Tuskegee Inst., 1939; M.A. in English, NYU, 1948; postgrad., U. Mich., 1940, Northwestern U., 1941, U. Paris, 1950; Litt. D. (hon.), Colgate U., 1975. Tchr. undergrad. composition and lit. Tuskegee Inst., 1940-43, 46-51, also dir. Coll. Little Theatre, cons. on jazz; lectr. Grad. Sch. Journalism, Columbia U., N.Y.C., 1968; O'Connor prof. lit. Colgate U., 1970, O'Connor lectr., 1973, prof. humanities, 1982; vis. prof. lit. U. Mass., Boston, 1971; Paul Anthony Brick lectr. U. Mo., 1972; writer-in-residence Emory U., 1978; adj. assoc. prof. creative writing Barnard Coll., N.Y.C., 1981-83; lectr., participant symposia in field; duPont vis. scholar Washington and Lee U., 1993. Author: The Omni Americans, 1970, South to a Very Old Place, 1972, The Hero and the Blues, 1973, Train Whistle Guitar, 1974 (Lillian Smith award for fiction), Stomping the Blues, 1976 (ASCAP Deems Taylor award for music criticism), Good Morning Blues: The Autobiography of Count Basie as told to Albert Murray, 1985, The Spyglass Tree, 1991, The Seven League Boots, 1996, The Blue Devils of Nada, 1996; also numerous articles. Served to maj. USAAF, World War II; ret. USAAF. Woodrow Wilson fellow Drew U., 1983, Lincoln Ctr. Dirs. Emeriti award, 1991.

MURRAY, ALLEN EDWARD, oil company executive; b. N.Y.C., Mar. 5, 1929; s. Allen and Carla (Jones) M.; m. Patricia Ryan, July 28, 1951; children: Allen, Marilyn, Ellen, Eileen, Allison. B.S. in Bus. Adminstrn, NYU, 1956. Trainee Pub. Nat. Bank & Trust Co., N.Y.C., 1948-49; acct. Gulf Oil Corp., 1949-52; various fin. positions Socony-Vacuum Overseas Supply Co. (Mobil), 1952-56; with Mobil Oil Corp. (subs. Mobil Corp.), 1956—, v.p. planning N.Am. div., 1968-69, v.p. planning, supply and transp. N.Am. div., 1969-74, exec. v.p. N.Am. div., 1974, pres. U.S. mktg. and refining div., exec. v.p., 1975-82, pres. worldwide mktg. and refining, 1979-82, corp. pres., 1983-84, COO, 1984-86, CEO, COO, chmn. exec. com., 1986—, chmn. bd., 1986—, also dir., 1976—; pres., chief operating officer Mobil Corp., N.Y.C., 1984-86, chmn., pres., chief exec. officer, 1986—, dir., 1977—; dir. Met. Life Ins. Co. Mem. adv. council Columbia U. Grad. Sch. Bus.; trustee Presbyn. Hosp., N.Y.C. Served with USNR, 1946-48. Mem. Nat. Fgn. Trade Council (dir.), Am. Petroleum Inst. (dir.), Council on Fgn. Relations. Club: Huntington Country. Office: Mobil Corp PO Box 2072 New York NY 10163-2072*

MURRAY, ANNE, country singer; b. Springhill, N.S., Can., June 20, 1945; d. Carson and Marion (Burke) M.; m. William M. Langstroth, June 20, 1975; children: William Stewart, Dawn Joanne. B.Phys. Edn., U. N.B., 1966, D.Litt. (hon.), 1978; D.Litt. (hon.), St. Mary's U., 1982. Rec. artist for, Arc Records, Can., 1968, Capitol Records, 1969—; appeared on series of TV spls., CBC, 1970-81, 88-93; star CBS spls., 1981-85; toured N. Am., Japan, England, Germany, Holland, Ireland, Sweden, Australia and New Zealand, 1977-82; released 31 albums including: A Little Good News, 1984, As I Am, 1988, Greatest Hits, vols. I, 1981, vol. II, 1989, Harmony, 1987, You Will, 1990, Yes I Do, 1991, Croonin', 1993, others. Hon. chmn. Can. Save the Children Fund, 1978-80. Recipient Juno awards as Can.'s top female vocalist, 1970-81; Can.'s Top Country Female Vocalist, 1970-86; Grammy award as top female vocalist-country, 1974; Grammy award as top female vocalist-pop, 1978; Grammy award as top female vocalist-country, 1980, 83; Country Music Assn. awards, 1983-84; named Female Rec. Artist of Decade, Can. Rec. Industry Assn., 1980, Top Female Vocalist 1970-86; star inserted in Hollywood Walkway of Stars, 1980; Country Music Hall of Fame Nashville; decorated companion Order of Can.; inducted Juno Hall of Fame, 1993. Mem. AFTRA, Assn. Canadian TV and Radio Artists, Am. Fedn. Musicians. Office: Balmur Ltd, 4950 Yonge St Madison Ctr 2400, Toronto, ON Canada M2N 6K1

MURRAY, ARTHUR G., food products executive; b. 1945. Asst. corp. contr. Mickelberry Corp., Chgo., 1967-71; pres. Mama Cookie Bakeries Inc., Chgo., 1971-79; pres., CEO Salerno Magowen Biscuit Co., Chgo., 1979-84; exec. v.p. of ops. Sunshine Biscuits Inc., Woodbridge, N.J., 1984-88, pres., COO, 1988—. With U.S. Army, 1963-66. Office: Sunshine Biscuits Inc 100 Woodbridge Center Dr Woodbridge NJ 07095-1125*

MURRAY, BARBARA ANN, banker; b. Mitchell, S.D., Apr. 17, 1953; d. John Richard and Shirley Ann (Larson) McNary; m. Wayne Allan Murray, Jan. 25, 1975; children: Corissa Ann, Rebecca Lea, Jeffrey Wayne, Katie Aileen. BS in Edn., Dakota State Coll., 1975. Substitute tchr. Sioux Falls Pub. Schs., S.D., 1975; assoc. Murray Constrn., Sioux Falls, 1975-82; telephone rep. Citibank S.D. NA, Sioux Falls, 1982-83, sr. svc. rep., 1983-84, unit mgr. customer svc., 1984-88, unit mgr. image processing, 1988-89, mgr. corr. svcs., 1989-90, unit mgr., chargeback specialist, 1990-91, unit mgr. cardmem. acctg., 1991-92, unit mgr. nat. accounts payable, 1992-94, mem. gen. ledger implementation mgmt. team, 1994—; owner-operator Hartford Café & Catering, 1994—. Supr. Sunday sch., 1988—, confirmation tchr., 1992-94; mem. bd. edn. First Luth. Ch. Mem. Nat. Assn. Female Execs. Democrat. Lutheran. Clubs: Mothers (pres. 1977-78), Christian Women's (prayer adviser 1980-82). Lodge: Order Eastern Star. Avocations: sewing, camping, hiking, sports. Home: Country Villa Estates 46466 267th St Hartford SD 57033-6917

MURRAY, BILL, actor, writer; b. Evanston, Ill., Sept. 21, 1950; m. Margaret Kelly, 1980; children: Homer, Luke. Grad., Loyola Acad.; attended, Regis Coll., Denver; student, Second City Workshop, Chgo. Formerly with improvisational theater group Second City, Chgo.; writer; performer off-broadway National Lampoon Radio Hour; regular on TV series Saturday Night Live, 1977-80, also writer; featured in 3 prodns. of. TVTV co.; played Johnny Storm, the Human Torch in radio series Marvel Comics' Fantastic Four; appeared in movies Meatballs, 1977, Mr. Mike's Mondo Video, 1979, Where the Buffalo Roam, 1980, Caddyshack, 1980, Stripes, 1981, Tootsie, 1982, Ghostbusters, 1984, The Razor's Edge, 1984, Nothing Lasts Forever, 1984, Little Shop of Horrors, 1986, Scrooged, 1988, Ghostbusters II, 1989, What About Bob?, 1991, Groundhog Day, 1993, Mad Dog and Glory, 1993, Ed Wood, 1994, Kingpin, 1996; co-producer, co-dir., actor film Quick Change, 1990; other TV appearances include Things We Did Last Summer. Recipient Emmy award for best writing for comedy series, 1977. Office: William Carroll Agency 139 N San Fernando Rd Ste A Burbank CA 91502

MURRAY, BILLY DWAYNE, SR., church administrator; b. Nash County, N.C., Apr. 8, 1930; m. Oma Lee Hensley; children: B. Dwayne, Jr., Susan Murray Duncan, Beth Murray Aukerman. Student, Kings Bus. Coll., Raleigh, N.C. Ordained to ministry, Ch. of God of Prophecy, 1950. Pastor Ch. God of Prophecy, Waynesville, N.C., 1950-51, Biltmore and Elk Mountain, N.C., 1951, Selma, N.C., 1954-58, Leaksville, N.C., 1958-61, Bethany, N.C., 1961-65, Greenville, S.C., 1965-66; served at N.C. state hdqs. Ch. God of Prophecy, 1951-54; gen. Sunday sch. sec. world hdqs. Ch. God of Prophecy, Cleveland, Tenn., 1966-72; state overseer Tenn. Ch. God of Prophecy, 1972-77; asst. editor White Wing Messenger, 1977-89; overseer Ill. Ch. God of Prophecy, 1989-90, gen. overseer, 1990—; chief usher Gen. Assembly, 1967-72; mem. questions and subjects com., mem. editorial com. ch. history, policy and doctrine, gen. properties com. Office: Church of God of Prophecy PO Box 2910 Cleveland TN 37320-2910

MURRAY, BRIAN WILLIAM, lawyer; b. Newton, Mass., Jan. 20, 1960; s. William Andrew and Arleen Veronica (Dagnese) M.; m. Emily Gottschling, Aug. 22, 1987; children: Alexandra Leland, John William. BA, Stonehill Coll., Newton, Mass., 1981; JD, New Eng. Sch. Law, Boston, 1984. Bar: Mass. 1985, R.I. 1985, U.S. Dist. Ct. Mass. 1985. Assoc. William A. Murray Law Office, Milford, Mass., 1985—; conveyancing atty. Milford Fed. Savs. & Loan, 1992—; mem. hearing com. Bd. Bar Overseers, Boston, 1993—. Mem., chmn. War Meml. Com., Milford, 1986-93, Milford Sch. Com., 1989—; mem. Milford Sch. Bldg. Com., 1991—; pres. Friends Milford Sr. Ctr., 1990—; pro bono atty. Vol. Lawyers Svc., Worcester, Mass., 1993—. Recipient Fenn award for leadership John F. Kennedy Libr., Boston, 1992, citation Milford Bd. Selectmen, 1993. Mem. Mass. Bar Assn., R.I. Bar Assn., Worcester County Bar Assn., Mass. Acad. Trial Lawyers. Democrat. Avocations: bicycling, skiing, home. Home: 23 Congress Ter Milford MA 01757-4021 Office: 260 Main St Milford MA 01757-2504

MURRAY, BRYAN, professional sports team executive; married; two children. Grad., McGill U., Montreal. Former athletic dir., hockey coach McGill U.; gen. mgr., head coach Detroit Red Wings, 1990-94; gen. mgr. Fla. Panthers, 1994—. Recipient Jack Adams award as NHL Coach of Yr., 1983-84. Office: Florida Panthers 10th Flr 100 Northeast Third Ave Fort Lauderdale FL 33301

MURRAY, BRYAN CLARENCE, professional sports team executive; b. Shawville, Que., Can., Dec. 5, 1942; came to U.S., 1980; s. Clarence Herbert and Rhoda (Schwartz) M.; m. Geraldine Frances Sutton, July 8, 1967; 1 dau., Heide Alicia. Grad., McGill U., 1964. Athletic dir. MacDonald Coll., Ste. Anne de Bellevue, Que., 1968-72; coach, tchr. Rockland Nat.-Pontiac High Sch., Rockland, Ont., 1974-76; coach Pembroke-Kings, Pembroke, Ont., 1976-79, Regina Pats, Sask., 1979-80, Hershey (Pa.) Bears, 1980-81; former coach Washington Capitals, Landover, Md., from 1981; coach, gen. mgr. Detroit Red Wings, 1990-94; gen. manager Florida Panthers, Fort Lauderdale, Flor., 1994—. Office: Florida Panthers 100 NE 3rd Ave Fl 10 Fort Lauderdale FL 33301-1176*

MURRAY, CAROLINE FISH, psychologist; b. Buenos Aires, Argentina, Mar. 28, 1920; came to U.S., 1924; d. Alfred Dupont and Caroline Johnston (Ramsay) Chandler; m. Henry A. Murray, May 17, 1969; children by previous marriages: Caroline D. Janover, Alexander M. Davis, Ann Kelso D. MacLaughlin, Quita D. Palmer, Maude I. Fish. AB magna cum laude, Smith Coll., 1942; MEd, U. N.H., 1962; EdD, Boston U., 1967. Exec. sec. to dir. Alfred I. duPont Inst., Wilmington, Del., 1953-55; tchr. Kingston (N.H.) Pub. Schs., 1962-63; instr. Boston U., 1966-67, asst. prof. psychology, 1967-71, co-dir. psycho-educational clinic, 1966-70, coord. headstart evaluation and rsch. ctr., 1966-69, cons., 1969-83; mem. clin. staff Mass. Mental Health Ctr., Boston, 1983-90; lectr. psychology dept. psychiatry Harvard Med. Sch., 1983-91; mem. profl. adv. com. Mass. Dept. Mental Health, 1983-85; cons. Indochinese Psychiatry Clinic, Brighton, Mass., 1987—, sch. consultation and treatment team Mass. Mental Health Ctr., 1987-90; mem. profl. adv. com. Mass. Dept. Mental Health, 1983-85, adolescent planning subcom., 1990—. Corporator Nantucket Cottage Hosp., 1993—; bd. dirs. Friends Nantucket Pub. Schs., 1993—, Wediko Children's Svcs., 1975-85, Shaker Village, Hancock, Mass., Douglas A. Thom Clinic, Boston, 1974-77, pres., 1977; chmn. bd. Ariel Chamber Music, Cambridge, 1979, Mass. Children's Lobby, 1978-82, pres., 1979-81, Nantucket Edn. Trust, Friends of Nantucket Atheneum; chmn. statewide adv. council Office for Children, 1980-82. Mem. APA, Am. Assn. Advancement Psychology, Mass. Psychol. Assn., Eastern Psychol. Assn., N.Y. Acad. Scis., Fedn. Am. Sci., Jean Piaget Soc., Pi Lambda Theta. Democrat. Home: 11 Lincoln Ave Nantucket MA 02554-3412

MURRAY, CHERRY ANN, physicist, researcher; b. Ft. Riley, Kans., Feb. 6, 1952; d. John Lewis and Cherry Mary (Roberts) M.; m. Dirk Joachim Muehlner, Feb. 18, 1977; children: James Joachim, Sara Hester. BS in Physics, MIT, 1973, PhD in Physics, 1978. Rsch. asst. physics dept. MIT, Cambridge, 1969-78; rsch. assoc. Bell Labs., Murray Hill, N.J., 1976-77; mem. tech. staff AT&T Bell Labs., Murray Hill, 1978-85, disting. mem. tech. staff, 1985-87, dept. head low-temperature and solid-state physics rsch., 1987-90, dept. head condensed matter physics rsch., 1990-93, dept. head semicond. physics rsch., 1993—; co-chair Gordon Rsch., Wolfeboro, N.H., 1982, chair, 1984. Contbr. numerous articles to profl. jours. and chpts. to books. NSF fellow, 1969; IBM fellow MIT, 1974-76. Fellow Am. Phys. Soc. (Maria Goeppart-Mayer award 1989), Sigma Xi. Office: Bell Labs Lucent Techs 700 Mountain Ave Rm 1D-334 New Providence NJ 07974

MURRAY, CHRISTOPHER CHARLES, III, architect; b. Bklyn., July 6, 1950; s. Christopher Charles and Gertrude Rose (Marr) M.; m. Ann Herring, Nov. 16, 1974. BArch, U. Notre Dame, 1973. Registered architect, N.Y., Md., D.C., Va., Ga. Project architect Hibner Architects, Garden City, N.Y., 1973-76; project mgr. BBM Architects, N.Y.C., 1976-79; project dir. Gensler & Assocs., N.Y.C., 1979-84, office dir., v.p., mem. nat. mgmt. com., 1984—. Prin. works include interior design Sidley & Austin Worldwide, Hewlett-Packard Regional HQ, Dept. Edn., First Am. Bankshares. Asst. scoutmaster Boy Scouts Am., also cubmaster, NCAC unit commr.; active Greater Washington Bd. Trade, 1986. Mem. AIA, N.Y. Soc. Architects, Md. Soc. Architects, Notre Dame Club, Club at Franklin Sq (bd. dirs.). Roman Catholic. Home: 12517 Knightsbridge Ct Rockville MD 20850-3732 Office: Gensler & Assocs 1101 17th St NW Washington DC 20036-4704

MURRAY, COLETTE MORGAN, healthcare executive, fundraising consultant; b. San Francisco, July 28, 1935; d. Thomas Ralph and Althea L. (Bail) Morgan; m. J. Roger Samuelsen, Sept. 14, 1959 (div. 1969); 1 child, Thea S. Kano; m. Richard Arlan Murray, Nov. 4, 1983. AB, U. Calif., Berkeley, 1959; JD, U. San Francisco, 1964; cert. in mgmt., U. Calif., Davis, 1975, U. Tex., 1989. Cert. fund raising exec. Pvt. practice law Walnut Creek, Calif., 1965-73; exec. dir. Calif. Alumni Assn., Berkeley, 1973-78; asst. chancellor univ. rels. U. Calif., Santa Cruz, 1978-85; v.p. for devel. and alumni U. Louisville, Ky., 1985-88; v.p. for devel. and univ. rels. Tex. Tech. U., Lubboch, 1988-90; corp. v.p. for philanthropy and community devel. Henry Ford Health System, Detroit, 1990-95; CEO Sharp Healthcare Found., San Diego, 1995—; cons. Coun. for the Advancement and Support of Edn., Washington, 1980—, NSFRE, Washington, 1992-93; bd. dirs. Leadership Detroit, 1992-95, pres. Leadership Am. Assn., Washington, 1993-94. Bd. dirs. CATCH, Detroit, 1990-95. Recipient Dorothy Shaw award Alpha Delta Pi, 1958; named Citizen of Yr., Santa Cruz C. of C., 1981. Mem. NSFRE (pres. 1994), Coun. for Advancement and Support of Edn. (chair bd. 1981-82, Hesburgh award 1984), Univ. Club, San Diego Country Club. Avocations: art and teddy bear collecting, music, travel, golf, cooking. Office: Sharp Healthcare Found Ste 302 8525 Gibbs Dr San Diego CA 92123

MURRAY, DANIEL RICHARD, lawyer; b. Mar. 23, 1946; s. Alfred W. and Gloria D. Murray. AB, U. Notre Dame, 1967; JD, Harvard U., 1970.

Bar: Ill. 1970, U.S. Dist. Ct. (no. dist.) Ill. 1970, U.S. Ct. Appeals (7th cir.) 1971, U.S. Supreme Ct. 1974. Ptnr. Jenner & Block, Chgo., 1970—; trustee Chgo. Mo. and Western Rlwy. Co., 1988—. Co-author: Illinois Code Comments, 1976, Secured Transactions, 1978. Bd. dirs. Big Shoulders Fund, Archdiocese of Chgo. Mem. Am. Bankruptcy Inst., Am. Law Inst., Am. Coll. Comml. Fin. Lawyers, Transp. Lawyers Assn., Assn. of Transp. Practitioners, Law Club, Legal Club. Roman Catholic. Home: 1307 N Sutton Pl Chicago IL 60610-2007 Office: Jenner & Block One IBM Plz Chicago IL 60611

MURRAY, DAVID, pastor, social worker; b. Chicago, Ill., Mar. 4, 1953; s. Julius and Alberta (Tolbert) M. m. Debra McKnight, Oct. 7, 1989; 3 foster children. BS in Criminal Justice, Wayne State U., Detroit, 1982; DDiv, God's Divine Emancipation Tng., 1975; cert. mktg., Detroit Bus. Inst., 1978; MA in Teaching, Wayne State U., 1989; MA in Criminal Justice Studies, U. Detroit Mercy, 1994. Pastor First Holy Temple Ch., Detroit, 1975—; asst. payments worker Mich. Dept. of Social Svcs., Detroit, 1981-85, social svcs. specialist, 1985—. Inventor cardiovascular display system. Pres., bd. dirs. Project Care, Detroit, 1975; mem. Detroit Police Res., 1978-83; instr. CPR ARC, Detroit, 1979, advanced 1st aid, 1980—; instr., trainer Am. Heart Assn., Detroit, 1983—; active Big Bros/Big Sisters Am.; chaplain Detroit Receiving Hosp.; asst. chaplain Wayne County Youth Home, 1978—; chmn. David Murray Scholarship Fund; chmn. com. help handicapped student Mary Grove Coll. Recipient Cert. Appreciation, IRS, Acctg. Aid Soc., 1987, Detroit City Clk. Disting Citizen award, 1988, Wayne County Commrs. Cert. Appreciation, Mich. Senate Spl. tribute, 1988, U.S. Senate proclamation, 1988, TV 2 Jefferson award 1991 Cert. Nomination, Life award Met. Youth Found., 1991. Mem. NAACP, NASW, AACD, Internat. Conf. Police Chaplains, Detroit Fedn. Tchrs., Eighth Point Investigations, Detroit Police Chaplains Corps, Detroit Police Officers Assn., Wayne County Sheriff Dept. (sheriff chaplain), Masons, Golden Key. Avocations: table tennis, music. Home: 18994 Oak Dr Detroit MI 48221-2264

MURRAY, DAVID GEORGE, architect; b. Tulsa, Nov. 9, 1919; s. Lee Cloyd and Marion (Bennett) M.; m. Margaret Elizabeth Oldham, Sept. 23, 1944; children: Michael Allen, Lucy Margaret (Mrs. Norman Scheer), Patrick David. BArch, Okla. State U., 1942. Registered architect, Okla. Ptnr. Atkinson & Murray, Tulsa, 1949-52; prin. David G. Murray & Assocs., Tulsa, 1952-56; pres. Murray, Jones, Murray, Inc., Tulsa, 1957-85, chmn., 1986-89; chmn., bd. govs. Licensed Architects, Oklahoma City, 1964-74. Prin. works include Cities Service Technology Ctr., Broken Arrow, Okla., Terminal Bldg. Tulsa Internat. Airport, St. Patrick's Ch., Oklahoma City, Coll. of Osteopathic Medicine and Surgery, Tulsa, First Nat. Tower, Tulsa, Hillcrest Med. Ctr., Tulsa, Thomas Gilcrease Mus., Tulsa, Tulsa Civic Ctr. Bldgs. Chmn., dir. Goodwill Industries of Tulsa, 1966-87; chmn., exec. com. Downtown Tulsa Unltd., 1975-87; v.p., exec. com., dir. Met. Tulsa C. of C., 1979-85. Served to 1st lt. USAF, 1942-45. Named to Hall of Fame Coll. Engrng. Okla. State U., 1969. Fellow AIA (pres. Tulsa chpt. 1964, mem. com. office practice 1983-87); mem. Southern Hills Country Club (dir. 1977-80). Republican. Methodist. Avocations: travel, golf.

MURRAY, DAVID GEORGE, orthopedic surgeon, educator; b. Ames, Iowa, July 1, 1930; s. William Gordon and Mildred (Furniss) M.; m. Lee McFarland, Dec. 27, 1952 (div. 1984); children: Christopher, Bruce, James; m. Judith M. Sayles, Aug. 4, 1984. Student, Cornell U., 1948-51; M.D., Washington U., St. Louis, 1955. Diplomate: Am. Bd. Orthopaedic Surgery. Intern Vancouver (B.C., Can.) Gen. Hosp., 1955-56; asst. resident in surgery Upstate Med. Center, Syracuse, N.Y., 1958-59; resident in orthopedics State U. Iowa, Iowa City, 1959-62; asst. prof. orthopaedic surgery Upstate Med. Center, Syracuse, 1962-66; asso. prof. Upstate Med. Center, 1966-69, prof., 1969—, Disting. prof., 1990—, chmn. dept., 1966-86, 91—, acting chmn. dept., 1990-91; mem. staff State Univ. Hosp., Syracuse, 1962—, Crouse-Irving Meml. Hosp., Syracuse, 1962—, Syracuse VA Hosp., 1962—; cons. Community Gen. Hosp., Syracuse, 1965—; hon. staff Charles A. Wilson Meml. Hosp., Johnson City, N.Y., 1972—; med. dir. Muscular Dystrophy Assn. Clinic, 1962-67; mem. Task Force for Oral Exams., Nat. Bd. Med. Examiners; examiner Am. Bd. Orthopaedic Surgery. Bd. asso. editors: Jour. Bone and Joint Surgery, 1969-78, Clin. Orthopaedics, 1968-78, Jour. Surg. Research, 1972-82, Orthopaedic Surgery, 1978-79; contbr. articles to profl. jours.; trustee Am. Jour. Bone and Joint Surgery, 1984-90, treas., 1986-90. Bd. dirs. Planned Parenthood Ctr. of Syracuse; chmn. affiliate med. com. Planned parenthood Ctr. of Syracuse, 1976-82; trustee Orthopaedic Rsch. Edn. Found., 1986-92, pres., 1988-91, Martin Momoriac Found., 1988-92, chmn., 1990-92; mem. med. adv. com. Shirners Hosps., 1989-93. Served to lt., M.C. USNR, 1956-57. Mem. AMA, ACS (bd. regents 1985-94, vice chmn. 1992-93, chmn. 1993-94, pres.-elect 1995-96), AAAS, Am. Orthopaedic Assn. (exec. com., chmn. program com. 1982), Am. Acad. Orthopaedic Surgeons (bd. dirs. 1980-86, pres. 1982-83), Assn. Acad. Surgery (sec.-treas., chmn. com. constn. and bylaws), N.Y. State Med. Soc., Onondaga County Med. Soc. (v.p. 1989-90, pres. 1992-93), Am. Rheumatism Assn., Orthopaedic Rsch. Soc., Assn. Bone and Joint Surgeons, Continental Orthopaedic Soc., Knee Soc. (pres. 1989), N.Y. State Soc. Orthopaedic Surgeons, Assn. Orthopaedic Chmn., Phi Beta Kappa, Sigma Xi, Alpha Omega Alpha. Home: 5 Quaker Hill Rd Syracuse NY 13224-2011 Office: 750 E Adams St Syracuse NY 13210-2306

MURRAY, DAVINA ANN, financial analyst; b. Sabetha, Kans., Nov. 12, 1951; d. Jim R. and Shirley A. (Ellington) Murphy; m. Brian C. Murray, July 2, 1981; 1 child, Bria Lynne. AS in Bus., Point Park Coll., 1992, BS in Acctg., 1992; postgrad., Robert Morris Coll., 1996—. With Integra Fin. Corp., Pitts., 1978-96, past acctg. clk., 1978-79, adminstrv. asst., 1980-86, fin. analyst, 1986-96; sr. acctg. officer fixed assets Pitts. Nat. Corp, 1996—. Mem. com. Pitts. City Sch. Redistricting, 1993. Mem. Inst. Mgmt. Accts., Alpha Sigma Lambda. Avocations: reading, sewing, music. Office: Pitts Nat Corp 2 PNC Plz Pittsburgh PA 15265

MURRAY, DIANE ELIZABETH, librarian; b. Detroit, Oct. 15, 1942; d. Gordon Lisle and Dorothy Anne (Stekelee) LaBoueff; m. Donald Edgar Murray, Apr. 22, 1968. AB, Hope Coll., 1964; MLS, Western Mich. U., 1968; MM, Aquinas Coll., 1982; postgrad., Mich. State U., East Lansing, 1964-66. Catalog libr., asst. head acquisitions sect. Mich. State U. Librs., East Lansing, 1968-77; libr. tech. and automated svcs. Hope Coll., Holland, Mich., 1977-88; dir. librs. DePauw U., Greencastle, Ind., 1988-91; acquisitions libr. Grand Valley State U., Allendale, Mich., 1991—; sec., vice chair, chairperson bd. trustees Mich. Libr. Consortium, Lansing, 1981-85. Vice pres. Humane Soc. of Putnam County, Greencastle, 1990-91. Mem. ALA. Methodist. Avocations: dog breeding and showing. Office: Grand Valley State U Zumberge Libr Allendale MI 49401

MURRAY, EDDIE CLARENCE, professional baseball player; b. L.A., Feb. 24, 1956. Student, Calif. State U., L.A. Player minor league teams Bluefield, Miami, Asheville, Charlotte, Rochester, 1973-76; player Balt. Orioles, 1973-88, L.A. Dodgers, 1988-91, N.Y. Mets, 1991-93, Cleveland Indians, 1993—. Named to All-Star Team, 1978, 81-86, 91; named Appalachian League Player of Yr., 1973, Am. League Rookie of Yr., Baseball Writers Assn. Am., 1977, First Baseman, Sporting News Am. League All-Star Team, 1983, 90, ; recipient Gold Glove award, 1982-84, Silver Slugger award, 1983-84, 90. Office: Cleve Indians 2401 Ontario St Cleveland OH 44115*

MURRAY, ELIZABETH DAVIS REID, writer, lecturer; b. Wadesboro, N.C., June 10, 1925; d. James Matheson and Mary Kennedy (Little) Davis; A.B. cum laude, Meredith Coll., Raleigh, N.C., 1946; postgrad. N.C. State U., 1967-68, 74-75; m. James William Reid, Feb. 7, 1948 (dec. June 1972); children: Michael Ernest, Nancy Kennedy Reid Baker, James William; m. Raymond L. Murray, May 12, 1979; stepchildren: Stephen, Ilah Murray Garton, Marshall. Continuity writer Sta. WPTF, Raleigh, 1946-47; program mgr., women's commentator Sta. WADE, Wadesboro, 1947-48; dir. news bur. Meredith Coll., 1948-51; state woman's news editor, columnist Raleigh News and Observer, 1951-52; exec. sec. Gov.'s Coordinating Com. on Aging, 1959-61; rsch. asst. to Dr. Clarence Poe, Raleigh, 1963-64; contbg. editor Raleigh Mag., 1969-72; local history corr. Raleigh Times, News and Observer, Spectator of Raleigh; lectr. art and local history; tchr. Wake history Wake Tech. Coll., Wake pub. schs. and librs.; rsch. cons. Wake County Pub. Libraries, Mordecai Historic Park, State Visitor Ctr., Exec. Mansion; resource person Wake Public Schs.; dir. Capital County Pub. Co.; writer; books include: From Raleigh's Past (cert. of commendation Am. Assn. State and Local History), 1965; Wake: Capital County of North Carolina, vol. 1, 1983 (W.P. Peace award for best book on N.C. history 1983); editor, compiler: North Carolina's Older Population: Opportunities and Challenges, 1960; editor, contbr. Wake County Hist. Soc. newsletter, 1965-69; History of Raleigh Fire Dept., 1970; guest editor Raleigh Mag. Wake County Bicentennial Issue, 1971; author, photographer filmstrip for Wake Pub. Schs., 1971; author sect. Windows of the Way, 1964; Am. arts slide lectures for pub. library; author instructional materials State Exec. Mansion and Mordecai Hist. Park docents; author monthly history page Raleigh Mag., 1969-72; contbr. biog. sketches Dictionary of North Carolina Biography, 1979; contbr. to newspapers and mags. Mem. Raleigh City Council, 1973; pres. Jr. Woman's Club, 1956-57; organizing pres. Arts Council Raleigh, 1965; exec. com. N.C. Humanities Found., 1974-76; dir., officer North Carolinians for Better Libraries, 1965-69; mem. Meredith Bd. Assocs., 1976-79; trustee Pub. Libraries, 1956-67, Meredith Coll., 1966-69; pres. Wake Meml. Hosp. Aux., 1962-63; mem. Raleigh Hist. Sites Commn., 1969-73; trustee Pullen Meml. Bapt. Ch., 1975-78, chmn., 1977-78, also deacon; chmn. Mayor's Com. to Preserve Hist. Objects, 1965—; mem. Tryon Palace Commn., 1967-78; adv. council WUNC-FM, 1976-80, N.C. Art Soc.; vis. lectr. N.C. Mus. History Assos., 1980; docent, lectr. N.C. Exec. Mansion, Mordecai Hist. Park, N.C. Mus. Art; bd. dirs. Raleigh-Wake County Symphony Orch. Devel. Assn., 1979-83, Estey Hall Found., 1980—, Friends of Meredith Library, 1980-83; mem. adv. bd. Raleigh City Mus., mem. task force on local history; bldg. adv. com. local history Wake County Pub. Libr.; com. 1000 to establish Children's Mus. About World. Recipient Outstanding Community Service award, 1952, best all-round Jr. Woman's Club mem., 1955, Disting. Alumna award Meredith Coll., 1970, recognition for service award Raleigh Hist. Sites Commn., 1973, Raleigh City Council, 1973; Community Service award Raleigh Bd. Realtors, 1983, Phi Beta Kappa award Wake County, 1985, Silver Bowl award N.C. Mus. of Art, 1987, Anthemion award Capital Area Preservation Inc., 1994. Mem. N. Caroliniana Soc., N.C. Soc. County and Local Historians (life), N.C. Lit. and Hist. Assn., Apex Hist. Soc. (charter), Yates Mill Assocs., Inc. (charter), N.C. Art Soc. (Disting. Service citation 1979), Docents N.C. Mus. Art (pres. 1980-81), Friends of N.C. State U. Library, Friends of Carlyle Campbell Library (charter, life), Wake County Hist. Soc. (Pres.'s Cup 1994), Wake County Genealogical Soc., N.C. African-Am. Genealogical and Hist. Soc., Friends of N.C. Archives (life), Kappa Nu Sigma. Democrat. Clubs: Carolina Country, Capital City (charter mem.). Home: 8701 Murrayhill Dr Raleigh NC 27615-2531

MURRAY, ERNEST DON, artist, educator; b. Asheville, N.C., Apr. 21, 1930; s. Ernest Burgin and Daisy Ann (Bishop) M. Student, Asheville-Biltmore Jr. Coll., 1950; A.A., B.A., U. Tenn., 1952; student, Art Students League, 1953; M.F.A., U. Fla., 1957, M.Ed., 1958. Instr. art Chipola Jr. Coll., Marianna, Fla., 1958; head div. humanities Chipola Jr. Coll., 1964-68; instr. humanities U. Fla., Gainesville, 1969-72; prof. humanities, asso. chmn. dept. humanities U. Fla., 1974-78, prof. fine art and humanities dept. fine art, 1978—; cons. Holt, Rinehart & Winston, Inc., N.Y.C., 1963-76, Harcourt Brace, Jovanovich, Inc., N.Y.C., 1964-76. One-man shows in Knoxville, Tex., 1952, N.Y.C., 1953, Gainesville, 1968, 71, 72, 75, 90, 93, Pub. Sculpture Commns., 1989, 90, 91, 93, 95, Fla. Mus. Natural History, Fla. State Fire Coll., Mathieson Hist. Ctr.; exhibited in group shows Asheville, 1949, Knoxville, 1951, 65, N.Y.C., 1953, 61, 67, Gainesville, Miami, Tallahassee, 1979—; represented in pvt. collections. With C.E. U.S. Army, 1954-56, USNR, 1949-54. Mem. So. Highlands Craftsman's Guild, Fla. Artists Assn., Phi Theta Kappa, Phi Kappa Phi, Phi Beta Kappa. Unitarian. Office: Univ of Florida 302C Architecture Bldg Gainesville FL 32611-2004

MURRAY, FLORENCE KERINS, state supreme court justice; b. Newport, R.I., Oct. 21, 1916; d. John X. and Florence (MacDonald) Kerins; m. Paul F. Murray, Oct. 21, 1943; 1 child, Paul F. AB, Syracuse U., 1938; LLB, Boston U., 1942; EdD, R.I. Coll. Edn., 1956; grad., Nat. Coll. State Trial Judges, 1966; LLD (hon.), Bryant Coll., 1956, U. R.I., 1963, Mt. St. Joseph Coll., 1972, Providence Coll., 1974, Roger Williams Coll., 1976, Salve Regina Coll., 1977, Johnson and Wales Coll., 1977, Suffolk U., 1981, So. New Eng. Law Sch., 1995. Bar: Mass. 1942, R.I. 1947, U.S. Dist. Ct. 1948, U.S. Tax Ct. 1948, U.S. Supreme Ct. 1948. Sole practice Newport, 1947-52; mem. firm Murray & Murray, Newport, 1952-56; assoc. judge R.I. Superior Ct., 1956-78; presiding justice Superior Ct. R.I., 1978-79; assoc. justice R.I. Supreme Ct., 1979—; staff, faculty adv. Nat. Jud. Coll., Reno, Nev., 1971-72, dir., 1975-77, chmn., 1979-87, chair emeritus, 1990—; mem. com. Legal Edn. and Practice and Economy of New Eng., 1975—; former instr. Prudence Island Sch.; legal adv. R.I. Girl Scouts; sec. Commn. Jud. Tenure and Discipline, 1975-79; apptd. by Pres. Clinton to bd. dirs. State Justice Inst., 1994—; participant, leader various legal seminars. Mem. R.I. Senate, 1948-56; chmn. spl. legis. com.; mem. Newport Sch. Com., 1948-57, chmn., 1951-57; mem. Gov.'s Jud. Coun., 1950-60, White House Conf. Youth and Children, 1950, Ann. Essay Commn., 1952, Nat. Def. Adv. Com. on Women in Service, 1952-58, Gov.'s Adv. Com. Mental Health, 1954, R.I. Alcoholic Adv. Com., 1955-58, R.I. Com. Youth and Children, Gov.'s Adv. Com. on Revision Election Laws, Gov.'s Adv. Com. Social Welfare, Army Adv. Com. for 1st Army Area; mem. civil and polit. rights com. Pres.'s Commn. on Status of Women, 1960-63; mem. R.I. Com. Humanities, 1972—, chmn., 1972-77; mem. Family Ct. Study Com., R.I. com. Nat. Endowment Humanities; bd. dirs. Newport YMCA; sec. Bd. Physicians Service; bd. visitors Law Sch., Boston U.; bd. dirs. NCCJ; mem. edn. policy and devel. com. Roger Williams Jr. Coll.; trustee Syracuse U.; pres. Newport Girls Club, 1974-75, R.I. Supreme Ct. Hist. Soc., 1988—; chair Supreme Ct. Mandatory Continuing Legal Edn. Com., 1993—. Served to lt. col. WAC, World War II. Decorated Legion of Merit; recipient Arents Alumni award Syracuse U., 1956, Carroll award R.I. Inst. Instn., 1956, Brotherhood award NCCJ, 1983, Herbert Harley award Am. Judicature Soc., 1988, Melvin Eggers Sr. Alumni award Syracuse U., 1992, Merit award R.I. Bar Assn., 1994; named Judge of Yr. Nat. Assn. Women Judges, 1984, Outstanding Woman, Bus. and Profl. Women, 1972, Citizen of Yr. R.I. Trial Lawyers Assn.; Newport courthouse renamed in her honor, 1990. Mem. ABA (chmn. credentials com. nat. conf. state trial judges 1971-73, chair judges adv. com. on standing com. on ethics and profl. responsibility 1991—, joint com. on jud. discipline of standing com. on profl. discipline 1991-94), AAUW (chmn. state edn. com. 1954-56), Am. Arbitration Assn., Nat. Trial Judges Conf. (state chmn. membership com., sec. exec. com.), New Eng. Trial Judges Conf. (com. chmn. 1967), Boston U. Alumni Coun., Am. Legion (judge adv. post 7, mem. nat. exec. com.), Bus. and Profl. Women's Club (past state v.p., past pres. Newport chpt., past pres. Nat. legis. com.), Auota Club (past gov. internat., past pres. Newport chpt.), Alpha Omega, Kappa Beta Pi. Office: RI Supreme Ct 250 Benefit St Providence RI 02903-2719

MURRAY, FRED F., lawyer; b. Corpus Christi, Tex., Aug. 1, 1950; s. Marvin Frank and Suzanne Louise M.; m. Susan McKeen. BA, Rice U., 1972; JD, U. Tex., 1974. Bar: Tex. 1975, U.S. Dist. Ct. (so. dist.) Tex. 1976, U.S. Ct. Claims 1976, U.S. Tax Ct. 1976, U.S. Ct. Appeals (5th, D.C. and fed. cirs.) 1976, U.S. Supreme Ct. 1978, U.S. Ct. Internat. Trade 1985, N.Y. 1987, D.C. 1987, U.S. Dist. Ct. (ea. dist.) Tex. 1987; CPA, Tex. Ptnr. Chamberlain, Hrdlicka, White, Williams & Martin, P.C., Houston, 1985-92; spl. counsel (legislation) U.S. Dept. Treasury, IRS, Washington, 1992—; mem. Tax Law Adv. Commn., Tex. Bd. Legal Specialization, 1984—, vice chmn., 1987-92; mem. Commn. Tax Law Examiners, 1984—, vice chmn., 1987-92; adj. prof. U. Houston Law Ctr., 1984-92, U. Tex. Sch. Law, 1987; faculty lectr. Rice U. Jones Grad. Sch. Adminstrn., 1987-92; spkr. various assns. and univs.; mem. bd. advisors Houston Jour. Internat. Law, 1986—, chmn., 1987-91; v.p. for tax policy Nat. Fgn. Trade Coun., Inc., 1996—. Author various publs. Del. Bishop's Diocesan Pastoral Coun., 1979-80; chmn. parish coun. Sacred Heart Cathedral, Cath. Diocese Galveston-Houston, 1979-81, 89, mem. Red Mass steering com., 1986-92; mem. exec. com., bd. dirs., 1987-91, chmn. deferred giving com. Houston Symphony Soc., 1987-88, chmn. govt. and pub. affairs com., 1988-91; co-trustee Houston Symphony Soc. Endowment Fund, 1987-91; mem. fund coun. Rice U., 1987—, exec. com. 1988-92, chmn. Major Gifts Com., 1988-92; gen. counsel, bd. dirs., com. on fin. and adminstrn. S.E. Tex. chpt. Nat. Multiple Sclerosis Soc.; mem. Red Mass com. Archdiocese Washington, 1993—. Fellow Am. Coll. Tax Counsel; mem. ABA (officer various coms.), FBA (mem. steering com. tax sect. 1995—), AICPA, Am. Arbitration Assn. (panels comml. and internat. arbitrators 1980—), Internat. Bar Assn., Houston Bar Assn., State Bar of Tex. (various coms.), N.Y. State Bar Assn., D.C. Bar Assn., Tex. Soc. CPAs, Internat. Tax Forum of Houston (sec. 1981-84, pres. 1984-92), Internat. Fiscal Assn., Am. Soc. Internat. Law, Am. Fgn. Law Assn., Am. Law Inst. (tax adv. group 1990—).

MURRAY, GREGORY S., lawyer; b. Phila., Apr. 19, 1949. AB, U. Notre Dame, 1971; JD, U. Va., 1974. Bar: Ill. 1974. Ptnr. Winston & Strawn, Chgo. Mem. ABA, Ill. State Bar Assn. Office: Winston & Strawn 35 W Wacker Dr Chicago IL 60601-1614*

MURRAY, GROVER ELMER, geologist, educator; b. Maiden, N.C., Oct. 26, 1916; s. Grover Elmer and Lucy (Lore) M.; m. Nancy Beatrice Setzer, June 21, 1941 (dec. Sept. 1985); children: Martha Murray Poag, Barbara Elizabeth Murray Baca; m. Sally Marie Sowell Williams, Oct. 26, 1986. BS, U. N.C., 1937; MS, La. State U., 1939, PhD, 1942. Rsch. geologist La. Geol. Survey, 1938-41; geologist Magnolia Petroleum Co., Jackson, Miss., 1941-48; prof. dept. geology La. State U., 1948-55, chmn. dept., 1950-53, Boyd prof. geology, 1955-66, cons. prof. geology, 1966—, v.p., dean acad. affairs, 1963-65; v.p. acad. affairs La. State U. System, 1965-66; pres., prof. geosci. Tex. Tech U., Lubbock, 1966-76; pres. Tex. Tech U. Sch. Medicine, 1969-76; Grover E. Murray Disting. prof., 1994; Univ. prof., prof. geosci. Tex. Tech U. Complex, 1976-87; Univ. prof. emeritus and pres. emeritus Tex. Tech. U. and Tex. Tech. U. Sch. Medicine, 1988—; founder Ranching Heritage Ctr. Tex. Tech U., dir. Niger Agrl. Project, 1976-78; prof. La. State U. geology camp, Colo., 1949, 51, La., 1961; dir. U. Tex. geology camp, East Tex., 1949, 51; vis. lectr. U. Tex., 1958; dir. Global Exploration Inc., now pres.; bd. govs. Icasals, Inc., 1967-76; mem. Internat. Sub commn. on Stratigraphic Classification, 1955—; cons. geologist, 1988—; chmn. U.S. Nat. Com. on Geology, 1964-68; dir. NSF project for basic geologic studies in, Northeastern Mex., 1956-66; mem. Nat. Sci. Bd., 1968-80, vice chmn., 1978-80; mem. Tex. Natural Fibers and Food Protein Commn., 1966-76; U.S. del. Internat. Geol. Congresses, Mex., 1956, Scandinavia, 1960, India, 1964, Czechoslovakia, 1968, Can., 1972, U.S.A., 1989, hon. mem.; bd. dirs. Ashland Oil Inc., 1977-87, dir. emeritus, 1987—. Author: Geology of Atlantic and Gulf Coastal Province of North America, 1961; Contbr. articles to edn., sci. jours. Bd. dirs. Africare, Inc., 1975-86, Tex. Ptnrs. with Peru. Recipient Disting. Alumnus award U. N.C., 1971, La. State U., 1988, Hollis D. Hedberg award in energy La. State U.-Inst. for Study of Earth and Man, So. Meth. U., 1986, Twenhofel medal Soc. Sedimentary Geology, 1996. Fellow Geol. Soc. Am. (chmn. symposium on sedimentary vols. in Coastal Plain, U.S. and Mex. 1952, commr. Am. Stratigraphic Commn. 1951-54, program chmn. New Orleans Meeting 1955, councilor 1961-64, gen. chmn. New Orleans meeting 1967, chmn. Southeastern sect. 1960); mem. Am. Assn. Petroleum Geologists (chmn. com. geol. names and nomenclature 1952-54, disting. lectr. com., Disting. lectr. 1954, editor 1959-63, pres. 1964-65, mem. Am. Stratigraphic Commn. 1957-63, hon. mem. 1972, Sidney Powers Meml. medal 1983), Soc. Econ. Paleontologists and Mineralogists (editor Jour. Paleontology 1952-54, chmn. rsch. com. 1958-59, pres. 1963-64, hon. mem. Gulf Coast sect. 1973, hon. mem. Permian Basin sect. 1992, hon. mem. nat. soc. 1981, mem. assn. found. 1986-89, designee W.H. Twenhofel medal 1996), Am. Inst. Profl. Geologists (hon. mem., pres. 1978-79, exec. com. 1979-80, inst. found. 1989-92, Ben H. Parker Meml. medal 1990), Am. Geol. Inst. (vis. geosci. lectr. 1959-60, v.p. 1979, pres. 1980, exec. com. 1981, Ian Campbell Meml. medal 1989, William B. Heroy, Jr. award, 1992), Orgn. for Tropical Studies (dir., exec. com.), Gulf Univs. Research Corp. (pres. 1965-66, chmn. bd. dirs. 1967), Tex. Acad. Scis. (Disting. Tex. Scientist 1986), Soc. Exploration Geophysicists, Paleontol. Research Inst. (dir. 1978-81), Geol. and Mining Soc., Norsk Geologisk Forening (life), Asociación Mexicana de Geólogos Petroleros, Sociedad Geológica Mexicana, AAAS, Am. Geophys. Union, Golden Key, Sigma Xi, Sigma Gamma Epsilon, Omicron Delta Kappa (designee Grover E. Murray chpt. Tex. Tech U.), Phi Kappa Phi. Home: 4609 10th St Lubbock TX 79416-4827

MURRAY, HAYDN HERBERT, geology educator; b. Kewanee, Ill., Aug. 31, 1924; s. Herbert A. and Ardis M. (Adams) M.; m. Juanita A. Appenheimer, Dec. 16, 1944; children: Steven, Marilyn, Lisa. B.S., U. Ill., 1948, M.S., 1950, Ph.D., 1951. Asst. prof. geology Ind. U., 1951-53, assoc. prof., 1953-57, prof., chmn. dept. geology, 1973-84, prof. geology, 1984-94, prof. emeritus, 1994—; dir. research Georgia Kaolin Co., Elizabeth, N.J., 1957-60; mgr. ops. Georgia Kaolin Co., 1960-62, v.p. ops., 1962-64, exec. v.p., 1964-73; dir. Oil-Dri Corp. Am. Contbr. numerous articles to profl. jours.; patentee in field. Trustee Union Found., E.J. Grassmann Trust. Served with AUS, 1943-46. Recipient Disting. Svc. award Ind. U., 1993. Fellow Geol. Soc. Am., Mineral Soc. Am., Am. Ceramic Soc. (v.p. 1974-75), Tech. Assn. Pulp and Paper Industry; mem. Clay Minerals Soc. (pres. 1965-66, Disting. mem. 1980), Soc. Mining Metallurgy and Exploration (dist. mem., pres. elect 1987, pres. 1988, Hal Williams Hardinge award 1976, found. bd. trustees 1993—), Internat. Clay Minerals Soc. (pres. 1993—), Am. Assn. Petroleum Geologists, Am. Inst. Profl. Geologists (pres.-elect 1990, pres. 1991), Am. Geol. Inst. Found. (dir. 1990—), Geol. Soc. Am. Fdn. Home: 3790 S Inverness Farm Rd Bloomington IN 47401-9141

MURRAY, HERBERT FRAZIER, retired federal judge; b. Waltham, Mass., Dec. 29, 1923; s. Arnold Howatt and Hilda (Frazier) M.; m. Jane Ward, Sept. 4, 1948; 1 child, Douglas Frazier. B.A., Yale U., 1947; postgrad., Harvard U., 1947-48; LL.B., U. Md., 1951. Bar: Md. 1951. Law clk. to presiding judge U.S. Dist. Ct., 1951-52; assoc. Ober, Grimes & Stinson, Balt., 1952-54; asst. U.S. atty. for Md., 1954-56; from assoc. to ptnr. Smith, Somerville & Case, Balt., 1956-71; judge U.S. Dist. Ct. Md., 1971-94. Past bd. dirs. Union Meml. Hosp., Legal Aid Bur., Inc. of Balt. Capt. USAAF, World War II, MTO. Decorated Air medal with 3 oak leaf clusters, D.F.C. Mem. ABA, Md. Bar Assn., Balt. Bar Assn., Fed Bar Assn. (hon.), Wednesday Law Club Balt., Nat. Lawyers Club of Washington (hon.).

MURRAY, JAMES CUNNINGHAM, JR., lawyer; b. Chgo., Feb. 11, 1944; s. James Cunningham and Marie Rose (Grady) M.; m. Sandra Jean Isbella, Sept. 12, 1970; children: Caroline E., James Cunningham III. BA, U. Notre Dame, 1966; JD, Northwestern U., Chgo., 1969. Bar: Ill. 1969, U.S. Dist. Ct. (no. dist.) Ill. 1970, U.S. Ct. Appeals (7th cir.) 1971. Assoc. Carey Filter White, Chgo., 1969-70; atty. Asst. U.S. Dept. Justice, Chgo., 1970-73; assoc. Burditt & Calkins, Chgo., 1973-74; spl. asst. U.S. Atty. Dept. Justice, Chgo., 1974-75; ptnr. Katten, Murchin, Zavis, Chgo., 1975—; dir. Mental Health Assn. Greater Chgo., 1985-89. Office: Katten Muchin Zavis 525 W Monroe St Ste 1600 Chicago IL 60661-3629

MURRAY, JAMES DICKSON, mathematical biology educator; b. Moffat, Scotland, Jan. 2, 1931; s. Peter and Sarah Jane (Black) M.; m. Sheila Todd Campbell, Oct. 1959; children: Mark Woodeaton, Sarah Corinne. BSc in Math. with 1st class honors, U. St. Andrews, Scotland, 1953, PhD in Applied Math., 1956; MA, U. Oxford, Eng., 1961, DSc in Math., 1968; DSc (hon.), U. St. Andrews, 1994. Lectr. applied math. King's Coll. Durham U., Newcastle, Eng., 1955-56; Gordon McKay lectr. and rsch. fellow Harvard U., Cambridge, Mass., 1956-59, rsch. assoc. engrng., applied physics, 1963-64; prof. engrng. mechanics U. Mich., Ann Arbor, 1965-67; prof. math. NYU, N.Y.C., 1967-70; lectr. Univ. Coll., London, 1959-61; fellow in math. Hertford Coll. U. Oxford, 1961-63, reader, 1972-86, prof. math. biology, 1986-92, fellow Corpus Christi Coll., 1970-92, dir. Ctr. Math. Biology, 1983-92, emeritus prof., 1992—; vis. prof. applied math. MIT, 1979, U. Utah, Salt Lake City, 1979, 85, Calif. Tech. U., 1983; vis. rsch. prof. Nat. Tsing Hua U., Republic of China, 1975, U. Florence, Italy, 1976, Winegard Guelph U., 1980; guest prof. U. Heidelberg, Fed. Republic Germany, 1980; disting. vis. prof., Scott Hawkins lectr. So. Meth. U., Dallas, 1984; adj. prof. zoology U. Wash., 1988—, prof. applied math., 1988—; ULAM scholar Los Alamos Nat. Lab., 1985; Robert F. Philip prof. U. Wash., 1988-94; Lansdowne lectr. U. Victoria, 1990, Ostram lectr. Wash. State U. Author: Asymptotic Analysis, 1974, Nonlinear Differential Equation Models in Biology, 1977, Russian translation, 1983, Theories of Biological Pattern Formation, 1981, Modelling Patterns in Space and Time, 1983, Mathematical Biology, 1989; contbr. numerous articles to learned jours. Recipient Naylor prize for applied math. London Math. Soc., 1989; vis. fellow St. Catherine's Coll., U. Oxford, 1967, Guggenheim fellow, 1967-68; La Chaire Européene, U. Paris, 1994, 95. Fellow Royal Soc., Royal Soc. Edinburgh, European Soc. for Math. and Theoretical Biology (pres. 1991-94). Office: U Wash Dept Applied Math Box 352420 Seattle WA 98195-2420

MURRAY, JAMES DOYLE, accountant; b. Rochester, N.Y., July 24, 1938; s. William Herbert and Mildred Frances (Becker) M.; m. Mary Louise Goodyear, June 22, 1962; children: William Doyle, Robert Goodyear. B.S.,

U. Rochester, 1961. CPA, N.Y. With Ernst & Whinney, Rochester, N.Y., 1963—, ptnr., 1977-86; pvt. practice Rochester, 1986—; mem. faculty Found. for Acctg. Edn., N.Y.C., 1979—. Contbr. articles to profl. jours. Treas. William Warfield Scholarship Fund, 1987—, bd. dirs. March of Dimes, Rochester chpt.; active fund raising Boy Scouts Am., Rochester Philharm., Rochester Mus. and Sci. Ctr., bd. dirs., treas. Downstairs Cabaret, 1985; mem. Eagle bd. of rev. Boy Scouts Am.; elder Presbyn. Ch., 1987—; pres. Egypt Vol. Fire Dept., 1975. Lt. USN, 1961-63. Mem. AICPA, N.Y. State Soc. CPAs (pres. Rochester chpt. 1982-83), Nat. Assn. Accts. (bd. dirs. 1978-80). Republican. Presbyterian. Home: 42 Blackwatch Trl Fairport NY 14450-3702 Office: 349 W Commercial St Ste 3000 East Rochester NY 14445-2402

MURRAY, JAMES JOSEPH, III, association executive; b. Boston, Dec. 31, 1933; s. James Joseph Jr. and Anne Louise (Gurvin) M.; children: James Arthur, Paul, Douglas Joseph, Laura Anne. AB, Harvard U., 1955. Regional editor Prentice Hall, Inc., 1957-60, editor, 1960-64, exec. editor, 1964-69; pres. Winthrop Pubs., Inc. subs. Prentice Hall, Cambridge, Mass., 1969-82; also bd. dirs. Winthrop Pubs., Inc. subs. Prentice Hall; spl. mng. cons. Am. Coun. Edn., Washington, 1983-84, dir. external affairs, 1984—; chmn. N.J. Heart Fund; spl. cons. NEH, 1975—. Mem. editorial bd. Capitol Pub., 1992—. Mem. Dem. Nat. Com. from N.J., 1968; del. Dem. Nat. Conv., 1968; mem. gov. bd. Marine Mil. Acad., 1995—. 1st lt. USMCR, 1955-57. Mem. Am. Polit. Sci. Assn., Assn. Physical Plant Adminstrs. (bd. dirs.), Am. Assn. of Higher Edn., Harvard Club, Varsity Club, Pi Eta. Office: One DuPont Circle Ste 800 Washington DC 20036

MURRAY, JAMES MICHAEL, librarian, law librarian, legal educator, lawyer; b. Seattle, Nov. 8, 1944; s. Clarence Nicholas and Della May (Snyder) M.; m. Linda Monthy Murray; MLaw Librarianship, U. Wash., 1978; JD, Gonzaga U., 1971. Bar: Wash., 1974. Reference/reserve libr. U. Tex. Law Libr. Austin, 1978-81; assoc. law libr. Washington U. Law Libr. St. Louis, 1981-84; law libr., asst. prof. Gonzaga U. Sch. Law, Spokane, 1984-91; libr. East Bonner County Libr., 1991—; cons. in field. Author: (with Gasaway and Johnson) Law Library Administration During Fiscal Austerity, 1992. Bd. dirs. ACLU, Spokane chpt., 1987-91; Wash. Vol. Lawyers for the Arts, 1976-78. Mem. ABA, Idaho Libr. Assn., Wash. State Bar Assn (law sch. liaison com., 1986-88). Mem. state adv. bd. National Reporter on Legal Ethics and Professional Responsibility, 1982-91; author: (with Reams and McDermott) American Legal Literature: Bibliography of Selected Legal Resources, 1985; editor Texas Bar Jour. (Books Appraisals Column), 1979-82; contbr. numerous articles and revs. to profl. jours., acknowledgements and bibliographies in field. Home: 921 W 29th Ave Spokane WA 99203-1318 Office: East Bonner County Libr 419 N 2nd Ave Sandpoint ID 83864-1501

MURRAY, SISTER JEAN CAROLYN, college president; b. Broadview, Ill., May 30, 1927. B.A., Rosary Coll., River Forest, Ill., 1949; Ph.D. in French Lang. and Lit., Fribourg, 1961. Instr. French Rosary Coll., 1961-66, asst. prof., 1966-68, assoc. prof., 1968—; pres. Rosary Coll., River Forest, Ill., 1981-94; bd. dirs. Fenwick Prep. High Sch., St. Paul Fed. Bank for Savings. Editor: La genese Dialogues des Carmelites, 1963; editor, translator: Correspondance, choisie et presentee, Vol. I, Combat pour la verite Vol. II, Comban pour la liberte, 1971. Bd. dirs. Am. Heart Assn.; active Leadership Greater Chgo. Assocs. Mem. MLA, Am. Assn. Tchrs. French, Ill. Fgn. Lang. Tchrs. Assn., Associated Colls. Ill., Univ. Club Chgo., Chgo. Network, Econ. Club. Chgo., Oak Park Country Club, Fedn. Ind. Colls. and Univs. (chair). Home and Office: Rosary Coll 7900 Division St River Forest IL 60305-1066

MURRAY, JEANNE See STAPLETON, JEAN

MURRAY, JEANNE MORRIS, scientist, educator, consultant; b. Fresno, Calif., July 6, 1925; d. Edward W. and Augusta R. (French) Morris; m. Thomas Harold Murray, June 19, 1964; children: Jeanne, Margaret, Barbara, Thomas, William. BS in Math., Morris Harvey Coll., 1957; MS in Info. and Computer Sci., Ga. Inst. Tech., 1966; PhD, in Pub. Adminstrn., Tech. Mgmt., Am. U., 1981, post doctoral student in internat. rels., 1993. Research scientist Ga. Inst. Tech., Atlanta, 1959-68; adj. prof. Am. U., Washington, 1968-73; computer scientist U.S. Dept. Def., Washington, 1968-69; staff scientist Delex Systems, Inc., Arlington, Va., 1969-70; mgmt. analyst GSA, Washington, 1971-74; assoc. prof. No. Va. Community Coll., 1975-76, U. Va., 1976—; guest lecturer, Computers and Soc., U. Md., 1986—, Govtl. Rels., Marymount U. Arlington Va., 1990; cons., TechDyn Systems, ABA Corp., OrKand Corp., 1978-80; pres. Sequoia Assocs., Arlington, Va., 1981—; panelist Inst. Agr., Akadamgorodok, Siberia, 1991, Inst. Nuclear Physics, 1991, M.Ulughbek Inst., Samarkand, Uzbekistan, 1991; chmn. confs. Future on Fin. Structure and Pvt. Industry for Uzbekistan, 1994; rschr., developer cons. large info. warfare project, 1995—; developer indirect personality profiles for spl. internat. persons, 1995—; pres. Sequoia Enterprises, Inc., Arlington, 1995—, R&D Alt. Med. Approaches, 1996; sponsor, mem. team devel. and testing vaccine for specific infectious diseases, 1995; active U.S. Global Strategy Coun., 1993—. Author: Development and Testing of a System of Encoding Visual Information Based on Optimization of Neural Processing in Man--with Application to Pattern Recognition in the Computer, 1966, Cybernetics and the Management of the Research and Development Function in Society, 1971, Cybernetics as a Tool in the Control of Drug Abuse, 1972, Development of a General Computerized Forecasting Model, 1971, Political Humankind and the Future of Governance, 1974, The Doctrine of Management Planning, 1973, Policy Design, 1980, Computer Futures, 1982, A Search for Positive Response Level Indicators (PRLI's) Under Stress, 1987, Strategic Planning: Pathfinder to the Future, Beijing, 1988, Strategic Planning: A Systems Perspective, Shanghai PRC 1988, Electronic Control Systems for Railroads, Wuhan PRC 1988, Technology Forecasting Methodologies for Use on Personal Computers, 1989, Japan's Burgeoning Rates of Economic Expansion in the U.S. and other Western Countries, 1990, Technology Transfer and National Security, 1992, Privatization Mechanism for the Former Soviet Union and Central European Countries, 1992, Curriculum Development for Privatization Training of Entrepreneurs in Siberia, 1993, Development of Training Courses for Automated Acquisition Management Systems, 1994, Presentations on Methods of Achieving More Effective, Less Costly Federal Government, 1994; co-developer TV program "Cybernetics and You", Fairfax County, Va., 1995. OPSEC and Info. Warfare, 1996—, Mem. Carter transition team, 1976-77, Arlington (Va.) Civil Def. Com., 1983—, Washington Met. Area Emergency Assistance Com., Arlington County Com. on Sci. and Tech. Mem. IEEE (sr. mem., vice chmn. Washington sect., chmn. panel on internat. mktg. high tech. in the presence of def. tech. controls 1983, nat. com. on a tech. transfer policy for the U.S. 1986, mem. land transp. com. Vehicular Tech. Soc. 1993-94), AAAS, N.Y. Acad. Scis., Assn. Computing Machinery, Washington Evolutionary Systems Soc., Inst. Noetic Scis., Soc. Gen. Rsch., Am. Soc. Pub. Adminstrn., World Future Soc., Better World Soc., Acad. Polit. Sci., Personality Assessment System Found., Soc. for the Advance of Socio-Econs.; Episcopalian. Home and Office: 2915 27th St N Arlington VA 22207-4922

MURRAY, JOHN A., orthopedist, medical association executive; b. Canton, Ohio, 1932. MD, U. Pitts., 1958. Diplomate Am. Bd. Orthop. Surgery. Intern Jefferson-Davis Hosp., Houston, 1958-59; resident in orthopedics Baylor Coll. Medicine, Houston, 1959-63; resident orthopedist M.D. Anderson Hosp., Houston, 1963—; prof., clin. orthopedics U. Tex. Med Sch., Houston, 1963—; pres. Am. Bd. Orthopedic Surgery; prof. surgery, chief orthopedic oncology MD Anderson Cancer Ctr., Houston. Office: MD Anderson Cancer Ctr.Dept Surgery PO Box 106 1515 Holcombe Houston TX 77030-4009*

MURRAY, JOHN DANIEL, lawyer; b. Cleve., Feb. 13, 1944; s. Clarence Daniel and Mary Anne (Bormann) M.; m. Pamela Mary Seese, Aug. 20, 1966 (div. Sept. 1978); children: Laura Jane, Joshua Daniel, Katherine Anne; m. Marilyn Noren, June 15, 1979. BA, Marquette U., 1965, JD, 1968. Bar: Wis. 1968, Ill. 1968, U.S. Dist. Ct. (ea. and we. dist.) Wis. 1968, U.S. Supreme Ct. 1971, U.S. Ct. Appeals (7th cir.) 1979. Assoc. Law Offices of Elmo Koos, Peoria, Ill., 1968-70; ptnr. Coffey, Lerner & Murray, Milw., 1970-72, Coffey, Murray & Coffey, Milw., 1972-76, Murray & Burke, S.C., Milw., 1983-85; pvt. practice Milw., 1976-83; shareholder Habush, Habush, Davis & Rottier, S.C., Appleton, Wis., 1985—; adj. prof. law Marquette U., Milw., 1993—; lectr. Law Sch. U. Wis., Madison, 1976-80. Mem. ABA, ATLA, Nat. Bd. Trial Advocacy (cert.), Am. Soc. Law and Medicine, Wis. State Bar (chmn. criminal law sect. 1977-78, tort law com. 1990—, bd. dirs. litigation sect. 1995—), Wis. Acad. Trial Lawyers (bd. dirs. 1990—). Roman Catholic. Avocations: golf, travel. Home: 3095 Fox Run Appleton WI 54914 Office: Habush Habush Davis Rottier 4100 Boardwalk Ct Appleton WI 54913-1915

MURRAY, JOHN EDWARD, JR., lawyer, educator, university president; b. Phila., Dec. 20, 1932; s. John Edward and Mary Catherine (Small) M.; m. Isabelle A. Bogusevich, Apr. 11, 1955; children: Bruce, Susan, Timothy, Jacqueline. BS, LaSalle U., 1955; JD scholar, Cath. U., 1958; SJD fellow, U. Wis., 1959. Bar: Wis. 1959, Pa. 1986. Assoc. prof. Duquesne U. Sch. Law, Pitts., 1963-64, prof., 1965-67; prof. Villanova U. Sch. Law, 1964-65; prof. U. Pitts. Sch. Law, 1967-84, dean, 1977-84; dean Sch. Law Villanova U., 1984-86; disting. svc. prof. U. Pitts., 1986-88; pres. Duquesne U., Pitts., 1988—; cons. to law firms; chmn. Pa. Chief Justice's com. on comprehensive jud. and lawyer edn. Author: Murray on Contracts, 1974, 90, Murray, Commercial Transactions, 1975, Murray, Cases & Materials on Contracts, 1969, 76, 83, 91, Purchasing and the Law, 1978, Problems & Materials on Sales, 1982, Murray, Problems & Materials on Secured Transactions, 1987, Sales & Leases: Problems and Materials in National/International Transactions, 1993. Mayor Borough of Pleasant Hills, Pa., 1970-74. Mem. Assn. Am. Law Schs. (life, editor Jour. Legal Edn.), mem. Am. Law Inst. Democrat. Roman Catholic. Office: Duquesne U Pres Office Adminstrn Bldg Pittsburgh PA 15282

MURRAY, JOHN EINAR, lawyer, retired army officer, federal official; b. Clifton, N.J., Nov. 22, 1918; s. Joseph Michael and Maru Elizabeth (Liljeros) M.; m. Elaine Claire Riehlmann (dec. 1970); 1 dau., Valerie Anne; m. Phyllis Irene Harris (div. 1989). Student, St. Johns U., 1938-41; LLB, N.Y. Law Sch., 1949, LLD, 1975; MA, George Washington U., 1961. lectr. U.S. Marine Corps Nat. Def. U.; mem. sci. panel of White House Agent Orange Working Group, Def. Intelligence Agy. Task Force on POWS and MIAS; participant Georgetown U. Panel on Crisis Mgmt. Drafted pvt. U.S. Army, 1941, advanced through grades to maj. gen., 1972; comdr. truck group Europe Mil. Ports, Vietnam and maj. logistic units, 1968; dir. Army Transp., 1969-70; chief logistics Pacific Command, 1970-72, Mil. Assistance Command, Vietnam, 1972-73; def. attache Vietnam, 1973-74; ret., 1974; v.p. Assn. Am. Railroads, Washington, 1974-84; spl. counsel Am. Internat. Underwriters, 1985; prin. dep. asst. sec. of def. for spl. ops. and low intensity conflict, 1988-89; with Am. Internat. Group Cos., Washington, 1989; spl. counsel Snavely, King & Assocs., Inc. (econ. cons.), Washington, 1990—; adv. bd. U.S. Army Transp. Mus.; lectr. Nat. Def. U.; mem. sci. panel of White House Agent Orange Working Group, Def. Intelligence Agy. Task Force on POWs and MIAs; participant Georgetown U. Panel on Crisis Mgmt. Author: (with A.M. Chester) Orders and Directive, 1952, (with V.F. Caputo) Quick on the Vigor, 1966, The Myths of Business and the Business of Myths, 1975, The Third Curse of Moses, 1975, The Military Mind and the New Mindlessness, 1976, Lawyers, Computers and Power, 1977, Pothole Plague and Knothole Outlook, 1978, Railroads, Terrorism and the Pinkerton Legacy, 1978, Raising Corn and Beans and Hell, 1979, Remembering Who You Are, 1979, Running A Muck—The Folly of Coal Slurry, 1979, The Railroads and the Energy Crisis, 1980, U.S. Security Assistance—The Vietnam Experience, 1980, Hopeless Cause or Cause of Hope, 1980, War, Transport and Show Biz, 1981, Forget Everything You Ever Knew About the Japanese Railroads, 1981, Sweet Adversity: The U.S. Army-How It Motivates, 1982, Random Danger: The Railroad Response, 1983, Vietnam Logistics: An American Debacle, 1984, Dead Headheads and Warheads, 1987 ; Operation Desert Shield: The Smart Way to War, 1991; He Was There, 1992, The Logistics of Limited Wars, 1992, The United Nations: Sizing Up Consultant Prospects, 1992; contbr.: book revs. to Nat. Def. Transp. Mag., Time-Life books. Decorated D.S.M., Legion of Merit with 4 oak leaf clusters, Bronze Star medal, Italian War Cross, Joint Services Commendation medal with oak leaf cluster, Army Commendation medal with 2 oak leaf clusters, Sec. of Def. medal for Outstanding Pub. Svc., Italian Cross of War, Knight Order of Crown of Italy, Korean Chung Mu with gold star, Vietnamese Kim Khanh medal 1st class, Vietnamese Army Distinguished Service Order 1st class, Vietnamese Navy Distinguished Service Order 1st class, Vietnamese Air Force Distinguished Service Order 1st class, Vietnamese Gallantry Cross with palm. Mem. Spl. Forces Assn., Nat. Def. Transp. Assn., Army War Coll. Grad. Assn., Army and Navy Club. Home: 3823 Bosworth Ct Fairfax VA 22031-3807 Office: Mullenholz & Brimsek 1150 Connecticut Ave NW Washington DC 20036-4104

MURRAY, JOHN PATRICK, psychologist, educator, researcher; b. Cleve., Sept. 14, 1943; s. John Augustine and Helen Marie (Lynch) M.; m. Ann Coke Dennison, Apr. 17, 1971; children—Jonathan Coke, Ian Patrick. PhD, Cath. U. Am., 1970. Rsch. dir. Office U.S. Surgeon Gen. NIMH, Bethesda, Md., 1969-72; assoc. prof. psychology Macquarie U., Sydney, Australia, 1973-79, U. Mich., Ann Arbor, 1979-80; dir. youth and family policy Boys Town Ctr., Boys Town, Nebr., 1980-85; prof., dir. Sch. Family Studies and Human Svcs. Kans. State U., Manhattan, 1985—. Author: Television and Youth: 25 Years of Research and Controversy, 1980, The Future of Children's TV, 1984, (with H.T. Rubin) Status Offenders: A Sourcebook, 1983, (with E.A. Rubenstein, G.A. Comstock) Television and Social Behavior, 3 vols., 1972, (with A. Huston and others) Big World, Small Screen: The Role of Television in American Society, 1992; contbr. articles to profl. jours. Mem. Nebr. Foster Care Rev. Bd., 1982-84 ; mem. Advocacy Office for Children and Youth, 1980-85 ; mem. Nat. Coun. Children and TV, 1982-87; trustee The Villages Children's Homes, 1986—. Fellow Am. Psychol. Assn. (pres. div. child youth and family svcs. 1990); mem. Am. Sociol. Assn., Soc. Rsch. in Child Devel. Clubs: Royal Commonwealth Soc. (London), Manhattan Country. Home: 1731 Humboldt St Manhattan KS 66502-4140 Office: Kans State U Sch Family Studies & Human Svcs Manhattan KS 66506-1403

MURRAY, JOHN RALPH, former college president; b. Alva, Okla., Apr. 17, 1916; s. John and Euna Vista (Young) M.; m. Fern Berniece Brauch, July 26, 1936; children: John Ralph III, Ann Elaine. A.B., Northwestern State U., 1937; A.M., U. So. Calif., 1939; Ph.D., U. Fla., 1952; L.H.D. (hon.), Elmira Coll., 1976. Prin., tchr. English Carrier and Gore high schs., Okla., 1936-38; teaching asst. U. So. Calif., 1939-41; instr. English U. Miami, Coral Gables, Fla., 1941; exec. asst. to pres. U. Miami, 1942, asst. prof. English, adminstrv. asst. dean, 1945, acting dean, dir. south campus, 1946-50, asst. to pres., assoc. prof. English, 1948-51; lectr., instr. English Ohio U., 1942-44; pres. Greenbrier Coll., Lewisburg, W.Va., 1952-54; pres. Elmira (N.Y.) Coll., 1954-72, chancellor, 1972-76, cons. to bd. trustees, 1976—; dir. Hardinge Bros.; Mem. N.Y. State Senate Adv. Com. on Higher Edn. Author: Secretary's Handbook, 1941; Editorial bd.: Learning Today; mem. pub. com.: The College and World Affairs; chmn. com. pub.: Non-Western Studies in Liberal Arts Colleges. Trustee Robert Packer Hosp., Coll. Center of Finger Lakes, Am. Center for Students and Artists, Paris; bd. mgrs. Arnot Ogden Hosp.; bd. regents Council on Tchr. Edn.; bd. dirs. Library Coll. Assocs.; mem. Pres.'s Task Force on Internat. Edn.; chmn. long range planning com. Friends of Weymouth; chmn. bd. dirs. Council on Internat. Ednl. Exchange; v.p. Given Meml. Library Bd.; chmn. dirs. Empire State Found., 1963-65, dir., mem. exec. com.; trustee Internat. Coll.; pres. World Golf Hall of Fame. Served as ensign USNR, 1944-45. Mem. Internat. Assn. U. Presidents, Assn. Am. Colls. (past chmn. com. on internat. understanding), Phi Sigma Pi, Kappa Delta Pi, Phi Kappa Phi, Epsilon Phi. Lodge: Rotary. Home: 6152 N Verde Trl Apt D 123 Boca Raton FL 33433-2419

MURRAY, JOSEPH JAMES, JR., zoologist; b. Lexington, Va., Mar. 13, 1930; s. Joseph James and Jane Dickson (Vardell) M.; m. Elizabeth Hickson, Aug. 24, 1957; children—Joseph James III, Alison Joan, William Lister. B.S., Davidson Coll., 1951; B.A., Oxford U., Eng., 1954, M.A., 1957, D.Phil., 1962. Instr. biology Washington & Lee U., Lexington, Va., 1956-58; asst. prof. biology U. Va., Charlottesville, 1962-67, assoc. prof., 1967-73, prof., 1973-77, Samuel Miller prof. biology, 1977—, chmn. dept. biology, 1984-87; co-dir. Mountain Lake Biol. Sta., Pembroke, Va., 1963-91. Author: Genetic Diversity and Natural Selection, 1972; contbr. articles to profl. jours. Served with U.S. Army, 1955-56. Rhodes scholar, 1951-54. Fellow AAAS, Va. Acad. Sci.; mem. Am. Soc. Naturalists, Genetics Soc. Am., Soc. Study Evolution, Am. Soc. Ichthyologists and Herpetologists, Va. Acad. Sci. (pres. 1986-87), Va. Soc. Ornithology (pres. 1976-79). Avocations: walking; mountaineering; shooting. Office: U Va Dept Biology Gilmer Hall Charlottesville VA 22901

MURRAY, JOSEPH WILLIAM, banker; b. Alamosa, Colo., July 20, 1944; s. Joseph A. and Virginia (Wood) M.; m. Helen Hoberg, Jan. 20, 1970; children: Brian, Beth, Meghan. BS in Bus. with hon., U. Colo., 1966; MBA with hon., Northwestern U., 1967. Various positions with Continental Ill. Nat. Bank, Chgo., 1967-82; sr. v.p. First Nat. Bank Md., Balt., 1982—; faculty mem. U. N.C. Exec. Programs on Cash Mgmt., Chapel Hill, 1982—; lectr. cash mgmt.; mem. corp. svcs. commn. Bank Adminstrn. Inst., 1992-94. Assoc. editor: Essentials of Cash Management, 4th edit., 1992, 5th edit., 1995. Pres. Wakefield Improvement Assn., Timonium, Md., 1987, 96, bd. dirs., 1996—; pres. Glen Ellyn (Ill.) Libr., 1978-82, trustee; pres. Glen Ellyn Tennis Assn., 1981, bd. dirs.; bd. trustees, sec. Ctr. Stage, 1987—. Mem. Treasury Mgmt. Assn., Mid-Atlantic Planning Assn., Beta Gamma Sigma. Club: L'Hirondelle (Ruxton, Md.). Avocations: tennis, jazz piano, reading, racewalking. Office: 1st Nat Bank Md PO Box 1596 Baltimore MD 21203-1596

MURRAY, JULIA KAORU (MRS. JOSEPH E. MURRAY), occupational therapist; b. Wahiawa, Oahu, Hawaii, 1934; d. Gijun and Edna Tsuruko (Taba) Funakoshi; m. Joseph Edward Murray, 1961; children: Michael, Susan, Leslie. BA, U. Hawaii, 1956; cert. occupational therapy U. Puget Sound, 1958. Therapist, Inst. Logopedics, Wichita, Kans., 1958; sr. therapist Hawaii State Hosp., Kaneohe, 1959; part-time therapist Centre County Ctr. for Crippled Children and Adults, State College, Pa., 1963; vice chmn. adv. bd. Hosp. Improvement Program, East Oreg. State Hosp., Pendleton, 1974; v.p. Ind. Living, Inc., 1976-79; job search instr.; mem. adv. com. Oreg. Ednl. Coordinating Commn., 1979-82; mem. Oreg. Bd. Engring. Examiners, 1979-87; supr., occupational therapist Fairview Tng. Ctr., Salem, Oreg., 1984-94; occupational therapist U.S. Naval Hosp., Okinawa, Japan, 1994—. Rep. from Umatilla County Commrs. to Blue Mountain Econ. Devel. Council, 1976-78; mem. Ashland Park and Recreation Bd., 1972-73; vice chmn. adv. bd. LINC, 1978; mem. exec. bd. Liberty-Boone Neighborhood Assn., 1979-83. Mem. Am. Occupational Therapy Assn., Oreg. Occupational Therapy Assn., Hawaii Occupational Therapy Assn. (sec. 1960) Occupational Therapy Assn., LWV (bd. dirs. Pendleton 1974, 77-78, pres. 1975-77; bd. dirs. Oreg. 1979-81, Ashland, Wis., 1967-71, Wis. v.p. 1970). Office: Medically Related Svcs US Naval Hosp Okinawa Japan Psc 482 FPO AP 96362-1600

MURRAY, LEONARD HUGH, railroad executive; b. Evanston, Ill., Sept. 26, 1913; s. Albert L. and Estelle A. (Matthews) M.; m. Virginia P. Dutcher, Aug. 23, 1940; children: Carole J., Linda P., John L. J.D., U. Minn., 1938. Bar: Minn. 1938. Legal sec. to assoc. justice Minn. Supreme Ct., 1938-40; pvt. practice law Mpls., 1940-42; chief price atty. dist. office OPA, Minn., 1942-44; pvt. practice law, specializing r.r. re-orgn. Mpls., 1944-54; asst. to pres. Duluth, S. Shore & Atlantic R.R., 1949-52, v.p., 1952-58, pres., dir., 1958-60; v.p., dir. Wis. Central R.R., 1954-60, v.p., gen. counsel, dir., 1958-60; counsel C.P. Ry. Co., 1958-60; pres., chief exec. officer, dir. Soo Line R.R. Co., 1961-78, chmn. bd., chief exec. officer, 1978-79, chmn. exec. com., 1980-83; former dir. First Bank System, Inc.; dir. Gt. No. Ins. Co., 1963-84; dir. emeritus 1st Nat. Bank Mpls. Pres. Jr. Achievement Mpls., 1964-66; former trustee Dunwoody Indsl. Inst., pres., 1966-67; bd. dirs. Minn. Council on Crime and Justice; pres. Correctional Service of Minn., 1976-79. Recipient Outstanding Achievement award U. Minn., 1971. Mem. Greater Mpls. C. of C. (pres. 1977-78), Beta Gamma Sigma. Republican. Episcopalian.

MURRAY, LOWELL, Canadian senator; b. New Waterford, N.S., Can., Sept. 26, 1936; s. Daniel and Evelyn (Young) M.; m. Colleen Elaine MacDonald; children: William, Colin. BA, St. Francis Xavier U., Antigonish, N.S., Can.; MA in Pub. Adminstrn., Queen's U., Kingston, Ont., Can. Chief of staff Minister of Justice and Minister of Pub. Works Can., Ottawa, Ont., Senator M. Wallace McCutcheon, Ottawa, Ont.; leader of opposition Can., Ottawa, Ont.; dep. minister Premier N.B. (Can.); mem. Senate of Can., Ottawa, Ont., 1979—, co-chmn. joint Senate-House of Commons com. ofcl. langs., 1980-84, chmn. standing Senate com. on banking, trade and commerce, 1984-86, chmn. standing Senate com. on nat. fin., 1995—; bd. dirs. SONY Can. Inc.; trustee Inst. Rsch. Pub. Policy, 1984-86, mem. Trilateral Commn., 1985-86. Nat. campaign chmn. gen. election Progressive Conservative Party Can., 1977-79, 81-83; sworn of the privy coun., appointed Leader of the Govt. in the Senate, 1986-94; Min. of the State Fed.-Provincial Rels., 1986-91; Min. Responsible for the Atlantic Can. Opportunities Agy., 1987-88. Roman Catholic. Office: The Senate, Ottawa, ON Canada K1A 0A4

MURRAY, MARY, early childhood and elementary educator; b. Beverly, Mass.; d. Edward James and Anne (Dowd) M. AS in Nursing, Endicott Coll.; AB, Boston Coll., 1985; MSEd in Early Childhood & Elem. Edn., Wheelock Coll., 1993. Cert. tchr., Mass. Tchr. Glen Urquhart Sch., Beverly Farms, Mass., 1982-87, kindergarten asst., 1982-83; kindergarten tchr., 1983-85, first grade tchr., 1985-87; dir. extended day program Glen Urquhart Sch., Beverly Farms, Mass., 1982-85, coord. summer camp program, 1984-86; lower sch. assoc. Shady Hill Sch., Cambridge, Mass., 1987-88; rsch. asst. Wheelock Coll., Boston, 1987-91; tchr. kindergarten, curriculum coord. Prospect Hill Parents' and Childrens' Ctr., Waltham, Mass., 1988-91; substitute tchr. Marblehead (Mass.) Mid. Sch., 1993—; ednl. cons. Beverly Farms, Mass., 1992—; substitute tchr. Shore Country Day Sch., Beverly, Mass., 1992—; mentor, tchr., faculty summer compass program Lesley Coll. Grad. Sch. of Edn., Cambridge, Mass., 1994—; founder, dir. Summer Enrichment at Lanesville, Mass., 1987-89; certification cons., adv. bd. Power Industries, Wellesley Hills, Mass., 1989—; cons. Activities Club, Inc., Waltham, 1989-91, NSA, Inc. Woburn, Mass., 1991-92; mem. Early Childhood Adv. Coun., Medford, Mass., 1990-93; lifeguard supr. West Beach Corp., 1980-86; mem. cert. team Nat. Assn. Educators Young Children, 1989-91, Ind. Sch. Assn. Mass., 1983-88; presenter workshops. Author curriculum materials, activity kits for children. Tchr. religious edn. program St. Margaret Parish, Beverly Farms, 1970—, dir., coord., 1989—; synod group leader Archdiocese of Boston, 1987; water safety instr. ARC; coach Christian Youth Orgn. Girls Basketball, St. Joseph Parish, Medford, Mass., 1991-93; active Mass. Spl. Olympics; mem. Youth Activities Coord., Farms/Prides Cmty. Orgn., Feed the Hungry Project, Beverly, Mass., Good Friday Walk Orgnl. Com.; adv. bd. Wenham (Mass.) Mus.; friends-of-com. Fitz Meml. Libr. Endicott Coll., Beverly, Mass. Wheelock Coll. grad. grantee, 1993. Mem. ASCD, Nat. Assn. Edn. Young Childen, Ind. Schs. Assn. Mass., Assn. Childhood Edn. Internat., Young Alumni Club Boston Coll. (program coord./spl. events 1988-90), Ste. Chretienne Acad. Alumnae Assn., Wheelock Coll. Alumni Assn. Democrat. Roman Catholic. Avocations: reading, photography, travel, seasonal sports, children's literature. Home: 650 Hale St Beverly Farms Beverly MA 01915-2117

MURRAY, MICHAEL PETER, economist, educator; b. N.Y.C., Sept. 15, 1946; s. Thomas John and Marie Fitzgerald; m. Rosanne Ducey, June 21, 1969; children: Sarah, Anna, Adam, Ben, Seth, Peter. BA, U. Santa Clara, 1968; MS, Iowa State U., 1971, PhD, 1974. Acting asst. prof. U. Calif., San Diego, 1972-73; asst. prof. U. Va., Charlottesville, 1973-77; vis. asst. prof. U. Calif., Berkeley, 1977-78; assoc. prof. Duke U., Durham, N.C., 1978-80; prof. Claremont (Calif.) Grad. Sch., 1980-86; sr. economist The RAND Corp., Santa Monica, Calif., 1980-86; Charles Franklin Phillips prof. econs. Bates Coll., Lewiston, Maine, 1986—; cons. HUD, Washington, 1973, The World Bank, Washington, 1981—. Author: Subsidizing Industrial Location, 1988, Building Organizational Decision Support Systems, 1992; contbr. articles to profl. jours. NDEA fellow U. Calif., San Diego, 1971; vis. scholar HUD, Washington, 1979. Mem. Am. Econ. Assn., Western Econ. Assn., Order of Silver Spade. Democrat. Roman Catholic. Avocations: soccer, bridge, theater. Home: 342 College St Lewiston ME 04240-6001 Office: Bates Coll Dept Econs Lewiston ME 04240

MURRAY, NEIL VINCENT, computer science educator; b. Schenectady, N.Y., July 14, 1948; s. Robert Emslie and Eileen Marie (Milano) M. BS in Engring. Physics, Cornell U., 1970; MS in Computer and Info. Sci., Syracuse U., 1974, PhD in Computer and Info. Sci., 1979. Rsch. asst. Syracuse (N.Y.) U., 1977-78; instr. computer sci. dept. LeMoyne Coll., Syracuse, 1978-79, asst. prof., 1979-82; asst. prof. computer sci. SUNY, Albany, 1982-87, assoc. prof. computer sci., 1987—; Sec.-treas. CADE, Inc., Assn. Automated Reasoning; presenter in field. Contbr. articles to profl. jours. Mem. IEEE

Computer Soc., Am. Assn. Artificial Intelligence, Assn. Automated Reasoning, Assn. Computing Machinery. Home: 1035 Onondaga Rd Niskayuna NY 12309 Office: SUNY Dept Computer Sci L1 # 67A Albany NY 12222

MURRAY, PATTY, senator; b. Seattle, Wash., Oct. 11, 1950; d. David L. and Beverly A. (McLaughlin) Johns; m. Robert R. Murray, June 2, 1972; children: Randy P., Sara A. BA, Wash. State U., 1972. Sec. various cos., Seattle, 1972-76; citizen lobbyist various ednl. groups, Seattle, 1983-88; legis. lobbyist Orgn. for Parent Edn., Seattle, 1977-84; instr. Shoreline Community Coll., Seattle, 1984—; mem. Wash. State Senate, Seattle, 1989-92, U.S. Senate, Washington, 1993—; ranking minority mem. Appropriations Legis Br.; vice chmn. Senate Dem. Policy Com.; mem. Com. on Banking, Housing and Urban Affairs, Budget Com., Senate Dem. Tech. and Comms. Com., Com. on Vets. Affairs, Select Com. on Ethics. Mem. bd. Shoreline Sch., Seattle, 1985-89; mem. steering com. Demonstration for Edn., Seattle, 1987; founder, chmn. Orgn. for Parent Edn., Wash., 1981-85; lst Congl. rep. Wash. Women United, 1983-85. Recipient Recognition of Svc. to Children award Shoreline PTA Coun., 1986, Golden Acorn Svc. award, 1989; Outstanding Svc. award Wash. Women United, 1986, Outstanding Svc. to Pub. Edn. award Citizens Ednl. Ctr. NW, Seattle, 1987. Democrat. Office: US Senate 111 Russell Senate Office Bldg Washington DC 20510-4704

MURRAY, PETER, metallurgist, manufacturing company executive; b. Rotherham, Yorks, Eng., Mar. 13, 1920; came to U.S., 1967, naturalized, 1974; s. Michael and Ann (Hamstead) M.; m. Frances Josephine Glaisher, Sept. 8, 1947; children: Jane, Paul, Alexander. BSc in Chemistry with honors, Sheffield (Eng.) U., 1941, postgrad., 1946-49; PhD in Metallurgy, Brit. Iron and Steel Research Bursar, Sheffield, 1948. Research chemist Steetley Co., Ltd., Worksop, Notts, Eng., 1941-45; with Atomic Energy Research Establishment, Harwell, Eng., 1949-67; head div. metallurgy Atomic Energy Research Establishment, 1960-64, asst. dir., 1964-67; tech. dir., mgr. fuels and materials, advanced reactors div. Westinghouse Electric Corp., Madison, Pa., 1967-74; dir. research Westinghouse Electric Europe (S.A.), Brussels, 1974-75; chief scientist advanced power systems divs. Westinghouse Electric Corp., Madison, Pa., 1975-81; dir. nuclear programs Westinghouse Electric Corp., Washington, 1981-92; sr. cons. Nuclear Programs, 1992—; mem. divisional rev. coms. Argonne Nat. Lab., 1968-73; Mellor Meml. lectr. Inst. Ceramics, 1963. Contbr. numerous articles to profl. jours.; editorial adv. bd.: Jour. Less Common Metals, 1968—. Recipient Holland Meml. Research prize Sheffield U., 1949. Fellow Royal Inst. Chemistry (Newton Chambers Research prize 1954), Inst. Ceramics, Am. Nuclear Soc.; mem. Brit. Ceramics Soc. (pres. 1965), Am. Ceramic Soc., Nat. Acad. Engring. Roman Catholic. Home: 20308 Canby Ct Gaithersburg MD 20879-4014 Office: Westinghouse Electric Corp One Montrose Metro 11921 Rockville Pike Ste 450 Rockville MD 20852

MURRAY, PETER BRYANT, English language educator; b. N.Y.C., Oct. 6, 1927; s. Frederick James and Florence (Leech) M.; m. Frances N. Pearson, Apr. 24, 1954 (div. Apr. 1970); children: Jean P., Stephen F., Susan C., Christopher J.; m. Karen Louise Olson, Aug. 14, 1970. Student, Va. Mil. Inst., 1945-47; A.B., Swarthmore Coll., 1950; M.A., U. Pa., 1959, Ph.D., 1962. Research chemist Sun Oil Co., Marcus Hook, Pa., 1950-57; instr. English U. Pa., 1961-63, asst. prof., 1963-67; assoc. prof. English U. Del., 1967-68; prof. Macalester Coll., St. Paul, 1968—; chmn. dept. Macalester Coll., 1971-77; Vice pres. Spencer-Murray Corp., Swarthmore, Pa., 1961—. Author: A Study of Cyril Tourneur, 1964, A Study of John Webster, 1969, Thomas Kyd, 1969, Shakespeare's Imagined Persons: The Psychology of Role-Playing and Acting, 1996. Served with AUS, 1946-47. Mem. Modern Lang. Assn. Am., Modern Humanities Research Assn., Am. Assn. U. Profs. (past chpt. pres.), Shakespeare Assn. Am., Nat. Council Tchrs. English. Patentee in petroleum chemistry field, 1953-57, games entertainment field, 1962-66. Office: Macalester Coll Dept English Saint Paul MN 55105

MURRAY, PHILIP JOSEPH, III, lawyer; b. Pitts., Sept. 20, 1961; s. Philip Joseph Jr. and Dorothy Cecelia (Hollinger) M.; m. Carol Jean Gibson, July 7, 1990; 1 child, Vanessa Lee. BS in Psychology, U. Pitt., 1985; JD, Duquesne U., 1988. Bar: Pa. 1988, U.S. Dist. Ct. (we. dist.) Pa. 1988, U.S. Ct. Appeals (3d cir.) 1992, U.S. Ct. Appeals (8th cir.) 1995. Law clk. to Hon. Barron P. McCune U.S. Dist. Ct. We. Dist., Pitts., 1988-90; assoc. Thorp, Reed & Armstrong, Pitts., 1990—. Exec. dir. William P. Fralic Found., Pitts., 1992—. Mem. Allegheney County Bar Assn. Republican. Roman Catholic. Avocations: golf, athletics. Office: Thorp Reed and Armstrong One Riverfront Ctr Pittsburgh PA 15222

MURRAY, RAYMOND HAROLD, physician; b. Cambridge, Mass., Aug. 17, 1925; s. Raymond Harold and Grace May (Dorr) M.; children—Maureen, Robert, Michael, Margaret, David, Elizabeth, Catherine, Anne. B.S., U. Notre Dame, 1946; M.D., Harvard U., 1948. Diplomate: Am. Bd. Internal Medicine, also Sub-bd. Cardiovascular Disease. Practice medicine Grand Rapids, Mich., 1955-62; asst. prof. to prof. medicine Ind. U. Sch. Medicine, 1962-77; prof. dept. medicine Mich. State U. Coll. Human Medicine, 1977-95, chmn. dept. medicine, 1977-89, emeritus, 1995—; chmn. aeromed-bioscis panel Sci. Adv. Bd., USAF, 1977-81. Contbr. numerous articles to profl. publs. Served with USNR, 1942-45; Served with USPHS, 1950-53. Fellow ACP (gov. Mich. chpt. 1994—); mem. Am. Heart Assn. (fellow coun. clin. cardiology), Am. Fedn. Clin. Rsch. Office: Mich State U 210B Clinical Ctr East Lansing MI 48824-1313

MURRAY, RAYMOND LE ROY, nuclear engineering educator; b. Lincoln, Nebr., Feb. 14, 1920; s. Ray Annis and Bertha (Mann) M.; m. Ilah Mae Rengler, June 16, 1941; children: Stephen, Maureen, Marshall; m. Quin Meyer, June 3, 1967; 1 stepdau., Tucker; m. Elizabeth Reid, May 12, 1979; stepchildren: Michael, Nancy, James. B.S., U. Nebr., 1940, M.S., 1941; Ph.D., U. Tenn., 1950; postgrad., U. Calif., Berkeley, 1941-43. Physicist U. Calif. Radiation Lab., Berkeley, 1942-43; asst. dept. supt. Tenn. Eastman Corp., Oak Ridge, 1943-47; research physicist Carbide & Carbon Chem. Co., Oak Ridge, 1947-50; prof. physics N.C. State U., 1950-57, Burlington prof. physics, 1957-80, prof. emeritus, 1980—, head dept. physics, 1960-63, head dept. nuclear engring., 1963-74; acting dir. Nuclear Reactor Project, 1956-57; cons. Oak Ridge Nat. Lab., 1950-68, Los Alamos Nat. Lab., 1988-92, also to industry and govt. Author: Introduction to Nuclear Engineering, 1954, 2d edit., 1961, Nuclear Reactor Physics, 1957, Physics: Concepts and Consequences, 1970, Nuclear Energy, 1975, 4th edit., 1993, Understanding Radioactive Waste, 1982, 4th edit., 1994; mem. edit. adv. bd., U.S. exec. editor Jour. Nuclear Energy, 1963-73; adv. editor Annals Nuclear Energy, 1973—; contbr. numerous articles to profl. jours. and encys. Mem. adv. com. on radiation N.C. Bd. Health, 1958-59; mem. Gov.'s Tech. Adv. Com. on Low Level Radioactive Waste, 1980-87; mem. N.C. Radiation Protection Commn., 1979-87, chmn., 1980-82; mem., vice chmn., chmn. N.C. Low Level Radioactive Waste Mgm. Authority, 1987-93. Recipient O. Max Gardner award U. N.C., 1965; Arthur H. Compton award, 1970, Donald G. Fink award IEEE, 1988, Eugene P. Wigner Reactor Physicist award, 1994. Fellow Am. Phys. Soc., Am. Nuclear Soc. (chmn. edn. div. 1966-67, chmn. Eastern Carolinas sect. 1976-77, mem. nominating com. 1989); mem. Am. Soc. Engring. Edn. (chmn. com. on relationships with AEC 1967-68, chmn. nuclear engring. div. 1970-71, Glenn Murphy award 1976), N.C. Soc. Engrs. (Outstanding Engring. Achievement award 1975), Atomic Indsl. Forum (edn. coun. 1970-73), Inst. Nuclear Power Ops. (adv. coun. 1985-87, 89-94), Phi Beta Kappa, Sigma Xi, Pi Mu Epsilon, Phi Kappa Phi. Home: 8701 Murray Hill Drive Raleigh NC 27615

MURRAY, RICHARD BENNETT, physics educator; b. Marietta, Ga., Dec. 5, 1928; s. William Moore and Ruth (Mozley) M.; m. Clella Bay, Apr. 1, 1956; children: Ada, Annette. BA, Emory U., 1947; MS, Ohio State U., 1950; PhD, U. Tenn., 1955. Rsch. asst. Gaseous Diffusion Plant, Oak Ridge, 1947-48; rsch. physicist Oak Ridge Nat. Lab., 1955-66; vis. assoc. prof. physics U. Del., Newark, 1962-63, assoc. prof., 1966-69, prof., 1969—, acting chmn. dept. physics, 1975-76, univ. coord. for grad. studies, 1979-85, assoc. provost for grad. studies, 1986-88, acting provost and v.p. for acad. affairs, 1988-91, provost, 1993-94; lectr. physics U. Tenn., Knoxville, 1963-66; vis. rsch. physicist U.S. Naval Rsch. Lab., 1991-92; vis. scientist Clarendon Lab., Oxford U., 1992; cons. to industry, 1957-93; councillor Oak Ridge Associated Univs., 1979-88, bd. dirs., 1983-94, vice chmn. coun., 1983-85, chmn. coun., 1985-88; sec.-treas. NE Assn. Grad. Schs., 1982-84; dir. U. Del. Press, 1979-82. Contbr. numerous articles on exptl. nuclear and solid state physics to profl. publs., 1948—. Trustee Sanford Sch., Hockessin, Del., 1981-85; chmn. bd dirs. Oak Ridge Associated Univs. Found., 1989-94; bd. dirs. Del. Inst. for Med. Edn. and Rsch., 1989-91. Predoctoral fellow Oak Ridge Inst. Nuclear Studies, 1953-55; grantee AEC, NSF, Dept. Energy, 1967-84. Fellow AAAS, Am. Phys. Soc.; mem. Southeastern Univs. Rsch. Assn. (bd. dirs. 1989—), Phi Beta Kappa, Sigma Xi, Sigma Pi Sigma, Phi Kappa Phi. Home: 4 Bridlebrook Ln Newark DE 19711-2058 Office: U Del Dept Physics & Astronomy Newark DE 19716

MURRAY, RICHARD MAXIMILIAN, insurance executive; b. Vienna, Austria, Nov. 21, 1922; came to U.S., 1955, naturalized, 1961; s. and Elizabeth Helen Peiker. Grad. in world commerce studies, U. Vienna; postgrad., Columbia U. Asst. sec. Sterling Offices Ltd. (reins. intermediaries), London, Toronto, N.Y.C., 1951-59; v.p. Guy Carpenter, Inc. (reins. intermediaries), N.Y.C., 1959-68; v.p. Travelers Ins. Cos., 1968-87, ret., 1987; mng. dir. La Metropole Ins. Co., Brussels, ret., 1987; chmn. bd. Nippon Mgmt. Corp., N.Y.C., ret., 1991; chmn. bd. Travelers Marine Corp., ret., 1987; pres. Travelers Reins Co. Bermuda Ltd., ret., 1987; pres. Travelers of Asia Ltd., Hong Kong, ret., 1987; vice-chmn. bd. La Prov Corp., N.Y.C.; bd. electors Ins. Hall of Fame; bd. dirs. SCOR U.S. Corp., N.Y., SCOR Reins Co., N.Y., Unity Fire and Gen. Ins. Co., N.Y.C., Gen. Security Ins. Corp. N.Y., Rockleigh Mgmt. Corp., N.Y.C., Preferred Life Ins. Co. N.Y., United Am. Inst. Co., United Am. Holdings Co., Inc.; mem. adv. bd. Firemark Global Ins. Fund, L.P.; chair audit com. Davis Internat. Total Return Fund. Contbr. articles to profl. publs. Decorated for promotion of pvt. ins. (Peru); Knight Order of St. John, Knights of Malta (ambassador at large). Mem. Internat. Ins. Coun. (chmn. 1979-81, award 1990), City Midday Club. Home: 60 Remsen St Brooklyn NY 11201-3453 Office: 80 Broad St Fl 35 New York NY 10004-2209

MURRAY, ROBERT BRUCE, theatre administrator; b. Evanston, Ill., Apr. 8, 1932; s. Robert Wolcott and Hazel (Clayton) M.; m. Erika Grob, Oct. 19, 1957 (dec. Feb. 1986); children: Christopher (dec.), Timothy, Molly, Gideon. BS, U. Wis., 1954; MFA, Yale U., 1961. Program dir. Aspen (Colo.) Inst. For Humanistic Studies, 1961-65; assoc. prof. dept. drama Emerson Coll., Boston, 1965-72; dir. cultural svcs. and bicentennial City of Salem (Mass.), 1972-78; dir. Aspen Community Sch., 1978-83; exec. dir. Wheeler Opera House, Aspen, 1983—; bd. dirs. League Hist. Am. Theatres, Washington, 1984—. Playwright: The Good Lieutenant, 1963 (PBS-TV award 1965), Donner, 1973 (Rockefeller Found. award 1975), Salem Chronicles, 1974 (U.S. Park Service award 1976). Mem. Hist. Salem Inc., 1970-76; bicentennial dir. City of Salem, 1973-77; pres. Aspen Hist. Soc., 1980-81; bd. mem. Mountain Valley Devel. Services, 1981—. Named Playwright in Residence Yale U., John Golden Found., 1963-65; recipient Bristol Myers Drama award, N.Y.C., 1963, Rockefeller Drama award Rockefeller Found., U. Calif. Davis, 1973. Office: Wheeler Opera House 320 E Hyman Ave Aspen CO 81611-1948

MURRAY, ROBERT EUGENE, coal company executive; b. Martins Ferry, Ohio, Jan. 13, 1940; s. Albert Edward and Mildred Etheline (Shepherd) M.; m. Brenda Lou Moore, Aug. 26, 1962; children: Sherri Sue (dec.), Robert Edward, Jonathan Robert, Ryan Michael. B in Engring., Ohio State U., 1962; postgrad. Case Western Res. U., 1968-70, Harvard U. Grad. Sch. Bus. Advanced Mgmt. Program, U. N.D., 1982-83. Registered profl. engr., Ohio. Asst. to mgr. indsl. engring. and coal preparation N.Am. Coal Corp., 1961-63, sect. foreman, plant foreman, gen. mine foreman, Ohio div., 1963-64, asst. supt., 1964-66, supt. 1966-68, asst. to pres., Cleve., 1968-69, v.p. operations, v.p. eastern div., 1969-74, pres. Western div., 1974-83; exec. v.p. and pres. coal ops. N.Am. Coal Corp., 1985-86, pres., chief operating officer, 1986-87, pres., chief exec. officer, 1987; pres. Coteau Properties Co., Falkirk Mining Co., Western Plains Mining Co., Mo. Valley Properties Co., N. Am. Constrn. and Reclamation Co.; v.p., bd. dirs. Nacco Mining Co.; bd. dirs. Sabine Mining Co. 1987-88; pres., chief exec. officer and owner Ohio Valley Resources Inc., Coal Resources Inc., Am. Coal Sales Co., Ohio Valley Coal Co., Ohio Valley Transloading Co., Maple Creek Mining, Inc., Energy Resources, Inc., Mill Creek Mining, Inc., Hocking Valley Resources, Inc., W.Va. Resources, Inc., 1988—; shareholder Oneida Coal Co., Inc., MonValley Transp. Ctr., Inc., Ken American Resources, Inc.; mining engring. departmental asst. Ohio State U., 1960-62; past pres., chmn. bd. N.D. Lignite Council; bd. dirs. Energy Resources, Inc., Energy Transp., Inc. Exec. bd. Greater Cleve. and No. Lights council Boy Scouts Am.; past pres., bd. dirs. United Way of Bismarck; bd. regents U. Mary; trustee, lay speaker, tchr., lay leader Meth. Ch., bd. dirs. Mining Electro-Mech. Assn. (pres. Ohio Valley br. 1967-68), Pitts. Coal Mining Inst. Am., Soc. Mining Engrs. AIME (bd. dirs., exec. com., past chmn. coal div., pres., past-pres. Howard N. Evenson award, Disting. Mem. award), Rocky Mountain Coal Mining Inst. (past pres., program chmn., chmn. adv. bd.), Nat. Mining Assn. (bd. dirs.), World Energy Conf., past chmn. ad hoc coalition on internat. electric power trade, research adv. com., generic mineral tech. ctr., Nat. Soc. Profl. Engrs. (pres. east Ohio chpt. 1966-67), Mining Hall Fame (dir.), Ohio Engrs. in Industry (mem. bd. govs. 1966-67). Republican. Lodges: Masons (32d degree), Shriners. Home: 32 Cotswold Ln Moreland Hills Chagrin Falls OH 44022 Office: Ohio Valley Resources Inc Coal Resources Inc 29525 Chagrin Blvd Suite 111 Pepper Pike OH 44122 also: N Am Coal Corp 13140 Coit Rd Dallas TX 75240-5755

MURRAY, ROBERT FULTON, JR., physician; b. Newburgh, N.Y., Oct. 19, 1931; s. Robert Fulton and Henrietta Frances (Judd) M.; m. Isobel Ann Parks, Aug. 26, 1956; children: Colin Charles (dec.), Robert Fulton III, Suzanne Frances, Dianne Akwe. B.S., Union Coll., Schenectady, 1953; M.D., U. Rochester, N.Y., 1958; M.S., U. Wash., Seattle, 1968. Diplomate Am. Bd. Internal Medicine, Am. Bd. Med. Genetics. Rotating intern Denver Gen. Hosp., 1958-59; resident in internal medicine U. Colo. Med. Center, 1959-62; staff investigator (service with USPHS) Nat. Inst. Arthritis and Metabolic Diseases, NIH, Bethesda, Md., 1962-65; NIH spl. fellow med. genetics U. Wash., 1965-67; mem. faculty Howard U. Coll. Medicine, Washington, 1967—; prof. pediatrics and medicine Howard U. Coll. Medicine, 1974—, grad. prof., 1976, prof. oncology, 1976, chief div. med. genetics, 1968—, chmn. dept. genetics and human genetics Grad. Sch., 1976—; nat. adv. gen. med. scis. coun. NIH, 1971-75, recombinant DNA adv. com., 1988-92; sci. adv. bd. Nat. Sickle Cell Anemia Found.; ethics adv. bd. to sec. HEW, 1978-80; chmn. Washington Mayor's Adv. Com. on Metabolic Disorders, 1980-89; active Med. Com. Human Rights. Co-author: Genetic Variation and Disorders in Peoples of African Origin, 1990; co-editor: Genetic, Metabolic and Developmental Aspects of Mental Retardation, 1972, Genetic Counseling: Facts, Values and Norms, 1979; assoc. editor Am. Jour. Clin. Genetics, 1977-93; mem. editorial adv. bd. Ency. Bioethics, 1975-77, 93-95; mem. editorial bd. Jour. Clin. Ethics, 1990. Trustee Union Coll., 1972-80. Rotary Found. fellow, 1955-56; research grantee NIH, 1969-75. Fellow ACP, AAAS, Inst. Medicine (coun. mem. 1983-85), Inst. Soc., Ethics and Life Scis. (bd. dirs.), Am. Coll. Med. Genetics; mem. AAUP, Assn. Acad. Minority Physicians, Am. Soc. Human Genetics, Genetics Soc. Am., Acad. Medicine Washington, Neighbors Inc. D.C., Sigma Xi, Alpha Omega Alpha. Unitarian. Home: 510 Aspen St NW Washington DC 20012-2740 Office: Coll Medicine Box 75 Howard Univ Washington DC 20059*

MURRAY, ROBERT GRAY, sculptor; b. Vancouver, B.C., Can., Mar. 2, 1936; s. John Gray and Vera (Meakin) M.; m. Cintra Wetherill Lofting, Jan. 23, 1971; children: Rebecca and Megan (twins), Claire, Hillary. Student, U. Sask., Can., 1956-58. One man shows Betty Parsons Gallery, N.Y.C., 1965, 66, 68, David Mirvish Gallery, Toronto, 1967, 68, 72, 73, 74, 75, Jewish Mus., N.Y.C., 1967, Hammarskjold Plaza, N.Y.C., 1971, Paula Cooper Gallery, N.Y.C., 1974, Janie Lee Gallery, Houston, 1977, Hamilton Gallery, N.Y.C., 1977, 79, 80, Klonaridis Inc., Toronto, 1979, 81, 82, Rice U., 1978, Dayton Mus., 1979, Columbus Mus., 1979, Lamont Gallery, Phillips Acad., Exeter, N.H., 1983, Art Gallery Greater Victoria, 1983, Gallery One, Toronto, 1985, Culturale Canadese Roma, 1985, Gallery 291, Atlanta, 1986, Richard Greene Gallery, N.Y.C.,1986, L.A., 1987, Del. Art Mus., Wilmington, 1990, Muhlenberg Coll., Allentown, Pa., 1992, Mira Godard Gallery, Toronto, Reading (Pa.) Pub. Mus., 1994, 96, Andre Zarre Gallery, N.Y.C., 1994; exhibited in group shows at Whitney Mus. 1996— Am., Art, N.Y.C., 1964-66, Tibor de Nagy Gallery, N.Y.C., 1965, Musée cantonal des Beaux Arts, Lausanne, Switzerland, 1966, World House Gallery, N.Y.C., 1966, Betty Parsons Gallery, 1966, Sch. Visual Arts, N.Y.C., 1967, Los Angeles County Mus., 1967, Nat. Gallery Can., Toronto, 1967, Inst. Contemporary Art, Boston, 1967, U. Toronto, 1967, Guggenheim Mus., N.Y.C., 1967, Inst. Torcuato Di Tella, Buenos Aires, 1967, Musée d'Art Moderne, Paris, 1968, Whitney Mus., 1967, Walker Art Gallery, 1969, X Sao Paulo Biennial, Brazil, 1969, Boston City Hall, 1971, Artist and Fabricator, Amherst, Mass., 1975, Met. Mus., N.Y.C., 1983, Del. Art Mus., 1990, GrandRapids (Mich.) Mus., 1994; represented in permanent collections, Montreal Mus. Fine Arts, Nat. Gallery Can., Joseph Hirshhorn Collection, Art Gallery Ont., Larry Aldrich Mus., Ridgefield, Conn., New Brunswick Mus., Whitney Mus. Am. Art, Met. Mus., N.Y.C., Columbus Mus., Dayton Art Inst., Storm King Art Centre, Del. Art. Mus., Wilmington, Muhlenberg Coll., Allentown, Pa., others; major commns. include, Everson Mus., Syracuse, N.Y., Fredonia (N.Y.) State Coll., Canadian Dept. External Affairs, Ottawa, Ont., U. Mass., U. Toronto, Ont., State Ct. Bldg., Juneau, Alaska, Honeywell Corp., Mpls., also others.

MURRAY, ROBERT J., think-tank executive. Grad., Suffolk Coll., Harvard U. Under sec. Navy U.S. Govt., dep. asst. sec. defense, asst. to the sec., dep. sec. defense; pol. mil. attaché Am. Embassy, London; dean Naval War Coll., 1981-83; dir. Ctr. Naval Warfare Studies, 1981-83; mem. faculty, dir. nat. security program John F. Kennedy Sch. Govt. Harvard U., 1983-90; with CNA Corp., 1990—, pres., CEO, also trustee; pres. Ctr. Naval Analyses; mem. bd. advisors Naval War Coll., Nat. War Coll., Washington. Served USMC. Recipient numerous awards for pub. svc. Fellow Nat. Inst. Pub. Affairs; mem. Internat. Inst. Strategic Studies. Office: Center for Naval Analyses 4401 Ford Ave Alexandria VA 22302-1432*

MURRAY, ROBERT WALLACE, chemistry educator; b. Brockton, Mass., June 20, 1928; s. Wallace James and Rose Elizabeth (Harper) M.; m. Claire K. Murphy, June 10, 1951; children: Kathleen A., Lynn E., Robert Wallace, Elizabeth A., Daniel J., William M., Padraic O'D. AB, Brown U., 1951; MA, Wesleyan U., Middletown, Conn., 1956; PhD, Yale U., 1960. Mem. tech. staff Bell Labs., Murray Hill, N.J., 1959-68; prof. chemistry U. Mo., St. Louis, 1968-81; chmn. dept. U. Mo., 1975-80, curators' prof., 1981—; vis. prof. Engler-Bunte Inst. U. Karlsruhe, Fed. Republic Germany, 1982, dept. chemistry Univ. Coll., Cork, Ireland, 1989; cons. to govt. and industry. Co-editor: Singlet Oxygen, 1979; contbr. articles to profl. jours. Mem. Warren (N.J.) Twp. Com., 1962-63, mayor, 1963; mem. Planning Com. and Bd. Health, 1962-64, Bd. Edn., 1966-68. Served with USNR, 1951-54. Grantee EPA, NSF, NIH, Office of Naval Research. Fellow AAAS, Am. Inst. Chemists, N.Y. Acad. Scis.; mem. Am. Soc. Photobiology, Am. Chem. Soc., The Oxygen Soc., Sigma Xi. Home: 1810 Walnutway Dr Saint Louis MO 63146-3659 Office: Univ Mo Dept Chemistry Saint Louis MO 63121

MURRAY, ROGER FRANKLIN, economist, educator; b. N.Y.C., Oct. 11, 1911; s. Walter Fletcher and Mary (Van Horne) M.; m. Agnes M. McDede, Oct. 19, 1934; 1 child, Roger Franklin III. Grad., Phillips Andover, 1928; BA, Yale U., 1932; MBA,. NYU, 1938, PhD, 1942; LLD, Hope Coll., Holland, Mich., 1960, Tulane U., 1992. Investment adminstr. Bankers Trust Co., N.Y.C., 1932-43, v.p., 1946-56; assoc. dean Grad. Sch. Bus. Columbia U., N.Y.C., 1956-58, S. Sloan Colt prof. banking and fin., 1958-65, 71-77; v.p. Tchrs. Ins. and Annuity Assn. and Coll. Retirement Equities Fund, 1965-67, exec. v.p., 1967-70; bd. dirs. Alliance Group Mut. Funds, 1966-88, Chgo. Bd. Options Exch., Putnam Group of Mut. Funds; pres. Fund for Mut. Depositors, 1970-77, Investor Responsibility Rsch. Ctr., Inc.; trustee N.Y. Bank for Savs., 1947-77, Common Fund for Nonprofit Orgns., 1969-81. Pres. alumni coun. Phillips Andover Sch., 1973; mem. N.Y. State Coun. Econ. Advisers, 1973-74, Pension Rsch. Coun.; mem. investment policy panel Pension Benefit Guaranty Corp., 1975-84; mem. President's Task Force on Aging, 1969-70; mem. investment adv. com. N.Y. State Tchrs. Retirement Sys., SEC Adv. Com. on Corp. Disclosure; life trustee Collegiate Sch., pres., 1968-72; trustee Smith Coll., 1969-70; trustee Mayhew program Wolfeboro Area Children's Ctr.; selectman Town of Wolfeboro, N.H. Capt. USAAF, 1943-45. Decorated Legion of Merit. Mem. Am. Econ. Assn., Am. Fin. Assn. (pres. 1964), SR, Phi Beta Kappa, Beta Gamma Sigma. Mem. United Ch. Christ. Home: 32 Pleasant Valley Rd PO Box 669 Wolfeboro NH 03894-0669

MURRAY, ROYCE WILTON, chemistry educator; b. Birmingham, Ala., Jan. 9, 1937; s. Royce Leeroy and Justina Louisa (Herd) M.; m. Judith Studinka, 1957 (div.); children: Katherine, Stewart, Debra, Melissa, Marion; m. Mirtha X. Umana, Dec. 11, 1982. BS in Chemistry, Birmingham So. Coll., 1957; PhD in Analytical Chemistry, Northwestern U., 1960. Instr. U. N.C., Chapel Hill, 1960-61, asst. prof., 1961-66, assoc. prof., 1966-69, prof., 1969—, vice chmn., 1970-75, acting chair dept. chemistry, 1970-71, dir. undergrad. studies, 1978-80, dept. chmn., 1980-85, chmn. curriculum applied scis., 1995—, div. chmn., 1987-93, Kenan prof., 1980—. Contbr. articles to jours. in field. Recipient award Japanese Soc. for Promotion Sci., 1978, Electrochem. Group medal Royal Soc. Chemistry, 1989; Alfred P. Sloan fellow, 1969-72, Guggenheim fellow, 1980-82. Fellow AAAS, Am. Inst. Chemists, Am. Acad. Arts and Scis., Electrochem. Soc.; mem. NAS, Soc. for Electroanalytical Chemistry (bd. dirs., co-founder 1982-84, Charles N. Reilley award 1988, pres. 1991-93), Am. Chem. Soc. (Electrochemistry award 1990, Analytical Chemistry award 1991, editor in chief Analytical Chemistry 1991—), Electrochem. Soc. (hon. life, Carl Wagner Meml. award 1987-95). Presbyterian. Office: U NC Dept Chemistry Chapel Hill NC 27599-3290

MURRAY, RUSSELL, II, aeronautical engineer, defense analyst, consultant; b. Woodmere, N.Y., Dec. 5, 1925; s. Herman Stump and Susanne Elizabeth (Warren) M.; m. Sally Tingue Gardiner, May 22, 1954; children: Ann Tingue, Prudence Warren, Alexandria Gardiner. BS in Aero. Engring, MIT, 1949, MS, 1950. Guided missile flight test engr. Grumman Aircraft Engring. Corp., Bethpage, N.Y., 1950-53, asst. chief operations analysis, 1953-62; prin. dep. asst. sec. of def. for systems analysis The Pentagon, Washington, 1962-69; dir. long range planning Pfizer Internat., N.Y.C., 1969-73; dir. review Center for Naval Analyses, Arlington, Va., 1973-77; asst. sec. of def. for program analysis and evaluation Dept. of Def., The Pentagon, Washington, 1977-81; prin. Systems Research & Applications Corp., Arlington, Va., 1981-85; spl. counsellor Com. on Armed Services U.S. Ho. of Reps., 1985-89, nat. security cons., 1989—. Served with USAAF, 1944-45. Recipient Sec. of Def. Medal for meritorious civilian service, 1968; Disting. Public Service medal Dept. Def., 1981. Home: 210 Wilkes St Alexandria VA 22314-3839

MURRAY, SANDRA ANN, biology research scientist, educator; b. Chgo., Oct. 7, 1947; d. Charles William and Muggie (Wise) M. BS, U. Ill., 1970; MS, Tex. So. U., 1973; PhD, U. Iowa, 1980. Instr. biology Tex. So. U., Houston, 1972-73; NIH rsch. fellow U. Calif., Riverside, 1980-82; asst. prof. anatomy U. Pitts., 1982-89, assoc. prof. cell biology and physiology, 1989—; assoc. prof. Health Officers Inst. Office Def., Addis Ababa, Ethiopia, 1996—; vis. scientist Scripps Rsch. Inst., La Jolla, Calif., 1991-92, INSERM-INRA Hosp. Debrousse, Lyon, France, 1995; cons. NIH, NSF; vis. sci. cons. Fedn. Am. Soc. Exptl. Biology; invited internat. rsch. lectr. at sci. confs. Contbr. articles to Jour. Cell Biology, Anat. Records, Endocrinology, Am. Jour. Anatomy, Molecular and Cellular Endocrinology, Cancer Rsch. Bd. dirs. NAACP, Riverside, 1980-81. Ford Found. fellow, 1978; Rsch. grantee NSF, 1984—, Beta Kappa Chi, Tri Beta Biol. Soc.; recipient Outstanding Achievment award in Sci., Omega Psi Chi; recipient Faculty award Student Nat. Med. Assn. Mem. Am. Soc. Cell Biology (mem. minority affairs com. 1980—, rsch. award to marine biol. lab. 1986, 87, 88, 89, rsch. presentation travel award 1984), Am. Soc. Biol. Chemists (rsch. presentation travel award 1985), Am. Assn. Anatomists, Tissue Culture Assn. (chairperson internat. sci. com. 1982), Endocrine Soc. (student affairs com.). Home: 5417 Coral St Pittsburgh PA 15206-3413 Office: Univ Pitts Scaife Hall 864A Pittsburgh PA 15261

MURRAY, TERESA MARIE, elementary education educator; b. Pottsville, Pa., July 7, 1950; d. Joseph John and Gloria Barbara (Mozloom) DeMarkis; m. William Bernard Murray, Sept. 21, 1974; children: Megan Gloria, William Gerard. BA in Elem. Edn., Kutztown U., 1990, postgrad. in Elem. Counseling, 1994—. 1st grade tchr. Holy Redeemer Sch., Minersville, Pa., 1990-92, 5th, 6th, 7th and 8th grade tchr., 1992—; sci., reading coord. Holy Redeemer Sch., Minersville, 1992-94. Mem. St. Clair Women Club. Roman Catholic. Avocations: reading, crafts, painting, golf. Home: 128 N Morris St Saint Clair PA 17970-1061 Office: Holy Redeemer Sch 301 Saint Francis St Minersville PA 17954-1524

MURRAY, TERRENCE, banker; b. Woonsocket, R.I., July 11, 1939; s. Joseph W. and Florence (Blackburn) M.; m. Suzanne Young, Jan. 24, 1960; children: Colleen, Paula, Terrence, Christopher, Megan. B.A., Harvard U., 1962. With Fleet Nat. Bank, Providence, 1962—, pres., 1978-86; with Fleet Fin. Group Inc., Providence, 1969—, pres., 1978—, chmn., pres., chief exec. officer, 1982-88, pres., 1988, chmn., pres., chief exec. officer, 1988—, also bd. dirs.; bd. dirs. Fleet Nat. Bank, A.T. Cross Co., State Mut. Assurance Co. Am., Fed. Res. Bank Boston, Stop & Shop Cos. Inc. Trustee R.I. Sch. of Design, Brown U. Recipient Outstanding Bus. Leader award Northwood Inst., 1986, Humanitarian award Nat. Jewish Ctr. for Immunology and Respiratory Medicine, 1988, Never Again award Jewish Fedn., 1989, New Englander of Yr. award New England Coun., 1990, New England Business-person of Yr. award New England Bus. Mag., 1991, Humanitarian award Fogarty Found., 1991. Mem. Am. Bankers Assn. (bd. dirs.), Assn. of Res. City Bankers (bd. dirs.), Harvard Alumni Assn. (bd. dirs.). Office: Fleet Bank 1 Federal Street Boston MA 02211*

MURRAY, TERRY (TERENCE RODNEY MURRAY), professional hockey team coach; b. Shawville, Que., Can., July 20, 1950; m. Linda Murray; children: Megan, Lindsey. Hockey player Calif. Golden Seals, 1972-75, Phila. Flyers, 1975-77, 78-81, Detroit Red Wings, 1977; hockey player Washington Capitals, 1981-82, asst. coach, 1982-88, head coach, 1990-94; head coach Balt. Skipjacks, 1988-90, Philadelphia Flyers, 1994—. Named to 3 Am. Hockey League all-star teams; named most valuable defenseman Am. Hockey League, 1978, 79. Office: Philadelphia Flyers Core States Spectrum 3601 S Broad St Philadelphia PA 19148*

MURRAY, THOMAS DWIGHT, advertising agency executive; b. Middletown, Ohio, May 1, 1923; s. Charles H. and Rose (Newbrander) M.; m. Barbara Helen Howlett, Oct. 5, 1946; children—Cynthia Helen, Susan Howlett; m. Carol Callaway Muehl, Apr. 13, 1968; children—David Rutherford, Piper Dee. Student, U. Va., 1941-43. Passenger relations agt. United Airlines, N.Y.C., 1946-47; tech. and advt. writer, copy supr. Frigidaire div. Gen. Motors Corp., Dayton, O., 1947-55; with Campbell-Ewald Co., Detroit, 1955-71; sr. v.p., creative dir. Campbell-Ewald Co., 1968-69, dir., mem. exec. com., 1968-71, exec. v.p., creative dir., 1969-71; chmn. bd., creative dir. Thomas Murray & Austin Chaney, Inc., Hudson, Ohio, 1971-80; Lectr. Wayne State U., U. Mich., Mich. State U., U. Ill., Art Center Los Angeles, Kent State U., Cleve. Advt. Sch., others; advt. adv. council Kent State U., 1976. Author: A Child to Change Your Life, 1976, A Look at Tomorrow, 1985, Tire Tracks Back, 1989; sr. editor Car Collector mag.; essayist Wall St. Jour., 1991—; wrote ad on Apollo 11 moonshot which was read into Congl. Record; contbr. articles to profl. jours. Vice pres., pres. local PTA, 1962-64; chmn. advt. com. United Found., 1966; Bd. dirs. Mich. Mental Health Soc., Big Bros. and Sisters of Greater Akron. Served with F.A. AUS, 1943-46, ETO. Recipient numerous advt. awards including Clio, Andy of N.Y. Mem. Detroit Copy Club (past pres., dir.). Clubs: Recess, Flying, Uptown Athletic Detroit, Birmingham Athletic. Home: 6650 Washington Cir # 18 Franklin OH 45005-5521

MURRAY, THOMAS HENRY, bioethics educator, writer; b. Phila., July 30, 1946; s. Thomas Henry and Colombia Rita (Lucci) M.; m. Sharon Marie Engelkraut, Jan. 1968 (div. Sept. 1975); children: Kathleen Elizabeth, Dominique Maria, Peter Albert; m. Cynthia Sarah Aberle, Apr. 1, 1978; 1 child, Emily Sarah Aberle. BA in Psychology, Temple U., 1968; PhD in Social Psychology, Princeton, 1976. Instr. New Coll., Sarasota, Fla., 1971-75; asst. prof. Interdisciplinary Studies Miami U., Oxford, Ohio, 1975-80, assoc. prof., 1980; assoc. social behavioral studies The Hastings Ctr., Hastings-on Hudson, N.Y., 1980-84; assoc. prof. Inst. Med. Humanities U. Tex Med. Br., Galveston, Tex., 1984-86, prof., 1986-87; prof., dir. Ctr. Biomed. Ethics Case We. Reserve U., Cleve., 1987—; mem. ethical, legal and social issues working group Human Genome Orgn. NIH/Dept. Energy, 1989-95. Author: The Worth of a Child, 1996; founder, editor Med. Humanities Rev.; mem. editl. bd. Social Sci. and Medicine, Physician and Sportsmedicine, Human Gene Therapy. Mem. U.S. Olympic com., com. sports medicine. Fellow NEH, 1977-78, 1979-80, Aspen Inst., 1989. Fellow Soc. Values in Higher Edn., Hastings Ctr., Environ. Health Inst.; mem. APHA, Assn. Practical and Profl. Ethics (exec. com.), Am. Soc. Law Medicine and Ethics (bd. dirs. 1993—), Assn. Integrative Studies (bd. dirs. 1980-87, pres. 1983), Soc. Health and Human Values (chair program dirs. sect. 1989-90, faculty assn. 1989-90, SHHV program com. 1990, pres.-elect 1992-93, pres. 1993-94), Am. Soc. Human Genetics (social issues com.), Am. Coll. Ob-Gyn. (com. on ethics), Human Genome Orgn. (ethical, legal and social issues com.). Office: Case Western Res U Sch Medicine Ctr Biomed Ethics 10900 Euclid Ave Cleveland OH 44106-1712

MURRAY, THOMAS JOHN (JOCK MURRAY), medical humanities educator, medical researcher; b. Halifax, N.S., Can., May 30, 1938; m. Janet Kathleen Pottie; children: Shannon, Bruce, Suellen, Brian. Grad. pre-med, St. Francis Xavier U., 1958, LLD (hon.), 1989; MD, Dalhousie U., 1963; DSc (hon.), Acadia U., 1991. Family physician, Nashwaaksis, N.S., 1963-65; chief of medicine Camp Hill Hosp., Halifax, N.S., 1974-79; chief of neurology Dalhousie U., Halifax, 1979-85, dir. multiple sclerosis rsch. unit, 1980—, dean of medicine, 1985-92; prof. med. humanities, 1992—. Co-author: (textbook) Essential Neurology; author over 200 pub. works, including contbns. to 7 textbooks. Bd. dirs. St. Francis Xavier U., Pictou Acad. Found., Robert Pope Found., Nat. Coun. on Bioethics and Health Rsch. Decorated officer Order Can. Fellow Royal Coll. Physicians (Can.), ACP (gov. 1985-90, chmn. bd. govs. 1990-91, bd. regents, chmn. 1995—); mem. Can. Neurol. Soc. (pres. 1982-84), Am. Acad. Neurology (v.p. 1981-83), Can. Med. Forum (chair), Can. Med. Assn., N.S. Med. Soc., Assn. Can. Med. Colls. (pres. 1991-92), Can. Med. Forum (chmn. 1992-95). Avocations: medical history, marathon running, piano, windsurfing, beer-making. Home: 16 Bobolink St. Halifax, NS Canada B3M 1W3 Office: Dalhousie Med Sch, Clin Rsch Ctr, Halifax, NS Canada B3H 4H7

MURRAY, THOMAS JOSEPH, advertising executive; b. Bridgeport, Conn., Mar. 12, 1924; s. Thomas and Mary (Diskin) M.; m. Mary Elizabeth Cull, Feb. 22, 1945; children: Joshua Francis, Mary Elizabeth, Katherine Diskin. A.B., Dartmouth Coll., 1947. Instr., Dartmouth Coll., 1947-48; with Warwick & Legler, N.Y.C., 1948-68; sr. v.p., mgmt. account supr. Warwick & Legler, 1964-68; sr. v.p. group supr. Gaynor & Ducas, Inc., 1968-74, exec. v.p., 1974—, chief fin. officer and gen. mgr., 1978-87; pres. TJM & Assn., 1987—. Pres., trustee Hillcrest Gen. Hosp., N.Y.C.; Westchester Inst. for tng. in Psychoanalysis and Psychotherapy, Mt. Kisco, N.Y. Served as 1st lt. USAAF, 1942-45. Decorated D.F.C., Air medal with 4 oak leaf clusters. Mem. Nat. Wholesale Druggists Assn., Propriety Assn., Nat. Assn. Chain Drug Stores, Am. Mktg. Assn. Home & Office: 65 Norfield Rd Weston CT 06883-2213

MURRAY, THOMAS MICHAEL, civil engineering educator, consultant; b. Dubuque, Iowa, May 22, 1944; s. Raymond M. and Laura R. (Juergens) M.; m. Margaret Ann Schrodt, July 13, 1964 (div. 1995); children: Matthew R., Elizabeth A., Nicholas P. BSCE, Iowa State U., 1962; MSCE, Lehigh U., 1966; PhD in Engring. Mechanics, U. Kans., 1970. Registered profl. engr., Iowa, Okla. Engr. trainee Pitts. Des Moines (Iowa) Steel Co., 1962-64; instr. civil engring. U. Omaha, 1966-67, U. Kans., Lawrence, 1967-69; asst. prof., assoc. prof., prof. U. Okla. Sch. Civil Engring., Norman, 1970-86; Disting. vis. prof. USAF Acad., Colorado Springs, Colo., 1986-87; Montague-Betts prof. structural steel design Va. Poly. Inst. and State U., Blacksburg, 1987—; pres. Structural Engrs. Inc., Radford, Va., 1973—. Author: Design Guide for Connections, 1990; also numerous articles; patentee in field. Recipient various teaching awards U. Okla., 1979, 81, 84. Fellow ASCE (numerous offices 1970—); mem. Am. Inst. Steel Constrn. (T.R. Higgins lectr. 1991), Am. Soc. for Engring. Edn., Structural Stability Rsch. Coun., also others. Republican. Roman Catholic. Avocations: skiing, spectator sports, railroads. Office: Va Poly Inst and State U Dept Civil Engring Blacksburg VA 24061

MURRAY, TY (THE KID MURRAY), professional rodeo cowboy; s. Harold "Butch" and Joy M. Student, Odessa (Tex.) Coll. Five-time world all-around world champion Profl. Rodeo Circuit Assn., 1989-93; world champion bull rider, 1993. Named Nat. H.S. Rodeo All-Around Champion, 1987, PRCA Rookie of the Year Profl. Rodeo Cowboy Assn., 1988, Nat. Intercollegiate Rodeo All-Around Champion, 1988. Record for single season earnings, 1991. Office: Profl Rodeo Cowboy Assn 101 Pro Rodeo Dr Colorado Springs CO 80919-2301*

MURRAY, WALLACE SHORDON, publisher, educator; b. Dorchester, Mass., May 9, 1921; s. Wallace Jennings and Ina (Shordon) M.; m. Eleanor Muriel Grandy, Oct. 30, 1948; children: Patricia Ann, William Howard. B.S., MIT, 1942; M.Ed., Boston U., 1949; Litt.D. (hon.), Western New Eng. Coll., 1965. Tchr. Bolles Sch., Jacksonville, Fla., 1945-46; head math. dept., asst. prin. Bolles Sch., 1946-49; headmaster Berwick Acad., South Berwick, Maine, 1949-50; sales rep. D.C. Heath & Co., Boston, 1950-52; editor D.C. Heath & Co., 1952-53, head elementary editorial dept., 1953-55, editor in chief, 1955-66, v.p., 1962-66, dir., 1956-66, sec. of corp., 1957-66; dir. Erica Corp., 1956-66; exec. v.p. Heath de Rochemont Corp., 1960-66, dir., 1960-66; editor-in-chief, mgr. materials devel. dept. Raytheon Edn. Co., 1966-68; v.p., editorial dir. domestic and internat. ops. Grolier Inc., 1968-80, dir., 1969-82, cons., 1980-82; dir. Grolier Edn. Corp., 1968-80, Scarecrow Press Inc., 1969-80; Chmn. elementary and high sch. research com. Am. Ednl. Pubs. Inst., 1966-68, chmn. elem. and high sch. sect., 1968-69. Lay leader Boston dist. Meth. Ch., 1952-56; mem. adv. bd. Boston U. Student Christian Assn., 1954-62, treas., 1957-59, chmn., 1959-61; mem. president's adv. council St. Joseph's Coll., North Windham, Maine, 1973-88; mem. corp. New Eng. Deaconess Assn., 1965-95, exec. com., 1965-68; mem. corp. New Eng. Deaconess Hosp., 1967-93; dir. Japan America Soc. of Maine, 1981-91, pres., 1984-86; merit badge counselor Pine Tree Coun., Boy Scouts Am., 1984—; dir. Children's Mus. of Maine, 1987-89; dir. Leisure Ctr. for the Handicapped, Inc., Portland, Maine, 1987-93, treas. 1988-93; mem. adv. council So. Maine Retired Sr. Vol. Program, 1987-90, chmn. fin. com., 1987-89; mem. Foster Care Case Review Panel Maine Dept. Human Services, 1987-91; dir. Foreside Common Condominium Assn., Falmouth, Maine, 1986-89, 1991-92, pres., 1987-89; vol. staff mem. Vol. Lawyers Project of Maine, 1987-90; vol. math. instr. Adult Basic Learning Exchange, Portland, 1987-91. Served to capt. AUS, 1942-46, to maj. USAR. Mem. Newcomen Soc., World Affairs Council of Maine, Phi Delta Kappa. Republican. Methodist. Lodges: Masons, Shriners. Home: PO Box 17 Sebago Lake ME 04075-0017

MURRAY, WARREN JAMES, philosophy educator; b. St. Paul, Dec. 3, 1936; s. James Bernard and Louise (Robertson) M.; m. Mary Ann McAulay, July 18, 1959; children: Mark, Anne, Kathleen. Student, St. Thomas Coll., 1954-55; B.A. in Chemistry, Wis. State Coll., River Falls, 1962; B.Ph. in Philosophy, Universite Laval, Que., Can., 1964, Ph.L., 1965, scolarite Ph.D., 1966. Analytical chemist 3M Co., St. Paul, 1957-61, research chemist, 1961-63; prof. philos. sci. U. Laval, Sainte-Foy, 1966—, vice dean, 1979—; invited prof. Faculte de philosophie Comparee, Paris, 1969, 72, Universite libre des sciences de l'homme, Paris, 1975—, Ecole des Hautes Etudes, Paris, 1976, Universidad Nacional de Tucuman, Argentina, 1991. fgn. exchange teaching grantee Province Que., 1969. Mem. Soc. Aristotelian Studies (pres.), Can. Soc. History and Philosophy Sci. Office: Faculte De Philosophie, Universite Laval, Sainte Foy, PQ Canada G1K 7P4

MURRAY, WILLIAM JAMES, anesthesiology educator, clinical pharmacologist; b. Janesville, Wis., July 20, 1933; s. James Arthur and Mary Helen (De Porter) M.; m. Therese Rose Dooley, June 25, 1955; children: Michael, James, Anne. BS, U. Wis., 1955, PhD, 1959; MD, U. N.C., 1962. Diplomate Am. Bd. Anesthesiology. Rsch. asst. U. Wis., Madison, 1955-59; instr. pharmacology U. N.C., Chapel Hill, 1959-62, resident and fellow in surgery (anesthesiology), 1962-64, instr., 1964-65, asst. prof., 1965-68; asst. to dir. for drug availability FDA, Washington, 1968-69; assoc. prof. pharmacology, clin. pharmacology and anesthesiology U. Mich., Ann Arbor, 1969-72; assoc. prof. anesthesiology Duke U., Durham, N.C., 1972-81, prof., 1981—; assoc. dir. Upjohn Ctr. for Clin. Pharmacology, Ann Arbor, 1969-72. Mem. AMA, Am. Soc. Anesthesiologists, Internat. Anesthesia Rsch. Soc., Soc. for Ambulatory Anesthesia, Am. Pharm Assn., N.Y. Acad. of Sci., N. C. Soc. Anesthesiologists, Am. Soc. Hosp. Pharmacists, U.S. Pharmacopeial Conv., Am. Coll. Clin. Pharmacology, Am. Soc. for Clin. and Therapeutic Pharmacology, Am. Soc. Pharmacology and Exptl. Therapeutics, N.C. Soc. Hosp. Pharmacists, So. Med. Assn., The Annals of Pharmacotherapy. Republican. Roman Catholic. Home: 135 Pinecrest Rd Durham NC 27705 Office: Duke U Med Ctr Dept Anesthesiology Box 3094 Durham NC 27710

MURRAY, WILLIAM JOHN, lawyer; b. N.Y.C., Sept. 21, 1948; s. William Edward and Louise Marie (Sgro) M.; m. Noreen McKenna, May 5, 1973 (div. Nov. 1981); m. Eileen Julie Finneran, Nov. 17, 1984; children: Fiona, Maeve, Bridget. BA, CUNY, 1977; JD, Fordham U., 1981. Assoc. Cole & Dietz, N.Y.C., 1981-82, J. Richard Williams, Albany, N.Y., 1983-85; asst. counsel N.Y. State Dept. Econ. Devel., Albany, 1985-88; counsel N.Y. State Lottery, Schenectady, 1988—. With U.S. Army, 1968-71. Office: NY State Lottery 1 Broadway Ctr Schenectady NY 12301

MURRELL, THOMAS W., III, lawyer; b. Nov. 28, 1948. BA, Yale U., 1971; JD, U. Va., 1974. Bar: Pa. 1974. Ptnr. Morgan, Lewis & Bockius, Phila. Office: Morgan Lewis & Bockius One Logan Sq Ste 2000 Philadelphia PA 19103*

MURRIAN, ROBERT PHILLIP, magistrate, judge, educator; b. Knoxville, Tenn., Apr. 1, 1945; s. Albert Kinzel and Mary Gilbert (Eppes) M.; m. Jerrilyn Sue Boone, Oct. 29, 1983; children—Kimberley Ann, Jennifer Rebecca, Albert Boone, Samuel Robert. B.S., U.S. Naval Acad., 1967; J.D., U. Tenn., 1974. Bar: Tenn. 1974, U.S. Dist. Ct. (ea. dist.) Tenn. 1975, U.S. Ct. Appeals (6th cir.) 1982. Law clk. to judge U.S. Dist. Ct. (ea. dist.) Tenn., 1974-76; assoc. Butler, Vines, Babb & Threadgill, Knoxville, 1976-78; magistrate, judge U.S. Dist. (ea. dist.) Tenn., Knoxville, 1978—; adj. prof. U. Tenn. Coll. Law, 1990-93, 95—. Lt. USN, 1967-71. Green Scholar, 1973-74; Nat. Moot Ct. scholar, 1974. Fellow Tenn. Bar Found.; mem. ABA, Knoxville Bar Assn. (bd. govs. 1994), Tenn. Bar Assn., Order of Coif, Am. Inn of Ct. (master of the bench). Presbyterian. Office: Howard Baker Jr Fed Courthouse 800 Market St Knoxville TN 37902

MURRILL, PAUL WHITFIELD, former utility executive, former university administrator; b. St. Louis, July 10, 1934; s. Horace Williams and Grace (Whitfield) M.; m. Nancy Williams, May 17, 1959; children: Paul Whitfield, John Parham, William Britton. BS, U. Miss., 1956; MS, La. State U., 1962, PhD, 1963. Registered profl. engr., La. Instr. chem. engring. La. State U., 1961-62, spl. lectr. chem., mech., indsl. and aerospace engring., 1962-63, asst. prof., 1963-65, assoc. prof., 1965-67, assoc. prof., head dept. chem. engring., 1967-68, prof., head dept. chem. engring., 1968-69, prof., 1968-80, vice chancellor, dean acad. affairs, 1969-70, provost, 1970-74, chancellor, 1974-80; sr. v.p. Ethyl Corp., Richmond, Va., 1980-82; chmn. bd., chief exec. officer Gulf States Utilities Co., Beaumont, Tex., 1982-87, spl. advisor to chmn., 1987-90; pres. Monarch Internat. Corp., 1978—; chmn. FMOL Health System Inc., 1991-94; chmn. bd. dirs. Burden Found., 1992—, Piccadilly Cafeterias, 1994—; cons. in field; project mgr. Dept. Def. project THEMIS, 1967-72; bd. dirs. First Miss. Corp., Tidewater Inc., New Orleans, Gulf State Utilities Co., First Miss Gold, Inc., Howell Corp. Piccadilly Cafeterias, Zygo, Inc., Entergy Corp., Pavilion Techs., Inc. Author: Automatic Control of Processes, 1967; co-author: Fortran IV Programming for Engineers and Scientists, 1968, The Development and Utilization of Mathematical Models, 1970, An Introduction to Fortran IV Programming: A General Approach, 1970, COBOL Programming, 1970, Basic Programming, 1970, PL/I Programming, 1973, Introduction to Computer Science, 1973, Fundamentals of Process Control, 1980, 2d edit., 1991, Application Concepts in Process Control, 1988; cons. editor: Chemical Engineering series, Internat. Textbook Co., 1966-72, Instrument Soc. Am., 1981—. Bd. dirs. local Boy Scouts Am., United Way; deacon Bapt. ch. Served to lt. comdr USNR, 1956-59. Recipient Faculty Service award Nat. U. Extension Assn., 1968, Halliburton Found. award for excellence in engring. teaching, 1966. Mem. La. Engring. Soc. (Tech. Accomplishment medal 1970, Andrew Lockett medal 1978), Am. Soc. Engring. Edn., Am. Inst. Chem. Engrs., Instrument Soc. Am. (Donald Eckman Nat. award 1976), Sigma Xi, Omicron Delta Kappa, Tau Beta Pi, Pi Kappa Pi, Phi Kappa Phi (Disting. Nat. medal 1976), Phi Eta Sigma, Phi Lambda Epsilon. Lodge: Rotary.

MURRIN, REGIS DOUBET, lawyer; b. Erie, Pa., June 2, 1930; s. John III and Gabrielle (Doubet) M.; m. Evelyn L. Alessio, Aug. 22, 1959; children: Catherine Shaw Murrin Hargenrader, Mary Murrin Smith, Elizabeth Murrin Talotta, Rebecca Fielding Lamanna. BA, U. Notre Dame, 1952; JD, Harvard U., 1959; LLM, Temple U., 1968. Bar: Pa. 1959, U.S. Supreme Ct. 1971. Assoc. Murrin & Murrin, Butler, Pa., 1959-62; atty. Housing & Home Fin. Agy., Phila., 1962-64; ptnr. Baskin & Sears, Pitts., 1964-84; ptnr. Reed Smith Shaw & McClay, Pitts., 1985-95, of counsel, 1995—. Trustee Pitts. Oratory, 1976-93; chmn. Zoning Bd. Adjustment, City of Pitts., 1994—; bd. dirs. Ellis Sch., 1991—. Served as lt. USNR, 1952-55, Korea, Vietnam. Mem. Pa. Bar Assn. (real estate and common interest ownership coms.), Edwin Sorin Soc. Democrat. Roman Catholic. Office: Reed Smith Shaw & McClay 435 6th Ave Pittsburgh PA 15219-1809

MURRIN, THOMAS EDWARD, insurance company executive; b. Bklyn., Sept. 12, 1923; s. Maurice Joseph and Agnes (O'Brien) M.; m. Marguerite Judge, Aug. 23, 1947; children—Maureen, Thomas, Rosemary, Ann, Patricia, Elizabeth, James, Marguerite. B.S. magna cum laude, St. John's U., 1944. Actuary Nat. Bur. Casualty Underwriters, N.Y.C., 1946-61; v.p., actuary Am. Ins. Group, Newark, 1961-63, Fireman's Fund Am. Ins. Cos., San Francisco, 1963-68; sr. v.p., actuary Fireman's Fund Am. Ins. Cos., 1968-76, exec. v.p. ins. services office, 1976-83; exec. cons. Coopers and Lybrand, San Francisco, 1984—. Served to lt. (j.g.) USNR, 1944-46. Fellow Casualty Actuarial Soc. (past pres.); mem. Am. Acad. Actuaries (past pres.), Internat. Congress Actuaries. Home: 275 Calle de la Selva Novato CA 94949-6084 Office: 333 Market St San Francisco CA 94105-2102

MURRISH, CHARLES HOWARD, oil and gas exploration company executive, geologist; b. Rochester, Mich., Dec. 27, 1940; s. Richard John and Emily Louise (Marsh) M.; m. Brigitte Marie Furlotte, Oct. 23, 1965; children: Stephanie, Stephen, Brian. Student Mexico City Coll., 1962; BS, Mich. State U., 1963, MS, 1966. Exploration geologist and geophysicist Chevron, New Orleans, 1966-71; mgr. exploration Odeco, New Orleans, 1971-77; v.p. McMoRan Offshore Exploration Co., Metairie, La., 1977-79, sr. v.p., 1979-81; pres. McMoRan-Freeport Oil Co., New Orleans, 1981-83; pres. McMoRan Exploration Co., Metairie, 1983-86 ; exec. v.p. McMoran Oil & Gas Co., 1986; sr. exec. v.p. McMoRan Oil & Gas Co., 1986-90; sr. exec. v.p. Freeport-McMoRan Oil & Gas Co., 1990-92, also bd. dirs.; ptnr. CLK Co., 1992-94; pres., COO McMoRan Oil & Gas Co., 1994—. Chmn. bd. Hysell Ballet Arts, Inc., New Orleans, 1982-83; bd. dirs. Lenpac, Metairie, 1983. Mem. New Orleans Geol. Soc., Geol. Soc. Am., Am. Assn. Petroleum Geologists, Petroleum Club of New Orleans (bd. dirs. 1988, 89, 90), Houston Geol. Soc., La. Assn. Ind. Producers, Mid-Continent Oil and Gas Assn. Office: McMoRan Oil & Gas Co 1615 Poydras St New Orleans LA 70112-1254 also: PO Box 60004 New Orleans LA 70160-0004

MURRY, CHARLES EMERSON, lawyer, official; b. Hope, N.D., June 23, 1924; s. Raymond Henry and Estelle Margarete (Skeim) M.; m. Donna Deane Kleve, June 20, 1948; children: Barbara, Karla, Susan, Bruce, Charles. B.S., U. N.D., 1948, J.D., 1950. Bar: N.D. 1950. Mem. firm Nelson and Heringer, Rugby, N.D., 1950-51; dir. N.D. Legis. Council, 1951-75; adj. gen. with rank of maj. gen. State of N.D., Bismarck, 1975-84; mgr. Garrison Diversion Conservancy Dist., 1985-93; cons. Council State Govts.; mem. res. forces policy bd. Sec. of Def. Vice-pres. Mo. Slope Luth. Home of Bismarck, 1965-66. Served with AUS, 1942-45. Decorated D.S.M., Legion of Merit, Meritorious Service medal, Bronze Star, Army Commendation medal; Fourragere Belgium; Orange Lanyard Netherlands; recipient Sioux award U. N.D., 1970; Gov.'s award of excellence, 1971; Nat. Leadership award Bismarck C. of C., 1971. Mem. Adjs. Gen. Assn. (exec. com., sec. 1983-84), Nat. Legis. Conf. (past chmn.), N.G. Assn., Am. Bar Assn., N.D. Bar Assn., Commrs. Uniform State Laws. Lutheran. Lodges: Elks, Masons. Office: HC 9 5505 Ponderosa Ave Bismarck ND 58501-9159

MURRY, HAROLD DAVID, JR., lawyer; b. Holdenville, Okla., June 30, 1943; s. Harold David Sr. and Willie Elizabeth (Dees) M.; m. Ann Moore Earnhardt, Nov. 1, 1975; children: Elizabeth Ann, Sarah Bryant. BA, Okla. U., 1965, JD, 1968. Bar: Okla. 1968, D.C. 1974. Asst. to v.p. U. Okla., Norman, 1968-71, legal counsel Research Inst., 1969-71; atty. U.S. Dept. Justice, Washington, 1971-74; spl. asst. U.S. Atty., Washington, 1972; assoc. Clifford & Warnke, Washington, 1974-78, ptnr., 1978-91; ptnr. Howrey & Simon, Washington, 1991—. Mem. ABA, Okla. Bar Assn., D.C. Bar Assn., Fed. Bar Assn., Met. Club (Washington), Chevy Chase Club (Md.), Phi Alpha Delta. Democrat. Home: 8931 Bel Air Pl Potomac MD 20854-1606 Office: Howrey & Simon 1299 Pennsylvania Ave NW Washington DC 20004-2400

MURTAGH, JOHN EDWARD, alcohol production consultant; b. Wallington, Surrey, Eng., Sept. 12, 1936; came to U.S., 1982; s. Thomas Henry and Elsie (Kershaw Paterson) M.; m. Eithne Anne Fawsitt, July 18, 1959; children: Catherine, Rhoda, Sean, Aidan, Doreen. BSc, U. Wales, 1959, MSc, 1970, PhD, 1972. Rsch. coord. House of Seagram, Long Pond, Jamaica, 1959-63; whisky distillery mgr. House of Seagram, Beaupre, Que., Can., 1963-65; rum distillery mgr. House of Seagram, Richibucto, N.B., Can., 1965-68; rsch. mgr. House of Seagram, Montreal, Que., 1968-70; alcohol prodn. cons. Murtagh & Assocs., Buttevant, Ireland, 1972-77, 79-82, Winchester, Va., 1982—; vodka distillery mgr. Iran Beverages, Tehran, 1977-79; ethanol tech. cons., adv. bd. Info. Resources, Inc., Washington, 1988—; lectr. Alltech Ann. Alcohol Sch., Lexington, Ky., 1982—. Author: Glossary of Fuel-Ethanol Terms, 1990; co-author, editor: The Alcohol Textbook, 1995; pub.: Worldwide Directory of Distilleries, 1996; contbr. articles to profl. jours. Adv. bd. Byrd Sch. Bus., Shenandoah U., Winchester, Va., 1989—. Recipient Millers Mutual prize, U. Wales, 1959. Fellow Am. Inst. Chemists, Inst. Chemistry of Ireland, Inst. Food Sci. and Tech. of Ireland; mem. Royal Soc. Chemistry (chartered), Am. Arbitration Assn. (arbitrator nat. comml. panel 1990—). Achievements include development of proprietary process for production of ethanol from cheese whey and the design of whey-ethanol production plants. Home and Office: 160 Bay Ct Winchester VA 22602-4700

MURTAUGH, CHRISTOPHER DAVID, lawyer; b. Darby, Pa., Oct. 25, 1945; s. John Michael and Rita (Sullivan) M.; m. Nancy R. Hanauer, Nov. 30, 1968; children: Jason C., Colin M., Alison M. AB, U. Ill., 1967, JD, 1970. Bar: Ill. 1970, Fla. 1973, U.S. Dist. Ct. (no. dist.) Ill. 1975. Ptnr. Winston & Strawn, Chgo., 1974—, capital ptnr., 1987—. Mem. Glen Ellyn (Ill.) Capital Improvements Com., 1985-89, Glen Ellyn Plan Com., 1989—, Met. Planning Coun., 1995—. Lt. USNR, 1971-74. Mem. ABA, Am. Coll. Real Estate Lawyers, Fla. Bar Assn., Ill. State Bar Assn., Chgo. Bar Assn., Order of Coif. Office: Winston & Strawn 35 W Wacker Dr Chicago IL 60601-1614

MURTHA, JOHN FRANCIS, history educator, priest; b. Mt. Pleasant, Pa., May 28, 1930; s. Francis Regis and Margaret Ellen (Kearns) M. BA cum laude, St. Vincent Coll., 1953; MA, Columbia U., 1960; PhD, Cath. U. Am., 1965; M Div., St. Vincent Sem., 1985. Ordained priest Roman Cath. Ch., 1957. Assoc. prof. history St. Vincent Coll., Latrobe, Pa., 1977-93, prof., 1993—, bd. dirs., 1978-81, pres., 1984-95; prior St. Vincent Archabbey, Latrobe, 1980-85, mem. coun. srs., 1978-88. Editor: America 200, Essays in American History, 1976; contbr. articles to New Cath. Ency., 1963. Mem. Am. Benedictine Acad., Elks. Democrat. Office: St Vincent Coll Fraser Purchase Rd Latrobe PA 15650

MURTHA, JOHN PATRICK, congressman; b. New Martinsville, W.Va., June 17, 1932; s. John Patrick and Mary Edna (Ray) M.; m. Joyce Bell; three children. B.A. in Econs., U. Pitts., 1961; postgrad., Indiana U. of Pa., 1962-65; H.H.D. (hon.), Mt. Aloysius Jr. Coll. Mem. Pa. Ho. of Reps., 1969-73, 93rd-103rd Congresses from 12th Pa. dist., Washington, D.C., 1974—; mem. appropriations com. Served to lt. USMC, 1952-55, as maj. 1966-67, Vietnam; ret. col. Res. Decorated Bronze Star, Purple Heart (2); Cross of Gallantry Vietnam; Pa. Disting. Svc. award, 1978, Pa. Meritorious Svc. medal, numerous service awards for work during Johnstown flood, 1977, Iron Mike award Marine Corps League, 1988, Disting. Am. award Nation's Capital chpt. Air Force Assn., 1989, Outstanding Veteran award Vets. Caucus of Am. Acad. Physician Assts., 1989, Man of Steel award Cold Finished Steel Bar Inst., 1989; named Man of Yr. Johnstown Jaycees, 1978. Office: US Ho of Reps 2423 Rayburn Ho Office Bldg Washington DC 20515-3812*

MURTHA, JOHN STEPHEN, lawyer; b. Hartford, Conn., Apr. 30, 1913; s. John J. and Agnes E. (Hennessey) M.; m. Winifred Garvan, July 7, 1939;

children—John Garvan, Leslie A., Brenda A. B.A., Yale, 1935, LL.B., 1938. Bar: Conn. bar 1938. Ptnr. Murtha, Cullina, Richter & Pinney, Hartford, 1946-88, of counsel, 1989—; asst. states atty., Hartford County, 1946-51; dir. Kaman Corp. Pres. Greater Hartford Cmty. Chest, 1968-70, Oxford Sch., Hartford, 1960-62; chmn. distbn. com. Hartford Found. for Pub. Giving, 1983-86; bd. dirs. emeritus Blue Cross and Blue Shield Conn., Boys Clubs Hartford; trustee emeritus St. Joseph Coll., West Hartford, Conn., St. Thomas More Corp., New Haven, pres., 1962-64. Served to lt. (j.g.) USNR, 1943-46. Fellow Am. Coll. Trial Lawyers; mem. ABA, Greater Hartford C. of C., Conn. Bus. and Industry Assn., Hartford Golf Club (pres. 1961-63). Republican. Roman Catholic. Home: 6 Shibah Way Bloomfield CT 06002-1527 Office: City Place Hartford CT 06103

MURTHY, SRINIVASA K., engineering corporation executive; b. Bangalore, Karnataka, India, June 12, 1949; came to U.S., 1979; s. Ramaswamy and Gowramma Kadur. BS in Physics, Bangalore U., India, 1967; MS in Physics, Bangalore U., 1969; MSEE, Mysore U., India, 1971. Mgr. project engrng. Indian Space Rsch. Orgn., Bangalore, 1971-79; asst. prof. Calif. State U., Pomona, 1979-80, Fullerton, 1981-82; mgr. project Systems and Applied Scis. Corp., Anaheim, Calif., 1980-83; dir. div. IMR Systems Corp., Arlington, Va., 1983-84; mgr. systems engrng. GE, Portsmouth, Va., 1984-85; bus. and program mgr. govt. rsch. programs AT&T Bell Labs, Homdel, N.J., 1985-94, Murray Hill, N.J., 1994—; area mgr. AT&T Bus. Comms. Svcs., Pleasaton, Calif., 1996—; bd. advisors IMR Sys. Corp., Roslyn, Va., 1988—; mem. editl. adv. bd. R&D Mag., Cahners Publs.; judge R&D 100 awards. Editorial adv. bd. Rsch. and Devel. Mag. Calvert Publs., Reed Publs. Group; contbr. articles to profl. jours. Recipient Disting. Achievement award Dept. Space, Indian Govt., 1975. Mem. IEEE (sr. mem., bd. govs. 1986—, standards bd. 1986—, bd. dirs. Electronics and Aerospace Systems conf. 1983-84, editorial bd. dirs. Network Jour. 1986—, area activities bd. and tech. activities bd. 1988, Computer Soc. 1987—, lectr. India, Singapore, Australia 1989, South Am. 1990, inducted into Nat. Rsch. Coun., Advt. Rsch. Found. and Engrng. Consortium, numerous other coms.), Engrng. Mgmt. Soc. of IEEE (bd. govs. 1986—, v.p.). Home: 13 Willow Ave Somerset NJ 08873-1426 Office: AT&T Bus Comms Svcs Rm 6296 4460 Rosewood Dr Pleasanton CA 94588-3050

MUSA, JOHN DAVIS, computer and infosystems executive, software reliability engineering researcher and expert; b. Amityville, N.Y., June 11, 1933; s. Khan Hussein and Ione Geraldine (Ryan) M.; m. Marilyn Laurene Allred, June 24, 1959. BA, Dartmouth Coll., 1954, MSEE, 1955. With AT&T Bell Labs., Murray Hill, N.J., 1958-96, mem. tech. staff, 1958-63, supr. guidance program devel., 1963-68, supr. command and control program devel., 1968-69, supr. mgmt. control and new software tech., 1969-72, supr. human factors test, 1972-74, supr. computer graphics, 1974-80, supr. computer measurements, 1980-85, supr. software quality, 1985-90, tech. mgr. software reliability engrng., 1991-96; mem. N.J. Coun. R&D; lectr., spkr. in field. Author: Software Reliability: Measurement, Prediction, Application, 1987; contbr. more than 80 articles to profl. jours. and books. Lt. USN, 1955-58. Fellow IEEE; mem. IEEE Computer Soc. (2d v.p. 1986, v.p. publs. 1984-85, v.p. tech. activities 1986, chair tech com. software engring. 1982-84, founding mem. editl. bd. IEEE Software Mag., Disting. lectr. 1980-83, Meritorious Svc. award 1984, 85, 87, founding officer com. on software reliability engring., mem. editl. bds. Spectrum mag., 1984-86, Proc. of the IEEE 1983-90, Technique et Science Informatiques jour., sr. editor Software Engring. Inst. book series, chair steering com. Internat. Conf. on Software Engring.), IEEE Reliability Soc., Assn. for Computing Machinery. Internat. leader in software engrng. and in creation new tech. software reliability engrng.; created two software reliability models; developed concepts and practice of operational profile and sofware-reliability engineered testing; reduced operation software (ROS) operational development. Office: 39 Hamilton Rd Morristown NJ 07960-5341

MUSA, MAHMOUD NIMIR, psychiatry educator; b. Arraba, Jenin, Palestine, Mar. 22, 1943; came to U.S., 1964; s. Nimir A. and Zarifa (Haseeb) M.; m. Wafaa M. Arafat, Mar. 24, 1991. BS, Am. U. Beirut, 1964; MS, U. Wis., 1966, PhD, 1972; MD, Med. Coll. Wis., 1979. Diplomate Am. Bd. Psychiatry. Rsch. assoc. U. Wis., Madison, 1972-75; asst. prof. Idaho State U., Pocatello, 1975-76; resident Ill. State Psychiat. Inst., Chgo., 1979-83; assoc. prof. psychiatry Chgo. Med. Sch., North Chicago, Ill., 1987-90; prof. psychiatry Loyola U., Maywood, Ill., 1990—; cons. Mus. Sci. & Industry, Chgo., 1985-90; editl. bd. Jour. Clin. Pharmacology. Editor: Pharmacikinetics and Monitoring Psychiatry Drugs, 1992; mem. editl. bd. Jour. Clin. Pharmacology. Cons. Kovler Ctr. for Treatment of Survivors of Torture, CHgo., 1989-92. Recipient Scientific Achievement award Ill. Psychiat. Soc., Chgo., 1982. Fellow Am. Coll. Clin. Pharmacology, Great Lakes Soc. Clin. Pharmacology (pres. 1991-92); mem. AAAS, Am. Psychiat. Assn. Avocations: reading, photography, theater. Home: 1115 S Plymouth Ct Apt 102 Chicago IL 60605-2027

MUSA, SAMUEL ALBERT, technology and manufacturing executive director; m. Judith Friedman; children: Gregory, Jeffrey. BA, Rutgers U., 1961, BSEE, 1961; MS in Applied Physics, Harvard U., 1962, PhD in Applied Physics, 1965. Rsch. scientist Gen. Precision Inc., Little Falls, N.J., 1965-66; asst. prof. elec. engring. U. Pa., Phila., 1966-71; project leader Inst. for Def. Analyses, Arlington, Va., 1971-78; dep. dir. Office of Under Sec. Def., Washington, 1978-83; dir. rsch. and advanced tech. E-Systems, Inc., Dallas, 1983-86, v.p. rsch. and advanced tech., 1986-95; exec. dir. Ctr. Display Tech. and Mfg. U. Mich., 1995—; cons. sci. adv. bd. USAF, 1987-91; mem. adv. bd. Def. Intelligence Agy. Contbr. articles to profl. jours. Fellow IEEE; mem. AIA (tech. and ops. coun. 1986-95, vice chmn. 1993, chmn. 1994), Sigma Xi, Tau Beta Pi, Pi Mu Epsilon. Office: 2360 Bonisteel Blvd Ann Arbor MI 48109

MUSACCHIA, X(AVIER) J(OSEPH), physiology and biophysics educator; b. Bklyn., Feb. 11, 1923; s. Castrense and Orsolina (Mazzola) M.; m. Betty Cook, Nov. 23, 1950; children: Joseph, Mary, Thomas, Laura Ann. BS, St. Francis Coll., Bklyn., 1944; MS, Fordham U., 1947, PhD, 1949. Instr. biology Marymount (N.Y.) Coll., 1948-49; from instr. to prof. biology St. Louis U., 1949-65; prof. physiology U. Mo., Columbia, 1965-78; prof. physiology and biophysics U. Louisville, 1978-91, prof. emeritus, 1991—, dean Grad. Sch., 1978-89, assoc. provost for rsch., 1985-89; bd. dirs. Coun. Grad. Schs., 1986-89. Author: Depressed Metabolism, 1969, Regulation of Depressed Metabolism and Thermogenesis, 1976, Survival in Cold, 1981; also articles. Bd. govs. J. Graham Brown Cancer Ctr., Louisville, 1978-83; bd. dirs. Oak Ridge Associated Univs. Served with AUS, 1943-45. Research grantee NIH; Research grantee NASA. Fellow AAAS; mem. Am. Physiol. Soc., Am. Soc. Zoologists, Am. Soc. for Space and Gravitational Biology (v.p. 1988-89, pres. 1989-90), Soc. Exptl. Biology and Medicine, Corp. Marine Biol. Lab., Sigma Xi. (past chpt. pres.). Address: PO Box 5054 Bella Vista AR 72714-0054

MUSACCHIO, MARILYN JEAN, nurse midwife, educator; b. Louisville, Dec. 7, 1938; d. Robert William and Loretta C. (Liebert) Poulter; m. David Edward Musacchio, May 13, 1961; children: Richard Peter, Michelle Marie. BSN cum laude, Spalding Coll., 1968; MSN, U. Ky., 1972, degree in Nurse-Midwifery, 1976; PhD, Case Western Res U., 1993. RN; cert. nurse-midwife; advanced registered nurse practitioner; registered nurse-midwife. Staff nurse gynecol. unit St. Joseph Infirmary, Louisville, 1959-60, staff nurse male gen. surgery unit, 1960; instr. St. Joseph Infirmary Sch. Nursing, Louisville, 1960-71; from asst. prof. to assoc. prof., dir. dept. nursing edn. Ky. State U., Frankfort, 1972-75; asst. prof. U. Ky. Coll. Nursing, Lexington, 1976-79, assoc. prof., coord., 1979-92, acting coordinator nurse-midwifery, 1982-84, coordinator for nurse-midwifery, 1987-92; assoc. prof., dir. nurse-midwifery U. Ala., Birmingham, 1992—; cons. in field. Mem. editorial bd. Jour. Obstet., Gynecol. and Neonatal Nursing, 1976-82; author pamphlet; contbr. articles to profl. jours. Active St. James Parish Coun., chmn., 1980-81; mem. Louisville Fire Prevention Coun., 1973-80, Louisville Safety Coun., 1973-80. Brig. Gen. Army Nurse Corps, USAR, 1992-95. Recipient Disting. Citizen award City of Louisville, 1977, Jefferson Cup award Jefferson County, Ky., 1991; named Outstanding Alumna, Mercy Acad., 1993; named to Hall of Disting. Alumni, U. Ky., 1995; recipient scholarships and fellowships, other awards. Fellow Am. Acad. Nursing; mem. AWHONN, NAFE, Am. Nurses Assn. (nurse rschr. coun. 1985—, maternal child coun. 1985—), Nurse Assn. Am. Coll. Ob-Gyn. (charter; nat. sec. 1970-72, chmn. dist. V 1969), Am. Coll. Nurse-Midwives, Internat. Childbirth Edn. Assn., Am. Soc. Psychoprophylaxis in Obstetrics, Nat. Assn. Parents and Profls. for Safe Alternatives in Childbirth, Res. Officers Assn., Assn. Mil. Surgeons U.S., Sr. Army Res. Commdr. Assn., Assn. U.S. Army, Retired Army Nurse Corps. Assn., Army War Coll. Alumni Assn. Roman Catholic. Avocations: reading, candy making, cake decorating, cooking, sewing. Home: 1318 Springs Ave Birmingham AL 35242-4862

MUSAH, AL-HASSAN ISSAH, reproductive physiologist; b. Pong-Tamale, Ghana, Aug. 3, 1954; came to U.S., 1980; s. Issah and Mariama (Adam) M.; m. Hadiyatu Seidu Al-Hassan, July 16, 1981 (div. Nov. 1989); children: Abdul-Razak, Ayisha, Abdul-Faruk. BSc with honors, U. Ghana, 1978; MS, Iowa State U., 1983, PhD in Physiology of Reprodn., 1980. Rsch. asst. U. Ghana, Legon, 1978-79; tng. officer IFCAT-URADEP, Narrongo, Ghana, 1979-80; postdoctoral rsch. assoc. Iowa State U., Ames, 1986-89; asst. prof. St. Cloud (Minn.) State U., 1990-94, assoc. prof. reproductive physiology, 1994—; cons. St. Cloud State U. Sci. Discovery Program, 1991—; pres. Allbest Enterprises, Inc., Takoradi, Ghana, 1989—. Contbr. articles to profl. jours. Recipient Excellence award Iowa State U., 1986, Holco award Holco Agrl. Products, Inc., 1986; rsch. grantee USDA, 1993—, NIH, 1994—; U. Ghana postgrad. fellow, 1980-86. Mem. Endocrine Soc., Soc. for Study of Reprodn., Soc. for Exptl. Biology and Medicine, Sigma Xi. Achievements include research on elucidating the role of relaxin and ANP in ovarian luteal function. Home: 1823 15th Ave SE Saint Cloud MN 56304-2385 Office: St Cloud State Univ 720 4th Ave S Saint Cloud MN 56301-4442

MUSANTE, TONY (ANTHONY PETER MUSANTE, JR.), actor; b. Bridgeport, Conn.; s. Anthony Peter and Natalie Anne (Salerno) M.; m. Jane Ashley Sparkes, June 2, 1962. B.A. (Baker scholar), Oberlin Coll., 1958; postgrad., Northwestern U., 1957; student, HB Studios, N.Y.C., 1961-65. Appearances include: (off Broadway prodns.) Borak, 1960, Zoo Story, Night of the Dunce, The Collection, Match-Play, Kiss Mama, L'Histoire du Soldat, A Gun Play, Falling Man, Cassatt, Grand Magic, The Big Knife, The Taming of the Shrew, Two Brothers, The Archbishop's Ceiling, Souvenir, A Streetcar Named Desire, Double Play, Dancing in the End Zone, Snow Orchid, Wait until Dark, Widows, Anthony Rose, Mount Allegro, Frankie and Johnny in the Clair de Lune, Breaking Legs, The Flip Side, Love Letters, The Sisters, Italian Funerals and Other Festive Occasions (Broadway prodns.) PS Your Cat is Dead, 1975 (N.Y. Drama Desk nomination), Memory of Two Mondays, 27 Wagons Full of Cotton, The Lady from Dubuque; films: Once a Thief, 1964, The Incident (Best Actor award Mar del Plata Internat. Film Festival), 1967, The Detective, The Mercenary, One Night at Dinner, Bird with the Crystal Plumage, Grissom Gang, Anonymous Venetian, The Last Run, Pisciotta Case, Goodbye and Amen, Break-Up, Collector's Item, The Repenter, Devil's Hill, Appointment in Trieste, Nocturne, The Pope of Greenwich Village; TV appearances include Ride with Terror, 1963, star series Toma, 1973-74 (Photoplay Gold medal award 1974), scriptwriter several episodes; also starred in TV miniseries and movies: High Ice, Breaking Up is Hard to Do, The Baron, Legend of the Black Hand, The Story of Esther, My Husband is Missing, Nowhere to Hide, The Quality of Mercy (Emmy nominee 1975), Court Martial of Lt. William Calley, Night Heat, Rearview Mirror, Nutcracker: Money, Madness and Murder, American Playhouse: Weekend, Last Waltz on a Tightrope; daytime TV (guest star): Loving, ABC, 1993. Mem. SAG, AFTRA, ATAS, Actors Equity Assn., Writers Guild Am. West, Acad. Motion Picture Arts and Scis.

MUSBURGER, BRENT WOODY, sportscaster; b. Portland, Oreg., May 26, 1939; s. C.C. and Beryl Ruth (Woody) M.; m. Arlene Clare Sander, June 8, 1963; children: Blake, Scott. BJ, Northwestern U., 1962. Profl. umpire Midwest Baseball League, 1959; sports columnist Chgo. Am., 1962-68; dir. sports WBBM Radio and TV, Chgo., 1968-74; sportscaster CBS-TV, 1974-90; dir. sports Sta. KNXT, Los Angeles, 1979-81; host Sports Time, NCAA Today, Saturday/Sports Sunday, CBS, from 1981; host, mng. editor NFL Today; now with ABC-TV Sports, 1990—. Served with AUS, 1960. Named Ill. Sportscaster of Yr., Nat. Assn. Sportswriters and Sportscasters, 1971, 74. *Hustle.*

MUSCATINE, CHARLES, English educator, author; b. Bklyn., Nov. 28, 1920; m. Doris Corn, July 21, 1945; children: Jeffrey, Alison. B.A., Yale U., 1941, M.A., 1942, Ph.D., 1948; L.H.D. (hon.), New Sch. for Social Research, 1982; Litt.D., SUNY, 1989, Rosary Coll., 1991. Mem. faculty dept. English U. Calif., Berkeley, 1948—; prof. U. Calif., 1960-91, prof. emeritus, 1991—, dir. Collegiate Seminar Program, 1974-80; vis. prof. Wesleyan U., 1951-53; Ward Phillips lectr. U. Notre Dame, 1969; mem. com. of selection J.S. Guggenheim Found., 1969-89, chmn. 1985-89. Author: Chaucer and the French Tradition, 1957, The Book of Geoffrey Chaucer, 1963, Poetry and Crisis in the Age of Chaucer, 1972, The Old French Fabliaux, 1986. Co-author, editor: Education at Berkeley, 1966, (with M. Griffith) The Borzoi College Reader, 1966, 7th edit., 1992, First Person Singular, 1973; co-editor Integrity in the Coll. Curriculum, 1985. Bd. dirs. No. Calif. chpt. ACLU, 1959-62, 63-66, Assn. Am. Colls., 1979-82, Ctr. for the Common Good, 1994—; bd. dirs. Fedn. State Humanities Couns., 1989-94, chair, 1991-93; mem. Commn. on Humanities, Rockefeller Found., 1978-79, Calif. Coun. Humanities, 1986-94. With USNR, 1942-45. Recipient Navy Commendation ribbon, 1945, Berkeley citation, 1991; Fulbright fellow, 1958, 62, ACLS Rsch. fellow, 1958, Guggenheim fellow, 1962, NEH Sr. fellow, 1968. Fellow Am. Acad. Arts and Scis., Medieval Acad. of Am.; mem. MLA, New Chaucer Soc. (pres. 1980-81), Aircraft Owners and Pilots Assn., Phi Beta Kappa. Club: Arts (Berkeley). Home: 2812 Buena Vista Way Berkeley CA 94708-2016

MUSCATO, ANDREW, lawyer; b. Newark, Aug. 28, 1953; s. Salvatore and Bertha (Kubilus) M.; m. Ann Marie Hughes, Aug. 19, 1978; children: Amy, Andrew Joseph, Amanda. AB magna cum laude, Brown U., 1975; JD, Seton Hall U., 1978. Bar: N.J. 1978, U.S. Dist. Ct. N.J. 1978, U.S. Ct. Appeals (3d cir.) 1981, N.Y. 1984, U.S. Dist. Ct. (so. and ea. dists.) N.Y. 1984. Law clk. to presiding judge, appellate div. N.J. Superior Ct., Somerville, 1978-79; staff atty. Adminstrv. Office of Cts., Trenton, N.J., 1979-80; assoc. Simon & Allen, Newark, 1980-86; ptnr. Kirsten & Simon, Newark, 1987-89, Whitman & Ransom, Newark, 1989-93, Whitman Breed Abbott & Morgan, Newark, 1993—; atty. Irvington (N.J.) Rent Leveling Bd., 1980—. Author: Executing on a Debtor's Interest in a Tenancy by the Entirety, 1986. Mem. ABA, Essex County Bar Assn., Trial Attys. N.J., N.J. Inst. Mcpl. Attys. Republican. Roman Catholic. Home: 66 Addison Dr Basking Ridge NJ 07920-2202 Office: Whitman Breed Abbott Et Al 1 Gateway Ctr Newark NJ 07102-5311

MUSCHEL, LOUIS HENRY, immunologist, educator; b. N.Y.C., July 4, 1916; s. Maurice and Betty (Tobey) M.; m. Anne Orzel, Oct. 22, 1946; 1 child, Ruth Josephine. B.S., NYU, 1936; M.S., Yale U., 1951, Ph.D., 1953. Joined U.S. Army, 1941, advanced through grades to lt. col., 1961; chief dept. serology (Walter Reed Army Inst. Research), Washington, 1958-62; faculty U. Minn., Mpls., 1962-70; prof. microbiology U. Minn., 1964-70; prof. bacteriology U. Calif., Berkeley, 1965, 67; with research dept. Am. Cancer Soc., 1970-88; adj. prof. microbiology Columbia U., 1977-83; adj. prof. pathology NYU, 1983—. Mem. Am. Assn. Immunologists, Brit. Soc. Immunology, N.Y. Acad. Scis., Am. Soc. Microbiology, Soc. Exptl. Biology and Medicine, Am. Assn. for Cancer Research, Phi Beta Kappa, Sigma Xi, Phi Lambda Upsilon. Research, publs. on bactericidal action of serum and its role in host defs., natural bactericidal and viral neutralizing antibodies, applications of complement fixation technique. Home: 3333 Henry Hudson Pky W Apt 8A Bronx NY 10463-3255

MUSCHENHEIM, FREDERICK, pathologist; b. N.Y.C., July 9, 1932; s. Carl and Haroldine (Humphreys) M.; m. Linda Alexander, Mar. 29, 1958; children: Alexandra Lydia, Carl William, David Henry. AB, Harvard U., 1953; MDCM, McGill U., Montreal, Can., 1963. Intern Santa Clara County Hosp., San Jose, Calif., 1963-64; resident pathology U. Colo. Med. Ctr., Denver, 1964-68, chief resident clin. pathology, 1968-69; pathologist Freeman, Hanske, Munkittrick & Foley PA, Mpls., 1969-77; clin. pathologist Union-Truesdale Hosp., Fall River, Mass., 1977-78; chief pathologist St. Clare's Hosp., Denville, N.J., 1978-83, Oneida Healthcare Ctr., 1984—; clin. asst. prof. SUNY Health Sci. Ctr., Syracuse, 1984-90, clin. assoc. prof., 1990—; chief med. staff Oneida City Hosps., 1991; pres. Sunderman Fund, Bermuda Biol. Sta. for Rsch.; v.p. Madison County (N.Y.) bd. health, 1995. Choir 1st Presbyn. Ch. of Cazenovia, N.Y., 1984—, trustee, 1985-89. Mem. Assn. Clin. Scientists (v.p. 1989, pres. 1990, rec. sec. 1995—, Diploma of Honor 1991), Coll. Am. Pathologists (mem. govt. affairs com. 1994—, nominating com. 1995), Med. Soc. State of N.Y. (mem. legis. com. 1991—), Med. Soc. Madison County (v.p. 1990-91, pres. 1991-93), N.Y. State Assn. Pub. Health Labs. (v.p. 1992-93, pres. 1993-94, edn. chmn. 1994-95), N.Y. Soc. Pathologists (councilor 2nd dist. 1991—), ARC Blood Svcs. (chmn. med. adv. coun. 1995—). Home: 5257 Owera Point Rd Cazenovia NY 13035-9340 Office: Oneida Healthcare Ctr 321 Genesee St Oneida NY 13421-2611

MUSE, EWELL HENDERSON, III, gas company executive; b. Fort Worth, Dec. 25, 1938; s. Ewell Henderson and Mary Haydon (Tucker) M.; m. Ellen Estelle Cassin, June 23, 1962; children—Mary Ellen, Robert Cassin. B.S. in Petroleum Engring., U. Tex., 1961; M.B.A. in Fin., U. So. Calif., 1963. Petroleum engr. Tenneco Oil E&P, Shreveport and Lafayette, La., 1963-69; mgr. econs. Tenn. Gas Transmission, Houston, 1969-74, dir. econs., 1974-77, v.p., 1977-80, sr. v.p., 1980-82, 1985—; v.p. Tenneco Inc., Houston, 1985—; pres. Tenneco Gas Latin Am., 1995—. Mem. Am. Petroleum Inst., Planning Execs. Inst., Nat. Soc. Profl. Engrs. Republican. Episcopalian. Clubs: Lakeside (Houston). Avocations: golf; fishing. Office: Tenn Gas PO Box 2511 1010 Milam St Houston TX 77002-5312

MUSE, MARTHA TWITCHELL, foundation executive; b. Dallas, Sept. 1, 1926; d. John Blackburn Muse and Kathryn (Poole) M. B.A., Barnard Coll., 1948; M.A., Columbia U., 1955; D.H.L., Georgetown U., 1981. Exec. dir. Tinker Found., N.Y.C., 1965-68, pres., 1968-95, chmn., 1975—; bd. dirs. The Bank of N.Y. Co., Inc., Bank of N.Y., Trust & Investment Ct., Audit & Examining Ct., Cmty. Reinvestment Act Ct.; chair audit com. Bank N.Y.; bd. dirs., pension adv. com. ASARCO. Bd. dirs. Am. Coun. Germany, Americas Found., Americas Soc. Inc., Coun. of the Ams.; trustee emeritus Columbia U., N.Y.C.; vice chmn., bd. dirs. Spanish Inst.; bd. visitors Edmund A. Walsh Sch. Fgn. Svc., Georgetown U., 1973—; bd. dir. Am. Portuguese Soc.; mem. Wilson coun. Woodrow Wilson Internat. Ctr. for Scholars; mem. coun. Internat. Exec. Svc. Corps; mem. adv. coun. Luso-Am. Devel. Found. Decorated Comdr. Orden del Sol del Peru, Comdr. Ordem Nacional do Cruzeiro Do Sul (Brazil), Comdr. Order of Bernardo O'Higgins (Chile), Comdr. Orden de Mayo al Merito (Argentina), Lazo de Dama de la Orden de Merito Civil (Spain), Assoc. Dame Orde St. John Jerusalem (Great Britain); recipient Alumni award for excellence Columbia U. Grad. Faculties, 1987. Mem. Huguenot Soc., Nat. Soc. Colonial Dames. Episcopalian. Clubs: Colony (N.Y.C.), Met (N.Y.C.). Home: 3664 SE Fairway E Stuart FL 34997 Office: Tinker Found Inc 55 E 59th St New York NY 10022-1104

MUSE, MCGILLIVRAY, lawyer; b. Bridgeport, Tex., Apr. 26, 1909; s. Robert Van and Helen (Bailey) M.; m. Leona McKie, Nov. 9, 1935; 1 son, Marshall McKie (dec.). A.B., Daniel Baker Coll., 1928; LL.B., U. Tex. at Austin, 1931. Bar: Tex. 1931. Assoc. firm Judge R.E. Lee, Brownwood, Tex., 1931-34; mem. firm McCartney, McCartney & Muse, 1934-36; practice in Brownwood, 1936-38, Dallas, 1945—; assoc. firm Locke, Locke, Dyer & Purnell, Dallas, 1938-45. Bd. dirs. Dallas Big Bros., 1945-49. Mem. ABA, Dallas Bar Assn., State Bar Tex., Tex. and Southwestern Cattle Raisers Assn., Highland Park Community League (exec. com. 1960-63), Daniel Baker Coll. Ex-Students Assn. (pres. 1932-33), U. Tex. Ex-Students Assn., Beta Theta Pi. Republican. Presbyterian (elder). Clubs: Dallas Petroleum. Lodges: Lions, Masons, K.T. Home: 4400 Fairfax Ave Dallas TX 75205-3028 Office: 4725 NCNB Tex Nat Bank Bldg Elm Pl 1401 Elm St Dallas TX 75202

MUSE, VONCEIL FOWLER (MRS. BERT C. MUSE), school librarian, educator; b. Tyler, Tex., July 12, 1915; d. Dennis Cleveland and Elva Mary (Wallace) Fowler; m. Bert Cromwell Muse, Dec. 28, 1938 (dec. Jan. 1983). B.A., Tex. Coll., 1936; M.S.L.S., U. So. Calif., 1953; postgrad. NDEA seminars (grantee) Tex. Women's U., 1965. Cert. profl. all levels, Tex. Elem. tchr. Jasper (Tex.) Schs., 1936-37, Trinidad (Tex.) Schs., 1937-39; tchr.-librarian Stanton Rural High Sch., Whitehouse, Tex., 1940-46; co-owner, Tyler (Tex.) Tribune, 1946-49; tchr.-librarian Tyler Schs., 1949-52; sch. librarian Dallas Pub. Schs., 1952-78; past dir. Women's Southwest Fed. Credit Union, Dallas, 1975-80; yearbook chmn. Dallas Sch. Librarians, 1976; mem. social com. Dallas Ret. Tchrs., 1979. Founder, Glenview Neighbors Assn., Dallas, 1980; mem. Mental Health Assn. Dallas County, 1978, Community Connection, Dallas, 1983, South Central Dallas Civic Group, 1984; mem. Maria Morgan br. YWCA, Friends Vis. Nurses Assn. (charter Dallas chpt.), Mus. African Am. Life and Culture, Women's Ctr. of Dallas, Dallas Classroom Tchrs. (bldg. rep. 1969-78), Dallas Ret. Tchrs. Assn., Am. Assn. Ret. Persons (Red Bird chpt. bd. dirs. 1984-85), United Tchrs. Tex. State Tchrs. Assn. (life), NEA (life), Tex. Ret. Tchrs. Assn. (life), Tex. Library Assn., ALA, Tex. and Southwestern Cattle Raisers Assn., Mitchell County Hist. Commn., Tex. Coll. Nat. Alumni (life), Tex. Coll. Alumni Assn. of Dallas, Alpha Kappa Alpha life). Democrat. Mem. Christian Methodist Episcopal Ch. Lodge: Court of Calanthe.

MUSE, WILLIAM VAN, academic administrator; b. Marks, Miss., Apr. 7, 1939; s. Mose Lee and Mary Elizabeth (Hisaw) M.; m. Anna Marlene Munden, Aug. 22, 1964; children: Amy Marlene, Ellen Elizabeth, William Van. B.S. (T.H. Harris scholar), Northwestern La. State U., 1960; M.B.A. (Nat. Def. Grad. fellow), U. Ark., 1961, Ph.D. (Nat. Def. Grad. fellow), 1966. Instr. U. Ark., 1962-63; field supr. Tau Kappa Epsilon Fraternity, 1963-64; asst. prof. Ga. Tech., 1964-65; assoc. prof., chmn., dir. rsch. Ohio U., 1965-70; dean Coll. Bus. Appalachian State U., Boone, N.C., 1970-73; dean Coll. Bus. Adminstrn. U. Nebr., Omaha, 1973-79; dean Coll. Bus. Adminstrn. Tex. A&M U., College Station, 1979-82, vice chancellor, 1983-84; former pres. U. Akron, Ohio, 1984-92; now pres. Auburn U., Ala., 1992—. Author: Business and Economic Problems in Appalachia, 1969, Management Practices in Fraternities, 1965; Contbr. articles to profl. jours. Found. for Econ. Edn. fellow, 1967. Mem. Blue Key, Omicron Delta Kappa, Phi Kappa Phi, Delta Sigma Pi, Beta Gamma Sigma, Pi Omega Pi, Tau Kappa Epsilon. Club: Rotarian. Office: Auburn U Office of Pres Auburn AL 36849

MUSFELT, DUANE CLARK, lawyer; b. Stockton, Calif., Sept. 14, 1951; s. Robert H. and Doris E. (Roth) M.; m. Linh T. To, Sept. 6, 1980. Student, U. Calif., Davis, 1969-71; BA in Econs., U. Calif., Berkeley, 1973; JD, UCLA, 1976. Bar: Calif. 1976, U.S. Dist. Ct. (cen. dist.) Calif. 1977, U.S. Ct. Appeals (9th cir.) 1980, U.S. Dist. Ct. (no. dist.) Calif. 1982, U.S. Dist. Ct. (ea. and so. dists.) Calif. 1983, U.S. Supreme Ct. 1987. Assoc. Haight, Dickson, Brown & Bonesteel, L.A., 1976-77, Mori & Ota, L.A., 1977-79, Lewis, D'Amato, Brisbois & Bisgaard, L.A., 1979-82; ptnr. Lewis, D'Amato, Brisbois & Bisgaard, San Francisco, 1982—. Mem. State Bar Calif., No. Calif. Assn. Defense Counsel, Bar Assn. San Francisco, Defense Rsch. Inst. Democrat. Presbyterian. Avocations: tennis, skiing, bridge. Office: Lewis D'Amato Brisbois & Bisgaard 601 California St Ste 1900 San Francisco CA 94108-2824

MUSGRAVE, CHARLES EDWARD, retired music director, correctional official; b. Alton, Ill., Nov. 17, 1932; s. Clay Everett and Fannie Adeline (Peek) M.; m. Barbara Jean Robertson, Aug. 11, 1952 (div. Feb. 1971); children: Michael David, Debra Ann; m. Toby Elaine Riley, Aug. 18, 1973. B in Mus. Edn., Shurtleff Coll., 1954; MS, U. Ill., 1957; postgrad., U. No. Colo., 1970. Cert. tchr., Ill., Ind. Tchr. music Alton (Ill.) Pub. Schs., 1953-67; v.p. Monticello Coll., Godfrey, Ill., 1967-69; asst. to v.p. U. No. Colo., Greeley, 1970; chmn. dept. music Duneland Sch. Corp., Chesterton, Ind., 1970-72; dir. devel. Interlochen (Mich.) Arts Acad., 1972-73; v.p. Musart Corp., Chgo., 1973-74; dir. music and coll. coord. Ind. State Prison, Michigan City, 1974-95; ret., 1995; asst. dir. music Willowbrook Meth. Ch., Sun City, Ariz., 1996—; vice chmn. La Porter Fed. Credit Union, Michigan City, 1975—; facility coordinator adult continuing edn. Ind. U. Author: Fussell's Individual Technique Guide, 1973, (music) Why Only on Christmas, 1981. Rep. committeeman, Chesterton, 1976-95, del. to state conv., Ind., 1978-89; mem. Porter County (Ind.) Planning Comm., 1984-85; chmn. govt. workers sect. United Way, Michigan City, 1981-90; mem. Ind. Gov.'s Adv. Com., 1983; minister of music 1st United Meth. Ch., Chesterton, 1978-91; bd. dirs. Five Lakes Conservation Club, Wolcottville, Ind., 1983-95; bd. dirs., v.p. Valparaiso Cmty. Concerts Assn., 1986-95. Grantee Systems Mgmt. U. W. Va., U. Chgo., 1979. Mem. Correctional Edn. Assn. (Internat. Tchr. of Yr. 1981), Ind. Soc. Chgo., LaGrange Country Club, Masons, Shriners, Scottish Rite, Phi Delta Kappa. Avocations: sailing, golf, photography, computers. Home: 750 Graham Dr Chesterton IN 46304-1620

MUSGRAVE, R. KENTON, federal judge; b. 1927. Student, Ga. Inst. Tech., 1945-46, U. Fla., 1946-47; BA, U. Wash., 1948; JD with distinction, Emory U., 1953. Asst. gen. counsel Lockheed Internat., 1953-62; v.p., gen. counsel Mattel, Inc., 1963-71; mem. firm Musgrave, Welbourn and Fertman, 1972-75; asst. gen. counsel Pacific Enterprises, 1975-81; v.p., gen. counsel Vivitar Corp, 1981-85; v.p., dir. Santa Barbara Applied Rsch., 1982-87; judge U.S. Ct. Internat. Trade, N.Y.C., 1987—. Trustee Morris Animal Found., The Dian Fossey Gorilla Fund, Dolphins of Sharks Bay (Australia); hon. trustee Pet Protection Soc.; mem. United Way, South Bay-Centinela Svc. Orgn., Save the Redwoods League; active LWV, Legal Aid, Palos Verdes Community Assn. Mem. ABA, Internat. Bar Assn., Pan Am. Bar Assn., State Bar Calif. (chmn. corp. law sect. 1965-66, del. 1966-67), L.A. County Bar Assn., State Bar Ga., Fng. Trade Assn. So. Calif. (bd. dirs.), Sierra Club. Office: US Ct Internat Trade 1 Federal Plz New York NY 10278-0001

MUSGRAVE, STORY, astronaut, surgeon, pilot, physiologist, educator; b. Boston, Aug. 19, 1935; children: Lorelei Lisa, Bradley Scott, Holly Kay, Christopher Todd, Jeffrey Paul, Lane Linwood. BS in Math. and Statis., Syracuse U., 1958; MBA, UCLA, 1959; BA in Chemistry, Marietta Coll., 1960; MD, Columbia U., 1964; MS in Biophysics, U. Ky., 1966; MA in Lit., U. Houston, 1987, MA in Humanities, 1989. Surg. intern U. Ky. Med. Ctr., Lexington, 1964-65; scientist-astronaut NASA, Houston, 1967—, backup sci.-pilot 1st Skylab mission, 1973, flew on first Challenger flight, STS-6, 1983, flew on Spacelab 2, 1985, flew on space shuttle mission STS-33, 1989, flew on STS-44, 1991; flew as payload comdr. STS61 Hubble Telescope Repair Mission STS61 Hubble Telescope Repair Mission, 1993; assigned to fly on STS-80, 1996. Contbr. articles to profl. jours. With USMC, 1953-56. Recipient Reese AFB Comdr.'s trophy, 1969, NASA exceptional svc. medal, 1974, 83, 90, NASA disting. svc. medal, 1992, 94, NASA spaceflight medal, 1983, 85, 89, 91, 93; USAF postdoctoral fellow, 1965-66, Nat. Heart Inst. postdoctoral fellow, 1966-67. Mem. AAAS, AAS, AIAA, Flying Physicians Assn. (Airman of Yr. award 1974, 83), Civil Aviation Med. Assn., N.Y. Acad. Sci., Nat. Geog. Soc., Soaring Soc. Am., U.S. Parachute Assn., Marine Corps Assn., Alpha Kappa Psi, Phi Delta Theta, Omicron Delta Kappa, Beta Gamma Sigma. Address: NASA Code CB Houston TX 77058 *From subatomic particles, to the stardust from which I was created, from the forming galaxies, to the universes beyond our own, I live to participate physically and spiritually in every aspect of this cosmic creation and evolution.*

MUSGRAVE, THEA, composer, conductor; b. Edinburgh, Scotland, May 27, 1928; m. Peter Mark, 1971. Ed., Edinburgh U., Paris Conservatory; Mus.D. (hon.). Composer: (opera) The Abbot of Drimock, 1955, The Decision, 1964-65, The Voice of Ariadne, 1972-73, Mary, Queen of Scots, 1975-77, (first performed Scottish Opera) A Christmas Carol, 1978-79 (first performed Va. Opera Assn., 1979), An Occurrence at Owl Creek Bridge, 1981, Harriet, The Woman Called Moses, 1981-84 (first performed Va. Opera 1985), Simon Bolivar, (ballet) Beauty and the Beast, 1969, (symphony and orchestral music) Obliques, 1958, Nocturnes and Arias, 1966, Concerto for Orch., 1967, Clarinet Concerto, 1968, Night Music, 1969, Scottish Dance Suite, 1969, Memento Vitae, 1969-70, Orfeo II, 1975, Soliloquy II and III, 1980, From One to Another, 1980, Peripeteia, 1981, The Seasons, 1988, (marimba concerto) Journey through a Japanese Landscape, (bass-clarinet concerto) Autumn Sonata, (oboe concerto) Helios, (chamber and instrumental music) String Quartet, 1958, Trio for flute, oboe and piano, 1960, Monologue, 1960, Serenade, 1961, Chamber concerto No. 1, 1962, Chamber Concerto No. 2, 1966, Chamber Concerto No. 3, 1966, Music for horn and piano, 1967, Impromptu No. 1, 1967, Soliloquy I, 1969, Elegy, 1970, Impromptu No. 2, 1970, Space Play, 1974, Orfeo I, 1975, Fanfare, 1982, Pierrot, 1985, Narcissus, 1987, Niobe, 1987, (vocal and choral music) Two Songs, 1951, Four Madrigals, 1953, Six Songs: Two Early English Poems, 1953, A Suite O'Bairnsangs, 1953, Cantata for a Summer's Day, 1954, Song of the Burn, 1954, Five Love Songs, 1955, Four Portraits, 1956, A Song for Christmas, 1958, Triptych, 1959, Sir Patrick Spens, 1961, Make Ye Merry for Him That Is to Come, 1962, Two Christmas Carols in Traditional Style, 1963, John Cook, 1963, Five Ages of Man, 1963-64, Memento Creatoris, 1967, Primavera, 1971, Rorate Coeli, 1973, Monologues of Mary, Queen of Scots, 1977-86, O Caro M'e Il Sonno, 1978, The Last Twilight, 1980, Black Tambourine, 1985, For the Time Being, 1986, Echoes Through Time, 1988, Wild Winter for Viols & Voices, 1993, On the Underground Sets 1, 2 & 3, 1994, 95, (Robert Burns' poems for soprano & orch.) Songs for a Winter's Evening, 1995. Office: VA Opera Assn PO Box 2580 Norfolk VA 23501-2580

MUSGROVE, RONNIE, state official; b. July 29, 1956; m. Melanie Ballard; children: Jordan, Carmen Rae. Grad., Northwest Miss. Jr. Coll., U. Miss.; JD, U. Miss. Ptnr. Smith, Musgrove & McCord, Batesville, Miss.; lt. gov. State of Miss., Jackson, 1996—. Fellow Miss. Bar Found.; mem. Am. Inns Ct., Miss. State Bar (bd. bar commrs. 1990), Miss. Bar Assn., Miss. Young Lawyers Assn. (bd. dirs.), Panola County Bar Assn. (v.p., pres.), Tri-County Bar Assn. (pres.), Phi Beta Lambda. Office: Office of Lt Governor New Capitol Rm 316 Jackson MS 39215

MUSHER, DANIEL MICHAEL, physician; b. N.Y.C., Feb. 27, 1938; s. Sidney and Hadassah (Kaplan) M.; m. Karol Sue Katz, June 17, 1967; children: Rebecca Leah, Benjamin Leon, Deborah Ann. AB magna cum laude, Harvard Coll., 1959; MD, Columbia U., 1963; postgrad., MIT, 1969-70. Diplomate Am. Bd. Internal Medicine, specialty infectious diseases. Intern, jr. med. resident first med. divsn. Bellevue Hosp., 1963-65; sr. med. resident Tufts-New Eng. Med. Ctr. Hosps., 1967-68; NIH trainee in infectious diseases New Eng. Med. Ctr. Hosps., 1968-71; instr. medicine Tufts U. Sch. Medicine, 1970-71; asst. prof. medicine, asst. prof. microbiology & immunology Baylor Coll. Medicine, Houston, 1971-73, assoc. prof., 1974-78, prof. microbiology and immunology, 1979—, prof. medicine, 1979—, chief infectious diseases, 1994—; chief infectious disease sect. VA Med. Ctr., Houston, 1971—; mem. Baylor House Staff Selection Com., 1973—; mem. infection control com. VA Med. Ctr., 1971—, chmn., 1971, mem. AIDS task force, 1987—; mem. Baylor Dept. Medicine Task Force, 1987—; mem. Baylor Dept. Medicine Exec. Faculty, 1992—. Mem. editl. bd.: Sexually Trasmitted Diseases, 1979-83, Infection and Immunity, 1996—; assoc. editor Jour. Infectious Diseases, 1983-88; contbr. numerous articles to profl. jours. Chmn. edn. William Malev Schs. of Congregation Beth Yeshurun, Houston, 1993—; bd. mem., past pres. I. Weiner Jewish Secondary Sch., Houston, 1979—; bd. mem. Congregation Beth Yeshurun, Houston, 1975—; bd. mem., v.p., pres. Houston Friends of Music, 1975—. With USAF, 1965-67. Recipient Physician's Recognition award AMA, 1991—, Dir.'s award for profl. leadership VA Med. Ctr., Houston, 1991. Fellow ACP; mem. AAAS, Am. Assn. Immunologists, Am. Fedn. Clin. Rsch., Am. Soc. Clin. Investigation, Am. Soc. Microbiology, Am. Thoracic Soc., Am. Venereal Disease Assn., Infectious Diseases Soc. Am., Med. Soc. for Study Venereal Diseases (Britain), So. Soc. Clin. Investigation, Soc. Exptl. Biology and Medicine, Sigma Xi, Phi Beta Kappa, Alpha Omega Alpha. Avocations: music (string quartet playing), reading. Office: VA Hosp 2002 Holcomb Houston TX 77030

MUSICK, GERALD JOE, entomology educator; b. Ponca City, Okla., May 24, 1940; s. Arlie A. and Leona (Beier) M.; m. Florene Ione Thompson, May 11, 1962; children: Linda Kaye, Mary Louise. BS, Okla. State U., 1962; MS, Iowa State U., 1964; PhD, U. Mo., 1969. Grad. asst. Iowa State U., 1962-64; instr. U. Mo., 1964-69; asst. prof. Ohio State U., Wooster, 1969-71, assoc. prof., 1971-76; dept. head U. Ga., Tifton, 1976-79; prof., dept. head U. Ark., 1979-86, interim dir. agrl. exptl. sta., 1986-87, dean, assoc. v.p. agrl. rsch., 1987-93, univ. prof. entomology, 1993—. Author and co-author numerous publs. Vice-chairperson com. Coop. States Rsch. Svc., 1993, So. Expt. Sta.; chairperson steering com. Midwest Food Safety Consortium, 1991-93. Mem. Entomol. Soc. Am. (pres. S.E. br. 1983-84), Ark. Acad. Sci., Sigma Xi, Gamma Sigma Delta. Lutheran. Avocation: golf. Office: University of Arkansas AG-321 Dept Entomology Fayetteville AR 72701

MUSKY, JANE MICHELLE, film production designer; b. N.J., May 27, 1954; d. John and Olga (Badaukus) M.; m. Anthony Howard Goldwyn, Apr. 18, 1987. BFA, Boston U., 1976. Asst. designer: (theatre) Barnum, 1980; set designer: (theatre) Marathon 1984, 1984; designer: (theatre) The News, 1985; art dir.: (short film) Split Cherry Tree, 1983 (Academy award nomination best short film 1983), (TV movies) Johnny Bull, 1986, Murrow, 1986; prodn. designer: (films) Blood Simple, 1984, Raising Arizona, 1987, Young Guns, 1988, Patty Hearst, 1988, When Harry Met Sally..., 1989, Ghost, 1990, Glengarry Glen Ross, 1992, Boomerang, 1992, City Hall, 1995, (TV movies) Rockabye, 1986, LBJ: The Early Years, 1987, (TV spls.) Alfred G. Graebner Memorial High School Handbook of Rules and Regulations, 1983 (Emmy award nomination outstanding art direction 1984). Recipient gold medal Nat. Women's Crew Championship, 1976, silver medal, 1978. Democrat. Office: care Gersn Agy 232 N Canon Dr Beverly Hills CA 90221

MUSOLF, LLOYD DARYL, political science educator, institute administrator; b. Yale, S.D., Oct. 14, 1919; s. William Ferdinand and Emma Marie (Pautz) M.; m. Berdyne Peet, June 30, 1944; children—Stephanie, Michael, Laura. B.A., Huron Coll., 1941; M.A., U. S.D., 1946; Ph.D., Johns Hopkins U., 1950. Mem. faculty Vassar Coll., Poughkeepsie, N.Y., 1949-59, assoc. prof. polit. sci., 1955-59; chief of party adv. group Mich. State U., Republic South Vietnam, 1959-61; prof. polit. sci. Mich. State U., East Lansing, 1961-63; prof. polit. sci. U. Calif.-Davis, 1963-87, dir. Inst. Govtl. Affairs, 1963-84, prof. emeritus, 1988—; vis. prof. Johns Hopkins U., Balt., 1953, U. Del., 1954, U. Mich., 1955-56; U.S. Nat. rapporteur for Internat. Congress Adminstrv. Scis., Berlin, 1983; cons. and lectr. in field. Author: Federal Examiners and the Conflict of Law and Administration, 1953, Public Ownership and Accountability: The Canadian Experience, 1959, Promoting the General Welfare, Government and the Economy, 1965, (with others) American National Government-Policies and Politics, 1971, Mixed Enterprise-A Developmental Perspective, 1972, (with Springer) Malaysia's Parliamentary System-Representative Politics and Policymaking in a Divided Society, 1979, Uncle Sam's Private Profitseeking Corporations-Comsat, Fannie Mae, Amtrak and Conrail, 1983; editor: (with Krislov) The Politics of Regulation, 1964, Communications Satellites in Political Orbit, 1968, (with Kornberg) Legislatures in Developmental Perspective, 1970, (with Joel Smith) Legislatures in Development-Dynamics of Change in New and Old States, 1979; contbr. monographs, chpts. to books, articles to profl. jours. Served to lt. USNR, 1942-45. Johnston scholar Johns Hopkins U., 1946-48; Faculty fellow Vassar Coll., 1954-55; sr. assoc. East-West Ctr., Honolulu, 1968-69; vis. scholar Brookings Instn., Washington, 1980. Mem. Am. Soc. Pub. Adminstrn. (exec. council 1967-70), Nat. Assn. Schs. Pub. Affairs and Adminstrn. (exec. council 1972-75), Western Govtl. Research Assn. (exec. bd. 1966-68), Am. Polit. Sci. Assn., Nat. Assn. State Univs. and Land Grant Colls. (rsch. com. fdiv. urban affairs 1980-81). Home: 844 Lake Blvd Davis CA 95616-2611 Office: U Calif Dept Polit Sci Davis CA 95616

MUSON, HOWARD HENRY, writer, editor; b. Mt. Vernon, N.Y., Mar. 19, 1935; s. Joseph Ernest and Beatrice (Hakmaier) M.; m. Dorothy Regina Tyor, May 21, 1967; children: Eve, Stephanie, Nickolas, Alice. A.B. magna cum laude, Harvard U., Cambridge, Mass., 1956; cert., Johns Hopkins Sch. Advanced Internat. Studies, Bologna, Italy, 1956-57; postgrad., U. Calif., Berkeley, 1957-58. Dir. program research CARE Inc., N.Y.C., 1960-62; bur. chief Hartford Courant, Conn., 1962; newsman, columnist AP, Boston, 1963-66; contbg. editor Time mag., N.Y.C., 1966-70; articles editor N.Y. Times mag., N.Y.C., 1970-77; exec. editor Psychology Today mag., N.Y.C., 1977-82; editor Across The Board, N.Y.C., 1983-89; editor, pub. Family Bus. mag., Phila., 1992—; vis. lectr. in residential colls. Yale U., New Haven, 1982-83; instr. in sci. & environ. reporting program NYU, 1992. Author: Media Violence, 1972, Triumph of the American Spirit: Johnstown, Pennsylvania, 1989; contbr. articles to profl. jours., popular mags. Dir. Project Concern/No. Westchester Walk for Mankind, Mt. Kisco, N.Y., 1985-86. Mem. Nat. Assn. Sci. Writers.

MUSPRATT, KIRK, conductor. Studied with Georg Mark and Reinhard Schwartz, Vienna (Austria) Conservatory, 1983-84; attended, Tanglewood Inst., 1987. Affiliate artist asst. condr. St. Louis Symphony, 1987-90; music dir. St. Louis Symphony Youth Orch., 1987-90; assoc. condr. Utah Symphony, Salt Lake City, 1990-92; affiliate condr. Pitts. Symphony Orch., 1991-92, resident staff condr., 1992-93, resident condr., 1994—; asst. condr. opera houses Monchengladbach and Krefeld, Germany, 1985-87; guest condr. Utah Opera, 1991, 93, L.A. Philharmonic, 1993, R.I. Philharm., Green Bay Symphony, Montreal Symphony, Que. Symphony, others; condr. Woodstock Mozart Festival, 1994; participant Leighton Artist Colony, Banff Ctr. for Fine Arts. Conducting fellow Aspen Music Festival, 1986, L.A. Philharmonic Inst., 1988; Can. Coun. grantee, Presser Found. grantee; recipient Johann Strauss prize for advanced study in Vienna, 1983, 84, Utah Up'n Comers award. Office: Pitts Symphony Orch Heinz Hall for Performing Arts 600 Penn Ave Pittsburgh PA 15222

MUSSEHL, ROBERT CLARENCE, lawyer; b. Washington, May 1, 1936; s. Chester Carl and Clara Cecelia (Greenwalt) Mussehl; children: Debra Lee, David Lee; spouse: Misook Chung, Mar. 22, 1987. BA, Am. U., 1964, JD, 1966. Bar: Wash. 1967, U.S. Dist. Ct. (we. dist.) Wash. 1967, U.S. Ct. Appeals (9th cir.) 1968, U.S Supreme Ct. 1971. Sr. ptnr. Thom, Mussehl, Navoni, Hoff, Pierson & Ryder, Seattle, 1967-78, Neubauer & Mussehl, Seattle, 1978-80, Mussehl & Rosenberg, Seattle, 1980—; speaker law convs. and other profl. orgns.; moot ct. judge Nat. Appellate Advocacy Competition, San Francisco, 1987; panel mem. ABA Symposium on Compulsory Jurisdiction of World Ct., San Francisco, 1987; chmn. bd., chief exec. officer The Seattle Smashers profl. volleyball club, 1976-80. Contbr. numerous articles to legal publs. Mem. Wash. Vol. Lawyers for Arts, 1976-80; statewide chair Lawyers for Durning for Gov., 1976; mem. task force on the single adult and ch. Ch. Coun. Greater Seattle, 1976-78; bd. dirs. Wash. State Pub. Interest Law Ctr., 1976-81; founder, chair Wash. State Lawyers Campaign for Hunger Relief, 1991—. Fellow Am. Bar Found., Am. Acad. Matrimonial Lawyers; mem. ABA (ho. of dels. 1979-91, spl. adv. com. on internat. activities 1989-91, chair marriage and family counseling and conciliation com. family law sect. 1981-83, mem. world order under law standing com. 1983-89, chair, 1986-89, chair ad hoc com. on the assembly 1986-89, mem. assembly resolutions com. 1979-91, mem. blue ribbon com. for world ct. 1987-88, mem. standing com. on dispute resolution, 1992-93; exec. coun. sect. dispute resolution 1993-95, asst. budget officer, 1995—, others, Achievement award), Wash. State Bar Assn. (exec. com. family law sect. 1973-75, chmn. internat. law com. 1974-76, sec.-treas., exec. com. world peace through law sect. 1980—, chair 1981-82, mem. edit. bd. Family Law Deskbook 1987-89), Wash. State Trial Lawyers Assn., Seattle-King County Bar Assn. (family law sect. 1971-90, other coms. 1970—, chmn. young lawyers sect. 1971-72, sec. 1972-73, trustee), Am. Arbitration Assn. (panel arbitrators), World Assn. Lawyers of World Peace Through Law Ctr. (founding mem.), Heritage Club YMCA Greater Seattle (charter 1977—), UN Assn. U.S.A. (bd. dirs. Seattle chpt. 1989-91). Avocations: biking, tennis, weight training, painting, religious studies. Home: One Pacific Towers 2000 1st Ave # 902 Seattle WA 98121 Office: 1111 3rd Ave Ste 2626 Seattle WA 98101-3210

MUSSELMAN, FRANCIS HAAS, lawyer; b. Utica, N.Y., Aug. 3, 1925; s. John Joseph and Kathryn Agnes (Haas) M.; m. Marjorie Louise Balme, June 22, 1948; children: Martha Musselman Sheridan, Kathryn Ann Musselman Bourbonniere, Carol Elizabeth Musselman Kuntz, John Francis. AB, Hamilton Coll., Clinton, N.Y., 1950; JD, Columbia U., 1953; LHD (hon.), Wadhams Hall Seminary/Coll., 1994. Bar: N.Y. 1954, D.C. 1980; U.S. Dist. Ct. (so. dist.) N.Y. 1956, U.S. Ct. Appeals (D.C. cir.) 1981, U.S. Supreme Ct. 1981. Assoc. firm Milbank, Tweed, Hadley & McCloy, N.Y.C., 1953-60; ptnr. Milbank, Tweed, Hadley & McCloy, 1960-90, ret., 1990—; pres., dir. Panfield Corp., N.Y.C., 1961-82; dir. Panfield Nurseries, N.Y.C., 1961-82; law firm mgmt. cons., 1991—; Bankruptcy trustee Finley, Kumble et al, 1988-93. Bd. dirs. Milbank Meml. Fund, 1960-94, chmn., 1985-90; bd. dirs. Memton Fund, 1958-90; trustee Kirkland Coll., Clinton, 1971-78, chmn., 1972-78, Nat. Ctr. for Automated Info. Retrieval, 1979-80, Hamilton Coll., 1978-91, life, 1991, Barnard Coll., 1979-81, Mater Dei Coll., 1991—; chmn. Mater Dei Coll. Found., 1993—; trustee emeritus Wadhams Hall Sem. Coll., vice chmn., 1979-90. With USN, 1943-46. Fellow Am. Bar Found., N.Y. State Bar Found., Am. Coll. Law Practice Mgmt.; mem. Am. Judicature Soc., Am. Law Inst., Union Internationale des Avocats, Internat. Am., Fed. Bar Assn., N.Y. State Bar Assn., D.C. Bar Assn., Assn. of Bar of City of N.Y., St. Lawrence County Bar Assn., World Trade Club (N.Y.C.), Union League (N.Y.C.), Capitol Hill Club (Washington), Coram Nobis (N.Y.C.), Phi Delta Phi, Lambda Chi Alpha. Roman Catholic. Clubs: World Trade (N.Y.C.), Union League (N.Y.C.); Capitol Hill (Washington), Coram Nobis (N.Y.C.). Home: Oak Point Hammond NY 13646 Office: PO Box 289 Hammond NY 13646-0289

MUSSELMAN, NORMAN BURKEY, retired editor; b. Arkansas City, Kans., Mar. 21, 1929; s. Norman Beachy and E. Ruth (Burkey) M.; m. Elizabeth Temple Henry, Oct. 26, 1957; children: Elizabeth Temple Whitson, Norman Henry, Robert Beachy. BA, U. Okla., 1951, MA, 1954. Columnist McGraw Hill Pub. Co., Washington, 1954-67; editor Nat. Assn. Electric Cos., Washington, 1967-80; dir. govt. com. Edison Electric Inst., Washington, 1980-94. Pres. Okla. U. Alumni Club, Washington, 1957-58; pres. men of ch. Presbyn. Meeting House, Alexandria, Va., 1962-63, clk. of session, 1980-82; precinct capt. Rep. Party, 1968-69; cubmaster, pack chmn., scout com. Boy Scouts, Alexandria, 1970-73, 78-82. 1st lt. U.S. Army, 1951-53. Mem. Nat. Press Club, Sigma Delta Chi (pres. Okla. U. chpt. 1953-54). Home: 700 Silver Oak Dr Glenwood Springs CO 81601-2804

MUSSENDEN, GERALD, psychologist; b. N.Y.C., June 1, 1941; s. Geraldo and Adele (Gimenez) M.; m. Iris Manuela Prado, Aug. 11, 1967; children: Gerald, Ricardo-Antonio, Gina. BA, Tarkio Coll., 1968; MS, Brigham Young U., 1971, PhD, 1974. Diplomate Am. Bd. Profl. Disability Cons., Am. Bd. Forensic Examiners. Dir. child program Albert Einstein Coll. Medicine, N.Y.C., 1974-76; psychologist Mental Health Ctr., Bartow, Fla., 1976-77, Norside Community Mentala Health Ctr., Tampa, Fla., 1977-80; pvt. practice Brandon (Fla.) Counseling Ctr., 1980—; criminal ct. psychologist Fla. Cts., Hillsborough, Fla., 1978—; with children's svcs. State Rehab., Hillsborough, 1977—; rehab. psychologist Vocat. Rehab., Hillsborough; psychologist Div. Blind Svcs., Hillsborough. Fellow Ford Found., 1972-73. Mem. APA, Fla. Psychol. Assn., Bay Area Psychol. Assn., Soc. Personality Assessment. Home: 317 Cactus Rd Seffner FL 33584-6105 Office: Brandon Counseling Ctr 134 N Moon Ave Brandon FL 33510-4420

MUSSER, C. WALTON, physical scientist, consultant; b. Mt. Joy, Pa., Apr. 5, 1909; s. Ezra Nissley and Cora Grace (Weidman) M.; m. Edna Mae Hoak, June 23, 1937; children: Lila Darle (Mrs. Richard Hackman), Yvonne Duane (Mrs. Harold Graham), Stanley Walton (dec.). Student, Chgo. Tech. Coll., 1926-28, Leavitt Sch. Psychology, 1928-29, Wharton Sch. Fin. and Commerce, 1929-30, U. Pa., 1930-32, MIT, 1957. Chief engr. product devel. Indsl. Improvement Corp., Phila., 1936-41; rsch. adviser Dept. Def., 1941-56; pres., dir. rsch. Sci. Rsch., Inc., Glenside, Pa., 1945-52; pvt. practice cons., adviser in rsch. and devel., 1936—. Holder of over 162 U.S. Patents in 32 different classes and more than 60 patents in over 28 countries. Recipient Exceptional Civilian Service award for First Working Recoilless Weapon, Sec. of War, 1945; John C. Jones medal for Disting. Svc., Am. Ordnance Assn., 1951; Machine Design award ASME, 1968; named to Ordnance Hall of Fame, 1976. Mem. Acad. Applied Scis., Am. Def. Preparedness Assn. (hon. life), Nat. Soc. Profl. Engrs., Sigma Xi. Address: 1206 Lela Ln Santa Maria CA 93454-6642 *Personal philosophy: Emphasize liking what you do rather than doing what you like. Limiting your activity to only those things you like rapidly decreases your personal universe and eventually assures that much of your activity becomes drudgery.*

MUSSER, SANDRA G., lawyer; b. Hollywood, Calif., July 23, 1944; d. Donald Godfrey Gumpertz and Gloria G. (Rosenblatt) King; m. Michael R.V. Whitman, Feb. 19, 1980. BA, UCLA, 1965; JD, Hastings Coll. of Law, 1970. Bar: Calif. 1971, U.S. Dist. Ct. (no. dist.) Calif. 1971, U.S. Ct. Appeals (9th cir.) 1971. Clk. 9th Cir. Ct. of Appeals, 1971-72; lawyer pvt. practice of family law, 1972-86; ptnr. Musser & Ryan, San Francisco, 1986—; judge pro tem San Francisco County Superior Ct., 1988—. Contbr. articles to profl. jours. Fellow Acad. Matrimonial Lawyers; mem. ABA (chair litig. sect. domestic rels. and family law com. 1993-94), State Bar Calif. (state bar family law sect. 1977—, chair 1982-83, advisor 1983-84), Bar Assn. San Francisco. Office: Musser & Ryan 361 Oak St San Francisco CA 94102-5615

MUSSER, THARON, theatrical lighting designer, theatre consultant; b. Roanoke, Va., Jan. 8, 1925; s. George C. and Hazel (Riddle) M. B.A., Berea Coll., 1946; H.H.D., 1979; M.F.A., Yale U., 1950; H.H.D., Emerson Coll., 1980. Lighting designer over 100 Broadway prodns.; lighting designer for repertory theatre including, Jose Limon Dance Co., 1953-56, Group 20 Players of Mass., 1954-56, Phoenix Theatre Co., 1957-60, Am. Theatre Festival, Boston, 1961, Boston Arts Festival, 1962, Empire State Music Festival, 1959, Nat. Repertory Theatre Co., 1961-68, Am. Shakespeare Festival Theatre and Acad., 1963-68, Lincoln Center Repertory Theatre, 1968, Dallas Civic Opera, 1969-77, New Phoenix Repertory Co., 1972, Miami Opera Guild, 1975-78, Wolf Trap Found., Filene Center for Performing Arts, 1977; staff designer, Mark Taper Forum, Los Angeles Center Theatre Group, 1970-86; lighting designer internat. prodns. including, Jose Limon Dance Co. State Dept. Tour, S. Am., 1953; London prodns. Golden Boy, 1968, Mame, 1969, Applause, 1972, A Little Night Music, 1975, They're Playing Our Song, 1979, London Ballet Festival Romeo and Juliet, 1977; London prodn. Ziegfeld, 1988; internat. prodn. A Chorus Line, 1976; lighting designer and cons. internat. prodn., Ford's Theatre Restoration and TV prodn., Washington, 1968, Man and the Universe at, Hemisfair, San Antonio, 1968, Chgo. Auditorium, 1968, Los Angeles Shubert Theatre, 1971, Dallas Music Hall, Berea Coll. Dramatic Arts Center, 1976-80; London prodn. Children of a Lesser God, 1981, 15 Neil Simon shows including, Broadway Bound, Rumors and Lost in Yonkers. Recipient Los Angeles Drama Critics' Circle award for Dream on Monkey Mountain, 1970, for Follies, 1972, for Pacific Overtures, a Chorus Line, 1976-77, for Terra Nova, 1979; Antoinette Perry award for Follies, 1971-72, for A Chorus Line, 1975-76, for Dreamgirls, 1981-82; Yale arts award, 1985; Theatre Hall of Fame award, 1985. Mem. United Scenic Artists, Soc. Brit. Theatrical Lighting Designers, U.S. Inst. Theatre Tech. Address: 21 Cornelia St New York NY 10014-4121

MUSSER, WILLIAM WESLEY, JR., lawyer; b. Enid, Okla., July 17, 1918; s. William Wesley Sr. and Ethel Rice (McElroy) M.; m. Estelle Bee Wiedeman, Jan. 19, 1947; children: James William, Mary Bee Clark. BA, U. Okla., 1939, LLB, 1941. Bar: Okla. 1941. Ptnr. Elam, Crowley & Musser, Enid, 1946-47; probate judge Garfield County, Okla., 1949-51; ptnr. Otjen, Carter & Musser, Enid, 1952-54; asst. county atty. Garfield County, 1955-56; sole practice Enid, 1957—; chmn. bd. dirs. Tax Roll Corrections, Garfield County, 1950-51; 6th congrl. dist. rep. Okla. Jud. Nominating Com., Enid, 1967-74; judge Okla. Ct. Appeals, Enid, 1982. Pres. Great Salt Plains council Boy Scouts Am., 1955; gen. chmn. St. Mary's Hosp. Bldg. Fund, 1949; bd. dirs. Enid Community Chest, 1950-51, N.W. Okla. Pastoral Care Assn., 1978-82; v.p. Phillips U., Enid, 1955-74, mem. exec. com., 1955-78, trustee, 1978-82; bd. dirs. Enid Estate Planning Council, 1971-74, sec., 1972, pres., 1973-74. Served to maj. AUS, 1941-45, ETO. Decorated Bronze Star. Fellow Okla. Bar Found.; mem. ABA, Okla. Bar Assn. (v.p. bd. govs. 1957), Garfield County Bar Assn. (pres. 1962), Am. Judicature Soc., U. Okla. Alumni Assn. (exec. bd. 1959-61), Sons and Daus. of Cherokee Strip Pioneers Assn. (exec. bd. dirs. 1967-70), Greater Enid C. of C. (bd. dirs. 1969-71), VFW, Am. Legion, Phi Delta Phi, Alpha Tau Omega. Republican. Mem. Christian Ch. (Disciples of Christ). Clubs: Am. Bus. (pres. 1947), Oakwood Country (Enid). Home: 1301 Indian Dr Enid OK 73703-7012 Office: Broadway Tower 3d Fl 114 E Broadway Ave Enid OK 73701-4126

MUSSEY, JOSEPH ARTHUR, health and medical product executive; b. Cleve., July 17, 1948; s. Arthur Glenn and Mary Jane (Silvaroli) M.; m. Mary Elizabeth Stone, July 11, 1975; 1 child, Joanna Lee. BS in Indsl. Engring. with distinction, Cornell U., 1970; MBA, Harvard U., 1976. Engring. mgmt. officer U.S. Navy Pub. Works Ctr., Pearl Harbor, Hawaii, 1971-75; mktg. exec. B.F. Goodrich, Akron, Ohio, 1976-80; fin. exec. B.F. Goodrich, 1980-84; v.p. fin. Combustion Engring., Stamford, Conn., 1984-85; v.p. ops. Combustion Engring., 1985-86; exec. v.p. Process Automation Bus. Combustion Engring., Columbus, Ohio, 1987-90; pres., CEO Danninger Med. Tech., Inc., Columbus, 1990—; treas., dir. Danninger Med. Tech. Inc. Served as lt. U.S. Navy, 1971-75. Decorated Disting. Naval Grad. (USN), 1971, Disting. Grad. U.S. Navy Civil Engring. Corps., 1971. Mem. Alpha Pi Mu, Tau Beta Pi, Phi Eta Sigma. Republican. Roman Catholic. Club: Skull & Daggar. Home: 8967 Dunskeath Ct Dublin OH 43017-9466 Office: Danninger Med Tech Inc 4140 Fisher Rd Columbus OH 43228-1022*

MUSSINA, MICHAEL COLE, professional baseball player; b. Williamsport, Pa., Dec. 8, 1968. BA Econs., Stanford U., 1990. Pitcher Balt. Orioles, 1990—; player Am. League All-Star Team, 1992-94. Named Internat. League Most Valuable Pitcher, 1991. Office: Balt Orioles 333 W Camden St Baltimore MD 21201-2435*

MUSTACCHI, PIERO, physician, educator; b. Cairo, May 29, 1920; came to U.S., 1947; naturalized, 1962; s. Gino and Gilda (Rieti) M.; m. Dora Lisa Ancona, Sept. 26, 1948; children: Roberto, Michael. BS in Humanities, U. Florence, Italy, 1938; postgrad. in anatomy, Eleve Interne, U. Lausanne, Switzerland, 1938-39; MB, ChB, Fouad I U., Cairo, Egypt, 1944, grad. in Arabic lang. and lit., 1946; D Medicine and Surgery, U. Pisa, 1986; D Honoris Causa, U. Aix-Marseilles, France, 1988; hon. degree, U. Alexandria, Egypt, 1985. Qualified Med. Examiner, Calif. Indsl. Med. Coun., 1994. House officer English Hosp., Ch. Missionary Soc., Cairo, Egypt, 1945-47; clin. affiliate U. Calif., San Francisco, 1947-48; intern Franklin Hosp., San Francisco, 1948-49; resident in pathology U. Calif., San Francisco, 1949-51; resident in medicine Meml. Ctr. Cancer and Allied Diseases, N.Y.C., 1951-53; rsch. epidemiologist Dept. HEW, Nat. Cancer Inst., Bethesda, Md., 1955-57; cons. allergy clinic U. Calif., San Francisco, 1957-70, clin. prof. medicine and preventive medicine, 1970-90, clin. prof. medicine and epidemiology, 1990—, head occupl. epidemiology, 1975-90, head divsn. internat. health edn. dept. epidemiology and internat. health, 1985-90; médecin agréé Consulate Gen. of France, San Fransisco, 1995—; med. cons., vis. prof. numerous edn. and profl. instns., including U. Marseilles, 1981, 82, U. Pisa, Italy, 1983, U. Gabon, 1984, U. Siena, Italy, 1985, work clinic U. Calif., 1975-84, Ctr for Rehab. and Occupl. Health U. Calif., San Francisco, 1984-93; cons. numerous worldwide govtl. agys.; ofcl. physician French Consulate Gen., San Francisco, 1995. Contbr. chpts. to books, articles to profl. jours. Editorial bd. Medecine d'Afrique Noire, Ospedali d'Italia. Served with USN, USPHS, 1953-55. Decorated Order of Merit (Commander) (Italy), Ordre de la Legion d'Honneur (France), Medal of St. John of Jerusalem, Sovereign Order of Malta, Order of the Republic (Egypt); Scroll, Leonardo da Vinci Soc., San Francisco, 1965; award Internat. Inst. Oakland, 1964; Hon. Vice Consul. Italy, 1971-90. Fellow ACP, Am. Soc. Environ. and Occupational Health; mem. AAAS, Am. Assn. Cancer Rsch., Calif. Soc. Allergy and Immunology, Calif. Med. Assn., San Francisco Med. Soc., West Coast Allergy Soc. (founding), Mex. Congress on Hypertension (corr.), Internat. Assn. Med. Rsch. and Continuing Edn. (U.S. rep.), Villa Taverna Club, Acad. Italiana della Cucina. Democrat. Avocations: mathematics, music, languages. Home: 3344 Laguna St San Francisco CA 94123-2208 Office: U Calif Parnassus Ave San Francisco CA 94143

MUSTAFA, MOHAMMAD GHULAM, biochemistry educator; b. Dhaka, Bangladesh, Mar. 1, 1940; came to U.S., 1963, naturalized, 1978; s. Mohammad and Quamerunnesa Yaseen; m. Sultana Begum Mustafa, Nov. 6, 1969; 1 child, George E. BS, Dhaka U., 1960, MS summa cum laude, 1962; MA, U. Calif., Berkeley, 1966; PhD, SUNY, Albany, 1969. Asst. research biochemist U. Calif., Davis, 1969-73, asst. adj. prof., 1973-75; adj. asst. prof. UCLA, 1975-78, assoc. prof. in residence, 1978-79, assoc. prof., 1979-84, prof. environ. and occupational health sci., 1984—. Co-editor: Biomedical Effects of Ozone, 1983; mem. editorial bd. Toxicology and Indsl. Health, Princeton, N.J., 1984—; contbr. articles to profl. jours. Recipient Research Career Devel. award NIH, 1976-81; grantee NIH, 1970—. Mem. Am. Chem. Soc., Am. Coll. Toxicology, Air Pollution Control Assn., AAAS, N.Y. Acad. Sci., Sigma Xi. Democrat. Muslim. Avocations: badminton, volleyball, swimming, bicycling. Home: 10534 Louisiana Ave Los Angeles CA 90025-5918 Office: UCLA Sch Pub Health 405 Hilgard Ave Los Angeles CA 90024-1772

MUSTARD, JAMES FRASER, research institute executive; b. Toronto, Oct. 16, 1927; s. Allan Alexander and Jean Ann (Oldham) M.; m. Christine Elizabeth Sifton, June 4, 1952; children: Cameron, Ann, Jim, Duncan, John, Christine. MD, U. Toronto, 1953; PhD, Cambridge U., 1956. Asst., then assoc. prof pathology U. Toronto, 1963-66, asst. prof. medicine, 1965-66, hon. prof. pathology, 1990—; prof. pathology McMaster U., Hamilton, Ont., Can., 1966-88, prof. emeritus, 1988—, chmn. pathology, 1966-72, dean faculty health. scis., 1972-80, v.p. faculty health scis., 1980-82; bd. dirs., pres., sr. fellow Can. Inst. Advanced Rsch., Toronto, 1982—; mem. Ont. Coun. Health, 1966-72; founder, chmn. Health Rsch. Com., 1966-73; chmn. Spl. Task Force Future Arrangements Health Edn., 1970-71, Task Force Health Planning for Ont., Ministry Health and Govt. Ont., 1973-74; mem. Ont. Coun. Univ Affairs, 1975-81; chmn. Adv. Coun. Occupl. Health and Safety, 1977-83; mem. Royal Commn. Matters Health and Safety Arising Use of Asbestos in Ont., 1980-83; mem. Bovey Commn. Study Future Devel. Univ. in Ont., 1984-85; mem. Premier's Coun. Ont., 1986-95, Premier's Coun. Health Strategy, 1988-91; chmn. ctrs. excellence com. Govt. Ont., 1987-91; mem. Prime Minister's Nat. Adv. Bd. on Sci. and Tech., 1987-91, Ottawa, vice chmn., 1988-91; rsch. and analysis adv. com. Stats. Can., Ottawa, 1986—; nat. adv coun. Can. Adv. Tech. Assn., Ottawa, 1988—; adv. coun. Ctr. Health Econs. and Policy Analysis, McMaster U., 1990-92; chmn. bd. dirs. Inst. Work & Health, 1990—; mem. adv. bd. Man. Ctr. for Health Policy and Evaluation, 1991—; pres. Assn. Can. Med. Colls., 1975-76; bd. dirs. Steel Co. Can., Hamilton, Atomic Energy Can. Ltd., 1990-95, Ballard Powers Sys., Inc., 1995—. Bd. dirs. Heart and Stroke Found. Can., 1971-82, Heart and Stroke Found. Ont., 1982-87; bd. govs. McMaster U., 1978-82; bd. dirs. McMaster U. Med. Centre, 1972-82; trustee Advanced Systems Inst. Found., Vancouver, 1986—, Aga Khan U., Karachi, Pakistan, 1985—; mem. chancellor's commn. Aga Khan U., 1992-95. Decorated Officer Order of Can., 1986, Order of Ont., 1992, Companion Order of Can., 1994; recipient Disting. Svc. award Can. Soc. Clin. Investigation, J. Allyn Taylor Internat. prize, 1988, Internat. award Gairdner Found., 1967, James F. Mitchell award, 1972, Izaak Walton Killam prize in health sci. Can. Coun., 1987, Robert P. Grant award for contbns. to progress Internat. Congress on Thrombosis and Haemostasis, 1987, Disting. Career award for contbns. Internat. Soc. Thrombosis and Haemostasis, 1989, Pvt. Sector Leadership award Can. Advanced Tech. Assn., 1989, R & D Mgmt. award Can. Rsch. Mgmt. and Assn., 1989, Man of Yr. award Can. High Tech. Coun., 1989, Xerox Can.-Forum award Corp. Higher Edn. Forum, 1990, Royal Bank award, 1993, Order of Ont., 1992. Fellow Royal Coll. Physicians Can., Royal Soc. Can., Internat. Soc. Thrombosis and Haemostasis (pres. 1965-66); mem. Am. Soc. Clin. Investigation, Assn. Am. Physicians, Am. Assn. Pathologists, Am. Soc. Hematology (pres. 1970), Can. Atherosclerosis Soc. (councillor exec. com. 1986—), Can. Soc. Clin. Investigation (pres. 1965-66). Home: 422 Sumach St, Toronto, ON Canada M4X 1B5 Office: Can Inst Advanced Rsch, 179 John St Ste 701, Toronto, ON Canada M5T 1X4

MUSTIAN, MIDDLETON TRUETT, hospital administrator; b. Texarkana, Tex., Mar. 27, 1921; s. Thomas William and Hattie (Cornelius) M.; m. Jackie Cain, Dec. 3, 1955; children—Mark Thomas, John Perry, Janet Louise. B.B.A., Baylor U., 1949. Asst. adminstr. Bapt. Hosp., Alexandria, La., 1950-54; asst. adminstr. Miss. Bapt. Hosp., Jackson, 1954-55; adminstr. Meml. Hosp., Panama City, Fla., 1955-60, Alachua Gen. Hosp., Gainesville, Fla., 1960-64, Cen. Unit Meml. Bapt. Hosp., Houston, 1964; asst. dir. Meml. Bapt. Hosp. System, Houston, 1964; pres., chief exec. officer Tallahassee Meml. Regional Med. Center Hosp., 1964-89, pres. emeritus, 1990—; pres., CEO TMH Reg. Med. Ctr. Found., Inc., 1976-89; clin. instr. dept. health adminstrn. U. Gainesville; mem. Hosp. Cost Containment Bd., State of Fla. Contbr. articles to hosp. jours. Bd. dirs. Blue Cross of Fla.; mem. Fla. Statewide Health Coordinating Council. Served to capt. Med. Adminstrv. Corps U.S. Army, 1940-45. Decorated Purple Heart. Fellow Am. Coll. Hosp. Adminstrs. (regent); mem. Am. Hosp. Assn., Fla. Hosp. Assn. (past pres.). Democrat. Baptist. Clubs: Kiwanis, Masons. Home: 6325 Velda Dairy Rd Tallahassee FL 32308-6308

MUSTO, DAVID FRANKLIN, physician, educator, historian, consultant; b. Tacoma, Jan. 8, 1936; s. Charles Hiram and Hilda Marie (Hanson) Musto; m. Emma Jean Baudendistel, June 2, 1961; children: Jeanne Marie, David Kyle, John Baird, Christopher Edward. BA, U. Wash., 1956, MD, 1963; MA, Yale U., 1961. Lic. physician, Conn., Pa. Clerk Nat. Hosp. for Nervous Disease, London, 1961; intern Pa. Hosp., Phila., 1963-64; resident Yale U. Med. Ctr., New Haven, 1964-67; spl. asst. to dir. NIMH, Bethesda, Md., 1967-69; vis. asst. prof. Johns Hopkins U., 1968-69; asst. prof. Yale U., 1969-73, assoc. prof., 1973-78, sr. rsch. scientist, 1978-81, prof., 1981—, exec. fellow Davenport Coll., 1983-88; mem. adv. editorial com. Yale Edits. Private Papers James Boswell, 1975—; cons. Exec. Office of Pres., 1973-75; mem. White House Strategy Coun., 1978-81; mem. panel on alcohol policy NAS, Washington, 1978-82; cons. White House Conf. on Families, 1979-80; vis. fellow Clare Coll., Cambridge U., 1994; mem. alcohol adv. com. Nat. Assn. Broadcasters, 1994—; DuMez lectr. U. Md.; Walter Reed meml. lectr. Richmond Acad. Medicine. Author: The American Disease: Origins of Narcotic Control, 1973, expanded edit., 1987. Historian Pres.'s Commn. on Mental Health, 1977-78; adv. U.S. Del. to UN Commn. Narcotic Drugs, Geneva, 1978-79; mem. nat. coun. Smithsonian Instn., Washington, 1981-90, hon. mem., 1991—; hist. cons. Presdl. Commn. Human Immuno-deficiency Virus Epidemic, 1988; mem. nat. adv. com. on anti-drug program Robert Wood Johnson Found., 1989—; mem. nat. adv. com. on internat. narcotic policy UN Assn. of U.S.A., 1991; mem. adv. com. causes drug abuse Office Tech. Assessment, Congress U.S., 1992-94; commr. Conn. Alcohol and Drug Abuse Commn., 1992-93; bd. dirs. Coll. on Problems of Drug Dependence, 1990-94; trustee Assocs. of Cushing-Whitney Med. Libr., 1994—. With USPHS, 1968-69. Fellow Am. Psychiat. Assn., Coll. Problems of Drug Dependence; mem. New Haven County Med. Assn. (chmn. bicentennial com. 1983), Am. Inst. History of Pharmacy (chmn. Urdang Medal com. 1978, Kraemers award), Am. Hist. Assn., Am. Assn. History of Medicine (chmn. edn. com. 1985, William Osler medal), English-Speaking Union (pres. New Haven br. 1995—), Soc. of Cin. in the State of Conn., Beaumont Med. Club (pres. 1985-87), Acorn Club, Cosmos Club, Yale Club (N.Y.C.), Athenaeum Club (London). Office: Yale U 333 Cedar St New Haven CT 06520-7900

MUSTO, DOREEN, interior designer; b. Rochester, N.Y., Oct. 18; d. Nunzio Edward and Ann (Iaculli) Musto; m. Douglas L. Wink; 1 stepdaughter, Melissa Lynn; 1 child, Douglas III. AAS in Psychology cum laude, Monroe C.C., 1973; BSW cum laude, SUNY, Brockport, 1975. Social worker, dir. mental health Cobbs Hill Nursing Home, Rochester, N.Y., 1975-78; social worker Rochester, N.Y., 1980-89; interior designer for retail stores Washington, 1989-91; CEO Three-D-Wink Inc., Washington, 1991—. Mem. Peerless Rockville (Md.) Hist. Soc.; judge, mem. 4-H Orgn., 1985—; vol. to staff White House, Washington, 1994—; head art dept. Young Reps. Club, Rochester, 1964-69; organizer, pres. Rockshire New Comers Club, Rockville, Md.; active nat., local politics; chmn. Rockshire Arch. Com. Named Most Popular High Schooler in City of Rochester, Times Union Newspaper, 1964. Mem. NOW, Nat. Trust for Hist. Preservation, White House Hist. Soc., Decorative Arts Trust (cons.), Nat. Mus. of Women in the Arts (charter), Tex. State Soc. (inaugural ball com. 1985-94), Nat. Am. Italian Found., Smithsonian Instn., Md. Design, Space Planning and Props Soc. (founder, dir.). Avocations: painting, biking, crochet, walking, reading. Office: 2205 Newton Dr Ste 201 Rockville MD 20850-3023

MUSTOE, THOMAS ANTHONY, physician, plastic surgeon; b. Columbia, Mo., June 29, 1951; s. Robert Moore and Carolyn (Swett) M.; m. Kathryn Claire Stallcup, Aug. 13, 1977; children: Anthony, Lisa. BA cum laude in biology, Harvard Coll., 1973, MD cum laude, 1978. Diplomate Am. Bd. Otolaryngology, Am. Bd. Plastic Surgery. Rsch. assoc. dept. microbiology Harvard Med. Sch., Cambridge, Mass., 1976-77; intern in medicine Mass. Gen. Hosp., Boston, 1978-79; resident in surgery Peter Bent Brigham Hosp., Boston, 1979-80; resident in otolaryngology Mass. Eye and Ear Infirmary, Boston, 1980-82, chief resident, 1982-83; resident in plastic surgery Brigham and Women;s Hosp., Children's Hosp., Boston, 1983-84, chief resident, 1984-85; asst. prof. in surgery Wash. U. Sch. Medicine, St. Louis, 1985-89, assoc. prof., 1989-91; prof., chief divsn. plastic surgery Northwestern U. Med. Sch., Chgo., 1991—; plastic surgeon Northwestern Meml. Hosp., 1991—, Evanston Hosp., 1991—, Children's Meml. Hosp., 1992—, Shriner's Hosp. Chgo., 1994—; co-chmn. Gorden Rsch. Conf., 1995; spl. cons. Fed. Drug Adminstrn., 1994-95. Editl. bd. Archives of Surgery, 1992—, Plastic and Reconstructive Surgery, 1993—, Wound Repair and Regeneration, 1992—; contbr. articles to profl. jours., more than 125 publs., book chpts.; book reviewer. Harvard Nat. scholar, 1969-73; Rhodes scholar candidate, Harvard Coll., 1973. Fellow Am. Coll. Surgeons (surg. biology club III); mem. AMA, Am. Soc. Plastic and Reconstructive Surgery (rsch. fund proposal com. 1987-92, sci. program com. 1993-95, co-chmn. gen. reconstruction subcom. 1995, plastic surgery device com. 1989-93, resource book for plastic surgery residents com. 1991-93, chmn. resource book com., socioecon., 1992-94, chmn. device and technique assessment com. 1994, domestic clin. symposia com. 1992-95, ednl. tech. com. 1994—, adv. implant group 1994-96, task force for outcomes and guidelines 1995-96, ultrasonic lipectomy task force 1995-96), Am. Assn. Plastic Surgery (rsch. and edn. com. 1994-96), Midwest Assn. Plastic Surgeons, Plastic Surgery Rsch. Coun. (com. indsl. rels. 1992, judge Snyder and Crikelair awards 1991, rep. Coun. Acad. Surgeons 1991-94, program com. 1992-94, 95), Soc. Head and Neck Surgeons (membership com. 1993-95), Soc. Univ. Surgeons, Assn. Acad. Chmn. Plastic Surgery (matching program and ctrl. application svc. com. 1994), Wound Healing Soc. (audit com. 1992, program com. 1990, 92, 94, 97, bd. dirs. 1993-96, fin. com. 1994-96), Chgo. Plastic Surg. Soc., Chgo. Surg. Soc., Double Boarded Soc. (pres. 1995—), Sigma Xi, Aesculapian Club. Avocations: reading, golf, gardening, sports. Home: 144 Greenwood Evanston IL 60201 Office: Northwestern U Med Sch 707 N Fairbanks Ct Ste 811 Chicago IL 60611

MUSZYNSKI, L. JANE, interior designer; b. Memphis, Dec. 4, 1950; d. George Logan and Laura (Wall) Sullivan; m. Jerry Muszynski, Aug. 23, 1975; children: Logan, Jaclyn. BA in Interior Design and Home Econs., Calif. State U., 1973. Profl. status Nat. Coun. Interior Design Qualification, 1986; cert. Calif. Coun. Interior Design, 1993. Graphic designer Stewart Woodard Arch., Irvine, Calif., 1973-74; interior designer Interior Space Design, Newport Beach, Calif., 1974-76; office mgr. purchasing Lockheed Marine Lab., Diablo Canyon, Calif., 1976-77; realtor assoc. Century 21 Real Estate, Los Osos, Calif., 1977-79, Sierra Madre, Calif., 1979-80; v.p. mktg., designer S.K. Young Assocs., Tustin, Calif., 1979-88; sales acct. exec. Entouch Bus. Interiors, Rancho Cucamonga, Calif., 1988-89; sr. interior designer Disneyland Design Studio, Anaheim, Calif., 1989—; mktg. exec., owner Staffease & Advance Concepts, Walnut, Calif., 1991—; realtor, sales assoc. Anthony Real Estate, Santa Maria, Calif., 1977—; instr. Mt. San Antonio Coll., Walnut, 1985, 87, Calif. Poly. U., Pomona, 1988-89, adv. bd. interior design, 1988-90; chmn. nominating com. Bus. Devel. Assn. Orange County, Irvine, 1988-89. Mem. host program Bear Mountain Ski Resort, Big Bear, Calif., 1993, 94; cookie chmn. Girl Scouts Am., Walnut, 1993. Mem. Am. Soc. Interior Designers, Network Exec. Women in Hospitality. Avocations: golf, snow skiing, camping, hiking. Office: Advance Concepts Employer Svcs 709 Brea Canyon Rd #11 Walnut CA 91789

MUTAFOVA-YAMBOLIEVA, VIOLETA NIKOLOVA, pharmacologist; b. Svishtov, Bulgaria, Apr. 18, 1954; d. Nikola Anastassov Mutafov and Bogdanka Ivanova (Boteva) Mutafova; m. Ilia Angelov Yamboliev, Mar. 24, 1984; children: Irena, Kalina. MD, Med. Acad., Sofia, Bulgaria, 1978, splty. Pharmacology, 1985, PhD, 1987. Physician Dept. Internal Medicine Dist. Hosp., Svishtov, Bulgaria, 1979-82; rsch. asst. prof. pharmacology Med. Acad., Sofia, 1982-87, Bulgarian Acad. Scis., Sofia, 1987-93; Fogarty Internat. fellow Sch. Medicine Univ. Nev. Reno, 1993-95. Co-author: Trends in Pharmacology and Pharmacotherapy; contbr. articles to profl. jours. Mem. AAAS, Bulgarian Pharmacol. Soc. (exec. com., Best Young Pharmacologist award 1988), Soc. Bulgarian Physicians, N.Y. Acad. Scis. Avocations: skiing, theater, opera, books, playing bridge.

MUTH, ERIC PETER, ophthalmic optician; b. Munich, Germany, July 25, 1940; s. Erich Walter and Anna Lisa (Pentenrieder) M.; came to U.S., 1948, naturalized, 1955; BS, Charter Oak Coll., 1978; MBA, PhD in Mgmt., Columbia Pacific U., 1983; degree (hon.) Anora-Hannipen Tech. Coll., 1995; m. Rachel Hubbard, Apr. 4, 1971; children: Eric Van, Karl George, Ellen Anna. Lic. optician, Conn. Pres. Park Lane Opticians, Inc., Milford, Conn., 1968—; cons. Nat. Acad. Ophthalmology Found. Mus., San Francisco, 1982-88, Nat. Mus. Hist., Smithsonian Inst., 1983-94, Gesell Inst. Human Devel., 1984, 89; mem. adv. com. South Cen. Community Coll., Seattle, 1984; mem. adv. bd. Internat. Scientific Inst., P.R., 1989, adv. bd. Middlesex C.C., 1989 (vice chmn.). Mem. editorial rev. bd. (U.S.A.) Dispensing Optician mag., 1984—; author: Management for Opticians, Butterworths Textbook, 1983; contbr. The Social History of Eyeglasses in Japan, 1991, die Brille, Leipzig, 1989, Thinking on the Edge, Agamennon, 1993; pub. over 200 papers in 6 langs.; contbg. editor Optical Mgmt., 1979-80, OpticScan Canada, 1981-82, Indian Optician, 1982, Prism Mag., Can., 1988; tech. editor Optical Index, 1980-82; reviewer optical books. Presdl. appointment U.S. Selective Svc. Sys., 1991-92; Scoutmaster Boy Scouts Am., 1962; bd. dirs. ARC, Conn. chpt., 1988; advisor Tri Hi-Y YMCA, 1964; chmn. Korea-Vietnam Meml. com., Milford, 1985-86; organizer WWII Monument Com. 1991; trustee Conn. Visual Health Ctr., 1982-84; mem. Soc. 3d U.S. INf. Div., 1987. Served with AUS, 1957-59, Conn. Army N.G., 1960-69. Recipient Eng. Nelson/Wingate prize, 1983, Service Above Self award Rotary, 1986, Optician of the Yr. Guild of Prescription Opticians Am., 1991. Fellow Nat. Acad. Opticianry (regional membership chmn., faculty speakers bur., citation 1988), Internat. Acad. Opticianry, Opticians Assn. Am. (historian citation 1993, diploma in refractometry 1995); mem. Conn. Opticians Assn. (pres. 1974, chmn. membership and ethics coms., Optician of Yr 1975), Conn. Guild Prescription Opticians (pres. 1980, Man of Yr 1981), Assn. Dispensing Opticians Eng., Nat. Commn. on Opticianry Accreditation (commr. 1989-93), Brit. Guild Dispensing Opticians, Ednl. Found. in Ophamalic Optics, Calif. Soc. Dispensing Opticians (hon.), Ariz. Soc. Dispensing Opticians (hon.), Am. Legion (citation 1986), Milford C. of C. (chmn. law and safety com. 1975, Community Service award 1986), Internat. Platform Assn., Am. Bd. of Opticianry and Nat. Contact Lens Examiners (cert.), Am. Bd. of Opticianry Master of Ophthalmic Optics, Charter Oak Coll. Alumni Assn. (bd. dirs. 1987, alumni citation 1995). Recipient Senate Citation State of Conn., 1993, German-Am. Friendship award, Germany, 1995, State of Conn. Justice of the Peace, 1995; sr. rsch. fellow Internat. Soc. for Philosophical Inquiry, 1991—, pers. cons., 1996. Lodges: Lions, Rotary. Avocations: skydiving, ballooning, motorcycling, Tae Kwan Do (presdl. sports award, 1973). Home: 25 Parkland Pl Milford CT 06460-7723 Office: Park Lane Opticians Inc 50 Broad St Milford CT 06460-3358

MUTH, GEORGE EDWARD, former art and drafting supply company executive; b. Washington, July 1, 1906; s. Edward Everhardt and Edna Elizabeth (Cassidy) M.; m. Lydagene Black, Apr. 19, 1930. A.B., George Washington U., 1931, J.D., 1934; LL.D. (hon.), Gallaudet Coll., 1965. Bar: D.C. 1933. With firm Pennie, Davis, Marvin and Edmonds (patent law), Washington, 1924-36; pres., treas. Geo. F. Muth Co., Inc., Washington, 1936-71; pres. Geo. F. Muth Co., Inc., 1971, 1972—; sec., treas. GFM, Inc., Woodville, Va., 1972-82. Past mem. zoning appeal bd. Rappahannock County, Va.; past mem. Rappahannock County Electoral Bd., Rappahannock County Planning Commn.; past chmn. bd. Gallaudet Coll., Washington; past trustee Westbrook Sch., Montgomery County, Md., George Washington U.; trustee Rappahannock County Libr., Washington, Va.; past mem. fine arts com. U.S. Agr. Grad. Sch.; past pres. Boys Club Washington, Travelers Aid Soc. Washington; past v.p. Nat. Travelers Aid Soc., Nat. Capital Area coun. Boy Scouts Am., Washington Soc. for Blind; bd. dirs., past vice chmn. Culpeper (Va.) Meml. Hosp.; past bd. dirs., past chmn. Rappahannock-Rapidan Cmty. Svcs. Bd. Mem. Nat. Art Materials Trade Assn. (past pres., dir.), Arts Club (past pres.), Rotary (past pres.), Rappahannock Hunt Club (past pres. Washington, Va.), Masons, Sigma Alpha Epsilon, Gamma Eta Gamma, Omicron Delta Kappa. Presbyterian (elder). Home: 424 Highlands Pl Harrisonburg VA 22801-8348

MUTH, JOHN FRANCIS, newspaper editor, columnist; b. N.Y.C., Sept. 18, 1918; s. Ernest and Mary (Bijot) M.; m. Helen Scanlan, Sept. 26, 1948. Student, Fordham Coll., evenings 1939-40. With King Features Syndicate, 1941—; now asso. editor; editor Nat. Press Photographer mag., 1963-67; syndicated columnist, science writer, 1967—. Served with the USAAF, 1942-45, ETO. Mem. Bellerose Civic Assn., VFW (John F. Prince post). Democrat. Roman Catholic. Club: Caterpillar. Home: 81-33 243rd St Bellerose NY 11426-1319 Office: 235 E 45th St New York NY 10017-3305

MUTH, JOHN FRASER, economics educator; b. Chgo., Sept. 27, 1930; s. Merlin Arthur and Margaret Fraser (Ferris) M. B.S.I.E., Washington U., St. Louis, 1952; M.S., Carnegie-Mellon U., 1954, Ph.D., 1962. Research fellow Carnegie-Mellon U., 1956-59, asst. prof. econs., 1959-62, assoc. prof., 1962-64; prof. Mich. State U., 1964-69, Ind. U., 1969-94; ret., 1994. Author: (with others) Planning Production, Inventories, and Work Force, 1960, (with G. K. Groff) Operations Management: Analysis for Decision, 1972; editor: (with G. L. Thompson) Industrial Scheduling, 1963, (with G. K. Groff) Operations Management: Selected Readings, 1969. Fellow Econometric Soc.; mem. Inst. Mgmt. Sci. Home: 21028 4th Ave Summerland Key FL 33042

MUTH, RICHARD FERRIS, economics educator; b. Chgo., May 14, 1927; s. Merlin Arthur and Margaret Ferris M.; m. Helene Louise Martin, Dec. 23, 1955; children: Lisa Helene, Laurianne Martin Love. Student, USCG Acad., 1945-47; A.B., Washington U., St. Louis, 1949, M.A., 1950; Ph.D., U. Chgo., 1958; M of Theol. Studies, Emory U., 1995. Lectr. polit. economy Johns Hopkins U., Balt., 1955-56; economist Resources for Future, Washington, 1956-58; assoc. prof. urban econs. U. Chgo., 1959-64; economist Inst. Def. Analyses, Arlington, Va., 1964-66, cons., 1966-69; prof. econs. Washington U., St. Louis, 1966-70, Stanford U., (Calif.), 1970-83; Callaway prof. econs. Emory U., Atlanta, 1983—, chmn. dept., 1983-90; vis. assoc. prof. econs. Vanderbilt U., 1958-59; vis. sr. fellow Urban Inst., Washington, 1976-77; vis. prof. Sch. Bus., U. Calif. Berkeley, 1991. Author: (with others) Regions, Resources and Economic Growth, 1960, Cities and Housing, 1969, Public Housing, 1974, Urban Economic Problems, 1975; (with Allen C. Goodman) The Economics of Housing Markets, 1989. Mem. Presdl. Task Force on Urban Renewal, 1969; mem. Presdl. Task Forces on Urban Affairs and on Housing, 1980-81, Presdl. Commn. on Housing, 1981-82. Served with USCG, 1951-52. Mem. Am. Econ. Assn., Am. Real Estate and Urban Econs. Assn., Regional Sci. Assn. (v.p. 1975-76), So. Econ. Assn. Libertarian. Methodist. Office: Emory U Dept Econs Atlanta GA 30322

MUTH, ROBERT JAMES, metal company executive, lawyer; b. Phila., May 13, 1933; s. James H. and Ruth M. (Will) M.; m. Shirley M. Carnes, Jan. 31, 1959; children: Christopher James, Jennifer Augusta. BA, Lafayette Coll., 1954; postgrad., Yale Div. Sch., 1954-55; LLB, Columbia U., 1960. Bar: D.C. 1961, N.Y. 1969. Atty. Covington & Burling, Washington, 1960-68; asst. gen. counsel Asarco, Inc., N.Y.C., 1969-71, assoc. gen. counsel, 1971-77, v.p., 1977—; chmn. Lead Industries Assn., N.Y.C., 1986-89, 93—; pres. Silver Inst., Washington, 1987-89; vice chmn. Nat. Legal Ctr. for Pub. Interest, Washington, 1986-90; bd. dirs. So. Peru Copper Corp. Mem. George Sch. Com., Newton, Pa., 1985—; bd. dirs. No. Lights Inst., Missoula, Mont. Lt. inf. U.S. Army, 1955-57, Korea. Mem. ABA, N.Y. State Bar Assn., Met. Club (Washington). Home: 1062 Washington Crossing Rd Newtown PA 18940

MUTI, RICCARDO, orchestra and opera conductor; b. Naples, Italy, July 28, 1941. Edn., Milan Conservatory; MusD (hon.), U. Pa., Curtis Inst. Music U. Bologna, Mt. Holyoke Coll.; LLD (hon.), Warwick U., Eng.; Doctor Honoris Causa, Westminster Choir Coll., Princeton, N.J. Prin. condr. Orch. Maggio Musicale Florentino, Florence, Italy, 1969-80; guest condr. numerous orchs., Europe and U.S.; music dir. Philharmonia Orch., London, 1973-82; prin. guest condr. Phila. Orch., 1967-78, music dir., 1980-92, laureate condr., 1992—; music dir. La Scala, 1986—, prin. condr., 1973-82; concerts at Salzburg, Edinburgh, Lucerne, Flanders, Vienna and Berlin Festivals; condr. operas at Vienna, Salzburg, La Scala, Milan, Munich, London. Decorated officer of merit Republica Tedesca, Commendatore and Grand Ufficiale Della Republica Italiana, Cavaliere Di Gran Croce; winner Guido Cantelli prize, 1967; recipient Verdienst Kreuz, Fed. Republic of Germany; recipient numerous internat. prizes for recordings. Hon. mem. Royal Acad. Music, Acad. Santa Cecilia, Acad. Luigi Cherubini. Office: Phila Orch Acad of Mus 1420 Locust St Ste 400 Philadelphia PA 19102-4223 also: Orch del Teatro alla Scala, Via dei Filodarmmatici, I-20121 Milan Italy

MUTO, SUSAN ANNETTE, religion educator, academic administrator; b. Pitts., Dec. 11, 1942; d. Frank and Helen (Scardamalia) M. BA in Journalism and English, Duquesne U., 1964; MA, U. Pitts., 1967, PhD in English Lit., 1970. Asst. dir. Inst. of Formative Spirituality, Duquesne U., Pitts., 1965-80, dir., 1980-88, faculty coordinator grad. programs in foundational formation, 1979-88, prof., 1981—; guest lectr. formative reading various colls. and community orgns., 1970—. Author: (with Adrian van Kaam) The Emergent Self, 1968, (with Adrian van Kaam) The Participant Self, 1969, Approaching the Sacred: An Introduction to Spiritual Reading, 1973, Steps Along the Way, 1975, A Practical Guide to Spiritual Reading, 1976, The Journey Homeward: On the Road of Spiritual Reading, 1977, Tell Me Who I Am, 1977, Celebrating the Single Life, 1982, Blessings That Make Us Be, 1982, Pathways of Spiritual Living, 1984, 89, Meditation in Motion, 1986, (with Adrian van Kaam and Richard Byrne) Songs for Every Season, 1989, (with van Kaam) Commitment: Key to Christian Maturity, 1989, Commitment: Key to Christian Maturity, A Workbook and Guide, 1990, John of the Cross for Today: The Ascent, 1990, Womanspirit, 1991, (with Adrian van Kaam) The Power of Appreciation: A New Approach to Personal and Relational Healing, 1992, John of the Cross for Today: The Dark Night, 1994, Stess and the Search for Happiness: A New Challenge for Christian Spirituality, 1993, Harnessing Stress: A Spiritual Quest, 1993,

Healthy and Holy Under Stress: A Royal Road to Wise Living, 1994, Divine Guidance: A Basic Directory to the God-Guided Life for All Believers, 1994, A Practical Guide to Spiritual Reading, 1994, Late Have I Loved Thee: The Recovery of Intimacy, 1995, The Commandments: Ten Ways to a Happy Life and a Healthy Soul, 1996, Words of Wisdom for our World: The Precautions and Counsels of St. John of the Cross, 1996; contbr. articles to religious and secular publs. Mem. Edith Stein Guild, Epiphany Assn. (exec. dir. 1988—), Phi Kappa Phi. Home: 2223 Wenzell Ave Pittsburgh PA 15216-3159 Office: Epiphany Assn 948 Tropical Ave Pittsburgh PA 15216-3032

MUTOMBO, DIKEMBE (DIKEMBE MUTOMBO MPOLONDO MUKAMBA JEAN JACQUE WAMUTOMBO), professional basketball player; b. Kinshasa, Zaire, June 25, 1966. Student, Georgetown U. Center Denver Nuggets, 1991—. NBA All-Star, 1992; NBA All-Rookie Team, 1992. Office: Denver Nuggets McNichols Sports Arena 1635 Clay St Denver CO 80204-1799*

MUTSCHLER, HERBERT FREDERICK, retired librarian; b. Eureka, S.D., Nov. 28, 1919; s. Frederick and Helena (Oster) M.; m. Lucille I. Gross, Aug. 18, 1945; 1 dau., Linda M. B.A., Jamestown Coll., 1947; M.A., Western Res. U., 1949, M.S., 1952. Tchr. history high sch. Lemmon, S.D., 1947-48; asst. librarian Royal Oak (Mich.) Libr., 1952-55; head librarian Hamtramck (Mich.) Libr., 1955-56; head public svcs. Wayne County Libr. System, Wayne, Mich., 1956-59; asst. county librarian Wayne County Libr. System, 1960-62; dir. King County Libr. System, Seattle, 1963-89; library bldg. cons. Wayne County Libr., 1956-62, Wash. State Libr., 1966—; cons. Salt Lake County Libr., Pierce County Libr., North Olympic Libr.; lectr. U. Wash. Sch. Librarianship, 1970-71; bldg. cons. Hoquiam (Wash.) Libr., Olympic (Wash.) Regional Libr., Camas (Wash.) Pub. Libr., N. Cen. (Wash.) Regional Libr., Spokane (Wash.) County Libr., Enumclaw (Wash.) Libr., Puyallup (Wash.) Pub. Libr., Kennewick (Wash.) Pub. Libr., Lopez Island (Wash.) Libr. Contbr. articles profl. jours. Mem. Foss Home and Village Bd. Trustees, 1989—; bd. dirs. King County Libr. Sys. Found. With AUS, 1941-45; to capt. 1950-52. Decorated Silver Star, Bronze Star with cluster, Purple Heart, Presdl. Unit Citation. Mem. ALA (councilor at large 1965-69, chpt. councilor 1971-75, pres. library adminstrv. div. 1974-75), Pacific N.W. Library Assn., Wash. Library Assn. (exec. bd. 1964-65, 69-71, pres. 1967-69). Republican. Lutheran. Club: City, Municipal League. Lodge: Kiwanis. Home: 5300 128th Ave SE Bellevue WA 98006-2952

MUTTI, ALBERT FREDERICK, minister; b. Hopkins, Mo., Feb. 13, 1938; s. Albert Frederick and Phyllis Margaret (Turner) M.; m. Etta Mae McClurg, June 7, 1959; children: Timothy Allen, John Frederick, Martin Kent. AB, Cen. Meth. Coll., 1960; MDiv., Garrett Theol. Sem., 1963; DMin., St. Paul Sch. Theology, 1975; DD, Baker U., 1993. Sr. pastor Union Star Charge, Mo., 1963-65, Crossroads Parish, Savannah, Mo., 1965-74; assoc. coun. dir. Mo. West Conf. UMC, Kansas City, 1974-80, coun. dir., 1980-82; sr. pastor First United Meth. Ch., Blue Springs, Mo., 1982-87; dist. supt. Cen. Dist. UMC, Mo., 1987-89; dist. supr. Kansas City N. Dist., 1989-92; bishop Kans. Area United Meth. Ch., Topeka, 1992—. Chair Savannah Cmty. Betterment, 1971; bd. mem. St. Mary's Hosp., Blue Springs, 1986; dir. ARC, Savannah, 1968; bd. Discipleship, Nashville, bd. Global Ministries, N.Y.; pres. Mo. Coun. Chs., Jefferson City, Dean Mo. Area Ministers Sch., Ctrl. Meth. Coll.; trustee St. Paul Sch. Theology; organizer Rural, Religion and labor Coun. Kans. Named Disting. Alumni Ctrl. Meth. Coll.; recipient Grad. award St. Paul Sch. Theology. Home: 6841 SW Dunstan Ct Topeka KS 66610-1406 Office: 4201 SW 15th St Topeka KS 66604-2412

MUTZ, OSCAR ULYSSES, manufacturing and distribution executive; b. Edinburg, Ind., Feb. 12, 1928; s. Harold Winterberg and Laura Belle (Sawin) M.; m. Jean Greiling, Aug. 22, 1948; children: Marcia, H. William. B.S., Ind. U., 1949. Vice pres. Peerless Corp., Indpls., 1954-63; v.p., gen. mgr. Space Conditioning, Inc., Harrisonburg, Va., 1964-66; v.p., treas. Cosco, Inc., Columbus, Ind., 1966-67; exec. v.p., 1967-69, pres., 1969-71; chmn. bd. Court Manor Corp., Columbus, 1971-73; pres. Jenn Air Corp., Indpls., 1973-75; pres., CEO Mutz Corp., 1975-81; pres. Forum Group, Inc. (merger Mutz Corp. and Excepticon, Inc.), Indpls., 1981-91; chmn., chief exec. officer Capital Industries, Inc., Indpls., 1991—, also bd. dirs.; bd. dirs. Ct. Manor Corp., Sargent & Greenleaf; pres. Sovereign Group, Inc., 1991—, also bd. dirs. Nat. trustee Fellowship Christian Athletes, 1985-91, chmn. nat. conf. ctr., 1994-96; mem. pres. coun. and dean's adv. coun. Ind. U. Mem. Ind. Mfrs. Assn. (chmn. 1980), Acad. Alumnae Fellows Ill. U. Sch. Bus. Republican. Mem. Christian Ch. Office: Capital Industries Inc 8900 Keystone Xing Ste 1150 Indianapolis IN 46240-2135

MUUSS, JOHN, public safety and emergency management executive; b. Bklyn., Mar. 8, 1940; s. Leona (Schwanzer; divorced; children: John. Lance, Diana. Student, C.W. Post Coll., Suffolk (N.Y.) C.C., N.Y.C. (N.Y.) Police Acad. Lab. technician Royaltone Photo Finishers, N.Y.C., 1958-59; comml. photographer A. Studley Inc., N.Y.C., 1962-64; police officer N.Y.C. (N.Y.) Police Dept., 1966-70, detective, 1970-78; bonded dep. sheriff Suffolk County, N.Y., 1979—; dir. pub. safety Town of Islip, N.Y., 1978—; dir. emergency mgmt. Town of Islip, 1981—; pvt. practice security cons. East Islip, N.Y., 1986—. Pres., mem. Lakeland Civic Assn., Ronkonkoma, N.Y., 1970-79, Connetquot Bd. Edn., Bohemia, N.Y., 1975-78; campaign chmn. various local and state polit. seats, Islip, 1970—; chmn., mem. MacArthur Airport Adv. Com., Ronkonkoma, 1975-78; vestry mem. St. Marks Episcopal Ch., Islip, 1982-89. With U.S. Army, 1959-62. Mem. Am. Soc. for Indsl. Security, Fire Island Law Enforcement Coun., Internat. Assn. Chiefs of Police, N.Y. State Assn. Chiefs Police, Kiwanis Club of the Islips (charter pres. 1986). Republican. Episcopalian. Avocation: golf. Office: Islip Twp Dept Pub Safety/Emergency 401 Main St Islip NY 11751-3533

MUUSS, ROLF EDUARD, retired psychologist, educator; b. Tating, Germany, Sept. 26, 1924; came to U.S., 1953, naturalized, 1992.; s. Rudolf A. and Else (Osterwald) M.; m. Gertrude Louise Kremser, Dec. 22, 1953; children: Michael John, Gretchen Elise. Diploma, Tchr. Coll., Flensburg, Germany, 1951; student, U. Hamburg, Germany, 1951, Ctrl. Mo. State Coll., 1951-52, Columbia Tchrs. Coll., 1952; MEd, Western Md. Coll., 1954; PhD, U. Ill., 1957. Tchr. pub. sch. Germany, 1945-46, 51, 52-53, substitute prin., 1952-53; tchr. trainee U.S. Office Edn., 1951-52; houseparent Child Study Ctr., Balt., 1953; grad. asst. U. Ill., 1954-57; rsch. assoc. prof. Iowa Child Welfare Rsch. Sta., State U. Iowa, 1957-59; rsch. cons., 1960, 61; mem. faculty Goucher Coll., 1959-95, prof. edn., 1964-95, chmn. dept., 1972-75, dir. spl. edn., 1977-92, Elizabeth C. Todd disting. prof., 1980-85, chmn. dept. sociology and anthropology, 1983-85, prof. emeritus, 1995—; rsch. assoc. edn. Johns Hopkins, 1962-63; part-time or summer tchr. U. B.C., 1962, Johns Hopkins U., 1962, 65, U. Del., 1965, Towson U., 1967, U. Ill., 1967; tchg. assoc. Sheppard and Enoch Pratt Hosp., 1969-80; guest lectr. Tchrs. Coll., Kiel, Fed. Republic Germany, 1977-78; hearing officer spl. edn. cases State of Md., 1980—. Author: First-Aid for Classroom Discipline Problems, 1962, Theories of Adolescence, 1962, 5th edit., 1988, 6th edit., 1996, Grundlagen der Jugendpsychologie, 1982; also numerous articles; editor: Adolescent Behavior and Society: A Book of Readings, 1971, 4th edit., 1990. Served with German Air Force, 1942-45. Recipient award for disting. scholarship Goucher Coll., 1979; grantee Andrew W. Mellon Found., 1976-77. Fellow Am. Psychol. Soc., Am. Psychol. Assn., Md. Psychol. Assn. (treas. 1971-73); mem. Balt. Psychol. Assn. (chmn. membership com. 1966, v.p. 1970-71), Soc. Rsch. Child Devel., Soc. Rsch. on Adolescence, Coun. for Exceptional Children, Kappa Delta Pi (v.p. Alpha chpt. 1956-57), Phi Delta Kappa. Home: 1540 Pickett Rd Lutherville Timonium MD 21093-5822

MUZYKA, DONALD RICHARD, specialty metals executive, metallurgist; b. Northampton, Mass., Aug. 23, 1938; s. Stephen S. and Mary (Paul) M.; m. Eileen J. Hannigan, June 10, 1961; children: Steven Richard, James Paul, David Joseph. Supr. high temperature alloy research Carpenter Tech. Corp., Reading, Pa., 1966-73, mgr. alloy research and devel., 1973-76, mgr. high temperature alloys research, 1975-76, gen. mgr. research and devel. labs., 1976-77, gen. mgr. distbn., 1977-79, v.p. tech. div., 1979-82; dir. tech. Cabot Corp., Boston, 1982-85; gen. mgr. refractory metals Cabot Corp., Boyertown, Pa., 1985-87, gen. mgr. elec. and refractory metals, 1987-88; v.p., gen. mgr. Cabot Corp., Boyertown, 1988-89; v.p. rsch. and devel. Cabot Corp., 1989; pres. Spl. Metals Corp., New Hartford, N.Y., 1990—; bd. dirs. Aviall, Inc., CSM Holdings, Inc. Contbr. articles to profl. jours.; patentee in field. Bd. dirs. Wilson Sch. Bd., West Lawn, Pa., 1960-63, Montessori Country Day Sch., Wyomissing, Pa., 1960-63. Recipient Engring. Alumni award U. Mass., 1984. Fellow Am. Soc. Metals (trustee 1982-84, Bradley Stoughton award 1981); mem. The Metall. Soc., Indsl. Research Inst., Am. Ceramic Soc., Am. Soc. Quality Control. Republican. Roman Catholic. Avocation: antique clock collector. Home: 6824 Reservoir Rd Clinton NY 13323-4816 Office: Spl Metals Corp Middle Settlement Rd New Hartford NY 13413

MYCIELSKI, JAN, mathematician, educator; b. Wisniowa, Poland, Feb. 7, 1932; s. Jan and Helena (Bal) M.; m. Emilia Przezdziecka, Apr. 25, 1959. MS, U. Wroclaw, Poland, 1955, PhD, 1957. With Inst. Math., Polish Acad. Scis., Wroclaw, 1956-68; prof. math. U. Colo., Boulder, 1969—; vis. prof. Case Western Res. U., Cleve., 1967, U. Colo., 1967, Inst. des Hautes Etudes Scientifiques, Bures-sur-Yvette, 1978-79, dept. math. U. Hawaii, 1987; attache de recherche Centre National de la Recherche Scientifique, Paris, 1957-58; asst. prof. U. Calif., Berkeley, 1961-62, 70; long-term vis. staff mem. Los Alamos Nat. Lab., 1989-90. Author over 140 rsch. papers. Recipient Stefan Banach prize, 1965, Alfred Jurzykowski award, 1977, Waclaw Sierpinski medal, 1990. Mem. Am. Math. Soc., Polish Math. Soc., Assn. for Symbolic Logic. Office: U Colo Dept Math Boulder CO 80309-0395

MYDLAND, GORDON JAMES, judge; b. nr. Hetland, S.D., May 12, 1922; s. Jacob and Anna (Hetl) M.; m. Lorrie Grange, May 29, 1958; 1 child, Gabriel. BS, S.D. State U., 1947; JD, U. S.D., 1956. Bar: S.D. 1956. Pvt. practice law Brookings, S.D., 1956-69, Lake Preston, S.D., 1973; S.D. circuit judge, 1973-87; presiding judge (3d Jud. Circuit), 1975, 79-80; S.D. state's atty. Brookings County, 1959-62; mem. S.D. State Senate, 1963-68; atty. gen. S.D., 1968-72; ret., 1987; part-time instr. constl. and bus. law S.D. State U., 1956-65. Mem. S.D. Code Compilation Commn., 1964-68; mem. S.D. Planning and Adv. Commn. Crime and Juvenile Delinquency, 1970-72; adv. com. S.D. Alcohol Safety Action Project, 1971-72. Served with USNR, 1943-46. Mem. Am. Legion. Lutheran.

MYERBERG, MARCIA, investment banker; b. Boston, Mar. 25, 1945; d. George and Evelyn (Lewis) Katz; m. Jonathan Gene Myerberg, June 4, 1967 (div. Mar. 1994); 1 child, Gillian Michelle. BS, U. Wis., 1966. Corp. trust adminstr. Chase Manhattan Bank, N.Y.C., 1966-67; asst. cashier Glore Forgan, Wm. R. Staats, Phoenix, 1967-68; bond portfolio analyst Trust Co. of Ga., Atlanta, 1969-72; asst. v.p. 1st Union Nat. Bank, Charlotte, N.C., 1973-78; dir. cash mgmt. Carolina Power & Light Co., Raleigh, N.C., 1978-79; sr. v.p., treas. Fed Home Loan Mortgage Corp., Washington, 1979-85; dir. Salomon Bros. Inc., N.Y.C., 1985-89; sr. mng. dir. Bear, Stearns & Co. Inc., N.Y.C., 1989-93; mng. dir. Bear, Stearns Home Loans, London, 1989-93; chief exec. Myerberg & Co., L.P., N.Y.C., 1994—. Home: 201 E 87th St Apt 16R New York NY 10128-1101 Office: 780 3rd Ave New York NY 10017-2024

MYEROWITZ, P. DAVID, cardiologist, surgeon, educator; b. Balt., Jan. 18, 1947; s. Joseph Robert and Merry (Brown) M.; B.S., U. Md., 1966, M.D., 1970; M.S., U. Minn., 1977; m. Susan Karen Macks, June 18, 1967 (div.); children—Morris Brown, Elissa Suzanne, Ian Matthew. Intern in surgery U. Minn., Mpls., 1970-71, resident in surgery, 1971-72, 74-77; resident in cardiothoracic surgery U. Chgo., 1977-79; practice medicine, specializing in cardiovascular surgery, Madison, Wis., 1979—; asst. prof. thoracic and cardiovascular surgery U. Wis., Madison, 1979-85, assoc. prof., 1985, chief sect. cardiac transplantation, 1984-85, Karl P. Klassen prof., chief thoracic and cardiovascular surgeon Ohio State Univ. and Hosps., Columbus, 1985—. Served with USPHS, 1972-74. Mem. ACS, Am. Coll. Cardiology, Assn. for Acad. Surgery, Soc. Univ. Surgeons, Soc. Thoracic Surgeons, Am. Soc. Artificial Internal Organs, Am. Coll. Chest Physicians, Am. Heart Assn., Internat. Soc. Heart Transplantation, Internat. Soc. Cardiovascular Surgery, Am. Assn. Thoracic Surgeons. Jewish. Author: Heart Transplantation; contbr. articles to profl. jours. Office: Ohio State Univ Hosps Doan N # 825 Columbus OH 43210

MYERS, AL, realtor, property manager, mayor; b. Oakland, Calif., Aug. 6, 1922; s. Alvi A. and Emma (Thoren) M.; student Oreg. Inst. Tech., 1940-41; m. Viola Doreen Wennermark, Sept. 11, 1954; children: Susan Faye, Pamela Ann, Jason Allen. Supt.'s asst. Aluminum Co. Am., Troutdale, Oreg., 1942-44; asst. mgr. Western Auto Supply Co., Portland, 1944-46; owner, operator Al Myers Auto & Electric, Gresham, Oreg., 1946-53; realtor, broker Al Myers Property Mgmt., 1954—; v.p., sec. Oreg. Country, Inc.; faculty Mt. Hood Community Coll. Chmn., Indsl. and Econ. Devel. Com. for Multnomah County, Oreg. Real Estate Ednl. Program, 1961. Mayor Gresham, Oreg., 1972-83. Pres. East Multnomah County Dem. Forum, 1965—, mem. exec. com., 1958—. With AUS, 1943. Mem. Portland Realty Bd., Nat. Assn. Real Estate Bds., Christian Bus. Men's Com. Internat., Internat. Platform Assn., Rho Epsilon Kappa (pres. Oreg.). Mem. Evang. Ch. (trustee, treas.). Home: 935 NW Norman Ave Gresham OR 97030-6966 Office: 995 NE Cleveland Ave Gresham OR 97030-5707

MYERS, ALBERT G., JR., textile manufacturer; b. Charlotte, N.C., Feb. 15, 1917; s. Albert Gallatin and Elfreida (Nail) M.; m. Kittie Brownlee, Feb. 7, 1942; children—Albert Gallatin III, Barbara Brownlee Melvin. Student, Davidson Coll.; B.S., Erskine Coll., 1940; grad., Exec. Program U. N.C., 1959; LLD (hon.), Belmont Abby Coll., 1995. With Textiles-Inc. (name changed to Ti-Caro Inc., 1978), Gastonia, N.C., 1939-82; successively mfg. dept., asst. v.p., sec.-treas., v.p., treas. Textiles-Inc. (name changed to Ti-Caro Inc., 1978), 1939-61, pres., 1961-70, chmn. bd., 1971-82, also dir.; ret., 1982; with Threads-Inc. (now Threads USA), 1946-82, successively purchasing agt., sec., asst. treas., v.p. and sec., v.p. and treas., 1946-61, pres., 1961-70, chmn. bd., 1971-82, also dir.; ret., 1982; past chmn. bd. Carolina Motor Club. Past pres. Piedmont council Boy Scouts Am., regional chmn.; past mem. adv. bd. Red Shield Boys Club; past pres. Gaston County YMCA; past pres. N.C. Textile Found., Inc., 1967-69; past chmn. bd. First Gaston Found.; past treas., dir. Schiele Mus. Natural History; past trustee Gaston Coll.; trustee Brevard Coll.; past mem. bd. advisers Belmont Abbey Coll.; past chmn. bd. trustees Gaston Meml. Hosp.; trustee Crossnore (N.C.) Sch. Served with USAAF, 1942-46. Mem. Gastonia C. of C. (past pres.), Combed Yarn Spinners Assn. (past pres.), N.C. Textile Mfgrs. Assn. (past dir., 1st v.p. 1970-71), Am. Textile Mfrs. Inst. (dir. 1964-68), Am. Legion, Gaston Country Club, Grandfather Golf and Country Club (Linville, N.C.), Linville Golf Club, Key Largo (Fla.) Anglers Club. Methodist (ofcl. bd.).

MYERS, ALFRED FRANTZ, state education official; b. Crooked Creek State Park, Pa., Feb. 19, 1936; s. Jacob Alfred Jr. and Ida Gertrude (Schaeffer) M. BA, Lehigh U., 1958, MA, 1966; postgrad. George Peabody Coll., 1971-72. Instr., Grand River Acad., Austinburg, Ohio, 1966, Culver (Ind.) Mil. Acad., 1966-68, Kiskiminetas Springs Sch., Saltsburg, Pa., 1968-71; asst. prof. social studies Ind. State U., Terre Haute, 1972-73; div. trainer Ency. Britannica, Rochester, N.Y., 1973-75; mgr. Rupp's, Kittanning, Pa., 1976-77; criminal justice system planner Pa. Commn. on Crime and Delinquency, Harrisburg, 1977-80; rsch. assoc. Pa. Dept. Edn., Harrisburg, Pa., 1980-89, basic edn. assoc., 1989—. Social work Dominican Rep., 1958. 1st lt. USAF, 1958-63, 1st. lt., capt. USAFR, 1963-71. Mem. ACLU, AAUP, ASCD, Nat. Coun. Social Studies, Am. Acad. Polit. and Social Sci., Am. Evaluation Assn., Am. Ednl. Rsch. Assn., Am. Hist. Assn., Caribbean Studies Assn., Acad. Polit. Sci., Conf. Latin Americanist Geographers, Mid. States Coun. for Social Studies (pres. 1987-88), Nat. Braille Assn., People for Am. Way., Am. Legion, Orgn. Am. Historians, Phi Beta Kappa, Phi Delta Kappa. Home: 849 Melissa Ct Enola PA 17025-1551

MYERS, ALLEN RICHARD, rheumatologist; b. Balt., Jan. 14, 1935; s. Ellis Benjamin and Rosina (Blumberg) M.; m. Ellen Patz, Nov. 26, 1960; children: David Joseph, Robert Todd, Scott Patz. BA, U. Pa., 1956; MD, U. Md., 1960. Diplomate Am. Bd. Internal Medicine, Am. Bd. Rheumatology. Intern Univ. Hosp., Balt., 1960-61; resident in medicine Univ. Hosp., Ann Arbor, Mich., 1961-64; fellow in rheumatology Mass. Gen. Hosp. and Harvard Med. Sch., Boston, 1966-69; dir. clin. tng. rheumatology U. Pa. Sch. Medicine, Phila., 1969-72, chief rheumatology sect., 1972-78; dep. chair medicine Temple U. Sch. Medicine, Phila., 1978-84, acting chmn. medicine, 1984-86, dean, 1991-95, prof. medicine, 1978—, assoc. v.p. Health Scis. Ctr., 1988-95; vis. prof. Cardiothoracic Inst., U. London, 1988; med. adv. bd. Scleroderma Rsch. Found., Santa Barbara, Calif., 1986. Mem. editorial bd. Arthritis & Rheumatism, 1985-90, Brit. Jour. Rheumatology, 1989-94; editor: Systemic Scleroderma, 1985, Medicine, 1986, 93. Mem. exec. com. Phila. Health Care Congress, 1990—, chmn., 1994—; mem. adv. com. Pa. Lupus Found., 1976. With USPHS, 1964-66. Recipient Margaret Whitaker prize U. Md. Sch. Medicine, 1960, Lindback Found. award Temple, 1981; named Physician of Yr. Temple U. Hosp., 1986. Fellow Phila. Coll. Physicians (councillor 1994—), ACP, Am. Coll. Rheumatolog; mem. Phila. Rheumatism Soc., Am. Fedn. CLin. Rsch., N.Y. Acad. Scis., Brit. Soc. Rheumatology. Avocations: walking, classical music, reading. Office: Temple U Sch Medicine 3400 N Broad St Philadelphia PA 19140-5196

MYERS, ANDREW S., lawyer; b. N.Y.C., Oct. 13, 1952; m. Robin S. Merrill, June 27, 1978; 1 child, Alan Stewart Harry. BA in Polit. Sci., San Diego State U., 1976; MPH, UCLA, 1978; JD, Washburn U., 1988. Bar: Nev. 1988, Colo. 1989, Kans. 1989, U.S. Dist. Ct. Kans. 1989, U.S. Dist. Ct. Nev. 1989, U.S. Supreme Ct. 1995. Hosp. adminstr. various hosps., Calif., 1978-85; jud. clk. Hon. Michael Wendell, Las Vegas, Nev., 1988-89, Hon. Joseph Pavlikowski, Las Vegas, 1989-90; dep. pub. defender Clark County Pub. Defender, Las Vegas, 1991; law ptnr. Bell, Davidson & Myers, Las Vegas, 1992-94, Davidson & Myers, Las Vegas, 1994—; mem. State Bar So. Nev. Disciplinary Com., 1993—, State Bar Fee Dispute Com., 1994—; hearing master for civil commitments 8th Jud. Dist. Ct., 1993-95, URESA hearing master, 1994—. Fund raiser Stewart Bell for Dist. Atty., Las Vegas, 1994. Mem. ABA, ATLA, Nat. Assn. Criminal Def. Lawyers, Clark County Bar Assn., Am. Coll. Legal Medicine, Nat. Health Lawyers Assn. Avocation: travel. Office: Davidson & Myers 601 Bridger Ave Las Vegas NV 89101-5805

MYERS, ANNE M., church administrator. Sec. Ch. of the Brethren. Office: Church of Brethren 1451 Dundee Ave Elgin IL 60120-1674

MYERS, ARTHUR B., journalist, author; b. Buffalo, Oct. 24, 1917; s. Edward A. and Isabelle (Baker) M.; m. Irma H. Ashley, 1972. BA, Hobart Coll., 1939. Journalist Rochester (N.Y.) Times Union, 1948-52, Washington Post, 1956-57, Berkshire (Mass.) Eagle, 1957-64; contbg. editor Coronet mag., 1965-68; columnist Bergen Record, Hackensack, N.J., 1969-71; exec. editor Berkshire Sampler, Pittsfield, Mass., 1971-77; tchr. writing Mass. U. extension program and Berkshire Community Coll., Pittsfield, 1958-62, Fairleigh Dickinson U., Teaneck, N.J., 1970, Cambridge (Mass.) Coll., 1989. Author: (with J. O'Connell) Safety Last: An Indictment of Auto Industry, 1966, Journalism Careers for the 70's, 1971, Analysis: The Short Story, 1975, Analysis: The Personal Profile Magazine Article, 1976, Kids Do Amazing Things, 1980, The Ghost Hunters, 1980, Sea Creatures Do Amazing Things, 1981; (with Irma Myers) Why You Feel Down and What You Can Do About It, 1982, The Ghostly Register, 1986, Ghosts of the Rich and Famous, 1988, The Ghostly Gazetteer, 1990, Ghost Hunter's Guide, 1993, The Cheyenne, 1992, The Pawnee, 1993, The First Movies, 1993, The First Baseball Game, 1993, The First Football Game, 1993, Drugs and Peer Pressure, 1995; also short stories, articles. Mem. PEN, Nat. Writers Union, Mensa. Home: 60 Grove St Apt 6202 Wellesley MA 02181-7716

MYERS, BARTON, architect; b. Norfolk, Va., Nov. 6, 1934; s. Barton and Meeta Hamilton (Burrage) M.; m. Victoria George, Mar. 7, 1959; 1 child, Suzanne Lewis. BS, U.S. Naval Acad., 1956; MArch with honors, U. Pa., 1964. Commd. 2d lt. USAF, 1956, resigned, 1961; architect Louis I. Kahn, Phila., 1964-65, Bower, Fradley, Phila., 1967-68; architect, prin. A.J. Diamond & Barton Myers, Toronto, Ont., Can., 1968-75; architect, prin. Barton Myers Assocs., Toronto, 1975—, Los Angeles, 1981—; disting. vis. prof. Ariz. State U., Tempe, 1986; sr. prof. UCLA, 1981—; Thomas Jefferson Prof. U. Va., Charlottesville, 1982; vis. prof., lectr., Harvard U., U. Pa., other univs. U.S. and Can., 1968—. Prin. works include Myers Residence, Toronto (Ont. Assn. Architects Toronto Chpt. Annual Design award, 1971, Can. Housing Design Coun. award, 1971), Wolf Residence, Toronto (Archtl. Record: Record Houses of 1977, Twenty-five Yrs. of Record Houses, 1981), Housing Union Bldg., Edmonton (Can. Housing Design Coun. award, 1974, Design in Steel award, 1975), Citadel Theatre, Edmonton (City of Edmonton Design award, 1978, Stelco Design award, 1978), Seagram Mus., Waterloo, Ont. (Gov. Gen.'s Medal for Architecture, 1986), Howard Hughes Ctr. Master Plan and Wang Tower, L.A., 1986, Phoenix Mcpl. Govt. Ctr. (Winning Competition Entry, 1985), Portland Ctr. for the Performing Arts, Portland (Progressive Architecture Design award, 1984, USITT Merit award, 1994), Art Gallery Ont. expansion (Winning Competition Entry, 1987), Film and Drama Facility York U., Toronto, 1987, Cerritos (Calif.) Ctr. Performing Arts, 1987 (USITT Honor Award, 1994), N.J. Performing Arts Ctr., Newark, 1991, Ivan Reitman Prodn. Studio, 1994, Scripps Ocean Atmosphere Rsch. Facility, 1995; others. Recipient Gov. Gen.'s award for Architecture Woodsworth Coll., 1992, RAIC Gold Medal, 1994, Royal Archtl. Inst. Canada. Fellow AIA, Royal Archtl. Inst. Can.; mem. Soc. Archtl. Historians, Royal Can. Acad. Art, Tau Sigma Delta. Avocations: travel, reading. Office: Barton Myers Assocs Inc 9348 Civic Ctr Dr Ste 450 Beverly Hills CA 90210-3624

MYERS, CLARK EVERETT, retired business administration educator; b. Rossville, Kans., Oct. 19, 1915; s. Thad James and Rose I (Page) M.; m. Cora Henley Hepworth, May 7, 1942; children—Clark Everett, Richard G. Hepworth. B.S., U. Kans., 1939, M.B.A., 1946; D.C.S., Harvard, 1956. Tchr. Auburn (Kans.) Sch., 1932-34, prin., 1934-36; instr. U. Kans., 1939-41; asst. prof. U. Tex., 1947-49, assoc. prof., 1949-53, chmn. dept. mgmt., 1950-53; lectr. Harvard Grad. Sch. Bus. Adminstrn., 1953-54; dean Coll. of Commerce, prof. bus. adminstrn. Ohio U., 1954-57; dir. mgmt. devel. inst. Lausanne, Switzerland, 1957-60; lectr. Harvard Grad. Sch. Bus., 1960-61; dean Sch. Bus. Adminstrn., prof. mgmt. U. Miami, Coral Gables, Fla., 1961-68; dean Grad. Sch. Bus. Adminstrn., Emory U., Atlanta, 1968-75; prof. bus. adminstrn. Grad. Sch. Bus. Adminstrn., Emory U., 1975-85, prof. emeritus, 1985—. Editor: (with William R. Spriegel) The Writings of the Gilbreths, 1953. Served as lt. USNR, 1942-45. Fellow Acad. Mgmt.; mem. Am. Assn. Collegiate Schs. Bus. (exec. com. 1965-68, 1969-70, pres. 1970-71), Phi Kappa Phi, Sigma Iota Epsilon, Delta Sigma Pi, Beta Gamma Sigma, Phi Gamma Delta, Beta Alpha Psi. Home: 1082 Vistavia Cir Decatur GA 30033-3413

MYERS, CLAY, retired investment management company executive; b. Portland, Oreg., May 27, 1927; s. Henry Clay and Helen (Mackey) M.; m. Elizabeth Lex Arndt, Oct. 1, 1955; children: Richard Clay (dec.), Carolyn Elizabeth, David Hobson. B.S., U. Oreg., 1949; postgrad., Northwestern Coll. Law, 1950-52; LHD (hon.), Ch. Div. Sch. of the Pacific, 1992. With 1st. Nat. Bank, Portland, 1949-53; with Conn. Gen. Life Ins. Co., Hartford and Portland, 1953-62; state mgr. Conn. Gen. Life Ins. Co., 1960-62; v.p. Ins. Co. Oreg., Portland, 1962-65; asst. sec. state State of Oreg., Salem, 1965-67; sec. state State of Oreg., 1967-77, state treas., 1977-84; v.p. J.P. Morgan Investment Mgmt. Co., N.Y.C., 1984-89, Capital Cons. Inc., Portland, Oreg., 1989-92; chmn. Oreg. House Adv. Com. Legis. Reapportionment, 1961; chmn. Oreg. Gov.'s Commn. on Youth, 1969-74. Author: (with others) Population Reapportionment Initiative Constitutional Amendment, 1952. Bd. dirs., treas. Ch. Divinity Sch. of Pacific, 1977-83; trustee Pacific U., 1989-92; vestryman Trinity Parish, Wall St., 1986-93; pres. Nat. Interfrat. Conf., 1986-87; mem. social responsibility in investing com. Nat. Episcopal Ch., 1983-87; trustee Ch. Pension Fund; bd. dirs. Ch. Life Ins. Co. Mem. Nat. Assn. State Treas. (past pres.), Multnomah Athletic Club (Portland), DeMolay Club (Legion of Honor), Lambda Chi Alpha (nat. pres. 1974-78), Sigma Nu Phi. Republican. Episcopalian. Home: 10456 NW 2d St Portland OR 97231-1072

MYERS, DANIEL N., lawyer, association executive; b. Independence, Kans., Sept. 17, 1942; s. James Kenneth and Evalyn Clair Petty (Feather) M.; m. Eileen Carruthers, Dec. 14, 1966; children: Yvette Christine, John Joseph. AA, Coffeyville Coll., 1961; BA, U. Okla., 1963; JD, Georgetown U., 1975. Bar: Va. 1976, U.S. Ct. Customs and Patent Appeals 1977, Ill. 1991. Asst. to pres. J.V. Hurson Assoc., Inc., Washington, 1968-74; mgr. fed. legis. affairs AICPA, Washington, 1974-77; dir. legis. svcs., assoc. counsel Nat. LP-Gas Assn., Arlington, Va., 1977-79; gen. counsel, v.p. govt. relations Nat. Propane Gas Assn., Arlington, Va., 1979-88; exec. v.p. Nat. Propane Gas Assn., Lisle, Ill., 1989—. Contbr. articles on good samaritan laws and genealogy to various publs. Bd. dirs. Washington Area State Rels. Group, 1980-82, mem. energy task force White House Conf. on Small Bus., 1980; chmn. good samaritan coaliton hazardous materials Adv. Coun., Washington, 1982-88; mem. motor carrier adv. com. Fed. Hwy. Adminstrn., Washington, 1982-88. Sgt. U.S. Army, 1964-68. Mem. Am. Soc. Assn.

Execs. (legal sect. coun. 1980—, chmn. legal sect. 1991-92, bd. dirs. 1991-92), Spl. Indsl. Radio Svc. Assn. (bd. dirs. 1979-88), Indsl. Telecomm. Assn. (bd. dirs. 1995—), Chgo. Soc. Assn. Execs., Nat. Vol. Firefighters Coun. Found. (bd. dirs. 1995—). Avocations: golf, genealogy, racquetball. Office: 1600 Eisenhower Ln Lisle IL 60532

MYERS, DANIEL WILLIAM, II, lawyer; b. Camden, N.J., Mar. 21, 1931; s. Charles Rudolph II and Myrtle Henrietta (Kress) M.; m. Eileen Ethel Kohn, Nov. 22, 1959; children: Susan Leigh, Meredith Ann Myers Winner, Kathryn Kress. BS in Commerce, U. Va., 1952, LLB, 1957. Bar: Va. 1957, N.J. 1958, U.S. Dist. Ct. N.J. 1958, U.S. Supreme Ct. 1980. Assoc. Lewis & Hutchinson, Camden, 1958-60; ptnr. Myers, Matteo, Rabii, Norcross & Landgraf, predecessors, Camden, 1960—, Cherry Hill, N.J., 1960-89; ptnr. Montgomery, McCracken, Walker & Rhoads, 1989-94, of counsel, 1994—. 1st lt. U.S. Army, 1952-54. Mem. ABA, N.J. Bar Assn., Va. Bar Assn., Camden County Bar Assn., Am. Arbitration Assn., Exch. Club (pres. Cherry Hill chpt. 1969). Republican. Lutheran. Home: 325 Rhoads Ave Haddonfield NJ 08033-1468 Office: Montgomery McCracken Walker & Rhoads 1010 Kings Hwy S Cherry Hill NJ 08034-2524

MYERS, DAVID N., construction executive; b. June 22, 1900; s. Robert H. and Annie May (Gosberg) M.; m. Inez Pink, Mar. 27, 1929; children: Hal, Dieter. MBA, Dyke Coll., 1922, LHD (hon.), 1981; LHD (hon.), Cleve. State U. Pres. Byerlyte Corp., Cleve., 1931-1965; chmn. bd. Consol. Coatings Corp., 1965-89, Hastings Pavement Co., N.Y.C., 1965—. Life trustee Mt. Sinai Hosp., 1946—; pres. emeritus Menorah Home for Aged; pres. Jewish comty. Fedn., 1964-69; mem. internat. adv. coun. World Jewish Congress, 1966—; chmn. exec. com. Asphalt Inst., 1953-55; hon. life trustee ARC; chmn. Ohio State Commn. on Aging, 1983-87; founder Hebrew U. in Jerusalem, Albert Einstein Coll. Medicine, N.Y.C., David N. Myers Coll. Recipient United Appeal Disting. Svc. award Eleanor Roosevelt Humanities award, Charles Eisenman award of Jewish Community Fedn., Philos. award ARC, Ollie A. Randall award Nat. Coun. on Aging, 1992; mem. Ohio Sr. Hall of Fame, 1985. Mem. ASTM, Mus. of Art (life), Mus. Natural History, Assn. Asphalt Technologists (life), Am. Ordnance Assn. (life), Oakwood Club, Masons (32 degree). Home: 16900 S Park Blvd Cleveland OH 44120-1643 Office: Investment Plz 1801 E 9th St Cleveland OH 44114-3103 *Retirement at 60 or 65 is folly. Older men are blessed with a perception which allows them, through a recollection of decisions in their past years, to judge things well, whether they be in business or in a profession; or in daily life.*

MYERS, DEBRA TAYLOR, elementary school educator, writer; b. Balt., Feb. 5, 1953; d. James Zachary and Gene Elizabeth (Blubaugh) Taylor; m. Kenneth Lee Myers Jr., June 18, 1977; children: Kenneth Andrew, Katherine Elizabeth. BS in Elem. Edn., Towson State U., 1975, MEd, 1983. Cert. tchr., Md. 5th grade tchr. N.W. Mid. Sch., Taneytown, Md., 1975-80; home and hosp. sch. tchr. Balt. County Schs., 1992-93; tchr. educator in elem. edn. dept. Towson (Md.) State U., 1993-94; 2d grade tchr. Balt. County Pub. Schs., 1994—; workshop leader, guest lectr. Harford (Md.) County Schs., Balt. County Schs., United Meth. Commn. on the Young Child, Balt. Editor Kid's View; contbr. articles to children's mags. and jours. Mem. Renew, A Randallstown Cmty. Group Assn., Balt., 1993—; bd. dirs. Child Devel. Ctr., Milford Mill United Meth. Ch., 1992—. Recipient Outstanding Vol. award Balt. County PTA, 1992, 93, 94. Mem. Kappa Delta Pi. Avocations: travel, reading, writing for children, volunteering, spending time with family. Home: 3607 Blackstone Rd Randallstown MD 21133-4213 Office: Randallstown Elem Sch 9103 Liberty Rd Randallstown MD 21133-3521

MYERS, DEE DEE See MYERS, MARGARET JANE

MYERS, DENYS PETER, JR., architectural historian; b. Boston, Apr. 23, 1916; s. Denys Peter and Ethel May (Johnston) M.; m. Anne Buchonis, Aug. 24, 1940. S.B., Harvard U., 1940; grad. studies, Fogg Art Mus., 1949-50; M.A., Columbia U., 1948. Asst. reference dept. N.Y. Public Library, 1941-42, charge exbhns., 1942-43; instr. Hunter Coll., N.Y.C., 1947; dir. Art Inst., Zanesville, Ohio, 1947-55, Philbrook Art Center, Tulsa, 1955-58, Des Moines Art Center, 1958-59; asst. dir. Balt. Mus. Art, 1959-64; dir. No. Va. Fine Arts Assn., 1964-66; vis. lectr. Johns Hopkins U., 1962-64; historian Nat. Park Service, U.S. Dept. Interior, 1966-68; prin. archtl. historian Historic Am. Bldgs. Survey, Office of Archaeology and Historic Preservation, Washington, 1968-73; pvt. practice cons. archtl. historian Washington, 1973-78; cons. Faulkner, Fryer and Vanderpool (Architects), Washington, 1975-83; archtl. historian Historic Am. Bldgs. Survey, Nat. Park Service, Dept. Interior, Washington, 1978-85; lectr. Smithsonian Instn., 1974-78, 91, Cath. U. Am., 1966-67. Co-author: A Preservation Index for the Federal Hill Historic District, 1973, Nashville, A Short History and Selected Buildings, 1974, Maine Forms of American Architecture, 1976, Alexandria - A Towne in Transition 1800-1900, 1977, Historic America, 1983; author: Maine Catalog: The Historic Architecture of Maine, 1974, American Gas Lighting: A Guide for Historic Preservation, 1978; introduction to Minard Lafever's Beauties of Modern Architecture, (1835), 1968, Introduction to 1876 Mitchell, Vance & Co. catalog reprint; contbr. articles to MacMillan Ency. Arch., 1982, Dictionary of Art, American National Biography and profl. jours. Ordained perpetual deacon Episcopal Ch., 1954. Served with AUS, 1943-46. Mem. Am. Archtl. Found. (mem. adv. com.), Soc. Archtl. Historians (founding mem., dir. 1962-65, pres. Latrobe chpt. 1975-77), Alexandria Assn. (pres. 1968-69), Victorian Soc. in Am. (dir. 1970-72), Alexandria Library Co. (pres. 1982-83), Alexandria Hist. Soc., Steamship Hist. Soc., Preservation Round Table, Soc. for Preservation New Eng. Antiquities, Hist. Alexandria Found. Club: Cosmos (Washington). Home and Office: 201 N Columbus St Alexandria VA 22314-2411

MYERS, DONALD ALLEN, university dean; b. Nebraska City, Nebr., Dec. 17, 1932; s. Merle D. and Ruth Irene (Potter) M.; m. Dixie Lois Ashton, Aug. 10, 1957; 1 son, Eric; m. Lilian Rose Bautista, Apr. 18, 1966; children: Sherri, Johnny, David; m. Alice L. Twining, July 15, 1990; 1 child, Aaron. B.A., Mcpl. U. Omaha, 1956; M.A., U. Chgo., 1957, Ph.D., 1962. Asst. supt. Sch. Dist. Riverview Gardens, Mo., 1962-65; research assoc. NEA, Washington, 1965-66; curriculum and research specialist Inst. for Devel. of Ednl. Activities, Los Angeles, 1966-70; assoc. prof. SUNY, Albany, 1970-73; head dept. curriculum and instrn. Olka. State U., Stillwater, 1973-79; dean Coll. Edn., U. Nebr., Omaha, 1979-85; dean Sch. Edn. Old Dominion U., Norfolk, Va., 1985—. Author: Teacher Power, 1973, Open Education Reexamined, 1973; contbr. articles, chpts. to profl. jours., books. Washington intern in edn. Ford Found., 1965-66. Democrat. Home: 1272 Belvoir Ln Virginia Beach VA 23464-6746 Office: Old Dominion U Coll Edn 5215 Hampton Blvd Norfolk VA 23508-1506

MYERS, DOUGLAS GEORGE, zoological society administrator; b. L.A., Aug. 30, 1949; s. George Walter and Daydeen (Schroeder) M.; m. Barbara Firestone Myers, Nov. 30, 1980; children: Amy, Andrew. BA, Christopher Newport Coll., 1981. Tour and show supr. Annheuser-Busch (Bird Sanctuary), Van Nuys, Calif., 1970-74, mgr. zool. ops., 1974-75, asst. mgr. ops., 1975-77, mgr. ops., 1977-78; gen. services mgr. Annheuser-Busch (Old Country), Williamsburg, Va., 1978-80, park ops. dir., 1980-81; gen. mgr. wild animal park Zool. Soc. San Diego, 1981-83, dep. dir. ops., 1983-85, exec. dir., 1985—; cons. in field. Bd. dirs. San Diego Conv. and Visitors Bur.; mem. adv. com. of pres.' assn. Am. Mgmt. Assn. Fellow Am. Assn. Zool. Parks and Aquariums (profl.), Internat. Union Dirs. Zool. Gardens; mem. Internat. Assn. Amusement Parks and Attractions, Calif. Assn. Zoos and Aquariums, Mus. Trustee Assn. Lodge: Rotary. Office: San Diego Zoo PO Box 551 San Diego CA 92112-0551

MYERS, EDWIN, think-tank executive. Exec. dir. WESTED (formerly Southwest Regional Lab), Los Alamitos. Office: WESTED 4665 Lampson Ave Los Alamitos CA 90720-5139*

MYERS, ELISSA MATULIS, publisher, association executive; b. Munich, Aug. 4, 1950; (parents Am. citizens); d. Raymond George and Anne Constance (Moley) Matulis; m. John Wake Myers, Sept. 13, 1967 (div. 1972); 1 child, Jennifer Anne Myers Bick. BA in English Lit., George Mason U., 1972, MA in English Lit., 1982. Dir. rsch. and info. Am. Soc. Assn. Execs., Washington, 1972-80, dir. mem. svcs., 1980-88, v.p., pub. Assn. Mgmt. mag., 1988—. Pub. Principles of Association Management, 1976, 3d edit., 1996; columnist Footnotes, 1988—. Bd. dirs. Ethics Resource Ctr., Washington, 1982-86. Mem. Am. Soc. Assn. Execs. (cert.), Assn. Conv. Mktg. Execs. (bd. dirs. 1994—), Nat. Coalition Black Mktg. Planners, Greater Washington Soc. Assn. Execs. Roman Catholic. Avocations: running, scuba diving. Home: 5315 Moultrie Rd Springfield VA 22151 Office: Am Soc Assn Execs 1575 I St NW Washington DC 20005

MYERS, EUGENE EKANDER, art consultant; b. Grand Forks, N.D., May 5, 1914; s. John Q. and Hattye Jane (Ekander) M.; m. Florence Hutchinson Ritchie, Sept. 9, 1974. BS in Edn., U. N.D., 1936, MS in Edn., 1938; postgrad., U. Oreg., 1937; MA, Northwestern U., 1940, Columbia U., 1947; grad., Advanced Mgmt. Program, Harvard U., 1953; cert., Cambridge (Eng.) U., 1958; postgrad., U. Md., 1958-61, Oxford (Eng.) U., 1964; diploma, various mil. schs. Student asst. U. N.D., 1935-36, instr. summer sessions, 1936, 37, asst., 1936-37; prof., head dept. N.D. Tchrs. Coll., 1938-40; instr. Columbia U. Tchrs. Coll., 1940-41; vis. prof. U. Vt., summers, 1941, 42; commd. 1st lt. USAAF, 1942, advanced through grades to col., 1951; dir. personnel plans and tng. Hdqrs. Air Force Systems Command Washington, 1959-60; dir. personnel research and long-range plans Hdqrs. Air Force Systems Command, 1960-62; head dept. internat. relations Air War Coll., Air U. Maxwell AFB, Ala., 1962-63; dir. curriculum, dean (Air War Coll., Air U.), 1963-65; dir. res. affairs Hdqrs. Air Res. Personnel Center Denver, 1965-66; ret., 1966; dean Corcoran Sch. Art, Washington, 1966-70; founder Corcoran Sch. Art Abroad, Leeds, Eng., 1967; v.p. mgmt. Corcoran Gallery Art, Washington, 1970-72; vis. art dir. Washington, also Palm Beach, Fla.; art cons., 1972—; adv. Washington chpt. Nat. Soc. Arts and Letters.; bd. assos. Artists Equity. Author: (with Paul E. Barr) Creative Lettering, 1938, (with others) The Subject Fields in General Education, 1939, Applied Psychology, 1940; contbr. articles, reports to mags. and profl. publs. bd. dirs. Columbia (Md.) Inst. Art, World Arts Found., N.Y., Court Art Center, Montgomery, Ala. and Palm Beach, Fla., Order of Lafayette, Boston, English-Speaking Union, Palm Beach; mem. Hamilton St. Vol. Fire Dept. and Lit. Soc., Balt., Pundits, Palm Beach. Recipient Sioux award U. N.D., 1978. Mem. Internat. Communication Assn. (hon.), U. N.D. Alumni Assn. (pres. Washington chpt. 1959), Mil. Classics Soc., Titanic Soc., Mil. Order Carabao, Order of St. John of Jerusalem, Knightly Assn. St. George the Martyr, Co. Mil. Historians, Mil. Order World Wars, Ancient Order United Workmen, Saint Andrews Soc., Clan Donnachaidh (Perthshire, Scotland), Soc. Friends St. Andrews (Scotland) U., Delta Omicron Epsilon, Lambda Chi Alpha, Delta Phi Delta, Phi Delta Kappa, Phi Alpha Theta. Republican. Presbyterian. Clubs: Union (Manchester, Eng.) (hon.); Royal Scottish Automobile (Glasgow, Scotland); Royal Overseas (London); New (Edinburgh, Scotland) (assoc.); Army and Navy (Washington), Nat. Aviation (Washington), City Tavern (Washington), Harvard Business School (Washington); Army and Navy Country (Arlington, Va.); Metropolitan (N.Y.C.), Wings (N.Y.C.), Explorers (N.Y.C.) (fellow), Harvard (N.Y.C.); Minneapolis; Everglades (Palm Beach, Fla.), Beach (Palm Beach, Fla.), Sailfish of Fla. (Palm Beach, Fla.); Liitle (Gulf Stream, Fla.); Fairmont (W.Va.) Field Country, Lions. Home: 1 Royal Palm Way Palm Beach FL 33480 also: 3320 Volta Pl NW Washington DC 20007-2733 also: 721 Mount Vernon Ave Fairmont WV 26554-2522

MYERS, EUGENE NICHOLAS, otolaryngologist, otolaryngology educator; b. Phila., Nov. 27, 1933; s. David and Rosalind (Nicholas) M.; m. Barbara Labov, June 10, 1956; children: Marjorie Rose, Jeffrey N. BS in Econs., U. Pa., 1954; MD, Temple U., 1960. Diplomate Am. Bd. Otolaryngology. Intern Mt. Sinai Hosp., N.Y.C., 1960-61; resident Mass. Eye and Ear Infirmary, Boston, 1963-65; asst. prof. clin. otolaryngology U. Pa., 1968-72; prof. clin. oncology dept. oral pathology U. Pitts. Sch. Dental Medicine, Pitts., 1975-82, prof. dept. diagnostic services, 1982—; prof., chmn. dept. otolaryngology U. Pitts. Sch. Medicine, 1972—; chief dept. otolaryngology U. Pitts. Med. Ctr., 1972—; cons. VA Med. Ctr., Pitts., 1972—, Children's Hosp., Pitts., 1972—. Editor: Cancer of the Head and Neck, 1981, 2d edit., 1989, 3d edit., 1996, Tracheotomy, 1985; mem. editorial bd. Laryngoscope, 1973—, Jour. Head and Neck Surgery, 1978-92, AMA Archives of Otolaryngology, 1983-91, Annals of Otology Rhinology and Laryngology, 1984—, Oncology, 1986—, European Archives of Oto-Rhino-Laryngology, 1990—; editor-in-chief Advances in Orolaryngology, Yr. Book Med. Pubs., 1985—; co-editor Butterworth's Intern Med. Revs., Eng., 1981. Mem. adv. bd. Pa. Lion Hearing Research Found., Pitts., 1983—. Served to capt. M.C., U.S. Army, 1965-67. Recipient Cert of Merit Com. Research, Am. Acad. Otolaryngology-Salicylate Otoxicity, 1965; recipient Award of Merit Am. Acad. Otolaryngology-Head and Neck Surgery Inc., 1978, Robert E. Shoemaker Research award Pa. Acad. Ophthalmology and Otolaryngology, 1979. Fellow ACS (mem. bd. govs. 1981-87, mem. adv. coun. 1985-87), Am. Laryngol. Assn. (sec. 1982-88, pres. 1989-90, mem. coun. 1990-93, James Newcomb award 1993), Am. Acad. Otolaryngology (chmn. com. on head and neck surgery 1981-83, bd. dirs. 1985-88, 90—, pres. 1994-95); mem. Am. Bd. Otolaryngology (bd. dirs 1981—, pres.-elect 1994-96, pres. 1996—), Assn. Acad. Depts. Otolaryngology (mem. coun. 1978-80), Nat. Cancer Inst. (chmn. upper aerodigestive tract working group 1986-89), am. Soc. Head and Neck Surgery (mem. coun. 1977-93, pres. 1988-90), Triological Soc. (mem. coun. 1989-92, v.p. Ea. sect. 1994-95), Pitts. Athletic Assn. Republican. Jewish. Office: U Pitts Sch Med Eye & Ear Inst Ste 500 200 Lothrop St Pittsburgh PA 15213-2588

MYERS, EVELYN STEPHENSON, editor, writer; b. N.Y.C.; d. William and Gertrude Maud (Pickett) Stephenson; m. Charles Bogart Myers, June 1, 1946 (dec. Nov. 1990); children—Cynthia Myers Marquardt, Meredith Myers Ballard. Student Simmons Coll., 1940-42; B.A., Barnard Coll., 1943-45; MA in Liberal Studies, Georgetown U., 1976; postgrad. New Sch. Soc. Research, 1945-49, George Washington U., 1977-78. Mng. editor Advance, N.Y.C., 1947-50; editor, Pres.'s Water Resources Policy Commn., Washington, 1950-51; editorial cons. Viet Nam Press, Saigon, 1958-60; chief joint info. service Am. Psychiat. Assn., Nat. Assn. Mental Health, Washington, 1961-63; writer, editor NIMH, Bethesda, Md., 1963-65; mng. editor Am. Jour. Psychiatry, Washington, 1965-87; editor, Eco-Facts, Washington, 1987-91; editorial cons. Am. Psychiat. Assn., Washington, 1993—. Author: (with others) Facing Facts: A Handbook for Reporters in Viet Nam, 1959, Health Insurance and Psychiatric Care: Utilization and Cost, 1972, Health Insurance and Psychiatric Care: Update and Appraisal, 1984, Ethics and Policy in Scientific Publication, 1990. NEH Summer Seminar fellow, 1981. Mem. Council Biology Editors (bd. dirs. 1981-84, editorial policy com. 1984-91), Soc. Scholarly Pub. (program com. 1983-84), LWV, Woman's Nat. Dem. Club, Barnard Club (Washington). Unitarian. Home: 15107 Interlachen Dr Apt 512 Silver Spring MD 20906-5630

MYERS, FRANCES, artist; b. Racine, Wis., Apr. 16, 1938; d. Stephen George and Bernadette Marie (Gales) M.; m. Warrington Colescott, Mar. 15, 1971. MFA, U. Wis., 1965. lectr. St. Martin's Sch. Art, London, 1967; disting. prof. printmaking Mills Coll., Oakland, Calif., 1979; vis. lectr. U. Calif., Berkeley, 1982; currently prof. art U. Wis., Madison. One-woman shows include Horwich Gallery, Chgo., 1977, 81, Haslem Gallery, Washington, 1981, 88, Madison Art Center, 1981, Carnegie Inst., Pitts., 1982, Wis. Acad. Arts, 1985, Perimeter Gallery, Chgo., 1986, 88, 91, 93, Natasha Nicholson Works of Art, 1989, Dittmar Gallery, Northwestern U., Evanston, Ill., 1989, Peltz Gallery, Milw., 1990, 91, 94; group shows include U.S. Pavilion, World's Fair, Osaka, Japan, 1970, Biennale of Prints Musée d'Art Moderne, Paris, 1970, Bklyn. Mus. 20th Biennale Exhbns. of Prints, 1976, 23d Biennale, 1982, 14th and 16th Internat. Biennial Graphic Arts, Ljubljana, Yugoslavia, 1981, 85, Am. Biennial Graphic Arts, Cali, Colombia, 1981, Brit. Internat. Print Biennale, Bradford, Eng., 1984, Bklyn. Mus. 25th Print Biennale, 1986, prints displayed in Am. Consulate, Leningrad, USSR, 1987, USIA, Yugoslavia, 1989-90, Pace Gallery, N.Y.C., 1990, Figurative Graphics, Amerikahaus, Cologne, Fed. Rep. Germany, 1991, Portland (Oreg.) Art Mus., 1992, Milw. Mus. Art, 1990, Nat. Mus. Am. Art, Washington, 1991, Duke U. Mus. Art, Durham, N.C., 1993, Internat. Biennial of Prints, Bhopal, India, 1995; represented in permanent collections Met. Mus. of Art, Victoria and Albert Mus., London, Chgo. Art Inst., Library of Congress, Phila. Mus. Art, Mus. Fine Arts, Boston. Nat. Endowment for the Arts fellow, 1974-75, 85-86, H.I. Romnes fellow U. Wis., 1991. Mem. Nat. Acad. Design, Am. Print Alliance, Nat. Womens Forum, Phila. Print Club. Home: 8788 County Road A Hollandale WI 53544-9423

MYERS, FRANKLIN, lawyer, oil service company executive; b. Pensacola, Fla., Nov. 2, 1952; s. T.F. Sr. and D. Bernice (Brewer) M.; m. Melinda Munson, Aug. 9, 1974; children: Amanda C., Adam F., Anne Marie M. BS, Miss. State U., 1974; JD, U. Miss., 1977. Bar: Miss. 1977, Tex. 1978. Ptnr. Fulbright and Jaworski, Houston, 1978-88; sr. v.p., gen. counsel Baker Hughes Inc., Houston, 1988-95; sr. v.p., gen. counsel, corp. sec. Cooper Cameron Corp., Houston, 1995—; adj. prof. U. Tex. Sch. Law, 1990-95; bd. dirs. Convest Energy, Reunion Resources Co. Bd. dirs. U. St. Thomas, Houston. Fellow Houston Bar Found., Tex. Bar Assn., Miss. Bar Assn., Houston Bar Assn. Baptist. Office: Cooper Cameron Corp 515 Post Oak Blvd Ste 1200 Houston TX 77027

MYERS, GEORGE CARLETON, sociology and demographics educator; b. Bklyn., Apr. 8, 1931; s. Francis Murdock and Ruth Emily (Hassinger) M.; m. Pauline Dorothy Kraebel, Apr. 24, 1954; children: George C., Marie E., Peter D., Kathleen A. BA, Yale U., 1953; postgrad., dipl., U. Stockholm, 1956; MA, U. Wash., Seattle, 1960; PhD, U. Wash., 1963. Instr. U. Wash., 1957-59, UCLA, 1960-62; asst. prof. Cornell U., Ithaca, N.Y., 1962-66; assoc. prof. Cornell U., 1966-68; sr. scientist WHO, Geneva, Switzerland, 1968-70; prof. sociology Duke U., Durham, N.C., 1968—; dir. Ctr. for Demographic Studies, 1972—; mem. Nat. Com. on Vital and Health Stats., Washington, 1985-88; mem. com. on aging Nat. Acad. Sci., Washington, 1982-85; mem. Census Adv. Com., 1977-83, WHO Program on Aging, 1988—, NIH Nat. Adv. Com. on Aging, 1991-95; vis. lectr. UN China Nat. Demographic Tng. Ctr., Beijing, 1991; advisor ECE Population Act. Unit, 1992—; vis. prof. U. Geneva Med. Sch., 1994, Flinders U. Med. Sch., 1994. Editor: Jour. of Gerontology, 1986-89; contbr. articles to profl. jours. With U.S. Army, 1953-55. NIH grantee, 1969—; sr. vis. fellow Australian Nat. U., 1984; vis. scholar Can. Soc. Human Coun., 1982; sr. internat. fellow Fogarty Ctr., NIH, London, 1978-79. Fellow Gerontol. Soc. Am.; mem. Population Assn. Am. (bd. dirs. 1977-79), So. Demographic Assn. (pres. 1974-76), Triangle Area Population Soc. (pres. 1988-89), Duke Faculty Club (pres. 1972-74). Avocations: sailing, skiing, golf. Home: 12 Scott Pl Durham NC 27705-5719 Office: Duke U Ctr for Demographic Studies 2117 Campus Dr Box 90408 Durham NC 27708-0408

MYERS, GERALD E., humanities educator; b. Central City, Nebr., June 19, 1923; s. Harold W. and Mary (Ferguson) M.; m. Martha Coleman, Aug. 7, 1948; 1 son, Curt. B.A., Haverford Coll., 1947; M.A., Brown U., 1949, Ph.D., 1954. Instr. Smith Coll., 1950-52; asst. prof. Williams Coll., 1952-61; assoc. prof. Kenyon Coll., 1961-65; prof. C.W. Post Coll., L.I. U., 1965-67, Queens Coll. and Grad. Center, City U. N.Y., 1967—; also dep. exec. officer Ph.D. program Queens Coll. and Grad. Center, City U. N.Y. (Grad. Center); dir. intro. philosophy into N.Y.C. High Schs. project.; dir. humanities-and-dance projects Am. Dance Festival, Durham, N.C., 1979; project dir. African-Am. Perspectives in Am. Moslem Dance, Am. Dance Festival/NEH. Author: Self, Religion and Metaphysics, 1961, Self: An Introduction to Philosophical Psychology, 1969, The Spirit of American Philosophy, 1970, William James: His Life and Thoughts, 1986; editor: The Aesthetic and Cultural Signigicance of Modern Dance, 1984, The Black Tradition in American Modern Dance, 1988, African American Genius in Modern Dance, 1992; co-editor: Emotion Philos. Studies, 1983, Echoes from the Holocaust, 1988; contbr. articles to profl. jours. NEH fellow, 1981-82. Mem. Am. Philos. Assn. (past sec.-treas. Western div.), Metaphys. Soc. Am., Soc. Phenomenology and Existential Philosophy, Phi Beta Kapa. Home: 36 Gardner Ave New London CT 06320-4313 Office: 33 W 42nd St New York NY 10036-8003

MYERS, HAROLD MATHEWS, academic administrator; b. Doylestown, Pa., Apr. 13, 1915; s. Carl and Alice W. Myers; m. Margaret F. Smith, July 19, 1946 (dec. Sept. 1963); children: Donald Smith, Dean Chappell, Deborah Kay; m. L. Marjorie Bellau, Nov. 28, 1964. BS in Commerce, Drexel Inst. Tech., 1938, DSc in Commerce (hon.), 1983; postgrad., Temple U., 1940-41, U. Omaha, summer 1957. Instr. coop. edn., dir. grad. placement Drexel U., Phila., 1938-46, asst. dean men, dir. student bldgs., adj. instr. labor econs., 1946-52, dean of men, 1952-55, treas., 1955-57, v.p., treas., 1957-80, sr. v.p., 1980-82, sr. v.p. emeritus, 1982-87, interim pres., 1987-88, pres. emeritus, 1988—, life trustee, 1986—; regional dir. First Pa. Banking and Trust Co., 1959-76; dir. Sadtler Rsch. Labs., Inc., 1963-69, Almo Indsl. Elecs., Inc., 1966-68; dir., treas. Uni-Coll Corp., 1974-81; bd. dirs. Beulah Cemetary Assn., asst. treas., 1984-89, treas., 1989-90, v.p. and treas., 1990—; bd. dirs., mem. exec. com. Univ. City Sci. Ctr., 1974-90, dir. emeritus, 1991—, chmn. fin. com., 1976-88, vice chmn., 1988-90. Contbr. articles to profl. jours. Bd. dirs. Internat. House of Phila. Inc., 1954-81, exec. com., 1972-81; active Phila. council Boy Scouts Am., 1953—, hon. chmn., 1985—, pres., 1982, 83; mem. citizens fire prevention com. Phila. Fire Dept., 1970-86; bd. dirs. United Fund Greater Phila., 1983-87, Luth. Ch. of Am. Common Investing Fund, 1976-82, Nat. Conf. of Christians and Jews, Inc., Phila. and S. Jersey region NCCJ, 1959-65; dir. Phila. Coun. of Chs., 1954-61; bd. dirs., pres. Ea. Assn. Coll. and Univ. Bus. Officers, 1967-68; pres. Nat. Assn. Coll and Univ. Bus. Officers, 1971-72; trees. Lambda Chi Alpha Found., 1970-84, dir. emeritus, 1984—; pres. Broadmoor Pines Home Owners Assn., 1993-94. Served to comdr. USNR, ret. Recipient Silver Beaver award Boy Scouts Am., 1963, Mary M. Hart award Phila. coun. Boy Scouts Am., 1986, Drexel Alumni Varsity Club award, 1966, Drexel U. Evening Coll. Alumni Assn. award, 1973, Drexel U. Anthony J. Drexel Paul award, 1988, Dept. of Army Cert. of Appreciation for Patriotic Civilian Svc., 1979, Disting. Bus. Officer award Nat. Assn. Coll. and Bus. Officers, 1989, Disting. Svc. in Trusteeship award Assn. Governing Bd. Univs. and Colls., 1989; named Educator of Yr., Phila. coun. Boy Scouts Am., 1989; named to Legion of Honor, Chapel of Four Chaplins; Drexel U. student dormitory named Myers Hall in his honor, 1984; 1 of 100 alumni honored Centennial of Drexel U., 1992. Mem. AARP, Am. Legion, Mil. Order World Wars (perpetual, comdr. Phila. chpt. 1958-59), Ret. Officers Assn. (life), Swedish Colonial Soc. Phila. (sec. 1968), Welsh Soc. Phila. (life), Internat. Frat. Lambda Chi Alpha (pres. 1966-70), Vet. Corps 1st Regiment Infantry, N.G.P. (hon.), Penn Club, Union League Phila. (pres. 1980-81), Sarasota Yacht Club, Masons, Rotary (Paul Harris fellow), Gulf Coast Corvair Club.

MYERS, HARRY CHARLES, national monument administrator; b. Pontiac, Ill., June 6, 1950; s. John Vincent and Kathryn Louise (Distlehorst) M. BS, Western Ill. U., 1977. Dir. Ft. Scott (Kans.) Nat. Hist. Site, 1978-79, mgmt. asst. Nat. Pk. Svc., 1979; review coord., budget asst. midwest regional office Nat. Pk. Svc., Omaha, 1979-81; supt. Perry's Victory and Internat. Peace Meml., Put-in-Bay, Ohio, 1981-88, Ft. Union Nat. Monument, Watrous, N.Mex., 1988—; acting supt. Chaco Culture Nat. Hist. Pk., Bloomfield, N.Mex., 1993, Amistad Nat. Recreation Area, Del Rio, Tex., 1994; spkr. in field. Contbr. articles to profl. jours. Bd. dirs. N.Mex. Endowment for Humanities, 1992-93. Mem. Kans. State Hist. Soc. (life), Nat. Pks. and Conservation Assn., Santa Fe Trail Assn. (chmn. 175th Anniversary of Santa Fe Trail 1993—, Award of Merit 1993, named Santa Fe Trail Assn. ambassador 1995). Home: Ft Union Nat Monument Box 7 Watrous NM 87753 Office: Ft Union Nat Monument Watrous NM 87753

MYERS, HARRY J., JR., retired publisher; b. Denver, Aug. 7, 1931; s. Harry J. and Edith M. (Reed) M.; m. Mary Kay Racine, June 21, 1958; children: Harry J., Hans R. (dec.), Peter C. BA, Colo. U., 1957; postgrad., U. Mo., 1959-60. Pub., or pub. dir. Geo, Archtl. Digest, Bon Appetit, Home, Sci. Am., Cowles Mag, 1970-95. Served with USMC, 1953-56. Mem. Kappa Tau Alpha, Phi Gamma Delta. Home: 46 W Ranch Trl Morrison CO 80465-9504

MYERS, HELEN PRISCILLA, music educator; b. Palo Alto, Calif., June 5, 1946; d. Henry Alonzo Myers and Elsie (Phillips) Myers-Stainton; children: Ian Alister Woolford, Adam Robert Woolford, Sean Patrick Woolford. MusB, Ithaca Coll., 1967; M in Mus. Edn., Syracuse U., 1971; MA, Ohio State U., 1975; PhD, U. Edinburgh, Scotland, 1984; MPhil, Columbia U., 1993. Cert. instrumental mus. K-12, N.Y. Clarinettist Am. Wind Symphony Orch., Pitts., 1966-67; rsch. fellow Columbia U., N.Y.C., 1973-75, lectr., 1975-76; lectr. Goldsmiths' Coll. U. London, 1981-89; assoc. prof. Trinity Coll., Hartford, Conn., 1989—, St. Anthony Hall prof., 1994—; Ford Found. lectr. ethnomusicology Nat. Ctr. Performing Arts, Bombay, India, 1988; vis. assoc. prof. music Columbia U., N.Y.C., 1993; ethnomusicologist cons. Oxford U. Press, London, 1981-83, The New Grove Dictionary of Music, 7th edit., London, 1993—; resident ethnomusicologist Grove's Dictionaries of Music and Musicians, 1976-89; guest lectr. Guildhall Sch. of Music, London, 1982-89. Author: Felicity, Trinidad: Musical Portrait of a Hindu Village, 1984, (with Bruno Nettl) Folk Music in the United States: An Introduction, 1976; author introductions to facsimile reprints of Alice Cunningham Fletcher's Omaha Indian Music, 1994, Indian Games and Dances,

1994, Native Songs, 1994, others; editor, contbr.: Ethnomusicology: An Introduction, 1992, Ethnomusicology: Historical and Regional Studies, 1993; gen. editor, contbr. South Asia Vol. VI, The Garland Ency. of World Music. Grantee Am. Inst. Indian Studies, 1986-87, 88-89, Brit. Acad., 1988-89, Ford Found., 1988, Am. Philosophical Soc., 1989-90, Wenner-Gren Found. for Anthropological Rsch., 1989-90. Mem. Am. Anthropol. Assn., Am. Musicological Soc., Soc. Ethnomusicology (coun. mem. 1992—), Assn. Asian Studies, Internat. Coun. Traditional Music, Indian Musicological Soc., Sangeet Natak Akademi, Earthwatch, English Folk Dance and Song Soc. (editorial bd. Polk Music Jour.), Phi Kappa Lambda. Home: 207 Old Main St Rocky Hill CT 06067-1505 Office: Trinity Coll Music Dept 300 Summit St Hartford CT 06106-3100 also: Grove Dictionaries, Macmillan Press, 4 Little Essex St, London WC2R 3LF, England

MYERS, HOWARD MILTON, pharmacologist, educator; b. Bklyn., Dec. 12, 1923; s. Charles and Rose (Nassberg) M.; m. Louise Perry, Mar. 14, 1972; children by previous marriage: Clifford Raymond, Nancy Rose, Stephen Andrew. D.D.S., Western Res. U., 1949; Ph.D., U. Rochester, 1958; M.A. (hon.), U. Pa., 1974; M.A., San Francisco State U., 1964. Prof. oral biology U. Calif., San Francisco, 1965-71; prof. biochemistry U. Pacific Sch. Dentistry, San Francisco, 1971-74; dir. Center for Oral Health Research, U. Pa., Phila., 1974-78; prof. pharmacology Sch. of Dental Medicine, 1974-86; dir. research/tchr. tng. grant U. Calif., San Francisco, 1965-71; prof. emeritus pharmacology U. Pa.; adj. prof. pharmacology U. Calif.-San Francisco Sch. Medicine, Calif. Coll. Podiatric Medicine; adj. prof. oral biology U. Calif.-San Francisco Sch. Dentistry, 1987-95; pharmacology cons. Nat. Bd. Podiatric Examiners, 1992-95; reviewer U.S.-Israel Binat. Sci. Found., 1982-95. Contbr. articles to profl. jours.; editor: Monographs in Oral Science, 1972-95. Served with U.S. Army, 1942-45. NIH fellow Karolinska Inst., Stockholm, 1964-65; Fogarty Sr. Internat. Research fellow U. Geneva, 1980-81. Mem. AAAS (chmn. sect. dentistry 1974), Am. Assn. Dental Research (pres. 1973-75), Council Biology Editors., Am. Chem. Soc. Home and Office: 3649 Market St Apt 601 San Francisco CA 94131-1307 *Intellectual maturity is the realization that there is more misinformation in the world than there is information.*

MYERS, IRA LEE, physician; b. Monrovia, Ala., Feb. 9, 1924; s. Ira W. and Azelea Juanita (Cobbs) M.; m. Dorothy Will Foust, Sept. 4, 1943; children: Martha Crystal, Ira Grady, Stephen Allen, Joanna Lynn. B.S., Howard Coll., Birmingham, Ala., 1945; M.D., U. Ala., 1949; postgrad., Harvard U. Sch. Public Health, 1953. Diplomate: Am. Bd. Preventive Medicine. Commd. officer USPHS, 1949-55; intern USPHS Marine Hosp., Seattle, 1949-50; epidemic intelligence officer Charleston, W.Va., 1950-52, Erie County Health Dept., Buffalo, 1952, Center Communicable Disease, Atlanta, 1952-55; resigned, 1955; adminstrv. health officer Ala. Dept. Health, Montgomery, 1955-63; state health officer Ala. Dept. Health, 1963-86; sec. Ala. Bd. Med. Examiners, 1962-73; chmn. Ala. Bd. Registration Sanitarians, 1964-81, Ala. Air Pollution Control Commn., 1969-82; v.p. Ala. Pollution Control Fin. Authority, 1971-81; assoc. clin. prof. preventive medicine and pub. health U. Ala. Med. Sch.; mem. Ala. vol. med. adv. com. SSS, 1968-86. Pres. Ala. div. Am. Cancer Soc., 1991-93; chmn. bd. dirs. Dalraida Health Ctr., 1992—. Recipient Ala. Sr. Citizens Hall of Fame Golden Eagle award, 1986, St. George medal Nat. Divisional award Am. Cancer Soc., 1989, 1st Ann. Vol. award Montgomery Bapt. Assn., 1993. Mem. AMA, Med. Assn. Ala. (William Henry Saunders award 1968, 1st annual Ira L. Myers Service award, 1986), Montgomery County Med. Soc., Ala. Pub. Health Assn. (D.G. Gill award 1967, established Ira L. Myers Scholarship Endowment), Am. Assn. Pub. Health Physicians, Assn. State and Territorial Health Officers (Arthur N. McCormick award 1976), Ala. Hosp. Assn. (hon.), State. Ala. Acad. Honor. Republican. Baptist. Lodge: Montgomery Kiwanis. Initiated state narcotic control program, 1967, state hosp. service for indigent, 1958. Home and Office: 925 Green Forest Dr Montgomery AL 36109-1515

MYERS, JACK DUANE, physician; b. New Brighton, Pa., May 24, 1913; s. Louis Albert and Esther Fern (McCabe) M.; m. Jessica Helen Lewis, Aug. 31, 1946; children: Judith (dec.), John, Jessica, Elizabeth, Margaret. AB, Stanford, 1933, MD, 1937. Residency tng. medicine Stanford U. Hosps., Peter Bent Brigham Hosp., Boston, 1937-42; asst. prof. medicine Emory U., 1946-47; from instr. to asso. prof. medicine Duke, 1947-55; prof. medicine, chmn. dept. U. Pitts., 1955-70, univ. prof., 1970-85, univ. prof. emeritus, 1985—; Sec.-treas. Am. Bd. Internal Medicine, 1964-67, chmn., 1967-70; chmn. Nat. Bd. Med. Examiners, 1971-75; chmn. gen. medicine study sect. Nat. Inst. Arthritis and Metabolic Diseases, 1963-65, research career program com., 1966-69, mem. nat. adv. council, 1970-74. Served from capt. to lt. col. M.C. AUS, 1942-46. Mem. Assn. Am. Physicians, Am. Physiol. Soc., Am. Soc. Clin. Investigation (sec. 1954-57), A.C.P. (regent 1971-78, pres. 1976-77), Inst. Medicine of Nat. Acad. Scis. Home: 220 N Dithridge St Pittsburgh PA 15213

MYERS, JACK EDGAR, biologist, educator; b. Boyds Mills, Pa., July 10, 1913; s. Garry Cleveland and Caroline (Clark) M.; m. Evelyn DeTurck, June 19, 1937; children: Shirley Ann, Jacqueline, Linda Caroline, Kathleen. BS, Juniata Coll., 1934, DSc, 1966; MS, Mont. State Coll., 1935; PhD, U. Minn., 1939. NRC fellow Smithsonian Instn., Washington, 1940-41; asst. prof. zoology U. Tex., 1941-45, assoc. prof., 1945-48, prof., 1948—, prof. botany, 1955—, prof. emeritus, 1980—. Author: (with F.A. Matsen and N.H. Hackerman) Premedical Physical Chemistry, 1947; sci. editor Highlights for Children, 1960—; contbg. author: Algal Culture: from Laboratory to Pilot Plant, 1953, proc. of the World Symposium on Applied Solar Energy, 1956; contbr. articles to profl. jours. Guggenheim fellow, 1959. Mem. Soc. Gen. Physiologists, Am. Soc. Plant Physiologists, Phycol. Soc., AAAS, Nat. Acad. Sci., Tex. Acad. Sci., Am. Soc. Photobiology (pres. 1975), Sigma Xi.

MYERS, JAMES CLARK, advertising and public relations executive; b. Chgo., Aug. 26, 1941; s. Herbert George Myers and Lenore (Goldberg) Levi; m. Judy Anne Schnitzer, Feb. 9, 1964; children: Jeffrey Stephan, Jeremy H. BA, Washington U., St. Louis, 1964. Acct. exec. Nahas, Blumberg, Zelikow, Houston, 1967-69; mgr. spl. events Houston Post, 1969-73; pres., creative dir. Motivators, Inc., Houston, 1973—; vice-chmn. Internat. Sci. and Engring. Fair Coun., Washington, 1972-73; bd. dirs. Sci. Engring. Fair of Houston, 1969-73; spl. corrs. Navy Times Newspaper. Contbr. articles to newspapers. Chmn. Boy Scouts Am., Houston Chpt. Served to capt. USNR, 1964—. Recipient Wood Badge award, Boy Scouts Am., 1979, Shofar award, 1981. Mem. Pub. Relations Soc. Am. (Silver Anvil award 1983, 87). Jewish. Avocations: model railroading, square dancing, photography. Home: 8006 Duffield Ln Houston TX 77071-2017 Office: Motivators Inc 7171 Harwin Dr Ste 206 Houston TX 77036-2119

MYERS, JAMES DAVID, municipal government official; b. Salt Lake City, Sept. 16, 1944; s. James William and Pauline (Winsor) M.; m. Carmen Kay Forsland, Mar. 28, 1979 (div.); stepchildren: James Christopher, Jesse Robin; m. Cleo Ester Evitt, Sept. 20, 1986; stepchild: Jennifer Michelle. Student, U. Calif., Berkeley, 1965; BSBA, Calif. State U., Chico, 1968; MPA, Golden Gate U., 1979. Mgr. Unishops, Inc. (Monte Mart), Del Rey Oaks, Calif., 1968-69; acct.-adminstrv. asst. City of Pacific Grove, 1969-79; gen. mgr. Monterey Regional Waste Mgmt. Dist., Marina, Calif., 1979—; dir., sec. Monterey Fed. Credit Union, 1979-91, vice chmn., 1986-87, chmn. supervisory com., 1976-87. Mem. Monterey County Integrated Waste Mgmt. Task Force, Salinas, Calif., 1979—, chmn. tech. com.; dir. Ecology Action of Monterey Peninsula, 1979-82, Milne Home, Residential Treatment Facility for Boys, Carmel Valley, Calif., 1985-87. Staff sgt. USAFR, 1966-72. Mem. Nat. Solid Waste Mgmt. Assn., Calif. Resource Recovery Assn., Solid Waste Assn. N.Am. (dir. No. Calif. chpt. 1988—, internat. landfill gas steering com. 1984-91, internat. conf. chmn. 1989, chpt. pres. 1992-93, legis. task force), Calif. Integrated Waste Mgmt. Bd. (local govt. adv. com. 1992—, chmn. 1996—), Commonwealth Club (San Francisco), Marines Meml. Club (San Francisco). Democrat. Avocations: bicycling, tennis, record collecting, numismatics. Office: Monterey Regional Waste PO Box 609 Marina CA 93933-0609

MYERS, JAMES NELSON, dean; b. Buffalo, Aug. 24, 1941; s. James N. and Frances M. (Lennon) M.; m. Victoria A. Montavon; children: James N., Molly P. Houghton, Elizabeth L. Makela. B.A., Canisius Coll., 1963; M.S., U. Ill., 1968; JD, Temple U., 1993. Tchr. Latin Lancaster Central Sch. Dist., N.Y., 1963-65; acquisitions-circulation librarian Canisius Coll., Buffalo, 1965-66; acquisitions librarian Oakland U., Rochester, Minn., 1968-70; assoc. dir. libraries Eastern Wash. State Coll., Cheney, 1970-74; asst. dir. libraries U. Ariz., Tucson, 1974-79; assoc. dir. libraries Stanford U., Calif., 1979-85; libr. Temple U., Phila., 1985-95; dean Temple Univ. Japan, Tokyo, 1995—. Co-editor: Disasters: Prevention & Coping, 1981; bd. of rev. Temple U. Press, 1987-89. Bd. dirs. Friends Free Libr. Phila., 1986-88; mem. libr. com. Balch Inst., 1993-95, Gov.'s Adv. Coun. on Libr., 1989-93; trustee Balch Inst., 1994-95. Office: Temple Univ Japan, 2 8 12 Minami Azabu, MinatoKu Tokyo 106, Japan

MYERS, JAMES R., lawyer; b. Valdosta, Ga., Aug. 29, 1952; s. J. Walter Jr. and Mary (Gallion) M.; m. Monica Faeth Myers, Sept. 19, 1992. BA cum laude, Harvard U., 1972, JD, 1975. Bar: Mass. 1975, U.S. Dist. Ct. (D.C. dist.) 1976, D.C. 1977, U.S. Ct. Appeals (D.C. cir.) 1977, U.S. Supreme Ct. 1983, U.S. Ct. Appeals (fed. cir.) 1991, Va. 1992, U.S. Ct. Appeals (4th cir.) 1992. Assoc. Wald, Harkrader & Ross, Washington, 1976-77; assoc. solicitor U.S. Dept. Energy, Washington, 1977-79; assoc. Andrews & Kurth, Washington, 1980-85; ptnr. Steele, Simmons & Fornaciari, Washington, 1985-86, Robbins & Laramie, Washington, 1986-89, Venable, Baetjer, Howard & Civiletti, Washington, 1990—. Author Jour. Space Law, 1984, Space Mfg., 1983. Office: Venable Baetjer Howard & Civiletti 1201 New York Ave NW Ste 1000 Washington DC 20005

MYERS, JESSE JEROME, lawyer, construction company executive; b. Anthony, Kans., Sept. 30, 1940; s. Claud Lewis and Lucille S. (Robertson) M.; m. Claire H. Conni, Nov., 1966; children: Timothy Todd, Jessica Joy. B.S., McPherson Coll., 1963; J.D., Washburn U., 1970. Bar: Kans. 1970, U.S. Dist. Ct. Kans. 1970. Law clk. U.S. Dist. Ct. Judge Frank Theis, Wichita, KS, 1970-72; individual practice law Wichita, KS, 1972-74; lawyer Cessna Aircraft Co., Wichita, KS, 1974-75; v.p., dir., gen. counsel Martin K. Eby Constrn. Co., Wichita, Kans., 1975-95; pvt. practice Wichita, 1995—. Served with USN, 1963-67. Mem. Am. Bar Assn., Kans. Bar Assn.

MYERS, JIM, church administrator. Chmn. of the bd. Division for Congregational Ministries of the Evangelical Lutheran Church in America, Chicago, Ill.

MYERS, JOHN HERMAN, investment management executive; b. Queens, N.Y., July 2, 1945; s. John Howard and Edna May (Strodthoff) M.; m. JoAnn Barbara Eikamp, Sept. 29, 1973; children: Jennifer Ann, David John, Christina Marie, Kimberly Grace. BS in Math., Wagner Coll., 1967. With GE, 1970—; fin. program trainee GE Internat. GE, N.Y.C. and Frankfurt, Fed. Republic Germany, 1970-74; fin. mgr. Compagnia Generale di Elettricita GE, Milan, 1974-77; fin. mgr. GE, Fairfield, Conn., 1977-81, dep. treas., 1981-84; group fin. mgr. GE, N.Y.C., 1984-86; exec. v.p. GE Investments GE, Stamford, Conn., 1986—; bd. dirs. Butler Capital Corp., N.Y.C., Doubletree Hotel Corp., Phoenix Grimes Aerospace Co., Columbus Hispaland S.A., Madrid, Spain. Bd. trustees Wagner Coll., 1993—. Lt. (j.g.) USN, 1967-70, Vietnam. Mem. Aspetuck Valley Country Club. Republican. Lutheran. Avocations: tennis, basketball, golf.

MYERS, JOHN JOSEPH, bishop; b. Ottawa, Ill., July 26, 1941; s. M.W. and Margaret Louise (Donahue) M. BA maxima cum laude, Loras Coll., 1963; Licentiate in Sacred Theology, Gregorian U., Rome, 1967; Doctor of Canon Law, Cath. U. Am., 1977; DD (hon.), Apostolic See, Vatican City, 1987. Ordained priest Roman Cath. Ch., 1966, bishop, 1987. Asst. pastor Holy Family Parish, Peoria, Ill., 1967-70; asst. dept. internat. affairs U.S. Cath. Conf., Washington, 1970-71; asst. pastor St. Matthew Parish, Champaign, Ill., 1971-74; vice chancellor Cath. Diocese Peoria, 1977-78, vocation dir., 1977-87, chancellor, 1978-87, vicar gen., 1982-90, co-adjutor bishop, 1987-90; bishop of Peoria, 1990—; bd. govs. Canon Law Soc. Am., Washington, 1985-87; bd. dirs. Pope John XXIII Ctr. for Med.-Moral Rsch. and Edn., Boston; mem. sem. com. Mt. St. Mary's Sem., Md., 1989—. Author: (commentary) Book V of the Code of Canon Law, 1983; contbr. numerous articles to religious publs. Mem. Canon Law Soc. Am., Nat. Conf. Cath. Bishops. Roman Catholic. Office: Cath Diocese Peoria PO Box 1406 607 NE Madison Ave Peoria IL 61603-3832*

MYERS, JOHN LYTLE, historian; b. Findlay, Ohio, June 13, 1929; s. Robert James and Doris Lucille (Lytle) M.; m. Ardene Harriet Muller, June 30, 1957; children: John Lytle II, Jennifer Lucile Myers Hathaway, Jeffrey Lawrence. BS in Edn., Bowling Green U., 1951; MA, U. Mich., 1954, PhD, 1961. Asst. to assoc. prof. Southeast Mo. State Coll., Cape Girardeau, 1957-64; assoc. prof., prof. SUNY, Plattsburgh, 1964—; chmn. faculty senate SUNY, Plattsburgh, 1968-70, 77, 86-88, dean social scis., 1970, acting asst. to pres., 1972. Pres. Clinton-Essex-Franklin Libr. System, Plattsburgh, 1981-84, bd. dirs., 1977-94; bd. dirs. Clinton County Hist. Assn., 1986—, pres., 1988-89; session Presbyn. Ch., Plattsburgh, 1966-69, 82-85, 87-89, 91-95, clk., 1983-85, 92-95. With U.S. Army, 1951-53. Rackham fellow U. Mich., 1956; SUNY fellow, 1965, 67; Penrose fellow Am. Philos. Soc., 1979. Mem. Orgn. Am. Historians, United Univ. Profls. (local pres. 1970), AAUP (local pres. 1963), Soc. Historians of Early Am. Reps. Home: 17 Newell Ave Plattsburgh NY 12901-6418 Office: SUNY Dept History Plattsburgh NY 12901

MYERS, JOHN THOMAS, congressman; b. Covington, Ind., Feb. 8, 1927; m. Carol Carruthers; children: Carol Ann, Lori Jan. B.S., Ind. State U., 1951. Cashier, trust officer Fountain Trust Co.; owner, operator farm; mem. 90th-104th Congresses from 7th Dist. Ind., 1967—; chmn. subcom. on energy & water, appropriations com. Served with AUS, World War II, ETO. Mem. Am. Legion, VFW, Wabash Valley Assn., Res. Officers Assn., C. of C., Sigma Pi. Republican. Episcopalian. Clubs: Mason, Elk, Lion. Office: US Ho of Reps 2372 Rayburn Bldg Washington DC 20515-0005*

MYERS, JOHN WESCOTT, aviation executive; b. L.A., June 13, 1911; s. Louis Wescott and Blanche (Brown) M.; m. Lucia Raymond, Mar. 21, 1941; children: Louis W., Lucia E. A.B., Stanford U., 1933; J.D., Harvard U., 1936. Bar: Calif. 1936. Ptnr. law firm O'Melveny & Myers, L.A., 1936-42; from test pilot to sr. v.p., dir. Northrop Corp., 1942-54, 1954-79; chmn. bd. Pacific Airmotive Corp., 1954-79, Airflite, Long Beach, Calif., 1970-89, Flying M Assocs., Long Beach, 1989—; owner Flying M Ranches, Merced, Calif., 1959—. Mem. Calif. Bar Assn., Los Angeles Bar Assn., Soc. Exptl. Test Pilots, Inst. Aerospace Scis. Republican. Clubs: Bohemian, California, Los Angeles Country, Los Angeles Yacht, Sunset, Aviation Country, Conquistadores del Cielo. Home: 718 N Rodeo Dr Beverly Hills CA 90210-3210 Office: 3200 Airflite Way Long Beach CA 90807-5312

MYERS, JOHN WILLIAM, minister, poet, editor, publisher; b. Huntington, W.Va., Dec. 1, 1919; s. Condon William and Mary Olive (Fox) M.; m. Nancy Hortense Paxton, July 6, 1942 (div. Feb. 22, 1961); children: Martha Ann, Lenora Ellen, Nancy Louise, John Charles; m. Helen Donna File, Nov. 28, 1981. BA, Ohio Wesleyan U., 1951; MA, Bowling Green State U., 1952; STD (hon.), Kletzing Coll. (name now Vannard Coll.), 1951. Ordained to ministry Meth. Ch., 1948, transferred to Unitarian Universalist Ch., 1954. Min. Meth. Ch., Stockport, Ohio, 1944-46, Bradner, Ohio, 1946-50; gen. evangelist Ohio Conf., Toledo, 1954-74; min. First Universalist Ch., Pataskala, Ohio, 1974-78, First Unitarian Universalist, Lyons, Ohio, 1978-81, Horton (Mich.) Universalist Ch., 1981-91; editor, pub. Humanist Edn. Press, Toledo, 1957—; ed.-at-large Dasein, the Quar. Rev., 1962-93. Author: (poetry) Evening Exercises, 1956, These Mown Dandelions, 1959, My Mind's Poor Birds, 1963, Alley to An Island, 1963, Green Are My Words, 1964 (nominated for a Pulitzer prize 1964), Sun Bands and Other Poems, 1964, Anatomy of a Feeling, 1966, Variations on a Nightingale, 1968, A Greene County Ballad, 1979, Annotations, 1951, 82, The Sky is Forever, 1986, Something Will Be Mine, 1991; editor Ohio Poetry Soc. Bull., 1957-59, Ohio Poetry Rev., 1957-59, Poetry Dial, 1959; poetry editor The Humanist, 1958-59. Promoter Fulton County Dem. Com., Wauseon, Ohio, 1978—, Lyons-Royanton United Fund. Recipient London Lit. Cir. citation for Achievement in Poetry, Ohio Ho. of Reps., 1993. Mem. Am. Acad. Poets, Poetry Soc. Am., Ohio Poetry Soc. (editor 1958-93), Masons (lodge edn. officer 1979-93, chaplain Lyons chpt. 1980-91), Beta Theta Pi. Avocations: cooking, walking, reading philosophy. Home: 105 Fulton St Lyons OH 43533-0105 Office: Humanist Edn Press Inc 109 N Adrian St Lyons OH 43533

MYERS, KATHERINE DONNA, writer, publisher; b. L.A., Nov. 10, 1925; d. John Allen Myers and Eulah Caldwell (Myers) Harris; m. Thomas Miller, Feb. 2, 1944 (div. 1963); children: Kathleen JoAnn Content, David Thomas. Teaching credential in bus. edn., U. So. Calif., L.A., 1975; postgrad., Loyola U., Paris, 1980. Cert. pub. adminstr. Dep. field assessor L.A. County Tax Assessor, L.A., 1944-60; sec. L.A. Unified Sch. Dist., 1960-70; br. sec. bank Crocker Nat. Bank, L.A., 1970-78; instr. legal sec. Southland Coll., L.A., 1975-78; exec. sec. ABC, L.A., 1978-89; v.p. spl. projects Glendale (Calif.) TV Studios, 1990-92; writer, publisher Eagles Wings Publishing Co., L.A., 1992—; owner, pres. Success Secretarial Seminar, L.A., 1980-84; pub., author Eagle's Wings Pub. Co., L.A., 1992—; wedding cons., counselor Crenshaw United Meth. Ch., L.A., 1993—. Author, pub.: Wedding Bells, A New Peal, 1994; (instrnl. book) Productivity Guide, Bilingual Special Education, 1980; (biography) The Eagle Flies on Friday, 1988, (hist. newsletter) Eagle Reader's Newsletter, 1993; author: (tech. booklet) Ronnie Knows about Sickle Cell, 1973 (Founder's award 1973). Troop leader, adminstr. Girl Scouts Am., L.A., 1956; chmn. sickle cell com. MLK Hosp. Guild, L.A., 1974; den mother Boy Scouts Am., 1960; lifetime mem. PTA, L.A., 1960. Recipient THANKS badge Girl Scouts Am., 1959, Founder's award MLK Jr. Hosp. Guild, 1974. Mem. Photo Friends Ctrl. Libr., Wilshire C. of C. (bd. dirs. 1980). Democrat. United Methodist. Avocations: health walking, supporting illiteracy programs, short story writing. Home: # 122 4215 W Slauson Ave Apt 122 Los Angeles CA 90043-2831 Office: Eagles Wings Publishing Co PO Box 361263 5350 Wilshire Blvd Los Angeles CA 90036

MYERS, KENNETH ELLIS, hospital administrator; b. Battle Creek, Mich., Jan. 1, 1932; s. Orlow J. and Kathryn (Brown) M.; m. Nancy Lee Lindgren, June 9, 1956; children—Cynthia Lynn, Anne Lisa, Thomas Scot, Susan Elaine. BBA, U. Mich., 1956, MBA, 1957. Research analyst Bur. Bus. Research, U. Mich., 1956-57; in financial mgmt. Burroughs Corp., Detroit, 1957-66; controller William Beaumont Hosp., Royal Oak, Mich., 1966-68; assoc. dir. William Beaumont Hosp., 1968-69, hosp. dir., 1969-80, exec. v.p., 1976-80, pres., 1981—; pres. Trinity Loss Prevention Systems, 1980-81; bd. dirs. Chateau Properties, Inc. Elder Bloomfield Hills Christian Ch., 1979-82, Grace Chapel, 1988-92, 95—; bd. visitors Oakland Sch. Bus. Adminstrn., 1978-92; adv. bd. Salvation Army, 1985—; bd. dirs. William Tyndale Coll., 1992—, West Bloomfield Bldg. Authority, 1978—; trustee St. Mary's Hosp., 1992—. Mem. Mich. Hosp. Assn. (past chmn.), Vol. Hosps. Am. Enterprises (bd. dirs. 1984-87), Full Gospel Businessmen's Fellowship, Bloomfield Hills Country Club, Old Club, Phi Delta Theta, Beta Gamma Sigma. Home: 5085 Lakebluff Rd West Bloomfield MI 48323-2430 Office: William Beaumont Hosp Corp 3601 W 13 Mile Rd Royal Oak MI 48073-6712

MYERS, KENNETH L(EROY), secondary education educator; b. Auburn, Nebr., Oct. 5, 1954; s. Kenneth E. and Erma F. (Hardwick) M.; m. Willo Kay Dykstra, July 1, 1995. BS in Edn., Peru State Coll., 1985, mid. sch. endorsement, 1990, MS in Edn., 1992. Cert. tchr., Nebr., Mo., S.D. Tchr. math., coach Nodaway-Holt High Sch., Graham, Mo., 1985-87, Nebraska City (Nebr.) Lourdes High Sch., 1987-89; tchr. math., social studies, coach Newcastle (Nebr.) High Sch., 1989—; chair Newcastle Math. Curriculum Team, 1991—; master tchr. N.E. Nebr. Masters Tchrs. Project, 1991—; mem. N.E. Nebr. Math. Cadre. Mem. NEA, ASCD, Nat. Coun. Tchrs. Math., Nebr. Assn. Tchrs. Math., Nebr. Coaches Assn., Nebr. State Edn. Assn., Newcastle Faculty Orgn. (pres. 1992-95). Office: Newcastle Pub Schs PO Box 187 Newcastle NE 68757-0187

MYERS, KENNETH M., lawyer; b. Miami, Fla., Mar. 11, 1933; s. Stanley C. and Martha (Scheinberg) M.; div. 1973. AB, U. N.C., 1954; JD, U. Fla., 1957. Bar: Sept. 1957, Colo. 1986, N.Y. 1987. Ptnr. Myers, Kenin Levinson & Richards, Miami, 1957-87, Shea & Gould, N.Y.C., 1987-88, Squire, Sanders & Dempsey, Miami, 1988—; mem. Fla. Ho. Reps., 1965-69, mem. Fla. Senate, 1969-80. Trustee U. Miami, 1985—. Mem. ABA, Fla. Bar Assn., Colo. Bar Assn., N.Y. State Bar Assn., Am. Law Inst., Nat. Assn. Bond Lawyers, Dade County Bar Assn., Greater Miami C. of C. (bd. govs.). Democrat. Jewish. Office: Squire Sanders & Dempsey 2900 Miami Ctr 201 S Biscayne Blvd Miami FL 33131-4332

MYERS, KENNETH RAYMOND, lawyer; b. N.Y.C., Apr. 14, 1939; s. Cyril Burleigh and Dorothy (Podolyn) M.; m. Susan Kay Plotnick, Sept. 9, 1962; children: Lisa R., Jonathan S., Andrew C. SB, MIT, 1960; JD, Harvard U., 1963. Bar: Ill. 1963, Pa. 1968. Assoc. Ross, Hardies & O'Keefe, Chgo., 1963-68; assoc. Morgan, Lewis & Bockius, Phila., 1968-71, ptnr., 1972—; mem. rules com. Environ. Hearing Bd., Harrisburg, Pa., 1984-89. Editor: Environmental Spill Reporting Handbook, 1992; contbg. author: Environmental Law Practice Guide, 1992; contbr. articles to profl. jours. Mem. exec. com. Water Resources Assn. Del. River Basin, Valley Forge, Pa., 1975—, Am. Jewish Congress, Phila., 1987—, mem. nat. comm., N.Y.C., 1984—, v.p., 1991—. Mem. ABA (rep. to U.S. Office Personnel Mgmt. 1975—), Pa. Bar Assn., Phila. Bar Assn., Fed. Energy Bar Assn., Eta Kappa Nu. Office: Morgan Lewis & Bockius 2000 One Logan Sq Philadelphia PA 19103*

MYERS, LAWRENCE STANLEY, JR., radiation biologist; b. Memphis, Apr. 29, 1919; s. Lawrence Stanley and Jane Myers; m. Janet Vanderwalker, June 13, 1942; children: David Lee, Frederick Lawrence, Lee Scott. BS, U. Chgo., 1941, PhD, 1949. Jr. chemist Metall. Lab. of Manhattan Engring. Dist., U. Chgo., 1942-44; asst. chemist Clinton Labs. of Manhattan Engring. Dist., Oak Ridge, Tenn., 1944-46; chemist Inst. for Nuclear Studies, U. Chgo., 1947-48; assoc. chemist Argonne (Ill.) Nat. Lab., 1948-52; asst. prof. radiology UCLA, 1953-70, assoc. rsch. phys. chemist Atomic Energy project, 1952-59, lectr. in radiol. scis., 1970-76, adj. prof. radiol. scis., 1976-82; rsch. radiobiologist, chief radiobiology div. UCLA Lab. Nuclear Medicine and Radiation Biology, 1959-76; prof. radiology and nuclear medicine Uniformed Svcs. Univ. of Health Scis., 1982-88; sci. advisor Armed Forces Radiobiology Rsch. Inst., 1982-87; cons. Oak Ridge Assoc. Univs., 1987-94; vis. scientist AFRRI, 1987-93; adj. biophysicist Radiation Biology Br. Nat. Cancer Inst. NIH, 1993—; co-organizer UCLA Internat. Conf. on Radiation Biology, 1957, 59; participant in three major Fed. Govt. planning exercises related to energy rsch. and devel. in U.S., 1973-74; mem. adv. com. Ctr. for Fast Kinetic Rsch. U. Tex., Austin, 1975-81, chmn., 1977-81; mem. adv. bd. Radiation Chemistry Data Ctr., U. Notre Dame, 1976-84, sec. 1979-81, chmn. 1981-83; chmn. Long Range Planning Com., Radiation Rsch. Soc., 1976-78; dir. Issues and Requirements Workshop for Analysis of the 1976 "Inventory of Fed. Energy Related Environ. and Safety Rsch.", 1977. Contbr. more than 100 sci. articles and abstracts to profl. jours. Com. mem. Boy Scouts of Am., Pacific Palisades and Malibu, Calif., 1956-67. Fellow AAAS; mem. Radiation Rsch. Soc., Biophys. Soc., N.Y. Acad. Sci., Am. Inst. Biol. Scis., Am. Soc. for Photobiology, Soc. for Free Radical Rsch., European Soc. for Photobiology, Sigma Xi. Home: 11810 Coldstream Dr Potomac MD 20854-3612 Office: NIH Nat Cancer Inst Radiation Biology Br Bethesda MD 20892-1002

MYERS, LONN WILLIAM, lawyer; b. Rockford, Ill., Nov. 14, 1946; s. William H. and Leona V. (Janvrin) M.; m. Janet L. Forbes, May 14, 1968; children: Andrew, Hillary, Corwin. BA, Mich. State U., 1968; MBA, Ind. U., 1973; JD, Harvard U., 1976. Bar: Ill. 1976, U.S. Ct. of Fed. Claims 1977, U.S. Tax Ct. 1977, U.S. Ct. Appeals (7th cir.) 1977. Ptnr. McDermott, Will & Emery, Chgo., 1976—. Served to maj. USAR, 1968-80. Mem. ABA (chair intangibles com. of capital recovery and leasing com. tax sect. 1994—), Union League Club (Chgo.). Episcopalian. Home: 1711 Highland Ter Glenview IL 60025-2284 Office: McDermott Will & Emery 227 W Monroe St Chicago IL 60606-5016

MYERS, MALCOLM HAYNIE, artist, art educator; b. Lucerne, Mo., June 19, 1917; s. Clyde Emmet and Kathleen M.; m. Roberta Bernice King, May 6. B.F.A., Wichita State U., 1940; M.A., U. Iowa, 1941, M.F.A., 1946. Instr. U. Iowa, 1946-48; prof. art U. Minn., Mpls., 1948—; chmn. dept. art U. Minn., 1957-61. Retrospective print exhbns. include Mr. Possum and Friends, Univ. Art Mus., U. Minn., 1983; traveling exhbn. Worcester (Mass.) Art Mus., 1990-91, The Katherine Nash Gallery, U. Minn., 1996; paintings also exhibited at Amon Carter Mus., Fort Worth and Nelson-Atkins Mus. Art, Kansas City, Mo.; one-man shows include Dolly Fiterman Gallery, Mpls., 1983, 85, 87; represented in permanent collections Bibliotheque Nationale, Paris, Libr of Congress, Washington, L.A. County Art Mus., Mpls.

Inst. Art, St. Louis Art Mus., Seattle Art Mus., Walker Art Ctr., Mpls., Phoenix Art Mus., Am. Embassy, Bonn, Germany, Mus. Am. Art, Smithsonian Instn., Ulrich Art Mus., Wichita, Wichita Art Mus., Fredrick Weiseman Mus., Mpls., Mpls. Art Inst.; contbr. art and articles to book, Am. Prints and Printmakers (Una Johnson). Served with U.S. Mcht. Marines, 1943-45. Recipient Alumni Achievement award Wichita State U., 1973; John Simon Guggenheim fellow Paris, 1950; Guggenheim fellow Mexico City, 1954; trustee Minn. Mus. Art, St. Paul, 1975-78. Mem. Alumni Club U. Minn., Artist Equity (past pres.), Mid-Am. Coll. Art Assn. (past pres.). Presbyterian. Home: 1715 James Ave S Minneapolis MN 55403-2826 Office: U Minn Studio Arts Dept Minneapolis MN 55455

MYERS, MARGARET JANE (DEE DEE MYERS), television personality, editor; b. Quonset Pt., R.I., Sept. 1, 1961; d. Stephen George and Judith Ann (Burleigh) M. BS, U. Santa Clara, 1983. Press asst. Mondale for Pres., L.A., 1984; deputy Senator Art Torres, L.A., 1985; dep. press sec. to press sec. Mayor Tom Bradley, L.A., 1985-87; deputy press sec. Tom Bradley For Gov., L.A., 1986; Calif. press sec. Dukakis for Pres., L.A., 1988; press sec. Feinstein for Gov., L.A. and San Francisco, 1989-90; campaign dir. Jordan for Mayor, San Francisco, 1991; comm. cons. DeeDee Myers Assocs., Valencia, Calif., 1991; press sec. Clinton for Pres., Little Rock, 1991-92, White House, Washington, 1993-94; co-host Equal Time, CNBC, Washington, 1995—; mag. editor Vanity Fair, Washington, 1995—. Recipient Robert F. Kennedy award Emerson Coll., Boston, 1993. Democrat. Roman Catholic. Avocations: running, cycling, music, major league baseball. Office: CNBC 1233 20th St NW Ste 302 Washington DC 20036

MYERS, MARJORIE LORA, educational administrator; b. Waco, Tex., Jan. 12, 1950; d. Duncan Clark and Dorothy (Love) M.; m. Larry Lee Brannon, Dec. 19, 1975 (div. 1979). BA in Edn. and Spanish, U. Fla., 1972; MA in Bilingual and Multicultural Edn., George Mason U., 1985; postgrad., Georgetown U., 1986-88. Cert. bilingual tchr., pub. sch. adminstrn., D.C. Lead tchr. Rock Springs Multicultural Adult Edn. Ctr., Atlanta, 1977-81; composite K-12 tchr., adminstr. Bechtel Corp., Andes Mountains, Siberia, Venezuela, 1981-83; rsch. asst. NSF, Washington, 1983-84; bilingual and ESL tchr. Lincoln Jr. H.S., Washington, 1984-88; bilingual counselor Deal Jr. H.S., Washington, 1988-89; Leadership in Ednl. Adminstrn. Devel. participant Francis Jr. H.S., Washington, 1989-90; coord. programs and instrn. lang. minority affairs D.C. Pub. Schs., Washington, 1990-93; asst. prin. Cardozo Sr. H.S., Washington, 1993-94; prin. H.D. Cooke Elem. Sch., Washington, 1994-95; prin. Key Spanish Immersion Sch., Arlington (Va.) Pub. Schs., 1995—; mem. adv. bd. Ctr. for Immigration Policy & Refugee Assistance, Georgetown U., Washington, 1986-88; adj. prof. George Washington U., 1991, George Mason U., 1992-94, Marymount U., summer 1995. Mem. ASCD, TESOL, Nat. Assn. Bilingual Educators. Republican. Episcopalian. Avocations: tennis, hunting, biking, horseback riding, skiing. Home: 1840 California St NW Washington DC 20009 Office: Key Spanish Immersion Sch 2300 Key Blvd Arlington VA 22201

MYERS, MARY CATHERINE, geriatrics nurse, medical surgery nurse, mental health nurse; b. Marion, Ohio, June 3, 1942; d. Clarence Roy and Josephine Rita (Irvin) Anderson; m. Stephen J. Myers, June 13, 1964 (div. Apr. 1973); children: Stephen, Kevin, Eric, Ivan. Diploma, St. Joseph Sch. Nursing Purdue U., 1963; student, Northwestern Community Jr. Coll., 1974-79; BSN, Marian Coll., Indpls., 1988; postgrad., Ball State U. Cert. CPR, BLS. Mem. pediatric, med./surg. staff Marion Gen. Hosp.; staff pediatric, ICU Sinai Hosp., Detroit; pediatric staff Munson Med. Ctr., Traverse County, Mich.; admission children's units, devel., supervision Traverse County Regional Psychiatric Hosp.; psychiatric staff, cardiac unit Borgress Hosp., Kalamazoo, Mich.; psychiatric nurse counselor, cons. for pvt. physician Kokomo, Ind.; staff nurse St. Vincents Stress Ctr., Indpls.; agy. nurse Favorite Nurses; float staff Birchwood Nursing Home Traverse City; mem. psychiat. staff, admission unit VA Med. Ctr. Vol. ARC. Fellow Ball State U. Mem. Grand Traverse County Nurses (pres. 1979). Home: 226 Wenonah St Traverse City MI 49686-3054

MYERS, MARY KATHLEEN, publishing executive; b. Cedar Rapids, Iowa, Aug. 19, 1945; d. Joseph Bernard and Marjorie Helen (Huntsman) Weaver; m. David F. Myers, Dec. 30, 1967; children: Mindy, James. BA in English and Psychology, U. Iowa, 1967. Tchr. Lincoln H.S., Des Moines, 1967-80; editor Perfection Learning Corp., Des Moines, 1980-87, v.p., editor-in-chief, 1987-93; pres., founding ptnr. orgn. to promote Edward de Bono Advanced Practical Thinking Tng., Des Moines, 1992—. Editor: Retold Classics, 1988-91, (ednl. program) Six Thinking Hats, 1991, Lateral Thinking, 1993; originator numerous other ednl. products and programs. Mem. Gov.'s Commn. to Enhance Ednl. Leadership Iowa, Dept. of Edn., 1991-93. Mem. ASTD, Am. Soc. Quality Control, Assn. for Quality and Participation. Home: 4315 Urbandale Ave Des Moines IA 50310-3460 Office: APTT 10520 New York Ave Des Moines IA 50322-3775

MYERS, MICHELE TOLELA, university president; b. Rabat, Morocco, Sept. 25, 1941; came to U.S., 1964; d. Albert and Lilie (Abecassis) Tolela; m. Pierre Vajda, Sept. 12, 1962 (div. Jan. 1965); m. Gail E. Myers, Dec. 20, 1968; children: Erika, David. Diploma, Inst. Polit. Studies, U. Paris, 1962; MA, U. Denver, 1966, PhD, 1967; MA, Trinity U., 1977; LHD, Wittenberg U., 1994. Asst. prof. speech Manchester Coll., North Manchester, Ind., 1967-68; asst. prof. speech and sociology Monticello Coll., Godfrey, Ill., 1968-71; asst. prof. communication Trinity U., San Antonio, 1975-80, assoc. prof., 1980-86, asst. v.p. for acad. affairs, 1982-85, assoc. v.p., 1985-86; assoc. prof. sociology, dean Undergrad. Coll. Bryn Mawr (Pa.) Coll., 1986-89; pres. Denison U., Granville, Ohio, 1989—; comm. analyst Psychology and Commn., San Antonio, 1974-83; bd. dirs. Am. Coun. on Edn., chair elect. Nat. Assn. Ind. Colls. and Univs., Sherman Fairchild Found.; mem. Fed. Res. Bank of Cleve., 1995—; pres.'s commn. Na. Collegiate Athletic Assn., 1993—. Author: (with Gail Myers) The Dynamics of Human Communication, 1973, 6th and internat. edits., 1992, transl. into French, 1984, Communicating When We Speak, 1975, 2d edit., 1978, Communication for the Urban Professional, 1977, Managing by Communication: An Organizational Approach, 1982, transl. into Spanish, 1983, internat. edit., 1982. Trustee Phila. Child Guidance Clinic, 1988-89; trustee assoc. The Bryn Mawr Sch., Balt., 1987-89; v.p., bd. dirs. San Antonio Cmty. Guidance Ctr., 1979-83. Am. Coun. Edn. fellow in acad. adminstrn., 1981-82, Bank One Columbus, 1990-94. Mem. Am. Coun. Edn. (commn. on women in higher edn. 1990-92, bd. dirs. 1993—, chmn.-elect 1996—). Home: 204 Broadway W Granville OH 43023-1120 Office: Denison U Office of the President Granville OH 43023

MYERS, MIKE, actor, writer; b. Toronto, Ont., Can., May 25, 1963; s. Eric and Bunny (Hind) M.; m. Robin Ruzan, 1993. Stage appearences: The Second City, Toronto, 1986-88, Chgo., 1988-89; actor, writer: Mullarkey & Myers, Can., 1984-86, (TV show) Saturday Night Live, 1989-94 (Emmy award for outstanding writing in a comedy or variety series 1989), (film) Wayne's World, 1992, So I Married an Axe Murderer, 1993, Wayne's World II, 1993; actor: (TV movie) John and Yoko, 1985. *

MYERS, MILES A., educational association administrator; b. Newton, Kans., Feb. 4, 1931; s. Alvin F. and Katheryn P. (Miles) M.; m. Celeste Myers; children: Royce, Brant, Roslyn. BA in Rhetoric, U. Calif., Berkeley, 1953, MAT in English, 1979, MA in English, 1982, PhD in Lang. and Literacy, 1982. Cert. secondary tchr. English, vocat. tchr., adminstrn. Tchr. English Washington Union High Sch., Fremont, Calif., 1957-59, Oakland (Calif.) High Sch., 1959-67, 69-74, Concord High Sch., Mt. Diablo, Calif., 1967-69; sec. Alpha Plus Corp., Piedmont, Calif., 1968—; tchr. English Castlemont High Sch., Oakland, 1975-76; mem. faculty U. Calif., Berkeley, 1965-76, 84-85; exec. dir. Nat. Coun. Tchrs. of English, Urbana, Ill., 1989—; co-dir. Bay Area writing project Sch. of Edn., Berkeley, 1976-82; adminstrv. dir. nat. writing project sch. edn. U. Calif., Berkeley, 1979-85; adj. prof. English U. Ill., Champaign-Urbana, 1991—; vis. lectr. U. Okla., U. So. Calif., Calif. State U. at Northridge, U. Calif. at Irvine, U. Calif. at Santa Barbara, San Francisco State U., Mills Coll., U. Calgary, U. of the Pacific; tchr. English for adult night sch. Washington Union High, 1958-59, Oakland High Sch., 1959-61, 63-66; cons., lectr. and rschr. in field. Author: The Meaning of Literature, 1973; co-author: Writing: Unit Lessons in Composition, Book III, 1965, The English Book-Composition Skills, 1980; author (with others) Men and Societies, 1968, Teacher as Learner, 1985, The Teaching of Writing, 1986; editor Calif. Tchr., 1966-75, 1981—; contbr. articles to profl. jours.; pub. monographs. Sgt. U.S. Army, 1953-56. Recipient cert. of Merit, Ctrl. Calif. Coun. Tchrs. of English, 1969, commendation, 1970, First Place award Internat. Labor Assn., 1971. Fellow Nat. Conf. Rsch. in English; mem. Nat. Coun. Tchrs. of English, Nat. Conf. on Rsch. in English, Am. Fedn. of Tchrs. (legis. dir. Calif. Fedn. of Tchrs. 1971-72, pres. 1983-85, 90, Union Tchr. Press awards 1969-75, 86, 87, 89, Ben Rust award Calif. Fedn. of Tchrs. 1994), Am. Edn. Rsch. Assn., Calif. Assn. Tchrs. of English (Disting. Svc. award 1984, 86), Calif. Reading Assn., Internat. Reading Assn., Assn. Childhood Edn., Secondary Tchrs. Assn. of Reading of the East Bay, English 300 Soc., U. Calif./Berkeley Alumni Assn., Phi Delta Kappa. Home: 137 Lake Rd Seymour IL 61875-9600 Office: Nat Coun Tchrs English 1111 W Kenyon Rd Urbana IL 61801-1010

MYERS, MINOR, JR., academic administrator, political science educator; b. Akron, Ohio, Aug. 13, 1942; s. Minor and Ruth (Libby) M.; m. Ellen Achin, Mar. 21, 1970; children—Minor III, Joffre V.A. B.A., Carleton Coll., Northfield, Minn., 1964; M.A., Princeton U., 1967, Ph.D., 1972. From instr. to assoc. prof. Conn. Coll., New London, 1968-81, prof. govt., 1981-84; provost, dean of faculty, prof. polit. sci. Hobart and William Smith Colls., Geneva, N.Y., 1984-89; pres., prof. polit. sci. Ill. Wesleyan U., Bloomington, 1989—; adv. Numismatic Collection Yale U., 1975-84; chmn. adv. coun. Lyman Allyn Mus., 1976-81, 82-84, pres., 1982-84. Author: Liberty Without Anarchy: A History of the Society of the Cincinnati, 1983; (with others) New London County Furniture, 1974, (with others) The Princeton Graduate School: A History, 1978, (with others) American Interiors: A Documentary History from the Colonial Era to 1915, 1980. Asst. sec. gen. Soc. of the Cin., 1983-86, sec.-gen., 1986-89; trustee Inst. for European Study, 1992—. Mem. Princeton Club (N.Y.C.), University (Chgo.). Office: Ill Wesleyan U PO Box 2900 Bloomington IL 61702-2900

MYERS, MOREY MAYER, lawyer; b. Scranton, Pa., Aug. 5, 1927; s. Samuel Z. and Libbye (Kaplan) M.; m. Sondra Gelb, Nov. 25, 1956; children: Jonathan S., David N. AB, Syracuse U., 1949; LLB, Yale U., 1952. Bar: Pa. 1953, U.S. Dist.Ct. (mid. dist.) Pa. 1953, U.S. Ct. Appeals (3rd cir.) 1958, U.S. Supreme Ct. 1960, U.S. Dist. Ct. (ea. dist.) Pa. 1981, U.S. Dist. Ct. (we. dist.) Pa. 1988. Asst. solicitor City of Scranton, Pa., 1957-61; asst. atty. gen. Commonwealth of Pa., Harrisburg, 1962-63, chief coun. milk control comn., 1962-63; mng. ptnr. Gelb, Myers, Bishop & Warren, Scranton, 1982-85; sr. ptnr. Hourigan, Kluger, Spohrer, Quinn & Myers, 1985-87; chief coun. Commonwealth of Pa., Harrisburg, 1987-89; ptnr. Schnader, Harrison, Segal & Lewis, Scranton, 1990-95, Myers, Brier & Kelly, Scranton, 1995—; vis. lectr. Hamilton Coll., Clinton, N.Y., 1982-84, Yale U., 1986, 89, 91, 95, Haverford (Pa.) Coll., 1990; chief counsel Gov. of Pa., Harrisburg, 1987-89. Contbr. articles to profl. jours. with USN, 1945-46. Fellow Am. Bar Found.; mem. Nat. Conf. Commrs. Uniform State Laws (commr.). Office: Myers Brier & Kelly 108 N Washington Ave Scranton PA 18503-1818

MYERS, NORMAN ALLAN, marketing professional; b. Beeville, Tex., Dec. 10, 1935; s. Floyd Charles and Ruby (Lee) Myers; m. Suzanne Carlile, Oct. 11, 1935; children: Lisa Leigh Myers Nowlin, Matthew Scott. BS in Banking and Fin., Okla. State U., 1958. Salesman Jones and Laughlin Steel Corp., Houston, 1958-64; agt. Acacia Mutual Life Ins., Houston, 1964-69; with Browning-Ferris Industries, Houston, 1969—, exec. v.p., 1976-81, chief mktg. officer, 1981—, vice chmn., 1982—; also bd. dirs. Bd. dirs. My Friends-A Neuenschwander Found. for Children in Crisis. 2d lt. U.S. Army, 1958-59. Named to Okla. State Univ. Coll. of Bus. Adminstrn. Hall of Fame, 1996. Mem. Lakeside Country Club, Hills of Lakeway Club, Barton Creek Lakeside Country Club, Shriners, Holland. Republican. Avocation: golf. Office: Browning-Ferris Ind Inc 757 N Eldridge Pky Houston TX 77079-4435

MYERS, ORIE EUGENE, JR., university official; b. Hagan, Ga., Oct. 14, 1920; s. Orie Eugene and Betty (Shuman) M.; m. Margaret Elizabeth Nesbit, June 7, 1941; children: Orie Eugene III, Curtis Alan, Adrian Marvyn. Student, Ga. Inst. Tech., 1937-38; A.B., Emory U., 1941, M.A., 1957. Personnel asst. Atlanta Personnel Bd., 1940-41; personnel officer Nat. Youth Adminstrn., 1941-43, Office Emergency Mgmt., 1943-44, VA, 1946-48; dir. personnel Emory U., 1948-61, bus. mgr., 1961, dean adminstrn., dir. health services, 1961-64, v.p. bus., 1973-89, sr. bus. analyst, 1989-91; v.p. bus., dir. Woodruff Med. Center, 1964-73; past chmn. bd. Prime Bancshares, Inc., Prime Bank FSB. Trustee, chmn. med. com. Wesley Homes; bd. dirs., past chmn. DeKalb County unit Am. Cancer Soc. Served to 1st lt. USAAF, 1944-46. Mem. Coll. and Univ. Personnel Assn. (past pres.), Nat. Assn. Coll. and Univ. Bus. Officers (past pres.), So. Assn. Coll. and Univ. Bus. Officers (past pres.), DeKalb C. of C. (past pres.), Sigma Nu. Democrat. Baptist. Home: 236 Mt Vernon Dr Decatur GA 30030-1607

MYERS, PHILLIP FENTON, financial services and technology company executive; b. Cleve., June 24, 1935; s. Max I. and Rebecca (Rosenbloom) M.; m. Hope Gail Strum, Aug. 13, 1961. B in Indsl. Engring., Ohio State U., 1958, MBA, 1960; D in Bus. Adminstrn., Harvard U., 1966. Staff indsl. engr. Procter & Gamble Co., Cin., 1958; sr. cons. Cresap, McCormack & Paget, N.Y.C., 1960-61; staff assoc. Mitre Corp., Bedford, Mass., 1961; cons. Sys. Devel. Corp., Santa Monica, Calif., 1963-64; dir. long range planning Electronic Specialty Co., Los Angeles, 1966-68; chmn. Atek Industries, 1968-72; pres. Myers Fin. Corp., 1973-82; chmn. Amvid Comm. Svcs., Inc., 1975-79, Omni Resources Devel. Corp., 1979-83; chmn., pres. Am. Internat. Mining Co., Inc., 1979-83; pres. Advent Internat. Mgmt. Co., Inc., 1982—; chmn. Global Bond Mktg. Svcs., Inc., 1987-90; pres., CEO Whitehall Container Mfg. Corp., 1988-91; pres. Whitehall Motors Co., 1989—, Allied Metamatter Tech. Corp., 1994—; chmn U.S. Water Resources, Inc., 1994—; pres. Am. Tech. Venture Fund Mgmt., Inc., Advent Internat. Realty Corp., 1996—; pres. Turbogon, Inc., 1995—, pres. Advent Internat. Realty Corp., 1996—, pres. First Internet Capital Corp., 1996—; founding dir. Warner Ctr. Bank, 1980-83; lectr. bus. adminstrn. U. So. Calif., L.A., 1967-74; prof. Grad. Sch. Bus. Adminstrn. Pepperdine U., 1974-81. Trustee, treas. Chamber Symphony Soc. Calif., 1971-78; pub. safety commr. City of Hidden Hills, Calif., 1977-83, chmn., 1982-83; co-chmn. budget adv. com. Las Virgenes Sch. Dist., 1983-86; mem. Mayor's Blue Ribbon Fin. Com., 1981-82; mem. dean's select adv. com. Coll. Engring., Ohio State U., 1984-94; mem. state exec. com. Calif. Libertarian Party, chmn. region 61, 1989-90, chmn. strategic planning com.; dep. chmn. Los Angeles County Libertarian Party, 1991-92; chairperson campaign sisues com. Marrou for Pres., 1991-92; chmn. bd. trustees WWII Hist. Soc., 1992—. Capt. USAF, 1958-60. Ford Found. fellow, 1961-64. Mem. Harvard Bus. Sch. Assn., Ohio State Alumni Assn., Harvard Club (bd. dirs. 1970-74, treas. 1971-73); pres. Harvard Bus. Sch. Club Columbus, 1996—; dir. Ohio State Alumni Club Franklin County, 1996—. Office: 682 Laurel Ridge Dr Gahanna OH 43230-2196 *Personal philosophy: All out all the time. I stand for the creation of a new system of global governance which stresses individual liberty, freedom and responsibility, and which leads to a world that works for everyone with no one left out. In business, I stand for exceptional vision, creativity, innovation, and success.*

MYERS, PHILLIP SAMUEL, mechanical engineering educator; b. Webber, Kans., May 8, 1916; s. Earl Rufus and Sarah Katharine (Breon) M.; m. Jean Frances Alford, May 26, 1943; children: Katharine Myers Muirhead, Elizabeth Myers Baird, Phyllis Myers Rathbone, John, Mark. BS in Math. and Commerce, McPherson Coll., 1940; BSME, Kans. State Coll., 1942; PhDME, U. Wis., 1947. Registered profl. engr., Wis. Instr. mech. engring. Ind. Tech. Coll., Ft. Wayne, summer 1942; instr. U. Wis., Madison, 1942-47, asst. prof., 1947-50, assoc. prof., 1950-55, prof., 1955-86, emeritus prof., 1986—, chmn. dept. mech. engring., 1979-83; cons. Diesel Engine Mfrs. Assn., U.S. Army, various oil and ins. cos.; bd. dirs. Nelson Industries, Echlin Mfg. Corp., Digisonix, Inc. Contbr. articles to profl. jours. Chmn. Pine Lake com. W. Wis. Conf. Meth. Ch., 1955-60; Mem. Village Bd., Shorewood Hills, 1962-67. Recipient B.S. Reynolds Teaching award, 1964, McPherson Coll. Alumni citation of merit, 1971; Dugald Clerk award, 1971. Fellow ASME (Diesel Gas Power award 1971, Soichiro Honda award 1993), Soc. Automotive Engrs. (Colwell award 1966, 79, Horning award 1968, nat. pres. 1969, hon. mem.); mem. AAAS, NAE, Am. Soc. for Engring. Edn., Blue Key, Sigma Xi, Phi Kappa Phi, Sigma Tau, Pi Tau Sigma (Gold medal 1949), Tau Beta Pi (Ragnar Onstad Svc. to Soc. award 1978). Mem. Brethren Ch. Achievements include patents in field.

MYERS, PHILLIP WARD, otolaryngologist; b. Evanston, Ill., Nov. 11, 1939; s. R. Maurice and Vivian (Ward) M.; m. Lynetta Sargent, Dec. 22, 1963; children: Andrea, Ward, Alycia, Amanda, Andrew. B.S., Western Ill. U., 1961; M.D., U. Ill., 1965. Diplomate: Am. Bd. Otolaryngology. Intern St. Paul-Ramsey Hosp., 1965-66; resident in otolaryngology U. Louisville, 1966-68; resident Northwestern U., 1968-70, fellow, 1970-71; practice medicine specializing in otolaryngology Springfield, Ill., 1973—; clin. assoc. prof. otolaryngology So. Ill. U., Springfield, 1973—. Served to maj. M.C. AUS, 1971-73. Fellow Am. Soc. for Head and Neck Surgery, Am. Acad. Facial Plastic and Reconstructive Surgery; ACS, Am. Acad. Otolaryngology-Head and Neck Surgery. Research perilymphatic fistulas. Home: 111 Oak Hill Rd Rochester IL 62563-9229 Office: 331 W Carpenter St Springfield IL 62702-4901

MYERS, R. DAVID, library director, dean; b. Hutchinson, Kans., Mar. 27, 1949; s. William Raymond and Elizabeth (Haas) M.; m. Barbara Jean Burridge, Sept. 15, 1973; 1 child, John David. BA, U. No. Colo., 1972, MA, 1974; ABD, U. Mich., 1976; MA, U. Denver, 1979. Manuscript curator Western History Collection, Denver, 1976-79; rsch. assoc. Colo. Legis. Coun., Denver, 1979-81; reference specialist Libr. of Congress, Washington, 1981-84, reference supr., 1984-88; libr. dir. State Hist. Soc. of Wis., Madison, 1988-94; assoc. dean univ. libr. N.Mex. State U., Las Cruces, 1994—; editor Am. history Macmillan Pub., N.Y.C., 1991-94; cons. history of medicine dept. U. Wis., Madison, 1993-94. Author bibliographies for Libr. of Congress, 1987, 88. Mem. ALA, Am. Hist. Assn., Orgn. Am. Historians, Wis. Libr. Assn. Avocations: research, writing, baseball, mysteries. Office: N Mex State U Dept 3475 PO Box 3006 Las Cruces NM 88003-3006

MYERS, R(ALPH) CHANDLER, lawyer; b. Los Angeles, Jan. 9, 1933; s. Ralph Cather and Winifred (Chandler) M.; m. Rebecca Blythe Borkgren, Jan. 11, 1963. BA, Stanford U., 1954, JD, 1958; LLD (hon.), Whittier Coll., 1988. Bar: Calif. 1959, U.S. Dist. Ct. (cen. dist.) Calif. 1959, U.S. Supreme Ct. 1971. Law clk., then assoc. Parker, Stanbury, Reese & McGee, Los Angeles, 1958-63; assoc. Nicholas, Kolliner & Van Tassel, Los Angeles, 1963-65; ptnr. Myers & D'Angelo and predecessors, Los Angeles and Pasadena, Calif., 1965—; nat. panelist Am. Arbitration Assn., Los Angeles, 1964—; bd. visitors Stanford U. Law Sch., Calif., 1970-73; mem. judge pro tem panel Los Angeles Mcpl. Ct., 1971-81; mem. Los Angeles County Dist. Atty.'s Adv. Council, Calif., 1976-83. Bd. dirs. Opera Guild So. Calif., Los Angeles, 1971-83, pres., 1980-82,. Guild Opera Co. Los Angeles, 1974-83, pres., 1975-77, Western Justice Ctr. Found., 1993—; pres. Los Angeles Child Guidance Clinic, 1977-79, bd. dirs., 1972-83; nat. vice chmn. Keystone Gifts, Stanford Centennial Campaign, 1987-92; trustee Whittier Coll., Calif., 1973—, chmn. bd. trustees, 1981-87; bd. dirs. Opera Assocs. of the Music Ctr., Los Angeles, 1976-78; trustee Flintridge Prep. Sch., La Canada Flintridge, Calif., 1981-88, chmn. bd. trustees, 1985-88; bd. vis. Whittier Coll. Sch. Law, 1988—. Served to 1st lt. AUS, 1955-57. Recipient Stanford Assocs. award, 1984, Centennial Medallion award, 1991, Gold Spike award Stanford U., 1989, Disting. Svc. award Whittier Law Sch., 1993, Outstanding Achievement award Stanford Assocs., 1995. Mem. Wilshire Bar Assn. (bd. govs. 1972-81, pres. 1979-80), L.A. County Bar Assn. (trustee 1979-81), Stanford Law Soc. So. Calif. (bd. dirs. 1967-72, pres. 1970-71), Stanford Assocs. (bd. govs. 1992-97, treas. 1995—), Jonathan Club, University Club (Pasadena), Stanford Club of L.A. (bd. dirs. 1963-70, pres. 1968-69). Home: 5623 Burning Tree Dr La Canada Flintridge CA 91011-2861 Office: Myers & D'Angelo 301 N Lake Ave Ste 800 Pasadena CA 91101-4107

MYERS, RANDALL KIRK (RANDY MYERS), professional baseball player; b. Vancouver, Washington, Sept. 19, 1962. Student, Clark C.C., Washington. Baseball player N.Y. Mets, 1982-89, Cin. Reds, 1989-91, San Diego Padres, 1991-92, Chicago Cubs, 1992—. Named Calif. League Pitcher of the Yr., 1984, Nat. League Fireman of Yr., Sporting News, 1993. All-Star, 1990, 94; 2d in Nat. League in Saves, 1992. Office: Chicago Cubs Wrigley Field 1060 W Addison St Chicago IL 60613-4305*

MYERS, RAYMOND IRVIN, optometrist, researcher; b. Mishawaka, Ind., Nov. 19, 1943; s. Raymond E. Myers and Adeline S. (Hiler) M.; m. Paulette K. Emerine, July 9, 1966; 1 child, Christopher Raymond. BS, U. Notre Dame, 1966, Ind. U., 1968; OD, Ind. U., 1970. Dir. edn. and manpower div. Am. Optometric Assn., St. Louis, 1970-73; mgr. internat. profl. services Bausch & Lomb, Inc., Rochester, N.Y., 1973-77; research fellow Moorfields Eye Hosp., London, 1977-78; pvt. practice optometry St. Louis, 1979—; mem. faculty U. Mo., St. Louis, 1986—; mem. faculty, dir. dept. contact lenses La. State U., New Orleans, 1992-93; faculty dept. ophthalmology Washington U., 1978-86; adj. faculty La. State U. and U. Houston; rsch. cons. various contact lens mfrs. Contbr. more than 35 articles to profl. jours. Fellow Am. Acad. Optometry; mem. Am. Optometric Assn., Mo. Optometric Assn., Assn. for Rsch. on Vision and Ophthalmology, St. Louis Optometric Soc. (pres. 1985-86), Internat. Soc. for Contact Lens Rsch. (co-founder, v.p. 1980-93), Am. Optometric Student Assn. (co-founder, pres. 1967). Office: U Mo Sch Optometry 8001 Natural Bridge Rd Saint Louis MO 63121-4401

MYERS, REX CHARLES, history educator, retired college dean; b. Cleve., July 1, 1945; s. Charles F. and Merial W. (Jones) M.; m. Susan L. Richards, Jan. 10, 1987; children: Gary W., Laura M. BA, Western State Coll., 1967; MA, U. Mont., 1970, PhD, 1972; postgrad., U. Wash., 1983; Mgmt. Devel. Program, Harvard U., 1990. Instr. Palo Verde Coll., Blythe, Calif., 1972-75; reference librarian Mont. Hist. Soc., Helena, 1975-78; prof., div. chmn., dean Western Mont. Coll., Dillon, 1979-86; dean S.D. State U., Brookings, 1986-91; acad. dean Lyndon State Coll., Lyndonville, Vt., 1991-95; lectr. Western State Coll., Gunnison, Colo., 1995—. Author: Montana Symbols, 1976, Montana Trolleys, 1970, Lizzie, 1989; co-author: Marble Colorado, 1970, Montana: Our Land and People, 1978, Montana and the West, 1984; contbr. articles to profl. jours. Bd. dirs. Ctr. for Western Studies, Sioux Falls, S.D., 1990—, Gunnison Arts Ctr., Gunnison County Libr. Summer stipend NEH, 1973; fellow James J. Hill Library, 1985. Mem. AAUW, Western History Assn. (chmn. membership com. 1980-83), Am. Conf. Acad. Deans, Mont. Oral History Assn. (chmn. 1980-83), N.E. Kingdom C. of C. (bd. dirs.), Phi Kappa Phi. Lutheran. Lodges: Kiwanis (pres. Dillon 1983, lt. gov. 1984), Masons (master 1984). Home: PO Box 931 Gunnison CO 81230-0931

MYERS, ROBERT DAVID, judge; b. Springfield, Mass., Nov. 20, 1937; s. William and Pearl (Weiss) M.; m. Judith G. Dickenman, July 1, 1962; children—Mandy Susan, Jay Brandt, Seth William. A.B., U. Mass., 1959; J.D., Boston U., 1962. Bar: Ariz. 1963. Practice in Phoenix, 1963-89; presiding judge civil dept. Superior Ct. of Arizona in Maricopa County, 1991-92; presiding judge probate and mental health dept. Superior Ct. of Ariz., Maricopa County, Ariz., 1992-95; presiding judge Superior Ct. of Ariz., Maricopa County, 1995—; pro tem judge Ariz. Ct. Appeals; judge Ariz. Superior Ct., 1989—; chmn. com. on exams and admissions Ariz. Supreme Ct., 1974-75, chmn. com. on character and fitness, 1975-76, mem. multi-state bar exam. com., 1976-85. Pres. Valley of Sun chpt. City of Hope, 1965-66, Cmty. Orgn. for Drug Abuse Control, 1972-73, Valley Big Bros., 1975; chmn. Mayors Ad Hoc Com. on Drug Abuse, 1974-75; bd. dirs. Maricopa County Legal Aid Soc., 1978, Phoenix Jewish Cmty. Ctr. Mem. ATLA (nat. chmn. gov.), Ariz. Bar Assn. (gov., com. chmn., sect. pres.), Maricopa County Bar Assn. (dir., pres. 1979-80), Ariz. Trial Lawyers Assn. (pres., dir., co-editor newsletter), Phoenix Trial Lawyers Assn. (pres., dir.), Western Trial Lawyers Assn. (pres. 1977), Am. Judicature Soc. (spl. merit citation outstanding svc. improvement of adminstrn. justice 1986), Am. Bd. Trial Advocates, Sandra Day O'Connor Inn of Ct. (pres. 1991-92). Office: Justice Ctr 201 W Jefferson St Phoenix AZ 85003-2205

MYERS, ROBERT JAY, retired aerospace company executive; b. Bklyn., Oct. 15, 1934; s. John J. and Clara S. (Martinsen) M.; m. Carolyn Erland, Aug. 10, 1963; children—Susan, Kenneth. BCE, NYU, 1955, postgrad., 1957-65; P.M.D., Harvard U., 1972. With Grumman Corp., Bethpage, N.Y., 1964-94, v.p. resources, 1980-83, sr. v.p. bus. and resource mgmt., 1983-85, sr. v.p. corp. svcs., 1985-86; pres. Grumman Data Systems Corp., Bethpage, 1986-90; pres., chief operating officer, bd. dirs. Grumman Corp., 1991-94, ret., 1994; mem. sci. adv. coun. Ala. Space and Rocket Ctr., 1986-91. Mem. adv. panel on econ. devel. N.Y. State Project 2000, 1985-86; mem. L.I. Project 2000; mem. adv. bd. L.I. Youth Guidance, 1986-91; vice chmn., bd. dirs. Huntington Hosp., Poly. U., 1991—, North Shore Health System, 1994—, L.I. Mus. of Sci. and Technology, 1994—. 1st lt. U.S. Army, 1955-57. Fellow Poly. U., 1987, Disting. Alumni award, 1989. Mem. Am. Def.

Preparedness Assn. (dir. 1992—), Navy League, Industry Exec. Bd., Nat. Space Club (bd. govs. 1986-89), Huntington Country Club. Lutheran. Home: 7 Heather Ln Huntington NY 11743-1011

MYERS, ROBERT MANSON, English educator, author; b. Charlottesville, Va., May 29, 1921; s. Horwood Prettyman and Matilda Manson (Wynn) M. B.A. summa cum laude, Vanderbilt U., 1941; M.A., Columbia, 1942, Harvard, 1943; Ph.D., Columbia, 1948. Instr. English Yale, 1945-47; asst. prof. Coll. William and Mary, 1947-48, Tulane U., 1948-54; tchr. English Brearley Sch., N.Y.C., 1954-56; chmn. dept. English Osbourn High Sch., Manassas, Va., 1956-59; mem. faculty U. Md., College Park, 1959—; prof. English U. Md., 1968-86, prof. emeritus, 1986—. Author: Handel's Messiah, 1948, From Beowulf to Virginia Woolf, 1952, rev., 1984, Handel, Dryden, and Milton, 1956, Restoration Comedy, 1961, The Children of Pride, 1972, abridged edit., 1984 (Nat. Book award 1973), A Georgian at Princeton, 1976, Quintet: Five Plays, 1991. Fulbright Postdoctoral Research fellow U. London, 1953-54; Fulbright lectr. Rotterdam, Netherlands, 1958-59. Mem. Modern Lang. Assn. Am., Am. Soc. 18th Century Studies, Jane Austen Soc. N.Am., Phi Beta Kappa. Home: 3900 Connecticut Ave NW Washington DC 20008-2412

MYERS, ROLLAND GRAHAM, investment counselor; b. St. Louis, Aug. 30, 1945; s. Rolland Everett and Lurilien (Graham) M. Diploma, St. Louis Country Day Sch., 1963; AB cum laude in History and Lit., Harvard U., 1966; postgrad. Faculties of Scis. and Law, U. Edinburgh, Scotland, 1966-67; postgrad. Fondation Nationale des Sciences Politiques and Faculte de Lettres et des Sciences Humaines, U. Paris, 1967-68. Trainee global credit dept. The Chase Manhattan Bank, N.A., N.Y.C., 1968-69, mem. 32nd spl. devel. program, 1969, strategic planner internat. dept., 1969-70, securities analyst, mktg. rep., fiduciary investment dept., 1970; assoc. Smith, Barney & Co., Inc., N.Y.C., 1971, account exec. N.Y. sales dept., 1971-72, instl. account exec. N.Y. internat. sales dept., 1972-74, 2nd v.p., stockholder, 1975-76; v.p., stockholder Smith Barney, Harris Upham & Co., Inc. (subs. SBHU Holdings, Inc.), N.Y.C., 1976-78; prin. W.H. Graham & Sons, family investment office, 1977-82, investment counsel, 1982—; ltd. ptnr. Croke Patterson Campbell, Ltd., Denver, 1975—; joint founder, gen. ptnr. Mansion Disbursements, Denver, 1979—; pres., chmn. exec. com., bd. dirs. Fifty-Five Residents Corp., N.Y.C., 1980-84; bd. dirs. Fifty-Six Danbury Rd. Assn., Inc., New Milford, Conn. Trustee, mem. corp. Bishop Rhinelander Found. (Episcopal Chaplaincy at Harvard and Radcliffe Colls.), Cambridge, 1973-75; v.p., treas., bd. dirs. The Whitehill Graham Found., St. Louis, 1976—; bd. dirs., fin. com., bylaws com., mem. corp. Eliot Pratt Edn. Ctr., Inc., The Pratt Ctr.: Your Connection with the Natural World, New Milford, 1987-94; bd. dirs., mem. corp. Kent (Conn.) Land Trust, Inc., 1989—, treas., 1989-93; project financier Restoration of 1851 Samuel Curtiss Hosford House, Nat. Register Historic Dist., Falls Village, Conn., 1984-86; commr. Housatonic River Commn., Warren, Conn., 1985-93, vice chmn., 1986-87, chmn., 1988-92; commr. Conservation, Inland Wetlands and Watercourses Commn., Kent, 1988-92, vice chmn., 1988-93; mem. schs. and scholarships com., Office of Admissions and Fin. Aid, Harvard and Radcliffe Colls., 1991—. Mem. Cum Laude Soc., Mary Inst. and St. Louis Country Day Sch. Alumni Assn., Harvard Alumni Assn., Capitol Hill Club (Washington), Harvard Club (N.Y.C.), Hasty Pudding-Inst. of 1770 (Cambridge), Wyoming Heritage Found. and Soc. Republican. Episcopalian. Office: W H Graham & Sons Investment Counsel 1818 Evans Ave Ste 207 Cheyenne WY 82001-4664

MYERS, SHARON DIANE, auditor; b. Lawrence, Kans., Sept. 18, 1955; d. Richard Paul and Helen Carol (Overbey) M. AA, Mt. San Antonio Coll., Walnut, Calif., 1981; BSBA, Calif. State U., Pomona, 1983, MBA, 1986. Cert. fraud examiner; cert. govt. fin. mgr. Revenue agt. IRS, Glendale, Calif., 1984-85; auditor Def. Contract Audit Agy., L.A., 1985-92; auditor Office Inspector Gen. FDIC, Newport Beach, Calif., 1992—; instr. Azusa (Calif.) Pacific U., 1987, 88, West Coast U., San Diego, 1992. Musician, Sunday sch. supt. Covina (Calif.) Bapt. Temple, 1975-95, Liberty Bapt. Ch., Irvine, Calif., 1995—. Mem. Assn. Govt. Accts. Republican. Avocations: piano, traveling. Home: 4885 NW Gustafson Rd Silverdale WA 98383

MYERS, SHELLEY LYNN, elementary education educator; b. Williamsport, Pa., May 11, 1967; d. John Franklin and Sandra Mae (Johnson) M. BS, Shippensburg U., 1989; MEd summa cum laude, Bloomsburg (Pa.) U., 1992; postgrad., Indiana U. Pa., 1993—. Cert. elem. edn. and reading specialist. Tchr. 5th grade Williamsport Sch. Dist., 1990-91, tchr. 1st grade, 1991-93, tchr. kindergarten, 1993—; instr. reading Pa. Coll. Tech., Williamsport, 1992-93; mem. adv. com. Lang. Arts Com., Williamsport, 1993-94; mem. various sch. coms.; presenter in field. Summer day camp dir. YMCA, Williamsport, 1989. Mem. Internat. Reading Assn., North Ctrl. Reading Coun. (v.p. 1993-94, pres. 1994-95), Keystone State Reading Assn., Delta Kappa Gamma. Methodist. Avocations: reading, travel.

MYERS, SHIRLEY DIANA, art book editor; b. N.Y.C., Jan. 6, 1916; d. Samuel Archibald and Regina (Edelstein) Levene; m. Bernard Samuel Myers, Aug. 11, 1938 (dec. Feb. 1993); children: Peter Lewis, Lucie Ellen. BA, NYU, 1936, MA, 1938. Editorial asst. Am. Dancer mag., N.Y.C., 1936-38; asst. to dir. Nat. Art Soc., N.Y.C., 1938-42; freelance, art book editor N.Y.C. and Austin, Tex., 1947—. Editor: Modern Art in the Making, 1950, 59, Mexican Painting in Our Time, 1956, The German Expressionists, 1957, 63, Understanding the Arts, 1958, 63, Bruegel, 1976, Manet, 1977, (with B.S. Myers) Dictionary of 20th Century Art, 1974; asst. editor Ency. of Painting, 1955, 70, 79; asst. editor, contbr. McGraw-Hill Dictionary of Art, 5 vols., 1960-69; contbg. editor: Art and Civilization, 1956, 67; coord., picture editor Ency. World Art: Supplement, Vol. XVI, 1982, 83. Vol. archives New Sch. for Social Rsch. Libr., 1993-95. Mem. NOW, Older Women's League (rec. sec. Greater N.Y. chpt. 1993-95, v.p. 1995-97), Quest (coord. archaeology 1995-97, the city in history 1996-97).

MYERS, STEPHANIE E., publishing company executive; b. L.A., Mar. 7, 1950; d. Robert Wilson and Estella Elizabeth (Halle) Lee; m. Roy J. Myers, July 13, 1991. BA, Calif. State U.-Dominquez Hills, 1971; MA, Occidental Coll., 1975. Cons. Coro Found., Los Angeles, 1973-77; fundraiser Legal Def. Fund NAACP, Los Angeles, 1978-79; owner, mgr. Contact Calif., Beverly Hills, 1979-81; spl. asst. Dept. Commerce, Washington, 1981-83; asst. sec. pub. affairs HHS, Washington, 1983-89; dir. Office Comml. Space Transp. Dept. Transportation, Washington, 1989-95; v.p. R.J.Myers Pub. Co., Washington, 1995—; mem. U.S. del. to Internat. Women's Conf., Nairobi, Kenya, 1985, UN Commn. on Status of Women, 1987. Co-author: The Rescue of Robby Robo, Can Do Kids (kits). Named Woman of Yr. Women's Transp. Seminar, 1990. Mem. Nat. Links, Inc., Delta Sigma Theta (Outstanding Leader in Govt. 1994). Office: RJ Myers Pub Co PO Box 70427 SW Washington DC 20024

MYERS, SUE BARTLEY, artist; b. Norfolk, Va., Aug. 22, 1930; d. Louis and Rena M. Bartley; m. Bertram J. Myers, Nov. 24, 1949; children: Beth R., Mark F., Alyson S. Student, Stephens Coll., Va. Wesleyan. V.p. Jamson Realty Inc., Myers Realty Inc.; ltd. ptnr. Downtown Plaza Shopping Ctr., Warwick Village Shopping Ctr., Suburban Park Assocs. Solo shows at Village Gallery, Newport News, 1988, Artist at Work Gallery, Virginia Beach, Va., 1991, Va. Wesleyan U., Virginia Beach, 1991, 92, Will Richardson Gallery, Norfolk, Va., 1993, 94. Pres. adv. coun. Va. Wesleyan U., 1982-94; mayor's del. Sister Cities, Norwich, Eng., 1984, Kidikushu, Japan, 1982, Edinburgh, Scotland, 1991, Toulon, France, 1992; mem. entertainment com. Azalea Festival Norfolk, 1984; founder art scholarship Va. Wesleyan; active corporate campaign Va. Zool. Soc. Mem. Tidewater Artists Assn., Art Odyssey. Jewish. Avocations: travel, physical fitness, reading, golf. Home: 7338 Barberry Ln Norfolk VA 23505-3001

MYERS, WALTER DEAN, young adult book author; b. Martinsburg, W.Va., Aug. 12, 1937; foster s. Herbert Dean and Florence Brown; children from previous marriage: Karen, Michael Dean; m. Constance Brendel, June 19, 1973; 1 child, Christopher. BA, Empire State Coll., 1984. Employment supr. N.Y. State Dept. Labor, Bklyn., 1966-69; sr. trade book editor Bobbs-Merrill Co., Inc., N.Y.C., 1970-77. Author: (for children) Where Does the Day Go?, 1969 (Coun. Interracial Books for Children award 1968), The Dragon Takes a Wife, 1972, The Dancers, 1972, Fly, Jiimy, Fly!, 1974, The World of Work: A Guide to Choosing a Career, 1975, Fast Sam, Cool Clyde, and Stuff, 1975 (Woodward Park Sch. Ann. Book award 1976), Social Welfare, 1976, Brainstorm, 1977, Mojo and the Russians, 1977, Victory for Jamie, 1977, It Ain't All for Nothin', 1978 (ALA Best Books for Young Adults citation 1978), The Young Landlords, 1979 (ALA Best Books for Young Adults citation 1979, Coretta Scott King award 1980), The Black Pearl and the Ghost; or, One Mystery After Another, 1980, The Golden Serpent, 1980, Hoops, 1981 (ALA Best Books for Young Adults citation 1982), The Legend of Tarik, 1981 (Notable Children's Trade Book in Social Studies citation 1982), Won't Know Till I Get There, 1982, The Nicholas Factor, 1983, Tales of a Dead King, 1983, Mr. Monkey and the Gotcha Bird, 1984, Motown and Didi: A Love Story, 1984 (Coretta Scott King award 1984), The Outside Shot, 1984, Adventure in Granada, 1985, The Hidden Shrine, 1985, Duel in the Desert, 1986, Ambush in the Amazon, 1986, Sweet Illusions, 1986, Crystal, 1987, Shadow of the Red Moon, Fallen Angels, 1988, Scorpions, 1988 (Newbery Honor Book 1989), Me, Mop and the Moondance Kid, 1988, The Mouse Rap, 1990, Now Is Your Time!: The African American Struggle for Freedom, 1991 (Coretta Scott King award 1991), Somewhere in the Darkness, 1992 (Newbery Honor book 1993), A Place Called Heartbreak: A Story of Vietnam, 1992, The Righteous Revenge of Artemis Bonner, 1992, Mop, Moondance and the Nagasaki Knights, 1992, Young Martin's Promise, 1992, Malcolm X: By Any Means Necessary, 1993, The Test, 1993, Intensive Care, 1993, Fashion by Tasha, 1993, Dangerous Games, 1993, Brown Angels: An Album of Pictures and Verse, 1993, The Glory Field, 1994, Darnell Rock Reporting, 1994, The Story of the Three Kingdoms, 1995, One More River to Cross, 1995, How Mr. Monkey Saw the Whole World, 1996. Recipient Margaret A. Edwards award ALA's Young Adult Library Services Assn., 1994.

MYERS, WARREN POWERS LAIRD, physician, educator; b. Phila., May 2, 1921; s. John Dashiell and Mary Hall (Laird) M.; m. Katharine Van Vechten, July 1, 1944; children: Warren Powers Laird, Jr., Anne Van Vechten Myers Evans, Duncan McNeir, Sara Myers Gormley. Grad., Episcopal Acad., 1939; B.S., Yale U., 1943; M.D., Columbia U., 1945; M.S. in Medicine, U. Minn., 1952; postgrad. (Eleanor Roosevelt Found. fellow), U. Cambridge, Eng., 1962-63. Diplomate: Am. Bd. Internal Medicine. Rotating intern Phila. Gen. Hosp., 1945-46; intern medicine Maimonides Hosp., N.Y.C., 1948-49; resident fellow in medicine Mayo Clinic, Rochester, Minn., 1949-52; clin. asst. Meml. Hosp., N.Y.C., 1952-54; asst. attending physician Meml. Hosp., 1954-58, assoc. attending physician, 1959, attending physician, 1959-90; instr. Cornell U. Med. Coll., 1955-56, asst. prof., 1956-59, asso. prof., 1959-68, prof. medicine, 1968-86, prof. emeritus, 1986—, assoc. dean, 1977-86; chmn. dept. medicine Meml. Sloan-Kettering Cancer Ctr., N.Y.C., 1967-77; v.p. for ednl. affairs Meml. Hosp., 1977-81, Eugene W. Kettering prof., 1979-86; attending physician N.Y. Hosp., N.Y.C., 1968-86; mem. Sloan-Kettering Inst. Cancer Rsch., N.Y.C., 1969-90; mem. emeritus Meml. Sloan-Kettering Cancer Ctr., N.Y.C., 1990—; cons. Rockefeller U. Hosp., N.Y.C., 1977-86; Mem. clin. cancer tng. com. Nat. Cancer Inst., 1970-73, chmn., 1971-73, chmn. clin. cancer edn. com., 1975-78; adj. prof. medicine Dartmouth Med. Sch., 1987—; cons. staff Mary Hitchcock Meml. Hosp., Hanover, N.H., 1987—. Contbr. articles on cancer, bone metabolism, internal medicine, and med. edn. to med. jours. Bd. dirs. Rye (N.Y.) United Fund, 1969-72, chmn. budget com., 1968-69; bd. dirs. Damon Runyon-Walter Winchell Cancer Fund, 1976-86, pres., 1985-86; trustee Hitchcock Clinic, Hanover, N.H., 1983-96, Dartmouth-Hitchcock Med. Ctr., Hanover, 1983-95, chmn. exec. com., 1992-95, tchr.'s coll. Columbia U., 1980-86. With M.C., USNR, 1946-47. Recipient Alumni award for research Mayo Clinic, 1952, Margaret Hay Edwards Achievement medal Am. Assn. Cancer Edn., 1993. Fellow ACP, N.Y. Acad. Medicine (v.p. 1983-85); mem. Am. Clin. and Climatological Assn., Am. Assn. Cancer Research, Endocrine Soc., Harvey Soc., Am. Fedn. Clin. Research, Practioners' Soc. of N.Y., AMA, Am. Assn. Cancer Edn. (pres. 1984-85), Am. Soc. Clin. Oncology, Founders and Patriots Pa., Alpha Omega Alpha. Presbyterian (elder 1969—). Clubs: Yale, Charaka, Century Assn. (N.Y.C.). Address: 376 Jericho St White River Junction VT 05001

MYERS, WAYNE ALAN, psychiatrist, educator; b. N.Y.C., Dec. 13, 1931; s. Harry and Eve Myers; m. Joanne Jackson, Mar. 23, 1969; children: Tracy Victoria, Blake Andrew. BS with high honors, U. Ark., 1952; MD, Columbia U., 1956. Cert. in psychiatry and psychoanalysis. Intern Bellevue Hosp., N.Y.C., 1956-57; resident Payne Whitney Clinic, N.Y. Hosp., N.Y.C., 1957-59, 61-62; instr. psychiatry Cornell U. Med. Ctr., N.Y.C., 1962-72; clin. asst. prof. psychiatry Cornell U. Med. Ctr., 1972-77, clin. assoc. prof. psychiatry, 1977-84, clin. prof. psychiatry, 1984—; tng. and supervising admitting psychoanalyst Columbia U. Ctr. for Psychoanalytic Tng. & Research, N.Y.C., 1983—; sec. Assn. for Psychoanalytic Medicine, N.Y.C., 1987-89. Author: Dynamic Therapy of the Older Patient, 1984, Shrink Dreams, 1992; editor: New Concepts in Psychoanalytic Psychotherapy, 1987, New Techniques in the Psychotherapy of Older Patients, 1991, The Perverse and the Near Perverse in Clinical Practice, 1991, contbr. articles to profl. jours. Capt. U.S. Army, 1959-61. Fellow Am. Psychiat. Assn. (life), Am. Psychoanalytic Assn.; mem. Assn. for Psychoanalytic Medicine (sec.), N.Y. State Med. Soc., N.Y. County Med. Soc., PEN, Author's Guild. Avocations: skiing, squash, creative writing. Office: 60 Sutton Pl S Ste ICN New York NY 10022

MYERS, WENDY SUZANNE, editor; b. North Kansas City, Mo., Sept. 1, 1966; d. F. Dale and Fran L. (Bellinger) Richmond; m. Douglas G. Myers, June 11, 1988. BS in Journalism & Broadcasting, Cen. Mo. State U., 1988; postgrad., Webster U., 1991—. Reporter, photographer Decorah (Iowa) Newspapers, 1988-89; editor Women in Bus. mag., Kansas City, Mo., 1989—. Mem. Soc. Profl. Journalists (nat. bd. dirs. 1994-95), Kansas City Soc. Mag. Editors (pres. 1992-93), Kansas City Press Club (treas. 1990-92, membership chmn. 1990-92, pres.-elect 1992-93). Office: Women in Business 9100 Ward Pky Kansas City MO 64114-3306

MYERS, WILLIAM GERRY, III, advocate, lawyer; b. Roanoke, Va., July 13, 1955; s. William Gerry and Ruby Grey (Pollard) M.; m. Susan Louise Benzer, Aug. 27, 1988; children: Katherine Coulter, Molly Benzer. AB, Coll. of William and Mary, 1977; JD, U. Denver, 1981. Bar: Colo. 1981, Wyo. 1982, D.C. 1987, U.S. Supreme Ct. 1990. Assoc. Davis & Cannon, Sheridan, Wyo., 1981-85; legis. counsel U.S. Sen. Alan K. Simpson, Wyo., 1985-89; asst. to atty. gen. U.S. dept. Justice, Washington, 1989-92; dep. gen. counsel for programs U.S. Dept. Energy, Washington, 1992-93; corp. counsel The Cattlemen Advocating Through Litigation Fund, 1993—; dir. fed. lands Nat. Cattlemen's Assn., 1993—; exec. dir. Pub. Lands Coun., Washington, 1993—; guest lectr. Yale U., Georgetown U. Sch. Law, Am. U., U. Colo. Sch. Law, Nat. Park Svc. Tng. Ctr., Nat. Acad. Scis., Grazing Lands Forum, Wyo. State Bar. Editl. staff Denver Law Jour., Denver Jour. Internat. Law and Policy; contbr. articles to profl. jours. Office: Public Lands Council 1301 Pennsylvania Ave NW Washington DC 20004-1701

MYERS, WILLIAM S., magazine publishing executive; m. Aleksandra Myers; 3 children. BA, Colgate U., 1958. From sales and mktg. rep. to N.Y. divsn. sales mgr. Life Mag., until 1972; advt. sales rep. Sports Illustrated Mag., 1972-74, N.Y. advt. sales mgr., 1976-82; v.p. mktg. HBO, 1974-75; advt. sales dir. People Mag., 1982-85, assoc. pub., 1985-88; pub. Money Mag., N.Y.C., 1988—. With USN. Office: Money Mag Time & Life Bldg Rockefeller Ctr 33rd fl New York NY 10020*

MYERS, WOODROW AUGUSTUS, JR., physician, health care management director; b. Indpls., Feb. 14, 1954; s. Woodrow Augustus Sr. and Charlotte T. (Tyler) M.; m. Debra Jackson, June 23, 1973; children: Kimberly Leilani, Zachary Augustus. BS, Stanford (Calif.) U., 1973, MBA, 1982; MD, Harvard U., 1977. Intern in internal medicine Stanford U. Med. Ctr., 1977-78, resident in internal medicine, 1978-80, fellow, critical care medicine, 1980-81; asst. prof. critical care medicine San Francisco Gen. Hosp., 1982-84; physician health advisor com. on labor and human resources U.S. Senate, Washington, 1984; commr. Ind. Dept. of Health, Indpls., 1985-90; health commr. N.Y.C. Dept. of Health, 1990-91; corp. med. dir. Assoc. Group, Indpls., 1991-95; dir. health care mgmt. Ford Motor Co., Dearborn, Mich., 1996—; asst. prof. medicine Cornell Med. Coll., N.Y.C., 1990-91; bd. trustees Stanford U., 1987-92; assoc. prof. medicine Ind. U. Sch. Medicine, 1992-95. Bd. dirs. Stanford Health Systems, 1994—. Robert Wood Johnson clin. scholar, Stanford U., 1980-82. Fellow ACP; mem. AMA, Nat. Med. Assn., Soc. Critical Care Medicine. Office: Ford Motor Co The American Rd WHQ-1148 Dearborn MI 48121-1899

MYERSON, ALAN, director, film and television writer; b. Cleve., Aug. 8, 1936; s. Seymour A. and Vivien I. (Caplin) M.; m. Irene Ryan, June 2, 1962; 1 son, Lincoln; m. Leigh French, Apr. 15, 1977; children: Sierra Jasmine French-Myerson, Darcy Anna French-Myerson. Student, Pepperdine Coll., 1956-57, UCLA, 1957. mem. acting faculty U. Calif., Berkeley, 1966, San Francisco State U., 1967. Dir. N.Y. and Off Broadway Prodns., 1958-64, including This Music Crept By Me Upon the Waters, The Committee; dir.: Second City, N.Y.C. and Chgo., 1961, 62; founder, producer, dir. The Committee, San Francisco, L.A. and N.Y., 1963-74; dir.: (films) Steelyard Blues, 1972, Private Lessons, 1981, Police Academy 5, 1988; numerous TV shows, 1975—, including Laverne and Shirley, Rhoda, Bob Newhart Show, Welcome Back, Kotter, Fame, Crime Story, Dynasty, Miami Vice, Hunter, Sisters, Picket Fences, The Larry Sanders Show, Frazier, Friends; TV films The Love Boat, 1976, Hi, Honey, I'm Dead, 1991, Bad Attitudes, 1991; writer It's Showtime. Active in civil rights, anti-war, anti-nuclear power movements, 1957—. Mem. Acad. Motion Picture Arts and Scis., Acad. TV Arts and Scis., Dirs. Guild Am., Writers Guild Am. West.

MYERSON, ALBERT LEON, physical chemist; b. N.Y.C., Nov. 14, 1919; s. Myer and Dora (Weiner) M.; m. Arline Harriet Rosenfield, May 10, 1953; children: Aimee Lenore, Lorraine Patrice, Paul Andrew. BS, Pa. State U., 1941; postgrad., Columbia U., 1942-45; PhD, U. Wis., 1948. Rsch. asst. Manhattan Project Columbia U., N.Y.C., 1941-45; sr. rsch. chemist Franklin Inst. Labs., Phila., 1948-56; mgr. phys. chemistry Gen. Electric Co., Phila., 1956-60; prin. phys. chemist Aero. Lab. Cornell U., Buffalo, 1960-68; rsch. assoc. Exxon Rsch. and Engring. Co., Linden, N.J., 1969-79; head phys. chemistry sect. Mote Marine Lab., Sarasota, Fla., 1979-85; sr. scientist Princeton (N.J.) Sci. Enterprises, Inc., 1985—; cons. in field. Violinist in Venice Symphony; co-editor: Physical Chemistry in Aerodynamics and Space Flight, 1961; contbr. articles in field to profl. jours.; patentee in field. Fellow Am. Phys. Soc.; mem. Am. Chem. Soc., Combustion Inst., Pa. State U. Alumni Assn., Sigma Xi, Phi Lambda Upsilon. Home and Office: 4147 Rosas Ave Sarasota FL 34233-1614 *It has always seemed to me that one's satisfacion with life can be expessed as an integral of the intensity of his or her pursuit of contributions to the world as a function of time, throughout one's life.*

MYERSON, HARVEY DANIEL, lawyer; b. Phila., Aug. 1, 1939; s, Morris and Rachel (Cohen) M.; m. Anne Borish, Aug. 20, 1961 (div. 1975); children: Karen Michelle, Jill Diane, Jessica Ann; m. Diane Clare Stukelman, Oct. 17, 1975; children: Rachel Clare, Emily Alicia. Student, U. Chgo., 1957-59; BS, Temple U., 1961; LLB, Columbia U., 1964. Bar: N.Y. 1964, U.S. Ct. Appeals (2d cir.) 1965, U.S. Dist. Ct. (so. dist.) N.Y. 1965, U.S. Supreme Ct. 1975, U.S. Ct. Appeals (4th cir.) 1975. Assoc. Hughes, Hubbard & Reed, N.Y.C., 1964-70; mng. ptnr. Webster & Sheffield, N.Y.C., 1970-84, Finley, Kumble, Wagner, Heine, Underberg, Manley, Myerson & Casey, N.Y.C., 1984-88; chmn. exec. com. Myerson & Kuhn, N.Y.C., 1988-89; lectr. seminars. Mem. Fed. Bar Council, Assn. Bar City N.Y. Republican. Jewish. Clubs: University (N.Y.C.); Tryall Golf and Beach (Jamaica, W.I.).

MYERSON, JACOB MYER, former foreign service officer; b. Rock Hill, S.C., June 11, 1926; s. Solomon and Lena (Clein) M.; m. Nicole Neuray, June 10, 1965 (dec. Oct. 1968); 1 child, Sylvie Anne; m. Helen Hayashi, Mar. 9, 1974 (dec. Jan. 1995). Student, Pa. State Coll., 1944; B.A. with distinction, George Washington U., 1949, M.A., 1950; grad., Fgn. Service Inst., 1953. Joined U.S. Fgn. Service, 1950; 3d sec. (Office U.S. High Commr. Germany), Berlin, 1950-52; 2d sec. (U.S. Mission to NATO and European Regional Orgn.), Paris, France, 1953-55; also mem. U.S. permanent del. to coordinating com. InterGovtl. Consultative Group on EastWest Trade; internat. economist, internat. relations officer State Dept., 1956-60; adviser U.S. del. GATT session, Geneva, Switzerland, 1958; ministerial session OEEC, Paris, 1958; 1st sec., chief polit. section U.S. Mission to European Communities, Brussels, Belgium, 1960-65; spl. asst. to under sec. state, 1965-66; officer-in-charge NATO Polit. Affairs, Dept. State, 1966-68; adviser U.S. delegation ministerial sessions North Atlantic Council, 1966-67; dep. polit. adviser, counselor U.S. Mission to NATO, Brussels, Belgium, 1968-70; counselor econ. affairs U.S. Mission to European Communities, Brussels, 1970-74; minister counselor U.S. Mission to European Communities, from 1974; U.S. rep. to UN Econ. and Social Council with rank of ambassador, 1975-77; alt. U.S. del. 30th and 31st sessions UN Gen. Assembly, 1975, 76; alt. U.S. rep. 4th session UN Conf. on Trade and Devel., 1976; minister-counselor for econ. and comml. affairs Am. Embassy, Paris, 1977-80; ret., 1980; dep. sec. gen. OECD, Paris, 1980-88. Served with inf. AUS, 1944-46, ETO. Decorated Bronze Star; Order of the Sacred Treasure Gold and Silver medal (Japan). Recipient Meritorious Service award State Dept., 1960. Mem. Fgn. Service Assn. (Rivkin award 1969), Phi Beta Kappa, Artus, Pi Gamma Mu, Phi Eta Sigma. Address: 2 rue Lucien Gaulard, 75018 Paris France

MYERSON, JOEL ARTHUR, English language educator, researcher; b. Boston, Sept. 9, 1945; s. Edward Yale and Gwenne (Rubenstein) M. AB, Tulane U., 1967; MA, Northwestern U., 1968, PhD, 1971. Asst. prof. English U. S.C., Columbia, 1971-76, assoc. prof., 1976-80, prof., 1980-90, Carolina Rsch. prof. Am. Lit., 1990—, chmn. English dept., 1987-90. Author: Margaret Fuller: An Annotated Secondary Bibliography, 1977, Brook Farm: An Annotated Bibliography and Resources Guide, 1978, Margaret Fuller: A Descriptive Bibliography, 1978, The New England Transcendentalists and the Dial: A History of Magazine and Its Contributors, 1980, Theodore Parker: A Descriptive Bibliography, 1980, Ralph Waldo Emerson: A Descriptive Bibliography, 1982, Emily Dickinson: A Descriptive Bibliography, 1984, Walt Whitman: A Descriptive Bibliography, 1993; co-author: Melville Dissertations: An Annotated Directory, 1972, Emerson: An Annotated Secondary Bibliography, 1985, Ralph Waldo Emerson: An Annotated Bibliography of Criticism, 1980-91, 1994; editor: The American Renaissance in New England, 1978, Margaret Fuller: Esssays on American Life and Letters, 1978, Antebellum Writers in New York and the South, 1979, Critical Essays on Margaret Fuller, 1980, Margaret Fuller, Woman in the Nineteenth Century, 1980, Emerson Centenary Essays, 1982, The Transcendentalists: A Review of Research and Criticism, 1984, The Brook Farm Book: A Collection of First-Hand Accounts of the Community, 1987, The American Transcendentalists, 1988, Critical Essays on Henry David Thoreau's Walden, 1988, Whitman in His Time, 1991, Emerson and Thoreau: The Contemporary Reviews, 1992, The Walt Whitman Archive, 1993, The Cambridge Companion to Henry David Thoreau, 1995, Studies in the American Renaissance, 1977-96; co-editor: Critical Essays on American Transcendentalism, 1982, Critical Essays on Ralph Waldo Emerson, 1983, The Selected Letters of Louisa May Alcott, 1987, A Double Life: Newly Discovered Thrillers of Louisa May Alcott, 1988, The Journals of Louisa May Alcott, 1989, Louisa May Alcott: Selected Fiction, 1990, Freaks of Genius: Unknown Thrillers of Louisa May Alcott, 1991, Three Children's Novels by Christopher Pearse Cranch, 1993, Emerson's Antislavery Writings, 1995. Mem. Mass. Hist. Soc., Am. Antiquarian Soc. Woodrow Wilson Dissertation Yr. fellow, 1970, summer fellow NEH, 1976, rsch. grantee, 1978-81, 88-91, 94-97; Guggenheim Found. fellow, 1981; rsch. grantee Am. Philos. Soc., 1982, 84. Mem. MLA (del. assembly 1978-80), Assn. for Documentary Editing (pres. 1989-90, Disting. Svc. award 1986, Lyman H. Butterfield award 1996), Philol. Assn. of Carolinas (pres. 1987-88), Thoreau Soc. (pres. 1992-96), Emerson Soc. (pres. 1994-95). Democrat. Home: 6310 Goldbranch Rd Columbia SC 29206-3340 Office: U of SC Dept of English Columbia SC 29208

MYERSON, PAUL GRAVES, psychiatrist, educator; b. Boston, Sept. 15, 1914; s. Abraham and Dorothy (Loman) M.; children: Peter P., Deborah L. Myerson-Kaup, Andrew A., Nancy E. Myerson-Shield. B.S., Harvard, 1935, M.D., 1939. Diplomate Am. Bd. Psychiatry and Neurology. Intern Beth Israel Hosp., Boston, 1939-40; resident neurology Mt. Sinai Hosp., N.Y.C., 1941-42; resident psychiatry N.Y. Psychiat. Inst., 1942-43; tng. analyst Boston Psychoanalytic Soc. and Inst., 1959-85, tng. analyst emeritus, 1985—; prof. psychiatry Tufts U. Sch. Medicine, 1962-85, prof. emeritus, 1985—, chmn. dept. psychiatry, 1963-79, area dir. Mental Health Ctr., 1968-74; psychiatrist-in-chief New Eng. Med. Ctr. Hosp., 1963-79; vis. prof. psychiatry Harvard Med. Sch., 1979-86; Pres. Boston Psychoanalytic Soc. and Inst., 1972-74. Served to lt. USNR, 1943-46. Fellow Am. Psychiat. Assn. (life); mem. Am. Psychoanalytic Assn., AAAS. Home and Office: 25 Larch Rd Newton MA 02168-1413

MYERSON, ROBERT J., radiologist, educator; b. Boston, May 12, 1947; s. Richard Louis and Rosemarie (Farkas) M.; m. Carla Wheatley, Aug. 8, 1970; 1 child, Jacob Wheatley. BA, Princeton U., 1969; PhD, U. Calif., Berkeley, 1974; MD, U. Miami, 1980. Diplomate Am. Bd. Radiology. Asst. prof. dept. physics Pa. State U., State Coll., 1974-76; fellow Inst. Advanced Studies, Princeton, N.J., 1976-78; resident U. Pa. Hosp., Phila., 1981-84; assoc. prof. radiology Washington U. Sch. Medicine, St. Louis, 1984—, assoc. dir. residency tng. radiation oncology, 1989—. Contbr. articles to profl. jours. Recipient Career Devel. award Am. Cancer Soc., 1985. Mem. Am. Coll. Radiation, Am. Soc. Therapeutic Radiologists, Am. Phys. Soc. Democrat. Jewish. Avocation: bicycling. Office: Washington U Radiation Oncology Ctr Box 8224 4939 Audubon Ave Ste 5500 Saint Louis MO 63110

MYERSON, ROGER BRUCE, economist, game theorist, educator; b. Boston, Mar. 29, 1951; s. Richard L. and Rosemarie (Farkas) M.; m. Regina M. Weber, Aug. 29, 1982; children: Daniel, Rebecca. AB summa cum laude, Harvard U., 1973, SM, 1973, PhD, 1976. Asst. prof. decision scis. Northwestern U., Evanston, Ill., 1976-78, assoc. prof., 1979-82, prof., 1982—, Harold Stuart prof. decision scis., 1986—, prof. econs., 1987—; guest researcher U. Bielefeld, Federal Republic of Germany, 1978-79; vis. prof. econs. U. Chgo., 1985-86. Author: Game Theory: Analysis of Conflict, 1991; mem. editorial bd. Internat. Jour. Game Theory, 1982-92, Games and Econ. Behavior, 1988—; assoc. editor Jour. Econ. Theory, 1983-93; also articles. Guggenheim fellow, 1983-84; Sloan rsch. fellow, 1984-86. Fellow Econometric Soc., Am. Acad. Arts and Scis. Office: Northwestern U Kellogg Grad Sch Mgmt 2001 Sheridan Rd Evanston IL 60208-2009

MYERSON, TOBY SALTER, lawyer; b. Chgo., July 20, 1949; s. Raymond King and Natalie Anita (Salter) M. BA, Yale U., 1971; JD, Harvard U., 1975. Bar: N.Y. 1977, Calif. 1977. Assoc. Coudert Bros., N.Y.C., 1975-77, 81, San Francisco, 1977-81; assoc. Paul, Weiss, Rifkind, Wharton & Garrison, N.Y.C., 1981-83, ptnr., 1983-89; mng. dir. Wasserstein Perella & Co., Inc., N.Y.C., 1989-90; ptnr. Paul, Weiss, Rifkind, Wharton & Garrison, N.Y.C., 1990—; lectr. U. Calif. Berkeley, 1979-81, Harvard U., Cambridge, Mass., 1982-83; visiting lectr. Yale U., New Haven, 1983-84; bd. dirs. Myerson, Van Den Berg & Co., Santa Barbara, Calif. Contbg. editor: Doing Business in Japan, 1983, Council on Foreign Rels., 1993—, Foreign Policy Assn., 1995—. Sec. Japan Soc., Inc., N.Y.C., 1985-89; bd. dirs. 1056 Fifth Ave. Corp., N.Y.C., 1985-88. Mem. ABA (subcom. internat. banking, corp. and bus. law sect.), Internat. Bar Assn., N.Y. State Bar Assn., Assn. Bar City N.Y. (com. on fgn. and comparative law, chmn. 1988-89), Calif. Bar Assn. Avocations: art, music, literature, tennis, golf. Home: 1056 5th Ave New York NY 10028-0112 Office: Paul Weiss Rifkind Wharton & Garrison 1285 Avenue Of The Americas New York NY 10019-6064

MYGATT, SUSAN HALL, lawyer; b. Stamford, Conn., Sept. 29, 1947; d. Eben Clarke and Jane Elizabeth (Terhune) Hall; m. Samuel G. Mygatt, June 11, 1977; children: Elizabeth, Jenny, Catherine. BA, Smith Coll., 1969; JD, Boston U., 1977. Bar: Mass. 1977. Adminstrv. asst. HUD, Washington, 1969-73; exec. asst. Urban Devel. Corp., N.Y.C., 1973-74; ptnr. Goodwin, Procter & Hoar, Boston, 1977—. Mem. ABA, Mass. Bar Assn., New Eng. Women in Real Estate. Office: Goodwin Procter & Hoar Exchange Pl Boston MA 02109

MYHAND, WANDA RESHEL, paralegal, legal assistant; b. Detroit, Aug. 15, 1963; d. Ralph and Geraldine (Leavell) M. Office mgr./adminstrv. asst. Gregory Terrell & Co., CPA, Detroit, 1987-90; legal sec. Ford Motor Co., Detroit, 1990-91; office mgr. M.G. Christian Builders, Inc., Detroit, 1991; paralegal, legal asst. Law Office of Karri Mitchell, Detroit, 1991—. Vol. UNCF Telethon Detroit, 1988. Mem. NAFE. Avocations: jigsaw puzzles, crossword puzzles.

MYHRE, BYRON ARNOLD, pathologist, educator; b. Fargo, N.D., Oct. 22, 1928; s. Ben Arnold and Amy Lillian (Gilbertson) M.; m. Eileen Marguerite Scherling, June 16, 1953; children: Patricia Ann, Bruce Allen. B.S., U. Ill., 1950; M.S., Northwestern U., 1952, M.D., 1953; Ph.D., U. Wis., 1962. Intern Evanston (Ill.) Hosp., 1953-54; resident Children's Meml. Hosp., Chgo., 1956-57, U. Wis. Hosp., Madison, 1957-60; assoc. med. dir. Milw. Blood Center, 1962-66; sci. dir. Los Angeles Red Cross Blood Center, 1966-72; dir. Blood Bank Harbor-UCLA Med. Center, Torrance, 1972-85; chief clin. pathology Harbor-UCLA Med. Center, 1985—; prof. pathology UCLA, 1972—. Author: Quality Control on Blood Banking, 1974, (with others) Textbook of Clinical Pathology, 1972, Paternity Testing, 1975; editor seminar procs.; contbr. articles to med. jours., chpts. to books. Served with USAF, 1954-56. Mem. AMA, Am. Soc. Clin. Pathology (dep. commr. commn. on continuing edn.), Am. Assn. Blood Banks (pres. 1978-79), Coll. Am. Pathologists (chmn. blood bank survey com.), Assn. Clin. Scientists (pres. 1993), Calif. Med. Assn., Calif. Blood Bank Systems (past pres.), Wis. Blood Bank Assn. (past pres.), L.A. Acad. Medicine (past pres.), Harbor-UCLA Faculty Soc. (past pres.), Palos Verdes Breadfast Club (v.p. 1995). Home: 4004 Via Larga Vis Pls Vrds Est CA 90274-1122 Office: Harbor-UCLA Med Center 1000 W Carson St Torrance CA 90509-2910

MYHRE, KATHLEEN RANDI, nurse; b. Everett, Wash., Apr. 18, 1952; d. Richard Alvin and Beverley Jeanette (Nesbit) M. LPN, Bellingham (Wash.) Tech. Sch., 1970; ADN, Lane C.C., Eugene, Oreg., 1988. RN, Oreg. LPN night charge nurse Island's Convalescent Ctr., Friday Harbor, Wash., 1970-75; LPN float Sacred Heart Gen. Hosp., Eugene, Oreg., 1975-87; charge nurse urgent care unit Eugene Clinic, 1987—. Democrat. Avocations: fishing, hiking, stained glass, gardening. Home: 80687 Lost Creek Rd Dexter OR 97431-9742

MYHRE, ROGER L., agricultural products executive; b. 1938. Sr. v.p. Agrex, Inc., Shawnee Mission, Kans. Office: AGREX Inc 9300 W 110th St Ste 500 Overland Park KS 66210*

MYHREN, TRYGVE EDWARD, communications company executive; b. Palmerton, Pa., Jan. 3, 1937; s. Arne Johannes and Anita (Blatz) M.; m. Carol Jane Enman, Aug. 8, 1964; children: Erik, Kirsten, Tor; m. 2d Victoria Hamilton, Nov. 14, 1981; 1 stepchild, Paige. BA in Philosophy and Polit. Sci., Dartmouth Coll., 1958, MBA, 1959. Sales mgr., unit mgr. Procter and Gamble, Cin., 1963-65; sr. cons. Glendinning Cos., Westport, Conn., 1965-69; pres. Auberge Vintners, 1970-73; exec. v.p. Mktg. Continental, Westport, 1969-73; v.p., gen. mgr. CRM, Inc., Del Mar, Calif., 1973-75; v.p. mktg. Am. TV and Communications Corp., Englewood, Colo., 1975-78, sr. v.p. mktg. and programming, 1978-79, exec. v.p., 1980, pres., 1980, chmn. bd., chief exec. officer, 1981-88; v.p., then exec. v.p. Time Inc., N.Y.C., 1981-88; treas., vice chmn., then chmn. bd. dirs., mem. exec. com. Nat. Cable TV Assn., Washington, 1982-91; mem. adv. com. on HDTV, FCC, 1987-89; bd. dirs. Advanced Mktg. Sys., Inc., LaJolla, Citizens Bank Corp., Providence, Providence Jour. Co., Continental Cablevision, Inc., Boston, Peopod, Ltd., Chgo.; pres. Myhren Media, 1989—, Greenwood Cable Mgmt., 1989-91, Providence Jour. Co., 1990—; pres., CEO King Broadcast Co., 1991-96. Vice chmn. Pub. Edn. Coalition; mem. Colo. Forum, 1984-91, chmn. higher edn. com., 1986; bd. dirs., founder Colo. Bus. Com. for the Arts, 1985-91; mem. exec. coun. Found. for Commemoration U.S. Constn., 1987-90; mem. Nat. GED Task Force, 1987-90, Colo. Baseball Commn., 1989-91, Colo. Film Commn., 1989-91; trustee Nat. Jewish Hosp., 1989— (Humanitarian award 1996), R.I. Hosp., 1991-95, Lifespan Health Sys., 1994—; chmn. Looc 1995 NCAA Hockey Championship. Lt. (j.g.) USNR, 1959-63. Recipient Disting. Leader award Nat. Cable TV Assn., 1988, ann. humanitarian award Nat. Jewish Hosp., 1996. Mem. Cable TV Adminstrn. and Mktg. Soc. (pres. 1978-79, Grand Tam award 1985, One of a Kind award 1994), Cable Adv. Bur. (founder 1978), Chrons and Colitis Found. Am. (trustee Rocky Mountain chpt.). Episcopalian.

MYLES, KEVIN MICHAEL, metallurgical engineer; b. Chgo., July 18, 1934; s. Michael J. and Ursula (May) M.; m. Joan Christine Ganczewski, Dec. 16, 1967; children: Kathleen, Gary, Jennifer. BS in Metallurgical Engring., U. Ill., 1956, PhD in Phys. Metall. Engring., 1963. Asst. mgr. nuclear fuel reprossing program Argonne (Ill.) Nat. Lab., 1977-79, dep. dir. fossil energy program, 1982-87, mgr. fuel cell program, 1987-88, mgr. electrochemical tech. program, 1988—, assoc. dir. chem. tech. div., 1992—; adj. prof. materials sci. U. Ill., Chgo., 1967-69; prof. materials sci. Midwest Coll. Engring., Lombard, Ill., 1969-81. Contbr. articles to Jour. Phys. Chemistry, Chem. Engring. Sci., Jour. Electrochemical Soc., Jour. Fusion Energy, Jour. Power Sources. Mem. Sch. Bd. Dist. #58, Downers Grove, Ill., 1964-70. Capt. USAR, 1956-68, Korea. Mem. Am. Soc. for Metals, AIME, Alpha Sigma Mu. Achievements include 8 patents in field. Office: Argonne Nat Lab 9700 Cass Ave Argonne IL 60439-4803

MYLROIE, WILLA WILCOX, transportation engineer, regional planner; b. Seattle, May 30, 1917; d. Elgin Roscoe and Ruth B. (Begg) Wilcox; m. John Ellis Mylroie (dec. 1947); children: Steven Wilcox Mylroie, Jo Mylroie Sohnerone; m. Donald Gile Fassett, Dec. 30, 1966. BS in Civil Engring., U. Wash., 1940, MS in Regional Planning, 1953. Lic. profl. civil engr. Civil engr. U.S. Engring. Dept. C.E., Seattle, 1941-46; affiliate prof. civil engring. U. Wash., Seattle, 1948-51, research asst. prof. civil engring., 1951-56; assoc. prof. civil engring. Purdue U., Lafayette, Ind., 1956-58; research engr. and planner Wash. State Dept. Hwys., Olympia, 1958-69, head research and spl. assignment div., 1969-81; cons. civil engring. and regional planning Olympia, 1981—; cons. King County Design Commn., Seattle, 1981-89; advisor Coll. Engring. U. Wash., 1978-86, affiliate prof. civil engring., 1981-84; advisor Wash. State U. Coll. Engring., Pullman, 1977-85. Active Girls Scouts U.S. coun., Boy Scouts Am., Olympia, Renton, 1950-66; pres. high sch. PTA, Olympia; commr. Thurston County Planning Commn., Olympia; U.S. Coast Guard Auxilliary, 1982-89, U.S. Power Squadron, 1967—; citizen amb. People to People Trip, Moscow, St. Petersburg, Russia and Muensk, Bolarus. Recipient Profl. Recognition award Women's Transp., Spokane, Spl. Svc. award Transp. Rsch. Bd. Coun., Washington, U. Wash. Coll. Engring. Alumni Achievement award, 1993. Fellow ASCE (ad hoc vis. com. engring. coun. for profl. devel., Edmund Friedman Profl. Recognition award 1978), Inst. Transp. Engrs. (hon. mem., internat. bd. dirs., Tech. Coun. award 1982); mem. Planning Assn. Wash. (bd. dirs.), Sigma Xi. Avocations: sailing, gardening, travel, music, vol. community activities. Home and Office: 7501 Boston Harbor Rd NE Olympia WA 98506-9720

MYRA, HAROLD LAWRENCE, publisher; b. Camden, N.J., July 19, 1939; s. John Samuel and Esther (Christensen) M.; m. Jeanette Austin, May 7, 1966; children: Michelle, Todd, Gregory, Ricky, Joshua, Lindsey. B.S., East Stroudsburg State Coll., 1961; Litt.D., John Wesley Coll., 1976; D.Lit., Biola U., 1984; DLitt, Gordon Coll., 1992. Tchr. Pocono Mountain Jointure, Cresco, Pa., 1961; editorial asst. Youth for Christ Internat., Wheaton, Ill., 1961-62; asso. editor Youth for Christ Internat., 1962-64, mng. editor, 1964-65, dir. of lit., 1965-66; v.p. lit. div., pub. Campus Life, Wheaton, 1966-75; pres., chief exec. officer Christianity Today, Inc., Carol Stream, Ill., 1975—. Author: No Man in Eden, 1969, Michelle, You Scallawag, I Love You, 1972, The New You, 1972, The Carpenter, 1972, Elsbeth, 1975, Is There a Place I Can Scream?, 1976, Santa, Are You For Real?, 1979, Love Notes to Jeanette, 1979, The Choice, 1980, Halloween, 1982, Your Super-Terrific Birthday, 1985, Living By God's Surprises, 1988, Children in the Night, 1991, The Shining Face, 1993, Morning Child, 1994. Presbyterian. Home: 1737 Marion Ct Wheaton IL 60187-3319 Office: Christianity Today 465 Gundersen Dr Carol Stream IL 60188-2415

MYRBERG, ARTHUR AUGUST, JR., marine biological sciences educator; b. Chicago Heights, Ill., June 28, 1933; s. Arthur August and Helen Katherine (Stelle) M.; divorced; children—Arthur August III, Beverly Priscilla. A.B., Ripon Coll., 1954; M.S., U. Ill., 1958; Ph.D. (NIH fellow), UCLA, 1961. Research asst. Ill. Natural History Survey, Champaign-Urbana, 1957; mem. faculty U. Miami, Fla., 1964—; assoc. prof. Sch. Marine and Atmospheric Sci., 1967-72, prof., 1972—; chmn. div. marine biology and fisheries U. Miami, Fla., 1991, academic chmn. div. marine biology and fisheries, 1991-93. Contbr. articles to profl. jours., chpts. to books; assoc. editor Bull. Marine Sci, 1964-73. Mem. Khoury League, 1967-75. Served to 1st lt., inf. U.S. Army, 1954-57. Recipient Disting. Alumni award Ripon Coll., 1991; NIH postdoctoral fellow Max Planck Inst. Behavioral Physiology, Seewiesen, Germany, 1961-64. Fellow Animal Behavior Soc. (Disting. Fellow Lecture award 1993), Am. Inst. Fishery Rsch. Biologists; mem. Am. Soc. Ichthyologists and Herpetologists, Am. Soc. Zoologists, Ecol. Soc. Am., Am. Inst. Biol. Scis., N.Y. Acad. Scis., Internat. Assn. Fish Ethologists, Am. Elasmobranch Soc. (gov. 1985-90), Sigma Xi (nat. lectr. 1980-81), Phi Sigma, Omicron Delta Kappa. Achievements include demonstration of the importance of sound production for survival and reproduction in fishes, that sharks are attracted to specific types of underwater sound; reported on the social behavior of sharks. Home: 6001 SW 65th Ave Miami FL 33143-2031

MYRDAL, ROSEMARIE CARYLE, state official, former state legislator; b. Minot, N.D., May 20, 1929; d. Harry Dirk and Olga Jean (Dragge) Lohse; m. B. John Myrdal, June 21, 1952; children: Jan, Mark, Harold, Paul, Amy. BS, N.D. State U., 1951. Registered profl. first grade tchr., N.D. Tchr. N.D., 1951-71; bus. mgr. Edinburg Sch. Dist., 1974-81; mem. N.D. Ho. of Reps., Bismarck, 1984-92, mem. appropriations com., 1991-92; lt. gov., State of N.D., Bismarck, 1992—; sch. evaluator Walsh County Sch. Bds. Assn., Grafton, N.D., 1983-84; evaluator, work presenter N.D. Sch. Bds. Assn., Bismarck, 1983-84; mem. sch. bd. Edinburg Sch. Dist., 1981-90; adv. com. Red River Trade Corridor, Inc., 1989—. Co-editor: Heritage '76, 1976, Heritage '89, 1989. Precinct committeewoman Gardar Twp. Rep. Com., 1980-86; leader Hummingbirds 4-H Club, Edinburg, 1980-83; bd. dirs. Camp Sioux Diabetic Children, Grand Forks, N.D., 1980-90, N.D. affiliate Am. Diabetes Assn., Families First-Child Welfare Reform Initiative, Region IV, 1989-92; dir. N.D. Diabetes Assn., 1989-91; chmn. N.D. Ednl. TelecommunicationsCoun., 1989-90; vice chmn. N.D. Legis. Interim Jobs Devel. Commn., 1989-90. Mem. AAUW (pres. 1982-84 Pembina County area), Pembina County Hist. Soc. (historian 1976-84), Northeastern N.D. Heritage Assn. (pres. 1986-92), Red River Valley Heritage Soc. (bd. dirs. 1985-92). Lutheran. Club: Agassiz Garden (Park River) (pres. 1968-69). Avocations: gardening, architectural history, ethnic foods, historic/cultural preservation. Home: 121 E Arikara Ave Apt 302 Bismarck ND 58501-2638 Office: 600 E Boulevard Ave Bismarck ND 58505

MYREN, RICHARD ALBERT, criminal justice consultant; b. Madison, Wis., Aug. 9, 1924; s. Andrew Olaus and Olyanna (Olson) M.; m. Patricia Ross Hubin, June 12, 1948; children: Nina Ross Schroepfer, Tania Ellis Zobel, Kristina Albee Myren Sheldon, Andrew James. BS, U. Wis., 1948; LLB, Harvard U., 1952; LLD (hon.), U. New Haven, 1976. Bar: N.C. 1954. Research chemist U.S. Dept. Agr., No. Regional Research Lab., Peoria, Ill., 1948-49; asst. to assoc. research prof. pub. law and govt. Inst. Govt., Chapel Hill, N.C., 1952-56; asst. to assoc. prof. Ind. U., 1956-66; dean, prof. Sch. Criminal Justice, State U. N.Y., Albany, 1966-76; dean, prof. Sch. Justice, Am. U., Washington, 1976-86, prof. emeritus, 1986—; cons. Washington, 1987—; vis. prof. Inst. Criminology, Cambridge (Eng.) U., 1973-74, East China Inst. for Politics and Law, Shanghai, People's Republic of China, 1988; cons. law enforcement programs for children and youth Children's Bur., HEW, Washington, 1960-62; cons. Pres.'s Com. on Juvenile Delinquency and Youth Crime, 1962-64, Pres.'s Commn. on Law Enforcement and Adminstrn. Criminal Justice, 1966, U.S. Law Enforcement Assistance Adminstrn., 1968-82, N.Y. State Temp. Commn. on Constl. Conv., 1967, N.Y. State Dept. Edn., 1967, 69, Calif. Coordinating Council for Higher Edn., 1969-70, Nat. Adv. Commn. on Criminal Justice Standards and Goals, 1971-72, Tenn. Higher Edn. Commn., 1976, Ky. Dept. Justice, 1977-78, NSF, 1978—, U.S. Civil Rights Commn., 1978, others. Author: Coroners in North Carolina: A Discussion of Their Problems, 1953, Indiana Sheriffs' Manual of Law and Practice, rev. edit, 1959, Indiana Conservation Officers' Manual of Law and Practice, 1961; (with Lynn D. Swanson) Police Work With Children, 1962; (with Carroll L. Christenson) The Walsh-Healey Public Contracts Act: A Critical Review of Prevailing Minimum Wage Determinations, 1966, Education in Criminal Justice, 1970, Law and Justice: An Introduction, 1988, Investigation for Determination of Fact: A Primer on Proof, 1989; contbr. to: Bases for Justice Systems: Law and the Social Sciences (Gordon E. Misner), 1980, Five Year Outlook: Problems, Opportunities and Constraints in Science and Technology, 1980; assoc. editor: Jour. Criminal Justice; contbr. articles to profl. jours. Bd. dirs. Sex Info. and Edn. Council U.S., 1972-75. Served with inf. AUS, 1943-46, ETO; with USNR, 1954-68. Fulbright research scholar to Argentina Cordoba, 1964-65. Mem. N.C. Bar Assn., Sociedad Argentina de Sociologia. Home: 1051 S Highland St Apt 6D Mount Dora FL 32757-6323

MYRICK, BISMARCK, diplomat; b. Portsmouth, Va., Dec. 23, 1940; children: Bismarck, Jr., Wesley Todd, Allison Elizabeth. BA, U. Tampa, 1972; MA, Syracuse U., 1973, postgrad., 1979-80. Enlisted U.S. Army, 1959, advanced through grades to fgn. area officer; desk officer U.S. Dept. of State, Somalia, 1980-82; polit. officer U.S. Dept. of State, Monrovia, 1982-84; action officer office strategic nuclear policy bur. politico-milit. affairs U.S. Dept. of State, 1985-87, dep. dir. policy plans and coordination bur. inter-Am. affairs, 1987-89, Una Chapman Cox fellow US-African Policy, 1988-90; consul gen. U.S. Dept. of State, Durban, South Africa, 1990-93, Capetown, South Africa, 1993-95; amb. to Kingdom of Lesotho U.S. Dept. of State, Maseru, 1995—. Author: Three Aspects of Crisis in Colonial Kenya, 1975. Decorated Silver Star, Purple Heart, 4 Bronze Stars. Office: Lesotho Dept of State Washington DC 20521-2340*

MYRICK, SUE, congresswoman, former mayor; b. Tiffin, Ohio, Aug. 1, 1941; d. William Henry and Margaret Ellen (Roby) Wilkins; m. Jim Forest (div.); children: Greg, Dan; m. Wilbur Edward Myrick Jr., Sept. 11, 1977. Student, Heidelberg Coll., 1959-60, HHD (hon.). Exec. sec. to mayor and city mgr. City of Alliance, Ohio, 1962-63; dir. br. office Stark County Ct. of Juvenile and Domestic Rels., Alliance, 1963-65; pres. Myrick Agy., Charlotte, N.C., 1971-95; mayor of Charlotte, 1987-91; mem. 104th Congress from 9th N.C. District, Washington, D.C., 1995—; candidate for U.S. Senate from N.C., 1992; active Heart Fund, Multiple Sclerosis, March of Dimes, Arts and Scis. Coun. Fund Dr.; past mem. adv. bd. Uptown Shelter, Uptown Homeless Task Force, bd. dirs. N.C. Inst. Politics; v.p. Sister Cities Internat.; mem. Pres. Bush's Affordable Housing Commn.; founder, coord. Charlotte vol. tornado relief effort; former bd. dirs. Learning How; former mem. adv. bd. U.S. Conf. Mayors; mem.-at-large Charlotte City Coun., 1983-85, Strengthening Am. Commn.; lay leader, Sunday sch. tchr. 1st United Meth. Ch.; treas. Mecklenburg Ministries; former trustee U.S. Conf. of Mayors. Recipient Woman of Yr. award Harrisonburg, Va., 1968; named one of Outstanding Young Women of Am., 1968. Mem. Women's Polit. Caucus, Beta Sigma Phi. Republican. Home: 310 W 8th St Charlotte NC 28202-1704 Office: US House Reps 509 Cannon House Office Bldg Washington DC 20515-3309 also: Myrick Enterprises 505 N Poplar St Charlotte NC 28202-1729

MYSAK, LAWRENCE ALEXANDER, oceanographer, climatologist, mathematician, educator; b. Saskatoon, Sask., Can., Jan. 22, 1940; s. Stephen and Nettie (Trojan) M.; m. Diane Mary Eeles, Aug. 15, 1974; children: Paul Alexander, Claire Anastasia. BSc, U. Alta., Can., 1961; MSc, U. Adelaide, Australia, 1963; AM, Harvard U., 1964, PhD, 1967. Rsch. fellow Harvard U., 1966-67; mem. faculty U. B.C., Vancouver, 1967-86, prof. math. and oceanography, 1976-86; Atmospheric Environ. Svc./Natural Scis. Engring. Rsch. Coun.; sr. indsl. rsch. prof. climatology McGill U., Montreal, Que., Can., 1986-96, dir. Climate Rsch Group, 1986-90, Can. Steamship Lines prof. meteorology, 1989—, founding dir. Ctr. for Climate and Global Change Rsch., 1990-96; vis. rsch. assoc. Oreg. State U., summer 1968; sr. visitor Cambridge (Eng.) U., 1971-72; vis. scientist Inst. Ocean Sci., Sidney, B.C., fall 1976, Nat. Ctr. Atmospheric Rsch., Boulder, Colo., 1977; vis. prof. U.S. Naval Postgrad. Sch., Monterey, Calif., summer 1981, Swiss Fed. inst., Tech., Zurich, 1982-83; George's Lemaître vis. prof. Cath. U. Louvain, Belgium, 1995. Co-author: Waves in the Ocean, 1978; also articles in profl. jours.; assoc. editor Jour. Phys. Oceanography, 1977-92, Atmospheric-Ocean, 1988-91, Climatol. Bull., 1992-93; contbg. editor Am. Geophys. Union books on coastal and esturaine studies, 1987—; mem. editl. bd. Geophys. and Astrophys. Fluid Dynamics, 1983-96. Fellow Acad. of Sci. of Royal Soc. Can. (v.p. Acad. of Sci. 1991-93, pres. 1993-96); mem. Can. Meteorol. and Oceanog. Soc. (co-recipient Pres.'s prize 1980), Royal Soc. Can. (life), Am. Meteorol. Soc., Am. Geophys. Union, Oceanography Soc., European Geophys. Soc. Office: McGill U, 805 Sherbrooke St W, Montreal, PQ Canada H3A 2K6

MYSEL, RANDY HOWARD, publishing company executive; b. Bronx, N.Y., July 26, 1954; s. Sam and Esther (Sinsheimer) M.; m. Rosemary Eileen Vaccari, July 25, 1987; children: Steven, Samantha, Sophia. AA, Queensboro C.C., Queens, N.Y., 1975; BA in Acctg., Queens Coll., 1977; MBA, Adelphi U., 1986; grad., Warwick Sch. Bus., London. Mktg./acctg. profl. CBS, Inc., N.Y.C., 1981-86; mktg. analyst Reed Reference Pub., N.Y.C., 1986, bus. mgr., 1987; v.p., planning, in-house sales Reed Reference Pub., New Providence, N.J., 1988—; creator in-house sales dept. Reed Reference pub., creator all advt. revenue. Avocations: tennis, golf, softball, bowling, reading. Home: Reed Reference Publishing 63 Lawrence Dr Berkeley Heights NJ 07922 Office: Reed Reference Pub 121 Chanlon Rd New Providence NJ 07974*

NABERS, DRAYTON, JR., insurance company executive; b. Birmingham, Ala., Dec. 2, 1940; s. Drayton Sr. and Jane (Porter) N.; m. Fairfax Smathers, Dec. 31, 1965; children: Drayton III, Mary James, Fairfax Virginia. BA, Princeton U., 1962; LLB, Yale U., 1965. Law clk. to justice Hugo Black U.S. Supreme Ct., Washington, 1965-66; assoc. Cabaniss, Johnston, Gardner, Dumas & O'Neal, 1967-71, ptnr., 1971-79; sr. v.p. ops., gen. counsel Protective Life Ins. Co., 1979; pres. Empire Gen. Life Ins. Co., 1980-82; pres., COO Protective Life Corp./Protective Life Ins. Co., 1982-92; pres., CEO Protective Life Ins. Co, Birmingham, Ala., 1992-94, chmn., pres., CEO, 1994—; bd. dirs. Protective Life Corp., Protective Life Ins. Co., Am. Found. Life Ins. Co., Energen, Inc., Nat. Bank of Commerce. Mem. steering com. Leadership Birmingham; bd. dirs. Ala. Assn. Ind. Colls.; pres., bd. dirs. Birmingham Alive; trustee So. Rsch. Inst., Berry Coll. Mem. Birmingham Bar Assn., Ala. Bar Assn. Office: Protective Life Corp 2801 Highway 280 S Birmingham AL 35223-2407 Office: PO Box 2606 Birmingham AL 35202-2606

NABHOLZ, JOSEPH VINCENT, biologist, ecologist; b. Memphis, Nov. 3, 1945; s. Martin Peter and Helen Kathleen (Garbacz) N.; m. Sue Ann Winterburn, Aug. 12, 1972; children: Karen Stacey, Pamela Michelle. BS, Christian Bros. U., Memphis, 1968; MS, U. Ga., 1973, PHD, 1978. Sr. biologist U.S. EPA, Washington, 1979—; reviewer NSF and profl. jours., 1973—, Standards Methods Com., Am. Water Works Assn., Denver 18th through 20th edits.; evaluator Office Exptl. Learning U. Md., College Park, Md., 1984-86. Co-author: Methods of Ecological Toxicology, 1981, Testing for Effects of Chemicals on Ecosystems, 1981; author: Estimating Toxicity of Industrial Chemicals to Aquatic Organisms Using Structure Activity Relationships, 1988; contbr. over 20 articles to profl. jours. Bd. dirs. Community Assn. Rollingwood Village (4th sect.), Woodbridge, Va., 1981-90, v.p. 1981-82, pres. 1983-90, maintainence chmn. 1990—. Decorated Army Commendation medal with oak leaf cluster, U.S. Army, Vietnam, 1969, '70. Mem. AAAS, Am. Inst. Biol. Scis., Assn. Southeastern Biologists, Internat. Assn. Ecology, Ecol. Soc. Am. (life), Phi Kappa Phi (life). Roman Catholic. Achievements include pragmatic application of theory of chemical structure activity relationships for routine risk assessment of industrial chemicals for environmental toxicity. Home: 13627 Bentley Cir Woodbridge VA 22192-4340 Office: US EPA 7403 ET 427 401 M St SW Washington DC 20460-0001

NABHOLZ, MARY VAUGHAN, rehabilitation nurse; b. Memphis, July 4, 1938; d. George E. Jr. and Anna Marie (Hannifin) Vaughan; m. William James Nabholz, Jr., May 30, 1959; children: Kathleen Marie, William James III, Michael Vaughan. Diploma, St. Joseph Hosp., Memphis, 1959; BA, Webster U., 1978. Cert. CIRS, CCM. Staff nurse St. Joseph Hosp., St. Charles, Mo., 1965-77; supr. Always Care Nursing Svc., St. Louis, 1977-78; home care nurse Jewish Hosp., St. Louis, 1979-81; regional med. mgr. Md. Casualty Co., St. Louis, 1981-88; case mgr. Am. Health Network, St. Louis, 1988-91; regional mgr., 1990; cons., owner Nabholz & Assocs., Bridgeton, Mo., 1991—. Bd. dirs. Ctr. Head Injury Svcs. Mem. Nat. Head Injury Assn., Nat. Spinal Cord Assn., Assn. Rehab. Nurses, Nat. Rehab. Assn.

NABI, STANLEY ANDREW, investment executive; b. Baghdad, Iraq, Sept. 17, 1930; came to U.S., 1947; s. Moshi S. and Victoria T. (Mukamal) N.; m. Bette E. Miller, Mar. 31, 1968; children: Deborah Susan, Lisa Meryl. B.A., Columbia U., 1952; postgrad., NYU, 1954-58. Gen. ptnr. Schweickart & Co., N.Y.C., 1954-72; gen. ptnr., chief investment officer Lazard Freres & Co., N.Y.C., 1973-84; exec. v.p. Bessemer Trust Co., N.A., 1985—; pres., CEO, Bessemer Investors Svcs., 1985-95; vice chmn., chmn. investment policy com. Wood, Struthers & Winthrop, N.Y.C., 1995—; lectr. New Sch. Social Research, N.Y.C., 1963-68; investment cons. U.S. Steel and Carnegie Pension Fund, N.Y.C., 1979—; dir. Bargain Town U.S.A., N.Y.C., 1962-69; mem. Pres.'s Coun. New Sch. Social Rsch., N.Y.C., 1989—; adj. prof. fin. Grad. Sch. Bus. Fordham U., N.Y., 1992—. Editor: weekly jour. The Analyst, 1957-72; assoc. editor: jour. The Fin. Analysts Jour., 1971-83.

Trustee NABI Found., 1964—. Served with U.S. Army, 1952-54. Mem. N.Y. Soc. Security Analysts (pres. 1971-72), Inst. Chartered Fin. Analysts, Fin. Analysts Fedn. (dir. 1972-74). Home: 83 Beach Rd Great Neck NY 11023-1019 Office: 630 Fifth Ave New York NY 10111-0001

NABRIT, SAMUEL MILTON, retired embryologist; b. Macon, Ga., Feb. 21, 1905. BS, Morehouse Coll., 1925; MS, Brown U., 1928; 13 hon. degrees, various U.S. univs. Instr. zoology Morehouse Coll., 1925-27, prof., 1928-31; prof. Atlanta U., 1932-55; pres. Tex. So. U., 1955-66; commr. US AEC, 1966-67; exec. dir. So. Fellows Fund, 1967-81; exch. prof. Atlanta U., 1930, dean Grad. Sch.; gen. edn. bd. fellow Columbia U., 1943; rsch. fellow U. Brussels, 1950; coord. Carnegie Exp. Grant-in-Aid Rsch. Program; mem. sci. bd. NSF, 1956-60; mem. corp. Marine Biol. Lab., Woods Hole; mem. Marine Biol. Labs., AEC, 1966-67; exec. dir. Nat. Fellows Fund, 1967-81; interim dir. Atlanta U. Ctr., 1989-91. Fellow AAAS; mem. Inst. Medicine-NAS, Soc. Devel. Biology, Nat. Assn. Rsch. Sci. Tchg., Nat. Inst. Sci. (pres. 1945), Am. Soc. Zoology, Sigma Xi.

NACE, BARRY JOHN, lawyer; b. York, Pa., Nov. 28, 1944; s. John Harrison and Mildred Louise (Orwig) N.; m. Andrea Marcia Giardini, Apr. 28, 1973; children: Christopher Thomas, Jonathan Barry, Matthew Andrew. BS, Dickinson Coll., 1965, JD, 1969, LLD, 1994. Bar: Md. 1970, D.C. 1971, Pa. 1972, U.S. Ct. Appeals (3d, 4th and D.C. cirs.), U.S. Supreme Ct. Ptnr. Davis & Nace, Washington, 1972-78, Paulson & Nace, Bethesda, Md., 1978-85; sr. ptnr. Paulson, Nace & Norwind, Washington, 1986—. Fellow Roscoe Pound Found. (trustee); mem. Am. Law Inst., D.C. Bar Assn., Montgomery County Bar Assn., Assn. Trial Lawyers Am. (gov. 1976-87, pres. 1993-94), Met. D.C. Trial Attys. (pres. 1977, 87, Atty. of Yr. 1976), Trial Lawyers for Pub. Justice, Civil Justice Found. (trustee), Internat. Acad. Trial Lawyers, Lambert Soc., Am. Inns of Ct., Am. Law Inst. Am. Bd. of Profl. Liability Attorneys. Avocations: golf, tennis, reading, racquetball. Home: 6208 Garnett Dr Bethesda MD 20815-6618 Office: Paulson Nace & Norwind 1814 N St NW Washington DC 20036-2404

NACHMAN, FREDERICK J., public relations executive. Sr.v.p., dir. investor rels. Golin/Harris Comms., Inc., Chgo.; formerly ptnr. Fin. Rels. Bd., Chgo. Office: Golin/Harris Comm Inc 500 N Michigan Ave Chicago IL 60611

NACHMAN, GERALD WEIL, columnist, critic, author, lecturer; b. Oakland, Calif., Jan. 13, 1938; s. Leonard Calvert and Isabel (Weil) N.; m. Mary Campbell McGeachy, Sept. 3, 1966 (div. 1979). Student, Merritt Coll., 1955-57; BA in Journalism, San Jose State U., 1960. TV and humor columnist San Jose (Calif.) Mercury, 1960-63; feature writer N.Y. Post, N.Y.C., 1963-66; drama critic Oakland (Calif.) Tribune, 1966-71; syndicated humor columnist N.Y. Daily News, 1973-79; critic and columnist San Francisco Chronicle, 1979-93; author, 1995—; humor columnist N.Y. Times Syndicate, 1996—; juror Pulitzer Prize Com. to choose best play, 1991. Author: The Portable Nachman, 1960, Playing House, 1978, Out on a Whim, 1983, The Fragile Bachelor, 1989; contbr. to (book) Snooze, 1986; contbr. articles to newspapers, mags.; author, co-lyricist (revues) Quirks, 1979, Aftershocks, 1992. Recipient Page One award N.Y. Newspaper Guild, 1965, Deems Taylor award ASCAP, 1989. Home: 281 Juanita Way San Francisco CA 94127-1744

NACHMAN, MERTON ROLAND, JR., lawyer; b. Montgomery, Ala., Dec. 21, 1923; s. Merton Roland and Maxine (Mayer) N.; children: Nancy Nachman Yardley, Linda Nachman Connelly, Betsy Wild, Amy N. DeRoche, Karen Vann; m. Martha Street, June 8, 1968. AB cum laude, Harvard U., 1943, JD, 1948. Bar: Ala. 1949, U.S. Supreme Ct. 1953, U.S. Ct. Appeals (5th and 11th cirs.), U.S. Ct. Claims, U.S. Tax Ct. Asst. atty. gen. State of Ala., 1949-54; ptnr. Knabe & Nachman, Montgomery, 1954-59; adminstrv. asst. to Senator John Sparkman of Ala., 1956; ptnr. Steiner, Crum & Baker, Montgomery, 1959-86; ptnr. Balch & Bingham, 1986-94, coun. 1994—. Chmn. human rights com. Ala. Prison System, 1976-78. With USN, 1943-46. Recipient award of merit Ala. State Bar, 1974; cert. of appreciation Supreme Ct. Ala., 1974. Fellow Am. Coll. Trial Lawyers; mem. ABA (com. on fed. judiciary 1982-88, bd. govs. 1978-81), Ala. State Bar (pres. 1973-74), Am. Judicature Soc. (dir. 1976-80, Herbert Lincoln Harley award 1974), Am. Law Inst., Ala. Law Inst., Unity Club (Montgomery), Am. Acad. Appellate Lawyers. Episcopalian. Office: 2 Dexter Ave PO Box 78 Montgomery AL 36101

NACHMAN, NORMAN HARRY, lawyer; b. Chgo.; s. Harry and Mary (Leibowitz) N.; m. Anne Lev, June 19, 1932; children: Nancy Nachman Laskow, James Lev, Susan Lev. PhB, U. Chgo., 1930, JD, 1932. Bar: Ill. 1932, U.S. Dist. Ct. (no. dist.) Ill. 1932, U.S. Dist. Ct. (we. dist.) Tex. 1978, U.S. Ct. Appeals (7th cir.) 1942, U.S. Ct. Appeals (4th cir.) 1978, U.S. Ct. Appeals (8th cir.) 1994, U.S. Supreme Ct. 1942. Assoc. Michael Gesas, Chgo., 1932-35; assoc. Schwartz & Cooper, Chgo., 1936-40, ptnr., 1940-46; pvt. practice, Chgo., 1947-67; founder, sr. ptnr. Nachman, Munitz & Sweig, Ltd., Chgo., 1967-87; ptnr. Winston & Strawn, 1987-94; counsel McDermott, Will & Emery, 1994—; mem. adv. com. bankruptcy rules Jud. Conf. U.S., 1960-76, 78-88; mem. Nat. Bankruptcy Conf., 1952—, mem. com. bankruptcy reorganization plans and securities problems, 1977-85; mem. faculty numerous bankruptcy seminars throughout U.S. Contbg. editor: Collier on Bankruptcy, 1981, 84. Chmn. appeals bd. Chgo. Dept. Environ. Control, 1960-80. Served to lt. USN, 1943-46. Mem. ABA (past chmn. comml. bankruptcy com.), Chgo. Bar Assn. (pres. 1963-64), Ill. Bar Assn., Standard Club, Law Club. Jewish. Office: McDermott Will & Emery 227 W Monroe St Chicago IL 60606-5016

NACHMAN, RALPH LOUIS, physician, educator; b. Bayonne, N.J., June 29, 1931; s. Samuel Nachman and Ethel Nelson; m. Nancy Rubin; children: Susan, Steve. BA, Vanderbilt U., 1953, MD, 1956. Lic. physician N.Y.; diplomate Am. Bd. Internal Medicine; subsplty. hematology, med. oncology. Intern in medicine Vanderbilt U. Hosp., 1956-57; asst. resident in medicine Montefiore Hosp., 1960-62; asst. resident in pathology N.Y. Hosp.-Cornell U. Med. Ctr., N.Y.C., 1957-58, rsch. fellow in medicine, 1962-63; dir. labs. for clin. pathology N.Y. Hosp., 1963-69, assoc. attending physician, 1968-72, attending physician, 1972—; from instr. to asst. prof. to assoc. prof. medicine Cornell Med. Ctr., 1963-72, chief divns. hematology, 1968-93, prof. medicine, 1972—; vice chmn. dept. medicine Cornell U. Med. Coll., 1974-78, acting chmn. dept. medicine, 1974-75, dir. Specialized Ctr. Rsch. in Thrombosis, 1976—, acting co-chmn. dept. medicine, 1980-81, bd. overseers, 1987-89, chmn. Dept. of Med., 1990; physician-in-chief New York Hospital, 1990; guest investigator Rockefeller U., 1969-70; Wiessberg lectr. Case Western Res. U., 1978; Aggeler lectr. U. Calif., San Francisco, 1981; Patek lectr. Boston U., 1981; Rosenthal lectr. Mt. Sinai, 1982; Beaumont lectr. Wash. U., 1983; Wiener lectr. N.Y. Blood Ctr., 1983; chmn. Gordon Conf. on Hemostasis, 1984; Alpha Omega Alpha lectr. N.Y. Med. Coll., 1985; Sharp lectr. Wayne State U., 1986; Roon lectr. Scripps Rsch. Inst., 1987; Johnson lectr. Internat. Soc. on Thrombosis, 1987; Merck lectr. Cleve. Clinic, 1987; vis. prof. Harvard U., 1991; E. Stanley Emery Jr. Meml. lectr, physician-in-chief pro tempore, 1991; chief resident's vis. prof. Baylor Coll. Medicine, 1991; Samuel S. Riven vis. prof. Vanderbilt U., 1992; Hymie Nossel Meml. lectr. Columbia U., 1992; Pfizer vis. prof. Royal Soc. Medicine, 1992; disting. lectr. Am. Heart Assn., 1994; Seckler lectr. Mt. Sinai Med. Ctr., 1994; Runme Shaw Meml. lectr. Acad. Medicine, Singapore, 1994; chmn. hematology study panel Health Rsch. Coun., N.Y.C., 1973-75; mem. NIH-Program Project Com., Heart and Lung Inst., 1975-79; bd. govs. Am. Bd. Internal Medicine, 1985-88; cons. Manhattan VA Hosp.; vis. physician Rockefeller U. Hosp. Author: Genetics of Coronary Heart Disease, 1992, Systemic Lupus Erythematosus, 1993, (jours.) Blood, 1994, Ann. Internal Medicine, 1993; assoc. editor: Beeson McDermott Textbook of Medicine, XIV edit., 1975, XV edit., 1979, Blood, 1976-82, Am. Jour. Medicine, 1978; adv. editor: Jour. Exptl. Medicine, 1976; editl. bd. Arteriosclerosis, 1983; contbr. articles to med. jours. With USN, 1958-60. Fellow ACP; mem. AAAS, Assn. Am. Physicians, Am. Soc. Clin. Investigation, Am. Fedn. Clin. Rsch., Am. Clin. and Climatol. Assn., N.Y. Acad. Sci., N.Y. Soc. for Study of Blood (pres. 1975), Am. Soc. Hematology (exec. coun. 1978-79), Harvey Soc. (coun. 1980), Am. Physiol. Assn., Internat. Soc. Thrombosis and Hemostasis (coun. 1986-92), Soc. Exptl. Biology and Medicine, Am. Soc. Biol. Chemists, Inst. Medicine of NAS, N.Y. Acad. Medicine, Cornell Med. Alumni (hon.), Nat. Blood Club (pres. 1981-82), Peripatetic Club, Alpha Omega Alpha, Phi Beta Kappa. Home: 657 Floyd St Englewd Clfs NJ 07632-2049 Office: NY Hosp-Cornell Med Ctr F-433 525 E 68th St # F-433 New York NY 10021-4873*

NACHMAN, RONALD JAMES, research chemist; b. Takoma Park, Md., Feb. 1, 1954; s. Joseph Frank and Rosemary (Anderson) N.; m. Lita Rose Wilson, Dec. 18, 1976 (div. 1987); m. Isidora Austria Panis, May 6, 1989. BS in Chemistry, U. Calif., San Diego, 1976; PhD in Organic Chemistry, Stanford U., 1981. Rsch. asst. Scripps Inst. Oceanography, La Jolla, Calif., 1974-76; chemist Western Regional Rsch. Ctr., USDA, Berkeley, Calif., 1981-89, Vet. Toxicology and Entomology Rsch. Lab., College Station, Tex., 1989—; vis. scientist dept. molecular biology The Salk Inst., La Jolla, 1985, Scripps Rsch. Inst., La Jolla, 1988-89. Contbr. sci. articles to profl. jours. Recipient USDA Cert. of Merit, 1988, 91, Arthur S. Flemming award for sci. achievement, 1994. Fellow Sci. and Humanities Symposia; mem. AAAS, Am. Chem. Soc., N.Y. Acad. Scis., Sigma Xi. Avocations: travel, photography, jogging, racketball. Home: 14891 Pollux Willis TX 77378-0014 Office: USDA Vet Toxicology Entomology Rsch Lab 2881 F and B Rd College Station TX 77845-9594

NACHT, DANIEL JOSEPH, architect; b. Chgo., Sept. 22, 1915; s. George Carl and Hattie (Zaylor) N.; m. Mary Alice Belcher, Nov. 19, 1960; 1 dau., Pamela Jean. B.S., U. Ill., 1940. Mem. faculty U. Ill., 1940-42; with Skidmore, Owings & Merrill, Chgo., 1946-53; designer Rogers Engring. Co., San Francisco, 1953-55; architect Starks, Jozens & Nacht, Sacramento, 1956-70, Nacht & Lewis, 1970. Prin. works include Consumnes River Coll, Sacramento County Courthouse. Mem. Capitol Bldg. and Planning Commn., 1959-67; mem. Core Area Com., 1962-64; mem. adv. bd. Salvation Army Sacramento area. With USNR, 1942-46. Fellow A.I.A.; mem. Crocker Art Gallery, Alpha Chi Rho. Club: Mason (Shriner). Home: 7604 Pineridge Ln Fair Oaks CA 95628-4855 Office: 7300 Folsom Blvd Sacramento CA 95826-2622

NACHT, SERGIO, biochemist; b. Buenos Aires, Apr. 13, 1934; came to U.S., 1965; s. Oscar and Carmen (Scheiner) N.; m. Beatriz Kahan, Dec. 21, 1958; children: Marcelo H., Gabriel A., Mariana S., Sandra M. BA in Chemistry, U. Buenos Aires, 1958, MS in Biochemistry, 1960, PhD in Biochemistry, 1964. Asst. prof. biochemistry U. Buenos Aires, 1960-64; asst. prof. medicine U. Utah, Salt Lake City, 1965-70; rsch. scientist Alza Corp., Palo Alto, Calif., 1970-73; sr. investigator Richardson-Vicks Inc., Mt. Vernon, N.Y., 1973-76; asst. dir., dir. rsch. Richardson-Vicks Inc., Mt. Vernon, 1976-83; dir. biomed. rsch. Richardson-Vicks Inc., Shelton, Conn., 1983-87; sr. v.p. rsch. and devel. Advanced Polymer Systems, Redwood City, Calif., 1987-93, sr. v.p. sci. and tech., 1993—; lectr. dermatology dept. SUNY Downstate Med. Ctr., Blkyn., 1977-87. Contbr. articles to profl. jours.; patentee in field. Mem. Soc. Investigative Dermatology, Soc. Cosmetic Chemists (award 1981), Dermatology Found., Am. Physiological Soc., Am. Acad. Dermatology. Democrat. Jewish. Home: 409 Wembley Ct Redwood City CA 94061-4308

NACHTIGAL, PATRICIA, equipment manufacturing company executive, general counsel; b. 1946. BA, Montclair State U.; JD, Rutgers U.; LLM, NYU. Tax atty. Ingersoll-Rand Co., Woodcliff Lake, N.J., 1979-83, dir. taxes and legal, 1983-88, sec., mng. atty., 1988-91, v.p., gen. counsel, 1991—. Office: Ingersoll-Rand Co 200 Chestnut Ridge Rd Westwood NJ 07675

NACHTWEY, JAMES ALAN, photojournalist; b. Syracuse, N.Y., Mar. 14, 1948; s. James Vincent and Jean (Stockton) N. BA cum laude, Dartmouth Coll., 1970. Contract photographer Time mag., N.Y.C., 1984—; mem. Magnum Photos, N.Y.C., 1986—; tchr. Internat. Ctr. Photography, N.Y.C., 1993, 94, 95, 96, Santa Fe Workshop, 1994, Photography at the Summit, Jackson Hole, Wyo., 1994. Author, photographer: Deeds of War, 1989 (Leica award 1989), The Inferno, 1995; contbg. photographer (books) War Torn, El Salvador, In Our Time-40 Years of Magnum, The Indelible Image, Odyssey-Photography at the National geographic, National Geographic, The Photographs, (mags.) Time, Life, Nat. Geographic, N.Y. Times mag., George Stern; one-man shows Internat. Ctr. Photography, 1989, Hasszeblad Ctr., Goteborg, Sweden, 1992, Canon Gallery, Amsterdam, The Netherlands, 1992, Carolinum, Prague, Czech republic, 1994, Nieuwe Kerk, Amsterdam, 1995, Hood Mus., Dartmouth Coll., 1995. Recipient Robert Capa gold medal Overseas Press Club, 1983, 84, 86, 94, Olivier Rebbot award, 1992, 93; photography award World Press Photo Found., 1992, 94, Mag. Photographer of Yr. award Nat. Press Photographers Assn., 1983, 86, 88, 90, 92, 94, Canon Photog. essayist award, 1992; Infinity award Internat. Ctr. Photography, 1991, 93, Leica award New Sch. for Social Rsch., 1990, award Budapest Photgraphic Festival, 1985, Nikon award Maine Workshop, 1985, Nikon World Image award New Sch.-Parsons Sch. Design, 1991; Eugene Smith Meml. grantee, 1994. Avocations: fly fishing, skiing. Office: Magnum Photos 151 W 25th St New York NY 10001-7204

NACHWALTER, MICHAEL, lawyer; b. N.Y.C., Aug. 31, 1940; s. Samuel J. Nachwalter; m. Irene, Aug. 15, 1965; children: Helynn, Robert. BS, Bucknell U., 1962; MS, L.I. U., 1967; JD cum laude, U. Miami, 1967; LLM, Yale U., 1968. Bar: Fla. 1967, D.C. 1979, U.S. Dist. Ct. (so. dist.) Fla. 1967, U.S. Dist. Ct. (mid. dist.) Fla. 1982, U.S. Ct. Appeals (5th and 11th cirs.) 1967, U.S. Supreme Ct. 1975. Law clk. to judge U.S. Dist. Ct. (so. dist.) Fla.; shareholder Kelly, Black, Black & Kenny; now shareholder Kenny Nachwalter Seymour Arnold Critchlow & Spector, P.A., Miami; lectr. Law Sch. U. Miami. Fellow Am. Coll. Trial Lawyers; mem. Judicial Qualifications Commn.; mem. ABA, Am. Bd. Trial Advocates, Fla. Bar Assn. (bd. govs. 1982-90), Fed. Bar Assn., Internat. Soc. Barristers, Dade County Bar Assn., Omicron Delta Kappa, Phi Kappa Phi, Phi Delta Phi, Iron Arrow, Soc. Wig and Robe. Editor-in-chief U. Miami Law Rev., 1966-67. Office: Kenny Nachwalter Seymour Arnold Critchlow & Spector PA 201 S Biscayne Blvd Ste 1100 Miami FL 33131-4332

NACKEL, JOHN GEORGE, health care consulting director; b. Medford, Mass., Nov. 4, 1951; s. Michael and Josephine (Maria) N.; m. Gail Helen Becker, Oct. 30, 1976; children: Melissa Anne, Allison Elizabeth. BS, Tufts U., 1973; MS in Pub. Health and Indsl. Engring., U. Mo., 1975, PhD, 1977. Sr. mgr. Ernst & Young, Chgo., 1977-83; nat. dir. health care cons. Cleve., 1983-87, regional dir. health industry svcs., 1987-91; mng. dir. health care Ernst & Young, Cleve., 1991-93; nat. dir. Health Care Cons., L.A., 1994—; editorial bd. Jour. Med. Systems, 1983—. Author: Cost Management for Hospitals, 1987 (Am. Hosp. Assn. book award 1988); contbr. articles to profl. jours. Grantee Dept. Health Edn. Welfare, Washington, 1973-76. Fellow Am. Coll. Healthcare Execs., Healthcare Info. and Mgmt. Systems Soc. (articles award); mem. Inst. Indsl. Engrs. (sr.), U. Mo. health Svcs. Mgmt. Alumni Assn. (pres.), Canterbury Golf Club (Cleve.), La Canada-Flintridge Country Club, Annandale Golf Club, Jonathan Club. Republican. Avocations: golf, tennis, squash, paddle, photography. Home: 666 Linda Vista Ave Pasadena CA 91105-1145

NACLERIO, ROBERT M., Otolaryngologist, educator; b. N.Y.C., Mar. 30, 1950; s. Albert Paul and Lee Ann (Rabinowitz) N.; m. Sharon Ann Silhan, Mar. 30, 1983; children: Jessica, Daniel. BA, Cornell U., 1972; MD with honors, Baylor U., 1976. Diplomate Am. Bd. Otolaryngology. Intern in surgery Johns Hopkins Hosp., Balt., 1976-77, resident in surgery, 1977-78; resident in otolaryngology Baylor Coll. Medicine, Houston, 1978-80, chief resident in otolaryngology, 1982-83; fellow in clin. immunology divsn. Johns Hopkins U. Sch. Medicine, Balt., 1980-82, asst. prof. medicine and otolaryngology, 1983-87, asst. prof. pediatrics, 1986-87, dir. divsn. pediatric otolaryngology, 1986-94, assoc. prof. otolargyngology, medicine and pediatrics, 1987-92, prof. otolaryngology, medicine and pediatrics, 1992-94; chief of otolaryngology, head and neck surgery U. Chgo., Chgo., 1994—; cons. Richardson-Vicks Inc., 1986-89, 90, NIH, 1987, Proctor & Gamble, 1987, 94, Sandoz Rsch. Inst., 1988, Schering Rsch., 1988, Wallace Labs., 1989, Joint Rhinologic Conf., 1989, Internat. Congress Rhinology, 1991, Norwich-Eaton Pharm. Inc., 1991-92, Ciba-Geigy Corp., 1991-92, Mktg. Corp. Am., 1993—, others; mem. med. bd. Children's Ctr., 1991-94, other local comms.; reviewer Am. Jour. Rhinology, others; lectr. in field. Editor: Rhinoconjunctivitis: New Perspectives in Topical Treatment, 1988; asst. editor: Am. Jour. Rhinology, 1986—, Rhinology, 1988—; mem. editorial bd. Otolaryngology-Head and Neck Surgery, 1990—, Laryngoscope, 1990—, Jour. Allergy and Clin. Immunology, 1992-97; contbr. numerous chpts. to books, papers and abstracts to profl. jours. and procs. Fellow ACS, Am. Acad. Otolaryngology-Head and Neck Surgery (mem. com. 1985-90, 90-92, subcom. 1987-92), Am. Laryngol., Rhinol. and Otol. Soc., Inc.; mem. Am. Acad. Allergy and Immunology (mem. com. 1983-88, 88-89, 88-95, chmn. com. 1990-91, 91—, Jerome Glazer Meml. lectureship), Am. Fedn. Clin. Rsch., Am. Soc. Pediatric Otolaryngology (rsch. com. 1990-94, chmn. subcom. 1990), Md. Soc. Otolaryngology-Head and Neck Surgery, Soc. Univ. Otolaryngologists-Head and Neck Surgeons, Pan-Am. Assn. Otorhinolaryngology, Internat. Symposium on Infection and Allergy of the Nose (v.p.). Office: U Chgo MC1035 5841 S Maryland Ave MC 1035 Chicago IL 60637

NACOL, MAE, lawyer; b. Beaumont, Tex., June 15, 1944; d. William Samuel and Ethel (Bowman) N.; children: Shawn Alexander Nacol, Catherine Regina Nacol. BA, Rice U., 1965; postgrad., S. Tex. Coll. Law, 1966-68. Bar: Tex. 1969, U.S. Dist. Ct. (so. dist.) Tex. 1969. Diamond buyer/appraiser Nacol's Jewelry, Houston, 1961—; pvt. practice law, Houston, 1969—. Author, editor ednl. materials on multiple sclerosis, 1981-85. Nat. dir. A.R.M.S. of Am. Ltd., Houston, 1984-85. Recipient Mayor's Recognition award City of Houston, 1972; Ford Found. fellow So. Tex. Coll. Law, Houston, 1964. Mem. Houston Bar Assn. (chmn. candidate com. 1970, chmn. membership com. 1971, chmn. lawyers referral com. 1972), Assn. Trial Lawyers Am., Tex. Trial Lawyers Assn., Am. Judicature Soc. (sustaining), Houston Fin. Coun. Women, Houston Trial Lawyers Assn. Presbyterian. Office: 600 Jefferson St Ste 850 Houston TX 77002-7326

NADAS, JULIUS ZOLTAN, data processing educator; b. Ried, Austria, Oct. 1, 1945; came to U.S., 1951; s. Julius Zoltan and Ibolya (Szollosy) N.; m. Erika Marta Vietorisz, Sept. 25, 1971; children: Krisztina, Gyula, Zsolt, Tas. BS, Case Inst. Tech., Cleve., 1966; MA, U. Wis., 1968. Staff cons. Sperry Univac, Chgo., 1968-74; prof. data processing and dept. chair Wilbur Wright Coll., Chgo., 1974—; grievance chair Cook County Coll. Tchrs. Union, Chgo., 1990; chair Dist.-Wide Faculty Coun. Com. for Distance Learning, 1993-94. Scoutmaster Hungarian Scout Assn. Troop 19, Chgo., 1981-89. Recipient Disting. Svc. Prof. award Bd. Trustees of Chgo. City Colls., 1994. Mem. Math. Assn. Am. Office: Wilbur Wright College 4300 N Narragansett Ave Chicago IL 60634-1591

NADASKAY, RAYMOND, architect; b. Newark, Aug. 26, 1938; s. Charles and Marie (Roncskevitz) N.; m. Nancy Searle, June 29, 1962; 1 child, Cathy. BArch, Washington U., St. Louis, 1962. Registered architect, N.J., Conn., Vt., Mass., Ill., Ohio; registered planner; cert. NCARB. Designer Rotwein and Blake, Architects, Union, N.J., 1962-63, I.M. Pei, N.Y.C., 1963-64; designer, assoc. McDowell Goldstein, Morristown, N.J., 1964-72; pres. Nadaskay Kopelson Architects, P.A., Morristown, 1972—. Mem. Mendham (N.J.) Twp. Hist. Preservation Commn., Mendham Twp. Roadscape Commn. Recipient numerous spl. commendations, awards of merit for variety of works. Mem. N.J. Soc. Archs. (conv. chmn. 1985-86, past pres. Newark Suburban chpt. 1984, recipient of 30 awards for architecture from 1979-95), Porsche Club (No., N.J.). Avocations: woodworking, sailing, auto rally events, swimming. Office: Nadaskay Kopelson Architects 95 Washington St Morristown NJ 07960-6816

NADEAU, BERTIN F., diversified company executive; b. May 26, 1940; s. J.-D. and Irene (Daigle) N.; m. Juliette Angell, July 24, 1971; children: Eric, Shahn, Stephanie. BA, Coll. St-Louis, 1961; grad., Ecole des Hautes Etudes Commerciales de Montreal, 1964; postgrad., Harvard U.; DBA, Ind. U., 1969. Chmn., CEO Unigesco Inc., 1982-94; chmn., CEO, Unigesco, Inc., Montreal, 1994—; bd. dirs. Sun Life Can., Lafarge Corp., The Banff Ctr. Office: GescoLynx Inc, 606 Cathcart Ste 1035, Montreal, PQ Canada H3B 1K9

NADEAU, EARL RAYMOND, electronics executive; b. Conrad, Mont., June 8, 1926; s. Raymond Joseph and Marvel Mae (Hunter) N.; m. Frances Ann Gambale, June 30, 1962; children: Nicole Mary, Christopher Earl. Student, Carroll Coll., 1944, U. Wash., 1945, Mont. State U., 1946-48. Supr. method engring., mgr. major subcontracting Boeing Airplane Co., Seattle and Wichita, 1950-55; adminstr. Atlas program Convair div. Gen. Dynamics, San Diego, 1955-57; chief plans and proposals Boeing Co., Seattle, 1958-59; mgmt. planning and applications cons. Waldwick, N.J., 1960-65; mgr. project engring/applications engring. Lockheed Electronics Co. Inc., Plainfield, N.J., 1966-69, dir. engring., 1970-76, dir. advanced devel., 1976-83; gen. ptnr. Nadeau Assocs., Watchung, N.J., 1984—. Served with USNR, 1943-46, PTO. Electrd to Mont. State U. Athletes Hall of Fame, 1992. Mem. AIAA, Instrument Soc. Am. (sr.), Marine Tech. Soc. Roman Catholic. Home: 132 Sunbright Rd Watchung NJ 07060-6045

NADEAU, JOSEPH EUGENE, health care management consultant, information systems consultant; b. Portland, Maine, Sept. 23, 1937; s. Edwin Tustin and Beatrice Margaret (Spiller) N.; m. Mary Lou Prendible, Dec. 2, 1961; children—Laura, Keith, Michael. B.S. in Math., Boston Coll., 1960. Dir. systems devel. Mass. Hosp. Assn., Burlington, 1967-72; S.E. regional mgr. Automatic Data Processing, Miami, Fla., 1972-73; S.E. regional mktg. mgr. Space Age Computer Systems, Louisville, 1973-74; prin. COMPUTERx Cons., Miami, 1974—. Asst. scoutmaster South Fla. council Boy Scouts Am., 1972-81. Served to 1st lt. U.S. Army, 1960-64; Germany. Mem. Am. Hosp. Assn., Soc. Computer Medicine, Data Processing Mgmt. Assn., Hosp. Mgmt Systems Soc., Assn. Systems Mgmt. (pres. 1971-72), Hosp. Fin. Mgmt. Assn. (chmn. data processing com. 1967-84), Am. Arbitration Assn. (arbitrator 1980—). Cert. Computer profl. Home: 7750 SW 118th St Miami FL 33156-4433 Office: COMPUTERx Consulting 9719 S Dixie Hwy # 1 Miami FL 33156-2806

NADEAU, MICHAEL JOSEPH, college service assistant; b. Glens Falls, N.Y., Dec. 19, 1949; s. John Long and Mary Catherine (Cimo) N. Student of Eli Siegel's Aesthetic Realism, N.Y.C., 1977-81; AA in English with honors, Borough of Manhattan C.C., N.Y.C., 1992. Orderly Glens Falls (N.Y.) Hosp., 1969-72; record storage clk. Continental Ins. Co., Glens Falls, 1972-75; purchasing agt. Maersk Inc., Madison, N.J., 1975-93; coll. svc. asst. Passaic County C.C., Paterson, N.J., 1993—. Author: The Adventures of Prudence Longface, 1993. Actor, singer Elbee Audio Players, N.Y.C., 1979-81. With USN, 1969-70. Mem. Am. Legion. Democrat. Roman Catholic. Avocations: bowling, swimming, boating, woodworking, singing. Home: 15 Overlook Ave Mine Hill NJ 07803

NADEAU, REGINALD ANTOINE, medical educator; b. St. Leonard, N.B., Can., Dec. 18, 1932; married, 1957; 2 children. BA, Loyola Coll., Can., 1952; MD, U. Montreal, 1957. From asst. prof. to assoc. prof. Faculty Medicine, U. Montreal, 1964-70, prof. physiology, 1972-75, prof. medicine, 1975—; career investigator Med. Rsch. Coun. Can., 1965; dir. rsch. Cardiol. Hosp. Sacre Coeur, Montreal. Fellow Royal Coll. Physicians (Can.); mem. Can. Physiol. Soc., Can. Cardiovasc. Assn., Am. Coll. Cardiology. Achievements include research in clinical cardiology. Office: Sacre Coeur Hosp Montreal, 5400 Gouin Blvd W, Montreal, PQ Canada H4J 1C5*

NADEL, ELLIOTT, investment firm executive; b. N.Y.C., Nov. 23, 1945; s. Archie and Faye (Braverman) N.; children: Lindsey, Amanda. BBA, Baruch Coll., 1969, MBA, 1971. Portfolio mgr. SwissRe Advisors, N.Y.C., 1973-74; v.p., stockbroker E. F. Hutton, N.Y.C., 1975-84, Shearson Lehman Bros., N.Y.C., 1984-85, Oppenheimer & Co., N.Y.C., 1985, Rooney Pace Inc., N.Y.C., 1986-87, Philips Appel & Walden, N.Y.C., 1987-88; sr. v.p. investments Moore, Schley & Cameron, N.Y.C., 1988-90, Prudential-Securities, N.Y.C., 1990-94; sr. v.p. Gilford Securities, N.Y.C., 1994—. With U.S. Army, 1969-74. Jewish. Avocations: tennis, reading, cars, golf, travel. Office: SFI Investments 88 Pine St New York NY 10005

NADEL, ETHAN RICHARD, epidemiology educator; b. Washington, Sept. 3, 1941. BA, Williams Coll., 1963; MA, U. Calif., Santa Barbara, 1966, PhD in Biology, 1969. From asst. prof. to prof. epidemiology Yale U., New Haven, 1970—; from asst. fellow to assoc. fellow John D. Pierce Found. Lab., 1970—; environ. physiol. commn. Internat. Union Physiol. Sci., 1977—; Hall meml. lectr. U. Louisville, 1979. Fellow NIH, 1969-70; grantee USPHS, 1970—. Fellow Am. Coll. Sports Medicine; mem. AAAS, Am. Physiol. Soc. Office: John B Pierce Lab Inc 290 Congress Ave New Haven CT 06519-1403*

NADEL, NORMAN ALLEN, civil engineer; b. N.Y.C., Apr. 10, 1927; s. Louis and Bertha (Julius) N.; m. Cynthia Esther Jereski, July 6, 1952; children: Nancy Sarah Frank, Lawrence Bruce. B.C.E., CCNY, 1949; postgrad., Columbia U., 1949-50. Registered profl. engr., N.Y., Conn. Engr. Arthur A. Johnson Corp., N.Y.C., 1950-53; engr. Slattery Contracting Corp., N.Y.C., 1953-56; mgr., estimator Hartsdale Constrn. Corp., Hartsdale, N.Y., 1956-59; engr. MacLean Grove & Co., Inc., Greenwich, Conn., 1959-63, project mgr., 1963-66, v.p., 1966-70, pres., 1970-94; chmn. Nadel Assocs., Inc., Brewster, N.Y., 1988—; cons. tunnel and underground constrn.; chmn., bd. dirs. United Am. Energy Corp., PB-KBB Inc.; mem. com. on tunneling Transp. Rsch. Bd., Washington, 1974-75; mem. U.S. Nat. Com. on Tunneling Tech., Washington, 1976-82, chmn., 1980-81; chmn. adv. com. Superconducting Super Collider Underground Tech., 1992-94. Trustee Tunnel Workers Welfare Fund, N.Y.C., 1976-88; mem. exec. coun. Pace U., N.Y.C., 1984—; mem. CCNY Engring. Sch. bd. adv., 1992—. Served with USNR, 1945-46. Named Heavy Constrn. Man of Yr., United Jewish Appeal, 1984; Benjamin Wright award Conn. Soc. Civil Engrs., 1984, Townsend Harris medal City Coll. of N.Y. Alumni Assn., 1987. Fellow ASCE (Constrn. Mgmt. award 1986); mem. Nat. Acad. Engring., Conn. Acad. Sci. and Engring., The Moles (pres. 1982-83, Outstanding Achievement in Constrn. award 1985), Am. Arbitration Assn., Tau Beta Pi, Chi Epsilon. Home: Reynwood Manor Greenwich CT 06830

NADELL, ANDREW THOMAS, psychiatrist; b. N.Y.C., Nov. 3, 1946; s. Samuel Tyler and Bertha Elaine (Trupine) N.; m. Eleanore Edwards Ramsey, July 24, 1993. MA, Columbia U., 1968; MSc, U. London, 1973; MD, Duke U., 1974. Diplomate Am. Bd. Psychiatry and Neurology. Resident in psychiatry U. Calif., Davis, 1974-77; clin. instr. psychiatry Stanford (Calif.) U. Sch. Medicine, 1979-84, clin. asst. prof. psychiatry, 1984-93. Trustee Calif. Hist. Soc., 1989-95. Fellow Royal Soc. Medicine; mem. Am. Psychiat. Assn., Am. Assn. History Medicine, Am. Osler Soc., Calif. Med. Assn., Bay Area History Medicine Soc. (sec. 1984-88, v.p. 1988-90, pres. 1990-92, bd. govs. 1992—), Soc. Social History Medicine, Assn. Internat. de Bibliophilie, Soc. Internat. d'Histoire de la Medicine, Stanford Univ. Librs. Assocs. (adv. coun. 1988-94), Univ. Club, Olympic Club, Grolier Club, Roxburghe Club, Colophon Club, Book Club of Calif. Avocation: book collecting. Office: 1515 Trousdale Dr Burlingame CA 94010

NADELSON, CAROL COOPERMAN, psychiatrist, educator; b. Bklyn., Oct. 13, 1936; m. Theodore Nadelson, July 16, 1965; children—Robert, Jennifer. B.A. magna cum laude, Bklyn. Coll., 1957; M.D. with honors, U. Rochester, N.Y., 1961. Dir. med. student edn. Beth Israel Hosp., Boston, 1974-79, psychiatrist, 1977; assoc. prof. psychiatry Harvard U. Med. Sch., Boston, 1976-79; research scholar Radcliffe Coll., Cambridge, Mass., 1979-80; prof. psychiatry Tufts Med. Sch., Boston, 1979-95; vice chmn., dir. tng. and edn. dept. psychiatry Tufts-New Eng. Med. Ctr., Boston, 1979-93; clin. prof. psychiatry Harvard Med. Sch., Boston, 1995—. Editor: The Woman Patient, Vols. 1, 2 and 3, 1978, 82; Treatment Interventions in Human Sexuality, 1983; Marriage and Divorce: A Contemporary Perspective, 1984, Women Physicians in Leadership Roles, 1986, Training Psychiatrists for the '90s, 1987; editor-in-chief Am. Psychiatric Press, Inc., 1986—, pres., CEO, 1995—; contbr. articles to profl. jours. Trustee Menninger Found., 1988—. Recipient Gold Medal award Mt. Airy Psychiat. Ctr., 1981, award Case Western Res. U., 1983; Picker Found. grantee, 1982-83. Fellow Ctr. for Advanced Study in the Behavioral Scis., Am. Psychiat. Assn. (pres. 1985-86, Seymour D. Vestermark award 1992, Disting. Svc. award 1995); mem. Am. Coll. Psychiatrists (bd. regents 1991-94), AMA (impaired physicians com. 1984), Group for Advancement of Psychiatry (bd. dirs. 1984). Avocation: travel. Office: 30 Amory St Brookline MA 02146-3909

NADER, RALPH, consumer advocate, lawyer, author; b. Winsted, Conn., Feb. 27, 1934; s. Nadra and Rose (Bouziane) N. AB magna cum laude, Princeton U., 1955; LLB with distinction, Harvard U., 1958. Bar: Conn. 1958, Mass. 1959, U.S. Supreme Ct. 1959. Practiced law in Hartford, Conn., from 1959; lectr. history and govt. U. Hartford, 1961-63; founder Center for Responsive Law, Pub. Interest Research Group, Center for Auto Safety, Pub. Citizen, Clean Water Action Project, Disability Rights Ctr., Pension Rights Ctr., Project for Corporate Responsibility; lectr. to colls. and univs.; lectr. Princeton U., 1967-68; co-founder Princeton Project 55, 1989. Author: Unsafe at Any Speed, 1965, rev., 1972; sponsor: Working on the System: A Manual for Citizen's Access to Federal Agencies, 1972; co-author: Action for a Change, 1972, You and Your Pension, 1973, Taming the Giant Corporation, 1976, Menace of Atomic Energy, 1977, The Lemon Book, 1980, The Big Boys, 1986, Winning The Insurance Game, 1990; editor: Whistle Blowing: The Report on the Conference on Professional Responsibility, 1972, The Consumer and Corporate Accountability, 1973; co-editor: Corporate Power in America, 1973, Verdicts on Lawyers, 1976, Who's Poisoning America, 1981; contbg. editor: Ladies Home Jour., 1973—, also articles. With U.S. Army, 1959. Recipient Nieman Fellows award, 1965-66; named One of 10 Outstanding Young Men of Year U.S. Jr. C. of C., 1967. Mem. ABA, AAAS, Phi Beta Kappa. Address: PO Box 19367 Washington DC 20036-9367*

NADER, ROBERT ALEXANDER, judge, lawyer; b. Warren, Ohio, Mar. 31, 1928; s. Nassef J. and Emily (Nader) N.; m. Nancy M. Veauthier. B.A., Western Res. U., 1950, LL.B., 1953. Bar: Ohio 1953. Ptnr. Paul G. Nader, Warren, 1953-83. Pres. Warren City Police and Fire Pension Bds., 1960-66; trustee Office Econ. Opportunity, 1970-72; mem. Warren City Coun., 1960-66, pres. pro tem, 1964-66; mem. Ohio Ho. of Reps., 1971-83, chmn. reference com., 1977-81, chmn. judiciary com., 1981-83; presiding judge Trumbull County Ct. Common Pleas, 1983-91; judge Ohio 11th Dist. Ct. Appeals, 1991—; trustee Family Svc. Assn., 1959-65. With AUS, 1946-48. Recipient Outstanding Young Man of Yr. award, 1964, award Am. Arbitration Assn., 1965, Community Action award Warren Area Bd. Realtors, 1967, Outstanding Svc. award Kent State U., Trumbull campus. 1978, Outstanding Svc. award Children's Rehab. Ctr., 1980; named to Warren High Sch. Disting. Alumni Hall of Fame, 1993. Mem. Ohio State Bar Assn., Trumbull County Bar Assn. (past pres.), Ct. Appeals Judges Assn. (chmn. legis. com.), Trumbull County Law Libr. Assn. (trustee 1958-72), Trumbull New Theatre (past pres.), KC, Elks, Lambda Chi Alpha (v.p. 1958). Roman Catholic. Home: 798 Wildwood Dr NE Warren OH 44483-4458 Office: 11th Dist Ct # Appeals Warren OH 44481 *My parents provided me with a strong moral background and the inspiration to improve. I will never feel that I have achieved success and thus may continue to improve.*

NADHERNY, FERDINAND, executive recruiting company executive. Sr. mng. dir. Russell Reynolds Assocs. Inc., Chgo. Office: Russell Reynolds Assocs Inc 200 S Wacker Dr Suite 3600 Chicago IL 60606*

NADICH, JUDAH, rabbi; b. Balt., May 13, 1912; s. Isaac and Lena (Nathanson) N.; m. Martha Hadassah Ribalow, Jan. 26, 1947; children: Leah N. (Mrs. Aryeh Meir), Shira A. (Mrs. James L. Levin), Nahma M. Nadich (Mrs. David Belcourt). B.A., CCNY, 1932; M.A., Columbia U., 1936; rabbi, M.H.L., Jewish Theol. Sem. Am., 1936, D.H.L., 1953, D.D. (hon), 1966. Rabbi Temple Beth David, Buffalo, 1936-40; co-rabbi Anshe Emet Synagogue, Chgo., 1940-42; lecture tour U.S., South Africa and Rhodesia, 1946-47; rabbi Kehillath Israel Congregation, Brookline, Mass., 1947-57; rabbi Park Ave. Synagogue, N.Y.C., 1957-87, rabbi emeritus, 1987—; conducted first Bat Mitzvah in People's Republic of China, 1990. Author: Eisenhower and the Jews, 1953, Jewish Legends of the Second Commonwealth, 1983, Legends of the Rabbis, 2 vols., 1994; editor, translator: (Menachem Ribalow) The Flowering of Modern Hebrew Literature, 1959; editor: (Louis Ginzberg) Al Halakha v'Aggada, 1960. Pres. Rabbinical Assembly, 1972-74; pres. Jewish Book Coun. Am., 1968-72; bd. dirs., exec. com. Jewish Theol. Sem. Am.; past bd. dirs., mem. exec. com. Nat. Jewish Welfre Bd., Fedn. Jewish Philanthropies N.Y.; mem. hospice com. Beth Israel Med. Ctr.; mem. N.Y.C. Holocaust Meml.; hon. v.p. bd. dirs. Jewish Braille Inst.; bd. dirs. Friends of Jewish Hist. Mus., Warsaw; past pres. Assn. Jewish Chaplains Armed Forces; adv. to Gen. Eisenhower on Jewish affairs, ETO, 1945; com. 50th anniversary World War II U.S. Dept. Defense. Lt. col., chaplain AUS, 1942-46, ETO. Decorated Order Brit. Empire; Croix de Guerre France; Ittur Lohamai Hamdinah Israel; fellow Herbert Lehman Inst. Talmudic Ethics, 1958. Mem. Mil. Chaplains Assn., Phi Beta Kappa. Lodge: Masons. Home: 1040 Park Ave New York NY 10028-1032 Office: Park Ave Synagogue 50 E 87th St New York NY 10128-1002 *Live so that your life will make a difference for the better in the lives of other people.*

NADIG, GERALD GEORGE, manufacturing executive; b. Astoria, N.Y., May 9, 1945; s. Charles Edwin and Louise (Hahn) N.; m. Nancy Hanford Stewart, June 20, 1970; children: Sara Hanford, Jennifer Stewart. AB cum laude, Harvard Coll., 1967, MBA, 1974. Fin. mgr. Rockwell Internat., Hopedale, Mass., 1974-76; materials mgr. Rockwell Internat., Oshkosh, Wis., 1976-78, Marysville, Ohio, 1978-79; ops. mgr. Rockwell Internat., Marysville, 1979-80, plant mgr., 1980-82; regional mgr. Rockwell Internat., Atlanta, 1984-85; mng. dir. Rockwell Maudslay Ltd., Great Alne, Eng., 1982-84; dir. mfg. Toyoda Machinery USA, Arlington Heights, Ill., 1985-87; v.p., gen. mgr. Toyoda Machinery USA, Arlington Heights, 1987-88; v.p., gen. mgr. Littell div. Allied Products Corp., Chgo., 1988-89; exec. v.p. pre finish metals Material Scis. Corp., 1989-90; pres. Pre Finish Metals Materials Scis. Corp., 1990-91; pres., chief oper. officer Material Scis. Corp., Chgo., 1991—. Trustee Village of Lake Barrington, 1989-91. With U.S. Army, 1966-70. Mem. Soc. Mfg. Engrs. (sr.), Biltmore Country Club. Avocations: golf, tennis, game theory. Home: 24354 N Grandview Dr Barrington IL 60010-6218 Office: Material Scis Corp 2300 Pratt Blvd Elk Grove Village IL 60007-5919

NADIRI, M. ISHAQ, economics educator, researcher, lecturer, consultant; b. Kabul, Afghanistan, Oct. 16, 1936; s. M. Alam and Gul-Nasa N.; m. Tahira Homayun, Sept. 9, 1978; children: Youssof, Khalid. B.S. with highest distinction, U. Nebr., 1958; M.A., U. Calif.-Berkeley, 1960, Ph.D., 1965; postgrad., Yale U., 1962-63. Asst. prof. Northwestern U., Evanston, Ill., 1964-66, U. Chgo. Bus. Sch., 1966-67; research fellow Nat. Bur. Econ. Research, N.Y.C., 1968-70; research assoc. Nat. Bur. Econ. Research, 1969—; full prof. econs. NYU, 1970—, Jay Gould prof. econs., 1975—, chmn. dept. econs., 1972-78; Disting. vis. prof. Am. U. Cairo, 1993; cons. in field; participant seminars NSF Ctr Strategic Studies, UN Assn. Author: books, including A Disequilibrium Model of Demand for Factors of Production, 1974; research, numerous publs. in field; editor books including The Importance of Technology and the Permanence of Structure in Industrial Growth, 1978, Commodity Markets and Latin American Development: A Modeling Approach, 1980; editorial bd.: Annals of Econs. and Social Measurement. Mem. Com. to Upgrade Central Park, N.Y.C.; mem. Com. to Help Afghan Refugees in the U.S. C. Miller fellow, 1958-59; U. Calif. fellow, 1959-60; Earnhart fellow, 1962-63, 63-64; grantee NSF, Ford Found., IBM Corp., AT&T. Mem. Am. Econs. Assn., Econometrica Soc., Univs.-Nat. Bur. Econ. Research, Internat. Assn. Research in Income and Wealth; mem. AAAS, Am. Statis. Assn., Council Fgn. Relations, Phi Beta Kappa, Pi Sigma Alpha, Beta Gamma Sigma. Office: NYU Dept Econs 269 Mercer St 7th Fl New York NY 10003

NADLER, ALLAN LAWRENCE, institute director; b. Montreal, May 8, 1954; came to U.S., 1976; s. Joseph Y. and Doris (Josevlefsky) N. BA, McGill U., 1976; MA, Harvard U., 1980, PhD, 1988. Ordained rabbi, 1978. Rabbi Charles River Park Synagogue, Boston, 1980-84; asst. prof. McGill U., Montreal, 1982-90; rabbi Congregation Shaar Hashomayim, Montreal, 1984-90; dir. rsch. Yivo Inst. for Jewish Rsch., N.Y.C., 1991—; vis. prof. Cornell U., Ithaca, N.Y., 1993—; adj. prof. NYU. Author: A Religion of Limits, 1995; contbr. articles to profl. jours. Lady Davis fellow Hebrew U., Jerusalem, 1987. Mem. Assn. Jewish Studies. Office: Yivo Inst 555 W 57th St New York NY 10019-2925

NADLER, GEORGE L., orthodontist; b. Bklyn., Jan. 13, 1939; s. Rudolph M. and Hannah (Helfman) N.; m. Essie Rubinstein, June 4, 1961; children: Rudolph M., Eric Marc. Student, Bkly. Coll., 1956-59; DDS, NYU Coll. of Dentistry, 1963, postgrad., 1966-70. Diplomate Am. Bd. Orthodontia, 1979. Intern L.I. Coll. Hosp., Bklyn., 1963-64; pvt. practice Bklyn., 1966-70, Tucson, Ariz., 1970—; cons. El Rio Health Ctr., Tucson, 1973—. Contbr. articles to profl. jours. Cons. Ariz. Crippled Children Svc., Tucson, 1973—; exec. bd. Congregation Anshei Israel, 1988—. With USPHS, 1964-66. Fellow NIH, 1961, 62. Mem. ADA, Ariz. Dental Assn., So. Ariz. Dental Assn., Am. Assn. Orthodontists, Pacific Coast Orthodontic Assn., Ariz. Orthodontic Study Club, Tucson Orthodontic Study Club, Tucson Orthodontic Soc. (pres. 1980-81), Ariz. State Orthodontic Soc. (pres. 1988-90), Angle Orthodontic Soc., Golden Key, Skyline Country Club, Omicron Kappa Upsilon. Avocations: tennis, golf, gardening. Home: 6822 N Longfellow Dr Tucson AZ 85718-2422 Office: 5610 E Grant Rd Tucson AZ 85712-2239

NADLER, GEORGIA JANE, healthcare executive; d. John Patrick and Georgia (Snook) McCarthy; children: Meredith, Lauren. Diploma, Easton (Pa.) Hosp. Sch. Nurisng, 1970; AAS, NYU, 1981; BSN, Hunter Coll., 1983; MBA in Mgmt., Fairleigh Dickinson U., 1986. Staff nurse NYU Med. Ctr., N.Y.C., 1970-71, oper. rm. supr., 1973-82; staff nurse U. Minn. Hosp., Mpls., 1971-73; oper. rm. dir. Manhattan Eye and Ear Hosp., N.Y.C., 1982-85; dir. Surg. Ctr. Med. Ctr. Princeton, N.J., 1985—; v.p. patient svcs. Med. Ctr., Princeton, 1989; presenter, spkr. in field. Co-author, spkr. Health in Law and Ethics, Electronic Patient Care Documentation, 1992; contbr. articles to profl. publs. Recipient Nursing Incentive Reimbursement award N.J. State Dept. Health, 1989, 90, Tribute to Women in Bus. award YWCA, 1996. Mem. Am. Orgn. Nurse Execs., Nat. League Nursing. Avocations: skiing, jogging. Home: 60 Dogwood Ln Skillman NJ 08558-1301 Office: Med Ctr Princeton 253 Witherspoon St Princeton NJ 08540-3211

NADLER, GERALD, engineering educator, management consultant; b. Cin., Mar. 12, 1924; s. Samuel and Minnie (Krumbein) N.; m. Elaine Muriel Dubin, June 22, 1947; children: Burton Alan, Janice Susan, Robert Daniel. Student, U. Cin., 1942-43; BSME, Purdue U., 1945, MS in Indsl. Engring, 1946, PhD, 1949. Instr. Purdue U., 1948-49; asst. prof. indsl. engring. Washington U., St. Louis, 1949-52, assoc. prof., 1952-55, prof., head dept. indsl. engring., 1955-64; prof. U. Wis., Madison, 1964-83, chmn. dept. indsl. engring., 1964-67, 71-75; prof., chmn. dept. indsl. and systems engring. U. So. Calif., L.A., 1983-93, IBM chair engring. mgmt., 1986-93, IBM chair emeritus, prof. emeritus, 1993—; v.p. Artcraft Mfg. Co., St. Louis, 1956-57; dir. Intertherm Inc., St. Louis, 1969-85; pres. Ctr. for Breakthrough Thinking Inc., L.A., 1989—; vis. prof. U. Birmingham, Eng., 1959, Waseda U., Tokyo, 1963, Ind. U., 1964, U. Louvain, Belgium, 1975, Technion-Israel Inst. Tech., Haifa, 1976; speaker in field. Author: The Planning and Design Approach, 1981; (with S. Hibino) Breakthrough Thinking, 1990, 2d edit., 1994, Creative Solution Finding, 1995; (with G. Hoffherr, J. Moran) Breakthrough Thinking in Total Quality Management, 1994; contbr. articles to profl. jours.; reviewer books, papers, proposals. Mem. Ladue Bd. Edn., St. Louis County, 1960-63; acting exec. dir. Higher Edn. Coordinating Coun. Met. St. Louis, 1962-63; chmn. planning com. Wis. Regional Med. Program, 1966-69, mem. steering com., 1969-73. Served with USN, 1943-45. Recipient Gilbreth medal Soc. Advancement Mgmt., 1961, Editorial award Hosp. Mgmt. Mag., 1966, Disting. Engring. Alumnus award Purdue U., 1975; Book of Yr. award Inst. Indsl. Engrs., 1983, Frank and Lillian Gilbreth award, 1992; Phi Kappa Phi Faculty Recognition award U. So. Calif., 1990. Fellow AAAS, Inst. Indsl. Engrs. (pres. 1989-90), Inst. for Advancement Engrs., Am. Soc. Engring. Edn.; mem. NAE, Inst. Operations Rsch. and Mgmt. Scis., Japan Work Design Soc. (hon. adv. 1968—), World Futurs Soc. Acad. Mgmt. Strategic Leadership forum Engring. Mgmt. Soc., Sigma Xi, Alpha Pi Mu (nat. officer), Pi Tau Sigma, Omega Rho, Tau Beta Pi. Office: Univ Park GER 240 Dept of I&SE Los Angeles CA 90089-0193

NADLER, HENRY LOUIS, pediatrician, geneticist, medical educator; b. N.Y.C., Apr. 15, 1936; s. Herbert and Mary (Kartiganer) N.; m. Benita Weinhard, June 16, 1957; children: Karen, Gary, Debra, Amy. A.B., Colgate U., 1957; M.D., Northwestern U., 1961; M.S., U. Wis., 1965. Diplomate: Am. Bd. Pediatrics, Am. Bd. Med. Genetics. Intern NYU Med. Ctr., 1961-62, sr. resident pediatrics, 1962-63, chief resident, 1963-64; teaching asst. NYU Sch. Medicine, 1962-63, clin. instr., 1963-64; clin. instr. U. Wis. Sch. Medicine, 1964-65; practice medicine specializing in pediatrics Chgo., 1965—; fellow Children's Meml. Hosp. dept. pediatrics Northwestern U., 1964-65; assoc. in pediatrics Northwestern U. Med. Sch., 1965-66, asst. prof., 1967-68, assoc. prof., 1968-70, prof., 1970-81, chmn. dept. pediatrics, 1970-81; prof. Northwestern U. Med. Sch. (Grad. Sch.), 1971-80; mem. staff Children's Meml. Hosp., 1965-81, head div. genetics, 1969-81, chief of staff, 1970-81; dean, prof. pediatrics, ob-gyn Wayne State U. Med. Sch., Detroit, 1981-88; prof. U. Chgo., 1988-89, U. Ill., 1989—; pres. Michael Reese Hosp. and Med. Ctr., Chgo., 1988-91; market med. dir. Aetna Health Plans, Phoenix, 1993-94, mktg. v.p., CEO, 1994-95; v.p. managed care/physician integration, med. dir. Am. Healthcare Sys., San Diego, 1995; mem. vis. staff, div. medicine Northwestern Meml. Hosp., 1972-81; staff Children's Hosp. of Mich., 1981-88. Mem. editorial bd. Comprehensive Therapy, 1973-84, Am. Jour. Human Genetics, 1979-83, Pediatrics in Rev., 1980-83, Am. Jour. Diseases of Children, 1983-91; contbr. articles to profl. jours. Recipient E. Mead Johnson award for pediatric rsch., 1973, Meyer O. Cantor award for Disting. Svc. Internat. Coll. Surgeons, 1987; Irene Heinz Given and John La Porte Given rsch. prof. pediatrics, 1970-81. Fellow Am. Acad. Pediatrics; mem. Am. Soc. for Clin. Investigation, Am. Soc. Human Genetics, Am. Pediatric Soc., Soc. for Pediatric Rsch., Midwest Soc. for Pediatric Rsch., Pan Am. Med. Assn., Alpha Omega Alpha. Home & Office: 25150 N Windy Walk Dr # 23 Scottsdale AZ 85255

NADLER, JERROLD LEWIS, congressman, lawyer; b. Brooklyn, N.Y., June 13, 1947; s. Emanuel and Miriam (Schreiber) N.; m. Joyce L. Miller, 1976; 1 child, Michael. JD, Fordham U., 1978; AB, Columbia Coll., 1969. Mem. Community Planning Bd. No. 7, Manhattan, 1967-71; Dem. leader 67th Assembly Dist. Part C, 1969-71; exec. dir. Community Free Dem., 1972; law clerk Morgan, Finnegan, Pine, Foley & Lee, 1976; Dem. dist. leader 69th Assembly dist. Part A, 1973-77; assemblyman N.Y. State 69th dist., 1977-82, 67th dist., 1983-92; mem. 102d Congress from 17th N.Y. dist., Washington, 1992; mem. 103d and 104th Congress 8th N.Y. Dist., Washington, 1993—; subcoms. comml./adminstrv. law, cts. intellectual property U.S. Ho. Reps., 1995—; mem. coms. on judiciary and pub. works and transp. U.S. Ho. Reps., 1995—, subcom. on constitutional law and immigration, 1993-94, chmn. Assembly Com. on Corps, Authorities and Commn., 1991-92, Assembly Consumer Affairs and Protection Com., 1987-89, Assembly Com. on Ethics and Guidance, 1985-86, Assembly Subcom. on Mass Transit and Rail Freight, 1979-86, mem. Assembly Com. on Judiciary, Gov. Ops., Legis. Tax Study Commn.; mem. Assembly Com. Ways and Means, Housing, Real Property Tax, Health, Election Law, Ins. Founder, chmn. West Side Peace Com., 1969-71; former mem. exec. coun. N.Y. State New Dem. Coalition; pres. Zionist Orgn. Am. dist. 7A; active Common Cause, Met. Coun. on Housing, West Side Tenants Union, Community Free Dems.; mem. nat. governing coun. Am. Jewish Congress; former bd. dirs. N.Y. State Nat. Abortion Rights Action League, Women's InterArts Ctr. Recipient hon. recognition award N.Y. State Nurses Assn., 1982, Disting. Svc. award Coalition on Domestic Violence, 1989; named Assembly Mem. of Yr. N.Y. chpt. NOW, 1980; Pulitzer scholar Columbia U. Mem. NOW, NAACP, N.Y. Bar Assn., N.Y. Civil Liberties Union (honor roll), Citizens Union, League Conservation Voters, New Dem. Coalition, Ams. for Dem. Action (bd. dirs., nat. v.p.). Office: US Ho of Reps Office of Ho Mems Washington DC 20515

NADLER, MARK B., executive editor; b. N.Y.C., Aug. 2, 1951; s. Leonard and Sylvie (Moret) N.; m. Jan Griffin, Aug. 21, 1978; children: Chloe, Jessica, Charles. BA in English, George Washington U., 1973. Staff writer The Record, Havre de Grace, Md., 1973-74, news editor, 1974-76, mng. editor, 1976-77; staff reporter The Charlotte (N.C.) Observer, 1977-80; city/state editor The Lexinton (Ky.) Herald-Leader, 1980-82, asst. mng. editor, 1982, dep. mng. editor, 1983; second front page The Wall Street Jour., N.Y.C., 1983-84, asst. news editor, 1984-85, editor, spl. reports, 1985-86; mng. editor The Pioneer Press, St. Paul, 1986-90; exec. editor, v.p. The Chicago Sun Times, 1990—. Recipient First Place award N.C. Press Assn., First Place award Md.-Del.-D.C. Press. Assn., Grand prize and First prize awards Edn. Writers Assn., 1980. Office: Chicago Sun-Times 401 N Wabash Ave Rm 356 Chicago IL 60611-3532

NADLER, MYRON JAY, lawyer; b. Youngstown, Ohio, July 22, 1923; s. Murray A. and Jean (Davis) N.; m. Alice Blue, Nov. 4, 1951; children: Jed M., Wendy D., John M.S. Student, N.Mex. State Coll., 1943-44; B.S. in Econs, U. Pa., 1947; J.D. with distinction, U. Mich., 1949. Bar: Ohio 1950. Pres., shareholder Nadler, Nadler & Burdman Co., L.P.A., Youngstown, 1950-95, pres., 1950-95; asst. editor Mich. Law Rev., 1949; instr. Youngstown U. Law Sch., 1952-59. Author: (with Saul Nadler) Nadler on Bankruptcy, 1965, April's Bankruptcy Forms and Practice, 1964; contbr. articles profl. jours. Chmn. exec. budget com. United Appeal, Youngstown, 1964-66, v.p., 1967-70; co-chmn. Mayor's Commn. Human Rights, 1957; mem. Mahoning County Planning Commn., 1965-71, Nat. Budget and Consultation Com., 1967-70; trustee Community Corp., Youngstown, v.p., 1977-82, chmn. pers. com., 1974-92; bd. dirs. Ctr. for Learning, Villa Maria, Pa., 1969-95, pres., 1981-89, chmn. bd., 1989-94, chmn. emeritus, 1994—. With AUS, 1943-45. Decorated Purple Heart with oak leaf cluster. Mem. Fellows of Ohio Bar Assn. Found., Am., Ohio, Mahoning County bar assns., Scribes Assn. Legal Writers, Comml. Law League Am. Clubs: Youngstown, Squaw Creek Country (pres. 1966-68); Hamlet Country. Home: 601 Pine Lake Dr Delray Beach FL 33445 Home: 1313 Virginia Trl Youngstown OH 44505-1641 Office: 20 Federal Plz W Ste 600 Youngstown OH 44503-1423

NADLER, SIGMOND HAROLD, physician, surgeon; b. Bklyn., May 16, 1932; s. Morris and Rose (Levine) N.; m. Beverly Melcher, June 20, 1954; children: Geoffrey, Shail, Tamara, Kimberly. B.A., State U. Iowa, 1955, M.D., 1957. Intern Menorah Med. Center, Kansas City, Mo., 1957-58; surg. resident Menorah Med. Center, 1958-61; surg. resident Roswell Park Meml. Inst., 1961-63, mem. staff, 1962-68, clin. coordinator Eastern region clin. drug evaluation program, 1966-68, project dir. nat. adj. studies, 1966-68, asso. chief cancer research surgery, 1966-68; asso. prof. surgery Jefferson Med. Coll., Phila., 1968-70; also dir. clin. cancer tng.; asst. clin. prof. surgery SUNY-Buffalo, 1970—. Mem. Am. Soc. Clin. Oncology. Research in human tumor immunotherapy. Home: 9513 Preston Trl W Ponte Vedra Beach FL 32082-3311

NADLEY, HARRIS JEROME, accountant, educator, author; b. Phila., July 6, 1926; s. Michael and Celia (Millman) N.; BS, U. Pa., 1950; MA, PhD, Harvard U., 1952; m. Barbara A. Malone, June 28, 1953; children—Jennifer Beth, Amy Jane, Adam Christopher. Asst. trust officer Provident Trust Co., Phila., 1949; exec. trainee Merrill, Lynch, Pierce, Fenner & Smith, N.Y.C., 1950; ptnr. Michael Nadley Co., CPAs, Phila., 1952—. Teaching fellow Harvard, 1952; instr. fin. Wharton Sch., Phila., 1953-54; adj. prof. bus. adminstrn. St. Joseph's Coll., Phila., Acad. Food Mktg., Pa. Inst. CPAs, N.J. Soc. CPAs, AICPA; cons. Control Data Corp., 1971; participant Current Strategy Forum, Naval War Coll., 1978, Naval War Coll. Found., 1979. Gen. chmn. Marine Corps Birthday Ball, Phila., 1973. Bd. dirs. Montgomery County Assn. for Retarded Children, Cruiser Olympia Assn., ea. Pa. chpt. Arthritis Found.; trustee Lesley Coll., Cambridge, Mass.; pres. adv. council Wharton Sch., U. Pa., 1950; del. White House Conf. on Small Bus., 1986; mem. pres.'s council Chestnut Hill Coll.; mem. Benjamin Franklin Assocs., U. Pa.; chmn. bd. advisors USMC Tun's Tavern Commn., 1991. Served with USMCR, 1944-46; PTO. Mem. Am. Radio Relay League, Fraternal Order Police (hon.), Econometric Soc., Am. Econ. Soc., Mil. Order Fgn. Wars, Brit. Officers' Club, Preservation Soc. Newport County, St. Joseph's Coll. Acad. Food Mktg. (founder), Quarter Century Wireless Assn., World Affairs Coun. of Phila., The Libr. Co. of Phila., Marine Corps Res. Officers Assn., Sixth Marine Div. Assn., Marine Raiders Assn., Navy League, Pa. Soc., Beta Gamma Sigma, Pi Gamma Mu, Beta Sigma Rho. Clubs: Masons, Union League, Harvard, Harvard Faculty, Mercedes-Benz, Urban (Phila.). Author: A Covey of Peacocks, 1969. Contbr. articles to profl. jours.; fin. columnist Phila. mag., Welcomat Newspaper, Phila. Bus. Jour.; cons. Fin. News Network, Phila. Home and Office: 325 S 3rd St Philadelphia PA 19106-4304

NADZICK, JUDITH ANN, accountant; b. Paterson, N.J., Mar. 6, 1948; d. John and Ethel (McDonald) N. BBA in Acctg., U. Miami (Fla.), 1971. CPA, N.J. Staff acct., mgr. Ernst & Whinney, C.P.A.s, N.Y.C., 1971-78; asst. treas. Gulf & Western Industries, Inc., N.Y.C., 1979-83, asst. v.p., 1980-82, v.p., 1982-83; v.p., corp. controller United Mchts. and Mfrs. Inc., N.Y.C., 1983-85, sr. v.p., 1985-86, exec. v.p., CFO, 1986—, also bd. dirs. 1987—. Mem. AICPAs, Nat. Assn. Accts., N.Y. State Soc. CPAs, U. Miami Alumni Assn., Delta Delta Delta. Roman Catholic. Home: 280 Lincoln Ave Elmwood Park NJ 07407

NAEF, WESTON JOHN, museum curator; b. Gallup, N.Mex., Jan. 8, 1942; s. Weston John and Kathleen Winifred (Skerry) N.; m. Mary Dawes Meghan, Apr. 4, 1964; children: Edward Weston, Ella Dawes. B.A., Claremont Men's Coll., 1964; M.A., Ohio State U., 1966; postgrad., Brown U., 1966-69. Vis. scholar Boston Pub. Library, 1968; dir. art gallery Wheaton Coll., Mass., 1969; staff dept. prints and photographs Met. Mus.

Art, N.Y.C., 1970-84; asst. curator Met. Mus. Art, 1971-81, curator, 1981-84; curator photographs J. Paul Getty Mus., Malibu, Calif., 1984—; cons. in field. Author, exhbn. dir. Behind the Great Wall of China, 1971, The Painterly Photograph, 1973, The Truthful Lens: A Survey of Victorian Books Illustrated with Photographs, 1974, Era of Exploration, The Rise of Landscape Photography in the American West 1860-1885, 1975, Pioneer Photographers of Brazil 1939-1914, 1976, The Collection of Alfred Stieglitz, 1978, Georgia O'Keeffe by Alfred Stieglitz, 1978, Eliot Porter, The Intimate Landscapes, 1979, After Daguerre: Masterworks of 19th Century French Photography from the Bibliotheque Nationale, Paris, 1980, Counterparts: Form and Emotion in Photographs, 1982, Whisper of the Muse: Photographs by Julia Margaret Cameron, 1986, Edward Weston in Los Angeles: The Home Spirit and Beyond, 1986, Rare States and Unusual Subjects: Photographs by Paul Strand, Andre Kertesz and Man Ray, 1987, Capturing Shadows: Notable Acquisitions, 1985-1990, 1990; August Sander: Faces of the German People, 1991; Atget's Magical Analysis; Photographs, 1915-27, 91, Two Lives: O'Keeffe by Stieglitz, 1917-23, 1992, Being and Becoming: Photographs by Edmund Teske, 1993, André Kentesz: A Centennial Tribute, 1994, Palette of Light: Handcrafted Photographs, 1898-1914, 1994, Frederick Sommer: Poetry and Logic, 1994, Hidden Witness: African Americans in Early Photography, 1995, Carrie Mae Weems Reacts to Hidden Witness, 1995, Alfred Stieglitz: Seen and Unseen, 1995, The J. Paul Getty Museum Handbook of the Photographs Collection, 1995, The Focus: Andre Kentesz, 1994, In Focus: Alfred Stieglitz, 1995. Kress fellow, 1968. Club: Grolier (N.Y.C.). Office: J Paul Getty Mus Dept Photographs PO Box 2112 Santa Monica CA 90406

NAEGELE, CARL JOSEPH, university academic administrator, educator; b. Newark, Jan. 1, 1939; s. Carl Joseph Sr. and Mabel (Flood) N.; m. Elizabeth C. McVey, June 19, 1971; children: Jennifer, Erin. BS, Kean Coll., 1965; MS, Syracuse U., 1969; PhD, Cornell U., 1974. Tchr. physics Summit (N.J.) High Sch., 1965-68; instr. physics Kean Coll., Union, N.J., 1968-70; research assoc. Cornell U., Ithaca, N.Y., 1973-75; prof. Mich. State U., East Lansing, 1975-79; program dir. NSF, Washington, 1979-81, 91-92; dean coll. arts and scis. U. San Francisco, 1981-91; dir. Sci. Inst., 1984—; prof. physics and computer sci. U. San Francisco, 1981—; computer cons. San Rafael, Calif., 1981—. Author: Physics for the Life and Health Sciences, 1974, Laboratory Experiment in General Physics, 1976, Electronic Mail and Communications Networks, 1984, Computer Systems and Applications, 1989, Experiments in Physical Science, 1995; contbr. articles to profl. jours. Served with U.S. Army, 1959-61, Korea. Recipient Outstanding Tchg. award Mich. State U., 1978, Leadership award U. San Francisco, 1985; grantee NSF, 1968, 78, 94, 95, 96, Coun. for Basic Edn., 1984-89. Mem. Am. Phys. Soc., Am. Assn. Physics Tchrs., Am. Assn. Univ. Adminstrs., Assn. for Computing Machinery. Avocations: flying, boating, skiing, tennis, running. Office: U San Francisco Coll Arts and Scis Ignatian Heights San Francisco CA 94117-1080

NAEGELE, PHILIPP OTTO, violinist, violist, music educator; b. Stuttgart, Fed. Republic Germany, Jan. 22, 1928; came to U.S., 1940; s. Reinhold and Alice (Nordlinger) N.; m. Susanne Russin (div. 1980); 1 child, Matthias Dominic; m. Barbara Wright, Mar. 1992. BA, Queens Coll., 1949; MFA, Princeton U., 1950, PhD, 1955. Violinist, violist Marlboro (Vt.) Music Festival, 1950—; violinist Cleve. Orch., 1956-64; from asst. prof. to assoc. prof. to prof. violin dept. music Smith Coll., Northampton, Mass., 1964-78; William R. Kenan Jr. prof. music Smith Coll., 1978—; violist Cantilena Piano Quartet, 1980—; mem. Boccherini Ensemble, 1980-84; mem. Resident String Quartet, Kent (Ohio) State U., 1960-64, violin faculty Cleve. Inst. Music, 1961-64, Vegh String Quartet, 1977-79; rec. artist Columbia Mus. Heritage Soc., Pro Arte., Nonesuch Records, Bis Records, Marlboro Rec. Soc., Arabesque Records, Da Camera, Spectrum Records, Bayer Records, Sony Classical, Philomusica. Contbr. to New Groves Dictionary of Music, also articles to profl. jours. Served to cpl. U.S. Army, 1955-56. Fellow Am. Council Learned Socs., 1949-50, Proctor, 1952-53, Fulbright, 1953-54. Home: 57 Prospect St Northampton MA 01060-2130 Office: Smith Coll Dept Music Northampton MA 01060

NAEGLE, MADELINE ANNE, mental health nurse, educator; b. Penn Yan, N.Y., Feb. 2, 1942; d. Lester Lawrence and Nona Caroline (Muir) N.; m. James Michael McGowan, Aug. 6, 1966 (div. 1984); children: Amanda Allen, Benjamin Logan. BS, Nazareth Coll. Rochester, 1964; MA, NYU, 1967, PhD, 1980. Staff nurse Syracuse (N.Y.) Meml. Hosp., summer 1964; staff nurse, asst. head nurse Payne Whitney Clinic, N.Y.C., 1964-65; instr. nursing Herbert H. Lehman Coll., Bronx, N.Y., 1972-75, part-time instr. nursing, 1975-78; asst. clin. prof. Sch. Nursing U. Pa., Phila., 1979-83; pvt. practice N.Y.C., 1980—; assoc. prof. Leinhard Sch. Nursing Pace U., Pleasantville, N.Y., 1983-85; assoc. prof. div. nursing NYU, N.Y.C., 1985—; cons. The Day Sch., 1980-84; mem. N.Y. State Gov.'s Health Care Adv. Bd., 1991-94. Author: Nursing Process with Clients Using Drugs, 1993, Patterns of Substance Abuse, 1996; author, editor: (model curriculum) Substance Abuse Education in Nursing, 1991; editor Addictions Nursing Network, 1988—; contbr. articles to profl. jours. Recipient Presdl. Citation award N.Y. County RN Assn., 1986, Lavinia Dock Disting. Svc. award N.Y. County RN Assn., 1994; inducted into Acad. Women Achievers, YWCA, 1991; USPHS fellow, 1978-79; grantee Nat. Inst. Alcohol Abuse and Alcoholism, Nat. Inst. Drug Abuse, 1989-90, Ctr. for Substance Abuse Prevention, 1990-95; Fulbright scholar U. Malta, 1995. Fellow Am. Acad. of Nursing; mem. ANA (com. chair 1987-89, com. on addiction 1990, nominating com. 1996—), N.Y. State Nurses Assn. (chair com. on impaired nursing practice 1986-88, pres. elect. 1987-89, pres. 1989-91), Assn. Med. Educators and Rschrs. in Substance Abuse, Sigma Theta Tau (Upsilon chpt.). Democrat. Avocations: hiking, running, dancing, theatre, music. Office: NYU Div Nursing 50 W 4th St New York NY 10012

NAESER, MARGARET ANN, linguist, medical researcher; b. Washington, June 22, 1944; d. Charles Rudolph and Elma Mathilda (Meyer) N. BA in German, Smith Coll., 1966; PhD in Linguistics, U. Wis., 1970. Chief speech pathology sect. Martinez (Calif.) VA Med. Ctr., 1972-74, Palo Alta (Calif.) VA Med. Ctr., 1974-77; rsch. linguist Boston VA Med. Ctr., 1977—; dir. Ct scan/MRI scan Aphasia Rsch. Lab. Boston U. Aphasia Rsch. Ctr., Boston U. Sch. Medicine, asst. rsch. prof. neurology, 1978-84, assoc. rsch. prof., 1984—; mem. adv. bd. CT scan/aphasia VA Nat. Task Force, Washington, 1990-91; panel mem. Office Alternative Medicine NIH, 1994. Contbr. articles to Neurology, Archives of Neurology, Brain; author: Outline Guide to Chinese Herbal Patent Medicines in Pill Form, 1990, Laser Acupuncture: An Introductory Textbook, 1994. NDEA fellow, 1967, AAUW fellow, 1970. Mem. Acoustical Soc. Am., Am. Speech, Lang., Hearing Assn., Acad. Aphasia, AAAS, Am. Assn. Acupuncture and Oriental Medicine. Office: Boston VA Med Ctr 150 S Huntington Ave Boston MA 02130-4817

NAESER, NANCY DEARIEN, geologist, researcher; b. Morgantown, W.Va., Apr. 15, 1944; d. William Harold and Katherine Elizabeth (Dearien) Cozad; m. Charles Wilbur Naeser, Feb. 6, 1982. BS, U. Ariz., 1966; PhD, Victoria U., Wellington, New Zealand, 1973. Geol. field asst. U.S. Geol. Survey, Flagstaff, Ariz., 1966; sci. editor, New Zealand Jour. Geology and Geophysics, New Zealand Dept Sci. and Indsl. Research, Wellington, 1974-76; postdoctoral rsch. assoc., U. Toronto, Ont., Can., 1976-79; postdoctoral rsch. assoc. U.S. Geol. Survey, Denver, 1979-81, geologist, 1981—; adj. prof. Dartmouth Coll., Hanover, N.H., 1985—, U. Wyo., Laramie, 1984—. Editor: Thermal History of Sedimentary Basins - Methods and Case Histories, 1989; contbr. articles on fission-track dating to profl. jours., 1977—. Docent Denver Zoo. Fulbright fellow New Zealand, 1967-68. Fellow Geol. Soc. Am.; mem. Am. Assn. Petroleum Geologists, Geol. Soc. New Zealand, Mortar Bd., Phi Kappa Phi. Methodist. Office: US Geol Survey Mail Stop 926 A 12201 Sunrise Valley Dr Herndon VA 22092

NAEVE, MILO MERLE, museum curator; b. nr. Arnold, Kans., Oct. 9, 1931; s. Bernhardt and Fern (Yasmer) N.; m. Nancy Jammer, July 18, 1954. B.F.A., U. Colo., 1953; M.A., U. Del., 1955. Curatorial asst. Henry Francis duPont Winterthur Mus., 1957, asst. curator, 1958, sec. of mus., 1959-63, registrar, 1963-65; editor Winterthur Portfolio, 1965-66; asst. dir. dept. collections Colonial Williamsburg, 1967-69, curator, dir. dept. collections, 1970; dir. Colorado Springs (Colo.) Fine Arts Center, 1971-74; curator Am. Arts, Art Inst. Chgo., 1975-91, ret., 1991; curator emeritus Field McCormick. Author: The Classical Presence in American Art, 1978, Identifying American Furniture: A Pictorial Guide to Styles and Terms, Colonial to Contemporary, 1981, 2d edit., 1989, John Lewis Krimmel: An Artist in Federal America, 1987; mem. editorial bd. Am. Art Jour.; contbr. articles to profl. jours. Trustee Sewell C. Biggs Mus., Skowhegan Sch. Painting and Sculpture, Nat. Coun. of the Fine Arts Mus. of San Francisco, Calif. Fellow Royal Soc. Arts; mem. Coll. Art Assn. Am., Nat. Trust Historic Preservation, Am. Assn. Museums, Museums Assn. (Eng.), Ill. Acad. Fine Arts (Lifetime Achievement award 1991). Home: 24 Ingleton Cir Kennett Square PA 19348-2000

NAEYE, RICHARD L., pathologist, educator; b. Rochester, N.Y., Nov. 27, 1929; s. Peter John and Gertrude Ellen (Lookup) N.; m. Patricia Ann Dahl, June 4, 1955; children: Nancy Ellen, Susan Amy, Robert Peter. A.B., Colgate U., 1951; M.D., Columbia U., 1955. Diplomate: Am. Bd. Pathology. Intern N.Y. Hosp., N.Y.C., 1955-56; resident Columbia-Presbyn. Med. Center, 1956-58, Mary Fletcher Hosp., Burlington, Vt., 1958-60; practice medicine, specializing in pathology Burlington, 1960-67, Hershey, Pa., 1967—; asst. attending pathologist Mary Fletcher Hosp., 1960-63; assoc. prof. U. Vt., 1963-67, prof. pathology, 1967; prof., chmn. dept. pathology M.S. Hershey Med. Center, Pa. State U. Coll. Medicine, 1967—; mem. NIH study sect. USPHS, 1968-72. Editorial bd. Human Pathology, 1982—, Pediatric Pathology, 1983—, Pediatric and Perinatal Epidemiology, 1987-94, Modern Pathology, 1993—; contbr. articles to med. jours. Markle scholar in acad. medicine, 1960-65. Mem. Am. Soc. Exptl. Pathology, U.S. Can. Acad. Pathology, Am. Soc. Pathologists, Am. Soc. Clin. Pathologists, Coll. Am. Pathologists, Pediatric Pathology Soc., Pa. Soc. Clin. Pathologists, Investigative Pathology. Home: 50 Laurel Ridge Rd Hershey PA 17033-2513 Office: Pa State U Coll Medicine Dept Pathology 500 University Dr Hershey PA 17033

NAFFAH, ELI A., law school dean; b. Youngstown, Ohio, Dec. 9, 1950; s. Assad Farris and Odette Amin Naffah; m. Cynthia Marie Hunter, May 26, 1985. BA, John Carroll U., 1973; JD, Southland U., Pasadena, Calif., 1983. Grad. Realtors Inst. Dean Law Sch., N.Am. Coll., Anaheim, Calif., 1983-87, Newport U., Newport Beach, Calif., 1987—. Pres. Windrift Homeowners Assn., Laguna Niguel, Calif., 1986-88, Fieldstone Homeowners Assn., Laguna Niguel, 1991-93; mem. Laguna Niguel Community Coun., 1988-89. Mem. Am. Soc. for Pub. Adminstrn., Calif. Law Sch. Assembly, Laguna Niguel C. of C. Roman Catholic. Avocations: photography, golf, bicycling. Office: Newport U 2220 University Dr Newport Beach CA 92660-3319

NAFIE, LAURENCE ALLEN, chemistry educator; b. Detroit, Aug. 9, 1945; s. Marvin Daniel and Edith Allman (Fletcher) N.; m. Dorothy Bondurant Butler, Dec. 28, 1968; children: Bree Lauren, Jordan Wright. B in Chemistry, U. Minn., 1967; MS, U. Oreg., 1969, PhD, 1973. Postdoctoral assoc. U. So. Calif., L.A., 1973-75; asst. prof. chemistry Syracuse (N.Y.) U., 1975-79, assoc. prof., 1979-82, prof., 1982—, chmn. dept., 1984—, assoc. dean Coll. Arts and Scis., 1993-94. Editor BioSpectroscopy; contbr. chpts. to books. With U.S. Army, 1969-71. Alfred P. Sloan Found. fellow, 1978. Mem. Am. Chem. Soc., Am. Phys. Soc., Soc. for Applied Spectroscopy, Coblentz Soc. (pres. 1993-95, Coblentz award 1981). Avocations: running; golf; biking. Home: 208 Crawford Ave Syracuse NY 13224-1712 Office: Syracuse U Dept Chemistry 1-014 CST Syracuse NY 13244-4100

NAFT, BARRY NIEL, waste management administrator, chemical engineer; b. N.Y.C., Mar. 26, 1945; s. Albert A. and Hattie (Cutler) N.; m. Rochelle Susan Weiner, Dec. 26, 1966; children: Jason, David, Rachel. BSChemE, Clarkson U., 1965, MSChemE, 1967; PhD, Purdue U., 1969; AMP, U. Pa., 1988. Registered profl. engr. Calif. Sr. engr. Westinghouse Electric Co., Pitts., 1969-71; br. mgr. Getty Oil Corp., Rockville, Md., 1971-73; dept. mgr. Sci. Applications Inc., McLean, Va., 1973-74; v.p., group exec. NUS Corp., Gaithersburg, Md., 1974-89; pres., chief exec. officer Dow Environ. Inc., Rockville, 1989—. Contbr. numerous articles to profl. jours. Chmn. Potomac (Md.) Citizens Assn., 1979. USAEC fellow, 1967-70. Mem. Am. Nuclear Soc. (chmn. fuel cycle and waste mgmt. divsn. 1978-79), Potomac Squash Club (chmn. 1975). Office: Dow Environ Inc 15204 Omega Dr Rockville MD 20850-4601

NAFTALIS, GARY PHILIP, lawyer, educator; b. Newark, Nov. 23, 1941; s. Gilbert and Bertha Beatrice (Gruber) N.; m. Donna Arditi, June 30, 1974; children: Benjamin, Joshua, Daniel, Sarah. AB, Rutgers U., 1963; AM, Brown U., 1965; LLB, Columbia U., 1967. Bar: N.Y. 1967, U.S. Dist. Ct. (so. dist.) N.Y. 1969, U.S. Ct. Appeals (2d cir.) 1968, U.S. Ct. Appeals (3d cir.) 1973, U.S. Ct. Appeals (D.C. cir.) 1993, U.S. Supreme Ct. 1974. Law clk. to judge U.S. Dist. Ct. So. Dist. N.Y., 1967-68; asst. U.S. atty. So. Dist. N.Y., 1968-74, asst. chief criminal div., 1972-74; spl. asst. U.S. atty. for V.I., 1972-73; spl. counsel U.S. Senate Subcom. on Long Term Care, 1975, N.Y. State Temp. Commn. on Living Costs and the Economy, 1975; ptnr. Orans, Elsen, Polstein & Naftalis, N.Y.C., 1974-81, Kramer, Levin, Naftalis & Frankel, N.Y.C., 1981—; lectr. in law Law Sch. Columbia U., 1976-88; vis. lectr. Law Sch. Harvard U., 1979; mem. dept. disciplinary com. Appellate div. 1st Dept., 1980-86. Author: (with Marvin E. Frankel) The Grand Jury: An Institution on Trial, 1977, Considerations in Representing Attorneys in Civil and Criminal Enforcement Proceedings, 1981, Sentencing: Helping Judges Do Their Jobs, 1986, SEC Actions Seeking to Bar Securities Professionals, 1995; editor: White Collar Crimes, 1980. Trustee Boys Brotherhood Rep., 1978—, Blueberry Treatment Ctr., 1981-91, Joseph Haggerty Children's Fund, 1991—. Fellow Am. Coll. Trial Lawyers; mem. ABA (white collar crime com. criminal justice sect. 1985—), Assn. of Bar of City of N.Y. (com. criminal cts. 1980-83, com. judiciary 1984-87, com. on criminal law 1987-90, coun. criminal justice 1985-88), Fed. Bar Coun. (com. cts. 2d cir. 1974-77), N.Y. Bar Assn. (com. state legis. 1974-76, exec. com. comml. and fed. litigation sect.), Internat. Bar Assn. (bus. crimes com. 1988—). Home: 1125 Park Ave Apt 7B New York NY 10128-1243 Office: Kramer Levin Naftalis Nessen Kamin & Frankel 919 Third Ave New York NY 10022

NAFTOLIN, FREDERICK, physician, reproductive biologist educator; b. Bronx, N.Y., Apr. 7, 1936; s. Nathan and Jean (Pesacov) N.; children: Michael Eugene, Joshua Joseph; m. Marcie Myerson, Nov. 1, 1987. A.A., UCLA, 1957; B.A. with honors, U. Calif., Berkeley, 1958; M.D. with honors, U. Calif., San Francisco, 1961; D.Phil., U. Oxford, 1970. Intern King County Hosp., Seattle, 1961-62; resident in ob-gyn UCLA, 1962-66; asst. chief gynecology, endocrine fellow USPHS, Seattle, 1966-68; NIH fellow Oxford (Eng.) U., 1968-70; asst. prof. ob-gyn U. Calif., San Diego Sch. Medicine, 1970-73; asso. prof. ob-gyn Harvard Med. Sch., 1973-75; prof., chmn. ob-gyn dept. McGill Faculty Medicine, Montreal, 1975-78; prof., chmn. dept. ob-gyn Yale Med. Sch., New Haven, Conn., 1978—, prof. dept. biology, 1983—; dir. Yale U. Ctr. for Research in Reproductive Biology, 1986—; vis. prof. U. Geneva, 1982-83, Weizmann Inst., 1991-92. Author 15 books including: Subcellular Mechanisms in Reproductive Neuroendocrinology, 1976, Abnormal Fetal Growth, 1978, Clinical Neuroendocrinology, 1979, Dilatation of the Uterine Cervix, 1980; 2-vol. series Basic Reproductive Medicine, Vol. I, Basis of Normal Reproduction, Vol. II, 1981, Male Reproduction, Vol. III, Metabolism of Steroids by Neuroendocrine Tissues, Follicle Stimulation and Ovulation Induction, 1986; mem. editorial bd. Jour. Soc. Gynecologic Investigation, Menopause, Endocrine Revs.; contbr. over 400 papers, articles to med. jours. Fogarty Internat. fellow, 1982, John Simon Guggenheim fellow, 1983; Berlex Internat. scholar, 1991. Mem. Am. Gynecol. and Obstet. Soc., Soc. Gynecol. Investigation (pres. 1991-92), Endocrine Soc., Internat. Soc. Neuroendocrinology, New Haven Ob-Gyn. Soc., Can. Fertility Soc., Soc. for Neurosci., N.Am. Menopause Soc., Pituitary Soc. Office: Yale Med Sch Dept Ob-Gyn 333 Cedar St New Haven CT 06520-8063

NAFZIGER, DEAN H., special education research executive. CEO WestEd. Office: WESTED 730 Harrison St San Francisco CA 94107-1242

NAFZIGER, ESTEL WAYNE, economics educator; b. Bloomington, Ill., Aug. 14, 1938; s. Orrin and Beatrice Mae (Slabaugh) N.; m. Elfrieda Nettie Toews, Aug. 20, 1966; children: Brian Wayne, Kevin Jon. B.A., Goshen Coll., 1960; M.A., U. Mich., 1962; Ph.D., U. Ill., 1967. Rsch. assoc. Econ. Devel. Inst., Enugu, Nigeria, 1964-65; asst. prof. Kans. State U., Manhattan, 1966-73, assoc. prof., 1973-78, prof., 1978—; Fulbright prof. Andhra U., Waltair, India, 1970-71; fellow East West Ctr., Honolulu, 1972-73; vis. scholar Cambridge U., 1976; vis. prof. Internat. U. Japan, Yamato-machi, 1983; external rsch. fellow World Acad. Devel. and Coop., College Park, Md., 1984-85; Indo-Am. Found. scholar Andura U., Waltair, India, 1993; World Inst. for Devel. Econ. Rsch., UN Univ., Helsinki, Finland, 1996. Author: African Capitalism, 1977, Class, Caste and Entrepreneurship, 1978, (with others) Development Theory, 1979, Economics of Political Instability, 1983, Economics of Developing Countries, 1984, 2d edit., 1990, Entrepreneurship Equity and Economic Development, 1986, Inequality in Africa, 1988 (named one of Outstanding Acad. Books, Choice 1989-90), The Debt Crisis in Africa, 1993, Poverty and Wealth, 1994, Learning From the Japanese, 1995. Sec. bd. overseers Hesston Coll., Kans., 1980-85; chmn. Lou Douglas Lecture Series, 1984-91, 92-93; pres. faculty senate Kans. State U., 1990-92. Recipient Honor Lectr. award Mid Am. State U.'s Assn., 1984-85; grantee Social Sci. Found., 1969. Mem. Am. Econ. Assn., AAUP (pres. chpt. 1981-82), African Studies Assn., Soc. Internat. Devel., Assn. Comparative Econ. Studies, Omicron Delta Epsilon (hon.), Phi Kappa Phi (hon.). Democrat. Avocations: reading; running. Home: 1919 Bluestem Ter Manhattan KS 66502-4508 Office: Kans State U Dept Econs Waters Hall Manhattan KS 66506-4001

NAGAMIYA, SHOJI, physicist, educator; b. Mikage-shi, Hyogo-Ken, Japan, May 24, 1944; came to U.S., 1973; s. Takeo and Masako Nagamiya; m. Tae Nagamiya, Nov. 9, 1969; children: Masahiko, Kenji. BSc, U. Tokyo, 1967; DSc, Osaka (Japan) U., 1972. Rsch. assoc. U. Tokyo, 1972-75; staff scientist Lawrence Berkeley (Calif.) Lab., 1975-82; assoc. prof. U. Tokyo, 1982-88; prof. Columbia U., N.Y.C., 1986—, chmn. dept. physics, 1991-94; adj. prof. Waseda U., 1994—, U. Tokyo, 1996—; chmn. Internat. Conf. on Quark Matter, Lennox, Mass., 1987-88; mem. Sci. Coun. GSI, 1994—. Author: Advances in Nuclear Physics, 1984, Annual Review of Nuclear & Particle Science, 1984; mem. editorial bd. Il Nuovo Cimento, 1989—, Jour. Phys. Soc. Japan, 1984-86; mem. adv. com. Jour. Phys. G., 1992—, Internat. Jour. Modern Phys. E., 1992—. Mem. evaluation com. Swedish Natural Rsch. Coun., 1987; mem. vis. com. Lawrence Berkeley Lab., Oak Ridge Nat. Lab., Brookhaven Nat. Lab., others; mem. sci. coun. GSI, Germany, 1994—; chmn. Nuclear Physics Com. of Japan, 1985-87. U.S. Dept. of Energy grantee, 1986—, Yamada Sci. Found. grantee, 1989-91; recipient Inoue prize, 1992. Fellow Am. Phys. Soc. Home: 29 Claremont Ave New York NY 10027 Office: Columbia U Dept Physics W 120th St New York NY 10027

NAGAN, PETER SEYMOUR, publisher; b. N.Y.C., Dec. 18, 1920; s. Arthur and Anna (Janis) N.; m. Gloria Mesinoff, Dec. 23, 1951; children: Laura Evelyn Brown, Michael Jay. BA, Columbia Coll., 1942; MS in Journalism, Columbia U., 1943, MA in Econs., 1948. Wire editor AP, Newark, N.J., 1943-44; staff writer Sunday dept. New York Times, 1944-45; staff writer Fortune Mag., N.Y.C., 1946-47; corr. Bus. Week Mag., Washington, 1948-52; mng. editor newsletters Bur. Nat. Affairs, Washington, 1952-60; editor, pub. Bond and Money Market Letter, 1960—; bd. chmn. Newsletter Svcs., Inc., Lanham, Md., 1972—. Author: Medical Alamanac, 1961, Fail-Safe Investing, 1981. Recipient Loeb award for Bus. Journalism U. Conn., 1965. Office: Newsletter Svcs Inc 9700 Philadelphia Ct Lanham Seabrook MD 20706

NAGANO, KENT GEORGE, conductor; b. Morro Bay, Calif.. B.A. Sociology & Music (high honors), U of Calif., Santa Cruz; MA in Composition, San Francisco State U.; studied with, Laszlo Varga. Former asst. Opera Co. Boston; former prin. guest condr. Ensemble InterContemporain & the Dutch Radio Orch.; mus. dir. & condr. Berkeley Symphony, 1978—; mus. dir. Opéra de Lyon, 1989—; assoc. prin. & guest condr. LSO, London, England, 1990; mus. dir., prin. condr. designate Hallé Orch., England, 1991-94; mus. dir., prin. condr. Hallé Orch., 1994—. has performed with numerous orchestras around the world; recordings include: Songs of the Auvergne, Peter and the Wolf, Turandot and Arlecchino (Grammy nom.), La Boheme, Dialogues of the Carelites, The Death of Klinghoffer (Grammy nom.), Love for Three Oranges (Grammy nom.), Susannah (Grammy award), La damnation de Faust, The Rite of Spring, Rodrgue et chimene. Recipient Seaver/NEA Conducting award, 1985; Record of Yr. award Gramophone; named "officer" of France's Order of Arts and Letters, 1993. Office: care Stephen Marcus Pub Rels 110-8 Suburban Ct Rochester NY 14620

NAGATA, AKIRA, publishing executive; b. Tokyo, Aug. 8, 1929; s. Koichi and Mikiko (Minami) N.; m. Tomoko Iida, Apr. 21, 1958; children: Junko, Hidehiko, Kazuhiko. BS in Econs., Jiyu-Gakuen Coll., Tokyo, 1953. Gen. mgr. for N.Am. Nihon Keizai Shimbun, Inc., Tokyo, 1973-77, spl. asst. to pres., 1977-80; dir. Nikkei-McGraw-Hill, Inc., Tokyo, 1980-88; sr. exec. dir. Nikkei Bus. Publs., Inc., Tokyo, 1988-90, pres., CEO, 1990-94, chmn., 1995—; vice chmn. Internat. Fedn. Periodical Press, London, 1994—; chmn. Postal Coop. Assn. of Shin-Tokyo, 1992—; chmn. Postal Coop. Assn. of Harumi, Tokyo, 1983-90. Co-author: Japanese Agriculturl Industry Off for a New Start, 1961, Revaluation of the Japanese Yen, 1971, Business Culture in the U.S., 1978, The Nine Years in New Delhi, London and New York, 1980. Mem. Japan Mag. Pubs. Assn. (exec. dir. 1993—), Rotary (Tokyo Club). Avocations: golf, tennis, opera. Office: Nikkei Bus Publs Inc, 2 7 6 Hirakawa cho, Tokyo 102, Japan

NAGATANI, PATRICK ALLAN RYOICHI, artist, art educator; b. Chgo., Aug. 19, 1945; s. John Lee and Diane Yoshiye (Yoshimura) N.; m. Rae Jeanean Bodwell, June 17, 1979; children: Methuen, Hart Gen, Louis-Thomas. BA, Calif. State U., L.A., 1967; MFA, UCLA, 1980. Cert. tchr. K-12, Calif. Instr. Alexander Hamilton High Sch., L.A., 1968-80, West. L.A. C.C., 1980-83; artist in residency Calif. Arts Coun., Juvenile Ct. and Cmty. Schs., L.A., 1986-87; instr. Otis Art Inst. Parson Sch. of Design, L.A., 1987; asst. prof. dept. art/art history Loyola Marymount U., L.A., 1980-87; prof. dept. art & art history U. N.Mex., Albuquerque, 1987—; instr. Fairfax Cmty. Adult Sch., L.A., 1976-79; vis. artist/instr. The Sch. of the Art Inst., Chgo., 1983; conductor numerous seminars and workshops; lectr. in field. One man shows include Pal Gallery, Evergreen State U., Olympia, Wash., 1976, BC Space, Laguna Beach, Calif., 1978, Cityscape Gallery, Pasadena, Calif., 1978, Exploratorium Gallery, Calif. State U., L.A., 1979, Orange Coast Coll., Costa Mesa, Calif., 1980, Susan Spiritus Gallery, Newport Beach, Calif., 1981, 83, 85, Canon Photo Gallery, Amsterdam, The Netherlands, 1982, John Michael Kohler Arts Ctr., Sheboygan, Wis., 1983, 86, Arco Ctr. Visual Arts, L.A., 1983, Clarence Kennedy Gallery, Boston, 1984, Colo. Mountain Coll., Breckenridge, 1984, Jayne H. Baum Gallery, N.Y.C., 1985, 87, 89, 91, 94, Torch Gallery, Amsterdam, 1985, 87, Fotografie Forum Frankfurt, Fed. Rep. Germany, 1986, Frederick S. Wight Art Gallery, U. Calif., L.A., 1987, San Francisco Cameraworks, 1988, Koplin Gallery, L.A., 1988, 90, 92, 95, Shadai Gallery, Tokyo Inst. Polytech., 1989, Lubbock (Tex.) Fine Arts Ctr., 1990, Haggerty Mus. Art, Marquette U., Milw., 1991, Richard Levy Gallery, Albuquerque, 1992, Stanford (Calif.) Mus. Art, 1993, numerous others; exhibited in group shows at Friends of Photography, Carmel, Calif., 1976, 81, 85, Ctrl. Wash. State Coll., Ellensburg, 1977, Humboldt State U., Arcata, Calif., 1977, Soho/Cameraworks Gallery, L.A., 1978, Libra Gallery, Claremont (Calif.) Grad. Sch., 1978, Cirrus Gallery, L.A., 1979, Skidmore Coll. Art Gallery, Saratoga, N.Y., 1980, Tortue Gallery, Santa Monica, Calif., 1981, Palos Verdes (Calif.) Cmty. Art Ctr., 1982, Fine Arts Gallery, Cypress (Calif.) Coll., 1982, Fay Gold Gallery, Atlanta, 1982, Mus. Photographic Arts, San Diego, 1983, 84, Jayne H. Baum Gallery, N.Y.C., 1983, 87, Arco Ctr. Visual Art, L.A., 1984, Alt. Mus., N.Y.C., 1984, 88, Black Gallery, L.A., 1985, Mus. N.Mex., Santa Fe, 1986, Whitney Mus. Am. Art, Stamford, Conn., 1986, Balt. Mus. Art, 1987, Ctr. Photography, Woodstock, N.Y., 1988, Oakland Mus., Calif., 1989, Alinder Gallery, Gualala, Calif., 1990, 92, Coll. Santa Fe, 1990, Art Ctr., Waco, Tex., 1991, Lintas Worldwide, N.Y.C., 1991, Dirs. Guild of Am., L.A., 1992, Burden Gallery, N.Y.C., 1992, Nat. Arts Club, N.Y.C., 1992, Knoxville (Tenn.) Art Mus., 1993, G. Ray Hawkins Gallery, L.A., 1994, Houston FotoFest, 1994, Riverside (Calif.) Art Mus., 1994, Mass. Coll. Art, Boston, 1994, numerous others; represented in permanent collections Albuquerque Mus., Balt. Art Mus., Continental Ins., N.Y.C., Chrysler Mus. Art, Norfolk, Va., Denver Art Mus., Ga. Power Co., Atlanta, Honolulu Advertiser, L.A. County Mus. Art, Loyola Marymount U., L.A., Mass. Coll. Art, Boston, Met. Mus. Art, N.Y.C., Mus. Fine Arts, Houston, Mus. N.Mex., Santa Fe, Nev. Mus. Art, Reno, Oakland (Calif.) Mus., Prudential Ins. Co. Am., Newark, Roswell (N.Mex.) Mus., St. Louis Art Mus., Shearson/Am. Express, N.Y.C., Tampa (Fla.) Mus. Art, Tokyo Inst. Polytech., numerous others. Travel grantee Ford Found., 1979; Faculty Rsch. grantee Loyola Marymount U., L.A., 1981, 83, U. N.Mex., 1988, 90; Artist-In-Residence grantee Calif. Arts Coun., 1982-83; Visual Artist fellow Nat. Endowment for the Arts, 1984-85, 92-93; Brody Arts Fund fellow, 1986; Polaroid fellow, 1983-90; named Art Waves competition and exhbn. finalist Cmty. Redevel. Agy. L.A., 1987;

recipient Calif. Disting. Arist award Nat. Art Edn. Assn. Conv., Mus. Contemporary Art, L.A., 1988, Kraszna-Krausz award and Photographic Book Innovation award Kraszna-Krausz Found., 1992. Avocations: gardening, gambling. Office: U NMex Dept Art & Art History Albuquerque NM 87131

NAGATOSHI, KONRAD R., anthropology educator, information systems specialist; b. Chgo., Jan. 18, 1951; s. Paul A. and Dorothea E. (Przybilla) N. BS in Anthropology with honors, Loyola U., 1973; MA in Anthropology, U. Chgo., 1976, PhD in Anthropology, 1984; cert. in data processing-tech., Harper Coll., 1990. Lic. realtor, Ill. Instr. anthropology Loyola U., Chgo., 1979-81; sr. rsch. specialist Ctr. for Craniofacial Anomalies U. Ill., Chgo., 1985-86, clin. asst. prof. biomed. visualization dept., 1987-88, adj. prof. anthropology dept., 1988; comml. real estate sales Samuel Spiro & Assocs., Chgo., 1989; computer micro-asst. Harper Coll., Palatine, Ill., 1990-91, instr. anthropology, 1991—; instr. anthropology Northeastern U., Chgo., 1991; computer programmer and analyst Ill. Dept. Employment Security, Chgo., 1992—, Kemper Nat. Ins., Long Grove, Ill., 1994—. Abstract reviewer Internat. Jour. Primatology, N.Y.C., 1990, Am. Jour. Physical Anthropology, N.Y.C., 1987; abstract reviewer, organizer U. Ill. Rsch. Forum, 1988; contbr. articles to profl. jours. Organist, song leader Our Lady of Mercy Roman Cath. Ch., Chgo., 1983-88. Found. for Rsch. Into the Origins of Man grantee, 1978-84, NSF Found. grantee, 1978-79, Sigma Xi grantee, 1978-79. Fellow Am. Anthropol. Assn.; mem. AAAS, Am. Assn. Phys. Anthropologists. Avocations: piano, art history, fishing, hiking, bicycling. Office: Harper Coll Div Bus/Social Sci 1200 W Algonquin Rd Palatine IL 60067-7373

NAGEL, DARYL DAVID, retail executive; b. Arlington, Minn., Apr. 13, 1939; s. Paul Charles and Frieda L. (Oldenburg) N.; m. Joan Clare Dacey, Dec. 23, 1961; children: Kelly, Andrew, Maureen. BME, U. Minn., 1962; diploma in Advanced Mgmt. Program, Harvard U., 1978. Asst. mdse. mgr. Res. Supply Co., Mpls., 1962-65; sr. mdse. mgr. Reserve Supply Co., Mpls., 1965-66, v.p., gen. mgr., 1966-69; v.p. area gen. mgr. United Bldg. Ctrs., Winona, Minn., 1969-78, exec. v.p., chief ops. officer, 1978-84, pres., chief exec. officer, 1984-87; pres., CEO Lanoga Corp., Seattle, 1987—; bd. dirs. Lanoga Corp., Seattle, 1987—, Badger Foundry, Winona, 1984-87. Bd. dirs. United Way, Winona, 1978-84, Home Ctr. Inst., 1996. Mem. Home Ctr. Leadership Coun., C. of C. (bd. dirs. 1964-69, 73, 78), Sahalee Country Club. Republican. Lutheran. Avocations: golf, gardening, skiing. Office: Lanoga Corp 17946 NE 65th St Redmond WA 98052-4963

NAGEL, EDWARD MCCAUL, lawyer, former utilities executive; b. Geneva, N.Y., Sept. 6, 1926; s. Edward Samuel and Helen Veronica (McCaul) N.; m. Mary Elizabeth Klein, Sept. 11, 1950; children—Christopher, Linda, Michael, Jeffrey, Ellen. A.B., Harvard, 1949; LL.B., U. Pa., 1952; postgrad., Cornell U. Bus. Sch., 1962. Bar: Pa. 1953. Assoc. Simpson, Thacher & Bartlett, N.Y.C., 1953-54; atty. Pa. Power & Light Co., Allentown, 1952, 54-62; asst. counsel Pa. Power & Light Co., 1962-68, asst. gen. counsel, 1968-71, gen. counsel, 1971-85, sec., 1971-89, v.p., 1973-91; prin. Edward M. Nagel Atty. at Law, 1991—; bd. dirs. Exec. Svc. Corps of Lehigh Valley. Chmn. Mayor's Citizens Adv. Com., Allentown, 1968-72; assoc. counsel, bd. dirs. Minsi Trails council Boy Scouts Am. Served with USNR, 1945-46. Mem. Pa. Bar Assn., Lehigh County Bar Assn. Home: 417 N 28th St Allentown PA 18104-4838

NAGEL, JOACHIM HANS, biomedical engineer, educator; b. Haustadt, Saarland, Feb. 22, 1948; came to U.S., 1986; s. Emil and Margarethe Nagel; m. Monika Behrens. MS, U. Saarbruecken, Fed. Republic Germany, 1973; DSc, U. Erlangen, Fed. Republic Germany, 1979. Rsch. assoc., lectr., instr. U. Saarbruecken, 1973-74; rsch. assoc., lectr., instr. Dept. Biomed. Engring., U. Erlangen-Nuernberg, 1974-75, asst. prof., 1975-79, dir. med. electronics and computer div., 1976-85, assoc. prof., 1980-86; assoc. prof. radiology Med. Sch. U. Miami, Coral Gables, Fla., 1990-91, assoc. prof. psychology Sch. Arts and Scis., 1988-91, assoc. prof. biomed. engring. Coll. Engring., 1986-91, prof. biomed. engring, radiology and psychology, 1991—. Editor Annals of Biomedical Engineering, Section Instrumentation, 1989-94, Inst. of Physics Physiological Measurement, 1994—; contbr. articles numerous articles to profl. jours. NIH grantee since 1986. Mem. IEEE (sr.), IEEE/Engring. in Medicine and Biology Soc. (chmn. Internat. Conf. 1991, chmn. Internat. Progr. Com. Conf. 1989, 90, 92), IEEE/Acoustics, Speech, and Signal Processing Soc., Biomed. Engring. Soc. (sr.), N.Y. Acad. Scis., Internat. Soc. Optical Engring., Romanian Soc. for Clin. Engring. and Med. Computing (hon.), Sigma Xi. Roman Catholic. Achievements include numerous U.S., German and European patents; invention and development of procedure for Sub-Nyquist Sampling of signals for statistic signal processing, NMR imaging of electric currents, passive telemetry for analogue signals, ECG detection; invention of Macro programming; portable drug infusion systems; new techniques for impedance cardiography and perinatal monitors; new techniques for medical image registration and U.S. Doppler analysis; neural network classification of Alzheimer's disease. Office: U Miami PO Box 248294 Miami FL 33124-0621

NAGEL, PAUL CHESTER, historian, writer, lecturer; b. Independence, Mo., Aug. 14, 1926; s. Paul Conrad and Freda (Sabrowsky) N.; m. Joan Peterson, Mar. 19, 1948; children: Eric John, Jefferson, Steven Paul. B.A., U. Minn., 1948, M.A., 1949, Ph.D., 1952. Historian SAC, USAF, Omaha, 1951-53; asst. prof. Augustana Coll., Sioux Falls, S.D., 1953-54; asst. prof., then assoc. prof. Eastern Ky. U., Richmond, 1954-61; mem. faculty U. Ky., 1961-69, prof. history, 1965-69; dean U. Ky. (Coll. Arts and Scis.), 1965-69; spl. asst. to pres. for acad. affairs U. Mo., 1969-71, v.p. acad. affairs, 1971-74, prof. history, 1969-78; prof., head dept. history U. Ga., 1978-80; dir. Va. Hist. Soc., Richmond, 1981-85; Disting. Lee scholar Lee Meml. Found., 1986-90; vis. prof. Amherst Coll., 1957-58, Vanderbilt U., 1959, U. Minn., 1964; vis. scholar, Duke U., 1991-92, U. Minn., 1992—, Carleton Coll., 1993—. Author: One Nation Indivisible, 1964, 2d edit., 1980, This Sacred Trust, American Nationality, 1798-1898, 1971, 2d edit., 1980, Missouri: A History, 1977 (Best Book award 1977), 2d edit., 1988, Descent from Glory, Four Generations of the John Adams Family, 1983 (Book of the Month Club main selection), The Adams Women: Abigail and Louisa Adams, Their Sisters and Daughters, 1987, The Lees of Virginia: Seven Generations of an American Family, 1990; co-author: Extraordinary Lives, 1986, George Caleb Bingham, 1989, Massachusetts and the New Nation, 1992; contbg. editor American Heritage. Mem. Coun. Colls. Arts and Scis., 1965-69, Ky. Arts Commn., 1966-69; trustee Colonial Williamsburg Found., 1983-95, disting. rsch. assoc., 1995—; vice-chmn. bd. dirs. Ctr. for Rsch. Librs., Chgo., 1973-74. Elected a Laureate of Va., 1988. Fellow Soc. Am. Historians, Pilgrim Soc.; So. Hist. Assn. (pres. 1984-85), Mass. Hist. Soc., Elder Learning Inst. (v.p. 1994—). Home: 1314 Marquette Ave Apt 2206 Minneapolis MN 55403-4114

NAGEL, SIDNEY ROBERT, physics educator; b. N.Y.C., Sept. 28, 1948; s. Ernest and Edith (Haggstrom) N.; married. BA, Columbia U., 1969; MA, Princeton U., 1972, PhD, 1974. Rsch. assoc. Brown U., Providence, R.I., 1974-76; asst. prof. physics U. Chgo., 1976-81, assoc. prof., 1981-84, prof., 1984—. Dir. U. Chgo. Materials Research Lab., 1987-91. Contbr. articles to profl. jours. Alfred Sloan Found. fellow, 1978-82. Fellow AAAS, Am. Phys. Soc. Home: 4919 S Blackstone Ave Chicago IL 60615-3003 Office: U Chgo 5640 S Ellis Ave Chicago IL 60637-1433

NAGEL, STUART SAMUEL, political science educator, lawyer; b. Chgo., Aug. 29, 1934; s. Leo I. and Florence (Pritikin) N.; m. Joyce Golub, Sept. 1, 1957; children: Brenda Ellen, Robert Franklin. Student, U. Chgo., 1954-55; BS, Northwestern U., 1957, JD, 1958, PhD, 1961. Bar: Ill. 1958. Instr. Pa. State U., 1960-61; asst. prof. U. Ariz., 1961-62; prof. polit. sci. U. Ill., 1962—; law and social sci. vis. fellow Yale Law Sch., 1970-71; vis. fellow Nat. Inst. Law Enforcement and Criminal Justice, 1974-75; Sr. scholar East-West Center, Honolulu, 1965; fellow Behavioral Scis. Center, Palo Alto, Calif., 1964-65; dir. O.E.O. Legal Services Agy. of Champaign, 1966-69; vol. atty. Lawyers Constl. Def. Com., Miss., 1967; asst. counsel U.S. Senate Jud. Com., 1966. Author: The Legal Process from a Behavioral Perspective, 1969, Law and Social Change, 1970, New Trends in Law and Politics Research, 1971, Rights of the Accused, 1972, Comparing Elected and Appointed Judicial Systems, 1973, Minimizing Costs and Maximizing Benefits in Providing Legal Services to the Poor, 1973, Improving the Legal Process: Effects of Alternatives, 1975, Operations Research Methods: As Applied to Political Science and The Legal Process, 1976, The Application of Mixed Strategies: Civil Rights and Other Multiple Activity Policies, 1976, Legal Policy Analysis: Finding an Optimum Level or Mix, 1977, Too Much or Too Little Policy: The Example of Pretrial Release, 1977, The Legal Process: Modeling the System, 1977, Decision Theory and the Legal Process, 1979, Policy Analysis: In Social Science Research, 1979, Policy Studies Handbook, 1980, Policy Evaluation: Making Optimum Decisions, 1982, Public Policy: Goals, Means and Methods, 1984, Contemporary Policy Analysis, 1984, Prediction Causation and Legal Analysis, 1986, Law, Policy and Optimizing Analysis, 1986, Evaluation Analysis with Microcomputers, 1988, Policy Studies: Integration and Evaluation, 1988, Higher Goals for America, 1988, Decision-Aiding Software and Legal Decision-Making, 1988, Introducing Decision-Aiding Software, 1989, Multi-Criteria Dispute Resolution, 1989, Evaluative and Explanatory Reasoning, 1990, Legal Scholarship and Microcomputers, 1990, Decision-Aiding Software: Skills, Obstacles and Applications, 1990, Judicial Decision-Making and Decision-Aiding Software, 1991, Legal Process Controversies and Super-Optimum Solutions, 1991, Public Policy Substance and Super-Optimum Solutions, 1991, Teach Yourself Decision-Aiding Software, 1991, Social Science, Law, and Public Policy, 1991, Policy Analysis Methods and Super-Optimum Solutions, 1992, Professional Developments in Policy Studies, 1992, Developing Nations and Super-Optimum Policy Analysis, 1993, The Policy Process and Super-Optimum Solutions, 1994, others; editor: Policy Studies Jour., The Policy Studies Directory, 1973, Environmental Politics, 1974, Policy Studies in America and Elsewhere, 1975, Policy Studies and the Social Sciences, 1975, Sage Yearbooks in Politics and Public Policy, 1975—, Lexington-Heath Policy Studies Orgn. Series, 1975—, Political Science Utilization Directory, 1975, Policy Studies Review Annual, 1977, Policy Grants Directory, 1977, Modeling the Criminal Justice System, 1977, Policy Research Centers Directory, 1978, Policy Studies Personnel Directory, 1979, Improving Policy Analysis, 1980, Policy Publishers and Associations Directory, 1980, Encyclopedia of Policy Studies, 1982, The Political Science of Criminal Justice, 1982, Productivity and Public Policy, 1983, The Policy Studies Field: It's Basic Literature, 1983, Public Policy Analysis and Management, 1986, Law and Policy Studies, 1987, Social Science and Computers, 1988, Decision-aiding Software and Decision Analysis, 1990, Decision-aiding Software and Public Administration, 1990, Global Policy Studies, 1990, Law, Decision-making and Microcomputers, 1990, Policy Theory and Policy Studies, 1990, Advances in Developmental Policy Studies, 1991—, Applications of Decision-Aiding Software, 19, Applications of Super-Optimum Solutions, 1991, Decision-Aiding Software and Decision Analysis, 1991, Law, Decision-Making, and Microcomputers, 1991, Policy Studies and Developing Nations: A Multi-Volume Treatise, 1991, Public Administration, Public Policy, and The People's Republic of China, 1991, Systematic Analysis in Dispute Resolution, 1991, Computer-Aided Decision Analysis, 1992, Resolving International Disputes Through Win-Win or SOS Solutions, 1992, Computer-Aided Judicial Analysis, 1992, Developing Nations and Super-Optimum Policy Analysis, 1992, Evaluative and Explanatory Reasoning, 1992, Developing Nations and Super-Optimum Policy Analysis, 1993, Legal Scholarship, Super-Optimizing, and Microcomputers, 1993, Encyclopedia of Policy Studies, 1993, African Development and Public Policy, 1994, Asian Development and Public Policy, 1994, East European Development and Public Policy, 1994, Latin American Development and Public Policy, 1994, Policy Studies in Developing Nations, 1994—, Political Reform and Developing Nations, 1995, Policy Studies in Developing Nations, 1994, India Development and Public Policy, 1995, others; mem. editorial bd.: Law and Soc. Assn. 1966—, Law and Policy Studies, 1986—, Pub. Policy Analysis and Mgmt., 1986—. Grantee Social Sci. Research Council, 1959-60; Grantee Am. Council Learned Socs., 1964-65; Grantee NSF, 1970-73; Grantee Rockefeller Found., 1976; Grantee Dept. Transp., 1976; Grantee Ford Found., 1975—; Grantee ERDA, 1977; Grantee Dept. Agr., 1977; Grantee NIE, 1976; Grantee HUD, 1978; Grantee ILEC, 1978; Grantee Dept. Labor, 1978; Grantee NIJ, 1979; Grantee Am. Bar Assn., 1980. Fellow AAAS; mem. ABA, Am. Polit. Sci. Assn., Law and Soc. Assn. (trustee), Policy Studies Orgn. (sec.-treas.). Home: 1720 Park Haven Dr Champaign IL 61820-7153 *There is a need for social scientists to show more interest in applying their knowledge and skills to important policy problems. There is also a need for policy-makers and policy-appliers to become more aware of the relevant knowledge and skills that social scientists have developed. I have tried to stimulate closer relations between social science and public policy by such relevant activities as writing articles, authoring books, editing journals, and founding associations. Those activities will hopefully result in promoting more applications of social science to important public policy problems. I am especially interested in developing solutions to public policy problems whereby liberals, conservatives, and other major viewpoints can all come out ahead of their initial best expectations simultaneously. Such solutions are facilitated by decision-aiding software which enables one to systematically process goals to be achieved, alternatives available for achieving them, and relations be*

NAGEL, THOMAS, philosopher, educator; b. Belgrade, Yugoslavia, July 4, 1937; came to U.S., 1939, naturalized, 1944; s. Walter and Carolyn (Baer) N.; m. Doris Blum, June 18, 1958 (div. 1973); m. Anne Hollander, June 26, 1979. B.A., Cornell U., 1958; B.Phil., Oxford (Eng.) U., 1960; Ph.D., Harvard, 1963. Asst. prof. philosophy U. Calif., Berkeley, 1963-66; asst. prof. Princeton U., 1966-69, assoc., 1969-72, prof., 1972-80; prof. N.Y. U., 1980—, prof. philosophy and law, 1986—; vis. prof. Rockefeller U., 1973, U. Mex., 1977, U. Witwatersrand, 1982, UCLA, 1986; Tanner lectr. Stanford U., 1977, Oxford (Eng.) U., 1979, Howison lectr. U. Calif., Berkeley, 1987, Thalheimer lectr. Johns Hopkins U., 1989, John Locke lectr. Oxford U., 1990, Hempel lectr. Princeton U., 1995, Whitehead lectr. Harvard U., 1995, Kant lectr. Stanford U., 1995. Author: The Possibility of Altruism, 1970, Mortal Questions, 1979, The View from Nowhere, 1986, What Does It All Mean?, 1987, Equality and Partiality, 1991, Other Minds, 1995, The Last Word, 1996; assoc. editor: Philosophy and Public Affairs, 1970-82. Guggenheim fellow, 1966, NSF fellow, 1967-69, NEH fellow, 1978, 84-85, vis. fellow All Souls Coll., Oxford, Eng., 1990. Mem. Am. Philos. Assn., Am. Acad. Arts and Scis., Brit. Acad.

NAGERA, HUMBERTO, psychiatrist, psychoanalyst, educator, author; b. Havana, Cuba, May 23, 1927; m. Gloria Maria Hernandez, Sept. 8, 1952; children: Lisette Maria, Humberto Felipe, Daniel. B.Sc., U. Havana, 1945; M.D., Havana Med. Sch., 1952. Intern, resident in psychiatry Havana U. Hosp., 1950-55; sr. staff, chmn. research Anna Freud's Clinic, London, 1958-68; prof. psychiatry U. Mich., Ann Arbor, 1968-87; chief youth services U. Mich., 1973-79, prof. emeritus, 1987; prof. psychiatry U. South Fla., 1987—, dir. adolescent inpatient unit and children's inpatient unit, 1987—. Author: Early Childhood Disturbances, Problems of Developmental Psychoanalytic Psychology, 1966, Vincent Van Gogh, 1966, Basic Psychoanalytic Concepts on the Libido Theory, 1969, Basic Psychoanalytic Concepts on the Theory of Instincts, 1970, Basic Psychoanalytic Concepts of Metapsychology Conflicts, Anxiety, and Other Subjects, 1970, Female Sexuality and the Oedipus Complex, 1975, Obsessional Neurosis: Developmental Psychopathology, 1977, 2nd edit., 1993, The Developmental Approach in Child Psychopathology, 1981; Contbr. articles to profl. jours. Mem. Am. Psychiat. Assn., Internat. Psychoanalytic Assn., Mich. Psychoanalytic Inst. (pres. 1975-77), Am. Assn. Child Psychoanalysis, Cuba Med. Assn. in Exile, South Fla. Tampa Bay Psychoanalytic Soc. (pres. 1992-93). Home: 5202 Dwire Ct Tampa FL 33647-1016 Office: U South Fla Dept Psychiatry 3515 E Fletcher Ave Tampa FL 33613-4706

NAGLE, ARTHUR JOSEPH, investment banker; b. Allentown, Pa., Sept. 11, 1938; s. Paul Arthur and Frances Helene (Kline) N.; m. Paige Carlton, Sept. 12, 1970; children: Kathryn Elizabeth, Christopher Paul. BS in Math., Pa. State U., 1961; MBA in Fin., Columbia U., 1967. Systems engr., mktg. rep. IBM, Pitts., 1961-62; trainee to mng. dir. First Boston Corp., N.Y.C., 1967-88; mng. dir. Vestar Capital Ptnrs., Inc., 1988—; bd. dirs. Chart House Restaurant, Solana Beach, Calif., Super D. Drugs, Inc., Memphis, Russell Stanley Corp., Woodbridge, N.J., La Petite Acad., Inc., Overland Park, Kans., Hampshire Chem. Corp., Danbury, Conn., Cabot Safety Corp., Boston. Active Community Fund, Bronxville, N.Y.; bd. govs. Lawrence Hosp., Bronxville, Nat. Devel. Coun., Pa. State U., Bronxville Sch. Found. Lt. USN, 1962-66, Vietnam. Office: Vestar Capital Ptnrs Inc 245 Park Ave 41st Fl New York NY 10017

NAGLE, JAMES FRANCIS, lawyer; b. Jersey City, Aug. 5, 1948; s. James Francis and Cecile Marie (Dorgan) N.; m. Ann Marie Thomas, Dec. 28, 1974; children: James, John, Stephen. BS, Georgetown U., 1970; JD, Rutgers U., 1973; LLM, George Washington U., 1981, SJD, 1986. Bar: N.J. 1973, U.S. Ct. Mil. Appeals 1979, U.S. Supreme Ct. 1979, U.S. Ct. Appeals (fed. cir.) 1982, U.S. Ct. Appeals (D.C. cir.) 1983. Enlisted U.S. Army, 1970, advanced through grades to lt. col., 1987; chief of criminal law Presidio of San Francisco, 1974-75; command judge adv. U.S. Army 8th Army, Korea, 1975-76; chief of administrv. law U.S. Army Electronics Command, Ft. Monmouth, N.J., 1976-79; br. chief Army Def. Appellate Div., Falls Church, Va., 1982-85; team chief Army Chief Trial Atty.'s Office, Falls Church, 1982-85; contracts atty. U.S. Army Forces Command, Ft. McPherson, Ga., 1985-88; chief adminstrv. law U.S. Third Army, Ft. McPherson, 1986-88; chief logistic and contract law dept. U.S. Army, Washington, 1988-90; ret. U.S. Army, 1990; ptnr. Oles, Morrison & Rinker, Seattle, 1990—. Author: Procurement Regulations, 1987, A History of Government Contracting, 1992, How to Review Federal Contracts, 1990, Federal Construction Contracting, 1992; contbr. articles to profl. jours. Mem. Fed. Bar Assn., Wash. State Bar Assn., D.C. Bar Assn. Roman Catholic. Avocations: gardening, karate. Home: 5196 Lynwood Center Rd NE Bainbridge Island WA 98110

NAGLEE, ELFRIEDE KURZ, medical nurse; b. Phila., Mar. 13, 1932; d. Emil and Frida (Keppler) Kurz; m. David I. Naglee, Sept. 6, 1952; children: Joy, Miriam, Deborah, Joanna, David. Diploma, Phila. Gen. Hosp., 1952. RN, Ga. Dir. nursing City County Hosp., LaGrange, Ga.; house supr. West Ga. Med. Ctr., LaGrange; staff nurse med. fl. West Ga. Med. Ctr., LaGange. Mem. Ga. Nursing Assn. Home: 804 Piney Woods Dr La Grange GA 30240-2020

NAGLER, ARNOLD LEON, pathologist, scientist, educator; b. N.Y.C., 1935; s. Max and Esther (Finkel) N.; m. Rosalie Groden, Feb. 18, 1961; children: Stephen Marc, Melissa Sue. B.S., CCNY, 1953; M.D., NYU, 1958, Ph.D., 1960. Lic. dir. labs., N.Y. Postgrad. tng. NYU-Bellevue Med. Ctr., 1958-61; research assoc. Mt. Sinai Hosp., N.Y.C., 1960-61; mem. faculty Albert Einstein Coll. Medicine, Bronx, N.Y., 1961—, assoc. prof. pathology, surgery, 1975—; cons., prof., chmn. pathology dept., dean pre-clin. medicine N.Y. Coll. Osteo Medicine, 1978—; trustee Robert Chambers Microsurgery Research Labs., 1978—; founder, trustee Esther Nagler Dystrophy Research Fund, N.Y. Coll. Osteo. Medicine. Mem. editorial bd.: Circulatory Shock; contbr. articles to profl. jours. Chmn. Jericho council Boy Scouts Am., 1971-73; mem. Pres.'s Task Force, 1981—, Nat. Republican Congressional Com., U.S. Senatorial Club; trustee Liberal Jewish Day Sch., N.Y.C.; corp. mem. Nassau-Suffolk Health Systems Agy., mem. Primary Care Task Force. Served with U.S. Army, 1953-55. NIH grantee, 1961—. Fellow Am. Soc. Clin. Pathologists; mem. N.Y. Acad. Sci., N.Y. Acad. Medicine, AAAS, Am. Trauma Soc. (founder), Sigma Xi. Jewish. Home: 72 Hazelwood Dr Jericho NY 11753-1704 Office: Albert Einstein Coll Medicine 1300 Morris Park Ave Bronx NY 10461-1926 *I was guided by my parents when they were alive and directed by their teachings and precepts after their death to strive to do the best that I possibly may, in any and every endeavor that I undertake. They provided the armoury: Do no harm to anyone—achieve by dedicating yourself to excellence/performance. Do not rally in relegating someone to a lesser state; this is only relative success and is neither satisfying nor worthwhile to the soul, nor is it real.*

NAGLER, LEON GREGORY, management consultant, business executive; b. Buenos Aires, Argentina, Jan. 29, 1932 (parents Am. citizens); s. Morris and Jennie (Golden) N.; BS cum laude, Boston U., 1953, MBA, 1954; J.D., Cleve. State U., 1961; m. F. Elise Charness, Dec. 20, 1953; children: Jeri Lynn, Sandra Michelle. Bar: Ohio 1961. Tchr. psychology Cameron State Agrl. Jr. Coll., Lawton, Okla., 1956-57; supr. employment and tng. Jones & Laughlin Steel Corp., Cleve., 1957-65; exec. dir. indsl. relations Charles Corp., Cleve., 1965-67; dir. personnel ITT Service Industries Corp., Cleve., 1967-72; v.p. personnel Builder Services Corp., Clearwater, Fla., 1972-73; v.p. adminstrn. Damon Corp., Needham Heights, Mass., 1973-77; pres. Nagler & Co., Inc., Wellesley Hills, Mass., 1977-95; pres. Nagler, Robins & Poe, Inc., 1995—. Mem. Mayfield Heights (Ohio) Planning and Zoning Commn., 1965-67; sec. Mayfield Heights Zoning Bd. Appeals, 1963-65; chmn. Combined Health Fund, Mayfield Heights, 1963; pres. N.E. Ohio region, mem. nat. gov. coun. Am. Jewish Congress, 1972-73; bd. dirs. New Eng. region Anti-Defamation League, 1977-80; bd. dirs. Jewish Vocat. Svc., Boston, 1977—, sec., 1980-83, v.p., 1983-88; bd. dirs. Jewish Community Ctr. Greater Boston, 1988—, Am. Friends Wingate Inst., 1987—, v.p. fin., 1987—; trustee Temple Beth Avodah, Newton, 1978—, v.p., 1979-83, pres., 1983-85; trustee Combined Jewish Philanthropies, Boston, 1985-92; bd. overseers Combined Jewish Philanthropies, 1992—. Served with AUS, 1955-57. Mem. Ohio, Cleve. bar assns., Soc. for Human Resource Mgmt., Internat. Assn. Corp. and Exec. Recruiters, Boston U. Alumni Assn. (pres. N.E. Ohio 1969-73, nat. council 1973—). Democrat. Lodge: Masons. Office: Nagler Robins & Poe Inc 65 William St Wellesley MA 02181-3802

NAGLER, MICHAEL NICHOLAS, classics and comparative literature educator; b. N.Y.C., Jan. 20, 1937; s. Harold and Dorothy Judith (Nocks) N.; m. Roberta Ann Robbins (div. May 1983); children: Jessica, Joshua. BA, NYU, 1960; MA, U. Calif., Berkeley, 1962, PhD, 1966. Instr. San Francisco State U., 1963-65; prof. classics, comparative lit. dept. U. Calif., Berkeley, 1966-91, prof. emeritus, 1991—. Author: Spontaneity and Tradition, 1974, America Without Violence, 1982; co-author: The Upanishads, 1987; contbr. articles to profl. publs. Pres. bd. dirs. METTA Ctrs. for Nonviolence Edn. Fellow Am. Coun. Learned Socs., NIH; MacArthur Found. grantee, 1988. Mem. Am. Philolog. Soc. (editor Oral Tradition). Office: U Calif Classics Dept Berkeley CA 94720

NAGLER, STEWART GORDON, insurance company executive; b. Bklyn., Jan. 30, 1943; s. Henry and Mary N.; m. Bonnie Lawrence, Aug. 9, 1964; children: David, Ellen. B.S. summa cum laude, Poly. U., 1963. With Met. Life Ins. Co., N.Y.C., 1963—, exec. v.p., 1978-85, sr. exec. v.p., 1985—. Fellow Soc. Actuaries, Acad. Actuaries. Office: Met Life Ins Co 1 Madison Ave New York NY 10010-3603

NAGLESTAD, FREDERIC ALLEN, legislative advocate; b. Sioux City, Iowa, Jan. 13, 1929; s. Ole T. and Evelyn Elizabeth (Erschen) N.; student (scholar) U. Chgo., 1947-49; m. Beverly Minnette Shellberg, Feb. 14, 1958; children—Patricia Minnette, Catherine Janette. Pub. affairs, pub. relations, newscaster, announcer KSCJ-radio, Sioux City, Iowa, 1949-51; producer, dir., newscaster, announcer WOW-TV, Omaha, 1953-57; program mgr. WCPO-TV, Cin., 1957-58; mgr. KNTV-TV, San Jose, Calif., 1958-61; owner Results Employment Agy., San Jose, 1961-75; legis. advocate Naglestad Assocs., Calif Assn. Employers, Calif. Automotive Wholesalers Assn., Air Quality Products, Calif. Assn. Wholesalers-Distbrs., State Alliance Bd. Equalization Reform, Quakemaster, many others, 1969—. Pres. Calif. Employment Assn., 1970-72. Asst. concertmaster Sioux City Symphony Orch., 1945-47. Sgt. AUS, 1951-53. Recognized for outstanding contbn. to better employment law, Resolution State Calif. Legislature, 1971. Office: 3991 Fair Oaks Blvd Sacramento CA 95864-7254 *Personal philosophy: Tell the truth, perservere and follow through.*

NAGOURNEY, HERBERT, publishing company executive; b. N.Y.C., Jan. 30, 1926; s. Isidor and Tillie (Burstein) N.; children: Adam, Beth, Eric, Sam. BS, Columbia U., 1946, MS, 1947. Pres. Profl. and Tech. Programs, N.Y.C., 1951-65; v.p. Macmillan Co., N.Y.C., 1965-69; pres. Quadrangle/New York Times Book Co., N.Y.C., 1969-76, New York Times Book Co., N.Y.C., 1971-76, Quartet Books, Inc., N.Y.C. and London, 1976-81, Knowledge Tree Group Inc., 1979-89; v.p., dir. Sci. DataLink, 1981-88, Comtex Sci., 1981-90; pres. Profl. and Tech. Pub. Inc., 1989—, Sci. Datalink, 1990—. Served with AUS, 1944. Home: 320 Joshuatown Rd Lyme CT 06371-3000 Office: 45 Christopher St New York NY 10014

NAGRIN, DANIEL, dancer, educator, choreographer, lecturer, writer; b. N.Y.C., May 22, 1917; s. Harry Samuel and Clara (Wexler) N.; m. Helen Tamiris, 1946 (dec. 1966); m. Phyllis A. Steele, Jan. 24, 1992. BS in Edn., CCNY, 1940; DFA, SUNY, Brockport, 1991; LHD, Ariz. State U., 1992; studied dance with Martha Graham, Anna Sokolow, Helen Tamiris, Mme. Anderson-Ivantzova, Nenette Charisse and Edward Caton, 1936-56, studied acting with Miriam Goldina, Sanford Meisner and Stella Adler, 1936-56. Tchr. Silvermine Guild Art, New Canaan, Conn., 1957-66, SUNY, Brockport, 1967-71, U. Md., College Park, 1970, Davis Ctr. Performing Arts, CCNY, 1973-75, Nat. Theatre Inst., Eugene O'Neill Found.,

Waterford, Conn., 1974, Hartmann Theatre Conservatory, Stamford, Conn., 1975-77; long-term resident tchr., Nat. Endowment for Arts sponsorship U. Hawaii, 1978-80, tchr., 1981; tchr. Bill Evans Dance Workshop, Seattle, 1981; prof. dance dept. Ariz. State U., Tempe, 1982-92; tchr. grad. liberal studies program Wesleyan U., Middletown, Conn., 1984, Dance Workshop for Movement Rsch., N.Y.C., 1984, Improvisation Workshop, Seattle, 1985, Improvisation, Choreography and Acting Technique for Dancers, Seattle, 1985, Dance Workshop, Glenwood Springs, Colo., 1990; prof. emeritus dance Ariz. State U., 1992; tchr. summer sessions Conn. Coll., New London, 1959, 74; Am. Dance Festival at Conn. Coll., 1960, 77, Duke U., Durham, N.C., 1978, 80, 82, 87, 88, 92; summer dance program Conn. Coll., 1979, E. La Tour Dance Workshop, Sedgewick, 1982, 83; dance workshop U. Minn. at Mpls., 1984, Stanford U., 1990; co-dir. Tamiris-Nagrin Summer Dance Workshop, Sedgewick, 1960-61, (with Tamiris) summer dance session C. W. Post Coll., Greenville, N.Y., 1962-63; dir. summer dance workshop Johnson (Vt.) State Coll., 1972, 73, 75, 76. Featured dance soloist on Broadway: Annie Get Your Gun, Lend an Ear, Touch and Go, Plain and Fancy (Billboard Donaldson award 1954-55), 1940-56; appearance in film, Just for You; adapted and performed one-man theatre piece The Fall, from novel by Albert Camus, 1977-79, choreographer (solo works) Spanish Dance, 1948, Man of Action, 1948, Strange Hero, 1948, Indeterminate Figure, 1957, With My Eye and With My Hand, 1968, Jazz: Three Ways, 1958, 66, Path-Silence, 1965, Not Me, But Him, 1965, The Peloponesian War, 1967-68, Untitled, 1974, Ruminations, 1976, Getting Well, 1978, Poems Off the Wall, 1981, Apartment 18C, 1993, others; (for groups) Faces from Walt Whitman, 1950, An American Journey, 1962; asst. choreographer original Broadway prodns.: Up in Central Park, Stovepipe Hat, Show Boat, Annie Get Your Gun, By the Beautiful Sea, others; dir. off-Broadway: Volpone, 1957, The Firebugs, 1960, The Umbrella, 1961, Emperor Jones, (Boston), 1963, others; film choreography: His Majesty O'Keefe: acted in video The Art of Memory, 1985, play, Three Stories High, others; extensive touring U.S., Europe, The Pacific, and Japan, 1957-84; conceived and directed videos: Steps, 1972, The Edge is Also a Circle, 1973, Nagrin Videotape Library of Dances, 1985; author: How to Dance Forever: Surviving Against the Odds, 1988, Dance and the Specific Image: Improvisation, 1993. With spl. svcs. Army Airforce, 1942-43. Grantee Rebekah Harkness Found., 1962, Logan Found., 1965, N.Y. State Coun. on Arts and Nat. Found. for Arts and Humanities, 1967-68, N.Y. State Coun. on Arts, 1971-72, 73-74, 75-76, 76-77, 78-79, 80-81, Anne S. Richardson Fund, 1971, 73, 74, 75, 76, 78, Nat. Endowment for Arts, 1975, 79, 81, 83, Ariz. State U., 1983, 84, 85, 86, 88; CAPS fellow N.Y. State Coun. on Arts, 1977-78; fellow Nat. Endowment for Arts, 1977-78, 80, 82, 83, 90, 91; comsd. ballet Rebekah Harkness Ballet Found., 1986. Mem. Actors' Equity, Phi Kappa Phi (hon.). Avocation: reading. Home and Office: 208 E 14th St Tempe AZ 85281-6707

NAGTALON-MILLER, HELEN ROSETE, humanities educator; b. Honolulu, June 27, 1928; d. Dionicio Reyes and Fausta Dumbrigue (Rosete) N.; m. Robert Lee Ruley Miller, June 15, 1952. BEd, U. Hawaii, 1951; Diplôme, The Sorbonne, Paris, 1962; MA, U. Hawaii, 1967; PhD, Ohio State U., 1972. Cert. secondary education educator. Tchr. humanities Hawaii State Dept. Edn., Honolulu, 1951-63; supr. student tchrs. French lab. sch. Coll. of Edn. U. Hawaii, Honolulu, 1963-66, instr. French, coord. French courses Coll. Arts and Scis., 1966-69; teaching asst. Coll. Edn. Ohio State U., Columbus, 1970-72; instr. French lab. sch. Coll. Edn. U. Hawaii, Honolulu, 1974-76; adminstr. bilingual-bicultural edn. project Hawaii State Dept. Edn., Honolulu, 1976-77; coord. disadvantaged minority recruitment program Sch. Social Work, U. Hawaii, Honolulu, 1977-84; coord. tutor tng. program U. Hawaii, Honolulu, 1984-86; program dir. Multicultural Multifunctional Resource Ctr., Honolulu, 1986-87; vis. prof. Sch. Pub. Health, ret. U. Hawaii, Honolulu, 1987-92, 92—; bd. dirs. Hawaii Assn. Lang. Tchrs., Honolulu, 1963-66, Hawaii Com. for the Humanities, 1977-83; mem. statewide adv. coun. State Mental Health Adv. Com., Honolulu, 1977-82; task force mem. Underrepresentation of Filipinos in Higher Edn., Honolulu, 1984-86. Author: (with others) Notable Women in Hawaii, 1984; contbr. articles to profl. jours. Chairperson edn. and counseling subcom. First Gov.'s Commn. on Status of Women, Honolulu, 1964; vice chairperson Honolulu County Com. on the Status of Women, 1975-76, Hawaii State Dr. Martin Luther King Jr. Commn., Honolulu, 1982-85; pres. Filipino Hist. Soc. of Hawaii, 1980—; mem. Hawaii State Adv. Com. to U.S. Commn. on Civil Rights, 1981—, chairperson, 1982-85; bd. dirs. Japanese Am. Citizens League Honolulu chpt., 1990—, mem. Hawaiian Sovereignty com., 1994—. Women of Distinction, Honolulu County Com. on Status of Women, 1982; recipient Nat. Edn. Assn. award for Leadership in Asian and Pacific Island Affairs, NEA, 1985, Alan F. Saunders award ACLU in Hawaii, 1986, Disting. Alumni award U. Hawaii Alumni Affairs Office, 1994. Mem. Filipino Am. Nat. Hist. Soc., Filipino Coalition for Solidarity, Gabriela Network (Hawaii chpt.), FIlipino Cmty. Ctr., NOW. Democrat. Avocations: social-political advocacy, reading, classical music, theater, literary presentations. Home and Office: 3201 Beaumont Woods Pl Honolulu HI 96822-1423

NAGY, ANDREW FRANCIS, engineering educator; b. Budapest, Hungary, May 2, 1932; came to U.S., 1957, naturalized, 1968; s. Bela and Lilly (Dekany) N.; children: Robert Bela, Susan Elizabeth. BE, U. New South Wales, 1957; MSc, U. Nebr., 1959; MS, U. Mich., 1960, PhD, 1963. Design engr. Electric Control and Engring. Co., Ltd., Sydney, Australia, 1956-57; instr. elec. engring. U. Nebr., 1957-59; research engr. U. Mich., Ann Arbor, 1959-63; asst. prof. elec. engring. U. Mich., 1963-67, assoc. prof., 1967-71, prof. space sci., prof. elec. engring., 1971—, assoc. v.p. for rsch., 1987-90; vis. assoc. prof. engring. U. Calif. at, San Diego, 1969-70; vis. prof. physics Utah State U., 1976-77. Past editor: Revs. of Geophysics and Space Physics, Geophys. Rsch. Letters. Fulbright scholar, 1957. Fellow Am. Geophys. Union (pres. SPR sect.); mem. IEEE (sr.), Internat. Radio Sci. Union (commns. 3 and 4), Hungarian Acad. Scis., Sigma Xi, Eta Kappa Nu. Home: 338 Rock Creek Dr Ann Arbor MI 48104-1860

NAGY, BALINT, biologist; b. Szabadszallas, Hungary, Feb. 29, 1956; came to U.S., 1991; s. Balint and Julia (Bajnoczi) N.; m. Maria Vegh, Jan. 30, 1982; children: Balint Miklos, Balazs Gabor. MS, Attila Jozsef U., 1980; PhD, Semmelweis Med. U. Sch., 1986. Biologist Human Inst. for Serobact Prodn., Budapest, 1980-85; rsch. fellow Semmelweis U. Med. Sch., Budapest, 1986—; vis. fellow NIH Clin. Ctr., Bethesda, Md., 1992—. Contbr. articles to profl. jours. Recipient Young Investigator awrd Acad. for Clin. Physicians and Scientists, 1995. Mem. Am. Assn. Clin. Chemistry, N.Y. Acad. Scis., Assn. Hungarian Ob.-Gyn., Assn. Hungarian Microbiologists. Achievements include research in downward transfer of proteins, pulsed field electrophoresis applicable for proteins. Office: NIH Clin Ctr Dept Pathology Bldg 10 Rm 2C-407 9000 Rockville Pike Bethesda MD 20892

NAGY, CHRISTINE LEE, rehabilitation, home care and geriatrics nurse, nursing educator; b. N.Y.C., July 11, 1961; d. Augustus Richard Monturo and Martha Kay Childress Ferris; m. William John Nagy, Aug. 19, 1989; 1 child, Alexander Christopher; 1 stepchild, Angeline Nicole. BA in Communications, BSN, Cleve. State U., 1990. Cert. in gerontology, rehab. and nursing adminstrn. Staff/charge nurse Metrohealth Med. Ctr., Cleve., 1988-90; charge nurse Jackson Meml. Hosp., Miami, Fla., 1990-92; unit mgr. geriatric rehab. and long term care Saginaw (Mich.) Community Hosp., 1992; charge nurse, nursing home care and rehab. unit Saginaw VA Hosp., 1992-93; unit mgr. geriatric rehab. unit Mt. Sinai Med. Ctr., Miami Beach, Fla., 1993-94; home care rehab. coord. Marymount Hosp., Garfield Heights, Ohio, 1994—; mem. policy, procedure, nurses wk., long term care coms. and behavior modification team Saginaw Community Hosp., 1992—. BLS instr. ARC/Am. Heart Assn., Cleve., Miami, 1990, 91, continuing edn./insvc. educator, 1990—; active Broward County Schs. PTA, 1993, 94, Garfield Heights Schs. PTA, 1994, Black River Schs. PTA; cub scout den leader, coach Seminole Dist. and Greater Cleve. Dist. Boy Scouts Am.; vol. Lakewood Meals on Wheels, Ohio, 1987-90, Garfield Heights Meals on Wheels; mem. St. Stephen's Ch. Ladies Guild, West Salem, Ohio; coaching asst. youth/boys divsn. Ashland Soccer Assn. Mem. ANA, Nat. League for Nursing, Assn. Rehab. Nurses, Mich. Nurses Assn., Fla. Nurses Assn., Ohio Nurses Assn., Nat. Spinal Cord Nurses. Republican. Roman Catholic. Avocations: camping, traveling, fishing, reading, journal writing.

NAGY, JOE HOWARD, lawyer; b. Pearsall, Tex., Dec. 17, 1928; s. Joe H. and Pauline (Howard) N.; m. Dorothy Fay Shelton, May 6, 1951; children: Margaret Nagy Dobbs, Joe Howard Jr. BS, Tex. A&M U., 1950; JD, U. Tex., 1958. Bar: Tex. 1958, U.S. Dist. Ct. (no. and we. dists.) Tex. 1958, U.S. Supreme Ct. 1975. Ptnr. Crenshaw, Dupree & Milam, Lubbock, Tex., 1958-65, 1965—. 1st lt. U.S. Army, 1951-53, Korea. Fellow Tex. Bar Found., Tex. Assn. Def. Counsel; mem. State Bar of Tex. (bd. dirs. 1975-78, pres. elect 1986-87, pres. 1987-88), Lubbock County Bar Assn. (pres. elect 1971-72, pres. 1972-73, bd. dirs.), Am. Coll. Trial Lawyers, Tex. Assn. Mediators. Republican. Methodist. Avocation: hunting. Office: Crenshaw Dupree & Milam 1500 Broadway St Ste 9000 Lubbock TX 79401-3106

NAGY, LOUIS LEONARD, engineering executive, researcher; b. Detroit, Jan. 15, 1942; s. Alex and Helen (Marth) N.; m. Dianna M. Skarjune, Aug. 5, 1961; children: Tammy, Kimberly, Kristine, Amanda. BSEE, U. Mich., Dearborn, 1965; MSEE, U. Mich., Ann Arbor, 1969, PhDEE, 1974. Rsch. engr. U. Mich., Ann Arbor, 1962-69; staff rsch. engr. GM Rsch. Labs., Warren, Mich., 1969—. Contbr. articles to profl. jours.; patentee in field. Bd. dirs. Convergence Ednl. Found., Birmingham, Mich., 1990—, Convergence Transp. Electronics Assn., Birmingham, 1990—. Fellow IEEE; mem. Convergence Fellowship (bd. dirs. 1988—), Vehicular Tech. Soc. (Spl. Recognition award 1979, Avant Garde award 1986, Paper of Yr. 1975), Soc. Automotive Engrs., Tau Beta Pi, Eta Kappa Nu. Avocations: electronics, antennas, radar, automotive radar, microwaves. Office: GM Rsch Labs Dept 3 Engineering Warren MI 48090

NAGY, ROBERT DAVID, tenor; b. Lorain, Ohio, Mar. 3, 1929; s. John Robert and Helen Elizabeth (Polesko) N.; m. Vincenza Rose Ianni, May 1, 1954; children—Robert John, Helena Jean, Gina Kati. Student, Cleve. Inst. Music, 1952-55. tchr., cons. to young opera students. Soloist Met. Opera, 1957-88, ret.; appeared in opera houses throughout U.S., World. Served with U.S. Army, 1950-52, Korea. Weyer Hauser scholar, 1957; Ford Found. scholar, 1959. Winner Met. Opera audition, 1956. Home: 5996 Case Rd North Ridgeville OH 44039-1030

NAGY, STEVEN, biochemist; b. Fords, N.J., Apr. 7, 1936; s. Steven and Martha (Moberg) N.; m. Suzanne Nagy; children: Lacey, Nicolette, Steven. BS in Chemistry, La. State U., 1960; MS in Physiology and Biochemistry, Rutgers U., 1962, PhD in Biochemistry, 1965; MEngring. in Indsl. Engring., U. South Fla., 1977. Analytical chemist USPHS, Metuchen, N.J., 1962-65; rsch. assoc. Lever Bros., Edgewater, N.J., 1965-67; rsch. chemist Dept. Agr., Winter Haven, Fla., 1968-79; rsch. scientist Fla. Dept. Citrus, Lake Alfred, 1979—; adj. prof. U. Fla., 1979—; treas. AgScience Inc. Mem. Am. Chem. Soc. (chmn. div. agrl. and food chemistry, disting. svc. award 1988, fellow, 1990), Phytochem. Soc. N. Am. (chmn.), Inst. Food Technologists (chmn. citrus products div.), Am. Soc. for Hort. Sci., Internat. Soc. Citriculture, Fla. Hort. Soc. (v.p.), Sigma Xi. Republican. Author: Citrus Science and Technology, 2 vols., 1977; Tropical and Subtropical Fruits, 1980; Citrus Nutrition and Quality, 1980; Fresh Citrus Fruits, 1986, Adulteration of Fruit Juice Beverages, 1988, Fruits of Tropical and Subtropical Origin, 1990, Fruit Juice Processing Technology, 1993, Methods To Detect Adulteration of Fruit Juice Beverages, 1995; editorial bd. Food Chemistry, Jour. Agrl. and Food Chemistry; contbr. articles to profl. jours. Home: 103 Arietta Shores Dr Auburndale FL 33823-9336 Office: 700 Experiment Station Rd Lake Alfred FL 33850-2243

NAGY, SUZANNE CSIKOS, artist, gallery owner; b. Budapest, Hungary, Mar. 2, 1947; came to U.S., 1979; d. Bela Csikos-Nagy and Lili Kneppo; m. Steve Mati, May 11, 1977 (dec. May 1990); m. R. Edward Townsend, Jr., May 18, 1991; 1 child, Lina N. Degree in econs., Budapest U., 1967; degree in media and art, Acad. of Art and Film, Budapest, 1977. Economist Technoimpex, Budapest, 1968-69; head internat. bus. BUBIV, Budapest, 1969-72; owner Gallery Les Looms, N.Y.C., 1984—. One woman shows include Madison Ave. Matignon Gallery; exhibited in group shows in N.Y., Pa., Conn.; represented in permanent collections Budapest Nat. Gallery, Budapest Mus. Contemporary Art; contbr./exhibitor 5 major 15th-19th century tapestries Fed. Res. Bd. Exhbn.; author, artist: (art book) Tale of the Clock, 1994; contbr. articles to mags. Mem. Yale Club. Home: 22 W 26th St New York NY 10010-2023 Office: Gallery Les Looms 1050 2nd Ave New York NY 10022-4063

NAHARY, LEVIA L., campus programming director; b. Scranton, Pa., Apr. 21, 1965; d. Haim and Bracha (Seri) N. BA in Liberal Arts, U. Scranton, 1986; MS in Higher Edn. Counseling, West Chester U., 1995. Admissions counselor Widener U., Chester, Pa., 1987-89; admissions rep. Thomas Jefferson U., Phila., 1989-92; dir. on campus programming U. Pa., Phila., 1992—; advisor, interviewer health professions adv. bd. U. Pa., 1994—, mem. new student orientation com., 1992—; presenter in field. Mem. ACA, Pa. Assn. Secondary Sch. and Coll. Admissions Counselors (mem. conf. planning com. 1992-93, 94-95, profl. devel. com. 1992-93), Nat. Assn. Coll. Admissions Counselors, Nat. Collegiate Vis. Svcs. Assn. Office: U Pa 1 College Hall Philadelphia PA 19104

NAHAS, GABRIEL GEORGES, pharmacologist, educator; b. Alexandria, Egypt, Mar. 4, 1920; came to U.S., 1947, naturalized, 1962; s. Bishara and Gabrielle (Wolff) N.; m. Marilyn Cashman, Feb. 13, 1954; children: Michele, Anthony, Christiane. BA, U. Toulouse, France, 1937, MD, 1944; MS, U. Rochester, 1949; PhD, U. Minn., 1953; DSc (hon.), U. Uppsala, 1988. Rockefeller Found. fellow U. Rochester, 1947-48; Mayo Found. fellow Mayo Clinic, 1949-50; rsch. fellow U. Minn., 1950-53, mem. faculty, 1955-57; mem. staff Walter Reed Army Inst. Rsch., 1957-59; faculty George Washington U. Med. Sch., 1957-59; mem. faculty Columbia U. Coll. Physicians and Surgeons, N.Y.C., 1959-92, prof. anesthesiology, 1962-92; rsch. prof. anesthesiology NYU Med. Sch., N.Y.C., 1992—; disting. vis. scientist Addiction Rsch. Ctr., NIDA, 1987; adj. rsch. prof. anesthesiology U. Paris, 1968-71; fellow Coun. Circulation and Basic Sci., Am. Heart Assn., 1961—; mem. com. on trauma NRC, 1964-66; mem. adv. bd. Cousteau Soc.; cons. commn. on narcotics, drug control program UN. Author 700 sci. publs. and 30 books and monographs in English and French. Decorated Presdl. Medal of Freedom with gold palm Govt. of U.S.; comdr. Legion of Honor, Croix de Guerre with 3 palms (France), Order Brit. Empire, Order Orange Nassau Netherlands, Silver medal City of Paris; recipient Medal of Honor, Statue of Liberty Centennial, 1986; Fulbright scholar, 1966. Fellow AAAS, N.Y. Acad. Sci.; mem. Am. Physiol. Soc., Harvey Soc., Am. Soc. Pharmacology and Exptl. Therapeutics, Am. Soc. Clin. Pharmacology, Soc. Physiol. Langue Française, French Acad. Medicine (laureate), Brit. Pharm. Soc., Sigma Xi. Research on med. instrumentation, pharmacology Tham, acid-base regulation, pharmacology of cannabis and cocaine, drug dependence. Home: 40 E 74th St New York City NY 10021-2732 Office: NYU Med Ctr Dept Anesthesiology 550 1st Ave New York NY 10016-6481 *COURAGE - To have the courage to stand by one's own conviction unheeding the trends of fashion or pressure groups. It is to suffer alone and be scorned for a lifetime. But, in the end, one will hear "he was right!".*

NAHAT, DENNIS F., artistic director, choreographer; b. Detroit, Feb. 20, 1946; s. Fred H. and Linda M. (Haddad) N. Hon. degree, Juilliard Sch. Music, 1965. Prin. dancer Joffrey Ballet, N.Y.C., 1965-66; prin. dancer Am. Ballet Theatre, N.Y.C., 1968-79; founder, artistic dir. Cleve. Ballet, 1976—; co-chair Artists Round Table Dance USA, 1991; mem. bd. trustees Cecchetti Council of Am., 1991; adv. bd. Ohio Dance Regional Dance Am. Pin. performer Broadway show Sweet Charity, 1966-67; choreographer Two Gentlemen of Verona (Tony award 1972), 1969-70; (ballet) Celebrations and Ode (resolution award 1985), 1985, Green Table, Three Virgins and a Devil (Isadora Duncan award 1985); co-founder Sch. of Cleve. Ballet, 1972, Cleve. Ballet, 1976; founder, artistic dir. San Jose Cleve. Ballet; choreographer, dir. Blue Suede Shoes, 1996. Grantee Nat. Endowment Arts, 1978, Andrew Mellow Found., 1985; recipient Outstanding Achievement award Am. Dance Guild, 1995. Avocation: master chef. Office: Cleve Ballet 1375 Euclid Ave Cleveland OH 44115-1808 also: Cleve San Jose Ballet PO Box 1666 San Jose CA 95109-1666

NAHAVANDI, AMIR NEZAMEDDIN, retired engineering firm executive; b. Tehran, Iran, Apr. 6, 1924; came to U.S., 1956, naturalized, 1970; s. Ahmad and Fatima (Razaghi) N. Electromech. Engring. degree, Tehran U., 1947; M.S. in Mech. Engring, Carnegie Inst. Tech., 1957, Ph.D., 1960. Registered profl. engr., Pa. Engr. Tehran U., 1948-50; head design group Nat. Iranian Oil Co., Tehran, 1950-56; adv. engr. Westinghouse Electric Corp., Pitts., 1957-66; prof., chmn. dept. mech. engring. U. Vt., 1967-68; research prof. N.J. Inst. Tech., 1969-77; prof. engring. and applied Sci. Columbia U., N.Y.C., 1977-81; chief scientist Electronic Assocs., Inc., West Long Branch, N.J., 1981-82; pres. Mazen, Inc., Long Branch, N.J., 1982-92. Decorated Sci. medal 1st degree Iran). Fellow ASME; mem. N.Y. Acad. Scis., Phi Kappa Phi, Sigma Xi, Tau Beta Pi. Research and devel. in dynamics of steam generators and boiling systems, dynamic and accident analysis of conventional and nuclear power plants, vibration of reactor structures, thermal pollution of lakes and rivers, solid-fluid interaction. Home: 168 Seabreeze Cir Jupiter FL 33477

NAHIGIAN, ALMA LOUISE, technical documentation administrator; b. Peabody, Mass., Sept. 17, 1936; d. Walter Daniel and Alma Edith (Knowles) Higgins; m. Franklin Roosevelt Nahigian, April 30, 1961; daus.: Ellen Elise, Dana Leigh, Catherine Elizabeth. AA, Boston U., 1956, BS, 1958, MS in Journalism, 1963. Editor nat. and spl. projects Boston U. News Bur., 1959-61, 63-64; writer, editor Nutrition Found., N.Y.C., 1961-63; writer, editor, cons. Cambridge (Mass.) Communicators, Tech. Edn. Research Ctr., Harvard U., Cambridge, Smart Software, Inc., Belmont, Mass., 1970-82; tech. editor Digital Equipment Corp., Bedford, Mass., 1979-84; prin. tech. writer, editor Wang Labs, Inc., Lowell, Mass., 1984—, documentation sect. mgr. editorial, 1984-93; sr. adv. tech. editor Dun & Bradstreet Software, Westborough, Mass., 1993-95; prin. tech. editor Info. Resources, Inc., Waltham, Mass., 1995—; instr. Harvard U., Cambridge, 1988, Radcliffe Coll., Cambridge, 1979; mem. adj. faculty Northeastern U., Boston, 1989—, guest lectr., 1979, 88. Contbr. numerous articles to profl. pubs. Active LWV, Arlington, Mass., 1963-73. Mem. Soc. for Tech. Comm. (bd. dirs., Boston chpt. pres. 1992-93, co-mgr. soc.-level com. 1993-95, mem. 1995—, judge internat. level competitions 1993—, Tech. Pubs. Competition Excellence award 1989, 93; 95, Art Competitions Excellence award 1992). Democrat. Roman Catholic. Home: 30 Venner Rd Arlington MA 02174-8028 Office: Info Resources Inc 200 5th Ave Waltham MA 02154

NAHMAN, NORRIS STANLEY, electrical engineer; b. San Francisco, Nov. 9, 1925; s. Hyman Cohen and Rae (Levin) N.; m. Shirley D. Maxwell, July 20, 1968; children: Norris Stanley, Vicki L., Vance W., Scott T. B.S. in Electronics Engring, Calif. Poly. State U., 1951; M.S.E.E., Stanford U., 1952; Ph.D. in Elec. Engring, U. Kans., 1961. Registered profl. engr., Colo. Electronic scientist Nat. Security Agy., Washington, 1952-55; prof. elec. engring., dir. electronics rsch. lab. U. Kans., Lawrence, 1955-66; sci. cons., chief pulse and time domain sect. Nat. Bur. Standards, Boulder, Colo., 1966-73; chief time domain metrology, sr. scientist Nat. Bur. Standards, 1975-83, group leader field characterization group, 1984-85; v.p. Picosecond Pulse Labs, Inc., Boulder, 1986-90; cons. elec. engr., 1990—; prof., chmn. dept. elec. engring. U. Toledo, 1973-75;; prof. elec. engring. U. Colo., Boulder, 1966—; Disting. lectr., prin. prof. Ctr. Nat. d' Etude des Telecomm. Summer Sch., Lannion France, 1978; disting. lectr. Harbin Inst. Tech., Peoples Republic China, summer 1982; mem. faculty NATO Advanced Study Inst., Castelvecchio, Italy, 1983, Internat. Radio Sci. Union/NRC; chmn. Internat. Intercomm. Group Waveform Measurements, 1981-90, chmn. Commn. A, 1985-86; affiliate Los Alamos Nat. Lab., 1990—. Contbr. rsch. articles profl. jours.; patentee in field. Asst. scoutmaster Longs Peak coun. Boy Scouts Am., 1970-73, 75-89. With U.S. Mcht. Marine, 1943-46, U.S. Army, 1952-55. Ford Found. faculty fellow MIT, 1962; Nat. Bur. Standards sr. staff fellow, 1978-79; recipient Disting. Alumnus award Calif. Poly. State U., 1972, Order of Arrow Boy Scouts Am., 1976. Fellow IEEE (life), Internat. Sci. Radio Union; mem. Instrumentation and Measurement Soc. of IEEE (admstrv. com. 1982-84, editorial bd. Trans., 1982-86, Andrew H. chi Best Tech. Paper award 1984, Tech. Leadership and Achievement award 1987), Am. Assn. Engring. Edn., U.S. Mcht. Marine Veterans World War II, Am. Legion, Calif. Poly. State U. Alumni Assn. (life), Stanford U. (life), U. Kans. (life), Am. Radio Relay League Club (life), Sigma Pi Sigma, Tau Beta Pi, Eta Kappa Nu, Sigma Tau, Sigma Xi.

NAHRWOLD, DAVID LANGE, surgeon, educator; b. St. Louis, Dec. 21, 1935; s. Elmer William and Magdalen Louise (Lange) N.; m. Carolyn Louise Hoffman, June 14, 1958; children: Stephen Michael, Susan Alane, Thomas James, Anne Elizabeth. AB, Ind. U., 1957, MD, 1960. Diplomate Am. Bd. Surgery, Am. Bd. Thoracic Surgery. Intern, then resident in surgery Ind. U. Med. Ctr., Indpls., 1960-65; postdoctoral scholar in gastrointestinal physiology VA Ctr., UCLA, 1965; asst. prof. surgery Med. Sch. Ind. U., 1968-70; assoc. prof. Coll. Medicine Pa. State U., 1970-73; vice chmn. dept. surgery Pa. STate U., 1971-82, assoc. provost, dean health affairs, 1981-82, prof., chief divsn. gen. surgery, 1974-82; Loyal and Edith Davis prof., chmn. dept. surgery Med. Sch. Northwestern U., Chgo., 1982—; surgeon-in-chief Northwestern Meml. Hosp., Chgo., 1982—; pres., CEO Northwestern Med. Faculty Found., Inc., 1996—; mem. Nat. Digestive Disease Adv. Bd., 1985-89; bd. dirs. Am. Bd. Surgery; vice chmn. 1994-95, chmn. 1995-96. Editor-in-chief Jour. Laparoendoscopic Surgery, 1993—; mem. editl. bd. Surgery, 1981-94, Archives of Surgery, 1983-93, Digestive Surgery, 1986—, Am. Jour. Surgery, 1994—, Current Opinion in Gen. Surgery, Jour. Lithotripsy and Stone Disease, 1988-92; contbr. articles to profl. jours. With M.C., U.S. Army, 1966-68. Fellow ACS (bd. govs. 1992—, vice-chmn. bd. govs. exec. com. 1994—); mem. AMA, Am. Bd. Med. Specialties, Accreditation Coun. for Grad. Med. Edn., Am. Phys. Soc., Am. Surg. Assn. (2d v.p. 1993-94), Assn. Acad. Surgery, Assn. for Surg. Edn., Ctrl. Surg. Assn. (sec. 1994—), Chgo. Med. Soc., Chgo. Surg. Soc. (pres. 1993-94), Collegium Internat. Chirurgiae Digestive (pres. U.S. chpt. 1988-90), Gastroenterology Rsch. Group, Ill. State Med. Soc., Ill. Surg. Soc., Internat. Biliary Assn., Soc. Clin. Surgery (sec. 1984-88, pres. 1989-90, trustee), Soc. Univ. Surgeons, Soc. Surg. Chairmen, We. Surg. Assn., Sigma Xi, Alpha Omega Alpha. Office: Northwestern U Med Sch Dept Surgery 250 E Superior St Ste 201 Chicago IL 60611-2914

NAIBURG, IRVING B., JR., publisher; b. Chgo., Oct. 3, 1942; s. Irving B. and Bobette (Mayer) N. B.A., Harvard U., 1964. Asst. to gen. mgr. Free Press div Macmillan Co., N.Y.C., 1964-66, paperback editor, 1966-68, editor, 1968-72; exec. editor profl. and reference div. Appleton Century Crofts, N.Y.C., 1972-73, editorial dir., 1973-74; founder, pres., editorial dir. Irvington Pubs., Inc., N.Y.C., 1974—. Mem. N.Y. Polit. Action Com., 1978-80. Mem. Tarrytown Group, Soc. Scholarly Pub., Inst. Advancement Health, Network Ind. Pubs. Democrat. Club: Harvard (N.Y.C.). Home and Office: Irvington Pubs Inc 522 E 82nd St New York NY 10028-7118*

NAIDORF, LOUIS MURRAY, architect; b. Los Angeles, Aug. 15, 1928; s. Jack and Meriam (Abbott) N.; m. Dorise D. Roberts, June 1948 (div.); children: Victoria Beth Naidorf-Slifer; m. Patricia Ann Shea, June 1, 1968 (div.); m. Patricia Ruth Allen, Dec. 6, 1992. BA, U. Calif., Berkeley, 1949, MA, 1950. Registered architect, Calif. Designer Welton Becket Assocs., L.A., 1950-51, Pereira and Luckman, L.A., 1951-52; project designer Welton Becket Assocs., L.A., 1952-55, sr. project designer, 1955-59, v.p. asst., dir. design, 1959-70, sr. v.p., dir. rsch., 1970-73; sr. v.p., design prin. Ellerbe Becket Assocs., L.A., 1973-95; dean Sch. Architecture and Design Woodbury U., L.A., 1990—; mem. peer rev. panel Nat. Endowment Arts, 1995—; vis. lectr. Calif. Poly. Sch. Architecture, San Luis Obispo, 1975-82; instr. UCLA Sch. Architecture, 1985, UCLA Landscape Archtl. Program, 1980-85, Otis-Parsons, L.A., 1986—. Prin. works include Capitol Records Bldg., Century City, Los Angeles, Hyatt Regency, Dallas, Restoration Calif. State Capitol Bldg. Bd. dirs. Inst. for Garden Studies, L.A., 1986—. Recipient Honor award Nat. Trust for Hist. Preservation, 1985. Fellow AIA (bd. dirs. Los Angeles chpt. 1977-79, Silver Medal 1950, Nat. Honor award 1985). Office: Woodbury Univ 7500 Glenoaks Blvd Burbank CA 91510-7846 *Leadership often requires decisions based on limited information. Course corrections can be made but only after action is taken because you can't steer a car that isn't moving.*

NAILOR, RICHARD ANTHONY, SR., research company executive; b. New Haven, July 27, 1935; s. Earl Edward and Theresa Mary (Massaro) N.; m. Sandra Louise Grace, Jan. 16, 1960; children: Richard, Michele, Keith. Student, Fairfield U., 1952-54; AA, USN Exec. Officers, 1964. Enlisted, terrier MSL fire control technician USMC, Egypt, Lebanon and Cuba, 1954-62; radar maintenance officer 9th MEB USMC, Vietnam, 1965, 69-70; project officer Hdqs. USMC, 1966-74; logistics analyst Potomac Rsch., Inc., Alexandria, Va., 1974-79, head publs. br., 1978-80, dir. ILS dept., 1980-82, dir. ILS div., 1982-83, v.p. OPS, 1983-86; sr. v.p. OPS Potomac Rsch. Internat., Alexandria, 1986-94, exev. v.p., COO, 1994-96, pres., CEO, 1996—. Troop leader Boy Scouts Council, Woodbridge, Va., 1968-69; pres. Woodbridge Parks Assn., 1978-81; park authority rep. Pr. William County (Va.) Park Authority, 1982-86. Mem. VFW, Ret. Officers Assn., Marine Corps Mustang Assn. (charter), Soc. Logistics Engrs., 1st Marine Aircraft

Wing Assn. Republican. Roman Catholic. Avocations: golf, bowling, fishing, genealogy. Home: 12307 Beaver Lodge Rd Stafford VA 22554-3427 Office: Potomac Rsch Internat 11320 Random Hills Rd Ste 300 Fairfax VA 22030-6001

NAIMARK, ARNOLD, medical educator, physiologist, educator; b. Winnipeg, Man., Can., Aug. 24, 1933; s. Harvey and Lisa N.; m. Barbara Jean Alder, Feb. 28, 1960; children: David, Mila. MD, U. Man., Winnipeg, 1957, BSc in Medicine, 1957, MSc, 1960; postgrad., U. London, 1962-63, U. Calif., 1960-62; LLD (hon.), Mt. Allison U., 1986. Registrar in medicine Hammersmith Hosp., London, 1962-63; asst. prof. physiology U. Man., 1963-64, asso. prof., 1965-66, prof., 1967-71, acting head dept. physiology, 1966-67, head dept., 1967-71, dean Faculty of Medicine, 1971-81, pres. and vice chancellor, 1981-96; prof. medicine, physiology U. Manitoba, Winnipeg, Man., Can., 1996—; bd. govs. St. Boniface Gen. Hosp., Health Scis. Ctr.; cons. to govt. agys. and founds.; chmn. North Portage Devel. Commerce, Urban Idea Ctr., North Portage Theater Corp., Inspiraplex Ltd.; mem. adv. coun. Order of Can., 1988-89; v.p., Can., Inter-Am. Orgn. for Higher Edn., 1993-95. Contbr. articles to profl. jours. Mem. nat. hon. bd. dirs. Juvenile Diabetes Fedn. Internat. Can.; trustee Alcoholic Beverage Med. Rsch. Found., 1994—. Lt. Royal Can. Arty., 1950-53. Decorated officer Order of Can.; recipient Queen Elizabeth Silver Jubilee medal; medal in physiology U. Man., 1955; Stefansson Meml. prize, 1957; Prowse prize in clin. rsch., 1959; Isbister scholar, 1950-53, 54-56. Fellow Royal Coll. Physicians, AAAS, Roayal Soc. Can. (G. Malcolm Brown award 1987, com. univ. rsch. 1989-91); mem. Can. Med. Assn., Can. Physiol. Soc., Am. Physiol. Soc., Can. Soc. Clin. Investigation, Med. Rsch. Soc. Gt. BRit., Assn. Chairmen Depts. Physiology, Can. Tb and Respiratory Disease Assn., Can. Assn. Univ. Tchrs., Assn. Commmonwealth Univs. (coun. 1985-91), Assn. Univs. and Colls. Am. (pres. 1986-88), Am. Heart Assn., Assn. Commonwealth Univs. (chmn. 1988), Can. Soc. for Acad. Medicine, Nat. Inst. Nutrition (bd. dirs. 1990—). Office: U Manitoba, Ctr Advancement of Medicine, 730 William Ave Ste 230, Winnipeg, MB Canada R3E 3J7

NAIMARK, GEORGE MODELL, marketing and management consultant; b. N.Y.C., Feb. 5, 1925; s. Myron S. and Mary (Modell) N. BS, Bucknell U., 1947, MS, 1948; PhD, U. Del., 1951; m. Helen Anne Wythes, June 24, 1946; children: Ann, Richard, Jane. Rsch. biochemist Brush Devel. Co., Cleve., 1951; dir. quality control Strong, Cobb & Co., Inc., Cleve., 1951-54; dir. sci. svcs. White Labs., Inc., Kenilworth, N.J., 1954-60; v.p. Burdick Assocs., Inc., N.Y.C., 1960-66; pres. Rajah Press, Summit, N.J., 1963—; pres. Naimark and Barba, Inc., Florham Park, N.J., 1966—; pres. Naimark & Assocs., Inc., Florham Park, N.J., 1994—. With USNR, 1944-46. Fellow AAAS, Am. Inst. Chemists; mem. Am. Chem. Soc., N.Y. Acad. Scis., Am. Mktg. Assn. Author: A Patent Manual for Scientists and Engineers, 1961, Communications on Communication, 1971, 3d edit., 1987, A Man Called Skeeter, 1996; patentee in field; contbr. articles in profl. jours. Home: 87 Canoe Brook Pky Summit NJ 07901-1404 Office: Naimark & Barba Inc 248 Columbia Tpke Florham Park NJ 07932-1210

NAIMI, SHAPUR, cardiologist; b. Tehran, Iran, Mar. 28, 1928; s. Mohsen and Mahbuba (Naim) N.; came to U.S., 1959; MB, ChB, Birmingham (Eng.) U., 1953; m. Amy Cabot Simonds, May 11, 1963; children: Timothy Simonds, Susan Lyman, Cameron Lowell. House physician Royal Postgrad Med. Sch. London, 1955; sr. house officer Inst. Diseases of the Chest, London, 1956; fellow in grad. tng. New Eng. Med. Center and Mass. Inst. Tech., 1961-64; cardiologist Tufts New Eng. Med. Center, Boston, 1966—, dir. intensive cardiac care unit, 1973—, assoc. prof. 1970-93, prof. 1993—. Recipient Distinguished Instr. award, 1972, Teaching citation, 1976, Excellence in Teaching award, 1982 (all Tufts Med. Sch.); diplomate Royal Coll. Physicians London, Royal Coll. Physicians Edinburgh, Am. Bd. Internal Medicine (subsplty. bd. cardiovascular disease). Fellow Royal Coll. Physicians (Edinburgh), A.C.P., Am. Coll. Cardiology; mem. Am. Soc. Exptl. Biology and Medicine, Am. Heart Assn., Mass. Med. Soc. Clubs: Country Brookline; Cohasset Yacht. Contbr. to profl. jours. Home: 265 Woodland Rd Chestnut Hill MA 02167-2204 Also: 55 Lothrop Ln Cohasset MA 02025 Office: 750 Washington St Boston MA 02111-1533

NAIMOLI, RAYMOND ANTHONY, infosystems specialist, financial consultant; b. Paterson, N.J., Apr. 16, 1942; s. Ralph A. and Margaret Rita (Calabrese) N.; children: Lisa Marie, Dianne, Dolors, Raymond . B.B.A., U. Notre Dame, 1963; M.S., Columbia U., 1976. C.P.A., N.J. Sr. auditor Arthur Young & Co., Newark, 1963-68; asst. controller Universal Mfg. Co., Paterson, 1968-70; corp. controller Scholastic Mags., Inc., N.Y.C., 1970-80; v.p. fin., treas. U.S. News & World Report, Washington, 1980-84; also dir. U.S. News & World Report; exec. v.p. EBM Systems, Inc., Greenbelt, Md., 1986-90; pres. Naimoli & Assocs., Arlington, Va., 1984—; pres. MedLine, Inc., 1991-93, also bd. dirs.; chief fin. officer Ladish Co., Inc., Milw., 1993-94; sr. v.p., CFO Tampa Bay Devil Rays, 1995—; dir. Parkway Communications Corp., Publishers Service Internat., Madana Realty Co., U.S. News Investment Co.; adj. prof. Grad. Sch., Fairleigh Dickinson U., Rutherford, N.J., 1976-80. Mem. Am. Inst. C.P.A.s, Planning Execs. Inst., N.J. Soc. C.P.A.s. Roman Catholic. Office: Thunderdome 1 Stadium Dr Saint Petersburg FL 33705

NAIMOLI, VINCENT JOSEPH, diversified operating and holding company executive; b. Paterson, N.J., Sept. 16, 1937; s. Ralph A. and Margaret R. (Calabrese) N.; children—Christine, Tory Ann, Alyson, Lindsey. B.S.M.E., U. Notre Dame, 1959; M.S.M.E., N.J. Inst. Tech., 1962; M.B.A., Fairleigh Dickinson U., 1964; grad. Advanced Mgmt. Program, Harvard Bus. Sch., 1974. With Continental Group, 1965-77, v.p., gen. mgr. ops., 1975-77; pres., chief oper. officer Allegheny Beverage Corp., Balt., 1977-78; sr. v.p., group exec. Jim Walter Corp., Tampa, Fla., 1978-81; group v.p. packaging Anchor Hocking Corp., Lancaster, Ohio, 1981-83; chmn. bd., pres., chief exec. officer Anchor Glass Container Corp., Lancaster, 1983-89; chmn., pres., CEO Anchor Industries Internat., Tampa, Fla., 1990—; chmn., chief exec. officer Electrolux Corp., Atlanta, 1990-91; chmn., CEO Doehler Jarvis Corp., Toledo, 1991-95; mng. gen. ptnr., CEO Tampa Bay Devil Rays, 1992—; chmn., CEO Ladish, Inc., Milw., 1992-95; chmn., pres., CEO Harvard Industries, 1993—; bd. dirs. Simplicity Pattern, New River Industries, Russell-Stanley Corp., Fla. Progress. Roman Catholic. Office: Anchor Industries Internat 2502 N Rocky Point Dr Ste 960 Tampa FL 33607-1421

NAIPAUL, VIDIADHAR SURAJPRASAD, author; b. Trinidad, Aug. 17, 1932. Student, Queen's Royal Coll., Trinidad, 1943-48; B.A., University Coll., Oxford, Eng., 1953; D.Litt. (hon.), St. Andrews Coll., Scotland, 1979, Columbia U., 1981, Cambridge U., 1983, London U., 1988; DLitt (hon.), Oxford U., 1992. Author: Miguel Street, 1959, A House for Mr. Biswas, 1961, An Area of Darkness, 1964, In a Free State, 1971, Guerrillas, 1975, India: A Wounded Civilization, 1977, A Bend in the River, 1979, Among the Believers, 1981, The Enigma of Arrival, 1987, A Turn in the South, 1989, India: A Million Mutinies Now, 1990, A Way in the World, 1994. Office: Aitken & Stone Ltd, 29 Fernshaw Rd, London SW10 0TG, England

NAIR, RAGHAVAN D., accountant, educator; b. Dehradun, United Provinces, India, Oct. 23, 1951; came to U.S., 1973; s. Keshavan R. and Parvati Nair; m. Ruth Marie Nair, 1976; 1 child, Andrea. BA, U. Madras, India, 1970, MA, 1972; MBA, U. Mich., 1974, PhD, 1977. CPA, Wis. Prof. U. Wis., Madison, 1978—, sr. assoc. dean acad. affairs Sch. Bus., 1994—; faculty fellow Fin. Acctg. Standards Bd., Norwalk, Conn., 1984-86; faculty resident Arthur Andersen & Co., Chgo., 1991—, dir. PhD Program, 1987-90, chmn. dept. acctg., 1991-94; dir. Arthur Andersen Ctr. Fin. Reporting, 1992-93; prof. acctg. and info. systems Price Waterhouse, 1993—; invited speaker various corps., pub. acctg. firms, mgmt. and exec. edn. groups, 1982—. Contbr. articles to profl. jours. Pres. John Muir PTO, Madison, Wis., 1988-89. Recipient Excellence in Teaching award Lawrence J. Larson Sch. Bus., 1992. Mem. AICPA, Parkwood Hills Community Assn. (treas. 1987-89), Am. Acctg. Assn., Wis. Inst. CPAs (Outstanding Educator award 1989), Bascom Hill Soc., Blackhawk Country Club (bd. dirs. 1994-96). Avocation: golf.

NAIR, VELAYUDHAN, pharmacologist, medical educator; b. India, Dec. 29, 1928; came to U.S., 1956, naturalized, 1963; s. Parameswaran and Ammini N.; m. Jo Ann Burke, Nov. 30, 1957; children: David, Larry, Sharon. Ph.D. in Medicine, U. London, 1956, D.Sc., 1976. Research assoc. U. Ill. Coll. Medicine, 1956-58; asst. prof. FUHS/Chgo. Med. Sch., 1958-63; dir. lab. neuropharmacology and biochemistry Michael Reese Hosp. and Med. Center, Chgo., 1963-68; dir. therapeutic research Michael Reese Hosp. and Med. Center, 1968-71; vis. assoc. prof. pharmacology FUHS/Chgo. Med. Sch., 1963-68, vis. prof., 1968-71, prof. pharmacology, 1971—, vice chmn. dept. pharmacology and therapeutics, 1971-76, dean Sch. Grad. and Postdoctoral Studies, 1976—. Contbr. articles to profl. publs. Recipient Morris Parker award U. Health Scis./Chgo. Med. Sch., 1972. Fellow AAAS, N.Y. Acad. Scis., Am. Coll. Clin. Pharmacology; mem. AAUP, Internat. Brain Rsch. Orgn., Internat. Soc. Biochem. Pharmacology, Am. Soc. Pharmacology & Exptl. Therapeutics, Am. Soc. Clin. Pharmacology & Therapeutics, Radiation Rsch. Soc., Soc. Toxicology, Am. Chem. Soc., Brit. Chem. Soc., Royal Inst. Chemistry (London), Pan Am. Med. Assn. (council on toxicology), Soc. Exptl. Biology & Medicine, Soc. Neurosci., Internat. Soc. Chronobiology, Am. Coll. Toxicology, Internat. Soc. Developmental Neurosci., Sigma Xi, Alpha Omega Alpha. Club: Cosmos (Washington). Office: FUHS/Chgo Med Sch 3333 Green Bay Rd North Chicago IL 60064-3037 *Success like happiness is relative and can only be gauged by one's own standards and ideals. There is probably no universal formula for either of them, but I have been guided by the following tenets: Dedication and commitment to one's responsibilities and in the conduct of everyday life, honesty and sincerity in personal relations. One must have tolerance for those in less fortunate situations. As one grows older, one recognizes that no one makes it alone. As for me, I have received help from many: some of whom I can never repay except by passing on the gift which I was privileged to share. Above all, a faith that looks beyond the immediate helps to bear the inevitable ups and downs in life.*

NAITOH, YUTAKA, biology educator; b. Tokyo, Japan, Mar. 23, 1931; s. Hisao and Emiko (Gotoh) N.; 1 child, Takuya. BS, U. Tokyo, Japan, 1955, MS, 1957, DSc, 1960. Rsch. assoc. U. Tokyo, Faculty of Sci., Japan, 1960-71; rsch. assoc. dept. biology UCLA, 1972, adj. assoc. prof., 1972-75; prof. Tsukuba (Japan) U., 1975-94, prof. emeritus, 1994—; guest prof. U. Hawaii, Japan, 1994-95. Author: Behavior of Unicellular Animal, 1990; contbr. sci. articles to profl. jours. Recipient Fulbright grant U.S.-Japan Exch. Progamme, 1966-69, Mitsubishi Rsch. grant, 1976, The Zool. Soc. prize, 1973. Mem. Zool. Soc. Japan, AAAS, Soc. Gen. Physiologist, Japanese Soc. Comparative Physiology and Biochemistry. Avocations: butterfly collection, radio amateur. Office: University of Hawaii at Manoa Dept of Microbiology Snyder Hall 207, 2538 The Mall Honolulu HI 96822

NAJARIAN, HAIGAZOUN, church administrator. Viscar gen. Ea. Diocese of the Armenian Ch. Am. Office: Ea Diocese of the Armenian Ch Am 630 2nd Ave New York NY 10016-4806

NAJARIAN, JOHN SARKIS, surgeon, educator; b. Oakland, Calif., Dec. 22, 1927; s. Garabed L. and Siranoush T. (Demirjian) N.; m. Arlys Viola Mignette Anderson, Apr. 27, 1952; children: Jon, David, Paul, Peter. AB with honors, U. Calif., Berkeley, 1948; MD, U. Calif., San Francisco, 1952; LHD (hon.), Univ. Athens, 1980; DSc (hon.), Gustavus Adolphus Coll., 1981; LHD (hon.), Calif. Luth. Coll., 1983. Diplomate Am. Bd. Surgery. Surg. intern U. Calif., San Francisco, 1952-53, surg. resident, 1955-60, asst. prof. surgery, dir. surg. research labs., chief transplant service dept. surgery, 1963-66, prof., vice chmn., 1966-67; spl. research fellow in immunopathology U. Pitts. Med. Sch., 1960-61; NIH sr. fellow and assoc. in tissue transplantation immunology Scripps Clinic and Research Found., La Jolla, Calif., 1961-63; Markle scholar Acad. Medicine, 1964-69; prof., chmn. dept. surgery U. Minn. Hosp., Mpls., 1967-93; med. dir. Transplant Ctr., clin. chief surgery Univ. Hosp., 1967-94; chief hosp. staff U. Minn. Hosp., Mpls., 1970-71, Regents' prof., 1985-95, Jay Phillips Disting. Chair in Surgery, 1986-95; prof. emeritus, clin. prof. surgery, 1995—; spl. cons. USPHS, NIH Clin. Rsch. Tng. Com., Inst. Gen. Med. Scis., 1965-69; cons. U.S. Bur. Budget, 1966-68; mem. sci. adv. bd. Nat. Kidney Found., 1968; mem. surg. study sect. A div. rsch. grants NIH, 1970; chmn. renal transplant adv. group VA Hosps., 1971; mem. bd. sci. cons. Sloan-Kettering Inst. Cancer Rsch., 1971-78; mem. screening com. Dernham Postdoctoral Fellowships in Oncology, Calif. div. Am. Cancer Soc. Editor: (with Richard L. Simmons) Transplantation, 1972; co-editor: Manual of Vascular Access, Organ Donation, and Transplantation, 1984; mem. editorial bd. Jour. Surg. Rsch., 1968—, Minn. Medicine, 1968—, Jour. Surg. Oncology, 1968—, Am. Jour. Surgery, 1967—, assoc. editor, 1982—; mem. editorial bd. Year Book of Surgery, 1970-85, Transplantation, 1970—, Transplantation Procs, 1970—, Bd. Clin. Editors, 1981-84, Annals of Surgery, 1972—, World Jour. Surgery, 1976—, Hippocrates, 1986—, Jour. Transplant Coordination, 1990—; assoc. editor: Surgery, 1971; editor-in-chief: Clin. Transplantation, 1986—. Bd. dirs., v.p. Variety Club Heart Hosp., U. Minn.; trustee, v.p. Minn. Med. Found. Served with USAF, 1953-55. Hon. fellow Royal Coll. Surgeons of Eng., 1987; hon. prof. U. Madrid, 1990; named Alumnus of Yr., U. Calif. Med. Sch., San Francisco, 1977; recipient award Calif. Trudeau Soc., 1962, Ann. Brotherhood award NCCJ, 1978, Disting. Achievement award Modern Medicine, 1978, Internat. Gt. Am. award B'nai B'rith Found., 1982, Uncommon Citizen award, 1985, Sir James Carreras award Variety Clubs Internat., 1987, Silver medal IXth Centenary, U. Bologna, 1988, Humanitarian of Yr. award, U. Minn., 1992, Najarian Festschrift award Am. Jour. Surgery, 1993, Jubilee medal Swedish Soc. Medicine, 1994. Fellow ACS; mem. Soc. Univ. Surgeons, Soc. Exptl. Biology and Medicine, AAAS, Am. Soc. Exptl. Pathology, Am. Surg. Assn. (pres. 1988-89), Am. Assn. Immunologists, AMA, Transplantation Soc. (v.p. western hemisphere 1984-86, pres. 1994-96), Am. Soc. Nephrology, Internat. Soc. Nephrology, Am. Assn. Lab. Animal Sci., Assn. Acad. Surgery (pres. 1969), Internat Soc. Surgery, Soc. Surg. Chairmen, Soc. Clin. Surgery, Central Surg. Assn., Minn., Hennepin County med. socs., Mpls., St. Paul, Minn., Howard C. Naffziger, Portland, Halsted surg. socs., Am. Heart Assn., Am. Soc. Transplant Surgeons (pres. 1977-78), Council on Kidney in Cardiovascular Disease, Hagfish Soc., Italian Research Soc., Minn. Acad. Medicine, Minn. Med. Assn., Minn. Med. Found., Surg. Biology Club, Sigma Xi, Alpha Omega Alpha, others. Office: U Minn Surgery Dept Mayo Meml Bldg Box 195 420 Delaware St SE Minneapolis MN 55455-0374

NAKAE, HIDEO, metallurgical engineering educator, researcher; b. Tokyo, Sept. 11, 1941; s. Nobutaro and Sumiko (Sugiyama) Nakae; m. Komumi Yuhki, Dec. 8, 1970. B of Engring., Waseda U., Tokyo, 1964, M of Engring., 1966, D of Engring. (hon.), 1970. Rschr. Hitachi Ltd., Ibaragi, Japan, 1971-77, sr. rschr., 1977-83; prof. Waseda U., Tokyo, 1983-96, rsch. fellow Lab. for MS&T, 1984-96. Author: Solidification Processing, 1987, Casting Technology, 1995; editor Jour. Japan Foundrymen's Soc., 1992-94; editl. dir. Jour. Iron and Steel Inst., 1990-92, Japan Foundryman's Soc., 1992-94; co-editor Trans. Japan Inst. Metals, 1991-93, 95-96. Mem. com. Bur. of Jour. Indsl. Std., Tokyo, 1987—. Avocations: travel, photography, golf. Home: 3.3.3-214 Hikarigaoka Nerima, Tokyo 179, Japan Office: Waseda U Dept Material Sci & Engring, 3-4-1 Okubo Shinjuku, Tokyo 169, Japan

NAKAGAKI, MASAYUKI, chemist; b. Tokyo, Apr. 19, 1923; s. Sengoro and Shizue N.; m. Hisako Yoshitake, May 3, 1951. BSc, Imperial U., Tokyo, 1945; DSc, U. Tokyo, 1950. Instr. Imperial U., Tokyo, 1945-51; lectr. U. Tokyo, 1951-54; prof. Osaka (Japan) City U., 1954-60; prof. Kyoto (Japan) U., 1960-87, emeritus prof., 1987—; vis. prof. Wayne State U., Detroit, 1955-57, 68-69; dean faculty pharm. sci. Kyoto U., 1978-80; prof. Hoshi U., Tokyo, 1987-92; dir. Tokyo Inst. Colloid Sci., 1992—. Regional editor: Colloid and Polymer Sci., Darmstadt, Germany, 1982—. Recipient rsch. award Takeda Found. 1971. Mem. Membrane Soc. Japan (inspector 1988—, prse. 1978-88), Pharm. Soc. Japan (Rsch. award 1970, merit mem. 1990—). Home: 354 Kotokujicho Teramachi, Kamigoryo, Kyoto 602, Japan Office: Tokyo Inst Colloid Sci, 502 Higashi-Nakano 4-4-3, Tokyo 164, Japan

NAKAGAWA, ALLEN DONALD, radiologic technologist; b. N.Y.C., Mar. 14, 1955; s. Walter Tsunehiko and Alyce Tsuneko (Kinoshita) N. BS in Environ. Studies, St. John's U., Jamaica, N.Y., 1977; MS in Marine Biology, C.W. Post Coll., 1980. Cert. radiologic technologist, in fluoroscopy, Calif.; cert. Am. Registry Radiol. Technologists. Research asst. environ. studies St. John's U., 1976-78; lab. asst. Bur. Water Surveillance, Nassau Co. of Health Dept., Wantaugh, N.Y., 1978; clin. endocrinology asst. U. Calif. VA Hosp., San Francisco, 1981-83; student technologist St. Mary's Hosp., San Francisco, 1985-86; radiologic technologist Mt. Zion Hosp., San Francisco, 1986-88; sr. radiologic technologist U. Calif., San Francisco, 1989—, urosurg. radiologic technologists, 1988-89; attendee U. Calif. San Francisco Trauma and Emergency Radiology Conf., 1995, U. Calif. San Francisco Musculoskeletal MRI Conf., 1996. Mem. AAAS, ACLU, Calif. Soc. Radiologic Technologists, Marine Mammal Ctr., Calif. Acad. Scis., Japanese-Am. Nat. Mus., World Affairs Coun., San Francisco, Sigma Xi. Democrat. Methodist. Avocations: assisting handicapped, photography, music, computer illustration, studying advanced technology. *If you know, believe and have faith in yourself first, only then can you endeavor to assist someone else. Otherwise, you have wasted your efforts and may have even caused a loss of life.*

NAKAGAWA, JEAN HARUE, diversified corporation executive; b. Honolulu, Sept. 21, 1943; d. Herbert Haruo and Dorothy Mitsue (Nishimura) Yorita; m. Melvin Katsumi Nakagawa, July 16, 1966; 1 child, Lisa. BBA, U. Hawaii, 1965, MBA, 1968. Rsch. asst. First Hawaiian Bank, Honolulu, 1965-68; dir. planning AMFAC, Inc., Honolulu, 1968-73; v.p. Island Fed. Savings and Loan, Honolulu, 1973-75; dir. rsch. and planning Servco Pacific Inc., Honolulu, 1975—, asst. v.p., 1975-77, v.p., 1977-79, group v.p., 1979-84, sr. v.p., 1984-88, exec. v.p., 1988—; bd. dirs. Servco Pacific Inc., Servco Fin. Corp. Trustee Honolulu Theater for Youth, 1982-89, Hawaii Pub. Employees Health Fund, 1985-89; mem. devel. com. Hawaii Baptist Acad.; bd. dirs. ARC; mem. Pacific Asian Affairs Coun., Hawaii Econ. Edn. Coun., Hawaii Fgn. Rels. Coun. Mem. Hawaii Soc. Corp. Planners (v.p., pres.), Hawaii Econ. Assn. (pres., v.p.), Planning Execs. Inst. (pres.), Orgn. Women Leaders (v.p.). Club: Plaza.

NAKAGAWA, KOJI, endocrinologist, educator; b. Sapporo, Hokkaido, Japan, June 5, 1932; s. Satosu and Michi (Yokoyama) N.; m. Keiko Hirato, Oct. 20, 1962; children: Shin, Tamao Yamaguchi. MD, Hokkaido U., 1957, PhD, 1962. Lic. endocrinologist, Japan. Staff scientist Worcester Found. for Experimental Biology, Shrewsbury, Mass., 1964-65; rsch. staff Syntex Rsch. Ctr., Palo Alto, Calif., 1965; rsch. fellow U. Utah Med. Ctr., Salt Lake City, 1965-66; rsch. assoc. 2d dept. medicine Hokkaido U. Sch. Medicine, Sapporo, 1967-83, asst. prof., 1983-89; prof. Health Adminstrn. Ctr., Hokkaido U. Edn., Sapporo, 1989-96, dir. Health Adminstrn. Ctr., 1990-96; retired; lectr. Hokkaido U. Sch. of Medicine, Sapporo, 1989—. Contbr. articles to profl. jours., including Jour. Clin. Endocrinology and Metabolism, Endocrinology, Acta Endocrinologica. Fellow Japan Endocrine Soc.; mem. Endocrine Soc., Japanese Soc. Internal Medicine, Japan Diabetes Soc. Home: 2-8 4-chome Yamanote 1-jo, Nishi-ku, Sapporo 063, Japan Office: Health Adminstrn Ctr, Hokkaido U of Edn, 1-5 3 chome 5-jo Ainosato, Kita-ku Sapporo 002, Japan

NAKAJIMA, YASUKO, medical educator; b. Osaka, Japan, Jan. 8, 1932; came to U.S., 1962, 69; d. Isao and Taeko Nakagawa; m. Shigehiro Nakajima; children: Hikeko H., Gene A. MD, U. Tokyo, 1955, PhD, 1962. Intern U. Tokyo Sch. Medicine, 1955-56, resident, 1956-57, instr., 1962-67; assoc. prof. Purdue U., West Lafayette, Ind., 1969-76, prof., 1976-88; prof. anatomy and cell biology U. Ill. Coll. Medicine, Chgo., 1988—; vis. rsch. fellow Coll. Physicians and Surgeons, Columbia U., N.Y.C., 1962-64; asst. rsch. anatomist UCLA Sch. Medicine, 1964-65; vis. rsch. fellow Cambridge U., 1967-69. Contbr. articles to sci. jours. Fulbright travel grantee, 1962-65. Mem. AAAS, Am. Physiol. Soc., Soc. Neurosci., Am. Soc. Cell Biology, Am. Assn. Anatomists, Biophys. Soc., Marine Biol. Lab. Corp. Office: U Ill Coll Medicine at Chgo Dept Anatomy-Cell Biology m/c 512 808 S Wood St Chicago IL 60612-7300

NAKAKUKI, MASAFUMI, physician, psychiatry educator; b. Shimotsuma, Ibaragi, Japan, Mar. 1, 1930; came to U.S., 1969, naturalized 1975; s. Keisuke and Toi (Saito) N.; m. Ritsuko Oka, May 25, 1957; children: Mari, Emma; m. Michael McAndrewes, Sept. 1988. MS, U. Ibaragi, 1949; MD, U. Tokyo, 1953. Diplomate Am. Bd. Psychiatry and Neurology. Intern U. Tokyo Hosp., 1953-54, dir. psychiat. inpatient service, 1966-69; resident in psychiatry U. Tokyo, 1954-60, U. Colo.-Denver, 1962-66; asst. prof. psychiatry U. Colo. Med. Ctr., Denver, 1969-73; staff psychiatrist Ft. Logan Mental Health Ctr., Denver, 1973-74, Arapahoe Mental Health Ctr., Englewood, Colo., 1974-76; med. dir. Park East Mental Health Ctr. Denver, 1977-83; pres. Masafumi Nakakuki, M.D., P.C., Denver, 1977—; pres. med. staff Bethesda Hosp., Denver, 1982-83; psychiat. cons. Asian Pacific Devel. Ctr., Denver, 1983—; vis. prof. psychiatry St. Mariana U., Tokyo, 1995—. Author: Textbook of Psychiatry for the General Practitioner, 1968; New Parenting and Culture, 1982. Recipient Letter of Appreciation for Mental Health Svcs. and Leadership from Gov. Romer, 1995. Bd. dirs. Asian Human Service Assn., Denver, 1982. Fulbright scholar, 1961. Fellow Am. Psychiat. Assn.; mem. AAAS, Colo. Med. Soc. Office: 4770 E Iliff Ave Denver CO 80222-6061 also: 2-1-15-705 Takanawa, Minato-ku Tokyo 108, Japan

NAKAMOTO, FAYE, public health officer. Asst. to dir. Dept. of Health State of Hawaii, Honolulu. Office: Health Dept State of Hawaii 1250 Punchbowl St Honolulu HI 96813*

NAKAMURA, HIDEO, law educator; b. Tokyo, Mar. 2, 1926; s. Muneo and Fumiko (Mitani) N.; m. Mitsuko Terai, Feb. 25, 1958; children: Eri, Akiyoshi. LLB, Waseda U., Tokyo, 1947, LLD, 1980; Dr. honoris causa, Athens U., 1995. Assoc. prof. Faculty of Law Waseda U., tokyo, 1955-60, prof., 1960, dean Grad. Sch. Law, 1980-82, dir. Inst. Comparative Law, 1984-88, pres. Law Assn., 1990-94; dir. Inst. Comparative Civil Law, tokyo, 1975—. Author: (in German) The Japanese Criminal Procedure Code, 1970, Japan and German Civil Procedure, 1995, (in Japanese) Collected Works on Civil Procedure, Vols., 1-5, 1975-86; Civil Procedure, 1987co-author: (in German) The Japanese Civil Procedure Code, 1978; editor: Family Law Litigation, 1984. Mem. Japanese Assn. of Law of Civil Procedure (exec. com. 1960-80), Japanese Assn. of Law of Pub. Notary (coun. 1978—), Japan Fedn. of Bar Assn. (commr. disciplinary com. 1984-87), Acad. Assn. of Law of Internat. Procedure. Avocation: photography. Home: 2-6-6 Kamitakata Nakano-ku, Tokyo 164, Japan Office: Inst Comparative Civil Law, 43 Waseda-Minamicho Shinjuku, Tokyo 162, Japan

NAKAMURA, HIROSHI, urology educator; b. Tokyo, Mar. 22, 1933; s. Yataroh and Hideko (Tanaka) N.; m. Miyoko Kodachi, Aug. 13, 1966. MD, Keio U., Tokyo, 1960; PhD, Grad. Sch. Medicine, Keio U., 1966. Med. diplomate. Asst. resident Mt. Sinai Hosp., N.Y.C., 1962-63; rsch. fellow Cornell U. Med. Coll., N.Y.C., 1966-68; asst. Sch. Medicine Keio U., Tokyo, 1968-70; chmn. urology dept. Tokyo Elec. Power Hosp., 1970-73; vis. asst. prof. surgery Cornell U. Med. Coll., N.Y.C., 1973; chmn. urology Kitasato Inst. Hosp., Tokyo, 1973-77; chmn. dept., prof. urology Nat. Def. Med. Coll., Tokorozawa, Saitama, Japan, 1977—, dir. dept. acad. affairs, 1994—. Author: New Clin. Urology, 1982, Practice of Renal Transplantation, 1985, Bedside Urology, 1991; editor: Up-to-date Urology, 1983. Recipient Tamura award Keio U. Sch. Medicine, 1967, All-around Med. award, Igaku-Shoin, Ltd., Tokyo, 1967. Buddhist. Avocations: jazz, audiophile, travel, fishing, baseball. Home: 4-403 Boei Idai 3-2 Namiki, Tokorozawa 359 Saitama, Japan Office: Nat Def Med Coll Dept Urol, 3-2 Namiki, Tokorozawa 359 Saitama, Japan

NAKAMURA, JAMES I., economics educator; b. Toppenish, Wash., Mar. 16, 1919; s. Ichihei and Suya (Hirayama) N.; m. Tetsuko Fujii; children—Richard Ken, Leonard Isamu. A.A., Santa Maria Jr. Coll., 1939; B.S., Columbia U., 1952, Ph.D., 1964. Asst. prof. Columbia U., N.Y.C., 1964-68, assoc. prof., 1968-80, prof. econs., 1980-89, prof. emeritus, 1989—; vis. research scholar Kobe U., Japan, 1971-72; co-founder, co-dir., sec.-treas. Japan Econ. Seminar (supported by Columbia U., Harvard U.,, George Washington U.), 1965—. Author: Agricultural Production and Economic Development of Japan, 1966, Nihon no Keizai Hatten to Nogyo, 1968; mem. editorial bd. Japan Econ. Studies, 1972—; contbr. numerous articles to profl. jours. Editor newspaper War Relocation Ctr., Gila River, Ariz., 1943-44; legal researcher Shanks Village Com. to Fight Closure, Orangeburg, N.Y., 1952. Served to lt. U.S. Army, 1945-48, PTO. Ford Found. fellow 1952-55, 62-63; Fulbright-Hays fellow, 1967. Mem. Econ. History Assn., Am. Econ. Assn., Assn. for Asian Studies, Japan Econ. Research Ctr., Phi Beta Kappa. Buddhist. Home: 35 Claremont Ave New York NY 10027-6823 Office: Columbia U Dept Econ 935 IAB New York NY 10027

NAKAMURA, KAZUO, artist; b. Vancouver, Can., Oct. 13, 1926; s. Toichi and Yoshiyo (Uyemoto) N.; m. Lillian Yuriko Kobayakawa, Sept. 15, 1967;

children—Elaine Yukae, Bryan Kazuto. Student, Central Tech. Sch., Toronto, 1948-51. Exhibited in one man shows at, Picture Loan Soc., 1952, Hart House, U. Toronto, 1953, Gallery of Contemporary Art, Toronto, 1956, 58, Jerrold Morris Gallery, Toronto, 1962, 65, 67-70, R. McLaughlin Gallery, Oshawa and Can. Tour, 1974-75, Christopher Cutts Gallery, Toronto, 1991; exhibited in group shows at, Fifth Internat. Hallmark Art Award Exhbn., N.Y.C., 1960, Canadian Prints, Drawings and Watercolor, Am. Fedn. Arts Tour, 1960, Seconde Biennale, Musee d'Art Moderne, Paris, France, 1961, Canadian Painting, Polish Tour, 1962, Canadian Painting, Central Africa, 1962, Nineteen Canadian Painters, Louisville, 1962, Commonwealth Painting, London, Eng., 1962, Recent Acquisitions, Mus. Modern Art, N.Y.C., 1963, Canadian Painting, London, 1963, Member's Loan Gallery Acquisitions, Albright-Knox Gallery, Buffalo, 1963, World Show, Washington Sq. Gallery, N.Y.C., 1964, Cardiff Commonwealth Exhbn. of Drawings, Wales, 1965, Centennial Exhbn. of Canadian Prints and Drawings, Australian Tour, 1967, Painters Eleven in Retrospect, Can. tour, 1979-81, Ont. Heritage Found. Firestone Collection, European tour, 1983-84, Nat. Gallery Can., Ottawa, 1989, Nat. Gallery Can., Ottawa, Can. tour, 1993, Mead Mus., Amherst Coll., 1994; others; represented in permanent collections at Nat. Gallery Can., Mus. Modern Art, N.Y.C., Art Gallery of Ont., Toronto, Musée d'Art contemporain, Montreal, R. McLaughlin Gallery, Oshawa, Hirshhorn Mus., Washington, British Mus., London, Art Gallery of Hamilton, Winnipeg Art Gallery, Beaverbrook Art Gallery, Fredericton, N.B., Windsor (Ont.) Art Gallery, Lugano Collection, Hart House, U. Toronto, Victoria Coll., U. Toronto, U. Western Ont., U. Guelph, Concordia U., Univ. Club Montreal, commd. 2 sculptures, Toronto Internat. Airport. (Recipient prize 4th Internat. Exhbn. Drawings and Engravings, Lugano, Switzerland 1956, Purchase award 5th Internat. Hallmark Art Award Exhbn., N.Y.C. 1960).

NAKAMURA, MITSURU JAMES, microbiologist, educator; b. L.A., Dec. 17, 1926; s. Jingo and Michie (Inadomi) N.; m. Judith Ann Frohreich; children: Monica Suzan, Nancy Midori, Mark James. Student, Drake U., 1944-45; AB, UCLA, 1949, postgrad., 1950-52; MS, U. So. Calif., 1950; PhD, Boston U., 1956; ScD (hon.), Albert Szent-Gyorgyi Med. U., 1991. Diplomate: Am. Bd. Microbiology. Research asst. U. Calif., San Francisco, 1950-52; asst. prof. Northeastern U., 1952-54, assoc. prof., 1954-56; assoc. prof. U. Mont., Missoula, 1956-62; prof. U. Mont., 1962-86, prof. emeritus, 1986—, chmn. dept., 1963-85; assoc. prof. rsch. Wash. State U., summers 1957, 58; internat. vis. prof. Med. U. Pecs, Hungary, 1987; vis. prof. Yang Ming Med. Coll., Taipei, Taiwan, 1988, Albert Szent Gyorgyi Med. U., Szeged, Hungary, 1989, U. West Indies, Trinidad, 1990, Barbados, 1990, Jozsef Attila U. Scis., Szeged, 1991, Inst. Microbiol. Bulgarian Acad. Scis., 1992; rsch. fellow La. State U. Sch. Medicine, 1959, 60. Contbr. articles profl. jours. With AUS, 1945-47, capt. USPHS, 1959—. U.S. Army rsch. grantee 1959-62, NSF grantee, 1959-67, HEW grantee, 1960-67, Dept. Interior grantee 1964-67; Nat. Acad. Sci. awardee Poland, 1976, Yugoslavia, 1978, Hungary, 1982, 84, 89, Bulgaria, 1985, Czechoslovakia, 1987, ProCultura grantee, Hungary, 1991, 93. Fellow AAAS, APHA, Royal Soc. Tropical Medicine (London), Am. Acad. Microbiology, Bulgarian Acad. Scis., Elks. Home: PO Box 2068 Missoula MT 59806-2068

NAKAMURA, ROBERT MOTOHARU, pathologist; b. Montebello, Calif., June 10, 1927; s. Mosaburo and Haru (Suematsu) N.; m. Shigeyo Jane Hayashi, July 29, 1957; children: Mary, Nancy. AB, Whittier Coll., 1949; MD, Temple U., 1954. Cert. of spl. qualification in pathologic anatomy, clin pathology, immunopathology, Am. Bd. Pathology. Prof. pathology U. Calif., Irvine, 1971-74, adj. prof. pathology, 1974-75; chmn. dept. pathology Scripps Clinic and Rsch. Found., La Jolla, Calif., 1974-92; sr. cons., 1992—; pres. Scripps Clinic Med. Group, La Jolla, 1981-91; adj. prof. pathology U. Calif., San Diego, 1975-93. Author, editor profl. publs.; co-editor Jr. Clin. Lab. Analysis, 1989—. Fellow: Coll. Am. Pathologists, Am. Soc. Clin. Pathologists, Assn. Clin. Scientists, Am. Coll. Nutrition; mem. Internat. Acad. Pathology. Avocation: reading. Home: 8841 Nottingham Pl La Jolla CA 92037-2131

NAKAMURA, YOSHIO, professional sports team executive; b. Japan, 1950; s. of Nagayoshi Nakamura; m. Keiko, d. Yuri. Political Law, Keio U., Tokyo, 1973. Prof. sports exec. Fukuoka Lions (later Seibu Lions 1979—), Japan, 1969-87; mgr. operations Lodi Lions, USA, 1971-73; v.p. Seibu Lions, Japan, 1979-87; pres. Kokusai Green Co., Ltd., Japan, 1987—, Lightning Partners Ltd., Tampa Bay, FL, 1991—. Office care Tampa Bay Lightning 1 Mack Center 501 E Kennedy Blvd Ste 175 Tampa FL 33602-5200

NAKANISHI, DON TOSHIAKI, Asian American studies educator, writer; b. L.A., Aug. 14, 1949; m. Marsha Hirano; 1 child, Thomas. BA in Polit Sci. cum laude, Yale U., 1971; PhD in Polit. Sci., Harvard U., 1978. Prof., dir. Asian Am. Studies Ctr. UCLA; researcher Social Sci. Rsch. Coun. of N.Y. and the Japan Soc. for the Promotion of Sci. of Tokyo Joint-Project on Am.-Japanese Mut. Images, 1971-73; mem. Asian Am. task force for social studies guideline evaluation, Calif. State Dept. Edn., 1973; guest spkr. Ctr. for the Study of Ednl. Policy, Grad. Sch. Edn., Harvard U., 1974, Metropathways, Ethni-City Sch. Desegregation Program, Boston, 1974; researcher, co-project chair Hispanic Urban Ctr., Project Sch. Desegregation, L.A., 1974. Author: (with others) Mutual Images: Essays in American-Japan Relations, 1975, Eliminating Racism, 1988, Racial and Ethnic Politics in California, 1991; author: In Search of a New Paradigm: Minorities in the Context of International Politics, 1975, The Education of Asian and Pacific Americans: Historical Perspectives and Prescriptions for the Future, 1983, The UCLA Asian Pacific American Voter Registration Study, 1986; contbr. articles to profl. jours. Chair Yale U. Alumni Schs. Com. of So. Calif., 1978—; bd. dirs. Altamed and La Clinica Familiar Del Barrio of East L.A., 1982—; commr. Bd. Transp. Commrs., City of L.A., 1984-90; v.p. Friends of the Little Tokyo Pub. Libr., 1986-88; co-chair nat. scholars adv. com. Japanese Am. Nat. Mus., 1987—; mem., bd. govs. Assn. of Yale Alumni, 1988-91; mem. exec. coun. Mayor's LA's Best Aftersch. Program, City of Los Angeles, 1988-90. Rsch. fellow Japan Soc. for the Promotion of Sci., 1978; recipient Nat. Scholars awrd for Outstanding Rsch. Article on Asian Pacific Am. Edn., Nat. Assn. for Asian and Pacific Am. Edn., 1985, Civil Rights Impace award Asian Am. Legal Ctr. of So. Calif., 1989; grantee Chancellors' Challenge in the Arts and Humanities, 1991, Calif. Policy Seminar, 1992, U. Calif. Pacific Rim Studies, 1992. Mem. Nat. Assn. for Interdisciplinary Ethnic Studies (bd. dirs. 1976-79), Assn. Asian Am. Studies (nat. pres. 1983-85), Nat. Assn. for Asian and Pacific Am. Edn. (exec. bd. dirs., v.p. 1983—). Office: UCLA Asian Am Studies Ctr Los Angeles CA 90024

NAKANISHI, KOJI, chemistry educator, research institute administrator; b. Hong Kong, May 11, 1925; came to U.S., 1969; s. Yuzo and Yoshiko (Sakata) N.; m. Yasuko Abe, Oct. 25, 1947; children: Keiko, Jun. B.Sc., Nagoya U., Japan, 1947; Ph.D., Nagoya U., 1954; DSc (hon.), Williams Coll., 1987, Georgetown U., 1992. Asst. prof. Nagoya U., 1955-58; prof. Tokyo Kyoiku U., 1958-63, Tohoku U., Sendai, Japan, 1963-69; prof. chemistry Columbia U., N.Y.C., 1969-80; Centennial prof. chemistry Columbia U., 1980—; dir. research Internat. Ctr. Insect Physiology and Ecology, Nairobi, Kenya, 1969-77; dir. Suntory Inst. for Bioorganic Research, Osaka, Japan, 1979-91; hon. prof. Shanghai Inst. Materia Medica, 1995. Author: Infrared Spectroscopy-Practical, 1962, rev. edit., 1977, Circular Dichroic Spectroscopy-Exciton Coupling in Organic Stereochemistry, 1983, A Wandering Natural Products Chemist, 1991. Recipient Asahi cultural prize, 1968, Sci. Workers Union medal, Bulgaria, 1978, E.E. Smissman medal U. Kan., 1979, H.C. Urey award Columbia U., 1980, Alcon ophthalmology award, 1986, Paul Karrer gold medal U. Zurich, 1986, E. Havinga medal Havinga Found., Leiden, 1989, Impreial prize Japan Acad., 1990, Japan Acad. prize, 1990, R.T. Major medal U. Conn., 1991, L.E. Harris award U. Nebr., 1991, award in chem. scis. NAS, 1994, J. Heyrovsky hon. gold medal Czech Acad. Scis., 1995, Robert A. Welch award in chemistry, 1996. Fellow N.Y. Acad. Scis., Nat. Acad. Sci. Italy (fgn.); mem. Chem. Soc. Japan (award in pure chemistry 1954, award 1979, Nakanishi prize established 1996), Am. Chem. Soc. (E. Guenther award 1978, Remsen award Md. sect. 1981, A.C. Cope award 1990, Nichols medal N.Y. sect. 1992, Mosher award Santa Clara Valley sect. 1995, internat. award in agrochems. 1995, Nakanishi prize established 1996), Brit. Chem. Soc. (Centenary medal 1979), Swedish Acad. Pharm. Scis. (Scheele award 1992), Am. Acad. Arts and Scis., Am. Soc. Pharmacognosy (rsch. achievement award 1985), Internat. Chirality Symposium (Chirality gold medal 1995), Pharm. Sc. Japan (hon.). Home: 560 Riverside Dr New York NY 10027-3202 Office: Columbia U Dept chemistry Mail Code 3114 3000 Broadway New York NY 10027

NAKANO, TATSUHIKO, chemist, educator; b. Osaka, Japan, Feb. 4, 1925; s. Denichi and Shie (Kubo) N.; m. Toshiko Kitagawa, Apr. 23, 1965. BA, Kyoto U., 1950, PhD, 1955. Rsch. fellow Kyoto (Japan) U., 1950-55, assoc. prof., 1960-65; rsch. assoc. Wayne State U., Detroit, 1956-59, Stanford (Calif.) U., 1959-60; prof. Inst. Venezolano de Investigaciones Cientificas, Caracas, Venezuela, 1965-94, investigador emerito, 1994; prof. U. Ctrl. de Venezuela, Caracas, 1981—; disting. prof. Inst. de Tecnologia y Estudios Superiores, Monterrey, Mex., 1979; vis. prof. U. N.C., Chapel Hill, 1990, 91, 93, 95; regional editor Revista Latinoamericana de Quimica, Mexico City, 1970—. Contbr. 200 articles to Jour. Chem. Soc., Jour. Chem. Rsch., Tetrahedron, Tetrahedra Letters, etc.; author: Studies in Natural Products Chemistry, 1989, 90. Recipient Spl. Rsch. fwllowship IKUEIKAI, 1950, Fulbright Vis. Scientist Travel award, 1956, Rsch. award Rockefeller Found., 1961, NIH, 1962, Fundación José Maria Vargas, 1969, 80, ABI Twentieth Century Achievement award 1995; decorated Order Andrés Bello, 3rd class, 1979, 2nd class 1989, 1st class 1996; investigador emérito, 1994, Miembro Emérito, PPI Consejo Nacional de Investigaciones Cientificas y Technológicas, 1994. Mem. AAAS, Am. Chem. Soc., Royal Soc. Chemistry, N.Y. Acad. Scis., L.Am. Acad. Scis. (acad. mem., diploma outstanding scientific investigation 1995), Japan Fulbright Alumni Assn. Office: Centro de Quimica IVIC, Apartado 21827, Caracas 1020-A, Venezuela

NAKASONE, ROBERT C., retail toy and game company executive; b. 1947; married. BA, Claremont Coll., 1969; MBA, U. Chgo., 1971. With Brighams Ice Cream Parlor & Sandwich Shops, 1979-82; v.p., gen. mgrs. Jewel Food Stores, 1982-84; Midwest stores v.p. Toys R Us Inc., 1986-89; pres. Toys R Us, USA, 1989—; pres., vice chmn. Toys R Us Worldwide Toy Stores, 1989—; now chmn., CEO Toys R Us Inc.; also bd. dirs. 1st lt. U.S. Army, 1979-82. Office: Toys R US Inc 461 From Rd Paramus NJ 07652-3526 Address: 395 W Passaic St Rochelle Park NJ 07662-3016*

NAKHLEH, EMILE A., governmental sciences educator; b. Galilee, Palestine, May 25, 1938; came to U.S., 1960; s. Abdullah J. and Labibeh (Shiban) N.; m. Mary Bird, Dec. 25, 1965 (div. Aug. 1993); children: Charles, Richard; m. Ilonka Lessnau, Dec. 30, 1993. BA in Polit. Sci., St. John's U., 1963; MA in Polit. Sci., Georgetown U., 1966; PhD in Internat. Relation, Am. U., 1968. From asst. prof. to prof. Mt. St. Mary's Coll., Emmitsburg, Md., 1967-93, chmn. dept., 1975-89, dir. internat. studies, 1981-93, chmn. dept. govt. and internat. studies, 1989-93, John L. Morrison prof. in internat. studies, 1990-93; exec. dir. Inst. for Internat. and Contemporary Affairs, 1990-93; scholar-in-residence, sr. analyst U.S. Govt., Washington, 1993—; adj. scholar Am. Enterprise Inst., Washington, 1981-90, Ctr. for Strategic and Internat. Studies, Washington, 1986-90. Author: Gulf Cooperation Council: Policies, Problems and Prospects, 1986, Persian Gulf and American Policy, 1982, A Palestinian Agenda for West Bank and Gaza, 1980, Bahrain: Political Development in a Modernizing Society, 1976. Founding mem. Cumberland Valley Fgn. Policy Study Group, Waynesboro, Pa., 1981-93, Soc. for Gulf Arab Studies, 1989-93; commr. Town of Emmitsburg Coun., 1977; chmn. City Bd. Commrs., Emmitsburg, 1978-79. Fulbright Sr. Rsch. fellow, Bahrain, 1972-73, Jerusalem, Israel, 1987, Sr. Rsch. fellow NEH, Washington, 1979-80; resident scholar Woodrow Wilson, Washington, 1979, U.S. Govt., Washington, 1990-91, 93-94. Mem. Md. Assn. for Higher Edn. (Outstanding Educator award 1989), Coun. for Advancement and Support of Edn., Soc. for Gulf Arab Studies (founding mem., pres. 1992-93), Am. Polit. Sci. Assn. Roman Catholic. Avocations: reading, traveling, gardening. Home: 11415 Bedfordshire Ave Potomac MD 20854-2009 Office: US Govt Washington DC 20505

NAKONECZNY, MICHAEL MARTIN, artist; b. Detroit, Oct. 30, 1952; s. Michael and Edithe (Pheil) N.; 1 child, Alysha. Student, Kent State U., 1972-74; BA, Cleve. State U., 1979; MFA, Univ. Cin., 1981. Artist in residence Pub. Sch. 1, Long Island City, N.Y., 1986; instr. Cuyahoga C.C., Cleve., 1987, Cleve. Inst. of Art, 1988; vis. artist Herron Sch. of Art Ind. U., Indpls., 1990, Kansas City (Mo.) Art Inst., 1991; artist in residence Bemis Found., Omaha, Nebr., 1992; vis. artist Tamarind Inst., Albuquerque, N. Mex., 1995. Artist: solo exhibitions include: Graham Modern Gallery, N.Y.C., 1988, Cleve. Ctr. for Contemporary Art, 1993, Zolla Lieberman Gallery, Chgo. 1991, 92, 93, Horwitch LewAllen Gallery, Santa Fe, N. Mex., 1995, Purdue U., West Lafayette, Ind., 1995; exhibited in group shows at Corcoran Gallery of Art, Washington, 1985, The Alternative Mus., N.Y., 1986, LA County Mus. of Art, 1987 (travelling exhibition), Graham Modern Gallery, N.Y.C., 1989, Machida City Mus. of Graphic Arts, Tokyo, 1993, Galleria De Arte, Sao Paulo, Brazil, 1994, Weatherspoon Art Gallery, U. N.C., 1995 (travelling exhibition). Recipient fellowship U. Cin., 1979-81, Ohio Arts Coun., 1990, Arts Midwest NEA Regional fellowship, 1994-95, Ill. Arts Coun., 1995, Summerfair Aid to Artists award, Cin., 1984, Visual Arts 7 in Conjunction with Travelling Exhibition, 1987. Home: 2010 Wesley Ave Evanston IL 60201

NALCIOGLU, ORHAN, physics educator, radiological science educator; b. Istanbul, Feb. 2, 1944; U.S., 1966, naturalized, 1974; s. Mustafa and Meliha N. BS, Robert Coll., Istanbul, 1966; MS, Case Western Res. U., 1968; PhD, U. Ore., 1970. Postdoctoral fellow dept. physics U. Calif.-Davis, 1970-71; Rsch. assoc. dept. physics U. Rochester, N.Y., 1971-74, U. Wis., Madison, 1974-76; sr. physicist EMI Med. Inc., Northbrook, Ill., 1976-77; prof. depts. radiol. scis., elec. engring., medicine and physics U. Calif.-Irvine, 1977—, head divsn. physics and engring., 1985—; dir. Biomedical Magnetic Resonance Rsch., 1987—, dir. Rsch. Imaging Ctr., 1992—; cons. UN, 1980-86. Editor several books; contbr. articles to profl. jours. Mobil scholar, 1961-66. Fellow IEEE, Am. Assn. Physicists in Medicine; pres. IEEE NPSS, 1993-94; mem. Internat. Soc. Magnetic Resonance. Republican. Subspecialty: medical physics. Office: U Calif Irvine Coll Medicine Dept Radiol Sci Irvine CA 92717-5000

NALDER, ERIC CHRISTOPHER, investigative reporter; b. Coulee Dam, Wash., Mar. 2, 1946; s. Philip Richard and Mibs Dorothy (Aurdal) N.; m. Jan Christiansen, Dec. 20, 1968; 1 child, Britt Hillary. BA in Communications, U. Wash., 1968. News editor Whidbey News-Times, Oak Harbor, Wash., 1971; reporter Lynnwood (Wash.) Enterprise, 1972, Everett Herald, Lynnwood, 1972-75; gen. assignment reporter Seattle Post-Intelligencer, 1975-78, edn. writer, 1977-78, investigative reporter, 1978-83; chief investigative reporter Seattle Times, 1983—. Author: Tankers Full of Trouble, 1994. Recipient Edn. Writers Assn. award Charles Stewart Mott Found., 1978, Hearst Comty. Svc. award, 1978, C.B. Blethen awards (13), Outstanding Govt. Reporting award Seattle Mcpl. League, Pub. Svc. in Journalism award Sigma Delta Chi, 1987, Edward J. Meeman award Scripps Howard Found., 1987, Thomas Stokes award, Washington Journalism Ctr., 1990, Pulitzer prize for nat. reporting, 1990, Nat. Headline award, 1991, Pub. Svc. award AP Mags. Editors Assn., 1992, Pub. Svc. award AP Mags. Editors Assn., 1992, Goldsmith prize for investigative reporting, 1992, Worth Bingham prize for investigative reporting, 1992, Headliner award, 1992, Investigative Reporters and Editors award, 1992, 95, Silver Gavel award ABA, 1995. Mem. Investigative Reporters and Editors, Pacific N.W. Newspaper Guild. Avocation: downhill skiing. Office: Seattle Times Fairview Avenue St N Seattle WA 98109

NALDRETT, ANTHONY JAMES, geology educator; b. London, June 23, 1933; emigrated to Can., 1957; s. Anthony George and Violet Ethel (Latham) N.; m. Sylvia Robb Clark, Apr. 23, 1960 (div.); children: Anne, Jennifer, Penelope; m. Galina Stanislavovna Rylkova, July 6, 1991. B.A., U. Cambridge, 1956, M.A., 1962; M.Sc., Queens U., Can., 1961, Ph.D., 1964. Geologist Falconbridge Nickel Mines, Ltd., Sudbury, 1957-59; fellow Carnegie Inst. Washington, Geophys. Lab., 1964-67; asst. prof. U. Toronto, Ont., 1967-68; assoc. prof. U. Toronto, 1968-72, prof. mineral deposits geology, 1972-84, univ. prof., 1984—; mine geologist Falconbridge Nickel, 1957-59, exploration geologist, summers 1959-63, sr. prin. rsch. officer CSIRO, Australia, 1972-73; vis. prof. U. Pretoria, South Africa, 1979-80; chercheur associé CNRS, Orleans, France, 1986-87; stagiére BRGM, Orleans, France, 1993-94. Contbr. articles to profl. jours.; editor: Jour. Petrology, 1974-82. Served with Royal Air Force, 1951-53. Recipient Barlow medal Can. Inst. Mining/Metallurgy, 1974, Duncan Derry medal Geol. Assn. Can., 1980, Logan medal Geol. Assn. Can., 1994, Bownocker gold medal Ohio State U., 1986. Fellow Royal Soc. Can., Mineral. Soc. Am., European Union Geoscientists (hon. fgn.), Geol. Assn. Can., Soc. Econ. Geologists (v.p. 1982, pres. 1991-92, medal 1982, Disting. lectr. 1996), Geol. Soc. Am., Mineral. Assn. Can. (pres. 1982, 83, Past Pres.'s medal 1991), Societè de Mineralogie et Crystallograhie (v.p. 1987), Internat. Mineral. Assn. (1st v.p. 1994—). Avocations: sailing, skiing, carpentry. Home: 33 Harbour Sq Ste 1210, Toronto, ON Canada M5J 2G2 Office: Dept Geology, University of Toronto, Toronto, ON Canada M5S 1A1

NALEN, CRAIG ANTHONY, government official; b. Montclair, N.J., Apr. 17, 1930; s. Paul Anthony and Mildred A. (Tucker) N.; m. Katherine Andrews, Dec. 30, 1953; children: Katherine M., David A., Peter H. BA, Princeton U., 1952; MBA, Stanford U., 1957. Mktg. exec. Procter & Gamble, Cin., 1957-62, Foremost-McKesson, San Francisco, 1962-64; divisional gen. mgr., corp. v.p. Gen. Mills Inc., Mpls., 1964-72; pres., also bd. dirs. Am. Photograph Corp., Great Neck, N.Y., 1972-75; pres., chmn. bd. dirs. STP Corp., Ft. Lauderdale, Fla., 1975-80; pres., chief exec. officer Overseas Pvt. Investment Corp. (govt. agy.), Washington, 1981-89, also bd. dirs.; chmn. AES Transpower, Washington, 1989—; bd. dirs. Firan Corp., Ont., Can., Sonex Corp. Bd. dirs., founder Children's World, Denver; bd. dirs. Washington Tennis Found. Lt. USNR, 1952-55. Mem. Woodhill Country Club (Wayzata, Minn.), Liks Club, Chevy Chase (Md.) Club, Gulf Stream Golf Club (Fla.), Ocean Club (Delray Beach, Fla.), Valley Golf Club (Sun Valley, Idaho). Republican. Home: 532 Banyan Rd Gulf Stream FL 33483 also: 4419 Chalfont Pl Bethesda MD 20816-1812 also: PO Box 2439 Ketchum ID 83340-2439 Office: AES Transpower 1001 19th St N Arlington VA 22209-1722

NALEWAKO, MARY ANNE, corporate secretary; b. Johnstown, Pa., Aug. 15, 1934; d. Charles and Margaret (Timothy) Rooney; m. Michael S. Nalewako, Apr. 8, 1961; 1 child, Michael. BSBA, Coll. St. Elizabeth, Convent Station, N.J., 1987. Adminstrv. asst. to chmn. Gen. Pub. Utilities, Parsippany, N.J., 1975-88, corp. sec., 1988—. Recipient Twin award Central (N.J.) YWCA, 1989, award Exec. Women of N.J., 1992. Mem. Am. Soc. Corp. Secs., Seraphic Soc., Spring Brook Country Club. Office: Gen Pub Utilities Corp 100 Interpace Pky Parsippany NJ 07054-1149

NALL, LUCIA LYNN, controller; b. Jackson, Miss., Nov. 22, 1954; d. Aldert S. and Jean (Eaves) Nall. BA in History, Belhaven Coll., 1975, BS in Acctg., 1981; MBA, Miss. Coll., 1994. Acct. Miss. State Bd. Health, Jackson, 1979-85; asst. contr. Miller-Wills Aviation, Jackson, 1985-87; contr. Alston, Rutherford, Tardy & Van Slyke, Jackson, 1987-96; owner Freight Brokers, Brandon, Miss., 1996—. Mem. NAFE, IMA. Home: 930 N Livingston Rd Jackson MS 39213-9207 Office: Freight Brokers 108 Office Park Dr Brandon MS 39043

NALLE, PETER DEVEREUX, publishing company executive; b. N.Y.C., July 26, 1947; s. Peter Borie and Margaret Graham (Josephs) N.; m. Eleanor Jo Graham, June 14, 1969; 1 child, Graham Devereux. B.A., Brown U., 1969. Salesman and mem. sales mgmt. dept. McGraw-Hill Book Co., N.Y.C., 1970-76, editor, mem. editorial mgmt. dept., 1976-81, mktg. dir., 1981-82, gen. mgr., 1982-84, group v.p., 1984-87; pres., chief exec. officer J.B. Lippincott Co., Phila., 1987-90; pres. Simon and Schuster Profl. Info. Group, Englewood Cliffs, N.J., 1990-93; COO Grolier, Inc., Danbury, Conn., 1994—. Bd. dirs. Schuylkill River Devel. Coun. Mem. Assn. Am. Pubs. (exec. council profl. and scholarly div. 1985-87, bd. dirs. 1995-96), Soc. Scholarly Pub., Washington Square Assn. (bd. dirs.), Am. Med. Pubs. Assn. (bd. dirs.), Info. Industry Assn., Friends of Schuylkill River Park (v.p.), Athenaeum of Phila. Club: Brown U. Avocations: sailing; windsurfing; tennis. Home: 2113 Delancey St Philadelphia PA 19103-6511

NALLEY, ELIZABETH ANN, chemistry educator; b. Catron, Mo., July 8, 1942; d. Arthur E. and Thelma L. (King) Frazier; m. Robert L. Mullican, Jan. 2, 1986; 1 child, George Ray. BS, Northeastern Okla. State U., 1965; MS, Okla. State U., 1969; PhD, Tex. Woman's U., 1975. High sch. tchr. Muskogee (Okla.) Ctrl. High Sch., 1964-65; instr. Cameron U., Lawton, Okla., 1969-72; asst. prof. Cameron U., Lawton, 1972-75, assoc. prof., 1975-78, prof., 1978—. Contbr. articles to profl. jours. Recipient Disting. Svc. award Cameron U., 1995. mem. AAAS, Assn. for Advancement of Computers in Edn., Am. Chem. Soc. (councilor 1980—, sec. div. profl. rels. 1987—, sec. divsn. profl. rel. 1987-96, chair-elect divsn. profl. rels. 1996, Okla. Chemist award 1992, divsn. profl. rels. Henry Hill award, 1996), Am. Inst. Chemists (nat. bd. dirs.), Phi Kappa Phi (regent 1981-89, nat. v.p. 1989-92, nat. pres.-elect 1992-95, nat. pres. 1995—, Disting. Faculty award 1978), Sigma Xi, Sigma Pi Sigma, Iota Sigma Pi. Home: RR 3 Box 176-1 Chickasha OK 73018-9544 Office: Cameron U Dept of Chemistry 2800 W Gore Blvd Lawton OK 73505-6320

NALLS, GAYIL LYNN, artist; b. Washington, July 17, 1953; d. Hampton Roberts and Doris Winifred (Fields) N.; m. Winfred Overholser III, Feb. 17, 1979 (dec. Oct. 1983); m. John William Steele, Aug. 15, 1992; 1 child, Morgan Nalls. Student, Va. Commonwealth U., 1971-72, Parsons Sch. Design, 1972-74, Am. U., Washington, 1974, Corcoran Sch. Art, 1975-76. Tchr. Parsons Sch. Design, N.Y.C., 1986—; ptnr. Election Satellite Network, Tribeca Film Ctr., N.Y.C., 1991-94; co-founder Digital Network TV, N.Y.C., 1993—. One-person shows include Susan Caldwell Gallery, N.Y.C., 1983, U. Richmond, Va., 1988, Baumgartner Galleries, Washington, 1990, Phillipe Staib Gallery, N.Y.C., 1992, Downtown Cmty. TV Ctr., N.Y.C., 1992; exhibited in group shows at Indpls. Mus. Art, 1984, Corcoran Gallery Art, Washington, 1988, U.S. Mission, Berlin, West Germany, 1988, Bruce Mus., Greenwich, Conn., 1988, Southeastern Ctr. Contemporary Art, Winston-Salem, 1989, Monastery of Santa Clara, Seville, Spain, 1992, Pretoria Art Mus., South Africa, 1994, Hand Workshop, Richmond, 1995, NGO Forum on Women '95 Film Festival, Huairou, China, 1995, (internet exhibition) Inst. Studies in the Arts Ariz. State U., 1995, Internat. Ctr. N.Y., 1996; represented in permanent collections at Met. Mus.Art, Nat. Mus. Am. Art, Corocoran Gallery; author: The Laments, 1990, (screenplay) X-tips, 1994; author, producer: Permutatude, 1988-94, Gal Gaia/Mother Right, 1990; producer, dir. The Laments, 1994; dir., prodr. (documentary) A Common Destiny: Thomas Banyacya, The Hopi Prophecy, Jewell Praying Wolfe James, (Talking Head documentary) Walking in Both Worlds, 1989, Tom Doston Speaking for Traditional Chief William Commanda: Message from the Elders of the Seven Fires Prophecy, 1995; choreographer (video) Wheels Over Indian Trails, 1993. Conceiver, designer, constructor Commn. Fine Arts and Landmark, Winfred Overholser III Meml. Sculpture Garden, Georgetown U. Hosp., Washington, 1983-85; conceier The Lab Sch. Portfolio for Lab. Sch. Washington, 1986; bd. dirs., curator 10thAnniversary Exhbn. Washington Project for the Arts, 1985-88. Recipient award EarthPeace Internat. Film Festival, Burlington, Vt., 1991, award of merit 20th Biennial Exhbn., U. Del., Newark, 1982, Purchase award Richard B. Russell Bldg. and U.S. Ct. House, Atlanta, 1982, Bay Bank Valley Trust Co. award 66th Nat. Exhbn. George Walter Vincent Smith Art Mus., Springfield, Mass., 1985; D.C. Commn. Arts. and Humanities fellow, Washington, 1987.

NAM, CHARLES BENJAMIN, sociologist, demographer, educator; b. Lynbrook, N.Y., Mar. 25, 1926; s. Samuel and Yetta (Huff) N.; m. Marjorie Lee Tallant, Jan. 1, 1956; children: David Wallace, Rebecca Jane. BA, NYU, 1950; MA, U. N.C., 1957, PhD, 1959. Statistician U.S. Bur. Census, Washington, 1950-53; chief edn. and social stratification br. U.S. Bur. Census, 1957-64; statistician USAF, Montgomery, Ala., 1953-54; rsch. asst. U. N.C., Chapel Hill, 1954-57; prof. sociology Fla. State U., Tallahassee, 1964-96; chmn. dept. sociology Fla. State U., 1968-71; dir. Center for Study of Population, 1967-82; disting. rsch. prof. Fla. State U., Tallahassee, 1994-96, disting. rsch. prof. emeritus, 1996—; mem. population adv. com. U.S. Bur. Census, 1978-81; cons. population divsn. Orgn. for Econ. Coop. and Devel., 1968-70, UNESCO, 1978-83, Indonesian Ministry of Population and Environment, Jakarta, 1988-90; Social Sci. Rsch. Coun., 1981-88. Author: (with John K. Folger) Education of the American Population, 1967, (with Susan Gustavus) Population: The Dynamics of Demographic Change, 1976, Nationality Groups and Social Stratification, 1981, (with Susan Philliber) Population: A Basic Orientation, 1983, (with Mary Powers) The Socioeconomic Approach to Status Measurement, 1983, Our Population: The Face of America, 1988, Understanding Population Change, 1994; editor: Demography, 1972-75; co-editor: (with David Sly, William Serow) International Handbook of Internal Migration, 1990, Handbook of International Migration, 1990; assoc. editor jour. Population Research and Policy Review, 1993-94. Bd. dirs. Soc. Study Social Biology, 1996—. Mem. Am. Sociol.

Assn. (chmn. sect. on population 1976-78), Population Assn. Am. (pres. 1979), Internat. Union for Sci. Study Population, Am. Statis. Assn. (chmn. social statistics sect. 1974), So. Sociol. Soc. (pres. 1981-82), So. Regional Demographic Group (vice chmn. 1974-75), Soc. Study Social Biology (bd. dirs. 1996—). Home: 820 Live Oak Plantation Rd Tallahassee FL 32312-2413

NAM, SANG BOO, physicist; b. Kyung Nam, Korea, Jan. 30, 1936; came to U.S., 1959, naturalized, 1978; s. Sai Hi and Boon Hi (Kim) N.; m. Wonki Kim, June 1, 1969; children—Sae Woo, Jean Ok. BS, Seoul Nat. U., Korea, 1958; MS, U. Ill., 1961, PhD, 1966. Rsch. assoc. U. Ill., Urbana, 1966; rsch. fellow Rutgers U., New Brunswick, N.J., 1966-68; asst. prof. physics U. Va., Charlottesville, 1968-71; vis. prof. physics Seoul Nat. U., 1970, Belfer Grad. Sch., Yeshiva U., N.Y.C., 1971-74; sr. rsch. fellow in physics Nat. Acad. Sci.-NRC, Washington, 1974-76, 84-86; rsch. prof. physics U. Dayton, Ohio, 1976-80; prof. physics Univ. Rsch. Ctr., Wright State U., Dayton, 1980—. With Korean Army, 1958-59. U. Ill. fellow, 1961. Fellow Am. Phys. Soc., Korean Phys. Soc.; mem. AAAS, N.Y. Acad. Scis., Sigma Xi. Home: 7735 Peters Pike Dayton OH 45414-1713

NAMATH, JOSEPH WILLIAM, entertainer, former professional football player; b. Beaver Falls, Pa., May 31, 1943; s. John Andrew and Rose (Juhasz) N.; m. Deborah Lynn Mays, 1984; 1 child, Jessica Grace. Grad., U. Ala., 1965. Quarterback N.Y. Jets, Am. Football League (merged with NFL 1969), 1965-77, Los Angeles Rams Nat. Football Conf., 1977-78; co-owner Joe Namath Instructional Football Camp, Dudley, Mass. Appeared in films C.C. and Company, 1970, Avalanche Express, 1978, Chattanooga Choo Choo, 1984; TV appearances include The Waverly Wonders, NBC, 1978; frequent guest on Tonight Show; stage appearances include Picnic, 1979, Li'l Abner, 1980, The Caine Mutiny Court-Martial, 1983, Sugar, 1984; leading role in musical Damn Yankees, 1981; author (autobiography): Namath—A Matter of Style; commentator ABC Monday Night Football, 1985-86, TV series The Waverly Wonders, TV Movie Marriage is Alive Well, TV appearances Here's Lucy, The Bradu Bunch. The Love Boat, Kate and Allie. Past chmn. Leukemia Soc. Coin Campaign; hon. chmn. Am. Hungarian Soc.; established scholarship for women athletes U. Ala. Named Am. Football League Rookie of Yr., Sporting News, 1965, to Am. Football League All-Star team, 1968, 72, Most Valuable Player of Super Bowl, 1969, Dodge Man of Yr., N.Y. Jets, to Ala. Sports Hall of Fame, 1981; recipient Hickock Belt for Profl. Athlete of Yr., George Halas Most Courageous Athlete award; named to Pro Football Hall of Fame. Office: care Lantz Office 888 7th Ave New York NY 10106

NAMBA, TATSUJI, physician, medical researcher; b. Changchun, China, Jan. 29, 1927; came to U.S., 1959, naturalized, 1968; s. Yosuke and Michino (Hinata) N. MD, Okayama U., Japan, 1950, PhD, 1955. Asst., lectr. medicine Okayama U. Med. Sch. and Hosp., 1955-62; rsch. assoc. Maimonides Med. Ctr., Bklyn., 1959-66; dir. neuromuscular labs. Maimonides Med. Ctr., 1966-70, dir. neuromuscular disease div., head electromyography clinic, 1966—; instr., asst. prof., assoc. prof. medicine SUNY, Bklyn., 1959-76, prof., 1976—; mem. med. adv. bd. Myasthenia Gravis Found., 1968—. Recipient commendation for rsch. and clin. activities on insecticide poisoning Minister Health and Welfare, Japanese Govt., 1958; Fulbright scholar, 1959-62. Fellow ACP, Royal Soc. Medicine; mem. AMA, Am. Acad. Neurology, Am. Soc. Pharmacology and Exptl. Therapeutics, Am. Soc. Clin. Pharmacology and Therapeutics, Am. Assn. Electrodiagnostic Medicine. Home: 4114 9th Ave Brooklyn NY 11232 Office: 4802 10th Ave Brooklyn NY 11219-2916

NAMBOODIRI, KRISHNAN, sociology educator; b. Valavoor, Ind., Nov. 13, 1929; s. Narayanan and Parvathy (Kutty) N.; m. Kadambari Kumari, Sept. 7, 1954; children: Unni (dec.), Sally. B.Sc., U. Kerala, 1950, M.Sc., 1953; M.A., U. Mich., 1962, Ph.D., 1963. Lectr. U. Kerala, India, 1953-55, 58-59; tech. asst. Indian Statis. Inst., Calcutta, 1955-58; reader demography U. Kerala, 1963-66; asst. prof. sociology U. N.C., Chapel Hill, 1966-67; asso. prof. U. N.C., 1967-73, prof., 1973-84, chmn. dept., 1975-80; Robert Lazarus prof. population studies Ohio State U., Columbus, 1984—, chmn. dept. sociology, 1989-93. Author: (with L.F. Carter and H.M. Blalock) Applied Multivariate Analysis and Experimental Designs, 1975; editor: Demography, 1975-78, Survey Sampling and Measurement, 1978, Auth. Matrix Algebra: An Introduction, 1984, (with C.M. Suchindran) Life Table Techniques and Their Applications, 1987, (with R.G. Corwin) Research in Sociology of Education and Socialization: Selected Methodological Issues, 1989, Demographic Analysis: A Stochastic Approach, 1991, The Logic and Method of Macrosociology, 1993, Methods for Macrosociological Research, 1994, A Primer of Population Dynamics, 1996; contbr. articles to profl. jours. Fellow Am. Statis. Assn.; mem. Population Assn. Am. (dir. 1975-76), Internat. Union Sci. Study Population, Am. Sociol. Assn., Indian Sociol. Assn., Am. Statis. Assn., Sociol. Research Assn. Home: 3107 N Star Rd Columbus OH 43221-2366

NAMBU, YOICHIRO, physics educator; b. Toyko, Jan. 18, 1921; came to U.S., 1952; m. Chieko Hida, Nov. 3, 1945; 1 child, Jun-ichi. Research asst. U. Tokyo, 1945-49; prof. physics Osaka City U., Japan, 1950-56; mem. Inst. Advanced Study, 1952-54; research assoc. U. Chgo., 1954-56, mem. faculty, 1956—, prof. physics, 1958, Disting. prof., 1971—; emeritus, 1991—. Contbr. articles to profl. jours. Recipient J.J. Sakurai prize Am. Physical Soc., 1994, Wolf Prize in Physics, 1994. Mem. Nat. Acad. Scis., Am. Acad. Arts and Scis., Am. Phys. Soc. Office: Univ of Chicago Dept of Physics 5720 S Ellis Ave Chicago IL 60637-1434

NAMDARI, BAHRAM, surgeon; b. Oct. 26, 1939; s. Rostam and Sarvar Namdari; M.D., 1966; m. Kathleen Diane Wilmore, Jan. 5, 1976. Resident in gen. surgery St. John's Mercy Med. Ctr., St. Louis, 1969-73; fellow in cardiovascular surgery with Michael DeBakey, Baylor Coll. Medicine, Houston, 1974-75; practice medicine specializing in gen. and vascular surgery and surg. treatment of obesity, Milw., 1976—; mem. staff St. Mary's, St. Luke's, St. Michael, St. Francis hosps. (all Milw.); founder, pres. Famous Mealwaukee Foods Enterprises. Diplomate Am. Bd. Surgery. Fellow ACS, Internat. Coll. Surgeons; mem. Med. Soc. Milw. County, Milw. Acad. Surgery, Wis. Med. Soc., Wis. Surg. Soc., Royal Soc. Medicine Eng. (affiliate), Am. Soc. for Bariatric Surgery, AMA, World Med. Assn., Internat. Acad. Bariatric Medicine (founding mem.), Michael DeBakey Internat. Cardiovascular Soc. Contbr. articles to med. jours.; patentee med. instruments and other devices. Office: Great Lakes Med and Surg Ctr 6000 S 27th St Milwaukee WI 53221-4805

NAMIAS, JEROME, meteorologist; b. Bridgeport, Conn., Mar. 19, 1910; s. Joseph and Saydie (Jacobs) N.; m. Edith Paipert, Sept. 15, 1938; 1 child, Judith Ellen. Student, MIT, 1932-34, M.S., 1941; M.S., U. Mich., 1934-35; Sc.D. (hon.), U. R.I., 1972, Clark U., 1984. Research asst. Blue Hill Meteorol. Obs., Milton, Mass., 1933-35; research assoc. MIT, Boston, 1936-41, Woods Hole (Mass.) Oceanographic Inst.; mgr. extended forecast br. U.S. Weather Bur., Washington, 1941-64; assoc. dir. Nat. Meteorol. Ctr., 1964-66, chief extended forecast div., 1966-71; vis. scientist NYU, N.Y.C., 1966; research meteorologist Scripps Inst. Oceanography, La Jolla, Calif., 1968—; vis. scholar Rockefeller Study and Conf. Center, Bellagio, Italy, 1977; frequent cons. USAAF, USN; developer of system for extending time range of gen. weather forecasts up to a season. Author: An Introduction to the Study of Air Mass and Isentropic Analysis, 1936, Extended Forecasting by Mean Circulation Methods; monograph, 1947, Thirty-Day Forecasting, 1953; Short Period Climatic Variations, Collected Works of Jerome Namias, 1934-74, 1975-82, 83, Namias Symposium Volume, 1986; also tech. articles to sci. jours.; Editorial bd.: Geofisica Internacional, Mexico. Recipient citation for weather forecasts North African invasion Sec. of Navy, 1942; Dept. Commerce Meritorious Service award, 1950; Rockefeller Pub. Service award, 1955; Gold medal for disting. achievement Dept. Commerce, 1965; Chancellor's Assocs. award excellence in research U. Calif.-San Diego; Compass award for research Marine Tech. Soc., 1984; Rossby fellow Woods Hole (Mass.) Oceanographic Instn., 1972. Fellow AAAS, Am. Geophys. Union, Washington Acad. Scis., Am. Meteorol. Soc. (Meisinger award 1983, extraordinatry achievement award 1955, Sverdrup Godl medal 1981, Lifetime Achievement award So. Calif. chpt. 1991, councilor 1940-42, 50-53, 60-63, 70-73); mem. NAS, Am. Acad. Arts and Sci., Royal Meteorol. Soc. Great Britain (hon. mem.), Explorers Club. Home: 240 Coast Blvd Apt 2C La Jolla CA 92037-4669 Office: Scripps Inst Oceanography Poss # A-024 La Jolla CA 92093 *I was stimulated by a few exceptionally capable high school teachers to pursue a career in meteorology. This subject became both a vocation and a most challenging hobby and never has ceased to fascinate me. My guiding philosophy has been that one is rewarded if he contributes fundamental ideas which are reasonable and at least partially verifiable. It is not necessary to be highly aggressive to get ahead.*

NANAVATI, GRACE LUTTRELL, dancer, choreographer, instructor; b. Springfield, Ill., Oct. 2, 1951; d. Curtis Loren and Mary Grace (Leaverton) Luttrell; m. P.J. Nanavati, May 11, 1985; 1 child, William P. BA, Butler U., 1973; MA, Sangamon State U., 1978. Owner, dir. Dance Arts Studio, Springfield, 1973—; artistic dir. Springfield (Ill.) Ballet Co., 1975—; compulsory arts programming com. Sch. Dist. 186, Springfield, 1990—; dance panel Ill. Arts Coun., 1990-92, 94-96. Vol. Meml. Med. Ctr., Springfield, 1980-88. Named Women of Yr., YMCA, Springfield, 1982; recipient Mayor award for Arts, City of Springfield, 1985, Best of Springfield award Ill. Times, Springfield, 1990. Home: 1501 Williams Blvd Springfield IL 62704-2346 Office: Dance Arts Studio Inc 2820 Macarthur Blvd Springfield IL 62704-5017

NANCE, ALLAN TAYLOR, lawyer; b. Dallas, Jan. 31, 1933; s. A.Q. and Lois Rebecca (Taylor) N. BA, So. Meth. U., 1954, LLB, 1957; LLM, NYU, 1978. Bar: Tex. 1957, N.Y. 1961. With Simpson Thacher & Bartlett, N.Y.C., 1960-65; asst. counsel J.P. Stevens & Co., Inc., N.Y.C., 1965-70, sec., 1970-78, asst. gen. counsel, 1970-89; counsel J.P. Stevens & Co. Inc. and WestPoint-Pepperell Inc., 1989-93; asst. gen. counsel WestPoint Stevens Inc., N.Y.C., 1993—. With USNR, 1957-59. Woodrow Wilson fellow Columbia U., 1959-60. Mem. Phi Beta Kappa. Home: 201 E 66th St New York NY 10021-6451 Office: WestPoint Stevens Inc 1185 Ave of the Americas New York NY 10036-2601

NANCE, BETTY LOVE, librarian; b. Nashville, Oct. 29, 1923; d. Granville Scott and Clara (Mills) Nance. BA in English magna cum laude, Trinity U., 1957; AM in Library Sci., U. Mich., 1958. Head dept. acquisitions Stephen F. Austin U. Library, Nacogdoches, Tex., 1958-59; librarian 1st Nat. Bank, Fort Worth, 1959-61; head catalog dept. Trinity U., San Antonio, 1961-63; head tech. processes U. Tex. Law Library, Austin, 1963-66; head catalog dept. Tex. A&M U. Library, College Station, 1966-69; chief bibliographic services Washington U. Library, St. Louis, 1970; head dept. acquisitions Va. Commonwealth U. Library, Richmond, 1971-73; head tech. processes Howard Payne U. Library, Brownwood, Tex., 1974-79; library dir. Edinburg (Tex.) Pub. Library, 1980-91; pres. Edinburg Com. for Salvation Army. Mem. ALA, Pub. Library Assn., Tex. Library Assn., Hidalgo County Library Assn. (v.p. 1980-81, pres. 1981-82), Pan Am. Round Table of Edinburg (corr. sec. 1986-88, assoc. dir. 1989-90), Edinburg Bus. and Profl. Womens Club (founding bd. dirs., pres. 1986-87, bd. dirs. 1987-88), Alpha Lambda Delta, Alpha Chi. Methodist. Club: Zonta Club of San Antonio (bd. dirs. 1996—). Home: 5359 Fredericksburg Rd Apt 806 San Antonio TX 78229-3549

NANCE, CECIL BOONE, JR., lawyer; b. Marion, Ark., Feb. 14, 1925; s. Cecil Boone and Virginia (Essary) N.; m. Harriet Jane McGee, Aug. 7, 1948; children: Janet E., Cecil Boone III. J.D., U. Ark., 1951. Bar: Ark. 1951. Since practiced in West Memphis; mem. firm Nance, Nance & Fleming (named changed to Nance & Nance P.A.), 1951—; Chmn. bd. Fidelity Nat. Bank West Memphis, 1966-71; dir., gen. counsel E. Ark. Savs. & Loan Assn., 1970-83; spl. asso. justice Ark. Supreme Ct. Contbr. articles to profl. jours. Mem. Ark. Ho. of Reps., 1957-68; v.p. Ark. Constl. Conv., 1969. Served with AUS, 1943-46, 52-53. Decorated Bronze Star. Mem. Am. Bar Assn., Ark. Bar Assn. (chmn. jr. bar sect. 1957-58, dir. Ark. Law Rev. and Bar Assn. Jour. 1975), Am. Judicature Soc. Methodist. Club: Rotarian (West Memphis) (pres. 1970-71). Home: 506 Roosevelt Ave West Memphis AR 72301-2961 Office: 203 W Broadway St West Memphis AR 72301-3903

NANCE, JAMES CLIFTON, company executive; b. Bryan, Tex., Sept. 2, 1957; s. Joseph Milton and Eleanor Glenn (Hanover) N.; m. Eileen Bonner, June 14, 1980; children: Jordan Eleanor, Robert Clifton, Kira Liane, Sarina Jenet. BS, U.S. Naval Acad., 1980. Registered quality sys. lead auditor Registrar Accreditation Bd. U.S.; cert. lead assessor Internat. Register of Cert. Auditors U.K.; cert. head auditor Internat. Register Cert. Auditors U.K. Quality assurance engr. Tex. Instruments, Inc., Dallas, 1985-86; people and asset effectiveness coord. Tex. Instruments, Inc., Plano, Tex., 1986-87; mgmt. cons. KPMG, Newport, R.I., 1987-88; sr. compliance auditor Litton Corp. Office, Beverly Hills, Calif., 1989; dir. continuous process improvement Litton Aero Products, Moorpark, Calif., 1989-93; v.p. P-E Handley-Walker, Inc., Independence, Ohio, 1993—; mem. Malcolm Baldridge Nat. Quality Award Bd. Examiners, 1993, 94. Troop com. chmn. Boy Scouts Am., Orlando, 1980-81, unit commr., Vallejo, Calif., 1984-85, varsity coach, McKinney, Tex., 1985-87, scouting coord., Newport, R.I., 1988, chmn. advancement com., Thousand Oaks, Calif., 1989-93, Medina, Ohio, 1994, asst. blazer leader, Medina, 1995—. Recipient Adult Varsity Letter, Boy Scouts Am., Circle Ten Coun., 1986, Scouter's Tng. award, 1987. Mem. Assn. for Quality and Participation (chpt. pres. 1992-93), Am. Soc. Quality Control (sr.), U.S. Naval Acad. Alumni Assn. (life), Sons of the Republic of Tex. (life). Avocations: golf, squash, running, genealogy, photography. Home: PO Box 259 9103 Westfield Rd Westfield Center OH 44251-0259 Office: P-E Handley-Walker Inc 6000 Freedom Square Dr Ste 140 Independence OH 44131-2554

NANCE, JOSEPH MILTON, history educator; b. Kyle, Tex., Sept. 18, 1913; s. Jeremiah Milton and Mary Louise (Hutchison) N.; m. Eleanor Glenn Hanover, Mar. 19, 1944; children: Jeremiah Milton, Joseph Hanover, James Clifton. B.A., U. Tex., 1935, M.A., 1936, Ph.D., 1941; cert. in naval communications, Harvard U., 1944. Tex. supr. Am. imprints, manuscripts and newspaper inventories U.S. Hist. Records Survey, 1938-40; instr. history Tex. A&M U., 1941-42, 46-47, asst. prof., 1947-51, assoc. prof., 1951-57, prof., 1957-58, prof., head dept. history and govt., 1958-68, head dept. history, 1968-73, prof., 1973—; instr. U.S. Naval Tng. Sch., College Station, 1942-43; vis. prof. history SW Tex. State Coll., San Marcos, summers 1956, 58. Author: Checklist of Texas Newspapers, 1813-1939, 1941, 3d edit., 1963, The Early History of Bryan and the Surrounding Area, 1962, After San Jacinto: The Texas-Mexican Frontier, 1836-1841, 1963, Attack and Counter-Attack, The Texas Mexican Frontier, 1842, 1964; co-author: Heroes of Texas, 1964; student guide to accompany A History of the American People (Graebner, Fite, White), 1971; also instr.'s man.; editor: Some Reflections upon Modern America, 1969, A Mier Expedition Diary: A Texan Prisoner's Account (Joseph D. McCutchan), 1978, Dare-Devils All: The Texas Mier Expedition, 1842-1844; mem. editl. bd.: Ariz. and the West, 1980-83; sr. editor: Handbook of Texas, 1983—; co-editor: The Handbook of Texas, 6 vols., 1996. Mem. Hood's Brigade-Bryan Centennial Com., 1960-62; panel participant Tex. Legis. Assembly, 1967; mem. Ann. Faculty seminar Standard Oil Co. Calif., summer 1959, Brazos County Hist. Commn., Tex., 1972—. Served to lt. (j.g.) USNR, 1943-46. Recipient 15th Ann. Writers Roundup award Theta Sigma Phi, 1963, Tex. Inst. Letters award, 1964, Walter Prescott Webb award in history U. Tex., 1967, AMOCO Disting. Research award Tex. A&M U., 1979, History award and medal DAR, 1985; 3 ann. scholarships established in his name at Baylor U. Coll. Law, 1979—; ann. lectureship established in his honor Tex. A&M U., 1980—; named Knight of San Jacinto Sons of Republic, 1983. Fellow Tex. State Hist. Assn. (exec. coun.), East Hist. Assn., East Tex. Hist. Assn. (dir. 1980-83); mem. Tex. Inst. Letters, Am. Hist. Assn., So. Hist. Assn., W. Tex. Hist. Assn. (exec. coun., book rev. editor 1975-81, v.p. 1978-81, pres. 1981-82), Orgn. Am. Historians, Western History Assn., Am. Heritage Soc., Am. Studies Assn. Tex. (pres. 1969), Southwestern Social Sci. Assn., Central Tex. Area Writers Conf., Nat. Geog. Soc., Phi Beta Kappa, Phi Kappa Phi, Phi Alpha Theta. Home: 1403 Post Oak Cir College Station TX 77840-2322

NANCE, MARTHA MCGHEE, rehabilitation nurse; b. Huntington, W.Va., Jan. 24, 1944; d. Orme Winford and Sadie Mae (Dudley) McGhee; m. John Edgar Nance, Mar. 17, 1990; children: Laura Beckner, Suzie Brickey. RN, St. Mary's Sch. Nursing, Huntington, W.Va., 1980; student, Marshall U., Huntington, W.Va., 1978-88. Cert. rehab. nurse, cert. case mgr. Surg. head nurse Huntington Hosp. Inc., nursing supr.; quality assurance dir. Am. Hosp. for Rehab., Huntington, 1988-89, DON, 1989-90; rehab. charge nurse Am. Putnam Nursing and Rehab. Ctr., Hurricane, W.Va., 1990—; mgr. health svcs. Mountain State Blue Cross/Blue Shield, Charleston, W.Va., 1995—, mgr. precert., case mgmt. and med. rev., 1995—. Mem. Assn. for Practitioners in Infection Control. Home: RR 4 Box 100 Hurricane WV 25526-9351

NANCE, MARY JOE, secondary education educator; b. Carthage, Tex., Aug. 7, 1921; d. F. F. and Mary Elizabeth (Knight) Born; m. Earl C. Nance, July 12, 1946; 1 child, David Earl. BBA, North Tex. State U., 1953; post-grad., Northwestern State U. La., 1974; ME, Antioch U., 1978. Tchr., Port Isabel (Tex.) Ind. Sch. Dist., 1953-79; tchr. English, Tex., 1965, Splendora (Tex.) High Sch., 1979-80, McLeod, Tex., 1980-81, Bremond, Tex., 1981-84. Vol. tchr. for Indian students, 1964-65, 79. Served with WAAC, 1942-43, WAC 1945. Recipient Image Maker award Carthage C. of C., 1984; cert. bus. educator. Mem. ASCD, NEA, Nat. Bus. Edn. Assn., Tex. Tchrs. Assn., Tex. Bus. Tchrs. Assn. (cert. of appreciation 1978), Nat. Women's Army Corps Vets. Assn., Air Force Assn. (life), Gwinnett Hist. Soc., Hist. Soc. Panola County, Panola County Hist. & Geneal. Assn., Coun. for Basic Edn., Nat. Hist. Soc., Tex. Coun. English Tchrs. Baptist.

NANCE, ROBERT LEWIS, oil company executive; b. Dallas, July 10, 1936; s. Melvin Renfro Nance and Ruth Natlie (Seibert) Nowlin; m. Penni Jane Warfel; children: Robert Scott, Amy Louise, Catherine Leslie. BS, So. Meth. U., 1959; LLD (hon.), Rocky Mountain Coll., 1989. V.p. geology Oliver & West Cons., Dallas, 1960-66; ptnr. Nance & Larue Cons., Dallas, 1966-69; pres., CEO Nance Petroleum Corp., Billings, Mont., 1969—; bd. dirs. First Interstate Bank Commerce, MDU Resources, Rocky Mountain Coll., Billings, chmn., 1986-91; mem. Nat. Petroleum Coun., 1992-94; chmn. Petroleum Technology Transfer Coun. Coun. pres. Am. Luth. Ch., Billings, 1980; trustee, chmn. Deaconess Med. Ctr., Billings; chmn. Deaconess Billings Clinic Healty Sys. Recipient Hall of Fame award Rocky Mountain Coll. Alumni, 1987, Disting. Svc. Trusteeship, Assn. Governing Bds. Univs. Colls., 1988. Mem. Am. Assn. Petroleum Geologists, Ind. Petroleum Assn. Am. (exec. com., nat. bd. govs.), Ind. Petroleum Assn. Mountain States (v.p. Mont. 1977-79), Mont. Petroleum Assn., Hilands Golf Club, Billings Petroleum Club. Avocations: fly fishing, scuba diving, skiing. Office: Nance Petroleum Corp PO Box 7168 550 N 31st St Billings MT 59103

NANCE, TONY MAX-PERRY, designer, illustrator; b. Montclair, N.J., Feb. 25, 1955; s. Perry Hedgeman and Ida Delea (King) N.; m. June Anne Percival, Oct. 31, 1986 (div. May 1994); children: Jack Anthony, Jacqlene Angela, Jihad Conan. Student, U. Denver, 1975; BA, N.Y. Sch. Visual Arts, 1976, postgrad., 1980-81; postgrad., N.J. Inst. Tech., 1977-78, Rutgers U., 1980-82. Design engr. Automation Controls, Montclair, 1975-77; artist, designer Greg Copeland, Inc., Fairfield, N.J., 1976-79; owner, designer Stalhaus, Inc., Montclair, 1976-80; editor contemporary ads Graphics Mag., N.Y.C., 1977-79; illustrator, artist L.C. Graphics, Inc., Clifton, N.J., 1979-80; carrier supr. Montclair Post Office, 1980-93; owner, design engr. Decotech Alternations, Orange, N.J., 1984—, Electronics Tech-Atlas Soundolier, 1993—, Machine Tech-Atlas Soudolier, 1995—. Editor Graphis mag.; artist, art dir. (album covers) Bhang, 1984 Ron Smyth I, 1986; artist, illustrator (album cover, tour and advt. promotion) Passport Greatest Hits/Doldinger, 1977 (album cover, internat. poster) Zap and the Wires-The Saga of the Black Silk Jetmen; producer, illustrator (album cover) The Little Things by Dogs Eating Glass with Loren Tindall; one man shows include Discovery Galleries, Montclair, 1978, The Gallery, Fairfield, 1979, Broghton Galleries, Bloomfield, N.J., 1983, Scotland Galleries, Laurinburg, N.C., 1993; contbr. artist mags. Verotika, 1996, Hard Core, 1996; various musical and graphic copyrights; mem. Southern Ambition band, 1993—, Southern Fried Dogs band, 1996—; creator comic strip Appliances, 1995—. Art dir. Montclair Coalition for Performing Arts, Montclair, 1982. Mem. Soc. for Creative Anachronism (founding assoc.), Local Musicians Union, Nat. Rifle Assn., Mensa, Scotland County Art Guild, Porsche Club Am., N.C. SCCA. Avocations: music, prop and special effect design, collecting plastic toys, computer software design, collecting guitars. Office: Decotech Alternations Nanceart 1209 N Main St Laurinburg NC 28352

NANCE, WILLIAM BENNETT, economic development specialist; b. Garland, N.C., Nov. 18, 1944; s. Lemon Francis Nance and Hattie McCoy Jones; m. Mildred Elaine McKiever, Dec. 26, 1971; children: William Bennett, David Christopher. BA in Polit. Sci., N.C. Ctrl. U., Durham, 1966; postgrad., Swarthmore Coll., 1966-67; MA in Internat. Affairs, George Washington U., 1979; MA in Pub. Adminstrn., Harvard U., 1989. Asst. program officer, Turkey AID, Ankara, 1971-75; asst. desk officer, Syria AID, Washington, 1975-77, officer-in-charge, Lebanon, 1977-79; chief Office of Program/Planning AID, Kathmandu, Nepal, 1979-83; officer-in-charge, Thailand AID, Washington, 1983-86, officer-in-charge, Philippines, 1986-88, officer-in-charge, Bangladesh, 1989-90; chief Office of Program AID, Rabat, Morocco, 1990-92; rep. to Mongolia AID, Ulaanbaatar, 1992-94; pres. The AMIDA Group, Inc., Chevy Chase, Md., 1994—. Recipient Presdl. award Pres. of U.S., 1993. Avocations: reading, chess, tennis. Home: 4105 Oliver St Chevy Chase MD 20815

NANDA, CHITTA RANJAN, industrial hygienist, metallurgical engineer; b. Puri, Orissa, India; s. Janardan and Sulakhyana (Rath) N.; m. Gita Rani Devi, Mar. 13, 1970; children: Nellie, Tusar Kanti. BS, Banaras Hindu U., Varanasi, India, 1964; MS, U. Ill., 1966; PhD, U. Wis., 1969. Cert. indsl. hygienist, safety profl. Asst. prof. U. Roorkee, India, 1969-71, Rourkela (India) Engring. Coll., 1972-76; resident in phys. sci. Touro Infirmary, New Orleans, 1977-78; rsch. assoc. La. State U., New Orleans, 1978-79; adj. faculty Sch. of Engring. & APP Sci., Portland, Oreg., 1980-81; indsl. hygienist VA Med. Ctr., Saginaw, Mich., 1986-87; chief safety & indsl. hygiene VA Med. Ctr., Danville, Ill., 1987-91; regional indsl. hygienist Dept. Vet. Affairs, Ann Arbor, Mich., 1991-92, Grand Prairie, Tex., 1992—. Contbr. articles to Jour. Am. Inst. of Metall. Engring., Metall. Transaction, The Eastern Metals Rev. and other profl. jours. Mem. Am. Indsl. Hygiene Assn., Am. Soc. Safety Engrs., Am. Conf. Govt. Indsl. Hygienists, Sigma Xi. Republican. Home: 3102 Voltaire Blvd Mc Kinney TX 75070-4248

NANDA, VED PRAKASH, law educator, university official; b. Gujranwala, India, Nov. 20, 1934; came to U.S., 1960; s. Jagan Nath and Attar (Kaur) N.; m. Katharine Kunz, Dec. 18, 1982; 1 child, Anjali. MA, Punjab U., 1952; LLB, U. Delhi, 1955, LLM, 1958; LLM, Northwestern U., 1962; postgrad., Yale U., 1962-65. Asst. prof. law U. Denver, 1965-68, assoc. prof., 1968-70, prof. law, dir. Internat. Legal Studies Program, 1970—, Thompson G. Marsh prof. law, 1987—, Evans Univ. prof., 1992—, asst. provost, 1993-94, vice provost, 1994—; vis. prof. Coll. Law, U. Iowa, Iowa City, 1974-75, Fla. State U., 1973, U. San Diego, 1979, U. Colo., 1992; disting. vis. prof. internat. law Chgo. Kent Coll. Law, 1981, Calif. We. Sch. Law, San Diego, 1983-84; disting. vis. scholar Sch. Law, U. Hawaii, Honolulu, 1986-87; cons. Solar Energy Rsch. Inst., 1978-81, Dept. Energy, 1980-81. Author: (with David Pansius) Litigation of International Disputes in U.S. Courts, 1987; editor: (with M. Cherif Bassiouni) A Treatise on International Criminal Law, 2 vols., 1973, Water Needs for the Future, 1977; (with George Shepherd) Human Rights and Third World Development, 1985; (with others) Global Human Rights, 1981, The Law of Transnational Business Transactions, 1981, World Climate Change, 1983, Breach and Adaption of International Contracts, 1992, World Debt and Human Conditions, 1993, Europe Community Law After 1992, 1993, International Environmental Law and Policy, 1995; (with William M. Evan) Nuclear Proliferation and the Legality of Nuclear Weapons, 1995; editor, contbr.: Refugee Law and Policy, 1989; editl. bd. Jour. Am. Comparative Law, Indian Jour. Internat. Law. Co-chmn. Colo. Pub. Broadcasting Fedn., 1977-78; mem. Gov.'s Commn. on Pub. Telecommunications, 1980-82. Mem. World Jurist Assn. (v.p. 1991—, pres. World Assn. Law Profs. 1987-93), UN Assn. (v.p. Colo. divsn. 1973-76, pres. 1986-88, 93—, nat. coun. UNA-USA 1990—, mem. governing bd. UNA-USA 1995—), World Fedn. UN Assns. (vice-chmn. 1995—), Am. Assn. Comparative Study Law (bd. dirs. 1980—), Am. Soc. Internat. Law (v.p. 1987-88, exec. coun. 1969-72, 81-84, bd. rev. and devel. 1988-91), Assn. Am. Law Schs., U.S. Inst. Human Rights, Internat. Law Assn. (mem. exec. com. 1986—), Colo. Coun. Internat. Orgns. (pres. 1988-90), Assn. U.S. Mems. Internat. Inst. Space Law (bd. dirs., mem. exec. com. 1980-88), Order St. Ives (pres.), Rotary, Cactus. Office: U Denver Coll Law 1900 Olive St Denver CO 80220-1857

NANDI, SATYABRATA, zoology educator; b. North Lakhimpur, Assam, India, Dec. 1, 1931; came to U.S., 1954; s. Kunja Bihari Nandi and Jyotirmoyee Sen-Gupta; m. Jean Brandt-Erichsen, July 5, 1957. B.S. with honors, U. Calcutta, India, 1949, M.S., 1951; Ph.D., U. Calif.-Berkeley, 1958. Asst. prof. zoology U. Calif.-Berkeley, 1962-64, assoc. prof., 1964-68, prof., 1968-89, prof. cell and devel. biology, dept. molecular and cell biology, 1989—, Miller prof., 1970-71, vice chmn. zoology, 1965-66, chmn. zoology, 1971-73, dir. cancer research lab., 1974-84; vis. scientist Kyoto U., Japan, 1965. Guggenheim fellow, 1967-68; recipient Spl. Honor for Outstanding Achievement, Ambassador of India, 1979. Mem. Assn. Indians in Am. (award 1980), Internat. Assn. for Breast Cancer Rsch. (chmn.). Office: U Calif Cancer Research Lab 447 Life Scis Addition Berkeley CA 94720

NANFELT, P. N., church administrator. V.p. for Overseas Ministries Christian and Missionary Alliance. Office: PO Box 35000 Colorado Springs CO 80935-3500

NANGLE, CAROLE FOLZ, counselor; b. Evansville, Ind.; d. Francis Jacob Jr. and Mary Josephine (Metzger) Folz; m. James Francis Nangle Jr., Nov. 21, 1953; children: Cynthia Nangle Bitting, Mary Nangle Boughton, Catherine Nangle Howland. BS, Maryville Coll. Sacred Heart, 1953; MA in Counseling, Webster U., 1985. Substitute tchr. All Saints Cath. Parish, 1962-66; counselor, tchr. Cath. Women's League Day Care Ctr., 1965-74; asst. tchr. art St. Joseph Inst. for Deaf, 1980-81; tutor, counselor St. Vincent German Home, 1979-82; counselor Cath. Family Svcs., 1985—; project Rachel Archdiocese of St. Louis, 1989—. Fundraiser Cath. Women's LEague, 1965-68, fundraiser chmn., 1966, bd. dirs., 1965-71; bd. dirs. Washington U. St. Louis-Newman Club, 1969-74; mem. aux. bd. St. Louis Hosp., 1981-83; mem. alumnae bd. Villa Duchesne Acad. of Sacred Heart, 1963-70, 80-86; weekly fin. accts. Christ the King Parish, 1958-60; bd. govs. Lake Forest Subdivsn., 1982-84, directory, 1982; alumnae class rep. Maryville Coll., 1960-69; bd. dirs. Scholar Program St. Louis, 1966-68, co-chmn., 1967. Mem. Am. Counseling Assn., Assn. Adult Devel. and Aging, Mensa (nat. scholar program 1981-82, chmn. nat. scholar program 1981). Roman Catholic. Avocations: bridge, interior decoration, child care.

NANGLE, JOHN FRANCIS, federal judge; b. St. Louis, June 8, 1922; s. Sylvester Austin and Thelma (Bank) N.; m. Jane Adams, June 7, 1986; 1 child, John Francis Jr. AA, Harris Tchrs. Coll., 1941; BS, U. Mo., 1943; JD, Washington U., St. Louis, 1948. Bar: Mo. 1948. Pvt. practice law Clayton, 1948-73; judge U.S. Dist. Ct., St. Louis, 1973—, chief judge, 1983-90, sr. judge, 1990—. Mem. Mo. Rep. Com., 1958-73; mem. St. Louis County Rep. Cen. Com., 1958-73, chmn., 1960-61; pres. Mo. Assn. Reps., 1961, Reps. Vets. League, 1960; mem. Rep. Nat. Com., 1972-73; bd. dirs. Masonic Home Mo. With AUS, 1943-46. Named Mo. Republican of Year John Marshall Club, 1970, Mo. Republican of Year Mo. Assn. Reps., 1971; recipient Most Disting. Alumnus award Harris-Stowe Coll., Most Disting. Alumnus award Washington U. Sch. Law, 1986. Mem. ABA, Am. Judicature Soc., Legion of Honor DeMolay, Mo. Bar Assn., St. Louis Bar Assn., St. Louis County Bar Assn., 8th Cir. Jud. Coun., Jud. Conf. U.S. (apptd. mem. exec. com.), Jud. Panel on Multidist. Litigation (chmn.).

NANJI, AMIN AKBARALI, biochemist, clinical pathologist, educator; b. Mombasa, Kenya, Feb. 21, 1954; came to U.S., 1988; s. Ebrahim Akbarali and Gulbanu (Velji) N.; m. Zenobia Sherali Jaffer, June 10, 1978; children: Azra, Afshan. MD, U. Nairobi, Kenya, 1977. Med. biochemist, asst. prof. Vancouver (B.C., Can.) Gen. Hosp. and U. B.C., 1981-84; head clin. biochemistry, assoc. prof. Ottawa (Ont.) Gen. Hosp. and U. Ottawa, 1984-88; chief clin. biochemistry, assoc. prof. Deaconess Hosp./Harvard Med. Sch., Boston, 1988—; cons. Aga Khan U., Karachi, Pakistan, 1986-87; external examiner King Saud U., Riyadh, Saudi Arabia, 1987; cons. Govt. of Can., Ottawa, 1984-88. Contbr. more than 200 articles to profl. jours. Mem. Aga Khan Edn. Bd., 1993—. Recipient Wild-Leitz Rsch. award Can. Assn. Pathologists, 1989, merit award AgaKhan Health Svcs., 1996; rsch. grantee various pvt. founds. and NIH, 1982—. Fellow Royal Coll. Physicians and Surgeons of Can.; mem. Am. Assn. for Study of Liver Disease, Am. Soc. for Investigative Pathology, Rsch. Soc. for Alcoholism, Soc. for Exptl. Biology and Medicine, Royal Coll. Pathologists. Ismaili Muslim. Achievements include patents on novel methods for drug detection and treatment of alcoholic liver disease; evaluation of role of dietary components in alcoholic liver disease. Avocations: hiking, walking, reading, travel. Office: Deaconess Hosp Harvard Med Sch One Deaconess Rd M323 Boston MA 02215

NANNA, ELIZABETH ANN WILL, librarian, educator; b. Rahway, N.J., Nov. 21, 1932; d. Rudolph Julius and Dorothy Ada (Haulenbeck) Will; m. Antonio Carmine Nanna, June 15, 1963. Cert. in bus. with honors, Stuart Sch. Bus. Adminstrn., 1963; AA, Ocean County Coll., 1980; BA with honors, Georgian Ct. Coll., 1984, MA, 1984, postgrad., 1984-85; postgrad., Jersey City State Coll., 1988, Montclair State Coll., 1988-89. Cert. art, early childhood and spl. edn., media specialist, supr., N.J. Entrepreneur Ye Olde Cedar Inn, Toms River, N.J., 1963-78; tchr. art and history Monsignor Donovan High Sch., Toms River, 1980-82; tchr. art Whiting (N.J.) Elem. Sch./Manchester Twp. Sch. Dist., 1983-84, Ridgeway Elem. Sch./ Manchester Twp. Sch. Dist., Manchester, 1985-87; gifted and talented program tchr., coord., 1984-86; tchr. spl. edn. New Egypt (N.J.) Elem. Sch./ Plumsted Twp. Sch. Dist., 1988, libr. media specialist, 1988—. Author: Fostering Cognitive Growth Through Creativity, 1984; contbr. articles to profl. jours. Mem. Mounmouth Park Ball Com., Monmouth County, N.J., 1974—; dir. teen charm sch. Rutgers U. Extension Svc., Ocean County, N.J., 1965; chmn. Ocean County Fair Queen, 1967-84, Ocean County Heart of Hearts Charity Ball, 1976. Recipient Leadership and Svcs. award Ocean County Fair, Ocean County Heart Fund Assn., 1977. Mem. N.J. Reading Assn. (state coun.), N.J. Libr. Assn., N.J. Edn. Assn., Ednl. Media Assn. N.J., Ocean County Artists Guild, Edn. Media Assn. N.J., Georgian Ct. Coll. Alumni Assn. Republican. Roman Catholic. Avocations: international travel, studying arts, cultures, skiing. Home: 15 Mitchell Dr Toms River NJ 08755-5179 Office: Plumsted Twp Sch Dist 44 N Main St New Egypt NJ 08533-1316

NANNA, MICHELE, cardiologist, educator; b. Mola di Bari, Puglia, Italy, Mar. 21, 1953; came to U.S., 1981; naturalized, 1985; s. Giovanni and Maria (Francese) N.; m. Barbara Luise McKnight, Aug. 5, 1981 (div. Feb. 1991); children: Michael Giovanni Jr., Anna Maria; m. Nancy J. Konovalov, Nov. 14, 1991; 1 child Giovanni Jacob Michele. MD summa cum laude, U. Bari, Italy, 1978. Lic. physician, Italy, Calif., N.Y. Intern Ospedale Conzorziale, Bari, 1978-81; clin. clerkship U. Soc. Calif. Med. Ctr., L.A., 1982-83; instr. medicine, fellow in cardiovascular disease U. So. Calif., 1983-86; asst. prof. medicine U. Rochester, N.Y., 1986-88, Albert Einstein Coll. Medicine, Bronx, N.Y., 1988-94; assoc. prof. of med., 1994—; dir. care unit Bronx Mcpl. Hosp. Ctr., 1988-92; dir. lab. Montefiore Med. Ctr., Bronx, N.Y., 1988—; cardiology cons. Monroe Community Hosp., Rochester, 1987-88; mem. coms. Bronx Mcpl. Hosp. Ctr., 1988—, chmn. com., 1990-92. Editor jour. Ultrasound in Medicine and Biology, 1986—; editor-in-chief Jour. Cardiovascular Diagnosis and Procedures, 1993—; contbr. chpts. to books and articles to profl. jours. Grantee NIH, 1987, Whitaker Found., Genetech Inc., Bristol-Myers Squibb, Inc. Mem. AMA, Am. Heart Assn., Am. Coll. Cardiology, N.Y. Athletic Club. Republican. Roman Catholic. Avocations: boating, swimming, jogging. Office: Albert Einstein Coll Med Montefiore Med Ctr 111 E 210th St Bronx NY 10467-2490

NANNE, LOUIS VINCENT, professional hockey team executive; b. Sault Ste. Marie, Ont., Can., June 2, 1941; s. Michael and Evelyn N.; m. Francine Yvette Potvin, Aug. 27, 1962; children: Michelle, Michael, Marc, Marty. B.S. in Mktg., U. Minn., 1963. Mem. Minn. North Stars hockey club, 1967-78, v.p., gen. mgr., 1978-88, pres., 1988-91; sr. v.p. Piper Capital Mgmt., Mpls., 1991—; bd. govs. Nat. Hockey League, 1981-91; mem. internat. com. USA Hockey. Bd. dirs. Mpls. Community Coll. Found., 1986-90. Recipient Lester Patrick award NHL, 1989; inducted into U. Minn. Hall of Fame, U.S. Hockey Heritage Hall of Fame award. Mem. Interlachen Country Club (bd. dirs. 1992—). Roman Catholic. Office: Voyageur Asset Mgmt 90 S 7th St Minneapolis MN 55402

NANNEY, DAVID LEDBETTER, genetics educator; b. Abingdon, Va., Oct. 10, 1925; s. Thomas Grady and Pearl (Ledbetter) N.; m. Jean Kelly, June 15, 1951; children: Douglas Paul, Ruth Elizabeth Beshears. A.B., Okla. Bapt. U., 1946; Ph.D., Ind. U., 1951; Laurea honoris causa, U. Pisa, Italy, 1994. Asst. prof. zoology U. Mich., Ann Arbor, 1951-56; asso. prof. U. Mich., 1956-58; prof. zoology U. Ill., Urbana-Champaign, 1959-76; prof. genetics and devel. U. Ill., 1976-86, prof. ecology, ethology and evolution, 1987-91, prof. emeritus, 1991—; sr. postdoctoral fellow Calif. Inst. Tech., 1958-59; predoctoral fellow NIH, Ind. U., 1949-51. Author: (with Herbert Stern) The Biology of Cells, 1965, Experimental Ciliatology, 1980. Recipient Disting. Alumnus award Okla. Bapt. U., 1972; named Disting. Lectr. Sch. Life Scis., U. Ill., 1981; Preisträger, Alexander von Humboldt Stiftung, Fed. Republic Germany, 1984. Fellow AAAS, Am. Acad. Arts and Scis.; mem. Genetics Soc. Am., Am. Genetic Assn. (pres. 1982), Soc. Protozoologists. Home: 703 W Indiana Ave Urbana IL 61801-4835 Office: U Ill Dept Ecology Ethology and Evolution 505 S Gregory St Urbana IL 61801

NANNEY, SONDRA TUCKER, dance school executive, small business owner; b. Knoxville, Tenn., Dec. 11, 1937; d. Willard Woodrow and Mary Lou (Pollard) Tucker; m. Red Celestine Nanney, March 11, 1960; children: Stacy Leigh Nanney Courtney, Kristin Kaye. Grad. high sch., Knoxville, 1955. Bookkeeper Miles Siegel, CPA, Knoxville, 1955-56; sales sec. Sta. WBIR-TV, Knoxville, 1956-64, Knoxville News Sentinel, 1965-67; owner Concord Farragut Sch., Knoxville, 1974-79, Knoxville Sch. Dance, 1979-95, Images Dancewear, Knoxville, 1989-95; pres. Knoxville Met. Dance, 1982-95. Mem. Knoxville Symphony League (officer 1982-95, pres. 1989-90, chmn. showcase 1993, nominating com. 1992), Knoxville Met. Dance Theatre (pres. 1995). Republican. Avocations: reading, bridge, the arts.

NANTS, BRUCE ARLINGTON, lawyer; b. Orlando, Fla., Oct. 26, 1953; s. Jack Arlington and Louise (Hulme) N. BA, U. Fla., 1974, JD, 1977. Bar: Fla. 1977. Asst. state's atty. State Atty.'s Office, Orlando, 1977-78; pvt. practice, Orlando, 1979—. Columnist The Law and You, 1979-80. Auctioneer pub. TV sta., 1979; campaign coord. cen. Fla. steering com. Bob Dole for Pres., 1988; bd. dirs. Cystic Fibrosis Found. Mem. Acad. Fla. Trial Lawyers, Am. Arbitration Assn., Fellowship Christian Athletes (past bd. dirs. Cen. Fla.), Tiger Bay Club Cen. Fla., Orlando Touchdown Club, Fla. Blue Key, Omicron Delta Kappa, Phi Beta Kappa, Phi Delta Theta. Democrat. Baptist. Avocations: tennis, golf, swimming, scuba diving. Home: 1112 Country Ln Orlando FL 32804-6934 Office: PO Box 547871 Orlando FL 32854-7871

NANZ, ROBERT HAMILTON, petroleum consultant; b. Shelbyville, Ky., Sept. 14, 1923; s. Robert Hamilton and Willie Virginia (O'Brien) N.; m. Norma Lee Peters, Dec. 21, 1944; children—Robert H., Loren P. B.A. in Geology, Miami U., Oxford, Ohio, 1944; Ph.D., U. Chgo., 1952. With Shell Oil Co., 1947-83; exploration mgr. Shell Oil Co., Denver, 1964-66; exploration mgr. Pacific Coast area Shell Oil Co., Los Angeles, 1966-67; dir. exploration research Shell Oil Co., Houston, 1959-64, v.p. exploration and prodn. research center, 1967-70; v.p. exploration Shell Oil Co., N.Y.C., Houston, 1970-75; v.p. Western exploration and prodn. ops. Shell Oil Co., Houston, 1975-81, v.p. tech., 1982-83. Fellow Geol. Soc. Am.; mem. Am. Petroleum Inst. (past chmn. gen. com. exploration affairs, chmn. public lands task force), Am. Assn. Petroleum Geologists (select com. on OCS). Presbyterian. Clubs: Lakeside Country (Houston); Dearborn Country (Ind.). Home: 10102 Briar Dr Houston TX 77042-1209

NAPADENSKY, HYLA SARANE, engineering consultant; b. Chgo., Nov. 12, 1929; d. Morris and Minnie (Litz) Siegel; m. Arnaldo I. Napadensky; children: Lita, Yafa. BS in Math., U. Chgo., MS in Math. Design analysis engineer Internat. Harvester Co., Chgo., 1952-57; dir. rsch. Ill. Inst. Tech. Rsch. Inst., Chgo., 1957-88; v.p. Napadensky Energetics Inc., Evanston, Ill., 1988-94; engring. cons., Lutsen, Minn., 1994—. Contbr. numerous articles to profl. jours. Bd. overseers Armour Coll. Engring. Ill. Inst. Tech., 1988-93. Mem. NAE, Combustion Inst., Sigma Xi. Home and Office: HC 3 Box 458 Lutsen MN 55612-9705

NAPARSTEK, ARTHUR J., social work educator; b. N.Y.C., June 1, 1938; s. Abe and Clara (Meltzer) N.; m. Belleruth Krepon, Sept. 5, 1965; children: Aaron, Keila, Abram. BS, Ill. Wesleyan U., Bloomington, 1960; MSW, NYU, 1962; PhD, Brandeis U., 1972. Sr. health educator USPHS, Chgo., 1962-65; dir. Urban Devel. Inst. Purdue U., Hammond, Ind., 1965-69; dir. rsch. Cath. U., Nat. Ctr. Ethnic Affairs, Washington, 1972-76; dir., prof. Washington Pub. Affairs Ctr. U. So. Calif., Washington, 1976-83; dean, prof. Mandel Sch. Applied Social Sci., Case Western Res. U., Cleve., 1983-88, prof. social work, 1988—; Grace Longwell Coyle prof. Case Western Res. U., Cleve., 1989—; pres. Premier Indsl. Found., Cleve., 1987-89, cons. 1989—. Author: Neighborhood Networks, 1982, Community Support, 1982; author legislation for city govt., 1976-78. Mem. White House Commn. on Neighborhoods, Washington, 1979-80; trustee Corp. for Nat. Svc. Cleve. Found. sr. fellow, 1993-95; sr. assoc. Urban Inst., 1995—. Democrat. Jewish. Office: Case Western Res U Mandel Sch Applied Social Scis Cleveland OH 44106

NAPIER, CAMERON MAYSON FREEMAN, historic preservationist; b. Shanghai, China, Dec. 5, 1931; d. Hamner Garland and Cameron Middleton (Brame) Freeman; m. John Hawkins Napier III, Sept. 11, 1964. Student, L'Ecole des Artes Municipale, Paris, 1950-51; BA, U. Ala., 1955. Photographer's asst. Scott, Demott & Perry, Montgomery, Ala., 1951; art dir. WCOV-TV, Montgomery, 1955; self-employed graphic designer Dallas, 1956-64; self-employed designer Alexandria, Va., 1965-71; restoration chmn. White House Assn. Ala., Montgomery, 1973-76, 1st vice regent, 1976-80, regent, 1980—; co-founder Friends of Stratford Hall for No. Va., Alexandria, late 1960s; docent chmn. Lee's Boyhood Home, Alexandria, late 1960s; bd. dirs. Landmarks Found., Montgomery, 1971-75; advisor Conde Charlotte House, Mobile, Ala., 1994-95. Author, designer booklet: The First White House of the Confederacy, 1978 (nat. printers award 1979). Bd. dirs. English Speaking Union, Montgomery, 1980-83. Recipient awards of excellence Advt. Artists Assn., Dallas, 1960, 61, 62, disting. svc. award Ala. Hist. Commn., Montgomery, 1977, cert. commendation Gov. Ala., 1986; named hon. first lady the Gov.'s wife, Montgomery, 1985. Mem. Nat. Soc. Colonial Dames in Am. (hist. properties com. 1994-95), Antiquarian Soc. (pres. 1981-82), Sojourners Lit. Club (past pres.), United Daus. of the Confederacy (Jefferson Davis award, Winnie Davis award), Am. Soc. Most venerable Order of the Hosp. of St. John of Jerusalem (assoc. officer sister 1995), Sovereign Mil. Order Temple of Jerusalem (aumoniere 1995, dame comdr. 1996), Militi Templi Scotia (dame 1993), Daus. of Barons Runnymede, Nat. Soc. Magna Carta Dames, Soc. descendants of Colonial Clergy, Kappa Delta. Episcopalian. Avocations: crossword puzzles, afternoon tea. Office: First White House Confed 644 Washington Ave Montgomery AL 36130

NAPIER, JOHN, set designer; b. London, England, Mar. 1, 1944; s. James Edward Thomas and Florence (Godbold) N; m. Andreane Neofitou (div.); m. Donna King; children: Julian, Elise, James. Assoc. designer Royal Shakespeare Co., London, England. stage work includes: (with the RSC) Macbeth, The Comedy of Errors, King Lear, Once in a Lifetime, Nicholas Nickleby (Tony award), Hedda Gabler, Peter Pan, Mother Courage, (with the Royal National Theatre) Equus, Trelawny of the Wells, (operas) Lohengrin, Macbeth, Idomeneo, The Devils, (musical theater) Cats (Tony award), Starlight Express (Tony award), Miss Saigon, Les Misérables (Tony award), Sunset Boulevard (Tony award); film work includes: Captain EO, Hook. Office: ML Representaion, 194 Old Brompton Rd, London SW5 0AS, England

NAPIER, JOHN LIGHT, lawyer; b. Blenheim, S.C., May 16, 1947; s. John Light and Miriam (Keys) N.; m. Pamela Ann Caughman, June 12, 1971; 1 child, Page. A.B., Davidson (N.C.) Coll., 1969; J.D., U. S.C., 1972. Bar: S.C. 1972, U.S. Dist. Ct. 1972, U.S. Ct. Appeals 1975, U.S. Tax Ct. 1975, U.S. Supreme Ct. 1978, D.C. 1983, U.S. Ct. Fed. Claims 1987. U.S. senatorial counsel and asst., 1972-78; atty. Goldberg, Cottingham Easterling & Napier, P.A., Bennettsville, S.C., 1978-80, 83-84; mem. 97th Congress 6th Dist. S.C., mem. agr. com., asst. whip, mem. vets. affairs com., 1981-83; ptnr. Napier & Jennings, Bennettsville, S.C., 1984-86; judge U.S. Ct. Fed. Claims, Washington, 1986-89; ptnr. McNair Law Firm, P.A., Washington and Columbia, S.C., 1989-95; of counsel Winston & Strawn, Washington, 1995—; mem. Commn. on Grievance and Discipline, S.C. Supreme Ct., 1984-86; chmn. fee dispute panel 4th Jud. Cir. S.C., 1984-86; nat. adv. coun. U.S. Ct. Fed. Claims, 1989—; pvt. judge The Pvt. Adjudication Ctr., Inc., Duke U., 1992; outside spl. counsel U.S. House Reps. House Adminstrn. Com., 1992. Active local United Way, Boy Scouts Am.; pres. Marlborough Hist. Soc., 1978-80. Served as officer USAR, 1969-77. Recipient Disting. Service award Marlboro County Jaycees, 1980. Mem. ABA, S.C. Bar Assn., Marlboro County Bar Assn., D.C. Bar Assn. Republican. Presbyterian. Office: Winston & Strawn Madison Office Bldg 1400 L St NW Washington DC 20005

NAPIER, RICHARD STEPHEN, electrical engineering manager; b. Clarksburg, W.Va., May 13, 1949; s. Richard Arthur and Lois Jane (Silcott) N.; m. Barbara Elaine Deems, June 13, 1970; 1 child, Stephen Michael. BSEE, W.Va. U., 1971; MSEE, Stanford U., 1973. Tech. staff mem. Bell Telephone Labs., Holmdel, NY, 1972-73; tech. staff mem. Watkins Johnson Co., San Jose, Calif., 1973-77, head synthesizer equipment sect., 1977-85, mgr. radio frequency automatic test equipment, 1985-88, mgr. antenna dept., 1988—. Author: various newspaper and profl. jour. articles, TV editorials. Mem. Sunnyvale (Calif.) City Coun., 1987—, vice mayor, 1990, mayor, 1990-91; voting mem. Pub. Safety Com. League Calif. Cities, Sacramento, 1987-92; active United Way, Santa Clara County, 1986-87, South Bay Discharges Authority, Santa Clara County, 1987—, Intergovtl. Coun. Solid Waste Com., Santa Clara County, 1988—; mem. Transp. Commn., Santa Clara County, 1989-91; mem. congestion mgmt. planning agy., Santa Clara County, 1990—. Western Electric Fund scholar, 1973. Mem. Assn. Old Crows, W.Va. U. Alumni Assn., Stanford U. Alumni Assn., Albemerle Hist. Soc., Sunnyvale Hist. Soc., Calif. Theatre Ctr., Tau Beta Pi. Republican. Methodist. Avocations: bicycling, camping, sailing, computers, geneology. Home: 754 Carlisle Way Sunnyvale CA 94087-3429 Office: Watkins Johnson Co 2525 N 1st St San Jose CA 95131-1003

NAPIER, WILLIAM JAMES, JR., marine oil and gas construction consultant; b. Dallas, July 19, 1952; s. William James and Frankie (Hanchey) N.; m. Christine Ann Douget, June 18, 1977; children: Jay, Stephanie, George, Catherine. BS in Marine Biology, U. So. Miss., 1974; BS in Civil Engring., La. Tech. U., 1976. Project engr., field engr. inland svcs. divsn. McDermott Internat. Inc., Harvey, La., 1976-80; project coord. McDermott Internat. Inc., New Orleans and Houston, 1982-86; sr. project coord./project coord. worldwide bus. devel. McDermott Internat. Inc., New Orleans, 1986-89; project engr. McDermott Nigeria, Ltd., Warri, 1980-82; mgr. marine sales/dir. marine sales, nat. accounts mgr. Bailey Controls Co., New Orleans, 1989-92; pres. COO Balehi Marine, Inc., Lacombe, La., 1992-94; pres., owner Fairwinds Internat. Inc. (formerly IVX of La.), Mandeville, La., 1994—. Elder Lakeview Christian Ctr., New Orleans, 1985-92. Mem. Soc. Naval Architects and Marine Engrs., Franco's Athletic Club. Republican. Presbyterian. Avocations: weight lifting, racquetball, bicycling. Home and Office: Fairwinds Internat Inc 913 Beau Chene Dr Mandeville LA 70471-1505

NAPIERSKI, EUGENE EDWARD, lawyer; b. Albany, N.Y., Jan. 9, 1944; s. Eugene J. and Elizabeth (Doran) N.; children: Christine, Eugene, Michelle, Daniel. BA, Siena Coll., 1965; JD, Union U., 1968. Bar: N.Y. 1968, U.S. Dist. Ct. (ed. dist.) N.Y. 1968, U.S. Supreme Ct. 1975. Atty. Forsyth, Howe & O'Dwyer, Rochester, N.Y., 1968-69; staff atty. Rsch. Found. SUNY, Albany, N.Y., 1969-70; assoc. Carter & Conboy, Albany, 1970-76; ptnr. Carter, Conboy, Case, Blackmore, Napierski & Maloney, Albany, 1976—. Mem. Am. Bd. Trial Advocates (mem. sect. upstate N.Y.), N.Y. State Bar Assn., Capitol Dist. Trial Lawyers Assn. (v.p., dir.), Ft. Orange Club, Wolferts Roost Country Club. Avocations: reading, golf, travel. Home: 7 Woodridge St Albany NY 12203 Office: Carter Conboy Case Blackmore Napierski & Maloney PC 20 Corporate Woods Blvd Albany NY 12211-2350

NAPLES, CAESAR JOSEPH, public policy educator, lawyer, consultant; b. Buffalo, Sept. 4, 1938; s. Caesar M. and Fannie A. (Occhipinti) N.; children: Jennifer, Caesar; m. Sandra L. Harrison, July 16, 1983. AB, Yale U., 1960; JD, SUNY, 1963. Bar: N.Y. 1963, Fla. 1977, Calif. 1988, U.S. Supreme Ct. 1965. Assoc. Moot & Sprague, Buffalo, 1965-69; asst. dir., employee rels. N.Y. Gov. Office, Albany, 1969-71; asst. v. chancellor SUNY, Albany, 1971-75; vice chancellor and gen. counsel Fla. State U. System, 1983-92; v. chancellor Calif. State U. System, Long Beach, 1983-92; vice chancellor emeritus Calif. State U., 1992—; prof. law and fin. Calif. State U. System, Long Beach, 1983—; gen. counsel Walden U., Mpls. and Naples, Fla., 1993—; cons. Govt. of Australia, U. Nev. Sys., Assn. Can. Colls. and Univs., Que., also other univs. and colls. Contbr. articles to profl. jours.; co-author: Romanov Succession, 1989 with J.Victor Baldridge. Mem. Metlife Resources Adv. Bd., 1986—, chmn., 1992—; mem. heart bd. Long Beach Meml. Hosp., 1993—; bd. dirs. Calif. Acad. Math. and Scis., 1995—. Capt. U.S. Army, 1963-65. Mem. Acad Pers. Adminstrn. (founder), Nat. Ctr. for Study Collective Bargaining Higher Edn. (bd. dirs.). Avocations: opera, tennis. Office: 816 N Juanita Ave Ste B Redondo Beach CA 90277-2200

NAPLES, RONALD JAMES, manufacturing company executive; b. Passaic, N.J., Sept. 10, 1945; s. James V. and Lee A. N.; B.S., U.S. Mil. Acad., 1967; M.A., Fletcher Sch. Law and Diplomacy, 1972; M.B.A. with distinction (Walter Heller fellow), Harvard U., 1974; m. Suzanne Lorraine Shoudy, June 17, 1967; children—Regen Jeffrey, Marcus Jamison, Tiffany Marie. Assoc. in corp. fin. Loeb Rhoades Co., 1974; White House fellow, asst. to counselor to Pres., 1974-75; exec. dir. Presdl. Task Force on Energy, Washington, 1975-76; v.p. internat. Hunt Mfg. Co., Phila., 1976, exec. v.p., 1980-81, vice chmn., pres., chief exec. officer, 1981-86, chmn., chief exec. officer, 1987—, also dir.; pres. Hunt Internat. Co., 1977-82. Mem. regional commn. Pres.'s Com. on White House Fellows, 1980—, Fletcher Sch. Law and Diplomacy Adv. Bd., 1982—; chmn.; vice chmn. Greater Phila. 1st Corp., Free Libr. of Phila. Fedn.; bd. dirs. Univ. of the Arts, Pa.-Milw. Ballet, Free Library Phila., Fgn. Policy Research Inst., Childrens Hosp., Phila., Phila. Mus. of Art, Eisenhower Exchange fellowships. Served with U.S. Army, 1967-71. Decorated Bronze Star with oak leaf cluster, Army Commendation medal with oak leaf cluster, Air medal (U.S.); Cross of Gallantry (Vietnam); recipient Mil. Order World Wars award U.S. Mil. Acad., 1967, Phila. Inc. Community Leadership award, 1990; named Outstanding Young Man Am., U.S. Jaycees, 1977, Chief Exec. Officer of decade bus. equipment, 1989-90. Mem. White House Fellows Assn., Young Pres.'s Orgn., Assn. Grad. U.S. Mil. Acad., Harvard Bus. Sch. Alumni Assn. Club: Racquet, Harvard Bus. Sch. (Phila.). Office: Quaker Chemco Elm & Lee Sts Conshohocken PA 19428*

NAPODANO, RUDOLPH JOSEPH, internist, medical educator; b. Rochester, N.Y., Oct. 16, 1933. B.A., U. Buffalo, 1955; M.D., SUNY-HSC, Syracuse, 1959. Diplomate Am. Bd. Internal Medicine, Am. Bd. Cardiovascular Diseases. Intern, asst. resident Highland Hosp., Rochester, 1959-61; fellow in cardiology SUNY-Upstate, Syracuse, 1961-62; chief resident in medicine Highland Hosp., 1962-63; spl. trainee in cardiology U. Rochester, 1968, clin. asst. prof. medicine, 1969-70, asst. prof. medicine, 1970-72, assoc. prof., 1972-79, prof., 1979-93, prof. emeritus, 1993—; with U. Rochester Sch. Medicine and Dentistry, 1970-93; retired 1993; prof. medicine SUNY, Syracuse, N.Y., 1994—. Fellow ACP, Am. Coll. Cardiology; mem. AAAS, Soc. Gen. Internal Medicine, Rochester Acad. Medicine (trustee 1976—, pres. 1980-81), Alpha Omega Alpha.

NAPOLES, VERONICA KLEEMAN, graphic designer, consultant; b. N.Y.C., July 9, 1951; d. Florencio Andres and Elena (Colomar) N.; m. Michael Jeffrey Kleeman, May 5, 1985; 1 child, Samuel Andres. BA, U. Miami, 1972; BArch, U. Calif., Berkeley, 1979. Account supr. Marsh & McLennan, Miami, Fla., 1974-76; designer Mus. of Anthropology, San Francisco, 1977-79; project dir. Landor & Assocs., San Francisco, 1979-81; prin. Communications Planning, Kentfield, Calif., 1981—; bd. dirs. Mind Fitness, Mill Valley, Calif., Main Arts Coun., Mykytyn Cons. Group; instr. U. Calif.-Berkeley, San Francisco, 1983—, Sonoma State U., Santa Rosa, Calif., 1983-84; tchr. Dynamic Graphics Ednl. Found., San Francisco. Author: Corporate Identity Design, 1987; exhibited at San Francisco Airport, 1992. Bd. dirs. Marin Arts Coun. Recipient Bay Area Hispanic Bus. Achiever award, 1988, Design award PRINT, 1988, Excellence award Am. Corp. Identity, 1989, 90, 91, 92, 93, 94, 95, Excellence award N.Y. Art Dirs. Show, 1989; finalist Sundance Inst., 1991. Mem. Am. Inst. Graphic Arts, Women in Communications. Avocations: painting, writing. Office: Napoles Design 189 Madrone Ave Larkspur CA 94939

NAPOLIELLO, MICHAEL JOHN, psychiatrist; b. Feb. 14, 1942; s. Frank J. and Anne M. (Palazzo) N. BS, Fordham U., 1962; MD, NYU, 1966; MBA, Xavier U. Grad. Sch. of Bus., 1980. Diplomate Am. Bd. Psychiatry and Neurology. Attending psychiatrist Bernalillo County Med. Ctr., Albuquerque, 1973-74; dir. behavioral medicine U. N.Mex. Sch. of Medicine,

Albuquerque, 1973-74; attending psychiatrist Mary Hitchcock Meml. Hosp., Hanover, N.H., 1974-76; assoc. group dir. Merrell Nat. Labs., Cin., 1976-79; assoc. group dir. clin. pharm. Merrell-Nat. Labs., Cin., 1979-84; dir. clin. investigation Merrell-Dow Research Inst., Cin., 1979-84; sci. dir. Bristol-Myers Internat. Group, N.Y.C., 1984-85, dir. med. & sci. affairs, 1986, v.p. med. & sci. affairs, 1986-90; v.p., cen. nervous system clin. planning Bristol-Myers Squibb, Princeton, N.J., 1990-91; sr. dir. clin. rsch. and prodn. devel. Bristol-Myers Squibb, Tokyo, Japan, 1991-93; exec. dir. internat. clin. devel. Bristol-Myers Squibb, Tokyo, 1993-94, exec. dir. worldwide med. affairs, 1994—; clin. asst. prof. psychiatry Cornell U. Med. Coll., N.Y.C., 1985—; asst. clin. prof. U. Cin. Coll. Medicine, 1976-80, assoc. prof., 1980-84; lectr. in field. Contbr. 30 articles to profl. med. jours. Maj. U.S. Army, 1970-73. Recipient Physicians Recognition award AMA, 1969, 72, 76, 79, 82, 85, 88, 91, 94. Mem. Am. Psychiat. Assn., Am. Coll. Neuropsychopharmacology. Roman Catholic. Avocations: foreign languages, creative writing, basketball. Home: 27 Richard Ct Princeton NJ 08540-3802 Office: Bristol-Myers Squibb PO Box 4000 Princeton NJ 08543-4000

NAPOLITANO, GRACE F., state legislator; b. Brownsville, Tex., Dec. 4, 1936; d. Miguel and Maria Alicia Ledezma Flores; m. Frank Napolitano, 1982; 1 child, Yolando M., Fred Musquiz Jr., Edward M., Michael M., Cynthia M. Student, Cerritos Coll., L.A. Trade Tech, Tec Southwest Coll. Mem. Calif. Assembly, 1993—. Councilwoman City of Norwalk, Calif., 1986-92, mayor, 1989-90; active Cmty. Family Guidance. Mem. Cerritos Coll. Found., Lions Club. Democrat. Roman Catholic. Home: 12946 Belcher St Norwalk CA 90650-3328 Office: Calif Assembly State Capitol Sacramento CA 95814-4906 also: PO Box 942849 Sacramento CA 94249-0001*

NAPOLITANO, LEONARD MICHAEL, anatomist, university administrator; b. Oakland, Calif., Jan. 8, 1930; s. Filippo Michael and Angela (De Fiore) N.; m. Jane M. Winer, July 9, 1955; children—Leonard M., Janet Ann, Nancy Angela. B.S., Santa Clara U., 1951; M.S., St. Louis U., 1954, Ph.D., 1956. Instr. anatomy Cornell Med. Coll., N.Y.C., 1956-58; instr. U. Pitts. Sch. Med., 1958-59, asst. prof., 1959-64; asso. prof. U. N.Mex., 1964-68; prof. dept. anatomy U. N.Mex. (Sch. Medicine), 1968—, acting chmn. dept., 1971-72, dean pro tem, 1972-73, dean, 1973—, interim v.p. for health scis., 1976—; dir. U. N.Mex. (Med. Center); dean U. N.Mex. (Sch. Medicine), 1977—; Mem. NIH Rsch. Resource Coun., 1988-91, ret. cons., 1994. Contbr. articles on lipid research and ultra structure of cholesterol to profl. jours.; Asso. editor: Anatomical Record, 1968-74. Mem. Am. Assn. Anatomists, Am. Soc. Cell Biology, Electron Microscope Soc. Am., Albuquerque, Bernalillo county Med. Assn. (hon.), Assn. Am. Med. Colls. Council of Deans. Home: 2308 Calle De Panza NW Albuquerque NM 87104-3070 Office: Dean Sch of Medicine U of N Mex Health Sci Center Albuquerque NM 87131

NAQUIN, PATRICIA ELIZABETH, employee assistance consultant; b. Houston, Jan. 28, 1943; d. Louie Dee and Etha Beatrice (English) Price; m. Hollis James Naquin, Mar. 23, 1961; children: Price Naquin, Holli Campbell. BS, U. Houston, 1969, MS, 1982; PhD, Tex. Woman's U., 1988. Lic. profl. counselor; lic. chem. dependency counselor; nat. cert. counselor; cert. chem. dependency specialist; cert. employee assistance profl. Purchasing agt. Internat. Affairs U. Houston, 1966-68; elem. sch. tchr. Pasadena (Tex.) Ind. Sch. Dist., 1969-82; spl. edn. counselor Alvin (Tex.) Ind. Sch. Dist., 1982-85, drug-free schs. coord., 1988-92; marriage and family therapist Lifespan Counseling, Pasadena, 1985-92; employee assistance cons. DuPont, LaPorte, Tex., 1992—; adv. com. mem. Sam Houston U., Huntsville, Tex., 1983; trainer and instr. Bay Area Coun. on Drugs and Alcohol, Houston, 1988-92; cons. Alvin Ind. Sch. Dist., 1989-92, DuPont Valuing People Core Team, 1993—; supr. State Bd. of Profl. Counselors, Houston, 1988—. Co-author: Life is for Everyone Manual, 1990. Com. co-chair Alvin S.A.P. Task Force, 1988-92; com. mem. Tri-Dist. Task Force, Alvin, 1990-91; com. chmn. Alvin Bus./Edn. Partnership, 1992; bd. dirs. Brazoria (Tex.) County Coun. Drugs and Alcohol, 1991. Mem. Am. Assn. Marriage and Family Therapists, Tex. Assn. Counselors of Alcohol and Drug Abuse, Am. Counseling Assn., Employee Assistance Program Assn., Nat. Disting. Svc. Registry/Libr. of Congress, Phi Delta Kappa. Republican. Methodist. Avocations: quilting, playing piano, playing with grandchildren, computer games.

NAQVI, SHEHLA HASNAIN, pediatric infectious disease specialist, pediatrician; b. Karachi, Pakistan, July 21, 1950; came to U.S., 1974; d. Syed Zulfiqar and Akhtar Fatima (Khwaja) Hasnain; m. Nazar H. Naqvi, Dec. 15, 1973 (div. Jan. 1986); children: Erum, Yusuf. MB, BS, U. Karachi, 1973. Diplomate Am. Bd. Pediatrics, Am. Bd. Pediat. Infectious Disease. Asst. prof. pediat. St. Louis U., 1980-86; assoc. prof. pediat. Aga Khan U., Karachi, 1986-90; assoc. prof., acting dir. pediat. infectious diseases St. Louis U., 1990-92; physican-in-charge pediat. infectious diseases Brookdale Hosp. Med. Ctr., Bklyn., 1992—; assoc. prof. SUNY, Bklyn., 1992—; cons. N.Y. Bur. TB Control, N.Y.C., 1994—. Mem. editl. bd. Jour. Islamic Med. Assn., 1994—. Mem. Am. Soc. for Microbiology. Islam. Avocation: poetry. Home: 52 Hickory Ln Roslyn NY 11577 Office: Brookdale Univ Hosp Med Ctr 1 Brookdale Plz Brooklyn NY 11212

NARA, LOUISA AUGUSTA, engineering executive; b. Charleston, W.Va., Oct. 21, 1958; d. Raymond F. and Regina L. (Cunningham) Nolte; m. Geoffrey Bruce Nara, Apr. 17, 1982. BS in Chem. Engring., W.Va. U., 1981; postgrad., U. Houston, 1983-85; MS in Water Resources & Environ. Engr., Villanova (Pa.) U., 1989. Engr.-in-tng., Pa., 1992. Process engr. I and II Diamond Shamrock Chem. Co., Deer Park, Tex., 1981-85; process design engr. The PQ Corp., Valley Forge, Pa., 1985-89; sr. chem. engr. SMC Environ. Svcs. Group, Valley Forge, 1989-90, mgr. indsl. svcs., 1990-91; engring. mgr. chem. process safety Baker Environ., Inc., Coraopolis, Pa., 1991-95; prin. LakeRidge Tech. Group Inc., Cranberry Twp., Pa., 1995—. Sponsor Jr. Achievement, Houston, 1984. Mem. AIChE, Internat. Inst. Ammonia Refrigeration (mem. codes and standards com. 1994). Roman Catholic. Avocations: volleyball, music, hiking, raquetball, landscaping. Home: 540 Callery Rd Cranberry Township PA 16066 Office: LakeRidge Tech Group Inc 540 Callery Rd Cranberry Township PA 16066

NARAHASHI, TOSHIO, pharmacology educator; b. Fukuoka, Japan, Jan. 30, 1927; came to U.S., 1961; s. Asahachi and Itoko (Yamasaki) Ishii; m. Kyoko Narahashi, Apr. 21, 1956; children: Keiko, Taro. BS, U. Tokyo, 1948, PhD, 1960. Instr. U. Tokyo, 1951-65; research assoc. U. Chgo., 1961, asst. prof., 1962; asst. prof. Duke U., Durham, N.C., 1962-63, 65-67, assoc. prof., 1967-69, prof., 1969-77, head pharmacology div., 1970-73, vice chmn. dept. physiology and pharmacology, 1973-75; prof., chmn. dept. pharmacology Northwestern U. Med. Sch., Chgo., 1977-94; Alfred Newton Richards prof. Med. Sch. Northwestern U., Chgo., Ill., 1983—; John Evans prof. Northwestern U., Evanston, Ill., 1986—; mem. pharmacology study sect. NIH, 1976-80; mem. rsch. rev. com. Chgo. Heart Assn., 1977-82, vice chmn. rsch. coun., 1986-87, chmn., 1988-90; mem. Nat. Environ. Health Scis. Coun., 1982-86; rev. com. Nat. Inst. Environ. Health Scis., 1991-95. Editor: Cellular Pharmacology of Insecticides and Pheromones, 1979, Cellular and Molecular Neurotoxicology, 1984, Insecticide Action: From Molecule to Organism, 1989, Ion Channels, 1988—; specific field editor Jour. Pharmacology and Exptl. Therapeutics, 1972—; assoc. editor Neurotoxicology, 1994—; contbr. articles to profl. jours. Recipient Javits Neurosci. Investigator award NIH, 1986. Fellow AAAS; mem. Am. Soc. for Pharmacology and Exptl. Therapeutics, Am. Physiol. Soc., Soc. for Neurosci., Biophys. Soc. (Cole award 1981), Soc. Toxicology (DuBois award 1988, Merit award 1991), Agrochem. Div. Am. Chem. Soc. (Burdick L. Jackson Internat. award 1989). Home: 175 E Delaware Pl Apt 7911 Chicago IL 60611-1727 Office: Northwestern U Med Sch Dept Mol Pharmaco Biol Chem 303 E Chicago Ave Chicago IL 60611-3008

NARASIMHAN, PADMA MANDYAM, physician; b. Bangalore, India, Mar. 19, 1947; came to U.S., 1976; d. Alasingracher Mandyam and Alamela Mandyam Narasimhan; m. Mandyam N. Venkatesh, Mar. 28, 1981 (div.) 1 child, Ravi. Student, Delhi U., New Delhi, 1964, MBBS, 1969; MD, Maulana Azad Med. Coll., New Delhi, 1970. Diplomate Am. Bd. Internal Medicine. Intern in internal medicine Flushing Hosp., N.Y.C., 1976-77; resident in internal medicine Luth. Med. Ctr., N.Y.C., 1977-79; fellow hematology, oncology Beth-Israel Med. Ctr., N.Y.C., 1979-81; asst. prof. King Drew Med. Ctr., L.A., 1983-87, Harbor UCLA, Torrance, 1987—. Mem. editorial bd. Jour. Internal Medicine, 1986—. Mem. ACP, Am. Soc. Clin. Oncology, So. Calif. Acad. Clin. Oncology. Hindu. Avocations: travel, reading, meeting people, music, walking. Home: 6604 Madeline Cove Dr Palos Verdes Peninsula CA 90275-4608 Office: Harbor UCLA 100 W Carson St Torrance CA 90509

NARATH, ALBERT, laboratory administrator; b. Berlin, Mar. 5, 1933; came to U.S., 1947; s. Albert Narath and Johanna Agnes Anne (Bruggeman) Bruckmann; m. Worth Haines Scattergood (div. 1976); children: Tanya, Lise, Yvette; m. Barbara Dean Camp (div. 1983); 1 child, Albert; m. Shanna S. Lindeman. BS in Chemistry, U. Cin., 1955; PhD in Phys. Chemistry, U. Calif., Berkeley, 1959. Mem. tech. staff, mgr. phys. sci. Sandia Nat. Labs., Albuquerque, 1959-68, dir. solid state sci., 1968-71, mng. dir. phys. sci., 1971-73, v.p. rsch., 1973-82, exec. v.p. rsch. and adv. weapons sys., 1982-84, pres., 1989-95; pres. energy and environ. sect. Lockheed Martin Corp., Albuquerque, 1995—. Contbr. sci. articles to profl. jours. Fellow AAAS, Am. Phys. Soc. (George E. Pake prize 1991); mem. NAE. Office: Lockheed Martin Corp 1155 University Blvd SE Albuquerque NM 87106

NARAYAN, BEVERLY ELAINE, lawyer; b. Berkeley, Calif., June 19, 1961; d. Jagjiwan and Alexandra (Mataras) N.; m. James Dean Schmidt, Jan. 7, 1989; children: Sasha Karan, Kaiya Maria. Student, San Francisco State U., 1979-80; BA, U. Calif., Berkeley, 1983; JD, U. Calif., San Francisco, 1987. Bar: Calif. 1987, U.S. Dist. Ct. (no. dist.) Calif. 1987, U.S. Dist. Ct. (ctrl. dist.) 1988. Atty. Daniels Barratta & Fine, L.A., 1988-89, Kornblum Ferry & Frye, L.A., 1990-91, Clapp Moroney Bellagamba Davis & Vucinich, Menlo Park, Calif., 1991-93, pvt. practice, Burlingame, Calif., 1993—; arbitrator Nat. Assn. Securities Dealers, San Francisco, 1987—, Pacific Stock Exch., San Francisco, 1994—; mediator Peninsula Conflict Resolution Ctr., San Mateo, Calif., 1995—; judge pro tem San Mateo Superior Ct., Redwood City, Calif., 1994—. Candidate Sch. Bd. San Mateo (Calif.) Unified Sch. Dist., 1993. Recipient U. Calif. Hastings Coll. Law Achievement award, 1986. Mem. ABA, San Mateo County Bar Assn. (co-chair women lawyers 1995, bd. dirs. 1994-96), Nat. Women's Polit. Caucus (bd. dirs., diversity chair 1993—), San Mateo County Barristers Club (bd. dirs. 1993—, child watch chair 1995—). Avocations: baking, cooking, reading, travel, motorcycles, family. Office: 1508 Howard Ave Burlingame CA 94010

NARAYAN, K(RISHNAMURTHI) ANANTH, biochemist; b. Secunderabad, India, Oct. 1, 1930; came to U.S., 1954, naturalized, 1970; s. Ananthnarayan and Rukmani (Sreenivasan) Krishnamurthi; m. Suhasini Naik, Sept. 3, 1961; children—Krishnamuthi, Sheila. B.S. in Chemistry, Christian Coll., India, 1949; M.S. in Chem.Tech., Osmania U., India, 1951; Ph.D. in Food Tech., U. Ill., 1957. Research assoc. Wash. State U., Pullman, 1957-61; asst. prof. U. Ill., Urbana, 1962-71; research biochemist U.S. Army Natick Research and Devel. Ctr., Mass., 1971—. Contbr. chpts. to books. Grantee NIH, 1966-70, Am. Cancer Soc., 1968-70, Am. Heart Assn., 1967-71. Mem. Am. Oil Chemists Soc., Am. Inst. Nutrition, N.Y. Acad. Scis., Inst. Food Tech. Hindu. Avocations: photography; woodworking; jogging. Home: 84 Indian Head Rd Framingham MA 01701-7920 Office: US Army R and D Ctr SusD/RSD/AFB Natick MA 01760-5018

NARAYAN, RAMESH, astronomy educator; b. Bombay, India, Sept. 25, 1950; came to U.S., 1983; s. G.N. and Rajalakshmi (Sankaran) Ramachandran; m. G.V. Vani, June 6, 1977. BS in Physics, Madras U., 1971; MS in Physics, Bangalore U., 1973, PhD in Physics, 1979. Rsch. scientist Raman Rsch. Inst., Bangalore, India, 1978-83; postdoctoral fellow Calif. Inst. Tech., 1983-84, sr. rsch. fellow, 1984-85; assoc. prof. U. Ariz., Tucson, 1985-90, prof. astronomy, 1990-91; prof. astronomy Harvard U., Cambridge, Mass., 1991—. Contbr. articles to profl. jours. Named NSF Presdl. Young Investigator, 1989. Mem. AAAS, Am. Astronomical Soc., Internat. Astronomical Union, Astronomical Soc. India. Achievements include research in the general area of theoretical astrophysics, specializing in accretion disks, collapsed stars, gravitational lenses, hydrodynamics, image processing and scintillation. Office: Harvard-Smithsonian Ctr Astrophysics 60 Garden St # 51 Cambridge MA 02138-1516

NARAYANAMURTI, VENKATESH, research administrator; b. Bangalore, Karnataka, India, Sept. 9, 1939; came to U.S., 1961; s. Duraiswami and Janaki (Subramaniam) N.; m. Jayalakshmi Krishnayya, Aug. 23, 1961; children: Arjun, Ranjini, Krishna. BSc, MSc, St. Stephen's Coll., Delhi, India, 1958; PhD, Cornell U., 1965. Instr., rsch. assoc. Cornell U., Ithaca, N.Y., 1965-68; mem. tech. staff AT&T Bell Labs., Murray Hill, N.J., 1968-76, dept.head, 1976-81, dir., 1981-87; v.p. rsch. Sandia Nat. Labs., Albuquerque, 1987-92; dean engring. U. Calif., Santa Barbara, 1992—; chmn. microelectric bd. Jet Propulsion Lab., Pasadena, Calif., 1988—; chair Dept. of Energy Inertial Confinement Fusion Adv. Com., 1992—, NSF Engring. Directorate Adv. Bd., 1992—; mem. NAE Pub. Info. Adv. Bd., 1993—, NSF Dir.'s Strategic Planning Bd., 1994—, Los Alamos Nat. Lab. Adv. Bd. for Materials and Indsl. Partnerships, 1994—. Author more than 120 publs.; patentee in field. Fellow IEEE, AAAS, Am. Phys. Soc., Indian Acad. Scis.; mem. NAE, Royal Swedish Acad. Engring. Scis. (fgn.). Avocations: long distance running, squash. Office: U Calif Dept Engring Santa Barbara CA 93106

NARDELLI-OLKOWSKA, KRYSTYNA MARIA, ophthalmologist, educator; b. Myslowice, Poland, June 23, 1939; d. Walerian and Stefania (Jasinska) Nardelli; m. Zbigniew L. Olkowski, Apr. 15, 1963. M.D., Silesian U. Med. Sch., 1964. Diplomate: Am. Bd. Ophthalmology; 1983. Intern, resident ophthalmology Emory U. Med. Sch., Atlanta, 1977-80; fellow in glaucoma Emory U. Med. Sch., 1980-81; asst. prof. dept. ophthalmology Emory U. Med. Sch., Atlanta, 1972—; pvt. practice ophthalmology, 1982—. Postdoctoral fellow Fight for Sight, 1974-75. Mem. Am. Soc. Research in Ophthalmology, Royal Micros. Soc. (Eng.). Home: Villa Sadyba 1018 Mcconnell Dr Decatur GA 30033-3402 Office: Bldg 4 724 Holcomb Bridge Rd Norcross GA 30071-1325 Office: Bldg 4 724 Holcomb Bridge Rd Norcross GA 30071-1325

NARDINI, RITA LYNN, mental health nurse; b. Chgo., Nov. 21, 1947; d. Arthur and Julia Rae (Edbrooke) N. ADN, Southwestern Mich. Coll., 1985; student, Mennonite Bibl. Sem., 1987, U. Indpls., 1994—. RN, Ind., Mich.; cert. BLS Am. Heart Assn., crisis prevention intervener, Ind. Staff nurse Michiana Community Hosp., South Bend, Ind., 1985-86; charge nurse psychiat. unit St. Jopseph's Hosp., Mishawaka, Ind., 1986-87, Elkhart (Ind.) Gen. Hosp., 1987-88, Oaklawn Hosp., Goshen, Ind., 1988-90; evening supr., charge nurse adolescent psychiat. unit Charter Hosp., Indpls., 1990-92; weekend charge nurse geriatric psychiat. unit Lockerbie Healthcare, Indpls., 1992—; charge nurse child and adolescent psychiatry Midwest Med. Ctr. (Winona Hosp.), Indpls., 1992-93; child/adolescent psychiat. nurse Koala Hosp., Indpls., 1994—; nurse cons. Growth Innovations, Inc., Berrien Springs, Mich., 1988-89. Mem. ANA (cert. psychiat. nurse), Nat. League Nursing (cert. addictions nurse), Am. Psychiat. Nurses' Assn., Amnesty Internat. Republican. Episcopalian. Avocations: art, foreign languages, travel. Office: Koala Hosp 1404 S State Ave Indianapolis IN 46203-2009

NARDINO, GARY, television and motion picture producer; b. Garfield, N.J., Aug. 26, 1935; s. Louis and Phyllis (Iacovino) N.; m. Florence Peluso, May 1, 1965; children: Caroline, Gary Charles Frank, Teresa. B.S.B.A., Seton Hall U., 1957, LL.D. (hon.), 1983. Agt. William Morris Agy., Ashley Famous Agy., 1959-76; pres. TV prodn. div. Paramount Pictures Corp., Hollywood, Calif., 1977-83; pres. Gary Nardino Prodns., L.A., 1983-89; chmn., chief exec. officer Orion TV Entertainment, L.A., 1989-91, Lorimar TV, Gary Nardino Prodn., Burbank, Calif., 1991—, Warner Bros., 1993—; now exec. prod. Warner Bros. Television. Exec. producer film Star Trek III; producer film Fire with Fire: producer TV series Brothers (Showtime Cable), Hard Knocks (Showtime Cable), Marblehead Manor (1st run synd.), Time Trax (1st run synd. 2nd yr.). Served to 1st lt. inf. U.S. Army, 1957-59. Named Man of Yr., WAIF, Inc., 1983, TV Showman of Yr., Publicist Guild of Am., 1985; recipient Sword of Truth award for Winds of War B'naie B'rith, 1982. Mem. Acad. TV Arts and Scis., Hollywood Radio and TV Soc. (pres. 1981-83), Caucus of Producers, Writers & Dirs., WAIF (nat. chmn.), Alpha Kappa Psi. Roman Catholic. Clubs: N.Y. Athletic; Burning Tree Country (Greenwich, Conn.); Bel Air Country (Los Angeles). Office: Warner Bros TV Producers Bldg 8 #109 300 Television Plz Burbank CA 91505

NARDI RIDDLE, CLARINE, association administrator, judge; b. Clinton, Ind., Apr. 23, 1949; d. Frank Jr. and Alice (Mattioda) Nardi; m. Mark Alan Riddle, Aug. 15, 1971; children: Carl Nardi, Julia Nardi. AB, Ind. U., 1971, JD, 1974; LHD (hon.), St. Joseph Coll., 1991. Bar: Ind. 1974, Conn. 1979, U.S. Dist. Ct. Ind. 1974, Fed. Dist. Ct. Conn. 1980, U.S. Ct. Appeals (2d cir.) 1986, U.S. Ct. Appeals (D.C. cir.) 1994, U.S. Supreme Ct. 1980. Staff atty. Ind. Legis. Svc. Agy., Indpls., 1974-78, legal counsel, 1978-79; dep. corp. counsel City of New Haven, 1980-83; counsel to atty. gen. State of Conn., Hartford, 1983-86, dep. atty. gen., 1986-89, acting atty. gen., 1989, atty. gen., 1989-91; judge Superior Ct. State of Conn., 1991-93; sr. v.p. for govtl. affairs, gen. counsel Nat. Multi-Housing Coun., Nat. Apartment Assn., 1995—; asst. counsel state majority Conn. Gen. Assembly, Hartford, 1979, legal rsch. asst. to prof. Yale U., New Haven, 1979; legal counsel com. on law revision Indpls. State Bar Assn., 1979; mem. Chief Justice's Task Force on Gender Bias, Hartford, 1988-90; mem. ethics and values com. Ind. Sector, Washington, 1988-90. Bd. visitors Ind. U., Bloomington, 1974-92; mem. Gov.'s Missing Children Com., Hartford, Conn. Child Support Guidelines Com., Gov.'s Task Force on Justice for Abused Children, Hartford, 1988-90. Named Conn. History Maker Women's Bur. & Permanent Commn. on Status of Women, U.S. Dept. Labor, 1989; recipient Citizen award Nat. Task Force on Children's Constl. Rights. Mem. ABA, Conn. Bar Assn. (chair com. on gender bias, Citation of Merit women and law sect. 1989), Nat. assn. Attys. Gen. (chair charitable trusts and solicitation 1988-90), New Haven Neighborhood Music Sch. (bd. dirs.), Am. Arbitration Assn. (arbitration panel 1994). Democrat. Presbyterian.

NARDONI, ENRIQUE, priest, theology educator; b. Rosario, Argentina, Nov. 15, 1924; came to U.S., 1974; s. Francisco and Enriqueta (Piermarini) N. MA in Theology, Cath. U., Buenos Aires, 1948; MA in Bibl. Studies, Pontifical Biblicas Inst., Rome, 1953, PhD in Bibl. Studies, 1975. Ordained priest Roman Cath. Ch., 1948. Tchr. theology Major Sem., Rosario, 1954-70, dean studies, 1958-70; tchr. anthropology State U., Rosario, 1960-70; tchr. Bibl. interpretation St. Thomas Sem., Seattle, 1974-77, St. Mary's Sem., Balt., 1977-78; tchr. Bibl. interpretation U. Dallas, Irving, Tex., 1978—, prof., 1980—, chmn. theology, 1985-90. Author: El Hijo del Hombre, 1961, La Transfiguracion, 1977; (art) Catholic Biblical Quarterly, 1993, New Testament Studies, 1991, Theologicas Studies, 1992, Revista Biblica, 1994-96. Recipient Scholarships Argentinian Govt., Rome, 1949-52, Adveniat, German Inst., Rome, 1971-74; resident fellow Ctr. for Study Religion in Greek-Roman World, 1983-94. Mem. Cath. Bibl. Assn., Soc. Bibl. Lit. Roman Catholic. Avocation: photography. Office: U Dallas 1845 E Northgate Dr Irving TX 75062-4799

NARDULLI, PETER F., political science educator; b. Chgo., May 20, 1947; s. Peter F. and Catherine Rose N.; m. Ann Marie Wannemacher, Oct. 24, 1943. BA, No. Ill. U., 1969; MA, Northwestern U., 1972, JD, 1973, PhD, 1975. Asst. prof. Inst. Pub. Affairs and Dept. Political Sci. U. Ill., Urbana, 1975-80, assoc. prof. Inst. Pub. Affairs and Dept. Political Sci., 1980-85, vis. prof. Coll. of Law, 1985-86, acting dir. Inst. Govt. and Pub. Affairs, 1985-86, prof. Inst. Govt. Pub. Affairs and Dept. Political Sci., 1985—, dir. grad. studies Dept. Political Sci., 1987-91, dept. head and prof. Dept. Political Sci., 1992—. Co-author: (books) The Contours of Justice: Communities and Their Courts, 1987, The Tenor of Justice: Felony Courts & The Guilty Plea Process, 1988, The Constitution and American Political Development: An Institutional Perspective, 1991, The Craft of Justice, 1992. Office: U Ill-Dept Political Sci 361 Lincoln Hall 702 S Wright St Urbana IL 61801

NARENDRA, KUMPATI SUBRAHMANYA, electrical engineering educator, association administrator; b. Madras, India, Apr. 14, 1933; came to U.S., 1954, naturalized, 1974; s. Subrahmanya and Sarada (Alladi) Kumpati; m. Barbara Lamb, Nov. 3, 1961. BEE with honors, U. Madras, 1954; MS, Harvard U., 1955, PhD, 1959; MA (hon.), Yale U., 1968; DSc (hon.), Anna U., Madras, India, 1995. Lectr., postdoctoral asst. Harvard U., Cambridge, Mass., 1959-61, asst. prof., 1961-65; assoc. prof. Yale U., New Haven, Conn., 1965-68, prof. elec. engring., 1968—, chmn. dept. elec. engring., 1984-87, dir. Neuroengring. and Neurosci. Ctr., 1995—; cons. to comml. firms, 1961—; dir. Ctr. for Systems Sci., 1981—; disting. vis. sci. Jet Propulsion Lab., 1994—; honorary vis. prof. Anna Univ., Madras, India, 1993; mem. adv. bd. Inst. Advanced Engring, Korea; mem. sci. adv. bd. Ctr. for Engring. Sys. Advanced Rsch. Oakridge Nation Lab. Author: Frequency Domain Criteria For Absolute Stability, 1973, Stable Adaptive Systems, 1989, Learning Automata: An Introduction, 1989; editor: Applications of Adaptive Control, 1980, Adaptive and Learning Systems: Theory and Applications, 1987, Advances in Adaptive Control, 1991; editor issue on learning automata Jour. Cybernetics and Info. Sci., vol. I, 1977. Recipient Edn. award Am. Automatic Control Coun., 1990, Leadership award Neural Network Soc., 1994, Hendrik W. Bode Prize/Lectr. award Control Sys. Soc., 1995. Fellow AAAS, Inst. Elec. Engrs. (U.K.), IEEE (Franklin V. Taylor award 1973, George S. Axelby award, 1988, Outstanding Paper of neural network coun. 1991); mem. Conn. Acad. Sci. and Engring., Sigma Xi. Home: 35 Old Mill Rd Woodbridge CT 06525-1523 Office: Yale U Ctr Systems Sci PO Box 2157 New Haven CT 06520-2157

NARIN, STEPHEN B., lawyer; b. Phila., Nov. 23, 1929; s. Bernard E. and Anne (Lipsius) N.; m. Sandra C. Goldberg, Sept. 29, 1963; children: Howard Glen, Brenda Teri. B.S., Temple U., 1951, LL.B., 1953; LL.M. in Taxation, NYU, 1960. Bar: Pa. 1954, U.S. Supreme Ct. 1958; CPA, Pa. Dep. atty. gen. Commonwealth of Pa., Harrisburg, 1955-57; instr. acctg. Temple U., Phila., 1954-55; lectr. in law grad. legal studies div. Temple U. Sch. Law, Phila., 1976-85; lectr. Practicing Law Inst., 1967-69; ptnr. Narin & Chait, Phila., 1970-89, Predecessor Ptnrships., Phila., 1955-70; v.p., gen. counsel Travelco Assocs., Phila., 1989-90; of counsel Krekstein, Wolfson & Krekstein, Phila., 1989-92; v.p., gen. counsel Eagle Nat. Bank, 1990-91; counsel Schachtel, Gerstley, Levine & Koplin, Phila., 1993—; mem. Phila. County Bd. Law Examiners, 1961-65. Mem. nat. governing council Am. Jewish Congress, 1963-84, nat. exec. com., 1978-84, pres. Greater Phila. council, 1965-67; mem. Nat. Commn. on Law and Social Action, 1964-84. Mem. ABA, Am. Judicature Soc., Am. Inst. CPA's, Pa. Inst. CPA's, Pa. Bar Assn., Phila. Bar Assn., Phi Alpha Delta. Office: Schachtel Gerstley et al 4 Penn Center Plz Philadelphia PA 19103-2514

NARITA, HIRO, cinematographer; b. Seoul, Republic of Korea, June 26, 1941; came to Japan, 1945, came to U.S., 1957; s. Masao Morikawa and Masako (Kojima) Morikawa; m. Barbara Parker, Sept. 9, 1971. BFA in Design, San Francisco Art Inst., 1964. lectr. Mill Valley Film Festival, 1984, Hawaii Internat. Film Festival, 1984. Dir. photography for films: Farewell to Manzanar, 1976 (Emmy nomination 1976), Never Cry Wolf, 1983 (Best Cinematography award 1983), Solomon Northrup's Odyssey, 1984, Go Tell It on the Mountain, 1985, Amerika, 1987, Honey, I Shrunk the Kids, 1989, The Rocketeer, 1991, Star Trek VI, 1992, Hocus Pocus, 1993, White Fang II, 1994, James & The Giant Peach, 1995, The Arrival, 1995. Served with U.S Army, 1964-66. Mem. Internat. Photographers Guild, Am. Soc. Cinematographers, Acad. Motion Picture Arts and Scis.

NARITA, YUTAKA, advertising executive; b. Japan, Sept. 19, 1929; s. Kiyoomi and Some Narita; m. Michi Narita; children: Chiaki, Akira. BA in Law, U. Tokyo, 1953. Exec. dir. Dentsu Inc., Tokyo, 1981-83, mng. dir., 1983-89, sr. mng. dir., 1989-93, pres., 1993—. Office: Dentsu Inc, 1-11 Tsukiji Chuo-ku, Tokyo 104, Japan

NARKIS, ROBERT JOSEPH, bank executive, lawyer; b. Nashua, N.H., May 23, 1934; s. Joseph John and Stephanie (Kamieneki) N.; m. Mary Ellen Gardner Morris, Oct. 26, 1962 (div. 1974); 1 child Sally Gardner; m. JoAnn Georgetson, Feb. 1975. BA cum laude, U. N.H., 1956; LLB, Yale U., 1961. Sr. ptnr. Gager, Henry and Narkis, Waterbury, Conn., 1961-89; chmn., chief exec. officer Centerbank, Waterbury, Conn., 1989—. Pres., chmn. exec. com. Waterbury Hosp., Conn., 1973-75; bd. dirs. Conn. Bar Assn., Hartford, 1985; trustee Mattatuck Hist. Soc., Waterbury, 1975-78, Waterbury Found., 1984-89, Post Coll., 1984-90, Quinnipiac Coll., Hamden, 1992—. Mem. ABA, Conn. Bar Assn., Supreme Ct. USA Bar, Yale Law Sch. Assn. (exec. com. 1989—), Metropolitan Club, Waterbury Country Club. Avocations: antique collecting, golf, foreign travel, sailing. Home: PO Box 385 625 Charcoal Ave Middlebury CT 06762-0385 Office: Centerbank 60 N Main St Waterbury CT 06702-1403

NARMONT, JOHN STEPHEN, lawyer; b. Auburn, Ill., June 24, 1942; s. Stephen and Luriel (Welle) N.; m. Sondra J. Nicholls, Feb. 12, 1978. BBA magna cum laude, U. Notre Dame, 1964; JD, U Ill., Champaign, 1967. Bar: Ill. 1967, U.S. Tax Ct. 1978, U.S. Supreme Ct. 1973, U.S. Dist. Ct. (so. dist.) Ill., U.S. Ct. Appeals (7th cir.). Prt. practice law Springfield, Ill.; owner Richland Stables, Auburn; originator, pres. The Solid Gold Futurity, Ltd. Mem. ABA, Sangamon County Bar Assn., Ill. State Bar Assn., Assn. Trial Lawyer Am., Am. Agrl. Law Assn., Ill. Inst. for Continuing Legal Edn. Office: 209 N Bruns Ln Springfield IL 62702-4612

NARSAVAGE, GEORGIA ROBERTS, nursing educator, researcher; b. Pittston, Pa., Jan. 1, 1948; d. George H. Roberts and Betty (Smith) Lanphear; m. Peter P. Narsavage, Oct. 26, 1969; children: Peter A., Paul J., Marea L. BSN, U. Md., Washington DC, 1969; MSN, Coll. Misericordia, 1984; PhD in Nursing, U. Pa., Phila., 1990. RN, Pa.; cert. CPR instr. Staff nurse Mercy Hosp., Scranton, Pa., 1970-72; pvt. duty nursing Pa., 1972-79; pvt. duty nurse Community Med. Ctr., Scranton, Pa., 1979; clinical instr. Lackawanna County Vo-Tech Practical Nursing Program, Dunmore, Pa., 1979-82; clinical and theoretical instr. Mercy Hosp. Sch. of Nursing, Scranton, Pa., 1982-84; asst. prof. nursing Dept. of Nursing, U. Scranton, Pa., 1984-93; assoc. prof. U. Scranton, Pa., 1993—, chmn. dept., 1991-94; dir. RN program Dept. of Nursing U. Scranton, Pa., 1990-92; postdoctoral fellow U. Pa., Phila., 1995-96; cons. in field. Contbr. articles to profl. jours. Gifted program mentor Scranton Sch. Dist.; active in ch. and civic choirs. U. Scranton grantee, 1989, 91, 94, 95; Ea. Nursing Rsch. Soc. Am. Nurses Found. rsch. grantee, 1994, NIH NRSA grantee, 1995-96. Mem. ANA, APHA, Am. Thoracic Soc./Am. Lung Assn., Pa. Nurses Assn. (bd. dirs., chmn. com., conv. del.), Lackawanna Nurses Assn. (bd. dirs., com. chmn., dist. pres.), Nat. League for Nursing, Coun. Nursing Informatics (chair nominating com. 1993-95), Pa. League for Nursing (chair nominating com.), U. Md. Nurses Alumnae Assn., Cmty. Health Nurse Educators Assn., Ea. Nursing Rsch. Soc. (mem.-at-large bd. dirs.). Lutheran. Office: U Scranton O'Hara Hall 118 Scranton PA 18510-4595

NARVER, JOHN COLIN, business administration educator; b. Portland, Oreg., Aug. 5, 1935; s. Ursel Colin and Merle (Wells) N.; children: Gregory, Allison Ann, Colin. B.S., Oreg. State U., 1957; M.B.A., U. Calif.-Berkeley, 1960; Ph.D., 1965. With Boise Cascade Corp., Portland, 1960-61; asst. prof. U. B.C., Can., 1964-66; asst. prof. dept. mktg. and internat. bus. U. Wash., Seattle, 1966-68; assoc. prof. U. Wash., 1968-71, prof., 1971—, chmn. dept., 1974-78; vis. prof. Norwegian Sch. Econs., 1973, Bogazici U., Istanbul, Turkey, 1974, U. Helsinki, 1995; cons. in field. Author: Conglomerate Mergers and Market Competition, 1967, (with R. Savitt) The Marketing Economy: An Analytical Approach, 1971, (with S. Slater) The Effect of a Market Orientation on Business Profitability, 1990. Served to lt. U.S. Army, 1957-59. Mem. Am. Mktg. Assn., AAUP, Phi Delta Theta. Democrat. Episcopalian. Home: 2015 Federal Ave E Seattle WA 98102-4141 Office: U Wash Sch Bus Adminstrn Seattle WA 98195

NARWOLD, LEWIS LAMMERS, paper products manufacturer; b. Cleve., Sept. 4, 1921; s. Lewis Lammers and Dorothy Marie (Andrus) N.; m. Marilyn Ebner, Oct. 26, 1944; 1 dau., Christine. BBA, Western Res. U., 1942; MBA, Harvard, 1947. Salesman Hoerner Boxes, Inc., 1950-54, gen. sales mgr., 1954-57, v.p., gen. mgr., 1957-62; v.p. So. div. Hoerner Waldorf Corp., St. Paul, 1962-70; sr. v.p., container div. Hoerner Waldorf Corp., 1970-72; CEO, founder, pres. SouthWest Packaging Inc., Tulsa, 1972—; dir. UNCA Bankshares, Utica Nat. Bank & Trust, Thermo Chem. Corp., Sooner Box Corp., Hoerner Boxes, Inc., So. Mo. Container Corp.; organizer 1st Bank & Trust Co. of Okla. Chmn. United Fund of Sand Springs, Okla.; pres., trustee Tulsa Charity Horse Show.; Trustee Children's Med. Center of Tulsa, Tulsa Psychiat. Clinic, U. of the Ozarks. Capt. USMC, 1943-45. Decorated Purple Hearts; recipient Presdl. Citation. Mem. Sand Springs C. of C. (dir.), Tulsa C. of C. (dir.), N.A.M., Tulsa Mfg. Club, Mason Club, Summit Club (dir.), So. Hills Country Club, Union League Club (Chgo.), Coves Golf Club. Home: 7116 S College Ave Tulsa OK 74136-5601 Office: 6106 W 68th St Tulsa OK 74131-2429

NARY, JOHN HENRY, interior designer; b. Rochester, N.Y., Oct. 14, 1948; s. Robert John and Edna Gertrude (Gessner) N.; A.A., Erie County Community Coll., 1974; m. Jacqueline Marie Steiger, Jan. 13, 1970. Staff artist, regional mgr. The Birge Co., Buffalo, 1969-71; v.p. Heinzelman Interiors, Inc., Buffalo, 1971-72; dir. design McMullen Dental, Buffalo, 1972-80; v.p. design and sales William H. Prentice, Inc., Buffalo, 1980-91; pres. Corning (N.Y.) Office Interiors, Inc., 1991—; guest lectr. Sch. Dentistry SUNY, Buffalo. Bd. dirs. S.E. Steuben County Habitat for Humanity, 1993-94, v.p., 1995; mem. Community Services Pilot Program, 1982. Cert., Nat. Council Interior Design Qualification. Mem. Am. Soc. Interior Designers (past pres. N.Y. Upstate/Can. East chpt., bd. dirs., nat. ethics com. 1987, 88, assessment task force 1990, nominating com. 1994), Corning Country Club, Corning Rotary Club. Author: Dental Office Design, 1974. Home: 109 W Hill Ter Painted Post NY 14870-1001 Office: 19 Denison Pky Ste 100 Corning NY 14830

NASAR, SYED ABU, electrical engineering educator; b. Gorakhpur, Uttar Pradesh, India, Dec. 25, 1932; came to U.S., 1956; s. Syed M. and Syeda (Begum) Y.; m. Sara Samad, Sept. 3, 1961; children—Naheed, Sajida. BSc, Agra U., 1951; BSEE, Dacca U., 1955; MSEE, Tex. A&M U., 1957; PhD, U. Calif., Berkeley, 1963. Chartered elec. engr., U.K. Assoc. prof. U. Ky., Lexington, 1968-70, prof. elec. engring., 1970—, Univ. Rsch. prof., 1989—, chmn., 1980-87, dir. grad. studies, 1980-87; visitor Brit. Council, London, 1964. Author or co-author 30 books on elec. engring., 1970-93; editor Elec. Machines and Power Systems Jour., 1976—; contbr. articles to profl. jours. Recipient Aurel Vlaicu award Romanian Nat. Acad., 1978; NSF rsch. grantee, 1966-87, 92—. Fellow IEEE (life), Instn. Elec. Engrs. London. Office: U Ky 453 Anderson Hall Lexington KY 40506

NASGAARD, ROALD, museum curator; b. Denmark, Oct. 14, 1941; s. Jens Larsen and Petra (Guldbaek) N.; m. Susan Ursula Watterson, Sept. 8, 1967 (divorced). B.A., U. B.C., 1965, M.A., 1967; Ph.D., Inst. Fine Arts, N.Y. U., 1973. Lectr., asst. prof. U. Guelph, 1971-75; curator contemporary art Art Gallery of Ont., Toronto, 1975-78, chief curator, 1978-89, deputy dir., chief curator, 1989-93, sr. curator rsch., 1993; chair dept. art Fla. State U., Tallahassee, 1995—; co-dir. programming Inst. of Modern and Contemporary Art, Calgary, Alta., Can.; vis. lectr. U. Guelph, York U., U. Toronto; adj. prof. U. Toronto. Author: Ron Martin: World Paintings, 1976, Structures for Behavior, 1977, Garry Neill Kennedy: Recent Work, 1978, Ten Canadian Artists in the 1970's, 1980, Yves Gaucher: A Fifteen Year Perspective, 1978, The Mystic North: Symbolist Landscape Painting in Northern Europe and North America, 1890-1940, 1984, Gerhard Richter: Paintings, 1988, Individualites: 14 Contemporary Artists from France, 1991, Free Worlds: Metaphors and Realities in Contemporary Hungarian Art, 1991, Free Worlds: Metaphors and Realities in Contemporary Hungarian Art, 1991; co-organizer The European Iceberg: Creativity in Germany and Italy Today, 1985. Mem. Toronto Pub. Art Commn., Gershon Iskowitz Found. Can. Council fellow, 1967-68, 70-71. Mem. Coll. Art Assn., Univ. Art Assn. Can., Internat. Art Critics Assn.

NASH, BOB J. (BOB NASH), under-secretary agriculture rural and small development; b. Texarkana, Ark., 1947. ABA Sociology, U. Ark., 1969; MA Urban Studies, Howard U., 1972. Asst. to dep. mayor Washington, 1970-71; asst. to city mgr. Fairfax, Va., 1971-72; adminstrv. officer Nat. Tng. and Devel. Svc., Washington, 1972-74; dir. community and regional affairs Ark. Dept. Planning, 1974-75; v.p. Winthrop Rockefeller Found., Little Rock, 1975-83; sr. exec. asst. econ. devel. Office Ark. gov., 1983-89; pres. Ark. Devel. Fin. Authority, Little Rock, 1989-92; assoc. dir. personnel White House; dep. dir. personnel Clinton Adminstrn. Transition; under sec. agriculture small community and rural devel. with USDA, Rural Devel. Adminstrn., Farmers Home Adminstrn., Alternative Rsch. & Commercialization Ctr., Rural Electrification Adminstrn., Washington, 1993-1995. Office: Dept of Agriculture Small Cmty & Rural Devel 14th & Independence Ave SW Washington DC 20250 Office: The White House Office Presidential Personnel Old Executive Office Bldg Washington DC 20503*

NASH, BRADLEY DELAMATER, transportation executive; b. Boston, Apr. 7, 1900; s. Edward R. and Allie (DeLamater) N.; m. Ruth B. Cowan, June 30, 1956 (dec. 1993); m. Virginia Josie Ingram, Aug. 3, 1995. A.B. cum laude, Harvard, 1923, postgrad., 1924; LHD (hon.), Shepherd Coll., Shepherdstown, W.Va. Banker N.Y.C., 1929-32, 35-40, Washington, 1949-51; sec. to Herbert Hoover, 1927-29; financial adviser RFC, 1932-35, WPB, 1941-42; cons. Pres.'s Adv. Com. Govt. Orgn., 1953; dep. asst. sec. Dept. of Air Force, 1953-56; dep. under sec. transp. Dept. Commerce, 1957-61; cons. U.S. Weather Bur., 1961-63; historian, cons. Nat. Park Svc., Dept. Interior, 1963-64; mayor of Harper's Ferry, W.Va., 1971-77, 81-86; mem. W.Va. R.R. Maintenance Authority, 1977—. Author: Investment Banking in England, 1924, A Hook in Leviathan, 1950, Staffing the Presidency, 1952, (with Milton S. Eisenhower et al) Organizing and Staffing the Presidency, 1980. Bd. advs. Nat. Trust for Historic Preservation; trustee Center for Study Presidency, 1975-84, Storer Coll., Alderson Broaddus Coll. Lt. col. AUS, 1942-45, MTO and Italian campaigns. Decorated Bronze Star, Commendation medal War Dept. Mem. Harvard Club (N.Y.C.), Metropolitan Club (Washington), Nat. Press Club (Washington), Chevy Chase Club (Md.). Address: High Acres Farm RR 3 Box 122 Harpers Ferry WV 25425-9728

NASH, CHARLES PRESLEY, chemistry educator; b. Sacramento, Calif., Mar. 15, 1932; s. Clarence and Mildred Vida (Johnson) N.; m. Lois Olive Brown, May 29, 1955; children: Nancy Caroline, Sandra Lee, James Roy. BS, U. Calif., Berkeley, 1952; PhD, UCLA, 1958. Instr. chemistry UCLA, 1956-57; from instr. to assoc. prof. U. Calif., Davis, 1957-70, prof., 1970-93; prof. emeritus, 1993—; chmn. acad. senate U. Calif., Davis, 1987-90, chmn. faculty assn., 1993-96; vis. sr. lectr. Imperial Coll., London, 1968-69; disting. vis. prof. USAF Acad., Colorado Springs, 1979-80. Contbr. numerous articles to profl. jours. Bd. pres. Explorit Sci. Ctr., 1995—. Recipient Disting. Teaching award U. Calif. Davis, 1978. Mem. Am. Chem. Soc., Sigma Xi, Phi Lambda Upsilon. Office: U Calif at Davis Dept Chemistry Davis CA 95616

NASH, CYNTHIA JEANNE, journalist; b. Detroit, Dec. 24, 1947; d. Frederick Copp and Carolyn (Coffin) N.; 1 child, Lydia Anne Maza; m. Richard Zahler, July 22, 1994. BA, U. Mich., 1969. Reporter, Detroit News, 1970-75, sports columnist, 1975-77, Life Style columnist, 1977-79, Life Style editor, 1979-82; news features editor Seattle Times, 1983, asst. mng. editor Sunday Seattle Times, 1983-86, assoc. mng. editor, 1986—. Mem. Harbor Sq. Club. Office: Seattle Times PO Box 70 Fairview Ave N & John St Seattle WA 98111-0070

NASH, DONALD GENE, commodities specialist; b. Paris, Ill., July 20, 1945; s. Lelan and Mildred (Washburn) N.; m. Jo Ann Bellew, Aug. 29, 1964; children—Stacey Alan, Ryan Christopher, Shaun Christian. B.S., So. Ill. U., 1967, M.S., 1969; postgrad., DePaul U., 1970-71. Farm mgr., test farms So. Ill. U., Carbondale, 1968-69; economist Commodity Futures Trading Commn., Chgo., 1969-77; v.p.-ops. Mid. Am. Commodity Exchange, Chgo., 1977-86, Div. Enforcement, Commodity Futures Trading Commn., Chgo., 1986—. With Ill. Army N.G., 1968-74. Recipient Outstanding Mktg. award Wall St. Jour., 1966, award of merit Am. Farm Econ. Assn., 1967, cert. of merit Commodity Exch. Authority, merit award Naperville Art League, 1994, Honorable Mention award Danada Nature Show, 1995. Methodist. Avocations: photography; woodworking; sketching. Home: 923 Bainbridge Dr Naperville IL 60563-2002 Office: Commodity Futures Trading Commn 300 S Riverside Plz Ste 1600N Chicago IL 60606-6615

NASH, EDWARD L., advertising agency executive; b. N.Y.C., Nov. 8, 1936; s. Irving and Mina (Koppel) N.; m. Diana R. Kithcart, June 2, 1968; 1 child, Amelia. B.A., CCNY, 1953. Dir. advt. Crowell, Collier, Macmillan, Inc., N.Y.C., 1961-62; v.p. mktg. LaSalle Extension U., Chgo., 1962-64; pres. Capitol Record Club, Inc., Los Angeles, 1964-69; founder, pres. Nash Pub., Los Angeles, 1969-74; exec. v.p. Rapp & Collins, N.Y.C., 1975-82; pres., chief exec. officer BBDO Direct, N.Y.C., 1982-86; owner, pres. Nash Direct Inc., N.Y.C., 1986-91; chmn. Nash, Wakeman & de Forrest, Inc., 1991-92; exec. v.p. Bozell, Jacobs, Kenyon & Eckhardt, N.Y.C., 1992-95; CEO, mng. ptnr. Team Nash, Inc., N.Y.C., 1996—; lectr. in field; chmn. Direct Mktg. Day, N.Y.C., 1985, Internat. Direct Mktg. Conf., 1996. Author: Direct Marketing: Strategy/Planning/Execution, 1982, 2d edit., 1986, 3d edit., 1995; editor: The Direct Marketing Handbook, 1984, 2d edit., 1991, Database Marketing, 1993. Mem. Direct Mktg. Assn. (chmn. mktg. coun. 1980-82). Home: Team Nash Inc 162 Fifth Ave New York NY 10010

NASH, E(DWARD) THOMAS, physicist; b. N.Y.C., July 31, 1943; s. Edward Thomas and Lili Maria (Schvarcz) N.; m. Jessie Madeleine Berry, June 9, 1970. AB, Princeton U., 1965; MA, Columbia U., 1967, PhD, 1970. Rsch. assoc. Nevis Labs., Columbia U., Irvington, N.Y., 1970, MIT, Cambridge, 1970-72; assoc. scientist, then scientist Fermi Nat. Accelerator Lab., Batavia, Ill., 1972—, dep. chmn. dept. physics, 1979-83, head advanced computer program, 1983-89, head computing div., 1989-93; assoc. dir. for tech., info. planning Fermi Nat. Accelerator Lab., 1994—; mem. rsch. briefing panel on computer architectures NAS, 1984, assoc. dir. scientific tech. and lab. info.; chmn. organizing com. Symposium on Recent Devels. in Computing, Processor and Software Rsch. for High-Energy Physics, Guanajuato, Mex., 1984; mem. internat. adv. com. Computing in High Energy Physics Conf., Asilomar, Calif., 1987, Oxford, Eng., 1989, Santa Fe, 1990, Tsukuba City, Japan, 1991, Annecy, France, 1992, Rio de Janeiro, 1995, sci. adv. com. Conf. on Impact Digital Microelectronics and Microprocessors on Particle Physics, Trieste, Italy, 1988; mem. computing/networking rev. panel Ill. Tech. Challenge Grant Program, State of Ill., 1990; sci. and tech. adv. com. Office Non-Proliferation and Nat. Security U.S. Dept. Energy; rschr. in field. Specialist editor Computer Physics Communications, 1986-93; editorial cons. Ency. Applied Physics, 1988—; contbr. numerous articles, revs. to profl. jours. Carnegie Sci. fellow Ctr. for Internat. Security and Arms Control, Stanford U., 1988-89. Fellow Am. Phys. Soc.; mem. Sigma Xi. Office: Fermi Nat Accelerator Lab PO Box 500 Batavia IL 60510-0500

NASH, FRANK ERWIN, lawyer; b. Pendleton, Oreg., Feb. 27, 1916; s. Frank Lee and Gertrude (Walbridge) N.; m. Elizabeth Ann Kibbe, Apr. 20, 1943; children: Thomas K., Robert L., Carl F., Frances L. B.S., U. Oreg., 1937, J.D., 1939. Bar: Oreg. 1939. Since practiced in Portland; with firm Miller, Nash, Wiener, Hager & Carlsen (and predecessors), 1939-91, ptnr., 1948-91, ret., 1991. Bd. dirs. Tri-County United Good Neighbors, 1961-66, pres., 1963-64; pres. U. Oreg. Found., 1979-81; bd. dirs. Med. Research Found., pres., 1980-81; bd. dirs. Library Assn. Portland, pres., 1978-81; bd. visitors U. Oreg. Law Sch. Served to lt. col., inf. AUS, 1941-46, PTO. Recipient Pioneer award U. Oreg., 1980, Meritorious Svc. award., 1992. Fellow Am. Bar Found.; mem. ABA, Multnomah Bar Assn. (pres. 1964-65), Oreg. State Bar, Order of Coif, Phi Delta Phi, Phi Delta Theta. Republican. Methodist (past chmn. ofcl. bd.). Clubs: Arlington (Portland) (dir. 1963-65), Multnomah Amateur Athletic (Portland) (dir. 1963-65, pres. 1965-66), Waverley (Portland) (pres. 1979-80). Home: 1885 NW Ramsey Dr Portland OR 97229-4240 Office: 111 SW 5th Ave Fl 35 Portland OR 97204-3604

NASH, GARY BARING, historian, educator; b. Phila., July 27, 1933; s. Ralph C. and Edith (Baring) N.; m. Mary Workum, Dec. 20, 1955 (div.); children—Brooke, Robin, Jennifer, David; m. Cynthia Shelton, Oct. 24, 1981. B.A., Princeton U., 1955, Ph.D., 1964. Asst. to dean Grad. Sch., Princeton (N.J.) U., 1959-61, instr., 1964-65, asst. prof. history, 1965-66; asst. prof. history UCLA, 1966-68, assoc. prof., 1969-72, prof., 1972—, dean undergrad. curriculum devel., 1984-91; assoc. dir. Nat. Ctr. for History in the Schs., 1988-94, dir. 1994—; co-chair Nat. Hist. Stds. Project, 1992-95. Author: Quakers and Politics: Pennsylvania, 1681-1726, 1968, rev. edit., 1993, Class and Society in Early America, 1970, The Great Fear: Race in the Mind of America, 1970, Red, White, and Black: The Peoples of Early America, 1974, 2d edit., 1982, 3d edit., 1991, The Urban Crucible, 1979, Struggle and Survival in Colonial America, 1981, Race, Class and Politics: Essays on American Colonial and Revolutionary Society, 1986, (with others) The American People: Creating a Nation and a Society, 1986, 3d edit., 1994, Forging Freedom: The Formation of Philadelphia's Black Community, 1720-1840, 1988, Race and Revolution, 1990, (with Jean R. Soderlund) Freedom by Degrees: Emancipation and Its Aftermath in Pennsylvania, 1991, American Odyssey: The United States in the 20th Century, 1991, rev. edit., 1993; mem. editorial bd. William and Mary Quar., 1974-77, Jour. of Black Studies, 1971-73, Am. Indian Culture and Rsch. Jour., 1978—, Am. Quar., 1980-84, Pa. Mag. History and Biography, 1987—, Social History/Histoire Sociale, 1990—. Served with USN, 1955-58. Guggenheim fellow, 1969-70, Am. Council Learned Socs. fellow, 1973-74. Mem. Am. Hist. Assn., Inst. Early Am. History and Culture, Orgn. Am. Historians (exec. com. 1988-91, pres. 1994-95), Soc. Am. Historians, Am. Antiquarian Soc. Home: 16174 Alcima Ave Pacific Palisades CA 90272-2408

NASH, GERALD DAVID, historian; b. Berlin, July 16, 1928; came to U.S., 1938, naturalized, 1944; s. Alfred and Alice (Kantorowicz) N.; m. Marie L. Norris, Aug. 19, 1967; 1 dau., Stephanie Ann. B.A., NYU, 1950; M.A., Columbia U., 1952; Ph.D., U. Calif., Berkeley, 1957. Instr. history Stanford U., 1957-58, vis. asst. prof., 1959-60; asst. prof. No. Ill. U., DeKalb, 1958-59; postdoctoral fellow Harvard U., 1960-61; mem. faculty U. N.Mex., Albuquerque, 1961—; prof. history U. N.Mex., 1968—, chmn. dept., 1974-80, Presdl. prof., 1985-90, Disting. prof., 1990—; faculty rsch. lectr., 1970; vis. assoc. prof. NYU, 1965-66; George Bancroft prof. Am. History U. Goettingen, Fed. Republic Germany, 1990-91. Author: State Government and Economic Development, 1964, U.S. Oil Policy, 1968, Perspectives on Administration, 1969, The Great Transition, 1971, American West in 20th Century, 1973, Great Depression and World War II, 1979, The American West Transformed: The Impact of World War II, 1985, World War II and the West: Reshaping the Economy, 1990; editor: Issues in American Economic History, 3d edit., 1980, F.D. Roosevelt, 1967, Urban West, 1979 (with Noel Pugach and Richard Tomasson) Social Security in the U.S.-The First Half Century, 1988, (with Richard Etulain) Perspectives on the 20th Century West, 1989, Creating the West: Historical Interpretations, 1991, A.P. Giannini and the Bank of America, 1992, The Crucial Era, 1992; editor: (with Richard Etulain) Research Opportunities in 20th Century Western History, 1996; editor The Historian, 1974-84. Fellow Newberry Library, 1959, Huntington Library, 1979; sr. fellow NEH, 1981; Project 87 fellow, 1982-83. Mem. Am. Hist. Assn., Orgn. Am. Historians, Bus. History Soc., Agrl. History Soc., Western History Assn., Phi Beta Kappa. Club: Commonwealth. Office: U NMex Dept History Albuquerque NM 87131 *Anyone reflecting on major trends in the 20th century must conclude that the greatest challenge is to preserve freedom and democratic processes in the effort to achieve greater economic and social equality in America.*

NASH, GRAHAM WILLIAM, singer, composer; b. Blackpool, Lancashire, Eng., 1942. Mem.: Brit. group The Hollies, 1963-68; joined David Crosby and Stephen Stills to form group Brit. group, Crosby, Stills & Nash, 1969, then with Neil Young, to 1971, now soloist and duo (with David Crosby), then regrouped (with Stephen Stills), 1977; (with Hollies) albums include Bus Stop, 1966, Stop, Stop, Stop, 1967, Hollies' Greatest Hits, 1967, Evolution, 1967, Dear Eloise/King Midas in Reverse, 1967, (with Crosby and Stills) Crosby, Stills & Nash, 1969, CSN, 1977, (with Crosby, Stills and Young) Deja Vu, 1970, 4 Way Street, 1971, (with Crosby) Graham Nash and David Crosby, 1972, Wind on the Water, 1975, Whistling Down the Wire, 1976, Crosby/Nash Live, 1977, After The Storm, 1994; solo albums Songs for Beginners, 1971, Wild Tales, 1974, Earth & Sky, Innocent Eyes, 1986; appeared in film Woodstock, 1970. Recipient Grammy award (with Crosby and Stills) for Best New Artist of Year, 1969. Office: Atlantic Records 75 Rockefeller Plz New York NY 10019-6908

NASH, HENRY WARREN, marketing educator; b. Tampa, Fla., Sept. 19, 1927; s. Leslie Dikeman and Mildred (Johnson) N.; m. Frances Lora Venters, Aug. 20, 1950; children: Warren Leslie, Richard Dale. B.S. in Bus. Adminstrn, U. Fla., 1950, M.B.A., 1951; postgrad., Ind. U., 1951-53; Ph.D., U. Ala., 1965. Student asst. U. Fla., 1948-50, grad. asst., 1950-51; grad. asst. Ind. U., 1951-53; salesman Field Enterprises, Inc., Chgo., 1953; assoc. prof. bus. and econs. Miss. Coll., 1953-57; assoc. prof. marketing Miss. State U., 1957-66, prof., head dept., 1966—; ptnr. Southland Cons. Assos., 1968-84; bd. dirs. Govt. Employees Credit Union, 1969-92, v.p., 1969-73, pres., 1973-78. Author: (with others) Principles of Marketing, 1961. Served with USNR, 1945-46. Loveman's Merchandising fellow U. Ala., 1961-62. Mem. Am. Mktg. Assn., Am. Acad. Advt., Acad. Internat. Bus., So. Econ. Assn., So. Mktg. Assn. (sec. 1974-75, pres. 1976-77), Sales and Mktg. Execs. (internat. chmn. educators com. 1967-70), Miss. Retail Mchts. Assn. (bd. dirs.), Pi Sigma Epsilon (Nat. educator, v.p. 1967-69, nat. pres. 1967-71), Kiwanis (treas. Starkville club 1969-70, v.p. 1973-74, pres. 1974-75, lt. gov. 1977-78, gov. 1982-83), Blue Key, Beta Gamma Sigma, Omicron Delta Kappa, Mu Kappa Tau (nat. v.p. 1977-79, 86-88, pres. 1979-81, 88-90), Alpha Kappa Psi, Phi Kappa Phi (v.p. Miss. State U. 1990-91, pres. 1991-92). Baptist (tchr., deacon). Home: 114 Forest Hill Dr Starkville MS 39759-3127 Office: Miss State U Dept Mktg Mississippi State MS 39762

NASH, HOWARD ALLEN, biochemist, researcher; b. N.Y.C., Nov. 5, 1937; s. Harvey and Harriet (Ratner) N.; m. Dominie Maria Shortino, Aug. 31, 1963; children: Janet Elisabeth, Emily Julia. BS, Tufts U., 1957; MD, U. Chgo., 1961, PhD, 1963. Intern U. Chgo. Clinics, 1963-64; rsch. assoc. NIMH, Bethesda, Md., 1964-68, med. officer (res), 1968-84, chief, sec. molecular genetics, 1984—; chmn. Gordon Conf. on Nucleic Acids, 1988; vice-chair FASEB Conf. on Genetic Recombination, 1993, chair, 1995. Assoc. editor: Cell Jour., 1985-91; editorial bd.: Current Biology Jour., 1993—. Lt. comdr. USPHS, 1964-68. Recipient Superior Svc. award USPHS, 1985, Disting. Svc. award HHS, 1990, Alumni award for Disting. Svc., U. Chgo., 1994. Fellow Am. Acad. Arts and Sci.; mem. NAS. Office: Lab Molecular Biology NIMH 36 Convent Dr Bethesda MD 20892-4034

NASH, JOHN ARTHUR, bank executive; b. Indpls., Mar. 12, 1938; s. Basil and Harriet Nash; m. Susan Moss; children: John, Bill, Stacia. BS, Ind. U., 1960, MBA, 1961. Account officer Nat. City Bank, Cleve., 1961-66; v.p. Irwin Union Bank, Columbus, Ind., 1966-71, exec. v.p., 1971-75, pres., 1975-79; pres. Irwin Fin. Corp., Columbus, 1979—; also bd. dirs. Irwin Fin. Corp., Columbus, Ind.; bd. dirs. Irwin Union Bank, Irwin Union Investor Svcs., Inc., Inland Mortgage Corp., Affiliated Capital Corp., Irwin Home Equity Corp. Bd. dirs., trustee Columbus Regional Hosp. Found., Columbus Econ. Devel. Bd.; past chmn. Heritage Fund Bartholomew County, Columbus; mem. steering com. Columbus 2000; mem. adv. bd. Ind. U.-Purdue U., Indpls. 2d lt. U.S. Army, 1961-63. Recipient Sagamore of Wabash award Gov. of Ind., 1991. Mem. Am. Bankers Assn. (mem. bank leadership coun.), Ind. Bankers Assn. (bd. dirs., past chmn., chmn. govt. rels. com.), Ind. U. Alumni Assn. (pres. 1991-92). Office: Irwin Fin Corp 500 Washington St Columbus IN 47201-6230

NASH, JOHN FORBES, JR., research mathematician; b. Bluefield, W.Va., 1928. BS in Math., Carnegie-Mellon U., 1945, MS, 1948; PhD, Princeton U., 1950. Rsch. asst., instr. Princeton (N.J.) U., 1950-51; Moore instr. MIT, 1951-53, asst. prof., 1953-57, assoc. prof., 1957-59; vis. rsch. collaborator math. dept. Princeton U.; cons. RAND Corp., summers 1950, 52, 54; vis. mem. Inst. Advanced Study, Princeton, 1956-57, 61-62, 63-64; rsch. assoc. math. MIT, 1966-67. Co-recipient Nobel Prize in Econ. Scis., 1994; recipient von Neumann Theory prize Ops. Rsch. Soc. Am.; Sloan fellow, NSF fellow; Westinghouse scholar. Fellow Econometric Soc. Office: Princeton U Dept Math Fine Hall Princeton NJ 08544

NASH, JOHN N., professional basketball team executive; b. Phila., Nov. 28, 1946; s. John N. and Rosemary K. (Noon) N.; m. Anne Kelly (div.); children: Andrea, Carolyn; m. Ann Raley, Oct. 27, 1978; children: Brian, Barbara. Dir. group sales Phila. 76ers, 1969-71, asst. gen. mgr., 1981-86, gen. mgr., 1986-90; ticket mgr. athletic dept. U. Pa., Phila., 1971-72, Phila. Blazers, 1972-73, Phila. Flyers, 1973-75; exec. sec. Big 5 Basketball, 1975-81; asst. gen. mgr., bus. mgr. Phila. 76ers, 1981-86, gen. mgr., 1986-90; v.p. and gen. mgr. Washington Bullets, 1990—. Office: Washington Bullets USAir Arena Landover MD 20785*

NASH, JONATHON MICHAEL, program manager, mechanical engineer; b. Little Rock, Aug. 10, 1942; s. Bertram B. and Nora B. (Shed) N.; m. Meta W. Smith, Aug. 12, 1972; children: Lillian Kendrick, Caroline Michael. BS in Mech. Engring., U. Miss., 1966, MS in Engring. Sci., 1970, PhD in Engring. Sci., 1973. Registered profl. engr., Ala., Miss., Md. Jr. engr. IBM Fed. Systems div., Huntsville, Ala., 1967-68, Saturn/Apollo manned spacecraft programs sr. assoc. engr., 1973-74, staff engr., 1975-77, solar energy programs project engr., 1977-78, devel. engr., Gaithersburg, Md., 1978-80, adv. engr. synthetic fuels program, 1980-81, tech. planning mgr., 1981-83, sr. engr. FAA programs, Rockville, Md., 1983-88, sr. engr., program mgr. internat. air traffic control programs, 1988-94; program mgr. air traffic control LORAL Fed. Systems, Rockville, Md., 1994—; rsch. assoc. U. Miss., 1970-72, adj. assoc. prof. mech. engring., 1983—; aerospace engr., sci. intern

NASA Manned Space Craft Center, summers 1970, 71; instr. U. Ala., Huntsville, 1977-78. Bd. dirs. Arts Council of Frederick City and County, Md., 1981-84, v.p., 1982-83; mem. Lafayette County (Miss.) Rep. Exec. Com., 1972-73. With C.E., U.S. Army, 1968-70, Vietnam; maj. USAR. Decorated Bronze Star; recipient NASA New Tech. award, 1979; NASA Apollo Achievement award 1971; Ala. Young Engr. of Yr. award, Nat. Soc. Profl. Engrs., 1978; Tudor medal for engring. contbns. Soc. Am. Mil. Engrs., 1978; Engring. Achievement award, Huntsville chpt. Soc. Am. Mil. Engrs., 1977; Outstanding Young Engr. of Yr. award Huntsville chpt. Ala. Soc. Profl. Engrs., 1976, others; U. Miss. fellow, 1970-73. Fellow AIAA (assoc.), ASME (exec. com. solar energy div. 1981-86, sec./treas. 1982-83, vice chmn. 1983-84, chmn. 1984-85, mem. coun. engring. 1992—, mem. operating bd. energy resources group 1984—, Cert. of Appreciation, solar engery div. 1982, 85, chpt. chmn., 1978, vice chmn. 1977-78, treas. 1976-77, mem. nat. bur. standards interaction com., chmn. nat. com. tech. planning 1992—, nat. nominating com. 1988-90, nat. sattelite programs com.. 1990-92); mem. NSPE, VFW, ASHRAE (nat. tech. com. on solar energy utilization 1977-80), Am. Inst. Chem. Engrs., Soc. Am. Mil. Engrs. (chpt. pres. 1976-77, bd. dir. 1977-78), Md. Engring. Soc., Ala. Soc. Profl. Engrs. (chpt. dir. 1978), Internat. Solar Energy Soc., Ala. Solar Energy Assn. (chpt. dir. 1978), Am. Def. Preparedness Assn., Sigma Xi (chpt. pres. 1977-78), Omicron Delta Kappa, Alpha Tau Omega (pres. Huntsville alumni 1976-77), Res. Officers Assn. Editor: (with Smok, Thomas and Jenkins) Modeling, Simulation, Testing and Measurements for Solar Energy Systems, 1978; assoc. editor: (jour.) Applied Mechanics Revs., 1985-87, Mfg. Rev., 1987—; contbr. articles to profl. jours.; inventor in field. Home: 300 Rockwell Ter Frederick MD 21701-4912 Office: 9211 Corporate Blvd Rockville MD 20850-3202

NASH, JUNE CAPRICE, anthropology professor; b. Salem, Mass., May 30, 1927; d. Joseph and M. Josephine Bousley; children: Eric, Laura; m. Herbert Menzel, July 1, 1972. BA, CUNY, 1948; MA, U. Chgo., 1953, PhD, 1960. Asst. prof. Chgo. Tchrs. Coll., Chgo., Ill., 1960-63, Yale U. New Haven, Conn., 1963-68; assoc. prof. NYU, 1968-72; prof. CUNY, 1972—; disting. vis. prof. Am. U., Cairo, 1978, U. Colo., Boulder, 1988—; vis. prof. SUNY, Albany, 1988-89; disting. prof. CUNY, N.Y.C., 1990. Author: In the Eyes of the Ancestor, 1970, We Eat the Mines and the Mines Eat Us: Dependency and Exploitation in Bolivian Mining Communities, 1979, From Tank Town to High Tech: The Clash of Community and Industrial Cycles, 1989; editor: Crafts in the World Market: The Impact of Global Exchange on Middle American Artisans, 1993, La explosion de comunidades en chiapas, México, 1995; co-editor: (with Helen I. Safa) Sex and Class in Latin America, 1976, Women and Change in Latin America, 1986, (with Juan Carradi and Hobard Spaldine) Ideology and Change in Latin America, 1976, (with Jorge Dandler and Nicholas Hopkins) Ideology and Change in Latin America, 1976. Mem. Soc. for the Anthropology of Work (pres. 1988—), Assn. Polit. and Legal Activities (pres. 1983), Am. Anthropology Assn. (Disting. Svc. award 1995), Am. Ethnographic Soc., Assn. for Feminist Anthropology (pres. 1990-93). Avocations: skiing, hiking. Home: 2166 Broadway 18D New York NY 10024 Office: CUNY 137th Convent New York NY 10031

NASH, LEE J., banker; b. Elgin, Ill., Aug. 17, 1939; s. Richard Lee and Pearl Kepler (June) N.; m. Ruth Ann Ebeling, June 16, 1963; children—Joanne Elizabeth, J.R.; m. Sandra Gail Clegg, Feb. 16, 1980; children—Jason Lee, Jessica Gail. A.B. with honors, Harvard Coll., 1961; M.B.A., Columbia U., 1963. Mgmt. trainee Bankers Trust Co., N.Y.C., 1963-64; v.p. Pitts. Nat. Bank, 1964-70, Crocker Nat. Bank, San Francisco, 1970-75; sr. v.p. Shawmut Corp., Boston, 1975-79; exec. v.p., treas. Mfrs. Hanover Trust Co., N.Y.C., 1979-87; pres., chief exec. officer Mfrs. Hanover Securities Corp., N.Y.C., 1988-90; exec. v.p. Fed. Farm Credit Banks Funding Corp., 1990—. Mem. Am. Bankers Assn. (chmn. fund mgmt. and fin. markets divsn. 1985-87), Pub. Securities Assn. (bd. dirs. 1982-84), Treas. Securities Luncheon Club, Harvard Club (N.Y.C.), Beta Gamma Sigma. Office: Fed Farm Credit Banks Funding Corp 10 Exchange Pl Jersey City NJ 07302-3905

NASH, LEONARD KOLLENDER, chemistry educator; b. N.Y.C., Oct. 27, 1918; s. Adolph and Carol (Kollender) N.; m. Ava Byer, Mar. 3, 1945; children—Vivian C., David B. B.S., Harvard, 1939, M.A., 1941, Ph.D., 1944. Rsch. asst. Harvard U., Cambridge, Mass., 1943-44, instr., 1946-48, asst. prof., 1948-53, assoc. prof., 1953-59, prof. chemistry, 1959-86, chmn. dept., 1971-74; rsch. assoc. Columbia, 1944-45; instr. U. Ill., 1945-46; ret.; staff Manhattan Project, 1944-45. Author: Elements of Chemical Thermodynamics, 1962, The Nature of the Natural Sciences, 1963, Stoichiometry, 1966, Elements of Statistical Thermodynamics, 1968, ChemThermo, 1972. Recipient Mfg. Chemists' award, 1966; James Flack Norris award, 1975. Home: 11 Field Rd Lexington MA 02173-8014

NASH, MARY ALICE, nursing educator; b. Erie, Pa., Nov. 13, 1957; d. Robert Stuart and Jean Marie (Clark) N. BSN, Duquesne U., 1979; post-grad., Edinboro U., 1988-95. RN, Pa.; cert. CPR instr. Clin. educator St. Vincent Health Ctr., Erie, 1984, asst. nurse educator, 1988—. Mem. ANA, AACCN, Nat. Nurses Assn., Pa. Nurses Assn., Sigma Theta Tau. Home: 917 W 30th St Erie PA 16508-1645 Office: St Vincent Health Ctr 232 W 25th St Erie PA 16544-0002

NASH, NICHOLAS DAVID, retailing executive; b. Mpls., June 11, 1939; s. Edgar Vanderhoef and Nancy (Van Slyke) N. A.B., Harvard U., 1962; M.Ed., Bowling Green State U., 1970; Ph.D., U. Minn., 1975. Head lower sch. Maumee Valley (Ohio) Country Day Sch., 1965-71; assoc. dir. Univ. Council for Ednl. Adminstrn.; adj. asst. prof. Ohio State U., 1975-78; v.p. programming Minn. Public Radio, St. Paul, 1978-82, Am. Pub. Radio, St. Paul, 1982-85; pres. The Nash Co., 1985—; bd. dirs. Sta. WCAL-FM. Author works in field. Bd. dirs. Schubert Club, Sigurd Olson Environ. Inst., 1992—, Nash Found., 1975—. Mem. University Club St. Paul. Episcopalian. Home: 1340 N Birch Lake Blvd Saint Paul MN 55110-6716 Office: 2179 4th St # 2-h Saint Paul MN 55110-3028

NASH, PAUL LENOIR, lawyer; b. Poughkeepsie, N.Y., Jan. 29, 1931; s. George Matthew and Winifred (LeNoir) N.; m. Nancy Allyn Thouron, Dec. 30, 1961; children—Andrew Gray, Laurie LeNoir, Daphne Thouron. B.A., Yale U., 1953; LL.B., Harvard U., 1958. Bar: N.Y. 1959. Assoc., Dewey, Ballantine, Bushby, Palmer & Wood, N.Y.C., 1958-66, ptnr., 1966—. Pres. bd. trustees Peck Sch., Morristown, N.J., 1978-82. Served to capt. USMC, 1953-55; Japan. Mem. ABA, N.Y. State Bar Assn., Assn. Bar City of N.Y. Republican. Home: 4 Westminster Pl Morristown NJ 07960-5810 Office: Dewey Ballantine 1301 Avenue Of The Americas New York NY 10019-6022

NASH, PETER HUGH JOHN, geographer, educator, planner; b. Frankfurt-on-Main, Germany, Sept. 18, 1921; came to U.S., 1938, naturalized, 1943; s. John Hans Joseph and Alice (Heuman) N.; m. Inez Mae Frost, July 30, 1955 (dec. Apr. 1988); children: Carina Frost Nash Lawrence, Peter Hugh John Jr. A.A. in Earth Scis, Los Angeles City Coll., 1941; B.A. (Gruen Fellow), UCLA, 1942, M.A. in Geography, 1946; Certificat D'Etudes, U. Grenoble, France, 1945; postgrad., U. Wis., 1946-47; M. City Planning (Holtzer fellow), Harvard U., 1949, M.Pub. Adminstrn., 1956, Ph.D. in Archtl. Scis, 1958; postgrad., U. Cin. Law Sch., 1961-63; hon. degree, Aligarh Muslim U., India, 1968. Prin. planning asst. Boston Planning Bd., 1949-50; sr. planner City of Worcester, Mass., 1950-51; asst. chief urban redevel. div. Boston Housing Authority, 1951-52; dir. planning dept. City of Medford, Mass., 1952-56; vis. critic Harvard Grad. Sch. Design, 1955-57, 66-68; assoc. prof. city and regional planning U. N.C., 1957-59; prof., head dept. geography and regional planning U. Cin., 1959-63; dean Grad. Sch., U. R.I. Kingston, 1963-68, prof. geography and regional planning, dir. grad. curriculum in community planning and area devel., 1963-70; dean faculty of environ. studies U. Waterloo, Ont., Can., 1970-75; prof. architecture, geography and planning U. Waterloo, 1970-93, disting. prof. emeritus, 1993—; instr. Center for Adult Edn., Cambridge, Mass., 1949-57; lectr. Northeastern U., Boston, 1954-56; lectr., acting asst. prof. Boston U., 1956-57; vis. prof. summers U. So. Calif., 1959, 62, Aroostook State Coll., Maine, 1961, Grad. School Ekistics, Athens, Greece, 1967, 70, Inst. Human Scis. Boston Coll., 1969-70; cons. Brookings Inst., 1960-61, ACTION, Inc., 1959-61, Battelle Meml. Inst., Columbus, Ohio and Cleve., 1967-73; corr. Ekistics, 1960-73; Western hemisphere rep. commn. applied geography Internat. Geog. Union, 1964-76. Author 3 books; contbr. over 200 articles, chpts. and revs. in profl. and scholarly jours.; pub. in his honor Peter Nash Festschrift- Abstract Thoughts: Concrete Solutions: Essays, 1987. Participant Delos Symposion, Greece, 1967, 70, 74; mem. alumni council Harvard Sch. Design, pres., 1967-70; mem. exec. coun., sec.-treas. Kennedy Sch. govt., Harvard U., 1982-87; chmn. bd. dirs. K/W Philharm. Choir, 1976-80. Served with AUS, 1942-45. Decorated Purple Heart with oak leaf cluster, Bronze Star; Croix de Guerre (France); recipient Sci. Achievement medal U. Liege, Belgium, 1967; Social Sci. Research Council grantee, 1960; NSF grantee, 1960; Am. Council of Learned Socs. grantee, 1968; Can. Council grantee, 1974, 80, 82; Can. Social Scis. and Humanities Research Council fellow U. Grenoble, France, 1984-85, research grantee, Athens, Greece, 1985, Barcelona, Spain, 1986, research fellowship grantee, 1986-88. Fellow Am. Geog. Soc. (life), Assn. Am. Geographers (life); mem. Inst. Alpine Geography, Grenoble (hon.), Am. Inst. Planners, Internat. City Mgmt. Assn., AAAS, Am. Soc. Pub. Adminstrn., Can. Assn. Geographers, Can. Inst. Planners, Regional Sci. Assn., World Future Soc. (life), New Eng. Conf. on Grad. Edn. (sec.-treas. 1966-68), Assn. Collegiate Schs. Planning (treas. 1968-70), World Soc. Ekistics (v.p. 1994—), Sigma Xi, Sigma Nu, Kappa Delta Pi. Clubs: Mason (Boston and Toronto) (K.T.), Harvard (Boston and Toronto); Rotary Internat. (Kitchener, Ont., Paul Harris fellow). Home: 588 Sugarbush Dr, Waterloo, ON Canada N2K 1Z8 *I have never felt constrained by boundaries, whether geographical, intellectual, disciplinary, or any other type. One has to follow those avenues where one's intellectual curiosity points the way, even if these paths lead to entirely different territories. The world of reflective thinkers is inhabited primarily by splitters and lumpers, but the lumpers and spreaders are increasing rapidly in this era of knowledge explosion, and I am a standard bearer of this salient group as I help to create better futures.*

NASH, RONALD HERMAN, philosophy educator; b. Cleve., May 27, 1936; s. Herman Nash and Viola McAlpin; m. Betty Jane Perry, June 8, 1957; children: Jeffrey A., Jennifer A. BA, Barrington (R.I.) Coll., 1958; MA, Brown U., 1960; PhD, Syracuse U., 1964. Instr. philosophy Barrington Coll., 1958-60, Houghton (N.Y.) Coll., 1960-62; prof. philosophy Western Ky. U., Bowling Green, 1964-91; prof. philosophy religion Ref. Theol. Sem., Orlando, Fla., 1991—; dept. head Western Ky. U., Bowling Green, 1964-84; mem. adv. bd. CEBA, Lynchburg, Va., 1989—. Author: 25 books, including: Poverty and Wealth, 1986, Faith and Reason, 1988, The Closing of the American Heart, 1990, The Gospel and the Greeks, 1992, Beyond Liberation Theology, 1992, World Views in Conflict, 1992, Great Divides, 1992; contbg. editor: The Freeman, 1993—, Christian Rsch. Jour., 1993—; mem. bd. editors Durell Jour. Money and Banking, 1988-91. Advisor U.S. Civil Rights Commn., Washington, 1988-91. Fellow NEH, 1969. Office: Ref Theol Sem PO Box 945120 Maitland FL 32794-5120

NASH, SYLVIA DOTSETH, religious organization executive, consultant; b. Montevedio, Minn., Apr. 25, 1945; d. Owen Donald and Selma A. (Tollefson) Dotseth; divorced; 1 child, Elizabeth Louise; m. Thomas L. Nash, Dec. 20, 1986. Grad., Calif. Luth. Bible Sch., 1965; doctorate (hon.), Pilgrims Theol. Seminary, 1994. Office mgr. First Congl. Ch., Pasadena, Calif., 1968-75; adminstrv. asst. Pasadena Presbyn. Ch., 1975-78; dir. adminstrv. svcs. Fuller Theol. Sem., Pasadena, 1978-81; CEO Christian Mgmt. Assn., Diamond Bar, Calif., 1981-94; pres. Christian Healthcare Network, La Mirada, Calif., 1994-95; sr. cons. Lillestrand and Assocs., La Mirada, Calif., 1996—; cons. various orgns., 1985—. Author: Inspirational Management, 1992 (Your Church Mag. award 1992); editor: The Clarion, 1975-78, The Christian Mgmt. Report, 1981-94; mem. editl./adv. bd. Your Church Mag.; mem. editl. bd. Jour. Ministry Mktg. and Mtmg.; contbr. articles to profl. jours. Bd. dirs. Evang. Coun. for Fin. Accountability, Campus Crusade for Christ Internat. Sch. Theology, Nat. Network of Youth Ministries, The Mustard Seed, Inc., Nat. Assn. of Ch. Bus. Adminstrn., Found. for His Ministry, Lamb's Players, Gospel Lit. Internat., Rosemead, Calif. Mem. NAFE, Nat. Assn. Ch. Adminstrs. (sec. 1979-81), Am. Soc. Assn. Execs. Office: Lillestrand and Assocs PO Box 1361 La Mirada CA 90637-1361

NASH, WILLIAM ARTHUR, civil engineer, educator; b. Chgo., Sept. 15, 1922; s. William A. and Rose (Keck) N.; m. Verna Lucile Baer, Aug. 8, 1953; children: Rebecca Ann, Phillip Arthur. B.S. in Civil Engring, Ill. Inst. Tech., 1944, M.S., 1946; Ph.D., U. Mich., 1949. Research engr. David W. Taylor Model Basin, Navy Dept., Washington, 1949-54; mem. faculty U. Fla., Gainesville, 1954-67; head dept. engring. mechanics U. Fla., 1964-67; prof. civil engring. U. Mass., Amherst, 1967—; cons. to govt. and industry; hon. prof. Shanghai Inst. Tech., 1985; pres. Cons. Engring., Amherst, 1992—. Author: Theory and Outline of Strength of Materials, 2d edit., 1973, 3d edit., 1994, Statics and Mechanics of Materials, 1991, Hydrostatically Loaded Structures, 1995; contbr. 105 rsch. articles to profl. jours.; editor Internat. Jour. Nonlinear Mechanics. Recipient Humboldt U.S. Sr. Scientist award to Fed. Republic Germany, 1986; named Outstanding Sr. Faculty Mem. in Engring., U. Mass., 1987. Fellow ASME; mem. Internat. Assn. Shell and Spatial Structures, Am. Soc. Engring. Edn. (Curtis W. McGraw Research award 1961), AIAA, Earthquake Engring. Research Inst. Congregationalist. Office: 235 Marston Hall U Mass Amherst MA 01003

NASHE, CAROL, association executive, public relations consultant; b. Boston; d. Max and Sarah Ida (Litcofsky) Naselsky; m. Russell Weinberg (dec. Aug. 1980); children: Richard Dana, Harold Mark (dec.). Student, Mass. Sch. of Art, Boston, 1949. Asst. fashion editor Boston Herald Traveler, 1951; pres., founder Carol Nashe Sch. & Model Agy., Boston, 1951-74; dir. pub. rels. Sheraton Boston Hotel & Tower, 1974-84; cons. Blue Cross and Blue Shield of Mass., Boston, 1984-93; state chmn. U.S. Olympic Com., Mass., 1986-92; bd. dirs. World Trade Ctr., 1987-96; exec. dir., exec. v.p. Nat. Assn. Radio Talk Show Hosts. Bd. dirs. Morgan Meml. Goodwill Industries, Boston, 1986-93, Wang Ctr., Mass. Spl. Olympics, Pub. Action for Arts, Boys and Girls Clubs, Friends of John F. Kennedy Libr.; chmn. bd. Nat. Kidney Found.; advisor Boston organizing com., Mayors Drug Rally; chmn., founder Harold Weinberg Meml. Found., Friends of Mateo's Ballet Theatre of Boston. Named Woman of Yr., Nat. Kidney Found., 1983, Woman of Achievement, Big Sisters, 1986, Nat. Humanitarian of Yr., Heaven's Children, 1989; recipient Matrix award Women in Communications, Inc., 1988. Mem. Publicity Club, New Eng. Broadcasters Assn. (bd. dirs. 1985-90), Mass. Women's Polit. Caucus, Internat. Inst. Women's Polit. Leaders, Greater Boston C. of C. (bd. dirs. 1986-93), Exec. Club Boston (pres. 1991-92), Boston Club (pub. rels. com. 1987-95). Avocations: travel, photography, reading, home decorating, collectables. Home and Office: 134 Saint Botolph St Boston MA 02115-4819

NASON, CHARLES TUCKEY, financial services executive; b. Pitts., Apr. 22, 1946; s. Raymond W. and Helen (Tuckey) N.; m. Marlane L. Mulac, Nov. 20, 1967; children—Rebecca Ann, Jill Nicole. B.A., Washington and Jefferson Coll., 1968; M.B.A., U. Pitts., 1969. Cert. fin. planner; chartered fin. cons.; CLU. Dist. sales mgr. Met. Life Ins. Co., Pitts., 1971-77; mng. dir. Acacia Group Cos., Pitts., 1977-88; chmn., pres., chief exec. officer Acacia Mut. Life Ins. Co. , Washington, 1988—; founder, pres. Coordinated Capital Ltd., Pitts., 1982-85. Chmn. exec. com. Washington and Jefferson Coll. Devel. Coun., 1982-85; bd. trustees Washington and Jefferson Coll., 1988—; chmn. Nat. Annual Giving Fund Washington and Jefferson Coll., 1992-94; trustee Washington Federal City Coun., 1988—; bd. dirs. Greater Washington Bd. Trade, 1990—, pres.-elect, 1993, pres., 1994, chmn. 1994; bd. dirs. Blue Cross Blue Shield of Washington, 1991-93, Greater Washington Boys and Girls Clubs, 1991—, Am. Coun. of Life Ins., 1993—. Lt. USAF, 1970-71, Korea. Mem. Gen. Agts. and Mgrs. Assn. (pres. 1984-85), Am. Soc. CLUSs (pres. 1981-82), Estate Planning Coun. (bd. dirs.), Nat. Assn. Securities Dealers, Inst. Cert. Fin. Planners (bd. dirs.), Burning Tree Club, Congl. Country Club, Met. Club (Washington), Wexford Plantation Club (Hilton Head, S.C.), Melrose Club. Republican. Roman Catholic. Avocations: reading, golf, guitar. Home: 18 Beman Woods Ct Potomac MD 20854-5481 Office: Acacia Group 51 Louisiana Ave NW Washington DC 20001-2105

NASON, JOHN WILLIAM, retired college president, educational consultant; b. St. Paul, Feb. 9, 1905; s. Albert John and Mary Ethel (Eaton) N.; m. Bertha Deane White, June 15, 1935 (dec. Dec. 1955); children: Charles Kirby, Robert White; m. Elizabeth Mercer Knapp, June 29, 1957; stepchildren: Whitman E. Knapp, Caroline Knapp Hines, Marion E. Knapp. BA, Carleton Coll., 1926, LLD, 1948; postgrad., Yale U., 1926-27; MA, Harvard U., 1928; BA, Oxford (Eng.) U., 1931; LLD, U. Pa., 1941; LittD, Muhlenberg Coll., 1943, Hahnemann Med. Coll. and Hosp., 1943; LHD, Dropsie Coll., 1952, Coll. of Wooster, 1961, St. Olaf Coll., 1970, SUNY, 1992; LLD, Swarthmore Coll., 1953, Hamilton Coll., 1955, Brandeis U., 1958, Johns Hopkins U., 1960. Instr. philosophy Swarthmore Coll., 1931-34, asst. prof., 1934-40, asst. to pres., 1937-38, 39-40, acting chmn. dept. philosophy, 1938-39, pres., 1940-53; asst. to Am. sec. Rhodes Trustees, 1934-40; pres. Fgn. Policy Assn., 1953-62, Carleton Coll., Northfield, Minn., 1962-70; dir. studies Assn. Governing Bds., 1973-75, dir. study presdl. selection and assessment, 1977-79; dir. study on found. trustees Coun. on Founds., 1975-77; ednl. cons., 1979—. Author: American Higher Education in 1980—Some Basic Issues, 1965, Crises in the University, 1970, The Future of Trusteeship: The Role and Responsibilities of College and University Boards, 1975, Trustees & the Future of Foundations, 1977, Presidential Search: A Guide to the Process of Selecting and Appointing College and University Presidents, 1979, Presidential Assessment: Challenge to College and University Leadership, 1980, The Nature of Trusteeship, 1982, Foundation Trusteeship: Service in the Public Interest, 1989; various articles, revs. Chmn. Nat. Japanese-Am. Student Relocation Coun., 1942-45; pres. UN Coun. Phila., 1942-45, World Affairs Coun. Phila., 1949-51, 52-53; mem. Fulbright-Hays Com. Internat. Exchange Persons, 1963-66; mem. educators adv. com. Esso Edn. Found., 1964-68; trustee Edward W. Hazen Found., 1945-67, 68-78; Trustee Phillips Exeter Acad., 1946-50, 52-62, Vassar Coll., 1954-62, Danforth Found., 1961-68, United Negro Coll. Fund, 1966-70, Adirondack Conservancy, 1977-90, N.Y. State Conservancy, 1983-90; bd. govs. Bruce L. Crary Found., 1979-93; bd. dirs. Eisenhower Exchange Fellowship, 1953-65, Fgn. Policy Assn., 1953-62, 71-80 ; mem. adv. coun. Inst. Ednl. Mgmt., Harvard U., 1975-76; mem. vis. com. Harvard Grad. Sch. Edn., 1977-82. Rhodes scholar Oxford U., 1931. Fellow Nat. Coun. Religion in Higher Edn. (pres. 1943-49); mem. Soc. Values in Higher Edn., Phi Beta Kappa (senator united chpts. 1967-73), Delta Sigma Rho. Mem. Soc. of Friends. Home: 12 Crosslands Dr Kennett Square PA 19348-2039

NASON, ROBERT E., accountant; b. Sioux Falls, S.D., July 29, 1936; s. Earl V. and Eileen P. (Henegar) N.; m. Carol Ann Nason, Oct. 6, 1962; children: Steven, Jill. BS, U. S.D., 1958. Staff acct., mgr. Grant Thornton, Mpls., 1958-69, audit ptnr., 1969-71; mng. ptnr. Grant Thornton, Cleve., 1971-76; mng. ptnr. Grant Thornton, Chgo., 1976-88, midwest regional mng. ptnr., 1980-90, exec. ptnr., chief exec. officer, 1990—. Governing mem. Chgo. Symphony Orchestral Assn., 1985—. Mem. AICPA, Ill. CPA Soc., Chgo. Assn. Commerce & Industry, Exmoor Country Club (pres. 1988-90), Mid-Am. Club (bd. dirs. 1988-90), The Plaza Club, Econ. Club Chgo. Avocation: golf. Office: Grant Thorton LLP 1 Prudential Plaza Ste 800 130 E Randolph Dr Chicago IL 60601*

NASON, ROCHELLE, conservation organization administrator; b. Oakland, Calif., May 21, 1959; d. Milton and Ann Frances (Reed) N. BA, U. Calif., Berkeley, 1984; JD, U. Calif., San Francisco, 1987. Bar: Calif. 1987. Law clk. to Chief Justice Malcolm Lucas Supreme Ct. of Calif., San Francisco, 1987-88; litigation assoc. Morrison & Foerster, San Francisco, 1988-92; staff lawyer League to Save Lake Tahoe, South Lake Tahoe, Calif., 1992-93, exec. dir., 1993—; adj. instr. Sierra Nev. Coll., Incline Village, 1992-94, Lake Tahoe C.C., 1992—. Editor: The Traynor Reader, 1987; sr. rev. editor Hastings Law Jour., 1986-87; editor jour. Keep Tahoe Blue, 1992—; columnist (newspaper) Tahoe Daily Tribune; contbr. articles to profl. jours. V.p., bd. dirs. Jewish Cmty. South Lake Tahoe/Temple Bat Yam, 1992—; mem. leadership coun. Tahoe-Truckee Regional Econ. Coalition, Stateline, Nev., 1992-94; bd. dirs. Tahoe Ctr. for Sustainable Future, Glenbrook, Nev., 1995—. Mem. AAUW, Thurston Soc., Order of Coif. Jewish. Avocations: back-packing, skiing. Office: League to Save Lake Tahoe 955 Emerald Bay Rd South Lake Tahoe CA 96150

NASR, SALAH, sales executive; b. Alexandria, Egypt, May 31, 1952; came to U.S., 1972; s. Nasreldin and Fawzia (Shahata) Mohamed; m. Elizabeth A., July 15, 1982; children: Adam K., Amanda E., Adrian S. Student, Alexandria U. Commerce, Egypt, 1968-72. Waiter Theodore's Restaurant, N.Y.C., 1974-75; waiter, mgr. Astera Food's, N.Y.C., 1975-77; free-lance photographer N.Y.C., 1977-78; mgr. Jay Dee Restaurant, Troy, N.Y., 1979-80; sales rep. Cooley VW Corp., Rensselaer, N.Y., 1980-84; sales mgr. Paine Webber, Albany, N.Y., 1984-90; chmn.,CEO Alexandria Group of N.J. Corp., Lakewood, 1987—. Appearances on local TV fin. talk shows, 1986-88. Republican. Moslem. Avocation: power yachts. Home: 2 Shore Dr Waretown NJ 08758-2029 Office: Alexandria Group NJ Corp Exel Bus Park 525 Prospect St Lakewood NJ 08701

NASRALLAH, HENRY ATA, psychiatry researcher, educator; b. Apr. 30, 1947; came to U.S., 1972; s. Ata George and Rose G. (Yameen) N.; m. Amelia C. Tebsherani, June 6, 1972; children: Ramzy George, Rima Alice. BS in Biology, Am. U. of Beirut, 1967; MD, Am. U. Coll Medicine, Beirut-Lebanon, 1971. Intern Am. U. Med. Ctr., Beirut, Lebanon, 1972; resident in psychiatry U. Rochester, N.Y., 1975; rsch. assoc. NIMH, Washington, 1975-77; asst. prof. psychiatry U. Calif., San Diego, 1977-79; from assoc. prof. to prof. psychiatry U. Iowa, Iowa City, 1979-85; prof., chmn. dept. psychiatry Ohio State U., Columbus, 1985—; staff psychiatrist VA Med. Ctr., La Jolla, Calif., 1977-79; chief psychiatry svc. VA Med. Ctr., Iowa City, 1979-85. Editor: (5 vol. book series) Handbook of Schizophrenia, 1986-90; co-editor: NMR Spectroscopy in Psychiatric Brain Disorders, 1995; editor-in-chief Schizophrenia Rsch., 1987—, Psychiatry Watch, 1996—; author and co-author over 200 published articles, 1976—. Pres. Psychiat. Rsch. Found. of Columbus, 1985—; mem. Alliance for the Mentally Ill, Columbus, 1987—. Recipient VA grants, 1979-84, NIMH, 1983—. Fellow Am. Psychiat. Assn. (coun. on rsch.), Am. Coll. Neuropsychopharmacology (chmn. pubs. com. 1992-95), Am. Coll. Psychiatrists (Deans Award com. 1996—), Am. Acad. Clin. Psychiatrists (pres. 1989-90), Soc. Biol. Psychiatry (awards com. 1988-90). Avocations: photography, tennis, poetry. Office: Ohio State U Dept Psychiatry 1670 Upham Dr Columbus OH 43210-1252

NASSAU, MICHAEL JAY, lawyer; b. N.Y.C., June 3, 1935; s. Benjamin and Belle (Nassau) N.; m. Roberta Bluma Herzlich, June 26, 1971; children: Stephanie Ellen, William Michael. BA summa cum laude, Yale U., 1956, LLB cum laude, 1960. Bar: N.Y. 1960, D.C. 1992, U.S. Dist. Ct. (so. dist.) N.Y. 1978, U.S. Tax Ct. 1963, U.S. Ct. Appeals (2d cir.) 1963, U.S. Supreme Ct. 1965. Asst. instr. in constl. law Yale U., 1959-60; law clk. to judge U.S. Ct. Appeals 2d. Cir., 1960-61; assoc. tax dept. Paul, Weiss, Rifkind, Wharton & Garrison, N.Y.C., 1961-73; ptnr. Kramer, Levin, Naftalis & Frankel, and predecessor, N.Y.C., 1974—; mem. adv. bd. Matthew Bender Fed. Pension Law Service, 1975-76; mem. adv. com. NYU Ann. Inst. Employee Plans and Exec. Compensation, 1976-79; mem. steering com. Am. Pension Conf., 1981-83; lectr. in field; panelist various seminars on employee benefits. Mem. ABA (sect. taxation, employee benefits com. 1993—), N.Y. State Bar Assn. (co-chmn. employee benefits sect. taxation 1976-78, mem. exec. com. sect. taxation 1976-79), Assn. of Bar of City of N.Y. (chmn. subcom. pension legis. of com. taxation 1975-76, employee benefits com. 1987-92), WEB (N.Y. chpt. bd. dirs. 1990—, pres. 1993-94), Phi Beta Kappa. Mem. editorial bd. Bank and Corp. Governance Law Reporter, 1989—; contbr. chpts., articles to law publs.; panelist Pension Video Seminar, 1983. Office: Kramer Levin Naftalis & Frankel 919 3rd Ave New York NY 10022

NASSBERG, RICHARD T., lawyer; b. N.Y.C., Mar. 30, 1942; s. Jules and Rhea (Steinglass) N.; m. Kathryn S. Lynn, May 2, 1981; children: Schuyler M. L., Kathryn Cupp. BS in Econs., Wharton Sch., U. Pa., 1963; JD, U. Pa., 1968. Bar: N.Y. 1969, U.S. Ct. Appeals (2d cir.) 1970, Pa. 1972, Tex. 1983. With Milbank, Tweed, Hadley & McCloy, N.Y.C., 1968-70; with Schnader, Harrison, Segal & Lewis, Phila., 1971-78, ptnr., 1978-82; ptnr. Mayor, Day & Caldwell, Houston, 1982-90; pvt. practice law, 1990-92; of counsel Mannino & Griffith, Phila., 1992-95; planning chmn. courses of study on banking and comml. lending law Am. Law Inst.-ABA, 1979—, mem. adv. com. to subcom. on continuing legal edn., 1982-90 . Served with Army N.G., 1963-65, USAR, 1965-66, USAFR, 1966-69. Mem. NYCOC (standing com. on Nat. Security 1968-71), Am. Law Inst. (advisor comml. law 1985—), ABA, Tex. Bar Assn., Houston Bar Assn. Clubs: Franklin Inn (Phila.). Author: The Lender's Handbook. 1986; editor resource books on banking law; contbr. articles on banking law to profl. publs.; editor U. Pa. Law Rev., 1967-68, assoc. editor, 1966-67. Office: PO Box 5055 Jersey Shore PA 17740

NASSERI, TOURAJ, engineering executive; b. Tehran, Iran, Feb. 28, 1944; married; two children. BSc, Manchester U., 1967; MSc, Imperial Coll.,

1969; PhD in Structural Engring., London U., 1974. From mgr. offshore tech. to pres. Det Norske Veritas Ltd., Calgary, Can., 1982-89; pres. Centre Frontier Engring. Rsch., Edmonton, Can., 1989—; subcom. nat. strategies Premier's Coun. Sci. & Tech., 1990—; mem. Polartech Conf. Internat. Com., 1991. Mem. Assn. Prof. Engrs., Geologists and Geophysicists Alta, Inst. Civil Engrs. London, Can. Standard Assn. (steering com. 1984—, tech. com. 1984—). Office: Ctr for Frontier Engineer Rsch, 200 Karl Clark Rd, Edmonton, AB Canada T6N 1E2*

NASSIF, THOMAS ANTHONY, business executive, former ambassador; b. Cedar Rapids, Iowa, July 22, 1941; s. George Joseph and Clara Christine (Nofal) N.; m. Zinetta Marie Meherg, Sept. 14, 1968; children—Jaisa Diane, Matthew Christian. BS, Calif. State U.-Los Angeles, 1965; JD, Calif. Western Sch. Law, 1969, LLD (hon.), 1988. Ptnr. Gray, Cary, Ames & Frye, El Centro, Calif., 1980-81; dep. and acting chief of protocol Dept. State, Washington, 1981-83; dep. asst. sec. Bur. Near Eastern and South Asian Affairs, Dept State, Washington, 1983-85; U.S. ambassador to Morocco, 1985-88; chmn. bd. Gulf Interstate Internat. Corp., San Diego, 1988-95; chmn. of bd. Gulf Intern. Inc., Houston, 1988-95, Gulf Internat. Consulting Inc., San Diego, 1992—; chmn. Am. Task Force for Lebanon, Washington, 1991—. Active campaign Reagan for Pres., 1980; mem. Calif. State Rep. Cen. Com. Served with U.S. Army and USNG, 1960-67. Recipient Disting. Profl. Achievement award Attiyeh Benevolent Soc., Ellis Island Congl. Medal of Honor, 1993. Office: Gulf Internat Consulting Inc Ste 1025 4660 La Jolla Village Dr San Diego CA 92122-4606

NASSIKAS, JOHN NICHOLAS, lawyer; b. Manchester, N.H., Apr. 29, 1917; s. Nicholas John and Constantina (Gagalis) N.; m. Constantina Andreson, Feb. 21, 1943; children: Kira Hohenadel, Marcy (Mrs. Wade B. C. Weathers, Jr.), Elizabeth (Mrs. Watson Lowery), John Nicholas III. A.B., Dartmouth Coll., 1938; M.B.A., Harvard U., 1940, J.D., 1948; LL.D. (hon.), Notre Dame Coll., Manchester, N.H., 1972. Bar: N.H. and Mass. 1948, D.C. 1968, U.S. Supreme Ct. 1953, Va. 1986. Asst., dep. atty. gen. N.H., 1950-53; sr. partner firm Wiggin, Nourie, Sundeen, Nassikas & Pingree, Manchester, 1953-69; chmn. Fed. Power Commn., 1969-75; partner firm Squire, Sanders & Dempsey, Washington, 1975-86; spl. commr., presiding chmn. N.H. Pub. Utilities Commn., 1984-86; spl. commr., presiding chmn. procs. for reorgn. of Pub. Svc. Co. N.H., N.H. Pub. Utilities Commn., 1989-92; arbitrator Duke Power Co., NCEMC and SALVDA River Elect. Coops., 1992-94. Mem. Adminstrv. Conf. U.S., 1969-75; bd. dirs. U.S. Nat. Com. of World Energy Conf., 1970-74, 77-87; mem. Water Resources Council, 1969-75; mem. exec. com. NARUC, 1970-75; mem. Pres.'s Cabinet Task Force on Oil Import Control, 1969-70; mem. energy subcom. domestic council, 1969-73; mem. Pres.'s Joint Bd. on Fuel Supply and Transport, 1970-73, Pres.'s Energy Resources Council, 1974-75, Nat. Petroleum Council, 1975-79; bd. dirs. Ams. for Energy Independence, 1975-84; trustee Pathfinder Mines Corp., 1976-82; mem. adv. council Gas Research Inst., 1977-87; bd. dirs. corp. Madeira Sch., 1972-80. Served to lt. USNR, 1942-46. Mem. ABA, N.H. Bar Assn., Mass. Bar Assn. (spl. commr. Seabrook Nuclear Fin. Hearings), D.C. Bar Assn., Fed. Bar Assn., Va. Bar Assn., Fed. Energy Bar Assn., Cosmos Club, Met. Club, Farmington Country Club, Ahepa, Kappa Kappa Kappa. Republican. Home and Office: 1131 Litton Ln Mc Lean VA 22101-1823

NASSOURA, NANCY KATHRYN, special education educator; b. N.Y.C., Oct. 16, 1968; d. Robert Emmett and Winifred Kathryn (Flynn) Bozzomo; m. Khaled Nassoura, July 8, 1995. BA, Coll. St. Elizabeth, 1991; MA in Spl. Edn., Kean Coll. N.J., 1994. Tchr. handicapped, elem. edn., secondary English. Permanent substitute Clifton (N.J.) Pub. Schs., 1992; resource ctr. tchr. Bedwell Elem. Sch., Bernardsville, N.J., 1992-94, Hilltop Elem. Sch., Mendham, N.J., 1994—; head tchr. summer program, YMCA, Livingston, N.J., 1991—, morning program, Basking Ridge, N.J., 1992-94. Mem. Coun. Exceptional Children, Coun. for Children with Behavioral Disorders, Coun. for Children with Learning Disabilities, Orton Dyslexia Soc., N.J. Edn. Assn., N.J. Coun. for Social Studies, Kappa Delta Pi. Avocations: writing, reading, rollerblading, mountain biking, music. Office: Hilltop Elem Sch 12 Hilltop Rd Mendham NJ 07945-1215

NATALICIO, DIANA SIEDHOFF, academic administrator; b. St. Louis, Aug. 25, 1939; d. William and Eleanor J. (Biermann) Siedhoff. BS in Spanish summa cum laude, St. Louis U., 1961; MA in Portuguese lang., U. Tex., 1964, PhD in Linguistics, 1969. Chmn. dept. modern langs. U. Tex., El Paso, 1973-77, assoc. dean liberal arts, 1977-79; acting dean liberal arts, 1979-80; dean Coll. Liberal Arts U. Tex., El Paso, 1980-84, v.p. acad. affairs, 1984-88, pres., 1988—; bd. dirs. El Paso br. Fed. Res. Bd. Dallas, chmn., 1989; mem. Presdl. Adv. Commn. on Ednl. Excellence for Hispanic Ams., 1991; bd. dirs. Sandia Corp., Enserch Corp.; bd. dirs. Nat. Action Coun. for Minorities in Engring., 1993-96; mem. Nat. Sci. Bd. 1994-2000; mem. NASA adv. coun., 1994—; bd. mem. Fund for Improvement of Post-Secondary Edn., 1993-97; bd. dirs. Fogarty Internat. Ctr. of NIH, 1993—; ; bd. chair Am. Assn. Higher Edn., 1995-96; bd. dirs. U.S.-Mexico Commn. for Edn. and Cultural Exch., 1994-96. Co-author: Sounds of Children, 1977; contbr. articles to profl. jours. Bd. dirs. United Way El Paso, 1990-93, chmn. needs survey com., 1990-91, chmn. edn. divsn., 1989; chmn. Quality Edn. for Minorities Network in Math. Sci. and Engring., 1991-92; chairperson Leadership El Paso, Class 12, 1989-90, mem. adv. coun., 1987-90, participant, 1980-81; mem. Historically Black Colls. and Univs./Minority Instns. Consortium on Environ. Tech. chairperson, 1991-93. Recipient Torch of Liberty award Anti-Defamation League B'nai B'rith, 1991, Conquistador award City of El Paso, 1990, Humanitarian award Nat. Coun. Christians and Jews, El Paso chpt., 1990; mem. El Paso Women's Hall of Fame, 1990. Mem. Philos. Soc. Tex. Avocations: hiking, bicycling, skiing, skating. Home: 711 Cincinnati Ave El Paso TX 79902-2616 Office: U Tex at El Paso Office of the President El Paso TX 79968-0500

NATALIE, RONALD BRUCE, lawyer; b. Lynn, Mass., Nov. 29, 1935; s. John Richard and Cecelia Lucy (Fish) N.; m. Betty Ann McEnteggart, Aug. 22, 1958; children: Ronald Bruce Jr., Karen Lorraine, Donna Leslie, John Francis. AB, Tufts Coll., 1957; JD with highest honors, George Washington U., 1962. Bar: D.C. 1962, U.S. Ct. Appeals (D.C. cir.) 1964, U.S. Ct. Appeals (2d cir.) 1970, U.S. Ct. Appeals (5th cir.), 1991, U.S. Ct. Appeals (3d cir.) 1992. Atty. Office of Gen. Counsel, U.S. Commn. on Civil Rights, Washington, 1962-64; assoc. Verner, Liipfert, Bernhard, McPherson and Hand, Washington, 1964-68, ptnr., 1968-81; shareholder Verner Liipfert, Bernarhd, McPherson & Hand, Washington, 1981—; chief counsel Pres.'s Commn. to Investigate the Accident at Three Mil Island, Washington, 1979; vice chmn. Close Up Found., Alexandria, Va., 1971—. Lt. USN, 1957-62. Mem. ABA, D.C. Bar Assn., Ba Assn. of D.C., Assn. for Transp., Law, Logistics and Policy, Phi Alpha Delta. Democrat. Home: 3307 39th St NW Washington DC 20016-3711 Office: Verner Liipfert Bernarhd McPherson & Hand 901 15th St NW Washington DC 20005-2327

NATCHER, STEPHEN DARLINGTON, lawyer, business executive; b. San Francisco, Nov. 19, 1940; s. Stanlus Zoch and Robena Lenore Collie (Goldring) N.; m. Carolyn Anne Bowman, Aug. 23, 1969; children: Tanya Michelle, Stephanie Elizabeth. A.B. in Polit. Sci., Stanford U., 1962; J.D., U. Calif., San Francisco, 1965. Bar: Calif. 1966. Assoc. firm Pillsbury, Madison & Sutro, San Francisco, 1966-68; counsel Douglas Aircraft div. McDonnell Douglas Corp., Long Beach, Calif., 1968-70; v.p., sec. Security Pacific Nat. Bank, 1971-79; asst. gen. counsel Security Pacific Corp., 1979-80; v.p., sec., gen. counsel Lear Siegler, Inc., Santa Monica, Calif., 1980-87; v.p., gen. counsel Computer Scis. Corp., El Segundo, Calif., 1987-88; exec. v.p., gen. counsel, sec. CalFed Inc., 1989-90; sr. v.p. adminstrn., gen. counsel, sec. Wyle Electronics, Irvine, Calif., 1991—. With USCG, 1965-71. Mem. St. Francis Yacht Club (San Francisco), The Pacific Club (Newport Beach). Republican.

NATELSON, NINA BETH, non-profit organization administrator; b. N.Y.C., Nov. 12, 1948; d. Samuel and Ethel Doris (Nathan) N.; m. Murry Joseph Cohen. BA in French, German, NYU, 1968, postgrad., 1969; postgrad., George Washington U., 1974-76. Sales asst. Merrill Lynch, Pierce, Fenner & Smith, Inc., Washington, 1971; investment broker Baxter, Blyden, Selheimer, Inc., Washington, 1971-73; mgmt. intern Gen. Svcs. Adminstr., Washington, 1974-76; program analyst Gen. Svcs. Adminstrn., Insp. Gen.'s Office, Office Audits, Washington, 1975-80; program analyst Dept. Labor Insp. Gen.'s Office, Office of Loss Analysis and Prevention, Washington, 1980-82; freelance writer, 1985-92; founder, pres. Concern for Helping Animals in Israel, Alexandria, Va., 1984—. Contbr. articles to profl. jours. Vol. People for the Ethical Treatment of Animals, Washington, 1982-84. Recipient awards U.S. Dept. Health and Human Svcs. and Carroll County Md. Mem. Nat. Fedn. Bus. and Profl. Women (editor local newsletter 1973-74, Disting. Vol. award 1984). Avocation: parapsychology. Home and Office: Concern for Helping Animals Israel PO Box 3341 Alexandria VA 22302

NATELSON, STEPHEN ELLIS, neurosurgeon; b. N.Y.C., Dec. 23, 1937; s. Samuel R. and Ethel D. (Nathan) N.; B.A. magna cum laude, Carleton Coll., 1958; Fulbright scholar in Math., Westfälische-Wilhelms U., Germany, 1958-59; M.D., U. Rochester, 1963; m. Laurie Lou Acred, 1990; children from previous marriage: Lea Jane, Jamie Ann, Jessica Ilana, Benjamin Henry, Marissa Claire. Intern, USAF Hosp., Wright-Patterson AFB, 1963-64; resident in neurosurgery Ohio State U., 1967-71; chief resident in neurology U. N.Mex., 1971-72; pvt. practice specializing in neurosurgery, Knoxville, Tenn., 1972—; clin. assoc. prof. U. Tenn. Served with USAF, 1962-67. Decorated Air Force Commendation medal; diplomate Am. Bd. Neurol. Surgery. Fellow ACS; mem. Am. Assn. Neurol. Surgeons, Congress Neurol. Surgeons, AMA, Knoxville Acad. Medicine, Tenn. Neurosurg. Soc. (past press.), Am. Physicians Fellowship, Undersea Med. Soc., Phi Beta Kappa, Sigma Xi, Alpha Omega Alpha. Republican. Jewish. Contbr. articles to profl. jours. Office: 103 Newland Profl Bldg Knoxville TN 37916

NATH, JOGINDER, genetics and biology educator, researcher; b. Joginder Nagar, Panjab, India, May 12, 1932; came to U.S. 1957; s. Moti Ram and Vira Wali (Khorana) N.; m. Charlotte Lynn Reese, Apr. 5, 1969; children—Pravene, Brian. B.S. with honors, Panjab U, Amritsar, India, 1953; M.S. with honors, Panjab U, 1955; Ph.D., U. Wis., 1960. Research assoc. Am. Inst. Biol. Research, Madison, Wis., 1960-63; asst. prof. So. Ill. U., Carbondale, Ill., 1964-66; from asst. to assoc. prof. W.Va. U., Morgantown, 1966-72, prof., chmn. dept. genetics and devel. biology, 1972—. Contbr. articles on cytogenetics, mutagenesis, biochem. genetics and cryobiology to profl. jours. Chmn. bd. Morgantown Day Sch., 1977-79. Grantee NSF, 1967-68, DOE, 1992-95, Nat. Inst. Occupational Safety & Health, 1985-95. Mem. Soc. Cryobiology, Environ. Mutagen Soc., Electron Microscopy Soc., Sigma Xi. Office: WVa U Coll Agr Dept Genetics & Devel Biology Morgantown WV 26506

NATHAN, ANDREW JAMES, political science educator; b. N.Y.C., Apr. 3, 1943; s. Paul S. and Dorothy (Goldeen) N.; 1 child, Chloe; 1 stepchild Alexandra Witke. B.A. summa cum laude, Harvard U., 1963, M.A. in East Asian Regional Studies, 1965, Ph.D. in Polit. Sci., 1971. Lectr. U. Mich., Ann Arbor, 1971; research assoc. Ctr. for Chinese Studies, 1970; asst. prof. polit. sci. Columbia U., N.Y.C., 1971-75, assoc. prof., 1975-82, prof., 1982—; dir. East Asian Inst. Columbia U., N.Y.C., 1991-95; mem. steering com. China Internat. Bus. Project, 1978—; mem. nat. com. on U.S.-China rels., 1987—; chair adv. com. Human Rights Watch/Asia, 1995—; cons. U.S. Dept. State, U.S. Ho. Fgn. Affairs Com., Security Pacific Nat. Bank, Charles of the Ritz, Brown U., U. Iowa, Ambrica Prodns., WNYC Comms. Group, Commn. on Broadcasting to People's Republic of China, Levi-Strauss & Co., Nat. Endowment for Democracy, Pfizer Internat., Carnegie Coun. for Ethics in Internat. Affairs, Immigration and Naturalization Svcs., others; lectr. in feild; external examiner Australian Nat. U., 1994. Author: A History of the China International Famine Relief Commission, 1965, Modern China, 1840-1972, An Introduction to Sources and Research Aids, 1973, Peking Politics, 1918-1923: Factionalism and the Failrue of Constitutionalism, 1976, Chinese Democracy, 1985 (Levenson prize 1987), (with others) Human Rights in Contemporary China, 1986, China's Crisis, 1990; co-editor Popular Culture in Late Imperial China, 1985; contbr. book revs. to publs.; manuscript reviewer U. Calif. Press., Columbia U. Press, Harvard U. Press, others; contbr. numerous articles to profl. jours. and current popular pubs. Chair Zoning Bd. of Appeal, Village of Grand View-on-Hudson, N.Y., 1985-93, zoning adminstr. and dep. zoning adminstr., 1978-85; bd. dirs. Cmty. Playgroup, Piermont, N.Y., 1984-88. Guggenheim fellow, 1973-74; fellow Am. Coun. Learned Soc.- Social Sci. Rsch. Coun., 1977-78, NEH fellow 1986-87, 1992-93; grantee Luce Found., 1979-82, 91-93, 92-95, Chiang Ching-Kuo Found., 1992, 1995-96, 1995-97, NSF, 1993-96 and others. Mem. Am. Polit. Sci. Assn., Assn. for Asian Studies. Home: 35 Claremont Ave Apt 6N New York NY 10027-6823 Office: East Asian Inst Columbia U 420 W 118th St New York NY 10027-7213

NATHAN, ANDREW JONATHAN, lawyer, real estate developer; b. Honolulu, Mar. 20, 1957; s. Joel Joseph and Wendy Barbra (Bernstein) N.; m. Bonnie Lynn Raymond, Aug. 16, 1981 (div. Sept. 1987); m. Holly Lorraine Marshall, Feb. 17, 1990; children: Jake, Tyler. BA cum laude, Brandeis U., 1978; JD with distinction, Hofstra U., 1981. Assoc. Schulte Roth & Zabel, N.Y.C., 1981-87; counsel Tishman Speyer Properties, N.Y.C., 1987, gen. counsel, 1990, gen. counsel, mng. dir., 1993—. Articles editor Hofstra Law Rev., 1981. Mem. ABA, N.Y. State Bar Assn. Office: Tishman Speyer Properties 520 Madison Ave New York NY 10022-4213

NATHAN, DAVID GORDON, physician, educator; b. Boston, May 25, 1929; s. E. Geoffrey and Ruth (Gordon) N.; m. Jean Louise Friedman, Sept. 1, 1951; children: Deborah, Linda, Geoffrey. BA, Harvard U., 1951; MD, Harvard Med. Sch., 1955. Diplomate Am. Bd. Internal Medicine, Am. Bd. Pediatrics. Intern dept. medicine Peter Bent Brigham Hosp., Boston, 1955-56, sr. resident, 1958-59; jr. assoc. in medicine Brigham and Women's Hosp., Boston, 1961-67, sr. assoc. in medicine, 1967—; assoc. in medicine, hematology Childrens Hosp., Boston, 1963-68, chief, div. hematology, 1968-73, chief div. hematology and oncology, 1974-84; pediatrician-in-chief Dana Farber Cancer Inst., Boston, 1974-85; Robert A. Stranahan prof. pediatrics Harvard Med. Sch., Boston, 1977-95; physician-in-chief Childrens Hosp., Boston, 1985-95; pres. Dana-Farber Cancer Inst., Boston, 1995—; Richard and Susan Smith prof. medicine Harvard Med. Sch., Boston, 1996—, prof. of pediatrics, 1996—. Author: Genes, Blood and Courage, 1994; editor: Hematology in Infancy and Childhood, 4th edit., 1993. With USMC, 1948-49. Recipient Nat. Medal Sci. NSF, 1990. Fellow AAAS; mem. Inst. of Medicine of NAS, Am. Acad. Arts & Scis., Am. Pediatric Soc., Soc. Pediatric Rsch., Assn. Am. Physicians, Am. Soc. Clin. Investigators, Am. Soc. Hematology (pres. 1986), Phi Beta Kappa (hon.). Avocations: tennis, hiking. Office: Dana-Farber Cancer Inst 44 Binney St Boston MA 02115

NATHAN, EDWARD SINGER, lawyer; b. Newark, Aug. 14, 1954; s. Emanuel and Evelyn (Lachter) N.; m. Merridith Elaine Cramer, Feb. 23, 1995. BA, U. Rochester, 1976; JD, Rutgers U., 1986. Bar: N.J. 1986. Assoc. McCarter & English, Newark, 1986—. V.p. The Children's Inst., Livingston, N.J., 1993—; life mem. South Orange (N.J.) Rescue Squad, 1976—. Mem. N.J. Bar Assn., Vanderbilt Inn of Ct. Avocations: bicycling, fitness. Home: 768 Springfield Ave B-8 Summit NJ 07901 Office: 100 Mulberry St Newark NJ 07102

NATHAN, FREDERIC SOLIS, lawyer; b. N.Y.C., June 24, 1922; s. Edgar Joshua and Mabel (Unterberg) N.; m. Frances E., Oct. 28, 1956; children: JEan E., Frederic S. Jr., William E. BA, Williams Coll., Williamstown, Mass., 1943; LLD, Yale U., 1948. Bar: N.Y. 1948, U.S. Dist. Ct. (so. and ea. dists) N.Y. 1948, U.S. Ct. Appeals (2d cir.) 1953, U.S. Supreme Ct. 1968. Instr. Williams Coll., Williamstown, 1948; assoc. Rathbone Perry Kelley & Drye, N.Y.C., 1948-53; asst. U.S. atty. U.S. Attys.' Office (so. dist.), N.Y.C., 1953-56; assoc. Greenbaum, Wolff & Ernst, N.Y.C., 1956-58, ptnr., 1959-65, 70-82; 1st asst. corp. counsel N.Y.C. Law Dept., N.Y.C., 1966-69; ptnr. Kelley, Drye & Warren, N.Y.C., 1982—. Mem. N.Y. Rep. County Com., N.Y.C., 1948-66; trustee Mt. Sinai Hosp. and Med. Sch., N.Y.C., 1970—; chmn. bd. FOJP Svc. Corp., N.Y.C., 1977-85, bd. dirs., 1979—; bd. dirs., v.p. Am. Jewish Soc. for Svc., N.Y.C., 1950—. With U.S. Army, 1943-45, ETO. Fellow Am. Coll. Trial Lawyers; mem. ABA, Assn. of Bar of City of N.Y. (exec. com. 1979-81), Fed. Bar Council (pres. 1975-76), N.Y. State Bar Assn. Republican. Jewish. Clubs: Century Assn., Yale of N.Y.C.; Sunningdale Country. Home: 180 East End Ave New York NY 10128-7763 Office: Kelley Drye & Warren 101 Park Ave New York NY 10178

NATHAN, IRWIN, business systems company executive; b. N.Y.C., June 24, 1932; s. Albert Y. and Sarah (Abrams) N.; m. Sandra Alpert, June 18, 1955 (dec. June 1989); children: Alan Bradley, Mitchell Jordan; m. Phyllis Davis, Feb. 16, 1992. BSME, Stevens Inst. Tech., Hoboken, N.J., 1953; MSEE, N.Y.U., 1955, MS in Indsl. Engring., 1960; PhD, Poly. U., Bklyn., 1984. Registered profl. engr., N.Y. Rsch. and devel. engr. Dynamics Corp. of Am., Garden City, N.Y., 1953-56; sr. systems engr. Am. Bosch ARMA, Inc., Garden City, N.Y., 1956-63; prin. engr. Gen. Precision, Inc., Totowa, N.J., 1963-66; from section mgr. to mgr. svc. maintenance strategy Xerox Corp., Stamford, Conn., 1967-94; ret., 1994, cons. in reliability and svc., 1994—; guest lectr. George Washington U., 1969, UCLA, 1971, The Wharton Sch., 1985. Mem. IEEE, Ops. Rsch. Soc. Am. Avocations: boating, fishing, woodworking. Home: 12 Linda Ln Westport CT 06880-3945

NATHAN, JAMES ROBERT, hospital administrator; b. Albuquerque, Nov. 23, 1946; married. B, Miami U., 1968; M, Xavier U., 1974, MHA, 1976. Adminstrv. resident Lee Meml. Hosp., Ft. Myers, Fla., 1975-76, v.p., 1976-81, pres., 1982—. Mem. Fla. Hosp. Assn. Home: 3333 Hibiscus Dr Fort Myers FL 33901-6720 Office: Lee Meml Hosp PO Box 2218 Fort Myers FL 33902-2218*

NATHAN, LAURA E., sociology educator; b. L.A., Oct. 28, 1951; d. Monroe and Sheila (Solomon) Engelberg; m. Mark D. Nathan, April 9, 1978; children: Justin. BA in Sociology, U. Calif., Santa Barbara, 1973; MA in Sociology, U. Calif., L.A., 1975, PhD in Sociology, 1981. Teaching assoc. in sociology Univ. Calif., L.A., 1975-76; acting asst. prof. sociology Calif. State Univ., Fullerton, Calif., 1977-81; coord., instr. Univ. Calif., L.A., 1979-80; assoc. prof. sociology and psychology Antelope Valley Coll., Lancaster, Calif., 1981-82; asst. prof. sociology Mills Coll., Oakland, Calif., 1982-87; assoc. prof. sociology Mills Coll., Oakland, 1987-93; prof. of sociology Mills Coll., Oakland, Calif., 1993—, Robert J. and Ann B. Wert prof. of sociology, 1993—; lectr. in sociology and womens studies Calif. State Univ., Long Beach, 1978; program evaluator U.S. Dept. Health, Edn. and Welfare, L.A., 1974-75, program dir. 1975-76; mem. conf. planning com. Womens Leadership Conf., Mills Coll., also com. chair, 1992-93; bd. dirs. Am. Cancer Soc., Alameda County, Calif., 1985—. Author: (with others) Secondary Analysis of Survey Data, 1985; contbr. chpts. to books. Regents Rsch. grantee, 1979, Mellon Found. grantee, 1983, Faculty Devel. Rsch. grantee Mills. Coll., 1985, 86, 87, 90, 91, 94, 95l W.K. Kellogg Nat. fellow, 1988, Thornton Bradshaw Humanities fellow Claremont Grad. Sch., 1990; recipient Disting. Leadership award Am. Cancer Soc., 1995, ten Broek Soc. award for Excellence in Teaching, 1996. Mem. Pacific Sociol. Assn. (mem. nominating com. 1985-88, mem. program com. 1995—), Am. Sociol. Assn. (membership com. 1988-92), Soc. for the Study of Social Problems (chmn. poverty, class inequality div. 1987-88). Jewish. Avocations: traveling, mysteries, vol. work. Office: Mills Coll 5000 Macarthur Blvd Oakland CA 94613-1301

NATHAN, LEONARD EDWARD, writer, educator; b. Los Angeles, Nov. 8, 1924; s. Israel and Florence (Rosenberg) N.; m. Carol Gretchen Nash, June 27, 1949; children: Andrew Peter, Julia Irene, Miriam Abigail. Student, Ga. Tech., 1943-44, UCLA, 1946-47; BA summa cum laude, U. Calif.-Berkeley, 1950, MA, 1952, PhD, 1961. Instr. Modesto (Calif.) Jr. Coll., 1954-60; prof. dept. rhetoric U. Calif., Berkeley, 1960-91, ret., 1991, chmn. dept., 1968-72. Author: Western Reaches, 1958, The Glad and Sorry Seasons, 1963, The Matchmaker's Lament, 1967, The Day The Perfect Speakers Left, 1969, The Tragic Drama of William Butler Yeats, 1963, Flight Plan, 1971, Without Wishing, 1973, The Likeness, 1975, Coup, 1975, Returning Your Call, 1975, The Transport of Love: The Meghaduta by Kalidasa, 1976, Teachings of Grandfather Fox, 1977, Lost Distance, 1978, Dear Blood, 1980, Holding Patterns, 1982, Carrying On: New and Selected Poems, 1985; also record: Confessions of a Matchmaker, 1973, De Meester van Het WinterLandschap, Selected Poems in Dutch transl. by Cees Nooteboom, Uitgeverij de Arbiedspers, Amsterdam, 1990; translator: Songs of Something Else, 1982, Grace and Mercy in Her Wild Hair, 1982, (with Czeslaw Milosz) Happy As a Dog's Tail: Poems by Anna Swir, 1985, (with Czeslaw Milosz) With the Skin: Poems of Aleksander Wat, 1989 (with Arthur Quinn) The Poet's Work: Study of Czeslaw Milosz, 1991, Diary of Left Handed Bird Watcher, 1996. With U.S. Army, 1943-45, ETO. Recipient Phelan award, 1955; Longview prize, 1961; award in lit. Nat. Inst. Arts and Letters, 1971; Poetry medal Commonwealth Club, 1976, 81; U. Calif. Creative Arts fellow, 1961-62, 73-74; U. Calif. Humanities research fellow, 1983-84; Am. Inst. Indian Studies fellow, 1966-67; Guggenheim fellow, 1976-77. Mem. Assn. of Lit. Scholars and Critics. Avocation: birdwatching. Home: 40 Beverly Rd Kensington CA 94707-1304

NATHAN, MARSHALL IRA, electrical engineering educator; b. Lakewood, N.J., Jan. 22, 1933; s. Benjamin Charles and Ruth (Blumenthal) N.; m. Nancy Jennens, June 7, 1955 (div. Feb. 1970); children: Eric, Barbara; m. Rosalie Mary Lanzarone, Apr. 10, 1971. BS, MIT, 1954; MA, Harvard U., 1956, PhD, 1958. Mem. rsch. staff, then mgr. IBM, Yorktown Heights, N.Y., 1958-87; prof. dept. elec. engring. U. Minn., Mpls., 1987—, Centennial chair dept. elec. engring., 1990—; vis. prof. Cornell U., Ithaca, N.Y., 1984. Contbr. articles to profl. jours. Recognition award for semiconductor laser Laser and Electro-Optic Soc., 1986. Fellow IEEE (David Sarnoff award 1980), Am. Physical Soc. Office: Univ of Minn Dept Elec Engring 200 Union St SE Minneapolis MN 55455-0154

NATHAN, MARTIN, publishing company executive. Pres. Reed Travel Pub., Secaucus, N.J. Office: Reed Travel Pub 500 Plaza Dr Secaucus NJ 07096*

NATHAN, PAUL S., editor, writer; b. Oakland, Calif., Apr. 2, 1913; s. Alfred Jacobs and Frances (Strause) N.; m. Dorothy Goldeen, July 14, 1935 (dec. Dec. 1966); children: Andrew J., Carl F., Janet D.; m. Ruth Wilk Notkins, May 26, 1972. BA, U. Calif., Berkeley, 1934. Reporter Oakland Post-Enquirer, 1929-36; asst. play editor Paramount Pictures, N.Y.C., 1937-48; hosp. pub. relations Will, Folsom & Smith, N.Y.C., 1948-61; sci. editor Nat. Cystic Fibrosis Research Found., N.Y.C., Atlanta, 1963-73; contbg. editor column Rights and Permissions (now Rights), Pubs. Weekly, N.Y.C., 1946—; U.S. liaison Jerusalem Internat. Book Fair, 1976-77. Author: (play) Ricochet, 1980 (Edgar Allan Poe award of Mystery Writers Am. for best play of 1980), Texas Collects: Fine Arts, Furniture, Windmills & Whimseys, 1988; co-editor: (anthology) View: Parade of the Avant-Garde, 1991; author: (novels) Protocol for Murder, 1994, No Good Deed, 1995; contbr. fiction and articles to Story, N.Y. Times mag., Saturday Evening Post, Saturday Rev., others. Mem. P.E.N., Dramatists Guild, Authors Guild, Authors League, Mystery Writers Am., Phi Beta Kappa. Office: care Pubs Weekly 249 W 17th St New York NY 10011-5300

NATHAN, PETER E., psychologist, educator; b. St. Louis, Apr. 18, 1935; s. Emil and Kathryn (Kline) N.; m. Florence I. Baker, Nov. 26, 1959; children: David Edward, Anne Miller, Laura Carol, Mark Andrew. A.B., Harvard U., 1957; Ph.D., Washington U., 1962. Research fellow psychology Harvard U., 1962-64, research asso., 1964-68, asst. prof. psychology, 1968-69; research psychologist Boston City Hosp., 1964-68, dir. alcohol study unit, 1967-70; prof. Rutgers U., New Brunswick, N.J., 1969-89; dir. clin. psychology tng. Rutgers U., 1969-87, dir. Alcohol Behavior Research Lab., 1970-87, chmn. dept. clin. psychology, 1976-87, dir. Ctr. Alcohol Studies, 1983-89, Henry and Anna Starr prof. psychology, 1983-89; sr. program officer, health program MacArthur Found., 1987-89; v.p. acad. affairs, found. disting. prof. psychology U. Iowa, 1990—, dean faculties, 1990-93, provost, 1993-95, acting pres., 1995; mem. advisory council VA, 1972-76; chmn. alcoholism com. Nat. Inst. on Alcohol Abuse and Alcoholism, 1973-76, co-chmn. spl. rev. com., 1985, mem. nat. adv. coun., 1990-94; mem. psychol. scis. fellowship rev. com. NIMH, 1977-79; chmn. N.J. State Community Mental Health Bd., 1981-84; mem. working group substance use disorders, DSM-IV. Author: Cues, Decisions, and Diagnoses, 1967, Psychopathology and Society, 1975, 2d edit., 1980, Experimental and Behavioral Approaches to Alcoholism, 1978, Alcoholism: New Directions in Behavioral Treatment and Research, 1978, Clinical Case Studies in the Behavioral Treatment of Alcoholism, 1982, Professionals in Distress, 1987, Neuropsychological Deficits in Alcoholism, 1987, Introduction to Psychology, 1987, 2d edit., 1990, Abnormal Psychology, 1992, 2d edit., 1996; exec. editor Jour. Studies Alcohol, 1983-90; assoc. editor Am. Psychologist, 1977-85, Contemporary Psychology, 1991—; mem. numerous editl. bds. including Jour. Clin. Psychology, 1969—, Jour. Cons. Clin. Psychology, 1973—, Profl. Psychology, 1976-89. Fellow Am. Psychol. Assn. (chmn. sect. 3 div. 12 1976-77, rep. to council 1976-79, 82-85, pres. div. 12

1984-85). Democrat. Jewish. Home: 248 Black Springs Cir Iowa City IA 52246-3800 Office: Univ Iowa E119 Seashore Hall Iowa City IA 52242-1316

NATHAN, RICHARD ARNOLD, technology company executive; b. N.Y.C., Sept. 25, 1944; s. Joseph and Mildred (Heller) N.; m. Shelly Ann Michaels, Sept. 5, 1966 (div. Mar. 1992); children: Wendy Beth, Daniel Scott; m. Onalee Louise Bodi, Apr. 27, 1994. BS in Chemistry, MIT, 1965; PhD in Chemistry, Poly. U., Bklyn., 1969. Researcher Polaroid Corp., Cambridge, Mass., 1969; chemist Battelle Meml. Inst., Columbus, Ohio, 1970-74, project mgr., 1974-76, mgr. environ. chem. sect., 1976-79, dir. programs, 1979-80, mgr. nuclear tech. dept., 1980-85, dir. tech. mgmt., 1985-86, div. gen. mgr., 1986-87, corp. v.p., div. pres., 1987-89, group v.p., gen. mgr., 1989-92; sr. v.p. Mason & Hanger-Silas Mason Co. Inc., Lexington, Ky., 1993—. Editor: Fuels from Sugar Crops, 1976; contbr. articles to profl. publs.; patentee in field. Bd. dirs. Ctrl. Ohio coun. Boy Scouts Am., 1981-90, Ctrl. Sci. and Industry, Columbus, 1988—; chmn. Ohio Sci. Tech. and Industry Hall of Fame, 1989-93. Recipient award Indsl. Rsch. Mag., 1976. Mem. Am. Soc. Macro-Engrng. (bd. dirs. 1986—), Am. Nuclear Soc., Am. Mgmt. Assn., Ohio Acad. Sci., Sigma Xi, Phi Lambda Upsilon. Avocations: golf, reading. Office: Mason & Hanger-Silas Mason Co 2355 Harrodsburg Rd Lexington KY 40504-3324

NATHAN, RICHARD P(ERLE), political scientist, educator; b. Schenectady, N.Y., Nov. 24, 1935; s. Sidney Robert and Betty (Green) N.; m. Mary McNamara, June 5, 1957; children: Robert Joseph, Carol Hewit. AB, Brown U., 1957; M in Pub. Adminstrn., Harvard U., 1959, PhD, 1966. Legis. asst. U.S. Senator Kenneth B. Keating, Washington, 1959-62; dir. domestic policy rsch. for Nelson A. Rockefeller, 1963-64; rsch. assoc. The Brookings Instn., Washington, 1966-69, sr. fellow, project dir. monitoring studies gen. revenue sharing, community devel. block grant and pub. svc. employment programs, 1972-79; associated staff The Brookings Inst., Washington, 1980-85; asst. dir. U.S. Office of Mgmt. and Budget, Washington, 1969-71; dep. undersec. U.S Dept. Health, Edn. and Welfare, Washington, 1971-72; prof. pub. and internat. affairs Woodrow Wilson Sch. Pub. and Internat. Affairs Princeton (N.J.) U., 1979-89, also dir. Princeton Urban and Regional Rsch. Ctr., 1979-89; Disting. prof. polit. sci. and pub. policy SUNY, Albany, 1989—, provost Rockefeller Coll. Pub. Affairs and Policy, dir. Rockefeller Inst. Govt., 1989—; assoc. dir. Nat. Adv. Commn. on Civil Disorders, 1967-68; vis. prof. govt. and fgn. affairs U. Va., 1972-77; chmn. Nixon Adminstrn. Transition Task Forces on Poverty and Intergovtl. Fiscal Rels., 1968, Domestic Coun. Com. on Welfare Reform Planning, 1969-70; mem. Commn. on Orgn. Govt. of D.C., 1970-72; bd. overseers New Sch. for Social Rsch., 1982-88; mem. working seminar on family and welfare Marquette U., 1986-87; mem. selection com. Rockefeller Pub. Svc. Awards Program, 1976-78; mem. income maintenance task force Nat. Urban Coalition, 1975-78; treas. Manpower Demonstration Rsch. Corp., 1974-81, chmn., 1981—; mem. coun. scholars U.S. Libr. of Congress, 1989—; mem. N.Y. State Temp. Commn. Constl. Revision, 1993-94; mem. U.S. Adv. Commn. on Intergovtl. Rels., 1994—; bd. dirs. Fleet Bank N.Y. Author: Jobs and Civil Rights, The Role of the Federal Government in Promoting Equal Opportunity in Employment and Training, 1969, The Plot That Failed: Nixon and the Administrative Presidency, 1975, Monitoring Revenue Sharing, 1975, Revenue Sharing, The Second Round., 1977, Monitoring the Public Service Employment Program, 1978, America's Government: A Fact Book of Census Data on the Organization, Finances, and Employment of Federal, State, and Local Governments, 1979, Public Service Employment: A Field Evaluation, 1981, The Administrative Presidency, 1983, Reagan and the States, 1987, Social Sciences in Government Uses and Abuses, 1988, A New Agenda for Cities, 1992, Turning Promises into Performance: The Management Challenge of Implementing Workfare, 1993; contbr. chpts. to books; editor: (with Harvey S. Perloff) Revenue Sharing and the City, 1968, (with John D. DiJulio, Jr.) The View From the States, Making Health Reform Work, Brookings Instn., 1994; mem. editl. bd. Urban Affairs Quar., 1978-85. Eisenhower fellow European Econ. Commn., 1977. Mem. ASPA (intergovtl. mgmt. award 1985), Na.t Acad. Social Inst., Nat. Acad. Pub. Adminstrn. (James E. Webb award 1986), Am. Polit. Sci. Assn. (Charles E. Merriam award 1987), Assn. for Pub. Policy Analysis and Mgmt., Princeton Club (N.Y.C.), Phi Beta Kappa, Theta Delta Chi. Republican. Jewish. Avocations: reading, travel, movies. Home: 9 Pasture Gate Ln Delmar NY 12054-4329 Office: SUNY Rockefeller Coll Provost Office 135 Western Ave Albany NY 12203-1011

NATHANS, DANIEL, molecular biology and genetics educator; b. Wilmington, Del., Oct. 30, 1928; s. Samuel and Sarah (Levitan) N.; m. Joanne E. Gomberg, Mar. 4, 1956; children: Eli, Jeremy, Benjamin. B.S., U. Del., 1950; M.D., Washington U., 1954. Intern Presbyn. Hosp., N.Y.C., 1954-55; resident in medicine Presbyn. Hosp., 1957-59; clin. assoc. Nat. Cancer Inst., 1955-57; guest investigator Rockefeller U., N.Y.C., 1959-62; prof. microbiology Sch. Medicine, Johns Hopkins, 1962-72, prof., dir. dept. microbiology, 1972-82, Univ. prof. molecular biology and genetics, 1982—; mem. Pres. Coun. Advisers on Sci. & Tech., 1990-93; sr. investigator Howard Hughes Med. Inst., 1982—. Recipient Nobel prize in physiology or medicine, 1978, Nat. Medal of Sci., 1993. Fellow Am. Acad. Arts and Scis.; mem. NAS. Office: Johns Hopkins U-Sch Med Dept Molecular Biology & Genetics 725 N Wolfe St Baltimore MD 21205-2105*

NATHANSON, CONSTANCE A., health science organization administrator, sociology educator. Dir. Hopkins Ctr. on the Demography of Aging, Balt. Office: Johns Hopkins U Hopkins Population Ctr 615 N Wolfe St Baltimore MD 21205-2103*

NATHANSON, HARVEY CHARLES, electrical engineer; b. Pitts., Oct. 22, 1936; s. David Benjamin and Ella (Sachs) N.; m. Esther Janet Mishelevich, Oct. 13, 1963; children: Marc Elliot, Elinor Sharon. B.S.E.E., Carnegie Inst. Tech., 1958, M.S.E.E., 1959, Ph.D., 1962. Sr. engr. Junction Device Physics, Westinghouse, Research/Devel. Center, Pitts., 1962-67; fellow engr. Junction Device Physics, Westinghouse, Research/Devel. Center, 1968-72, mgr. silicon junction physics, 1972-77, mgr. microelectronics dept., 1978-90, chief scientist electronic div., 1990-95; chief scientist Northrop Grumman Sci. Tech. Ctr., Pitts., 1996—; instr. Carnegie Inst. Tech., Pitts., 1959-60; chmn. Westinghouse Sat. Sci. Honors Inst. for High Sch. Students, 1970-76; mem. adv. group on electron devices Dept. Def., 1976-86; adviser to Nat. Materials Bd., 1986-87. Contbr. articles to profl. jours.; mem. editorial bd. Solid State Electronics, 1985—. Bd. dirs. Temple Sinai, 1981-83, 95—; pres. Brotherhood, 1993-95. Recipient IR100 award, 1965, hon. mention Outstanding Young Engr. award Eta Kappa Nu, 1967, Best Display Paper award Soc. Info. Display, 1972, Carnegie-Mellon Alumni award, 1982, Westinghouse Top Corp. Patent award, 1990; named to Westinghouse Order of Merit, Westinghouse Electric Corp., 1987. Fellow IEEE (mem. editorial bd. Spectrum mag. 1989-91); mem. IEEE Electron Device Soc. (pres. 1978-80), Fedn. Materials Socs. (bd. dirs. 1987-90), Sigma Xi, Eta Kappa Nu. Democrat. Jewish. Patentee in field. Home: 5635 Marlborough Rd Pittsburgh PA 15217-1404 Office: Northrup Grumann Sci & Tech Ctr 1310 Beulah Rd Pittsburgh PA 15235-5068

NATHANSON, KIM, computer support executive; b. 1956. Buyer, in-store mgmt. Sattlers Dept. Store, Buffalo, 1975-84; with Computers Plus, Frederick, Md., 1984—; chmn. FCP Technologies, Inc. (formerly Computers Plus), Frederick, Md., 1995—. Office: FCP Technologies Inc 5726 Industry Ln Frederick MD 21704

NATHANSON, MELVYN BERNARD, university provost, mathematician; b. Phila., Oct. 10, 1944; s. Israel and Sophia (Manstein) N.; m. Marjorie Jane Frankel, Jan. 29, 1978; children: Alexander Philip, Rebecca Anne. BA, U. Pa., 1965; postgrad., Harvard U., 1965-66; MA, U. Rochester, 1968, PhD, 1972. Prof. So. Ill. U., Carbondale, 1971-81; dean Rutgers U., Newark, N.J., 1981-86; provost, v.p. acad. affairs Lehman Coll. CUNY, Bronx, 1986-91; prof. math. Grad. Sch. Lehman Coll. CUNY, 1986—; vis. prof. Moscow State U., USSR, 1972-73, Inst. for Advanced Study, Princeton U., N.J., 1974-75, 76, 90-91, Harvard U., Cambridge, Mass., 1977-78, Rockefeller U., 1982-85, Rutgers U., 1991-93. Author, editor fifteen books; contbr. articles to profl. jours. Fellow N.Y. Acad. Sci.; mem. AAAS, Am. Math. Soc., Math. Assn. Am., Assn. Mems. Inst. for Advanced Study (v.p.). Home: 123 Maplewood Ave Maplewood NJ 07040-1233 Office: CUNY Lehman Coll Dept Math Bronx NY 10468

NATHANSON, MICHAEL, film company executive. Pres. world wide prodn. Columbia Pictures Entertainment Inc., N.Y.C., from 1989, former exec. v.p. prodn.; pres. worldwide prodn. Columbia Pictures Entertainment Inc., Culver City, Calif., to 1993. Office: Columbia Pictures 10202 Washington Blvd Culver City CA 90232-3119

NATHANSON, NEAL, virologist, epidemiologist, educator; b. Boston, Sept. 1, 1927; s. Robert B. and Leah (Rabinowitch) N.; m. Constance Allen, June 8, 1954; children—Katherine L., John A., Daniel R.; m. Phoebe Starfield, Oct. 7, 1984. B.A., Harvard, 1949, M.D., 1953. Chief polio surveillance unit USPHS, 1955-57; research asso., asst. prof. anatomy Johns Hopkins, Balt., 1957-63; asso. prof. epidemiology Johns Hopkins, 1963-68, prof., 1968-79; chmn. dept. microbiology U. Pa., Phila., 1979-93, vice dean rsch., 1993-95. Editor-in-chief: Am. Jour. Epidemiology, 1964-79, Microbial Pathogenesis, 1985-88. Research, publs. pathogenesis, immunology, and epidemiology of viral infections. Home: 1600 Hagys Ford Rd Apt 9W Narberth PA 19072-1049

NATHENSON, STANLEY GAIL, immunology educator; b. Denver, Aug. 1, 1933; s. Abe and Esther (Kurland) N.; m. Susan L., Oct. 16, 1959; children: Matthew, John. BA, Reed Coll., 1955; MD, Washington U. Sch. Medicine, 1959. From asst. to prof. Albert Einstein Coll. Medicine, Bronx, N.Y., 1966—. With USPHS, 1962-64. Mem. AAAS, NAS, Am. Assn. Immunologists. Office: A Einstein Coll of Medicine Dept Microbiology & Immunology Bronx NY 10461

NATHWANI, BHARAT NAROTTAM, pathologist, consultant; b. Bombay, Jan. 20, 1945; came to U.S., 1972; s. Narottam Pragji and Bharati N. (Lakhani) N. MBBS, Grant Med. Coll., Bombay, 1969, MD in Pathology, 1972. Intern Grant Med. Coll., Bombay U., 1968-69; asst. prof. pathology Grant Med. Coll., 1972; fellow in hematology Cook County Hosp., Chgo., 1972-73; resident in pathology Rush U., Chgo., 1973-74; fellow in hematopathology City of Hope Med. Ctr., Duarte, Calif., 1975-76, pathologist, 1977-84; prof. pathology, chief hematopathology U. So. Calif., L.A., 1984—. Contbr. numerous articles to profl. jours. Recipient Grant awards Nat. Libr. Medicine, Bethesda, Md., Nat. Cancer Inst., 1991. Mem. AAAS, Internat. Acad. Pathology, Am. Soc. Clin. Pathology, Am. Soc. Hematology, Am. Soc. Oncology. Office: U So Calif Sch Medicine HMR 209 2011 Zonal Ave Los Angeles CA 90033-4526

NATION, EARL F., retired urologist, educator; b. Zephyr, Tex., Jan. 16, 1910; s. Joseph Madison and Alma Emily (Johnson) N.; m. Evelyn Stapp Poynter, Aug. 11, 1936; children: William Earl, Robert Joseph. BA, San Diego State U., 1931; MD, Western Res. U., 1935. Lic. urologist, Calif.; diplomate Am. Bd. Urology. Internship, resident in urology Los Angeles County Gen. Hosp., 1935-39; pvt. practice Pasadena, Calif., 1941-90, ret., 1990; instr., assoc. prof. urology U. So. Calif., L.A., 1941-55; sr. attending staff Huntington Meml. Hosp., Pasadena, 1941—, St. Luke Hosp., Pasadena, 1941—, also past pres.; pres. Pasadena Dispensary, 1946; lectr. Coll. Med. Evangelists (now Loma Linda U.), 1941-48. Mem. editorial bd. Jour. of Urology, 1958-66, Calif. Medicine, 1965-69, Forum on Medicine; contbr. articles to profl. jours., contbg. author to numerous books. Sec.-treas. Pasadena Breakfast Forum, 1970-73, pres. 1974-75. Crile rsch. scholar Western Res. U., 1931. Mem. ACS, AMA, Am. Urological Assn. (past pres.), Am. Osler Soc. (past pres.), L.A. County Med. Assn., Calif. Med. Assn., Pasadena Hist. Soc., So. Calif. Hist. Soc., Am. Soc. Clin. Urologists, Pasadena U. Club, Zamorano Club (v.p. L.A. chpt. 1991), Alpha Omega Alpha. Republican. Avocations: book collecting, reading, writing, gardening, fishing. Home: 311 E Sierra Madre Blvd Sierra Madre CA 91024-2675

NATION, JAMES EDWARD, retired speech pathologist; b. Springfield, Ill., Aug. 22, 1933; s. John Herbert and Margaret Josephine (Weiss) N. B.S., Ill. State U., 1959; M.S., U. Wis., 1960, Ph.D., 1964. Asst. prof. U. Ga., 1964-66; asst. prof., assoc. prof., prof. Case Western Res. U., Cleve., 1966-86; prof., chmn. dept. communication scis. Case Western Res. U., 1979-85; dir. speech pathology Cleve. Hearing and Speech Center, 1970-74; sr. clin. instr. dept. pediatrics Case Western Res. Sch. Medicine, 1979-86; speech-lang. pathologist Tucson Unified Sch. Dist. #1, 1985-95; ret., 1995; chief speech-lang. pathologist craniofacial defects team Rainbow Babies and Childrens Hosp., Univ. Hosps., Case Western Res. U., 1978-85; exec. bd. Nat. Council Grad. Programs in Speech-Lang. Pathology and Audiology; cons. in field. Author: Diagnosis of Speech and Language Disorders, 1977, Child Language Disorders, 1982, 2d rev. edit., 1984; editorial cons.: Cleft Palate Jour.; contbr. chpts. to books; editor: Ohio Speech and Hearing Jour., 1969-73; contbr. articles to profl. jours. Served with U.S. Army, 1953-55. Recipient Wittke award for disting. undergrad. teaching, 1977, Outstanding Service award Ill. State U. Alumni Assn., 1982. Fellow Am. Speech-Lang. and Hearing Assn. (cert. speech-lang. pathologist); mem. Am. Cleft Palate Assn., Ohio Speech and Hearing Assn., Aphasiology Assn. Ohio, Nat. Council Grad. Programs in Speech-Lang. Pathology and Audiology. (Disting. Service award 1982). Home: Apt 19 2600 E Skyline Dr Unit 19 Tucson AZ 85718-3065

NATION, LAURA CROCKETT, electrical engineer; b. Ft. Worth, Dec. 1, 1957; d. Donald Ray and Cora Lee (Holt) Crockett; m. David Hunter Nation, Aug. 23, 1986. BA, U. Tex., Arlington, 1980, BSEE, 1984. Registered profl. engr., Tex. With engrng. coop. TU Electric, Dallas, 1981-84; assoc. engr. TU Electric, Euless, Tex., 1984-85, Irving, Tex., 1985-87; engr. TU Electric, Dallas, 1987-91; staff engr. TU Electric, Ft. Worth, 1991-92, Ctr. for Electron Devices and Systems, U. Tex., Arlington, 1993—. Vol. United Way, Ft. Worth, 1992, Muscular Dystrophy Assn., Dallas, 1987-91. Scholar Mogul Corp., Canton, Ohio, 1976. Mem. IEEE (vol. Discover "E"), NSPE. Republican. Missionary Alliance. Home: 1303 Brittany Ln Arlington TX 76013-2320 Office: U Tex at Arlington Elec Engrng Dept 416 Yates St Arlington TX 76010-1539

NATIONS, HOWARD LYNN, lawyer; b. Dalton, Ga., Jan. 9, 1938; s. Howard Lynn and Eva Earline (Armstrong) Lamb; m. Ella Lois Johnson, June 4, 1960 (div. Nov. 1976); 1 child, Cynthia Lynn Nations Garcia. BA, Florida State U., 1963; JD, Fla. State U., 1966. Bar: Tex. 1966. Assoc. Butler, Rice Cook & Knapp, Houston, 1966-71; pres. Nations & Cross, Houston, 1971—; v.p., dir./co-founder Ins. Corp. Am., Houston, 1972—; pres. Caplinger & Nations Galleries, Houston, 1973—, Nations Investment Corp., Houston, 1975—, NCM Trade Corp., Houston, 1975; v.p. Delher Am. Inc., Houston, 1975—; pres. Howard L. Nations, P.C., Houston, 1971—; adj. prof. So. Tex. Coll. Law, Houston, 1967—; speaker in field. Author: Structuring Settlements, 1987; co-author: Texas Workers' Compensation, 1988, (with others) The Anatomy of a Personal Injury Lawsuit, 3rd rev. edit. 1991; editor: Maximizing Damages in Wrongful Death and Personal Injury Litigation, 1985; contbr. articles to profl. jours. Chair, trustee Nat. Coll. Advocacy, Washington, 1985-92. With M.I. Corps, U.S. Army, 1957-60. Fellow Tex. Bar Found., Houston Bar Found. (life); mem. ATLA (exec. com. 1991-95), Nat. Bd. Trial Advocacy (diplomate civil trial advocacy), So. Trial Lawyers Assn. (pres. 1994-95), Tex. Trial Lawyers Assn. (pres. 1992-93), Tex. Assn. Cert. Trial Lawyers (past pres.). Office: 3000 Post Oak Blvd # 1400 Houston TX 77056

NATKIN, ALVIN MARTIN, environmental company executive; b. Bklyn., Feb. 4, 1928; s. Max Harvey and Rebecca (Rubenstein) N.; m. Lorraine Rothchild, Aug. 26, 1950; children: Jeff Warren, Stacy Ellen, Marcy Caren. B in Chem. Engrng., Poly. Inst. Bkyln., 1952; MBA, Rutgers U., 1954. Engr. Standard Oil Devel. Co., Linden, N.J., 1952-57; mgr. exploratory mktg. Esso Standard Oil Co., N.Y.C., 1957-60, mgr. mktg. rsch., 1960-63; gen. mgr. Esso East Africa, Inc., Nairobi, Kenya, 1963-66; v.p. Esso Philippines, Inc., Manila, 1966-68; mgr. mktg. Esso East, Inc., Houston, 1968-77; environ. mgr. Exxon Corp., N.Y.C., 1977-84; Disting. fellow World Resources Inst., Washington, 1984-86; pres. Continental Environment Co., Summit, N.J., 1986—; internat. chmn. Petroleum Environment Inst., London, 1980-84; dir. World Industry Environment Conf., N.Y.C., 1982-86; cons. Environment & Safety Audit Corp., Midland, Mich., 1986-90. Author: Guidelines for Growth, 1984, Improving Environmental Cooperation, 1985; contbr. articles to profl. jours.; patentee in field, 1958. Served as cpl. U.S. Army, 1946-48. Recipient Disting. Service award U. Tex., 1985; named Hunter of Yr. Profl. Hunters Assn., 1965. Mem. Am. Inst. Chem. Engrs., Am. Assn. Radon Scientists, Am. Chem. Soc., Air Pollution Control Assn., Nat. Assn. Environ. Profls., Explorers Club, Chemists Club (N.Y.C.), Masons, Shriners. Republican. Jewish. Avocations: golf, fishing, hunting. Home: 21567 Villanova Dr Boca Raton FL 33433 Office: 2800 S Ocean Blvd Boca Raton FL 33432

NATKIN, ROBERT, painter; b. Chgo., Nov. 7, 1930; s. Phillip and Betty Natkin; m. Judith Dolnick; children: Joshua, Leda. B.A., Art Inst. Chgo., 1952. Exhibited paintings in numerous one-man shows, including André Emmerich Gallery, N.Y.C., Holburne of Menstrie Mus., Bath, Eng., Art Inst. Chgo., Moore Coll. Art, Phila., Ivory/Kimpton Gallery, San Francisco, Gimpel Fils Gallery, London, Gimpel & Weitzenhoffer Gallery, N.Y.C., A.B.C.D. Gallery, Paris, Tortue Gallery, Santa Monica, Calif., Galerie Brusberg, Hannover, Fed. Republic Germany, Hirshhorn Mus. and Sculpture Garden, Washington, Okla. Art Ctr., Oklahoma City, 1982 , Gloria Luria Gallery, Miami, 1984, Klonarides Gallery, Toronto, 1985; group shows include Mus. Art, Pa. State U., 1973, Poindexter Gallery, N.Y.C., 1976; represented in permanent collections, including Art Inst. Chgo., Mus. Modern Art, N.Y.C., Solomon R. Guggenheim Mus., N.Y.C., Whitney Mus. Am. Art, Hirshhorn Mus. and Sculpture Garden, Smithsonian Instn., Washington, Mus. Fine Arts, Houston, Mus. Art, R.I. Sch. Design, San Francisco Mus. Art, Mus. Art, Carnegie Inst., Duke U. Mus. Art, Centre Georges Pompidou (Beaubourg), Paris, Milw. Art Ctr., Fogg Mus. Harvard U., Met. Mus. Art, N.Y.C.

NATOLI, JOE, newspaper publishing executive. Pres. The Miami Herald, Fla. Office: The Miami Herald 1 Herald Plz Miami FL 33132-1609*

NATORI, JEFFREY KAZUO, lawyer; b. Honolulu, Aug. 15, 1958; s. Shigeo and Gertrude Keiko (Miyamoto) N.; m. Eriko Sudo, June 24, 1989; 1 child, Gemma Reina. BA, Am. U., 1980; JD, Del. Law Sch., 1983; MBA, Drexel U., 1986; cert. completion, Japan-Am. Inst. Mgmt. Sci., Honolulu and Tokyo, 1986-87. Bar: Pa. 1983, U.S. Dist. Ct. (ea. dist) Pa. 1983, Hawaii, 1987. Pvt. practice law Jeffrey K. Natori, Esquire, Phila., 1983-86; intern Seiko Instruments Inc., Tokyo, 1987; in-house counsel Chiyoda Corp., Yokohama, Japan, 1988-92; assoc. Cades Schutte Fleming & Wright, Honolulu, 1993—. Mem. ABA (speaker, Hawaii state chair, regions divsn., Fidelity and Surety law com., tort and ins. practice sect.), Internat. Bar Assn. (speaker), Japanese Soc. Internat. Transactions, Inter-Pacific Bar Assn. (vice chair com. on internat. constrn. projects 1991-93, chair, 1993-95, com. coord. 1995—), Internat. Forum Drexel U. Office: Cades Schutte Fleming & Wright 1000 Bishop St Honolulu HI 96813

NATOW, ANNETTE BAUM, nutritionist, author, consultant; b. N.Y.C., Jan. 30, 1933; d. Edward and Gertrude (Jackerson) Baum; m. Harry Natow, Nov. 30, 1955; children: Allen, Laura, Steven. BS, CUNY Bklyn. Coll., 1955; MS, SUNY Coll. Plattsburg, 1960; PhD, Tex. Women's U., 1963. Registered dietitian, N.Y. Asst. prof. SUNY Coll. Plattsburg, 1967-69, CUNY Coll. Lehman, N.Y.C., 1969-70; assoc. prof., chmn. dept. SUNY Downstate Med. Ctr., Bklyn., 1970-76; prof., dir. nutrition programs Adelphi U., Garden City, N.Y., 1976-90, prof. emerita, 1991—; intern Montreal Diet Dispensary, March of Dimes, 1980; pres., writer, cons. NRH Nutrition Cons., Inc., Valley Stream, N.Y., 1980—. Author: No-Nonsense Nutrition, 1978, Geriatric Nutrition, 1980, Nutrition for the Prime of Your Life, 1983, No-Nonsense Nutrition for Kids, 1985, Megadoses: Vitamins as Drugs, 1985, Nutritional Care of the Older Adult, 1986, Pocket Encyclopedia of Nutrition, 1986, The Cholesterol Counter, 1989, 1988, 2d edit., 1989, The Fat Counter, 1989, The Fat Attack Plan, 1990, The Diabetes Carbohydrate and Calorie Counter, 1991, The Pregnancy Counter, 1992, The Iron Counter, 1993, The Sodium Counter, 1993, The Antioxidant Vitamin Counter, 1994, The Fast Food Counter, 1994, The Supermarket Nutrition Counter, 1995; editor Jour. Nutrition for Elderly, 1983—; mem. editorial bd. Environ. Nutrition Newsletter, 1985—; mem. editorial adv. bd. Prevention, 1984-86; contbr. numerous articles to profl. jours. United Hosp. Fund grantee, 1978. Mem. Am. Dietetic Assn., N.Y. State Dietetic Assn., N.Y. State Nutrition Coun. (sec. 1973-74). Avocations: square dancing, music. Home: 100 Rosedale Rd Valley Stream NY 11581-2802 Office: NRH Nutrition Cons Inc 100 Rosedale Rd Valley Stream NY 11581-2802

NATOWITZ, JOSEPH B., chemistry educator, research administrator; b. Saranac Lake, N.Y., Dec. 24, 1936. BS in Chemistry, U. Fla., 1958; Cert. in Meteorology, UCLA, 1959; PhD in Nuclear Chemistry, U. Pitts., 1965. Staff meteorologist, 1st lt. USAF, 1958-61; grad. teaching asst. U. Pitts., 1961-62, grad. rsch. asst., 1962-65; postdoctoral rsch. assoc. SUNY, Stony Brook, 1965-67; rsch. collaborator Brookhaven Nat. Lab., 1965-67; asst. prof. Tex. A&M U., College Station, 1967-72, assoc. prof., 1972-76, prof., 1976—, head dept. chemistry, 1981-85, dir. Cyclotron Inst., 1991—; part-time instr. SUNY-Stony Brook, 1966-67; rsch. collaborator Lawrence Radiation Lab., Berkeley, Calif., 1966, Los Alamos (N.Mex.) Nat. Lab., 1973-74; Alexander Von Humboldt sr. scientist Max Planck Inst. für Kernphysik, Heidelberg, Germany, 1978; vis. prof. Inst. for Nuclear Studies, U. Tokyo, 1979, U. Claude Bernard, Inst. de Physique Nucleaire, 1983, U. de Caen, 1985, Ctr. des Etudes Nucleaires de Saclay, 1986, U. Cath. de Louvain, 1987; with accelerator review com. TASCC, Chalk River, Can.; former mem. adv. com. LBL Superhilac, ORNL Cyclotron, Nat. Superconducting Cyclotron Lab. Contbr. over 130 articles to profl. jours., also to approx. 40 books and procs. Chmn. Cub Scout Pack 802, 1973-75; v.p. College Hills PTO, 1974-75; mem. A&M Consol. Sch. Bd., 1975-78, pres., 1977-78; pres. A&M Consol. Band Boosters, 1980-81. NSF summer fellow, 1962; NASA predoctoral fellow, 1964-65; recipient Disting. Achievment award-rsch. Tex. A&M U., 1988, Am. Chem Soc. award for Nuc. Chemistry, 1995. Fellow Am. Phys. Soc.; mem. Am. Chem. Soc. (vice chmn. div. nuclear chemistry and tech. 1993, chmn. 1994, award in nuclear chemistry 1995), Sigma Xi, Phi Lambda Upsilon. Office: Tex A&M U Cyclotron Inst College Station TX 77843

NATSIOS, NICHOLAS ANDREW, retired foreign service officer; b. Lowell, Mass., July 31, 1920; s. Andrew and Fanny (Papageorgiou) N.; m. Mitzi Peterson, Sept. 2, 1951; children: Christine Daphne, Deborah Diane, Valerie Sophia, Alexandra Roxanne. Student, Lowell Technol. Inst., 1939-40; B.A. cum laude, Ohio State U., 1948; M.A.L.D., Fletcher Sch. Law and Diplomacy, 1983. Civilian spl. adviser polit. problems U.S. Mil. Mission, Salonika, Greece, 1948-50; polit. adviser mil. secretariat U.S. Mil. Mission, Athens, Greece, 1951-56; polit. officer, 1st sec. embassy, spl. asst. to ambassador Am. embassy, Saigon, Viet Nam, 1956-60; attache Am. embassy, Paris, 1960-62; spl. asst. to ambassador Am. embassy, Seoul, 1962-65; 1st sec. American embassy, Buenos Aires, Argentina, 1965-69; spl. asst. to ambassador Am. embassy, The Hague, The Netherlands, 1969-72; regional affairs officer. Am. embassy, Tehran, Iran, 1972-74; mgmt. cons., 1977—. Served to capt. AUS, 1942-47; comdg. officer Italian Frontier Control Detachment, U.S. Occupation Forces, 1945-47, Milan, Italy. Decorated medal of Merit; decorated Bronze Star U.S.; knight comdr. of Italy; Knight comdr. Order of St. George; medal of Mil. Valor Italy; D.S.C. 1st class Knights of Malta; Order of Eagle Yugoslavia; Distinguished Service medal Greece; Order of Service Merit Korea). Mem. Phi Beta Kappa, Phi Eta Sigma. Address: 77 Lincoln Pky Lowell MA 01851-3405

NATTEL, STANLEY, cardiologist, research scientist; b. Haifa, Israel, Jan. 28, 1951; arrived in Can., 1952; s. William and Julie (Zwirek) N.; m. Celia Anne Reich, Sept. 25, 1973; children: Jonathan, Ilana, Daniel, Sarah. BSc magna cum laude, McGill U., 1972, MD, 1974. Diplomate Am. Bd. Internal Medicine, Am. Bd. Cardiology. Intern in medicine Royal Victoria Hosp., 1974-75, resident in internal medicine, 1975-76; resident in clin. pharmacology Montreal (Que., Can.) Gen. Hosp., 1976-78, cardiologist, clin. pharmacologist, 1981-87, dir. coronary care unit, 1983-87; fellow in cardiology Ind. U., 1978-80; fellow in physiology U. Pa., 1980-81; asst. prof. medicine, pharmacology, medicine McGill U., Montreal, 1981-87, assoc. prof., 1987—; cardiologist Montreal Heart Inst., 1987—, dir. rsch. ctr., 1990—; prof. Dept. Medicine, U. Montreal, 1995—; external reviewer Med. Rsch. Coun., 1981—, Ont. Health Ministry, 1983-84, NSF, 1992, others; chmn. libr. com. dept. pharmacology McGill U., 1982-86, mem. grad. com., 1984-89, chmn. grad. tng. com., 1986-89, departmental rep. grad. faculty coun., 1989-91, coord. grad. teaching pharmacology, 1989-91; mem. oper. grants com. Can. Heart Found., 1983-86; chmn. clin. trials com. Montreal Gen. Hosp., 1983-87, chmn. pharmacy and therapeutics com., 1984-87, sec. clin. chemistry rev. com., 1984, course dir. drug therapy, 1984-87, acting dir. divsn. clin. pharmacology, 1984-85, mem. various coms., 1985-87; mem. fellowship awards com. FRSQ, 1988-90, mem. ctr. grants pharmacology/pharmacy com., 1989-90; chmn. pharmacology com. Montreal Heart Inst., 1988-90, mem. search com. pharmacist-in-chief, 1989-90, mem. ethics com., 1991—, chmn. internal rsch. com., 1991—, mem. consultative com. exec. dir., 1991—, chmn. consultative com. rsch. ctr., 1991—; consulting coun. pharmacology Province of Quebec, 1989-90; mem. safety monitoring com. CAMIAT Study, 1990—; assoc. prof. medicine U. Montreal, 1991-95, prof. 1995—, chmn. search com. dir. rsch. Sacré-Coeur Hosp., 1991, mem. rsch. com. CoRMES faculty medicine, 1991—, mem. rsch. com. dept. medicine, 1991—; mem. site visit team program project grant NIH, 1991, cons. program project grant, 1993, spl. reviewer cardiovascular study sect., 1993, 95; mem. oper. grants com. Med. Rsch. Coun. Can., 1988-93; mem. sr. personnel awards com. Can. Heart Found., 1994—; lectr. in field. Assoc. editor Can. Jour. Physiology and Pharmacology, 1990—; mem. editl. bd. Jour. Cardiovasc. Electrophysiology, 1991—, Drugs, 1993—, Cardiovasc. Drugs and Therapy, 1993—, Circulation Rsch., 1995—, JACC, 1995—; manuscript reviewer Am. Jour. Cardiology, Can. Med. Assn. Jour., European Jour. Pharmacology, New Eng. Jour. Medicine, others; contbr. chpts. to books and articles to profl. jours. Chmn. edn. com. Hebrew Acad. Sch., Montreal, 1991-92. Grantee Que. Heart Found., 1981—, Nordic Pharms., 1985-87, Knoll Pharms., 1991-93, others; fellow Med. Rsch. Coun. Can., 1979-81; McGill U. scholar, 1967-74, Sir Edward Beatty scholar McGill U., 1967-70, Rsch. scholar Med. Rsch. Coun., 1982-87, Sr. Rsch. scholar Fonds de la Recherche en Santé du Quebec, 1990-93. Fellow Am. Coll. Cardiology, Royal Coll. Physicians Can. (cert. medicine, cardiology); mem. Am. Heart Assn. (coun. basic sci.), Am. Soc. Pharmacology and Exptl. Therapeutics, Can. Cardiovasc. Soc. (councilor 1992-95), Can. Soc. Clin. Pharmacology (Kenneth M. Piafsky Young Investigator award 1985), Pharm. Soc. Can. Biophys. Soc. Avocations: studying Jewish religious works, sports. Home: 5609 Alpine Ave, Côte Saint Luc, PQ Canada H4V 2X6 Office: Montreal Heart Inst, 5000 Belanger St E, Montreal, PQ Canada H1T 1C8

NATTRAS, RUTH A(NN), school nurse; b. Wilkes-Barre, Pa., June 30, 1946; d. George James and Jean Harriet (LeGault) Willis; m. John D. Nattras, Aug. 23, 1969; children: John R., Laura R. Diploma, Nesbitt Meml. Hosp., Kingston, Pa., 1967. RN, Pa., N.Y. Operating room staff nurse Morristown (N.J.) Meml. Hosp., 1967-69, Horton Meml. Hosp., Middletown, N.Y., 1969-70; sch. nurse Middletown City Sch. Dist., 1986—; substitute sch. nurse, 1982-86; summer sch. nurse Pine Bush (N.Y.) Cen. Sch. Dist., 1984,86. Vol. Am. Heart Assn., Am. Cancer Soc.; den leader Boy Scouts Am., 1978-80, den leader coach, 1981, awards chmn., 1981, com. mem., 1976-84; mem. planning com. Lienhard Sch. Nursing Pace U., 1994—. Mem. N.Y. State United Tchrs. (bldg. rep. 1993—), Nat. Assn. Sch. Nurses (cert. sch. nurse), N.Y. State Assn. Sch. Nurses, Orange County Sch. Nurses, Middletown Sch. Nurses Assn., Nesbitt Meml. Hosp. Alumni Assn. (life), Order Ea. Star (matron 1991).

NATZLER, OTTO, ceramic artist; b. Vienna, Austria, Jan. 31, 1908; came to U.S., 1938, naturalized, 1944; s. Sigmund and Frieda (Loewy) N.; m. Gertrud Amon, June 1938; m. Gail Reynolds, Sept. 7, 1973. Author: (with others) Form and Fire—Natzler Ceramics 1939-72, 1973; one man exhbns. include, Fine Art Gallery, San Diego, 1940, 42, San Francisco Mus. Art, 1943, 63, Los Angeles County Mus. Art, 1944, 66, Art Inst. Chgo., 1946, 63, La Jolla Mus. Art, Calif., 1953, Cin. Art Mus., 1954, 60, Joslyn Art Mus., Omaha, 1955, Springfield Mus., Mo., 1955, Jewish Mus., N.Y.C., 1958, Bezalel Nat. Mus., Jerusalem, 1959, Mus. Modern Art, Haifa, Israel, 1959, Kunstgewerbemuseum, Zurich, Switzerland, 1959, Stedelijk Mus., Amsterdam, Holland, 1959, Tulane U., 1961, St. Paul Art Center, 1963, Mus. Contemporary Crafts, N.Y.C., 1963, Birger Sandzen Meml. Gallery, Lindsborg, Kans., 1964, Palm Springs Mus., Calif., 1968, George Walter Vincent Smith Art Mus., Springfield Mass., 1970, Carleton Coll., Northfield, Minn., 1970, retrospective, M.W. deYoung Meml. Mus., San Francisco, 1971, Renwick Gallery, Smithsonian Instn., Washington, 1973, Contemporary Crafts Gallery, Portland, 1975, Craft and Folk Art Mus., Los Angeles, 1977, Scottsdale Center for Arts, Ariz., 1977, No. Ariz. U., Flagstaff, 1978, Los Angeles County Mus. Art, 1980; retrospective show Am. Craft Mus, 1993, Juedisches Museum der Stadt, Wien, 1994; works represented in permanent collections, Renwick Gallery, Smithsonian Inst., Am. Craft Mus., N.Y.C., Cooper-Hewitt Mus., N.Y.C., Fine Arts Gallery, San Diego, Everson Mus. Art, Syracuse, N.Y., Cin. Art Mus., Los Angeles County Mus. Art, Walker Art Center, Mpls., Art Inst. Chgo., Dallas Mus. Fine Arts, Tucson Art Mus., Joselyn Art Mus., Met. Mus. Art, U. Nebr., San Francisco Mus. Art, Kantonales Gewerbemuseum, Bern, Switzerland, Phoenix Art Mus., Nat. Mus. Design, Smithsonian Instn., E.B. Crocker Art Gallery, Sacramento, Balt. Mus. Art, Detroit Inst. Art, Fort Worth Mus. Art, U. Minn., Cranbrook Acad. Art, Bloomfield Hills, Mich., Kunstgewerbemuseum, Zurich, Calif. State Fair, Sacramento, Springfield Art Mus., St. Paul Art Center, Phila. Mus. Art, Seattle Art Mus., Slater Meml. Mus., Norwich, Conn., Museo Internazionale delle Ceramiche, Faenza, Italy, Portland Mus. Art, Oreg., U. Wis., UCLA, Ariz. State Coll., Houston Mus. Fine Art, Krannert Art Mus. at U. Ill., Northwestern U., Oakland Art Mus., Calif., La Crosse State Coll., Ind., Birger Sandzen Meml. Gallery, Mus. Modern Art, N.Y.C., Mills Coll., Oakland, Palm Springs Desert Mus., Newark Mus. Art, George Walter Vincent Smith Mus., Springfield, Mass., U. Oreg., Eugene, Victoria and Albert Mus., London, Minn. Mus. Art, St. Paul, Nat. Mus. Am. History, Smithsonian Instn., Washington, Des Moines Art Center, Santa Barbara Mus. Art, Calif., Maurice Spertus Mus. Judaica, Chgo., Staatliche Museen Preussischer Kulturbesitz, Kunstgewerbemuseum, Berlin, Utah Mus., U. Utah, Salt Lake City, Jewish Mus., N.Y.C., Contemporary Crafts Gallery, Portland, Honolulu Acad. Art, Oesterreichisches Mus fuer Angewandte Kunst, Vienna, Austria, Mus. Bellerive, Zurich Switzerland, Bklyn. Mus., Nelson-Atkins Mus. Art, Kansas City, Mo., Skirball Mus., Los Angeles, Mus. Fine Arts, Boston, Va. Mus. Fine Arts, Richmond, others. Fellow Am. Craft Coun., Internat. Inst. Arts and Letters. Address: 7837 Woodrow Wilson Dr Los Angeles CA 90046-1213

NAUERT, PETER WILLIAM, insurance company executive, lawyer; b. Rockford, Ill., May 3, 1943; s. Robert W. and Irene H. (Hippenbecker) N.; B.S., Marquette U., 1965; J.D., George Washington U., 1968. children: Heather, Justin, Jonathan. Bar: D.C. 1968, Ill. 1969, U.S. Ct. Appeals (7th cir.) 1969, U.S. Supreme Ct. 1971. Vice pres. Pioneer Life Ins. Co. of Ill., Rockford, 1968-75, pres., chmn., CEO, 1975—; chmn., CEO Pioneer Fin. Svcs., Inc.; Mem. ABA, Ill. Bar Assn., Winnebago County Bar Assn., Rockford C. of C., Young Pres. Orgn., World Pres. Assn., University Club, Rockford Country Club. Office: Pioneer Fin Svcs Inc 1750 E Golf Rd Schaumburg IL 60173-5835

NAUERT, ROGER CHARLES, healthcare executive; b. St. Louis, Jan. 6, 1943; s. Charles Henry and Vilma Amelia (Schneider) N.; B.S., Mich. State U., 1965; J.D., Northwestern U., 1969; M.B.A., U. Chgo., 1979; m. Elaine Louise Harrison, Feb. 18, 1967; children: Paul, Christina. Bar: Ill. 1969. Asst. atty. gen. State of Ill., 1969-71; chief counsel Ill. Legis. Investigating Commn., 1971-73; asst. state comptroller State of Ill., 1973-75; dir. adminstrn. and fin. Health and Hosps. Governing Commn. Cook County, Chgo., 1975-79; nat. dir. health care services Grant Thornton, Chgo., 1979-88; exec. v.p. Detroit Med. Ctr., 1988-91; exec. v.p. Columbia-Presbyn. Med. Ctr., N.Y.C., 1991-93; sr. v.p. Mt. Sinai Med. Ctr., N.Y.C., 1993—; vis. lectr. healthcare mgmt. & fin. Columbia U., Vanderbilt U., U. Chgo., 1978—; preceptor Wharton Sch., U. Pa. Ford Found. grantee, 1968-69. Mem. Am. Hosp. Assn., Am. Public Health Assn., Am. Coll. Healthcare Execs., Nat. Health Lawyers Assn., Health Care Fin. Mgmt. Assn. (faculty mem.), Alpha Phi Sigma, Phi Delta Phi, Delta Upsilon. Clubs: N.Y. Athletic, Mt. Kisco Country. Author: A Sociology of Health, 1977; The Demography of Illness, 1978; Proposal for a National Health Policy, 1979; Health Care Feasibility Studies, 1980; Health Care Planning Guide, 1981; Health Care Strategic Planning, 1982; Overcoming the Obstacles to Planning, 1983; Principles of Hospital Cash Management, 1984; Healthcare Networking Arrangements, 1985; Strategic Planning for Physicians, 1986; HMO's: A Once and Future Strategy, 1987, Mergers, Acquisitions and Divestitures, 1988, Tax Exempt Status Under Seige, 1989, Governance in Multi-Hospital Systems, 1990, Planning Alternative Delivery Systems, 1991, Direct Contracting: The Future is Now, 1992, The Rise and Fall of the U.S. Healthcare System, 1993, A Proposal for National Healthcare Reform, 1994, Academic Medical Centers and the New Age of Managed Care, 1995, The Quest For Value in Healthcare, 1996. Home: 461 Haines Rd Bedford Corners NY 10549 Office: Mt Sinai Med Ctr 1 Gustave L Levy Pl New York NY 10029-6504

NAUGHTON, JAMES, actor; b. Middletown, Conn., Dec. 6, 1945; s. James Joseph and Rosemary (Walsh) N.; m. Pamela Parsons, Oct. 1968; children: Gregory J., Keira P. BA, Brown U., 1967; MFA, Yale U., 1970. Broadway appearances include Edmund in Long Day's Journey Into Night, 1971 (Theatre World award, N.Y. Drama Critics award, Vernon Rice award 1971), Stone in City of Angels (Tony award 1990, Drama Desk award), I Love My Wife, 1977, Whose Life Is It Anyway, 1980. Feature films include Paper Chase, 1972, Second Wind, 1975, A Stranger is Watching, 1981, Cat's Eye, 1982, The Glass Menagerie, 1987, The Good Mother, 1988; TV appearances include: (series) Faraday and Company, 1973-74, Planet of the Apes, 1974, Making the Grade, 1982, Trauma Center, 1983; (movies) F. Scott Fitzgerald and "The Last of the Belles", 1974, The Last 36 Hours of Dr. Durant, 1975, The Bunker, 1981, My Body, My Child, 1982, Parole, 1982, The Last of the Great Survivors, 1984, Between Darkness and the Dawn, 1985, Sin of Innocence, 1986, Necessity, 1988, The Cosby Mysteries, 1994. *

NAUGHTON, JAMES LEE, internist; b. 1946. AB, Dartmouth Coll., 1968; MD, Harvard U., 1972. Intern U. Calif. Moffitt Hosp., San Francisco, 1972-73; resident in medicine U. Calif. Affiliated Hosps., San Francisco, 1973-75, San Francisco Gen. Hosp., 1975-76; fellow in nephrology U. Calif., San Francisco, 1976-77, assoc. clin. prof. medicine, 1982—; pvt. practice, ptnr. Pinole Med. Group, Pinole, Calif. Office: Pinole Med Group 2160 Appian Way Pinole CA 94564

NAUGHTON, JAMES MARTIN, journalist; b. Pitts., Aug. 13, 1938; s. Francis Patrick and Martha Ann (Clear) N.; m. Diana Marie Thomas, Sept. 5, 1964; children—Jenifer Mary, Lara Marie, Michael Thomas, Kerry Marie. B.A. cum laude, U. Notre Dame, 1960. Reporter, photographer Painesville (Ohio) Telegraph, summer, 1955-60; reporter Cleve. Plain Dealer, 1962-69; Washington corr. N.Y. Times, 1969-77; nat. editor Phila. Inquirer, 1977-79, met. editor, 1979-83, assoc. mng. editor, 1980-86, dep. mng. editor, 1986-90, mng. editor, 1990-91, exec. editor, 1991-96; pres. The Poynter Inst. for Media Studies, St. Petersburg, Fla., 1996—; Marsh prof. U. Mich., 1977. Served with USMC, 1960-62. Recipient Disting. Service award Sigma Delta Chi, 1973. Roman Catholic. Club: Franklin Inn (Phila.). Home: 8870 Norwood Ave Philadelphia PA 19118-2711 Office: 801 Third St S Saint Petersburg FL 33701

NAUGHTON, JOHN M., insurance company executive; b. Holyoke, Mass., Dec. 18, 1936; s. James Leo and Catherine (Looney) N.; m. Frances Elaine Willard, Sept. 15, 1962; children: Michael, Matthew. BS, U. Mass., 1959. Pension cons. N.E. Life, Boston, 1959-65; pension cons. Mass. Mut. Life, Los Angeles and Phila., 1965-76; regional sales dir. Mass. Mut. Life, Boston, 1976-78; v.p. Mass. Mut. Life, Springfield, 1978, sr. v.p., 1981, exec. v.p., 1984—; bd. dirs. MML Pension Ins. Co., Oppenheimer Mgmt. Corp., Concert Capital Mgmt., Colebrook Group, APPWP; trustee SIS Bank. Chmn. Greater Springfield United Way, 1987; trustee Am. Internat. Coll., Baystate Med. Ctr.; mem. chancellor's exec. com. U. Mass.; past chmn. ERISA adv. coun. Dept. Labor. Served to capt. U.S. Army, 1960-61. Mem. Am. Soc. Pension Actuaries, Charter Life Underwriters. Republican. Roman Catholic. Clubs: Colony, Longmeadow Country, StageWest (bd. dirs.). Avocations: reading; skiing; golf; tennis. Office: Mass Mut Life Ins Co 1295 State St Springfield MA 01111-0001*

NAUGHTON, JOHN PATRICK, cardiologist, medical school administrator; b. West Nanticoke, Pa., May 20, 1933; s. John Patrick and Anne Frances (McCormick) N.; children: Bruce, Marcia, Lisa, George, Michael, Thomas. AA, Cameron State Coll., Lawton, Okla., 1952; BS, St. Louis U., 1954; MD, Okla. U., 1958; MD (hon.), Kosin U., 1995. Intern George Washington U. Hosp., Washington, 1958-59; resident U. Okla. Med. Center, 1959-64; asst. prof. medicine U. Okla., 1966-68; assoc. prof. medicine U. Ill., 1968-70; prof. medicine George Washington U., 1970-75, dean acad. affairs, 1973-75, dir. div. rehab. medicine and Regional Rehab. Research and Tng. Center, 1970-75; dean Sch. Medicine, SUNY, Buffalo, 1975—; prof. medicine and physiology Sch. Medicine, SUNY, 1975—, lectr. in rehab. medicine, 1975; acting v.p. for health scis. SUNY, 1983-84, v.p. clin. affairs, 1984—; dir. Nat. Exercise and Heart Disease Project, 1972—; chmn. policy adv. bd. Beta-blocker Heart Attack Trial Nat. Heart, Lung and Blood Inst., 1977-82; pres. Western N.Y. chpt. Am. Heart Assn., 1983-85, v.p. N.Y. State affiliate, 1985, pres. N.Y. State affiliate, 1988-90; chmn. clin. applications and preventions adv. com. Nat. Heart, Lung and Blood Inst., 1984; mem. Fed. COGME working group on consortia, 1996, N.Y. Gov.'s Commn. on Grad. Med. Edn., 1985, N.Y. State Coun. on Grad. Med. Edn., 1988-90, chmn. 1996—; pres. Assoc. Med. Schs. N.Y., 1982-84, mem. adminstrv. com. Coun. of Deans, 1983-89; mem. N.Y. State Dept. of Health Adv. Com. on Physician Recredentialing; mem. exec. coun. Nat. Inst. on Disability and Rehab. Rsch. 1991-92. Author: Exercise Testing and Exercise Training in Coronary Heart Disease, 1973, Exercise Testing: Physiological, Biomechanical, and Clinical Principles, 1988. Career devel. awardee Nat. Heart Inst., 1966-71; recipient Brotherhood-Sisterhood award in medicine NCCJ, N.E. Minority Educators award, 1990, Acad. Alumnus of Yr. award Okla. U., 1990, award for svc. to minorities in med. edn., 1991, Honorary Doctor of Medicine award, Kosin U., 1995, Frank Sindelar award N.Y. State Am. Heart Assn., 1995, James Platt White Soc. award, 1995, Outstanding Contbns. in the field of Health Care award Sheehan Meml. Hosp., 1995. Fellow ACP, Am. Coll. Cardiology, Am. Coll. Sports Medicine (pres. 1970-71), Am. Coll. Chest Physicians; mem. N.Y. State Heart Assn. (pres.), Am. Coll. Cardiology (coun. N.Y. chpt.). Office: SUNY Buffalo Sch Medicine Biomed Scis 3435 Main St Buffalo NY 14214-3001

NAUGHTON, PATRICIA J., gerontological nurse, administrator, consultant; b. Blair, Nebr., Aug. 31, 1938; d. J. Merton and Emily J. (Spanggaard) Kuhr; m. John Naughton, Sept. 1, 1986; children: Jeff Kloster, Tara Schnack, Anne LaBrie, Neal Kloster. Diploma N.E. Nebr. Meth. Hosp., Sch. Nursing, Omaha, 1974; student, U. Nebr., Omaha, Iowa Lakes Community Coll., Spencer. Cert. gerontology ANCC. DON Bapt. Meml. Home, Harlan, Iowa, Sunny View Care Ctr., Ankeny, Iowa, Quality Health Care Ctr., Des Moines, Regency Care Ctr., Norwalk, Iowa, 1990-91; nurse cons. The Britwill Co., Dallas, 1991-92; DON Good Shepherd Luth. Home, 1992—. Mem. Nebr. Commn. for Hearing Impaired; sec. Network for the Elderly; mem. Iowa Tri-Coun. Nursing Summit. Mem. Iowa Coun. Gerontol. DONs (sec., pres.), Nebr. Health Care Assn., Omaha Dist. Nursing Soc. (pres.), Liaison Group Nebr. Nurses Orgn., Lions (v.p.), Beta Sigma Phi (past pres., Woman of Yr. 1984, 91, 95).

NAUGHTON, PAUL FRANCIS, financial executive; b. Port Monmouth, N.J., Sept. 1, 1942; s. John Paul and Gertrude (Sheehan) N.; m. Jean Connell, Sept. 18, 1965; children: Thomas, Brian, Jacqueline Ann. BS, LaSalle U., 1964; MBA, St. John's U., 1969. Sr. analyst Dean Witter & Co., N.Y.C., 1968-70; ptnr., sr. analyst F.S. Smithers & Co., N.Y.C., 1970-72; v.p. 1st Boston Corp., N.Y.C., 1972-75; treas. Am. Natural Svc. Co., Detroit, 1975-79; v.p. Dean Witter Reynolds Inc., 1979-81; v.p. fin. Mich. Consol. Gas Co., Detroit, 1981-86, also dir.; sr. v.p. chief fin. officer Primark Corp., McLean, Va.; pres., chief exec. officer Primark Fin. Svcs., Inc., McLean, 1984-86; mng. ptnr. Fin. Resource Enterprises, 1986-87; sr. v.p., chief fin. officer Potomac Capital Investment Corp., 1987-91, pres., COO, dir., 1991—; bd. dirs., treas. Recording for the Blind, 1990. Mem. Fin. Execs. Inst., N.Y. Soc. Security Analysts, Hidden Creek Country Club (Va.), Univ. Club (Washington), Delta Sigma Pi. Home: 1058 Harriman St Great Falls VA 22066-2533 Office: Potomac Capitol Investment Corp 900 19th St NW Washington DC 20006-2105

NAUHEIM, STEPHEN ALAN, lawyer; b. Washington, Nov. 17, 1942; s. Ferdinand Alan and Beatrice Lillian (Strasburger) N.; children: Terry Beth, David Alan. BS in Acctg., U. N.C., 1964; JD, Georgetown U., 1967; LLM, George Washington U., 1970. Bar: D.C. 1968, U.S. Ct. Claims 1968, U.S. Tax Ct. 1971. Atty. adviser office chief counsel IRS, Washington, 1967-71, asst. br. chief, 1970-71; assoc. Surrey & Morse, Washington, 1971-75, ptnr., 1975-81; prin. Anderson, Hibey, Nauheim & Blair, Washington, 1981-91, Schall, Boudreau & Gore, Washington, 1991-93; pres., gen. counsel CMW Group, Ltd., Washington, 1994—; internat. adviser Price Waterhouse LLP, 1996—; mem. adv. bd. World Trade Inst., N.Y.C., 1978—, Tax Mgmt. Adv. Bd., Washington, 1980—; internat. adv. Price Waterhouse LLP, 1996—. Mem. editl. bd. Internat. Tax Jour., N.Y.C., 1982—; contbr. to profl. publs. Mem. ABA (former com. chmn. taxation sect.), Internat. Fiscal Assn., D.C. Bar Assn. (mem. steering com. tax sect. 1987-92, chmn. tax sect. 1990-92), Am. Coll. of Tax Counsel. Avocations: travelling, sailing. Office: CMW Group Ltd 1350 Eye St NW Ste 820 Washington DC 20005

NAULEAU, HEIDI A., holding company executive, metal products executive; b. 1957. Grad., U. Pa., 1978. With Aarque Sec. Corp., Jamestown, N.Y., 1978—, pres.; also bd. dirs. Aarque Mgmt. Corp.; bd. dirs., sec. Cold Metal Products, Youngstown, Ohio. Office: Aarque Sec Corp 111 W 2nd St Jamestown NY 14701-5207

NAULT, FERNAND, choreographer; b. Montreal, Dec. 27, 1921. Leading character dancer, ballet master Am. Ballet Theatre, N.Y.C., 1944-65; dir. ABT's Sch. of Classical Ballet, N.Y.C., 1960-64; co-artistic dir., resident choreographer Les Grands Ballets Canadiens, 1965-73, resident choreographer, 1973-90, artistic advisor, 1987-90, choreographer emeritus, 1990—; adv. dir. L'Écle Supérieure de Danse du Québec, 1973-90; guest choreographer Colorado Ballet, 1978-81, artistic dir., 1981-82. Choreographer works, Am. Ballet Theatre, Joffrey Ballet Co., Harkness Co., Colo. Concert Ballet Co., Md. Ballet Co., Atlanta Ballet, Ballet Fedn. Phillipines; works choreographed include Claytonia, 1960, The Lonely Ones, 1960, Iskushenye, 1960, Giosco, 1961, Latin American Symphoniette, 1961, Cyclic, 1962, Roundabout, 1962, The Sleeping Beauty, 1963, Carmina Burana, 1966, Pas d'Eté, 1966, La Lettre, 1966, Hip and Straight, 1970, Tommy, 1970, Coppelia, 1971, Cantique des cantiques, 1974, Liberté Temperée, 1976, La Scouine, 1977. Other choreographed works include Aurki, Ceremonie, Casse-Noisette/The Nutcracker, Chants de douleur chants d'allégresse/Songs of Joy and Sorrow, Gehenne, Incohérence, L'Oiseau de feu, La fille mal gardée, Les sept péchés capitaux/The Seven Deadly Sins, Les sylphides, Miribilia, Mobiles, Paquita (Pas de deux), Pas d'époque, Pas rompu, Quintan, Quintessence, Symphonie de psaumes, Ti-Jean, Try, Ready, Go, Visages. Recipient Silver medal for choreography 7th Internat. Ballet Competition Varna, Bulgaria, 1976; Order of Canada, 1977, Prix Denise-Pelletier, Quebec, 1985, Chevalier de l'ordre national du Quebec, 1990. Office: Les Grands Ballets Canadiens, 4816 rue Rivard, Montreal, PQ Canada H2J 2N6

NAULT, WILLIAM HENRY, publishing executive; b. Ishpeming, Mich., June 9, 1926; s. Henry J. and Eva (Perrault) N.; m. Helen E. Matthews, Nov. 28, 1946; children: William Henry, Rebecca Nault Marks, Ronald, George, Peter, Julia Nault Doyle, Robert, David. AB, No. Mich. U., 1948, LittD (hon.), 1988; MA, U. Mich., 1949; EdD, Columbia U., 1953, LittD (hon.), LLD (hon.), LHD (hon.). Dir. adult edn. Battle Creek, Mich., 1948-49; guidance counselor, 1949-50; prin. W.K. Kellogg High Sch., Battle Creek, 1950-53; research assoc. Columbia U., 1953-54; asst. supt. Ridgewood, N.J., 1954-55; adj. prof. Patterson State Coll., N.J., 1954-55; dir. research World Book, Inc. (formerly Field Enterprises Edn. Corp.), Chgo., 1955-63; v.p. World Book, Inc. (formerly Field Enterprises Edn. Corp.), 1963-66, sr. v.p., editorial dir., 1966-68, exec. v.p. and editorial dir., 1968-83; pres., pub., chief operating officer World Book, Inc., 1983-84, gen. chmn. editorial adv. bds., 1968—, pub., 1983—; past vice chmn. Govt. Adv. Com. on Internat. Library and Book Programs, U.S. Dept. State; past mem. nat. adv. bd. Ctr. on Ednl. Media and Materials for Handicapped; past mem. exec. bd. Commn. Instns. Higher Edn., North Central Assn. Colls. and Secondary Schs.; mem. dean's adv. council Coll. Bus. and Pub. Adminstrn., U. Mo., Columbia; mem. nat. council Inst. Internat. Edn. Author material on courses of study. Mem. alumni com. Columbia Tchrs. Coll. Capital Campaign; mem. White House Conf. on Youth; pres. Oak Park (Ill.) Bd. Edn., 1960-63; bd. regents Lincoln Acad., Ill.; past trustee Adler Planetarium, De Paul U., Chgo. Geol. Soc.; trustee No. Mich. U. Devel. Fund; bd. dirs. H.V. Phalin Found. Grad. Study; mem. adv. bd. Rosary Coll.; liberal arts and scis. adv. council De Paul U. Served with F.A., AUS, 1944-45. Recipient Columbia U. Tchrs. Coll. medal for disting. svc. in edn.; named Disting. Alumnus No. Mich. U., U. Mich. Fellow AAAS; mem. ALA, Chgo. Planetarium Soc. (trustee), Chgo. Geog. Soc. (dir.), Am. Acad. Polit. and Social Sci., Am. Edn. Research Assn., Am. Assn. Sch. Adminstrs., Assn. Supervision and Curriculum Devel., Chgo. Pubs. Assn. (past pres.), Ill. Assn. Sch. Adminstrs., Ill. Acad. Sci., Nat. Sci. Tchr. Assn., Nat. Council Tchrs. English, Assn. Am. Geographers, Assn. Childhood Edn. Internat., Nat. Assn. Elementary Sch. Prins., Nat. Assn. Secondary Sch. Prins., Council for Advancement Sci. Writing, Internat. Platform Assn., Nat. Council Social Studies, Nat. Soc. Study Edn. Roman Catholic. Clubs: Mid-Am, Mchts. and Mfrs. Office: World Book Inc 525 W Monroe St Chicago IL 60661-3629

NAULTY, SUSAN LOUISE, archivist; b. Abington, Pa., May 28, 1944; d. Charles J. and Ruth E. (Schick) N. BA, Whittier Coll., 1967; MA, Loyola U., L.A., 1972. Tchr. history and English, Whittier (Calif.) H.S., 1968-70; from libr. asst. to asst. curator Huntington Libr., San Marino, Calif., 1972-91; archivist Richard Nixon Libr. and Birthplace, Yorba Linda, Calif., 1991—. Republican. Roman Catholic. Office: Richard Nixon Libr & Birthplace 18001 Yorba Linda Blvd Yorba Linda CA 92686

NAUMANN, HANS JUERGEN, manufacturing company executive; b. Fed. Republic Germany, May 5, 1935; came to U.S., 1960; s. Herbert and Elfriede (Heydenreich) N.; m. Edith Huempel; children: Irene, Michelle, Jacqueline, John. MME, U. Hamburg, Fed. Rep. Germany, 1960; MBA, Rochester (N.Y.) U., 1965. Registered profl. engr., N.Y. Mgr. engring. Farrell Corp., Rochester, 1961-66; exec. v.p. Hegenscheidt Corp., Troy, Mich., 1966-70; pres., chief exec. officer, stockholder Hegenscheidt GmbH, Erkelenz, Fed. Republic Germany, 1970-82; chmn., chief exec. officer Internat. Knife Corp., Erlanger, Ky., 1982-84; chmn. bd., chief exec. officer, stockholder Simmons Machine Tool Corp., Albany, N.Y., 1984—; chmn., CEO, stockholder Niles-Simmons Industrieanlagen, GmbH, Chemnitz, Germany, 1992—; chmn. bd. dirs., CEO Constant Velocity Systems, Inc., Ballston Spa, N.Y., 1993—. Author: Tool and Manufacturing Engineering Handbook, 1976; patentee roller finishing and deep rolling. Bd. dirs. U. Albany Fund, Inc., 1986—. Mem. ASME, SAE, Am. Inst. Mgmt. (pres.'s coun.), Am. Mgmt. Assn., Am. Pub. Transit Assn., Verein Deutscher Ingenieure, Soc. Mech. Engrs., Capital Region Tech. Devel. Coun., Capital Region World Trade Coun., Assn. for Mfg. Tech. (formerly Nat. Machine Tool Builders Assn.), Albany Colonie Regional C. of C., Rwy. Supply Assn., N.Y. R.R. Club Inc., Lions (past pres.). Avocations: sailing, tennis, golf, skiing. Home: 26 Folmsbee Dr Albany NY 12204-1206 Office: Simmons Machine Tool Corp 1700 Broadway Albany NY 12204-2701

NAUMANN, ROBERT BRUNO ALEXANDER, chemistry and physics educator; b. Dresden, Germany, June 7, 1929; came to U.S., 1932, naturalized, 1951; s. Eberhard Bruno and Elsa Henriette (Haege) N.; m. Marina Grot Turkevich, Sept. 16, 1961; children: Kristin Ragnhild Naumann Juros, Andrew John Bruno. B.S., U. Calif., Berkeley, 1949; M.A., Princeton U., 1951, Ph.D., 1953. Mem. faculty Princeton U., 1953—, prof. chemistry and physics, 1973-92, prof. emeritus chemistry and physics, 1992—; mem. vis. staff Los Alamos Nat. Lab., 1970-86; rsch. collaborator Brookhaven Nat. Lab., 1984-87; sci. assoc. CERN, Geneva, 1985-96; vis. prof. physics dept. Tech. U. Munich, 1988; vis. scholar physics Dartmouth Coll., 1992-96, adj. prof. physics and astronomy, 1996—. Author articles electromagnetic isotope separation, nuclear structure via radioactive and charged particle nuclear spectroscopy, implantation radioactive isotopes into solids, formation and properties of muonic atoms. Recipient Alexander von Humboldt Stiftung Sr. U.S. Scientist award, 1978, 83; Allied Chem. and Dye Corp. fellow, 1951-52, Procter and Gamble faculty fellow, 1959-60; Deutsche Forschungsgemeinschaft grantee, 1988. Fellow Am. Phys. Soc., AAAS; mem. Am. Chem. Soc. (chmn. Princeton U. sect. 1975, Chmn. Div. Nuclear Chemistry and Technology 1984), Sierra Club, Phi Beta Kappa, Sigma Xi (chmn. Princeton, N.J. sect. 1986-87). Episcopalian. Home: 387 Hawk Pine Hills Norwich VT 05055-9516

NAUMANN, WILLIAM CARL, consumer products company executive; b. Peoria, Ill., Mar. 25, 1938; s. William Louis and Emma (Bottin) N.; m. Polly Roby, May 20, 1962 (div. 1980); children: Jeff, Heather, Derek; m. Patricia Gallagher, Sept. 9, 1993. BSCE, Purdue U., 1960; MBA, U. Chgo., 1975. With Inland Steel Products Co., Chgo., 1960-74, N.Y. dist. mgr., 1968-70, div. gen. mgr., 1971-74; group v.p., bd. dirs. Inryco, Melrose Park, Ill., 1974-81; asst. chief engr. Inland Steel Co., Chgo., 1981-82, asst. gen. mgr. corp. planning, 1982-83, asst. gen. mgr. sales, 1983-85, gen. mgr. sales and mktg., 1985-87; exec. v.p. internat. ops. Hussmann Corp., Bridgeton, Mo., 1987; exec. v.p. sales and mktg. Hussmann Corp., Bridgeton, 1987; pres. Hussmann Food Svc. Co., Bridgeton, 1987-89; corp. v.p., chief quality officer

Whitman Corp., Chgo., 1989-91; CEO Ranger Industries, 1992; sr. v.p., COO Pexco Holdings, Inc., Tulsa, 1993—; also bd. dirs. Pexco Holding Inc., , Tulsa; bd. dirs. Nat. Tobacco Co., Crosman Air Rifle, Voit Sports, Fla. Orthopedics and Worldwide Sports and Recreation. Mem. U. Chgo. Exec. Program Club (past pres.), Cedar Ridge Country Club (Tulsa), U. Chgo. Alumni Assn. (past pres., bd. govs. 1986-95), Beta Gamma Sigma. Avocations: sailing, travel, tennis. Home: 5146 E 107th Pl Tulsa OK 74137 Office: 7130 S Lewis Ave Ste 850 Tulsa OK 74136-5490

NAUMOFF, PHILIP, physician; b. Pitts., Feb. 16, 1914; s. Louis and Celia (Rubenstein) N.; m. Esther Zuckerman, Aug. 21, 1937; children—Carolyn Naumoff Lerner, Susan Naumoff Southern, Lawrence Jay, Elizabeth Anne Naumoff McCarthy, Deborah Jane Naumoff Flynn. B.S., U. Pitts., 1934; M.D., Duke U., 1937. Intern U. Pitts. Hosps., 1937-38; resident Bradford (Pa.) Hosp., 1938-39; gen. practice medicine Charlotte, N.C., 1946—; chmn. dept. family practice Meml. Hosp., 1964-79; Asst. clin. prof. community health scis. Duke Med. Center, Durham, N.C., 1973-79. Served to maj. M.C. AUS, 1942-46. Mem. AMA, Am. Acad. Family Physicians, N.C. Acad. Family Physicians (past pres.), Mecklenburg County Med. Soc. (past pres.), Heart Assn. Mecklenburg County (past pres.), B'nai B'rith (past pres. N.C.). Home: 4214 Woodglen Ln Charlotte NC 28226-7247 Office: 1012 S Kings Dr Charlotte NC 28283-0001

NAUNTON, RALPH FREDERICK, surgeon, educator; b. London, Sept. 26, 1921; came to U.S., 1954, naturalized, 1962; s. Frederick and Violet (Leader) N.; m. Mary Beatrice Ball, Aug. 25, 1945 (div.); children—Phillip, David; m. Natasha Tjonamon Cofield, Aug. 3, 1978. M.B., B.S., U. Coll., U. London, 1945. Intern U. Coll. Hosp., London, 1945-46; resident in otolaryngology U. Coll. Hosp., 1946-49; mem. Med. Research Council Eng., 1949-54; mem. faculty U. Chgo. Med. Sch., 1954—, prof. surgery, 1964-80, chmn. otolaryngology sect., 1966-79; dir. div. communicative disorders Nat. Inst. Neurol., Communicative Disorders and Stroke, NIH, 1980—. Contbr. articles on physiology and pathology, also treatment hearing and hearing disorders to profl. jours. Fellow ACS, Royal Soc. Medicine; mem. Royal Coll. Surgeons, Am. Otol. Soc., Collegium Oto-Rhino-Laryngol. Soc., Sigma Psi. Home: 3303 Pauline Dr Bethesda MD 20815-3919 Office: NIH Nat Inst Deafness & Comm Disorder 6120 Executive Blvd # 400 C Rockville MD 20852-4909

NAUS, JAMES H., accountant; b. 1944. Ptnr. Cowe Chizek & Co. Office: Cowe Chizek & Co 2100 Market Tower 10 West Market St Indianapolis IN 46204-2970*

NAUSEDA, ANN JURA See **JILLIAN, ANN**

NAVA, CYNTHIA D., state legislator. BS, Western Ill. U.; MA, Ea. Ill. U. Dep. supt. Gadsden Schools; mem. N.Mex. Senate; mem. rules com., fin. com. Home: 3002 Broadmoor Dr Las Cruces NM 88001-7501 Office: N Mex Senate State Capitol Santa Fe NM 87503*

NAVA, ELOY LUIS, financial consultant; b. N.Y.C., May 19, 1942; s. Eloy and Dolores Nava; m. Diane Margret Binder, Dec. 21, 1968; children: Alyson Beth, David Eloy. BMgmt Engring., Rensselaer Poly. Inst., 1964, BMech. Engring., 1965, MSMgmt., 1970. Cert. fund specialist. Indsl. engr. Johnson & Johnson Inc., Troy, N.Y., 1965-66; nuclear project engr. and chief nuclear test engr. to ops. analysis project mgr. Electric Boat Div., Gen. Dynamics Corp., Groton, Conn., 1966-78; ptnr., chief fin. officer Collado Ozamiz Co., N.Y.C., 1978-88; pres., chmn. bd. JB Apparel Corp., N.Y.C., 1984-93; v.p., sr. fin. cons. Cruice Investment Advisors, Ltd., 1994-95; sr. assoc. Fleming, Relyea & Cox, Inc., Stamford, Conn., 1996—; bd. dirs. Jose Blanco Inc., Santo Domingo, Dominican Republic; mgmt., fin. cons. various orgns. in Dominican Republic. Chmn. water, sewer com. City of Waterford, Conn., 1975-77; mem. Rep. Nat. Com.; swimming ofcl. YMCA, USS. Mem. Midwest Decoy Collectors Assn., NRA, Am. Philatelic Soc., Country Club of Darien (Conn.). Roman Catholic. Avocations: fishing, golf, skiing, stamp and antique decoy collecting. Home: 15 Pasture Ln Darien CT 06820-5618

NAVAJAS, GONZALO, foreign language educator; b. Barcelona, Spain, May 14, 1946; came to U.S., 1970; s. Jose and Carmen (Navarro) N.; 1 child, Paul. PhD, UCLA, 1975. Prof. SUNY, Stony Brook, 1980-83, Tulane U., New Orleans, 1983-85; prof. dept. Spanish and Portuguese U. Calif., Irvine, 1985—; lectr., mem. editorial bd. various jours. in field. Author 8 books; contbr. articles to profl. jours. Mem. Modern Assn. Am., Internat. Assn. Hispanists.

NAVALKAR, RAMCHANDRA GOVINDRAO, microbiologist, immunologist; b. Bombay, May 7, 1924; s. Govindrao Narayan and Shantabai Navalkar; m. Shubhangi Navalkar, Dec. 27, 1966; children: Sushant, Sudevi. BS, Bombay U., 1946, STC, 1952, PhD, 1956. Research asst. Acworth Leprosy Hosp., Bombay, 1952-56, field and research officer, 1959-60; biologist Stanford Research Inst., Menlo Park, Calif., 1956-58; vis. fellow sch. pub. health Harvard U., Cambridge, Mass., 1958; postdoctoral fellow dept. med. microbiology Stanford (Calif.) U., 1956-58; project assoc. dept. med. microbiology U. Wis., Madison, 1960-63, 66-67; research engr. assoc. Inst. Med. Microbiology, U. Gothenburg, Sweden, 1964-65; asst. prof. microbiology Meharry Med. Coll., Nashville, 1967-72, assoc. prof. microbiology, 1972-76, prof. microbiology, 1976-80; prof., chmn. dept. microbiology and immunology Morehouse Sch. Medicine, Atlanta, 1980—; mem. site visit com. NIH for tuberculosis rsch. programs, India, 1975; prin. co-ord. Immunology of Leprosy Project, Al-Azhar U., Cairo, 1977; mem. ad hoc rev. com. NIH, 1978, 1979, Internat. Leprosy Assn. Workshop on Microbiology, Mexico City, 1978; mem. project site visit com. NIH, Atlanta, 1978, exec. com. Sci. Rsch. Inst., Atlanta Univ. Ctr.; cons. MARC program Tenn. State U., Nashville, 1981; disting. guest and cons. to Inst. Dermatology, People's Republic of China, 1982; chmn., mem. NIH spl. study sect. on AIDS-related infectins, 1990, on tuberculosis present in lung, 1993; mem. AIDS and related-rsch. study sect., DRG, NIH, 1995—. Guest reviewer Internat. Jour. Leprosy, 1984; contbr. numerous articles and rsch. papers to profl. jours. Recipient Golden Apple award Meharry chpt. Student Am. Med. Assn., 1972, Maj. Gen. Sahib Singh Sokhey Outstanding Researcher award, 1976; grantee NIH, 1966-82, 83-87, 89-92, 92-97, PI WHO, 1983-84. Fellow Am. Acad. Microbiology; mem. Am. Soc. Microbiology, The Soc. for Exptl. Biology and Medicine, Internat. Leprosy Assn., Indian Assn. of Leprologists, Acworth Leprosy Hosp. Soc. for Research and Rehab. (life mem.), Assn. Med. Sch. Microbiology Chairmen. Avocations: reading, cooking. Office: Morehouse Sch of Medicine Dept of Microbiology and Immunology Atlanta GA 30310-1495

NAVAR, LUIS GABRIEL, physiology educator, researcher; b. El Paso, Tex., Mar. 24, 1941; s. Luis and Concepcion (Najera) N.; m. Randa Ann Bumgarner, Oct. 15, 1965; children: Tonia, Tess, Gabriel, Daniel. BS, Tex. A&M U., 1962; PhD, U. Miss., 1966, postdoctoral study, 1966-69. Instr. dept. physiology/biophysics U. Miss., Jackson, 1966-67, asst. prof., 1967-71, assoc. prof., 1971-74; assoc. prof. U. Ala., Birmingham, 1974-76, prof., 1976-88, assoc. prof. Nephrology Rsch. and Tng. Ctr., 1979-83, prof., 1983-88; prof., chmn. dept. physiology Tulane U. Med. Sch., New Orleans, 1988—; vis. scientist Duke U. Med. Ctr., Durham, N.C., 1972-73. Assoc. editor: News in Physiol. Scis., 1994—, Am. Jour. Physiology, 1983-89, mem. editorial bd., 1982-83; assoc. editor Hypertension, 1993—; mem. editorial bd. Kidney Internat., 1976-87, Hypertension, 1980-83, assoc. editor, 1993—; editorial bd. Kidney, 1992—, Clinical Science, 1994—; contbr. sci. papers, book chpts., slides and tapes to profl. publs. Chmn. cardiorenal rsch. study com. Am. Heart Assn., 1994-95, mem. nat. rsch. com. 1994-99. Recipient Rsch. Career Devel. award Nat. Heart, Lung and Blood Inst., 1974-79; Merit award, 1988. Mem. AAAS, Am. Physiol. Soc. (coun. 1991-94), Am. heart Assn. (kidney, high blood pressure couns., nat. rsch. com. 1994—), N.Y. Acad. Sci., Am. Soc. Nephrology, Internat. Soc. Nephrology, Am. Soc. Hypertension (coun. 1992-94), Internat. Soc. Hypertension, Assn. Chmn. Depts. Physiology (councillor 1993-95, pres.-elect 1995-96, pres. 1996-97). Democrat. Roman Catholic. Home: 10020 Hyde Pl River Ridge LA 70123-1522 Office: Tulane U Med Sch Dept Physiology 1430 Tulane Ave New Orleans LA 70112-2699

NAVARRE, ROBERT WARD, manufacturing company executive; b. Monroe, Mich., May 21, 1933; s. Joseph Alexander N.; m. Barbara Anne Navarre, June 26, 1953; children—Veo Anne, Robert Ward, Jan Louise. B.S. in Commerce, U. Notre Dame, 1955; grad., exec. program Stanford U., 1979. Sales mgr. Marben Corp., Jackson, Mich., 1958-64; mktg. adminstr. Simpson Industries, Litchfield, Mich., 1964-67; pres., CEO Simpson Industries, 1967-89, chmn., 1989—, also bd. dirs.; bd. dirs. Webster Industries, Kysor Insl. Corp., Cadillac, Mich., Libertyville Toyota, Ill. Chmn. Jackson/Hillsdale Mental Health Service Bd., 1972-78; mem. Hillsdale Schs. Bd. Edn., 1972-76. Mem. NAM (regional vice chmn. 1978-79, chmn. membership com. 1979-80, bd. dirs.), Mich. Mfg. Assn. (bd. dirs., chmn. 1991—). Roman Catholic. Office: Simpson Industries Inc 47603 Halyard Dr Plymouth MI 48170-2429

NAVARRETE, YOLANDA, lawyer; b. Havana, Cuba, May 12, 1960; came to U.S., 1962; d. Concepcion (Bernardez) N.; children: Kristopher Suris, Adam Suris. BA in Bilingual/Bicultural Edn., Kean Coll., 1983; JD, Rutgers U., 1991. Bar: N.J. 1991. Tchr. Eliz (N.J.) Bd. Edn., 1983-85, Dover (N.J.) Bd. Edn., 1990-91; atty. Jose Navarette, Union City, N.J., 1991—; linguistic cons. Aguirre Internat., Calif., 1985-87. Bd. mem. Cesarean Prevention Movement, N.J., 1985. Mem. ABA, North Hudson Lawyers. Office: Navarrete & Navarrete 3916 Bergenline Ave Union City NJ 07087-4820

NAVARRO, ANTONIO (LUIS), public relations executive; b. Havana, Cuba, Sept. 26, 1922; came to U.S., 1940; s. Antero Navarro and Aurora (Pérez-Zuazo) Todd; m. Avis Hedges, Dec. 28, 1954; children: Antonio, Avis, Alexander. B.S. in Chem. Engring., Ga. Tech., 1944. With Shell Chem. Corp., Calif., 1944-50, Lobo Sugar Trading, Cuba, 1950-54, Textilera Ariguanabo (Hedges Family Textile Bus.), Cuba, 1954-61; mgr. Peruvian ops. W.R. Grace & Co., Lima, Peru, 1961-73; v.p. corp. adminstrn. group, mgr. corp. communications W.R. Grace & Co., N.Y.C., 1973-78, corp. v.p., 1978-82, sr. v.p., 1982-87, group exec., corp. relations group, corp. communications, govt. relations, investor relations, 1986-87; vice chmn. Jack Hilton Inc., 1987-88; dir. Office of Cuba Broadcasting (Radio Marti and TV Marti) USIA, Washington, 1990-93; pub. rels. cons., 1994—; bd. dirs. Radio Free Europe/Radio Liberty Fund, 1986. Author: (memoir of Cuban revolution) Tocayo, 1981 (Conservative Club Selection award 1981). Bd. dirs. Accion, N.Y.C., 1973-91; mem. Coun. of Ams. (now Ams. Soc.), 1976-86; bd. dirs. Radio Broadcasting to Cuba (Radio Marti), 1985-90; mem. Blue Ribbon panel on minority affairs and indsl. rels. Am. Chem. Soc., 1993—. Recipient Liberty medal N.Y.C., 1986, USIA Superior Honor award, Dir.'s award for superior achievment, 1993, Cuban-Am. Engr. of Yr. award, Fla., 1994; named to Ga. Tech. Engring. Hall of Fame, 1994. Democrat. Roman Catholic. Avocations: tennis, classical music, writing. Home: 151 Crandon Blvd Key Biscayne FL 33149-1573

NAVARRO, ARTURO VILLEGAS, biomedical researcher; b. Puebla, Mex., Sept. 26, 1947; s. Fermin Villegas Lopez and Amelia Navarro Dias; m. Carmen Sanchez Perez, July 31, 1974; children: Andrea, Arturo, Carmen Amelia, Adolfo, Ignacio Manuel. BS in Pharmacobiology and Chemistry, Puebla Autonomous U., 1975; MS, Nat. Poly. Inst. of Mex., 1976. Cert. nat. rsch. scientist, Mex. Prof. Nat. Poly. Inst. Mex., 1979-82, Autonomous U. Nuevo Leon, Monterrey, Mex., 1982-94, Autonomous U. Puebla, Mex., 1984—; biomed. rschr. Instituto Mexicano del Seguro Social, Puebla, 1979—; counselor Envjron. Contamination, Puebla, 1994, Nat. Coun. Sci. and Tech. of Mex., 1992-94. Co-author: QSAR in Design of Bioactive Compounds, 1984; contbr. articles to profl. jours. Grantee Pub. Edn. Sec. Mex., 1991, Instituto Mexicano del Seguro Social, 1993. Mem. AAAS, Mex. Assn. Physiol. Scis., Mex. Assn. Pharmacology, Mex. Assn. Chemistry. Home: 95 Oriente No 1649 Col Granjas San Isidro Puebla Pue 72590, Mexico Office: Inst Mex del Seguro Social, 2 Norte 2004 2o Piso Sur, Puebla 72000, Mexico

NAVARRO, BRUCE CHARLES, lawyer; b. West Lafayette, Ind., Oct. 30, 1954; s. Joseph Anthony and Dorothy Gloria (Gnazzo) N.; m. Nancy Elizabeth Pryor; children: Philip Joseph, Joanna Christina, Kelly Finnegan, Ian Chandler Finnegan. BA, Duke U., 1976; JD, Ind. U., 1980. Bar: D.C. 1980. Asst. counsel U.S. Senate Labor Subcom., Washington, 1981-84; acting dep. undersec. for legis. affairs Dept. Labor, Washington, 1984-85; atty. advisor EEOC, Washington, 1985-86; dir. Office of Congl. Rels. Office of Pers. Mgmt., Washington, 1986-89; prin. dep. asst. atty. gen. for legis. U.S. Dept. of Justice, Washington, 1989-91; spl. asst. to gen. counsel U.S. Dept. HHS, Washington, 1991; expert cons. U.S. Dept. Def., Washington, 1992; counsel to the vice chmn. U.S. Consumer Product Safety Commn., Bethesda, Md., 1992-95; prin. Bruce C. Navarro Regulatory and Legis. Affairs, Washington, 1995—. Mem. Arlington County Republican Com. (Va.), 1983. Mem. D.C. Bar Assn. Roman Catholic. Avocation: music, golf. Home: 4277 Berwick Pl Woodbridge VA 22192-5119 Office: Ste 550 1201 Connecticut Ave NW Washington DC 20036

NAVARRO, JOSEPH ANTHONY, statistician, consultant; b. New Britain, Conn., July 6, 1927; s. Charles C. and Josephine V. (Bianco) N.; m. Dorothy G. Gnazzo, Feb. 6, 1929; children: Kenneth M., Bruce C., Joseph S. BS, Cen. Conn. State U., 1950; MS, Purdue U., 1952, PhD, 1955. Rsch. staff, cons. GE, 1955-59; rsch. staff, mgmt. IBM, 1962-64; sr. staff mem., asst. dir. Inst. Def. Analyses, Alexandria, Va., 1964-72; pres., chief oper. officer System Planning Corp., Arlington, Va., 1972-86; dep. undersec. test and evaluation Dept. Defense, Washington, 1986-87; now pvt. practice cons., 1987—; pres. Wackenhut Applied Technologies Ctr., Fairfax, Va., 1989-90. Contbr. articles to profl. jours. Mem. Bd. Trade, Washington, 1983-85. Mem. Internat. Test and Evaluation Assn. Republican. Roman Catholic. Club: COSMOS (Washington). Office: JAN Assocs Inc 7825 Fulbright Ct Bethesda MD 20817-3119

NAVAS, WILLIAM ANTONIO, JR., military officer, civil engineer; b. Mayaguez, P.R., Dec. 15, 1942; s. William Antonio Sr. and Ethel Ines (Marin) N.; m. Wilda Margarita Cordova Navas, Aug. 7, 1965; children: William Antonio III, Gretchen Maria. BSCE, U. P.R., 1965; MS in Engring. Mgmt., U. Bridgeport, 1979. Registered profl. engr., P.R. Commd. 2d. lt. U.S. Army, 1966, advanced through grades to maj. gen., 1990; served in U.S. Army Corps of Engrs., 1966-70; project engr. Empresas Navas, Inc., Mayaguez, P.R., 1970-72; ptnr., prin. W.A. Navas Jr. & Assocs., Mayaguez, 1972-80; dir. Navas & Moreda, Inc., Mayaguez, 1973-81; with Interamerican Def. Coll., Washington, 1981-82; dir. ops. P.R. Army Nat. Guard, San Juan, 1982-84, 84-87; comdr. Engr. Task Force, Panama, 1984; dep. dir. Army Nat. Guard Bur., Washington, 1987—; vice chief Nat. Guard Bur., 1990; mil. exec. res. forces policy bd. Office of Sec. of Def., 1992-94, dep. asst. sec. of def., 1994-95; dir. Army Nat. Guard, 1995—; chmn. Dept. of Army Hispanic Employment Commn., Washington, 1988. Decorated Knight Eq. Order of Holy Sepulchre. Mem. Nat. Guard Assn. of the U.S. (del. 1980-86), Nat. Guard Assn. of P.R., Soc. of Am. Mil. Engrs. Roman Catholic. Avocations: militaria collection, reading, running, travel. Home: Qtrs # 16A Fort Myer VA 22211 Office: Army Nat Guard The Pentagon Washington DC 20013

NAVASKY, VICTOR SAUL, magazine editor, publisher; b. N.Y.C., July 5, 1932; s. Macy and Esther Blanche (Goldberg) N.; m. Anne Landey Strongin, Mar. 27, 1966; children: Bruno, Miri, Jenny. A.B., Swarthmore Coll., 1954; LL.B., Yale U., 1959. Spl. asst. to Gov. G. Mennen Williams, Mich., 1959-60; editor-in-chief, pub. Monocle Mag., 1961-65; editor N.Y. Times mag., 1970-72; editor-in-chief The Nation mag., N.Y.C., 1978-94; editl. dir. and pub., 1995—; vis. scholar Russell Sage Found., 1975-76; Ferris prof. journalism Princeton U., 1976-77. Author: Kennedy Justice, 1971 (Nat. Book Award nominee), Naming Names, 1980 (Am. Book award 1981), rev. edit., 1991; editor: (with C. Cerf) The Experts Speak, 1984. Mem. bd. govs. Swarthmore Coll., 1991—. Served with U.S. Army, 1954-56. Guggenheim fellow, 1974-75; fellow Inst. of Politics, Harvard U., 1994; Sr. fellow Freedom Forum, 1994. Mem. Author's Guild (coun.), PEN (exec. com.), Com. To Protect Journalists (exec. com.), Phi Beta Kappa. Democrat. Jewish. Home: 33 W 67th St New York NY 10023-6224 Office: The Nation 72 Fifth Ave New York NY 10011-8004

NAVEJA-ELLIS, FRANCESCA ANGELA, mental health clinic administrator; b. N.Y.C., June 23, 1939; d. Antonio and Jeannette Marie (Thomas) Naveja; m. David H. Ellis, Oct. 21, 1957; children: Theresa Fae Ann Zendejas, David Cary. AA with Honors, Allan Hancock Coll., 1985; BS, Columbia Pacific U., 1988; MA, U. San Francisco, 1989. Adminstr. Community Ministry Ctr., Chino, Calif., 1977-79; bus. mgr. Humanistic Mental Health, Santa Maria, Calif., 1984-85; med. sec. A. Edward Hoctor, MD., Santa Maria, 1985; bus. mgr. Affiliated Psychotherapist, Santa Maria, 1985-87; founder, exec. dir., psychotherapist, C.E.O. AP Inst., Inc. Community Counseling Ctr., Santa Maria, 1988—; program dir. Safe Interventions, Santa Maria, Case Mgmt. and Consulting Assocs., Santa Maria; mem. adj. faculty Columbia Pacific U., Sierra U.; founder, dir. Trias Inst., Santa Maria, 1984—, AP Inst., Santa Maria, 1986-87, AP Inst. Valley Counseling Ctr., 1986-95; bd. dirs. Friends of Ruth Women's Shelter, Santa Maria, 1985; cons. St. Joseph's High Sch., 1990; CEO Cen. Coast Cons. Assocs., 1991—. Editor, author quar. newsletter Pride, 1990—. Vol. Dem. Women's Caucus 1986; mem. Women's Network, Santa Maria, 1986-89; mental health adv. coun. Santa Barbara County, 1990, with Domestic violence Edn./Elimination Svcs., 1992-95. Mem. Am. Mental Health Counseling Assn., Assn. Christian Therapists (regional coord., 1988-90), Calif. Assn. Marriage Family Therapists, Cen. Coast Jung Soc., Western Assn. Spiritual Dirs., Cen. Coast Hypnosis Soc. Mem. Am. Assn. Prof. Hypnotherapists. Avocations: vocalist, actress, walking, theatre, dancing. Office: Lovelock Mental Health PO Box 1046 Lovelock NV 89419

NAVIA, JUAN MARCELO, biologist, educator; b. Havana, Jan. 16, 1927; came to U.S., 1961; s. Juan and Hortensia (DeLaCampa) N.; m. Josefina Blanca Bonich, Aug. 20, 1950; children: Juan, Carlos, Ana, Beatriz. BS, MIT, 1950, MS, 1951, PhD, 1965; DDSc (hon.), Chiang Mai U., Thailand, 1996. Sr. scientist Inst. Dental Rsch. U. Ala., Birmingham, 1969-88; dir. nutrition and oral health tng. program U. Ala., Birmingham, 1968-88, dir. rsch. tng. Sch. Dentistry, 1971-81, dir. clin. rsch. tng. program - MD, PhD, 1972-75, dir Sparkman Ctr., 1981-94, prof. comparative medicine, 1973-94, prof. biochemistry, 1976-86, prof. nutrition scis., 1977-94; ret., prof. emeritus, 1994—; adv. bd. mem. Fogarty Internat. Ctr., Bethesda, Md., 1985-88, Princeton (N.J.) Dental Resource Ctr., 1987-90; dean U. Ala. Sch. Pub. Health, 1989-92. Author: Animal Models in Dental Research, 1977; editor: The Biologic Basis of Dental Caries, 1980; contbr. Encyclopedia Americana, 1968. Am. Inst. Nutrition fellow, 1995, Sr. Internat. Fogarty fellow, 1979, AAAS fellow, 1982; recipient H. Trendley Dean Meml. award Internat. Assn. Dental Rsch., 1990, U. Ala. Birmingham's Pres.'s medal, 1992. Mem. Internat. Assn. Dental Rsch. (pres. cariology 1983-84), Am. Assn. Dental Rsch., Am. Chem. Soc., European Orgn. Caries Rsch., Inst. Food Technologists, Nat. Coun. Internat. Health, Sociedad Latinoamericana de Nutricion, N.Y. Acad. Scis., Internat. Serra Club, Sigma Xi, Sigma Delta Pi. Republican. Roman Catholic. Avocations: walking, writing. Office: U Ala at Birmingham Dept Comparative Medicine Volker Hall 403 Birmingham AL 35294

NAVON, IONEL MICHAEL, mathematics educator; b. Bucharest, Romania, Apr. 28, 1940; s. David and Sarah (Schwartzman) N.; m. Lily Marcu, May 11, 1967; children: Daria, Livia. BSc in Math., Hebrew U. Jerusalem, 1967, MSc in Atmospheric Scis., 1971; PhD in Applied Math., U. Witwatersrand, Johannesburg, South Africa, 1979. Sr. rsch. meteorologist Israel Meteorol. Office, Tel Aviv, 1973-74; head applied math. sect. Tamam/Israel Aircraft Industry, Tel Aviv, 1974-76; sr. rsch. officer Counc. Sci. and Indsl. Rsch., Pretoria, South Africa, 1976-78, chief rsch. officer, 1979-80, sr. chief rsch. officer, 1981-83; sr. vis. scientist NASA/Goddard Space Flight Ctr., Greenbelt, Md., 1983-84; cons. NASA/Goddarad Space Flight Ctr., Greenbelt, Md., 1984-85; sr. specialist researcher Coun. Sci. and Indsl. Rsch., Pretoria, 1984-85; assoc. rsch. scientist Supercomputer Rsch. Inst., Tallahassee, Fla., 1985-87; assoc. prof. math. Fla. State U., Tallahassee, 1987-1990, prof., 1991—, program dir. optimization and optimal control, 1993—, hon. prof. dept. meteorology Supercomputer Rsch. Inst., 1987—, faculty assoc. Supercomputer Computation Rsch. Inst., 1988—, faculty assoc. Geophys. Fluid Dynamics Inst., 1989—; cons. Ctr. Analysis Prediction of Storms, Norman, Okla., 1989, French Navy, 1995; leader Argonne Nat. Lab.; co-organizer Internat. Conf. Element Methods in Geophysics, Tallahassee, 1991; summer lecture series scientist NASA, 1991—; mem. panel nat. experts to rev. and conduct site visiting Okla. Sci. and Tech. Ctr.; keynote spkr. Internat. Conf. on Finite Element Methods, South Africa, 1992, Internat. Conf. on Optimization Techniques and Applications, Singapore, 1992, Assimilation of Meteorological and Oceanographic Observations, France, 1993. Editor spl. issues Computer and Math. with Applications; editor Monthly Weather Rev., 1991-94, Jour. for Numerical Linear Algebra with Applications, 1991, Computational Fluid Dynamics Jour., 1992; contbr. 86 refereed articles. Lt. Israel Civil Def., 1960-63. Grantee NSF, 1988, 91, 94—, NASA, 1991, 94, Rsch. grantee Air Force Office Sci., 1989, 91, 94. Mem. Am. Meteorol. Soc., Am. Math. Soc., Am. Geophys. Union, Soc. Indsl. and Applied Math., Israel Assn. Profl. Engrs., Am. Computing Machinery Assn. Avocations: ping-pong, photography, books. Home: 3138 Ferns Glen Dr Tallahassee FL 32308-2304 Office: Fla State U Love Building Rm 111 Tallahassee FL 32306

NAVRATIL, GERALD ANTON, physicist, educator; b. Troy, N.Y., Sept. 5, 1951; s. Lloyd George and Frances Mary (Scalise) N.; m. Joan Frances Etzweiler, Sept. 4, 1976; children: Frances, Alexis, Paula. BS, Calif. Inst. Tech., 1973; MS, U. Wis., 1974, PhD, 1976. Project assoc. dept. physics U. Wis.-Madison, 1976-77; asst. prof. engring. sci. Columbia U., N.Y.C., 1977-78, asst. prof. applied physics, 1978-83, assoc. prof., 1983-88, prof., 1988—, chmn. 1988-94, vice dean Sch. Engring. and Applied Sci., 1994—; vis. fellow Princeton U., 1985-86; cons. MIT, 1984-86, Fusion Systems, Inc., 1988, Inst. Def. Analysis, 1992—, com.; mem. Nat. Adv. Coun. TPX Tokomak Project and chair TPX Program Adv. Com., 1993—. Assoc. editor Physics of Plasmas, 1994—. Patentee in field. Cottrell Rsch. grantee, 1978; U.S. Dept. Energy High Beta Tokomak Research contract, 1982—; NSF grantee, 1978-88; Alfred P. Sloan rsch. fellow, 1984. Fellow Am. Phys. Soc., Univ. Fusion Assn. (sec./treas. 1988-89, v.p. 1990, pres. 1991), Sigma Xi. Office: Columbia U Dept Applied Physics 500 W 120th St Rm 215 Mudd New York NY 10027-6623

NAVRATILOVA, MARTINA, former professional tennis player; b. Prague, Czechoslovakia, Oct. 18, 1956; came to U.S., 1975, naturalized, 1981; d. Miroslav Navratil and Jana Navratilova. Student, schs. in Czechoslovakia; Hon. doctorate, George Washington U., 1996. Profl. tennis player, 1975-94. Author: (with George Vecsey) Martina, 1985, (with Liz Nickels) The Total Zone, 1995, (with Liz Nickels) The Breaking Point, 1996. Vol. Rainbow Found. Winner Czechoslovak Nat. singles, 1972-74, U.S. Open singles, 1983, 84, 86, 87, U.S. Open doubles, 1977, 78, 80, 83, 84, 87, 90, U.S. Open mixed doubles, 1987, Va. Slims Tournament, 1978, 83, 84, 85, 86, Va. Slims doubles, 1991, Wimbledon singles, 1978, 79, 82, 83, 84, 85, 86, 87, 90, Wimbledon women's doubles, 1976, 79, 81, 82, 83, 84, 86, Wimbledon mixed doubles, 1985, 94, 95, French Open singles, 1982, 84, Australian Open singles, 1981, 83, 85, Australian Doubles (with Nagelsen) 1980, (with Shriver), 1982, 84, 85, 87, 88, 89, Grand Slam of Women's Tennis, 1984, Roland Garros (with Shriver), 1985, 87, 89, Italian Open doubles (with Sabatini), 1987, (with Shriver) COREL WTA Tour doubles team of yr., 1981-89, triple Crown at U.S. Open, 1987; recipient Women's Sports Found. Flo Hyman award, 1987; named Female Athlete of the Decade (1980s) The Nat. Sports Review, UPI, and AP, WTA Player of Yr., 1978-79, 82-86, Women's Sports Found. Sportswoman of Yr., 1982-84, Hon. Citizen of Dallas, AP Female Athlete of Yr., 1983, Chgo. Hall of Fame, 1994; Martina Navratilova Day proclaimed in Chgo., 1992. Mem. Women's Tennis Assn. (dir., exec. com., pres.). Holder of 167 singles titles and 165 doubles titles; holder of record of singles-match wins which is 1,309, 1991. Address: IMG 1 Erieview Plz Cleveland OH 44114-1715

NAWY, EDWARD GEORGE, civil engineer, educator; b. Baghdad, Iraq, Dec. 21, 1926; came to U.S., 1957, naturalized, 1966; s. George M. and Ava (Marshall) N.; m. Rachel E. Shebbath, Mar. 23, 1949; children: Ava Margaret, Robert M. DIC, Imperial Coll. Sci. and Tech., London, 1951; CE, MIT, 1959; D of Engring., U. Pisa, Italy, 1967. Registered profl. engr. (P.E.), N.J., N.Y., Pa., Calif., Fla. Head structures Israel Water Planning Authority, Tel-Aviv, 1952-57; mem. faculty Rutgers U., New Brunswick, N.J., 1959—; mem. grad. faculty Rutgers U., 1961—, prof. civil engring., 1966-72, Distinguished prof. (prof. II), 1972—, chmn. dept. civil and environ. engring., dir. grad. programs, 1980-86; chmn. Coll. Engring. Del Assembly, 1969-72; mem. Univ. Senate, 1973-80, also mem. exec. com., also faculty rep., mem. bd. govs., trustee; guest prof. Nat. U. Tucuman, Argentina, summer 1963, Imperial Coll. Sci. and Tech., summer 1964; vis. prof. Stevens Inst. Tech., Hoboken, N.J., 1968-72; hon. prof. Nanjing Inst. Tech., China, 1987; mem. N.J. Chancellor Higher Edn. for Higher Edn. Master Plan; mem. Rutgers U. rep. Transp. Rsch. Bd. Bridge Com.; cons. to industry; U.S. mem. commn. on cracking Comitè EuroInternat. du Beton; mem. Civil Engring. Tech. Adv. Coun. N.J., 1966-72; concrete sys. cons. FAA, Washington; cons. energy divsn. U.S. Gen. Acctg. Office, Washington; gen. chmn. Internat. Symposium on Slabs and Plates, 1971; hon. presidium internat. conf. Reunion Internationale des Laboratories d'Essais et de Recherches sur Les Materiaux et les Constructions, Budapest, 1977; mem. Accreditation Bd. Engring. and Tech. Author: Reinforced Concrete, 1985, 3d edit., 1996, Simplified Reinforced Concrete, 1986, Prestressed Concrete, 2d edit., 1996, High Strength High Performance Concrete, 1996; contbr. more than 125 articles to profl. jours. Vice pres. Berkeley Twp. Taxpayers Assn., Ocean City, N.J., 1966-70. Recipient merit citation and award N.J. Concrete Assn., 1966; C. Gulbenkian Found. fellow, 1972. Fellow ASCE (mem. joint com. on slabs), Instn. Civil Engrs. (London), Am. Concrete Inst. (pres. N.J. chpt. 1966, 77-78, chmn. nat. com. on cracking 1966-73, bd. com. chpts. 1969-72, ACI rep. internat. commn. fractures, H.L. Kenneday award 1972, award of recognition N.J. chpt. 1972, chpt. activities award 1978, chmn. nat. com. on deflection 1989—); mem. NSPE, AAUP (chmn. budget and priorities com. Rutgers U. chpt. 1972), Am. Soc. Engring. Edn., Prestressed Concrete Inst. (Bridge Competition award 1971, mem. tech. activities com.), N.Y. Acad. Scis., Tall BBldgs. Coun., N.J. Contractors Assn. (cons. ednl. com., tall bldgs. coun.), Rotary, Sigma Xi, Tau Beta Pi, Chi Epsilon (hon.). Office: Rutgers State U of NJ Civil Engring Dept New Brunswick NJ 08855 *Success is normally the result of honesty and continuous setting and updating of high goals which have to be perseverely pursued.*

NAY, HOWARD RILEY, surgeon, educator; b. Wheeling, W.Va., Apr. 13, 1930; s. Howard Erwin and Agnes Ellen (Gauld) N.; m. Geraldine Tullock, Oct. 26, 1956 (dec. 1995); children: Kathryn Nay Clay, Elizabeth Denby Nay Schwengel, Jennifer Hunt. BA, Va. Mil. Inst., 1952; MD, Columbia U., 1956. Diplomate Am. Bd. Surgery; cert. advanced traumal life support, laparoscopic laser cholecystectomy, clin. laparoscopic cholecystectomy, advanced laparoscopic surgery, advanced operative laparoscopy for gen. surgery. Axting asst. attending surgeon St. Luke's Hosp., N.Y.C., 1964-65, asst. attending surgeon, 1965-72, assoc. attending surgeon, 1972-76, attending surgeon, 1976—; sr. attending surgeon St. Luke's/Roosevelt Hosp. Ctr., 1982—, chief surgery A svc., 1985—, chief surgery A trauma svcs., 1989—; attending srugeon Dr.'s Hosp., N.Yu.C., 1982—, Beth Isreal North Hospice Ctr., 1989—; instr. surgery Columbia U., N.Y.C., 1964-72, asst. clin. prof. surgery, 1972-80, assoc. clin. prof. surgery, 1980—. Contbr. numerous articles to profl. jours. With M.C., USAF, 1959-61, hon. disharge, 1961, USAFR, 1961-70. Fellow ACS; mem. AMA, N.Y. Med. Soc., N.Y. County Med. Soc., N.Y. Surg. Soc., N.Y. Soc. Cardiovascular Surgery, Internat. Soc. Angiology, Internat. Cardiovascular Soc. Office: 925 Park Ave New York NY 10028-0210

NAYAR, BALDEV RAJ, political science educator; b. Gujrat Dist., India, Oct. 26, 1931; emigrated to Can., 1964; s. Jamna Das and Durga Devi (Marwah) N.; m. Nancy Ann Skinner, Aug. 27, 1961; children—Sheila Jane, Kamala Elizabeth, Sunita Maria. B.A., Punjab U., 1953; M.A., 1956, U. Chgo., 1959; Ph.D., U. Chgo., 1963. Asst. prof. Calif. State Coll., Hayward, 1963-64; mem. faculty dept. polit. sci. McGill U., 1964-94, assoc. prof., 1966-71, prof., 1971-94, prof. emeritus, 1996—, assoc. chmn., 1990-93; research assoc. Internat. Devel. Research Centre, 1978. Author: Minority Politics in the Punjab, 1966, National Communication and Language Policy, 1969, The Modernization Imperative and Indian Planning, 1972, American Geopolitics and India, 1976, India's Quest for Technological Independence, 1983, India's Mixed Economy, 1989, The Political Economy of India's Public Sector, 1990, Superpower Dominance and Military Aid, 1991, The State and International Aviation in India, 1994. Bd. dirs. Shastri Indo-Canadian Inst., 1970-72, sr. fellow, 1978, 86. Recipient Watumull prize Am. Hist. Assn., 1966; Charles E. Merriam fellow, 1957; Carnegie Study New Nations fellow, 1962; Can. Council sr. fellow, 1967, 74; SSHRC leave fellow, 1982. Mem. Can. Polit. Sci. Assn., Assn. Asian Studies, Assn., Can. Asian Studies Assn. Office: McGill Univ, Dept Polit Sci, Montreal, PQ Canada H3A 2T7

NAYDAN, MICHAEL M., foreign language educator; b. Trenton, N.J., Oct. 20, 1952; s. William and Anna (Yaremko) N.; m. Roxanne Robak; 1 child Liliana Marika. BA magna cum laude, The American U., Washington, 1973, MA, 1975; MPh, Columbia U., 1980, PhD, 1984. Asst. prof. Yale U., New Haven, Conn., 1982-86; vis. asst. prof. Rutgers U., New Brunswick, N.J., 1986-88; asst. prof. Pa. State U., Univ. Park, 1988-90, assoc. prof., 1990—; gen. asst. Columbia U. Bakhmeteff Archive of Russian and East European History and Culture, 1979-81; adj. instr. Russian Rutgers U., Newark, 1982; preceptor and instr. Russian, Columbia Univ., 1980-82; acting instr. Russian Yale U., 1982-84; head of instruction Yale Russian and Slavic Summer Lang. Inst., 1984-86; panelist, lectr. on Russian and Slavic poets at convs. and meetings of nat. and internat. orgns. Translator: (books) The Poetry of Lina Kostenko: Wanderings of the Heart, 1990, Marina Tsvetaeva's After Russia, 1992; contbr. articles and reviews to profl. jours. and encyclopedias, translations in book chpts., journals and periodicals; contbr. poetry to Monmouth Review, 1975, Poet Lore, 1977, Bitterroot, 1979; editor-in-chief Slavic and East European Journal, 1993—; assoc. editor Comparative Literature Studies, 1990—; assoc. editor and co-founder Ulbandus Review: A Jour. of Slavic Langs. and Lits., 1977-84. Recipient Pushkin prize, 1975, 76, 81, Columbia U., Eugene Kayden Meritorious Achievement award in translation, U. Colo., 1993, Mihaly-Nigukat fellowship, Columbia U., 1979; grantee Schevchenko Scholarly Soc., 1980, Moore Fund, 1983-84, N.J. Dept Higher Edn., 1987-88 (2), Woskob Fellow in Humanities, Nat. Endowment for the Humanities, 1991-92, 95. Mem. Am. Assn. for Advancement of Slavic Studies, Am. Assn. Tchrs. of Slavic and East European Langs., Am. Assn. Ukranian Studies (v.p.), Phi Kappa Phi. Ukranian Catholic. Avocations: tennis, squash. Home: Box 8006 State College PA 16803 Office: Pa State Univ Slavic Studies Dept 211 Sparks Bldg University Park PA 16802

NAYLON, MICHAEL EDWARD, military officer; b. Rochester, N.Y., Jan. 15, 1943; s. Edward M. and Patricia (Brennan) N.; m. Beverly Marzano, Mar. 27, 1965; children: Michelle A., Colleen M. BA, John Carroll U., 1965; MBA, Marymount U., 1986; grad., U.S. Army War Coll., 1989. Indsl. rels. specialist Gen. Railway Signal Co., Rochester, N.Y., Farrell Co., Rochester; manpower adminstr. City of Rochester; employment mgr. U. Rochester; personnel dir. Interstate Brands Corp., Rochester; office mgr., dir. adminstrn., regional tng. coord. Nat. Machine Tool Builders Assn., McLean, Va.; chief U.S Army Res. Hdqs. Dept. of Army, Washington; staff officer Joint Chiefs of Staff, col. sr. res. advisor Dept. Def., Washington; with U.S. Southern Command, Panama City, Panama; dir. ops. Nat. Asssn. Retired Fed. Employees. Mem. Am. Soc. Assn. Execs., Am. Soc. Pers. Adminstrn., U.S. Army War Coll. Alumni Assn., John Carroll U. Alumni Assn., Res. Officers Assn. USA. Home: 1434 Aldenham Ln Reston VA 22090-3901 Office: The Pentagon J 3 JOD Washington DC 20318-3000

NAYLOR, AUBREY WILLARD, botany educator; b. Union City, Tenn., Feb. 5, 1915; s. Harry Joseph and Clara Mae (Isbell) N.; m. Frances Valentine Lloyd, Dec. 26, 1940; children: Virginia Dawson Naylor Kirby, Edith-Margaret Naylor Eastman DeWitt. BS, U. Chgo., 1937, MS, 1938, PhD, 1940. Mem. staff, bur. plant industry U.S. Dept. Agr., Chgo., 1938-40; instr. botany U. Chgo., 1940-44, Northwestern U., Evanston, Ill., 1944-45; asst. prof. U. Wash., Seattle, 1946-47, Yale U., 1947-52; assoc. prof. Duke U., 1952-59, prof., 1959-72, James B. Duke prof., 1972-85, James B. Duke prof. emeritus, 1985—; program dir. for metabolic biology NSF, Washington, 1961-62, cons., 1960-63; chmn. com. examiners for Grad. (Sch.) Record Examination on Biology, Edn. Testing Svc., Princeton, N.J., 1966-72; cons. Oak Ridge Nat. Lab., 1957-58, Rsch. Triangle Inst., N.C., 1968—, TVA, 1969-75, Schaper and Brümmer Pharm. Co., Salzgitter, Fed. Republic of Germany, 1986-92, Akzo Salt Co., 1991—; mem. summer faculties U. N.C., Chapel Hill, 1960-61, Greensboro, 1964-65; mem. summer faculties Bennett Coll., Greensboro, N.C.; vis. prof. U. Bristol, Eng., 1958-59, U. Tex., Austin, 1977. Contbr. chpts. to books, articles and book revs. to profl. jours. NRC fellow Boyce Thompson Inst. for Plant Rsch., Yonkers, N.Y., 1945-46, Guggenheim fellow, 1958-59; NSF sr. fellow, 1958-59; grantee, 1956-86, Am. Cancer Soc. grantee, 1953-57, Herman Frasch Found. grantee, 1957-72. Fellow AAAS (life mem.); mem. Am. Soc. Plant Physiologists (life, chmn. bd. trustees 1962-74, pres. 1961, exec. com. 1959-60, 62-74, 81-82, Disting. Svc. award So. sect. 1981, Charles Reid Barnes life membership 1981, archivist 1987—), Am. Inst. Biol. Scis., Am. Soc. Cell Biologists, Bot. Soc. Am. (life, cert. of merit 1988), Scandinavian Soc. Plant Physiologists, Japanese Soc. Plant Physiologists, Australian Soc. Plant Physiologists, Cosmos Club (Washington), Sigma Xi (life, pres. chpt. 1968-69). Home: 2430 Wrightwood Ave Durham NC 27705-5802 *Almost everything interests me. For this reason, I am seldom bored. Channeling my curiosity has been best achieved through a burning desire to learn how living things grow from a single cell, differentiate into a distinct multicellular organism and reproduce. The joy of discovery feeds upon itself and motivates me to work, work, and work some more.*

NAYLOR, BRIAN, news correspondent; b. Mt. Kisco, N.Y., Aug. 7, 1955. BA in Broadcasting/Film, U. Maine, 1978. Gen. assignment reporter, anchor, announcer Sta. WLBZ, Bangor, Maine, 1976-78; statehouse reporter Capital News Svc., Augusta, Maine, 1978; gen. assignment reporter, anchor Sta. WLAM, Lewiston, Maine, 1978-79; statehouse reporter, host Sta. WOSU Radio, Columbus, Ohio, 1979-82; prodr., co-host Sta. WOSU-TV, Columbus, 1979-82; newscaster, gen. assignment reporter, White House reporter Nat. Pub. Radio, Washington, 1982-92, Congl. corr., 1992—; adj. prof. Am. U., Washington, 1991. Named Winner Silver Baton, DuPont-Columbia awards, 1996.; Jefferson fellow, 1990. Office: Nat Pub Radio 635 Massachusetts Ave NW Washington DC 20001-3752

NAYLOR, BRUCE GORDON, museum director; b. Midale, Sask., Can., Aug. 19, 1950; s. John Raymond Naylor and Mary Lynn (Frisby) Redeberg; m. Marlene Johnstone, Dec. 19, 1981 (dec. July 1992); m. Judith Jeune, June 11, 1994. BS with high honors, U. Sask., 1972; PhD, U. Alta., 1978. Postdoctoral fellow U. Toronto, Ont., 1978-80; lectr. U. Calif., Berkeley, 1979; asst. prof. U. Alta., Edmonton, 1980-82; curator Tyrrell Mus., Drumheller, Alta., 1982-86; asst. dir. Royal Tyrrell Mus., Drumheller, 1986-92, dir., 1992—; adj. prof. U. Alta., 1983—; sen. U. Calgary, Alta., 1989-90; bd. dirs. Yoho-Burgess Shale Rsch. Found. Contbr. articles to sci. publs. Operating grantee Nat. Sci. & Engring. Rsch. Coun., Ottawa, 1981-82. Fellow Geol. Assn. Can.; mem. Soc. Vertebrate Paleontology, Rotary Club Drumheller. Avocations: horseback riding, gardening. Office: Royal Tyrrell Mus, Box 7500, Drumheller, AB Canada T0J 0Y0

NAYLOR, FRANK WESLEY, JR., financial executive; b. Mulvane, Kans., Feb. 7, 1939; s. Frank Wesley Sr. and Hildred Ethel (Reed) N.; m. Marilyn Everest, May 16, 1987; children: Mary Allison, Frank Wesley III, Erin, Mark. BA, U. Kans., Lawrence, 1961; postgrad., Rockhurst Coll., Kansas City, Mo., 1966-68. Staff mgr. Met. Life Ins. Co., Grand, Kans., 1965-69; dep. mgr. Fed. Crop Ins. Corp., USDA, Washington, 1969-72; exec. asst. to adminstr. VA, Washington, 1972-74; assoc. adminstr. Farmers Home Adminstrn., USDA, Washington, 1974-77; sr. v.p. Farm Credit Banks, Sacramento, 1977-81; under sec. USDA, Washington, 1981-86; chmn. Farm Credit Adminstrn., Washington, 1986-88; pres., chief exec. officer U.S. Agricredit Inc., Washington, 1988—. Mem. Community Services Dist. Bd., Shingle Springs, Calif., chmn. Eldorado County Fin. Com., Shingle Springs; bd. dirs. Sacramento C. of C., 1977; active Presdl. campaigns, Washington, 1968, 72. Mem. Kansas City (Kans.) Jr. C. of C. Republican. Home: 2 Clapham Ct Sterling VA 20165-5653*

NAYLOR, GEORGE LEROY, retired lawyer, rail transportation executive; b. Bountiful, Utah, May 11, 1915; s. Joseph Francis and Josephine Chase (Wood) N.; student U. Utah, 1934-36; student George Washington U., 1937; J.D. (Bancroft Whitney scholar), U. San Francisco, 1953; m. Maxine Elizabeth Lewis, Jan. 18, 1941; children: Georgia Naylor Price, RoseMaree Naylor Hammer, George LeRoy II. Bar: Calif. 1954, Ill. 1968. V.p., sec., legis. rep. Internat. Union of Mine, Mill & Smelter Workers, CIO, Dist. Union 2, Utah-Nevada, 1942-44; examiner So. Pacific Co., San Francisco, 1949-54, chief examiner, 1955, asst. mgr., 1956-61; carrier mem. Nat. R.R. Adjustment Bd., Chgo., 1961-77, chmn., 1970-77; atty. Village of Fox River Valley Gardens, Ill., 1974-77; practice law, legal cons., Ill. and Calif., 1977—, ret. from pvt. practice, 1991; gen. counsel for Can-Veyor, Inc., Mountain View, Calif., 1959-64; adj. instr. dept. mgmt. U. West Fla., 1981. Active Rep. Nat. Com., 1992-95. Served with AUS, World War II. Mem. ABA, Ill. Bar Assn., Calif. Bar Assn., Chgo. Bar Assn., San Francisco Bar Assn. Mormon. Author: Defending Carriers Before the NRAB and Public Law Boards, 1969, Choice Morsels in Tax and Property Law, 1966, Underground at Bingham Canyon, 1944; National Railroad Adjustment Board Practice Manual, 1978. Home and Office: Virginia Lee Rd RR 1 Box 570 Cotter AR 72626

NAYLOR, HARRY BROOKS, microbiologist; b. Hewitt, Minn., Mar. 30, 1914; s. George Brooks and Anna Elmira (Larsen) N.; m. Ellen Florence Haanela, Sept. 8, 1940; children—Lynn Brooks, Roy Allen, Gail Ann. B.S., U. Minn., 1938; Ph.D., Cornell U., 1943. Mem. tech. dept. Sheffield Farms Dairy, Inc., N.Y.C., 1946-47; mem. faculty dept. microbiology Cornell U., Ithaca, N.Y., 1947—; prof. emeritus Cornell U., 1977—; cons. Pasco Labs., Inc., Wheat Ridge, Colo., 1978-86; mem. grant review bd. USPHS, 1967-70; OAS lectr., Brazil, 1972, 73; teaching fellow Fed. U. of Rio de Janeiro, 1978. Contbr. articles to profl. jours. Served with USNR, 1943-46. Fulbright-Hayes fellow, 1966-67. Mem. Am. Soc. Microbiology, Am. Acad. Microbiology. Home: 5390 Belfern Dr Bellingham WA 98226-9063

NAYLOR, JAMES CHARLES, psychologist, educator; b. Chgo., Feb. 8, 1932; s. Joseph Sewell and Berniece (Berg) N.; m. Georgia Lou Mason, Feb. 14, 1953; children—Mary Denise, Diana Darice, Shari Dalice. B.S., Purdue U., 1957, M.S., 1958, Ph.D., 1960. Asst. prof. Ohio State U., 1960-63, asso. prof., 1963-67, prof. vice chmn. dept. psychology, 1967-68; prof. Purdue U., Lafayette, Ind., 1968-86, head dept. psychol. scis., 1968-79; prof., chmn. dept. psychology Ohio State U., Columbus, 1986—; Fulbright rsch. scholar, Umea, Sweden, 1976; Disting. scholar, vis. scientist Flinders U., South Australia, 1982-83, UNESCO ednl. cons. to Hangzhou U., Peoples Republic of China, 1984; chmn. Coun. Grad. Depts. Psychology, 1993-94. Author: Industrial Psychology, 1968, A Theory of Behavior in Organizations, 1980; founder, editor: Organizational Behavior and Human Decision Processes; mem. editorial bd.: Prof. Psychology; Contbr. articles to profl. jours. Served with USN, 1950-54. Fellow AAAS, Am. Psychol. Soc., Am. Psychol. Assn.; mem. Psychonomic Soc., Psychmetric Soc., Internat. Assn. Applied Psychology, Soc. Organizational Behavior (founder), Phi Beta Kappa, Sigma Xi. Home: 176 Tucker Dr Columbus OH 43085-3064 Office: Ohio State U Dept Psychology Columbus OH 43210

NAYLOR, JOHN THOMAS, telephone company executive; b. Orillia, Ont., Can., Jan. 30, 1913; s. Fred Addison and Ethel (Thompson) N.; m. Ruth Louisa Tissot, Dec. 21, 1934; children: Joan Crosby, Carol Manka. BSEE, Oreg. State U., 1934. Registered profl. engr., Calif., Oreg., Wash. Chief accountant McKesson & Robbins, Inc., Portland, Oreg., 1934-38; engr. Pub. Service Commn. Oreg., 1938-41; v.p. Gen. Telephone Co. Calif., 1941-50; v.p., gen. mgr. Philippine Long Distance Telephone Co., Manila, 1950-56; also dir.; v.p. United Utilities, Inc., 1956-59; pres., dir. United Telephone Co.; v.p. Internat. Tel. & Tel. Corp., N.Y.C., 1959-61; pres., dir. Telectronic Systems, Inc., Manila, Philippines, 1962-73; cons., 1973—. Author articles on engring., finance, mgmt., pub. service. Active Boy Scouts Am., YMCA; pres. Am. Sch., Manila; mem. coun. regents Oreg. State U., 1981—. Mem. IEEE, NSPE, Philippine Assn. Mech. and Elec. Engrs., Phi Kappa Phi, Tau Beta Pi, Eta Kappa Nu. Club: Army and Navy. Address: 1451 NE Meier Dr Grants Pass OR 97526-3805

NAYLOR, PHYLLIS REYNOLDS, author; b. Anderson, Ind., Jan. 4, 1933; d. Eugene Spencer and Lura Mae (Schield) Reynolds; m. Thomas A. Tedesco, Jr., Sept. 9, 1951 (div. 1960); m. Rex V. Naylor, May 26, 1960; children: Jeffrey, Michael. Diploma, Joliet Jr. Coll., 1953; BA, Am. U., 1963. Author: 90 books including Crazy Love: An Autobiographical Account of Marriage and Madness, 1977, Revelations, 1979, A String og Chances, 1982 (ALA notable book), Tha Gaony of Alice, 1985 (ALA notable book), The Keeper, 1986 (ALA notable book), Unexpected Pleasures, 1986, Send No Blessings, 1990 (YASD best book for young adults), Shiloh, 1991 (ALA notable book, John Newbery medal 1992). Recipient Golden Kite award Soc. Children's Book Writers Am., 1985, Child Study award Bank St. Coll., 1983, Edgar Allan Poe award Mystery Writers Am., 1985, Internat. book award Soc. Sch. Librs., 1988, Christopher award, 1989, Newbery award ALA, 1992, Nat. Endowment of Arts Creative Writing fellow, 1987. Mem. Children's Book Guild of Washington (pres. 1974-75, 83-84), Soc. Children's Book Writers, Authors Guild, PEN, Council for a Livable World, SANE, Physicians for Social Responsibility, Amnesty Internat. Unitarian. Avocations: theater, madrigal singing, swimming. Home and Office: 9910 Holmhurst Rd Bethesda MD 20817-1618

NAYLOR, THOMAS HERBERT, economist, educator, consultant; b. Jackson, Miss., May 30, 1936; s. Thomas Hector and Martha (Watkins) N.; m. Magdalena Raczkowska, Dec. 14, 1985; children: Susanne, Alexander. B.S. in Math., Millsaps Coll., 1958; B.S. in Indsl. Engring., Columbia U., 1959; M.B.A., Ind. U., 1961; Ph.D. in Econs., Tulane U., 1964. Instr. Sch. Bus. Adminstrn. Tulane U., 1961-63; asst. prof. econs. Duke U., 1964-66, assoc. prof., 1966-68, prof. econs., 1968-93, prof. emeritus, 1994—; vis. prof. Middlebury Coll., 1993—; pres. Social Systems, Inc., 1971-80; mng. dir. Naylor Group, 1980; cons., lectr. worldwide. Co-author: Computer Simulation Techniques, 1966, Strategies for Change in the South, 1975, Managerial Economics, 1983, The Abandoned Generation, 1995, The Search for Meaning in the Workplace, 1996; author of 27 books including: Corporate Planning Models, 1978, Strategic Planning Management, 1980, The Corporate Strategy Matrix, 1986, The Gorbachev Strategy, 1988, The Cold War Legacy, 1991, The Search for Meaning, 1994; contbr. numerous articles to profl. publs.; mem. editl. bd. jours. Founder. L.Q.C. Lamar Soc., Washington. Mem. Beta Gamma Sigma, Lambda Chi, Omicron Delta Kappa.

NAYLOR-JACKSON, JERRY, public relations consultant, retried; b. Chalk Mountain, Tex., Mar. 6, 1939; s. William Guy and Mary Bernice (Lummus) Jackson; m. Pamela Ann Robinson, Jan. 30, 1966; children: Geoffrey K. Naylor, Kelli A. Naylor, Gregory K. Naylor. Grad., Elkins Electronics Inst., Dallas, 1957; student, U. Md., Fed. Republic of Germany, 1957-58. Life first class radio/TV engring. lic. FCC. Broadcaster various local TV and AM radio stas., San Angelo, Texas, 1955-57; mem. Buddy Holly and the Crickets, 1957-65, lead singer, 1960-65; solo entertainer, performer, recording artist and producer, 1965-83; sr. v.p. corp. devel. Newslink Internat. Satellite Broadcast Comms. Co., Inc., Washington, 1986-88; pres. Internat. Syndications, Inc. subs. Newslink, Inc., Washington, 1986-88; pres., CEO, owner The Jerry Naylor Co., Inc., Agoura, Calif., 1984—; v.p. capital programs, sr. cons. Calif. Luth. Univ., Thousand Oaks, 1990-92; sr. cons., dir. ann. fund Calif. Luth. Univ., 1989-90; polit./media cons. various Rep. candidates and orgns., 1968—; spl. cons. to Violeta Barrios de Chamarro, Pres. of Republic of Nicaragua, 1990-92; disc jockey Sta. KHEY-AM, Sta KINT-AM, El Paso, Tex., 1959; on-air personality Sta. KRLA-AM, Sta. KDAY-AM, L.A., 1960, on-air disc jocky/air personality/celebrity host, KLAC-AM, L.A., Calif., 1974-83; on-camera and voice-over spokesman for Safeway Stores, Inc., Avis Rent-a-Car, Mutual of Omaha, Wrigley Co., 1968-83; U.S. presdl. appointee, chmn. Job Tng. Partnership Act work group/youth at risk subcom. Nat. Commn. for Employment Policy, 1985-92; nat. dir. spl. events Reagan For Pres., 1979-81; apptd. mem. commn. for employment policy Pres. Ronald Reagan, 1985-91. Recording artist maj. labels including CBS Records, Motown Records, Warner Bros. Records, EMI Records, 1965-84; host weekly nat. and internat. radio program Continental Country (Number 1 syndicated country music radio show in Am., Billboard Mag., Country Music Assn., 1974, 77). Nat. dir. spl. events Reagan for Pres., 1975-76, 79-80; sr. cons. to White House, 1981-88, 89-92. With U.S. Army, 1957-58. Named to Top 40 Male Vocalists of Yr., Billboard Mag., 1970, named #1 Rock Group (Crickets), Billboard Mag./New Musical Express Mag., 1958, 62. Mem. NARAS, Country Music Assn., Acad. Country Music (Telly award for TV documentary 1991, 92), Phi Kappa Phi (alumni). Avocation: writing prose and poetry. Home and Office: Jerry Nalor Co Inc 5308 Ambridge Dr Agoura Hills CA 91301 *Know no boundaries. Experience the world and become enriched from its varied inhabitants.*

NAYOR, CHARLES FRANCIS, lawyer; b. Boston, Dec. 28, 1913; s. Harry H. and Rose (Rofelsohn) N.; m. Phyllis Joyce Ponn, June 28, 1959; 1 child, Nancy. AB, Dartmouth Coll., 1935; LLB, Harvard U., 1938, JD, 1964. Bar: Mass. 1935, N.Y. 1946. counsel Mass. Speech & Hearing Found., Boston, 1960-92; atty. Les Dames d'Escoffier, Boston, 1970-91. Chmn. Mass. Outdoor Advt. Authority, Boston, 1975. Lt. (j.g.) USCG, 1942-46. Republican. Jewish. Home: 205 Gardner Rd Brookline MA 02146

NAZAIRE, MICHEL HARRY, physician; b. Jérémie, Haiti, Sept. 29, 1939; s. Joseph and Hermance N.; m. Nicole N., Dec. 28, 1968 (div.); children: Hanick and Carline (twins). Grad., Coll. St. Louis de Gonzague, 1959; MD Faculty of Medicine and Pharmacology, State U. Haiti, 1966. Intern, State U. Hosp., Port-Au-Prince, Haiti, 1965-66; resident physician Sanitarium, Port-Au-Prince, Haiti, 1966-68; practice medicine specializing in pneumophysiology, Port-Au-Prince, 1966—; physician fellow Klinik Havelhohe, West Berlin, 1969-70, 89-91; attending physician Sanitarium, Port-Au-Prince, 1976-91. Dep. mem. Internat. Parliament for Safety and Peace; envoy-at-large Internat. State Parliament; mem. global environ. technol. network Who. Contbr. articles to Jour. Indsl. Hygiene, Pneumology and Respiratory Protection. Fellow Internat. Soc. for Respiratory Protection, Am. Coll. Chest Physicians (assoc.); mem. Am. Pub. Health Assn., Am. Conf. Govtl. Indsl. Hygienists, Internat. Union Against Tuberculosis. Address: 6407 S 12th St Apt 1711 Tacoma WA 98465

NAZARIAN, JOHN, academic administrator, mathematics educator; b. Pawtucket, R.I., Sept. 6, 1932; s. Zakie and Amenia (Nahas) N. EdB, R.I. Coll., 1954; AM, Brown U., 1956; MA, U. Ill., 1961; PhD, NYU, 1967. Instr. math. R.I. Coll., Providence, 1954-58, asst. prof., 1958-67, assoc. prof., 1967-71, prof., 1971—, assoc. dean Arts and Scis., 1970-72, spl. asst. to pres., 1971-77, v.p. adminstrn. and fin., 1977-90, pres., 1990—. Chmn., vice-chmn. Arabic Ednl. Found., Pawtucket, 1966-72; chmn. Sargeant Rehab. Ctr, Providence, 1983-86, Diocesan Pastoral Coun., West Newton, Mass., 1974-78. Recipient Cross of Jerusalem, Patriarch of Melkite Ch., 1976. Avocations: music, golf, reading. Office: RI Coll 600 Mt Pleasant Ave Providence RI 02908-1924

NAZEM, FEREYDOUN F., venture capitalist, financier; b. Tehran, Iran, Dec. 29, 1940; came to U.S., 1960, naturalized, 1976; s. Hassan and Afsar N.; m. Susie Gharib, Jan. 20, 1973; children: Alexander, Taraneh. BSc, Ohio State U., 1964; MSc, U. Cin., 1967; MBA, Columbia U., 1971. Sr. rsch. chemist Matheson Coleman & Bell, Norwood, Ohio, 1967-68; asst. v.p., investment analyst Irving Trust Co., N.Y.C., 1969-74; v.p., venture capital officer Charter N.Y., N.Y.C., 1974-75; mng. dir. Collier Enterprises, N.Y.C., 1976-81; mng. ptnr. Nazem & Co., N.Y.C., 1981—; bd. dir. Tegal Corp., Petaluma Calif., Svc. Corp., Wallingford, Conn., Genesis Health Venture Inc., Kennott Square, Pa., Spatial Tech. Inc., Boulder, Colo., Oxford Health, Darien, Conn., Genetix Corp., Tarrytown, N.Y., Consep Corp., Bend, Oreg. Author: The Chemical Industry and Energy Shortage, 1973; contbr. articles to profl. jours. Mem. N.Y. Soc. Security Analysts, N.Y. Venture Capital Forum. Office: Nazem & Co 645 Madison Ave New York NY 10022-1615 *Don't take activity for progress or comfort for civility. Set aside a peaceful hour a day to get in touch with the divinity within you.*

NAZETTE, RICHARD FOLLETT, lawyer; b. Eldora, Iowa, July 27, 1919; s. Hilmer H. and Genevieve A. (Follett) N.; m. Joan Chehak, June 20, 1942; children—Ronald D., Randall A. B.A., U. Iowa, 1942, J.D. with distinction, 1946. Bar: Iowa bar 1946. Practiced in Cedar Rapids, 1946—; partner firm Nazette, Marner, Good, Wendt & Knoll, 1968—; asst. atty. Linn County, Iowa, 1951-56; county atty., 1957-63; dir. United States Bank, Cedar Rapids, 1968-91, State Surety Co., Des Moines, 1966-78. Bd. dirs. Linn County Health Center, 1968-73, chmn., 1968-69; mem. Iowa Bd. Parole, 1981-84. Served with AUS, 1942-44. Fellow Am. Bar Found., Iowa Bar Assn. (bd. govs. 1972-76), Iowa State Bar Found.; mem. Linn County Bar Assn. (pres. 1963), Iowa County Attys. Assn. (pres. 1959), Iowa Acad. Trial Lawyers (pres. 1964), Sigma Phi Epsilon. Republican. Presbyterian. Clubs: Masons, Shriners, Jesters, Elks, Optimists (internat. v.p. 1955). Home: 2224 Country Club Pky SE Cedar Rapids IA 52403-1639 Office: 100 1st St SW Cedar Rapids IA 52404-5701

NDIMBA, CORNELIUS GHANE, language educator; b. Ngeptang-din, Cameroon, Sept. 5, 1953; came to the U.S., 1981; s. Dominic Kimah and Sabina (Meilo) N.; 1 child, Melvynne Meilo. BS in Econs. and Mgmt., S.E. Okla. State U., 1984, M in Adminstrv. Studies, 1989; postgrad., Tex. Woman's U. Cert. tchr. bus. adminstrn. and mgmt., Tex. Customer svc. rep. Internat. Bank of West Africa, Cameroon, 1979-81; storeroom clk. S.E. Okla. State U., Durant, 1981-84, student counselor, 1989-90; purchasing asst. Las Colinas Sports Club, Irving, Tex., 1985-88; assembler GM Corp.,

Arlington, Tex., 1988; admissions rep. ATI Career Tng., Dallas, 1991-92; ESL tchr. Dallas Ind. Sch. Dist., 1992—; sales cons. Am. Foods, Irving, 1989-94. Mem. com. Boy Scouts Am., Dallas, 1992, Cmty. Adv. Com., East Dallas, 1994. Mem. Internat. Reading Assn., Parent-Tchr. Assn., Sasse Old Boys Assn. (pres. 1989—). Republican. Roman Catholic. Avocations: tennis, outdoor soccer, travel, manufacturing. Home: 3113 W Northgate Dr Apt 1045 Irving TX 75062-3104 Office: 4800 Ross Ave Dallas TX 75204

NDUBIZU, CHUKWUKA CLEMENT, mechanical engineer; b. Uruala, Nigeria, Feb. 14, 1945; s. Simon and Virginia (Ochuehi) N.; m. Nwakaego Theresa Obidegwu, Nov. 25, 1977; children: Osita, Obioma, Goziem, Ejiogu. BS with distinction, Cornell U., 1975, MS, 1976; PhD, Ga. Inst. Tech., 1980. Registered profl. engr., Nigeria. Grad. rsch. ast. Cornell U., Ithaca, N.Y., 1975-76; grad. rsch. asst. Ga. Inst. Techs., Atlanta, 1976-80; rsch. engr. George Washington U., Washington, 1980-83; lectr. A.T.B. U., Bauchi, Nigeria, 1983-85; assoc. prof. Fed. U. Techs., Owerri, Nigeria, 1985-94; sr. engr. I Geo-Ctrs., Inc., Ft. Washington, Md., 1994—. Contbr. articles to Jour. Heat Transfer, Combustion and Flame, Combustion Sci. and Tech., Internat. Jour. Heat and Tech. Chmn. Chaplaincy Coun., Owerri, Nigeria, 1990-94. Mem. N.Y. Acad. Scis., Nigerian Soc. Engrs., Compustion Inst., Rotary (v.p. 1993-94), Sigma Xi, Tau Beta Pi. Home: 13217 Schubert Pl Silver Spring MD 20904-6865 Office: Geo-Ctrs Inc 10903 Indian Head Hwy Fort Washington MD 20744-4018

NEACSU, MARIA, artist; b. Manoleasa, Romania, Aug. 15, 1948; d. Ioan and Valeria (Busuioc) Grosu; m. Marius C. Neacsu, Aug. 15, 1970; 1 child, George Mircea. BSBA, Acad. Econ. Study, Bucharest, 1973; BS in Art, U. Calif., Berkeley, 1993; MFA, U. Calif., 1995. Econ. Iprochim, Bucharest, 1973-81; sr. acct. Bechtel, Inc., San Francisco, 1981-83; acctg. mgr. West Mgmt. Co., Oakland, Calif., 1983-86; sr. acct. Kaiser Engring. Inc., Oakland, 1986-89; artist Walnut Creek, Calif., 1989—. Jack K. and Gertrude Murphy fine arts fellow San Francisco Found., 1994. Republican. Avocations: travel, ballet, political study. Home: 505 Pimlico Ct Walnut Creek CA 94596-3677

NEAGLE, DENNIS EDWARD (DENNY NEAGLE), professional baseball player; b. Gambrills, Md., Oct. 13, 1968. Grad. high sch., Gambrills, Md.; student, U. Minn. With Minn. Twins, 1991; pitcher Pitts. Pirates, 1992—. Selected to N.L. All-Star Team, 1995. Mem. Pitts. Pirates N.L. East Champions, 1992. Office: Pittsburgh Pirates 600 Stadium Circle Pittsburgh PA 15212*

NEAL, A. CURTIS, retired lawyer; b. Nacogdoches, Tex., Nov. 25, 1922; s. Berry W. and Mattie E. (Shepherd) N.; m. Martha E. Bishop, Apr. 16, 1942; children: Curtis Jr., Patricia Ann, Dick (dec. 1968). BBA, U. Tex. 1948, LLB 1952. Bar: Tex. 1951; CPA., Tex.; soc. lic., Tex.; lic. E.M.T., Tex., 1983. With Office of Tex. Sec. of State 1948-52; pvt. practice, Amarillo, Tex., 1952-90; ret., 1990. Counsel, exec. com., advancement chmn. Boy Scouts Am., 1957-67; mem. Kids, Inc. (bd. dirs. 1954-68, pres. 1960), Western Merchandisers (bd. dirs. 1970-90), Hastings Books, Music, Video (bd. dirs.1971-93); mem. Key Presdl. Legion of Merit (Rep. Presdl. award 1994); formerly active Amarillo Jaycees, Amarillo C. of C., Amarillo Symphony, United Fund, Nat. Com. Rep. Presdl. Task Force, Barber Shop Quartett Singing in Am., Inc.; deacon, bd. mem. and vol. Paramount Ter. Christian Ch.; vol. High Plains Bapt. Hosp., Amarillo Garden Club, Hospice and ch. work. With USN, 1942-45. Decorated with 12 Combat Stars USN, South Pacific. Fellow Tex. Bar Found. (life); mem. ABA, DRV, Am. Inst. Accts., State Bar Tex. Assn. (com. assistance to local bar assns. 1979-84, chmn. 1982-83, com. on coordination with accts. 1977-79, spl. services to membership div. 1982, state bar coll. law 1981-90), Tex. Soc. CPAs, Amarillo Bar Assn. (pres. 1981-82), Amarillo Jaycees, Amarillo C. of C., Disabled Am. Vets., Masons, York Rite (comdr. 1961) Scottsh Rite Masons, Amarillo Club, Starlighters Dance Club, Amarillo Knife & Fork Club (dir. 1995—), Tex. Shrine Assn. (all-state dir. gen. 1962, Khiva Temple potentate 1970), Cabiri (pres. 1974), Khiva Stage Band (pres. 1978), Downtown Lions Club, Delta Theta Phi, Beta Alpha Psi. Republican. Home: 6205 Jameson Rd Amarillo TX 79106-3518

NEAL, ANN PARKER See **PARKER, ANN**

NEAL, AVON, artist, author; b. Morgantown, Ind., July 16, 1922; s. Orval Francis and Goldie Agnes (Prather) N.; m. Ann Russell Parker, Oct. 31, 1964. Student, Long Beach Coll., Calif.; M.F.A., Escuela de Bellas Artes, Mex., 1949. Artist-in-residence Altos de Chavon, Dominican Republic, 1983, 84; mem. advisory bd. Mus. Am. Folk Art, 1968-71, Dublin Seminar for New Eng. Folklife, 1976-78; pres. Thistle Hill Press; lectr., radio and TV appearances. Exhibited stone rubbings in one and two man shows, Am. embassy, London, 1965, Hallmark Gallery, N.Y.C., 1968, Amon Carter Mus., Ft. Worth, 1968, 71, Mus. Am. Folk Art, 1970, Mus. Fine Arts, Springfield, Mass., 1972, Altos de Chavon, 1984, Princeton U. Library, N.J., 1986, others; represented in permanent collections at Met. Mus. Art, N.Y.C., Library of Congress, Smithsonian Instn., Washington, Abby Aldrich Rockefeller Mus. Am. Folk Art, Williamsburg, Va., Winterthur Mus., Wilmington, Del.; author: Rubbings From Early American Stone Sculpture, 1963, Ephemeral Folk Figures, 1969, Molas: Folk Art of the Cuna Indians, 1977, Pigs and Eagles, 1978, Scarecrows, 1978, Early American Stone Sculpture Found in the Burying Grounds of New England, 1981, Los Ambulantes, 1982, Hajj Paintins, Folk Art of the Great Pilgrimage, 1994; contbr. articles to profl. jours. Served with USN, World War II. Ford Found. grantee, 1962-64; fiction writing fellow Mass. Artists Found., 1979. Home: Thistle Hill North Brookfield MA 01535

NEAL, CHARLIE, sports broadcaster; b. Phila., Oct. 28, 1944; s. Robert Parrish and Elizabeth Neal; m. Jody Lynn Manns, Oct. 27, 1995. BA in Psychology, Villanova U., 1966. Sportscaster Sta. WRC-TV, Washington, 1971-73, Sta. WPVI-TV, Phila., 1973-75, Sta. WJBK-TV, Detroit, 1975-82, Sta. BET-TV, Washington, 1980—; cons. Greyhound Bus Lines, Dallas, 1990—, Md. State Police, Forrestville, 1994—. Avocations: model railroading, motorcycles. Office: Sta BET-TV 1899 9th St NE Washington DC 20018

NEAL, DARWINA LEE, government official; b. Mansfield, Pa., Mar. 31, 1942; d. Darwin Leonard and Ina Belle (Cooke) N. BS, Pa. State U., 1965; postgrad., Cath. U, 1968-70. Registered landscape architect. Landscape architect nat. capital region Nat. Pk. Svc., 1965-69, office of White House liaison, 1969-71, office of profl. services, 1971-74, div. design svcs., 1974-89, chief design svcs., 1989-95; landscape architect office of stewartship & partnership Nat. Pk. Svc., Washington, 1996—; judge numerous award juries. Contbr. articles to profl. jours.; co-author sects. of profl. bull., mag.; author introduction to book Women, Design and the Cambridge School; columnist: Land monthly, 1975-79. Mem. Women's Coun. on Energy in Environment. Recipient Merit award Landscape Contractors Met. Washington; recipient hon. mention Les Floralies Internationales de Montreal, 1980 Alumni Achievement award Pa. State U. Arts and Architecture Alumni Soc., 1981. Fellow Am. Soc. Landscape Architects (v.p. 1979-81, pres. elect 1982-83, pres. 1983-84, trustee 1976-77, nat. treas. 1977-79, legis. coordinator 1975-79, sec. Coun. Fellows 1988-90, (del. to Internat. Fedn. Landscape Architects, del. 1989—, ex-officio rep. to U.S./internat. com. on monuments and sites, liaison to historically black coll. and univ. program Dept. Interior, recipient Pres.' medal 1987); mem. Landscape Archtl. Accreditation Bd. (roster vis. evaluators), Nat. Recreation and Parks Assn., Nat. Soc. Park Resources (bd. dirs. 1978-80), Nat. Trust Hist. Preservation, Pa. State U. Alumni Assn. (Washington met. chpt. trustee 1972-74), Am. Arbitration Assn. (nat. panel arbitrators), Com. 100 for the Fed. City, Preservation Action, Nat. Assn. Olmsted Parks, Beekman Pl. Condominium Assn. (bd. dirs. 1985-91, archtl. control com.), Nat. Parks and Conservation Assn., Alliance for Historic Preservation, World Watch, Worldwide. Office: Nat Pk Svc Nat Capitol Reg Dept Interior Divsn Design Svcs 1100 Ohio Dr SW Washington DC 20242

NEAL, FRED WARNER, political scientist, educator; b. Northville, Mich., Aug. 5, 1915; s. Frank Stephenson and Bertha (Fendt) N.; m. Grace Irene Repine, Feb. 14, 1952; children: Susan Victoria, Frank Stephenson, Alexander Frederick (dec.); m. Marian Katherine Walker, Jan. 2, 1969; m. Mary Caroline Hall, Jan. 10, 1982. B.A., U. Mich., 1937, Ph.D., 1955; student (Nieman fellow), Harvard U., 1942-43, U. Karlova, Prague, Czechoslovakia, 1949; Fulbright research fellow, U. Paris, 1950. Washington corr. UP and Wall St. Jour., 1938-43; cons. Russian affairs, chief fgn. research State Dept., 1946-48; asst. to pres. Univ. State of N.Y., 1948-49; asst. to chmn. Com. on Present Danger, 1951; asst. prof. polit. sci. U. Colo., 1951-56; asso. prof. UCLA, 1956-57; asso. prof. internat. relations and govt. Claremont (Calif.) Grad. Sch., 1957-60, prof., 1960-83, prof. emeritus, 1983—; Rockefeller prof. internat. rels. U. W.I., 1965-66; vis. lectr. U. Mich., 1950, 53-54; assoc. Am. U. Field Staff, 1954-55; co-dir. Twentieth Century Fund Study on Yugoslavia, 1958-61; Fulbright fellow, Paris, 1961-62; cons. Ctr. for Study of Dem. Instns.; organizer, dir. Pacem in Terris convocations; chmn. Am. Com. on U.S.-Soviet Rels., 1974-77, exec. v.p., 1977-93. Author: Titoism in Action: The Reforms in Yugoslavia after 1948, 1958, U.S. Foreign Policy and the Soviet Union, 1961, War and Peace and Germany, 1962; co-author: Yugoslvia and the New Communism, 1962; editor: Pacem in Terris III: New Opportunities for American Foreign Policy, 1974, Pacem in Terris IV: American Foreign Policy at Home and Abroad, 1976, Detente or Debacle, 1979; author: A Survey of Detente—Past, Present, Future, 1977. Democratic nominee for Congress 24th Dist. Calif., 1968; Pres. Albert Parvin Found., 1969-70. Served with A.C., USNR, 1943-46, Russia, Siberia. Recipient Decoration of Yugoslav Flag with Golden Wreath, highest honor of Yugoslvia, 1987; Japan Found. fellow, 1978. Mem. Am., Internat., Western polit. sci. assns., Internat. Studies Assn., Am. Assn. Advancement Slavic Studies, AAUP, Soc. Nieman Fellows, Los Angeles Com. Fgn. Relations. Home: 910 N Oxford Ave Claremont CA 91711-3712 *I have become convinced of the essential similarity in human motivations and, also, the essential differences in their expression imposed by different cultures; of the oneness of nature; of the unlikeliness and, usually, the undesirability of extreme solutions; of the difficulties of one generation imparting values to another; of the honor of patriotism and its moral dangers; of the tendency of power to corrupt; and of the incomprehensibility of life as well as the joy of engaging in the struggle to comprehend it.*

NEAL, HOMER ALFRED, physics educator, researcher, university administrator; b. Franklin, Ky., June 13, 1942; s. Homer and Margaret Elizabeth (Holl) N.; m. Donna Jean Daniels, June 16, 1962; children: Sharon Denise, Homer Alfred. BS in Physics with honors, Ind. U., 1961; MS in Physics (John Hay Whitney fellow), U. Mich., 1963, PhD in Physics, 1966. Asst. prof. physics Ind. U., 1967-70, assoc. prof., 1970-72, prof., 1972-81, dean research and grad. devel., 1976-81; prof. physics SUNY, Stony Brook, 1981-87, provost, 1981-86; prof. physics, chmn. U. Mich., Ann Arbor, 1987-93, v.p. rsch., 1993—, interim pres., 1996—; mem. Nat. Sci. Bd., 1980-86; chmn. Argonne Zero Gradient Synchrotron Users Group, 1970-72; trustee Argonne Univs. Assn., 1971-74, 77-80; NSF physics adv. panel , 1976-79, chmn. NSF physics adv. panel, 1987-89; high energy physics adv. panel U.S. Dept. Energy, 1977-81; bd. dirs. Ogden Corp. Contbr. articles to profl. jours. Bd. dirs. N.Y. Sea Grant Inst., 1982-86; mem. bd. overseers Superconducting Super Collider, 1989-93; mem. bd. regents Smithsonian Instn., 1989—; trustee Ctr. for Strategic and Internat. Studies, 1990—; trustee Environ. Rsch. Inst. of Mich., 1994-96; mem. adv. bd. Oak Ridge (Tenn.) Nat. Lab., 1993—. NSF fellow, 1966-67; Sloan fellow, 1968; Guggenheim fellow, 1980-81. Fellow Am. Phys. Soc., AAAS, Am. Acad. Arts and Scis.; mem. Univs. Research Assn. (trustee 1983-87), Sigma Xi. Office: Office VP for Rsch 4080 Fleming Adminstrn 503 Thompson Ann Arbor MI 48109-1340

NEAL, IRENE COLLINS, artist, educator; b. Greensburg, Pa., May 14, 1936; d. Oliver Shupe and Betsey Cowap (Mann) Collins; m. Paul Whitaker Neal, Nov. 24, 1960; children: Paul Collins Gordon, Betsey Whitaker. BA, Wilson Coll., 1958. guest spkr. Coll. Santa Fe, Albuquerque, N.Mex., 1994. Solo exhbns. include Allied Chem. Corp., Morristown, N.J., 1975, Planetarium of Rio de Janeiro, 1977, The Pat Ackerman Gallery, Mphs., 1980, Westmoreland Mus. Art, Greensburg, 1986, Wilson Coll., 1993; group exhbns. include Jersey City Mus., 1975, N.J. State Mus., 1975, Somerset (N.J.) Tri-State Mus., 1975, Nat. Arts Club, N.Y.C., 1975, Garden State Watercolor Soc., 1975, Salao de Marinhas, Rio de Janeiro, 1977, Stamford (Conn.) Mus., 1984, 85, 89, Branchville Soho Gallery, Ridgefield, Conn., 1984, Silvermine Guild, New Canaan, Conn., 1984, Stamford Libr., 1985, Shippee Gallery, N.Y.C., 1986, 110 Greene St., N.Y.C., 1986, Wilton (Conn.) Libr., 1986, Aldrich Mus. Contemporary Art, Ridgefield, 1987, Ariel Gallery, N.Y.C., 1988, 89, Visual Arts Festival, Edmonton, Can., 1989, Mus. Art., Ft. Lauderdale, Fla., 1991-92, Salander-o'Reilly Galleries, Inc., N.Y., 1994, Vanderleelie Gallery, Edmonton, Can., 1996, Galerie Piltzer, Paris, France, 1996; represented in collections Planetarium Rio de Janeiro, Internat. Paper, N.Y.C., Westmoreland Mus. Art, Greensburg, Pepperdine U., Malibu, Calif., Newport Harbor Art Mus., Newport Beach, Calif., Hoover Instn. Stanford (Calif.) U., St. Matthew's Episcopal Ch., Wilton, Conn., Columbia U., N.Y.C., Ctr. Arts, Vero Beach, Fla., Mus. Art., Ft. Lauderdale, Alamo Rent A Car, Ft. Lauderdale, Denver Ctr. Performing Arts, Louis P. Cabot, Boston. Republican. Episcopalian. Avocations: ocean diving, tennis, golf, gardening. Home and Studio: 700 River Rd Cos Cob CT 06807

NEAL, JAMES AUSTIN, architect; b. Greenville, S.C., Nov. 23, 1935; s. Charles Albert Neal and Jane (Anderson) Cole; m. Leonette Dedmond, Apr. 13, 1963; 1 child, Heather Anderson. B. Arch., Clemson U., 1959. Registered arch., S.C. Designer McMillan Architects, Greenville, S.C., 1960-62; project mgr. W.E. Freeman Architects, Greenville, 1963-64; project architect J.E. Sirrine Co., Greenville, 1964-68; pres., prin. Neal, Prince & Browning, Greenville, 1969—; vis. prof. Clemson U. Coll. Architecture, 1974-75; mem. bd. advisors Wachovia Nat. Bank. Pres. Leslie Meyer Devel. Ctr., Greenville, 1980-82. Recipient Leadership award Greenville C. of C., 1983. Mem. AIA (Merit Design award 1978, pres. S.C. chpt. 1991, regional dir. S.C., Ga., N.C., mem. nat. bd. 1994—), Greenville Council Architects (past pres.), Interfaith Forum of Religious Art and Architecture (mem. nat. bd.). Baptist. Club: Poinsett (pres. 1985-86). Avocations: jogging; flying. Office: Neal Prince & Ptnrs 110 W North St Greenville SC 29601-2727

NEAL, JAMES MADISON, JR., editor; b. Oklahoma City, Aug. 6, 1925; s. James Madison and Tillie Belle (Milliken) N.; m. Caroline Dorothy Becker (dec. Dec. 1974); children: Charles, James W., Jody, Carolyn. BA, U. Colo., 1949; MA, S.D. State U., 1970. Editor various newspapers, Colo., Nebr. and Okla., 1949-59; wire editor Rapid City Journal, Rapid City, S.D., 1959-67; instr. S.D. State U., Brookings, S.D., 1967-71; asst. prof. U. Nebr., Lincoln, 1971-73, assoc. prof., 1973-90; S.D. chmn. AP Mng. Editors Assn., 1962-64. Mem. Soc. Profl. Journalists, Investigative Reporters and Editors, ACLU (bd. dirs. Nebr. chpt. 1979-82), VFW. Unitarian. Avocations: painting, travel. Home: 4700 N Kolb Rd Apt 7207 Tucson AZ 85150-6187

NEAL, JAMES PRESTON, state senator, project engineer; b. Cin., July 1, 1935; s. James Preston and Desha Frank (Thompson) N.; m. Nancy Joan Tyner, June 11, 1961; children: Leslie, Neal Driscoll, Karen Desha, James P. BSME, U. Ill., 1960. Registered profl. engr., Del. Tech. svc. engr. DuPont Co., Parlin, N.J., 1960-62; engr DuPont Co., Waynesboro, Va., 1962-64; instrument engr. DuPont Co., Newburgh, N.Y., 1964-68, Newark, 1966-78; project engr. DuPont Co., 1978-92; dir. Tetra Tech Inc., Christiana, Del., 1992—; pres. Tech. Mgmt., 1994—; mem. Del. Ho. of Reps., 1978-80; mem. Del. Senate, 1980-94. Patentee in field. Councilman City of Newark, 1973-78. With U.S. Army, 1954-56. Recipient Disting. Svc. award Forum to Advance Minorities in Engring., 1989, Disting. Svc. citation Del. Libr. Assn., 1994. Fellow Am. Legis. Exch. Coun. (sr. fellow, nat. officer 1991-94, Outstanding Leader 1989, Outstanding Legis. mem. 1994), Conf. World Regions (sr. fellow); mem. IEEE (sr.), Del. Engring. Soc. (Engr. of Yr. 1989), Instrument Soc. Am. Republican. Presbyterian. Avocations: photography, reading. Home: 50 Bridlebrook Ln Newark DE 19711-2061 Office: Tetra Tech Inc 56 W Main St Newark DE 19702-1501

NEAL, JOSEPH C., JR., church administrator. Sec. of fin. Christian Methodist Episcopal Church, L.A. Address: Christian Methodist Episcopal Ch PO Box 75058 Los Angeles CA 90075-0058

NEAL, LEORA LOUISE HASKETT, social services administrator; b. N.Y.C., Feb. 23, 1943; d. Melvin Elias and Miriam Emily (Johnson) Haskett; m. Robert A. Neal, Apr. 23, 1966; children: Marla Patrice, Johnathan Robert. BA in Psychology and Sociology, City Coll. N.Y., 1965; MS in Social Work, Columbia U., 1970, cert. adoption specialist, 1977; IBM cert. community exec. tng. program, N.Y., 1982. Cert. social worker N.Y. state. Caseworker N.Y.C. Dept. Social Service, 1965-67, Windham Child Care, N.Y.C., 1967-73; exec. dir. Assn. Black Social Workers Child Adoption Counseling and Referral Service, N.Y.C., 1975—; cons. adoption, adoption tng. N.Y. State Dept. Social Svc., Columbia U. Sch. Social Work, N.Y.C. Human Resources Adminstrn., U. La., New Orleans; founder Haskett-Neal Publs., Bronx, N.Y., 1993. Co-author: Transracial Adoptive Parenting: A Black/White Community Issue, 1993; contbr. articles in field to profl. jours. Child Welfare League Am. fellow, 1976; recipient cert. No Time to Lose cert. N.Y. State Dept. Social Svcs., 1989. Mem. NAFE, Columbia U. Alumni Assn., CCNY Alumni Assn., Missionary Com. Revival Team (outreach chairperson 1982-88). Democrat. Avocations: writing, history and religious studies, traveling, cultural activities. Office: Assn Black Social Workers 1969 Madison Ave New York NY 10035-1549

NEAL, LOUISE KATHLEEN, life insurance company executive, accountant; b. Seattle, Nov. 25, 1951; d. Paul Bradford and Ruth Catherine (Park) Johnson; m. William Steven Neal, Oct. 25, 1974. B.A. in Bus. Adminstrn. and Acctg., U. Wash., 1974. Sr. acct. Touche Ross & Co., Seattle, 1974-77; internal auditor No. Life Ins. Co., Seattle, 1977-83; auditor Northwestern Nat. Life Ins. Co., Mpls., 1983-84, 2d v.p., auditor, 1984-88; sr. v.p., gen. auditor Transam. Occidental Life Ins. Co., L.A., 1988-89, sr. v.p., 1990-92, sr. v.p., chief adminstrv. officer, 1992-95; pres. USA Admin. Svcs. Inc. sub. Transam. Occidental Life Ins. Co., Overland Park, Kans., 1995—. Fellow Life Mgmt. Inst.; mem. AICPA. Office: USA Admin Svcs Inc PO Box 2948 Overland Park KS 66201-1348

NEAL, MARCUS PINSON, JR., radiologist, medical educator; b. Columbia, Mo., Apr. 22, 1927; s. M. Pinson and Mathilda (Evers) N.; m. Gail S. Fallon, May 27, 1961; children: Sandra G., M. Pinson III, Ruth-Catherine E. AB, U. Mo., 1949, BS, 1951; MD, U. Tenn., 1953. Intern Med. Coll. Va., Richmond, 1953-54; resident U. Wis. Hosp., Madison, 1954-57; instr. dept. radiology Sch. Medicine U. Wis., Madison, 1957-59; mem. staff U. Wis. Hosps., Madison, 1957-63; asst. prof. radiology, dir. dept. radiology Cen. Wis. Colony, Madison, 1959-63; radiologist Wis. Diagnostic Ctr., Madison, 1962-63; mem. staff Med. Coll. Va. Hosps., Va. Commonwealth U., 1963—; assoc. prof. radiology Med. Coll. Va., Va. Commonwealth U., 1963-66, prof. radiology, 1966—, dir. postgrad. edn. dept. radiology, 1964-73, chmn. divsn. diagnostic radiology, 1965-68, asst. dean Sch. Medicine, dir. grad. med. edn., dir. regional med. program, 1968-71, dir. continuing edn. Sch. Medicine,, 1969-72, interim dean Sch. Medicine,, 1971, asst. v.p. for health scis., 1971-73, provost Health Scis. campus, 1973-78, assoc. dean for continuing med. edn. and quality assurance Sch. Medicine,, 1978-79, dir. housestaff edn. Dept. Radiology,, 1979-93, dir. section genitourinary radiology, Dept. Radiology,, 1981-92; bd. dirs. Common Wealth Bank, Richmond; cons., radiologist Va. Hosp., Madison, 1962-63, USAF Hosp., Truax Field, Madison, 1962-63, McGuire VA Hosp., Richmond, 1963—; bd. forestry Commonwealth of Va., 1990-94, chmn. bd. forestry, 1993-94. Editor: Emergency Interventional Radiology: Practical Aspects, 1988; contbr. articles to profl. jours. Pres. Oxford Civic Assn., Richmond, 1965-67, Three Ridges Condominium Assn., Wintergreen, Va., 1979-84. Served as pharmacist mate USNR, 1945-47. Fellow Oak Ridge Inst. Nuclear Studies, Am. Coll. Radiology (councilor Va. chpt. 1977-83, 85-91, 93—); mem. AMA, Radiol. Soc. N.Am., Am. Roentgen Ray Soc., Med. Soc. Va., So. Med. Assn. (pres. 1982-83), Richmond Acad. Medicine, Capital Club (bd. dirs.), Commonwealth Club, Bull and Bear Club, Willow Oaks Country Club, Sigma Xi. Avocations: hunting, fishing, gardening, skiing. Home: 4607 Stratford Rd Richmond VA 23225-1066 Office: Med Coll Va PO Box 980295 Richmond VA 23298-0295

NEAL, MARGARET SHERRILL, writer; b. Memphis, Apr. 13, 1950; d. Wilburn Franklin and Merle Aileen (Willis) N. BA, Memphis State U., 1972, postgrad., 1973; MS, Columbia Pacific U., 1984. Air traffic controller FAA, Memphis, 1974-76, New Bern, N.C., 1976-81, Vero Beach, Fla., 1981-83; detection systems specialist U.S. Customs Service, Miami, 1983-87, intelligence rsch. specialist, 1987-89; ret., 1989. Mem. NOW, Smithsonian Instn., Mensa, Nat. Trust Hist. Preservation, Greenpeace, Clan Macneil Soc., Nature Conservancy, Save the Manatee Club. Republican. Presbyterian. Avocations: genealogy, needlework, traveling, sketching, growing orchids.

NEAL, PHIL HUDSON, JR., manufacturing company executive; b. Birmingham, Ala., Nov. 17, 1926; s. Phil Hudson and Amy (Gross) N.; m. Sarah Swift Britton, Sept. 19, 1959; children: Amy Neal Ager, Phil Hudson, III, Samuel Abney Britton. A.B., Duke U., 1950; M.B.A., Harvard U., 1952. Investment analyst First Nat. Bank, Birmingham, 1952-55; procedures analyst Gen. Electric Co., Hendersonville, N.C., 1955-58; with Ala. By-Products Corp., Birmingham, 1958-79; asst. treas. Ala. By-Products Corp., 1964-68, treas., 1968-79; dir., v.p. Utility Tool Co., Birmingham, 1979-86; dir., pres. Nutec Metal Finishing Inc., Birmingham, 1986-92, chmn., 1992—; dir. Pounds Ins. Corp., 1986—. Trustee Advent Episcopal Day Sch., 1967—, pres., 1968-89, trustee charitable endowment trust, 1981—; treas. Cathedral Ch. of Advent, 1981-82, mem. chpt., 1983-85, 86-89; bd. dirs. Greater Birmingham Ministries, 1975-77, Advent Episcopal Assn. for Edn., 1968-89, Jefferson County chpt. Ala. Soc. Crippled Children and Adults, Inc., 1977-79; trustee Ala. Found. for Hearing and Speech, 1967-74, v.p., 1968-69, pres., 1969-71. Served with USNR, 1945-46. Mem. Newcomen Soc. N.Am., Phi Beta Kappa, Sigma Nu, Phi Eta Sigma. Episcopalian (vestryman, sr. warden). Clubs: Birmingham Country, The Club. Home: 3336 Hermitage Rd Birmingham AL 35223-2004 also: 81 Old Duck Hole Rd East Orleans MA 02643 Office: 3669 Indsl Pkwy PO Box 170746 Birmingham AL 35217-0746

NEAL, PHILIP, dancer. Grad. magna cum laude, St. Paul's Sch., 1986; trained, Sch. Royal Danish Ballet, Copenhagen, Denmark. With corps. de ballet N.Y.C. Ballet, 1987-91, soloist, 1991-92, prin. dancer, 1992—. Featured in ballets (Balanchine) Divertimento No. 15, Walpurgisnacht, Slaughter on Tenth Avenue, Western Symphony, Swan Lake, Coppelia; (Robbins) Interplay, The Four Seasons, The Goldberg Variations, Glass Pieces, Mother Goose; (Martins) Les Gentilhommes, Ecstatic Orange, Black & White, Fearful Symmetries, The Sleeping Beauty; also appeared in N.Y.C. Ballet's Balanchine Celebration, 1993. Recipient silver medal Internat. Prix de Lausanne ballet competition; summer scholar N.Y.C . Sch. Am. Ballet; named Presdl. scholar of the Arts Nat Found. Advancement of the Arts. Office: New York City Ballet NY State Theater Lincoln Ctr Plaza New York NY 10023

NEAL, PHILIP MARK, diversified manufacturing executive; b. San Diego, Aug. 28, 1940; s. Philip Mark and Florence Elizabeth (Anderson) N.; children: Brian, Kevin. B.A., Pomona Coll., 1962; M.B.A., Stanford U., 1964. Mgr. financial planning and analysis CBS, Hollywood, 1964-66; cons. McKinsey & Co., Los Angeles, 1966-73; v.p., controller Avery Internat. Corp., Los Angeles, 1974-78; sr. v.p. fin. Avery Internat. Corp., Pasadena, 1979-88, group v.p. materials group, 1988-90; exec. pres. Avery Internat. Corp., 1990, pres., chief operating officer, 1990—; bd. dirs. Ind. Colls. of So. Calif. Trustee Pomona Coll; gov. Town Hall of Calif. Bd. Govs. Mem. Fin. Execs. Inst. Republican. Episcopalian. Office: Avery Dennison Corp PO Box 7090 Pasadena CA 91109-7090

NEAL, RICHARD, protective services official; b. Phila.; m. Dolores Neal; children: Richard, Jason. Grad., Bok Vocat.-Tech. Sch.; student, Temple U. From police officer to chief inspector Phila. Police Dept., 1962-92, commr., 1992—. Pres. Police Athletic League; asst. treas. Hero Scholarship Fund; bd. dirs. Corp. Alliance for Drug Edn., Boy Scouts Am. Phila. Coun., ARC, Jr. Achievement Delaware Valley, Crime Prevention Assn., Pa. Automobile Theft Prevention Authority. Recipient Citation Pa. Ho. Rep., Phila. City Coun., Award Korean Assn., Wolf Baron Lodge of Overbrook, Phila. Housing Authority. Mem. Nat. Orgn. Black Law Enforcement Execs., Guardian Civic League, Fraternal Order Police, Prince Hall Masons. Baptist. Office: Office Police Commr Police Adminstrn Bldg 8th & Race Sts Philadelphia PA 19106

NEAL, RICHARD EDMUND, congressman, former mayor; b. Worcester, Mass., Feb. 14, 1949; s. Edmund J. and Mary H. (Garvey) N.; m. Maureen Conway, Dec. 20, 1975; children—Rory, Brendan, Maura, Sean. B.S., Am. Internat. Coll., Springfield, Mass., 1972; M.P.A., U. Hartford, Conn., 1976; postgrad., U. Mass., Amherst, 1982. Adminstrv. aide to Mayor City of Springfield, Mass., 1973-78, mem. city council, 1978-83, mayor, 1984-88; mem. 101st-103rd Congresses from 2nd. Mass. dist., Washington, DC,

1989—; mem. ways and means com.; lectr. history and politics Springfield Tech. Community Coll., Mass., 1973-83; lectr. bus. and govt. Western New Eng. Coll., Springfield, 1979-82; project dir. Springfield Tech. Community Coll., 1979-82. Trustee ARC, YMCA, Springfield. Named to Outstanding Young Men in Am., U.S. Jr. C. of C., Springfield. Mem. Am. Internat. Coll. Alumni Assn. (pres. 1980, Alumni Achievement award 1985). Springfield Library and Mus. Assn. (trustee). Democrat. Roman Catholic. Clubs: Valley Press. John Boyle O'Reilly (Springfield). Office: US House of Reps 2431 Rayburn Washington DC 20515-2102*

NEAL, STEVEN GEORGE, journalist; b. Coos Bay, Oreg., July 3, 1949; s. Ernest L. and Ellen Louise (Williams) N.; m. Susan Christine Simmons, May 8, 1971; children: Erin, Shannon. BS in Journalism, U. Oreg., 1971; MS in Journalism, Columbia U., 1972. Reporter Oreg. Jour., Portland, 1971, Phila. Inquirer, 1972-78; gen. assignment reporter, White House corr., polit. writer Chgo. Tribune, 1979-87; polit. editor Chgo. Sun-Times, 1987-92, polit. columnist, 1987—; bd. govs. White House Corrs. Assn., Washington, 1981-83. Co-author: Tom McCall: Maverick, 1977; author: The Eisenhowers, 1978, Dark Horse: A Biography of Wendell Willkie, 1984, McNary of Oregon, 1985; editor: They Never Go Back to Pocatello: The Essays of Richard Neuberger, 1988; contbr. to Am. Heritage, The Nation, The N.Y. Times Books Rev., Dictionary of Am. Biography. Recipient William H. Jones award Chgo. Tribune, 1984; Robert W. Ruhl lectr. U. Oreg., Eugene, 1984; Col. Robert R. McCormick fellow, McCormick Found., Chgo., 1989; Hoover Libr. Assn. scholar, West Branch, Iowa, 1989. Roman Catholic. Home: 411 N Elm St Hinsdale IL 60521-3709 Office: Chgo Sun-Times Inc 401 N Wabash Ave Rm 110 Chicago IL 60611-3532

NEALE, E(RNEST) R(ICHARD) WARD, retired university official, consultant; b. Montreal, Que., Can., July 3, 1923; s. Ernest John and Mabel Elizabeth (McNamee) N.; m. Roxie Eveline Anderson, June 3, 1950; children—Richard Ward, Owen Curtis. B.Sc., McGill U., Montreal, 1949; M.S., Yale U., 1950, Ph.D., 1952; LL.D. (hon.), Calgary U., Alta., Can., 1977; DSc (hon.), Meml. U., Nfld., Can., 1989. Asst. prof. geology U. Rochester, N.Y., 1952-54; sect. chief Geol. Survey Can., Ottawa, Ont., 1954-63; div. chief Geol. Survey Can., 1965-68, Calgary, 1976-81; commonwealth geol. liaison officer London, 1963-65; prof., head geology Meml. U., St. John's, Nfld., Can., 1968-76; v.p. Meml. U., 1982-87; cons., Calgary, Alta., Can., 1987—; chmn. nat. adv. bd. on sci. publs. NRC-Natural Scis. and Engring. Rsch. Coun., Ottawa, 1982-88. Author: Geology and Geophysics in Canadian Universities, 1980. Editor: Some Guides to Mineral Exploration, 1967, Geology in the Atlantic Region, 1968, The Geosciences in Canada, 1968; Editor: Can. Jour. of Earth Science, 1974-79, Science and the Public, 1988. Bd. dirs. Unitarian Ch. Calgary, 1993—, pres., 1995-96. Petty officer Royal Can. Navy, 1943-45. Decorated officer Order of Can., 1990; recipient Queen's Jubilee medal Govt. of Can., 1977, Can. 125 medal, 1992. Fellow Royal Soc. Can. (coun. 1972-75, chmn. com. pub. awareness of sci. 1987-91, Bancroft medal 1975), Geol. Assn. Can. (pres. 1973-74, Ambrose medal 1986, 1st E.R. Ward Neale medal 1995), Can. Geosci. Coun. (pres. 1975-76, R.T. Bell medal Can. Mining Jour. 1977), Geol. Soc. Am.; mem. Assn. Earth Sci. Editors, Nat. Def. (chmn. biol. and chem. def. rev. com. 1990-93), Calgary Elks Golf Club, Chancellor's Club, Crows Nest Club, Calgary Sci. Network (pres. 1989), Sigma Xi (nat. lectr. New Haven 1976, chmn. Avalon chpt. 1986). Avocations: golf, cross-country skiing, hiking, canoeing. Home and Office: 5108 Carney Rd NW, Calgary, AB Canada T2L 1G2

NEALE, GARY LEE, utilities executive; b. Lead, S.D., Mar. 3, 1940; s. Vearl J. and Gladys M. (Trenkle) N.; m. Sandra C. Lovell, June 16, 1962; children: David G., Julie C. BA in Econs., U. Wash., 1962, MBA, 1965. Loan examiner Wells Fargo, 1966-69; sr. fin. analyst Kaiser Industries, 1969-70; chmn., pres., chief exec. officer Planmetrics, Chgo., 1970-89; pres., chief oper. officer No. Ind. Pub. Svc. Co., Hammond, 1989-93, chmn., pres., CEO, 1993—; bd. dirs. Modine Mfg., Racine, Wis., Am. Gas Assn., Arlington, Va., Ind. Gas Assn./Ind. Electric Assn., Indpls., Nipsco Industries Inc., Hammond. Bd. dirs. N.W. Ind. Symphony, 1990; mem. Ind. Energy Policy Forum, 1991. Lt. (j.g.) USN, 1962-64. Mem. Econ. Club Chgo., Chgo. Univ. Club, NYU Club. Office: No Ind Pub Svc Co 5265 Hohman Ave Hammond IN 46320-1722*

NEALE, HENRY WHITEHEAD, plastic surgery educator; b. Richmond, Va., July 18, 1940; s. Richard C. and Eva W. Neale; m. Margaret C. Neale, June 20, 1964; children: Leigh, Jennifer, Henry Whitehead Jr., William. BS, Davidson Coll., 1960; MD, Med. Coll. Va., 1964. Diplomate Am. Bd. Surgery, Am. Bd. Plastic Surgery (guest examiner 1986-90, dir. 1990-96, mem. com. on plans and qualifying exam. com. 1993-96, exec. com. 1993—, chmn. certifying examing com. 1993-95, mem. ethics com. 1993, liaison to Am. Bd. Surgery 1993-96, pres.-elect 1995—). Rotating intern Mercy Med. Ctr., Springfield, Ohio, 1964-65; resident in gen. surgery U. Cin. Med. Ctr., 1965-71, dir. div. plastic, reconstructive and hand surgery, 1974—; resident in plastic surgery Duke U. Med. Ctr., Durham, N.C., 1971-74; fellow in hand surgery, Christine Kleinert hand fellow U. Louisville, 1973; asst. prof. surgery U. Cin. Coll. Medicine, 1974-77, assoc. prof., 1977-82, prof., 1982—; active staff, dir. hand surgery and plastic surgery clinics U. Cin. Med. Ctr. Hosp. Group, 1974—; dir. burn reconstructive and plastic surgery, co-dir. hand surgery svc. Shriners Burns Inst., Cin., 1983—; dir. div. plastic, reconstructive and hand surgery and plastic surgery clinic Childrens Hosp. Med. Ctr., Cin., 1983—; assoc. attending staff Good Samaritan Hosp.; courtesy staff Christ Hosp., Jewish Hosp.; numerous presentations in field. Mem. editl. bd. Jour. Plastic and Reconstructive Surgery, 1989—; contbr. numerous articles to med. jours. Capt. M.C., USAF, 1965-70. Rsch. grantee Eli Lilly Co., 1979-91. Fellow ACS; mem. AMA, Am. Assn. Plastic Surgeons, Am. Burn Assn., Am. Cleft Palate Assn., Am. Soc. for Aesthetic Plastic Surgery, Am. Soc. Plastic and Reconstructive Surgeons, Am. Soc. for Surgery of Hand, Acad. Medicine Cin., Assn. Acad. Chairmen in Plastic Surgery, Cin. Surg. Soc., Grad. Surg. Soc. Cin., Greater Cin. Soc. Plastic and Reconstructive Surgeons (pres. 1988-89), Ohio Med. Assn., Ohio Valley Soc. Plaastic and Reconstructive Surgery (pres. 1985-86), Plastic Surgery Rsch. Coun. Home: 2970 Alpine Ter Cincinnati OH 45208-3408 Office: U Cin Coll Medicine Div Pl Reconst Hand Surgery 231 Bethesda Ave Cincinnati OH 45229-2827

NEALON, WILLIAM JOSEPH, JR., federal judge; b. Scranton, Pa., July 31, 1923; s. William Joseph and Ann Cannon (McNally) N.; m. Jean Sullivan, Nov. 15, 1947; children: Ann, Robert, William, John, Jean, Patricia, Kathleen, Terrence, Thomas, Timothy. Student, U. Miami, Fla., 1942-43; B.S. in Econs, Villanova U., 1947; LL.B., Cath. U. Am., 1950; LL.D. (hon.), U. Scranton, 1975. Bar: Pa. 1951. With firm Kennedy, O'Brien & O'Brien (and predecessor), Scranton, 1951-60; mem. Lackawanna County Ct. Common Pleas, 1960-62; U.S. dist. judge Middle Dist. Pa., 1962—, chief judge, 1976-88, sr. status, 1989—; mem. com. on adminstrn. of criminal law Jud. Conf. U.S., 1979—; lectr. bus. law and labor law U. Scranton, 1951-59; mem. jud. council 3d Cir. Ct. Appeals, 1984—; dist. judge rep. from 3d Cir. Jud. Conf. of U.S., 1987—. Mem. Scranton Registration Commn., 1953-55; hearing examiner Pa. Liquor Control Bd., 1955-59; campaign dir. Lackawanna County chpt. Nat. Found., 1961-63; mem. Scranton-Lackawanna Health and Welfare Authority, 1963—; assoc. bd. Marywood Coll., Scranton; pres. bd. dirs. Cath. Youth Center; pres. Father's Club Scranton Prep. Sch., 1966; chmn. bd. dirs. Mercy Hosp., 1991—; chmn. bd. trustees U. Scranton; vice chmn. bd. trustees Lackawanna Jr. Coll., Scranton; bd. dirs. St. Joseph's Children's and Maternity Hosp., 1963-66, Lackawanna County unit Am. Cancer Soc., Lackawanna County Heart Assn., Lackawanna County chpt. Pa. Assn. Retarded Children, Scranton chpt. ARC, Lackawanna United Fund, Mercy Hosp., Scranton, 1975—; trustee St. Michael's Sch. Boys, Hoban Heights; adv. com. Hosp. Service Assn. Northeastern Pa. Served to lt. USMCR, 1942-45. Recipient Americanism award Amos Lodge B'nai B'rith, 1975; Cyrano award U. Scranton Grad. Sch., 1977; Disting. Service award Pa. Trial Lawyers Assn., 1979; named one of 50 Disting. Pennsylvanians Greater Phila. C. of C., 1980, Outstanding Fed. Trial Judge Assn. Trial Lawyers Am., 1983. Mem. Pa. Bar Assn., Lackawanna County Bar Assn. (Chief Justice Michael J. Eagen award 1987), Friendly Sons St. Patrick (pres. Lackawanna County 1963-64), Pi Sigma Alpha. Club: Scranton Country (Clarks Summit, Pa.) (bd. dirs.). Lodge: K.C. Office: US Courthouse PO Box 1146 Scranton PA 18501-1146

NEAL-VITTIGLIO, CYNTHIA KAREN, clinical psychologist; b. Detroit, Dec. 30, 1952; d. Gaston O. and Evelyn Jewel (Dunn) N.; m. Thomas Anthony Vittiglio, July 10, 1988; 1 child, Anthony. BA, Wayne State U., 1975, MA, 1977, PhD, 1983. Licensed psychologist. Clin. researcher Sinai Hosp., Detroit, 1977-78; clin. asst. Dept. Neuropsychology Lafayette Clinic, 1974-75; faculty mem. Inst. for Sex Rsch., Bloomington, Ind., 1975, 80; sch. psychologist Lakeshore Pub. Schs., St. Clair Shores, Mich., 1979-80; staff psychologist Evergreen Counseling Ctr., St. Clair Shores, 1979—; consulting psychologist St. John Hosp., Detroit, 1983—. Mem. Jr. Coun., Founders Soc., Detroit, 1985—, Cranbrook Women's Soc., Bloomfield Hills, Mich., 1987—, Am. Ballet Soc., N.Y.C., 1980—. Recipient Grad. Fellowship Wayne State U., 1988. Mem. APA, DAR (Louise St. Clair chpt.). Republican. Avocations: exercise, boating, downhill skiing. Home: PO Box 250628 Franklin MI 48025-0628 Office: Evergreen Counseling Svcs 19900 Ten Mile Saint Clair Shores MI 48009

NEAMAN, MARK A., health facility administrator. With Riverside Methodist Hosp., Columbus, 1971-74; with Evanston Hosp. Corp., Evanston, Ill., 1974—, now pres., CEO. Office: Evanston Hosp Corp 1301 Central St Evanston IL 60201-1613*

NEAMAN, MARK ROBERT, hospital administrator; b. Buffalo, Oct. 22, 1950; married. B, Ohio State U., 1972, MHA, 1974. Adminstrv. asst. Evanston (Ill.) Hosp., 1974-76, asst. to v.p., 1976-78, asst. v.p., 1978-80, v.p., 1980-84, sr. v.p., 1984-85, pres., exec. v.p., 1985-90, pres., 1990-92, pres., CEO, 1992—. Fellow Am. Coll. Healthcare Execs. (regent northern Cook County, Ill. 1990—, RS Hudgens award 1988). Home: 263 W Onwentsia Rd Lake Forest IL 60045-2826 Office: Evanston Hosp 2650 Ridge Ave Evanston IL 60201-1718*

NEAME, RONALD, director, producer; b. Hendon, Middlesex, Eng., Apr. 23, 1911; s. Stuart Elwin and Ivy Lillian (Close) N.; m. Beryl Yolanda Heanly, Oct. 15, 1933; 1 son, Christopher Elwyn; m. Dona Friedberg, Sept. 12, 1993. Student pvt. schs., London and Sussex, Eng. Asst. cameraman Brit. Internat. Pictures, Estree, Eng., 1928-35; chief cameraman Brit. Internat. Pictures, 1935-45. Dir.: photography, prodn. supr. various films, including In Which We Serve, 1942, This Happy Breed, 1943, Blithe Spirit, 1944; co-writer, producer: films Brief Encounter, 1945, Great Expectations, 1946; producer: film Oliver Twist, 1947; dir.: films Take My Life, 1948, Golden Salamander, 1949, The Promoter, 1952, Man with a Million, 1953, The Man Who Never Was, 1954, Windom's Way, 1957, The Horse's Mouth, 1958, Tunes of Glory, 1960, I Could Go On Singing, 1962, The Chalk Garden, 1963, Mr. Moses, 1964, Gambit, 1966, The Prime of Miss Jean Brodie, 1968, Scrooge, 1970, The Poseidon Adventure, 1972, The Odessa File, 1974, Meteor, 1978, Hopscotch, 1979, First Monday in October, 1980-81, Foreign Body, 1985, The Magic Baloon, 1989; co-founder film co. Cineguild Co., Denham, Eng., 1943-44. Mem. Dirs. Guild Am., Am. Film Inst., Acad. Motion Picture Arts and Scis. (gov. 1977-79), Brit. Acad. Film and TV Arts (London and Los Angeles), Savile Club (London). *When I am asked which film I consider to be my best, I reply, "I haven't made it yet. Perhaps next time."*

NEAR, JAMES W., restaurant and franchise executive; b. 1938; married. Student, Hanover Coll., 1961. V.p. BBF Restaurants, 1965-69; exec. v.p., then pres. retail sales Borden, Inc., 1969-74; with Sisters Internat., Inc., 1979-86; pres., chief oper. officer Wendy's Internat., Inc., Ohio, 1986-89, past pres., chief exec. officer, chmn. With USNG. Office: Wendy's Internat Inc 4288 W Dublin Granville Rd Dublin OH 43017-1442*

NEARINE, ROBERT JAMES, educational psychologist; b. Fitchburg, Mass., May 15, 1930; s. Raymond Johns and Beatrice Aileen (Strickland) N.; children: Luke, Martha, Amy. BS, Fitchburg State Coll., 1951; EdM, Tufts Coll., 1952; cert. of advanced grad. specialization, Boston U., 1961; MA, U. Conn., 1965; EdD, Boston U., 1972. Tchr. pub. schs., Holbrook, Mass., 1952-54, Groton, Mass., 1954-55, Winchester, Mass., 1955-59; supr. pub. schs., Inverness, Mont., 1959-60; guidance counselor pub. schs., Manchester, Conn., 1961-66, supr. of evaluation, 1966-73, adminstr. for funding and evaluation, 1973-76; spl. asst. for funding pub. schs., Hartford, Conn., 1976-78; spl. asst. for evaluation rsch. and testing Bd. Edn., Hartford, 1978-93; ednl. cons. Glastonbury, Conn., 1993—; mem. practitioners com. Chpt. I, Com. of N. Sch. Dist. Reporting, State of Conn., 1988-92, mem. requirements adv. com., 1991-92. Contbr. articles to profl. jours. Col. USAR, A.D., 1953-54. NDEA fellow Boston U., 1960-61, Gen. Electric fellow Syracuse U., 1971, Ednl. Policy Inst. fellow for ednl. leadership, 1979-80. Mem. APA, Am. Evaluation Assn., Res. Officers Assn. (nat. councilman 1994—), Phi Delta Kappa. Avocations: military history, travel.

NEARY, PATRICIA ELINOR, ballet director; b. Miami, Fla.; d. James Elliott and Elinor (Mitsitz) N. Corps de ballet Nat. Ballet of Can., Toronto, Ont., 1957-60; prin. dancer N.Y.C. Ballet, 1960-68; ballerina Geneva Ballet (Switzerland), 1968-70, ballet dir., 1973-78; guest artist Stuttgart Ballet, Germany, 1968-70; asst. ballet dir., ballerina West Berlin Ballet, 1970-73; ballet dir. Zurich Ballet (Switzerland), 1978-86, La Scala di Milano ballet co., Italy, 1986-88; tchr., Balanchine ballets, Balanchine Trust, 1987—.

NEAS, JOHN THEODORE, petroleum company executive; b. Tulsa, May 1, 1940; s. George and Lillian J. (Kaspar) N.; BS, Okla. State U., 1967, MS, 1968; m. Sally Jane McPherson, June 10, 1966; children: Stephen, Gregory, Matthew. CPA, Okla. With acctg. dept. Rockwell Internat., 1965; with controller's dept. Amoco Prodn. Co., 1966-67; mem. audit and tax staff Deloitte, Haskins & Sells, 1968-75; pres. Nat. Petroleum Sales, Inc., Tulsa, 1975—, John Neas Tank Lines, Inc., 1986—; pres. McPherson Fuels & Asphalts, Inc., 1981-88, sec., 1989—; mem. NPS/Hallmark LLC, 1994—; mem. Bailey Ranch Estates LLC, 1994—; asst. instr. U. Tulsa, 1974; bd. dirs. Waterways Bd. Okla. Dept. Transp. Mem. AICPA, Inst. Mgmt. Accts. (v.p. membership 1976-77), Okla. Soc. CPAs, Am. Petroleum Inst., McClellan-Kerr Arkansas River Navigation System Hist. Soc., Okla. Heritage Assn., Okla. State U. Pres.'s Club, Okla. State U. Coll. Bus. Adminstrn. Assocs. (v.p. memberships 1989-91, Hall of Fame 1991, Acctg. Dept. Hall of Fame, 1993), Oaks Country Club, The Golf Club Okla. Republican. Lutheran. Home: 2943 E 69th St Tulsa OK 74136-4541 Office: Nat Petroleum Sales Inc 5401 S Harvard Ave Ste 200 Tulsa OK 74135-3861

NEASE, STEPHEN WESLEY, college president; b. Everett, Mass., Jan. 15, 1925; s. Floyd William and Madeline Anzelette (Nostrand) N.; m. Dorothy Christine Hardy, June 17, 1946; children: Linda Carol Nease Scott, Floyd William II, Stephen Wesley Jr., David Wayne, Melissa Jo Nease Wallace. A.B., Brown U., 1946; Th.B., Eastern Nazarene Coll., 1947, D.D., 1966; Ed.M., Boston U., 1956; postgrad., Harvard Div. Sch., 1946-48. Ordained to ministry Ch. of the Nazarene, 1951; pastor East Side Ch. of the Nazarene, Newark, Ohio, 1948-50; dean men, instr. religion Ea. Nazarene Coll., Wollaston, Mass., 1950-53, dir. devel., 1953-66, pres. emeritus; founding pres. Mt. Vernon (Ohio) Nazarene Coll., 1966-72, pres. emeritus; pres. Bethany (Okla.) Nazarene Coll., 1973-76, Nazarene Theol. Sem., Kansas City, Mo., 1976-80, Eastern Nazarene Coll., Wollaston, Mass., 1981-89; edn. commr. Ch. of the Nazarene, 1989-94; exec. dir. Capital and Endowment Devel., Mt. Vernon, Ohio, 1994—. Served with USNR, 1943-46. Office: Capital and Endowment Devel 17012 Glen Rd Mount Vernon OH 43050-9501

NEAVES, NANCY J., lawyer; b. Elmhurst, Ill., May 18, 1966. BA, U. So. Fla., 1987; JD, Stetson U., St. Petersburg, Fla., 1992. Bar: Fla. Law clk., program atty. Guardian Ad Litem, Tampa, Fla., 1990-93; juvenile/misdemeaner atty. Pub. defenders Office, Tampa, 1993-94; assoc. Hendrix Law Firm, Tampa, 1994—. Mem. Hillbrook Bar Assn. Avocations: skiing, boating, scuba. Office: Hendrix Tampa Theatre Bldg 707 N Franklin St Ste 750 Tampa FL 33602-4430

NEAVES, WILLIAM BARLOW, cell biologist, educator; b. Spur, Tex., Dec. 25, 1943; s. William Fred and Revvie Lee (Hefner) N.; m. Priscilla Wood, Jan. 28, 1965; children: William Barlow, Clarissa D'laine. AB magna cum laude, Harvard U., 1966; postgrad., Med. Sch., 1966-67, PhD, 1969. Lectr. vet. anatomy U. Nairobi, 1970-71, vis. prof., 1978; lectr. anatomy Harvard U., 1972; asst. prof. cell biology U. Tex. Health Sci. Ctr., Dallas, 1972-74; assoc. prof. U. Tex. Health Sci. Ctr., 1974-77, prof., 1977—, Doris and Brian Wildenthal Prof. of Biomed. Sci., 1993—, dean Grad. Sch. Biomed. Scis., 1980-88, interim dean Southwestern Med. Sch., 1986-88, dean Southwestern Med. Sch., 1989—; rsch. assoc. herpetology Los Angeles County Mus., 1970-73; vis. lectr. U. Chgo., 1976-77. Assoc. editor Anat. Record, 1975-87; mem. editl. bd. Biology of Reprodn., 1983-86, Jour. Andrology, 1987-89; contbr. chpts. to books, articles to profl. jours. Bd. dirs. Dallas Zool. Soc., 1989-94, Dallas Mus. Natural History, 1993—, Damon Runyan-Walter Winchell Cancer Fund, 1986-92, v.p., 1990-92. Rockefeller Found. fellow, 1970-71; Milton Fund grantee, 1970-71; Population Council grantee, 1973-75; NIH grantee, 1973-89; Ford. Found. grantee, 1976-78. Fellow AAAS; mem. Am. Assn. Anatomists, Am. Soc. Andrology (Young Andrologist award 1983), Dallas Assembly, N.Y. Acad. Scis., Soc. Study of Reprodn., Liaison Com. on Med. Edn. (joint com. of AMA and Assn. Am. Med. Colls.), Sigma Xi, Alpha Omega Alpha. Methodist. Office: 5323 Harry Hines Blvd Dallas TX 75235-7200

NEAVOLL, GEORGE FRANKLIN, newspaper editor; b. Lebanon, Oreg., Aug. 20, 1938; s. Jesse Hunter and Mazie Maude (Meyer) N.; m. Laney Lila Hunter Hough, June 21, 1969. BS, U. Oreg., 1965. Reporter, photographer Lebanon Express, 1969-70; state editor Idaho State Jour., Pocatello, 1970-72; editorial writer The Jour.-Gazette, Ft. Wayne, Ind., 1972-75, Detroit Free Press, 1975-78; editorial page editor The Wichita (Kans.) Eagle, 1978-91, Portland (Maine) Press Herald, Maine Sunday Telegram, 1991—. Vol. Peace Corps, India, 1967-69; bd. councilors Save-the-Redwoods League, 1980—. Recipient Edward J. Meeman award Scripps-Howard Found., 1973, Honor Roll award, Izaak Walton League Am., 1974; named Hon. Pk. Ranger, Nat. Pk. Svc., 1988. Mem. Inter Am. Press Assn. (bd. dirs. 1985—, Jamaica Daily Gleaner award 1985), Am. Soc. Newspaper Editors, Nat. Conf. Editorial Writers, Soc. Profl. Journalists, Nat. Press Club, Cumberland Club. Home: Unit 7D 45 Eastern Promenade Portland ME 04101-4820 Office: The Portland Newspapers 390 Congress St Portland ME 04101-3514

NEBEKER, FRANK QUILL, federal judge; b. Salt Lake City, Apr. 23, 1930; s. J. Quill and Minnie (Holmgren) N.; m. Louana M. Visintainer, July 11, 1953; children: Caramaria, Melia, William Mark. Student, Weber Coll., 1948-50; B.S. in Polit. Sci, U. Utah, 1953; J.D., Am. U., 1955. Bar: D.C. 1956. Corr. sec. The White House, 1953-56; trial atty. Internal Security div. Justice Dept., Washington, 1956-58; asst. U.S. atty., 1958-69; assoc. judge D.C. Ct. Appeals, 1969-87; dir. Office Govt. Ethics, Washington, 1987-89; chief judge U.S. Ct. of Vets. Appeals, Washington, 1989—; cons. Nat. Commn. on Reform of Fed. Criminal Laws, 1967-68; adj. prof. Am. U. Washington Coll. Law, 1967-85. Mem. Am., D.C. Bar Assn., Am. Law Inst. Office: US Court of Veterans Appeals 625 Indiana Ave NW Ste 900 Washington DC 20004-2901

NEBEKER, STEPHEN BENNION, lawyer; b. Salt Lake City, Feb. 21, 1929; s. Acel Hulme and Lora (Bennion) N.; m. June Wilkins, June 18, 1951; children: Jeanne N. Jardine, Mary N. Larson, Stephen W., Ann. JD, U. Utah, 1954. Bar: Utah 1957, U.S. Dist. Ct. Utah 1957, U.S. Ct. Appeals (10th cir.) 1957. Assoc. Ray Quinney & Nebeker, Salt Lake City, 1957-63, ptnr., 1963—, mem. exec. com., 1972—, pres., 1992—. Bd. editors Utah Law Rev., 1953-54. Mem. S.J. and Jessie Quinney Found., Salt Lake City, 1982—; chmn. nat. adv. coun. U. Utah; trustee Ray Quinney & Nebeker Found., Salt Lake City, 1982—. 1st lt. U.S. Army, 1954-57. Recipient Disting. Alumnus award U. Utah, 1992, named Lawyer of Yr. by Law Sch., 1988. Fellow Am. Coll. Trial Lawyers (bd. regents 1984-87), Am. Bd. Trial Advocates, Internat. Assn. Ins. Counsel, Fedn. Ins. Counsel, Am. Bar Found., Utah Bar Found. (trustee 1988-95), Utah State Bar (outstanding lawyer of yr. 1986, trial lawyer of yr. 1994), Legal Aid Soc., Am. Inn of Ct. II (pres. 1982-83), Alta Club, Rotary, Salt Lake City Area C. of C. (bd. govs. 1986-89, U. Utah Law Sch. Alumni Assn. (pres. 1985-86). Republican. Mormon. Avocations: skiing, golf, fly fishing, tennis, hunting. Home: 746 16th Ave Salt Lake City UT 84103-3705 Office: Ray Quinney & Nebeker 400 Deseret Bldg Salt Lake City UT 84111

NEBEL, HENRY MARTIN, JR., literature historian, educator; b. N.Y.C., Sept. 29, 1921; s. Henry Martin and Margaret (Naumann) N.; m. Sylvia Sue Fuller, July 13, 1967; children—Althea, Keith, Grant, Blake. B.A., Columbia U., 1943, M.A., 1950, Ph.D., 1960. Researcher analyst Nat. Security Agy., Arlington, Va., 1949-50, U.S. Mcht. Marine Acad., Kings Point, N.Y., 1955-56, Duke U., Durham, N.C., 1956-57; mem. faculty Northwestern U., Evanston, Ill., 1957—, prof. Russian lit., 1960-86, prof. emeritus, 1986—. Author: N.M. Karamzin, A Russian Sentimentalist, 1966, Selected Prose of N.M. Karamzin, 1967, Selected Aesthetic Works of Sumarokov and Karamzin, 1981, others; author articles and translations of Russian topics; editor, contbg. editor various jours. Served with USAF, 1943-45. Mem. Am. Assn. Tchrs. Slavic and East European Langs., Soc. for Eighteenth-Century Lit., AAUP.

NEBEL, KAI ALLEN, lawyer; b. Geneva, N.Y., July 9, 1932; s. Bernard Rudolph and Mabel (Ruttle) N.; m. Maria Agnese Marini, Sept. 15, 1958; children: Natalia, Silvia, Isabella, Erik. BA, Princeton U., 1954; LLB, Harvard U., 1957. Bar: Ill. 1958, U.S. Dist. Ct. (no. dist.) Ill. 1958. Assoc. Clausen, Miller, Caffrey, Witous, Gorman, Chgo., 1958-63; ptnr. Nisen, Elliott, Meier & Bowles, Chgo., 1963-71; ptnr. Boodell, Sears, Giambalvo & Crowley, Chgo., 1971-84, chmn. exec. com., 1982-83; ptnr. Keck, Mahin & Cate, Chgo., 1984—. Contbr. chpt. in profl. jours. Chmn. com. Ill. Gov., 1965, Hyde Park Kenwood Community Org., Chgo., 1968-69; pres. Parents Assn. of Lab. Schs. of U. Chgo., 1970; bd. dirs., mem. adv. bd. Friends of Downtown Chgo., 1982-83; pres. Skokie Sch. Found., Winnetka, Ill., 1984—; mem. design rev. bd. Village of Winnetka, 1988—. Named Man of Yr. Winnetka C. of C., 1986, Vol. of Yr. North Shore Mag. and Neiman Marcus, 1986. Mem. ABA, Ill. Bar Assn., Chgo. Bar Assn., Ill. Tax Increment Assn. (bd. dirs. 1987—), Union League Club. Avocations: photography, gardening, hiking. Home: 362 Hawthorn Ln Winnetka IL 60093-4217 Office: Keck Mahin & Cate 77 W Wacker Dr Ste 4900 Chicago IL 60601-1629*

NEBENZAHL, KENNETH, rare book and map dealer, author; b. Far Rockaway, N.Y., Sept. 16, 1927; s. Meyer and Ethel (Levin) N.; m. Jocelyn Hart Spitz, Feb. 7, 1953; children: Kenneth (dec.), Patricia Suzanne Nebenzahl Frish, Margaret Spitz Nebenzahl Quintong, Suzanne Spitz Nebenzahl Nichol. Student, Columbia U., 1947-48; L.H.D. (hon.), Coll. William and Mary, 1983. Solicitor new bus. United Factors Corp., N.Y.C., 1947-50; sales rep. Fromm & Sichel, Inc., N.Y.C., 1950-52; v.p. Cricketeer, Inc., Chgo., 1953-58; pres. Kenneth Nebenzahl, Inc., Chgo., 1957—; bd. dirs. Imago Mundi, Ltd., London, 1976—; cons. Rand McNally and Co., 1966—. Author: Atlas of the American Revolution, 1974, Bibliography of Printed Battle Plans of the American Revolution, 1975, Maps of the Holy Land, 1986, Atlas of Columbus and the Great Discoveries, 1990, also edits. in Spanish, German, Italian, Portugese and French langs.; contbr. articles to profl. jours. and monographs. Trustee Glencoe Pub. Libr., 1963-69, pres., 1966-69; bd. dirs. North Suburban Libr. System, 1966-69, Beverly Farm Found., Godfrey, Ill., 1961-67, Nature Conservancy of Ill., 1980-88; trustee Adler Planetarium, 1969—, chmn., 1977-81; mem. exec. com. Northwestern U. Libr. Coun., 1973-75; sponsor Kenneth Nebenzahl Jr. lectures history cartography Newberry Libr., Chgo., 1965—; mem. assoc. coun. John Crear Libr., Chgo., 1972—, trustee, 1976-84, mem. vis. com. to libr., 1978—, chmn., 1987—; trustee U. Chgo., 1982—; co-chair Phillips Soc.-Libr. of Congress, Washington, 1995—; bd. dirs. Evanston Hosp. Corp., 1978-85, Am. Himalayan Found., 1994—; mem. U.S. nat. adv. coun. World Wildlife Fund, 1993—. With USMCR, 1945-46. Recipient IMCoS-Tooley award (London), 1984. Fellow Royal Geog. Soc., Am. Geog. Soc.; mem. Manuscript Soc. (dir. 1965-71), Am. Library Trustees Assn. (nat. chmn. com. intellectual freedom 1967-68), Bibliog. Soc. Am., Newberry Library Assocs. (bd. govs. 1965-78, chmn. 1976-78), Newberry Library (trustee 1978—, vice chmn. 1994—), Antiquarian Booksellers Assn. Am. (bd. govs. 1965-67, v.p. 1975-77), Am. Antiquarian Soc. (gov. 1981-85), Soc. History Discoveries (dir. 1974-76), Chgo. Map Soc. (dir. 1976-86), Ill. Ctr. for the Book (pres. 1986-88). Clubs: Caxton (Chgo.) (bd. govs. 1961-68, 74-80, pres. 1964-66), Wayfarers (Chgo.) (pres. 1979-80); Lake Shore Country (Glencoe); Century (N.Y.C.), Grolier (N.Y.C.). Office: PO Box 370 Glencoe IL 60022-0370

NEBERGALL, DONALD CHARLES, investment consultant; b. Davenport, Iowa, Aug. 12, 1928; s. Ellis W. and Hilda (Bruhn) N.; m. Shirley Elaine Williams, Apr. 12, 1952; children: Robert W., Nancy L. Nebergall Bosma. BS, Iowa State U., 1951. With Poweshiek County Nat. Bank, 1958-72, sr. v.p., to 1972; founding pres., CEO Brenton Bank and Trust Co., Cedar Rapids, Iowa, 1972-82, chmn. bd., 1982-86; v.p. Chapman

Co., 1986-88; bd. dirs. Telephone & Data Systems, Inc., chmn. audit com., 1977—; bd. dirs. Guaranty Bank and Trust, Barlow Investment Co.; former vice chmn. bd. Iowa Transfer Svc. V.p., bd. dirs. Iowa 4-H Found., 1972-76; div. campaign chmn. United Way; former bd. dirs., past pres. Methwick Retirement Community; founding trustee Cedar Rapids Community Sch. Dist. Found.; past pres. Cedar Rapids Greater Downtown Assn. With AUS, 1946-48. Recipient Ptnr. in 4-H award Iowa 4-H, 1983, charter 4-H Found. Ct. of Honor, 1989. Mem. Rotary, Alpha Zeta, Gamma Sigma Delta, Delta Upsilon. Republican. Methodist. Office: 2919 Applewood Pl NE Cedar Rapids IA 52402-3323

NEBERT, DANIEL WALTER, molecular geneticist, research administrator; b. Portland, Oreg., Sept. 26, 1938; s. Walter Francis Nebert and Marie Sophie (Schick) Kirk; m. Myrna Sisk, Mar. 12, 1960 (div. 1975); children: Douglas Daniel, Dietrich Andrew; m. Kathleen Dixon, Aug. 15, 1981; children: Rosemarie Dixon, Rebecca Frances, David Porter, Lucas Daniel. BA, Wesleyan U., 1959; BS and MS in Biochemistry, U. Oreg., MD, 1964. Lic. physician, Calif., Ohio; bd. qualified in pediats. and human genetics; Am. Bd. Pediat. and Human Genetics. Pediat. intern UCLA Hosps., 1964-65, resident in pediat., 1965-66; postdoctoral fellow Nat. Cancer Inst., NIH, Bethesda, Md., 1966-68; sr. investigator Nat. Inst. Child Health and Human Devel., Bethesda, 1968-71, sect. head, 1971-74, lab. chief, 1974-89; prof. dept. environ. health U. Cin. Med. Ctr., 1989—, prof. dept. pediatrics, 1991—; dir. Ctr. Environ. Genetics, 1992—; mem. faculty bd. cert. in human genetics NIH, 1981-89; coord. med. genetics program U.S.-China Coop. Med. Health Protocol, 1982-89; Pfizer lectr. U. Vt., Burlington, 1978, Stanford U., 1979; Wellcome vis. prof. biochemistry and molecular biology U. S.D., Vermillion, 1991. Mem. editl. bd.: Archives Biochemistry and Biophysics, 1973-76, Archieves Internationales de Pharmacodynamie et de Therapie, 1975-81, Jour. Environ. Scis. and Health, 1976-81, Teratogenesis, Carcinogenesis and Mutagenesis, 1980-86, Anticancer Research, 1981-83, Chemico-Biol. Interactions, 1977-83, Molecular Pharmacology and Therapeutics, 1979-87, Biochem. Pharmacology, 1972—, Jour. Exptl. Pathology, 1986—, DNA and Cell Biology, 1986—, Molecular Endocrinology, 1988-91, Endocrinology, 1989—, Pharmacogenetics, 1991—, N.Am. Assoc. Ed. for Biochem. Pharmacology, 1994—, assoc. editor DNA Cell Biology, 1994—; contbr. more than 420 articles to profl. jours. Capt. USPHS, 1966-89. Recipient Meritorious Svc. medal USPHS, 1978, Frank Ayrey fellow award in clin. pharmacology, U.K., 1984, Bernard B. Brodie award, 1986, Ernst A. Sommer Meml. award, 1988; GM scholar, 1956-59, Lawrence Selling scholar, 1961, 63. Fellow AAAS; mem. Am. Soc. Pharmacology and Exptl. Therapeutics, Am. Soc. Biochemistry and Molecular Biology, Am. Soc. Clin. Investigation, Soc. Pediatric Rsch., Am. Soc. Microbiology, Genetics Soc. Am., Endocrine Soc., Soc. Toxicology, Sigma Xi. Republican. Unitarian. Avocations: gardening, golf, piano, skiing, squash, art. Home: 65 Oliver Rd Cincinnati OH 45215-2630 Office: U Cin Med Ctr Dept Environ Health PO Box 670056 Cincinnati OH 45267-0056

NEBLETT, CAROL, soprano; b. Modesto, Calif., Feb. 1, 1946; m. Philip R. Akre; 3 children. Studies with, William Vennard, Roger Wagner, Esther Andreas, Ernest St. John Metz, Lotte Lehmann, Pierre Bernac, Rosa Ponselle, George London, Jascha Heifetz. Soloist with Roger Wagner Chorale; performed in U.S. and abroad with various symphonies; debut with Carnegie Hall, 1966, N.Y.C. Opera, 1969, Met. Opera, 1979; sung with maj. opera cos. including Met. Opera, N.Y.C., Lyric Opera Chgo., Balt. Opera, Pitts. Opera, Houston Grand Opera, San Francisco Opera, Boston Opera Co., Milw. Florentine Opera, Washington Opera Soc., Covent Garden, Cologne Opera, Vienna (Austria) Staatsoper, Paris Opera, Teatro Regio, Turin, Italy, Teatro San Carlo, Naples, Italy, Teatro Massimo, Palermo, Italy, Gran Teatro del Liceo, Barcelona, Spain, Kirov Opera Theatre, Leningrad, USSR, Dubrovnik (Yugoslavia) Summer Festival, Salzberg Festival, others; rec. artist RCA, DGG, EMI; appearances with symphony orchs., also solo recitals, (film) La Clemenza di Tito; filmed and recorded live performance with Placido Domingo, La Fancivila del West; numerous TV appearances. Office: New Century Artist Mgmt Inc PO Box 802 Tuxedo Park NY 10987-0802

NEBORSKY, STEPHANIE JOY, reading and language arts consultant, educator; b. Putnam, Conn., June 14, 1950; d. Stephen Frank and Dorothy Elizabeth (Angelott) N. AS, Manchester Cmty Coll., Manchester, Conn., 1968-70; BS in intermediate edn., Eastern Conn. State U., 1972, MS in language arts, 1978; cert. supervision and adminstrn., Sacred Heart U., 1991. Cert. reading and lang. arts cons., supervision and adminstrn., Conn. English, reading tchr. Dr. Helen Baldwin Sch., Canterbury, Conn., 1972-86, 94-95, 5th grade tchr., 1986-89, 95—, 5th grade tchr., writing coach, 1989-90, language arts coord., 1990-94; adult edn. instr. Putnam (Conn.)-Thompson Cmty. Coun., 1975-76; tchr. Summer Youth Employment Tng. Program East Conn./Brandeis U., Hampton, 1993; adj. instr. Sacred Heart U., Lisbon, Conn., 1993—; presenter numerous edn. confs.; scorer and resolution reader Conn. State Dept. Edn., 1980-90. Contbr. articles to profl. jours. Named Dist. Tchr. of Yr., Canterbury Pub. Schs., Canterbury, Conn., 1989, Finalist Conn. Tchr. of Yr., 1989. Mem. ASCD, Ea. Conn. Reading Assn. (pres. 1995-96), Canterbury Edn. Assn. (governing bd. sec. 1995-96), Internat. Reading Assn., New Eng. Reading Assn., Nat. Coun. Tchrs. English, Delta Kappa Gamma (rec. sec. 1994-96). Avocations: collecting childrens books, travel, Tunis sheep, judging and promoting youth sheep shows. Home: 314 Main St Hampton CT 06247-1416 Office: Dr Helen Baldwin Mid Sch PO Box 100 45 Westminister Rd Canterbury CT 06331

NECARSULMER, HENRY, investment banker; b. N.Y.C., Mar. 6, 1914; s. Edward and Manuela Fortlouis (Maas) N.; m. Elizabeth Louise Borden, Mar. 21, 1946; children: Susan N. Dallin, John B., Peter B. A.B., Dartmouth Coll., 1934. With Kuhn, Loeb & Co., N.Y.C., 1935-77; gen. partner Kuhn, Loeb & Co., 1956-77, mng. partner, 1969-77; vice chmn. Kuhn, Loeb & Co., Inc., 1977; mng. dir. Lehman Bros. Kuhn Loeb Inc., 1977-81, adv. dir., 1981-84; adv. dir. Shearson Lehman Bros. Inc., 1984-85, mng. dir., 1986-88, adv. dir., 1988-90, cons., 1990-93; cons. Lehman Bros., Inc., 1993—; dir. Polaroid Corp.; past dir. various corps.;. Mem. Am. Stock Exchange, 1973-78; mem. governing council Securities Industry Assn., 1972-75; mem. State of N.Y. Judiciary Relations Com., Appellate Div., 1st Jud. Dept., 1973-77; Trustee Jewish Child Care Assn. N.Y. Served to capt. AUS, 1942-46. Office: Lehman Bros Inc 3 World Fin Ctr 17th Fl New York NY 10285

NECCO, E(DNA) JOANNE, school psychologist; b. Klamath Falls, Oreg., June 23, 1941; d. Joseph Rogers and Lillian Laura (Owings) Painter; m. Jon F. Puryear, Aug. 25, 1963 (div. Oct. 1987); children: Laura L., Douglas F.; m. A. David Necco, July 1, 1989. BS, Cen. State U., 1978, MEd, 1985; PhD in Applied Behavioral Studies, Okla. State U., 1993. Med.-surg. asst. Oklahoma City Clinic, 1961-68; spl. edn. tchr. Oklahoma City Pub. Schs., 1978-79, Edmond (Okla.) Pub. Schs., 1979-83; co-founder, owner Learning Devel. Clinic, Edmond, 1983-93; asst. prof. profl. tchr. edn. U. Ctrl. Okla., Edmond, 1993—; adj. instr. Ctrl. State U., Edmond, 1989-93, Oklahoma City U., 1991-93; mem. rsch. group Okla. State U., Stillwater, 1991-93; presenter in field. Contbr. articles to profl. jours. Com. Boy Scouts of Am., SCUBA Post 604, Oklahoma City, 1981-86; mem. Edmond Task Force for Youth, 1983-87, Edmond C. of C., 1984-87; active Okla. Ctr. for Neurosci., 1991; evaluator for Even Start Literacy Program, 1994—. Mem. ASCD, Nat. Assn. for Sch. Psychologists, Am. Bus Women's Assn., Coun. for Exceptional Children, Learning Disabilities Assn., Am. Assn. for Gifted Underachieving Students, Okla. Learning Disabilities Assn., Okla. Assn. for Counseling and Devel., Golden Key Nat. Honor Soc., Internat. Soc. for Scientific Study of Subjectivity, Am. Coun. on Rural Spl. Edn., Ctrl State U. (Okla., life), Phi Delta Kappa. Republican. Avocations: scuba diving, underwater photography, water skiing, travel. Home: 17509 Woodsorrel Rd Edmond OK 73003-6951 Office: U Ctrl Okla Coll Edn 100 N University Dr Edmond OK 73034

NECHEMIAS, STEPHEN MURRAY, lawyer; b. St. Louis, July 27, 1944; s. Herbert Bernard and Toby Helen (Wax) N.; m. Marcia Rosentein, June 19, 1966, (div. Dec. 1981); children: Daniel Jay, Scott Michael; m. Linda Adams, Aug. 20, 1983. BS, Ohio State U., 1966; JD, U. Cin., 1969. Bar: Ohio 1969. Ptnr., Taft, Stettinius & Hollister, Cin., 1969— ; adj. prof. law No. Ky. U., Chase Coll. Law. Tax comment author: Couse's Ohio Form Book, 6th edit., 1984. Mem. Ohio State Bar Assn. (chmn. taxation com.), Cin. Bar Assn. (chmn. taxation sect. 1985), Legal Aid Soc. Cin. (pres., trustee). Democrat. Jewish. Home: 777 Cedar Point Dr Cincinnati OH 45230-3755 Office: 1800 Star Bank Ctr 425 Walnut St Cincinnati OH 45202-3904

NECHIN, HERBERT BENJAMIN, lawyer; b. Chgo., Oct. 25, 1935; s. Abraham and Zelda (Benjamin) N.; m. Susan Zimmerman (div.); 1 child, Jill Rebecca; m. Roberta Fishman, Oct. 24, 1976; 1 child, Stefan. BA with distinction, honors in History, Northwestern U., 1956; JD, Harvard U., 1959. Bar: Ill. 1960. From assoc. to ptnr. Brown Fox & Blumberg, Chgo., 1960-75; ptnr. Taussig Wexler & Shaw, Chgo., 1975-79, Fink Coff Stern, Chgo., 1979-81, Holleb & Coff, Chgo., 1981—. Contbr. articles to profl. jours. Pres. Emanuel Congregation, Chgo., 1994—. Staff sgt. USAR, 1960-66. Mem. ABA, Ill. Bar Assn., Chgo. Bar Assn. (chmn. trust law com. 1990-91), Am. Coll. Trust and Estate Counsel, Univ. Club, Cliff Dwellers Club, Phi Beta Kappa. Office: Holleb & Coff 55 E Monroe St Ste 4100 Chicago IL 60603-5803

NECKERMANN, PETER JOSEF, insurance company executive; b. Wuertzburg, Fed. Republic Germany, Oct. 26, 1935; came to U.S., 1977; s. Josef and Annemarie (Brueckner) N.; m. Jutta Voelk, Feb. 10, 1960; children: Susanne, Christian. Grad., J.W. Goethe U., Frankfurt, Fed. Republic Germany, MA, 1962; PhD, Ohio State U., 1990. Pres. Neckermann Versand KGaA, Frankfurt, 1962-77; dir. econ. analysis and systems Nationwide Ins. Cos., Columbus, Ohio, 1977-79, v.p. econ. and investment services, 1979—. CIV. Mem. Columbus Assn. Bus. Economists, Columbus Coun. on World Affairs (bd. dirs.), Rotary Club of Columbus, Univ. Club of Columbus (pres.). Avocations: tennis, skiing. Home: 1261 Fountaine Dr Columbus OH 43221-1519 Office: Nationwide Ins Cos 1 Nationwide Plz Columbus OH 43215-2220

NEDELMAN, DOROTHY O'FLAHERTY, primary care nurse; b. N.Y.C., Nov. 9, 1945; d. John Joseph Sr. and Dorothy Mary (Walsh) O'Flaherty; m. Philip B. Nedelman, Aug. 27, 1977; 1 child, Kathryn Hannah. Diploma, St. Elizabeth's Hosp., Boston, 1966; BS, St. Joseph's Coll., North Windham, Maine, 1979. Cert. adult nurse practitioner. DON Franvale Extended Care Facility, Braintree, Mass.; adult nurse practitioner, researcher Braintree Family Physician, Inc. Active Braintree Sch. Com., 1993, vice chair, 1994, chair, 1995. Mem. ANA (coun. primary health care nurse practitioners), Soc. Tchrs. Family Medicine.

NEDERHOOD, JOEL H., church organization executive, minister; b. Grand Rapids, Mich., Dec. 22, 1930; s. Arthur William and Dena (Homan) N.; m. Mary Lou Nederhood, July 1, 1954; children: Maria, Carol, David. AB, Calvin Coll., 1952; MDiv, Calvin Sem., Grand Rapids, 1957; ThD, Free U. Amsterdam, The Netherlands, 1959. Ordained to ministry Christian Ref. Ch. Broadcast min. Back to God Hour, Christian Ref. Ch., Chgo., 1960-66, dir. Back to God Hour, 1966-81, dir. ministries Back to God Hour, 1981—; host Faith 20 TV, 1980—. Author: God Is Too Much, 1969, The Holy Triangle, 1975, Promises, Promises, 1980; editor monthly devotional Today. With U.S. Army, 1952-54. Fulbright scholar, 1957. Office: Back to God Hour 6555 W College Dr Palos Heights IL 60463-1770

NEDERLANDER, JAMES LAURENCE, theater owner, producer; b. Detroit, Jan. 23, 1960; s. James Morton and Barbara (Smith) N. Student, Cranbrook Prep, Boston U. Asst. mgr. Pinchnob, Clarkston, Mich.; producer Pineknob, N.Y.C.; v.p. Nederlander, N.Y.C. Assoc. producer plays including The Tragedy of Carmen, 1984 (Tony award 1984), Starlight Express, 1989, Cafe Crown, 1989; assoc. producer musicals On Your Toes, 1987, Legs Diamond, 1988, Barry Manilow on Broadway, 1989; producer show Mort Sahl on Broadway, 1988, Kenny Loggins on Broadway, 1988; coproducer Billy Joel at Yankee Stadium, 1990, Harry Connick Jr. on Broadway, 1990, Yanni on Broadway, 1993, Pink Floyd at Yankee Stadium, 1994, Basia on Broadway, 1994, Shari Lewis and Lambchop on Broadway, 1994, Laurie Anderson on Broadway, 1995, How to Succeed.., 1995. Mem. Com. Am. Candlelite Vigil, 1990, Nat. Hyptertension Benefit, N.Y.C., 1988; bd. trustees Entrepid Museum, 1990. Mem. League N.Y. Theatres, Roundabout Theatre Group, City Athletic Club, LaCosta Country Club.

NEDERLANDER, JAMES MORTON, theater executive; b. Detroit, Mar. 31, 1922; s. David T. and Sarah L. (Applebaum) N.; m. Charlene Saunders, Feb. 12, 1969; children: James Laurence, Sharon, Kristina. Student, Detroit Inst. Tech. Chmn., former pres. Nederlander Orgn., Inc. (formerly Nederlander Producing Co. Am., Inc., N.Y.C., 1966—. Owner and operator of numerous theaters including Palace Theatre, Lunt-Fontanne Theatre, Biltmore Theatre, Nederlander Theatre, Brooks Atkinson Theatre, Biltmore Theatre, Gershwin Theatre, Neil Simon Theatre, Marquis Theatre, Minskoff Theatre, Richard Rodgers Theatre, N.Y.C., Greek Theatre, Pantages Theatre, Henry Fonda Theatre, L.A., Shubert Theatre, Chgo., Fisher Theatre, Masonic Temple, Detroit, Poplar Creek, Hoffman Estates, Ill., Merriweather Post Pavilion, Columbia, Md., Aldwych Theatre, London, Dominion Theatre, London, Adelphi Theatre, London; producer numerous shows for Broadway including She Loves Me, Will Rogers Follies, Me and My Girl, Orpheus Descending, Les Liaisons Dangereuses, Nicholas Nickleby, Annie, La Cage aux Folles, Nine, Applause, Not Now Darling, See Saw, Oliver, Abelard and Heloise, Sherlock Holmes, Treemonisha, Habeus Corpus, Otherwise Engaged, Whose Life is it Anyway?, Betrayal, Woman of the Year, Lena Horne: The Lady and Her Music, The Dresser, Noises Off, Merlin, Night and Day, My Fat Friend, Shirley MacLaine on Broadway, Sweet Charity, Benefactors, Breaking the Code; numerous road show prodns.; revivals: Peter Pan, She Loves Me, Hello Dolly, Porgy and Bess, The Music Man, I Do! I Do!, Oklahoma, On a Clear Day You Can See Forever, Fiddler on the Roof. Office: Nederlander Orgn Inc 810 7th Ave New York NY 10019-5818

NEDERLANDER, ROBERT E., entertainment and television executive, lawyer; b. Detroit, Apr. 10, 1933; s. David T. and Sarah (Applebaum) N.; m. Caren Berman (div.); children: Robert E. Jr., Eric; Gladys Rackmil, Jan. 1, 1988. BA in Econs., U. Mich., 1955, JD, 1958, LLD (hon.), 1990. Ptnr. Nederlander, Dodge & Rollins, Detroit, 1960-90; pres. Nederlander Orgn., Inc., N.Y.C., 1981—, Nederlander TV & Film Prodns., N.Y.C., 1985—; mng. gen. ptnr. N.Y. Yankees, 1990-91. Regent U. Mich., Ann Arbor, 1969-84; trustee Am. Health Found., 1989—; chmn. Gateway Am., 1991—. Recipient Disting. Alumni Svc. award U. Mich., 1985; named Man of Yr. by Gov.'s Com. on Scholastic Achievement, N.Y.C., 1991. Fellow ABA, Mich. Bar Assn. Avocations: tennis, baseball. Office: Nederlander Orgn 810 7th Ave New York NY 10019-5818

NEDOM, H. ARTHUR, petroleum consultant; b. Lincoln, Nebr., Aug. 19, 1925; s. Henry Arthur and Pearle Bertrick (Swan) N.; m. Patricia Margaret Rankin, July 4, 1974; children: Richard A., Robert L., Nicole C. B.S., U. Tulsa, 1949, M.S., 1950; postgrad. in bus. adminstrn., Northwestern U., Evanston, Ill., 1968. Chief engr. Amerada Petroleum Corp., Tulsa, 1961-65; v.p. Amerada Petroleum Corp., 1965-70, Natomas Co., San Francisco, 1971-74; also dir.; pres. Norwegian Oil Co., Houston, 1974-75; pres., mng. dir. Weeks Petroleum Ltd., Westport, Conn., 1975-82; cons., 1982—; chmn. bd. arbitration Prudhoe Bay Unit, 1983-85; chmn. Offshore Tech. Conf., 1971; bd. dirs. Engrs. Joint Council, 1978. Contbr. articles to profl. jours. Served with inf. U.S. Army, 1943-45, ETO. Decorated Bronze Star; named Disting. Alumnus U. Tulsa, 1972. Mem. Soc. Petroleum Engrs. (dir. 1965-68, pres. 1967, Disting. Lectr. 1973, Disting Svc. award 1978, DeGolyer Disting. Svc. medal 1981, Disting. mem. 1983, Disting. lectr. emeritus 1989, v.p. SPE Found. 1988-89), AIME (dir. 1966-69, 76-79, pres. 1977, hon. mem. 1982, Disting. Svc. award 1993), Am. Assn. Engring. Soc. (dir. 1980-82, chmn. 1981, Spl. award 1979, Engring. Svc. award 1980). Episcopalian. Home: 21 Deerwood Ln Westport CT 06880-2648

NEE, SISTER MARY COLEMAN, college president emeritus; b. Taylor, Pa., Nov. 14, 1917; d. Coleman James and Nora Ann (Hopkins) N. AB, Marywood Coll., 1939, MA, 1943; MS, Notre Dame U., 1959. Joined Order of Sisters, Servants of Immaculate Heart of Mary, 1941; assoc. prof. math. Marywood Coll., Scranton, Pa., 1959-68; pres. Marywood Coll., 1970-88, pres. emerita, 1988—; apostolic cord. Sisters, Servants Immaculate Heart of Mary, Scranton, Pa., 1968-70. Home and Office: Cathedral Convent 333 Wyoming Ave Scranton PA 18503-1223

NEE, OWEN D., JR., lawyer; b. Bronxville, N.Y., Nov. 22, 1943; s. Owen D. and Elisabeth (Osborne) N.; m. Amber W., Dec. 11, 1971. BA, Princeton U., 1965; JD, Columbia U., 1973. Bar: N.Y. 1973, Eng. and Wales, 1995, Hong Kong, 1996. Ptnr. Coudert Bros., N.Y.C and Hong Kong, 1981—. Author: CHINA, 1986; Commercial, Business and Trade Laws of PRC, 3 vols., 1991. Capt. U.S. Army, 1969-71, Vietnam. Decorated Bronze Star. Mem. Apawamis Club. Office: Coudert Bros, Nine Queen's Rd, Central, Hong Kong Hong Kong

NEECK, BERNARD J., insurance company executive; b. 1927. Sr. acct. Price Waterhouse & Co., N.Y.C., 1951-56; corp. mgr. gen. acctg. Kennecott Cooper Corp., N.Y.C., 1956-66; contr. Conrock Machinery, Clifton, N.J., 1967; v.p., contr. The Okonite Co., Ramsey, N.J., 1967-73; v.p. fin. HIP-NY, N.Y.C., 1973-82; med. dir. Staten Island Med. Group; now exec. v.p, CFO Health Ins. Plan of Greater N.Y., N.Y.C. Office: Health Insur Plan of Grter NY 7 W 34th St New York NY 10001-8100*

NEEDELS, CHRISTOPHER JAMES, sports association administrator; b. Martinez, Calif., 1942. BS in Engring., U.S. Mil. Acad.; MS in Ops. Rsch., Navy Postgrad. Sch.; M Mil. Arts and Scis., U.S. Command & Gen. Staff Coll. Commd. 2d lt. U.S. Army, 1965, advanced through grades to col., 1988, dir. internat. programs Nat. Security Coun., ret., 1992; mgmt., pub. rels. and land use cons., 1992—; v.p. Piedmont Environ. Coun.; v.p., chair fin. and budget com. U.S. Parachute Assn., 1974-80, exec. dir., 1980—; sr. fellow Ctr. for Strategic and Internat. Studies Georgetown U. Recipient Silver Star, DFC, Bronze Star, Purple Heart. Mem. Nat. Aero. Assn. (bd. dirs.). Office: US Parachute Assn 1440 Duke St Alexandria VA 22314

NEEDHAM, CHARLES WILLIAM, neurosurgeon; b. Bklyn., Oct. 14, 1936; s. William and Jeanne (Studioso) N.; m. Constance Taft, June 15, 1958; children: Susan, Andrew, Jennifer, Sarah, Benjamin. B.S. cum laude Wagner Coll., 1957; M.D., Albany Med. Coll., 1961; M.Sc., McGill U., 1969. Cert. Am. Bd. Neurol. Surgery; lic. physician Conn. Asst. prof. neurol. surgery UCLA Sch. Medicine, 1969-71; clin. assoc. prof. neurol. surgery U. Ariz., Tucson, 1971-84; staff neurosurgeon Norwalk (Conn.) Hosp., Greenwich (Conn.) Hosp., 1984—; clin. instr. neurosurgery Yale U. Sch. Medicine, 1989—; postdoctoral fellow Nat. Inst. Neurol. Diseases & Blindness, 1967-69. Author: Neurosurgical Syndromes of the Brain, 1973, Cerebral Logic, 1978, Principles of Cerebral Dominance, 1982, Neurosurgical Signs, 1986; contbr. articles to profl. jours. Served to capt. USAF MC, 1963-65. Recipient numerous awards for excellence in medicine including AMA Continuing Edn. awards, 1978—, Yale U. Sch. Medicine award, 1986. Fellow ACS; mem. AAAS, Am. Assn. Neurol. Surgeons, Congress Neurol. Surgeons, Brain and Behavioral Scis. Assn., N.Y. Acad. Scis., New Eng. Neurosurg. Soc., Conn. State Neurosurg. Soc. (pres. 1992—), Fairfield (Conn.) County Med. Soc. Avocations: philosophy, physics, anthropology, writing. Home: 1 Sipperleys Hill Rd Westport CT 06880-1245 Office: 5 Elmcrest Ter Norwalk CT 06850-3938

NEEDHAM, GEORGE AUSTIN, investment banker; b. Beverly, Mass., Jan. 27, 1943; s. Everett Austin and Edith Strode (Walton) N.; m. Ellen Ann Levin, July 9, 1978; children—Michael Austin, Sarah Elisabeth, Paul Everett. B.S. in Bus. Adminstrn., Bucknell U., 1965; M.B.A., Stanford U., 1971. Portfolio mgr. Bankers Trust Co., N.Y.C., 1967-69; mng. dir. First Boston Corp., N.Y.C., 1971-84; chmn., CEO Needham & Co. Inc., N.Y.C., 1985—. Trustee Stanford Bus. Sch. Trust, Palo Alto, Calif., 1983-89. Served to 1st lt. U.S. Army, 1965-67. Mem. Fin. Analysts Fedn., Bond Club N.Y. Republican. Clubs: University (N.Y.C.); Sleepy Hollow County (Scarborough, N.Y.); Coral Beach Club (Bermuda). Home: 79 E 79th St New York NY 10021-0202 Office: Needham & Co Inc 445 Park Ave New York NY 10022

NEEDHAM, GEORGE MICHAEL, library association executive; b. Buffalo, July 3, 1955; s. Paul James and Dolores Ann (Duffy) N.; m. Joyce Elaine Leahy, Nov. 28, 1992; 1 stepchild, Katherine Wallace. BA in English, SUNY, Buffalo, 1976, MLS, 1977. Various profl. positions Charleston (S.C.) County Libr., 1977-84; dir. Fairfield County Dist. Libr., Lancaster, Ohio, 1984-89; mem. svcs. dir. Ohio Libr. Assn., Columbus, 1990-92; exec. dir. Pub. Libr. Assn., Chgo., 1993—; cons. Wright Meml. Libr., Oakwood, Ohio, 1992; mem. adv. bd. Southeastern Correctional Inst., Lancaster, Ohio, 1984-89; cons. Reference Point Found., Columbia, Md., 1994—. Co-author: A Director's Checklist for connecting Public Libraries to the Internet, 1995; author (book revs.) Booklist, 1994—, (video revs.), Libr. Jours., 1979—. Bd. dirs. Fairfield County chpt. ARC, Lancaster, 1984-88, Mt. Prospect Theatre Soc., Mt. Prospect, Ill., 1993-95. Mem. ALA, ACLU, Am. Soc. Assn. Execs., Pub. Libr. Assn. Democrat. Avocations: acting, traditional folk music, writing, 2-time Jeopardy champion. Office: Pub Libr Assn 50 E Huron St Chicago IL 60611

NEEDHAM, HAL, director, writer; b. Memphis, Mar. 6, 1931; s. Howard and Edith May (Robinson) N.; m. Dani Janssen, June 28, 1981 (separated); children: Debra Jean, Daniel Albert, David Allyn. Student pub. schs. Founder Stunts Unltd., Los Angeles, 1956; stuntman Stunts Unltd., 1956-68, dir. and stunt coordinator second unit, 1968-76, dir., writer, 1976—; chmn bd. Camera Platforms Internat., Inc., 1986—. Dir., writer films Smokey and The Bandit, 1977, Hooper, 1978, The Villain, 1979, Smokey and The Bandit, II, 1980, The Cannonball Run, 1981, Mega Force, 1982, Stroker Ace, 1983, Cannonball Run Part 2, 1984, Rad, 1986, Body Slam, 1987; dir., writer, exec. prodr. Bandit, 1993; dir. pilot TV series Stunts Unltd.; movie of the week Death Car on the Freeway, B.L. Stryker, 1989. Served with Paratroopers U.S. Army, 1951-54. Mem. Screen Actors Guild, Dirs. Guild Am., Writers Guild Am., AFTRA. Owner Budweiser Rocket Car (fastest car in the world) displayed at Smithsonian Inst. Office: c/o Laura Lizer & Assocs 12711 Ventura Blvd Ste 440 Studio City CA 91604-2431 *I feel that if I can become successful with less than ten years of education, anyone in this country is capable of the same goals with positive thinking and total dedication.*

NEEDHAM, JAMES JOSEPH, retired financial services executive; b. Woodhaven, N.Y., Aug. 18, 1926; s. James Joseph and Amelia (Pasta) N.; m. Dolores A. Habick, July 1, 1950 (dec. Feb. 1993); children: James Joseph, Robert, Ravenna, Michael, Catherine; m. Patricia Henry Campo, May 24, 1995. Student, Cornell U., 1946; BBA, St. John's U., 1951, LLD (hon.), 1972. CPA, N.Y. Acct. Price Waterhouse & Co., N.Y.C, 1947-54; ptnr. R. T. Hyer & Co., Port Washington, N.Y., 1954-57; ptnr., mem. exec. com. A. M. Pullen & Co., N.Y.C., 1957-69; commr. SEC, Washington, 1969-72; chmn., chief exec. officer N.Y. Stock Exch., 1972-76; v.p. Internat. Fedn. Stock Exchs., 1973-75; pres. Internat. Fedn. Stock Exchanges, 1976-90; councilman Town of Southampton, N.Y., 1986—; Disting. prof., grad. div. Coll. Bus. Adminstrn., St. John's U., Jamaica, N.Y.; U.S. amb. to Japan Expo '85, 1982-85; bd. dirs. Axe-Houghton Mut. Funds, Standard Register Co. Treas. Central Sch. Dist. 4, 1951-52, mem. budget and finance com., 1951, 63, chmn. high sch. planning com., 1947; active local Boy Scouts Am., 1962-65; mem. bishop's com. of laity Catholic Charities, Rockville Center, N.Y., 1960-68; mem. lay adv. bd. Cath. Youth Orgn., 1964-67; bd. advs. Coll. Bus. Adminstrn., St. John's U.; mem. hon. com. Am. Cancer Soc.; N.Y. State co-chmn. fin. Reagan for Pres. Campaign, 1980; Past pres., auditor Plainview (N.Y.) Republican Club.; Bd. govs. Fed. Hall Meml. Assos.; trustee N.Y. Foundling Hosp. Served with USNR, 1944-46. Recipient Disting. Citizen award N.Y. U. Law Sch., Disting. Service award in investment edn. Nat. Assn. Investment Clubs; named Bus. Person of Year Bus. Adminstrn. Soc. St. John's U., 1975; fellow Aspen Inst. for Humanistic Studies. Mem. N.Y. Soc. CPA's (past dir., treas., past pres. Nassau-Suffolk chpt., recognition award), Am. Inst. CPA's (past mem. council), L.I. Assn., N.Y. Chamber Commerce and Industry, Internat. C. of C. (U.S. council), Downtown-Lower Manhattan Assn. (dir., mem. exec. com.), N.Y. Credit and Fin. Mgmt. Assn. (Laurel award), Cath. Accountants Guild (past pres.), Accountants Club Am., NYU Fin. Club (adv. council), Bond Club N.Y., Beta Alpha Psi. Clubs: Serra (Nassau) (past pres.); Cornell of Nassau County, Wheatley Hills Golf (past treas.), Siwanoy Country; Economic, University, Board Room , Downtown A.C. (N.Y.C.); Burning Tree, Capitol Hill (Washington); Blind Brook (Port Chester, N.Y.). Home: PO Box 1229 Bridgehampton NY 11932-1229

NEEDHAM, LILLIE DULCENIA, secondary school educator; b. Chgo., June 12, 1949; d. Clarence R. Sr. and Deborah Lee (Morris) Needham; 1 child, Aston R. Needham-Watkins. BS in Edn., Chgo. State Coll., 1970, MS in Edn., 1974. Tchr. Chgo. Pub. Schs., 1970—, office occupations coord., 1976-77, 78-90, 91—, S.W.A.T. shop founder, coord., 1992—, bus./computer dept. chair. Mem. NAFE, ASCD, Am. Entrepreneur Assn., Chgo. Bus. Edn. Assn. (sec. 1994-95, v.p. 1995—), Nat. Bus. Edn. Assn. Internat. Soc. Bus. Educators, Chgo. Computer Soc., Bus. Profls. Am. (adv.). Home: 6801 S Paxton Ave Chicago IL 60649-1654 Office: Manley Career and Prep Acad 2935 W Polk St Chicago IL 60612-3904

NEEDHAM, LUCIEN ARTHUR, musician, educator; b. Hull, Yorkshire, Eng., Apr. 5, 1929; s. Arthur and A. Nita (Sims) N.; m. Louise Chapman, Aug. 16, 1974 (dec. Oct. 1988); m. Marilyn J. Goldfinch, May 28, 1995. Student, Guildhall Sch. Music, London, 1952-56. Condr. Winnipeg (Man., Can.) Philharm. Choir, 1956-60, Winnipeg Male Voice Choir, 1957-60; vis. instr. voice and theoretical subjects Brandon (Man.) U. Sch. Music, 1959-62, asst. prof. voice, organ and theoretical subjects, 1962-64, asso. prof., 1964-67; founding condr., mus. dir. Western Man. Philharm. Choir, 1965-67; assoc. prof. U. Lethbridge, Alta., 1967-69, prof. voice and theoretical subjects, 1970-87; chmn. dept. music U. Lethbridge, 1967-71, condr. Univ. Choir, 1968-74; condr. Lethbridge Symphony Orch., 1970-76; lectr., speaker, condr. master classes, 1956-87; examiner Western Bd. Music, 1957-87; adjudicator regional, interstate, provincial and local music festivals, scholarship competitions, 1957-87; mem. Alta. Registered Music Tchrs. Assn., 1967-87, pres., 1980-81. Tchr. singing, pianist, accompanist, condr. public concerts and on radio and TV, 1952-87; composer: Christmas Gradual, 1963, The Fields Abroad, 1967; contbr. articles, monographs to music jours. Served with RAF, 1948-50. Fellow Guildhall Sch. Music, 1965; grantee Nuffield Found., 1965; grantee Can. Council, 1966, 71; grantee U. Lethbridge, 1974, 85.

NEEDHAM, NANCY JEAN, management consultant; b. Chgo., July 21, 1941; d. Robert Leonard and Grace Irene (Bennett) N.; children: Thomas, Charles, Catharine, Jessica. BA, Wellesley Coll., 1964; MBA, Harvard U., 1972, DBA, 1977. Pubs. specialist MIT, Cambridge, Mass., 1964-65; editor SRA, Chgo., 1966; sr. editor Ency. Britannica, Chgo., 1967; cons. ABT Assocs., Cambridge, 1968; program mgr. Am. Sci. & Engring., Boston, 1969; faculty Harvard Bus. Sch., Cambridge, 1973-75; cons. CRI, Cambridge, 1977-78; prof. mgmt. Poly. U. N.Y., N.Y.C., 1986—; assoc. dir. Ctr. for Advanced Tech. in Telecommunications, N.Y.C., 1986—; pres. ICGS Inc., Boston, 1978—. Contbr. articles to profl. jours. Mem. Am. Soc. Macro Engring. (bd. dirs. 1984-92), C.G. Jung Found. (bd. dirs. 1988-94), Phi Beta Kappa. Presbyterian. Home: RR 2 Box 191 B Delhi NY 13753-9643

NEEDHAM, RICHARD LEE, magazine editor; b. Cleve., Jan. 16, 1939; s. Lester Hayes and Helen (Bender) N.; m. Irene Juechter, Aug. 7, 1965; children—Margaret, Richard, Trevor. B.A., Denison U., 1961; M.A., U. Mo., 1967. Copy editor Sat. Rev., N.Y.C., 1967-68; editor-in-chief Preview Internat., N.Y.C., 1968-69; financial and N.Y. editor Instns. mag.; also editor Service World Internat., N.Y.C., 1969-70; copy dir. American Home mag., N.Y.C., 1970-71; exec. editor Ski Mag., N.Y.C., 1971-74, editor, 1974-92, editor-in-chief, 1992-94, editor-at-large, 1994-96, eastern editor, 1996—; contbg. editor Yachting Mag., N.Y.C., 1996—; editor Ency. of Skiing, 1978, Ski Fever, 1995; editl. dir. Times Mirror Mags. Conservation Coun., 1994-96. Broadcaster: Ski Spot, CBS Radio, N.Y.C., 1978-83, On the Slopes, Audio Features Syndicate, 1984-87; author: Ski--50 Years in North America, 1992, Ski Fever!, 1995. Served to lt. USNR, 1961-65. Recipient Lowell Thomas award, 1985. Mem. N.Am. Ski Journalists Assn., Internat. Assn. Ski Journalists, Internat. Motor Press Assn. Home: 115 Old Post Rd Croton On Hudson NY 10520 Office: SKI mag Times-Mirror Mags 2 Park Ave New York NY 10016-5603

NEEDLEMAN, ALAN, mechanical engineering educator; b. Phila., Sept. 2, 1944; s. Herman and Hannah (Goodman) N.; m. Wanda Sapolsky, Apr. 12, 1970; children—Deborah, Daniel. B.S., U. Pa., 1966; M.S., Harvard U., 1967, Ph.D., 1970. Instr. applied math. MIT, Cambridge, 1970-72, asst. prof., 1972-75; asst. prof. engring. Brown U., Providence, 1975-78, assoc. prof., 1978-81, prof., 1981—, dean engring., 1988-91; Florence Price Grant Univ. prof.; vis. asst. prof. Tech. U. Denmark, Lyngby, 1973; vis. fellow Clare Hall, U. Cambridge, Eng., 1978; vis. prof. MIT, Cambridge, 1991. Contbr. articles to profl. jours. Guggenheim fellow, 1977. Fellow ASME, Am. Acad. Mechanics, Danish Ctr. for Applied Math. and Mechanics (fgn.), Groupe Francais de Macanique des Materiaux (hon.). Home: 24 Elton St Providence RI 02906-4106 Office: Brown U Div Engring Providence RI 02912

NEEDLEMAN, HARRY, lawyer; b. N.Y.C., Oct. 13, 1949; s. Jack and Sarah (Friar) N.; m. Roseann Marie Eppolito, Jan. 15, 1971. BA, Bklyn. Coll., 1970; JD, St. John's U., Queens, N.Y., 1975. Bar: N.Y. 1976, U.S. Dist. Ct. (so. dist.) N.Y. 1979, U.S. Supreme Ct. 1980. Staff atty. Merrill Lynch, N.Y.C., 1975-80; gen. counsel Cantor Fitzgerald, L.P., N.Y.C., 1980-93; with Furman Selz, N.Y.C., 1995—. Address: 13 Crestview Dr Pleasantville NY 10570-1426

NEEDLEMAN, HERBERT LEROY, psychiatrist, pediatrician; b. Phila., Dec. 13, 1927; s. J. Joseph and Sonia Rita (Shupak) N.; m. Shirley Weinstein, Sept. 12, 1948 (div. 1957); 1 child, Samuel; m. Roberta Pizor, June 2, 1963; children Joshua, Sara. BS, Muhlenberg Coll., Allentown, Pa., 1948; MD, U. Pa., 1952. Intern Phila. Gen. Hosp., 1952-54; resident in pediatrics Children's Hosp. of Phila., 1957-58, chief resident in pediatrics, 1958-59; resident in psychiatry Temple U. Med. Ctr., Phila., 1962-65, asst. prof. psychiatry, 1967-71; spl. fellow in psychiatry NIMH, Bethesda, Md., 1965-67; assoc. prof. psychiatry Harvard Med. Sch., Boston, 1971-81; prof. psychiatry and pediatrics U. Pitts. Sch. Medicine, 1981—; cons. air lead criteria document EPA, Washington, 1977; editor Ctrs. for Disease Control, Atlanta, 1978; mem. adv. com. on childhood lead poisoning prevention, 1990; chmn. devel. toxicology subpanel NAS, 1986. Editor: Low Level Lead Exposure: The Clinical Implications of Current Research, 1980, contbr. articles to profl. jours. Chmn. Com. of Responsibility, Boston, 1966-75, Alliance to End Childhood Lead Poisoning, Washington, 1991-92; bd. dirs. Mass. Advocacy Ctr., Boston, 1972-80. Capt. U.S. Army, 1955-57. Recipient Sarah L. Poiley Meml. award N.Y. Acad. Scis., 1985, The Charles A. Dana award, 1989; NAS IOM, 1990, H. John Heinz award, 1995. Fellow Am. Acad. Pediatrics; mem. Soc. of Toxicology, Am. Pediatric Soc., Am. Acad. of Child and Adolescent Psychiatry, Am. Acad. of Pediatrics Com. on Environ. Hazards, Phi Beta Kappa, Sigma Xi. Democrat. Jewish. Avocations: trout fishing, carpentry. Home: 5734 Aylesboro Ave Pittsburgh PA 15217-1412 Office: Univ Pitts Sch Medicine 305 Iroquois Ave Pittsburgh PA 15237-4724

NEEDLEMAN, JACOB, philosophy educator, writer; b. Phila., Oct. 6, 1934; s. Benjamin and Ida (Seltzer) N.; m. Carla Satzman, Aug. 30, 1959 (div. 1989); children: Raphael, Eve; m. Gail Anderson, Dec. 1990. BA, Harvard U., 1956; grad., U. Freiburg, 1957-58; PhD, Yale U., 1961. Clin. psychology trainee West Haven (Conn.) Veterans Hosp. Adminstrn., 1960-61; rsch. assoc. Rockefeller Inst., N.Y., 1961-62; from asst. prof. to assoc. prof. philosophy San Francisco State U., 1962-66, prof philosophy, 1967—, chair dept. philosophy, 1968-69; vis. scholar Union Theol. Seminary, 1967-68; dir. Ctr. Study New Religions, 1977-83; lectr. psychiatry, cons. med. ethics U. Calif., 1981-84. Author: Being-in-the-World, 1963, The New Religions, 1970, Religion for a New Generation, 1973, A Sense of the Cosmos, 1975, On the Way to Self-Knowledge: Sacred Tradition and Psychotherapy, 1976, Lost Christianity, 1980, Consciousness and Tradition, 1982, The Heart of Philosophy, 1982, Sorcerers, 1986, Sin and Scientism, 1986, Lost Christianity: A Journey of Rediscovery to the Centre of Christian Experience, 1990, Money and the Meaning of Life, 1991, Modern Esoteric Spirituality, 1992, The Way of the Physician, 1993, The Indestructible Question, 1994, A Little Book on Love, 1996; (trans.) The Primary World of Senses, 1963, Essays on Ego Psychology, 1964; editor Care of Patients with Fatal Illness, 1969, The Sword of Gnosis, 1973, Sacred Tradition and Present Need, 1974, Understanding the New Religions, 1978, Speaking of My Life: The Art of Living in the Cultural Revolution, 1979, Real Philosophy: An Anthology of the Universal Search for Meaning, 1991; contbr. Death and Bereavement, 1969, To Live Within, 1971, My Life with a Brahmin Family, 1972, The New Man, 1972, The Universal Meaning of the Kabbalah, 1973, The Phenomenon of Death. Grantee Religion in Higher Edn., 1967-68, Marsden Found., Ella Lyman Cabot Trust, 1969, Marsda Found, Far West Inst., 1975; Fulbright scholar Germany, 1957-58; Fels Found. fellow Munich, 1959; fellow Rockefeller Found. Humanities, 1977-78. Office: San Francisco State U Dept Philosophy 1600 Holloway Ave San Francisco CA 94132-1722

NEEDLEMAN, PHILIP, cardiologist, pharmacologist; b. Bklyn., Feb. 10, 1939. BS, Phila. Coll. Pharm. & Sci., 1960; MS, U. Md. Med. Sch., 1962, PhD in Pharmacology, 1964. Fellow Sch. Medicine Washington U., St. Louis, 1965-67, from asst. prof. to prof. Sch. Medicine, 1967-75, prof. Sch. Medicine, 1975—, with dept. pharmacology, 1976—, corp. v.p. R&D, chief scientist, 1991—. Contbr. numerous articles to profl. jours. Recipient Rsch. Career Devel. award NIH, 1974, 76, Wellcome Creesy award in clin. pharmacology, 1977, 78, 80, 87, Cochems Thrombosis Rsch. prize, 1980. *

NEEDLER, GEORGE TREGLOHAN, oceanographer, researcher; b. Summerside, P.E.I., Can., Feb. 2, 1935; s. Alfred Walker Holinshead and Alfreda Alice (Berkeley) N.; m. Catherine Lebedoff de Badrihaye, June 11, 1984; 1 child, Frederick Hoelbl; children from previous marriage: Mary Catherine, Kirstie Ann, Ian Berkeley, Peter Alfred. BS in Math. and Physics with honours, MS in Theoretical Physics, U. B.C., 1958; PhD in Theoretical Physics, McGill U., 1963. Research scientist dept. fisheries and ocean Bedford Inst. Oceanography, Dartmouth, N.S., Can., 1962-75, head ocean circulation div., 1975-79, dir., 1979-85, rsch. scientist, 1992-95, emeritus scientist, 1995—; scientific dir. World Ocean Circulation Experiment Inst. Oceanographic Scis., Deacon Lab., Wormley, Godalming, Surrey, Eng., 1985-89, chief scientist, 1989-92; rsch. assoc. Dalhousie U., Halifax, N.S., 1965-85; mem. UN body Joint Group of Experts on Scientific Aspects of Marine Pollution, 1980-85, chmn. working group on oceanographic model of wastes disposed in the deep sea, 1980-83; mem. Can. Nat. Com. Internat. Union Geodesy and Geophysics, 1979-83, chmn., 1983-85; mem. Can. Nat. Com. for Sci. Com. Oceanographic Rsch., 1978-79; bd. dirs., rsch./policy com. Can. Global Change Program. Rossby Meml. fellow Woods Hole Oceanographic Instn., 1970. Fellow Royal Soc. Can.; mem. Can. Meteorological and Oceanographic Soc. (scientific com. 1977-80). Avocations: golf, squash. Office: Bedford Inst Oceanography, PO Box 1006, Dartmouth, NS Canada B2Y 4A2

NEEDLES, BELVERD EARL, JR., accounting educator; b. Lubbock, Tex., Sept. 16, 1942; s. Belverd Earl and Billie (Anderson) N.; BBA, Tex. Tech U., 1964, MBA, 1965; PhD, U. Ill., 1969; m. Marian Powers, May 23, 1976; children: Jennifer Helen, Jeffrey Scott, Annabelle Marian, Abigail Marian. CPA, Ill.; cert. mgmt. acct. Asst. prof., assoc. prof. acctg. Tex. Tech U., Lubbock, 1968-72; dean Coll. Bus. and Adminstrn., Chgo. State U., 1972-76; prof. acctg. U. Ill., Urbana, 1976-78; dir. Sch. Accountancy, DePaul U., Chgo., 1978-86, prof. acctg., 1976-88, Arthur Andersen & Co. Alumni Disting. prof. acctg., 1988—. Author: Accounting and Organizational Control, 1973, Modern Business, 2d edit., 1977, Principles of Accounting, 1980, 6th edit., 1996, Financial Accounting, 1982, 6th edit., 1996, The CPA Examination: A Complete Review, 7th edit., 1986, Comparative International Auditing Standards, 1985, Financial and Managerial Accounting, 4th edit., 1996, Managerial Accounting, 4th edit, 1996; editor Accounting Instructor's Report, 1981—, The Accounting Profession and the Middle Market, 1986, Creating and Enhancing The Value of Post-Baccalareate Accounting Education, 1988, A Profession in Transition: The Ethical and Responsibilities of Accountants, 1989, Comparative International Accounting Educational Standards, 1990, Accounting Education for the 21st Century: The Global Challenges, 1994. Treas., bd. dirs. CPAs for Pub. Interest, 1978-86. Gen. Electric fellow, 1965-66; Deloitte Haskins and Sells fellow, 1966-68; named Disting. Alumnus Tex. Tech U., 1986; recipient Award of Merit DePaul U., 1986, Faculty Award of Merit Fedn. of Schs. of Accountancy, 1990. Fellow Am. Acctg. Assn. (sec. internat. sect. 1984-86, vice chmn. 1986-87, chmn. 1987-88); mem. AICPA (named Outstanding Educator 1992), Fedn. Schs. Accountancy (bd. dirs. 1980-87, pres. 1986), Acad. Internat. Bus., Ill. CPA Soc. (bd. dirs. 1994—, Outstanding Acctg. Educator 1990), European Acctg. Assn. (exec. com. 1986-89), Fin. Execs. Inst., Nat. Assn. Accts., Internat. Assn. for Edn. & Rsch. in Acctg. (v.p. 1989-92, sec.-treas. 1992—), Phi Delta Kappa, Phi Kappa Phi, Beta Alpha Psi (named Acct. of Yr. for Edn. 1992), Beta Gamma Sigma. Club: Chgo. Athletic.

NEEL, HARRY BRYAN, III, surgeon, scientist, educator; b. Rochester, Minn., Oct. 28, 1939; s. Harry Bryan and May Birgitta (Bjornsson) N.; m. Ingrid Helene Vaga, Aug. 29, 1964; children: Carlton Bryan, Harry Bryan IV, Roger Clifton. BS, Cornell U., 1962; MD, SUNY-Bklyn., 1966; PhD, U. Minn., 1976. Diplomate Am. Bd. Otolaryngology. Intern Kings County Hosp., Bklyn., 1966-67; resident in gen. surgery U. Minn. Hosps., Mpls., 1967-68; resident in otolaryngology Mayo Grad. Sch. Medicine Mayo Clinic, Rochester, Minn., 1970-74, cons. in otohinolaryngology, 1974—, cons. in cell biology, 1981—, assoc. prof. otolaryngology and microbiology Med. Sch., 1979-84, prof., 1984—, also chmn. dept. otolaryngology. Author: Cryosurgery for Cancer, 1976; contbr. chpts. to books, articles to profl. jours. V.p. bd. dirs. Minn. Orch. in Rochester, Inc., 1982, pres., chmn., 1983-84; mem. devel. com. Minn. Orchestral Assn., 1983, Mayo Found. bd. devel., 1983-86; bd. dirs. Mayo Health Plan, 1986-92, chmn., 1990-92; mem. bd. Mayo Mgmt. Svcs., Inc., 1992—; mem. bd. regents U. Minn., 1991—, chair faculty staff, student affairs com., 1993-95, vice chmn. bd., 1995—; bd. dirs. Greater Rochester Area Univ. Ctr., 1993—. With USPHS, 1968-70. Recipient travel award Soc. Acad. Chmn. Otolaryngology, 1974, Ira J. Tresley rsch. award Am. Acad. Facial and Reconstructive Surgery, 1982, Notable award Nat. Assn. Collegiate Women Athletic Admisntrs., 1992, The Best Doctors in Am. award Woodward/White, 1992-93, 94-95. Mem. AMA, ACS (bd. govs. 1985-90, devel. bd. 1988—, treas. 1990—, sec.-treas. Minn. chpt. 1983-85, pres. 1988-89), Am. Acad. Otolaryngology-Head and Neck Surgery (prize for basic rsch. in otolaryngology 1972, bd. dris. 1988-91, established Neel Disting. Rsch. Lectureship Endowment Fund 1994), Minn. Med. Assn., Zumbro Valley Med. Soc., Am. Broncho-Esophagological Assn. (pres.-elect 1988, pres. 1989-90), Am. Laryngological, Rhinological and Oto. Sco. (Mosher award 1980, pres.-elect 1995—), Am. Laryngological Assn. (Casselberry award 1985, sec. 1988-93, v.p. 1994, pres. 1994—, Newcomb award 1996), Assn. for Rsch. in Otolaryngology, Assn. Acad. Depts. in Otolaryngology (sec.-treas. 1984-86, pres.-elect 1986, pres. 1988-9), Alumni Assn. Cornell U. (Outstanding Alumni award 1985, Collegium ORL Amicitiae Sacrum 1990—), Am. Bd. Otolaryngology (bd. dirs. 1986—, most admired man of decade 1992). Republican. Presbyterian. Club: Rochester Golf and Country. Home: 828 8th St SW Rochester MN 55902-6310 Office: Mayo Clinic 200 1st St SW Rochester MN 55905-0001

NEEL, JAMES VAN GUNDIA, geneticist, educator; b. Hamilton, Ohio, Mar. 22, 1915; s. Hiram Alexander and Elizabeth (Van Gundia) N.; m. Priscilla Baxter, May 6, 1943; children—Frances, James Van Gundia, Alexander Baxter. A.B., Coll. Wooster, 1935, D.Sc. (hon.), 1959; Ph.D., U. Rochester, 1939, M.D., 1944, D.Sc. (hon.), 1974; D.Sc. (hon.), Med. Coll. Ohio, 1981. Instr. zoology Dartmouth, 1939-41; fellow zoology NRC, 1941-42; intern, asst. resident medicine Strong Meml. Hosp., 1944-46; asso. geneticist lab. vertebrate biology, asst. prof. internal medicine U. Mich. Med. Sch., 1948-51, geneticist Inst. Human Biology, asso. prof. med. genetics, 1951-56, prof. human genetics, chmn. dept., 1956-85, prof. internal medicine, 1957-85, Lee R. Dice U. prof. human genetics, 1966-85, prof. emeritus, 1985—; Galton lectr. U. London,, 1955; Cutter lectr. Harvard U., 1956; Russel lectr. U. Mich., 1966; Wilhemene E. Key lectr. Am. Genetic Assn., 1982; Jacobson lectr. U. Newcastle upon Tyne, 1988; Baker lectr. Pa. State U., 1989; Andros lectr. U. Chgo., 1991; Lederberg lectr. Rockefeller U., 1995; cons. USPHS, AEC, NRC, WHO, EPA, VA; pres. 6th Internat. Congress Human Genetics; chmn. 7th Internat. Symposium Smithsonian Instn., Washington, 1981. Author med. articles; mem. editorial bd.: Blood, 1950-62, Perspectives in Biology and Medicine, 1956—, Human Genetics Abstracts, 1962—, Mutation Research, 1964-75. Served to 1st lt. M.C. AUS, 1943-44, 46-47; acting dir. field studies Atomic Bomb Casualty Commn., 1947-48. Recipient Albert Lasker award, 1960, Allan award Am. Soc. Human Genetics, 1965, Nat. Medal of Sci., 1974, medal Smithsonian Instn., 1981, Conte award Conte Inst. for Environ. Health, 1991, James D. Bruce award ACP, 1995; named Mich. Scientist of Yr., 1984. Fellow Am. Coll. Med. Genetics (hon.), Royal Soc. Medicine; mem. Am. Philos. Assn., Am. Acad. Arts and Scis., Inst. of Medicine, Nat. Acad. Scis. (mem. coun. 1970-72), Genetics Soc. Am., Am. Soc. Human Genetics (v.p. 1952-53, pres. 1953-54), Internat. Genetic Epidemiology Soc. (pres. 1992-93), Am. Fedn. Clin. Rsch., Am. Soc. Naturalists, Assn. Am. Physicians, ACP (Laureate award 1987), Brazilian Soc. Human Genetics, Phi Beta Kappa, Sigma Xi, Alpha Omega Alpha. Avocation: orchid cultivation.

NEEL, JASPER PHILLIP, English educator; b. Florence, Ala., Nov. 14, 1946; s. Jasper Peaster and Jessie Alice (Wright) N.; m. Faye Richardson, July 10, 1982; 1 child, Elizabeth Faye. BA, Miss. Coll., 1968; MA, U. Tenn., Knoxville, 1972, PhD, 1975. Asst. prof. Baylor U., Waco, Tex., 1975-76, NYU, 1976-79; assoc. prof. Francis Marion Coll., Florence, S.C., 1979-84; prof. No. Ill. U., DeKalb, 1984-89, U. Waterloo, Ont., Can., 1989-90, Vanderbilt U., Nashville, 1990—. Author: Plato, Derrida, and Writing, 1988, Aristotle's Voice: Rhetoric, Theory, and Writing in America, 1994. Office: Vanderbilt U English Dept Nashville TN 37235

NEEL, JOHN DODD, memorial park executive; b. McKeesport, Pa., Aug. 7, 1923; s. Harry Campbell and Anna (Dodd) N.; m. Jean Wyatt, Feb. 11, 1948; children: Harry C., John Dodd II, W. Wyatt, Jeffrey J. BA, Pa. State U., 1946. From salesman to pres. Jefferson Meml. Park, Pitts., 1946-88, chmn. bd. dirs., 1988—. Mem. Zoning Hearing Bd., Pleasant Hills, Pa., 1970—. Mem. adv. bd. Pa. State U., McKeesport; former campus mem. Pa. State Real Estate Commn. 1st lt. USAAF, 1943-45. Decorated Air medal with 4 clusters, D.F.C. Recipient George Washington cert. Freedom Found., 1974. Mem. Cemetery Assn. Pa. (pres. 1963-65), Am. Cemetery Assn. (pres. 1973-74), West Jefferson Hills C. of C. (pres. 1984), VFW, Am. Legion, 57th Bomb Wing Assn., South Hills Country Club, Indian Lake Golf Club, Aero Club, Kiwanis (pres. 1959), Masons, Shriners, Tau Kappa Epsilon. Presbyterian. Avocations: golf, travel, reading, hunting. Office: 401 Curry Hollow Rd Pittsburgh PA 15236-0808

NEEL, JUDY MURPHY, trade association administrator; b. Rhome, Tex.; d. James W. and Linna B. (Vess) Neel; m. Ellis F. Murphy, Jr., Dec. 30, 1975; children from previous marriage: Mary B. Schmidt, Janet E. Wescott, Susan E. Salinas. BS, Northwestern U., 1976; MBA, Roosevelt U., 1983. V.p. Murphy, Tashjian & Assocs., Chgo., 1960-73; exec. dir. Automotive Affiliated Rep. Assn., Chgo., 1973-78; mgr. Automotive Svc. Ind. Assn., Chgo., 1978-80; exec. dir. Am. Soc. Safety Engrs., Des Plaines, Ill., 1980—. Mem. Chgo. Soc. Assn. Execs. (bd. dirs. 1979—, pres. 1985—, Shapiro award 1991), Am. Soc. Assn. Execs. (sec.-treas. 1994, found. dir. 1986-90, bd. dirs. 1990-95, Key award 1986). Republican. Office: Am Soc Safety Engrs 1800 E Oakton St Des Plaines IL 60018-2112

NEEL, RICHARD EUGENE, economics educator; b. Bluefield, Va., Jan. 7, 1932; s. Charles Richard and Zell LaVerne (Bowling) N.; m. Binnie Jo LeFever, June 10, 1961; children: Jeffrey Richard, Cynthia Jo. BS, U. Tenn., 1954, MS, 1955; PhD, Ohio State U., 1960. Instr. econs. Ohio State U., 1958-60; asst. prof. econs. Coll. William and Mary, 1960-61; asst. prof. U. South Fla., 1961-63, assoc. prof., 1963-66, chmn. econs. and fin. programs, 1964-66, acting chmn. grad. program Coll. Bus Adminstrn., 1965-66; dir. instl. planning Fla. Tech. U., 1966-68, chmn. dept. econs., prof. econs., 1968-69; assoc. dean Sch. Bus. Adminstrn. Ga. State U., 1969-77, dean grad. studies Sch. Bus. Adminstrn., 1973-77, prof. econs. Sch. Bus. Adminstrn., 1969-78; dean Coll. Bus. Adminstrn. U. N.C., Charlotte, 1978-93, econ. prof., 1993—. Contbg. author: The Case Study of Off-Campus Postsecondary Education on Military Bases, 1980; contbr. numerous articles, monographs to profl. publs.; editor: Readings in Price Theory, 1973. Sec., bd. dirs. Charlotte Fgn. Trade Zone; mem. fin. and adminstrn. com. United Way Ctrl. Carolinas, Inc.; mem. Urban League/Nations Bank Loan Rev. Bd. Mem. Charlotte Sales and Mktg. Execs., Phi Kappa Phi, Beta Gamma Sigma. Presbyterian. Office: U NC at Charlotte Charlotte NC 28223

NEEL, SAMUEL ELLISON, lawyer; b. Kansas City, Mo., Feb. 22, 1914; s. Ellison Adger and Serena (Smith) N.; m. Mary Wilson, Oct. 11, 1941; children: James Adger, Amy Bowen, Wilson (dec. 1947), Wendy Busselle, Mary Ellison, Sophia Talbot. BA, Westminster Coll., Mo., 1935, LLD, 1995; LLB, Yale U., 1938. Bar: Mo. 1938, D.C. 1946, Va. 1953. Spl. asst. to atty. gen. anti-trust div. U.S. Dept. Justice, Washington, 1938-40, rep. State-War Dept. Mission on Japanese Combines, 1946; legal staff adv. commn. Coun. Nat. Def., OPM, WPB, 1940-42; pvt. practice Washington and McLean, Va., 1946-93; bd. dirs. emeritus Rouse Co. Mem. Fed. City Coun., Washington, 1954-58; pres. McLean Citizens Assn., 1953-54, Pub. Utilities Commn., Fairfax County, Va., 1956-57, The Squam Lakes Assn., N.H., 1987-89; chmn. Fairfax County Water Authority, 1957-63, Fairfax County Housing Authority, 1970-72; mem. adv. com. mortgage fin. FHA, 1956-66; pres. Neel Found.; trustee Westminster Coll. Lt. comdr. USNR, 1942-46; comdr. air forces Pacific Fleet. Mem. Mortgage Bankers Assn. Am. (exec. v.p. 1965-66, gen. counsel 1946-74), Soc. Cin., Beta Theta Pi, Omicron Delta Kappa. Democrat. Episcopalian (past trustee). Clubs: Lawyers (Washington), Metropolitan (Washington); N.Y. Yacht. Home: 1157 Chain Bridge Rd Mc Lean VA 22101-2215 Office: PO Box 385 Mc Lean VA 22101-0385

NEEL, SPURGEON HART, JR., physician, retired army officer; b. Memphis, Sept. 24, 1919; s. Spurgeon Hart and Pyrle (Womble) N.; m. Alice Glidewell Torti, Nov. 18, 1939; children: Spurgeon Hart III, Alice Leah Neel Zartarian. Student pre-med., Memphis State U., 1939; M.D., U. Tenn., 1942; M.P.H., Harvard U., 1958; M.S.B.A., George Washington U., 1965. Diplomate: Am. Bd. Preventive Medicine. Intern Meth. Hosp., Memphis, 1943; resident x-ray Santa Ana (Calif.) AFB, 1944; resident aviation medicine USAF Sch. Aerospace Medicine, 1960; commd. 2d lt. U.S. Army, 1942, advanced through grades to maj. gen., 1970; various assignments U.S., 1943-44, 47-48, ETO, 1944-47; chief surgeon service Ft. McPherson, Ga., 1949; med. service, 1949; div. surgeon (82d Airborne Div.), Ft. Bragg, N.C., 1949-51; comdr. (30th Med. Group), Korea, 1953-54; dep. dir. div. physiology and pharmacology (WRAIR, WRAMC), 1956; chief aviation br. (OTSG), 1957; chief aviation medicine Ft. Rucker, Ala., 1960; comdg. officer U.S. Army Hosp., post surgeon, 1961-64; stationed in Vietnam, 1965-66, 68-69; dep. surgeon gen. U.S. Army, Washington, 1969-73; comdr. (U.S. Army Health Services Command), 1973-77; clin. assoc. prof. family practice U. Tex. Health Sci. Ctr., San Antoniko, now prof. emeritus occupl. and aerospace medicine U. Tex. Sch. Pub. Health; med. cons. U.S. Automobile Assn., other industries, San Antonio. Contbr. articles med. jours. Decorated D.S.M. with oak leaf cluster, Legion of Merit with 4 clusters, Bronze Star with oak leaf cluster, Air medal with 3 oak leaf clusters, Joint Service Commendation medal, USAF Commendation medal, Purple Heart, others.; Recipient Seaman award Assn. Mil. Surgeons U.S., 1950, Gary Wratten award, 1967; McClelland award Army Aviation Assn. Am., 1962; named to U.S. Army Aviation Hall Fame, 1976; recipient Lyster award Aerospace Med. Assn., 1977. Fellow A.C.P., Am. Coll. Preventive Medicine (past v.p.), Royal Soc. Health, Aerospace Med. Assn. (past pres.), Internat. Acad. Aviation and Space Medicine, Am. Acad. Med. Adminstrs., Am. Coll. Health Care Execs.; mem. AMA (past-sec. sect. mil. medicine), Assn. Mil. Surgeons U.S., Assn. U.S. Army, Army Aviation Assn. Am.; asso. mem. Phi Chi. Home: 1321 Spanish Oaks San Antonio TX 78213-1606

NEELANKAVIL, JAMES PAUL, marketing educator, consultant, researcher; b. Anjoor, India, May 29, 1940; came to U.S., 1973, naturalized, 1985; s. Paul V. and Mary (Velara) N.; m. Salvacion Querol Pena, July 15, 1973; children: Mary Angel, Jacques Prince. BS, St. Thomas Coll., India, 1961; MBA, Asian Inst. Mgmt., Philippines, 1972; PhD, NYU, 1976. Asst. prof. N.Y. Inst., 1976-78; assoc. prof. Montclair State Coll., N.J., 1978-80; asst. prof. NYU, 1980-84; chmn. mktg. and internat. bus. dept. Hofstra U., Hempstead, N.Y., 1984-86, assoc. dean sch. bus., 1986-89, acting dean, 1989-91, prof. mktg. and internat. bus., 1991—; supr. Firestone, Bombay, India, 1961-70; cons. Internat. Advt. Assn., N.Y.C., 1979-88, GTE Inc., Stamford, Conn., 1980-85, Healthchem Inc., N.Y.C., 1980-83. Author: Self-Regulation, 1980, Agency Compensation, 1982, Advertising Regulation, 1985, Advertising Regulations in Selected Countries, 1987; co-author Advertising Self-Regulation: A Global Perspective, 1980, Global Business: Contemporary Issues, Problems and Challenges; also articles. Min. Resurrection Ascension Ch., N.Y.C., 1990—. Mem. Internat. Advt. Assn., Am. Mktg. Assn., Acad. Internat. Bus., Advt. Research Found. Avocations: reading, tennis, travel.

NEELD, ELIZABETH HARPER, author; b. Brooks, Ga., Dec. 25, 1940; d. Tommie Frank and Rachel (Leach) Harper; m. Gregory Cowan, Feb. 24, 1975 (dec. 1979); m. Jerele Don Neeld, 1983. BS, U. Chattanooga, 1962, MEd, 1966; PhD, U. Tenn., Knoxville, 1973. Dir. English programs MLA, N.Y.C., 1973-76; prof. English Tex. A&M U., College Station, 1976-83; exec. prof. Coll. Bus. Adminstrn., U. Houston, 1990—. Author: Seven Choices: Taking the Steps to New Life After Losing Someone You Love, 1990, Sister Bernadette: Cowboy Nun From Texas; author, editor 14 additional books;

author: (audiocassette series) Yes! You Can Write; anchor and subject of PBS documentary The Challenge of Grief, 1991. Big sister Big Sister Orgn., Houston, 1991. Democrat. Methodist. Avocations: cooking, opera, gardening. Home: 716 Euclid St Houston TX 77009-7229

NEELEY, DELMAR GEORGE, human resources executive; b. Charleston, Ill., June 4, 1937; s. Glenn Truman and Gladys Bernice (Dittman) N.; m. Yvonne Tamara Penrod, Mar. 2, 1957 (div. Feb. 1969); children: Timothy Del, Kimberly Yvonne, Terry; m. Terry Anne Barbour, Aug. 28, 1971; children: Robert James, Stephen Edward. BA in Philosophy, Olivet Nazarene U., 1965, MA in Lit., 1969; EdD, U. Sarasota, 1996. Cert. mediator and arbitrator. Mgr. mgmt. devel. Rauland Divsn. Zenith Corp., Chgo., 1967-70; sr. personnel cons. Mid. West Svc. Co., Chgo., 1971-73; dir. human resources Nichols-Homeshield Inc., West Chicago, Ill., 1974-76, Gould Inc./Ind. Battery Divsn., Langhorne, Pa., 1976-81; pres., owner Barbour-Neeley Inc., Sarasota, Fla., 1982-91. Counselor Chgo., 1967-70, Sarasota, 1982-85. Recipient Meritorious Svc. award Chgo. Boys Club, 1970, Svc. award Chgo. Jaycees, 1967-71. Mem. Ctr. for Study of Presidency, The Century Club (life), Libr. of Congress Assocs. (charter mem.), Am. Counseling Assn., Coll. of Chaplains, Fla. Acad. Profl. Mediators. Independent. Methodist. Avocations: tchg., bus. cons., marital and mental health counseling hosp. chaplain. Home: 5161 Cedar Hammock Dr Sarasota FL 34232-2243

NEELEY, KATHLEEN LOUISE, librarian; b. Pitts., Feb. 22, 1946; d. George Edward Jr. and Mildred Jane (Snellbacher) Kratt; m. James Dalton Neeley, July 20, 1968; children: Laura Elizabeth, Alan Dalton. BS in Chemistry, Chatham Coll., Pitts., 1968; MS in LS, Syracuse U., 1972. Analytical chemist U.S. Plant, Soil and Nutrition Lab., Cornell U., Ithaca, N.Y., 1968-69, libr. asst. Olin Libr., 1969-70; libr. Syracuse (N.Y.) U. Sch. Nursing Libr., 1971; libr. Logan Lewis Libr., Carrier Corp., Syracuse, 1971-72; med. libr. Health Sci. Libr., U. Minn., Duluth, 1973-74; tech. libr. Nuclear Energy Sys. Libr., Westinghouse Electric Corp., Pitts., 1974-77; asst. sci. libr. U. Kans. Librs., Lawrence, 1977-85, acting head sci. librs., 1985-86, head sci. librs., 1986—; mem. access to health info. task force Kans. Libr. Network Bd. Contbr. articles to profl. jours. Mem. ALA (programming planning com. sci. and tech. sect.), Am. Chem. Soc., Assn. Coll. and Rsch. Librs., Beta Phi Mu. Avocations: reading, gardening, travel. Office: U Kans 424 Anschutz Sci Libr University Of Kansas KS 66045

NEELY, CAMERON MICHAEL, professional hockey player; b. Comox, B.C., Can., June 6, 1965. Hockey player Vancouver Canucks, 1983-86, Boston Bruins, 1986—; player NHL All-Star Game, 1988-91. Recipient Bill Masterton Meml. trophy, 1993-94; named to Sporting News All-Star Team, 1987-88, 93-94. Office: Boston Bruins 1 Fleet Ctr Ste 250 Boston MA 02114-1310*

NEELY, CHARLES LEA, JR., retired physician; b. Memphis, Aug. 3, 1927; s. Charles Lea and Ruby Perry (Mayes) N.; m. Mary Louise Buckingham, Mar. 30, 1957; children: Louise Mayes, Charles Buckingham. A.B., Princeton U., 1950; M.D., Washington U., St. Louis, 1954. Diplomate: Am. Bd. Internal Medicine. Intern Cornell Service, Bellevue Hosp., N.Y.C., 1954-55; resident Barnes Hosp., St. Louis, 1955-57; fellow in hematology Barnes Hosp., 1957-58; dir. U. Tenn. Cancer Clinic, 1979-87; mem. staffs Bapt. Meml. Hosp., Regional Med. Ctr. at Memphis, U. Tenn. Med. Center; prof. medicine and pathology U. Tenn., 1971-87. Served with USNR, 1945-47. Fellow A.C.P.; mem. AMA, Am. Soc. Clin. Oncology, Am. Soc. Hematology, Am. Fedn. Clin. Research, Sigma Xi, Alpha Omega Alpha. Home: 4743 Mint Dr Memphis TN 38117-4010

NEELY, J. RANDALL, public relations executive; b. Houston, Jan. 16, 1943. BS in Journalism, U. Tenn., 1966. PI spec. NASA, 1966-68; A/E Holder-Kennedy, 1968-69, v.p., 1969-70; exec. v.p. Wenz-Neely Co., 1970-85, pres., 1985-95; sr. con., 95—. Mem. PRSA, PRSA/Bluegrass (pres., v.p., sec., treas.). Address: The Wenz-Neely Co PO Box 1363 Louisville KY 40201-1363*

NEELY, MARK EDWARD, JR., writer; b. Amarillo, Tex., Nov. 10, 1944; s. Mark Edward and Lottie (Wright) N.; m. Sylvia Eakes, June 15, 1966. BA, Yale U., 1966, PhD, 1973; LHD (hon.), Lincoln Coll., 1981. Former dir. Louis A. Warren Lincoln Library and Museum, Ft. Wayne, Ind.; vis. instr. Iowa State U., Ames, 1971-72; editor Lincoln Lore, 1973—; mem. adv. bd. Ind. Historical Bureau, 1980—; mem. editorial adv. com. Ind. Mag. of History, 1981—; mem. editorial bd. Ulysses S. Grant Assn., 1981—. Author: The Abraham Lincoln Encyclopedia, 1981, The Lincoln Family Album: Photographs From The Personal Collection of a Historic American Family, 1990, The Fate of Liberty: Abraham Lincoln and Civil Liberties, 1991 (Pulitzer Prize for history 1992), The Last Best Hope on Earth: Abraham Lincoln and the Promise of America, 1993; (with Harold Holzer and Gabor S. Boritt) The Lincoln Image: Abraham Lincoln and the Popular Print, 1984, The Confederate Image: Prints of the Last Cause, 1987; (with R. Gerald McMurty) The Insanity File: The Case of Mary Todd Lincoln, 1986; (with Holzer) Mine Eyes Have Seen the Glory: The Civil War in American Art, 1993. Mem. Abraham Lincoln Assn., Soc. Ind. Archivists (pres. 1980-81), Ind. Assn. of Historians (pres. 1987-88). *

NEELY, PAUL, newspaper editor; b. San Francisco, July 30, 1946; s. Ralph and Virginia (Gaylord) N.; m. Linda Borsch, Oct. 6, 1977; children: David King, Michael Paul. BA, Williams Coll., 1968; MS in Journalism, Columbia U., 1970, MBA, 1970. Reporter, editorial writer Press Enterprise, Riverside, Calif., 1970-73; copy editor, asst. mng. editor Courier Jour., Louisville, 1973-79; news features editor St. Petersburg Times (Fla.), 1980-83; mng. editor Chattanooga Times, 1983-91, editor, dep. pub., 1991-92, pub. 1992—; mem. Commn. on Future Tenn. Judicial Sys., bd. trustees Williams Coll. Mem. Am. Assn. Sunday and Feature Editors (pres. 1981-82), Am. Soc. Newspaper Editors. Home: 1000 Skillet Gap Chattanooga TN 37419 Office: The Chattanooga Times Po Box 951 100 E 10th St Chattanooga TN 37402-4230

NEELY, RICHARD, lawyer; b. Aug. 2, 1941; s. John Champ and Elinore (Forlani) N.; m. Carolyn Elaine Elmore, 1979; children: John Champ, Charles Whittaker. AB, Dartmouth Coll., 1964; LLB, Yale U., 1967. Bar: W.Va. 1967. Practiced in Fairmont, W.Va., 1969-73; chmn. Marion County Bd. Pub. Health, 1971-72; mem. W.Va. Ho. of Dels., 1971-73; justice, chief justice W.Va. Supreme Ct. of Appeals, Charleston, 1973-95; ptnr. Neely & Hunter, Charleston, 1995—; chmn. bd. Kane & Keyser Co., Belington, W.Va., 1970-88. Author: How Courts Govern America, 1980, Why Courts Don't Work, 1983, The Divorce Decision, 1984, Judicial Jeopardy: When Business Collides with the Courts, 1986, The Product Liability Mess: How Business Can Be Rescued from State Court Politics, 1988, Take Back Your Neighborhood: A Case for Modern-Day Vigilantism, 1990, Tragedies of our Own Making: How Private Choices have Created Public Bankruptcy, 1994; contbr. articles to nat. mags. Capt. U.S. Army, 1967-69. Decorated Bronze Star, Vietnam Honor medal 1st Class. Mem. Am. Econ. Assn., W.Va. Bar Assn., Fourth Cir. Jud. Conf. (life), Internat. Brotherhood Elec. Workers, VFW, Am. Legion, Moose, Phi Delta Phi, Phi Sigma Kappa. Episcopalian. Office: Neely & Hunter 159 Summers St Charleston WV 25301

NEELY, SALLY SCHULTZ, lawyer; b. L.A. BA Stanford U., 1970, JD, 1971. Bar: Ariz. 1972, Calif. 1977. Law clk. to judge U.S. Ct. Appeals (9th cir.), Phoenix, 1971-72; assoc. Lewis and Roca, Phoenix, 1972-75; asst. prof. Harvard U. Law Sch., Cambridge, Mass., 1975-77; assoc. Shutan & Trost, P.C., Los Angeles, 1977-79, ptnr., 1979-80, Sidley & Austin, L.A., 1980—; faculty Am. Law Inst.-ABA Chpt. 11 Bus. Reorgns., 1989-95, Bankruptcy Law Inst. and Bankruptcy Litigation Inst., 1987-92, Nat. Conf. Bankruptcy Judges, 1988, 90, 95, Fed. Jud. Ctr., 1989, 90, 94-95, Workshop Bankruptcy and Bus. Reorganization NYU, 1992—; rep. 9th cir. jud. conf., 1989-91; mem. Nat. Bankruptcy Conf., 1993—. Chair Stanford Law Sch. Reunion Giving, 1986; bd. visitors Stanford Law Sch., 1990-92. Fellow Am. Coll. Bankruptcy; mem. ABA, Calif. State Bar Assn. (debtor-creditor rels. and bankruptcy subcom. bus. law sect. 1985-87). Office: Sidley & Austin 555 W 5th St Ste 4000 Los Angeles CA 90013-3000

NEELY, THOMAS EMERSON, lawyer; b. Pitts., Oct. 19, 1943; s. William Homer and Frances Elizabeth (Curtis) N.; m. Janice Elaine Fay, July 6, 1968; children: Daniel, Morgan, Benjamin. BA, Williams Coll., 1965; JD, Harvard U., 1968. Bar: Mass. 1968. Assoc. Hale and Dorr, Boston, 1971-80, ptnr., 1980—. With U.S. Army, 1969-71, Vietnam. Office: Hale and Dorr 60 State St Boston MA 02109-1803

NEELY, VICKI ADELE, legal assistant, poet; b. Dallas, Nov. 29, 1962; d. Robert Theodore and Linda Carolyn (Vogtsberger) Kissel. Attended, Richland Coll., Austin C.C., San Antonio Coll., Am. Coll. Real Estate. Asst. mgr., leasing cons. Nash Phillips/Copus, Inc., 1983-85; loan processor Univ. Nat. Bank, 1985-87; co-owner Reels on Wheels, 1987; loan sec. Tex. Am. Bank/Richardson, N.A., 1987-88; legal sec., paralegal Clements, Allen & Warren, 1988-89; legal sec. Jackson & Walker, A Profl. Corp., 1989-90, Robins, Kaplan, Miller & Ciresi, 1990-91; freelance litigation sec. Smith & Underwood, 1991-92, legal asst., 1992-94; legal asst. Collins, Norman & Basinger, P.C., Dallas, 1994—, Law Offices of Arlen D. (Spider) Bynum, 1995—. Author: (poems) Animal Love, Believe, 1993; co-author: Texas Rent-A-Bank, 1993. Methodist. Avocations: sailing, reading, dancing, painting. Home: 1911 Eastfield Dr Richardson TX 75081-5435 Office: Hampton Ct 4311 Oak Lawn Ste 444 Dallas TX 75219

NEENAN, THOMAS FRANCIS, association executive, consultant; b. Kansas City, Mo., Apr. 3, 1923; s. Emmet Joseph and Mary Helen (Liebst) N.; m. Eileen Margaret Vala, Aug. 4, 1951; children: Nancy, Tom Jr., Pamela, Kathleen, Maureen. BA, Iowa U., 1948; MA, Iowa State U., 1978. Trademark researcher Lampa Christopherson, Chgo., 1948-50; sales mgr. Cedar Rapids (Iowa) Block Co., 1950-53; owner Tywal Co., Center Point, Iowa, 1953-60; mem. sales staff Capp Homes, Center Point, Iowa, 1960-78; property mgr. Center Point, Iowa, 1978-86; exec. dir. Iowa Trails Coun., Center Point, Iowa, 1984—. Editor: (mag.) Trails Advocate, 1986—. Mayor City of Center Point, 1959-61, 65-69; chmn. City Planning an dzoning Com., Center Point, 1970—; active County Dem. Ctrl. Com., Linn County, Iowa, Linn County Conservation Bd., 1972-83; vice chair state legis. com. AARP, Des Moines, 1988-93; active leader Boy Scouts Am. Recipient Silver Beaver award Boy Scouts Am., 1961, St. George award Cath. Archdiocese Dubuque, 1973; named to Iowa's Vol. Hall of Fame, 1995. Mem. Am. Hiking Soc. (bd. dirs., Kern award 1986), Rails to Trails Conservancy, Am. Trails (treas., bd. dirs., award of excellence 1992). Democrat. Roman Catholic. Avocation: trail acquisition, development, and promotion. Home: 1201 Central Ave Center Point IA 52213-9638 Office: Trails Coun Inc PO Box 131 Center Point IA 52213-0131

NEER, CHARLES SUMNER, II, orthopedic surgeon, educator; b. Vinita, Okla., Nov. 10, 1917; s. Charles Sumner and Pearl Victoria (Brooke) N.; m. Eileen Meyer, June 12, 1990; children: Charlotte Marguerite, Sydney Victoria, Charles Henry. BA, Dartmouth Coll., 1939; MD, U. Pa., 1942. Diplomate Am. Bd. Orthopaedic Surgery (bd. dirs. 1970-75). Intern U. Pa. Hosp., Phila., 1942-43; asso. in surgery N.Y. Orthopedic-Columbia-Presbyn. Med. Center, N.Y.C., 1943-44; instr. in surgery Coll. Physicians and Surgeons, Columbia U., N.Y.C., 1946-47; instr. orthopaedic surgery Coll. Physicians and Surgeons, Columbia U., 1947-57, asst. prof. clin. orthopaedic surgery, 1957-64, asso. prof., 1964-68, prof. clin. orthopaedic surgery, 1968-90, prof. clin. orthopaedic surgery emeritus, spl. lectr. orthopaedic surgery, 1990—; attending orthopaedic surgeon Columbia-Presbyn. Med. Ctr., N.Y.C.; chief adult reconstructive svc. N.Y. Orthopaedic Hosp.; chief shoulder and elbow clinic Presbyn. Hosp.; cons. orthopaedic surgeon emeritus N.Y. Orthopaedic-Columbia-Presbyn. Med. Ctr., 1991—; chmn. 4th Internat. Congress Shoulder Surgeons; chmn. Internat. Bd. Shoulder Surgery, 1992—. Founder, chmn. bd. trustees Jour. Shoulder and Elbow Surgery, 1990—; contbr. articles to books, tech. films, sound slides. Served with U.S. Army, 1944-46. Recipient Disting. Svc. award Am. Bd. Orthopaedic Surgeons 1975. Fellow ACS (sr. mem. nat. com. on trauma), Am. Acad. Orthop. Surgeons (com. on upper extremity, shoulder com.); mem. AMA, ACS (mem. com. trauma), Am. Bd. Orthop. Surgeons (bd. dirs. 1970-75, Disting. Svc. award 1975), Am. Shoulder and Elbow Surgeons (inaugural pres.), Am. Assn. Surgery Trauma, Am. Orthop. Assn., Mid-Am. Orthop. Assn. (hon.), N.Y. Acad. Medicine, Allen O. Whipple Surg. Soc., N.Y. State Med. Soc., N.Y. County Med. Soc., Pan Am. Med. Assn., Am. Trauma Soc., Soc. Latino Am. Orthop. y Traumatology, Internat. Soc. Orthop. Surgery and Traumatology, Va. Orthop. Soc. (hon.), Carolina Orthop. Alumni Assn. (hon.), Conn. Orthop. Club (hon.), Houston Orthop. Assn. (hon.), Soc. Française de Chirurgie Orthop. et Traumatology (hon.), Soc. Italiana Orthop. Etravmatologia; patron, Shoulder and Elbow Soc. Australia, South African Shoulder Soc., Giraffe Club, Internat. Bd. Shoulder Surgery (chmn. 1992—), Alpha Omega Alpha, Phi Chi. Home and Office: 231 S Miller St Vinita OK 74301-3625 *Forever grateful I could be a doctor and especially to work in the exciting area of shoulder surgery.*

NEERHOUT, JOHN, JR., petroleum company executive; b. 1931. BSME, U. Calif., 1953. With Bechtel Petroleum, Inc. (now Bechtel, Inc.), San Francisco, 1966—; pres. Bechtel Petroleum, Inc. (now Bechtel, Inc.), 1983-86, also dir. Bechtel Group, Inc., v.p. Office: Bechtel Group Inc 50 Beale St San Francisco CA 94105-1813*

NEESON, LIAM, actor; b. Ballymena, No. Ireland, June 7, 1952; s. Barney and Kitty N.; m. Natasha Richardson, July 3, 1994; 1 son: Micheál Richard Antonio. Theatrical appearances include (Broadway) Anna Christie, 1993; films include Excalibur, 1981, Krull, 1983, The Bounty, 1984, The Innocent, 1984, Lamb, 1986, Duet for One, 1986, The Mission, 1986, A Prayer for the Dying, 1987, Suspect, 1987, Satisfaction, 1988, The Dead Pool, 1988, High Spirits, 1988, The Good Mother, 1988, Next of Kin, 1989, Darkman, 1990, Crossing the Line, 1990, Ruby Cairo, 1991, Shining Through, 1992, Under Suspicion, 1992, Husbands and Wives, 1992, Leap of Faith, 1992, Ethan Fromme, 1992, Schindler's List, 1993 (Best Actor Acad. award nominee 1994), Nell, 1994, Rob Roy, 1995, Before and After, 1996, Michael Collins, 1996. Office: c/o Susan Culley & Assocs 150 S Rodeo Dr Ste 220 Beverly Hills CA 90212

NEEVES, ARTHUR EDWARD, optics scientist; b. White Plains, N.Y., June 21, 1956; s. Arthur Ernest and Marcella (Myer) N. AS, Dutchess C.C., 1981; BS, Rensselaer Poly. Inst., 1983, MS, 1986, PhD, 1988. Postdoctoral fellow AT&T Bell Labs., Murray Hill, N.J., 1988-90; mem. tech. staff AT&T Advanced Tech. Systems, Whippany, N.J., 1990-95; disting. mem. tech. staff advanced tech. sys. Lucent Techs., Whippany, 1996—; Pres. Neeves Airmotive Corp., Morristown, N.J., 1990—. Contbr. articles to profl. jours. Mem. Optical Soc. Am. Achievements include following patents: nonlinear optical materials, adjustable filter for tuning multimode optical signals, bending process for optical coupling of glass optical fibers, and evanescent field coupler. Office: Lucent Techs Advanced Sys 67 Whippany Rd Whippany NJ 07981-1406

NEF, EVELYN STEFANSSON, psychotherapist, author, editor, specialist polar regions; b. N.Y.C., July 24, 1913; d. Jeno and Bella (Klein) Schwartz; m. Bil Baird, 1932 (div. 1938); m. Vilhjalmur Stefansson, 1941 (dec. 1962); m. John Ulric Nef, Apr. 21, 1964 (dec. Dec. 1988). Student, Traphagen Art Sch., N.Y.C., summer 1927, Art Student League, 1931, Inst. Study Psychotherapy, N.Y.C., 1974-77, Advanced Psychoanalytic Seminar, 1977-83. Librarian Stefansson Polar Library, N.Y.C., 1941-52; librarian Stefansson collection Baker Library, Dartmouth Coll., 1952-63, also lectr. polar studies program, 1960-61; adminstrv. officer Am. Sociol. Assn., Washington, 1963-64; freelance writer book reviews, newspaper articles N.Y. Times Book Review, also Washington Post, 1942-72; research assoc. dept. dermatology Washington Hosp. Ctr., 1976—, coordinator psoriasis social adjustment study, 1977-80; guest worker Inst. Brain Evolution and Behavior, NIHM; guest on radio and TV programs; mem. vis. com. U. Chgo. Libr., 1973-84, vice chmn., 1977-84; mem. vis. com. on social scis. U. Chgo., 1978-83; bd. dirs. MacDowell Colony, 1992—, fellow, summer 1993. Author: Within the Circle, 1945, Here is the Far North, 1957, Here is Alaska, 4th rev. edit. (with Linda C. Yahn), 1983, also contbg. author other books; editor-in-chief: Beyond the Pillars of Heracles (Rhys Carpenter), 1966, South from the Spanish Main (Earl Hanson), 1967, Silk, Spices and Empire (Owen and Eleanor Lattimore), 1968, West and By North (Louis B. Wright and Elaine Fowler), 1971, The Moving Frontier (Louis B. Wright and Elaine Fowler), 1972; foreward writer for Eleanor Lattimonew's Turkestan Reunion, 1995; editor, contbr.: Polar Notes, 1960-63, Eleanor Holgate Lattimore, 1895-1970, 1970, Jour. of Polar Studies, 1984; contbr. to: A Chronological Bibliography of the Published Works of Vilhjalmur Stefansson, 1978, Vilhjalmur Stefansson and The Development of Arctic Terrestial Science, 1984. Pres. Evelyn S. Nef Found., 1992—; trustee Corcoran Gallery Art, Washington, 1974-89; bd. dirs. Reginald S. Lourie Ctr. for Infants and Young Children, 1989-93, Washington Opera, 1993—, Nat. Symphony, MacDowell Colony, 1991—, Paget Found.; mem. adv. coun. dept. geriatrics Mt. Sinai Hosp., N.Y.C., 1988—. Recipient Vol. Activist award, 1978, recognition award Young Audiences, 1992. Mem. Washington Acad. Scis., Smithsonian Assocs. (mem. women's com. 1971-74), Soc. Women Geographers (nat. v.p., chmn. Washington chpt. 1969-71, nat. pres. 1972-75), Explorers Club, Sulgrave Club, Cosmos Club. Research on psychosomatic skin diseases, progressive aging. Home: 2726 N St NW Washington DC 20007-3323

NEFF, BLAKE J., college president, clergyman; b. Warsaw, Ind., Jan. 18, 1952; s. Billy Liggett and Mary Louise (Brown) N.; m. Nancy J. Meeks, June 21, 1974; children: Jay, Jannette, Joanna. BSIA, Gen. Motors Inst., Flint, Mich., 1975; MDiv, Asbury Theol. Sem., Wilmore, Ky., 1980; PhD, Bowling Green State U., 1982. Ordained to ministry United Meth. Ch., 1980. Pastor United Meth. Chs., Ohio, 1980-86; dir. Sch. of Comm. Toccoa Falls Coll., Toccoa, Ga., 1988-92; pastor New Liberty United Meth. Ch., Clarksville, Ga., 1988-92; pres. Vennard Coll., University Park, Iowa, 1992—; bd. dirs. World Gospel Mission, Marion, Ind., 1993—; mem. bd. adminstrn. Christian Holiness Assn., Wilmore, 1993—. Author: A Complete Handbook of Religious Education Volunteers, 1993; contbr. chpt. to book; contbr. articles to profl. jours. Mem. Wesleyan Theol. Soc., Speech Comm. Assn., Rotary Internat. Office: Vennard Coll PO Box 29 University Park IA 52592

NEFF, CRAIG, periodical editor. Student, Colgate U. Mng. editor Sports Illustrated for Kids, N.Y.C. Office: Sports Illustrated for Kids Rockefeller Ct Time & Life Building New York NY 10020-1393

NEFF, DIANE IRENE, naval officer; b. Cedar Rapids, Iowa, Apr. 26, 1954; d. Robert Mariner and Adeline Emma (Zach) N. BA in Psychology and Home Econs., U. Iowa, 1976; MA in Sociology, U. Mo., 1978; MEd in Ednl. Leadership, U. West Fla., 1990. Contract compliance officer, dir. EEO, City of Cedar Rapids, 1979-81; commd. ensign USN, 1981, advanced through grades to lt. comdr.; asst. legal officer Naval Comm. Area Master Sta., Guam, 1982-83; comm. security plans and requirements officer Comdr.-in-Chief US Naval Forces in Europe, London, 1983-85; dir. standards and evaluation dept. Recruit Tng. Command, Orlando, Fla., 1985-89; rsch. and analysis officer Naval Res. Officers Tng. Corps Office Chief Naval Edn. and Tng., Pensacola, Fla., 1989-91; tech. tng. officer Recruit Tng. Command, Great Lakes, Ill., 1991-92, mil. tng. officer, 1992-93, dir. apprentice tng., 1993-95; coord. ednl. and tng. programs U. Ctrl. Fla., Orlando, 1995—. Founding mem. Unity of Gulf Breeze, Fla., 1990; performer various benefits for chs., mus., others, Orlando, 1988, 91, 95, 96. Fellow Adminstrn. on Aging, 1977. Unitarian. Avocation: piano.

NEFF, DONALD LLOYD, news correspondent, writer; b. York, Pa., Oct. 15, 1930; s. Harry William and Gertrude Marie N.; m. Abigail Trafford; 1 son, Gregory Harry. Student, Trinity Coll., San Antonio, 1949, York Coll., 1950-52, N.Y. U., 1953. Reporter York Dispatch, 1954-56, L.A. Mirror-News, 1956-57, UPI, L.A., 1957-61; with L.A. Times, 1961-64; bur. chief L.A. Times, Tokyo, 1964; with Time mag., 1965-81; corr. Time mag., Vietnam, 1965-66; writer Time mag., N.Y.C., 1966-68; bur. chief Time mag., Houston, 1968-70, L.A., 1970-73, Jerusalem, 1975-78; bur. chief Time mag., N.Y.C., 1978-79, sr. editor, 1973-75; news svcs. editor Washington Star, 1979-80; Washington corr. Middle East Internat., 1989—. Author: Warriors at Suez: Eisenhower Takes America into the Middle East, 1981, Warriors for Jerusalem, The Six Days That Changed the Middle East, 1984; Warriors Against Israel, 1988, Fallen Pillars; U.S. Policy Toward Palestine and Israel since 1945, 1995. Served with AUS, 1948-50. Recipient Theta Sigma Phi Matrix award, 1962, Calif.-Nev. AP Writing Contest best met. spot news story award, 1962, Overseas Press Club award for best fgn. article in a mag., 1979; finalist Am. Book Award History category, 1982. Mem. Fgn. Press Assn. (Israel pres. 1977, v.p. 1978).

NEFF, EDWARD AUGUST, manufacturing company executive; b. Chgo., Feb. 7, 1947; s. Russell Jack and Betty Rae (Heins) N.; m. Janet Irene Picerno; children: Kathleen Rae, David Russell. BA, Ohio Wesleyan U., 1969. Mgmt. trainee Phoenix Trimming Co., Chgo., 1970-73, dir. research and devel., 1973-77; dir. research and devel. Phoenix Trimming Co., Tarboro, N.C., 1977-86, v.p. mfg., 1986-87; v.p. mfg. Murdock Webbing Co., Central Falls, R.I., 1987-95, sr. v.p. ops., 1995—. Deacon, treas. Howard Meml. Presbyn. Ch., Tarboro, N.C., 1984-88; treas. Christ Ch., East Greenwich, R.I., 1994—. Mem. Narrow Fabrics Inst. (pres. 1985-88), Web Sling Assn. (v.p. 1974-76). Republican. Avocations: golf, bridge. Home: 1065 South Rd East Greenwich RI 02818-1435 Office: Murdock Webbing Co 27 Foundry St Pawtucket RI 02863-2317

NEFF, FRANCINE IRVING (MRS. EDWARD JOHN NEFF), former federal government official; b. Albuquerque, Dec. 6, 1925; d. Edward Hackett and Georga (Henderson) Irving; m. Edward John Neff, June 7, 1948; children: Sindle, Edward Vann. A.A., Cottey Coll., 1946; B.A., U. N.Mex., 1948. Div. and precinct chmn. Republican Party, Albuquerque, 1966-71; mem. central com. Bernalillo County (N.Mex.) Republican Party, 1967-74, mem. exec. bd., 1968-70; mem. N.Mex. State central com. Republican Party, 1968-74, 77-82, mem. exec. bd., 1970-74, 81-83; Rep. nat. committeewoman State of N.Mex., 1970-74; also mem. exec. com.; Treas. of U.S. U.S. Dept. Treasury, Washington, 1974-77; nat. dir. U.S. Savs. Bonds, 1974-77; mktg. v.p. Rio Grande Valley Bank, Albuquerque, 1977-81; dir. Hershey Foods Corp., Pa., E-Systems Inc., Dallas, La.-Pacific Corp., Portland, Oreg., D.R. Horton, Inc., Arlington, Tex. N.Mex. state adviser Teenage Reps., 1967-68; del. Rep. Nat. Conv., Miami, 1968, 72; campaign coordinator Congressman Lujan of N.Mex., 1970; pres. Albuquerque Federated Rep. Women's Club, 1977; Leader Camp Fire Girls, Albuquerque, 1957-64; pres. Inez (N.Mex.) PTA, 1961; den mother Cub Scouts Am., Albuquerque, 1964-65; former mem. exec. bd. United Way of Albuquerque; former mem. adv. council Mgmt. Devel. Center, Robert O. Anderson Grad. Sch. Bus. and Adminstrv. Scis., U. N.Mex.; former mem. Def. Adv. Com. on Women in the Services, 1980-83; trustee Cottey Coll., Nevada, Mo., 1982-89. Recipient Exceptional Service award Dept. Treasury, 1976, Horatio Alger award, 1976. Mem. P.E.O. (pres. Albuquerque chpt. 1958-59, 63-64), Albuquerque City Panhellenic Assn. (pres. 1959-60), Greater Albuquerque C. of C. (bd. dirs. 1978-81), Alpha Delta Pi, Sigma Alpha Iota, Phi Kappa Phi, Pi Lambda Theta, Phi Theta Kappa. Episcopalian.

NEFF, FRED LEONARD, lawyer; b. St. Paul, Nov. 1, 1948; s. Elliott Ira and Mollie (Poboisk) N.; m. Christa Ruth Powell, Sept. 10, 1989. BS with high distinction, U. Minn., 1970; JD, William Mitchell Coll. Law, 1976. Bar: Minn. 1976, N.D. 1994, U.S. Dist. Ct. Minn. 1977, U.S. Ct. Appeals (8th cir.) 1985, U.S. Supreme Ct. 1985, Wis. 1986, U.S. Dist. Ct. (ea. and we. dists.) Wis. 1992. Tchr. Hopkins (Minn.) Pub. Schs., 1970-72; instr. U. Minn., Mpls., 1974-76; pvt. practice law Mpls., 1976-79; asst. county atty. Sibley County, Gaylord, Minn., 1979-80; mng. atty. Hyatt Legal Svcs., St. Paul, 1981-83, regional ptnr., 1983-85, profl. devel. ptnr., 1985-86; pres. Neff Law Firm, P.A., Mpls., 1986—; CEO Profl. Devel. Inst. Inc., Edina, Minn., 1994—, also bd. dirs.; instr. Inver Hills Coll., 1973-77; counsel Am. Tool Supply Co., St. Paul, 1976-78; cons. Nat. Detective Agy., Inc., St. Paul, 1980-83; CEO A Basic Legal Svc., Bloomington, 1990—; CEO, bd. dirs. Profl. Devel. Inst., Inc., Edina, Minn., 1994—; lectr., guest instr. U. Wis., River Falls, 1976-77; spl. instr. Hamline U., St. Paul, 1977; vis. lectr. Coll. St. Scholastica, Duluth, Minn., 1977; program. faculty, cons. Employment Law Seminar for Colo., Fla., La., Oreg., Employment and Labor Law Seminar for Ala., Alaska, Calif., Conn., Ind., N.C., Ohio, Va., N.C. Safety and Health at the Workplace, S.C. Labor Law, Ohio Safety at the Workplace; bd. dirs. Acceptance Ins. Holdings, Inc., Omaha; active Internat. Confederation Jurists, 1993; mem. faculty sem. Ariz. Safety at Workplace, Hawaii Employment & Labor, Miss. Employment & Labor Law, Del. Employment & Labor, Alaska Employment and Labor Law, Ga. Employment & Labor Law, N.J. Employment & Labor, Wash. Employment Law, Mass. Employment & Labor Law, 1995—, Ark. Employment and Labor Law, Mo. Employment and Labor Law, Iowa Employment and Labor Law, Utah Employment and Labor Law. Author: Fred Neff's Self-Defense Library, 1976, Everybody's Self-Defense Book, 1978, Karate Is for Me, 1980, Running Is for Me, 1980, Lessons from the Samurai, 1986, Lessons from the Art of Kempo, 1986, Lessons from the Western Warriors, 1986, Lessons from the Fighting Commandos, 1990, Lessons from the Ancient Japanese Masters of

Self-Defense, 1990, Lessons from the Eastern Warrors, 1990, Mysterious Persons of the Past, 1991, Great Mysteries of Crime, 1991; host TV series Great Puzzles In History; co-host TV series Great Unsolved Crimes, Minn.; asst. editor: Hennepin County Lawyer, 1992—. Advisor to bd. Sibley County Commrs., 1979-80; speaker civic groups, 1976-82; mem. Hennepin County Juvenile Justice Panel, 1980-82, Hennepin County (Minn.) Pub. Def. Conflict Panel, 1980-82, 86—, Hennepin County Bar Assn. Advice Panel Law Day, 1987, mem. dist. ethics com., 1990—; mem. Panel Union Privilege Legal Svcs. div. AFL-CIO, 1986—, Montgomery Wards Legal Svcs. Panel, 1986—, Edina Hist. Soc., Decathlon Athletic Club; charter mem. Commn. for the Battle of Normandy Mus.; founding sponsor Civil Justice Found., 1986—; mem. com. for publ. Hennepin County Lawyer, 1992. Recipient Outstanding Tchr. award Inver Hills Coll. Student Body, 1973, St. Paul Citizen of Month award Citizens Group, 1975, Kempo Club award U. Minn., 1975, U. Minn. Student Appreciation award Kempo Club, 1978, Sibley County Atty. Commendation award, 1980, Good Neighbor award WCCO Radio, 1985, Lamp of Knowledge award Twin Cities Lawyers Guild, 1986, N.W. Cmty. TV Commendation award, 1989-91, Presdl. Merit medal Pres. George Bush, 1990, N.W. Cmty. TV award, 1991, HLS Leadership award, 1984, Mng. Attys. Guidance award, 1985, Creative Thinker award Regional Staff, 1986, HLS Justice award, 1986, Honors cert. for Authors, Childrens Reading Round Table of Chgo., 1988. Fellow Roscoe Pound Found., Nat. Dist. Attys. Assn.; mem. ABA, ATLA, Minn. Bar Assn. (com. on ethics, 1994—, com. on alternative dispute resolution, 1994—), Minn. Trial Lawyers Assn., Hennepin County Bar Assn. (dist. ethics com. 1990—), Minn. Bar Assn. (co994, com. on alternative dispute resolution 1994), Wis. Bar. Assn., Ramsey County Bar Assn., Am. Judicature Soc., Internat. Platform Assn., Am. Arbitration Assn. (panel of arbitrators 1992), Minn. Martial Arts Assn. (pres. 1974-78, Outstanding Instr. award 1973), Nippon Kobudo Rengokai (bd. dirs. North Cen. States 1972-76, regional dir. 1972-76), Internat. Confederation Jurists, Edina C. of C., Southview Country Club, Masons, Kiwanis, Scottish Rite, Sigma Alpha Mu. Avocations: reading, Far Eastern and Oriental studies, civic activities, physical conditioning, gardening. Home: 4515 Andover Rd Minneapolis MN 55435-4031 also: 7250 France Ave S Ste 107 Edina MN 55435-4311 also: 5930 Brooklyn Blvd Ste 206 Brooklyn Center MN 55429-2518 also: 1711 W County Rd B Ste 340N Roseville MN 55113 also: 1751 W County Rd B Ste 104 Roseville MN 55113

NEFF, GARY VERYL, mathematics educator, consultant; b. Altoona, Pa., Sept. 2, 1943; s. Donald Eugene and Florence Ione (Ross) N.; m. Mary Ellen Andre, Oct. 1964; children: Gary Jr., Traci. BS, Ind. U., 1964; MEd, U. Pitts., 1969; M in Math. Edn., Ind. U., 1970; MS in Math., Ohio U., 1971. Cert. tchr. math., driver's edn., prin., Pa.; tchr. math., Ohio. Tchr. West Allegheny Schs., Imperial, Pa., 1964-65; tchr., coach Greater LSD, Latrobe, Pa., 1965-87; asst. prof. Salem (W.Va.) Coll., 1987-88, Bethany Coll., W.Va., 1988-90, Ohio U. Eastern, Athens, 1990—; mem. steering com., interim dir. S.E. region Project Discovery, Columbus, Ohio, 1992—; cons. Zanesville (Ohio) City Schs., 1992—, Cambridge (Ohio) City Schs., 1992—, Hamilton (Ohio) City Schs., 1994—, K-6 Math. Tchr. Tng., Athens, 1991-94, S.E. Region Ohio, St. Clairesville, 1991—; mem. textbook selection com. St. Clairsville Schs., 1994, curriculum writer, 1993. Councilman Latrobe Boro, 1975-80; committeeman 2d ward Latrobe Boro, 1976-82. Prison Edn. grantee Ohio State Correctional Facility, 1994. Mem. Nat. Coun. Tchrs. Math., Ohio Coun. Tchrs. Math., Pa. Coun. Tchrs. Math. (chmn. state conf. software sales 1995), Ohio Math. Educators Leadership Coun., Rural Systemic Initiative, Elks. Avocation: antiques. Home: PO Box 71 Belmont OH 43718-0071 Office: Ohio U Eastern 45425 National Rd W Saint Clairsville OH 43950-9764

NEFF, GREGORY PALL, manufacturing engineering educator, consultant; b. Detroit, Nov. 23, 1942; s. Jacob John and Bonnie Alice (Pall) N.; m. Bonita Jean Dostal, Apr. 27, 1974; 1 child, Kristiana Dostal Neff. BS in Physics, U. Mich., 1964, MA in Math., 1966, MS in Physics, 1967; MSME, Mich. State U., 1982. Registered profl. engr., Ind.; cert. mfg. engr.; cert. mfg. technologist; cert. sr. indsl. technologist. Rsch. asst. cyclotron lab U. Mich., Ann Arbor, 1968-72, teaching fellow physics dept., 1973; instr. sci. dept. Lansing (Mich.) C.C., 1976-82; guest lectr. Purdue U. Calumet, Hammond, Ind., 1982-83, asst. prof., 1984-91, assoc. prof. mech. engring. tech., 1991—; cons. Inland Steel Co., Indsl. Engring., East Chicago, Ind., 1984-86, Polyurethane div. Pinder Industries, East Chicago, 1990-92, Elevated div. Pitts. Tank & Tower, Henderson, Ky., 1990-91. Contbr. articles to profl. jours. County commr. Ingham County Bd. of Commr., Mason, Mich., 1977-80, Tri-County Regional Planning Commn., Lansing, 1978-80, chair, non-motorized adv. coun. Mich. Dept. Transp., Lansing, 1982-83. Mem. ASME, AAUP, Soc. Mfg. Engrs. (chpt. 112 bd. dirs. 1986—, Appreciation award 1990, 92, Outstanding Faculty Advisor award 1991,), Ind. Soc. Profl. Engrs., Am. Soc. for Engring. Edn. (Merl K. Miller award 1994), Nat. Assn. Indsl. Tech., Order of the Engr. Democrat. Roman Catholic. Office: Purdue U Calumet 2200 169th St Hammond IN 46323-2068

NEFF, HOWARD, bank executive; b. 1933. Pres. Thunderbird Bank, Phoenix; with Bluebonnet Savings Bank FSB, Dallas, 1989—, now vice chmn., chmn., 1993. Office: Bluebonnet Savs Bank FSB 3100 Monticello Ave Dallas TX 75205-3442*

NEFF, JACK KENNETH, apparel manufacturing company executive; b. N.Y.C., Feb. 23, 1938; s. William K. and Rose T. N.; m. Barbara Joan Neff, Nov. 4, 1961; 1 son, Craig William. A.A.S., Queens Coll., 1968; postgrad., Stanford Advanced Mgmt. Coll., 1973. Gen. mdse. mgr. youthwear Levi Strauss & Co., 1973-78, v.p. mktg., 1978-80; pres. Salant & Salant Co., N.Y.C., 1980-81; exec. v.p. Salant Corp., N.Y.C., 1981-84; pres., chief exec. officer Thomson Co., N.Y.C., 1984-87; exec. v.p., chief operating officer Stanley Blacker Co., N.Y.C., 1987-90; with Inside Mgmt. Assocs., N.Y.C., 1991-93; v.p. and gen. mgr. Reebok Worldwide Apparel Div., 1993-94; sr. v.p., 1994—. Served in USN, 1956-59.

NEFF, JOHN, recording engineer, producer; b. Birmingham, Mich., Mar. 13, 1951; s. Robert Leslie Joseph and Mary Therese (McElvarr) N.; m. Nancy Louise Boocks, Aug. 29, 1987; children: Jennifer Lyn Neff, Bryan C. Groves, Kenneth John Neff. Student, Oakland Community Coll., Auburn Hills, Mich., 1970-72. Freelance recording artist, session musician Detroit, 1965-73; freelance record producer Toronto, Phoenix, L.A., 1974-79; radio announcer, engr. Stas. KVIB, KHEI, KMVI, KLHI, KAOI, 1981-88; record producer Maui Recorders, Kula, Hawaii, 1986-92; cons. studio design Roadrunner Audio Svcs., Glendale, Ariz., 1993—; rec. engr. for Walter Becker, Donald Fagen (Steely Dan), Buffy Ste Marie, Willie Nelson, Sagan Lewis; touring musician Detroit, Toronto, Phoenix, L.A., 1969-79. Recipient Grammy award nomination for Kamakiriad, 1994. Mem. ASCAP, Audio Engring Soc. (cert.), Am. Fedn. Musicians. Avocations: photography, hiking, travel. Home and Office: Roadrunner Audio Svcs 23846 N 38th Dr Glendale AZ 85310-4113

NEFF, KENNETH D., realtor; b. Montpelier, Ind., Oct. 19, 1929; s. Clyde A. and Cora I. N.; m. Nancy Stiffler, Dec. 26, 1951; children: David, Susan, Julie, Bradley. BS in Bus., Ball State U. Owner Neff Realty, Montpelier, 1983-95; mayor City of Montpelier, 1983-95. Mem. air pollution bd. Ind. Dept. Environ Mgmt., Indpls., 1991-95; mem. Purdue Hwy. Extension and Rsch. Project, Ind. Counties and Cities Bd., West Lafayette, 1991-95; chmn. adminstrv. coun. Montpelier United Meth. Ch. Lt. col. USAF, 1958-81. Mem. Ind. Dem. Editl. Assn., Ind. Assn. Cities and Towns (exec. bd., legis com. 1988-96), North Ctrl. Mayors' Roundtable (pres. 1991-92), Kiwanis (past state lt. gov.). Democrat. Home: 129 S Washington St Montpelier IN 47359-1331 Office: 109 W Huntington St Montpelier IN 47359-1123

NEFF, MICHAEL ALAN, lawyer; b. Springfield, Ill., Sept. 4, 1940; s. Benjamin Ezra and Ann (Alpert) N.; m. Lin Laghi, Mar. 26, 1977; 1 son, Aaron Benjamin. Student U. Ill., 1958-61; B.A., U. Calif.-Berkeley, 1963, postgrad. 1963-64; J.D., Columbia U., 1967. Bar: N.Y. 1967, U.S. Dist. Ct. (so. and ea. dists.) N.Y. 1969, U.S. Ct. Appeals (2nd cir.) 1988, U.S. Supreme Ct. 1988. Assoc., Sage Gray Todd & Sims, N.Y.C., 1967-74, Fellner & Rovins, N.Y.C., 1974-75; ptnr. Polier Tulin Clark & Neff, N.Y.C., 1976-77; sole practice, N.Y.C., 1977—; counsel St. Dominic's Home, 1971-74, Louise Wise Services, 1976-77, Edwin Gould Service for Children, 1969-74, 76—, Family Services of Westchester, Inc., 1977—, The Children's Village, 1977-84, Puerto Rican Assn. for Community Affairs, Inc., 1979-92, Brookwood Child Care, 1980—, Forestdale, 1988—, Cen. Bklyn. Coord. Counsel, 1989—, Miracle Makers, 1989—, Fam. Support Systems Unlimited, 1990—; teaching asst. U. Calif., 1963-64; congl. intern U.S. Ho. of Reps., summer 1965; instr. Marymount Manhattan Coll., 1973; mem. Indigent Defendant's Legal Panel, Appellate Div., First Dept., 1974-84; participant N.Y. State Conf. on Children's Rights, 1974; asst. sec. Edwin Gould Services for Children, 1977—; cons. N.Y. Task Force on Permanency Planning For Children in Foster Care, 1985-90, N.Y. State Foster and Adoptive Parent Assn., Inc., 1988—, N.Y. Spaulding for Children, 1988-90, Ct. Appointed Spl. Advocates, 1988-91. Mem. ABA, Assn. Bar City of N.Y. Contbr. articles to profl. jours. Home: 5 W 86th St Apt 6B New York NY 10024-3664 Office: 36 W 44th St Ste 1212 New York NY 10036

NEFF, P. SHERRILL, health care executive; b. Balt., Dec. 18, 1951; s. Paul Heston and Mary (Poulnot) N.; m. Sarah B. Barrett, June 20, 1976 (div. 1985); 1 child, Jacob Colin; m. Alicia Phyll Felton, May 26, 1988; 1 child, Michael Felton. BA, Wesleyan U., 1974; JD magna cum laude, U. Mich., 1980. Bar: Pa. 1980. Atty. Morgan Lewis & Bockius, Phila., 1980-84; investment banker Alex Brown & Sons, Inc., Balt., 1984-93, mng. dir., 1992-93; sr. v.p. corp. devel. U.S. Healthcare, Blue Bell, Pa., 1993-94; pres., CFO Neose Techs., Inc., Horsham, Pa., 1994—, also bd. dirs.; bd. dirs. Jeff Banks, Inc., Phila. Trustee Zero Moving Dance Co., Phila., 1984-93. Mem. Pa. BIotech. Assn. (bd. dirs.). Democrat. Jewish. Home: 619 Revere Rd Merion Station PA 19066-1007 Office: Neose Techs. Inc PO Box 1109 102 Witmer Rd Horsham PA 19044

NEFF, PETER JOHN, chemicals, mining and metal processing executive; b. New Brunswick, N.J., Oct. 31, 1938; s. Peter and Carrie (Colasurdo) N.; m. Joan Ruth Knapp, June 18, 1960; children: Lisa, Kristopher, Greg. BS in Chemistry, Rutgers U., 1969; MBA, Rider Coll., Lawrenceville, N.J., 1978. Rsch. chemist Exxon Chems., Linden, N.J.; product mgr. Standard Brands Chem. Industries, Edison, N.J., 1970-73; sales mgr. St. Joe Minerals Corp., N.Y.C., 1973-77; dir. planning St. Joe Zinc Co., Pitts., 1977-80; v.p. St. Joe Internat. Corp., N.Y.C., 1980-83, pres., 1983-85; pres., chief exec. officer St. Joe Minerals Corp., St. Louis, 1985-89; pres., chief oper. officer Rhone-Poulenc Inc., Princeton, N.J., from 1987, now pres., chief exec. officer, also bd. dirs.; pres. Interchem., Inc., New Castle, Del. With USN, 1956-59. Mem. Chem. Mfg. Assn. (bd. dirs.), French. Am. C. of C. Avocations: furniture design and construction. Home: 47 Dogwood Ln Skillman NJ 08558-1302*

NEFF, RAY, insurance company executive. MS in Actuarial Sci., U. Mich. With Mich. and Fla. ins. depts.; dir. divsn. workers compensation Fla. Dept. Labor and Security; with FCCI Mut. Ins. Co., Sarasota, Fla., now pres., CEO. Office: Fla Constr Commerce Ind 2601 Cattlemen Rd Sarasota FL 34232-6214

NEFF, RAY QUINN, electric power educator, consultant; b. Houston, Apr. 29, 1928; s. Noah Grant and Alma Ray (Smith) N.; m. Elizabeth McDougald, Sept. 4, 1982. Degree in Steam Engring., Houston Vocat. Tech., 1957; BSME, Kennedy Western U., 1986. Various positions Houston Lighting & Power Co., 1945-60, plant supr., 1960-70, plant supt. asst., 1970-80, tech. supr., 1980-85, tng. supr., 1985-87; owner, operator Neff Enterprises, Bedias, Tex., 1987—; tng. supr. Tex. A&M U., 1991—; cons. Houston Industries, 1987-89. Author: Power Plant Operation, 1975, Power Operator Training, 1985, Power Foreman Training, 1986. Judge Internat. Sci. and Engring. Fair, Houston, 1982, Sci. Engring. Fair Houston, 1987. Mem. ASME, Assn. Chief Operating Engrs., Masons. Republican. Methodist. Avocations: farming, ranching, classic cars. Home: Hwy 90 Rte 2t Box 193-A Bedias TX 77831 Office: Tex A&M U Power Plant College Station TX 77843

NEFF, RICHARD B., consumer products company executive; b. 1948. BS, Fairleigh Dickinson U., 1970. CPA. With Arthur Andersen & Co., 1970-73; various exec. positions including exec. v.p., CFO and dir. Transco Group, Inc., 1973-86; mng. ptnr. Greenwood Meadows Devel. Co., 1988—; exec. v.p., CFO, dir. Di Giorgio Corp., 1990—; pres. Las Plumas Lumber, 1991—; officer White Rose Foods, Inc., 1992—. Office: Di Giorgio Corp 380 Middlesex Ave Carteret NJ 07008

NEFF, ROBERT ARTHUR, business and financial executive; b. Woodbury, N.J., June 20, 1931; s. Arthur Adelbert and Esther Augusta (Fosdick) N.; m. Cristina Archila, Nov. 10, 1961 (div.); children: Robert Arthur, Phillip Adam; m. Julie Ann Ebers, Nov. 23, 1974; 1 child, William Savidge. A.B., Cornell U., 1953, B.P.E., 1954, LL.B., 1956, LL.D., 1969. Bar: N.Y. 1958. Asst. to chmn. bd. Internat. Basic Economy Corp., N.Y.C., 1958-59, v.p. S.Am., 1960-64; v.p. adminstrn., corp. sec. Seaboard World Airlines, Inc., Jamaica, N.Y., 1964-77, sr. v.p., dir., 1977-80; v.p. adminstrn. Flying Tiger Lines, 1980-81; sr. v.p. Vanguard Ventures, Inc., N.Y.C., 1982-85; pres. Icarus, Inc., Lake Success, N.Y., 1985-87; chmn. Greenway Capital Corp., N.Y.C., 1991-95. Mem. coun. Cornell U.; trustee Blair Acad., 1993—. Served to capt. USAF, 1956-58. Mem. Phi Delta Phi, Psi Upsilon. Home: Arreton Rd Princeton NJ 08540 Office: 45 Broadway 19th Fl New York NY 10006-3007

NEFF, ROBERT CLARK, lawyer; b. St. Marys, Ohio, Feb. 11, 1921; s. Homer Armstrong and Irene (McCulloch) N.; m. Betty Baker, July 3, 1954 (dec.); children: Cynthia Lee Neff Schifer, Robert Clark, Abigail Lynn (dec.); m. Helen Picking, July 24, 1975. BA, Coll. Wooster, 1943; postgrad. U. Mich., 1946-47; LLB, Ohio No. U., 1950. Bar: Ohio 1950, U.S. Dist. Ct. (no. dist.) Ohio 1978. pvt. practice law, Bucyrus, Ohio, 1950—; law dir. City of Bucyrus, 1962-95. Chmn. blood program Crawford County (Ohio) unit ARC, 1955-89; life mem. adv. bd. Salvation Army, 1962—; clk. of session 1st Presbyterian Ch., Bucyrus, 1958—; bd. dirs. Bucyrus Area Cmty. Found, Crawford County Bd. Mental Retardation and Devel. Disabilities, 1977-82 . With USNR, World War II; comdr. Res. ret. Recipient "Others" plaque for 30 yrs. adv. bd. svc. Salvation Army, Ohio No. U. Coll. Law Alumni award for cmty. svc. Mem. Ohio Bar Assn., Crawford County Bar Assn., Naval Res. Assn., Ret. Officers Assn., Am. Legion, Bucyrus Area C. of C. (past bd. dirs., Outstanding Citizen award, 1973, Bucyrus Citizen of Yr., 1981). Republican. Clubs: Kiwanis (life mem., past pres.), Masons. Home: 1085 Mary Ann Ln # 406 Bucyrus OH 44820-0406 Office: 840 S Sandusky Ave Box 406 Bucyrus OH 44820-0406

NEFF, ROBERT MATTHEW, lawyer; b. Huntington, Ind., Mar. 26, 1955; s. Robert Eugene and Ann (Bash) N.; m. Lee Ann Loving, Aug. 23, 1980; children: Alexandra, Graydon, Philip. BA in English, DePauw U., 1977; JD, Ind. U., Indpls., 1980. Bar: Ind. 1980, U.S. Dist. Ct. (so. dist.) Ind. 1980, U.S. Supreme Ct., 1993. Assoc. Krieg, DeVault, Alexander & Capehart, Indpls., 1980-85, ptnr., 1986-88; ptnr. Baker & Daniels, Indpls., 1988-92; of counsel, 1993—; dept. to chmn. Fed. Housing Fin. Bd., Washington, 1992-93; pres., CEO Circle Investors, Inc., Indpls., 1993—, also bd. dirs.; mem. faculty Grad. Sch. of Banking of South, 1988-90; chmn. Liberty Bankers Life Ins. Co., 1995—. Exec. editor Ind. Law Rev., 1979-80. Participant Lacy Exec. Leadership Conf., Indpls., 1985-86; trustee DePauw U., 1977-80. Mem. Ind. Bar Assn. (chmn. corps. banking and bus. law sect. 1987-88), ABA (chmn. bus. law com. young lawyers div. 1988-90, mem. banking law com. 1990-92), DePauw Alumni Assn. (bd. dirs. 1982-88), Phi Kappa Psi, Phi Beta Kappa. Avocations: tae kwon do, golf. Home: 6455 N Olney St Indianapolis IN 46220-4436 Office: Circle Investors Inc 251 N Illinois St Ste 1680 Indianapolis IN 46204 also: Baker and Daniels 300 N Meridian St Indianapolis IN 46204-1755

NEFF, ROBERT WILBUR, academic administrator, educator; b. Lancaster, Pa., June 16, 1936; s. Wilbur Hildebr and Hazel Margaret (Martin) N.; m. Dorothy Rosewarne, Aug. 16, 1959; children: Charles Scott, Heather Lynn. BS, Pa. State U., 1958; BD, Yale Div. Sch., 1961, MA, 1963, PhD, 1969; DD, Juniata Coll., 1978, Manchester Coll., 1979; DHL, Bridgewater Coll., 1979. Asst. prof. Bridgewater Coll., 1964-65; mem. faculty dept. Bibl. studies Bethany Theol. Sem., 1965-77, prof., 1973-77; gen. sec. Ch. of the Brethren, Elgin, Ill., 1978-86; pres. Juniata Coll., 1986—; mem. faculty North Park Sem., No. Bapt. Sem., Theol. Coll. No. Nigeria; bd. dirs. Mellon Bank (Ctrl.) Nat. Assn., exec. com., 1989, chair exec. com., 1993, chair CRA com., 1994—; mem. pres.'s com. NCAA, 1996—. Mem. governing bd. Nat. Coun. Chs. of Christ, 1976-86, mem. exec. com., 1979-86; mem. Mid-East panel, 1980, 2d v.p., 1985-86; mem. ctrl. com. World Coun. Chs., 1983-92; rep. Assembly of World Coun. Chs., 1983, mem. exec. com. on interch. rels., 1980-84, mem. del. to China, 1981, chmn. presdl. panel, 1982-84; bd. dirs. Bethany Theol. Sem., 1978-86; campaign chmn. United Way, Huntington County, 1989; chair higher edn. com. Ch. of Brethren, 1993—. Danforth fellow, 1958-69. Mem. Soc. Bibl. Lit., Soc. Old Testament Study, Chgo. Soc. Bibl. Rsch., Soc. Values in Higher Edn., Coun. Ind. Colls. (nat. bd. dirs. 1991-94, treas. 1995—), Pa. Coun. Ind. Colls. and Univs. (exec. com. 1988-90, 92—, chair ann. conf. nominating com. 1993-94), Mid Atlantic Athletic Conf. (sec., mem. exec. com. 1994—). Democrat. Home: 2201 Washington St Huntingdon PA 16652-9762 Office: Juniata Coll 1700 Moore St Huntingdon PA 16652-2119

NEFF, THOMAS JOSEPH, executive search firm executive; b. Easton, Pa., Oct. 2, 1937; s. John Wallace and Elizabeth Ann (Dougherty) N.; m. Susan Culver Paull, Nov. 26, 1971 (dec.); children: David Andrew, Mark Gregory, Scott Dougherty; m. Sarah Brown Hallingby, Jan. 20, 1989; stepchildren: Brooke, Bailey. BS in Indsl. Engring., Lafayette Coll., 1959; MBA, Lehigh U., 1961. Assoc. McKinsey & Co., Inc., N.Y.C. and Australia, 1963-66; dir. mktg. planning Trans-World Airlines, N.Y.C., 1966-69; pres. Hosp. Data Scis., Inc., N.Y.C., 1969-74; prin. Booz, Allen & Hamilton, Inc., N.Y.C., 1974-76; regional ptnr. Spencer Stuart, Inc., N.Am., 1976-79; bd. dirs. Spencer Stuart & Assocs., N.Y.C., 1976-79, pres., 1979—, also bd. dirs.; bd. dirs. Lord Abbett & Co. Mut. Funds, Affiliated Fund; chmn. Brunswick Sch. Trustee Lafayette Coll. Served with U.S. Army, 1961-63. Mem. Links Club, Sky Club, Racquet and Tennis Club, Blind Brook Club, Quogue (N.Y.) Beach Club, Quogue Field Club, Round Hill Club, Mill Reef Club, Coral Beach Club. Republican. Roman Catholic. Home: 25 Midwood Rd Greenwich CT 06830-3807 Office: Spencer Stuart & Assocs Park Ave Plz 277 Park Ave New York NY 10172

NEFF, WALTER PERRY, financial consultant; b. Madison, Wis., Apr. 2, 1927; s. Ezra Eugene and Ruth (Perry) N.; m. Diane Michele Dubois, Mar. 12, 1963; children: Christopher (dec.), Taylor E., Stewart P. (by previous marriage), Michael W.P., Laura D. B.A., Williams Coll., 1950; LL.B., U. Wis., 1954; grad. advanced mgmt. program, Harvard U., 1969. Bar: Wis. 1954. Practiced in Madison, 1954-57; with Chem. Bank N.Y. Trust Co. (now Chem. Bank), N.Y.C., 1957-71; v.p. personal trust dept. Chem. Bank N.Y. Trust Co. (now Chem. Bank), 1965-68, sr. v.p., head fiduciary adminstrn. dept., 1968-71; exec. v.p. Chem. Bank, N.Y.C., 1971-73; sr. operating officer, adminstrv. head trust and investment Chem. Bank, 1973-82; fin. cons., 1983—; bd. dirs. Petroleum & Resources Corp., Balt., Adams Express Corp., Balt.; fin. dir. Manulife, Toronto; dir. Vista Mutual Funds; police justice Village of Centre Island, Oyster Bay, N.Y., 1965-74. Served with USNR, 1945-46. Mem. N.Y. State Bankers Assn. (exec. com. trust div.), Seawanhaka Corinthian Yacht Club (former commodore) (Oyster Bay), Royal Bermuda Yacht Club, Ekwanok Country Club (Manchester, Vt.), Phi Alpha Delta, Psi Upsilon. Home and Office: Holden Hill Rd Weston VT 05161

NEFT, DAVID SAMUEL, marketing professional; b. N.Y.C., Jan. 9, 1937; s. Louis and Sue (Horowitz) N.; m. Naomi Silver, May 31, 1964; children: Michael Louis, Deborah Isabel. BA, Columbia U., 1957, MBA, 1959, PhD, 1962. Dir. info. pub. Info. Concepts, Inc., N.Y.C., 1965-68, treas., chief exec. officer, 1968-70; gen. mgr. Sports Illustrated Enterprises, N.Y.C., 1970-73; pres. Sports Products Inc., Ridgefield, Conn., 1973-76; chief statistician Louis Harris and Assocs., N.Y.C., 1963-65, sr. v.p., 1977-78, exec. v.p., chief exec. officer, 1978-85; dir. research Gannett Co., Inc., N.Y.C., 1985-90, v.p. rsch., 1990—; cons. Fed. Energy Adminstrn., Washington, 1973-75. Author: Statistical Analysis for Areal Distributions, 1966; editor: The Baseball Encyclopedia, 1969; author (with others) The World Book of Odds, 1978, The Sports Encyclopedia: Baseball, 1974, 76-77, 81-82, 85, 87-89, 90—, The Sports Encyclopedia: Pro Football, 1974, 76, 78, 83, 87, 88-89, 90—, Pro Football: The Early Years, 1978, 83, 87, The World Series, 1976, 79, 86, The Sports Encyclopedia: Pro Basketball, 1975, 89, 90-91, All-Sports World Record Book, 1974, 75, 76, The Scrapbook History of Pro Football, 1976, 77, 79, The Scrapbook History of Baseball, 1975, The Notre Dame Football Scrapbook, 1977, The Ohio State Football Scrapbook, 1977, The University of Michigan Football Scrapbook, 1978, The Football Encyclopedia, 1991, 94; contbr. articles to profl. and acad. jours. Served with U.S. Army, 1961-63. Mem. Am. Assn. Pub. Opinion Rsch., Profl. Football Rsch. Assn. (v.p. 1985-87), Soc. for Am. Baseball Rsch. Jewish. Home: 525 E 86th St New York NY 10028-7512

NEGELE, JOHN WILLIAM, physics educator, consultant; b. Cleve., Apr. 18, 1944; s. Charles Frederick and Virgil Lea (Wettich) N.; m. Rose Anne Meeks, June 18, 1967; Janette Andrea, Julia Elizabeth. B.S., Purdue U., 1965; Ph.D., Cornell U., 1969. Research fellow Niels Bohr Inst., Copenhagen, 1969-70; vis. asst. prof. MIT, Cambridge, 1970-71, faculty mem., 1971—, prof. physics, 1979—, William A. Coolidge prof., 1991—, assoc. dir. Ctr. for Theoretical Physics, 1988-89, dir. Ctr. for Theoretical Physics, 1989—; cons. Los Alamos Sci. Lab., Brookhaven Nat. Lab., Lawrence Livermore Nat. Lab., Oak Ridge Nat. Lab.; mem. physics div. rev. com. Argonne Nat. Lab., (Ill.), 1977-83; mem. nuclear sci. div. rev. com. Lawrence Berkeley Lab., (Calif.), 1982—; mem. adv. bd., steering com. Inst. for Theoretical Physics, U. Calif.-Santa Barbara, 1982-86; mem. adv. bd. inst. for Nuclear Theory U. Washington, 1990—, chair 1992-94; program adv. com. Tandem Van de Graaff Accelerator, Brookhaven Nat. Lab., 1977-78, Bates Linear Accelerator, 1977-80, Los Alamos Meson Prodn. Facility, 1986-89, Brookhaven Alternating Gradient Synchraton, 1987-90. Author: Quantum Many Particle Systems, 1987; contbr. articles to profl. jours.; editor: Advances in Nuclear Physics, 1977—. Grantee NSF, 1965-69; grantee Danforth Found., 1965-69, Woodrow Wilson Found., 1965, Alfred P. Sloan Found., 1979, Japan Soc. for Promotion Sci., 1981, John Simon Guggenheim Found., 1982. Fellow Am. Phys. Soc. (exec. com. 1982-84, program com. 1980-82, editorial bd. Phys. Rev. 1980-82, exec. com. topical group on computational physics 1992-93, chair divsn. of computational physics 1992-93, exec. com. 1992-94, Bonner prize com. 1984-85), AAAS (nominating com. 1987-91, mem. physics sect. com. 1991—), Fedn. Am. Scientists. Home: 70 Buckman Dr Lexington MA 02173-6000 Office: MIT Dept Physics 6-308 77 Massachusetts Ave Cambridge MA 02139-4301

NEGLIA, JOHN PETER, chemical engineer, environmental scientist; b. Passaic, N.J., Dec. 30, 1957; s. Anthony John and Claire Ann (Graglia) N.; m. Deborah Ann Rean, Apr. 5, 1981; children: Kimberlee Claire, Anthony Richard. BSChemE, N.J. Inst. of Tech., 1981, MS in Environ. Sci., 1992. Cert. hazardous materials mgr. Process engr. Am. Cyanamid Co., Wayne, N.J., 1981-85; mfg./environ. mgr. Powder Tech. Co., Fairfield, N.J., 1985-86; facility/environ. engring. mgr. Curtiss Wright Fligh Systems Inc., Fairfield, 1986-89; plant supt. Dubois Chem. Divsn. of Molson Breweries, East Rutherford, N.J., Toronto, 1989-92; mgr. environ. and safety engring. Becton Dickinson and Co., Franklin Lakes, N.J., 1992—; adj. asst. prof. N.J. Inst. of Tech., Fairleigh Dickinson Sch. of Continuing Edn. Author: Encyclopedia of Environmental (vol. 5), 1992, Control Technology (vol. 8), 1992; contbr. articles to profl. jours. Vice chmn. Hazardous Material Control Bd., Clifton, N.J., 1990—; chmn. of edn. subcom. Local Emergency Planning Com., Clifton, 1990—. Mem. AIChe, Am. Soc. of Safety Engrs., Water Pollution Control Fedn. Republican. Roman Catholic. Avocations: music, recreational sports, reading. Home: 9 Glenwood St Clifton NJ 07013 Office: Becton Dickinson & Co 1 Becton Dr Franklin Lakes NJ 07417

NEGREPONTIS, MICHAEL (TIMOTHY), bishop; b. Athens, Greece, June 7, 1930; s. Anastasios and Maria Negrepontis. Sacred Theology, U. Thessalonika, Greece; M.Div., Holy Cross Greek Orthodox Theol. Sch., Boston; B.A. with honors, Hellenic Coll. Ordained deacon Greek Orthodox Ch., 1950, ordained priest, 1952. Pastor St. Nicholas Ch., Bethlehem, Pa., 1955-61, Parish of Sts. Constantine and Helen, Middletown, Ohio, 1961-62; pastor Holy Trinity Ch., London, Ont., Can., 1962-67, Harrisburg, Pa.; pastor Dionysios Ch., Kansas City, Kans., St. Barbara; dean Holy Trinity Archdiocesan Cathedral, N.Y.C., until 1969; spl. asst. to chancellor and personnel dir. archdiocesan staff Archdiocesan Hdqrs., N.Y.C., from 1969; pastor St. Anargyroi Ch., Marlboro, Mass., until 1973, Ch. Holy Ascension, Fairview, N.J.; elevated to Titular Bishop of Pamphilos, 1973, consecrated bishop, 1974; bishop Greek Orthodox Diocese in S.Am., 1974-79; aux. bishop to the Archbishop 7th Archdiocesan Dist. Detroit, 1979; bishop Greek Orthodox Diocese of Detroit, 1979—; apptd. pastor Greek Orthodox Communities of Republic of Panama. Decorated Grand Master of Order of Vasco Nuñez de Balboa, Republic of Panama; Grand Taxiarch, Order

Orthodox Crusaders of Holy Sepulcher. Address: 19405 Renfrew Rd Detroit MI 48221-1835

NEGRON, JAIME, academic administrator; b. San Juan, P.R., Dec. 23, 1939; came to U.S., 1952; s. Rito and Tomasa (Otero) N.; m. Barbara Charlotte Stovall, Nov. 5, 1959; children: Jeannette Michelle, Victoria Frances. BA in Econs., Howard U., 1987. Lic. realtor. Chief receiving & shipping Am. Univ., Washington, 1960-62; book dept. mgr. Am. U., Washington, 1968-71; bookstore mgr. Follett Corp., Chgo., 1962-68, Cath. U., Washington, 1971-74; dir. Howard U. stores Howard Univ., Washington, 1974-87; dir. aux. enterprises Howard U., Washington, 1987-91; real estate agt. Shannon & Luchs, Vienna, Va., 1988-92; asst. dir. aux. enterprises DeKalb Coll., Atlanta, 1992—; cons. U. Del., Newark, 1988, Wesley Sem., Washington, 1984, R.R. Moton Meml. Inst., N.Y.C., 1974-79. Active Vienna Jaycees, 1970-80. With USN, 1958-60. Mem. Middle Atlantic Coll. Stores (pres. 1984), Nat. Assn. Coll. Stores, Nat. Bd. Realtors, Va. Bd. Realtors. Episcopalian. Avocation: dancing. Office: DeKalb Coll 555 N Indian Creek Dr Bldg S Clarkston GA 30021-2361

NEGROPONTE, JOHN DIMITRI, diplomat; b. London, July 21, 1939; s. Dimitri John and Catherine (Coumantaros) N.; m. Diana Mary Villiers, Dec. 14, 1976; children: Marina, Alexandra, John, George, Sophia. B.A., Yale U., 1960. Commd. fgn. service officer Dept. of State, 1960; vice consul Hong Kong, 1961-63; 2d sec. Saigon, 1964-68; mem. U.S. Del. to Paris Peace Talks on Viet-Nam, 1968-69, Nat. Security Council Staff, 1970-73; polit. counselor Quito, Ecuador, 1973-75; consul gen. Thessaloniki, Greece, 1975-77; dep. asst. sec. of state for oceans and fisheries affairs Washington, 1977-79; dep. asst. sec. for East Asian and Pacific affairs Dept. State, Washington, 1980-81; U.S. amb. to Honduras, 1981-85, asst. sec. for oceans and internat. environ. and sci. affairs, 1985-87; dep. asst. Pres. for Nat. Security Affairs, 1987-89; U.S. amb. to Mexico, 1989-93, U.S. amb. to The Philippines, 1993—. Mem. Am. Fgn. Service Assn., Council on Fgn. Relations. Greek Orthodox. Office: US Embassy APO AP 96440

NEHAMAS, ALEXANDER, philosophy educator; b. Athens, Greece, Mar. 22, 1946; came to U.S., 1964; s. Albert and Christine (Yannuli) N.; m. Susan Glimcher, June 22, 1983; 1 child, Nicholas Albert Glimcher. BA, Swarthmore Coll., 1967; PhD, Princeton U., 1971, D in Philosophy (hon.) Athens, 1993. Asst., then assoc. prof. philosophy U. Pitts., 1971-81, prof., 1981-86; prof. philosophy U. Pa., 1986-90; vis. prof. Princeton U., N.J., 1978-79, 89, Edmund Carpenter prof. humanities, prof. philosophy and comparative lit., 1990—, chair humanities coun., 1994—, chmn. program in Hellenic studies, 1994—; Mills vis. prof. U. Calif., Berkeley, 1983, Sather vis. prof., 1993; vis. prof. U. Calif., Santa Cruz, 1988; bd. dir. Princeton Univ. Press; bd. trustees Nat. Humanities Ctr. Author: Nietzsche: Life as Literature, 1985; translator: Plato's Symposium, 1989, Plato's Phaedrus, 1995; co-editor: Aristotle's Rhetoric: Philosophical Essays, 1994; contbr. articles to profl. jours.; mem. editorial bd. Am. Philos. Quar., 1981-86, History of Philosophy Quar., 1983-88, Ancient Philosophy, 1984—, Jour. Modern Greek Studies, 1986—, Arion, 1989—, Philosophy and Lit., 1989—, Philosophy and Phenomenological Rsch., 1990—. Recipient Lindback Found. Teaching award, U. Pa., 1989; Guggenheim fellow 1983; NEH grantee, 1978. Mem. MLA, Am. Philos. Assn. (chmn. program 1982-83, exec. com. 1990-92), Modern Greek Studies Assn. (exec. com. 1983-89), Am. Soc. Aesthetics, North Am. Nietzsche Soc. (exec. com. 1988-91), Phi Beta Kappa (vis. scholar 1995). Office: Princeton U Dept Philosophy Princeton NJ 08544

NEHER, LESLIE IRWIN, engineer, former air force officer; b. Marion, Ind., Sept. 15, 1906; s. Irvin Warner and Lelia Myrtle (Irwin) N.; m. Lucy Marion Price; 1 child, David Price; m. Cecelia Marguerite Hayworth, June 14, 1956; BS in Elec. Engring., Purdue U., 1930. Registered profl. engr., Ind., N.Mex. Engr. high voltage rsch., 1930-32; engr. U.S. Army, Phila., 1933-37; heating engr. gas utility, 1937-40; commd. 2d lt. U.S. Army, 1929, advanced through grades to Col., 1947; dir. tng., Tng. Command, Heavy Bombardment, Amarillo (Tex.) AFB, 1942-44; dir. mgmt. tng., 15th AF, Colorado Springs, Colo., 1945-46; mgr. Korea Electric Power Co., Seoul, 1946-47, ret., 1960; engr. Neher Engring. Co., Gas City, Ind., 1960—; researcher volcanic materials, 1948-49. Chmn. Midwest Indsl. Gas Coun., 1969; historian Grant County, Ind., 1982-95. Named Outstanding Liaison Officer, Air Force Acad., 1959; Ambassador for Peace, Republic of Korea, 1977; recipient Republic of Korea Svc. medal, 1977. Mem. Ind. Soc. Profl. Engrs. (Outstanding Engr. 1982, Engr. of Yr. Ind. 1986), Nat. Soc. Profl. Engrs., Midwest Indsl. Gas Assn. (chmn. 1969), Am. Assn. of Retired Persons (pres. Grant County chpt. 1986, 87, 89, 90, dir. dist. 5 1992-93), NAUS (pres. Grissom chpt. 1992—). Republican. Methodist. Lodge: Kiwanis (Disting. sect. 1979-85, lt. gov. 1964; Disting. Svc. award 1962).

NEHER, TIMOTHY PYPER, cable company executive; b. Jersey City, Sept. 9, 1947; s. Harry Paul and Alice (Pyper) N.; m. Mary Ann King, June 13, 1970; children: Amy, Victoria. BA in Math., Cornell U., 1969; MBA in Fin., Boston U., 1971. Loan officer Bank New Eng., Boston, 1971-74; regional mgr. Continental Cablevision, Boston, 1974-77, v.p., gen. mgr., 1977-80, v.p., treas., 1980-82, exec. v.p., 1982-85, pres., chief operating officer, 1985-90, vice chmn., 1991—, also bd. dirs.; bd. dirs. Turner Broadcasting Inc., Atlanta, Viewers' Choice Network Inc., N.Y.C. Mem. Weston Golf Club (Mass.), Boston Racquet Club, Old Marsh Golf Club, Lost Tree Golf Club (North Palm Beach, Fla.), Oyster Harbors Club (Osterville, Mass.). Republican. Office: Continental Cablevision Inc 5 Niblick Rd Enfield CT 06082-4443

NEHLS, ROBERT LOUIS, JR., school system administrator; b. Berkeley, Calif., Dec. 27, 1944; s. Robert Louis and Inda May (Kean) N.; m. Diana Jean Smith, June 17, 1967; 1 child, Patrick Robert. AA, Coll. Marin, 1965; BS, San Jose State U., 1967, MA, 1976; EdD, U. San Francisco, 1991. Cert. tchr., sch. adminstr., Calif. Tchr. Diablo Valley Coll., Pleasant Hill, Calif., 1979-86; acct. Kelly and Tama, CPAs, Walnut Creek, Calif., 1978-79; tchr. Pleasanton (Calif.) Unified Sch. Dist., 1970-78, 79-81, dir. fiscal svcs., 1981-83; dep. supt. San Leandro (Calif.) Unified Sch. Dist., 1983-87, 90—; asst. supt. Acalanes Union High Sch. Dist., Lafayette, Calif., 1987-89; supt. Orinda (Calif.) Union Sch. Dist., 1989-90; exec. adv. com. Calif. Found. Improvement of Employee/Employer Relationships, Sacramento, 1992—. Contbr. articles to profl. jours. Mem. Assn. Calif. Sch. Adminstrs. (comptroller 1992-95, pres. 1996), Calif. Assn. Sch. Bus. Ofcls. (bd. dirs. no. sect. 1984-89), No. Calif. Sch. Bus. Ofcls. (past pres.), Acad. of Sci., Phi Kappa Phi. Avocations: fishing, skiing. Home: 1004 Leland Dr Lafayette CA 94549-4130 Office: San Leandro Unified Sch Dist 14735 Juniper St San Leandro CA 94579-1222

NEHMER, STANLEY, economics consultant; b. N.Y.C., Dec. 8, 1920; s. Alexander and Laura (Kessler) N.; m. Phyllis Fleishman, Nov. 30, 1946; children: Sheryl Rae, Jonathan Craig. BSS, CCNY, 1941; MA, Columbia U., 1942; postgrad., George Washington U., 1943-44, Am. U., 1946-47. Faculty CCNY, 1941-42; with OSS, 1942-45; economist Dept. State, 1945-57; dep. dir. Office Internat. Resources, Washington, 1961-64, dir., 1964-65; dep. asst. sec. for resources Dept. Commerce, 1965-73; sr. economist IBRD, 1957-61; prin. and dir. econ. cons. services Wolf & Co., Washington, 1973-78; pres. Econ. Cons. Services Inc., Washington, 1978-88, chmn., 1988-95; chmn. emeritus, 1995—; adj. prof. Am. bus. history Am. U., 1948-63; U.S. rep. commodities com. UN Conf. on Trade and Devel., Geneva, 1965; chmn. Interagy. Textile Adminstrv. Com., 1965-72; chmn. U.S. rep. OECD Textiles Com., 1971-73; mem. U.S. Oil Import Appeals Bd., 1965-73; chmn. Com. for Implementation of Textile Agreements, 1972-73; alt. mem. Oil Policy Com., 1970-73; mem. U.S. Govt. Industry Sector Adv. Com. for Trade Negotiations, 1976-88, Treasury Dept. Adv. Com. on Comml. Ops. of Customs Svc., 1988-92. Contbr. to: Ency. Americana, Ency. Brit., U.S. Competiteveness in the World Economy, 1985. Served with AUS, 1943-45. Recipient Commendable Service award Dept. State, 1956, Superior Honor award, 1964; certificate appreciation Sec. Commerce, 1967; Gold medal Dept. Commerce, 1971; N.Y. Bd. Trade Ann. Textile award, 1972; No. Textile Assn. Distinguished Service award, 1973. Fellow Am. Council Learned Socs., mem. Nat. Economists Club, Am. Econ. Assn. Home: 15100 Interlachen Dr Silver Spring MD 20906-5611 also: 2600 S Ocean Blvd Boca Raton FL 33432 Office: 1225 19th St NW Washington DC 20036-2411

NEHRA, GERALD PETER, lawyer; b. Detroit, Mar. 25, 1940; s. Joseph P. and Jeanette M. (Bauer) N.; children: Teresa, Patricia; m. Peggy Jensen, Sept. 12, 1987. B.I.E., Gen. Motors Inst., Flint, Mich., 1962; J.D., Detroit Coll. Law, 1970. Bar: Mich. 1970, U.S. Dist. Ct. (ea. dist.) Mich. 1970, N.Y. 1972, U.S. Dist. Ct. (so. dist.) N.Y. 1972, U.S. Dist. Ct. (no. dist.) N.Y. 1976, U.S. Ct. Appeals (6th cir.) 1978, Colo. 1992. Successively engr., supr., gen. supr. Gen. Motors Corp., 1958-67; mktg. rep., to regional counsel IBM Corp., 1967-79; v.p., gen. counsel Church & Dwight Co., Inc. 1979-82; dep. chief atty-Amway Corp., 1982-83, dep. gen. counsel, 1983-92; dir. legal div., 1989-91, sec. and dir. corp. law, 1991-92; v.p. gen. counsel Fuller Brush, Bolder, Colo., 1991-92; pvt. practice, 1992—; adj. instr. Dale Carnegie Courses, 1983-91. Recipient Outstanding Contbn. award Am. Cancer Soc., 1976. Mem. Mich. Bar Assn., Colo. Bar Assn., N.Y. State Bar Assn., ABA. Contbr. chpt. to book. Home and Office: 1710 Beach St Muskegon MI 49441

NEHRBASS, SETH MARTIN, patent lawyer; b. Lafayette, La., Nov. 10, 1960; s. Neil Martin and Janet (Himbert) N.; m. Isabel Hortelano, July 10, 1982 (div. Feb. 1993); children: Gabriel, Fabian. Student, U. Catholique de l'Ouest, Angers, France, 1980, U. Paul Valéry, Montpellier, France, 1981; BS in Physics summa cum laude, U. Southwe. La., 1982; JD cum laude, Loyola U., 1990. Bar: U.S. Patent & Trademark Office 1984, La. 1990, U.S. Dist. Ct. (ea., mid., and we. dists.) La. 1990, U.S. Ct. Appeals (5th and fed. cirs.) 1990; cert. notary public, La. Patent examiner U.S. Patent & Trademark Office, 1982-84; patent agt. with law firm New Orleans, 1986-87; assoc. Pravel, Hewitt, Kimball & Krieger, New Orleans, 1987—; judge practice round moot ct. teams Loyola Law Sch., 1992—; preparer questions patent bar exam PTO Q & A Bd., 1992-93; presenter in field. Contbr. articles to profl. jours. Den leader 2d grade Cub Scouts, Boy Scouts Am., Lusher Sch., Audubon Dist., 1991-92, 3d grade, 1994-95, asst. den leader 3d grade, 1992-93, 4th grade, 1993-94; soccer coach Carrollton Booster Club, New Orleans, 1993—, Lakeview Soccer Club, New Orleans, 1995—. Recipient Hornbook award West Pub. Co., 1986-87, 87-88, Corpus Juris Secundum award, 1986-87, Am. Jurisprudence awards (2), 1986; scholar La. State U. Alumni Fedn., 1978, Coun. Devel. French La./French Govt., 1980-81, Loyola Law Sch., 1986. Mem. ABA (sect. law, sci., tech. 1988-91, law student divsn. liaison patent trademark and copyright law 1988-90, intellectual property law sect. 1988—, student law com. 1989—, chmn. spl. com. drug crisis 1990-93, co-chmn. ann. meeting arrangements com. 1993-94, internat. treaties and laws com. 1994—), Am. Intellectual Property Law Assn. (ADR com., internat. and fgn. law com., patent law com. 1994—), La. State Bar Assn. (internat. law sect. 1992-94), New Orleans Bar Assn. (interim chmn. ad hoc com. drug crisis 1991-92, chmn. charter mem. intellectual property law com. 1991-95, chmn. law related edn. com., 1995—), Loyola Law Sch. Moot Ct. Alumni Assn., Sigma Pi Sigma, Pi Delta Phi, Alpha Sigma Nu. Democrat. Roman Catholic. Avocations: gardening, dancing, traveling, hunting, fishing. Office: Pravel Hewitt Kimball & Krieger PO Box 24788 New Orleans LA 70184-4788

NEHRING, LISA MARIE, secondary school educator; b. Charleston, S.C., June 30, 1966; d. Roy Andrew and Lilian (Nunnen) Olson; m. C. Mark Nehring, June 15, 1991. BA in Math., Lake Forest Coll., 1988; MEd in Adminstrn. summa cum laude, Nat.-Louis U., 1994. Cert. tchr., Ill.; cert. supr. adminstrn., Ill. H.S. math. tchr. Wykeham Rise, Washington, Conn., 1988-89, Wamogo Regional H.S., Litchfield, Conn., 1989-90; math. tchr. Waukegan (Ill.) H.S., 1990-94, Adlai E. Stevenson H.S., Lincolnshire, Ill., 1994—. Mem. Nat. Coun. Tchrs. Math., Ill. Coun. Tchrs. Math. Avocations: skiing, tennis, travel, dance. Office: Adlai E Stevenson HS Two Stevenson Dr Lincolnshire IL 60069

NEHRT, LEE CHARLES, management educator; b. Baldwin, Ill., Sept. 12, 1926; s. Martin William and Amanda Fredarika (Tillock) N.; m. Ardith Ann Saltzman, Mar. 26, 1952; children: Chadwick Charles, Philip Lee, Dana Ann. BS, USCG Acad., 1949; certificat d'Etudes Politiques, U. Paris, 1955; MBA, Columbia U., 1956, PhD, 1962. Fgn. ops. supr. Atomics Internat., Canoga Park, Calif., 1956-60; prof. internat. bus. Ind. U., 1962-65, 67-69, 71-74; Ford Found. adv. to minister planning, economy and industry Tunisia, 1965-67; chief adv. group U. Dacca, E. Pakistan, 1969-71; R.P. Clinton prof. internat. mgmt. Wichita (Kans.) State U., 1974-78; pres. World Trade Inst., N.Y.C., 1978-81; Owens-Ill. prof. internat. mgmt. Ohio State U., Columbus, 1981-86; cons. UN, World Bank, advisor Ministry Planning Govt. Indonesia, 1987-89; dir., curator The Blacksmith Mus., 1991-92. Author monographs, books, papers, reports in field. Served to lt. (j.g.) USCG, 1949-53. Mem. Acad. Internat. Bus. (pres. 1972-74, dean fellows 1978-81), Soc. Internat. Devel. (gov. 1968-71).

NEIDELL, MARTIN H., lawyer; b. Bklyn., Apr. 5, 1946; s. Sidney B. and Sophie (Goldstein) N.; m. Suzan C. Rucker, June 23, 1968; children: Michael, Sari. BA magna cum laude, Lehigh U., 1968; JD cum laude, NYU, 1971. Bar: N.Y. 1972, U.S. Dist. Ct. (ea. and so. dists.) N.Y. 1973, U.S. Ct. Appeals (2d cir.) 1973. Law clk. to presiding justice U.S. Dist. Ct. (ea. dist.) N.Y., Bklyn., 1971-73; assoc. Stroock & Stroock & Lavan, N.Y.C., 1973-79, ptnr., 1980—; sec. Page Am. Group, Hackensack, N.J., 1983—. Editor NYU Law Rev., 1971. Trustee North Shore Synagogue, Syosset, N.Y., 1984-90. Mem. ABA. Office: Stroock & Stroock & Lavan 7 Hanover Sq New York NY 10004-2616

NEIDERT, KALO EDWARD, accountant, educator; b. Safe, Mo., Sept. 1, 1918; s. Edward Robert and Margaret Emma (Kinsey) N.; m. Stella Mae Vest, June 22, 1952; children—Edward, Karl, David, Wayne, Margaret. B.S. in Bus. Adminstrn. with honors, Washington U., St. Louis, 1949, M.S. in Bus. Adminstrn, 1950; postgrad., U. Minn., 1950-54. CPA, Nev. Mem. faculty U. Minn., 1950-54; mem. faculty U. Miss., 1954-57, U. Tex., Austin, 1957-61, Gustavus Adolphus Coll., St. Peter, Minn., 1961-62; prof. acctg. and info. systems U. Nev., 1962-90, prof. emeritus, 1990—; auditor Washoe County Employee Fed. Credit Union, 1969-82, dir., treas., 1982-86. Author: Statement on Auditing Procedure in Decision Tree Form, 1974. Asst. scoutmaster local Boy Scouts Am.; Bd. dirs. Tahoe Timber Trails, 1980-82, treas., 1981-82, v.p. fin., 1982-84; Bd. dirs. St. Johns Child Care Center, 1982-84; cen. com. mem. Washoe County Rep. Party, Reno, 1986-88, 90—. Mem. AICPA, Assn. System Mgmt. (treas. Reno chpt. 1984—), Am. Acctg. Assn., Am. Econ. Assn., Am. Fin. Assn., Fin. Mgmt. Assn., Nev. Soc. CPAs, Western Fin. Assn., Oddfellows, Beta Alpha Psi, Beta Gamma Sigma. Presbyterian. Office: U Nev Coll Bus Adminstrn Reno NV 89557 *I am the descendent of a second generation American. In addition I was raised on a farm in rural America. Early in life, I learned that achievements come only with hard work and taking advantage of each opportunity that comes along, not waiting to see if there was a better opportunity around the corner. All through life this has been my philosophy; take advantage of each opportunity and work hard to make it succeed.*

NEIDHARDT, FREDERICK CARL, microbiologist; b. Phila., May 12, 1931; s. Adam Fred and Carrie (Fry) N.; m. Elizabeth Robinson, June 9, 1956 (div. Sept. 1977); children: Richard Frederick, Jane Elizabeth; m. Germaine Chipault, Dec. 3, 1977; 1 son, Marc Frederick. BA, Kenyon Coll., 1952, DSc (hon.), 1976; PhD, Harvard U., 1956; DSc (hon.), Purdue U., 1988, Umea U., 1994. Research fellow Pasteur Inst., Paris, 1956-57; H.C. Ernst research fellow Harvard Med. Sch., 1957-58, instr., then assoc., 1958-61; mem. faculty Purdue U., 1961-70, assoc. prof. then prof., assoc. head dept. biol. scis., 1965-70; mem. faculty U. Mich., Ann Arbor, 1970—, chmn. dept. microbiology and immunology, 1970-82, F.G. Novy disting. univ. prof., 1989—, assoc. dean faculty affairs, 1990-93, assoc. v.p. for rsch., 1993—; Found. for Microbiology lectr. Am. Soc. Microbiology, 1966-67; cons. Dept. Agr., 1964-65; mem. grant study panel NIH, 1965-69, 88-92; mem. commn. scholars Ill. Bd. Higher Edn., 1973-79; mem. test com. for microbiology Nat. Bd. Med. Examiners, 1975-79, chmn., 1979-83; mem. sci. adv. com. Neogen Corp., 1982-92; mem. basic energy scis. adv. com. U.S. Dept. Energy, 1994—; Wellcome vis. prof. in microbiology U. Ky., 1986. Author books and papers in field; mem. editorial bd. profl. jours. Recipient award bacteriology and immunology Eli Lilly and Co., 1966; Alexander von Humboldt Found. award for U.S. sr. scientist, 1979; NSF sr. fellow U. Copenhagen, 1968-69. Mem. Am. Soc. Microbiology (pres. 1981-82), Am. Acad. Arts and Scis., Am. Soc. Biochemistry and Molecular Biology, Am. Inst. Biol. Scis., Genetics Soc. Am., Soc. Gen. Physiology, Phi Beta Kappa, Sigma Xi. Office: U Mich Med Sch Dept Microbiology and Immunology Ann Arbor MI 48109-0620

NEIDHART, JAMES ALLEN, physician, educator; b. Steubenville, Ohio, Aug. 30, 1940; s. James Leonard and Mary Jane (Daniels) N.; m. Patricia Irene Harpkamp, Aug. 16, 1966 (div. Apr. 1985); children—James, Jeffrey, Jennifer; m. Mary Gagen, Feb. 1986; children: Andrew, Rae Ann. B.S., Union Coll., Alliance, Ohio, 1962; M.D., Ohio State U., 1966. Diplomate Am. Bd. Internal Medicine, Am. Bd. Hematology and Oncology. Intern Bronson Hosp., Kalamazoo, Mich., 1966-67; resident Ohio State U., Columbus, Ohio, 1969-71; postdoctoral fellow Coll. Medicine, Ohio State U., Columbus, 1972-74, asst. prof. medicine, 1974-78, assoc. prof., 1978-84, dir. interdisciplinary oncology unit Comprehensive Cancer Ctr., 1975-80, dep. dir. Comprehensive Cancer Ctr., 1980-84; prof. medicine U. Tex.-Houston-M.D. Anderson Hosp. and Tumor Inst., 1984-86, Hubert L. and Olive Stringer prof. oncology, 1984-86, dep. head div. medicine, 1984-86, chmn. dept. med. oncology, 1984-86; dir. Cancer Rsch. and Treatment Ctr., U. N.Mex., Albuquerque, 1986—, chief hematology and oncology, 1986-91. Contbr. chpts. to Recent Advances in Clinical Therapeutics, Clinical Immunotherapy. Former mem. bd. dirs. Am. Cancer Soc., Columbus; former v.p. Ohio Cancer Research Assocs. Served to lt. USN, 1967-69, Vietnam. Mem. Am. Soc. Hematology, Am. Soc. Clin. Oncology, Am. Assn. Cancer Research, ACP, S.W. Oncology Group, Wilderness Soc., Sierra Club. Home: 21 Rd 3285 Aztec NM 87410 Office: San Juan Regional Cancer Ctr Farmington NM 87401

NEIDICH, GEORGE ARTHUR, lawyer; b. N.Y.C., Feb. 22, 1950; s. Hyman and Rosalyn (Eisenberg) N.; m. Alene Wendrow, Jan. 10, 1982. BA, SUNY, Binghamton, 1971; JD magna cum laude, SUNY, Buffalo, 1974; MLT, Georgetown U., 1981. Bar: N.Y. 1975, D.C. 1979, U.S. Ct. Appeals (2d cir.) 1975, U.S. Dist. Ct. (we. dist.) N.Y. 1975, U.S. Tax Ct. 1976, Conn. 1990. Assoc. Runfola & Birzon, Buffalo, 1973-75, Duke, Holzman, Yaeger, & Radlin, Buffalo, 1975-77; gen. counsel subcom. on capital, investments and bus. opportunity, com. on small bus. U.S. Ho. of Reps., Washington, 1977-79, subcom. on gen. oversight, 1979-80; sr. legal advisor Task Force Product Liability and Accident Compensation, Office of Gen. Counsel, Dept. Commerce, Washington, 1980-81; assoc. Steptoe & Johnson, Washington, 1981-86, of counsel, 1986-89; gen. counsel, sr. v.p. Preferred Health Care, Ltd., Wilton, Conn. (now Value Behavioral Health, Inc.), 1989-93, COO, 1993-95, cons., 1995—; adj. prof. Georgetown U. Law Ctr., 1985-87. Author: Report on Product Liability, 1980. Contbr. articles to profl. jours. Mem. N.Y. State Bar Assn. Home: 9301 Morison Ln Great Falls VA 22066-4153 Office: PO Box 536 Great Falls VA 22066

NEIGHMOND, PATRICIA, reporter; b. Boston, Sept. 25, 1949; d. Howard Francis and Joyce (Ghiglia) N. BA, U. Md., 1971. Researcher Community Nutrition Inst., Washington, 1974-77; news reporter Sta. WPFW- FM, Washington, 1977-78; bur. chief Pacific Found., Washington, 1978-80; reporter Nat. Pub. Radio, Washington, 1981-84, editor/producer, 1984-87, reporter, 1987—; lectr. Am. Soc. of Journalists and Authors; U.S. Indo Subcommn., Bangalore, India, 1986, U.S. Inf. Agy, Recife, Sao Paulo, Brazil, 1989. Recipient George Polk award L.I. U., 1989, Best Consumer Journalism award Nat. Press Club, Washington, 1988, Radio Documentary award Pol. Inst., Washington, 1984, 87, Best Radio Documentary award Corp. for Pub. Broadcasting, 1982. Democrat. Avocation: creative writing. Office: Nat Pub Radio 635 Massachusetts Ave NW Washington DC 20001-3752

NEIKIRK, WILLIAM ROBERT, journalist; b. Irvine, Ky., Jan. 6, 1938; s. Lewis Byron and Nancy Elizabeth (Green) N.; m. Ruth Ann Clary, Sept. 10, 1960; children: Paul Gregory, John Stuart, Christa Lynn. B.A. in Journalism, U. Ky., 1960. Reporter Lexington (Ky.) Herald, 1959-60; state capital corr. AP, Frankfort, Ky., 1961-66, Baton Rouge, 1966-69; econ. corr. AP (Washington Bur.), 1970-74; nat. econ. writer Chgo. Tribune, Washington, 1974-83, White House corr., 1977, 94—, econ. columnist, 1980—, news editor Washington bur., 1983, fin. editor, 1988-91, sr. writer, 1991—. Author: The Work Revolution, 1983, Volcker: The Money Man, 1987. Recipient Beck award Chgo. Tribune, 1975, Bus. Writing award U. Mo., 1978, 80, Bus. Writing award Amos Tuck Grad. Sch. Bus., Dartmouth Coll., 1980, John Hancock Bus. Writing award Wharton Sch. Fin., U. Pa., 1979, finalist, 1990, 91, John Hancock Bus. Writing award U. Houston, 1980, Loeb Bus. Writing award UCLA Grad. Sch. Mgmt., 1979, Chgo. Headliner Club award, 1979, 84, Raymond Clapper Meml. award, 1981, Barnet Nover award, 1994, Merriman Smith award, 1995, White House Correspondents Assn. Mem. Gridiron Club. Mem. United Ch. of Christ. Home: 5121 38th St N Arlington VA 22207-1827

NEIL, FRED APPLESTEIN, public relations executive; b. Balt., Nov. 26, 1933; s. Frank and Mollie (Schapiro) Applestein; m. Sheila Tilles, Aug. 30, 1959 (div. May 1980); children: Jay Alan, Brian Mark Applestein, Gail Renee Applestein; m. Dawn Francis Fisher, July 6, 1986. BA, U. Md., 1959. News and sports editor Sta. WITH, Balt., 1959-60; dir. news and sports Sta. WCBM, Metromedia, Balt., 1960-69; press officer Mayor William Donald Schaefer, Balt., 1970-71; gen. mgr. Balt. Banners World Team Tennis League, 1971-72; pres. Fred Neil Assocs., Pub. Rels., Balt., 1972—; staff specialist pub. info. Md. Rehab. Ctr., Balt., 1980-91; owner Cruising for Mems., Ellicott City, 1987—, Dir. Office of Comm. and Community Rels., Divsn. Rehab. Svcs., Balt., 1980—; co-owner Carrolltowne Card & Gift Shop. Author: It's a Very Simple Game!, The Life and Times of Charles Eckman and More, 1995; editor, contbr. Lafayette Sq. Newsletter, 1974-82, Fed. Hill Newsletter, 1974-82, Greater Penn Ave. Newsletter, 1974-82, MPCA News Letter, 1982—, Md. Rehab. Assn. News Letter, 1985—, Front and Center newsletter, 1980-92, Rehab Digest, 1992—; contbr. articles to mags., newspapers, and newsletters. Bd. dirs. Liberty Showcase Theater, 1985-87, Howard County Summer Theatre, 1992—, pres. 1995. With U.S. Army, 1956-58. Recipient award for spot reporting Chesapeake AP, 1967, award for in-depth sports reporting, 1967, 69, Media Appreciation award U.S. Intercollegiate Lacrosse Assn., 1970, Humanitarian award Md. Rehab. Assn., 1982, Appreciation award 1986, Profl. Svc. award Md. Rehab. Counseling Assn., 1985, Ams. with Disabilities Act award The Task Force on the Rights and Empowerment of Ams. with Disabilities, 1991, Outstanding Contbns. award, 1994, Md. Gov.'s Com. on Employment of People with Disabilities Print Media award, 1996, Golden Radio Buffs' Golden Mike award, 1996. Mem. Md. Rehab. Assn. (pres. 1985, 87), Md. Press Club (pres. 1988-89, bd. dirs. 1990-91), Balt. Sports Reporters Assn. (pres. 1964), Balt. Press Reporters Assn. (pres. 1965), Mid-Atlantic Rehab. Adminstrs. Assn. (pres. 1990). Home: 4029 Pebble Branch Rd Ellicott City MD 21042-5348

NEILL, DENIS MICHAEL, government relations consulting executive; b. Grand Rapids, Mich., Apr. 27, 1943; s. Thomas Patrick and Agnes Josephine (Weber) N.; m. Mary Kathleen Golden, June 11, 1966; children: Mark, Erin. AB cum laude, St. Louis U., 1964, JD cum laude, 1967. Bar: Mo. 1967, D.C. 1969. Gen. atty. Office of Asst. Regional Counsel IRS, Newark, 1967-68; assoc. Arent, Fox, Kintner, Plotkin & Kahn, Washington, 1969-71, Morgan, Lewis & Bockius, Washington, 1971-72; atty. advisor office gen. counsel AID, Washington, 1972-73, asst. gen. counsel legis. and policy coordination, 1973-75, asst. adminstr. legis. affairs, 1975-77; sr. v.p., gen. counsel Aeromaritime Internat. Corp., Washington, 1977-80; counsel Surrey & Morse, Washington, 1980-81; sr. ptnr. Neill & Shaw, Washington, 1981-92; sr. law ptnr. Dalley, Neill, Assevero, Carroll & Nealer, Washington, 1992-93; pres. Neill & Co., Inc., Washington, 1981—. Bd. dirs. Barker Found., 1981-86, Fed. City Nat. Bank, Washington, 1987. Lt. USCG, 1968-71. Recipient Superior Unit Citation AID, 1976, Disting. Honor award, 1977. Mem. ABA, FBA, D.C. Bar Assn., Mo. Bar Assn., Nat. Security Indsl. Assn. (bd. dirs. 1982-90), Capitol Hill Club, Columbia Country Club (Chevy Chase, Md.), Jefferson Islands Club. Democrat. Home: 5945 Searl Ter Bethesda MD 20816-2022 Office: Neill & Co 5945 Searl Ter Bethesda MD 20816-2022

NEILL, RICHARD ROBERT, retired publishing company executive; b. N.Y.C., June 20, 1925; s. Robert Irving and Mildred Mary (Hall) N.; m. Patricia Mae Robinson, Dec. 27, 1952; 1 son, Robert Kenneth. A.B. summa cum laude, Princeton U., 1948; M.A., N.Y. U., 1953. With Prentice-Hall, Inc., N.Y.C. and Englewood Cliffs, N.J., 1948-85, advt. mgr., 1953-58, v.p. advt., 1958-62; pres. Executive Reports Corporation, 1962-85, ret., 1985; Regional chmn. Princeton Alumni Giving, Yonkers, N.Y., 1960-63, Tarrytown-Irvington, N.Y., 1977-80. Pres. Tarrytown (N.Y.) Jr. High Sch. PTA, 1971-72; bd. dirs. Martling Owners, Tarrytown, 1980-84, 89-93. Lt.

(j.g.) USNR, 1943-46, PTO. Mem. USN Meml. Found., Princeton Terrace Club (bd. govs. 1986-92), Great Harbour Cay Club (Bahamas), Phi Beta Kappa. Republican. Mem. Reform Ch. Home: 222 Martling Ave Tarrytown NY 10591-4756 *A thought acquired from one of my first bosses: "Everything happens for the best - or can be made to do so." This has been a lifelong help.*

NEILL, ROLFE, newspaper executive; b. Mount Airy, N.C., Dec. 4, 1932; s. Kenneth A. and Carmen (Goforth) N.; m. Rosemary Clifford Boney, July 20, 1952 (div.); children: Clifford Randolph, Sabrina Ashley, Dana Catlin, Jessica Rosemary Ingrid, Quentin Roark Robinson; m. Ann Marshall Snider, Sept. 24, 1988. A.B. in History, U. N.C., 1954. Reporter Franklin (N.C.) Press, 1956-57; reporter Charlotte (N.C.) Observer, 1957-58, bus. editor, 1958-61; editor, pub. Coral Gables (Fla.) Times and The Guide, 1961-63, Miami Beach (Fla.) Daily Sun, 1963-65; asst. to pub. N.Y. Daily News, 1965-67, suburban editor, 1967-68, asst. mng. editor, 1968-70; editor Phila. Daily News, 1970-75; v.p., dir. Phila. Newspapers Inc., 1970-75; chmn., pub. Charlotte (N.C.) Observer, 1975—. Served with AUS, 1954-56. Office: Knight Pub Co 600 S Tryon St PO Box 32188 Charlotte NC 28232

NEILL, SAM, actor; b. Northern Ireland, Sept. 14, 1947; m. Noriko Watanabe; 3 children. Student, U. Canterbury, Eng. Appearances include (film) Land Fall, 1976, Sleeping Dogs, 1977, The Journalist, 1979, Just Out of Reach, 1979, My Brilliant Career, 1980, Attack Force Z, 1981, The Final Conflict, 1981, Possession, 1981, Enigma, 1983, The Country Girls, 1983, Robbery Under Arms, 1984, Plenty, 1985, For Love Alone, 1986, The Good Wife, 1987, A Cry in the Dark, 1988, Dead Calm, 1989, La Révolution Française, 1989, The Hunt for Red October, 1990, Death in Brunswick, 1990, Until the End of the World, 1991, Memoirs of An Invisible Man, 1992, The Piano, 1993, Jurassic Park, 1993, In the Mouth of Madness, 1993, Country Life, 1993, Rudyard Kipling's Jungle Book, 1994, Restoration, 1994, Sirens, 1994, In the Mouth of Madness, 1995, Country Life, 1995, (TV miniseries) Kane and Abel, 1985, Reilly Ace of Spies, 1986, Amerika, 1987, (TV movies) From a Far Country: Pope John Paul II, 1981, Ivanhoe, 1982, The Blood of Others, 1984, Arthur Hailey's Strong Medicine, 1986, Leap of Faith, 1988, Fever, 1991, One Against the Wind, 1991, The Sinking of the Rainbow Warrior, 1991, Family Pictures, 1993. Recipient O.B.E. award, 1991. Office: Internat Creative Mgmt 8942 Wilshire Blvd Beverly Hills CA 90211-1934*

NEILL, VE, make-up artist; b. Riverside, Calif., May 13, 1951; d. Charles and Eileen Anne (Bernasco) Flores. Grad., Louisville H.S., Woodland Hills, Calif. Credits include (TV movies) Cry for Help, 1978, The London Affair, 1978, Sultan and the Rock Star, 1979, Muppets Go to the Movies, 1981, First Lady of the World, 1982, Money on the Side, 1982, Jane Doe, 1986; (TV Spls.) Sold Out-Lily Tomlin, 1981, Lily for President, 1982, Comedy Store 15th Yr. Reunion, 1988; (TV pilots) One Night Band, 1981, T.J. Hooker, 1981, Madeline (Madeline Kahn), 1982, Girls Life, 1982, A-Team, 1982, Rock & Roll Mom, 1987, Kowalski Loves, 1987; (TV show) Pee Wee's Playhouse (Emmy award 1988, Emmy award nominee 1989); (feature films) Star Trek: The Motion Picture (Saturn award 1981), The Incredible Shrinking Woman, 9 to 5, Monty Python at the Hollywood Bowl, Sword and the Sorcerer, The Last Star Fighter, All of Me, The Lost Boys, 1986 (Saturn award 1987), Beetlejuice, 1987 (Acad. award 1987, Saturn award 1988, Brit. Acad. award nominee 1988), Cocoon II, 1988, Big Top Pee Wee, 1988, Dick Tracy, 1989, Flatliners, 1989, Edward Scissorhands, 1990 (Acad. award nominee 1989, Brit. Acad. award nominee 1990), Curly Sue, 1990, Hook, 1991, Batman Returns, 1991 (Saturn award 1992, Acad. award nominee 1992, Brit. Acad. award nominee 1992), Hoffa, 1992 (Acad. award nominee 1992), Rising Sun, 1992, Mrs. Doubtfire, 1993 (Acad. award 1993), Ed Wood, 1993 (Acad. award 1994), Cobb, 1994, Junior, 1994, Batman Forever, 1995. Mem. Acad. Motion Picture Arts and Scis. (mem. exec. bd.), Brit. Acad. Film and TV. Avocations: collecting antiques, beading with antique Am. trade beads, hiking, traveling the U.S. Office: IATSE Local 706 11519 Chandler Blvd North Hollywood CA 91607

NEILL, WILLIAM HAROLD, JR., biological science educator and researcher; b. Wynne, Ark., Oct. 21, 1943; s. William H., Sr. and Shirley A. (Ellis) N.; m. Charlotte A. Jackson, Dec. 20, 1964; 1 child, Amanda K. BS in Zoology, U. Ark., 1965, MS in Zoology, 1967; PhD in Zoology/Statis., U. Wis., 1971. Rsch. fishery biologist Southwest Fisheries Ctr. Nat. Marine Fisheries Svc., Honolulu, 1971-74; assoc. prof. Tex. A&M U./Tex. Agrl. Expt. Sta., College Station, 1975-83; prof. Tex. A&M U./TAES, College Station, 1983—; interim head Dept. Wildlife and Fisheries Sci., College Station, 1992-93; mem. organizing com. Advanced Rsch. Inst. on Mechanisms Fish Migration, NATO, 1980-82; mem. tech. com. So. Regional Aquaculture Ctr., USDA, 1987-89; mem. sci.-tech. adv. com. Corpus Christi Bay Nat. Estuary Program, 1994—. Editor Tex. Jour. Sci., 1983-85; mem. editl. adv. bd. Critical Revs. in Aquatic Sci., 1986-90; assoc. editor Transactions of the Am. Fisheries Soc., 1995—; contbr. articles to sci. jours. and books. Grantee numerous orngs., 1975—. Fellow Tex. Acad. Sci.; mem. AAAS, Am. Fisheries Soc. (life, Award of Excellence com. 1987, 89, chair Publ. Awards com. 1993, editl. bd. 1995), Am. Inst.. Fishery Rsch. Biologists, Internat. Soc. Ecol. Modelling, World Aquaculture Soc., Phi Beta Kappa, Sigma Xi, Phi Sigma. Office: Texas A&M U Dept Wildlife & Fisheries Sci College Station TX 77843-2258

NEILSON, BENJAMIN REATH, lawyer; b. Phila., July 11, 1938; s. Harry Rosengarten and Alberta (Reath) N.; m. Judith Rawle, June 20, 1959 (div. May 1983); children: Benjamin R. Jr., Theodora C., Johanna K., Alberta R., Marshall R.; m. Meta B. Grace, Dec. 26, 1983. AB magna cum laude, Harvard U., 1960, LLB, 1963. Bar: Pa. 1964. Law clk. to chief justice Pa. Supreme Ct., Phila., 1963-64; assoc. Ballard, Spahr, Andrews & Ingersoll, Phila., 1964-71, ptnr., 1971—. Bd. dirs. WHYY, Inc., Phila; sec.-treas. The Chanticleer Found., Wayne, Pa.; bd. trustees St. Paul's Sch., Concord, N.H. Mem. ABA, Pa. Bar Assn., Phila. Bar Assn., Phi Beta Kappa. Episcopalian.

NEILSON, ELIZABETH ANASTASIA, health sciences educator, association executive, author, editor; b. Medford, Mass., Oct. 13, 1913; d. William H. and Anastasia (Mahony) N. Diploma, Tufts U., 1933; B.S. in Edn, Boston U., 1934, M.Ed., 1945, Ed.D., 1957. Tchr. pub. schs. Medford, 1934-43; instr. health and phys. edn. Boston Coll., 1954-55; mem. faculty State Coll., Lowell, Mass., 1944-72; prof. edn., chmn. dept. health and phys. edn. State Coll., 1966-72; dir. continuing edn. Am. Sch. Health Assn., Kent, Ohio, 1972—; adj. prof. Kent State U., 1971-77; adj. prof. health edn. Boston-Bouvé Coll. Human Devel. Professions, Northeastern U., 1974—; lectr. extension div. Harvard U., 1975—; vis. prof. Boston U., 1960-62, Ind. U., summers 1966-72, Utah State U., summer 1968; del. Internat. Conf. Health and Edn., Madrid, 1965, Pa., 1962, Dusseldorf, Germany, 1959; health edn. cons. to govt. agys., industry, ednl. instns.; del. White House Conf. Children and Youth, 1970; mem. membership com. Am. Nat. Council for Health, 1967-73; chmn. resources council Mass. Sch. Health Council, 1964-69; mem. Nat. Adv. Council on Smoking and Health Edn., 1966-74, Gov.'s Council for Health and Fitness, 1964-69, Gov.'s Council for Nutrition Edn., 1971-74; mem. program evaluation team N.H. State Bd. Edn. Author: Health Living Program, 1977, also school health textbooks; contbg. author: coll. text Personal and Community Health; editor in chief coll. text Journal-Health Values: Achieving High Level Wellness, 1976—; contbr. articles to profl. jours. V.p. bd. dirs. March Against Dental Disease Found.; bd. dirs. Middlesex TB and Health Assn., Mass. Cancer Soc., Lowell MEntal Health Assn., Lowell Heart Assn., Lowell Diabetes Assn., New Hampshire Lung Assn.; mem. Jackson Sch. Bd.; trustee Jackson Libr.; pres., bd. dirs. Flintlock Village Assn.Inc., Wells, Maine, 1988—; founder Elizabeth A. Neilson-George H. Neilson Advanced Grad. Endowed Scholarship Fund for the Promotion of Health Edn., dept. physiology and health scis., Ball State U., 1992. Recipient William A. Howe award Am. Sch. Health Assn., 1969, Disting. Svc. award 1965, Disting. Svc. award ea. dist. AAHPER, 1967, Profl. Svc. award Mass. chpt. 1965, Svc. award Nat. ARC, 1960, Disting. Alumni award Northeastern U., Boston, 1983, Profl. Svc. award Am. Alliance for Health Edn., 1987; inducted into Mass. Hall of Fame, Medford High, 1990; hon. fellow Ball State U., Muncie, Ind., 1993, named to Fellows Soc. and Pres.'s Cir., 1996. Fellow Am. Sch. Health Assn. (life, pres. 1964-66, chmn. study coms. 1969-72, mem. governing assn. 1960-65, Howe award), Royal Soc. Health; mem. Am. Assn. Higher Edn., Am. Soc. Assn. Execs., Nat. Bus. and Profl. Women's Club, Assn. Supervision and Curriculum Devel., UN Assn. U.S.A., Internat. Union for Health, Smithsonian Assos., Nat. Parks and Conservation Assn., New Eng. Health Assn., Am. Coll. Health Assn. (research council 1954-57), Am. (editorial bd. 1958-60, chmn. coll. health com. Eastern dist. 1948-51, chmn. resolutions com. sch. health div. 1951-53), Mass. assns. health, phys. edn. and recreation, Am. Pub. Health Assn., Soc. Pub. Health Educators, Phi Lambda Theta. Home and Office: PO Box 890 Wells ME 04090-0890 *Since childhood my life has been guided by the concept that it is best to prevent illness by healthful living. On this premise I have devoted my life toward achieving a high level of wellness for myself and my family. As a professor of health education and an exemplar of the concepts associated with the daily application of scientific health information, I have worked toward helping others achieve the level of health their inherited potential would permit.*

NEILSON, ERIC GRANT, physician, educator, health facility administrator; b. Bklyn., Sept. 14, 1949; s. Jack Drew and Lynette Elsie (Lundquist) N.; m. Linda Rae Apolzon, May 27, 1972; children: Tinsley, Sigrid. BS magna cum laude, Denison U., 1971; MD magna cum laude, U. Ala., 1975; MD (hon.), U. Pa., 1987. Asst. prof. U. Pa., Phila., 1980-87, assoc. prof., 1987-91, prof., 1991—, C. Mahlon Kline prof., 1993—, chief renal-electrolyte & hypertension divsn. dept. medicine, 1988—; attending physician Hosp. of U. Pa., 1980—; cons. in field. Med. editorial bds. on sci. jours.; contbr. numerous articles to profl. jours. Chmn. med. adv. bd. Lupus Found. of Phila., 1985-95; chmn. pathology A study sect. NIH, Bethesda, Md., 1990-92; chmn. grant rev. com. Nat. Kidney Found. of Delaware Valley. Recipient Clin. Scientist award Am. Heart Assn., 1980, Young Investigator award Am. Soc. Nephrology/Am. Heart Assn., 1985, Established Investigator award Am. Heart Assn., President's medal Am. Soc. Nephrology, 1994. Fellow ACP; mem. Am. Soc. Clin. Investigation, Assn. Am. Physicians, Am. Soc. Nephrology, Am. Assn. Immunologists, Am. Fedn. Clin. Rsch., Assn. Subsplty. Profs. (pres. 1994-96). Mem. Soc. of Friends. Office: U Pa Renal Electrolyte Sect 700 Clin Rsch Bldg 415 Curie Blvd Philadelphia PA 19104-6140

NEILSON, WINTHROP CUNNINGHAM, III, communications executive, financial communications consultant; b. N.Y.C., Jan. 7, 1934; s. Winthrop Cunningham, Jr. and Frances Fullerton (Jones) N.; m. Ilse Rossenbeck, Jan. 4, 1957; children: Luise R., Victoria F.; m. Demaris King Hetrick, July 5, 1985; 1 child, Whitney C.; stepchildren: Norman P. Hetrick Jr., D. Page Hetrick. BA, Harvard U., 1956; grad. in security analysis, N.Y. Inst. Finance, 1963. Asst. producer, asst. dir. Rangley Lakes Theater, 1955; gen. assignment reporter Albany (N.Y.) Times-Union, 1959-60; pub. info. writer, speaker Consol. Edison, 1960-61; asst. dir. pub. relations Union Service Corp., 1962; with Georgeson & Co., N.Y.C., 1962-81, prin., 1969-81; sr. v.p. D.F. King & Co. Inc., N.Y.C., 1982-86; founder, mng. dir. Krone Communications, Harrisburg, Pa., 1986-89; pres. Krone Group Inc., Harrisburg, 1987-89; mng. dir. Neilson/Hetrick Group, Montclair, N.J., 1990—, Harrisburg, Pa., 1993—; chmn. Neilson/Hetrick Group, Montclair, N.J., 1993—; mng. dir. Corp. Investor Communications, Carlstadt, N.J., 1991-93; guest lectr. NYU, 1991; bd. dirs. Guardman Products. Author: series Aunt Jane, 1971, 73, The Reluctant Marriage, 1978, Investorism, 1981, Annual Reports, The Agony and the Ecstasy, 1985, Individual Investors, a Counterbalance to Institutional Investors, 1986; writer, assoc. editor: Trends, 1965-81; contbr. articles to profl. jours. Mem. Mountain Lakes (N.J.) Econ. Devel. Council, 1974-79, chmn., 1977-79; pres. Robert A. Taft Republican Club, Queens, N.Y., 1964-65, chmn., 1966-67; treas. 23d Assembly Dist. Rep. Party, 1966-67; county committeeman, 1964-67; del. N.Y. State Nominating Conv., 1966; campaign mgr. for 2 assemblymen and state senator. Served with AUS, 1956-59. Recipient Investor Edn. Disting. Service award Nat. Assn. Investors Clubs, 1986. Mem. Nat. Investor Rels. Inst. (dir. 1980-84, v.p. manpower 1980-81, v.p. long-range planning 1981-84), Pub. Rels. Soc. Am. (charter, exec. com., investor rels. 1982-90, hmn. 1987, Pres. award 1987, inducted into Hall of Fame for Investor Rels.), Corp. Rels. Soc. Ctrl. Pa. (v.p. 1986-89, pres. 1994-95), Ctrl. Pa. Entrepreneurial Assn. (bd. dirs. 1988-89, adv. bd. tech. coun. Ctrl. Pa. 1994-96), Colonial Country Club, DU Club, Hasty Pudding Club, Ausable Club. Mem. Soc. of Friends. Home: 5778 Nesbit Dr Harrisburg PA 17112-2200 Office: 5778 Nesbit Dr Ste 12 Harrisburg PA 17112-2200

NEIMAN, JOHN HAMMOND, lawyer; b. Des Moines, Jan. 8, 1917; s. Donald Edwin and Bessie A. (White) N.; m. Madeline Clare Flint, July 2, 1941; children—Richard F., Donald F., Nancy J. Student, Grinnell Coll., 1935-37; B.A., Drake U., 1939, J.D., 1941. Bar: Iowa 1941. Ptnr. Neiman, Neiman, Stone & Spellman, Des Moines, 1946-92, Neiman, Stone, McCormick & Wendl, Attys., Des Moines, 1992—; exec. v.p., sec. Nat. Assn. Credit Mgmt., Des Moines, 1956-83; mem. ethics com. Iowa Senate, 1969-73, probate rules com. Iowa Supreme Ct., 1977-81; mem., chmn. Client Security and Atty. Disciplinary Commn., Iowa, 1974-85. Pres. bd. councilors Drake U. Law Sch., 1968; pres. Northwest Community Hosp., Des Moines, 1974-77. Recipient Centennial award Drake U., 1981. Fellow Am. Bar Found., Comml. Law Found., Iowa State Bar Found. (50 Yr. award 1995); mem. ABA (bd. govs. 1984-85, ho. of dels. 1978-87, profl. discipline com. 1979-84, forum com. 1985-89, responsibility for clients protection 1989-90), Iowa Bar Assn. (bd. govs. 1963-67, pres. 1967-68, award of merit 1975), Polk County Bar Assn. (pres. 1960-61), Comml. Law League Am., Iowa State Bar Found. (sec. 1975-78, pres. 1988-92), Wakonda Club (pres. 1973), Met. Club (pres. 1981-82, 84-86). Republican. Methodist. Home: 3514 Wakonda Ct Des Moines IA 50321-2648 Office: Neiman Stone McCormick & Wendl 2910 Westown Pky Ste 104 West Des Moines IA 50266-1308 *There are talkers and doers, it's more important to be a doer. Their accomplishments live long after they are gone.*

NEIMAN, LEROY, artist; b. St. Paul, June 8, 1927; s. Charles and Lydia (Serline) Runquist; m. Janet Byrne, June 22, 1957. Student, Sch. Art Inst., Chgo., 1946-50, U. Ill., 1951, DePaul U., 1951; LittD (hon.), Franklin Pierce Coll., 1976; hon. doctorate, St. John's U., 1980; hon. Doctorate, Iona Coll., 1985. Instr. Sch. Art Inst. Chgo., 1950-60, Saugatuck (Mich.) Summer Sch. Painting, 1957-58, 63, Sch. Arts and Crafts, Winston-Salem, N.C., 1963; instr. painting Atlanta Youth Council, 1968-69; printmaker-graphics, 1971—; artist Olympics, ABC-TV, Munich, 1972; ofcl. artist Olympics, ABC-TV, Montreal, 1976, U.S. Olympics, 1980, 84; computer artist CBS-TV (Superbowl), New Orleans, 1978; ofcl. artist Goodwill Games CNN-TV, Moscow, USSR, 1986; mem. adv. com. LeRoy Neiman Ctr. for Print Studies Sch. of the Arts Columbia U., 1995; mem. adv. com. for N.Y.C. Commn. for Cultural Affairs, 1995. Exhibited one-man shows, Oehlshlaeger Gallery, Chgo., 1959, 61, O'Hana Gallery, London, Gallerie O. Bosc, Paris, 1962, Hammer Gallery, N.Y.C., 1963, 65, 67, 70, 72, 76, 78, 79, 81-83, 85-87, 89, 92, Huntington-Hartford Gallery Modern Art, N.Y.C., 1967, Heath Gallery, Atlanta, 1969, Abbey Theatre, Dublin, Ireland, 1970, Museo de Bellas Artes, Caracas, Indpls. Inst. Arts, 1972, Hermitage Mus., Leningrad, Tobu Gallery, Tokyo, 1974, Springfield (Mass.) Mus. Fine Arts, 1974, 84, Knoedler Gallery, London, 1976, Casa gratica, Helsinki, 1977, Renée Victor, Stockholm, 1977, Okla. Art Ctr., Oklahoma City, 1981, Harrod's, London, 1982; retrospective show, Minn. Mus. Art, St. Paul, 1975, Meredith Long Galleries, Houston, 1978, Hanae Mori Gallery, Tokyo, 1988, New State Tretyakov Mus., 1988, Butler Inst., Youngstown, Ohio, 1990, Galerie Marcel Bernheim, Paris, 1993, Ky. Derby Mus., Louisville, 1995, two man show, Neiman-Warhol, Los Angeles Inst. Contemporary Art, 1981; exhibited in group shows, Art Inst. Chgo., 1954-60, Carnegie Internat., 1956, Corcoran Gallery Am., Washington, Walker Art Center, Mpls., 1957, Ringling Mus., Sarasota, Fla., 1959, Salon d'Art Mus., Paris, 1961, Nat. Gallery Portraiture, Smithsonian Instn., Washington, Minn. Mus. Art, 1969, Rotunda Della Basana, Milan, Italy, 1971, Royal Coll. Art, London, 1971, Minn. Mus. Art Nat. Tour, 1976-77, Whitney Mus., 1985 ; Master Prints of 19th and 20th Centuries, Hammer Galls., N.Y., 1987, Salon d'Automne, Paris, 1992, 93; represented in permanent collections, Mpls. Inst. Arts, Ill. State Mus., Springfield, Joslyn Mus., Omaha, Wodham Coll., Oxford, Eng., Nat. Art Mus. Sport, N.Y.C., Museo De Ballas Artes Caracas, Hermitage Mus., Indpls. Inst. Arts, U. Ill., Balt. Mus. Fine Art, The Armand Hammer Collection, Los Angeles; executed murals at, Merc. Nat. Bank, Hammond, Ind., Continental Hotel, Chgo., Swedish Lloyd Ship S.S. Patricia, Stockholm, ceramic tile mural, Sportsmans Park, Chgo.; author: LeRoy Neiman—Art and Life Style, 1974, Horses, 1979, LeRoy Neiman. Posters, 1980, LeRoy Neiman. Catalogue Raisonné, 1980, Carnaval, 1981, LeRoy Neiman: Winners, 1983, Japanese translation, 1985, LeRoy Neiman, Monte Carlo Chase, 1988, The Prints of LeRoy Neiman, 1980-90, Big Time Golf, 1992, LeRoy Neiman, An American in Paris, 1994; illustrator: 12 paintings deluxe edit. Moby Dick, 1975. Served with AUS, 1942-46. Recipient 1st prize Twin City Show, 1953, 2d prize Minn. State Show, 1954, Clark Meml. prize Chgo. Show, 1957, Hamilton-Graham prize Ball State Coll., 1958, Municipal prize Chgo. Show, 1958, Purchase prize Miss. Valley Show, 1959, Gold medal Salon d'Art Modern Paris, 1961; award of merit as nation's outstanding sports artist AAU, 1976; Olympic Artist of Century award, 1979, Gold Medal award St. John's U., 1985. Address: 1 W 67th St New York NY 10023-6200

NEIMANN, ALBERT ALEXANDER, mathematician, business owner; b. Torrington, Wyo., Nov. 29, 1939; s. Alexander and Lydia (Temple) N.; m. Barbara Jean Maw, May 6, 1962; children: Debbie, Todd, Amy, Kelly,. BA, Willamette U., 1967. Mathematician Keyport (Wash.) Naval Torpedo Sta., 1968-70; math. statistician Concord (Calif.) Naval Weapons Sta., 1970-85, engrng. statistician, 1985-94; bus. owner Antioch Sports Cards and Collectibles, Calif., 1994—. Mgr. Little League Baseball, Antioch, Calif., 1977-84, Little League Softball, Antioch, 1984-87; Sunday sch. tchr. Grace Bapt. Ch., 1979-90; statistician Antioch H.S., 1985-89. Recipient Performance award Concord Naval Weapons Sta., 1978, 88-89. Mem. Am. Statis. Assn., Math. Assn. Am., Am. Soc. for Quality Control, Nat. Coun. Tchrs. Math. Avocations: jogging, electronics, reading, gardening, basketball. Office: Antioch Sports Cards & Collectibles 2550 Somersville Rd Ste 51 Antioch CA 94509

NEIMARK, PHILIP JOHN, financial consultant, editor; b. Chgo., Sept. 13, 1939; s. Mortimer William and Hortense (Peters) N.; m. Vassa Lynn; children: Tanya Lee, Joshua Daniel, Dashiel Charles, Darq-Amber. Student U. Chgo., 1956-58, Northwestern U., 1958-59; D in Bus. Mgmt. (hon.), Ricker Coll., Houlton, Maine, 1976. Ordained minister Babalawo of IFA Ch. of Nigeria, 1989. Mem. Chgo. Mercantile Exchange, 1968-74; owner Josephson Neimark Trading Co., Chgo., 1972-73; ptnr. Rosenthal & Co., Chgo., 1973-77; owner, prin. Philip J. Neimark Investments, Miami, Fla., 1977-79, Chgo., 1979—; pres. Neimark Fin. Pub. Co., 1985—; pres., Croesus Assocs., 1988-90; prin. TBFB, Inc., 1995—; editor, pub. Philip J. Neimark Viewpoint, N.Y.C., 1976-85, editor Pro Trade, 1984—, Low Priced Stock Edit., 1984-91; fin. editor Money Maker mag., 1979-85; mem. Internat. Monetary Market, 1971-74, N.Y. Mercantile Exchange, 1973-74, Chgo. Bd. of Options Exchange, 1973-75; editor, Low Priced Stock Edition, 1984-91, Pro Trade, 1985—; instr. Omega Inst., 1994, Esalen Inst., 1994. Author: How to Be Lucky, 1975, Way of the Orisa, 1992, The Sacred Ifa Oracle, 1995; syndicated columnist Ask the Shaman, 1994—; contbg. editor Consumers Digest mag., 1977-85. Bd. dirs. Luth. Gen. Med. Found. (emeritus), Principal Vassa Inc.; chmn. IFA Found N.Am., 1989—. Mem. Fla. Exec. Planning Assn., South Fla. Fin. Planners Assn., Investment Co. Inst., Nat. Paso Fino Assn. (founder).

NEIMARK, SHERIDAN, lawyer; b. Youngstown, Ohio, Apr. 7, 1935; s. David and Anne (Kamisar) N.; m. Dana Ellen Perlzweig, Jan. 5, 1963; children: David, Rebecca, Matthew. B.S. in Chem. Engring, Carnegie-Mellon U., 1957; J.D., George Washington U., 1961. Bar: Va. 1962, D.C. 1962, U.S. Ct. of Customs and Patent Appeals 1963, U.S. Ct. Appeals (Fed. cir.) 1982, U.S. Supreme Ct. 1973. Patent examiner U.S. Patent Office, Washington, 1957-62; practiced in Washington, 1962—; patent atty. firms K. Flocks and A. Browdy, Washington, 1962-68; mem. firm Browdy and Neimark, Washington, 1969—, sr. ptnr., 1989—. Contbr. articles, papers to profl. jours. Charter mem. Gov.'s Planning and Adv. Coun. on Devel. Disabilities, State of Md., 1971-86, vice chmn., 1975-77; mem. Legal and Human Rights Task Force, Montgomery County (Md.) Com. for Employment of Handicapped, 1972-73; bd. dirs., co-founder Cmty. Svcs. for Autistic Adults and Children; past bd. dirs. Tifereth Israel Congregation. Recipient Gov.'s citation State of Md., 1986. Mem. Am. Bar Assn. (mem. adv. bd. developmental disabilities model legis. project 1977-81, mem. adv. bd. mental and phys. disabilities law reporter 1979—), D.C. Bar, Va. State Bar, Am. Intellectual Property Law Assn. (mem. com. patent law 1965-69, chem. practice 1970—), Md. Patent Law Assn., Internat. Assn. Jewish Lawyers and Jurists, Patent Office Soc., Autism Soc. Am. (nat. dir. 1973-77, dir. Montgomery County chpt. 1970-72, nat. Plaque awards 1972, 77), Md. State Soc. for Autistic Children (founder, dir. 1971-73), Am. Jewish Com., Am. Jewish Congress, B'nai Brith. Home: 12908 Ruxton Rd Silver Spring MD 20904-5278 Office: 419 7th St NW Suite 300 Washington DC 20004

NEIMS, ALLEN HOWARD, univeristy dean, medical scientist; b. Chgo., Oct. 24, 1938; s. Irving Morris and Ruth (Geller) N.; m. Myrna Gay Robins, June 18, 1961; children: Daniel Mark, Susan Roberta, Nancy Elizabeth. B.A., B.S., U. Chgo., 1957; M.D., Johns Hopkins U., 1961, Ph.D., 1966. Intern, resident in pediatrics Johns Hopkins Hosp., 1961-62, 66-68; research asso. Lab. Neurochemistry, NIH, 1968-70; asst. prof. physiol. chemistry and pediatrics Johns Hopkins Med. Sch., 70-72; assoc. prof. McGill U., 1972-77, prof. pharmacology and pediatrics, 1977-78; dir. Roche developmental pharmacology unit, 1972-78; prof., chmn. dept. pharmacology and therapeutics, prof. pediatrics U. Fla., Gainesville, 1978-89, dean Coll. Medicine, 1989—; Fulton Bequest prof. U. Melbourne, Australia, 1974; mem. human embryology and devel. study sect. NIH, 1979-83; sci. cons. Can. Found. for Study of Sudden Infant Death, 1974-77, Nat. Soft Drink Assn., 1976-78, Internat. Life Scis. Inst., 1978-89; bd. sci. counsellors Nat. Inst. Child Health and Human Devel., 1984-89. Contbr. chpts. to books, articles to med. jours. Served to comdr. USPHS, 1968-70. NIH, Can. Med. Research Council grantee. Mem. Can. Assn. Research in Toxicology (pres. 1976-78), Am. Soc. Pharmacology and Exptl. Therapeutics (past mem. exec. coms. clin. pharmacology and drug metabolism), Pediatric Research Soc., Am. Soc. Clin. Pharmacology and Therapeutics, Assn. Am. Med. Colls, Coun. of Deans, Am. Pediatric Soc., Am. Acad. Pediatrics. Office: U Fla Coll Medicine PO Box 100215 Gainesville FL 32610-0215

NEINAS, CHARLES MERRILL, athletic association executive; b. Marshfield, Wis., Jan. 18, 1932; s. Arthur Oscar and Blanche Amelia (Reeder) N.; children: Andrew, Toby. B.S., U. Wis., 1957. Asst. exec. dir. Nat. Collegiate Athletic Assn., Kansas City, Mo., 1961-71; commr. Big Eight Conf., Kansas City, 1971-81; exec. dir. Coll. Football Assn., 1981—; Dr. Patricia L. Pacey prof. econs. U. Colo., Boulder, 1981—, econ. cons., 1981—. Served with USNR, 1952-54. Home: 4977 Idylwild Trl Boulder CO 80301-3651 Office: College Football Assoc 6688 Gunpark Dr Boulder CO 80301-3372*

NEIS, ARNOLD HAYWARD, pharmaceutical company executive; b. N.Y.C., Feb. 13, 1938; s. Harry H. and Mary Ruth (Bishop) N.; m. Lucy de Puig, Dec. 8, 1989; children by previous marriage: Nancy R., Robert C. B.S. cum laude, Columbia U., 1959; M.B.A., N.Y.U., 1967. With Scott Chem. Co., 1959-64; v.p. mktg., then v.p. Odell, Inc., N.Y.C., 1964-71, pres. Knomark div., 1969-71; pres., chief exec. officer E.T. Browne Drug Co., Inc., Englewood Cliffs, N.J., 1971—; dir. Esquire A.B. Stockholm, Knomark Can. Ltd., E.T. Browne Internat. Fellow Royal Soc. Chemists, Royal Geog. Soc., Am. Inst. Chemists, N.Y. Acad. Scis.; mem. AAAS, Am. Chem. Soc., Am. Pharm. Assn., New Eng. Soc. (bd. dirs.), Explorers Club (v.p., bd. dirs.), Chemists Club, Lotos Club, Soldiers, Sailors and Airmans Club (bd. dirs.), St. Georges Soc. Episcopalian. Home: 898 Park Ave New York NY 10021-0234 Office: PO Box 1613 140 Sylvan Ave Englewood NJ 07632-2502

NEIS, ARTHUR VERAL, healthcare and development company executive; b. Lawrence, Kans., May 30, 1940; s. Veral Herbert and Louise (Schlegel) N.; m. Fleeta Weigel, Apr. 12, 1969; children: Frederich Arthur, Benjamin Jason, Sarah Louise. BS in Bus., U. Kans., 1962, MS in Acctg., 1963. CPA, Kans., Iowa. Mgmt. cons. Arthur Andersen & Co., Kansas City, Mo. and Mpls., 1963-74; chief corp. acctg. Carlson Co., Mpls., 1974-76; controller The Fullerton Cos., Mpls., 1976-78; asst. treas. Fru-Con Corp., St. Louis, 1978-80, asst. controller, 1981, controller, 1982-86; corp. contr. LCS Holdings, Inc. (Weitz Corp. and Subsidiaries), Des Moines, 1986-87; treas., chief fin. officer The Weitz Corp., Des Moines, 1987—; treas., CFO Weitz Co., Des Moines, 1987-93, Life Care Services Corp., Des Moines, 1987—; bd. dirs. LCS Holdings, Inc. (Weitz Corp.); mem. adv. group NAIC, 1990-93. Bd. dirs. Inst. Humane Studies George Mason U., Fairfax, Va., 1973—, exec. com., 1975-83, chmn., 1978-83; bd. dirs. Lake Country Sch., Mpls., 1973-78; treas. Villa de Maria Montessori Sch., St. Louis, 1982-86, bd. dirs.; trustee Crossroads Sch., St. Louis, 1984-86, exec. com. bd., 1984-86; vice chair, bd. dirs. Alliance for Arts and Understanding, 1993—; trustee Fin. Execs. Rsch. Found., 1994—; trustee Plymouth Congrl. United Ch. of Christ, 1993—. Mem. AICPA, Kans. Soc. CPAs, Iowa Soc. CPAs, Fin. Execs. Inst. (bd.

dirs. Iowa chpt. 1986, 88-94, sec. 1988-90, v.p. 1990-91, pres. 1991-92). Avocations: bibliophile, Kans. history, orientalia. Home: 1575 NW 106th St Clive IA 50325-6604 Office: Life Care Svcs Corp 800 2nd Ave Des Moines IA 50309-1328

NEIS, JAMES MICHAEL, lawyer; b. Chgo., Mar. 3, 1946. BA, DePaul U., 1969, JD, 1973. Bar: Ill. 1973, U.S. Tax Ct. 1974. Mng. ptnr. Winston & Strawn, Chgo., 1977—; adj. prof. law DePaul U., 1979-86. Mem. ABA, Ill. State Bar Assn., Chgo. Bar Assn. Office: Winston & Strawn 35 W Wacker Dr Chicago IL 60601-1614

NEISER, BRENT ALLEN, public affairs consultant; b. Cin., Sept. 16, 1954; s. Rodger John and Hazel Jean Neiser; m. Marion Alice Hutton, Apr. 1, 1978; children: Christy Jean, Steven José, April Reneé. BA in Pub. Affairs, George Washington U., 1976; MA in Urban Studies, Occidental Coll., 1978; MBA, U. Louisville, 1979; postgrad. in internat. affairs, U. Denver, 1987—. Cert. fin. planner, 1985; cert. assn. exec., 1994; cert. mut. fund counselor, 1996. Project mgr., analyst Legis. Research Com., Frankfort, Ky., 1978-84; pres. Moneyminder, Denver and Frankfort, 1983-91; dir. edn., govt. affairs and ethics Inst. Cert. Fin. Planners, Denver, 1985-91, exec. dir., 1991-94; pub. affairs, telecomms., govt. rels. bus. strategies cons. The Brent Neiser Co., Englewood, Colo., 1994—; dir. Nat. Endowment for Fin. Edn., 1995—; mng. dir. Fin. Products Stds. Bd., Denver, 1985-91; co-creator Personal Econ. Summit '93, Washington; dir. Nat. Endowment for Fin. Edn. Author: EPCOT/World Showcase External Directions, Walt Disney Imagineering, 1977; co-inventor: Trivia Express (game) Denver, 1986. Vol., v.p. Big Bros./Big Sisters, Frankfort, 1982; del. Colo. Model Constrnl. Conv., 1987; mem. citizens budget rev. com. Greenwood Village; parent trainer The Adoption Exch., Denver, 1988, mem. long range planning com., 1992-93, bd. dirs., 1993—; polit. action dir. Frankfort NAACP, 1983, legis. chmn. state conf., 1984; troop com. mem., asst. scoutmaster Boy Scouts Am., Englewood, 1993—; bd. dirs. Young Ams. Bank Edn. Found., 1993—, Leadership Denver, 1993. Lt. (j.g.) USNR, 1985-92. Recipient Outstanding Service award Frankfort NAACP, 1981; named Man of Yr., Frankfort NAACP, 1983; Pub. Affairs fellow Coro Found., 1976-77. Mem. Investors Edn. Assn. Colo. (bd. dirs.), Nat. Assns. in Colo., Denver C. of C. (pub. affairs coun.), Adoptive Families of Am., Inst. Cert. Fin. Planners, Assn. for Fin. Counseling and Planning Edn., Am. Soc. Assn. Execs., Inst. Mgmt. Cons., Nat. Coun. La Raza, Internat. Assn. Fin. Planners (bd. dirs. Rocky Mountain chpt. 1990-92), N.Am. Securities Adminstrs. Assn. (investment adviser and fin. planner adv. com.), Nat. Soc. Compliance Profls. (bd. dirs. 1987-89), Am. Film Inst. (writers workshop). Office: 5860 Big Canyon Dr Englewood CO 80111-3516

NEISSER, ULRIC, psychology educator; b. Kiel, Germany, Dec. 8, 1928; came to U.S., 1933; s. Hans Philip and Charlotte (Schroeter) N. BA, Harvard U., 1950, PhD, 1956; MA, Swarthmore Coll., 1952; Laurea Honoris Causa, U. Rome, 1988, U. Aarhus, Denmark, 1993, U. Cluj, Romania, 1994. Instr. Swarthmore (Pa.) Coll., 1953-54, Harvard U., Cambridge, Mass., 1956-57; from asst. to assoc. prof. Brandeis U., Waltham, Mass., 1957-66; prof. psychology Cornell U., Ithaca, N.Y., 1967-80, Susan Linn Sage prof. psychology, 1980-83; Robert W. Woodruff prof. psychology Emory U., Atlanta, 1983-96; prof. psychology Cornell U., Ithaca, N.Y., 1996—. Author: Cognitive Psychology, 1967, Cognition and Reality, 1976; editor: Memory Observed, 1982, The School Achievement of Minority Children, 1987, Concepts and Conceptual Development, 1987, Remembering Reconsidered, 1988, The Perceived Self, 1993. Ctr. for Advanced Study in Behavior Scis. fellow, 1973-74, Guggenheim fellow, 1987-88. Fellow APA; mem. NAS, Am. Acad. Arts and Scis., Cognitive Sci. Soc., Internat. Soc. Ecol. Psychology, Psychonomic Soc. Office: Cornell U Dept Psychology Ithaca NY 14853

NEITER, GERALD IRVING, lawyer; b. L.A., Nov. 11, 1933; s. Harry and Ida Florence (Alperin) N.; m. Margaret P. Rowe, Mar. 5, 1961; children: David, Karen, Michael. BSL, U. So. Calif., 1957, JD, 1957. Bar: Calif. 1958. Judge pro tem Mcpl. Cts., L.A. and Beverly Hills, 1970-94; judge pro tem and mediator Calif. Superior Ct., L.A. County, 1974-94, family law mediator, 1976—; prin. Gerald I. Neiter, P.C., L.A., 1981—; lectr. State Bar of Calif., 1968, 76, 79, 81; former referee State Bar Ct.; arbitrator Am. Arbitration Assn. Mem. Am., Los Angeles County (arbitrator), Beverly Hills, Century City bar assns., State Bar Calif. Office: 1925 Century Park E Ste 200 Los Angeles CA 90067-2701

NEJELSKI, PAUL ARTHUR, judge; b. Chgo., Feb. 24, 1938; s. Leo Lawrence and Rena Grace (Martin) N.; m. Marilyn Ray Mills, Oct. 2, 1965; children: Nicole Rena, Stephen Downing. BA magna cum laude, Yale U., 1959, LLB, 1962; MPA, Am. U., 1969; cert. of theol. studies, Georgetown U., 1989. Bar: N.J. 1963. Law clk. appellate div. N.J. Superior Ct., 1962-63; asst. U.S. atty. U.S. Dist. Ct. N.J., 1964-65; atty., later chief immigration unit Dept. Justice, Washington, 1965-69; chief cts. desk Nat. Inst. Justice, Washington, 1969-70; asst. dir. Criminal Justice Ctr., Harvard U., 1970-71; dir. planning phase Inst. Jud. Adminstrn.-ABA Juvenile Justice Standards Project, N.Y.C., 1971-73; dir. Inst. Jud. Adminstrn., NYU, 1973-76; dep. ct. adminstrn. Conn. Jud. Dept., Hartford, 1976-77; dep. asst. atty. gen. Office for Improvements in Adminstrn. Justice, Dept. Justice, Washington, 1977-79; dir. Action Commn. to Reduce Ct. Costs and Delay, ABA, Washington, 1979-81; cir. exec. 3rd Cir., Phila., 1981-84; ct. adminstr. U.S. Tax Ct., 1984-89; immigration judge Dept. Justice, Arlington, Va., 1989—; mem. faculty law NYU, 1972-74, U. Conn., 1976-77, U. Md., 1981-82; cons. Author: (with C.O. Philip) Where Do Judges Come From?, 1976; editor: Social Research in Conflict With Law and Ethics, 1976; contbr. articles to profl. jours. With U.S. Army, 1963-64. Office: 901 N Stuart St Ste 1300 Arlington VA 22203-1853

NELKIN, DOROTHY, sociology and science policy educator; b. Boston, July 30, 1933; d. Henry and Helen (Fine) Wolfers; m. Mark Nelkin, Aug. 31, 1952; children: Lisa, Laurie. B.A., Cornell U., 1954. Research assoc. Cornell U., Ithaca, N.Y., 1963-69, sr. research assoc., 1970-72, assoc. prof., 1972-76, prof. sci. tech. sociology program, 1976-90, prof. sociology, 1977-90; univ. prof., prof. sociology, affiliate prof. law NYU, 1990—, Clare Boothe Luce vis. prof., 1988-90; cons. OECD, Paris, 1975-76, Inst. Environ., Berlin, 1978-79; maitre de conference U. Paris, 1975-76; maitre de recherche Ecole Polytechnique, Paris, 1980-81. Author: The Atom Besieged, 1981, The Creation Controversy, 1982, Science as Intellectual Property, 1983, Workers at Risk, 1984, Selling Science: How the Press Covers Science and Technology, 1987, 2d edit., 1995, Dangerous Diagnostics: The Social Power of Biological Information, 1989, 2d edit., 1994, A Disease of Society: Cultural Impact ofAIDS, 1991, The Animal Rights Crusade, 1991, Controversy: Politics of Technical Decision, 3d edit., 1992, The DNA Mystique: The Gene as Cultural Icon, 1995. Adviser Office Tech. Assessment, 1977-79, 82-83; expert witness ACLU, Ark., 1982; mem. Nat. Adv. Coun. to NIH Human Genome Project, 1991-95. Vis. scholar Resources for the Futures, 1980-81; vis. scholar Russell Sage Found., N.Y.C., 1983; Guggenheim fellow, 1983-84. Fellow AAAS (bd. dirs.), Hastings Inst. Soc. Ethics and Life Scis.; mem. NAS Inst. of Medicine, Soc. for Social Studies Sci. (pres. 1978-79). Home: 3 Washington Square Vlg New York NY 10012-1836 Office: NYU Dept Sociology 269 Mercer St New York NY 10003-6633

NELLERMOE, LESLIE C., lawyer; b. Oakland, Calif., Jan. 26, 1954; d. Carrol Wandell and Nora Ann (Conway) N.; m. Darrell Ray McKissic, Aug. 9, 1986; 1 child, Devin Anne. BS cum laude, Wash. State U., 1975; JD cum laude, Willamette U., 1978. Bar: Wash. 1978, U.S. Dist. Ct. (ea. dist.) Wash. 1979, U.S. Dist. Ct. (we. dist.) Wash. 1983. Staff atty. Wash. Ct. Appeals, Spokane, 1978-79; asst. atty. gen. Wash. Atty. Gen. Office, Spokane, 1979-83, Olympia, 1983-85; assoc. Syrdal, Danelo, Klein, Myre & Woods, Seattle, 1985-88; ptnr. Heller Ehrman White & McAuliffe, Seattle, 1989—. Bd. dirs. Campfire Boys & Girls, Seattle, 1991—. Mem. ABA, Wash. State Bar Assn., King County Bar Assn. Wash. Environment Industry Assn. (bd. dirs.). Office: Heller Ehrman White & McAuliffe 701 5th Ave 6100 Columbia Ctr Seattle WA 98104

NELLES, MAURICE, mechanical engineer, author; b. Madison, S.D., Oct. 19, 1906; s. Hubert Tilman and Anne (Benson) N.; m. Cecelia Nelson, Aug. 28, 1929; 1 son, Maurice Tilman; foster daus., Sally Sue Hopkins, Merrill Sherwin. A.B., U. S.D., 1927, A.M., 1928; Ph.D., Harvard, 1932; D.Sc., U. S.D., 1955. Prof. physics Columbus Coll., 1928-29; instr. chemistry U. S.D., 1929-30; research chemist Nat. Aniline Chem. Co., 1932-34, Union Oil Co., 1934-36; camp dir. Civilian Conservation Corps, Ft. Lewis, 1936-37; research engr. Riverside Cement Co., 1937-39; engr. Permanente Corp., 1939-40; staff asst. Lockheed Aircraft, 1940-46; prof. aero. engring., mgr. Allan Hancock Found., U. So. Calif., 1947-50; prof., dir. engring. expt. sta. Pa. State U., 1950-51; dir. research Borg-Warner, also v.p. petro-mechanics div., 1951-54; dir. research and diversification, mgr. graphic arts div. Technicolor Corp., 1954-57; v.p. engring. Crane Co., Chgo., 1957-59; v.p. Am. Electronics, Inc., 1959-62, Quail Products, Inc.; pres. Corwith Co. div. Crane Co., Locked-Lattice Steel Co.; dir. Merd Corp., Lamb-Weston, Inc., Scientia Corp., Hydro-Aire Co., Crane, Ltd., Can., Western Optics, Inc., Radix Corp.; Rust prof. bus. adminstrn. U. Va.; exec. dir. Tayloe Murphy Inst.; prof. Grad. Sch. Bus. Adminstrn., 1966-70, Christian Heritage Coll.; cons. Nat. Acad. Sci.; Dep. dir. WPB; mem. war metall. com. NACA; dir. Sch. Ministry World Evangelism, Inc., 1977-81; chief engr. Office Prodn. Research and Devel. Author: Satan's 20th Century Strategy, 1971, Precious Christian Thought Patterns, 1973, The Deal, 1976, also articles mgmt. research and engring., new research technique. Trustee Midwest Research Inst., Marine Studies Inst.; commr. to synod United Presbyn. Ch. Charles Coffin fellow; George H. Emerson scholar; Harvard U. fellow. Fellow Am. Inst. Chemists; mem. Am. Soc. M.E., Soc. Automotive Engrs., Inst. Aero. Scis., I.E.E.E., Am. Chem. Soc., Am. Soc. Naval Engrs., Am. Soc. Metals, AIAA, Am. Soc. Motion Picture and TV Engrs., Internat. Soc. Visual Literacy, Optical Soc. Am., Am. Mgmt. Assn., A.A.A.S., Sigma Xi, Tau Beta Pi, Alpha Tau Omega, Tau Kappa Alpha, Sigma Phi Delta, Gamma Alpha, Alpha Chi Sigma. Presbyn. (elder, mem. San Diego Presbytery). Clubs: Mason, Los Angeles Athletic; Montecito (Santa Barbara); Chemists (N.Y.C.); Farmington Country (Charlottesville, Va.). Sci. expdns. aboard U. So. Calif. Marine Lab. Ship Sci. expdns. aboard U. So. Calif. Marine Lab. Ship. Home: 5522 Rutgers Rd La Jolla CA 92037-7821 *I have walked with God since I was eight years of age. While in college I made the decision not to work with any one organization in any one field for more than three years. As a result I have an unusually diverse set of thought patterns and material in my memory that makes it possible to quickly accomplish much by analogical actions and to use for creative planning.*

NELLETT, GAILE L., mental health nurse; b. Ottawa, Ill., Nov. 5, 1941; d. Edwin Edward and Mabel Delia (Higgins) Hausaman; children: Anne Marie, James, Sarah, Susan, Julie; m. Henry H. Nellett, Aug. 8, 1988. BSN, Governors State U., University Park, Ill., 1993; MS in Nursing Adminstrn., Loyola U., Chgo., 1995, postgrad., 1996—. RN, Ill. Staff nurse med.-surg. and psychiat. units Cmty. Hosp. Ottawa, 1974-75, asst. head nurse, 1975-77, head nurse psychiat. unit, 1977-79, head nurse psychiat. and chem. dependency units, 1979-84, nursing mgr. psychiat. and chem. dependency units, 1984-92, program mgr. psychiat. and chem. dependency units, 1987-92, part-time home health nurse, 1992-94; rsch. asst. Loyola U., 1993-96. Bd. dirs. Ottawa area United Way, 1976-92, v.p., 1985, sec., 1984, 86. Nursing Adminstrn. fellow Edward Hines Jr. VA, Hines, Ill., 1994, tuition fellow Loyola U., 1993-96. Mem. ANA, Nat. Nurses Soc. on Addictions, Ill. Nurses Assn. (bd. dirs. dist. 4 1974-80), Peer Assistance Network for Nurses (regional support person dist. 2 1988-96), Am. Psychiat. Nurses Assn., Sigma Theta Tau. Roman Catholic. Avocations: archery, hunting, handcrafts, reading. Home: PO Box 730 108 S Wabena Ave Minooka IL 60447

NELLI, D. JAMES, business school executive, accountant; b. Seneca Falls, N.Y., Feb. 19, 1917; s. Thomas and Vita N.; m. Victoria Margaret Serino, Aug. 31, 1941 (dec. May 1980); children: Thomas, Diane, Joseph, John; m. 2d, Carmel L. Dowd, Sept. 19, 1981. BS, Syracuse U., 1948. CPA, N.Y. Staff acct. Seidman & Seidman, N.Y.C., 1948-49, Stover, Butler & Murphy, Syracuse, N.Y., 1949-55; instr. Syracuse U., 1953; instr. acctg. Central City Bus. Inst., Syracuse, 1955-58, pres., 1958—, also pvt. practice acctg., Syracuse. Served with USNR, 1943-46. CPA, N.Y. Mem. Am. Inst. CPAs, N.Y. State Soc. CPAs, Am. Acctg. Assn., AAUP. Roman Catholic. Clubs: Lakeshore Yacht and Country (Clay, N.Y.), Italian Am. Athletic (Syracuse). Home: 7929 Boxford Rd Clay NY 13041-8606 Office: Cen City Bus Inst 224 Harrison St Syracuse NY 13202-3052

NELLIGAN, KATE (PATRICIA COLLEEN NELLIGAN), actress; b. London, Ont., Can., Mar. 16, 1951; d. Patrick Joseph and Alice (Dier) N. Attended, York U., Toronto, Ctrl. Sch. Speech and Drama, London. Appeared in plays in Bristol, London, and New York: Barefoot in the Park, 1972, Misalliance, A Streetcar Named Desire, The Playboy of the Western World, London Assurance, Lulu, Private Lives, Knuckle, 1974, Heartbreak House, 1975, Plenty, 1975, As You Like It, A Moon for the Misbegotten, 1984, Virginia, 1985, Serious Money, 1988, Spoils of War, 1988, BAd Habits; films include: The Count of Monte Cristo, 1979, The Romantic Englishwoman, 1979, Dracula, 1979, Mr. Patman, 1980, Eye of the Needle, 1980, Agent, 1980, Without a Trace, 1983, Eleni, 1985, Frankie and Johnnie, 1991, The Prince of Tides, 1991, Shadows and Fog, 1992, Fatal Instinct, 1993, Wolf, 1994, How to Make an American Quilt, 1995; TV appearances include: The Onedin Line, The Lady of the Camellias, Licking Hitler, Measure for Measure, Therese Raquin, 1980, Forgive Our Foolish Ways, 1980, Love and Hate: A Marriage Made in Hell, 1990, Terror Strickes the Class Reunion, 1992, The Diamond Fleece, 1992, Liar Liar, 1993. Recipient Best Actress award Evening Standard, 1978. Avocations: reading, cooking. Office: Internat Creative Mgmt c/o Joe Funicello 8942 Wilshire Blvd Beverly Hills CA 90211*

NELLIGAN, WILLIAM DAVID, professional association executive; b. Halstead, Kans., Aug. 10, 1926; s. William D. and Katherine (Roberts) N.; m. Dorothy Meyer, Aug. 17, 1952; children: Richard, Arthur, Mark. Student, U. Wichita, 1944-46; BS, U. Kans., 1949. Display advt. salesman Kansas City Star and Times, Mo., 1949-51; mgr. SW Kans. Extension Ctr. U. Kans., Garden City, 1951-55; exec. dir. dept. postgrad. med. edn. Sch. Medicine U. Kans., Kansas City, Kans., 1955-64; asst. to pres. Med. Coll. Ga., Augusta, 1964-65; exec. v.p. Am. Coll. Cardiology, Bethesda, Md., 1965-92; v.p. Marion Merrell DOW, Inc., Kansas City, Mo., 1992-94; exec. dir. Am. Soc. Nuc. Cardiology, Bethesda, 1994—. mem. Nat. Commn. Diabetes, 1975-76, adv. council Nat. Diabetes and Digestive and Kidney Diseases, 1987-88; bd. dirs. Arthur E. Hertzler Research Found., Halstead, Kans., 1961—. Recipient Man with a Heart award N.Y. Cardiol. Soc., 1970, Presdl. citation Am. Coll. Cardiology, 1975, Disting. Service award Am. Coll. Cardiology, 1986, CLC Hall of Leaders award, 1986. Fellow Am. Coll. Cardiology; mem. AMA (citation of layman for disting. svc. 1993), Profl. Conv. Mgmt. Assn. (pres. 1974-75, Disting. Svc. award 1990), Am. Med. Writers Assn. (dir., exec. com., treas. 1970-78, Harold Swanberg Disting. Svc. award), Am. Soc. Assn. Execs. (cert., dir. 1975-78, sec.-treas. 1987-88, Key award 1984), Am. Assn. Med. Soc. Execs. (pres. 1986-87), Brit. Cardiac Soc. (hon.), Alliance for Continuing Med. Edn. (Pres.'s award 1994), Masons. Office: 9111 Old Georgetown Rd Bethesda MD 20814-1699

NELMS, CHARLIE, academic administrator; b. Crawfordsville, Ark., Sept. 11, 1946. BS in Agronomy, U. Ark., Pine Bluff, 1968; MS, Ind. U., 1971, EdD, 1977. Various collegiate positions to lectr. and counselor Lehman Coll./CUNY, Pine Bluff, 1971-73; assoc. dean, asst. prof. edn. Earlham Coll., Richmond, Ind., 1973-77; assoc. dir. Ctr. Human Devel. and Edn. Svcs., asst. prof. U. Ark., Pine Bluff, 1977-78; assoc. dean for acad. affairs Ind. U., Northwest Gary, Ind., 1978-84; v.p. student svcs. Sinclair C.C., Dayton, Ohio, 1984-87; chancellor, prof. edn. Ind. Univ., 1987-94; chancellor and prof. edn., pub. adminstrn. Univ. Mich., Flint, 1994—; cons., evaluator N.Cen. Assn. Schs. & Colls., 1987—, Middle States Assn., 1994—. Contbr. articles to profl. jours. Recipient Outstanding Svc. award NASPA, 1990, I-MAEOPP, 1990, Disting. Svc. award Negro Edn. Review, 1990, Nat. Alliance Bus., 1984, Wall Street Joun. Student Achievement award, 1968, Rockefeller Student Leadership award, 1968. Office: U Mich Office of Chancellor 221 University Pavilion Flint MI 48502 Home: 915 Woodlawn Pk Dr Flint MI 48503

NELSEN, HART MICHAEL, sociologist, educator; b. Pipestone, Minn., Aug. 3, 1938; s. Noah I. and Nova (Ziegler) N.; m. Anne Kusener, June 13, 1964; 1 dau., Jennifer. B.A., U. No. Iowa, 1959, M.A., 1963; M.Div., Princeton Theol. Sem., 1963; Ph.D. (NSF faculty fellow), Vanderbilt U., 1972. Asst. prof. sociology Western Ky. U., Bowling Green, 1965-70; assoc. prof. Western Ky. U., 1970-73; assoc. prof. Catholic U. Am., 1973-74, prof., 1974-81, chmn. dept. sociology, 1974-77, mem. Boys Town Ctr. for Study Youth Devel., 1974-81; prof. sociology La. State U., Baton Rouge, 1981-84, chmn. dept. sociology, head dept. rural sociology, 1981-84, coordinator rural sociology research, 1981-84; dean Coll. Liberal Arts Pa. State U., 1984-90, prof. sociology, 1984—. Author: (with Anne K. Nelsen) Black Church in the Sixties, 1975; co-author: The Religion of Children, 1977, Religion and American Youth, 1976; editor: (with others) The Black Church in America, 1971; adv. editor: Sociol. Quar, 1976-82; assoc. editor: Sociol. Analysis, 1977-80, Rev. Religious Research, 1977-80, 84—, editor, 1980-84; mem. editorial bd.: Social Forces, 1983-86. Co-rec. sec. Capitol Hill Restoration Soc., 1979-80, v.p., 1980-81; mem. exec. bd. Lafitte Hills Assn., 1983-84. Presbyterian Chs. grantee, 1966-69; NIMH co-grantee, 1969-72; Russell Sage Found. co-grantee, 1972-73; La. Gov.'s Commn. on Alcoholism and Drug Abuse grantee, 1982. Mem. Assn. Sociology Religion (exec. council 1974-76, 78-82, v.p. 1978-79, pres. 1980-81), Religious Research Assn. (dir. 1977-80, pres.-elect 1985-86, pres. 1987-88), Soc. Sci. Study Religion (council 1981-83, exec. sec. 1984-87), Am. Sociol. Assn., So. Sociol. Soc. (chmn. membership com. 1983-85), AAAS (rep. 1984—). Presbyterian. Office: Pa State U Oswald 306 Dept Sociology University Park PA 16802

NELSEN, TIMOTHY ALAN, lawyer; b. Chgo., Nov. 14, 1947; s. Theodore Allen and Betty Jane (Freeman) Nelsen. BA, Carleton Coll., 1969; JD, U. Mich., 1972. Bar: N.Y. 1973, U.S. Dist. Ct. (so. and ea. dists.) N.Y. 1973, U.S. Ct. Appeals (2d cir.) 1973, U.S. Tax Ct. 1981, U.S. Ct. Appeals (5th cir.) 1985, Ill. 1986, U.S. Dist. Ct. (no. dist.) Ill. 1986, U.S. Ct. Appeals (7th cir.) 1986, U.S. Supreme Ct. 1987, U.S. Dist. Ct. (ea. dist) Mich. 1992, U.S. Ct. Appeals (6th cir.) 1992, U.S. Dist. Ct. Ariz. 1993; cert. ICC, 1982. Ptnr. Skadden, Arps, Slate, Meagher & Flom, N.Y.C., 1972-85, Chgo., 1985—. Home: 2800 N Lake Shore Dr Apt 3601 Chicago IL 60657-6253 Office: Skadden Arps Slate et al 333 W Wacker Dr Chicago IL 60606-1218

NELSEN, WILLIAM CAMERON, foundation president, former college president; b. Omaha, Oct. 18, 1941; s. William Peter and Ellen Lucella (Cameron) N.; m. Margaret Leone Rossow, May 30, 1981; children by previous marriage: William Norris, Shawna Lynn; 1 adopted dau., Sarah Ruth. B.A., Midland Lutheran Coll., Fremont, Nebr., 1963; M.A. (Danforth Grad. fellow 1963, Woodrow Wilson fellow 1963), Columbia U., 1966; Ph.D., U. Pa., 1971; Fulbright scholar, U. Erlangen, W. Ger., 1964; D (hon.), Midland Luth. Coll., 1995. Program exec. Danforth Found., St. Louis, 1970-73; asst. dean, then v.p., dean coll. St. Olaf Coll., Northfield, Minn., 1973-80; pres. Augustana Coll., Sioux Falls, S.D., 1980-86, Citizens' Scholarship Found. of Am., St. Peter, Minn., 1986—; bd. dirs. 1st Nat. Bank, St. Peter, Minn., Coun. of Ind. Colls.; adv. bd. Consortium for Advancement of Pvt. Higher Edn., 1988—. Author: Effective Approaches to Faculty Development, 1980, Renewal of the Teacher Scholar, 1981, also articles. Bd. dirs. S.D. Symphony, 1980-85, Sioux Falls YMCA, 1980-86, Luth. Ednl. Conf. N.Am., 1982-86, Sioux Falls United Way, 1983-86. Mem. Am. Assn. Higher Edn., Assn. Am. Colls. (bd. dirs. 1984-86, dir. project faculty devel. 1979), Shoreland Country Club (pres. 1996—). Republican. Lutheran. Home: 804 Spruce Pl Saint Peter MN 56082-1598 Office: Citizens' Scholarship Found Am PO Box 297 Saint Peter MN 56082-0297

NELSON, ALAN CURTIS, government official, lawyer; b. Oakland, Calif., Oct. 18, 1933; s. Albert C. and Martha (Peters) N.; m. JoAnn Wallen, Jan. 31, 1960; children: Kristine Ann, Kathryn Donna, Karin Martha. BS, U. Calif., Berkeley, 1955, JD, 1958. Bar: Calif. 1959, U.S. Dist. Cts. Calif. 1959, U.S. Supreme Ct. 1984. Atty. Rogers, Clark & Jordan, San Francisco, 1959-64; dep. dist. atty. Alameda County (Calif.), 1964-69; asst. dir. State of Calif. Human Resource Dept., Sacramento, 1969-72; dir. State of Calif. Dept. Rehab., Sacramento, 1972-75; gen. atty. Pacific Telephone & Telegraph, San Francisco, 1975-81; dep. commr. Immigration and Naturalization Service, Washington, 1981-82, commr., 1982-89; cons. fed. Am. immigration reform U.S. Dept. Justice, Washington, 1989-90, 91-94; gen. counsel Employment Devel. Dept. State of Calif., 1990-91; atty. and cons. on immigration Sacramento, 1994—; adj. prof. McGeorge Sch. Law, U. Pacific. Chmn. Calif. Gov. Com. for Employment of Handicapped, 1981-82. Recipient Alumnus of Yr. award Tau Kappa Epsilon, 1987; Border Patrol Sta., Imperial Beach, Calif. dedicated to Commr. Nelson, 1988. Mem. State Bar Calif., Assn. Calif. Tort Reform (dir.), Bar Assn. San Francisco, Legal Aid Soc. San Francisco (dir.), Assn. Fed. Investigators (pres. 1987). Republican. Club: Commonwealth. Office: Law Offices of Alan Nelson 835 Shoreside Dr Sacramento CA 95831-1422 *Four Key Personal and Management Concepts: Pride, Integrity, Innovation and Persistence. Pride: pride in ones country, family and traditions are a foundation for all meaningful personal actions. Integrity: most individuals have an innate sense of integrity; this plus integrity which is learned in one's life experience must also form the foundation for all actions. Innovation: constantly pursue new challenges and approaches; innovation, which makes our system so effective, is essential in all business and government. Persistence: in any bureacratic setting a lack of persistence can often equate to failure because most obstacles must be overcome with some difficulty.*

NELSON, ALAN RAY, internist, medical assocation executive; b. Logan, Utah, June 11, 1933; s. Ray J. and Leah B. (Olson) N.; m. Gwen L. Sparrow, Jan. 2, 1959; children: John R., Shannon, Alan L. Student, Utah State U., 1951-54; MD, Northwestern U., 1958. Diplomate Am. Bd. Internal Medicine, Am. Bd. Endocrinology and Metabolism. Intern Highland Alameda County Hosp., Oakland, Calif., 1958-59; resident in internal medicine U. Utah, Salt Lake City, 1959-62, assoc. clin. prof., 1964-89; clin. prof. U. Utah, 1989-92; practice medicine specializing in internal medicine and endocrinology Salt Lake City, 1964-91; assoc. Meml. Med. Ctr., Salt Lake City, 1964-91; exec. v.p. Am. Soc. Internal Medicine, Washington, 1992—; mem. Nat. Profl. Standard Rev. Coun., 1973-77; pres. Utah Profl. Rev. Orgn., 1971-75; mem. AMA Coun. on Legis., 1977-80, trustee 1980—, chmn. 1986-88, pres.-elect 1988-89, pres. 1989-90; commr. Joint Commn. on Accreditation of Hosps., 1982-86, sec.-treas., 1985-86. Chair Health Care Quality Alliance, 1992-96. With M.C. USAF, 1962-64. Recipient Spl. Recognition award Am. Soc. Internal Medicine, 1973, Disting. Internist award, 1989. Fellow ACP; mem. Utah Med. Assn. (pres. from 1976, award 1973, 79), Inst. Medicine of NAS, (governing coun. 1984-87), World Med. Assn. (pres.-elect 1990-91, pres. 1992-92). Home: 11905 Parkside Dr Fairfax VA 22033-2648 Office: ASIM 2011 Pennsylvania Ave NW Washington DC 20006-1813

NELSON, ALFRED JOHN, retired pharmaceutical company executive; b. Dalmuir, Scotland, Jan. 24, 1922; came to U.S., 1972; s. John and Mary Catherine (Duncan) N.; m. Frances C. Hillier, Dec. 5, 1952; children: J. Stuart, Andrew D. MBChB, U. Glasgow, Scotland, 1945, MD with commendation, 1957; DPH, Royal Inst. Pub. Health and Hygiene, London, 1948. Resident Ayr County Hosp., 1945, Belvidere Fever Hosp., Glasgow, Scotland, 1948; cons. N.Y. State Dept. Health, Albany, 1950-51; dir. venereal disease control B.C. Dept. Health and Welfare, Vancouver, Can., 1952-54, cons. epidemiology, 1954-55; assoc. dean medicine U. B.C., Can., 1955-57, clin. assoc. prof. pub. health, 1952-70; dir. health services B.C. Hydro and Power Authority, Vancouver, Can., 1957-70; v.p. Hoechst-Roussel Pharm., Inc., Somerville, N.J., 1972-81, sr. v.p., med. dir., 1981-87, ret., 1987; hon. mem. staff Vancouver Gen. Hosp. Served with RCAF, 1953-56. Recipient John J. Sippy Meml. award APHA, 1959, Spl. award, 1960; named officer brother Order St. John of Jerusalem, 1966. Fellow ACP, Royal Coll. Physicians and Surgeons Can., Am. Coll. Preventive Medicine, N.Y. Acad. Medicine; mem. Can. Med. Assn. (sec. com. 1954-57). Presbyterian. Home: 29436 Port Royal Way Laguna Niguel CA 92677-7947

NELSON, ARTHUR HUNT, real estate management development company executive; b. Kansas City, Mo., May 21, 1923; s. Carl Ferdinand and Hearty (Brown) N.; m. Eleanor Thomas, Dec. 27, 1954; children: Carl F., Frances, Pamela. AB, U. Kans., 1943; JD, Harvard U., 1949. Bar: Mass. 1949. Staff radiation lab. MIT, 1943-44; sr. engr., cons. Raytheon Mfg. Co., Boston, 1948-52; pvt. practice Boston, 1949; v.p., treas., dir. Gen. Electronic Labs., Inc., Cambridge, Mass., 1951-64, chmn. bd., 1959-63; treas., dir. Sci. Electronics, Inc., Cambridge, 1955-64; treas., dir. Assocs. for Internat. Rsch., Inc., Cambridge, 1954—, pres., 1968—; treas., dir. Victor Realty Devel., Inc., Cambridge, 1959-76, pres., 1972-76, gen. ptnr., 1976—; gen. ptnr. Prospect Hill Exec. Office Park, Waltham, Mass., 1977—; chmn. Nelson Cos., 1990—, Cambridge Devel. Lab., 1994—; Bd. dirs. Internat. Data Group, Inc., Sterling Bank; chmn. Cambridge Devel. Lab., Inc., 1994—.

Pres., trustee Tech. Edn. Rsch. Ctrs., Inc., 1965—; trustee Winsor Sch., Boston, 1978-88, treas., 1978-82; bd. dirs. Charles River Mus. Industry, Waltham, 1986—, pres. 1994. Lt. USRN, 1944-46. Mem. ABA, Mass. Bar Assn., Boston Bar Assn., Boston Computer Soc. (bd. dirs. 1985—, chmn. 1994), Greater Boston C. of C., Harvard Club Boston, Beta Theta Pi, Phi Beta Kappa, Sigma Xi. Home: 75 Robin Rd Weston MA 02193-2436 Office: 100 5th Ave Waltham MA 02154-8703

NELSON, BARBARA JONES, food service and theatre professional; b. Augusta, Ga., Feb. 3, 1954; d. Robert F. and Margaret H. (Hill) Jones; divorced; children: Candice, Russell. Diploma, Dallas Fashion Mdse. Coll. Pres. Bo-Mar, Inc., Gallup, N.Mex., Cinebar, Inc. Mem. McKinley County Rep. Party, Gallup, 1991—; treas., sec. Gallup Downtown Devel. Group; sec. McKinley County Crimestoppers Bd. Named Employer of Yr. by Connections/Nat. Assn. Retarded Citizens, Durango, Colo., 1991, N.Mex. Mainstreet Vol. of Yr., 1995, Woman of Yr., AAUW, 1995. Mem. NAFE, soroptimist, Am. Mgmt. Assn., Nat. Restaurant Assn., Nat. Fedn. Ind. Bus., Gallup C. of C. Episcopalian. Avocations: travel, photography. Office: Bo-Mar Inc 914 E 66 Ave Gallup NM 87301

NELSON, BEN, JR., retired air force officer; b. Ft. Lewis, Wash., Jan. 31, 1942; s. Ben and Marie (Warn) N.; m. Suzanne Wiseman, Dec. 22, 1963; 1 child, William Bryant. BBA, U. Tex., 1964; MPA, Golden Gate U., 1976. Commd. 2d lt. USAF, 1964, advanced through grades to brig. gen., 1988; instr. pilot 3525th Fighter Tng. Squadron, Williams AFB, Ariz., 1965-70; flight comdr. 390th Tactical Fighter Squadron, DaNang, Vietnam, 1970-71, Sheppard AFB, Tex., 1971-74; chief pers. tng. br. Office Dep. Chief of Staff for Pers., Hdqrs. Tactical Air Command, Langley AFB, Va., 1974-77; ops. officer, comdr. 428th Tactical Fighter Squadron, Nellis AFB, Nev., 1977-81; student Naval War Coll., Newport, R.I., 1981-82; chief fighter plans br. Office Dep. Chief of Staff Ops., Hdqrs. USAF, Washington, 1982-84; vice comdr. 32d Tactical Fighter Squadron, Soesterberg Air Base, The Netherlands, 1984-85; vice comdr., then comdr. 50th Tactical Fighter Wing, Hahn Air Base, Fed. Republic Germany, 1985-88; asst. dep. chief of staff for plans Hdqrs. Tactical Air Command, Langley AFB, 1988-89; comdr. 56th Fighter Wing, MacDill AFB, Fla., 1989-92; dep. comdr. 5th Allied Tactical Air Forces (NATO), Vicenza, Italy, 1992-94; CEO regional office ARC, Tampa Bay, Fla., 1994—. Recipient Phoenix award Dept. Def., 1987, O'Malley award Dept. Air Force. Mem. Air Force Assn., Tampa C. of C. (bd. dirs. 1989-92), Order of Daedalians. Episcopalian. Avocation: golf.

NELSON, BERNARD EDWARD, lawyer; b. Miles City, Mont., May 9, 1950; s. Theodore M. and Lucille K. Nelson; m. Jane Walker, Sept. 8, 1978; children: Iain, Colin, Stuart. BA, Yale U., 1972; JD, Harvard U., 1975. Bar: N.Y. 1976. Assoc. White & Case, N.Y.C., 1975-84; ptnr. White & Case, N.Y.C. and London, 1984—, London, 1988—. Mem. Union Internationale Des Avocats (U.S. rep. permanent tax commn.). Democrat. Avocations: antique map collecting, antiquarian books. Office: White & Case, 7 Moorgate, London EC2R 6HH, England

NELSON, BERNARD WILLIAM, foundation executive, educator, physician; b. San Diego, Sept. 15, 1935; s. Arnold B. and Helene Christina (Falck) N.; m. Frances Davison, Aug. 9, 1958; children—Harry, Kate, Anne, Daniel. A.B., Stanford U., 1957, M.D., 1961. Asst. prof., asst. dean medicine Stanford U., Palo Alto, Calif., 1965-67, assoc. dean medicine, 1968-71, cons. assoc. prof., 1980-86; assoc. dean U. Wis., Madison, 1974-77, acting vice chancellor, 1978-79; exec. v.p. Kaiser Family Found., Menlo Park, Calif., 1979-81, 1981-86; chancellor U. Colo. Health Sci. Ctr., Denver, 1986—; mem., v.p., pres. Nat. Med. Fellowships, 1969-77. Trustee Morehouse Med. Sch., 1981-83. Fellow Inst. Medicine; mem. Calif. Acad. Sci., Alpha Omega Alpha (bd. dirs. 1978—). Avocations: fishing; photography; gardening; carpentry. Office: U Colo Health Sci Ctr Office of Chancellor 4200 E 9th Ave Denver CO 80220-3706*

NELSON, BERTHA MAE, psychiatric nurse; b. Alexandria, La., Aug. 26, 1935; d. Dennie and Mary (Price) Matthews; m. Robert Lee Nelson Sr., Jan. 25, 1953; children: Patsy Faye Henderson, Robert Lee Jr., Bennie Ray. ADN, Galveston Coll., 1978. RN, Tex.; lic. vocat. nurse. Charge nurse-11-7 U. Tex. Med. Br., Galveston, 1962-78, staff nurse, 1978-83, asst. head nurse, 1983-93, nurse clinician III, 1993—. Mem. Cts. of Calanthe, Texas City, Tex., 1993-94. Mem. Order Ea. Star (Silver Cir.). Baptist. Avocations: bicycle riding, singing, church activities, missionary work. Home: 6618 Park Ave Texas City TX 77591-3740

NELSON, BRIAN JAMES, broadcast journalist; b. Montreal, Que., Can., Oct. 11, 1948; s. Charles Gordon and Mary (Timlin) N.; m. Joan Lynn Osborne, July 31, 1971 (div.); m. Louise Antoinetta Zambon, June 28, 1985. BA cum laude in Comm. Arts, Loyola of Montreal, 1970. News and sports announcer Sta. CJAD Radio, Montreal, 1969-70; news announcer Sta. CFRA Radio, Ottawa, Ont., Can., 1970-71; parliamentary bur. chief, corr. Std. Broadcast News, Ottawa, 1971-77; sr. polit. reporter CFCF-TV, Montreal, 1977-81; corr. CTV Network, Montreal and Ottawa, 1981-83; comm. dir. Don Johnston Liberal Party Leadership Campaign, Ottawa, 1984; news anchor, exec. prodr., corr. CNN, Atlanta, Miami, Fla., and Tokyo, 1984—. Host, exec. prodr. news mag. show This Week in Japan, 1989-90, East Meets West, 1990; host, prodr. news documentary The Everglades, 1994; host, corr. news mag. show The CNN Computer Connection, 1995—. Mem. Atlanta Press Club, Can. Am. Assn. Southeastern U.S. (bd. dirs., comm. dir.). Avocations: tennis, fishing, travel, fitness, reading. Office: CNN Box 105366 One CNN Ctr Atlanta GA 30348-5366

NELSON, BRUCE SHERMAN, advertising agency executive; b. Lansing, Mich., Nov. 3, 1951; s. Max and Blanche (Sherman) N.; m. Minette Raskin. AB, UCLA, 1973. Sr. copywriter Ogilvy & Mather, Los Angeles, 1977-78, Young & Rubicam, N.Y.C., 1978-79; assoc. creative dir. McCann Erickson, Inc., N.Y.C., 1979-80, v.p., 1980-81, sr. v.p., 1981-83, exec. v.p., creative dir., 1983-86, exec. v.p., worldwide dir. strategic creative devel., 1987-93; exec. v.p., creative dir. worldwide accounts, 1993-94, exec. v.p., creative dir. worldwide accts., 1994—; founder, chief exec. officer Ira Madris, Bruce Nelson & Colleagues, 1986-87; lectr. Columbia Bus. Sch. Exec. Programs, N.Y.C., 1993—. Mgmt. fellow Sch. orgn. and Mgmt. Yale U., 1993—. Office: McCann-Erickson Worldwide 750 3rd Ave New York NY 10017-2703

NELSON, CARL ROGER, retired lawyer; b. Gowrie, Ia., Dec. 26, 1915; s. Carl Helge and Inez Olivia (West) N.; m. Elizabeth Boswell Campbell, Apr. 27, 1946; children: Thomas C., Nancy L. AB, Grinnell Coll., 1937; MA, Columbia, 1938, LLB, 1941. Bar: N.Y. 1941, D.C. 1947, U.S. Supreme Ct. 1947. Law clk. to Chief Justice Stone, 1941-42; Washington asso. firm Root, Ballantine, Harlan, Bushby & Palmer, 1946-51; mem. firm Purcell & Nelson, Washington, 1951-80; firm Reavis & McGrath, 1980-83, Nelson Thurston Jones & Blouch, 1984-88; Mem. Adminstrv. Conf. U.S., 1967-73. Served to capt. AUS, 1942-46. Fellow Am. Bar Found.; mem. ABA (mem. ho. dels. 1964-66, mem. coun. 1960-66, chmn. sect. adminstrv. law 1963-64), D.C. Bar Assn. (chmn. corp. law, com. 1954-55, 58-60), Mediation Panel U.S. Ct. Appeals (D.C. cir.), Chevy Chase (Md.) Club, Lawyers Club (Washington), Met. Club (Washington), Phi Beta Kappa. Mem. United Ch. of Christ.

NELSON, CARLON JUSTINE, engineering and operations executive; b. Siloam Springs, Ark., May 26, 1960; d. Robert F. and Jean (Carson) Toenges. BS in Indsl. Engring., U. Ark., 1982; MBA, Houston Bapt. U., 1988. Registered profl. engr., Tex. Supr. codes and regulatory compliance Tex. Ea., Houston, 1982-85, supr. ops. spl. projects, 1985-87, mgr. project devel., 1987-90; dir. spl. projects, tech. asst. to pres. Enron, Houston, 1990-91, dir. throughput engring., 1991-92, project dir., 1992-95; v.p. engring. So. Union Gas Co., Austin, Tex., 1995-96; v.p. ops. Mo. Gas Energy, Kansas City, Mo., 1996—. Mem. NSPE, Tex. Soc. Profl. Engrs. Home: 5601 NE Northgate Crossing Lees Summit MO 64064 Office: Mo Gas Energy 3420 Broadway Kansas City MO 64111

NELSON, CHARLES ARTHUR, publisher, consultant; b. Berwyn, Ill., Dec. 21, 1922; s. Arthur A.R. and Florence Dorothy (Lagergren) N.; m. Anne Ballou Higgins, July 1946; children: Christopher, Janet, Colin, Edward. BA, St. John's Coll., Annapolis, Md., 1947. Dir. liberal arts program, humanities lectr. U. Chgo., 1947-52; exec. dir. Am. Found. For Polit. Edn., Chgo., 1947-56; sr. cons. Cresap, McCormick & Paget, N.Y.C., 1956-58; pres. Nelson Assocs., N.Y.C., 1958-68; prin. Peat Marwick Mitchell & Co., N.Y.C., 1968-83; pres. Exec. Search, Croton-on-Hudson, 1983—; pub. Croton-Cortlandt Gazette, Croton-on-Hudson, 1986—. Author: Developing Responsible Public Leaders, 1963; co-author: The University, The Citizen, & World Affairs, 1956, Financial Management for the Arts, 1975, Ratio Analysis in Higher Education, 1980, Ethics, Leadership and the Bottom Line, 1991; contbr. articles to jours. Chmn. bd. Exec. Council on Fgn. Diplomats, N.Y.C.; chmn. bd. St. John's Coll., Annapolis, Md., Santa Fe, 1978-83, trustee, 1952-91, Linfield Coll., McMinville, Oreg., 1983-88. Mem. N.Y. Press Assn. Democrat. Home and Office: PO Box 247 Croton On Hudson NY 10520-0247

NELSON, CHARLES J., university administrator, international consultant, diplomat, consultant; b. Mich., Mar. 5, 1920; m. Maureen Tinsley. A.B., Lincoln U., 1942; M.P.A., NYU, 1948. Research assoc. state govt., 1949-52; program asst. MSA Manila, 1952-53; pub. adminstrn. analyst FOA, 1953-54, pub. adminstrn. specialist, 1954-55; dep. spl. asst. for community devel. ICA, 1955-57; chief community devel. adviser Tehran, 1958; community devel. adviser Dept. State, 1960, chief Africa-Latin Am. br., 1960-61, detailed African br., 1961; assoc. dir. Office Program Devel. and Coordination PC, Washington, 1961-63; dir. Office Devel. Resources, AID, 1963-64, dir. North African affairs, 1964-66; dep. mission dir. Addis Ababa, 1966-68; mission dir. Dar es Salaam, 1968-71; ambassador to Botswana, Lesotho and Swaziland, 1971-74; mission dir. counsellor internat. devel. AID, Nairobi, Kenya, 1974-78; adminstr. program in internat. studies Sch. Human Ecology, Howard U., 1978-81. Mem. Overseas Devel. Coun.; chair Mayor's Internat. Adv. Council; bd. dirs. Nations Capital council Girl Scouts U.S.A., 1981-87, also mem. retention extension outreach com.; bd. dirs. D.C. Council Internat. Programs, 1981-87; v.p. nat. bd. dirs. Sister Cities Internat.; mem. U.S. D.C.-Beijing Friendship Council; mem. Thai-Am. Assn. Coun. Am. Ambassadors, U.S.-Dakar Capital Cities Friendship Council; co-chmn. Soc. for Internat. Devel., Africa Roundtable. Served to capt. AUS, 1942-47. Mem. Georgetown Citizens Assn., Voice of Informed Cmty. Expression, Smithsonian Instn., Overseas Devel. Coun., The Atlantic Coun., Am. Polit. Sci. Assn., UN Assn., Diplomatic and Counselor Officers Ret., Friends of Ethiopia, Univ. Club (Washington). Address: 1401 35th St NW Washington DC 20007-2806

NELSON, CONNIE RAE, pharmacy education director, educator; b. Lewistown, Mont., Aug. 19, 1950; d. Ward Wallace and Violet May (Charette) Dickson; m. Alan C. Nelson, July 23, 1977; children: Russell Robert, Nicole Elaine. Pharmacy asst. level A degree, Clover Park Vocat. Tech. Inst., Tacoma, 1979; student in pharmacology Bates Vocat. Tech. Inst., Tacoma, 1982. Lic. pharmacy asst. level A. Druggist clk. Thrifty Drugs, Tacoma, 1972-79; intern in hematology, oncology, pediatrics Madigan Army Med. Ctr., Tacoma, 1979-80; pharmacy asst. A, St. Joseph Hosp., Tacoma, 1979-84; pharmacy instr. Clover Park Vocat. Tech. Inst., Tacoma, 1984-93; pharmacy dept. dir. Eton Tech. Inst., Federal Way, Wash., 1993-94; ednl. task force pharmacy bd. Wash. State, 1993-95, co-chmn. Wash. State Ednl. Task Force, 1995; pharmacy curriculum cons., 1993—. Archtl. and land development West Tapps Maintenance Co., Sumner, Wash., 1979-86, legal and pub. affairs mem., 1984-86, pres., 1985-90. Mem. Wash. State Soc. Pharmacy Assts., Pharmpac (legis. rep. for assts. 1986), Wash. State Soc. Hosp. Pharmacists (pres. Pharmacy Asst. chpt. 1984-95), Wash. State Soc. Pharmacy Assts. (founder, pres. 1985—, legal and pub. affairs chmn. 1987—, legis. chmn. 1987-95, exec. dir. 1991—). Avocations: lecturing, camping, horticulture. Home: 18710 58th St E Sumner WA 98390-6808

NELSON, CRAIG ALAN, management consultant; b. San Rafael, Calif., July 11, 1961; s. Kenneth Alfred and Anne Catherine (Laurie) N. BS in Fin., San Diego State U., 1984. Loan assoc. Union Bank, San Diego, 1984-85, comml. loan officer, 1985-86, corp. banking officer, 1986-87, asst. v.p., 1987-89, v.p. corp. banking, 1989-93; v.p. Alexander & Alexander, San Diego, 1993-95; sr. assoc. Goreham-Moore & Assocs., San Diego, 1995—. Corp. recruiter United Way, San Diego, 1988; community group chair San Diego chpt. Am. Cancer Soc., 1989; mem. com. Juvenile Diabetes Assn.; bd. dirs. San Diego State Found., 1989—. Mem. San Diego State U. Young Alumni Assn. (pres. 1988-89, bd. dirs. emeritus 1989). Home: 1233 San Dieguito Dr Encinitas CA 92024-5116 Office: Gordham-Moore & Assocs 1331 Morena Blvd San Diego CA 92110-1550

NELSON, CRAIG T., actor; b. Spokane, Wash., Apr. 4, 1944. Appeared in (feature films) And Justice for All, 1979, The Formula, 1980, Where the Buffalo Roam, 1980, Private Benjamin, 1980, Stir Crazy, 1981, Poltergeist, 1982, Man, Woman, and Child, 1983, The Osterman Weekend, 1983, All the Right Moves, 1983, The Killing Fields, 1984, Silkwood, 1984, Poltergeist II: The Other Side, 1986, Red Riding Hood, 1987, Action Jackson, 1988, Me and Him, 1988, Troup Beverly Hills, 1989, Rachel River, 1989, Turner & Hooch, 1989; (stage prodn.) Friends, 1983-84, (TV movies) How the West Was Won, 1978, Diary of a Teenage Hitchiker, 1979, Rage, 1980, Inmates: A Love Story, 1981, Murder in Texas, 1981, Paper Dolls, 1983, Alex: The Life of a Child, 1986, The Ted Kennedy, Jr. Story, 1986, Murderers Among Us: The Simon Wiesenthal Story, 1989, Extreme Close-Up, 1990, Drug Wars: The Camarena Story, 1990, The Josephine Baker Story, 1991, The Fire Next Time, 1993; (TV series) Heroes: Made in the U.S.A. (host), 1986, Coach, 1993— (Emmy award, Leading actor in a comedy series, 1992); producer (film documentaries) American Still; screenwriter (TV shows) The Lohman and Barkley Show, The Tim Conway Show, The Alan King Special. Office: care Brian Mann - ICM 8942 Wilshire Blvd Beverly Hills CA 90211*

NELSON, CRAIG WAYNE, academy administrator; b. Mpls., Mar. 8, 1932; s. Clarence August and Blanche Adeline (Nordell) N.; m. Betty Ann McLouth, Oct. 27, 1956; children: Cynthia Ann, Jon Craig. AA, North Pk. Coll., 1951; student, Trinity Coll., Hartford, Conn., 1951-52; BA, Northwestern U., 1955, MA in History, 1959; BD, North Pk. Theol. Sem., 1956; postgrad., Ea. Mich. U., 1970-71. Ordained clergyperson Covenant Ch. Am. Intern pastor Queen St. Congl. Ch., Bristol, Conn., 1952-53; pastor Evang. Covenant Ch., Villa Park, Ill., 1956-61, 1st Covenant Ch., Red Wing, Minn., 1961-66, Dearborn (Mich.) Evang. Covenant Ch, 1966-71, Bloomington (Minn.) Covenant Ch., 1971-77; pres. Minnehaha Acad., Mpls., 1977-94; ednl. cons., 1995—; tchr. North Pk. Coll., 1958-59, Minnehaha Acad., 1979-90; chaplain Mpls. Police Dept., 1972-77, Bloomington Police Dept., 1973-77; area co-dir. Evangelism N.W. conf., mem. exec. bd.; sec. N.W. Covenant Ministerium; active Covenant Bd. Minstry, Covenant Stewardship Commn.; dir. Lake Minnetonka Conservation Dist., 1995—; chmn. Minn. Ind. Sch. Forum, 1993-95; ednl. cons., 1994—. Active Bloomington Bd. Health, 1975-77; trustee Minn. Ind. Sch. Fund, 1979-91, v.p., 1980-81, 92-93, treas., 1991-92, chair, 1993-95. Named Disting. Alumni, North Pk. Coll., 1985. Mem. Coun. for Advancement and Support of Edn., North Ctrl. Assn., Bloomington Ministerial Assn. (chmn. 1974-75), Mpls. Ministerial Assn. (chmn. 1976-77), Minn.Ind. Sch. Fund. Avocations: fishing, hunting, boating, reading. Home and Office: 3888 Park Ln Spring Park MN 55384

NELSON, DARRELL WAYNE, university administrator, scientist; b. Aledo, Ill., Nov. 28, 1939; s. Wayne Edward and Olive Elvina (Peterson) N.; m. Nancyann Hyer, Aug. 27, 1961; children: Christina Lynne, Craig Douglas. BS in Agriculture, U. Ill., 1961, MS in Agronomy, 1963; PhD in Agronomy, Iowa State U., 1967. Cert. profl. soil scientist. Div. chief U.S. Army Chem. Corps., Denver, 1967-68; asst. prof. Purdue U., West Lafayette, Ind., 1968-73, assoc. prof., 1973-77, prof. agronomy, 1977-84; dept. head U. Nebr., Lincoln, 1984-88, dean for agr. rsch. and dir. Nebr. Agrl. Experiment Sta., 1988—; cons. U.S. EPA, Washington, 1977-79, Ind. Bd. of Health, Indpls., 1977-83, Eli Lilly Co., Indpls., 1976. Editor: Chemical Mobility and Reactivity in Soils, 1983. Served to capt. U.S. Army, 1967-68. Fellow AAAS, Am. Soc. Agronomy (bd. dirs., CIBA-Geigy award 1975, Agronomic Achievement award 1983, Environ. Quality Rsch. award 1985), Soil Sci. Soc. Am. (bd. dirs., pres. elect 1992, pres. 1993, past. pres. 1994); mem. Internat. Soil Sci. Soc., Lions Lodge (treas. 1980-83, Lafayette, Ind. chpt.). Presbyterian. Avocations: fishing, skiing, jogging. Office: Univ of Nebr Agrl Rsch Div Lincoln NE 68583-0704

NELSON, DAVID ALDRICH, federal judge; b. Watertown, N.Y., Aug. 14, 1932; s. Carlton Low and Irene Demetria (Aldrich) N.; m. Mary Dickson, Aug. 25, 1956; 3 children. A.B., Hamilton Coll., 1954; postgrad., Cambridge U., Eng., 1954-55; LL.B., Harvard U., 1958. Bar: Ohio 1958, N.Y. 1982. Atty.-advisor Office of the Gen. Counsel, Dept. of the Air Force, 1959-62; assoc. Squire, Sanders & Dempsey, Cleve., 1958-67, ptnr., 1967-69, 72-85; cir. judge U.S. Ct. Appeals (6th cir.), Cin., 1985—; gen. counsel U.S. Post Office Dept., Washington, 1969-71; sr. asst. postmaster gen., gen. counsel U.S. Postal Svc., Washington, 1971; mem. nat. coun. Coll. Law, Ohio State U., 1988—. Trustee Hamilton Coll., 1984-88. Served to maj. USAFR, 1959-69. Fulbright scholar, 1954-55; recipient Benjamin Franklin award U.S. Post Office Dept., 1969. Fellow Am. Coll. Trial Lawyers; mem. Fed. Bar Assn., Ohio Bar Assn., Cleve. Bar Assn., Cin. Bar Assn., Emerson Lit. Soc., Ct. of Nisi Prius (sgt. emeritus), Phi Beta Kappa. Office: US Ct Appeals 6th Cir Potter Stewart US Ct House 5th and Walnut St Cincinnati OH 45202-3988

NELSON, DAVID EDWARD, lawyer; b. Passaic, N.J., Oct. 26, 1930; s. David Charles and Ann Ellen (Pardoe) N.; m. Stuart McKenna, May 28, 1953; children: Douglas, Kathryn, Ann; m. Elizabeth A. Carlston, Dec. 28, 1974; children: Lynn, Kathleen. A.B., UCLA; LL.B., U. Calif.-Berkeley; Diploma in Comparative Legal Studies, U. Cambridge, Eng., 1960. Bar: Calif. Assoc. Morrison & Foerster, San Francisco, 1960-65, ptnr., 1965—. Bd. dirs. Berkeley Bd. Edn., 1967-69; chmn. bd. Head-Royce Sch., Oakland, Calif., 1974-79. Served to lt. (j.g.) U.S. Navy, 1952-56. Mem. San Francisco Bar Assn. (pres. Barrister Club), ABA (chmn. bus. law sect. 1988-89), Calif. Bar Assn. (com. bar examiners 1973-77, chmn. 1976-77), Southwestern Legal Found., Bankers Club. Office: Morrison & Foerster 345 California St San Francisco CA 94104-2635

NELSON, DAVID LEONARD, process management systems company executive; b. Omaha, May 8, 1930; s. Leonard A. and Cecelia (Steinert) N.; m. Jacqueline J. Zerbe, Dec. 26, 1952; 1 child, Nancy Jo. BS, Iowa State U., 1952. Mktg. adminstr. Ingersoll Rand, Chgo., 1954-56; with Accuray Corp., Columbus, Ohio, 1956-87, exec. v.p., gen. mgr., 1967, pres., 1967-87, chief exec. officer, 1970-87; pres. process automation bus. unit Combustion Engring., Inc., Columbus, 1987-90; pres. bus. area process automation Asea Brown Boveri, Stamford, Conn., 1990-91, v.p. customer satisfaction Ams. region, 1991-93, v.p. customer support Ams. region, 1994-95; chmn. bd. dirs. Herman Miller Inc., Zeeland, Mich., 1995—. Patentee in field. Bd. dirs. Cardinal Govt. Obligations Fund, Columbus, Cardinal Govt. Securities Trust, Columbus, Cardinal Tax Exempt Money Trust, Columbus, Cardinal Govt. Guaranteed Fund, Columbus, Cardinal Aggressive Growth Fund, Columbus, Cardinal Balanced Fund, Columbus. Served to capt. USMCR, 1952-54. Mem. IEEE, Instrument Soc. Am., Newcomen Soc. N.Am., Tau Beta Pi, Phi Kappa Phi, Phi Eta Sigma, Delta Upsilon. Home: 295 Whispering Way Holland MI 49424

NELSON, DAVID LOREN, geneticist, educator; b. Washington, June 25, 1956; s. Erling Walter and Marlys Joan (Jorgenson) N.; m. Claudia Jane Hackbarth, July 31, 1982; children: Jorgen William, Erik Alexander. BA, U. Va., 1978; PhD, MIT, 1984. Staff fellow NIH, Bethesda, Md., 1985-86; sr. assoc. Baylor Coll. Medicine, Houston, 1986-89, instr., 1989-90, asst. prof., 1990-94, assoc. prof., 1994—; dir. Human Genome Ctr., 1995-96. Editor: Genome Data Base, 1992—; assoc. editor Genomics, 1994—. Achievements include development of Alu PCR; discovery of fragile X syndrome gene (FMR-1), new form of genetic mutation (simple repeat expansion). Office: Baylor Coll Med Dept Molecular & Human Genetics 1 Baylor Plz Houston TX 77030-3411

NELSON, DAVID ROBERT, physics educator; b. Stuttgart, Federal Republic of Germany, May 9, 1951; came to U.S., 1953; s. Robert Charles and Faye Scott (Abernethy) N.; m. Patricia Schneider, Dec. 30, 1975; children: Meredith, Leigh, Christopher David, Peter Charles. AB, Cornell U., 1972, MS, 1974, PhD, 1975; MA (hon.), Harvard U., 1980. Jr. fellow Harvard Soc. Fellows, Cambridge, Mass., 1975-78; assoc. prof. physics Harvard U., 1978-80; prof. Harvard U., Cambridge, 1980-91, Mallinckrodt prof. physics, 1992—; cons. IBM, Yorktown Heights, N.Y., 1976-82, Mitre Corp., Bedford, Mass., 1985—, AT&T Bell Labs., Murray Hill, N.J., 1988—, Exxon Rsch. & Engring., 1994-95. Co-author: Phase Transitions and Critical Phenomena, Vol. 7, 1983; co-author, editor: Statistical Mechanics of Membranes and Interfaces, 1989. A.P. Sloan Found. fellow, 1979-83, MacArthur Found. Prize fellow, 1984-89, Guggenheim fellow, 1993—; recipient award for initiatives in rsch. NAS, 1986, Ledlie prize, 1995. Fellow Am. Phys. Soc., Harvard Soc. Fellows (sr.); mem. APS, AAAS, NAS, Am. Acad. Arts and Scis. Office: Harvard U Dept Physics Cambridge MA 02138

NELSON, DAWN MARIE, elementary school educator; b. Norristown, Pa., Mar. 29, 1960; m. Peirce Watson Nelson, Aug. 12, 1978; children: Adam Christopher, Joshua Peirce. Student, Montgomery County C.C., Blubell, Pa., 1977-78, Temple U., 1979-80, Ursinus Coll.; BS in Edn. summa cum laude, Cabrini Coll., Radnor, Pa., 1992, postgrad., 1996—; postgrad., St. Joseph's U., 1995. Cert. elem. tchr., Pa.; cert. ASCI. Tchr. Penn Christian Acad., Norristown, 1992—; asst. curriculum and program developer; accreditation steering com.; supr. Math. Olympics, co-chmn.; mentor, student tchr. supr. Vol. pub. and pvt. schs., ch. orgns. Mem. ASCD, Alpha Sigma Lambda. Avocations: reading, travel, quilting, writing. Office: Penn Christian Acad 50 W Germantown Pike Norristown PA 19401-1565

NELSON, DEWEY ALLEN, neurologist, educator; b. Eldrado, Ark., Dec. 2, 1927; s. Herman Eugene and Pearl Estelle (Shirley) N.; m. E. Jem Nolt, Oct. 7, 1951; children: Allen, Stephen, John, Daniel. BS, Cornell U., 1948, MD, 1951. Diplomate Am. Bd. Psychiatry and Neurology, Am. Bd. Neurophysiology. Resident Bellevue Hosp., N.Y.C., 1951-52, 54-57; chief neurology Med. Ctr. Del., Wilmington, 1957-83, sr. neurology, 1983-88, hon. sr. neurology, 1988—; chief neurology St. Francis Hosp., Wilmington, 1957-83; founder, neurologist Neurology Assocs., Wilmington, 1957-85; assoc. clin. prof. neurology Thomas Jefferson U. Med. Ctr., Phila., 1971-75, prof. neurology, 1975—; med. expert, advisor to ct. Social Security Adminstrn., 1982—. Contbr. 70 articles to profl. jours., poetry to periodicals. 1st lt. U.S. Army, 1952-54, Korea. Decorated Bronze Star, United Nations Svc. medal with 2 battle stars, Nat. Def. Svc. medal; recipient Bronze Hope Chest award Nat. Multiple Sclerosis Soc., 1960, Plaque award Multiple Sclerosis Clinic, 1979; Teagle Found. scholar, 1946-51. Republican. Presbyterian (ruling elder). Avocations: metal work cast iron, antique cars, choir. Home: 206 N Spring Valley Rd Wilmington DE 19807-2427

NELSON, DON JEROME, electrical engineering and computer science educator; b. Nebr., Aug. 17, 1930; s. Irvin Andrew and Agnes Emelia (Nissen) N. BS, U. Nebr., 1953, MSc, 1958; PhD, Stanford U., 1962. Registered profl. engr., Nebr. Mem. tech. staff AT&T Bell Labs., Manhattan, N.Y., 1953, 55; instr. U. Nebr., Lincoln, 1955-58, from asst. to assoc. prof., 1960-63, dir. computer ctr., 1963-72, prof. electrical engring., 1967—, prof. computer sci., 1969—, co-dir. Ctr. Comm. & Info. Sci., 1988-91, dir. rsch. computing group, 1993—; cons. Union Life Ins., Lincoln, 1973, Nebr. Pub. Power Dist., Columbus, 1972-83, Taiwan Power Co., Taipei, 1974. 1st lt. USAF, 1953-55. Mem. IEEE (sr., Outstanding Faculty award 1989), Assn. Computing Machinery. Republican. Home: 4911 Concord Rd Lincoln NE 68516 Office: U Nebr Dept Computer Sci 209N Wsec Lincoln NE 68588

NELSON, DOREEN KAE, mental health counselor, reserve military officer; b. Duluth, Minn., Oct. 18, 1957; d. Norman G. Nelson and Carola Gerene (Sunneli) Cooper. B Applied Scis., U. Minn., 1983; MS in Human Resources Mgmt. Devel., Chapman U., 1988; MAEd in Mental Health Counseling, Western Ky. U., 1995. Commd. 2nd lt. U.S. Army, 1983, advanced through grades to capt., 1987; pers. officer 62nd Med. Group U.S. Army, Ft. Lewis, Wash., 1987-88; med. pers. officer Acad. Health Scis. U.S. Army, Ft. Sam Houston, Tex., 1989, chief adminstrv. svcs. div. Med. Dept. Ctr. and Sch., 1989-92; med. advisor Readiness Group Knox, Ft. Knox, Ky., 1992-94; counselor intern Ireland Army Hosp., Ft. Knox, 1995; mental health counselor IV Mental Health Svcs., Inc., Gainesville, Fla., 1995—. Lutheran. Avocations: designing specialty clothing, computer applications. Home: PO Box 807 Newberry FL 32669-0807

NELSON, DOROTHY WRIGHT (MRS. JAMES F. NELSON), federal judge; b. San Pedro, Calif., Sept. 30, 1928; d. Harry Earl and Lorna Amy Wright; m. James Frank Nelson, Dec. 27, 1950; children: Franklin Wright,

Lorna Jean. B.A., UCLA, 1950, J.D., 1953; LL.M., U. So. Calif., 1956; LLD honoris causa, Western State U., 1980, U. So. Calif., 1983, Georgetown U., 1988, Whittier U., 1989, U. Santa Clara, 1990; LLD (honoris causa), Whittier U., 1989. Bar: Calif. 1954. Research assoc. fellow U. So. Calif., 1953-56; instr., 1957, asst. prof., 1958-61, assoc. prof., 1961-67, prof., 1967, assoc. dean., 1965-67, dean., 1967-80; judge U.S. Ct. Appeals (9th cir.), 1979—; cons. Project STAR, Law Enforcement Assistance Adminstrn.; mem. select com. on internal procedures of Calif. Supreme Ct., 1987—; co-chair Sino-Am. Seminar on Mediation and Arbitration, Beijing, 1992; dir. Dialogue on Transition to a Global Soc., Weinacht, Switzerland, 1992. Author: Judicial Adminstration and The Administration of Justice, 1973, (with Christopher Goelz and Meredith Watts) Federal Ninth Circuit Civil Appellate Practice, 1995; Contbr. articles to profl. jours. Co-chmn. Confronting Myths in Edn. for Pres. Nixon's White House Conf. on Children, Pres. Carter's Commn. for Pension Policy, 1974-80, Pres. Reagon's Madison Trust; bd. visitors U.S. Air Force Acad., 1978; bd. dirs. Council on Legal Edn. for Profl. Responsibility, 1971-80, Constnl. Right Found., Am. Nat. Inst. for Social Advancement; adv. bd. Nat. Center for State Cts., 1971-73; chmn. bd. Western Justice Ctr., 1986—; mem. adv. com. Nat. Jud. Edn. Program to promote equality for woman and men in cts. Named Law Alumnus of Yr. UCLA, 1967; recipient Profl. Achievement award, 1969; named Times Woman of Yr., 1968; recipient U. Judaism Humanitarian award, 1973; AWARE Internat. award, 1970; Ernestine Stalhut Outstanding Woman Lawyer award, 1972; Pub. Svc. award Coro Found., 1978, Pax Orbis ex Jure medallion World Peace thru Law Ctr., 1975, Hollzer Human Rights award Jewish Fedn. Coun., L.A., 1988, Medal of Honor UCLA, 1993; Lustman fellow Yale U. 1977. Fellow Am. Bar Found., Davenport Coll., Yale U.; mem. Bar Calif. (bd. dirs. continuing edn. bar commn. 1967-74), Am. Judicature Soc. (dir., Justice award 1985), Assn. Am. Law Schs. (chmn. com. edn. in jud. adminstrn.), Am. Bar Assn. (sect. on jud. adminstrn., chmn. com. on edn. in jud. adminstrn. 1973-89), Phi Beta Kappa, Order of Coif (nat. v.p. 1974-76), Jud. Conf. U.S. (com. to consider standards for admission to practice in fed. cts. 1976-79). Office: US Ct Appeals Cir 125 S Grand Ave Ste 303 Pasadena CA 91105-1652

NELSON, DOUGLAS A., pathologist, educator; b. Windom, Minn., 1927. MD, U. Minn., 1954. Diplomate Am. Bd. Pathology (trustee 1979-90, pres. 1988), Am. Bd. Hematology. Intern Phila. Gen. Hosp., 1954-55; resident in pathology Mallory Inst. Pathology, Boston, 1955-58; chief resident Boston City Hosp., 1957-58; med. fellow Affiliated Hosps. U. Minn. Hosps., 1958-60; instr., lab. medicine U. Minn., 1960-63, asst. prof., 1963-64; assoc. prof., dep. dir. clin. pathology SUNY, Syracuse, 1964-69, prof., dep. dir. clin. pathology, 1969-93, prof. emeritus, 1993—; mem. Res. Rev. Com. for Pathology, 1985-90. With USNR, 1945-46. Mem. AMA, Am. Soc. Clin. Pathologists, Am. Soc. Hematology, Acad. Clin. Lab. Physicians and Scientists, Phi Beta Kappa, Sigma Xi, Alpha Omega Alpha. Office: SUNY Health Sci Ctr 750 E Adams St Syracuse NY 13210-2306*

NELSON, DOUGLAS LEE, insurance company executive; b. Washington, Mar. 7, 1944; s. John Jacob and Sharett L. (Legreid) N. BA, U. So. Calif., 1967. Planning USAID/MACV, Republic of Vietnam, 1968-69; life mgmt. staff Prudential Ins. Co., L.A., 1971-75; planning cons. Prudential Ins. Co., Roseland, N.J., 1975-77; small group health staff Prudential Ins. Co., L.A., 1978-82; svc. support staff Prudential Ins. Co., Mpls., 1983-87, mutual funds staff, 1988-90; quality svc. exec. Prudential Ins. Co., Newark, 1990-93; quality officer Prudential Direct, Newark, 1993-95; dir. Prudential Policyowner Rels., 1995—. Bd. dirs., treas. Self Reliance Ctr., Mpls., 1986-88, Pax World Found., Washington, 1991—; mem. aviation adv. coun. NJDOT, 1994—. Mem. Am. Soc. Quality Control, Internat. Svc. Quality Assn. (edn. com. 1991—), Quality Productivity Mgmt. Assn., Assn. Quality and Participation, Life Ins. Mktg. Rsch. Assn. (quality bus. com. 1991—, examiner, N.J. Quality Achievement award 1993-94, Exptl. Aircraft Assn. (chpt. pres. 1991—), Conf. Bd., Sierra Club (exec. com. Northstar chpt. 1989-90). Avocations: skiing, sailing, flying, airplane building and restoration. Office: Prudential Ins Co Am Newark NJ 07102

NELSON, DREW VERNON, mechanical engineering educator; b. Elizabeth, N.J., Oct. 11, 1947; s. Andrew K. and Myra G. (Kempson) N. BSME, Stanford U., 1968, MSME, 1970, PhDME, 1978. Research asst. Stanford U., Calif., 1971-74, asst. prof., 1978-83, assoc. prof., 1983-96; prof. Stanford U., 1996—; engr. Gen. Electric Co., Sunnyvale, Calif., 1975-76, sr. engr., 1977-78; cons. in field. Co-editor: Fatigue Design Handbook, 1989; contbr. articles to profl. jours. Recipient Spergel Meml. award for Most Outstanding Paper, 32d Internat. Wire and Cable Symposium, 1984, Hetenyi award for Best Rsch. Paper Pub in 1994 in the jour. Exptl. Mechanics. Mem. ASTM, Soc. Automotive Engrs., Soc. for Exptl. Mechanics, Sigma Xi, Tau Beta Pi. Avocations: tennis, jogging. Home: 840 Cabot Ct San Carlos CA 94070-3464 Office: Stanford U Dept Mech Engring Stanford CA 94305-4021

NELSON, E. BENJAMIN, governor; b. McCook, Nebr., May 17, 1941; s. Benjamin Earl and Birdella Ruby (Henderson) N.; B.A., U. Nebr., 1963, M.A., 1966, J.D., 1970; LLD (hon.) Creighton U., 1992, Peru State Coll., 1993; m. Diane C. Gleason, Feb. 22, 1980; children by previous marriage—Sarah Jane, Patrick James; stepchildren—Kevin Michael Gleason, Christine Marie Gleason. Bar: Nebr. 1970. Instr. dept. philosophy U. Nebr., 1963-65; supr. Dept. Ins., State of Nebr., Lincoln, 1965-72, dir. ins., 1975-76; asst. gen. counsel, gen. counsel, sec., v.p. The Central Nat. Ins. Group of Omaha, 1972-75, exec. v.p., 1976-77, pres., 1978-81, CEO, 1980-81, of counsel, Kennedy, Holland, DeLacy & Svoboda, Omaha, 1985-90; gov. State of Nebr., Lincoln, 1991—. Co-chmn. Carter/Mondale re-election campaign, Nebr., 1980; chair Nat. Edn. Goals Panel, 1992-94, Gov.'s Ethanol Coalition, 1991-94, chair 1991, 94; pres. Coun. of State Gov's., 1994. Named Amb. Plenipotentiary, 1993. Mem. Consumer Credit Ins. Assn., Nat. Assn. Ind. Insurers, Nat. Assn. Ins. Commissioners (exec. v.p. 1982-85), Nebr. Bar Assn., Am. Bar Assn., Midwestern Gov's. Assn. (chair 1994), Western Gov.'s Assn. (vice chair 1994), Happy Hollow Club, Omaha Club, Hillcrest Country Club. Democrat. Methodist. Home: 1425 H St Lincoln NE 68508-3759 Office: State Capitol 2nd Floor Lincoln NE 68509

NELSON, EDITH ELLEN, dietitian; b. Vicksburg, Mich., Sept. 26, 1940; d. Edward Kenneth and Anna (McManus) Rolffs; m. Douglas Keith Nelson; children: Daniel Lee, Jennifer Lynn. BS, Mich. State U., 1962; MEd in Applied Nutrition, U. Cin., 1979. Lic. dietitian, Fla. Clin. dietitian Macon (Ga.) Gen. Hosp., Blodgett Meml. Hosp., Grand Rapids, Mich.; grad. teaching asst. U. Cin., 1978-79; dir. nutrition svcs. Dialysis Clinic, Inc., Cin., 1979-88; cons. dietitian Panama City Devel. Ctr., Ft. Walton Beach Devel. Ctr., Fla., 1988-94, N.W. Fla. Community Hosp., Chipley, Fla., 1993-94, Beverly Enterprises, Panama City Beach, 1994—; renal dietitian Dialysis Svcs. Fla., Ft. Walton Beach, 1989-92. Mich. Edn. Assn. scholar, 1958; Nat. Kidney Found. grantee, 1986. Mem. Am. Dietetic Assn., Fla. Dietetic Assn., Panhandle Dist. Dietetic Assn., Nat. Kidney Found. (coun. on renal nutrition, Fla. coun. on renal nutrition), Omicron Nu. Home: 150 Grand Lagoon Shores Dr Panama City FL 32408

NELSON, EDWARD GAGE, merchant banking investment company executive; b. Nashville, May 17, 1931; s. Charles and Polly (Prentiss) N.; m. Carole Olivia Frances Minton, Sept. 17, 1960; children—Carole Gervais, Emily Minton, Ellen Prentiss. B.A. in Polit. Sci., U. of South, Sewanee, 1952. Exec. v.p. Clark, Landstreet & Kirkpatrick, Inc., Nashville, 1955-64; exec. v.p. Commerce Union Bank, Nashville, 1968-72, pres., 1972-82, cons., 1985—, chmn., chief exec. officer, 1982-84; chmn., pres. Nelson Capital Corp., Nashville, 1985—; hon. consul gen. Japan; bd. dirw. Werthan Packaging, SouthCap Corp., Franklin Industries, Osborn Comm., Trans Arabian Investment Bank, ClinTrials, Inc., Berlitz Internat., Inc. Ctrl. Parking Sys., Advocat Inc., Micro Craft, Inc., NAshville Scene; mem. 1st adv. coun. Japan/Tenn. Soc. Trustee Vanderbilt U., Nashville, 1979—, chmn. med. ctr. bd., 1984—; vice chmn. Pub. Edn. Nashville Citizens; mem. De Tocqueville Soc. of United Way. Spl. agt. U.S. Army, 1955, Japan. Mem. Belle Meade Country Club, Cumberland Club, River Club (N.Y.C.). Republican. Episcopalian. Home: 1305 Chickering Rd Nashville TN 37215-4521 Office: Nelson Capital Corp 3401 W End Ave Ste 300 Nashville TN 37203-1069

NELSON, EDWARD HUMPHREY, architect; b. Winchester, Mass., Sept. 2, 1918; s. Richard MacDonald and Evelyn Miller (Humphrey) N.; m. Lois Whitaker Renouf, Sept. 24, 1948 (dec.); children: Susan, David, Sarah; m. Miriam P. Ketcham, Jan. 2, 1988. Grad., Lenox Sch., 1936; B.Arch., Yale, 1950. Pvt. archtl. practice Tucson, 1953-61; sr. v.p. CNWC Architects, Tucson, 1961-88, pres., 1989-94; ret., 1994; bd. dirs. CNWC & Steppe Archs.; mem. adv. com. U. Ariz. Coll. Arch., 1984-93. Works include: design for Tucson Community Ctr. Pres. Tucson Cmty. Coun., 1969-71, Tucson Art Ctr., 1960, Tucson Housing Found., 1969-92; bd. dirs. Tucson Trade Bur., 1976-91, pres., 1984; bd. dirs. Tucson Symphony, 1977-84, Tucson United Way, 1980; trustee Green Fields Sch., 1960-74, Tucson Art Mus.; vestry St. Philips Episc. Ch., 1967-69, sr. warden, 1987-90, parish warden, 1993-94; convenor Episcopal Interparish Coun., 1990-92; mem. Episcopal Diocese of Ariz., W.W. Regional Parish. Served to capt. AUS, 1940-41, WWII, ETO. Decorated Bronze Star with oak leaf cluster, Purple Heart; recipient Disting. Citizen award U. Ariz., 1981. Fellow AIA (emeritus, pres. So. Ariz. chpt. 1962, chmn. Ariz. fellows 1986-90); mem. Ariz. Soc. Architects (pres. 1963), Yale Club (pres. Tucson chpt. 1962, 83, dir. 1979—), U. Ariz. Pres.'s Club. Home: 2020 E 4th St Tucson AZ 85719-5114

NELSON, EDWARD SHEFFIELD, lawyer, former utility company executive; b. Keevil, Ark., Feb. 23, 1941; s. Robert Ford and Thelma Jo (Mayberry) N.; m. Mary Lynn McCastlain, Oct. 12, 1962; children: Cynthia, Lynn (dec.), Laura. BS, U. Cen. Ark., 1963; LLB, Ark. Law Sch., 1968; JD, U. Ark., 1969. Mgmt. trainee Ark. La. Gas Co., Little Rock, 1963-64; sales engr. Ark. La. Gas Co., 1964-67, sales coordinator, 1967-69, gen. sales mgr., 1969-71, v.p., gen. sales mgr., 1971-73, pres., dir., 1973-79, pres., chmn., chief exec. officer, 1979-85; ptnr., chmn. bd., chief exec. officer House, Wallace, Nelson & Jewel, Little Rock, 1985-86; pvt. practice law Little Rock, 1986—; of counsel Jack, Lyon & Jones, P.A., 1991—; bd. dirs. Fed. Res. Mem. N.G., 1957-63; bd. dirs. U. Ark., Little Rock, vice chmn. bd. visitors, 1981; bd. dirs. Philander Smith Coll., 1981; chmn. Ark. Indsl. Devel. Commn., 1987, 88; past chmn. Little Rock br. Fed. Res. Bd. St. Louis; chmn. Econ. Expansion Study Commn., 1987—; bd. dirs. Ark. Ednl. TV Found., Ark. Game and Fish Commn. Found.; founder, 1st pres. Jr. Achievement Ark., 1987-88; Rep. nominee for Gov. of Ark., 1990, 94; co-state chmn. Ark. Reps., 1991-92, nat. committeeman Ark. GOP, 1993—. Named Ark.'s Outstanding Young Man Ark. J. C. of C., 1973; One of Am.'s Ten Outstanding Young Men U.S. Jr. C. of C., 1974; Citizen of Yr. Ark. chpt. March of Dimes, 1983; Humanitarian of Yr. NCCJ, 1983; Best Chief Exec. Officer in Natural Gas Industry Wall Street Transcript, 1983; recipient 1st Disting. Alumnus award U. Cen. Ark., 1987. Mem. Am., Ark., Pulaski County bar assns., Ark. C. of C. (dir.), Little Rock C. of C. (dir., pres. 1981), Sales and Mktg. Execs. Assn. (pres. 1975, Top Mgmt. award 1977), U. Ark. Law Sch. Alumni Assn. (pres. 1980). Methodist. Office: 6th and Broadway 3400 Tcby Bldg Little Rock AR 72201

NELSON, EDWIN CLARENCE, academic administrator, emeritus; b. Dallas, S.D., Apr. 19, 1922; s. Clifford and Vera (Usher) N.; m. Avis Hedrix, Nov. 15, 1941; children—Judy, Roger. A.B., Kearney (Nebr.) State Coll., 1950; M.E., West Tex. State U., 1953; Ed.D., U. Nebr., 1959; postgrad., U. Minn., 1959; LHD (hon.), U. Nebr., Kearney, 1993. Tchr. math. and sci. pub. schs. Nebr., 1947-50; supt. schs. Huntley, Nebr., 1950-52, Wilcox, Nebr., 1953-56, Red Cloud, Nebr., 1956-59; tchr. aircraft mechanics Amarillo (Tex.) AFB, 1952-53; asso. prof. edn. Kearney State Tchrs. Coll., 1959-61; dean coll., dir. grad. studies Chadron (Nebr.) State Coll., 1961-67, pres., 1967-73, 75-86, pres. emeritus, Disting. Service prof., 1986—; community devel. specialist, 1988—; pres. Leadership Seminars, 1988—; exec. officer bd. trustees Nebr. State Colls., 1973-75; pres. Nebr. Ednl. TV Council for Higher Edn., 1967, 85. Served with AUS, 1942-45. Recipient Disting. Svc. award Kearney State Coll., 1968, Disting. Svc. award Chadron State Coll., 1989, Nebr. Statewide Citizen's award, 1996, Disting. Svc. award Nebr. Schoolmasters Club, 1996; named Boss of Yr., Chadron Jaycees, 1971, Chadron Citizen of the Yr., 1985, AK-SAR-BEN Ike Friedman Cmty. Leader, 1994; bldg. on Chadron State Coll. Campus named Edwin and Avis Nelson Phys. Activity Ctr., 1996. Mem. Nebr. Edn. Assn. (pres. 1967), Chadron C. of C. (Magic Key award 1988), Phi Delta Kappa. Republican. Methodist. Clubs: Elk, Kiwanian. *I have appreciated my opportunities to serve education at all levels.*

NELSON, EDWIN L., federal judge; b. 1940. Student, U. Ala., 1962-63, Samford U., 1965-66; LLB, Samford U., 1969. Mem. firm French & Nelson, Ft. Payne, Ala., 1969-73; pvt. practice Ft. Payne, Ala., 1974—; magistrate U.S. Dist. Ct. (no. dist.) Ala., Birmingham, 1974-90, judge, 1990—. With USN, 1958-62. Mem. Ala. Bar Assn., Birmingham Bar Assn., 11th Cir. Assn. U.S. Magistrates, Nat. Coun. Magistrates, Phi Alpha Delta. Office: US Dist Ct Hugo L Black Courthouse 1729 5th Ave N Fl 7 Birmingham AL 35203-2000

NELSON, ELMER KINGSHOLM, JR., educator, writer, mediator, consultant; b. Laramie, Wyo., Sept. 14, 1922; s. Elmer Kingsholm and Alice (Downey) N.; m. Jane Beckwith Oliver, Aug. 4, 1945; 1 son, Elmer Kingsholm III (Kirk). BA, U. Wyo., 1943, JD, 1948, MA, 1949; Dr. Pub. Adminstrn., U. So. Calif., 1959. Instr. psychology U. Wyo., 1947-49; psychologist, staff psychologist dept. probation Contra Costa County, Calif., 1949-51; sr. psychologist Cal. State Dept. Corrections, San Quentin and Chino Prisons, 1951-52; asst. prof. criminology U. B.C., Can., 1952-54; assoc. prof. U. B.C., 1954-56, head criminology div., 1953-56; warden Haney Correctional Instn., B.C., 1956-58; assoc. dir. Youth Studies Ctr. U. So. Calif., 1958-59, dir. Youth Studies Ctr., 1959-64, assoc. prof. pub. adminstrn., 1958-61, prof., 1961—, dean Sch. Pub. Adminstrn., 1971-76, prof., co-dir. Sacramento Pub. Affairs Ctr.; head Bay Area Research Center, Berkeley, 1979—; dep. adminstr. Youth and Adult Corrections Agy., State of Calif., Sacramento, 1964-65; interim exec. dir. Office Criminal Justice Planning, spring 1975; dir. Nat. Study Probation and Parole, 1976-77; chmn. task force on corrections, asso. dir. Pres.'s Commn. on Law Enforcement and Adminstrn. of Justice, Washington, 1966-67; dir. nat. study of correctional adminstrn. U. So. Calif. for Joint Commn. on Correctional Manpower and Tng., 1967-69. Co-author: Corrections in America, 1975; contbr. articles, monographs, research reports to profl. jours. Advisor on mgmt. Boys Republic, Chino, Calif., 1967—; bd. dirs., v.p. Am. Justice Inst., Sacramento; bd. dirs. Human Interaction Rsch. Inst., L.A. Recipient Disting. Alumnus award U. Wyo., 1975, Exemplary Alumni award U. Wyo. Coll. Arts and Scis., 1994; Ford Found. Travel Study grantee, 1970-71; E. Kim Nelson endowed doctoral fellowship established at U. So. Calif., 1987. Mem. Nat. Acad. Pub. Adminstrn., Wyo. Bar Assn., Alpha Tau Omega, Phi Beta Kappa, Phi Kappa Phi. Home: 716 Ivinson Ave Laramie WY 82070

NELSON, FREDA NELL HEIN, librarian; b. Trenton, Mo., Dec. 16, 1929; d. Fred Albert and Mable Carman (Doan) Hein; m. Robert John Nelson, Nov. 1, 1957 (div. Apr. 1984); children: Thor, Hope. Nursing diploma, Trinity Luth. Hosp., Kansas City, Mo., 1950; B. Philosophy, Northwestern U., 1961; MS in Info. and Libr. Sci., U. Ill., 1986. RN. Operating rm. nurse Trinity Luth. Hosp., Kansas City, Mo., 1950-52, Johns Hopkins Hosp., Balt., 1952, Wesley Meml. Hosp., Chgo., 1952-58, Tacoma Gen. Hosp., 1958-59, Chgo. Wesley Hosp., 1959-61; libr. asst. Maple Woods Campus Met. Community Colls., Kansas City, 1987-89, libr., libr. mgr. Blue Springs Campus, 1989—; co-founder Coll. for Kids, Knox Coll., Galesburg, Ill., 1982. Nurses scholar Edgar Bergen Found., 1947; recipient Award of Merit, Chgo. Bd. Health, 1952. Avocations: swimming, walking, cross-word puzzles. Home: 7000 N Elm St Pleasant Valley MO 64068 Office: Blue Springs Campus Libr 1501 W Jefferson St Blue Springs MO 64015-7242

NELSON, FREDERICK CARL, mechanical engineering educator; b. Braintree, Mass., Aug. 8, 1932; s. Carl Edwin and Marjorie May (Miller) N.; m. Delia Ann Dwaresky; children: Jeffrey, Karen, Richard, Christine. BSME, Tufts U., 1954; MS, Harvard U., 1955, PhD, 1961. Registered profl. engr., Mass. Instr. Tufts U., Medford, Mass., 1955-57, asst. prof. mech. engring., 1957-64; assoc. prof. mech. engring., 1964-71; prof. mech. engring. Tufts U., Medford, 1971—, dean engring., 1980-94; bd. dirs. Mass. Tech. Park Corp., Westboro. Translator: (book) Mechanical Vibrations for Engineers, 1983. Fellow ASME (centennial medal award 1980), AAAS, ASA; mem. Nat. Inst. Applied Scis. of Lyon (medal 1988), Korea Advanced Inst. Sci. and Tech. (medal 1988), Tufts U. Alumni Assn. (medal 1991. Office: Tufts U Coll Engring Medford MA 02155-5555

NELSON, FREDERICK DICKSON, lawyer; b. Cleve., Oct. 19, 1958; s. David Aldrich and Mary Ellen (Dickson) N. AB, Hamilton Coll., 1980; JD, Harvard U., 1983. Bar: Ohio 1984, D.C. 1985. Majority counsel subcom. on criminal law U.S. Senate Judiciary Com., Washington, 1983-85; spl. asst. to asst. atty. gen., Office of Legal Policy U.S. Dept. Justice, Washington, 1985-86, dep. asst. atty. gen., Office of Legal Policy, 1986-87; assoc. Taft, Stettinius & Hollister, Cin., 1988-89, of counsel, 1991-93; assoc. counsel to Pres. of U.S. The White House, Washington, 1989-90; advisor to govts. of Ukraine and Russia, ABA Ctrl. and East European Legal Law Initiative, 1992-93; adj. prof. constl. law Salmon P. Chase Coll. Law, U. No. Ky., 1994; chief of staff U.S. Rep. Steve Chabot, 1995—. Exec. editor Harvard Jour. of Law and Pub. Policy, 1982-83. Dir. issues and rsch. Nahra for Congress campaign, Cleve., 1980; mem. Hamilton County Rep. Leadership Coun., 1992; cons. Chabot for Congress Campaign, Cin., 1994. Harry S. Truman Found. scholar, 1978-81. Mem. Federalist Soc., Harvard Club of Cin. (bd. dirs. 1989), Phi Beta Kappa. Republican. Home: 7900 Brill Rd Cincinnati OH 45243-3944

NELSON, FREDERICK HERBERT, lawyer; b. Ft. Bragg, N.C., Sept. 19, 1960; s. Grant H. II Nelson and Sandra J. (Dexter) Bergen. BA magna cum laude, Toccoa Falls (Ga.) Coll., 1989; JD, Stetson U., 1993. Bar: Fla. 1993, U.S. Dist. Ct. (ea. dist.) Wis. 1993, U.S. Ct. Appeals (11th cir.) 1993, U.S. Dist. Ct. (mid. dist.) Fla. 1994, U.S. Ct. Appeals (D.C., 6th, 7th, 9th, 10th cirs.) 1994, U.S. Dist. Ct. (no. and so. dists.) Fla. 1995, U.S. Ct. Appeals (2d, 3d, 4th, 5th, 8th cirs.) 1995. Rsch. asst. Stetson U. Coll. Law, St. Petersburg, Fla., 1992-93; exec. counsel Liberty Counsel, Orlando, Fla., 1993—; pres., gen. counsel Am. Liberties Inst., Orlando, 1994—. contbg. editor: The International Sale of Goods, 1994; contbr. articles to profl. jours. Bd. dirs. Cmty. Issues Forum, Orlando, 1994—, Ctrl. Fla. CLS, Orlando, 1994—. Mem. ABA (mem. bd. dirs.), ATLA (Fla. bar appellate practice & advocacy sect., Fla. bar fed. appellate practice com.), Phi Delta Phi. Avocations: scuba diving, snow skiing, sky diving. Home: 528 Terracview Cove Altamonte Springs FL 32714 Office: Liberty Counsel 1900 Summit Tower Blvd Ste 560 Orlando FL 32810

NELSON, GARY, county councilman, engineer; b. Spokane, Wash., Apr. 11, 1936; s. Nels Alfred and Laura Marie (Winberg) Nelson; m. JoAnne Laura Knudson, Nov. 27, 1959; children: Grant, Geoffrey, Gregory. BSEE, Wash. State U., 1958; MSEE, U. Wis., 1963. Engr. RCA, Camden, N.J., 1958-59; officer USAF, Madison, Wis., 1959-62; mgr. U.S. West, Seattle, 1963-90; pvt. practice Edmonds, Wash., 1990-94; bd. dirs. Stevens Hosp. Found., Edmonds, Olympic Ballet, Snohomish County Health Dist., 1994—, United Way of Snohomish County, Everett, 1986-92; Wash. State Legislator, 1972-94. planning commn. City of Edmonds, 1964-67, city coun., 1968-74. Capt. USAF, 1959-62. Mem. Sons of Norway, Rotary. Republican. Lutheran. Home: 9710 Wharf St Edmonds WA 98020-2363 Office: Snohomish County Coun 3000 Rockefeller M/S 609 Everett WA 98201

NELSON, GAYLORD ANTON, former senator, association executive; b. Clear-Lake, Wis., June 4, 1916; s. Anton and Mary (Bradt) N.; m. Carrie Lee Dotson, Nov. 14, 1947; children—Gaylord, Cynthia, Jeffrey. Grad., San Jose State Coll., Calif., 1939, U. Wis. Law Sch., 1942. Bar: Admitted Wis. bar 1942. Practiced in Madison, 1946-58; mem. Wis. Senate, 1949-58, Democratic leader, 1948-52; gov. Wis., 1958-62, U.S. senator from Wis., 1963-81; mem. finance com., chmn. subcom. on Social Security; chmn. employment, poverty and migratory labor subcom. of human resources com.; chmn. select com. on small bus., chmn. monopoly subcom. Author: Environmental Education Act, 1970, Nat. Environmental Education Act, 1972; co-author: The National Teacher Corps, 1965. Counselor Wilderness Soc., Washington, 1981—; founder Earth Day. 1st lt. AUS, World War II. Recipient Conservationist of the Year Award, Nat. Wildlife Fedn., 1989, Only One Earth Award, Environmental Leadership Award, UN Environment Prog., 1992, Presdl. Freedom medal, 1995. Mem. State Bar Assn. Wis. Home: 3611 Calvend Ln Kensington MD 20895-3154 Office: Wilderness Soc 900 17th St NW Washington DC 20006-2501

NELSON, GLEN DAVID, medical products executive, physician; b. Mpls., Mar. 28, 1937; s. Ralph and Edna S. Nelson; m. Marilyn Carlson, June 30, 1961; children: Diana, Curtis, Wendy. AB, Harvard U., 1959; MD, U. Minn., 1963. Diplomate Am. Bd. Surgery, also sub-bd. bariatric and peripheral vascular surgery. Intern Hennepin County Gen. Hosp., Mpls., 1963-64, resident in gen. surgery, 1964-69; staff surgeon Park Nicollet Med. Ctr. (formerly St. Louis Park Med. Ctr.), Mpls., 1969-86, pres., chmn. bd. trustees, 1975-86; chmn., CEO Am. Med Ctrs., Mpls., 1984-86; exec. v.p. Medtronic, Inc., Mpls., 1986-88, vice chmn., 1988—, also bd. dirs.; clin. prof. dept. surgery U. Minn.; bd. dirs. ReliaStar Fin. Corp. (formerly Northwestern Nat. Life Inst. Co.), Mpls., Carlson Holdings, Inc., Mpls., St. Paul Cos., Medtronic, Inc., Mpls. Fellow ACS (ed.); mem. AMA, Am. Acad. Med. Dirs., Am. Coll. Physician Execs., Hennepin County Med. Assn., Greater Mpls. C. of C. (chmn. 1987), Jackson Hole Group. Office: Medtronic Inc 7000 Central Ave NE Minneapolis MN 55432-3568

NELSON, GORDON LEIGH, chemist, educator; b. Palo Alto, Calif., May 27, 1943; s. Nels Folke and Alice Virginia (Fredrickson) N. BS in Chemistry, U. Nev., 1965; MS, Yale U., 1967, PhD, 1970; DSc (hon.), William Carey Coll., 1988. Staff research chemist corp. research and devel. Gen. Electric Co., Schenectady, N.Y., 1970-74; mgr. combustibility tech. plastics div. Gen. Electric Co., Pittsfield, Mass., 1974-79, mgr. environ. protection plastics div., 1979-82; v.p. materials sci. and tech. Springborn Labs. Inc., Enfield, Conn., 1982-83; prof., chmn. dept. polymer sci. U. So. Miss., Hattiesburg, 1983-89; dean Coll. Sci. and Liberal Arts, prof. chemistry Fla. Inst. Tech., Melbourne, 1989—, mem. coun. sci., soc. pres., sec., 1989-90, chair-elect, 1991, chair, 1992; cons. in field. Author: Carbon-13 Nuclear Magnetic Resonance for Organic Chemists, 1972, 2d edit., 1980; co-author: Polymer Materials--Chemistry for the Future, 1989,Carbon Monxide and Human Lethality, 1993; editor: Fire and Polymers--Hazard Identification and Prevention, 1990; editor: Fire and Polymers II-Materials and Tests for Hazard Prevention, 1995; editor books on coating sci. tech.; contbr. articles to profl. jours. Mem. ASTM (E5 cert. of appreciation 1985), Am. Inst. Chemists (Mems. and Fellows Lectr. award 1989), Soc. Plastics Engrs., Am. Chem. Soc. (pres. 1988, bd. dirs. 1977-85, 87-89, 92-94, Henry Hill award 1986), Info. Tech. Industry coun. (chmn. plastics task group), Ctr. Sci., Tech. and the Media (bd. dirs. 1991-94), So. Soc. for Coatings Tech., Internat. Electrotech. Commn. (U.S. tech. adv. group on info. processing equipment), Soc. of Plastics Industry (structural plastics divsn., Man of Yr. 1979), Coun. Colls. Arts and Scis., Yale Chemists Assn. (pres. 1981—), Nev. Hist. Soc., Sigma Xi. Republican. Presbyterian. Avocations: travel, western U.S. history. Office: Fla Inst Tech Coll Sci & Liberal Arts 150 W University Blvd Melbourne FL 32901-6982

NELSON, GRANT STEEL, lawyer, educator; b. Mitchell, S.D., Apr. 18, 1939; s. Howard Steel and Clara Marie (Winandy) N.; m. Judith Ann Haugen, Sept. 22, 1962; children: Mary Elizabeth, Rebekah Anne, John Adam. BA magna cum laude, U. Minn., 1960; JD cum laude, 1963. Bar: Minn. 1963, Mo. 1971. Assoc. Faegre & Benson, Mpls., 1963-67; mem. law faculty U. Mo., Columbia, 1967-91, assoc. prof., 1970-72, prof., 1972-91, Enoch H. Crowder prof. law, 1974-91; prof. UCLA, 1991—; mem. bd. legal advisors Gt. Plains Legal Found., 1978-85; vis. asst. prof. U. Mich., Ann Arbor, 1969-70, Brigham Young U., Provo, Utah, summer 1976; vis. prof. U. Minn., Mpls., 1981-82, UCLA, 1989-90; disting. vis. prof. Pepperdine U., 1987-88; commr. Nat. Conf. Commrs. Uniform State Laws, 1983-91; mem. West Pub. Law Sch. Adv. Bd. Author: (with Van Hecke and Leavell) Cases and Materials on Equitable Remedies and Restitution, 1973, (with Whitman) Cases and Materials on Real Estate Finance and Development, 1976, Cases and Materials on Real Estate Transfer, Finance and Development, 1981, (with Osborne and Whitman) Real Estate Finance Law, 1979, (with Leavell and Love) Cases and Materials on Equitable Remedies and Restitution, 1980, (with Whitman) Land Transactions and Finance, 1983, rev. edit., 1988, (with Whitman) Real Estate Finance Law, 1985, rev. edit., 1994, (with Leavell and Love) Cases and Materials on Equitable Remedies, Restituion and Damages, 1986, rev. edit., 1994 (with Whitman) Cases and Materials on Real Estate Transfer, Finance and Development, 1987, (with Browder, Cunningham, Stoebuck and Whitman) Basic Property Law, 1989, (with Stoebuck and Whitman) Contemporary Property, 1996, (with Whitman) Cases and Materials on Real Estate Transfer, Finance and Development, 1992; co-reporter ALI Restatement of Land Security; contbr. articles to profl. jours. 1st lt. AUS, 1964-65. Recipient award for meritorious service and achievement U. Mo. Law Sch. Found., 1974; recipient Disting. Faculty Service award U. Mo.-Columbia Alumni Assn., 1978, Disting. Faculty award, 1986, Disting. Non-Alumnus award, 1991. Fellow Am. Bar Found.; mem. ABA, Am. Law Inst., Assn. Am. Law Schs. (sect. chmn. 1976-77), Am. Coll. Real Estate Lawyers, Mo. Bar Assn. (vice chmn. property law com. 1974-75, chmn. 1975-77), Order of Coif, Phi Beta Kappa, Phi Delta Phi. Home: 24609 Plover Way Malibu CA 90265-4718 Office: UCLA Sch Law Hilgard Ave Box 951476 Los Angeles CA 90095-1476

NELSON, H. H. RED, insurance company executive; b. Herman, Nebr., June 2, 1912; m. Ruth Hansen; children: John, Steve. B.A., U. Nebr., 1934, J.D., 1937. Bar: Iowa, Nebr. 1938; C.L.U., 1948. Asst. mgr. life accident group depts. Travelers Inc. Co., Omaha, 1939-44; chmn. bd. Redlands Ins. Co., 1945—, Ins. Agts. Inc., Council Bluffs, Iowa, 1945—, Am. Agrisurance Co., 1969—, Am. Growers Ins., 1995—, Acceptance Ins., Texas, 1988—; chmn. Redland Group Cos. Pres. United Fund, Western Iowa council Boy Scouts Am.; bd. dirs. Nat. Scout Council; pres. Christian Home Orphanage, Council Bluffs Indsl. Found. Mem. Ind. Ins. Agts. Am. (pres. 1964-65, Woodworth Meml. award 1966), Iowa Assn. Ins. Agts. (nat. dir., pres. 1957-60, Heritage award 1986), C. of C. (bd. dirs.). Lodges: Elks (past exalted ruler), Masons, Shriners. Office: Redland Group Inc 535 W Broadway Council Bluffs IA 51503-0812

NELSON, HAROLD BERNHARD, museum director; b. Providence, R.I., May 14, 1947; s. Harold B. and Eleanor (Lavina) N. BA, Bowdoin Coll., 1969; MA, U. Del., 1972. Rsch. fellow NMAA Smithsonian Inst., Washington, 1976-77; curator Am. art Mus. Art & Archeol., U. Mo., Columbia, 1977-79; registrar Solomon R. Guggenheim Mus., N.Y.C., 1979-83; exhibition program dir. Am. Fedn. Arts, N.Y.C., 1983-89; dir. Long Beach (Calif.) Mus. of Art, 1989—; juror Annual Art Exhibition Mus. Art, Sci. & Industry, Bridgeport, Conn., 1988, Annual Art Exhibition, Clark County Dist. Libr., Las Vegas, Nev., 1984; speaker Am. Assn. Mus. Annual Conf., Detroit, 1985, annual meeting Western Mus. Conf., Portland, Oreg., 1987, Grantmakers in Art Symposium, N.Y.C., 1986, annual meeting Western Mus. Conf., Salt Lake City, 1985; mem. adv. com. APA, Assn. Sci. and Tech. Ctrs.; panelist Aid to Spl. Exhibitions, NEA, Washington, 1986; participant Am. Legal Assn., ABA Conf., San Francisco, 1986; observer, respondent Mus. Symposium, NEA, Dallas, 1985. Author: Sounding the Depths: 150 Years of American Seascape, 1989. Office: Long Beach Mus Art 2300 E Ocean Blvd Long Beach CA 90803-2442

NELSON, HARRY, journalist, medical writer; b. Interlachen, Fla., Apr. 18, 1923; s. Knut Alfred and Edith Farr (Wilkes) N.; m. Diane Gabriella Meerschaert, Aug. 29, 1948 (div. 1977); children—Tanya Ann, Lawrence Stephen, Ronald Gerard, James Anthony, John Christopher; m. Gita Doris Wheelis, Jan. 29, 1984. B.A., U. So. Calif., 1949. Reporter, photographer Bakersfield Press, Calif., 1949; reporter, photographer Bakersfield Community Chest, Calif., 1949; promotion writer Los Angeles Times, 1949-57, reporter, 1957-58, med. writer, 1958-88, sr. writer, 1977-80; freelance med. writer, 1988—; staff writer Milbank Meml. Fund, 1993—. Charter mem. bd. dirs. Los Angeles County Comprehensive Health Planning Assn., Los Angeles, 1968-69. Served with USAAF, 1941-45. Recipient spl. commendation AMA, 1974, John Hancock award John Hancock Ins. Co., 1978, Journalism award Am. Acad. Pediatrics, 1979, Disting. Svc. by non-physician award Calif. Med. Assn., 1988, Lifetime Achievement in med. writing award AMA, 1988, Peter Lisagor award for exemplary journalism Chgo. Headliners Club, 1988. Mem. Nat. Assn. Sci. Writers (pres. 1966). Avocations: sailing; hiking; ceramics. Address: Med Writers Internat PO Box N 14016 Yellowstone Dr Frazier Park CA 93222

NELSON, H(ARRY) DONALD, communications executive; b. Chgo., Nov. 23, 1933; s. Harry Emmanual and Elsie Ina (Liljedahl) N.; m. Carol Jacqueline Stewart, Mar. 31, 1956; children: Donald S., David S., Sharon Nelson Arnold. BS in Bus., Northwestern U., 1955, MBA with distinction, 1959. Salesperson Procter & Gamble, Chgo., 1955-58; product mgr. Gen. Electric Corp., Syracuse, N.Y., 1959-72; mktg. mgr. Tex. Instruments, Dallas, 1972-74; v.p. mktg. Rockwell Internat., Anaheim, Calif., 1974-75, HMW-Pulsar, Lancaster, Pa., 1975-77; mgr. market and product devel. Gen. Electric Corp., Louisville, 1977-80; v.p. mktg. Genesco, Nashville, 1981-83; v.p. cellular bus. Telephone and Data Systems, Chgo., 1983-85; pres., chief exec. officer U.S. Cellular, Chgo., 1986—; mem. mgmt. alumni adv. bd. dirs. Kellogg Grad. Sch. With U.S. Army. Mem. Cellular Telecomm. Industry Assn. (bd. dirs. 1984—, com. chmn. 1985-89, exec. com. 1991—, treas.), Am. Stock Exch. (listed co. adv. coun.). Republican. Baptist. Office: US Cellular 8410 W Bryn Mawr Ave Ste 700 Chicago IL 60631-3402

NELSON, HARVEY FRANS, JR., retired foreign service officer; b. Long Beach, Calif., Jan. 26, 1924; s. Harvey Frans and Marian (Norris) N.; m. Celia Anne Kendrick, June 27, 1947 (dec. June 1985); children—Erik Frans, Kai David, Peter Norris, Annika Di Vittorio; m. Esta Harrie de Fossard, May 31, 1987; children: Granville, Beatrice. B.A., Occidental Coll., 1948; postgrad., Stockholm U., 1948-49; M.A., Fletcher Sch. Internat. Law and Diplomacy, Medford, Mass., 1950. Commd. fgn. service officer Dept. State, 1951; dep. chief of mission Am. embassy, Pretoria, Republic of South Africa, 1976-79; diplomat in residence Ariz. State U., Tempe, 1979-80; dep. commandant U.S. Army War Coll., Carlisle, Pa., 1980-84; ambassador Am. embassy, Mbabane, Swaziland, 1985-88; sr. advisor U.S. Del. to UN, 1988, 90. Served to lt. (j.g.) USN, 1942-46.

NELSON, HELAINE QUEEN, lawyer; b. Hamtramck, Mich., Mar. 15, 1945; d. Willard Myron and Helen Victoria (Nebraska) Bowers; m. William Michael Nelson, Apr. 19, 1970; 1 child, Lindsey Paige. BS, Western Mich. U., 1969, MS, 1971; JD, U. Detroit, 1977. Bar: Ohio 1977, U.S. Dist. Ct. (no. and so. dists.) Ohio 1978, Ill. 1985, Mich. 1996. Corp. counsel Beverage Mgmt., Inc., Columbus, Ohio, 1977-79, assoc. gen. counsel, 1979-80, gen. counsel, 1980-84; sr. atty. Abbott Labs., Abbott Park, Ill., 1984-87; sr. counsel Abbott Labs., Abbott Park, 1995—; divsn. counsel Abbott Labs., Columbus, 1987-95; sr. counsel Abbott Labs., Abbott Park, Ill., 1995—; pvt. practice Mich., 1996—. Mem. Ohio Bar Assn., Am. Corp. Counsel Assn. Unitarian. Avocations: freelance writing, jogging, reading. Office: 16940 Riley St Holland MI 49424-6018

NELSON, HERBERT LEROY, psychiatrist; b. Eddyville, Iowa, June 15, 1922; s. Albert and Bessie Mae (Durham) N.; m. Carol Lorayne Hofert, Dec. 23, 1943; children—Richard Kent, Vicki Lurae, Thadeus Leroy, Cylda Vermae. B.A., U. Iowa, 1943, M.D., 1946. Diplomate Am. Bd. Psychiatry and Neurology. Intern Univ Hosps. of U. Iowa, Iowa City, 1946-47; resident Brooke Army Med. Ctr, Fort Sam Houston, Tex, 1947-49, U.S. VA Hosp., Knoxville, Iowa, 1949-51; resident Oreg. State Hosp., Salem, 1951-52, clin. dir., 1952-63; asst. prof. psychiatry U. Iowa, Iowa City, 1963-66; assoc. prof. U. Iowa, 1966-73, prof., 1973-84, prof. emeritus, 1984—; dir. Iowa Mental Health Authority, Iowa City, 1968-82; med. dir. Mideast Iowa Community Mental Health Ctr., Iowa City, 1969-84; adj. prof. Tulane U., New Orleans, 1974-77. Co-author 4 monographs; also articles, 1965-83. Served as capt. M.C., U.S. Army, 1947-49. Fellow Am. Psychiat. Assn.; mem. Iowa Psychiat. Soc. (pres. 1970-71, chmn. subcom. on psychiat. care 1973-77), AMA, Johnson County Med. Soc., Am. Assn. Psychiat. Adminstrs., Am. Coll. Mental Health Adminstrs. Republican. Methodist. Avocations: gardening; fishing; woodworking; painting; travel. Home and Office: 1400 Laura Dr Iowa City IA 52245-1539

NELSON, HOWARD JOSEPH, geographer, educator; b. Gowrie, Iowa, Jan. 12, 1919; s. Joseph A. and Hannah (Swanson) N.; m. Betty Marie Garlick, June 18, 1944; children: Linda Ann, James Allan. B.A. with high honors, Iowa State Tchrs. Coll., 1942; M.A., U. Chgo., 1947, Ph.D., 1949. Mem. faculty UCLA, 1949—, prof. geography, 1963-86, prof. emeritus, 1986—, chmn. dept., 1966-71. Author: (with W.A.V. Clark) Los Angeles, The Metropolitan Experience, 1976, The Los Angeles Metropolis, 1983. Served with AUS, 1943-46. Mem. Assn. Am. Geographers (regional councillor 1968-71), Sigma Xi. Home: 6136 Kentland Ave Woodland Hills CA 91367-1719 Office: Univ Calif Dept Geography Los Angeles CA 90024

NELSON, IVORY VANCE, academic administrator; b. Curtis, La., June 11, 1934; s. Elijah H. and Mattie (White) N.; m. Patricia Robbins, Dec. 27, 1985; children: Cherlyn, Karyn, Eric Beatty, Kim Beatty. BS, Grambling (La.) State U., 1959; PhD, U. Kans., 1963. Assoc. prof. chemistry So. U., Baton Rouge, 1963-67, head div. sci., 1966-68; prof. chemistry Prairie View (Tex.) A&M U., 1968-83, asst. acad. dean, 1968-72, v.p. rsch., 1972-82, acting pres., 1982-83; exec. asst. Tex. A&M U. System, College Station, 1983-86; chancellor Alamo C.C. Dist., San Antonio, 1986-92; pres. Cen. Wash. U., Ellensburg, 1992—; DuPont teaching fellow U. Kans., 1959; rsch. chemist Am. Oil Co., 1962; sr. rsch. chemist Union Carbide Co., 1969; vis. prof. U. Autonomous Guadalajara, Mex., 1966, Loyola U., 1967; Fulbright lectr., 1966; cons. evaluation coms. Oak Ridge (Tenn.) Assoc. Univs., NSF, Nat. Coun. for Accreditation Tchr. Edn., So. Assn. Colls. and Schs.; mem. regional policy coms. on minorities Western Interstate Com. on Higher Edn., 1986-88; mem. exec. com. Nat. Assn. State Univs. and Land Grant Colls., 1980-82. Contbr. articles to profl. jours. Bd. dirs. Target 90, Goals San Antonio, 1987-89, coun. of pres.NAIDA,(1993-96) Commn. on Student Learning, Wash., 1992—, United Way San Antonio, 1987-89, Alamo Area coun. Boy Scouts Am., 1987-89, San Antonio Symphony Soc., 1987-91, Key Bank of Wash.; mem. bd. dirs. assn. Western U., (1995—) mem. com. fir jud. reform State of Tex., 1991; mem. edn. adv. bd. Tex. Rsch. Park, 1987-89; bd. givs. Am. Inst. for character Edn., Inc., 1988-91; mem. adv. com. Tex. Ho. of Reps., 1978; chmn. United Way Campaign Tex. A&M U. System, 1984, others. Staff sgt. USAF, 1951-55, Korea. T.H. Harris scholar Grambling State U., 1959; fellow Nat. Urban League, 1969. Mem. AAAS, Am. Chem. Soc., Tex. Acad. Sci., NAACP, Phi Beta Kappa, Sigma Xi, Phi Lambda Upsilon, Beta Kappa Chi, Alpha Mu Gamma, Kappa Delta Pi, Sigma Pi Sigma, Omega Psi Phi, Sigma Pi Phi, Phi Kappa Phi. Avocations: fishing, photography, sports. Home: 211 E 10th Ave Ellensburg WA 98926-2911 Office: Office of Pres Cen Wash U Ellensburg WA 98926

NELSON, J. GORDON, geography educator. Prof. dept. geography U. Waterloo, Ont., Can. Recipient Massey medal Royal Can. Geog. Soc., 1993. Office: U Waterloo, Dept Geography, Waterloo, ON Canada N2L 3G1

NELSON, JACK LEE, education educator; b. Cheyenne, Wyo., Nov. 2, 1932; s. Myron Alfred and Mary Elizabeth (Baker) N.; m. Gwen Margret Names, Mar. 13, 1953; children: Barbara Louise Nelson Vollmer, Steven Lee. B.A., U. Denver, 1954; M.A., Calif. State U.-Los Angeles, 1958; Ed.D., U. So. Calif., 1961. Tchr. pub. schs., Riverside, Calif., 1956-58; instr. Calif. State U., Los Angeles, 1958-59, asst. prof., 1959-63; instr. Citrus Community Coll., Glendora, Calif., 1959-63; assoc. prof. SUNY, Buffalo, 1963-68, chmn. dept., 1966-68; prof. edn. Rutgers U., New Brunswick, N.J., 1968—, Disting. prof., 1975; dean, prof. Sch. Edn. San Jose (Calif.) State U., 1986-87; chmn. dept. sci. and humanities edn. Rutgers U., 1972-75; vis. prof. Cambridge U., Eng., 1974, 75, 79, 80, 83, 84, 85; vis. scholar U. Calif., Berkeley, 1975-76, Stanford U., 1982-83, Western Australia Inst. Tech., 1985, U. Colo., 1989, U. Wash., 1993, U. Sydney, Australia, 1994-95; cond. editor Random House Inc., McGraw-Hill Inc.; mem. adv. coun. New World Dictionary. Author: (with J. Michaelis) Secondary Social Studies, 1980, (with V. Green) International Human Rights, 1980, (with Frank Besag) Foundations of Education, 1984, (with S. Palonsky and K. Carlson) Critical Issues in Education, 1990, 2d edit., 1993, 3d edit., 1996; contbr. numerous articles to profl. jours.; editor: Social Sci. Rsch., 1964-68, Theory and Rsch. in Social Edn., 1982-85. Mem. exec. bd. ACLU, Middlesex County, N.J., 1968-83; mem. Erie County Dem. Com., 1967-68, N.J. Gov.'s Task Force on Rehab. Edn. for Prisoners, 1970-74; mem. Highland Park Bd. Edn., N.J., 1972-75, pres., 1974-75; mem. Highland Park Hist. Commn., 1980-86; mem. nat. panel Project Censored, 1976—; mem. N.J. Rural Adv. Commn., 1992—. Robert Taft Found. grantee Inst. in Govt., 1970, 86; Inst. for World Order grantee Rutgers U., 1973—; Rutgers U. grantee; SUNY-Buffalo grantee, 1967-68; ACLU of N.J. grantee, 1972-73; U.S. Office Edn. grantee, 1967-68; N.J. Dept. Higher Edn. grantee, 1985-86. Mem. Am. Acad. Polit. and Social Sci., AAUP (editorial bd. 1977-80, rep. nat. council 1982-85, com. on acad. freedom and tenure 1983-86, com. on legis. affairs 1992-95), Am. Ednl. Research Assn., Internat. Studies Assn., Nat. Council for Social Studies, Social Sci. Edn. Consortium (bd. dirs. 1983-85), Phi Delta Kappa. Home: 299 Woodbridge Ave Metuchen NJ 08840-2039 Office: Rutgers U Grad Sch Edn Rutgers U Grad Sch Edn New Brunswick NJ 08903

NELSON, JAMES ALBERT, librarian, state official; b. Grand Junction, Colo., June 13, 1941; s. Gerhardt Melvin and Lettie Louise (Sanders) N.; m. Judith Ann Brown, Sept. 5, 1965 (div. July 1972); children: Colm Corbett, Rebekah Sanders; m. Carol Stern, Aug. 8, 1982 (div. Apt. 1992); 1 child, Michael Leland. B.A. in English, U. Colo., 1965; M.S. in L.S., U. Ky., 1969. Head librarian Hardin County Pub. Library, Elizabethtown, Ky., 1969-70; dir. interlibrary coop. Ky. Dept. Libraries and Archives, Frankfort, 1970-72; state libr., commr. Ky. Dept. Librs. and Archives, Frankfort, 1980—; speech writer Gov. Ky., Frankfort, 1972-73; dir. continuing edn. Coll. Libr. Sci., U. Ky., Lexington, 1973-77; asst. prof. libr. sci. U. Wis., Madison, 1977-80; vol. U.S. Peace Corps, Bulan, Sorsogon, Philippines, 1965-66; mem. Ky. Sci. and Tech. Coun., 1990—, Ky. Task Force on Open Meetings and Open Records, 1990—. Editor column Jour. Edn. for Librarianship, 1976-79, Gateways to Comprehensive State Information Policy, 1990; contbr. articles to jours. Pres. Increase Lapham Community Edn., Madison, 1979; mem. Ky. Gov.'s Commn. on Literacy; mem. exec. bd. Ky. Oral History Commn.; mem. KISC Comm. Adv. Coun., 1991—. Recipient Outstanding Alumnus award U. Ky. Coll. Library and Info. Sci., 1985. Mem. ALA (chmn. continuing edn. com. 1976-78, pres. 1984-85, chair 1988-89), Assn. Coop. and Specialized Libr. Agys., Ky. Info. Systems Commn. (chair info. policy spl. com. 1991-96), Continuing Libr. Edn. Network and Exch. (pres. 1979-80), Soc. Am. Archivist (task force archives and soc.), Chief Officers State Libr. Agys. (treas. 1989-91, chair legis. com. 1991-92), ALA Office for Info. Tech. Policy Adv. Com., Beta Phi Mu (chpt. pres. 1969). Democrat. Home: 222 Raintree Rd Frankfort KY 40601-4459 Office: Ky Dept Libr and Archives PO Box 537 Frankfort KY 40602-0537

NELSON, JAMES ALONZO, radiologist, educator; b. Cherokee, Iowa, Oct. 20, 1938; s. Joe George and Ruth Geraldine (Jones) N.; m. Katherine Metcalf, July 16, 1966; children: John Metcalf, Julie Heaps. AB, Harvard U., 1961, MD, 1965. Asst. prof. radiology U. Calif. San Francisco, 1972-74; assoc. prof. U. Utah, Salt Lake City, 1974-79, prof., 1979-86; prof. U. Wash., Seattle, 1986—; dir. radiol. rsch. U. Calif.-San Francisco/Ft. Miley VAH, 1973-74, U. Utah, 1984-85, U. Wash., 1986—. Contbr. chpts. to books, articles to Am. Jour. Roentgenology, Radiology, Investigative Radiology, others. Capt. USAF, 1967-69. John Harvard scholar, 1957-61, James Picker Found. scholar, 1973-77; recipient Mallinkrodt prize Soc. Body Computerized Tomagraphy, 1990, Roscoe Miller award Soc. Gastrointestinal Radiology, 1991. Fellow Am. Coll. Radiology (diplomate); mem. Radiol. Soc. N.Am., Assn. Univ. Radiology. Achievements include patents (with others) for Non-Surgical Peritoneal Lavage, Recursive Band-Pass Filter for Digital Angiography, for Unsharp Masking for Chest Films, Improved Chest Tube, Oral Hepatobiliary MRI Contrast Agent. Office: U Wash Dept Radiology Diagnostic Imaging Sci Ctr Box 357115 Seattle WA 98195

NELSON, JAMES AUGUSTUS, II, real estate executive, architect, banker; b. Damrascotta, Maine, July 26, 1947; s. Robert Maynard and Margret Rebbeca (Harmision) N.; m. Linda Ray, Aug. 15, 1975 (div. 1985); m. Tina Nides, Oct. 22, 1986 (div. 1991); 1 child, Jennifer Alexandria. BArch, Columbia U., 1973, MBA, 1974. Resident v.p. Citibank, N.Y.C., 1974-77; group v.p. Bank of Am., San Francisco, 1977-82; assoc. John Portman and Assocs., Atlanta, 1983-85; pres. J.A. Nelson and Assocs., L.A., 1986-88; dir. real estate planning and devel. MCA Devel. Co., L.A., 1988-94; founder Mother Co., Hollywood, Calif., 1995. Author: Banker's Guide to Construction, 1978, Doing Business in Saudi Arabia, 1979. Chmn. Laurel Canyon Coalition, L.A.; bd. dirs. Laurel Canyon Area Assn., Hollywood Heritage, Hillside Fedn., L.A., Lookout Mountain Assocs., L.A. Avocations: gardening, architecture. Home: 8306 Grandview Dr Los Angeles CA 90046 Office: Mother Co 8306 Grandview Dr Los Angeles CA 90046-1918

NELSON, JAMES CARMER, JR., advertising executive, writer; b. Denver, Nov. 10, 1921; s. James Carmer and Helen (McClelland) N.; m. Mary-Armour Ransom, Sept. 9, 1950; children—James Carmer III, Marie-Louise Nelson Masters, Jeffrey Armour, Rebecca McClelland Nelson Sylla. A.B., Yale, 1943. Mktg. editor Bus. Week mag., N.Y.C., 1946-48; illustration editor Bus. Week mag., 1948-52; freelance author Sonoma, Calif., 1952-57; copy chief Hoefer, Dieterich & Brown, Inc., San Francisco, 1957-59; v.p., creative dir. Hoefer, Dieterich & Brown, Inc., 1959-66, exec. v.p., 1966-76, pres., 1976-79, vice chmn., 1979-80; ptnr. John H. Hoefer & Assocs., 1972—; vice chmn. Chiat/Day/Hoefer, 1980; pvt. advt. cons., 1980—; bd. dirs. McKinney, Inc., Phila.; instr. Golden Gate Coll., San Francisco, 1958-59; alternate mem. Nat. Advt. Rev. Bd., 1971-75. Author: The Trouble With Gumballs, 1957, Great Cheap Wines: A Poorperson's Guide, 1977, Great Wines Under $5, 1983; contbr. articles and fiction to popular mags. Mem. Harold Brunn Soc. for Med. Research, Mt. Zion Hosp., San Francisco; bd. assos. Linus Pauling Inst. Sci. and Medicine, Palo Alto, Calif.; mem. Colony Found., New Haven; trustee Coro Found., 1965-75, Marin Art Complex; bd. mgrs. Marin County YMCA. Served with USNR, 1942-46. Mem. ASCAP. Club: Villa Taverna (San Francisco). Home: 649 Idylberry Rd San Rafael CA 94903-1231

NELSON, JAMES F., judge, religious organization administrator. BS, U. Calif., LLB, Loyola U., Los Angeles. Bar: Calif. 1954. Judge, Los Angeles Mcpl. Ct. Chmn. Baha'i Faith Nat. Spiritual Assembly Bahais of the U.S., Wilmette, Ill. Address: Nat Spiritual Assembly Bahai Faith 536 Sheridan Rd Wilmette IL 60091-2849*

NELSON, JAMES SMITH, pathologist, educator; b. St. Louis, Mar. 19, 1933; s. Victor Paul and Dorothy Gertrude (Smith) N.; children: Paul F., Andrew S. BS, St. Louis U., 1950-53, MD, 1957. Pathology intern, resident St. Louis U. Hosps., 1957-59, 60-61; neuropathology fellow Columbia U. Coll. Phys. & Surgery, N.Y.C., 1959-60; neurochemistry fellow Washington U. Med. Sch., St. Louis, 1961-63, instr. in pathology, 1963-64, assoc. prof., prof. pathology & pediatrics, 1973-87; asst. prof., assoc. prof. pathology St. Louis U. Med. Sch., 1964-73; head divsn. neuropathology Henry Ford Hosp., Detroit, 1987-89; clin. prof. neuropathology U. Mich. Med. Sch., Ann Arbor, 1988-89; prof. pathology La. State U. Med. Ctr., New Orleans, 1989—; chmn. dept. neuropathology Armed Forces Inst. Pathology, Washington, 1990-94; ad hoc cons. NIH, Washington, 1973-92; mem. Nat. Cancer Inst. CNS Oncology Working Group, Washington, 1986-89; mem. neuropathology test com. Am. Bd. Pathology, Tampa, Fla., 1984-90; mem. WHO Brain Tumor Working Group, Zurich, Switzerland, 1990—; adv. mem. neuropathology com. Coll. Am. Pathologists, Chgo., 1992—. Author: Medical School Admission: A Systematic Guide, 1974; author, editor: Principles and Practice of Neuropathology, 1993; contbr. over 150 articles to profl. jours. Col. M.C., U.S. Army, 1990-94. Decorated Legion of Merit; recipient U.S. Sr. Scientist award Alexander von Humboldt Found., Free U. Berlin, 1979-80, Cert. of Achievement, U.S. Surgeon Gen., 1985, Res. Components Achievement medal U.S. Army, 1986; NIH spl. rsch. fellow in neurochemistry, 1961-63; NIH grantee, 1966-87, 95—. Mem. AMA, Coll. Am. Pathologists (com. mem.), Am. Soc. Clin. Pathologists, Am. Assn. Neuropathologists, U.S. & Can. Acad. Pathology, Am. Inst. Nutrition. Roman Catholic. Avocations: sailing, fishing, photography, skydiving. Home: 3443 Esplanade Ave Apt 415 New Orleans LA 70119-2956 Office: Dept of Pathology La State Univ Med Ctr 1901 Perdido St New Orleans LA 70112-1328

NELSON, JOHN HOWARD, food company research executive; b. Chgo., May 29, 1930; s. Harold Eugene and Zoe (Peters) N.; m. Jacqueline Raff, Apr. 30, 1952; children: Keith E., Kevin E., Kristen E. BS in Horticulture and Food Tech., Purdue U., 1952, MS in Food Tech. and Microbiology, 1953; PhD in Biochemistry and Microbiology, U. Minn., 1961. From rsch. biochemist to head R&D dept. Gen. Mills., Mpls., 1955-67; dir. R&D to v.p. R&D Peavey Co., Mpls., 1968-76; ptnr. Johnson Powell & Co., Mpls., 1976-78; v.p. R&D, then v.p. mktg. and product devel. Am. Maize Products Co., Hammond, Ind., 1978-82; v.p. corp. devel., then chief oper. officer Roman Meal Co., Tacoma, Wash., 1982-86; corp. dir. R&D, then v.p. R&D McCormick & Co. Inc., Hunt Valley, Md., 1986-88, v.p. sci. and tech., 1988-94; ret., 1994; prof. food sci. dept. Purdue U., West Lafayette, Ind., 1994—; sci. program advisor Charles F. Kettering Rsch. Lab., Dayton, Ohio, 1976-77. Trustee St. Joseph Hosp., Towson, Md., 1989-95; mem. chancellor's adv. com. U. Md., 1989-96; chmn. Ind./Acad. bd. Towson State U., 1990-92. Visking fellow Visking Corp., 1958. Fellow League for Internat. Food Edn. (pres. 1981-82, chmn. Project SUSTAIN 1988-94); mem. Am. Assn. Cereal Chemists (pres. 1974-75, William F. Geddes award 1979, Geddes lectr. 1991), Am. Chem. Soc., Inst. Food Technologists, Elks, Sigma Xi, Gamma Sigma Delta, Alpha Zeta. Republican. Avocations: travel, golf, gardening. Office: Purdue Univ 1160 Smith Hall West Lafayette IN 47907-1160

NELSON, JOHN HOWARD (JACK HOWARD NELSON), journalist; b. Talladega, Ala., Oct. 11, 1929; s. Howard Alonzo and Barbara Lena (O'Donnell) N.; m. Virginia Dare Dickinson, Aug. 4, 1951 (div. Nov. 1974); children: Karen Dare, John Michael, Steven Howard; m. Barbara Joan Matusow, Dec. 7, 1974. Student econs., Ga. State Coll., 1953-57; Nieman fellow, Harvard U., 1961-62. Reporter, Biloxi (Miss.) Daily Herald, 1947-51; Reporter Atlanta Constitution, 1952-65; So. bur. chief Los Angeles Times, Atlanta, 1965-70; with Washington bur. Los Angeles Times, 1970—, Washington bur. chief, 1975-96, chief Washington corr., 1996—. Author: (with Gene Roberts, Jr.) The Censors and the Schools, 1963, (with Jack Bass) The Orangeburg Massacre, 1970, (with R.J. Ostrow) The FBI and the Berrigans, 1972, Captive Voices, Shocken Books, 1974, Terror in the Night, 1993. Mem. vis. com. U. Md. Sch. Journalism, U. Miami Sch. Communications. With AUS, 1951-52. Recipient Pulitzer prize for local reporting under deadline pressure, 1960; Drew Pearson award for gen. excellence in investigative reporting, 1974. Mem. Fgn. Policy Coun., The Gridiron Club. Home: 4 Wynkoop Ct Bethesda MD 20817-5936 Office: 1875 I St NW Ste 1100 Washington DC 20006-5409

NELSON, JOHN KEITH, electrical engineering educator; b. Oldham, Lancashire, Eng., July 3, 1943; s. John Collins and Joyce Palfrey (Simmons) N.; m. Christine Anne Baker, Feb. 10, 1968; children: David John, Peter Mark. BS in Engring., U. London, 1965, PhD, 1969. Rsch. fellow U. London, 1966-69, lectr., 1969-78, reader, 1978-79; rsch. mgr. Gen. Electric, Schenectady, 1979-82; prof. elec. power engring. Rensselaer Poly. Inst., Troy, N.Y., 1982—, head dept.; examiner U. Sri Lanka, 1970-85; cons. in field. Contbr. articles to profl. jours. Patentee in field. Recipient Snell Premium, IEE, London, 1972, J.R. Beard award, 1976, Rsch. award, Brit. Council, 1974, 76; Travel award, Royal Soc., London, 1976, Power Engring. Educator award Edison Electric Inst., 1994. Fellow Inst. Elec. Engrs. (U.K.), IEEE (tech. v.p. Dielectrics and Elect. Insulation Soc. 1991-92, administrv. v.p., 1993-94, pres. 1995—, Meml. lectr. 1993); mem., Council of Engring. Inst. Episcopalian. Avocations: squash, sailing, scuba diving, flying. Office: Rensselaer Poly Inst Dept Elec Power Engring Troy NY 12180-3590

NELSON, JOHN MARSHALL, medical information services company executive; b. Madison, Wis., Oct. 28, 1941; s. Russell Arthur and Dorothea (Smith) N.; m. Linda Taylor, Oct. 13, 1962 (div. June 1968); children: Ann, David; m. Katherine Dianne Hoagland, Sept. 24, 1972; children: James, George. AB, Harvard Coll., 1963; MD, Case Western Reserve U., 1967; MBA, U. Chgo., 1983. Diplomate Am. Bd. Internal Medicine. Staff assoc. NIH, Bethesda, Md., 1968-71; rsch. assoc., asst. prof. medicine Promis Lab. Med. Sch. Univ. Vt., 1973-76; med. dir. Madison Gen. Hosp., 1976-84; assoc. clin. prof. Med. Sch. U. Wis., 1976-84; v.p. corp. med. affairs Gen. Health Mgmt. Co., Madison, 1984-86; dir. med. and ednl. affairs Washington Hosp. Ctr., 1986-87; pres. Nelson Info. Systems, Bethesda, Md., 1987—; cons. Med. Sch. U. Utah, Salt Lake City, 1985-86; med. reviewer FDA, 1990-91. Contbr. articles to profl. jour. Coach youth soccer, 1984-85; merit badge counselor Boy Scouts Am., 1987; mem. Harvard Schs. Com., Md., 1988-91; vestry St. John's Episcopal Ch., Bethesda, 1988-91. Harvard Hon. Nat. Scholar, 1959-62; recipient Steuer Meml. award Case Western Reserve U., Cleve., 1967. Fellow ACP, Am. Coll. Physician Execs.; mem. AMA, Univ. Club Chgo., Harvard Club (Washington), Alpha Omega Alpha. Republican. Episcopalian. Avocations: swimming, reading, cycling. Home: 6616 Millwood Rd Bethesda MD 20817-6058 Office: 4740 Chevy Chase Dr Chevy Chase MD 20815-6461

NELSON, JOHN MARTIN, corporate executive; b. N.Y.C., Aug. 9, 1931; s. Martin H. and Margaret (Larkin) N.; m. Linda Crocker Moore, Aug. 30, 1992; children: Murrey E., Christopher L. A.B., Wesleyan U., 1953; M.B.A., Harvard U., 1959. With Norton Co., Worcester, Mass., 1959-90; pres., chief exec. officer Norton Christensen Inc. subs. Norton Co., Salt Lake City, 1978-86; pres., chief operating officer Norton Co., Worcester, 1986-88, chmn., chief exec. officer, 1988-90; chmn., chief exec. officer Wyman-Gordon Co., Worcester, 1991-94; chmn., 1994—, The TJX Cos., Inc., Framingham, Mass., 1995—; bd. dirs. Browne and Sharpe Mfg. Co., Kingstown, R.I., Cambridge Biotech., Corp., Worcester, Mass., Stockery & Yale, Inc., Beverly, Mass. Trustee Wesleyan U., 1978-81, Worcester Poly. Inst., 1986—, chmn. 1995—; bd. dirs. Worcester Mcpl. Rsch. Bur., 1989—, Greater Worcester Cmty. Found., 1990, Alliance for Edn., 1991—, U. Mass. Med. Ctr. Found., Inc., 1991—, United Way Ctrl. Mass., 1993; trustee Worcester Found. for Biomed. Rsch., 1993—; mem. Worcester Airport Commn., 1993—, chmn. 1996. Home: 7 Massachusetts Ave Worcester MA 01609-1622 Office: Wyman-Gordon Co 244 Worcester St # 8001 North Grafton MA 01536-1260

NELSON, JOHN ROBERT, theology educator, clergyman; b. Winona Lake, Ind., Aug. 21, 1920; s. William John and Agnes Dorothy (Soderborg) N.; m. Dorothy Patricia Mercer, Aug. 18, 1945; children: Eric Mercer, William John. AB, DePauw U., 1941, LHD, 1960; BD, Yale U., 1944; DTheol, U. Zürich, Switzerland, 1951; LLD, Wilberforce U., 1954; DD, Ohio Wesleyan U., 1964; LHD, Loyola U., 1969; DH, Hellenic Coll., 1985. Ordained to ministry Meth. Ch., 1944; dir. Wesley Found., Chapel Hill, N.C., 1946-48; assoc. dir. Wesley Found., Urbana, Ill., 1950-51; study sect. United Student Christian Council, N.Y.C., 1951-53; sec. commn. on faith and order World Council Chs., Geneva, Switzerland, 1953-57, chmn. working com., 1967-75; dean, prof. theology Vanderbilt Div. Sch., 1957-60; vis. prof. ecumenics Princeton Theol. Sem., 1960-61; vis. prof. United Theol. Coll., Bangalore, India, and Leonard Theol. Coll., Jabalpur, India, 1961-62; Fairchild prof. Christian theology Grad. Sch. Theology, Oberlin Coll., Ohio, 1962-65; prof. systematic theology Boston U. Sch. Theology, 1965-84, dean, 1972-74; Peyton lectr. So. Meth. U., 1961; Merrick lectr. Ohio Wesleyan U., 1964; Lowell lectr., 1966; Burke lectr. U. Calif.-San Diego, 1985; Willson lectr. Centenary Coll., 1985; Nobel lectr. Gustavus Adolphus U., 1985; vis. prof. Pontifical Gregorian U., Rome, 1968-69; Mendenhall lectr. DePauw, 1974; Russell lectr. Tufts U., 1976, Wattson lectr., Cath. U., 1989; cons. Pres.'s Commn. for Study Ethical Problems in Biomed. Research, 1980-82; dir. Inst. Religion, Tex. Med. Ctr., Houston, 1985-92, sr. rsch. fellow 1992—; adj. prof. medicine Baylor Coll. Medicine, 1985—, adj. prof. religious studies Rice U., 1987-91; program dir. Genetics, Religion and Ethics, Baylor Coll. Medicine, 1990—. Author: The Realm of Redemption, 1951, One Lord, One Church, 1958, Overcoming Christian Divisions, rev. edit, 1962, Criterion for the Church, 1963, Fifty Years of Faith and Order, (with J. Skoglund), 1963, Crisis in Unity and Witness, 1968, Church Union in Focus, 1968, Science and Our Troubled Conscience, 1980, Human Life: a Biblical Perspective for Bioethics, 1984, On the New Frontiers of Genetics and Religion, 1994; editor: The Christian Student and the World Struggle, 1952, Christian Unity in North America, 1958, No Man Is Alien, 1971, Life as Liberty, Life as Trust, 1992; editor-at-large, The Christian Century, 1958-91; assoc. editor: Jour. Ecumenical Studies; mem. editorial bd. Human Gene Therapy. Del. all 7 assemblies World Coun. Chs., 5th World Conf. on Faith and Order, 1993, United Meth. Gen. Conf., 1968, 72; mem. commn. on faith and order Nat. Coun. Chs.; mem. U.S. Commn. for UNESCO, 1974-80; bd. dirs. Value of Life Com. Fellow Am. Acad. Arts and Scis.; mem. Am. Theol. Soc. (past pres.), N.Am. Acad. Ecumenists (past pres.), Soc. Europeenne de Culture (v.p.), Houston Philosophy Soc., Country Club of Brookline (Mass.), Rotary, Phi Beta Kappa, Beta Theta Pi. Home: 1111 Hermann Dr Apt 19 A Houston TX 77004-6930 Office: Inst of Religion Tex Med Ctr 1129 Wilkins St Houston TX 77030-2805 *The sequence of my persuasions and commitments has been from Christian unity to human unity to basic concern for the value of human life itself; and these are cumulative convictions from which I cannot deviate.*

NELSON, JOHN THILGEN, retired hospital administrator, physician; b. Aurora, Ill., Feb. 11, 1921; s. George William and Margaret Mary (Thilgen) N. Student, Wheaton (Ill.) Coll., 1941-44; M.D., Chgo. Med. Sch., 1949. Intern Macon (Ga.) Hosp., 1948-49; resident anesthesiology U. Ill. Sch. Medicine, 1949-51, clin. instr., 1949-57; attending physician VA Hosp., Hines, Ill., 1951-57; pvt. practice medicine, specializing in anesthesiology Chgo., 1951-52, Elgin, Ill., 1954-69; chief of dept. St. Joseph Hosp., Elgin, 1954-69; sec. med. staff St. Joseph Hosp., 1966, v.p. med. staff, 1967, pres., 1968; supt. Chgo.-Read Mental Health Center, 1969-74; med. dir. Elgin Mental Health Center, 1974-87; coordinator med. services Ill. Dept. Health and Devel. Disabilities, 1976-87; ret., 1985. Served with AUS, 1952-54. Fellow Am. Coll. Anesthesiology; mem. Am., Ill., Chgo., Kane County med. socs., Am., Ill., Chgo. socs. anesthesiology. Home: RR 1 Box 313 11 N 070 Rohrssen Rd Elgin IL 60120

NELSON, JOHN WILTON, symphonic conductor; b. San Jose, Costa Rica, Dec. 6, 1941; came to U.S., 1953; s. Wilton Mons and Thelma (Agnew) N.; m. Anita Christine Johnsen, Sept. 4, 1964; children: Kirsten, Kari. B. Music, Wheaton Coll., 1963; M.M. (Teaching fellow), Juilliard Sch., 1965, postgrad. diploma (teaching fellow), 1967. Conducting faculty Juillard Sch., N.Y.C., 1968-72; dir. Aspen Choral Inst., 1968-73; music dir. Indpls. Symphony Orch., 1976-87; conductor prodns. at Met. Opera and City Opera in N.Y., Santa Fe, Chgo. Lyric Opera, Rome Opera, Lyon Opera, Geneva Opera, The Bastille, la Monnaie in Brussels and Welsh Nat. Opera; recordings include Berlioz' Beatrice and Benedict, 1992, a disc of works by Paul Schoenfield, 1994, and Gorecki's Miserere with Chgo. Symphony and Lyric Opera choruses. Music dir., ProArte Chorale, Ridgewood, N.J., 1965-75; condr., N.Y. Mozart Festival, 1967, Juilliard Opera Theatre, N.Y.C., 1968; music dir., Greenwich Philharmonica Orch., N.Y.C., 1966-74; condr., N.Y.C. Opera, 1973-75, Santa Fe Opera, 1973, Geneva Grand Theatre, 1974, Met. Opera, N.Y.C., 1974—, Lyon Opera, 1991, Geneva Opera, 1992; condr., music dir., Indpls. Symphony Orch., 1976-87; music adviser, Nashville (Tenn.) Symphony, 1975; conducted, Chgo. Symphony, N.Y. Philharm., Boston Symphony, Phila. Orch., Indpls. Symphony Orch., Cin. Orch., L.A. Philharmonic, London Royal Philharmonic, Suiss Romande, Dresden Staatskapelle, Leipzig Lewardhaus, Orch. de Paris; music dir. St. Louis Opera, 1981-91, prin. guest condr., 1991—. Recipient Irving Berlin Conducting award, 1967, Diapason d'Or award recording Beatrice & Benedict, 1993, Best Operatic Rec. Grammy award for Handel's Semele with English Chamber Orch./Kathleen Battle, 1993. Office: care IMG Artists Media House, 3 Burlington Ln, London Chiswick W4 2TH, England

NELSON, JOHN WOOLARD, neurology educator, physician; b. Hagerstown, Ind., Mar. 9, 1928; s. John Hans and Marvel May (Woolard) N.; m. Nancy Louise Elam, July 21, 1966; 1 son, John Hancock. A.B., Earlham Coll., 1950; M.D., Ind. U., 1953. Diplomate: Am. Bd Psychiatry and Neurology (clin. neurophysiology). Instr. neurology U. Tenn. Coll. Medicine, 1959-61; asst. prof. neurology W. Va. U. Sch. Medicine, 1961-63; assoc. prof. neurology U. Tenn., 1963-66; assoc. prof. to prof. Med. Coll. Wis., Milw., 1966-72; clin. prof. neurology U. Minn., Duluth, 1972-73; prof., head dept. neurology U. Okla. Coll. of Medicine, Oklahoma City, 1973-88, prof. emeritus neurology, 1989—. Served with M.C. U.S. Army, 1955-56. Mem. Okla. County Med. Soc., Okla. Med. Soc., AMA, Am. Acad. Neurology, Am. Electroencephalographic Soc., Am. Med. Electroencephalographic Soc. Home: 2608 Greenfield Dr Edmond OK 73003-6528

NELSON, JUDD, actor; b. Portland, Maine, Nov. 28, 1959. Student, Bryn Mawr Coll., Stella Adler Conservatory. mem. Shoestring Theatre Co. Performances include: (stage prodns.) Mozart and Salieri, Domino Courts; (feature films) Making the Grade, 1984, Fandango, 1985, The Breakfast Club, 1985, St. Elmo's Fire, 1986, Blue City, 1986, (voice only) Transformers: The Movie, 1986, From the Hip, 1987, Relentless, 1989, Far Out Man, 1990, New Jack City, 1991, The Dark Backward, 1991, Every Breath, 1993, Blindfold, 1993; (TV episode) Moonlighting; (TV movies) Billionaire Boys Club, 1987, Hiroshima: Out of the Ashes, 1990. Office: C/O Stephen Siebert/Lighthouse Entertainment 409 N Camden Dr Ste 202 Beverly Hills CA 90210*

NELSON, JULIE D., lawyer; b. N.Y.C., Sept. 8, 1954; d. John D. and Eileen M. (Canning) Krohn; m. James L. Nelson, Dec. 29, 1973; children: Morgan, Max, Byron. BS, U. Iowa, 1975, JD, 1978. Bar: D.C., Colo., Tex. Law clk. to presiding justice Iowa Supreme Ct., Des Moines, 1978-79; assoc. Sidley & Austin, Washington, 1979-84; atty. AT&T Info. Systems, Denver, 1984-87, AT&T Communications, Austin, Tex., 1987-91, AT&T Fed. Sys., 1991-92; sr. v.p., counsel AT&T Universal Card Svcs. Corp., 1993—; instr. U. Iowa Sch. Law, summer 1983, U. Phoenix, 1986-87. Mem. Order of Coif, Phi Beta Kappa. Democrat. Office: AT&T Universal Card 8787 Baypine Rd 3-2-A720 Jacksonville FL 32256

NELSON, KARIN BECKER, child neurologist; b. Chgo., Aug. 14, 1933; d. George and Sylvia (Demansly) Becker; m. Phillip G. Nelson, Mar. 20, 1955; children: Sarah Nelson Hammack, Rebecca Nelson Miller, Jenny Nelson Walker, Peter. MD, U. Chgo., 1957; Student, U. Minn., 1950-53. Cert. child neurology Am. Bd. Psychiatry and Neurology. Intern rotating Phila. Gen. Hosp., 1957-58; asst. resident neurology U. Md. Sch. Medicine, Balt., 1958-59; resident neurology George Washington U. Sch. Medicine, Washington, 1959-62; cons. in med. neurology St. Elizabeth's Hosp., Washington, 1960-62; registrar to outpatients Nat. Hosp., Queen Sq., London, 1963; med. officer perinatal rsch. br. Nat. Inst. of Neurol. Disorders and Blindness, NIH, 1964-67; asst. prof. neurology George Washington U., Washington, 1970-72; assoc. neurologist Children's Hosp. of D.C., Washington, 1967-71; instr. neurology George Washington U., Washington, 1967-70; attending neurologist Children's Hosp., Washington, 1971-73, 78—; assoc. clin. prof. neurology George Washington U., Washington, 1972—; cons. Nat. Inst. Child Health and Human Devel., 1975-80, orphan products devel. initial rev. group FDA, 1983-86, Boston Collaborative Drug Surveillance Group, 1985-86, vaccine Am. Acad. Pediatrics, 1985, 87, Dept. Health, State of Calif. Birth Monitoring Group, 1986—, Ctr. for Disease Control Birth Defects Monitoring Com., 1987; med. officer Nat. Inst. Neurol. Disorders and Blindness, NIH, Bethesda, 1972—; med. staff Children Hosp., Washington, 1962—; mem. adv. bd. Internat. Sch. Neurosci., Venice, Italy, Little Found./World Fedn. Neurology, 1992—, rev. bd. Nat. Inst. Aging; mem. epidemiology steering com. NIH, 1993—. Editor: Workshop on the Neurobiological Basis of Autism, 1979, (with J.H. Ellenberg) Febrile Seizures, 1981; editorial bd. Pediatric Neurology, 1984-90, Brain and Development, 1984—, Neurology, 1985-88, Paediatric and Perinatal Epidemiology, 1987—, Developmental Medicine and Child Neurology, 1988; field editor Epilepsy Advances; contbr. papers to profl. jours. Recipient Spl. Recognition award USPHS, 1977, Spl. Achievement award 1981, United Cerebral Palsy Weinstein-Goldenson Rsch. award 1990, Dirs. award NIH, 1992. Fellow Am. Acad. Neurology (exec. bd. 1989-91, councillor); mem. Soc. Perinatal Obstetricians (hon.), Child Neurology Soc. (program chmn. 1973, liaison nat. Inst. of Neurol. and Communicative Disorders and Blindness 1975-80, ethics com. 1985-87, by-laws com. 1990—, ad hoc com. for concensus statement of DPT immunications and the cen. nervous system 1990, long range planning com. 1991—, Hower award 1991), Am. Acad. for Cerebral Palsy and Devel. Medicine (program chmn. 1985), Am. Epilepsy Soc. (Disting. Basic Neuroscientist Epilepsy Rsch. award 1992), Am. Neurol. Assn. (membership com. 1994—), Internat. Child Neurology Assn. (sci. selection com. 1993-94), Can. Assn. Child Neurology (hon.), Soc. Perinatal Obstetricians (hon.), Baltic Child Neurology Soc., Dana Alliance Brain Initiatives, Alpha Omega Alpha. Democrat. Jewish. Office: NIH 7550 Wisconsin Ave Rm 700 Bethesda MD 20892-9130

NELSON, KAY ELLEN, speech and language pathologist; b. Milw., Apr. 14, 1947; d. John A. and Margaret B. (Janke) Strobel; m. Kuglitsch Dale, Mar. 2, 1974 (div. Dec. 1981); 1 child, Ashley Lara. BA with distinction, U. Wis., Madison, 1969; MA, U. Wis., Milw., 1972. Speech and lang. pathologist Sch. Dist. 146, Dolton, Ill., 1970-71, Waukesha County Handicapped Children's Edn. Bd., Waukesha, Wis., 1972-77, 79-80, Kettle Moraine Area Schs., Wales, Wis., 1980-94; dir. speech/lang. pathology MJ Care, Inc., Fond du Lac, Wis., 1994-96; speech-lang. pathologist NovaCare, Inc., New Berlin, Wis., 1996—; pvt. practice Dousman, Wis., summers 1991-93. Fellow Herb Kohl Found., 1993. Mem. Am. Speech, Lang. and Hearing Assn. (cert. of clin. competence, ACE award 1990, 91, 92, 94, 95), Wis. Speech, Lang. and Hearing Assn. (sch. rep. dist. VII 1991—, chmn. sch. svcs. com. 1992-94, v.p. sch. svcs. 1994-95, rep. at large 1995-96), Internat. Soc. Augumentive and Alternative Comm., U.S. Soc. Augumentive and Alternative Comm., Wis. Soc. Augumentive and Alternative Comm. (sec. 1990-92, membership chmn. 1990-93, v.p. profl. affairs 1993). Unitarian. Avocations: sewing, computers, nature activities, travel. Office: NovaCare Inc 13700 W National Ave New Berlin WI 53151

NELSON, KEITH ADAM, chemistry educator; b. N.Y.C., Dec. 8, 1953; s. Sidney and Doris Nelson; m. Martha Leticia Cortes, Oct. 5, 1981; children: Hannah, Dylan. BS in Chemistry, Stanford U., 1976, PhD in Phys. Chemistry, 1981. Postdoctoral scholar UCLA, 1981-82; asst. prof. chemistry MIT, Cambridge, 1982-87, assoc. prof., 1987-92, prof., 1992—. Contbr. over 150 articles to profl. jours. Recipient Presdl. Young Investigator award NSF, 1985-90, Coblentz prize Coblentz Soc., 1988; fellow Alfred P. Sloan Found., 1987-89. Fellow Am. Phys. Soc., Japan Soc. Promotion Sci.; mem. Am. Chem. Soc., Optical Soc. Am., Materials Rsch. Soc., Inter-Am. Photochem. Soc. Avocations: chess, soccer, topless coed roller derby. Office: MIT Dept Chemistry 77 Massachusetts Ave Cambridge MA 02139-4301

NELSON, KEITHE EUGENE, lawyer, state court administrator; b. Grand Forks, N.D., Mar. 23, 1935; s. Herman William and Hannah Marie (Anderson) N.; m. Shirley Jeanne Jordahl, June 10, 1955; children: Kirsti Lynn Nelson Hoerauf, Scott David, Kenen Edward, Karen Lee Nelson Strandquist. PhB, U. N.D., 1958, JD, 1959. Bar: N.D. 1959, U.S. Ct. Mil. Appeals 1967., U.S. Supreme Ct. 1967. With Armour & Co., Grand Forks, 1958-59; commd. 2d lt. USAF, 1958, advanced through grades to maj. gen., 1985; judge advocate USAF, N.D. and, Fed. Republic Germany and Eng., 1959-73; chief career mgmt. USAF, Washington, 1973-77; comdt. USAF JAG Sch., Montgomery, Ala., 1977-81; staff judge adv. Tactical Air Command USAF, Hampton, VA., 1981-82, SAC, Omaha, 1984-85; dir. USAF Judiciary, Washington, 1982-84; dep. JAG USAF, Washington, 1985, JAG., 1988-91, JAG, 1988, ret. JAG, 1991; dir. jud. planning Supreme Ct. N.D.; state ct. administr., 1992—. Chmn. editorial bd. USAF Law Rev., 1977-81. Decorated D.S.M., Legion of Merit with two oak leaf clusters. Mem. ABA. Lutheran. Avocations: skeet shooting, hunting, tennis, theater. Home: 800 Munich Dr Bismarck ND 58504-7050

NELSON, KENT C., delivery service executive; b. 1937. BS, Ball State U., 1959. With United Parcel Svc. Am., Inc., 1959-80, exec. v.p. fin., 1980-86, exec. v.p., 1986-88, vice chmn., 1988-89, chmn. bd., CEO, 1989—; chmn. bd., CEO United Parcel Svc. Inc., N.Y., Ohio. Office: United Parcel Svc AM Inc 55 Glenlake Pky NE Atlanta GA 30328*

NELSON, KENT C., foundation administrator. Chmn. Annie E. Casey Found., Balt. Office: Annie E. Casey Found 701 St Paul St Baltimore MD 21202

NELSON, KIRK N., insurance company executive. Pres., coo Federated Mutual Ins. Co., Owatonna, Minn. Office: Federated Mutual Insurance Co 121 E Park Sq Owatonna MN 55060-3046*

NELSON, LARRY A., statistics educator, consultant; b. Omaha, Oct. 28, 1932; s. Rudolph Lawrence and Elizabeth Coleman (Lewis) N. BS in Agronomy, Iowa State U., 1954; MS in Soil Sci., Tex. A&M U., 1958; PhD in Soil Sci.-Stats., N.C. State U., 1961. Soil scientist Iowa Agrl. Exptl. Sta., Ames, 1954-55; soils instr. Tex. A&I Coll., Kingsville, 1955; rsch. soil scientist Tex. A&M Rsch. Found., College Station, 1956; soils lab. instr. Tex. A&M U., College Station, 1956-58; rsch. asst. N.C. State U., Raleigh, 1959-61, asst. prof. exptl. stats., 1964-66, assoc. prof. exptl. stats., 1966-71, prof. stats., 1971-89, prof. emeritus stats., 1989—; asst. specialist in land classification Land Study Bur., U. Hawaii, Honolulu, 1961-63; lectr., tchr., cons. in field; spl. advisor head dept. stats. Kasetsart U., Bangkok, Thailand, 1973; evaluator quantitative skills IADS, Bangladesh, 1984; mem. rev. team Ctr. for Agrl. Econs. and Ctr. for Data Processing, Winrock Internat., Indonesia, 1985; statis. cons. PROCAFE, El Salvador, 1993—, ICRAF, Nairobi, Kenya, 1991—; ptnr. Statis. Rsch. Assocs., Honolulu, 1962-63. Assoc. editor Geoderma, 1976-84, Agronomy Jour., 1981-87; contbr. numerous articles to profl. publs. NATO fellow Data Analysis Lab., Lynbgy, Denmark, 1978. Fellow AAAS, Am. Statis. Assn. (mem. biometrics sect. com. 1989-90, mem. com. on internat. rels. in stats. 1996—), Am. Soc. Agronomy, Soil Sci. Soc. Am.; mem. Statis. Assn. Thailand (life), Internat. Biometric Soc. (bus. mgr. and treas. 1969-79, awards com. 1987-94, chmn. 1990-93), Sigma Xi, Gamma Sigma Delta (internat. pres. 1984-86, award of merit 1973-74, rep. to AAAS 1978-86), Phi Kappa Phi. Baptist. Avocations: music, genealogy, diving, bicycling, travel. Home: 1422 Banbury Rd Raleigh NC 27607-3711 Office: NC State U Dept Stats Box 8203 Raleigh NC 27695-8203

NELSON, LARRY DEAN, telecommunications and computer systems company executive, consultant; b. Newton, Kans., Aug. 5, 1937; s. Carl Aaron and Leta V. (Van Eaton) N.; m. Linda Hawkins, June 2, 1972. BA, Phillips U., 1959; MS, Kans. State U., 1962; PhD, Ohio State U., 1965. From rsch. asst. to rsch. assoc. Rsch. Found., Ohio State U., Columbus, 1962-65; mathematician II, Batelle Meml. Inst., Columbus, 1962-65; from mem. tech. staff to supr. math. dept. and data systems devel. Bellcomm, Inc., Washington, 1965-72; supr. mgmt. info. systems dept. Bell Telephone Labs., Murray Hill, N.J., 1972-77; supr. rate and tariff planning div. AT&T, N.Y.C., 1977-79; dep. adminstr. rsch. and spl. programs adminstrn. U.S. Dept. Transp., Washington, 1979-81; pres. MCS, Inc., Washington, 1981—; supr. govt. communications ctr. AT&T Bell Labs., 1985-89; mgr. govt. mktg. AT&T Network Systems, 1989-90; supr. secure info. system engring. AT&T Bell Labs., 1990-94; disting. mem. tech. staff, secure systems engring., 1995—; cons. Contel Info. Systems, Denver, 1982-85, Martin Marietta Corp., Denver, 1982-85; mem. info. assurance task force Nat. Security Telecomms. Advisory Com. Contbr. articles to profl. jours. Organizer, sponsor Odd Jobs Club, Washington, 1967-72; pres. Mountain County Condominiums Assn., Dillon, Colo., 1975-83, 85—; treas. Chris' Landing Condominium Assn., 1986-90; mem. Am. del. 5th Meeting of U.S.-USSR Joint Commn. on Cooperation in Field of Transp., Moscow, 1979; head Am. del. 5th Meeting of U.S.-USSR Working Group on Transport of Future, Moscow, 1979. Mem. ABA (info. security com.), Am. Nat. Stds. Inst. (info. tech. security tech. stds. com.), IEEE (sec. D.C. sect. 1982, cert. appreciation 1968), Systems, Man and Cybernetics Soc. (sec. 1981, v.p. 1982-83), Math. Programming Soc., Am. Math. Soc., N.Y. Acad. Scis., Assn. Computing Machinery, Sigma Xi, Phi Kappa Phi, Pi Mu Epsilon. Democrat. Mem. Disciples of Christ. Current work: requirements definition, analysis, design and development of secure information movement and management systems, networks and network management, digital signature, public key infrastructure, and electronic commerce technology. Subspecialties: secure distributed systems and networks; Systems engineering. Office: AT&T 2020 K St NW Ste 550 Washington DC 20006-1806

NELSON, LARS-ERIK, newspaperman; b. N.Y.C., Oct. 15, 1941; s. Arthur and Freda (Rappaport) N.; m. Mary Elizabeth Cantwell, Dec. 28, 1963; children—Peter, Amanda. A.B., Columbia U., 1964. Editorial asst. N.Y. Herald Tribune, N.Y.C., 1959-63; Russian translator Current Digest, N.Y.C., 1963-64; rewriteman The Record, Hackensack, N.J., 1965-66; corr. Reuters, London, Moscow, Prague and Washington, 1966-77, Newsweek, Washington, 1977-79; corr. N.Y. Daily News, Washington, 1979—, bur. chief, 1981-93; columnist Newsday, Washington, 1993-95, N.Y. Daily News, Washington, 1995—. Mem. State Dept. Corrs. Assn. (pres. 1978-79), Overseas Writers, White Ho. Corrs. Assn. (Merriman Smith award 1980), Gridiron Club (Washington). Office: NY Daily News 1615 M St NW Washington DC 20036

NELSON, LAWRENCE EVAN, business consultant; b. Chgo., Dec. 3, 1932; s. Evan Thomas and Elizabeth Marie (Stettka) N.; m. Jean H. Clayton, July 11, 1953; children: Lori Jean, Lawrence Evan. BS with honors, So. Ill. U., 1959; MBA, U. Chgo., 1969. CPA, Ill. Sr. acct. Price Waterhouse & Co., CPA's, Chgo., 1959-65; sec.-treas. Bradner Cen. Co., Chgo., 1965-73; pres. Protectoseal Co., Bensenville, Ill., 1973-84, Plan Ahead Inc., Palos Park, Ill, 1984—. Author: (book) Personal Financial Planning, 1985. Treas. City of Palos Heights, Ill., 1964-68, alderman, 1970-71; trustee Palos Heights FPD, 1977—. Served with USNR, 1952-56. Mem. Am. Inst. CPA's, Ill. Soc. CPA's. Office: Plan Ahead Inc PO Box 164 Palos Park IL 60464-0164

NELSON, LINDA CAROL, corporate chief executive; b. Knoxville, Tenn., Feb. 18, 1954; d. Solon Morris and Dorothy Thelma (Randles) Woods. BA in Polit. Sci. and Psychology magna cum laude, U. Tenn., 1975; BS in Acctg. summa cum laude, Ga. State U., 1978. Cert. of mgmt. acct.; enrolled agt. Pvt. investigator Hanover Security Systems, Knoxville, 1968-74; office mgr. Dale Carnegie Inst., Knoxville, 1969-75; instr. Dale Carnegie course and profl. devel. series Dale Carnegie Inst., Atlanta, 1980-88; legal asst. office of regional atty. H.E.W., Atlanta, 1975; tech. support staff Dist. Conf. U.S. Treasury Dept., Atlanta, 1976, instr., tng. analyst continuing profl. edn., 1976-88, recruiter, 1979-86, team coord. large case exam, 1980-85, resident lead instr. S.E. Region, 1984, fed. racketeering investigator, 1985-86, coord. Joint Com. Taxation in Congress, 1986-87; internal revenue agt., tax technician of exam. div. IRS, Atlanta, 1976-79; consolidations tax dept. staff mgr. Bellsouth, Atlanta, 1984-85; ind. mgmt. cons. Ga., 1980-86; pres., CEO Exec. Svcs. Inc., Atlanta, 1988—; active Speakers' Bur., Atlanta, 1993—. Hospitality com. mem. Atlanta Women's Network, 1990-92; vol. worker Eagles Boy's Ranch, Atlanta, 1986—; River of Life Family Ch.; vol. counselor Atlanta Home for Abused Children, 1980-83; Sunday sch. tchr., choir, nursery, various chs., 1975—; fundraiser Atlanta Symphony Orch., 1985-86; cons. adopt-a-student program, 1985-86; vol. missions program 1st Bapt. Ch., Atlanta, 1986; key person United Way Atlanta Combined Fed. Campaign, 1978-84; calling com. Norcross (Ga.) United Meth. Ch., 1983-84; coord. blood drive ARC, Atlanta, 1984; vol. counselor Helen Ross McNabb Ctr., Knoxville, 1970-72; campaign com. mem. Senator Paul Coverdell. Recipient citation U.S. Sec. Labor Brennan, Superior Instr. award Dale Carnegie, 1988; named one of Outstanding Young Women of Am., 1984. Mem. ASTD (vol. placement com. 1988-92), NAFE, Inst. Mgmt. Accts. (program speaker Atlanta chpt., bd. dirs. 1989), High Mus. Art Young Career Mems. Guild, Young Women of the Arts, Nat. Assn. Enrolled Agts., Nat. Soc. Tax Profls., Profl. Info. Network (mem. spkr.'s bur.), Gwinnett County Leads Network (founder), Women's Life Underwriters' Assn. (program spkr.), Altanta C. of C., Ga. State U. Alumni Assn., U. Tenn. Alumni Assn., Golden Key Nat. Honor Soc., Mortar Bd., U.S. Tennis Assn., Atlanta Lawn Tennis Assn., So. Bicycle League, Sierra Club, Phi Beta Kappa, Beta Alpha Psi, Pi Sigma Alpha, Pi Kappa Phi, Alpha Lambda Delta, Delta Gamma (social chair), Chi Phi Little Sisters (pres.). Avocations: serving others, cooking, public speaking, outdoor activities, tennis. Home: 6001 Meadowbrook Dr Norcross GA 30093-3729 Office: Exec Svcs Inc PO Box 450822 Atlanta GA 31145-0822

NELSON, LINDA SHEARER, child development and family relations educator; b. New Kensington, Pa., Dec. 8, 1944; d. Walter M. and Jean M. (Black) Shearer; m. Alan Edward Nelson, Dec. 29, 1973; children: Amelia (Amy), Emily. BS in Home Econs. Edn., Pa. State U., 1966; MS in Child Devel. and Family Rels., Cornell U., 1968; PhD in Higher Edn. and Child Devel., U. Pitts., 1982. Head tchr.-lab. nursery sch. Dept. of Psychology, Vassar Coll., Poughkeepsie, N.Y., 1968-69; instr. child devel. dept. home econs. edn. Indiana U. Pa., 1969-72, asst. prof., 1972-77, assoc. prof., 1977-84, prof. child devel. and family rels. Coll. Health/Human Svcs., 1984—, dept. chair, 1991-93; prof. child devel. and family rels. Indiana U. Pa. Coll. Health and Human Svcs., 1993—; mem. values task force Indian U. Pa. Coll. Health and Human Svcs., 1995-96; cons. trainer Head Start programs, Pa., 1970—, child care programs and agys., Pa., 1970—; child devel. assoc. rep. Coun. for Early Childhood Profl. Recognition, Washington, 1988-91; field rep. Keystone U. Rsch. Corp., Erie, 1990-91; keynote, guest spkr. on child devel., child care and home econs. confs., Pa. and nationally, 1985—. Mem. adv. bd. Early Childhood Edn., Annual Edits., 1985—; mem. adv. bd. Interface: Home Economics and Technology Newsletter, 1993—; contbr. articles to profl. jours. Bd. dirs. Indiana County Child Care Program, 1970-92; guest spkr. Dalta Kappa Gamma, Indiana, 1990, Bus. and Profl. Women, Indiana, 1991, AAUW, 1996, The Marriage Project, Indiana U. Pa., 1996. Grantee in field, 1985—. Mem. AAUW (guest spkr. 1996), Nat. Assn. for Edn. Young Children, Pitts. Assn. for Edn. Young Children (conf. co-chair 1983-85, in-svc. tng. spkr. 1995), Assn. Pa. State Coll. and Univ. Faculties, Kappa Omicron Nu, Phi Upsilon Omicron. Democrat. Presbyterian. Avocations: photography, reading, Chautauqua Instn. programs. Office: Indiana U of Pa Human Devel and Environ Studies Dept 207 Ackerman Hall Indiana PA 15705

NELSON, LLOYD STEADMAN, statistics consultant; b. Norwich, Conn., Mar. 29, 1922; s. Ronald Richbourg and Marion Shapley (Rogers) N.; m. Almeda Christine Ponder, Feb. 21, 1947; children: Peter Reid, Fay Hulett-Nelson, Barbara Nelson Ramey; m. Frances Betty Pallant, Mar. 13, 1982. BS, U. N.C., 1943; PhD, U. Conn., 1950. Registered profl. engr., Calif. Instr. physics U. Conn., Storrs, 1943-44; instr. chemistry Ill. Inst. Tech., Chgo., 1949-51; research chemist Gen. Electric Co., Waterford, N.Y., 1951-53; research assoc. Gen. Electric Research Lab., Schenectady, N.Y., 1953-56; cons. statistician Gen. Electric Lamp Div., Cleve., 1956-68; lectr. in math. Case Inst. Tech., Cleve., 1963-64; mgr. applied math. lab. Gen. Electric Major Appliance Group, Louisville, 1968-80; dir. statis. methods Nashua (N.H.) Corp., 1980-92; pvt. practice statis. cons., 1992—. Editor: Indsl. Quality Control, 1966-68; founding editor: Jour. Quality Tech., 1969-71;

contbr. over 100 articles to sci. jours. Served with USN, 1944-46. Fellow AAAS, Am. Soc. Quality Control (Shewhart medal, 1978, Deming medal 1985), Am. Statis. Assn. (outstanding statistician of yr. award 1983). Home: 17 Jefferson Dr Londonderry NH 03053-3647

NELSON, LYLE MORGAN, communications educator; b. Yamhill, Oreg., Feb. 28, 1918; s. Guy Calvin and Bessie Alzine (Morgan) N.; m. Corrine Marlis Wignes, Oct. 2, 1941; children: Gayle Kathryn, Judith Lee. AB, U. Oreg., 1941; LHD (hon.), Linfield (Oreg.) Coll., 1981; Dr. honoris causa, U. Autónoma de Guadalajara, Mex., 1981. Acting dir. Univ. News Service, U. Oreg., 1941-43, asst. to pres., asso. prof. journalism, 1947-53; with U.S. Army Ordnance Dept., 1943-45; asst. regional info. officer Bur. Reclamation, Boise, Idaho, 1945-47; asst. to pres., sec. bd. dirs. Ednl. TV and Radio Center, Ann Arbor, Mich., 1953-55; asst. to pres., prof. communications San Francisco State Coll., 1955-57; v.p., prof. journalism U. Mich., 1957-60, v.p., 1960-62; dir. univ. relations Stanford, 1962-72, prof. communications, chmn. dept., 1968-78, dir. John S. Knight profl. journalism fellow program, 1972-86, Thomas M. Storke distinguished prof. emeritus, 1986—; hon. prof. journalism Autonomous U. Guadalajara; cons. edn. Ford Found., 1962-63, 65, Meyer Meml. Trust, 1982—; acad. cons. Xiamen U. Author: (with W. Schramm) Financing of Public Television, Bold Experiment: The Impact of Television on American Samoa; Editor: (with Dan Lerner) Communication Research: A Half Century Appraisal. Exec. dir. White House Conf. Edn., 1965; spl. cons. U.S. Commr. Edn., 1963, 67-70; cons. USIA, 1966-69; cons. higher edn. master plans, Ohio, N.Y., Kans.; mem. Greenbrier Conf. Higher Edn., 1958, U.S. ednl. del. to USSR, 1959; UNESCO ednl. TV Study Team; chmn. UNDP/UNESCO team to Evaluate TV Tng. in India, 1973; 1st vice chmn., bd. govs. Nature Conservancy, 1972-74; chmn. bd. fgn. scholarships State Dept., 1973-76; chmn. bd. trustees Alliance for Devel. of Latin Am. Higher Edn., 1974-79; trustee Hewlett Found., 1975-94. Recipient award for disting. svc. to higher edn. Am. Coll. Pub. Rels. Assn., 1953, 66, award for exceptional svc. to Stanford U., 1984, Disting. Svc. award U. Oreg., 1994; sr. Fulbright scholar, Australia, New Zealand, 1978. Mem. Am. Coll. Pub. Rels. Assn. (bd. dirs. 1956-65, pres. 1959-60), Bohemian Club (San Francisco), Lamplighters Club, Phi Kappa Phi, Sigma Delta Chi, Sigma Chi. Clubs: Bohemian (San Francisco); Lamplighters. Home: 732 San Rafael Pl Stanford CA 94305-1007

NELSON, MARK BRUCE, interior designer; b. Los Angeles, Dec. 8, 1921; s. Mark Bruce and Rubie (Henrionnet) N. B.A. in Art, U. Calif., Los Angeles, 1943, postgrad., 1949-50; postgrad., Art Center Sch., Los Angeles, 1946-49. Tchr. Pasadena (Calif.) City Coll., 1950-54; propr. Mark Nelson Interiors, Los Angeles, 1954—; designer DuPont Corp. exhibit N.Y. World's Fair, 1964; co-chmn. Los Angeles show com. Am. Inst. Interior Designers, 1960-67, Living with Famous Paintings, 1964-65; Mem. Los Angeles adv. council Am. Arbitration Assn., 1971-72; chmn. Los Angeles N.C.I.D.Q., 1973-80, Design House West, 1978. Mem. Los Angeles Beautiful Com., 1966. Served as officer USNR, 1942-46, 52-53, ETO, Korea. Fellow Am. Soc. Interior Designers (life mem., exam. chmn. 1972—, chmn. nat. by-laws com. 1973, pres. Los Angeles 1969-71, Calif. regional v.p. 1970-73, pres. Los Angeles found. 1980, Presdl. citation 1973); mem. Phi Kappa Sigma. Home and Office: 554 Lillian Way Los Angeles CA 90004-1106 *During my thirty years as a interior designer, I have enjoyed many successes, while watching the profession grow and improve. Designing the homes of rich and famous Americans has not altered my concept that it is the middle class American consumer who needs and can afford the services of professional designers.*

NELSON, MARTHA JANE, magazine editor; b. Pierre, S.D., Aug. 13, 1952; d. Bernard Anton and Pauline Isabel (Noren) N. BA, Barnard Coll., 1976. Mng. editor Signs: Jour. of Women in Culture, N.Y.C., 1976-80; editor Ms. Mag., N.Y.C., 1980-85; editor-in-chief Women's Sports and Fitness Mag., Palo Alto, Calif., 1985-87; exec. editor Savvy, N.Y.C., 1988-89, editor-in-chief, 1989-91; asst. mng. editor People, 1993; editor In Style Mag., N.Y.C., 1993-96. Editor: Women in the American City, 1980; cons. editor Who Weekly, Sydney, 1992; contbr. articles to profl. publs. Bd. dirs. Painting Space 122, N.Y.C., 1982-85, Urban Athletic Assn. Mem. Am. Soc. Mag. Editors, Women in Film.

NELSON, MARVIN RAY, retired life insurance company executive; b. Thornton, Iowa, Aug. 29, 1926; s. Clarence Anton and Rose Bessie (Nicolet) N.; m. Juanita Mae Brown, May 26, 1951; children: Nancy, Kenneth. BS, Drake U, 1951. Actuary Security Mut. Life Ins. Co., Lincoln, Nebr., 1951-58; assoc. actuary Life Ins. Co. N.Am., Phila., 1958-59; group actuary Bankers Life of Nebr., Lincoln, 1959-66; actuary Mut. Service Life Ins. Co., St. Paul, 1966-68; sr. v.p. Horace Mann Educators Corp., Springfield, Ill., 1968-77; sr. v.p. Security Life of Denver, 1977-83, exec. v.p., 1988-91; pres., chief oper. officer, dir., mem. investment com. Midwestern United Life Ins. Co., Ft. Wayne, Ind., 1983-89; ret., 1991. Bd. dirs., treas. Ft. Wayne Urban League, 1983-87; bd. dirs. Taxpayers Research Assn., Ft. Wayne, 1984-88. Served with U.S. Army, 1946-47. Fellow Soc. Actuaries; mem. Am. Acad. Actuaries, Pi Kappa Phi. Home: 7636 E Windford St Parker CO 80134-5927

NELSON, MERLIN EDWARD, international business consultant, company director; b. Fargo, N.D., Jan. 30, 1922; s. Theodore G. and Eva C. (Hultgren) N.; m. Nancy Ellen Craig, June 1952 (div. June 1962); children: Craig Edward, Brian Anthony; m. Janet April Pope, Aug. 30, 1963; children: Claudia Jane, Rolf Merlin. BS in Polit. Sci., U. Oreg., 1943; postgrad., Fordham U., 1943-44; JD, Yale U., 1948. Bar: Oreg. 1948, N.Y. 1954, U.S. Dist. Ct. D.C. 1954. Atty. Office Gen. Counsel, ECA, Washington and Paris, 1949-52; assoc. Davis, Polk, Wardwell, Sunderland & Kiendl, 1952-59; exec. asst. to v.p. AMF, Inc., N.Y.C., 1960-62; chmn., mng. dir. AMF Internat., Ltd., London, 1962-63; v.p., group exec. AMF, Inc., 1963-70, exec. v.p., vice chmn., dir., 1970-84, now cons., 1984—; ret., 1984; bd. dirs. Indsl. Bank Japan Trust Co., Derby Internat. Corp., S.A., Exeter Internat. Corp., S.A., Mitsui Found.; chmn. IBJ Found.; chmn. adv. coun. Trust for Pub. Land; chmn. Econ. Literacy Project, Ltd. Mem. Coun. Fgn. Rels., Overseas Devel. Coun., Avon Internat. Adv. Coun. Decorated Purple Heart. Mem. Phi Beta Kappa. Home and Office: 16 W 77th St # 12E New York NY 10024-5126

NELSON, MICHAEL UNDERHILL, aerospace company executive, association executive; b. Balt., May 5, 1932; s. Cyril Arthur and Elise (Macy) N.; m. Barbara Gail Hutchins, June 25, 1960; children: Kevin Underhill, Bronwyn Hastings, Gayle Hutchins, Corey Williams. AB, Rutgers U., 1957, EdM, 1968. Salesman J & N Distbg. Co., New Brunswick, N.J., 1957-59; extension assoc. Univ. Coll., Rutgers U., New Brunswick, 1959-61; asst. dir. summer session Rutgers U., 1961-68; asst. dean sch. continuing edn., dir. summer sch. Washington U., St. Louis, 1969-81, dir. div. of profl. and community programs sch. continuing edn., 1975-78; exec. sec. N.Am. Assn. Summer Sessions, 1979—; account exec. Trio Printing Co., 1982-84; sr. procedures analyst McDonnell Douglas Corp, St. Louis, 1984—. Bd. dirs. Adult Edn. Council of Greater St. Louis, 1975-78. Served with USMC, 1951-54. Mem. North Ctrl. Conf. Summer Schs. (pres. 1974-75), Am. Assn. Univ. Adminstrs., Assn. Univ. Summer Sessions, Am. Summer Sessions Senate, N.Am. Assn. Summer Sessions (pres. 1978), Alpha Sigma Lambda, Phi Delta Kappa. Episcopalian. Home: 11728 Summerhaven Dr Saint Louis MO 63146-5444 Office: McDonnell Douglas Corp Mailcode 306 4168 Dept 804 Saint Louis MO 63166-0516

NELSON, NANCY ELEANOR, pediatrician, educator; b. El Paso, Apr. 4, 1933; d. Harry Hamilton and Helen Maude (Murphy) N. BA magna cum laude, U. Colo., 1955, MD, 1959. Intern, Case Western Res. U. Hosp., 1959-60, resident, 1960-63; pvt. practice medicine specializing in pediats., Denver, 1963-70; clin. prof. U. Colo. Sch. Medicine, Denver, 1988—, asst. dean Sch. Medicine, 1982-88, assoc. dean, 1988—. Mem. Am. Acad. Pediats., AMA (sect. med. schs. governing coun. 1994—), Denver Med. Soc. (pres. 1983-84), Colo. Med. Soc. (bd. dirs. 1985-88, judicial coun. 1992—). Home: 1265 Elizabeth St Denver CO 80206-3241 Office: 4200 E 9th Ave Denver CO 80262

NELSON, NEVIN MARY, interior designer; b. Cleve., Nov. 5, 1941; d. Arthur George Reinker and Barbara Phyllis (Gunn) Parks; m. Wayne Nelson (div. 1969); children: Doug, Brian. BA in Interior Design, U. Colo., 1964. Prin. Nevin Nelson Design, Boulder, Colo., 1966-70, Vail, Colo., 1970—; program chmn. Questers Antique Study Group, Boulder, 1969. Coord. Bob Kirscht for Gov. campaign, Eagle County, Colo., 1986; state del. Rep. Nat. Conv., 1986-88; county coord. George Bush for U.S. Pres. campaign, 1988, 92; chmn. Eagle County Reps., 1989-93; v.p. bd. dirs. Park Lane Condo Assn., Denver, 1995-96. Mem. Am. Soc. Interior Designers. Episcopalian. Avocations: party planning, cooking, reading, travel, skiing. Home: PO Box 1212 Vail CO 81658-1212 Office: 2498 Arosa Dr Vail CO 81657-4276

NELSON, NORMAN CROOKS, surgeon, academic administrator, educator; b. Hibbing, Minn., July 24, 1929; s. Sander Noble and Lillian Olive (Olsen) N.; m. Annie Lee Pitre, June 25, 1955; children—Norman, Charles, Jennifer. B.S., Tulane U., 1951, M.D., 1954. Diplomate: Am. Bd. Surgery. Intern Charity Hosp. La., New Orleans, 1954-55; resident Charity Hosp. La., 1958-62; USPHS fellow Nat. Inst. Arthritis and Metabolic Diseases, Harvard and Mass. Gen. Hosp., 1962-63; pvt. practice Houston, 1955-56; instr. surgery, Sch. Medicine La. State U., New Orleans, 1963-65; asst. prof., Sch. Medicine La. State U., 1965-68, assoc. prof., Sch. Medicine, 1968-71, prof., assoc. dean Sch. Medicine, 1969-71, dean Sch. Medicine, 1971-73; vice chancellor health affairs, dean Sch. Medicine, prof. surgery U. Miss. Med. Ctr., Jackson, 1973-94, vice chancellor health affairs emeritus, prof. surgery emeritus, 1993-94. Capt. AUS, 1956-58. John and Mary Markle scholar in acad. medicine, 1965-70; recipient Outstanding Alumnus award Tulane U. Sch. Medicine, 1989, laureate Miss. Bus. Hall of Fame, 1995; named to U. Miss. Alumni Hall of Fame, 1994. Fellow ACS, Southeastern Surg. Congress; mem. AAAS, AMA, Assn. Acad. Surgery, Assn. Am. Med. Colls., Central Med. Soc. Miss., Endocrine Soc., James D. Rives Surg. Soc. (founders group), Miss. Acad. Scis., Miss. Med. Assn., Miss. Hosp. Assn. (hon.), New Orleans Surg. Soc., N.Y. Acad. Scis., Soc. Exptl. Biology and Medicine, Soc. Head and Neck Surgeons, Soc. Univ. Surgeons, Am. Surg. Assn., So. Surg. Assn., Soc. Internationale de Chirurge, Surg. Assn. La. (pres. 1973), Allen O. Whipple Surg. Soc., Univ. Club (Jackson), Sigma Xi, Alpha Omega Alpha, Phi Kappa Phi, Omicron Delta Kappa, Omicron Kappa Upsilon (hon.), Alpha Eta Soc. Home: 109 Cardinal Cir Brandon MS 39042-6418

NELSON, NORMAN DANIEL, career officer; b. Dec. 30, 1968. BSBA, U. Fla., 1991; MBA, U. Miami, 1997. Intern internat. trade and commerce dept. ctrl. Europe office Fla. Dept. Commerce, Frankfurt, Germany, 1992; intern corp. fin. divsn. mergers and acquisitions Commerzbank AG, Frankfurt, 1992; intern corp. fin. divsn. internat. leasing and new stock issues Deutsche Bank AG, Frankfurt, 1992; commd. 2d lt. disting. mil. grad. USAR, 1991; advanced through grades to capt. U.S. Army, 1995; platoon leader 44th engr. bn., 2d inf. divsn. U.S. Army, Republic of South Korea, 1993-94; exec. officer 497th Port Constrn. Engr. Co., Ft. Eustis, Va., 1994-96; 52 - intel/ security officer 841st engr. bn. USAR, 1996—. Vol. Amer-Asian orphanage, Seoul, Republic of Korea, 1993-94; asst. scout master Boy Scouts Am., 1994-95. Decorated 2 Army Commendation medals, Army Achievement medal; scholar Army ROTC, 1987-91, Acad. scholar State Fla., 1987-91, Fed. Chancellor scholar Alexander-von-Humboldt Found., 1991-92. Mem. Masons, Phi Kappa Phi. Home: 1010 Ridgefield Dr Valrico FL 33594-6630 also: PO Box 248529 Coral Gables FL 33124

NELSON, OLIVER EVANS, JR., geneticist, educator; b. Seattle, Aug. 16, 1920; s. Oliver Evans and Mary Isabella (Grant) N.; m. Gerda Kjer Hansen, Mar. 28, 1963. A.B., Colgate U., 1941; M.S., Yale, 1943, Ph.D., 1947. Asst. prof. genetics Purdue U., 1947-49, assoc. prof., 1949-54, prof., 1954-69; prof. genetics U. Wis., Madison, 1969—, Brink prof. genetics, 1982-91, Brink prof. emeritus, 1991—, chmn. Lab. of Genetics, 1986-89; vis. investigator Biochem. Inst., U. Stockholm and Nat. Forest Research Inst., Stockholm, 1954-55; NSF, sr. postdoctoral fellow Calif. Inst. Tech., Pasadena, 1961-62. Contbr. articles on controlling elements, genes affecting starch synthesis and genes affecting storage protein synthesis to profl. publs. Recipient John Scott medal City of Phila., 1967; Hoblitzelle award Tex. Research Found., 1968; Browning award Am. Soc. Agronomy, 1974; Donald F. Jones medal Conn. Agrl. Exptl. Sta., 1976. Mem. NAS, AAAS, Am. Acad. Arts and Scis., Genetics Soc. Am., Am. Genetics Assn., Am. Soc. Plant Physiologists (Stephen Hales award, 1988), Sigma Xi. Home: Apt 325 325 S Yellowstone Dr Madison WI 53705-4355 Office: U Wis Lab Genetics Madison WI 53706

NELSON, PAUL EDWARD, science educator; b. Franklin Township, Wis., May 26, 1927; s. John Richard and Zella Mae (Merritt) N.; m. Barbara Jean Enyeart, June 18, 1950; children: Kathryn, John, Nancy. AA in Plant Sci., Fullerton Jr. Coll., 1949; BS in Plant Pathology, U. Calif., Berkeley, 1951, PhD in Plant Pathology, 1955. Asst. prof. plant pathology Cornell U., Ithaca, 1955-61, assoc. prof., 1961-65; assoc. prof. Pa. State U., University Park, 1965-67, prof., 1967—, interim dept. head, 1981-82; adj. prof. Cornell U., 1975—; hon. assoc. dept. plant pathology and agrl. entomology U. Sydney, Australia, 1981; mem. various coms. Pa. State U.; cons. med. mycology sect. M.D. Anderson Cancer Ctr., Houston; mem. rev. panel USDA, Southeast Area, Agrl. Rsch. rev. culture collection rsch. No. Regional Rsch. Ctr., Peoria, Ill., Coop. States Rsch. Svc. rev. grad. program and rsch. and tng. programs dept. entomology and plant pathology U. Tenn., Knoxville, comprehensive program rev.. Contbr. articles to profl. jours. Recipient Alex & Jessie C. Black award Coll. Agrl. Scis., Pa. State U., 1992. Fellow Am. Phytopathological Soc. (northeastern divsn., mem. various coms., asst. editor Phytopathology 1970, sr. editor 1970-72, Award of Merit 1986); mem. Mycological Soc. Am., U.S. Fedn. Culture Collections, Am. Soc. Microbiology. Home: 535 Outer Dr State College PA 16801-7936 Office: Pa State U Fusarium Rsch Ctr 211 Buckhout Lab University Park PA 16802

NELSON, PAUL WILLIAM, real estate broker; b. Mpls., Mar. 7, 1952; s. William H. and Jean (Darrington) N.; m. Jill Brownson, Oct. 18, 1986 (dec. Nov. 1990); 1 child, Emily J.; m. Robin K. Carpenter, Aug. 14, 1993. BS, U. Colo., 1974. Lic. real estate broker, Colo. Advt. dir. Denver Beechcraft, 1976-77; real estate broker Coldwell Banker, Grand Junction, Colo., 1977—; bd. dirs. Colo. Assn. Realtors, Denver, 1981-83. Mem. Grand Junction City Coun., 1985-93, also mayor pro tem; mem. Downtown Devel. Authority, Grand Junction, 1985-91; bd. dirs. Mesa County Planning Commn., Grand Junction, 1980-85, Colo. Nat. Monument Assn., 1989-91, Grand Junction Visitors and Conv. Bur., 1993-96, bd. dirs. Club 20 (20 counties west of continental divide), 1994—; Lobbying Group; mem. Mesa County Uranium Mill Tailings Removal Citizens Com.; mem. co-chmn. Mesa County Riverfront Commn.; mem. dist. resource adv. coun. Bur. Land Mgmt., 1990-92, Grand Junction Visitors and Conv. Bur. bd. dirs., 1992-96. Recipient Citizen Svc. award Mesa County, 1985. Mem. Mesa County Assn. Realtors (bd. dirs. 1981-83), Rotary. Republican. Avocations: pvt. pilot, skiing. Office: Coldwell Banker PO Box 3117 Grand Junction CO 81502-3117

NELSON, PHILIP EDWIN, food scientist, educator; b. Shelbyville, Ind., Nov. 12, 1934; s. Brainard R. and Alta E. (Pitts) N.; m. Sue Bayless, Dec. 27, 1955; children: Jennifer, Andrew, Bradley. BS, Purdue U., 1956, PhD, 1976. Plant mgr. Blue River Packing Co., Morristown, Ind., 1956-60; instr. Purdue U., West Lafayette, Ind., 1961-76, head dept. food sci., 1984—; cons. PEN Cons., West Lafayette, 1974; chair Food Processors Inst., Washington, 1990-93. Editor: Fruit Vegetable Juice Technology, 1980, Principles of Aseptic Processing and Packaging, 1992. Fellow Inst. Food Techs. (Indsl. Achievement award 1976, Nicholas Appert award 1995, 49'er Svc. award 1995); mem. AAAS, Sigma Xi, Phi Tau Sigma (pres. 1976-77). Achievements include 11 U.S. and foreign patents. Office: Purdue U Dept Food Sci 1160 Smith Hall West Lafayette IN 47907-1160

NELSON, PHILIP FRANCIS, musicology educator, consultant, choral conductor; b. Waseca, Minn., Feb. 17, 1928; s. Elmer Philip and Frances (Bretzke) N.; m. Georgia Ann Yelland, June 5, 1950; children: Curtis Ann, Philip Francis Jr. AB, Grinnell Coll., 1950; AM, U. N.C., 1956, PhD, 1958; Diplome (Fulbright scholar), U. Paris, 1957; student, Conservatoire Nat. de Paris, 1956-57; MA (hon.), Yale U., 1971; LHD (hon.), Grinnell Coll., 1981. Asst. prof. Ariz. State U., 1958-62, assoc. prof., 1962-63; prof., chmn. dept. music SUNY, Binghamton, 1963-70; prof., dean Sch. Music, Yale U., 1970-81; prof., provost, dean U. Calif., Santa Cruz, 1981-83; chmn. trustee com. Curtis Inst., 1982-83; sr. v.p. AED, N.Y.C., 1984-87; v.p. Aspen Inst. for Humanistic Studies, 1987-89; interim chancellor Sch. Arts, U. N.C., 1989-90; assoc. fellow Nat. Humanities Ctr., 1990-91; interim vice chancellor U. N.C., Chapel Hill, 1991; cons. edn., arts, 1992-93; chmn. grad. sch. adv. coun. U. N.C., Chapel Hill, 1993—; music critic Phoenix Gazette, 1959-62; music cons. Taliesin West, 1959-63; chmn. Nat. Screening Com. for Fulbright Awards in Musicology, 1965-68; cons. Nat. Endowment for Arts, 1984—. Contbg. editor: College and Adult Reading List, 1962, Nicolas Bernier, Principles of Composition, 1964, Recherches sur la musique Française classique, 1979, 80; contbr. to Groves Dictionary of Music, 6th edit.; editor publs. in the arts for The Aspen Inst. for the Humanities, 1987-89. Bd. dirs. various symphonies, chamber music socs., arts groups; trustee Curtis Inst. Music, Phila., 1980-83; mem. exec. com. Conn. State Golf Assn., 1975-81; founder Seven Springs Soc., 1975; bd. dirs. Conn. Hospice, 1983-87, Nat. Soc. to Prevent Blindness, 1987-93;, bd. dirs., v.p., 1987-93; mem. Chapel Hill Arts Ctr., 1992—; mem. Triangle J. Coun. Govt., 1992-95. Served from ensign to lt. comdr. USCGR, 1952-72. Found. grantee. Mem. Am., Internat. musicol. socs., Coll. Music Soc. (nat. council, editor jour. 1966-69), Société Française de Musicologie, Soc. Ethnomusicology, U.S. Srs. Golf Assn. Clubs: Mory's (New Haven); Yale (N.Y.C.); Elizabethan Grads., New Haven Country, Yale Golf, Finley Golf, Chapel Hill Country. Home: 621 Greenwood Rd Chapel Hill NC 27514-5921 *Keep casting bread on the waters-it may come back as French toast.*

NELSON, PRINCE ROGERS See PRINCE

NELSON, RALPH ALFRED, physician; b. Mpls., June 19, 1927; s. Alfred W. and Lydia (Johnson) N.; m. Rosemary Pokela, Aug. 7, 1954; children—Edward Ancher, Audrey Anne, Elizabeth Marie, Andrew William, Evan Robert. B.A., U. Minn., 1949, M.D., 1953, Ph.D., 1961. Diplomate Am. Bd. Internal Medicine. Intern Cook County (Ill.) Hosp., 1953-54; resident U. Minn. Hosps., Mpls., 1954-55, U. Minn., Mpls., 1955-56; fellow in physiology Mayo Grad. Sch., Rochester, Minn., 1957-60, resident in internal medicine, 1976-78; practice medicine specializing in internal medicine and clin. nutrition Sioux Falls, S.D., 1978-79, Urbana, Ill., 1979—; bd. dirs. Scott Research Lab., Fairview Park Hosp., Cleve., 1962-67; assoc. in physiology Western Res. U., Cleve., 1962-67; asst. prof. physiology Mayo Grad. Sch., 1967-73, Mayo Med. Sch., 1973, assoc. prof. nutrition, 1974; cons. in nutrition Mayo Clinic, 1967-76; assoc. prof. medicine U. S.D. Sch. Medicine, Sioux Falls, 1978-79; prof. nutrition U. Ill. Coll. Medicine, Urbana-Champaign, 1979—, chmn. dept. medicine prof. nutritional sci., physiology, biophysics dept. food sci. Sch. Agr., 1979—, also prof. medicine, exec. head dept. internal medicine , 1989—; dir. research Carle Found. Hosp., Urbana, 1979—; head nutritional support service Danville (Ill.) VA Hosp., 1980—. Co-author: The Mayo Clinic Renal Diet Cookbook, 1974; contbr. articles on nutrition, physiology, and hibernation to sci. jours.; editor: Geriatrics, 1980—, The Physician and Sportsmedicine, 1980-88, Am. Jour. Clin. Nutrition, 1980-83. Cons. in nutrition Nat. Cancer Inst., 1976; cons. in nutrition HEW, 1976, 79, 89, Nat. Heart and Lung Inst., 1976. Served with USAF, 1945-47. Fulbright scholar, Morocco, 1988. Mem. Am. Physiol. Soc., Am. Inst. Nutrition, Am. Soc. Clin. Nutrition, Central Soc. Clin. Research, Am. Gastroent. Assn. Lutheran. Home: 2 Illini Cir Urbana IL 61801-5813 Office: Carle Foundation Hospital 611 W Park St Urbana IL 61801-2529

NELSON, RALPH LOWELL, economics educator; b. St. Paul, June 9, 1926; s. Ralph Edward and Beulah (Pierce) N.; m. Ann Eileen Carson, Apr. 18, 1954; children—David Lowell, Rachel Jean. B.S., U. Minn., 1949; M.A., Columbia U., 1953, Ph.D., 1955. Instr. econs. Adelphi Coll., 1950-54; asst. prof. fin. Northwestern U., 1956-59; econ. census monographist Social Sci. Research Council, 1958-59; research staff Nat. Bur. Econ. Research, 1959-72; dir. Found. Investment Study, Found. Library Ctr., 1962-64; assoc. prof. econs. Queens Coll., CUNY, 1964-67, prof. econs., 1968—, acting assoc. dean grad. div., 1969-70; acad. visitor London Sch. Econs. and Polit. Sci., 1970-71; mem. securities industry task force 20th Century Fund, 1972-74; spl. cons. Commn. on Pvt. Philanthropy and Pub. Needs, 1974-76; cons. Dept. Treasury, 1977; mem. rsch. staff Philanthropic Found. rsch. project, program on non-profit orgn. Yale U., 1982-87; cons. Am. Assn. Fund-Raising Counsel, 1984—; bd. dirs. trust for philanthropy, 1985-90. Author: Merger Movements in American Industry, 1959, Concentration in the Manufacturing Industries of the United States, 1963, The Investment Policies of Foundations, 1967, Economic Factors in Corporation Giving, 1970, Total Personal Giving in the United States, 1986, An Economic History of Large Foundations, 1987; contbr. articles to profl. jours. Bd. govs. Caroline Veatch Assistance and Extension Program, 1974-76. Served with USNR, 1944-46. Mem. AAUP, Am. Econ. Assn., Royal Econ. Soc., Phi Beta Kappa, Beta Gamma Sigma. Unitarian. Home: 346 Millspring Rd Manhasset NY 11030-3622 Office: Queens Coll Econs Dept Flushing NY 11367

NELSON, RALPH STANLEY, lawyer; b. Mpls., Mar. 15, 1943; s. Stanley L. and Louise M. Nelson; m. Judy E. Nelson, July 8, 1867; children: Sara C., Amy E., David A. BS in Bus. Adminstrn., U. Minn., 1966; JD with honors, Drake U., 1972. Bar: Minn. 1973, Wash. 1982, Tex. 1985, Ind. 1993. Assoc. Wiese and Cox, Ltd., Mpls., 1973-76; atty. Burlington No. R.R., St. Paul, Minn., 1976-81; sr. corp. counsel Burlington No. Inc., Seattle, 1981-85; v.p. law and adminstrn. Burlington Motor Carriers Inc., Ft. Worth, Tex., 1985-88; exec. v.p. and gen. counsel Burlington Motor Carriers Inc., Ft. Worth, 1988-93; sr. v.p., gen. counsel Burlington Motor Carriers Inc., Daleville (Indpls.), Ind., 1992—. Mem. law rev. Drake U. Capt. USMC, 1966-70. Mem. Order of the Coif.

NELSON, RANDY J., psychology educator; b. Detroit, Mich., Jan. 13, 1954; s. Ralph Edward and Ada B. (Morganstein) N.; m. Anne Courtney DeVries. AB in Psychology wit honors, U. Calif., Berkeley, 1978, MA in Psychology, 1980, PhD in Psychology, 1983, PhD in Endocrinology, 1984. Rsch. asst. Dr. F.A. Beach U. Calif., Berkeley, 1978, Dr. I Zucker U. Calif., Berkeley, 1978-84; post doctoral fellow U. Tex., Austin, 1984-86; asst. prof. psychology The Johns Hopkins Univ., Balt., 1986-91, assoc. prof. psychology, 1991—, assoc. prof. population dynamics, 1991—; grant application reviewer NIH, 1986-87, 95, NSF, 1986—, program officer, 1995-96; jour. reviewer Animal Behaviour, Brain Rsch., Biology of Reproduction, Jour. Biol. Rhythyms, Jour. Comparative Neurology, Jour. Comparative Psychology, Jour. Mammology, Jour. of Reproduction & Fertility, Jour. Exptl. Psychology, Jour. Reproduction, Fertility & Devel., Jour. Pineal Rsch., Neuroendocrine Letters, Nature, Neurobehavioral Toxicology and Teratology, Neuroendocrinology, Physiology and Behavior, Sci., Procs. of NAS. Author: An Introduction to Behavioral Endocrinology, 1995; contbr. numerous articles to profl. jours. including Nature, Jour. of Nervous and Mental Disease, Jour. Comparative Psychology, Jour. Exptl. Zoology, Biology of Reproduction, Jour. of Urology, Physiology and Behavior, Am. Jour. Physiology, Physiological Zoology, Behavioral and Brain Scis., Can. Jour. Zoology, others. Recipient post-doctoral fellowship NIH, 1984-86, James A. Shannon award Nat. Cancer Inst., 1992-94. Mem. Soc. for Neurosci., Am. Soc. Mammalogists, Animal Behavior Soc., Soc. for Study of Biolog. Rhythyms, Soc. for the Study of Reproduction (mem. edn. com. 1982-83, 85-86, chairperson edn. com. 1986-87, editor newsletter 1986-88, membership com. 1990-94), Phi Beta Kappa, Sigma Chi, Psi Chi. Office: Johns Hopkins Univ Dept Psychology Behavioral Neuroendo Group Baltimore MD 21218

NELSON, RAYMOND JOHN, mathematics and philosophy educator; b. Chgo., Oct. 8, 1917; s. Emil and Florence (Anderson) N.; m. Hendrieka Rinkema, Aug. 11, 1942; children: Susan Nelson McGuire, Steven, Peter. AB, Grinnell Coll., 1941; PhD, U. Chgo., 1949. Prof. philosophy U. Akron, 1946-52; mathematician IBM, 1952-55; staff engr. Link Aviation Corp., 1955-56; prof. math., dir. Computing Ctr. Case Western Res. U., 1956-65, prof. math. and philosophy, 1965-72, Truman P. Handy prof. philosophy, 1972-81; prof. emeritus, 1981—; Rockefeller Scholar, Belagio, 1982; cons. to industry, 1956—; spl. rsch. on computer logic, philosophy of sci.; bd. dirs. CHI Corp.; adj. prof. of computer sci. U. N.C., 1986—. Author: Introduction to Automata, 1967, The Logic of Mind, 1982, 2d edit., 1989, Naming and Reference, 1992; contbr. articles to profl. jours.; patentee electronic switching device, large data processing device. Mem. Ohio Environ. Health Com. Capt. AUS, 1942-46. Mem. AAUP, Am. Philos. Assn., Am. Math. Soc., Assn. Symbolic Logic, Assn. Computing Machinery, Philos. Sci. Assn., Sigma Xi. Home: 2400 Demington Dr Cleveland OH 44106-3652

NELSON, RAYMOND JOHN, English literature educator, university dean, author; b. Waterbury, Conn., Sept. 5, 1938; s. Raymond John and Eileen (McGrath) N.; m. Claudine Eva Ligot, Aug. 20, 1972; children: Sylvie, Christopher. BA, U. Conn., 1965; MA, Stanford U., 1967, PhD, 1969. Prof. English U. Va., Charlottesville, 1969—, dean faculty arts and scis.,

1989—. Author: Van Wyck Brooks: A Writer's Life, 1981, Kenneth Patchen and American Mysticism, 1984 (Melville Cane award Poetry Soc. Am. 1984); also articles. With USCG, 1958-62. Woodrow Wilson fellow, 1965-66, fellow NEH, 1971-72. Mem. Colonnade Club (U. Va.), Phi Beta Kappa. Avocation: photography. Home: RR 3 Box 14 Earlysville VA 22936-9756 Office: U Va Dean of Faculty Office 419 Cabell Hall Charlottesville VA 22903

NELSON, RICHARD, writer; b. 1950. Literary mgr. BAM Theatre Co., Bklyn., 1979-81; assoc. dir. Goodman Theatre, Chgo., 1980-83; dramaturg Guthrie Theatre, Mpls., 1981-82. Author The Vienna Notes (in World Plays I), 1980, Il Campiello (adaptation), 1981, An American Comedy and Other Plays, 1984, Between East and West (in New Plays USA 3), 1986, Principia Scriptoriae, 1986, (editor) Strictly Dishonorable and Other Lost American Plays, 1986, Rip Van Winkle, 1986, Jungle Coup (in Plays from Playwrights Horizons), 1987, Accidental Death of an Anarchist (adaptation), 1987, Sensibility and Sense, 1989, Some Americans Abroad, 1989. Recipient Lannan Literary award, 1995. Office: William Morris Agy 1350 Ave of Americas New York NY 10019

NELSON, RICHARD ARTHUR, lawyer; b. Fosston, Minn., Apr. 8, 1947; s. Arthur Joseph and Thelma Lillian Nelson; m. Kathryn Louise Sims, Sept. 25, 1976; children: Jennifer Kathryn, Kristen Elizabeth. BS in Math., U. Minn., 1969, JD, 1974. Bar: Minn. 1974, U.S. Ct. Appeals (D.C. cir.) 1975, U.S. Dist. Ct. Minn. 1975. Law clk. U.S. Ct. Appeals (D.C. cir.), Washington, 1974-75; ptnr. Faegre and Benson, Mpls., 1975—; seminar lectr. in employee benefits and labor laws, 1983—. Note and articles editor Minn. Law Rev., 1973-74. Active Dem.-Farmer-Labor State Cen. Com., Minn., 1976—, del. dist. and local coms. and convs., 1970—, state exec. com., 1990—; student rep. bd. regents U. Minn., Mpls., 1973-74; v.p. Minn. Student Assn., 1968-69. Served with U.S. Army, 1970-72. Mem. ABA, Minn. Bar Assn., Order of Coif, Tau Beta Pi. Lutheran. Office: Faegre and Benson 2200 Norwest Ctr 90 S 7th St Minneapolis MN 55402-3903

NELSON, RICHARD BURTON, physicist, former patent consultant; b. Powell, Wyo., Dec. 10, 1911; s. Severt A. and Sedona Lenora (Fesenbeck) N.; m. Maxine Caroline George, Feb. 25, 1950 (div. June 1963); 1 child, Anna Afton Ghandour; m. Pauline Wright, Dec. 29, 1969. Student, San Diego State Coll., 1930-32; BS in Physics with honors, Calif. Inst. Tech., 1935; PhD, MIT, 1938. Registered patent agt. Physicist R.C.A. Mfg. Co., Harrison, N.J., 1938-41, NRC, Ottawa, Ont., Can., 1941-42; rsch. assoc. GE Rsch. Lab., Schenectady, 1942-50; div. mgr. Varian Assocs., Palo Alto, Calif., 1960-63, chief engr., 1963-74, patent agt., 1974-77, cons., 1977-91; bd. dirs. 1st Nat. Bank, Powell (Wyo.), 1st Co., Powell. Author of numerous tech. papers; patentee in field. Fellow IEEE; mem. N.W. Wyo. Coll. Found. Home and Office: Villa 28 23350 Sereno Ct Cupertino CA 95014-6507

NELSON, RICHARD COPELAND, hotel executive; b. Millington, Md., May 12, 1930; s. Roland H. and Marion (Beauchamp) N.; m. Helen Kowaleski, Feb. 22, 1964 (dec.). B.A., Duke, 1952; B.S., Cornell U., 1957. Food and beverage mgr. Hilton Inn, New Orleans, 1960-63; mgr. Hilton Inn, Seattle, 1963-64; exec. asst. mgr. Hilton Inn, San Francisco, 1964; gen. mgr. Hilton Inn, New Orleans, 1964-66; resident mgr. Statler Hilton, Dallas, 1966-68, Palmer House, Chgo., 1968-69; asst. to sr. v.p. Hilton Hotels Corp., 1969; gen. mgr. Capitol Hilton, Washington, 1969-72, Hyatt Regency Hotel, Houston, 1972-80; regional v.p., mng. dir. Hyatt Regency Washington, 1980-86, Grand Hyatt Washington, 1986—. Bd. dirs. exec. com. U.S. Navy Meml. Found. Served as lt. (j.g.) USNR, 1952-54. Mem. Hotel Assn. Washington (pres.), Washington Conv. & Visitors Assn. (pres.), Greater Washington Bd. Trade (bd. dirs., Leader of Yr. award 1994), Cornell Soc. Hotelmen (regional v.p.), Am. Hotel & Motel Assn. (sec.-treas. 1989, v.p. 1990, pres. 1991), Skal Club, Chaine des Rotisseurs, Alfalfa Club, Washington Golf and Country Club, Burning Tree Club. Republican. Roman Catholic. Address: 1000 H St NW Washington DC 20001-4310

NELSON, RICHARD DAVID, lawyer; b. Chgo., Jan. 29, 1940; s. Irving E. and Dorothy (Apolsky) N.; m. Davida Distenfield, Dec. 17, 1960; children: Cheryl, Laurel. BS in Acctg., U. Ill., 1961, LLB, 1964. Bar: Ill. 1964. Ptnr. Defrees & Fiske Law Offices, Chgo., 1964-81; ptnr., counsel, CFO, chief adminstrv. officer Heidrick & Struggles, Inc., Chgo., 1981—; bd. dirs., exec. com. Heidrick & Struggles, Inc., Chgo., 1981—. Pres. Jewish Cmty. Ctrs. of Chgo., 1987-89; chmn. Sign Graphics Task Force, Highland Park, Ill., 1986-88, Bus. and Econ. Devel. Commn., Highland Park; chmn. Econ. Devel. Commn. Highland Park, 1993—. Mem. ABA, Ill. State Bar Assn., Chgo. Bar Assn., Standard Club, Northmoor Country Club. Office: Heidrick & Struggles Inc 125 S Wacker Dr Ste 2800 Chicago IL 60606-4501

NELSON, RICHARD HENRY, manufacturing company executive; b. Norfolk, Va., May 24, 1939; s. Irvin Joseph and Ethel Blair (Levy) N.; m. Carole Ellen Rosen, Mar. 12, 1966; children: Christopher, Karin. BA, Princeton U., 1961; postgrad., Georgetown U., 1962-63. Spl. asst. to dir. Peace Corps, Washington, 1961-62; mil. aide to U.S. v.p. Office of the V.P., Washington, 1962-63; asst. to U.S. Pres. Office of the Pres., Washington, 1963-66; spl. asst. to sec. HUD, Washington, 1966-68; v.p. Am. Internat. Bank, N.Y.C., 1968-70, Studebaker-Worthington, N.Y.C., 1970-73; pres. Sartex Corp., N.Y.C., 1973-80; pres., CEO Cogenic Energy Systems, Inc., N.Y.C., 1981-91; CEO U.S. Envirosystems, Inc., West Palm Beach, Fla., 1992—; bd. dirs. Nelco Corp., Laurel, Md.; chmn. bd. Powersave, Inc., N.Y.C., 1984-92. Bd. dirs. Nat. Hypertension Assn., N.Y.C., 1982-90; exec. com. Southampton Assn., N.Y., 1983—. 1st lt. U.S. Army, 1962-64. Recipient Presdl. Medal Office of Pres. of U.S., 1965. Mem. Internat. Cogeneration Assn., Am. Gas Assn., Am. Cogeneration Coalition, Ind. Power Producers, Princeton Club, Doubles Club, Southampton Hunt and Polo Club (chmn. bd.), Palm Beach Polo and Country Club, U.S. Polo Assn., Meadow Club. Democrat. Avocations: horseback riding, trap and skeet shooting. Home: 12012 Longwood Green Dr West Palm Beach FL 33414-7070 Office: US Envirosystems Inc 515 N Flagler Dr Ste 202 West Palm Beach FL 33401

NELSON, RICHARD JOHN, playwright; b. Chgo., Oct. 17, 1950; s. Richard Finis and Viola (Garbriel) N.; m. Cynthia Blair Bacon, May 21, 1972; children: Zoe Elizabeth, Jocelyn Anne. BA, Hamilton Coll., 1972. Literary mgr. Bklyn. Acad. Music Theater Co., 1979-81; assoc. dir. Goodman Theatre, Chgo., 1980-83; dramaturg Tyrone Guthrie Theater, Mpls., 1981-82. Author: (plays) The Killing of Yablonski, 1975, Conjuring an Event, 1976, Scooping, 1977, Jungle Coup, 1978, The Vienna Notes, 1978 (Obie award for disting. playwriting 1979), Bal, 1980, Rip Van Winkle or 'The Works', 1981, The Return of Pinocchio, 1983, Between East and West, 1985 (HBO Playwrights USA award 1986), Principia Scriptoriae, 1985 (ABC-TV Playwriting award 1985, Timeout London Theatre award 1987), An American Comedy, 1986, Roots in the Water, 1989, Some Americans Abroad, 1989, Sensibility and Sense, 1989, Two Shakespearean Actors, 1990, Columbus and the Discovery of Japan, 1992, (with Alexander Gelman) Misha's Party, 1993, Life Sentences, 1993, New England, 1994, The General From America, 1996, The American Wife, 1996; (radio plays) Languages Spoken Here, 1987 (Giles Cooper award 1988), Eating Words, 1989 (Giles Cooper award 1990), Advice to Eastern Europe, 1990; (book of musical) Chess, 1988; (teleplays) The End of a Sentence, 1991; (screenplay) Ethan Frome, 1993; contbr., editor: Strictly Dishonorable and Other Lost American Plays, 1986; translator: Don Juan (Moliere) 1979, The Wedding (Brecht) 1980, The Suicide (Erdman) 1980, Il Campiello (Goldoni) 1980, Jungle of Cities (Brecht) 1981, The Marriage of Figaro (Beaumarchais) 1982, Three Sisters (Chekhov) 1984, Accidental Death of an Anarchist (Dario Fo) 1984, Jitterbugging, 1989, The Father (Strindberg) 1995. Thomas J. Watson Travelling fellow, 1972, Creative Writing fellow NEA, 1979, Guggenheim fellow, 1983, Playwriting fellow NEA, 1986-87; Office of Advanced Drama Rsch. grantee, 1976, Rockefeller grantee, 1979, 88; recipient Obie award for innovative programming, 1980, Lila Wallace Writers award Readers Digest Fund, 1991-93. Office: care William Morris Agy 1350 Avenue Of The Americas New York NY 10019-4702

NELSON, RICHARD LAWRENCE, public relations executive; b. Chgo., Nov. 13, 1953; s. Stanley Eric and Joan Carol (Greif) N. BS in Speech, Northwestern U., 1975. Dep. dir. radio/TV Dem. Nat. Com., Washington, 1975-76; press sec. U.S. Ho. of Reps., Washington, 1976-78; spl. asst. office of media liasion The White House, Washington, 1978-80, asst. press sec. office of media liasion, 1980-81; acct. supr. Hill & Knowlton, Inc., Chgo., Ill., 1981-82; dir. corp. pub. rels. Playboy Enterprises, Inc., Chgo., 1982-84; v.p. pub. rels. First Chgo. Corp., Chgo., 1984-87; prin. Richard Nelson Pub. Rels., Chgo., 1987-89; v.p. pub. rels. The NutraSweet Co., Deerfield, Ill., 1989-94, v.p. integrated mktg. comm., 1994-95; v.p. pub. affairs The NutraSweet Kelco Co., Deerfield, Ill., 1996—; mem. exec. com. Internat. Food Info. Coun., Washington, 1991—; dir. Calorie Control Coun., Atlanta, 1990—. Dir., past pres. Nat. Runaway Switchboard, Chgo., 1987—; dir. AIDS Found. Chgo., 1993—, treas., 1995—. Recipient Silver Trumpet award Publicity Club Chgo., 1991, 94. Trustee Arthur W. Page Soc.; mem. Chgo. Pub. Rels. Forum. Democrat. Avocations: piano, bicycling. Home: 1220 Noyes St Evanston IL 60201-2636 Office: The NutraSweet Co 1751 Lake Cook Rd Deerfield IL 60015-5615

NELSON, RICHARD M., lawyer; b. Newark, N.J., July 19, 1961; m. Jackie Orth, Feb. 28, 1996; children: J.C., Erika, Michael, Daniel, Sean. BA, U. Fla., 1983; JD, Nova Law Sch., 1986. Bar: Fla. 1986, U.S. Dist. Ct. (so. dist.) Fla. 1987. Assoc. Bunnel & Woulfe, Fort Lauderdale, Fla., 1986-88, Barnett & Clark, Miami, Fla., 1988-92; ptnr. Clark, Sparkman, Robb, Nelson and Mason, Miami, Fla., 1992-95, mng. ptnr., 1995—. Review editor: Nova Law Review, 1984, editor, 1985, 86. Recipient Goodwin Rsch. fellow Nova Law, 1984, 85, 86. Avocations: roller hockey, fishing, reading, volunteer work, boxing. Office: Sparkman Robb & Nelson 19 W Flager St # 1003 Miami FL 33136

NELSON, RICHARD PHILIP, medical educator, dean; b. Bloomington, Ill., Dec. 28, 1946; s. Edward Philip and Dorothy Emma (Bergquist) N.; m. Phyllis Nelson, June 22, 1969; children: Elyse, Emily. BA, Northwestern U., Evanston, Ill., 1968; MD, Northwestern U., Chgo., 1972. Diplomate Am. Bd. Pediatrics. Resident pediat. Children's Meml. Hosp., Chgo., 1972-75, chief resident, 1975-76; clin. fellow pediatrics Harvard U., Boston, 1976-78; dir. Minn. Svcs. for Children with Handicaps/Minn. Dept. Health, Mpls., 1978-82; asst. prof. U. Minn. Med. Sch., Mpls., 1982-87; dir. developmental disabilities Gillette Children's Hosp., St. Paul, 1982-87; assoc. prof. pediatrics U. Iowa, Iowa City, 1987-94, prof. pediatrics, 1994—, dir. Child Health Specialty Clinics, 1987—, assoc. dean, 1992—. Editor: Maternal and Child Health Practices, 1994; co-author chpts. in books. Mem. Iowa Health Care Reform Coun., 1993; bd. dirs. Health Policy Corp. of Iowa, 1993; mem. Inst. of Medicine, Nat. Forum on Future of Children and Families, MCH Health Care Reform, 1991. James Patton scholar Northwestern U. Med. Sch., 1968-72. Mem. Am. Acad. Pediatrics (com. on child health care financing 1992—), Beta Beta Beta. Office: Child Health Specialty Clin 247 Hospital School Iowa City IA 52242-1011

NELSON, ROBERT BRUCE, retired lawyer; b. Chgo., Feb. 21, 1935; s. Albert G. and Julia (Stevens) N.; m. Jeanne Bambas Denton, June 21, 1986. BA in Econs., U. Mich., 1957, JD, 1960. Bar: Ohio 1961, Fla. 1976. Assoc. Jones, Day, Reavis & Pogue, Cleve., 1960-68, ptnr., 1968-95. Spl. counsel to atty. gen. Ohio for Litigation regarding Battelle Meml. Inst., Columbus, 1973-75; v.p. Children's Aid Soc., Cleve., 1977-79, pres., 1979-81, trustee, 1970-95, hon. trustee 1995—; chmn. Inner City Renewal Soc., Cleve., 1971-73, trustee, 1965-89; trustee Cleve. Playhouse, 1987-94. Mem. Fla. Bar Assn., Cleve. Bar Assn., Am. Coll. Trust and Estate Counsel, Order of Coif, Phi Beta Kappa, Phi Kappa Phi, Phi Eta Sigma. Congregationalist. Avocation: swimming. Home: 4614 L Honoapiilani Rd La Haina HI 96761

NELSON, ROBERT CHARLES, newspaper executive; b. Phila., Dec. 10, 1924; s. Charles Emil and Florence E. (Kelly) N.; m. Jeanne H. Wallace, Mar. 10, 1945; children—John R., Barbara J., Nancy A. Student, The Citadel, 1942-43; M.E., Stevens Inst. Tech., 1949. Asst. mech. supt. N.Y. News, N.Y.C., 1949-52; with Detroit News, 1952—, prodn. mgr., 1952-69, ops. mgr., 1969-75, v.p., 1973-79, gen. mgr., 1975-81, pres., 1981-87, pres., pub., 1982-87, spl. asst. to chmn., 1987—; exec. v.p. newspaper div. Evening News Assn., Detroit, 1978-87; dir. Evening News Assn., 1985-90, ret., pub. emeritus, 1990—; Bd. dirs., sec. Greater Detroit Safety Council, 1973—; bd. dirs. Engrng. Sci. Fair, Detroit, 1975—; bd. dirs., mem. exec. com. Better Bus. Bur., Detroit, 1976—. Trustee New Detroit, 1980—. Served with USNR, 1943-46, PTO. Mem. Engrng. Soc. Detroit, Greater Detroit C. of C. (bd. dirs. 1980—, vice chmn. 1985—), Acad. Sr. Profls. at Eckerd Coll., Detroit Club, Orchard Lake Country Club, Adcraft Club of Detroit, Econ. Club, St. Petersburg Yacht Club.

NELSON, ROBERT E., public relations executive, political consultant; b. Jefferson, Wis., Oct. 25, 1951; s. Clifford H. and Mary Ann (Lundquist) N.; m. Heidi Nelson. Fiscal svcs. officer Orange (Calif.) County Med. Ctr., 1968-73; exec. asst. Orange County Bd. Suprs., Santa Ana, 1973-75; sr. assoc. Butcher-Forde Cons., Newport Beach, Calif., 1976-77; chmn., CEO Nelson Comm. Group, Irvine, Calif., 1979—. dep. asst. dir. pub. outreach presdl. transition, Little Rock, 1993; presdl. appointee U.S. Competitiveness Policy Coun., Washington, 1994—. Recipient Rocky Mountain regional Emmy award TV. advt., 1986. Mem. Internat. Assn. Polit. Cons. (bd. dirs. 1992—), Young Pres. Orgn. (bd. dir.s 1994—), Pacific Club. Avocations: fly fishing, scuba, horses, skiing. Office: Nelson Comm Group 2600 Michelson Dr Ste 1570 Irvine CA 92715

NELSON, ROBERT EARL, JR., financial services company executive; b. Mobile, Ala., May 15, 1938; s. Robert Earl Sr. and Frances Lucille (Till) N.; m. Sandra Anne Berry, Aug. 3, 1964; children: Robin Lynne, Robert Earl III, Patricia Anne. BS in Indsl. Mgmt., Ga. Inst. Tech., 1960; MBA, U. Ala., 1963. CPA, Ga., N.Y. Prodn. mgr. Borg Warner Corp., Chgo., 1963-65; mgr., mgmt. cons. Peat, Marwick, & Mitchell, Atlanta, 1965-71; corp. controller VF Corp., Reading, Pa., 1971-73; ptnr., mgmt. services Arthur Young & Co., N.Y.C., 1973-81; sr. v.p., CFO Cable Am. Inc., Atlanta, 1981-84; exec. v.p., chief ops. officer Kroh Bros. Devel. Co., Kansas City, Mo., 1984-87; chief exec. officer Nelson & Co., Atlanta, 1987—. Contbr. articles to profl. jours. Served to 1st lt. USMC, 1960-62. Mem. AICPA, Am. Inst. Indsl. Engrs., Fin. Execs. Inst., Bus. and Tech. Alliance, Venture Forum, Union League Club (N.Y.C.), Cherokee Town and Country Club (Atlanta). Republican. Episcopalian. Avocations: golf, tennis, biking, scuba diving. Home: 5100 Jett Forest Trl NW Atlanta GA 30327-4560 Office: Nelson & Co 1100 Circle 75 Pky NW Ste 800 Atlanta GA 30339-3097

NELSON, ROBERT GARY, textile executive; b. Queens, N.Y., Oct. 12, 1948; s. HOrace T. and Irene A. (Robertson) N.; m. Marla A. Svoboda, May 20, 1989; children: Ian A., Jessica L., Robert G. Jr. BBA, Dowling Coll., 1971. Various mktg. positions Springs Industries, N.Y.C., 1972-85, dir. bus. planning, 1985-88; pres. Walton Fabrics divsn. Avondale Mills Inc., Monroe, Ga., 1988-1996, Avondale Yarn Division, Sylacauga, AL, 1996—. Program chair Leadership Ga., Athens, 1994; elder Lawrenceville (Ga.) Presbyn. Ch., 1992—. Mem. Ga. Textile Manufacturers Assn. (bd. dirs. 1992—), Am. Textile Mfg. Assn. (advisor, com. mem. 1986-87). Avocations: skiing, golf, boating. *

NELSON, ROBERT LOUIS, lawyer; b. Dover, N.H., Aug. 10, 1931; s. Albert Louis and Alice (Rogers) N.; m. Rita Jean Hutchins, June 11, 1955; children: Karen, Robin Andrea. B.A., Bates Coll., Lewiston, Maine, 1956; LL.B., Georgetown U., 1959. Bar: D.C. 1960. With U.S. Commn. Civil Rights, 1958-63, AID, 1963-66; program sec. U.S. Mission to Brazil, 1965-66; exec. dir. Lawyers Com. Civil Rights Under Law, 1966-70; dep. campaign mgr. Muskie for Pres., 1970-72; v.p. Perpetual Corp., Houston, 1972-74; sr. v.p., gen. counsel Washington Star, 1974-76; pres. broadcast div. Washington Star Communications, Inc., 1976-77; asst. sec. of army U.S. Dept. Def., 1977-79; spl. advisor to chief N.G. Bur., Dept. Def., 1980-85; pres., dir. Mid-Md. Communications Corp., 1981-85; ptnr. Verner, Liipfert, Bernhard, McPherson and Hand,, 1979-87; gen. counsel Paralyzed Vets. Am., 1988—. Vice chmn. D.C. Redevel. Land Agy., 1976-77; bd. dirs. Community Found. Greater Washington, 1977-78 ; bd. dirs. Friends of Nat. Zoo, 1975—, pres., 1982-84; bd. dirs. Downtown Progress, 1976-77, Fed. City Council, 1976-77, 83-87, Pennsylvania Ave. Devel. Corp., 1976-77. Served with AUS, 1953-54. Mem. ABA, D.C. Bar Assn., Army Navy Club (Washington). Democrat. Episcopalian. Home: 1001-E 4201 Mass Ave NW Washington DC 20016 Home (summer): Robins Nest Orrs Island ME 04066 Office: 801 18th St NW Washington DC 20006-3517

NELSON, ROGER HUGH, management educator, business executive; b. Spring City, Utah, Mar. 7, 1931; s. Hugh Devere and Maudella Sarah (Larsen) N.; m. DeEtte Munk, Aug. 26, 1955; children—Steven R., Deanne, Mark L. B.S., U. Utah, 53, M.S., 1953; Ed.D., Columbia U., 1958. Mem. faculty U. Utah Coll. Bus., 1953—, prof. mgmt., 1970—; pres. faculty David Eccles Sch. Bus., 1995-96; dir. programs in emerging bus. U. Utah Coll. Bus., 1989—, chmn. mgmt. dept., 1976-82, asst. dean, 1969-74; dir. MBA integrative field studies, 1993-96; pres. David Eccles Sch. of Bus. Faculty, 1995-96; mem. faculty Utah Mgmt. Inst., 1968-75; v.p. Computer Logic Corp., 1970-73; pres. Am. Leisure & Sports Investment Corp., 1973-75, Oil Resources, Inc., 1980-88, Puma Energy Corp., 1981-88, The Ultimate Choice Catalog Co., 1986—; fin. and mgmt. cons., 1965—; founder Utah Small Bus. Devel. Center, U. Utah, 1979. Author: Personal Money Management, 1973, The Utah Entrepreneur's Guide, 1995, also articles, reports, manuals. Active local Am. Heart Assn., Am. Cancer Soc. campaigns; mem. exec. bd. Utah Opera Co., 1981-85, gen. bd., 1985-89. Danforth Teaching fellow, 1957. Mem. Acad. Mgmt., Adminstrv. Mgmt. Soc., NEA, AAUP, Phi Kappa Phi, Beta Gamma Sigma, Phi Delta Kappa, Delta Phi Epsilon. Inventor comml. color separation camera and related dye-transfer processes. Home: 2662 Skyline Dr Salt Lake City UT 84108-2855 Office: U Utah David Eccles Sch Bus Salt Lake City UT 84112

NELSON, RON, composer, conductor, educator; b. Joliet, Ill., Dec. 14, 1929; s. Walter E. and Lois (Fulton) N.; m. Helen Mitchell, 1954 (dec. 1967); children: Marc W., Kristen R. Mus.B., Eastman Sch. Music, 1952, Mus.M., 1953, Mus.D., 1956; postgrad., L'École Normale, Normale, Paris, 1954-55; M.A., Brown U., 1959. Prof. Brown U., Providence, chmn. dept. music, 1963-73, Acuff chair of excellence in creative arts, 1991; prof. emeritus Brown U., 1993—. film composer, HEW, Eastman Kodak, ARC, Columbia Pictures, commns. from, Cin. Symphony, Lima Symphony, Rochester Philharmonic, R.I. Philharm., Am. Bapt. Soc., U. Minn., Dartmouth Coll., Brown U., New Music Ensemble, LaSalle Coll., Western Mich. U., Classic Chorale, U.S. Air Force Band, Nat. Symphony Orch.; composer (for orch.) Savannah River Holiday, 1954, Sarabande: For Katherine in April, 1954, (opera) The Birthday of the Infanta, 1956; (cantata) The Christmas Story, 1958: (for orch.) Tocatta for Orchestra, 1963; (oratorio) What is Man?, 1964; (orch./wind ensemble) Rocky Point Holiday, 1968-69; This is the Orchestra; (orch. and tape trilogy) Trilogy: JFK-MLK-RFK, 1969; (choral) Prayer of Emperor of China, 1973; (choral) Thy Truth is Great, 1973; (choral) Psalm 95, 1974; (orch.) Five Pieces for Orchestra after Paintings by Andrew Wyeth, 1975; (choral) Prayer of St. Francis of Assisi, 1976; (orch.) Meditation and Dance for Orch., 1976; (choral) Six Pieces for Chamber Ensemble, 1977, Four Choral Pieces After the Seasons, 1978, Three Autumnal Sketches, 1979, Here We Come As in The Beginning, 1979, Mass in Honor of St. LaSalle, 1981, Three Nocturnal Pieces, 1982, Three Seasonal Reflections, 1982; composer: Fanfare for a Celebration, 1982; (choral) On Christmas Night, 1982; Medieval Suite, 1983; (choral) Dreams, 1982; (band) Fanfare for a Celebration, 1983; (cello-piano) And the Moon Rose Golden, 1983; (band) Medieval Suite, 1983; composer: Aspen Jubilee, 1984; (organ-brass) Pebble Beach Sojourn, 1984; (chorus-band) Te Deum Laudamus, 1985; (choral) Lost and Found, 1985, Light Years, 1985, Three Settings of the Moon, 1985, (strings-trumpet) Elegy, 1986, (brass) Brevard Fanfare, 1986, (chorus/band) Prime: The Hour of Sunrise, 1987, (choral) White, 1987, (choral) Another Spring, 1987, (choral) Miniatures from a Bestiary Parts I and II, 1988, (saxophone-band) Danza Capriccio, 1988, (choral) Three Pieces after Tennyson (1988), (choral) Three Mountain Ballads, 1989, (brass-winds-percussion) Fanfare for the Hour of Sunrise, 1989, (band) Morning Alleluias for the Winter Solstice, 1989, (band) Resonances, 1990; (chorus) And This Shall Be for Music, 1990, Invoking the Powers, 1991, Songs of Praise and Reconciliation, 1991, The Meadow, 1991, (band) Lauds: Praise High Day, 1992, To the Airborne, 1991, Passacaglia (Homage on B-A-C-H), 1992, Chaconne (In Memoriam), 1994, Sonoran Desert Holiday, 1994, (orch.) Fpiphanies, 1993, Epiphanies (Fanfares and Chorales), 1995, Courtly Airs and Dances, 1995, (orch.) Resonances II, 1996, (orch., band) Resonances III, 1996. Recipient ASCAP awards, 1962-95, Found. award for World tour, 1965-66, Nat. Band Assn. award, 1992, John Philip Sousa medal of merit, 1994; Fulbright fellow, 1954; Ford Found. commn., 1962, NEA grantee, 1973, 76, 79; awarded Acuff Chair of Excellence on the Creative Arts, 1991; winner Am. Bandmasters Assn. Ostwald Contest, 1993, Am. Band Assn. contest, 1992, Sudler Internat. Wind Band Competition, 1993. Office: Brown U Dept Music Providence RI 02912

NELSON, RONALD HARVEY, animal science educator, researcher; b. Union Grove, Wis., Aug. 10, 1918; s. Harvey August and Myra Frances (Sheen) N.; m. Elizabeth Jane Lappley, Apr. 13, 1940; children: David Peter, Marjorie Jean, Linda Louise, Ronda Elizabeth. BS, U. Wis., 1939; MS, Okla. A&M U., 1941; PhD, Iowa State U., 1943. Mem. faculty Mich. State U., 1946-85, prof., head, animal sci. dept., 1950-84, prof. emeritus, 1985—; chief of party Mich. State U. tech. assistance project Balcarce, Pcia, Buenos Aires, 1966-68. Recipient Grad. Distinction award Okla State U., 1987, Nat. Saddle and Sirloin Portrait award, 1990. Fellow Am. Soc. Animal Sci. (Internat. Animal Agr. award 1978, Animal Industry award 1984); mem. Am. Angus Assn. (chmn. research advisory com. 1956-60), Mich. Angus Assn. (pres. 1977-78), Animal Sci. Assn., Sigma Xi, Phi Kappa Phi, Alpha Zeta. Home: 1545 N Harrison Rd East Lansing MI 48823-1801

NELSON, RUSSELL MARION, surgeon, educator; b. Salt Lake City, Sept. 9, 1924; s. Marion C. and Edna (Anderson) N.; m. Dantzel White, Aug. 31, 1945; children: Marsha Nelson McKellar, Wendy Nelson Maxfield, Gloria Nelson Irion, Brenda Nelson Miles, Sylvia Nelson Webster, Emily Nelson Wittwer (dec.), Laurie Nelson Marsh, Rosalie Nelson Ringwood, Marjorie Nelson Helsten, Russell Marion Jr. BA, U. Utah, 1945, MD, 1947; PhD in Surgery, U. Minn., 1954; ScD (hon.), Brigham Young U., 1970; DMS (hon.), Utah State U., 1989; LHD (hon.), Snow Coll., 1994. Diplomate: Am. Bd. Surgery, Am. Bd. Thoracic Surgery (dir. 1972-78). Intern U. Minn. Hosps., Mpls., 1947; asst. resident surgery U. Minn. Hosps., 1948-51; first asst. resident surgery Mass. Gen. Hosp., Boston, 1953-54; sr. resident surgery U. Minn. Hosps., Mpls., 1954-55; practice medicine (specializing in cardiovascular and thoracic surgery), Salt Lake City, 1959-84; staff surgeon Latter-day Saints Hosp., Salt Lake City, 1959-84; dir. surg. research lab. Latter-day Saints Hosp., 1959-72, chief cardiovascular-thoracic surg. div., 1967-72, also bd. govs., 1970-90, vice chmn., 1979-89; staff surgeon Primary Children's Hosp., Salt Lake City, 1960; attending in surgery VA Hosp., Salt Lake City, 1955-84, Univ. Hosp., Salt Lake City, 1955-84; asst. prof. surgery Med. Sch. U. Utah, Salt Lake City, 1955-59, asst. clin. prof. surgery, 1959-66, asso. clin. prof. surgery, clin. prof., 1966-69, research prof. surgery, 1970-84, clin. prof. emeritus, 1984—; staff services Utah Biomed. Test Lab., 1970-84; dir. tng. program cardiovascular and thoracic surgery at Univ. Utah affiliated hosps., 1967-84; mem. policyholders adv. com. New Eng. Mut. Life Ins. Co., Boston, 1976-80. Contbr. articles to profl. jours. Mem. White House Conf. on Youth and Children, 1960; bd. dirs. Internat. Cardiol. Found.; bd. govs. LDS Hosp., 1970-90, Deseret Gymnasium, 1971-75, Promised Valley Playhouse, 1970-79. 1st lt. to capt. M.C., AUS, 1951-53. Markle scholar in med. scis., 1957-59; Fellowship of Medici Publici U. Utah Coll., 1967; Gold Medal of Merit, Argentina, 1974; named Hon. Prof. Shandong Med. U., Jinan, People's Republic of China, 1985; Old People's U., Jinan, 1986; Xi-an (People's Republic of China) Med. Coll., 1986, Legacy of Life award, 1993. Fellow A.C.S. (chmn. adv. council on thoracic surgery 1973-75), Am. Coll. Cardiology, Am. Coll. Chest Physicians; mem. Am. Assn. Thoracic Surgery, Am. Soc. Artificial Internal Organs, AMA, Dirs. Thoracic Residencies (pres. 1971-72), Utah Med. Assn. (pres. 1970-71), Salt Lake County Med. Soc., Am. Heart Assn. (exec. com. cardiovascular surgery 1972, dir. 1976-78, chmn. council cardiovascular surgery 1976-78), Utah Heart Assn. (pres. 1964-65), Soc. Thoracic Surgeons, Soc. Vascular Surgery (sec. 1968-72, pres. 1974), Utah Thoracic Soc., Salt Lake Surg. Soc., Samson Thoracic Surg. Soc., Western Soc. for Clin. Research, Soc. U. Surgeons, Am., Western, Pan-Pacific surg. assns., Inter. Am. Soc. Cardiology (bd. mgrs.), Phi Beta Kappa, Sigma Xi, Alpha Omega Alpha, Phi Kappa Phi, Sigma Chi. Mem. Ch. of Jesus Christ of Latter-day Saints (pres. Bonneville Stake 1964-71, gen. pres. Sunday sch. 1971-79, regional rep. 1979-84, Quorum of the Twelve Apostles 1984—). Home: 1347 Normandie Cir Salt Lake City UT 84105-1919 Office: 47 E South Temple Salt Lake City UT 84150

NELSON, SANDRA KAY, foundation administrator; b. Hicksville, Ohio, July 12, 1961; d. Deloy LaVerl and B. Lucille (Wonderly) Osmun; m. Gregory Lynn Thompson, May 22, 1982 (div. Aug. 1988); 1 child, Andrew Braden; m. Dean Marshall Nelson, July 17, 1993; 1 child, Tanner Marshall. Student, Internat. Bus. Coll., Ft. Wayne, Ind., 1979-80, N.W. State

C.C., 1990—. Supr. Ohio Art Co., Bryan, 1984-87; nat. devel. dir. Nat. Reye's Syndrome Found., Bryan, 1987-93, acting exec. dir., 1993-94, exec. dir., 1994—. Editor (newsletter) In The News, 1989—. Den leader Cub Scout Pack 3186, Fremont, Ind., 1993-95. Mem. Nat. Voluntary Health Agys. (chairperson 1994-95, trustee 1993—, nat. com. rep. 1989—), Clear Lake Yacht Club (social chair 1993-94), Steuben County Bus. and Profl. Women's Orgn. Lutheran. Avocations: sailing races, bike treks. Office: Reyes Syndrome Found 426 N Lewis PO Box 829 Bryan OH 43506

NELSON, SARAH MILLEDGE, archaeology educator; b. Miami, Fla., Nov. 29, 1931; d. Stanley and Sarah Woodman (Franklin) M.; m. Harold Stanley Nelson, July 25, 1953; children: Erik Harold, Mark Milledge, Stanley Franklin. BA, Wellesley Coll., 1953; MA, U. Mich., 1969, PhD, 1973. Instr. archaeology U. Md. extension, Seoul, Republic Korea, 1970-71; asst. prof. U. Denver, 1974-79, assoc. prof., 1979-85, prof. archaeology, 1985—, chair dept. anthropology, 1985-95, dir. women's studies program, 1985-87; vis. asst. prof. U. Colo., Boulder, 1974; resident Rockefeller Ctr. in Bellagio, Italy, 1996. Co-editor: Powers of Observation, 1990, Equity Issues for Women in Archaeology, 1994; author: Archaeology of Korea, 1993; editor: The Archaeology of Northeast China, 1995. Active Earthwatch, 1989. Recipient scholarly comm. award from China, NAS, 1988, Outstanding Scholar award U. Denver, 1989; grantee S.W. Inst. Rsch. on Women, 1981, Acad. Korean Studies, Seoul, 1983, Internat. Cultural Soc. Korea, 1986, Colo. Hist. Fund, 1995-97. Fellow Am. Anthrop. Assn.; mem. Soc. Am. Archaeology, Assn. Asian Studies, Royal Asiatic Soc., Sigma Xi (sec.-treas. 1978-79), Phi Beta Kappa. Democrat. Avocations: skiing, gardening. Home: 5878 S Dry Creek Ct Littleton CO 80121-1709 Office: U Denver Dept Anthropology Denver CO 80208

NELSON, SCOTT LEE, physical education educator; b. St. Louis, July 3, 1964; s. Charles Lenorad and Ola Fay (Sherrod) N.; m. Gina Brewer, June 11, 1988; 1 child, Natalie. BE, Freed-Hardeman U., Henderson, Tenn., 1986; MEd, U. Memphis, 1994. Social studies, phys. edn. specialist Mt. Dora (Fla.) Sch., 1987-88; phys. edn. specialist Nova Elem. Sch., Jackson, Tenn., 1990—. Recipient part-time Masters fellowship U. Memphis, 1994, project mentor grant U. Tenn., 1993. Mem. AAHPERD, NEA, Tenn. Assn. Health, Phys. Edn., Recreation and Dance, Tenn. Edn. Assn., Jackson-Madison County Edn. Assn. Home: 52 Driftwood Dr Jackson TN 38305-7700 Office: Nova Elem Sch 248 Bedford White Rd Jackson TN 38305-9503

NELSON, STEVEN CRAIG, lawyer; b. Oakland, Calif., May 11, 1944; s. Eskil Manfred and Florence Lucille (Boatman) N.; m. Kathryn Cassel Stoltz, Nov. 30, 1974; children: Carleton Philip, Whitney Cassel. BA in Econs. with exceptional distinction, Yale U., 1966, LLB, 1969. Bar: DC 1969, Minn. Supreme Ct. 1975, U.S. Supreme Ct. 1973. From atty. adviser to asst. legal adviser U.S. Dept. State, Washington, 1969-74; from assoc. to ptnr. Oppenheimer, Wolff, Foster, Shepard & Donnelly, St. Paul and Mpls., 1975-85; ptnr. Dorsey & Whitney, Mpls., 1985—; mem. bd. appeals NATO, Brussels. 1977—; adj. prof. law U. Minn, 1980—; speaker in field. Contbr. articles to profl. jours. Mem. ABA (chmn. internat. law and practice 1988-89), Minn. Bar Assn., Am. Fgn. Law Assn., Am. Soc. Internat. Law, Internat. Bar Assn., Union Internat. des Avocats (1st v.p. 1991-94), Minikahda Club. Presbyterian. Avocations: golf, tennis, skiing, sailing. Office: Dorsey & Whitney 220 S 6th St Minneapolis MN 55402-4502*

NELSON, STEVEN DOUGLAS, lawyer; b. Houston, Oct. 13, 1950; s. Stewart L. and Jean (Boyd) N.; m. Elizabeth (Betsy) Lane Brown, Mar. 25, 1972; children: Elizabeth K., D. Andrew, Allison L., Amanda J. BA in Econs., So. Meth. U., 1972, JD, 1976. Bar: Tex. 1976, U.S. Dist. Ct. (no. dist.) Tex. 1980, U.S. Ct. Claims 1980, U.S. Ct. Appeals (5th cir.) 1979, U.S. Ct. Appeals (fed. cir.) 1982, U.S. Supreme Ct. 1980; fellow Am. Coll. Constrn. Lawyers. Shareholder, chmn. constrn. law practice group Winstead, Sechrest & Minick, P.C., Dallas, 1976-95; ptnr. Ford & Nelson, P.C., 1995; gen. counsel Capital Adminstrv. Svcs., Austin, 1995-96; CEO Faulkner Constrn. Co., Austin, 1996—; participant Surety Claims Inst., Mo., 1982, 84-86, 89, 91; leader constrn./fidelity/surety sect. Winstead, Sechrest & Minich, 1983-85, 89-95, mem. mgmt. com., 1985-86, compensation com., 1991-93, co-chmn. bus. devel. com., 1986-87, practice and procedures com., 1990-91, chmn. facilities, systems and tech. com., 1988-90; mem. AIA/AGC liaison com. Dallas chpt. Associated Gen. Contractors, 1984-88, legis. com. Dallas bldg. br., 1988-90, bd. dirs. 1991—. Author: Bonds and Liens in Texas, 1991; co-author: Texas Lien Law Digest, 1984; contbg. editor: Design and Construction Market Strategist, 1993, Mexican Business Review, 1993, Dallas Construction Industry Practices, 1986-89; author: (audiovisual presentations) Insurable Risks, 1985. Mem. adv. com. magnet ctr. pub. svcs., govt. and law Dallas Ind. Sch. Dist., 1989—, adv. coun. Ctr. Non-Profit Mgmt., 1992-93, Pub. Safety Com., City University Park, Tex., 1992-93; bd. dirs. Greater Dallas Crime Comsn., 1990—, chmn. legis. com., 1990, v.p. crime stoppers, 1990-91, pres., 1992, gen. counsel, 1993; bd. dirs. and v.p. The City Club, Dallas, 1992—; asst. scoutmaster Boy Scout Troop # 72, Dallas, 1992—. Staff sgt. USAR, 1971-77. Mem. ABA (fidelity and surety subcommittee tort and ins. practice sect., pub. contract law sect., forum com. construction law), Am. Surety Assn. (vice-chmn. claims com. 1981-82, chmn. 1982-83, dir. 1983-84, 86-90, v.p. 1988-90), Am. Arbitration Assn. (nat. panel arbitrators), U.S. Arbitration and Mediation, Inc. (nat. constrn. panel), State Bar Tex. (co-founder constrn. law sect., various offices, editor Constrn. Law Newsletter 1992-93), Def. Rsch. Inst., Dallas Bar Assn. Republican. Presbyterian. Avocations: backpacking, genealogy, computers. Home: 4011 Amherst Ave Dallas TX 75225-7004 Office: Capital Adminstrv Svcs Inc 3901 S Lamar Austin TX 78767

NELSON, STUART OWEN, agricultural engineer, researcher, educator; b. Pilger, Nebr., Jan. 23, 1927; s. Irvin Andrew and Agnes Emilie (Nissen) N.; m. Carolyn Joye Fricke, Dec. 27, 1953 (dec. Nov. 1975); children: Richard Lynn, Jana Sue; m. Martha Ellen White Fuller, Apr. 8, 1979. BS in Agrl. Engring., U. Nebr., 1950, MSc in Agrl. Engring., 1952, MA in Physics, 1954; PhD in Engring., Iowa State U., 1972, hon. DSc U. Nebr., 1989. Grad. asst. U. Nebr., Lincoln, 1952-54, rsch. assoc., 1954-60, assoc. prof., 1960-72, prof., 1972-76; project leader Farm Electrification Rsch., Agrl. Rsch. Svc., USDA, Lincoln, 1954-59, rsch. investigations leader, 1959-72, rsch. leader, 1972-76, rsch. agrl. engr. Russell Rsch. Ctr., Athens, Ga., 1976—; adj. prof. U. Ga., 1976—; sci. adv. council Am. Seed Rsch. Found.; mem. CAST Task Force on Irradiation for Food Preservation and Pest Control; adv. com. grain moisture measurement Nat. Council Weights and Measures; mem. sci. bd. 4th Internat. Conf. on Phys. Properties Agrl. Materials, Prague, 1985. Served with USN, 1946-48. Recipient HM Crops and Soils award Am. Soc. Agronomy, 1966; recipient Founders Gold medal as named Fed. Engr. of Yr., NSPE, 1985; Superior Svc. award USDA., 1986; Profl. Achievement Citation Engring. award Iowa State U., 1987. Fellow Am. Soc. Agrl. Engrs. (Tech. Paper award 1965, 94, Engr. of Yr. award Ga. sect. 1988, chmn. Ga. sect. 1988-89). Fellow Internat. Microwave Power Inst. (Decade award 1981); mem. AAAS, IEEE (sr.), The Electromagnetics Acad., Internat. Soc. Agrometarials Sci. and Engring., Ga. Soc. Profl. Engrs. (Engr. of Yr. in Govt. award 1991), Nat. Acad. Engring., Nat. Soc. Profl. Engrs., Orgn. Profl. Employees of Dept. of Agr. (pres. Athens area chpt. 1984-86, nat. coun. rep. 1988-95, Profl. of Yr. award 1987), Sigma Xi, Sigma Tau, Gamma Sigma Delta, Tau Beta Pi. Methodist. Club: Athens Optimist (pres. 1980-81, lt. gov. Ga. dist. 1983-84, Optimist of Yr. award 1982, disting. and outstanding lt. gov. Ga. dist. 1985), Assoc. editor Jour. Microwave Power, 1975-76; contbr. more than 300 articles to sci. and tech. jours. Home: 270 Idylwood Dr Athens GA 30605-4635 Office: Russell Rsch Ctr USDA ARS PO Box 5677 Athens GA 30604

NELSON, SYDNEY B., lawyer, state senator; b. Mar. 12, 1935; BBA, U. Okla.; JD, La. State U.; m. Gail Anderson. Law clk. U.S. Dist. Ct., 1963-64; pvt. practice law, Shreveport, La., 1964—; Mem. La. Senate, 1980-92. Mem. adminstrv. bd. 1st Meth. Ch., Shreveport; mem. adv. bd. Norwella coun. Boy Scouts Am. Served as officer USN, 1957-60. Assoc. editor La. Law Rev. Mem. ABA, La. Bar Assn., Shreveport Bar Assn. (pres. 1989), Order of Coif. Republican. Office: 705 Milam St Ste A Shreveport LA 71101-3507

NELSON, TERI LYNN, social worker; b. Anderson, Ind., Jan. 22, 1956; d. Gordon Dey and Carolyn Jean (Hasler) N. BA, Anderson (Ind.) U., 1978; MSW, Ind. U., Indpls., 1985. Cert. clin. social worker, Ind.; cert. criminal justice specialist. Pub. liaison A Better Way, Inc., Muncie, Ind., 1979-80; substance abuse counselor Aquarius House, Inc., Muncie, 1980-85; staff therapist Community Mental Health Ctr., Inc., Lawrenceburg, Ind., 1985; program dir. Cmty. Mental Health Ctr., Inc., Lawrenceburg, Ind., 1985-95; pres., CEO New Directions, Inc., Lafayette, Ind., 1995—; mem. Ind. Substance Abuse Task Force, Indpls., 1985—, co-chair, 1991-94; co-chair Ind. State Ann. Addictions Conf., 1992—; mem. adv. bd. Gov.'s Commn. for a Drug-Free Ind., Jeffersonville, 1988-92; clin. supr. Cmty. Mental Health Ctr., Inc., Lawrenceburg, 1989-95; ad. faculty Union Inst., Cin., 1993—; tng. cons. Fairbanks Rsch. and Tng. Inst., Indpls., 1994—; mem. conf. faculty Midwest Inst., Kalamazoo, 1992—; mem. adv. bd. Addiction Counselor Tng. Partnership, Indpls., 1993—; v.p. Ind. Addictions Treatment Providers, Indpls., 1995—; v.p. Addications Resource Network of Ind., 1995—; presenter in field. Contbr. articles to profl. jours. Vol. Crisis Intervention Ctr., Muncie, 1979-84, bd. sec., 1979-82; bd. sec. Family Svcs. Delaware County, Muncie, 1980-84; chairperson Dearborn County Citizens Against Substance Abuse, Lawrenceburg, Ind., 1990. Recipient Citations, VA Med. Ctr., 1985, Am. Bus. Women's Assn., 1985. Mem. NASW, Acad. Cert. Social Workers, Nat. Forensic Counselor Assn., Native Am. Legal Def. Assn. Avocations: photography, acoustic guitar, creative writing, crewel embroidery. Office: New Directions Inc 360 N 775E Lafayette IN 47905

NELSON, THOMAS G., federal judge; b. 1936. Student, Univ. Idaho, 1955-59, LLB, 1962. Ptnr. Parry, Robertson, and Daly, Twin Falls, Idaho, 1965-79, Nelson, Rosholt, Robertson, Tolman and Tucker, Twin Falls, from 1979; judge U.S. Cir. Ct. (9th cir.), San Francisco, Calif., 1990—. With Idaho Air N.G., 1962-65, USAR, 1965-68. Mem. ABA (ho. of dels. 1974, 87-89), Am. Bar Found., Am. Coll. Trial Lawyers, Idaho State Bar (pres., bd. commrs.), Idaho Assn. Def. Counsel, Am. Bd. Trial Advocates (pres. Idaho chpt.), Phi Alpha Delta, Idaho Law Found. Office: US Ct Appeals 9th Circuit PO Box 1339 Boise ID 83701-1339

NELSON, THOMAS WILLIAM, former management consultant, government official; b. Rupert, Idaho, June 9, 1921; s. John Glenn and Jessie Olive (Wise) N.; m. Frances Grace Rotanzi, Oct. 17, 1948; children: Janet, Neal, Eric, Karen. A.B., San Diego State U., 1948; grad., Fed. Exec. Inst., 1968. Personnel technician U.S. Air Force, 1948-61; chief civilian salary and wage adminstrn. Hdqrs. U.S. Air Force, 1961-66; chief mgmt. div. Office of Sec. of Air Force, 1966-69; dep. adminstrv. asst. to Sec. Air Force, 1969-71, adminstrv. asst., 1971-80; pres., mgmt. cons. Thomas W. Nelson & Assoc. Inc., 1981-96; mgmt. cons. ManTech Internat. Corp., 1981-85. With U.S. Army, 1943-45, ETO. Decorated Purple Heart, Bronze Star; recipient Meritorious Service award Dept. Air Force, 1961, Exceptional Civilian Service award, 1971, 73, 75, 77, 79, 80; Disting. Civilian Service medal Dept. Def., 1980. Mem. Sigma Phi Epsilon. Home: 6344 Nicholson St Falls Church VA 22044-1912

NELSON, VIRGINIA SIMSON, pediatrician, educator; b. L.A.; d. Jerome and Virginia (Kuppler) Simson; children: Eric, Paul. AB, Stanford U., 1963, MD, 1970; MPH, U. Mich., 1974. Diplomate Am. Bd. Pediatrics, Am. Bd. Phys. Medicine and Rehab. Pediatrician Inst. Study Mental Retardation and Related Disabilities, U. Mich., Ann Arbor, 1973-80; mem. faculty phys. medicine and rehab. dept. U. Mich. Med. Ctr., Ann Arbor, 1980-83, resident PM&R, 1983-85, chief pediatric PM&R, 1985—. Contbr. articles to profl. jours. Office: Univ Mich Med Ctr F7822 Mott Hospital Ann Arbor MI 48109-0230

NELSON, WALDEMAR STANLEY, civil engineer, consultant; b. New Orleans, July 8, 1916; s. Bernard Stanley and Mary Lockett (Hutson) N.; widowed; children: Mary Sue Nelson Roniger, Martha Nelson Frost, Charles W., Virginia Nelson Dodge, Kenneth H. BS in Mech. and Elec. Engring., Tulane U., 1936. Registered civil, elec. and mech. engr., 44 states. Jr. engr. A. M. Lockett & Co., 1936-37; civil engr. Jeff. Lake Sulphur Co., Brazoria, Tex., 1937-38; chief survey party N.O. Pub. Belt. R.R., New Orleans, 1938; resident engr. James M. Todd, Buras, La., 1938-39; pvt. practice New Orleans, 1939-40; asst. chief engr. W. Horace Williams Co., Camp Claiborne, La., 1940-41; sr. engr. U.S. Engr. Dept., Camp Claiborne, 1941-44; prin. Waldemar S. Nelson and Co. Inc., New Orleans, 1945—, chmn. bd. dirs.; past chmn. La. State Bd. Registration Profl. Engrs. and Land Surveyors; founding mem., pres. bd. advisors sch. engring. Tulane U. Chmn. Tulane Alumni Fund, Mems' Coun., 1984; mem. bd. visitors Tulane U.; active The Chamber/New Orleans, Boy Scouts Am.; past chmn. Com. of 50; past pres. bd. commrs. NewOrleans City Pk. Improvement Assn.; mem. exec. bd. Christmas New Orleans, 1988; past sr. warden of vestry St. Andrew's Episcopal Ch.; past chmn. bd. dirs. St. Andrew's Episcopal Sch.; past pres. bd. trustees St. Martin's Protestant Episcopal Sch.; trustee Tulane Engring. Found.; bd. dirs. River Region, MetroVision. Recipient Outstanding Engring. Alumnus award Tulane U., 1976, Honor award Constrn. Industry Assn. New Orleans, Inc., 1982, Role Model of Yr. award Young Leadership Coun., 1987, Vol. of Yr. award Tulane U. Alumni Affairs, 1992. Fellow ASCE (life), ASME (life, past chmn. New Orleans sect.); mem. IEEE, NSPE (past v.p., past chmn. bd. ethical rev.), Am. Pub. Works Assn. (life), Am. Acad. Environ. Engrs. (diplomate), Nat. Coun. Engring. Examiners (past treas., Disting. Svc. award), Soc. Am. Mil. Engrs., La. Engring. Soc. (hon., past pres., Charles M. Kerr Pub. Rels. award, Leo M. Odom Profl. Svcs. award, A.B. Paterson medal, Andrew M. Lockett medal), La. Engring. Found. (trustee 1990, treas. 1991, sec. 1994—, pres. 1995-96), Soc. Tulane Engrs. (past pres.), French-Am. C. of C. (pres. La. chpt. 1992-93, chmn. 1994, pres. 1996—), Tulane Alumni Assn. (past pres.), Engrs. Club New Orleans (past pres.), Tau Beta Pi, Pi Tau Sigma, Eta Kappa Nu, others. Avocations: fishing, boating, gardening, shop work, photography. Office: Waldemar S Nelson & Co Inc 1200 Saint Charles Ave New Orleans LA 70130-4334

NELSON, WALLACE BOYD, economics and business administration educator; b. Oilton, Okla., Mar. 17, 1923; s. Frank and Notie (Ferguson) N.; m. Merietta Josephine Lair, Sept. 1, 1942; 1 child, Larry Frank. BS, So. Ill. U., 1947; MA, U. Ia., 1948; PhD, U. Iowa, 1950. From asst. to prof. econs. Kans. State U., 1950-61; prof., chmn. dept. bus. adminstrn. Arlington (Tex.) State Coll., 1961-65; prof. econs. and bus. adminstrn., dean U. Tex. Sch. Bus. Adminstrn., Arlington, 1965-73; prof. econs. and bus. adminstrn. U. Tex., Arlington, 1973-93, prof. emeritus, 1993—; pres. Nelson Assocs., 1974—; co-chmn. regional devel. com. N. Tex. Commn., 1972-77, bd. dirs. commn., 1973-77; personal injury litigation cons. Contbr. articles to profl. jours. With USAAF, 1943-46, USAF, 1951-53. Honor guest Brazil at Celebration Brazil's 150th Anniversary, 1972; Ford Motor Co. fellow, 1955, rsch. fellow Claremont Men's Coll., 1957. Mem. Am. Arbitration Assn., Fed. Mediation Conciliation Service, Nat. Acad. Arbitrators, Arlington, Dallas, Ft. Worth C. of C., Am. Econ. Assn., Indsl. Relations Research Assn., Southwestern Social Sci. Assn., Order of Artus (pres. 1948). Presbyn. (trustee). Club: Rotarian. Home: 917 Sherwood Dr Arlington TX 76013-1571

NELSON, WALLACE WARREN, retired superintendent experimental station, agronomy educator; b. Tracy, Minn., Feb. 17, 1928; s. Elmer R. and Mabel K. (Anderson) N.; m. Arlene S. Michelson, June 18, 1949; children: Thomas W., Kathryn J. BS, U. Minn., 1950, PhD, 1956. Asst. supt., agronomist N.E. Exptl. Sta. U. Minn., Duluth, 1953-59; supt., agronomist S.W. Exptl. Sta. U. Minn., Lamberton, 1959-72, supt., prof., 1972-95; ret.; bd. dirs. North Star Ins., Cottonwood, Minn. Bd. dirs. Minn . Pollution Control Agys., 1980-83. Recipient Outstanding Alumni award U. Minn., 1989. Fellow Am. Soc. Agronomists (chmn. A-7 1988). Lutheran.

NELSON, WALTER GERALD, retired insurance company executive; b. Peoria, Ill., Jan. 2, 1930; s. Walter Dennis and Hazel Marie (Tucker) N.; m. Mary Ann Olberding, Jan. 28, 1952 (dec. Nov. 1989); children—Ann (Mrs. Michael Larkin), Michael, Susan (Mrs. Jay Boor), Patrick, Thomas, Timothy, Molly (Mrs. David Edwards); m. Mary Jo Sunderland, Apr. 6, 1991. Student, St. Benedict's Coll., Atchison, Kans., 1947-49, Bradley U., Peoria, Ill., 1949; JD, Creighton U., Omaha, 1952. Bar: Nebr. 1952, Ill. 1955; CLU. Practice in Peoria, 1955-56; with State Farm Life Ins. Co., Bloomington, Ill., 1956—; counsel State Farm Life Ins. Co., 1968—, v.p., 1970—; past dir. Ill. Life Ins. Coun.; past chmn. legal sect. Am. Coun. Life Ins.; speaker in field. Contbr. articles to profl. jours. Community bd. dirs. St. Joseph Med. Ctr., Bloomington, Ill., 1994. Mem. ABA, Ill. Bar Assn., Nebr. Bar Assn., Assn. Life Ins. Counsel (bd. govs., past pres.), Nat. Orgn. Life and Health Ins. Guaranty Assns. (past chmn., bd. dirs.), Bloomington Country Club, KC. Republican. Roman Catholic.

NELSON, WENDEL LANE, medicinal chemist, educator; b. Mason City, Nebr., Apr. 7, 1939; s. Clayton W. and Joyce E. (Wilson) N.; m. Karen A. Hansen, June 14, 1968; children—Christopher E., Timothy D. B.S., Idaho State U., 1962; Ph.D., U. Kans., 1965. Asst. prof. med. chemistry U. Wash., Seattle, 1965-70; asso. prof., 1970-76, prof., 1976—. NSF fellow, 1963-65; recipient career devel. award NIH, 1971-76. Mem. Am. Chem. Soc., N.Y. Acad. Sci., Am. Assn. Colls. Pharmacy. Office: Dept Med Chem U Wash Seattle WA 98195

NELSON, WILLARD GREGORY, veterinarian, mayor; b. Lewiston, Idaho, Nov. 21, 1937; s. Donald William and Eve Mae (Boyer) N.; m. Mary Ann Eklund, Apr. 3, 1965 (div.); children: Elizabeth Ann, John Gregory. BS in Premedicine, Mont. State U., 1959; DVM, Wash. State U., 1961. Lic. veterinarian, Wash., Oreg., Idaho, Mont. Pvt. practice vet. medicine, Kuna, Idaho, 1963-66; asst. to dir. Idaho Dept. Agr., Boise, 1966-78; asst. chief Idaho Bur. Animal Health, 1978-80, chief, 1980-81; adminstr., state veterinarian Idaho Div. Animal Industries, 1981-90; dir. Idaho Dept. Agr., 1990-95; dir. pub. affairs Idaho Farm Bur. Fedn., 1995—; mayor City of Kuna (Idaho), 1984—; chmn. Idaho Gov.'s Human and Animal Health Consortium, 1983-90. Kuna city councilman, 1964-68, pres. Planning and Zoning Commn., 1968-72; mem. bd. trustees Joint Sch. Dist. 3, 1970-71, pres., 1972-76; mem. adv. bd. Mercy Med. Hosp., Nampa, Idaho, 1986-96; mem. adv. com. Wash., Oreg., Idaho Coll. Vet. Medicine, 1983—; mem. ADA Planning Assn., 1986—, vice chmn., 1991-92, chmn. 1993-94; mem. Western U.S. Trade Assn., 1990-95, treas., 1992, v.p. 1993, pres. 1994; mem. Idaho Emergency Response Commn., 1992-95, Idaho Export Coun., 1992—, Idaho Rural Devel. Coun., 1992—, vice-chair, 1993, chair 1994; bd. dirs S.W. Idaho Rsch. and Devel., 1993—. Served as capt. U.S. Army Vet Corps, 1961-63; lt. col. Idaho Army N.G., 1979-88, col., 1988—. Mem. Idaho Vet. Med. Assn. (v.p. 1987, pres.-elect 1988, pres. 1989, Idaho Veterinarian of Yr. 1989), S.W. Idaho Vet. Med. Assn., U.S. Animal Health Assn. (chmn. anaplasmosis com. 1987-90), AVMA (mem. coun. on pub. health and regulatory medicine 1988-94, chmn. 1993, pres. nat. assembly 1988), Western States Livestock Assn., USDA (nat. damage control adv. com. 1992-94, nat. dir. animal welfare coalition 1992—), Am. Legion, Nat. Animal Damage Control and Com. Lutheran. Club: Lions (Kuna). Home: 793 W 4th St Kuna ID 83634-1941 Office: 2270 Old Penitentiary Rd Boise ID 83712-8266

NELSON, WILLIAM EDWARD, lawyer, educator; b. 1940. A.B., Hamilton Coll., 1962; LL.B., NYU, 1965; Ph.D., Harvard U., 1971. Bar: N.Y. 1966. Law clk. to assoc. justice, Byron R. White, U.S. Supreme Ct., Washington, 1970-71; asst. prof. U. Pa., Phila., 1971-74, assoc. prof., 1974-75; assoc. prof. Yale U., New Haven Conn., 1975-80; prof. NYU, N.Y.C., 1980—. Mem. Order of Coif. Author: Americanization of the Common Law: The Impact of Legal Change on Massachusetts Society, 1760-1830, 1975; The Roots of American Bureaucracy, 1830-1900, 1982, The Fourteenth Amendment: From Political Principle to Judicial Doctrine, 1988. Office: NYU Law Sch 40 Washington Sq S New York NY 10012-1005*

NELSON, WILLIAM GEORGE, IV, software company executive; b. Phila., May 26, 1934; s. William George III and Eleanor (Boyle) N. BA in Chemistry, Swarthmore Coll., 1956; MBA in Finance, U. Pa., 1958; PhD in Econs., Rice U., 1965. Various positions Du Pont Co., 1957-62, Monsanto Co., St. Louis, 1965-76; vis. asst. prof. Washington U., St. Louis, 1966-75; sr. v.p. Chase Econs./Interactive Data, Waltham, Mass., 1976-83; pres. Pansophic Systems, Lisle, Ill., 1983-90; pres., CEO OnLine Software, Ft. Lee, N.J., 1990-91, bd. dirs.; pres., CEO Pilot Software, Boston, 1992-94; CEO Harris Data Corp., 1990—; pres., CEO Clarendon Capital Corp., Boston, 1995—; bd. dirs. GEAC, Toronto, Manugistics, Rockville, Md., Harris Data, Waukesha, Wis., HPR, Inc., Boston, Project Software and Devel. Inc., Cambridge, Mass. Bd. dirs. Swarthmore Coll., Hampton U. NFS fellow in econs., 1963-65. Office: Clarendon Capital Corp 267 Clarendon St Boston MA 02116

NELSON, WILLIAM RANKIN, surgeon, educator; b. Charlottesville, Va., Dec. 12, 1921; s. Hugh Thomas and Edith (Rankin) N.; m. Nancy Laidley, Mar. 17, 1956 (div. 1979); children: Robin Page Nelson Russel, Susan Kimberly Nelson Wright, Anne Rankin Nelson Cron; m. Pamela Morgan Phelps, July 5, 1984. BA, U. Va., 1943, MD, 1945. Diplomate Am. Bd. Surgery. Intern Vanderbilt U. Hosp., Nashille, 1945-46; resident in surgery U. Va. Hosp., Charlottesville, 1949-51; fellow surg. oncology Meml. Sloan Kettering Cancer Ctr., N.Y.C., 1951-55; instr. U. Colo. Sch. Medicine, Denver, 1955-57; asst. clin. prof. U. Colo. Sch. Medicine, 1962-87, clin. prof. surgery, 1987—; asst. prof. Med. Coll. Va., Richmond, 1957-62; mem. exec. com. U. Colo. Cancer Ctr.; mem. nat. bd., nat. exec. com. Am. Cancer Soc. Contbr. articles to profl. jours. and chpts. to textbooks. Capt. USAAF, 1946-48. Recipient Nat. Div. award Am. Cancer Soc., 1979. Fellow Am. Coll. Surgeons (bd. govs. 1984-89); mem. AMA, Internat. Soc. Surgery, Brit. Assn. Surg. Oncology, Royal Soc. Medicine (U.K.), Soc. Surg. Oncology (pres. 1975-76), Soc. Head and Neck Surgeons (pres. 1986-87), Am. Cancer Soc. (pres. Colo. div. 1975-77, exec. com., nat. bd. dirs., del. dir. from Colo. div. 1975—), Am. Soc. Clin. Oncology, Western Surg. Assn. Colo. Med. Soc., Denver Med. Soc., Denver Acad. Surgery, Rocky Mt. Oncology Soc., Univ. Club, Rotary. Republican. Episcopalian. Avocations: skiing, backpacking, travel, bicycling, fly fishing.

NELSON, WILLIE, musician, songwriter; b. Abbott, Tex., Apr. 30, 1933; children: Jacob, Lukas, Paula Carlene, Amy, Lana, Susie, Billy. Student, Baylor U. Worked as salesman; announcer, host country music shows local Tex. stas.; bass player, Ray Price's band; then formed own band, personal appearances at Grand Ole Opry, Nashville and throughout U.S., 1964—; rec. artist, Atlantic, Columbia and RCA records; albums include One for the Road, Here's Willie Nelson, 1963, Country Willie, 1973, Red Headed Stranger, 1975, The Troublemaker, 1976, Willie Nelson and His Friends, 1976, Willie Before His Time, Wanted/The Outlaw, The Willie Way, The Best of Willie Nelson, Stardust, 1978, Family Bible, 1980, Tougher Than Leather, 1983, City of New Orleans, 1984, Me and Paul, 1985, (with Johnny Cash, Kris Kristofferson and Waylon Jennings) Highwayman, 1985, The Promise Land, 1986, Partners, 1986, Island in the Sea, 1987, Seashores of Old Mexico, 1987, What a Wonderful World, 1988, A Horse Called Music, 1989, Highwayman II, 1990, Born for Trouble, 1990, Clean Shirt Waylon and Willie, 1991, Across the Borderline, 1993, Across the Borderline, 1993, Moonlight Becomes You, 1993, Healing Hands of Time, 1994, Super Hits, 1994, Just One Love, 1995, The Road Goes on Forever (The Highwaymen), 1995; film appearances include: Electric Horseman, 1979, Honeysuckle Rose, 1980, Thief, 1981, Barbarosa, 1982; star, co-writer mus. score TV film Stagecoach, 1986; theme song performed, film Welcome Home, 1989; TV films include Where the Hell's That Gold, 1988, Once upon a Texas Train, 1989, A Pair of Aces, 1990, Born for Trouble, 1990, Another Pair of Aces: Three of a Kind, 1991; author: (autobiography) I Didn't Come Here and I Ain't Leading, 1988. Served in USAF. Recipient Grammy award for song Blue Eyes Crying in the Rain 1975, for Georgia on My Mind 1978, for Mammas Don't Let Your Babies Grow Up to Be Cowboys (with Waylon Jennings) 1978, Billboard mag. citation for Top Album Artist 1976, Country Music Assn. award for single Good Hearted Woman, for vocal duo with Waylon Jennings and for album Wanted: The Outlaws, Grammy award for Best Album, 1984, Special Humanitarian award Nat. Farmers Orgn., 1986, (with Julio Iglesias) Best Vocal Duo award Country Music Assn., Grammy Lifetime Achievement award, 1989; named to Nashville Songwriters Assn. Hall of Fame, 1973, CMA Entertainer of Yr., 1979, Country Music Hall of Fame, 1993. Office: care Mark Rothbaum & Assocs Inc PO Box 2689 Danbury CT 06813-2689

NELSON-HUMPHRIES, TESSA (TESSA UNTHANK), English language educator, writer, lecturer; b. Yorkshire, Eng.; came to U.S., 1955; m. Kenneth Nelson Brown, June 1, 1957 (dec. 1962); m. Cecil H. Unthank, Sept. 26, 1963 (dec. 1979). BA, U. London, 1953; MA, U. N.C., 1965; PhD in English, U. Liverpool (Eng.), 1973. Head English dept. Richard Thomas Girls Sch., Elmore Green Sch., Walsall, Eng., 1956-58, 59-60; dir. English studies Windsor Coll., Buenos Aires, Argentina, 1958-59; prof. English, Cumberland Coll., Williamsburg, Ky., 1964-90; prof. dept. English, N.Mex. State U., 1990-91. Best Actress award Carlsbad (N.Mex.) Little Theatre, 1962, Cumberland Coll., 1979; Fulbright fellow, 1955-56, Danforth fellow, 1971, James Still fellow, 1983; Mellon travel/study grantee, China, 1981, 87; recipient awards for fiction Eng., 1986, 87, 88, Clemence Dane trophy, 1995, Third prize Cairns Poetry Competition, 1995. Fellow AAUW; mem. Soc. Women

Writers and Journalists (Short Story prize 1975, 87, Poetry prize 1988, 89, Julia Cairns Silver trophy for Poetry, 1978, article prize, London, 1986, poetry prizes, 1994, Fiction award U.K. 1995), Soc. Women Writers and Journalists Eng., Soc. Children's Book Writers, Vegetarian Soc. (life), Mensa. Episcopalian. Contbr. articles to Cats Mag., Let's Live, The Lookout, Child Life, Children's Digest, Vegetarian Times, Alive!, The Dalesman, Mich. Quar. Rev., Bull. of Soc. Children's Book Writers, Bull. Soc. Women Writers and Journalists, others; columnist, British Vegetarian mag., 1976-85; contbr. poetry to various mags. including Joycean Lit. Arts Guild, Z-Miscellaneous, Blue Unicorn, Appalachian Heritage, Aireings-U.K., ENVOI (HardBack Anthology)-U.K., Negative Capability, McCann's Alaska Jour. Poetry Philosophy, Array, New Frontiers of N.Mex.

NELSON-MAYSON, LINDA RUTH, art museum curator; b. Vincennes, Ind., Jan. 9, 1954; d. Robert Arthur and Darleen Marie (Andrews) N.; m. William A. Mayson, June 12, 1982; 1 child, Eric Nelson. BFA, Miami U., Oxford, Ohio, 1976; MFA, Ohio State U., 1981. Co-dir. Artreach Gallery, Columbus, Ohio, 1980-82; art instr., gallery asst. Ohio U., Chillicothe, 1982-83; asst. curator Ross County Mus., Chillicothe, 1982-83; art dir. Aaron Copland Music & Arts Program, White Plains, N.Y., 1982-85; artist-in-edn. Nebr. Arts Council, Omaha, 1983-85; curator Art Mus. South Tex., Corpus Christi, 1985-89; curator collections Columbia (S.C.) Mus. Art, 1989-92, dep. dir. curatorial svcs., 1992-94; supr. curatorial projects Minn. Mus. Am. Art, St. Paul, 1994—; juror art exhibits Corpus Christi Arts Found., 1986-88, Hardin Simmons U., 1987, Anderson Coll., 1989, Hilton Head Art League, 1994; mem. pub. art selection panel S.C. Arts Coun., 1990; mem. steering com. South Tex. Regional Arts Conf., 1986-88; adj. lectr. art history U. S.C., 1989-94; chmn. curators com. S.E. Mus. Conf., 1991-93, chmn. local program com., 1992, mem. program com., 1992-93. Grantee NEA, S.C. Arts Coun., Tex. Coun. on Arts, Kress Found., Inst. Mus. Svcs. Mem. am. Assn. Mus. (co-chmn. exhibits competition 1991-93, chmn. curator's com. 1993-95, chmn. of SPC com. 1994-95, nominating com. 1994-95), Minn. Assn. Mus., Midwest Mus. Assn., Coll. Art Assn. Democrat. Avocations: dogs, gardening, camping. Office: Minn Mus Am Art Landmark Ctr 75 W 5th St Saint Paul MN 55102

NELSON-WALKER, ROBERTA, company executive; b. N.Y.C., Sept. 1, 1936; d. Richard E. and Esther (McBride) Martin; m. Robert L. Nelson, July 20, 1957 (div.); children: Carol, Craig, Robert H.; m. Dan Walker, Nov. 1978 (div.). BA, DePaul U., 1976, MS in Mgmt. with distinction, 1977. Dir. devel. Ray Graham Assocs., Elmhurst, Ill., 1970-76; dir. human resources Nat. Easter Seal Soc., Chgo., 1979-81; v.p. Butler Walker Inc., Oak Brook, Ill., 1981-85; pres. CNR, Inc., Oak Brook, Ill., 1985-91; spl. agt. Prudential Ins., Oak Brook, Ill., 1991-95; mng. dir. Visimark L.L.C., Oak Brook, Ill. Author: Creating Acceptance for Handicapped People, 1975, Creating, Planning, and Financial Housing for Handicapped People, 1979. Founder, organizer Found. for Handicapped, 1970-76,; pres. DuPage County Pub. Health Coun., 1974; bd. dirs. DuPage County Mental Health Assocs., 1970, Forest Found. DuPage County, 1976-86, Shakespeare Globe, London and Chgo., 1982—; mem. DuPage County Bd. Health, 1975, Ill. Gov.'s Com. for Handicapped, 1976, women's coun. Chgo. Heart Assn., 1979—. Recipient Meritorious Svc. award, Chgo. Heart Assn., 1968, 70, Fond du Coer award AHA, 1968, Cursade of Mercy Achievement awards, 1974-76, State of Ill. procalmation by Gov. James Thompson, Ill. Epilepsy Assn., 1978. Office: Visimark LLC 2100 Clearwater Dr Oak Brook IL 60521

NELTNER, MICHAEL MARTIN, lawyer; b. Cin., July 31, 1959; s. Harold John and Joyce Ann (Schell) N.; m. Barbara Ann Phair, July 9, 1988; children: Brandon August, Alexandra Nicole. BA, Mercy Coll., 1981; MA, Athenaeum of Ohio, 1987; JD, U. Cin., 1994. Bar: Ohio 1994, U.S. Dist. Ct. (so. dist.) Ohio 1995. Tchr. Elder H.S., Cin., 1985-91; ins. agt. Ky. Ctrl., Cin., 1987-91; mediator City of Cin., 1992-94; tchg. asst. Ohio Gov.'s Inst., Cin., 1992; legal extern to Chief Justice Thomas Moyer Ohio Supreme Ct., 1993; assoc. Cash, Cash, Eagen & Kessel, Cin., 1994—. Editor-in-chief Mercy Coll. Lit. Mag., 1980-81, U. Cin. Law Rev., 1993-94. Campaign coord. Rep. Orgn. Detroit, 1980. Recipient Merit scholarship Cin. Enquirer, 1977-81, Sage scholarship Mercy Coll., 1980, Am. Jurisprudence award Lawyers Coop. Publishing, 1994. Mem ABA, Ohio Bar Assn., Cin. Bar Assn. (acad. medicine com. 1995—, ct. appeals com. 1995—). Home: 3317 Felicity Dr Cincinnati OH 45211 Office: Cash Cash Eagen & Kessel 432 Walnut St Cincinnati OH 45202

NEMAN, DANIEL LOUIS, movie critic; b. Cin., May 18, 1960; s. Albert Henry and Beth Maxine (Smilansky) N.; m. Mary Anne Pikrone. BA in English Lang. and Lit., U. Chgo., 1982. Movie critic, entertainment writer Bryan-College Sta., Eagle, Tex., 1983-86; movie critic, features writer Richmond (Va.) News Leader, 1986-92, Richmond Times-Dispatch, 1992—. Mem. Soc. Profl. Journalists, Va. Press Assn. Office: Richmond Times-Dispatch 333 E Grace St Richmond VA 23293-1000

NEMAN, THOMAS EDWARD, advertising and marketing executive, researcher; b. Milw., Aug. 7, 1940; s. Edward Louis and Helen (Lawler) N.; m. Jo Ann Spahn, Oct. 14, 1967. A.B., Marquette U., 1962; M.A., Ind. U.-Bloomington, 1963, Ph.D., 1967. Sr. economist, Smith Kline and French, Phila., 1967-69; corp. mgr. statis. applications Gen. Foods Corp., White Plains, N.Y., 1969-72; v.p., assoc. research dir. J. Walter Thompson, N.Y.C., 1972-76; v.p., research dir. Leber, Katz Ptnrs., N.Y.C., 1976-79; sr. v.p., dir. planning and research BBDO, Worldwide Inc., N.Y.C., and Detroit, 1979—; mem. council Advt. Research Found., N.Y.C., 1972—. Mem. Advt. Research Found., Am. Acad. Advt., Econ. Club Detroit, Am. Mktg. Assn., Am. Statis. Assn. (sec. N.Y. chpt. 1977-78). Republican. Roman Catholic. Home: 21590 E Valley Woods Dr Franklin MI 48025-2633 Office: BBDO Detroit 26261 Evergreen Rd Southfield MI 48076-4447

NEMEC, JOSEPH C., III, production designer. Prodn. designer: (TV movies) Blind Justice, 1986, Amerika, 1987, (films) Extreme Prejudice, 1987, Fatal Beauty, 1987, Alien Nation, 1988, The Abyss, 1989, Another 48 Hours, 1990, Fear, 1990, Patriot Games, 1993, The Getaway, 1993. Office: care Marty Barkin CNA & Associates 1801 Ave of the Stars Ste 1250 Los Angeles CA 90067

NEMECEK, ALBERT DUNCAN, JR., retail company executive, investment banker, management consultant; b. Helena, Mont., Mar. 10, 1936; s. Albert Duncan and Geneva (Reindle) N.; m. Marilyn Ann Shaughnessy, Sept. 7, 1963 (div.); children: Maureen Ann, Steven Mathew; m. Judith Eileen Swift, Sept. 18, 1981 (div.); 1 child, Jennifer Eileen. B.S., U. Md., 1960, postgrad. in econs., 1961. Agt. IRS, Washington, 1961-65; tax dir. Macke Co., Washington, 1965-69; tax dir., then sec. Garfinckle, Brooks Bros., Miller & Rhoads, Inc., Washington, 1969-76; treas. Garfinckle, Brooks Bros., Miller & Rhoads, Inc., 1976—, v.p., 1979—; mng. ptnr. Nemecek & Falleroni, 1987, Nemecek & Jacknis, investment bankers, mgmt. cons., Falls Church, Va., 1989; founder Nemecek & Co., Inc., Falls Church, 1990; founder Entrepreneurial Growth Fund, Falls Church, 1990. Home: 18724 Walkers Choice Rd Apt 5 Gaithersburg MD 20879-2621 *A man's success is measured by the respect he has gained from his peers, his understanding and compassion, respect for the feelings of others, appreciation of the world's beauty, and his attempts to leave the world better than he found it.*

NEMECEK, GEORGINA MARIE, molecular pharmacologist; b. Mineola, N.Y., Aug. 27, 1946; d. George and Frances Valerie (Masaryk) N. AB, Mt. Holyoke Coll., 1968; PhD, U. Pa., 1972. Rsch. assoc. dept. biochemistry U. Mass. Med. Sch., Worcester, 1972-73, postdoctoral fellow of Am. Heart Assn., dept. biochemistry, 1974, asst. prof., 1974-80, assoc. prof., 1981-83; sr. scientist platelet dept. Sandoz Pharm. Corp., East Hanover, N.J., 1983-85, mem. sr. sci. staff, platelet dept., 1986, fellow, sect. head molecular biology, 1987-91, fellow diabetes, 1991-93; fellow regulatory toxicology Sandoz Pharm. Corp., East Hanover, 1993—; vis. scientist dept. molecular biology, Princeton (N.J.) U., 1987, Sea Pharm. Inc., 1984, NATO, U. Libre, Brussels, 1979, biotechnology dept. Sandoz AG, Basel, Switzerland, 1988. Contbr. articles to profl. jours. Named Nat. Heart, Lung, and Blood Inst. Young Investigator, NIH, 1977-81. Mem. Am. Soc. Pharmacol. Exptl. Therapeutics, N.Y. Acad. Scis. (chmn. biochem. sect. 1992-94), Tissue Culture Assn., Sigma Xi. Avocations: boating, gardening, riding, needlework. Office: Sandoz Pharm Corp 59 State Route 10 East Hanover NJ 07936-0180

NEMEROFF, CHARLES BARNET, neurobiology and psychiatry educator; b. Bronx, N.Y., Sept. 7, 1949; s. Philip Peace and Sarah (Greenberg) N.; m. Melissa Ann Pilkington, May 24, 1980; children: Matthew P., Amanda P., Sarah-Frances P. B.S., CCNY, 1970; M.S., Northeastern U., 1973; Ph.D., U. N.C., 1976, M.D., 1981. Diplomate Am. Bd. Psychiatry and Neurology; lic. physician, N.C., Ga. Research asst. ichthyology Am. Mus. Natural History, N.Y.C., 1968-71, neurochemistry lab. McLean Hosp., Belmont, Mass., 1971-72; research assoc. surgery Beth Israel Hosp., Boston, 1972-73; teaching asst. biology Northeastern U., 1972-73; postdoctoral fellow Biol. Scis. Research Ctr., U. N.C., Chapel Hill, 1976-77, research fellow, 1977-83, clin. instr. psychiatry, 1983; resident in psychiatry N.C. Meml. Hosp., Chapel Hill, 1981-83; asst. prof. dept. psychiatry and pharmacology Duke U., Durham, N.C., 1983-85, assoc. prof. psychiatry, 1985-89, assoc. prof. pharmacology, 1986-89, prof. depts. psychiatry and pharmacology, 1989-91; chief div. biological psychiatry, 1988-91, prof., chmn. dept. psychiatry and behavioral scis. Emory U. Sch. Medicine, 1991—, Reunette W. Harris prof. psychiatry and behavioral scis., 1994—; vis. prof. physiology Cath. U., Santiago, Chile, 1978. Predoctoral fellow Schizophrenia Research Found., Soc. Scottish Rite, Lexington, Mass., 1975-76; postdoctoral fellow Nat. Inst. Neurol., Communicative Disorders and Stroke, 1977; recipient Michiko Kuno award U. N.C., 1978, 79, Merck award for acad. excellence, 1981; grantee Nat. Inst. Aging, 1982-83, NIMH, 1983—; Merck award for young investigators Am. Geriatrics Soc., 1985, 2d prize Anna Monica Found. for Research in Endogenous Depression, 1987, Merit award NIMH, 1987; Nanaline Duke fellow Duke U. Med. Ctr., 1985-87; Rsch. prize World Fedn. Societies of Biol. Psychiatry, 1991; recipient Edward J. Sachar award Columbia U., 1993, Edward A. Strecker prize Inst. Pa. Hosp., 1993, Outstanding Alumni award in health scis. Northeastern U., 1995. Fellow Am. Coll. Neuropsychopharmacology (Mead Johnson travel award 1982, coun. 1993—), Am. Coll. Psychiatrists (chmn. contbns. com. 1991-93, edn. com. 1993—, bd. regents 1994—); mem. Soc. Neurosci. (program com. 1993-95), AAAS, N.Y. Acad. Scis., Internat. Soc. Psychoneuroendocrinology (pres. 1993—, Curt P. Richter award 1985), Internat. Soc. Neurochemistry, Am. Soc. Neurochemistry (Jordi-Folch-Pi award 1987), Endocrine Soc., Internat. Soc. Neuroendocrinology, Soc. Biol. Psychiatry (A.E. Bennett award 1979, gold medal award 1996), Am. Fedn. Clin. Research, AMA, Am. Pain Soc., Am. Psychiat. Assn. (Kempf award 1989, Samuel Hibbs award 1991, coun. rsch. 1993—, chmn. 1994-95, rsch. prize 1996), Argentine Assn. Psychoneuroendocrinology (sci. council), Sigma Xi. Democrat. Jewish. Editor: (with A.J. Prange, Jr.) Neurotensin, a Brain and Gastrointestinal Peptide, 1982, (with A.J. Dunn) Peptides, Hormones and Behavior, 1984, (with P.T. Loosen) Handbook of Clinical Psychoneuroendocrinology, Neuropeptides in Psychiatric and Neurological Disorders, 1987, Neuropeptides in Psychiatric Disorders, 1991, Neuroendocrinology, 1992, (with P. Kitabgi) The Neurobiology of Neurotensin, 1992, (with A.F. Schatzberg) Textbook of Psychopharmacology, 1995; editor-in-chief: Depression, 1993—; co-editor-in-chief: Critical Revs. in Neurobiology, 1992—; contbr. numerous articles and abstracts to profl. jours., chpts. in books. Office: Emory U Sch Medicine Dept Psychiatry 1639 Pierce Dr Atlanta GA 30322

NEMEROFF, MICHAEL ALAN, lawyer; b. Feb. 16, 1946; s. Bernard Gregor and Frances (Gotleib) N.; m. Sharon Lynn Leininger, Sept. 22, 1974; children: Theodore, Patrick, James. BA, U. Chgo., 1968; JD, Columbia U., 1971. Asst. counsel Subcom. on Juvenile Delinquency of Senate Jud. Com., Washington, 1971-73; assoc. Sidley & Austin, Washington, 1973-78, ptnr., 1978—. Treas. Friends of Jim Sasser, 1978—, Andy Ireland Campaign Com., 1984-92. Office: Sidley & Austin 1722 I St NW Washington DC 20006-3705

NEMEROVSKI, STEVEN H., lawyer; b. Oak Park, Ill., Nov. 9, 1951. BA, U. Pa., 1972; JD, U. Ill., 1976. Bar: Ill. 1977, U.S. Dist. Ct. (no. dist.) Ill. 1977; CPA, Ill. Parliamentarian Ill. Ho. of Reps., Springfield; ptnr. Lavin & Waldon, Chicago; instr. Roosevelt U., 1979. Mem. Chgo. Bar Assn. Office: Lavin & Waldon 111 E Wacker Dr Ste 2800 Chicago IL 60601-4208*

NEMETZ, NATHANIEL THEODORE, lawyer, former chief justice of British Columbia; b. Winnipeg, Man., Can., Sept. 8, 1913; s. Samuel and Rebecca (Birch) N.; m. Bel Newman, Aug. 10, 1935 (dec.); 1 son, Peter Newman. B.A. with 1st class honors, U. B.C., 1934; LL.D. (hon.), Notre Dame, Nelson, B.C., 1972, U. B.C., 1975, Simon Fraser U., 1975, U. Victoria, 1976; PhD honoris causa, Tel Aviv U., 1991. Bar: Created King's Counsel 1950. Spl. counsel Public Utilities Commn., 1958-61; spl. counsel to cities of Vancouver, Burnaby, New Westminster, Can., 1959-63; justice Supreme Ct. B.C., 1963-68, Ct. Appeal, 1968-73; chief justice B.C. Supreme Ct., 1973-78, B.C., 1979-88; assoc. counsel Russell & DuMoulin, Vancouver, 1990—; mem. Royal Commn. to investigate election irregularities, 1965; arbitrator fishing, lumber and hydro industries West Coast shipping dispute, 1966-73; del. Govt. Can. to Internat. Labor Orgn., Geneva, 1973; chmn. Legal Conf., Stanford U., 1986; co-chmn. 1st Can.-Australasian Legal Conf., Canberra, Australia, 1988; mem. appeal bd. Can.-U.S. Free Trade Agreement; chmn. Japan-Can. Coal Dispute Arbitration, 1988; hon. consul gen. Singapore, 1989; commr. Nanaimo Commonwealth Holding Soc., 1996. Contbr. articles in field to profl. publs. Mem. senate, chmn. bd. govs. U. B.C., 1957-68, chancellor, 1972-75; chmn. Can. edn. del. to China, 1974; chmn. Univ. Dist. Sch. Bd., 1957-59; hon. chmn. Crusade Against Cancer, 1988; hon. trustee B.C. Govt. Ho. Found., 1988; mem. Freeman City of Vancouver, 1988; hon. chm. Vancouver Sun Children's Fund, 1990, 91. Named hon. fellow Hebrew U., Jerusalem, 1976; recipient award Can. Council Christians and Jews, 1958; Great Trekker award U.B.C., 1969; Beth Emeth Brotherhood award, 1969; Canada medal, 1967; award of distinction U. B.C. Alumni, 1975; Queen Elizabeth medal, 1977, 125th Can. medal, Alumni award U. B.C., 1988; medal of Flag of Yugoslavia with ribbon, 1989; Companion Order of Can., 1990; Order of Brit. Columbia; Nathan T. Nemetz chair in Legal History created in his honor U. B.C., 1988. Mem. Can. Jud. Coun. (exec. 1973-88, vice chmn. 1988), Can. Bar Assn. (George Goyer Meml. award B.C. br. 1994), Faculty Assn. U. B.C. (hon.), Alumni Assn. U. B.C. (pres. 1957). Jewish. Clubs: Faculty (U. B.C.); Vancouver. Office: Russell & DuMoulin, 2100-1075 W Georgia St, Vancouver, BC Canada V6E 3G2

NEMFAKOS, CHARLES PANAGIOTIS, federal official; b. Athens, Greece, Oct. 21, 1942; s. Panagiotis Soterios and Mirka (Kyriakakis) N.; m. Suzanne Marie Ertel, Oct. 2, 1965; children: Mirka Leigh, Charles Jr. BA, Pan Am. U., 1964; MA, Georgetown U., 1982. Cert. in nat. security. Health advisor Dept. Pub. Health, Washington, 1965-66; fed. mgmt. intern Dept. Navy, Washington, 1966-67; budget analyst Naval Ordnance Systems Command, Washington, 1967-71; supervisory budget analyst Naval Ship Systems Command, Washington, 1971-73; sr. budget analyst Office of Sec. of Def., Washington, 1973-75; divsn. dir. Office of Budget and Reports, Washington, 1975-76; assoc.dir. Office of Budgets and Reports, Washington, 1976-93; dep. asst. sec. Dept. of Navy, Washington, 1994-95, dep. under sec., 1995—; lectr. Naval Postgrad. Sch., Monterey, Calif., 1984—, Georgetown U., Washington, 1987—; mem. base structure com. Dept. Navy, Washington, 1990-91, mem. sr. advisors group, 1991-92, vice chmn. base structure com., 1992-95. Contbr. articles to profl. jours. Coach McLean (Va.) Youth Soccer, 1978-93, chmn., 1982-85; bd. dirs. McLean Youth, Inc., 1980-84; registrar Va. Youth Soccer Assn., 1984-86. Recipient Dept. Navy Superior Civilian Svc. award Asst. Sec. of Navy, 1980, Dept. Navy Disting. Civilian Svc. award Sec. of Navy, 1985, 87, 93, Dept. Def. Disting. Civilian Svc. award Sec. of Def., 1990, Dept. Navy Disting. Pub. Svc. award Sec. of Navy, 1995; named to Rank of Disting. Exec. Pres. of U.S., 1986, 95, to Rank of Meritorious Exec., Pres. of U.S., 1981, 91. Mem. Am. Assn. Budget and Program Analysis (dir.-at-large 1980-83), Am. Soc. of Mil. Comptrs. (v.p. 1988-90), Fed. Execs. Inst. Alumni Assn., Tau Kappa Epsilon (chpt. pres. 1964-65). Greek Orthodox. Avocations: golf, tennis, coaching soccer. Office: Under Sec of Navy Pentagon 4E 775 Washington DC 20350-1000 Office: 6060 Tower Ct Alexander VA 22304

NEMHAUSER, GEORGE L., industrial, systems engineer, operations research educator; b. N.Y.C., July 27, 1937; s. Martin and Rose (Schwartz) N.; m. Ellen Krupsaw, Sept. 14, 1959; children: Wendy, Dennis. B.Chem.Engring., CCNY, 1958; M.S., Northwestern U., 1959, Ph.D., 1961. Prof. ops. research Johns Hopkins U., Balt., 1961-69; prof. Cornell U., Ithaca, N.Y., 1969-84, Leon C. Welch prof. engring., 1984-85, dir. Sch. Ops. Research and Indsl. Engring., 1977-83; Chandler prof. indsl. and systems engring. Ga. Inst. Tech., 1985—, inst. prof., 1992—; vis. prof. U. Leeds, U.K., 1963-64; vis. prof., dir. research Center for Ops. Research and Econometrics, U. Louvain, Belgium, 1975-77; cons. NSF (others.). Author: Introduction to Dynamic Programming, 1966, Integer Programming, 1972, Integer and Combinatorial Optimization, 1988; editor-in-chief: Ops. Research, 1975-78, Ops. Research Letters, 1981—; contbr. articles to profl. jours. NSF faculty fellow, 1969-70. Mem. NAE, Ops. Research Soc. Am. (pres. 1981-82, Lanchester prize 1977, 89, Kimball medal 1988), Inst. Mgmt. Sci., Soc. Indsl. and Applied Math., Am. Inst. Indsl. Engrs., Math. Programming Soc. (chmn. 1989-1992). Home: 1208 Villa Dr NE Atlanta GA 30306-2567

NEMIR, DONALD PHILIP, lawyer; b. Oakland, Calif., Oct. 31, 1931; s. Philip F. and Mary (Shavor) N. AB, U. Calif., Berkeley, 1957, JD, 1960. Bar: Calif. 1961. Pvt. practice, San Francisco, 1961—; pres. Law Offices Donald Nemir. Mem. ABA, ATLA, Calif. State Bar Assn., Phi Delta Phi. Home: PO Box 1089 Mill Valley CA 94942-1089

NEMIROW, ARNOLD MYLES, manufacturing executive; b. Hartford, Conn., Mar. 25, 1943; s. Benjamin and Elsie (Nozik) N.; m. Barbro Sandberg, Dec. 22, 1967 (dec. Aug. 1983); children: Matthew, Adam; m. Sharon Green, April 23, 1988. AB cum laude, Harvard U., 1966; JD, U. Mich., 1969. Bar: N.Y. Atty. Carter, Ledyard & Milburn, N.Y.C., 1969-73; asst. gen. counsel Coleco Industries Inc., Hartford, 1973-74; atty., asst. gen. counsel Gt. No. Nekoosa Corp., Stamford, Conn., 1974-80, dir. indsl. rels., 1981-83, v.p., 1984-90; pres. Gt. Southern Paper Co., Cedar Springs, Ga., 1984-87, Nekoosa Papers Inc., Port Edwards, Wis., 1988-90; pres., CEO Wausau Papers, Wausau, Wis., 1990-94; CEO, pres. Bowater Inc., 1995—; chmn. Bowater, 1996—. Office: 55 E Camperdown Way Greenville SC 29601-3511

NEMSER, EARL HAROLD, lawyer; b. N.Y.C., Jan. 17, 1947; s. Harold Summers and Eleanor Patricia (Beckerman) N.; m. Randy Lynn Lehrer, June 17, 1974 (div.); children: Eliza Sarah, Maggie Lehrer. B.A., NYU, 1967; J.D. magna cum laude, Boston U., 1970. Bar: N.Y. 1970, U.S. Supreme Ct. 1975, U.S. Claims Ct. 1979, U.S. Tax Ct. 1985. Law clk. Hon. Collins J. Seitz, Chief Judge U.S. Ct. appeals 3rd Cir., 1970-71; ptnr. Cadwalader, Wickersham & Taft, N.Y.C., 1971-95, Shereff, Friedman, Hoffman & Goodman, L.L.P., N.Y.C., 1996—; mng. dir. Interactive Brokers, Inc., Valhalla, N.Y., 1995—; dir. Timber Hill, Inc., Valhalla, N.Y., 1989—. Mem. ABA, Assn. Bar City of N.Y., Fed. Bar Council, Boston U. Law Sch. Alumni Assn. (pres. 1984). Clubs: Downtown Assn.; Contbr. note to legal rev. Office: Shereff Friedman Hoffman & Goodman 919 3d Ave New York NY 10038

NEN, ROBERT ALLEN (ROBB NEN), professional baseball player; b. San Pedro, Calif., Nov. 28, 1969; s. Dick Nen. Grad. high sch., Los Alamitos, Calif. With Tex. Rangers, 1993; pitcher Fla. Marlins, 1993—. Office: Fla Marlins 2267 N.W. 199th St. Miami FL 33056*

NENNER, VICTORIA CORICH, nurse, educator; b. Marshall, Tex., Jan. 17, 1945; d. Bernard Paul and Mary DeLayne (Bowen) Corich; BSN (Regents scholar, Krost-Freeman scholar, Mary Gobbs Jones Nursing scholar), Tex. Women's U., 1966; cert. U. Paris, summer 1966; MSN, U. San Diego, 1984; m. Paul Edwin Nenner, Aug. 12, 1970. Mem. nursing staff St. Thomas Hosp., London, 1966-67, Parkland Meml. Hosp., Dallas, 1967-68; coord. nursing continuing edn. Scripps Meml. Hosp., La Jolla, Calif., 1974-85; owner, pres. Marvik Ednl. Svcs., Inc., 1985—; mem. part-time faculty U. Calif., San Diego; mem. vis. faculty U. B.C.; mem. Inservice Council San Diego and Imperial Counties, 1974-80, pres., 1976-77; mem. San Diego Community Colls. Health Edn. Adv. Bd., 1976-84. Served to capt. Nurse Corps, USAF, 1968-73. Named Tex. Student Nurse of Year, 1966. Mem. ANA, Am. Soc. Health Edn. and Tng., Nat. League Nursing (Leadership award 1995), Calif. League for Nursing (pres. 1993-94), Sigma Theta Tau. Author articles in field; contbg. author in healthcare software; producer oncology nursing ednl. videotapes. Home: 167712 Los Altos Rd San Diego CA 92109

NEPPL, WALTER JOSEPH, retired retail store executive; b. Halbur, Iowa, June 15, 1922; s. Frank and Anna (Halbur) N.; m. Marian Maher, Oct. 15, 1945; children: Eugenie Neppl Kauffman, Marilee Neppl Cumming, Deborah Neppl Johnson, John, Thomas (dec.), Christina Neppl Totino, Nancy Neppl Tripucka. Grad. h.s., Carrol, Iowa. With J.C. Penney Co., Inc., 1940—; mgr. store J.C. Penney Co., Inc., Albuquerque, 1954-55; dist. mgr. J.C. Penney Co., Inc., Pitts., 1955-61; store coordination mgr. J.C. Penney Co., Inc., N.Y.C., 1961-64; asst. to dir. dist. mgmt. dept. J.C. Penney Co., Inc., 1964-65, gen. mdse. mgr. hard lines, 1965-67, v.p., 1967-68, gen. sales and mdse. mgr., 1968-71, dir. merchandising, 1971-72, exec. v.p., 1972-76, pres., chief operating officer, 1976-81, vice-chmn. bd., 1981-82, ret., 1982, dir., 1968-85; bd. dirs. emeritus J.C. Penney Co. Inc. Trustee emeirtus Geraldine R. Dodge Found. Served to capt. USAAF, 1943-45. Decorated D.F.C. Roman Catholic. Home: The Enclave 5345 Annabel Ln Plano TX 75093-3428

NEPTUNE, JOHN ADDISON, chemistry educator, consultant; b. Barnesville, Ohio, Nov. 27, 1919; s. George Addison and Lola Mae (Skinner) N.; m. Ruth Elizabeth Dorsey, Aug. 24, 1947; 1 child, Benjamin. BS summa cum laude, Muskingum Coll., 1942; MS, U. Wis., 1949, PhD, 1952. Instr. chemistry Muskingum Coll., New Concord, Ohio, 1943-44, 45-48; foreman Tenn. Eastman Corp., Manhattan Project, 1944-45; asst. prof. chemistry Bowling Green State U., Ohio, 1949-50; instr. pharm. chemistry U. Wis.-Madison, 1952-55; asst. prof. chemistry San Jose State U., Calif., 1955-58, assoc. prof., 1958-61, prof., 1961-90, chmn. dept., 1973-86. Mem. Am. Chem. Soc., AAUP. Methodist. Home: 50 Cherokee Ln San Jose CA 95127-2513 Office: San Jose State U Dept Chemistry San Jose CA 95192

NEQUIST, JOHN LEONARD, retired food company executive; b. Sparta, Mich., July 31, 1929; s. John Ormond and Leola Irene (Fessenden) N.; m. Patricia Ann Kelley, Jan. 7, 1950; children: Eric Martin, Kelley Jo; m. Donna Jean Williams, 1990. B.B.A., U. Mich., 1956. With Kellogg Co., Battle Creek, Mich., 1957-88; chief accountant, then asst. controller Kellogg Co., 1967-75, controller, 1975-79, v.p., controller U.S. Foods Products div., 1979-84, dir. spl. assignments McCanly Sq. div., hotel and retail area, 1984-88. Chmn. planning and budget com. Battle Creek United Fund, 1969-70, Battle Creek Family/Childrens Service, 1973, Battle Creek United Arts Council, 1975; dir. spl. assignments Gov.'s Exec. Corps, 1984-85; bd. dirs. ARC, Battle Creek; chmn. bd. Downtown Bus. Assn., Battle Creek., 1987-88; mem. South Haven (Mich.) City Council. Served with USAF, 1948-52. Mem. Beta Alpha Psi. Home: 36 Lake Shore Dr South Haven MI 49090-1131 Home (winter): 196 Furse Lakes Cir Naples FL 33942-6436

NEREM, ROBERT MICHAEL, engineering educator, consultant; b. Chgo., July 20, 1937; s. Robert and Borghild Guneva (Bakken) N.; m. Jill Ann Thomson, Dec. 21, 1958 (div. 1977); children: Robert Steven, Nancy Ann Nerem Chambers; m. Marilyn Reed, Oct. 7, 1978; stepchildren: Christina Lynn Maser, Carol Marie Maser. BS, U. Okla., 1959; MS, Ohio State U., 1961, PhD, 1964; D (honoris causa), U. Paris, 1990. Asst. prof. Ohio State U., Columbus, 1964-68, assoc. prof., 1968-72, prof., 1972-79, assoc. dean Grad. Sch., 1975-79; prof. mech. engring., chmn. dept. U. Houston, 1979-86; Parker H. Petit prof. Ga. Inst. Tech., Atlanta, 1987—, Inst. prof., 1991—, dir. Inst. for Bioengring. and Biosci., 1995—; mem. Ga. Gov.'s Adv. Coun. on Sci. and Tech. Devel., Atlanta, 1992-95; ALZA disting. lectr. Biomed. Engring. Soc., 1991, ASME Thurston lectr., 1994. Contbr. over 100 articles to profl. jours. Fellow Am. Inst. Med. and Biol. Engring. (founding pres. 1992-94), ASME, AAAS; mem. NAE, Biomed. Engring. Soc., Inst. Medicine, Internat. Union for Phys. and Engring. Scis. in Medicine (pres. 1991-94), Internat. Fedn. for Med. and Biol. Engring. (pres. 1988-91), U.S. Nat. Com. on Biomechanics (1988-91 chmn.), Polish Acad. Scis. Home: 2950 Waverly Ct NW Atlanta GA 30339-4200 Office: Ga Inst Tech Inst Bioentring & Biosci 281 Ferst Dr Atlanta GA 33032-0363

NERENBERG, AARON, lawyer; b. Phila., Sept. 22, 1940; s. Jacob and Rose (Solominsky) N.; m. Adrianne Daufman, May 30, 1965; children: Jeffrey, Kimberly. BSME, Pa. State U., 1963; MSME, Villanova U., 1967; JD, Temple U., 1971. Bar: Pa. 1971, U.S. Dist. Ct. (ea. dist.) Pa., 1973, U.S. Ct. Appeals (3d cir.),1973, U.S. Supreme Ct., 1974, U.S. Patent Office, 1972. Devel. engr. Naval Air Engring. Ctr., Phila., 1963-71; sole practice Phila., 1971-72; patent advisor Naval Air Devel. Ctr., Warminster, Pa., 1972-74;

patent atty, SPS Techs. Inc., Jenkintown, Pa., 1974-78, patent counsel, 1978-82, assoc. gen. counsel, Newtown, Pa., 1982-86, gen. counsel, 1986—, sec., 1986—, v.p., 1988. Mem. ABA, Phila. Patent Law Assn. (chmn. placement com. 1977-85), Pa. State Alumni Assn. (v.p. 1982-86, Disting. Alumni award 1982). Republican. Jewish. Avocations: golf, swimming. Office: SPS Techs Inc Jenkintown Plz 101 Greenwood Ave Ste 470 Jenkintown PA 19046-2627

NERENZ, TIMOTHY THEODORE, accounting executive; b. Mpls., June 22, 1954; s. Kenneth Lester and Janet (Wray) N.; m. Joanne s. Schleicher, Sept. 8, 1984. Student, Carthage Coll., 1972-75, U. Wis., Madison, 1975-84. Warehouse supr. Gettys Mfg., Racine, Wis., 1975-78, prodn. mgr., 1978-81; materials mgr. Rayovac Corp., Madison, Wis., 1981-84; dir. bus. sys. Rayovac Corp., Portage, Wis., 1984-90; dir. info. sys. Lake Shore, Inc., Kingsford, Mich., 1990-92, dir. info. sys. and contract acctg., 1992-95, gen. mgr. mining products, 1995—; mfg. sys. cons. I.S.S., Inc., Racine, 1978-81; bd. dirs. SST Contractors, LaCrosse, Wis., 1986-89; ptnr. H.O.T.D. Assocs., Kingsford, 1993-94. Vol. Middleton (Wis.) Fire Dept., 1986-90; bd. dirs. Ducks Unltd., Kingsford, 1990-94; scout leader Cub Scouts, Middleton, 1984-87. Mem. Am. Prodn. and Inventory Control Soc., Data Processing Mgmt. Assn., Wis. Firefighters Assn., Oak Crest Country Club. Avocations: golf, hunting, skiing, hiking, photography. Home: 1509 Woodward Ave Iron Mountain MI 49801-4318 Office: Lake Shore Inc 900 W Breitung Ave Iron Mountain MI 49801-5316

NERLINGER, JOHN WILLIAM, trade association administrator; b. Detroit, June 22, 1920; s. John W. and Bessie Prudence (Beith) N.; m. Pearl Pauline Procup, Nov. 4, 1943; children: John Charles, Ruth Marie Nerlinger Blazevich. Grad., Detroit Bus. Inst., 1939; BA, Detroit Inst. Tech., 1950; LLD (hon.), Northwood U., Midland, Mich., 1990. Bus. mgr. Retail Gasoline Dealers Assn. Mich., Detroit, 1939-51; exec. sec. Retail Gasoline Dealers Assn. Mich., 1951-63, Nat. Congress Petroleum Retailers, Detroit, 1951-63; asst. exec. v.p. Automotive Service Industry Assn., Chgo., 1963-73; exec. v.p. Automotive Service Industry Assn., 1973-80, pres., 1981-91; ret., 1991; Vice chmn. Automotive Hall of Fame; advisor Nat. Hwy. Users Fedn. Served with AUS, 1942-45, PTO. Recipient Petroleum Man of Yr. award Gasoline News, 1961, Automotive Replacement Edn. award Northwood U., Midland, Mich., 1975, Disting. Svc. citation Automotive Hall of Fame, 1978, Industry Leadership award Automotive Svc. Industry Assn., 1978. Mem. Am. Soc. Assn. Execs. (mem. edn. com.), Chgo. Soc. Assn. Execs., Automotive Old Timers, Automotive Info. Council (dir.), Automotive Boosters Clubs Internat., Chgo. Assn. Commerce and Industry (mem. govt. relations com.), Nat. Assn. Wholesaler-Distbrs. (exec. com., dir. distbn. research and edn. found), Automotive Acad. Lutheran. Clubs: Mid-America, Inverness Golf. Lodge: Masons (32 deg.), Shriners. Home: 601 E Fairview St Arlington Heights IL 60005-2770

NERLOVE, MARC LEON, economics educator; b. Chgo., Oct. 12, 1933; s. Samuel Henry and Evelyn (Andelman) N.; children: Susan, Miriam. BA, U. Chgo., 1952; MA, Johns Hopkins U., 1955, PhD, 1956. Analytical statistician USDA, Washington, 1956-57; assoc. prof. U. Minn., Mpls., 1959-60; prof. Stanford (Calif.) U., Stanford U., 1960-65, Yale U., 1965-69; prof. econs. U. Chgo., 1969-74; F.W. Taussig rsch. prof. Harvard Coll., Cambridge, Mass., 1967-68; vis. Cook prof. Northwestern U., Evanston, Ill., 1973-74, Cook prof., 1974-82; prof. econs. U. Pa., Phila., 1982-86, Univ. prof., 1986-93; prof. agriculture and resource econs. U. Md., College Park, 1993—. Author: Dynamics of Supply, 1958, Distributed Lags and Demand Analysis, 1958, Estimation and Identification of Cobb-Douglas Production Functions, 1965, Analysis of Economic Time Series: A Synthesis, 1979, Household and Economy: Welfare Economics of Endogenous Fertility, 1987; contbr. numerous articles to profl. jours. 1st lt. AUS, 1957-59. Recipient award Am. Farm Econ. Assn., 1956, 58, 61, 79, P.S. Mahalanobis medal Indian Econ. Soc., 1975. Fellow Am. Statis. Assn., Econometric Soc. (v.p. 1980, pres. 1981), Am. Acad. Arts and Scis., Am. Agrl. Econ. Assn.; mem. NAS, Am. Econ. Assn. (mem. exec. com. 1977-79, John Bates Clark medal 1969), Royal Econ. Soc., Phi Beta Kappa, others. Achievements include research on economics of agriculture with particular reference to developing countries, population and economic growth; analysis of categorical data, particularly business and household surveys. Office: U Md Dept Agri & Rsch Econs College Park MD 20742-5535

NERO, ANTHONY VINCENT, JR., physicist, environmental scientist; b. Salisbury, Md., Apr. 11, 1942; s. Anthony V. Nero and Anna Elizabeth Coladonato. BS summa cum laude, Fordham U., 1964; PhD in Physics, Stanford U., 1971. Rsch. fellow physics dept. Fordham U., summers 1962-63; grad. rsch. asst. Nuclear Physics Lab., Stanford (Calif.) U., 1966-70; postdoctoral rsch. fellow Kellogg Radiation Lab., Calif. Inst. Tech., Pasadena, 1970-72; asst. prof. physics Princeton (N.J.) U., 1972-75; physicist energy and environ. div. Lawrence Berkeley (Calif.) Lab., 1975—, leader indoor radon group, 1980-86, sr. scientist, 1986—, dep. leader indoor environ. program, 1986-94; visitor nuclear power div. Electric Power Rsch. Inst., summers 1974-75; phys. sci. officer Non-Proliferation Bur., ADCA, 1978; lectr. dept. mech. engring. U. Calif., Berkeley, 1979, lectr. energy and resources program, 1980, lectr. Sch. Pub. Health, 1989, mem. environ. health scis. ctr., 1992-94, acad. coord. energy and resources program, 1993-94; mem. adv. com. 3d Internat. Conf. on Indoor Air Quality and Climate, Stockholm, 1984, symposium organizer, rapporteur for radon 4th Conf., Berlin, 1987; mem. various adv. and rev. panels EPA, 1984—; mem. program com. 4th Internat. Symposium on Natural Radiation Environ, Lisbon, 1987, 5th internat. syposium, Salzburg, Austria, 1991. Author: A Guidebook to Nuclear Reactors, 1979; co-author: Instrumentation for Environmental Monitoring, Vol. 1, 1983, Radon and Its Decay Products in Indoor Air, 1988; contbr. articles to profl. and popular publs., chpts. to books. Gen. Motors Corp. nat. scholar, 1960-64; NSF undergrad. summer rsch. fellow, 1962, 63, NSF grad. fellow, 1964-68. Fellow Am. Physics Soc. (panel on pub. affairs 1981-83, Leo Szilard award of Physics in the Pub. Interest 1989, exec. com. forum on physics and soc. 1988-90, vice-chair forum on physics and soc. 1992-93, chair-elect 1993-94, chair 1994-95); mem. AAAS, Health Physics Soc., Fedn. Am. Scientists, Soc. Risk Analysis, Phi Beta Kappa, Sigma Xi. Office: Lawrence Berkeley Lab 1 Cyclotron Rd Rm 3058 Berkeley CA 94720

NERO, PETER, pianist, conductor, composer, arranger; b. N.Y.C., May 22, 1934; s. Julius and Mary (Menasche) N.; m. Marcia Dunner, June 19, 1956; children—Beverly, Jedd; m. Peggy Altman, Aug. 31, 1977. Student, Juilliard Sch., N.Y.C. Nat. tour with Paul Whiteman on TV and in concert, 1953-57, appearances concert halls, theatres, colls., TV and supper clubs throughout U.S., Eng., France, Holland, Italy, Scandinavia, 1962—; appeared at Grand Gala du Disque, Amsterdam, The Netherlands, 1964, five TV specials on BBC-TV; arranged, appeared and recorded with Boston Pops Orch.; pops music dir. Tulsa Philharm., 1987—; music dir., Philly Pops Orch., 1979—, Fla. Philharm., 1981—; rec. artist for Arista Records, Pro Arte, Columbia; albums include Peter Nero Now, The Sounds of Love, Anything But Lonely and Peter Nero and Friends, 1993; appeared in film Sunday in New York; composer, condr. more than 150 symphony orchs., 1971—; recordings include (with the Rochester Philharmonic) Classic Connections. Honored by Internat. Soc. Performing Arts Adminstrs., 1986; recipient 8 Grammy nominations, 2 Grammy awards; named #1 Instrumentalist Cashbox Mag. Office: Tulsa Philharm 2901 S Harvard Ave Tulsa OK 74114-6119 also: care Gurtman & Murtha Assoc 450 7th Ave # 603 New York NY 10123-0101 also: Pro Arte 90 Intersound Internat Inc P O Box 1724 Roswell GA 30077

NEROD, STEVE (SCHEZEPAN ALEXANDER NEROD), entrepreneur, designer; b. Anchorage, June 15, 1952; s. Steve (Schezepan) and Eleanor (Maytak) Nierodzik. Student, U. Wash., 1970-72, U. Alaska, 1978-82, U. Calif., Berkeley, 1983-85. Owner Eldorado Placers, Eldorado Creek, Alaska, 1970-83, Nerod & Assocs. Apparel, San Francisco, Seattle, N.Y., 1971-82, Nerod Orthopedics, San Francisco and Seattle, 1982—, DoNots ATV, 1991—, RadGear Bicycles, 1992—, VAS-Comp, Hong Kong, 1993—, OrthoSys, Everett, Wash., 1994—, N.A.S.T.I., Everett, 1994—; cons. OrthoTech, San Leandro, Calif., Orthopedic Systems, Hayward, Calif., Med. Device Engring., Hayward, Israel Med. Products Devel., Tel Aviv, 1991—. Patentee in field. Mem. Am. Acad. Cosmetic Surgery, Am. Soc. Plastic and Reconstructive Surgery, Am. Orthopedic and Prosthetic Assn., Am. Assn. Orthopaedic Medicine, Am. Acad. Orthopaedic Surgeons, Alaska Miners Assn. Avocations: writing, art, archaeology, travel. Office: PO Box 5461 Everett WA 98206-5461

NERODE, ANIL, mathematician, educator; b. L.A., June 4, 1932; s. Nirad Ranjan and Agnes (Spencer) N.; m. Sondra Raines, Feb. 12, 1955 (div. 1968); children: Christopher Curtis, Gregory Daniel; m. Sally Riedel Sievers, May 16, 1970; 1 child, Nathanael Caldwell. B.A., U. Chgo., 1949, B.S., 1952, M.S., 1953, Ph.D., 1956. Group leader automata and weapons systems Lab. Applied Sci., U. Chgo., 1954-57; mem. Inst. for Advanced Study, Princeton, 1957-58, 62-63; vis. asst. prof. math. U. Calif. at Berkeley, 1958-59; mem. faculty Cornell U., 1959—, prof. math., 1965—, Goldwin Smith prof. math., 1990—, chmn. dept. math., 1982-87, dir. Math. Sci. Inst., 1986—; acting dir. Center for Applied Math., 1965-66; vis. prof. Monash U., Melbourne, Australia, 1970, 74, 78, 79, U. Chgo., 1976, M.I.T., 1980, U. Calif., San Diego, 1981; disting. vis. scientist EPA, 1985-87; prin. investigator numerous grants; CEO Sagent Corp., 1995—; mem. sci. adv. bd. EPA, 1988—, chair tech. adv. panel Global Change, 1990-92; mem. sci. adv. bd. Ctr. for Intelligent Control, Harvard-MIT-Brown U., 1988-94; cons. to govt. and industry. Author: (with John Crossley) Combinatorial Functors, 1974, (with Richard Shore) Logic for Applications, 1993; editor Advances in Mathematics, 1967-70, Jour. Symbolic Logic, 1967-82, Annals of Pure and Applied Logic, 1983—, Future Generation Computing Systems, 1983—, Jour. Pure & Applied Algebra, 1988—, Annals of Math. and Artificial Intelligence, 1989—, Logical Methods in Computer Sci., 1991—, Computer Modelling and Simulation, 1991—, Constraints, 1995—. Mem. AIII, IEEE, Assn. Computing Machinery, Am. Math. Soc. (assoc. editor procs. 1962-65, v.p. 1992-95), Soc. Indsl. and Applied Math., Math. Assn. Am., Assn. Symbolic Logic, European Assn. for Theoretical Computer Sci. Home: 406 Cayuga Heights Rd Ithaca NY 14850-1402 Office: Cornell U Math Sci Inst 409 College Ave Ithaca NY 14850-4694

NERREN, GEORGE N., school system administrator. Supt. Dyersburg (Tenn.) City Schs. State finalist Nat. Supt. Yr., 1993. Office: Dyersburg City Schs PO Box 1507 1025 Phillips St Dyersburg TN 38024-4114

NESBIT, ROBERT CARRINGTON, historian; b. Ellensburg, Wash., July 16, 1917; s. Sidney Shaw and Verna Mildred (Carrington) N.; m. Marie Richert, Nov. 24, 1942. B.A., Central Wash. Coll., 1939; M.A., U. Wash., 1947, Ph.D., 1957. Tchr. Cashmere (Wash.) Pub. Schs., 1939-41; state archivist Wash., 1951-57; adminstrv. asst. Wash. Dept. Gen. Adminstrn., 1958-59, supr. state purchasing, 1959-62; assoc. prof. U. Wis., Madison, 1962-68; prof., assoc. chmn. dept. history U. Wis., 1967-80. Author: He Built Seattle: A Biography of Judge Thomas Burke, 1961, Wisconsin, A History, 1973 (award of merit Am. Assn. State and Local History 1975), rev. edit. (with William F. Thompson Jr.), 1990; The History of Wisconsin, Vol. III, Industrialization and Urbanization, 1873-1893, 1985. Served with USAAF, 1941-46. Named Hon. fellow State Hist. Soc. Wis., 1986. Wis. History Found. grantee, 1971-72; NEH grantee, 1980-82. Home: 2406 Fir St SE Olympia WA 98501-3048

NESBIT, ROBERT GROVER, management consultant; b. Scranton, Pa., Feb. 8, 1932; s. George Archibald and Mildred Maude (Bohl) N.; m. Nancy Elizabeth Wilson, June 17, 1961; children: Robert, Jonathan. B.S., U. Scranton, 1957; M.S., NYU, 1958. Asst. to dean NYU, N.Y.C., 1960-64; mdse. mgr. Associated Merchandising Corp., N.Y.C., 1964-67; dir. corp. mktg. Genesco, Inc., Nashville, 1968-77; v.p., div. gen. mgr. Levi Straus & Co., San Francisco, 1977-79; sr. partner Korn/Ferry Internat., N.Y.C., 1979—. Trustee Rollins Coll., 1992-95, U. Scranton, 1995—. With U.S. Army, 1953-55. Mem. Nat. Retail Mchts. Assn., Am. Apparel Mfrs. Assn., Sigma Nu. Presbyterian. Club: N.Y. Athletic. Home: 71 Bank St New Canaan CT 06840-6203 Office: 237 Park Ave New York NY 10017-3142

NESBIT, WILLIAM TERRY, small business owner, consultant; b. Pitts., Jan. 30, 1945; s. William Frank and Glenna (Cleeton) N.; divorced. Owner, CEO Narrow Gauge Car Shop, Evergreen Outdoor Ctr., Shiremanstown, Pa., 1972-81; mem. faculty Millersville (Pa.) U., 1976-81, Temple U., Phila., 1979, Nat. Aquatic and Small Craft Sch., Bemis Point, N.Y., 1980, Harrisburg (Pa.) Area C. C., 1981-82, 91, Dickinson Coll., Carlisle, Pa., 1982-83; judge 32d Capital Area Sci., Engring. Fair, Dickinson Coll., Carlisle, Pa., 1989. Co-developer ARC basic and whitewater canoeing programs for instrn., 1977-79; developer The Z Drag for Boat Rescues, 1980; developer, mfr. first HOn3 ready-to-run plastic rolling stock having NMRA warrant. Vol. ARC, 1961—; contbr. A.C. Kalmbach Meml. Libr., Chattanooga. Recipient award for Humanity ARC, 1967, award for 30 Yrs. Vol. Svc., 1991; named Class I Radiological Protection Officer, U.S. Dept. of Defense, 1993. Mem. Math. Assn. Am., Nat. Assn. Canoe Liveries and Outfitters (founding), Nat. Model Railroad Assn. (life). Episcopalian. Avocations:. Office: Evergreen Outdoor Ctr PO Box 3081 Shiremanstown PA 17011-3081

NESBITT, ARTHUR WALLACE, mail order and manufacturing executive; b. Enon Valley, Pa., July 29, 1927; s. William and Frances Mildred (Gilmore) N.; m. Donna Saviers Fox, Aug. 19, 1967; children: Warren P., David G.; stepchildren: Marsha, Marilyn, William, Leann, Sandra Fox. B.S., Pa. State U., 1950. Asst. county agt. Pa. State U., Clarion, 1950-51; exec. sec. Pa. Holstein Assn., State College, 1952-59; v.p. sales Nasco, Fort Atkinson, Wis., 1959-71; exec. v.p. Nasco Internat., Inc., 1972-74, pres., CEO, 1974—; bd. dirs., v.p. World Dairy Expo, 1967-90; bd. dirs., treas. Nat. Dairy Shrine, 1969-93; chmn. bd., dir. Gehl Co., Bank Ft. Atkinson, Geneve Corp. Bd. govs. Agrl. Hall of Fame; bd. dirs. Wis. 4-H Found., Competitive Wis., Blue Cross-Blue Shield United Wis., 1990—, United Wis. Svc., 1991—; trustee Pa. State U., 1987-88. With U.S. Army, 1945-46. Recipient Nat. 4-H Alumni award, 1979, Fellow award Pa. State U., Disting. Alumnus award, Pa. State U., 1987; named Hon. County Agt., 1988, Person of Yr. World Dairy Expo. Industry, 1989, Guest of Honor Nat. Dairy Shrine, 1993. Mem. Dairy and Food Industries Supply Assn. (bd. dirs., past pres. 1974—), Wis. Mfg. and Commerce Assn. (bd. dirs. 1980—, chmn. 1990-91), Nat. Speakers Assn., Am. Dairy Sci. Assn., Holstein-Friesian Assn. Am., Pa. State U. Soc. for Disting. Alumni (pres. 1993—), Delta Theta Sigma (past pres.), Gamma Sigma Delta. Mem. United Ch. of Christ. Home: 711 Blackhawk Dr Fort Atkinson WI 53538-1047 Office: Nasco Internat Inc 901 Janesville Ave Fort Atkinson WI 53538-2402

NESBITT, CHARLES RUDOLPH, lawyer, energy consultant; b. Miami, Okla., Aug. 30, 1921; s. Charles Rudolph and Irma Louise (Wilhelmi) N.; m. Margot Dorothy Lord, June 6, 1948; children: Nancy Margot Nesbitt Nagle, Douglas Charles, Carolyn Jane Nesbitt Gresham. B.A., U. Okla., 1942; LL.B., Yale, 1947. Bar: Okla. 1947, U.S. Supreme Ct. 1957. Pvt. practice Oklahoma City, 1948-62, 67-69;, 75-91, 95—; atty. gen. Okla., 1963-67; mem. Okla. Corp. Commn., 1968-75, chmn., 1969-75; sec. of energy State of Okla., Oklahoma City, 1991-95; pvt. practice Oklahoma City, 1995—; Okla. rep., v.p. Interstate Oil and Gas Compact. Bd, dirs., trustee endowment fund St. Gregory's Coll.; trustee Oklahoma City U.; pres. Hist. Preservation, Inc.; pres. bd. trustees Okla. Mus. Art; v.p., bd. dirs. Western History Collections Assocs., U. Okla. Librs.; mem. panel arbitrators Am. Arbitration Assn., NASD, NYSE; mem. Ecclesiastical Ct., Diocese Okla. With AUS, 1942-46. Mem. Am., Okla. bar assns., Oklahoma City C. of C., Phi Beta Kappa, Phi Delta Phi. Episcopalian. Home: 1703 N Hudson Ave Oklahoma City OK 73103-3428 Office: 125 NW 6th St Oklahoma City OK 73102

NESBITT, LEE TERRELL, JR., dermatologist; b. Gaffney, S.C., May 2, 1941. MD, Tulane U., 1966. Intern Charity Hosp., Tulane U., New Orleans, 1966-67, resident in dermatology, 1969-72; prof., head dept. dermatology La. State U. Sch. Medicine, New Orleans; attending physician Univ. Hosp., New Orleans. Fellow ACP; mem. Am. Acad. Dermatology, Am. Dermatology Assn. Office: La State U Med Ctr 1542 Tulane Ave New Orleans LA 70112-2825*

NESBITT, LENORE CARRERO, federal judge; m. Joseph Nesbitt; 2 children: Sarah, Thomas. A.A., Stephens Coll., 1952; BS, Northwestern U., 1954; student U. Fla. Law Sch., 1954-55; LLB, U. Miami, 1957. Rsch. asst. Dist. Ct. Appeal, 1957-59, Dade County Cir. Ct., 1963-65; pvt. practice Nesbitt & Nesbitt, 1960-63; spl. asst. attorney gen., 1961-63; with Law Offices of John Robert Terry, 1969-73; counsel, Fla. State Bd. Med. Examiners, 1970-71; with Petersen, McGowan & Feder, 1973-75; judge Fla. Cir. Ct., 1975-82, U.S. Dist. Ct. (so. dist.) Fla., Miami, 1983—. Bd. trustees U. Miami; bd. dirs. Miami Children's Hosp. Mem. FBA, Fla. Bar Assn., U.S. Jud. Conf. Com. on Criminal Law and Probation Adminstrn. Office: US Dist Ct 301 N Miami Ave Miami FL 33128-7702*

NESBITT, LEROY EDWARD, inventor, design specialist; b. Phila., Sept. 14, 1925; s. Lonnie Reynolds and Josephine Elvira N.; student Temple U., 1965-69; m. Vivian Elizabeth Lee, June 27, 1952; 1 son, Warren Eric. Founder, pres. Incentives, Inc., Wilmington, Del., 1975—; design specialist Sperry Corp., Blue Bell, Pa. Served with U.S. Army, 1943-46. Decorated Bronze Star (4). Home and Office: 6213 Gardenia St Philadelphia PA 19144-1608

NESBITT, LLOYD IVAN, podiatrist; b. Toronto, Ont., Can., Sept. 24, 1951; s. Allan Jay and Rose (Shuster) N.; m. Marlene Cindy Wegler, May 13, 1984; children: Hilary Liza, Andrea Eve, Jeffrey Ryan. D in Podiatric Medicine, Calif. Coll. Podiatric Medicine, San Francisco, 1975. Diplomate Internat. Soc. Podiatric Laser Surgery. Residency program Vancouver (B.C.) Gen. Hosp., Can., 1975-76; pvt. practice podiatric medicine Toronto; cons. podiatry Alan Eagleson Sports Medicine Clinic, Toronto, 1979—; lectr. numerous colls., fitness ctrs. and sports medicine confs., Ont., 1979—. Contbr. numerous articles to sports medicine books and jours; editor Canadian Podiatrist Jour., 1979-88. Fellow Can. Podiatric Sports Medicine Acad. (pres. 1979-89, editor newsletter 1977-89), Am. Acad. Podiatric Sports Medicine; mem. Internat. Soc. Podiatric Laser Surgery (diplomate), Am. Podiatric Med. Assn., Sierra Club. Avocations: skiing, in-line skating, sailing, cycling, gardening. Home: 122 Argonne Crescent, Willowdale, ON Canada M2K 2K1 Office: Madison Ctr Office Tower, 4950 Yonge St Ste 2414, Toronto, ON Canada M2N 6K1

NESBITT, MARK, management consultant; b. Ottawa, Ont., Can., Dec. 31, 1952; s. William Alonzo and Barbara (Ellis) N.; 1 child, Karen Elizabeth. BSc, Carleton U., Ottawa, 1973, BA, 1974; MBA, Harvard U., 1978. Cert. Mgmt. Cons. Cons. Peat Marwick & Ptnrs., Ottawa, 1978; assoc./mgr. Veritas Cons. Inc., Toronto, Ont., Can., 1978-86, pres., 1986-93; pres., CEO Vertex Cons. Inc., Toronto, 1993—; IS com. mem. YMCA Metro Toronto, 1992-93; bd. dirs. Inst. Cert. Mgmt. Cons. Can. Mem. Am. Mktg. Assn., Inst. Cert. Mgmt. Cons. Ont. (vice-chmn. firms com.), Assn. for Creative Change, Internat. Mgmt. Devel. (1st v.p., sec.-treas.). Anglican. Avocations: bicycling, photography, programming. Office: Vertex Cons Inc, 14 Dundonald St, Toronto, ON Canada M4Y 1K2

NESBITT, PAUL EDWARD, historian, author, educator; b. Balt., Dec. 25, 1943; s. William Ervin and Margaret Caroline (Shaw) N.; m. Donna Jean Coppock, Aug. 15, 1966 (dec. 1972); children: Erik-Paul A., Janelle M., m. Pamela Jean Lichty, May 25, 1974 (div. 1983); m. Anita Louise Wood, Dec. 8, 1984 (div. 1989); m. Paula Jane Sawyer, May 7, 1994. AB, U. Wash., 1965; MA, Wash. State U., 1968, PhD (hon.), 1970; PhD, U. Calgary, 1972. Reader in Anthropology, U. Wash., 1965, grad. research-tchr. Wash. State U., 1966-68, instr., Tacoma Community Coll., Wash., 1968-69; grad. research-tchr. U. Calgary, Alta., Can., 1969-71; exec. Hudson's Bay Co., Calgary, 1971; prof. Western Oreg. U., Monmouth, 1971-74; state historian State of Calif., Sacramento, 1974—; dir. Am. Sch. of Interior Design, San Francisco, 1974, HBC Bow Fort Rsch., Morley, Atla., 1970-71; instr. Am. River Coll., Sacramento, 1980-86; exec. mgr. Calif. State Govt. United Way Campaign, 1986, 87, also bd. dirs., mem. fiscal and communication coms., El Dorado County and Sacramento chpts., 1988—; designer, cultural rsch. cons. pvt. contracts western states, 1960—; exec. dir. Heritage Areas Assn., 1993—, pres. bd. dir., 1994—. Contbr. articles to prof. jours. Fellow Am. Anthropl. Assn.; mem. Calif. Hist. Soc., Am. Inst. of Interior Designers (profl. 1974-77, bd. dirs. energy planning and devel. cos. 1986-88), AIA (Cen. Valley chpt. 1975-77), Rotary. Home: 3177 Clark St Placerville CA 95667-6405 Office: PO Box 942896 Sacramento CA 94296-0001

NESBITT, ROBERT EDWARD LEE, JR., physician, educator; b. Albany, Ga., Aug. 21, 1924; s. Robert E.L. and Anne Louise (Hill) N.; m. Ellen Therese Morrissey. B.A., Vanderbilt U., 1944, M.D., 1947. Diplomate: Am. Bd. Ob-Gyn (asso. examiner). Asst. prof. Johns Hopkins U., 1954-56, chief obstetric pathology lab., acting chief obstetrics, 1955-56; prof., chmn. dept. ob-gyn Albany (N.Y.) Med. Coll., Union U., 1956-61; prof., chmn. dept. ob-gyn SUNY Health Sci. Ctr., Syracuse, 1961-81, dir. gen. gynecology service, 1982-84, prof. and chmn. emeritus dept. ob-gyn; obstetrician-gynecologist-in-chief Albany Hosp., 1956-61; obstetrician, gynecologist-in-chief Syracuse Meml. Hosp., 1961-65; obstetrician-gynecologist-in-chief Crouse-Irving Hosp., 1963-70, attending staff, 1970-84; prof. surgery U. South Fla., Tampa, 1988-92, prof. ob.-gyn., 1988-92; chief ob-gyn State U. Hosp., 1964-81, chmn. med. staff and med. bd., 1964-66; attending staff St. Joseph's Hosp.; cons., chief gynecology sect. surg. service Syracuse VA Hosp., 1984-88; chief gynecology sect., asst. chief surgery, dir. urogynecology VA Med. Ctr., Bay Pines, Fla., 1988-92, acting chief of staff, 1990, interim chief surgery, 1991-92, chmn. O.R. com. surg. svc., 1988-92, chmn. patient care evaluation com., 1989-90, chmn. clin. exec. bd., 1990, chmn. drug usage evaluation com., 1990-91, chmn. profl. standards bd., 1990; cons. Syracuse Psychiat. Inst.; mem. cancer tng. grants and edn. com. Nat. Cancer Insts.; mem. adv. com. Bur. Maternal and Child Health, N.Y. State Dept. Health, 1957-61; nat. adviser to Children, publ. of Children's Bur., HEW, 1959-63; cons. Children's Bur., 1959-62; mem. prenatal care guide subcom. Am. Pub. Health Assn., 1962-64; cons. to regional adviser in maternal and child health Pan Am. San. Bur., WHO, 1963-65; numerous guest professorships including univs. in Mex., Chile, Uruguay, Colombia, St. Vincent (W.I.), Venezuela, People's Republic of China; numerous guest professorships including univs. in others. Author: Perinatal Loss in Modern Obstetrics, 1957; sect. on ob-gyn in Rypin's Med. Licensure Exams; also chpts. in numerous anthologies; co-author: Infant, Perinatal, Maternal and Childhood Mortality in U.S, 1968; editor: sect. on obstetrics and gynecology Stedman's Medical Dictionary, 1958-64; sect. on fetus Funk and Wagnalls Universal Standard Ency, 1959; 1st guest editor: sect. on fetus Clinics in Perinatology, 1974; 1st editor: sect. on fetus Clinical Diagnosis Quiz for Obstetrics and Gynecology, 1976, Clini-Pearls in Obstetrics and Gynecology, 1977; contbr. to: sect. on fetus Attorneys' Textbook of Medicine. Capt. M.C., U.S. Army, 1952-54. Named One of Ten Outstanding Young Men in Am., U.S. Jr. C. of C., 1957; Robert E.L. Nesbitt Jr. scholarship, Sr. Resident in Ob-Gyn, and Robert E.L. Nesbitt Jr. student scholarship established in his honor, SUNY Health Sci. Ctr. at Syracuse, 1987. Fellow Am. Assn. Maternal and Child Health, Am. Coll. Obstetricians and Gynecologists (chmn. com. mental retardation and perinatal health 1966), A.C.S. (com. forum fundamental surg. problems 1962-67), Venezuelan Obstetrics-Gynecol. Soc. (hon.), N.Y. Acad. Scis.; mem. AMA, Soc. for Gynecol. Investigations (council), Pan Am. Med. Assn. (med. ambassador goodwill, life mem. sect. on cancer), Med. Soc. N.Y. State (regional obstetrics chmn., subcom. Maternal and Child Welfare), Onondaga County Med. Soc., Am. Soc. Cytology, Pub. Health Council N.Y. State, Alpha Omega Alpha; hon. mem. Southwest, Fla. obstet. and gynecol. socs., others. Research and 230 publs. on cytologic, cytochem. and histochem. study of early cervical cancer, perinatal and placental pathology, cytologic and hormonal studies in normal and high-risk obstet. patiens, exptl. prodn. of abruptio placentae, reproductive endocrinology, animal experimentation, induced endocrine insults upon pregnant and nonpregnant ewes and hormonal influence on placentation, invitro placenta perfusion, fetal growth and devel., female urology, new surgical technique for restoration of female pelvic floor integrity while preserving the uterus (published 1989); creation science. Home: 11639 Grove St North Seminole FL 34642-7137

NESBITT, ROSEMARY SINNETT, theatre educator; b. Syracuse, N.Y., Oct. 12, 1924; d. Matthew A. and Mary Louise (Kane) Sinnett; m. George R. Nesbitt, June 18, 1955 (dec. Nov. 1971); children: Mary, Anne, George R., Elizabeth. BS magna cum laude, Syracuse U., 1947, MS, 1952. Instr. in speech Wells Coll., Aurora, N.Y., 1949-52, Syracuse U., 1952-57; asst. prof. SUNY, Oswego, 1965-68, assoc. prof., 1968-72, prof. theatre, 1972-77, Disting. teaching prof., 1977—, dir. children's theatre, 1969—; cons., lectr. pub. schs., N.Y. and New Eng., 1965—; lectr. in field. Author: The Great Rope, 1968, Colonel Meacham's Giant Cheese, 1971; (play) The Great Rope, 1975 (George Washington medal Freedom Found. 1975); plays for children. Founding mem. Oswego Heritage Found., 1963; historian City of Oswego, 1973-80, 88—; founder, bd. dirs. H. Lee White Marine Mus., Oswego, 1983—; chmn. bd. dirs. Port of Oswego Authority, 1986-88, bd. dirs., 1978-88. Recipient George R. Arents Disting. Alumnus award Syracuse U., 1975,

Jefferson award Jefferson Award Com., 1984, Svc. to Arts award Cultural Resources Coun. Onondaga County, 1985, Franklin award for Disting. Svc. in Transp. Syracuse U. Sch. mgmt., 1989, Amelia Earhart Woman of the Yr. award Zonta Club of Oswego; named Woman of Yr. in Cultural Devel., Syracuse Post Standard, 1971, Citizen of Yr., City of Oswego, 1974. Mem. AAUW, Alpha Psi Omega. Democrat. Roman Catholic. Avocations: history, reading, travel. Home: 119 W 4th St Oswego NY 13126-2002 Office: SUNY Theatre Dept Oswego NY 13126

NESBITT, VANCE GORDON, computer software company executive; b. Apr. 27, 1959. Student in computer sci., U. Tex., 1977-82. Operator Seismic Data Ctr. Tex. Instruments, Austin, 1983-84; facilities and tech. svcs. assoc. Microelectronics & Computer Tech. Corp., Austin, 1984-85; v.p. product devel. Kent * Marsh Ltd., Houston, 1985-90; chmn., CEO Kent & Marsh Ltd., Houston, 1990—. Author: (comml software) MacSafe, 1990, FolderBolt, 1992. Mem. IEEE Computer Soc., Computer Security Inst., Nat. Computer Security Assn., Assn. Computing Machinery, Electronic Frontier Found., Computer Profls. for Social Responsibility, Info. Systems Security Assn., South Tex. Info. Systems Security, Houston Area Apple Users Group, Houston Area League of PC Users, Boston Computer Soc., Apple Programmers and Developers Assn., Assn. Corp. Computing Tech. Profls., Data Processing Mgmt. Assn., Optimist Club, Alpha Phi Omega. Office: Kent & Marsh Ltd 3260 Sul Ross St Houston TX 77098-1930

NESHEIM, DENNIS WARREN, art educator, instructional materials producer; b. Decorah, Iowa, Nov. 24, 1948; s. Kenneth H. and Adelle T. (Amundson) N.; m. Lavonne Selene Jones, Mar. 29, 1968. AA, Rochester State Jr. Coll., Minn., 1970; BS in Art/Art Edn., Winona (Minn.) State U., 1972. cert. art tchr. K-12, Minn., Wis., Dept. Def. Dependent Schs. Tchr. art Cassville (Wis.) Pub. Schs., 1972-74, Franklin Mid. Sch., Shawano, Wis., 1974-76; substitute tchr., tchr. 4th grade Dept. Def. Dependent Schs., Neu Ulm, Germany, 1977-78; tchr. art Ulm. Am. Sch. Dept. Def. Dependent Schs., Neu Ulm, 1978-80, tchr. art and video arts, 1980-87; tchr., artist art ctrs., Fla., 1987-89; owner, producer Nesheim Arts & Video, Lakeland Fla., Lakewood, Colo., 1989—; tchr. art, tchr. aide Synergy Sch., Denver, Colo.; presenter workshops and seminars, 1980-86; video tng., cons., Lakeland, 1988-93. Author, illustrator: (workbook) Making Waves, An Imagination Starter, 1994; creator, producer: (instrnl. video/handbook kits) Look and Draw series, 1990—; editor lit. quar. Onionhead, 1989-93, others. Mem. Arts on Park, Lakeland Ctr. for Creative Arts, 1987-95, bd. dirs., 1991-93. Recipient various commendations and appreciation awards from schs. and cmty. orgns. Mem. Nat. Art Edn. Assn., Fine Art Forum, Compuserve, Amnesty Internat. Avocations: hiking, reading, creative cooking. Office: Synergy Sch 4123 S Julian Way Denver CO 80236

NESHEIM, MALDEN C., academic administrator. Provost emeritus Cornell U., Ithaca, N.Y. Office: Cornell U 376 Uris Hall Ithaca NY 14853

NESHEIM, ROBERT OLAF, food products executive; b. Monroe Center, Ill., Sept. 13, 1921; s. Olaf M. and Sena M. (Willms) N.; m. Emogene P. Sullivan, July 13, 1946 (divorced); children: Barbara Mowry, Susan Yost (dec.), Sandra Rankin; m. doris Howes Calloway, July 4, 1981. BS, U. Ill., 1943, MS, 1950, PhD, 1951; postgrad. in advanced mgmt. program, Harvard U., 1971. Farm mgr. Halderman Farm Mgmt. Svc., Wabash, Ind., 1946-48; instr. U. Ill., 1951; mgr. feed rsch. The Quaker Oats Co., Barrington, Ill., 1952-64; prof., head of dept. animal sci. U. Ill., 1964-67; dir. nutrition rsch. The Quaker Oats Co., Barrington, Ill., 1967-69, v.p. R & D, 1969-78; v.p. sci. & tech. The Quaker Oats Co., Chgo., 1978-83; sr. v.p. sci. & tech. Avadyne, Inc., Monterey, Calif., 1983-85; pres. Advanced Healthcare, Monterey, 1985-91; ret., 1991. Capt. U.S. Army, 1943-46, South Pacific. Fellow Am. Inst. Nutrition (treas. 1983-86), AAAS; mem. Inst. Food Technologists, Fed. Socs. Exptl. Biologists (treas. 1973-79), APHA, Corral de Tierra Club (Salinas, Calif.). Avocations: gardening, golf.

NESIN, JEFFREY D., academic administrator; b. N.Y.C.; m. Diane Garvey, 1968; children: Kate Dillon, Sarah Grace. BA in Eng. Lit., Hobart Coll., 1966; MA in Eng. Lit, SUNY, Buffalo, 1971, MA in Am. Studies, 1973. Faculty dept. humanities & scis. Sch. Visual Arts, N.Y.C., 1974-91; pres. Memphis Coll. Art, 1991—; adj. lectr. CCNY, Hunter Coll.; advisor dept. fine arts Sch. Visual Arts, 1975-82, dir. spl. programs, 1978-91, asst. to pres., 1982-91; cons. Smithsonian Instn., IBM, 1st Tenn. Bank; panelist, speaker in field. Contbg. editor: High Fidelity, Creem; contbr. reviews, interviews, essays to mags.; adv. editor Jour. Popular Music and Society. Mem. Am. Studies Assn., Met. Am. Studies Assn. (past pres.), Assn. Ind. Colls. Art & Design (bd. dirs. 1991—), Memphis Rotary, Nat. Assn. Schs. Art & Design (commn. accreditation 1993—). Avocations: mystery novels, barbecue, baseball. Office: Memphis Coll Art Office of President 1930 Poplar Ave Memphis TN 38104-2756 Home: 1545 Vinton Ave Memphis TN 38104-4923

NESMITH, MICHAEL, film producer, video specialist; b. Houston, Dec. 30, 1942; s. Warren and Bette Nesmith; m. Phyliss Nesmith; children: Christian, Jonathan, Jessica; m. 2d, Kathryn Nesmith. Chmn., chief exec. officer Pacific Arts Corp. (div. Nesmith Enterprises), L.A., 1987—. Author, producer, performer various records, 1968-77; mem. (rock group) The Monkees; co-author, exec. producer: (films) including Timerider; actor: (films) Head, 1968, Burglar, 1987, (TV series) The Monkees; exec. producer: (films) Repo Man, 1984, Square Dance, 1986, Tapeheads, 1988; exec. producer, actor: (video) Dr. Duck's Super Secret All-Purpose Sauce; producer: (series) Television Parts, 1985; co-author, producer: (pilot) for TV Pop Clips, original concept for MTV.; creator PBS Home Video. Trustee Gihon Found., 1970—, McMurray Found., 1970—. Recipient 1st Video Grammy for Elephant Parts. Christian Scientist. Office: Pacific Arts Corp 11858 La Grange Ave Ste 210 Los Angeles CA 90025-5230

NESMITH, RICHARD DUEY, clergyman, theology educator; b. Belleville, Kans., Jan. 9, 1929; s. Eugene Gordon and Edith Mae (Duey) N.; m. Patricia N. Nichols, Aug. 24, 1985; children: Leslie Ann, Lisa Lorraine, Laurel Sue, Lana Louise, Christopher Toscano. B.A., Nebr. Wesleyan U., 1950; M.Div., Garrett Evang. Sem., 1953; Ph.D., Boston U., 1957. Ordained to ministry United Methodist Ch., 1953; dean students MacMurray Coll., Jacksonville, Ill., 1957-61; prof. sociology of religion St. Paul's Sch. Theology, Kansas City, 1961-67; dir. planning Nat. div. Methodist Bd. of Global Ministries, N.Y.C., 1967-73; pastor Trinity Ch., Lincoln, Nebr., 1973-77; dean Sch. Theology Boston U., 1977-88, prof., 1988—; bd. dirs. State Line Farms, Inc.; pres. Nesmith Inc. Producer religious TV program, Perspectives. Office: Boston U Sch Theology 745 Commonwealth Ave Rm 438 Boston MA 02215-1401

NESS, ALBERT KENNETH, artist; b. St. Ignace, Mich., June 21, 1903; s. Albert Klingberg and Violet Matilda (Sutherland); m. Lenore Consuelo Chrisman, Aug. 4, 1926; children: Peter, James Kenneth, Jane Lenore. Student U. Detroit, 1923-24, Detroit Sch. of Applied Art, 1924-26, Wicker Sch. of Fine Art, 1926-28; Diploma, Sch. of Art Inst., 1932. Show-card writer, window display man S.S. Kresge Co., Detroit, 1923-24; artist poster and advt. Cunningham Drugs, Detroit, 1924-26; artist layout lettering and design W.L. Flemming Studios, Detroit, 1926-28, McAleer Displays, Chgo., 1929-32; artist, design asst. Layman-Whitney Assocs., 1933 World's Fair, Chgo.; layout artist, poster designer Elevated Advt. Co., Chgo., 1934-37; instr., art dir. Sch. of Applied Art, Chgo., 1938-40; Carnegie resident artist U. N.C., Chapel Hill, 1941-43, dir. War Art Ctr., 1942-43, resident artist, assoc. prof. art, 1943-49, acting head, dept. art, acting dir. Person Hall Art Gallery, 1944-45, resident artist, prof. art, 1949-73, acting head dept. of art, acting dir. Person Hall Art Gallery, 1955, 57-58, resident artist, prof. emeritus, 1973—. One man shows include: Chester Johnson Galleries, Chgo., 1932, Evanston Art Ctr., Ill., 1940, Person Hall Art Gallery, 1941, N.C. Art Soc. Gallery, Raleigh, 1942, Duke U. Art Gallery, Durham, N.C., 1955, Louisburg Coll. Gallery, N.C., 1964, Ackland Art Mus., U.N.C. Chapel Hill, 1973; Internat. Water Color Exhbn. Chgo. Art Inst., 1934-39; Golden Gate Internat. Exposition, San Francisco, 1939, exhibited in group shows: Whitney Mus., N.Y.C., 1933, U. Chattanooga, Tenn., 1946, Centennial Exhbn. U. Fla., Gainesville, 1953, Jacksonville Art Mus, Fla., 1960; exhibited nationally Am. Artists' Anns., Chgo. Art Inst., 1935-37, Butler Art Inst., Youngstown, Ohio, 1951, Pa. Acad. Am. Annuals, Phila., 1953-54, Optique Gallery, Lambertville, N.J., 1991—, Ross-Constantine Gallery, N.Y.C., 1991—, Marita Gilliam Gallery, Raleigh, N.C., 1993—, others; works in pub. collections include: N.C. Mus., Raleigh, Ackland Art Mus., Reynolds Found., Winston Salem, Duke U. Art Mus., Durham. Contbr. to local and state newspapers. Editor, designer, photographer: A brochure on art study, 1964. Recipient Jenkins Meml. prize 38th Ann. Chgo. Artists' Exhbn., 1934, Purchase award N.C. Artists' Ann., Raleigh, 1953; 2-Star award Movie Maker Competition, London, 1970, N.C. award in Fine Arts, 1973, Purchase award Reynolds Competition, Winston Salem, 1977. Home: PO Box 14 Chapel Hill NC 27514-0014

NESS, ANDREW DAVID, lawyer; b. San Francisco, Oct. 29, 1952; s. Orville Arne and Muriel Ruth (Trendt) N.; m. Rita M. Kobylenski, May 25, 1980; children: Katherine, Austin, Emily. BS, Stanford U., 1974; JD, Harvard U., 1977. Bar: Calif. 1977, D.C. 1979, Va. 1986, U.S. Dist. Ct. (no. dist.) Calif. 1977, U.S. Dist. Ct. D.C. 1983, U.S. Dist. Ct. (ea. dist.) Va. 1988, U.S. Ct. Appeals (4th cir.) 1989. Law clk. U.S. Dist. Ct., San Francisco, 1977-78; assoc. Lewis, Mitchell & Moore, Vienna, Va., 1979-82, ptnr., 1982-87; ptnr. Morgan, Lewis & Bockius LLP, Washington, 1987—; instr. U. Md., College Park, 1987-90; mem. faculty constrn. exec. program Stanford (Calif.) U., 1984-87. Contbr. chpt. to book, 1990, also articles to profl. jours. Mem. ABA (forum on constrn. industry, vice-chair environ. restoration com., pub. contract law sect.). Avocations: hiking, bicycling. Office: Morgan Lewis & Bockius LLP 1800 M St NW Washington DC 20036-5802

NESS, FREDERIC WILLIAM, former academic administrator, educator, consultant; b. York, Pa., Feb. 2, 1914; s. Harry and Rosalyn Barbara (Eichelberger) N.; m. Dore Roberts, June 30, 1943 (dec. May 1959); children: Lynne, Diane, Merryl, Melanie Barbara; m. Eleanor H. Hedge, Sept. 1, 1962 (dec. May 1994); 1 child, Brook H. A.B., Dickinson Coll., 1933, LL.D., 1973; student, Cin. Conservatory Music, 1930, 31, 33-35; A.M., U. Cin., 1935; Ph.D., Yale U., 1940; Litt.D., Ursinus Coll., 1971, Coll. Idaho, 1972, Monmouth Coll., 1976; L.H.D., Beaver Coll., 1972, Millikin U., 1972, Coll. St. Scholastica, 1972, Ottawa U., 1976, York Coll., 1978, Moravian Coll., 1984; Ped. D., Hofstra U., 1975; H.H.D., Rider Coll., 1975, Bridgewater Coll., 1977; LL.D., Elizabethtown Coll., 1976, New Eng. Coll., 1982. Instr. English, dean men Cin. Conservatory Music, 1938-39; instr. English U. Cin., 1939, Yale U., 1939-42; fellow Berkeley Coll., Yale U., 1940-42; asst. to vice chancellor/sec. NYU, 1945-52; dean, prof. English Dickinson Coll., 1952-60, acad. v.p., 1955-60, chmn. dept. English, 1956-58, William W. Edel prof. humanities, 1959-60; v.p., provost, dean Grad. Sch. L.I. U., 1960-62; v.p. Hofstra U., 1962-64; pres. Fresno (Calif.) State Coll., 1964-69, pres. emeritus, 1975—; pres. Assn. Am. Colls., Washington, 1969-78, pres. emeritus, 1978—; founding dir. Presdl. Search Consultation Svc., 1979-86, sr. cons., 1986-94; vis. prof. Poly. Inst., San German, P.R., 1955; mem. Pa. Gov.'s Com. Edn., 1958-60; pres. Western Colls. Assn., 1967-69. Author: The Use of Rhyme in Shakespeare's Plays, 1941; co-author: Graduate Study in the Liberal Arts College, 1961; editor, author: The Role of the College in the Recruitment of Teachers, 1958, A Guide to Graduate Study, 1957, 61, A Regional Faculty Orientation Program, 1961, An Uncertain Glory, 1970. Chmn. bd. dirs. Cmty. Chest, Carlisle, Pa., 1960; bd. dirs. Bklyn. Acad., 1960-62, Fresno Philharmonic Orch., 1965-69, Am. Coun. Edn., 1968-69, Change, 1970-72, Common Fund, 1970-76, Catalyst, 1974-78, Ind. Coll. Fund Am., 1976-86, Moravian Coll., 1976-84, Am. U., 1980-88, Annapolis Life Care, 1994—, Md. Hall for Creative Arts, 1990-95; bd. dirs., pres. Tchg. Film Custodians, 1970-73; mem. acad. adv. bd. U.S. Naval Acad., 1978-86. Lt. commdr. USNR, 1942-46. Mem. Elizabethan Club, Cosmos Club, Annapolis Yacht Club, Phi Beta Kappa, Beta Gamma Sigma, Omicron Delta Kappa, Phi Mu Alpha, Beta Theta Pi. Presbyterian. Office: 3105 River Crescent Dr Annapolis MD 21401-7719

NESS, JAMES MCCULLIE, JR., sales and marketing executive; b. Trenton, N.J., Nov. 4, 1940; s. James McCullie and Genevieve (O'Neill) N. Student, Loyola U., Montreal, 1959-60, Loyola U., Chgo., 1970-73, Rutgers U., 1970. Salesperson Rheem Mfg., Linden, N.J., 1966-70; dist. sales mgr. Imco divsn. Ethyl Corp., Richmond, Va., 1970-82; dir. devel. Continental Glass & Plastic, Chgo., 1982-85; dir. sales/mktg. Dana Plastic Container Corp., Arlington Heights, Ill., 1985—. Bd. dirs. Edgewater Community Coun., Chgo., 1991—, Edgewater Devel. Corp., Chgo., 1992—. With USN, 1961-66. Mem. Inst. Packaging Profls., Chgo. Perfumers, Am. Mgmt. Assn., East Bank Club (Chgo.). Republican. Roman Catholic. Home: 6334 N Sheridan Rd Chicago IL 60660-1754 Office: Dana Plastic Container Corp 6 N Hickory Ave Arlington Heights IL 60004-6205

NESS, NORMAN FREDERICK, astrophysicist, educator, administrator; b. Springfield, Mass., Apr. 15, 1933; s. Herman Hugo and Eva (Carlson) N.; children: Elizabeth Ann, Stephen Andrew. B.S., Mass. Inst. Tech., 1955, Ph.D., 1959. Space physicist, asst. prof. geophysics UCLA, 1959-61; Nat. Acad. Sci.-NRC post doctoral research assoc. NASA, 1960-61; research physicist in space scis. Goddard Space Flight Center, Greenbelt, Md., 1961-86; head extraterrestrial physics br. Goddard Space Flight Center, 1968-69; chief Lab. for Extraterrestrial Physics, 1969-86; pres., prof. Bartol Research Inst., U. Del., 1987—; lectr. math. U. Md., 1962-64, assoc. research prof., 1965-67. Contbr. articles profl. jours. Recipient Exceptional Sci. Achievement award NASA, 1966, 81, 86, Arthur S. Flemming award, 1968, Space Sci. award AIAA, 1971, Disting. Svc. medal NASA, 1986, Nat. Space Club Sci. award, 1993, Emil Wiechert medal German Geophys. Soc., 1993. Fellow Am. Geophys. Union (John Adam Fleming award 1968), Royal Astron. Soc.; mem. NAS, Accademia Nazionale dei Lincei, Royal Ocean Racing Club. Achievements include research, experimental studies of interplanetary and planetary magnetic fields by satellites and space probes. Home: 9 Wilkinson Dr Landenberg PA 19350-9359 Office: U Del Bartol Research Inst Newark DE 19716-4793

NESSE, MARK A., library director; b. Redwing, Minn., Mar. 10, 1943; s. Marvin Edgar and Ruth (Huus) N.; m. Sheila Joan Powers, Apr. 5, 1967; children: Rachel, Eric, John. BA in Edn., Pacific Luth. U., Tacoma, 1965; MS in LS, U. N.C., 1971. Cert. libr., Wash. Secondary tchr. U.S. Peace Corps, Yrgalem and Hosanna, Ethiopia, 1965-67; tng. instr. at U. Utah U.S. Peace Corps, Salt Lake City, summer 1967; tchr. jr. h.s. Tacoma Pub. Schs., 1967-69; extension head Durham County Libr., Durham, N.C., 1971-73; dir. Beverly (Mass.) Pub. Libr., 1973-77, Everett (Wash.) Pub. Libr., 1977—. Contbr. chpt. to book. Bd. dirs. Marie Weeks Varley Campfire Found., Everett, 1985-88, Snohomish chpt. ARC, Everett, 1991-94; mem. Everett Sch. Bd., 1993—. Mem. ALA, Rotary Club of Everett (pres. 1988-89). Avocations: restoring Jeepster automobiles, antiques. Office: Everett Pub Libr 2702 Hoyt Ave Everett WA 98201

NESSELROADE, JOHN RICHARD, psychology educator; b. Silverton, W.Va., Mar. 13, 1936; s. John S. and Emma E. (Suck) N.; m. Carolyn S. Boyles, July 12, 1959; children: Cynthia Anne, Jennifer Sue. BS, Marietta Coll., 1961; MA, Univ. Ill., 1965, PhD, 1967. Asst. prof. W. Va. U., Morgantown, 1967-70, assoc. prof., 1970-72; assoc. prof. human devel. Pa. State U., University Park, 1972-75, prof., 1975-83, rsch. prof., 1983-90, disting. rsch. prof., 1990-91, dir. Ctr. for Devel. and Health Rsch. Methodology, 1989-91; Hamilton prof. psychology U. Va., Charlottesville, 1991—. Editor: Handbook of Multivariate Exptl. Psychology, 1988. Sgt. USMC, 1954-57, Japan. Recipient Cattell award Soc. of Multivariate Exptl. Psychology, 1972. Fellow AAAS, APA (Disting. Contbns. award Divsn. 20, 1994), Am. Psychol. Soc. (charter), Gerontol. Soc. Am. Avocations: music, tennis, golf. Home: 116 Chestnut Ridge Rd Charlottesville VA 22901-8544

NESSEN, RONALD HAROLD, public affairs executive; b. Washington, May 25, 1934; s. Frederick E. and Ida Edith (Kaufman) N.; m. Johanna Neuman, Feb. 14, 1988; children: Caren Jayne, Edward Song. B.A., Am. U., 1959; LL.D. (hon.), Heidelberg Coll., 1975, Ursinus Coll., 1977. News announcer Sta. WEPM, Martinsburg, W.Va., 1952-54, Sta. WARL, Arlington, Va., 1954-55; writer Montgomery County (Md.) Sentinel, Rockville, 1955-56; editor UPI, Washington, 1956-62; news corr. NBC News, Washington, 1962-74; press sec. to Pres. Gerald R. Ford, 1974-77; freelance writer, lectr., 1977-80; exec. v.p. Marston & Rothenberg Public Affairs, Inc., Washington, 1980-84; sr. asso. Robert Marston & Assos., N.Y.C., 1980-84; moderator Pro-Con TV series Pa. Pub. Broadcasting System, 1983-84; v.p. MBS, Arlington, Va., 1984-92; sr. v.p. pub. affairs comm. Cellular Telecom. Industry Assn., 1992—. Author: It Sure Looks Different from the Inside, 1978, The First Lady, 1979, The Hour, 1984, (with J. Neuman) Knight and Day, 1995, Press Corpse, 1996; contbr. articles to popular publs. Recipient George Foster Peabody Broadcasting award, 1964, George Polk Meml. award Overseas Press Club, 1967, Edward R. Murrow Brotherhood award, 1988, 1989, Grand award Internat. Radio Festival, 1988, Nat. Headliner award, 1989. Mem. Nat. Press Club. Home: 6409 Walhonding Rd Bethesda MD 20816-2264

NESSEN, WARD HENRY, typographer, lawyer; b. Empire, Mich., Nov. 29, 1909; s. Henry L. and Louise (Stecher) N.; m. Jane Randall, Apr. 4, 1959. AB, U. Mich., 1931; JD, John Marshall Law Sch., Chgo., 1937; course in acctg. Northwestern U. Grad. Sch., 1946. Bar: Ill. 1937. With trust dept. No. Trust Co., Chgo., 1934-41; sales planning Am. Home Products, 1946-51; sales exec. Permacel Tape Corp., 1951-55; pres. The Highton Co., Newark, 1955-75; sr. v.p. Arrow Typographers, Newark, 1975-84; chmn. Coll. Communications Seminar, 1973. Mem. Civic Clubs Council Greater Newark Area, 1957-59, Bd. Comml. Arbitration N.Y.C., 1982-86; pres. Dale Carnegie course, 1964; chmn. selection com. Advt. Hall of Fame of N.J., 1983. Lt. col. AUS, 1941-46, ETO, assigned ETOUSA. Decorated Bronze Star with oak leaf cluster, Army Commendation medal; recipient Svc. to Industry award Printing Industries, N.J., 1973, recipient award of Excellence for Exhbn. Insides Am. Inst. Graphic Arts, 1974, Elmer G. Voigt award, 1975; named to Advt. Hall of Fame N.J., 1990. Mem. Internat. Platform Assn., Typographers Internat. Assn. (pres. 1970-71), N.J. Typographers Assn. (pres. 1957-59), Print/N.J. (pres. 1967-69), Assn. Graphic Arts N.Y. (bd. govs. 1967-69), Advt. Club N.J. (chmn. com. Constnl. by-laws 1980-81), John Monteith Soc., Pres.'s Club of U. Mich., Order of John Marshall, Sigma Phi. Republican. Episcopalian. Clubs: Type Dirs.; Advt. N.J. (bd. govs 1972-84). Home: 11 Euclid Ave Summit NJ 07901

NESSON, CHARLES R., lawyer, educator; b. 1939. A.B., Harvard U., 1960, LL.B., 1963. Bar: D.C. 1964, Mass. 1971. Law clk. to assoc. justice Harlan, U.S. Supreme Ct., Washington, 1964-65; spl. asst. Civil Rights Div., Dept. Justice, 1965-66; asst. prof. Harvard U., Cambridge, Mass., 1966-69, prof., 1969—. Author: (with E. Green) Federal Rules of Evidence, 1984, 94. Office: Law Sch Harvard U Cambridge MA 02138

NESSON, H. RICHARD, medical administrator, physician; b. Boston, May 6, 1932; s. Edward Donald and Ruthe (Zakon) N.; m. Lois Feinberg, Aug. 25, 1957; children—Edward D., Sara F. A.B., Harvard Coll., 1954; M.D., Boston U., 1959. Med. dir. Harvard Community Health Plan, Boston, 1967-73; dir. Office of Extramural Health Programs Harvard Sch. Pub. Health, Boston, 1973-76; dir. div. Gen. Medicine and Primary Care, dept. medicine Brigham & Woman's Hosp., Boston, 1976-82, v.p. ambulatory and community health services, 1976-82, pres., 1982—; CEO Partners HealthCare System, Inc., 1994—; sr. program cons. Robert Wood Johnson Found., Princeton, N.H., 1979-82; bd. dirs. Mercy Hosp. Sys. Contbr. articles to profl. jours. Chmn. Brookline Adv. Council of Pub. Health, Mass., 1971-76; mem. adv. com. of Radcliffe Seminars Program, Cambridge, Mass., 1975-82; bd. dirs. United Way, Boston, 1985-90; mem. policy adv. com. Mass. Supreme Judicial Ct., 1991. Recipient Disting. Alumni award Boston U. Sch. Medicine, 1983. Mem. AAAS, APHA, Assn. Am. Med. Colls., Mass. Pub. Health Assn., Med. Adminstrs. Conf. (sec. 1982), Soc. Med. Adminstrs., Am. Fedn. Clinic Rsch., Mass. Med. Soc., Am. Hosp. Assn. (mem. coun. of mgmt. 1984-87, chmn. 1994-95), Mass. Hosp. Assn. (chmn. 1994-95), Group Health Assn. Am., Harvard Club of Boston, Alpha Omega Alpha. Avocation: tennis. Office: Ptnrs HealthCare Sys Inc Ste 1150 800 Boylston St Boston MA 02199-8001*

NESTER, EUGENE WILLIAM, microbiology educator; b. Johnson City, N.Y., Sept. 15, 1930; married, 1959; 2 children. BS, Cornell U., 1952; PhD, Western Reserve U., 1959. Am. Cancer Soc. rsch. fellow genetics Stanford U., 1959-62, instr. microbiology, 1962-63, from asst. to assoc. prof. microbiology and genetics, 1963-72; prof. microbiology U. Wash., Seattle, 1972—, chmn. microbiology, 1982-96. Recipient Chiron Corp. Biotechnology Rsch. award, Australia prize, 1990. Fellow NAS, AAAS, Am. Acad. Microbiology; mem. Am. Soc. Microbiology. Achievements include bacterial-plant relationships. Office: Univ Wash Microbiology Dept Box 357242 Seattle WA 98195-7242

NESTER, WILLIAM RAYMOND, JR., retired academic administrator and educator; b. Cin., Feb. 19, 1928; s. William Raymond and Evelyn (Blettner) N.; m. Mary Jane Grossman, Aug. 21, 1950; children: William Raymond, Mark Patrick, Brian Philip, Stephen Christopher. BS, U. Cin., 1950, EdM, 1953, EdD, 1965. Tchr. high sch. English and history Cin., 1950-52; dir. student union U. Cin., 1952-53, asst. dean of men, 1953-60, dean of men, 1960-67, assoc. prof. edn., 1965-70, dean of students, 1967-69, vice provost student and univ. affairs, 1969-76, prof. edn., 1970-78, assoc. sr. v.p., assoc. provost, 1976-78; v.p. student svcs. Ohio State U., Columbus, 1978-83, prof. edn., 1978-83; pres. Kearney State Coll., Nebr., 1983-91, prof. edn., 1983-93; chancellor U. Nebr., Kearney, 1991-93, prof. emeritus, chancellor emeritus, 1993—; pres. emeritus Mus. Nebr. Art, 1991—; cons. on edn., 1993—. Pres. Metro-Six Athletic Conf., 1975-76, Cen. States Intercollegiate Conf., 1986-89. Mem. AAUP, Am. Assn. State Colls. and Univs. (bd. dirs.), Nat. Assn. Intercollegiate Athletics (pres.), Nat. Assn. Student Pers. Adminstrs. (past regional v.p., mem. exec. com.), Am. Assn. Higher Edn., Ohio Assn. Student Pers. Adminstrs. (past pres.), Nat. Intrafrat. Conf. (pres. 1991-92), Frat. Scholarship Officers Assn. (past pres.), Mortar Bd., Pi Kappa Alpha (nat. pres. 1978-80, past pres. edni. found.), Omicron Delta Kappa, Phi Delta Kappa, Phi Alpha Theta, Phi Eta Sigma, Sigma Sigma. Episcopalian. Home: 7674 Coldstream Dr Cincinnati OH 45255-3932

NESTVOLD, ELWOOD OLAF, information technology company executive; b. Minot, N.D., Mar. 19, 1932; came to Netherlands 1979; s. Ole Enevold and Ragnhilda (Quanbeck) N.; m. Simone Chriqui, Dec. 6, 1955 (dec. Jan. 1990); children: Rebecca Lynn, Paul Stephen; m. Jeannette Garvin, Mar. 23, 1991; stepchildren: Michele Marie, Jennifer Ann, Michael Dennis. BA, Augsburg Coll., Mpls., 1952; postgrad., U. Wash., 1952-53; MS, U. Minn., 1959, PhD, 1962. Physics instr. U. Minn., Mpls., 1956-61; physicist and section leader Shell EP Rsch. Lab., Houston, 1962-68, mgr. geophysics rsch., 1968-71; mgr. geophysics Shell Western Div., Denver, Houston, 1971-74, Pecten Internat., Houston, 1974-77; chief geophysicist Woodside Petroleum, Perth, Australia, 1977-78; mgr. EP processing ctr. Shell EP Rsch. Lab., Rijswijk, Netherlands, 1979-81; chief geophysicist Shell Internat. Petroleum, The Hague, 1981-86, dir. geophysics and topography, 1986-92; chief geophysicist Geco-Prakla div. Schlumberger Ltd., Paris, 1992-94, v.p. mktg. Geco-Prakla div., 1993-94; sr. geophysics cons. Schlumberger Oilfield Svcs., Houston, 1994-95; exploration and prodn. sector exec. IBM Corp., Houston, 1995—; cons. Lighting and Transients Rsch. Inst., Mpls., 1957-61; lectr. Australian Petroleum Exploration Assn, 1991, Internat. Assn. Geophysical Contractors, 1992, European Assn. Exploration Geophysicists, 1994 and others. Presenter keynote addresses; contbr. articles to profl. and trade jours. 1st lt. USAF, 1952-56. Recipient award of appreciation Internat. Assn. Geophys. Contractors, 1992. Mem. IEEE, Am. Assn. Petroleum Geologists (Disting. lectr. 1993-94), Am. Assn. Physics Tchrs., European Assn. Petroleum Geoscientists, European Assn. Exploration Geophysicists, Soc. Exploration Geophysicists, N.Y. Acad. Scis., Soc. Petroleum Engrs. (Disting. lectr. 1994-95), Sigma Xi. Avocations: hiking, museums. Home: 9059 Briar Forest Houston TX 77024 Office: 2 Riverway Houston TX 77056

NETER, JOHN, statistician; b. Germany, Feb. 8, 1923; m. Dorothy Rachman, June 24, 1951; children: Ronald J., David L. B.S., U. Buffalo, 1943; M.B.A., U. Pa., 1947; Ph.D., Columbia U., 1952. Asst. prof. Syracuse (N.Y.) U., 1949-55, chmn. dept. bus. stats., 1952-55; prof. U. Minn., Mpls., 1955-75; chmn. dept. quantitative analysis U. Minn., 1961-65; C. Herman and Mary Virginia Terry prof. mgmt. sci., stats. U. Ga., Athens, 1975-89, prof. emeritus, 1990—; supervisory math. statistician U.S. Bur. Census, 1959-60; chmn. panel on quality control of fed. assistance programs Nat. Acad. Scis., 1986-87; cons. in field. Co-author: Statistical Sampling for Auditors and Accountants, 1956, Fundamental Statistics for Business and Economics, 4th edit., 1973, Applied Linear Statistical Models, 1974, 4th edit., 1996, Applied Statistics, 1978, 4th edit., 1993, Applied Linear Regression Models, 1983, 3d edit., 1996; editor: Am. Statistician, 1976-80; assoc. editor: Decision Scis., 1973-74; contbr. articles to profl. jours. Chmn. citizens adv. com., City of St. Louis Park, Minn., 1972, mem. planning commn., 1974-75. Served with AUS, 1943-45. Ford Found. faculty research fellow, 1957-58. Fellow Am. Statis. Assn. (council 1963-64, 67-70, dir. 1975-80, pres. 1985), AAAS (chmn., sec. on statistics 1991), Decision Scis. Inst. (pres. 1978-79); mem. AAUP (chpt. pres. 1969-70), Inst. Mgmt. Scis., Inst. Math. Stats., Internat. Statis. Inst. Home: 310 St George Dr Athens GA 30606-3910 Office: Terry Coll Bus Univ Ga Athens GA 30602-6255

NETH, JERRY, publishing company executive. Exec. v.p. pub. ops. Cahners Pub. Co., Newton, Mass. Office: Cahners Pub Co 275 Washington St Newton MA 02158*

NETHERCUT, PHILIP EDWIN, honorary consul; b. Indpls., Apr. 3, 1921; s. William Richard and Ruth Salome (Habbe) N.; m. Leah Teresa Diehl, Apr. 9, 1949; children: Bruce Philip, Gail Ellen, Anne Louise. B.S., Beloit Coll., 1942; M.S., Lawrence Coll., 1944, Ph.D., 1949. With Watervliet Paper Co., Mich., 1949-50; research mgr. Scott Paper Co., 1951-56; with TAPPI, N.Y.C., now Atlanta, 1957-86; sec.-treas. TAPPI, 1959-60, exec. sec., 1960-75, treas., 1964-75, exec. dir., 1975-82, vice. chmn. bd., 1983-86; hon. consul for Finland in Ga., 1976—; trustee Inst. Paper Chemistry, 1979-83, TAPPI Found., 1990—. Bd. dirs. Met. Atlanta Boys' and Girls' Club, 1979—. Served to lt. (j.g.) USNR, 1944-46. Recipient Distinguished Service citation Beloit Coll., 1967; Clarke award Ga. Soc. Assn. Execs., 1979; decorated Knight Finnish Order of White Rose, 1987. Fellow TAPPI; mem. Am. Soc. Assn. Execs. (CAE award 1968, Key award 1981), Inst. Paper Chemistry Alumni Assn. (chmn. 1960), Council Engring. and Sci. Soc. Execs. (pres. 1968), Finnish-Am. C. of C. S.E., Atlanta Consular Corps, Phi Beta Kappa, Beta Theta Pi. Club: Mountain View. Home: 9240 Huntcliff Trce Atlanta GA 30350-1603

NETHERCUTT, GEORGE RECTOR, JR., congressman, lawyer; b. Spokane, Wash., Oct. 4, 1944; s. George Rector and Nancy N.; m. Mary Beth Socha Nethercutt, Apr. 2., 1977; children: Meredith, Elliott. BA in English, Wash. State U., 1967; JD, Gonzaga U., 1971. Bar: D.C. 1972. Law clk. to Hon. Raymond Plummer U.S. Dist. Ct. Alaska, Anchorage, 1971; staff counsel to U.S. Senator Ted Stevens Washington, 1972, chief of staff to U.S. Senator Ted Stevens, 1972-76; pvt. practice Spokane, Wash., 1977-94; mem. 104th Congress from 5th Wash. dist., Washington, 1994—. Chmn. Spokane County Rep. Party, 1990-94, co-founder Vanessa Behan Crisis Nursery, pres. Spokane Juvenile Diabetes Found., 1993-94. Mem. Masons (lodge #34), Lions Club (Spokane Ctrl.), Sigma Nu. Republican. Presbyterian. Avocations: running, handball, squash. Office: US House Reps 1527 Longworth House Office Bldg Washington DC 20515-4705

NETHERY, JOHN JAY, government official; b. Mpls., June 4, 1941; s. Ronald Jay and Mary Vesta (McVeety) N.; m. Sonya Elisabeth Magin, July 27, 1968; children: William Jay, Mary Elisabeth (dec.), Sarah Ann. BA, U. Denver, 1963, MPA, 1968. Mgmt. intern USAF Logistics Command, San Antonio, 1969-71; budget analyst USAF Logistics Command, Dayton, Ohio, 1971-72; chief, fiscal analysis USAF Hdqrs., Washington, 1973-80, chief, investment div., 1980-81, chief budget mgmt., 1981-85; dep. asst. sec. Dept. of USAF, Washington, 1986-88, asst. to undersecretary, 1988-89, dep. asst. sec., 1989—; mem. Air Force bd. for the correction of mil. records, Washington, 1980—. Recipient Gov.'s Scholastic award Gov. of Colo., 1968, Presdl. Rank award, 1988. Mem. Sr. Execs. Assn., Air Force Assn. Presbyterian. Avocations: history, military minatures. Home: 12349 Coleraine Ct Reston VA 22091-1627 Office: Dept USAF SAF/FM The Pentagon Washington DC 20330-1130

NETI, SUDHAKAR, mechanical engineering educator; b. Bapatla, India, Sept. 27, 1947; came to U.S., 1968, naturalized, 1977; s. Chiranjeeva Rao and Meenakshi (Yanamandra) N.; BME, Osmania U., 1968; MS, U. Ky., 1970, PhD, 1977; m. Kathy Gibson, Jan. 11, 1974. Research asst. U. Ky., 1968-77; asst. prof. mech. engring. Lehigh U., Bethlehem, Pa., 1978-83, assoc. prof., 1983-92, prof., 1992—; vis. fellow Wolfson Coll., Oxford U., Eng.; vis. rsch. assoc. U.K. Atomic Energy Rsch. Establishment, Harwell, Eng.; fallout shelter analyst Fed. Emergency Mgmt. Adminstrn.; mem. county joint planning commn.; cons. to industry. Summer faculty fellow NASA-Am. Soc. Engring. Edn., 1978; grantee Electric Power Research Inst., 1979, NSF, 1980, NRC, 1981. Mem. ASME, AAAS, Sigma Xi. Contbr. articles to profl. jours. Office: Lehigh U Mech Engring Dept 19 Memorial Dr W Bethlehem PA 18015

NETRAVALI, ARUN N., communications executive; b. Bombay, May 26, 1946; m. Chitra Netravali; 2 children. BS in Tech. with honors, Indian Inst. Tech., Bombay, 1967; MS, Rice U., 1969, PhD, 1970; PhD (hon.), Ecole Polytechnique Federale, Lausanne, Switzerland, 1994. With NASA, Orlando, Fla., 1970-72; mem. tech. staff AT&T Bell Labs., Holmdel, N.J., 1972-78; head visual comm. rsch. dept. AT&T Bell Labs., Murray Hill, N.J., 1978-83, dir. computing systems rsch., 1983-92, exec. dir. rsch., comm. scis. divsn., 1992-94; v.p. AT&T Bell Labs., 1994—; adj. prof. media lab. MIT, Cambridge, Mass., 1984—; lectr. City Coll. N.Y., Columbia U., MIT, Rutgers U.; advisor Ctr. for Telecomm. Rsch. of Columbia U., 1987—, EPFL Swiss Fed. Inst. Tech., Lausanne, 1986—, Beckman Inst. of U. Ill. Co-author: Digital Pictures: Representation and Compression, 1987, Visual Communication Systems, 1989; contbr. 100 tech. papers to sci. jours.; patentee for 64 inventions. Mem. N.J. Govs. Com. on Schs. Program. Recipient Journal award Soc. of Motion Pictures and TV Engrs., 1982, Ann. Asian Am. Corp. Employees award Orgn. Chinese Ams., 1991, Engr. of Yr. award Assn. Engrs. of India, 1992. Fellow IEEE (editor Communications 1984—, mem. editorial bd. Proceedsings of IEEE 1980-84, Fink prize 1980, L.G. Abraham prize 1985, 91, Alexander Graham Bell medal 1991, mem. digitals TV com.), AAAS; mem. NAE, Tau Beta Pi, Sigma Xi. Avocation: tennis. Home: 10 Byron Ct Westfield NJ 07090-2250 Office: AT&T Bell Labs 600 Mountain Ave New Providence NJ 07974

NETT, LOUISE MARY, nursing educator, consultant; b. Sept. 25, 1938. Diploma, St. Cloud Sch. Nursing, 1959; cert. in therapy program, Gen. Rose Hosp., Denver, 1967. Staff nurse med. unit Mt. Sinai Hosp., Mpls., 1959-60; staff nurse nursing registry San Francisco, 1960-61; emergency rm. staff nurse Colo. Gen. Hosp., Denver, 1961-62; head nurse Outpatient Clinic Charity Hosp., New Orleans, 1962-64; dir. respiratory care U. Colo. Health Scis. Ctr., Denver, 1965-85, pulmonary program specialist Webb-Waring Lung Inst., 1985-89; rsch. assoc. Presbyn./St. Luke's Ctr. for Health Scis. Edn., Denver, 1989—; clins. assoc. prof. nursing U. Colo. Sch. Nursing, Denver; adj. asst. prof. U. Kans. Sch. Allied Health; instr. medicine pulmonary divsn. U. Colo. Sch. Medicine, Denver, 1980-89; mem. Nat. Heart, Lung, and Blood Inst. adv. coun., NIH, 1979-82, mem. safety and data monitoring bd. for early intervention for chronic obstructive pulmonary disease, lung divsn., 1985-91; mem. clin. practice guidelines for smoking cessation and presentation panel Agy. for Health Care Policy and Rsch., 1994; dir. numerous courses, confs. in field; worldwide lectr. assns., symposia, confs., TV, convs., meetings, workshops; internat. cons. hosps., health depts., 1975—; local, regional lectr. through med. programs Am. Lung Assn., Am. Cancer Soc. Colo., cmty. hosps., businesses. Author: (with T.L. Petty) For Those Who Live and Breathe with Emphysema and Chronic Bronchitis, 1967, 2d edit., 1971, Enjoying Life with Emphysema, 1984, 2d edit., 1987 (Am. Jour. Nursing Book of Yr. award 1987), Rational Respiratory Therapy, 1988; mem. editl. bd. Heart and Lung Jour., 1972-87, Respiratory Times Newsletter, 1986-88, Jour. Home Health Care Practice, 1988; contbr. articles to profl. jours., chpts. to books. Mem. subcom. on nursing Am. Lung Assn., 1975-76; mem. exec. bd. dirs. Colo. divsn. Am. Cancer Soc., 1984—, chairperson pub. edn. com., 1985-86; mem. exec. com. Am. Stop Smoking Intervention Study, 1991-94, mem. alliance bd. Recipient Rocky Mountain Tobacco Free Challenge Regional award for treatment of nicotine addiction program, 1989, award for ednl. seminars, 1989, award in profl. end., 1992, award for outstanding work in developing and promoting smoking cessation, 1992, profl. educator award, 1993, award for nicotine treatment network, 1993. Mem. ANA, Am. Assn. for Respiratory Care (health promotion com. 1987—, internat. liaison com. 1987-90, Charles H. Hudson Pub. Respiratory Health award 1991), Am. Assn. of Cardio Vascular and Pulmonary Rehab., Am. Thoracic Soc. (ad hoc com. role of nonphysician in respiratory care 1972, respiratory therapy com. 1972-74, program planning com. 1989), Behavioral Medicine Soc., Colo. Trudeau Soc. (v.p. 1981, pres.-elect 1982, pres. 1983), Colo. Pub. Health Assn., Internat. Oxygen Club, Internat. Soc. for Humor Studies, Soc. of European Pnemonology. Office: Presbyn/St Lukes Ctr Health Clin Rsch Divsn 1719 E 19th Ave Denver CO 80218-1235

NETTELS, ELSA, English language educator; b. Madison, Wis., May 25, 1931; d. Curtis Putnam and Elsie (Patterson) N. BA, Cornell U., 1953; MA, U. Wis., 1955, PhD, 1960. From instr. to asst. prof. English Mt. Holyoke Coll., South Hadley, Mass., 1959-67; asst. prof. to prof. English Coll. William and Mary, Williamsburg, Va., 1967—. Author: James and Conrad, 1977 (South Atlantic Modern Lang. Assn. award 1975), Language, Race and Social Class in Howells' America, 1988; contbr. articles to profl. jours. NEH fellow, 1984-85. Mem. Modern Lang. Assn., South Atlantic Modern Lang. Assn. (edit. bd. 1977-83), Henry James Soc. (edit. bd. 1983—), Am. Studies Assn. Home: 211 Indian Springs Rd Williamsburg VA 23185-3940 Office: Coll William and Mary Dept English Williamsburg VA 23185

NETTELS, GEORGE EDWARD, JR., mining executive; b. Pittsburg, Kans., Oct. 20, 1927; s. George Edward and Mathilde A. (Wulke) N.; m. Mary Joanne Myers, July 19, 1952; children: Christopher Bryan, Margaret Anne, Katherine Anne, Rebecca Jane. B.S. in Civil Engring, U. Kans., Lawrence, 1950. With Black & Veatch Engrs., Kansas City, Mo., 1950-51, Spencer Chem. Co., Kansas City, Mo., 1951-55, Freeto Constrn. Co., Pittsburg, 1955-57; pres. Midwest Minerals, Inc., Pittsburg, 1957—; chmn. bd. McNally Pittsburg Mfg. Corp., 1970-76, pres., chief exec. officer, 1976-87; ret. McNally Pitts. Inc., 1987; bd. dirs. Bank IV, Pitts., Kansas City Power & Light Co.; past chmn. bd. Nat. Limestone Inst.; bd. dirs. Pitts. Indsl. Devel. Com. Bd. advisers Kans. U. Endowment Assn.; mem. Kans. U. Chancellor's Club, Kans., Inc.; past pres. Bd. Edn. 250, Pittsburg; past chmn. bd. trustees Mt. Carmel Hosp.; past mem. Kans. Commn. Civil Rights; chmn. Kans. Republican Com., 1966-68; Kans. del. Rep. Nat. Conv., 1968, Kans. Bus. and Industry Com. for Re-election of the President, 1972. Served with AUS, 1946-47. Recipient Disting. Service citation U. Kans., 1980, Disting. Engring. citation U. Kans., 1985; named Kansan of Yr., 1986. Mem. ASCE, NAM (past. dir.), Kans. C. of C. and Industry (dir., chmn. 1983-84), Kans. Right to Work (dir.), Pittsburg C. of C. (past dir.), Kans. U. Alumni Assn. (pres. 1977), Kans. Leadership Com., Tau Beta Pi, Omicron Delta Kappa, Beta Theta Pi. Presbyterian. Clubs: Crestwood Country (Pittsburg); Wolf Creek Golf (Olathe). Office: Midwest Minerals Inc 509 W Quincy St Pittsburg KS 66762-5531

NETTER, KURT FRED, retired building products company executive; b. Mannheim, Fed. Republic Germany, Dec. 3, 1919; came to U.S., 1941, naturalized, 1944; s. Arthur and Kate (Gruenfeld) N.; m. Alice Dreyfus, May 26, 1942; children: Nadine, Ronald, Alfred. Student, Swiss Inst. Tech., 1938-39, U. Toronto, 1939-41; BS, Columbia U., 1942. Ptnr. Interstate Engring. and Machinery Co., N.Y.C., 1942-44; officer, dir. Supradur Cos., Inc., 1946-95, pres., CEO, 1953-93; chmn., 1986-95. Bd. dirs. Selfhelp Community Svcs., Inc., treas., 1970-85, pres., 1985-90, chmn., 1990—. With AUS, 1944-46. Home: 203 Griffen Ave Scarsdale NY 10583-7905

NETTER, VIRGINIA THOMPSON, produce company owner; b. Hardyville, Ky., Nov. 2, 1931; d. Duluth Sydnor and Vera (Asbury) Thompson; m. S. Mitchell Netter, Oct. 4, 1947; children: Ronald Lee, Candace Netter Harrison. BA, U. Louisville, 1982; MA in Counseling/Clin. Psychology, Spalding U., 1989. Owner, Netter Produce Co., Louisville, 1954—, Big Four Farms, Belmont, Ky., 1959—. Named to Hon. Order Ky. Cols., 1982. Mem. AAUW, Woodcock Soc., Psi Chi, Phi Kappa Phi. Avocations: ballroom dancing, riding, golf, travel. Home: 1029 Alta Vista Rd Louisville KY 40205-1727 Office: Netter Produce Co 331-335 Produce Plz Louisville KY 40202

NETTL, BRUNO, anthropology and musicology educator; b. Prague, Czechoslovakia, Mar. 14, 1930; s. Paul and Gertrud (Hutter) N.; m. Wanda Maria White, Sept. 15, 1952; children: Rebecca, Gloria. A.B., Ind. U., 1950, Ph.D., 1953; M.A. in L.S, U. Mich., 1960; LHD (hon.), U. Chgo., 1993, U. Ill., 1996. Mem. faculty Wayne State U., Detroit, 1953-64; asst. prof. Wayne State U., 1954-64, music librarian, 1958-64; mem. faculty U. Ill., Urbana, 1964—; prof. music and anthropology U. Ill., 1967—, chmn. div. musicology, 1967-72, 75-77, 82-85; vis. lectr., Fulbright grantee U. Kiel, Fed. Republic of Germany, 1956-58; cons. Ency. Britannica, 1969—, also on ethomusicology to various univs.; vis. prof. Williams Coll., 1971, Wash. U., 1978, U. Louisville, 1983, U. Wash., 1985, 88, 89, 93, 95, Fla. State U., 1988, Harvard U., 1989, U. Alta., 1991, Colo. Coll., 1992, Northwestern U., 1993, U. Minn., 1994, U. Chgo., 1996, Carleton Coll., 1996. Author: Theory and Method in Ethnomusicology, 1964, Music in Primitive Culture, 1956, Folk and Traditional Music of the Western Continents, 1965, 2d edit., 1973, Eight Urban Musical Cultures, 1978, The Study of Ethnomusicology, 1983, The Western Impact on World Music, 1985, The Radif of Persian Music, 1987, rev. edit., 1992, Blackfoot Musical Thought, 1989, Comparative Musicology and Anthropology of Music, 1991, Heartland Excursions, 1995; co-author Excursions in World Music, 1992; editor Ethnomusicology, 1961-65, Yearbook of the International Folk Music Council, 1975-77; contbr. articles to profl. jours. Recipient Koizumi prize in ethnomusicology, Tokyo, 1994. Mem. Soc. Ethnomusicology (pres. 1969-71), Am., Internat. musicol. socs., Internat. Coun. for Traditional Music. Home: 1423 Cambridge Dr Champaign IL 61821-4958 Office: Sch Music U Ill Urbana IL 61801

NETTLES, JOHN BARNWELL, obstetrics and gynecology educator; b. Dover, N.C., May 19, 1922; s. Stephen A. and Estelle (Hendrix) N.; m. Eunice Anita Saugstad, Apr. 28, 1956; children: Eric, Robert, John Barnwell; m. 2d, Sandra Williams, Sept. 14, 1991; stepchildren: Steven Williams, Clayton Williams. B.S., U. S.C., 1941; M.D., Med. Coll. S.C., 1944. Diplomate: Am. Bd. Obstetrics and Gynecology. Intern Garfield Meml. Hosp., Washington, 1944-45; research fellow in pathology Med. Coll. Ga., Augusta, 1946-47; resident in ob-gyn. U. Ill. Rsch. and Ednl. Hosps., Chgo., 1947-51; instr. to asst. prof. ob-gyn. U. Ill. Coll. Medicine, Chgo., 1951-57; asst. prof., assoc. prof., prof. ob-gyn. U. Ark. Med. Ctr., Little Rock, 1957-69; dir. grad. edn. Hillcrest Med. Ctr., Tulsa, 1969-73; prof. ob-gyn Coll. Medicine, U. Okla., Oklahoma City, 1969—; chmn. dept. ob-gyn. U. Okla.-Tulsa Med. Coll., 1975-80, prof., 1980—, mem. coun. on residency edn. in ob-gyn., 1974-79; dir. Tulsa Obstet. and Gynecol. Edn. Found., 1969-80; Coordinator med. edn. Nat. Def., Ark., 1961-69; mem. S.W. regional med. adv. com. Planned Parenthood Fedn. Am., 1974-78; mem. adv. com. Health Policy Agenda Am. People, 1982—, rev. com. Accrediation Council for Continuing Med. Edn., 1987-92. Contbr. articles on uterine malignancy, kidney biopsy in pregnancy, perinatal morbidity and mortality, human sexuality sch. age pregnancy to profl. jours. Served as lt. (j.g.) M.C. USNR, 1945-46; as lt. 1953-54. Fellow Am. Coll. Obstetricians and Gynecologists (dist. sec.-treas. 1964-70, dist. chmn. exec. bd. 1970-73, v.p. 1977-78), A.C.S. (bd. govs. 1969-71, program com. 1970-71, Surg. forum 1977-84, adv. com. gyn/ob 1985—), Royal Soc. Health, Royal Soc. Medicine; mem. Ark. Obstet. and Gynecol. Soc. (exec. sec. 1959-69), Central Assn. Obstetrics and Gynecology (exec. com. 1966-69, pres. 1978-79), Internat. Soc. Advancement Humanistic Studies in Gynecology, Assn. Mil. Surgeons U.S., AMA (sect. council on obstetrics and gynecology 1975—, chmn. 1982—, del. from Am. Coll. Obstetricians and Gynecologists 1987—, Young at Heart award Young Physicians sect. 1994), Nurses Assn. Am. Coll. Obstetricians and Gynecologists (exec. bd. 1970-73, assoc. 1980—), So. Med. Assn. (chmn. obstetrics 1973-74), Okla. Med. Soc., Tulsa County Med. Soc., Chgo. Med. Soc., Am. Assn. for Maternal and Infant Health, Assn. Am. Med. Colls., Am. Public Health Assn., Am. Assn. Sex Edn. Counselors and Therapists (S.W. regional bd. 1976-79), Soc. for Gynecol. Investigation, AAAS, Am. Soc. for Study Fertility and Sterility, Internat. Soc. Gen. Semantics, Aerospace Med. Assn., So. Gynecol. and Obstet. Soc. (pres. 1981-82), Am. Cancer Soc. (pres. Okla. div. 1979-83, St. George's medal 1991), Com. on In-Tng. Exam. in Obstetrics and Gynecology, Am. Coll. Nurse Midwives (governing bd. examiners 1979-83), Sigma Xi (pres. Tulsa chpt. 1992-93), Phi Rho Sigma. Lutheran. Office: U Okla Tulsa Med Coll 2808 S Sheridan Rd Tulsa OK 74129-1014 *To live life fully, with faith and trust in God and his people, working with others to make our world a little better, and willing to fill the gaps wherever they are.*

NETZEL, PAUL ARTHUR, fund raising management executive, consultant; b. Tacoma, Sept. 11, 1941; s. Marden Arthur and Audrey Rose (Jones) N.; BS in Group Work Edn., George Williams Coll., 1963; m. Diane Viscount, Mar. 21, 1963; children: Paul M., Shari Ann. Program dir. S. Pasadena-San Marino (Calif.) YMCA, 1963-66; exec. dir. camp and youth programs Wenatchee (Wash.) YMCA, 1966-67; exec. dir. Culver-Palms Family YMCA, Culver City, Calif., 1967-73; v.p. met. fin. devel. YMCA Met. Los Angeles, 1973-78, exec. v.p. devel., 1979-85; pres. bd. dirs. YMCA Employees Credit Union, 1977-80; chmn. N.Am. Fellowship of YMCA Devel. Officers, 1980-83; adj. faculty U. So. Calif. Coll. Continuing Edn., 1983-86, Loyola Marymount U., L.A., 1986-90, Calif. State U., L.A., 1991-92, UCLA Extension, 1991—; chmn., CEO Netzel Assocs., Inc., 1985—; pvt. practice cons., fund raiser. Chmn. Culver-Palms YMCA, Culver City, 1991-93, chmn. 1989-91, bd. mgrs. 1985—; pres. bd. Culver City Guidance Clinic, 1971-74; mem. Culver City Bd. Edn., 1975-79, pres., 1977-78; mem. Culver City Edn. Found., 1982-91; bd. dirs. Los Angeles Psychiat. Svc., 1971-74, Goodwill Industries of So. Calif., 1993—; mem. Culver City Council, 1980-88, vice-mayor, 1980-82, 84-85, mayor, 1982-83, 86-87; mem. Culver City Redevel. Agy., 1980-88, chmn., 1983-84, 87-88, vice chmn, 1985-86; bd. dirs. Los Angeles County Sanitation Dists., 1982-83, 85-87, Western Region United Way, 1986-93, vice chmn, 1991-92; chmn. bd. dirs. Calif. Youth Model Legislature, 1987-92; mem. World Affairs Coun., 1989—; mem. adv. bd. Automobile Club of So. Calif., 1996—. Recipient Man of Yr. award Culver City C. of C., 1972. Mem. Nat. Soc. Fund Raising Execs. (nat. bd. dirs. 1989-91, vice chmn. 1994, v.p. bd. dirs. Greater L.A. chpt. 1986-88, pres. bd. dirs. 1989-90, Profl. of Yr. 1983), Calif. Club, Rotary (L.A. # 5, pres. 1992-93, treas. L.A. found. 1995—), Mountain Gate Country. Address: Netzel Assocs Inc 9696 Culver Blvd Ste 204 Culver City CA 90232-2753

NETZER, DICK, economics educator; b. N.Y.C., May 14, 1928; s. Solomon and Sue (Dick) N.; m. Carol Risika, Dec. 30, 1945; children: Jenny, Katherine. B.A., U. Wis., 1946; M.A., M.P.A., Harvard U., 1948, Ph.D., 1952. Successively economist, sr. economist, asst. v.p. Fed. Res. Bank Chgo., 1948-60; econ. cons. Regional Plan Assn., N.Y.C., 1960-80; assoc. prof. N.Y. U., 1961-64, prof. econs., 1964—, dean Grad. Sch. Pub. Adminstrn., 1969-82, dir. Urban Research Center, 1981-86; cons. in field, 1960—. Author: Economics of the Property Tax, 1966, The Economics of Public Finance, 1974, The Subsidized Muse, 1978, Urban Politics New York Style, 1990; editor: N.Y. Affairs, 1973-88. Mem. Mayor N.Y.C. Fiscal Adv. com., 1969-73; treas. Colony-South Bklyn. Houses, 1968-73; mem. Mcpl. Securities Rulemaking Bd., 1978-81, vice chmn., 1980-81; bd. dirs. Mcpl. Assistance Corp., N.Y.C., 1975—, Citizens Union Found., 1981—; bd. dirs., treas. Adolph and Esther Gottlieb Found., 1975—, v.p., 1979-88, pres. 1989—. Mem. Am. Econs. Assn., Regional Sci. Assn., Nat. Tax Assn., Am. Inst. Cert. Planners, Assn. Cultural Econs. Internat. (pres. 1993-94). Home: 227 Clinton St Brooklyn NY 11201-6144 Office: 4 Washington Sq N New York NY 10003-6635

NETZER, LANORE A(GNES), retired educational administration educator; b. Laona, Wis., Aug. 27, 1916; d. Henry N. and Julia M. (Niquette) Netzer; m. Glen G. Eye, 1979. Diploma, Oconto County Normal Sch., 1935; BS, State Tchrs. Coll., Oshkosh, Wis., 1943; MS, U. Wis., 1948, PhD, 1951. Tchr. Goldhorn Rural Sch., Pound, Wis., 1935-36; tchr. Goldfield Sch., Pound, 1936-37, tchr., acting prin., 1937-39; tchr., prin. Spruce (Wis.) Grade Sch., 1939-41; tchr. pub. schs. Neenah, Wis., 1943-46; demonstration and critic tchr. Campus Sch. State Tchrs. Coll., Oshkosh, 1946-48; supr. student tchrs.' coll. instrn. State Tchrs. Coll., Milw., 1950-55; teaching asst. U. Wis., Madison, 1948-50; assoc. prof. edn. U. Wis., Milw., 1955-63; prof. ednl. adminstrn. U. Wis., Madison, 1963-77, emeritus prof., 1977—; rsch. assoc. U.S. Office Edn., 1963-66; supr. student tchrs. coll. instrn. State Tchrs. Coll., Milw., 1950-55; mem. curriculum adminstrn. com. Wis. Coop. Curriculum Planning Program, 1945-52; mem. Wis. Joint Com. on Edn., 1957-59, E.B. Fred Fellowship Com., U. Wis., 1966—; ednl. cons. Educators Progress Svc., 1970—. Author: The Use of Industry Aids in Schools, 1952, (with Glen G. Eye) Supervision of Instruction: A Phase of Administration, 1965, 2d. edit., 1971, (with others) Interdisciplinary Foundations of Supervision, 1969, (with G. Eye) School Administrators and Instruction, 1969, (with others) Education Administration and Change, 1970, (with others) Supervision of Instruction, 1971, Strategies for Instructional Management, 1977; contbr. articles to profl. jours. Rsch. grantee Hill & Knowlton, Inc., N.Y.C., 1949; grantee Wis. Mfrs. Assn., 1954; recipient award of Distinction Nat. Coun. of Adminstrv. Women in Edn., 1975. Mem. AAUP, Wis. Edn. Assn. (life), So. Wis. Edn. Assn., Nat. Assn. Supervision and Curriculum Devel., Wis. Assn. Supervision and Curriculum Devel., Southwestern Assn. Supervision and Curriculum Devel., Wis. Elem. Sch. Prins. Assn., Am. Assn. Sch. Adminstrs., Wis. Assn. Sch. Dist. Adminstrs., Am. Edn. Rsch. Assn., Wis. Edn. Rsch. Assn., Univ. Coun. Ednl. Adminstrn., U. Wis. Alumni Assn. (life), U. Wis. Meml. Union (life), Phi Beta Sigma, Kappa Delta Pi, Pi Lambda Theta, Phi Delta Kappa. Home: 110 S Henry St Apt 1506 Madison WI 53703-3168 Office: U Wis Dept Ednl Adminstrn 1025 W Johnson St Madison WI 53706-1706 *My life achieves meaning as I help people to appreciate, reinforce, and serve each other. Kindness may be a goal, a process of living, or a product of effort, but to me it is the main road to self-realization.*

NETZLOFF, MICHAEL LAWRENCE, pediatric educator, endocrinologist; b. Madison, Wis., Sept. 11, 1942; s. Harold Harvey Netzloff and Garnet Lucille (Wilson) MacFarlane; m. Cheryl Lynne Crandall, July 20, 1963; children: Michelle Lynne, Rochelle Anne, Cherie Lucille. BS with high honors, Eckert Coll., 1964; MS, U. Fla., 1968, MD, 1969. Diplomate Am. Bd. Pediatrics, Diplomate Am. Bd. Pediatric Endocrinology. Rsch. fellow, rsch. trainee dept. of anat. scis. U. Fla. Coll. Medicine, Gainesville, 1965-69, intern and resident in pediatrics, 1969-71, clin. and rsch. fellow div. genetics, endocrinology and metabolism, dept. pediatrics, 1971-73, instr. in pediatrics, 1973-74, asst. prof. of pediatrics, 1974-79; assoc. prof. of pediatrics and human devel. Mich. State U. Coll. of Human Medicine, East Lansing, 1979-85, dir. of pediatric endocrinology, pediatrics and human devel., 1981-89, dir. div. of human genetics, genetic toxicology, endocrinology and oncology, pediatrics and human devel., 1982-89, prof. dept. pediatrics and human devel., 1985—, chmn. dept., 1987-91; vis. prof. dept. pediatrics U. Mich., 1992-93; cons. Juvenile Diabetes Found., Lansing, 1981—; mem. diabetes adv. coun. Mich. State Dept. Pub. Health and Chronic Disease Control, Lansing, 1980-90. Recipient Carithers award for Child Health and Human Dev., U. Fla. Coll. Medicine, 1969, Edward Bogen fellowship U. Fla. Coll. Med., 1972, Basil O'Connor rsch. grant Nat. Found. March of Dimes, 1973, pediatric residency teaching award, Grad. Med. Edn., Inc., Mich. State U.. Affiliated Residency program, 1982, 86. Fellow Am. Acad. Pediatrics; mem. Assn. Clin. Scis. Inst. (sci. com. 1979—), Am. Diabetes Assn. (coun. on diabetes in youth 1979—), Am. Pediatric Soc., Lawson-Wilkins Pediatric Endocrine Soc., Mich State Med. Soc., Ingham County Med. Soc., Soc. for Pediatric Rsch., Sigma Xi. Democrat. Lutheran. Home: 4432 Greenwood Dr Okemos MI 48864-3044 Office: Mich State U Dept Pediatrics B240 Life Scis East Lansing MI 48824-1317

NEU, CARL HERBERT, JR., management consultant; b. Miami Beach, Fla., Sept. 4, 1937; s. Carl Herbert and Catherine Mary (Miller) N.; BS, MIT, 1959; MBA, Harvard U., 1961; m. Carmen Mercedes Smith, Feb. 8, 1964; children—Carl Bartley, David Conrad. Cert. profl. mgmt. cons. Indsl. liaison officer MIT, Cambridge, 1967-69; coord. forward planning Gates Rubber Co., Denver, 1969-71; pres., co-founder Dyna-Com Resources, Lakewood, Colo., 1971-77; pres., founder Neu & Co., Lakewood, 1977—; mng. dir. Pro-Med Mgmt. Systems, Lakewood, 1981—; lectr. Grad. Sch. Pub. Affairs, U. Colo. Denver, 1982-84. Mem. exec. coun. Episcopal Diocese Colo., 1974; mem. Lakewood City Coun., 1975-80, pres., 1976; chmn. Lakewood City Charter Commn., 1982, Lakewood Civic Found., Inc., 1986—; pres. Lakewood on Parade, 1978, bd. dirs., 1978-80; pres. Classic Chorale, Denver, 1979, bd. dirs., 1978-83; pres. Lakewood Pub. Bldg. Authority, 1983—; bd. dirs. Metro State Coll. of Denver Found., 1990—, treas., 1994—; bd. dirs. Kaiser Permanente Health Adv. Com., 1990—. With U.S. Army, 1961-67. Decorated Bronze Star medal, Army Commendation medal; recipient Arthur Page award AT&T, 1979; Kettering Found. grantee, 1979-80. Mem. World Future Soc., Internat. City Mgrs. Assn., Lakewood-So. Jefferson County C. of C. (bd. dirs. 1983-89, chmn. 1988, chmn. 1987-88), Jefferson County C. of C. (chmn. 1988). Republican. Episcopalian. Contbr. articles to profl. jours. Home: 8169 W Baker Ave Denver CO 80227-3129

NEU, CHARLES ERIC, historian, educator; b. Carroll, Iowa, Apr. 10, 1936; s. Arthur Nicholas and Martha Margaret (Frandsen) N.; m. Deborah Dunning, Sept. 2, 1961 (div. 1978); children: Hilary Adams, Douglas Bancroft.; m. Susan Jennifer Kane, May 14, 1983 (div. 1991). B.A., Northwestern U., 1958; Ph.D., Harvard U., 1964. Instr. history Rice U., 1963-64, asst. prof., 1964-67, asso. prof., 1968-70; asso. prof. history Brown U., Providence, 1970-76; prof. Brown U., 1976—, chmn. dept. history, 1995—; fellow Charles Warren Center for Studies in Am. History, 1971-72; dir. summer seminar NEH, 1979, 86-87, 89, 92. Author: An Uncertain Friendship: Theodore Roosevelt and Japan, 1906-1909, 1967, The Troubled Encounter: The United States and Japan, 1975; co-editor: The Wilson Era: Essays in Honor of Arthur S. Link, 1991. Woodrow Wilson fellow, 1958-59; NEH younger scholar, 1968-69; Am. Council Learned Socs. fellow, 1975-76; Howard Found. fellow, 1976-77; Guggenheim fellow, 1981-82; guest scholar Woodrow Wilson Ctr., summer 1988. Mem. Am. Hist. Assn., Orgn. Am. Historians, Soc. Historians of Am. Fgn. Policy, Phi Beta Kappa. Democrat. Club: Agawam Hunt (Providence). Home: 346 Rochambeau Ave Providence RI 02906-3516 Office: Brown U Dept History Providence RI 02912

NEUBAUER, CHARLES FREDERICK, investigative reporter; b. Berkeley, Ill., Feb. 13, 1950; s. Fred Charles and Dolores Jeanne (Pries) N.; m. Sandra Carol Bergo, Oct. 4, 1975; 1 child, Michael Frederick. B.S.J., Northwestern U., 1972, M.S.J., 1973. Investigator Better Govt. Assn., Chgo., 1971-73; investigative reporter Chgo. Today, 1973-74, Chgo. Tribune, 1974-83, Chgo. Sun Times, 1983—. Recipient Pulitzer prize local reporting, 1976; Edward Scott Beck award for domestic reporting Chgo. Tribune, 1980. Office: 401 N Wabash Ave Chicago IL 60611-3532

NEUBAUER, JOSEPH, food services company executive; b. Oct. 19, 1941; s. Max and Herta (Kahn) N.; children: Lawrence, Melissa. B.S. in Chem. Engring, Tufts U., 1963; M.B.A. in Fin, U. Chgo., 1965. Asst. treas. Chase Manhattan Bank, 1965-68, asst. v.p., 1968-70, v.p., 1970-71; asst. treas. Pepsico Inc., Purchase, N.Y., 1971-72; treas. Pepsico Inc., 1972-73, v.p., 1973-76; v.p. fin. and control Wilson Sporting Goods Co., River Grove, Ill., 1976-77, sr. v.p., gen. mgr. team sports div., 1977-79; exec. v.p. fin. and devel., chief fin. officer, dir. ARA Svcs., Inc., Phila., 1979-81; pres., chief operating officer, dir. ARA Services, Inc., Phila., 1981-83, pres., chief exec. officer, 1983-84; chmn., CEO ARA Svcs., Inc. (in 1994, name changed to Aramark Corp.), Phila., 1984—; bd. dirs. 1st Fidelity Bancorp, Bell Atlantic, Federated Dept. Stores; trustee Penn Mut. Life Ins. Co. Chmn., CEO Phila. Orch. Assn., Mann Music Ctr., Inroads/Phila., Inc.; trustee Hahnemann U., Tufts U., Mus. Am. Jewish History, Greater Phila. First Corp., Com. for Econ. Devel., U. Chgo.; bd. govs. Joseph H. Lauder Inst. Mgmt. and Internat. Studies, U. Pa. Mem. Phila. C. of C., Union League Club, Locust Club, Phila. Club, Bus. Coun., Bus. Roundtable. Office: ARAMARK Corp ARAMARK Tower 1101 Market St Philadelphia PA 19107-2934*

NEUBAUER, PETER BELA, psychoanalyst; b. Krems, Austria, July 5, 1913; came to U.S., 1941, naturalized, 1946; s. Samuel and Rose (Blau) N.; m. Susan Rachlin, Nov. 25, 1953 (dec.); children—Joshua Rachlin, Alexander Lewis. M.D., U. Berne, 1938. Intern Lawrence Meml. Hosp., New London, Conn., 1941, Beth-El Hosp., Bklyn., 1942; resident in psychiatry Bellevue Hosp., N.Y.C., 1943-45; dir. Child Devel. Ctr., Jewish Bd. Family and Children's Services, N.Y.C., 1951-83; clin. prof. psychiatry Psychoanalytic Inst., N.Y. U., 1979—; lectr. child psychoanalysis Psychoanalytic Inst. for Tng. and Research Columbia U., 1973. Author: Children in Collectives: Child Rearing Aims and Practices in Kibbutzim, 1965, Early Child Day Car, 1974, Process of Child Development, 1976, (with Alexander Neubauer) Nature's Thumbprint, 1990; contbg. author: Fathers and Their Families, 1989; mem. editorial bd. Psychoanalytic Study of the Child, 1978. Recipient Hulse award N.Y. Council Child Psychiatry, 1975, Heinz Hartmann award N.Y. Psychoanalytic Soc., 1981, Mary S. Sigourney award, 1994. Mem. Am. Psychoanalytic Assn., Am. Acad. Child Psychiatry, Assn. Child Psychoanalysis, Internat. Assn. Child and Adolescent Psychiatry, Assn. for Child Psychoanalysis (pres. 1974-76). Office: 33 E 70th St New York NY 10021-4946

NEUBAUER, RICHARD A., library science educator, consultant; b. Meadville, Pa., Oct. 9, 1933; s. Carl Gustave and Velma Winston (Watson) N.; m. Janice Ernest; children: David, Lynda, Karl, Jennifer; m. Carol Barton. BS, Clarion U., 1955; MLS, SUNY, Geneseo, 1966; attended, Kent St. U., 1966-68, Simmons Coll., 1970-72. Cert. profl. libr., sch. libr., tchr. Tchr. geography Franklin (Pa.) Sch. Dept., 1957-58, N. Bedford County Schs., Woodbury, Mass., 1958-60; tchr. history Hornell (N.Y.) Jr. High Sch., 1960-62, sch. libr., 1962-65; prof. libr. sci. Edinboro (Pa.) U., 1965-68, assoc. libr. Hamilton Libr., 1965-68; dir. sch. librs. Duxbury (Mass.) Sch. Dept., 1968-69; dir., cons. Pub. Libr., Lincoln, Mass., 1969-70; prof. libr. sci. Bridgewater (Mass.) State Coll., 1969-78, chair dept. libr. sci., 1978-80, prof. libr. sci., 1980-91, coord. libr. media program, 1991-95; prof. emeritus libr. sci., 1996—; adj. prof. libr. sci. U. R.I., Kingston, 1975-88; cons. Tabor Acad., Marion, Mass., 1970-71, Abington (Mass.) Pub. Libr. Trustees, 1973-76, Duxbury Free Libr., 1968-72. Author: Planning the Elementary School Library, 1968; author, editor Exploring the U.S.-Northeast, 1994. Chmn. Mass. Dept. Edn. Cert., Quincy, 1989-90; resource cons. Project Contemporary Competitiveness, Bridgewater, Mass., 1973-83. 1st lt. USMC, 1955-57. Inst. grantee HEA of 1965 Edinboro U., 1968. Mem. NEA, Am. Libr. Assn., Intellectual Freedom Found., Mass. Assn. of Edn. Media, Mass. Sch. Libr. Media Assn., Mass. Tchrs. Assn. Democrat. Avocations: gardening, woodworking, reading. Home: 22 Pleasant St Carver MA 02330-1013

NEUBERGER, EGON, economics educator; b. Zagreb, Croatia, Yugoslavia, Feb. 27, 1925; came to U.S., 1940; s. Paul and Ann (Freund) N.; m. Florence Perlmutter, Dec. 22, 1949; children: Leah Ruth, Marc Joseph. BA, Cornell U., 1947; MA, Harvard U., 1949, PhD, 1958. Econ. analyst State Dept., Washington, 1949-54; asst. prof. econ. Amherst (Mass.) Coll., 1957-60; economist RAND Corp., Santa Monica, Calif., 1960-67; prof. econ. SUNY, Stony Brook, 1967-81, leading prof. econs., 1982—, dean social and behavioral scis., 1982-88; vice provost for undergraduate studies SUNY, 1989-90; econ. officer Am. Embassy, Moscow, 1952-53; vis. prof. U. Mich., Ann Arbor, 1965-66, U. Konstanz, Germany, 1995, U. Tuebingen, Germany, 1996. Served with U.S. Army, 1943-46, ETO. Mem. Assn. Comparative Econ. Studies (mem. exec. com. 1974-76, pres. 1990-91), Am. Econ. Assn., Assn. Study of Grants Economy (adv. bd.), Omicron Delta Epsilon (pres. 1979-81, exec. bd., Disting. Ser. award 1981). Democrat. Jewish. Home: 5 Somerset Ct East Setauket NY 11733-1831 Office: SUNY Dept Econs Stony Brook NY 11794

NEUBERGER, ROY R., investment counselor; b. Bridgeport, Conn., July 21, 1903; s. Louis and Bertha (Rothschild) N.; m. Marie Salant, June 29, 1932; children—Ann Marie Neuberger Aceves, Roy S., James A. Ed., NYU, U. Sorbonne; DFA (hon.), SUNY, Purchase, 1982; LHD (hon.), Parsons Sch. Design, New Sch. for Social Research, N.Y.C., 1985; DHL (hon.), Bar-Ilan U., Israel, 1987. Buyer B. Altman & Co., 1922-25; art student Paris, 1925-29; broker Halle & Stieglitz, N.Y.C., 1929-40; sr. partner Neuberger & Berman, N.Y.C., 1940—; pres. Guardian Mut. Fund, Inc., 1950-79, chmn. bd., 1979-91, chmn. emeritus, 1991—; chmn. bd. Genesis Fund, Inc., 1988-91; chmn. emeritus, 1991—; chmn. bd., dir. Neuberger & Berman Asset Mgmt., Inc. (formerly Neuberger & Berman Pension Mgmt. Inc.), 1976-87, chmn. emeritus, 1991—; chmn. bd., dir. Neuberger & Berman Mgmt. Inc. (formerly Cedar St. Cons.), 1970—. Art collector, collection exhibited museums throughout, U.S. and abroad, 1936—. Bd. dirs. Bard Coll. Ctr., 1979-91, City Ctr. Music and Drama, N.Y.C., 1957-74, trustee, 1974—, fin. chmn., 1971-74; chmn. adv. coun. on arts N.Y.C. Housing Authority, 1960-70; trustee Whitney Mus. Am. Art, 1961-69, trustee emeritus, 1969-94, hon. trustee, 1994—; collectors com. Nat. Gallery Art, Washington, 1975—; trustee, exec. com. New Sch. Social Rsch., 1967-75; hon. trustee Met. Mus. Art, N.Y.C., 1968—; coun. friends Inst. Fine Arts/NYU, 1961—; pres. coun. Mus. City N.Y.; trustee Purchase Coll. Found., 1971-85, chmn., 1974-85; donor Neuberger Mus. Art/SUNY, Purchase, 1969—. Recipient award Artists Equity Assn., 1972; Gari Melchers medal Artists Fellowship, Inc., N.Y.C., 1984, Arts award Council for Arts in Westchester, 1985, Art in Am. award, 1959, North Shore Com. Arts Ctr. award, 1971; Benjamin Franklin fellow Royal Soc. Arts, 1969—; fellow R.I. Sch. Design, 1981. Fellow in perpetuity NAD; mem. Am. Fedn. Arts (pres. 1955-67, hon. pres. 1968—), N.Y. Soc. Security Analysts, Soc. Ethical Culture N.Y.C. (treas. 1956-64, pres. 1965-68), Century Assn. Club, City Athletic Club, Harmonie Club. Home: 795 5th Ave New York NY 10021-8402 Office: Neuberger & Berman 605 3rd Ave New York NY 10158-3698

NEUDECK, GEROLD WALTER, electrical engineering educator; b. Beach, N.D., Sept. 25, 1936; s. Adolph John and Helen Annette (Kramer) N.; m. Mariellen Kristine MacDonald, Sept. 1, 1962; children: Philip Gerold, Alexander John. BSEE, U. N.D., 1959, MSEE, 1960; PhD in Elec. Engring., Purdue U., 1969. Asst. prof. U. N.D., Grand Forks, 1960-64; grad. instr. Purdue U., West Lafayette, Ind., 1964-68; asst. prof. Purdue U., 1968-71, assoc. prof., 1971-77, prof. elec. engring., 1977—; asst. dean engring. Purdue U., West Lafayette, 1988-90, assoc. dir. NSF/ERC Engring., 1988-94, dir. Optoelectronics Rsch. Ctr., 1993-96; cons. in field. Author: Electric Circuit Analysis and Design, 1976, 2d edit., 1987, Junction Diode/Bipolar Transisters, 1983, 2d edit., 1989; author, editor: Modular Series on Solid State Devices, 1983; contbr. over 220 articles to profl. jours.; inventor/holder 13 U.S. patents in field. Bd. dirs. W. Lafayette Devel. Commn., 1990—, Greater Lafayette Pub. Transp., 1975-80; pres. Lafayette Tennis, 1976-78. Recipient Dow Outstanding Faculty award Am. Soc. Engring. Edn., 1972, Western Elec. Fund award, 1974-75, D.D. Ewing award Purdue U., 1973, A.A. Potter award, 1973, Honeywell Teaching award, 1995. Fellow IEEE (Harry S. Nyquist award 1992); mem. Am. Vacuum Soc., Sigma Xi, Eta Kappa Nu, Sigma Tau, Sigma Pi Sigma. Avocations: tennis, backpacking, fishing, woodworking, baking. Office: Purdue U Elec Engring Bldg West Lafayette IN 47907

NEUEFEIND, WILHELM, economics educator, university administrator; b. Viersen, Germany, Mar. 6, 1939; came to U.S., 1977; m. Ingrid Leuchtenberg, Mar. 30, 1966; children: Nicole, Bettina. MBA, U. Cologne, Germany, 1962, MA in Math., 1969; PhD in Econs., U. Bonn, 1972. Lectr. econs. U. Bonn, 1973-77; prof. Washington U., St. Louis, 1977—; chmn. dept. econs. Wash. U., St. Louis, 1983—; Contbr. articles to profl. jours. Mem. Econometric Soc., Am. Econ. Assn., Assn. for Advancement Econ. Theory. Office: Washington U Dept Econs 1 Brookings Dr # 1208 Saint Louis MO 63130-4899

NEUENSCHWANDER, PIERRE FERNAND, medical educator. BS in Chemistry, 1985; PhD in Chemistry and Molecular Biology, SUNY, Stony Brook, 1990. Lab. tchg. asst. SUNY, Stony Brook, 1985-86, lecture tchg. asst. in biochemistry, 1986, 87; assoc. rsch. scientist Cardiovascular Biology Rsch. Program Okla. Med. Rsch. Found., Oklahoma City, 1990-93, sr. rsch. scientist, 1993-94, found. rsch. scientist, 1994-95, asst. mem., 1995—. Co-editor Trigger newsletter; rev. Jour. Biol. Chemistry; contbr. articles to profl. jours. Recipient Am. Heart Assn. Travel stipend, 1994, Internat. Soc. Haematology Travel award, 1992, Am. Soc. Hematology Travel award, 1989, 90. Mem. Am. Heart Assn. (coun. on thrombosis), Am. Chem Soc. (divsn. biol. chemistry), Internat. Soc. Thrombosis and Haemostasis, Sigma Xi, Alpha Chi Sigma. Office: Okla Med Rsch Found 825 NE 13th St Oklahoma City OK 73104

NEUFELD, ELIZABETH FONDAL, biochemist, educator; b. Paris, Sept. 27, 1928; U.S. citizen; m. 1951. Ph.D., U. Calif., Berkeley, 1956; D.H.C. (hon.), U. Rene Descartes, Paris, 1978; D.Sc. (hon.), Russell Sage Coll., Troy, N.Y., 1981, Hahnemann U. Sch. Medicine, 1984. Asst. research biochemist U. Calif., Berkeley, 1957-63; with Nat. Inst. Arthritis, Metabolism and Digestive Diseases, Bethesda, Md., 1963-84, research biochemist, 1963-73, chief sect. human biochem. genetics, 1973-79, chief genetics and biochem. br., 1979-84; prof., chmn. dept. biol. chemistry UCLA Sch. Medicine, 1984—. Passano Found. sr. laureate, 1982; named Calif. Scientist of Yr., 1990; recipient Dickson prize U. Pitts., 1974, Hillenbrand award, 1975, Gairdner Found. award, 1981, Albert Lasker Clin. Med. Rsch. award, 1982, William Allan award, 1982, Elliott Cresson medal, 1984, Wolf Found. prize, 1988, Christopher Columbus Discovery award for biomed. rsch., 1992, Nat. Medal of Sci., 1994. Fellow AAAS; mem. NAS, Inst. Medicine of NAS, Am. Acad. Arts and Scis., Am. Soc. Human Genetics, Am. Chem. Soc., Am. Soc. Biochemistry and Molecular Biology (pres. 1992-93), Am. Soc. Cell Biology, Am. Soc. Clin. Investigation. Office: UCLA Sch Medicine Dept Biol Chemistry Los Angeles CA 90024-1737

NEUFELD, MACE, film company executive; b. N.Y.C., July 13, 1928; s. Philip M. and Margaret Ruth (Braun) N.; Feb. 28, 1954; children: Bradley David, Glenn Jeremy, Nancy Ann. B.A., Yale U., 1948; postgrad., NYU, 1958-60. Photographer various N.Y. pubs., 1943-45; prodn. asst. Raymond E. Nelson, 1949-50; founder, owner Ray Bloch Assocs., Inc., N.Y.C., 1951-59; ptnr. BNB Prodns., N.Y.C., 1959-70, Neufeld-Davis Prodns., Inc., Beverly Hills, Calif., 1981—; Trustee Am. Film Inst., 1978—; chmn. life achievement award nominating com. and scholarship fund. Producer in assn. with Harvey Bernhard The Omen, 1976, Damien - Omen II, 1977, Omen III - The Final Conflict, 1980; producer: The Frisco Kid, 1979, Angel on My Shoulder, 1980, The American Dream, 1980; ABC-TV mini-series East of Eden, 1981; CBS-TV series Cagney and Lacey, 1984; MGM film The Aviator, 1984, ABC-TV A Death in California, 1985; producer films Transylvania 6-5000, 1985, No Way Out, 1987, The Hunt for Red October, 1989, Flight of the Intruder, 1990, Necessary Roughness, 1991, Patriot Games, 1992, Clear and Present Danger, 1994, Gettysburg, 1994, Beverly Hills Cop 3, 1994. Photograph entitled Sammy's Home voted Picture of Yr. N.Y. World Telegram-Sun, 1955; recipient Grand prize Eastman Kodak's First Nat. Salon of Photography, 1945; named N.A.T.O./Showest Producer of the Yr., 1993. Mem. Acad. TV Arts and Scis., Acad. Motion Picture Arts and Scis., ASCAP, Am. Film Inst. Democrat. Clubs: Friars, Yale of N.Y. Home: 624 N Arden Dr Beverly Hills CA 90210-3510 Office: Paramount Pictures 5555 Melrose Ave Los Angeles CA 90038-3149

NEUFELD, MICHAEL JOHN, curator, historian; b. Edmonton, Alta., Can., July 7, 1951; s. Henry John and Isabel Grace (Mitchell) N.; m. Sheila Faith Weiss, May 29, 1983 (div. Dec. 1992); m. Karen Lee Levenback, June 14, 1994. BA with 1st class honors, U. Calgary, Alta., 1974; MA, U. B.C., Vancouver, Can., 1976, Johns Hopkins U., 1980; PhD in History, Johns Hopkins U., 1984. Hist. rschr. Dept. Supply and Svcs., Ottawa, Ont., Can., summer 1973, 74; teaching asst. Johns Hopkins U., Balt., 1979-80; instr. Clarkson U., Potsdam, N.Y., 1983-84, from part-time instr. to part-time asst. prof., 1983-85; vis. asst. prof. SUNY, Oswego, 1985-86, Colgate U., Hamilton, N.Y., 1986-88; Verville fellow Nat. Air and Space Mus., Washington, 1988-89, Smithsonian postdoctoral fellow, 1989-90, curator dept. aeronautics, 1990—; curator Air Power in WWII series, 1991-94. Author: The Skilled Metalworkers of Nuremberg, 1989, The Rocket and the Reich, 1995; contbr. articles and book revs. to profl. jours. Recipient History Manuscript award AIAA, 1995, NSF Scholar's award History of Sci. and Tech. Program, 1989-90. Mem. Am. Hist. Assn., Conf. Group on Ctrl. European History, Soc. Mil. History, Soc. for History in Tech., History of Sci. Soc. Avocation: amateur astronomy. Office: Nat Air & Space Mus Dept Aeronautics Smithsonian Instn Washington DC 20560

NEUGARTEN, BERNICE LEVIN, social scientist; b. Norfolk, Nebr., Feb. 11, 1916; d. David L. and Sadie (Segall) Levin; m. Fritz Neugarten, July 1, 1940; children: Dail Ann, Jerrold. B.A., U. Chgo., 1936, Ph.D., 1943; D.Sc. (hon.), U. So. Calif., 1980; PhD (hon.), Cath. U., Nijmegen, 1988. Rsch. assoc. Com. on Human Devel., U. Chgo., 1948-50; asst. prof. U. Chgo., 1951-60, assoc. prof., 1960-64, prof., 1964-80, chmn., 1969-73, prof. social svc. adminstrn., 1978-80, mem. com. on policy studies, 1979-80, Rothschild disting. scholar, prof. emeritus, 1988—; prof. emerita Northwestern U., 1980-88; mem. council U. Chgo. Senate, 1968-71, 72-75, 78-80, chmn. council com. on univ. women, 1969-70; nat. adv. council Nat. Inst. on Aging, 1975-76, 78-81, Fed. Council on Aging, 1978-81; dep. chmn. White House Conf. on Aging, 1980-81. Author: (with R.J. Havighurst) American Indian and White Children: A Social-Psychological Investigation, 1955, reprint, 1969, (with R.J. Havighurst) Society and Education, 1957, rev., 1962, 67, 75, (with Assocs.) Personality in Middle and Late Life, 1964, reprint, 1980, (with J.M.A. Munnichs et al) Adjustment to Retirement, 1969, (with R.P. Coleman) Social Status in the City, 1971, Middle Age and Aging, 1968; co-editor: (with H. Eglit) Age Discrimination, 1981, Age or Need? Public Policies for Older People, 1982; assoc. editor Jour. Gerontology, 1958-61, Human Devel., 1962-68; adv. or cons. editor other profl. jours., 1959—; author monographs, research papers and reports. mem. various adv. bodies. Recipient Am. Psychol. Found. Disting. Tchg. award, 1975, Disting. Psychologist award Ill. Psychol. Assn., 1979, Sandoz Internat. Prize for Gerontol. Rsch., 1987, Ollie Randall award Nat. Coun. on Aging, 1993, Gold Medal award for lifetime contbn. as a psychologist in the public interest Am. Psychol. Found., 1994. Fellow AAAS, Am. Psychol. Assn. (coun. rep. 1967-69, 73-76, Disting. Sci. Contbn. award 1980, honoree Women's Heritage Exhibit 1992, Gold Medal award 1994), Am. Sociol. Assn., Gerontol. Soc. Am. (pres. 1968-69, Kleemeier award 1971, Brookdale award 1982, Disting. Mentor award 1988), Am. Acad. Arts and Scis., Internat. Assn. Gerontology (governing coun. 1975-78, chmn. N.Am. exec. com. 1983-85, disting. creative contbrn. to gerontology award); mem. Inst. Medicine of NAS. Home: # 1202 1551 Larimer St Denver CO 80202

NEUGEBAUER, MARCIA, physicist, administrator; b. N.Y.C., Sept. 27, 1932; d. Howard Graeme MacDonald and Frances (Townsend) Marshall; m. Gerry Neugebauer, Aug. 25, 1956; children: Carol, Lee. B.S., Cornell U., 1954; M.S., U. Ill., 1956. Grad. asst. U. Ill., Urbana, 1954-56; vis. fellow Clare Hall Coll., Cambridge, Eng., 1975; sr. research scientist Jet Propulsion Lab. Calif. Inst. Tech., Pasadena, 1956—; vis. prof. planetary sci. Calif. Inst. Tech., Pasadena, 1986-87; mem. com. NASA, Washington, 1960—, NAS, Washington, 1981—; Regents lectr. UCLA, 1990-91. Contbr. numerous articles on physics to profl. jours. Named Calif. Woman Scientist of Yr. Calif. Mus. Sci. and Industry, 1967; recipient Exceptional Sci. Achievement medal NASA, 1970, Outstanding Leadership medal NASA, 1993. Fellow Am. Geophys. Union (sec., pres. solar planetary relationships sect. 1979-84, editor-in-chief Rev. Geophysics 1988-92, pres.-elect 1992-94, pres. 1994-96)mem. governing bd. Amer. Inst. Physics, 1995—. Democrat. Home: 1720 Braeburn Rd Altadena CA 91001-2708 Office: Calif Inst Tech Jet Propulsion Lab/MS 169-506 4800 Oak Grove Dr Pasadena CA 91109-8001

NEUGROSCHEL, ARNOST, electrical engineering educator; b. Prešov, Czechoslovakia, June 18, 1942; came to U.S., 1973; s. Ludovit and Irene (Gottfried) Neugröschl; m. Susan M. Pertz, June 20, 1982. Diploma in engring., Slovak Tech. U., Bratislava, Czechoslovakia, 1965; PhD, Technion-Israel Inst. Tech., Haifa, 1973. Engr. Tesla, Inc., Piešťany, Czechoslovakia, 1966-67; instr. Technion-Israel Inst. Tech., 1969-73; postdoctoral rsch. assoc. dept. elec. engring. U. Ill., Urbana, 1973-75; asst. prof. U. Fla., Gainesville, 1975-79, assoc. prof., 1979-83, prof., 1983—; on leave Interuniv. Microelectronic Ctr., Leuven, Belgium, 1986; mem. summer faculty IBM T.J. Watson Rsch. Ctr., Yorktown Heights, N.Y., 1982. Contbr. over 75 articles to profl. jours.; patentee in field. Fellow IEEE. Avocations: tennis, travel. Office: U Fla Dept Elec Engring Gainesville FL 32611

NEUGROSCHL, GAIL E. (PENNY NEUGROSCHL), geriatrics nurse, educator; b. Chgo., May 27, 1938; d. Rudolph and Leona (Zurakov) Edelstein; m. J. Gilston Neugroschl, Dec. 27, 1959; children: Cynthia, Scott, Lori Jo. Diploma, Los Angeles Pierce Coll., Woodland Hills, Calif., 1978; BS, Boston U., 1959; MS, U. La Verne, Calif., 1985. Cert. gerontological nurse, BCLS instr. Charge nurse West Valley Community Hosp., Encino, Calif., 1978-79; head nurse Canoga Park (Calif.) Hosp., 1979-80; instr. nursing Valley Coll. of Med.-Dental Careers, North Hollywood, Calif., 1980-82; dir. insvc. Jewish Home for the Aging, Grancell Village, Reseda, Calif., 1982-85; instr. nursing Pacific Coast Coll., West Los Angeles, Calif., 1985-89; asst. dir. nursing edn. Concorde Career Inst. Valley Coll. Campus, North Hollywood, Calif., 1989-92; dir. nursing Country Villa Wilshire, L.A., 1992, West L.A. Pavillion, 1992; dir. edn. Cmty. Hospice Care, L.A., 1993-95; dir. nursing Nicksan Home Healthcare, L.A., 1995—. Pres., Jewish Marriage Enhancement So. Calif. Home: 21900 Marylee St Apt 245 Woodland Hills CA 91367-4821

NEUHARTH, ALLEN HAROLD, newspaper publisher; b. Eureka, S.D., Mar. 22, 1924; s. Daniel J. and Christina (Neuharth) N.; m. Loretta Fay Helgeland, June 16, 1946 (div. 1972), m. Lori Wilson, Dec. 31, 1973 (div. 1982), m. Rachel Fornes, March 21, 1993; children: Daniel J. II, Jan, Alexis Rae Fornes-Neuharth; . BA cum laude, U. S.D., 1950. Reporter Rapid City (S.D.) Jour., 1948; sports writer Mitchell (S.D.) Daily Republic, 1949; staff writer AP, Sioux Falls, S.D., 1950-52; editor, pub. SoDak Sports, Sioux Falls, 1952-54; with Miami (Fla.) Herald, 1954-60, asst. mng. editor, 1958-60; asst. exec. editor Detroit Free Press, 1960-63; gen. mgr. Times-Union and Democrat and Chronicle, Rochester, N.Y., 1963-66; exec. v.p. Gannett Co., Inc., Washington, 1966-70, pres., chief operating officer, 1970-73, pres., chief exec. officer, 1973-79, chmn., chief exec. officer, 1979-86; founder, chmn. USA Today, 1982; chmn. Gannett Co., Inc., Washington, 1986-89, Gannett Found., Arlington, Va., 1989-91, Freedom Forum, 1991—. Author: Confessions of an S.O.B., 1989. Trustee, chmn. Gannett Found. Served with inf. AUS, 1943-46, ETO, PTO. Decorated Bronze Star; recipient Horatio Alger award, 1975; named Outstanding Chief Exec. of Yr. in Pub. and Printing Industry for 3 consecutive yrs. Mem. Am. Newspaper Pubs. Assn. (bd. dirs. 1968-82, chmn., pres. 1979-80), Jockey Club (Miami), Ocean Reef Club (Key Largo, Fla.), Sky Club, Sigma Delta Chi (past nat. region I dir.). Office: Freedom Forum 1101 Wilson Blvd Arlington VA 22209-2248

NEUHAUS, OTTO WILHELM, biochemistry educator; b. Zweibrucken, Germany, Nov. 18, 1922; came to U.S., 1927, naturalized, 1931; s. Clemens Jakob and Johanna Amalie (Schnorr) N.; m. Dorothy Ellen Rehn, Aug. 30, 1947; children: Thomas William, Carol Alida, Joanne Marie. B.S., U. Wis., 1944; M.S., U. Mich., 1947, Ph.D., 1953. Research chemist Huron Milling Co., 1951-54; mem. faculty Wayne State U., Detroit, 1954-66; assoc. prof. Wayne State U., 1965-66; prof., chmn. dept. biochemistry U. S.D., Vermillion, 1966-76, acting chmn. dept. physiology and pharmacology, 1975-76, 82-83, prof., chmn. div. biochemistry, physiology and pharmacology, 1976-82, prof., 1982-88, chmn. dept. biochemistry, 1982-86; prof. emeritus U. S.D., 1988—. Author: (with John Halver) Fish in Research, 1969, (with James Orten) Human Biochemistry, 1982; also research articles. NATO Research fellow, 1961-62. Fellow AAAS; mem. Am. Chem. Soc., Am. Soc. Biol. Chemists, Sigma Xi, Phi Sigma, Alpha Chi Sigma, Phi Lambda Upsilon. Lutheran. Home: 1090 Valley View Dr Vermillion SD 57069-3587

NEUHAUS, PHILIP ROSS, investment banker; b. Houston, Dec. 25, 1919; s. Hugo Victor and Kate Padgitt (Rice) N.; m. Elizabeth Lacey Thompson, Oct. 31, 1942 (div. 1967); children: Philip Ross (dec.), Lacey Neuhaus Dorn, Elizabeth Neuhaus Armstrong, Joan Thompson Neuhaus; m. Barbara R. Haden, Aug. 14, 1968; 5 stepchildren. Grad., St. Mark's Sch., Southborough, Mass., 1938; BA, Yale, 1942. With Nat. City Bank of Cleve., 1946-47, McDonald & Co., Cleve., 1947; with Neuhaus & Co., 1947; chmn. Underwood, Neuhaus & Co., Inc., Houston, 1948-89; hon. chmn. Lovett Underwood Neuhaus & Webb, Houston, 1989-92; sr. v.p. Kemper Securities Inc., Houston, 1992-95, Everen Securities, Inc., Houston, 1995—; chmn. bd. Voss-Woodway, Inc., 1994—. Trustee Tex. Childrens Hosp.; assoc. Rice U.; advisory bd. Salvation Army, Houston, 1969-91. Served to capt., cav. AUS, 1942-45. Mem. Securities Industry Assn. Am. (bd. govs., chmn. Tex. dist. 1973, exec. com. 1975), Houston Soc. Financial Analysts (pres. 1959), Stock and Bond Club Houston (past pres.), Nat. Fedn. Financial Analysts (v.p. 1963, dir.). Clubs: Bayou, Houston Country, Houston, Eagle Lake Rod and Gun. Home: 407 Thamer Ln Houston TX 77024-6939 Office: Everen Securities Inc 909 Fannin St Houston TX 77010

NEUHAUS, WILLIAM OSCAR, III, architect; b. Houston, Mar. 16, 1944; s. W. Oscar and Betty Palmer (Bosworth) N.; m. Kay Ficklen; children: Kimberly Sautelle, Sara Palmer. BArch, Ga. Inst. Tech., 1967. Registered architect, Tex., N.Mex. Intern architect Caudill Rowlett Scott, Houston, 1967-69; assoc. Charles Tapley Assocs., Houston, 1969-72; prin. W.O. Neuhaus Architecture/Planning, Houston, 1972-83; owner, mgr. W.O. Neuhaus Assocs., Houston, 1984—. Co-author trading Toilets: The Subterranean Zoning of Houston, 1982; author Foreword, 1992. Pres. Rice Design Alliance, Houston, 1982-83, bd. dirs. 1978-84; pres. Armand Bayou Nature Ctr. Found., 1986-90, Stages Repertory Theatre, Houston, 1988-89; mem. Mayor's Land Use Strategy com., Houston, 1990. Fellow Am. Leadership Forum, AIA (pres. 1990-91, chair design com. 1988-89); mem. Tex. Soc. Architects (mem. design com. 1989-90). Office: WO Neuhaus Assocs 4100 Montrose Blvd Ste D Houston TX 77006-4912

NEUHAUSEN, BENJAMIN SIMON, auditor, accountant; b. Urbana, Ill., Apr. 23, 1950; s. Stanley Edward and Dolores Renee (Epstein) N.; m. Madeline Cohen, Sept. 6, 1987; 3 children. BA, Mich. State U., 1971; MBA, NYU, 1973. CPA, Ill. Staff auditor Arthur Andersen & Co., N.Y.C., 1973-75, sr. auditor, 1975-78, audit mgr., 1978-79, 81-85; audit ptnr. Arthur Andersen LLP, Chgo., 1985—; practice fellow Fin. Acctg. Standards Bd., Stamford, Conn., 1979-81. Contbr. articles to profl. jours. Bd. dirs. The Renaissance Soc., Chgo., 1987-90. Recipient Charles W. Haskins medal N.Y. Soc. CPAs, 1974. Mem. AICPA, Ill. Soc. CPAs, Chgo. Athletic Assn. Jewish. Office: Arthur Andersen LLP 69 W Washington St Chicago IL 60602-3004

NEUHAUSER, DUNCAN VON BRIESEN, health services educator; b. Phila., June 20, 1939; s. Edward Blaine Duncan and Gernda (von Briesen) N.; m. Elinor Toaz, Mar. 6, 1965; children: Steven, Ann. B.A., Harvard U., 1961; M.H.A., U. Mich., 1963; M.B.A., U. Chgo., 1966, Ph.D., 1971. Research assoc. U. Chgo., 1965-70; asst. prof. Sch. Pub. Health, Harvard U.,

Boston, 1970-74; assoc. prof. Sch. Pub. Health, Harvard U., 1974-79; cons. in medicine Mass. Gen. Hosp., Boston, 1975-80; assoc. dir. Health Systems Mgmt. Ctr. Case Western Res. U., Cleve., 1979-85, prof. epidemiology, biostats. and orgnl. behavior, 1979—, prof. medicine, 1981—, prof. family medicine, 1990—, Charles Elton Blanchard prof. health mgmt., 1995—, co-dir. Health Systems Mgmt. Ctr., 1985—; cons. in medicine Cleve. Met. Gen. Hosp., 1981—; adj. mem. med. staff Cleve. Clinic Found., 1984—. Author numerous books, sci. papers; editor: jours. Health Matrix, 1982-90, Med. Care, 1983—. Vice chmn. bd. dirs. Vis. Nurse Assn. Greater Cleve., 1983-84, chmn., 1984-85; bd. dirs. New Eng. Grenfell Assn., Boston, 1972—, Braintree (Mass.) Hosp., 1975-86; trustee Internat. Grenfell Assn., St. Anthony, Nfld., Can., 1975-83, Blue Hill (Maine) Hosp., 1983-89; trustee Hough Norwood Health Ctr., 1983-94, chmn., 1993-94. Recipient E.F. Meyers Trustee award Cleve. Hosp. Assn., 1987, Hope award Nat. Multiple Sclerosis Soc., 1992; Kellogg fellow, 1963-65; Keck Found. scholar, 1982—; Neuhauser lectr. Soc. Pediatric Radiology, 1982; Freedlander lectr. Ohio Permanente Med. Group, 1986. Mem. Inst. Medicine of NAS, Soc. for Clin. Decision Making, Cleve. Skating Club, St. Botolph Club (Boston), Kollegewidgwok Yacht Club (Blue Hill, Maine, commodore 1991-93), Beta Gamma Sigma. Home: 2655 N Park Blvd Cleveland Heights OH 44106-3622 Office: Case Western Reserve U Med Sch 10900 Euclid Ave Cleveland OH 44106-4945

NEUMAIER, GERHARD JOHN, environment consulting company executive; b. Covington, Ky., July 27, 1937; s. John Edward and Elli Anna (Raudies) N.; m. Ellen Elaine Klepper, Oct. 24, 1959; children: Kevin Scott, Kirsten Lynn. BME, Gen. Motors Inst., 1960; MA in Biophysics, U. Buffalo, 1963. Research ecologist, project mgr. Cornell Aero. Lab., Buffalo, 1963-70; pres., chief exec., chmn. bd. Ecology and Environment Inc., Buffalo, 1970—. Recipient Theodore Roosevelt Citizen of Yr. award City of Buffalo, 1990. Mem. APHA, Air Pollution Control Assn., Internat. Assn. Gt. Lakes Research, Inst. Environ. Scis., Ecol. Soc. Am., Am. Inst. Biol. Scis., Urban Land Inst., Arctic Inst. N.Am., Nat. Parks and Conservation Assn., Defenders of Wildlife, Nat. Wildlife Fedn., Wilderness Soc., Am. Hort. Soc., Smithsonian Assocs., Nat. Audubon Soc. Home: 284 Mill Rd East Aurora NY 14052-2805 Office: Ecology & Environment Inc 368 Pleasant View Dr Lancaster NY 14086-1316

NEUMAN, CHARLES P., electrical and computer engineering educator; b. Pitts., July 26, 1940; s. Daniel and Frances G. Neuman; m. Susan G. Neuman, Sept. 4, 1967. B.S. in Elec. Engring. with honors, Carnegie Inst. Tech., 1962; S.M., Harvard U., 1963, Ph.D. in Applied Math., 1968. Tchg. fellow Harvard U., Cambridge, Mass., 1962-64, rsch. asst., 1964-67; mem. tech. staff Bell Telephone Labs., Whippany, N.J., 1967-69; asst. prof. elec. engring. Carnegie-Mellon U., Pitts., 1969-71, assoc. prof., 1971-78, prof. elec. engring., 1978-83, prof. elec. and computer engring., 1983—, undergrad. advisor, 1994—. Mem. editorial bd. Internat. Jour. Modelling and Simulation, Control and Computers; contbr. numerous articles to profl. jours. Mem. IEEE (sr., assoc. editor Trans. on Systems, Man and Cybernetics), Inst. Mgmt. Scis., AAAS, Instrument Soc. Am. (sr.), Soc. Harvard Engrs. and Scientists, Soc. Indsl. and Applied Math., Sigma Xi, Phi Kappa Phi, Tau Beta Pi, Eta Kappa Nu. Office: Carnegie-Mellon U Dept Elec & Computer Engring Pittsburgh PA 15213

NEUMAN, NANCY ADAMS MOSSHAMMER, civic leader; b. Greenwich, Conn., July 24, 1936; d. Alden Smith and Margaret (Mevis) Mosshammer; BA, Pomona Coll., 1957, LLD, 1983; MA, U. Calif. at Berkeley, 1961; LHD, Westminster Coll., 1987; m. Mark Donald Neuman, Dec. 23, 1958; children: Deborah Neuman Metzler, Jennifer Neuman Joye, Jeffrey Abbott. William A. Johnson Disting. lectr. Am. govt. Pomona Coll., 1990; disting. vis. prof. Washington and Jefferson Coll., 1991, 94, Bucknell U., 1992. Pres., Lewisburg (Pa.) area League Women Voters, 1967-70; bd. dirs. LWV Pa., 1970-77, pres., 1975-77; bd. dirs. LWV U.S., 1977-90, 2d v.p., 1978-80, 1st v.p., 1982-84, pres., 1986-90; bd. dirs. Pathmakers, Inc., 1993—, pres. 1993-95; mem. Pa. Gov.'s Commn. on Mortgage and Interest Rates, 1973, Pa. Commonwealth Child Devel. Com., 1974-75, Nat. Commn. on Pub. Svc., 1987-90; bd. dirs. Housing Assistance Council, Inc., Washington, 1974—, pres., 1978-80; bd. dirs. Nat. Council on Agrl. Life and Labor, 1974-79, Nat. Rural Housing Coalition, 1975-95, Pa. Housing Fin. Agy., 1975-80, Jud. Inquiry and Rev. Bd. Pa., 1989-93; Disciplinary Bd. Supreme Ct. Pa., 1980-85; mem. Pa. Gov.'s Task Force on Voter Registration, 1975-76, Nat. Task Force for Implementation Equal Rights Amendment, 1975-77; mem. adv. com. Pa. Gov.'s Interdepartmental Council on Seasonal Farmworkers, 1975-77; mem. Appellate Ct. Nominating Commn. Pa., 1976-79; mem. Fed. Jud. Nominating Commn. Pa., 1977-85, chmn., 1978-81, 82-83; mem. Pa. Gov.'s Study Commn. on Pub. Employee Relations, 1976-78; del. Internat. Women's Yr. Conf., 1977; bd. dirs. ERAmerica, Inc., 1st v.p., 1977-79, Nat. Low Income Housing Coalition, 1979-82; Rural Am., 1979-81, Fed. Home Loan Bank Pitts., 1979-82; mem. Nat. Adv. Com. for Women, 1978-79; mem. nat. adv. com. Pa. Neighborhood Preservation Support System, 1976-77; bd. dirs. Pa. Women's Campaign Fund, 1984-86, 92—, pres., 1992—, Rural Coalition, Washington, 1984-90, Com. on the Constitutional System, 1988-90, Am. Judicature Soc., 1989-93; exec. com. Leadership Conf. Civil Rights, 1986-90; bd. dirs. Pennsylvanians for Modern Cts., 1986— trustee Citizen's Rsch. Found., 1989—; mem. mid. dist. Pa. adv. com. judicial and U.S. atty nominations, 1993-94. Editor: A Voice of Our Own: Leading American Women Celebrate the Right to Vote, 1996. Virginia Travis lectureship Bucknell U., 1982. Recipient Disting. Alumna award MacDuffie Sch. for Girls, 1979, Liberty Bell award Pa. Bar Assn., 1983, Barrows Alumni award Pomona Coll., 1987, Thomas P. O'Neill Jr. award for exemplary pub. svc., 1989; named Disting. Daughter of Pa., 1987 Woodrow Wilson vis. fellow, 1993—. Mem. ABA (com. election law and voter participation, 1986-90, accreditation com. 1990—). Home: 132 Verna Rd Lewisburg PA 17837-8747

NEUMAN, ROBERT HENRY, lawyer; b. N.Y.C., Oct. 14, 1936; s. Sydney A. and Ethel (Pekelner) N.; m. Emily Mann, Dec. 30, 1960 (div. 1975); children: David Marshall, Anthony Howard, Amanda Sarah; m. Joyce Thompson, May 5, 1975; 1 child, Nicole Sydney. AB magna cum laude, Harvard U., 1958, JD, 1961. Bar: N.Y. 1962, D.C. 1962. Ford Found. fellow West Africa, 1961-62; assoc. Meyers & Batzell, Washington, 1962-64; asst. legal adviser U.S. Dept. of State, Washington, 1964-70; ptnr. Arent, Fox, Kintner, Plotkin & Kahn, Washington, 1970-93, Baker & Hostetler, Washington, 1993—. U.S. rep. to UN Conf. on Marine Pollution, 1969. Recipient Superior Honor award Dept. State, 1965. Mem. ABA, Fed. Internat. Bar Assn., Am. Soc. Internat. Law, Phi Beta Kappa. Avocation: sailing. Home: 3408 34th Pl NW Washington DC 20016-3136 Office: Baker & Hostetler 1050 Connecticut Ave NW Washington DC 20036-5303

NEUMAN, ROBERT STERLING, art educator, artist; b. Kellogg, Idaho, Sept. 9, 1926; s. Oscar C. and Katherine (Samuelson) N.; m. Helen Patricia Feddersen, Apr. 6, 1947 (div. 1971); children—Ingrid Alexandra, Elizabeth Catherine; m. Sunne Savage, June 3, 1979; 1 dau., Christina Mary. Student, U. Idaho, 1944-46; B.A.A., M.F.A., Calif. Coll. Arts and Crafts, 1947-51; student, San Francisco Sch. Fine Arts, 1950-51, Mills Coll., 1951. Assoc. prof. art Brown U., 1962-63; lectr. drawing Carpenter Center for Visual Arts, Harvard, 1963-72; prof. art, chmn. dept. Keene (N.H.) State Coll., 1972-90. Exhbns. include, Mus. Modern Art, Whitney Mus. Am. Art, Carnegie Internat., San Francisco Mus. Art, Boston Mus. Fine Arts, Worcester (Mass.) Art Mus., also Japan and Europe. Served with AUS and USAAF, 1945-46. Recipient Howard Found. award for painting, 1967; Fulbright grantee, 1953-54; Guggenheim fellow, 1956-57; Bender grantee San Francisco Art Assn., 1952. Home: 135 Cambridge St Winchester MA 01890-2411

NEUMAN, SHLOMO P., hydrology educator; b. Zilina, Czechoslovakia, Oct. 26, 1938; came to U.S., 1963, naturalized, 1970; s. Alexander Neumann and Klara (Pikler) Lesny; m. Yael B. Boritzer, Jan. 30, 1965; children: Gil, Michal, Ariel. BSc in Geology, Hebrew U., Jerusalem, 1963; MS in Engring. Sci., U. Calif., Berkeley, 1966, PhD in Engring. Sci., 1968. Cert. profl. hydrogeologist. Acting asst. prof., asst. rsch. engr. dept. civil engring. U. Calif., Berkeley, 1968-70, vis. assoc. prof. dept. civil engring., 1974-75; sr. scientist, assoc. rsch. prof. Inst. Soil and Water Agrl. Rsch. Orgn., Bet-Dagan, Israel, 1970-74; prof. hydrology dept. hydrology and water resources U. Ariz., Tucson, 1975-88, Regents' prof. dept. hydrology and water resources, 1988—; vis. scientist dept. isotope Weizmann Inst. Sci., Rehovot, Israel, 1976; maitre de rsch. Ctr. d'Informatique Geologique, Ecole Mines Paris, Fountainebleau, France, 1978, dir. rsch., 1981; vis. prof. dept. fluid mechanics and heat transfer Tel-Aviv U., 1981; disting. lectr. in field. Mem. editorial adv. bd. Jour. Hydrology, 1977-84, Water Sci. and Tech. Libr. (The Netherlands), 1983-86, Stochastic Hydrology and Hydraulics, 1992—; assoc. editor Water Resources Rsch. Jour., 1987-93; contbr. articles to profl. jours. Hebrew U. scholar, 1962-63, Edwin Letts Oliver scholar, 1965-66; Jane Lewis fellow, 1966-68; recipient Cert. of Appreciation award USDA, 1975, C.V. Theis award Am. Inst. Hydrology, 1990. Fellow Geol. Soc. Am. (O.E. Meinzer award 1976, Birdsal Disting. Lectr. 1987), Am. Geophys. Union (Robert E. Horton award 1969, assoc. editor Water Resources Rsch. 1987—); mem. Soc. Petroleum Engrs. of AIME, U.S. Nat. Acad. Engring., Assn. Groundwater Scientists and Engrs. of Nat. Well Water Assn. (Sci. award 1989), Ariz. Hydrol. Soc., Internat. Assn. Hydrogeologists, Sigma Xi. Jewish. Office: U Ariz Dept Hydrology & Water Resources Tucson AZ 85721

NEUMAN, TED R., principal. Prin. Duluth (Ga.) High Sch. Recipient Blue Ribbon award U.S. Dept. Edn., 1990-91. Office: Duluth High Sch 3737 Brock Rd Duluth GA 30136-2724

NEUMAN, TOM S., emergency medical physician, educator; b. N.Y.C., July 23, 1946; s. Otto and Susan Ann (Baltaxe) N.; m. Doris Rubin, Aug. 24, 1969; children: Allison Rachel, Russell Solomon. AB, Cornell U., 1967; MD, NYU, 1971. Diplomate Nat. Bd. Med. Examiners, Am. Bd. Internal Medicine, Am. Bd. Preventative Medicine, Am. Bd. Emergency Medicine. Intern Bellevue Hosp., N.Y.C., 1971-72, resident, 1972-73; commd. med. officer USN, 1973; advanced through grades to capt. USNR, 1990; instr. Naval Undersea Med. Inst., New London, Conn., 1973-74; staff med. officer Submarine Devel. Group One, San Diego, 1974-76, 78-80; emergency room physician Chula Vista (Calif.) Community Hosp., 1975-80; attending physician VA Med. Ctr., La Jolla, Calif., 1976-78; fellow in pulmonary medicine and physiology U. Calif. Sch. Medicine at San Diego, 1976-78, clin. instr., 1978-80, asst. clin. prof., 1980-84, flight physician Life Flight Aeromed. Program, 1980-86, asst. dir. dept. emergency medicine, 1980-94; assoc. dir. dept. emergency medicine, 1994—; attending physician pulmonary divsn. U. Calif. Sch. Medicine at San Diego, 1980—, assoc. clin. prof. medicine and surgery, 1984-87, base hosp. physician, 1984—, dir. Hyperbaric Med. Ctr., 1984—; med. officer UDT/SEAL Res. Unit 119, San Diego, 1980-84, Mobile Diving and Salvage Unit One, USNR, San Diego, 1984-86, PRIMUS Unit 1942-A, U. Calif. at San Diego, 1988-90; sr. med. officer Seal Teams 1/3/5, USNR, Coronado, Calif., 1986-87; asst. officer in charge Med. Unit 1942-A U. Calif. at San Diego, 1990-95; mem. med. adv. bd. western regional underwater lab. program U. So. Calif. Marine Sci. Ctr., Catalina, 1982-85; assoc. adj. prof. medicine and surgery U. Calif. Sch. Medicine at San Diego, 1987—; mem. San Diego Coroner's com. for investigation of diving fatalities, 1974—; mem. diving cons. Vocat. Diver Tng. Facility, Calif. Inst. Med., Chino, Calif., 1967; mem. task force City Mgr. on Carbon Monoxide Poisoning, San Diego, 1991; active Am. Nat. Stds. Inst. com. for minimal course content for recreational scuba instr. cert., 1992-94; chmn. emergency med. physician quality improvement com., 1992-94; spkr. in field. Author book chpts.; contbr. articles to profl. jours. Fellow ACP, Am. Coll. Preventive Medicine; mem. Am. Thoracic Soc., Am. Lung Assn., Undersea and Hyperbaric Med. Soc. (program com. 1981-82, nominations com. 1982-83, chmn. 1988-89, mem. edn. com. 1982-87, chmn. awards com. 1983-84, v.p. exec. com. 1983-84, co-chmn. credentials com. 1984-85, editor-in-chief Undersea and Hyperbaric Medicine 1995—), Profl. Assn. Diving Instrs. (emeritus). Avocations: scuba diving, fishing, photography. Office: Dept Emergency Medicine UCSD Med Ctr 200 W Arbor Dr Bldg 8676 San Diego CA 92103-1911

NEUMANN, ANDREW CONRAD, geological oceanography educator; b. Oak Bluffs, Mass., Dec. 21, 1933; s. Andrew Conrad Neumann and Faye Watson (Gilmore) Gilmour; m. Jane Spaeth, July 7, 1962; children: Jennifer, Christopher, Jonathan. BS in Geology, Bklyn. Coll., 1955; MS in Oceanography, Tex. A&M U., 1958; PhD in Geology, Lehigh U., 1963. Asst. prof. marine geology Lehigh U., Bethlehem, Pa., 1963-65; asst. prof. marine sci. U. Miami, Fla., 1965-69, assoc. prof. marine sci., 1969-72; prof. marine sci. U. N.C., Chapel Hill, 1972-85, Bowman and Gray prof. geol. oceanography, 1985—; program dir. NSF, Washington, 1969-70; Kenan prof. U. Edinburgh, Scotland, 1978; summer vis. investigator U.S. Geol. Survey, Woods Hole, Mass., 1981—, Woods Hole Oceanographic Inst., 1981—; vis. prof. U. Naples, Italy, 1984, Eötvös U., Budapest, Hungary, 1991. Contbr. articles to profl. jours. Trustee Bermuda Biol. Sta. for Research Inc., 1972-76. Recipient Disting. Alumni award Bklyn. Coll., 1987. Fellow Geol. Soc. Am.; mem. Soc. Econ. Paleontologists and Mineralogists, N.C. Acad. Sci. Avocations: fishing, gardening, sailing. Office: U NC Dept Marine Scis 1205 Venable Hall 045a Chapel Hill NC 27599-3300

NEUMANN, CHARLES HENRY, mathematics educator; b. Washington, Jan. 30, 1943; s. Bernhardt Walter and Emma (Habitz) N.; m. Cheryl Elaine Girard, June 18, 1965; children: Matthew Roy, Kristen Elizabeth. AS, Alpena (Mich.) C.C., 1962; BS in Math., Mich. State U., 1964, M.A.T. in Math., 1965. Sci. tchr. Alpena Pub. Schs., 1965-66; instr. math. Alpena C.C., 1966-84, math. sci. dept. chair, 1969-84; instr. math. Oakland C.C., Bloomfield Hills, Mich., 1984—; mem. fin. com. Luth. Social Svcs. of Mich. Scoutmaster troop 92 Boy Scouts Am., Alpena, 1981-84; bd. dirs. Mich. Vision Svc. Assn., Columbus, 1988-89; mem. exec. com. Oakland County (Mich.) Dem. Com., 1995; mem. fin. com. Luth. Social Svcs. Mich., 1995—; bd. dirs., 1996—. Mem. NEA (del. 1974-80, adv. com. on membership 1993—), Math. Assn. Am., Am. Math. Assn. of Two-Yr. Colls., Mich. Edn. Assn. (bd. dirs. 1974-80), Mich. Edn. Spl. Svcs. (trustee 1975-93, pres. 1976-93), Mich. Math. Assn. of Two-Yr. Colls., Mich. Assn. Higher Edn. (v.p. two-yr. colls. 1970—), Oakland C.C. Faculty Assn. (v.p. 1994-95, pres. 1995—), Phi Kappa Phi. Lutheran. Avocations: collecting antique books, racquetball, cross country skiing. Home: 5871 Warbler Clarkston MI 48346-2973 Office: Oakland CC 2900 Featherstone Rd Auburn Hills MI 48326-2817

NEUMANN, FORREST KARL, retired hospital administrator; b. St. Louis, Oct. 7, 1930; s. Metz Earl and Ruth (McGhee) N.; m. Erika Stefanie Turkl, Feb. 11, 1955; children: Tracey Neumann Liberson, Karen Neumann Kruger, Scott, Lisa. B.S., Roosevelt U., 1953; M.S. in Hosp. Adminstrn., Northwestern U., 1955. Adminstrv. resident Louis A. Weiss Hosp., Chgo., 1954-55; mem. staff Sparrow Hosp., Lansing, Mich., 1958-90; CEO, dir. Edward W. Sparrow Hosp., Lansing, 1962-90; pres., chief exec. officer, dir. Mason Gen. Hosp., Mich., 1973-85; chmn. bd. Caymich Ins. Co. Ltd., Cayman Islands, 1979-91; emeritus dir. Caymich Ins. Co. Ltd., Cayman Islands, 1991—; chmn. bd. Caymich Ins. Co. (Barbados) Ltd., 1986-91; pres., CEO, Mich. Hosp. Assn. Ins. Co., 1990-96; dir. Mich. Hosp. Assocs. Ins. Co., 1976—; pres., CEO, Sparrow, Inc., 1984-90. Chmn. hosp. div. United Community Chest, 1965-68, chmn. budget steering com., 1970-71, bd. dirs., mem. exec. com., 1969-75; mem. adv. com. Capitol Area Comprehensive Health Planning Assn., 1969, bd. dirs., 1971-75, treas., 1974-75; mem., vice chmn. Mich. Arbitration Adv. Com., 1975-80; bd. dirs. Grad. Med. Edn., Inc., 1971-80, pres., 1972-73, treas. 1973. Fellow Am. Coll. Hosp. Adminstrs.; mem. Southwestern Mich. Hosp. Council (trustee 1968-73, pres. 1970-71), Am. Hosp. Assn. (del. 1979-87), Mich. Hosp. Assn. (1st v.p. 1972-73, bd. dirs., exec. com., treas. 1974-75, chmn. 1976-77, Meritorious Key award 1979). Lodge: Rotary (Lansing). Office: Mich Hosp Assn Ins Co 6215 W St Joseph Hwy Lansing MI 48917-4852

NEUMANN, FREDERICK LOOMIS, accounting educator, academic administrator, consultant; b. New Britain, Conn., Nov. 16, 1930; s. Carl Samuel and Rachel Louise (Clark) N.; m. Elizabeth Ann Robinson, Sept. 10, 1960; children: Bradford E., Carla C., Marshall G. A.B. magna cum laude, Dartmouth Coll., 1952; M.B.A. with highest distinction, Amos Tuck Sch. Bus. Adminstrn., 1953; M.B.A., U. Chgo., 1965, Ph.D., 1967. CPA, Ill., Conn.; cert. internal auditor. Sr. acct. Arthur Andersen & Co., N.Y.C., 1956-62; mem. faculty U. Ill., Urbana-Champaign, 1965—, asst. prof. accountancy, 1965-70, assoc. prof., 1970-75, prof., 1975—, Price Waterhouse prof. auditing, 1979—, head dept. accountancy, 1981-86, assoc. dean acad. affairs, 1992—; cons. in field; pres. Fedn. Schs. of Accountancy, 1987—; sec. Adminstrs. of Accountancy Programs, 1986. Author: Case Studies in Computer Control and Auditing, 1975, Questions and Problems in Auditing, 11th edit., 1995; editor: Issues in Accounting Education, 1991-95; contbr. numerous articles to profl. jours., chpts. to books. Cons. Champaign County Headstart and Child Devel. Corp., 1970-87; treas. Weslye Meth. Ch., 1987—; chmn. com. Champaign County Regional Blood Ctr., 1982—; bd. govs. Univ. YMCA, 1990-96, chmn., 1992-95; mem. Univ. Senate. Lt. (j.g.) USNR, 1953-56, comdr. Res. Ford Found. fellow, 1962-65, Ernst & Whinney fellow, 1972-73. Mem. Inst. Decision Scis., Am. Acctg. Assn. (chmn. auditing sect. 1976-77, chmn. tchg. and curriculum sect. 1991-92, named Outstanding Audit Educator 1991, named for Disting. Svc. in Auditing 1994, dir. pubs. 1995—, exec. com. 1995), Ill. CPA Soc. (bd. dirs. 1983-85), AICPAs, Inst. Internal Auditors (Leon Radde Outstanding Educator award 1986), Info. Systems Audit and Control Assn., Acctg. Historians, Inst. Mgmt. Accts., Fin. Execs. Inst., Phi Beta Kappa (treas. local chpt. 1981-96, v.p. 1996—), Beta Gamma Sigma, Beta Alpha Psi. Home: 2211 S Cottage Grove Ave Urbana IL 61801-6815 Office: U Ill 1206 S 6th St Champaign IL 61820-6915

NEUMANN, HARRY, philosophy educator; b. Dormoschel, Germany, Oct. 10, 1930; came to U.S., 1937, naturalized, 1948; s. Siegfried and Frieda (Lion) N.; m. Christina Sopher, Sept. 25, 1959. B.A., St. John's Coll., 1952; M.A., U. Chgo., 1954; Ph.D., Johns Hopkins U., 1962; postgrad., U. Heidelberg, Germany, 1956-58. Mem. faculty Mich. State U., 1962-63, Lake Forest Coll., 1963-65; prof. philosophy, and govt. Claremont Grad. Sch. Scripps Coll., Claremont (Calif.) Grad. Sch., 1966—; research assoc. Rockefeller Inst., N.Y.C., 1963. Author: Liberalism, 1991; contbr. articles profl. jours. With AUS, 1954-56. Classical Philosophy fellow Ctr. Hellenic Studies, Dumbarton Oaks, Washington, 1965-66, rsch. fellow Salvatori Ctr. for Study of Individual Freedom in the Modern World, 1970; rsch. fellow Earhart Found., 1973-74, 78, 82, 86, 90, 94. Mem. AAUP, Univ. Ctrs. Rational Alternatives, Univ. Profs. for Acad. Order, John Brown Cook Assn. for Freedom (advisor). Home: Scripps Coll Claremont CA 91711

NEUMANN, HERSCHEL, physics educator; b. San Bernardino, Calif., Feb. 3, 1930; s. Arthur and Dorothy (Greenhood) N.; m. Julia Black, June 15, 1951; 1 child, Keith. BA, U. Calif., Berkeley, 1951; MS, U. Oreg., 1959; PhD, U. Nebr., 1965. Theoretical physicist Gen. Electric Co., Richland, Wash., 1951-57; instr. physics U. Nebr., Lincoln, 1964-65; asst. prof. physics U. Denver, 1965-71, assoc. prof. physics, 1971-85, prof., chmn. physics, 1985—. Contbr. over 20 articles to profl. jours. Dir. numerous pub. outreach programs in physics. Mem. Am. Phys. Soc., Am. Assn. Physics Tchrs. Home: 2425 S St Paul St Denver CO 80210-5516 Office: U Denver Dept Physics and Astronomy Denver CO 80208-0202

NEUMANN, L. N., grain company executive; b. 1941. With Ctrl. Soya Co., Inc., Fort Wayne, Ind., 1964-73, Cook Grain Co. of Minnesota, Mpls., 1973-76, Porr Corp., Mpls., 1976-79; chmn. bd., CEO Benson-Quinn Co., Mpls., 1979—. Office: Benson-Quinn Co 301 S 4th Ave Ste 1075 Grain Exchange Bldg Minneapolis MN 55415*

NEUMANN, MARK W., congressman; b. Waukesha, Wis., Feb. 2, 1954; m. Sue; 3 children. BS, U. Wis., 1975. Real estate developer Neumann Devels., 1980—; mem. 104th Congress from 1st Wis. dist., 1994—. Office: US House Reps 1725 Longworth House Office Bldg Washington DC 20515-4901*

NEUMANN, ROBERT GERHARD, ambassador, consultant; b. Vienna, Austria, Jan. 2, 1916; s. Hugo and Stephanie (Taussky) N.; m. Marlen Eldredge, July 27, 1941; children: Ronald E., Gregory W. Diplome superieur, U. Rennes, France, 1936; diploma Consular Acad. Vienna, Geneva Sch. Internat. Studies, 1937; student, U. Vienna, 1938; M.A., Amherst Coll., 1940; Ph.D. (Shevlin fellow 1940-41), U. Minn., 1946. Instr. State Tchrs. Coll., Oshkosh, Wis., 1941-42; lectr. U. Wis., 1946-47; asst. prof. UCLA, 1947-52, asso. prof., 1952-58, prof., 1958-70, dir. Inst. Internat. and Fgn. Studies, 1959-65, chmn. Atlantic and West European Program, 1965-66; U.S. ambassador to Afghanistan Kabul, 1966-73; to Morocco Rabat, 1973-76; dir. transition team Dept. State, 1980-81; to Saudi Arabia Jidda, 1981; sr. staff assoc. Center for Strategic and Internat. Studies, 1976-80, vice chmn., 1980-81, cons., 1980-81, sr. advisor, 1982—, cons. to bus. and govt., 1983—. Author: The Government of the German Federal Republic, 1966, European and Comparative Government, 4th edit, 1968, Toward a More Effective Executive-Legislative Relationship in the Conduct of America's Foreign Policy, 1977; contbr.: The Austrian Solution, 1982; Contbr. articles to jours.; Editorial writer: Los Angeles Times, 1952-59. Chmn. internat. relations sect. Town Hall, 1956-62; mem. Calif. Rep. Cen. Com., 1954-60; bd. dirs. Coun. Am. Ambs., 1982—; vice chmn., trustee Moroccan-Am. Found., 1982-90; vice chmn. Am.-Saudi Bus. Roundtable, 1982-83, chmn., 1984-91; mem. exec. com. Islam and the West, 1984-88; v.p. Am. Friends of Afghanistan, 1985-93; hon. dir. Afghanistan Relief Com., 1985-93; mem. regional task force Am.-Russian Rels., 1984—; mem. adv. bd. Nat. Coun. U.S.-Arab Rels., 1989—; founding mem. Reps. Abroad. Served from pvt. to lst lt. AUS, 1942-46. Haynes Found. fellow, 1950-51; Social Sci. Research Council fellow, 1950-51; Fulbright fellow France, 1954-55; Nat. Woodrow Wilson Found. fellow, 1984-93; recipient hon. medal U. Brussels, 1955; decorated Legion of Honor (France), 1957; officers cross Order of Merit (Fed. Republic of Germany), 1963; Comdr.'s Cross, 1974; Order of the Star (Afghanistan), 1973; grand officier Order and Star of Ouissam Alaoui (Morocco), 1976; Knight Comdr.'s Cross and Star (Austria), 1991. Mem. Atlantic Coun. U.S. (sponsor), Am. Polit. Sci. Assn., Internat. Polit. Sci. Assn., Internat. Law Assn., Univ. Club (Washington). Roman Catholic. Home: 4986 Sentinel Dr Apt 301 Bethesda MD 20816-3580 *The following thoughts and principles, forged on the ladder to success, took their roots earlier when I was a prisoner in Nazi concentration camps and then a penniless immigrant to America: 1. When in doubt, choose the road of courage. The dynamics of action will carry others with you and confound your opponents. 2. While action must be carefully considered, it is generally better to act than not to act. It is easier to correct the course of action than to move from inaction to action. 3. Dream big and without restraint. There will always be time afterwards to reduce the scope of your action in the light of confining realities. But if you start dreaming small, you shackle your imagination from the outset. 4. Have some reasonable and constant ideas as to what you will not put up with and examine your conscience from time to time to check the possible corrosion success might have wrought. It might keep you honest, or, at least—humble.*

NEUMANN, RONALD ELDREDGE, diplomat; b. Washington, Sept. 30, 1944; s. Robert G. and Marlen (Eldredge) N.; m. Margaret Elaine Grimm, 1966; children: Helen, Brian. BA, U. Calif., Riverside, 1966, MA, 1967; postgrad., Army Officers Candidate Sch., 1968, Nat. War Coll., 1991. Joined Fgn. Svc.; vice consul U.S. Dept. State, Dakar, Senegal, 1971-72, Tabriz, Iran, 1973-76; desk officer Office So. European Affairs U.S. Dept. State, 1976-77, aide to asst. sec. Near Ea and South Asian Affairs, 1977-78; desk officer U.S. Dept. State, Jordan, 1978-81; dep. chief of mission U.S. Dept. State, Sanaa, Yemen, 1981-83; dep. dir. Office Arabian Peninsula Affairs U.S. Dept. State, 1983-86; dep. chief of mission U.S. Dept. State, Abu Dhabi, United Arab Emirates, 1987-90; dir. Office No. Gulf Affairs (Iran-Iraq) U.S. Dept. State, 1991-94; amb. to Algeria U.S. Dept. State, Algiers, 1994—. 1st lt. U.S. Army, 1967-70, Vietnam. Decorated Bronze Star. Mem. Am. Fgn. Svc. Assn., U. Calif.-Riverside Alumni Assn., Nat. War Coll. Alumni Assn., Phi Beta Kappa. Office: Algeria Dept of State Washington DC 20521-6030*

NEUMANN, ROY COVERT, architect; b. Columbus, Nebr., Mar. 1, 1921; s. LeRoy Franklin and Clara Louise (Covert) N.; m. Hedy Charlotte Schultz, Aug. 28, 1948; children: Tali, Scott. Student, Midland Coll., 1939-40, U. Calif.-Berkeley Armed Forces Inst., overseas, 1942-43; AB, U. Nebr., 1948, BArch, 1949; MA, Harvard U., 1952; postgrad., U. Wis., Iowa State U. Registered profl. architect, Iowa, Nebr., Kans., Minn., S.D., N.Y., N.J., Mass., Ohio, Pa., Tenn., Ky., Va., W.Va., Ga., Mich., Mo., Ill., Wis., Tex., Colo. Ptnr., architect R. Neumann Assocs., Lincoln, Nebr., 1952-55; officer mgr. Sargent, Webster, Crenshaw & Folley, Schenectady, N.Y., 1955-59; dir. architecture, ptnr. A.M. Kinney Assocs., Cin., 1959-65; officer mgr. Hunter, Campbell & Rea, Johnstown, Pa., 1965-66; dir. architecture, ptnr. Stanley Cons., Muscatine, Iowa, 1966-76; pres., chmn. bd. Neumann Monson P.C., Iowa City, 1976—; ptnr. Clinton St. Ptnrs., Iowa City, 1983—, Iris City Devel. Co. Mt. Pleasant, Iowa, 1986. Prin. works include Harbour Facilities, Antigua, W.I., S.C. Johnson Office Bldg., Racine, Wis., Iowa City Transit Facility Bldg., addition to Davenport Ctrl. High Sch., V.A. Adminstrv. Office Bldg., Iowa City, Johnson County Office Bldg., Iowa City Mercer Park Aquatic Ctr., Iowa City, Coll. Bus. U. Iowa, Iowa City, renovation Lawrence County Courthouse, Deadwood, S.D. Mem. bd. edn. Muscatine

Community Sch. Dist., 1974-76. Served with USN, 1942-46, PTO. Recipient Honor award Portland Cement Assn., 1949. Mem. AIA (Honor award 1975), Constrn. Specifications Inst. (pres. 1974-76, Honor award 1983, 84, 85, 86), Soc. Archtl. Historians, Archtl. Assn. London, U. Nebr. Alumni Assn., Harvard U. Alumni Assn., Iowa City C. of C., Phi Kappa Psi, Univ. Athletic Club (Iowa City), Masons, Ea. Star, Elks. Republican. Presbyterian. Avocations: golf, fishing, medieval history, big band music. Home: 2014 Burnside Dr Muscatine IA 52761-3510 Office: Neumann Monson Architects 111 E College St Iowa City IA 52240-4002

NEUMANN, THOMAS WILLIAM, archaeologist; b. Cin., Aug. 30, 1951; s. William Henry and Virginia Marie (Walz) N.; m. Mary Louise Spink, Sept. 3, 1988. BA in Anthropology, U. Ky., 1973; PhD in Anthropology, U. Minn., 1979. Instr. U. Minn., Mpls., 1977-79; asst. prof. Syracuse U., 1979-86, dir. archaeology field program, 1979-86; sr. ptnr. Neumann & Sanford Cultural Resource Assessments, Syracuse, 1985-87; sr. scientist R. Christopher Goodwin & Assocs., Inc., Frederick, Md., 1987-92; rsch. assoc. Terrestrial Environ. Specialists, Phoenix, N.Y., 1980-83, SUNY Rsch. Found., Potsdam, 1985-87; external reviewer NSF, Washington, 1982-85; dir. Ctr. for Archaeol. Rsch. and Edn., Houston, Minn., 1982-84; vis. assoc. prof. Emory U., 1991-93, 96; ind. cons., 1991—. Author, co-author more than 70 monographs including 2 winners of the Anne Arundell County Hist. Preservation award; asst. editor Amanuensis, 1972-73; contbr. more than 30 articles to profl. jours. Nat. Trust Historic Preservation honor award. Grantee, Am. Philos. Soc., 1981, Appleby-Mosher Found., 1983, Landmarks Assn. Cen. N.Y., 1984; recipient Oswald award, U. Ky., 1973. Mem. AAAS, N.Y. Acad. Sci., Soc. for Am. Archaeology, Ea. States Archaeol. Fedn., Mid. Atlantic Archaeol. Conf., Phi Beta Kappa. Roman Catholic. Achievements include development of use of vegetation successional stages for cultural resource assessments; identification of cause of passenger pigeon extinctions, microlithic compound tool industry in the eastern prehistoric U.S., contingency planning budget system for Archdiocese of Atlanta. Home: 3859 Wentworth Ln SW Lilburn GA 30247-2260 Office: Ind Archeol Cons 3859 Wentworth Ln SW Lilburn GA 30247-2260

NEUMARK, MICHAEL HARRY, lawyer; b. Cin., Oct. 28, 1945; s. Jacob H. and Bertha (Zubor) N.; m. Sue Daly, June 5, 1971; children: Julie Rebecca, John Adam. BS in Bus., Ind. U., 1967; JD, U. Cin., 1970. Bar: Ohio 1970, D.C. 1972. Atty. chief counsel's office IRS, Washington, 1970-74; acting br. chief IRS, 1974-75; sr. atty. regional counsel's office IRS, Cin., 1975-77; assoc. Paxton & Seasongood Legal Profl. Assn., Cin., 1977-80; ptnr. Thompson, Hine & Flory, 1980—, mem. mgmt. com., 1993—; chmn. So. Ohio Tax Inst., 1987; mem. IRS and Bar Liaison Com.; speaker at profl. confs. Contbr. articles to profl. jours. Bd. dirs. 1987 World Figure Skating Chamionship, Cin., 1986-89; precinct exec. Hamilton County Rep. Orgn., 1980-86; vol. referee Hamilton County Juvenile Ct., 1980-86; adv. bd. Cin. Entrepreneurship Inst.; trustee St. Rita Sch. for Deaf, 1991—. Recipient Commendation Resolution Sycamore Twp., 1987. Mem. ABA (tax sect. S corp. subcom. chmn. 1981-88), Ohio State Bar Assn. (pres. 1996—), Cin. Bar Assn. (recognition award 1985, treas., bd. trustees 1988-91, trustee 1992—, chair tax sect., 1990-91), Leadership Cin., Kenwood Country Club, Indian Hill Club. Republican. Avocations: golf, travel. Office: Thompson Hine & Flory 312 Walnut St Cincinnati OH 45202-4024

NEUMEIER, JOHN, choreographer, ballet company director; b. Milw., Feb. 24, 1942; s. Albert and Lucille N. BA, Marquette U., 1961, DFA (hon.), 1987; student, Stone-Camryn Ballet Sch., Chgo., 1957-62, Royal Ballet Sch., London, 1962-63; student of Vera Volkova, Copenhagen, 1962-63. Dancer Sybil Shearer Co., Chgo., 1960-62, Stuttgart (Fed. Republic Germany) Ballet, 1963-69; artistic dir. Frankfurt (Fed. Republic Germany) Opera Ballet, 1969-73, Hamburg (Fed. Republic Germany) State Opera Ballet, 1973—; prof. City of Hamburg, 1987; found. ballet sch. Hamburg State Opera, 1978; found. ballet ctr. John Neumeier, ballet sch., Hamburg State Opera co. tng. under one roof., 1989. Guest choreographer for various cos. including Am. Ballet Theatre, Royal Ballet London, Royal Danish Ballet, Nat. Ballet Can., Royal Winnipeg Ballet, Stuttgart Ballet, Munich Opera, Vienna Opera, Ballet du XX siecle, Brussels, Opera de Paris, Opera of Stockholm; guest opera dir.: Otello, Munich Opera, Hamburg State Opera, ballet dir.: films Rondo, 1971 (Prix Italia 1972), Third Symphony of Gustav Mahler (Golden Camera award 1978), Legend of Joseph, Wendung (String Quintet in C major by Schubert), 1979, Scenes of Childhood, The Lady of the Camellias, 1986, Othello, 1987. Decorated knight's cross Danebrog Order (Denmark); recipient Dance mag. award, 1983, Fed. German Cross of Merit, 1987, German Dance prize, 1988; title of Prof. conferred by City of Hamburg, 1987, Deutscher Tanzpreis, Fed. Republic of Germany, 1988; recipient Prix Diaghilev award, France, 1988, Order Des Arts et des Lettres award French Minister Culture, 1991, Carina Ari award, Stockholm, 1994. Mem. Acad. der Kuenste Hamburg, Acad. der Kuenste Berlin. Roman Catholic. Office: Ballettzentrum Hamburg, Caspar-Voght-Strasse 54, D-20535 Hamburg Germany

NEUMEIER, MATTHEW MICHAEL, lawyer; b. Racine, Wis., Sept. 13, 1954; s. Frank Edward and Ruth Irene (Effenberger) N.; m. Lori Gerard Nantelle, Sept. 4, 1976 (div. 1985); m. Annmarie Prine, Jan. 31, 1987; children: Ruthann Marie, Emilie Irene. B in Gen. Studies with distinction, U. Mich., 1981; JD magna cum laude, Harvard U., 1984. Bar: N.Y. 1987, Mich. 1988, Ill. 1991, U.S. Dist. Ct. (ea. dist.) Mich. 1988, U.S. Dist. Ct. (ea. and no. dists.) Ill. 1991, U.S. Ct. Appeals (7th cir.) 1992, U.S. Supreme Ct. 1991. Sec.-treas. Ind. Roofing & Siding Co., Escanaba, Mich., 1973-78; mng. ptnr. Ind. Roofing Co., Menominee, Mich., 1977-78; law clk. to presiding justice U.S. Ct. Appeals (9th cir.), San Diego, 1984-85; law clk. to chief justice Warren E. Burger U.S. Supreme Ct., Washington, 1985-86; spl. asst. to chmn. U.S. Constn. Bicentennial Commn., Washington, 1986; assoc. Cravath, Swaine & Moore, N.Y.C., 1986-88; spl. counsel Burnham & Ritchie, Ann Arbor, Mich., 1988; assoc. Schlussel, Lifton, Simon, Rands, Galvin & Jackier, P.C., Ann Arbor, 1988-90, Skadden, Arps, Slate, Meagher & Flom, Chgo., 1990-96; ptnr. Jenner & Block, Chgo., 1996—. Editor Harvard Law Rev., 1982-84. Pres., bd. dirs. Univ. Cellar Inc., Ann Arbor, 1979-81; bd. dirs. Econ. Devel. Corp., Menominee, 1978-79, Midwestern divsn. Am. Suicide Foun., sec. 1992—. Mem. ABA, State Bar Mich., Assn. of Bar of City of N.Y., Ill. State Bar Assn., Chgo. Bar Assn. Republican. Avocations: classic automobiles, piano, choir. Office: Jenner & Block Ste 4100 One IBM Plz Chicago IL 60611

NEUMEYER, JOHN LEOPOLD, research company administrator, chemistry educator; b. Munich, Germany, July 19, 1930; came to U.S., 1945, naturalized, 1950; s. Albert and Martha (Stern) N.; m. Evelyn Friedman, June 24, 1956; children: Ann Martha, David Alexander, Elizabeth Jean. BS, Columbia U., 1952; PhD, U. Wis., 1961. Rsch. chemist Ethicon Inc., New Brunswick, N.J., 1952-57, FMC Corp., Princeton, N.J., 1961-63; sr. staff chemist Arthur D. Little Inc., Cambridge, Mass., 1963-69; prof. medicinal chemistry, chemistry Northeastern U., Boston, 1969-91, dir. grad. sch., 1978-85, disting. emeritus prof., 1992—; chmn. bd., chief sci. officer, co-founder Rsch. Biochem. Internat., Natick, Mass., 1981—; mem. com. of revision U.S. Pharmacopeia, 1970-85; cons. in field. Patentee in field. Contbr. articles to profl. jours., also chpts. to books in field. Mem. Bd. Health, Wayland, Mass., 1968-75, Pesticide Bd., Mass., 1972-75; mem. panel to sec. HEW Commn. on Pesticides and their Relationship to Environ. Health, 1969. Served to cpl. U.S. Army, 1953-55. Recipient Lunsford Richardson award, 1961, Marie Curie award in Nuclear Medicine, 1992; Sr. Hayes Fulbright fellow, 1975-76. Fellow AAAS (mem. at large 1983-87, chmn. pharm. sci. sect. 1992-93), Am. Assn. Pharm. Scis. (rsch. achievement award in medicinal chemistry 1982, Northeastern U. faculty lectr. award 1978, U. disting. prof. 1982-92); mem. Am. Soc. Neurosci., Am. Soc. Exptl. Pharm. & Exptl. Therapeutics, Am. Chem. Soc. (councilor 1985—, trustee 1989-93, bd. editors Jour. Medicinal Chemistry 1974-88, chmn. div. med. chem. 1982). Office: Rsch Biochems Internat 1 Strathmore Rd Natick MA 01760-2418

NEUNZIG, CAROLYN MILLER, elementary, middle and high school educator; b. L.I., May 5, 1930; kd. Stanley and Grace (Walsh) Miller; m. Herbert Neunzig, May 28, 1955; children: Kurt Miller, Keith Weidler. BA, Beaver Coll., Glen Side, Pa., 1953; MSSc, Syracuse U., 1989; postgrad., Adelphi U.; Cert., N.C. State U., Raleigh. Cert. in elem. edn., reading, history and English, N.C. Reading tchr. grades K-6 St. Timothy's Sch., Raleigh, N.C., 1971-83, 5th grade tchr., 1983-88, 5th grade lead tchr., 1986-88; tchr. English and geography 7th grade St. Timothy's Mid. Sch., Raleigh, 1991—; tchr Am. govt. 12th grade St. Timothy's Mid. Sch./Hale High Sch., Raleigh, 1991-93; instr. continuing edn. program history Meredith Coll., Raleigh, 1990-91, spl. high sch. registration commr., 1991-93, instr. continuing edn. program in history, 1995-96. Mem. Am. Acad. Polit. and Social Sci., Acad. Polit. Sci., Nat. Coun. for Social Studies, Nat. Coun. Tchrs. English.

NEUREUTHER, ANDREW R., electrical engineer, educator; b. July 30, 1941. BS, U. Ill., 1963, MS, 1964, PhD, 1966. Prof. dept. electronics U. Calif., Berkeley. Fellow IEEE. Office: Univ of Calif Dept Elect Eng & Computer Sci Berkeley CA 94720*

NEUSCHEL, ROBERT PERCY, educator, former management consultant; b. Hamburg, N.Y., Mar. 13, 1919; s. Percy J. and Anna (Becker) N.; m. Dorothy Virginia Maxwell, Oct. 20, 1944; children—Kerr Anne Zipríck, Carla Becker Neuschel Wyckoff, Robert Friedrich (Fritz). B.A., Denison U., 1941; M.B.A., Harvard U., 1947. Indsl. engr. Sylvania Elec. Products Co., Inc., 1947-49; with McKinsey & Co., Inc., 1950-79, sr. partner, dir., 1967-79; prof. corp. governance, assoc. dean J. L. Kellogg Grad. Sch. Mgmt.; former dir. Northwestern U., assoc. dean J.L. Kellogg Sch. Mgmt.; mem. exec. coun. Internat. Air Cargo Forum, 1988—; mem. com. study air passenger svc. and safety NRC, 1989—; bd. dirs. Butler Mfg. Co., Combined Ins. Co. Am., Templeton, Kenly & Co., TNT Freightways Co.; lectr. in field; mem. McKinsey Found. Mgmt. Research, Inc.; transp. task force Reagan transition team. Contbr. to profl. jours. Pres. Bd. Edn., Lake Forest, Ill., 1965-70; rep. Nat. council Boy Scouts Am., 1970—, mem. N.E. exec. coun., 1969—; chmn. bd. Lake Forest Symphony, 1973; bd. dirs. Loyola U., Chgo., Chgo. Boys' Club, Nat. Ctr. Voluntary Action, Inst. Mgmt. Consultants; trustee N. Suburban Mass Transit, 1972-73, Loyola Med. Ctr.; mem. adv. coun. Kellogg Grad. Sch. Mgmt., Northwestern U., White House conferece Drug Free Am.; mem. Nat. Petroleum Coun. Transp. and Supply Com. Served to capt. USAAF, World War II. Named Transporation Man of Yr. Chitransp. Assoc., 1994. Fellow Acad. Advancement Corp. Governance; mem. Transp. Assn. Am., Nat. Def. Transp. Assn. (mem. subcom. transp. tech. agenda 1990—). Presbyterian (ruling elder). Clubs: Harvard Bus. Sch. (pres. 1964-65), Economic, Executive, Chicago, Mid America, Mid-Day (Chgo.); Onwentsia (Lake Forest). Home: 101 Sunset Pl Lake Forest IL 60045-1834 Office: 1936 Sheridan Rd Evanston IL 60208-0849 *My observations and experiences with corporate executives convince me that leadership is based less on sheer intelligence and more on fundamental qualities of character. By traits of character I would suggest such things as trust, staying power, guts, fairness, maturity, and the capacity to be 'big'. And the primary task of the individual leader is, above all else, to manage himself—his time, talents, emotions, sense of values, and priorities, as a living example to those who follow his leadership.*

NEUSNER, JACOB, humanities and religious studies educator; b. Hartford, Conn., July 28, 1932; m. Suzanne Richter, Mar. 15, 1964; children: Samuel Aaron, Eli Ephraim, Noam Mordecai Menahem, Margalit Leah Berakhah. AB in History magna cum laude, Harvard U., 1953; postgrad. (Henry fellow), Lincoln Coll., Oxford, Eng., 1953-54; postgrad. (Fulbright scholar), Hebrew U., 1957-58; M.H.L., Jewish Theol. Sem. Am., 1960; Ph.D. in Religion (Univ. scholar), Columbia U., 1960; A.M. ad eudem, Brown U., 1969; L.H.D., U. Chgo., 1978; D.Phil. (hon.), U. Cologne, 1979; Hon. Doctorate, U. Bologna, Tulane U., St. Louis U., U. Rochester. Instr. religion Columbia U., 1960-61; asst. prof. Hebrew U. Wis.-Milw., 1961-62; research asso. Brandeis U., 1962-64; asst. prof. religion Dartmouth Coll., 1964-66; assoc. prof. Dartmouth Coll., Providence, 1966-68; prof. religious studies Brown U., Providence, 1968-75, prof. religious studies, Ungerleider Disting. scholar Judaic studies, 1975-82, Univ. prof., Ungerleider Disting. scholar, 1982-90; Disting. Rsch. prof. religious studies U. S. Fla., Tampa, 1990—; vis. prof. Jewish Theol. Sem. Am., summer 1977, Iliff Sch. Theology, Denver, summer 1978, U. Frankfurt, 1991, Cambridge (Eng.) U., 1992, Abo Akademi U., 1993, U. Canterbury, Eng., 1994, U. Goettingen, Germany, 1995; Hill vis. prof. U. Minn., 1978; pres. Max Richter Found., 1969—; mem. Nat. Coun. for Humanities; governing bd. Nat. Endowment Humanities, 1978-84, Nat. Coun. for the Arts, 1984-90; lectr. in field. Author 650 books including: A Life of Yohanan ben Zakkai, 1962 (Abraham Berliner prize in Jewish History), A History of the Jews in Babylonia, 1965-70, Development of a Legend: Studies on the Traditions Concerning Yohanan ben Zakkai, 1970, Aphrahat and Judaism: The Christian-Jewish Argument in Fourth Century Iran, 1971, The Rabbinic Traditions about the Pharisees before 70, 1971, Eliezer ben Hyrcanus: The Tradition and the Man, 1973, The Idea of Purity in Ancient Judaism, 1973, A History of the Mishnaic Law of Purities, 1974-80, Judaism: The Evidence of the Mishnah, 1981, others; author numerous textbooks including American Judaism, Adventure in Modernity, 1972, From Politics to Piety: The Emergence of Pharisaic Judaism, 1973, 78, Invitation to the Talmud: A Teaching Book, 1974, Between Time and Eternity: The Essentials of Judaism, 1976, Form-Analysis and Exegeis: A Fresh Approach to the Interpretation of Mishnah, 1980; editor numerous books including Studies in Judaism in Late Antiquity, 1973—, Studies in Judaism in Modern Times, 1975—, Library of Judaic Learning, 1975—, Brown Judaic Studies, 1976-90, Chicago Studies in the History of Judaism, 1980-90; founder, editor-in-chief Brown Studies on Jews and Their Societies, 1985-90. Kent fellow Nat. Council for Religion in Higher Edn., 1957-60; Lown fellow, 1962-64; Guggenheim Found. fellow, 1973-74, 79-80; Am. Council Learned Socs. fellow, 1966-67, 70-71; research grantee Am. Philos. Soc., 1965, 67; recipient Univ. Medal for Excellence Columbia U., 1974, Von Humboldt prize Von Humboldt Found., 1981, Disting. Humanitarian award Ohio State U., 1983. Fellow Royal Asiatic Soc.; mem. Am. Acad. Religion (v.p., program chmn. 1967-68, pres. 1968-69, chmn. sect. on history of Judaism 1979-81, dir. 1981—), Soc. Bibl. Lit., Phi Beta Kappa. Home: 735 14th Ave NE Saint Petersburg FL 33701-1413 Office: U South Fla Dept Religious Studies Tampa FL 33620

NEUSTADT, BARBARA MAE, artist, illustrator, etcher; b. Davenport, Iowa, June 21, 1922; d. David and Cora (Wollensky) N.; children: Diane Elizabeth Walbridge Wheeler, Laurie Barbara Meyer Hall. B.A., Smith Coll., 1944; postgrad., U. Chgo., 1945-46; Art Student's League scholar, Ohio U. Sch. Fine Arts, 1952. Art dir., designer Shepherd Cards, Inc., N.Y.C., 1956-63; dir., instr. Studio Graphics Workshop, Woodstock, N.Y., 1970—; lectr. on printmaking; participant artist in schs. program N.Y. State Schs., 1972-74; Bd. dirs., editor bull. LWV of Woodstock, 1969-70. Illustrator: The First Christmas, 1960, A Dream of Love (by Joseph Langland), 1986 (exhibited in Sarasota, Fla., 1986, Ga. So. Coll., Statesboro, 1987), Nat. Mus. Women in the Arts, Washington, 1993-94; commd. etching edits to Collectors Am. Art, N.Y.C., 1956, 58, 61, Internat. Graphic Arts Soc., N.Y.C., 1960, N.Y. Hilton Art Collection, N.Y.C., 1961; one-man shows include Ruth White Gallery, N.Y.C., 1958, Phila. Art Alliance, 1959, Portland (Maine) Mus. Art, 1965, L.I. U., Bklyn., 1973, Smith Coll., Northampton, Mass., 1974, Manatee Art League, Bradenton, Fla., 1980, 91, Sarasota, Fla., 1985, 86, Unity Gallery, Sarasota, 1994; group shows include Mus. Modern Art, N.Y.C., 1958-59, Yale U. Art Gallery, New Haven, 1960, Soc. Am. Graphic Artists nat. and internat. exhbns., 1954, 55, 57, 59, 60, 61, 73, 75, 76, 78, L'Antipoete Galerie Librairie, Paris, 1961, Quito, Ecuador, S.Am., 1987, Fla. Printmakers, 1987, 88, So. Printmakers, U. of S. Ala., 1988, Springfest '89, Bradenton, Fla., 1989, Invitational Manatee Art League, Bradenton, 1992, 93, 94, Soc. Exptl. Artists, Longboat Key, juried 1992, juried Shreveport, La., 1993, Nat. Mus. Women Arts, Washington, 1993-94, Longboat Key Art Ctr., 1994; represented in permanent collections including Met. Mus. Art, N.Y.C., Library of Congress, Nat. Gallery Art, Washington, Phila. Mus. Art, USIA, Bonn, Germany, N.Y. Public Library N.Y.C., Rare Book Rm., William A. Neilson Libr., Smith Coll., Henderson Libr., Ga. So. Coll. Found., Statesboro, Ga., McFarlin Libr., Spl. Collections, U. of Tulsa, 1990, Ward Meml. Collection, Gilkey Ctr. for Graphic Arts, Portland (Oreg.) Art Mus., 1992, Nat. Mus. Women Arts. Recipient prize Boston Printmakers, 1957, Joseph Pennell Meml. medal Phila. Watercolor Club, 1972; Yasuo Kuniyoshi Meml. award, 1978; Am. the Beautiful Fund of N.Y. of Natural Area Council grantee, 1973. Mem. Soc. Am. Graphic Artists (prize 1954, 78), Phila. Water Color Club (prize 1972), Fla. Printmakers, The So. Graphics Coun., Art Uptown Inc. Gallery (Sarasota, Fla.), Gallery Two (Rockville, Md.). Studio: Pleiades Press/ Studio Graphics 3014 Ave C Holmes Beach FL 34217

NEUSTADT, DAVID HAROLD, physician; b. Evansville, Ind., Dec. 2, 1925; s. Mose and Leah (Epstein) N.; m. Carolyn Jacobson, June 15, 1952; children: Susan Miriam, Jeffrey Bruce, Robert Alan. Student, DePauw U., 1943-44, 46-47; M.D., U. Louisville, 1950. Intern Morrisania City Hosp., N.Y.C., 1950-51; resident in internal medicine Lenox Hill Hosp., N.Y.C., 1951-52; NIH trainee in rheumatic diseases Lenox Hill Hosp., 1952-53, resident in gastroenterology, 1953-54; practice medicine specializing in rheumatic diseases Louisville, 1954—; chief arthritis clinic Louisville Gen. Hosp., 1960-76; asst. prof. medicine Sch. Medicine, U. Louisville, 1963-67, asso. prof. clin. medicine, 1967-75, clin. prof. medicine, 1974—, head sect. rheumatic diseases, 1960-76; chief dept. medicine Jewish Hosp., Louisville, 1965-67; pres. med. staff Jewish Hosp., 1967-69; cons. in rheumatology VA, 1970—; advisor Network for Continuing Med. Edn., 1983—. Author: The Chemistry and Therapy of Collagen Diseases, 1963, (with other) Aspiration and Injection Therapy in Arthritis and Musculoskeletal Disorders, 1972; editor: (with other) Arthritis Abstracts, References Indexes, 1970-75; contbr. articles to profl. jours. Former pres., chmn. bd. med. sci. com. Ky. chpt. Arthritis Found. Served with AUS, 1944-46. Master Am. Coll. Rheumatology (formerly Am. Rheumatism Assn.; mem. editl. bd. 1989-94, exec. com., pres. ctrl. region 1982-84); fellow Am. Med. Writers Assn., ACP; mem. AMA, N.Y. Acad. Sci., N.Y. Rheumatism Soc., Ky. Rheumatism Assn. (pres. 1956-57), Internat. Soc. Internal Medicine, So. Med. Assn. (edn. com., sect. rheumatology), Am. Physicians Fellowship (nat. trustee 1984—), Spondylitis Assn. (adv. bd. 1986—, contbg. editor 1989—, mem. editl. bd. Arthritis Care and Rsch. Newsletter 1989—), Mason, Shriner. Jewish. Home: 216 Smithfield Rd Louisville KY 40207-1267 Office: Med Towers Louisville KY 40202 *I believe the qualities necessary to achieve success include a combination of ability, commitment to hard work, enthusiasm or enjoyment of your work, plus a liberal chunk of optimism, faith, luck, and a supporting family and co-workers.*

NEUSTADT, RICHARD ELLIOTT, political scientist, educator; b. Phila., June 26, 1919; s. Richard Mitchells and Elizabeth (Neufeld) N.; m. Bertha Frances Cummings, Dec. 21, 1945 (Dec. 1984); children: Richard Mitchells (Dec. 1995), Elizabeth Ann; m. Shirley Williams, Dec. 19, 1987. AB, U. Calif., Berkeley, 1939; MA, Harvard U., 1941, PhD, 1951. Economist OPA, 1942; mem. staff Bur. Budget, 1946-50, White House, 1950-53; prof. pub. adminstrn. Cornell U., 1953-54; prof. govt. Columbia U., 1954-64; prof. govt. Harvard U., 1965-78, Lucius N. Littauer prof. pub. adminstrn., 1978-87, Douglas Dillon prof., 1987-89, assoc. dean John Fitzgerald Kennedy Sch. Govt., 1965-75, dir. Inst. Politics, 1966-71, prof. emeritus, 1989—; spl. cons. subcom. on nat. policy machinery U.S. Senate, 1959-61; mem. adv. bd. Commn. Money and Credit, 1960-61; spl. cons. to Pres. elect Kennedy, 1960-61; to subcom. on nat. security staffing and ops. U.S. Senate, 1962-68; cons. to Pres. Kennedy, 1961-63, Pres. Johnson, 1964-66, Dept. State, 1962-69, Bur. Budget, 1961-70, AEC, 1962-68, Rand Corp., 1964-79, Pres.'s Reorgn. Project, Office Mgmt. and Budget, 1977-79; vis. lectr. Nuffield Coll., Oxford, Eng., 1961-62, assoc. mem., 1965-67, 90-92; vis. prof., Princeton U., 1957, U. Calif., Berkeley, 1986, Cornell U., 1992, U. Essex, UK, 1994—. Author: Presidential Power, 1960, rev., 1990, Alliance Politics, 1970; (with Harvey V. Fineberg) The Swine Flu Affair, 1978, reissued as The Epidemic That Never Was, 1983; (with Ernest R. May) Thinking in Time, 1986; contbr. articles to mags., revs. Mem. staff Dem. Platform Com., 1952, 56, chmn., 1972; trustee Radcliffe Coll., 1976-80; mem. exec. bd. Coll. Letters & Scis., U. Calif., Berkeley, 1994—. With USNR, 1942-46. Fellow Ctr. Advanced Study in the Behavioral Scis., 1978-79. Fellow Am. Acad. Arts Scis; mem. Am. Polit. Sci. Assn., Nat. Acad. Pub. Adminstrn., Council Fgn. Rels., Inst. Strategic Studies, Am. Philos. Soc., Cosmos Club. Office: Kennedy Sch Govt Harvard U Cambridge MA 02138

NEUTHALER, PAUL DAVID, publisher; b. N.Y.C., Nov. 2, 1942; s.Jacob and Frances (Poses) N.; m. Paula Diane Wool, Nov. 20, 1965 (div.) 1976; m. Abbi Mae Greenfield, Dec. 19, 1982; children: Mindy, Howard, Jamie, Jacob. BA, Columbia U., 1964, MA, 1965, PhD, 1972. Pres., pub. Gen. Health Pub. Corp., N.Y.C., 1977-79; pres., chief exec. officer Warren Gorham & Lamont Inc., N.Y.C., 1980-84; pres., chief exec. officer, prof. and tech. pub. Bertelsmann Pub. Co., N.Y.C., 1984-86; exec. v.p. JPT Pub. Group, N.Y.C., 1986-90; chmn., chief exec. officer Bantam Doubleday Pub. Group, N.Y.C., 1990-91; pres., chief exec. officer prof. and tech. pub. Bertelsmann Pub. Group Internat., N.Y.C., 1991—. Honoree United Jewish Appeal, N.Y.C., 1991. Mem. Assn. Am. Publishers (bd. dirs. 1990-91), University Club (N.Y.C.). Office: Bertelsmann Pub Group Internat 1540 Broadway New York NY 10036-4039

NEUTRA, DION, architect; b. Los Angeles, Oct. 8, 1926; s. Richard Joseph and Dione (Niedermann) N.; children: Gregory, Wendy, Haig, Nicholas. Student, Swiss Inst. Tech., 1947-48; B.Arch. cum laude, U. So. Calif., 1950. With Richard J. Neutra (architect), Los Angeles, 1942-55; assoc. Neutra & Alexander, Los Angeles, 1955-60; asso. Robert E. Alexander, Los Angeles, 1960-62; prin. Dion Neutra and Assos., Los Angeles, 1962-65; ptnr. Richard & Dion Neutra, Architects and Assos., Los Angeles, 1965—; pres. Richard J. Neutra, Inc., 1970—; exec. con. Inst. for Survival Through Design, L.A.; lectr. Calif. State U., L.A., Sacramento City Coll., Mira Costa State U., Cabrillo State U., Soka U., Tokyo, San Diego City Coll., Germany, Switzerland, Eng., Austria; vis. prof. Calif. State U.-Pomona, 1970, 85-86, now vis. lectr.; vis. lectr. U. So. Calif. Prin. works include various residential, ednl., religious and instnl. facilities including Am. Embassy Karachi, Pakistan, Gettysburg Meml., Simpson Coll. Libr., Adelphi Coll. Libr., Libr. and Resource Ctr. for City of Huntington Beach, Calif., Treetops Townhouses, 1980; exhbns. "View from Inside", 1984, 86, 92, "Visions & Exiles", Vienna, 1995. Mem. Silver Lake-Echo Park Dist. Plan Adv. Com., Master Plan City of Los Angeles, 1970-71; mem. Citizens to Save Silver Lake, 1973-76; Dir. Child Care and Devel. Services, 1970-71. Served with USNR, 1944-46. Neutra Place A St. named in firm's honor, Silverlake, 1992; Neutra Centennial, 1992. Mem. AIA, Nat. Council Archtl. Registration Bds., Alpha Rho Chi. Studio: Richard & Dion Neutra 2440 Neutra Pl Los Angeles CA 90039-4205

NEUWIRTH, ALAN JAMES, lawyer; b. N.Y.C., July 4, 1943; s. Bernard and Audrey (Hattenbach) N.; m. Patricia E. Neuwirth, Sept. 4, 1966; children: John A., Daniel P. BA, Lehigh U., 1965; JD, NYU, 1969. Bar: N.Y. 1970, U.S. Dist. Ct. (so. and ea. dists.) N.Y. 1972, U.S. Ct. Appeals (2d cir.) 1972, U.S. Ct. Internat. Trade 1983, U.S. Ct. Appeals (Fed. cir.) 1984, U.S. Supreme Ct. 1988. Assoc. Miller & Summit, N.Y.C., 1970-72, Ratheim, Hoffman, Kassel & Silverman, N.Y.C., 1973-75; ptnr. Kassel, Neuwirth & Geiger, N.Y.C., 1976-86, Webster & Sheffield, N.Y.C., 1987-90; sr. ptnr. Morgan, Lewis & Bockius, N.Y.C., 1990—; bd. dirs. various cos. With U.S. Army, 1969-74, USAR. Mem. ABA, Assn. of Bar of City of N.Y., N.Y. County Lawyers Assn., Internat. Trade Commn., Trial Lawyers Assn. Office: Morgan Lewis & Bockius 101 Park Ave New York NY 10178

NEUWIRTH, BEBE, dancer, actress; b. Newark, Dec. 31; d. Lee Paul and Sydney Anne Neuwirth. Student, Juilliard Sch., 1976-77. Appeared on Broadway and internationally as Sheila in A Chorus Line, 1978-81; other stage appearances include West Side Story, 1981, (on Broadway) Little Me, 1982, Upstairs at O'Neal's, 1982-83, The Road to Hollywood, 1984, Just So, 1985, (on Broadway) Sweet Charity, 1985-87 (Tony award for Best Supporting Actress in a Musical 1985-86), Waiting in the Wings: The Night the Understudies Take the Stage, 1986, Showing Off, 1989, Chicago, 1992 (L.A. Drama Critics Circle award), Kiss of the Spider Woman (London), 1993, (on Broadway) Damn Yankees, 1994, Pal Joey, 1995; prin. dancer on Broadway Dancin', 1982; leading dance role Kicks, 1984; TV series Cheers, 1984-93 (Emmy award for Best Supporting Actress in a Comedy Series 1990, 91); TV guest appearances Frasier, 1994, Aladdin, 1994; TV movies Without Her Consent, 1990, Unspeakable Acts, 1990, Wild Palms, 1993; films Say Anything, 1989, Green Card, 1990, Bugsy, 1991, Painted Heart, 1992, Malice, 1993, Jumanji, 1994, Pinocchio, 1995. Vol. performances for March of Dimes Telethon, 1986, Cystic Fibrosis Benefit Children's Ball, 1986, Ensemble Studio Theater Benefit, 1986, Circle Repertory Co. Benefit, 1986, all in N.Y.C. Democrat. Office: Internat Creative Mgmt 8942 Wilshire Blvd Beverly Hills CA 90211-1934 Office: Internat Creative Mgmt 40 W 57th St New York NY 10019-4001

NEUWIRTH, JESSICA ANNE, lawyer; b. N.Y.C., Dec. 10, 1961; d. Robert Samuel and Gloria (Salob) N. BA, Yale U., 1982; JD, Harvard U., 1985. Bar: Mass. 1986, N.Y. 1987. Prodr. Concerts for Human Rights Found., N.Y.C., 1987-90; assoc. Cleary, Gottlieb, Steen & Hamilton, N.Y.C., 1990-93, Kridel & Neuwirth, N.Y.C., 1993-94; exec. dir., pres. Equality

Now, N.Y.C., 1992-94; legal officer UN, 1994—. Mem. nat. adv. com. Physicians for Human Rights, Boston, 1986—. Mem. Assn. Bar City N.Y. (mem. com. on sex and law 1992-95, mem. com. on internat. human rights 1988-91).

NEUWIRTH, ROBERT SAMUEL, obstetrician, gynecologist; b. N.Y.C., July 11, 1933; s. Abraham Alexander and Phyllis Neuwirth; children from previous marriage: Susan, Jessica, Laura, Michael, Alexander. BS, Yale U., 1954, MD, 1958. Intern Presbyn. Hosp., N.Y.C., 1958-59, resident, 1959-64; asst. prof. ob-gyn. Columbia U., 1964-68, assoc. prof., 1968-71, prof., 1972—, Babcock prof., 1977—; dir. ob-gyn. Bronx Lebanon Hosp., N.Y.C., 1967-72, Woman's Hosp., N.Y.C., St. Luke's Hosp. Ctr., 1974—; prof. Albert Einstein Coll. Medicine, 1971-72; cons. WHO, NIH, AID, FDA. Author: Hysteroscopy, 1975; contbr. articles to profl. jours. Mem. Am. Coll. Obstetricians and Gynecologists, Soc. Gynecologic Investigation, N.Y. Obstet. Soc., Am. Assn. Profs. Ob-Gyn., Assn. Vol. Sterilization (chmn. biomed. com. 1971—). Office: 1090 Amsterdam Ave Fl 6 New York NY 10025-8107

NEVA, FRANKLIN ALLEN, physician, educator; b. Cloquet, Minn., June 8, 1922; s. Lauri Albin and Anna (Lahti) N.; m. Alice Hanson, July 5, 1947; children: Karen, Kristin, Erik. SB, U. Minn., 1944, MD, 1946; AM (hon.), Harvard U., 1964. Diplomate Am. Bd. Internal Medicine. Intern Harvard Med. Services, Boston City Hosp., 1946-47, resident, 1949-50; research fellow Harvard Med. Sch., 1950-53; asst. prof. U. Pitts. Med. Sch., 1953-55; mem. faculty Harvard Sch. Pub. Health, 1955-69, John LaPorte Given prof. tropical pub. health, 1964-69; chief Lab. Parasitic Diseases Inst. Allergy and Infectious Diseases, NIH, 1969-95, acting sci. dir., 1994-95; mem. commn. parasitic diseases, assoc. mem. commn. virus infections Armed Forces Epidemiol. Bd., 1963-68; mem. Latin Am. sci. bd. Nat. Acad. Scis.-NRC, 1963-68; bd. sci. counselors Inst. Allergy and Infectious Diseases, NIH, 1966-69. Served to lt. (j.g.) USNR, 1947-49. Mem. Soc. Exptl. Biology and Medicine, Infectious Diseases Soc. Am. (Joseph Smadel lectr. 1985), Am. Soc. Tropical Medicine and Hygiene (Bailey K. Ashford award 1965, Craig lectr. 1986, Ben Kean award 1995), Assn. Am. Physicians (Presdl. Meritorious Exec. Rank award 1985). Achievements include special research infectious diseases especially tropical, parasitic and virus infections. Home: 10851 Glen Rd Potomac MD 20854-1401 Office: NIH Inst Allergy & Infectious Diseases Bethesda MD 20892

NEVANS-PALMER, LAUREL SUZANNE, rehabilitation counselor; b. N.Y.C., Aug. 1, 1964; d. Roy N. and Virginia (Place) Nevans; m. Russell Baird Palmer III, Oct. 12, 1991. BA in English, Secondary Edn. cum laude, U. Richmond, 1986, postgrad., 1989-92; MA in Edn. & Human Devel., George Washington U., 1991, cert. in job devel. and placement, 1992. Group leader S.E. Consortium for Spl. Svcs., Larchmont, N.Y., 1980-85; vocat. instr. Assn. for Retarded Citizens Montgomery County, Rockville, Md., 1986-89; edn. specialist George Washington U. Out of Sch. Work Experience Program, Washington, 1989-90; rsch. asst. George Washington U. Dept. Tchr. Prep. & Spl. Edn., Washington, 1989-91; employability skills tchr., rsch. intern Nat. Rehab. Hosp. Rehab. Engring. Dept., Washington, 1991; vocat./ind. living skills specialist The Independence Ctr., Rockville, Md., 1991-93; leadership team mgr. Career Choice project The Endependence Ctr. of No. Va., Arlington, 1993-94; program dir. United Cerebral Palsy of D.C. and No. Va., Washington, 1994—; teaching asst. Rehab. Counseling Program, George Washington U., 1991. Recipient traineeship GWU Counseling Dept., 1990, 91. Mem. Nat. Rehab. Assn., Nat. Rehab. Counselors Assn., D.C. Met. Area Assn. Person's in Supported Employment (editor newsletter 1995—), Nat. Career Devel. Assn., Nat. Employment Counseling Assn., Nat. Assn. Ind. Living, Am. Assn. Counseling and Devel., Am. Rehab. Counseling Assn. Democrat. Avocations: writing, photography, music, travel, jewelry making. Home: 611 Woodside Pky Silver Spring MD 20910 Office: United Cerebral Palsy 3531 8th St NE Washington DC 20017

NEVAS, ALAN HARRIS, federal judge; b. Norwalk, Conn., Mar. 27, 1928; s. Nathan and Eva (Harris) N.; m. Janet S. Snyder, Sept. 13, 1959; children: Andrew, Debra, Nathaniel. B.A., Syracuse U., 1949; LL.B., NYU, 1951. Bar: Conn. 1951, U.S. Dist. Ct. Conn. 1955, U.S. Supreme Ct. 1959, U.S. Ct. Appeals for 2d circuit 1967, U.S. Tax. Ct. 1981. Ptnr. firm Nevas Nevas & Rubin, Westport, Conn., 1954-81; U.S. atty. for Dist. of Conn., 1981-85; judge U.S. Dist. Ct., Hartford, 1985—. Mem. Conn. Ho. Reps., 1971-77, dep. house majority leader, 1973-75, dep. house minority leader, 1975-77; justice of the peace, Westport, Conn., 1976-81. Served with AUS, 1952-54. Named One of 10 Most Outstanding Mems. Conn. Gen. Assembly Conn. Mag., 1975-77. Mem. Conn. Bar. Assn. (gov. 1978-81). Republican. Jewish. Office: US Dist Ct 915 Lafayette Blvd Bridgeport CT 06604-4706*

NEVELOFF, JAY A., lawyer; b. Bklyn., Oct. 11, 1950; s. Cydelle (Weber) Elrich; m. Arlene Sillman, Aug. 26, 1972; children: David, Kevin. BA, Bklyn. Coll., 1971; JD, NYU, 1974. Bar: N.Y. 1975, D.C. 1992, U.S. Dist. Ct. (so. and ea. dists.) N.Y. 1975, U.S. Ct. Appeals (2d cir.) 1975, U.S. Supreme Ct. 1982. Assoc. Marshall, Bratter, Greene, Allison & Tucker, N.Y.C., 1974-82; assoc. Rosenman, Colin, Freund, Lewis & Cohen, N.Y.C., 1982-83, ptnr., 1983-88; ptnr. Kramer, Levin, Naftalis, Nessen, Kamin & Frankel, N.Y.C., 1988—. Editor N.Y. Real Property Service. Mem. planning bd. Briar Cliff Manor, 1995—. Mem. ABA (vice chmn. com. partnerships, joint ventures and other investment vehicles 1988-95), Am. Law Inst., Am. Coll. Real Estate Attys., N.Y. State Bar Assn. (financing com.), Practising Law Inst. (lectr. 1988—, mem. adv. bd. 1991—), N.Y. County Lawyers Assn. (lectr. 1984—), Assn. of Bar of City of N.Y. (real property law com., chmn. condominium resale contract com., lectr. 1984-88), Cmty. Assns. Inst. (lectr. 1986), Law Jours. Seminars (lectr. 1987—), Strategic Resources Inst. (lectr. 1994—), Internat. Health Network Soc. (vice chmn. 1995—). Home: 134 Alder Dr Briarcliff Manor NY 10510-2218 Office: Kramer Levin Naftalis Nessen Kamin & Frankel 919 Third Ave New York NY 10022

NEVES, KERRY LANE, lawyer; b. San Angelo, Tex., Dec. 19, 1950; s. Herman Walter and Geraldine (Ball) N.; m. Sharon Lynn Briggs, July 28, 1973; 1 child, Erin Lesli. BBA, U. Tex., 1975, JD, 1978. Bar: Tex. 1978, U.S. Dist. Ct. (so. and ea. dists.) Tex. 1979, U.S. Ct. Appeals (5th cir.) 1979, U.S. Dist. Ct. (we. dist.) 1980; cert. personal injury trial law, Tex. Bd. Legal Specialization, 1994. Ptnr. Mills, Shirley, Eckel & Bassett, Galveston, Tex., 1978-93, Neves & Crowther, Galveston, Tex., 1993—. Vice-chmn. Bldg. Stnds. Commn., Dickinson, Tex., 1991—. Sgt. USMC, 1969-72. Fellow Tex. Bar Found.; mem. ABA, State Bar Tex. (grievance com. 1989-92, disciplinary rules profl. conduct com. 1990-92), Galveston County Bar Assn. (pres. 1989-90), U. Tex. Law Alumni Assn. (pres. 1991-92). Avocations: gardening, bicycling, wine, books. Home: RR 2 Box 95 Dickinson TX 77539-9204 Office: Neves & Crowther 1802 Broadway St Ste 206 Galveston TX 77550-4953

NEVEU, JEAN, printing company executive. Chmn., CEO, Quebecor Printing Inc., Montreal, Que., Can. Office: Quebecor Printing Inc 612 Saint-Jacques St, Montreal, PQ Canada H3C 4M8

NEVIASER, ROBERT JON, orthopedic surgeon, educator; b. Washington, Nov. 21, 1936; s. Julius Salem and Jane Frances (Gibbons) N.; m. Anne Maclean Shedden, Dec. 3, 1966; children: Jeanne Nicole, Robert Jon Jr., Ian Maclean, Andrew Shedden. Grad., Phillips Acad., Andover, Mass., 1954; AB, Princeton U., 1958; MD, Jefferson Med. Coll., 1962. Diplomate Am. Bd. Orthopaedic Surgery with cert. of added qualification in surgery of hand. Intern N.Y. Hosp., Cornell Med. Center, N.Y.C., 1962-63; asst. resident N.Y. Hosp., Cornell Med. Center, 1963-64; asst. resident in orthopaedic surgery N.Y. Orthopaedic Hosp., Columbia-Presbyn. Med. Center, N.Y.C., 1964-66; resident N.Y. Orthopaedic Hosp., Columbia-Presbyn. Med. Center, 1966-67; fellow in surgery of the hand Orthopaedic Hosp., Los Angeles, 1969-70; asst. prof. div. orthopaedic and hand surgery, chmn. dept. U. Conn., Hartford, 1970-71; assoc. prof. orthopaedic surgery George Washington U., Washington, 1971-76; prof. George Washington U., 1976—, dir. orthopaedic edn., assoc. chmn. dept. orthopedic surgery, 1984-87, chmn. dept. orthopedic surgery, 1987—; chmn. governing bd., CEO, med. faculty assocs. George Washington U. Med. Ctr., 1995—; chmn. governing bd., CEO Med. Faculty Assocs., George Washington U. Contbr. articles in field to profl. jours. Served to lt. comdr. USNR, 1967-69. Fellow Am. Soc. Surgery of the Hand, Am. Acad. Orthopaedic Surgeons, Ea. Orthopaedic Assn., Am. Shoulder and Elbow Surgeons, Am. Orthopaedic Assn.; mem. Alpha Kappa Kappa. Republican. Clubs: Princeton (N.Y. and Washington); Darnestown Swim and Racquet, Cosmos. Office: 2150 Pennsylvania Ave NW Washington DC 20037-2396

NEVILL, WILLIAM ALBERT, chemistry educator; b. Indpls., Jan. 1, 1929; s. Irwin Lowell and Mary Marie (Barker) N.; m. Nancy Neiman Roll, May 19, 1979; children: Paul David, John Michael, Steven Joseph, Anne Marie, Deborah Ruth. BS magna cum laude, Butler U., 1951; PhD, Calif. Inst. Tech., 1954. Research chemist Proctor-Gamble, Cin., 1954; prof. chemistry, chmn. dept. Grinnell Coll., 1956-67; prof. chemistry Ind. U.-Purdue U., Indpls., 1967-83, chmn. dept., 1967-72; dean Sch. Sci. Ind. U.-Purdue U., 1972-79, dir. grad. studies, 1979-83; pres. B&N Cons. Co., 1972-93; vice chancellor acad. affairs La. State U., Shreveport, 1983-85; prof. La. State U., 1983-94; pres. Catoctin Assocs., 1993—; arbitrator, mediator Ind. Employment Rels. Bd., 1975-83. Author: General Chemistry, 1967, Experiments in General Chemistry, 1968. Bd. dirs. Indpls. Sci. and Engring. Found., 1972-75, 79-82, Westminster Found., Lafayette, Ind., 1972-74, Am. Chem. Soc., 1986-92. With U.S. Army, 1954-56; col. USAR, 1956-84. Grantee NSF, 1959-74; Grantee NIH, 1963-70; Grantee Office Naval Research, 1953. Mem. Ind. Acad. Sci., Am. Chem. Soc. (chmn. sect. 1972, counselor 1973-92). Presbyterian. Home: 2229 Greenpark Dr Richardson TX 75082-4219

NEVILLE, AARON, musician; m. Joel; 1 d., Ernestine; 3 s., Aaron, Jr., Ivan, Jason. Singer (singles): Over You, 1959, Tell It Like It Is, 1966, 91; (albums): Orchid in the Storm, 1990, The Classic: My Greatest Gift, 1990, Warm Your Heart, 1991, The Grand Tour, 1993, Aaron Neville's Soulful Christmas, 1993; singles (with Linda Ronstadt) Don't Know Much, 1990 (Grammy award), All My Life, 1990, albums (with Neville Brothers) The Neville Brothers, 1978, Fiyo On the Bayou, 1980, Neville-ization, 1984, Uptown, 1987, Treacherous: A History of the Neville Brothers, 1987, Yellow Moon, 1989, Brother's Keeper, 1990, Treacherous Too, 1991, Family Groove, 1992, Live on Planet Earth, 1994. Recipient Down Beat Blues, Soul, R&B Group award, 1990; 2 Grammy nominations, 1994. Office: care A&M Records Inc 1416 N La Brea Ave Los Angeles CA 90028-7563

NEVILLE, ART, musician. Albums include: Mardi Gras Rock 'N' Roll, 1987, (with Neville Brothers) The Neville Brothers, 1979, Treacherous: A History of the Neville Brothers, 1987, Brother's Keeper, 1990, Fiyo On the Bayou, 1980, Neville-ization, 1984, Uptown, 1987, Yellow Moon, 1989, Treacherous Too, 1991, Family Groove, 1992, Live on Planet Earth, 1994; (with The Meters) Sophisticated Sissy, 1968, Sissy Strut, Look-Ka Py Py, Chicken Strut, Cabbage Alley, also backup for many groups until 1980's. Recipient Down Beat Blues, Soul, R&B Group award, 1990. Office: care A & M Records Inc 1416 N La Brea Ave Los Angeles CA 90028-7563

NEVILLE, CHARLES, musician. Albums include: (with Neville Brothers) The Neville Brothers, 1979, Fiyo on the Bayou, 1980, Neville-ization, 1984, Uptown, 1987, Treacherous: A History of the Neville Brothers, 1987, Yellow Moon, 1989, Brother's Keeper, 1990, Treacherous Too, 1991, Family Groove, 1992, Live on Planet Earth, 1994. Recipient Down Beat Blues, Soul, R&B group award, 1990. Office: care A & M Records Inc 1416 N La Brea Ave Los Angeles CA 90028-7563

NEVILLE, CYRIL, musician. Albums include: (with Neville Brothers) The Neville Brothers, 1979, Fiyo on the Bayou, 1980, Neville-ization, 1984, Uptown, 1987, Treacherous: A History of the Neville Brothers, 1987, Yellow Moon, 1989, Brother's Keeper, 1990, Treacherous Too, 1991, Family Groove, 1992, Live on Planet Earth, 1994. Recipient Down Beat Blues, Soul, R&B Group award, 1990. Office: care A & M Records Inc 1416 N La Brea Ave Los Angeles CA 90028-7563

NEVILLE, GWEN KENNEDY, anthropology educator; b. Taylor, Tex., Mar. 23, 1938; d. Matthew Ranken and Gwendolyn (Harrison) Kennedy; m. William Gordon Neville (div.); children: Katherine, Mary Grace, William Kennedy; m. Jack Gregory Hunnicutt, Jr., 1975. BA, Mary Baldwin Coll., Staunton, Va., 1959; MA, U. Fla., 1968, PhD, 1971. Asst. prof. Emory U., Atlanta, 1971-78, assoc. prof., 1978-79; assoc. prof. Southwestern U., Georgetown, Tex., 1979-84, prof. anthropology, 1984—, Elizabeth Root Paden chairholder, 1979—; cons. Wenner-Gren Conf., Mt. Kisco, N.Y., 1983; grant holder NEH, Washington, 1972, 89; researcher, writer Lilly Endowment, Indpls., 1988—; bd. dirs. Soc. for Anthropology of Europe, 1988—. Author: Kinship and Pilgrimage, 1987, The Mother Town, 1994; co-author: Generation to Generation, 1973, Learning Through Liturgy, 1978; contbr. articles to profl. jours. Fellow Am. Anthropol. Assn.; mem. Am. Ethnological Soc., Am. Folklore Soc., Soc. for Anthropology of Europe (bd. dirs. 1989-92), Assn. for Scottish Ethnography, Coun. on Anthropology and Edn. (bd. dirs. 1971-74), So. Anthropol. Soc. (editor 1974-77). Methodist. Office: Southwestern Univ University Ave at Maple St Dept Anthropolgy Georgetown TX 78626

NEVILLE, JAMES MORTON, food company executive, lawyer; b. Mpls., May 28, 1939; s. Philip and Maurene (Morton) N.; m. Judie Martha Proctor, Sept. 9, 1961; children: Stephen Warren, Martha Maurene. BA, U. Minn., JD magna cum laude, 1964. Bar: Minn. 1964, Mo. 1984. Assoc. firm Neville, Johnson & Thompson, Mpls., 1964-69, ptnr., 1969-70; assoc. counsel Gen. Mills, Inc., Mpls., 1970-77, sr. assoc. counsel, 1977-83, corp. sec., 1976-83; v.p., sec., asst. gen. counsel Ralston Purina Co., St. Louis, 1983-84, v.p., gen. counsel, sec., 1984—; lectr. bus. law. U. Minn., 1967-71. Named Man of Yr. Edina Jaycees, 1967. Mem. ABA, Minn., Mo. Bar Assns., U.S. Supreme Ct. Bar Assn., Hennepin County Bar Assn., St. Louis Bar Assn., U. Minn. Law Sch. Alumni Assn., Am. Soc. Corp. Secs., Old Warson Country Club, Ladue Racquet Club, Noonday Club, Order of Coif, Phi Delta Phi, Psi Upsilon. Episcopalian. Home: 9810 Log Cabin Ct Saint Louis MO 63124-1133 Office: Ralston Purina Co Checkerboard Sq Saint Louis MO 63164-0002

NEVILLE, MARGARET COBB, physiologist, educator; b. Greenville, S.C., Nov. 4, 1934; d. Henry Van Zandt and Florence Ruth (Crozier) Cobb; m. Hans E. Neville, Dec. 27, 1957; children: Michel Paul, Brian Douglas. BA, Pomona Coll., 1956; PhD, U. Pa., 1962. Asst. prof. physiology U. Colo. Med. Sch., Denver, 1968-75, assoc. prof., 1975-82, prof., 1982—, dir. med. scientist tng. program, 1985-94. Editor: Lactation: Physiology, Nutrition, Breast Feeding, 1983 (Am. Pubs. award 1984), Human Lactation I, 1985, The Mammary Gland, 1987, Jour. Mammary Gland Biology and Neoplasia, 1995—; contbr. numerous articles to profl. jours. Recipient Rsch. Career Devel. award NIH, 1975, NIH merit award, 1993. Mem. AAAS, Am. Physiol. Soc., Am. Soc. Cell Biology, Internat. Soc. Rsch. in Human Milk and Lactation, Phi Beta Kappa. Office: U Colo Dept Physiology PO Box 240C Denver CO 80262

NEVILLE, PHOEBE, choreographer, dancer, educator; b. Swarthmore, Pa., Sept. 28, 1941; d. Kennith R. and Marion (Eberbach) Balsley. Student, Wilson Coll., 1959-61. Cert. practitioner body-mind centering; registered movement therapist. Instr. Bennington (Vt.) Coll., 1981-84, 87-88; vis. lectr. UCLA, 1984-86. Dancer, choreographer Judson Meml. Ch., N.Y.C., 1966-70, Dance Uptown Series, N.Y.C., 1969, Cubiculo Theatre, N.Y.C., 1972-75, Delacorte Dance Festival, N.Y.C., 1976, Dance Umbrella Series, N.Y.C., 1977, Riverside Dance Festival, N.Y.C., 1976, 78, N.Y. Seasons, 1979—; dancer, artistic dir. Phoebe Neville Dance Co., N.Y.C., 1975—, Jacob's Pillow Splash! Festival, 1988, Dance Theater Workshop Winter Events, 1988. Recipient Creative Artist Public Svc. award, 1975; Nat. Endowment for Arts fellow, 1975, 79, 80, 85-87, 92-94, Choreographic fellow N.Y. Found. for Arts, 1989. Mem. Laban Inst. Movement Studies, Dance Theater Workshop, Body-Mind Centering Assn. (cert. practitioner and tchr.), Internat. Movement Therapy Assn. (registered), Internat. Assn. Healthcare Practitioners. Buddhist. Club: Recluse.

NEVILLE, ROBERT CUMMINGS, philosophy and religion educator; b. St. Louis, May 1, 1939; s. Richard Perry and Rose Naomi (Cummings) N.; m. Elizabeth Egan, June 8, 1963; children: Gwendolyn (dec.), Naomi, Leonora. BA, Yale U., 1960, MA, 1962, PhD, 1963. Ordained as elder United Meth. Ch., 1966. Instr. philosophy Yale U., New Haven, Conn., 1963-65; from asst. to assoc. prof. philosophy Fordham U., Bronx, 1965-71; assoc. prof. philosophy SUNY-Purchase, 1971-74, prof. 1974-77; prof. philosophy and religion, chair religion dept. SUNY-Stony Brook, N.Y., 1978-82, dean humanities and arts, 1982-85, chmn. dept. religion, 1986-87; prof. religion, philosophy and theology, chmn. religion dept. Boston U., 1987-88, dean Sch. of Theology, 1988—. Author: God the Creator, 1968, 2d edition, 1992, The Cosmology of Freedom, 1974, reprinted, 1995, Soldier, Sage, Saint, 1978, reprinted, 1995, Creativity and God, 1980, Reconstruction of Thinking, 1981, The Tao and the Daimon, 1982, The Puritan Smile, 1987, Recovery of the Measure, 1989, Behind the Masks of God, 1991, A Theology Primer, 1991, The Highroad around Modernism, 1992, Eternity and Time's Flow, 1993, Normative Cultures, 1995, The Truth of Broken Symbols, 1996; editor: (with Gaylin and Meister) Operating on the Mind, 1975; New Essays in Metaphysics, 1987; contbr. articles to profl. jours. Mem. Mo. E. Ann. Conf., United Meth. Ch., 1963—. Mem. Am. Acad. Religion (bd. dirs. 1982-93, chmn. rsch. com. 1984-89, v.p., pres. elect, pres. 1990-92), Am. Theol. Soc. (exec. com. 1980-83), Am. Philos. Assn. (exec. com. 1983-85), Metaphys. Soc. Am. (pres. 1988), Internat. Soc. Chinese Philos. (pres. 1992-93). Democrat. Avocations: t'ai chi ch'uan, singing. Office: Boston U Sch Theology Boston MA 02215

NEVILLE, ROY GERALD, scientist, chemical management and environmental consultant; b. Bournemouth, Dorsetshire, Eng., Oct. 15, 1926; came to U.S., 1951, naturalized, 1957; s. Percy Herbert and Georgina Lallie (Jenkins) N.; m. Jeanne Frances Russ, July 26, 1952; children: Laura Jean, Janet Marilyn. BSc with honors, U. London, 1951; MSc, U. Oreg., 1952, PhD, 1954; FRIC, Royal Inst. Chemistry, London, 1963, DSc (hon.), 1973. Research chemist Monsanto Chem. co., Seattle, 1955-57; sr. chem. engr. Boeing Co., Seattle, 1957-58; sr. research scientist Lockheed Missiles & Space Co., Palo Alto, Calif., 1958-61; sr. staff scientist Aerospace Corp., El Segundo, Calif., 1961-63; prin. scientist Rockwell Internat. Corp., Los Angeles, 1963-67; head dept. materials Scis. Lab., Boeing Sci. Research Labs. Boeing Co., Seattle, 1967-69; sr. environ. engring. specialist Bechtel Corp., San Francisco, 1969-73; pres. Engring. & Tech. Cons., Inc., Redwood City, Calif., 1973—. Contbr. numerous sci. articles on organic synthesis, polymers, pollution control processes to profl. jours. and books; many U.S. and fgn. patents in field. Fulbright scholar to U.S., 1951; USPHS fellowship, 1951-52, Research Corp. fellow, 1952-54; chartered chemist, London. Fellow Royal Soc. Chemistry (London), Am. Inst. Chemists, AAAS; mem. Am. Chem. Soc., Am. Inst. Chem. Engrs., History Sci. Soc., Soc. Study Early Chemistry, Royal Instn. Great Britain, Research Soc. Am., Soc. Mining Engrs. of AIME, Calif. Mining Assn., Sigma Xi. Office: ETC Inc 1068 Eden Bower Ln Redwood City CA 94061-1806

NEVIN, CROCKER, investment banker; b. Tulsa, Mar. 14, 1923; s. Ethelbert Paul and Jennie Crocker (Fassett) N.; m. Mary Elizabeth Sherwin, Apr. 24, 1952 (div. 1984); children: Anne, Paul, Elizabeth, Crocker; m. Marilyn Elizabeth English, Nov. 3, 1984; 1 child, Jennie Fassett. Grad. with high honors, St. Paul's Sch., 1942; A.B. with high honors, Princeton U., 1946. With Vick Chem. Co., 1949-50, John Roberts Powers Cosmetic Co., 1950-52; with Marine Midland Grace Trust Co. of N.Y., 1952—, exec. v.p., 1964-66, pres., 1966-70, chmn. bd., chief exec. officer, 1968-73; also dir.; vice chmn. bd. Evans Products Co., N.Y.C., 1974-76, Drexel Burnam Lambert Co., investment bankers, N.Y.C., 1976-88; chmn. bd., chief exec. officer CF & I Steel Corp., Pueblo, Colo., 1985-93; dir. Magnatck, Inc. Chmn. exec. com. ACCION Internat. Lt. (j.g.) AC USN, 1942-46. Mem. Riverside Yacht Club, N.Y. Yacht Club (N.Y.C.), Blind Brook Club. Home: 20 Hope Farm Rd Greenwich CT 06830

NEVIN, JOHN ROBERT, business educator, consultant; b. Joliet, Ill., Jan. 27, 1943; s. Robert Charles and Rita Alice (Roder) N.; m. Jeanne M. Conroy, June 10, 1967; children: Erin, Michael. BS, So. Ill. U., 1965; MS, U. Ill., 1968, PhD, 1972. Asst. prof. bus. U. Wis., Madison, 1970-77, assoc. prof. bus., 1977-83, prof. bus., 1983—, Wis. disting. prof. bus., 1988-89, Grainger Wis. disting. prof. bus., 1989—, dir. Grainger Ctr. for Distbn. Mgmt., 1992—; mem. editorial bd. Jour. of Mktg. Channels, The Haworth Press, Inc., 1991—; mem. investment adv. com. Venture Investors of Wis., Inc., Madison, 1986—. Author: International Marketing: An Annotated Bibliography, 1983; contbr. articles to profl. jours. Bd. dirs. Madison Civic Ctr., 1983—. Mem. Am. Mktg. Assn. (bd. dirs. PhD consortium 1979, editorial bd. Jour. of Mktg. Chgo. chpt. 1983—), Am. Coun. on Consumer Interests, Assn. for Consumer Rsch. Avocations: golf, skiing, running. Home: 7514 Red Fox Trl Madison WI 53717-1860 Office: U Wis 975 University Ave Madison WI 53706-1324

NEVIN, JOSEPH FRANCIS, computer systems engineer; b. Washington, Mar. 20, 1947; s. John Joseph and Mary Frances (O'Donnell) N.; m. Kathleen Cecelia Ridgell, Mar. 16, 1991; children: Christopher, Andrew, Amy, Megan. BA, Georgetown U., 1969; MS, Am. U., 1977. Chief of systems devel. USPHS, BPHC, Bethesda, Md., 1980—; historian Smithsonian Assocs., Washington, 1982—. Pres. Balt. and Ohio RR Hist. Soc., 1982-83, 94—, v.p., 1984-94. Recipient Adminstrs. award Health Resources and Svcs., 1983; Pub. Health Spl. Recognition award USPHS, 1984. Avocations: railroad and transportation history. Office: Balt and Ohio RR Hist Soc PO Box 13578 Baltimore MD 21203

NEVIN, ROBERT CHARLES, information systems executive; b. Dayton, Ohio, Nov. 4, 1940; s. Robert Steely and Virginia (Boehme) N.; m. Linda Sharon Fox, Apr. 16, 1966; children: Heather, Andrew. B.A., Williams Coll., 1962; M.B.A., U. Pa., 1970. Fin. planning mgr. Huffy Corp., Dayton, Ohio, 1971-72, asst. treas., 1972-73, treas., 1973-75, v.p. fin., 1975-79, exec. v.p., 1982-85; pres., gen. mgr. Frabill Sporting Good, Milw., 1979-82; exec. v.p. Reynolds & Reynolds, Dayton, Ohio, 1985-88, pres. bus. forms div., 1988—; bd. dirs. Reynolds & Reynolds, Olympic Title Ins. Co. Bd. dirs., pres. Camp Fire Girls, Dayton, 1975; bd. dirs. ARC, 1977; participant, then trustee Leadership Dayton, 1986-95; vice chmn. Med Am. Corp.; trustee, treas. Victory Theater Assn., 1985-91, Dayton Mus. Natural History, 1982-96; trustee Alliance for Edn., Dayton Art Inst. 1st lt. USN, 1962-70. Mem. Beta Gamma Sigma, Racquet (Dayton), Dayton Country, Country Club of the North. Republican. Episcopalian. Office: Reynolds & Reynolds 3555 S Kettering Blvd Dayton OH 45439

NEVINS, ALBERT J., publisher, editor, author; b. Yonkers, N.Y., Sept. 11, 1915; s. Albert J. and Bessie (Corcoran) N. Ed., Venard Coll., Clarks Summit, Pa., 1936, Maryknoll (N.Y.) Sem., 1942; LHD (hon.), St. Benedict's Coll., Atchinson, Kans., 1963, Universidad Catolica de Puerto Rico, 1978. Ordained priest Roman Catholic Ch., 1942. Dir. social communications Cath. Fgn. Mission Soc. Am., 1960-69; v.p., pub., editor-in-chief Our Sunday Visitor, Inc., 1969-80; editor The Pope Speaks, 1980—, Diaconate Mag., 1985-91, Nova, 1989—; editor Maryknoll mag., 1955-69, World Campus mag., 1958-67; dir. World Horizon Films, 1945-68; cons. internat. visitors office U.S. Cath. Conf.; treas. Inter-Am. Tech. Ctr., 1972-88. Author: The Catholic Year, 1949, Adventures of Wu Han of Korea, 1951, Adventures of Kenji of Japan, 1952, Adventures of Pancho of Peru, 1953, Adventures of Ramon of Bolivia, 1954, St. Francis of the Seven Seas, 1955, The Adventures of Duc of Indochina, 1955, The Meaning of Maryknoll, 1956, Adventures of Men of Maryknoll, 1957, The Maryknoll Golden Book, 1956, The Making of a Priest, 1958, Away to Africa, 1959, The Maryknoll Book of Peoples, 1959, The Young Conquistador, 1960, Aways to the Lands of the Andes, 1962, Maryknoll Catholic Dictionary, 1964, Church in the Modern World, 1964, Away to Mexico, 1966, Away to Central America, 1967, Maryknoll Book of Treasures, 1968, Away to Venezuela, 1969, The Prayer of the Faithful, 1970, Our American Catholic Heritage, 1972, General Intercessions, 1977, A Saint for Your Name, 1980, Life After Death, 1983, The Sunday Readings, 1984, Builders of Catholic America, 1985, The Life of Jesus Christ, 1987, American Martyrs, 1987, Strangers at Your Door, 1988, Ask Me a Question, 1989, Answering a Fundamentalist, 1990, Scriptures of Faith, 1991, Catholicism, 1994, Indulgences, 1995; prodr., author, photographer numerous films, from 1946, including The Story of Juan Mateo (Film Festival award), 1957, A Problem of People (Film Festival award), 1961, The Gods of Todos Santos (Film Festival awards 1966, 67). Comdr. Westchester group Civil Air Patrol; pres. Cath. Journalism Scholarship Fund; bd. dirs. Cath. League for Religious and Civil Rights, 1975—. Recipient Nat. Brotherhood award NCCJ, 1958, Maria Moors Cabot prize Columbia, 1961, St. Augustine award Villanova U., 1962, Benemerenti gold medal Holy See, 1980. Mem. Inter-Am. Press Assn. (treas. tech. ctr., bd. dirs. 1965-94), Cath. Press Assn. (pres.

1959-61, bd. dirs., award 1961), Cath. Inst. Press (co-founder, mem. exec. bd. 1945-60), U.S. Cath. Hist. Soc., Latin Am. Studies Assn., Cath. Assn. Internat. Peace, Fellowship of Cath. Scholars, Overseas Press Club. Address: 4606 W Loughman St Tampa FL 33616-1826

NEVINS, JOHN J., bishop; b. New Rochelle, N.Y., Jan. 19, 1932. Student, Iona Coll. (N.Y.), Cath. U. Washington. Ordained priest, Roman Catholic Ch., 1959. Ordained titular bishop of Rusticana and aux. bishop Diocese of Miami, Fla., 1979-84; first bishop Diocese of Venice, Fla., 1984—. Office: PO Box 2006 1000 Pinebrook Rd Venice FL 34292-1426*

NEVINS, JOSEPH R., medical educator; b. June 21, 1947. BS, U. Okla., 1970, MS, 1972; PhD, Duke U., 1976. Asst. prof. molecular cell biology Rockefeller U., 1979-82, assoc. prof., 1982-87, investigator Howard Hughes Med. Inst., 1986-87; prof. microbiology Duke U. Med. Ctr., 1987—, investigator Howard Hughes Med. Inst., 1987—, prof. genetics and head, sect. genetics, 1990-94, chmn. dept. genetics, 1994—; lectr. in field. Dept. Microbiology and Immunology fellow Duke U. Med. Ctr., 1972-76, Postdoctoral fellow Rockefeller U., 1976-79; guest scholar Inst. Virus Rsch., Kyoto U., 1986. Mem. Am. Soc. Microbiology, Am. Soc. Virology, Am. Assn. Cancer Rsch. Office: Howard Hughes Med Inst Duke U Med Ctr Dept Genetics Durham NC 27710

NEVINS, LYN (CAROLYN A. NEVINS), educational supervisor, trainer, consultant; b. Chelsea, Mass., June 9, 1948; d. Samuel Joseph and Stella Theresa (Maronski) N.; m. John Edward Herbert, Jr., May 1, 1979; children: Chrissy, Johnny. BA in Sociology/Edn., U. Mass., 1970; MA in Women's Studies, George Washington U., 1975. Cert. tchr., trainer. Tchr. social studies Greenwich (Conn.) Pub. Schs., 1970-74; rschr. career/vocat. edn. Conn. State Dept. Edn., Hartford, 1975-76; rschr., career/vocat. edn. Area Coop. Edn. Svcs., Hamden, Conn., 1976-77; program mgr., trainer career edn. and gender equity Coop. Ednl. Svcs., Norwalk, Conn., 1977-83; trainer, mgr., devel., Beginning Educator Support and Tng. program Coop. Ednl. Svcs., Fairfield, Conn., 1987—; state coord. career edn. Conn. State Dept. Edn., Hartford, 1982-83; supr. Sacred Heart U., Fairfield, 1992—; mem. bias com. Conn. State Dept. Edn., Hartford, 1981—; mem. vision com. Middlesex Mid. Sch., Darien, Conn., 1993-95; mem. ednl. quality and diversity com. Town of Darien, 1993-95; cons., trainer career devel./pre-retirement planning Cohen and Assocs., Fairfield, 1981—, Farren Assocs., Annandale, Va., 1992—, Tracey Robert Assocs., Fairfield, 1994—; freelance cons., trainer, Darien, 1983-87; presenter Nat. Conf. GE, 1980, Career Edn., 1983, Am. Edn. Rsch. Assn., 1991; lectr. in field. Coach Spl. Olympics, 1993—, Darien (Conn.) Girls' Softball League, 1992—. Mem. NOW (founder, state coord. edn. 1972-74), ASCD. Avocations: tennis, running, walking, golf, travel. Home: 4 Hollister Ln Darien CT 06820-5404 Office: Coop Ednl Svcs 25 Oakview Dr Trumbull CT 06611

NEVINS, SHEILA, television programmer and producer; b. N.Y.C.; d. Benjamin and Stella N.; B.A., Barnard Coll., 1960; M.F.A. (Three Arts fellow), Yale U., 1963; m. Sidney Koch; 1 son, David Andrew. TV producer Great Am. Dream Machine, NET, 1970-72, The Reasoner Report, ABC, 1973, Feeling Good, Children's TV Workshop, 1975-76, Who's Who, CBS, 1977-78; v.p. documentary and family programming HBO, N.Y.C., 1978-82, dir. documentary programming Home Box Office, N.Y.C., 1986-95, sr. v.p. documentary and family programming, 1995—. Bd. dirs. Women's Action Alliance. Recipient Peabody award, 1986, 92, Acad. Award Documentary, 1993, Emmy award, 1994, 1995; named Woman of Achievement YWCA, 1991. Mem. Writers Guild Am., Women in Film.

NEW, ANNE LATROBE, public relations, fund raising executive; b. Evanston, Ill., May 10, 1910; d. Charles Edward and Agnes (Bateman) N.; m. John C. Timmerman, Sept. 30, 1933; 1 child, Jan LaTrobe. AB, U. S.C., 1930; postgrad., Hunter Coll., 1930-31, NYU, 1932-33. APR (Accredited Pub. Relatons Practitioner). Editorial asst. Pictorial Review Mag., N.Y.C., 1930-32; copy asst. J. Walter Thompson Co., N.Y.C., 1932-33; sub editor Cosmopolitan Mag., N.Y.C., 1933-37; with Girl Scouts of the U.S., N.Y.C., 1937-57, chief pub. rels. officer, 1945-57; dir. pub. info. edn. Nat. Recreation and Park Assn., 1957-66; special asst. gen. dir. Internat. Social Svc. Am. Branch, N.Y.C., 1966-68; dir. devel. Nat. Accreditation Coun. for Agys. Serving Blind and Visual Handicapped, N.Y.C., 1969-78; pres. Timmerman & New Inc., Mamaroneck, N.Y., 1980—; cons. dept. pub. adminstrn. Baruch Coll., CUNY, 1987-94, Sch. Pub. Affairs, 1994—. Author: Service For Givers, The Story of the National Information Bureau, 1983, Raise More Money for Your Nonprofit Organization, 1991; contbr. articles to profl. jours. Mem. Westchester Dem. Com. Westchester County, 1963-67, 89—; bd. dirs. Mamaroneck (N.Y.) United Fund, 1963-64; chmn. nominating com. LWV, Mamaroneck, 1988, chmn. by-law com., 1989; warden emerita, vestry mem. St. Thomas' Episc. Ch., Mamaroneck. Recipient Marzella Garland award for outstanding achievement in promotion of improved housing conditions in Mamaroneck Village, 1995. Mem. Pub. Rels. Soc. Am. (bd. dirs. N.Y. chpt. 1958-72), Women Execs. Pub. Rels. (sec. 1962--63), Nat. Soc. Fund Raising Execs. (bd. dirs. greater N.Y. chpt. 1978-84), Phi Beta Kappa (Scarsdale/Westchester Phi Beta Kappa Assn.). Democrat. Avocations: tennis, dancing, swimming. Office: Timmerman & New Inc 235 S Barry Ave Mamaroneck NY 10543-4104

NEW, ELOISE OPHELIA, special education educator; b. Jeffersonville, Ind., Jan. 14, 1942; d. Ivan Foster and Nellie Katherine (Harman) Baugh; m. Paul Eugene New, Nov. 23, 1961; children: Paula, Paul Jr. BS in Elem. Edn., Eastern Ky. U., 1963; MA in Edn., Coll. Mt. St. Joseph, 1987. Cert. elem. K-8, and developmentally handicapped tchr. K-12, Ohio. Tchr. Newport (Ky.) City Schs., 1963-69, Ross County and Chillicothe (Ohio) City Schs., 1977-78; developmentally handicapped tchr. Mt. Logan Middle Sch., Chillicothe, 1979—. Tchr. Sunday sch. Tabernacle Bapt. Ch., Chillicothe, 1987-93, chmn. elem. edn. com., 1988-93, Sunday sch. supt., 1994—, mem. christian Bd. Edn., 1988—; spokesperson for edn. selectin Chillicothe Edn. Found., 1989. Recipient Excellence in Edn. award Pllasco-Ross Adminstrn. Conf. for Spl. Educators, 1984, Ohio Jennings Scholar award, 1991-93. Mem. NEA, Ohio Edn. Assn., Chillicothe Edn. Assn. (rep. 1986-88). Baptist. Home: 828 Orange St Chillicothe OH 45601-1340 Office: Mt Logan Mid Sch 841 E Main St Chillicothe OH 45601-3509

NEW, MARIA IANDOLO, physician, educator; b. N.Y.C.; d. Loris J. and Esther B. (Giglio) Iandolo; m. Bertrand L. New, 1949 (dec. 1990); children: Erica, Daniel, Antonia. B.A., Cornell U., 1950; M.D., U. Pa., 1954. Diplomate: Am. Bd. Pediatrics. Med. intern Bellevue Hosp., N.Y.C., 1954-55; resident pediatrics N.Y. Hosp., 1955-57; fellow NIH, 1957-58, 61-64; practice medicine specializing in pediatrics N.Y.C., 1955—; mem. staff N.Y. Hosp., N.Y.C.; dir. Pediatric Metabolism Clinic, N.Y. Hosp., 1964—, attending pediatrician, 1971-80, pediatrician-in-chief, 1980—; asst. prof. dept. pediat. Cornell U. Med. Coll., N.Y.C., 1963-68, assoc. prof., 1968-71, prof., 1971—, Harold and Percy Uris prof. pediatric endocrinology, 1978—, prof., chmn. dept. pediat., 1980—; assoc. dir. Pediatric Clin. Rsch. Ctr., 1980-88; adj. prof. Rockefeller U., 1981—; career scientist N.Y.C. Health Rsch. Coun., 1966-75; adj. attending pedatrician dept. pediat. Meml. Sloan-Kettering Cancer Ctr., 1979—; cons. United Hosp., Port Chester, N.Y., 1977—, North Shore Univ. Hosp., 1982—, dept. pediat. Cath. Med. Ctr. Bklyn. and Queens, N.Y., 1987; vis. physician Rockefeller U. Hosp., N.Y.C., 1973—; mem. endocrine study sect. NIH, 1977-81, Gen. Clin. Rsch. Ctrs. Adv. Com.; chmn. Divsn. Rsch. Resources Gen. Clin. Rsch. Ctrs. Com. NIH, 1987-88; bd. dirs. Robert Wood Johnson Clin. Scholars Program; mem. N.Y. State Gov.'s Task Force on Life and Law, 1985—; mem. NIH Reviewers Res.; mem. FDA endocrinology and metabolism drug adv. com., 1994—; panelist ACGME bd. appeals, 1994—. Editor-in-chief Jour. Clin. Endocrinology and Metabolism, 1994—; mem. editorial adv. coun. Jour. Endocrinol. Investigation, 1995—; mem. editorial bd. Jour. Women's Health, 1993; corr. editor Jour. Steroid Biochemistry, 1985; mem. adv. bd. pediatric anns., assoc. editor Metabolism, 1981—. Trustee Irma T. Hirschl Trust. Recipient Mary Jane Kugel award Juvenile Diabetes Found., 1977, Katharine D. McCormick Disting. Lectureship, 1981, Robert H. Williams Disting. Leadership award, 1988, Albion O. Bernstein award Med. Soc. State N.Y., 1988, medal N.Y. Acad. Medicine, 1991, Disting. Grad. award U. Pa. Sch. Medicine, 1991, Optimate Recognition award Assn. Student-Profl. Italian-Ams., 1991, Outstanding Woman Scientist award N.Y. chpt. Am. Women in Sci., 1986, Maurice R. Greenberg Disting. Svc. award, 1994, Humanitarian award Juvenile Diabetes Found., 1994, Rhône Poulenc Rorer Clinical Investigator Lecture award, 1994; grantee. Fellow Italian Soc. Endocrinology (hon.); mem. AAAS, Am. Soc. Human Genetics, Am. Acad. Pediatrics, Soc. for Pediatric Research, Harvey Soc., Endocrine Soc. (mem. coun. 1981-84, pres. 1991-92), Lawson Wilkins Pediatric Endocrine Soc. (pres. 1985-86), Am. Soc. Nephrology, Am. Soc. Pediatric Nephrology, Am. Pediatric Soc., Am. Fedn. Clin. Research, Am. Diabetes Assn., European Soc. Pediatric Endocrinology, Am. Coll. Clin. Pharmacology, Am. Clin. & Climatol. Assn., N.Y. Acad. Scis., Pan Am. Med. Assn., Assn. Am. Physicians, Am. Fertility Soc., U.S. Pharmacopeial Conv. (elected), Am. Acad. of Arts and Scis. (elected 1992), Alpha Omega Alpha. Office: New York Hosp-Cornell Med Ctr Dept Pediatrics 525 E 68th St New York NY 10021-4873

NEW, ROSETTA HOLBROCK, home economics educator, nutrition consultant; b. Hamilton, Ohio, Aug. 26, 1921; d. Edward F. and Mabel (Kohler) Holbrock; m. John Lorton New, Sept. 3, 1943; 1 child, John Lorton Jr. BS, Miami U., Oxford, Ohio, 1943; MA, U. No. Colo., 1971; PhD, The Ohio State U., 1974; student Kantcentrum, Brugge, Belgium, 1992, Lesage Sch. Embroidery, Paris, 1995. Cert. tchr., Colo. Tchr. English and sci. Monahans (Tex.) H.S., 1943-45; emergency war food asst. U.S. Dept. Agr., College Station, Tex., 1945-46; dept. chmn. home econs., adult edn. Hamilton (Ohio) Pub. Schs., 1946-47; tchr., dept. chmn. home econs. East H.S., Denver, 1948-59, Thomas Jefferson H.S., Denver, 1959-83; mem. exec. bd. Denver Pub. Schs.; also lectr.; exec. dir. Ctr. Nutrition Info. U.S. Office of Edn. grantee Ohio State U., 1971-73. Mem. Cin. Art Mus., Nat. Trust for Historic Preservation. Mem. Am. Home Econs. Assn., Am. Vocat. Assn., Embroiders Guild Am., Hamilton Hist. Soc., Internat. Old Lacers, Ohio State U. Assn., Ohio State Home Econs. Alumni Assn., Fairfield (Ohio) Hist. Soc., Republican Club of Denver, Internat. Platform Assn., Phi Upsilon Omicron. Presbyterian. Lodges: Masons, Daughters of the Nile, Order of Eastern Star, Order White Shrine of Jerusalem. Home and Office: 615 Crescent Rd Hamilton OH 45013-3432

NEW, WILLIAM NEIL, physician, retired naval officer; b. Atoka, Okla., Oct. 24, 1908; s. Robert Calvin and Nommar Bell (Willmore) N.; m. Ruth Anderson Pride, Mar. 30, 1940. B.A., Central State Tchrs. Coll., Edmond, Okla., 1931; B.S. in Medicine, U. Okla., 1932, M.D., 1934; postgrad., Northwestern U. Med. Sch., 1947-48. Diplomate: Am. Bd. Dermatology and Syphilology. Intern So. Pacific R.R. Hosp., San Francisco, 1934-35; commd. lt. (j.g.), M.C. U.S. Navy, 1935, advanced through grades to rear adm., 1963; resident dermatology and syphilology Naval Hosp., Phila., 1946-47; med. officer on gunboat and USMC Hosp., Shanghai, 1937-39; regtl. surgeon 7th Marines in Guadalcanal; later div. surgeon 5th Marine Div. (Japanese occupation), 1945; established Naval Med. Field Research Lab., Camp Lejeune, 1943; chief dermatology services naval hosps. Great Lakes, Ill., 1948-51, Phila., 1951-53, San Diego, 1956-59; force surgeon Fleet Marine Force, Pacific, 1954-56; comdg. officer U.S. Naval Hosp., Yokusuka, Japan, 1959-62; dir. staff Office Dep. Asst. Sec. Def. for Health and Med., 1962-66; pvt. practice dermatology Dallas Med. and Surg. clinic, 1968-91; ret., 1991; clin. assoc. prof. dermatology Southwestern Med. Sch., U. Tex., Dallas, 1966-92. Mem. ACP (life), Am. Acad. Dermatology (life), Pacific Dermatol. Assn. (life), Assn. Mil. Dermatologists (past pres.), N.Am. Clin. Dermatol. Soc. (co-founder, life), Space Dermatol. Found. (co-founder), Cutaneous Therapy Soc. (co-founder, life). Home: 3310 Fairmount St Apt 17C Dallas TX 75201-1241 *Love and live today as we plan a rewarding tomorrow.*

NEWACHECK, DAVID JOHN, lawyer; b. San Francisco, Dec. 8, 1953; s. John Elmer and Estere Ruth Sybil (Nelson) N.; m. Dorothea Quandt, June 2, 1990. AB in English, U. Calif., Berkeley, 1976; JD, Pepperdine U., 1979; MBA, Calif. State U., Hayward, 1982; LLM in Tax, Golden Gate U., 1987. Bar: Calif. 1979, U.S. Dist. Ct. (no. dist.) Calif. 1979, U.S. Ct. Appeals (9th cir.) 1979, U.S. Supreme Ct. 1984, Washington D.C. 1985. Tax cons. Pannell, Kerr and Forster, San Francisco, 1982-83; lawyer, writer, editor Matthew Bender and Co., San Francisco, 1983—; instr. taxation Oakland (Calif.) Coll. of Law, 1993—; lawyer, tax cons., fin. planner Castro Valley, Calif., 1983—; bd. dirs. Aztec Custom Co., Orinda, Calif., 1983—; cons. software Collier Bankruptcy Filing Sys., 1984. Author/editor: (treatises) Ill. Tax Service, 1985, Ohio State Taxation, 1985, N.J. Tax Service, 1986, Pa. Tax Service, 1986, Calif. Closely Held Corps., 1987, Texas Tax Service, 1988; author: (software) Tax Source 1040 Tax Preparation, 1987, Texas Tax Service 1988, California Taxation, 1989, 2d edit., 1990, Bender's Federal Tax Service, 1989, Texas Litigation Guide, 1993, Family Law: Texas Practice & Procedure, 1993, Texas Transaction Guide, 1994, Ohio Corporation Law, 1994, Michigan Corporation Law, 1994, Massachusetts Corporation Law, 1994. Mem. youth com. Shepherd of the Valley Luth. Ch., Orinda, 1980-85, ch. coun., 1980-82. Mem. ABA, Internat. Platform Assn., State Bar Assn. Calif., Alameda County Bar Assn., U. Calif. Alumni Assn., U. Calif. Band Alumni Assn., Mensa. Republican. Club: Commonwealth (San Francisco). Avocations: music, competitive running, sports. Home and Office: 5141 Vannoy Ave Castro Valley CA 94546-2558

NEWBAUER, JOHN ARTHUR, editor; b. Newport, R.I., Apr. 24, 1928; s. John Arthur and Theo Caroline (Trewhella) N.; m. Marilyn Mahler, Oct. 14, 1956; children: April, Dana, Miranda. B.A., U. Calif.-Berkeley, 1951. Sr. editor and writer sci. and engring., rocket devel. dept. U.S. Naval Ordnance Test Sta., China Lake, Calif., 1951-56; editor in chief Astronautics and Aeronautics jour., N.Y.C., 1963-83; adminstr. sci. publs. AIAA, 1983-91, cons. editor, 1991—; editor in chief Aerospace Am., 1983-87, aquisitions editor, 1987-89. Fellow AIAA (assoc.), Brit. Interplanetary Soc. Home: 356 Bay Ridge Ave Brooklyn NY 11220-5315

NEWBERG, DOROTHY BECK (MRS. WILLIAM C. NEWBERG), portrait artist; b. Detroit, May 30, 1919; d. Charles William and Mary (Labedz) Beck; student Detroit Conservatory Music, 1938; m. William C. Newberg, Nov. 3, 1939; children: Judith Bookwalter Bracken, Robert Charles, James William, William Charles. Trustee Detroit Adventure, 1967-71, originator A Drop in Bucket Program for artistically talented inner-city children. Cmty. outreach coord. Reno Police Dept.; bd. dirs. Bloomfield Art Assn., 1960-62, trustee 1965-67; bd. dirs. Your Heritage House, 1972-75, Franklin Wright Settlement, 1972-75, Meadowbrook Art Gallery, Oakland U., 1973-75; bd. dirs. Sierra Nevada Mus. Art, 1978-80; bd. dirs. Nat. Conf. Christians and Jews, Gang Alternatives Partnership. Recipient Heart of Gold award, 1969; Mich. vol. leadership award, 1969, Outstanding Vol. award City of Reno, 1989-90. Mem. Nevada Mus. Art, No. Nev. Black Cultural Awareness Soc. (bd. dirs.), Hispanic 500 C. of C. No. Nev. Roman Catholic. Home: 2000 Dant Blvd Reno NV 89509-5193

NEWBERN, WILLIAM DAVID, state supreme court justice; b. Oklahoma City, May 28, 1937; s. Charles Banks and Mary Frances (Harding) N.; m. Barbara Lee Rigsby, Aug. 19, 1961 (div. 1968); 1 child, Laura Harding; m. Carolyn Lewis, July 30, 1970; 1 child, Alistair Elizabeth. B.A., U. Ark., 1959, J.D., 1961; LL.M., George Washington U., 1963; M.A., Tufts U., 1967. Bar: Ark. 1961, U.S. Dist. Ct. (we. dist.) Ark. 1961, U.S. Supreme Ct. 1968, U.S. Ct. Appeals (8th cir.) 1983. Commd. 1st lt. advanced to maj. U.S. Army JAGC, 1961-70; Prof. law U. Ark., Fayetteville, 1970-84; adminstr. Ozark Folk Ctr., Mountain View, Ark., 1973; judge Ark. Ct. Appeals, Little Rock, 1979-80; assoc. justice Ark. Supreme Ct., Little Rock, 1985—; mem. faculty sr. appellate judges seminar NYU, 1987-91. Editor Ark. Law Rev., 1961; author: Arkansas Civil Practice and Procedure, 1985, 2d edit., 1993. Mem. Fayetteville Bd. Adjustment, 1972-79; bd. dirs. decision Point, INc., Springdale, Ark., 1980-85, Little Rock Wind Symphony, 1993, pres. 1993-95. Fellow Ark. Bar Found.; mem. Am. Judicature Soc. (bd. dirs. 1985-89), Washington County Bar Assn., Inst. Jud. Adminstrn., Ark. IOLTA Found. (bd. dirs. 1985-87). Democrat. Avocation: string band-guitar, mandolin, banjo and brass quintet-tuba. Office: Ark Supreme Ct 625 Marshall St Little Rock AR 72201-1020

NEWBERRY, CONRAD FLOYDE, aerospace engineering educator; b. Neodesha, Kans., Nov. 10, 1931; s. Ragan McGregor and Audra Anitia (Newmaster) N.; m. Sarah Louise Thonn, Jan. 26, 1958; children: Conrad Floyde Jr., Thomas Edwin, Susan Louise. AA, Independence Jr. Coll., 1951; BEME in Aero. Sequence, U. So. Calif., 1957; MSME, Calif. State U., Los Angeles, 1971, MA in Edn., 1974; D.Environ. Sci. and Engring., UCLA, 1985. Registered profl. engr., Calif., Kans., N.C., Tex. Mathematician L.A. divsn. N.Am. Aviation Inc., 1951-53, jr. engr., 1953-54, engr., 1954-57, sr. engr., 1957-64; asst. prof. aerospace engring. Calif. State Poly. U., Pomona, 1964-70, assoc. prof. aerospace engring., 1970-75, prof. aerospace engring., 1975-90, prof. emeritus, 1990—; staff engr. EPA, 1980-82; engring. specialist space transp. systems div. Rockwell Internat. Corp., 1984-90; prof. aeronautics and astronautics Naval Postgrad. Sch., Monterey, Calif., 1990—, acad. assoc. space systems engring., 1992-94. Recipient John Leland Atwood award as outstanding aerospace engring. educator AIAA/Am. Soc. Engring. Edn., 1986. Fellow AIAA (dep. dir. edn. region VI 1976-79, dep. dir. career enhancement 1982-91, chmn. L.A. sect. 1989-90, chmn. Point Lobos sect. 1990-91, chmn. acad. affairs com. 1990-93, dir. tech.-aircraft sys. 1990-93), Inst. Advancement Engring., Brit. Interplanetary Soc.; mem. IEEE, AAAS, ASME, NSPE, Royal Aero. Soc., Calif. Soc. Profl. Engrs., Am. Acad. Environ. Engrs. (cert. air pollution control engr.), Am. Soc. Engring. Edn. (chmn. aerospace divsn. 1979-80, divsn. exec. com. 1976-80, 89-94, exec. com. ocean and marine engring. divsn. 1982-85, 90—, program chmn. 1993-95, chmn. 1993-95, chmn. PIC II 1995—), Am. Soc. Pub. Adminstrn., Am. Meteorol. Soc., U.S. Naval Inst., Am. Helicopter Soc., Soc. Naval Architects and Marine Engrs., Air and Waste Mgmt. Assn., Inst. Environ. Scis., Exptl. Aircraft Assn., Water Environ. Fedn., Soc. Automotive Engr., Soc. Allied Weight Engrs., Assn. Unmanned Vehicle Sys., Calif. Water Pollution Control Assn., Nat. Assn. Environ. Profls., Am. Soc. Naval Engrs., Planetary Soc., Tau Beta Pi, Sigma Gamma Tau, Kappa Delta Pi. Democrat. Mem. Christian Ch. (Disciples of Christ). Achievements include research on aircraft, space, missile and engine design and related impacts on exergy, quality, concurrent engineering, cost and environmental controls. Home: 9463 Willow Oak Rd Salinas CA 93907-1037 Office: Naval Postgrad Sch Dept Aeronautics and Astronautics AA/Ne 699 Dyer Rd Monterey CA 93943-5106

NEWBERRY, ROBERT CURTIS, SR., communications executive, newspaper editor; b. Port Arthur, Tex., Feb. 20, 1945; s. Ira and Nona (Houston) N.; m. Carolyn Annette Ponder, Dec. 21, 1968; children: Renita, Renona, Robert Jr.; m. Jackolyn Cone, Oct. 8, 1994. BA, U. Houston, 1967. Sports editor The Houston Informer, 1964-65, Sports World, Houston, 1965; asst. news editor, columnist The Houston Post, 1967-87, columnist, 1987-95; exec. editor The Houston Reader, 1995; owner, pres. Newberry Comm.; editor, pub. newsletter Stress-Less. Bd. dirs. I Have a Dream, Houston, Citizens for Better Health, Houston Child Guidance Ctr., 1988-92, tutor and mentor, 1991—. Recipient Life Svc. award Tex. So. U., Houston, 1972, Print Media award Mental Health Assn., 1987, Print Media award Tex. Mental Health Assn., 1988, Julia C. Hester Achievement award Trailblazer, 1988, Awards of Excellence Dallas Press Club, 1989, Houston Press Club, 1990, 1st Pl. award UPI Regional Awards, 1990, 2d Pl. award commentary newspapers over 100,000 circulation, 1995, Disting. Alumnus award U. Houston, 1990. Fellow Am. Leadership Forum (sr., bd. dirs. 1990—); mem. Nat. Assn. Black Journalists, Soc. Profl. Journalists (bd. dirs. 1968), Houston Assn. Black Journalists, U. Houston Alumni Orgn. (bd. dirs. 1991—). Democrat. Avocations: writing, fishing, boating. Office: Newberry Communications Box 44 3700 Wakeforest Houston TX 77098

NEWBILL, KAREN MARGARET, elementary school educator, education educator; b. East Orange, N.J., Oct. 6, 1945; d. Richard Oliver and Edna Mae (Crook) Jacobson; m. Gary C. Newbill, Aug. 18, 1965; children: Kari L., Erick D. BA, Seattle Pacific U., 1968; MEd, City U., Bellevue, Wash., 1993. Cert. tchr., Wash. Tchr. Shoreline Pub. Schs., Seattle, 1969-71, Northshore Sch. Dist., Bothell, Wash., 1971-74; tutor, substitute tchr. Issaquah (Wash.) Sch. Dist., 1980-89, tchr., 1989—, tech. and curriculum integration cons., 1991—; adj. prof. N.W. Coll., Kirkland, Wash., 1994—, mem. profl. edn. adv. bd., 1994—; adj. prof. Seattle Pacific U., 1994—; student tchr. supr. U. Wash., Seattle, 1991—. Children's choir dir. Westminster Chapel, Bellevue, Wash., 1980-88; children's worship leader Evergreen Christian Fellowship, Issaquah, 1993-94. Mem. ASCD, NEA, Wash. Edn. Assn., Nat. Coun. Tchrs. Math., Internat. Reading Assn. Avocations: decorative painting, reading, traveling, music. Home: 420 Kalmia Pl NW Issaquah WA 98027-2619 Office: Issaquah Sch Dist. 565 NW Holly St Issaquah WA 98027-2834

NEWBLATT, STEWART ALBERT, federal judge; b. Detroit, Dec. 23, 1927; s. Robert Abraham and Fanny Ida (Grinberg) N.; m. Flora Irene Sandweiss, Mar. 5, 1965; children: David Jacob, Robert Abraham, Joshua Isaac. B.A. with distinction, U. Mich., 1950, J.D. with distinction, 1952. Bar: Mich. bar 1953. Ptnr. firm White & Newblatt, Flint, Mich., 1953-62; judge 7th Jud. Cir. Mich., 1962-70; ptnr. firm Newblatt & Grossman (and predecessor), Flint, 1970-79; judge U.S. Dist. Ct. (ea. dist.) Mich., Flint, 1979—; adj. instr. U. Mich.-Flint, 1977-78, 86. Mem. Internat. Bridge Authority Mich., 1960-62. Served with AUS, 1946-47. Mem. Fed. Bar Assn., State Bar Mich., Dist. Judges Assn. 6th Circuit. Jewish. Office: US Dist Ct 140 Federal Bldg 600 Church St Flint MI 48502-1214

NEWBOLD, ARTHUR, lawyer; b. Harrisburg, Pa., 1942. AB cum laude, Harvard U., 1964; LLB magna cum laude, U. Pa., 1967. BAr: Pa. 1967. Ptnr. Dechert Price & Rhodes, Phila. Comment editor U. Pa. Law review, 1966-67. Fellow Am. Coll. Trial Lawyers; mem. Order of Coif. Office: Dechert Price & Rhoads 4000 Bell Atlantic Tower 1717 Arch St Philadelphia PA 19103-2793

NEWBOLD, HERBERT LEON, JR., psychiatrist, writer; b. High Point, N.C., Nov. 3, 1921; s. Herbert Leon and Mary Temperance (Sherrod) N.; m. Susan Deena Hecht; children: Lucile, Susan. Student, U. Chgo., 1941, Coll. William and Mary, 1941; B.S., Duke U., 1945, M.D., 1945; postgrad., Northwestern U., 1951, New Sch. Social Research, 1960-61. Intern U. Chgo. Clinics, 1945-46, U. Minn., 1949-50; resident Woodlawn Hosp., Chgo., 1946; resident in internal medicine Vanderbilt U. and associated VA Hosp., Nashville, 1946-47; resident in psychiatry U. Ill. and associated VA Hosp., Hines, Ill., 1955-58; practice medicine specializing in internal medicine Newton, N.C., 1947-48; practice medicine specializing in psychiatry Chgo., 1950-55, 1958-60; Asheville, N.C., 1961-70; N.Y.C., 1970—, pvt. practice specializing in psychiatry and neurology, 1976—; instr. neurology and psychiatry Sch. Medicine, Northwestern U., Chgo., 1958-61; freelance writer, 1950—. Author: (novels) 1/3 of an Inch of French Bread, 1961, Long John, 1979, Dr. Cox's Couch, 1979, others under pseudonym, 1950-60; (sci. books) Psychiatric Programming of People, 1972, Mega-Nutrients for Your Nerves, 1975, Doctor Newbold's Revolutionary New Discoveries about Weight Loss, How to master hidden allergies that make you fat, 1977, Physicians Handbook on Orthomolecular Medicine, 1977, Vitamin C Against Cancer, 1979, Mega-Nutrients, 1987, Dr. Newbold's Type A/Type B Weight Loss Book, 1991, Dr. Newbold's Nutrition for Your Nerves, 1993, Dr. Newbold's Diet To Cure Incurable Diseases, 1994; (with others) The New Chemotherapy in Mental Illness, 1958; contbr. articles to profl. jours.; numerous appearances radio and TV. Served with U.S. Army, 1943-45, 46-47. Mem. AMA. Address: 21 E 10th St Apt 10C New York NY 10003-5922 *There are only two horses that win. One is called luck and the other persistence, and you can't count on the one called luck.*

NEWBOLD, JOHN LOWE, banker; b. Washington, Dec. 26, 1935; s. John Lowe and Katharine Emily (Wilkins) N.; m. Judith Allen Bourne, June 20, 1959; children: Jennifer Hathaway, Timothy Bourne, Michael Fleming. BS, Yale U., 1957; MBA, NYU, 1963; sr. execs. program cert. MIT, 1970. Asst. v.p., credit instr. Citibank, N.A., N.Y.C., 1968-69, v.p. retail trade unit, 1969-70, v.p. info. svcs. dept., 1970-72, v.p., corp. bank head, Tokyo, 1972-73, v.p., country head, Singapore, 1974-76, sr. v.p., shipping dept. head, N.Y.C., 1976-85, div. exec. Global Shipping Div., 1985-89, Global Transp. Div., 1989—; pres., dir. Mchts. Fund, Inc., Silver Spring, Md., 1981—; bd. dirs. First Olsen Tankers Ltd., Bermuda. Trustee Summit Area Community Coun., N.J., 1983-86, United Way, Summit, 1984-92; pres. PTA Presidents' Coun., Summit, 1981-83. Served as lt. (j.g.) USNR, 1957-60. Mem. Yale of Cen. N.J. Club (trustee 1980—), Met. Club (Washington), Beacon Hill Club (Summit). Episcopalian. Home: 47 Hillcrest Ave Summit NJ 07901-2011 Office: Citibank NA 399 Park Ave New York NY 10022-4614

NEWBORG, GERALD GORDON, historical agency administrator; b. Ada, Minn., Dec. 13, 1942; s. George Harold and Olea (Halstad) N.; m. Jean Annette Gruhl, Aug. 14, 1964; children: Erica, Annette. BA, Concordia Coll., Moorhead, Minn., 1964; MA, U. N.D., 1969; MBA, Ohio State U., 1978. Cert. archivist. Tutor, preceptor Parsons Coll., Fairfield, Iowa, 1964-67; state archivist Ohio Hist. Soc., Columbus, 1968-76; v.p. Archival Systems Inc., Columbus, 1978-81; state archivist State Hist. Soc. of N.D., Bismarck, 1981—; instr. Franklin U., Columbus, 1974; adj. prof. Bismarck State Coll.,

1985-86. Co-author: North Dakota: A Pictorial History, 1988. Recipient Resolution of Commendation Ohio Ho. of Reps., Columbus, 1976. Mem. Soc. Am. Archivists, Nat. Assn. Govt. Archives & Records Adminstrs. (bd. dirs. 1984-86, sec. 1994—), Midwest Archives Conf., N.D. Libr. Assn. (exec. bd. 1985-86). Home: 1327 N 18th St Bismarck ND 58501-2827 Office: State Hist Soc 612 E Boulevard Ave Bismarck ND 58505-0660

NEWBORN, IRA, composer. Scores include (films) The Blues Brothers, 1980, All Night Long, 1981, Sixteen Candles, 1984, Into the Night, 1985, Weird Science, 1985, Ferris Bueller's Day Off, 1986, Wise Guys, 1986, Dragnet, 1987, Amazon Women on the Moon, 1987, Planes, Trains and Automobiles, 1987, Caddyshack II, 1988, The Naked Gun, 1988, Uncle Buck, 1989, Short Time, 1990, My Blue Heaven, 1990, The Naked Gun 2 1/2: The Smell of Fear, 1991, Brain Donors, 1992, Innocent Blood, 1992, The Opposite Sex and How to Live with Them, 1993, Naked Gun 33 1/3: The Final Insult, 1994, Ace Ventura, Pet Detective, 1994, (TV movies) Cast the First Stone, 1989. Office: The Robert Light Agency 6204 Wilshire Blvd Ste 900 Los Angeles CA 90048-5104

NEWBORN, JUD, anthropologist, writer, lyricist; b. N.Y.C., Nov. 8, 1952; s. Solomon and Rita (Cohen) N. BA magna cum laude in Anthropology and English, NYU, 1974; postgrad., Clare Hall, Cambridge U., 1974-75; MA in Anthropology, U. Chgo., 1977, PhD with distinction, 1994. Free-lance writer N.Y.C., Munich, Chgo., 1974—; publicist Oxford U. Press, N.Y.C., 1975-76; mus. historian, curatorial cons. Mus. Jewish Heritage (N.Y. Holocaust Meml. Commn.), N.Y.C., 1986-92; cons. Sci. Inst. for Pub. Info., N.Y.C., 1987-90; cons., spkr., lectr. in field. Author: Shattering the German Night: The Story of the White Rose Anti-Nazi Resistance, 1986; freelance writer, lyricist. Fulbright fellow, 1980-82; Newcombe fellow, 1984-85. Mem. ASCAP, Am. Anthrop. Assn., The Am. Hist. Assn., The Authors' Guild, Phi Beta Kappa.

NEWBORN, KAREN B., lawyer; b. Cleve., Oct. 30, 1944. BA, Goucher Coll., 1966; JD summa cum laude, Cleve. State U., 1976. Bar: Ohio 1976, U.S. Dist. Ct. (no. dist.) Ohio 1976, U.S. Ct. Appeals (6th cir.) 1978, U.S. Dist. Ct. (ea. dist.) Mich. 1984, U.S. Supreme Ct. 1988. Ptnr. Baker & Hostetler, Cleve.; asst. law dir. City Cleve., 1976-79; adj. instr. teaching trial advocacy, 1987. Mem. ABA, Ohio State Bar Assn., Cleve. Bar Assn. (bd. trustees 1989-92, chair commn. women in the law 1987-90), Inn of Ct. Office: Baker & Hostetler 3200 Nat City Ctr 1900 E 9th St Cleveland OH 44114-3401*

NEWBRAND, CHARLES MICHAEL, advertising firm executive; b. Staten Island, N.Y., May 2, 1944; s. Charles Henry and Edith (Kotte) N.; m. Clare Ann Holmes, Aug. 26, 1967; 1 child, Alexis Christina. B.A., U. Notre Dame, 1965; J.D., U. Pa., Phila., 1968. Bar: N.J. 1968. Media planner Ogilvy & Mather, N.Y.C., 1968-71, account exec., 1971-74, account supr., 1974-77, v.p. mgmt. supr., 1977-82, sr. v.p. mgmt. supr., 1982-85, sr. v.p., group dir., 1985-89; mem. N.Y. oper. bd. Ogilvy & Mather, 1987-89; sr. v.p., group acct. dir., mem. exec. com. Foote, Cone & Belding, Inc., Chgo., 1990; sr. v.p. The Martin Agy., Richmond, Va., 1991—. Recipient Stephen E. Kelly award Mag. Pubs. Assn., 1981, Golden Effie Am. Mktg. Assn., N.Y. chpt., 1982, 87. Office: The Martin Agy 500 N Allen Ave Richmond VA 23220-2904

NEWBRANDER, WILLIAM CARL, health economist, management consultant; b. Irumagawa, Japan, Sept. 14, 1951; parents Am. citizens; s. Virgil Ray and Ella Jeannette (Rae) N.; m. Nancy Sharon Wilson, June 15, 1974; children: Sharon, Billy, Andrew, Jonathan, Daniel. BA, Wheaton Coll., 1973; M of Hosp. Adminstrn., 1975; M of Applied Econs., U. Mich., 1981, PhD, 1983. Teaching/rsch. asst. U. Mich., Ann Arbor, 1979-83; mgmt. specialist V-HSR&D, Ann Arbor, 1980-83; hosp. adminstr. Whittaker Corp., Tabuk, Saudi Arabia, 1983-85; health economist WHO, Geneva, Switzerland, 1985-92; sr. assoc. Mgmt. Scis. for Health, Boston, 1992—. Author: Health Policy and Planning, 1988, 89, 90, 91, 94, Health Planning and Mgmt., 1988, 90, 91, Decentralization in a Developing Country, 1991, Hospital Economics and Financing in Developing Countries, 1992, World Health Forum, 1994, Health Sector Reform in Asia: Issues and Experiences Related to Private Sector Growth, 1996. Eagle Scout advisor Boy Scouts Am., Geneva and Hopkinton, Mass., 1990—; mgr. Little League baseball team, Geneva and Hopkinton, 1990—; elder First Congl. Ch., Hopkinton, 1995—. Capt. U.S. Army, 1975-79. VA Rsch. fellow, 1981-83. Fellow Am. Coll. Healthcare Execs. Office: Health Fin Program Mgt Sciences Health 165 Allandale St Boston MA 02130-3400

NEWBROUGH, EDGAR TRUETT, retired management consultant; b. Madison, Ill., June 22, 1917; s. Edgar M. and Iris M. (Webb) N.; m. Muriel E. Amos, Nov. 26, 1936; children—Sherrill (Mrs. T.D. McIntyre), Sandra (Mrs. D. S. Cole), Arthur T. B.A., San Diego State U., 1938. Registered profl. engr., Pa., Mo., Ill., Mich. cert. mgmt. cons. With Solar Aircraft Co., San Diego, 1937-43; supt. Des Moines plant, 1942-43; mem. staff Albert Ramond & Assos., Chgo., 1943-72, v.p., 1956-61, pres., 1962-72; spl. cons. Theodore Barry & Assocs., L.A., 1977-82, ind. mgmt. cons., 1982-89, cons. fellow; ret. Author: Effective Maintenance Management; also articles. Mem. Inst. Indsl. Engrs., Assn. Cons. Mgmt. Engrs. (dir. 1964-66), Am. Inst. Plant Engrs., Inst. Mgmt. Cons.'s (charter), St. Joe Valley Golf Club, Masons, Shriners. Presbyterian. (elder). Home: 24664 Ridgewood Dr Sturgis MI 49091

NEWBURGER, BETH WEINSTEIN, medical telecommunications company executive; b. Schenectady, July 8, 1937; d. H. Edward and Shirley (Diamond) Weinstein; m. Alan C. Newburger, Jan. 23, 1963 (dec. Oct. 1980); children: Mark, Lori, Eric, Jill; m. Richard Schwartz, May 26, 1989. BA, Cornell U., 1959. Dir. advt. New Republic, Washington, 1974-77; mktg. mgr. Washington Post, 1977-84; pres. Owlcat/Digital Rsch., Inc., Monterey, Calif., 1984-86; pres., chief exec. officer Corabi Internat. Telemetrics, Inc., Alexandria, Va., 1986-94; chmn. bd. Health Street, Inc., Bethesda, Md., 1985-95, assoc. adminstr. gen. svc. adminstrn., 1996—; bd. dirs. Tysons Nat. Bank, Vienna, Va.; apptd. to tech. adv. coun. NASA, 1995, mem. NASA adv. coun. TCAC, 1995—. Bd. dirs. Arena Stage, Washington, 1993—; chmn. bd. Nat. Learning Ctr./Capital Children's Mus., Washington, 1984—. Named Woman of Yr., Svc. Guild, Washington, 1972, 73. Mem. Women in Advt. and Mktg. (bd. dirs. 1986-89). Home: 1401 N Oak St Arlington VA 22209-3648

NEWBURGER, FRANK L., JR., retired investment broker; b. Phila., Nov. 26, 1908; s. Frank L. and Helen (Langfeld) N.; m. Dorothy Hess, Nov. 7, 1946 (dec.); children: Patricia S. (dec.), Frank L., III; m. Jane Berger, Aug. 19, 1973. AB, Cornell U., 1929. Ptnr. Newburger, Loeb & Co., Phila., 1930-46, Newburger & Co., 1946-70, Advest Co.; mng. partner Newburger & Co. div. Advest, 1970-77; sr. v.p. Newburger & Co. div. Advest, Phila., 1977-84; Bd. govs. N.Y. Stock Exchange, 1959-62; bd. govs. Phila.-Balt. Stock Exchange, 1946-56, pres., 1954-57. Vice chmn. United Fund, 1957-63; dir. Fedn. Jewish Agys., 1950—, pres., 1966, 67; emeritus bd. dirs., past treas., trustee (hon.) Acad. Natural Scis.; emeritus trustee Albert Einstein Med. Center, treas., 1957-60; mem. council Cornell U., 1965-71, 74-77, emeritus, 1978-88, life mem., 1989; mem. Health and Welfare Council, 1965-70. Mem. Bond Club Phila. (pres. 1966). Home: 8302 York Rd Apt B-63 Elkins Park PA 19027 Office: # 807 Benj Fox Pavilion 261 York Rd Jenkintown PA 19046

NEWBURGER, HOWARD MARTIN, psychoanalyst; b. N.Y.C., May 16, 1924; s. Bernhard and Bertha (Travers) N.; m. Doris Schekter, July 3, 1949; children: Amy, Barry, Cary. B.A., N.Y. U., 1948, M.A., 1950, Ph.D., 1952; tng. in Jungian, Neo-Freudian and Horneyian psychoanalysis. Cert. in group psychotherapy and psychodrama. Rotating intern N.J. Dept. Instns. and Agys., 1948-49; chief psychologist N.J. State Instn., Annandale, 1949-52; dir. psychoanalysis Div. Social Def. UN, 1952; pvt. practice in psychoanalysis and group psychotherapy, 1952—; dir. rsch. HEW, 1958; rsch. assoc. Beth Israel Hosp., 1958-69; staff mem. St. Agnes Hosp., White Plains, 1991—; lectr., adj. assoc. prof. NYU, 1951-60, chmn. dept. exceptional child and youth, 1954-62; chmn. faculty and supr. treatment Inst. Applied Human Dynamics, 1960—; lectr., cons. in field; prelect prof. psychology John Jay Coll. Criminal Justice, 1969-72; chmn. bd. dirs. Inst. Applied Human Dynamics, N.Y.C. and Westchester, N.Y., 1960-81, exec. v.p., 1983-85; cons. Police Dept., Harrison, N.Y., 1970—. Co-author: Winners and Losers. Assoc. editor: Excerpta Medica, 1951-62. Contbr. articles and papers to tech. jours. Trustee Acad. Jewish Religion, 1991—. Served with AUS, World War II, ETO; with AUS, MTO. Recipient Outstanding Service to Humanity award Inst. Applied Human Dynamics for Handicapped, 1970. Mem. Am. Psychol. Assn., Am. Soc. Group Psychotherapy and Psychodrama (sec.-treas. 1954-55). Office: Timber Trail Rye NY 10580-1935 *Our country affords tremendous opportunity. Through the development of our inner resources, and their assertion, we can all have happy and effective lives.*

NEWBY, JOHN ROBERT, metallurgical engineer; b. Kansas City, Mo., Nov. 17, 1923; s. Merritt Owen and Gladys Mary (McCleery) N.; m. Audry Marie Loniker, Sept. 21, 1963 (div. 1980); children: Deborah A., Walter J., William F., Matthew O., Robert J. BA, U. Mo., Kansas City, 1947; BS in Metall. Engring., Colo. Sch. Mines, 1949; MS, U. Cin., 1963. Cert. profl. engr. Chemist Bar Rusto Plating Corp., Kansas City, 1949; supr. United Chromium, Ferndale, Mich., 1949-52; prin. rsch. metallurgist Armco Inc., Middletown, Ohio, 1952-85; prin. John Newby Cons., Middletown, 1985—; cons. Phoenix Cons., Inc., Cin., 1988—. Author, editor: Formability 2000, 1982, Metallic Materials, 1978, Sheet Metal Forming, 1976; editor: Mechanical Testing, Vol. 8, 9th edit., 1985. Scoutmaster Boy Scouts Am., Middletown, 1952-86; chmn. Safety Coun., Middletown, 1978-80. Staff sgt. USAF, 1943-46, PTO. Fellow ASTM (chmn. 1963—, Award of Merit 1984), ASM (chpt. chmn. 1970, Award of Merit 1980); mem. SAE (sect. chmn. 1984). Democrat. Achievements include patent for high strength formable steel sheet; development of interstitial free steel, strain analysis process for metallic sheet formability. Home and Office: 100 Marymont Ct Middletown OH 45042-3735

NEWBY, TIMOTHY JAMES, education educator, researcher; b. Nampa, Idaho, Oct. 9, 1955; s. Neal Arthur and Margy Lou (Hooker) N.; m. Deedra Diane Hays, May 3, 1978; children: Timbre, Landon, Alexis, Brayden. BS, Brigham Young U., 1979, PhD, 1984. Assoc. prof. Purdue U., West Lafayette, Ind. Mem. Am. Edn. Rsch. Assn. Home: 216 Berwick Dr Lafayette IN 47905 Office: Purdue U Curriculum and Instruction 1442 LAEB West Lafayette IN 47907

NEWCOMB, DANFORTH, lawyer; b. Tarrytown, N.Y., Jan. 24, 1943; s. Russell Ladd and Louise Munroe (Blazer) N.; m. Elizabeth W. Newcomb, Nov. 25, 1966; children—Alexander, Thomas. B.A., U. Vt., 1965; LL.B., Columbia U., 1968. Bar: N.Y. 1968, D.C. 1990, U.S. Dist. Ct. (so. and ea. dists.) N.Y. 1971, U.S. Ct. Claims 1971, U.S. Tax Ct. 1971, U.S. Ct. Appeals (2d and 3d cir.) 1971, U.S. Supreme Ct. 1981, U.S. Dist. Ct. (ea. dist.) Mich. 1983, U.S. Ct. Appeals (11th cir.) 1983, U.S. Ct. Appeals (6th cir.) 1986. Assoc., Shearman & Sterling, N.Y.C., 1968-69, 71-78, ptnr., 1979—; mem. panel of mediators U.S. Dist. Ct. (so. dist.) N.Y. Served to capt. U.S. Army, 1969-70. Decorated Bronze Star. Mem. ABA, Fed. Bar Council, Am. Arbitration Assn. (panel of arbitrators). Office: 153 E 53rd St New York NY 10022-4602

NEWCOMB, ELDON HENRY, retired botany educator; b. Columbia, Mo., Jan. 19, 1919; s. Ernest Henry and Ruby Josephine (Anderson) N.; m. Joyce Bright Rieling, June 21, 1949; children—Norman Robert, Barbara Pauline, Cynthia Irma. Student, U. Kansas City, 1936-38; A.B., U. Mo., 1940, A.M., 1942; Ph.D., U. Wis., 1949; DS honoris causa, U. Mo., Columbia, 1993. Asst. prof. botany U. Wis.-Madison, 1949-54, assoc. prof., 1954-58, prof., 1958-90, prof. emeritus, 1990—; dir. Inst. Plant Devel., 1979-88; chmn. dept. botany U. Wis.-Madison, 1982-88, Folke Skoog prof. botany, 1987—; cons. Shell Devel. Co., 1954-59. Sr. author: Plants in Perspective, 1963; mng. editor Protoplasma, 1969-73; mem. editorial bd. Ann. Rev. Plant Physiology, 1965-69, Protoplasma, 1973—, Planta, 1981-90; contbr. articles to profl. jours. Served with AUS, 1942-45. NRC predoctoral fellow U. Wis., 1946-49; Guggenheim Found. fellow U. Calif. at Berkeley, 1951-52; Sci. Faculty fellow Harvard, 1963-64; Fulbright Sr. Research scholar Australian Nat. U., Canberra, 1976. Mem. NAS, Am. Soc. Cell Biologists, Am. Acad. Arts and Scis., Bot. Soc. Am., Am. Soc. Plant Physiologists, Soc. Devel. Biology, Phi Beta Kappa (pres. Wis. Alpha chpt. 1978-79), Sigma Xi. Mem. expdn. to Great Barrier Reef, 1973. Home: 52 Oak Creek Trl Madison WI 53717-1510

NEWCOMB, JONATHAN, publishing executive; b. Chappaqua, N.Y., June 12, 1946; s. Russell L. and Louise B. N.; m. Deborah Small, Dec. 11, 1970; children: Thaddeus, Zachary. AB in Econs., Dartmouth Coll., 1968; MBA, Columbia U., 1970. Mgr. Dun & Bradstreet, N.Y.C., 1972-74; mgr. Standard & Poor's Corp, N.Y.C., 1974-75, dir., 1976-79, v.p., 1979-80, sr. v.p., 1980-82, group v.p., 1982-84, exec. v.p., 1984-85; pres. McGraw-Hill Fin. & Econ. Info. Co., N.Y.C., 1985-88, Simon & Schuster Profl. Info. Group, N.Y.C., 1989-91; pres., CEO, Simon & Schuster, N.Y.C., 1991-94, pres., chief executive officer, 1994—; bd. dirs. CorpTech, Boston, Teltech, Mpls. Bd. overseers Amos Tuck Sch. Bus. Dartmouth Coll. Tuck Sch.; bd. dirs. Bklyn. Acad. of Music. 1st lt. U.S. Army, 1969-71, Vietnam. Club: Heights Casino (Bklyn.). Home: 35 Pierrepont St Brooklyn NY 11201-3359 Office: Simon & Schuster Inc 1230 Ave of Americas New York NY 10020-1513

NEWCOMB, LAWRENCE HOWARD, agricultural educator; b. Chase City, Va., July 20, 1947; s. George W. and Doris A. (Ashworth) N.; m. Beverly Hope Spain, July 12, 1968; children: Rodney, Angela. BS, Va. Poly. Inst., 1969, MS, 1971; PhD, Ohio State U., 1973. Vocat. agriculture tchr. Pulaski County (Va.) Sch. Bd., 1969-71; asst. prof. agrl. edn. Ohio State U., Columbus, 1973-81, prof., 1981—, chmn. dept., 1986-89, assoc. dean Coll. Agr., 1989—; cons. Coll. Agriculture U. Wis., Madison, U. Fla., Gainesville, Dept. Animal Sci., Okla. State U., Stillwater. Co-author: The FFA and You, 1979, Methods of Teaching Agriculture, 1986. Lay leader Northwest United Meth. Ch., Columbus, 1984-87, chairperson adminstrv. bd., 1988-90. Mem. Am. Assn. tchr. Educators in Agr. (chmn. nat. agrl. edn. rsch. meeting 1982-83, outstanding paper award 1985, editing-mng. bd., Author of Yr. award 1984), Am. vocat. Assn., Nat. Future Farmers Am. Alumni Coun., Gamma Sigma Delta (pres. 1984-85), Nat. Assn. State Univs. and Land Grant Colls. (chmn. acad. programs com. on orgn. and policy, bd. on agrl. 1995-96). Home: 4146 Checkerberry Ct Hilliard OH 43026-3017 Office: Ohio State Univ 2120 Fyffe Rd Columbus OH 43210-1010

NEWCOMB, MARTHA FREEMAN, lawyer; b. R.I., Aug. 4, 1955; d. Peter Hendrix and Juliette Adams (Freeman) N. AB, Smith Coll., Northampton, Mass., 1976; JD, Northeastern U., Boston, 1984. Bar: Mass. 1984, R.I. 1985, U.S. Supreme Ct. 1993. Editor, reporter Phoenix-Times Newspapers, Bristol, R.I., 1976-79; reporter The New Review, Clackamas County, Oreg., 1979-80; staff writer RIOICC, Providence, 1981; staff atty. R.I. Supreme Ct., Providence, 1984-86, chief staff atty., 1986—. Mem. ABA (chair Nat. Coun. Appellate Staff Attys. 1992-93), R.I. Bar Assn. Avocations: long-distance bicycling, sailing, traveling. Office: RI Supreme Ct 250 Benefit St Providence RI 02903-2719

NEWCOMB, ROBERT WAYNE, electrical engineering educator; b. Glendale, Calif., June 27, 1933; s. Robert Dobson and Dorothy Opal (Bissinger) N.; m. Sarah Eleanor Fritz, May 22, 1954; children: Gail E., Robert W. BSEE, Purdue U., 1955; MS, Stanford U., 1957, PhD, U. Calif., Berkeley, 1960. Registered profl. engr., Calif. Rsch. intern Stanford Rsch. Inst., Menlo Park, Calif., 1955-57; teaching assoc. U. Calif., Berkeley, 1957-60; asst. and assoc. prof. Stanford U., 1960-70; prof. elec. engring. U. Md., College Park, 1970—; bd. dirs. PARCOR Rsch. program, Universidad Politecnica de Madrid, Spain. Author: Linear Multiport Synthesis, 1966, Active Integrated Circuit Synthesis, 1968, Concepts of Linear Systems and Control, 1968, Network Theory, 1967. Fulbright fellow, 1963; Fulbright-Hays fellow, 1976; Robert Wayne Newcomb Lab. opened U. Politecnica Madrid, 1995. Fellow IEEE; mem. Soc. Indsl. and Applied Math., Math. Assn. Am., Acad. Am. Poets. Avocations: film, literature, poetry. Home: 13120 Two Farm Dr Silver Spring MD 20904-3418 Office: Univ Md Microsystems Lab Elec Engring Dept College Park MD 20742

NEWCOMBE, ALAN GEORGE, plant pathologist; b. Toronto, Aug. 11, 1953; came to the U.S., 1991; s. Alan G. and Hanna (Hammerschlag) N.; m. Frances Schips, July 30, 1977; children: Felice G., Claire L. BS, McGill U., 1983; PhD, U. Guelph, 1988. Postdoctoral rsch. assoc. Agriculture Canada, Winnipeg, 1988-91; rsch. assoc. in plant pathology Washington State U., Puyallup, 1991—. Contbr. articles to profl. jours. Grantee USDA, 1992—, DOE, 1995—. Mem. Am. Phytopathological Soc. Achievements include research in hybrid poplar pathogens and the genetics of resistance to them. Office: Wash State U 7612 Pioneer Way E Puyallup WA 98371

NEWCOMBE, GEORGE MICHAEL, lawyer; b. Newark, Nov. 11, 1947; s. George Anthony and Mary Hellen Newcombe; m. Joan Sharon Hanlon, May 30, 1969; children: Sean Michael, Scott Ryan, Jennifer Leigh. B-SChemE, N.J. Inst. Tech., 1969; JD, Columbia U., 1975. Bar: N.J. 1975, N.Y. 1976, U.S. Dist. Ct. N.J. 1975, U.S. Ct. Appeals (2d cir.) 1975, U.S. Dist. Ct. (so. dist.) N.Y. 1976, U.S. Dist. Ct. (we. dist.) Tex. 1985, U.S. Ct. Appeals (5th cir.) 1986, U.S. Ct. Appeals (3d cir.) 1992, U.S. Ct. Appeals (fed. cir.) 1995, U.S. Supreme Ct. 1987. Ptnr. Simpson, Thacher & Bartlett, N.Y.C., 1975—; dir. Columbia Law Sch. Assn., Inc., Columbia Jour. Environ. Law; dir., legal sec. Am. Ditchley Found., 1994. Mem. coun. com. law offices vol. divsn. Legal Aid Soc., N.Y.C., 1980-86. Lt. USPHS, 1970-72. James Kent scholar Columbia Law Sch., 1974, Harlan Fiske Stone scholar Columbia Law Sch., 1975. Mem. Am. Law Inst., ABA, AICE, Assn. of Bar of City of N.Y., Tau Beta Epsilon, Omicron Delta Kappa. Office: Simpson Thacher & Bartlett 425 Lexington Ave New York NY 10017-3903

NEWCOMBE, HOWARD BORDEN, biologist, consultant; b. Kentville, N.S., Can., Sept. 19, 1914; s. Edward Borden and Mabel Elsie (Outerbridge) N.; m. Beryl Honor Callaway, Feb. 14, 1942; children—Kenneth Donald, Charles Philip, Richard William. B.Sc., Acadia U., Wolfville, N.S., 1935; Assoc., Imperial Coll. Tropical Agr., Trinidad, 1938; Ph.D., McGill U., Montreal, P.Q., Can., 1939; D.Sc. (hon.), McGill U., 1966, Acadia U., 1970. Sci. officer Brit. Ministry of Supply, London, 1940-41; research assoc. Carnegie Instn. Washington, 1946-47; research sci. Atomic Energy of Can. Ltd., Chalk River, Ont., 1947-79; head biology br. Atomic Energy of Can. Ltd., 1949-70, head population research br., 1970-79; vis. prof. genetics Ind. U., Bloomington, 1963; mem. Internat. Commn. on Radiol. Protection, 1965-77, chmn. com. on biol. effects, 1965-72. Contbr. articles to profl. jours. Served to lt. Brit. Royal Naval Vol. Res., 1941-46. Fellow Royal Soc. Can.; mem. Genetics Soc. Am. (sec. 1956-58), Am. Soc. Human Genetics (pres. 1965), Genetics Soc. Can. (pres. 1964-65). Home: 67 Hillcrest Ave, PO Box 135, Deep River, ON Canada K0J 1P0

NEWCOMER, CLARENCE CHARLES, federal judge; b. Mount Joy, Pa., Jan. 18, 1923; s. Clarence S. and Marion Clara (Charles) N.; m. Jane Moyer Martin, Oct. 2, 1948; children: Judy (Mrs. Kenneth N. Birkett Jr.), Nancy Jane Newcomer (Mrs. Edward H. Vick), Peggy Jo Pollack. A.B., Franklin and Marshall Coll., 1944; LL.B., Dickinson Sch. Law, 1948. Bar: Pa. 1950. Practiced law Lancaster, 1950-57; partner firm Rohrer, Honaman, Newcomer & Musser, Lancaster, 1957-60; with Office of Dist. Atty., Lancaster, 1960-64; 1st asst. dist. atty. Office of Dist. Atty., 1964-68, dist. atty., 1968-72; partner Newcomer, Roda & Morgan, 1968-72; fed. dist. judge Eastern Dist. Pa., Phila., 1972—; Spl. dep. atty. gen. Pa. Dept. Justice, 1953-54. Served to lt. (j.g.) USNR, 1943-46, PTO. Office: US Dist Ct 13614 US Courthouse 601 Market St Philadelphia PA 19106-1510*

NEWELL, BARBARA WARNE, economist, educator; b. Pitts., Aug. 19, 1929; d. Colston E. and Frances (Corbett) Warne; m. George V. Thompson, June 15, 1954 (dec. 1954); m. George S. Newell, June 9, 1956 (dec. 1964); 1 dau., Elizabeth Penfield. BA, Vassar Coll., 1951; MA, U. Wis., 1953, PhD, 1958, D. Pub. Svc.; LHD, Trinity Coll., 1973, Lesley Coll., 1978; LLD, Central Mich. U., 1973, Williams Coll., 1974, Rollins Coll., 1981, Butler U., 1983, Monmouth Coll., 1986; DLitt, Northeastern U., 1974, Mt. Vernon Coll., 1975, Lesley Coll., 1978, Denison U., 1978, Eckerd Coll., 1982, Gettysburg Coll., 1982, Dennison U., 1978; D.Adminstrn., Purdue U., 1976; DSc, Fla. Inst. Tech., 1981; LHD, Eckerd Coll., 1982; LLD, Butler U., 1983; D Pub. Service, Alaska Pacific U., 1986; DsPS, U. Md., 1987. Asst. to chancellor U. Wis., 1965-67; research, teaching asst., assoc. U. Ill., 1954-59; asst. prof., then assoc. prof. econs. Purdue U., 1959-65; asst. to pres., assoc. prof. econs. U. Mich., Ann Arbor, 1967-71, acting v.p. student affairs, 1968-70; prof. econs., assoc. provost grad. study and research U. Pitts., 1971; pres. Wellesley (Mass.) Coll., 1972-79; U.S. rep. with rank ambassador to UNESCO, Paris, 1979-81; chancellor State U. System Fla., Tallahassee, 1981-85; Regents prof. Fla. State U., 1985—; vis. scholar Harvard U., 1985-86, vis. lectr., 1986-87. Author: Chicago and the Labor Movement, 1961, (with Lawrence Senesh) The Pulse of the Nation, 1961, Our Labour Force, 1962; editorial bd.: (with Lawrence Senesh) Labor History, 1975—; mem. editorial bd. Jour. for Higher Edn. Mgmt., 1984—; contbr. articles and revs. to profl. jours. and mags. Trustee Carnegie Endowment for Internat. Peace, 1973—; bd. dirs. Americans for the Universality of UNESCO, 1984—; mem. Fla. State Job Tng. com., 1991—, mem. Fla. Edn. and Employment Coun. for Women and Girls, 1992—. Wells fellow, 1981. Office: Florida State U Dept of Econ Tallahassee FL 32306-2045

NEWELL, BYRON BRUCE, JR., theological seminary dean, clergyman; b. Long Beach, Calif., July 31, 1932; s. Byron Bruce and Eleanor Whitaker (Davis) N.; m. Ingrid Charlotte Asche, June 11, 1955 (dec. July 1989); children: Thomas, Susan, Robert, Michael; m. Theresa Ann Troncale, Sept. 1, 1990. Student, Wesleyan U., 1950-51; BS, U.S. Naval Acad., 1955; MSEE, U.S. Naval Postgrad. Sch. Monterey, 1962; postgrad. nuclear power tng., 1964-65; MDiv, Va. Theol. Sem., 1987. Ordained priest, Episcopal Ch., 1988. Commd. ensign U.S. Navy, 1955, advanced through grades to rear adm., 1980; weapons officer U.S.S. Lowry, Hull (destroyers), 1955-58; comdg. officer salvage ship, 1962-64, exec., comdg. officer nuclear cruisers, 1968-77, manpower/tng. surface ship personnel, 1977-79; with Nat. Mil. Command Center, Washington, 1979-80, chief navy info., 1980-82, chief navy legis. affairs, 1982-84; assoc. dean Trinity Episcopal Sch. for Ministry, Ambridge, Pa., 1990—; chmn., trustee Breakthrough, Inc. Decorated Legion of Merit, D.S.M. Mem. Naval Inst., Naval Hist. Soc., Met. Club. Home: 256 Thorn St Sewickley PA 15143-1204

NEWELL, CHARLDEAN, public administration educator; b. Ft. Worth, Oct. 14, 1939; d. Charles Thurlow and Mildren Dean (Looney) N. BA, U. North Tex., 1960, MA, 1962; PhD, U. Tex., 1968; cert., Harvard U., 1988. Instr. U. North Tex., Denton, 1965-68, asst. prof., 1968-72; assoc. prof., dir. Fedn. North Tex. Area Univs., Denton, Dallas, 1972-74; assoc. prof., assoc. v.p. acad. affairs U. North Tex., Denton, 1974-76, assoc. prof., chair dept. polit. sci., 1976-80, prof. polit. sci., 1980-92, assoc. v.p., spl. asst. to chancellor, 1982-92, regents prof. pub. adminstrn., 1992—; cons. Miss. Bd. Trustees State Instns. Higher Learning, Jackson, 1983-84, Ednl. Testing Svc., Princeton, N.J., 1980, 82, 85, Spear, Down & Judin, Dallas, 1994-95, North Tex. Inst. Edn. in Visual Arts, Denton, 1993-94; bd. dirs. Mcpl. Clks. Ednl. Found., San Dimas, Calif.; bd. regents Internat. City/County Mgmt. Assn., Washington. Author: (with others) City Executives: Leadership Roles, Work Characteristics and Time Management, 1989, The Effective Local Government Manager, 1993, Essentials of Texas Politics, 1995, Texas Politics, 1996; contbr. articles to profl. jours. Chmn. Denton Charter Rev. Com., 1978-79; mem. Denton CSC, 1989—, chmn., 1992—; mem. adv. com. Ann's Haven Hospice, Denton, 1981-85; mem. exec. coun. Episcopal Diocese Dallas, 1985-88; mem. Denton Blue Ribbon Capital Improvements Com., 1995-96. Recipient Elmer Staats Career Pub. Svc. award Nat. Assn. Sch. Pub. Affairs Adminstrn., 1993. Mem. ASPA (sect. chmn. 1982-83, mem. editl. bd. 1985-88), Internat. Pers. Mgmt. Assn. (regional program com. 1982-83), Am. Polit. Sci. Assn., Southwestern Polit. Sci. Assn. (sec., treas. 1975-79), Denton C. of C., Denton Tennis Assn., Pi Sigma Alpha (exec. coun. 1988-92), Pi Alpha Alpha (exec. coun. 1995—). Democrat. Avocations: walking, reading. Home: 709 Mimosa Dr Denton TX 76201-8814 Office: U North Tex PO Box 5367 Denton TX 76203-0367

NEWELL, ERIC JAMES, financial planner, tax consultant, former insurance executive; b. Toronto, Ont., Can., Sept. 24, 1930; came to U.S., 1959, naturalized, 1970; s. James and Anne (Brown) N.; m. Essie Miskelly, Sept. 30, 1950; 1 son, Eric Wayne. Student, U. Toronto, 1951-53. Pub. acct. W.J. Wilcox & Co., Toronto, 1949-53; chief acct. Toronto Mut. Life Ins. Co., 1953-57; asst. sec. Holland Life Ins. Co., Toronto, 1957-59; with Penn Mut. Life Ins. Co., Phila., 1959-86; assoc. controller Penn Mut. Life Ins. Co., 1965-70, 2d v.p., controller, 1970-84, v.p., controller, 1984-86, ret., 1986; fin., tax cons., 1986—; dir. Hotel Brunswick, Lancaster, Pa., 1982-85. Mem. Traffic and Transp. Bd., Cherry Hill, N.J., 1971-73, Zoning Bd., 1975-78; vice chmn. Cherry Hill Econ. Devel. Bd., 1973-75; pres. Greater Kingston Civic Assn., Cherry Hill, 1970-76; Democratic committeeman, Camden County, 1976-79; vice chmn. Dem. Party, Cherry Hill, 1976. Fellow Life

Mgmt. Inst., Royal Commonwealth Soc.; mem. Fin. Execs. Inst., Am. Inst. Corp. Contrs., N.Y. Ins. Accts. Club (chmn. 1984), Nat. Soc. Tax Profls., Royal Black Knights of Ireland, Loyal Orange Assn. (past master), Scotch-Irish Soc. of U.S. (mem. coun.), Am. Legion. Presbyterian (deacon 1969—). Home and Office: 137 E Partridge Ln Cherry Hill NJ 08003-4407

NEWELL, FRANK WILLIAM, ophthalmologist, educator; b. St. Paul, Jan. 14, 1916; s. Frank John and Hilda (Turnquist) N.; m. Marian Glennon, Sept. 12, 1942; children: Frank William, Mary Susan Newell O'Connell, Elizabeth Glennon Newell Murphy, David Andrew Newell. M.D., Loyola U., Chgo., 1939; M.Sc., U. Minn., 1942. Diplomate Am. Bd. Ophthalmology (chmn. bd. 1967-69). James and Anna Raymond prof. dept. ophthalmology U. Chgo., 1953—; prof. extraordinario Autonomous U. Barcelona, Spain, 1972—; hon. prof. Tech. U., Japan, 1986—; sci. counselor Nat. Inst. Neurol. Diseases and Blindness, 1959-62, chmn., 1961-62; mem. nat. adv. eye coun. NIH, 1972-75; mem. Internat. Council Ophthalmology, 1977-85; bd. dirs. Heed Ophthalmic Found., 1965-93, chmn., 1975-90; dir. Ophthalmic Pub. Co., 1962—, sec., treas., 1971-95. Author: Ophthalmology: Principles and Concepts, 1965, 8th edit., 1996, The American Ophthalmological Society 1864-89, 1989; also articles; editor in chief Am. Jour. Ophthalmology, 1965-91, pub., 1972-95; editor: Trans Glaucoma Conf., Vols. 1-5, 1955-61, Amblyopia and Strabismus, 1975, Hereditary Diseases of the Eye, 1980, Stedman's Medical Dictionary, 25th edit., 1990, Documenta Ophthalmologica Historia, 1996—. Trustee Loyola U., Chgo., 1977-81. Served from 1st lt. to maj. M.C. AUS, 1942-46. Recipient Alumni Citation award Loyola U., 1962, Stritch medal, 1966, Outstanding Achievement award U. Minn., 1975, 92, Gold Key U. Chgo., 1981, Lang medal Royal Soc. Medicine, London, 1974, medal honor Soc. Eye Surgeons, 1975, Vail medal Internat. Eye Found., 1986, medalla André Bello U. Chile, 1977, medalla de Oro Instituto Barraquer, Barcelona, Spain, 1982; Disting. Svc. award Physicians Edn. Network, 1983; decorated knight Order of St. John. Mem. Nat. Soc. Prevention Blindness (dir., v.p. 1970-81, pres. 1981-83, chmn. bd. 1983-85, Dunnington medal 1976), AMA (chmn. sect. ophthalmology 1964-65, Howe prize 1968), Am. Acad. Ophthalmology and Otolaryngology (pres. 1975), Inst. Barraguer (pres. 1970-88, hon. pres. 1988—), Assn. Univ. Profs. Ophthalmology (trustee 1966-69, pres. 1968-69), Assn. Research Ophthal. (chmn. bd. trustees 1967-68), Pan-Am. Assn. Ophthalmology (dir. 1969—, pres. 1981-83), Am. Ophthal. Soc. (pres. 1986-87, Howe medal 1979), Chgo. Ophthal. Soc. (pres. 1957-58), Oxford (Eng.) Ophthal. Congress (hon. mem., dep. master 1980), Hellenic Ophthal. Soc. (hon.), Royal Soc. Medicine (hon.), Academia Ophthalmologica Internationalis (pres. 1980-84), Columbia Ophthal. Soc. (hon.), Sigma Xi, Alpha Omega Alpha. Roman Catholic. Clubs: Literary (Chgo.), Quadrangle (Chgo.). Home: 4500 N Mozart St Chicago IL 60625-3817 Office: 939 W 57th St Chicago IL 60637

NEWELL, HAROLD JOE, quality assurance engineer; b. Fernbank, Ala., Dec. 31, 1945; s. Homer Isaiah and Beulah Mae (Tomlin) N.; m. Brenda Kay Guin, Sept. 24, 1966 (div. Jan. 1993); m. Kathy Lane Vaughn, Oct. 2, 1995; children: Tyrena Kay, Wesley Joe. Student, E. Miss. Jr. Coll., 1976, Miss. U. for Women, 1984, 86, U. Ala., 1990—. lic. rep. Franklin Life Ins. Co. Lineman Four-County Elec. Power Assn., 1964-65; tool and die apprentice Quality Tooling, Fayette, Ala., 1965-66; quality assurance engr., quality control supr. United Techs. Motor Sys., Columbus, Miss., 1966-95. Pastor S.C. Bapt. Ch., Vernon, Ala., Mt. Olive Bapt. ch., Millport, Ala.; conducts weekly radio program Sta. WVSA, Vernon; mgr. five mem. band, 1968-73. Recipient award of excellence in photography Photographer's Forum Mag., Santa Barbara, Calif., 1984, 87. Mem. Am. Soc. Quality Control (sr. mem., pub. rels. com.). Republican. Avocations: music, photography, collector. Home: 6215 Hwy 18 W Vernon AL 35592

NEWELL, KEITH DOUGLAS, paralegal; b. Kingston, Pa., Aug. 3, 1968; m. Mary Kay D. Riscavage, July 23, 1989; 1 child, Alexzander H. Assoc. in Bus. Adminstrn., St. Petersburg Jr. Coll., 1990; paralegal cert., Blackston Sch. Law, Tex., 1995. Account resolution specialist Sallie Mae, Washington, 1991—. Mem. Nat. Capital Area Assn. Paralegals. Avocation: British car restorations. Home: PO Box 1213 Herndon VA 22070 Office: Sallie Mae 397 Herndon Pkwy #16 Herndon VA 22070

NEWELL, NORMAN DENNIS, paleontologist, geologist, museum curator, educator; b. Chgo., Jan. 27, 1909; s. Virgil Bingham and Nellie (Clark) N.; m. Valerie Zirkle, Feb. 25, 1928 (dec. 1972); m. Gillian Wendy Wormall, Apr. 28, 1973. B.S., U. Kans., 1929, M.A., 1931; Ph.D. in Geology, Yale U., 1933. Faculty mem. U. Kans., Lawrence, 1934-37; assoc. prof. geology U. Wis.-Madison, 1937-45; prof. geology Columbia U., N.Y.C., 1945-77, prof. emeritus, 1977—; curator Am. Mus. Nat. History, N.Y.C., 1945-77, curator emeritus, 1977—; geologist Kans. Geol. Survey, Lawrence, 1929-37; cons. on petroleum geology Peruvian Govt., 1942-45. Author: Permian Reef Complex of the Guadalupe Mountains Region, Texas and New Mexico, 1953, Creation and Evolution: Myth or Reality?, 1982, also numerous sci. articles and papers. Recipient Disting. Svc. Alumni award Kans. U., 1961, Hayden award Phila. Acad. Sci., 1965, Verrill medal Yale U., 1966, Gold medal for achievment in sci. Am. Mus. Natural History, 1978, Raymond C. Moore medal Soc. Econ. Paleontologists and Mineralogists, 1980, Scientific Freedom and Responsibility award AAAS, 1987. Mem. Nat. Acad. Scis. (Mary Clark Thompson medal 1960), Am. Philos. Soc., Am. Acad. Arts and Scis., Geol. Soc. Am. (Penrose medal 1990), Soc. Study Evolution (pres. 1949), Soc. Systematic Zoology (pres. 1972-73), Paleontol. Soc. (pres. 1960-61, medal 1979), Can. Soc. Petroleum Geologists (hon.). Avocations: geologic field expeditions. Home: 135 Knapp Ter Leonia NJ 07605-1216 Office: Am Mus Natural History Central Park St W New York NY 10026

NEWELL, PAUL HAYNES, JR., engineering educator, former college president; b. Nashville, July 1, 1933; s. Paul Haynes Newell; m. Martha A. Newell; children—Paul Haynes III, Mike, Nan. B.M.E., U. Tenn., 1958, M.M.E., 1961; Mech.E., Mass. Inst. Tech., 1964, Ph.D., 1966. Registered profl. engr., Ala., Tenn., Tex., N.J. Student asst. mech. engring. U. Tenn., 1957, instr. mech. engring., 1958-62; NSF Sci. faculty fellow Mass. Inst. Tech., 1962-65; asso. prof. mech. engring. U. Ala. Coll. Engring., 1966-69; prof. mech. engring. Tex. A. and M. U., 1969-72, asso. dean engring., 1972; prof. biomed. engring., dept. phys. medicine Baylor Coll. Medicine, 1969-74, prof. biomed. engring., dept. physiology, 1970-74, prof. biomed. engring., dept. community medicine, 1972-74, prof. biomed. engring., dept. rehab., 1972—, mem. grad. faculty, 1970-74; prof., head indsl. engring. dept. Tex. A. & M. U., 1972-74, prof., head combined programs of behavioral engring., bioengring., cybernetic engring., hygiene and safety engring., indsl. engring., 1972-74; pres., prof. Newark Coll. Engring., N.J. Inst. Tech., 1974-78; prof. Adminstrn. Prosthetics Ctr., N.Y., 1973-75, VA Hosp., Houston, 1972-75, Baylor Coll. Medicine, Houston, from 1971; pres. Newell Engring., Greenbrier, Tenn., 1979—; dir. N.J. Bell Telephone Co., Mid Atlantic Nat. Bank, Thomas-Betts Corp. Contbr. articles to profl. jours., chpts. to books. Mem. NSF liaison com., Newark Transp. Council, N.J. Safety Council; sec. exec. com. council Boy Scouts Am., Birmingham, Ala., 1966-68; bd. dirs. N.J. State Opera, United Hosps. Newark. Served with USMCR, Korean Conflict. Recipient NSF Sci. Faculty fellowship. Mem. Am. Soc. Tool and Mfg. Engrs., N.Y., Ala. acads. scis., AAAS, Am. Congress Rehab. Medicine, Am. Heart Assn., Am. Inst. Indsl. Engrs., Am. Soc. Artificial Internal Organs, Am. Soc. Engring. Edn., ASME, Biomed. Engring. Soc., Inst. Engring. Deans, Internat. Soc. Prosthetics and Orthotics, Nat. Soc. Profl. Engrs., Soc. Advanced Med. Systems, Soc. Engring. Sci., Pres.'s Assn., Am. Fluid Power Soc., N.J. Soc. Engrs., Sigma Xi, Tau Beta Pi, Phi Kappa Phi, Pi Tau Sigma. Club: Rotary. Address: 1855 Lake Rd Greenbrier TN 37073-4619 Office: Newell Engring Greenbrier TN 37073-4619

NEWELL, REBECCA GAIL, psychiatric nurse; b. Savannah, Ga., July 4, 1953; d. Henry Morgan and Julia (Rogers) Grimes; m. E. Andrew Newell, June 14, 1980. AA, Armstrong State Coll., 1973, BS in Nursing, 1980; postgrad. Sch. Grad. Nursing, Med. Coll. Ga., 1980-81; cert. psychiat. nurse. RN, Ga. Staff nurse Charter Behavioral Health Sys., Savannah, 1973-74, head nurse, 1974-75, coord. utilization rev. and staff devel., 1975-80, asst. dir. nursing, dir. quality assurance and risk mgmt., 1980-82, dir. nursing, 1982-89, adminstr. adult psychiat. svcs., 1989-91, nursing adminstr., 1991-93, chief nursing officer and adminstr. patient care svcs., 1993, adminstr. clin. svcs., chief nursing officer, 1993—, COO, 1995—; mem. adj. faculty Armstrong Coll. Sch. Nursing, 1982, Coun. Recruitment and Retention of Nurses, 1978—; profl. staff exchange cons. Named one of Outstanding Young Women Am., 1984, 85; mem. adv. coun. Sta. WGEC-FM Radio; mem. pers. com. Calvary Bapt. Temple. Recipient Leadership award Vocat. Indsl. Clubs Am., 1971, cert. of merit U. Ga. Mem. Ga. Orgn. Nurse Execs., Ga. Hosp. Assn., Armstrong State Coll. Hon. Soc. for Nursing, Ga. So. Coll. Hon. Soc. for Nursing, Concerned Women For Am., Ga. Right to Life Assn., Am. Ctr. for Law and Justice, Sigma Theta Tau. Baptist. Home: 11 Ramsgate Rd Savannah GA 31419-3215 Office: 1150 Cornell Ave Savannah GA 31406-2702

NEWELL, REGINALD EDWARD, physics educator; b. Peterborough, Eng., Apr. 9, 1931; came to U.S., 1954, naturalized, 1969; s. Harold Aubrey and Edith (Swiffin) N.; m. Maireen W. Lees, Sept. 6, 1954; children: Madeleine, Elizabeth, Oliver, Nicholas. B.S. in Physics, U. Birmingham, Eng., 1954; M.S., Mass. Inst. Tech., 1956, Sc.D., 1960. With Brit. Meteorol. Office, 1947-50; successively research staff asst., asst. prof., asso. prof., prof. MIT, Cambridge, 1954—; mem IUGG Internat. Commn. Meteorology Upper Atmosphere, 1967-75; mem. Internat. Commn. Atmospheric Chemistry and Global Pollution, 1971-83; pres. Internat. Commn. on Climate, 1977-83. Joint author: The General Circulation of the Tropical Atmosphere, Vol. 1, 1972, Vol. 2, 1974, Global Ocean Surface Temperature Atlas, 1990; contbr. articles to profl. jours. Served with RAF, 1950-51. Fellow Royal Meteorol. Soc., Am. Meteorol. Soc.; mem. Am. Geophys. Union. Home: 45 Jason St Arlington MA 02174-6446 Office: MIT 54-1824 77 Massachusetts Ave # 54-1824 Cambridge MA 02139-4301

NEWELL, ROBERT LINCOLN, retired banker; b. Hartford, Conn., Dec. 2, 1922; s. Robert B. and Helen C. (Lincoln) N.; m. Sally C. Erdman, July 28, 1944; children: Sally Newell Huss, Helen Newell Douglas, Robert Lincoln, Katharine Newell Chiodo, William Henry II. Student, Wesleyan U., Middletown, Conn. With Conn. Nat. Bank, Hartford, 1946-88, exec. v.p., 1967-72, 1st exec. v.p., 1972-75, pres., 1975-78, chmn., 1978-87, ret., 1987; former chmn. Hartford Nat. Corp. Corporator Hartford Hosp., Mt. Sinai Hosp.; bd. dirs. Mystic Seaport Mus. Lt. USNR, 1943-46. Home: 42 Mountain View Dr West Hartford CT 06117-3029

NEWELL, WILLIAM JAMES, educator American sign language and of the deaf; b. Port Jefferson, N.Y., Sept. 13, 1947; s. William James and Mary Louise (Pinder) N.; m. Beverly Jo Beller, June 18, 1971; children: Eric James, Christopher Ian. BA, St. Edwards U., Austin, Tex., 1970; MS, St. Cloud State U., 1977; PhD, Greenwich U., 1994. Cert. tchr. Am. Sign Lang.; cert. Coun. on Edn. of the Deaf. Houseparent, tchr. aide Tex. Sch. for the Deaf, Austin, 1969-70; tchr. of the deaf Harris County Pub. Schs., Houston, 1970-72, Dade County Pub. Schs., Miami, Fla., 1972-74; supervising tchr. of the deaf Hennepin Tech. Ctrs., Mpls., 1974-78; instr. Am. Sign Lang. Rochester (N.Y.) Inst. Tech., 1978-81; chairperson sign communication dept. Nat. Tech. Inst. for the Deaf, Rochester, 1981-91, rsch. assoc., 1991-96, assoc. prof. Am. sign lang. and deaf studies, 1996—; proprietor Sign Lang. Consulting Svcs., Ednl. Cons., Adult Edn. Resource, Cyberpreneur, Freedomstarr Comm., Inc., Canandaigua. Co-developer: Sign Communication Proficiency Interview, 1981—; author: Basic Sign Communication, 1983. Recipient Outstanding Svc. award Sign Instrs. Guidance Network, Silver Spring, Md. Mem. Am. Sign Lang. Tchrs. Assn. (pres. 1986-90, chairperson evaluation and cert. com. 1990—, Veditz award 1996), Conv. of Am. Instrs. for the Deaf. Avocations: home brewing, walking for fitness, backyard birdfeeding. Home: 5259 Lower Egypt Rd Canandaigua NY 14424-9311 Office: Nat Tech Inst for the Deaf 52 Lomb Memorial Dr Rochester NY 14623-5604

NEWELL, WILLIAM TALMAN, JR., hospital administrator; b. Newport News, Va., Apr. 4, 1932; s. William Talman and Helen Louise (Woolfolk) N.; m. Mary Hill Chilton, Feb. 11, 1956; children—William Talman III, John Chilton, Anne Caroline. B.S. in Hotel Adminstrn., Cornell U., 1954; M.B.A. in Health Care Adminstrn., George Washington U., 1967. Asst. mgr. Dayton (Ohio) Biltmore Hotel, 1956-57; restaurant mgr. Marriott Corp., Washington, 1957-60; food service mgr. The Fairfax Hosp., Falls Church, Va., 1960-63, asst. dir. gen. services div., 1963-64, dir. gen. services div., 1964-66, asst. to the adminstr., 1966-67; asst. dir. Yale-New Haven (Conn.) Hosp., 1967-70, assoc. dir., 1970-75; chief exec. officer U. Miss. Hosp., 1975-83; exec. dir. Univ. Hosp., SUNY, Stony Brook, 1983-94, ret., 1994; lectr. Sch. Epidemiology and Pub. Health, Yale U. Sch. Medicine, 1969-75; dir. Miss. Blue Cross & Blue Shield, 1979-83; mem. Appalachian Council Teaching Hosps., 1979; mem. Miss. Gov.'s Health Care Task Force on Children and Youth, 1982-83. Chmn. bd. Vocat. Rehab. Ctr. for Blind, Jackson, Miss.; adminstrv. bd. Nassau-Suffolk Hosp. Council Bd.; v.p. ops. Suffolk County council Boy Scouts Am.; bd. dirs. U. Hosp. Consortium; pres. bd. dirs. Miss. Blood Services, 1977-83; bd. dirs. Hosp. Assn. N.Y. Served to 1st lt. U.S. Army, 1954-56. Mem. Am. Coll. Health Care Adminstrs. Episcopalian.

NEWEY, PAUL DAVIS, lawyer; b. Mpls., July 4, 1914; s. Paul S. and Mary (Yonan) N.; m. Viola W. Raymond, Dec. 16, 1943 (dec. June 1982); children: Paul S. Newey II, Davis Raymond, Dean Alan, Arthur Tyler. AA, Cen. YMCA, 1935; LLB, JD, John Marshall Law Sch., 1940; AB, Detroit Inst. Tech., 1947; diploma, U.S. Treasury Dept. Law Enforcement Sch., 1943; spl. courses, U.S. Gov. and Mil. Intelligence Schs., 1951-53. Bar: Ill. 1946. Squad leader Bur. Census, Dept. Commerce, 1940; officer Uniformed Force U.S. Secret Svc., 1940-42; agt. Bur. Narcotics, Treasury Dept., 1942-47; pvt. practice law, real estate and ins. broker Chgo., 1948-51; spl. rep. CIA, 1951-57; asst. state's atty.-investigator County of Cook, Ill., 1957-58; asst. state's atty.-chief investigator, chief state's atty.'s police County of Cook, 1958-60; pvt. practice law Chgo., 1961-65, spl. investigator, 1961—; ptnr. Adamowski, Newey & Adamowski, Chgo., 1965-82; spl. atty. Ill. Sec. of State, 1975-80; ptnr. firm Adamowski & Newey, Chgo., 1982-89; ret., 1989; sec., dir. Master Fishing Gear, Inc., 1956-57. Pvt. AUS, 1941; 1st lt. Counter Intelligence Corps. USAR, 1949-54. Recipient Medal of Merit and elected to Hall of Fame Nat. Police Officers Assn. Am., 1960, Disting. Citizen award Assyrian-Am. Welfare Council, 1970, Hammurabi award Assyrian Heritage Orgn., 1985; recipient Outstanding Svc. citation John Marshall Law Sch., 1975, Disting. Alumnus merit citation, 1970; honored by proclamation by Ill. gov., resolution by City of Chgo. aldermen and granted by mayor of Chgo. setting June 8, 1985 as Paul D. Newey Day. Mem. ABA, Fed. Bar Assn., Ill. Bar Assn., Chgo. Bar Assn., Internat. Assn. Investigators and Spl. Police (chmn. bd. dirs.), N. Am. Inst. Police Sci. (bd. dirs.), N.Am. Detective Agy. (bd. dirs.), Spl. Agts. Assn. (3d v.p. and legal counsel 1977—), U.S. Treasury Agts. Assn. (pres. 1970-71), John Marshall Law Sch. Alumni Assn. (treas. 1973-75, bd. dirs. 1966-84), Internat. Assn. Chiefs of Police (life), Spl. Agts. Assn. Chgo. (life), Amvets, Am. Legion, Assn. Former Fed. Narcotic Agents, Fed. Criminal Investigators Assn., Edward T. Lee Found. John Marshall Law Sch. (life), Amvets, Am. Legion, Smithsonian Assocs., Congl. Club (pres. 1963-64, bd. dirs., trustee 1962-65), Masons (32 degree, life), Medina Temple, Shriners (life), Lawyers Shrine Club (life). Mem. United Ch. of Christ. Home: 1034 W Altgeld St Chicago IL 60614-2209 *Life is an interlude in eternity, and material gain, by itself, makes it a nullity. The Master's admonition, "whatsoever ye have done for the least of these thy brethren, ye have done it unto me!" demands pro bono conduct; or perish without paying your debt for existence. I know that "man does not live by bread alone!" and try to shape my sojourn here accordingly.*

NEWFIELD, JACK, columnist. Columnist N.Y. Post, N.Y.C. Office: NY Post Corp 210 South St New York NY 10002-7807

NEWHALL, DAVID, III, former federal government official; b. Phila., Dec. 6, 1937; s. David Jr. and Jane Martyn (Dunn) N. AB in Politics, Princeton U., 1961. Mgr. Bell Tel. Co. of Pa., Norristown, 1961-63; adminstrv. asst. to U.S. Rep. R.S. Schweiker Washington, 1963-69, chief of staff to U.S. Senator R.S. Schweiker, 1969-81; chief of staff HHS, Washington, 1981-83; pres. Marmion Plantation Co., King George, VA., 1983-91; prin. dep. asst. sec. def.(health affairs) U.S. Dept. Def., Washington, 1985-90, acting asst. sec. def. (health affairs), 1989-90; gen. ptnr. Marmion Partnership Restorations, 1990—; bd. dirs. Western Healthcare Alliance, Phoenix; mem. nat. adv. bd. Am. Compliance Inst., Alexandria, Va. Republican. Episcopalian. Club: Princeton Tower. Avocation: beef cow-calf operation. Home and Office: 7382M Marmion Ln King George VA 22485-7300

NEWHALL, DAVID SOWLE, history educator; b. Burlington, Vt., July 26, 1929; s. Chester Albert and Nella Perry (Tillotson) N.; m. Edna Irene Newton, Mar. 25, 1952; children: Rebecca, John Newton, Jesslyn, Melissa, David Chester. BA, U. Vt., 1951; postgrad., Boston U., 1951; AM, Harvard U., 1956, PhD, 1963. Instr., asst. prof. U. Vt., Burlington, 1959-66; asst. prof., assoc. prof. history Centre Coll., Danville, Ky., 1966, prof., 1970, disting. prof. humanities, 1987, Pottinger disting. prof. history, 1994-95; Pottinger disting. prof. history emeritus, 1995—; mem. adv. com. Danville High Sch., 1980-81; cons. dept. history Berea (Ky.) Coll., 1983; rep. Ky. Coun. on Internat. Edn., Lexington, 1984-85. Author: Clemenceau: A Life at War, 1991; contbr. to Historical Dictionary of the Third French Republic, 1988, Kentucky Ency., 1992, Historic World Leaders, 1994. Elder Presbyn. Ch., U.S.A., Danville, 1969—; officer Danville H.S. Band Parents Assn., 1968-82; bd. dirs. Project Opportunity, Lee and Breathitt Counties, Ky., 1968-74; mem. Citizens Com. on Coal-Hauling Traffic, Boyle County, Ky., 1982—; mem. adv. bd. Ky. Elderhostel, 1996—. With U.S. Army, 1951-53, Korea. Recipient Acorn award Ky. Advocates for Higher Edn., 1994; Nat. Meth. scholar Boston U., 1953-55. Mem. Soc. for French Hist. Studies, World History Assn., Phi Beta Kappa (officer Centre Coll. 1971-95), Omicron Delta Kappa, Phi Alpha Theta. Avocations: church choir, railroading. Home: 634 N 3rd St Danville KY 40422-1125 Office: Centre Coll Danville KY 40422

NEWHALL, JEFFREY ROBERT, religious organization administrator; b. Washington, July 14, 1946; s. Robert Moody and Shirley Emily (Raw) N.; m. Sarah Elisabeth Studenmund, Sept. 25, 1971; children: Sarah E., Jeremiah R. BA, George Washington U., 1969; MA, Hartford Seminary, 1972, MDiv, 1972; DMin, Andover/Newton, 1975. Assoc. pastor Ctrl. Bapt. Hartford, Conn., 1972-73, First Calvary, Lawrence, Mass., 1974-78; sr. pastor Palisades Cmty. Ch., Washington, 1978-85; pastor Orchard Park (N.Y.) Cmty. Ch., 1985-91; exec. dir. Internat. Coun. Cmty. Chs., Mokena, Ill., 1991—; therapist Samaritan Counseling Ctr., Buffalo, 1985-91; exec. com. Nat. Coun. Chs., N.Y., 1991—, Consultation on Ch. Union, Princeton, N.J., 1991—; bd. dirs. U.S. chpt. World Coun. Chs., N.Y. Editor, writer newsletter Christian Cmty., 1991-95. Mem. Am. Assn. Pastoral Counselors. Democrat. Avocations: reading, writing, hiking, gardening. Office: Internat Coun Cmty Chs 21116 Washington Pkwy Frankfort IL 60423-3112

NEWHALL, JOHN HARRISON, management consultant; b. Phila., Sept. 29, 1933; s. Blackwell and Mary Large (Harrison) N.; m. Jane Carol Ward, July 15, 1961; children: Carol Newhall Neilson, Thomas Blackwell, Daniel Ward. BA, Williams Coll., 1955; MBA, Harvard U., 1960. Dir. corp. planning, gen. mgr. Europe H.J. Heinz Co., Pitts., 1970-77; v.p. mktg. Sun Co., Phila., 1977-81; chmn., chief exec. officer Aitkin-Kynett Co. (subs. Foote Cone & Belding), Phila., 1981-84; mng. dir., exec. v.p. Campbell-Ewald Co., N.Y.C., 1984-86; prin. mgmt. cons. SRI Internat., Menlo Park, Calif., 1987-90; mng. dir. Strategic Directions, Narberth, Pa., 1990—; pres. Advanced Promotion Techs., Deerfield Beach, Fla., 1992-93; pres. Harvard Bus. Sch. Club of Phila., 1994—. Mem. devel. council Williams Coll., Williamstown, Mass., 1977-87, Reg. v. chmn. Capital Campaign, 1991-93; mem. Com. of 70, Phila., 1981-84; bd. dirs. Bryn Mawr (Pa.) Hosp., 1982-88, The Haverford (Pa.) Sch., 1980-86, Headmaster sel. comm., 1992, Strategic Planning Comm., 1994, World Affairs Council, Phila., 1982-86, Found. for Vascular Hypertension Research, Phila., 1982—, chmn., 1987, Jr. Achievement, Phila., 1977-81, vice chmn., 1981, SE chpt. ARC, Phila., 1981-84, Pa. Economy League, 1981-84; vestryman, lay reader Episc. Ch., 1964-70. Served to lt. USN, 1955-58. Recipient Cert. of Merit Chapel of Four Chaplains, 1983, 85. Mem. Assn. Nat. Advertisers (exec. com. 1977-81). Republican. Episcopalian. Clubs: Union League (Phila.); Merion Cricket (Haverford); Gulph Mills (Pa.) Golf; Harbor (Seal Harbor, Maine). Avocations: skiing, tennis, sailing. Home and Office: Strategic Directions 414 Righters Mill Rd Narberth PA 19072-1423

NEWHART, BOB, entertainer; b. Oak Park, Ill., Sept. 29, 1929; m. Virginia Quinn, Jan. 12, 1963; 4 children. BS, Loyola U., Chgo., 1952. Acct. U.S. Gypsum Co.; copywriter Fred Niles Film Co.; appeared on Jack Paar Show, 1960; TV performer numerous guest appearances, 1961—; star TV series Newhart, 1982-90. Rec. artist (album) Button Down Mind on TV; royal command performance, London, 1964, appeared in films Hot Millions, 1968, Catch 22, 1970, Cold Turkey, 1971, First Family, 1980, Little Miss Marker, 1982; TV films include Thursday's Game, 1978, Marathon, 1980. Grand marshall Tournament Roses Parade, 1991. Served with U.S. Army, 1952-54. Recipient Emmy award, 1961, Peabody award, 1961, Sword of Loyola award, 1976, Legend to Legend award, 1993; named to Acad. Hall of Fame, 1993. Office: c/o David Capell 1875 Century Park E Ste 2250 Los Angeles CA 90067-2523

NEWHOUSE, ALAN RUSSELL, retired federal government executive; b. N.Y.C., Feb. 27, 1938; s. Russell Conwell and Clara Lucille (Scovell) N.; m. Margo Stiles Hicks, Feb. 3, 1960; children: Daryl, Jeffrey, William. BEE, Cornell U., 1960. Engr. Bur. of Ships, Washington, 1964-66; nuclear power engr., chief West Milton field office AEC, Schenectady, N.Y., 1966-69; sr. exec. AEC, ERDA, U.S. Dept. Energy, Washington, 1969-92; dep. asst. sec. Space and Def. Power Systems Office Nuclear Energy, Washington, 1992-93; dir. Office Space and Def. Power Systems, 1993-95, retired, 1995, ind. cons., 1995—; cons. Energy Conversion Techs. Composer numerous musical works. Bd. trustees River Road Unitarian Ch., Bethesda, Md., 1973-75; mem. McLean Symphony Orchestra, Washington Men's Camerata, Musica Antiqua, Interamerican Chamber Singers, Continuum Chamber Singers, U. Md. Chorus. Lt. USN, 1960-64. Mem. IEEE, AIAA, Am. Nuclear Soc., Am. Soc. Naval Engrs., Soc. Naval Architects and Marine Engrs., Am. Astronautical Soc. Republican. Unitarian. Home and Office: 11108 Deborah Dr Potomac MD 20854-2721

NEWHOUSE, BRIAN E., lawyer; b. Galion, Ohio, Feb. 22, 1953. BA with honors, Denison U., 1975; JD cum laude, U. Mich., 1978. Bar: Conn. 1978, Ill. 1984, Calif. 1985. Ptnr. Mayer, Brown & Platt, L.A.; lectr. Banking Law Inst., 1985. Mem. ABA (mem. corp., banking and bus. law sects.), State Bar Calif. Office: Mayer Brown & Platt 350 S Grand Ave Los Angeles CA 90071-3406*

NEWHOUSE, DONALD E., newspaper publishing executive; b. 1930; s. Samuel N. Student, Syracuse U. With Advance Publs., Staten Island, N.Y., 1951—, now pres.; co-founder Newhouse Newspapers, N.Y.C., 1963, now v.p.; pres. Newark (N.J.) Star-Ledger; v.p. Times Picayune Pub. Corp., New Orleans; treas. Herald Am., Syracuse, 1960—, The Post Standard, Syracuse, 1960—, The Syracuse Herald Journal, 1960—, The Herald Co. Inc., 1960—; co-founder Metro-Suburbia, Inc., N.Y.C., 1963; prin. The Trenton (N.J.) Times, Times of Trenton Pub. Corp. Office: Star-Ledger 1 Star Ledger Plz Newark NJ 07102-1200*

NEWHOUSE, IRVING RALPH, state legislator; b. Mabton, Wash., Oct. 16, 1920; s. John and Tina (Bos) N.; m. Ruth Martha Gardner, July 14, 1945; children: Joyce, James, Linda, Laura, Daniel, Dorothy. BS, Wash. State U., 1943. County agt. Egrl. Extension Svc., Ellensburg, Wash., 1946; farmer Mabton, 1947—; mem. Wash. Ho. of Reps., Olympia, 1964-80; mem. Wash. State Senate, Olympia, 1980—, Rep. floor leader. Lt. (j.g.) USNR, 1943-45, PTO. Republican. Mem. Christian Reformed Ch. Home: 1160 Murray Rd Mabton WA 98935-9714 Office: Wash State Sen 403 Legislative Bldg Olympia WA 98504

NEWHOUSE, JOSEPH PAUL, economics educator; b. Waterloo, Iowa, Feb. 24, 1942; s. Joseph Alexander and Ruth Linnea (Johnson) N.; m. Margaret Louise Locke, June 22, 1968; children: Eric Joseph, David Locke. BA, Harvard U., 1963, PhD, 1969; postgrad (Fulbright scholar), Goethe U., Frankfort, Germany, 1963-64. Staff economist Rand Corp., Santa Monica, Calif., 1968-72, dep. program mgr., health and biosci. rsch., 1971-88, sr. staff economist, 1972-81, head econs. dept., 1981-85, sr. corp. fellow, 1985—; John D. MacArthur prof. health policy and mgmt., dir. div. Health Policy Rsch. and Edn., Harvard U., 1988—; lectr. UCLA, 1970-83, adj. prof., 1983-88; mem. faculty Rand Grad. Sch., 1972-88; dir. Rand-UCLA Ctr. for Study Health Care Fin. Policy, 1984-88, co-dir., 1988-92; prin. investigator health ins. study grant HHS, 1971-86; chmn. health svcs. rsch. study sect. HHS-Agy. for Health Care Policy and Rsch., 1989-93; mem. Nat. Commn. Cost Med. Care, 1976-77; mem. health svcs. devel. grants study sect. HEW, 1978-82, Inst. Medicine of NAS, 1978—, mem. coun., 1992—; mem. Physician Payment Rev. Commn., 1993-96, chmn. Prospective Payment Assessment Com., 1996—. Author: The Economics of Medical Care, 1978, The Cost of Poor Health Habits, 1991, A Measure of Malpractice,

1993, Free for All?, 1993; editor Jour. Health Econs., 1981—; assoc. editor Jour. Econ. Perspectives, 1992—; contbr. articles to profl. jours. Recipient David Kershaw award and prize Assn. Pub. Policy and Mgmt., 1983, Baxter Am. Found. prize, 1988, Adminstr.'s citation Health Care Fin. Adminstrn., 1988, Hans Sigrist Found. prize, 1995, Elizur Wright award, 1995. Fellow Am. Acad. Arts and Scis.; mem. Assn. for Health Svcs. Rsch. (Article of Yr. award 1989, bd. dirs. 1991—, pres. 1993-94), Am. Econ. Assn., Royal Econ. soc., Econometric Soc., Phi Beta Kappa. Office: Harvard U Health Policy Rsch and Edn 25 Shattuck St Fl 1 Boston MA 02115-6027

NEWHOUSE, MARK WILLIAM, publishing executive; b. N.Y.C., Oct. 14, 1948; s. Norman Nathan and Alice (Gross) N.; m. Lorry A. Whitehead, June 1, 1974; children: Jesse Louis, Charlotte Ann. BA, Yale U., 1969. V.p., gen. mgr. The Star-Ledger, Newark, N.J., 1980—. Bd. dirs. N.Y.C. Opera, 1992—, pres., 1993—; bd. dirs. Audit Bur. of Circulations, 1995—. Office: Newark Morning Star Ledger Co One Star Ledger Plz Newark NJ 07102-1200

NEWHOUSE, NANCY RILEY, newspaper editor; b. Bellingham, Wash.; d. Fenwick Charles and Elizabeth (Grace) Riley; m. John Newhouse, Sept. 27, 1961 (div. 1970); m. Michael Iovenko, Mar. 6, 1983. BA, Vassar Coll., 1958. Sr. editor N.Y. Mag., N.Y.C., 1970-75, House & Garden Mag., N.Y.C., 1976; successively home editor, style editor and travel editor N.Y. Times, N.Y.C., 1976—. Editor: Hers: Through Women's Eyes, 1985; editor Hers column N.Y. Times, 1976-92; mem. adv. bd. Vassar Quar., Poughkeepsie, N.Y., 1985—. Recipient Penney-Mo. Newspaper award U. Mo. Sch. Journalism, 1982-83. Mem. The Century Assn., Women's Forum N.Y. Office: NY Times Co 229 W 43rd St New York NY 10036-3913

NEWHOUSE, ROBERT J., JR., insurance executive. Ret. vice chmn. bd. Marsh & McLennan Cos., Inc.; chmn. bd. Mid Ocean Reins. Co. Ltd., Bermuda; dir., chm. exec. comm. ACE. Ltd., Bermuda, dir., Trident Corp., Bermuda. Office: 55 Madison Ave Ste 450 Morristown NJ 07960-7397

NEWHOUSE, SAMUEL I., JR., publishing executive; b. 1928; m. Victoria Newhouse. Chmn. Condé Nast Publs. Inc., N.Y.C.; also chmn. bd. dirs., CEO Advance Publs. Inc., S.I., N.Y. Recipient Henry Johnson Fisher award Mag. Pubs. Assn., 1985. Office: Condé Nast Publs Inc 350 Madison Ave New York NY 10017-3704 also: Advance Pubs Inc 950 Fingerboard Rd Staten Island NY 10305-1453*

NEWICK, CRAIG DAVID, architect; b. Orange, N.J., Feb. 14, 1960; s. Russel Forester and Helen (Welch) N.; m. Linda Hammer Lindroth, June 6, 1987; 1 child, Zachary Eran. BA in Architecture, Lehigh U., 1982; MArch, Yale U., 1987. Registered architect, Conn. Designer, draftsman The Archtl. Studio, Easton, Pa., 1983-84; job capt., project designer Svigals & Assocs., New Haven, 1985; designer, draftsman Centerbrook (Conn.) Architects, 1986; job capt., project designer Allan Dehar Assocs., Architects & Planners, New Haven, 1988-90; ptnr. Lindroth & Newick, New Haven, 1991—; designer Cesar Pelli & Assocs., Inc., New Haven, 1992; project arch. Tai Soo Kim Ptnrs., Hartford, Conn., 1995—; vis. faculty Vis. Critics Studio, Lehigh U., 1993; vis. critic Wesleyan U., 1990-93, R.I. Sch. Design, 1988; faculty Creative Arts Workshop, New Haven, 1991, 92. Out Of Bounds (fisrt prize artists books 1994). Recipient 1st place award Am. Visionary Set Design Competition, 1989, 3d place award Astronauts Meml. Design Competition, 1988, ID Mag. Ann. Design Rev. award, 1990, 2d prize African Burial Ground Competition Mcpl. Arts Soc. N.Y., 1994; grantee New Eng. Found. for Arts, 1992, NEA Interarts grantee Rockefeller Found., 1989-90, Found. for Contemporary Performance Art, 1989, 90, Humanities Coun. of Fairfield U., 1995; New Eng. Found. for Arts Regional fellow, 1993, others. Mem. Architecture League N.Y. (young architects forum 1991, emerging voices, 1996). Office: Lindroth & Newick 219 Livingston St New Haven CT 06511-2209

NEWKIRK, JOHN BURT, metallurgical engineer, administrator; b. Mpls., Mar. 24, 1920; s. Burt Leroy and Mary Louise (Leavenworth) N.; m. Carolyn Mae Jordan, Aug. 4, 1951; children: Jeffrey Burt (dec.), John Jordan, Victoria Louise Lierheimer, Christina Brooks. B. Metall. Engring, Rensselaer Poly. Inst., Troy, N.Y., 1941; M.S., Carnegie Inst. Tech., 1947, Sc.D., 1950. Metall. investigator Bethlehem Steel Co., Pa., 1941-42; Fulbright postdoctoral fellow Cambridge (Eng.) U., 1950-51; research metallurgist research lab. Gen. Electric Co., Schenectady, 1951-59; prof. Cornell U., 1959-65; Phillipson prof. U. Denver, 1965-74, prof. phys. chemistry, 1975-84, Phillipson prof. emeritus, 1984—; pres. Colo. Biomed., Inc., 1969—, ret. Editor Rews. on High Temperature Materials, 1973-78; 16 ann. volumes Advances in X-Ray Analysis; contbr. over 75 articles profl. jours. With USNR, 1942-46. Fellow Am. Soc. Metals (life); mem. Sigma Xi, Tau Beta Pi, Phi Kappa Phi, Alpha Sigma Mu (internat. pres. 1950), Alpha Tau Omega. Republican. Presbyterian. Office: Colo Biomed Inc 6851 Highway 73 Evergreen CO 80439-6558

NEWKIRK, RAYMOND LESLIE, management consultant; b. Shreveport, La., July 13, 1944; s. Raymond Clay and Dorothy Emily (Parker) N.; m. Felicisima Guese Calma, Jan. 19, 1985. AA, Dayton Community Coll., 1973; BS in Behavioral Sci., N.Y. Inst. Tech., 1976; MS in Philosophy, Columbia Pacific U., 1980, PhD in Behavioral Sci., 1982; PhD in Human Sci., Saybrook Inst., 1992. Clin. intern Fielding Inst., 1995; chief exec. officer, cons. Newkirk & Assocs., Ft. Lauderdale, Fla., 1980-84; head dept. ADP Royal Saudi Naval Forces, Jeddah, 1984-86; pres., cons. Internat. Assn. Info. Mgmt., Santa Clara, Calif., 1984; cert. quality analyst Quality Assurance Inst., Orlando, Fla., 1986—; prin. cons. Info. Impact Internat., Nashville, 1988—; pres., CEO Sys. Mgmt. Inst., Pleasant Hill, Calif., 1987; pres., COO P.Q. Info. Group, Egmont ann Hoeff, The Netherlands, 1992-94; pres., CEO Systems Mgmt. Inst., 1994—; prin. Forum 2000, 1996—; dep. gov. Am. Biog. Inst., 1995. Author: Chronicles of the Making of A Philosopher, 1983; contbr. articles to profl. jours. Speaker, mem. Union for Concerned Scientists, San Francisco, 1988. Fellow Brit. Inst. Mgmt., Internat. Biog. Assn.; mem. Assn. Systems Mgmt., Assn. Profl. Cons., Planetary Soc., Columbia Pacific Alumni Assn. (pres. Mid-east chpt. 1985), Assn. Computing Machinery, IEEE Computer Soc., Am. Biograph. Inst. (dep. gov. 1995), Phi Theta Kappa (outstanding scholar award 1973), Confedn. of Chivalry (knight). Roman Catholic. Avocations: writing, classical guitar, tennis, weight lifting. Home: 803 Treehaven Ct Pleasant Hill CA 94523-2473

NEWLAND, CHESTER ALBERT, public administration educator; b. Kansas City, Kans., June 18, 1930; s. Guy Wesley and Mary Virginia (Yoakum) N. BA, U. N. Tex., Denton, 1954; MA, U. Kans., 1955, PhD, 1958. Social Sci. Rsch. Coun. fellow U. Wis. and U.S. Supreme Ct., 1958-59; instr. polit. sci. Idaho State U., Pocatello, 1959-60; mem. faculty U. North Tex., Denton, 1960-66, prof. govt., 1963-66, dir. dept. govt., 1963-66; prof. polit. sci. U. Houston, 1967-68; dir. Lyndon Baines Johnson Libr., Austin, Tex., 1968-70; prof. pub. adminstrn. U. So. Calif., 1966-67, 68-71, 76-82, 84-92, Duggan disting. prof. pub. adminstrn., 1992—; prof. George Mason U., Fairfax, Va., 1982-84; mem. faculty Fed. Exec. Inst., 1971-76, dir. 1973-76, 80-81; mgr. task force on fed. labor-mgmt. rels. U.S. Pers. Mgmt. Project, Pres.'s Reorgn., Washington, 1977-78. Editor in chief Pub. Adminstrn. Rev., 1984-90; contbr. articles to profl. jours. Chmn. Mcpl. Rsch. Coun., Denton, 1963-64; city councilman, Denton, 1964-66; mem. Pub. Sector Commn. on Productivity and Work Quality, 1974-78; trustee Sacramento (Calif.) Mus. History, Sci. and Tech., 1993-95; mem. UN Devel. Program, Moldova, 1994, Kuwait, 1995-96. Mem. Nat. Acad. Pub. Adminstrn., Southwestern Social Sci. Assn. (chmn. govt. sect. 1964-65), Am. Soc. Pub. Adminstrn. (pres. Dallas-Ft. Worth chpt. 1964-65, nat. coun. 1976, 78-81, editorial bd. jour. 1972-76, chmn. publ. com. 1975-79, program chmn. 1977, nat. pres. 1981-82, Dimock award 1984), Am. Polit. Sci. Assn., Internat. Pers. Mgmt. Assn. (program chmn. 1978, Stockberger award 1979), Am. Acad. Polit. and Social Sci., Internat. City Mgmt. Assn. (hon.), Nat. Assn. Schs Pub. Affairs and Adminstrn. (Staats Pub. Svc. award 1989). Office: Univ Southern California 1201 J St Sacramento CA 95814-2906

NEWLAND, JANE LOU, nursing educator; b. Toledo, July 18, 1931; d. Clarence Charles Meinen and Bernice Isabell (Floyd) Scott; m. Byron Merle Newland, Aug. 4, 1962; children: Jeffrey Bruce, Brian James. Diploma in nursing, Lima (Ohio) Meml. Hosp., 1952; BSN, Ohio State U., 1959; M Vocat. Edn., U. South Fla., 1983, EdS in Vocat. Edn., 1989. RN, Ohio, Fla.; cert. tchr., Fla. Stewardess nurse Balt. & Ohio R.R., Cin., 1953-56; dir. nursing Lima State Hosp., 1960-67, dir. nursing edn., 1967-72; renal nurse children's svc. Health and Rehabilitative Svcs. Fla., Ft. Myers, 1975-78; practical nursing instr. Lee High-Tech. Ctr. Ctrl., Ft. Myers, 1979—; mem. adv. bd. Practical Nurse Assn., Lima, 1966-71. Mem., sec. St. James City Civic Assn., 1973-76; den leader Boy Scouts Am., St. James City, 1970-76; treas. PTA Pine Island Elem. Sch., Pine Island Center, Fla., 1973-75. Recipient Assoc. Master Tchr. award Fla. State Bd. Edn., 1986. Mem. Assn. Practical Nurse Educators Fla., Nat. Assn. health Occupations Tchrs., Lee County Vocat. Assn. (Outstanding Health Occupation Tchr. award 1985, Outstanding Vocat. Edn. Tchr. award 1990), Fla. Vocat. Assn., Health Occupation Educators Assn. Fla., Ladies Aux. VFW, Ladies Oriental Shrine, Order Ea. Star, Newbians of Cape Coral (Fla.), Kappa Delta (v.p. 1983-85, pres. 1993—), Phi Kappa Phi. Lutheran. Avocations: crafts, stamp collecting, history. Home: 2261 Carambola Ln Saint James City FL 33956 Office: Lee County High Tech Ctr 3800 Michigan Ave Fort Myers FL 33916-2202

NEWLAND, LARRY J., orchestra conductor; b. Winfield, Kans., Jan. 24, 1935; s. Roy E. and Frances M. (Hammond) N.; m. Paula Kahn, Feb. 18, 1977; children: Lee Ann, Sara. MusB, Oberlin Conservatory, 1955; MusM, Manhattan Sch. Music, 1957. artistic adminstr. Sr. Concert Orch., N.Y.C., 1987-89. Asst. condr., musician N.Y. Philharm., N.Y.C., 1960-85; music dir., condr. Harrisburg (Pa.) Symphony, 1978-94, Philharm. Chamber Orch. (formerly Diabolus Musicus Chamber Orch.), N.Y.C., 1974—; music dir. Sr. Concert Orch. N.Y., 1987-89; regular guest condr. Seoul (Republic of Korea) Philharm.; prof., dir. ensembles Adelphi U., Garden City, N.Y., 1990—, acting chair music dept., 1993-94, chair music dept., 1994—. Served with U.S. Army, 1957-60. REcipient Harold Bauer Meml. award, 1957, Koussevitzky Conducting prize, 1963, Pa. Gov.'s citation, 1982, Pa. Ho. of Reps. citation, 1988, Disting. Pub. Svc. award City of Harrisburg, 1982, Golden Baton award Harrisburg Symphony, 1994, Pa. State Senate commendation, 1994; Leonard Bernstein conducting fellow, 1964. Mem. Am. Symphony Orch. League, Am. Fedn. Musicians, Condrs. Guild (pres. 1993-95). Avocations: tennis, sailing, mountain climbing, hiking, reading.

NEWLAND, MATTHEW JOHN, state legislator; b. Middletown, Conn., Dec. 6, 1967; s. Marshall Lee Jr. and Arline Ann (Stafford) N.; Heather Catherine Clough, Oct. 2, 1993. A Bus. Mgmt., N.H. Tech. Inst., 1990; BBA, U. N.H., 1993. Mem. N.H. Ho. of Reps., Concord, 1992—. Trustee U. Sys. of N.H., Lee, 1991-92; mem. Civic Ctr. Commn., Concord, 1994; mem. N.H. State Dem. Com., Concord, 1993-94; bd. mem. Cmty. Svc. Coun., 1994—. Mem. Sachem Soc., World Wildlife Fund. Democrat. Roman Catholic. Avocations: reading, skiing, movies, hiking, mountain biking. Home: 81 Fisherville Rd Apt 28 Concord NH 03303-4155 Office: State House Rm 306 Concord NH 03301

NEWLAND, RON, airport executive. Mgr. of airport svcs. Rickenbacker Internat Airport, Columbus, OH. Office: Rickenbaker Intl Airport 7400 Alum Creek Dr Columbus OH 43217-1232*

NEWLAND, RUTH LAURA, small business owner; b. Ellensburg, Wash., June 4, 1949; d. George J. and Ruth Marjorie (Porter) N. BA, Cen. Wash. State Coll., 1970, MEd, 1972; EdS, Vanderbilt U., 1973; PhD, Columbia Pacific U., 1981. Tchr. Union Gap (Wash.) Sch., 1970-71; ptnr. Newland Ranch Gravel Co., Yakima, Wash., 1970—, Arnold Artificial Limb, Yakima, 1981-86; owner, pres. Arnold Artificial Limb, Yakima and Richland, Wash., 1986—; ptnr. Newland Ranch, Yakima, 1969—. Contbg. mem. Nat. Dem. Com., Irish Nat. Caucus Found.; mem. Pub. Citizen, We The People, Nat. Humane Edn. Soc.; charter mem. Nat. Mus. Am. Indian. George Washington scholar Masons, Yakima, 1967. Mem. NAFE, NOW, Am. Orthotic and Prosthetic Assn., Internat. Platform Assn., Nat. Antivisection Soc. (life), Vanderbilt U. Alumni Assn., Peabody Coll. Alumni Assn., Columbia Pacific U. Alumni Assn., World Wildlife Fund, Nat. Audubon Soc., Greenpeace, Mus. Fine Arts, Humane Soc. U.S., Wilderness Soc., Nature Conservancy, People for Ethical Treatment of Animals, Amnesty Internat., The Windstar Found., Rodale Inst., Sierra Club (life), Emily's List. Democrat. Avocations: reading, gardening, sewing, handcrafts, people. Home: 2004 Riverside Rd Yakima WA 98901-9564 Office: Arnold Artificial Limb 9 S 12th Ave Yakima WA 98902-3106 *Personal philosophy: God first. Then be politically and socially conservative but liberal in your concern for others.*

NEWLIN, CHARLES FREMONT, lawyer; b. Palestine, Ill., Nov. 18, 1953; s. Charles Norris and Regina Helen (Correll) N.; m. Jean Bolt, Jan. 6, 1975; children: Christian N., Charles W., Ethan A. BA in Polit. Sci. summa cum laude, Ill. Wesleyan U., 1975; JD cum laude, Harvard U., 1978. Bar: Ill. 1978, U.S. Dist. Ct. (no. dist.) Ill. 1978, U.S. Tax Ct. 1980. Law clk. Sugarman, Rogers, Barshak & Cohen, Boston, 1976-78; assoc. Mayer, Brown & Platt, Chgo., 1978-84, ptnr., 1985—; ptnr. Sonnenschein, Nath & Rosenthal; adj. prof. law DePaul U., Chgo., 1986-90; lectr. in field. Contbg. author: Am. Law of Property, 1975, Trust Adminstrn. Ill., 1983, 87, 92, Bogert on Trusts, 1986-91, The Lawyer's Guide to Retirement, 1991, 94; contbr. articles to profl. jours. Scouting coord. DuPage area coun. Boy Scouts Am., Woodridge, Ill., 1984-86; bishop's counselor Mormon Ch., Woodridge, 1984-86; mem. planned giving com. Ill. div. Am. Cancer Soc., 1988—, Boys and Girls Clubs of Chgo., 1993—; vol. legal cons. The Tower Chorale, Western Springs, Ill., 1989-91. Fellow Am. Coll. Trust and Estate Counsel; mem. Chgo. Bar Assn., Chgo. Estate Planning Coun. Democrat. Methodist. Office: Sonnenschein Nath & Rosenthal 7600 Sears Tower Chicago IL 60606*

NEWLIN, LYMAN WILBUR, bookseller, consultant; b. Buda, Ill., May 26, 1910; s. Fred Matheny and Maude Lillian (Potter) N.; m. Evy Ottonia Magnusson, 1966; children: Fred M. II, Erik B.M. Student, Coll. Emporia, Kans., 1928-30, U. Chgo., 1930-32. Buyer, bus. mgr. Follett Book Co., Chgo., 1934-44; mgr. Minn. Book Store and Macalester Coll. Book Store, Mpls. and St. Paul, 1944-48; co-owner Broadwater Lodge, Hackensack, Minn., 1948-65; founder, owner Broadwater Books, Lewiston, N.Y., 1948—; buyer, dept. mgr. Kroch's & Brentano's Book Store, Chgo., 1951-65; regional mgr. Richard Abel and Co., Portland, Oreg. and Zion, Ill.,, 1966-69, asst. to pres., 1969-75; founder, prin. counselor Lyman W. Newlin Book Trade Counsellors, Lewiston, N.Y., 1975—; mdse. mgr. Coutts Library Services, Inc., Lewiston, 1976-90; pub. rels. advisor The Charleston (Coll. Libr.) Conf., 1985—; pub. liaison Book News, Inc., Portland, 1989—; program coord. Acad. of Scholarly Pub. seminar Coll. of Charleston, 1995—; cons. Rutgers U. Press, New Brunswick, N.J., 1975-81; panelist and lectr. to acad. librs. and schs., booksellers. Pub. Rev. Index Quar. Guide to Profl. Revs., 1941-43; pub. rels. advisor, contbr. Quar. Publ. Against the Grain, 1985—; contbr. articles to profl. jours. Founder, 1st pres. Boy River Chain of Lakes Improvement Assn., Cass County, Minn., 1961-65, Concerned Parents Orgn., Freehold, 1976-79; trustee, v.p., sec., chmn. new libr. bldg. com. Lewiston Pub. Libr., 1985—; committeeman Niagara County Dem. Party, 1987—, sec., 1988-90; mem. coun. Luth. Ch. Messiah, Lewiston, 1982-93, deacon, 1992—; mem. Town of Lewiston Sr. Citizens Adv. Bd., 1992—. Mem. ALA, Assn. Book Travelers (50 Yr. award 1984), Am. Booksellers Assn., Soc. Scholarly Pub. (program com. 1985), Book Industry Study Group, Pi Kappa Delta. Lutheran. Democrat. Avocations: amateur ornithology, Am. folk music, New Orleans jazz, book collecting. Office: PO Box 278 Lewiston NY 14092-0278 *If the Golden Rule is truly one's rule in living, no other rule is needed.*

NEWLIN, STEPHEN DORE, chemical company executive; b. Pierre, S.D., Feb. 8, 1953; s. Douglas M. and Mary Newlin; m. Terry Ochsner, Aug. 17, 1975; children: Grant, Scott. BSCE, S.D. Sch. Mines & Tech., 1975; Advanced Mgmt. Program, Harvard U., 1990. Dist. rep. Nalco Chem. Co., Naperville, Ill., 1976-80, sales rep., 1980-82, dist. mgr. Watergy group, 1982-84, sales mgr. Watergy group, 1984-87, gen. mgr. Watergy group, 1987-90, gen. mgr. Unisolv group, 1990-92, gen. mgr. pulp & paper group, 1992-93, v.p.-pres. Nalco Pacific, 1993-94; chmn./mem. various bds. of subs. and affiliates. With USPHS. Mem. Paper Industry Mgrs., Triangle Alumni Assn. Avocation: sports. Office: Nalco Europe, PO Box 627, Leiden 2300 AP, The Netherlands

NEWMAN, ANDREA HAAS, school counselor, educator; b. N.Y.C., Nov. 17, 1947; d. Charles and Miriam (Kasdan) Haas; m. Arthur Robert Newman, July 5, 1970; children: Aaron Charles, Andrew Benjamin, Alan Jacob. BS, Ohio State U., 1970; MEd, Cleve. State U., 1985. Cert. sch. counselor. English spl. edn. tchr. Roosevelt H.S., Dayton, Ohio, 1970-71; counselor Parma (Ohio) H.S., 1985-86, occupational work adjustment, sch. counselor, 1986-88; sch. counselor Hillside Jr. H.S., Seven Hills, Ohio, 1988-95, Parma Sr. H.S., 1995—; mem. strategic planning team Parma City Schs., 1992-93, tchr. svc. planning com., 1993-94; personality fitness trainer Personality Fitness for Youth, L.A., 1987-88; advisor S.A.D.D. (Students Against Drunk Dribing), Seven Hills, 1992—. Instr., group leader Systematic Tng. for Effective Parenting, Hillside Jr. High Sch., 1992-93. Mem. Ohio Sch. Counselors Assn. Jewish. Avocations: hiking, golf, fitness walking, cycling. Office: Parma Sr HS 6285 West 54th St Parma OH 44129

NEWMAN, ANDREW EDISON, restaurant executive; b. St. Louis, Aug. 14, 1944; s. Eric Pfeiffer and Evelyn Frances (Edison) N.; m. Peggy Gregory, Feb. 14, 1984; children: Daniel Mark, Anthony Edison. BA, Harvard U., 1966, MBA, 1968. With Office of Sec. Def., Washington, 1968-70; with Edison Bros. Stores, Inc., St. Louis, 1970-95, v.p. ops. and adminstrn., 1975-80, dir., 1978—, exec. v.p., 1980-86, chmn., 1987-95; chmn., CEO Race Rock Internat., St. Louis, 1995—; bd. dirs. Edison Bros. Stores, St. Louis, Sigma-Aldrich Corp., St. Louis, Lee Enterprises, Davenport, Iowa, Dave and Buster's, Dallas. Trustee Washington U. Office: 501 N Broadway Saint Louis MO 63102-2196

NEWMAN, BARBARA MAE, retired special education educator; b. Rockford, Ill., July 16, 1932; d. Greene Adam and Emma Lorene (Fields) N. BS Edn., No. Ill. U., 1973. Cert. elem. edn. K-8 tchr., spl. edn. (blind and p.s.) K-12 tchr. Exec. sec. Rockford Art Assn., 1961-70; tchr. Title 1 Rockford Pub. Sch. Dist. #205, 1975-76, tchr. vision impaired, 1977-91. Feature editor (Rock Valley Coll. newspaper) The Valley Forge, 1970; contbg. writer (Rockford Coll. history) A Retrospective Look, 1980. St. Bernadette adult choir, 1958-95, Cathedral Chorale, 1995—; holder 5 offices Am. Bus. Women's Assn., Forest City chpt., 1963-70; vol. Winnebago Ctr. for the Blind, Rockford, 1965-70; mem. Rockford Diocesan Chorale, 1969—. Named Woman of Yr., Am. Bus. Women's Assn., Forest City chpt., Rockford, 1966; scholar Ill. State Scholarship Commn., No. Ill. U., 1970-73. Mem. Ill. Ret. Tchrs. Assn. Roman Catholic. Avocations: writing, swimming, gardening.

NEWMAN, BARRY INGALLS, retired banker, lawyer; b. N.Y.C., Mar. 19, 1932; s. M.A. and T.C. (Weitman) N.; BA, Alfred U., 1952; JD, NYU, 1955; m. Jean Short, Mar. 6, 1965; children: Suzanne, Cathy, David. Bar: N.Y. 1957, Ohio 1957, U.S. Supreme Ct. 1967, Calif. 1990; practiced in N.Y.C., 1957; assoc., then ptnr. firm Shapiro Persky Marken & Newman, Cleve., 1957-63; asst. v.p. Meinhard & Co. (now Meinhard Comml. Corp.), N.Y.C., 1963-65; v.p. Amsterdam Overseas Corp., N.Y.C., 1966-68; pres. No. Fin. Corp., L.A., 1968-72; sr. v.p. Aetna Bus. Credit, Inc., Hartford, Conn., 1972-78; exec. v.p. Security Pacific Fin. Group, San Diego, 1978-81, chmn., pres., chief exec. officer, 1981-82; sr. exec. v.p. Gt. Am. First Savs. Bank, 1982-88; ret. 1988; chmn. bd. dirs. San Diego County Capital Asset Leasing Corp. With U.S. Army, 1955-57. Recipient Disting. Svc. award Cleve. Jr. C. of C., 1961. Mem. ABA, N.Y. State Bar Assn., Ohio Bar Assn., Calif. Bar Assn., San Diego Bar Assn., Masons. Republican. Home: 3308 Avenida Sierra Escondido CA 92029-7937

NEWMAN, BARRY MARC, pediatric surgeon; b. N.Y.C., Dec. 13, 1951; s. Sheldon and Miriam (Jasphy) N.; m. Jane Post, July 2, 1989; 1 child, Alexander Ross. BA, U. Pa., 1973; MD, SUNY, Stony Brook, 1976. Diplomate Nat. Bd. Med. Examiners, Am. Bd. Surgery, Am. Bd. Pediatric Surgery. Resident in surgery N.Y. Med. Coll., N.Y.C., 1976-78; sr. resident in surgery SUNY, Stony Brook, 1978-81; chief resident pediatric surgery Childrens Hosp. of Buffalo, 1981-83, fellow pediatric surgery and gastroenterology, 1983-84; asst. prof. surgery U. Va., Charlottesville, 1984-88, U. Ill., Chgo., 1988-93; dir. pediatric surgery Luth. Gen. Children's Hosp., Park Ridge, Ill., 1991-96; clin. assoc. prof. surgery U. Chgo., 1993-95; dir. pediatric surg. svcs. Loyola U. Med. Ctr., Maywood, Ill., 1996—, co-dir. surg. laparoscopy lab., 1996—, assoc. prof. surgery and pediatrics, 1996—; instr. Adv. Trauma and Life Support, ACS, Chgo., 1984—. Contbr. articles to profl. jours., chpts. to books. NIH grantee, 1982-83, 87-88. Fellow Am. Acad. Pediatrics, ACS; mem. Am. Gastroenterol. Assn., Am. Pediatric Surg. Assn. Democrat. Jewish. Avocations: wine collecting, scuba diving, underwater photography, personal computing. Office: Loyola U Med Ctr Dept Surgery 2160 S First Ave Maywood IL 60153

NEWMAN, BERNARD, federal judge; b. N.Y.C., Oct. 28, 1907; s. Isidor J. and Sarah C. (Berkowitz) N.; m. Kathryn Bereano, Apr. 3, 1932; children: Phyllis Newman Cechini, Helene Newman Bernstein. BS, NYU, 1928, LLB, 1929. Bar: N.Y. 1930. With Newman & Newman, intermittently 1930-65; asst. corp. counsel N.Y.C., 1936-42; law sec. to N.Y. Supreme Ct. Justice Samuel H. Hofstadter, 1942-48; ofcl. referee appellate div. N.Y. Supreme Ct., 1948-62, spl. referee, 1963-65, justice, 1962; judge Family Ct. N.Y., N.Y.C., 1965-68, U.S. Customs Ct., 1968—; now sr. judge U.S. Ct. Internat. Trade; lectr. motion practice N.Y. U. Law Sch., Practicing Law Inst.; speaker colls., univs., civic assns.; mem. spl. panel examiners N.Y. State Labor Relations Bd.; spl. panel arbitrators N.Y. State Mediation Bd.; govt. appeals agt. Selective Service. Pres. PTA High Sch. of Sci., N.Y.C., 1953-56, Bentley High Sch., 1955-56; mem. exec. com. Fedn. Jewish Philanthropies; Rep. dist. leader, 1955-62; counsel N.Y. Rep. County Com., 1957-58, chmn., 1958-62; mem. exec. com. N.Y. Rep. State Com., 1958-62; del. to jud., state, nat. convs.; bd. dirs. Met. adv. bd. Anti-Defamation League, LaGuardia Meml. Assn., Civic Ctr. Synagogue, Community Synagogue Ctr., N.Y.C.; dir. congregations Jewish synagogue, 1950—; patron Met. Opera Assn., 1962—. Served with USCG, World War II. Recipient Silver medal Nat. Essay Contest; named Merit Man for N.Y.C.; cited by Internat. Trade Bd., N.Y. U. Mem. ABA, N.Y. State Bar Assn., Assn. of Bar of City of N.Y., Fed. Bar Coun., Am. Judicature Soc., Nat. Legal Aid Assn., NYU Law Rev. Alumni Assn. (pres. 1958-61, gov. and bd. dirs. 1956—). Office: US Ct Internat Trade 1 Federal Plz New York NY 10278-0001

NEWMAN, BRUCE MURRAY, antiques dealer; b. N.Y.C., Jan. 27, 1930; s. Meyer and Evelyn (Kantor) N.; m. Judith S. Brandus, June 26, 1965; 1 child, Emily Rachel. BA, Pratt Inst., 1953. Pres. Newel Art Galleries Inc., N.Y.C., 1975—; lectr. mus. and univs.; regional adv. bd. Chase Manhattan Bank. Author: Fantasy Furniture, 1989; featured on numerous TV & radio programs, mags. and other publs.; guest CBS Morning Show, 1988; prime time host PBS Chanel 13, N.Y.C. Bd. dirs. N.Y.C. Ctr., 1988-90; assoc. mem. Mt. Sinai Med. Ctr., 1988-90; trustee Pratt Inst., Bklyn., 1983—; mem. regional adv. bd. Chem. Bank. Recipient Designer award Art Dirs. Club, 1984, Man of Yr. award Pratt Inst., 1993; featured on Lifestyles of the Rich and Famous, 1991, other TV programs, Cover Connoisseur Mag., 1989, (story) Architectural Digest, 1989, N.Y. Times, 1983, 84, (2) 89, 92, 95, Internat. Herald Tribune, 1992, others. Mem. Am. Soc. Interior Designers (bd. dirs. 1989—), Victorian Soc. Am. Avocations: golfing, reading, jogging, traveling. Office: Newel Art Galleries Inc 425 E 53rd St New York NY 10022-5122

NEWMAN, CAROL L., lawyer; b. Yonkers, N.Y., Aug. 7, 1949; d. Richard J. and Pauline Frances (Stoll) N. AB/MA summa cum laude, Brown U., 1971; postgrad. Harvard U. Law Sch., 1972-73; JD cum laude, George Washington U., 1977. Bar: D.C., 1977, Calif., 1979. With antitrust div. U.S. Dept. Justice, Washington and L.A., 1977-80; assoc. Alschuler, Grossman & Pines, L.A., 1980-82, Costello & Walcher, L.A., 1982-85, Rosen, Wachtell & Gilbert, 1985-88, ptnr., 1988-90; ptnr. Keck, Mahin & Cate, 1990-94; pvt. practice, L.A., 1994—; adj. prof. Sch. Bus., Golden Gate U., spring 1982. Candidate for State Atty. Gen., 1986; L.A. city commr. L.A. Bd. Transp. Commrs., 1993—, v.p., 1995—. Mem. ABA, State Bar Calif., L.A. County Bar Assn., L.A. Lawyers for Human Rights (co. pres. 1991-92), Log Cabin (bd. dirs. 1992—, pres. 1996—), Calif. Women Lawyers (bd. dirs., bd. govs. 1991-94), Order of Coif, Phi Beta Kappa.

NEWMAN, CHARLES A., lawyer; b. L.A., Mar. 18, 1949; s. Arthur and Gladys (Barnett) N.; m. Joan Kathleen Meskiel, Aug. 8, 1971; children: Anne R., Elyse S. BA magna cum laude, U. Calif., 1970; JD, Washington U., 1973. Bar: Mo. 1973, D.C. 1981, U.S. Dist. Ct. (ea. dist.) Mo. 1973, U.S. Ct. Appeals (8th and 11th cirs.) 1973, U.S. Tax Ct. 1981, U.S. Claims Ct. 1981, U.S. Supreme Ct. 1976. From assoc. to ptnr. Thompson Coburn, St. Louis, 1973—; lectr. law Washington U., St. Louis, 1976-78. Trustee Mo. Bar Found., 1990—, mem. Mo. Bar Bd. Govs, 1980-84; bd. dirs. United

Israel Appeal, N.Y.C., 1990-93, Coun. Jewish Fedns., N.Y.C., 1992-95, United Jewish Appeal Young Leadership Cabinet, N.Y.C., 1985-88, Ctr. for Study of Dispute Resolution, 1985-88, Legal Svcs. Ea. Mo., 1985-94, St. Louis Community Found., 1992—, St. Louis chpt. Young Audiences 1993-95, Planned Parenthood St. Louis, 1986-89, Jewish Fedn., St. Louis, 1986—, asst. treas., 1989-90, v.p. fin. planning, 1990-93, asst. sec., 1994—; v.p. Repertory Theatre, St. Louis, 1986-89, sr. v.p., 1990-91; pres. St. Louis Opportunity Clearinghouse, 1974-78. Recipient Lon O. Hocker Meml. Trial award Mo. Bar Found., 1984. Mem. Bar Assn. Met. St. Louis (Merit award 1976). Democrat. Avocations: golf, tennis, reading, music. Office: Thompson & Mitchell 1 Mercantile Ctr Ste 3000 Saint Louis MO 63101-1643

NEWMAN, CLAIRE POE, corporate executive; b. Jacksonville, Fla., Dec. 12, 1926; d. Leslie Ralph and Gertrude (Criswell) Poe; student Fla. State Coll. for Women, 1944-45, Tulane U., 1971-73; m. Robert Jacob Newman, July 3, 1948; children—Leslie Claire, Robert, Christopher David. Co-owner Vineyards in Burgundy, France. Mem. various coms. New Orleans Mus. Art. Mem. Women's com. New Orleans Philharmonic Symphony Assn., 1961—, chmn. orch. rels. com., 1961-63; chmn. New Orleans Easter Seal Drive, 1963; La. trustee Nat. Soc. Crippled Children and Adults, 1963-65. Mem. Women's Aux. C. of C., New Orleans Soc. Archeol. Inst. Am. (v.p. 1972-74), Confrérie des Chevaliers du Tastevin, Sigma Kappa. Club: Metairie Country, Kitzbuehel (Austria) Golf, Golden Skibook (Kitzbuehel), Pass Christian (Miss.) Yacht; Ski (Arlberg). Home: 1111 Falcon Rd Metairie LA 70005-4129 Other: Tiemberg, Kitzbuehel Austria

NEWMAN, DAVID, composer; b. L.A., Mar. 11, 1954; s. Alfred N. music dir. Sundance Inst. Film scores include Critters, 1985, Vendetta, 1986, The Kindred, 1987, The Brave Little Toaster, 1987, Malone, 1987, My Demon Lover, 1987, Dragnet, 1987, Throw Momma from the Train, 1987, Pass the Ammo, 1988, Heathers, 1989, Bill & Ted's Excellent Adventure, 1989, Disorganized Crime, 1989, Little Monsters, 1989, The War of the Roses, 1989, Gross Anatomy, 1989, Madhouse, 1990, Fire Birds, 1990, The Freshman, 1990, Mr. Destiny, 1990, Duck Tales: The Movie, 1990, Meet the Applegates, 1991, The Marrying Man, 1991, Don't Tell Mom the Babysitter's Dead, 1991, Bill & Ted's Bogus Journey, 1991, Rover Dangerfield, 1991, Talent for the Game, 1991, Paradise, 1991, Other People's Money, 1991, Honeymoon in Vegas, 1992, The Runestone, 1992, The Mighty Ducks, 1992, That Night, 1992, Hoffa, 1992, The Sandlot, 1993, Coneheads, 1993, Undercover Blues, 1993, The Air Up There, 1994, My Father, the Hero, 1994, The Flintstones, 1994, The Cowboy Way, 1994, I Love Trouble, 1994, Boys On the Side, 1995. Office: Marks and Vangelos Mgt 19301 Ventura Blvd Ste 206 Tarzana CA 91356-3041

NEWMAN, DAVID WHEELER, lawyer; b. Salt Lake City, Apr. 5, 1952; s. Donnell and Vera Mae (Siratt) N.; m. Mahnaz Navai, Mar. 14, 1981; 1 child, Anthony Dara. BA cum laude, Claremont Men's Coll., 1973; JD, UCLA, 1977; LLM in Taxation, NYU, 1979. Bar: Calif. 1978, U.S. Dist. Ct. Calif. 1978, U.S. Tax Ct. 1979. Tax ptnr. Mitchell, Silberberg & Knupp, L.A., 1982—; bd. dirs. Indsl. Bank, Nat. Com. on Planned Giving; mem. exec. com. tax sect. L.A. County Bar, 1991—. Mem. Calif. Club. Avocations: tennis, skiing. Office: Mitchell Silberberg & Knupp 11377 W Olympic Blvd Los Angeles CA 90064-1625

NEWMAN, EDGAR LEON, historian, educator; b. New Orleans, Jan. 21, 1939; s. Isidore and Anna (Pfeifer) N.; children: Jonathan, Suzanne; m. Linda Loeb Clark, Apr. 21, 1989. BA, Yale U., 1962; PhD, U. Chgo., 1969. Asst. prof. N.Mex. State U., Las Cruces, 1969-75, assoc. prof. history, 1975—; lectr. U. Peking, 1985. Fulbright fellow, 1965-66; Am. Philos. Soc. fellow, 1971; Nat. Endowment for Humanities fellow, 1975-76. Mem. Western Soc. for French History (pres. 1977-78, governing coun. 1990-92, 96—), Societe d'histoire de la Revolution de 1848 (comite directeur), Soc. Scis. History Assn., French Hist. Studies Assn., Am. Hist. Assn. (annotator for France bibliographical survey 1815-52). Editor: Historical Dictionary of France from the 1815 Restoration to the Second Empire; author: (with others) Dictionnaire de Biographique; contbr. Dictionnaire de Biographie Française, Dictionnaire du Movement Ouvrier Français. Office: NMex State U PO Box 3H Las Cruces NM 88004-0003

NEWMAN, EDWARD HENRY, judge, lawyer; b. Providence, Nov. 21, 1947; m. Dinae J. Newman. BA, Providence Coll., 1969; JD, Suffolk Coll., Boston, 1972. Vis. lectr. Providence Coll., 1975-85; probate judge Richmond, R.I., 1988—; town solicitor, Richmond, 1975-81. Chmn. Richmond Dem. Town Com., 1984-86; bd. dirs. Olean Ctr., Westerly, R.I., 1983-87; treas. Woodriver Health Ctr., Hopkinton, R.I., 1984-93. Mem. R.I. Trial Lawyers (v.p. 1980-84), Washington County Bar (pres. 1991—). Office: 42 Granite St Westerly RI 02891-2250

NEWMAN, EDWIN HAROLD, news commentator; b. N.Y.C., Jan. 25, 1919; s. Myron and Rose (Parker) N.; m. Rigel Grell, Aug. 14, 1944; 1 child, Nancy (Mrs. Henry Drucker). BA, U. Wis., 1940; postgrad. (fellow), La. State U., 1940. With Washington bur. Internat. News Svc., 1941, U.P., 1941-42, 45-46, N.Y. Daily PM, 1946-47; ind. Washington news bur., 1947; asst to Eric Sevareid at Washington bur. CBS, 1947-49; freelance writer, broadcaster London, 1949-52; with European Recovery Program, 1951-52, NBC, 1952—; chief news bur. NBC, London, 1956-57, Rome, 1957-58, Paris, 1958-61; news commentator NBC, N.Y.C., 1961-83; columnist King Features Syndicate, 1984-89; moderator 1st Ford-Carter Debate, 1976, 2d Reagan-Mondale debate, 1984; moderator ann. conf. former secs. of state, 1983—, former secs. of def., 1987—. Narrator: TV spls. including Japan: East is West, 1961, Orient Express, 1964, Who Shall Live?, 1965, Pensions-The Broken Promise, 1972, Violence in America, 1977, I Want It All Now, 1978, Spying for Uncle Sam, 1978, Oil and American Power, 1979, The Billionaire Hunts, 1981, Congress: We the People, 1983-84, On Television, 1985-86, Freud, 1987, The Borgias, 1988; host Saturday Night Live, 1984; drama critic WNB C-TV, 1965-71 (Emmy awards 1966, 68, 70, 72, 73, 74, 82, Peabody award 1966); author: Strictly Speaking: Will America Be The Death of English?, 1974, A Civil Tongue, 1976, Sunday Punch, 1979, I Must Say, 1988; contbr. articles and revs. to various periodicals, U.S., Can. and Eng.; chmn. usage panel Am. Heritage Dictionary, 1975-80. Served from ensign to lt. USNR, 1942-45. Decorated chevalier Legion of Honor France; recipient awards Overseas Press Club, 1961, awards U. Wis. Sch. Journalism, 1967, awards U. Mo. Sch. Journalism, 1975. Mem. AFTRA, Authors Guild, Screen Actors Guild. Address: care Richard Fulton Inc 66 Richfield St Plainview NY 11803-1441

NEWMAN, ELIAS, artist; b. Staszow, Poland, Feb. 12, 1903; came to U.S., 1913, naturalized, 1928; s. Simon and Rebecca (Becker) N.; m. Lillian Judith Tesser, Feb. 26, 1945 (dec. June 1990). Student, N.A.D., 1919-20, Edn. Alliance Art Sch., 1920-25, Academie du Chaumiere, Paris, 1929. Art instr. Ednl. Alliance Art Sch., 1946-48; instr. painting YMHA 92nd St. Art Sch., 1949-51, Elias Newman Sch. of Art, Rockport, Mass., 1951-64; art dir. Palestine Pavilion, N.Y. World's Fair, 1939-40; cons. Internat. Exposition, Cleve., 1941; chmn. Conf. Am. Artists, 1971-75; exec. officer Artists Welfare Fund, Inc., 1975-88, prse. emeritus, 1988—; lectr. art of Israel, trends in Am. art; consul for cultural affairs in the U.S. for the State of Israel, 1996. Editor: Improvisations, 1950, 51, 52, Artists' Equity, N.Y.; author: Art in Palestine, 1939; one-man shows, 1927—, including Salon Henri Brendle, Zurich, Switzerland, 1929, High Mus. Art, Atlanta, 1928, Yorke Gallery, Washington, 1929, Balt. Mus. Art, 1928, 30, 34, 41, The Art Ctr., N.Y.C., 1931, Montross Gallery, N.Y.C., 1932, Sears Roebuck & Co. Art Gallery, Washington, 1932, Md. Art Inst., Balt., 1932, 35, 36, Maxwell Galleries, San Francisco, 1945, Modernage Art Gallery, N.Y., 1945, Phila. Art Alliance, 1946, Jewish Mus., N.Y.C., 1949, Babcock Galleries, N.Y.C., 1947, 49, 51, 53, 60, Tel Aviv Mus., (Israel), 1934, 38, 49, 62, Werbe Galleries, Detroit, 1956, Doll & Richards Galleries, Boston, 1947, 50, 60, Rubin Mus. Found., Tel viv, Israel, 1986; participated juried exhbns. including Ohel Group of Modern Artists, Tel Aviv, 1927, The Group of Palestinian Artists, Tel Aviv, 1930, N.A.D., Am. Acad. Arts and Letters, Am. Watercolor Soc., Nat. Soc. Painters in Casein and Acrylics, Audubon Artists, Rockport Art Assn., Am. Soc. Contemporary Artists, Butler Mus. Art, Youngstown, Ohio, The Currier Gallery of Art, Manchester, N.H., Cape Ann Soc. Modern Artists; works in permanent collections Nat. Mus. Am. Art of Smithsonian Instn., Washington, Jewish Mus., N.Y.C., San Francisco Mus. of Art, Balt. Art Mus., John Herron Mus. Art, Indpls., Denver Mus. Art, Tel Aviv Mus. (Israel), Bklyn. Mus. Art, Haifa Mus. Modern Art, Israel, Histadruth House, Tel Aviv, Butler Mus. Am. Art, Youngstown, Ohio, Boston Mus. Fine Arts, Nebr. U. Gallery, Inst. Man and Sci., Rensselaerville, N.Y., Brandeis U., Hillel House, Boston U., Jasper Rand Art Mus., Westfield, Mass., Joslyn Mus., Omaha, Addison Gallery Am. Art, Andover, Mass., George Washington Carver Mus., Tuskegee, Ala., Arnot Art Mus., Elmira, N.Y., Everson Mus. Art, Syracuse, N.Y., Ga. Art Mus., Athens, Slater Meml. Mus., Norwich, Conn., Norfolk (Va.) Mus. Arts and Scis., Phoenix Mus. Art, Met. Ins. Co., Newark, DeCordova Mus., Lexington, Mass., Tel Aviv Municipality, Israel, Mishkan Le'omanut Mus. Art, Ein Harod, Israel, others. Served with C.A.C. AUS, 1942-43. Recipient Minnie R. Stern Meml. medal and prize Audubon Artists 18th Ann. Exhibit, N.Y., 1960, Pauline Mintz Meml. award 28th Ann. Exhibit, 1970, Stanley Grumbacher Meml. medal and prize 35th Ann. Exhibit, 1977, Elaine and James Hewitt award, 1988, awards Nat. Soc. Painters in Casein and Acrylics, Joseph Meyer Co. prize, 1966, Gramercy prize, 1968, M.J. Kaplan Meml. prize, 1970, Today's Art mag. medal merit, 1971, Shiva award for casein painting, 1980, 91, The Elizabeth Erlanger Meml. award, 1992, Beatrice S. Katz prize Am. Soc. Contemporary Artists, 1971, Morrilla Co. award, 1981, Grumbacher art award, 1983, Philip Reisman Meml. award, 1994, Municipality Tel-Aviv-Jaffo, Israel medal, 1987, Pres.'s Spl. citation of merit 47th Ann. Exhibit, 1989, Audubon Artists, Cert. Achievement for cultural contbn. and the outstanding accomplishments in the field of art award of lifetime achievement, Rubin Mus., Tel Aviv. Mem. Palestine Artists and Sculptors Assn. (organizer 1935), Am. Artists for Israel (chmn. 1949), Cape Ann Soc. Modern Artists (pres. 1958-59), Am. Soc. Contemporary Artists (bd. dir. 1970, 87), Artists Equity Assn. (nat. sec. 1954, exec. dir. 1959-60, pres. N.Y. chpt. 1960-62, v.p. 1963-64, 67, 68), N.Y. Artists Equity Assn. (pres. 1970-75, pres. emeritus 1975—), Audubon Artists (bd. dir. 1971-74, treas. 1976-77, bd. dir. 1977-78, v.p. 1978-82), Nat. Soc. Painters in Casein and Acrylics (bd. dir. 1963, chmn. ways and means com. 1966, pres. 1967-71, hon. pres. 1971—), Am. Jewish League for Israel. Club: Overseas Press. Home: 215 Park Row New York NY 10038-1149 *I have tried in the course of my life in art to be guided by the following concepts: Art is a continuum that expresses the time in which we live. I am involved with the phenomenon of nature, the changing scene and the life around me. I believe that each painting should be the result of an experience deeply felt. I try to absorb influences, refine them and recreate them in my own image. I believe great works of art always have affinity with humanity, nature, and the soul of mankind.*

NEWMAN, ERIC PFEIFFER, retail chain store executive; b. St. Louis, May 25, 1911; s. Samuel Elijah and Rose (Pfeiffer) N.; m. Evelyn Edison, Nov. 29, 1939; children: Linda Newman Schapiro, Andrew Edison. B.S., Mass. Inst. Tech., 1932; J.D., Washington U., St. Louis, 1935; D.H.L. (hon.), U. Mo., 1980. Bar: Mo. 1935. Practice in St. Louis, 1935-43; with Edison Bros. Stores, Inc., St. Louis, 1944, sec., 1951-87, v.p., 1964-68, exec. v.p., 1968-87, retired, now bd. dirs. Author: Coinage for Colonial Virginia, 1957, The Secret of the Good Samaritan Shilling, 1959, The Fantastic 1804 Dollar, 1962, The Early Paper Money of America, 1967, rev. edit., 1976, 90; editor: Studies on Money in Early America, 1976. Pres. Community Sch., 1952-53, Mark Twain Summer Inst., 1963-67; treas. Jefferson Nat. Expansion Meml. Assn., 1970-77; chmn. U.S. Assay Commn., 1967; chmn. coins and medals panel Am. Revolution Bicentennial Commn., 1972-74; trustee Harry Edison Found., 1959—, pres., 1988—; pres. Eric P. Newman Numis. Edn. Soc. (operator Mercantile Money Mus., St. Louis), 1959—. Recipient Farran Zerbe award, 1969, Archer M. Huntington medal, 1978, Royal Numismatic Soc. medal, 1991. Mem. Am. Numis. Soc. (council (dir.) 1963—), Am. Numism. Assn. (16 Heath Lit. awards), Am. Antiquarian Soc. Club: Explorers. Home: 6450 Cecil Ave Saint Louis MO 63105-2225 Office: 501 N Broadway Saint Louis MO 63102-2102

NEWMAN, FRANK NEIL, bank executive; b. Quincy, Mass., Apr. 20, 1942; m. Lizabeth Newman. B.A. in Econs. magna cum laude, Harvard U., 1963. Exec. v.p., CFO Wells Fargo & Co. and Wells Fargo Bank, San Francisco, 1980-86; CFO, vice-chmn. bd. dirs. Bank Am. Corp, Bank of Am., San Francisco, 1986-93; under sec. domestic fin. Dept. Treasury, Washington, 1993-94, dep. sec., 1994-95; sr. v.p. Bankers Trust, 1995, pres., 1995—, CEO, chmn., 1996—. Office: Bankers Trust 130 Liberty St New York NY 10006*

NEWMAN, FREDRIC SAMUEL, lawyer, business executive; b. York, Pa., June 22, 1945; s. Nat. Howard and Josephine (Farkas) N.; m. Mary E. Kiley, May 19, 1973; children: Lydia Ann, Anne Marie, Pauline. AB cum laude, Harvard U., 1967; JD, Columbia U., 1970; cert. the exec. program, U. Va., 1984. Bar: N.Y. 1971, U.S. Dist. Ct. (so. and ea. dists.) N.Y. 1972, U.S. Ct. Appeals (2d cir.) 1974, U.S. Ct. Claims 1993. Assoc. White & Case, N.Y.C., 1970-80; asst. gen. counsel Philip Morris Cos., N.Y.C., 1981-87; gen. counsel, v.p., sec. Philip Morris, Inc., N.Y.C., 1987-90; chief exec. officer TeamTennis, Inc., 1991; prin. Law Office of Fredric S. Newman, N.Y.C., 1992-95; founding ptnr. Hoguet Newman & Regal, LLP, 1996—; pres., CEO, Pathe Comm. Corp., N.Y.C., 1993—; bd. dirs. Exel Ins. Co., Bermuda. Trustee Calhoun Sch., N.Y.C., 1985-88; bd. dirs. N.Y. Fire Safety Found., N.Y.C., 1985-88. Fellow Am. Bar Found. Office: 10 E 40th St New York NY 10016-0200

NEWMAN, GARY, lawyer; b. Paterson, N.J., June 13, 1948; s. Arthur Oscar and Helen (Bloom) N.; m. Gara, Dec. 6, 1986; 1 child, Griffin Hayes. BA in Polit. Sci., Syracuse U., 1969; JD, Am. U., 1972. Bar: N.J. 1972, Fla. 1975, N.Y. 1980. Law sec. Judge Edward F. Broderick, Morristown, N.J., 1972-73; asst. prosecutor Hudson County Prosecutors Office, Jersey City, N.J., 1973-76; assoc. Skoloff & Wolfe, Livingston, N.J., 1976-78; ptnr. Newman & Carey, East Orange, N.J., 1978-85, La Bue Farber Newman, West Orange, N.J., 1985-87; atty. pvt. practice, Roseland, N.J., 1987—; dir. N.Y. Susquehanna & W. Rlwy., Rodgefield Park, N.J., 1980—. Mem. exec. com. Martini for Congress, Cedar Grove, N.J., 1994. Fellow Am. Acad. Matrimonial Lawyers; mem. Nat. Assn. R.R. Trial Counsel, N.J. State Bar Assn. (mem. exec. com. family law sect. 1988-90), Essex County Bar Assn. (mem. exec. com. family law sect. 1988-91). Jewish.

NEWMAN, GERALDINE ANNE, advertising executive; b. Boston, Apr. 1; d. Joseph M. and Clara (Bistry) N. BS, UCLA; postgrad., Alliance Francaise, Paris, Los Angeles Sch. Fine Arts, NYU. Writer Tinker Dodge and Delano, N.Y.C., 1970-72, Ketchum Advt., N.Y.C., 1972-75, Advt. to Women, N.Y.C., 1975-78; v.p., creative supr. Young and Rubicam, N.Y.C., 1978-83; v.p., assoc. creative dir. Backer Spielvogel Bates Worldwide Internat. Div., N.Y.C., 1983-90; pres. Geraldine Newman Comm., Inc., N.Y.C., 1990—. County committeewoman Dem. Party, N.Y.C., 1972; advt. adviser Youth at Risk, Breakthrough Found., Food Bank, Food for All, Gifts that Give Back. Featured in Adweek mag., 1986; winner Andy award 1975, 78, 82, 84, Clio award 1982, numerous others. Mem. Ad-net (bd. dirs. 1984-89, creative dir. 1986-89, Pres.'s award 1988). Avocations: painting, travel. Home and Office: 315 E 72nd St New York NY 10021-4625

NEWMAN, HARRY RUDOLPH, urologist, educator; b. Russia, Sept. 10, 1909; naturalized, 1919, came to U.S., 1935, naturalized, 1944; s. Abraham and Mary (Rudolph) N.; m. Lillian Lear, Aug. 18, 1942; children: Nancy Ellen, Robert Lear, Suzanne Mary. M.D., U. Toronto, 1935; M.S., U. Pa., 1940. Diplomate: Am. Bd. Urology. Resident urology U. Minn. Hosps., 1936-37, All Saints Hosp., London, Eng., 1937-38; sr. resident urology N.Y. Postgrad. Med. Sch. and Hosp., 1939-40, Boston Long Island Hosp., 1941-42; resident surgery N.Y. Postgrad. Hosp., 1942; resident gen. surgery Prince of Wales Hosp., Plymouth, Eng.; asst. clin. prof. urology N.Y. Postgrad. Med. Sch. & Hosp., 1946-54; sr. attending urologist Bellevue Hosp., N.Y.C., 1946-54; attending urologist Yale New-Haven Hosp.; attending univ. service Yale U., asst. clin. prof. urology, 1949—; dir. urology Albert Einstein Coll. Medicine, also clin. prof. surgery, chief urology, 1957—, clin. prof. urology, 1957-62, prof. urology, 1963-65, 66-80, emeritus chmn. and prof. urology, 1980—, chmn. dept., 1966-80; prof. history; chief urology Bronx Mcpl. Hosp., 1966—; chief urology community div. Grace New Haven Hosp., 1965-66; cons. urologist Stamford (Conn.) Hosp., St. Joseph Hosp., Stamford, 1965—; former asst. clin. prof. urology NYU; dir. urology City N.Y. Bronx Mcpl. Med. Center, 1954-65; chief urology Regional Hosp., Hunter Field, Savannah, Ga. Served from capt. to maj. USAAF, 1942-46. Fellow ACS, N.Y. Acad. Medicine, Royal So. of Health (Great Britian); mem. Soc. Univ. Urologists, Masons (32 deg.), Shriners, Yale Club (N.Y.), Sigma Xi. Clubs: Masons (New Haven) (32 deg.), Shriners (New Haven), Yale (New Haven); Woodbridge (Conn.) Country. Home: 95 Broadfield Rd Hamden CT 06517-1543 Office: 2 Church St S New Haven CT 06519-1717

NEWMAN, HOWARD NEAL, law educator, lawyer; b. N.Y.C., June 11, 1935; s. Herman and Sarah (Steinsaltz) N.; m. Carol Redstone, Dec. 25, 1960; children: Leslie, Amy. A.B., Dartmouth Coll., 1956, M.B.A., 1957; M.S., Columbia U., 1959; J.D., Temple U., 1970. Trainee to asst. v.p. Roosevelt Hosp., N.Y.C., 1957-65; assoc. adminstr. Pa. Hosp., Phila., 1965-70; commr. Med. Services Adminstrn., Washington, 1970-74; pres. Dartmouth-Hitchcock Med. Center, Hanover, N.H., 1974-80; adminstr. Health Care Financing Adminstr., Dept. Health and Human Services, Washington, 1980-81; ptnr. Memel, Jacobs, Pierno & Gersh, Washington, 1982-86, Powell, Goldstein, Frazer & Murphy, Washington, 1986-88; deam, prof. health policy and mgmt. NYU, 1988-94, prof. health policy and mgmt., 1994—. Served with USAR, 1959. White House fellow, 1967-68. Mem. Nat. Inst. for Dispute Resolution, D.C. Bar Assn. Jewish. Office: 4 Washington Square N New York NY 10003-6635

NEWMAN, JAMES WILSON, business executive; b. Clemson, S.C., Nov. 3, 1909; s. Charles Carter and Grace (Strode) N.; m. Clara Collier, July 1934; children: Clare Adelaide, Mildred Bledsoe, James Wilson, Charles Carter II. B.S., Clemson U., 1931, also LL.D. (hon.); student, Am. Inst. Banking, 1931-32; J.D., N.Y. U., 1937. Bar: N.Y. bar 1937. Reporter R.G. Dun & Co., 1931-46; v.p. Dun & Bradstreet, Inc., 1946-52, pres., chief exec. officer, 1952-60, chmn., chief exec. officer, 1960-68, chmn. finance com., 1968-80, dir., to 1980; adv. bd. Chem. Bank, Gen. Foods Corp., 1963-81, Internat. Paper Co., until 1982; trustee Atlantic Mut. Ins. Co., Mut. Life Ins. Co. Am., until 1982; chmn. spl. rev. com. Lockheed Corp., 1976-78. Chmn. Pres.'s Task Force on Small Bus., 1969; mem. Commn. on Bankruptcy Laws U.S., 1970-73; chmn. Nat. Bur. Econ. Rsch., 1974-78; trustee Com. Econ. Devel., Va. Mus. Fine Arts, 1978-94; mem. coun. Miller Ctr. Pub. Affairs, U. Va., 1983-94; mem. Price Commn., 1971-72; chmn. Sweet Briar Coll., 1963-69. Mem. ABA, Ocean Club (Fla.), Farmington Country Club (Va.), Commonwealth Club (Richmond, Va.), Army and Navy Club (Washington), Phi Delta Phi. Home: 4 Apple Tree Ln Charlottesville VA 22901-1903 Office: 503 Falconer Dr Madison Park Suite 4A Charlottesville VA 22903

NEWMAN, JANE, advertising agency executive; b. Woking, Surrey, Eng., Oct. 22, 1947; came to U.S., 1978; d. Ronald William and Victoria (Brady) N.; 1 child. BA, Sussex U., Eng., 1969; MA, Lancaster U., Eng., 1970. Account planner Boase Massimi & Pollitt, London, 1970-78; account mgr. Needham Harper & Steers, Chgo., 1978-79, Ammirati & Puris, N.Y.C., 1979-81; vice chmn. Chiat/Day Advt., N.Y.C., 1981-93; ptnr. Merkley Newman Harty Advt. Agy., N.Y.C., 1993—. Avocation: gardening. Office: Merkley Newman Harty 12th Fl 200 Varick St New York NY 10014-4810

NEWMAN, JOAN MESKIEL, lawyer; b. Youngstown, Ohio, Dec. 12, 1947; d. John F. and Rosemary (Scarmuzzi) Meskiel; m. Charles Andrew Newman, Aug. 8, 1971; children: Anne R., Elyse S. BA in Polit. Sci., Case-Western Reserve U., 1969; JD, Washington U., St. Louis, 1972, LLM in Taxation, 1973. Bar: Mo. 1972. Assoc. Lewis & Rice, St. Louis, 1973-80, ptnr., 1981-90; ptnr. Thompson Coburn, St. Louis, 1990—; adj. prof. law Washington U. Sch. Law, St. Louis, 1975-92; past pres., mem. Midwest Pension Conf., St. Louis chpt.; lectr. in field. chmn. bd. dirs. Great St. Louis coun. Girl Scouts U.S., 1988-92, officer, 1978-92; mem. bd. dirs. and exec. com. Girl Scouts U.S., 1993—; chmn. bd. dirs. Met. Employment and Rehab. Svcs., 1994—; bd. dirs. Jewish Fedn. St. Louis, 1991—, Jewish Ctr. Aged, 1990-92; chmn. bd. dirs. Women of Achievement, 1993-96; mem. cmty. wide youth svcs. panel United Way Greater St. Louis, 1992-96; fin. futures task force Kiwanis Camp Wyman, 1992-93; mem. nat. coun. Washington U. Sch. Law, 1988-91; chmn. staff blue ribbon fin. com. Sch. Dist. Clayton, 1986-87; vol. Women's Self Help Ctr. Named Woman of Achievement St. Louis, 1991. Mem. Mo. Bar Assn. (staff pension and benefits com. 1991—), Bar Met. St. Louis (past chmn. taxation sect.), St. Louis Forum, Order of Coif (hon.). Office: Thompson Coburn 1 Mercantile Ctr Ste 3300 Saint Louis MO 63101-1643

NEWMAN, JOHN KEVIN, classics educator; b. Bradford, Yorkshire, Eng., Aug. 17, 1928; came to U.S., 1969, naturalized, 1984; s. Willie and Agnes (Shee) N.; m. Frances M. Stickney, Sept. 8, 1970; children: Alexandra, John, Victoria. B.A. in Lit.-Humaniores, Exeter Coll., Oxford U., 1950, B.A. in Russian, 1952, M.A., 1953; Ph.D., Bristol U., 1967. Classics master St. Francis Xavier Coll., Liverpool, Eng., 1952-54, Downside Sch., Somerset, Eng., 1955-69; mem. faculty U. Ill., Urbana, 1969—, prof. classics, 1980—, chmn. dept., 1981-85. Author: Augustus and the New Poetry, 1967, Latin Compositions, 1976, Pindar's Art, 1984, The Classical Epic Tradition, 1986, Roman Catullus, 1990, Lelio Guidiccioni, Latin Poems, 1992; co-author: (with A.V. Carozzi) Horace-Benedict de Saussure, 1995; editor: Ill. Classical Studies, 1982-87; contbr. The New Princeton Encyclopedia of Poetry and Poetics, 1993. mem. sr. common room Corpus Christi Coll., Oxford U., 1985-86. Recipient silver medals Vatican, Rome, 1960, 62, 65. Roman Catholic. Home: 703 W Delaware Ave Urbana IL 61801-4806 Office: Dept Classics U Ill 4072 Fgn Lang Bldg 707 S Mathews Ave Urbana IL 61801-3625

NEWMAN, JOHN KEVIN, broadcast journalist; b. Toronto, Ont., Can., June 2, 1959; came to U.S., 1994; s. George Edmund and Sheila Lorraine (Stevenson) N.; m. Catharine Erica Kearns, June 15, 1985; children: John Alexander, Erica Louise. BA, U. Western Ont., 1981. Atlantic bur. chief CTV Nat. News, Halifax, N.S., Can., 1987; parliament reporter CTV Nat. News, Ottawa, Ont., Can., 1987-89, CBC Nat. News, Ottawa, 1990-92; anchor CBC Midday, Toronto, 1992-94, ABC World News This Morning, N.Y.C., 1994-96, Good Morning America-Sunday, N.Y.C., 1996—; corr. ABC World News Tonight, N.Y.C., 1996—; instr. in journalism Ryerson U., Toronto, 1992-94. Avocations: skiing, canoeing, camping. Office: ABC News 47 W 66th St New York NY 07901

NEWMAN, JOHN M., JR., lawyer; b. Youngstown, Ohio, Aug. 15, 1944. BA, Georgetown U., 1966; JD, Harvard U., 1969. BAr: Ill. 1970, Calif. 1972, Ohio 1976. Law clerk ctrl. dist. U.S. Dist. Ct., Calif., 1969-70, asst. U.S. Atty. ctrl. dist., 1970-75; ptnr. Jones, Day, Reavis & Pogue, Cleve. Fellow Am. Coll. Trial Lawyers; mem. Phi Beta Kappa. Office: Jones Day Reavis & Pogue North Point 901 Lakeside Ave E Cleveland OH 44114-1116

NEWMAN, JOHN MERLE, lawyer; b. Cleve., June 25, 1934; s. Emanuel Robert and Theresa Esther (Dreissinger) N.; 1 child, Thomas Edward; m. Thelma Aitken, July 10, 1992; 1 child, Jennifer Ann Newman-Brazil. AB, Miami U., Oxford, Ohio, 1957; LLB, Cornell U., 1957. Bar: N.J. 1971, U.S. Ct. Appeals (3d cir.) 1961, U.S. Dist. Ct. N.J. 1983, U.S. Dist. Ct. (so. and ea. dists.) N.Y. 1983; cert. civil atty. Supreme Ct. of N.J. Assoc. Bertram Polow, Morristown, N.J., 1960-62; ptnr. Porzio Bromberg & Newman P.C., Morristown, 1962-76, 80—; presiding judge chancery/family divsn. Superior Ct. of N.J., Morristown, 1976-80. Trustee, officer Cmty. Med. Ctr., Randolph Libr., Morristown, 1970-74, Hist. Speedwell Mus., Morristown, 1991—, Family Svc., Morristown, 1988-91; trustee Occupational Tng. Ctr., Morristown, 1965-69. Recipient Cert. of Acad. Performance U. Edinburgh, Scotland, 1956, various certs. for bar and cmty. svcs. Mem. ABA (litigation sect., environ. subcom., environ. law sect. corp. counsel subcom., vice chair various coms.), N.J. State Bar Assn., Morris County Bar Assn., Omicron Delta Kappa. Avocations: cycling, tennis. Office: Porzio Bromberg & Newman 163 Madison Ave Morristown NJ 07960

NEWMAN, JOHN NICHOLAS, naval architect educator; b. New Haven, Mar. 10, 1935; s. Richard and Daisy (Neumann) N.; m. Kathleen Smedley Kirk, June 16, 1956; children—James Bartram, Nancy Kirk, Carol Ann. B.S. Mass. Inst. Tech, 1956, M.S., 1957, Sc.D., 1960; postgrad., Cambridge (Eng.) U., 1958-59; D Technicae honoris causa, U. Trondheim, Norway, 1992. Research naval architect David Taylor Model Basin, Navy Dept., Washington, 1959-67; assoc. prof. naval architecture MIT, Cambridge, 1967-70, prof., 1970—; vis. prof. U. New South Wales, Australia, 1973, U. Adelaide, Australia, 1974, Tech. U. Norway, 1981-82; cons. Navy Dept., Dept. Justice, pvt. firms. Author: Marine Hydrodynamics, 1977; Contbr.: articles to profl. jours., including Sci. Am. Recipient prize Am. Bur. Shipping, 1956; Walter Atkinson prize Royal Instn. Naval Architects, 1973, also Bronze medal, 1976; Guggenheim fellow, 1973-74; research grantee Office Naval Research: NSF. Mem. AAAS, NAE, Soc. Naval Architects and Marine Engrs. (Davidson medal 1988), Norwegian Acad. Sci. Home: 60 Campbell Rd Wayland MA 01778-1024 Office: MIT Dept Naval Architecture Cambridge MA 02139

NEWMAN, JOHN SCOTT, chemical engineer, educator; b. Richmond, Va., Nov. 17, 1938; s. Clarence William and Marjorie Lenore (Saucerman) N.; m. Nguyen Thanh Lan, June 30, 1973; children—Natalie Diane, Michael Alexander. B.S., Northwestern U., 1960; M.S., U. Calif., Berkeley, 1962, Ph.D., 1963. Asst. prof. chem. engring. U. Calif., Berkeley, 1963-67, assoc. prof., 1967-70; prof. U. Calif., 1970—; prin. investigator energy & environ. divsn. Lawrence Berkeley Nat. Lab., 1963—; vis. prof. U. Wis., Madison, 1973; summer participant Oak Ridge Nat. Lab., 1965, 66. Author: Electrochemical Systems, 1973, rev. edit. 1991; assoc. editor Jour. Electrochem. Soc., 1990—; contbr. articles to profl. jours. Fellow Electrochem. Soc. (Young Author's prize 1966, 69, David C. Grahame award 1985, Henry B. Linford award 1990, Olin Palladium medal 1991); mem. Am. Inst. Chem. Engrs. Home: 114 York Ave Kensington CA 94708-1045 Office: U Calif Dept Chem Engring Berkeley CA 94720-1462

NEWMAN, JON O., federal judge; b. N.Y.C., N.Y., May 2, 1932; s. Harold W. Jr. and Estelle L. (Ormond) N.; m. Martha G. Silberman, June 19, 1953; children: Leigh, Scott, David. Postgrad., Hotchkiss Sch., 1949; AB magna cum laude, Princeton U., 1953; LLB, Yale U., 1956; LLD (hon.), U. Hartford, 1975, U. Bridgeport, 1980. Bar: Conn. 1956, D.C. 1956. Law clk. to Hon. George T. Washington U.S. Ct. Appeals, 1956-57; sr. law clk. to chief justice Hon. Earl Warren, U.S. Supreme Ct., 1957-58; ptnr. Ritter, Satter & Newman, Hartford, Conn., 1958-60; counsel to majority Conn. Gen. Assembly, 1959; spl. counsel to gov. Conn., 1959-61; asst. to sec. HEW, 1961-62; adminstrv. asst. to U.S. senator, 1963-64; U.S. atty. Dist. of Conn., 1964-69; pvt. practice law, 1969-71; U.S. dist. judge Dist. of Conn., 1972-79; U.S. cir. judge 2d Cir. Ct. of Appeals, 1979-93, chief judge, 1993—. Co-author: Politics: The American Way. With USAR, 1954-62. Recipient Learned Hand medal Fed. Bar Coun., 1987. Fellow Am. Bar Found.; mem. ABA, Am. Law Inst., Conn. Bar Assn., Am. Judicature Soc. Democrat. Office: US Ct Appeals 450 Main St Hartford CT 06103-3002

NEWMAN, JOSEPH HERZL, advertising executive; b. N.Y.C., Dec. 1, 1928; s. Max A. and Tillie C. (Weitzman) N.; m. Ruth Z. Marcus, Dec. 19, 1954 (div. Feb. 1987); children: Deborah Lynn, David Alan, Mark Jonathan; m. Nancy K. Deutschman, Aug. 19, 1990; stepchildren: Pamela Sue Deutschman, Douglas Hayes Deutschman, Cindi Elaine Deutschman. AB, Bethany Coll., W.Va., 1949; MS, Columbia U., 1956. With 20th Century Fox Film Corp., N.Y.C., 1949-53; media supr. Fred Wittner Advt. Agy. (now Hammond Farrell Inc.), N.Y.C., 1953-56; media dir. O.S. Tyson & Co. (now Poppe Tyson, Inc.), N.Y.C., 1956-64; v.p., media dir. Marsteller Inc. (now Lord, Dentsu and Ptnrs.), N.Y.C., 1965-85; v.p., assoc. media dir. HBM/Creamer, N.Y.C., 1985-87, Della Femina, McNamee, Inc., N.Y.C., 1987-89; pres. Newman and Assocs., Cleve., 1989—; mem. faculty Advt. Age Media Workshop, 1972; past chmn. media mgrs. adv. com. Bus. Publs. Audit of Circulation Inc., N.Y.C.; conducted profl. media planning seminars, 1989—. Contbr. articles to profl. jours. Past chmn. bus.-to-bus. media com. Am. Assn. Advt. Agys.; mem. tax incentive rev. coun. City of Mayfield Heights, Ohio, 1994—. With U.S. Army, 1950-52. Mem. Bus. Mktg. Assn. (mem. media comparability coun., media data form com. and rsch. resource com., Agy. Exec. of Yr., N.Y. chpt. 1960, 66, 71, 73). Home and Office: 6338 Woodhawk Dr Cleveland OH 44124-4153

NEWMAN, JOYCE KLIGERMAN, sculptor; b. Atlantic City, July 7, 1927; d. Louis and Anne (Levine) Kligerman; m. Melvin Micklin Newman, Sept. 11, 1949; children—Rebecca, Morris Henry. B.A., Cornell U., 1948; Ph.D. in Biochemistry, U. Chgo., 1955; student, Art Students League, N.Y.C., 1962. Research asso. biochemistry U. Colo. Med. Center, Denver, 1963-70; mem. faculty dept. chemistry Met. State Coll., 1976-77. Profl. sculptor, Denver, 1968-84, Pasadena, Calif., 1984—, sculpture installed, Douglas County (Colo.) Pub. Library, 1971; commd. public sculpture, City of Littleton (Colo.), 1979, U. No Colo., Greeley, 1981, City of Chandler, Ariz., 1986; Contbr. numerous articles on biochemistry, also artists' rights to profl. jours. Mem. Artists Equity Assn. (pres. Colo. chpt. 1970-72, nat. pres. 1973-75), U. Chgo. Alumni Assn. (bd. govs. 1995-97, pres. Denver club 1967-84, bd. dirs. L.A. club 1985—, v.p. 1987-91, pres. 1992-94). Address: 1750 E Mountain St Pasadena CA 91104-3937

NEWMAN, JULLIANA, marketing executive; b. Huntington, N.Y., June 5, 1957; d. Coleman and Lillian (Saboe) Newell; m. John Sherfy Newman, Nov. 7, 1988; children: Ana, Anders, Hayley. AA, Suffolk County Community, Selden, N.Y., 1978; BA, Queens (N.Y.) Coll., 1980; postgrad., CUNY, 1980-82. Prodn. editor Plenum Press, N.Y.C., 1982-83; mng. editor LeJacq Pub., N.Y.C., 1984-86; mng. editor/project dir. Audio Visual Med. Mktg., N.Y.C., 1986-88; editorial dir. Haymarket Doyma, N.Y.C., 1988-90; dir. healthcare communication Macmillan Healthcare Info., Florham Park, N.J., 1990-91; communications specialist PCS, Inc., Scottsdale, Ariz., 1991-93; v.p. mktg. ValueRx, Albuquerque, 1993—; founder Jour. of Outcomes Mgmt., 1994; developer software Pro Tracker; editorial dir. Diagnostek Report, 1993—, PRN: Information As Needed, 1993—; cons. Nat. Asthma Edn. Program, Bethesda, Med., 1991, Asthma and Allergy Found., Washignton, 1991, Pres.'s Coun. on Phys. Fitness and Sports, Washington, 1991. Cert. editor of Life Scis. Vol. Pres.'s Coun. on Phys. Fitness and Sports, Washington, 1991—. Ednl. grantee Connaught Labs., 1991, Allen & Hanburys, Research Triangle Park, N.C., 1991, 92. Mem. Coun. of Biology Editors, Am. Med. Writers Assn., NAFE, Am. Heart Assn., Arthritis Found., Nat. Council on Prescription Drug Programs. Democrat. Lutheran. Avocations: traveling, creative writing, gourmet cooking. Office: Diagnostek Inc 4500 Alexander Blvd NE Albuquerque NM 87107-6805

NEWMAN, LAWRENCE WALKER, lawyer; b. Boston, July 1, 1935; s. Leon Bettoney and Hazel W. (Walker) N.; m. Cecilia Isette Santos, Nov. 29, 1975; children: Reynaldo W., Timothy D., Virginia I.S., Isabel B., Thomas H. A.B., Harvard U., 1957, LL.B., 1960. Bar: D.C. 1961, N.Y. 1965. Atty. U.S. Dept. Justice, 1960-61, Spl. Study of Securities Markets and Office Spl. Counsel on Investment Co. Act Matters, U.S. SEC, 1961-64; asst. U.S. atty. So. Dist. N.Y., 1964-69; assoc. Baker & McKenzie, N.Y.C., 1969-71, ptnr., 1971—; mem. internat. adv. coun. World Arbitration Inst., 1984-87; mem. adv. com. Asia Pacific Ctr. for Resolution of Internat. Trade Disputes, 1987—; mem. adv. bd. Inst. for Transnational Arbitration, 1988—; chmn. U.S. Iranian Claimants Com., 1982—; mem. adv. bd. World Arbitration and Mediation Report, 1993—; mem. bd. adv. to Corporate Counselor Internat. Adviser, 1995—. Co-author: The Practice of Internat. Litigation, 1992, 93, Litigating Internat. Commercial Disputes, 1996; columnist N.Y. Law Jour., 1982—; adv. bd. World Arbitration and Mediation Report; contbr. articles to profl. jours. and books on litigation and internat. arbitration. Mem. ABA (internat. litigation com., internat. arbitration com.), Internat. Bar Assn. (com. dispute resolution, com. constrn. litigation), Inter-Am. Bar Assn., Fed. Bar Coun., Am. Fgn. Law Assn., Maritime Law Assn. U.S., Assn. Bar City N.Y. (com. on arbitration & alternative dispute resolution 1991-94), Am. Arbitration Assn. (corp. counsel com. 1987—, panel comml. arbitrators), U.S. Coun. Internat. Bus., Ct. Arbitration of Polish Chamber Fgn. Trade (panel of arbitrators), Brit. Col. Internat. Comml. Abitration Ctr. Home: 1001 Park Ave New York NY 10028-0935 Office: Baker & McKenzie 805 3rd Ave New York NY 10022-7513

NEWMAN, LAWRENCE WILLIAM, financial executive; b. Chgo., Jan. 14, 1939; s. Eskil William and Adele Diane (Lawnicki) N.; m. Christine Harriet Jaronski, Sept. 22, 1962; children: Paul, Scott, Ron. BBS, U. Ill., 1965; MBA, Northwestern U., 1970. CPA, Ill. Controller ECM Corp., Schaumburg, Ill., 1966-70; controller Nachman Corp., Des Plaines, Ill., 1970-76, v.p., treas., controller, 1976-79; v.p. fin. P & S Mgmt. Inc., Schiller Park, Ill., 1979-83; controller Underwriters Labs., Northbrook, Ill., 1983-85, asst. treas., 1985-89; v.p., treas. Underwriters Labs., 1990—. Mem. Fin. Execs. Inst., Am. Inst. CPA's. Club: Exec. of Chgo. Office: Underwriters Labs 333 Pfingsten Rd Northbrook IL 60062-2002

NEWMAN, MALCOLM, civil engineering consultant; b. N.Y.C., June 29, 1931; s. George and Evelyn (Weber) N.; m. Estelle Ruth Glotzer, June 11, 1955; children: Roberta Gail, Leonard Scott, Alisa Gwen. BSCE, CCNY, 1952; MS in Civil Engring., Columbia U., 1957; D in Engring. Sci., NYU, 1962. Registered profl. engr., N.Y. Chief structural mechanics Republic-Fairchild Hiller Corp., Farmingdale, N.Y., 1962-65, staff cons., 1970-71; dir. structural mechanics Harry Belock Assocs. Inc., Great Neck, N.Y., 1965-69; dir. structural mechanics and design Analytical Mechanics Assn., Jericho, N.Y., 1969-70; prof. mech. engring. Tel Aviv U., 1972-75; pres., tech. dir. Inter-City Testing and Cons., Mineola, N.Y., 1976—; pres. Athletic Safety Products Inc., Mineola, 1985—. Contbr. over 80 articles to profl. jours.; patentee in field. Bd. dirs. Cinema Arts Ctr., Huntington, N.Y., 1989—. Mem. NSPE, Am. Soc. Safety Engrs., Nat. Assn. Profl. Accident Reconstruction Specialists, Soc. Automotive Engrs., System Safety Soc. (pres. 1983-85). Office: Inter-City Testing & Cons 167 Willis Ave Mineola NY 11501-2621

NEWMAN, MARGARET ANN, nursing educator; b. Memphis, Oct. 10, 1933; d. Ivo Mathias and Mamie Love (Donald) N.; BSHE, Baylor U., 1954; BSN, U. Tenn., Memphis, 1962; MS, U. Calif., San Francisco, 1964; PhD, NYU, 1971. Dir. nursing, asst. prof. nursing Clin. Research Center, U. Tenn., 1964-67; asst. prof. N.Y.U., 1971-75, assoc. prof., 1975-77; prof. in charge grad. program and research dept. nursing Pa. State U., 1977-80, prof. nursing, 1977-84; prof. nursing U. Minn., 1984-96, prof. emeritus 1996—; disting. resident Westminster Coll., Salt Lake City Utah, 1991. Travelling fellow New Zealand Nursing Ednl. & Rsch. Fund, 1985; Am. Jour. Nursing scholar, 1979-80; recipient Outstanding Alumnus award U. Tenn. Coll. Nursing, 1975, Disting. Alumnus award NYU Div. Nursing, 1984; Disting. Scholar in Nursing award NYU Div. Nursing, 1992, Sigma Theta Tau Founders Rsch. award, 1993, Nursing Scholar award St. Xavier U., 1994. Fellow Am. Acad. Nursing. Author: Theory Development in Nursing, 1979, Health as Expanding Consciousness, 1986, 2nd edit., 1994, A Developing Discipline, 1995; editor: (with others) Source Book of Nursing Research, 1973, 2d edit., 1977. Research on patterns of person-environment interaction as indices of health as expanding consciousness; also models of profl. practice. Home: 289 5th St E Saint Paul MN 55101-1995 Office: 6-101 Health Scis 308 Harvard St SE Unit F Minneapolis MN 55455

NEWMAN, MARY THOMAS, communications educator, management consultant; b. Howell, Mo., Oct. 15, 1933; d. Austin Hill and Doris (McQueen) Thomas; m. Grover Travis Newman, Aug. 22, 1952 (div. 1967); 1 child, Leah Newman Lane; m. Rodney Charles Westlund, July 18, 1981. BS, S.F. Austin State U., 1965; MA, U. Houston, 1956; PhD, Pa. State U., 1980. Cert. permanent tchr., Tex. Instr. communications South Tex. Coll., Houston, 1965-70; assoc. prof. communications Burlington County Coll., Pemberton, N.J., 1970-72; teaching asst. in communications Pa. State U., University Park, 1972-73; asst. prof. Ogontz Campus Pa. State U., Abington, 1973-80; lectr. mgmt. and communications U. Md., Europe and Asia, 1980-83; mem. vis. faculty dept. communications U. Tenn., Knoxville, 1984-85; asst. prof. human factors U. So. Calif., L.A., 1985-88; assoc. prof. human factors, dir. profl. devel. U. Denver Coll. Systems Sci., 1988-92; assoc. prof. USC, Berlin, Germany, 1992-93; assoc. prof., assoc. dir. Whitworth Coll., Spokane, Wash., 1993-95; assoc. prof. comms. Houston Baptist U., 1995—; pres. Human Resource Communications Group, Easton, Md., 1984—; lectr. Bus. Rsch. Inst., Toyo U., Tokyo, 1983, Saitama Med. U., Japan, 1983; scholar in residence U.S. Marine Corps., Quantico, Va., 1990-92; mem. final phase faculty USC MSSM Troop Draw Down, Berlin, Germany, 1992-93; team mem. Spokane Inter-Collegiate Rsch. & Tech. Inst., 1993-95; dir. Women's Leadership Conf., Moses Lake, Wash., 1993; mem. world svcs. com. YWCA, Spokane; Lilly fellow 1996. Author: Introduction to Basic Speech Communication, 1969; contbr. articles to profl. jours. Program developer U.S. Army Hdqrs. Sch. Age Latch Key Program, Alexandria, Va., 1987; mem. Govt. of Guam Women's Issues Task Force, 1985. Lilly fellow in humanities and arts, summer 1996. Mem. Human Factors Soc., Speech Communication Assn. (legis. coun. 1970-73, editl. bd. jour. 1970-76), Ea. Communication Assn. (editl. bd. jours. 1975-80), Univ. Film Assn. (publicity dir. 1978-80), Indsl. Comm. Coun., Chesapeake Women's Network, Easton Bus. and Profl. Women, Alpha Chi, Alpha Psi Omega, Pi Kappa Delta, Delta Kappa Gamma. Avocations: military history and women's issues research. Office: Houston Baptist U Dept Comms 7502 Fondren Houston TX 77074

NEWMAN, MICHAEL RODNEY, lawyer; b. N.Y.C., Oct. 2, 1945; s. Morris and Helen Gloria (Hendler) N.; m. Cheryl Jeanne Anker, June 11, 1967; children: Hillary Abra, Nicole Brooke. BA, U. Denver, 1967; JD, U. Chgo., 1970. Bar: Calif. 1971, U.S. Dist. Ct. (cen. dist.) Calif. 1972, U.S. Ct. Appeals (9th cir.) 1974, U.S. Dist. Ct. (no. dist.) Calif. 1975, U.S. Dist. Ct. (so. dist.) Calif. 1979, U.S. Dist. Ct. (ea. dist.) Calif. 1983, U.S. Tax Ct. 1979, U.S. Supreme Ct. 1978. Assoc. David Daar, 1971-76; ptnr. Daar & Newman, 1976-78, Miller & Daar, 1978-88, Miller, Daar & Newman, 1988-89, Daar & Newman, 1989—; judge pro tem L.A. Mcpl. Ct., 1982—, L.A. Superior Ct., 1988—. Lectr. Eastern Claims Conf., Eastern Life Claims Conf., Nat. Health Care Anti-Fraud Assn., AIA Conf. on Ins. Fraud; mem. L.A. Citizens Organizing Com. for Olympic Summer Games, 1984, mem. govtl. liaison adv. commn. 1984; mem. So. Calif. Com. for Olympic Summer Games, 1984; cert. ofcl. Athletics Congress of U.S., co-chmn. legal com. S.P.A-T.A.C, chief finish judge; trustee Massada lodge B'Nai Brith. Recipient NYU Bronze medal in Physics, 1962, TAC Disting. Svc. award, 1988, Maths. award USN Sci., 1963. Mem. ABA (multi-dist. litigation subcom., com. on class actions), L.A. County Bar Assn. (chmn. attys. errors and omissions prevention com.), Conf. of Ins. Counsel, So. Pacific Assn., TAC (bd. dirs.), Porter Valley Country Club. Office: 865 S Figueroa St Ste 2500 Los Angeles CA 90017-2567

NEWMAN, MONROE, retired economist, educator; b. Bklyn., Jan. 31, 1929; s. David A. and Ida Mary (Leight) N.; m. Ruth Zielinski, Feb. 6, 1951. BA, Antioch Coll., 1950; MA, U. Ill., 1953, PhD, 1954. Mem. rsch. staff AFL, 1947-48; examiner NLRB, 1949-50; rsch. analyst U. Ill., 1950-54; research analyst Assn. Casualty and Surety Cos., 1954-55; mem. faculty Pa. State U., University Park, 1955-86; prof. econs. Pa. State U., 1961-86, prof. emeritus, 1986—, head dept., 1958-62, 78-85, chmn. grad. program regional planning, 1971-72, dir. Ctr. for Study of Environ. Policy, 1972-73; vis. rsch. prof. econs. U. Pitts., 1964-65; economist Appalachian Regional Commn., Washington, 1964-65, rsch. dir., 1965-66, spl. cons., 1966-86, sr. econ. advisor, 1986-93. Co-author: Insurance and Risk, 1964, Acid Mine Drainage in Appalachia, 1969, Experiment in Appalachia, 1973; author: Political Economy of Appalachia, 1972, also articles. Mem. So. Regional Sci. Assn. (pres.), Am. Econ. Assn., Regional Sci. Assn. Home: 4101 Cathedral Ave NW Washington DC 20016-3585

NEWMAN, MORRIS, mathematician; b. N.Y.C., Feb. 25, 1924; s. Isaac and Sarah (Cohen) N.; m. Mary Aileen Lenk, Sept. 18, 1948; children: Sally Ann, Carl Lenk. A.B., N.Y.U., 1945; M.A., Columbia U., 1946; Ph.D., U. Pa., 1952. Mathematician applied math div. Nat. Bur. Standards, Washington, 1951-63, chief numerical analysis sect., 1963-70, sr. rsch. mathematician, 1970-76; prof. math. U. Calif., Santa Barbara, 1976-94, prof. emeritus, 1994—; dir. Inst. Interdisciplinary Applications of Algebra and Combinatorics, 1976-80; lectr. U. B.C., 1960, U. Calif.-Santa Barbara, 1965, Am. U., Cath. U., U. Md. Author: Matrix Representations of Groups, 1968, Integral Matrices, 1972; editor: Jour. Research Nat. Bur. Standards, 1966-76, Math. of Computation, 1975-86; assoc. editor: Jour. Linear and Multilinear Algebra, 1973—, Letters in Linear Algebra, 1979—; contbr. articles to profl. jours. Recipient Gold medal U.S. Dept. Commerce, 1966. Mem. Am. Math. Soc. (council 1980-86), London Math. Soc., Math. Assn. Am., Washington Acad. Scis., AAAS, sigma Xi. Home: 1050 Las Alturas Rd Santa Barbara CA 93103-1608 Office: U Calif Dept Math Santa Barbara CA 93106

NEWMAN, MURIEL KALLIS STEINBERG, art collector; b. Chgo., Feb. 25, 1914; d. Maurice and Ida (Nudelman) Kallis; m. Albert H. Newman, May 14, 1955; 1 son by previous marriage, Glenn D. Steinberg. Student, Art Inst. Chgo., 1932-36, Ill. Inst. Tech., 1947-50, U. Chgo., 1958-65. hon. life trustee, benefactor Met. Mus. Art, N.Y.C., mem. vis. com. dept. 20th Century Art, mem. acquisitions com., 1981—, mem. decorative arts com., 1989; also Costume Inst. Dir., 20th Century Painting and Sculpture Com., Art Inst. Chgo., 1955-80, governing mem. inst., 1955—, major benefactor, 1979—; pioneer collector Am. abstract expressionist art, 1949—, major show of collection, Met. Mus. Art, N.Y.C., 1981, also show of personal collection of costumes and jewelry, 1981. Bd. govs. Landmarks Preservation Council, Chgo., 1966-78; mem. woman's bd. U. Chgo., 1960-81, Art Inst. Chgo., 1953—; trustee Mus. Contemporary Art, 1970—, benefactor, 1970—; trustee Chgo. Sch. of architecture Found., 1971—, Archives Am. Art, 1976—; mem. bd. Bright New City Urban Affairs Lecture Series, 1966—. Recipient Scroll Recognition of Public Service U.S. Dept. State, 1958. Mem. Antiquarian Soc. of Art Inst. Chgo., Chgo. Hist. Soc. (mem. guild 1958—). Clubs: Arts (Chgo.), Casino (Chgo.). *Searching for truth is a given for a life of value. For me visual art ontologically reveals the truth of the search. Striving for excellence is the spearhead with which to proceed.*

NEWMAN, MURRAY ARTHUR, aquarium administrator; b. Chgo., Mar. 6, 1924; emigrated to Can., 1953, naturalized, 1970; s. Paul Jones and Virginia (Murray) N.; m. Katherine Greene Rose, Aug. 8, 1952; 1 child, Susan. B.Sc., U. Chgo., 1949; postgrad., U. Hawaii, 1950; M.A., U. Calif., Berkeley, 1951; Ph.D., U. B.C. (Can.), Vancouver, 1960. Curator fisheries UCLA, 1951-53, Ichthyology Museum, U. B.C., 1953-56; curator Vancouver Public Aquarium, 1956-66, dir., 1966-93; pres. Mana Aquarium Cons.; fgn. adv. Nat. Mus./Aquarium Project, Taiwan, Republic of China; past chmn. adv. com. western Can. Univs. Marine Biol. Soc. Author: Life in a Fishbowl: Confessions of an Aquarium Director, 1994. Served with USN, 1943-46. Decorated Order of Can.; recipient Man of Yr. award City of Vancouver, 1964; Centennial award Govt. Can., 1967, cert. of merit, 1988; Harold J. Merilees award Vancouver Visitors Bur., 1976, 75 Achievers award, 1987, Silver Bravery medal Royal Soc. Canada, 1992, Canada 125 medal, 1992. Mem. Am. Assn. Zool. Parks and Aquariums, Internat. Union Dirs. Zool. Gardens, Can. Assn. Zool. Pks. and Aquariums (pres. 1978-79), Vancouver Club (bd. dirs.), Round Table Club. Office: Vancouver Pub Aquarium, PO Box 3232, Vancouver, BC Canada V6B 3X8

NEWMAN, NANCY MARILYN, ophthalmologist, educator, consultant, inventor, entrepreneur; b. San Francisco, Mar. 16, 1941. BA in Psychology magna cum laude, Stanford U., 1962, MD, 1967. Diplomate Am. Bd. Ophthalmology. NIH trainee neurophysiology Inst. Visual Scis., San Francisco, 1964-65; clin. clk. Nat. Hosp. for Nervous and Mental Disease, London, 1966-67; intern Mount Auburn Hosp., Cambridge, Mass., 1967-68; NIH trainee neuro-ophthalmology, from jr. asst. resident to sr. asst. resident to assoc. resident dept. ophthalmology sch. medicine Washington U., St. Louis, 1968-71; NIH spl. fellow in neuro-ophthalmology depts. ophthalmology and neurol. surgery sch. medicine U. Calif., San Francisco, 1971-72, clin. asst. prof. ophthalmology sch. medicine, 1972; asst. prof., chief divsn. neuro-ophthalmology Pacific Med. Ctr., San Francisco, 1972-73, assoc. prof., chief, 1973-88; physician, cons. dept. neurology sch. medicine U. Calif., VA Med. Ctr., Martinez, Calif., 1978—; prof. dept. spl. edn. Calif. State U., San Francisco, 1974-79; vis. prof. Centre Nat. D'Ophtalmologie des Quinze-Vingts, Paris, 1980; clin. assoc. prof. sch. optometry U. Calif., Berkeley, 1990—; bd. dirs., adv. bd. Frank B. Walsh Soc., 1974-91, Rose Resnick Ctr. for the Blind and Handicapped, 1988-92, Fifer St. Fitness, Larkspur, 1990-92; Internat. Soc. for Orbital Disorders, 1983—, North Calif. Soc. Prevention of Blindness, 1978-88, North African Ctr. for Sight, Tunis, Tunisia, 1988—; pres., CEO Minerva Medica; cons. in field. Author: Eye Movement Disorders; Neuro-ophthalmology: A Practical Text, 1992; mem. editoral bd. Jour. of Clin. Neuro-ophthalmology, Am. Jour. Opthalmology, 1980-92, Soc. Francaise d'Ophtalmogie, Ophthalmology Practice, 1993—; contbr. numerous articles to profl. jours. Recipient NSPI award Self Instrnl. Materials Ophthalmology, Merit award Internat. Eye Found., fellow 1971; Smith-Kettlewell Inst. Vis. Scis. fellow , 1971-72. Mem. AMA (leader Calif. del. continuing med. edn. 1982, 83), San Francisco Med. Soc., Calif. Med. Assn. (sub com. med. policy coms. 1984—, chair com. on accreditation continuing med. edn. 1981-88, chair quality care rev. commn. 1984), Assn. for Rsch. in Vision and Ophthalmology, Pan Am. Assn. of Ophthalmology, Soc. of Heed Fellows, Pacific Coast Oto-Ophthalmology Soc., Lane Medical Soc. (v.p. 1975-76), Internat. Soc. of Neuro-Ophthalmology (founder), Cordes Soc., Am. Soc. Ophthalmic Ultrasound (charter), Orbital Soc. (founder), West Bay Health Systems Agy., Oxford Opthalmology Soc., Pacific Physician Assocs., Soc. Francaise D'Ophtalmologie (mem. editorial bd. jour.). Home: 819 Spring Dr Mill Valley CA 94941-3924

NEWMAN, NORMAN, lawyer; b. Bklyn., Nov. 7, 1952; s. Irving and Rachel (Manheim) N.; m. Gitta Stern, Feb. 4, 1981; children: Evan Michael, Jennifer Danielle, Stephanie Gabrielle, Adam Jay. BA, Yeshiva U., N.Y., 1974; JD, Columbia U. Sch. of Law, N.Y., 1977. Bar: N.Y. 1978, U.S. Supreme Ct. N.Y. 1978, U.S. Tax Ct. 1978. Student clk. Roberts & Holland, N.Y., 1976-77; summer clk. Hale and Dorr, Boston, 1976; assoc. Mudge, Rose, Guthrie, Alexander & Ferdon, N.Y., 1977-79, Zimet, Haines et al, N.Y., 1979-82, Baer, Marks & Upham, N.Y., 1982-86; ptnr., chmn. Baer, Marks & Upham Employee Benefits Dept., N.Y., 1986-92; ptnr. Winston & Strawn, N.Y.C., 1992—, chmn. employee benefits dept., 1994—; mem. mgmt. com., bus. devel. com. Baer Marks & Upham, N.Y., 1990-92; mem. commrs. ad-hoc adv. com. exempt plans IRS, Washington, 1988-91. Contbr. editor: Compensation and Benefit Management Journal, United States Employee Benefit Plans and Executive Compensation, New Business Law mag., 1989. Bd. dirs. Hartmann YMHA, N.Y., 1989-91, Peninsula Counseling Ctr., 1991—, Minyan for the Stars, 1991-92; dir. v.p. exec. com. Yeshiva Toras Chaim, N.Y., 1989-91, pres. 1991—. Mem. N.Y.S. Bar Assn., Am. Bar Assn., Bar Assn. of N.Y.C. Avocations: tennis, biking. Home: 180 Lakeside Dr S Lawrence NY 11559-1721 Office: Winston & Strawn 175 Water St New York NY 10038-4918*

NEWMAN, PAUL, actor, professional race-car driver, food company executive; b. Cleve., Jan. 26, 1925; s. Arthur S. and Theresa (Fetzer) N.; m. Jacqueline Witte, Dec. 1949; children: Scott (dec.), Susan, Stephanie; m. Joanne Woodward, Jan. 1958; children: Elinor, Melissa, Clea. BA, Kenyon Coll., 1949; postgrad., Yale U. Sch. Drama, 1951; studied with Lee Strasberg, Actor's Studio; LHD (hon.), Yale U., 1988. Pres. Newman's Own Found., Inc., Westport, Conn. Appeared on Broadway in: Picnic, 1953-54, Desperate Hours, 1955, Sweet Bird of Youth, 1959, Baby Want a Kiss, 1964; motion pictures include Somebody Up There Likes Me, 1956, The Long Hot Summer, 1958 (Best Actor award Cannes Internat. Film Festival 1958), Cat on a Hot Tin Roof, 1958, From the Terrace, 1960, Exodus, 1960, The Hustler, 1961, Sweet Bird of Youth, 1962, Hud, 1963, The Outrage, 1964, The Prize, 1964, Lady L, 1965, Harper, 1966, Hombre, 1967, Cool Hand Luke, 1967, Winning, 1969, Butch Cassidy and the Sundance Kid, 1969, WUSA, Sometimes a Great Notion, 1971, Pocket Money, 1972, The Life and Times of Judge Roy Bean, 1972, The MacIntosh Man, 1973, The Sting, 1973, The Towering Inferno, 1974, Drowning Pool, 1975, Buffalo Bill and the Indians, 1976, Slap Shot, 1977, Quintet, 1979, Fort Apache, The Bronx, 1980, When Time Ran Out, 1980, Absence of Malice, 1981, The Verdict, 1982, The Color of Money, 1986, (Acad. award for best actor, 1987), Blaze, 1989, Mr. and Mrs. Bridge, 1989, The Hudsucker Proxy, 1994, Nobody's Fool, 1994; dir. motion pictures including: Rachel, Rachel, The Effect of Gamma Rays on Man-in-the-Moon Marigolds, 1973, Glass Menagerie, 1987; dir., screenwriter, actor in film Harry and Son, 1984. Served with AC USNR, 1943-46. Recipient Best Actor Acad. award nominee Acad. Motion Picture Arts and Scis., 1959-61, 63, 81, 82, Man of Yr. award Hasty Pudding Theater, Harvard U., 1968, D.W. Griffith Best Actor award Nat Bd. Rev. Motion Pictures, 1986, Hon. Acad. award for career achievement Acad. Motion Pictures Arts and Scis., 1986, Jean Hersholt Humanitarian award Acad. Motion Pictures Arts and Scis., 1994; named World Film Favorite, Golden Globe award, 1967, Best Motion Picture Prodr. of Yr., Prodrs. Guild of Am., 1968.

NEWMAN, PAULINE, federal judge; b. N.Y.C., N.Y., June 20, 1927; d. Maxwell Henry and Rosella N. B.A., Vassar Coll., 1947; M.A., Columbia U., 1948; Ph.D., Yale U., 1952; LL.B., NYU, 1958. Bar: N.Y. 1958, U.S. Supreme Ct. 1972, U.S. Ct. Customs and Patent Appeals 1978, Pa. 1979, U.S. Ct. Appeals (3d cir.) 1981, U.S. Ct. Appeals (fed. cir.) 1982. Research chemist Am. Cyanamid Co., Bound Brook, N.J., 1951-54; mem. patent staff FMC Corp., N.Y.C., 1954-75; mem. patent staff FMC Corp., Phila., 1975-84, dir. dept. patent and licensing, 1969-84; judge U.S. Ct. Appeals (fed. cir.), Washington, 1984—; bd. dir. Research Corp., 1982-84; program specialist Dept. Natural Scis. UNESCO, Paris, 1961-62; mem. State Dept. Adv. Com. on Internat. Indsl. Property, 1974-84; lectr. in field. Contbr. articles to profl. jours. Bd. dirs. Med. Coll. Pa., 1975-84, Midgard Found., 1973-84; trustee Phila. Coll. Pharmacy and Sci., 1983-84. Mem. ABA (council sect. patent trademark and copyright 1983-84), Am. Patent Law Assn. (bd. dirs. 1981-84), U.S. Trademark Assn. (bd. dirs. 1975-79, v.p. 1978-79), Am. Chem. Soc. (bd. dirs. 1972-81), Am. Inst. Chemists (bd. dirs. 1960-66, 70-76), Pacific Indsl. Property Assn. (pres. 1979-80). Clubs: Vassar,

Yale. Office: US Ct Appeals Nat Cts Bldg 717 Madison Pl NW Washington DC 20439-0001*

NEWMAN, PETER CHARLES, journalist; b. Vienna, Austria, May 10, 1929; emigrated to Can., 1940, naturalized, 1945; s. Oscar C. and Wanda (Newman) N. Ed., Upper Can. Coll., 1948; M.A., U. Toronto, 1951; LL.D. (hon.), Brock U., 1974; D.Litt. (hon.), York U., 1975; LL.D. (hon.), Wilfrid Laurier U., 1983, Royal Mil. Coll., 1986, Queens U., 1986. Asst. editor The Financial Post, 1951-55; Ottawa editor Maclean's Mag., 1955-64; Ottawa editor Toronto Daily Star, 1964-69, editor-in-chief, 1969-71; editor Maclean's, Toronto, 1971-82, sr. contbg. editor, 1982; Dep. chmn. for Can. Internat. Press Inst., 1970-74; vis. assoc. prof. polit. sci. McMaster U., Hamilton, Ont., 1970—; adj. prof. Sask. Indian Federated Coll., 1985; prof. creative writing U. Victoria, 1986; vis. prof. York U., 1979; dir. Maclean Hunter Ltd., 1972-82, Key Radio Ltd., 1982. Author: Flame of Power, 1959, Renegade in Power, 1963, The Distemper of Our Times, 1968, Home Country, 1973, The Canadian Establishment, 1975, Bronfman Dynasty, 1978, The Acquisitors, 1981, The Establishment Man, 1982, True North: Not Strong and Free, 1983, The Debrett's Guide to the Canadian Establishment, 1983, Company of Adventurers, 1985, Caesars of the Wilderness, 1987, Sometimes a Great Nation, 1988, Empire of the Bay, 1989, Merchant Princes, 1992, Canada: 1892-Portrait of a Promised Land, 1994, The Canadian Revolution: From Deference to Defiance, 1995. Gov. Shaw Festival, 1984; bd. dirs. Can. Coun. Native Bus., 1985, Can. Coun. Econ. Edn., 1985; dir. St. Paul's Hosp. Capt. Royal Can. Navy Res. Decorated companion Order of Can., knight comdr. St. Lazarus; recipient Nat. Newspaper award for feature writing, 1966, Wilderness award CBC, 1967, Michener award for journalism, 1971, Pres.'s medal U. We. Ont., 1974, Quill award-Journalist of Yr., 1977, Best TV Program of Yr. award Assn. Can. TV and Radio Artists, 1981, Nat. Bus. Writing award for disting. svc., 1986; elected to News Hall of Fame, 1989.

NEWMAN, PETER KENNETH, economist, educator; b. Mitcham, Eng., Oct. 5, 1928; s. Charles Francis and Harriet Anne (Newbold) N.; m. Jennifer Mary Hugh-Jones Steed, Sept. 30, 1974; children by previous marriage: Jean Ellen, John Lincoln, Kenneth Richard, Alan Peter. B.Sc. in Econs, Univ. Coll. U. London, Eng., 1949, M.Sc. in Econs, 1951, D.Sc. in Econs, 1962. Lectr. U. West Indies, Jamaica, 1957-59, sr. lectr., 1959-61; prof. econs. U. Mich., Ann Arbor, 1961-63; prof. econs. Johns Hopkins U., Balt., 1964-65, 66-90, prof. emeritus, 1990—; sr. assoc. Robert R. Nathan Assocs., Washington, 1965-66. Author: British Guiana, 1964, Malaria Eradication and Population Growth, 1965, Theory of Exchange, 1965; co-editor: The New Palgrave: A Dictionary of Economics, 4 vols., 1987; chief editor: The New Palgrave: Dictionary of Money and Finance, 3 vols., 1992.

NEWMAN, RACHEL, magazine editor; b. Malden, Mass., May 1, 1938; d. Maurice and Edythe Brenda (Tichell) N.; m. Herbert Bleiweiss, Apr. 6, 1973 (div. Apr. 1989). BA, Pa. State U., 1960; cert., N.Y. Sch. Interior Design, 1963. Accessories editor Women's Wear Daily, N.Y.C., 1964-65; designer, publicist Grandoe Glove Corp., N.Y.C., 1965-67; assoc. editor McCall's Sportswear and Dress Merchandiser mag., N.Y.C., 1967; mng. editor McCall's You-Do-It Home Decorating, 1968-70, Ladies Home Jour. Needle and Craft mag., N.Y.C., 1970-72; editor-in-chief Am. Home Crafts mag., N.Y.C., 1972-77; fashion dir. Good Housekeeping mag., N.Y.C., 1977-78, home bldg. and decorating dir., 1978-82; editor-in-chief Country Living mag., N.Y.C., 1978—; founding editor Country Cooking mag., 1985—, Dream Homes mag., 1989—, Country Kitchens mag., 1990—, Country Living Gardener Mag., 1993—, Healthy Living mag., 1996—. Pa. State U. Alumni fellow, 1986; recipient Cir. of Excellence award IFDA, 1992, YMCA Hall of Fame, 1992; named Disting. Alumni Pa. State U., 1988. Mem. N.Y. Fashion Group, Nat. Home Fashions League, Am. Soc. Interior Designers, Am. Soc. Mag. Editors. Office: Country Living 224 W 57th St New York NY 10019-3212

NEWMAN, RALPH GEOFFREY, literary scholar historian; b. Chgo., Nov. 3, 1911; s. Henry and Dora (Glickman) N.; m. Estelle Hoffman, 1934 (div.); children: Maxine (Mrs. Richard G. Brandenburg), Carol (Mrs. John Fox); m. Patricia Lyons Simon, 1972. Litt.D., James Milliken U. (Lincoln Coll.), 1950, Knox Coll., Rockford Coll.; LL.D., Iowa Wesleyan Coll.; Litt. D., Meisei U., Tokyo. Founder Abraham Lincoln Book Shop, Inc., Chgo., 1933-84; pres. Americana House, Inc., 1946-89, Lincoln's New Salem Enterprises, Inc., 1952-92, Ralph Geoffrey Newman, Inc., 1967—, Civil War Enterprises, Ltd., 1985-90; cons. Broadcast Music, Inc., 1941-89, Chgo. Sports Hall of Fame, 1989—. Author: (with Otto Eisenschiml) The American Iliad, 1947, Abraham Lincoln: An Autobiographical Narrative, 1970; Editor: The Diary of a Public Man, 1945, The Railsplitter, 1950, (with Otto Eisenschiml, E.B. Long) The Civil War, 1956; radio series The Abraham Lincoln Story, 1958-59; Lincoln for the Ages, 1960, (with Otto Eisenchiml) Evewitness, 1960, (with E.B. Long) The Civil War Digest, 1960, Pictorial Autobiography of Abraham Lincoln, 1962, Time-Table for the Lincoln Funeral, 1965, Abraham Lincoln: His Story in His Own Words, 1975, Abraham Lincoln's Last Full Measure of Devotion, 1981, The Lincoln Academy: A History, 1984, rev. edit., 1994, We Shall Pay Any Price, 1988, The General's Greatest Victory, 1989, (with G. N. Wiche) Great and Goods Books, 1989, Preserving Lincoln for the Ages, 1989, Lincoln: Day by Day, 1992; contbr. The Continuing Civil War, 1992, A Vermont 14, 1992, The Death of Your Kind and Brave Father, 1994; mem. editorial bd.: Civil War History, 1955-75. Chmn. Ill. com. N.Y. World's Fair, 1963-65; chmn. Ill. Sesquicentennial Commn., 1965-69; mem. Ill. Spl. Events Commn., 1969-73, Book and Libr. Commn., USIA, 1983—; past pres. Adult Edn. Council Greater Chgo.; bd. regents Lincoln Acad. Ill.; city archivist, City of Chgo., 1979-80; pres. bd. dirs. Chgo. Public Library, 1964-79; trustee Lincoln Coll.; past chmn. bd. dirs. Ford's Theatre Soc., Washington; pres. Urban Libraries Council, 1970-78; bd. dirs. Chgo. Fund on Ageing and Disability, 1987-89. Served with USNR, 1944-45. Recipient diploma of honor Lincoln Meml. U., 1952; Am. of Year award Independence Hall Assn., 1958; Nevins-Freeman award, 1975; laureate Lincoln Acad. Ill., 1983, Barondess award Lincoln Group of N.Y., 1987. Mem. Civil War Round Table Chgo. (founder 1940, Harry S. Truman award Kansas City chpt. 1966), Royal Arts Soc. (London), Abraham Lincoln Assn. (dir.), Stephen A. Douglas Assn. (chmn., bd. dirs.), Ulysses S. Grant Assn. (pres. 1962-90, pres. emeritus 1990—), Am., Ind., Ill., Iowa, Kans., Chgo. hist. socs., Am. Legion, ALA, Am. Booksellers Assn., Bibliog. Socs. Am., U.S. Info. Agy. (book and library com.), Soc. Am. Historians, Newberry Library Assocs. Chgo., Phi Alpha Theta. Clubs: Arts, Casino, Caxton, Internat. Tavern (Chgo.), Sangamo (Springfield, Ill.), Union League. Address: 175 E Delaware Pl Chicago IL 60611-1756 Office: Fine Arts Bldg 410 S Michigan Ave Chicago IL 60605-1302 *I believe opportunity exists wherever you are if you are willing to work hard enough to achieve it. No goal is impossible. If you are willing to forego dependence on anyone else and realize that your own, and only your own, efforts will bring success, you can be successful.*

NEWMAN, RANDY, singer, songwriter, musician; b. Los Angeles, Calif., Nov. 28, 1943; s. Irving and Adele N.; m. Roswitha Newman; children: Amos, Eric, John. Degree, U. Calif. Arranger, singer, songwriter, musician various record firms; singer-composer: (albums) including Randy Newman, 1968, Twelve Songs, 1969, Live, 1971, Sail Away, 1972, Good Old Boys, 1974, Little Criminals, 1977, Born Again, 1979, Trouble In Paradise, 1983, Land of Dreams, 1988; appeared in film: Ragtime, 1981; also TV and concert engagements; music composer for films: Performance, 1970, Pursuit of Happiness, 1971, Cold Turkey, 1971, Ragtime, 1981, The Natural, 1984, Three Amigos (also co-wrote screenplay), 1986, Parenthood, 1989, Avalon, 1990, Awakenings, 1990, Toy Story, 1995 (Acad. award nominee for best original score 1996, Acad. award nominee for best original song 1996). Recipient Grammy award for best instrumental composition, 1984.

NEWMAN, RICHARD ALAN, publisher, editor and consultant; b. Watertown, N.Y., Mar. 30, 1930; s. Gordon Leon and Belle (Burton) N.; m. Ann Cowan Meredith, 1955 (div. 1960); m. Peggy J. Hoyt, 1964 (div. 1978); stepchildren: David W. Bauer, Paul W. Bauer, Nancy E. Beck; m. Belynda Blair Bady, 1996. B.A., Maryville Coll., 1952; M.Div., Union Theol. Sem., 1955; postgrad., Syracuse U., 1959-61, Harvard U., 1966. Ordained to ministry Presbyn. Ch., 1955, demitted, 1977; minister Westminster Presbyn. Ch., Syracuse, N.Y., 1955-59; instr. religion Vassar Coll., Poughkeepsie, N.Y., 1962-63; prof., chmn. dept. social scis. Boston U., 1964-73; sr. editor G.K. Hall Co., Boston, 1973-79; exec. editor Garland Pub. Co., N.Y.C., 1978-81; mgr. publs. N.Y. Pub. Libr., 1981-92; cons. Columbia U., N.Y.C., 1992-93; publs. officer, mng. editor The Harvard Guide to African-Am. History, W.E.B. DuBois Inst., Harvard U., 1993-95, fellows officer, 1995—. Author: Black Index, 1981, Bless All Thy Creatures, Lord, 1982, Lemuel Haynes, 1984, Afro-American Education, 1984, Black Access: A Bibliography, 1984, Black Power and Black Religion, 1987, Words Like Freedom, 1989, Black Preacher to White America, 1990; editor: Treasures From the New York Public Library, 1985, This Far By Faith, 1996, Everybody Say Freedom, 1996; contbr. articles to profl. jours. Dem. candidate for N.Y. State Assembly from Onondaga County, 1960. Mem. Friends of Union Sem. Libr., Boston Athenaeum, Studio Mus. in Harlem, Friends of Amistad Rsch. Ctr., Schomburg Commn. for Preservation of Black Culture. Home: 160 Commonwealth Ave Apt 614 Boston MA 02116-2744

NEWMAN, ROBERT GABRIEL, physician; b. The Netherlands, Oct. 26, 1937; came to U.S., 1939; s. Randolph H. and Eva E. (Feilchenfeld) N.; m. Seiko Kusuba, Oct. 26, 1968; children—Henry Seiji, Hana Marie. B.A., NYU, 1958; M.D. with honors, U. Rochester, 1963; M.P.H., U. Calif.-Berkeley, 1969. Intern and resident in surgery Univ. Hosps., Cleve., 1963-65; dist. health officer N.Y.C. Health Dept., 1968; dir. Nat. Nutrition Survey of N.Y.C., 1969-70; asst. commr. N.Y.C. Health Dept., 1970-74; health cons., 1974-76; assoc. gen. dir. Beth Israel Med. Ctr., N.Y.C., 1976-78; chief exec. officer, pres. Beth Israel Med. Ctr., 1978—; prof. dept. community medicine Mt. Sinai Sch. Medicine, N.Y.C., 1982-94; prof. depts. epidemiology and social medicine/psychiatry Albert Einstein Coll. of Medicine, 1994—; cons. addiction problems Govt. of Hong Kong, 1975-85. Author book in field of methadone treatment; contbr. articles to profl. jours. Trustee Univ. of Rochester, N.Y., 1994—. With USAF, 1965-67. WHO fellow, 1972. Fellow N.Y. Acad. Medicine, Am. Coll. Preventive Medicine; mem. Public Health Assn. N.Y.C., Hosp. Assn. N.Y. State (past chmn. 1992), Greater N.Y. Hosp. Assn. (past chmn. bd.), Am. Public Health Assn. Office: Beth Israel Med Ctr 1st Ave # 16th St New York NY 10003

NEWMAN, ROGER, lawyer; b. Newnan, Ga., Sept. 11, 1954; s. James Taylor and Flora Mae (Rogers) N.; m. Brenda Susan Fleming, Nov. 13, 1993; children: Marisa Len Edge, Samantha Fleming Edge. AAS, Fayetteville Tech. C.C., 1988; BA in Polit. Sci., Fayetteville State U., 1990; JD, Campbell U., 1993. Bar: N.C. 1993, U.S. Dist. Ct. (ea., ctrl. and we. dists.) N.C. 1993. Police officer Fayetteville (N.C.) Police Dept., 1975-79; paralegal Rand, Finch & Gregory, Fayetteville, 1988-90, law clk., 1990-93, atty., 1993-94; atty., sole practitioner Roger Newman, Atty., Fayetteville, 1994—. Bd. dirs. Cumberland County Hospice Assn., Fayetteville, 1994, Cumberland County Health Occupl. Bd., Fayetteville, 1994. Mem. ABA, N.C. Assn. Trial Lawyers Am. Democrat. Avocations: golf, bowling, firearms safety. Home: 5024 Shimmer Dr Fayetteville NC 28304 Office: 2000 Fort Bragg Rd Ste 3 Fayetteville NC 28303-7000

NEWMAN, RUTH TANTLINGER, artist; b. Hooker, Okla., May 28, 1910; d. Walter Warren and Jean Louise (Hayward) Tantlinger; m. John Vincent Newman; children: Peter Vincent, Michael John. Student, Pomona Coll; BFA, UCLA, 1932; postgrad., Instituto Allende, U. Guanajuato, Mex. Art tchr. Santa Ana (Calif.) Schs., 1933-34, Santa Ana Adult Edn., 1934-40; watercolor tchr. Ventura (Calif.) Recreation Ctr., 1941-50; pvt. tchr. watercolor Calif., 1950-85. One-woman shows include Ventura County Mus. History and Art, 1993, Santa Barbara Art Assn., Ojai Art Ctr., Ventura Art Club, Oxnard (Calif.) Art Club, Art Club of Westlake Village, Thousand Oaks (Calif.) Art Club, others; commd. to paint 12 Calif. Missions, 1958, watercolors at San Juan Bautista Retreat House, Calif., oils at Ch. of San Bernardino, Mallorca, Spain; book featuring reproductions of selected works, Ruth Newman: A Lifetime of Art, introduced at her solo show in Ventura Mus., 1993. Mem. Westlake Village Art Guild, Thousand Oaks Art Club, Buena Ventura Art Club (charter). Home: 32120 Oakshore Dr Westlake Village CA 91361

NEWMAN, SAMUEL, trust company executive; b. N.Y.C., Mar. 12, 1938; s. Aaron and Rachel (Hershkowitz) N.; m. Carolyn Gropper, Oct. 27, 1963; children: Marci Ann, Jodi Robin, Michael David. BBA, CUNY, 1971; grad. Advanced Mgmt. Program, Harvard U., 1982. Methods analyst Bankers Trust Co., N.Y.C., 1960-67; project leader Clark O'Neill SVC Corp., Fairview, N.J., 1967-68; sr. v.p. Irving Trust Co., N.Y.C., 1968-85; sr. v.p., gen. mgr. trade svcs. and GEOSERVE legal and regulatory support Mfrs. Hanover Trust (merger with Chem. Bank 1992), N.Y.C., 1985-92; sr. v.p., gen. mgr. funds transfer and trade svcs. Chem. Bank, N.Y.C., 1992-93; sr. v.p. and bus. head payment products First Fidelity Bank NA, Newark, 1993-95; head dept. project support Fleet Pa. Svcs. Inc., Scranton, Pa., 1995—; past chmn. bd. dirs. S.W.I.F.T. Terminal Svcs.; past chmn. N.Y. Clearing House funds transfer com.; speaker industry confs. Contbr. articles to profl. jours. Advisor Nat. Conf. of Commrs. on Uniform State Laws; former mem. U.S. coun. Internat. Banking Exec. Com., U.S. del. to Uncitral Working Group on Internat. Payments; former chief U.S. del. to tech. com. 168 Internat. Standards Orgn. Mem. Soc. Worldwide Fin. Telecom. (bd. dirs. 1978-92, dep. chmn 1989-92). Avocations: numismatist; collecting Hummel figurines and plates. Office: Fleet Pa Svcs Inc PO Box 5600 Scranton PA 18505-5600

NEWMAN, SHARON LYNN, elementary education educator; b. Lewisburg, Tenn., Jan. 9, 1946; d. Hermit Taft and Martha Elizabeth (Pardue) Simmons; m. George Wynne Newman Sr., June 11, 1967; 1 child, George Wynne Jr. BS in Edn., Athens State Coll., 1979. Substitute tchr. Giles County Bd. Edn., Pulaski, Tenn., 1979-81; chpt. 1 reading tchr. Giles County Bd. Edn., Pulaski, 1981-91, chpt. 1 math. tchr., 1991—; chpt. 1 coord. Elkton (Tenn.) Elem. Sch., 1989—, mem. steering com., 1989—, chair math. dept., 1993-95, chpt. title I com., 1995—, mem. disaster preparedness team. Ch. libr. Elkton (Tenn.) Bapt. Ch., 1992—. Mem. Nat. Coun. Tchrs. Math., Giles County Edn. Assn. (rsch. chairperson 1993-95). Home: 1758 Old Stage Rd Ardmore TN 38449 Office: Elkton Elem Sch Elkton TN 38455

NEWMAN, SHELDON OSCAR, computer company executive; b. N.Y.C., June 25, 1923; s. Morris and Anna (Schlanger) N.; m. Miriam Jasphy, July 30, 1950; children: Barry Marc, Amy Stacy, Andrew Eric. BS in Elec. Engring., CUNY, 1944. Project engr. NASA, Sunnyvale, Calif., 1946-47; gen. mgr. info. and communications div. Sperry Corp., Gt. Neck, N.Y., 1947-67; chmn. bd., chief exec. officer Algorex Corp., Hauppauge, N.Y., 1968-93. Chmn. bd. trustees Hosp. for Joint Diseases, Orthopaedic Inst., N.Y.C.; trustee NYU Med. Ctr.; bd. dirs. HJD Rsch. and Devel. Found., Sjogrens Syndrome Found., Woodbridge Assn., Boca Raton, Fla.; pres. Pine Lake Park Coop. Assn., Peekskill, N.Y. Patentee in field. Lt. (j.g.), USN, 1944-46. Recipient Disting. Trustee award United Hosp. Fund, 1995. Mem. IEEE (sr.), Archaeol. Inst. Am. (pres.), L.I. Soc., Masons, Tau Beta Pi, Eta Kappa Nu.

NEWMAN, SLATER EDMUND, psychologist, educator; b. Boston, Sept. 8, 1924; s. Max and Gertrude (Raphael) N.; m. Corrine Lois Silfen, June 18, 1950 (div. 1968); children—Kurt Douglas, Jonathan Mark, Eric Bruce; m. Patricia Ellen Christopher Thomas, July 2, 1969; 1 stepchild, Arthur C. Thomas III. B.S., U. Pa., 1947; M.A., Boston U., 1948; Ph.D., Northwestern U., 1951. Research psychologist U.S. Air Force, 1951-57; mem. faculty N.C. State U., Raleigh, 1957—; now prof. psychology N.C. State U.; vis. fgn. mem. Exptl. Psychology Soc. U.K., 1973-74, 82-83, 90. Contbr. chpts. to books, articles to profl. publs. Bd. dirs. ACLU, 1992—, mem. biennial conf. com., 1994—, mem. task force internat. human rights, 1994—; pres. N.C. Civil Liberties Union, 1980-82, exec. com., 1986-87, bd. dirs., 1969-73, 76-82, 84-90, 91ú; chmn. Com. on Internat. Human Rights, 1988—; mem. steering ocm. ACLI-Affiliate Leadership Network, 1991-95; mem. Mayor's Com. UN Week, Raleigh, 1986-95; active Amnesty Internat.; coord. Com. to Reverse Arms Race, 1982—; mem. steering com. North Carolinians Against Apartheid, 1985-87; mem. Wake County com. Bicentennial U.S. Constn., 1987-89; co-chair N.C. Com. for Celebration of Human Rights, 1989—. Served to 2nd lt. USAF, 1943-46, 52-53. USPHS spl. rsch. fellow U. Calif.-Berkeley, 1965-66; U. London hon. rsch. fellow, 1973-74, 82-83, 90. Fellow AAAS, APA, Am. Psychol. Soc.; mem. NAACP, Psychonomic Sc., UN Assn. (bd. dirs. Wake County chpt. 1991-95), People for the Am. Way, Southeastern Psychol. Assn., So. Soc. Philosophy and Psyachology, Cognitive Sci. Soc., Soc. Rsch. in Child Devel., Southeastern Workers in Memory (fournder, N.C. Cognition Group (founder), Ea. Psychol. Assn., AAUP (pres. N.C. State U. chpt. 1968-69), Carolinas Conf. for Undergrad. Rsch. in Psychology (co-founder 1976), Sigma Xi, Psi Chi (v.p. southeastern region 1990-94, nat. pres. elect. 1996—, mem. nat. coun. 1990-94, 96). Home: 315 Shepherd St Raleigh NC 27607-4031 Office: Dept Psychology NC State U Raleigh NC 27695-7801

NEWMAN, STANLEY RAY, oil refining company executive; b. Milo, Idaho, Mar. 5, 1923; s. Franklin Hughes and Ethel Amelda (Crowley) N.; student Tex. A&M U, 1944-45; B.S., U. Utah, 1947, Ph.D., 1952. m. Rosa Klein, May 27, 1961 (div. Mar. 1980); children: Trudy Lynn, Susan Louise, Karen Elizabeth, Paul Daniel, Phillip John; m. Madelyn Wycherly, Jan. 10, 1991; children: Heidi, Heather, Amy. With Texaco Res. Ctr., Beacon, N.Y., 1951-82, technologist, 1973-77, sr. technologist research mfg.-fuels, 1977-82, profl. cons. on fuels and chems., 1983—. Chmn., Planning Bd., Village of Fishkill, N.Y., 1973- 77; village trustee, 1990-92; mem. Dutchess County Solid Waste Mgmt. Bd., 1974-76. With inf. Signal Corps U.S. Army, 1944-46. Mem. AAAS, N.Y. Acad. Sci., Dutchess County Geneal. Soc. (pres. 1981-87, exec. v.p. 1987-88), N.Y. Fruit Testing Assn., Sigma Xi (pres. Texaco Res. Ctr. br. 1980-81). Republican. Mormon. Patentee in field. Home: 285 Plantation Cir Idaho Falls ID 83404-7990 *I was born of humble parents in Idaho. Life was hard and difficult so early in my life at considerable sacrifice I went the extra distance to go to a good high school to prepare for college. By working at night and weekends, I was able to complete college with a Ph.D. Blessed with an inquiring mind, a strong will to work, and a desire to learn, I moved to the east coast, worked hard both at my job and in the community, always retaining the honesty, integrity and strong religious values taught by my humble parents. At retirement, I had numerous patents, publications, and had world wide responsibility for fuels for Texaco.*

NEWMAN, STEPHEN MICHAEL, lawyer; b. Buffalo, Jan. 12, 1945; s. Howard A. and Mildred (Ballow) N.; m. Gayle Mallon, May 24, 1969; children: Holly, Deborah. AB, Princeton U., 1966; JD, U. Mich., 1969. Bar: N.Y. 1969, Fla. 1976. Assoc. Hodgson, Russ, Andrews, Woods & Goodyear, Buffalo, 1969-73, ptnr., 1973—; lectr. various seminars, confs., profl. groups throughout the U.S. Bd. dirs. Leukemia Soc., United Jewish Fedn. Buffalo Inc., Jewish Ctr. Greater Buffalo Inc., Temple Beth Zion; bd. dirs., chpt. chmn., exec. com. Am. Jewish Com., Buffalo chpt.; active Vol. Action Ctr. United Way of Buffalo and Erie County. Fellow Am. Coll. Trusts and Estates Coun.; mem. ABA (personal svc. corps. com. tax sect.), N.Y. State Bar Assn. (exec. com. trusts and estates law sect.), Princeton Club of Western N.Y. (sch. com.). Office: Hodgson Russ Andrews Woods & Goodyear 1 Montana Ave Ste 1800 Buffalo NY 14211-1638

NEWMAN, STEVEN HARVEY, insurance company executive; b. Bklyn., Apr. 26, 1943; s. Charlotte (Segal) Newman Bart; m. Lenore Blaustein, June 14, 1964; children: Richard, Michael, Stephanie. B.S., Bklyn. Coll., 1963. Actuarial asst. Royal Globe Ins. Co., N.Y.C., 1963-65; asst. sec. Ins. Rating Bd., N.Y.C., 1965-69; v.p., sr. casualty actuary Am. Internat. Group, N.Y.C., 1969-82; exec. v.p. Home Ins. Co., N.Y.C., 1982-85, also dir., pres., 1985-86; chmn., CEO Underwriters Reinsurance Co., Woodland Hills, Calif., 1987—; chmn. GCR Holdings, 1993—, Reins. Assn. Am., 1995—; bd. dirs. Capital Corp., 1995—. Fellow Casualty Actuarial Soc. (pres. 1981-82); mem. Am. Acad. Actuaries, Internat. Actuarial Assn.

NEWMAN, STUART, lawyer; b. Hackensack, N.J., June 7, 1947; s. Joseph and Rose (Wilenski) N.; m. Tina Gilson; children: Leslie, Dara, Mindy, Robert. BA, SUNY, Cortland, 1971; JD cum laude, Albany Law Sch., 1974. Bar: N.Y. 1975, Ga. 1978. Assoc. Dewey, Ballantine, Bushby, Palmer & Wood, N.Y.C., 1974-76; from assoc. to ptnr. Jackson, Lewis, Schnitzler & Krupman, Atlanta, 1976—; lectr. U. Ala., Tuscaloosa, 1980-84, Auburn U., 1986—. Dir. Ruth Mitchell Dance Co. of Atlanta, 1986-88. Mem. ABA, Atlanta Bar Assn., Ga. Bar Assn., Shakerag Hounds, Inc., Midlands Fox Hounds, Inc., Live Oak Hounds, Ansley Golf Club. Office: Jackson Lewis Schnitzler & Krupman 2400 Peachtree Ctr Harris Tower 233 Peachtree St NE Atlanta GA 30303

NEWMAN, TERRY E., lawyer; b. Chgo., Jan. 15, 1947. BA, Loyola U., Ill., 1969; JD, DePaul U., 1977. Bar: Ill. 1977, U.S. Dist. Ct. (no. dist.) Ill. 1977, D.C. 1991. Asst. states atty. Cook County, 1977-78; ptnr. Katten Muchin & Zavis, Chgo. Sec. bd. trustees City Coll. Chgo., 1989. Mem. ABA, Ill. State Bar, D.C. Bar, Chgo. Bar Assn. (real estate tax sect.). Address: Katten Muchin & Zavis 525 W Monroe St Ste 1600 Chicago IL 60661-3629*

NEWMAN, THEODORE ROOSEVELT, JR., judge; b. Birmingham, Ala., July 5, 1934; s. Theodore R. and Ruth L. (Oliver) N. A.B., Brown U., 1955, LL.D., 1980; J.D., Harvard U., 1958. Bar: D.C. 1958, Ala. 1959. Atty. civil rights div. Dept. Justice, Washington, 1961-62; practiced law in Washington, 1962-70; assoc. judge D.C. Superior Ct., 1970-76; judge D.C. Ct. Appeals, 1976-91, chief judge, 1976-84, sr. judge, 1991—; bd. dirs. Nat. Center for State Cts., v.p., 1980-81, pres., 1981-82. Trustee Brown U. With USAF, 1958-61. Fellow Am. Bar Found.; mem. Nat. Bar Assn. (past pres. jud. coun., C. Francis Stradford award 1984, William H. Hastie award 1988).

NEWMAN, THOMAS, composer. Scores include: (films) Grandview, U.S.A., 1984, Reckless, 1984, Revenge of the Nerds, 1984, Girls Just Want to Have Fun, 1985, Desperately Seeking Susan, 1985, The Man with One Red Shoe, 1985, Real Genius, 1985, Gung Ho, 1986, Jumpin' Jack flash, 1986, Quicksilver, 1986, Light of Day, 1987, The Lost Boys, 1987, Less Than Zero, 1987, The Great Outdoors, 1988, The Prince of Pennsylvania, 1988, Cookie, 1989, Men Don't Leave, 1990, Naked Tango, 1990, Welcome Home, Roxy Carmichael, 1990, Career Opportunities, 1991, Deceived, 1991, The Rapture, 1991, Fried Green Tomatoes, 1991, The Linguini Incident, 1992, The Player, 1992, Whispers in the Dark, 1992, Scent of a Woman, 1992, Flesh and Bone, 1993, Josh and S.A.M., 1993, The Favor, 1994, Threesome, 1994, The Shawshank Redemption, 1994 (Acad. award nominee for best original score 1994), Little Women, 1994 (Acad. award nominee for best original score 1994), Unstrung Heroes, 1995 (Acad. award nominee for best original score 1996); (TV movies) The Seduction of Gina, 1984, Heat Wave, 1991, Those Secrets, 1992, Citizen Cohn, 1992. Office: Gorfaine Schwartz Agency 3301 Barham Blvd Ste 201 Los Angeles CA 90068-1477

NEWMAN, W. JOE, financial planner, municipal official; b. Phenix City, Ala., Mar. 29, 1948; s. William Harvey and Lena Belle (Mancil) N.; m. M. Jackie Olah, Dec. 15, 1984; children: Sara, Susan. B in Bus. Adminstrn., Mktg. and History, Troy State U., 1970. Prin. W. Joe Newman and Assocs., Chesapeake, Va. Councilman City Chesapeake, Va., 1994—. Republican. Baptist. Office: W Joe Newman & Assocs 528 Forest Rd Chesapeake VA 23322-4327

NEWMAN, WADE DAVIS, trade association executive; b. Chgo., June 23, 1936; s. Clifford and Mary Gwendolyn (Parsons) N.; m. Rita Esmoer, Apr. 30, 1960; children—Erik Parsons, Sherrill Susan. Student, Northwestern U., 1954-57. Sales mgr. Schramm Fiberglass Products, Inc., Chgo., 1958-65; sales promotion mgr. Monogram Models, Inc., Morton Grove, Ill., 1965-68; dir. info. Nat. Sch. Supply & Equipment Assn., Chgo., 1968-72; product mgr. Skillcraft Corp., Chgo., 1972-73; dir. communications and convs. Nat. Bldg. Material Distbrs. Assn., Chgo., 1973-79; exec. dir. Nat. Assn. Floor Covering Distbrs., Chgo., 1979-91, Steel Plate Fabricators Assn., Des Plaines, Ill., 1992—. Bd. dirs. Edison Park (Ill.) Community Council, 1973—, pres., 1975. Mem. Am. Soc. Assn. Execs. (con. mgmt. cert.), Chgo. Soc. Assn. Execs., Assn. Econ. Coun. Republican. Methodist. Home: 7300 W Ibsen St Chicago IL 60631-1151 Office: Steel Plate Fabricators Assn 3158 Des Plaines Ave Des Plaines IL 60018-4211

NEWMAN, WILLIAM, real estate executive; b. N.Y.C., July 6, 1926; s. Morris B. and Ida (Singer) N.; m. Anita Eagle, Dec. 12, 1948; children: Steven (dec.), Sharon (dec.), Debra Newman Bernstein. BBA, CCNY, 1947. CPA, N.Y. Ptnr. Morris B. Newman & Co., N.Y.C., 1947-61; pres. New Plan Realty Corp., N.Y.C., 1961-72; chief exec. officer New Plan Realty Trust, N.Y.C., 1972—, also chmn. bd. trustees. Trustee Baruch Coll. Fund.; founder Steven L. Newman Real Estate Inst. at Baruch Coll., 1996. Recipient Gold award Wall St. Transcript, 1986, Bronze award, 1989, Silver award, 1990, 91, Outstanding Achievement award Baruch Coll. Alumni Assn., 1991; Baruch Coll. Libr. designated William and Anita Newman Libr.

Mem. Nat. Assn. Real Estate Investment Trusts (chmn. 1990-92, Industry Leadership award 1995), Chief Execs. Orgn., Met. Pres.'s Orgn., Aspinal-Curzon Club (London), Brae Burn Country Club, Boca Rio Golf Club, Princeton Club. Office: New Plan Realty Trust 1120 Ave Of The Americas New York NY 10036-6700

NEWMAN, WILLIAM BERNARD, JR., railroad executive; b. Providence, Nov. 16, 1950; s. William Bernard and Virginia (Crosby) N.; m. Karen O'Connor, Jan. 11, 1951. B.A., Ohio Wesleyan U., 1972; J.D., George Mason U., Arlington, Va., 1977; attended advanced mgmt. program, Harvard U., 1987. Bar: Va. 1977, D.C. 1978. Atty. com. energy Ho. of Reps., Washington, 1978-81; v.p., Washington counsel Consol. Rail Corp. Dept. Govt. Affairs, Washington, 1981—. Bd. dirs. Nat. Coun. for Adoption. Mem. ABA, Va. Bar Assn., D.C. Bar Assn. Home: 1009 Priory Pl Mc Lean VA 22101-2134 Office: Consol Rail Corp 990 Lenfant Plz SW Washington DC 20024-2116 also: Consol Rail Corp 6 Penn Center Plz Philadelphia PA 19103-2919

NEWMAN, WILLIAM C., bishop; b. Balt., Aug. 16, 1928. Student, St. Mary Sem., Cath. U., Loyola Coll. Ordained priest Roman Cath. Ch., 1954. Aux. bishop Archdiocese of Balt., 1984—. Address: 5300 N Charles St Baltimore MD 21210-2023 Office: Chancery Office 320 Cathedral St Baltimore MD 21201-4421

NEWMAN, WILLIAM E., naval officer; b. Chgo., Dec. 27, 1939; s. William Benedict and Florence Vivian (Skorup) N.; m. Judith Ann Morgan; children: Elizabeth, Matthew, David, Joseph. BS, U.S. Naval Acad., 1961; grad., Brit. Empire Test Pilot's Sch., Farnborough, Eng., 1966. Cert. pilot, test pilot, material profl. Commd. ensign USN, 1961, advanced through grades to rear adm., 1990; test pilot Naval Air Test Ctr. NAS, Patuxent River, Md., 1966-69; commanding officer Attack Squadron 195 USS Kitty Hawk NAS, Lemoore, Calif., 1975-77; commanding officer, flight leader The Blue Angels flying team NAS, Pensacola, Fla., 1978-79; comdr. Carrier Air Wing 9 USS Constellation, 1980-81; head air weapons requirements Chief of Naval Ops. Staff Washington, 1981-84; commanding officer USS White Plains Guam, 1984-86; maj. program mgr. Naval Air Systems Command Washington, 1987-89, dir. tactical aircraft programs, 1989-90; comdr. Pacific Missile Test Ctr. USN, Point Mugu, Calif., 1990—; now asst. comdr. rsch. engring. Arlington, VA. Contbr. articles to profl. jours. Decorated Legion of Merit, D.F.C. Mem. Soc. Exptl. Test Pilots, Assn. Naval Aviation, U.S. Naval Inst., D.C. Masters Swimming Club (pres. 1987-89). Republican. Roman Catholic. Competitive masters swimmer, 1987, 90. Home: 7808 Valleyfield Dr Springfield VA 22153-4118 Office: Naval Air Systems Command Commander 1421 Jefferson Davis Hwy Arlington VA 22243-5120*

NEWMAN, WILLIAM LOUIS, geologist; b. Rockford, Ill., July 14, 1920; s. Lyle Winfred and Carrie (Waterman) N.; m. Lucille Mary Hagen, Feb. 21, 1946; children: William Dwight, Christopher. BS, Beloit Coll., 1942; postgrad., Mont. Sch. Mines, 1946, U. Mont., 1948-50. Geologist Anaconda Mining Co., Butte, Mont., 1946-48; geologist U.S. Geol. Survey, 1950-80; uranium exploration U.S. Geol. Survey, Colo. Plateau, 1950-57; staff asst. to asso. dir. U.S. Geol. Survey, 1957-59; chief Metallogenic Map Project, 1959-62; staff asst. Office of Chief Geologist, 1962-63, staff geologist, 1963-67, chief nontech. reports, 1967-78; dep. chief Office Sci. Publs., 1978-80; cons., 1981—. Served with AUS, 1942-46. Recipient Superior Performance awards, 1963, 70; Superior Service award, 1972. Fellow AAAS, Geol. Soc. Am., Soc. Econ. Geologists; mem. Am. Assn. Petroleum Geologists (rep. Capital dist. 1966-68), Geochem. Soc., Fed. Editors Assn., Assn. Earth Sci. Editors, Am. Geol. Inst. (sec.-treas., bd. dirs. 1971-72), Geol. Soc. Washington (program chmn. 1963, sec. 1968-69), Geol. Soc. Grand Junction (Colo.) (sec. 1954), SAR, KC, Sigma Chi. Home and Office: 5624 E Wethersfield Rd Scottsdale AZ 85254-4317

NEWMAN, WILLIAM STEIN, music educator, author, pianist, composer; b. Cleve., Apr. 6, 1912; m. Claire Louise Murray, Dec. 20, 1947; 1 son, Craig William (dec. 1983). B.S., Cleve. Inst. Music, 1933, hon. doctorate, 1986; B.S. in Mus. Edn. (Cleve. Pub. Sch. Music scholar), Western Res. U., 1933, M.A. in Musicology (grad. fellow), 1935, Ph.D., 1939; postgrad. in Europe, Columbia U., 1940. Pvt. tchr. piano and theory, 1926—; fed. relief adminstr. Cleve., 1933-34; asst. choral dir. Western Res. U., 1934-36, instr. undergrad., grad. music courses, summer 1942; music tchr. Wilson Jr. High Sch., Cleve., 1935-37, Collinwood High Sch., 1937-42, Cleve. Music Sch. Settlement, 1937-38; vocal coach, accompanist Juilliard Sch. Music, Chautauqua, summer 1937; lectr. recitalist Juilliard Sch. Music, summer 1948; instr. music history Bennington Coll., summer 1940; instr. grad. courses Columbia Tchrs. Coll., summer 1941, asst. prof., summers 1946-48; asst. to librarian Cleve. Pub. Library System, 1941-42; asst. prof. U. N.C., 1945-46, mem. grad. faculty, 1946—, Carnegie research grantee, 1947, 48, asso. prof. music, chmn. piano instrn., 1949-69, prof., 1955-62, Alumni Disting. prof., 1962—, dir. grad. studies in music, 1966—, prof. emeritus, 1977—; prof. music summers U. Colo., 1956, U. Mont., 1963, U. Oreg., 1965, 69, Harpur Coll., 1966, Northwestern U., 1974, U. Mo., 1978, U. Alta., 1982; piano recitals, lectrs. throughout U.S. Author: The Pianists' Problems, rev. edit, 1956 (London 1952), 1974, 84, Understanding Music, rev. edit, 1961, 67, The Sonata in the Baroque Era, rev. edit, 1966, 72, 83, Sonata in the Classic Era, 1963, 72, 83, The Sonata Since Beethoven, (vols. 1, 2, and 3 of a History of the Sonata Idea, 1969, rev. edit., 1972, 83), Performance Practices in Beethoven's Piano Sonatas, 1971; Beethoven on Beethoven-Playing His Piano Music His Way, 1988; editor: Thirteen Keyboard Sonatas of the 18th and 19th Centuries, 1947, Two-Part Inventions of J.S. Bach, 1957, A Chopin Anthology, 1957, Diabelli Variations, 16 Contemporaries of Beethoven on a Waltz Tune, 1958, Six Keyboard Sonatas from the Classic Era, 1965; Contbg. editor: Piano Quar; contbr. numerous articles to profl. jours., reference works. Served with USAAF, 1943-45. Recipient Ann. Composition award Fortnightly Mus. Club, Cleve., 1935, Disting. Alumnus award Cleve. Inst. Music, 1986; scholarship Concord (Mass.) Sch. Music, 1935; Kenan rsch. leave U. N.C., 1956; Ford Found.-U. N.C. Rsch. grantee, 1958; Ford Found. Teaching grantee WUNC-TV, 1959; Guggenheim fellow musicology, 1960-61; Am. Council Learned Socs. grantee-in-aid, 1960, 61, 66-67, 80-81; sr. fellow NEH, 1973; summer seminars, 1975, 79; dir. year-long seminar, 1977-78; fellow Nat. Humanities Ctr., 1983-84. Mem. Music Tchrs. Nat. Assn. (chmn. theory forum 1940, membership chmn. N.C. 1949, chmn. sr. piano com. 1950-53, exec. bd. 1952-56), Am. Musicological Soc. (hon. life, exec. coun. 1955-57, nat. v.p. 1968-69, pres. 1969-70, program chmn. 1958, 66, editor jour. summer 1959), Internat. Musicological Soc. (U.S. rep. on directorium 1971-82), N.C. Music Educators, Music Libr. Assn., Coll. Music Soc. Home: 808 Old Mill Rd Chapel Hill NC 27514-3928

NEWMAN-GORDON, PAULINE, French language and literature educator; b. N.Y.C., Aug. 5, 1925; d. Bernard and Eva Newman; m. Sydney A. Gordon, Sept. 13, 1959 (dec.). BA, Hunter Coll., 1947; MA, Columbia U., 1948; PhD, Sorbonne U., Paris, 1951. Instr. French Wellesley (Mass.) Coll., 1952-53; mem. faculty Stanford (Calif.) U., 1953—, prof. French lit., 1969-93, prof. emerita, 1994—. Author: Marcel Proust, 1953, Eugene Le Roy, 1957, Corbiere, Laforgue and Apollinaire, 1964, Helen of Troy Myth, 1968, (poetry) Mooring to France, (prose poem) Sydney: editor: Dictionary of Ideas in Marcel Proust, 1968, also articles in field; contbr. articles to profl. jours. Scholar Internat. Inst. Edn., 1948-51, MLA, 1956-57, AAUW, 1962-63, Am. Philos. Soc., 1970-71, NEH, 1989; elected to Hall of Fame, Alumni Assn. Hunter Coll. of CUNY, 1990. Mem. MLA, Am. Assn. Tchrs. French, Soc. Friends Marcel Proust. Office: Stanford U Dept French and Italian Stanford CA 94305

NEWMARK, EMANUEL, ophthalmologist; b. Newark, May 25, 1936; s. Charles Meyer and Bella (Yoskowitz) N.; m. Tina Steinberg, Aug. 25, 1957; children: Karen Beth, Heidi Ellen, Stuart Jeffry. BS in Pharmacy, Rutgers U., 1959; postgrad., U. Amsterdam, The Netherlands, 1960-63, Armed Forces Inst. Pathology, Washington, 1971; MD, Duke U., 1966; Lancaster course in ophthalmology, Harvard U., 1967. Diplomate Am. Bd. Ophthalmology. Intern George Washington U. Hosp., Washington, 1966; trainee NIH rsch. Univ. Fla., Gainesville, 1967-70; resident ophthalmology U. Fla. Hosp., 1967-70; instr. dept. ophthalmology Univ. Fla., 1970; cons. ophthalmology Gainesville VA Hosp., 1970; clin. instr. ophthalmology U. Tex. Med. Sch., San Antonio, 1971-72; cons. ophthalmology Kerrville (Tex.) VA Hosp., 1971-72; asst. chief ophthalmology svc. Brooke Army Gen. Hosp., Fort Sam, Tex., 1971-72; clin. prof. Bascom Palmer Eye Inst., Miami, Fla., 1995—; clin. asst. prof. ophthalmology Bexar County Hosp. and Clinics, San Antonio, 1971-72; tchg. faculty Joint Com. Allied Health Pers. Ophthalmology, St. Paul, 1981—; chief ophthalmology svc. JFK Med. Ctr., Atlantis, Fla., 1982; cons. Bascom Palmer Eye Inst., 1983—; dir., sec., treas. Palm Beach Eye Assocs., Atlantis, 1973—; mem. pharm. adv. com. Agy. for Health Care Adminstrn. Bd. Optometry, 1991; mem. med. adv. bd. Fla. east coast chpt. Nat. Sjorgren's Syndrome Assn., 1990—; bd. dirs. Fla. Eye Injury and Disease Registry. Contbr. chpts. to 4 textbooks, over 12 articles to med. jours. Alumni assoc. Rutgers Coll. Pharmacy, 1960—; chmn. reunion 1986 Duke U. Med. Alumni Assn., N.C., 1967—; centurian Davison Club-Duke U. Med. Sch., N.C., 1982—; campaign chmn., nat. vice chmn. Israel Bonds, Palm Beach County, Fla., 1988—; participant charitable orgns.; v.p. Palm Beach Liturgical Culture Found., 1987-94, treas., trustee, 1987-94. Decorated Lion of Judea State of Israel, 1984; recipient Gates of Jerusalem medal, 1991, Jerusalem 3000 medal, 1996. Fellow ACS, Am. Acad. Ophthalmology (del. coun., Fla. state chmn. ednl. trust), Am. Castroveiejo Cornea Soc.; mem. AMA, Internat. Platform Assn., Assn. for Rsch. in Vision and Ophthalmology, Am. Orgn. for Rehab. Through Tng. Fedn. (nat. exec. com.-campaign cabinet 1987, pres. 1990—, Palm Beach Men's Achievement award 1988, Pres. award 1989), Fla. Med. Assn. (ho. dels. 1993-96), Palm Beach County Ophthal. Soc. (pres. 1984-85), Fla. Soc. Ophthalmology (ethics chmn. 1985-90, pres. 1990-91, James. W. Clower Jr. Cmty. Svc. award 1995), Founder's Soc. Duke U. Jewish. Avocations: travel, radio broadcasting, teaching. Home: 335 Glenbrook Dr Atlantis FL 33462-1009 Office: Palm Beach Eye Assocs 140 JFK Dr Atlantis FL 33462-1159

NEWMARK, HOWARD, surgeon, entrepreneur; b. Perth Amboy, N.J., Mar. 12, 1944; s. Carl and Ruth (Kestenbaum) N.; m. Mary Ella Adkins, Feb. 19, 1989. BA, Duke U., 1966; MD, Meharry Med. Coll., 1970; MBA, Ohio U., 1988. Diplomate Am. Bd. Abdominal Surgery. Intern Cook County Hosp., Chgo., 1971; resident in surgery Med. Coll. of Ohio, Toledo, 1975; resident in thoracic surgery U. Louisville, 1979; chief exec. officer, pres. Summa Med. Systems, Ashland, Ky., Ironton, Ohio, Huntington, W.Va., 1987—; pvt. practice surgeon Portsmouth, Ohio, 1979-81, Ashland, 1981-83, Ironton, 1983—, Huntington, 1990; surgeon Lawrence County Med. Ctr., Ironton, Cabell-Huntington Hosp., Huntington ; med. dir. dept. of emergency medicine Vets. Meml. Hosp., Pomeroy, Ohio, 1996—. Maj. USAF, 1975-77. Named Eagle Scout Boy Scouts Am. Fellow Am. Soc. Phlebology, Am. Soc. Abdominal Surgeons, Am. Coll. Angiology, Internat. Coll. Angiology, Internat. Coll. Surgeons; mem. AMA, ASPCA, PETA, Am. Thoracic Soc., N.Am. Soc. Pacing and Electrophysiology, Soc. Vascular Tech., Internat. Endovascular Soc., Am. Coll. Chest Physicians, Am. Coll. Physicians Execs. (alt. del.), Ohio State Med. Assn. (pres.), Lawrence County Med. Assn., Am. Mgmt. Assn., Pres.'s Assn., Greenpeace, Costeau Soc. Democrat. Jewish. Avocations: golf, stamp collecting, art collecting, writing. Office: 207 S 7th St Ironton OH 45638-1621 also: 1631 Offnere St Portsmouth OH 45662-3537

NEWMARK, LEONARD DANIEL, linguistics educator; b. Attica, Ind., Apr. 8, 1929; s. Max Jacob and Sophie (Glusker) N.; m. Ruth Broessler, Sept. 16, 1951; children: Katya, Mark. AB, U. Chgo., 1947; MA, Ind. U., 1951, PhD, 1955. Instr. English U. Ill., Urbana, 1951; vis. asst. prof. linguistics U. Mich., Ann Arbor, 1961; assoc. prof. English Ohio State U., 1954-62; assoc. prof. linguistics Ind. U., Bloomington, 1962-63; prof. linguistics U. Calif., San Diego, 1963-91, prof. emeritus, 1992—, chmn. dept., 1963-71, 79-85, head program in Am. lang. and culture, 1979-84, rsch. linguist Ctr. for Rsch. in Lang., 1992—. Author: Linguistic History of English, 1963, Spoken Albanian, 1981, Standard Albanian, 1982; inventor memory aid device. Mem. Linguistics Soc. Am., Dictionary Soc. N.Am., Phi Beta Kappa. Home: 2643 St Tropez Pl La Jolla CA 92037-3541 Office: U Calif San Diego Dept Linguistics La Jolla CA 92093

NEWMARK, MILTON MAXWELL, lawyer; b. Oakland, Calif., Feb. 24, 1916; s. Milton and Mary (Maxwell) N.; m. Marion Irene Johnson, July 31, 1941 (dec.); children—Mari Newmark Anderson, Lucy Newmark Sammons, Grace Newmark Lucini; m. Aylene Pruett Rosselli, June 21, 1991. A.B., U. Calif.-Berkeley, 1936, J.D., 1947. Bar: Calif. 1940, U.S. Supreme Ct. 1944. Ptnr. Milton Newmark, San Francisco, 1941-56; sole practice, 1956-62; sole practice, Lafayette, Calif., 1962-80, Walnut Creek, Calif., 1980-94; lectr. bankruptcy State Bar of Calif. Continuing Edn. Program. Served with U.S. Army, 1942-46; to lt. col. USAR. Mem. Alameda County Rep. Cen. Com., 1940-41; pres. Alameda Rep. Assembly, 1950. Mem. Am. Legion, ABA, San Francisco Bar Assn., Contra Costa Bar Assn., Alameda County Bar Assn., Scabbard and Blade. Lodges: Masons, Shriners, Rotary. Home: 609 Terra California Dr Apt 6 Walnut Creek CA 94595-3344

NEWMEYER, FREDERICK JARET, linguist, educator; b. Phila., Jan. 30, 1944; s. Alvin S. and Fritzie B. (Nisenson) N.; m. Carolyn V. Platt, Apr. 28, 1968 (div. 1974); m. Marilyn M. Goebel, Dec. 25, 1993. BA, U. Rochester, 1965, MA, 1967; PhD, U. Ill., 1969. Asst. prof. linguistics U. Wash., Seattle, 1969-75, assoc. prof., 1975-81, prof., 1981—; chair, 1990—; vis. prof. U. London, 1979, Cornell U., 1981, U. Md., 1982, UCLA, 1982-83, La Trobe U., Australia, 1987. Author: English Aspectual Verbs, 1975, Linguistic Theory in America, 1980, Grammatical Theory, 1983, Politics of Linguistics, 1986, Generative Linguistics, 1995; editor: Linguistics: The Cambridge Survey, 1988, Natural Language and Linguistic Theory, 1987—; assoc. editor: Language, 1980-85. NEH fellow, 1973-74. Mem. Linguistic Soc. Am. (sec.-treas. 1989-94). Avocations: gardening. Home: 4621 NE 107th St Seattle WA 98125-6947 Office: Univ of Wash Dept Linguistics Seattle WA 98195

NEWPORT, JOHN PAUL, philosophy of religion educator, former academic administrator; b. Buffalo, Mo., June 16, 1917; s. Marvin Jackson and Mildred (Morrow) N.; m. Eddie Belle Leavell, Nov. 14, 1941; children: Martha Ellen, Frank M., John P. Jr. BA, William Jewell Coll., Liberty, Mo., 1938; ThM, So. Bapt. Theol. Sem., Louisville, 1941, ThD, 1946; PhD, U. Edinburgh, Scotland, 1953; MA, Tex. Christian U., 1968; LittD, William Jewell Coll., 1967. Assoc. prof. Baylor U., 1949-51, New Orleans Bapt. Theol. Sem, 1951-52; prof. Southwestern Bapt. Theol. Sem, Ft. Worth, 1952-76, Rice U., 1976-79; v.p. acad. affairs, provost Southwestern Bapt. Theol. Sem., 1979-90, v.p. emeritus, spl. asst. to pres., 1990—, disting. prof. philosophy of religion, 1990—; vis. prof. Princeton Theol. Sem., 1982. Author: Theology and Contemporary Art Forms, 1971, Demons, Demons, Demons, 1972, Why Christians Fight over the Bible, 1974, Christ and the New Consciousness, 1978, Christianity and Contemporary Art Forms, 1979, Nineteenth Century Devotional Thought, 1981, Paul Tillich, 1984, What Is Christian Doctrine? 1984, The Lion and the Lamb, 1986, Life's Ultimate Questions, 1989; contbr. numerous articles to jours. and mags. Sealantic fellowship Rockefeller Found., Harvard U., 1958-59. Mem. Am. Acad. Religion (pres. S.W. div. 1967-68), Soc. Bibl. Lit. and Exegesis, Southwestern Philos. Assn., N.Am. Paul Tillich Soc. (dir. 1984-86), Southside C. of C. (Ft. Worth), Downtown Rotary Cub (Ft. Worth), Ft. Worth Club. Democrat. Avocations: golf, swimming, tennis. Office: Southwestern Bapt Theol Sem PO Box 22000 Fort Worth TX 76122

NEWPORT, L. JOAN, clinical social worker, psychotherapist; b. Ponca City, Okla., July 5, 1932; d. Crawford Earl and Lillian Pearl (Peden) Irvine; m. Don E. Newport, July 9, 1954 (div. July 1971); children: Alan Keith, Lili Kim. BA cum laude, Wichita State U., 1955; MSW, U. Okla., 1977. Bd. cert. diplomate in clin. social work Acad. Cert. Social Workers; lic. social worker, Okla. Dir. children's work Wesley United Meth. Ch., Oklahoma City, 1969-71; social worker Dept. Human Svcs., Newkirk, Okla., 1972-77; in-sch. suspension counselor Kay County Youth Svcs., Ponca City, Okla., 1977; med. social worker St. Joseph Med. Ctr., Ponca City, 1977-78, dir. social work, 1978-83; pvt. practice Ponca City, 1979—; med. social worker Healthcare Svcs., Ponca City, 1983-84; cons. Blackwell, Perry, Pawhuska, O'Keene Hosps., 1978-85; cons. social work Bass Meml. Hosp., Enid, Okla., 1985; sponsor, organizer Kay County Parents Anonymous, Ponca City, 1976-83; vice chair Okla. State Bd. Lic. Social Workers, Oklahoma City, 1988-90; presentor, lectr. in field; supr. students Okla. U. Sch. Social Work. Mem. Okla. Women's Network, 1989—; mem. adv. bd. Displaced Homemakers, Ponca City, 1985-89; mem. adv. bd. Kay County Home Health, 1979-83, chair, 1979-81. Named Hon. State Life Mem. Burbank PTA, Oklahoma City, 1971; scholar Wichita (Kans.) Press and Radio Women, 1953, Conoco, Inc., Houston, 1951-54. Mem. NASW (Okla. del. Del. Assembly Washington 1987, chmn. vendorship com. 1985-87, pres. Okla. chpt. 1988-90, Social Worker of Yr. 1987), Child Abuse Prevention Task Force (pres. dist. 17 1986-88, mem. grant evaluation com. 1986-96), Zeta Phi Eta. Democrat. Methodist. Home: 109 N Walnut Ave Newkirk OK 74647-2036 Office: 619 E Brookfield Ave Ponca City OK 74601-2804

NEWQUIST, DON, federal agency administrator; b. Stamford, Tex., Aug. 23, 1943. BBA, McMurry U., 1966; postgrad., Tex. Tech U. Farmer Jones County, 1973—; asst. gen. mgr. C. of C., Corpus Christi, Tex., 1969-72; gen. mgr. C. of C., Denver, 1972-74; asst. v.p. Valero Energy Corp., San Antonio, 1974-80, v.p., then sr. v.p., dir. subs. cos., 1980—; commr. U.S. Internat. Trade Commn., Washington, 1988—, chmn., 1991-94. With USN, 1967-69, Vietnam. Mem. South Tex. C. of C. (past pres.). Office: US Intl Trade Commn 500 E St NW Ste 704 Washington DC 20436-0003

NEWS, KATHRYN ANNE, editor, educator, writer; b. McPherson County, Kans., Mar. 16, 1934; d. Henry J. and Mary J. (Kauffman) Goering; m. Albert D. Klassen Jr. (div. June 1976); children: Teresa C., Jean A., Eric P., Rachel S.; m. Francis W. News, Mar. 4, 1982. Student, Bethel Coll., 1952-54, Washburn U., 1964-67; BA, Roosevelt U., 1968; MA, Ind. U., 1971. Assoc. editor Holiday mag. Curtis Pub. Co., Indpls., 1973-74, mng. editor, 1974-77; travel page cons. Sat. Evening Post, 1976-77, Country Gentleman, 1976-77; editor Going Places mag. Chilton Publs., Radnor, Pa., 1977-79; mng. editor Réalités mag., 1979-81, Spring mag. Rodale Press, 1981-82; assoc. prof. communications Temple U., Phila., 1982—. Author: Great Escapes: An Executive's Guide to Fine Resorts, 1980. Recipient cert. of merit Atlantic Monthy, 1958; 1st Place Fellowship award Ind. U. Writers Conf., 1970, Golden Basset award, 1973, Chilton Editorial award, 1978. Office: Temple U Dept Journalism Philadelphia PA 19122

NEWSOM, CAROLYN CARDALL, management consultant; b. South Weymouth, Mass., Feb. 27, 1941; d. Alfred James and Bertha Virginia (Roy) Cardall; m. John Harlan Newsom, Feb. 4, 1967; children: John Cardall, James Harlan. AB, Brown U., 1962; MBA, Wharton Sch., 1978; PhD, U. Pa., 1985. Systems engr. IBM, Seattle, 1964-70, Newsom S.E. Services, Seattle, 1970-76; instr. U. Pa. Wharton Sch., Phila., 1978-81; v.p., prin. sr. cons. PA Cons. Group, Princeton, N.J., 1981-88; pres. Newsom Assocs., Yardley, Pa., 1988; ptnr. Bus. Strategy Implementation, Princeton, N.J., 1989-90; pres. Strategy Implementation Solutions, Yardley, Pa., 1990—; examiner N.J. Quality Achievement Award, 1993-94, sr. examiner, 1995-96. Trustee St. Mary Hosp., Langhorne, Pa., 1986-94; bd. dirs. Chandler Hall. Mem. AAUW, Acad. Mgmt., Am. Mgmt. Assn., Am. Soc. for Quality Control, Am. Bus. Women's Assn., Brown Alumni Assn. (pres.-elect 1993-95, pres. 1995-97), Quality N.J. Office: Strategy Implementation Solutions 1588 Woodside Rd Yardley PA 19067-2611

NEWSOM, DAVID DUNLOP, foreign service officer, educator; b. Richmond, Calif., Jan. 6, 1918; s. Fred Stoddard and Ivy Elizabeth (Dunlop) N.; m. Jean Frances Craig, Nov. 17, 1942; children: John, Daniel, Nancy, David, Catherine. AB, U. Calif., 1938; MS, Columbia U., 1940; LLD, U. Pacific, 1979. Pulitzer traveling scholar, 1940-41; pub. Walnut Creek (Calif.) Courier-Jour., 1946-47; 3d sec., info. officer Am. embassy, Karachi, Pakistan, 1948-50; 2d sec., vice consul Oslo, 1950-51; pub. affairs officer Baghdad, Iraq, 1952-55; officer-in-charge Arabian peninsula affairs Dept. State, Washington, 1955-59; with Nat. War Coll., 1959-60; 1st sec. Am. embassy, London, 1960-62; dep. dir. Office No. African Affairs, Dept. State, Washington, 1962-63; dir. Office No. African Affairs, Dept. State, 1963-65; U.S. ambassador Libya, 1965-69; asst. sec. state for African affairs, 1969-74; U.S. ambassador Indonesia, 1974-77, Philippines, 1977-78; undersec. state of polit. affairs Washington, 1978-81; dir. Inst. Study of Diplomacy, Sch. Fgn. Svc., Georgetown U., 1981-90, Marshall Coyne rsch. prof. diplomacy, 1989-91; interim dean Sch. Fgn. Svc. Georgetown U., 1995-96; Cumming Meml. prof. internat. rels. U. Va., 1991—; spl. adviser U.S. del. UN Gen. Assembly, 1972, 78, 79, 80. Served to lt. USNR, 1942-46. Recipient Commendable Service award USIS, 1955; Dept. State Meritorious Service award, 1958; Nat. Civil Service League award, 1972; Rockefeller Pub. Service award, 1973. Mem. U.S. Fgn. Svc. Assn., Coun. Fgn. Rels., Cosmos Club. Presbyterian. Home: 2409 Angus Rd Charlottesville VA 22901

NEWSOM, DOUGLAS ANN JOHNSON, author, journalism educator; b. Dallas, Jan. 16, 1934; d. J. Douglas and R. Grace (Dickson) Johnson; m. L. Mack Newsom, Jr., Oct. 27, 1956 (dec.); children: Michael Douglas, Kevin Jackson, Nancy Elizabeth, William Macklemore; m. Bob J. Carrell, 1993. BJ cum laude, U. Tex., 1954, BFA summa cum laude, 1955, M in Journalism 1956, PhD, 1978. Gen. publicity State Fair Tex., 1955; advt. and promotion Newsom's Women's Wear, 1956-57; publicist Auto Market Show, 1961; lab. instr. radio-tv news-writing course U. Tex., 1961-62; local publicist Tex. Boys Choir, 1964-69, nat. publicist, 1967-69; pub. rels. dir. Gt. S.W. Boat Show Dallas, 1966-72, Family Fun Show, 1970-71, Horace Ainsworth Co., Dallas, 1966-76; pres. Profl. Devel. Cons., Inc., 1976-89; faculty Tex. Christian U., Ft. Worth, 1969—, prof. dept. journalism, chmn. dept., 1979-86, adviser yearbook and mag., 1969-79; dir. ONEOK Inc., diversified energy co., 1980—; Fulbright lectr. in India, 1988. Author: (with Alan Scott) This is PR, 1976, 3d edit., 1984, (with Alan Scott and Judy Van Slyke Turk) 4th edit., 1989, 6th edit., 1995, (with Judy Van Slyke Turk and Dean Kruckeberg), 1996, (with Bob Carrell) Writing for Public Relations Practice, 4th edit., 1994, (with Jim Wollert) Media Writing, 1984, 2d edit., 1988; editor (with Carrell) Silent Voices, 1995; mem. editorial bd. Pub. Rels. Rev., 1978—. Sec.-treas. Pub. Rels. Found. Tex., 1979-80, also trustee; pub. rels. chmn. local Am. Heart Assn., 1973-76, state pub. rels. com. 1974-82, chmn., 1980-82; trustee Inst. for Pub. Rels. Rsch. and Edn., 1985-89; mem. Gas Rsch. Adv. Coun., 1981—. Fellow Pub. Rels. Soc. Am. (chmn. Coll. Fellows 1992, nat. edn. com. 1975, chmn. 1978, nat. faculty adviser, chmn. edn. sect.); mem. Assn. Edn. in Journalism and Mass Communication (pres. pub. rels. div. 1974-75, nat. pres. 1984-85), Women in Communications (nat. conv. treas. 1967, nat. pub. rels. chmn. 1969-71), Tex. Pub. Rels. Assn. (dir. 1976-84, v.p. 1980-82, pres. 1982-83), Mortar Bd. Alumnae (adviser Tex. Christian U. 1974-75), Phi Kappa Phi, Kappa Tau Alpha, Phi Beta Delta. Episcopalian. Home: 4237 Shannon Dr Fort Worth TX 76116-8043 Office: Tex Christian U Dept Journalism PO Box 298060 Fort Worth TX 76129

NEWSOM, ERIC DAVID, diplomat; b. Wetumka, Okla., Apr. 5, 1943; s. Harley Johnson and Margaret Louise (Roberts) N.; m. Evea Souza, Sept. 8, 1963; children: Joel Andrew, James Eric. BA in History, U. Calif., Berkeley, 1965, MA in European History, 1967. Fgn. svc. officer Dept. of State, Washington, 1967-79; profl. staff mem. Senate Fgn. Rels. Com., Washington, 1979-81; asst. to former Sec. of State Cyrus Vance Washington, 1981-82; profl. staff mem. Senate Intelligence Com., Washington, 1982-85, minority staff dir., 1985-87; legis. dir. Office of Sen. Patrick Leahy, Washington, 1987-89; staff dir fgn. ops. subcom. Senate Appropriations Com., Washington, 1989-94; prin. dep. asst. sec. of state for polit.-mil. affairs Dept. of State, Washington, 1994—. Asst. to author (Cyrus Vance) Hard Choices, 1982. Avocations: fly fishing, family history, computers.

NEWSOM, GERALD HIGLEY, astronomy educator; b. Albuquerque, Feb. 11, 1939; s. Carroll Vincent and Frances Jeanne (Higley) N.; m. Ann Catherine Bricker, June 17, 1972; children: Christine Ann, Elizabeth Ann. BA, U. Mich., 1961; MA, Harvard U., 1963, PhD, 1968. Research asst. McMath-Hulbert Obs., Pontiac, Mich., summers 1959, 61; research asst. astronomy dept. U. Mich., Ann Arbor, 1959-61; research asst. Shock Tube Lab. Harvard U., Cambridge, Mass., 1962, 64-68; research asst. dept. physics Imperial Coll., London, 1968-69; asst. prof. astronomy Ohio State U., Columbus, 1969-73, assoc. prof., 1973-82, prof., 1982—, acting chmn. dept. astronomy, 1991-93, vice chmn. dept. astronomy, 1993—, acting asst. dean, 1985-86; sr. post-doctoral research asst. Physikalisches Institut, Bonn, Fed. Republic of Germany, 1978. Author: Astronomy, 1976, Exploring the Universe, 1979; contbr. articles to profl. and scholarly jours. Fellow Woodrow Wilson Found., 1961-62, NSF, 1961-63; grantee Noble Found., 1961-64. Mem. Internat. Astron. Union, Am. Astron. Soc. Home: 46 W Weisheimer Rd Columbus OH 43214-2545 Office: Ohio State U Dept Astronomy 174 W 18th Ave Columbus OH 43210-1106

NEWSOM, JAMES T., lawyer; b. Carrollton, Mo., Oct. 6, 1944; s. Thomas Edward and Hazel Love (Mitchell) N.; m. Sherry Elaine Retzloff, Aug. 9, 1986; stepchildren: Benjamin A. Bawden, Holly K. Bawden. AB, U. Mo., 1966, JD, 1968. Bar: Mo. 1968, U.S. Supreme Ct. 1971. Assoc. Shook,

Hardy & Bacon, London and Kansas City, Mo., 1972, ptnr., 1976—. Mem. Mo. Law Rev., 1966-68. Lt. comdr. JAGC, USNR, 1968-72. Mem. ABA, Internat. Bar Assn., Kansas City Met. Bar Assn., Lawyers Assn. Kansas City, U. Mo. Law Sch. Law Soc., Kansas City Club, U. Mo. Jefferson Club, Order of Coif. Avocations: skiing, sailing, car racing. Office: Shook Hardy & Bacon One Kansas City Pl 1200 Main St Ste 3100 Kansas City MO 64105-2100

NEWSOM, MELVIN MAX, retired research company executive; b. El Paso, Tex., Dec. 27, 1931; s. Melvin William and Dorthy Maxine (Kinnison) N.; m. Rose Marie Neill, June 5, 1953; children—Terri Laine, Cherri Leigh, Michael Dirk, Thomas Cody. B.S. in Elec. Engring, Tex. A. and M. U., 1955, M.S. in Elec. Engring. (Tex. Power & Light fellow), 1956. Mem. tech. staff Sandia Lab., Albuquerque, 1956—; sect. supr. Sandia Lab., 1961-64, div. supr., 1964-77, dept. mgr., 1977-92, dir. Ctr. for Applied Def. Tech., 1992-94; cons. Dept. Energy; mem. U.S. group on petroleum tech. Joint U.S./USSR Energy Program; participant several programs Nat. Acad. Engring. Contbr. numerous articles to profl. jours. Dist. chmn. Rep. Party, 1960-61, asst., 1963-64. With USN, 1951-53. Decorated Am. Spirit Honor medal; Dept. Energy grantee. Mem. Am. Inst. Mining Engrs., Am. Rose Soc., Tau Beta Pi, Etta Kappa Nu. Presbyterian. Club: Coronado (chmn. bd. 1965-66, 69-70, 73-74, 76-79, dir.). Research in improved drilling tech. for petroleum, geothermal and sci. drilling, and on high temperature well logging. Home: PO Box 856 304 Calle del Corte Elephant Butte NM 87935

NEWSOME, EDWARD BALDWIN, retired real estate broker, retired insurance agent; b. Utica, Miss., Dec. 1, 1920; s. Baldwin Mims and Tommie Effie (Pickett) N.; m. Mary Janet Kirkwood, June 11, 944; children: Janet Therese, Kirk Edward. BS, Miss. State U., 1941. Cert. ins. agent, real estate agent; CPCU, GRI. Ins. agent Jim Newsome Ins., Moscow, Idaho, 1948-88; real estate broker, owner Jim Newsome Real Estate, Moscow, 1988-95; ret., 1995; adj. prof. ins. U. Idaho, Moscow, 1975-87, Wash. State U., 1989-90. Bd. mem. Moscow Cemetary Bd. Lt. USN, 1942-45. Mem. VFW, Am. Legion (dept. state commdr. 1967-68, local commdr.), Elks (bd. trustees chmn. 1948); Moose, Moscow C. of C. (pres., bd. trustees). Republican. Avcoations: hunting, fishing, billiards.

NEWSOME, GEORGE LANE, JR., education educator; b. Bessemer, Ala., Oct. 5, 1923; s. George Lane and Mary Viola (Mobbs) N.; m. Martha Cornelia Merchant, June 8, 1947; children: George Lane III, Mary Virginia, Elizabeth Ann. BS, U. Ala., 1949, MA, 1950; PhD, Yale, 1956. Asst. prof. edn. U. Bridgeport, 1955-57, assoc. prof., 1957-58; assoc. prof. philosophy edn. U. Ga., 1958-63, prof., head dept., 1963-85, prof. emeritus philosophy edn., 1990—, mem. dept. curriculum and supervision, 1985-90; guest prof. Philosophy Inst., No. Ill. U., U. Pacific, 1970; guest lectr. U. Bridgeport, 1954-55. Author: Philosophical Perspectives, 1961; editor: Philosophy of Education Proces., 1968, (with William T. Blackstone) Education and Ethics, 1969; mem. editorial bd. Ga. Rev., 1973-75, Ednl. Theory, 1976-78; co-editor Jour. R & D in Edn., 1982-85, editor, 1985-89, bd. cons., 1991—. With AUS, 1943-46. Mem. Philosophy of Edn. Soc. (sec.-treas. 1964-66, pres. 1981-82), Southeastern Philosophy of Edn. Soc. (sec.-treas. 1961, v.p. 1962), U. Ga. Ret. Tchrs. Assn. (v.p. 1994-95, pres. 1995-96), Phi Kappa Phi, Kappa Delta Pi. Home: 145 Tuxedo Rd Athens GA 30606-3133

NEWSOME, GEORGE MARVIN, lawyer; b. Phenix City, Ala., June 30, 1919; s. Thomas L. and Mary E. (Spivey) N.; m. Norma Elizabeth Hollomon, Aug. 19, 1941; children—Keith, Glenn, Carol. AA, George Washington U., LLB, 1948. Bar: D.C. Dist. Ct. 1949, Va. 1990. With IBM 1945-83, office adminstrn., Washington, 1945-49, atty., N.Y.C., 1949-51, plant counsel, Poughkeepsie, Kingston, N.Y., 1951-59, div. counsel, White Plains, N.Y., 1959-68, staff counsel, Armonk, N.Y., 1968-79, staff counsel, Washington, 1979-83; pvt. practice law, Washington, 1983-89, Fairfax, Va., 1989—. Pres., United Way No. Westchester, 1974-79, v.p., 1977-79. Sgt. USAF, 1942-45; 1st lt. (JAG) Res., 1951-56. Recipient Marshall award United Way No. Westchester, 1977. Mem. ABA, Fairfax Bar Assn., D.C. Bar Assn., Va. Bar Assn., Nat. Security Indsl. Assn. Home: 10520 Wickens Rd Vienna VA 22181-3032 Office: 10623 Jones St Ste 301-B Fairfax VA 22030-5116

NEWSOME, RANDALL JACKSON, judge; b. Dayton, Ohio, July 13, 1950; s. Harold I. and Sultana S. (Stony) N.; B.A. summa cum laude, Boston U., 1972; J.D., U. Cin., 1975. Bar: Ohio 1975, U.S. Dist. Ct. (so. dist.) Ohio 1977, U.S. Ct. Appeals (6th cir.) 1979, U.S. Supreme Ct. 1981. Law clk. to chief judge U.S. Dist. Ct., So. Dist. Ohio, 1975-77; assoc. Dinsmore & Shohl, Cin., 1978-82; judge U.S. Bankruptcy Ct., So. Dist. Ohio, Cin., 1982-88, No. Dist. Calif., Oakland, 1988—. Faculty mem. Fed. Jud. Ctr., ALI-ABA, 1987—; mem. Nat. Conf. of Bankruptcy Judges, 1983—, mem. bd. govs., 1987-88. Fellow Am. Coll. Bankruptcy; mem. Am. Bankruptcy Inst., Phi Beta Kappa. Democrat. Mem. United Ch. of Christ. Office: US Bankruptcy Ct PO Box 2070 Oakland CA 94604-2070

NEWSOME, SANDRA SINGLETON, elementary education educator, assistant principal; b. Bayboro, N.C., Apr. 4, 1948; d. John Wilson Singleton and Cora Lee (Beasley) Hatchel; m. Edward Newsome Jr., Feb. 14, 1971. BS, Elizabeth City State U., 1970; MS, Bowie State U., 1979; EdD, Pensacola Christian Coll., 1992. Cert. tchr., Washington. Tchr. D.C. Pub. Schs., Washington, 1970-80, reading tchr., 1980-82, reading specialist, 1982—; asst. prin. Calvary Temple Christian Sch., Sterling, Va., 1985-86; prof. Bowie State U., 1994—; adminstrv. intern Roper Mid. Sch. of Math. Sci. and Tech., Washington, 1993-95; cons. Bowie State Spl. Interest Coun., 1991-92, D.C.-Dakar Friendship Coun., 1991-92; mem. adv. bd. Walk In Faith mag., Washington, 1991-92; dir. Acad. Tutorial Program, Temple Hills, Md., 1990-91. Contbr. to profl. publs. Mentor Teen Parenting, Inc., Hyattville, Md., 1989, Valuettes, Washington, 1990-92; dir. Adult Literacy Coun., Temple Hills, 1990; asst. dir. Jr. Toastmasters, Brightwood, 1993; program developer, dir. Visions: A Tour into Values, Washington, 1993; pres. Hellen Lee Dr. Civic Assn., Clinton, 1994-95; dir. Christian Edn., Alexandria (Va.) Christian Ctr., 1994—. Recipient Save Our Youth Am. award Soya, Inc., Washington, 1989, Literacy award Bowie State U., 1991; Teacher-to-Teacher grantee, 1990-92; fellow Cafritz Found., 1991. Mem. ASCD, AFT, AAUW, LEAD Program, Nat. Black Child Devel. Inst., Bowie State Spl. Interest Orgn., Alexandria Christian Ctr., Hellen Lee Dr. Civic Assn. (pres. 1994-96). Avocations: interpretative poetry reading, travel, African studies, photography. Home: 2319 Parkside Dr Mitchellville MD 20721 Office: Roper Mid Sch Math Sci Tech 4800 Meade St NE Washington DC 20019

NEWSOME, WILLIAM ROY, JR., state official; b. Asheville, N.C., July 8, 1934; s. William R. and Mary (Morgan) N.; m. Mary Grace Daniel, Dec. 22, 1958; children: William Daniel, Bo Nathan. Cert., Tollare Folkhögskola, Stockholm, 1959; BS, U. Tenn., 1960; M in Regional Planning, U. N.C., 1962. Planner Tenn. State Planning Commn., Knoxville, 1959-62; city planner Athens (Tenn.) City Govt., 1962-64; campus planner U. Tenn., Knoxville, 1964-66; regional planner Atlanta Regional Planning Commn., 1966-68; planner Pa. State Planning Bd., Harrisburg, 1968-70; spl. advisor Pa. Dept. Community Affairs, Harrisburg, 1970-77; spl. asst. Fed. Emergency Mgmt. Agy., Washington, 1977-81; ptnr. The GNP Firm, Harrisburg, 1982-87; dir. Gov.'s Policy Office, Harrisburg, 1987-88; spl. asst. Pa. Housing Fin. Agy., Harrisburg, 1988—; bd. dirs. Pa. Community Devel. and Fin. Corp., Harrisburg. Pres., bd. dirs. Ctrl. Pa. Literacy Coun., Harrisburg, 1992—; bd. dirs. Cmty. Rsch. and Devel. Group, Burlington, Vt., 1994—; elected voting official Dauphin County, 1990—; mem. planning commn. Lower Paxton Twp., 1994—, sec. 1996. With USMC, 1954-57. Bd. dirs. Cen. Pa. Literary Coun., Harrisburg, 1992—; mem. Gov.'s Bldg. Energy Conservation Com., Harrisburg, 1989—; elected voting official Dauphin County, 1990—; mem. planning commn. Lower Paxton Twp., 1994—, sec. 1996. Served with USMC, 1954-57. Mem. Am. Inst. Cert. Planners (charter). Democrat. Home: 112 Maple Rd Harrisburg PA 17109-2730 Office: Pa Housing Fin Agy 2101 N Front St Harrisburg PA 17110-1036

NEWSTEAD, ROBERT RICHARD, urologist; b. Detroit, Sept. 16, 1935; s. Oran Henry and Agnes Audery (Lewandowski) N.; m. Marie Carmela LiPuma, Aug. 5, 1961; children: Elizabeth Marie, Peter Joseph, Angela Agnes, Paul Michael. Student, Coll. Idaho, 1955-57, Quincy Coll., 1957-58; MD, Loyola U., Chgo., 1963. Intern Walter Reed Gen. Hosp., Washington, 1963-64; resident U. Iowa, Iowa City, 1967-71; urologist Urology Clinic Yakima, Wash., 1971-84, pres., 1984—; chief of staff Yakima Valley Meml. Hosp., 1995—; chief of surgery St. Elizabeth Med. Ctr., Yakima, 1980-81, Yakima Valley Hosp., 1978-79. Bd. dirs. St. Elizabeth Found., Yakima, 1983-93, The Capital Theater, 1987-93, Boy Scouts Am., Yakima, 1982-86. Capt. U.S. Army, 1962-67. Fellow Am. Cancer Soc., Iowa City, 1969-70, Am. Cancer Soc., 1961; named one of Outstanding Young Men Am., 1968. Fellow Am. Bd. Urology, ACS, Am. Urol. Assn., Wash. State Urol. Bd. (mem. at large exec. com.); mem. AMA, Rubin Flocks Soc. (pres. 1985-86), Yakima Surgical Soc. (pres. 1982-83), Yakima County Med. Soc. (pres. 1989-90), Rotary. Roman Catholic. Avocations: art, skiing, golf. Home: 814 Conestoga Blvd Yakima WA 98908-2419 Office: Urology Clinic Yakima 206 S 11th Ave Yakima WA 98902-3205

NEWTON, BLAKE TYLER, III, lawyer; b. Richmond, Va., June 21, 1942; s. Blake Tyler Jr. and Anne Rodgers (Walker) N.; m. Belle Carter Blanchard, May 12, 1979; 1 child, Samuel Tyler Blanchard. AB, Coll. William & Mary, 1964; LLB, U. Va., 1967. Assoc. Hall, McNicol, Hamilton & Clark, N.Y.C., 1969-75, ptnr., 1975-92; ptnr. Keck, Mahin & Cate (previously Hall McNicol), N.Y.C., 1992—; bd. dirs. Roothbert Fund, N.Y.C. With U.S. Army, 1967-69, Korea. Mem. ABA, N.Y. Bar Assn., Assn. Bar City N.Y. Office: Keck Mahin & Cate 220 E 42nd St New York NY 10017-5806*

NEWTON, CHARLES CHARTIER, architect; b. Albuquerque, Feb. 18, 1933; s. Charles Edward and Aileen (Chartier) N.; m. Patricia Clarke, Sept. 6, 1958; children: Heather Ann, Amy Marie, April Chartier. BArch, Tex. A&M U., 1956; MArch, Cranbrook Acad. of Art, 1957. Lic. architect, Tex. Designer Caudill, Rowlett & Scott, Architects, Bryan, Tex., 1958, Eero Saarinen & Assocs., Birmingham, Mich., 1959-60; head design dept. Harrell & Hamilton, Architects, Dallas, 1960-63; project architect Matthews and Assocs., Bryan, 1963-66; assoc. prof. design, dir. Basic Architecture Program Tex. A&M U., College Station, 1963-68; assoc. prof. Sch. Architecture Rice U., Houston, 1968-70; designer Rapp, Tacket, Fash, Houston, 1968; assoc. Van Ness and Mower, Houston, 1969-70; ptnr. Emerson, Fehr, Newton, Austin, Tex., 1970-74; pres. Chartier Newton & Assocs., Austin, 1975-89; prin., v.p. Jessen, Inc., Austin, 1989-91; prin. Chartier Newton & Assocs., Austin, 1991—. Major projects include Clear Lake Grad. Ctr., 1972 (Houston AIA merit award), additions to Robert Mueller Airport, 1976 (Austin AIA design award), Chartier Newton family residence, 1976 (Austin AIA hon. award), Pecan Sq. Splty. Shopping Ctr. (Austin AIA design citation), restoration Henry Hirshfield House and Cottage, 1980 (Austin AIA design award with others), South Austin Multi-Purpose Ctr., 1980 (Austin AIA design award with others), Cedar St. Ct., 1981 (Austin Heritage Soc. award, Austin AIA design award, Tex. Soc. Architects award 1983, Carl W. Burnett award Austin Devel. Found. 1983), office Moore Trust Group, 1982 (Austin AIA design award), Seay House, 1982 (Austin AIA award), renovation Sutton Hall U. Tex. Austin, 1983 (Tex. Soc. Architects design award with others), Riverbend Bapt. Ch., 1985 (merit award ch. architecture dept. Sun. Sch. Bd. So. Bapt. Conv.), Goldsmith Hall U. Tex. (Tex. Soc. Architects honor award with others 1989), Corps of Cadets Ctr. Tex. A & M U. Pres. Environ. Conservancy Austin and Cen. Tex., 1978-79; vice chmn. Sierra Club Austin, 1973-75; mem. Rollingswood (Tex.) Planning and Zoning Commn., 1980-83; mem. guild bd. Austin History Ctr., 1981-82; sr. warden St. Michael's Episc. Ch., 1990. 1st lt. USAR, 1957-58. Fellow AIA (pres. Austin chpt. 1981, mem. Loop 361 Bridge Task Force 1978); mem. Tex. Soc. Archs. (chmn. educators liaison com. 1989-90), Rotary (bd. dirs. Austin 1982-83, 95—). Episcopalian. Avocations: backpacking, sketching, fishing. Office: 3001 S Lamar Blvd Ste 301 Austin TX 78704

NEWTON, CHRISTOPHER, artistic director. BA with honors, Univ. Leeds; MA, U. Ill.; LLD (hon.), Brock U., U. Guelph. Founder, artistic dir. Theatre Calgary, 1968-71; artistic dir. Vancouver Playhouse, 1971-79, Shaw Festival, 1979—. Dir. Sherlock Holmes; Busman's Honeymoon, The Silver King, Candida, Pointe Valaine, Lulu, Pygmalion, Misalliance, Man and Superman, Don Juan in Hell, Saint Joan, You Never Can Tell, Caesar and Cleopatra, Heartbreak House, Major Barbara, The Millionairess, (opera) Barber of Seville, Madama Butterfly, Die Fledermaus, Patria I, Porgy and Bess, I Due Foscari, Candida, The Silver King; actor (stage) The Marrying of Ann Leete, Charley's Aunt, Peter Pan, Private Lives, Camille, A Flea in Her Ear, Present Laughter; writer (stage plays) Slow Train to St. Ives, You Stay Here, The Rest Come With Me, Trip, The Sound of Distant Thunder, Where Are You When We Need You Simon Fraser. Recipient Queen's Silver Jubilee medal, 1977, Dora award, 1986; Royal Conservatory of Music, fellow (hon.), 1993. Office: Shaw Festival Theatre Found, PO Box 774, Niagara on the Lake, ON Canada L0S 1J0

NEWTON, DAVID GEORGE, diplomat; b. Boston, Nov. 13, 1935; s. Charles Paul and Gladys Emelda (Moore) N.; m. Christa Margarete Rathay, Dec. 16, 1961; children: Mark Andrew, Lesley Christina. BA cum laude, Harvard U., 1957; MA with honors, U. Mich., 1970; diploma, Arabic Lang. Sch., Fgn. Service Inst., Beirut, 1966, Nat. War Coll., Washington, 1978. Vice consul Am. consulate gen., Zurich, Switzerland, 1962-64; econ. officer Am. embassy, Sanaa, Yemen, 1966-67; econ. officer for Arabian Peninsula affairs Dept. State, Washington, 1967-69; polit. officer Am. embassy, Jeddah, Saudi Arabia, 1970-72; dep. chief of mission Sanaa, Yemen, 1972-75; div. chief Near East div. intelligence and research bur. Dept. State, Washington, 1975-77; dep. chief of mission Am. embassy, Damascus, Syria, 1978-81; polit. counselor Am. embassy, Jeddah, 1981-84; prin. officer U.S. Interests Sect., Baghdad, Iraq, 1984; ambassador to Iraq Baghdad, 1985-88; dir. Office for Lebanon, Jordan & Syria Near East Bur. Dept. State, 1988-90; internat. affairs advisor, chmn. Dept. Nat. Security Policy, Nat. War Coll., Washington, 1990-93; sr. inspector, team leader Office of Inspector Gen. Dept. State, Washington, 1993-94; ambassador to Yemen Sanaa, 1994—. Served to 1st lt. U.S. Army, 1958-61. Recipient awards Dept. State, 1967, 75, 83-90, Dept. Army, 1993. Mem. Middle East Inst., Middle East Studies Assn. Mem. United Ch. of Christ. Avocations: philately, book collecting, running. Office: Am Embassy Sanaa Dept of State Washington DC 20521-6330

NEWTON, DON ALLEN, foundation administrator; b. Laurel, Miss., Oct. 19, 1934; s. Wilfred L. and Mary (McMullan) N.; m. Coleta Farrell, Oct. 11, 1958; children: Don Jr., Coleta Midge. AA, Meridian C.C., 1954; BA in Journalism, U. Ala., 1956; postgrad. bus. mgmt., U. N.C.; postgrad., U. Okla. Asst. mgr. Meridian C. of C., Miss., 1956; mgr. Winston County C. of C., Louisville, Miss., 1960-61; asst. dir. Delta Council Indsl. and Community Devel. Bd., Stoneville, Miss., 1961-62; dir. Delta Coun. Indsl. and Cmty. Devel. Bd., Stoneville, Miss., 1963-70; exec. v.p. Met. Devel. Bd., Birmingham, Ala., 1970-74; exec. v.p. Birmingham Area C. of C., 1974-88, pres., 1988—; pres. Birmingham Area C. of C. Found., Inc., 1988—; pub. Birmingham Mag., Birmingham Bus. Mag. Contbr. articles to profl. jours., newspapers. Appointee Ala. Export Coun.; bd. dirs. Met. Devel. Bd., Birmingham, Ala. Sports Found. Lt. USNR, 1957-60. Named Ala. Mktg. Man of Yr., 1972. Mem. Ala. C. of C. Execs., Econ. Devel. Assn. Ala., Am. C. of C. Execs., U. Ala. Commerce Execs. Soc., Sigma Chi. Home: 2541 Canterbury Rd Birmingham AL 35223-1909 Office: Birmingham Area C of C PO Box 10127 2027 First Ave N Birmingham AL 35202-0127

NEWTON, GEORGE ADDISON, investment banker, lawyer; b. Denver, Apr. 2, 1911; s. George Addison and Gertrude (Manderson) N.; m. Mary Virginia Powell, Sept. 18, 1937; children: George Addison IV, Nancy Ella Newton Shaxer, Virginia Powell Newton Jacobi. AB, U. Colo., 1933; LLB, Harvard U., 1936. Bar: Ill. 1937, Mo. 1946. Asso. firm Scott, MacLeish & Falk, Chgo., 1936-42; partner G.H. Walker & Co., St. Louis, 1946-62; mng. partner G.H. Walker & Co., 1962-72; chmn. bd. Stifel Nicolaus & Co., Inc., St. Louis, 1972-82, chmn. emeritus, 1982—; chief exec. officer Stifel Nicolaus & Co., Inc., 1974-78. Bd. govs. Greater St. Louis Cmty. Chest; mem. Coun. on Civic Needs; bd. dirs. Goodwill Industries, 1963—, chmn. bd., 1980-82; bd. dirs. U. Colo. Improvement Corp., U. Colo. Found., St. Louis Conservatory Music; dir. devel. fund U. Colo., 1954-55, chmn., 1955; trustee Fontbonne Coll., 1972-80, chmn., 1974-77; trustee Govtl. Rsch. Inst.; trustee Whitfield Sch., 1978—, chmn., 1986-88, 89-90. Served to maj., USAAF, 1942-45. Decorated Order of the Rising Sun, Gold Rays and Rosette, Emperor of Japan, 1991; recipient C. Fobb award U. Colo., 1955, alumni Recognition award, 1958, named to C Club Hall of Fame, 1968, Silver Ann. All Am. award Sports Illustrated, 1957, Norlin award U. Colo., 1968; U. Colo. medal, 1984. Mem. Investment Bankers Assn. Am. (pres. 1961), Nat. Assn. Securities Dealers (gov. 1954-56, vice chmn. 1956), Assn. Stock Exchange Firms (gov. 1969-72), Sales Execs. Assn. (dir. 1955-60), U. Colo. Assn. Alumni (dir. 1965-67), Japan-Am. Soc. St. Louis (dir. 1980—, pres. 1982-85), The Robert Burns Club of St. Louis (pres. 1993), Phi Beta Kappa, Phi Gamma Delta. Episcopalian (treas. diocese of Mo., 1958-69; sr. warden; trustee diocesan investment trust). Clubs: Racquet (St. Louis), Noonday (St. Louis), St. Louis (St. Louis), Bellerive Country (St. Louis). Home: 6428 Cecil Ave Saint Louis MO 63105-2225 Office: Stifel Nicolaus & Co Inc 500 N Broadway Saint Louis MO 63102-2110 *A reward of one's own accomplishment is realizing how help of others made it possible.*

NEWTON, JAMES QUIGG, JR., lawyer; b. Denver, 1911; s. James Quigg and Nelle (Singleton) N.; m. Virginia Shafroth, June 6, 1942; children: Nancy Grusin, Nelle Grainger, Abby Hornung, Virginia Rice. AB, Yale U., 1933, LLB, 1936, MA (hon.), 1951; DPS (hon.), U. Denver, 1952; LLD, Adams State Coll., 1960, Colo. Coll., 1962, U. Colo., 1975. Bar: Colo. 1938. Legal sec. to W.O. Douglas SEC, 1936-37; practiced in Denver, 1938-42, 46-47; lectr. U. Denver, 1938-41; with Ford Found., N.Y.C., 1955-56; v.p. Ford Found., 1956; pres. U. Colo., 1956-63, Commonwealth Fund, N.Y.C., 1963-75; vice chmn. Commonwealth Fund, 1975-76, dir., 1951-55, 57-78; sr. cons. Henry J. Kaiser Family Found., Menlo Park, Calif., 1978-80; of counsel firm Davis, Graham & Stubbs, 1981—; dir. N.Y. Life Fund, 1972-95, Kaiser Found. Hosps./Health Plan, 1972-80; trustee Dry Dock Savs. Bank; mem. Yale Corp., 1951-55, Western Interstate Com. Higher Edn., 1957-63; mem. nat. adv. mental health coun. NIH, 1964-68; mem. Inst. Medicine, Nat. Acad. Scis., 1972—, VA Spl. Med. Adv. Group, 1968-74; fellow Ctr. for Advanced Study in Behavioral Scis., 1977-78. Mayor, City and County of Denver, 1947-55; Sec. bd. trustees U. Denver, 1938-42, pres., 1946-47; pub. trustee Nutrition Found.; chmn. bd. YMCA Greater N.Y., 1976-77. Served with USNR, 1942-46. Fellow Acad. Arts and Scis.; mem. Am. Municipal Assn. (pres. 1950), Am. Council Edn. (dir. 1959-62), Am. Arbitration Assn. (dir., exec. com.), Fgn. Bondholders Protective Council (dir. 1975—), Phi Delta Phi, Alpha Delta Phi. Home: 2552 E Alameda Ave Denver CO 80209-3320 Office: Davis Graham & Stubbs 370 17th St Denver CO 80202-5656

NEWTON, JOHN MILTON, acadmeic administrator, psychology educator; b. Schenectady, Feb. 25, 1929; s. Harry Hazleton and Bertha A. (Lehmann) N.; m. Elizabeth Ann Slattery, Sept. 11, 1954; children: Patricia, Peter, Christopher. B.S., Union Coll., Schenectady, 1951; M.A., Ohio State U., 1952, Ph.D., 1955. Lic. psychologist, Nebr. Research psychologist Electric Boat div. Gen. Dynamics Corp., Groton, Conn., 1957-60; mem. faculty U. Nebr., Omaha, 1960—; prof. psychology U. Nebr., 1966—, chmn. dept., 1967-74; dean U. Nebr. (Coll. Arts and Scis.), 1974-94; acting vice chancellor academic affairs U. Nebr., Omaha, 1994-95; cons. in field, 1960-72. Author research papers in field. Served to 1st lt. Med. Service Corps, AUS, 1955-57. Mem. Am. Psychol. Assn., Psychonomic Soc., Midwestern Psychol. Assn., Omaha-West Rotary. Home: 5611 Jones St Omaha NE 68106-1232 Office: Univ of Nebr-Omaha Dept Psychology Omaha NE 68182

NEWTON, JOHN WHARTON, III, lawyer; b. Beaumont, Tex., Feb. 18, 1953; s. John Wharton and Katherine (King) N.; children: Martha Garrison, John Wharton IV, Stephen King. BA, U. Tex., 1975; JD, U. Houston, 1978. Bar: Tex. 1979, U.S. Dist. Ct. (ea. dist.) Tex. 1979, U.S. Ct. Appeals (5th cir.) 1981, U.S. Dist. Ct. (so. dist.) Tex. 1987. Ptnr. Orgain, Bell & Tucker, Beaumont, 1984—. Mem. ABA, Tex. State Bar Assn., Tex. Assn. Def. Counsel, Jefferson County Bar Assn., Coll. of State Bar of Tex., Beaumont Club (pres. 1988-89). Episcopalian. Office: Orgain Bell & Tucker 470 Orleans St Beaumont TX 77701-3000

NEWTON, LISA HAENLEIN, philosophy educator; b. Orange, N.J., Sept. 17, 1939; d. Wallen Joseph and Carol Bigelow (Cypiot) Haenlein; m. Victor Joseph Newton, June 3, 1972; children: Tracey, Kit, Cynthia Perkins, Daniel Perkins, Laura Perkins. Student, Swarthmore Coll., 1957-59; BS in Philosophy with honors, Columbia U., 1962, PhD, 1967. Asst. prof. philosophy Hofstra U., Hempstead, N.Y., 1967-69; asst. prof. philosophy Fairfield U., Conn., 1969-73, assoc. prof., 1973-78, prof., 1978—, dir. program in applied ethics, 1983—, dir. program in environ. studies, 1986—; lectr. in medicine Yale U., 1984—; lectr., cons. in field. Author: Ethics in America; co-author: Watersheds, 1994, Wake-Up Calls, 1996; co-editor: Taking Sides: Controversial Issues Business Ethics, 4th edit., 1996; contbr.a rticles to profl. jours. Mem. exec. bd. Conn. Humanities Council, 1979-83. Mem. Am. Soc. Value Inquiry (past pres.), Am. Philos. Assn., Am. Soc. Polit. and Legal Philosophy, Acad. Mgmt., Am. Soc. Law and Medicine, Soc. Bus. Ethics (past pres.), Phi Beta Kappa. Home: 4042 Congress St Fairfield CT 06430-2041 Office: Fairfield U Dept Philosophy Fairfield CT 06430-7524

NEWTON, MICHAEL DAVID, lawyer; b. Dearborn, Mich., Feb. 1, 1967; s. Nicholas and Dorothy Marlene (Falk) N. BS, Birmingham-So. Coll., 1989; JD, U. Memphis, 1992. Bar: Tenn. 1992, U.S. Dist. Ct. (ea. dist.) Tenn. 1993. Assoc. J. Troy Wolfe & Assoc., Chattanooga, 1992-93; pvt. practice Chattanooga, 1993—; staff atty. Tenn. Mediation Group, Inc., Chattanooga, 1994—; guest lectr. U. Tenn., Chattanooga. Mem. sponsorship com. March of Dimes, Chattanooga, 1994. Mem. ABA, ATLA, Tenn. Bar Assn., Tenn. Trial Lawyers, Chattanooga Bar Assn. Avocations: golf, hunting, guitar, skiing, music. Home: 2035 Rock Bluff Rd Hixson TN 37343 Office: University Tower Ste 401 651 E 4th St Chattanooga TN 37403

NEWTON, NATE, professional football player; b. Orlando, Fla., Dec. 20, 1961. Student, Fla. A&M U. Guard Tampa (Fla.) Bay Bandits, U.S. Football League, 1984-85, Dallas Cowboys, 1986—. Selected to Pro Bowl, 1992-94; mem. Dallas Cowboys Super Bowl Champions XXVII, 1992, XXVIII, 1993. Office: Dallas Cowboys One Cowboys Pkwy Irving TX 75063*

NEWTON, RHONWEN LEONARD, writer, microcomputer consultant; b. Lexington, N.C., Nov. 13, 1940; d. Jacob Calvin and Mary Louise (Moffitt) Leonard; children: Blair Armistead, Newton Jones, Allison Page, William Brockenbrough III. AB, Duke U., 1962; MS in Edn., Old Dominion U., 1968. French tchr. Hampton (Va.) Pub. Schs., 1962-65, Va. Beach (Va.) Pub. Schs., 1965-66; instr. foreign lang. various colls. and univs., 1967-75; foreign lang. cons. Portsmouth (Va.) Pub. Schs., 1973-75; dir. The Computer Inst., Inc., Columbia, S.C., 1983; pres., founder The Computer Experience, Inc., Columbia, 1983-88, RN Enterprises, Columbia, 1991—. Author: WordPerfect, 1988, All About Computers, 1989, Microsoft Excel for the Mac, 1989, Introduction to the Mac, 1989, Introduction to DOS, 1989, Introduction to Lotus 1-2-3, 1989, Advanced Lotus 1-2-3, 1989, Introduction to WordPerfect, 1989, Advanced WordPerfect, 1989, Introduction to Display/Write 4, 1989, WordPerfect for the Mac, 1989, Introduction to Microsoft Works for the Mac, 1990, Accountant, Inc for the Mac, 1992, Introduction to Filemaker Pro, 1992, Quicken for the MAC, 1993, Quicken for Windows, 1993, WordPerfect for Windows, 1993, Advanced WordPerfect for Windows, 1993, Lotus 1-2-3 for Windows, 1993, Introduction to Quick Books, 1994, Quick Book for Windows, 1994, Introduction to Word for Windows, 1995. Mem. Columbia Planning Commn., 1980-87; bd. dirs. United Way Midlands, Columbia, 1983-86; bd. dirs. Assn. Jr. Leagues, N.Y.C., 1980-82; trustee Heathwood Hall Episcopal Sch., Columbia, 1979-85. Republican. Episcopalian. Avocations: golf, walking. Home and Office: 1635 Kathwood Dr Columbia SC 29206-4509

NEWTON, RICHARD AARON, lawyer; b. Lyons, Ga., Jan. 11, 1935; s. Boyd Brymbrick and Emolyn (Mobley) N.; m. Josephine Reid Bogle, Aug. 10, 1957; children: Richard Aaron Jr., Malcolm Reid, Boyd Bogle. AB, Emory U., 1957; LLB, U. Ga., 1961. Bar: Ga. 1961, U.S. Dist. Ct. Ga. (no. dist.) 1964. Assoc. Kilpatrick & Cody, Atlanta, 1961-65; ptnr. Troutman Sanders, Atlanta, 1965—; bd. dirs. SouthTrust Bank Atlanta, 1989—, chmn., 1989-92. Chmn. bd. trustees Andrew Coll., Cuthbert, Ga., 1987-92. Mem. ABA, Ga. Bar Assn., Atlanta Bar Assn. Republican. Presbyterian. Home: 3661 Hadden Hall Rd NW Atlanta GA 30327-2627 Office: Troutman Sanders 600 Peachtree St NE Atlanta GA 30308-2220

NEWTON, ROBERT EUGENE, mechanical engineering educator; b. St. Louis, Oct. 16, 1917; s. H. Melville and Lily C. (Peterson) N.; m. Dorothy M. Fairbank, Jan. 31, 1942; children: Peggy D. (Mrs. Alan L. Rector), Gary Fairbank. B.S. in Mech. Engring, Washington U., St. Louis, 1938, M.S., 1939; Ph.D., U. Mich., 1951. From asst. applied math. to assoc. prof. Washington U., 1938-51; head structural methods unit Curtiss-Wright Corp.,

1941-45; sr. engr. McDonnell Aircraft Corp., 1945; prof. mech. engring. Naval Postgrad. Sch., Monterey, Calif., 1951-86; prof. emeritus Naval Postgrad. Sch., Monterey, 1986—, chmn. dept., 1953-67; vis. prof. U. Wales, Swansea, 1968-69, Universite de Nantes, 1981-82; cons. to industry, 1938—. Author articles, chpt. in book. Trustee Carmel (Calif.) Unified Sch. Dist., 1961-68, pres., 1962-67; Gov. Cmty. Theatre Monterey Peninsula, 1971-73; dir. Cypress Fire Protection Dist., 1993—. Recipient Distinguished Service award St. Louis County Jr. C. of C. Fellow ASME (life, Jr. award 1940); mem. Am. Soc. Engring. Edn., Soc. for Exptl. Mechanics, Sigma Xi, Tau, Beta Pi, Omicron Delta Kappa. Home: 3810 Whitman Cir Carmel CA 93923-8326 Office: Naval Postgrad Sch Monterey CA 93943

NEWTON, V. MILLER, medical psychotherapist, neuropsychologist, writer; b. Tampa, Fla., Sept. 6, 1938; s. Virgil M. Jr. and Louisa (Verri) N.; m. Ruth Ann Klink, Nov. 9, 1957; children: Johanna, Miller, Mark. BA, U. Fla., 1960; MDiv, Princeton Theol. Sem., 1963; postgrad., U. Geneva, Switzerland, 1962; PhD in Med. Anthropology, The Union Inst., 1981, PhD in Clin. Neuropsychology, 1993. Min. dir. Flectcher Pl. Urban Social Ministry, Indpls., 1963-65; coord. staff tng. and community rels. Breckinridge Job Corps Ctr., Ky., 1965-66; asst. prof., program dir. social scis. Webster Coll., St. Louis, 1966-69; assoc. prof., program dir. edn. U. South Fla., Tampa, 1969-73; clk. of the cir. ct. Pasco County, Fla., 1973-76; exec. dir. Fla. Alcohol Coalition, Inc., 1979-80; program and nat. clin. dir. Straight, Inc., St. Petersburg, Fla., 1980-83; dir. KIDS of North Jersey, Inc., 1983—; mem. Sec. Task Force Confidentiality and Client Info. System, Fla. Dept. of Health and Rehab. Svcs., 1979-80; chmn. pres.'s adv. Coun. Webster Coll., 1968-69; guest lectr. at the Grad. Inst. of Community Devel. So. Ill. U., 1968-69; cons. Tampa Model Cities Program, 1969-70; chmn. planning com. Tchr. Corps. Nat. Conf.; faculty mem. Internat. U. for Pres., Munich; co-chmn. Mayor's com. on Pre-sch. Edn., Indpls., 1964-65; speaker in field. Author: Gone Way Done: Teenage Drug-Use is a Disease, 1981, Kids, Drugs, and Sex, 1986, Adolescence: Guiding Youth Through the Perilous Ordeal, 1995; co-author: Not My Kid: A Parent's Guide to Kids and Drugs, 1984; appeared on TV programs NBC Mag., 1982, 1986 NBC, 1986, Drugs: A Plague upon America with Peter Jennings ABC, 1988; contbr. articles to profl. jours. Member drug abuse adv. coun. State of N.J., 1985-91; chmn., bd. dirs. Adjustment Madeira Beach, Fla., 1981—, Alcohol Community Treatment Svcs., Inc., Tampa, 1979; pres. Pasco County Coun. on Aging, 1977-79; chmn. bd. San Antonio Boys Village, 1975-76; chmn. Pasco County Data Ctr. Bd., 1973-75, Cen. Pasco Urban Planning Commn., 1972-73; adult del. White House Conf. on Youth, 1971; chmn. Nat. Tchr. Corps Field Coun., 1970-71; pres. Christian Inner City Assn., Indpls., 1964-65; mem. Gov. Ashew's Adv. Com., Pasco County, 1974-76. Aldersgate fellow, 1962; recipient Honor award Nat. LWV, 1963, Cert. Appreciation Pinellas County Bd. of County Commrs., 1982; named Outstanding Young Man of Yr., Indpls. Jaycees, 1965, Outstanding Govt. Leader, Dade City Jaycees, Fla., 1973-74. Mem. ACA, APHA, APA, Am. Bd. Med. Psychotherapists, Am. Anthrop. Assn., Nat. Acad. Neuropsychology (assoc.), Soc. Med. Anthropology, Ea. Psychol. Assn., Psychol. Anthropology, Soc. Behavioral Medicine, Soc. Adolescent Medicine, Phi Delta Theta, Rotary Internat., Order of DeMolay (state master counselor 1957). Democrat. Methodist. Office: KIDS of North Jersey PO Box 2455 Secaucus NJ 07096-2455

NEWTON, WAYNE, entertainer, actor, recording artist; b. Norfolk, Va., Apr. 3, 1942; s. Patrick and Evelyn (Smith) N.; m. Elaine Okamura, 1968 (div.); 1 child, Erin; m. Kathleen McCrone, April 9, 1994. L.H.D. (hon.), U. Nev.-Las Vegas, 1981. Owner Tamiment Internat. Resort. Appearances include Sands, Caesar's Palace, Desert Inn, Flamingo and Frontier hotels, Las Vegas, Harrah's Club, Reno and Lake Tahoe, I Love N.Y. Concert, Americana Hotel, N.Y.C., Talk of the Town, London, London Paladium, Grand Ole Oprey House, Nashville, 4th of July, Washington, Astrodome, Houston, Hollywood (Calif.) Bowl, Melodyland, Anaheim, Calif., Circle Star, San Francisco, Sea World, Orlando, Fla., Sherman House, Chgo., Wis. State, Iowa State fairs, Valley Forge Music, Westbury Music fairs, Deauville and Eden Roc hotels, Miami Beach, Carlton Club, Bloomington, Minn., hotels Atlantic City, N.J., before U.S. troops, Beirut; TV appearances on shows of Red, White & Wow, A Christmas Card, miniseries North and South: Book II, 1986; film appearance in 80 Steps to Jonah, 1969, The Adventures of Ford Fairlane, 1990; numerous recs. including Moods and Moments, Greatest Hits; author (with Dick Maurice): Once Before I Go, 1989. A supporter St. John's Indian Mission, Levene, Ariz. Recipient citation as distinguished recording artist and humanitarian, 1971; Freedom Lantern award Commonwealth of Mass., 1979; Entertainer of Yr. award Variety Clubs So. Nev., 1973; Gov.'s award Commonwealth of Mass., 1976; cert. of appreciation Gov. of Nev., 1978; Outstanding Indian Entertainer of Yr. Navajo Nation, 1980; Founders award St. Judes Childrens Hosp.; Humanitarian award AMC Cancer Research Ctr.; Recipient award for Daddy Don't Walk So Fast ASCAP; platinum record for Danke Schoen, also gold album and gold records; also others.; named One of 10 Outstanding Young Men of Am. Nat. Jaycees, 1976, Most Disting. Citizen of Yr. NCCJ.

NEWTON, WILLIAM ALLEN, JR., pediatric pathologist; b. Traverse City, Mich., May 19, 1923; s. William Allen and Florence Emma (Brown) N.; m. Helen Patricia Goodrich, Apr. 21, 1945; children: Katherine Germain, Elizabeth Gale, William Allen, Nancy Anne. B.Sc. cum laude, Alma (Mich.) Coll., 1943; M.D., U. Mich., 1946. Diplomate: Am. Bd. Pathology, Am. Bd. Pediatrics. Intern Wayne County Gen. Hosp., Detroit, 1947; resident in pediatric pathology/pathology/hematology Children's Hosp. Mich., Detroit, 1948-50; res. in pediatrics Children's Hosp. Phila., 1950; dir. labs. Children's Hosp. Columbus, Ohio, 1952-88, rsch. pathologist, 1989—; mem. faculty Coll. Medicine, Ohio State U., 1952—, prof., 1965—, chief pediatric pathology, 1952-89, chief div. pediatric hematology, 1952-88, prof. emeritus, 1989—; chmn. pathology com. Children's Cancer Study Group, 1965-91; chmn. Pathology Com. Intergroup Rhabdomyosarcoma Study Group; chmn. pathology com. Late Effects Study Group. Contbr. articles to med. jours. Trustee, mem. exec. com. Am. Cancer Soc., Ohio div., 1972-86; mem. adv. com. on childhood cancer Am. Cancer Soc.; chmn. exec. com. Consortium for Cancer Control of Ohio, 1982-86; mem. sci. adv. com. Armed Forces Inst. Pathology. Served to capt. M.C. U.S. Army, 1950-52, brig. gen. Res. ret. Mem. Ohio State Med. Assn. (com. on cancer), Midwest Soc. Pediatric Research (mem. council 1960-63, pres. 1964-65), Soc. Pediatric Research, Am. Pediatric Soc., Pediatric Pathology Club (pres. 1968-69), Am. Soc. Clin. Oncology, Internat. Soc. Pediatric Oncology, Sigma Xi, Phi Sigma Pi. Republican. Baptist. Home: 2500 Harrison Rd Johnstown OH 43031-9540 Office: 700 Childrens Dr Columbus OH 43205-2666

NEWTON-JOHN, OLIVIA, singer, actress; b. Cambridge, Eng., Sept. 26, 1948; d. Brin and Irene (Born) N.-J.; m. Matt Lattanzi; 1 child, Chloe. Student pub. schs. Co-owner Koala Blue, 1982—. Singer, actress in Australia, Eng. and U.S., 1965—; actress: (films) Grease, 1978, Xanadu, 1980, Two of a Kind, 1983; albums include: Let me Be There, 1973, If You Love Me Let Me Know, 1974, Long Live Love, 1974, First Impressions, 1974, Have You Ever Been Mellow, 1975, Clearly Love, 1975, Come on Over, 1976, Don't Stop Believing, 1976, Making a Good Thing Better, 1977, Greatest Hits, 1977, Totally Hot, 1978, Grease, 1978, Xanadu, 1980, Physical, 1981, Greatest Hits, 1982, (with John Travolta) Two of a Kind, 1984, Soul Kiss, 1985, The Rumour, 1988, Warm And Tender, 1989, Back To Basics-The Essential Collection, 1992; TV prodn. In Australia, 1988. Decorated Order Brit. Empire; recipient Acad. Country Music, 1973, Country Music Assn. U.K., 1974-75, Country Music Assn. award, 1974, Grammy award, 1973-74, AGVA award, 1974, Billboard Mag. award, 1974-75, People's Choice award 1974, 76, 79, Record World award, 1974-76, 78, Nat. Assn. Retail Merchandisers/Cashbox, 1974-75, Am. Music award 1974-76, Nat. Juke Box award, 1980. Address: care Bill Sammeth Orgn PO Box 960 Beverly Hills CA 90213-0960

NEXSEN, JULIAN JACOBS, lawyer; b. Kingstree, S.C., Apr. 14, 1924; s. William Ivey and Barbara (Jacobs) N.; m. Mary Elizabeth McIntosh, Jan. 28, 1948; children: Louise Ivey (Mrs. Heyward Harles Bouknight, Jr.), Julian Jacobs Jr. Student, The Citadel, 1941-43; BS magna cum laude, U. S.C., 1948, JD magna cum laude, 1950. Bar: S.C. 1950, U.S. Supreme Ct. 1960. Partner firm Nexsen Pruet Jacobs & Pollard, Columbia, S.C., 1950—. Trustee Richland County Pub. Libr., chmn., 1976-77; trustee Providence Hosp., chmn., 1984-86; trustee Providence Found., Sisters of Charity of St. Augustine Health Sys.; past bd. dirs. Columbia Music Festival Assn., ARC Richland-Lexington Counties, Ctrl. Carolina Cmty. Found.; mem. U.S.C. Law Sch. partnership bd.; elder Presbyn. Ch., trustee Congaree Presbytery, 1967-87, Synod, S.C., 1969-74, mem. Trinity Presbytery Coun., 1991-95. Lt. inf. AUS, 1943-46, ETO, capt., 1950-51, Korea. Decorated Bronze Star with oak leaf cluster. Mem. ABA, S.C. Bar (treas., bd. govs. 1974-79, ho. of dels. 1980-92), Richland County Bar Assn. (pres. 1974-75, Disting. Svc. award 1987), Am. Bar Found., S.C. Bar Found. (pres. 1971-72), S.C. Law Inst. (coun., exec. com. 1986—), Am. Law Inst., Am. Coll. Trust and Estate Counsel (regent 1973-82), Am. Judicature Soc., Forest Lake Country Club, Palmetto Club, Kiwanis (bd. dirs. 1972-74, 77-79), Phi Beta Kappa. Home: 2840 Sheffield Rd Columbia SC 29204-2332 Office: Nexsen Pruet Jacobs & Pollard Drawer 2426 1441 Main St Columbia SC 29201-2848

NEY, EDWARD N., ambassador, advertising and public relations company executive; b. St. Paul, May 26, 1925; s. John Joseph and Marie (Noonan) N.; m. Suzanne Hayes, 1950 (div. 1974); children: Nicholas, Hilary, Michelle; m. Judith I. Lasky, May 24, 1974. B.A. (Lord Jeffrey Amherst scholar 1942), Amherst Coll., 1947. With Young & Rubicam, Inc., N.Y.C., 1951-86; chmn., pres. CEO Young & Rubicam, Inc., 1970-86; chmn. Paine Webber/Young & Rubicam Ventures, N.Y.C., 1987-89; vice-chmn. Paine Webber, Inc., N.Y.C., 1987-89; amb. to Can., Am. Embassy, Ottawa, Ont., 1989-92; chmn. bd. advisors Burson-Marsteller, N.Y.C., 1992—; bd. dirs. Barrick Gold Corp., Toronto, Ont., Horsham Corp., Toronto, Mattel Corp., L.A., Power Fin. Corp., Montreal, Que., Bar Tech, Johnston, Pa. Trustee Amherst Coll., 1979—, Mus. of Broadcasting, 1982—; mem. adv. bd. Ctr. for Strategic and Internat. Studies, 1986—, Coun. on Fgn. Rels., 1975—. Lt. (j.g.) USNR, 1943-46. Office: Burson-Marsteller 230 Park Ave S New York NY 10003

NEY, JAMES WALTER EDWARD COLBY, English language educator; b. Nakaru, Kenya, July 28, 1932; came to U.S., 1951; s. Reginald Osborne and Elizabeth Grace Colby (Aikins) N.; m. Joan Marie Allen, June 12, 1954; children: Cheryl Lynn, James Allen Colby, Peter Cameron. AB, Wheaton Coll., 1955, AM, 1957; EdD, U. Mich., 1963. Cons. Dade County (Fla.) schs., 1961-62; mem. Faculty U. Ryukyus, Okinawa, 1962-64; asst. prof. Mich. State U., Hunt Valley, 1964-69; prof. English Ariz. State U., Tempe, 1969—; vis. prof. U. Montreal, 1962, George Peabody Coll., Nashville, 1965, U. Hawaii, 1967, Western N.Mex. U., 1971; pres. Ariz. Bilingual Council, 1973-74; appointed to council on practice The Am. Assn. Nurse Anesthetists, 1976-83. Author: Readings on American Society, 1969, Exploring in English, 1972, Discovery in English, 1972, American English for Japanese Students, 1973, Linguistics, Language Teaching and Composition in the Grade, 1975, Semantic Structures for the Syntax of the Modal Auxiliaries and Complements in English, 1982, Transformational Grammar: Essays for the Left Hand, 1988, American College Life in English Communication, 1991, GMAT Study Guide and Time Saver, 1993, English Proficiency through American Culture, 1994, others. Instr. workshop Community Assn. Inst. Tech. Writing, 1988; cons. TESL and bilingual edn. with Sta. KFYI, 1986-88. Recipient Best Pedagogical Article award Am. Assn. Tchrs. of Spanish and Portuguese and Hispania mag., 1976. Mem. Am. Linguistic Assn., Nat. Council Tchrs. English, Can. Linguistic Assn., Nat. Assn. Fgn. Student Affairs. Home: 13375 N 96th Pl Scottsdale AZ 85260-4406 Office: Ariz State U Dept English College and University Sts Tempe AZ 85287-0302

NEY, ROBERT TERRENCE, lawyer; b. Pensacola, Fla., July 18, 1944; s. Robert Jackson and Maybelle (Carriere) N.; m. Ursula Christa Deutsch, Sept. 17, 1983; children: Ashley Chamberlain, Shaler Brooke Lindsay. BA, Harvard U., 1966; JD, U. Tex., 1969. Bar: Va. 1970, U.S. Ct. Appeals (4th cir.) 1971, U.S. Supreme Ct. 1975. Atty. Bauknight, Prichard, McCandlish & Williams, Fairfax, Va., 1969-71; ptnr. Boothe, Prichard & Dudley, Fairfax, McLean, Va., 1971-87, McGuire Woods Battle & Boothe, McLean, Va., 1987—. Editor, chpt. author: Appellate Practice, 1986, 2d edit., 1992. Mem. Va. Bar Assn. (pres. 1995). Home: Rte 734 Box 206 Philomont VA 22131 Office: McGuire Woods Battle & Boothe Box 206 36878 Snickersville Tnpk Mc Lean VA 22102-3807

NEY, ROBERT W., congressman; b. Wheeling, W. Va., July 5, 1954; m. Candy; children: Bobby, Kayla Marie. BS in Edn., Ohio State U., 1976. Am. Embassy tchr., supr. affiliate school of Shiraz (Iran), 1978; health and edn. program mgr. Ohio Office of Appalachia, 1979; safety dir. City of Bellaire, Ohio, until 1980; mem. Ohio Ho. of Reps., 1980-84, Ohio Senate, 1984-94, 104th Congress from 18th Ohio dist., 1995—; mem. banking and fin. svc. com., mem. vets. affairs com., mem. house oversight com., dep. whip, mem. subcom. on fin. instns. and consumer credit, mem. subcom. on domestic and internat. monetary policy, mem. subcom. on housing/cmty. opportunity. Mem. Kiwanis, Elks, Lions, Sportsmen clubs, NRA. Office: US House of Reps 1605 Longworth HOB Washington DC 20515-3518 also: 3201 Belmont St Rm 504 Bellaire OH 43908*

NEY, WILLIAM ROSS ARNOLD, executive assistant; b. Stratford, Ont., Can., Mar. 31, 1948; s. Ross Arnold and Helen Ruth (Buckley) N.; m. Diane Mildred Luckhardt, Sept. 4, 1970; children: Michelle Diane, Paul William Ross. AA, Concordia Coll., 1967; BA, Concordia Sr. Coll., 1969; MDiv, Concordia Sem., 1973. Pastor St. Matthew Luth. Ch., Stony Plain, 1973-74; dir. student activities Concordia Coll., Ann Arbor, 1974-77; pastor Peace Luth. Ch., Saginaw, Mich., 1977-83, Redeemer Luth. Ch., Waterloo, Ont., Can., 1983-87; exec. asst., parish svcs. ABC Dist. of Luth. Ch.-Can., Edmonton, Alb., 1987—; v.p. Luth. Ch.-Can., Winnipeg, Man., Can., 1990-93, sec., 1993—; chair edn. dept. Ont. Dist. Luth. Ch.-Can., Kitchener, Ont., 1984-87. Contbr. articles to profl. jours. Avocations: antique auto restoration, organ, piano, choir director. Home: 4906-55 Ave, Stony Plain, AB Canada T7Z 1B5 Office: ABC Dist Luth Ch-Can, 7100 Ada Blvd, Edmonton, AB Canada T5B 4E4

NEYER, JEROME CHARLES, consulting civil engineer; b. Cin., July 15, 1938; s. Urban Charles and Marie Helen (Hemsteger) N.; m. Judy Ann Drolet, June 17, 1961; children: Janet, Karen. B.C.E., U. Detroit, 1961; M.C.E., U. Wash., 1963. Registered profl. engr. 16 states. Facilities engr. Boeing Co., Seattle, 1961-62; found. engr. Metro Engrs., Seattle, 1962-65; project engr. Hugo N. Helpert Assocs., Detroit, 1965-70; pres. NTH Cons. Ltd., Farmington Hills, Mich., 1970—; adj. prof. U. Detroit, 1973-79. Contbr. articles to profl. jours. Chmn. bldg. appeals bd. City of Farmington Hills, 1983; mem. mineral well adv. bd., Lansing, Mich., 1975, mem. constrn. safety standards bd., 1982. Mem. ASTM, ASCE (br. pres. 1973-74), Engring. Soc. of Detroit, Cons. Engrs. of Mich. (pres. 1981), Mich. Soc. Profl. Engrs. (bd. dirs. 1980), Assn. Engring. Firms Practicing in the Geoscis, (pres. 1991). Roman Catholic. Avocations: golfing; tennis. Home: 37972 Tralee Trl Northville MI 48167 Office: Neyer Tisco & Hindo Ltd 38955 Hills Tech Dr Farmington MI 48331-3434

NEYLON, MARTIN JOSEPH, bishop; b. Buffalo, Feb. 13, 1920; s. Martin Francis and Delia (Breen) N. PhL, Woodstock Coll., 1944, ThL, 1951; MA, Fordham U., 1948. Ordained priest Roman Cath. Ch., 1950. Bishop Roman Cath. Ch., 1970; mem. Soc. of Jesus; tchr. Regis High Sch., N.Y.C., 1952-54; master Jesuit novices Poughkeepsie, N.Y., 1955-67; chaplain Kwajalein Missile Range, Marshall Islands, 1967-68; superior Residence for Jesuit Students, Guam, 1968-70; coadjutor bishop Caroline and Marshall Islands, 1970-80; Vicar apostolic, 1971—; residential bishop New Diocese of Carolines-Marshalls, 1980—. Address: PO Box 250 Chuuk FM 96942*

NG, ALBERT YOUNG, city manager; b. Kaiping, Kwangtung, China, Oct. 1, 1934; came to U.S., 1952; s. George Yuck Ng and May Tak-Ching Tan; m. Jean Lee; children: Nolan R., Ronald W., Linda J. BS, U. Calif., L.A., 1960. With City of Torrance, Calif., 1960—, asst. city mgr., 1986—; mem. adv. bd. Am. Internat. Bank, Torrance, 1990-92, Internat. Bank Calif., L.A., 1992—. Mem. fundraising campaign YMCA, Torrance, 1978-80; vol. 1985 Olympic Com., L.A.; bd. dirs. Vol. Ctr., Torrance, 1990-93, 95—. Mem. Am. Soc. Pub. Adminstrsn., Am. Heart Assn. (bd. dirs. 1992—), Internat. City Mgmt. Assn., Internat. Assn. Budget Officers (charter), Govt. Fin. Officers Assn., UCLA Asian-Pacific Alumni Assn. (bd. dirs. 1993—), Optimist Internat. (charter, life, past pres., sec.-treas., bd. dirs.). Democrat. Baptist. Avocations: snow skiing, golfing, tennis, dancing, traveling. Home: 23329 Henry Ct Torrance CA 90505-3127 Office: City of Torrance 3031 Torrance Blvd Torrance CA 90503-5015

NG, LAWRENCE MING-LOY, pediatric cardiologist; b. Hong Kong, Mar. 21, 1940; came to U.S., 1967, naturalized, 1977; s. John Iu-cheung and Mary Wing (Wong) N.; m. Bella May Ha Kan, June 25, 1971; children: Jennifer Wing-mui, Jessica Wing-yee. B in Medicine, U. Hong Kong, 1965, B in Surgery, 1965. House physician Queen Elizabeth Hosp., Hong Kong, 1965-66, med. officer, 1966-67; resident physician Children's Hosp. of Los Angeles, 1967-68; resident physician Children's Hosp. Med. Center, Oakland, Calif., 1968-70, fellow in pediatric cardiology, 1970-72, now mem. teaching staff; practice medicine, specializing in pediatrics and pediatric cardiology, San Leandro, Calif., 1972—, Oakland, Calif., 1982—; mng. ptnr. Pediatric Med. Assocs. of East Bay, 1990—; chief of pediatrics Oakland Hosp., 1974-77; chief of pediatrics Vesper Meml. Hosp., 1977-79, sec. staff, 1984, v.p. staff, 1985; chief pediatrics Meml. Hosp., San Leandro, 1986-88; founder Pediatric Assocs. of East Bay, 1990. Active Republican Party. Diplomate Am. Bd. Pediatrics. Fellow Am. Acad. Pediatrics; mem. AMA, Calif. Med. Assn., Am. Heart Assn., Alameda County Assn. Primary Care Practitioners (membership chmn. 1993—, sec. treas 1994—), Los Angeles Pediatric Soc., East Bay Pediatric Soc., Smithsonian Assocs., Nat. Geog. Soc., Orgn. Chinese Ams. (chpt. pres. 1984), Chinese-Am. Physicians Soc. (co-founder, sec. 1980, pres. 1983), Chinese-Am. Polit. Assn. (life), Oakland Mus. Assns., Oakland Chinatown C. of C. (bd. dirs. 1986-91); Oakland Asian Cultural Cntr. (dir. 1996—), Hong Kong U. Alumni Assn. (sec. No. Calif. chpt. 1992—), Stanford U. Alumni Assn. (life), Chancellor's Assocs. U. Calif. at Berkeley, Commonwealth Club, Consumers' Union (life); Chinese Am. Golf Club. Buddhist. Office: 345 9th St Ste 204 Oakland CA 94607-4206 also: 101 Callan Ave Ste 401 San Leandro CA 94577-4519

NGAI, SHIH HSUN, physician; b. Wuchang, China, Sept. 15, 1920; came to U.S., 1946, naturalized, 1953; s. Chih F. and Shen (Shih) N.; m. Hsueh-hwa Wang, Nov. 6, 1948; children: Mae, Janet, John. M.B., Nat. Central U. Sch. Medicine, China, 1944. Mem. staff Presbyn. Hosp., N.Y.C., 1949-88; attending anesthesiologist Presbyn. Hosp., 1965-88; faculty Columbia Coll. Phys. and Surg., 1949—, prof. anesthesiology, 1965-88, prof. pharmacology, 1974-88, prof. emeritus, 1988—, chmn. dept. anesthesiology, 1970-73; mem. com. on anesthesia NRC-Nat. Acad. Scis., 1961-70; cons. NIH, 1963-67, 78-82. Author: Manual of Anesthesiology, 1959, 62, Metabolic Effects of Anesthesia, 1962, Highlights of Clinical Anesthesiology, 1971; contbr. to: Physiol. Pharmacology, 1963, Handbook of Physiology, 1964, Modern Trends in Anesthesia, 1966, Advances in Anesthesiology-Muscle Relaxants, 1967, Handbook of Experimental Pharmacology XXX, Modern Inhalation Anesthetics, 1972, Muscle Relaxants, 1975, Enzymes in Anesthesiology, 1978; editor: Anesthesiology, 1967-77. Mem. Am. Physiol. Soc., Am. Soc. Pharmacology and Exptl. Therapeutics, Assn. Univ. Anesthetists, Am. Soc. Anesthesiologists, Academia Sinica. Home: 281 Edgewood Ave Teaneck NJ 07666-3023

NGO, DAVID QUAT, electrical engineer; b. Bac-Giang, Vietnam, Jan. 9, 1947; came to U.S., 1975; m. Hang Mong, July 8, 1978; children: Nancy, Lynda. BSEE, Phu-Tho Inst. Tech., Saigon, South Vietnam, 1971, Lehigh U., 1979; MSEE, Pa. State U., 1981. Chief engr. Dept. Pub. Works & Comm., Saigon, 1971-75; rsch. asst. Pa. State U., State College, 1979-81; sr. engr. Allied-Bendix Aerospace, Columbia, Md., 1981-87; sr. system engr. E-Systems, Inc., Greenville, Tex., 1987-94; staff engr. Motorola, Inc., Scottsdale, Ariz., 1994—. Recipient Silver Snoopy award NASA, 1984. Mem. IEEE. Avocations: jogging, fishing, tennis, reading. Office: Motorola Inc 8201 E McDowell Rd Scottsdale AZ 85252

NGUYEN, KING XUAN, language educator; b. Hue, Vietnam, Dec. 20, 1930; came to U.S., 1975; s. Duong Xuan Nguyen and Thi Thi Ton-Nu. BA, U. Saigon, 1960, LLB, 1963; MEd, Boise State U., 1980. Tchr. Boise Sch. Dist., 1975—; lectr. S.E. Asian Studies Summer Inst./U. Wash., 1992-93, SEASSI, U. Wis., 1994—; spl. lectr. Boise State U., 1975-77. Col. Vietnamese Air Force to 1975. Recipient Red Apple Award for Outstanding Svc. to Edn., Boise, 1990. Mem. NEA, Idaho Edn. Assn., Boise Edn. Assn., Consortium Tchrs. Southeast Asian Langs., Assn. of TESOL. Home: 9674 W Pattie Ct Boise ID 83704-2824

NGUYEN, TAI ANH, minister. Supt. Vietnamese Ministry Dist. of the Christian and Missionary Alliance. Office: 2275 W Lincoln Anaheim CA 92801

NGUYEN, VUNG DUY, radiologist, educator; b. Nhatrang, Vietnam, Dec. 25, 1938; came to U.S., 1975; s. Con Duy and Duc Thi Nguyen; m. Quy Tran, Nov. 10, 1963; children: Khanh Duy, Phong Duy, Lam Duy, Linhda. MD with honors, Saigon (Vietnam) U., 1964; cert., U. Tex. Health Sci. Ctr., San Antonio, 1979. Lic. radiologist, Tex. Radiologist chief Draftee Ctr., Gia Dinh, Vietnam, 1967-69; staff radiologist Cong Hoa Hosp., Saigon, 1969-74; asst. chief radiology dept. Saigon Med. Sch., Saigon, 1974-75; instr. radiology U. Tex. Health Sci. Ctr., San Antonio, 1977-79, asst. prof. radiology, 1980-84, assoc. prof. radiology, 1985—; cons. skeletal radiology Med. Hosp. Ctr., San Antonio, 1979—; cons., chief of svc. Audie Murphy VA Hosp., San Antonio, 1979—. Contbr. chpts. to books, 30 articles to profl. jours. Advisor Vietnamese med. students, San Antonio, 1980—. maj. South Vietnamese Army Med. Corps, 1958-74. Recipient Am. Physician Recognition award AMA, 1983. Mem. U. Radiologists Assn., Radiol. Soc. N.Am., Internat. Skeletal Soc., N.Y. Acad. Scis. Avocations: soccer, swimming, fishing, gardening, traveling. Home: 3511 Hunters Sound San Antonio TX 78284 Office: U Tex Health Scis Ctr 7703 Floyd Curt Dr San Antonio TX 78284

NGUYEN-TRONG, HOANG, physician, consultant; b. Hue, Republic of Vietnam, Sept. 4, 1936; s. Nguyen-Trong Hiep and Nguyen-Phuoc Ton-nu-Thi Sung. B in Math., Lycée d'Etat Michel Montaigne, Bordeaux, 1956; state diploma of medicine, Sch. Medicine, Paris, 1966, also cert. aeronautical medicine and health and sanitation, 1965, diploma Health and Smoking, 1993; diploma post traumatic stress disorder, crises and disasters, The Am. U. and Centre Internat. de Scis. Criminelles de Paris, Washington, 1995. Resident surgeon Compiegne State Hosp., 1963-64, Meaux State Hosp., 1964-66, Lagny State Hosp., 1966; specialist in health and sanitation Paris Sch. Medicine, 1965—; specialist in family planning French Action of Family Planning, Paris, 1968—; practice medicine, Nanterre, France, 1969—; cons. physician various pharm. labs., Paris, 1987; investigator physician WHO regional office for Europe, 1991. Contbr. articles to profl. jours. Active mem. task force on tobacco dependency Biomed. Saints Péres Rsch. Unit, Paris, 1993, AIDS treatment assn. Le Val de Seine, 1993. Recipient World Decoration of Excellence, 1990, Commemorative Medal of Honor, 1990, Internat. Order of Merit, 1990. Mem. French Soc. Aviation and Space Physiology and Medicine (titulary, specialist in aviation medicine), Assn. Nanterre Physicians, Assn. Vietnamese Practitioners in France, Assn. Le Val de Seine, Chambre Syndicale des Medecins des Hauts de Seine, Ordre des Medecins des Hauts de Seine, Les Ex du XIV Shooting Club. Avocations: painting, poetry, classical and modern jazz music, riflery, martial arts. Home: 3 Rue Gazan, 75014 Paris France Office: Cabinet Med Privé, 38 Rue des Fontenelles, 92000 Nanterre France

NIBLEY, ANDREW MATHEWS, editorial executive; b. Maxwell AFB, Ala., May 25, 1951; s. Owen Smoot and Frances Elizabeth (Browder) N.; m. Mary Elizabeth Michael, Nov. 24, 1984; children: Kevin Mathews, Carlyle Gower, Leath Michael. Attended, Montgomery Coll, Rockville, Md., 1970-72, Univ. Md., 1973. Legis. corr. UPI, Hartford, Conn., 1975-78; bur. chief UPI, Concord, N.H., 1979; Treasury corr. UPI, Washington, 1980; Treasury corr. Reuters N.Am., Washington, 1980-82, editor-in-charge, 1982, news editor, 1982-85; news editor Reuters N.Am., N.Y.C., 1985-87; news editor Europe Reuters Holdings, London, 1987-89; editor, America Reuters America Inc., N.Y.C., 1989-94; sr. v.p., news and TV Reuters America Inc., 1993-94; editor, exec. v.p., bd. dirs. Reuters New Media Inc., N.Y.C., 1994—; mem. Knight-Bagehot editl. panel Columbia U., 1995—; bd. dirs. InGenius Inc., Sportsline USA, Inc.; bd. advisors Red Herring Mag. Mem. Gov.'s Coun. on Alcoholism and Drug Abuse, mem. media subcom., 1991-92; trustee N.J. Ctr. for Family Studies; bd. advisors Grad. Sch. Journalism U. Calif., Berkeley; patron Met. Opera, Birds of Vt. Mus.; mem. bd. dirs. Knight-Baghest fellow Columbia U. Recipient Meritorious Service award Nat. Press Club. Mem. Am. Soc. Newspaper Editors (editl. bd. 1992-93), Overseas Press Club (program vice chmn. 1990-93, bd. govs. 1993—), Fgn. Press Assn., Internat. Platform Assn., N.Y. New Media Assn., Triathlon Fedn. Am., Montclair Golf Club (Verona, N.J.), Essex Running Club, The

Athletic and Swim Club (N.Y.C.). Avocations: golf, tennis, jogging, racquetball, triathlons. Office: Reuters New Media Inc 1700 Broadway New York NY 10019-5905

NIBLEY, ROBERT RICKS, retired lawyer; b. Salt Lake City, Sept. 24, 1913; s. Joel and Teresa (Taylor) N.; m. Lee Allen, Jan. 31, 1945 (dec.); children—Jane, Annette. A.B., U. Utah, 1934; J.D., Loyola U., Los Angeles, 1942. Bar: Calif. bar 1943. Accountant Nat. Parks Airways, Salt Lake City, 1934-37, Western Air Lines, Los Angeles, 1937-40; asst. mgr. market research dept. Lockheed Aircraft Corp., Burbank, Calif., 1940-43; asso. firm Hill, Farrer and Burrill, Los Angeles, 1946-53; partner Hill, Farrer and Burrill, 1953-70, of counsel, 1971-78. Served from ensign to lt. comdr. USNR, 1943-46. Mem. ABA, L.A. Bar Assn., Calif. Club, Phi Delta Phi, Phi Kappa Phi, Phi Delta Theta. Home: 4860 Ambrose Ave Los Angeles CA 90027-1866

NIBLOCK, WILLIAM ROBERT, manufacturing executive; b. Phila., Aug. 15, 1928; s. William and Grace Neary (Rennie) N.; m. Barbara Ann Parsons, Sept. 26, 1956; children: Elizabeth Ann, Christopher Parsons. BSChemE, Drexel U., 1951; MBA, U. Chgo., 1956. Dir. corp. devel. and planning Pitts. Coke and Chem. Co., 1956-68, U.S. Chems., Inc., Pitts., 1966-70; v.p. corp. devel. Courtaulds Coatings, Inc., Louisville, 1970-95; v.p. investments Courtaulds Coatings Inc. (Porter Paint Co.), Louisville, 1995—; bd. dirs. Internat. Paint of Am. Inc., v.p., 1988; chmn., bd. dirs. The Hanseatic Group Inc., Louisville, 1990. Bd. dirs. Ky. Ednl. Found., Lexington, 1984—; bd. dirs. Jr. Achievement of Kentuckiana; pres., co-dir. Porter Paint Found. Inc; pres., dir. Porter Paint Found., Inc. Lt. USN, 1952-55. Mem. Wynn-Stay Club, Jefferson Club. Republican. Episcopalian. Avocations: sailing, skiing, coins, computers. Home: 2210 Wynnewood Cir Louisville KY 40222-6342 Office: Courtaulds Coatings Inc 400 S 13th St Louisville KY 40203-1714

NICANDROS, CONSTANTINE STAVROS, retired oil company executive; b. Port Said, Egypt, Aug. 2, 1933; came to U.S., 1955, naturalized, 1963; s. Stavros Constantine and Helen (Lianakis) N.; m. Tassie Boozalis, May 24, 1959; children: Steve Constantine, Vicky Ellen. Diploma, HEC Ecole des Hautes Etudes Commerciales, 1954; lic. en droit, Law Sch. U. Paris, 1954, doctorate in econ. sci., 1955; MBA, Harvard U., 1957. With planning dept. Conoco Inc., Houston, 1957-61; with planning dept. Conoco Inc., N.Y.C., 1961-64, with land acquisition internat. exploration-prodn. dept., 1964-66, dir. planning ea. hemisphere, 1966-71, gen. mgr., then v.p. supply and transp. ea. hemisphere, 1971-74, exec. v.p. ea. hemisphere refining, mktg., supply, transp., 1974-75; exec. v.p. worldwide supply and transp. Conoco Inc., Stamford, Conn., 1975-78; group exec. v.p. petroleum products Conoco Inc., Houston, 1978-83, pres. petroleum ops., 1983-87, pres., CEO, 1987-96; chmn. CNS and Co., 1996—; pres., CEO CSN & Co.; bd. dirs. strategic direction com. E.I. duPont de Nemours & Co., 1983-96; bd. dirs. Tex. Commerce Bank, Cooper Industries, Inc., Mitchell Energy and Devel., Keystone Internat.; active mem. adv. bd. Tex. Ctr. for Superconductivity, U. Houston, 1989-91. Bd. dirs., chmn. Houston Symphony; bd. dirs. Greater Houston Partnership, 1989-95; bd. dirs. Tex. Gulf Coast affiliate United Way, 1986-91, campaign chmn., 1988; trustee Mus. Fine Arts, Houston, 1987-94, 95—, Houston Ballet Found., Baylor Coll. Medicine; sr. chmn. bd. trustees Houston Grand Opera; bd. govs. Rice U.; chmn. Tex. chpt. Am. Com. on French Revolution Bicentennial, 1989. Mem. Am. Petroleum Inst. (bd. dirs.), Tex. Rsch. League (bd. dirs.), The Houston Forum (mem. bd. govs.), Nat. Petroleum Coun. Greek Orthodox. Office: CSN and Co 10000 Memorial Dr Houston TX 77024

NICASTRO, FRANCIS EFISIO, defense electronics and retailing executive; b. N.Y.C., Apr. 21, 1942; s. Louis and Janet Amaloa (Onnis) N.; m. Rosalind Piperno, Nov. 22, 1972 (div. Aug. 1995); 1 child, Jason. BS in Econs., U. Pa., 1964. Audit analyst ops., coordinator audit and procedures S.H. Kress and Co., N.Y.C., 1967-68; mgr. audit and acctg. Singer Co., N.Y.C., 1968-76, dir. acctg. and budgets, 1976-77, dir. cons. acctg., 1977-79; dir. domestic treasury ops. Singer Co., Stamford, Conn., 1979-80, asst. treas., 1980-86, treas., 1986-89; corp. v.p., treas. Grand Union Co., Wayne, N.J., 1989—. Served to 1st lt. U.S. Army, 1964-66. Republican. Home: 11 Moshier St Greenwich CT 06831 Office: The Grand Union Co 201 Willowbrook Blvd Wayne NJ 07470-7025

NICASTRO, NEIL DAVID, business executive, lawyer; b. N.Y.C., Oct. 25, 1956; s. Louis Joseph and Rosalie Laura (Vanson) N.; m. Kimberly Ann Hyland, May 23, 1981; children: Nicholas L., Mark T., Kelly Ann. BA, Kenyon Coll., Gambier, Ohio, 1978; JD, John Marshall Law Sch., 1981. Dir. stockholder rels. WMS Industries, Inc., N.Y.C., v.p., treas., 1986-88, exec. v.p., 1988-90, COO; pres. WMS Industries, Inc., Chgo., 1991—. Office: WMS Industries Inc 3401 N California Ave Chicago IL 60618*

NICE, CARTER, conductor, music director; b. Jacksonville, Fla., Apr. 5, 1940; s. Clarence Carter and Elizabeth Jane (Hintermister) N.; m. Jennifer Charlotte Smith, Apr. 4, 1983; children: Danielle, Christian, Olivia. MusB, Eastman Sch. Music, 1962; MusM, Manhattan Sch. Music., 1964. Asst. condr., concert master New Orleans Philharm., 1967-79; condr., music dir. Sacramento Symphony, 1979-92; music dir., conductor Bear Valley Music Fest., 1985—. Office: 18 Rivershore Ct Sacramento CA 95831

NICE, CHARLES MONROE, JR., physician, educator; b. Parsons, Kans., Dec. 21, 1919; s. Charles Monroe and Margaret (McClenahan) N.; m. Mary Ellen Cranmer, Dec. 21, 1940; children: Norma Jane Nice Murphy, Pamela, Deborah, Julianne, Charles Monroe III, Thomas, Mary Ellen, Rebecca. AB, U. Kans., MD, 1943; MSc in Medicine, U. Colo., 1948; PhD, U. Minn., 1956. Intern Grasslands Hosp., 1943-44; resident in radiology U. Minn. Hosp., 1948-50; mem. faculty U. Minn. Hosp., Mpls., 1951-58; prof. radiology Tulane U. Sch. Medicine, New Orlens, 1958—; chmn. dept. Tulane U. Sch. Medicine, 1960-85; mem. staff Charity Hosp., New Orleans, 1958—; mem. tng. com.investigative radiology NIH, 1967-69, mem. subcom. Sickle Cell, heart, lung, blood com., 1982-83; mem. com. on radiology NRC, 1965-67; chmn. tng. adv. com. Bur. Radiol. Health, 1970-72; guest lectr. Congress of Radiology, Japan, Colombian Radiol. Soc.; U.S. counselor Inter Am. Coll. Radiology, 1985-90. Author: Roentgen Diagnois of Abdominal Tumors in Childhood, 1957, Clinical Roentgenology of Collagen Disease, 1966, Differential Diagnosis of Cardiovascular Disease by X-ray, 1966, Cardiovascular Roentgenology; a validated program, 1967, Cerebral Computed Tomography; contbr. articles to profl. jours. Served with AUS, 1944-46, PTO. Fellow Am. Coll. Chest Physicians (bd. gov's 1975-81), Am. Coll. Radiologists. Home: 508 Millaudon St New Orleans LA 70118-3805 Office: 1415 Tulane Ave New Orleans LA 70112-2699

NICE, WILMA OGDEN, executive recruiter; b. Stockton, Mo., Dec. 25, 1930; d. Lyman R. and Ida C. (Boss) VanBuskirk; children: Michael, Bruce Neil; m. Dean Nice, Oct. 3, 1992. BSN, Avila Coll., Kansas City, Mo., 1951. Nursing supr. St. Joseph Hosp., Kansas City, 1950-74; owner/mgr. Arrow Employment Svc., Kansas City, 1980-92; post-polio coord. Rehab. Inst., Kansas City, 1992—. Mayor, city counvilman City of Gladstone, Mo.; bd. trustees Platte Ray Mental Health; active Clay County Health Bd. Named Gladstone Citizen of the Yr. Mem. Law Enforcement Asst. Assn., Soroptimist Internat. (pres.). Home: 14514 W 58th St Shawnee Mission KS 66216-4663

NICELY, DENISE ELLEN, elementary education educator; b. Fort Carson, Colo., Apr. 28, 1966; d. Dallas Lorenzo and Elizabeth Mae (Thurston) Nicely. BS, Radford U. Cert. elem./mid. sch. tchr., Va. Tchr. kindergarten Basics Primary Sch., Chesapeake, Va., 1989-90; tchr. third grade B.M. Williams Elem., Chesapeake, 1990-91, tchr. second grade, 1991—; math. curriculum devel., Chesapeake Pub. Schs., 1992—; sci. lead tchr. B.M. Williams Primary, 1992—, math. lead tchr., 1992—. Spl. Olympics Vol., Chesapeake Spl. Olympics, 1990—; supporter Va. Paralyzed Vets. Assn., 1992—. Mem. Chesapeake Edn. Assn., Nat. Coun. Tchrs. Math., PTA. Presbyterian. Avocations: volleyball, softball. Office: BM Williams Primary 1100 Battlefield Blvd Chesapeake VA 23320

NICELY, OLZA M., insurance company executive. Pres., CEO GEICO Corp., Washington. Office: GEICO 5260 Western Ave Washington DC 20076*

NICELY, ROBERT FRANCIS, JR., education educator, administrator; b. Greensburg, Pa., Jan. 10, 1940; s. Robert Francis and Jean Isabelle (Baird) N.; m. Donna Comnale, Dec. 29, 1962; children: Lisa Ann, Scott Alan. BS, Pa. State U., 1961; MEd, Indiana U. of Pa., 1965; PhD, U. Pitts., 1970. Cert. tchr. math. and sci., Pa. Tchr. math. and chemistry Norwin and Gateway Schs., 1961-67; instructional cons. Pitts. Sch. Dist., 1967-68; lectr., asst. prof., research assoc. U. Pitts., 1968-72; asst. prof. edn. Pa. State U., University Park, 1972-76, assoc. prof., 1976-86, prof., 1986—, also asst. dean, 1987-90, acting dean, 1989, assoc. dean edn., 1990—. Contbr. articles to profl. jours.; speaker in field. Mem. ASCD (bd. dirs. 1981-85, 95-96, chair nominating com. 1986-87, chair conf. com. 1990, assoc. editor, coeditor, mem. editorial bd. Jour. Curriculum and Supervision 1985-92, Outstanding Affiliate Newsletter and Jour. awards 1993, 94, 96), Pa. ASCD (pres. 1982-84, exec. bd. 1978—, editor PASCD, Pa. Ednl. Leadership, Outstanding Research and Publ. award 1985, Disting. Service award 1986, Spl. Leadership award 1990), Cen. Pa. ASCD, Council Profs. Instructional Supervision, Nat. Council Tchrs. Math. (chair instrnl. issues adv. com. 1992-94), Pa. Council Tchrs. Math. (pres. 1988-90, Outstanding Leadership and Service award 1983, Outstanding Contbns. to Math. Edn. award 1991, coeditor 4 PCTM Yearbooks), Pa. Edn. Research Assn. (pres. 1987-88, 94-95, editor Pera-Scope), Phi Delta Kappa (pres. Pa. State chpt. 1984-85). Avocations: aerobic conditioning, golf, Landscape design and construction. Home: 109 Cherry Ridge Rd State College PA 16803-3309 Office: Pa State U 277 Chambers Bldg University Park PA 16802

NICEWANDER, WALTER ALAN, psychology educator; b. Eagle River, Wis., Sept. 23, 1939; s. B. Walter and Dorothy (Shirley) N.; children: David, Brent, Karen. BS, Purdue U., 1961, PhD, 1971. Prof. psychology U. Okla., Norman, 1970-93; dir. of statis. rsch. Am. Coll. Testing, 1994—. Recipient Okla. Bd. of Regent's award for Superior Teaching, 1988. Mem. Soc. Multivariate Exptl. Psychology. Democrat. Achievements include research on latent trait based reliability estimate and upper bound and symmetric, invariant measures of multivariate association. Home: 1512 1st Ave Apt 203A Iowa City IA 52241-1139 Office: ACT PO Box 168 Iowa City IA 52243-0168

NICHOL, FRED JOSEPH, federal judge; b. Sioux City, Iowa, Mar. 19, 1912; s. Ralph Edwin and Florence (Young) N.; m. Evelyn Parrish, June 2, 1939; children: Allen H., Janet M. A.B., Yankton Coll., 1933; J.D., U. S.D., 1936; LL.D. (hon.), Dakota Wesleyan U., 1975. Bar: S.D. bar 1936. Mem. firm Hitchcock, Nichol & Lasegard, Mitchell, 1938-58; mem. S.D. Ho. of Reps. from, Davison County, 1951-52, 57-58; state's atty. Davison County, 1947-51; circuit judge 4th Jud. Circuit S.D., 1959-65; U.S. dist. judge for S.D., 1965-66; chief judge, 1966-80, sr. judge, 1980—; Mem. exec. com. Legis. Research Council, 1951; S.D. del. Nat. Trial Judges Conv., 1962, 63, 64. Mem. sch. bd. and library bd., Mitchell, 1958-64; del. White House Conf. on Aging, 1961; Sec. S.D. delegation Democratic Nat. Conv., 1956; Mem. corp. bd., also trustee Yankton Coll., from 1954. Served to lt. USNR, World War II. Mem. ABA, Am. Judicature Soc., Phi Delta Phi. Congregationalist (past chmn.). Clubs: Elk, Mason (32 Shriner, K.T.), Rotarian. Address: 8842 West Piute Ave Peoria AZ 85382

NICHOL, HENRY FERRIS, former government official, environment consultant; b. Charleston, S.C., Jan. 21, 1911; s. A. Ferris and Ella (Humphrey) N.; m. Elizabeth B. Holmes, Apr. 15, 1944; children: Susan (Mrs. William C. Thompson), Elizabeth (Mrs. Robert McC. McConnell III), David, Peter. AB, Davidson Coll., 1933; postgrad., Georgetown U. Law Sch., 1936-37. Clk. HOLC, 1934-37; adminstrv. asst. FSA, 1937-46; fgn. affairs specialist Dept. State, 1946-63, fgn. service officer, 1955-63; conf. attache Geneva, Switzerland, 1952-58; consul Liverpool, Eng., 1958-63; acting prin. officer, 1958-59; sec. U.S. delegations to numerous confs.; adviser U.S. delegations, exec. com. Internat. Refugee Fund, Geneva, 1956-57; asst. dir., asst. to adminstr. Rural Community Devel. Service, U.S. Dept. Agr., 1963-66; staff rep. to Pres.'s Recreation Adv. Council, 1963-66, vice chmn. staff, 1964-66; mem. staff Pres.'s Council on Recreation and Natural Beauty, 1966-69; asst. to asso. adminstr. Soil Conservation Service, 1966-70; environ. cons., 1970—; Liaison officer Dept. Agr. to White House Conf. Natural Beauty, 1965; sr. warden Am. Ch., Geneva, Switzerland; Eastern rep. Nat. Outdoor Leadership Sch. Chmn. Montgomery County Citizens Adv. Com. on Bikeways and Trails; chmn. Potomac Com. Bikeways and Trails; trustee Potomac Conservation Found., Wilderness Edn. Assn.; v.p. Potomac Appalachian Trail Club; founder Potomac Clean and Green. Served to comdr. USNR, 1942-45. Recipient Pres. Theodore Roosevelt Conservation award Pres. of U.S., 1990, Community Svc. award Potomac Almanac, 1990; named Outstanding Citizen of Yr. Potomac C. of C., 1976. Mem. Explorers Club, Diplomatic and Consular Officers Ret., Am. Fgn. Svc. Assn., Phi Beta Kappa. Presbyterian. Home: Plantation Village 7809 Blue Heron Dr Villa 2 Wilmington NC 28405

NICHOL, NORMAN J., manufacturing executive; b. East Cleveland, Ohio, Feb. 12, 1944; s. Norman George and Irene Josephine (Peters) N.; m. Janice E. Nichol, Oct. 19, 1968; children: Gerard, Katherine. B.B.A., Kent State U. Mktg. trainee A.B. Dick Co., Chgo., 1968, sales rep., supr.-spl. markets mgr., 1971-75, br. mgr. Indpls. and Chgo., 1975-80, dir.-gen. mgr. internat., 1980-82, pres., 1982—; pres. Rycoline Products Co., 1985—, Sun Graphic Inc., Robersol Inc. Served with U.S. Army, 1968-70. Home: 1021 Dover Ct Libertyville IL 60048-3509 Office: Rycoline Products Inc 5540 N Northwest Hwy Chicago IL 60630-1116

NICHOLAS (RICHARD G. SMISKO), bishop; b. Perth Amboy, N.J., Feb. 23, 1936; s. Andrew and Anna (Totin) S. Grad., Christ the Saviour Sem., Johnstown, Pa., 1959; student, Patriarchal Theol. Acad., Istanbul, Turkey; BA, U. Youngstown, 1961; BTh, U. Pitts. Ordained priest Am. Carpatho-Russian Orthodox Greek Cath. Diocese, 1959. Pastor Sts. Peter and Paul Ch., Windber, 1959-62; prefect of discipline, tchr. Christ the Saviour Sem., Johnstown, 1963-65; pastor Sts. Peter and Paul Ch., Homer City, 1965-71, St. Michael's Ch., Clymer, 1971-72, St. Nicholas Ch., N.Y.C., 1972-78; elevated to archimandrite Am. Carpatho-Russian Orthodox Greek Cath. Diocese, 1976; abbot Monastery of Annunciation, Tuxedo Park, N.Y., 1978-82; elected titular bishop of Amissos, aux. bishop Ukrainian Orthodox Diocese of Ecumenical Patriarchate, 1983; consecrated bishop Am. Carpatho-Russian Orthodox Greek Cath. Diocese, 1985, bishop, 1985—; asst. Christ the Saviour Cathedral, 1963-65; chmn. XIV Diocesan Coun., New Brunswick, N.J., 1985, XV Diocesan Coun., Pitts., 1991. Office: 312 Garfield St Johnstown PA 15906-2122

NICHOLAS, ARTHUR SOTERIOS, manufacturing company executive; b. Grand Rapids, Mich., Mar. 6, 1930; s. Samuel D. and Penelope A. (Kalapodes) N.; m. Bessie Zazanis, Aug. 25, 1957; children: Niki Stephanie, Arthur S., Thomas. B.S. in Chem. Engring, U. Mich., 1953; B.A. in Indsl. Mgmt, Wayne State U., 1957. Registered profl. engr., Mich. Project engr. B.F. Goodrich Co., 1953-54; plant mgr. Cadillac Plastics and Chem. Co., 1954-69; pres., chief exec. officer Leon Chem. and Plastics, Inc., Grand Rapids, 1960-69; with U.S. Industries, Inc., 1969-73, pres., chief operating officer, 1973; now pres. The Antech Group; bd. dirs. ERO Industries, Inc. Judge Jr. Achievement, Chgo. Served with USNR, 1948-49. Recipient Distinguished Alumni award Grand Rapids Jr. Coll., 1970. Mem. Young Pres. Orgn., Soc. Plastic Engrs., Mich. Acad. Sci., Arts and Letters, Chgo. Coun. on Fgn. Rels., Pres.' Assn. Mem. Greek Orthodox Ch. Clubs: Chgo. Athletic Assn. (Chgo.), Executives (Chgo.). Patentee in field. Home: 655 Oak Rd Barrington IL 60010-3135 Office: 135 S La Salle St Ste 1150 Chicago IL 60603-4204

NICHOLAS, DAVID ROBERT, minister, academic administrator; b. L.A., May 10, 1941; s. Robert Grant and Pearl Elizabeth (Pickard) N.; m. Donna Lynn Roberts, June 28, 1969; children: Joy Lynn, Faith Elizabeth. AB, Azusa Pacific U., 1963; MS, U. So. Calif., 1967; MDiv., L.A. Bapt. Theol. Sem., 1966; ThM, Talbot Theol. Sem., 1971; ThD, Grace Theol. Seminary, 1982. Ordained to ministry Gen. Assn. Regular Bapt. Chs., 1970. Dir. admissions, mem. faculty L.A. Bapt. Coll., Newhall, Calif., 1966-71; dean, pres. Van Nuys (Calif.) Christian Coll., 1972-76; pastor Tri-Lakes Bapt. Ch., Columbia City, Ind., 1977-78; acad. dean, assoc. prof. Southwestern Coll., Phoenix, 1978-80; sr. pastor, acad. supt. Grace Bapt. Ch., Yuba City, 1980-82; sr. pastor Placerita Bapt. Ch., Newhall, 1982-84; pres., prof. theology Shasta Bible Coll., Redding, Calif., 1985—; chmn. Greater Redding Area Christian Edn. Conv., 1988—; mem. accreditation commn. Transnat. Assn. Christian Colls. and Schs., 1994—; trustee Regular Bapt. Conf. So. Calif., 1983-85, pres., 1963-65; dir. Bapt. Youth Assn., So. Calif., 1969-71. Author: Foundations of Biblical Inerrancy, 1978, What's A Woman to Do ... In the Church?, 1979, Church Discipline: Option or Obligation, 1991; contbr. articles to religious jours.; recordings include Trombone Testimonies, 1990; Bible tchr. broadcast program Truth for Today, 1988—, Bible Answer Man, 1978-80. Trustee Christian Heritage Coll., El Cajon, Calif., 1981-85; mem. steering com. Calif. Activists Network, Los Altos, Calif., 1991; del. Conf. on the Preservation of the Family, 1991; gov. Am. Coalition for Trad. Values, Washington, 1984; chaplain Los Angeles County Bd. Suprs., 1984. Recipient Svc. award Am. Legion, 1955. Mem. Evang. Theol. Soc., Creation Rsch. Soc., Shasta County Evang. Ministerial Assn. (pres. 19920-95), Kappa Tau Epsilon. Republican. Home: 8264 Taylor Ln Redding CA 96001-9530 Office: Shasta Bible Coll 2980 Hartnell Ave Redding CA 96002-2312

NICHOLAS, FAYARD ANTONIO, dancer, actor, entertainer; b. Mobile, Ala., Oct. 20, 1914; s. Ulysses Domonick and Viola (Harden) N.; m. Geraldine Pate (div. 1955); children: Anthony Fayard, Paul Didier; m. Barbara January, Sept. 17, 1967. Pvt. ed. in, high sch. and coll. related courses. Owner, dancer Cotton Club, Phila., from 1932; guest lectr. San Francisco State U., UCLA, U. So. Calif., U. Hawaii. Appeared in films Kid Millions, 1934, The Big Broadcast, 1936, Down Argentine Way, 1940, Tin Pan Alley, 1940, The Great American Broadcast, 1941, Sun Valley Serenade, 1941, Orchestra Wives, 1942, Stormy Weather, 1943, The Pirate, 1948, others; Broadway shows include Ziegfield Follies, 1936, Babes in Arms, 1937, St. Louis Woman, 1946; actor The Liberation of L.B. Jones, 1970; choreographer Broadway musical Black and Blue (Tony award), 1989; starred in ballet Nutcracker, San Diego Ballet Co., 1990; commd. Japan Satellite Broadcasting Co., 1991; performer maj. TV shows; entertainer (with Bob Hope) troops in Vietnam. Supporter numerous charity events including Danny Thomas-St. Jude Hosp., Jerry Lewis Telethon, Negro Coll. Fund, Drug Abuse, Spl. Concern with the Plights of Homeless. With U.S. Army, 1943-44. Recipient Emmy award, 1965, Bumps Blackwell Life Achievement award, 1980, Ellie award Nat. Film Soc., 1984, City of L.A. award, 1984, resolution, 1991, City of Hope award, 1986, Golden Angel award, 1986, Josephine Baker award, 1986, Ebony Life Achievement award, 1987, Jeanne Golden Halo award, 1988, Tony award, 1989, Lafayette Players West award, 1991, Paul Robeson award Black Am. Cinema Soc., 1992, Dance Mag. award, 1995, numerous others; named to Black Filmmakers Hall of Fame, 1989; with brother Harold honored at White House and Kennedy Ctr., 1991; honored TV Documentary, 1992; honored Lincoln Ctr., N.Y.C., 1993. Mem. Acad. Arts and Sci. (life), Dance Gallery, Friars Club (life), San Fernando Valley Art Coun. Home: 23388 Mulholland Dr Woodland Hills CA 91364-2733

NICHOLAS, FREDERICK M., lawyer; b. N.Y.C., May 30, 1920; s. Benjamin L. and Rose F. (Nechols) N.; m. Eleanore Berman, Sept. 2, 1951 (div. 1963); children: Deborah, Jan, Tony; m. Joan Fields, Jan. 2, 1983. AB, U. So. Calif., 1947; postgrad., U. Chgo., 1949-50; JD, U. So. Calif., 1952. Bar: Calif. 1952, U.S. Dist. Ct. Calif. 1952, U.S. Ct. Appeals (9th cir.) 1952. Assoc. Loeb & Loeb, L.A., 1952-56; ptnr. Swerdlow, Glikbarg & Nicholas, Beverly Hills, Calif., 1956-62; pvt. practice Beverly Hills, 1962-80; pres., atty. Hapsmith Co., Beverly Hills, 1980—; bd. dirs. Malibu Grand Prix, L.A., 1982-90; gen. counsel Beverly Hills Realty Bd., 1971-79; founder, pres. Pub. Counsel, L.A., 1970-73. Author: Commercial Real Property Lease Practice, 1976. Chmn. Mus. Contemporary Art, L.A., 1987-93, chmn. com. Walt Disney Concert Hall, L.A., 1987-95; trustee Music Ctr. L.A. County, 1987-95, L.A. Philharm. Assn., 1987-95; chmn. Calif. Pub. Broadcasting Commn., Sacramento, 1972-78; pres. Maple Ctr., 1977-79. Recipient Citizen of Yr. award Beverly Hills Bd. Realtors, 1978, Man of Yr. award Maple Ctr., 1980, Pub. Svc. award Coro Found., 1988, The Medici award L.A. C. of C., 1990, Founders award Pub. Counsel, 1990, Trustees award Calif. Inst. Arts, 1993, City of Angels award L.A. Ctrl. Bus. Assn.; named Outstanding Founder in Philanthropy, Nat. Philanthropy Day Com., 1990. Mem. Beverly Hills Bar Assn. (bd. govs. 1970-76, Disting. Svc. award 1974, 81, Exceptional Svc. award 1986), Beverly Hills C. of C. (Man of Yr. 1983). Home: 1011 Cove Way Beverly Hills CA 90210-2818 Office: Hapsmith Co 9300 Wilshire Blvd Beverly Hills CA 90212

NICHOLAS, LYNN HOLMAN, writer; b. New London, Conn., Nov. 11, 1939; d. William Grizzard Holman and Carol (Ackiss) Wakelin; m. Robert Carter Nicholas III, Dec. 20, 1965; children: William C., R. Carter, Philip H. Student, Radcliffe Coll., 1957-59; diploma, U. Madrid, 1960; BA, Oxford (Eng.) U., 1964. Author: The Rape of Europa, 1994 (Nat. Book Critics Circle award 1995).

NICHOLAS, PETER, medical educator; b. Little Falls, N.Y., June 5, 1942; s. Peter Sr. and Helen K. N.; m. Joan Marie Popadak, 1970. BS magna cum laude, Union Coll., 1964; MD, Yale U., 1968. Intern Mt. Sinai Hosp., N.Y.C., 1968-69, resident, 1969-70, 70-71, chief resident, 1971-72; instr. assoc., asst. prof. medicine, assoc. prof. CCNY, Mt. Sinai Sch. Medicine, 1971—; attending physician City Hosp. Ctr. Mt. Sinai Svcs., 1987—; assoc. dean; Lic. physician N.Y., 1969. Contbr. articles to profl. jours. Fellow Am. Coll. Physicians, N.Y. Acad. Medicine; mem. Am. Soc. Microbiology, AMA, Assn. Asm. Med. Colls., Soc. Hosp. Epidemiologists Am., N.Y. Heart Assn., N.Y. Sco. Tropical Medicine, Soc. Health and Human Values, Assn. Practitioners in Infection Control.

NICHOLAS, RALPH WALLACE, anthropologist, educator; b. Dallas, Nov. 28, 1934; s. Ralph Wendell and Ruth Elizabeth (Oury) N.; m. Marta Ruth Weinstock, June 13, 1963. B.A., Wayne U., 1957; M.A., U. Chgo., 1958, Ph.D., 1962. Asst. prof. to prof. Mich. State U., East Lansing, 1964-71; prof. anthropology U. Chgo., 1971—, chmn. dept., 1981-82, dep. provost, 1982-87, dean of coll., 1987-92, dir. Ctr. Internat. Studies, 1984-95, William Rainey Harper prof. of Anthropology and Social Scis., 1992—; pres. Internat. House of Chgo., 1993—; cons. Ford Found., Dhaka, Bangladesh, 1973. Author: (with others) Kinship Bengali Culture, 1977; editor: Jour. Asian Studies, 1975-78. V.p. Am. Inst. Indian Studies, 1974-76, treas., 1993—; trustee Bangladesh Found. Ford Found. fgn. area tng. fellow, India, 1960-61; Sch. Oriental and African Studies research fellow, London, 1962-63; sr. Fulbright fellow, West Bengal, India, 1968-69. Fellow AAAS, Am. Anthrop. Assn., Royal Anthrop. Inst. (Eng.); mem. Assn. Asian Studies, India League of Am. Found. (trustee). Home and Office: Internat House of Chicago 1414 E 59th St Chicago IL 60637-2940

NICHOLAS, ROBERT B., lawyer; b. N.Y.C., June 7, 1944. AB, St. Lawrence U., 1966; JD, Boston U., 1969. Bar: Mass. 1969, Pa. 1971, D.C. 1982. Spl. asst. to Atty. Gen. U.S. Atty. Gen. Office, Pa., 1971-73, dep. atty. gen., 1974-77; counsel toxic substances and environ. health U.S. Pres. Coun. on Environ. Quality, 1977-79, sr. staff mem., 1979-81; chief counsel, staff dir. Subcom. on Investigations and Oversight, Com. on Sci. and Tech., Ho. of Reps., Washington, 1982-85; ptnr. McDermott, Will & Emory, Washington; mem. U.S. Expert Group on Chem. Data Confidentiality OECD, 1978-81; chmn. Superfund-Nat. Contingency Plan Revision Com., 1980-81. Mem. editorial bd. Biotechnology Law Reporter, 1984—. Mem. ABA (mem. natural resources, energy and environ. law sects., vice chair spl. com. on biotechnology 1990—), Fed. Bar Assn. Office: McDermott Will & Emery 1850 K St NW Ste 500 Washington DC 20006-2213*

NICHOLAS, ROBERT LEON, foreign language educator; b. Lebanon, Oreg., Dec. 10, 1937; s. Elmer Leon Nicholas and Luella Lillian (Haberling) Haffner; m. Carole Anne Roberts, June 11, 1967; children: Scott Alan, Paul Elliot. BA, U. Oreg., 1959, MA, 1963, PhD, 1967. Instr. U. Wis., Madison, 1965-67, asst. prof., 1967-71, assoc. prof., 1971-76, prof., 1976—, chair dept. Spanish and Portuguese, 1979-82, 93-96. Author: (textbooks) En camino, 1977, 81, 85, 89, Adelante, 1977, 81, 85, Motivos de conversación, 1984, 88, 92 and several books of literary criticism written in Spanish. Mem. Am. Assn. Tchrs. Spanish and Portuguese, Kiwanis Club (pres. 1989). Democrat. Unitarian. Avocations: gardening, singing, piano and guitar, cycling, traveling. Home: 2126 Chadbourne Ave Madison WI 53705

NICHOLAS, THOMAS ANDREW, artist; b. Middletown, Conn., Sept. 26, 1934; s. Michael and Lena (Sequenzia) N.; m. Gloria R. Spencer, Oct. 11, 1958; 1 child, Thomas Michael. Student of Ernst Lohrmann, 1949-53; scholarship student, Sch. Visual Arts, N.Y.C., 1953-55. Instr. Famous Artists Schs., Inc., Westport, Conn., 1958-60; instr. painting, Rockport, Mass.,

1963-66. Commd. by Franklin Mint Gallery Am. Art to produce lithographs of Am. coastline, 1977; one-man shows include Grand Cen. Galleries, N.Y.C., 1962, 64, 66, 68, 70, 78, I.F.A. Galleries, Washington, 1964-92, A. Huney Gallery, San Diego, 1980, 82;, Carolyn Hill Gallery, Soho, N.Y.C., 1988-89, 3 person show, 1992; represented in permanent collections Butler Inst. Am. Art, Youngstown, Ohio, Ga. Mus., Athens, New Britain (Conn.) Art Mus., U. Utah, Adelphi U., Greenshields Mus., Montreal, Can., Farnsworth Mus., Rockland, Maine, Springfield (Mo.) Art Mus., Ranger Collection at NAD (2 works), Peabody Mus., Salem, Mass.; author articles; recipient numerous awards 1957—, including, Emile Lowe award for watercolor Am. Watercolor Soc. 1961, watercolor prize 1964, Gold medal honor 1969, Clare Stout award 1971, Mary S. Litt award 1972, medal honor for watercolor Knickerbocker Artists 1962, Purchase award watercolor Butler Inst. Am. Art 1962, Henry Ward Ranger Fund purchase watercolor NAD 1962, 71, Obrig prize watercolor 1964, 66, 79, 87, gold medal honor watercolor Allied Artists Am. 1962, Grumbacher prize 1978, Today Mag. Art medal 1970, 74, gold medal honor watercolor Am. Artists Profl. League 1964, best landscape award 1974, gold medal 1978, Edwin S. Webster award honor watercolor Boston Soc. Watercolor 1964, gold medal honor watercolor Hudson Valley Art Assn. 1964, DuMond Meml. award 1971, Isabel Stinschneider Meml. award 1972, Herman Wick Meml. award Salmagundi Club, N.Y.C. 1966, 2d prize 1966, June Justin J. Impasto award 1972, Arthur T. Hill prize 1973, Arthur T. Hill Meml. prize 1975, Louis Z. Seley prize 1978, Gwynne Lennon prize 1979, Gold medal honor oil Rockport Art Assn. 1966, 69, 76, 86, cash award Wichita Centennial Watercolor 1970, Providence Art Club prize 1972, gold medal Franklin Mint Competition 1974, Gold medal Honor Acad. Assn. 1976, others. Elizabeth Greenshields grantee, 1961, 62; recipient Gold medal of Honor New Eng. Watercolor Soc., Boston, 1985, Acad. Artists Assn., 1985; named Knickerbocker Honoree Artist of Yr., 1989; recipient Grumbacher award watercolor, Acad. Artists Assn., 1990, Grumbacher Gold medal Gouache New Eng. Watercolor Soc., 1992. Mem. NAD (cert. merit watercolor 1992), Am. Watercolor Soc. (ea. v.p. 1994—, Dolphin fellow), Boston Watercolor Soc., Conn. Watercolor Socs., Allied Artists Am., Knickerbocker Artists (dir.'s prize 1971, Gold medal 1989), Boston Guild Artists (Grumbacher Gold medallion award for Watercolor 1988, No. Shore Arts Assn. award for Oil 1991), Rockport Art Assn. (Silver medal 1988, 94, Darrand award for Oil 1992, Cirino award 1st prize Gouache 1992, Clark Polupar award Gouache 1992), Hudson Valley Artists (Gold medal 1974, 85, 94). Home: 7 Wildon Hts Rockport MA 01966-2007 Office: Tom Nicholas Gallery 71 Main St Rockport MA 01966-1512 *I have been fortunate to have been encouraged by my family at an early age and have a number of people to thank for their support, especially my wife. I feel artists must never compromise their ideals and principles, no matter how high their standards. Originality and professional ethics with one's work make goals achieved meaningful. On the one hand, an artist should inwardly feel that there is little he can't accomplish, and yet he must learn to work within his realized limitations.*

NICHOLAS, THOMAS PETER, library administrator, community television consultant, producer; b. Laramie, Wyo., Dec. 6, 1948; s. Thomas Lloyd Nicholas and Frances (Collins) Chambers; m. Tanya Michelle Villont; 1 child, Ja'el Michelle. AA in Fine Arts, Cabrillo Coll., 1970; BA in English, U. Colo., 1972; MS in Librarianship and Info. Sci., U. Denver, 1982. Real estate salesperson Sun Country, Lakewood, Colo., 1972-74; v.p. Nicholas Properties, Denver, 1971-77; libr. City of Aurora, Colo., 1975-80, system support mgr., 1981-83, dir. libr. and TV svcs., 1984—; dir. Libr., Recreation & TV Svcs. City of Aurora, 1995—; pres. bd. Irving Libr. Network Inc., Denver, 1985—; adv. CL System Inc., Boston, 1985—; acting pers. dir. City of Aurora; Denver Regional Coun. of Govt. award for Cmty. Svc. and Govt. Coop., 1995. Exec. producer TV programs: Election Night 85 (Franny award 1986), Miss Plumjoy's Place, 1988 (Starwards 1988), Aurora's Can't Afford Not To, 1988 (Starwards 1988). Mem. exec. bd., chmn. Arapahoe Pub. Access to Librs., 1984-85; site coordinator Am. Cancer Soc., Aurora, 1988; adv. Youth at Risk, Aurora, 1989; bd. dirs. Cen. Colo. Libr. System, Lakewood, 1985-87; mem. exec. bd. Colo. Libr. Legis. Com., Denver, 1988—; pres. Greater Metro Cable Consortium, 1992—; acting dep. city mgr. City of Aurora, 1993—. Mem. ALA, Colo. Libr. Assn. (advisor 1982-83, Programming award 1982, 1st Colo. Childrens Program award 1983, 88), Nat. Assn. Telecommunications Officers and Advisors (regional pres. 1983-84, T.V. Program award 1986), Rotary (program chmn. 1987-88), Eastgate Lions Club (pres. 1989-90). Democrat. Greek Orthodox. Avocations: fine art, poetry, automobile restoration, martial arts (Black Belt). Office: Aurora Pub Libr 14949 E Alameda Dr Aurora CO 80012-1544

NICHOLAS, WILLIAM RICHARD, lawyer; b. Pontiac, Mich., June 19, 1934; s. Reginald and Edna Irene (Bartlett) N.; m. Diana Lee Johnson, Aug. 20, 1960; children: Susan Lee, William Richard Jr. BS in Bus., U. Idaho, 1956; JD, U. Mich., 1962. Bar: 1963. Ptnr. Latham & Watkins, Los Angeles, 1962—. Contbr. numerous articles on taxation. Served to lt. (j.g.) USN, 1956-59. Mem. Calif. Bar Assn., Los Angeles County Bar Assn., Am. Coll. Tax Counsel. Home: 1808 Old Ranch Rd Los Angeles CA 90049-2207 Office: Latham & Watkins 633 W 5th St Ste 4000 Los Angeles CA 90071-2005

NICHOLAW, GEORGE, communications executive; b. Salinas, Calif., Nov. 17, 1927; s. Costas and Anna G. (Melissa) N.; m. Betty Baron. B in Fgn. Trade, Am. Grad. Sch. Internat. Mgmt.; BS, U. Calif., Berkeley. Program dir. Sta. KDON, Salinas, 1953-55; asst. dir. promotion, publicity Sta. KNXT-TV, Los Angeles, 1955-63; dir. info. services and community relations Sta. WBBM-TV, Chgo., 1963-66; dir. community services Sta. WCBS-TV, N.Y.C., 1966-67; v.p. CBS radio div., gen. mgr. Sta. KNX, Los Angeles, 1967—. Commr. Los Angeles Energy Commn.; active Communications Task Force Greater Los Angeles Urban Coalition., Calif. Air Pollution Emergency Traffic Control Com. Served with U.S. Army. Recipient Abe Lincoln award, Peabody award, Ohio State award, Alfred I DuPont award, Columbia U. Mem. Nat. Assn. Broadcasters, Calif. Broadcasters Assn. (dir. Los Angeles chpt.), Hollywood Radio and TV Soc. (dir. Los Angeles chpt.), Arbitron Radio Adv. Council (past chmn.), Calif. Inst. Cancer Research (bd. dirs.), Permanent Charities Com. Entertainment Industries (bd. dirs.). Office: Sta KNX-AM 6121 W Sunset Blvd Los Angeles CA 90028-6455*

NICHOLLS, DAVID G., editor, scholar; b. Indpls., Oct. 6, 1965; s. Thomas G. and Natalie A. (Keinonen) N. AB, Bowdoin Coll., 1988; MA, U. Chgo., 1989, PhD, 1995. Nonfiction editor Chgo. Rev., 1989-91, editor, 1991-96; Rockefeller resident postdoctoral fellow Ctr. for Afroamerican and African Studies, U. Mich., Ann Arbor, 1996-97. Co-editor: The Penguin New Writing in India, 1994. Javits fellow U.S. Dept. Edn., 1989-93, Mellon fellow U. Chgo., 1993-94; Witter Bynner Found. grantee, 1991. Office: Chicago Review 5801 S Kenwood Ave Chicago IL 60637-1766

NICHOLLS, RICHARD ALLEN, middle school social studies educator; b. Chgo., Sept. 1, 1944; s. Harry Allen and Rita Mae (O'Connell) N.; m. Linda Lee Soderberg, Mar. 27, 1969 (div. 1979). AA, Lincoln Coll., 1964; BA, MacMurray Coll., 1966; postgrad., Loyola U., 1967; MA, Nat. Lewis U., 1991. Cert. volleyball coach. 6th grade tchr. Chgo. Pub. Schs., 1966-67; 7th & 8th grades tchr. Palos Sch. Dist. 118, Palos Park, Ill., 1967—; sponsor student govt. Palos Sch. Dist. 118, 1971-73, sponsor pompon squad, 1971-73, mem. curriculum devel. com., 1970-72; writer (with others) curriculum for devel. of thematic units for transition of Palos South Jr. H.S. to Palos Mid. Sch., summer 1995; volleyball coach Palos South Jr. H.S. (now Palos South Mid. Sch.), 1977-90, Victor J. Andrew H.S., 1981-84, Carl Sandburg H.S., 1985-91; mem. IGAP com. for sch. stds., 1992-93. Mem. NEA, Ill. Edn. Assn., U.S. Volleyball Assn., Palos Edn. Assn., Am. Athletic Union (volleyball coach, nat. champions 1981, 82, finalists 1984, 85, 87 jr. Olympics Nat. Tournament, 5th pl. jr. Nats., 1994) Am. Legion (Citizenship award 1964), Phi Theta Kappa. Avocations: coaching volleyball, sponsoring school trips, personal training for physical fitness. Office: Palos Sch Dist 118 8800 W 119th St Palos Park IL 60464-1004

NICHOLLS, RICHARD H., lawyer; b. Toronto, Ont., Can., Oct. 27, 1938; s. Richard S. and Roberta T.; m. Judy Carter, Apr. 15, 1963; children: Christopher T., Jamie C.; m. Anne Delaney, June 10, 1978. BA cum laude, Amherst Coll., 1960; LLB, Stanford U., 1963; LLM, NYU, 1964. Bar: Calif. 1964, N.Y. 1965, D.C. Assoc. Mudge Rose Guthrie, Alexander & Ferdon and predecessor, N.Y.C., 1964-70, ptnr., 1971-94; of counsel Orrick, Herrington & Sutcliffe, N.Y.C., 1995—. Mem. ABA, N.Y. State Bar Assn., Nat. Assn. Bond Lawyers, Stamford Yacht Club. Home: 159 Ocean Dr W Stamford CT 06902-8004 Office: Orrick Herrington & Sutcliffe 666 Fifth Avenue New York NY 10103

NICHOLS, ALAN, newspaper publishing executive. CFO San Francisco Chronicle, 1993—. Office: San Francisco Chronicle 901 Mission St San Francisco CA 94103*

NICHOLS, ALBERT L., economics consultant; b. Poughkeepsie, N.Y., Feb. 13, 1951; s. Albert and Margaret (Schaefer) N.; m. Eve Kaufman, June 16, 1973; children: Matthew, Elizabeth. AB, Stanford U., 1973; M of Pub. Policy, Harvard U., 1975, PhD, 1981. Assoc. prof. Harvard U., Cambridge, Mass., 1977-83, 85-88, dir. adminstrv. planning, 1988-89; dir. econ. analysis EPA, Washington, 1983-85; v.p. Nat. Econ. Rsch. Assocs., Cambridge, 1989—; cons. various corps., 1976-89. Author: Targeting Economic Incentives for Environmental Protection, 1984; contbr. numerous articles to profl. jours. Nat. Merit scholar, 1969. Mem. Am. Econ. Assn., Soc. for Risk Analysis, Assn. Environ. and Resource Economists, Phi Beta Kappa. Avocation: woodworking. Home: 14 Baskin Rd Lexington MA 02173-6929 Office: Nat Econ Rsch Assocs 1 Main St Cambridge MA 02142-1517

NICHOLS, C. WALTER, III, retired trust company executive; b. N.Y.C., Aug. 25, 1937; s. Charles Walter and Marjorie (Jones) N.; B.A., U. Va., 1959; m. Anne Sharp, Aug. 8, 1959; children—Blair, Sandra, Walter, Hope. Vice pres. Citibank, N.Y.C., 1962-78, Morgan Guaranty Trust Co. N.Y., N.Y.C., 1979-93; 1st v.p. Republic Nat. Bank N.Y., N.Y.C., 1994—; mng. dir. Fissell, Laidlaw & Co. Inc., 1995—. Bd. dirs. Nichols Found., Inc., 1969—, pres. 1988-90; bd. dirs. Greenwich House, 1969-94, pres., 1984-90; bd. dirs. Choate Rosemary Hall, 1972-77, 82-89, Westover Sch., 1979-81, Lower Hudson (N.Y.) chpt. Nature Conservancy, 1978-87, hon. trustee, 1988—, John Jay Homestead, 1980—, Nat. Audubon Soc., 1983-87; mem. adv. bd. N.Y. Zool. Soc. (Bronx Zoo), 1987-94; mem. adv. bd. Caramoor Music Festival, 1994—. Served to 1st lt. U.S. Army, 1960-62. Decorated Army Commendation medal. Mem. Naturist Soc., Nat. Assn. Railroad Passengers (bd. dirs. 1996—), Am. Sunbathing Assn. Clubs: Bedford (N.Y.) Golf and Tennis, Pilgrims of U.S. Office: 42 Main St Bedford Hills NY 10507-1814

NICHOLS, CARL WHEELER, retired advertising agency executive; b. Ottawa, Kans., Oct. 9, 1923; s. Carl Wheeler and Cora Merle (Hanks) N.; children: Christine, Carl Wheeler, Nancy, Matthew; m. Anna Norris, Apr. 18, 1992. Student, Baker U., 1940-41, U. Mo., 1941-43; B.A., U. Mich., 1944. Research analyst Cunningham & Walsh, Inc. (advt. agy.), N.Y.C., 1946-49; copywriter Cunningham & Walsh, Inc. (advt. agy.), 1949-56, co-creative dir., v.p., 1956-59, dir. account mgmt., 1959-61, pres., 1961-69, chmn., chief exec. officer, 1969-85, chmn. emeritus, 1986. Capt. USMCR, 1943-46, 50-52, Korea. Named to Advt. Hall of Fame, 1986. Mem. N.Y. Advt. Coun. (bd. dirs. 1974-85), Am. Advt. Fedn. (dir. 1972-75, chmn. 1975-76), Advt. Ednl. Found. (bd. dirs., sec., treas. 1983-91), Woodway Country Club, John's Island Club, Bent Pine Club, Sigma Xi. Presbyterian (elder). Home: 241 Island Creek Dr Vero Beach FL 32963-3304

NICHOLS, CAROL D., real estate professional, association executive. BA, U. Pitts., 1964; cert. in advanced mgmt., U. Chgo. From mgmt. trainee to buyer May Dept. Stores Co., Pitts., 1964-70; various mgmt. positions, then mng. dir. mortgage and real estate div. Tchrs. Ins. and Annuity Assn. Am., N.Y.C., 1970—; instr. real estate div. continuing edn. Marymount Manhattan Coll., N.Y.C., 1975-76, Woman's Sch. Adult Edn. Ctr., N.Y.C., 1976-77; v.p. instn. owners div. Real Estate Bd. N.Y., past chmn. fin. com., mem. seminar and gen. meetings coms. Trustee, mem. investment com. Nat. Jewish Ctr. for Immunology and Respiratory Medicine. Recipient Nat. Humanitarian award Nat. Jewish Ctr. for Immunology and Respiratory Medicine, Nat. Brotherhood award NCCJ. Mem. Assn. Real Estate Women (past pres.), Urban Land Inst. (trustee, chmn. urban devel. and mixed use coun., coun. coord. and inner city). Home: 165 Winfield St East Norwalk CT 06855-1622 Office: Teachers Ins & Annuity Assn 730 3rd Ave New York NY 10017-3206

NICHOLS, COLIN GRAHAM, bioscience educator; b. Leicester, Eng., Aug. 27, 1960; came to U.S., 1985; s. Graham P. and Margaret Ann Nichols; m. Diana L. Coleman, Oct. 17, 1992. BSc, Leeds (Eng.) U., 1982, PhD, 1985. Postdoctoral fellow U. Md., Balt., 1985-90; vis. rsch. assoc. Baylor Coll. Medicine, Houston, 1990-91; asst. prof. cell biology Washington U., St. Louis, 1991—; established investigator Am. Heart Assn., 1993—. Contbr. numerous articles to sci. jours. Mem. Biophys. Soc., Soc. Gen. Physiologists. Avocations: avid cricket player. Office: Washington U Sch Medicine Dept Cell Biology 660 S Euclid Ave Saint Louis MO 63110-1010

NICHOLS, DAVID, production designer. Prodn. designer: (films) Box Car Bertha, 1972, The Wild Party, 1975, (with Robb Wilson King) Swamp Thing, 1982, Testament, 1983, Heartbreaker, 1983, Reckless, 1984, The Best of Times, 1986, Hoosiers, 1986, The Serpent and the Rainbow, 1988, Great Balls of Fire!, 1989, A Midnight Clear, 1992, Groundhog Day, 1993, Airheads, 1994, (TV movie) Finnegan Begin Again, 1985; visual cons.: (films) Mean Streets, 1973. Office: care Spyros Skouras Sanford Skouras Gross & Assocs 1015 Gayley Ave Fl 3 Los Angeles CA 90024-3424

NICHOLS, DAVID ARTHUR, mediator, retired state justice; b. Lincolnville, Maine, Aug. 6, 1917; s. George E. and Flora E. (Pillsbury) N. A.B. magna cum laude, Bates Coll., 1942; J.D., U. Mich., 1949. Bar: Maine bar 1949, Mass. bar 1949, U.S. Supreme Ct 1954. Pvt. practice Camden, Maine, 1949-75; justice Maine Superior Ct., 1975-77, Maine Supreme Jud. Ct., 1977-88; mediator, 1988—; Mem. Maine Exec. Council, 1955-57; moderator Lincolnville Town Meeting, 1950-74. Mem. editorial bd. Picton Press, 1989—; contbr. to legal and geneal. publs. Chmn. Maine Republican Com., 1960-64; mem. Rep. Nat. Com., 1960-68; chmn. Maine council Young Reps., 1950-54; New Eng. council Young Reps., 1952-54; trustee, past pres. Penobscot Bay Med. Center. Served with USAAF, 1942-45. Fellow Am. Bar Found., Am. Coll. Trial Lawyers; mem. Am. Law Inst., Camden-Rockport C. of C. (past pres.), Maine Hist. Soc., Camden Hist. Soc. (past pres.), Camden Bus. Men's Assn. (past pres.), ABA (bd. govs. 1960-63, ho. dels. 1957-78), Maine Bar Assn., Am. Judicature Soc. (dir. 1960-64), New Eng. Historic Geneal. Soc. (trustee), Bates Coll. Alumni Assn. (past pres.), Maine Trial Lawyers Assn. (past pres.), Phi Beta Kappa, Delta Sigma Rho. Clubs: Odd Fellows, Rotary (past pres.). Home: PO Box 76 Lincolnville ME 04849-0076

NICHOLS, DAVID HARRY, gynecologic surgeon, obstetrics and gynecology educator, author; b. Utica, N.Y., July 30, 1925; s. Harry Harrison and Katherine Valentine (Belknap) N.; m. Lorraine Elizabeth Landel, June 23, 1948; children: David L., Laurie L., Nancie L., Daniel A., Julie L. MD, U. Buffalo, 1947; MA (hon.), Brown U., 1982. Diplomate Am. Bd. Ob-Gyn. Intern E.J. Meyer Meml. Hosp., Buffalo, 1947-48; resident in ob-gyn Millard Fillmore Hosp., Buffalo, 1948-51; assoc. cancer rsch. gynecologist Roswell Pk. Meml. Inst., Buffalo, 1953-60; asst. clin. prof. ob-gyn. SUNY, Buffalo, 1958-68, clin. prof., 1968-75, prof., 1975-80; prof. Brown U., Providence, 1980-92, chmn. dept. ob-gyn., 1980-91, dir. Ctr. for Women's Surgery, 1990-91; chief of pelvic reconstructive surgery Mass. Gen. Hosp., Boston, 1991—; pres. Erie County unit Am. Cancer Soc., 1962-68, Buffalo Ob/Gyn. Soc., 1975-76; vis. prof. ob-gyn., reproductive biology Harvard U. Sch. Med., 1991—. Author: Atlas of Gynecological Pathology, 1951, Vaginal Surgery, 1976, 4th edit., 1996; author, editor: (med. monograph) Clinical Problems, Injuries, and Complications of GYN Surgery, 1983, 3d edit., 1995, Ambulatory Gynecology, 1985, 2d edit., 1995, Reoperative Gynecologic Surgery, 1991, Gynecologic and Obstetric Surgery, 1993. Maj. M.C., USAF, 1949-53. Fellow ACS, Am. Coll. Ob-Gyn., Internat. Coll. Surgeons, Boston Obstet. Soc.; mem. Soc. Pelvic Surgeons, Soc. Gynecol. Surgeons (nat. pres. 1984-85), N.E. Obstet. Soc., Boston Obstet. Soc., Am. Gyn. Club (pres. 1993-94), Harvard Club. Republican. Roman Catholic. Avocations: travel, music, literature. Office: Mass Gen Hosp Vincent 1 Boston MA 02114 Address: 101 Prospect St Providence RI 02906-1440

NICHOLS, DAVID L., retail executive; b. Toledo, Sept. 1, 1941; s. Lee Roy and Marianne (smith) N.; children: Fredericka, JoLynn, Jennifer, Laurie, Martha, Meredith; m. Lenore Grotke Nichols, Sept. 15, 1990. BA in Bus., U. Toledo, 1990. With The McAlpin Co., Cin., 1963-76; store mgr. McAlpin's Northgate, Cin., 1976-78; gen. mdse. mgr. Mercantile Stores Co., Inc., N.Y.C., 1978-82, v.p., CFO, treas., 1989-91, exec. v.p., CFO, treas., 1991-92, chmn., CEO, 1992—; pres. Lion Store, Toledo, 1982-89. Active Cin. Bus. Com., 1992. Recipient Green Thumb award Am. Apparel Mfr. Assn., 1993. Avocations: golf, gourmet cooking. Office: Mercantile Stores Co Inc 9450 Seward Rd Fairfield OH 45014*

NICHOLS, DONALD ARTHUR, economist, educator; b. Madison, Conn., Dec. 20, 1940; s. Edward Charles and Ruth (Nilson) N.; m. Linda Powley, Aug. 19, 1962 (dec. Oct. 1982); children: Charles Spencer, Elizabeth Clarke.; m. Barbara Jakubowski Noel, May 22, 1983. B.A., Yale U., 1962, M.A., 1963, Ph.D., 1968. Mem. faculty dept. econs. U. Wis., Madison, 1966—, prof., 1977—, chmn. dept. econs., 1983-86, 88-90, mem. exec. com. faculty senate, 1987-90, chmn., 1989-90; lectr. Yale U., 1970-71; sr. economist Senate Budget Com., Washington, 1975-76; dep. asst. sec. for econ. policy and rsch. Dept. Labor, Washington, 1977-79; dir. Ctr. for Rsch. on Wis. Economy; econ. advisor to gov. State of Wis., 1983-86; exec. sec. Gov.'s Coun. Econ. Advisors, 1983-86; mem. Gov.'s Export Strategy Commn., 1994-95; bd. dirs. Thompson, Plumb Funds; bd. dirs. PROFS, 1987-90, treas., 1987-88, pres., 1988-89; cons. in field. Author: (with Clark Reynolds) Principles of Economics, 1970, Dollars and Sense, 1994; contbr. articles to profl. jours. Trustee U. Wis. Bookstore, 1990-95; bd. advisors Am. Players Theatre, Spring Green, Wis., 1993—. NSF fellow, 1963-66, 70-72; Nat. Commn. Employment Policy rsch. grantee, 1980-82; recipient William H. Kiekhofer Meml. Teaching prize U. Wis., 1973. Mem. Am. Econ. Assn., Econometric Soc., Royal Econ. Soc. Office: U Wis 1180 Observatory Dr Madison WI 53706-1320

NICHOLS, DONALD RICHARDSON, medical educator; b. Mpls., Feb. 22, 1911; s. Arthur R. and Agusta (Fisher) N.; m. Margery Spicer, Mar. 5, 1942 (dec.); children: Virginia (Mrs. Gregory Blanchfield), John; m. Mary Jean Scholberg, Mar. 2, 1957 (dec.); children: Arthur, Edwin, Mary Jean (Mrs. Vincent Grimaldi), Barbara (Mrs. Todd McCallister). AB, Amherst Coll., 1933; MD, U. Minn., 1938, MS in Medicine, 1942. Diplomate: Am. Bd. Internal Medicine. Intern Milw. County Hosp., 1939; fellow medicine Mayo Found., 1939-42; mem. faculty Mayo Grad. Sch. Medicine, U. Minn., 1948-72, prof. clin. medicine, 1965-72; prof. medicine Mayo Med. Sch., 1972-81; cons. medicine Mayo Clinic, 1942-81, chmn. divsn. infectious diseases, 1963-73, sr. cons. medicine, 1973-81; dir. health svc. Rochester (Minn.) C.C. (Minn.), 1981-86. Treas. Rochester Human Rights Commn., 1983-89. Surgeon U.S. Mcht. Marines, 1941. Fellow Infectious Diseases Soc. Am., ACP; mem. AMA, Minn. State Med. Assn., Central Soc. Clin. Research, Mayo Alumni Assn., Sigma Xi, Nu Sigma Nu, Theta Delta Chi. Methodist. Home: 207 5th Ave SW Rochester MN 55902-3100

NICHOLS, EDIE DIANE, executive recruiter; b. Grahamstown, Eastern Cape Province, Republic of South Africa, Mar. 28, 1939; came to U.S., 1963; d. Cyril Doughtry and Dorothy Ethel (Nottingham) Tyson; m. John F. Nichols, Dec. 16, 1962; 1 child, Ian Tyson. Adminstrv. asst. Am. Acad. Medicine, N.Y.C., 1963-64, Jack Lenor Larsen, Inc., N.Y.C., 1964-70; v.p. John Scott Fones, Inc., N.Y.C., 1971-76, Howard J. Rubenstein Assocs. Inc., N.Y.C., 1976-80; dir. communications Carl Byoir & Assocs., N.Y.C., 1981-83; account supr. Hill and Knowlton, N.Y.C., 1983-85; broker Cross & Brown Co., N.Y.C., 1986-88; v.p. Marc Nichols Assocs., Inc., N.Y.C., 1989-95; mng. ptnr. Nichols Brown Internat., N.Y.C., 1995—. Trustee Cen. Park Hist. Soc., N.Y.C., 1978-80. Mem. NOW, N.Y. Women in Comm. (pub. rels. chair 1980-81, v.p., programs bd. dirs 1985-87), Fin. Women's Assn. of N.Y. Republican. Episcopalian. Club: City of N.Y. (trustee, v.p., fin. and devel. 1987-89). Home: 155 W 20th St Apt 2K New York NY 10011-3612 Office: Nichols Brown Internat 330 Madison Ave 11th fl New York NY 10017

NICHOLS, ELIZABETH GRACE, nursing educator, administrator; b. Tehran, Iran, Feb. 1, 1943; came to U.S., 1964; d. Terence and Eleanor Denny (Payne) Quilliam; m. Gerald Ray Nichols, Nov. 20, 1965; children: Tina Lynn, Jeffrey David. BSN, San Francisco State U., 1969; MS, U. Calif.-San Francisco, 1970, Dr. Nursing Sci., 1974, MA Idaho State U., 1989. Staff nurse Peninsula Hosp., Burlingame, Calif., 1966-72; asst. prof. U. Calif.-San Francisco Sch. Nursing, 1974-82; chmn. dept. nursing Idaho State U., Pocatello, 1982-85; assoc. dean Coll. Health Scis. Sch. Nursing U. Wyo., Laramie, 1985-91, asst. to pres. for program reviews, 1991-95, dean Coll. Nursing, U. N.D., 1995—; cons. U. Rochester, N.Y., 1979, Carroll Coll., Mont., 1980, div. Nursing Dept. HHS, Washington, 1980, 84, 85, 86, 87, Stanford Hosp. Nursing Service, Calif., 1981-82, Ea. N.Mex. U., 1988. Contbr. articles on nursing to profl. jours. Mem. adv. bd. dirs. Ombudsman Service of Contra Costa Calif., 1979-82, U. Calif. Home Care Service, San Francisco, 1975-82, Free Clinic of Pocatello, 1984. ACE fellow U. Maine system 1990-91. Fellow ACE, Gerontol. Soc. Am., Am. Acad. Nursing; mem. Gerontol. Soc. Am. (chmn. clin. medicine section 1987, sec. 1990-93), Am. Nurses Assn., Wyo. Nurses Assn., Idaho Nurses Assn. (dist. 51 adv. bd. dirs. 1982-84), Western Inst. Nursing (chair, 1990-92, bd. govs.). Club: Oakland Ski (1st v.p. 1981-82). (Calif.).

NICHOLS, EUGENE DOUGLAS, mathematics educator; b. Rovno, Poland, Feb. 6, 1923; came to U.S., 1946, naturalized, 1951; s. Alex and Anna (Radchuk) Nichiporuk; m. Alice Bissell, Mar. 31, 1951. BS, U. Chgo., 1949, postgrad., 1949-51; MEd, U. Ill., 1953, MA, 1954, PhD, 1956. Instr. math. Roberts Wesleyan Coll., North Chili, N.Y., 1950-51, U. Ill., 1951-56; assoc. prof. math. edn. Fla. State U., 1956-61, prof., head dept., 1961-73; dir. Project for Mathematical Devel. of Children, 1973-77; dir. math program NSF, 1958-61; dir. Math. Inst. Elem. Tchrs., 1961-70; pres. Nichols Schwartz Pub., 1992—; prof. math. edn. Fla. State U., 1974-90; Chmn. U. Ill. Com. on Sch. Math., 1954-55; cons. editor math McGraw-Hill Book Co., summer 1956. Co-author: Modern Elementary Algebra, 1961, Introduction to Sets, 1962, Arithmetic of Directed Numbers, 1962, Introduction to Equations and Inequalities, 1963, Introduction to Coordinate Geometry, 1963, Introduction to Exponents, 1964, Understanding Arithmetic, 1965, Elementary Mathematics Patterns and Structure, 1966, Algebra, 1966, Modern Geometry, 1968, Modern Trigonometry, 1968, Modern Intermediate Algebra, 1969, Analytic Geometry, 1973, Holt Algebra 1, 1974, 78, 82, 86, 92, Holt Algebra 2, 1974, 78, 82, 86, 92, Holt Geometry, 1974, 78, 82, 86, Holt School Mathematics, 1974, 78, 81, Holt Pre-Algebra Mathematics, 1980, 86, Holt Mathematics, 1981, 85, Elementary School Mathematics and How to Teach It, 1982, Geometry, 1991, Holt Pre-Algebra, 1992, Mathematics Dictionary and Handbook, 1993, 95; author: Pre-Algebra Mathematics, 1970, Introductory Algebra for College Students, 1971, Mathematics for the Elementary School Teacher, 1971, College Mathematics, 1975, College Mathematics for General Education, rev. edit., 1975. Named Fla. State U. Disting. Prof., 1968-69; recipient Disting. Alumni award U. Ill. Coll. Edn., 1970. Mem. Am. Math. Soc., Math. Assn. Am., Sch. Sci. and Math. Assn., Nat. Coun. Tchrs. Math., Coun. Basic Edn., Text and Acad. Authors Assn., Pi Mu Epsilon, Phi Delta Kappa. Home: 3386 W Lakeshore Dr Tallahassee FL 32312-1305 *Do not look for a career--look for opportunities to do kind things for others. Be honest with yourself and with those around you.*

NICHOLS, GERRY LYNN, occupational therapist; b. Larned, Kans., Nov. 18, 1951; d. James H. and Dorthea (Griffith) Sooby; m. William P. Hesley, July 1975 (div. July 1981); m. Douglas J. Nichols, Oct. 9, 1987; 1 child, Rebecca. BS in Occupl. Therapy, San Jose State U., 1980; MBA, U. Dallas, Irving, Tex., 1990. Lic. occupl. therapist; cert. case mgr. Mgr. occupl. therapy Meth. Med. Ctr., Dallas, 1985-87; pvt. practice Dallas, 1981-89; occupl. therapist Progressive Rehab. Inst. of Dallas for Ergonomics, Dallas, 1987-88; v.p. bus. devel./strategic planning and devel., dir. rehab., dir. ops., occupl. therapist Am. Rehab. Ctr./Rehab. Sys., Inc., Dallas, 1989-91; pres. GSN Cons., Inc., Carrollton, Tex., 1991—; pres., CEO WorkWell Sys., Inc., Carrollton, 1994—. Contbr. articles to profl. jours. Mem. adv. bd. Home Health Svcs., Inc., 1990—. Mem. Am. Occupl. Therapy Assn. (roster of evaluators 1993—), Tex. Occupl. Therapy Assn. (dist. chairperson, bd. dirs. 1984-88, Cert. of Appreciation 1989), Metrocrest C. of C. Democrat. Avocations: snow skiing, camping, needlework, reading. Home: 2208 Sunrise Ln Carrollton TX 75006-2754

NICHOLS, GUY WARREN, retired institute executive, utilities executive; b. Colchester, Vt., Oct. 27, 1925; s. Guy W. and Gladys (Tomlinson) N.; m. Shirley Hibbard, June 21, 1947; children: Pamela, Gail, Sally. BSCE, U. Vt.,

1947; postgrad., Worcester Poly. Inst. Sch. Indsl. Mgmt., 1953-56; MS in Bus. Adminstrn., MIT, 1961. With New. Eng. Electric System, Westborough, Mass., 1947-84, exec. v.p., 1968-70, pres., 1970-84, chief exec. officer, 1972-84, chmn. bd., 1978-84; bd. dirs. Allmerica Fin. Corp., Allmerica Property & Casualty Cos. Inc., Noble Affiliates. Chmn., trustee Woods Hole Oceanographic Instn., 1985-95. Sloan fellow, MIT, 1961. Fellow Am. Acad. Arts and Scis. Office: Ste 2115 One International Pl Boston MA 02110

NICHOLS, HAROLD JAMES, theatre educator; b. Mitchell Field, N.Y., July 27, 1945; s. Harold J. and Ruth (McCain) N.; m. Mary Frances Lutes, Nov. 25, 1967 (div. 1992); children: Ruth, David, Debra; m. Anna Marie Douet, July 4, 1992. BS, Iowa State U., 1967; MA, Ind. U., 1969, PhD, 1971. Assoc. instr. Ind. U., Bloomington, 1970-71; asst. prof. Kans. State U., Manhattan, 1971-75, assoc. prof., 1975-81, prof., 1981-84, prof., head speech dept., 1985-93; dean coll. fine arts and humanities U. Nebr., Kearney, 1993—; guest scholar DePauw U. Undergrad. Honors Conf., Greencastle, Ind., 1988; cons. Commonwealth of Va. Dept. Edn., 1988, Nebr. Wesleyan U., Lincoln, 1989, So. Ill. U., 1989, U. Va., 1992, U. No. Iowa, 1992. Co-editor: Status of Theatre Research-1984, 1986; contbr. articles to profl. jours. Named Outstanding Coll. Tchr., Kans. Speech Communications Assn., 1985. Mem. Assn. Theatre in Higher Edn. (pres. 1987-88), Am. Coll. Theatre Festival (region chair 1987-88, Kennedy Ctr. medallion 1990), Mid-Am. Theatre Conf. (chief regional officer 1978-81). Home: 1418 8th Ave Kearney NE 68847-6637 Office: Univ Nebr at Kearney Coll Fine Arts Humanities Kearney NE 68849

NICHOLS, HAROLD NEIL, corporate executive, former pipeline company executive; b. Digby, N.S., Can., June 15, 1937; s. Harold A. and Lillian (Nielsen) N.; m. Doris E. Outhouse, Mar. 2, 1957; children—Michael, Dale, Sherri, Susan, Lori. Grad. high sch. Cert. Mgmt. Acct. Various fin. positions TransCan. PipeLines Ltd., Toronto, Ont., from 1956, chief fin. officer, from 1983, exec. v.p., 1988-89; mgmt. cons. Unionville, Ont., 1989-92; chmn. Battery Techs., Inc., 1993-95; bd. dirs. Union Bank Switzerland (Can.); pres. Corrosion Interventions Ltd., Metocean Data Sys. Ltd. Mem. Fin. Execs. Inst. Home: 7 Blackwell Ct, Unionville, ON Canada L3R 0C2

NICHOLS, HENRY ELIOT, lawyer, savings and loan executive; b. N.Y.C.; m. Frances Griffin Morrison, Aug. 12, 1950 (dec. July 1978); children: Clyde Whitney, Diane Spencer; m. Mary Ann Wall, May 31, 1987. BA, Yale U., 1946; JD, U. Va., 1948. Bar: D.C. 1950, U.S. Dist. Ct. 1950, U.S. Ct. Appeals 1952, U.S. Supreme Ct. 1969. Assoc. Frederick W. Berens, Washington, 1950-52; sole practice, Washington, 1952—; real estate columnist Washington Star, 1966-81; pres., gen. counsel Hamilton Fed. Savs. & Loan Assn., 1971-74; vice chmn. bd. Columbia 1st Bank (formerly Columbia 1st Fed. Savs. & Loan Assn.), Washington, 1974-90, bd. dir.; pres. Century Fin. Corp., 1971-90; regional v.p. Preview, Inc., 1972-78; bd. dir., exec. com. Columbia Real Estate Title Ins. Co., Washington, 1968-78; bd. dir. Greater Met. Bd. Trade, 1974-78, Dist. Realty Title Ins. Co., 1978-86. Nat. adv. bd. Harker Prep. Sch., 1975-80; exec. com. Father Walter E. Schmitz Meml. Fund, Cath. U., 1982-83; bd. dirs. Vincent T. Lombardi Cancer Rsch. Ctr., 1979-84; del. Pres. Johnson's Conf. Law and Poverty, 1967; vice chmn. Mayor's Ad Hoc Com. Housing Code Problems, Washington, 1968-71; mem. Commn. Landlord-Tenant Affairs Washington City Coun., 1970-71; vice chmn. Washington Area Realtors Coun., 1970; exec. com., dir. Downtown Progress, 1970; bd. dirs. Washington Mental Health Assn., 1973, Washington Med Ctr., 1975. Capt. USAAF, 1942-46. Mem. Am. Land Devel. Assn., Nat. Assn. Realtors, Nat. Assn. Real Estate Editors, Washington Bd. Realtors (pres. 1970, Realtor of Yr. 1970, Martin Isen award 1981), Greater Met. Washington Bd. Trade (bd. dirs. 1974-80), U.S. League Savs. Assns. (attys. com. 1971-80), Washington Savs. and Loan League, ABA, D.C. Bar Assn., Internat. Real Estate Fedn., Omega Tau Rho. Episcopalian. Clubs: Yale, Cosmos, Rolls Royce, Antique Auto, St. Elmo. Patentee med. inventions; contbr. articles profl. jours. Address: 1 Kittery Ct Bethesda MD 20817-2137 Office: 1112 16th St NW Washington DC 20036-4823

NICHOLS, HENRY LOUIS, lawyer; b. Collin County, Tex., Nov. 7, 1916; s. Jesse Cleveland and Leva (Stiff) N.; m. Elaine Guentherman, May 17, 1949; children: David Michael, Martha Marie. LL.B., So. Meth. U., 1940. Bar: Tex. 1939. Asst. city atty. Dallas, 1946-50, sole practice, 1951—; bd. dirs. Southwestern Legal Found; mem. adv. bd. Ctr. for Legal Mcpl. Studies. Served to lt. col. AUS, 1941-46; col. USAR ret. Rsch. fellow Southwestern Legal Found., 1964. Fellow Am. Bar Found.; mem. ABA, Dallas Bar Assn. (pres. 1963-64), State Bar Tex., Tex. Bar Found. (charter). Club: Lakewood Country. Home: 3131 Maple Ave Apt 4F Dallas TX 75201-1204 Office: 1800 Lincoln St Dallas TX 75226-2248 *As a night-school graduate (Law School), I believe the opportunities in America are unlimited for anyone willing to work. Nowhere in the world are such opportunities available. We who live in the U.S.A. are blessed and the most fortunate of all people. We should strive to maintain that which our fathers preserved for us.*

NICHOLS, HORACE ELMO, state justice; b. Elkmont, Ala., July 16, 1912; s. William Henry and Lou Ella (Bates) N.; m. Edith Bowers, Oct. 20, 1945; children: Nancy (Mrs. Lewis Glenn), Carol (Mrs. Scott Henwood), Horace Elmo Jr. Mus.B., Columbia U., 1933, postgrad. in constnl. law, 1937-38; LL.B., Cumberland Law Sch., 1936. Bar: Ga. 1935. Practice in Canton, Ga., 1938-40, Rome, Ga., 1940-48; judge Superior Ct., Rome, 1948-54; mem. Ct. Appeals Ga., 1954-66; justice Supreme Ct. Ga., Atlanta, 1966-80; chief justice Supreme Ct. Ga., 1975-80. Vocal soloist, World's Fair, Chgo., 1933. Mem. Sigma Alpha Epsilon, Blue Key. Democrat. Presbyterian. Clubs: Coosa Country (Rome); Piedmont Driving (Atlanta), Capitol City (Atlanta), Atlanta City (Atlanta). Lodge: Elks (Rome). Home: 13 Virginia Cir Rome GA 30161-4473 Office: 28 Jud Bldg Atlanta GA 30334

NICHOLS, IRIS JEAN, illustrator; b. Yakima, Wash., Aug. 2, 1938; d. Charles Frederick and Velma Irene (Hacker) Beisner; (div. June 1963); children: Reid William, Amy Jo; m. David Gary Nichols, Sept. 21, 1966. BFA in Art, U. Wash., 1978. Freelance illustrator, graphic designer Seattle, 1966—; med. illustrator, head dept. illustration Swedish Hosp. Med. Ctr., Seattle, 1981-86; owner, med. and scientific illustrator Art for Medicine, Seattle, 1986—; part-time med. illustrator U. Wash., Seattle, 1966-67; part-time med. illustrator, graphic coord. dept. art The Mason Clinic, 1968-78; instr. advanced illustration Cornish Coll. Arts, Seattle, 1988—. Illustrator various books including Bryophytes of Pacific Northwest, 1966, Microbiology, 1973, 78, 82, 94, Introduction to Human Physiology, 1980, Understanding Human Anatomy and Physiology, 1983, Human Anatomy, 1984 Regional Anesthesia, 1990, and children's books on various subjects; exhibited in group shows at Seattle Pacific Sci. Ctr., summer 1979, 82, Am. Coll. Surgeons (1st prize 1974), N.W. Urology Conf. (1st prize 1974, 76, 2d prize 1975). Pres. ArtsWest (formerly West Seattle Arts Coun.), 1983; active Seattle Art Mus. Named to West Seattle H.S. Alumni Hall of Fame, 1986, Matrix Table, 1986-96. Mem. Assn. Med. Illustrators (Murial McLatchie Fine Arts award 1981), Nat. Mus. Women in the Arts (Wash. state com., bd. dirs. 1987-95, pres. 1993-94), Women Painters of Wash. (pres. 1987-89), U. Wash. Alumni Assn., Lambda Rho (pres. 1995-96). Avocations: artwork, printmaking small books, entering juried art exhibitions.

NICHOLS, J. LARRY, energy company executive, lawyer; b. Oklahoma City, July 6, 1942; s. John Whiteman and Mary (Davis) N.; m. Polly Puckett, Oct. 16, 1971; children: Tyler, Sally. BA in Geology, Princeton U., 1964; JD, U. Mich., 1967. Bar: Okla. 1967. Law clk. to chief justice U.S. Supreme Ct., Washington, 1967-68; spl. asst. to asst. atty. gen. U.S. Dept. Justice, Washington, 1968-70; pres. Devon Energy Corp., Oklahoma City, 1970—. Commr. Urban Renewal Authority Bd., Oklahoma City, 1989; pres. domestic petroleum coun. Okla. Nature Conservancy. Mem. Okla. Bar Assn. (bd. dirs., v.p.), Ind. Petroleum Assn. Am. (bd. dirs.), NAM (bd. dirs.), Oklahoma City C. of C., Econ. Club (pres. 1988-89). Office: Devon Energy Corp 20 N Broadway Ave Oklahoma City OK 73102-8202

NICHOLS, JAMES RAYMOND, JR., civil engineer; b. Holyoke, Mass., Mar. 14, 1966; s. James Raymond and Donna Jean (Riley) N. BSCE, Northeastern U., 1989; MS in Environ. Engring., U. Conn., 1994. Registered profl. engr., Conn., Wash. Staff engr. N.L. Jacobson & Assocs., Chester, Conn., 1989-95; project engr. II City of Olympia (Wash.) Pub. Works Dept., 1995—; speaker Am. Filtration & Separations Soc. conf., Nashville, 1995, Impervious Surface Reduction Rsch. Symposium, Olympia, Wash., 1996. Contbr. articles to profl. jours. Mem. Chester Inland Wetlands Commn., 1993-95. Mem. ASCE, Nat. Soc. Profl. Engrs. Achievements include research in the area of recirculating sand filters for wastewater treatment. Home: 5500 Park Pl Lacey WA 98503 Office: City Olympia Pub Works Dept 520 Pear St P O 1967 Olympia WA 98507

NICHOLS, JAMES RICHARD, civil engineer, consultant; b. Amarillo, Tex., June 29, 1923; s. Marvin Curtis and Ethel (Nichols) N.; m. Billie Louise Smith, Dec. 24, 1944; children: Judith Ann, James Richard Jr., John M. B.S. in Civil Engring., Tex. A&M U., 1949, M.S. in Civil Engring., 1950. Registered profl. engr., Tex., Okla., N.Mex. Ptnr. Freese & Nichols, Inc., Cons. Engrs., Fort Worth, 1950-76; pres. Freese & Nichols, Inc., Cons. Engrs., 1977-88, chmn., 1988—; bd. dirs. Cornerstone Investment Group, Kentex Jales, Inc. Chmn. Ft. Worth Conv. and Visitors Bur.; bd. dirs. United Way Tarrant County, Pub. Comm. Found. North Tex., Tex. A&M Rsch. Found., Tex. Wesleyan U. With U.S. Army, 1943-46. Fellow Am. Cons. Engrs. Council; mem. Cons. Engrs. Coun., Nat. Soc. Profl. Engrs., Tex. Water Conservation Assn. (pres.), Exchange Club, Fort Worth Club, Fort Worth C. of C. (bd. dirs., mem. adv. coun.), Newcomen Soc., Mason, Rotary. Methodist. Home: 4821 Overton Woods Dr Fort Worth TX 76109-2429 Office: Freese & Nichols Inc 4055 Internat Plz Ste 200 Fort Worth TX 76109-4895

NICHOLS, JAMES ROBBS, university dean; b. Jackson, Tenn., May 30, 1926; s. William Ed and Buelha (Robbs) N.; m. Johnnie Jones; 1 dau., Tina Jean Nichols Benson. BS, U. Tenn., 1949; MS, U. Minn., 1955, PhD, 1957. Former mem. faculty Pa. State U., U. Tenn.; mem. faculty Va. Poly. Inst. and State U., Blacksburg, 1964-71, 73—; head dairy sci. dept. Va. Poly. Inst. and State U., 1964-69; assoc. dean Va. Poly. Inst. and State U. (Coll. Agr.), 1969-71, 73-75; dean Coll. Agr. & Life Scis., dir. Va. Agr. Exptl. Sta., 1975-91; dean emeritus Va. Poly. Inst. and State U., 1991—; exec. v.p., gen. mgr. Select Sires, Inc., Columbus, Ohio, 1971-73. Served with USAAF, World War II. Named Man of Yr. in Agr. in Va. Progressive Farmer mag., 1975; hon. state farmer Tenn. Mem. AAAS, Am. Dairy Sci. Assn., Sigma Xi, Phi Kappa Phi, Alpha Zeta, Gamma Sigma Delta. Methodist. Clubs: Rotary.

NICHOLS, JOHN D., church administrator. Dir. of ministry to the military Ch. of God. Office: Church of God PO Box 2430 Cleveland TN 37320-2430

NICHOLS, JOHN DOANE, diversified manufacturing corporation executive; b. Shanghai, China, 1930; m. Alexandra M. Curran, Dec. 4, 1971; children: Kendra E., John D. III. BA, Harvard U., 1953, MBA, 1955. Various operating positions Ford Motor Corp., 1958-68; dir. fin. controls ITT Corp., 1968-69; exec. v.p., chief operating officer Aerojet-Gen. Corp., 1969-79; exec. v.p., COO Ill. Tool Works Inc., Chgo., 1980-81; chief exec. officer, dir. Ill. Tool Works Inc., 1982—, chmn., 1986—; bd. dirs. Household Internat., Philip Morris Cos., Inc., Rockwell Internat., Stone Container Corp.; overseer Harvard U. Trustee U. Chgo., 1987-93, Chgo. Symphony Orch., 1986-94, Lyric Opera Chgo., Mus. Sci. and Industry, Jr. Achievement Chgo., Chgo. Commerce Civic Com., Bus. Roundtable, Art Inst. Chgo.; bd. govs. Argonne (Ill.) Nat. Lab., 1988-93. Mem. Harvard Club (N.Y., Chgo.), Indian Hill Club (Winnetka, Ill.), Chgo. Club, Comml. Club, Econ. Club Chgo. Home: 900 Mount Pleasant Rd Winnetka IL 60093-3613 Office: Ill Tool Works Inc 3600 W Lake Ave Glenview IL 60025-1215

NICHOLS, KENNETH DAVID, consulting engineer; b. Cleve., Nov. 13, 1907; s. Wilbur Loren and Minnie May (Colbrunn) N.; m. Jacqueline Darrieulat, Dec. 15, 1932; children: Jacqueline Anne Thompson, K. David. BS, U.S. Mil. Acad., 1929; CE, Cornell U., 1932, MCE, 1933; postgrad., Technische Hochschule, Charlottenburg, Fed. Republic Germany, 1934-35; PhD in Hydraulics, U. Iowa, 1937. Commd. 2d lt. C.E. U.S. Army, 1929, advanced through grades to maj. gen., 1948, various mil. positions, 1929-41, dep. and dist. engr., Manhattan Engr. Dist., 1942-46; prof. mechanics U.S. Mil. Acad., West Point, N.Y., 1947-48; chief armed forces spl. weapons project (atomic) Pentagon, Va., 1948-50; dep. dir. guided missiles Office of Sec. of Def., Pentagon, Va., 1951-53; chief R&D Office of Chief of Staff, U.S. Army, Pentagon, Va., 1952-53; ret. U.S. Army, 1953; gen. mgr. U.S. AEC, Washington, 1953-55; cons. engr. Md., 1955-92; with World War II prodn. plants plutonium and uranium U-235, 1942-46; Cold War chief Armed Forces Spl. Weapons Project, 1948-50; cons. Yankee Atomic Power Plant, Conn. Atomic Power Plant, 1955-71. Author: The Road to Trinity, 1987. Trustee Thomas Alva Edison Found., Detroit, 1963-76; bd. dirs., v.p. Army Distaff Found., Washington, 1965-69; mem. at large engring. and indsl. rsch. divsn., NRC, Washington, 1954-58. Decorated DSM, 1945 and DSM with oak leaf cluster, 1954; named to Comdr. Brit. Empire Order, Brit. Amb., 1946, Disting. Grad. U.S. Mil. Acad., Assn. Graduates, 1996; recipient Presdl. Medal of Merit, Pres. of Nicaragua, 1931, Disting. Svc. medal Commn. AEC, 1955, Chiefs of Engrs. award for Outstanding Pub. Svc. Fellow Am. Nuclear Soc.; mem. ASME (hon.), Nat. Acad. Engring., ASCE (Collinwood Prize 1938). Republican. Home: Knollwood 6200 Oregon Ave NW Apt 345 Washington DC 20015-1542

NICHOLS, KYRA, ballerina; b. Berkeley, Calif., July 2, 1958. Studied with Alan Howard, Pacific Ballet, Sch. Am. Ballet, N.Y.C. With N.Y.C. Ballet, 1974—, prin. dancer, 1979—. Created roles in Tricolore, 1978, A Sketch Book, 1978, Jerome Robbins' Four Seasons, 1979, John Taras' Concerto for Piano and Wind Instruments, Stravinsky Centennial Celebration, 1982, Jacques d'Amboise's Celebration, 1983; performed in N.Y.C. Ballet's Balanchine Celebration, 1993. Ford Found. scholar; recipient Dance Mag. award, 1988. Office: Peter S Diggins Assocs 133 W 71st St New York NY 10023-3834 also: NYC Ballet Inc NY State Theater Lincoln Ctr Pla New York NY 10023

NICHOLS, LEE ANN, library media specialist; b. Denver, Apr. 27, 1946; d. Bernard Anthony and Margaret Mary (Pughes) Wilhelm; m. Robert Joseph Nichols, July 12, 1975; children: Rachel, Steven, Sarah. BS in Edn., St. Mary of the Plains, Dodge City, Kans., 1968; MA in Edn., Colo. U., 1978. Cert. type B profl. tchr., Colo. Tchr. So. Tama Sch. Dist. Montour, Iowa, 1968-70, Strasburg (Colo.) Sch. Dist., 1970-73; svc. rep. Montain Bell, Denver, 1973-75; libr., tchr. Simla (Colo.) Sch. Dist., 1976-78; dir. Simla Br. Libr., 1978-81; dir. Christian edn. St. Anthony's Ch/, Sterling, Colo., 1983-84; libr. cons. Rel Valley Sch., Iliff, Colo., 1984—, Plateau Sch. Dist., Peetz, Colo., 1986—; mem. Colo. Coun. for Libr. Devel., Denver, 1986-92, chmn. 1991; instr. Northeastern Jr. Coll., Sterling; del. Gov.'s Conf. on Libr. and Info. Scis., 1990. Contbr. articles to profl. jours. Active Sterling Arts Coun., sec., 1982-85, v.p., 1985, pres., 1986-87; chair Northeastern Jr. Coll. Found., Sterling, 1983-87, mem. 1981-91; mem. community adv. coun. Northeastern Jr. Coll., 1991-93, chair, 1993; bd. dirs. Wagon Wheel chpt. Girl Scouts Am., 1975-78. Mem. ALA, Am. Assn. Sch. Librs., Assn. Libr. Svcs. to Children, Colo. Ednl. Media Assn., Colo. Libr. Coun., Internat. Reading Assn. (Colo. Coun.). Avocations: reading, sewing. Home: 12288 County Road 370 Sterling CO 80751-8421 Office: Caliche Jr High Sch RR 1 Iliff CO 80736-9801

NICHOLS, MARCI LYNNE, gifted education coordinator, educator, consultant; b. Cin., July 7, 1948; m. James G. Nichols, June 19, 1970; children: Lisa, Jeannette. B in Arts & Sci., Miami U., 1970, MEd, 1990, postgrad. Cert. Secondary English, elem. gifted edn., computer edn., Ohio. Secondary English tchr. West Clermont Local Schs., Cin., 1970-71; coord. gifted edn. and tchr. Batavia (Ohio) Local Schs., 1981—; speaker, cons. Local Gifted Orgns., Cin., 1988—; vis. instr. dept. ednl. psychology Miami U., Oxford, Ohio, 1991—; presenter Nat. Rsch. Symposium on Talent Devel., 1991. Author, presenter: (videotape series) Parenting the Gifted Parts I and II, 1992; columnist, contbr. Resources for Everyday Living; contbr. articles to profl. jours. Speaker Christian Women's Club, Ohio, Ind., Ky., W.Va., 1981—; deacon First Presbyn. Ch. of Batavia, Ohio, 1986-88. Recipient Douglas Miller Rsch. award Miami U., 1991. Mem. ASCD, Am. Ednl. Rsch. Assn., Nat. Assn. for Gifted Children, Consortium Ohio Coords. of Gifted, Midwest Ednl. Rsch. Assn. (presenter), Internat. Platform Assn., Phi Kappa Phi. Home: 110 Wood St Batavia OH 45103-2923 Office: Batavia Local Schs 800 Bauer Ave Batavia OH 45103-2837

NICHOLS, MELVIN RAY, financial planner; b. Highland Park, Mich., May 18, 1952; s. Oather M. and Betty Fay (Miller) N.; m. Joan L. Bonanno, Oct. 26, 1979; children: Blake Christopher, Grant Daniel. AA, Oakland C.C., 1973; student, Oakland U., 1978. Cert. fin. planner; lic. securities dealer; lic. for health, life, disability and accident ins., Mich. Mgr. John Hancock Mut. Ins. Co., Bloomfield Hills, Mich., 1977-79, 82-85; with Gold Leaf Fin. Planning Inc., Troy, Mich., 1985—; founder, pres. The Nichols Group, Bloomfield Hills, Mich., 1995—. Mem. Internat. Bd. Cert. Fin. Planners. Avocations: bicycling, walking, backpacking, golf. Home: 6390 Livernois Rd Troy MI 48098-1567 Office: The Nichols Group 1533 N Woodward Ave Ste 343 Bloomfield Hills MI 48304

NICHOLS, MIKE, stage and film director; b. Berlin, Nov. 6, 1931; s. Nicholaievitch and Brigitte (Landauer) Peschowsky; m. Patricia Scott, 1957 (div.); m. Margot Callas, 1974 (div.); m. Annabel (div.); m. Diane Sawyer, Apr. 29, 1988. Student, U. Chgo., 1950-53; student acting, Lee Strasberg. Ptnr. with Elaine May in comedy act; first appeared at Playwrights Theatre Club, Compass Theatre, Chgo.; N.Y. debut An Evening with Mike Nichols and Elaine May, 1960; acted in A Matter of Position, Phila., 1962; dir.: (plays) Barefoot in the Park, 1963 (Tony award), The Knack, 1964, Luv, 1964 (Tony award), The Odd Couple, 1965 (Tony award for best dir.), The Apple Tree, 1966, The Little Foxes, 1967, Plaza Suite, 1968 (Tony award), The Prisoner of 2d Avenue, 1971 (Tony award), Uncle Vanya (co-adapted), 1973, Streamers, 1976, Comedians, 1976, The Gin Game, 1977, Billy Bishop Goes to War, Lunch Hour, 1980, Fools, 1981, The Real Thing, 1984 (Tony award 1984,), Hurlyburly, 1984, Social Security, 1984, Elliot Loves, 1990, Death and the Maiden, 1992; (films) Who's Afraid of Virginia Woolf?, 1966, (Academy award nomination best director 1966), The Graduate, 1967 (Academy award best director 1967), Catch-22, 1970, Carnal Knowledge, 1971, The Day of the Dolphin, 1973, The Fortune, 1975, Gilda Live, 1980, Silkwood, 1983 (Academy award nomination best director 1983), Heartburn, 1986, Biloxi Blues, 1987, Working Girl, 1988 (Academy award nomination best director 1988), Postcards From the Edge, 1990, Regarding Henry, 1991, Wolf, 1994; producer: (musical) Annie, 1977; performed at N.Y. musical Pres. Johnson's Inaugural Gala, 1965; TV appearances include Today Show. Office: care Mike Ovitz CAA 9830 Wilshire Blvd Beverly Hills CA 90212-1804

NICHOLS, RALPH ARTHUR, lawyer; b. Clinton, N.Y., Jan. 27, 1919; s. Arthur Britcher and Carrie Lena (Pitcher) N.; m. Pamela Crow Bermingham, May 3, 1947 (dec. Feb. 1980); children: Jeremy Nichols Pierce, Ralph A. Jr., Melinda Nichols Mayer; m. Victoria Requa Lalli, Sept. 5, 1981. AB, Hamilton Coll., 1940; LLB, Yale U., 1947. Bar: Conn. 1949, N.Y. 1947, U.S. Dist. Ct. (so. dist.) N.Y. 1949, U.S. Dist. Ct. Conn. 1950, U.S. Supreme Ct. 1959. Assoc. Burke & Burke, N.Y.C., 1947-49, Maguire, Walker & Middleton, Stamford, Ct., 1949-54; assoc., then ptnr. Cummings & Lockwood, Stamford, 1954—. Founder, former bd. dirs. Stamford Land Conservation Trust; former bd. dirs. Conservationists Stamford, Inc., Stamford YMCA; former bd. dirs., sec. Stamford Area Commerce and Industry; trustee Stamford YMCA. Lt. USNR, 1942-46, ETO, PTO. Fellow Am. Coll. Trust and Estate Counsel; mem. ABA, Woodway Country Club (Darien, Conn.), Yale Club (N.Y.C.), Phi Delta Phi. Republican. Episcopalian. Home: 656 Den Rd Stamford CT 06903-3824 Office: Cummings & Lockwood PO Box 120 10 Stamford Forum Stamford CT 06901-3215

NICHOLS, RICHARD DALE, former congressman, banker; b. Ft. Scott, Kans., Apr. 29, 1926; s. Ralph Dale and Olive Marston (Kittell) N.; m. Constance Weinbrenner, Mar. 25, 1951; children: Philip William, Ronald Dale, Anita Jane Nichols Bomberger. BS in Agr. and BS in Journalism, Kans. State U., 1951. Info. counsel Kans. State Bd. Agr., Topeka, 1951-54; assoc. far, dir. Sta. WIBW, WIBW-TV, Topeka, 1954-57; agr. rep. to v.p. Hutchinson (Kans.) Nat. Bank and Trust, 1957-69; pres., CEO Home State Bank, McPherson, Kans., 1969-79, chmn., pres., CEO, 1979-91; chmn. Home State Bank & Trust, McPherson, Kans., 1985-91, 93—; mem. 102d Congress from 5th Kans. dist., 1991-92. Pres. Arts Coun., McPherson, 1979; 5th Dist. chmn. Kans. Rep. Party, 1986-89; bd. dirs. Camp Wood YMCA Camp, Elmdale, Kans., 1995; Meth. Ch. lay spkr., 1994—; bd. trustees Ctrl. Coll., McPherson. Ensign USNR, 1944-47; ATO. Named Hon. Citizen N.Y.C., 1988. Mem. VFW, Kans. Bankers Assn. (pres. 1985-86), Am. Bankers Assn. (advisor 1986-88), Kans. Assn. Banking Ag. Reps. (pres. 1965), Am. Legion, McPherson C. of C. (pres. 1977), Optimist (pres. Hutchinson club 1965), Rotary (pres. McPherson club 1978), Kans. Cavalry (cmdg. gen. 1986-89). Methodist. Home: 404 N Lakeside Dr Mc Pherson KS 67460-3600 Office: Home State Bank and Trust PO Box 1266 Mc Pherson KS 67460-1266

NICHOLS, ROBERT E(DMUND), editor, writer, journalist; b. Daytona Beach, Fla., Feb. 14, 1925; s. Joe D. and Edna A. (Casper) N.; m. Diana R. Grosso; children by previous marriage: Craig S., Kim S., Robin K. Student, San Diego State Coll., 1942-43, St. John's Coll., 1944-45, George Washington U., 1948-49. Reporter San Diego Union, 1942-44; corr. Washington bur. N.Y. Herald Tribune, 1945-48, CBS, 1948-51, Time, Inc., 1951-61; contbg. editor Time, asst. edn. dir. Life mag., N.Y.C., 1951-52; corr. representing Time, Life, Fortune, Sports Illus. mags., San Diego area, 1952-61; Sunday editor San Diego Union, 1952-61; fin. editor Los Angeles Times, 1961-68, mem. editorial bd., 1965-68; spl. asst. to bd. govs. Fed. Res. System, 1968-70; v.p., dir. various editorial svcs. Bank of Am., 1970-85; prin. Robert E. Nichols Communications, San Francisco, 1985—. Writer, dir. film and radio documentaries. Mem. U.S. Antarctic Expedition, 1946-47. Recipient Loeb Newspaper Spl. Achievement award, 1963, Loeb award disting. fin. reporting, 1964. Fellow Royal Geog. Soc., Explorers Club; mem. Am. Polar Soc., Calif. Scholarship fedn. (hon., life), Soc. Am. Bus. Editors and Writers (hon., life, pres. 1967-68), South Polar Press Club. Home and Office: 38 Ord Ct San Francisco CA 94114-1417

NICHOLS, ROBERT LEE, food company executive; b. Clarksburg, W.Va., Nov. 4, 1924; s. Clarence Garfield and Reatha Maude (Berry) N.; m. Vianne Hope Demaray, Oct. 21, 1973; children: Donna Beth, Michael Alan, Jeffrey Mark. Student, Bus. Coll., 1944, U. Detroit, 1959. Sales rep. Kellogg Sales Co., Battle Creek, Mich., 1944-50; dist. mgr. Kellogg Sales Co., 1950-61, asst. div. mgr., 1961-64, sales promotion dir., 1964-69, exec. v.p., gen. sales mgr., 1969-71, pres., 1976-78; pres. Fearn Internat., 1971-76, dir., 1971-82; group exec. v.p. Kellogg Co., Battle Creek, 1979-82, dir., 1977-89, vice chmn., 1983-89; pres., dir. Mrs. Smith's Frozen Foods Co., 1979-82, McCamly Square Corp., 1983-89; dir., pres. Battle Creek Unltd., 1985-87; bd. dirs. Cereal Inst., 1976-79, Am. Frozen Food Inst., 1979-82, Cereal City Devel. Corp., 1986; bd. govs. Acad. Food Mktg., St. Joseph U., 1976-79. Exec. v.p., bd. dirs. Jr. Achievement, Battle Creek, 1970-71; trustee Mich. Colls. Found., 1985-89, Thomas Jefferson Found., Lakeview Schs., 1986-89, Mich. Biotechnology Inst., 1985-89, Citizens Rsch. Coun. Mich., 1985-90; mem., bd. dirs. United Way of Greater Battle Creek Area, 1984-89, campaign chmn., 1985; pres. Battle Creek Unltd., 1985-87; vice chmn. Battle Creek Airport Adv. Com., 1984-89; mem. Nat. Corp. Coun. Interlochen Ctr for the Arts, 1986-89; mem. adminstrv. bd. 1st United Meth. Ch., Stuart, Fla., 1990-94. Mem. Svc. Core Ret. Execs. (vice chair 1991-93), Snug Harbor Yacht Club (vice commodore 1990-92, commodore 1992-93), First Nat. Bank & Trust of the Treasure Coast (adv. bd. 1993-96), Martin County Coun. for Arts (dir. 1990-96), Masons. Office: Kellogg Co 1 Kellogg Sq PO Box 3599 Battle Creek MI 49016-3599

NICHOLS, ROBERT LEIGHTON, civil engineer; b. Amarillo, Tex., June 24, 1926; s. Marvin Curtis and Ethel N.; m. Frances Hardison, June 8, 1948; children—Eileen, William C., Michael L. B.S.C.E., Tex. A&M U., 1947, M.S.C.E., 1948. Grad. asst., instr. Tex. A&M U., 1947-48; assoc. Freese & Nichols (and predecessors), Ft. Worth, 1948-50; partner Freese & Nichols (and predecessors), 1950-77, v.p., 1977-88, pres., 1988-91, vice chmn., 1991-92, pres. emeritus, 1992—; mem. Bldg. Standards Commn., 1956-62. Chmn. Horn Frog dist. Boy Scouts Am., pres. Longhorn coun., 1990-93. Mem. ASCE, NSPE (pres. 1977-78), Tex. Soc. Profl. Engrs. (pres. 1965-66, Engr. of Yr. award Ft. Worth chpt. 1966), Am. Water Works Assn., Tex. Water Conservation Assn., Water Environ. Fedn., Water Environ. Assn. Tex. (pres. 1962-63), Am. Pub. Works Assn., Tex. Water Utilities Assn., Tex. Pub. Works Assn., Nat. Inst. for Engring. Ethics (pres. 1995—), Masons, Tau Beta Pi, Chi Epsilon. Methodist. Office: One S Main St Ste 102 Webb City MO 64870

NICHOLS, RONALD LEE, surgeon, educator; b. Chgo., June 25, 1941; s. Peter Raymond and Jane Eleanor (Johnson) N.; m. Elsa Elaine Johnson,

Dec. 4, 1964; children: Kimberly Jane, Matthew Bennett. MD, U. Ill., 1966, MS, 1970. Diplomate: Am. Bd. Surgery (assoc. cert. examiner, New Orleans, 1991), Nat. Bd. Med. Examiners. Intern U. Ill. Hosp., Chgo., 1966-67, resident in surgery, 1967-72, instr. surgery, 1970-72, asst. prof. surgery, 1972-74; assoc. prof. surgery U. Health Scis. Chgo. Med. Sch., 1975-77, dir. surg. edn., 1975-77; William Henderson prof. surgery Tulane U. Sch. Medicine, New Orleans, 1977—, vice chmn. dept. surgery, 1982-91, staff surgeon, 1977—, prof. microbiology and immunology, 1979—; vice chmn. dept. surgery Tulane U. Sch. Medicine, New Orleans, La., 1982-91; cons. surgeon VA Hosp., Alexandria, La., 1978-93, Huey P. Long Hosp., Pineville, La., 1978—, Lallie Kemp Charity Hosp., Independence, La., 1977-85, Touro Infirmary, New Orleans, Monmouth Med. Ctr., Long Branch, N.J., 1979-88; mem. VA Coop. Study Rev. Bd., 1978-81, VA Merit Rev. Bd. in Surgery, 1979-82; mem. sci. program com. 3d Internat. Conf. Nosocomial Infections, Ctr. Disease Control; bd. dirs. Nat. Found. Infectious Diseases, 1989—; hon. fellow faculty Kasr El Aini Cairo U. Sch. Medicine, 1989; mem. adv. com. on infection control Ctrs. for Disease Control, 1991-95; disting. guest, vis. prof. Royal Coll. Surgeons Thailand 14th Ann. Clin. Congress, 1989, 17th Ann. Clin. Congress, 1992; mem. infectious diseases adv. bd. Roche Labs., 1988-95, Abbott Labs., 1990-92, Kimberly Clark Corp., 1990—, SmithKline Beecham Labs., 1990-95, Fujisawa Pharm., chmn., 1990—, Bayer Pharm., 1994—, Merck Sharpe Dohme, 1996. Author: (with Gorbach, Bartlett and Nichols) Manual of Surgical Infection, 1984; author, guest editor: (with Nichols, Hyslop Jr. and Bartlett) Decision Mking in Surgical Sepsis, 1991; guest editor, author: Surgical Sepsis and Beyond, 1993; mem. editl. bd. Current Surgery, 1977—, Hosp. Physician, 1980—, Infection Control, 1980-86, Guidelines to Antibiotic Therapy, 1976-81, Am. Jour. Infection Control, 1981—, Internat. Medicine, 1983—, Confronting Infection, 1983-86, Current Concepts in Clin. Surgery, 1984—, Fact Line, 1984-91, Host/Pathogen News, 1984—, Infectious Diseases in Clin. Practice, 1991—, surg. sect. editor, 1992—, Surg. Infections: Index and Revs., 1991—, So. Med. Jour., 1992—, ANAEROBE, 1994—; mem. adv. bd. Physician News Network, 1991-95; patentee (with S.G. schoenberger and W.R. Rank) Helical-Tipped Lesion Localization Needle Device. Elected faculty sponsor graduating class Tulane Med. Sch., 1979-80, 83, 85, 87, 88, 91-92. Served to major USAR, 1972-75. Recipient House Staff teaching award U. Ill. Coll. Medicine, 1973, Rsch. award Bd. Trustees U. Health Scis.-Chgo. Med. Sch., 1977, Owl Club Teaching award, 1980-86, 90; named Clin. Prof. of Yr. U. Health Scis., Chgo. Med. Sch., 1977, Clin. Prof. of Yr., Tulane U. Sch. Medicine, 1979; Douglas Stubbs Lectr. award Surg. Sect. Nat. Med. Assn., 1987, Prix d'Elegance award Men of Fashion, New Orleans, 1993. Fellow Infectious Disease Soc. Am. (mem. FDA subcom. to develop guidelines in surg. prophylaxis 1989-93, co-recipient Joseph Susman Meml. award 1990), Am. Acad. Microbiology, Internat. Soc. Univ. Colon and Rectal Surgeons, ACS (chmn. operating room environment com. 1981-83, mem. 1984-87, 94—, internat. relations com. 1987-93, sr. mem. 1994—); mem. AMA, Nat. Found. for Infectious Diseases (bd. dirs. 1988—, v.p. 1994—), Joint Commn. on Accreditation of Health Care Orgn. (Infection Control adv. group, 1988—, sci. program com. 3d internat. conf. nosocomial infections CDC/Nat. Found. Infectious Diseases 1990, FDA Subcom. to Develop Guidelines in Surg. Prophylaxis, prophylactic antibiotic study group La. Health Care Rev. Inc. 1996—, AIDS commr. State of La. 1992-94), 5th Nat. Forum on AIDS (sci. program com.), U.S. Pharmacopeial Convention Inc. (adv. panel gen. drug info. divsn., surg. drugs anractitioners in Infection Control (physician adv. coun. 1991—), Internat. Soc. Anaerobic Bacteria, So. Med. Assn. (vice chmn. sect. surgery 1980-81, chmn. 1982-83), Assn. Acad. Surgery, N.Y. Acad. Sci., Warren H. Cole Soc. (pres.-elect 1988, pres. 1989-90), Assn. VA Surgeons, Soc. Surgery Alimentary Tract, Inst. Medicine Chgo., Midwest Surg. Assn., Cen. Surg. Assn., Ill. Surg. Soc., European Soc. Surg. Rsch., Collegium Internationale Chirugiae Digestivae, Chgo. Surg. Soc. (hon.), New Orleans Surg. Soc. (bd. dirs. 1983-87), Soc. Univ. Surgeons, Surg. Soc. La., Southeastern Surg. Soc., Phoenix Surg. Soc. (hon.), Hellenic Surg. Soc. (hon.), Cen. N.Y. Surg. Soc. (hon.), Tulane Surg. Soc., Alton Ochsner Surg. Soc., Am. Soc. Microbiology, Soc. Internat. de Chirugie, Surg. Infection Soc. (sci. study com. 1982-83, fellowship com. 1985-87, ad hoc sci. liaison com. 1986-89, program com. 1986-87, chmn. ad hoc com. rels. with industry 1990-93, mem. sci. liaison com. 1995—), Soc. for Intestinal Microbial Ecology and Disease, Soc. Critical Care Medicine, Am. Surg. Assn., Kansas City Surg. Soc., Bay Surg. Soc. (hon.), Cuban Surg. Soc. (hon.), Panhellenic Surg. Soc. (hon.), Sigma Xi, Alpha Omega Alpha. Episcopalian. Patentee in field. Home: 1521 7th St New Orleans LA 70115-3322 Office: 1430 Tulane Ave New Orleans LA 70112-2699

NICHOLS, RUSSELL JAMES, manufacturing company executive; b. Brockton, Mass., Nov. 12, 1943; s. Clarence Willard and Hattie Matilda (Harlow) N.; m. Patricia Anna Rogers, Aug. 1, 1964; children: James E., Sharon L., Deborah L. Student, Rutgers U., 1966-68, Marion (Ohio) Tech. Coll., 1973-75, Findlay (Ohio) Coll., 1979-80. Registered profl. engr., Ohio; cert. quality engr., cert. quality auditor, cert. reliability engr. Rsch. technician Princeton Rsch. Ctr. Columbian Carbon divsn. Cities Svc. Co., Cranberry, N.J., 1965-68; tech. svc. engr. HPM Corp., Mount Gilead, Ohio, 1969-71, rsch. engr., 1971-73, product engr., 1974, area sales mgr., 1975, product mgr., 1976-77; process engring. mgr. Hancor Inc., Findlay, 1977-80; dir. devel. and tech. dir. Welding Engrs., Inc., Blue Bell, Pa., 1981-88; v.p. engring. Farrel Corp., Ansonia, Conn., 1989-90, v.p. quality, 1991—. Contbr. articles to profl. jours.; patentee in field. With USN, 1961-64. Fellow Soc. Plastics Engrs.; mem. NSPE, Am. Mgmt. Assn., Am. Soc. Quality Control (sr. mem.), Am. Chem. Soc. (Akron Rubber Group divsn.). Avocations: computers, reading. Home: 292 Elmwood Cir Cheshire CT 06410-4211 Office: Farrel Corp 25 Main St Ansonia CT 06401-1605

NICHOLS, STEPHEN GEORGE, Romance languages educator; b. Cambridge, Mass., Oct. 24, 1936; s. Stephen George and Marjorie (Whitney) N.; m. Mary Winn Jordan, June 22, 1957 (div. 1972); children: Stephen Frost (dec.), Sarah Winn; m. Edith Karetzky, 1972; stepchildren: Laura Natalie Karetzky, Sarah Alexandra Karetzky. A.B. cum laude, Dartmouth Coll., 1958; Ph.D., Yale U., 1963; Docteur es lettres honoris causa, Université de Genève, 1992. Asst. prof. French UCLA, 1963-65; assoc. prof. comparative lit. U. Wis.-Madison, 1965-68, chmn. dept., 1967-68; prof. Romance langs. and comparative lit. Dartmouth Coll., 1968-84, chmn. dept. comparative lit., 1969-72, 74, 79-82, chmn. dept. Romance langs., 1974-77, Edward Tuck prof. French, 1984-85, chmn. dept. French and Italian, 1982-85, liaison officer Sch. Criticism and Theory, 1983-85; faculty Dartmouth Inst., 1980-85, faculty dir., 1984-85; prof. Romance langs. U. Pa., 1985-86, Edmund J. Kahn Disting. prof. humanities, 1986-92; James M. Beall prof. French and humanities Johns Hopkins U., Balt., 1992—; grad. group chmn. French and Italian U. Pa., 1986-88, chmn. dept. romance langs., 1987-88, assoc. dean for humanities, 1988-91; acting chair French, 1993-94; dir. grad. studies dept. French The Johns Hopkins U., Balt., 1992-94; R. Champlin and Debbie Sheridan interim dir. Eisenhower Libr., Johns Hopkins U., 1994-95, chair dept of French, 1995—; dir. sch. Criticism and Theory, 1995-2000; vis. prof. U. Tel Aviv, 1977, NYU, 1979-81, Exeter (Eng.) U., 1980, Ariz. State U., 1982, U. Calif., Irvine, 1985, Sch. Criticism and Theory, 1989, 95, Humanities Rsch. Inst. U. Calif., 1990, U. Pa., 1995, Dartmouth Coll., 1995-96; NEH fellow, 1978-79, rev. panelist 1979-81, 84, 91, Guggenheim fellow, 1987-88; Phi Beta Kappa vis. scholar, 1983-84; Lauder fellow Aspen Inst. for Humanistic Study, 1988; mem. adv. bd. Institut d'Etudes Francaises d'Avignon, Bryn Mawr Coll., 1965—; dir. seminar NEH, 1975-79, Mellon summer seminar in humanities Johns Hopkins U., 1993, 94; exec. com. Ea. Comparative Lit. Conf.; mem. adv. coun. dept. comparative lit. Princeton U., 1982-88, chmn., 1984-88; co-dir. Cultural Study, U. Pa., 1986-92; co-dir. Louis Marin Ctr. for French Studies, 1992—; advisor Waverly Consort, 1987—; adv. bd. Soc. Humanities Cornell U., 1993—; reviewer Guggenheim Fellowship applicaitons, medieval sect., 1995—, French, 1996—; dir. assoc. studies Ecole Patique des Hautes Etudes, Paris, 1994-95. Author: Formulaic Diction and Thematic Composition in the Chanson de Roland, 1961, The Songs of Bernard de Ventadorn, 1962, 2d edit., 1968, La Roman de la Rose, 1967, 72, Comparists at Work, 1968, The Meaning of Mannerism, 1972, Mimesis: From Mirror to Method, Augustine to Descartes, 1982, Medieval and Renaissance Theories of Representation: New, 1984, Romanesque Signs: Early Medieval Narrative and Iconography, 1983, 85, Images of Power: History/Text/Discourse, 1986, The Legitimacy of the Middle Ages, 1988, The New Philology, 1990, Boundaries and Transgressions, 1991, The New Medievalism, 1991, Commentary as Cultural Artifact, 1992, Medievalism and the Modernist Temper: On the Discipline of Medieval, 1996, The Whole Book: Miscellany and Order in the Medieval Manuscript, 1996; editor: (book series) Parallax: Revisions of Culture and Society, 1987—; asst. editor French Rev., 1968-88; mem. editl. bd. Olifant, 1974—, Medievalia et Humanistica, 1974—, Medievalia, 1975—, Comparative Lit. Studies, 1986, Publ. of the MLA, 1988-89, Recentiores, 1991—, Modern Lang. Notes, 1992; mem. adv. bd. Colleagues Press, 1986—, Exemplaria: A Jour. Medieval Theory, 1987—; mem. adv. com. PMLA, 1980-84; adv. editor Romanic Rev., 1986—, Storia della Storiographia, 1992—. Rotary Found. fellow U. d'Aix Marseilles, France, 1958-59; fellow Inst. Rsch. in Humanities, 1966-67; sr. fellow Sch. of Criticism and Theory, 1988—. Fellow Medieval Acad. Am.; mem. Acad. Lit. Studies (nominating com. 1974-78, sec.-treas. 1978-87), Dante Soc., Internat. CompaAssn., New Eng. Medieval Assn. (adv. com. 1981-85), MLA (chmn. com. on careers 1985-86, James Russell Lowell prize com. 1986-88, com. on profl. ethics 1987-88, del. assembly 1994—), Medieval Acad. Am., Société Rencesvals (sec.-treas. Am. sect. 1964-69). Home: 5 Saint Martins Rd Baltimore MD 21218-1815

NICHOLS, STEVEN PARKS, mechanical engineer, university official; b. Cody, Wyo., July 1, 1950; s. Rufus Parks Nichols and Gwen Sena (Frank) Keyes; m. Mary Ruth Barrow, Aug. 5, 1990; 1 child, Nicholas Barrow Nichols. PhD, U. Tex., Austin, 1975, JD, 1983. Assoc. dir. Tex. Space Grant Consortium, Austin, 1989-91; dep. dir. ctr. for energy studies U. Tex., Austin, 1988-91, dir. Ctr. for Energy Studies, 1991—, acting dir. ctr. for electromechanics, 1994—. Patentee (with others) railgun igniter, inert burner, rail thruster, other patents pending. Mem. NSPE, ASME, ABA, Am. Soc. Engring. Edn., Nat. Inst. Engring. Ethics (bd. govs. 1987-93). Home: 1400 Lorrain St Auston TX 78703 Office: U Tex Ctr for Energy Studies 10100 Burnet Rd Austin TX 78758-4445

NICHOLS, WILLIAM CURTIS, psychologist, family therapist, consultant; b. Fayette, Ala., Apr. 16, 1929; s. William Curtis and Eva (Hargett) N.; m. Alice Louise Mancill, May 29, 1954 (dec. 1990); children: Alice Camille, William Mancill, David Paul; m. Mary Anne Pace, Feb. 29, 1992. AB, U. Ala., 1953; EdD, Columbia U., 1960. Diplomate Am. Bd. Profl. Psychology. Asst. prof. sociology U. Ala., Birmingham, 1960-63; postdoctoral fellow Merrill-Palmer Inst., 1963-64, mem. psychotherapy faculty, 1965-69; prof. sociology Samford U., Birmingham, Ala., 1963-65; pvt. practice clin. psychology and marital and family therapy Grosse Pointe, Mich., 1969-73, 76-87; pvt. practice psychology, marital and family therapy Birmingham, Mich., 1976-87; prof. home and family life, dir. marriage and family counseling Fla. State U., 1973-76; exec. dir. Gov.'s Constituency Children, Fla., 1987-89; pvt. practice marital and family therapy S.E. Family Inst., 1989-90; pres. William Nichols Assocs., Organizational Cons., 1990-91; cons., marital and family therapist Atlanta, 1992—; adj. prof. clin. psychology U. Detroit, 1976-83; adj. prof. family therapy Fla. State U., 1990-91; adj. prof., grad. faculty child and family devel. dept. U. Ga., 1992—, founder, chair adv. com. Family Therapy Archives, 1993—. Author: Treating People in Families: An Integrative Framework, 1996, Marital Therapy: An Integrative Approach, 1988, Treating Adult Survivors of Childhood Sexual Abuse, 1992, The AAMFT: Fifty Years of Marital and Family Therapy, 1992; co-author: Systematic Family Therapy, 1986; editor: The Family Coord., 1970-75, Jour. Marriage and Family Counseling, 1974-76, Contemporary Family Therapy: An Internat. Jour., 1986—, Family Therapy News, 1986-91, The Internat. Connection, 1996—; mem. editl. bd. Internat. Jour. Family Therapy, 1977-85, Jour. Divorce and Remarriage, 1976-83, 85—, Internat. Jour. Family, Sage Family Studies Abstracts, 1977—, Family Systems Medicine, 1982—, Jour. Marital and Family Therapy, 1984—, Jour. Family Psychotherapy, 1990—, Jour. Family Psychology, 1986-90. Mem. mental health and health coms. Mayor's Commn. on Children and Youth, 1966-69; bd. dirs. Family and Children's Svc., Oakland, Mich., 1977-87, chmn., 1984-86, dir. emeritus, 1987—. With C.E., U.S. Army, 1948-49. Recipient Svc. award Ala. Assn. for Mental Health, 1962, Spl. award for Outstanding Contbns. Fla. Assn. Marriage and Family Therapy, 1977, 82, 90; NSF fellow U. Colo., 1963, Disting. Svc. to families award Southeastern Coun. on Family Rels., 1996. Fellow APA, Am. Psychol. Soc., Am. Assn. Marriage and Family Therapy (dir. 1969-72, 1979-83, chmn. accreditation com. 1976-77, co-chmn. Atlanta Multiregional Conf. 1975, 77, founding editor Jour. Marital and Family Therapy 1974-76, Spl. awards 1976, 78, Disting. Leadership awards 1982, 83, pres.-elect 1979-80, pres. 1981-82, Disting. Leadership award 1991, Orgnl. Contributions award 1992), Acad. of Clin. Psychology; mem. Am. Assn. Marriage and Family Therapy Edn. and Rsch. Found. (trustee 1992-94), Assn. Marital and Family Therapy Regulation Bds. (mem. MFT Examination Adv. bd. 1989-92), Mich. Inter-Profl. Assn. on Marriage, Divorce and Family (Orgnl. Contbn. award 1992, trustee 1977-80, com. chmn. 1968-71, 76—), Mich. Assn. Marriage Counselors (pres. 1969-71, chmn. profl. liaison com. 1972-73), Nat. Coun. on Family Rels. (pres. 1976-77, dir., mem. exec. com. 1969-78), Mich. Bd. Marriage Counselors (chair 1980-87), Ga. Assn. for Marriage and Family Therapy (pres.-elect 1994-95, pres. 1996—), Internat. Family Therapy Assn. (charter, editor Internat. Connections 1996—, bd. dirs. ex officio 1996—), Internat. Acad. Family Psychology. Home: 1041 Ferncreek Dr Watkinsville GA 30677-4212 Office: The Family Workshop 752 Houston Mill Rd NE Atlanta GA 30329-4210

NICHOLS, WILLIAM FORD, JR., foundation executive, business executive; b. Palo Alto, Calif., July 4, 1934; s. William Ford and Elizabeth (Woodyatt) N.; m. Rosemary Peterson, 1988; children: Deborah, John, Andrew. A.B., Stanford U., 1956, M.B.A., 1958. C.P.A., Calif. With Price Waterhouse, San Francisco, 1958-69, Price Waterhouse & Co., Sydney, Australia, 1966; asst. controller Saga Corp., Menlo Park, Calif., 1969-72; controller Saga Corp., 1972—, asst. treas., 1981-83; assoc. prof. San Jose State U., 1983-88; treas. William and Flora Hewlett Found., Menlo Park, 1985—; trustee Investment Fund for Founds., 1991—. Mem. AICPA, Calif. Soc. CPA's, Inst. Mgmt. Accts. (nat. v.p. 1974-75, bd. dirs.), Fin. Execs. Inst. (pres. Santa Clara Valley chpt. 1979-80). Home: 330 August Cir Menlo Park CA 94025-5829

NICHOLSON, BRADLEY JAMES, law clerk; b. Montebello, Calif., Sept. 22, 1958; s. Thomas Edwin and Charlotte Elizabeth (Knight) N.; m. Anne Marie Dooley, Oct. 6, 1990. BA, Reed Coll., 1983; JD, U. Pa., 1990. Bar: Calif. 1990, U.S. Ct. Appeals (9th cir.) 1990, U.S. Ct. Appeals (8th cir.) 1993, U.S. Dist. Ct. (no. dist.) Calif. 1990. Assoc. atty. Wilson, Sonsini, Goodrich & Rosati, Palo Alto, Calif., 1990-91; law clk. to Hon. Morris S. Arnold U.S. Dist. Ct., Ft. Smith, Ark., 1991-92; assoc. atty. Coudert Bros., San Jose, Calif., 1992-94; sr. law clk. to Hon. Morris S. Arnold U.S. Cir. Ct., Little Rock, 1994—. Contbr. articles to profl. jours. Mem. Federalist Soc., Am. Soc. for Legal History, Ninth Cir. Jud. Cir. Hist. Soc., Phi Beta Kappa (devel. chmn. no. Calif. chpt. 1990). Avocations: golf, fishing, music. Office: Chambers of Morris S Arnold PO Box 2060 Little Rock AR 72203

NICHOLSON, BRUCE, graphics expert, executive. With Ray Mercer & Co., Apogee, Future Gen.; from optical camera asst. to optical supr. Indsl. Light & Magic, San Rafael, Calif., 1976-83, visual effects supr., 1984—. Optical camera asst. (films) Close Encounters of the Third Kind, 1976, Star Wars, 1977; optical supr. (films) The Empire Strikes Back, 1980 (Oscar award), Raiders of the Lost Ark, 1981 (Oscar award), Dragonslayer, 1981, Poltergeist, 1982, Return of the Jedi, 1983, Indiana Jones and the Temple of Doom, 1984; visual effects supr. (films) Starman, 1985, Explorers, 1986, Batteries Not Included, 1987, Field of Dreams, 1989, Always, 1989, Ghost, 1990, Memories of An Invisible Man, 1991, Meteor Man, 1993, In The Mouth of Madness, 1994, (commls.) HDTV, 1988, Panasonic, 1988, Subaru, 1989, Honda, 1990, Choice Hotels, 1994. Office: Indsl Light and Magic PO Box 2459 San Rafael CA 94912-2459

NICHOLSON, BRUCE J., insurance company executive. With Ministers Life Ins. Co., Mpls., 1975-1984, Towers Perrin Co, Mpls., 1984-1990; now with Lutheran Brotherhood Inc., 1990—, now sr. exec. v.p. financial svcs. Office: Lutheran Brotherhood Inc 625 4th Ave S Minneapolis MN 55415*

NICHOLSON, DOUGLAS ROBERT, accountant; b. Avon, N.Y., Dec. 4, 1921; s. Robert William and Ruth (Neff) N.; m. Gertrude Jane Scott, Apr. 24, 1944; children—Laurie, Scott, Susan, Steven. A.B., U. Rochester, 1942, M.S., 1948. Baseball player St. Louis Cardinal Farm Teams, 1942, 46; Staff acct. Oliver & Clapp, 1948-49; sr. acct. Charles L. Clapp & Co., 1949-51; tchr. income taxes U. Rochester, 1950-61; office mgr. Williams, Clapp & Co., 1951-53, ptnr., 1953-56; prin. Haskins & Sells, CPA's, Rochester, N.Y., 1956-59, ptnr., 1959-67, ptnr.-in-charge Rochester office, 1967-82. Pres. Estate Planning Coun. Rochester; team capt. YMCA capital fund dr., 1961, Rochester Inst. Tech. new campus fund dr., 1964; chmn. spl. gifts com. U. Rochester, 1965, group leader 38 million capital fund campaign, 1966; mem. acctg. adv. bd. Syracuse U., 1968; adv. com. M.S. program Rochester Inst. Tech. Bd. Dirs.; treas. Highland Hosp., Rochester; bd. dirs. Hosp. Computer Ctr. Rochester, Rochester Regional Rsch. Libr. Coun.; mem. deferred giving adv. coun. Rochester Inst. Tech.; mem. N.Y. State Bd. Pub. Accountancy, 1977-82. Lt. USNR, 1942-45. Recipient Gannett Newspapers award, 1956. Mem. Am. Inst. C.P.A.'s, N.Y. State Soc. C.P.A.'s (past pres. Rochester), Nat. Assn. Accountants, Am. Accounting Assn., Am. Mgmt. Assn., Rochester C. of C., Beta Alpha Psi. Democrat. Unitarian (trustee). Clubs: Oak Hill Country, University, Genesee Valley. Home and Office: 663 Lake Rd Webster NY 14580-1552

NICHOLSON, GEORGE, judge; b. Dallas, Feb. 15, 1941; s. George William and Delighon (Ross) N.; m. Brenda Hommel, Nov. 14, 1959; children: Peggy, Christopher. AA, Oakland City Coll., 1962; BA in Polit. Sci., Calif. State U., Hayward, 1964; JD, U. Calif., San Francisco, 1967. Bar: Calif., U.S. Ct. Appeals (9th cir.), U.S. Dist. Ct. (ea. and no. dists.) Calif., U.S. Supreme Ct. Sr. trial dep. dist. atty. Alameda County, Oakland, Calif., 1966-76; exec. dir. Calif. Dist. Atty.'s Assn., Sacramento, 1976-79; sr. asst. atty. gen. Calif. Dept. Justice, Sacramento, 1979-83; legal and ednl. advisor Gov. Calif., Sacramento, 1983-84; dir. and chief counsel Nat. Sch. Safety Ctr., Sacramento, 1984-86; sole practice Sacramento, 1986-87; Judge Sacramento Mcpl. Ct., 1987-89; judge Sacramento County Superior Ct., 1989-90; assoc. justice Ct. of Appeal Third Appellate Dist., Sacramento, 1990—; adv. bds. Fed. Office Juvenile Justice and Delinquency Prevention-Nat. juvenile justice code project, Nat. restitution project; pres.'s adv. com. Victims of Crime, 1980-81; adj. prof. edn. Grad. Sch. Edn. Psychology, Pepperdine U., Malibu, Calif.; exec. com. Commn. on the Future of the Calif. Cts., 1991-1994 (chmn. tech. com., appellate cts. com.). Prin. author: Proposition 8, California Victims' Bill Rights, 1982, (with others) Forgotten Victims: An Advocate's Anthology, 1977, Crime Victims' Handbook, 1981, School Crime and Violence: Victims' Rights, 1986, 2d edit., 1992; editor School Safety Legal Anthology, 1985; contbr. articles to profl. jours. Vol. legal counsel Parents of Murdered Children, L.A., 1982, Laws at Work, L.A., 1980-82; Calif. Rep. exec. com., 1983-89; Rep. nominee Calif. Atty. Gen., 1982. Mem. ABA (jud. adminstrv. divsn.), Am. Judges Assn., Am. Judicature Soc., Calif. Judges Assn. Presbyterian. Avocations: legal edn. subjects, skiing, baseball. Office: Court of Appeal 914 Capitol Mall Sacramento CA 95814-4811

NICHOLSON, GEORGE ALBERT, JR., financial analyst; b. Baldwin City, Kan., May 7, 1908; s. George Albert and Nellie May (Ruthrauff) N.; m. Elizabeth Farnham, Sept. 1, 1933; children: George Albert III, Edwin F., John R., Elizabeth C. (Mrs. David D. Hamm). A.B., U. Mich., 1928; M.B.A., Harvard U., 1930; LL.D., Carthage Coll., 1972. Chartered fin. analyst. With Hudson Motor Co., 1930-31, Union Guardian Trust Co., 1931-33; fin. analyst Whitlock, Smith & Co., Detroit, 1933-37, Am. Industries, Detroit, 1937-41, Inc. Investors, Boston, 1941; civilian renegotiator USAF, 1942-45; fin. analyst Watling, Lerchen & Co., Detroit, 1945-58; rsch. dir. Smith, Hague & Co. Inc., Detroit, 1958-90; columnist Better Investing Mag.; cons. 1st of Mich. Merger, Detroit, 1990—; chmn. Investment Edn. Inst., Internat. Investment Edn. Inst., World Fedn. Investment Clubs. Nicholson awards for best ann. reports for individual investors established by Nat. Assn. Investors, 1978. Mem. Fin. Analyst Soc. Detroit (pres. 1957), Nat. Assn. Investment Clubs (chmn. adv. bd.), Delta Kappa Epsilon. Republican. Episcopalian. Clubs: Country (Detroit), Indian Village (Detroit). Home: 1017 Cadieux Rd Grosse Pointe MI 48230-1511

NICHOLSON, JACK, actor, director, producer; b. Neptune, N.J., Apr. 28, 1937; s. John and Ethel May N.; m. Sandra Knight, 1961 (div. 1966); children: Jennifer, Lorraine Broussard. Acting debut Hollywood stage prodn. Tea and Sympathy; films include Cry-Baby Killer, 1958, Studs Lonigen, 1960, Little Shop of Horrors, 1960, Ensign Pulver, 1964, The Trip, 1967, Easy Rider, (Acad. award nomination for best supporting actor), 1969, Five Easy Pieces, 1970, Carnal Knowledge, 1971, A Safe Place, 1971, The Last Detail, 1974 (Cannes Film Festival prize), Chinatown, 1974 (Acad. award nomination, N.Y. Film Critics Circle award), Tommy, The Passenger, 1975, The Fortune, 1975, One Flew Over the Cuckoo's Nest (Golden Globe award, Acad. award for best actor, N.Y. Film Critics Circle award), 1975, The Missouri Breaks, 1976, The Last Tycoon, 1976, The Shining, 1980, The Postman Always Rings Twice, 1981, Reds,1981 (Acad. award nomination for best supporting actor), The Border, 1982, Termsof Endearment (Acad. award for best supporting actor), 1983, Prizzi's Honor,1985 (Acad. award nomination for best actor), Heartburn, 1986, The Witches of Eastwick, 1987, Broadcast News, 1987, Ironweed, 1987 (Acad. award nomination for bestactor), Batman, 1989, Man Trouble, 1991, A Few Good Men, 1992, Hoffa, 1992, Wolf, 1994, The Crossing Guard, 1995, Mars Attacks!, 1996, The Evening Star, 1996, Blood and Wine, 1996; producer films Head, 1968, Ride the Whirlwind, The Shooting; dir. films Drive, He Said, 1971; dir., actor films Goin' South, 1978, The Two Jakes, 1990. Co-recipient (with Bobby McFerrin) Grammy award for best recording for children,1987. Office: Bresler Kelly Kipperman 15760 Ventura Blvd Ste 1730 Encino CA 91436*

NICHOLSON, JOSEPH BRUCE, real estate developer; b. San Jose, Calif., Jan. 21, 1940; s. Wilmot Joseph and Ruth (Russell) N.; m. Susan Knight, Nov. 1963 (div. 1972); children: Kelsey Erin, Craig Wilmot; m. Linda Mirassou, Aug. 1992. BArch, U. Oreg., 1963. Exec. v.p. Nicholson-Brown Inc., Santa Clara, Calif., 1967-80; prin. Nicholson Assocs., Aptos, Calif., 1977—; v.p., gen. mgr. Nicholson-Wilson Co., Santa Clara, 1980-83; prin. The Nicholson Co., Campbell, Calif., 1984—; v.p. Pacific Property Ventures Inc., Campbell, 1988—; pres. Nicholson Constrn. Inc., Campbell, 1989—; v.p. Nicholson Property Mgmt. Inc., Campbell, 1989—; bd. dirs. Transmetrics Inc., San Jose. Bd. dirs. Triton Mus., Santa Clara, 1979, Hope Rehab. Svc., San Jose, 1979, United Way Cen. Area, San Jose, 1991; pres. adv. bd. de Saisset Mus., Santa Clara U., 1991; trustee Art Mus. Santa Cruz County, 1993. Lt. USN, 1963-67. Mem. Rotary, Commonwealth Club (San Francisco), World Trade Club (San Francisco). Republican. Avocations: travel, reading, art collecting, cooking, tennis. Home: 218 Shoreview Dr Aptos CA 95003-4621 Office: The Nicholson Co 75 Cristich Ln Campbell CA 95008-5403

NICHOLSON, JUNE C. DANIELS, speech pathologist; b. Augusta, Maine, Dec. 28, 1938; d. Sumner T. and Bernadette (Dulac) Daniels; m. Kenneth E. Nicholson, June 27, 1964; children: Jeffrey Scott, Daren Patrick. BS, Abilene Christian U., 1963; MS, U. Vt., 1980. Cert. ASHA CCC, Vt. Dept. Edn. Speech pathologist, grades K-12 Arlington (Vt.) Pub. Sch. Mem. Am. Speech/Hearing Assn., Vt. Speech/Hearing Assn., Vt. Edn. Assn., NEA, Delta Kappa Gamma. Home: RR 3 Box 835 Arlington VT 05250-9712

NICHOLSON, LELAND ROSS, retired utilities company executive, energy consultant; b. Carrington, N.D., Feb. 21, 1924; s. Malcom and Lena May (Kerlin) N.; m. Virginia E. Blair, Mar. 16, 1946; children: Heather Le Nicholson Studebaker, Leland B., Holly Kay. Student, Northwestern U., 1940-41; BSEE, U. N.D., 1949; postgrad. in utility mgmt., U. Minn., 1952. Planning and mktg. engr. Minkota Power Coop., Grand Forks, N.D., 1949-54; dir. new bus. Kans. Power & Light Co., Topeka, 1954-64, v.p. mktg., 1964-76, sr. v.p., 1976-80, exec. v.p., 1980-83, also bd. dirs.; pres. Kans. Power & Light Gas Service, Topeka, 1985-88, ret., 1988; pres., chief operating officer The Gas Service Co., Kansas City, Mo., 1983-85; pres. Indsl. Devel. Corp., Topeka; chmn. Kans. Council on Electricity and Environment; exec. com. Kansas City Labor Mgmt. Council, 1986-89; mem. Mktg. Execs. Conf.; bd. dirs. Gas Service Energy Corp., Kansas City, Merchants Nat. Bank, Topeka. Idea innovator heat pump water heater, photo cell controlled yard light, electric grill. Bd. dirs., area relations com. Kansas City (Mo.) Area Econ. Devel. Council, 1983-89; bd. dirs. Kansas City Pvt. Industry Council, 1986-89, Kansas City Downtown Council; trustee U. Mo., Kansas City, 1984-91; mktg. chmn. Kansas City Full Employment Council; past chmn., mem. Topeka-Shawnee County Planning Commn.; adult adv. com. Sea Scouts. Served to master sgt. USMC, 1942-46. Mem. Am. Gas Assn., Midwest Gas Assn. (bd. dirs. 1985-89), Mo. Valley Electric Assn. (chmn. 1979-81), Edison Electric Inst. (mktg. chmn. 1978-80), Assoc. Industries of Mo., Kans. Assn. Commerce and Industry, Greater Kansas City (Mo.) C. of C. (bd. dirs. 1979-82), Shawnee Yacht Club (Topeka) (commodore 1972-74), Lake Gaston Assn. (pres. 1993—), Kansas City Club, Rotary. Republican.

Congregationalist. Avocations: sailing, canoeing, fishing, reading, electronics.

NICHOLSON, MORRIS EMMONS, JR., metallurgist, educator; b. Indpls., Feb. 15, 1916; s. Morris Emmons and Jessie (Cox) N.; m. Norma Story, Aug. 21, 1943; children: Morris Emmons III, Robert A., Richard A. BS, MIT, 1939; ScD, Mass. Inst. Tech., 1947. Registered profl. engr., Minn. Sect. head engring. research dept. Standard Oil Co., Ind., 1947-50; asst. prof. Inst. Study Metals, U. Chgo., 1950-55; prof. metallurgy U. Minn., 1956-85, prof. emeritus, 1985—, head dept., 1956-62, dir. continuing edn. in engring. and sci., 1973-85; mem. Materials Adv. Bd., 1960-62. Active Boy Scouts Am., 1952—, dist. commr., 1961-64, 70-71; trustee Ind. Dist. 623 Sch. Bd., 1959-65, treas., 1965-77; bd. dirs. 916 Area Vocat. Tech. Sch., 1976-83, 916 Found., 1984-95, sec., 1984-90; bd. dirs. Minn. Sch. bd. Assn., 1973-79; amb. N.W. Youth and Family Svcs., 1988-93; mem. Falcon Heights Parks and Recreation Commn., 1992-95. Recipient Silver Beaver, Boy Scouts Am., 1966; named Outstanding Sch. Bd. Mem., Minn. Sch. Bd. Assn., 1981. Mem. Am. Soc. Engring. Edn. (chmn. U. Minn. chpt. 1957-58, CPD divsn. 1962—, archivist 1985-94, Disting. Svc. award 1980), Am. Soc. Metals (chmn. Minn. chpt. 1958, mem. hist. sites com. 1989-92, chmn. 1991-92), Minerals, Metals and Materials Soc. (profl. registration com. 1982-93, chmn. 1986-93, Disting. Svc. award 1994), Assn. for Media-Based Continuing Edn. for Engrs. (bd. dirs. 1976-85), Sigma Xi, Theta Delta Chi, Tau Beta Pi, Alpha Chi Sigma. Mem. United Ch. Christ. Home: 1776 Pascal Ave N Saint Paul MN 55113-6259

NICHOLSON, MYREEN MOORE, artist, researcher; b. Norfolk, Va., June 2, 1940; d. William Chester and Illeen (Fox) Moore; m. Roland Quarles Nicholson, Jan. 9, 1964 (dec. 1986); children: Andrea Joy, Ross (dec. 1965); m. Harold Wellington McKinney II, Jan. 18, 1981; 1 child, Cara Isadora. AA, William and Mary Coll., 1960; BA Old Dominion U., 1962; MLS, U. N.C., 1971; postgrad. Old Dominion U. 1962-64, 64-67, 75-85, 86-92, 94-96. The Citadel, 1968-69, Hastie Sch. Art, 1968, Chrysler Mus. Art Sch., 1964. English tchr., Chesapeake, Va., 1962-63; dept. head, Portsmouth (Va.) Bus. Coll., 1963-64; tech. writer City Planning/Art Commn., Norfolk, 1964-65; art tchr. Norfolk pub. schs., 1965-67; prof. lit., art Palmer Jr. Coll., Charleston, S.C., 1968; tchr. Penn Sch. John's Island, S.C., 1968; librarian Charleston Schs., 1968-69; asst. to asst. dir. City Library Norfolk, 1970-72, art and audio-visual librarian, 1972-75, rsch. librarian, 1975-83, librarian dept. fiction, 1983-90; dir. W. Ghent Arts Alliance, Norfolk, 1978—. Poet-in-schs., Virginia Beach, Va., 1987. Book reviewer Art Book Revs., Library Jour., 1973-76; editor, illustrator Acquisitions Bibliographies, 1970—, West Ghent newsletter, 1995—; juried exhibits various cities including Grand Hyatt, Mayflower, Washington, by Joan Mondale, Nohra Haime, curator of Freer Gallery, by sr. curator Nat. Mus. Am. Art, curator Phillips Collection, asst. curator, White House; group shows include Yorktown Small Works Show, 1996, Hampton Arts Commn. and Tidewater Artists Assn. Portfolio Show, 1996, Suffolk Artists and Writers Invitational Exhibit, 1996, Virginia Beach Resort and Conference Ctr. Print Show; contbr. art and poetry to various publs. and anthologies. Mem. Virginia Beach Arts Ctr., 1978-93, Hampton Art League, 1990—, Suffolk Art League, 1990—; bd. dirs. W. Ghent Art/Lit. Festival, 1979; poetry reader Poetry Soc. Va., Va. Ctr. for Creative Arts, Sweetbriar, 1989, Walden Books, 1991, Christopher Newport U., 1994-95, Caberet Voltaire, 1994, J.M. Prince Books and Coffeehouse, 1995—, Statues St. Mark's Cath. Ch., 1991-92; graphics of hundreds of celebrities from life; curator Va. Winter Show Life Saving Mus., 1991-92; judge Bornstein art scholarship Chrysler Mus., 1992; mem. staff Mid-Atlantic Antiques Mag., 1993—. Recipient awards various art and poetry contests; Coll. William and Mary art scholar, 1958, Tricentenial award for Contbns. to the Arts in Va., 1993; recipient Cert. for Vol. Contbns. to Va. by Gov., 1994. Nat. Endowment Arts grantwriter, 1975; bd. dirs. Tidewater Literacy Coun., 1971-72; bd. dirs. West Ghent League. Mem. ALA (poster sessions rev. com. 1985-95, pub. relations judge, subcom. comm. 1988-90), Pub. Libr. Assn. (com. bylaws and orgns. 1988-90), Va. Libr. Assn. (pub. relations com. 1984-86, grievance and pay equity com. 1986-88, Logo award for Norfolk Pub. Libr., 1985, chair elect, 1991-92, chair Pub. Documents Forum, 1992-93, sec. 1994), Southeastern Libr. Assn. (Rothrock award com. 1986-88, com. on coms. 1991-92), Poetry Soc. Va. (ea. pres. 1986-89, nominating com. 1989-90, state corr. sec., editor newsletter 1990-93, dir. publicity 1993-95, 70th Anniversary plaque for Wren Bldg.), Art Librs. Soc. N.Am., Tidewater Artists Assn. (bd. dirs. 1989—, chair grantwriting com. 1990—, pres. 1991-92), Southeastern Coll. Art Assn., Acad. Am. Poets, Irene Leache Soc., Internat. Platform Assn. (artists assn.), Old Dominion U. Alumni Assn. (artistic dir. Silver Reunion), Southeastern Soc. Archtl. Historians, Ikara (pres. 1989—), D'Art Ctr. (Dockside art rev., bd. dirs. 1991—), Ex Libris Soc. (charter), Va. Writers Club. Home and Office: 1404 Gates Ave Norfolk VA 23507-1131

NICHOLSON, R. STEPHEN, organization administrator; b. Radford, Va., Mar. 4, 1926; s. Roy S. and Ethel Dovie (Macy) N.; m. Carol Peterson, 1987; 1 child, Suzanne Carpenter. A.B., Marion Coll., 1950; M.A., Syracuse U., 1956; Ph.D., Mich. State U., 1971. Prof. Lansing (Mich.) Community Coll., 1963-66, Acad. dean, 1966-69; pres. Daley Coll., Chgo., 1969-71, Clark County Community Coll., 1971-76, Mt. Hood Community Coll. Dist., 1976-85; chancellor Oakland Community Coll., 1985-90; vice chancellor Higher Colls. of Tech., United Arab Emirates, 1990-92; CEO Internat. Christian Leadership, 1992-93; pres. emeritus Mt. Hood Coll., 1993—; CEO Mercy Corps Internat., 1994-95. Rsch. advisor M.J. Murdock Trust, 1993-95, sr. fellow higher edn., 1996—. Mem. Am. Assn. Community and Jr. Colls. (pres. Pres.'s Acad. 1982, bd. dirs. 1985-87), N.W. Assn. Community and Jr. Colls. (pres. 1976), Am. Sch. Adminstrs. Assn., Am. Sociology Assn., Am. Acad. Polit. and Social Scis., Gresham C. of C. (dir. 1977-79), Japan-Am. Soc., World Affairs Council, Am. Futurist Soc., Phi Delta Kappa. Club: Rotary (pres. 1983, Paul Harris fellow 1986). Home: 3901 SW 22nd Dr Gresham OR 97080-8381

NICHOLSON, RALPH LESTER, botanist, educator; b. Lynn, Mass., Aug. 25, 1942; s. Nathan Aaron and Muriel Spinney (Buxton) N. BA, U. Vt., 1964; MS, U. Maine, 1967; PhD, Purdue U., 1972. Prof. dept. botany and plant pathology Purdue U., West Lafayette, Ind., 1972—; Contbr. chpts. to books, more than 100 articles to profl. jours. Active Big Bros./Big Sisters, Lafayette, Ind., 1974—. Fellow Am. Phytopathol. Soc. Office: Purdue U Botany and Plant Pathology Lafayette IN 47907

NICHOLSON, RICHARD JOSEPH, trust banking executive; b. N.Y.C., Feb. 19, 1932; s. Robert William and Mary Elizabeth (McShane) N.; m. Barbara Helen Malisky, Oct. 15, 1955; 1 child, Richard Jr. BS in Social Sci., Georgetown U., 1952; MBA, NYU, 1957. Asst. cashier Citibank Trust Div., N.Y.C., 1952-66; sr. v.p. 1st Fidelity Bank, Newark, 1966-90, ret., 1990; mem. exec. com. N.J. Bankers Assn. Trust Div., Princeton, 1983-85. Bd. dirs. Family Service Bur. of Newark, 1976—; mem. council Newark Mus., 1979-90. Served as cpl. U.S. Army, 1952-54. Mem. N.J. Bond Club. Republican. Roman Catholic. Avocations: tennis, travel, history.

NICHOLSON, RICHARD SELINDH, educational association administrator; b. Des Moines, Apr. 5, 1938; s. George Eugene and Margaret (Selindh) N.; m. Mary Lou Weisbrod, Aug. 1, 1958 (div. 1971) 1 child, Jeffrey Richard; m. Lois Ann Karls, Aug. 15, 1976; 1 child, Gregory Michael. BS, Iowa State U., 1960; PhD, U. Wis., 1964; LHD (hon.), CUNY, 1994, CUNY-Mt. Sinai Med. Ctr., 1994. Rsch. assoc. U. Wis., Madison, 1963-64; asst. prof. Mich. State U., East Lansing, 1964-67, assoc. prof., 1967-70; program dir. NSF, Washington, 1970-77, div. dir., 1977-82, chief of staff, 1983-85, asst. dir., 1985-89; exec. dir. Nat. Sci. Bd. Commn., Washington, 1982-83; exec. officer, pub. Science AAAS, Washington, 1989—; cons. on sci. affairs Pres. of U.S., Washington, 1978-79; exec. sec. Pres.' Com. on Nat. Medal Sci., Washington, 1976-84; mem. Pres.' Nat. Commn. on Superconductivity, 1989; vice chair Commn. on Phys. Scis., Math and Resources NRC, 1989—, Edn. Coordinating Coun., 1991—, com. on environ. rsch., 1991-92, co-chair coun. on competitiveness, 1993—; mem. statutory vis. com. Nat. Inst. of Stds. and Tech., 1990-93; vis. com. chemistry dept. Harvard U., 1989—; bd. dirs. Quality Edn. for Minorities Network, 1989—; trustee Gordon Rsch. Conf., 1989—; sci. policy adv. com. com. space, sci. and tech. U.S. Ho. Reps., 1992—; co-chair Coun. on Competitiveness, 1993—, Dept. of Energy Panel on Basic Rsch., 1995—; chmn. edn. adv. com. Genentech, 1993—. Mem. editorial bd. Analytical Chemistry, 1980-82, Chem. and Engring. News, 1985-88; contbr. articles to profl. jours. and chpts. to books. Served as seaman USN, 1956-63. Recipient Presdl. Disitng. Ranking, Pres. Reagan, 1982, Alumni Citation Merit award Iowa State U., 1983. Fellow AAAS; mem. Am. Chem. Soc. (chmn. Mich. State U. sect. 1968-70), Chem. Soc. Washington (nominations com. 1977), Cosmos Club, Nat. Press Club. Avocations: sports, tennis, reading. Home: 1020 Union Church Rd Mc Lean VA 22102-1115 Office: AAAS 1200 New York Ave NW Washington DC 20005-4707

NICHOLSON, ROBERT ARTHUR, college president; b. Pepin, Wis., Oct. 13, 1923; s. Arthur W. and Ethel (Weeden) N.; m. Dorothy Nelis, June 17, 1944; children: Paul, Gary. BS, Anderson U., Ind., 1944; MA, NYU, 1946, Ph.D., 1953. With Anderson U., 1945-90, successively instr., asst. prof., assoc. prof. music, chmn. dept., asst. to dean, 1945-58, dean, 1958-83, v.p., 1964-83, pres., 1983-90, pres. emeritus, 1990—. Author: Handbook to the Hymnal of the Church of God, 1953; Editor: Hymnal of the Church of God, 1953, 71. Mem. pub. bd. Ch. of God, 1955-80, chmn. commn. higher edn., 1963-70, 83-86, vice chmn., 1970-83, cons., 1990—; cons. Warner Pacific Coll., Oreg., 1990—, N.Ind. United Meth. Found., Inc., 1992-95, Anderson Pub. Libr., 1994-95, United Faith Housing Corp., 1994; bd. dirs. Anderson Symphony Orch., 1974-87, 93-94, United Way Madison County, 1985-89, 91-94, Minnetrista Cultural Found., 1988—; bd. dirs., v.p. Anderson Internat., 1990-93; bd. dirs. Comty. Hosp. Madison County, 1986-95, vice chmn., 1988-94, interim pres., CEO, 1991; pres. Madison County Comty. Found., Inc., 1991—. Mem. Associated Colls. of Ind., Ind. Colls. and Univs. of Ind. (chmn. 1988-89), Anderson Area C. of C. (bd. dirs. 1985-90, vice chmn. and chmn. elect 1988, chmn. 1989). Home: 721 Maplewood Ave Anderson IN 46012-3028

NICHOLSON, THEODORE H., educational administrator; b. Chgo., July 27, 1929; B.S., Loyola U., Chgo., 1951; M.S. (State of Ill. Vets scholar), No. Ill. U., 1955; postgrad., Rockford Coll., 1955; Ph.D. (NDEA fellow, 1966-67), U. Wis.-Madison, 1967; children—Craig, Kimberlee, Christine, Rhonda, Katrina, Alexandra. Tchr., Morris Kennedy Sch., Winnebago County, Ill., 1951-53, Rockford (Ill.) Public Schs., 1953-55, evening sch., 1955-59; prin. Marsh Schs., Dist. 58, Winnebago County, 1959-65, supt., 1959-66; supt. Dearborn Twp. Sch. Dist. 8, Dearborn Heights, Mich., 1967-68, Wilmington (Ohio) City Sch., 1968-72; supr. schs., Wausau, Wis., 1972-90; assoc. prof. edn. leadership U. No. Colo., 1990-93; vis. prof. Central State U., Wilberforce, Ohio, 1969-70; assoc. Univ. of Wis.-Madison, 1993-94; teaching asst., rsch. asst., lectr. U. Wis., summer 1976; assoc. prof. to assocs. U. Wis., Madison, 1993-94; lectr., cons. Univ. Council Ednl. Adminstrn.; mem. coordinating com. Partnership Schs.; v.p. N.C. Data Processing Ctr., 1974-81. Active Cen. Wausau Progress, 1973-82; mem. Pvt. Industry Coun.; bd. dirs. Wausau Performing Art Found., 1986-91, Wausau Area Community Found., 1988-91. Served with USN, 1943-46. Recipient Citizenship award City of Rockford, 1960, 64, Recognition award State Wis. Dept. Pub. Instr., 1989, Wausau Bd. Edn., 1989; Community Leader award Sta. WXCO, Wausau, 1974. Mem. Am. Assn. Sch. Adminstrs., Wis. Assn. Sch. Dist. Adminstrs. (state bd. dirs., Adminstr. of Yr. award spl. edn. dept., 1986, Recognition award 1989), Am. Assn. Supervision and Curriculum Devel., C. of C. (bd. dirs., edn com., Businessman's Roundtable), Phi Delta Kappa. Contbr. articles in field to profl. publs.

NICHOLSON, WILL FAUST, JR., bank holding company executive; b. Colorado Springs, Colo., Feb. 8, 1929; s. Will Faust and Gladys Olivia (Burns) N.; m. Shirley Ann Baker, Nov. 26, 1955; children: Ann Louise Nicholson Naughton, Will Faust III. S.B., M.I.T., 1950; M.B.A., U. Denver, 1956. V.p. Van Schaack & Co., Denver, 1954-66; pntr. N. G. Petry Constrn. Co., Denver, 1966-70; sr. v.p. Colo. Nat. Bankshares, Inc., Denver, 1970-75; pres. Colo. Nat. Bankshares, Inc., 1975-95, chmn. bd., chief exec. officer, 1985-95; chmn. Rocky Mountain Bankcard Sys., Denver, 1995—; bd. dirs. Pub. Svc. Co., Colo.; bd. dirs., chmn. VISA USA, Inc., VISA Internat. Bd. dirs. Boys and Girls Clubs of Metro Denver; active Downtown Denver, Inc., Colo. Assn. of Commerce and Industry, chmn. 1990-91, Denver Urban Renewal Authority, 1958-59, Denver Bd. Water Commrs., 1959-65, pres. 1964, 65; Nat. Western Stock Show; bd. Health One. With USAF, 1950-53. Mem. Assn. Bank Holding Cos. (bd. dirs. 1979-87, 89-91, exec. com. 1980-85, vice chmn. 1981-82, chmn. 1983-84), U.S. C. of C. (bd. dirs. 1990—), U.S. Golf Assn. (exec. com. 1974-82, v.p. 1978, 79, pres. 1980, 81), Denver Country Club, Denver Club, Univ. Club Colo., Univ. Club N.Y., Castle Pine Golf Club, Royal and Ancient Golf Club (St. Andrews, Scotland), Augusta (Ga.) Nat. Golf Club. Republican. Episcopalian. Home: 37 Polo Club Cir Denver CO 80209-3307 Office: Colo Nat Bankshares PO Box 5168 Denver CO 80217-5168

NICHOLSON, WILLIAM JOSEPH, forest products company executive; b. Tacoma, Aug. 24, 1938; s. Ferris Frank and Athyleen Myrtle (Fesenmaier) N.; m. Carland Elaine Crook, Oct. 10, 1964; children: Courtney, Brian, Kay, Benjamin. SB in ChemE, MIT, 1960, SM in ChemE Practice, 1961; PhD in ChemE, Cornell U., 1965; MBA, Pacific Luth. U., 1969. Registered profl. chem. engr., Wash. Sr. devel. engr. Hooker Chem. Co., Tacoma, 1964-69, Battelle N.W., Richland, Wash., 1969-70; planning assoc. Potlatch Corp., San Francisco, 1970-75, mgr. corp. energy service, 1976-94, dir. corp. energy and environ. svcs., 1994—; chmn. electricity com. Am. Forest and Paper Assn., 1977—, mem. solid waste task force, 1988-91, air quality com., 1989—, mem. environ. steering com., 1994—, vice-chmn. life cycle analysis work group, 1994—, chmn. wood products environ. task force, 1994—; chmn., mem. adv. bd. Forest Products Lab., U. Calif., Richmond, 1992-95; mem. adv. bd. Coll. of Natural Resources, U. Calif., Berkeley, 1993-95. Mem. AAAS, AIChE (assoc.), Am. Chem. Soc., Tech. Assn. Pulp and Paper Industry, Sigma Xi, Commonwealth Club (San Francisco), Cornell Club (N.Y.). Republican. Avocation: industrial history. Home: PO Box 1114 Ross CA 94957-1114 Office: Potlatch Corp 244 California St Ste 610 San Francisco CA 94111-4351

NICHOLSON-GUTHRIE, CATHERINE S. See **GUTHRIE, CATHERINE S. NICHOLSON**

NICITA, RICK, agent. Agent Creative Artists Agy. Office: Creative Artists Agy 9830 Wilshire Blvd Beverly Hills CA 90212-1804*

NICKA, BETTY LOU, secondary education educator; b. Madison, Wis., June 2, 1937; d. Marvin J. and Tilla S. (Haakinson) Lindberg; m. John George Nicka, June 27, 1970; 1 child, Karyn Theresa. BS, U. Wis., LaCrosse, 1959. Tchr. Mitchell Jr. High Sch., Racine, Wis., 1959-63, Cherokee Jr. High Sch., Madison, Wis., 1963-65, East High Sch., Madison, Wis., 1965-92; coach tennis, volleyball, basketball & track Madison East High Sch., 1965-73, dir. dance, performing arts, 1965-92, choreographer theatre plays and musicals, 1970-73. Coord. com. performing arts in dance Tower Twirler Dancers, Wis., 1978-92. Mem. NEA, Am. Assn. Health, Phys. Edn., Recreation and Dance, Wis. Edn. Assn. (coun. 1959—), Wis. Assn. Health, Phys. Edn., Recreation and Dance, So. Wis. Edn. Insvc. Orgn. (chair phys. sec. 1966-67), Madison Area Retired Educators Assn. Democrat. Lutheran. Home: 2105 Sheridan Dr Madison WI 53704-3844

NICKEL, ALBERT GEORGE, advertising agency executive; b. Pitts., July 12, 1943; s. Frank George and Dorothy (Wiefling) N.; children: Melissa, Mark. AB, Washington and Jefferson Coll., 1965; MBA, Ind. U., 1967. Mktg. rsch. analyst Pfizer, Inc., N.Y.C., 1967, profl. svc. rep., 1967-68, mktg. rsch. mgr., 1968-69, product mgr., 1969-70; product mgr. USV Internat., Tuckahoe, N.Y., 1970-71; account exec. J. Walter Thompson (Deltakos), N.Y.C., 1971-72, account supr., 1972-73; account supr. Sudler & Hennessey, N.Y.C., 1973-77; sr. v.p. mgmt. group supr. Young and Rubicam, N.Y.C., 1977-79; pres., COO Dorritie Lyons & Nickel, Inc., N.Y.C., 1979-94; pres., COO Lyons, Lavey, Nickel, Swift, Inc., 1994—. Trustee Wilton YMCA, Five Town Found.; bd. dirs., exec. com. Wilton LaCrosse Assn.; bd. dirs. Dominican Coll., Healthcare Businesswoman's Assn., Wilton H.S. Long Range Planning Team, Am. Coun. on Sci. and Health. Capt. USAF, 1969. Mem. Pharm. Rsch. and Mfrs. Assn. (bd. dirs.), Healthcare Mktg. and Comm. Coun. (bd. dirs.), Midwest Healthcare Mktg. Assn., Wilton Riding Club (pres.), Shore and Country Club, Silver Spring Country Club. Home: 65 Keelers Ridge Wilton CT 06897-4234

NICKEL, JANET MARLENE MILTON, geriatrics nurse; b. Manitowoc, Wis., June 9, 1940; d. Ashley and Pearl (Kerr) Milton; m. Curtis A. Nickel, July 29, 1961; children: Cassie, Debra, Susan. Diploma, Milw. Inst., 1961; ADN, N.D. State U., 1988. Nurse Milw. VA, Wood, Wis., 1961-62; supervising nurse Park Lawn Convalescent Hosp., Manitowoc, 1964-65; newsletter editor Fargo (N.D.) Model Cities Program, 1970-73; supervising night nurse Rosewood on Broadway, Luth. Hosps. and Homes, Fargo, 1973-92; assoc. dir. nursing Elim Nursing Home, Fargo, 1992-94, night supr., 1994—. Mem. Phi Eta Sigma. Home: 225 19th Ave N Fargo ND 58102-2352 Office: 3534 S University Dr Fargo ND 58104-6228

NICKEL, MELVIN EDWIN, metallurgical engineer; b. St. Louis, Aug. 24, 1915; s. Jacob William and Mary Anna (Madsen) N.; m. Mary Louise Breuer, Sept. 12, 1942; children: Elizabeth Ann Nickel Medve, Mary Patricia Nickel Hepburn, Sheila Breuer Nickel Stojak, William Louis. BS in Metall. Engring., U. Mo., Rolla, 1938, Profl. Degree of Metall. Engring., 1967. Mgmt. trainee Bethlehem (Pa.) Steel Corp., 1938-39; asst. to supt. blast furnaces Wis. Steel div. Internat. Harvester Co., Chgo., 1939-43, gen. foreman furnaces, blast furnaces, 1943-48, asst. supt. blast furnaces, 1948-49, supt. open hearths, 1949-61, supt. basic oxygen furnaces, mgr. steel prodn., 1961-68, mgr. primary ops., 1968-77; mgr. facilities planning and appropriations, works mgr. Envirodyne Industries, Inc., Wis. Steel Corp., 1977-80; pres. Melvin E. Nickel & Assocs., Inc., Chgo., 1980—. Contbr. articles to profl. jours.; developer early practices for prodn. of spl. bar quality and alloy steel in top blown basic oxygen furnace, 1962-64. Bd. trustees Iron and Steel Soc. Found., Warrensdale, Pa., 1980-91. Recipient Disting. Merit award U. Mo., Rolla, 1960; inducted Mo. Sch. Mines/U. Mo.-Rolla Athletic Hall of Fame U. Mo., Rolla, 1993. Mem. AIME (hon., nat. v.p., dir. 1974-76), Iron and Steel Soc. of AIME (nat. pres. 1974-75), Metall. Soc. of AIME (nat. chmn. iron and steel divsn. 1972-74), Assn. of Iron and Steel Engrs., Western States Blast Furnaces and Coke Assn., U. Mo., Rolla Alumni Assn. (pres. 1956-59, bd. dirs.), Triangle Fraternity, Jackson Hole Wildlife Soc., Ridge Country Club of Chgo., Beverly Hills Univ. Club. Republican. Roman Catholic. Avocations: hunting, fishing, carpentry, mineral collecting, boating. Home and Office: 10601 S Hamilton Ave Chicago IL 60643-3127

NICKELS, ROBERT EDWARD, plastic manufacturing company executive; b. Detroit, Jan. 23, 1943; s. William Edward and Winifred June (Hocking) N.; m. Carol Lee Johnson, Jan. 26, 1963; children: Tracy Lee, Robbie Lynn. BS in Mech. Engring., Mich. State U., 1966, MBA, 1967; postgrad., Stanford U., 1978. With Procter & Gamble, Chgo., 1967-69; prodn. mgr. Roper Lawn Products, Newark, Ohio, 1969-71; v.p., gen. mgr. Roper Lawn Products, Savannah, Ga., 1971-77; v.p. mfg. Roper Outdoor Products, Bradley, Ill., 1977-79, exec. v.p., 1979-81, pres., 1981-83; v.p. mfg. Sewell Plastics, Inc., Atlanta, 1983-84, exec. v.p., 1984-85, pres., chief exec. officer, 1985—; sr. v.p. Constar Internat. subs. Sewell Plastics, Inc., Chattanooga, 1986—; adv. bd. Allendale Ins., Johnson, R.I., 1986—; pres. MONTPLAS subs. Sewell Plastics, Inc.; bd dirs. Wellstar, Didam, the Netherlands. Mem. Nat. Assn. for Plastic Container Recovery (chmn. 1987-89), Flying Rebel Club. Republican. Presbyterian. Avocation: flying. Home: 646 Gunby Rd Marietta GA 30067-5132 Office: Constar Plastics Inc 5375 Drake Dr SW Atlanta GA 30336-2408*

NICKENS, JACKS CLARENCE, lawyer; b. McCamey, Tex., Feb. 7, 1949; s. Jacks C. Nickens and Elsie Louise (Jordan) Donohue; m. Linda M. Colangelo, June 13, 1970 (div.1984); 1 child, Marie Louise; m. Melinda Jo Hubbert, Oct. 13, 1990; 1 child, Charles Clay. AB magna cum laude, Harvard U., 1971, JD cum laude, 1975. Bar: Tex. 1975, U.S. Dist. Ct. (so. dist.) Tex. 1975. Assoc. Vinson & Elkins, Houston, 1975-79; ptnr. Scott Douglass & Keeton (now Miller, Bristow & Brown), Houston, 1979-90; prin. Jacks C. Nickens & Assocs., Houston, 1990-91; ptnr. Mayer, Brown & Platt, Houston, 1991-94, Clements, O'Neill, Pierce & Nickens, L.L.P., Houston, 1994—. Home: Clements O'Neill et al 1000 Louisiana Ste 1800 Houston TX 77002 Office: Mayer Brown & Platt 700 Louisiana St Ste 3600 Houston TX 77002-2730

NICKERSON, EUGENE H., federal judge; b. Orange, N.J., Aug. 2, 1918; m. Marie-Louise Steiner; children—Marie-Louise, Lawrie H., Stephanie W., Susan A. A.B., Harvard U., 1941; LL.B. (Kent scholar), Columbia U., 1943; LL.D. (hon.), Hofstra U., 1970, Bklyn. Law Sch., 1991. Bar: N.Y. 1944, U.S. Supreme Ct. 1948. Law clk. to Judge Augustus N. Hand, 2d circuit U.S. Ct. Appeals, 1943-44; to Chief Justice Harlan F. Stone U.S. Supreme Ct., 1944-46; county exec. Nassau County, N.Y., 1962-70; practice law N.Y.C., 1946-61, 71-77; judge U.S. Dist. Ct., Bklyn., 1977—; Counsel N.Y. Gov.'s Com. Pub. Employee Procedures, 1956-58; mem. N.Y. State Law Revision Commn., 1958-59, 77; mem. Met. Regional Council, 1962-70, chmn., 1969-70; mem. adv. council pub. welfare HEW, 1963-65; mem. pub. ofcls. adv. council OEO, 1968. Mem. ABA, Nassau County Bar Assn., Assn. Bar City N.Y. (com. fed. legislation 1971-74, com. on communications 1971-77, com. on judiciary 1974-77), Am. Law Inst., Phi Delta Phi. Office: US Dist Ct US Courthouse 225 Cadman Plz E Brooklyn NY 11201-1818*

NICKERSON, GUY ROBERT, lumber company executive; b. Salt Lake City, May 20, 1956; s. Charles Augustus and Florence May (Fogel) N.; m. Maggie Rose McDonnell, May 30, 1992; children: Melissa Marie, Rebecca Rose. B Acctg., U. Utah, 1977, M Profl. Accountancy, 1978. CPA, Utah. Sr. mgr. Deloitte Haskins & Sells, Salt Lake City and N.Y.C., 1978-87; v.p. fin. Anderson Lumber Co., Ogden, Utah, 1987—. Office: Anderson Lumber Co 4700 Harrison Blvd Ogden UT 84403

NICKERSON, JAMES FINDLEY, education consultant; b. Gretna, Nebr., Dec. 16, 1910; s. Elmer Samuel and Lulu Perkins (Patterson) N.; m. Juanita M. Bolin, Mar. 3, 1934; children: Ann Rogers Nickerson Lueck, Maria De Miranda. BS, Nebr. Wesleyan U., 1932; MA, Columbia Tchrs. Coll., 1940; PhD, U. Minn., 1948; ScD (hon.), Yankton (S.D.) Coll., 1971. Tchr. pub. schs. Giltner, Nebr., 1932-35; sch. music supr. Gordon, Nebr., 1936-38, Bayshore, L.I., 1939-41, Grand Island, Nebr., 1941-42; instr. Coll. Edn., music supr. high sch. U. Minn., 1942-46, vis. prof. Coll. Edn., summer 1948; asst. prof. music edn. U. Kans., 1946-48, assoc. prof., 1948-53; rsch. assoc. dept. psychology U. So. Calif., assigned human factors div. U.S. Navy Electronics Lab., San Diego, 1953-54; dean edn., dir. summer quar., prof. psychology Mont. State U., 1954-64, head dept. psychology, 1954-56, rsch. assoc. Electronics Rsch. Lab, 1958-64; v.p. acad. affairs N.D. State U., Fargo, 1964-66; pres. Mankato (Minn.) State U., 1966-73, then pres. emeritus, disting. svc. prof., 1973-76; dir. Svc. Mems. Opportunity Colls., Am. Assn. State Colls. and Univs., Washington, 1973-81; dir. Northwestern Nat. Bank, Mankato, 1967-69; cons. publ. edn. Office Gov. Wash., 1964; exec. sec., study dir. interim com. edn. Wash. Legislature, 1959-60; chmn. regional conf. womanpower Nat. Manpower Coun. and Mont. State Coll., 1957; mem. steering com. Pacific N.W. Con. Higher Edn., 1962; mem. nat. adv. com. sci. edn. NSF, 1968-71, chmn., 1970-71; mem. vis. com. Harvard Grad. Sch. Edn., 1970-76, Schola Cantorum, N.Y.C., 1938-39, Choral Arts Soc., Washington, 1969-71. Stringbass Mont. State Coll. Symphonette, 1959-63, Mankato Symphony Orch., 1967-73, 83—, bd. dirs., 1987-90. Recipient citation interim study Wash. Legislature and Gov., 1960, Outstanding Achievement award Bd. Regents U. Minn., 1968, Alumni award Nebr. Wesleyan U., 1968; Sec. Def. medal for outstanding pub. svc., 1981, citation Am. Coun. Edn., 1981; James F. Nickerson Medal of Merit for outstanding svc. to mil. edn. created by Am. Assn. Sr. Colls. and Univs., 1981; Danforth Found. adminstrn. grantee, 1969. Mem. Nat. Assn. State Univs. and Land Grant Colls. (senate, chmn. div. tchr. edn. 1962-65, sec. coun. acad. officers 1965), Am. Assn. State Colls. and State Univs. (bd. dirs. 1966-71), Am. Assn. Colls. Tchr. Edn. (bd. dirs. 1969-71), Am. Assn. Higher Edn. (chmn. resolutions com. 1974), Assn. Minn. Colls. (pres. 1972), Edn. Commn. States (commr. 1967-73, mem. task force on coordination, governance and structure postsecondary edn. 1973), Sigma Xi, Phi Mu Alpha Sinfonia. Home and Office: PO Box 204 Elysian MN 56028-0204

NICKERSON, JERRY EDGAR ALAN, manufacturing executive; b. North Sydney, N.S., Can., Apr. 28, 1936; s. Jeremiah Beldon and Jean Frances (Innes) N.; m. Jean Frances Ritcey, Sept. 20, 1958; children: Mark Alan, Jerry Ross. B.Commerce, Dalhousie U., 1958. Chmn. bd. H.B. Nickerson & Son, Ltd., North Sydney; bd. dirs. Gt. West Life & Annuity, Gt. West Life Assurance Co., Bank of Montreal, Seaside Cable TV Ltd. Mem. Zeta Psi. Office: HB Nickerson & Sons Ltd, PO Box 130, North Sydney, NS Canada B2A 3M2

NICKERSON, JOHN HENRY, artist, sculptor, designer; b. Mpsl., May 15, 1939; s. John and Lucile Ruth (Jones) Scott; m. Margie Lynette Hay, Sept. 9,

1962 (div. June 1970); 1 child, Shae Mikell Nickerson Elliott. BA, Mont. State U., 1964; MFA, Alfred (N.Y.) U., 1969. Ceramic designer Pacific Stoneware, Inc., Portland, Oreg., 1964; indsl. design sculptor GM Styling Staff, Warren, Mich., 1965-66; staff designer Shuron-Continental, Div. Textron Corp., Rochester, N.Y., 1967; asst. prof. ceramics and design Colo. State U., Ft. Collins, 1969-70; designer in residence Blenko Glass Co., Inc., Milton, W.Va., 1970-74; assoc. master design, drawing, sculpture, ceramics and glass Georgian Coll. Art and Technol., Barrie, Ont., Can., 1976-77; artist in residence Kanawha County Continuing Edn. Program, Charleston, W.Va., 1976-77; artist Cleve. Inst. Art Summer Sessions, 1989—, pvt. practice, 1979—. Numerous exhbtns. include Corning (N.Y.) Mus., 1979, Woodson Mus. Art, Wausaw, Wis., 1984, C. Corcoran Gallery, Muskegan, Mich., 1988, 89, Cartons, Cans, and Other Containers, Salem (Oreg.) Art Assn., 1989, Glassworks I Joan Robery Gallery, Denver, 1989, Sculptural Glass, Grohe Glass Gallery, Hyannis, Mass., 1990; permanent collections include Corning Mus., Del. Art Mus., Wilmington, Denver Art Mus., Muskegan (Mich.) Mus. Art, Musée des Arts Décortifs, Lausanne, Switzerland. Nat. Endowment for the Arts craftsman's fellow, 1981, creative fellow, 1986; Colo. Gov.;s Awards Commn., 1986. Home: PO Box 457 Sedalia CO 80135-0457 Office: Nickerson Glassworks 7327 Reynolds Dr Sedalia CO 80135-8805

NICKERSON, JOHN MITCHELL, political science educator; b. Lewiston, Maine, July 1, 1937; s. Elmer Winfield and Marion Gertrude (Howard) N. B.A., U. Maine, 1959; M.A., Wash. State U., 1966; Ph.D., U. Idaho, 1971. Commd. 2d lt. U.S. Army, 1959, advanced through grades to capt., resigned, 1967; rsch. assoc. Bur. Pub. Administrn. U. Maine, Orono, 1967-68, mem. grad. faculty, 1970-88; assoc. prof. polit. sci. U. Maine, Augusta, 1970-81, prof., 1981—, developer Baccalaureate program in pub. adminstrn.; dir. New Eng. Govtl. Research Inst., Inc., Waterville, Maine, 1971; lectr. Colby Coll., Waterville, Maine, 1979, Maine State Dedimus Justice; cons. in field. Author: The Control of Civil Disturbances, 1968, Municipal Police in Maine - A Study of Selected Personnel Practices with Emphasis on Recruit Selection and Training, 1969, (with others) A Study of Policy-Making: The Dynamics and Adaptability of the U.S. Federal System, 1971; editor, author foreward: Is the Municipality Liable for Insufficiently Trained Police? (James P. Murphy), 1968; contbr. articles to profl. jours. Mem. Maine State Police Planning Adv. Group, Maine State Bd. Assessment Rev., Maine Hwy. Safety Com.; vice chmn. adv. bd. Salvation Army, Augusta; trustee, treas. Lithgow Library; incorporator Kennebec Valley Med. Ctr., Augusta. Dept. Justice grantee, 1967. Mem. AAUP, Am. Polit. Sci. Assn., New Eng. Polit. Sci. Assn., Northeastern Polit. Sci. Assn., Acad. Polit. Sci. (life), Am. Acad. Polit. and Social Sci. (life), Am. Soc. for Pub. Adminstrn., ACLU (life), Kennebec Hist. Soc. (life), Kennebec Valley Humane Soc. (life), Maine Civil Liberties Union (life, legis. com.), Pi Sigma Alpha, Pi Alpha Alpha. Home: 192 Capitol St Augusta ME 04330-6236 Office: U Maine University Heights Augusta ME 04330

NICKERSON, WILLIAM MILNOR, federal judge; b. Balt., Dec. 6, 1933; s. Palmer Rice and Eleanor (Renshaw) N.; m. Virginia Arlen Bourne, Apr. 25, 1954; children: Carol Lee, Deborah, Susan, Wendy, Laura. BA, U. Va., 1955; LLB, U. Md., Balt., 1962. Bar: Md. 1962. Ptnr. Whiteford, Taylor & Preston, Balt., 1962-85; assoc. judge Cir. Ct. Baltimore County, Towson, Md., 1985-90; judge U.S. Dist. Ct. Md., Balt., 1990—. Served to lt. USCGR, 1955-59. Mem. ABA (judicial adminstrn. div.), Am. Judicature Soc., Fed. Judges Assn., Md. State Bar Assn.. Office: US Dist Ct 101 W Lombard St Baltimore MD 21201-2626

NICKFORD, JUAN, sculptor, educator; b. Havana, Cuba, Aug. 8, 1925; s. Basil and Maria (Hoshko) N.; m. Jene Rashkind, Aug. 16, 1952; children—Dena, Marc. M.F.A., Bellas Artes, Havana, 1945; postgrad., U. Havana, 1944-46. Head welding dept. Sculpture Center of N.Y., 1955-62; vis. artist Vasar Coll., 1962-63, Smith Coll., 1966-67, U. Hartford, 1965-66, Bklyn. Mus. Art Sch., 1968-70, Finch Coll., San Marino, 1975; prof. art CCNY, 1975-91, prof. emeritus, 1991—. One man shows, Leonard Gallery, Woodstock, N.Y., 1981, Emanuel Coll. Gallery, Boston, 1977, Sculpture Center, 1974, Art Glass Gallery, Toronto, Ont., Can., 1985, numerous others; retrospective Hopper House, Nyack, N.Y., 1986; group shows include, Thorpe Intermedia Gallery, Sparkill, N.Y., 1974, Hopper House, Nyack, N.Y., 1978, Sculpture Center, N.Y.C., 1978, Sculpture Gallery, Palo Alto, Calif., 1981, numerous museums; represented in permanent collection, Newberger Coll., N.Y., numerous pvt. collections. Cintas Found. grantee, 1970-71, CUNY Faculty Research Found. grantee, 1982-83; recipient Bronze medal N.Y. State Expn., 1964. Mem. Sculptors Guild. Home: 161 Old Tappan Rd Tappan NY 10983-2311

NICKLAS, ROBERT BRUCE, cell biologist; b. Lakewood, Ohio, May 29, 1932; s. Ford Adelbert and Marthabelle (Beckett) N.; m. Sheila Jean Counce, Sept. 17, 1960. B.A., Bowling Green State U., 1954; M.A. (Eugene Higgins fellow), Columbia U., 1956, Ph.D., 1958. Instr. in zoology Yale U., 1958-61, asst. prof. zoology, 1961-64, asso. prof., 1964-65; asso. prof. Duke U., 1965-71, prof., 1971—, chairperson dept., 1983-86; mem. NSF Postdoctoral Fellowship Panel, 1969-71, Am. Cancer Soc. Sci. Adv. Com. for Virology and Cell Biology, 1975-78; mem. adv. bd. 12th Internat. Chromosome Conf., 1994. Contbr. numerous articles to profl. publs.; mem. editorial bd. Chromosoma, 1966-83, Jour. Exptl. Zoology, 1970-72, Jour. Cell Biology, 1980-81, Jour. Cell Sci., 1984-91, European Jour. Cell Biology, 1985-89. Recipient award of disting. tchg. Duke Alumni, 1975; Yale fellow in scis., 1963-64; John Simon Guggenheim fellow, 1972-73, E.B. Wilson medal Am. Soc. Cell Biology, 1995, Inst. Gen. Med. Scis. USPHS grantee, 1960—. Fellow AAAS; mem. Am. Soc. Cell Biology (exec. com. 1976-78, coun. 1975-78, E.B. Wilson medal 1995), Am. Soc. Naturalists, Genetics Soc. Am., Sigma Xi. Home: 3101 Camelot Ct Durham NC 27705-5405 Office: Duke U Dept Zoology Durham NC 27708-1000

NICKLAUS, JACK WILLIAM, professional golfer; b. Columbus, Ohio, Jan. 21, 1940; s. Louis Charles, Jr. and Helen (Schoener) N.; m. Barbara Bash, July 23, 1960; children: Jack William II, Steven Charles, Nancy Jean, Gary Thomas, Michael Scott. Student, Ohio State U., 1957-62, D of Athletic Arts (hon.), 1972; LLD (hon.), U. St. Andrews, 1984. Chmn., chief exec. officer Golden Bear Internat., Inc. Author: My 55 Ways to Lower Your Golf Score, 1964, Take a Tip From Me, 1968, The Greatest Game of All, 1969, Jack Nicklaus' Lesson Tee, 1972, Golf My Way, 1974, Jack Nicklaus' Playing Lessons, 1976, On and Off the Fairway, 1978, Play Better Golf, Vols. 1-3, 1980, 81, 83, The Full Swing, 1982, My Most Memorable Shots in the Majors, 1988. Chmn. Ohio div. Am. Cancer Soc., 1967; chmn. sports div. Nat. Easter Seal Soc., 1967. Named PGA Player of Year, 1967, 72, 73, 75, 76, Dunlop Profl. Athlete of Yr., 1972, Golfer of Year Profl. Golfers Assn., 1973, Byron Nelson award, 1964, 65, 72, 73, Bob Jones award, 1975; named Sportsman of Year, Sports Illus. mag., 1978; named to World Golf Hall of Fame; named Athlete of the Decade for 1970-79, 1979, Golfer of the '70s, 1979, Golfer of the Century, 1988. Mem. President's Club Ohio State U., Phi Gamma Delta. Over 105 golf courses on 5 continents, 12 ranked in U.S. Top 100; hosted 185 profl. tournaments 1973—; won 71 tournaments including 20 maj. championships; maj. tournaments won include Tournament of Champions, 1963, 64, 71, 73, 77, U.S. Amateur, 1959, 61, U.S. Open, 1962, 67, 72, 80, U.S. Masters, 1963, 65, 66, 72, 75, 86, Brit. Open, 1966, 70, 78, PGA Championship, 1963, 71, 73, 75, 80, Internat. Pro-Amateur, 1973, Atlanta Golf Classic, 1973, Walt Disney World Golf Classic, 1971-73, 75, Hawaiian Open, 1974, Tournament Players Championship, 1974, 76, 78, Hawaiian Open, 1974, Doral-Eastern Open, 1975, Heritage Classic, 1975, Australian Open, 1964, 68, 71, 75, 76, 78, World Series of Golf, 1962, 63, 67, 70, 76, Gleason Inverrary Classic, 1976, 77, 78, Phila. Classic, 1965, 78, Colonial Nat. Invitational, 1982, PGA Seniors Championship, 1991, U.S. Senior Open, 1991, 93, Mercedes Sr. Championship, 1994, others. Office: Golden Bear Internat Inc 11780 US Hwy #1 North Palm Beach FL 33408*

NICKLE, DENNIS EDWIN, electronics engineer, church deacon; b. Sioux City, Iowa, Jan. 30, 1936; s. Harold Bateman and Helen Cecilia (Killackey) N. BS in Math., Fla. State U., 1961. Reliability mathematician Pratt & Whitney Aircraft Co., W. Palm Beach, Fla., 1961-63; br. supr. Melpar Inc., Falls Church, Va., 1963-66; prin. mem. tech. staff Xerox Data Systems, Rockville, Md., 1966-70; sr. tech. officer WHO, Washington, 1970-76; software tech. mgr. Melpar div. E-Systems, Inc., Falls Church, 1976-95; software process improvement mgr. Bell Atlantic, 1996—; lectr. in field. Ordained deacon Roman Catholic Ch., 1979. Chief judge for computers Fairfax County Regional Sci. Fair, 1964-88; mem. Am. Security Council; scoutmaster, commr. Boy Scouts Am., 1957-92; youth custodian Fairfax County Juvenile Ct., 1973-87; chaplain No. Va. Regional Juvenile Detention Home, 1978-88; moderator Nocturnal Adoration Soc.; parochial St. Michael's Ch., Annandale, Va., 1979-89, Christ the Redeemer, Sterling, Va., 1990-93. Served with U.S. Army, 1958-60. Recipient Eagle award, Silver award, Silver Beaver award, other awards Boy Scouts Am.; Ad Altare Dei, St. George Emblem, Diocese of Richmond. Mem. Assn. Computing Machinery, Computer Soc., Am. Soc. For Quality Control, CODSIA (mem., chmn working groups), ORLANDO II (Govt./industry working group), Old Crows Assn., Rolm Mil-Spec Computer Users Group (internat. pres.), San Antonio I (select industry coordination group), Nat. Security Indsl. Assn. (convention com. 1985-96, software quality assurance subcom., regional membership chmn. 1981-89, nat. exec. vice-chmn. 1989-94, chmn. 1994-96), Am. Security Coun., IEEE (sr., mem. standards working group in computers 1983—), Defense Software Devel. Standards Avd. Bd. (chmn. 1991-96), Soc. Software Quality, Hewlett Packard Users Group, Smithsonian Assn., Internat. Platform Assn., NRA (endowment), Nat. Eagle Scout Assn. (life), Alpha Phi Omega (life), Sigma Phi Epsilon. Club: KC (4 deg.). Author: Stress in Adolescents, 1986; co-author: Handbook for Handling Non-Productive Stress in Adolescence, Standard For Software Life Cycle Processes, IMPEESA Junior Leader Training Guide, Standard for Software Quality Assurance, 1984-91, Standard for Developing Software Life Cycle Processes, Configuration Management Procedures, Software Quality Assurance Procedures, Software Development Procedures; contbr. to profl. jours. Office: 1320 N Courthouse Rd Arlington VA 22201

NICKLES, DONALD (DON NICKLES), senator; b. Ponca City, Okla., Dec. 6, 1948; s. Robert C. and Coeweene (Bryan) N.; m. Linda L. Morrison, Sept. 5, 1968; children—Donald Lee II, Jennifer Lynn, Kim Elizabeth, Robyn Leigh. BA in Bus. Adminstrn., Okla. State U., 1971. Owner, operator Don Nickles Profl. Cleaning Svc., Stillwater, Okla., 1968-71; v.p., gen. mgr. Nickles Machine Corp., Ponca City, 1972—; mem. Okla. Senate, 1979-80; mem. U.S. Senate from Okla., 1981—, chmn. Senate Rep. policy com.; chem. Senate Rep. policy com., mem. com. on energy and natural resources,s com. on rules and adminstrn., com. on budget fin. and select com. on Indian affairs, mem. arms control observer group, coal caucus, rail caucus, rural health caucus, world climate conv. observer group, Rep. task force on nat. security and regulatory reform; passed legislation to provide for econ. and employment impact statement for all new laws and regulations. Chmn. platform com. Rep. Nat. Conv., 1992; bd. dirs. Ponca City United Way; bd. advisors Close Up Found.; mem. Kay Coun. for Retarded Children, Ponca City, St. Mary's Roman Cath. Parish Coun.; mem. adv. bd. Salvation Army, Ponca City. With USNG, 1970-76. Named one of Outstanding Young Men of Am., U.S. Jaycees, 1983. Mem. Fellowship Christian Athletes, Ponca City C. of C. Republican. Club: Rotary. Office: US Senate 133 Hart Senate Office Bldg Washington DC 20510*

NICKLIN, GEORGE LESLIE, JR., psychoanalyst, educator, physician; b. Franklin, Pa., July 25, 1925; s. George Leslie and Emma (Reed) N.; m. Katherine Mildred Aronson, Sept. 30, 1950. B.A., Haverford Coll., 1949; M.D., Columbia U., 1951; cert. in psychoanalysis, William A. White Inst., N.Y.C., 1962. Diplomate Am. Bd. Psychiatry and Neurology. Resident, then chief resident Bellevue Psychiat. Hosp., N.Y.C., 1953-56; pvt. practice specializing in psychoanalytic psychiatry, 1956—; staff Bellevue Hosp., 1956—; asst. clin. prof. psychiatry NYU Med. Sch., 1962-70, assoc. clin. prof. psychiatry, 1970—, dir. L.I. Inst. Psychoanalysis, 1978-88, dir. emeritus, 1988—; attending psychiatrist Nassau County Med. Center Clin. Campus; assoc. clin. prof. psychiatry SUNY-Stony Brook Health Sci. Ctr., 1976—; mem. Com. to Award Martin Luther King Peace Prize. Founder Friends World Coll., 1958, trustee, 1968-89. Served with AUS, 1943-46, ETO. Decorated Purple Heart with oak leaf cluster, Bronze Star with oak leaf cluster and three battle stars. Fellow Am. Acad. Psychoanalysis, Am. Psychiat. Assn.; mem. AAAS, NAACP, Soc. Med. Psychoanalysts (pres. 1986-87), White Psychoanalytic Soc., Assn. for World Edn. (charter trustee, treas. 1970-78), 9th Inf. Divsn. Assn., Vets. of the Bulge, Mil. Order of the Purple Heart. Mem. Soc. of Friends. Clubs: Gardiner's Bay Country (Shelter Island, N.Y.); Penn (London). Home and Office: 6 Butler Pl Garden City NY 11530-4603 *Education is essential to the future evolution of human society. But education alone is not enough. Integrity, creative thinking and informed action opens the path to the future.*

NICKON, ALEX, chemist, educator; b. Poland, Oct. 6, 1927; came to U.S., 1955, naturalized, 1961; s. Steve and Maria (Nickon); m. Beulah Monica Godby, Aug. 22, 1950; children—Dale Beverly, Linda Cheryl, Leanne Marie. B.Sc., U. Alta., 1949; M.A., Harvard U., 1951, Ph.D., 1953. Vis. lectr. Bryn Mawr Coll., 1953; postdoctoral fellow Birkbeck Coll., U. London, Eng., 1953-54, NRC, Ottawa, Can., 1954-55; NSF sr. fellow, Imperial Coll., London, 1963-64, U. Munich, Germany, 1971-72; mem. faculty Johns Hopkins, 1955—, prof. chemistry, 1964-94, Vernon K. Krieble prof. chemistry, 1975-94, prof. emeritus, 1994—; vis. assoc. Am. Chem. Soc. on Profl. Tng., 1975-95; mem. medicinal chem. panel NIH, 1966-70; postdoctoral panel NRC, 1968-69. Sr. editor Jour. Organic Chemistry, 1965-71; Am. exec. editor: Tetrahedron Reports, 1978-96. Recipient Md. Chemist award, 1990; Sloan Found. fellow, 1957-61. Fellow N.Y. Acad. Scis.; mem. Am. Chem. Soc. (nat. awards com. 1974-76), Brit. Chem. Soc. Home: 1009 Painters Ln Cockeysville Hunt Valley MD 21030-1729 Office: Dept Chemistry Johns Hopkins U Baltimore MD 21218-2685

NICKS, STEVIE (STEPHANIE NICKS), singer, songwriter; b. Calif., May 26, 1948. albums include: (with Lindsey Buckingham) Buckingham Nicks, 1973, (with Fleetwood Mac) Fleetwood Mac, 1975, Rumours, 1977 (co-winner, Billboard award for Album of the Year, Group of Year 1977), Tusk, 1979, Fleetwood Mac Live, 1980, Mirage, 1982, Tango in the Night, 1987, Greatest Hits, 1989, Behind The Mask, 1990, 25 Years-The Chain, 1992; (solo) Bella Donna, 1981, The Wild Heart, 1983, Rock a Little, 1985, The Other Side of the Mirror, 1989, Time Space, 1991, Street Angel, 1994; composer songs Rhiannon, 1975, Landslide, 1975, Leather and Lace, 1975, Dreams, 1977, Sara, 1979, Edge of Seventeen, 1981, If Anyone Falls (with Sandy Stewart), 1982, Stand Back (with Prince Rogers Nelson), 1983, I Can't Wait (with others), 1985, Seven Wonders (with Sandy Stewart). Office: Modern Records care WEA 111 N Hollywood Way Burbank CA 91505

NICLAS, KARL BERNHARD, electronics engineer; b. Ludenscheid, Germany, Nov. 11, 1930; came to the U.S., 1962; s. Karl Bernhard and Helene (Winterhoff) N.; m. Elka Bach, May 30, 1956; children: Joshua, Daniel. MS in Engring., Tech. U., Aachen, Germany, 1956, D in Engring., 1960. Project engr. Telefunken GmbH, Ulm, Germany, 1956-58, asst. mgr. lab., 1958-62; sr. project engr. GE Co., Palo Alto, Calif., 1962-63; mem. tech. staff Watkins-Johnson Co., Palo Alto, 1963-65, head low-noise tube sect., 1965-67, mgr. tube divsn., 1967-76, cons., 1976-90, prin. scientist, cons., 1990—. Contbg. author: Low-Noise Transistors and Amplifiers, 1981, Monolithic Microwave Integrated Circuits, 1985; mem. editl. bd.: Transactions, Microwave Theory and Techniques, 1987—. Recipient Outstanding Publs. award German Soc. Radio Engrs., 1962, Microwave prize IEEE, 1985. Mem. Microwave Theory and Techniques Soc. (sr.), Electron Devices Soc. (sr.), Solid-State Circuits Soc. (sr.). Achievements include eight patents in areas of microwave tubes, electromagnetic wave propagation and semiconductor devices; invented microwave matrix amplifier. Office: Watkins Johnson Co 3333 Hillview Ave Palo Alto CA 94304

NICOL, ROBERT DUNCAN, architect; b. La Jolla, Calif., Sept. 16, 1936; s. Duncan and Catherine (Muffly) N.; m. Susann Kay Larson; 1 child, Jennifer E. AA, Principia Coll., 1956; BArch, U. Calif., Berkeley, 1961. Registered arch., Ariz., Calif., Mont., Wash. Designer Kawneer Mfg. Co., Richmond, Calif., 1961-62, Claude Oakland, San Francisco, 1962-64; project arch. David T. Johnson, Oakland, Calif., 1964-68; pvt. practice Oakland, Calif., 1968—. Mem. bd. appeals City of Alameda, 1971-73, vice chair planning commn., 1973-77, founder, chair, vice chair design rev. bd., 1974-80, founder, chair, vice chair hist. adv. bd., 1976—, co-founder, chair, vice chair mayor's com. for handicapped, 1980-86; mem. Calif. State Access Bd., 1995—. Recipient Design award Am. Registered Archs., 1969, Harper Plz. Design award Calif. Bldg. Officials Assn., 1985. Fellow AIA; mem. Soc. Am. Registered Archs., Nat. Coun. Archtl. Registration Bds. (sr.), Alexander Graham Bell Assn. for Deaf (lectr.), Oral Hearing Impaired Sec., San Leandro Hist. Railway Soc. (founder, charter mem., chair, vice-chair), Alameda Jr. C. of C. (project dir. 1969), Alameda Victorian Preservation Soc. Republican. Office: 455 17th St Oakland CA 94612-2101

NICOLA, JAMES B., stage director, composer, playwright, lyricist; b. Worcester, Mass., Oct. 28, 1958; s. George Anthony and Settimia (Palumbo) Balko. BA cum laude, Yale U., 1980; studies with Maury Yeston, Lehman Engel. Script cons. Manhattan Theatre Club, 1980-82; assoc. dir. Am. Stage Festival, 1985; guest dir. Spokane (Wash.) Interplayers Ensemble, 1987-88; artistic dir. Youngstown Playhouse, 1988-89; vis. asst. prof., guest dir. U. Mont., Missoula, 1987, 91; dir. Ark. Reportory Theatre, 1992, Worcester Foothills Theatre, Mass., 1990-92, Heritage Repertory, Charlottesville, Va., 1990, Telluride (Colo.) Repertory Theatre, 1992, 93, 94, 95; dir. Indsl. Arts Theater, Denver, 1993, 94, 96; resident dir. Mint Theatre Co., N.Y.C., 1993—; dir. Nat. Shakespeare Co., 1995-96. Dir. (plays) (with Tony Musante) Italian Funerals and Other Festive Occasions, The Sunshine Boys, Hamlet, Madwoman of Chaillot, Tartuffe, Learned Ladies, Merry Wives of Windsor, Macbeth, Long Day's Journey Into Night, Lady Windermere's Fan, The Importance of Being Earnest, The House of Bernarda Alba, All My Sons, The Menaechmi, Amadeus (Pierrot award for Best Dir./Best Profn. 1987), Romeo and Juliet, The Attic, Children of a Lesser God, Steel Magnolias, Hannah Davis, Noises Off, Rapid Transit, The Elephant Man, Diary of Anne Frank, Measure for Measure, Uncle Vanya, Much Ado About Nothing, Fat Lucy; (mus.) Anything Goes, Kiss Me Kate, A Little Night Music, I Do!, Working, You're a Good Man Charlie Brown, My Fair Lady, Into the Woods; composer: Round for Four, 1987, The Tempest, Goodbye Columbus Ave.; playwright: Donuts, 1987. Madolin Cervantes grantee, SDC Workshop Found., 1984, 87, Meet the Composers grantee, 1987; semi-finalist Christina Crawford award, U. S.D., 1987. Mem. Soc. Stage Dirs. and Choreographers, Dramatists Guild. Home and Office: 484 W 43rd St Apt 45-0 New York NY 10036-6319

NICOLA, JAMES C., theater director; b. Hartford, Conn., July 5, 1950; s. Renato Nicola and Joyce Arlene Skates Bruckner. BA, Tufts U., 1972. Adminstrv. asst. Theatre Comms. Group, N.Y.C., 1973-75; casting asst. N.Y. Shakespeare Festival, N.Y.C., 1975-78, casting coord., 1978-80; NEA dir. fellow Arena Stage, Washington, 1980-81, producing assoc., 1981-88; artistic dir. N.Y. Theatre Workshop, N.Y.C., 1988—; freelance dir. WPA Theatre, N.Y.C., 1974-77, Studio Theatre, Washington, 1986, New Playwrights Theatre, Washington, 1981-85, Round House Theatre, Washington, 1987. Recipient Cmty. Svc. award League of Washington Theaters, 1988, Obie award Village Voice, 1991. Democrat. Office: NY Theatre Workshop 79 E 4th St New York NY 10003

NICOLAI, EUGENE RALPH, public relations consultant, editor, writer; b. Renton, Wash., June 26, 1911; s. Eugene George and Josephine (Heidinger) N.; student U. Wash., 1929, Whitman Coll., 1929-30; B.A., U. Wash., 1934; postgrad. Am. U., 1942; M.A., George Washington U., 1965; m. Helen Margaret Manogue, June 5, 1935; 1 son, Paul Eugene. Editor, U. Wash. Daily, Seattle, 1934; asst. city editor, writer, nat. def. editor Seattle Times, 1934-41; writer Sta. KJR, Seattle, 1937-39; writer, editor, safety edn. officer Bur. Mines, Washington, 1941-45; news dir. Grand Coulee Dam and Columbia Basin Project, Washington, 1945-50; regional info. dir. Bur. Mines, Denver and Pitts., 1950-55, asst. chief mineral reports, Washington, 1955-61, news dir. office of oil and gas, 1956-57; sr. info. officer, later sr. public info. officer Office Sec. Interior, Washington, 1961-71, staff White House Nat. Conf. on Natural Beauty, spl. detail to White House, 1971, ret.; now public relations cons., tech. editor, writer. Formerly safety policy adviser Interior Dept.; com. mem. Internat. Cooperation Year, State Dept., 1971. With George Washington U. Alumni Found.; founder, mng. dir. Josephine Nature Preserve; pres. Media Assocs. Bd. dirs. Wash. State Council on Alcoholism; adviser Pierce Transit Authority, Pierce County Growth Mgmt., Pierce County Ethics Commn. Named Disting. Alumnus, recipient Penrose award, both Whitman Coll., 1979. Mem. Nature Conservancy, Wash. Environ. Council, Nat. Audubon Soc. (Am. Belgian Tervuren dist. rep.), Crook County (Oreg.) Hist. Soc., Washington State Hist. Soc., Emerald Shores Assn, Sigma Delta Chi, Pi Kappa Alpha. Presbyn. Clubs: George Washington U., Purdy (pres.). Lodge: Masons. Author: The Middle East Emergency Committee; editor: Fed. Conservation Yearbooks. Home: 9809 N Seminole Dr Spokane WA 99208-8608

NICOLAÏ, JUDITHE, international business trade executive; b. Lawrence, Mass., Dec. 15, 1945; d. Victor and Evelyn (Otash) Abisalih. Student in photography, L.A. City Coll., 1967, UCLA, 1971; AA in Fgn. Langs., Coll. of Marin, 1983; hon. degree, Culinary Inst., San Francisco, 1981. Photographer Scott Paper Co., N.Y.C., 1975; owner, operator restaurant The Raincheck Room, West Hollywood, Calif., 1976; prin., pres., chief exec. officer, photographer fashion Photographie sub. Nicolaï Internat. Svcs., Nice, France, 1977—; prin., pres., chief exec. officer, instr. catering and cooking Back to Basics sub. Nicolaï Internat. Svcs., San Francisco, 1980—; chief photographer exhibit and trade show, chief of staff food div. Agri-Bus. U.S.A., Moscow and Washington, 1983; head transp. U.S. Summer Olympics, L.A., 1984, interpreter for Spanish, French, Portuguese, and Italian, 1985; prin., pres., chief exec. officer, interpreter Intertrans subs. (Nicolaï Internat. Svcs.), San Francisco, 1985—; founder, pres. Nicolaï Internat. Svcs., San Francisco, 1985—; pres., CEO Cyprus Personal Care Products, 1994—. Contbr. column on food and nutrition to jour., 1983-84. Mem. Alpha Gamma Sigma. Avocations: cooking, fencing, swimming, golf, photography. Office: Nicolai Internat Svcs 1686 Union St Ste 203 San Francisco CA 94123-4509 Mailing Address: 2269 Chestnut St Ste 237 San Francisco CA 94123-2607

NICOLAIDES, MARY, lawyer; b. N.Y.C., June 7, 1927; d. George and Dorothy Nicolaides. BCE, CUNY, 1947; MBA with distinction, DePaul U., 1975, JD, 1981. Bar: Ill. 1982, U.S. Dist. Ct. (no. dist.) Ill. 1982, U.S. Patent Office 1983. Sr. design engr. cement subs. U.S. Steel Corp., N.Y.C., then Pitts., 1948-71; sole practice Chgo., 1982—. Mem. ABA. Republican. Greek Orthodox. Address: 233 E Erie St Ste 1804 Chicago IL 60611

NICOLAOU, K. C., chemistry educator; b. Karavas, Kyrenia, Cyprus, June 5, 1946; came to U.S., 1972; s. Costa and Helen (Yettimi) N.; m. Georgette Karayianni, July 15, 1973; children: Colette, Alexis, Christopher, Paul. BSc, Bedford Coll., London, 1969; PhD, U. Coll., London, 1972; DSc, U. London, 1994; PhD (hon.), U. Athens, 1995. Rsch. assoc. Columbia U., N.Y.C., 1972-73, Harvard U., Cambridge, Mass., 1973-76; from asst. prof. to Rhodes-Thompson prof. chemistry U. Pa., Phila., 1976-89; Darlene Shiley prof. chemistry, chmn. dept. The Scripps Rsch. Inst., La Jolla, Calif., 1989—; prof. chemistry U. Calif. at San Diego, La Jolla, 1989—; vis. prof. U. Paris, 1986; mem. exec. com. Diann. Cyprus Conf. on Drug Design; mem. med. study sect. D, NIH, 1988-90; mem. internat. adv. bd. Angewandte Chemie, 1994—. Author: (with N. A. Petasis) Selenium in Natural Products Synthesis, 1984, (with E. J. Sorensen) Classics in Total Synthesis, 1996; co-editor: Synthesis, Germany, 1984-90, Chemistry and Biology, 1994; editl. bd. Prostaglandins, Leukotrienes and Medicine, 1978-88, Synthesis, 1990—, Accounts of Chem. Rsch., 1992—, Carbohydrate Letters, 1993—, Chemistry-A European Jour., 1994—, Perspectives in Drug, Discovery and Design, 1994—, Indian Jour. of Chemistry, Sect. B, 1995—; mem. bd. consulting editors Tetrahedron Publs., 1992—; mem. adv. bd. Contemporary Organic Synthesis, 1993—; mem. regional adv. bd. J. C. S. Chem. Comm., 189—, J. C. S. Perkin I, 1991—; contbr. articles to profl. jours.; patentee in field. Recipient Japan Soc. for Promotion Sci. award 1987-88, U.S. Sr. Scientist award Alexander von Humboldt Found., 1987-88, Alan R. Day award Phila. Organic Chemists Club, 1993, Pfizer Rsch. award, 1993-94, Paul Janssen Prize, 1994, Alexander the Great Award Hellenic Cultural Soc. of San Diego, 1994, Rhone-Poulenc medal Royal Soc. of Chemistry, 1995, Chem. Pioneer Am. Inst. of Chemists, 1996, Inhoffen Medal of Gesellscaft fur Biotechnologische Forschung mbH (GBF) Tech. U. of Braunschweig, 1996; fellow A.P. Sloan Found., 1979-83, J. S. Guggenheim Found., 1984; Camille and Henry Dreyfus scholar, 1980-84, Arthur C. Cope scholar, 1987. Fellow N.Y. Acad. Scis., AAAS; mem. Am. Chem. Soc. (Creative Work in Synthetic Organic Chemistry award 1993, William H. Nichols medal N.Y. sect. 1996, Ernest Guenther award in chemistry of natural products 1996), Chem. Soc. London, German Chem. Soc., Japanese Chem. Soc. Office: Scripps Rsch Inst Dept Chemistry 10550 N Torrey Pines Rd LaJolla CA 92037

NICOLAS, KENNETH LEE, international business executive; b. San Francisco, Feb. 7, 1944; s. Norman L. and Bernice L. (Hameister) N.; m. Anne Vanderwielen, July 5, 1992; children: Juliana M., Camille G. BA in Polit. Sci., Calif. State U., Fullerton, 1968; MA in Legis. Affairs/Econs., George Washington U., 1975. Exec. asst. Congressman Richard T. Hanna, Washington, 1970-72; sr. staff assoc. Nat. Assn. Ednl. Broadcasters, Washington, 1972-74; founder, pres. Nicolas Assocs. Internat., Inc., 1972; exec. dir. Am. Coll. Nuclear Physicians, Washington, 1974-77; aide to the Pres. White House, Washington, 1977-80; v.p. McSweeney & Co. Consulting, Newport Beach, Calif., 1980-83, L.E. Peterson & Co. Investment Banking, Costa Mesa, Calif., 1983-85; pres. Fin. Strategies Group, Inc., Newport Beach, 1985—; CEO Tradex Internat., Inc., Newport Beach, 1988-94; founder, CEO Trade Access Group, Inc., 1994—; bd. dirs. Amtrex Corp., Irvine, Calif.; adj. prof. Orange Coast Coll., Costa Mesa, 1984—, internat. MBA program U. So. Calif., 1989-90, Thunderbird Sch. Internat. Bus., Orange County, 1990-92; mem. exec. bd. Japan Am. Soc., 1995—. Author: (article series) Business to Business Mag., 1984-87 (Excellence award 1984-87). 10K race dir. Leukemia Soc. Am., Orange County, Calif., 1982-86, bd. dirs., v.p., 1982-88; chmn. Holiday Project, 1992-94. With U.S. Army, 1968-70, Vietnam. Recipient Outstanding Svc. award Nat. Holiday Project, 1993, Nat. Svc. Appreciation award Pres. Jimmy Carter, 1980, Excellence award Leukemia Soc. Am., 1988. Mem. Internat. Mktg. Assn. (corp. mem., Outstanding Export award 1993), Export Mgrs. Assn. Calif. (bd. dirs. 1990—, Excellence award 1992), World Trade Ctr. Assn. of Orange County (corp. mem., com. chmn. 1983-85, Outstanding Achievement award 1983, 84), Japan Am. Soc. of Orange County (exec. bd. dirs. 1995—). Avocations: karate (Shito-Ryu black belt 2d degree), sailing, travel, triathlons, chess. Office: Trade Access Group Inc 400 MacArthur Blvd Ste 500 Newport Beach CA 92660

NICOLAU, ALEXANDRU, educator; b. Bucharest, Romania, June 7, 1957; came to U.S., 1976; s. Frederick and Silvia (Pach) N.; m. Anca Arivei, Oct. 22, 1978; children, Danielle, Rebecca. BA, Brandeis U., 1980; MA, Yale U., 1982, PhD, 1984. Asst. prof. Cornell U., Ithaca, N.Y., 1984-88; assoc. prof. U. Calif., Irvine, 1988-92, prof., 1992—. Editor-in-chief Internat. Jour. Parallel Programming, 1993—; editor: Language and Compilers for Parallel Computing, 1994, Advanced in Languages and Compilers, 1994, Parallel Language and Compiler Research in Japan, 1995; contbr. articles to profl. jours. Mem. IEEE, Assn. for Computing Machinery. Office: U Calif Campus Dr Irvine CA 94717

NICOLETTI, PAUL LEE, veterinarian, educator; b. Goodman, Mo., Oct. 26, 1932; s. Felix and Clarice Nicoletti; m. Earlene Blackburn, June 6, 1954; children: Diana, Julie, Nancy. BS in Agr., U. Mo., 1956, DVM, 1956; MS, U. Wis., 1962. Diplomate Am. Coll. Vet. Preventative Medicine. Veterinarian, U.S. Dept. Agr., Mo., Wis., N.Y., 1956-68, UN Food and Agr. Orgn., Tehran, Iran, 1968-72, U.S. Dept. Agr., Jackson, Miss., 1972-75, Gainesville, Fla., 1973-78; prof. veterinarian medicine U. Fla., Gainesville, 1978—. Contbr. numerous articles to profl. jours. Recipient awards from Fla. Cattleman's Assn., 1978, Dairy Farmers, Inc., 1978, Borden award, 1979, Gold Star award Fla. Veterinary Medicine Assoc., 1981, 1986, Universidad Austral de Chile, 1981, Puerto Rico Dairy Assn., 1978, Faculty Alumni award U. Mo., 1987; named Basic Scis. Tchr. of Yr., Nat. Student Am. Veterinary Med. Assn., 1994; Veterinarian of the Yr. award, Fla. Veterinary Med. Assn., 1994, (pres. 1995—). Mem. Am. Veterinary Medicine Assn. (int. prize 1991), Am. Assn. Bovine Practice. Home: 2552 SW 14th Dr Gainesville FL 32608-2042 Office: Univ of Fla Coll Vet Medicine PO Box 110880 Gainesville FL 32611-0880

NICOSIA, JOSEPH A., transportation company executive; b. Phila., Mar. 16, 1943; s. Frank R. and Rose (Cola) N.; m. Janet A. Aldrich, Dec. 6, 1972. BS, Pa. State U., 1965. Traffic supr. Air Products & Chems. Inc., Allentown, Pa., 1965-67; mgr., leased equipment Roadway Express, Akron, 1969-70; prin. William Kordisemon & Assocs., Chgo., 1970-72; dir. nat. accts. Rollins Leasing Corp., Wlimington, Del., 1972-80; v.p. sales, mktg. McDonnell Douglas Truck Svcs., Phila., 1980-83, Leaseway Transp., Cleve., 1983-87, Customized Transp. Inc., Jacksonville, Fla., 1987—; pres., CEO GATX Logistics, Inc., Jacksonville, Fla. Lt. USN, 1967-69. Mem. Coun. Logistics Mgmt., Warehouse Edn. Rsch. Coun., Delta Nu Alpha, Marsh Landing Country Club, Rolling Green Golf Club. Home: 7525 Founders Way Ponte Vedra Beach FL 32082 Office: GATX Logistics Inc 1301 River Place Blvd Jacksonville FL 32207-9047*

NICOTRA, JOSEPH CHARLES, artist; b. Corona, N.Y., Aug. 9, 1931; s. Charles C. and Constanta (Maglienti) N.; m. Mary C. Losquadro, Sept. 9, 1951; children: Therese, Nanette, Marie. Student, Art Students League, N.Y.C., 1955-59, Art Students League, Woodstock, N.Y., 1959-60, Am. Art Sch., N.Y.C., 1960-61; diploma of merit, U. Art, Italy, 1982. Registered artist, N.Y.C., GSA, Met. Transp. Authority N.Y. Freelance easel painter N.Y.C., 1962—. One-man shows include Armstrong Mural Gallery, Flushing, N.Y., 1968, La Galerie Mouffe, Paris, 1976, Long Beach Artists Assn. Gallery, N.Y.C., 1978, 79, Long Beach Libr. Art Gallery, 1979, Cam Art Ctr., Bayshore, N.Y., 1982, Pricilla Redford Roe Gallery, Suffork, N.Y., 1982, Queens Mus., 1982, 84, Pla. Del Malfestazione, Italy, 1983, 6th Internat. Biennale, Garbo, Bulgaria, 1983, Flushing Coun. on Culture and Arts, 1986, Atlanta Gallery Generve, 1987 (Primo Milano Gold medal 1988), St. Paul's Ch., Beth Page, N.Y., 1992, "Time Capsule-Schedule Mail Call" from the People of the Borough of Queens, 1992 A.D., for 2292 A.D.; exhibited in group shows at Art Students League 57th St. Gallery, N.Y., 1957, A.S.L. Woodstock N.Y. Gallery, 1961, Long Beach (N.Y.) Mus., 1976, Flushing Coun. on Culture and Arts, 1986; represented in permanent collections Nat. Archives, Washington, Queens Mus. Art; prin. works include mural for Queens Mus. Title Wall for Nat. Travel Show; contbrs. Smithsonian Inst. Kennedy Gallery. Vol. Artist, tchr., docent, lectr. Queens Mus. Art, Flushing, N.Y., 1972—. With U.S. Army, 1952-54; mem. Queens Coun. Arts, Flushing Coun. Culture and Arts. Recipient Outstanding Svc. award Queens Mus. Art, 1972-91, 1st prize for Oil, Long Beach Mus., 1976; Bernsay scholar, 1958, scholar VA, 1959, 1st prize Long Beach Artists Assn., 1980, Accademia delle Art Gold medal, Italy, 1980, Gold medal for Safety, Peace & Artist Merit, Internat. Parliament, U.S.A., 1983, Accademia D'Europa award, 1983, Statue of Victory, Com. for World Culture, 1984, European Banner of Arts award 1985, Gold Plaque award Italian Accademia, 1987. Mem. Art Students League (life), Orgn. Ind. Artists, Internat. Confedn. Order of Artists (hon.), Queens Mus. Art (hon.), DAV (life). Home and Studio: 59-32 156th St Flushing NY 11355-5517

NIDA, JANE BOLSTER (MRS. DOW HUGHES NIDA), retired librarian; b. Chgo., July 19, 1918; d. Chalmer A. and Elsie R. (Sonderman) Bolster; m. Dow Hughes Nida, Sept. 1, 1946; 1 child, Janice Beth (Mrs. Robert M. Michaels). B.A., Aurora (Ill.) U., 1942; B.S. in Library Sci, U. Ill., 1943. Circulation librarian Aurora Pub. Library, 1940-42, 43-44, reference librarian, 1946; program dir. A.R.C., Eng., France, 1944-46; acquisitions librarian Ohio U., Athens, 1947; dir. Falls Church (Va.) Pub. Library, 1951-54; asst. dir. Arlington County Dept. Libraries, Arlington, Va., 1954-57; dir. Arlington County Dept. Libraries, 1957-80; on loan to AID, 1979-80; Mem. Va. Adv. Legis. Council, Com. to Revise State Library Laws, 1968-69, Women's Joint Congl. Com., 1968-80. Vol. Am. Cancer Soc., 1971-84, bd. dirs. Arlington chpt., 1974-84; mem. exec. com. Regional Adv. Group, Va. Regional Med. Program, 1971-76; v.p., founder, dir. Cultural Laureate Found. Recipient Meritorious Service award A.R.C., World War II, Outstanding Alumnus award Aurora U., 1979. Mem. AAUW, ALA, D.C. Libr. Assn., Va. Libr. Assn. (pres. 1969-70), Arlington Hist. Soc. (charter, bd. dirs. 1989-93), Army-Navy Country Club. Baptist. Home: 4907 29th St N Arlington VA 22207-2755 also: 1617 Bayhouse Ct #218 Sarasota FL 34231-6771

NIE, ZENON STANLEY, manufacturing company executive; b. Chgo., Nov. 19, 1950; m. Carol Ann Klockowski, Mar. 27, 1970; 1 child, Andrea Nicole. BS, U Ill., Chgo., 1971; MBA, Loyola U., Chgo., 1974. Mgr. sales stats. Zenith Electronics, Chgo., 1971-74; mktg. mgr. Hollister, Inc., Chgo., 1974-79; dir. market devel. Sealy, Inc., Chgo., 1979-81; sr. v.p. Serta, Inc., Chgo., 1981-89, exec. v.p., 1988-89, pres., 1989-91; pres. The Bibb Co., Macon, Ga., 1991-93; chm. pres. Ceo Simmons Co., 1993—; instr. Coll. of Lake County, Ill., 1978-81. Mem. Internat. Sleep Products Assn. (chmn. stats. com. 1985—). Avocations: scuba diving, fishing, skiing, jogging. Office: Simmons One Concourse Pky Ste 600 Atlanta GA 30328*

NIECE, RICHARD DEAN, academic administrator; b. Oberlin, Ohio, Nov. 1, 1946; s. Lewis H. and Dortha (Geyer) N. BS in Edn., Ohio State U., 1968; MEd, Kent State U., 1976, PhD, 1988. Cert. supt., prin., tchr. Curriculum dir. Brunswick (Ohio) City Schs., 1982-85; asst. prof. Kent (Ohio) State U., 1985-87; sr. v.p. and provost Walsh U., North Canton, Ohio, 1987—, assoc. prof. Contbr. articles to profl. jours. Mem. ASCD, Phi Delta Kappa. Home: 3311-E Mariners Island DrNW Canton OH 44708-3091 Office: Walsh U 2020 Easton St NW Canton OH 44720-3336

NIED, THOMAS H., publishing company executive; b. Queens, N.Y., May 4, 1942; s. Herman Joseph and Margaret (Jos) N.; m. Carol J. Thomas, June 6, 1964; children: Stacey, Allison. BA, Rutgers U., 1964, LLB, 1967; LLM in Taxation, NYU, 1972. CPA, N.J., Ga. Tax mgr. Ernst & Young, N.Y.C., Atlanta, Newark and Trenton, N.J., 1968-77, N.Y. Times Co., N.Y.C., 1977—. Mem. ABA, AICPA, Tax Execs. Inst. (bd. dirs. 1986-91, pres. N.Y. chpt. 1991-92, exec. com. 1992-93), Newspaper Assn. of Am. (chmn. tax com. 1995-96, mem. pub. policy com. 1995-96). Avocations: travel, reading, philately, tennis. Home: 31 Vreeland Ct Princeton NJ 08540-6760 Office: NY Times Co 229 W 43rd St New York NY 10036-3913

NIEDEL, JAMES E., pharmaceuticals executive; b. Milw., Mar. 30, 1944; m. Selaine Benaim, Mar. 11, 1969; children: Ian Edward, Felisa Ann, Shira Beth. BS, U. Wis., 1965; MD, U. Miami, 1973, PhD, 1974. Diplomate Am. Bd. Internal Medicine. Scientist Burroughs-Wellcome, Research Triangle Park, N.C., 1977-80; prof. medicine Duke U., Durham, N.C., 1980-89; v.p. rsch. Glaxo Rsch. Inst., Research Triangle Park, 1989-92, sr. v.p. R & D, 1992-95; bd. dirs. Glaxo Wellcome plc, London, 1995—; chmn., CEO Glaxo Wellcome R & D Ltd., Greenford, U.K., 1995—; chmn. Affymax Tech. N.V., 1995—. Bd. overseers Duke Cancer Ctr., Durham, 1990—. Searle scholar, 1981-84; recipient Career Devel. award NIH, 1981-84. Mem. Am. Soc. Clin. Investigation, Am. Soc. Biochemistry and Molecular Biology, Am. Soc. Immunology. Office: Glaxo Wellcome R&D PO Box 13408 5 Moore Dr Research Triangle Park NC 27709

NIEDERAUER, GEORGE H., bishop; b. Los Angeles, CA, June 14, 1936; s. George and Elaine N. B.A. Philosophy, St. John's Seminary, Camarillo, CA, 1959; B.A. Sacred Theology, Catholic U., Washington, DC, 1962; M.A. English Lit., Loyola U., Los Angeles, CA, 1962; Ph.D. English Lit., USC, 1966. ordained priest April 30, 1962; named prelate of honor (monsignor) 1984; named bishop of Diocese of Salt Lake City, Nov. 3, 1994. Asst. pastor Our Lady of the Assumption Parish, Claremont, CA, 1962-63; priest in residence Holy Name of Jesus Parish, Los Angeles, CA, 1963-65; instr. English Lit. St. John's Seminary Coll., Camarillo, CA, 1965-79; instr. of English Lit. Mt. St. Mary's Coll., Los Angeles, CA, 1967-74; English Dept. chmn. St. John's Seminary Coll., Camarillo, CA, 1968-77; spiritual dir. St. John's Seminary Coll., 1972-79; part-time instr. of Spiritual Theology St. John's Seminary Theologate, 1976-79, full-time instr. of Spiritual Theology, 1979-87; part-time instr. of English Lit. St. John's Seminary Coll., 1979-92; rector St. John's Seminary, 1987-92, spiritual dir., 1979—; co-dir. Cardinal Manning House of Prayer for Priests, Los Angeles, CA, 1992—; mem. Nat. Fedn. of Spiritual Dirs. (pres. 1975-77); mem. Alpha Sigma Nu (Jesuit Honor Soc. - LMU Chapter); pres. Western Assn. of Spiritual Dirs., 1973-75; mem. bd. of the Comm. of Priests' Retreat, Archdiocese of Los Angeles; mem. select comm. for the revision of the U.S. Catholic Conf. "Program for Priestly Formation" 3rd edition; mem. Vatican Visitation Team for Theologates; speaker World Vision Internat, Fuller Theological Seminary, Calif. Lutheran Coll.; mem. Camarillo Ministerial Assn. Avocations include: classical music, stamp collecting, reading, film appreciation. Office: Chancery Office 27 C St Salt Lake City UT 84103

NIEDERHUBER, JOHN EDWARD, surgical oncologist and molecular immunologist, university educator and administrator; b. Steubenville, Ohio, June 21, 1938; s. William Henry and Helen (Smittle) N.; m. Tracey J. Williamson; children: Elizabeth Ann, Matthew John. B.S., Bethany Coll., 1960; M.D., Ohio State U., 1964. Diplomate Am. Bd. Surgery. Internship, surgery Ohio State U. Hosp., Columbus, 1964-65; resident, surgery U. Mich. Med. Ctr., Ann Arbor, 1967-69, NIH acad. trainee in surgery, 1969-71, resident, surgery, 1971-72, chief resident surgery, 1972-73, asst. prof. surgery and asst. prof. microbiology, 1973-77, dir. transplantation program, 1975-76, assoc. prof. surgery and assoc. prof. microbiology, 1977-80, chief divsn. surg. oncology and transplantation, sect. gen. surgery, 1979-82, sr. assoc. dean med. sch., 1983-86, assoc. dean research, 1982-86, chief divsn. surg. oncology sect. gen. surgery, 1982-86, prof. surgery, prof. microbiology and immunology, 1980-87; cons. Wayne County Gen. Hosp. Mich., 1973-84; cons. surgery Ann Arbor VA Hosp., 1973-87; prof. surgery, oncology, molecular biology and genetics The Johns Hopkins U. Sch. Med., Baltimore, 1987-91; Emile Holman prof. surgery, chair, dept. surgery, head sect. surgical scis. Stanford (Calif.) U. Sch. Medicine., 1991—, prof. microbiology and immunology, 1991—; chief of surgery Stanford (Calif.) U. Hosp., 1991—; dir. Comp. Cancer Ctr. Stanford (Calif.) Med. Ctr., 1991—; vis. prof. Howard Hughes Med. Inst. Dept. Molecular Biology and Genetics The Johns Hopkins U. Sch. Medicine, Baltimore, 1986-87. Authored books on cancer; mem. editorial bd. Jour. Immunology, 1981-85, Jour. Surg. Res., 1989—, Current Opinion in Oncology, 1989—, Annals of Surgery, 1991—, Surg. Oncology, 1991—, Cancer, 1992—, Jour. Clin. Oncology, 1993, Annals of Surg. Oncology, 1993—, Jour. Am. Coll. Surgeons, 1994—; contbr. articles to profl. jours. Active NCI divsn. Cancer Treatment Bd. Scientific Councilors, 1986-91, chmn., 1987-91, Gen. Motors Cancer Rsch. Found. Awards Assembly, 1988-92. Served to capt. U.S. Army, 1965-67. Recipient USPHS Rsch. Career Devel. award Nat. Inst. Allergy and Infectious Disease, 1974-79, Disting. Faculty Svc. award U. Mich., 1978, Alumni Achievement award Ohio State U. Coll. Medicine, 1989, Alumni Achievement award in Medicine Bethany Coll., 1995; vis. rsch. fellow divsn. immunobiology Karolinska Inst., Stockholm, 1970-71, Am. Cancer Soc. Jr. Faculty Clin. fellow, 1977-79. Fellow ACS; mem. Am. Soc. Transplant Surgeons, Transplantation Soc., Am. Surg. Assn., Am. Assn. Immunologists, Coller Surg. Soc., Soc. Univ. Surgeons, Assn. Acad. Surgeons, Soc. Surg. Oncology, Ctrl. Surg. Soc., Am. Assn. Cancer Rsch., Am. Soc. Clin. Oncology, Soc. Clin. Surgery, Biology Club II, Robert M. Zollinger-Ohio State U. Surg. Soc., Pacific Coast Surg. Assn. Avocations: tennis, golf, gardening. Office: Stanford Univ Sch Medicine Dept of Surgery MSOB X300 Stanford CA 94304-5408

NIEDERJOHN, RUSSELL JAMES, electrical and computer engineering educator; b. Schenectady, June 13, 1944; s. Russell Kelly and Jeanette Ody (Burnison) N.; m. Susan A Swenson, June 7, 1969; children: Matthew Scott, Jeremy Michael. B.S. in Elec. Engring., U. Mass., Amherst, 1967, M.S. in Elec. Engring., 1968, Ph.D. in Elec. Engring., 1971. Registered profl. engr., Wis. Research asst. elec. engring. dept. U. Mass., Amherst, 1968-71; asst. prof. elec. engring. dept. Marquette U., Milw., 1971-75, assoc. prof., 1975-80, prof. elec. engring. and computer sci., dir. computer sci. and engring., 1980-87, prof., chmn. elec. and computer engring. dept., 1987-94; prof. elec. and computer engring. dept., 1994—; dir. speech and signal processing lab. Marquette U., Milw., 1973—, co-dir. signal processing rsch. ctr., 1991—; cons. William C. Brown Co. Pubs., Dubuque, Iowa, 1981-85, Eaton Corp., Milw., 1978-85, Seaman Nuclear Corp., Milw., 1979-81, 92-93, MacMillan Pubs., Encino, Calif., 1983-86. Contbr. articles to profl. jours. Mem. Milw. Ednl. TV Auction Com., 1978-81. Recipient Dow Outstanding Young Faculty award, 1977, award Western Electric Fund, 1981, Marquette U. Faculty award for teaching excellence, 1988. Fellow IEEE (mem. exec. com. Milw. sect. 1974-75, 76-79, 82-89, treas. 1982-83, sec. 1983-84, vice chmn. 1984-85, chmn. 1985-86, edn. chmn. 1977-80, chmn. nominating com. 1986-87, awards chmn. 1987-89, Meml. award 1979); mem. IEEE Signal Processing Soc., IEEE Computer Soc. (bd. dirs. Milw. chpt. 1981-85), IEEE Ind. Elec. Soc. (adminstrv. com. 1986—, edn. com. 1986-89, soc. chpt. coord. 1989-91, assoc. editor Trans. 1988—, v.p. for confs. 1992, v.p. for pubs. 1993, v.p. adminstrn. 1994-95, pres. 1996—, IEEE Systems, Man and Cybernetics Soc. (bd. dirs. Milw. chpt. 1975-79), Am. Soc. Engring. Edn. (exec. com. North Midwest sect. 1974-89), Acoustical Soc. Am., Milw. Symposium on Automatic Control (program chmn. 1975), Sigma Xi (pres. elect Marquette U. chpt. 1986-87, pres. 1987-88, sci. achievement award 1993), Eta Kappa Nu (C. Holmes MacDonald Outstanding Elec. Engring. Prof. in U.S. 1978, Marquette U. chpt. adv. 1986—, bd. dirs. 1993-95), Tau Beta Pi. Home: 2545 S Brookside Pky New Berlin WI 53151-2907 Office: 1515 W Wisconsin Ave Milwaukee WI 53233-2222

NIEDERMAN, JAMES CORSON, physician, educator; b. Hamilton, Ohio, Nov. 27, 1924; s. Clifford Frederick and Henrietta (Corson) N.; m. Miriam Camp, Dec. 12, 1951; children—Timothy Porter, Derrick Corson, Eliza Orton, Caroline Noble. Student, Kenyon Coll., 1942-45, D.Sc. (hon.), 1981; M.D., Johns Hopkins U., 1949. Intern Johns Hopkins Hosp., Balt., 1949-50; asst. resident in medicine Yale-New Haven Med. Center, 1950-51, assoc. resident, 1953-55; med. ctr. practice specializing in internal medicine, infectious disease and clin. epidemiology New Haven, 1955—; instr. Yale U., 1955-58, asst. prof., 1958-66, assoc. prof., 1966-76, clin. prof. medicine and epidemiology, 1976—; mem. Nat. Coun. for Johns Hopkins Medicine. Trustee Kenyon Coll.; bd. counselors Smith Coll., 1970-77; mem. Alumni Coun. Johns Hopkins U.; mem. Conn. Soc. of Arts and Scis. Served to 1st lt. M.C. U.S. Army, 1951-53. Fellow Silliman Coll., Yale U. Fellow Am. Coll. Epidemiology; mem. Infectious Diseases Soc. Am., Am. Epidemiol. Soc., Johns Hopkins Med. and Surg. Assn.,. Democrat. Episcopalian. Clubs: Yale (N.Y.C.); New Haven Lawn. Research in clin. epidemiology. Home: 429 Sperry Rd Bethany CT 06524-3544 Office: 60 College St New Haven CT 06510-3210

NIEDERREITER, HARALD GUENTHER, mathematician, researcher; b. Vienna, June 7, 1944; s. Simon and Erna (Emig) N.; m. Gerlinde Hollweger, Aug. 30, 1969. PhD, U. Vienna, 1969. Asst. prof. So. Ill. U., Carbondale, 1969-72, assoc. prof., 1972-73; mem. Inst. Advanced Study, Princeton, N.J., 1973-75; vis. prof. UCLA, 1975-76; prof. U. Ill., Urbana, 1976-78, U. W.I., Kingston, Jamaica, 1978-81; researcher Austrian Acad. Scis., Vienna, 1981-89, dir. Inst. Info. Processing, 1989—; mem. math. & info. scis. panel TMR Tng. Grants EU Commn., Brussels, 1995—, chmn., 1996—, TMR Networks, 1995—. Author: Uniform Distribution of Sequences, 1974, Russian transl., 1985, Finite Fields, 1983, Russian transl., 1988, Introduction to Finite Fields and Their Applications, 1986, rev. edit., 1994, Random Number Generation and Quasi-Monte Carlo Methods, 1992 (Outstanding Simulation Publ. award 1995), Monte Carlo and Quasi-Monte Carlo Methods in Scientific Computing, 1995; contbr. more than 210 rsch. articles to math. jours.; assoc. editor Maths. of Computation, 1988—, ACM Trans. Modeling and Computer Simulation, 1990—, Fibonacci Quar., 1995—; mem. editl. bd. Caribbean Jour. Math., 1982—, Applicable Algebra, 1990—, Stochastic Optimization and Design, 1991—, Jour. Ramanujan Math. Soc., 1991—, Acta Arithmetica, 1992—, Monatshefte Math., 1993—, Finite Fields and Their Applications, 1993—, Jour. Info. and Optimization Scis., 1995—, Jour. Complexity, 1996—. Named hon. prof. U. Vienna, 1986. Mem. Am. Math. Soc., Austrian Math. Soc., Austrian Acad. Scis., Internat. Assn. Cryptologic Rsch., Austrian Computer Soc., Gesellschaft für Informatik, Soc. Indsl. Applied Math. Home: Sieveringer Str 41, A1190 Vienna Austria Office: Austrian Acad Scis, Sonnenfelsgasse 19, A1010 Vienna Austria

NIEDZIELSKI, HENRI ZYGMUNT, French and English language educator; b. Troyes, France, Mar. 30, 1931; came to U.S., 1956, naturalized, 1963; s. Zygmunt and Anna (Pelik) N.; children: Henri Zygmunt, Daniel Domenic, Robert Nicholas, Anna-Pia Irene. B.A., U. Conn., 1959, M.A., 1963, Ph.D., 1964. Instr. U. Mass., 1962-64, asst. prof., 1965-66; free-lance interpreter, 1960—; asst. prof. U. Laval, Quebec, Can., 1964-65; assoc. prof. U. Hawaii, 1966-72, prof., 1972-90, chmn. div. French, 1968-70, prof. emeritus; linguistic specialist NDEA, Edn. Profl. Devel. Act, 1963-69; Fulbright lectr. linguistics and TESL Krakow, Poland, 1972-74, Bujumbura, Burundi, 1980-81, Poznan, Poland, 1990-92; guest prof. Avignon, France, 1983-84, Bonn, Fed. Republic Germany, 1986-87; Disting. fellow Auckland U., New Zealand, 1989. Author: Le Roman de Helcanus, 1966, Basic French: A Programmed Course, 1968, Handbook of French Structure; A Systematic Review, 1968, Intermediate French: An Individualized Course, 1972, The Silent Language of France, 1975, French Sound Visuals, 1976; Films on Polish Body Language, 1989; editor: Language and Literature in Hawaii, 1968-72, Jean Misrahi Memorial Volume: Studies in Medieval Languages and Literature, 1977, Studies on the Seven Sages of Rome, 1978; assoc. editor: The Phonetician, 1994—. Pres. Family Counseling Center Hawaii, 1968-70; chmn. bd. Family Edn. Centers Hawaii, 1969-72. Served with French Armored Cav., 1951-53. Mem. MLA, Am. Translators Assn., Am. Assn. Tchrs. French (pres. Hawaii chpt. 1981-83), Am. Coun. Tchg. Fgn. Langs. (dir. 1970-72), Internat. Sociol. Assn., Hawaii Assn. Lang. Tchrs. (pres. 1968-69), Chopin Soc. Hawaii (dir. 1990—), Alliance Française Hawaii (pres. 1978-80), Hawaii Assn. Translators (founding pres.s 1982—), Hawaii Second Lang. Articulation Com. (chmn. 1986-89), Rotary, Elks, Phi Beta Kappa, Pi Delta Phi, Phi Kappa Phi, Sigma Delta Pi. *There is more than one way to help people but there is only one way to live: Help people.*

NIEFELD, JAYE SUTTER, advertising executive; b. Mpls., May 27, 1924; s. Julius and Sophia (Rosenfeld) N.; m. Piri Elizabeth Von Zabrana-Szilagy, July 5, 1947; 1 child, Peter Wendell. Cert., London U., 1945; B.A., U. Minn., 1948; B.S., Georgetown U., 1949; Ph.D., U. Vienna, 1951. Project dir. Bur. Social Sci. Research, Washington, 1952-54; research dir. McCann-Erickson, Inc., N.Y.C., 1954-57; v.p., dir. mktg. Keyes, Madden & Jones, Chgo., 1957-60; pres., dir. Niefeld, Paley & Kuhn, Inc., Chgo., 1961-71; exec. v.p. Bozell, Inc., Chgo., 1971-89; pres. The Georgetown Group, Inc., 1991—; cons. U.S. Dept. State, Commerce, HEW, also others; lectr. Columbia U., Northwestern U., U. Chgo., 1989-94; chmn. Ctr. Advanced Comm. Rsch.; pres. Glencoe Angus Farms, J&J Enterprises, The Georgetown Group Inc., 1991; bd. dirs. Mktg. Decisions, Inc., E. Morris Comms., Inc. Author: The Making of an Advertising Campaign, 1989; (with others) Marketing's Role in Scientific Management, 1957, Advertising and Marketing to Young People, 1965, The Ultimate Overseas Business Guide for Growing Companies, 1990; contbr. articles to profl. jours. Mem. adv. bd. Glencoe Family Svc.; bd. dirs. Big Bros. Met. Chgo.; exec. v.p. City of Hope. Capt. AUS, 1942-46. Decorated Bronze Star. Mem. Am. Assn. Pub. Opinion Rsch., Am. Film Inst., Am. Mktg. Assn., Am. Sociol. Assn., Smithsonian Instn. Home: 1011 Bluff St Glencoe IL 60022-1120

NIEFORTH, KARL ALLEN, university dean, educator; b. Melrose, Mass., July 7, 1936; s. Reginald Lemuel and Mabel (Zeimetz) N.; children from previous marriage: Scott, Keith, Karla, Kraig; m. Joan Carolyn Whitney, Feb. 14, 1989. BS, Mass. Coll. Pharmacy, 1957; MS in Med. Chemistry, Purdue U., 1959, PhD, 1961. Lic. pharmacist, Conn., Mass. Asst. prof. med. chemistry Sch. Pharmacy, U. Conn., Storrs, 1961-68, assoc. prof., 1968-75, prof., 1975—, asst. dean, 1967-76, assoc. dean, 1976-81, dean, 1981-93; lectr. psychiatry Yale U., 1970-76; mem. evaluation panels NSF, 1974-76, NIH, 1972-75; bd. dirs. Ctr. Drug and Alcohol Studies, Farmington, Conn., 1976-78; mem. pharmacy educators com. Nat. Assn. Chain Drugstores, 1988-93. Mem. adv. com. Conn. Dept. Mental Health, 1972-75; bd. dirs. Ea. Conn. Drug Action Program, 1970-72; mem. pharm. tripartite com. Conn. Dept. Consumer Protection, 1979-82, 89-95. Mem. Am. Found. Pharm. Edn. (Charles Lynn Fellow 1960-61), Am. Chem. Soc., Am. Pharm. Assn., Am. Assn. Colls. Pharmacy, Conn. Pharm. Assn., Conn. Soc. Hosp. Pharmacists, Acad. Pharm. Scis., Sigma Xi, Kappa Psi, Phi Lambda Sigma, Phi Lambda Upsilon, Rho Chi, Phi Kappa Phi. Republican. Home: 83 Brookside Ln Mansfield Center CT 06250-1109 Office: U Conn Sch Pharmacy Storrs CT 06269

NIEHANS, DANIEL JURG, lawyer; b. Basel, Switzerland, July 9, 1949; came to U.S., 1966, naturalized, 1972; s. Jurg Max and Gertrud Helen (Heusler) N.; m. Patricia Delano Lazowska, July 14, 1979; 1 child, Christina Claire. BA, Johns Hopkins U., 1971; JD, U. Chgo., 1974. Bar: Calif. 1974, U.S. Dist. Ct. (no. dist.) Calif. 1974, U.S. Tax Ct. 1981. Assoc. Pillsbury, Madison & Sutro, San Francisco, 1974-81, ptnr., 1982—. Mem. ABA, Western Pension and Benefits Conf. Republican. Office: Pillsbury Madison & Sutro 235 Montgomery St San Francisco CA 94104-2902

NIEHAUS, LENNIE, composer, jazz saxophonist; b. St. Louis, Mo., June 1, 1929. Scores include (films) Tightrope, 1984, City Heat, 1984, Sesame Street: Follow That Bird, 1985, Pale Rider, 1985, Never Too Young to Die, 1986, Ratboy, 1986, Heartbreak Ridge, 1986, Emanon, 1987, Bird, 1988, Hot Men, 1989, White Hunter, Black Heart, 1990, The Rookie, 1990, Unforgiven, 1992, A Perfect World, 1993, The Bridges of Madison County, 1995, (TV movies) The Child Saver, 1988, Lush Life, 1994. Office: The Robert Light Agency 6404 Wilshire Blvd Ste 900 Los Angeles CA 90048-5511

NIEHAUS, MERLE H., agricultural educator, international agriculture consultant; b. Enid, Okla., Mar. 25, 1933; s. Roy H. and Hazel (Farris) N.;

m. Allene Rollier, Aug. 20, 1954; children: Lisa, Mark. BS, Okla. State U., 1955, MS, 1957; PhD, Purdue U., 1964. From asst. prof. to prof. agr. Ohio Agrl. Research and Devel. Ctr., Wooster, 1964-75, assoc. chmn. dept. agr., 1975-78; head dept. agronomy N.Mex. State U., Las Cruces, 1978-83, dir. agrl. exptl. sta., 1983-84; dean Coll. Agrl. Scis. Colo. State U., Ft. Collins, 1984-91, prof., 1991-92, dir. internat. R & D, 1993—; cons. FAO, UN, Rome, 1982. Contbr. articles to profl. jours. Mem. Wooster Sch. Bd., 1976-77. Fellow AAAS, Crop Sci. Soc. Am., Am. Soc. Agronomy. Office: Colo State U Internat R & D Fort Collins CO 80523

NIEHAUS, ROBERT JAMES, investment banking executive; b. Ann Arbor, Mich., Jan. 6, 1930; s. Julius Herman and Mary Johanna (Koch) N.; m. Jacqueline C. Mallier, Aug. 5, 1982. BBA, U. Mich., 1951; MBA, U. Detroit, 1958. Asst. sr. buyer Ford Motor Co., Dearborn, Mich., 1954-58; gen. purchasing agt. Hercules Motors Co., Canton, Ohio, 1959-60; v.p. procurement Schwitzer Corp., Indpls., 1960-66; sr. v.p. Wallace Murray Corp., N.Y.C., 1966-82; v.p. spl. projects Fischbach Corp., N.Y.C., 1983-84, sr. v.p., 1985-87; pres., chief exec. officer, vice chmn. Fischbach & Moore, Inc., Dallas, 1987-90; pres. Fischback Corp., 1989-90, 1st Phila. Corp., Radnor, Pa., 1991-92, Comutone corp., Atlanta, 1993; dir. Computone Corp., Atlanta, Ga., 1993-95; pres. Mile Marker, Inc., Pompano Beach, Fla., 1994-95; bd. dirs. Software Group, Barrie, Ont., Can. Served to lt. USN, 1951-54. Mem. Am. Mgmt. Assn. (gen. mgmt. council 1982—). Clubs: Union League (N.Y.C.); Greenwich (Conn.) Country. Avocations: boating, music, tennis, golf, swimming. Home: 5960 NE 28th Ave Fort Lauderdale FL 33308

NIEHM, BERNARD FRANK, mental health center administrator; b. Sandusky, Ohio, Feb. 7, 1923; s. Bernard Frank and Hedwick (Panzer) N.; m. Eunice M. Patterson, Oct. 4, 1924; children—Julie, Patti, Bernie. BA, Ohio State U., 1951, MA, 1955, PhD, 1968. Tchr. pub. schs. Sandusky, 1951-57; chief ednl., vocat. and occupational therapy svcs. Vineland (N.J.) Tng. Sch., 1957-61; exec. dir. Franklin County Coun. Retarded Children, Columbus, Ohio, 1962-64; dir. Ohio Sheltered Workshop Planning Project Mental Retardation, 1964-66; coordinator mental retardation planning Ohio Bur. Planning and Grants, Div. Mental Health and Mental Retardation, 1966-68; project dir. Ohio Gov.'s Citizen Com. on Mental Retardation Planning, 1966-68; adminstr. Franklin County Program for Mentally Retarded, 1968-70; supt. Gallipolis (Ohio) State Inst., 1970-76; tchr. spl. edn. Ohio U., 1975—; dir. consultation and edn. Gallia-Jackson-Meigs Community Mental Health Ctr. (now Woodland Ctrs. Inc.), Gallipolis, 1977-79, dir., 1979—; pres. Gallco, 1989-90; outreach bd. Woodland Ctr., Inc., Gallipolis, 1995. Contbr. articles to profl. jours. Active Foster Grandparents Adv. Coun., Gallia County, 1974-76, Gallipolis State Inst. Parent Vol. Assn., 1970-76, Franklin County Bd. Mental Retardation, 1967-68; chmn. MGM dist. Tri-State Boy Scout Coun.; chmn. Meigs, Gallia, Mason Counties Boy Scout Dist., 1972-94; pres. Gallipolis Girls Athletic Assn. Booster Club, 1976—, Gallia County Arthritis Unit, 1986—, Galleo Industries Bd. to Serve Handicapped Adults, 1987-94; bd. dirs. United Cerebral Palsy, Columbus, 1968-70. With U.S. Army, 1943-46. Mem. Am. Assn. Mental Deficiency (past chmn. Ohio chpt., chmn. Great Lakes region), Am. Mental Health Adminstrs. (nat., Ohio chpts.), Nat. Rehab. Assn., Ohio Rehab. Assn., Ohio Assn. Retarded Children (2d v.p. 1974-76, dir.), Vocat. Rehab. Assn., Ohio Coun. Community Mental Health Ctrs., Gallia County Arthritis Assn. (pres. 1991—), Gallipolis Area C. of C., Rotary. Lutheran. Home: 1525 Mill Creek Rd Gallipolis OH 45631-8616 Office: Woodland Ctr Inc 3086 State Rte 160 Gallipolis OH 45631-8418

NIEHOFF, KARL RICHARD BESUDEN, financial executive; b. Cin., May 11, 1943; s. Karl George and Jean (Besuden) N.; children: K. Richard B. Jr., Kelly B. B.A., U. Cin., 1967. Corp. trust officer 5th-3d Union Trust, Cin., 1968-74; v.p., gen. mgr. Sabina (Ohio) Water Co., 1974-76; v.p., sec. Weil, Roth and Irving, Inc., 1974-76; co-mgr., mcpl. fin. dept. Thomson McKinnon Securities, Cin. and N.Y.C., 1976-79; trustee Cin. Stock Exch., 1974-80, 87-90, chmn. bd. trustees, 1978-79, pres., chief oper. officer, 1979-90; exch. rep. Consol. Quote, Consol. Tape Oper. Coms., 1979-90, alt., 1991-92; pres. Fin. Instruments Svcs. Corp., Cin., Chgo., London, 1985-90; v.p. Trading Svcs. NASDAQ, Inc., 1991-92, D.E. Shaw & Co., N.Y.C., 1992-94; pres., mng. ptnr. Niehoff and Assocs., N.Y.C., 1994—; mgr. OTC Project, Warsaw, Republic of Poland, 1995—; voting mem. Inter-Market Trading Com., 1980-90, Stock Exch. Chief Execs. Com., 1988-90; mem. Cin. Stock Exch., 1974-89, P.B.W. Stock Exch., 1975-76; mgr. OTC Project for Mass Privatization for the Republic of Poland, 1995—. Trustee, sec. Contemporary Arts Ctr., Cin., 1975-83; mem. Young Mens Mercantile Libr. Assn., 1974-90, adv. com., 1974-77; mem. devel. com. Tangeman Gallery of Art, 1981-82. Mem. Securities Traders Assn. N.Y., Univ. Club (Cin.), Miami Club (Miamitown), Keeneland Assn. (Lexington, Ky.), European Assn. Securities Dealers (Laventem, Belgium), N.Y. Stock Exch. Luncheon Club, N.Y. Athletic Club, NYAC Yacht Club (Pelham Manor, N.Y.), Cin. Stock and Bond Club (trustee and 1st v.p. 1974-90), Queen City Mcpl. Bond Club (trustee 1974-80), India House, Phi Alpha Theta. Office: Niehoff and Assocs 2200 Star Bank Tower 5th and Walnut Sts Cincinnati OH 45202

NIELDS, MORGAN WESSON, medical supply company executive; b. Springfield, Mass., Jan. 25, 1946; s. Robert Littleton and Florence (Wesson) N.; m. Belinda Gammon, Aug. 14, 1968; children: William, Michael, Stefan, Morgan, Lindsey, Hunter. Cert. d'Etudes Francaises, Université de Lausanne, Switzerland, 1966; BA, Williams Coll., 1968; MBA, Dartmouth Coll., 1970. Mgr. mgmt. svcs. Graco Inc., Paris, 1970-73; chmn., chief exec. officer Fischer Imaging Corp., Denver, 1973—, also bd. dirs.; pres., chief operating officer Diasonics Inc., Milpitas, Calif., 1983-84; bd. dirs. Scinticor, Inc., Milw., Columbia Hosp. Corp., Ft. Worth. Trustee Humana, Mountain View Hosp., Thornton, Colo., 1988-89. Mem. Nat. Elec. Mfrs. Assn. (bd. govs. 1986-87, 91—, bd. dirs. diagnostic imaging and therapy systems div. 1976-89), U.S. Ski Assn. (masters div., pres. Rocky Mountain region 1987-88). Avocations: ski racing, tennis, golf. Office: Fischer Imaging Corp 12300 N Grant St Denver CO 80241-3120*

NIELSEN, ALDON DALE, retired government agency official, economist; b. Mason City, Nebr., Jan. 13, 1922; s. Seren and Sena (Nielsen) N.; m. Vivian Leola Lee, Mar. 26, 1944; children: Carol Ann, Aldon Lynn, Dennis Lee, Brian Paige. Student, Biarittz Am. U., France, 1945; B.Sc., U. Nebr., 1948, postgrad., 1951. With Bur. Reclamation, Dept. Interior, 1948-86; successively economist Bur. Reclamation, Dept. Interior, Grand Island, Nebr., 1948-60; regional agrl. economist Bur. Reclamation, Dept. Interior, Denver, 1960-63; contract and repayment specialist Bur. Reclamation, Dept. Interior, 1963-65; chief economics and program analysis br. Bur. Reclamation, Dept. Interior, Washington, 1965-77; asst. chief div. water and land Bur. Reclamation, Dept. Interior, 1977-78; dir. operation and maintenance policy staff Bur. Reclamation, Dept. Interior, Washington, 1978-83, dir. Office of Water Research, 1983-85; asst. chief div. fgn. activities Dept. Interior, 1985-86; mem. Internat. Commn. on Irrigation and Drainage. Pres. Nebr. Bapt. Men, 1957-59; bd. mgrs. Nebr. Bapt. Conv., 1957-59; mem. Nebr. Bapt. Lay Devel. Com., 1957-58; bd. dirs. Colo. Bapt. Conv., 1960-63; sec. Colo. Bapt. Men, 1961-63; exec. v.p. Am. Bapt. Men, 1962-65, pres., 1965-67; mem. exec. bd. D.C. Bapt. Conv., 1964-72, 76-78, 80-82, 88-96, v.p., 1989-90, pres., 1990-91. Served with AUS, 1944-46, ETO. Decorated Bronze Star; recipient Superior Service award Dept. Interior, 1958, 59, 61, 66, Meritorious Service award, 1973, Spl. Achievement award, 1978, Disting. Service award, 1985. Mem. Internat. Water Resources Assn. Home: 519 S Harrison St Arlington VA 22204-1217

NIELSEN, CHERIE SUE, elementary educator; b. Bingham Canyon, Utah, Nov. 9, 1947; d. Merrill Abindadi and Eva Elizabeth (Christensen) Nelson; m. Mark Andrew Nielsen, June 27, 1969; children: Travis, Jennifer, Trent, Denise, Marlene. AS, Snow Coll., 1968; BS, Brigham Young U., 1988. Cert. elem. tchr., gifted and talented endorsement, Utah. 4th grade tchr. Granite Sch. Dist., Salt Lake City, 1988-92, 5th grade tchr., 1992—; tchr. asst. Pioneer Elem. Sch., West Valley, Utah, 1992-94, art tchr., 1990—. V.p. coun. level PTA, Salt Lake City, 1993-94. Named Disting. Tchr. Utah State Senate, 1994. Republican. Mem. LDS Ch. Avocations: reading, quilting, watercolor, art, crafts. Home: 3836 S 3660 W West Valley City UT 84120-3310 Office: Pioneer Elem Sch 3860 S 3380 W Salt Lake City UT 84119-4442

NIELSEN, FORREST HAROLD, research nutritionist; b. Junction City, Wis., Oct. 26, 1941; s. George Adolph and Sylvia Viola (Blood) N.; m. Emily Joanne Currie, June 13, 1964; children: Forrest Erik, Kistin Emily. BS, U. Wis., 1963, MS, 1966, PhD, 1967. NIH grad. fellow, dept. biochemistry U. Wis., Madison, 1963-67; rsch. chemist, Human Nutrition Rsch. Inst. USDA, Beltsville, Md., 1969-70; rsch. chemist Human Nutrition Rsch. Ctr., USDA, Grand Forks, N.D., 1970-86, ctr. dir. and rsch. nutritionist, 1986—; rsch. assoc. dept. biochemistry, U. N.D., Grand Forks, 1971—, speaker in field. Assoc. editor Magnesium and Trace Elements Jour., 1990-93; mem. editl. bd. Jour. Trace Elements in Exptl. Medicine, 1988—, Biol. Trace Element Rsch. Jour., 1979—, Jour. Nutrition, 1984-88; contbr. articles to profl. jours. Capt. U.S. Army, 1967-69. Recipient Klaus Schwarz Commemorative medal and award Internat. Assn. of Bioinorganic Scientists; named Scientist of Yr. U.S. Dept. Agrl., 1993. Mem. Internat. Soc. Trace Element Rsch. in Humans (gov. bd. 1989—, pres. 1992-95), Internat. Assn. Bioinorganic Scis., Soc. for Exptl. Biology and Medicine, Am. Inst. Nutrition, N.D. Acad. Sci. (pres. 1988-89), Sigma Xi (pres. U. N.D. chpt. 1976-77). Lutheran. Achievements include patent for use of Boron Supplements to Increase in Vivo Production of Hydroxylated Steroids; discovery of the nutritional essentiality of the trace elements boron and nickel. Office: USDA ARS GFHNRC PO Box 9034 Grand Forks ND 58202-9034

NIELSEN, GEORGE LEE, architect; b. Ames, Iowa, Dec. 12, 1937; s. Verner Henry and Verba Lucile (Smith) N.; m. Karen Wall, Feb. 28, 1959; children: David Stuart, Kristina, Melissa. B.Arch., Iowa State U., 1961; M.Arch., M.I.T., 1962. Registered arch., Mass., Ohio, N.Y., Ill., Nat. Coun. Archtl. Registration Bds. Designer Perry, Shaw, Hepburn & Dean, Boston, 1961-64, F.A. Stahl & Assos., Cambridge, Mass., 1964-65; project architect Peirce & Pierce, Boston, 1965-70; project mgr. A.M. Kinney Assos., Cin., 1970—, partner, 1978—; sec. A.M. Kinney Assocs., Inc., Ill., 1993—; also dir. A.M. Kinney Assocs., Inc., Cin.; v.p. A.M. Kinney Inc., Cin., 1992-94, pres., 1994—, also dir. Architect assoc. with major projects for Avco Rsch. Lab., Children's Hosp. Med. Ctr., Square D. Corp., Nalco Chem. Co., Olin Corp., Mead Johnson/Bristol Myers Squib, Cin. Gas and Elec. Co., Sandoz Pharm. Corp., Hoechst Celanese, Witco Corp., Sotheby's, Shell Chem. Co., Bayer Corp. Served with U.S. Army, 1962-64. Mem. AIA (design awards 1970-71, 74, 78, 81, 91, 94, 95). Episcopalian. Home: 3419 Ault View Ave Cincinnati OH 45208-2518 Office: A M Kinney Inc 2900 Vernon Pl Cincinnati OH 45219-2436

NIELSEN, GLADE BENJAMIN, mayor, former state senator; b. Hyrum, Utah, Mar. 8, 1926; s. George Benjamin and Katie Ione (Jensen) N.; m. Alpha Fern Strempke, Oct. 15, 1955; children: Karen Lynn, Sharon Kay, Roger Glade, Laura Mae, Lance Eric. BS, Utah State U., 1949. Supt. various constrn. cos., Wyo., Nev., and Calif., 1949-55; pres. Glade Nielsen Builder, Roy, Utah, 1955-86; mem. Utah State Senate, Salt Lake City, 1987-92; may Roy City, 1994—. Pres. Weber Basin Homebuilders Assn., 1967-68, Home Builders Assn. Utah, 1972-73; v.p. Nat. Assn. Home Builders, Washington, 1974-75, mem. exec. com., 1976-79; exec. com. Weber Econ. Devel. Corp.; pres. Roy C. of C., 1980; bd. dirs. Utah Housing Fin. Agy., Salt Lake, 1975-83. With USN, 1944-46, PTO. Recipient Builder of Yr. award Home Builders Assn. Utah, 1988, Svc. award Utah State Com. Consumer Svcs., 1989, Recognition award Utah State Dept. Commerce, 1989, Hon. Commendation award Ogden Air Logistics Command, 1989, Roy City Outstanding Citizen award, 1993. Mem. U.S. Indiana Assn. (pres. 1996), VFW, Am. Legion, Thunderbird Motor Club Utah (pres.), Elks, Ogden/Weber C. of C. (dir.). Republican. Avocations: travel, antique cars.

NIELSEN, GREG ROSS, lawyer; b. Provo, Utah, Sept. 24, 1947; s. Ross T. and Carma (Peterson) N.; m. Jo Rita Beer, Sept. 3, 1971; children: Jennifer, Jerilyn, Eric Michael, Brittany Anne. BA in Polit. Sci. magna cum laude, Brigham Young U., 1971; JD cum laude, Harvard U., 1975. Bar: Ariz. 1975, U.S. Dist. Ct. Ariz. 1975, U.S. Ct. Appeals (9th cir.) 1977, Utah 1990. Assoc. Snell & Wilmer, Phoenix, 1975-80, ptnr., 1981-91; mng. ptnr. Snell & Wilmer, Salt Lake City, 1991—; adminstrv. coord. real estate practice group Snell & Wilmer, Phoenix, 1988-90. Mem. dist. com. Theodore Roosevelt coun. Boy Scouts Am., 1988-90, Valley Partnership, Phoenix, 1989-90. Hinckley scholar Brigham Young U., 1970; fellow Ford Found., 1970. Mem. ABA, State Bar Ariz., Utah Bar Assn. Republican. Mem. LDS Ch. Office: Snell & Wilmer 111 E Broadway Ste 900 Salt Lake City UT 84111-5235

NIELSEN, HARALD CHRISTIAN, retired chemist; b. Chgo., Apr. 18, 1930; s. Svend Aage and Seena (Hansen) N.; m. Eloise Wilma Soule, Dec. 19, 1953; children—Brenda Mae, Paul Erick, Gloria Lynn. B.A., St. Olaf Coll., 1952; Ph.D., Mich. State U., 1957. Cereal grain proteins chemist Nat. Ctr. for Agrl. Utilization Rsch. (formerly No. Regional Research Ctr.), Agrl. Research Service, USDA, Peoria, Ill., 1957-87. Contbr. articles to profl. jours. Pres. local 3247 Am. Fedn. Govt. Employees, AFL-CIO, 1977-86; mem. Peoria Area Combined Fed. Campaign Coordinating Com., 1980-87. Fellow AAAS; mem. ACLU, Am. Assn. Cereal Chemists, Nat. Assn. Ret. Fed. Employees (officer chpt. 268 1989-92, pres. chpt. 268 1991), Sigma Xi. Democrat. Lutheran. Home: 2318 N Gale Ave Peoria IL 61604-3229 *What useful thing have I accomplished this day? What did I learn today? These two questions I ask myself at the end of the day.*

NIELSEN, JENNIFER LEE, molecular ecologist, researcher; b. Balt., Mar. 21, 1946; d. Leo Jay and Mary Marriott (Mules) N.; divorced; children: Nadja Ochs, Allisha Ochs. MFA, Ecole des Beaux Arts, Paris, 1968; BS, Evergreen State Coll., 1987; MS, U. Calif., Berkeley, 1990, PhD, 1994. Artist Seattle, 1969-78; fish biologist Weyerhaeuser Co., Tacoma, Wash., 1978-89; resource cons. Berkeley, 1989-90; rsch. biologist USDA-Forest Svc., Albany, Calif., 1990—; vis. scientist Stanford U., Pacific Grove, Calif., 1994—; rsch. assoc. U. Calif., Santa Barbara, 1994—; rsch. assoc. U. Calif. Marine Sci. Inst., Santa Barbara, 1994—. Editor: Evolution and the Aquatic Ecosystem, 1995; contbr. articles to profl. jours.; paintings exhibited at Metro. Mus. Modern Art, 1966; represented in numerous pvt. collections, U.S. and Europe. Mem. Am. Fisheries Soc. (pres. chpt. 1993-94), Molecular Marine Biology and Biotech. (regional editor 1995), Animal Behaviour Soc. (policy com. 1993-94). Avocations: painting, cooking, gardening, rock climbing, sailing. Home: 84 Corona Rd Carmel Highlands CA 93923 Office: Hopkins Marine Sta Oceanview Blvd Pacific Grove CA 93950

NIELSEN, JOYCE, former state legislator; b. Askov, Minn., Nov. 20, 1933; d. Clarey Burnhardt and Dorothy Elaine (Saastad) Jensen; m. Eric Hans Nielsen, June 11, 1955; 1 child, Cindy. Grad., Cloquet (Minn.) H.S. Fin. cons. Nielsen Fin. Cons., Inc., Cedar Rapids, Iowa, 1984-88; mem. Iowa Ho. of Reps., Des Moines, 1989-93; facilitator Parenting Edn. Programs 1993—. Bd. dirs., Vice President, treas. Peoples Ch., Cedar Rapids, 1994—; bd. dirs., sec. UN Assn., Cedar Rapids, 1988; bd. dirs., mem. exec. com. United Way, Cedar Rapids. Named Woman of Yr., Coalition of Women's Groups; recipient Outstanding Svc. award YWCA, Community Action Agy. Mem. LWV (bd. dirs.). Democrat. Mem. Unitarian Ch. Home: 2702 Q Ave NW Cedar Rapids IA 52405-1439

NIELSEN, KENNETH RAY, academic administrator; b. Oct. 15, 1941; s. Frank and Elinor (Hansen) N.; children: Elizabeth, Mary. BEd, U. Wis., Whitewater, 1965; MS, U. Wis., Stout, 1966; EdD, U. Wyo., 1968. Dir. student activities Cornell U., Ithaca, N.Y., 1968-72; adminstr., prof. Tchr. Tng. Coll., San Juan, P.R., 1974-77; v.p. student affairs Northland Coll., Ashland, Wis., 1972-77; v.p. student life Seattle U., 1977-84; pres. Coll. St. Mary, Omaha, 1984—. Bd. dirs. Boy Scouts Am., Girl Scouts U.S.A., Nat. Coun. Christians and Jews, Providence Hosp. Found.; chmn. edn. sect. United Way Bd.; mem. Gov.'s Community Svcs. and Continuing Edn. Mem. Am. Coun. Edn., Am. Assn. Higher Edn., Am. Assn. Univ. Adminstrs., Coun. Ind. Colls. Roman Catholic. Avocations: reading, exercising. Office: Coll St Mary 1901 S 72nd St Omaha NE 68124-2301

NIELSEN, LELAND C., federal judge; b. Vesper, Kans., June 14, 1919; s. Carl Christian and Christena (Larson) N.; m. Virginia Garland, Nov. 27, 1958; 1 child, Christena. A.B., Washburn U., 1946; J.D., U. So. Calif., 1946. Bar: Calif. 1947. Practice law Los Angeles, from 1947; dep. city atty. City of Los Angeles, 1947-51; judge Superior Ct. Calif. San Diego County, 1968-71; judge, now sr. judge U.S. Dist. Ct. (so. dist.) Calif., San Diego, 1971—. Served to maj. A.C., U.S. Army 1941-46. Decorated Purple Heart, Disting. Svc. Cross, Air medal with oak leaf clusters. Mem. Am. Coll. Trial Lawyers. Republican. Presbyterian. Office: US Dist Ct Courtroom 10 940 Front St San Diego CA 92101-2960*

NIELSEN, LESLIE, actor; b. Regina, Sask., Can., Feb. 11, 1926; s. Ingvard and Maybelle N. Student, Neighborhood Playhouse, N.Y.C. Former announcer, disk jockey, Can. radio; feature films include The Vagabond King, 1956, Forbidden Planet, 1956, Ransom!, 1956, The Opposite Sex, 1956, Hot Summer Night, 1957, Tammy and the Bachelor, 1957, Night Train to Paris, 1964, Harlow, 1965, Dark Intruder, 1965, Beau Geste, 1965, Gunfight in Abilene, 1967, The Reluctant Astronaut, 1967, Rosie, 1967, Counterpoint, 1967, Dayton's Devils, 1969, How to Commit Marriage, 1969, Change of Mind, 1969, The Resurrection of Zachary Wheeler, 1971, The Poseidon Adventure, 1972, Viva, Knievel, 1977, City of Fire, 1979, Airplane!, 1980, Wrong is Right, 1982, Creepshow, 1983, Spaceship, 1983, Soul Man, 1986, The Patriot, 1986, Nuts, 1987, Nightstick, 1987, Home Is Where the Hart Is, 1987, The Naked Gun, 1988, Dangerous Curves, The Repossessed, The Naked Gun 2 1/2: The Smell of Fear, 1991, All I Want for Christmas, 1991, Surf Ninjas, 1993, The Naked Gun 33 1/3: The Final Insult, 1994; TV films include Crime Syndicated, 1952, Man Behind The Badge, 1954, See How They Run, 1964, Shadow Over Elveron, 1968, Hawaii Five-O, 1968, Companions in Nightmare, 1968, Trial Run, 1969, Deadlock, 1969, Night Slaves, 1970, The Aquarians, 1970, Hauser's Memory, 1970, Monty Nash, 1971, They Call It Murder, 1971, Incident in San Francisco, 1972, Snatched, 1973, The Letters, 1973, Can Ellen Be Saved?, 1974, Brinks! The Great Robbery, 1976, Little Mo, 1978, miniseries Back Stairs At the White House, 1979, Institute For Revenge, 1979, Ohms, 1980, The Night The Bridge Fell Down, 1980, Murder Among Friends, 1982, Cave-In, 1983, Blade in Hong Kong, 1985, The Loner, Fatal Confession: A Father Dowling Mystery, Chance of a Lifetime, 1991; numerous other TV appearances including dramatic series Studio One, Armstrong Circle Theater, Goodyear Playhouse; TV series include The New Breed, 1961, The Bold Ones, 1963-67, Peyton Place, 1965, Bracken's World, 1969-70, Shaping Up, 1984, Police Squad, 1982, The Golden Girls, 1992; toured country in one man show Darrow, 1979; co-author: The Naked Truth, 1993. Office: Bresler Kelly Kipperman 15760 Ventura Blvd Encino CA 91436-3002*

NIELSEN, LYNN CAROL, lawyer, educational consultant; b. Perth Amboy, N.J., Jan. 11, 1950; d. Hans and Esther (Pucker) N.; m. Russell F. Baldwin, Nov. 22, 1980; 1 child, Blake Nielsen Baldwin. BS, Millersville U., 1972; MA, NYU, 1979; JD, Rutgers U., 1984. Bar: N.J. 1984; cert. tchr. handicapped, reading specialist, learning disability tchr. cons., elem. edn. supr. Instr. Woodbridge (N.J.) Twp. Bd. Edn., 1972-83; legal intern appellate sect. divsn. criminal justice Atty. Gen. State N.J., Trenton, 1983, dep. atty. gen. divsn. civil law, 1985; assoc. Kantor & Kusic, Keyport, N.J., 1984-86, Kantor & Linderoth, Keyport, N.J., 1986-92. Officer Fords (N.J.) Sch. # 14 PTO, 1974-75; elder First Presbyn. Ch. Avenel, N.J., 1985-88; bd. dirs. New Beginnings Nursery Sch., Woodbridge, 1989-90, Flemington (N.J.) Presbyn. Nursery Sch., 1991-93. Mem. ABA, N.J. Bar Assn., Monmouth County Bar Assn., Hunterdon County Bar Assn. Avocations: reading, skiing, sailing. Home and Office: 3 Buchannan Way Flemington NJ 08822-3205

NIELSEN, NIELS CHRISTIAN, JR., theology educator; b. Long Beach, Calif., June 2, 1921; s. Niels Hansen and Frances (Nofziger) N.; m. Erika Kreuth, May 10, 1958; children—Camilla Regina, Niels Albrecht. BA, George Pepperdine Coll., L.A., 1942; BD, Yale U., 1946, PhD, 1951. Ordained to ministry Meth. Ch., 1946. Pastor Woodbury (Conn.) Meth. Ch., 1944-46; instr. religion Yale U., New Haven, 1948-51; faculty Rice U., Houston, 1951—; J. Newton Rayzor prof. religious studies. Rice U., prof. emeritus, 1991—; Amax presdl. prof. humanities Colo. Sch. Mines, Golden, 1982-83; scholar in residence St. Paul's United Meth. Ch., Houston. Author: Philosophy and Religion in Contemporary Japan, 1957, Geistige Landerkunde USA, 1960, A Layman Looks at World Religions, 1962, God in Education, 1966, Solzhenitsyn's Religion (Nelson), 1975, The Religion of Jimmy Carter, 1977, The Crisis of Human Rights, 1978, Religions of the World, 1982, Revolutions in Eastern Europe: The Religious Roots, 1991, Fundamentalism, Mythos and World Religions, 1993; editor: Religion After Communism in Russia, 1994; contbr. articles to profl. jours. Mem. Am. Acad. Religion, Am. Philos. Soc., Am. Soc. Study Religion (sec. 1977-89), Soc. European Culture, Soc. for Values in Higher Edn. Democrat. Home: 2424 Swift Blvd Houston TX 77030-1806

NIELSEN, STEVEN B., medical products executive; b. 1947. BA, Calif. State U., Long Beach, 1973. With Acme United Corp., 1973-76, Bergen Brunswig Med. Surgical Inc., 1976-78, 80-84, Hosp. Pharmacies Inc., 1978-80; exec. v.p. Gen. Med. Corp., Richmond, Va., 1984-88, pres., 1988-89, dir., 1989-93, chm. bd., CEO, 1993—. Office: General Medical Corp 8741 Landmark Rd Richmond VA 23228-2801*

NIELSEN, VERA BAGLEY, retired teacher, librarian; b. Greenwich, Utah, Oct. 13, 1916; d. James Alvin and Diantha Matilda (Anderson) Bagley; m. Byron Woodland, May 17, 1941 (dec. Feb. 1944); 1 child, Kathleen Myrle; m. Leland Nielsen, Sept. 12, 1952 (dec. Jan. 1993); 1 child, James Cary. AB magna cum laude, Brigham Young U., 1937, MA, 1949. Cert. tchr. 1st class elem., librarian, media specialist, supervisory/adminstrn. Tchr., librarian Franklin Sch., Provo, Utah, 1937, Maeser Sch., Provo, 1944-45, Wasatch Sch., Provo, 1952-58, Provost Sch., Provo, 1959-62; demonstraton tchr. Lab. Sch. Brigham Young U., Provo, 1945-49, tchr. film classics, 1957-58; media specialist Grandview Sch., Provo, 1949-52, Rock Canyon Sch., Provo, 1962-83; instr. libr. Coll. Edn., Provo, summers; instr. Coll. Edn. U. Utah, Salt Lake City, 1958-59; subtitute tchr. Cyprus High Sch., Magna, Utah, 1944; cons. workshops Salt Lake City Sch. Dist., 1957, Utah Edn. Assn., Salt Lake City, 1982-93. Contbr. articles to profl. publs.; editor Family Bull., Bagley Family Orgn., 1976-93; cons. Fascinating Tales Series, ARO Pub. Co., 1981-82. Sec. Orem (Utah) Boosters City Coun., 1970-80; with publicity Miss Orem Scholarship Pageant, 1984-94; sec. Utah County Dem. Party, 1984-92, treas., 1992-95. Recipient Disting. Svc. award Kiwanis Club, Provo, 1978, Vol. Svc. award Utah Gov.'s Commn., Salt Lake City, 1993. Mem. AAUW (br. pres., 1944, 76, state pres. 1968-70, regional dir. 1987-89, editor state bull. 1975-79, 90-94, Disting. Woman award Utah State chpt. 1986,), Assn. Childhood Edn. (pres., historian 1970), Ret. Sch. Employees (unit pres., 1983, , NRTA state coord. 1983-87, state pres. 1993-95), Gen. Federated Women's Clubs (state treas., 1992-94, v.p. 94—), Women's Divsn. C. of C. (sec. 1994, treas. 95), Women's Coun. Provo (pres. 1985-87, Delta Literary honor, 1991, parliamentarian, 1992), League of Women Voters, Phi Delta Kappa (treas., officer 1980, Kappan of Yr. Brigham Young U. chpt. 1987). Mormon.

NIELSEN, WILLIAM FREMMING, federal judge; b. 1934. BA, U. Wash., 1956, LLB, 1963. Law clk. to Hon. Charles L. Powell U.S. Dist. Ct. (ea. dist.) Wash., 1963-64; mem. firm Paine, Hamblen, Coffin, Brooke & Miller, 1964-91; judge U.S. Dist. Ct. (ea. dist.) Wash., Spokane, 1991—. Lt. col. USAFR. Fellow Am. Coll. Trial Lawyers; mem. ABA, Wash. State Bar Assn., Spokane County Bar Assn. (pres. 1981-82), Fed. Bar Assn. (pres. 1988), Spokane County Legal Svcs. Corp. (past pres.), Lawyer Pilot Bar Assn., Assn. Trial Lawyers Am., Wash. State Trial Lawyers Assn., Assn. Def. Trial Attys., Am. Inns of Ct., Charles L. Powell Inn (pres. 1987), The Spokane Club, Rotary, Alpha Delta Phi, Phi Delta Phi. Office: US Dist Ct PO Box 2208 920 W Riverside Ave Spokane WA 99210-2208

NIELSON, BARBARA BROADHEAD, special education administrator; b. Nephi, Utah, Apr. 9, 1931; d. Elmer Robert and Anna Else (Rassmussen) Broadhead; m. Gordon Leon Nielson, Jan. 5, 1953; children: Victoria, Ellen, Margo, Peggy, Thomas, Lyle, Clark. BS cum laude, Brigham Young U., 1965-67, MS, 1972-74, DEd, 1988-92. Cert. prof. elem., early childhood and spl. edn. tchr., adminstr. Elem. and kindergarten tchr. Tintic Sch. Dist., Eureka, Utah, 1966-68; spl. edn. tchr. Millard Sch. Dist., Delta, Utah, 1968-77, elem. prin., 1977-91, chpt. I dir., 1991-92, spl. edn. dir., coord. at-risk programs, 1992—; co-owner Booster Edn. Svc., Delta, 1973-75; mem. Utah Sch. Accreditation Com., Salt Lake City, 1980-85, Career Ladder Coun., Delta, 1984-92; dir. Millard Sch. Dist. Edn. Found., Delta, 1991-92. Author: A Systematic Instructional Reading Approach for Parent of School Ate Children, 1973, (games) Tic-Tac-Toe Phonics, 1973; co-author: Booster Math Materials, 1973; contbr. articles to profl. jours. Active Sierra club, Utah, 1990-94, Ashgrove Cement County Community Coun., Nephi-Delta, 1990-94, West Millard Recreation Coun., Delta, 1980-90; lobbyist, co-writer hazardous waste siting criteria Millard County Concerned Citizens for State of Utah, 1988-94. Named Outstanding Spl. Edn. Tchr., Utah State Office Edn., Salt Lake City, 1973, 74-75; recipient Disting. Svc. in Edn. award Utah

State Legis., Salt Lake City, 1991. Mem. Utah Edn. Assn. (profl. rights and responsibility com. 1977-79), So. Utah Educators Assn. (coun. mem. 1974-78), U. Adminstrv. Womens Assn., Delta Rotary, Prins. Acad. of Utah, Delta Kappa Gamma (regional dir. 1973-74). Republican. Mem. Latter Day Saints. Avocations: environmentalist, reading, gardening, travel, history/genealogy. Home: PO Box 38085 295 Juniper St Leamington UT 84638 Office: Millard Sch Dist 160 W Main PO Box 666 Delta UT 84624

NIELSON, HOWARD CURTIS, former congressman, retired educator; b. Richfield, Utah, Sept. 12, 1924; s. Herman Taylor and Zula May (Curtis) N.; m. Julia Adams, June 18, 1948; children: Noreen (Mrs. Stephen Astin), Elaine (Mrs. Stanley Taylor), John, Mary Lee (Mrs. Paul Jackson), James, Jean (Mrs. Clay Cundick), Howard Curtis Jr. BS in Math., U. Utah, 1947; MS in Math., U. Oreg., 1949; MBA, Stanford U., 1956, PhD in Bus. Adminstrn. and Stats., 1958. Statistician C & H Sugar Refining Corp., 1949-51; rsch. economist and statistician Stanford Rsch. Inst., 1951-57; mem. faculty Brigham Young U., Provo, Utah, 1957-82; prof. statistics Brigham Young U., 1961-82, chmn. dept., 1960-63; sr. devel. engr. Hercules, Inc., 1960-66; dir. Ctr. for Bus. and Econ. Rsch., 1971-72; sr. statistician, acting field mgr. C.E.I.R, Inc., 1963-64, mgr., cons., 1964-65; prin. scientist GCA Corp., 1965-67; dir. econ. rsch. Eyring Rsch. Inst., 1974-75; assoc. commr. higher edn. State of Utah, 1976-79; mem. 98th-101st Congresses from 3d dist. Utah; missionary LDS Ch., Australia, 1991-92, Hungary, 1993-94; econ. adviser Kingdom of Jordan, Ford Found., 1970-71; prof. Am. U., Beirut, 1970; adj. prof. U. Utah, 1972-76. Author: The Efficiency of Certain Truncated Order Statistics in Estimating the Mean of Various Distributions, 1949, Population Trends in the United States Through 1975, 1955, The Hows and Whys of Statistics, 1963, Experimental Designs Used in industry, 1965, Membership Growth of the Church of Jesus Christ of Latter-Day Saints, 1957, 67, 71, 75, 78, Evaluation of the Seven Year Plan for Economic Development in Jordan, 1971, Economic Analysis of Fiji, Tonga, Western and Am. Samoa, 1972; co-author: The Newsprint Situation in the Western Region of North America, 1952, America's Demand for Wood, 1954, also reports. Mem. Utah Gov.'s Econ. Rsch. Adv. Coun., 1967-72; dir. bur. ch. studies Ch. of Jesus Christ of Latter-day Saints, 1958-63; rsch. dir. Utah Republican Party, 1967-68; mem. Utah Ho. of Reps, 1967-75, majority leader, 1969-71, speaker, 1973-75, mem. legis. budget-audit com., 1967-73, chmn., 1971-73, chmn. legis. coun., 1973-75; mem. Utah 3d Dist., U.S. Ho. of Reps., 1983-91; chmn. Utah County Rep. Com., 1979-81. Mem. Am. Statis. Assn. (pres. Utah br. 1964-65, mem. nat. coun. 1967-70), Sci. Rsch. Soc. Am., Order of Artus, Phi Beta Kappa, Phi Kappa Phi, Sig,a Xi, Pi Mu Epsilon.

NIELSON, NORMA LEE, business educator; b. Augusta, Ga., Dec. 26, 1953; d. Norman Lyle and Betty Lou (Buckner) Parrott; m. Mark G. Nielson, Nov. 20, 1985 (div. 1988); 1 child, Eric Gordon. BS, Northwest Mo. State U., 1974; MA, U. Pa., 1976, PhD, 1979. CLU. Asst. prof. Iowa State U., Ames, 1977-79, U. So. Calif., L.A., 1979-84; cons. profl. Mercer-Meidinger, L.A., 1984-85; assoc. prof. Oreg. State U., Corvallis, 1985-90; prof. Oreg. State U., 1990—; bd. examiners Internat. Bd. Stds. and Practice for CFP, 1991-94. Developer software; contbg. author: Handbook for Corporate Directors, 1985; contbr. articles to profl. publs. Vol. Linn-Benton Food Share, Corvallis; bd. dirs. Corvallis Cmty. Dare Care, Inc., 1988-91; candidate for Oreg. Ho. of Reps., 1994. Andrus Found. rsch. grantee, 1989-91. Mem. Am. Risk and Ins. Assn. (bd. dirs. 1990—, officer 1993—), Western Risk and Ins. Assn. (officer 1981-84), Risk and Ins. Mgmt. Soc. Avocations: piano, stained glass, flying. Office: Oreg State U Coll Bus #200 Bexell Hall Corvallis OR 97331-2603

NIELSON, THEO GILBERT, law enforcement official, university official; b. Roosevelt, Utah, June 29, 1938; s. John Gilbert and Mazie (Alexander) N.; m. Martha Perez, May 22, 196l; children: Lucille Marie, Sherry Lou, Mark Andrew, Rex Alexander, Theo Gilbert Jr., Cristal Ina, Gregory Angus, Mazie Leah, Rosanna Alma. Grad., FBI Nat. Acad., 1970; BA, Ariz. State U., 1975, MS, 1977. Officer Univ. Police, Ariz. State U., Tempe, 1963-67, sgt., 1967-70, lt., 1970-79; chief police Douglas (Ariz.) Police Dept., 1979-82; div. adminstr. Ariz. Criminal Intelligence Systems Agy., Tucson, 1982-84; dir. campus safety and security No. Ariz. U., Flagstaff, 1984-92; chief police Ariz. Dept. Adminstrn., 1993—. Mem. Am. Soc. for Indsl. Security (chmn. No. Ariz. chpt. 1987), Internat. Assn. Chiefs Police, Internat. Assn. Campus Law Enforcement Adminstrs., Ariz. Assn. Campus Law Enforcement (pres. 1989-90). Republican. Mormon. Avocations: genealogy, hiking, grandchildren. Home: 3335 E Hampton Ave Mesa AZ 85204-6410 Office: Ariz State Capitol Police 1700 W Washington Ave Ste B15 Phoenix AZ 85007

NIELSON, WILLIAM BROOKS, clergyman; b. Jeffersonville, Vt., Nov. 26, 1949; s. John Bechtold and Marguerite Helene (Mann) N.; m. Susan Gail Walter, May 2, 1992; children: Anya Helene, Abigail Brooke, Aliece Gwen. AB in Religion, Ea. Nazarene Coll., Quincy, Mass., 1971; MDiv cum laude, Nazarene Theol. Sem., Kansas City, Mo., 1974. Ordained to ministry Ch. of Nazarene, 1979. Min. music St. Paul's Ch. of Nazarene, Kansas City, 1971-74, min. youth and music, 1974-75; min. youth and music Balt. 1st Ch. of Nazarene, Ellicott City, Md., 1975-81; sr. pastor Ch. of Nazarene, Concord, Ohio, 1981—; mem. bi-dist. camp bd. N.E. Camp, mem. program com., youth ministries rep., mem. bd. Christian life, dir. youth ministries, pres. Nazarene Youth Internat., Washington Dist. Ch. of Nazarene; mem. gen. coun. Nazarene Youth Internat., ea. regional rep. Ch. of Nazarene, 1977-80, gen. sec. Nazarene Youth Internat., 1980-85; spkr. team camps, retreats, revivals and Nazarene Youth Internat. convs., 1975—. Author: Unlocking the Bible, 1979, The Distinguishing Mark, 1980; contbr. to religious publs. Mem. alumni coun. bd. dirs. Ea. Nazarene Coll., 1979—; founder Painesville (Ohio) Christian Acad., 1983; bd. dirs., mem. founding bd. Painesville Counseling Ctr., 1985—; chaplain, capt. CAP, 1993—. Republican. Home: 6123 Chestnut St Concord OH 44077 Office: Ch of Nazarene 6235 Chestnut St Concord OH 44077

NIEMAN, JOHN FRANCIS, advertising executive; b. St. Louis, Jan. 8, 1949; s. John Francis and Virginia N.; m. Janice Seidel, Apr. 25, 1981; children: Lindsay Briana, John III, Scott Parker, James August. BA in English, U. Mo., 1971. From assoc. creative dir. to v.p. Gardner Advt. Co., St. Louis, 1971-79; from group creative dir. to sr. v.p. Young and Rubicam, N.Y.C., 1979-86, DDB Needham, Chgo., 1986; exec. creative dir., exec. v.p. McCann-Erickson, N.Y.C., 1986-89; vice chair, chief creative officer USA D'Arcy Masius Benton & Bowles, N.Y.C., 1989-91, vice chair, chief creative officer, N.Am., 1991—; dir.-at-large The Advt. Coun., N.Y.C. Chmn. Best of N.Y. Addy Awards, 1992; finalist judge Addy Awards, 1993; blue ribbon judge Andy Awards, 1990-93; mem. creative commn. Partnership for Drug Free Am., N.Y.C., 1991—. Recipient numerous Clios, Andy, Addy and Cannes awards. Office: D'Arcy Massius Benton & Bowles 1675 Broadway New York NY 10019-5820*

NIEMANN, BERNARD JOHN, JR., land and geographical system educator, researcher, consultant; b. Highland Park, Ill., July 23, 1937; s. Bernard J.. and Emma (Gaeble) N.; m. Sondra Sue, Dec. 29, 1962; 1 child, Ben. BA, U. Ill., 1960; MLA, Harvard U., 1964. Site planner Leo A. Daly Co., Omaha, 1960-63, Sasaki-Walker & Assocs., Watertown, Mass., 1963-64; asst. prof. dept. landscape architecture U. Wis., Madison, 1963-68, assoc. prof., 1969-71, chmn. dept., 1971-75, prof. dept. landscape architecture Inst. Environ.. Studies, adj. prof. urban and regional planning, 1976—, dir. land info. and computer graphics facility Sch. Natural Resources, 1988—; cons. resource and land investigations program U.S. Dept. Interior, Reston, Va., 1976-80; mem. com. on integrated land data mapping NRC, Washington, 1981-82, mem. com. mapping sci. NRC, Washington, 1990-94; prin. Landscapes Ltd., Madison, 1964-73; cons. Wis. Dept. Justice, Office Pub. Intervenor, Madison, 1978-84; mem. Lower Wis. Riverway Planning Task Force, Wis. Dept. Natural Resources, Madison, 1983-87; vice chair Wis. Gov.'s Land Records Com., 1985-87; adviser nat. geodetic survey U.S. Dept. Commerce. Author: (with others) Modernization of the Pubic Land Survey System, 1982; editor: Land Records Can and Should Be Improved, 1980, editor Wis. Land Info. Newsletter, 1983—; co-editor Jour. Urban and Regional Systems Assn., 1988—; editl. bd. Jour. Transactions in Wis., 1996—. Bd. dirs. Wis. Land Info. Bd., 1989—, chmn., 1989-90, vice chmn., 1990—; pres. Wis. Land Info. Assn., 1989-90. Recipient Educator of Yr. award Coun. Educators in Landscape Architecture, 1986, Wis. Idea award in natural resource policy, 1991, award of distinction and svc. Wis. Land Info. Assn., 1990, Pres. award, 1995. Mem. Am. Soc. Landscape Architects (award of achievement 1959, award of merit 1970, 74, 88, award of honor 1982, 84, 89, Horwood Merit award), Urban and Regional Info. Assn. (bd. dirs. 1986-88), Gamma Sigma Delta. Home: 2501 Marshall Pky Madison WI 53713-1030 Office: U Wis Land Info/Comp Graph B102 Steenbock Meml Libr 550 Babcock Dr Madison WI 53706-1522

NIEMANN, LEWIS KEITH, lamp manufacturing company executive; b. Alliance, Nebr., Dec. 10, 1930; s. William Grover and Vivian Zelma (Holloway) N. BS in Mktg. with honors (Standard Oil grantee), San Diego State Coll., 1956. Mdse. mgr. Fed Mart Corp., San Diego, 1954-61; store mgr. GEX, Atlanta, 1961-63; mdse. mgr. J. C. Penney Co., Pitts., 1963-67; mgr. sales planning and product devel. RCA Sales Corp., 1967-70; spl. asst. to pres. Magnavox Consumer Electronics Co., 1970-73, v.p. internat. and comml. sales, 1973-74; v.p. mktg., div. mfg. Beatrice Foods Co., Chgo., 1974-75; v.p. mktg., div. luggage Samsonite Corp., Denver, 1975-78; pres. Stiffel Co., Chgo., 1978-80, Westwood Lighting Group, Inc., Paterson, N.J., 1980-87, El Paso, Tex., 1987-90, Sunset-Richards Lighting, City of Commerce, Calif., 1990-91. Bd. dirs. Jr. Achievement, Denver, 1976-78, Pvt. Industry Council, Passaic County. Served with USMC, 1948-52, Korea. Recipient CLIO award for Best TV Comml. in class, 1978. Republican. Episcopalian.

NIEMANN, RICHARD HENRY, grocery executive; b. Quincy, Ill., Feb. 18, 1931; s. Ferdinand Elmer and Antoinette E. (Heckenkamp) N.; m. Constance M. Volm, Oct. 6, 1951; children—Linda M., Connie A., Richard Henry, Daniel M., Ted M., Christopher J., Margaret M., Amy E. B.S. in Mktg., Quincy Coll., 1953. Warehouse mgr. Niemann Bros., Quincy, 1953-69; pres., chief exec. officer Niemann Foods Inc., Quincy, 1969—; v.p. A'Village Land Corp., Quincy, 1969-82; mng. ptnr. FoodCo Land Trust, Quincy, 1973—; pres. Johannes Meats Inc., Quincy, 1979-83; ptnr. Niemann Farms, Quincy, 1953—; trustee Quincy Foods Profit Sharing Trust, 1971—; dir. State Street Bank & Trust, Quincy. Chmn. Ill. Food Distbrs. Polit. Action Com., Lombard, 1983—; dir., exec. com. Great River Econ. Devel. Found.; trustee Culver Stockton Coll.; mem. pres.'s bd. advisors Quincy Coll.; bd. dirs. Western Ill. U. Found., Quincy Area Project, Quincy Catholic Charities; past pres. bd. trustees St. Mary Hosp.; past pres. bd. edn. Quincy Pub. Sch.; past pres. Deanery Council Catholic Men. Mem. Ill. Food Retailers Assn. (dir., exec. com. 1972—), Ill. Retail Mchts. Assn. (dir. 1981—), Quincy Area C. of C. (dir.). Democrat. Roman Catholic. Club: Quincy Country. Lodges: K.C. (former master), Quincy Rotary (past pres.). Home: 2 Old Orchard Rd Quincy IL 62301-6524 Office: Niemann Foods Inc 1501 N 12th St Quincy IL 62301-1916*

NIEMETH, CHARLES FREDERICK, lawyer; b. Lorain, Ohio, Nov. 25, 1939; s. Charles Ambrose and Christine Cameron (Mollison) N.; m. Anne Marie Meckes, Oct. 12, 1968. B.A., Harvard U., 1962; J.D., U. Mich., 1965. Bar: Calif. 1966, N.Y. 1984. Assoc. O'Melveny & Myers, Los Angeles, 1965-72, ptnr., 1973—. Mem. nat. com. Mich. Law Sch. Fund; trustee Challengers Boys and Girls Club, 1968-83; mem. bus. adv. coun. UCLA, 1979-83; mem. exec. com. Internat. Student Ctr., 1979-83; bd. dirs. Olympic Tower Condominium, 1986-92; bd. visitors Mich. Law Sch., mem. Tri-Bar Opinion Com. Mem. Riviera Tennis Club, Regency Club, N.Y. Athletic Club, Field Club (Greenwich, Conn.), Bel-Air Bay Club. Democrat. Roman Catholic. Home: 10660 Bellagio Rd Los Angeles CA 90077-3713 also: 70 Oneida Dr Greenwich CT 06830-7131 Office: O'Melveny & Myers 1999 Avenue Of The Stars Los Angeles CA 90067-6022 also: O'Melveny & Myers 153 E 53rd St Fl 54 New York NY 10022-4611

NIEMEYER, GERHART, political science educator; b. Essen, Germany, Feb. 15, 1907; came to U.S., 1937, naturalized, 1943; s. Victor and Kaethe (Ley) N.; m. Lucie Lenzner, Sept. 18, 1931; children: A. Hermann, Lucian L., Paul V., Lisa M., Christian B. Student, Cambridge U., 1925-26, Munich U., 1926-27; J.U.D., Kiel U., 1932. Ordained priest Episcopal Ch. 1980, canon, 1987. Lectr., asst. prof. Princeton U., 1937-44; prof., head div. Oglethorpe U., 1944-50; fgn. affairs officer Dept. State, 1950-53; research analyst Council Fgn. Relations, 1953-55; prof. U. Notre Dame, 1955-76, emeritus, 1976—; mem. Bd. Fgn. Scholarships, 1981-84, chmn., 1982-84; vis. prof. Yale U., 1942, 46, 54-55, Columbia U., 1952, Vanderbilt U., 1962-66; faculty Nat. War Coll., 1958-59, 61; Fulbright prof. U. Munich, 1962-63; Distinguished vis. prof. Hillsdale Coll., 1976-82. Author: Law Without Force, 1941, An Inquiry into Soviet Mentality, 1956, Facts on Communism, vol. 1: The Communist Ideology, 1959, Handbook on Communism, 1962, Between Nothingness and Paradise, 1971, Deceitful Peace, 1971, Aftersight and Foresight, 1988, Within and Above Ourselves, 1996; assoc. editor Modern Age, 1965—. Mem. task force on fgn. policy Republican Nat. Com., 1965-68. Mem. Am. Polit. Sci. Assn. Roman Catholic. Home: Apt 5C 47 Lafayette Pl Greenwich CT 06830

NIEMEYER, GLENN ALAN, academic administrator, history educator; b. Muskegon, Mich., Jan. 14, 1934; s. John T. and Johanna F. (Walhout) N.; m. Betty Sikkenga, July 8, 1955; children: Kristin, Alexis, Sander. BA in History, Calvin Coll., 1955; MA in History, Mich. State U., 1959, PhD in History, 1962. Tchr. soc. sci. Grand Haven Christian Sch., Mich., 1955-58; teaching asst., asst. instr. Mich. State U., East Lansing, 1958-63; asst. prof. history Grand Valley State U., Allendale, Mich., 1963-66, assoc. prof., 1966-70, prof., 1970—, dean Coll. Arts and Scis., 1970-73, v.p. of colls., 1973-76, v.p. acad. affairs, 1976—, provost, 1980—; evaluator commn. on instns. of higher edn. North Ctrl. Assn., Chgo., 1974—, vice chair, 1994, chair, 1995, v.p., 1996; mem. Acad. Officers, Pres.'s Coun. State Univs. of Mich. Author: The Automotive Career of Ransom E. Olds, 1963; contbr. articles and book revs. to profl. publs. Trustee Calvin Coll., Grand Rapids, Mich., 1974-80; trustee Unity Christian High Sch., Hudsonville, Mich., 1978-80, pres. bd., 1979-80. Mem. Am. Coun. on Edn., Am. Assn. Higher Edn. Mem. Christian Ref. Ch. Office: Grand Valley State U Allendale MI 49401

NIEMEYER, PAUL VICTOR, federal judge; b. Princeton, N.J., Apr. 5, 1941; s. Gerhart and Lucie (Lenzner) N.; m. Susan Kinley, Aug. 24, 1963; children Jonathan K., Peter E., Christopher J. AB, Kenyon Coll., 1962; student, U. Munich, Federal Republic of Germany, 1962-63; JD, U. Notre Dame, 1966. Bars: Md. 1966, U.S. Dist. Ct. Md. 1967, U.S. Ct. Appeals (4th cir.) 1968, U.S. Supreme Ct. 1970, U.S. Dist Ct. (so. dist.) Tex. 1977, U.S. Ct. Appeals (5th cir.) 1978, U.S. Ct. Appeals (3d cir.) 1980. Assoc. Piper & Marbury, Balt., 1966-74, ptnr., 1974-88; U.S. dist. judge U.S. Dist. Ct. Md., Balt., 1988-90; fed. judge U.S. Ct. Appeals (4th cir.), Balt., 1990—; lectr. advanced bus. law Johns Hopkins U., Balt., 1971-75; lectr. Md. Jud. Conf., Md. Ct. Clks. Assn.; sr. lecturing fellow in appellate advocacy Duke U. Sch. of Law, 1994—; mem. standing com. on rules of practice and procedure cts. appeals, 1973-88, arty. grievance com.-hearing panel, 1978-81, select com.-profl. conduct, 1983-85, adv. com. on Fed. Rules of Civil Procedure, 1993—. Co-author: Maryland Rules Commentary, 1984, supplement, 1988, 2d edit., 1992; contbr. articles to profl. jours. Recipient Spl. Merit citation Am. Judicature Soc., 1987. Fellow Am. Coll. Trial Lawyers, Am. Bar Found., Md. Bar Found., Md. Bar Assn. (Disting. Svc. award litigation sect. 1981), Am. Law Inst.; mem. Wednesday Law Club, Lawyers' Round Table. Republican. Episcopalian. Office: US Cir Ct Md 101 W Lombard St Ste 910 Baltimore MD 21201-2611

NIEMI, BEATRICE NEAL, social services professional; b. Fitchburg, Mass., July 23, 1923; d. Albert G. and Florence E. (Copeland) Neal; m. Walter V. Niemi, Oct. 21, 1944 (div. 1970); children: Karen Smith-Gary, Gail Niemi Shaw. AS, Colby-Sawyer Coll., 1942; BS in Psychology, Northeastern U., 1972; MA in Counseling Psychology, Assumption Coll., 1974. Dir. homemaker svcs. Children's Aid and Family Svcs., Inc., Fitchburg, 1965-73; founder, exec. dir. Home Health Aide Svc. of North Cen. Mass., Inc., Fitchburg, 1973-85, Ctr. for Well Being, Inc., Fitchburg, 1985—; instr. Touch for Health Found., Pasadena, Calif., 1977—, The Radiance Technique Assn., St. Petersburg, Fla., 1986—; Outreach trainer The Monroe Inst., Faber, Va., 1990—; v.p. Mass. Coun. for Homemaker-Home Health Aide Svcs., Inc., 1973-81. Pres. Children's Aid and Family Svcs., Inc., Fitchburg, 1964-65; bd. dirs. United Way of Greater Fitchburg, Inc., 1964-70, Leominster (Mass.) Vis. Nursing Assn., 1972-78; chmn. adv. bd. Salvation Army, Fitchburg, 1970-72; v.p. Fitchburg Coun. of Girl Scouts. Fellow Acad. Holistic Health Practitioners; mem. ACA, Am. Mental Health Counselors Assn., Am. Holistic Health Assn., Am. Holistic Med. Found., Mass. Assn. Cmty. Health Agys. (bd. dirs. 1970-83), The Radiance Technique Assn. Internat., Mass. Mental Health Counselors Assn., Assn. for Transpersonal Psychology, Nat. Guild Hypnotists, N.E. Holistic Counselors Assn., others. Avocations: skiing, Yoga, meditation, travel. Office: Ctr for Well Being Inc 70 Bond St Fitchburg MA 01420-2251

NIEMI, JANICE, lawyer, former state legislator; b. Flint, Mich., Sept. 18, 1928; d. Richard Jesse and Norma (Bell) Bailey; m. Preston Niemi, Feb. 4, 1953 (divorced 1987); children—Ries, Patricia. BA, U. Wash., 1950, LL.B., 1967; postgrad. U. Mich., 1950-52; cert. Hague Acad. Internat. Law, Netherlands, 1954. Bar: Wash. 1968. Assoc. firm Powell, Livengood, Dunlap & Silverdale, Kirkland, Wash., 1968; staff atty. Legal Service Ctr., Seattle, 1968-70; judge Seattle Dist. Ct., 1971-72, King County Superior Ct., Seattle, 1973-78; acting gen. counsel, dep. gen. counsel SBA, Washington, 1979-81; mem. Wash. State Ho. of Reps., Olympia, 1983-87, chmn. com. on state govt., 1984; mem. Wash. State Senate, 1987-95; sole practice, Seattle, 1981-94; superior ct. judge King County, 1995—; mem. White House Fellows Regional Selection Panel, Seattle, 1974-77, chmn., 1976, 77; incorporator Sound Savs. & Loan, Seattle, 1975. Bd. dirs. Allied Arts, Seattle, 1971—, Ctr. Contemporary Art, Seattle, 1981-83, Women's Network, Seattle, 1981-84, Pub. Defender Assn., Seattle, 1982-84; bd. visitors dept. psychology U. Wash., Seattle, 1983-87, bd. visitors dept sociology, 1988— . Named Woman of Yr. in Law, Past Pres.'s Assn., Seattle, 1971; Woman of Yr., Matrix Table, Seattle, 1973, Capitol Hill Bus. and Profl. Women, 1975. Mem. Wash. State Bar Assn., Wash. Women Lawyers, Allied Arts of Seattle Bd. Democrat. Home: PO Box 20516 Seattle WA 98102-1516

NIEMI, RICHARD GENE, political science educator; b. Green Bay, Wis., Jan. 10, 1941; s. Eugene H. and Dorothy M. (Stevens) N.; m. Shirley A. Gill, Aug. 4, 1962; children: Nancy, Patricia, Jennifer, Julie. BA, Lawrence Coll., 1962; PhD, U. Mich., 1967. Asst. prof. polit. sci. U. Rochester, N.Y., 1967-71, assoc. prof., 1971-75, prof., 1975—, disting. grad. tchg. prof., 1983-86, chmn. dept. polit. sci., 1979-83, assoc. dean, 1986-89, sr. assoc. dean, 1989-91; vis. prof. U. Lund, Sweden, 1974, 81, U. Iowa, 1985; vis. rschr. Kobe U., Japan, 1991. Author: (with M. Kent Jennings) The Political Character of Adolescence, 1974, Generations and Politics, 1981, How Family Members Perceive Each Otehr, 1974; (with B. Grofman, L. Handley) Minority Representation and the Quest for Voting Equality, 1992; editor: (with Herbert Weisberg) Controversies in Voting Behavior, 1993; (with Harold Stanley) Vital Statistics in American Politics, 1988, 5th edit., 1995; co-author: Trends in Public Opinion; editor: (with L. LeDuc and P. Norris) Comparing Democracies. Rsch. grantee NIMH, 1969-70, NSF, 1974-77, 80-86, 94—, Ford Found., 1972-73; fellow Guggenheim Found., 1983-84, Ctr. for Advanced Study in Behavioral Sci., 1989. Mem. Am. Polit. Sci. Assn., Phi Beta Kappa. Lutheran. Home: 45 Boniface Dr Rochester NY 14620-3333 Office: U Rochester Dept Polit Sci Rochester NY 14627

NIEMIEC, DAVID WALLACE, investment company executive; b. Midland, Mich., Dec. 17, 1949; s. George G. and Eleanor (Yack) N.; m. Melanie Taveau Mason, Oct. 4, 1975; children—Elizabeth Street, Margaret Johnson. A.B., Harvard U., 1972, M.B.A., 1974. Assoc. Dillon, Read & Co., Inc., N.Y.C., 1974-78, v.p., 1979-81, sr. v.p., chief adminstrv. officer, 1982-83, mng. dir., chief adminstrv. officer, 1984—, vice chmn., 1991—; dir. Nat. Securities Clearing Corp., N.Y.C., 1989-92. Trustee Nightingale-Bamford Sch., N.Y.C., 1993—; bd. govs. The Mannes Coll. of Music, N.Y.C., 1996—. Republican. Unitarian. Clubs: Union, Down Town (N.Y.C.). Office: Dillon Read & Co Inc 535 Madison Ave New York NY 10022-4212

NIEMIEC, EDWARD WALTER, professional association executive; b. Detroit, Nov. 1, 1936; s. Walter A. and Mary N.; m. Nancy M. Bennett, Aug. 25, 1962; children: Lisa, Julie, Brenda. B.S., U. Detroit, 1959, M.B.A., 1961. With Paine Webber Jackson & Curtis, N.Y.C., 1959-80, exec. v.p., dir. adminstrv. div., to 1980; v.p., bd. dirs. Moseley, Hallgarten, Estabrook, Weeden, Inc., 1980-82; also bd. dirs. Moseley, Hallgarten, Estabrook & Weeden Holding Corp.; pres., chief exec. officer, dir., mem. exec. com. Securities Settlement Corp. (subs. The Travelers 1982), N.Y.C., 1980-87; pres., dir. Inc Trading Co. subs. Instinet Corp., 1988-89; chief oper. officer Instinet Corp. subs. Reuters Holdings Plc., 1988-89; group v.p. AICPA, N.Y.C., 1989—. Served with U.S. Army. Roman Catholic. Office: AICPA Harborside Fin Ctr 201 Plaza Three Jersey City NJ 07311-3801

NIEMIEC, PETER JUDE, lawyer; b. Yonkers, N.Y., Mar. 9, 1951; m. Ann Majchrzak. BA, Columbia U., 1973; JD, NYU, 1976. Bar: Calif. 1976, U.S. Dist. Ct. (cen. dist.) Calif. 1976, D.C. 1982, Ind. 1983. Sr. atty. U.S. EPA, Washington, 1980-83; dep. atty. gen. State of Ind., Indpls., 1983-86; sr. counsel Pacific Enterprises, L.A., 1986-89; ptnr. Greenberg, Glusker, Fields, Claman & Machtinger, L.A., 1990—; adj. prof. Ind. U. Sch. of Law, Indpls., 1984. Assoc. editor Ann. Survey of Am. Law, 1975. Mem. ABA (natural resources, energy and environ. law sect.), L.A. County Bar Assn. (exec. com. 1990-91), Nat. Rsch. Coun. (com. review and evaluation Army chem. stockpile disposal program, 1992-98). Office: Greenberg Glusker Fields Claman & Machtinger 1900 Avenue Of The Stars Los Angeles CA 90067-4301

NIENBURG, GEORGE FRANK, photographer; b. N.Y.C., Feb. 14, 1938; s. Carl George and Louise Elizabeth (Baum) N. Grad., Germain Sch. Photography, 1989. Veterinarian asst. Stamen Animal Hosp., New Rochelle, N.Y., 1966-70; trainer guard dogs Paradise Guard Dog Service, N.Y.C., 1970-71; animal care technician Am. Soc. for Prevention Cruelty to Animals, N.Y.C., 1971-82; security guard Cen. Nat. Investigation agy., New Rochelle, 1983-88; mem. rsch. bd. advisors Am. Biographical Inst., 1989—. Mem. Nat. Rep. Com., Washington, 1986—; mem. nat. leadership coalition Campaign Am., Washington, 1987—; mem. Nat. Rep. Sen. Com., 1989—; sustaining sponsor Ronald Reagan Found., 1987—; chartered founder Presdl. Trust Fund, 1992; charter mem., supporter Battle Normandy Mus., 1988—; sponsor Nat. Rep. Congl. Com., 1983; life mem. Rep. Presdl. Task Force, 1988; charter founder Ronald Reagan Ctr., 1988—; mem. Pres.'s Congl. Task Force, 1990, Rep. Campaign Com., 1991; supporter USN Meml. Owner Navy Plank, 1991. Recipient Congl. Order of Liberty award, 1993, Rep. Presdl. Legion of Merit; named in inscription in U.S. Pres. Bush's Spl. Honor Roll Commemorating the Reagan-Bush Adminstrn., 1991; included in the "Life Mem. Wall of Honor" at Ronald Reagan Rep. Ctr.; inducted to Rep. Nat. Senatorial com.'s full and complete presdl. commn., 1992, The Ronald Reagan Presdl. Libr. Register, 1991; named to Ronald Reagan Freed Flame, 1994, Election Registry, Washington, 1994. Mem. Washington Legal Found. (patron), U.S. Sen. Club, Internat. Freelance Photographer Orgn. (life), Westchester Photographic Soc., Nat. Fedn. Rep. Women, English First, Nat. Wildlife Fedn. (assoc.), Am. Mus. Natural History, Nat. Trust for Hist. Preservation, Am. Space Frontier Com. (sustaining mem.), Nat. Flag Found. (std. bearer 1987—), Internat. Platform Assn., Masons (master 1986—, royal arch and knight templer 1992), Golden Heart Club, Mil. Order Purple Heart Svc. Found., HeartHighlander Club, Oxford Club. Avocations: music, photography. Home: PO Box 511 65 Bayview Ave New Rochelle NY 10802-0511

NIENHUIS, ARTHUR WESLEY, physician, researcher; b. Hudsonville, Mich., Aug. 9, 1941; s. Willard M. and Grace (Prince) N.; m. Sheryl Ann Kalmink Nienhuis, Sept. 20, 1968; children: Carol Elizabeth, Craig Wesley, Kevin Robert, Heather Grace. Student, Cornell Coll., 1959-61; MD, U. Caif., L.A., 1963-68. Am. Bd. Internal Medicine, Am. Bd. Hematology. Intern Mass. Gen. Hosp., Boston, 1968-69, asst. resident, 1969-70; clin. assoc. NHLBI, NIH, Bethesda, Md., 1970-72; clin. fellow hematology Children's Hosp., Boston, 1972-73; chief. clin. svc. Molecular Hematology NIH, Bethesda, Md., 1973-77; dept. clin. dir. NHLBI, NIH, Bethesda, Md., 1976-93, chief clin. Hematology Branch, 1976-93; dir. St. Jude Children's Rsch. Hosp., Memphis, 1993—; editor BLOOD-J Am. Soc. Hematology, Bethesda, Md., 1988-92; chmn. Hematology Bd. Am. Bd. Internat Med., Phila., 1988-92; mem. bd. dirs. Am. Bd. Internat Med., Phila., 1988-92. Editor: Molecular Basis of Blood Diseases, 1986, 93. Mem. Am. Soc. Hematology (pres. 1994), Am. Soc. Clin. Investigation, Assn. Am. Physicians. Office: St Jude Children's Rsch Hosp 332 N Lauderdale St Memphis TN 38105-2729

NIERENBERG, ROGER, symphony conductor; b. N.Y.C., June 14, 1947; s. Gerard I. and Julliet L. N.; BA, Princeton U., 1969; postgrad. diploma Mannes Coll. Music, 1971; Mus.M., Juilliard Sch. Music, 1979. Mus. dir. Pro Arte Chorale, Paramus, N.J., 1976-85, Juilliard Pre-Coll. Orchestra, N.Y.C., 1979-84, Stamford (Conn.) Symphony Orchestra, 1980—, Jacksonville Symphony (Fla.), 1984—, also condr. Office: Stanford Symphony Orch 1 Stamford Plz 263 Tresser Blvd Stamford CT 06901

NIES, BOYD ARTHUR, hematologist, oncologist; b. Orange, Calif., Jan. 12, 1935; s. Arthur J. and Mary Dora (Sheffer) N.; m. Helen May Salter, July 28, 1957; children: Nancy, Linda, Boyd Jr. AB, Stanford U., 1956, MD, 1959. Diplomate Am. Bd. Internal Medicine, Am. Bd. Internal Medicine: Hematology, Med. Oncology. Intern UCLA, 1959-60, asst. resident, 1960-61; assoc. resident Wadsworth VA Hosp., L.A., 1961-62; clin. assoc. Nat. Cancer Inst., Bethesda, Md., 1962-64; fellow in hematology Stanford U., Palo Alto, Calif., 1964-65; pvt. practice internal medicine and hematology Redlands, Calif., 1965-68; pvt. practice hematology and med. oncology San Bernardino, Calif., 1968—. Contbr. articles to profl. jours. Bd. dirs. First United Meth. Ch., Redlands, 1985-88, St. Bernardine Hosp., San Bernardino, 1975-77, Riverside-San Bernardino Counties Blood Bank, 1984—, pres. 1988-90, bd. dirs. Inland Med. Providers, 1990-93. Fellow ACP; mem. AMA, Am. Soc. Internal Medicine, Am. Soc. Hematology, Am. Soc. Clin. Oncology, Internat. Soc. Hematology, Redlands Country Club, Redlands Swim and Tennis Club. Republican. Methodist. Avocations: tennis, golf, photography, stamp collecting. Home: 645 E Mariposa Dr Redlands CA 92373-7353 Office: Inland Hematology Oncology 401-C Highland Ave San Bernardino CA 92404-3801

NIES, HELEN WILSON, federal judge; b. Birmingham, Ala., Aug. 7, 1925; d. George Earl and Lida Blanche (Erckert) Wilson; m. John Dirk Nies ; children: Dirk, Nancy, Eric. BA, U. Mich., 1946, JD, 1948. Bar: Mich. 1948, D.C. 1961, U.S. Supreme Ct. 1962. Atty. Dept. Justice, Washington, 1948-51, Office Price Stblzn., Washington, 1951-52; assoc. Pattishall, McAuliffe and Hofstetter, Washington, 1960-66, resident ptnr., 1966-77; ptnr. Howrey & Simon, Washington, 1978-80; judge U.S. Ct. Customs and Patent Appeals, 1980-82; cir. judge U.S. Ct. Appeals Fed. Cir., 1982—; chief judge U.S. Ct. Appeals (fed. cir.), 1990-94, sr. status, 1995—; mem. jud. conf. U.S. Com. on Bicentennial of Constn., 1986-92; mem. pub. adv. com. trademark affairs Dept. Commerce, 1976-80; mem. adv. bd. BNA's Patent Trademark and Copyright Jour., 1976-78; mem. bd. visitors U. Mich. Law Sch., 1975-78; adv. for restatement of law and unfair competition Am. Law Inst., 1986—; speaker World Intellectual Property Orgn., Forum of Judges, Calcutta, 1987, European Judges Conf., Hague, 1991, Kyoto (Japan) Comparative Law Ctr., 1992, others. Recipient Athena Outstanding Alumna award U. Mich., 1987, Jefferson medal N.J. Patent Law Assn., 1991, Judicial Honoree award Bar Assn. D.C., 1992, D. of Laws, Honoris Causa, John Marshall Law Sch., Chgo., 1993. Mem. ABA (chmn. com. 203, 1972-74, com. 504, 1975-76), Bar Assn. D.C. (chmn. patent trademark copyright sect. 1975-76, dir. 1976-78), U.S. Trademark Assn. (chmn. lawyers adv. com. 1974-76, bd. dirs. 1976-78), Am. Patent Law Assn., Fed. Bar Assn., Nat. Assn. Women Lawyers, Women's Bar D.C. (Woman Lawyer of Yr. 1980), Order of Coif, Phi Beta Kappa, Phi Kappa Phi. Office: US Ct Appeals Fed Cir 717 Madison Pl NW Washington DC 20439-0001

NIESE, WILLIAM A., lawyer, newspaper publishing executive. BS, Cornell U., 1958; LLB, SUNY, Buffalo, 1961. Bar: N.Y. 1961, Ariz. 1963, Calif. 1966. Corp. counsel, asst. sec. Times Mirror Co., L.A., 1969-73, asst. gen. counsel, asst. sec., 1973-82; assoc. gen. counsel, asst. sec. L.A. Times, 1982-90, v.p., gen. counsel, 1985-90, sr. v.p. law and human resources, 1990—. Capt., JAGC, U.S. Army, 1961-66. Office: Times Mirror Co Times Mirror Sq Los Angeles CA 90053

NIESEN, JAMES LOUIS, theater director; b. St. Louis, Feb. 15, 1946; s. James Louis and Emily Elise (Brennecke) N. BFA, Ill. Wesleyan U., 1968; MFA, Ohio U., 1974. Actor Stage South, Columbia, S.C., 1974-75, Long Wharf Theatre, New Haven, 1977-78, Geva Theater, Rochester, N.Y., 1978-79; freelance dir., 1980-83; stage mgr. Roundabout Theater, N.Y., 1982-83; artistic dir. Irondale Ensemble Project, N.Y., 1983—; panelist N.Y. Found. on the Arts, N.Y., 1988-89. Author: (book) Game Guide, 1988; contbr. articles to profl. jours.; dir. (play) St. Joan of the Stockyards, 1993, Donton's Death, 1994. Mem. Actor's Equity Assn. Avocations: country music, tennis. Home: 419 Pacific St Brooklyn NY 11217-2204 Office: Irondale Ensemble Project 351 W 18th St New York NY 10011-4402

NIESZ, GEORGE MELVIN, tool and die company executive; b. Norwood, Ohio, Aug. 6, 1926; s. George John and Anita Agnes Lucille (Chialastri) N.; student pub. schs., Norwood and Deer Park; m. Evelyn Catherine Rayburn, Oct. 18, 1946; children—Nancy L., George J., Jr. Profl. baseball player St. Louis Cardinals Orgn., 1944-45; tool and die maker Steelcraft Mfg. Co., Cin., 1946-51; supt., mgr. Abco Tool & Die Co., 1951-70; founder, pres. Niesz Tool & Die Co., Cin., 1970-85; officer, dir. Pvt. Investment Co., 1985—. State dir., v.p. Sycamore-Deer Park Jr. C. of C., 1956-59. Ky. Col. Mem. Am. Soc. Metals, Soc. Mfg. Engring., Cin. C. of C., Anderson Twp. C. of C. Republican. Clubs: Masons (32 deg); Shriners. Patentee portable tool attachment; chess champion. Home: 4171 Winesap Ct Cincinnati OH 45236-1735 Office: DPHS Alumni Assn 8351 Plainfield Rd Cincinnati OH 45236

NIETO, BEATRIZ CHAVEZ, nursing educator; b. Edinburg, Tex., Apr. 14, 1958; d. Ruben and Amelia (Guerra) Chavez; m. Roy Munoz Nieto, June 17, 1983; 1 child, Vincent Michael. BSN, Incarnate Word Coll., 1981; MSN, U. Tex. Health Sci. Ctr., 1993. Cert. clin. nurse specialist in med.-surg. nursing. Charge nurse Santa Rosa Children's Hosp., San Antonio, 1981-82; asst. DON Beverly Enterprises Home Health, McAllen, Tex., 1982-83; staff nurse St. David's Comty. Hosp., Austin, Tex., 1983-84; instr. for nurse asst. program Tex. State Tech. Inst., Harlingen, 1984-87; insvc./infection control dir. Mission (Tex.) Hosp., Inc., 1987-90; specialist nursing dept. U. Tex. Pan Am., Edinburg, 1990-93, asst. prof. nursing, 1993—; adv. bd. nurse asst. program Tex. State Tech. Inst., Harlingen, 1987-88; mem. Am. Heart Assn./CPR Valley task force Rio Grande Valley, Tex., 1992-94; peer advisor U. Tex. Health Sci. Ctr., San Antonio, 1992-93; planning com. workshop in field, 1993. Instr., instr. trainer Am. Heart Assn., 1992-93. Mem. ANA, Assn. Practitioners in Infection Control (pres. 1987-90), Tex. Nurses Assn., 1984—, Sigma Theta Tau (Delta Alpha chpt. 1993—). Democrat. Avocations: reading, writing, needlepoint, spending time with family. Home: 518 E Fay St Edinburg TX 78539-4738 Office: U Tex Pan Am 1201 W University Dr Edinburg TX 78539-2909

NIETO, JOHN WESLEY, artist; b. Denver, Aug. 6, 1936; s. Simon and Natalia (Venegas) N.; m. Renay Hagin, Nov. 15, 1974; children: John Arthur, Laura Elizabeth, Anaya, Quint. Student, Pan Am. U., 1955-56, So. Meth. U., 1957-59. Artist: work has been reproduced in numerous publications including The Indian Trader, Tucson Mag., Austin (Tex.) Mag., Scottsdale Mag., Ariz. Daily Star, Art in the West, 1988, Nat. Geographic, 1990, New Mex. Mag., Horizon Mag., The Art Experience; featured on radio and TV shows including Japan Nat. TV, 1989, ABC TV Network, 1984, Nat. Pub. Radio, Washington, 1982, Voice of Am., 1981. Mem. adv. bd. Wheelwright Mus., Santa Fe, New Mex., 1985-86, Am. Indian Coll. Fund in N.Y., 1989, Native Am. Prep. Sch., Pecos, New Mex., 1991—; trustee Meadow Sch. of Arts So. Meth. U., Dallas, 1993-94, So. Meth. U., 1993-94; vol. lectr. sponsored tour for Navajo children of Wheelwright Mus., 1988, gallery talk at Ventana for Mescalero Apache children, Tularose Elem. Sch., 1991, six classes for children of migrant workers Guadalupe Sch., Salt Lake City, 1993; contbr. works to numerous benefits. Recipient Gov.'s award, New Mex., 1994. Home and Studio: PO Box 910 Corrales NM 87048-0910

NIETO DEL RIO, JUAN CARLOS, marketing executive; b. Mexico City, Mar. 1, 1962. BA, Tufts U., 1984. Latin Am. sales TELEVISA, Miami, Fla., 1984-86; rsch. assoc. UNIVISION, N.Y.C., 1986-87; asst. to v.p. UNIVISA, L.A., 1987-88; pres. Spanish Comm., A Divsn. of Western Media, L.A., 1989-93; pres. mktg. HES, L.A., 1993-95; founder Entertainment Comms. Mgmt. L.A., 1996—. Vol. Hermandad Mexicana, L.A. Avocations: travel, languages, multimedia computers. Home: 1208 S Chavez St Burbank CA 91506

NIEUWENDORP, JUDY LYNELL, special education educator; b. Sioux Center, Iowa, Jan. 3, 1955; d. Leonard Henry and Jenelda Faith (Van't Hul) N. BA in Religious Edn., Reformed Bible Coll., 1977; BA in Secondary Edn. and Social Scis., Northwestern Coll., 1980; degree edn. of emotional disabilities, Mankato State U., 1984; MEd, Marian Coll., 1989. Tutor, counselor The Other Way, Grand Rapids, Mich., 1976-77; sr. counselor Handicap Village, Sheldon, Iowa, 1978-79; florist Sheldon Greenhouse, 1979-80; K-6 summer sch. tchr. Worthington (Minn.) Sch. Dist., 1982-83; tchr. of emotional/behavioral disabilities class Worthington Sr. H.S., 1981-85, White Bear Lake (Minn.), 1985-89, Northland Pines H.S., Eagle River, Wis., 1989—; negotiator Coop. Edn. Svcs. Agy., Tomahawk, Wis., 1994—; instr. workshop Advanced Learning, Cedar Falls, Iowa, 1991-92; regional rep. for coun. of spl. program devel. Den. Coop. Svc. Unit, 1983-85; basketball/volleyball coach Worthington, White Bear Lake and Three Lakes, Wis., 1981-89. Mem. scholarship com. Profl. Bus. Women Am., Worthington, 1984-85; asst. devel. mem.Hosp. Mental Health Unit, Worthington, 1983-84; founder parent support group for parents of spl. edn. students Worthington Sch. Dist., 1983-84. Mem. Nat. Edn. Coun., Wis. Edn. Assn., Coun. for Exceptional Children, Minn. Educators for Emotionally Disabled, Eagle River Black Belt Acad. Avocations: kuy-ky-do, golf, gardening, reading, art, skiing. Home: 5148 Hwy G Eagle River WI 54521

NIEUWENDYK, JOSEPH, professional hockey player; b. Oshawa, Ontario, Can., Sept. 10, 1966. Student, Cornell U., 1984-87. Hockey player Calgary Flames, Calgary, Alberta, Can., 1987—. Ivy League Rookie of Yr., 1984-85, NCAA All Am. East 1st team 1985-86, 86-87, ECAC All-Star 1st team 1985-86--86-87, Player of Yr., 1986-87; named NHL Rookie of Yr. Sporting News, 1987-88; recipient Calder Meml. trophy, 1987-88, Dodge Ram Tough award, 1987-88, King Clancy trophy, 1994-95; named to NHL All-Rookie Team, 1987-88, NHL All-Star Game 1988, 90, 94. Office: Calgary Flames, PO Box 1540 Sta M, Calgary, AB Canada T2P 3B9*

NIEVERGELT, JURG, computer science educator; b. Luzern, Switzerland, June 6, 1938; came to U.S., 1962; s. Albert and Hedwig Nievergelt; m. Teresa Quiambao; children: Mark, Derek. Diploma in math., Swiss Fed. Inst. Tech. (ETH), Zurich, Switzerland, 1962; PhD in Math., U. Ill., 1965. Research fellow Dept. Computer Sci. and Math. U. Ill., 1962-65; asst. prof. computer sci. and math. U. Ill., Urbana, 1965-68, assoc. prof. computer sci., 1968-72, prof., 1972-77; prof. Swiss Fed. Inst. Tech. (ETH), Zurich, 1975-85, 89—; Kenan prof., chmn. dept. computer sci. U. N.C., Chapel Hill, 1985-89; rsch. scientist various rsch. labs. and univs., including U. Grenoble, U. Stuttgart, Keio U.; mem. Computing Rsch. Bd., 1987-89. Author: (with E.M. Reingold and N. Deo) Combinational Algorithms: Theory and Practice, 1977, (with A. Ventura and H. Hinterberger) Interactive Computer Programs for Education—Philosophy, Techniques and Examples, 1986, (with K. Hinrichs) Algorithms and Data Structures, with Applications to Graphics and Geometry, 1993; mem. editorial bd. Sci. Computer Programming, Jour. Symbolic Computation, Decision Support Systems, Informatik Spektrum; contbr. articles to profl. jours. Grantee NSF, 1972-76, 86-89, Office Naval Rsch., 1986-89. Fellow IEEE, AAAS, Assn. Computing Machinery. Research interests include algorithms and data structures, parallel computation, interactive systems. Office: ETH Informatik, CH-8092 Zurich Switzerland

NIEVES, JOESPHINE, federal agency administrator. BBA, CUNY; MS, Columbia U.; PhD, Union Grad. Sch. Assoc. asst. sec. employment and tng. Dept. of Labor, 1994—. Recipient Lifetime Achievement award Nat. P.R. Forum, Disting. Achievement Human Svcs. award Boricua Coll., Martin Luther Jr. medal Freedom; named Acad. Women Achievers YWCA, N.Y.C. Office: Dept of Labor Employment & Tng Adminstrn 200 Constitution Ave NW Washington DC 20210*

NIEWIAROSKI, TRUDI OSMERS (GERTRUDE NIEWIAROSKI), social studies educator; b. Jersey City, Apr. 30, 1935; d. Albert John and Margaret (Niemeyer) Osmers; m. Donald H. Niewiaroski, June 8, 1957; children: Donald H., Donna, Margaret Anne, Nancy Noel. AB in History and German, Upsala Coll., East Orange, N.J., 1957; MEd, Montgomery County Pub. Schs., Rockville, Md., 1992. Cert. tchr., Md. Tchr. geography Colego Americano, Quito, Ecuador, 1964-66; bd. dirs. Cotopaxi Acad., Quito, 1964-65; tchr. speed reading Escuela Lincoln, Buenos Aires, Argentina, 1966-67; substitute thcr. Montgomery County Pub. Schs., Rockville, 1978-83, tchr. social studies, 1984—; del. Eisenhower People to People Educators' Del. Vietnam, 1993. Author curricula; contbr. chpts. to books, articles to profl. jours.; lectr. at workshops. Bd. dirs. Cotopaxi Acad., Quito, 1964-65; pres. Citizens Assn., Potomac, Md., 1977-81; leader Girl Scouts U.S., 1975-76; adv. coun. Milken Found. Recipient Md. Tchr. of Yr. award State of Md. Edn. Dept., 1993, finalist nat. Tchr. of Yr., 1993, Disting. Alumni award Upsala Coll., 1993, Nat. Educator award Milken Found., 1994; Fulbright fellow, India, 1985, China, 1990, Japan Keizai Koho Ctr. fellow, 1992; UMBC-U. Mex. Art and Culture scholar, 1995. Mem. AAUW, ASCD, Nat. Coun. Social Studies, Md. Coun. for Social Studies, Asia Soc., Smithsonian Instn., Montgomery County Hist. Soc., Spl. Interest Groups-China, Japan and Korea, Md. Bus. Roundtable for Edn., Nat. Social Studies Suprs. Assn., Kappa Delta Pi. Avocations: cake and cookie decorating, travel. Office: R Montgomery High Sch Rockville MD 20852

NIEWIAROWSKI, STEFAN, physiology educator, biomedical research scientist; b. Warsaw, Poland, Dec. 4, 1926; came to U.S., 1972, naturalized, 1978; s. Marian and Janina (Sledzinska) N.; m. Marta Ciswicka (div. 1974); children: Agata, Tomasz. MD, Warsaw U., 1952, PhD, 1960, Dozent, 1961. Lic. physician, Pa.; cert. Ednl. Coun. Fgn. Med. Grads. Intern, med. resident Inst. Hematology, Warsaw, 1951-54; rsch. fellow, rsch. assoc. dept. physiol. chemistry Warsaw U. Med. Sch., 1948-54; rsch. assoc., sr. rsch. assoc. Lab. Clin. Biochemistry, Inst. Hematology, Warsaw, 1951-61; physician in charge Outpatient Dept. for Hemophiliacs, Warsaw, 1957-61; head dept., prof. physiol. chemistry Med. Sch., Bialystok, Poland, 1961-68; assoc. prof. pahtology dept. pathology McMaster U., Hamilton, Ont., Can., 1970-72; rsch. prof. medicine, head coagulation sect. Specialized Ctr. Thrombosis Rsch., Temple U. Sch. Medicine, Phila., 1972-78; prof. physiology Temple U. Sch. Medicine, Phila., 1975—, prof. physiology Thrombosis Rsch. Ctr., 1978—; cons. dept. infectious diseases Warsaw U. Med. Sch., 1954-60; vis. scientist Centre Nat. de Transfusion Sanguine, Paris, 1959; cons. dept. pediatrics Warsaw U. Med. Sch., 1961-65; vis. scientist Vascular Lab., Lemeul Shattuck Hosp., Boston, 1965, 68-70; vis. prof. medicine Tufts U. Sch. Medicine, Boston, 1968-70; dir. Blood Components Devel. Lab., Hamilton Red Cross and McMaster U., 1971-72; mem. sr. coun. Internat. Com. on Haemostatis and Thrombosis, 1973—; mem. NIH rsch. rev. coms., 1975—. Editor Thrombosis Rsch., 1972-80; mem. editorial com. Procs. of Soc. of Exptl. Biology and Medicine, 1980-82, mem. editorial bd., 1980—; reviewer Jour. Clin. Investigation, Jour. Lab. and Clin. Medicine, Blood, Biochimica et Biophysica Acta, Archives of Biochemistry and Biophysics, Jour. Biol. Chemistry, Am. Jour. Physiology; author, co-author 250 articles in the field of blood coagulation, platelet physiology and cell adhesion; contbr. articles to profl. jours. Ont. Heart Found. fellow, 1970-71; recipient Jurzykowski Found. award, 1990, rsch. awards NIH, 1972—. Mem. Internat. Soc. Hematology, Internat. Soc. Thrombosis and Hemostasis, Am. Physiology Soc., Am. Soc. Hematology, Coun. of Thrombosis of Am. Heart Assn., Soc. Exptl. Biology and Medicine, Polish Inst. Arts and Scis. in Am., Am. Soc. Exptl. Pathology, Polish Am. Med. Soc. (hon.). Achievements include patent for trigramin a platelet aggregation inhibiting polypeptide. Home: 445 S Woodbine Ave Narberth PA 19072-2027 Office: Temple U Sch Medicine 3400 N Broad St Philadelphia PA 19140-5196

NIEWYK, ANTHONY, lawyer; b. Utrecht, The Netherlands, Feb. 28, 1941; arrived in U.S., 1956; s. John and Anthonia B. (Thomassen) N.; m. Ruth Ann Hunderman, Aug. 20, 1965; children: Robert, Deborah. BS, Calvin Coll., 1961; BSEE, U. Mich., 1963, MSEE, 1964; JD, George Washington U., 1972. Engr. Whirlpool Corp., Benton Harbor, Mich., 1965-69; patent agt. Whirlpool Corp., Benton Harbor, 1969-72, patent atty., 1972-78, dir. labor rels., 1978-84; atty. Jeffers, Irish, Hoffman, Wayne, Ind., 1984-86; ptnr. Jeffers, Hoffman, Niewyk, Ft. Wayne, Ind., 1987-91, Baker & Daniels, Ft. Wayne, Ind., 1991—. Avocations: reading, golf, fishing, flying, gardening. Home: 12215 Glen Lake Dr Fort Wayne IN 46804-4572 Office: Baker & Daniels 2400 Ft Wayne Nat Bank Bldg Fort Wayne IN 46802

NIGAM, BISHAN PERKASH, physics educator; b. Delhi, India, July 14, 1928; came to U.S., 1952; s. Rajeshwar Nath and Durga (Vati) N.; m. Indira Bahadur, Nov. 14, 1956; children—Sanjay, Shobhna, Ajay. B.S., U. Delhi, 1946, M.S., 1948; Ph.D., U. Rochester, N.Y., 1955. Research fellow U. Delhi, 1948-50; lectr. in physics, 1950-52, 55-56; postdoctoral fellow Case Inst. Tech., Cleve., 1954-55; postdoctoral research fellow NRC, Ottawa, Can., 1956-59; research assoc. U. Rochester, 1959-60, asst. prof. physics, part-time 1960-61; prin. scientist Gen. Dynamics/Electronics, Rochester, N.Y., 1960-61; assoc. prof. physics SUNY, Buffalo, 1961-64; prof. physics Ariz. State U., Tempe, 1964—, U. Wis., Milw., 1966-67. Author: (with R.R. Roy) Nuclear Physics, 1967; also articles. Govt. of India scholar U. Rochester, 1952-54. Fellow Am. Phys. Soc. Office: Ariz State U Dept Physics Box 871504 Tempe AZ 85287-1504

NIGH, GEORGE, university administrator, former governor; b. McAlester, Okla., June 9, 1927; s. Wilber and Irene (Crockett) N.; m. Donna Mashburn, 1963; children: Mike, Georgeann. Student, Ea. A&M Coll., 1946-48; BA, E. Cen. State U., 1950. Ptnr. Nigh Grocery, McAlester, 1956-60; mem. Okla. Legislature, 1950-58; lt. gov. Okla., 1958-63, 67-79, gov., 1963, 79-87; pres. U. Cen. Okla., Edmond, OK, 1992—; bd. dirs. J.C. Penney Co., Boatmen's First Nat. Bank. Mem. Okla. Young Democrats (pres.), Okla. Jr. C. of C. (sec.), Am. Legion, V.F.W., Am. Vets. Presbyterian. Club: Mason (32 deg., Shriner). Office: U Ctrl Okla Office of President 100 N University Dr Edmond OK 73034

NIGHTINGALE, ELENA OTTOLENGHI, geneticist, physician, administrator; b. Livorno, Italy, Nov. 1, 1932; came to U.S., 1939; d. Mario Lazzaro and Elisa Vittoria (Levi) Ottolenghi; m. Stuart L. Nightingale, July 1, 1965; children—Elizabeth, Marisa. A.B. summa cum laude, Barnard Coll., 1954; Ph.D., Rockefeller U., 1961; M.D., NYU, 1964. Asst. prof. Cornell U. Med. Coll., N.Y.C., 1965-70, Johns Hopkins U., Balt., 1970-73; fellow in clin. genetics and pediatrics Georgetown U. Hosp., Washington, 1973-74; sr. staff officer NAS, Washington, 1975-79, sr. program officer Inst. Medicine, 1979-82, sr. scholar in residence, 1982-83; spl. advisor to pres. Carnegie Corp. N.Y., N.Y.C., 1983-94, sr. program officer, 1989-94; scholar-in-residence Nat. Acad. Scis., Washington, 1995—; vis. assoc. prof. Harvard U. Med. Sch., Boston, 1980-84, vis. lectr., 1984-95; adj. prof. pediatrics Georgetown U. Med. Ctr., 1984—, George Washington U. Med. Ctr., 1994—; mem. recombinant DNA adv. com. NIH, Bethesda, Md., 1979-83. Editor: The Breaking of Bodies and Minds: Torture, Psychiatric Abuse and the Health Professions, 1985, Prenatal Screening, Policies and Values: The Example of Neural Tube Defects, 1987; co-author: Before Birth: Prenatal Screening for Genetic Disease, 1990, Promoting the Health of Adolescents: New Directions for the 21st Century, 1993; contbr. numerous sci. articles to profl. publs. Bd. dirs. Ctr. for Youth Svcs., Washington, 1980-84, Sci. Svc. Inc., Washington, 1985-96, Amnesty Internat., U.S.A., 1989-91. Sloan Found. fellow, 1974-75. Fellow AAAS (chmn. com. on sci. freedom and responsibility 1985-88), N.Y. Acad. Scis., Royal Soc. Medicine; mem. Harvey Soc., Am. Soc. Microbiology, Am. Soc. Human Genetics (social issues com. 1982-85), Genetics Soc. Am., Inst. Medicine of NAS (chmn. com. on health and human rights 1987-90), Phi Beta Kappa, Sigma Xi. Office: Nat Acad Scis 2101 Constitution Ave NW Washington DC 20418-0007

NIGHTINGALE, GEOFFREY J., management and communications consultant; b. New Haven, Conn., Sept. 5, 1938; s. Louis M. and Evelyn G. (Carr) N.; m. Gisela I. Staats, Apr. 7, 1961; children: Alyssa M., Christopher G. BA, CCNY, 1963. Editor Trench Pubs., N.Y.C., 1961-64; pub. relations AE W. Alec Jordan Assocs., N.Y.C., 1964-68; pub. relations AE Burson-Marsteller, N.Y.C., 1968-71, group mgr., v.p. pub. relations, 1971-73, creative dir. pub. relations, v.p., 1973-78, exec. v.p., worldwide creative dir., 1983-93; pres. Syner Genics div. Burson-Marsteller, N.Y.C., The Hague (The Netherlands), 1986-93; pres. Syner Genics divsn. Young & Rubicam Inc., 1993-95; dir. strategy and devel. Nightingale & Ptnrs., Cold Spring Harbor, N.Y., 1991—; creative cons. N.Y.C., 1978-83; pres. Nightingale Mgmt. Sys., Inc., 1995—; cons. Port of Galveston, Tex., 1984-86; practice lader orgnl. comm. practice Burson-Marsteller. Author: The Highway Gourmet, 1992; contbr. articles to profl. jours. Cons. Conservative Party, 1977-78, USA for Africa, 1985-86. Served with U.S. Army, 1958-60. Mem. Internat. Assn. Bus. Communicators, Corp. Communication Cons., World Future Soc. Libertarian. Universalist-Unitarian. Avocations: dog breeding, travel, writing non-fiction. Office: Nightingale Mgmt Sys Inc 3 Harbor Rd Cold Spring Harbor NY 11724-1501 *In the end, nothing happens without communication. Failure to communicate means commitment goes unshared, action drifts, assessments and experience cannot be applied and the institution withers away. In a very real sense communication is management. And everything else is window dressing.*

NIGHTINGALE, RETHA LEE, federal agency administrator; b. Wichita, Kans., Dec. 15, 1954; d. L.D. and Barbara Louise (McClain) Figgins; m. William Boyd III, Dec. 30, 1982; children: Theodore Jacob, Katharine Ann. BA, U. Kans., 1977. Hydrologic technician U.S. Geol. Survey, Lawrence, Kans., 1975-78; personnel clk. U.S. Geol. Survey, Denver, 1978-79, position class specialist, 1979-80; personnel mgmt. specialist Office of Personnel Mgmt., Denver, 1980-81; personnel officer USDA Forest Service, Glenwood Springs, Colo., 1981-83; adminstrv. officer USDA Forest Service, Nemo, S.D., 1983-87, Bighorn Nat. Forest, Sheridan, Wyo., 1987-88; acting dist. ranger Ketchikan (Alaska) Ranger Dist., 1990; adminstrv. officer Tongass Nat. Forest, Ketchikan, Alaska, 1989—; mem. human resource investment coun. Ketchikan Gateway Borough, 1996—; chmn. exec. com. Regional Adminstrv. Team, 1987-88. Rep. Pres. Carter's Adv. Com. on the Status of Women, Denver, 1980, Civil Rights Commn., Custer, S.D., 1986-87; bd. dirs. Ketchikan Youth Svcs., 1989-91. Named one of Outstanding Young Women in Am., Jaycees, 1983, 87. Mem. Am. Soc. Pers. Adminstrn. (treas. 1975-76), Bus. and Profl. Women (dir. young career woman program 1984-85, Young Career Women award for Western Colo. 1983), Fed. Employed Women (sec. 1980-81), Rotary, Epsilon Sigma Alpha (dir. pub. rels. 1982-83), Alpha Delta Pi. Democrat. Presbyterian. Avocations: bicycling, swimming, hiking, reading.

NIGHTINGALE, STUART LESTER, physician, public health officer; b. N.Y.C., Jan. 26, 1938; s. Lester M. Nightingale and Beatrice L. N. (Liebowitz) Helpern; m. Elena Ottolenghi, July 1, 1965; children: Elizabeth S., Marisa O. BA, Yale U., 1959; MD, NYU, 1964. Diplomate Am. Bd. Internal Medicine. Intern in medicine and surgery Montefiore Hosp. and Med. Ctr., Bronx, N.Y., 1964-65, resident in internal medicine, fellow in adolescent medicine, 1965-66, 67-69, asst. attending physician, 1969-70; resident in anatomical pathology NYU Sch. Medicine, 1966-67; med. dir. drug abuse adminstrn. Dept. Health and Mental Hygiene State of Md., Balt., 1971-72; chief treatment and rehab., office of programs, spl. action office for drug abuse prevention Exec. Office of Pres., Washington, 1972-74, chief office treatment and rehab., spl. action office for drug abuse prevention, 1974-75; dir. divsn. resource devel. Nat. Inst. on Drug Abuse, Rockville, Md., 1974-76; asst. to dir. Bur. Drugs, Food and Drug Adminstrn., Rockville, 1976-79; dep. assoc. commr. for health affairs FDA, Rockville, 1979-82, acting assoc. commr. for health affairs, 1979-82, assoc. commr. for health affairs, 1982—; med. dir. The Fort Greene/Bklyn.-Cumberland Narcotic Detoxification Program, Bklyn., 1969-70; vis. physician Balt. City Hosps., 1970-72; clin. instr. dept. medicine Coll. Medicine SUNY, Bklyn., 1970; asst. physician out-patient dept., instr. dept. medicine Johns Hopkins U. Sch. Medicine, Balt., 1970-72, med. dir. drug abuse ctr., 1970-71, instr. dept. med. care and hosps. Sch. Hygiene and Pub. Health, 1971-74, rsch. program mgr. health svcs. rsch. and devel. ctr., 1970-71; chmn. rsch. involving human subjects com. FDA, 1979-84; liaison mem. Commn. on Fed. Drug Approval Process, U.S. Congress, 1980-81; mem.-at-large U.S. Pharmacopeial Conv., Inc., 1985-95; bd. trustees The Milton Helpern Libr. of Legal Medicine, N.Y.C., 1982—; bd. dirs. Nat. Coun. on Patient Info. and Edn., Washington; mem. forum on drug devel. and regulation Inst. Medicine, NAS, Washington, 1986—. Contbg. author Jour. AMA, 1985—, Am. Family Physician, 1986—. Capt. med. corps USAR, 1966-72; with USPHS. Recipient Disting. Svc. Spl. Action Office for Drug Abuse Prevention award Exec. Office of Pres., 1975, Pub. Health Superior Svc. award, 1983, Disting. Contbn. award Nat. Coun. Patient Info. and Edn., 1987, Achievement award Am. Assn. Physicians for Human Rights, 1990, Presdl. Meritorious Exec. Rank award, 1990, Pub. Health Svc. Spl. Recognition award, 1993. Fellow ACP (mem. clin. pharmacology subcom., health and pub. policy com. 1984-87, 87-88); mem. AMA, Sr. Execs. Assn., Cosmos Club, Yale Club of Washington. Office: FDA 5600 Fishers Ln Rockville MD 20857-0001

NIGHTINGALE, WILLIAM JOSLYN, management consulting company executive; b. Mpls., Sept. 16, 1929; s. William Issac and Gladys (Joslyn) N. B.A., Bowdoin Coll., 1951; M.B.A., Harvard U., 1953; children: Paul, Sara, William Joslyn, Margaret. Mktg. mgr. Gen. Mills Inc., Mpls., 1957-66; sr. assoc. Booz, Allen & Hamilton Inc., N.Y.C., 1966-68; v.p. fin. Hanes Corp., Winston-Salem, N.C., 1969; pres. Bali Co. Inc., N.Y.C., 1970-75; sr. advisor

Nightingale & Assocs. Inc., Stamford, Conn., 1975—; bd. dirs. Ring's End Lumber Inc., Spreckles Industries, Inc., GlassTec Inc.; trustee Naragansett Tax Free Bond Fund, Churchill Cash Reserves Fund, Churchill Tax Free Bd. Fund. Active numerous charitable orgns.; vestryman St. Luke's Episcopal Ch., 1975-78, sr. warden, 1989-91; mem. Darien Representative Town Meeting, 1971-74. Lt. (j.g.) USNR, 1953-57. Republican. Clubs: Wee Burn Country; Harvard (N.Y.C.); Noroton (Conn.) Yacht. Home: 195 Rowayton Ave Norwalk CT 06853-1237 Office: Soundview Plz 1266 E Main St Stamford CT 06902-3546

NIGUIDULA, FAUSTINO NAZARIO, surgeon; b. Pasay City, Philippines, June 27, 1926; s. Aquilino Uriarte and Encarnacion (Nazario) N.; MD, U. of Philippines, 1953; m. Barbara Ann Brooks, Dec. 17, 1977; children: Andrew, Nicole; children by previous marriage—David, Diane, Susan, John, Stephen, Daniel, Nancy, Kathy. Came to U.S., 1953, naturalized, 1970. Intern, Arnot-Ogden Meml. Hosp., Elmira, N.Y., 1953-54; resident surgery Strong Meml. Hosp., Rochester, N.Y., 1954-59; resident in thoracic surgery Buffalo Gen. Hosp., 1959-61; fellow pediatric cardiothoracic surgery Children's Hosp., Buffalo, 1961-62, Hosp. Sick Children, Toronto, Ont., Can., 1963-64; instr. surgery U. Rochester (N.Y.), 1958-59; clin. instr. surgery U. Buffalo, 1965-66; asst. prof. surgery Temple U., Phila., 1967-70, asso. prof. surgery, pediatrics, 1970-75; clin. assoc. prof. Rutgers U., 1979-83; prof. surgery, prof. pediatrics N.Y. Med. Coll., 1983—; dir. pediatric cardio-thoracic surgery Deborah Heart and Lung Center, Browns Mills, N.J., 1975-83; chief pediatric cardiothoracic surgery St. Christopher's Hosp. for Children, Phila., 1967-75, Westchester Med. Ctr., Valhalla, N.Y., 1983—. Mem. ACS, Soc. Thoracic Surgeons, Am. Heart Assn., Assn. Thoracic and Cardiovascular Surgeons Asia, Westchester County Med. Soc., N.Y. State Med. Soc., Westchester Acad. Medicine, AAAS, Soc. Philippine Surgeons in Am., N.Y. Acad. Scis., Cardiology Soc. Poland (hon., 7th commemorative medal 1982). Presbyterian. Home: 2 Pine Hill Ct Briarcliff Manor NY 10510-1742 Office: Westchester County Med Ctr Valhalla NY 10595

NIHART, FRANKLIN BROOKE, museum consultant, writer and editor; b. Los Angeles, Mar. 16, 1919; s. Claude Eugene and Vera Howard (Brooke) N.; m. Mary Helen Brosius, Feb. 11, 1945; children: Mary Catherine, Virginia Brooke Nihart-Martinez. BA, Occidental Coll., 1940. Commd. 2d lt. USMC, 1940, advanced through grades to col., 1957; dep. dir. Marine Corps. History and Mus. USMC, Washington, 1973-92; fellow, past gov., pres. Co. Mil. Historians, 1967-71; founder Marine Corps Hist. Found., 1979. Editor Jour. Am. Mil. Past; contbg. editor Almanac of Seapower. Bd. advisors Am. Mil. U. Decorated Navy Cross, Bronze Star with one gold star; named to Order del Mar Oceano; recipient Disting. Svc. award Co. Mil. Historians, 1982, Disting. Svc. award Marine Corps. Hist. Found., 1992. Mem. Am. Assn. Mus., Internat. Coun. Mus., Nat. Firearms Mus. (bd. dirs.), Nat. Hist. Intelligence Mus. (bd. dirs.), Va. Mus. Mil. Vehicles (bd. dirs.), Internat. Assn. Mus. Arms and Mil. History (hon. life), Orgn. Mil. Mus. Can. (hon. life), Washington Naval Corrs. Circle, Army and Navy Club, Mil. Order of Carabao (Disting. Svc. award 1987), Dacor House, Ends of the Earth Club, Masons. Republican. Presbyterian. Avocations: history, politics, travel, shooting, writing.

NIJENHUIS, ALBERT, mathematician, educator; b. Eindhoven, Netherlands, Nov. 21, 1926; came to U.S., 1952, naturalized, 1959; s. Hendrik and Lijdia (Koornneef) N.; m. Marianne Dannhauser, Aug. 14, 1955; children: Erika, Karin, Sabien, Alaine. Candidaat, U. Amsterdam, Netherlands, 1947, Doctorandus, 1950, Doctor cum laude, 1952. Assoc. Math. Ctr., Amsterdam, Netherlands, 1951-52; asst. Inst. Advanced Study, Princeton, N.J., 1955; mem. Inst. Advanced Study, 1953-55, 61-62; instr., rsch. assoc. U. Chgo., 1955-56; faculty U. Wash., Seattle, 1956-63, prof., 1961-63, affiliate prof., 1988—; prof. math. U. Pa., Phila., 1963-87, prof. emeritus, 1987—; Fulbright lectr. U. Amsterdam, 1963-64; vis. prof. U. Geneva, Switzerland, 1967-68, Dartmouth Coll., 1977-78; researcher and author publs. on subjects including differential geometry, deformation theory in algebra, combinatorics, especially tensors, holonomy groups, graded lie algebras, algorithms. Co-author: Combinatorial Algorithms, 1975, 78; editor: Jour. Algorithms. Postdoctoral fellow Princeton, 1952-53; Fulbright grantee, 1952-53, 63-64; Guggenheim fellow, 1961-62. Mem. Am. Math. Soc., Math. Assn. Am., Netherlands Math. Soc., Assn. for Computing Machinery, AAUP, Royal Netherlands Acad. Scis. (corr.). Office: U Wash Dept Math Box 354350 Seattle WA 98195-4350

NIKAIN, REZA, civil engineer; b. Tehran, Iran, Sept. 26, 1962; came to U.S., 1978; s. Heshmatalah and Maryam (Shahabadi) N.; m. Denise Maroon; 1 child, Cyrus A. BSCE, Rutgers U., 1985, MS, 1988. Registered profl. engr., N.J., Pa., Del., Ky., Fla., Ohio, Kans.; cert. project mgmt. profl. Asst. supt. Lefrak Orgn., New Brunswick, N.J., 1981-86; project mgr. N.J. Transit Corp., Newark, 1986-88; v.p. Mid-Atlantic region The Nielsen-Wurster Group, Inc., Princeton, N.J., 1988—. Mem. ASCE, NSPE, Am. Concrete Inst., Soc. Am. Value Engrs. Achievements include development of a computerized program for schedule delays analysis; methods to evaluate construction schedules and delays on construction projects. Office: The Nielsen-Wurster GroupInc 345 Wall St Princeton NJ 08540-1518

NIKIFORUK, PETER N., university dean; b. St. Paul, Alta., Can., Feb. 11, 1930; s. DeMetro N. and Mary (Dowhaniuk) N.; m. Eugenie F. Dyson, Dec. 21, 1957; children: Elizabeth, Adrienne. BSc, Queen's U., Ont., Can., 1952; PhD, Manchester U., Eng., 1955, DSc, 1970. Engr. A.V. Roe Ltd., Toronto, Ont., 1951-52; def. sci. service officer Def. Research Bd., Quebec, Que., Can., 1956-57; systems engr. Canadair Ltd., Montreal, Que., 1957-59; asst. prof. U. Sask., Saskatoon, 1960-61; assoc. prof. U. Sask., 1961-65, prof., 1965—, chmn. div. control engring., 1964-69, head mech. engring., 1966-73, dean engring., 1973—; mem. coun. NRC, 1973-78; mem. Def. Sci. Adv. Bd., 1993—; mem. coun., exec. and chmn. audit fin. com. Sask. Rsch. Coun., 1978—. Contbr. articles to profl. jours. Bd. dirs. Can. Inst. Indsl. Tech. Fellow Royal Soc. Arts, Inst. Physics, Inst. Elec. Engrs. (Kelvin Premium), Can. Acad. Engring., Engring. Inst. Can. (C. Julian Smith medal, Centennial medal), Can. Soc. Mech. Engr. (past. v.p.), RSC; mem. Assn. Profl. Engrs. Sask. (chmn. bd. examiners, Disting. Svc. award, IEEE Centennial medal). Home: 31 Bell Crescent, Saskatoon, SK Canada S7J 2W2

NIKKEL, RONALD WILBERT, social services administrator; b. Lethbridge, Alta., Can., June 8, 1946; came to U.S., 1978; s. Henry Peter and Katharine (Penner) N.; m. Celeste Carisa Friesen, June 11, 1970. BA, U. Winnipeg (Can.), 1970; MPS, Loyola U., Chgo., 1983. Nat. dir. YFC/Youth Guidance, Toronto, Ont., Can., 1973-78, Chgo., 1978-82; field dir. Prison Fellowship Internat., Washington, 1982-84, v.p., 1984-88, pres., 1988—. Editor: Guidelines for Volunteer Programs in Justice, 1988. Chmn. Non Govtl. Orgns. Alliance in Crime Prevention and Criminal Justice, N.Y.C., 1988-95; bd. dirs. Love and Action, Annapolis, Md., 1989—, Jericho Rd. Found., Chgo., 1992—, Advocates Internat., 1993—. Mem. Acad. Criminal Justice Scis. Episcopalian. Avocations: photography, hiking, gardening. Office: Prison Fellowship Internat PO Box 17434 Washington DC 20041-0434

NIKLAS, KARL J., plant biology educator. Prof. dept. plant biology Cornell U., Ithaca, N.Y. Recipient Cichan award Botanical Soc. Am., 1993. Office: Cornell U Dept Plant Biology 237 Plant Sci Bldg Ithaca NY 14853-0001

NIKOLAI, LOREN ALFRED, accounting educator, author; b. Northfield, Minn., Dec. 14, 1943; s. Roman Peter and Loyola (Gertrude) N.; m. Anita Carol Baker, Jan. 15, 1966; children: Trishia, Jay. BA, St. Cloud State U., 1966, MBA, 1967; PhD, U. Minn., 1973. CPA, Mo. Asst. prof. U. N.C., Chapel Hill, 1973-76; assoc. prof. U. Mo., Columbia, 1976-80, prof., 1980-82, Ernst & Young Disting. prof. Sch. Accountancy, 1982—. Author: Principles of Accounting, 3d edit., 1990, Financial Accounting: Concepts and Uses, 3d edit., 1995, Intermediate Accounting, 6th edit., 1994. Recipient Faculty award of merit Fedn. Schs. of Accountancy, 1989, Disting. Alumni award St. Cloud U., 1990, Coll. of Bus. Faculty Mem. of Yr. award, 1991, Mo. Outstanding Acctg. Educators award, 1993; Kemper fellow U. Mo., 1992. Mem. AICPA, Am. Acctg. Assn., Mo. Soc. CPAs, Fedn. Schs. of Acctg. (pres. 1994). Office: U Mo Sch Accountancy 326 Middlebush Columbia MO 65211

NILES, JOHN GILBERT, lawyer; b. Dallas, Oct. 5, 1943; s. Paul Dickerman and Nedra Mary (Arendts) N.; m. Marian Higginbotham, Nov. 21, 1970; children: Paul Breckenridge, Matthew Higginbotham. BA in History, Stanford U., 1965; LLB, U. Tex., 1968. Bar: Tex. 1968, Calif. 1969, U.S. Dist. Ct. (cen. dist.) Calif. 1973, U.S. Ct. Appeals (9th cir.) 1973, U.S. Dist. Ct. (so. dist.) Calif. 1977, U.S. Supreme Ct. 1979, U.S. Dist. Ct. (no. dist.) Calif. 1983. Assoc. O'Melveny & Myers, Los Angeles, 1973-77, ptnr., 1978—; judge pro tem mcpl. ct. L.A.; spkr., panel mem. Practicing Law Inst., Calif. C.E.B. Served to lt. comdr. USNR, 1968-72, Vietnam. Served to lt. comdr. USNR, 1968-72, Viet Nam. Mem. ABA, Los Angeles County Bar Assn., Am. Judicature Soc. Clubs: Bel-Air Bay (Pacific Palisades, Calif.); Calif. (Los Angeles). Avocation: sailing. Home: 1257 Villa Woods Dr Pacific Palisades CA 90272-3953 Office: O'Melveny & Myers 400 S Hope St Los Angeles CA 90071-2801

NILES, NICHOLAS HEMELRIGHT, publisher; b. Carbondale, Pa., Oct. 17, 1938; s. John Southworth and Helen (Hemelright) N.; m. Margaretta Linen Goodbody, Aug. 19, 1961; children—Jennifer Collett, Arthur David. B.S., Columbia U., 1965; M.B.A., Fordham U., 1976. With Time Inc., 1965-75; assoc. pub. New Times mag., N.Y.C., 1975-79, The Runner mag., 1978-79; pub. Changing Times mag., N.Y.C., 1979-88; v.p., pub. Food & Wine mag., N.Y.C., 1988-90; exec. v.p. Sprinhouse (Pa.) Corp., 1990-92; pres., CEO The Sporting News, N.Y.C., 1992—, Golf Mag. Properties, N.Y.C., 1995—; sr. v.p. Times Mirror Mags., N.Y.C., 1995; bd. dirs. Kiplinger Washington Editors, 1981-88; chmn. bd. Internat. Art of Jazz, Inc., 1985-89; mem. adv. bd. Cornell U. Alumni Mag., 1981-89; mem. exec. com. Times Mirror Mag., 1990—. Chmn. PTA Hinley Sch., Darien, Conn., 1974-76; bd. dirs., mem. exec. com. Urban League Southwestern Fairfield County, Conn., 1976-82; bd. dirs. Guthrie Clinic Found., Sayre, Pa., 1977, Call for Action, 1984-88, League for Hard of Hearing. Lt. U.S. Army, 1961-63. Mem. Met. Advt. Golf, Mag. Pub. Assn., Nat. Golf Found. (bd. dirs. 1995), Wee Burn Country Club, Union League, Blooming Grove Hunting and Fishing Club, Bohemian Club (San Francisco), Anglers Club, TPC Sawgrass Golf Club. Office: The Sporting News 2 Park Ave New York NY 10016-5603

NILES, THOMAS MICHAEL TOLLIVER, ambassador; b. Lexington, Ky., Sept. 22, 1939; s. John Jacob and Rena (Lipetz) N.; m. Carroll C. Ehringhaus, July 22, 1967; children: John Thomas, Mary Chapman. BA, Harvard U., 1960; MA, U. Ky., 1962. Commd. fgn. service officer Dept. State, Washington, 1962, U.S. ambassador to Can., 1985-1989; then permanent rep. EEC, Brussels; asst. sec. of state Europe and Can., 1991-93; amb. to Greece Athens, 1993—. Recipient Superior Honor award Dept. State, 1982, 85. Mem. Phi Beta Kappa. Office: Greece Psc 108 Box 56 APO AE 09842-5009

NILLES, JOHN MATHIAS (JACK NILLES), entrepreneur; b. Evanston, Ill., Aug. 25, 1932; s. Elmer Edward and Hazel Evelyn (Wickum) N.; m. Laila Padorr, July 8, 1957. BA magna cum laude, Lawrence Coll., 1954; MS in Engring., U. Calif., Los Angeles, 1964. Sr. engr. Raytheon Mfg. Co., Santa Barbara, Calif., 1956-58; section head. Ramo-Wooldridge Corp., L.A., 1958-59; project engr. Space Technology Lab., L.A., 1960; dir. The Aerospace Corp., L.A., 1961-67; sr. systems engr. TRW Systems, L.A., 1967-69; assoc. group dir. The Aerospace Corp., L.A., 1969-72; dir. interdisciplinary programs U. So. Calif., L.A., 1972-81, dir. info. technology program, 1981-89; pres. JALA Internat. Inc., L.A., 1980—; coord. EC Telework Forum, Madrid, 1992—; dir. Telecommuting Adv. Coun., L.A., 1991—, pres., 1993-94; chmn. Telecommuting Rsch. Inst., Inc., L.A., 1990—. Author: The Telecommunications Transportation Tradeoff, 1976, Japanese edit., 1977, Exploring the World of the Personal Computer, 1982, French edit., 1985, Micros and Modems, 1983, French edit., 1986, Making Telecommuting Happen, 1994. Capt. USAF, 1954-56. Recipient Rod Rose award Soc. Rsch. Adminstrs., 1976, Environ. Pride award L.A. Mag., 1993, Environ. Achievement award Renew Am., 1994. Mem. IEEE, IEEE Computer Soc., AAAS, Assn. Computing Machinery, Inst. Mgmt. Scis., World Future Soc., Calif. Yacht Club. Avocations: sailing, photography. Office: JALA Internat Inc 971 Stonehill Ln Los Angeles CA 90049-1400

NILLES, JOHN MICHAEL, lawyer; b. Langdon, N.D., Aug. 20, 1930; s. John Joseph and Isabele Mary (O'Neil) N.; m. Barbara Ann Cook, June 22, 1957; children: Trese M., Daniel J., Marcia L., Thomas M., Margaret J. BA cum laude, St. Johns U., 1955; JD cum laude with distinction, U. N.D., 1958. Bar: N.D. 1958, U.S. Dist. Ct. N.D. 1958, U.S. Ct. Appeals (8th cir.) 1958, Minn. 1991. Shareholder, dir., pres. Nilles, Hansen and Davies, Ltd., Fargo, N.D., 1958-90, of counsel, 1990—; exec. v.p., gen. counsel Met. Fin. Corp., Mpls., 1990-95, First Bank F.S.B., Mpls., 1995; pres., bd. dirs. Legal Aid Soc. N.D., Fargo, 1970-76, Red River Estate Planning Coun., 1980-87; vice-chmn. disciplinary bd. Supreme Ct. N.D., 1984-90. Bd. editors N.D. Law Rev., 1957-58. Mem. exec. bd. Red. River Valley coun. Boy Scouts Am., 1959-70; bd. regents U. Mary, Bismarck, N.D., 1967-77; pres., bd. dirs. Cath. Charities, Fargo, 1959-65, Southeast Mental Health Ctr., Fargo, 1972-80. Staff sgt. USAF, 1951-54. Fellow Am. Coll. Trust and Estate Counsel (state dir. 1979-90); mem. ABA, State Bar Assn. N.D., Minn. Bar Assn., Order of Coif. Republican. Roman Catholic. Avocations: tennis, downhill skiing, cross-country skiing, hunting. Home: 10412 Fawns Way Eden Prairie MN 55347-5117

NILSON, GEORGE ALBERT, lawyer; b. N.Y.C., Jan. 15, 1942; s. Howard Seth and Beatrice Ethyl (McCurdy) N.; m. Elizabeth Hughes Logan, July 18, 1942; children: Scott Logan, Douglas George. BA, Yale U., 1963, LLB, 1967, M of Urban Studies, 1967. Bar: Md. 1967, U.S. Dist. Ct. Md., U.S. Ct. Appeals (4th cir.), U.S. Supreme Ct. Assoc. Piper & Marbury, Balt., 1967-73, ptnr., 1982—; asst. atty. gen. Md. State Law Dept., Balt., 1973-76, dep. atty. gen., 1976-82; chmn. Gen. Assembly Compensation Commn., Annapolis, Md., 1984-93, Commn. to Rev. Md. Elections Laws, Annapolis, 1986-87. Pres. Guilford Assn., Balt., 1990-92. Mem. Rule Day Club, The Wranglers, Sergeants Inn. Democrat. Avocations: fishing, golf. Office: Piper & Marbury 36 S Charles St Baltimore MD 21201-3020

NILSON, PATRICIA, clinical psychologist; b. Boulder, Colo., Oct. 22, 1929; d. James William and Vera Maude (Peacock) Broxon; m. Eric Walter Nilson, Dec. 23, 1950; children: Stephen Daniel, Eric Jon, Christopher Lawrence. BA, U. Colo.; RPT, Med. Coll. Va.; MA in Clin. Psychology, L.I. U., 1972, PhD, 1973. Lic. psychologist, N.Y. Clin. psychologist Court Cons. Unit, Hauppauge, N.Y., 1972-92, Three Village Counseling Svc., Setauket, N.Y., 1974-75, Farmingville Mental Health Ctr., Commack, N.Y., 1992-95; pvt. practice Commack, N.Y., 1972—; adj. asst. prof. C.W. Post Coll., Brookdale, 1974-80; cons., supr. psychologist Wayside Sch. for Girls, Valley Stream, 1975-85; cons. L.I. Lighting Co., 1980; lectr. in field;. Author children's therapeutic stories; author therapeutic games: The Road to Problem Mastery; contbr. articles to profl. jours. Mem. APA, Suffolk County Psychol. Assn., Nat. Register Health Svc. Providers in Psychology, Soc. for Clin. and Exptl. Hypnosis (life), Am. Soc. Clin. Hypnosis (cert. and approved cons. in hypnosis). Office: 11 Montrose Dr Commack NY 11725-1312

NILSSON, A. KENNETH, investor; b. L.A., Mar. 16, 1933; s. Arthur V. and Esther (Dean) N.; m. Lesley Swanson, Sept., 1965; children: Kerstin, Keith. BA, U. So. Calif., 1955; MA, U. Calif., 1960; grad., U.S. Defense Language Inst., 1956. Founder Koken, Ltd., Tokyo, 1960-63; mng. dir. Pfizer Internat., Tokyo, 1963-66; pres. Pfizer Inc., Manila, The Philippines, 1966-68, Max Factor & Co. Japan Ltd., Tokyo, 1968-72, Cooper Labs Internat., Inc., Geneva and Brussels, 1972-80, Cooper Labs, Inc., N.Y.C. and Palo Alto, Calif., 1980-85, Cooper Lasersonics, Inc., Palo Alto, 1982-85; dir. Monterey County Bank, Monterey, Calif., 1982-86; vice chmn. The Cooper Cos., 1986-89; chmn. Monterey Inst. Internat. Studies, 1983—; dir. U.S. China Indsl. Exch., 1996—. Contbr. articles to profl. jours. Mem. Coun. on Foreign Rels., World Affairs Coun., Pacific Coun. on Internat. Policy. 1st lt. U.S. Army, 1955-58. Fellow Am. Soc. Laser Medicine, Internat. Inst. Stragetic Studies. Avocation: philology.

NILSSON, BIRGIT, soprano; b. Karup, Sweden, May 17, 1918; d. Nils P. and Justina (Paulsson) Svensson; m. Bertil Niklasson, Sept. 10, 1948. Student, Royal Musical Acad., Stockholm; MusD (hon.), Amherst U., Mass., Andover U., Manhattan Sch. Music, 1982, Mich. State U., 1982. Tchr. master classes Manhattan Sch. Music, N.Y.C., 1983—. Appeared opera and concert houses in Europe, N.Am., S.Am., Japan and Australia; most famous roles include: Isolde, Brünnhilde, Turandot, Elektra; now ret. Decorated 1st comdr. Order of Vasa (Sweden); comdr. Order of St. Olav 1st class (Norway); comdr. Arts et Lettres (France); recipient Swedish Golden medal Illis Quorum CL.18; Austrian and Bavarian Kammersaengerin; named Swedish Royal Court Singer. Hon. mem. Royal Acad. Music London, Royal Acad. Music Stockholm, Vienna State Opera.

NIMETZ, MATTHEW, lawyer; b. Bklyn., June 17, 1939; s. Joseph L. and Elsie (Botwinik) N.; m. Gloria S. Lorch, June 24, 1975; children: Alexandra Elise, Lloyd. B.A., Williams Coll., 1960, LL.D. (hon.), 1979; B.A. (Rhodes scholar), Balliol Coll., Oxford (Eng.) U., 1962; M.A., Oxford (Eng.) U., 1966; LL.B., Harvard U., 1965. Bar: N.Y. 1966, D.C. 1968. Law clk. to Justice John M. Harlan, U.S. Supreme Ct., 1965-67; staff asst. to Pres. Johnson, 1967-69; asso. firm Simpson Thacher & Bartlett, N.Y.C., 1969-71; partner Simpson Thacher & Bartlett, 1972-77; counselor Dept. of State, Washington, 1977-80; acting coordinator refugee affairs Dept. of State, 1979-80, under sec. of state for security assistance, sci. and tech., 1980; partner firm Paul, Weiss, Rifkind, Wharton & Garrison, N.Y.C., 1981—; commr. Port Authority N.Y. and N.J., 1975-77; dir. World Resources Inst., chmn., 1982-94; dir. Coun. for U.S. and Italy, Inc.; mem. N.Y. State Adv. Coun. on State Productivity, 1990-92; presdl. envoy Greed-Macedonian Negotiations, 1994-95. Trustee William Coll., 1981-96; chmn. UN Devel. Corp., 1986-94; bd. dirs. Charles H. Revson Found., 1990—. Mem. Assn. of Bar of City of N.Y., Coun. on Fgn. Rels. Club: Harvard (N.Y.C.). Office: Paul Weiss Rifkind Wharton & Garrison 1285 Avenue Of The Americas New York NY 10019-6028

NIMITZ, CHESTER WILLIAM, JR., manufacturing company executive; b. Bklyn., Feb. 17, 1915; s. Chester William and Catherine V. (Freeman) N.; m. Joan Leona Labern, June 18, 1938; children: Frances Mary, Elizabeth Joan, Sarah Catherine. BS, U.S. Naval Acad., 1936. Commd. ensign USN, 1936, advanced through grades to rear adm., 1957, principally assigned to submarines and destroyers, ret., 1957; with Tex. Instruments Co., 1957-61; with Perkin-Elmer Corp., Norwalk, Conn., 1961—, pres., chief exec. officer, 1965-73, chmn. bd., 1973—, chief exec. officer, 1973-78, chmn. exec. com., 1980-85. Decorated Navy Cross, Silver Star (3). Home: PO Box 1485 Boca Grande FL 33921-1485

NIMKIN, BERNARD WILLIAM, retired lawyer; b. N.Y.C., Apr. 15, 1923; s. Myron Benjamin and Anabel (Davidow) N.; m. Jean Horowitz, Feb. 9, 1947; children—David Andrew, Margaret Lee, Katherine. B.S. cum laude, Harvard U., 1943, LL.B. cum laude, 1949. Bar: N.Y. State bar 1949. Asso. firm Carter, Ledyard & Milburn, N.Y.C., 1949-58; asso. and partner firm Kaye, Scholer, Fierman, Hays & Handler, LLP, N.Y.C., 1958-91; lectr. Practising Law Inst., Banking Law Inst.; Mem. Am. Law Inst.; vis. com. U. Miami Law Sch.; mem. adv. bd. Rev. of Securities Regulation. Contbr. articles to profl. jours. Mem. Conservation Commn., Town of Mamaroneck, N.Y., 1970-74; bd. dirs., sec. United Way of Tri-State, 1985-91. Served to 1st lt. U.S. Army, 1943-46. Mem. ABA (mem. fed. regulation of securities com. 1975—, corp. laws com. 1984-92, legal opinions com. 1989—), N.Y. State Bar Assn. (chmn. sect. banking corp. and bus. law 1979-81, ho. of dels. 1981-84, chmn. corp. law com. 1976-79), Assn. Bar City of N.Y. (chmn. uniform state laws com. 1962-65), Tribar Opinion Com. Democrat. Jewish. Home: Kaye Scholer Fierman Et Al 116 E 63rd St New York NY 10021-7343 Office: Kaye Scholer Fierman Hays & Handler LLP 425 Park Ave New York NY 10022-3506

NIMMER, RAYMOND T., lawyer, law educator; b. Chgo., May 2, 1944; s. Raymond O. and Helen (Barscz) N. BA in Math., Valparaiso U., 1966, JD with distinction, 1968. Bar: Ill. 1968, Tex. 1984, U.S. Ct. Appeals (5th cir.) 1984, U.S. Supreme Ct. 1985. Rsch. atty. Am. Bar Found., 1968-75; assoc. dean U. Houston Law Sch., 1975-87, Childs prof. Law, 1979—; counsel Sheinfeld, Maley & Kay, Houston, 1985-91, Weil, Gotshal & Manges, Houston, 1991—; vis. prof. law U. Tex., Austin, 1985, U. Mich., Ann Arbor, 1987; mem. adv. com. U.S. State Dept., Washington, 1990—; vice chmn. computer law divsn., sect. sci. and tech. ABA, Chgo., 1991—; reporter UCC Art. 2 rev. com. Nat. Conf. Commrs. on Uniform State Laws, Chgo., 1992—. Author: Commercial Asset-Based Financing, 1989, The Law of Computer Technology, 2d edit., 1993; co-author: Secured Financing in Personal Property, 1992, Bankruptcy and Creditors Rights, 1992. Recipient 5th Nat. award Nathan Burkan Copyright Competition, ASCAP, 1970. Fellow Am. Coll. Comml. Fin. Lawyers; mem. Am. Intellectual Property Law Assn., Am. Law Inst., Licensing Law Execs. Soc., Law and Soc. Assn., Tex. Bar Found. Office: Weil Gotshal & Manges 700 Louisiana St Ste 1600 Houston TX 77002-2784*

NIMMONS, PHILLIP RISTA, composer, conductor, clarinetist, educator; b. Kamloops, B.C., Can., June 3, 1923; s. George Rista and Hilda Louise (McCrum) N.; m. Noreen Liese Spencer, July 5, 1950; children: Holly Jayne, Carey Jocelyn, Phillip Rista. BA, U. B.C., 1944; scholar, Juilliard Sch. Music, 1945-47, Royal Conservatory Music, U. Toronto, 1948-50. Performances include CBC radio and TV spls., 1948-79, CBC drama, mus. comedy, variety shows and own jazz program, 1953—; appearances include Royal Alexander Theatre, Crest Theatre, Toronto Symphony Orch., Expo 67, 1976 Olympics; composer numerous jazz works including: The Atlantic Suite, 1974, Transformations, 1975, Invocation, 1976, Contemporary Piano Suite/Jazz Band, 1980; commd. works: Duologue, 1985, PS42JS, 1985, L'Images Entre Nous, 1987, all by Ont. Arts Coun., Plateaux, 1986, by Can. Broadcasting Corp., The Torch, 1988, (Winter Olympics, Calgary); commd. works Trumpet Concerto, 1988, Skyscape, 1988, Bach in My Own Back Yard, 1988, Twosome: Concerto for Piano and Vibraphone, 1988, Of Moods and Contrasts: A Sound Poem, 1994, Riverscape, 1994; rec. artist; co-founder Advanced Sch. Contemporary Music, 1960, dir., 1961-66; on tour of Can. bases with CBC, 1965-72; tour of Atlantic Provinces, 1974, 77; dir. jazz program, prof. U. Toronto, 1970-80, adj. prof., 1980—, dir. emeritus Jazz Faculty, 1991; prof., dir. jazz program U. N.B., summers 1967—, Banff Sch. Fine Arts, 1972, U. Western Ont., 1968—; leader Nimmon 'n Nine Plus Six jazz ensemble, 1953—; pres. Nimmons 'N Music, Ltd., 1975—; lectr. schs., colls. and community groups; dir. Can. Stage Band Festival, 1981—; adjudicator numerous festivals. Mem. adv. bd. Humber Coll., Banff Sch. Fine Arts; trustee, then chmn. York Edn. Clinic, 1968-74; mem. parents adv. bd. Thornlea Secondary Sch., 1967-72; bd. dirs. Toronto Arts Award; artistic dir. Courtenay Youth Music Camp, B.C., 1985—, Jazz Camp, Manitouwabing, Ont., Can., 1986—. Decorated officer Order of Can., Order of Can.; recipient cert. for music contbn. to Expo '67 Govt. of Can., 1967, cert. of honor BMI, Can., 1968, cert. of recognition City of Fredericton, N.B., 1976, Juno award Can. Soc. Rec. Arts and Scis., 1976, Toronto Arts award for excellence, 1986, Best Jazz Clarinetist award Can. Jazz Report, 1994, 95, 96, Clarinetist of Yr. award Jazz Report, 1996. Mem. Am. Fedn. Musicians, Performance Rights Orgn. Can. (award 1980), Can. League Composers (charter), Can. Music Centre, Guild Can. Film Composers (dir. 1981—), Celebrity Club (Toronto), Performing Arts Lodge (adv. bd.). Home and Office: 114 Babcombe Dr, Thornhill, ON Canada L3T 1N1

NIMMONS, RALPH WILSON, JR., federal judge; b. Dallas, Sept. 14, 1938; s. Ralph Wilson and Dorothy (Tucker) N.; m. Doris Penelope Pickels, Jan. 30, 1960; children—Bradley, Paige, Bonnie. BA, U. Fla., 1960, JD, 1963. Bar: Fla. 1963, U.S. Dist. Ct. (mid. dist.) Fla. 1963, U.S. Ct. Appeals (5th cir.) 1969, U.S. Supreme Ct. 1970. Assoc. Ulmer, Murchison, Ashby & Ball, Jacksonville, Fla., 1963-65, ptnr., 1973-77; asst. pub. defender Pub. Defender's Office, Jacksonville, 1965-69; first asst. state atty. State Atty.'s Office, Jacksonville, 1969-71; chief asst. gen. counsel City of Jacksonville, 1971-73; judge 4th Jud. Cir. Ct., Jacksonville, 1977-83, First Dist. Ct. of Appeal Fla., Tallahassee, 1983-91; judge U.S. Dist. Ct. Mid. Dist. Fla., 1991—; mem. faculty Fla. Jud. Coll., Tallahassee, 1985, 86; mem. Fla. Bar Grievance Com., 1973-76, vice chmn., 1975-76; mem. Fla. Conf. Cir. Judges, 1977-83, mem. exec. com., 1980-83; mem. Met. Criminal Justice Adv. Council, 1977-79; mem. Fla. Gov.'s Task Force on Prison Overcrowding, 1983; mem. Trial Ct. Study Commn., 1987-88. Chmn. lay bd. Riverside Baptist Ch., Jacksonville, 1982; chmn. deacons First Bapt. Ch., Tallahassee, 1988—; trustee Jacksonville Wolfson Children's Hosp., 1973-83. Recipient Carroll award for Outstanding Mem. Judiciary Jacksonville Jr. C. of C., 1980, Disting. Svc. award Fla. Council on Crime and Delinquency, 1981; named Outstanding Judge in Duval County, Jacksonville Bar Assn. Young Lawyers Sect., 1981. Mem. Phi Alpha Delta (pres. chpt. 1962-63), Am. Inns of Ct. (master of bench), Delta Tau Delta (pres. chpt. 1959-60). Office: US Dist Ct 611 N Florida Ave Tampa FL 33602-4500

NIMNI, MARCEL EPHRAIM, biochemistry educator; b. Buenos Aires, Feb. 1, 1931; came to U.S., 1955; s. Sam and Sarah Dora (Freedman) N.; children: Elizabeth, Brian Sam. BS in Pharmacy, U. Buenos Aires, 1954, PhD, 1960; MS, U. So. Calif., 1957. Cert. nutrition specialist. Rsch. fellow U. So. Calif., L.A., 1960-61, asst. prof. biochemistry, 1963-66, assoc. prof., 1966-72, prof., 1972—; dir. biology Don Baxter Labs., Glendale, Calif., 1962; cons. Hancock Labs., Glendale, Calif., 1962; cons. Hancock Labs., Anaheim, Calif., 1970-78, pathobiochemistry study sect. NIH, 1980-85, orthopaedics and biomechanics study sect., 1987-90; dir. biochemistry rsch. Orthopaedic Hosp., L.A., 1980-91; cons. Tillots Pharma Labs., Basle, Switzerland, 1986-94; dir. surg. rsch. Chidlren's Hosp. of L.A., 1991—; mem. adv. bd. Maimonides U., Buenos Aires. Editor: Collagen: Biochemistry, Biotechnology and Molecular Biology, Vols. I-V,1987-91; editor Matrix, 1980-93, Connective Tissue Rsch., 1973-91, Jour. Orthopaedic Rsch., 1989-94; patentee collagen tech., transderman drug delivery. Recipient Merit award NIH, 1987; rsch. grantee NIH Arthritis Inst., 1966-94, NIH Aging Inst., 1982—. Fellow AAAS, Soc. Biomaterials (Founders award 1986); mem. Am. Inst. Nutrition, Am. Assn. Biochem. and Molecular Biology. Office: Childrens Hosp LA Mailstop # 35 4650 W Sunset Blvd Los Angeles CA 90027-6016

NIMOY, LEONARD, actor, director; b. Boston, Mar. 26, 1931; s. Max and Dora (Spinner) N.; m. Sandi Zober, Feb. 21, 1954 (div.); children: Julie, Adam; m. Susan Bay, 1988. Student (drama scholar), Boston Coll., Pasadena (Calif) Playhouse, Jeff Corey, 1960-63; M.A., Antioch U., Austin, Tex. Operator drama studio San Fernando Valley; tchr. Synanon; owner Adajul Music Pub. Co. Appeared in television including Eleventh Hour, Kraft Theatre, Profiles in Courage, Bonanza, The Twilight Zone, Wagon Train, The Virginian, The Outer Limits, Rawhide, Dr. Kildare, Night Gallery, Columbo, T.J. Hooker, Star Trek: The Next Generation; (series) Star Trek, 1966-69, Mission: Impossible, 1969-71, In Search Of..., 1976-80 (host); (movies) Assault on the Wayne, 1971, Baffled!, 1973, The Alpha Caper, 1973, The Missing Are Deadly, 1975, Seizure: The Story of Kathy Morris, 1979, The Sun Also Rises, 1984, A Woman Called Golda, 1982, Never Forget, 1991 (also co-producer); appeared in movies including: Queen for a Day, 1951, Rhubarb, 1951, Kid Monk Baroni, 1952, The Brain Eaters, 1958, The Balcony, 1963, Catlow, 1971, Invasion of the Body Snatchers, 1978, Star Trek: The Motion Picture, 1979, Star Trek II: The Wrath of Khan, 1982, Transformers: The Movie, 1986 (voice only), Star Trek V: The Final Frontier, 1989, The Pagemaster, 1994 (voice only); (dir., actor) Star Trek III: The Search for Spock, 1984; (dir., co-story, actor) Star Trek IV: The Voyage Home, 1986; (exec. producer, co-story, actor) Star Trek VI: The Undiscovered Country, 1991; (dir.) Three Men and a Baby, 1987, The Good Mother, 1988, Funny About Love, 1990, Holy Matrimony, 1994; appeared on stage in Dr. Faustus, Stalag 17, Streetcar Named Desire, Cat on a Hot Tin Roof, Deathwatch, Monserrat, Irma La Douce, Visit to a Small Planet, Fiddler on a Roof, The Man in the Glass Booth, 6 Rms Riv Vu, Equus, Vincent (dir., writer), Love Letters, others; composed, rec. albums including The New World of Leonard Nimoy; composer other songs; author poetry and photography Will I Think of You; biography I Am Not Spock, 1975, We Are All Children, 1977, Come Be With Me, 1979. Mem. ACLU; mem. sch. com. adv. bd. Parents for Peace Western Los Angeles.; del. Dem. Central Com., 1971, 72. Served with AUS, 1954-56. Office: care The Gersh Agy Inc 232 N Canon Dr Beverly Hills CA 90210-5320*

NIMS, ARTHUR LEE, III, federal judge; b. Oklahoma City, Jan. 3, 1923; s. Arthur Lee and Edwina (Peckham) N.; m. Nancy Chloe Keyes, July 28, 1950; children: Chloe, Lucy. B.A., Williams Coll., 1945; LL.B., U. Ga., 1949; LL.M. in Taxation, NYU, 1954. Bar: Ga. 1949, N.J. 1955. Practice law Macon, Ga., 1949-51; spl. atty. Office Chief Counsel, IRS, N.Y.C. and Washington, 1951-55; assoc. McCarter & English, Newark, 1955-61; ptnr. McCarter & English, 1961-79; judge U.S. Tax Ct., Washington, 1979-88, chief judge, 1988-92. Mem. standing com. Episcopal Diocese of Newark, 1971-75; pres. Colonial Symphony Soc., Madison, N.J., 1975-78. Served to lt. (j.g.) USNR, 1943-46. Recipient Kellogg award Williams Coll., 1990, Career Achievement award The Tax Soc. NYU, 1990. Fellow Am. Coll. Tax Counsel; mem. ABA (sec. sect. taxation 1977-79), N.J. Bar Assn. (chmn. sect. taxation 1969-71, Am. Law Inst., J. Edgar Murdock Am. Inn of Ct. (pres. 1988-92). Office: US Tax Ct 400 2nd St NW Washington DC 20217-0001

NIMS, JOHN FREDERICK, writer, educator; b. Muskegon, Mich., Nov. 20, 1913; s. Frank McReynolds and Anne (McDonald) N.; m. Bonnie Larkin, Sept. 11, 1947; children—John (dec.), Frank, George (dec.), Sarah Hoyt, Emily Anne. A.B., U. Notre Dame, 1937, M.A., 1939; Ph.D., U. Chgo., 1945. Mem. faculty U. Notre Dame, 1939-45, 46-52, 54-58, U. Toronto, 1945-46, Bocconi U., Milan, Italy, 1952-53, U. Florence, Italy, 1953-54, U. Madrid, 1958-60, Harvard U., 1964, 68-69, summer 1974, U. Ill.-Urbana, 1961-65, U. Ill., at Chgo., 1965-85, Bread Loaf Writers Conf., 1958-71, Bread Loaf Sch. English, 1965-69, U. Fla., fall 1972, 73-77; Margaret Scott Bundy prof. lit. Williams Coll., fall 1975; prof. lit. Coll. of Charleston, spring 1981; mem. editorial bd. Poetry mag., 1945-48, vis. editor, 1960-61, editor, 1978-84; Phi Beta Kappa poet Harvard U., 1978; Cockefair chair U. Mo., Kansas City, spring 1986; Kilby cons. in poetry Wheaton (Ill.) Coll., fall 1988. Author: The Iron Pastoral, 1947, A Fountain in Kentucky, 1950, The Poems of St. John of the Cross, 1959, rev., 1979, Knowledge of the Evening, 1960, Of Flesh and Bone, 1967, Sappho to Valéry: Poems in Translation, 1971, rev. edit., 1990, Western Wind, 1974, rev. edit., 1992, The Kiss: A Jambalaya, 1982, Selected Poems, 1982, A Local Habitation; Essays on Poetry, 1985, The Six Cornered Snowflake, 1990, Zany in Denim, 1990; contbr.: Five Young American Poets, 1944, The Complete Greek Tragedies, 1959; also anthologies, mags.; editor: Ovid's Metamorphoses, 1965, (James Shirley) Love's Cruelty, 1980, Harper Anthology of Poetry, 1981; assoc. editor: The Poem Itself, 1960; editorial adviser, Princeton U. Press, 1975-82. Recipient Harriet Monroe Meml. award Poetry mag., 1942, Guarantors prize, 1943, Levinson prize, 1944, Disting. fellowship Acad. Am. Poets, 1982; Fulbright grantee, 1952, 53; Smith Mundt grantee, 1958, 59; Nat. Found. Arts and Humanities grantee, 1967-68; award for creative writing Am. Acad. Arts and Letters, 1968, Aiken Taylor award, 1991, Melville Cane award 1992, Hardison Poetry prize, 1993; Creative Arts citation in Poetry Brandeis U., 1974; fellow Inst. Humanities U. Ill., 1983-84; Guggenheim fellow, 1986-87. Democrat. Roman Catholic. Address: 3920 N Lake Shore Dr Chicago IL 60613-3447

NIMS, MICHAEL A., lawyer; b. Manhattan, Kans., Oct. 18, 1946. AB, Murray State U., 1968; JD, U. Mich., 1971. Bar: Ohio 1971. Ptnr. Jones, Day, Reavis & Pogue, Cleve. Office: Jones Day Reavis & Pogue North Point 901 Lakeside Ave Cleveland OH 44114-1116*

NING, JOHN TSE-TSO, urologic surgeon; b. Tso-Ying, Taiwan, Aug. 25, 1951; came to U.S., 1963; s. Joseph Pei-Ying and Yuan-Chen (Chow) N.; m. Linda J. Ching, July 27, 1975; children: Lena, Jonathan. BS in Chemistry, MIT, 1978; MS in Pharmacology, Northeastern U., 1981, MS in Med. Lab. Sci., 1982; PhD Biochemistry & Molecular Biophysics, Med. Coll. of Va., 1988, MD, 1991. Diplomate Nat. Bd. Med. Examiners; lic. M.D., S.C.; cert. clin. chemist Nat. Registry Clin. Chemistry. Postdoctoral Va. Commonwealth Univ., Richmond, Va., 1988-91, Radiation Biology Br. Ctr. for Devices, FDA, Rockville, Md., 1991-92; affiliated rsch. assoc. Dept. of Biochemistry & Molecular BioPhysics Med. Coll. Va., Richmond, 1990-92; rsch. assoc. dept. of elect. engring. U. Md., College Park, 1991-92; vis. scholar Quindao (People's Rep. of China) Med. Coll. Affiliated Hosp., 1987-92; vis. scientist Peking (People's Rep. of China) Third Hosp., 1992; gen. surgery intern dept. surgery Med. U. of S.C., Charleston, 1992-93; gen. surgery resident dept. surgery Med. U. of S.C., 1993-94; urologic surgery resident dept. urology Brown U., Providence, R.I., 1994—; surgeon Indian Health Svc. U.S. Public Health Svc., Rockville, Md., 1992—. Editor: (proceedings) First World Congress: Electricity and Magnetism in Biology and Medicine, 1993; contbr. to Annals of N.Y. Acad. Sci., 1992. Cultural chmn. MIT Chinese Student Club, Cambridge, Mass., 1974; bd. dirs. South CDVC Cmty. Health Ctr., Boston, Mass., 1979. Recipient Commemorative medal of honor Am. Biographical Inst., 1987. Fellow Am. Inst. Chemists; mem. Bioelectromagnetics Soc., Biolect. Repair and Grwth Soc., Am. Med. Assn., Sigma Xi, Rho Chi (life), Phi Lambda Upsilon (life). Republican. Roman Catholic. Achievements include contributions to knowledge of effects of extremely low frequency electromagnetic fields on gene expression; effects of extremely low frequecy electromagnetic fields on genitourinary system in rabbits; health effects of electromagnetic field and potential therapeutic applications in medicine and surgery. Avocations: swimming, tennis, playing trumpet and saxophones, bowling. Home: 1 Columbia Ct Middletown RI 02842 also: Health Professions Support Indian Health Svc/ USPHS 5600 Fishers Ln Rockville MD 20857

NING, TAK HUNG, physicist, microelectronic technologist; b. Canton, China, Nov. 14, 1943; came to U.S., 1964; s. Hong and Kwai-Chan (Lee) N.; m. Yin Ngao Fan; children: Adrienne, Brenda. BA in Physics, Reed Coll., 1967; MS in Physics, U. Ill., 1968, PhD in Physics, 1971. IBM Rsch. Div., Yorktown Heights, N.Y., 1973-78, Mgr. bipolar devices and cirs., 1978-82, mgr. Advanced Silicon Technology Lab., 1982-83, mgr. silicon devices and technology, 1983-90; mgr. VLSI design and tech. IBM Rsch. Div., 1990-91; IBM fellow, 1991—. Patentee in field. Fellow IEEE (assoc. editor Trans. on Electron Devices 1988-90, J.J. Ebers award 1989, Jack a. Morton award 1991); mem. Nat. Acad. Engring. Home: 3085 Weston Ln Yorktown Heights NY 10598-1962 Office: IBM T J Watson Research Ct Yorktown Heights NY 10598

NING, XUE-HAN (HSUEH-HAN NING), physiologist, researcher; b. Peng-Lai, Shandong, People's Republic of China, Apr. 15, 1936; came to U.S., 1984; s. Yi-Xing and Liu Ning; m. Jian-Xin Fan, May 28, 1967; 1 child, Di Fan. MD, Shanghai 1st Med. Coll., People's Republic of China, 1960. Rsch. fellow Shanghai Inst. Physiology, 1960-72, leader cardiovasc. rsch. group, 1973-83, head, assoc. prof. cardiovasc. rsch. unit, 1984-87, prof. and chair hypoxia dept., 1988-90, vice chairperson academic com., 1988-90; NIH internat. rsch. fellow U. Mich., Ann Arbor, 1984-87, vis. prof., hon. prof., rsch. investigator, 1990-95; prof. and dir. Hypoxia Physiology Lab. Academia Sinica, Shanghai, 1989—; acting leader, High Altitude Physiology Group, Chinese mountaineering and sci. expdn. team to Mt. Everest, 1975; leader High Altitude Physiology Group, Dept. Metall. Industry of China and Ry. Engring. Corps, 1979; vis. prof. dept. physiology Mich. State U., East Lansing, 1989-90; vis. prof. dept. pediat. U . Wash., Seattle, 1994—. Author: High Altitude Physiology and Medicine, 1981, Reportson Scientific Expedition to Mt. Qomolungma, High Altitude Physiology, 1980, Environment and Ecology of Qinghai-Xizong (Tibet) Plateau, 1982; mem. editl. bd. Chinese Jour. Applied Physiology, 1984—, Acta Physiologica, 1988—; contbr. articles to profl. jours. Recipient Merit award Shanghai Sci. Congress, 1977, All-China Sci. Congress, Beijing, 1978, Super Class award Academia Sinica, Beijing, 1986, 1st Class award Nat. Natural Scis., Beijing, 1987, # 1 Best Article award Tzu-Chi Med. Jour., Taiwan, 1995. Mem. Am. Physiol. Soc., Internat. Soc. Heart Rsch., Royal Soc. Medicine, Shanghai Assn. Physiol. (bd. dirs. 1988—), Chinese Assn. Physiol. (com. applied physiology 1984—, com. blood, cardiovascular, respiratory and renal physiology 1988—), Chinese Soc. Medicine, Chinese Soc. Biomed. Engring. Achievements include research in predictive evaluation of mountaineering performance, paradox phenomenon of cardiac pump function injury after climbing or giving oxygen, blood flow-metabolism-function relationship of heart during hypoxia and ischemia, effect of medicinal herbs on cardiac performance, cardiovascular adaptation and resistance to hypoxia and ischemia; first electrocardiograph recording at summit of Mt. Everest. Home: 7033 43rd Ave NE Seattle WA 98115-6015 Office: U Wash Dept Pediatrics Box 356320 1959 NE Pacific St Seattle WA 98195

NINOS, NICHOLAS PETER, retired miliatry officer, physician; b. Chgo., May 11, 1936; s. Peter Spiros and Ann (Lesczynsky) N. BA in Art, Bradley U., 1958, BS in Chemistry, 1959; MD, U. Ill., Chgo., 1963. Diplomate Am. Bd. Internal Med., Am. Bd. Cardiology, Am. Bd. Critical Care Medicne. Intern Cook County Hosp., Chgo., 1963-64, resident in internal medicine, 1964-67, fellow in cardiology, 1967-68; commd. capt. U.S. Army, 1968, advanced through grades to col., 1979; chief dept. medicine U.S. Army Community Hosp. U.S. Army, Bremerhaven, Fed. Republic Germany, 1968-69, Wurzberg, Fed. Republic Germany, 1969-72; chief critical care Letterman Army Med. Ctr., San Francisco, 1976-91; dep. comdr. San Francisco med. command Letterman Army Med. Ctr./Naval Hosp. of Oakland, San Francisco and Oakland, Calif., 1988-90; ret., 1991; assoc. prof. medicine and surgery Uniformed Svcs. U. Health Scis., Bethesda, Md., 1981-91; critical care medicine cons. to U.S. Army Surgeon Gen., 1981-91; lectr. in field. Author: (jour.) Ethics, 1988; co-editor: Nutrition, 1988, Problems in Critical Care, Nutrition Support; mem. editl. bd. Jour. Critical Care Medicine, 1988-91; illustrator: Medical Decision Making, 1988. 2d v.p. Twin Springs Condominium Homeowners Assn., Palm Springs, Calif., 1993-94, sec., 1994-96; ch. bd. councilman St. George Orthodox Ch. of the Desert, Palm Desert, Calif., 1993-95; active Palm Springs Comm., 1993—. Decorated Legion of Merit, Meritorious Svc. medal with oak leaf cluster. Fellow Am. Coll. Critical Care Medicine (mem. bd. regents 1989-94, chmn. 1989-91); mem. AMA, Soc. Critical Care Medicine (pres. uniformed svcs. sect. 1987-90, Shubin/Weil award 1988), Soc. Med. Cons. to Armed Forces (assoc.), Inst. Critical Care Medicine (exec. v.p. 1991-92), Toastmasters Internat. (sec.-treas. Palm Springs chpt. 1993-94, pres. 1994, gov. area D-3 1994-95, divsn. gov. 1995-96). Avocations: art, skiing, jogging, traveling, music.

NINTEMANN, TERRI, legislative staff member; b. Rochester, Minn., Mar. 13, 1963; d. John F. and Janice A. (Blair) Nintemann; m. Vincent J. Kiernan, Aug. 27, 1994. BS, U. Minn., 1985. Legis. asst. Farm Credit Svcs., St. Paul, Minn., 1986; intern, receptionist U.S. Senator Rudy Boschwitz, Washington, 1985, legis. corr., 1986-87, legis. asst., 1987-91; legis. dir. U.S. Rep. Dave Camp, Washington, 1991-92; profl. staff mem. Senate Agrl. Com., U.S. Senate, Washington, 1992—. Mem. U. Minn. Alumni, FFA Alumni (life mem.). Republican. Roman Catholic. Avocations: movies, yoga, volunteer work. Office: Senate Agrl Com 328 A Russell Senate Office Bldg Washington DC 20510

NIRENBERG, LOUIS, mathematician, educator; b. Hamilton, Ont., Can., Feb. 28, 1925; came to U.S., 1945, naturalized, 1954; s. Zuzie and Bina (Katz) N.; m. Susan Blank, Jan. 25, 1948; children: Marc, Lisa. BSc, McGill U., Montreal, 1945, DSc (hon.), 1986; MS, NYU, 1947, PhD, 1949; DSc (hon.), U. Pisa, Italy, 1990, U. Paris Dauphine, 1990. Mem. faculty N.Y. U., 1949—, prof. math., 1957—, dir. Courant Inst., 1970-72; visitor Inst. Advanced Study, 1958; hon. prof. Nankai U., Zhejiang U. Author research articles. Recipient Crafoord prize Royal Swedish Acad., 1982, Nat. Medal of Science, 1995; NRC fellow, 1951-52; Sloan Found. fellow, 1958-60; Guggenheim Found. fellow, 1966-67, 75-76; Fulbright fellow, 1965; Leroy P. Steele prizes Am. Mathematical Society, 1994. Mem. NAS, Am. Acad. Arts and Scis., Am. Math. Soc. (v.p. 1976-78, M. Bôcher prize 1959, L. P. Steele prize 1994), Am. Philos. Soc., French Acad. Scis. (fgn. mem.), Accademia dei Lincei (fgn. mem.), Istituto Lombardo, Accad. de Scienze e Lettere (fgn. mem.), Ukrainian Acad. Sci. (fgn. mem.). Home: 221 W 82nd St New York NY 10024-5406 Office: Courant Inst 251 Mercer St New York NY 10012-1110

NIRENBERG, MARSHALL WARREN, biochemist; b. N.Y.C., N.Y., Apr. 10, 1927; s. Harry Edward and Minerva (Bykowsky) N.; m. Perola Zaltzman, July 14, 1961. B.S. in Zoology, U. Fla., 1948, M.S., 1952; Ph.D. in Biochemistry, U. Mich., 1957. Postdoctoral fellow Am. Cancer Soc. at NIH, 1957-59; postdoctoral fellow USPHS at NIH, 1959-60; mem. staff NIH, 1960—; research biochemist, chief lab. biochem. genetics Nat. Heart, Lung and Blood Inst., 1962—; researcher mechanism protein synthesis, genetic code, nucleic acids, regulatory mechanisms in synthesis macromolecules, and neurobiology. Recipient Molecular Biology award Nat. Acad. Scis., 1962, award in biol. scis. Washington Acad. Scis., 1962, medal HEW, 1964, Modern Medicine award, 1963, Harrison Howe award Am. Chem. Soc., 1964, Nat. Medal Sci. Pres. Johnson, 1965, Hildebrand award Am. Chem. Soc., 1966, Research Corp. award, 1966, A.C.P. award, 1967, Gairdner Found. award merit Can., 1967, Prix Charles Leopold Meyer French Acad. Scis., 1967, Franklin medal Franklin Inst., 1968, Albert Lasker Med. Research award, 1968, Priestly award, 1968; co-recipient Louisa Gross Horowitz prize Columbia, 1968, Nobel prize in medicine and physiology, 1968. Fellow AAAS, N.Y. Acad. Scis.; mem. Am. Soc. Biol. Chemists, Am. Chem. Soc. (Paul Lewis award enzyme chemistry 1964), Am. Acad. Arts and Scis., Biophys. Soc., Nat. Acad. Scis., Washington Acad. Scis., Soc. for Study Devel. and Growth, Soc. Devel. Biology, Harvey Soc. (hon.), Leopoldina Deutsche Akademie der Naturforscher, Pontificial Acad. Scis. Office: NIH Lab Biochemical Genetics Bldg 36 Rm 1C06 Bethesda MD 20892*

NISBET, JOANNE, ballet mistress; b. Karachi, Pakistan, July 15, 1931; d. James Maltman Wilson and Victoria (Dickie) Nisbet; m. David Robert Scott, Apr. 15, 1957. Studied with, Lubov Egorova, Paris, 1946-48, Anna Ivanova, London. Mem. corps de ballet Ballet Rambert, London, 1945-46; dancer Palladium Theatre, London, 1949; mem. corps de ballet Sadler's Wells Theatre, London, 1950-55, Festival Ballet, London, 1955-59; mem. corps de ballet Nat. Ballet Can., 1959-61, asst. ballet mistress, 1961-62, ballet mistress, 1962-83, prin. ballet mistress, 1983—. Staged (with David Scott) prodns. The Sleeping Beauty for Vienna State Opera, 1979, Etudes (by Harold Lander) for Am. Ballet Theatre, 1987. Office: Nat Ballet Can, 157 King St E, Toronto, ON Canada M5C 1G9

NISBET, JOHN STIRLING, electrical engineering educator; b. Darval, Scotland, Dec. 10, 1927; s. Robert George Jackson and Kathleen Agnes (Young) N.; m. J. Valerie Payne, Jan. 10, 1953; children: Robert John, Alexander Stevens. B.S., London U., 1950; M.S., Pa. State U., 1957, Ph.D., 1960. Trainee, engr. Nash & Thompson Ltd., Surbiton, Eng., 1944-51; engr. Decca Radar Ltd., Surbiton, 1951-53, Can. Westinghouse, Hamilton, Ont., 1953-55; research assoc. electric engring. dept. Pa. State U., University Park, 1955-60, prof., 1960—; Disting. Alumni prof. elec. engring. Pa. State U., 1985-90, Disting. Alumni prof. elec. engring. emeritus, 1990—, dir. Ionosphere Rsch. Lab., 1971-84, dir. Communications and Space Scis. Lab., 1984-86. Author numerous sci. papers; mem. editorial bd.: Jour. Atmospheric and Terrestrial Physics. NSF sr. postdoctoral fellow Brussels, 1965; Fulbright Hays lectr. Council Internat. Exchange Scholars, USSR, 1979; NRC-Nat. Acad. Sci. fellow Goddard Space Flight Ctr., 1980. Sr. mem. IEEE, Am. Geophys. Union, Sigma Xi, Phi Kappa Phi. Unitarian. Home: 618 Glenn Rd State College PA 16803-3474 Office: Communications & Space Scis Lab 316 Electrical Eng University Park PA 16802

NISBET, ROBERT A., historian, sociologist; b. Los Angeles, Sept. 30, 1913; s. Henry S. and Cynthia (Jenifer) N.; m. Emily P. Heron (div.); children: Martha Rehrman, Constance Field; m. Caroline Burks Kirkpatrick; 1 child, Ann Nash. AB, U. Calif., Berkeley, 1936, MA, 1937, PhD, 1939, Berkeley citation, 1970; LHD (hon.), Hofstra U., 1974. Instr. social instns. U. Calif. at Berkeley, 1939-43; asst. dean U. Calif. at Berkeley (Coll. Letters and Sci.), 1942-43, 46, asst. prof. social instns., 1943-48, asso. prof. sociology, 1948-52; prof. sociology U. Calif., Riverside, 1953-72; vice chancellor U. Calif., 1960-63; dean U. Calif. (Coll. Letters and Sci.), 1953-63; vis. prof. Columbia U., 1949, Albert Schweitzer prof. humanities, 1974-78, emeritus, 1978—; resident scholar Am. Enterprise Inst., Washington, 1978-80, adj. scholar, 1980-86; prof. history and sociology U. Ariz., 1972-74; vis. prof. U. Bologna, Italy, 1956-57; Rieker lectr. U. Ariz., 1956; lectr. all univs., Calif., 1961, Guggenheim fellow, 1963-64; Cooper lectr. Swarthmore Coll., 1966; John Dewey lectr. John Dewey Soc., 1970; William A. Neilson research prof. Smith Coll., 1971-72; Blazer lectr. U. Ky., 1971; Phi Beta Kappa Nat. vis. scholar, 1971-72; vis. fellow Princeton U., 1963-64; Johns Hopkins Centennial scholar, 1975-76; W.G. Sumner lectr. Yale U., 1976; Leon lectr. U. Pa., 1982; Benjamin Rush lectr. Am. Psychiat. Assn., 1983; Jefferson lectr. in Humanities NEH, 1988. Author: The Quest for Community, 1953, Human Relations in Administration, 1956, Emile Durkheim, 1965, The Sociological Tradition, 1966, Tradition and Revolt, 1968, Social Change and History, 1969, The Social Bond, 1970, The Degradation of the Academic Dogma, 1971, The Social Philosophers, 1973, rev. edit., 1983, The Sociology of Emile Durkheim, 1974, Twilight of Authority, 1975, Sociology as an Art Form, 1976, History of the Idea of Progress, 1980, Prejudices: A Philosophical Dictionary, 1982, Conservatism: Dream and Reality, 1986, The Making of Modern Society, 1986, The Present Age, 1988, Roosevelt and Stalin, 1989, Teachers and Scholars, 1992; editor: Social Change; co-editor: Contemporary Social Problems, 1961, 66, 71, 1976, History of Sociological Analysis, 1978; bd. editors Am. Jour. Sociology, 1970-74; mem. publ. com. The Public Interest, 1976-84; mem. editorial bd. The American Scholar, 1975-80; contbr. articles to profl. jours. Mem. Nat. Council Humanities, 1975-78; mem. N.Y. Gov.'s Health Adv. Council, 1975-76, Parkman Prize Com., 1978-80; bd. dirs. Am. Council Learned Socs., 1974-79, Council Acad. Advisers, Am. Enterprise Inst., Washington, 1972-86, Rockford Inst., 1978-84. Served with AUS, 1943-45, PTO. Decorated cavaliere ufficiale Order of Merit Italy; recipient Ingersoll award in humanities, 1985; Rockefeller Found. grantee, 1975-78. Fellow Am. Acad. Arts and Scis. (councillor 1977-80), Am. Philos. Soc. (councillor 1977-80, Penrose Meml. lectr. 1982), Soc. Am. Historians; mem. Société Européene de Culture, Columbia Soc. Fellows, Institut Internationale de Sociologie, Phi Beta Kappa. Address: 2828 Wisconsin Ave NW Apt 102 Washington DC 20007-4713

NISBETT, DOROTHEA JO, nursing educator; b. Lodi, Tex., May 16, 1940; d. Cecil Robey and Lola Ruby (Pippin) Lovett; m. Leonce Paul Lanoux Jr., June 10, 1966 (div. July 1984); 1 child, Cecil Lance Lanoux; m. James Harris Nisbett, May 12, 1990. Diploma in nursing, Tex. Ea. Sch. Nursing, 1963; BSN, Tex. Christian U., 1965; MS, Tex. Woman's U., 1977. RN, Tex. Asst. charge nurse med./surg. unit Med. Ctr. Hosp., Tyler, Tex., 1963-64, asst. dir. nursing, 1967; instr. nursing Tex. Ea. Sch. Nursing, Tyler, 1965-66; head nurse med./surg. unit Providence Hosp., Waco, Tex., 1966-67; dir. nursing Laird Meml. Hosp., Kilgore, Tex., 1967-69; instr. nursing Kilgore Coll., 1969-73, McLennan C.C., Waco, 1973—. Charter sec. Am. Heart Assn., Kilgore, 1968-69; bd. dirs. Heart of Tex. Soccer Assn., Waco, 1982-85. Mem. Nat. Orgn. Assoc. Degree Nursing, Tex. Jr. Coll. Tchr. Assn., Assn. Profl. and Staff Devel., Beta Sigma Phi (Outstanding Young Woman of Yr. 1981, Sweetheart 1970, 82, 91, Woman of Yr. 1990, Order of the Rose 1980, Silver Cir. award 1990). Methodist. Avocations: golf, arts and crafts. Office: McLennan CC 1400 College Dr Waco TX 76708-1402

NISBETT, RICHARD EUGENE, psychology educator; b. Littlefield, Tex., June 1, 1941; s. R. Wayne and Helen (King) N.; m. Susan Ellen Isaacs, June 29, 1969; children: Matthew, Sarah. A.B. summa cum laude, Tufts U., 1962; Ph.D., Columbia U., 1966. Asst. prof. psychology Yale U., New Haven, 1966-71; assoc. prof. psychology U. Mich., Ann Arbor, 1971-77, prof., 1977—, Theodore M. Newcomb prof. psychology, 1989-92, Theodore M. Newcomb disting. univ. prof. of psychology, 1992—. Author: (with others) Attribution: Perceiving the Causes of Behavior, 1972, Induction: Processes of Inference, Learning and Discovery, 1986, Rules for Reasoning, 1992, (with L. Ross) Human Inference: Strategies and Shortcomings of Social Judgment, 1980, The Person and the Situation, 1991, (with D. Cohen) Culture of Honor, 1996. Recipient Donald T. Campbell award for disting. rsch. in social psychology APA, 1982, Disting. Sci. Contbn. award APA, 1991, Disting. Sr. Scientist award Soc. Exptl. Social Psychology; fellow Ctr. for Advanced Studies in Behavioral Scis. Office: U Mich 5261 ISR Rsch Ctr Group Dynamics Ann Arbor MI 48106

NISENHOLTZ, MARTIN ABRAM, telecommunications executive, educator; b. Phila., Apr. 1, 1955; s. Louis William and Rhoda Greta (Koenig) N.; m. Anne Ermine Stockler, July 26, 1987; children: Johanna, Marjorie. BA, U. Pa., 1977, MA, 1979. Research scientist NYU, N.Y.C., 1979-83; mgr. Ogilvy & Mather, N.Y.C., 1983-84, v.p., 1984-89, sr. v.p., 1989-94; dir. content strategy Ameritech Corp., Chgo., 1994-95; pres. N.Y. Times Electronic Media Co., 1995—; mem. oper. com. Ogilvy & Mather Direct, 1992-94; adj. assoc. prof. NYU, 1983—. Grantee Nat. Endowment Arts, 1981. Mem. Interactive Svcs. Assn. (dir. 1985-94, chmn. 1991, Disting. Svc. award 1994). Office: The New York Times 229 W 43d St New York NY 10036

NISH, WAYNE PAUL, chef, restaurant owner; b. N.Y.C., July 23, 1951; s. John and Dorothy (Bugelli) N.; children: Caitlin Nicola, Alexandra Jane. Student, Long Island U., 1969-70, Cornell U., 1972-73, CCNY, 1973-74; diploma, N.Y. Restaurant Sch., 1983. Assoc. chef The Quilted Giraffe, N.Y.C., 1984-87; pvt. chef Anne Bass, N.Y.C., 1987-88; exec. chef La Colombe d'Or, N.Y.C., 1988-89; chef, co-owner March Restaurant, N.Y.C., 1990—; adv. bd. mem. N.Y. Restaurant Sch., 1991—. Fund raiser Women's Campaign Fund, 1992, 93, 94. Recipient Three Stars award N.Y. Times, 1988, 92, 95, Forbes Mag., 1989, Four Stars award Forbes Mag., 1993, 94; named Am.'s top Restaurant Zagat Survey, 1993, 94, 95. Mem. Am. Inst. Wine and Food, James Beard Found. Democrat. Roman Catholic. Avocations: cooking, photography, driving. Office: March Restaurant 405 E 58th St New York NY 10022-2302

NISHI, OSAMU, constitutional law educator; b. Toyama City, Japan, June 2, 1940; m. Masako Hanaoka, June 16, 1943; children: Sachiko, Hideji. B, Waseda (Japan) U., 1964, M, 1966. Lectr. Def. Acad., Yokosuka, 1970-74; assoc. prof. Komazawa U., Tokyo, 1974-80, prof., 1980—; lectr. Waseda U., 1990—, Keio (Japan) U., 1991-93. Author: The Constitution and the National Defense Law System in Japan, 1987, Ten Days Inside General Headquarters, 1989, Series of Constitutions of the Countries of the World, 1990. Exec. Japan Internat. Rescue Action Com., Tokyo, 1992—; mem. Yomiuri Constn. Study Coun., Tokyo, 1992—. Mem. Japan Comparative Constnl. Assn. (sec. gen. 1988—), Japan Def. Law Soc. (rep. 1996—), Japan Def. Acad. Soc. (exec. 1988—), Yokohama Internat. Soc. (rep. 1991—), Human Rights Advs. Internat. (v.p. 1990—), Phila. Constn. Found. (v.p. 1990—). Avocations: tennis, skiing. Office: Komazawa U, 1 23 1 Komazawa, Setagaya Tokyo 154, Japan

NISHIMURA, JOSEPH YO, retired retail executive, accountant; b. Berkeley, Calif., Nov. 4, 1933; s. Masamoto and Kimiko (Ishihara) N.; m. Joyce Toshiye Mori, Sept. 1, 1956; children: Brenda Joyce, Stephen Lloyd. AB cum laude, Princeton U., 1956; MBA, Stanford U., 1961. CPA, Calif., N.Y.; cert. Employee Benefit Specialist. Audit supr. Touche Ross & Co., San Francisco, 1961-66; contr. Scott Co. of Calif., Oakland, 1966-67, Purity Stores, Inc., Burlingame, Calif., 1967-69; pres. Cubit Systems Corp., Burlingame, 1969-72; sr. v.p. Golden West Fin. Corp., Oakland, 1972-73; exec. v.p. Victory Markets, Inc., Norwich, N.Y., 1973-90, dir., 1976-90; dir. Carl's Drug Co., Rome, N.Y., 1988-90; gen. ptnr. Mori Enterprises, 1994—. V.p., bd. dirs. Chenango Meml. Hosp., Norwich, 1981-87; bd. dirs. United Fund, Norwich, 1984-90, N.Y. State Food Mchts. Assn., 1988-90, Binghamton (N.Y.) Symphony Orch, 1988—, treas., 1990-93; gen. ptnr. Mori Enterprises, 1994—. Served to lt. (j.g.) USN, 1956-59; Japan. Mem. AICPA, N.Y. State Soc. CPA's, Calif. Soc. CPAs. Democrat. Presbyterian. Club: Princeton (N.Y.C.).

NISHIMURA, PETE HIDEO, oral surgeon; b. Hilo, Hawaii, Aug. 7, 1922; s. Hideichi and Satsuki N.; m. Tomoe Nishimura, June, 1949; children—Dennis Dean, Grant Neil, Dawn Naomi. Student, U. Hawaii, 1940-44; D.D.S., U. Mo., 1947; M.S.D., Northwestern U., 1949. Practice dentistry specializing in oral surgery Honolulu, 1952—; pres. Oral Surgery Group, 1978—; mem. coun. Nat. Bd. Dental Examination; dir. Hawaii Dental Svc., 1962-85, pres., 1970-72, 76-78; pres. State Bd. Dental Examiners, Delta Sigma Delta, Fedn. Dentaire Internat. Served with U.S. Army, 1952-54. Fellow Am. Coll. Dentists, Internat. Coll. Dentists; mem. Hawaii Dental Assn. (past pres.), Delta Dental Plans Assn. (dir.), Honolulu County Dental Soc., ADA, Hawaii Soc. Oral Surgeons, Am. Assn. Oral and Maxillofacial Surgeons, Western Soc. Oral and Maxillofacial Surgeons, Am. Assn. Dental Examiners, Pierre Fauchard Acad. Democrat. Home: 494 Halemaumau St Honolulu HI 96821-2135 Office: 848 S Beretania St Honolulu HI 96813-2551

NISHITANI, MARTHA, dancer; b. Seattle, Feb. 27, 1920; d. Denjiro and Jin (Aoto) N. B.A. in Comparative Arts, U. Wash., 1958; studied with, Eleanor King, Mary Ann Wells, Perry Mansfield, Cornish Sch., Conn. Coll. Sch. Dance, Long Beach State U. Founder, dir. Martha Nishitani Modern Dance Sch. and Co., Seattle, 1950—; dance dir. Helen Bush Sch. and Central YWCA, 1951-54; choreographer U. Wash. Opera Theater, 1955-65, Intiman Theater, 1972—; dance instr. Elementary and Secondary Edn. Act Program, 1966; dance specialist spl. edn. program Shoreline Pub. Schs., 1970-72; condr. workshops and concerts King County Youth Correctional Instns., 1972-73; Dance adv. counsel Wash. Cultural Enrichment Program; dance adv. bd. Seattle Parks and Recreation. Dancer Eleanor King Co., Seattle, 1946-50, dance films, 1946-51, Channel 9, Edl. TV, 1967-68; lectr. demonstrator numerous colls., festivals, convs., childrens theater.; author articles on dance; one of the subjects: A Celebration of 100 Years of Dance in Washington, 1989. Trustee Allied Arts Seattle, 1967. Recipient Theta Sigma Phi Matrix Table award, 1968, Asian Am. Living Treasure award Northwest Asian Am. Theater, 1984; listed Dance Archives, N.Y.C. Libr., 1991, N.Y.C. Lincoln Ctr. Dance Archives, 1991, U. Wash. Libr. Archives, 1993, exhibit of Japanese Am. Women of Achievement, Burke Mus., 1994, 42d Anniversary of Martha Nishitani Modern Dance Sch. Mem. Am. Dance Guild (exec. com. 1961-63), Com. Research in Dance, Seattle Art Mus., Internat. Dance Alliance (adv. council 1984), Smithsonian Assos., Progressive Animal Welfare Soc. Address: 4205 University Way NE PO Box 45264 Seattle WA 98145-0264 *Until a few years ago a compelling force within me would let nothing interfere with performing, teaching, and directing dance. My belief: "I must be selfish about that which means most to me." This dedication was in constant battle with loneliness, frugality and neglect of loved ones. My first solo dance was Credo in Conflict. I have earned a degree of success, satisfaction, joy and recognition. My thoughts are now that I have learned to pursue a balance in life as I battle. The scars of selfishness persist but the broader view brings validity to my beliefs.*

NISHIYAMA, CHIAKI, economist, educator; b. Fukuoka-ken, Japan, Aug. 9, 1924; s. Michiki and Teruko (Tsuji) N.; m. Shigeko Okabe, June 9, 1957; children: Keita, Mikiko. BA in Econs., Rikkyo U., Tokyo, 1950; MA in Polit. Sci., U. Chgo., 1952, PhD in Social Thought, 1960, postgrad. in econs., 1959-60. Lectr. U. Chgo., 1957-61; assoc. prof. Rikkyo U., 1962-64, prof. econs., 1964-90, prof. emeritus, 1990—; sr. rsch. fellow Hoover Instn., Stanford U., 1977—; prof. econs. Grad. Sch. Internat. Mgmt. Internat. U. Japan, 1994—; lectr. Tng. Inst., Ministry Trade and Industry, Japanese Govt., 1964-66, Gakushuin U., 1970-71, Waseda U., 1972-74; exec. dir. Assembly on U.S.-Japan Econ. Policy, 1972-76; prime minister's spl. envoy to U.S., 1971, 75; specialist counselor Japan Employers' Assn., 1975-85; del. European Assembly, Strasbourg, France, 1982; world travel for Japanese Ministry Fgn. Affairs, Japan External Trade Orgn., 1968-82; lectr. various univs., U.S. and Europe, 1976-94; mem. Am. Citizen to Citizen Econ. and Fin. Mgmt. Del. to the USSR, 1991; spl. envoy of Japan to Germany, Czechoslovakia, Hungary, Bulgaria, Ukraine, Russia, 1991. Author numerous books, including: Lecture on Modern Economics, 1964; Free Economy, Its Policies and Principles, 1974; The Price for Prosperity, 1974; A Monetary History and Analysis of the Japanese Economy, 1868-1970, 1974; Reflection on Japanese Economy, 1976; Monetarism, 1976; The Last Chance for Creativity, Liberty and Prosperity, 1981; Human Capitalims, 1982; The Fourth Philosophy, Vol. I, 1982, Vol. II, 1983; No Limits to Growth, 1984; The Essence of Hayek, 1984, The Japanese Economy, 1987, Panadigm Shift, 1987, Japanese Economy and Life Tomorrow, 1988, A New Economics Under a New Paradigm, 1991, The End of Recession, 1994; editorial bd. Jour. Internat. Money and Fin., 1981—. Bd. dirs. Inst. Econ. Affairs, London, 1976—; mem. adv. bd Econ. Inst. Paris, 1984-86, Carl Menger Inst. Wien, 1984; councilor The Daiwa Welfare Found., 1994—. Recipient Japan Econ. Lit. award Japan Econ. Jour., 1974; Earhart fellow, 1957-61; E. C. Nef fellow, 1958-59; fellow Woodrow Wilson Internat. Ctr. for Scholars, 1976-77; grantee Relm, 1964-67, Ford, 1965-66, Lilly, 1966-67, Bank of Japan, Bankers Assn. Japan, other fin. orgns., 1978-83. Mem. Am. Enterprise Inst. (adj. scholar), Am. Econ. Assn., Econometric Soc., Theoretical Econs. Assn., Internat. Econ. Assn., Statis. Soc., Mont Pelerin Soc. (pres. 1980-82, sr. v.p. 1982-85, hon. v.p. 1986-88). Episcopalian. Home: 5-15-18 Kamiuma, Setagaya-ku, 154 Tokyo Japan Office: Nishiyama-Kenkyushitsu, 5-15-18 Kamiuma Setagaya-ku, 154 Tokyo Japan

NISKANEN, PAUL MCCORD, travel company executive; b. Bend, Oreg., July 6, 1943; s. William Arthur and Nina Elizabeth (McCord) N.; m. Christine Campbell; 1 son, Tapio. Student U. Freiburg, Germany, 1963-64; BA, Stanford U., 1965; MBA, U. Chgo., 1966. Fin. analyst Kimberly-Clark Corp., Neenah, Wis., 1966-68; bus. mgr. Avent Inc. subs. Kimberly-Clark Corp., Tucson, 1968-70; v.p., gen. mgr. Pacific Trailways Bus. Line, Portland, Oreg., 1970-81; chmn. bd., owner Niskanen & Jones, Inc., Moab, Utah, 1982—, Perspectives, Inc., Portland; co-owner Cruise Holidays, Beaverton, Oreg., 1989—. Apptd. consul for Finland, 1980—; active Gov.'s Travel Adv. Com., Salem, Oreg., 1976-81; 1st pres. Oreg. Hospitality and Visitors Assn., Portland, 1977-78; bd. dirs. Suomi Coll., Hancock, Mich., 1981—; nat. co-chmn. Dole for Pres. Com., 1987; co-chmn. Vistory 88. Decorated knight 1st Class Order White Rose Republic of Finland. Mem. Travel Industry Assn. Am., Am. Assn. Travel Agts., Pacific Northwest Travel Assn. (chmn. 1978-79), Scandinavian Heritage Found. (bd. dirs. 1984). Republican. Home: 4366 SW Hewett Blvd Portland OR 97221-3107 Office: Cruise Holidays 2730 SW Cedar Hills Blvd Beaverton OR 97005-1356

NISKANEN, WILLIAM ARTHUR, JR., economist, think tank executive; b. Bend, Oreg., Mar. 13, 1933; s. William Arthur and Nina Elizabeth (McCord) N.; children—Lia, Pamela, Jaime. BA, Harvard U., 1954; MA, U. Chgo., 1955, PhD, 1962. Staff economist RAND Corp., Santa Monica, Calif., 1957-62; staff dir. Dept. Def., Washington, 1962-64; div. dir. Inst. Def. Analyses, Washington, 1964-70; asst. dir. Office of Mgmt. and Budget, Washington, 1970-72; prof. U. Calif., Berkeley, 1972-75; chief economist Ford Motor Co., Dearborn, Mich., 1975-80; prof. UCLA, 1980-81; mem. Coun. Econ. Advisers, Washington, 1981-85; chmn. CATO Inst., Washington, 1985—. Author: Bureaucracy and Representative Government, 1971, Reaganomics, 1988; editor Regulation mag., 1990—. Founder Nat. Tax Limitation Com. Mem. Am. Econ. Assn., Pub. Choice Soc., Atlantic Econ. Assn. (former pres.). Republican. Office: Cato Inst 1000 Massachusetts Ave NW Washington DC 20001-5400

NISONOFF, ALFRED, biochemist, educator; b. N.Y.C., Jan. 26, 1923; s. Hyman and Lillian (Klein) N.; m. Sarah Weiseman, July 17, 1946; children: Donald Michael, Linda Ann. B.S. (State scholar), Rutgers U., 1942; M.A., Johns Hopkins U., 1948, Ph.D. (AEC fellow), 1951. Postdoctoral fellow Johns Hopkins Med. Sch., 1951-52; research chemist U.S. Rubber Co., Naugatuck, Conn., 1952-54; sr. cancer research scientist Roswell Park Meml. Inst., Buffalo, 1954-57; assoc. cancer research scientist Roswell Park Meml. Inst., 1957-60; assoc. prof. microbiology U. Ill., Urbana, 1960-62; prof. U. Ill., 1962-66; prof. microbiology U. Ill. Coll. Medicine, Chgo., 1966-69; head dept. biol. chemistry U. Ill. Coll. Medicine, 1969-75; prof. biology Rosenstiel Research Center, Brandeis U., Waltham, Mass., 1975-93, prof. emeritus, 1993—; Mem. grant rev. bd. allergy and immunology study sect. NIH, 1965-67, 71-74, chmn., 1984-87; grant rev. bd. Nat. Multiple Sclerosis Soc., 1972-75, 77-80. Author: The Antibody Molecule, 1975, Introduction to Molecular Immunology, 1982; Editorial bd.: Jour. Immunology, 1962-67, 69-74, sect. editor, 1971-74, sr. editor, 1975-79; editorial bd.: Immunochemistry, 1964-70, Bacteriological Revs, 1968-70, Jour. Exptl. Medicine, 1974-78, Critical Reviews in Immunology, 1980—, European Jour. Epidemiology, 1986—; contbr. articles to profl. jours. Served to lt. (j.g.) USNR, 1943-46. Recipient Research Career award NIH, 1962-69; Pasteur Inst. medal, 1970. Fellow Am. Acad. Arts and Scis.; mem. NAS, Am. Assn. Immunologists (coun. 1985-92, pres. 1990-91), Belgian Royal Acad. Medicine (fgn. corr.), Phi Beta Kappa, Phi Lambda Upsilon. Home: 116 Florence St Apt I Chestnut Hill MA 02167-1938 Office: Brandeis Univ Rosenstiel Rsch Ctr Dept Biology Waltham MA 02254

NISONSON, IAN, urologist; b. Montreal, Que., Can., Jan. 10, 1937; came to U.S., 1947; s. Nathan and Rebecca (Etzkovich) N.; m. Myrna J. Goodman, Apr. 9, 1960; children: Evan J., Andrea B., Lauren R., Ronald S. BA, Columbia U., 1958, MD, 1962. Diplomate Am. Bd. Urology. Intern Strong Meml. Hosp.U. Rochester, 1962-64; resident Squire Urological Clinic Presbyn. Hosp. Columbia U., N.Y.C., 1966-70; NIH fellow in infectious diseases Columbia Presbyn. Hosp., N.Y.C., 1967-68; pvt. practice, Miami, Fla., 1970—; chief surgery Bapt. Hosp., Miami, 1986-87. Editor-in-chief Miami Medicine, 1987-90. Capt. M.C., USAF, 1964-66. Fellow ACS (pres. Greater Miami chpt. 1979-80, bd. govs. Fla. 1990-93), Greater Miami Urol. Soc. (pres. 1986). Office: South Fla Urology Assocs 7800 SW 87th Ave Miami FL 33173-3570

NISSEL, MARTIN, radiologist, consultant; b. N.Y.C., July 29, 1921; s. Samuel David and Etta Rebecca (Ostrie) N.; m. Beatrice Goldberg, Dec. 26, 1943; children: Philippa Lyn, Jeremy Michael. BA, NYU, 1941; MD, N.Y. Med. Coll., 1944. Diplomate Am. Bd. Radiology. Intern Met. Hosp., N.Y.C., 1944-45, Lincoln Hosp., N.Y.C., 1947-48; resident in radiology Bronx Hosp., 1948-50, attending radiologist, 1952-54; resident in radiotherapy Montefiore Hosp., Bronx, 1950-51, attending radiotherapist, 1954-65; attending radiologist Buffalo (N.Y.) VA Hosp., 1951-52; attending radiotherapist Univ. Hosp. Boston City Hosp., 1965-69; asst. prof. radiology Boston U. Sch. of Medicine, 1965-69; chief radiotherapist,dir. radiation ctr. Brookside Hosp., San Pablo, Calif., 1969-77; group leader, radiopharm. drugs FDA, Rockville, Md., 1977-86; pvt. cons. radiopharm. drug devel., 1986—. Contbr. articles to profl. jours. Lectr. Am. Cancer Soc., Contra Costa County, Calif., 1973-76. Capt. MC AUS, 1945-47, Korea. Recipient Contra Costa County Speakers Bur. award Am. Cancer Soc., 1973, 76, Responsible Person for Radiol. Health Program for Radiopharm. Drugs award FDA, 1980-86. Mem. Am. Coll. Radiology, Radiol. Soc. N.Am. Avocations; photography, model train building, travel. Office: PO Box 5537 Eugene OR 97405-0537

NISSEN, CARL ANDREW, JR., minister, retired procurement analyst; b. Manhattan, Kans., June 26, 1930; s. Carl Andrew and Bernice Lydia (Varney) N. Student, Denison U., 1948-49; BA, Ohio State U., 1960; postgrad., Grad. Sch. Theology, Oberlin, Ohio, 1959, Berkeley Bapt. Divinity Sch., 1960-61. Ordained to ministry Ohio Bapt. Conv. Supply pastor Ohio Bapt. Conv., various, 1958-61, 82-85; pastor Sinking Creek Bapt. Ch., Springfield, Ohio, 1985-90; chaplain gen. SAR, Louisville, 1989-90; ret., 1990; procurement analyst Def. Electronics Supply Ctr., Dayton, Ohio, 1963-90, ret., 1990. Sgt. U.S. Army, 1950-53, Korea; lt. col. Ohio Mil. Res., 1984-91. Recipient George Washington Honor medal Freedom's Found., 1972, Minute Man medal SAR, 1991. Home: 1001 Fordham Dr Ruskin FL 33573-5236 *Faith in the presence of Almighty God in our lives makes the challenges we face opportunities for change.*

NISSEN, WILLIAM JOHN, lawyer; b. Chgo., July 28, 1947; s. William Gordon Jr. and Ruth Carolyn (Banas) N.; m. Patricia Jane Press, Jan. 16, 1971; children: Meredith Warner, Edward William. BA, Northwestern U., 1969; JD magna cum laude, Harvard U., 1976. Bar: Ill. 1976, U.S. Dist. Ct. (no. dist.) Ill. 1976, U.S. Ct. Appeals (7th cir.) 1981. Assoc. Sidley & Austin, Chgo., 1976-83, ptnr., 1983—; gen. counsel Heinold Commodities, Inc., Chgo., 1982-84. Editor Harvard U. Internat. Law Jour., 1974-76. Served to lt. USN, 1969-73. Mem. ABA (co-chmn. futures regulation subcom. on internat. futures matters 1985—), Chgo. Bar Assn. (chmn. futures regulation com. 1985-86), Am. Legion (comdr. union league post 758 1994-95), Union League Club Chgo. Home: 348 Foss Ct Lake Bluff IL 60044-2753 Office: Sidley & Austin 1 First National Plz Chicago IL 60603

NISSINEN, MIKKO PEKKA, dancer; b. Helsinki, Finland, Mar. 4, 1962; came to U.S., 1987; s. Pekka and Pirkko (Pulkkinen) N. Grad., Finnish Nat. Ballet Sch., 1977; postgrad., Leningrad Acad. Ballet Sch., 1979-80. Mem. corps de ballet Finnish Nat. Ballet, Helsinki, 1977-79, soloist, 1980-82; grand sujete Dutch Nat. Ballet, Amsterdam, The Netherlands, 1982-84; soloist Basel (Switzerland) Ballet, 1984-87; soloist San Francisco Ballet, 1987-88, prin. dancer, 1988—; guest artist La Bayadere, Nat. Ballet Can., 1989, Oberlin Dance Collective, 1993; advisor to sch. dir. Nat. Ballet Sch., Toronto, Ont., Can., 1992; bd. dirs. Le Don Des Etoiles, 1989—; guest tchr. Royal Acad. of Dancing, 1993, Kennedy Ctr. Ednl. Program, 1994, Nat. Ballet Sch., Toronto, 1994; lectr. on dance history and state of dance today Standord U., St. Mary's Coll., Christensen Soc. Repertoire includes (with San Francisco Ballet) The Sleeping Beauty, Swan Lake, Bizet Pas de Deux, Handel-a Celebration, Haffner Symphony, Con Brio, Ballet d'Isoline, Giuliani: Variations on a Theme, Tchaikovsky Pas de Deux, Symphony in C, Theme and Variations, Ballo della Regina, The Nutcracker, Airs de Ballet, Variations de Ballet, Rodin, Rodeo, Maelstrom, Dark Elegies, Harvest Moon, Napoli, Job, The Wanderer Fantasy, In the middle, somewhat elevated, Calcium Light Night, Le Corsaire Pas de Deux, Dreams of Harmony, Pulcinella, The Dream; (with other cos.) Don Quixote, Giselle, A Midsummer Night's Dream, Les Biches, Sleeping Beauty, Pyrrich Dances, Masse, Le Tombeau de Couperin, Symphony in C, The Four Temperaments, The Prodigal Son, Rodin, Pierrot Lunaire, La Fille mal gardée, Swan Lake, Henze, Five Tangos, In and Out, Bits and Pieces, Jeu de Cartes; appeared in the Canadian Internat. Ballet Gala, 1989, 90, 91, 92, 93, 94, Reykjavik Arts Festival, 1990, Internat. Ballet Gala, Kuodio, Finland, 1992, Internat. Ballet Gala, Vail, Colo., 1993, Night of Stars Ballet Gala, Helsinki, 1993; profiled in nat. and internat. radio and TV programs, including CNN Worldwide Report, 1992; featured on cover of Dance Mag., 1992. Recipient 1st prize 1st Nat. Dance Competition Kuopio, Finland, 1978.

NITECKI, JOSEPH ZBIGNIEW, librarian; b. Dabrowa Górnicza, Poland, Jan. 31, 1922; came to U.S., 1951, naturalized, 1956; s. Henryk W. and Antonina S. N.; m. Sophie V. Zboinski, June 17, 1945; children: Zbigniew H., Danuta A. B.A. in Philosophy, Wayne State U., 1955; M.A., Roosevelt U., 1959; M.A. in L.S., U. Chgo., 1963. Various profl. and adminstrv. positions in libraries U. Chgo., 1961-63, Chgo. City Coll., 1963-66, U. Wis., Milw., 1967-70, Temple U., Phila., 1970-78; prof., exec. dir. libraries U. Wis., Oshkosh, 1978-80; dir. libraries SUNY, Albany, 1980-88, prof. Sch. Info Sci. and Policy, 1988-90, prof. emeritus, 1990—; cons. library issues. Author, editor compiler and reviewer in field; ref. and manuscript reader. Served with Polish Armed Forces under Brit. command, 1939-48. Mem. ALA, Beta Phi Mu. Home: 22 Shetland Dr Delmar NY 12054-3630

NITIKMAN, FRANKLIN W., lawyer; b. Davenport, Iowa, Oct. 26, 1940; s. David A. and Janette (Gordon) N.; m. Adrienne C. Drell, Nov. 28, 1972. BA, Northwestern U., 1963; LLB, Yale U., 1966. Bar: Ill. 1966, U.S. Dist. Ct. (no. dist.) Ill. 1967, U.S. Tax Ct. 1972, Fla. 1977, D.C. 1981. Assoc. McDermott, Will & Emery, Chgo., 1966-72, ptnr., 1973—. Co-author: Drafting Wills and Trust Agreements, 1990. Bd. dirs. Owen Coon Found., Glenview, Ill., 1985—, Spertus Inst. Jewish Studies, Chgo., 1991—, Jewish United Fund, Jewish Fedn. Metro. Chgo., 1994—. Fellow Am. Coll. Trust and Estate Coun., Am. Bar Found.; mem. Standard Club, Arts Club (Chgo.). Home: 365 Lakeside Pl Highland Park IL 60035-5371 Office: McDermott Will & Emery 227 W Monroe St Chicago IL 60606-5016

NITTA, EUGENE TADASHI, endangered species biologist; b. Lodi, Calif., Aug. 19, 1946; s. Kenji and Emiko (Taguchi) N.; m. Teresa Thelma Tanibe, Dec. 26, 1987; stepchildren: Sheri Y. Yokota, Tani-Lyn T. Yamamoto, Staci S. Yamamoto. BA, U. Calif., Santa Barbara, 1969. Observer Internat. Whaling Commn., Cambridge, England, 1972-75; marine mammal and endangered species program coord. NOAA Nat. Marine Fisheries Svcs. Southwest Region, Terminal Island, Calif., 1976-79; protected species program coord. NOAA Nat. Marine Fisheries Svcs. Southwest Region, Honolulu, 1980—; instr. coll. continuing edn. U. Hawaii, Honolulu, 1988-93. Mem. Soc. for Marine Mammalogy (charter mem.), Am. Soc. Mammalogists. Democrat. Episcopalian. Avocations: golf, surfing.

NITTA, KENJIRO, computer company executive. With NEC Corp., Tokyo, Japan, 1961-1991; chmn., ceo Nec Technologies Inc., Boxboro, Mass., 1991—. Office: Nec Technologies Inc 1414 Massachusetts Ave Boxboro MA 01719-2205*

NITTOLY, PAUL GERARD, lawyer; b. Bklyn., July 13, 1948; s. Edward Joseph and Philomena (Lorenzo) N.; m. Maryann Racioppi, May 31, 1970; children: Melissa Beth, Matthew Edward. AB, Rutgers U., 1970; JD, N.Y. Law Sch., 1973. Bar: N.J. 1973, U.S. Dist. Ct. N.J. 1973, U.S. Supreme Ct. 1979; cert. trial atty. (civil and criminal) N.J. Supreme Ct. Asst. prosecutor, sr. trial atty. Essex County Prosecutor's Office, Newark, 1974-79; ptnr. Shanley & Fisher, P.C., Morristown, N.J., 1984—; moot trial ct. judge Seton Hall Law Sch., Newark, 1982—; lectr. symposium on perinatal malpractice Am. Coll. Ob-Gyn and Rutgers U. Med. Sch., Morristown, N.J., 1984; mem. practitioner's adv. group to U.S. Sentencing Commn., 1992—. Author: Readings in White Collar Crime, 1991; contbr. chapts to books; mem. editorial adv. bd. Corporate Criminal Liability Reporter; pres. C. Willard Heckel Am. Inn of Court, master; del advocate Am. Bd. Trial Advocates. Served to capt. U.S. Army, 1972. Mem. ABA, N.J. Bar Assn., Essex County Bar Assn., Morris County Bar Assn., Nat. Assn. Criminal Defense Lawyers, Assn. Criminal Defense Attys. N.J., Trial Attys. N.J., Park Avenue Club (Morristown), Morristown Club, Delta Upsilon. Roman Catholic. Home: 275 Meetinghouse Ln Mountainside NJ 07092-1305 Office: Shanley & Fisher 131 Madison Ave Morristown NJ 07960-6086

NITZE, PAUL HENRY, international studies educator; b. Amherst, Mass., Jan. 16, 1907; s. William A. and Anina (Hilken) N.; m. Phyllis Pratt, Dec. 2, 1932 (dec.); children: Heidi, Peter, William II, Phyllis; m. Elisabeth Scott Porter, Jan. 23, 1993. AB cum laude, Harvard U., 1928; LLD (hon.), New Sch. Social Research, Pratt Inst., Johns Hopkins U., Holy Cross Coll., Harvard U., Amherst Coll., Williams Coll., Brown U. With Dillon, Read & Co. (investment bankers), N.Y.C., 1929-37; v.p. Dillon, Read & Co. (investment bankers), 1939-41; pres. P.H. Nitze & Co., Inc., 1938-39; U.S. govt. fin. dir., coord. Inter-Am. Affairs; chief metals and minerals br. Bd. Econ. Warfare; dir. fgn. procurement and devel. br. Fgn. Econ. Adminstrn.; dir., then vice chmn. U.S. Strategic Bombing Survey, 1944-46; dep. dir. Office Internat. Trade Policy, Dept. State, 1946; dep. to asst. sec. state for econ. affairs, 1948-49; dir. policy planning staff Dept. State, 1950-53; pres. Fgn. Service Ednl. Found., Washington, 1953-61; asst. sec. def. for Internat. Security Affairs, 1961-63; sec. of Navy, 1963-67, dep. sec. of def., 1967-69; mem. U.S. del. Strategic Arms Limitation Talks, 1969-74; head U.S. negotiating team Arms Control Talks, Geneva, 1981-84; spl. advisor to pres. and sec. state on arms control matters, 1984-89; founder, diplomat-in-residence, disting. rsch. prof. in strategic studies and Am. fgn. policy Paul H. Nitze Sch. Advanced Internat. Studies, Johns Hopkins U., Washington; mem. internat. adv. council Inst. Internat. Studies.; chmn. Washington Inst. Fgn. Affairs. Author: From Hiroshima to Glasnost: A Memoir, 1989 (Adolph Bentinck Lit. prize 1990), Tension Between Opposites: Reflections on the Practice and Theory of Politics, 1993. Recipient Medal for Merit, Medal of Freedom, George C. Marshall, Knight Comdrs. Cross (badge and star) Order of Merit (Fed. Republic Germany); grand officier de l'Ordre de la Couronne Royaume de Belgique, 1989, Grosse Goldene Ehrenzeiche des Landes Steiermark (Austria), 1991, other awards from The Netherlands, Italy, Sec. Gen. Atlantic award (NATO Man of Yr.), 1988, Sec. State Disting. Svc. award, 1988, Sylvanus Thayer award, 1991, Doolittle award, 1993. Home: 2416 Tracy Pl NW Washington DC 20008-1627 Office: Paul Nitze Sch Advanced Internat Studies John Hopkins U 1619 Massachusetts Ave NW Washington DC 20036-2213

NITZE, WILLIAM ALBERT, government official, lawyer; b. N.Y.C., Sept. 27, 1942; s. Paul Henry and Phyllis (Pratt) N.; m. Ann Kendall Richards, June 5, 1971; children: Paul Kendall, Charles Richards. BA, Harvard U., 1964, JD, 1969; BA, Oxford U., 1966. Bar: N.Y. 1970, U.S. Supreme Ct. 1987. Assoc. Sullivan and Cromwell, N.Y.C., 1970-72; v.p. London Arts, Inc., N.Y.C., 1972-73; counsel Mobil South, Inc., N.Y.C., 1974-76; gen. counsel Mobil Oil Japan, Tokyo, 1976-80; asst. gen. counsel exploration and producing div. Mobil Oil Corp., N.Y.C., 1980-87; dep asst. sec. for environment, health and natural resources U.S. Dept. State, Washington, 1987-90; pres. Alliance to Save Energy, Washington, 1990-94; asst. adminstr. for internat. activities U.S. EPA, Washington, 1994—; mem. adv. com. Sch. Advanced Internat. Studies, Washington, 1982-95, professorial lectr., 1993-94; vis. scholar Environ. Law Inst., Washington, 1990; dir. Charles A. Lindbergh Fund, Mpls., 1990-94, Nat. Symphony Orch. Assn., Washington, 1990—. Trustee Aspen Inst., Queenstown, Md., 1988—. Mem. Assn. of Bar of City of N.Y., Coun. on Fgn. Rels., Met. Club, Links Club. Republican. Episcopalian. Avocations: running, piano, collecting art. Home: 1336 30th St NW Washington DC 20007-3349 Office: US EPA 401 M St SW Washington DC 20460-0001

NITZSCHE, JACK, composer; b. Mich., 1937. music arranger Phil Spector, 1962-66, Specialty Records, Original Sound Records; session musician Rolling Stones, 1965-66, Buffalo Springfield, 1967; keyboardist, prodr. Crazy Horse, 1970-71; keyboardist Stray Gators, 1973; prodr. Lee Hazlewood, Rolling Stones, James Gang, Neil Young, Ringo Starr, Buffy Sainte-Marie, Rick Nelson, Graham Parker, Mink DeVille. Composer, music dir.: (films) Village of the Giants, 1965; composer, music dir., orchestrator: (films) When You Comin' Back, Red Ryder?, 1979; composer: (films) Performance, 1970, Greaser's Palace, 1972, The Exorcist, 1973, One Flew Over the Cuckoo's Nest, 1975 (Academy award nomination best original score 1975), (with Richard Hazard) Heroes, 1977, (with Ry Cooder) Blue Collar, 1978, Hardcore, 1979, Heart Beat, 1979, Melvin and Howard, 1980, Cruising, 1980, Cutter's Way, 1981, An Officer and a Gentleman, 1982 (Academy award nomination best original score 1982), Cannery Row, 1982, Personal Best, 1982, Without a Trace, 1983, Breathless, 1983, The Razor's Edge, 1984, Starman, 1984, Windy City, 1984, The Jewel of the Nile, 1985, (with Michael Hoenig) 9 1/2 Weeks, 1986, Stand By Me, 1986, Streets of Gold, 1986, (with Buffy Sainte-Marie) Stripper, 1986, The Whoopee Boys, 1986, The Seventh Sign, 1988, Next of Kin, 1989, Revenge, 1990, The Hot Spot, 1990, The Last of the Finest, 1990, Mermaids, 1990, The Indian Runner, 1991, (TV movies) Middle Ages, 1992, (TV series) Starman, 1986-86, (songs) (with Sonny Bono) Needles and Pins, 1963, The Lonely Surfer, 1963, Gone Dead Train, 1970, (with Cooder and Paul Schrader) Hard Working Man, 1978, No One Knows Better Than You, 1979, I Love Her

Too, 1979, We're Old Enough to Know, 1981, (with Will Jennings and Sainte-Marie) Up Where We Belong, 1982 (Academy award best original song 1983), Hit and Run Lovers, 1984; album: The Lonely Surfer, 1963, St. Giles Cripplegate, 1972. Office: Creative Artists Agency 9830 Wilshire Blvd Beverly Hills CA 90212-1804

NITZSCHKE, DALE FREDERICK, university president; b. Remsen, Iowa, Sept. 16, 1937; m. Linda Hutchinson, June 24, 1971; children: Mary Beth, Stephen, Lori, Eric, David. BA in Edn. cum laude, Lora Coll., 1959; MEd in Guidance and Counseling, Ohio U., 1960, PhD in Guidance and Counseling, 1964. Instr. edn. Loras Coll., Dubuque, Iowa, 1964-65, chmn. dept. edn., 1964-65; asst. prof., dir. ednl. placement bur. Ohio U., Athens, 1967-72; assoc. dean profl. and gen. studies, dean edn. State U. Coll. Arts and Sci., Plattsburgh, N.Y., 1972-76; prof. edn., dean Coll. Edn. U. No. Iowa, 1976-80; prof. edn., v.p. acad. affairs U. Nev., Las Vegas, 1980-84; pres. Marshall U., Huntington, W.Va., 1984-90, U. N.H., Durham, 1990—; workshop dir. Evaluation Elem. Schs.; dir. Martha Holden Jennings Founds. Lectureship Series; cons. Athens non-graded high sch.; cons. on personnel mgmt. U. Nev. Reno Med. Sch. Contbr. articles to profl. jours. Bd. dirs., blood chmn. Athens County Red Cross; v.p. Kootoga council Boy Scouts Am.; mem. N.Y. State Policy Bd. in Spl. Edn., 1975-76; nat. adv. com. Personalized Adult Counseling Experience (PACE); coordinator Coll. Drug Edn. Program, Ohio U.; dir. Student Tutors for Ednl. Progress (STEP); coordinator Preparation Program for Inner City and Appalachian Tchrs.; sec. State of Ohio Edn. Deans; bd. dirs. Elvis Presley Mus. and Entertainment Inst., Las Vegas; bd. acad. advisors Am. Inst. for Fgn. Study; chmn. bd. regents State Adv. Com. for Iowa Sch. for Deaf, Iowa Braille and Sight Saving Sch.; mem. State-wide Inter-Instl. Gerontology Com.; bd. dirs. W.Va. Council on Econ. Devel., W.Va. Roundtable, Cabell-Wayne United Way, River Cities Cultural Devel. Council, Community Players, W.Va. Edn. Fund, Inc., Boys Club Huntington, Ronald McDonald House, Huntington, W.Va. Com. on Employment Opportunities and Econ. Devel.; mem. com. on self regulation initiatives Am. Council on Edn.; mem. selection com. Harry S. Truman Scholarship Program; incorporator Trust for N.H. Lands, 1992—; bd. dirs. New Eng. Coun. Recipient Community Leader of Am. award, 1969; Disting. Service award Rotary, 1969; Alexander Meiklejohn award for acad. freedom AAUP, 1984. Mem. Assn. Higher Edn., Am. Personnel Guidance Assn., Nat. Vocat. Guidance Assn., Am. Counselor Edn. Assn., Student Personnel Assn. for Tchr. Edn., Nat. Assn. State Univs. and Land Grant Colls. (chmn. commn. on outreach and tech. transfer 1991—), Huntington C. of C. (bd. dirs.), Athens Jaycees (past pres., chmn. bd., Young Man of Yr. award 1969), Nature Conservancy (trustee N.H. chpt. 1992—). Home: 880 Wallace Ave Milford OH 45150-1158 Office: U NH Office of Pres Main St Durham NH 03824-2521

NIVISON, DAVID SHEPHERD, Chinese and philosophy educator; b. Farmingdale, Maine, Jan. 17, 1923; s. William and Ruth (Robinson) N.; m. Cornelia Green, Sept. 11, 1944; children—Louise, Helen Thom, David Gregory, James Nicholas. A.B. summa cum laude, Harvard U., 1946, M.A., 1948, Ph.D., 1953. Instr. Chinese Stanford U., 1948-52, Ford Found. faculty fellow, 1952-53, instr. Chinese and philosophy, 1953-54; Fulbright research scholar Kyoto, Japan, 1954-55; lectr. philosophy Stanford U., 1955-58, asst. prof. Chinese and philosophy, 1958-59, assoc. prof., 1959-66, prof., 1966-88, Walter Y. Evans-Wentz prof. Oriental Philosophies, Religions and Ethics, 1983-88, chmn. dept. philosophy, 1969-72, 75-76, acting chmn. dept. Asian langs., 1985-86; emeritus, 1988—. Author: The Life and Thought of Chang Hsüeh-ch'eng, 1738-1801, 1966, The Ways of Confucianism: Investigations in Chinese Philosophy, 1996; co-author: Chinese Language, Thought and Culture: Essays Dedicated to David S. Nivison, 1996; editor, co-compiler: Stanford Chinese Concordance Series, 1979; co-editor: Confucianism in Action, 1959; contbr. articles to profl. jours. and encys. Served with AUS, 1943-46. Recipient Prix Stanislas-Julien Inst. de France, 1967; Am. Council Learned Socs. fellow, 1973; John Simon Guggenheim fellow, 1973-74. Mem. Assn. Asian Studies, Am. Philos. Assn. (v.p. Pacific div. 1978-79, pres. 1979-80), Am. Oriental Soc. (Western br. v.p. 1964-65, sec. 1965-70, pres. 1971-72), AAUP (pres. No. Calif. Conf. 1964-66), Internat. Acad. Chinese Culture (Beijing, Peoples Republic of China), Phi Beta Kappa. Home: 1169 Russell Ave Los Altos CA 94024-5066 Office: Stanford U Philosophy Dept Stanford CA 94305

NIWA, NORIO, computer company executive. Pres., ceo Epson Am. Inc., Torrance, Calif., 1992—. Office: Epson AMerica Inc 20770 Madrona Ave Torrance CA 90503-3777*

NIX, EDMUND ALFRED, lawyer; b. Eau Claire, Wis., May 24, 1929; s. Sebastian and Kathryn (Keirnan) N.; m. Mary Kathryn Nagle Daley, Apr. 27, 1968; children: Kim, Mary Kay, Norbert, Edmund Alfred, Michael. B.S., Wis. State U., 1951; LL.B., U. Wis., 1954, postgrad. in speech, 1956-57. Bar: Wis. 1954. Practice in Eau Claire, 1954-65; dist. atty. Eau Claire County, 1958-64; U.S. atty. Western Dist. Wis., Eau Claire, 1965-69; U.S. magistrate Western Dist. Wis., 1969-70; dist. atty. La Crosse County, Wis., 1975-77; mcpl. judge City of La Crosse, 1992—. Co-chmn. United Fund, Eau Claire, 1958; Pres. Young Democrats Wis., 1951-53; mem. adminstrv. bd. Wis. Dem. party, 1953-54; chmn. 10th Congl. dist., 1965; sec. Kennedy for Pres. Club Wis., 1959-60. Served with AUS, 1954-56. Mem. Fed. Bar Assn., Wis. Bar Assn. (state chmn. crime prevention and control com.), La Crosse County Bar Assn. (pres.), Nat. Dist. Attys. Assn., KC. Roman Catholic. Office: 123 4th St N La Crosse WI 54601-3235

NIX, JAMES RAYFORD, nuclear physicist, consultant; b. Natchitoches, La., Feb. 18, 1938; s. Joe Ebbin and Edna (Guin) N.; m. Sally Ann Wood, Aug. 19, 1961; children—Patricia Lynne, David Allen. B.S. in Physics, Carnegie Inst. Tech., 1960; Ph.D. in Physics, U. Calif.-Berkeley, 1964. Summer physicist Lawrence Livermore Nat. Lab., Livermore, Calif., 1961; research asst. Lawrence Berkeley Lab., Berkeley, Calif., 1961-64, postdoctoral physicist, 1966-68; NATO postdoctoral fellow Niels Bohr Inst., Copenhagen, Denmark, 1964-65; staff mem. Los Alamos Nat. Lab., 1968-77, 89-94, group leader, 1977-89, fellow, 1994—; vis. prof. Centro Brasileiro de Pesquisas Fisicas, Rio de Janeiro, Brazil, 1974; cons. Calif. Inst. Tech., Pasadena, 1976, 79; chmn. Gordon Research Conf. Nuclear Chemistry, New London, N.H., 1976; chmn. physics div. adv. com. Oak Ridge Nat. Lab., 1976, chmn. nuclear sci. div. vis. com. Lawrence Berkeley Lab., 1979-80. Contbr. articles to numerous publs. Alfred P. Sloan Found. scholar, Pitts., 1956-60; Phi Kappa Phi fellow, Berkeley, Calif., 1960-61; Alexander von Humboldt Sr. U.S. Scientist award Univ. Munich and Max-Planck Inst. for Nuclear Physics, 1980-81. Fellow Am. Phys. Soc. (exec. com. 1973-75); mem. AAAS, Sigma Xi, Phi Kappa Phi. Democrat. Home: 12 Los Pueblos Los Alamos NM 87544-2659 Office: Los Alamos Nat Lab Nuclear Theory T-2 MS B243 Los Alamos NM 87545

NIX, ROBERT LYNN, minister; b. Belleville, Ark., Nov. 24, 1940; s. Huey Watson and Edna Mae (Johnson) N.; m. Patricia Sue Palmer, Aug. 27, 1961; children: Kevin Lynn, Robert Keith, Jonathan Kyle, Kelly Eugene. Diploma, Jackson (Miss.) Coll. Ministries, 1965. Ordained to ministry United Pentecostal Ch. Internat., 1963. Prof. Pentecostal Bible Inst., Tupelo, Miss., 1965-66; missionary to Peru, United Pentecostal Ch. Internat., 1966-69; missionary supt. United Pentecostal Ch., Peru, 1966-85; pres. United Pentecostal Sem., Peru, 1969-85; missionary supt. United Pentecostal Ch., Costa Rica, Cen. Am.; pres. United Pentecostal Sem. United Pentecostal Ch., Costa Rica, Cen. Am., 1983-85; pastor United Pentecostal Spanish Ch., Hilsboro, Oreg., 1985-86, Christian Apostolic Ch., San Antonio, 1987—. Bd. dirs. Tex. Bible Coll., Houston, 1993—. Home and Office: 12016 White Birch St San Antonio TX 78245-3350 *The Apostle Paul said, "For me to live is Christ." (Phil. 1:21). In this age of hedonism and materialism many believe that life consists of worldly goods and human achievements. How mistaken they are! People never really live until they die to self and allow Jesus Christ to become the Supreme Lord of their lives.*

NIX, ROBERT N(ELSON) C(ORNELIUS), JR., state supreme court chief justice; b. Phila., July 13, 1928; s. Robert Nelson Cornelius and Ethel (Lanier) N.; m. Renate Bryant; children from previous marriage: Dorthy Lewis (dec.), Robert Nelson Cornelius III, Michael, Anthony, S. Jude. A.B., Villanova U., LLD (hon.); J.D., U. Pa.; postgrad. bus. adminstrn. and econs., Temple U.; LLD (hon.), St. Charles Sem., Dickinson U. Sch. Law, Scranton U., Delaware Law Sch., Lafayette Coll. Bar: Pa. 1956, U.S. Dist. Ct. (ea. dist.) Pa., U.S. Ct. Appeals (3d cir.). Dep. atty. gen. Commonwealth of Pa., 1956-58; ptnr. Nix, Rhodes & Nix, Phila., 1958-68; judge Common Pleas Ct., Phila., 1968-71; justice Supreme Ct. Pa., Phila., 1972-84, chief justice, 1984—; chmn. bd. dirs. Nat. Ctr. for State Cts., 1990-91. Bd. dirs. Nat. Ctr. for State Cts., 1985—, Scranton U., Duquesne U., Lincoln U.; life mem. bd. consultors Villanova U., trustee, 1986—; bd. overseers U. Pa. Sch. Law, 1987—; bd. mgrs. Archdiocese of Phila. Served with AUS, 1953-55. Recipient First Pa. award, Benjamin Franklin award Poor Richard Club Pa., James Madison award Soc. Profl. Journalists; named Knight Comdr. Order of St. Gregory the Great. Fellow Am. Bar Found.; mem. ABA, Pa. Bar Assn., Phila. Bar Assn., Nat. Bar Assn. (past chmn. jud. coun.), Barristers Club, Am. Law Inst., Conf. of Chief Justices (bd. dirs., pres. 1990-91), The Legal Club, Omega Psi Phi. Lodge: KC. Office: Pa Supreme Ct Ea Dist Office City Hall Rm 468 Philadelphia PA 19107-3292 Office: 1 South Penn Sq Widener Building Rm 500 Philadelphia PA 19107-3519 *America is slowly becoming aware of the vast potential she possesses because of the varied backgrounds and cultures of her citizens. When this fact is fully appreciated and full advantage is taken of this resource, she will reach an unprecedented level of civilization.*

NIXON, AGNES ECKHARDT, television writer, producer; m. Robert Nixon; 4 children. Student, Sch. Speech, Northwestern U. Writer for radio and TV; freelance writer for: TV programs Hallmark Hall of Fame, Robert Montgomery Presents, Studio One; creator, packager, head writer: daytime TV series All My Children; creator nighttime mini-series The Manions of America; creator, packager daytime TV series One Life to Live; creator, packager: daytime TV series Loving; co-creator: daytime TV series As The World Turns; formerly head writer, The Guiding Light, daytime TV series Another World. Recipient Trustees award Nat. Acad. TV Arts and Sci., 1981, Super Achiever award Jr. Diabetes Found., 1981, Wilmer Eye Inst. award, 1981, Communicator award Am. Women in Radio & TV, 1984, Gold Plate award Am. Acad. Achievement, 1993, Popular Culture Lifetime Achievement award Popular Culture Assn., 1995, Pub. Svc. award Johns Hopkins Hosp., 1995; inducted into TV Hall of Fame, 1993. Mem. Internat. Radio and TV Soc. Nat. Acad. TV Arts and Scis., Harvard Found. (bd. dirs.), Mus. TV and Radio (bd. dirs.), The Friars Club. Address: 774 Conestoga Rd Rosemont PA 19010-1257

NIXON, DAVID, dancer; b. Windsor, Ont., Can.. Student, The Nat. Ballet Sch. With Nat. Ballet of Can., 1978-84, 1st soloist, 1982-84, prin. dancer, 1984-90; prin. dancer Berlin Opera Ballet, 1985-90, Bayerisches Staatsoper Ballet Munich, 1990-91; prin. dancer and 1st Ballet master Deutsche Opera Ballet Berlin, 1994-95; various guest appearances including Alexander Godunov and Stars, summer 1982, Milw. Ballet, 1984, Sydney Ballet Australia, 1984, World Ballet Festival Tokyo, 1985, 88, Hamburg Ballet, 1988, 89, Staatsoper Berlin, 1988-91, Bayerisches Staatsballet, 1988-90, Komische Opera Berlin, 1990-93; prodr. David Nixon's Dance Theatre, Hebbel Theatre, Berlin, 1990, 91; prodr., artistic dir. BalletMet, 1995—; choreographer Butterfly, 1983, La Follia, 1984, Dangerous Liaisons, 1990, African Fantasy, 1990, Celebrate Mozart, 1991, Sudden Impulse, 1994, A Summer's Nights Reflections, 1995, Full-Length Nutcracker, 1995.

NIXON, EUGENE RAY, chemist, educator; b. Mt. Pleasant, Mich., Apr. 14, 1919; s. William S. and Grace (Brookens) N.; m. Phyllis R. Jones, June 10, 1945; children—Cynthia L., Emily E. Sc.B. summa cum laude, Alma Coll., 1941; Ph.D., Brown U., 1947. Research chemist Manhattan Project, 1942-46; instr. chemistry Brown U., 1947-49; mem. faculty U. Pa., Phila., 1949—; prof. chemistry U. Pa., 1965—, vice dean grad. sch., 1958-62, acting chmn. dept. chemistry, 1965-66, dir. materials research lab., 1969-72; vis. prof. U. London, 1963-64; vis. lectr. Bryn Mawr Coll., 1957-58. Mem. Am. Chem. Soc., Am. Phys. Soc., Soc. Applied Spectroscopy (Jour. award 1965, Spectroscopist of Yr. award Del. Valley sect. 1988), Coblentz Soc. (bd. mgrs.), Sigma Xi. Research, publs. on phys. chemistry, molecular structure and molecular spectroscopy, properties of crystals, intermolecular interactions, laser spectroscopy and laser chemistry. Home: 35 Julio Dr Apt 106 Shrewsbury MA 01545-3049 Office: Univ Pa Dept Chemistry Philadelphia PA 19104

NIXON, JAMES ALEXANDER, cosmetic company executive; b. Detroit, Aug. 30, 1932; s. David S. and Kathleen (Garlick) N.; m. Elizabeth Fitzwater, Apr. 27, 1935; children: James Jeffery, Richard Scott. BA, Amherst Coll., 1954; MA, Harvard U., 1955. Mgr. advt. Campbell Soup Co., Camden, N.J., 1957-67; dir. mktg. Miles Labs., Elkhart, N.J., 1967-78; v.p. mktg. Keydata Corp., Boston, 1970-73, Bristol Myers Corp., N.Y.C., 1973-76; exec. v.p. Cosmair, Inc., N.Y.C., 1976—. Served with U.S. Army, 1955-57. Republican. Episcopalean. Clubs: Greenwich Country (Conn.); Pine Valley Golf (N.J.). Avocations: golf, squash, tennis. Home: 11 Hillside Rd Greenwich CT 06830-4834*

NIXON, JAMES GREGORY, economic development consultant; b. Kansas City, Mo., Dec. 7, 1962; s. Gerald Glen and Jane Ardis (Mountain) N.; m. Carol Ann Lake, June 21, 1986; 1 child, Kathryn Grace. BBA, U. Okla., 1985; MBA, Okla. State U., 1992. Cert. econ. developer. Govt. rels. aide Pub. Svc. Okla., Oklahoma City, 1985-86; info. analyst Pub. Svc. Okla., Tulsa, 1986-87, econ. devel. cons., 1987—. Mem. Am. Econ. Devel. Coun., So. Indsl. Devel. Coun. (alt. dir. 1986—), Order of Arrow (Vigil honor mem.). Republican. Mem. Disciples of Christ. Avocations: sailing, golf, water skiing, snow skiing, music. Office: Pub Svc Co Okla 212 E 6th St Tulsa OK 74119-1212

NIXON, JEREMIAH W. (JAY NIXON), state attorney general; b. DeSoto, Mo., Feb. 13, 1956; s. Jeremiah and Betty (Lea) N.; m. Georganne Nixon; children: Jeremiah, Will. BS in Polit. Sci., U. Mo., 1978, JD, 1981. Ptnr. Nixon, Nixon, Breeze & Roberts, Jefferson County, Mo., 1981-86; mem. Mo. State Senate from Dist 22, 1986-93; atty. gen. State of Mo., 1993—; chmn. select com. ins. reform.; created video internat. devel. and edn. opportunity program. Honoree, Conservation Fedn. Mo., 1992; named Outstanding Young Missourian, Mo. Jaycees, 1994, Outstanding Young Lawyer, Barrister's Mag., 1993. Mem. Nat. Assn. Attys. Gen. (antitrust com., chair FTC working group, criminal law com., consumer protection com.), Midwest Assn. Attys. Gen. (chmn.), Mo. Assn. Trial Attys. Democrat. Methodist. Office: Atty Gen Office PO Box 899 Jefferson City MO 65102-0899*

NIXON, JOAN LOWERY, writer; b. L.A., Feb. 3, 1927; d. Joseph Michael and Margaret Mary (Meyer) Lowery; m. Hershell Howard Nixon, Aug. 6, 1949; children: Kathleen Nixon Brush, Maureen Nixon Quinlan, Joseph Michael, Eileen Nixon McGowan. BA in Journalism, U. So. Calif., L.A., 1947; Elem. Edn. Credentials, Calif. State Coll., L.A., 1949. Tchr. L.A. Elem. Schs., 1947-50; free-lance writer Houston, 1944—; creative writing tchr. Midland (Tex.) Jr. Coll., 1971-73, U. Houston Continuing Edn., 1974-77; columnist The Houston Post, 1969-76. Author: The Mystery of Hurricane Castle, 1964, The Mystery of the Grinning Idol, 1965, The Mystery of the Hidden Cockatoo, 1966, The Mystery of the Haunted Woods, 1967, The Mystery of the Secret Stowaway, 1968, Delbert, The Plainclothes Detective, 1971, The Alligator under the Bed, 1974 (Tex. Inst. Letters award, 1975), The Secret Box Mystery, 1974 (Jr. Lit. Guild), The Mysterious Red Tape Gang, 1974 (Edgar scroll Mystery Writers of Am. 1975), The Mysterious Prowler, 1976, Who Is My Neighbor?, 1976, Five Loaves and Two Fishes, 1976, The Son Who Came Home Again, 1977, Writing Mysteries for Young People, 1977, The Boy Who Could Find Anything, 1978 (reprinted Scott Foresman text), Danger in Dinosaur Valley, 1978, (Jr. Lit. Guild), Muffie Mouse and the Busy Birthday, 1978, (Jr. Lit. Guild), When God Speaks, 1978, When God Listens, 1978, The Kidnapping of Christina Lattimore, 1979 (Edgar Allan Poe award Mystery Writers Am., 1980), The Grandmother's Book, 1979, The New Year's Day Mystery, 1978, The Halloween Mystery, 1979, The Butterfly Tree, 1979, Bigfoot Makes a Movie, 1979, The Valentine's Day Mystery, 1979, The Happy Birthday Mystery, 1979, The Seance, 1980 (Edgar Allan Poe award best juvenile mystery 1981), Gloria Chipmunk, Star! 1980, If You Say So, Claude, 1980 (Book of Month Club), Before You Were Born, 1980, Casey and the Great Idea, 1980, The Thanksgiving Day Mystery, 1980, The April Fools Day Mystery, 1980, Kleep, The Space Detective Series: Kidnapped on Astarr, The Mysterious Queen of Magic, The Mystery Dolls of Planet Ur, 1981, The Christmas Eve Mystery, 1981, The Easter Mystery, 1981, The Spotlight Gang and the Backstage Ghost, 1981, The Specter, 1982, The Gift, 1983, Days of Fear, 1983, Magnolia's Mixed-Up Magic, 1983 (Crabbery childrens choice award Prince George County, Md.), A Deadly Game of Magic, 1983 (Ind. Young Adult Hoosier award 1989), The Ghosts of Now, 1984 (Edgar Allan Poe award nomination), The House on Hackman's Hill (Mich. Children's Choice award 1987), The Stalker, 1985 (Calif. Young Readers medal 1989), Maggie, Too, 1987, Beats Me, Claude, 1986 (Lit. Guild), The Other Side of Dark, 1987 (Edgar award Mystery Writers Am., other awards, Calif. Young Readers medal 1990), And Maggie Makes Three, 1986, Haunted Island, 1987, Maggie Forevermore, 1987, Fat Chance, Claude, 1987, The Dark and Deadly Pool, 1987, Orphan Train Quartet: (vol. 1) A Family Apart, 1987 (Best Juvenile Western Book award Western Writers Am.), (vol. 2) Caught in the Act, 1988, (vol.3) In The Face Of Danger, 1988 (Best Juvenile Western Book award We. Writers of Am. 1989), (vol. 4) A Place to Belong, 1989, If You Were a Writer, 1988 (Jr. Lit. Guild), Secret, Silent Screams, 1988, The Island of Dangerous Dreams, 1989, You Bet Your Britches, Claude, 1989, Whispers From the Dead, 1989, Hollywood Daughters: A Family Triology: (vol. 1) Star Baby, 1989, (vol. 2) Overnight Sensation, 1990, (vol. 3) Encore, 1990, A Candidate for Murder, 1991, The Nic-Nacs and the Nic-Nac News Series (The Mystery Box, Watch Out for Dinosaurs, The Honeycutt Street Celebrities, and The Haunted House on Honeycutt Street), 1991, High Trail to Danger, 1991, The Deadly Promise, 1992, The Weekend Was Murder!, 1992, Ellis Island: Land of Hope, 1992, That's the Spirit, Claude, 1992, The Name of the Game Was Murder, 1993 (Edgar award Mystery Writers Am. 1994), Land of Promise, 1993, Land of Dreams, 1994, When I Am Eight, 1994, Will You Give Me A Dream?, 1994, A Dagerous Promise, 1994, Shadowmaker, 1994, Keeping Secrets, 1995, Spirit Seeker, 1995, The Statue Walks at Night, 1995, The Legend of Deadman's Mine, 1995, Backstage with a Ghost, 1995, Check in to Danger, 1995, The House Has Eyes, 1996, Secret of the Time Capsule, 1996, Beware the Pirate Ghost, 1996, Don't Scream, 1996, Search for the Shadowman, 1996; co-author textbooks: This I Can Be, 1975, People and Me, 1975; co-author: (with Hershell Nixon) Oil and Gas, from Fossils to Fuels, 1977, Volcanoes: Nature's Fireworks, 1978 (Outstanding Sci. Books for Children cert. Nat. Sci. Tchrs. Assn. and Children's Book Coun.), Glaciers: Nature's Frozen Rivers, 1980 (Outstanding Sci. Books for Children cert. Nat. Sci. Tchrs. Assn. and Children's Book Coun.), Earthquakes: Nature in Motion, 1981 (Outstanding Sci. Books for Children cert. Nat. Sci. Tchrs. Assn. and Children's Book Coun.), Land Under the Seas, 1985; author under pseudonym Jaye Ellen: The Trouble With Charlie, 1982; numerous of these books pub. in fgn. langs., paperbacks, reprints. Recipient Children's Choice awards in over 7 states, 1984-89, Best Children's Book award Tex. Inst. Letters, Austin, 1975, Outstanding Contbn. to Children's Lit. award Bishop Byrne Chpt. Cath. Librs. Am., 1980, Cen. Mo. State U. , 1982. Mem. Mystery Writers of Am., Inc. (regional v.p. southwest chpt. 1984-86, gen. awards chmn. N.Y. 1988-89, nat. bd. dirs. 1994—), Tex. Inst. Letters, Soc. Children's Book Writers (bd. dirs. 1974-78), Am. Crime Writers League, Western Writers Am., The Authors Guild, Sisters in Crime, Kappa Delta. Republican. Roman Catholic. Avocations: reading, travel. Home: 10215 Cedar Creek Dr Houston TX 77042-2049 Office: care Writers House Inc 21 W 26th St New York NY 10010-1003

NIXON, JOHN TRICE, judge; b. New Orleans, La., Jan. 9, 1933; s. H. C. and Anne (Trice) N.; m. Betty Chiles, Aug. 5, 1960 (div. Nov. 1985); children: Mignon Elizabeth, Anne Trice. A.B. cum laude, Harvard Coll., 1955; LL.B., Vanderbilt U., 1960. Bar: Ala. bar 1960, Tenn. bar 1972. Individual practice law Anniston, Ala., 1960-62; city atty. Anniston, 1962-64; trial atty. Civil Rights Div., Dept. Justice, Washington, 1964-69; staff atty., comptroller of Treasury State of Tenn., 1971-76; pvt. practice law Nashville, 1976-77; cir. judge, 1977-78, gen. sessions judge, 1978-80; judge U.S. Dist. Ct. (mid. dist.) Tenn., Nashville, 1980—, now chief judge, 1980. Served with U.S. Army, 1958. Democrat. Methodist. Clubs: D.U. (Cambridge); Harvard-Radcliffe (Nashville). Office: US Dist Ct 825 US Courthouse Nashville TN 37203

NIXON, JUDITH MAY, librarian; b. Gary, Ind., June 14, 1945; d. Louis Robert Sr. and Mable Sophia (Reiner) Vician; m. Cleon Robert Nixon III, Aug. 20, 1967; 1 child, Elizabeth Marie. BS in Edn., Valparaiso U., 1967; MA in LS, U. Iowa, 1974. Tchr. U.S. Peace Corps, Kingdom of Tonga, 1968-69; popular books libr. Lincoln Libr., Springfield, Ill., 1971-73; reference libr. Cedar Rapids (Iowa) Pub. Libr., 1974-76; reference coord. U. Wis., Platteville, 1976-82; bus. libr. U. Ariz., Tucson, 1982-84; consumer and family sci. libr. Purdue U., West Lafayette, La., 1984-93; Krannert mgmt. and econs. libr. Purdue U., West Lafayette, 1993—. Editor: Industry and Company Information, 1991, Organization Charts, 1992, Hotel and Restaurant Industries, 1993; editor quar. serial Lodging and Restaurant Index, 1985-93. Leader Girl Scouts U.S., Lafayette, 1985—. Recipient John H. Moriarty award Purdue U. Librs., 1989. Mem. ALA (chairperson bus. reference and svcs. sect. 1995-96, GALE Rsch. award for excellence in bus. librarianship 1994). Home: 2375 N 23rd St Lafayette IN 47904-1242 Office: Purdue U Mgmt and Econs Libr Krannert Grad Sch Mgmt West Lafayette IN 47907

NIXON, MARNI, singer; b. Altadena, Calif., Feb. 22, 1930; d. Charles and Margaret (Wittke) McEathron; m. Ernest Gold, May 22, 1950 (div. 1969); children: Andrew Maurice, Martha Alice, Melani Christine; m. Lajos Frederick Fenster, July 23, 1971 (div. July 1975); m. Albert David Block, Apr. 11, 1983. Student opera workshop, Los Angeles City Coll., UCLA, U. So. Calif., Tanglewood, Mass. Dir. vocal faculty Calif. Inst. Arts, Valencia, 1970-72; pvt. tchr., vocal coacn, condr. master classes, 1970—, pvt. voice tchr., coach, condr. master classes, 1970—; head apprentice div. Santa Barbara Music Acad. of West, 1980; formerly dir. opera workshop Cornish Inst. Arts, Seattle,; tchr. in field; judge Met. Opera Internat. Am. Music Awards, Nat. Inst. Music Theatre, 1984, 85-86, 87; panelist New Music, Nat. Assn. Tchrs. Singing, pres. (N.Y. chpt.), 1994—; dialect dir., opera recs. Child actress Pasadena (Calif.) Playhouse, 1940-45, soloist Roger Wagner chorale, 1947-53, appeared with New Eng. Opera Co., Los Angeles Opera Co., also Ford Found. TV Opera, 1948-63, San Francisco Spring Opera, 1966, Seattle Opera, 1971, 72, 73; classical recitals and appearances with symphony orchs. throughout U.S., Can., also Eng., Israel, Ireland; appeared on Broadway as Eliza Doolittle in My Fair Lady, 1964; in motion picture as Sister Sophia in Sound of Music, 1964; also in numerous TV shows and night clubs; star children's ednl. TV show Boomerang, ABC-TV, from 1975; off-Broadway show Taking My Turn, from 1983, Opal, from 1992; appeared in (stage plays) Romeo & Juliet, N.Y.C.; taped for Great Performances PBS-TV Role of Edna, 1994; voice dubbed in for musical motion pictures My Fair Lady, The King and I, An Affair to Remember, West Side Story, and others; rec. artist for Columbia, Mus. Heritage Records, Capital, RCA Victor, Ednl.Records, Reference Recs., Varese-Sarabande, Nonesuch; played violin at age 4; studied in youth orch., 10 yrs; studied voice at age 10. Recipient 4 Emmy awards for best actress, 2 Action for Childrens TV awards, 1977; nominee Drama Desk award; recipient Chgo. Film Festival award, 1977, Gold Record for Songs from Mary Poppins, 2 time Grammy award nominee Nat. Acad. Rec. Arts and Scis. (1st rec. Cabaret Songs and Early Songs by Arnold Schoenberg, RCA, 1977 and 1st rec. Emily Dickinson Songs by Aaron Copland, Reference Recs., 1988. Mem. Nat. Assn. Tchrs. Singing (pres. N.Y. chpt. 1994—).

NIXON, PHILIP ANDREWS, diversified company executive; b. Bklyn., Nov. 23, 1938; s. Philip A. and Hilda (Weidman) N.; m. Brooke Nichols, June 9, 1963; children: Lucia, Rachel, Eliot, Oliver, Preya, Malini, Biplab, Jasmine, Hilda. B.A., Yale U., 1960. Vol. Peace Corps, Sierra Leone, Africa, 1965-67; aide to gov. State of Maine, Augusta, 1967-70; asst. to chmn. Dead River Co., Bangor, Maine, 1970-71, v.p., 1971-73, exec. v.p., 1973, pres., chief exec. officer, 1974—; pres., chief exec. officer Dead River Group of Cos., Bangor, Maine, 1974-85; chmn. bd. Dead River Group of Cos., 1985—; dir. Fleet/Norstar Bank Maine, Forster Mfg. Co., Wilton, Maine. Sec. Maine Pulp & Paper Found., 1976-86; bd. dirs. New Eng. Council, 1978-86, Maine Community Found.; trustee Kenduskeag Found., Bangor, 1979—, Portland Sch. Art, 1983—; chmn. Maine Community Found., 1989-94. Served with USN, 1961-65. Mem. C. of C. of U.S., Conf. Bd. Democrat. Clubs: Union (Boston). Home: 71 Federal St Brunswick ME 04011-2114 Office: Dead River Co 1 Dana St Portland ME 04101-4014

NIXON, RALPH ANGUS, psychiatrist, educator, research neuroscientist; b. Somerville, Mass., Jan. 29, 1947; s. Ralph Angus and Eleanor Nixon; m. Katharine Sangree Faulkner, Aug. 20, 1974; children: Abigail, Rebecca. AB, Brandeis U., 1968; PhD in Cell and Devel. Biology, Harvard U., 1974; MD, U. Vt., 1976. Intern Mass. Gen. Hosp., 1976, Salem Hosp., 1977; resident in psychiatry Mass. Gen. Hosp., 1977-79, McLean Hosp.,

1979-80; clin. assoc. in psychiatry Mass. Gen. Hosp., Boston, 1980—; assoc. in neurosci. Children's Hosp Med. Ctr., Boston, 1982-88; staff physician Rehab. Ctr. for Aged, Boston, 1984-90; asst. prof. psychiatry Harvard Med. Sch., Boston, 1982-86, assoc. prof., 1986—; assoc. neuropathologist McLean Hosp., Belmont, Mass., 1982-90, assoc. psychiatrist, 1988-93, neuropathologist, 1991; psychiatrist, 1993—; mem. sci. rev. com. Am. Fedn. for Aging Rsch., 1990-92; mem. neurosci., behavior and sociology of aging rev. com., subcom. A, Nat. Inst. on Aging, NIH, 1991-95, chmn., 1994-95; dir. labs. for molecular neurosci. McLean Hosp., 1992. Mem. editl. bd. Jour. Neurochemistry, 1986—, Neurochem. Rsch., 1988—, Harvard Rev. Psychiatry, 1992—, Neurobiology of Aging, 1994—; contbr. numerous biol. articles to Sci. Jour. Cell Biology, Jour. Biol. Chem., Annals N.Y. Acad. Sci., Proc. NAS, chpts. to books; Proteases and protease Inhibitors Banner C Nixon R.A. eds. Annals Acad. Sci. vol. 67, 1992. Hon. bd. dirs. Ch. League for Civic Concerns, Boston, 1987-89. Recipient Merit award NIH, 1990, Leadership and Excellence in Alzheimer Disease award, Nat. Inst. Aging, 1992; Ethel DuPont Warren Fellow, 1979-80, rsch. fellw Med. Found., 1980-82, Alfred P. Sloan Found., 1981-83, Scottish Rite Schizophrenia Rsch. Program, 1983-85. Mem. AAAS, Soc. for Neurosci., Fedn. Am. Scientists, Am. Soc. for Neurochemistry, Internat. Soc. for Neurochemistry, Am. Psychiat. Assn., Am. Soc. for Cell Biology, Am. Assn. for Geriatric Psychiatry, Gerontol. Soc. Am., Am. Assn. Neuropathologists. Achievements include patents (with others) on cupric chloride spot test and neural calcium-activated neutral proteinase inhibitors; four patents pending. Office: McLean Hosp-Harvard Med Sch 115 Mill St Belmont MA 02178-1041

NIXON, ROBERT OBEY, SR., business educator; b. Pitts., Feb. 14, 1922; s. Frank Obey and Margurite (Van Buren) N.; m. Marilyn Cavanagh, Oct. 25, 1944 (dec. 1990); children: Nan Nixon Friend, Robert Obey, Jr., Dwight Cavanagh. BS in bus. adminstrn., U. Pitts., 1948; MS, Ohio State U., 1964; MBA, U. Phoenix, 1984. Commd. 2d lt. USAF, 1943, advanced through grades to col., 1970, master navigator WWII, Korea, Vietnam; sales, adminstrn. U.S. Rubber Corp., Pitts., 1940-41; asst. engr. Am. Bridge Corp., Pitts., 1941-42; underwriter, sales Penn Mutual Life Ins. Corp., Pitts., 1945-50; capt., nav. instr. USAF Reserves, 1945-50; ret. USAF Col., divsn. chief Joint Chiefs of Staff, 1973; educator, cons. U. Ariz., 1973-79; bus. dept. chmn., coord., founder weekend coll. Pima Community Coll., Tucson, 1979-90, prof. mgmt., coord. Weekend Coll. program, 1991—; founder, pres. Multiple Adv. Group edni. cons., Tucson, 1978—. Contbr. articles to profl. jours. Mem. Soc. Logistics Engrs. (sr., charter mem.), Phi Delta Theta. Presbyterian. Avocations: tennis, hiking, swimming. Home: 1824 S Regina Cleri Dr Tucson AZ 85710-8664

NIXON, SCOTT SHERMAN, lawyer; b. Grosse Pointe, Mich., Feb. 7, 1959; s. Floyd Sherman and Marjorie Jane (Querman) N.; m. Cathryn Lynn Starnes, Aug. 27, 1983; children: Jeffry Sherman, Kelsy Jane, James Robert. BABA, Mich. State U., 1981; JD, U. Denver, 1984. Bar: Colo. 1984, U.S. Dist. Ct. Colo. 1984, U.S. Ct. Appeals (10th cir.) 1984. Assoc. Pryor, Carney & Johnson, P.C., Englewood, Colo., 1984-89, shareholder, 1990-95; shareholder Pryor, Johnson, Montoya, Carney & Karr, P.C., Englewood, 1995—. Officer, bd. dirs. Luth. Brotherhood Br. 8856, Denver, 1993, Mark K. Ulmer Meml. Native Am. Scholarship Found., Denver, 1994—; officer, mem. coun. Bethan Luth Ch., Englewood, 1993-95. Mem. ABA, Colo. Bar Assn., Denver Bar Assn., Colo. Def. Lawyers Assn. Avocations: music, physical fitness, carpentry/construction. Home: 6984 S Pontiac Ct Englewood CO 80112-1127 Office: Pryor Johnson Montoya et al Ste 1313 6400 S Fiddlers Green Cir Englewood CO 80111

NIXON, SCOTT WEST, oceanography science educator; b. Phila., Aug. 24, 1943; s. Robert Scott West and Elizabeth (Wright) West Nixon; m. Pendleton Hall, (div.); children: Carter Hall, Elizabeth Pendleton; m. Virginia Lee. BA, U. Del., 1965; PhD, U. N.C., 1970. Prof. oceanography U. R.I., Kingston, 1970—, dir. sea grant coll. program, 1983—; owner Coastal Ecology, Wakefield, R.I., 1980—. Author: (with others) A Coastal Marine Ecosystem, 1978, The New England High Salt Marshes, 1982; editor-in-chief Estuaries, 1988—; also articles. Grantee NSF, NOAA, EPA, Office Water Resources Research, State of R.I. Mem. Am. Soc. Limnology and Oceanography (governing bd. 1984-87), Estuarine Research Fedn., Nat. Assn. State Univs. Land-Grant Colls. Office: Univ of RI Dept Of Oceanography Kingston RI 02881

NIZZE, JUDITH ANNE, physician assistant; b. L.A., Nov. 1, 1942; d. Robert George and Charlotte Ann (Wise) Swan; m. Norbert Adolph Otto Paul Nizze, Dec. 31, 1966. BA, UCLA, 1966, postgrad., 1966-76; grad. physician asst. tng. program, Charles R. Drew Sch. Postgrad., L.A., 1979; BS, Calif. State U., Dominguez, 1980. Cert. physician asst., Calif. Staff rsch. assoc. I-II Wadsworth Vet. Hosp., L.A., 1965-71; staff rsch. assoc. III-IV John Wayne Clinic Jonsson Comprehensive Cancer Ctr., UCLA, 1971-78; clin. asst. Robert S. Ozeran, Gardena, Calif., 1978; physician asst. family practice Fred Chasan, Torrance, Calif., 1980-82; sr. physician asst. Donald L. Morton prof., chief surg. oncology Jonsson Comprehensive Cancer Ctr., UCLA, 1983-91; adminstrv. dir. clin. rsch. John Wayne Cancer Inst., Santa Monica, Calif., 1991—. Contbr. articles to profl. jours. Fellow Am. Acad. Physician Assts., Am. Assn. Surgeons Assts., Calif. Acad. Physician Assts.; mem. Assn. Physician Assts. in Oncology, Am. Sailing Assn. Republican. Presbyterian. Avocations: sailing, tennis, skiing, photography, computers. Home: 13243 Fiji Way Unit J Marina Dl Rey CA 90292-7079 Office: John Wayne Cancer Inst St John's Hosp & Health Ctr 1328 22d St 2 West Santa Monica CA 90404-2032

NOAKES, BETTY L., retired elementary school educator; b. Oklahoma City, Okla., Aug. 28, 1938; d. Webster L. and Willie Ruth (Johnson) Hawkins; m. Richard E. Noakes, Apr. 22, 1962 (dec.); 1 child, Michele Monique. Student, Oklahoma City U., MEd, 1971; BS, Cen. State U., 1962; postgrad., Cen. State U., Okla. State U. Elem. tchr. Merced (Calif.) Pub. Schs., 1966-67, Oklahoma City Schs., 1971-73, Mid-Del Schs., Midwest City, Okla., 1973-95; owner Noakes-I Care Day Care, 1995—; founder I Care Day Care. 2d v.p. PTA, Pleasant Hill, 1991, cert. recognition, 1992-93; active Nat. PTA, 1991-92; charter mem. Nat. Mus. of Am. Indian-Smithsonian Instn. Recipient Cert. Appreciation YMCA, 1992-92, Disting. Svc. award Mid-Del PTA, 1992. Mem. NEA, AAUW, NAACP, Nat. Therapeutic Recreation Assn., Okla. Edn. Assn., Smithsonian Instn., Oklahoma City U. Alumni Assn., United Meth. Women Assn., Cen. State U. Alumni Assn., Okla. Ea. Star (Lilly of the Valley chpt. 7), Phi Delta Kappa (sgt.-at-arms), Zeta Phi Beta. Avocations: aerobics, singing, piano, clarinet, folk dancing. Home: 5956 N Coltrane Rd Oklahoma City OK 73121-3409

NOALL, ROGER, bank executive; b. Brigham City, Utah, Apr. 1, 1935; s. Albert Edward Noall and Mabel Clayton; m. Judith Ann Stelter, Mar. 16, 1962 (div.); children: Brennan, Tyler; m. Colleen Henrietta Mannion. BS, U. Utah, 1955; LLB, Harvard U., 1958; LLM, NYU, 1959. Legal asst. Donavan, Leisure, Newton & Irvine, N.Y.C., 1959-61; assoc. Olwine, Connelly, Chase, O'Donnell & Weyher, N.Y.C., 1961-65, ptnr., 1965-67; with Bunge Corp., N.Y.C., 1967-85, exec. v.p., 1975-83; exec. v.p., chief fin. officer Centran Corp., Cleve., 1985-85; vice chmn., chief adminstrv. officer Soc. Corp., Cleve., 1985—; sr. v.p., chief adminstrv. officer Key Corp., Cleve., 1994—. Served in USNG, 1959. Office: Society Corp 127 Public Sq Cleveland OH 44114-1216

NOBACK, CHARLES ROBERT, anatomist, educator; b. N.Y.C., Feb. 15, 1916; s. Charles Victor and Beatrice (Cerny) N.; m. Eleanor Louise Loomis, Nov. 23, 1938 (dec. Mar. 24, 1981); children: Charles Victor, Margaret Beatrice, Ralph Theodore, Elizabeth Louise. BS, Cornell U., 1936; MS, NYU, 1938; postgrad., Columbia U., 1936-38; PhD, U. Minn., 1942. Asst. prof. anatomy U. Ga., 1941-44; faculty L.I. Coll. Medicine, 1944-49, asso. prof., 1948-49; mem. faculty Columbia Coll. Phys. and Surg., 1949—, assoc. prof. anatomy, 1953-68, prof., 1968-86, prof. emeritus, 1986—, spl. lectr., 1986-92, acting chmn. dept., 1974-75. Author: The Human Nervous System, 1967, 75, 81, Spinal Cord, 1971, The Nervous System Introduction and Review, 1982, 77, 86, 91, (with R. Demarest) Human Anatomy and Physiology, 1990, 2d edit., 1992, 3d edit., 1995, (with D. Van Wyseberghe and R. Carola) Human Anatomy, 1992, (with N. Strominger and R. Demarest) The Human Nervous System, Structure and Function, 1996; editor: with R. Carola and H. Harley) The Primate Brain, 1970, Sensory Systems of Primates, 1978; sr. editor: Advances in Primatology: series editor: Contbns. to Primatology; contbr. articles to profl. jours., sects. to Ency. Britannica, McGraw Hill Ency. Sci. and Tech., Collier's Ency. Fellow N.Y. Acad. Scis. (past rec. sec.), AAAS; mem. Am. Assn. Anatomists, Histochem. Soc., Internat. Primatological Soc., Am. Soc. Naturalists, Cajal Club Am. (past pres.), Assn. Phys. Anthropologists, Harvey Soc., Am. Acad. Neurology, Soc. Neurosci., Sigma Xi. Home: 116 7th St Cresskill NJ 07626-2005 Office: Columbia U Anatomy And Cell Dept New York NY 10032

NOBACK, RICHARDSON KILBOURNE, medical educator; b. Richmond, Va., Nov. 7, 1923; s. Gustav Joseph and Hazel (Kilborn) N.; m. Nan Jean Gates, Apr. 5, 1947; children: Carl R., Robert K., Catherine E. MD, Cornell U., 1947; BA, Columbia U., 1993. Diplomate Am. Bd. Internal Medicine. Intern N.Y. Hosp., 1947-48; asst. resident Cornell Med. div. Bellevue Hosp., N.Y.C., 1958-50, chief resident, 1950-52; instr. medicine Cornell U., N.Y.C., 1950-53; asst. prof. medicine SUNY Upstate Med. Ctr., Syracuse, 1955-56; assoc. prof. medicine U. Ky. Med. Ctr., Lexington, 1956-64; exec. dir. Kansas City (Mo.) Gen. Hosp. and Med. Ctr., 1964-69; assoc. dean, prof. medicine U. Mo. Sch. Medicine, Columbia, 1964-69; founding dean U. Mo. Sch. Medicine, Kansas City, 1969-78, prof. medicine, 1969-90, prof. and dean emeritus, 1990—; cons. U. Tenn., U. Mich., U. Del., Northeastern Ohio Group, U. Mo., Eastern Va. Med. Sch., Tex. Tech. U. Contbr. numerous articles to profl. jours. Bd. dirs. Kansas City Gen. Hosp., Truman Med. Ctr., Wayne Miner Health Ctr., Jackson County Med. Soc., The Shepherd's Ctr., Am. Fedn. Aging Rsch., Mo. Gerontol. Inst., The Shepherd's Ctrs. of Am.; dir. Mo. Geriatric Edn. Ctr., 1985-88. Capt. USAF Med. Svcs. 1953-55. Recipient medal of honor Avila Coll., Kansas City, 1968, merit award Met. Med. Soc., 1991, recognition award Mo. Soc. Internal Medicine, 1993. Mem. AMA, Mo. Med. Assn. (former mem. ho. of dels., v.p. 1992), Am. Geriatric Soc., Alpha Omega Alpha, Phi Kappa Phi. Avocations: photography, writing, travel. Home: 2912 Abercorn Dr Las Vegas NV 89134-7440 Office: U Mo-Kansas City Sch Medicine Sch Medicine 2411 Holmes St Kansas City MO 64108-2741

NOBE, KEN, chemical engineering educator; b. Berkeley, Calif., Aug. 26, 1925; s. Sidney and Kiyo (Uyeyama) N.; m. Mary Tagami, Aug. 31, 1957; children: Steven Andrew, Keven Gibbs, Brian Kelvin. B.S., U. Calif., Berkeley, 1951; Ph.D., UCLA, 1956. Jr. chem. engr. Air Reduction Co., Murray Hill, N.J., 1951-52; asst. prof. chem. engrng. UCLA, 1957-62, assoc. prof., 1962-68, prof., 1968—, chmn. dept. chem., nuclear and thermal engrng., 1978-83, founding chmn. chem. engrng., 1983-84. Div. editor: Jour. Electrochem. Soc. 1967-91, Electrochimica Acta, 1977-85. Served with U.S. Army, 1944-46. Mem. Electrochem. Soc. (Henry B. Linford award 1992), Am. Chem. Soc., Nat. Assn. Corrosion Engrs., Internat. Soc. Electrochemistry, Sigma Xi. Office: UCLA Dept Of Chemical Engin Los Angeles CA 90095

NOBEL, JOEL J., biomedical researcher; b. Phila., Dec. 8, 1934; s. Bernard D. and Golda R. (Nobel) Judovich; m. Bonnie Sue Goldberg, June 19, 1960 (div.); children—Erika, Joshua; m. Loretta Schwartz, Oct. 28, 1979; 1 child, Adam. AB, Haverford Coll., 1956; MA, U. Pa., 1958; MD, Thomas Jefferson Med. Coll., Phila., 1963. Intern Presbyn. Hosp., Phila., 1963-64; resident in surgery Pa. Hosp., Phila., 1964-65; resident in neurosurgery U. Pa. Hosp., 1965-66; practice medicine specializing in biomed. engrng. rsch. and healthcare tech. assessment, Phila., 1968—; dir. research Emergency Care Research Inst., Plymouth Meeting, Pa., 1968-71; dir., pres. Emergency Care Research Inst., 1971—; pres. Plymouth Inst., 1979—; cons. in field; bd. dirs. Consumers Union, 1976-79, 80—, chmn. tech. policy com., exec. bd. Publisher Health Devices, 1971—, Health Devices Alerts, 1977—. Contbr. articles to profl. jours. Served with USNR, 1966-68. Smith, Kline & French fgn. fellow, 1962; grantee HEW, 1968-72; grantee Am. Heart Assn., 1965-66. Mem. AMA, APHA, Assn. Advancement Med. Instrumentation, Critical Care Med. Soc., Pa. Med. Assn., Navy League, U.S. Naval Inst., Sunday Breakfast Club. Home: 1434 Monk Rd Gladwyne PA 19035-1315 Office: ECRI 5200 Butler Pike Plymouth Meeting PA 19462-1241

NOBLE, DOUGLAS ROSS, museum administrator; b. Sturgis, Ky., Jan. 19, 1945; s. Roscoe and Robbie Rae (Martin) N.; m. Catherine Ann Richardson, Nov. 3, 1973; children: Kate Faxon, Jennifer Martin. BS, Okla. State U., 1967; MSA, Ga. Coll., 1978; D of Pub. Adminstrn., U. Ga., 1987. Asst. to dir. Savannah Sci. Mus., Ga., 1971-73; exec. dir. Mus. of Arts and Scis., Macon, Ga., 1973-80; dir. of museums Memphis Mus. System, 1980—; mem. mus. assessment program Inst. of Mus. Services, Washington, 1982—, grant reviewer, 1983—; cons. Mus. Mgmt. Program, Sarasota, Fla., 1985. Contbr. articles to profl. jours. Grad. Leadership Memphis, 1984; bd. dirs. Memphis in May Internat. Festival. 1st lt. U.S. Army, 1968-70; Vietnam. Decorated Bronze Star. Mem. Natural Sci. for Youth Found. (trustee 1980-87), Naumburg award 1978), Am. Assn. Museums (S.E. rep. 1984-87, chmn. mus. assessment program adv. com. 1987-89, treas., v.p. fin. 1990-92), chmn. nature ctr. accreditation com. 1985), Southeastern Museums Conf. (pres. 1982-84), Memphis Museums Roundtable (co-founder). Episcopalian. Home: 330 Belhaven St Memphis TN 38117-1602 Office: Memphis Pink Palace Mus & Planetarium 3050 Central Ave Memphis TN 38111-3316

NOBLE, ERNEST PASCAL, physician, biochemist, educator; b. Baghdad, Iraq, Apr. 2, 1929; came to U.S., 1946; s. Noble Babik and Barkev Grace (Kasparian) Babikian; m. Inga Birgitta Kilstromer, May 19, 1956; children—Lorna, Katharine, Erik. B.S. in Chemistry, U. Calif.-Berkeley, 1951; Ph.D. in Biochemistry, Oreg. State U., 1955; M.D., Case Western Res. U., 1962. Diplomate Nat. Bd. Med. Examiners. Sr. instr. biochemistry Western Res. U., Cleve., 1957-62; intern Stanford Med. Ctr., Calif., 1962-63, resident in psychiatry, 1963-66, research assoc., asst. prof., 1965-69; assoc. prof. psychiatry, psychobiology and pharmacology U. Calif.-Irvine, 1969-71, prof., chief neurochemistry, 1971-76, 79-81; dir. Nat. Inst. Alcohol Abuse and Alcoholism HEW, 1976-78, assoc. adminstr. sci., alcohol, drug abuse and mental health, 1978-79; Pike prof. alcohol studies, dir. Alcohol Research Ctr. UCLA Sch. of Medicine, 1981—. Mem. various med./sci. jour. editorial bds.; contbr. numerous articles to profl. jours., chpts. to books. v.p. Nat. Coun. on Alcoholism 1981-84; pres. Internat. Commn. for the Prevention of Alcoholism and Drug Dependency, 1988. Fulbright scholar, 1955-56; Guggenheim fellow, 1974-75; Sr. Fulbright scholar, 1984-85; recipient Career Devel. award NIMH, HEW, 1966-69. Fellow Am. Coll. Neuropsychopharmacology; mem. Internat. Soc. Neurochemistry, Am. Soc. Pharmacology and Exptl. Therapeutics, Research Soc. on Alcoholism. Office: UCLA 760 Westwood Plz Los Angeles CA 90024-8300

NOBLE, JAMES KENDRICK, JR., media industry consultant; b. N.Y.C., Oct. 6, 1928; s. James Kendrick and Orrel Tennant (Baldwin) N.; m. Norma Jean Rowell, June 16, 1951; children: Anne Rowell, James Kendrick III. Student, Princeton U., 1945-46; BS, U.S. Naval Acad., 1950; postgrad., USN Gen. Line Sch., 1955-56; MBA, NYU, 1961; postgrad., Sch. Edn., 1962-68. CFA. Commd. ensign USN, 1950; transferred to USNR, 1957; advanced through grades to capt. USNR, 1973; asst. gunnery officer in U.S.S. Thomas E. Fraser, 1950-51; student naval aviator USNR, 1951-52, pilot asst. ops. officer, 1952-55; instr. U.S. Naval Acad., 1956-57, Officer Candidate Sch., Newport, R.I., 1958; asst. to pres. Noble & Noble, Pub., Inc., N.Y.C., 1957-60, dir. spl. projects, 1960-62, v.p., 1962-65, exec. v.p., 1965-66, dir., 1957-65; dir., v.p. Transl. Pub. Co., N.Y.C., 1958-65, cons., 1965-66; v.p., dir. Elbon Realty Corp., Bronxville, N.Y., 1960-65; cons. Elbon Realty Corp., Bronxville, 1965-66; comdg. officer NAIRU R2, 1968-70; staff NARS W2, 1970-71, NRID 3-1, 1971-74; comdg. officer NRCSG 302, 1974-76; sr. analyst F. Eberstadt & Co., 1966-69; sr. analyst Auerbach, Pollak & Richardson, 1969-75, v.p., 1972-75, mgr. spl. rsch. projects, 1973-75, dir., 1975; v.p. rsch. Paine, Webber, Jackson & Curtis, Inc., 1975-77, assoc. dir. rsch., 1976-77; v.p. Paine Webber, N.Y.C., 1977-79; 1st v.p. Paine Webber, 1979-91; pres. Noble Cons., Bronxville, 1991—; bd. dirs. Curriculum Info. Center, Inc., Denver, 1972-78; instl. investor All Am. Rsch. Team, 1972-90. Author: Ploob, 1949, rev., 1956; editor pub.: The Years Between, 1966; also articles in various publs. Mem. Bronxville Bd. Edn., 1968-74, pres., 1970-72; Rep. co-leader 21st Dist., Eastchester, N.Y., 1961-65; dir. Merit; cons., dir. Space and Sci. Train, 1962-63; trustee St. John's Hosp., Yonkers, N.Y., 1972-92, com. chmn., 1980-92. Freedom Forum Ctr. for Media Studies fellow, 1993-94. Fellow emeritus AAAS; mem. Info. Industry Assn. (disting. profl. mem.), Nat. Inst. Social Scis., N.Y. Soc. Security Analysts (mem. com. 1971-91, dir. 1975-84, v.p. 1977-81, exec. v.p. 1981-82, pres. 1982-83), Am. Textbook Pub. Inst. (com. chmn. 1964-66), AIAA (mem. com. 1957-61), Media and Entertainment Analysts Assn. (pres. 1969-71), Fin. Analysts Fedn. (dir. 1984-87), Naval Res. Assn. (v.p. N.Y. Navy chpt. 1968-76), Wings Club, Siwanoy Country Club. Mem. Reformed Ch. Home: 45 Edgewood Ln Bronxville NY 10708-1946 Office: Noble Cons 45 Edgewood Ln Bronxville NY 10708-1946

NOBLE, JAMES WILKES, actor; b. Dallas, Mar. 5, 1922; s. Ralph Byrne and Lois Frances (Wilkes) N.; m. Carolyn Owen Coates, May 19, 1956; 1 child: Jessica Katherine. Student, North Tex. Coll., Arlington, 1939-41, So. Methodist U., Dallas, 1941-43, 1946-47. lectr. acting and mime Am. Acad. Dramatic Art, 1956-59. Mem. Lydia Tarnower Modern Dance Co., 1937-39; title role in 1st TV drama, The Egoist on Dumont TV, 1943; 1st N.Y. Stage appearance Helena's Room, 1947; 1st Broadway appearance: The Big Knife, 1949; others include: The Velvet Glove, 1949; Medea, 1951; Come of Age, 1952; A Far Country, 1961; Strange Interlude, 1963; 1776, 1971; The Runner Stumbles, 1976; mem. Am. Mime Theatre, 1952-59; appeared in numerous TV dramas and soap operas; appeared in more than 200 plays in theatres throughout the world most recent: Stratford Characters in Stratford-Upon-Avon, England, T.S. Eliot in The Poet's Theatre, Cambridge, Mass.; TV appearances include the role of the Governor on Benson, ABC-TV, 1979-86, series First Impressions, CBS-TV, 1987—, series Archies, NBC-TV, 1990—, Law and Order, 1991; movies include: Dragonfly, 1965; The Sporting Club, 1967; 1776, 1972; Promises in the Dark, 1978; Ten, 1979; Being There, 1979; Airplane II, 1983; You Talkin' To Me?, 1986; Tiger's Tale, 1987, Chances Are, 1988, Absent Minded Professor, 1989, Law and Order, 1991, All My Children, 1992; numerous other appearances. Author jour. article on Am. mime. Served as lt. USNR, 1943-46, P.T.O. Named Hon. Gov., N.J., N.Y., 1982; appreciation award Am. Heart Assn., 1983. Mem. Actors Studio (life), Actors Equity, SAG, AFTRA. Democrat. Roman Catholic. Avocation: Photography. Office: Paradigm Agy 10100 Santa Monica Blvd Los Angeles CA 90067

NOBLE, JOSEPH VEACH, fine arts administrator; b. Phila., Apr. 3, 1920; s. Joseph Haderman and Helen Elizabeth (Veach) N.; m. Olive Ashley Mooney, June 21, 1941 (dec. Sept. 1978); children: Josette, Ashley, Laurence; m. Lois Cook Cartwright, Oct. 27, 1979. Student, U. Pa., 1942. Cameraman, dir. DeFrenes and Co. Studios, Phila., 1939-41; studio mgr. WPTZ, Philco TV Sta., Phila., 1941-42, DeFrenes and Co. Studios, 1946-49; gen. mgr. Murphy-Lillis Prodns., N.Y.C., 1949-50; exec. v.p. Film Counselors, Inc., N.Y.C., 1950-56, dir., 1950-82; operating adminstr. Met. Mus. Art, 1956-67, vice dir. adminstrn., 1967-70; dir. Mus. City N.Y., 1970-85; exec. dir. Soc. Medalists, 1985-95; photog. salon exhibitor, from 1936; lectr. CCNY, 1949-51. Author: The Techniques of Painted Attic Pottery, 1965, The Historical Murals of Maplewood, 1961, Forgery of the Etruscan Terracotta Warriors, 1961; Contbr.: Ency. Brit, 1970. Trustee Corning Mus. of Glass, 1970—; mem. Morrow Meth. Ch., pres. trustees, 1972-77; chmn. N.Y. State Bd. Hist. Preservation 1972-76; co-chmn. Save Venice, Inc., 1972; trustee Brookgreen Gardens, 1971—, pres., 1976-90, chmn., 1990-95, chmn. emeritus, 1995—. With AUS, 1942-46. Recipient Venice Film Festival medal for photography in sci., 1948, Sigma Xi award 1963, Maple Leaf award Maplewood, N.J., 1966, 87, Gold medal for The Big Apple N.Y. Film Festival, 1979, Disting. Svc. award Maplewood C. of C., 1987. Fellow Soc. Antiquaries London; mem. N.Y. State Assn. Museums (pres. 1970-72), NAD (medal 1976), Nat. Sculpture Soc. (medal 1978, 91), Artists' Fellowship (medal 1978), Archeol. Inst. Am. (treas. 1963-70), Museums Council N.Y.C. (chmn. 1965-67), Am. Assn. Museums (pres. 1975-78, Disting. Svc. Awd., 1991), Cultural Instns. Group N.Y.C. (chmn. 1984-85), Soc. Promotion Hellenic Studies; Am. Watercolor Soc. (medal 1982). Clubs: Maplewood Country; Explorers (N.Y.C.), Century Assn. (N.Y.C.). Home: 107 Durand Rd Maplewood NJ 07040-2103 Office: Brookgreen Gardens Murrells Inlet SC 29576 *As a classical archaeologist I always have been guided by the ancient saying, "Let the light of the past illumine a pathway to the future.*

NOBLE, MERRILL EMMETT, retired psychology educator, psychologist; b. Las Vegas, N.Mex., July 25, 1923; s. Merrill Emmett and Martha (Van Petten) N.; m. Joy Lind, July 18, 1953; children: Margaret Lind, Eric Severin. B.A., N.Mex. Highlands U., 1947; M.A., Ohio State U., 1949, Ph.D., 1951. Research asso. Ohio State U., 1951-54, summers 1956, 58; mem. faculty Kans. State U., 1954-67, prof. psychology, 1961-67, chmn. dept., 1962-67; prof. psychology Pa. State U., 1967-89, chmn. dept., 1967-77, ret., 1989; Vis. scientist Inst. for Perception TNO, Soesterberg, Netherlands, 1973-74, 77-78, 80, also NATO vis. lectr. several univs. Mem. editorial bd. Psychol. Bull., 1963-64, Jour. Exptl. Psychology, 1967-78, Acta Psychologica, 1978-82, Human Performance, 1987-92. Bd. dirs. Environ. Research Found., Topeka, 1965-68. Fellow APA (com. on adv. svcs. for edn. and tng. 1967-70, accreditation com. 1979-82), AAAS, Psychonomic Soc., Midwestern Psychol. Assn. (mem. coun. 1967-70), Sigma Xi. Home: 2562 Calle Delfino Santa Fe NM 87505-6488

NOBLE, MICHAEL A., audit manager; b. Baton Rouge, La., May 26, 1953; s. Andrew Day and Elise (Prestridge) N.; m. Vickie Downs, Nov. 11, 1993; children: Andrew Joseph, Jill Mikelyn. BS in Acctg., Northwestern State U., 1975. CPA, La.; Cert. Fraud Examiner. Govtl. auditor II Legis. Auditor State of La., Baton Rouge, 1975-78, govtl. auditor III, 1978-79, sr. auditor I, 1979-82, sr. auditor II, auditor-in-charge, 1982-94; audit mgr. Shreveport, La., 1994—. Deacon Zoar Bapt. Ch., Baton Rouge, 1984—. Mem. AICPA, La. Soc. CPAs, Nat. Assn. Cert. Fraud Examiners, Govt. Fin. Officers Assn. La., Assn. La. Bass Clubs, Bass Anglers Sportsmen Soc., Hassle Free Bass Club (sec.-treas. 1992-94). Office: Office Legis Auditor 820 Jordan St Ste 306 Shreveport LA 71101-4518

NOBLE, NELDA KAYE, elementary education educator; b. Lumberton, N.C., Jan. 4, 1952; d. Albert T. and Nelle T. (Kizer) N. BS in Christian Edn., Atlanta Christian Coll., 1974; BA in Elem. Edn., Fla. Atlantic U., 1980, M in Counselor Edn., 1988. Cert. elem. tchr., early childhood tchr., guidance counseling, ESOL. Kindergarten tchr., asst. dir. Circle D Day Care and Kindergarten, College Park, Ga., 1974-76; tchr. Putnam County Schs., Palatka, Fla., 1980-84, Coral Springs Christian Sch., Coral Springs, Fla., 1984-85, Palm Beach County Schs., Boca Raton, Fla., 1985-95, Gwinnett County Pub Schs., Tucker, Ga., 1995—; chairperson Instructional Innovation Team-J.C. Mitchell Elem., Boca Raton, 1992-95, mem. sch. adv. coun., 1992-95. Bd. dirs. 1st Christian Pre-Sch., Boca Raton, 1985-88, 94. Mem. Palm Beach County Reading Coun. Avocations: reading, crafts. Home: 2103 Howell Blvd Duluth GA 30136 Office: Nesbit Elem Sch 6575 Cherokee Dr Tucker GA 30084

NOBLE, RICHARD LLOYD, lawyer; b. Oklahoma City, Oct. 11, 1939; s. Samuel Lloyd and Eloise Joyce (Millard) N. AB with distinction, Stanford, 1961, LLB, 1964. Bar: Calif. 1964. Assoc. firm Cooper, White & Cooper, San Francisco, 1965-67; assoc., ptnr. firm Voegelin, Barton, Harris & Callister, Los Angeles, 1967-70; ptnr. Noble & Campbell, Los Angeles, San Francisco, 1970—; dir. Langdale Corp., L.A., Gt. Pacific Fin. Co., Sacramento; lectr. Tax Inst. U. So. Calif., 1970; mem. bd. law and bus. program Stanford Law Sch. Contbr. articles to legal jours. Bd. govs. St. Thomas Aquinas Coll. Recipient Hilmer Dehlman Jr. award Stanford Law Sch., 1962; Benjamin Harrison fellow Stanford U., 1967. Mem. ABA, State Bar Calif., L.A. Bar Assn., San Francisco Bar Assn., Commercial Club (San Francisco), Petroleum Club (L.A.), Capitol Hill Club (Washington), Pi Sigma Alpha. Republican. Home: 2222 Ave of the Stars Los Angeles CA 90067-5655 Office: Noble & Campbell 333 N Grand Ave Los Angeles CA 90012-2622

NOBLE, RONALD KENNETH, government official, lawyer; b. Ft. Dix, N.J., Sept. 24, 1956. BA cum laude, U. N.H., 1979; JD, Stanford U., 1982. Bar: Pa. 1983, N.J., 1983. Sr. law clk. to Hon. A. Leon Higginbotham Jr. U.S. Ct. Appeals for 3d Cir., Phila., 1982-84; asst. U.S. atty. for ea. dist. Pa. Office Atty. Gen., Phila., 1984-88; with U.S. Dept. Justice, Phila., 1988-89, dep. asst. atty. gen., chief staff, spl. counsel criminal divsn., 1988-89; assoc. prof. law NYU Sch. Law, 1989-93; asst. sec. for enforcement U.S. Dept. Treasury, Washington, 1993-94, under sec. for enforcement, 1994—; pres. Fin. Action Task Force, 1994—; mem. exec. com. INTERPOL, 1994—; mem. Root-Tilden Scholar Selection Bd., 1990—; chmn. Customs Ops. Adv. Com., 1993—; chmn. Bank Secrecy Act Adv. Com., 1993—. Articles editor Stanford Law Rev., 1981-82. Mem. Am. Law Inst. Office: Dept of Treasury Ste 4330 1500 Pennsylvania Ave Washington DC 20220

NOBLE, (TERRY) THOM, film editor. Editor: (films) Fahrenheit 451, 1966, The Man Who Had Power over Women, 1970, Senza Ragione, 1972,

And Now for Something Completely Different, 1972, The Strange Vengeance of Rosalie, 1972, The Apprenticeship of Duddy Kravitz, 1974, (with Peter Thornton) Rosebud, 1975, Inside Out, 1976, Joseph Andrews, 1977, Black Joy, 1977, Who Is Killing the Great Chefs of Europe?, 1978, All Things Bright and Beautiful, 1979, Boardwalk, 1979, Improper Channels, 1981, Tattoo, 1981, Red Dawn, 1984, Witness, 1985 (Academy award best film editing 1985), Poltergeist II: The Other Side, 1986, The Mosquito Coast, 1986, Switching Channels, 1988, Winter People, 1989, Mountains of the Moon, 1990, Thelma and Louise, 1991 (Academy award nomination best film editing 1991), Body of Evidence, 1993, The Hudsucker Proxy, 1994; editor, visual cons.: (films) First Blood, 1982; editorial cons.: (films) North Dallas Forty, 1979, Uncommon Valor, 1983; editor, prodn. designer: (films) Final Analysis, 1992. Office: The Gersh Agency 232 N Canon Dr Beverly Hills CA 90210-5302

NOBLES, BRUCE R., transportation executive. BA in Bus. Adminstrn., U. So. Calif.; postgrad., Calif. State Coll., L.A. Passenger svc. agent Am. Airlines, 1966-79, mktg. contr., 1979-82; mktg. contr. Pan Am. World Airways, 1982-84; v.p. customer svc. Republic Airlines, 1984-86; pres., COO Pan Am Shuttle, Inc., 1986-88; pres., CEO Air Shuttle, L.P., 1988; sr. v.p. bus. mgmt. divsn. Continental Air Lines, 1988; pres., COO Trump Shttle, Inc., 1988-91; pres., CEO L'Express, Inc., New Orleans, 1991, Hawaiian Airlines, Honolulu, 1993—. Bd. dirs. Hawaii Visitors Bur.; bd. dirs., chmn. fin. com., mem. exec. com. Bishop Mus.; bd. govs. U. So. Calif. Alumni Assn., Young Pres. Orgn. Mem. Wings Club (v.p., bd. govs., chmn. nominating com.). Office: Hawaiian Airlines Inc PO Box 30008 Honolulu HI 96820*

NOBLES, DARLENE ADELE, elementary education educator; b. Chgo., Dec. 12, 1949; d. Mae Schaller; m. Joseph T. Nobles, Jan. 29, 1972; 2 children. AA, Fla. Jr. Coll., Jacksonville, 1974; BA, U. South Fla., Tampa, 1979; MA, U. South Fla., 1982; postgrad., U. Md., 1990—. Cert. early childhood, elem. tchr., supervision, adminstrn., Fla., Ga., Md. Tchr., kindergarten, 2d grade Hillsborough Pub. Sch., Dover, Fla., 1979-82; tchr., grades 1 & 2 Cobb County Pub. Sch., Marietta, Ga., 1982-87; magnet tchr. Wicomico County Pub. Schs., Salisbury, Md., 1987-88; tchr., 2d grade Wicomico County Pub. Schs., Salisbury, 1988—; cooperating tchr. for student tchrs. Salisbury State U. Dept. Edn., 1989—, first program facilitator. Mem. Mothers and Others for a Safe Planet, 1989, Jr. Woman's Club of Wicomico (edn. com. 1988-92). Named Suncoast Area Tchr. Training clin. tchr. for excellence in teaching U. South Fla., 1982. del. to Russia as part of U. Nebr. Tchrs. Coll. People to People Ednl. Orgn., 1995. Mem. AAUW, Nat. Assn. for Edn. of Young Children, Assn. for Childhood Edn. Internat. (pres. Betty Brantly br. 1980-82). Methodist. Avocations: oil painting, gardening.

NOBLES, LAURENCE HEWIT, retired geology educator; b. Spokane, Sept. 28, 1927; s. Harry and Florence (Giffin) N.; m. Barbara Joanne Smith, Aug. 28, 1948; children: Heather C., Laurence F. BS, Calif. Inst. Tech., 1949, MS, 1949; PhD, Harvard, 1952. Instr. geology Northwestern U., 1952-55, asst. prof., 1955-61, assoc. prof., 1961-67, prof., 1967-90, prof. emeritus, 1990—; also asst. dean Northwestern U. (Coll. Arts and Scis.), 1966-67, asso. dean, 1968-70, acting dean, 1970-72, dean adminstrn., 1972-81, v.p. adminstrn. and fin. planning, 1981-86. Trustee Adler Planetarium, 1980-86; faculty rep. Big Ten Conf., 1976-81; trustee Chgo. Acad. Scis., 1967-87, pres., 1973-78, hon. trustee, 1987—. Mem. Am. Geophys. Union, Geol. Soc. Am.

NOBLES, LEWIS, college president; b. Meridian, Miss., Sept. 11, 1925; s. Julius Sidney and Ruby Rae (Roper) N.; m. Joy Ford, Aug. 29, 1948; children—Sandra Jeanne (Mrs. Ben Nash), Glenda Suzanne (dec.). Student, Ursinus Coll., 1944-45; B.S. in Pharmacy, U. Miss., 1948, M.S., 1949; Ph.D., U. Kans., 1952; NSF postdoctoral fellow, U. Mich., 1958-59. Mem. faculty U. Miss., 1952-68, prof. pharm. chemistry, 1955-68; dean U. Miss. (Grad. Sch.), 1960-68, coordinator univ. research, 1964-68; pres. Miss. Coll., Clinton, 1968—. Co-author: Physical and Technical Pharmacy; contbr. to books; editorial adv. bd.: Jour. Pharm. Scis, 1965-71. Mem. regional adv. group Miss. Regional Med. Program 1969-76; chmn. 1971-76; mem. nat. adv. council on regional med. programs HEW, 1976-79; bd. grants Am. Found. Pharm. Ed., 1972-80; trustee New Orleans Baptist Theol. Sem., 1976-82. Served to lt. (j.g.) USNR, 1944-46. Am. Found. Pharm. Edn. fellow, 1949; Gustavus A. Pfeiffer Meml. Research fellow, 1955; recipient award for stimulation of research Am. Pharm. Assn. Found., 1966; named one of Top 18 Most Effective Coll. Pres. in U.S. Exxon Ednl. Found., 1986. Fellow AAAS; mem. Am. Chem. Soc., Chem. Soc. Gt. Britain, N.Y. Acad. Sci., Acad. Pharm. Scis. (chmn. medicinal chemistry sect. 1967-68), Am. Pharm. Assn. Internat. Platform Assn., Jackson C. of C., Am. Assn. Pres. Ind. Colls. and Univs. (trustee 1987—), Nat. Assn. Ind. Colls. and Univs. (bd. dirs. 1990-92), So. Assn. of Colls. and Schs. (mem. commn. on colls.), Rotary, Sigma Xi, Rho Chi, Kappa Psi, Phi Eta Sigma, Pi Kappa Pi. Baptist. Office: Miss Coll PO Box 4186 Clinton MS 39058

NOBLIN, CHARLES DONALD, clinical psychologist, educator; b. Jackson, Miss., Dec. 16, 1933; s. Charles Thomas and Margaret (Byrne) N.; m. Patsy Ann Beard, Aug. 12, 1989. BA, Miss. Coll., 1955; MS, Va. Commonwealth U., 1957; PhD, La. State U., 1962. Lic. psychologist, Miss., N.J., N.C. Instr. to asst. prof. La. State U., Baton Rouge, 1961-63; asst. to assoc. prof. U. N.C., Greensboro, 1963-66; assoc. prof. Rutgers Med. Sch., New Brunswick, N.J., 1966-69; dir. clin. training Va. Commonwealth U., Richmond, 1969-72; chmn. dept. psychology Va. Tech., Blacksburg, 1972-82; dir. clin. training U. So. Miss., Hattiesburg, 1982-85, chmn. dept. psychology, 1985-91, prof., 1991-93, dir. clin. tng., 1993—. Contbr. over 60 articles and presentations. Recipient Clin. Tng. grant NIMH, 1983-86, Victim Behavior & Personal Space rsch. grant U.S. Dept. Justice, 1970-71, Trubeck Found. Rsch. award, 1968-69. Baptist. Avocation: antique art glass. Home: 7 Cane Cv Hattiesburg MS 39402-8716 also: PO Box 10036 Hattiesburg MS 39406-0036 Office: U So Miss Dept Psychology Hattiesburg MS 39406

NOBLITT, HARDING COOLIDGE, political scientist, educator; b. Marion, N.C., Oct. 31, 1920; s. Walter Tate and Nellie Mae (Horton) N.; m. Louise Hope Lester, July 3, 1943; 1 son, Walter Thomas. B.A., Berea Coll., 1942; M.A., U. Chgo., 1947, Ph.D., 1955. Mem. faculty Concordia Coll., Moorhead, Minn., 1950-90, prof. polit. sci., 1956-90, Wije Disting. prof., 1979-82; chmn. dept. Concordia Coll., 1964-72, prof. emeritus, 1990. Mem. editorial bd.: Discourse: A Review of the Liberal Arts, 1957-67, acting editor, 1959-60. Democratic candidate Congress, 1962; del. Dem. Nat. Conv., 1964; chmn. Profs. for Johnson-Humphrey, Minn., 1964; chmn. platform com. Dem. State Conv., 1968; mem. Gov's Citizens Council on Aging, 1963-68; mem. City Charter Commn., Moorhead, 1985—; mem. Minn. Higher Edn. Coordinating Bd., 1971-81, sec., 1974-75, pres., 1979-80. Served with AUS, 1943-46, ETO. Recipient 1st ann. Great Tchr. award Concordia Coll., 1960; recipient Flaat Disting. Service award Concordia Coll., 1982. Mem. Am. Polit. Sci. Assn., Am. Legion, Phi Kappa Phi, Pi Gamma Mu, Tau Kappa Alpha, Pi Kappa Delta. Presbyterian (elder). Home: 2014 4th St S Moorhead MN 56560-4131 Office: Concordia Coll Dept Polit Sci Moorhead MN 56560

NOBLITT, NANCY ANNE, aerospace engineer; b. Roanoke, Va., Aug. 14, 1959; d. Jerry Spencer and Mary Louise (Jerrell) N. BA, Mills Coll., Oakland, Calif., 1982; M.S. in Indsl. Engring., Northeastern U., 1990. Data red specialist, Universal Energy Systems, Beaver Creek, Ohio, 1981; aerospace engr. turbine engine div. components br. turbine group aero-propulsion lab. Wright-Patterson AFB, Ohio, 1982-84, engine assessment br. spl. engines group, 1984-87; lead analyst cycle methods computer aided engr. Gen. Electric Co., Lynn Mass., 1987-90, Lynn PACES project coord., 1990-91; software systems analyst Sci. Applications Internat. Corp., with artificial intelligence Sci. Applications Internat. Corp., Mc Lean, Va., 1991-92, software engring. mgr., intelligence applications integration, Sci. Applications Internat. Corp., Hampton, Va., 1992-93, mgr. test engring. and systems support, 1993-94, mgr. configuration mgmt., 1994, mgmt. asst. to TBMCS program mgr., 1994-95; sr. simulation engr. Chem Demil, 1995—. Math and sci. tutor Centerville Sch. Bd., Ohio, 1982-86, math. and physics tutor Marblehead Sch. Bd., Mass., 1988-90; tutor math, chemistry & physics Poquoson Sch. Bd., Va., 1994—; rep. alumnae admissions Mills Coll., Boston area, 1987-91; mem. bd. trustees/bd. govs. Mills Coll., 1995—; mem. Citizens for Hilton Area Revitalization, 1994—. Recipient Notable Achievement award U.S. Air Force, 1984; recipient Special award Fed. Lab. Consortium, 1987. Mem. Soc. Mfg. Engrs. Avocation: book collecting. Home: 58 Hopkins St Newport News VA 23601-4034 Office: Sci Applications Internat Corp Hampton VA 23666

NOCAS, ANDREW JAMES, lawyer; b. Los Angeles, Feb. 2, 1941; s. John Richard and Muriel Phyliss (Harvey) N.; 1 child, Scott Andrew. B.S., Stanford U., 1962, J.D., 1964. Bar: Calif. 1965. Assoc. Thelen, Marrin, Johnson & Bridges, Los Angeles, 1964-71, ptnr., 1972-91; pvt. practice L.A., 1992—; del. Calif. Bar Conv., 1972-92. Served to capt. JAGC, USAR. Mem. Los Angeles County Bar Assn. (chmn. sect. law office mgmt. 1980-82, chair errors & ommissions com. 1987-88, chair litigation sect. 1988-89), ABA (chmn. arbitration com. 1981). Club: San Marino City. Office: 201 N Figueroa St Ste 1300 Los Angeles CA 90012-2636

NOCE, WALTER WILLIAM, JR., hospital administrator; b. Neptune, N.J., Sept. 27, 1945; s. Walter William and Louise Marie (Jenkins) N.; m. Cinda Ann Miller, Apr. 15, 1967; children: Krista Suzanne, David Michael. B.A., LaSalle Coll., Phila., 1967; M.P.H., UCLA, 1969. Regional coordinator USPHS, Rockville, Md., 1969-71; v.p. Hollywood Presbyn. Hosp., Los Angeles, 1971-75; sr. v.p. Hollywood Presbyn. Med. ctr., 1975-77; v.p. adminstrn. Huntington Meml. Hosp, Pasadena, Calif., 1977-83; pres., chief exec. officer St. Joseph Hosp., Orange, Calif., 1983-90; pres. so. Calif. region St. Joseph Health System, 1987-90, exec. v.p., 1990-94; pres., CEO Children's Hosp., L.A., 1995—; preceptor UCLA Health Services Mgmt. Program, 1977—; chmn. bd. Health Plan of Am., 1985-91; chmn. Hosp. Coun. So. Calif., 1989. Exec. v.p. Mental Health Assn. in Los Angeles County, 1979-82; regional v.p. Calif. Mental Health Assn., 1982-83. W. Glenn Ebersole finalist Assn. Western Hosp., 1969; recipient USPHS letter commendation, 1971. Mem. Am. Coll. Hosp. Adminstrs., Am. Hosp. Assn. (ho. of dels. 1994—), Calif. Assn. Cath. Hosps. (chmn. 1990-91), Calif. Assn. Hosps. and Health Sys. (chmn. 1992), UCLA Hosp. Adminstrn. Alumni Assn. (pres. 1979-80), Pasadena C. of C. (v.p. 1980-82). Home: 20388 Via Marwah Yorba Linda CA 92686-4522 Office: Children's Hosp Los Angeles 4650 Sunset Blvd Los Angeles CA 90027 *Ambition is necessary for success, but success achieved at the expense of others is failure.*

NOCHIMSON, DAVID, lawyer; b. Paterson, N.J., June 19, 1943; s. Samuel S. and Mildred (Singer) N.; m. Roberta Maizel, June 5, 1966 (div. 1972); m. Gail Burgess, May 26, 1978. BA, Yale U., 1965; LLB, Columbia U., 1968; LLM, Australian Nat. U., Canberra, 1969. Bar: N.Y. 1970, Calif. 1977. Assoc. Paul, Weiss, Rifkind, Wharton and Garrison, N.Y.C., 1970-72; sr. v.p. Comprop Equities Corp., N.Y.C., 1972-76; assoc. Mitchell, Silberberg and Knupp, L.A., 1977-80, ptnr., 1980-83; ptnr. Ziffren, Brittenham, Branca & Fischer, L.A., 1983—; mem. adv. com. UCLA Entertainment Symposium, 1979&, co-chmn., 1981-82. Contbr. articles to Encyclopedia of Investments, 1982, profl. jours. Pres. Friends of the L.A. Free Clinic, 1994-96; trustee Santa Monica (Calif.) Mus. of Art, 1995—. Fulbright scholar, Australia, 1968-69. Mem. ABA (forum com. on entertainment and sports industries 1982—, editor The Entertainment and Sports Lawyer 1982-89, chmn. 1989-92), Internat. Bar Assn. (Vice chmn. entertainment com. 1986-90), Am. Bar Found., Beverly Hills Bar Assn. Democrat. Jewish. Avocations: tennis, racquetball, playing piano, hiking. Office: Ziffren Brittenham Branca & Fischer #32D 2121 Avenue of the Stars Los Angeles CA 90067-5010

NOCHMAN, LOIS WOOD KIVI (MRS. MARVIN NOCHMAN), educator; b. Detroit, Nov. 5, 1924; d. Peter K. and Annetta Lois (Wood) Kivi; AB, U. Mich., 1946, AM, 1949; m. Harold I. Pitchford, Sept. 6, 1944 (div. May 1949); children: Jean Wood Pitchford Horiszny, Joyce Lynn Pitchford Undiano; m. Marvin A. Nochman, Aug. 15, 1953; 1 child, Joseph Asa. Tchr. adult edn., Honolulu, 1947, Ypsilanti (Mich.) H.S., 1951-52; spl. instr. English, Wayne State U., Detroit, 1953, 54; tchr. Highland Park (Mich.) Coll., 1950-51, instr. English, 1954-83. Mem. exec. bd. Highland Park Fedn. Tchrs., 1963-66, 71-72, mem. 1st bargaining team, 1965-66, 73, del. to Nat. Conv., 1964, 71-74, rep. higher edn. to Mich. Fedn. Tchrs. Exec. Com., 1972-76; mem. faculty adv. com. Gov.'s Commn. on Higher Edn., 1973—. Tchr. Baha'i schs., Davison, Mich., 1954-55, 58-59, 63-66, Beaulac, Que., Can., 1960, Greenacre, Maine, 1965; sec. local spiritual assembly Baha'is, Ann Arbor, 1953, sec., Detroit, 1954, chmn., 1955; mem. nat. com. Baha'is U.S., 1955-68; sec. Davison Bahai Sch. Com. and Council, 1956, 58, 63-68; Baha'i lectr. Subject of local TV show Senior Focus, 1992. Mem. NOW, Modern Lang. Assn., Nat. Coun. Tchrs. English, Mich. Coll. English Assn., Am. Fedn. Tchrs., Nat. Soc. Lit. and Arts, Women's Equity and Action League (sec. Mich. chpt. 1975-79), Alpha Lambda Delta, Alpha Gamma Delta. Contbr. poems to mags. Recipient Women's Movement plaque Women Lawyers Assn. Mich., 1975, Lawrence award Mich. Masters Swimming, 1991, 9 World Master Records In Age Group, Gresham, Oreg. Long Course Meters, 1995, 23 Nat. Masters Records, 1994-96, 6 Nat. YMCA records, 1995, 2 U.S. Nat. Sr. Sports Classic Records, 1995, 2 World Sr. Games Records, 1993, All-Am. award, 1990-96, 2 U.S. Nat. Sr. Sports Classic Records; named one of 10 Best of 1995 Swim Mag. Avocation: U.S. Swimming Master Champion.

NOCKS, JAMES JAY, psychiatrist; b. Bklyn., Apr. 17, 1943; s. Henry and Pearl (Klein) N.; m. Ellen Jane Leblang, June 21, 1964; children: Randy, Jason. BA in English Lit., U. Pa., 1964, MD, 1968. Diplomate Nat. Bd. Med. Examiners, Am. Bd. Psychiatry and Neurology (psychiatry and addiction psychiatry), Am. Bd. Med. Mgmt. Rotating intern Chgo. Wesley Meml. Hosp., Northwestern U., 1968-69; resident psychiatry U. Pa., Phila., 1969-73; chief alcoholism program VA Med. Ctr., West Haven, Conn., 1975-87; asst. chief psychiatry svc. VA Med. Ctr., 1978-87; chief staff VA Med. Ctr., Coatesville, Pa., 1987-95; network dir. Balt. VISN, 1995—; sr. resident psychiatry U. Pa., 1971-72, chief resident psychiatry, 1972-73, asst. instr. psychiatry, 1971-73; clin. asst. prof. psychiatry Health Sci. Ctr. U. Tex., San Antonio, 1973-75; asst. clin. prof. psychiatry Yale U. Sch. Medicine, New Haven, 1975-80, assoc. clin. prof. psychiatry, 1980-87; clin. prof. psychiatry and human behavior Jefferson Med. Coll., Phila., 1987-91; prof. psychiatry Temple U. Sch. Medicine, Phila., 1991—. Contbr. chpts. in Psychiatry: Pre-Test, Self-Assessment and Review, 2d edit., 1982, 3d edit., 1984, Alcoholic Liver Disease, 1985; contbr. articles to profl. jours. Mem. exec. com. Med. Alumni Soc., U. Pa., 1989—. Major Med. Corps, USAF, 1973-75. Fellow Am. Psychiat. Assn. (cert. adminstrv. psychiatry); mem. Pa. Psychiat. Soc., Phila. Psychiat. Soc., Am. Soc. of Addiction Medicine (cert.), Assn. for Med. Edn. & Rsch. in Substance Abuse, Am. Assn. for Social Psychiatry, Am. Acad. Psychiatrists in Alcoholism & Addictions. Jewish. Avocations: bicycling, tennis, music. Office: VA Med Ctr Ste 275 849 International Dr Linthicum Heights MD 21090

NODDINGS, NEL, education educator, writer; b. Irvington, N.J., Jan. 19, 1929; d. Edward A. Rieth and Nellie A. (Connors) Walter; m. James A. Noddings, Aug. 20, 1949; children: Chris, Howard, Laurie, James, Nancy, William, Sharon, Edward, Vicky, Timothy. BA in Math., Montclair State Coll., 1949; MA in Math., Rutgers U., 1964; PhD in Edn., Stanford U., 1973; PhD (hon.), Columbia Coll., S.C., 1995. Cert. tchr., Calif., N.J. Tchr. Woodbury (N.J.) Publ Schs., 1949-52; tchr. math. dept. Matawan (N.J.) High Sch., 1958-62, chair, asst. prin., 1964-69; curriculum supr. Montgomery Twp. Pub. Schs., Skillman, N.J., 1970-72; dir. precollegiate edn. U. Chgo., 1975-76; asst. prof. Pa. State U., State College, 1973; from asst. prof. to assoc. prof. Stanford (Calif.) U., 1977-86, prof., 1986—, assoc. dean, 1990-92, acting dean, 1992-94, Lee L. Jacks prof. child edn., 1992—; bd. dirs. Ctr. for Human Caring Sch. Nursing, Denver, 1986-92; cons. NIE, NSF and various other sch. dists. Author: Caring: A Feminine Approach to Ethics and Moral Education, 1984, Women and Evil, 1989, (with W. Paul Shore) Awakening the Inner Eye: Intuition in Education, 1984, (with Carol Witherell) Stories Lives Tell, 1991, The Challenge to Care in Schools, 1992, Educating for Intelligent Belief or Unbelief, 1993, (with Suzanne Gordon and Patricia Benner) Philosophy of Education, 1995, Voices of Care, 1996. Mem. disting. women's adv. bd. Coll. St. Catherine. NSF fellow Rutgers U., 1962-64; recipient Anne Roe award for Contbns. to Profl. devel. of Women, Harvard Grad. Sch. Edn., 1993, medal for disting. svc. Tchrs. Coll. Columbia, 1994. Fellow Philosophy of Edn. Soc. (pres. 1991-92); mem. Am. Ednl. Rsch. Assn., Am. Philos. Assn., John Dewey Soc. (pres. 1994-96), Phi Beta Kappa (vis. scholar), Kappa Delta Pi. Avocation: gardening. Office: Stanford U Sch of Edn Stanford CA 94305

NODDINGS, SARAH ELLEN, lawyer; b. Matawan, N.J.; d. William Clayton and Sarah Stephenson (Cox) Noddings; children: Christopher, Aaron. BA in Math., Rutgers U., New Brunswick, N.J., 1965, MSW, 1968; JD cum laude, Seton Hall U., Newark, 1975; postgrad., UCLA, 1979. Bar: Calif. 1976, Nev. 1976, N.J. 1975, U.S. Dist. Ct. (ctrl. dist.) Calif. 1976, U.S. Dist. Ct. N.J. 1975. Social worker Carteret (N.J.) Bd. Edn., 1970-75; law clk. Hon. Howard W. Babcock, 8th Jud. Dist. Ct., Las Vegas, Nev., 1975-76; assoc. O'Melveny & Myers, L.A., 1976-78; atty. Internat. Creative Mgmt., Beverly Hills, Calif., 1978-81, Russell & Glickman, Century City, Calif., 1981-83; atty. Lorimer Prodns., Culver City and Burbank, Calif., 1983-87, v.p., 1987-93; atty. Warner Bros. TV, Burbank, Calif., 1993—, v.p., 1993—. Dir. county youth program, rsch. analyst Sonoma County People for Econ. Opportunity, Santa Rosa, Calif., 1968-69; VISTA vol. Kings County Cmty. Action Orgn., Hanford, Calif., 1965-66; officer, PTA bd. Casimir Mid. Sch. and Arlington Elem. Sch. Mem. Acad. TV Arts and Scis. (nat. awards com. 1994—), L.A. Copyright Soc. (trustee 1990-91), Women in Film, L.A. County Bar Assn. (intellectual property sect.), Women Entertainment Lawyers. Avocations: travel, tennis, skiing, bicycling, swimming. Office: Warner Bros TV 300 Television Plz Burbank CA 91505-1372

NODEEN, JANEY PRICE, computer scientist; b. Scotland Neck, N.C., Nov. 7, 1959; d. Wade Hampton and Joyce Ann (Councill) P.; m. Thomas Nodeen. BS in Computer Sci., Christopher Newport Coll., 1987; grad., Def. Sys. Mgmt. Coll., 1994; grad. advanced mgmt. program, Nat. Def. U., 1995. Engring. analyst Newport News (Va.) Shipbldg., 1978-86; mgr. submarine info. resources and computer ops. Dept. of the Navy, Washington, 1986-93, mem. exec. devel. program, 1993-96, sr. staff Navy Acquisition Reform Exec., 1995, dep. program exec. officer Submarines for Acquisition, 1996—; mil. legis. fellow for Congressman Sam Gejdenson, 1994; sr. exec. fellow John F. Kennedy Sch. Govt. Harvard U., class officer, 1994; sr. staff mem., Navy acquisition reform exec., asst. sec. of Navy for rsch., devel. and acquisition, 1995, asst. program exec. officer for submarines, USN, 1996. Home: 6915 Ashbury Dr Springfield VA 22152-3221 Office: Naval Sea Systems Command PEO Subs Washington DC 20362

NODINE, LOREN L., critical care nurse, consultant; b. East St. Louis, Ill., Aug. 13, 1934; s. Hester Ruth Robinson (dec.); m. Billie R. Nodine, June 4, 1981 (dec.); children: Nancy, Kathy, Larry, Cynthia. BSN, So. Ill. U., 1973; M in Vocat. Edn., U. N.Mex., 1983. Cert. trauma nurse specialist, cardiovascular nurse. Charge nurse St. Elizabeth's Med. Ctr., Granite City, Ill.; staff and charge nurse Lovelace Med. Ctr., Albuquerque; paramedic clin. instr. Albuquerque Fire Dept.; staff nurse St. Joseph Med. Ctr., Albuquerque; elder choices nurse divsn. aging & adult svcs. Ark. Dept. Human Svcs. Mem. AACCN, Am. Heart Assn. Home: 1618 Hwy 63 Walnut Ridge AR 72476

NOE, ELNORA (ELLIE NOE), retired chemical company executive; b. Evansville, Ind., Aug. 23, 1928; d. Thomas Noe and Evelyn (West) Dieter. Student Ind. U.-Purdue U., Indpls. Sec., Pitman Moore Co., Indpls., 1946; with Dow Chem. Co., Indpls., 1960-90, pub. rels. asst. then mgr. employee comm., 1970-87, mgr. cmty. rels., 1987-90, DowBrands Inc., 1986-90; vice chmn. corp. affairs discussion group, 1988-89, chmn., 1989-90; mem. steering com. Learn About Bus. Recipient 2d pl. award as Businesswoman of Yr., Indpls. Bus. and Profl. Women's Assn., 1980, Indpls. Profl. Woman of Yr. award Zonta, Altrusa, Soroptomist & Pilot Svc. Clubs, 1985, DowBrands Great Things Cmty. Svc. award, 1991. Mem. Am. Bus. Women Assn. (Woman of Yr. award 1965, past pres.), Ind. Assn. Bus. Communicators (hon., Communicator of Yr. 1977), Women in Comm. (Louise Eleanor Kleinhenz award 1984), Zonta (dist. pub. rels. chmn. 1978-80, area dir. 1980-82, pres. Indpls. 1977-79, bd. dirs. 1993-95), Dow Indpls. Retiree Club (pres. 1995—).

NOE, FRED J., sports association administrator; m. Elizabeth Noe.; B Arts and Scis. in Fin., Northwestern U. Divsn. mgr. Eaton Corp.; CEO Stihl Inc., 1978-93; exec. v.p. U.S. Trotting Assn., Columbus, Ohio, 1993—. Office: US Trotting Assn 750 Michigan Ave Columbus OH 43215-1191

NOE, GUY, social services administrator; b. Brussels, Jan. 28, 1934; came to U.S., 1955, naturalized, 1961; s. Marinus Cornelis and Johana Dorothea (Beijne) N.; 1 dau., Jeanette Sue. B.S., Regional Agrl. Sch., Loiret, France, 1954. Social worker State of Wyo., Casper, 1962-66; dir. Natrona County (Wyo.) Dept. Public Assistance, Casper, 1966-79; dir. Wyo. Div. Mental Health, Cheyenne, 1979-82, asst. adminstr. Divsn. of Youth Svcs., 1992—; former mgr. Platte County Office Pub. Assistance and Social Services, Wheatland, Wyo., dir. low income energy assistance programs, 1994-95; lectr. in field. V.p. Wyo. chpt. Big Bros., 1976-77; chmn. adv. coun. social svcs. State of Wyo., 1969-79; bd. dirs. Casper United Way, 1970—, Casper Salvation Army, 1970—, Casper chpt. ARC, 1977—; mem. Gov.'s Drug Abuse Adv. Bd., 1992—; pres. State Employees Assn. Named Outstanding Adminstr. State of Wyo., 1976 ; recipient Youth Svcs. award Wyo. Human Resources Confederation, 1988. Mem. Am. Public Welfare Assn. (Wyo. membership chmn.), Am. Soc. Public Adminstrn. Democrat. Club: Toastmasters. Home: 2731 Deming Blvd Cheyenne WY 82001-5709

NOE, JAMES ALVA, judge; b. Billings, Mont., May 25, 1932; s. James Alva Sr. and Laura Madlen (Parmenter) N.; m. Patricia Arlene Caudill, Aug. 4, 1956; children: Kendra Sue, Jeffrey James, Bradley John, Kirkwood Merle. BA in Polit. Sci., U. Wash., 1954, LLB, 1957; LittD hon., Christian Theol. Sem., 1986. Bar: Wash. 1958, U.S. Dist. Ct. (we. dist.) Wash. 1958, U.S. Ct. Appeals (9th cir.) 1959. Dep. prosecuting atty. King County, Seattle, 1958-61; trial lawyer Williams, Kastner & Gibbs, Seattle, 1961-67; judge Seattle Mcpl. Ct., 1967-71, King County Superior Ct., 1971—. Moderator Christian Ch. (Disciples of Christ) in the U.S. and Can., 1977-79. Fellow Am. Bar Found.; mem. ABA (ho. of dels. 1976-78, 82-87, 91—, bd. govs. 1991-94, chmn. jud. adminstrn. div. 1988-89, nat. conf. state trial judges 1981-82), Wash. State Superior Ct. Judges Assn. (pres. 1984-85), Nat. Jud. Coll. (trustee 1988-91, 95—). Home: 8250 SE 61st St Mercer Island WA 98040-4902 Office: King County Courthouse 3rd Ave # 711 Seattle WA 98104-1802

NOE, JERRE DONALD, computer science educator; b. McCloud, Calif., Feb. 1, 1923; s. Charles J. and Mae H. (Linebarger) N.; m. Mary A. Ward, Oct. 20, 1943 (dec.); children: M. Sherill (Mrs. Michael F. Roberts), Jeffrey W., Russell H.; m. Margarete Wöhlert, Sept. 10, 1983. B.S., U. Calif., 1943; Ph.D., Stanford U., 1948. Rsch. assoc. Radio Research Lab. Harvard and Am. Brit. Lab., Malvern, Eng., 1943-45; devel. engr. Hewlett-Packard Co., Palo Alto, Calif., 1946-48; rsch. engr. Stanford Research Inst., Menlo Park, Calif., 1948-53; asst. dir. engring. rsch., 1954-60, exec. dir. info. sci. and engring., 1961-68; prof. computer sci. U. Wash., Seattle, 1968-89, prof. emeritus, 1990—; chmn. dept. U. Wash., 1968-76; lectr. Stanford U., 1955-68; vis. prof. Vrije Universiteit, Amsterdam, 1976-77; guest rsch. scientist Gesellschaft fur Mathematik und Datenverarbeitung (GMD), Bonn, Fed. Republic Germany, 1986-87; mem. Army Sci. Bd., 1984-90; trustee Internat. Computer Sci. Inst., 1991-93; panelist NRC, 1991-92. Mem. Assn. Computing Machinery, IEEE. (nat. chmn. profl. group electronic computers 1956-57), Sigma Xi, Eta Kappa Nu, Tau Beta Pi. Tech. dir., devel. 1st computer for banking industry Bank Am. ERMA system, 1950-56. Home: 7524 34th Ave NW Seattle WA 98117-4723 Office: U Wash Dept Computer Sci & Engring Sieg Hall Box 352350 Seattle WA 98195-2350

NOEHREN, ROBERT, organist, organ builder; b. Buffalo, Dec. 16, 1910; s. Alfred H. and Juliet (Egelhoff) N.; m. Eloise Southern, Aug. 27, 1938; children: Judith, Arthur. Student Inst. Mus. Art, N.Y.C., 1929-30, Curtis Inst. Music, Phila., 1930-31; BMus, U. Mich., 1948; DMus (hon.), Davidson Coll., 1957. Instr., Davidson Coll., 1946-49; prof., univ. organist U. Mich., 1949-77, prof. emeritus, 1977—; vis. prof. Eastman Sch. Music, 1967, U. Kans., 1975; organ builder; important instruments include organ in St. John's Roman Cath. Cathedral, Milw., 1st Unitarian Ch., San Francisco, 1st Presbyn. Ch., Buffalo, St. Andrew's Episc. Ch., Newport News, Va., Calvary Episc. Ch., Rochester, Minn.; designer, cons., 1954—; concert tours of Europe, 1948—; soloist Phila. Orch., Philharmonia Hungarica, New Sinfonia; rec. artist Lyrichord, Urania, Orion, Delos records; spl. research old organs Europe, 17th and 18th century organs in France. Recipient Grande Prix du Disque. Contbr. articles profl. jours. Composer pieces for organ, piano, voice, chorus. Patentee combination action for organs. Home: 17605 Drayton Hall Way San Diego CA 92128-2057

NOEL, CRAIG, performing arts company executive, producer. LHD (hon.), U. San Diego. Actor Old Globe Theatre, San Diego, 1937—, dir., 1939—, exec. prodr.; instituted Globe Ednl. Tours, 1974, Old Globe's multicultural theater component Teatro Meta, 1983; established Play Discovery Program, 1974—, Shakespeare Festival, 1949—; founder Calif. Theatre Coun.; former v.p. Calif. Confedn. Arts.; introduced various playwrights, such as Beckett, Ionesco, to San Diego at La Jolla Mus. Contemporary Art, then Falstaff Tavern renamed Cassius Carter Centre Stage, 1969; presenter original drama, 1939—. Dir. more than 200 works; prodr. 290 works; recent prodns. include Morning's at Seven, Shirley Valentine, The Norman Conquests, 1979, Taking Steps, 1984, Intimate Exchanges, 1987, The Night of the Iguana, 1987, The Boiler Room, 1987, The White Rose, 1991, Mr. A's Amazing Maze Plays, 1994. Recipient Gov.'s award for Arts, San Diego's Living Treasure award, Conservator Am. Arts award Am. Conservatory Theatre, Headliner award San Diego Press Club, San Diego Gentlemen of Distinction award, combined tribute Pub. Arts Adv. Coun. and San Diego County Bd. Suprs.; named Outstanding Citizen contbn. fine arts dept. U. Ariz. Alumni Assn., one of 25 persons who shaped city's history San Diego Union; year proclaimed in his honor Mayor Maureen O'Connor, San Diego, 1987. Office: Old Globe Theatre PO Box 2171 San Diego CA 92112-2171

NOEL, DON OBERT, JR., newspaper columnist; b. Elizabeth, N.J., Nov. 27, 1931; s. Don O. and Catherine (Pyle) N.; m. Elizabeth Bradford Foulds, Aug. 29, 1953; 1 child, Emily Rebecca. BA in Am. Studies, Cornell U., 1954. Reporter Hartford (Conn.) Times, 1958-68, asst. mng. editor, 1968-69, editorial page editor, 1969-74, editor in chief, 1974-75; sr. corr. WFSB-TV, host Face the State Post-Newsweek Stas., 1975-84; polit. columnist op-ed page Hartford Courant, 1984—. Bd. sec. Blue Hills Civic Assn., Hartford, 1988—. Served alt. mil. duty Am. Friends Svc. Com., Tokyo, 1954-56. Recipient Sevellon Brown Meml. award New England AP, 1964, Nat. Journalism award AMA, 1972, Nat. Journalism award Am. Soc. Planning Officials, 1972, 74; fellow Alicia Patterson Found., 1966-67; finalist Pulitzer Prize for non-deadline reporting, 1964. Mem. Soc. of Friends. Avocations: gardening, birdwatching, language study. Home: 141 Ridgefield St Hartford CT 06112-1837 Office: Hartford Courant Co Op-Ed Page 285 Broad St Hartford CT 06115-2500

NOEL, EDWIN LAWRENCE, lawyer; b. St. Louis, July 11, 1946; s. Thomas Currie and Christine (Jones) N.; m. Nancy Carter Simpson, Feb. 7, 1970; children: Caroline, Edwin C. BA, Brown U., 1968; JD cum laude, St. Louis U., 1974. Bar: Mo. 1974, U.S. Dist. Ct. (ea. dist.) Mo. 1974, U.S. Ct. Appeals (8th cir.) 1974, U.S. Ct. Appeals (6th cir.) 1978, U.S. Ct. Appeals (7th cir.) 1994, U.S. Supreme Ct. 1986. Ptnr. Armstrong, Teasdale, Schlafly & Davis, St. Louis, 1974—, mng. ptnr., 1993—; bd. dirs. Corley Printing Co., Elcom Industries, St. Louis, Home Fed. Savs. Bank of Mo., 1988-93. Bd. dirs. Edgewood Children's Ctr., St. Louis, 1982-92, St. Louis Assn. for Retarded Citizens, 1984-87, Churchill Sch., 1988-94, Whitfield Sch., 1991—; chmn. Mo. Clean Water Com., Jefferson City, 1982-86; chmn. environ. com. St. Louis Regional Commerce and Growth Assn., 1982-88. Mem. Mo. Bar Assn., Bar Assn. Met. St. Louis, Attys. Liability Assurance Soc. (bd. dirs. 1995—). Republican. Episcopalian. Home: 301 S Mcknight Rd Saint Louis MO 63124-1884 Office: Armstrong Teasdale Schlafly & Davis 1 Metropolitan Sq Saint Louis MO 63102-2733

NOEL, ELIZABETH ANNA (BETTY NOEL), geriatrics nurse; b. Columbus, Ohio, Dec. 11, 1937; d. Robert Willis and Gladys Emma (Stimpfle) Johnson; m. Bruce A. George (div. 1960); m. John D. Holt, 1963 (div.); children: Joni, McCourt, John R.; m. Robert Noel, July 1978 (div. 1980); children: Patti, George. Diploma, Miami Valley Hosp., 1958. RN Ky., Ohio. Staff nurse, asst. head nurse med./surg. unit Miami Valley Hosp., Dayton, Ohio, 1958-63; head nurse med. unit Grandview Hosp., Dayton, Ohio, 1963-67; head nurse med./surg. unit St. Rita's Hosp., Lima, Ohio, 1967-69; staff charge nurse med./surg. svcs. Ephraim McDowell Regional Med. Ctr., Danville, Ky., 1970-92, retired, 1992; relief instr. Danville Sch. Practical Nursing, 1978-79; field nurse (part time) Health Care Review, 1990-92; coord. patient care Harrodsburg (Ky.) Health Care Manor, 1992—, staff devel. coord., 1995—. Avocations: dancing, reading, movies, playing cards, TV quiz shows. Home: 227 Forrest Ave Danville KY 40422-1206 Office: Harrodsburg Health Care Manor 853 Lexington Rd Harrodsburg KY 40330-1260

NOEL, FRANKLIN LINWOOD, federal chief magistrate judge; b. N.Y.C., Dec. 7, 1951; s. Charles Alexander and Mayme (Loth) N.; m. Ellen Barbara Perl, Sept. 15, 1979; children: Kate Alexandra, Charles David. BA, SUNY, Binghamton, 1974; JD, Georgetown U., 1977. Bar: D.C. 1977, U. S. Dist. Ct. D.C. 1978, U.S. Ct. Appeals (D.C. cir.) 1978, Pa. 1979, Minn. 1983, U.S. Ct. Appeals (8th cir.) 1983, U.S. Dist. Ct. Minn. 1984. Assoc. Arnold & Porter, Washington, 1977-79; asst. dist. atty. Phila. Dist. Attys. Office, 1979-83; asst. U.S. atty. U.S. Attys. Office, Mpls., 1983-89; U.S. magistrate judge U.S. Dist. Ct., St. Paul, 1989—; legal writing instr. U. Minn., Mpls., 1989-92, adj. prof. Law Sch., 1996—. Mem. League of Am. Wheelman, Phi Beta Kappa. Episcopalian. Avocation: bicycling. Office: US Dist Ct 638 US Courthouse 316 Robert St N Saint Paul MN 55101-1423

NOËL, LAURENT, bishop, educator; b. St. Just de Bretenieres, Que., Can., Mar. 19, 1920; s. Remi and Albertine (Nadeau) N. B.A., Coll. de Levis, 1940; L.Th., Laval U., 1944, L.Ph., 1948; D.Th., Inst. Angelicum, Rome, 1951. Ordained priest Roman Catholic Ch., 1944; prof. theology Laval U., 1946-48, 52-63, prof. ethics Med. Sch., 1952-63; vice rector Grand Sem., Sch. Theology, 1961-63; aux. bishop Que., 1963-74; apostolic adminstr. Diocese of Hauterive, 1974-75; bishop Diocese of Trois-Rivieres, Que., 1975—; Provincial chaplain Assn. des Infirmieres Catholiques, 1958—; chaplain Syndicat Profl. des Infirmieres Catholiques, 1958-63. Author: Precis. de morale medicale, 1962. Address: Bishop's House, CP 879, Trois Rivieres, PQ Canada G9A 5J9

NOEL, RANDALL DEANE, lawyer; b. Memphis, Oct. 19, 1953; s. D.A. and Patricia G. Noel; m. Lissa Johns, May 28, 1977; children: Lauren Elizabeth, Randall Walker. BBA with honors, U. Miss., 1975, JD, 1978. Bar: Miss. 1978, U.S. Dist. Ct. (no. and so. dists.) Miss. 1978, Tenn. 1979, U.S. Dist. Ct. (we., mid. and ea. dists.) Tenn. 1979, U.S. Ct. Appeals (5th and 6th cirs.) 1984, U.S. Supreme Ct. 1986. Assoc. Armstrong, Allen, Braden, Goodman, McBride & Prewitt, Memphis, 1978-85; ptnr. Armstrong, Allen, Prewitt, Gentry, Johnston & Holmes, Memphis, 1985—, mgr. litigation practice group, 1990-94, mgmt. com., 1994-96. Mem. fin. com. Memphis in May Internat. Festival, 1980-81; sec., gen. counsel Carnival Memphis, 1981-94, v.p. 1995; bd. dirs. Christ United Meth. Ch., Memphis, 1984-87, 89-91, trustee, 1991-93; mem. Leadership Memphis, 1994-95. Fellow Am. Bar Found., Tenn. Bar Found.; mem. ABA (young lawyers divsn., fellow dir. 1988-90, editor The Affiliate newsletter 1987-88, dir. Affiliate Outreach project 1988—, vice chmn. Award of Achievement com. 1986, ALI-ABA bd. 1992-95, litigation sect. mem. chair), Am. Counsel Assn. (pres.-elect 1995), Tenn. Bar Assn. (pres. young lawyers conf. 1990—, pres. litigation sect. 1988, treas. 1986, mem. bd. govs. 1989—, Pres.'s Disting. Svc. award 1988, 89), Memphis and Shelby Bar Assn. (mem. jud. recommendations, law week nominations and membership coms.), Miss. Bar Assn., Def. Rsch. Inst., Tenn. Def. Lawyers Assn., Am. Judicature Soc . (bd. dirs. 1992—). Home: 2938 Tishomingo Ln Memphis TN 38111-2627 Office: Armstrong Allen Prewitt Gentry Johnston & Holmes Brinkley Plaza 80 Monroe Ave Ste 700 Memphis TN 38103-2467

NOËL HUME, IVOR, retired archaeologist, consultant; b. London, Eng., 1927; s. Cecil and Gladys Mary (Bagshaw Mann) Noël H. Student, Framlingham Coll., Suffolk, 1936-39, St. Lawrence Coll., Kent, 1942-44; LHD (hon.), U. Pa., 1976, Coll. William and Mary, 1983. Archaeologist Guildhall Mus. Corp., London, 1949-57; chief archaeologist Colonial Williamsburg, Va., 1957-64; dir. dept. archaeology Colonial Williamsburg, 1964-72, resident archaeologist, 1972-87, ret., 1987; consulting curator Winthrop Rockefeller Archaeology Mus., 1987—; guest curator Steuben Glass Co., 1990, dir. Roanoke Project, 1991-93; rsch. assoc. Smithsonian Instn., 1959—; archaeol. cons. to Govt. of Jamaica, 1967-69; vice chmn. gov.'s adv. com. Va. Rsch. Ctr. for Hist. Archaeology, 1967-70, mem., 1971-76; mem. Va. Historic Landmarks Bd., 1985-87; mem. rev. Panel NEH, 1973-77; mem. Coun. Inst. Early Am. History and Culture, 1974-77; chair Jamestown Rediscovery Adv. Bd., 1994-95. Author: Archaeology in Britain, 1953, (with Audrey Noël Hume) Tortoises, Terrapins and Turtles, 1954, Treasure in the Thames, 1956, Great Moments in Archaeology, 1957, Here Lies Virginia, 1963, 1994, 1775: Another Part of the Field, 1966, Historical Archaeology, 1969, Artifacts of Early America, 1970, All the Best Rubbish, 1974, Early English Delftware, 1977, Martin's Hundred, 1982, The Virginia Adventure, 1994, Shipwreck: History from the Bermuda Reefs, 1995, In Search of This and That, 1996; contbr. articles to profl. jours.; Writer-dir.: (film) Doorway to the Past, 1968; writer, narrator: (TV movie) The Williamsburg File, 1976, Search for a Century, 1981; author pseudonymous novels, 1971, 72. Bd. dirs. Jamestown-Yorktown Found., 1987-91, Flowerdew Hundred Found., 1988—, Bermuda Underwater Exploration Inst., 1992—. With Indian Army, 1944-45. Recipient spl. award for hist. archaeology U. S.C., 1975, Achievement award Nat. Soc. Daus. Founders and Patriots Am., 1989, Nat. Soc. Daus. of the Am. Colonists, 1990; named Officer of the Brit. Empire (OBE), 1992. Fellow Soc. Antiquaries London, Am. Antiquarian Soc., Zool. Soc. London; mem. Soc. Hist. Archaeology (Harrington medal 1991), Soc. for Post-Medieval Archaeology (v.p. 1967-76), Kent Archaeol. Soc. (Gt. Britain), Va. Archeol. Soc. (hon., Profl. Archaeologist of Yr. award 1980), English Ceramic Circle, Glass Circle. Home: 2 West Cir Williamsburg VA 23185-1426

NOELKE, PAUL, lawyer; b. La Crosse, Wis., Feb. 10, 1915; s. Carl Bernard and Mary Amelia (O'Meara) N.; m. Mary Jo Kamps, May 4, 1943; children: Paul William, Mary Nesius, Ann Witt, Kate Helms. A.B. magna cum laude, Marquette U., 1936, J.D. cum laude, 1938; LL.M., U. Chgo., 1947; D.H.L. (hon.), Mt. Senario Coll., 1976. Bar: Wis. 1938, D.C. 1975, U.S. Dist. Ct. (ea. dist.) Wis. 1938, U.S. Supreme Ct. 1960. Assoc. firm Miller, Mack & Fairchild, 1938-40; asst. prof. law Marquette U., 1940-42; spl. agt. FBI, 1942-45; assoc. Quarles & Brady and predecessor firms, Milw., 1943-52, ptnr., 1952-85, of counsel, 1985—. Trustee emeritus Viterbo Coll., LaCrosse, Wis.; mem. adv. bd. Cardinal Stritch Coll., Milw.; past chmn. Pres.'s Coun. Marquette U.; past pres. Serra Internat., Chgo.; past chmn. Bd. Tax Rev., Village of Shorewood, Wis. Recipient Alumnus of Yr. award Marquette U., 1980; recipient Conf. award NCCJ, 1967. Mem. ABA, Wis. State Bar Assn., Milw. Bar Assn., Am. Judicature Soc., Order Holy Sepulchre, Alpha Sigma Nu. Roman Catholic. Home: 2462 N Prospect Ave Milwaukee WI 53211-4462 Office: 411 E Wisconsin Ave Milwaukee WI 53202-4409

NOELKEN, MILTON EDWARD, biochemistry educator, researcher; b. St. Louis, Dec. 5, 1935; s. William Henry Noelken and Agnes (Westbrook) Burkemper; m. Carol Ann Agne, June 9, 1962. BA in Chemistry, Washington U., St. Louis, 1957, PhD in Chemistry, 1962. Rsch. chemist Ea. Regional Rsch., Dept. Agr., Phila., 1964-67; asst. prof. dept. biochemistry U. Kans. Med. Ctr., Kansas City, 1967-71, assoc. prof., 1971-81, acting chmn., 1973-74, prof., 1981—, interim chmn., 1993-94; vis. prof. Fed. U. Minas Gerais, Brazil, 1978; mem. rsch. proposal rev. panel Am. Heart Assn. Kans. Affiliate, Inc., 1989-93. Contbr. articles to profl. jours. Recipient Scholastic Achievement award Am. Inst. Chemists, Washington U., 1957; NSF fellow, Washington U., 1959. Mem. Am. Chem. Soc., Am. Soc. for Biochemistry and Molecular Biology, Biophys. Soc., Sigma Xi. Achievements include research in properties of antibody molecules related to antigen binding, stucture of collagen of basement membranes, and stability of proteins. Office: U Kans Med Ctr Dept Biochemistry 39th and Rainbow Kansas City KS 66160-7421

NOER, RICHARD J., physics educator, researcher; b. Madison, Wis., July 3, 1937; s. Rudolf J. and Anita M. (Showerman) N.; m. Raymonde Tasset, Aug. 17, 1967; children—Geoffrey, Catherine. B.A., Amherst Coll., 1958; Ph.D., U. Calif., Berkeley, 1963. Physicist Atomic Energy Research, Harwell, Eng., 1963-64; asst. prof. physics Amherst Coll., Mass., 1964-66; asst. prof. physics Carleton Coll., Northfield, Minn., 1966-68, assoc. prof. physics, 1968-72, prof. physics, 1972—, dept. chair, 1974-77, 89-92; vis. physicist U. Paris, Orsay, France, 1972-73; physicist Ames Lab., Iowa, summers 1977-80, 82-84; rsch. physicist U. Geneva, 1980-81, 84-85; vis. scientist Cornell U., summers 1986, 88-91; vis. physicist Centre d'Etudes Nucléaires, Saclay, France, 1992-93. Co-author: Revolutions in Physics, 1972; contbr. articles to profl. jours. Mem. Am. Phys. Soc., Am. Assn. Physics Tchrs., AAAS, Phi Beta Kappa, Sigma Xi. Home: 101 Winona St Northfield MN 55057-2232 Office: Carleton Coll Dept Physics Northfield MN 55057

NOETHER, EMILIANA PASCA, historian, educator; b. Naples, Italy; came to U.S., 1919; d. Guglielmo and Bianca (Dramis) Pasca; m. Gottfried E. Noether, Aug. 1, 1942; 1 dau., Monica Gail. AB, Hunter Coll., N.Y.C., 1943; MA, Columbia U., 1944, PhD, 1948. Instr., then asst. prof. history Douglass Coll., Rutgers U., 1947-52; research asso. Center Internat. Studies, Mass. Inst. Tech., 1952-54; from lectr. to prof. history Regis Coll., Weston., Mass., 1959-66; prof. history Simmons Coll., Boston, 1966-68, U. Conn., Storrs, 1968-87. Editor: Italian sect. Am. Hist. Rev, 1958-75, Recently Published Articles, 1976-90, Garland Modern History Dissertation Series (Italy), 1989— ; author: Seeds of Italian Nationalism, 2d edit, 1969, also articles.; co-editor, contbr.: Modern Italy: A Topical History Since 1861, 1974; contbg. editor: The American Constitution as a Symbol and Reality for Italy, 1989. AAUW fellow, 1946-47, 62-63; Bunting Inst. fellow, 1961-62; sr. Fulbright scholar Florence, Italy, 1965-66; Rome, 1982; research grantee Am. Philos. Soc., summer 1970; U. Conn. Research Found. grantee, 1969-71, 73-77, 81-86. Mem. Am. Hist. Assn. (council 1975-78, chmn. com. women historians 1976), Soc. Italian Studies (chmn. prize award and citation com. 1968-69, adv. council 1979-82, adv. council v.p. 1981-83, pres. 1983-85), Berkshire Conf. Women Historians (sec. 1962-64, pres. 1967-71), Coordinating Com. on Women in Hist. Profession, AAUW, Phi Beta Kappa, Pi Gamma Mu., Phi Kappa Phi. Home: 632 Fearrington Post Pittsboro NC 27312

NOETZEL, GROVER ARCHIBALD JOSEPH, dean emeritus, economist; b. Greenwood, Wis., June 14, 1908; s. August Herman and Coralie Marie (Van Den Bossche) N.; m. Anna B. Dobbins, June 11, 1953. A.B., U. Wis., 1929, Ph.D., 1934; certificate in econs., U. London, 1930, U. Geneva, 1936; fellow, Social Sci. Research Council, 1935-36; LL.D. (hon.), Embry-Riddle U., 1976. Instr. econs. U. S.D., 1930-32, U. Wis., 1934-35; economist Nat. Bur. Econ. Research, 1936-37; asst. prof. Temple U., 1937-40, assoc. prof., 1940-46; pvt. cons. econs. and investment counselor Phila. and N.Y.C., 1939-46; prof. econs. U. Miami, Fla., 1946-48; dean sch. bus. adminstrn. U. Miami, 1948-61, dean emeritus, 1961—, prof. econs., cons. economist, 1961-72. Author: Recent Theories of Foreign Exchange, 1934, Cooperation Entre L'Universite et Les Milieux Economiques, 1956, Objectives of a Management Center, 1956, Decisions That Affect Profits, 1957, Our Longest Peacetime BoomWhere Now?, 1966, Growth of the Investment Potential of Florida, 1966, What Price Pax Americana, 1967, Consequences of Imbalance In Our Maturing Boom, 1968, Approaching Maturing of The Florida Economy, 1968, The 1969 Economy—The Case for Discipline, Options Available to the U.S.A. in International Decision Making, The Boom of the 1960's Shapes 1970's Prospects, Keynes and Inflation: An Interpretation of the Early 1970's, The 1971 Economy: Prospects and Change, 1975-A Year of Economic Decline. Bd. dirs. Med. Service Bur. Miami; trustee emeritus Embry-Riddle U., Daytona Beach, Fla. Mem. Am. Econ. Assn., Am. Finance Assn., Econ. Soc. of South Fla. (dir., pres. 1956), Artus, Phi Kappa Phi, Alpha Phi Omega, Alpha Delta Sigma, Delta Sigma Pi, Beta Gamma Sigma. Clubs: Coral Gables Country (Coral Gables), Rivieria Country (Coral Gables), Century (Coral Gables) (past pres.). Home and Office: 2845 Granada Blvd Apt 1A Miami FL 33134-6359

NOFER, GEORGE HANCOCK, lawyer; b. Phila., June 14, 1926. B.A., Haverford Coll., 1949; J.D., Yale U., 1952. Bar: Pa. 1953. Pvt. practice Phila., 1953—; ret. ptnr. Schnader, Harrison, Segal & Lewis, Phila., 1961-91, sr. counsel, 1992—; lectr. probate law, 1955—. Pres. bd. sch. dirs. Upper Moreland Twp., Pa., 1965-73; trustee Beaver Coll., Glenside, Pa., 1969-76; bd. dirs. Fox Chase Cancer Ctr., Phila., 1989-94; elder, trustee, deacon Abington (Pa.) Presbyn. Ch.; vice chmn. bd. dirs. Phila. Presbyn. Homes, Inc.; bd. dirs. A.G. Bell Assn. for Deaf, Washington. Fellow Am. Coll. Trust and Estate Counsel (regent 1975—, pres. 1983-84, chmn. Pa. 1973-78), Am. Law Inst., Am. Bar Found.; mem. ABA (standing com. on specialization 1980-86, chmn. 1983-86), Pa. Bar Assn., Phila. Bar Assn., Internat. Acad. Estate and Trust Law, Phi Beta Kappa, Phi Delta Phi. Home: 241 Pine St Philadelphia PA 19106-4313 Office: Schnader Harrison Segal & Lewis 1600 Market St Ste 3600 Philadelphia PA 19103-7240

NOFFSINGER, ANNE-RUSSELL L., former nursing administrator, educator; b. Frankfort, Ky., Feb. 4, 1932; d. Charles Russell and Hettie Lee (Ward) Lillis; m. J. Philip Noffsinger, July 1, 1964; children: Ward, Gretchen, Hans. Diploma, Good Samaritan Hosp., Lexington, Ky., 1952; BA in English, U. Ky., 1966, MA in Counseling, 1968, EdD in Psychology, 1979; MSN, U. Tenn., 1986. Instr. fundamentals of nursing Good Samaritan Hosp., Lexington, 1955-56; assoc. dir. nursing St. Joseph Hosp., Lexington, 1958-61; instr. pediatric nursing Good Samaritan Hosp. Sch. Nursing, Lexington, 1961-68; prof., chmn. nursing Lexington Community Coll., 1968-94; asst. to pres. for instnl. advancement and rsch., 1994—. Co-author: Counseling: An Introduction for Health and Human Services, 1984. Recipient U. Ky. Alumni Great Teaching award; Helene Fuld grantee. Mem. ANA (del.), KNA (former pres.), Nat. League for Nursing, KLN (former pres.), ODK, KCADN, Sigma Theta Tau, Omicron Delta Kappa, Phi Delta Kappa.

NOFFSINGER, WILLIAM BLAKE, computer science educator, academic administrator; b. Atlanta, July 5, 1950; s. M.F. and Winifred (Blake) N.; m. Kathy A. Golden, Apr. 27, 1985; children: Margeaux Jones-Golden, William Blake Jr. BS in Exptl. Psychology, U. Fla., 1974, MS in Exptl. Psychology, 1984; postgrad., Fla. State U., 1993—. Sys. mgr. Santa Fe C.C., Gainesville, Fla., 1974-77, instnl. rschr., instr., 1977-79; sys. analyst U. Fla., Gainesville, Fla., 1979-82, sys. coord., 1982-88, sr. computer coord., 1988—, computer sci. instr., 1985—; computing and rsch. cons. Ctr. for Climacteric Studies, Gainesville, 1986, VA Hosp., Gainesville, 1986-87, U. Fla. Pediat. Neurology, Gainesville, 1991—. Contbr. articles to profl. jours. Judge computer sci. entries Alachua county Sci. Fair, Gainesville, 1981. Recipient Davis Productivity award State of Fla., 1992, 93; grantee Santa Fe C.C., 1978, U. Fla., 1989, 90. Mem. IEEE, Data Processing Mgmt. Assn. (chpt. v.p. 1982), Assn. for Computing Machinery, Phi Delta Kappa (chpt. treas. 1981). Episcopalian. Avocations: running, audio, electronics. Home: 131 SW 84th Ter Gainesville FL 32607-1434 Office: U Fla 33 Tigert Hall Gainesville FL 32611-3275

NOFSINGER, WILLIAM MORRIS, engineering executive; b. Orange, N.J., Sept. 11, 1932; s. Charles William and Grace Elizabeth (Morris) N.; m. Bonnie Jean Haisler, Nov. 6, 1965; children: Barry Jean, Betsy Jayne. BS in Chem. Engring., U. Kans., 1955. Registered profl. engr. With The C.W. Nofsinger Co., Kansas City, Mo., various positions to v.p., 1959-78, pres., 1978—; mem. adv. bd. U. Kans. Dept. Chem. and Petroleum Engring.; v.p., mem. exec. com. Fractionation Rsch., Inc., Bartlesville, Okla. Lt. USAF, 1955-58, capt. Res. Fellow Am. Inst. Chem. Engrs.; mem. NSPE, Am. Chem. Soc., Mo. Soc. Profl. Engrs., Kans. Engring. Soc. Republican. Lodge: Rotary (v.p. 1983-84, pres. elect 1984-85, pres. 1985-86). Home: 6645 Brookside Rd Kansas City MO 64113-1837 Office: The CW Nofsinger Co 4700 E 63rd St Kansas City MO 64130-4696

NOGALES, LUIS GUERRERO, communications company executive; b. Madera, Calif., Oct. 17, 1943; s. Alejandro Cano and Florence (Guerrero) N.; children: Alicia Fipp, Maria Cristina. BA in Polit. Sci., San Diego State U., 1966; JD, Stanford U., 1969. Asst. to pres. Stanford U., Calif., 1969-72; White House fellow, asst. to sec. U.S. Dept. Interior, Washington, 1972-73; exec. v.p., dir. Golden West Broadcasters, L.A., 1973-80; pres. Nogales, Bermudez, Chase and Tamayo, L.A., 1981-82; chmn., chief exec. officer UPI, Washington, 1983-86; pres. ECO Internat. News Svc., 1987, Univision, 1987-88; gen . ptnr. Nogales Castro Ptnrs., 1989-90; pres. Nogales Ptnrs., L.A., 1990—; bd. dir. The Bank of Calif., San Francisco, Stanford U. Ctr. for Pub. Svc., The Ford Found. Bd. dirs. State of Calif. Bd. Higher Edn., Sacramento, 1973-79, Los Angeles Redevel. Agy., 1973-76, United Way Am., Alexandria, Va., 1984-88; trustee Claremont U. Ctr. and Grad. Sch., 1987, Stanford U.; chmn. MALDEF, 1980-82. Office: 2049 Century Park E Bldg 39 Los Angeles CA 90067-3101

NOGELO, ANTHONY MILES, health care company executive; b. Framingham, Mass., Apr. 2, 1943; s. Anthony Joseph and Lillian Carol (Nowick) N.; m. Gerry C. Stugis, Mar. 20, 1965; children: Laura Elizabeth, Michael Joseph. B.A. in Econs., Tufts U., 1964; M.B.A., Harvard Bus. Sch., 1968. Mgr. fin. planning and analysis Gen. Foods Corp., White Plains, N.Y., 1968-73; ptnr. Paul E. Dean, Greenwich, Conn., 1973-74; asst. treas. Ludlow Corp., Needham Heights, Mass., 1974-80; v.p., treas. Nat. Med. Care Inc., Boston, 1980-85; v.p., chief fin. officer, treas. Nat. Med. Care Inc., 1985-95; v.p., treas. Nat. Med. Care, Inc., 1995—. Served to lt. j.g. USNR, 1964-66. Mem. Fin. Execs. Inst., Treas. Club Boston. Home: 19 Washington Dr Sudbury MA 01776-2935 Office: Nat Med Care Inc 1601 Trapelo Rd Waltham MA 02154-7333

NOGUCHI, THOMAS TSUNETOMI, author, forensic pathologist; b. Fukuoka, Japan, Jan. 4, 1927; came to U.S., 1952; s. Wataru and Tomika Narahashi N. D of Medicine, Nippon Med. Sch., Tokyo, 1951; LLD (hon.), U. Braz Cubas Fedn. Faculties Mogi Das Cruzes, Sao Paolo, Brazil, 1980; DSc (hon.), Worcester State Coll., 1985. Dep. med. examiner Los Angeles County Dept. Chief Med. Examiner, L.A., 1961-67, coroner, 1967-82; prof. forensic pathology U. So. Calif., L.A., 1982—. Author: Coroner, 1983 (N.Y. Times Bestseller 1984), Coroner At Large, 1985; (fiction) Unnatural Causes, 1988, Physical Evidence, 1990. Fellow Am. Acad. Forensic Sci. (chmn. sect. 1966); mem. Nat. Assn. Med. Examiners (pres. 1983), Calif. State Coroners Assn. (pres. 1974), World Assn. Med. Law (v.p.). Republican. Avocations: fine arts, gourmet Oriental cooking, painting stills and abstracts. Office: U So Calif Med Ctr 1200 N State St Rm 2520 Los Angeles CA 90033-1084

NOHA, EDWARD J., insurance company executive; b. N.Y.C., Aug. 25, 1927; married. BBA, Pace Coll. With Dept. Justice, 1944-52, Met. Life Ins. Co., 1952-55; exec. v.p. Allstate Ins. Co., 1955-74; chmn. bd., pres., CEO Continental Assurance Co., Chgo., 1955-74, CNA Ins. Cos., Chgo., 1975-92; chmn. bd. CNA Fin. Corp., Chgo., 1992—; chmn. bd. Nat. Fire Ins. Co. of Hartford, Inc., Transcontinental Ins. Co.; dir. Loews Corp.; mem. Property-Casualty Ins. Coun.; trustee Am. Inst. Property & Liability Underwriters, Ins. Inst. Am.; chmn. Chgo. Econ. Devel. Commn., 1992—. *

NOHRDEN, PATRICK THOMAS, lawyer; b. Santa Cruz, Calif., Mar. 7, 1956; s. Thomas Allen and Roberta Eugenia (Brydon) N.; m. Debora Ann Heintz, Sept. 19, 1981; children: Steven, Laura, Maranda, Wendy. AS, SUNY, Albany, 1980; BA in English, San Jose State U., 1984; JD, U. Akron, 1992. Bar: Nev. 1993, U.S. Dist. Ct. Nev. 1993. Regional dir. CareerPro, Inc., Roseville, Calif., 1984-91; cons. Patrick T. Nohrden & Assocs., Youngstown, Ohio, 1991-93; pvt. practice Las Vegas, Nev., 1993—; bd. dirs. Profl. Resume Svc., Inc., Las Vegas, Las Vegas Diamondbacks, Inc., Old Nev. Fin., Inc., Las Vegas. Sgt. U.S. Army, 1975-81. Mem. ATLA, ABA (family law sect.), Fed. Bar Assn., Nev. Trial Lawyers Assn., State Bar Nev. (family law and bankruptcy sects.), Clark County Bar Assn., Phi Kappa Phi. Republican. Roman Catholic. Office: 2601 W Charleston Blvd Las Vegas NV 89102-2107

NOHRNBERG, JAMES CARSON, English language educator; b. Berkeley, Calif., Mar. 19, 1941; s. Carson and Geneva Gertrude (Gibbs) N.; m. Stephanie Payson Lamport, June 14, 1964; children: Gabrielle L., Peter Carson L. Student, Kenyon Coll., 1958-60; BA, Harvard Coll., 1962, postgrad., 1965-68; PhD, U. Toronto, Ont., Can., 1970. Teaching fellow dept. English U. Coll., U. Toronto, 1963-64; jr. fellow Soc. of Fellows Harvard U., 1965-68; acting instr. dept. English Yale U., New Haven, 1968-69, lectr. dept. English, 1969-70, asst. prof. dept. English, 1970-75, assoc. prof., 1975; prof. English U. Va., Charlottesville, 1975—; adj. instr. English Harvard U., Cambridge, 1967; lectr. various univs., 1974-95; Gauss seminar in criticism lectr. Princeton U., 1987. Author: The Analogy of the Faerie Queene, 1976, 80, Like Unto Moses: The Constituting of an Interruption, 1995; mem. editl. bd. Spenser Ency., 1977-90, Bible, Homer, Dante, Boiardo, Spenser, Milton, Thomas Pynchon; contbr. articles to profl. jours. Woodrow Wilson fellow, 1962, jr. fellow Harvard U., 1965-68, Morse fellow Yale U., 1974-75, U. Va. Ctr. for Advanced Studies fellow, 1975-78, Guggenheim fellow, 1981-82, Ind. U. Inst. for Advanced Studies fellow, 1991. Mem. MLA, Spenser Soc. Presbyterian. Avocations: writing poetry, collecting books and records. Home: 1874 Wayside Pl Charlottesville VA 22903-1631 Office: U Va Dept English Bryan Hall Charlottesville VA 22903

NOIA, ALAN JAMES, utility company executive; b. Selbitz, Germany, Feb. 18, 1947; came to U.S., 1949; s. Fiore and Anneliese (Gossler) N.; m. Cynthia Dee Rathman. BSEE, U. Va., Charlottesville, 1969. Engr.

Potomac Edison Co., Hagerstown, Md., 1969-72, database adminstr., 1972-73; data base adminstr., supr. tech. svcs. Allegheny Power Svc. Corp., Greensburg, Pa., 1973-75; staff asst. Allegheny Power Svc. Corp., N.Y.C., 1975-79; asst. v.p., treas. Allegheny Power System, N.Y.C., 1979-80, treas., 1980-82, v.p., treas., 1983-84; v.p. bulk power supply, CFO Allegheny Power System, Inc. and Allegheny Power Svc. Corp., N.Y.C., 1984-87; pres. Potomac Edison Co., Hagerstown, Md., 1990-94; pres., COO Allegheny Power System, Inc., N.Y.C., 1994—, also bd. dirs.; bd. dirs. Allegheny Power Svc. Corp., Monongahela Power Co., Potomac Edison Co., West Penn Power Co., Allegheny Generating Co.; mem. Md. Econ. Devel. Com. Trustee East Ctrl. Nuclear Group, N.Y.C., 1979—; bd. dirs. Md. Symphony Orch., Southeastern Elec. Exch., Inc. Mem. Phi Eta Sigma, Eta Kappa Nu, Tau Beta Pi. Roman Catholic. Home: 9532 Childacrest Dr Boonsboro MD 21713 Office: Allegheny Power System Inc 12 E 49th St New York NY 10017-1028

NOKES, JOHN RICHARD, retired newspaper editor, author; b. Portland, Oreg., Feb. 23, 1915; s. James Abraham and Bernice Alfaretta (Bailey) N.; m. Evelyn Junkin, Sept. 13, 1936; children: Richard Gregory, William G., Gail (Mrs. William M. Hulden), Douglas J., Kathy E. BS., Linfield Coll., 1936, LHD (hon.), 1988. With The Oregonian, Portland, 1936-82, city editor, 1950-65, asst. mng. editor, 1965-71, mng. editor, 1971-75, editor, 1975-82; disting. vis. prof. journalism Linfield Coll., 1982-85; cons. editor The Hong Kong Standard, 1994. Author: American Form of Government, 1939, Columbia's River: The Voyages of Robert Gray 1787-1793, 1991; editor Oreg. Edn. Jour., 1944. Bd. dirs. Portland U.S.O., 1968-72, U.S. Coast Guard Acad. Found., 1972-74, Portland Opera Assn., 1976-78; trustee Linfield Coll., 1977-93; v.p. Oreg. UN Assn., 1983-85, chmn. Oreg. UN Day, 1983. Lt. (j.g.) USNR, 1944-46; comdr. Res. (ret.). Mem. Navy League U.S. (pres. Portland coun. 1969-71), Linfield Coll. Alumni Assn. (pres. 1940), World Affairs Coun. Oreg. (pres. 1973-74), AP Mng. Editors Assn. (dir. 1973-80), Am. Soc. Newspaper Editors, N.W. China Coun., Sigma Delta Chi (pres. Willamette Valley chpt. 1975-76). Republican. Methodist. Club: Multnomah Athletic (Portland). Home: 14650 SW 103rd Ave Tigard OR 97224-4740

NOLAN, ALAN TUCKER, retired lawyer; b. Evansville, Ind., Jan. 19, 1923; s. Val and Jeannette (Covert) N.; m. Elizabeth Clare Titsworth, Aug. 26, 1947 (dec. Nov. 1967); children: Patrick A., Thomas C., Mary F., Elizabeth T., John V.; m. Jane Ransel DeVoe, Feb. 7, 1970; adopted children: John C. DeVoe, Ellen R. DeVoe, Thomas R. DeVoe. AB in Govt., Ind. U., 1944, DHL (hon.), 1993; LLB, Harvard U., 1947. Bar: Ind. 1947. Law clk. U.S. Ct. Appeals (7th Cir.), Chgo., 1947-48; assoc. Ice, Miller, Donadio & Ryan, Indpls., 1948-58, ptnr., 1958-93, ret., 1993—; chmn. Disciplinary Commn. Supreme Ct. Ind., Indpls., 1966-73; vice-chmn. bd. dirs. Union City Body Co., Inc., 1982-92. Author: The Iron Brigade, 1961, As Sounding Brass, 1964, Lee Considered, 1991; contbg. editor The Civil War, 1985-89; contbr. numerous articles to profl. jours. Life mem. NAACP Indpls., v.p., 1950-54; bd. dirs., founder Ind. Civil Liberties Union, Indpls., 1953-60; bd. dirs. Indpls. Art League, 1981-87; chmn., bd. trustees Ind. Hist. Soc., Indpls., 1986—; trustee Eiteljorg Mus., Indpls., 1987-93. Fellow Co. Mil. Historians, Am. Bar Found.; mem. ABA, Ind. Bar Assn., Indpls. Bar Assn. (bd. mgrs. 1958-60, chmn. Grievance Com. 1960-64), Indpls. Civil War Round Table. Democrat. Roman Catholic. Avocations: travel, gardening, reading. Home: 4118 N Pennsylvania St Indianapolis IN 46205-2611 Office: PO Box 82001 1 American Sq Indianapolis IN 46282-0001

NOLAN, BARRY HANCE, publishing company executive; b. Easton, Pa., Sept. 15, 1942; s. Arthur James Nolan and Marion (Hance) Slater; m. Janet Lynch, Mar. 20, 1971 (dec. Mar. 1981); 1 child, Tracy; m. Catherine McDermott, Feb. 19, 1983; children: Craig, Kelsey. AB in Econs., Princeton U., 1964; MBA, Columbia U., 1966. Account exec. Papert, Koenig, Lois Advt., N.Y.C., 1966-68; group mgr. new bus.'s Butterick div. Am. Can, N.Y.C., 1969-72; dir. mktg. planning Current Inc. subs. Deluxe Check Printers, Colorado Springs, Colo., 1973-77, v.p. mktg., 1977-79, pres., chief exec. officer, 1980-89; pres., chief exec. officer ECM, Inc., Colorado Springs, Colo., 1991—; asst. to pres. Pacific Water Works Supply Co., Seattle, 1979-80. Pres. bd. dirs. Pikes Peak br. Cystic Fibrosis Found., Colorado Springs, 1984-89, nat. trustee-at-large, Washington, 1985-92. Mem. Parcel Shippers Assn. (bd. dirs. 1987-89). Republican. Presbyterian. Clubs: Cheyenne Mountain Country (Colorado Springs); Sahalee Country (Redmond, Wash.), Broadmoor Golf, Garden of the Gods. Avocations: golf, landscape architecture, photography. Home: 35 Elm Ave Colorado Springs CO 80906-3169 Office: ECM Inc PO Box 50065 Colorado Springs CO 80949-0065

NOLAN, CAROLE RITA, broadcasting executive; b. Chgo., Jan. 28, 1932; d. Martin Francis and Caroline Rita (Alton) N.; B.A., De Paul U., 1954, M.A., 1961. Tchr. Chgo. public schs., 1954-61, sci. cons., 1961-66, dir. instructional TV, 1966-71; dir. bur. telecommunications and broadcasting, mgr. Sta. WBEZ-FM, Chgo., 1971-90; pres, CEO, 1990-96, pres. emeritus 1996—; mem. faculty Northeastern U., 1964-65, De Paul U., 1975—; cons. Comptons Ency., 1964-65, Chgo. Area Sch. TV, 1964-72, Ill. TV Adv. Council, 1969. Bd. dirs. Chicagoland Radio Info. Services, Pub. Radio Internat., Ill. Arts Alliance, Bright New Cities. Mem. Chgo. Network, Nat. Pub. Radio, DePaul Univ. Women's Alumni Assn. (bd. dirs., treas.), Delta Kappa Gamma. Office: Sta WBEZ-FM 848 E Grand Chicago IL 60611

NOLAN, CARY J., medical products manufacturer; b. 1942. BA, Notre Dame, BS in Elec. Engring. With Xerox Corp.; pres. Xerox Med. Systems; pres., CEO Cooper Surgical subs The Cooper Co., Picker Internat. Inc., 1989—. Office: Picker Internat Inc 595 Miner Rd Cleveland OH 44143-2131*

NOLAN, EDITH ELLEN, research scientist, psychology educator; b. Brooklyn, N.Y., Sept. 21, 1951; d. Anthony Vincent and Sheila Frances (Whelan) Ventrice; m. Mark William Nolan jr., May 28, 1970 (div. May 1975); 1 child, Mark William; m. Gerard Michael Damm, Aug. 9, 1987. BA in psychology, SUNY, Stony Brook, 1981; PhD, 1988; MA in Exptl. Psychology, L.I. U.-C.W. Post, 1984. Clinician's asst. psychiatry dept. SUNY, Stony Brook, 1986, field coord. Medication Evaluations Program, 1986-90, sr. rsch. scientist, 1991—; field observer Devel. Disabilities Clinic, Stony Brook, 1987; adj. instr. L.I. U., Brookville, 1985-89, SUNY, Stony Brook, 1988, St. Joseph's Coll., Patchogue, N.Y., 1988-90; adj. asst. prof. Dowling Coll., Oakdale, N.Y., 1987—; behavioral intervention cons., Maryhaven Therapeutic Presch., Port Jefferson, N.Y., 1983-85; speaker in field. Mem. Brookhaven Village Assn., 1994. Rsch. grantee NIMH, 1994. Mem. APS, Sigma Xi. Achievements include field-testing modification of and extensive research with procedure for conducting school-based medication evaluations for hyperactive children, procedure for toilet training developmentally disabled children. Office: Dept Psychiatry Putnam Hall S Campus Stony Brook NY 11794-8790

NOLAN, JAMES PAUL, medical educator, scientist; b. Buffalo, June 21, 1929; s. James Paul and Isabel (Curry) N.; m. Christa Paul, July 23, 1956; children—Lisa, James, Christopher, Thomas. B.A., Yale U., 1951, M.D. cum laude, 1955. Diplomate Am. Bd. Internal Medicine. Instr. in medicine Yale U., New Haven, 1961-63; intern Grace-New Haven Hosp., 1955-56, resident, 1958-60, chief med. resident, 1961-62, asso. physician, 1962-63; asst. prof. medicine SUNY, Buffalo, 1963-67; asso. prof. SUNY, 1967-69, prof., 1969—, vice-chmn. dept. medicine, 1973-77, acting chmn. dept., 1978-79; chmn. dept., 1979-95; chief of medicine Buffalo Gen. Hosp., 1969-80, attending, 1969—; asso. attending Edward J. Meyer Meml. Hosp., Buffalo, 1963-68; attending Edward J. Meyer Meml. Hosp., 1968-71, cons., 1971—; cons. physician Millard Fillmore Hosp., 1981—, Deaconess Hosp., 1973—; attending Buffalo VA Hosp., Children's Hosp. Buffalo; cons. Roswell Park Meml. Inst., 1970—; acting dir. dept. medicine Erie County Med. Center, 1978-80, dir. dept., 1980—; Trustee Buffalo Gen. Hosp., 1974—. Editorial adv. bd. Jour. Medicine Exptl. and Clin, 1971—; reviewer: Gastroenterology, 1973—; contbr. numerous articles to med. and sci. jours. Served to lt. comdr., M.C. USN, 1956-58. NIH grantee, 1979-86; Hartford Found. grantee, 1981. Mem. ACP (master, chair bd. regents 1994-95), Am. Fedn. Clin. Rsch., AAAS, Am. Gastroent. Assn. (procedures com.), Am. Assn. Study of Liver Disease, Reticuloendothelial Soc., N.Y. Acad. Sci., Am. Clin. and Climatol. Assn., Interurban Club, Ctrl. Soc. Clin. Rsch., Internat. Assn. Study of Liver, Assn. Am. Physicians, Assn. Profs. Medicine (pres. 1993-94), Phi Beta Kappa, Alpha Omega Alpha. Home: 213 Burbank Dr Buffalo NY 14226-3938 Office: 462 Grider St Buffalo NY 14215-3075

NOLAN, JEAN, federal agency official; b. Collingdale, Pa., Oct. 25, 1959; d. John Thomas and Elizabeth (Gillan) N. BA, Temple U., 1981. Reporter Inside Radio, Cherry Hill, N.J., 1978-82; staff reporter Phila. Bus. Jour., 1982-84, Washington Bus. Jour., Tysons Corner, Va., 1984-85, Housing & Devel. Reporter, Washington, 1985-89; dir. publs. Enterprise Found., Columbia, Md., 1989-91, dir. comms., 1991-93; asst. sec. pub. affairs U.S. Dept. HUD, Washington, 1993—. Mem. Comms. Affinity Group Coun. Found. Democrat. Office: US Dept HUD 451 7th St SW Rm 10032 Washington DC 20410-0001

NOLAN, JOHN BLANCHARD, lawyer; b. Providence, Aug. 30, 1943; s. John O'Leary and Elizabeth Rita (Blanchard) N.; m. Marguerite Ruth Hartley, Mar. 1, 1969 (dec. Aug. 1988); children: Suzanne, Caroline, Danielle; m. Lillian B. Prestley, 1989. AB, Brown U., 1965; JD, Georgetown U., 1968. Bar: Conn. 1968, N.Y. 1974, U.S. Ct. Appeals (2d cir.) 1969, U.S. Dist. Ct. Conn.1969, U.S. Dist. Ct. (so. dist.) N.Y. 1973, U.S. Ct. Appeals (1st cir.) 1991, U.S. Dist. Ct. Ariz. 1994, U.S. Supreme Ct. 1995. Assoc. Day, Berry & Howard, Hartford, Conn., 1969-76, ptnr., 1976—; bd. dirs. Spiritus Wines, Inc., Hartford; chmn. Local Rules of Practice Adv. Com. to U.S. Bankruptcy Ct., 1981—. Corporator St. Francis Hosp. Med. Ctr., Hartford, 1982—; trustee St. Mary Home Found., 1983—, U. Hartford Art Sch., 1988-94; bd. dirs. Greater Hartford Arts Coun., Inc., 1993—; mem. parish coun. Ch. of St. Timothy. Mem. ABA, Am. Bankruptcy Inst., Conn. Bar Assn., Hartford County Bar Assn, Insolvency Internat., Hartford Golf Club. Democrat. Roman Catholic. Avocations: golf, skiing, travel, wines. Home: 150 Scarborough St Hartford CT 06105-1107 Office: Day Berry & Howard Cityplace Hartford CT 06103

NOLAN, JOHN EDWARD, retired electrical corporation executive; b. Bklyn., Apr. 15, 1925; s. John C. and Elizabeth (Reighton) N.; m. Dorothea Scheuermann, Aug. 23, 1952; children: Kathleen, Elizabeth, John Edward, James, Michael, Patricia, Maureen. BEE, Cooper Union, 1950; MSEE, U. Pitts., 1955. With Westinghouse Electric Corp., 1950-90, mem. staff Bettis Atomic Power Lab., 1951-69, with Advanced Reactors div., 1969-79, dir. Hanford Engring. Devel. Lab., 1980-87, pres. Westinghouse Hanford Co., 1988-90, ret., 1990. With U.S. Army, 1943-46, ETO. Mem. IEEE, ASME, Am. Nuclear Soc. Home: 411 Snyder Rd Richland WA 99352-1945

NOLAN, JOHN EDWARD, lawyer; b. Mpls., July 11, 1927; s. John E. and Teresa (Franey) N.; m. Joan Dobbins, June 3, 1950; children: Carol N. Klatt, John Edward III (dec.), Kelly N. Spencer, Richard Clark, Patricia N. McNeill. BS, U.S. Naval Acad., 1950; JD, Georgetown U., 1955. Bar: D.C. 1955, U.S. Supreme Ct. 1959, Md. 1961. Law clk. to Justice Clark U.S. Supreme Ct., 1955-56; adminstrv. asst. to Atty. Gen. Robert F. Kennedy, 1963-64; assoc. Steptoe & Johnson, Washington, 1956-62; ptnr. Steptoe & Johnson, 1962-63, 65—; assoc. counsel Cuban families com. Cuban Prisoners Exch., Havana, 1962-63; spl. counsel refugee subcom. Senate Jud. Com., Vietnam, 1967-68; mem. CPR Panel of Disting. Neutrals, Washington, U.S. Ct. Appeals mediator D.C. cir.; mem. exec. com. Lawyers Com. for Civil Rights Under the Law; bd. dirs. Hooper Holmes, Inc., Iomega Corp.; vis. fellow Wolfson Coll., Cambridge (Eng.) U., 1987, 92. Trustee Robert F. Kennedy Meml., 1969—; bd. dirs. Fund Dem. Majority; moderator Aspen Inst., 1980—. Capt. USMC, 1950-54, Korea. Decorated Silver Star, Bronze Star with Combat V, Purple Heart. Mem. ABA, D.C. Bar Assn. (gov.), Am. Law Inst. Democrat. Roman Catholic. Clubs: Met. (Washington); Congl. Home: 7830 Persimmon Tree Ln Bethesda MD 20817-4520 Office: 1330 Connecticut Ave NW Washington DC 20036-1704

NOLAN, JOHN MICHAEL, lawyer; b. Conway, Ark., June 21, 1948; s. Paul Thomas and Peggy (Hime) N. BA, U. Tex., 1970, postgrad., 1971, JD, 1973; LLM in Taxation, George Washington U., 1976. Bar: Tex. 1973, U.S. Ct. Mil. Appeals 1973, U.S. Ct. Appeals (D.C. cir.) 1975, U.S. Tax Ct. 1975, U.S. Supreme Ct. 1975. Chief counsel to chief judge U.S. Ct. Mil. Appeals, Washington, 1976-77; assoc. Winstead, McGuire, Sechrest & Minick P.C., Dallas, 1977-81; shareholder Winstead Sechrest & Minick P.C., Dallas, 1981—. Editor in chief The Advocate, 1973-76. Served as capt. JAGC, U.S. Army, 1973-76. Named one of Outstanding Young Men in Am., U.S. Jaycess, 1976. Mem. ABA (real property, probate and trust sect., real property com., partnerships, joint ventrues, and other investment vehicles), ALA (bd. dirs.), Tex. Bar Assn. (real property, probate and trust sect.), D.C. Bar Assn., Dallas Bar Assn. (real estate group), Tex. Coll. Real Estate Lawyers, Real Estate Coun., Salesmanship Club Dallas, Royal Oaks Country Club. Democrat. Presbyterian. Home: 6681 Crest Way Ct Dallas TX 75230 Office: Winstead Sechrest & Minick 5400 Renaissance Tower 1201 Elm St Dallas TX 75270

NOLAN, JOHN THOMAS, JR., retired oil industry administrator; b. Boston, Apr. 15, 1930; s. John T. Sr. and Margaret M. (Craig) N.; m. Mary Sharkey, May 7, 1955; children: Anne, Margaret, John T. III, Stephen, Michael. AB, Cath. U. Am., 1951; PhD, MIT, 1955. Chemist Texaco, Inc., Beacon, N.Y., 1955-59; group leader Texaco, Inc., Beacon, 1959-69, supr., 1969-79, asst. mgr., 1979-82, assoc. dir., 1982-87, dir. strategic rsch., 1987-92; mem. adv. bd. Dutchess County Sci. Fair, Poughkeepsie, N.Y., 1990—. Contbr. over 5 articles to profl. jours. Mem. blue ribbon panel Beacon Sch. Dist., 1987-92; chmn. bd. Dutchess C.C. Found., Poughkeepsie, 1989-92, chmn. planning com., 1992—. Mem. AAAS, Am. Chem. Soc., Greater So. Dutchess C. of C. (bd. dirs. 1989-92), Sigma Xi, Phi Beta Kappa. Achievements include patents in field. Home: 18 Relyea Ter Wappingers Falls NY 12590-5824

NOLAN, JOSEPH THOMAS, journalism educator, communications consultant; b. Waterbury, Conn., Apr. 11, 1920; s. Thomas Francis and Mary Margaret (Gaffney) N.; m. Virginia Theodate Tappin, May 6, 1943; children—Carol Nolan Rigolot, David J. A.B., Holy Cross Coll., 1942; MA in English Lit., Boston U., 1945; Ph.D. in Econs, NYU, 1973. Washington corr. UPI, 1943-49; writer, copy editor N.Y. Times, N.Y.C., 1949-55; mgr. editorial and press services RCA Corp., N.Y.C., 1955-62; sr. v.p. corporate communications Chase Manhattan Bank, N.Y.C., 1962-74; prof. journalism and pub. affairs U. S.C., Columbia, 1974-76; v.p. pub. affairs Monsanto Co., St. Louis, 1976-85; Gannett vis. prof. communications U. Fla., 1985-86; prof. communications U. North Fla., Jacksonville, 1986-92; adj. prof. bus. and comm. Flagler Coll., St. Augustine, Fla., 1992—. Contbr. articles to various mags. Fellow Pub. Rels. Soc. Am. Roman Catholic. Home: 30 Park Terrace Dr Saint Augustine FL 32084-5334

NOLAN, PATRICIA A., public health officer. MD, McGill U., Montreal, Que., Can., 1969; MPH, Columbia U., 1973. Cert. in pub. health Am. Bd. Prevention Medicine. Local pub. health adminstr. N.Y.C., Tucson, Ariz.; med. adminstr. Ariz. Health Care Cost Containment Sys.; state pub. health adminstr. Ill.; exec. dir. Colo. Dept. Pub. Health and Environ.; dir. R.I. Health Dept., 1995—; adj. prof. several med. schs. Mem. APHA. Office: RI Health Dept 3 Capitol Hill Providence RI 02908-5097

NOLAN, PATRICK JOSEPH, screenwriter, playwright, educator; b. Bronx, N.Y., Jan. 2, 1933; s. Patrick John and Catherine Katrina (O'Malley) N.; children: Patrick, Christian, Mark. BA, Villanova U., 1955; MA, U. Detroit, 1961; PhD, Bryn Mawr Coll., 1973. Teaching fellow and mem. faculty dept. English U. Detroit, 1959-62; instr. English Villanova (Pa.) U., 1962-80, prof., 1980—. TV playwright: The Hourglass Moment, 1968-69; playwright: Chameleons, 1980, Midnight Rainbows, 1991; TV screenwriter: The Hourglass Moment, 1968, The Jericho Mile, 1979 (Emmy award). Served to lt. (j.g.) USNR, 1955-59, PTO. Recipient teaching excellence award Philadelphia mag., 1980, Alumni Medallion award Villanova U., 1986. Mem. Writers Guild Am. (West chpt.), Dramatists Guild. Roman Catholic. Avocations: swimming, biking. Office: Dept English Villanova U Villanova PA 19085

NOLAN, PETER JOHN, physics educator; b. N.Y.C., Mar. 25, 1934; s. Peter John and Nora (Gleeson) N.; divorced 1978; children: Thomas, James, John, Kevin. BS in Physics, Manhattan Coll., 1956; cert. in meteorology, UCLA, 1958; MS in Physics, Adelphi U., 1966, PhD in Physics, 1974. Engr. various corps., N.J., N.Y., 1956-63; systems analysis engr. on lunar module Gruman Aircraft Engring. Corp., Bethpage, N.Y., 1963-66; asst. prof. Physics SUNY, Farmingdale, 1966-68, assoc. prof. Physics, 1968-71, prof. Physics, 1971—; chmn. Physics dept. SUNY, Farmingdale, 1970-77. Author: Experiments in Physics, 1982, 2d edit. 1995, Fundamentals of College Physics, 1993, 2d. edit. 1995, Electromagnetic Theory for Electrical Technology Students. Mem. Am. Assn. Physics Tchrs. Home: 47 Fairdale Dr Brentwood NY 11717-1337 Office: SUNY Dept Physics Farmingdale NY 11735

NOLAN, RICHARD THOMAS, clergyman, educator; b. Waltham, Mass., May 30, 1937; s. Thomas Michael and Elizabeth Louise (Leishman) N.; life ptnr. Robert C. Pingpank, Sept. 14, 1955. BA, Trinity Coll., 1960; cert. in clin. pastoral edn., Conn. Valley Hosp., 1962; diploma, Berkeley Divinity Sch., 1962; MDiv., Hartford Sem. Found., 1963; postgrad., Union Theol. Sem., N.Y.C., 1963; MA in Religion, Yale U., 1967; PhD, NYU, 1973; post doctoral, Harvard U., 1991. Ordained deacon Episcopal Ch., 1963, priest, 1965. Instr. Latin and English Watkinson (Conn.) Sch., 1961-62; instr. math. Choir Sch. of Cathedral of St. John the Divine, N.Y.C., 1962-64; instr. math. and religion, assoc. chaplain Cheshire (Conn.) Acad., 1965-67; instr. Hartford (Conn.) Sem. Found., 1967-68, asst. acad. dean, lectr. philosophy and edn., 1968-70; instr. Mattatuck C.C., Waterbury, Conn., 1969-70, asst. prof. philosophy and history, 1970-74, assoc. prof., 1974-78, prof. philosophy and social sci., 1978-92, prof. emeritus, 1992—; rsch. fellow in med. ethics Yale U., 1978, rsch. fellow in profl. and bus. ethics, 1987; vicar St. Paul's Parish, Bantam, Conn., 1974-88; pastor emeritus St. Paul's Parish, Bantam, 1988—; pres. Litchfield Inst., Conn. and Fla., 1984-96; mem. ethics com. Waterbury Hosp. Health Ctr., 1984-88; vis. and adj. prof. philosophy, theology and religious studies Trinity Coll., Conn., L.I. U., U. Miami, St. Joseph Coll., Conn., Pace U., Teikyo Post U., U. Conn., Hartford Grad. Ctr., Ctrl. Conn. State U., Barry U., Fla., Broward C.C., Fla., 1964-95; adj. assoc. in continuing edn. Berkeley Div. Sch. Yale U., 1987-89; Rabbi Harry Halpern Meml. lectr., Southbury, Conn., 1987; guest spkr. various chs. and orgns. including Cathedral of St. John the Divine, N.Y. and Trinity Cathedral, Miami; mem. faculty of consulting examiners Charter Oak State Coll., Conn., 1990-93; fellow Associated Fellows for Counseling and Psychotherapy, Inc., 1990-93; assoc. for edn. Christ Ch. Cathedral, Hartford, Conn., 1988-94, hon. canon, 1991—; cons. Dept. Def. Activity Non-Traditional Ednl. Support, Ednl. Testing Svcs., Princeton, 1990; vis. scholar Coll. Preachers Washington Nat. Cathedral, 1994; retired assisting priest Episcopal Ch. of Bethesda-by-the-Sea, Palm Beach, Fla., 1994—. Author: (with H. Titus and M. Smith) Living Issues in Philosophy, 7th edit., 1979, Indonesian edit., 1984, 8th edit., 1986, 9th edit., 1995, (with F. Kirkpatrick) Living Issues in Ethics, 1982; editor, contbr. Diaconate Now, 1968; host Conversations with ..., 1987-89. Founding mem. The Heritage Soc. of The Episcopal Ch. of Bethesda-by-the-Sea, Palm Beach. Mem. Am. Acad. Religion, Am. Philos. Assn., Authors Guild, Hemlock Soc., Boston Latin Sch. Alumni Assn., Tabor Acad. Alumni Assn., Cavalier King Charles Spaniel Club, Phi Delta Kappa. Avocation: Cavalier King Charles Spaniels. Home: 6342 Forest Hill Blvd # 350 West Palm Beach FL 33415-6158 *Who am I? By baptism I am a resurrected child of God born to love and be loved: my pilgrimage among others is lived within this baptismal identity, more enduring than any achievement.*

NOLAN, ROBERT, management consulting company executive; b. Hartford, Conn., Oct. 13, 1933; s. Robert Emmett and Marian (Sobanski) N.; m. Eileen Luke, July 7, 1955; children: Daniel, Kathleen, Michael, Pamela, Mary. BA, U. Conn., 1958. Sr. analyst Aetna Life & Casualty Co., Hartford, 1958-62; v.p. Serge A. Birn Co. Inc., Louisville, 1962-73; chmn., chief exec. officer Robert E. Nolan Co. Inc., Simsbury, Conn., 1973—; sr. examiner Malcolm Baldridge Nat. Quality Award, Gaithersburg, Md., 1988-89. Co-author: Work Measurement in Accounting, 1963, Office Work Measurement, 1970, Improving Productivity through Advanced Office Controls, 1980, White Collar Productivity, 1982. With USAF, 1950-54, Korea. Mem. Am. Soc. for Quality Control, Inst. Indsl. Engrs., Assn. for Systems Mgmt., Adminstrn. Mgmt. Soc. Office: Robert E Nolan Co Inc 90 Hopmeadow St Simsbury CT 06070-2413

NOLAN, STANTON PEELLE, surgeon, educator; b. Washington, May 29, 1933; s. James Parker and Ellen Dubose (Peelle) N.; m. Marion Faro, June 16, 1955; children—Stanton Peelle Jr., Tiphanie Ravenel. B.A., Princeton U., 1955; M.D., U. Va., 1959, M.S., 1962. Cert. Am. Bd. Surgery, Am. Bd. Thoracic Surgery. Intern U. Va. Med. Ctr., Charlottesville, 1959-60, asst. resident gen. surgery, 1960-61, research fellow surgery, 1961-62, sr. asst. resident gen. surgery, 1962-64, chief resident gen surgery, 1964-65, chief resident thoracic cardiovascular surgery, 1965-66; sr. rsch. assoc. Clinic of Surgery Nat. Heart Inst., NIH, Bethesda, Md., 1966-68; asst. prof. surgery U. Va. Med. Ctr., Charlottesville, 1968-70, assoc. prof. surgery, 1970-74, surgeon in charge div. thoracic cardiovascular surgery, 1970-93, prof. surgery, 1974—, Claude A. Jessup prof. surgery, 1981—, med. dir. Thoracic Cardiovascular post-operative unit, 1989-93; established investigator Am. Heart Assn., 1969-74; mem. surgery A study sect. NIH, Washington, 1972-76, surgery and bioengring. study sect. 1984-87, chmn. 1985-87; cons. thoracic cardiovascular surgery VA Hosp., Salem, Va., 1968—, Am. Bd. Surgery to qualifying examination com., 1988-91; surg. cons. Bur. Crippled Children, Charlottesville, 1968—; vis. cons. cardiothoracic surgery Aga Khan U., Karachi, Pakistan, 1995. Mem. editl. bd. Jour. Surg. Rsch., 1973-79, Annals of Thoracic Surgery, 1979-88; mem. sci. adv. bd. Jour. for Heart Valve Disease, 1993-94; mem. editl. adv. bd. ECRI Operating Rm. Risk Mgmt., 1992—; co-editor: Comprehensive Thoracic Surgery Curriculum, TSDA, 1995; contbr. numerous articles to profl. jours., chpts. to books. Recipient John Horsley Meml. prize U. Va. Med. Sch., 1962; Merit award Research Forum of Am. Coll. Chest Physicians, 1968; research fellow Va. Heart Assn., 1961-62, Am. Cancer Soc., 1963-64; grantee NIH, 1968-84, Am. Heart Assn., 1970-73, Medtronic Corp., 1975-81. Fellow ACS, Am. Coll. Cardiology, Am. Surg. Assn.; mem. Am. Assn. Thoracic Surgery (rep. to Assn. Am. Med. Colls., Am. Bd. Cardiovascular Perfusion, Am. Soc. Extracorporeal Tech., others), Am. Heart Assn. (coun. on cardiovascular surgery 1969—, anesthesiology, radiology and surgery study com. 1991-94), Andrew G. Morrow Soc., Assn. Acad. Surgery, Assn. Advancement of Med. Instrumentation (chair-elect 1996, co-chmn. cardiac valve prostheses stds. com. 1974—, mem. internat. stds. com. 1989—, bd. dirs. 1990—, stds. bd. 1991-94, edn. com. 1992-93), Internat. Stds. Orgn. (chmn. subcom. on cardiovascular surg. implants 1982—), Assn. Clin. Cardiac Surgeons, Halsted Soc. (exec. com. 1985-89), Coord. Com. on Perfusion Affairs (chmn. 1990—), Internat. Assn. Cardiac Biol. Implants (sci. com. 1994), Internat. Cardiovascular Soc., Muller Surg. Soc. (pres. 1979), Soc. Internat. de Cirurgie, Soc. Vascular Surgery, Soc. Thoracic Surgeons (ad hoc com. on industry rels. 1992—, stds. and ethics com. 1993-95, edn. and resources com. 1996—), Soc. Univ. Surgeons, Southeastern Surg. Congress, So. Surg. Assn. (2d v.p. 1982), Va. Surg. Soc. (v.p. 1980-83, pres. 1984), Va. Vascular Soc. (exec. com. 1985-86), Soc. Critical Care Medicine, Raven Soc., Assn. Am. Med. Colls. (rep. coun. acad. socs. 1992—), Alpha Omega Alpha, Omicron Delta Kappa. Clubs: Chevy Chase (Md.); Farmington Country (Va.); Princeton (N.Y.C.). Office: U Va Dept Surgery Box 181-6 Charlottesville VA 22908

NOLAN, TERRANCE JOSEPH, JR., lawyer; b. Bklyn., Mar. 29, 1950; s. Terrance Joseph Sr. and Antonia (Pontecorvo) N.; m. Irene M. Rush, Aug. 2, 1980; children: Maryjane Frances, David Anthony. BA, St. Francis Coll., Bklyn., 1971; JD, St. Johns U., Jamaica, N.Y., 1974; LLM, NYU, 1982. Bar: N.Y. 1975, U.S. Dist. Ct. (ea. and so. dists.) N.Y. 1975, U.S. Ct. Appeals (2d cir.) 1975, U.S. Supreme Ct. 1980. Atty. N.Y.C. Transit Authority, Bklyn., 1974-77; specialist labor rels. Pepsi-Cola Co., Purchase, N.Y., 1977-80; asst. gen. counsel, assoc. dir. labor rels. NYU, N.Y.C., 1980-89, assoc. gen. counsel, dep. dir. labor rels., 1989—. Mem. Am. Corp. Coun. Assn., N.Y. State Bar Assn., Indsl. Rels. Rsch. Assn., Nat. Assn. Coll. and Univ. Attys., Met. Arbitration Group. Home: 41 Russell St Lynbrook NY 11563-1135 Office: NYU 70 Washington Sq S New York NY 10012-1019

NOLAN, THEODORE JOHN, professional hockey coach; b. Sault Ste. Marie, Ont., Can., Apr. 7, 1958. Center Detroit Red Wings, 1978-85, Buffalo (N.Y.) Sabres, 1985, Pitts. Penguins, 1985-86, Buffalo Sabres, 1986; asst. coach Hartford (Conn.) Whalers, 1994-95; head coach Buffalo Sabres, 1995—. Office: Memorial Auditorium 140 Main St Buffalo NY 14202*

NOLAN, VAL, JR., biologist, lawyer; b. Evansville, Ind., Apr. 28, 1920; s. Val and Jeannette (Covert) N.; m. Susanne Howe, Dec. 23, 1946 (div. Aug. 29, 1980); children: Val, Ann Clare, William Alan; m. Ellen D. Ketterson, Oct. 17, 1980. A.B., Ind. U., 1941, J.D., 1949. Bar: Ind. 1949. Dep. U.S. marshal, 1941; agt. White House Detail, U.S. Secret Service, 1942; asst. prof. law Ind. U., 1949-52, assoc. prof., 1952-56, prof., 1956-85, prof. emeritus, 1985—, research scholar in zoology, 1957-68, prof. zoology, 1968-77, prof. biology, 1977-85; prof. emeritus, 1985—, acting dean Sch. Law, 1976, 80. Author: (with F.E. Horack, Jr.) Land Use Controls, 1955, Ecology and Behavior of the Prairie Warbler, 1978; editor Ind. Law Jour., 1945-46; co-editor Current Ornithology, 1994—. Served with USNR, 1942-46. Guggenheim fellow, 1957; recipient Ind. U. Disting. Alumni Svc. award, 1987; named to Acad. Law Alumni Fellows, Ind. U., 1988. Fellow AAAS, Am. Ornithologists Union (v.p. 1989-90, Brewster Meml. award 1986); mem. Brit. Ornithologists Union, Cooper Ornithol. Soc., Wilson Ornithol. Soc., Assn. Field Ornithologists, Ecol. Soc. Am., Am. Soc. Naturalists, Animal Behavior Soc., Deutsche Ornithologen-Gesellschaft, Nederlandse Ornithologische Unie, Soc. for Study of Reprodn., Phi Beta Kappa, Sigma Xi. Democrat. Home: 4675 E Heritage Woods Rd Bloomington IN 47401-9312

NOLAN, VICTORIA, theater director; b. Portland, Maine, June 15, 1952; d. Herbert Wallace and Diane Katharine (Kremm) N.; m. Clarkson Newell Crolius, Aug. 30, 1980; children: Covey Emmeline, Wilhelmina Adams. BA magna cum laude, U. Maine, 1976. Publicity asst. Loeb Drama Ctr. Harvard U., Cambridge, Mass., 1975; pub. rels. asst. to dir. Sch. for Arts Boston U., 1975-76; mgmt. asst. TAG Found., N.Y.C., 1976-77; mng. dir. Ram Island Dance Co., Portland, 1977-78; dir. devel. Ctr. Stage, Balt., 1979-81, assoc. mng. dir., 1981-87; mng. dir. Ind. Repertory Theatre, Indpls., 1988-93; mng. dir., assoc. prof. Yale Sch. Drama, Yale Repertory Theatre, New Haven, 1993—; cons. Fedn. for Ext. and Devel. Am. Profl. Theatre, N.Y.C., 1979-87; program evaluator Nat. Endowment for Arts, Washington, 1988—, panelist, 1991-95; mem. Indpls. Cultural Consortium, v.p., 1991-93; bd. dirs. Greater Indpls. Progress Com., Indpls. Urban League, Arts Coun. Indpls.; mem. nat. bd. Theatre Comm. Group, N.Y.C., treas., 1995—. Mem. exec. com. League Resident Profl. Theatres. Nat. Performing Arts Mgmt. fellow Exxon, Doner Fedn. and NEA, 1978. Home: 120 Rimmon Rd Woodbridge CT 06525-1915 Office: Yale Repertory Theater PO Box 208244 Yale Station 222 York St New Haven CT 06520-8244

NOLAN, WILLIAM JOSEPH, III, banker; b. N.Y.C., Apr. 6, 1947; s. William J. Jr. and Alice Nettleton (Edwards) N.; m. Wendy Collison French, Mar. 21, 1981; children: William J. IV, Anina Chrysler. Student, Hackley Sch., Tarrytown, N.Y., 1958-65; E.S.U. scholar, Eastbourne Coll., U.K., 1966; BA, Colgate U., 1970; MBA, Stanford U., 1973. V.p. Bankers Trust Co., N.Y.C., 1973-83; mng. dir. Becker-Paribas, N.Y.C., 1983-84, PaineWebber, N.Y.C., 1984—. Mem. Pub. Securities Assn. (money market exec. com. 1985-89, chmn. 1987, bd. dirs. 1988-91, treas. 1990), Adirondack League, Piping Rock Club, Union Club of N.Y.C. Home: 1088 Park Ave New York NY 10128-1132 Office: PaineWebber Inc 1285 6th Ave New York NY 10019-6028

NOLAND, CHRISTINE A., magistrate judge. BA, La. State Univ., JD. Law clk. to Hon. John V. Parker U.S. Dist. Ct. (La. mid. dist.), 5th circuit; magistrate judge U.S. Dist. Ct. (La. mid. dist.), 5th circuit, Baton Rouge, 1987—. Mem. ABA, La. State Bar, La. trial Lawyers Assn., Baton Rouge Bar Assn., Dean Henry George McMahon Inn of Ct. (counselor). Office: Russell B Long Fed Bldg & Courthouse 777 Florida St Rm 265 Baton Rouge LA 70801-1717

NOLAND, GARY LLOYD, vocation educational administrator; b. Lindsborg, Kans., July 29, 1942; s. Willard L. and Florence L. (Waggoner) N.; m. Deborah L. Homan, Mar. 20, 1981; children: Krista L., Timothy L. BSBA, Cen. Mo. State U., 1971, MEd, 1974. Cert. vocat. dir., Mo. V.p. sales First Nat. Land Co., Scottsdale, Ariz., 1961-66; student grad. asst. Cen. Mo. State U., Warrensburg, 1968-72; instr. State Fair CC., Sedalia, Mo., 1972-74, dir. job placement, 1974-79; dir. Statewide Job Placement Svc., Sedalia, 1979-84, State Fair Area Vocat. Sch., Sedalia, 1984—; dir. State Fair C.C. Found., Sedalia, 1986—; mgr. State Fair Coll. Farm, Sedalia, 1987-92. Author: Help Yourself to Successful Employment, 1980; author instructional modules. mem., chmn. ctrl. Mo. chpt. March of Dimes, Sedalia, 1979; v.p. Pettis County Farm Bur., Sedalia, 1987-91, pres., 1991-95; bd. dirs. Mo. Farm Bur., 1995—, Am. Cancer Soc., Sedalia, 1989-92. Named Outstanding Young Man Am., 1979, Outstanding Placement Specialist, Mo. Guidance and Placement, 1980, Outstanding Vocat. Program Area VII, U.S. Dept. Edn., 1982. Mem. VFW (life), Am. Simmental Assn., Am. Legion, Mo. Coun. Local Adminstrs., Mo. Assn. Secondary Prins., Mo. Cattleman's Assn., Pettis County Cattleman's Assn., Lions (pres. Sedalia 1979-80), Masons, Sedalia Area C. of C. (amb. 1975-92). Baptist. Avocations: farming, golfing, fishing. Home: 19776 Ridge Crest Pl Sedalia MO 65301-2199 Office: State Fair Area Vocat Sch 3201 W 16th St Sedalia MO 65301-2188

NOLAND, KENNETH CLIFTON, artist; b. Asheville, N.C., Apr. 10, 1924; s. Harry C. and Bessie (Elkins) N.; m. Cornelia Langer (div.); children: Cady, William L., Lyndon; m. Stephanie Gordon, 1967 (div.); m. Peggy Schiffer; children: Samuel Jesse (div.); m. Paige Rense, 1994. Student, Ozzip Zadkine, Paris, 1948-49; studied, Black Mountain Coll., N.C., summers, 1950, 51. Tchr. Inst. Contemporary Arts, 1950-52, Cath. U., 1951-60. One man shows include Galerie Creuze, Paris, 1949, Tibor de Nagy Gallery, N.Y.C., 1957, 58, Jefferson Pl. Gallery, 1958, French & Co., N.Y.C., 1959, Bennington Coll., 1961, Andre Emmerich Gallery, N.Y.C., 15 shows from 1960-83, Andre Emmerich Gallery, Zurich, Switzerland, 1973, 76, 79, 82, David Mirvish Gallery, Toronto, Can., 1965, 67, 74, 76, Jewish Mus., 1965, Salander O'Reilly Galleries, N.Y.C., 1989, also other galleries in Milan, Italy, Paris, Zurich, Dusseldorf, Hamburg and Cologne, Fed. Republic Germany, London, Montreal and Toronto, Can.; retrospective show Guggenheim Mus., N.Y.C., 1977; group shows include Kootz Gallery, N.Y.C., 1954, Norman Mackenzie Art Gallery, Regina, Sask., Can., 1963, Corcoran Gallery, Washington, 1956, 59, 63, 64, 67, 70, 75, Corcoran Gallery Biennial in Italy, 1964, Fogg Art Mus., Cambridge, Mass., 1965, 72, Mus. Modern Art, N.Y.C., 1965, 68, Nat. Gallery, Washington, 1968, U.S. Pavilion Expo 67, Montreal, Art Inst. Chgo., 1962, 70, 72, 76, Balt. Mus., 1957, 70, 77, Jewish Mus., 1963, Tate Gallery, London, 1964, 74, Guggenheim Mus., 1961, 66, 70, 73-74, 76-77, L.A. County Mus., 1964, Inst. Contemporary Art, Boston, 1964, 65, 67, Whitney Mus., N.Y.C., 1961-67, 69-73, 76, Met. Mus. N.Y.C., 1968, 70, Mus. Fine Arts, Boston, 1972, Albright-Knox Gallery, Buffalo, 1978, 80; represented in permanent collections Salander O'Reily Galleries, N.Y.C. Trustee Bennington (Vt.) Coll. Recipient 1st prize Premio Nacional Internat., Inst. Torcuato de Tella, Buenos Aires, 1964, Creative Arts award Brandeis U., 1965, 4th prize Corcoran Biennale, 1967. Home: Hall Farm RR 1 Box 45 North Bennington VT 05257-9703

NOLAND, MARCUS, economist, educator; b. Greensboro, N.C., Mar. 29, 1959. BA, Swarthmore Coll., 1981; PhD, Johns Hopkins U., 1985. Sr. fellow Inst. for Internat. Econs., Washington, 1985—; asst. prof. U. So. Calif., L.A., 1990-91; sr. economist Coun. Econ. Advisers, Washington, 1993-94; vis. prof. Saitama U., Urawa, Japan, 1988-89; vis. scholar Korea Devel. Inst., Swoul, 1991; vis. assoc. prof. Johns Hopkins U., Balt., 1991—; vis. prof. Tokyo U., 1996; cons. N.Y. Stock Exch., 1990, Adv. Com. on Trade Policy, Washington, 1989-92, World Bank, Washington, 1990—. Author: Pacific Basin Developing Countries, 1991; co-author: Japan in the World Economy, 1988, Reconcilable Differences?, 1993; co-editor: Pacific Economic Dynamism, 1993. Japan Soc. for Promotion of Sci. fellow, 1988; Internat. Affairs fellow Coun. on Fgn. Rels., 1993. Mem. Coun. on Fgn. Rels. Office: Inst for Internat Econs 11 Dupont Cir NW Washington DC 20036-1207

NOLAND, ROBERT LEROY, retired manufacturing company executive; b. Lawrence, Kans., Sept. 7, 1918; s. Harry L. and Angela (Scola) N.; m. Delpha Mae Mierndorf, June 16, 1962; children: Gary, Fabra Jeanine, Derice Elizabeth. B.S. in Mech. Engring, Calif. Inst. Tech., 1941. Design and devel. rocket propelled devices Calif. Inst. Tech., 1941-45; supr. propulsions Naval Ordnance Test Sta., China Lake, Calif., 1945-46; asst. chief engr. Aerojet Gen. Corp., 1946-52; cons. engr. plastic components, rockets and missiles, 1952-54; exec. v.p. Rienhold Engring. and Plastics Co., 1954-57, pres., 1957-59; exec. v.p. Haveg Industries, Wilmington, Del., 1959-66; exec. v.p. Ametek, Inc., Paoli, Pa., 1966-68, pres., bd. dirs., 1968-88; pres., chief exec. officer, dir. Ketema Inc., Bensalem, Pa., 1988-92; ret., ret., 1992; chmn. bd. Myricom, 1994—. Home: 5555 Eastlake Blvd Carson City NV 89704-9266

NOLAND, ROYCE PAUL, association executive, physical therapist; b. Walla Walla, Wash., Dec. 6, 1928; s. Homer Vernon and Mildred Bessie (Royce) N.; m. April Lynn Hawkes, Feb. 10, 1979; children—Royce Paul, Richard Mitchell. B.A., Whitman Coll., Walla Walla, Wash., 1951; Cert. in phys. therapy, Stanford U., 1952. Pvt. practice in phys. therapy Santa Cruz, Calif., 1961-68; exec. dir. Calif. chpt. Am. Phys. Therapy Assn., Santa Cruz, Calif., 1965-69; exec. dir. Am. Phys. Therapy Assn., Washington, D.C., 1969-87; pres., chief exec. officer Inst. Profl. Health Service Adminstrs., Alexandria, 1988-91; exec. dir., CEO Fedn. of State Bds. of Phys. Therapy, Arlington, Va., 1992—. Co-inventor phys. therapy device; contbr. articles to profl. publs. Mem. Am. Soc. Assn. Execs. (cert.), Presdl. Commn. Employment of Handicapped, Am. Pub. Health Assn. Republican. Club: Belle Haven Country (Alexandria). Avocation: golf. Home: 2302 Popkins Ln Alexandria VA 22306-2443 Office: Fedn of State Bds of Phys Therapy 2231 Crystal Dr Ste 500 Arlington VA 22202-3711

NOLD, CARL RICHARD, state historic parks and museums administrator; b. Mineola, N.Y., Nov. 26, 1955; s. Carl Frederick and Joan Catherine (Heine) N.; m. Mary Beth Krivoruchka (div.). BA in History magna cum laude, St. John's U., Jamaica, N.Y., 1977; MA in History Mus. Studies, SUNY, Oneonta, 1982. Pres. Gregory Mus., Hicksville, N.Y., 1977; registrar N.Y. State Hist. Assn., Cooperstown, 1978-80; dir., curator Gadsby's Tavern Mus., Alexandria, Va., 1980-84; dir. State Mus. Pa., Harrisburg, 1984-91; exec. dir. Mackinac State Hist. Parks, Lansing, Mackinac Island, Mich., 1992—; grant reviewer Inst. Mus. Svcs., Washington, 1982-90, 95—, mus. assessment prog. reviewer, 1985—, panelist, 1992-94; panelist mus. grant prog. Nat. Endowment for Humanities, 1990-93. Co-author: Gadsby's Tavern Mus. Interpretive Master Plan, 1984; contbr. articles to profl. jours. Mem. adv. bd. for Grad. History George Mason U., Fairfax, Va., 1982-84, adv. com. Susquehanna Mus. Art, Harrisburg, 189-91; bd. dirs. Harrisburg-Hershey-Carlisle Tourism and Visitor Bur., 1987-91, bd. sec., 1990-91; mem. mayor's adv. bd. city of Mackinac Island, 1993—. Mem. Midwest Mus. Assn., Mich. Mus. Assn. (bd. dirs. 1995—), Am. Assn. Mus. (vis. com. mus. accreditation 1989—), Am. Assn. for State and Local History (elections chmn. 1990), Cooperstown Grad. Assn. (bd. dirs. 1985-87).

NOLEN, JERRY AFTEN, JR., physicist; b. Washington, Nov. 17, 1940; s. Jerry Aften and Roxie Ann (Stout) N.; m. Geraldine Janet Meads, Oct. 4, 1980; children by previous marriage: Greer Roxanne, Joyce Lynne, Paige Hamilton; stepchildren: Jeffrey Brian, Tara Leigh, Christopher Allen. BS, Lehigh U., 1961; PhD, Princeton U., 1965. Instr. Princeton (N.J.) U., 1965-66; postdoctoral appointee Argonne (Ill.) Nat. Lab., 1966-68; asst. prof. U. Md., College Park, 1968-70; assoc. prof. Mich. State U., East Lansing, 1970-76; prof. physics Mich. State U., 1976-92, assoc. dir. Nat. Superconducting Cyclotron Lab, 1984-92; Max Planck fellow Heidelberg, Ger., 1977; dir. Atlas Argonne Nat. Lab., Argonne, Ill., 1992—. Contbr. articles to profl. jours.; editor: (with W. Benenson) Atomic Masses and Fundamental Constants, 1980. Woodrow Wilson grad. fellow, 1961-62. Fellow Am. Phys. Soc. (mem. exec. com. div. nuclear physics 1989-91); mem. Sigma Xi, Phi Beta Kappa, Tau Beta Pi. Home: # 4104 950 N Michigan Ave Chicago IL 60611 Office: Argonne Nat Lab Physics Div Bldg 203 Argonne IL 60439

NOLEN, ROY LEMUEL, lawyer; b. Montgomery, Ala., Nov. 29, 1937; s. Roy Lemuel Jr. and Elizabeth (Larkin) N.; m. Evelyn McNeill Thomas, Aug. 28, 1965; 1 child, Rives Rutledge. BArch, Rice U., 1961; LLB, Harvard U., 1967. Bar: Tex. 1968, U.S. Ct. Appeals (5th cir.) 1969. Law clk. to sr. judge U.S. Ct. Appeals (5th cir.), 1967-68; assoc. Baker & Botts, Houston, 1968-75, ptnr., 1976—; co-head Corp. Dept., 1985-90, mem. exec. com., 1988-91. Bd. dirs. Houston Ballet Found., 1980-92, Rice Design Alliance, 1995-96; exec. com. Contemporary Arts Mus., 1990-96; exec. com., gen. counsel Houston Symphony Soc., 1994—; sr. warden Christ Ch. Cathedral, 1991-92. 1st lt. USMC, 1961-64. Mem. ABA, State Bar of Tex., Houston Bar Assn., Coronado Club, Allegro, Paul Jones Club. Episcopalian. Office: Baker & Botts 3000 One Shell Plz 910 Louisiana St Houston TX 77002

NOLEN, WILFRED E., church administrator. Pres. Brethren Benefit Trust. Office: 1505 Dundee Ave Elgin IL 60120-1619

NOLEN, WILLIAM GILES, lawyer, accountant; b. Fayetteville, Ark., Aug. 4, 1931; s. William Jefferson and Marie (Giles) N.; m. Carole Turner, Aug. 25, 1957; children: Kathy, Thomas. B.S.B.A., U. Ark., 1960; J.D., U. Houston, 1980. Bar: Tex. 1980; C.P.A., Tex. Auditor Arthur Anderson & Co., Houston, 1960-66; sec., treas. Brown & Root (U.K.) Ltd., London, 1966-69; v.p. Highlands Ins. Co., Houston, 1969-73, sr. v.p., 1973-80, dir., 1973-88; v.p. Halliburton Co., Dallas, 1980-82; sr. v.p. Brown & Root, Inc., Houston, 1982-86; exec. v.p. Highlands Ins. Co., Houston, 1986-88; of counsel Whitmore, Sheppard & Pollicoff, Houston, 1988-92, Policoff, Smith & Myres LLP, Houston, 1992—. Maj. USAF, 1951-56. Mem. ABA, Am. Assn. Atty. CPAs (v.p., bd. dirs.), Tex. Soc. CPAs (Tex. CPA of Yr. 1961), Mensa. Presbyterian.

NOLF, DAVID MANSTAN, financial executive; b. Hartford, Conn., Nov. 25, 1942; s. Richard A. and Erreld I. (Manstan) N.; m. Linda J. Anderson, June 20, 1964; 1 child, Cristina E. BSChemE, Lafayette Coll., 1964; MBA, U. Conn., 1968. Prodn. engr. Am. Cyanamid, Wallingford, Conn., 1664-66; adminstrn. supr. Electric Boat Div. Gen. Dynamics, Groton, Conn., 1966-71; chief fin. and adminstrv. officer, corp. sec. Analysis and Tech. Inc., North Stonington, Conn., 1971—; bd. dirs. Analysis and Tech., Inc., North Stonington, Conn., Applied Sci. Assocs., Butler, Pa., Integrated Performance Decisions, Inc., North Stonington. Sec. Sch. Bldg. Com., Stonington, 1989-92; chmn. Ch. Fin. Com., Westerly, R.I., 1996—; trustee Westerly Hosp., 1993—. Mem. Nat. Contract Mgmt. Assn., Am. Mgmt. Assn., Def. Preparedness Assn., Tau Bet Pi, Beta Gamma Sigma. Avocations: fishing, golf. Home: 11 Meadow Rd Pawcatuck CT 06379-2013 Office: Analysis & Tech Inc Technology Park PO Box 220 North Stonington CT 06359-9801

NOLL, ANNA CECILIA, curator; b. Alexandria, Va., July 22, 1950; d. Louis Richard and Barbara Lucille (Curtice) N. BS in Psychology, Va. Poly. Inst. and State Univ., 1974; MA in Art History, George Washington U., 1983. Asst. curator Queens Mus., Flushing, N.Y., 1984-86; curator Fort Wayne (Ind.) Mus. Art, 1986-89, Heckscher Mus., Huntington, N.Y., 1989-95; curator of collections Tacoma Art Mus., 1995—; guest essayist June Kelly Gallery, N.Y.C., 1994, Bernice Steinbaum Gallery, N.Y.C., 1989; mem. benefit com. Ctr. for Book Arts Auction, N.Y.C., 1991. Vol. Gay Men's Health Crisis AIDS Dance-a-thon, N.Y.C., 1990, Cold Spring Harbor (N.Y.) Lab. Centennial Celebration, 1990. Hilla von Rebay fellow Solomon R. Guggenheim Mus., 1981, Univ. fellow George Washington U., 1981-83. Mem. Am. Assn. Mus. (mem. curators com., co-chair exhibit competition 1994-95), Coll. Art Assn. (presenter ann. meeting 1994), Alliance Française. Avocations: garden history, cooking, travel. Office: Heckscher Mus 2 Prime Ave Huntington NY 11743-2741

NOLL, CHARLES HENRY, former professional football coach; b. Cleve., Jan. 5, 1932; m. Marianne Noll; 1 son, Chris. BE, U. Dayton, 1953. Football player Cleve. Browns, 1953-59; asst. coach San Diego Chargers, 1960-65, Balt. Colts, 1966-68; head coach Pitts. Steelers, 1969-91; winner Super Bowl games, 1975-76, 79-80; now admn. advisor Pittsburgh Steelers. Named Am. Football Conf. Coach of Yr., UPI, 1972; inductee Pro Football Hall of Fame, 1993. Office: Pittsburgh Steelers 300 Stadium Cir Pittsburgh PA 15212-5729 Office: The Football Hall of Fame 2121 George Halas Dr NW Canton OH 44708-2630*

NOLL, JOHN F., sales and marketing executive, investment banker; b. Ft. Wayne, Ind., Feb. 2, 1945; s. Martin F. and Viola N.; m. Ann E. Files, Sept. 23, 1972; children: Eric, Scott. BA in Philosophy, Athanaeum of Ohio Coll., 1966; MA in English, Purdue U., 1968; MBA in Mktg., U. of Colo., 1970. From sales rep. to dist. mgr. Procter & Gamble, Cin., 1968-83; v.p. sales Software Distrbn. Svcs., Buffalo, 1983-85; adminstrv. v.p. trusts M&T Bank, Buffalo, 1985-88; dir. sales and mktg. Select Interior Door, Ltd., N. Java, N.Y., 1988-93; dir. corp. fin. Capital Formation Group, 1994—; co-founder, bd. dirs. NORAM Group, Ltd., Buffalo, 1988—; owner Sales Resources, Orchard Park, N.Y., 1989-90. Bd. dirs. Orchard Park Little League, 1973-85, Boys and Girls Club of Orchard Park, 1986-93; bd. dirs., pres. Eagle Ridge Recreation Assn., Orchard Park, 1986-88. Mem. Am. Mktg. Assn., Sales and Mktg. Execs. (bd. dirs. 1989-91), Resource Group (founder, bd. dirs. 1981—), Orchard Park Country Club. Republican. Presbyterian. Avocations: golf, skiing, tennis. Home and Office: 46 Knob Hill Rd Orchard Park NY 14127-3931

NOLL, ROGER GORDON, economist, educator; b. Monterey Park, Calif., Mar. 13, 1940; s. Cecil Ray and Hjordis Alberta (Westover) N.; m. Robyn Schreiber, Aug. 25, 1962; 1 child, Kimberlee Elizabeth. B.S., Calif. Inst. Tech., 1962; A.M., Harvard U., 1965, Ph.D. in Econs, 1967. Mem. social sci. faculty Calif. Inst. Tech., 1965-84, prof., 1973-82, Inst. prof., 1982-84, chmn. div. humanities and social scis., 1978-82; prof. econs. Stanford U., 1984—, dir. pub. policy program, 1986—, Morris M. Doyle centennial prof. of pub. policy, 1990—; Jean Monnet prof. European U. Inst., 1991; vis. fellow Brookings Instn., 1995-96; sr. staff economist Coun. of Econ. Advisors, Washington, 1967-69; sr. fellow Brookings Instn., Washington, 1970-73; mem. tech. adv. bd. Com. for Econ. Devel., 1978-82; mem. adv. coun. NSF, 1978-89, SERI, 1982-90, NASA, 1978-81; mem. Pres.'s Commn. for Nat. Agenda for the Eighties, 1980; chmn. L.A.Sch. Monitoring Com., 1978-79; mem. Commn. on Behavioral Social Scis. and Edn., NAS, 1984-90; mem. energy rsch. adv. bd. Dept. Energy, 1986-89; mem. Sec. of Energy Adv. Bd., 1990-94. Author: Reforming Regulation, 1971, The Economics and Politics of Deregulation, 1991; co-author: Economic Aspects of Television Regulation, 1973, The Political Economy of Deregulation, 1983, The Technology Pork Barrel, 1991; editor: Government and the Sports Business, 1974, Regulatory Policy and the Social Sciences, 1985; co-editor: Constitutional Reform in California, 1995; supervisory editor Info. Econs. and Policy Jour., 1984-92. NSF grantee, 1973-82; Recipient 1st ann. book award Nat. Assn. Ednl. Broadcasters, 1974; Guggenheim fellow, 1983-84. Mem. Am. Econ. Assn. Democrat. Home: 4153 Hubbart Dr Palo Alto CA 94306-3834 Office: Stanford U Dept Econs Stanford CA 94305

NOLLAU, LEE GORDON, lawyer; b. Balt., Feb. 6, 1950; s. E. Wilson and Carolyn G. (Blass) N.; m. Carol A. Haughney, Aug. 12, 1978; children: Ann G., Catherine E., Margaret C. BA, Juniata Coll., 1972; MAS, Johns Hopkins U., 1975; JD, Dickinson Sch. Law, 1976. Bar: Pa. 1976, U.S. Dist. Ct. (mid. dist.) 1982, U.S. Dist. Ct. (we. dist.) 1988, U.S. Ct. Appeals (3d cir.) 1980, U.S. Supreme Ct. 1982. Instr. Juniata Coll., Huntingdon, Pa., 1976-78; asst. dist. atty. Centre County, Bellefonte, Pa., 1978-80, dist. atty., 1981; assoc. Litke, Lee, Martin, Grine & Green, Bellefonte, 1981-83, Jubelirer & Assocs., State College, Pa., 1983-87; ptnr. Jubelirer, Nollau, Young & Blanarik, Inc., State College, 1988-89, Jubelirer, Rayback, Nollau, Walsh, Young & Blanarik, Inc., State College, 1989-94, Nollau & Young, State Coll., Pa., 1994—; mental health rev. officer Centre County, Bellefonte, 1982—; instr. Pa. State U. Smeal Coll. Bus. Adminstrn., 1995—; lectr. Pa. Bar Inst., 1995—. Mem. ABA, Pa. Bar Assn., Centre Co. Bar. Presbyterian. Office: Nollau & Young 2153 East College Ave State College PA 16801

NOLLER, HARRY FRANCIS, JR., biochemist, educator; b. Oakland, Calif., June 10, 1939; s. Harry Francis and Charlotte Frances (Silva) N.; m. Betty Lucille Parnow, Nov. 25, 1964 (div. 1969); 1 child, Maria Irene; m. Sharon Ann Sussman; 1 child, Eric Francis; stepchildren: Django Sussman, Seb Sussman. AB, U. Calif., Berkeley, 1960; PhD, U. Oreg., 1965. Postdoctoral fellow MRC Lab. of Molecular Biology, Cambridge, Eng., 1965-66, Inst. Molecular Biology, Geneva, Switzerland, 1966-68; asst. prof. biology U. Calif., Santa Cruz, 1968-73, assoc. prof., 1973-79, prof. biology, 1979—, Robert Louis Sinsheimer prof. molecular biology, 1987—; Harvey lectr. Rockefeller U., 1989; Sherman Fairchild Disting. scholar, Calif. Inst. Tech., 1990; dir. Ctr. Molecular Biology of RNA, 1992—. Mem. NAS. Office: Sinsheimer Labs U Calif Santa Cruz High St Santa Cruz CA 95064-1099

NOLLETTI, JAMES JOSEPH, lawyer; b. Portchester, N.Y., Sept. 20, 1953; s. James Louis and Anne Marie (Mandracchia) N.; m. Maryann Kathleen Bilka, June 5, 1976; children: Jay, Justin, Jamie-Lynn, Jeff. BA, Villanova U., 1975; JD, Fordham U., 1978. Bar: N.Y. 1979, U.S. Dist. Ct. (so. dist.) N.Y., U.S. Supreme Ct. Asst. dist. atty. Westchester County Dist. Atty.'s Office, White Plains, N.Y., 1978-81; assoc. Sirlin & Sirlin, Mamaroneck, N.Y., 1981-84; ptnr. Sirlin, Sirlin & Nolletti, Mamaroneck, 1984—; village atty. Village of Mamaroneck, 1985—; mem. adv. bd. Westchester Abstract Co., White Plains, 1985-88; bd. dirs., legal advisor Orienta Beach CLUB, iNC., mAMARONECK, 1986-90. Commr. ABC bd. Westchester County, White Plains, 1984-88, Westchester County Pub. Employees Rels. Bd., 1986-88. Mem. N.Y. State Bar Assn., Westchester County Bar Assn., Westchester County Col. Lawyers Bar Assn. (bd. dirs., v.p. 1989-93). Office: Sirlin Sirlin Nolletti 211 Mamaroneck Ave Mamaroneck NY 10543

NOLLY, ROBERT J., hospital administrator, pharmaceutical science educator; b. Amsterdam, N.Y., Jan. 8, 1947; m. Diera R. Lehtonen, June 21, 1969; children: Shelby Alexandra, Kirby Alycia, Kendall Alexis. BS in Pharmacy with honor, Albany Coll. Pharmacy, 1970; MSc in Hosp. Pharmacy, Ohio State U., 1979. Pharmacy extern Matt Pharmacy, Canajoharie, N.Y., 1967-70; pharmacy intern Park Row Drugs, Canajoharie, 1970-71, asst. mgr., 1971-72; staff pharmacist Mary Imogene Bassett Hosp., Cooperstown, N.Y., 1972-74, 75-77; med. svc. rep. Dista Products Co., Eli Lilly and Co., Indpls., 1974-75; resident hosp. pharmacy Grant Hosp., Columbus, Ohio, 1977-79; asst. dir. pharmacy svcs. City of Memphis Hosp., 1979-81; asst. dir. pharmacy svcs. U. Tenn. Bowld Hosp., Memphis, 1980-82, dir. pharmacy svcs. and materials mgmt., 1982-85, asst. adminstr. pharmacy svcs. and materials mgmt., 1985-91, adminstr., 1991—; asst. prof. dept. pharmacy practice Coll. Pharmacy U. Tenn., Memphis, 1979-83, asst. prof. dept. health sci. adminstrn. dept. pharmaceutics, 1983-92, assoc. prof. dept. clin. pharmacy divsn. pharmacy adminstrn., dept. pharm. scis., 1992—; attended confs., mgmt. tng. programs in field; lectr. Columbus Tech. Inst., 1978-79, City of Memphis Hosp., 1980-81; trustee Diversified Svcs., Inc., Tenn. Hosp. Assn., 1990-96, mem. pharmacy adv. com., 1990; bd. dirs. Ava Marie Nursing Home, chmn. nom. com., 1988, 89, mem. long-range planning com., 1989, 90, mem. constn. and by-laws com., 1990, mem. govtl. rels. com., 1991-93; presenter in field. Editor U. Tenn. Bowld Hosp. Pharmacy Newsletter, 1987-91; mem. editl. bd. Drug and Therapeutics Newsletter, U. Tenn. Coll. Pharmacy, 1989, 90. usher Ch. of Holy Spirit, 1988-96; mem. Am. Cancer Soc. Recipient Order of Sword award Am. Cancer Soc., 1992. Mem. Am. Soc. hosp. Pharmacists, Tenn. Soc. Hosp. Pharmacists (mem. com. 1980, constn. and by-laws com. 1985, 88, 89, 90, chmn. nominating com. 1989, orgn. and goals com. 1991, strategic planning com. 1992), Tenn. Pharmacists Assn. (pharmacy tech. task force 1988, 89, 90, ho. dels. 1988, 89, 90, 91, 92, 94, chmn. tech. curriculum com. 1991, tech. edn. accreditation com. 1991, 92, 94), Memphis Area Soc. Hosp. Pharmacists (pres.-elect 1984, pres. 1985, past pres. 1986, chmn. nominating com. 1991), Tenn. Hosp. Assn. (liaison Tenn. Med. Assn. com. 1991), Mid-South Healthcare Materials Mgmt. Assn. (co-chmn. founding orgnl. com. 1991), Kappa Psi, Rho Chi. Home: 2927 Mikeyair Dr Germantown TN 38138-7148 Office: UT Bowld Hosp 951 Court Ave Memphis TN 38103-2813

NOLTE, HENRY R., JR., lawyer, former automobile company executive; b. N.Y.C., Mar. 3, 1924; s. Henry R. and Emily A. (Eisele) N.; m. Frances Messner, May 19, 1951; children: Gwynne Conn, Henry Reed III, Jennifer Stevens, Suzanne. BA, Duke U., 1947; LLB, U. Pa., 1949. Bar: N.Y. 1950, Mich. 1967. Assoc. Cravath, Swaine & Moore, N.Y.C., 1951-61; assoc. counsel Ford Motor Co., Dearborn, Mich., 1961, asst. gen. counsel, 1964-71, assoc. gen. counsel, 1971-74, v.p., gen. counsel, 1974-89; v.p., gen. counsel Philco-Ford Corp., Phila., 1961-64; v.p., gen. counsel, sec. Ford of Europe Inc., Warley, Essex, Eng., 1967-69; gen. counsel fin. and ins. subs. Ford Motor Co., 1974-89; sr. ptnr. Miller, Canfield, Paddock & Stone, Detroit, 1989-93, of counsel, 1993—; bd. dirs. Charter One Fin., Inc. Trustee Cranbrook Ednl. Community; mem. Internat. and Comparative Law Ctr. of Southwestern Legal Found.; bd. dirs. Detroit Symphony Orch.; trustee Beaumont Hosp. Lt. USNR, 1943-46, PTO. Mem. ABA (past chmn. corp. law depts.), Mich. Bar Assn., Assn. Bar City N.Y., Assn. Gen. Counsel, Orchard Lake Country Club, Bloomfield Hills Country Club, Everglades Club (Fla.), Gulfstream Golf Club (Fla.), Ocean Club (Fla.). Episcopalian.

Office: Miller Canfield Paddock & Stone 1400 N Woodward Ave Ste 100 Bloomfield Hills MI 48304-2855

NOLTE, JUDITH ANN, magazine editor; b. Hampton, Iowa, Sept. 17, 1938; d. Clifford P. and Sigrid M. (Johnson) N.; m. Randers H. Heimer, May 7, 1971. BS, U. Minn., 1960; MA in English, NYU, 1965. Tchr. English Middletown (N.Y.) High Sch., 1960-62, High Sch. of Commerce, N.Y.C., 1962-64; merchandising editor Conde Nast Publs., N.Y.C., 1964-69; editor-in-chief Am. Baby Mag., Cahners Pub. Co., N.Y.C., 1969—, Weight Watchers mag., 1980-83; editorial dir. Cahners Childcare Group, N.Y.C., 1990—; hostess Am. Baby Cable TV Show. Chmn. media adv. bd. N.Y. chpt. March of Dimes. Mem. Am. Soc. Mag. Editors (pres. 1986-88), Mortar Bd., Delta Gamma (pres. 1960). Office: Am Baby/Healthly Kids Cahners Publishing Company 249 W 17th St New York NY 10011-5300

NOLTE, NICK, actor; b. Omaha, 1941; m. Rebecca Linger, Feb. 19, 1984 (div. 1995); 1 child, Brawley King. Student, Pasadena City Coll., Phoenix City Coll.; studies with, John Paul, Allen Dutton. Actor: (play) The Last Pad, 1973, (TV movies) Winter Kill, 1974, The California Kid, 1974, Death Sentence, 1974, Adams of Eagle Lake, 1975, The Treasure Chest Murder, 1975, The Runaways, 1975, (mini-series) Rich Man, Poor Man, 1976, (films) The Deep, 1977, Return to Macon County, 1975, Who'll Stop the Rain, 1978, North Dallas Forty, 1979, Heartbead, 1980, Cannery Row, 1982, 48 Hours, 1982, Under Fire, 1983, The Ultimate Solution of Grace Quigley, 1984, Teachers, 1984, Down and Out in Beverly Hills, 1986, Weeds, 1987, Extreme Prejudice, 1987, Farewell to the King, 1988, Three Fugitives, 1988, New York Stories, 1989, Everybody Wins, 1989, Q & A, 1990, Another 48 Hours, 1990, Prince of Tides, 1991, Cape Fear, 1991, Lorenzo's Oil, 1992, Blue Chips, 1994, I'll Do Anything, 1994, I Love Trouble, 1994, Jefferson in Paris, 1995, Mulholland Falls, 1996, Mother Night, 1996. Address: 6153 Bonsall Dr Malibu CA 90265-3824

NOLTE, RICHARD HENRY, political science researcher, consultant; b. Duluth, Minn., Dec. 27, 1920; s. Julius Mosher and Mildred (Miller) N.; m. Jeanne McQuarrie, Mar. 27, 1945; children: Charles McQuarrie, Roger Reed, Douglas Mitchell, Jameson Jay. A.B., Yale, 1943, M.A., 1947; B.A. (Rhodes scholar), Oxford (Eng.) U., 1950, MA, 1954. Inst. Current World Affairs fellow, 1948-54; D.Sc. (hon.), U. Wis., Milw., 1979. Assoc. on Middle East Am. Univs. Field Staff, 1953-58; asst. dir. humanities Rockefeller Found., Inc., N.Y.C., 1958-59; exec. dir. Inst. Current World Affairs, N.Y.C., 1959-78, Alicia Patterson Found., N.Y.C., 1965-78; exec. v.p. Hamilton, Johnston & Co., Inc., N.Y.C., 1978-81; cons. Middle East Dillon, Read & Co., Inc., N.Y.C., 1981-82; assoc. for Middle East HME Internat. Adv. Assocs., Inc., N.Y.C., 1982-90; gen. ptnr. Washburn Island Res. Ltd. Partnership, East Falmouth, Mass., 1981-89; pres. Near East Found., N.Y.C., 1984-87, now bd. dirs.; ambassador to Egypt Cairo, 1967. Editor: The Modern Middle East, 1963. Vice chmn. Stamford Forum for World Affairs; bd. dirs. Pro Bono, Inc., 1994—; hon. trustee Inst. Current World Affairs, 1995—. Pilot USNR, 1943-45. Mem. Am. Geog. Soc. (pres. 1973-80, now chmn. bd.), Nat. Aphasia Assn. (bd. dirs. 1990—, bd. dirs. Fund for Peace 1993—), Coun. on Fgn. Rels., Phi Beta Kappa. Clubs: Yale, Mid-Atlantic. Home and Office: 516 Harvest Commons Westport CT 06880-3950

NOLTE, WALTER EDUARD, retired retirement home executive, foundation counsel, former banker; b. Joplin, Mo., Oct. 28, 1911; s. Ernest Henry and Clara (Meyer) N.; m. Sara Elizabeth Mumford, Oct. 6, 1939 (dec. May 1990); children: Walter Eduard, Craig R. (dec.). AB, U. Nebr., 1934, JD, 1936. Bar: Nebr. 1936, Tex. 1952, U.S. Supreme Ct 1952. With firm Beghtol, Foe & Rankin, Lincoln, Nebr., 1936-48; asst. atty. gen. Neb., 1948-50; dep. atty. gen., 1950-52; pres. Nolte Nat. Bank, Seguin, Tex., 1952-59; v.p. 1st Nat. Bank & Trust Co., Lincoln, 1959-60; exec. v.p. 1st Nat. Bank & Trust Co., 1960-76; pres. Gateway Manor, Inc., 1976-89; dir. Am. Combined Life Ins. Co., Chgo. Co-editor: Nebraska Restatement of Trusts, 1941. Pres. Lincoln Better Bus. Bur., 1964-65; Past pres. Lincoln Gen. Hosp. and Lincoln Hosp. Assn.; gen. chmn. Lincoln United Fund, 1973-74; bd. dirs. Lincoln Symphony Assn.; pres. Tb Assn., 1970. Served to lt. comdr. USNR, 1943-45. Mem. Nebr. Bar Assn., State Bar Tex., Lincoln C. of C. (pres. 1967-68), Nebr. Assn. Commerce and Industry (pres. 1975-76), Lincoln U. Club, Ak-Sar-Ben Club, Lincoln Country Club, Beta Theta Pi, Phi Delta Phi. Republican. Episcopalian. Home and Office: 225 N 56th St Lincoln NE 68504-3515

NOLTE, WILLIAM HENRY, English language educator; b. Tulia, Tex., May 2, 1928; s. Eugene Arch Nolte and Myrtle (Burns) Goldman; m. Alice Froehling, June 12, 1954; 1 child, Katherine Ann. Student, Tex. Tech U., 1947-49; BA, U. Mo., 1951; MA, U. Tex., 1952; PhD, U. Ill., 1959. Teaching asst. U. Ill., Urbana, 1954-59; asst. prof. English U. Oreg., Eugene, 1959-65; assoc. prof. U. Mo., St. Louis, 1965-67; prof. U. S.C., Columbia, 1967-89, disting. prof. emeritus English, 1989—. Author: H.L. Mencken, Literary Critic, 1966, H.L. Mencken's Smart Set Criticism, 1968, Rock and Hawk: Robinson Jeffers and the Romantic Agony, 1978. Served to cpl. USAAF, 1946-47. Holder endowed chair U. S.C. Ednl. Found., Columbia, 1978. Democrat. Home: 4502 Storkland Ave Columbia SC 29206-1245 Office: Univ of SC Dept of English Lang & Lit Columbia SC 29208

NOMO, HIDEO, professional baseball player. Pitcher Kintetsu, Japan, 1990-94, L.A. Dodgers, 1995—; mem. Japanese Olympic Baseball team, 1988. Named Nat. League Rookie Pitcher of Yr. The Sporting News, 1995, Nat. League Rookie of Yr. Baseball Writers Assn., 1995; strikeout leader Japanese Pacific League, 1990-93, Nat. League, 1995. Office: 1000 Elysian Park Ave Los Angeles CA 90012*

NOMURA, MASAYASU, biological chemistry educator; b. Hyogo-Ken, Japan, Apr. 27, 1927; s. Hiromichi and Yaeko N.; m. Junko Hamashima, Feb. 10, 1957; children—Keiko, Toshiyasu. Ph.D., U. Tokyo, 1957. Asst. prof. Inst. Protein Research, Osaka (Japan) U., 1960-63; assoc. prof. genetics U. Wis., Madison, 1963-66, prof., 1966-70, Elvehejem prof. in Life Sci. genetics and biochemistry, 1970-84, co-dir. Inst. for Enzyme Research, 1970-84; prof. biol. chemistry, Grace Bell chair U. Calif., Irvine, 1984—. Recipient U.S. Steel award in molecular biology Nat. Acad. Scis., 1971; recipient Acad. award Japanese Acad. Arts and Sci., 1972. Mem. Am. Acad. Arts and Scis., Nat. Acad. Scis., Royal Danish Acad. Scis. and Letters, Royal Netherlands Acad. Arts and Scis., Japanese Biochem. Soc. Home: 74 Whitman Ct Irvine CA 92715-4066 Office: U Calif Dept Biol Chemistry Med Sci I # D240 Irvine CA 92717

NONET, PHILIPPE, law educator; b. Liège, Belgium, Feb. 25, 1939; s. Leon and Helene (Reginster) N.; m. Pamela Jean Utz, Mar. 21, 1978; children—Michael, Genevieve, Beatrice. Docteur en Droit, U. Liège, 1961; Ph.D., U. Calif., Berkeley, 1966. Prof. law U. Calif.-Berkeley, 1966—. Author: Administrative Justice, 1969; (with others) Law and Society in Transition, 1978. Mem. Am. Soc. for Polit. and Legal Philosophy, Amintaphil, Law and Soc. Assn. Home: 885 Creed Rd Oakland CA 94610-1853 Office: U Calif-Berkeley Sch Law Berkeley CA 94720

NONG, artist, sculptor; b. Seoul, Korea, Oct. 10, 1930; came to U.S., 1952, naturalized, 1958; Commr. Asian Art Commn. Asian Art Mus. San Francisco, The Avery Brundage Collection, City and County of San Francisco, 1981-84. One-man exhbns. paintings and/or sculpture include Ft. Lauderdale (Fla.) Mus. Arts, Santa Barbara (Calif.) Mus. Art, Crocker Art Mus., Sacramento, Calif., 1965, Ga. Mus. Art, Athens, 1967, El Paso (Tex.) Mus. Art, 1967, Juvisy (France) 10th Internat., 1969, Salon d'Automne, Paris, 1969, Salon d'Art Sacré, Musée d'Art Moderne, 1969, Salon Grands et Jeunes d'Aujourd'hui, Paris, 1970, Salon des Artistes Indépendents, Paris, 1970, Paris Galerie Vallombreuse, Biarritz, France, 1970, Nat. Mus. History, Taiwan, 1971, Nihonbashi Gallery, Tokyo, Japan, 1971, Shinsegye Gallery, Seoul, Korea, 1975, Nat. Mus. Modern Art, Seoul, 1975, San Francisco Zool. Garden, 1975, Tongin Art Gallery, Seoul, 1978, Consulate Gen. Republic of Korea, L.A., 1982, Choon Chu Gallery, Seoul, 1982, Mee Gallery, Seoul, 1984, 86, Leema Art Mus., Seoul, 1985, Tong-A Dept. Store, Taegu, Korea, 1986, Tongso Gallery, Masan, Korea, 1986, Han Kwang Art Mus., Pusan, Korea, 1986, Union de Arte, Barcelona, Spain, 1987, Acad. de Belles Arts, Sabadell, Spain, 1987, Nong Hyup Art Mus., Ft. Lee, N.J., 1995; numerous group exhibits Mus. and Art Ctr., Douglaston, N.Y., 1961, Nat. Collection Fine Arts, Smithsonian Instn., Washington, 1961, Mus. Fine Arts, Springfield, Mass., 1961, Conn. Acad. Fine Arts, Hartford, Conn., 1962, Charles and Emma Frye Art Mus., Seattle, 1962, The Denver Art Mus., 1965, Jersey City Mus., 1967, U. Santa Clara (Calif.) Mus., 1967, U. Calif., Berkeley, 1968, Maison de la Culture du Havre, Le Havre, France, 1970, Oakland (Calif.) Art Mus., 1971, Gallerie des Champs Elysees, Paris, 1971, Nat. Sculpture Soc., Lever House, N.Y.C., 1971, Taipei Provincial Mus., Republic of China, 1971, San Francisco Mus. Modern Art, 1972, Galerie Hexagramme, Paris, 1975, Galeria de Arte Misrachi, Mexico City, 1979, The Mun Ye Art Ctr., Seoul, 1986, Salon de Artistes Francais, Paris, France, 1971, Salon d'Automne, Paris, 1969-71, Salon Grands et Jeunes d'Aujourd'hui, Paris, 1971-77; represented in numerous permanent collections including, Santa Barbara Mus. Art, Anchorage (Alaska) Hist. and Fine Art Mus., Museo de Arte, Lima, Peru, Govt. Peru, Nat. Mus. History, Govt. of Republic of China, Oakland (Calif.) Art Mus., Ga. Mus. Art, Athens, Korean Embassy, Lima, Peru, Nat. Mus. of Modern Art, Nat. Mus. Korea, Govt. of Republic of Korea, Seoul, Nat. Gallery of Modern Art, New Delhi, India, Asian Art Mus. San Francisco, Govt. of People's Republic China, Beijing and Shanghai, Palacio de la Zarzuela, Madrid, Palacio de la Moncloa, Madrid, The Korean Embassy, Madrid, Mus. Art de Sabadell, Spain, Mus. Nat. des Beaux-Arts, Monte Carlo, Monaco, others; author: Nong Questions, 1982. Chmn. San Francisco-Seoul Sister City Com., City and County San Francisco, 1981-84. Served with U.S. Army, 1956-59; Served with USAF, 1959-60. Recipient numerous awards including citations from Republic of Korea, Cert. Disting. Achievement State of Calif., 1982, Proclamation City and County of San Francisco, 1982. Home: 13694 Bent Tree Cir #202 Centreville VA 22020 *Beauty and ugliness, good and bad, right and wrong. Which test should I choose to measure these? Then, how long can I rely on the test I choose?.*

NONNA, JOHN MICHAEL, lawyer; b. N.Y.C., July 8, 1948; s. Angelo and Josephine (Visconti) N.; m. Jean Wanda Cleary, June 9, 1973; children: Elizabeth, Caroline, Marianne, Timothy. AB, Princeton U., 1970; JD, NYU, 1975. Bar: N.Y. 1976, U.S. Dist. Ct. (so. dist.) N.Y. 1978, U.S. Ct. Appeals (2d cir.) 1978, U.S. Ct. Appeals (9th cir.) 1980, U.S. Dist. Ct. Conn. 1988. Law asst. to Hon. D.L. Gabrielli N.Y. Ct. Appeals, Albany, 1975-77; assoc. Reid & Priest, N.Y.C., 1977-84; ptnr. Werner & Kennedy, N.Y.C., 1984—. Contbr. articles to profl. jours. Dep. mayor, trustee Village of Pleasantville, N.Y., 1990-95, mayor, 1995—, acting justice, 1983-89. With USNR, 1970-75. U.S. Olympic Team, Munich, 1972, Moscow, 1980. Fellow Am. Bar Found.; mem. ABA (torts and ins. practice sect. com. chair 1986-87, 92-93), N.Y. State Bar Assn. (exec. com. comml. and fed. litigation sect. 1984—), Assn. Bar City N.Y., N.Y. Fencers Club (pres. 1990-93). Avocations: fencing, running, piano. Office: Werner and Kennedy 1633 Broadway Fl 46 New York NY 10019-6708

NOON, PATRICK, museum curator; b. Phila., Oct. 13, 1951; s. Francis Joseph and Marion (Henneberry) N.; m. Diane Meade Tsurutani, May 18, 1991. BA in Art History, Brown U., 1973; MA in Art History, U. Mich., 1974. Asst. curator Yale Ctr. for Brit. Art, New Haven, 1977-80, curator, 1980—; mem. adv. bd. Walpole Soc., London, 1989—. Author: English Portrait Drawings, 1979, English Miniatures, 1981, Richard Parkes Bonington, 1991; mem. editorial bd. Print Quar., 1986—, Master Drawings, 1989—; contbr. articles to profl. jours. Nat. Endowment of Art fellow, 1974, 86. Mem. Print Coun. Am. Democrat. Office: Yale Ctr for Brit Art Yale Sta PO Box 208280 New Haven CT 06520

NOONAN, FRANK R., business executive; b. Boston, July 21, 1942; s. Russell F. and Barbara (Yutronich) N.; m. Patricia Bernadette Saulnier, Aug. 22, 1964; children: Kathleen, Kelly, Kristin. BA, U. N.H., 1964. Fin. mgmt. trainee Gen. Electric Co., Lynn, Mass., 1966-69; corp. auditor Gen. Electric Co., Schenectady, N.Y., 1969-74, audit adminstr., 1974-76; fin. mgr. mechanical drive turbine dept. Gen. Electric Co., Fitchburg, Mass., 1976-78; fin. mgr. air conditioning div. Gen. Electric Co., Louisville, 1978-81; sr. v.p., chief fin. officer Union Mutual Ins. Co., Portland, Maine, 1981-86, UNUM Corp., Portland, 1986-89; sr. v.p., group fin. The Dun & Bradstreet Corp., N.Y.C., 1989-90; chmn., CEO Reuben H. Donnelly Corp., Purchase, N.Y., 1991—. Bd. dirs. United Hosp. Med. Ctr., 1995—, Maine Coll. Art; v.p. Found. Blood Rsch., Scarborough, Maine, 1982-89. Republican. Avocations: tennis, skiing, music, golf, model trains. Home: 8 Lincoln Ln Purchase NY 10577-2304 Office: Reuben H Donnelly Corp 287 Bowman Ave Purchase NY 10577-2517

NOONAN, GREGORY ROBERT, lawyer; b. Bridgeport, Conn., Dec. 15, 1960; s. John L. and Margaret B. (Petek) N. BA in Acctg. cum laude, N.C. State U., 1982; JD, Wake Forest U., 1985; LLM in Taxation, Villanova U., 1990. Bar: N.C. 1985, Pa. 1986, U.S. Dist. Ct. (ea. dist.) Pa. 1988, U.S. Ct. Claims 1991, N.J. 1995, U.S. Tax Ct. 1994, U.S. Ct. Appeals (3d cir.) 1994; CPA, N.C. Acctg. cons. Ernst & Whinney, Raleigh, N.C., 1985-86; tax atty. Fox, Differ, Norristown, Pa., 1987-90, Solomon Berschler & Warren, Norristown, 1990; tax/bankruptcy atty. Koresko & Noonan, Norristown, 1990-92, Pizonka, Reilley & Bello, King of Prussia, Pa., 1992-94, Deyoung, Walfish & Noonan, King of Prussia, 1994—; instr. acctg., tax and bus. law Pierce Jr. Coll., Phila., 1990-92, Paralegal Inst. Mainline, Phila., 1990; instr. 2d pl. team Mock Trials of Pa. Young Lawyers Divsn. ABA, Norristown, 1989. Mem. ABA, AICPA, Pa. Bar Assn., N.C. Bar Assn., N.J. Bar Assn., Montgomery County Bar Assn., Norristown Jaycees (dir. 1990-94). Republican. Roman Catholic. Avocations: tennis, boating, chess, golf, watching college basketball. Home: 109 Stony Way Norristown PA 19403-4210 Office: Deyoung Walfish & Noonan PC 144 E Dekalb Pike Ste 200 King Of Prussia PA 19406

NOONAN, JOHN T., JR., federal judge, legal educator; b. Boston, Oct. 24, 1926; s. John T. and Marie (Shea) N.; m. Mary Lee Bennett, Dec. 27, 1967; children: John Kenneth, Rebecca Lee, Susanna Bain. B.A., Harvard U., 1946, LL.B., 1954; student, Cambridge U., 1946-47; M.A., Cath. U. Am., 1949, Ph.D., 1951, LHD, 1980; LL.D., U. Santa Clara, 1974, U. Notre Dame, 1976, Loyola U. South, 1978; LHD, Holy Cross Coll., 1980; LL.D., St. Louis U., 1981, U. San Francisco, 1985; student, Holy Cross Coll., 1980, Cath. U. Am., 1980, Gonzaga U., 1986, U. San Francisco, 1986. Bar: Mass. 1954, U.S. Supreme Ct. 1971. Mem. spl. staff Nat. Security Council, 1954-55; pvt. practice Herrick & Smith, Boston, 1955-60; prof. law U. Notre Dame, 1961-66; prof. law U. Calif., Berkeley, 1967-86, chmn. religious studies, 1970-73, chmn. medieval studies, 1978-79; judge U.S. Ct. Appeals (9th cir.), San Francisco, 1985—; Oliver Wendell Holmes, Jr. lectr. Harvard U. Law Sch., 1972, Pope John XXIII lectr. Cath. U. Law Sch., 1973, Cardinal Bellarmine lectr. St. Louis U. Div. Sch., 1973, Baum lectr. U. Ill., 1988, Strassberger lectr. U. Tex., 1989; chmn. bd. Games Rsch., Inc., 1961-76; overseer Harvard U., 1991—. Author: The Scholastic Analyst of Usury, 1957; Contraception: A History of Its Treatment by the Catholic Theologians and Canonists, 1965; Power to Dissolve, 1972; Persons and Masks of the Law, 1976; The Antelope, 1977; A Private Choice, 1979; Bribes, 1984; editor: Natural Law Forum, 1961-70, Am. Jour. Jurisprudence, 1970, The Morality of Abortion, 1970. Chmn. Brookline Redevel. Authority, Mass., 1958-62; cons. Papal Commn. on Family, 1965-66, Ford Found., Indonesian Legal Program, 1968; NIH, 1973, NIH, 1974; expert Presdl. Commn. on Population and Am. Future, 1971; cons. U.S. Cath. Conf., 1979-86; sec., treas. Inst. for Research in Medieval Canon Law, 1970-88; pres. Thomas More-Jacques Maritain Inst., 1977—; trustee Population Council, 1969-76, Phi Kappa Found., 1970-76, Grad. Theol. Union, 1970-73, U. San Francisco, 1971-75; mem. com. theol. edn. Yale U., 1972-77; exec. com. Cath. Commn. Intellectual and Cultural Affairs, 1972-75; bd. dirs. Ctr. for Human Values in the Health Scis., 1969-71, S.W. Intergroup Relations Council, 1970-72, Inst. for Study Ethical Issues, 1971-73. Recipient St. Thomas More award U. San Francisco, 1974, Christian Culture medal, 1975, Laetare medal U. Notre Dame, 1984, Campion medal Cath. Book Club, 1987; Guggenheim fellow, 1965-66, 79-80, Laetare medal U. Notre Dame, 1984, Campion medal, 1987, Alemany medal Western Dominican Province, 1988; Ctr. for advanced Studies in Behavioral Scis. fellow, 1973-74; Wilson Ctr. fellow, 1979-80. Fellow Am. Acad. Arts and Scis., Am. Soc. Legal Historians (hon.); mem. Am. Soc. Polit. and Legal Philosophy (v.p. 1964), Canon Law Soc. Am. (gov. 1970-72), Am. Law Inst., Phi Beta Kappa (senator United chpts. 1970-72, pres. Alpha of Calif. chpt. 1972-73). Office: US Ct Appeals 9th Cir PO Box 547 San Francisco CA 94101*

NOONAN, NORINE ELIZABETH, academic administrator, researcher; b. Phila., Oct. 5, 1948; d. Alaric Edwin and Norine (Radford) Freeman. BA, summa cum laude, U. Vt., 1970; MA, Princeton U., 1972, PhD, 1976. Asst. prof. Coll. Vet. Medicine, U. Fla., Gainesville, 1976-81, assoc. prof., 1981; research assoc. prof. Georgetown U., Washington, 1981-82; Am. Chem. Soc. sci. fellow U.S. Senate Commerce Com., Washington, 1982-83; program and budget analyst Office Mgmt. and Budget, Washington, 1983-87, acting br. chief sci. and space programs, 1987-88, br. chief, 1988-92; v.p. rsch. Fla. Inst. Tech., Melbourne, 1992—, dean grad. sch., 1993—; bd. advisors U.S. Found. for the Internat. Space U., 1989-90; disting. lectr. MITRE Corp. Inst., 1991; vis. faculty Exec. Seminar Ctrs., Office Personnel Mgmt.; cons. Am. Chem. Soc. com. chem. and pub. affairs; mem. NASA space sci. adv. com.; mem. com. Antarctic policy & sci. NRC; mem. future of space sci. DOE environ. mgmt. sci. program NRC; councilor Oak Ridge Assn. Univs.; trustee Southeast Univs. Rsch. Assn., also chair finance com. Contbr. articles to sci. jours. Vol. Balt. City Fair, 1982-91. Bd. dirs. Brevard Symphony Orchestra, 1993-96, Wolf Trap Farm Pk. Assocs., Wolf Trap Farm Pk. for the Performing Arts, 1988-92, exec. com. 1990-92, exec. vice chmn., 1991-92, treas., 1992; mem. adv. coun. Brookings Instn. Ctr. for Pub. Policy Edn., 1989-93; treas. White House Athletic Ctr., 1990-92, Potomac Basset Hound Club, Space Coast Tiger Bay Club, bd. dirs 1996—. Recipient Spl. Performance award Office Mgmt. and Budget, 1987, 88; grantee Fla. div. Am. Cancer Soc., 1977, NIH, 1979, NSF, 1979. Fellow AAAS (mem. at large sect. gen. interest in sci. and tech. 1994—, mem. sci. engring. and pub. policy com.); mem. Am. Soc. Cell Biology, Sigma Xi, Phi Beta Kappa (pres. Fla. chpt. 1980-81). Mem. United Ch. of Christ. Avocations: running, purebred dogs, fishing, cooking, aerobics. Home: 2480 Grassmere Dr Melbourne FL 32904-9715 Office: Fla Inst Tech 150 W University Blvd Melbourne FL 32901-6982

NOONAN, PATRICK FRANCIS, conservation executive; b. St. Petersburg, Fla., Dec. 2, 1942; s. Francis Patrick and Henrietta (Donovan) N.; m. Nancy Elizabeth Peck, Aug. 15, 1964; children: Karen Elizabeth, Dawn Wiley. A.B., Gettysburg Coll., 1961-65; M.City and Regional Planning, Catholic U. Am., 1967; M.B.A., Am. U., 1971. Dir. ops. The Nature Conservancy, Arlington, Va., 1969-73; pres. The Nature Conservancy, 1973-80; chmn. The Conservation Fund, 1985—. Trustee Nat. Geographi Soc., 1990—, Gettysburg Coll., 1978-91, Duke U. Sch. Environment, 1979—, Ind. Sector, 1984-91, dir. Ashland, 1991—, Internat. Paper, 1993—, Saul Ctrs., 1993—, Rushmore Funds, 1987—; mem. Pres.' Commn. on Am. Outdoors, 1985-87, Pres.' Commn. on Environ. Quality, 1991-93; trustee Catholic Youth Orgn., 1975—, Am. Conservation Assn., 1986—, Am. Farmland Trust, 1987—. MacArthur Found. fellow, 1985-90. Home: 11901 Glen Mill Rd Potomac MD 20854-1920

NOONAN, SUSAN ABERT, public relations counselor; b. Lancaster, Pa., May 10, 1960; d. James Goodear and Carole (Althouse) Abert; m. David Lindsay Noonan, July 28, 1986; children: Caroline du Pont, Elizabeth Augusta. BA, Mt. Holyoke Col., 1982. Account exec. Merill Lynch, N.Y.C., 1982-83; sr. v.p. Cameron Assocs., N.Y.C., 1983-88; pres., founder Noonan/Russo Comm., N.Y.C., 1988—. Mem. Nat. Investor Rels. Inst. Office: Noonan/Russo Comm Inc 220 5th Ave New York NY 10001-7708

NOONAN, THOMAS SCHAUB, history educator, Russian studies educator; b. N.Y.C., Jan. 20, 1938; s. Thomas M. and Martha M. (Schaub) N.; m. Norma L. Corigliano, May 19, 1937; 1 child, Thomas R. AB, Dartmouth Coll., 1959; MA, Ind. U., 1962, PhD, 1965. Cert. Russian Inst., Ind. U. Asst. prof. Otterbein Coll., Westerville, Ohio, 1965-66; asst. prof. dept. history U. Minn.-Mpls., 1966-74, assoc. prof., 1974-79, prof., 1979—; chmn. dept. Russian and East European studies, 1981-91; assoc. chmn. dept. history U. Minn.-Mpls., 1992-93, 94—; acting chmn. dept. history, 1994-95. Co-editor Archivum Eurasiae Medii Aevi, 1980—, Russian and East European Studies, 1986-95; adv. bd. Russian History, 1980-88, Soviet Studies in History, 1986-89; contbr. articles to profl. jours. Recipient Royal medal Swedish Numismatic Soc., 1984; Kraay vis. fellow Oxford U., 1983; Social Sci. Rsch. Coun. fellow, 1980-81; Reference Tools grantee NEH, 1990-91. Fellow Am. Numismatic Soc., Royal Numismatic Soc.; mem. Am. Hist. Assn., Am. Assn. Advancement Slavic Studies, Assn. Advancement Baltic Studies. Home: 10224 Rich Rd Minneapolis MN 55437-2503 Office: Univ Minn Dept History 614 Social Sciences Bldg Minneapolis MN 55455

NOONE, ROBERT BARRETT, plastic surgeon; b. Scranton, Pa., Oct. 30, 1939; s. Robert Patrick and Margaret Ann (Barrett) N.; m. Barbara Ellen Atkins, May 29, 1965; children: Robert B. Jr., Megan J., Genevieve C., Rebecca B., Theresa Ann. BS, U. Scranton, 1961; MD, U. Pa., 1965. Diplomate Am. Bd. Surgery, Am. Bd. Plastic Surgery. Rotating intern Hosp. of U. Pa., Phila., 1965-66, resident in surgery, 1966-71, resident in plastic surgery, 1971-73; asst. prof. surgery Sch. Medicine, U. Pa., Phila., 1974-83, clin. assoc. prof. surgery, 1983-89; clin. prof. surgery Sch. Medicine, U. Pa., 1989—; head sect. on plastic surgery Pa. Hosp., Phila., 1974-80; chief svc. plastic surgery Bryn Mawr Hosp., Bryn Mawr, Pa., 1977—, Lankenau Hosp., Phila., 1980-91; chmn. dept. surgery Bryn Mawr (Pa.) Hosp., 1991—; bd. dirs. Am. Bd. Plastic Surgery, Phila., 1987-94, vice chmn. 1993-94; bd. dirs. Plastic Surgery Ednl. Found., Chgo., 1981-91, pres. 1989-90. Contbr. articles to profl. jours. Bd. dirs., trustee Rosemont (Pa.) Sch. of the Holy Child, 1983-87. Capt. USAF, 1967-69. Recipient Frank J. O'Hara Disting. Alumnus award U. Scranton, 1986. Fellow Am. Coll. Surgeons (bd. govs. 1994—); mem. AMA (del. plastic surgery 1986-88), Am. Soc. Plastic and Reconstructive Surgery (bd. dirs. 1989-90, 92-95, chmn. bd. trustees 1994—), Am. Assn. Plastic Surgeons (sec. 1995—), Northeastern Soc. Plastic Surgeons (pres. 1985-86), Robert H. Ivy Soc. (pres. 1982-83), Merion Cricket Club, Phila. Country Club. Republican. Roman Catholic. Avocations: golf, tennis, photography, swimming, fly fishing, reading. Home: 234 Cheswold Hill Rd Haverford PA 19041-1814 Office: Plastic & Reconstructive Surg Assocs 888 Glenbrook Ave Bryn Mawr PA 19010-2506

NOONE, STEPHEN J., educational association administrator; b. Indpls., Sept. 5, 1942; s. Dennis J. and Helen M. (McGinty) N.; m. Kathleen A. Thornburgh, June 18, 1966; children: Patrick (dec.), Lisa, Brendan. BA, Marian Coll., 1964; MS, Butler U., 1970. Cert. assn. exec., Am. Soc. Assn. Execs.; cert. secondary edn. tchr., adminstr., Ind. Tchr. Bishop Chatard High Sch., Indpls., 1964-70, prin., 1970-77; dir. schs. Office of Cath. Edn., Archdiocese of Indpls., 1977-84; exec. dir. Ind. Assn. of Osteo. Physicsians, 1984-92, Am. Acad. Osteopathy, 1992—. Contbr. articles to profl. jours. and pubis. Adv. bd. Our Lady of Grace Monastery, Beech Grove, Ind., 1989—; bd. dirs. Westview Osteopathic Hosp. Found., Indpls., 1988-92; mem. religious svcs. com. Pan Am. Games, Indpls., 1986-87; at-large del. and interviewer for Congress, Ind. Congress on Edn., 1983-84; rep. Nat. Forum on Excellence in Edn., 1983; mem. Christ the King Cath. Ch., 1968—, eucharistic minister, lector, choir mem., others; steering com. Sesquicentennial Celebration of the Archdiocese of Indpls., 1982-84, others. Mem. Am. Soc. Assn. Execs., Ind. Soc. Assn. Execs. (bd. dirs. 1989-93, Exec. Dir. of Yr. 1993), Am. Osteopathic Assn., Assn. Osteopathic State Exec. Dirs. Roman Catholic. Home: 5935 Hillside Ave W Dr Indianapolis IN 46220

NOONKESTER, JAMES RALPH, retired college president; b. Flatridge, Va., June 10, 1924; s. Reggie L. and Arcie (Parks) N.; m. Naomi Hopkins, June 10, 1947; children: Myron Craig, Lila. BA, U. Richmond, 1944, LLD, 1968; ThM, So. Bapt. Theol. Sem., 1947, PhD, 1949; LHD (hon.), Blue Mountain Coll., 1982; postgrad., Harvard U., 1980. Minister edn. 1st Bapt. Ch., Charlottesville, Va., 1950-52; prof., head div. religion and philosophy William Carey Coll., Hattiesburg, Miss., 1952-53; acad. dean William Carey Coll., 1953-56, pres., 1956-89, pres. emeritus, 1989—; pres. Miss. Found. Ind. Colls.; mem. Edn. commn. So. Bapt. Conv., chmn., 1983; bd. dirs. Miss. Sch. Bds. Assn. Workers Compensation Trust, 1993-95, chmn., 1994. Chmn. bd. dirs. Am. Cancer Soc., Miss. divsn., 1966; campaign chmn. United Givers Fund, 1975-76, pres. 1976-77; coun. chmn. Boy Scouts Am., dir. Planned Giving Pine Burr Area Boy Scouts Am., 1990-93; trustee Hattiesburg Pub. Schs., 1990-95, pres. bd. trustees, 1992-95. Recipient award Outstanding Grad. English U. Richmond, 1944; named Hattiesburg's Outstanding Young Man of 1956.; recipient Silver Beaver award Boy Scouts Am., 1981, HUB award, 1983; named Sales and Mktg. Execs. Man of Yr., 1983. Mem. NEA, Miss. Edn. Assn., Hattiesburg Concert Assn. (bd. dir.), So. Assn. Bapt. Colls. and Schs. (pres.), Miss. Assn. Colls. (pres.), Hattiesburg C. of C. (pres. 1966), Phi Beta Kappa, Phi Delta Kappa, Chi Beta Phi, Omicron Delta Kappa. Club: Kiwanian. Home: 100 Lesley Ln Hattiesburg MS 39402-2922

NOORDERGRAAF, ABRAHAM, biophysics educator; b. Utrecht, Netherlands, Aug. 7, 1929; s. Leendert and Johanna (Kool) N.; m. Geertruida Alida Van Nee, Sept. 6, 1956; children: Annemiek (Mrs. James A. Young), Gerrit Jan, Jeske Inette, Alexander Abraham. B.Sc., U. Utrecht, 1953, M.S., 1955, Ph.D., 1956; M.A. (hon.), U. Pa., 1971. Teaching asst. U. Utrecht, 1949-50, asst. dept. physics, 1951-53, research asst. dept. med. physics, 1953-55, research fellow dept. med. physics, 1956-58, sr. research fellow dept. med. physics, 1959-65; tchr. math. and physics Vereniging Nijverheidsonderwijs, Utrecht, 1951; research asst. U. Amsterdam, Netherlands, 1952; vis. fellow dept. therapeutic research U. Pa., Phila., 1957-58; assoc. prof. biomed. engrng. Moore Sch. Elec. Engring., 1964-70, acting head electromed. div., 1968-69, prof. biomed. engring., 1970—; prof. physiology Sch. Vet. Medicine, 1976—, prof. Dutch culture Sch. Arts and Scis., 1983—; prof. medicine Med. Sch. U. Pa., 1990—; assoc. dir. biomed. engring. tng. program Moore Sch. Elec. Engring., 1971-76, asso. dir. sch., 1972-74, chmn. grad. group in biomed. electronic engring., 1973-75, chmn. dept. bioengring., 1973-76, chmn. grad. group bioengring., 1975-76, dir. systems and integrative biology tng. program, 1979-84; vis. prof. biomed. engring. U. Miami, 1970-79, Erasmus U. Med. Sch., Rotterdam, The Netherlands, 1970-71, Tech. U., Delft, 1970-71, Polish Acad. Scis., Warsaw, 1975; hon. vis. prof. of physiology U. Ljubljana, 1994—; mem. cardiovascular study sect., 1985-89; cons. sci. affairs divsn. NATO, 1973—; participant numerous internat. confs. in field. Author: (with I. Starr) Ballistocardiography in Cardiovascular Research, 1967, Circulatory System Dynamics, 1978; contbg. author: Biological Engineering, 1969; Editor: (with G.N. Jager and N. Westerhof) Circulatory Analog Computers, 1963, (with G.H. Pollack) Ballistocardiography and Cardiac Performance, 1967, (with E. Kresch) The Venous System: Characteristics and Function, 1969, (with J. Baan and J. Raines) Cardiovascular System Dynamics, 1978, (with Reichenbach-Consten) Two Hundred Years of Netherlands-American Interaction; sci. editor Biophysics and Bioengring. Series, 1976-94; contbr. numerous articles to profl. jours.; Referee: Biophys. Jour., 1968—, Physics in Medicine and Biology, 1969—, Bull. Math. Biophysics, 1972-84, Circulation Research, 1973—; mem. editorial adv. bd.: Jour. Biomechanics, 1969-84; assoc. editor: Bull. Math. Biology, 1973-84. Vice pres. Haverford Friends Sch. PTA, 1968-70. Recipient S. Reid Warren Jr. award U. Pa. Sch. Engring. and Applied Sci., 1986, Christian and Mary Lindback award U. Pa., 1988. Fellow IEEE (mem. adminstrv. com. engring. in medicine and biology group 1967-70, mem. edn. com. group biomed. engring. 1968-70, sec. Phila. chpt. 1974-75, mem. regional council profl. group engring. in medicine and biology 1974-77), N.Y. Acad. Scis., AAAS, Explorers Club, Coll. Physicians Phila., Am. Coll. Cardiology, Royal Soc. Medicine London; mem. Nederlandse Natuurkundige Vereniging, Ballistocardiograph Research Soc. U.S.A. (sec.-treas. 1965-67, pres. 1968-70), Biophys. Soc. (charter), European Soc. for Noninvasive Cardiovascular Research (co-founder 1960, sec.-treas. 1960-61, mem. com. on nomenclature 1960-61, officer 1961-62, Herman C. Burger award 1978, Disting. Rsch. Award, 1993), Cardiovascular System Dynamics Soc. (co-founder 1976, pres. 1976-80, hon. life 1986), Franklin Inst., John Morgan Soc., Biomed. Engring. Soc. (founding mem., chmn. membership com. 1978-79, dir. 1972-75), Am. Heart Assn., Instrument Soc. Am. (sr. mem.), Soc. Math. Biology (charter mem.), Am. Physiol. Soc., Microcirculatory Soc., Am. Assn. Med. Systems and Informatics, Pa. Acad. Sci., Sigma Xi, Phi Zeta. Presbyterian. Home: 620 Haydock Ln Haverford PA 19041-1208 Office: U Pa 101 Hayden Hall Philadelphia PA 19104-6392

NORA, AUDREY HART, physician; b. Picayune, Miss., Dec. 5, 1936; d. Allen Joshua and Vera Lee (Ballard) H.; m. James Jackson Nora, Apr. 9, 1966; children: James Jackson Jr., Elizabeth Hart. BS, U. Miss., 1958, MD, 1961; MPH, U. Calif., 1978. Diplomate Am. Bd. Pediatrics, Am. Bd. Hematology and Oncology. Resident in pediatrics U. Wis. Hosp., Madison, 1961-64; fellow in hematology/oncology Baylor U., Tex. Childrens Hosp., Houston, 1964-66, asst. prof. pediatrics, 1966-70; assoc. clin. prof. pediatrics U. Colo. Sch. Medicine, Denver, 1970—; dir. genetics Denver Childrens Hosp., 1970-78; cons. maternal and child health USPHS, Denver, 1978-83, asst. surgeon gen. regional health adminstr., 1983-92; dir. maternal & child health bur., health resources and svc. adminstrn. USPHS, commd. med. officer, 1978, advanced through grades to asst. surgeon gen., 1983; adv. com. NIH, Bethesda, 1975-77; adv. bd. Metronet Health, Inc., Denver, 1986—, Colo. Assn. Commerce and Industry, Denver, 1985—. Author: (with J.J. Nora) Genetics and Counseling in Cardiovascular Diseases, 1978, (with others) Blakiston's Medical Dictionary, 1980, Birth Defects Encyclopedia, 1990, (with J.J. Nora and K. Berg) Cardiovascular Diseases: Genetics, Epidemiology and Prevention, 1991; contbr. articles to profl. jours. Recipient Virginia Apgar award Nat. Found., 1976. Fellow Am. Acad. Pediatrics; mem. Am. Pub. Health Assn. (governing coun. 1990-92, coun. mem. maternal and child health 1990—), Commd. Officers Assn., Am. Soc. Human Genetics, Teratology Soc., Western Soc. Pediatric Rsch. Presbyterian. Avocations: quilting, cooking, hiking. Office: USPHS Room 18-05 Parklawn Bldg 5600 Fishers Ln Rockville MD 20857-0001

NORA, JAMES JACKSON, physician, author, educator; b. Chgo., June 26, 1928; s. Joseph James and May Henrietta (Jackson) N.; m. Barbara June Fluhrer, Sept. 7, 1949 (div. 1963); children: Wendy Alison, Penelope Welbon, Marianne Leslie; m. Audrey Faye Hart, Apr. 9, 1966; children: James Jackson Jr., Elizabeth Hart Nora. AB, Harvard U., 1950; MD, Yale U., 1954; MPH, U. Calif., Berkeley, 1978. Intern Detroit Receiving Hosp., 1954-55; resident in pediatrics U. Wis. Hosps., Madison, 1959-61, fellow in cardiology, 1962-64; fellow in genetics McGill U. Children's Hosp., Montreal, Can., 1964-65; assoc. prof. pediatrics Baylor Coll. Medicine, Houston, 1965-71; prof. genetics, preventive medicine and pediatrics U. Colo. Med. Sch., Denver, 1971—; dir. genetics Rose Med. Ctr., Denver, 1980—; dir. pediatric cardiology and cardiovascular tng. U. Colo. Sch. Medicine, 1971-78; mem. task force Nat. Heart and Lung Program, Bethesda, Md., 1973; cons. WHO, Geneva, 1983—; mem. U.S.-U.S.S.R. Exchange Program on Heart Disease, Moscow and Leningrad, 1975. Author: The Whole Heart Book, 1980, 2d rev. edit., 1989; (with F.C. Fraser) Medical Genetics, 4th rev. edit., 1994, Genetics of Man, 2d rev. edit., 1986, Cardiovascular Diseases: Genetics, Epidemiology and Prevention, 1991; (novels) The Upstart Spring, 1989, The Psi Delegation, 1989, The Hemingway Sabbatical, 1996. Com. mem. March of Dimes, Am. Heart Assn., Boy Scouts Am. Served to lt. USAAC, 1945-47. Grantee Nat. Heart, Lung and Blood Inst., Nat. Inst. Child Health and Human Devel., Am. Heart Assn., NIH; recipient Virginia Apgar Meml. award. Fellow Am. Coll. Cardiology, Am. Acad. Pediatrics, Am. Coll. Med. Genetics; mem. Am. Pediatric Soc., Soc. Pediatric Rsch., Am. Heart Assn., Teratology Soc., Transplantation Soc., Am. Soc. Human Genetics, Authors Guild, Authors League, Acad. Am. Poets, Mystery Writers Am., Rocky Mountain Harvard Club. Democrat. Presbyterian. Avocations: writing fiction, poetry. Home: 3110 Fairweather Ct Olney MD 20832-3021 Office: Parklawn Bldg 5600 Fishers Ln Rm 18-05 Rockville MD 20857-0001

NORBACK, CRAIG THOMAS, writer; b. Pitts., Nov. 14, 1943; s. Howard George and Maybelle Veronica Montaigne (Cosse) N.; m. Judith Carol Shaul, Oct. 12, 1976. BS, Washington U., St. Louis, 1967; postgrad., Drew U., 1986—. Author, co-author, compiler, producer over 150 books, including: The Misspeller's Dictionary, 1972, Everything You Can Get from the Government for Free or Almost for Free, 1975, The Dream Machine: The Golden Age of American Automobiles 1946-65, 1976, Great Songs of Madison Avenue, 1976, Great North American Indians, 1977, The Health Care Directory, 1977, The Older American's Handbook, 1977, The Educational Marketplace, 1978, Famous American Admirals, 1978, Newsweek Travel Guide to the U.S., 1978, The Dow Jones-Irwin Guide to Franchising, 1979, The Horseman's Catalog, 1979, The Must Words, 1979, The Practical Inventor's Handbook, 1979, ABC Complete Book of Sports Facts, 1980, ABC Monday Night Football, 1980-81, 1980, The Bible Almanac, 1980, Check Yourself Out, 1980, The Signet Book of World Winners, 1980, The TV Guide Almanac, 1980, The World's Great News Photos (1840-1980), 1980, The Allergy Encyclopedia, 1981, American Expressions, 1981, The Computer Invasion, 1981, The Consumer's Energy Handbook, 1981, 500 Questions New Parents Ask, 1982, Business Week Almanac, 1982, The International Yellow Pages, 1982, The Puzzle King's Bafflers, 1982, The Associated Press Sunday Crossword Puzzle Book, 1983, Chilton's Job Textbook Series: Advertising Management, 1983, Office Management, 1983, It's a Fact, 1983, National Education Association Parent and Child Success Library: Helping Your Child Read, 1983, How Letters Make Words, 1983, How to Prepare Your Child for School, 1983, Learning the Alphabet, 1983, Learning to Add, 1983, The Ultimate Toy Catalog, 1983, U.S. Publicity Directory, various years, Advertising and Promotion Management, 1983, America Wants to Know, 1983, Certified Professional Secretary modules I through VI, 1984, East Coast Publicity Directory, 1984, Human Resources Yearbook, 1987, 88, 89, 90, Princeton Area Job Finder, 1986-87, Career Encyclopedia, 1987, Travel Publicity Directory, 1987, 88, 89, 90, Arthur Young Guide to Venture Capital, 1987, Hazardous Chemicals on File, 1988, Joint Ventures, 1992. Home: 131 S Mill Rd Princeton Junction NJ 08550-2005

NORBERG, ARTHUR LAWRENCE, JR., historian, physicist educator; b. Providence, Apr. 13, 1938; s. Arthur Lawrence Sr. and Margaret Helen (Riley) N.; m. Kerry J. Freedman. BS in Physics, Providence Coll., 1959; MS in Physics, U. Vt., 1962; PhD in History of Sci., U. Wis., 1974. Asst. prof. physics St. Michael's Coll., Winooski, Vt., 1961-63, 64-68; assoc. scientist Westinghouse Electric Co., Pitts., 1963-64; instr. in physics U. Wis., Whitewater, 1968-71; rsch. historian U. Calif., Berkeley, 1973-79; program mgr. NSF, Washington, 1979-81; dir. Charles Babbage Inst. for History of Info. Processing U. Minn., Mpls., 1981-93, prof. history of sci. and tech., 1995—, assoc. prof. computer sci., 1981-95, prof. computer sci., 1995—; del. Am. Coun. Learned Socs., N.Y.C., 1981-87; mem. adv. coun. NASA, Washington, 1988-93; endowed ERA Land Grant chair U. Minn., 1989-93. Editor: Annals of the History of Computing, 1982-93; adv. editor Tech. and Culture, 1985-92, (book) Transforming Technology: Information Processing for the Pentagon; contbr. articles to profl. jours. Founding pres. City Works-A Tech. Ctr., Mpls., 1987-90; bd. dirs. Charles Babbage Found., 1984-94; trustee Charles Babbage Found., 1993—. Fellow AAAS; mem. History of Sci. Soc. (treas. 1975-80), Brit. Soc. for History of Sci., Soc. for History of Tech., Sigma Xi. Office: U Minn Dept Computer Sci 4-192 EE/CS Bldg Minneapolis MN 55455-0290

NORBERG, CHARLES ROBERT, lawyer; b. Cleve., July 25, 1912; s. Rudolf Carl and Ida Edith (Roberts) N. B.S. in Adminstrv. Engring, Cornell U., 1934; M.A. in Internat. Econs, U. Pa., 1937; LL.B., Harvard U., 1939. Bar: Pa. bar 1940, U.S. Supreme Ct. bar 1946, D.C. bar 1947. Lab. research asst. Willard Storage Battery Co., Cleve., 1934-35; asso. firm Hepburn and Norris, Phila., 1939-42; with Office of Assn. Sec. State for Public Affairs, Dept. State, 1948-51; asst. dir. psychol. strategy bd. Exec. Office of the Pres., 1952-54; mem. staff U.S. Delegation to UN Gen. Assembly, Paris, 1951; adviser U.S. Delegation to UNESCO Gen. Conf., Montevideo, 1954; assoc. firm Morgan, Lewis and Bockius, Washington, 1955-56; individual practice law Washington, 1956—; treas., gen. counsel Inter-Am. Comml. Arbitration Commn., 1968-83, dir. gen., 1983-95, hon. dir. gen., 1995—; chief Spl. AID Mission to Ecuador, 1961; spl. Aid Mission to Uruguay, 1961; mem. U.S. delegation to Specialized Inter-Am. Conf. on pvt. internat. law, Panama, 1975. Chmn. Internat. Visitors Info. Service, Washington, 1965-69; chmn. Mayor's Com. on Internat. Visitors, 1971-78; chmn., pres. Bicentennial Commn. of D.C., Inc., 1975-81. Served with USAF, 1942-46. Mem. Phila. Bar Assn., Pa. Bar Assn., Inter-Am. Bar Assn., Washington Fgn. Law Soc. (pres. 1959-63), Am. Soc. Internat. Law, Am. Law Inst., Am. Bar Assn. (chmn. internat. legal exchange program 1974-79), Bar Assn. of D.C. (chmn. internat. law com. 1977-79), Inter-Am. Bar Found. (founder, dir. 1957, pres. 1969-84, chmn. bd. 1984—), Diplomatic and Consular Officers Retired (Washington), Washington Inst. Fgn. Affairs, Academia Colombiana de Jurisprudencia, Inter-Am. Acad. Internat. and Comparative Law, Colegio de Abogados de Quito. Clubs: Met. (Washington); Dacor (Washington); Racquet (Phila.); Harvard (N.Y.C.). Home: 3104 N St NW Washington DC 20007-3413 Office: 1819 H St NW Washington DC 20006-3603

NORBERG, RICHARD EDWIN, physicist, educator; b. Newark, Dec. 28, 1922; s. Arthur Edwin and Melita (Roefer) N.; m. Patricia Ann Leach, Dec. 27, 1947 (dec. July 1977); children—Karen Elizabeth, Craig Alan, Peter Douglas; m. Jeanne C. O'Brien, Apr. 1, 1978. B.A., DePauw U., 1943; M.A., U. Ill., 1947, Ph.D., 1951. Research assoc., control sytems lab. U. Ill., 1951-53, asst. prof., 1953; vis. lectr. physics Washington U., St. Louis, 1954—; mem. faculty Washington U., 1955—, prof. physics, 1958—, chmn. dept., 1962-91; dir. Technilab Inc. Mem. editorial bd. Magnetic Research Rev. Served with USAAF, 1943-46. Fellow Am. Phys. Soc., Internat. Soc. Magnetic Research. Home: 7134 Princeton Ave Saint Louis MO 63130-2308 Office: Washington U Dept Physics PO Box 1105 Saint Louis MO 63188-1105

NORBY, RONALD BRANDON, nurse executive; b. Jacksonville, Fla., Nov. 15, 1943; s. John K. and Corliss J. (Hisey) N. BS, Baylor U., 1965; MS in Nursing, U. Wash., 1970, postgrad., 1970-71; postgrad., U. Hawaii, 1973-74. Charge nurse, open heart surg. team Baylor U. Med. Ctr., Dallas, 1965; dir. nursing Mother Frances Hosp., Tyler, Tex., 1966; charge nurse, nursing dir. USN Nurse Corps., 1966-69; asst. dir. nursing U. Hosp., Seattle, 1972-73; asst. prof. U. Hawaii Sch. Nursing, Honolulu, 1972-74; dir. div. nursing Medicus Systems Corp., Chgo., 1974-77; v.p. nursing St. Francis Hosp., Evanston, Ill., 1977-79; dir. div. nursing Am. Hosp. Assn., Chgo., 1979-80; sr. v.p. Med. Scientific Internat., Corp., Washington, 1980-82; chief, nursing svc. Edward Hines, Jr. VA Hosp., Chgo., 1983-86; clin. svcs. mgr. Vets. Integrated Svc. Network So. Calif./Nevada, Long Beach, 1996—; asst. dean clin. nursing affairs Marcella Neiffoff Sch. Nursing, Loyola U., Chgo. 1983-86; assoc. chief of staff/nursing VA Med. Ctr., San Diego, 1986; adj. faculty San Diego State U., 1986; instr. Calif. State U. at Domenguez Hills; chair nat. devel. effort for expert panel-based nurse staffing methology for Dept. of Vets. Affairs; chair nursing conf., Las Vegas, 1992; dir. field support/clin. integration Nat. Hdqs. Dept. Vets. Affairs, Washington, 1994-96; cons. in field. Author: (with M. Mayers) Quality Assurance for Patient Care: Nursing Perspectives, 1977; Taking the Pain Out of Care Planning, 1976, A Realistic Approach to the Teaching and Implementation of Care Planning, 1976; (with others) Implementing Research in Nursing Practice, 1985, Identification of the Nursing Minimum Data Set, 1988, Positioning for Success, 1990. Chmn. hosp. disaster com. U. Hosp., 1970, mem. Nat. Commn. Nursing Implementation Project, 1985-86; treas. Being Alive, San Diego; mem. HIV Care Coalition, County of San Diego. Mem. Am. Hosp. Assn. (sr. staff coun. on nursing 1979-80, coord. Nat. Comm. Nursing 1980), Am. Orgn. Nurse Execs., (com. on nominations 1985), ANA, Nat. League Nursing, Calif. Soc. Nursing Svc. Conference Group, Calif. Nurses Assn., Hawaii Nurses Assn. (v.p. 1973), Ill. Nurses Assn., Chief Med. Dir. Clin. and Programs Adv. Coun. (chair VA western region ambulatory care and edn. nursing subcom.), Sigma Theta Tau (internat. treas. 1987-91, chmn. fin. com. 1987-91, chmn. membership enhancement task force 1988-91, pres. Gamma Gamma chpt. 1989-91). Home: 6104 Avenida de Castillo Long Beach CA 90803 Office: Integrated Svc Network of So Calif/Nevada 5901 E 7th St Long Beach CA 90822

NORBY, WILLIAM CHARLES, financial consultant; b. Chgo., Aug. 10, 1915; s. Oscar Maurice and Louise (Godejohann) N.; m. Camilla Edbrooke, June 12, 1943; children: Martha Norby Fraundorf, Richard James. AB, U. Chgo., 1935. With Harris Trust & Savs. Bank, Chgo., 1935-70, v.p., 1953-64, sr. v.p., 1964-70; exec. dir. Fin. Analysts Fedn., N.Y.C., 1970-72; sr. v.p., bd. dirs. Duff & Phelps, Inc., Chgo., 1973-81; mem. Fin. Acctg. Standards Adv. Coun., 1975-79. mem. Fin. Acctg. Stds. Adv. Coun., 1975-79. Mem. AICPA (com. on auditors responsibilities 1975-78), Fin. Analysts Fedn. (bd. dirs. 1962-68, pres. 1963-64, Disting. Svc. award 1973, Nicholas Molodovsky award 1979), Investment Analysts Soc. Chgo. (pres. 1955-56), U. Chgo. Alumni Assn. (citation 1961), Phi Beta Kappa. Congregationalist (trustee 1950-56, chmn. 1955-56). Home: 337 Blackstone Ave La Grange IL 60525-2107

NORCEL, JACQUELINE JOYCE CASALE, educational administrator; b. Bklyn., Nov. 19, 1940; d. Frederick and Josephine Jeanette (Bestafka) Casale; m. Edward John Norcel, Feb. 24, 1962. BS, Fordham U., 1961; MS, Bklyn. Coll., 1966; 6th yr. cert. So. Conn. State U., 1980; postgrad. Bridgeport U. Elem. tchr., pub. schs., N.Y.C., 1961-80; prin. Coventry Schs., Conn., 1980-84, Trumbull Schs., Conn., 1984—; guest lectr. So. Conn. State U., 1980—; cons. Monson Schs., Mass., 1984; mem. Conn. State Prin. Acad. Adv. Bd., 1986-88; mem. adj. faculty Sacred Heart U., Fairfield, Conn., 1985—, So. Conn. State U., summer 1991. Editor: Best of the Decade, 1980; mem. editorial adv. bd. Principal Matters; contbr. articles to profl. jours. Chmn. bldg. com. Trumbull Bd. Edn., 1978-80; chmn. Sch. Benefit Com., Trumbull, 1985-86; catechist Bridgeport Diocese, Roman Cath. Ch., Conn., 1975-85, youth minister, 1979-84, coord., evaluator leadership tng. workshops for teens and adults, 1979-84; mem. St. Stephen's Parish Coun., 1993—. Recipient Town of Trumbull Service award, 1982, Nat. Disting. Prin. award, 1988, Joseph Formica Disting. Svc. award EMSPAC, 1994. Mem. ASCD, N.E. Regional Elem. Prins. Assn. (rep. 1984-86, sec. 1986-87), Elem. Mid. Sch. Prins. Assn. (pres. 1985-86, Citizen of Year award, 1991, Pres.'s award 1981-85, state elected rep. 1989-90, fed. rels. coord. 1990-94, dist. dir. 1995-96),Adminstrn. and Supervision Assn. (sec. 1980-81, pres. 1981-82, exec. bd. 1982-93), Hartford Area Prins. and Suprs. Assn. (local pres. 1981-82), Nat. Assn. Elem. Sch. Prins. (zone I dir. 1987-90, del. to gen. assemblies 1984-90, bd. dirs. 1987-90), Conn. Assn. Supervision and Curriculum Devel., Trumbull Adminstrs. Assn. (pres.-elect 1989-91, pres. 1991-93), Eastern Conn. Council of Internat. Reading Assn., New Eng. Coalition Ednl. Leaders, Associated Tchrs. of Math. in Conn., Phi Delta Kappa (Disting. Fellow award 1992, v.p. rsch. and projects 1993-95), Pi Lambda Theta (Beta Sigma chpt.), Delta Kappa Gamma. Republican. Home: 5240 Madison Ave Trumbull CT 06611-1016 Office: Tashua Sch 401 Stonehouse Rd Trumbull CT 06611-1651

NORCIA, STEPHEN WILLIAM, advertising executive; b. N.Y.C., Jan. 21, 1941; s. William Matthew and Amelia (Marrone) N.; m. Martha Elizabeth Whelan, Apr. 22, 1978; children: Matthew F., Daniel P., Anne E. BA, U. Conn., 1962. Media planner and buyer SSC&B, N.Y.C., 1965-66; account exec. McCann-Erickson Co., Chgo., 1966-68; v.p., dep. mgr. McCann-Erickson Co., Milw., 1971-72; v.p., mgmt. supr. McCann-Erickson Co., N.Y.C., 1972-74; sr. v.p., gen. mgr. McCann-Erickson Co., Atlanta, 1974-78; exec. v.p., gen. mgr. McCann-Erickson Co., N.Y.C., 1978-81; exec. v.p., mem. exec. policy com., mem. mgmt. com. Lintas, N.Y.C., 1981—, exec. v.p., 1989-91, world wide client dir., dir. bus. devel., 1991—; also bd. dirs.; mng. ptnr. Earle Palmer Brown, N.Y.C., 1994-96; dir. global account DDB Needham, N.Y.C., 1996—; account exec. Needham, Harper & Steers, Chgo., 1968-70; dir. mktg. product devel. workshop Interpub., N.Y.C., 1970-71; bd. dirs. Communication Counselors Network. Bd. dirs. U. Ga. Master of Br. Mgmt. Program, 1985, 86, 87. 1st lt. U.S. Army, 1962-65. Recipient Robert E. Healy award Interpub. Group Cos., 1975, Effie award Am. Mktg. Assn., 1985, Grand Effie award Am. Mktg. Assn., 1984. Mem. Am. Assn. Advt. Agys., Advt. Club N.Y., Am. Yacht Club. Republican. Roman Catholic. Avocations: tennis, boating, skiing. Home: 1 Topsail Ln Rye NY 10580-3116 Office: DDB Needham 437 Madison Ave New York NY 10022

NORCROSS, DAVID FRANK ARMSTRONG, lawyer; b. Camden, N.J., Mar. 30, 1937; s. David Kincaid and Elizabeth S. (Norcross) Armstrong; m. Laurie Lee Michel, Nov. 11, 1988; children: Spencer Kincaid Cook, Victoria Lynn Armstrong. BA, U. Del., 1958; LLB, U. Pa., 1961. Bar: N.J. 1961, U.S. Ct. Appeals (3d cir.) 1971, U.S. Supreme Ct. 1987, D.C. 1993. Ptnr. Archer & Greiner, Haddonfield, N.J., 1965-71; exec. asst. to gov. State of N.J., Trenton, 1971-73; exec. dir. N.J. Election Law Enforcement Commn., Trenton, 1973-76; of counsel Brandt, Haughey, Penberthy & Lewis, Haddonfield, 1976; ptnr. Myers, Matteo, Rabil & Norcross, Cherry Hill, N.J., 1977-89, Montgomery, McCracken, Walker & Rhoads, Washington, Cherry Hill, 1989-94, Blank, Rome, Comisky & McCauley, Cherry Hill, 1994—; cons. Fed. Election Com., Washington, 1976, White House Conf. Drug Free Am., 1987-88; dir. Rep. Inst. Internat. Affairs, Washington, 1984—, gen. counsel, 1984-93; bd. dirs. Ctr. for Democracy, Washington, 1985-95; gen. counsel Rep. Nat. Com., 1993—. rep. candidate U.S. Senate, N.J., 1976; chmn. N.J. Rep. Party, 1977-81; counsel to chmn. Rep. Nat. Com., Washington, 1983-89, mem. 1977-81, 92—; vice chmn. Commn. on Presdl. Debates, 1988-93. Mem. N.J. Bar Assn., Burlington County Bar Assn., D.C. Bar Assn., Camden County Bar Assn., St. Andrews Soc. Washington, Capitol Hill Club, Moorestown Field Club, Univ. Club (Washington), Army-Navy Country Club. Episcopalian. Office: Blank Rome Comisky McCauley 1156 15th St NW Ste 550 Washington DC 20005-1704

NORCROSS, DAVID WARREN, physicist, researcher; b. Cin., July 18, 1941; s. Gerald Warren and Alice Elizabeth (Downey) N.; children: Joshua David, Sarah Elizabeth. AB, Harvard Coll., 1963; MSc, U. Ill., 1965; PhD, Univ. Coll., London, 1970. Research assoc. U. Colo., Boulder, 1970-74; physicist Nat. Bur. Standards, Boulder, 1974—; chief quantum physics divsn. Nat. Inst. Stds. and Tech., 1989-93, dir. Boulder Labs., 1994—; fellow Joint Inst. Lab. Astrophysics, Boulder, 1976—. Contbr. articles to profl. jours. Recipient Bronze medal Nat. Bur. Standards, 1982, Silver medal U.S. Dept. Commerce, 1994. Fellow Am. Phys. Soc. Office: Nat Inst Standards & Tech 325 Broadway Boulder CO 80303-3337

NORCROSS, MARVIN AUGUSTUS, veterinarian, government agency official; b. Tansboro, N.J., Feb. 8, 1931; s. Marvin A. and Katherine V. (McGuigan) N.; m. Diane L. Tuttle, Nov. 22, 1956 (div. 1991); children: James, Janet. Student, Rutgers U., 1954-55; VMD, U. Pa., 1959, PhD, 1966. Pathologist Merck Sharp & Dohme Research Labs., Rahway, N.J., 1966-69; dir. clin. research Merck Sharp & Dohme Research Labs., 1969-72, sr. dir. domestic vet. research, 1972-75; dir. div. vet. med. research Ctr. Vet. Medicine, FDA, Rockville, Md., 1975-78; assoc. dir. for research Ctr. Vet. Medicine, FDA, 1978-82, assoc. dir. for human food safety, 1982-84, assoc. dir. for new animal drug evaluation, 1984-87; asst. dep. adminstr., then dep. adminstr. Sci. and Tech., Food Safety and Inspection Svc. USDA, Washington, 1987-93, exec. asst. to the adminstr., 1993-94; U.S. coord. for Codex Alimentarius USDA, Washington, 1994-96, sr. sci. advisor to adminstr., 1996—; adj. prof. faculty Va.-Md. Regional Coll. Vet. Medicine, Blacksburg, Va., 1980-85. Contbr. articles to profl. jours. Trustee Scotch Plains (N.J.) Community Fund, 1969-72. Served to lt. AUS, 1952-54; col. Res., 1954-83 (ret.). Recipient FDA Merit award, 1978, Meritorious Presdl. Rank award, 1989. Mem. AVMA, AAAS, Am. Assn. Avian Pathologists, Assn. Mil. Surgeons U.S., Civil Affairs Assn., Inst. Food Technologists, Nat. Assn. Fed. Veterinarians, N.J. Acad. Sci., N.Y. Acad. Scis., Res. Officers Assn., Soc. Toxicologic Pathologists, Sigma Xi. Home: 14304 Brickhowe Ct Germantown MD 20874-3431 Office: USDA Food Safety Inspection West End Ct 1255 22nd St Rm 311 NW Washington DC 20250-3700

NORD, ELFRIDA HELENE, community health nurse; b. N.D., Oct. 8, 1933; d. Helmer Emil and Elfrida (Gjesbakk) N. Diploma, Sacred Heart Hosp., 1954; BS in Nursing, U. Wash., 1969; MPH, U. Hawaii, 1983. Staff nurse Sacred Heart Hosp., Havre, Mont., 1954-55; staff nurse oper. rm. Vancouver (Wash.) Meml. Hosp., 1955-58, 59-64; staff nurse Ulleval Hosp., Oslo and Hammerfest Hosp., Norway, 1958-59; nurse advisor USPHS/USAID, Cantho, Nha Trang, Vietnam, 1964-67; staff nurse Vancouver (Wash.) Meml. Hosp., 1970; head nurse Alaska Native Health Svcs. Hosp., Bethel, 1970-73; itinerant pub. health nurse Sect. of Nursing Div. Pub. Health, Bethel, 1973-76; nurse cons. Sect. of Communicable Disease Control Div. Pub. Health, Anchorage, 1976-82, 84; chief sect. of nursing Div. of Pub. Health, Juneau, Alaska, 1984—. Mem. Alaska Nurses Assn., Alaska Pub. Health Assn., Am. Pub. Health Assn., Am. Soc. Circumpolar Health (charter), Assn. State and Territorial Dirs. Nursing (sec.), Am. Assn. for the History of Nursing, Sigma Theta Tau. Home: 1135 Slim Williams Way Juneau AK 99801-8759 Office: Sect Pub Health Nursing PO Box 110611 Juneau AK 99811-0611

NORD, ERIC THOMAS, manufacturing executive; b. Amherst, Ohio, Nov. 8, 1917; s. Walter G. and Virginia C. (Greive) N.; m. Jane H. Baker; children: Virginia, Emily, Carlotte, Richard. BS in Mech. Engring., Case Inst. Tech., 1939. Pres., chief exec. officer Nordson Corp., Amherst, Ohio, 1954-73; chmn. Nordson Corp., Amherst, 1973—. Pres. Oberlin (Ohio) Bd. Edn., 1965; chmn. Oberlin City Council, 1959; bd. trustees Oberlin Coll., 1977—.

NORD, HENRY J., transportation executive; b. Berlin, May 1, 1917; came to U.S., 1937, naturalized, 1943; s. Walter and Herta (Riess) N.; children: Stephen, Philip. Student, U. Oxford, Eng., 1934, Northwestern U., 1938-40, Ill. Inst. Tech., 1942; JD, De Paul U., 1949. CPA, Ill. Apprentice in export Hamburg, Germany, 1935-37; with GATX Corp., Chgo., 1938-85; comptroller GATX Corp., 1961—, v.p., 1967-71, exec. v.p., 1971-78, sr. v.p., 1978-80, v.p., 1980-82, cons., 1982-84, fin. cons., 1982—, dir., 1964-78; dir. Planned Lighting, Inc. to 1988. Trustee DePaul U. Served to 1st lt. AUS, 1944-46. Mem. Internat. Law Assn. Club: Tavern (Chgo.). Home: 1000 N Lake Shore Plz Chicago IL 60611-1354 Office: 55 W Monroe St Ste 500 Chicago IL 60603-5003

NORD, PAUL ELLIOTT, accountant; b. Carona, N.Y., Mar. 22, 1936; s. Abe and Rose (Guss) N.; m. Marcia B. Gross, June 13, 1965; children: Howard, Aimee, Samuel. Student U. Utah, 1952-56; student, LaSalle Extension Inst., 1966. CPA, Calif.; accredited estate planner. Staff acct. Robinson, Nowell & Co. (merged with Muncy McPherson & Co., Muncy McPherson McCune Dieckman 1967), 1966-73, ptnr., 1973-81, mng. ptnr., 1981-87, ptnr. BDO Seidman, 1988-95, sr. ptnr., 1995—. Bd. dirs. Congregation Beth Sholom, San Francisco, 1969—, pres., 1979-81; mem. budget and allocations com. Jewish Fedn., East Bay, 1981-84. With U.S. Army, 1957-58, 61-62. Ford Found. scholar. Mem. Am. Inst. C.P.A.s (acctg. standards exec. com. 1979-81), Nat. Assn. Accredited Estate Planners, Calif. Soc. C.P.A.s (chmn. sub-com. acctg. principles 1981-83), C.P.A. Assocs. (bd. dirs. 1986-87) San Francisco Estate Planning Coun., Mensa, Club One Valley Vista Club. Jewish. Home: 931 Walnut Ave Walnut Creek CA 94598-3738 Office: 1 Sansome St Fl 11 San Francisco CA 94104-4430

NORD, ROBERT EAMOR, lawyer; b. Ogden, Utah, Apr. 11, 1945; s. Eamor Carroll and Ella Carol (Winkler) N.; m. Sherryl Anne Smith, May 15, 1969; children: Kimberly, P. Ryan, Debra, Heather, Andrew, Elizabeth. BS, Brigham Young U., 1969; JD, U. Chgo., 1972. Bar: Ill. 1972, U.S. Dist. Ct. (no. dist.) Ill. 1972, U.S. Ct. Appeals (D.C. cir.) 1974, U.S. Dist. Ct. (mid. dist.) Fla. 1976, U.S. Ct. Appeals (7th cir.) 1977, U.S. Dist. Ct. (no. dist.) Ind. 1978, U.S. Dist. Ct. (no. dist.) Fla. 1979, U.S. Supreme Ct. 1981, U.S. Dist. Ct. (ea. dist.) Mich. 1984, U.S. Ct. Appeals (11th cir.) 1985, U.S. Ct. Appeals (3d cir.) 1996. Assoc. Chadwell & Kayser, Chgo., 1972-75; from assoc. to ptnr. Hinshaw & Culbertson, Chgo., 1975—. Republican. Mormon. Club: University (Chgo.). Home: 481 Woodlawn Ave Glencoe IL 60022-2175 Office: Hinshaw & Culbertson 222 N La Salle St Ste 300 Chicago IL 60601-1005

NORD, THOMAS ALLISON, hospital administrator; b. Boise, Idaho, Dec. 29, 1934; s. Everett Oliver and Alice Susan (Sherry) N.; m. Kay Hahn, Apr. 19, 1958; children: Mark Allison, Matthew Brendan, Julia Christian Nord Jenkins, Christopher Thomas. BSBA, Denver U., 1957, MBA, 1971; postgrad., Cornell U., 1974. Office mgr. Mountain States Sprinkler Supply, Denver, 1957-61; owner, mgr. Desert Rain, Roswell, N.Mex., 1961-68; sheriff Chaves County, Roswell, 1966-71; adminstr. St. Vincent Gen. Hosp., Leadville, Colo., 1972-78, Grand River Hosp. Dist., Rifle, Colo., 1980-83; planner, coord. outreach St. Mary's Hosp. and Med. Ctr., Grand Junction, Colo., 1978-80, assoc. adminstr., 1980; pres., CEO, Ivinson Meml. Hosp., Laramie, Wyo., 1983—; Mem. Garfield County Human Svc. Commn., 1980-83, chmn., 1982-83; mem. governing bd. Western Colo. Health Sys. Agy., 1980; chmn. steering com. Southeastern Colo. Health Sys. Agy., 1975, chmn. governing bd., 1976-79; mem. liaison com. for U. Wyo. Sch. Nursing, 1984-85; mem. strategic planning com. U. Wyo., 1995—; mem. clin. faculty programs in health svcs. adminstrn. U. Minn. Sch. Pub. Health, 1984; bd. dirs. Blue Cross/Blue Shield Wyo., 1988—, mem. exec. com., 1993—, chmn. bd. dirs. 1996—; mem. Wyo. Healthcare Reform Commn., 1994; chmn. bd. VHA Mountain States. Active Boy Scouts Am., United Way. Fellow Am. Coll. Healthcare Execs. (Wyo. regent 1994—); mem. Am. Hosp. Assn. (Colo. Hosp. Assn. del. 1980-83, mem. task force for input price adjustments 1988, del. regional policy bd. 1994-96), Wyo. Hosp. Assn. (bd. dirs. 1984—, chmn. 1986), Healthcare Forum (membership com. 1985, bd. dirs. 1986-89), Laramie C. of C., Rotary, Lions, Elks. Republican. Avocations: skiing, hunting, hiking, fishing, woodworking. Home: PO Box 155 Centennial WY 82055-0155 Office: Ivinson Memorial Hospital 255 N 30th St Laramie WY 82070-5140

NORD, WALTER ROBERT, business administration educator, researcher, consultant; b. Mt. Kisco, N.Y., July 2, 1939; s. Arthur William and Elizabeth (Reimstedt) N.; m. Ann Feagan, June 10, 1967. BA in Econs., Williams Coll., 1961; MS in Organizational Behavior, Cornell U., 1963; PhD in Social Psychology, Washington U., St. Louis, 1967. Asst. prof. organizational psychology Washington U., 1967-70, assoc. prof., 1970-73, prof., 1973-89; prof. mgmt. U. South Fla., 1989—; vis. prof. faculty commerce U. B.C. (Can.), Vancouver, 1975-76, Northwestern U., 1981. Author: (with S. Tucker) Implementing Routine and Radical Innovations, 1987; editor: Concepts and Controversy in Organizational Behavior, 1972, rev. edit, 1976; (with P. Frost and V. Mitchell) Organizational Reality, 1978, rev. edit., 1982, 86, 92; (with H. Meltzer) Making Organizations Humane and Productive, 1982; (with P. Frost and V. Mitchell) Managerial Reality, 1989, HRM Reality, 1992; (with A. Brief) Meanings of Occupational Work, 1990. Fellow Am. Psychol. Assn.; mem. Acad. Mgmt., Union for Radical Polit. Econs. Home: 6004 Pratt St Tampa FL 33647-1043 Office: U South Fla Sch Bus Tampa FL 33620-5500

NORDBERG, JOHN ALBERT, senior federal judge; b. Evanston, Ill., June 18, 1926; s. Carl Albert and Judith Ranghild (Carlson) N.; m. Jane Spaulding, June 18, 1947; children: Carol, Mary, Janet, John. Student, Carleton Coll., 1943-44, 46-47; J.D., U. Mich., 1950. Bar: Ill. 1950, U.S. Dist. Ct. (no. dist.) Ill. 1957, U.S. Ct. Appeals (7th cir.) 1961. Assoc. Pope & Ballard, Chgo., 1950-57; ptnr. Pope, Ballard, Shepard & Fowle, Chgo., 1957-76; judge Cir. Ct. of Cook County, Ill., 1976-82; judge U.S. Dist. Ct. (no. dist.) Ill., Chgo., 1982-95, sr. judge, 1995—; lectr. Nat. Inst. Trial Advocacy, 1979. Editor-in-chief, bd. editors Chgo. Bar Record, 1966-74. Magistrate of Cir. Ct. and justice of peace Ill., 1957-65. Served with USN, 1944-46; PTO. Mem. ABA, Chgo. Bar Assn., Am. Judicature Soc., Law Club Chgo., Union League Club of Chgo., Legal Club Chgo., Order of Coif. Office: US Dist Ct 219 S Dearborn St Chicago IL 60604-1702

NORDBY, EUGENE JORGEN, orthopedic surgeon; b. Abbotsford, Wis., Apr. 30, 1918; s. Herman Preus and Lucille Violet (Korsrud) N.; m. Olive Marie Jensen, June 21, 1941; 1 child, Jon Jorgen. B.A., Luther Coll., Decorah, Iowa, 1939; M.D., U. Wis., 1943. Intern Madison Gen. Hosp., Wis., 1943-44, asst. in orthopedic surgery, 1944-48; practice medicine specializing in orthopedic surgery Madison, Wis., 1948—; pres. Bone and Joint Surgery Assocs., S.C. 1969-91; chief staff Madison Gen. Hosp., 1957-63; assoc. clin. prof. U. Wis. Med. Sch., 1961—; chmn. Wis. Physicians Svcs., 1979—; dir. Wis. Regional Med. Program, Chgo. Madison and No. RR; bd. govs. Wis. Health Care Liability Ins. Plan; chmn. trustees S.M.S. Realty Corp.; mem. bd. attys. Profl. Responsibility of Wis. Supreme Ct., 1992—. Assoc. editor Clin. Orthopaedics and Related Research, 1964—. Pres. Vesterheim Norwegian Am. Mus., Decorah, Iowa, 1968—. Served to capt. M.C., AUS, 1944-46. Decorated Knight 1st class Royal Norwegian Order St. Olav; named Notable Norwegian Dane County Norwegian-Am. Fest, 1995; recipient Disting. Svc. award Internat. Rotary,1 987, Den Hoyeste Aere award Vesterheim, 1993. Mem. Acad. Orthopaedic Surgeons (bd. dirs. 1972-73), Clin. Orthopaedic Soc., Assn. Bone and Joint Surgeons (pres. 1973), Internat. Soc. Study Lumbar Spine, State Med. Soc. Wis. (chmn. 1968-76, treas. 1976—, Coun. award 1976), Am. Orthopaedic Assn., N.Am. Spine Soc., Internat. Intradiscal Therapy Soc. (sec. 1987—), Wis. Orthopaedic Soc., Dane County Med. Soc. (pres. 1957), Nat. Exch. Club, Madison Torske Klubben (founder, pres. 1978—), Norwegian-Am. Orthopaedic Soc., Phi Chi. Lutheran. Home: 6234 S Highlands Ave Madison WI 53705-1115 Office: 2704 Marshall Ct Madison WI 53705-2256 *We must remember no matter how dedicated we are to the accumulation of knowledge, it isn't always what you know that matters but what you can think of in time.*

NORDBY, GENE MILO, engineering educator; b. Anoka, Minn., May 7, 1926; s. Bert J. and Nina Grace N.; m. Arlene Delores Anderson, Aug. 27, 1949 (dec. Nov. 1974); children: Susan Pamela, Brett Gene, Lisa Lea; m. Dusilla Anne Rycroft, July 8, 1975 (div. July 1988); m. Catherine Lynn Short, Dec. 23, 1992. BSCE, Oreg. State U., 1948; MSCE, U. Minn., 1949, Ph.D. in Civil Engring., 1955. Registered profl. engr., Colo. Ariz., Okla. Grad. asst. U. Minn., 1948-50; structural designer Pfeiffer and Shultz, Mpls., summer 1950; instr., then asst. prof. civil engring. U. Colo., Boulder, 1950-56; assoc. prof., rsch. engr. Joint Hwy. Rsch. Project Purdue U., East Lafayette, Ind., 1956; engr. program dir. engring. scis. NSF, Washington, 1956-58; lectr. civil engring. George Washington U., Washington, 1956-58; dir., then chmn. adv. com. Ariz. Transp. and Traffic Inst. at univ., 1959-62; prof. engring. U. Okla., Norman, 1962-77, dean Coll. Engring, 1962-70, v.p. for adminstrn. and fin. Coll. Engring, 1969-77; v.p. for bus. and fin., prof. civil engring. Ga. Inst. Tech., Atlanta, 1977-80; chancellor U. Colo., Denver, 1980-85; chancellor emeritus, 1985—; prof. civil engring. U. Colo., Denver and Boulder, 1985-86; prof. civil engring, head dept. civil engring. U. Ariz., 1958-62; prof. agrl. engring. U. Ariz., Tucson, 1986-94, prof. emeritus, 1994—, head dept. agrl. engring., 1986-91; mem. Reinforced Concrete Research Council Engring. Found., 1954-60; trustee Frontiers of Science Found., Okla., 1963-70; pres. Tetracon Assos., Inc., 1968-86; cons. structural engring., research financing and programming, ednl. facilities planning and constrn., reinforced concrete, also higher edn. adminstrn., engring. program accreditation, NSF, 1984-87, panel engring. ctrs. of excellence, 1983-87; bd. dirs. Higher Edn. and the Handicapped, Am. Council on Edn., 1980-83; pres. Accreditation Bd. for Engring. and Tech., 1985-86, fellow, mem. Related Accreditation Commn., 1986-95, chair, 1993-94; gen. chmn. Nat. Congress on Engring. Edn., Washington, 1986; commr. at large N. Cen. Assn. Schs. and Colls., 1988-92. Co-author: Introduction to Structural Mechanics, 1960; Cons. editor, MacMillan Co., 1962-70. Mem. bd. vis. Air Force Inst. Tech., 1985-87. With AUS, 1943-46. Recipient Citation for Svc., State of Okla. Ho. Reps., 1977, Linton E. Grinter Disting. Svc. award Accreditation Bd. for Engring. and Tech., 1982. Fellow ASCE (com. on engring edn., 1964-68, com. on research needs, 1965-70, com. on ednl. research, 1976-79, Edmund Friedman Profl. Devel. award 1982); mem. Am. Soc. Engring. Edn. (projects bd. 1969-70, chmn. Curtis W. McGraw award com. 1968, Dean's Inst. com. 1966-69, accreditation process com. 1979-81), Nat. Soc. Profl. Engrs., Am. Arbitration Assn., Am. Soc. Agrl. Engrs. (com. in egring. and tech. accreditation 1987-93), Engrs. Council for Profl. Devel. (chmn. engring. edn. and accreditation com. 1970, dir. 1976-79, 83-87), Ariz. Soc. Profl. Engrs., Okla. Soc. Profl. Engrs. (dir. 1966-69), Nat. Assn. State Univs. and Land Grant Colls. (commn. edn. engring. profession 1966, 70-73), Engring. Colls. Adminstrv. Council (mem. exec. bd. 1966), Ga. Soc. Profl. Engrs. (bd. dirs. Atlanta chpt. 1978-79), Nat. Assn. Coll. and Univ. Bus. Officers (chmn. personnel com. 1977-79), Sigma Tau, Omicron Delta Kappa, Tau Beta Pi, Chi Epsilon, Alpha Epsilon. Club: Mason. Office: U Ariz 403 Shantz Bldg 38 Tucson AZ 85721

NORDELL, HANS RODERICK, journalist, retired editor; b. Alexandria, Minn., June 26, 1925; s. Wilbur Eric and Amelia (Jasperson) N.; m. Joan Projansky, Apr. 30, 1955; children: Eric Peter, John Roderick, Elizabeth Sabin. AB magna cum laude, Harvard U., 1948; B Litt, U. Dublin, 1951. With Christian Sci. Monitor, Boston, 1948-93, arts editor, 1968-73, asst. chief editorial writer, 1973-83, home forum editor, 1983-85, feature editor, 1985-87; exec. editor World Monitor: The Chrstian Science Monitor Monthly, Boston, 1988-93. Bd. dirs. Community Music Ctr., Boston, 1970-94, corp. chair, 1994—; bd. dirs. Young Audiences, 1970-88; mem. Com. for Harvard Theatre Collection, 1977-91; trustee Berklee Coll. Music, 1970—. With USMCR, 1943-46. Fellowship Rotary Found., 1950-51. Mem. St. Botolph Club, Phi Beta Kappa. Christian Scientist. Home: 25 Meadow Way Cambridge MA 02138-4635

NORDENBERG, MARK ALAN, law educator, university official; b. Duluth, Minn., July 12, 1948; s. John Clemens and Shirley Mae (Tappen) N.; m. Nikki Patricia Pirillo, Dec. 26, 1970; children: Erin, Carl, Michael. BA, Thiel Coll., 1970; JD, U. Wis., 1973. Bar: Wis. 1973, Minn. 1974, U.S. Supreme Ct. 1976, Pa. 1985. Atty. Gray, Plant, Mooty & Anderson, Mpls., 1973-75; prof. law Capital U. Law Ctr., Columbus, Ohio, 1975-77; prof. law U. Pitts., 1977—, acting dean Sch. Law, 1985-87, dean Sch. Law, 1987-93, interim univ. sr. vice chancellor and provost, 1993-94, Univ. Disting. Svc. prof., 1994—, interim univ. chancellor, 1995—; mem. U.S. Supreme Ct. Adv. Com. on Civil Rules, Washington, 1988-93, Pa. Supreme Ct. Civil Procedure Rules Com., Phila., 1986-92; mem. large and complex case panel Am. Arbitration Assn.; reporter civil justice adv. group U.S. Dist. Ct., Pitts., 1991—. Author: Modern Pennsylvania Civil Practice, 1985, 2d edit., 1995. Trustee Thiel Coll., Greenville, Pa., 1987—; bd. dirs. Lawyers Concerned for Lawyers of Pa., Harrisburg, Inst. for Shipboard Edn.; vice chair Pitts.-Wuhan Friendship Com. Fellow Am. Bar Found.; mem. ABA, Pa. Bar Assn., Pa. Assn. Colls. and Univs. (bd. dirs.), Allegheny County Bar Assn., Acad. Trial Lawyers Allegheny County, Law Club Pitts., Univ. Club. Office: U Pitts 107 Cathedral of Learning Pittsburgh PA 15260-0001

NORDGREN, RONALD PAUL, engineering educator, researcher; b. Munising, Mich., Apr. 3, 1936; s. Paul A. and Martha M. (Busse) N.; m. Joan E. McAfee, Sept 12, 1959; children: Sonia, Paul. BS in Engring., U. Mich., 1957, MS in Engring., 1958; PhD, U. Calif., Berkeley, 1962. Rsch. asst. U. Calif., Berkeley, 1959-62; mathematician Shell Devel. Co., Houston, 1963-68, staff rsch. engr., 1968-74, sr. staff rsch. engr., 1974-80, rsch. assoc., 1980-90; Brown prof. civil and mech. engring. Rice U., Houston, 1989—; mem. U.S. nat. com. on theoretical and applied mechanics NRC, 1984-86, U.S. nat. com. for rock mechanics, 1991-95. Contbr. tech. papers to profl. jours.; assoc. editor Jour. Applied Mechanics, 1972-76, 81-85; patentee in field. Fellow ASME; mem. NAE, ASCE, Soc. Industrial and Applied Math., Soc. Engring. Sci., Sigma Xi. Office: Rice U 6100 Main St Houston TX 77005-1827

NORDHAUS, ROBERT RIGGS, lawyer; b. Albuquerque, Mar. 27, 1937; s. Robert J. and Virginia (Riggs) N.; m. Jean Friedberg, June 27, 1964; children: Ronald E., Hannah E. BA, Stanford U., 1960; LLB, Yale U., 1963. Bar: N.Mex. 1963, D.C. 1981, U.S. Supreme Ct. 1982. Asst. counsel U.S. House Reps., Washington, 1963-74, counsel interstate and fgn. commerce com., 1975-76; asst. adminstr. FEA, Washington, 1977; gen. counsel Fed. Energy Regulatory Commn., Washington, 1977-80; ptnr. Van Ness, Feldman & Curtis, Washington, 1981-93; gen. counsel Dept. of Energy, Washington, 1993—; adj. prof. Georgetown U. Law Ctr., Washington, 1980-85. Served to 2d. lt. U.S. Army, 1960-68. Mem. Fed. Energy Bar Assn. (bd. dirs. 1989—). Office: Gen Coun 1000 Independence Ave SW Washington DC 20585-0001

NORDIN, VIDAR JOHN, forestry educator, consultant; b. Ratansbyn, Sweden, June 28, 1924; s. John Herman and Beda Catherina (Wahlen) N.; m. Julianne Leona Zerr, Oct. 11, 1947; children: Christopher Eric, Katrin Anne. B.A., U. B.C., 1946, B.Sc.F., 1947; Ph.D., U. Toronto, 1951. Registered profl. forester, Ont. Officer in charge Forest Pathology Lab., Fredericton, N.B., Can., 1949-51; officer in charge Calgary, Alta., Can., 1952-57; asso. dir. forest biology div. Fed. Agr. Dept., 1958-65; research mgr. Fed. Environment Dept., Ottawa, Ont., Can., 1965-71; prof., dean faculty forestry U. Toronto, Ont., 1971-84, prof. emeritus, 1986—; chmn. bd. Algonquin Forestry Authority Corp., 1974-82; pres. U.J. Nordin Assocs. Ltd., 1974—; dir. Can. Forestry Accreditation Project, 1987-89; sr. cons. Assn. Univs. and Colls. of Can., 1989—; hon. lectr. U. N.B., 1949-51. Mem. editl. bd. European Jour. Forest Pathology, 1970-84; co-editor: Forestry Chronicle, 1995—; contbr. articles to profl. jours. Co-chmn. U. Toronto United Way Campaign, 1973-74; mem. Provincial Parks Adv. Council, 1974-77. Fellow Canadian Inst. Forestry (past pres.); mem. Internat. Union Forestry Research Orgns. (past subject group chmn.), Internat. Soc. Tropical Foresters (treas., dir., v.p.), Ont. Forestry Assn. (dir.), Ont. Profl. Foresters Assn., Soc. Am. Foresters, Assn. Univ. Forestry Schs. Can. (past pres.), Chinese Soc. Forestry (hon.), Can. Owners and Pilots Assn., Rockcliffe Flying Club. Home: 403-A Echo Dr, Ottawa, ON Canada K1S 1N5

NORDLAND, GERALD, art museum administrator, historian, consultant; b. Los Angeles. AB, U. So. Calif., JD. Dean of faculty Chouinard Art Sch., L.A., 1960-64; dir. Washington Gallery of Modern Art, 1964-66, San Francisco Mus. Art, 1966-72, Frederick S. Wight Art Galleries, UCLA, 1973-77, Milw. Art Mus., 1977-85; ind. curator, author, editor Chgo., 1985—. Author: Paul Jenkins, 1972, Gaston Lachaise/The Man and His Work, 1974, Richard Diebenkorn, 1987, Zhou Brothers, Chicago, 1994. Gaston Lachaise Found. grantee, 1973-74; John Simon Guggenheim Found. fellow, 1985-86. Home and Office: 645 W Sheridan Rd Chicago IL 60613-3316

NORDLEY, GERALD DAVID, writer, investor; b. Mpls., May 22, 1947; s. V. Gerald and Evelyn May (Whitesel) N.; (div. 1973); 1 child, Sharon; m. Gayle Ann Wiesner, May 9, 1976; children: Jeffrey Goldberg, Andrew Nordley. BA in Physics, Macalester Coll., 1969; MS in System Mgmt., U. So. Calif., L.A., 1980. Enlisted USAF, 1969, commd. 2nd lt., 1970, advanced through grades to maj., 1982; inter-range ops. officer Network Ops. Div., Sunnyvale AFB, Calif., 1973-76; chief orbital ops. br. Def. Satellite Communications Directorate, L.A. AFB, 1976-81; chief spacecraft engr. br. DSCS III Program Office, L.A. AFB, 1981-82; battle dir. Mangilsan Liason Annex, Mang Il San, South Korea, 1983; chief advanced propulsion br. A.F. Rocket Propulsion Lab., Edwards AFB, Calif., 1984-86; rsch. staff mgr. ARIES office Astronautics Lab., Edwards AFB, 1986-89; ret. USAF, 1989; writer, pvt. investor Sunnyvale, 1990—. Mem. dir. Macalester Coll. Rep. Club, St. Paul, 1967-68; pres. Park Knowles Estates Property Owners Assn., Boron, Calif., 1988; co-chair Silicon Valley Writers Workshop, Cupertino, Calif., 1992, 93. Decorated Air Force Commendation medal with 4 oak leaf clusters, Meritorious Svc. medal with 1 oak leaf cluster; recipient Anlab award Analog Mag., 1992, 93. Fellow Brit. Interplanetary Soc.; mem. AIAA (elec. propulsion com. 1984-86), Air Force Assn., Sci. Fiction Writers Am., Whensday People Writers Group, Ft. Mason's Officers Club, Am. Legion. Unitarian. Avocation: amateur astronomy.

NORDLIE, ROBERT CONRAD, biochemistry educator; b. Willmar, Minn., June 11, 1930; s. Peder Conrad and Myrtle (Spindler) N.; m. Sally Ann Christianson, Aug. 23, 1959; children: Margaret, Melissa, John. B.S. St. Cloud State Coll., Minn., 1952; M.S., U. N.D., 1957, Ph.D., 1960. Teaching and research asst. biochemistry U. N.D. Med. Sch., Grand Forks, 1955-60, Hill research prof. biochemistry, 1962-74, Chester Fritz disting. prof. biochemistry, 1974—, Cornatzer prof., chmn. dept. biochemistry and molecular biology, 1983—; hon. prof. San Marcos U., Lima, Peru, 1981, 82—; NIH fellow Inst. Enzyme Rsch., U. Wis., 1960-61; mem. biochemistry study sect. NIH; merit rev. com. VA, 1994—; cons. exzymology Oak Ridge, 1961—; vis. prof. Tokyo Biomed. Inst., 1984; mem. predoctoral fellowship rev. group Howard Hughes Inst., 1990-93. Mem. editorial bd.: Jour. Biol. Chemistry, Biochimca et Biophysica Acta. Research publs. on enzymology relating to metabolism of various carbohydrates in mammalian livers, regulation blood sugar levels. Served with AUS, 1953-55. Recipient Disting. Alumnus award St. Cloud State U., 1983; recipient Sigma Xi Rsch. award, 1969, Golden Apple award U. N.D., 1968, Edgar Dale award U. N.D., 1983, Burlington No. Faculty Scholar award, 1987, Thomas J. Clifford Faculty Achievement award for excellence in rsch. U. N.D. Found., 1993. Mem. Am. Soc. Biol. Chemistry and Molecular Biology, Am. Chem. Soc., AAAS, Internt. Union Biochemists, Am. Soc. Microbiology, Soc. Exptl. Biology and Medicine, Am. Inst. Nutrition, Brit. Biochem. Soc., Sigma Xi, Alpha Omega Alpha. Home: 162 Columbia Ct Grand Forks ND 58203-2947

NORDLING, BERNARD ERICK, lawyer; b. Nekoma, Kans., June 14, 1921; s. Carl Ruben Ebben and Edith Elveda (Freeburg) N.; m. Barbara Ann Burkholder, Mar. 26, 1949. Student, George Washington U., 1941-43; AB, McPherson Coll., 1947; JD, U. Kans., 1949. Bar: Kans. 1949, U.S. Dist. Ct. Kans. 1949, U.S. Ct. Appeals (10th cir.) 1970. Pvt. practice Hugoton, Kans., 1949—; ptnr. Kramer & Nordling, 1950-65; ptnr. Kramer, Nordling, Nordling & Tate, 1966-94, of counsel, 1994—; city atty. City of Hugoton, 1951-87; county atty. Stevens County, Kans., 1957-63; Kans. mem. legal com. Interstate Oil Compact Commn., 1969—; mem. supply tech. adv. com. nat. gas survey FPC, 1975-77. Editor U. Kans. Law Rev., 1949. Mem. Hugoton Sch. Bds., 1954-68, pres. grade sch. bd., 1957-63; trustee McPherson Coll., 1971-81, mem. exec. com., 1975-81; mem. Kans. Energy Adv. Coun., 1975-78, mem. exec. com., 1976-78. With AUS, 1944-46. Recipient Citation of Merit, McPherson Coll., 1987, Disting. Alumnus award Kans. U. Law Sch., 1993, Lifetime Achievement award Hugoton Kans. Area C. of C., 1994. Fellow Am. Bar Found. (Kans.); mem. ABA, Kans. Bar Assn., S.W. Kans. Bar Assn., Am. Judicature Soc., City Attys. Assn. Kans. (exec. com. 1975-83, pres. 1982-83), Nat. Assn. Royalty Owners (bd. govs. 1980—), S.W. Kans. Royalty Owners Assn. (exec. sec. 1968-94, asst. exec. sec. 1994—), U. Kans. Law Soc. (bd. govs. 1984-87), Kans. U. Endowment Assn. (trustee 1989—), Kans. U. Alumni Assn. (bd. dirs. 1992—), Order of Coif, Phi Alpha Delta. Home: 218 N Jackson St Hugoton KS 67951-2040 Office: 209 E 6th St Hugoton KS 67951-2613

NORDLUND, DONALD CRAIG, corporate lawyer; b. Chgo., May 23, 1949; s. Donald E. and Jane (Houston) N.; m. Sally Baum, Sept. 7, 1975; children: Courtney Elizabeth, Michael Andrew, Laurie Katherine. AB, Stanford U., 1971; JD, Vanderbilt U., 1974. Assoc. Ware & Freidenrich, Palo Alto, Calif., 1974-77; atty. Hewlett-Packard Co., Palo Alto, 1977-80, sr. atty., asst. sec., 1980-81, asst. sec., corp. counsel, 1981-85, sec., corp. counsel, 1985-86, sec., asst. gen. counsel, 1986-87, assoc. gen. counsel, sec., 1987—; bd. dirs. Hewlett-Packard Hellas, Palo Alto, Hewlett-Packard European Distbn., Ops., Inc., The Netherlands, Hewlett-Packard Labs. Japan, Inc., Hewlett-Packard Del. Holding Inc., Hewlett-Packard Employees Fed. Credit Union, other Hewlett-Packard subs.; sec. Hewlett-Packard Co. Found., Palo Alto, 1979—, Hewlett-Packard Fin. Co., Palo Alto, 1983—, Apollo Computer, Inc., 1989—; panelist disclosure documents seminar Practicing Law Inst., 1982-96, also contbg. author to course handbook; cons. pub. guide series, CEB, 1991. Chmn., bd. dirs. Santa Clara County chpt. Jr. Achievement, 1995—. Mem. Am. Soc. Corp. Secs. Inc. (pres. San Francisco region 1986-88, bd. dirs. 1987-90, mem. exec. com. 1988-89, chmn. securities law com. 1995—), Am. Corp. Counsel Assn. (bd. dirs. San Francisco chpt. 1984—, nat. bd. dirs. 1995—, pres. 1989-90), Foothills Tennis and Swimming Club (Palo Alto). Avocations: tennis, skiing, sailing, golf. Office: Hewlett-Packard Co 3000 Hanover St Palo Alto CA 94304-1112

NORDLUND, DONALD ELMER, manufacturing company executive; b. Stromsburg, Nebr., Mar. 1, 1922; s. E.C. and Edith O. (Peterson) N.; m. Mary Jane Houston, June 5, 1948; children: Donald Craig, William Chalmers, Sarah, James. A.B., Midland Coll., 1943; J.D., U. Mich., 1948. Bar: Ill. 1949. With Stevenson, Conaghan, Hackbert, Rooks and Pitts, Chgo., 1948-55, A.E. Staley Mfg. Co., Decatur, Ill., 1956-85; v.p., dir., mem. exec. com. A.E. Staley Mfg. Co., 1958-65, pres., chief operating officer, 1965-80, dir., mem. exec. com., 1965-85, also chmn., 1975-85; chief exec. officer Staley Continental, Inc., Rolling Meadows, Ill., 1985-88, chmn. and chief exec. officer, 1985-88; bd. dirs. Sentry Ins., Sundstrand Corp. Past chmn. bd. trustees Millikin U., now hon. trustee; trustee Vanderbilt U., Mus. Sci. and Industry, Chgo., Rush-Presbyn. St. Lukes Med. Ctr., Chgo.; bd. dirs. Lyric Opera Chgo.; mem. grad. dirs. coun. Decatur Meml. Hosp. Mem. ABA, Chgo. Bar Assn., Corn Refiners Assn. (bd. dirs., past chmn., now hon. dir.), Legal Club, Comml. Club, Chgo. Club, Tavern Club, Barrington Hills Club, Phi Alpha Delta.

NORDLUND, JAMES JOHN, dermatologist; b. St. Paul, Aug. 11, 1939; m. Mary Flanagan, Sept. 28, 1963; children: Christa, Michael, Marguerite. BA, St. John's U., 1961; BS, U. Minn., 1963, MD, 1965. Diplomate Am. Bd. Internal Medicine, Am. Bd. Dermatology. Clin. investigator VA, West Haven, Conn., 1977-80; assoc. prof. dermatology Yale U., New Haven, 1978-82, prof. dermatology, 1982-83; prof., chmn. U. Cin., 1983—; mem. nat. adv. com. St. John's U., Collegeville, Minn. Editor: Dermatology Resource Manual, 1988, Pigmentary Disorders, 1988, Cutaneous Aging, 1988. Lt. comdr. USPHS, 1967-69. Mem. Soc. Investigative Dermatology, Am. Dermatol. Assn., Pan Am. Soc. for Pigment Cell Rsch. (pres. 1986-91), Am. Acad. Dermatology (bd. dirs. 1987-91), N.Y. Acad. Sci., Assn. Profs. Dermatology, Internat. Fedn. Pigment Cell Socs. (sec.-treas. 1989-92), Sigma Xi. Avocations: scuba, hiking, woodworking, gardening. Office: U Cin Coll Medicine 231 Bethesda Ave # 592 Cincinnati OH 45229-2827

NORDLUND, JAMES ROBERT, state agency director; b. St. Paul, Minn., Dec. 23, 1952; s. Leonard Gustav and Catherine Ann (Lindow) N. BS, St. John U., 1975; MPA, U. Colo., 1982. Journeyman carpenter Carpenter's Locals Denver and Anchorage, 1981-85; housing rehab. specialist Anchorage Neighborhood Housing Svcs., 1983-86; legis. asst. Alaska State Legislature, Anchorage, Juneau, 1986-92, state legislator, 1993-95; dir. divsn. pub. assistance State of Alaska, Juneau, 1995—; pres., CEO Macuir Co. Inc., Anchorage, 1990—; comml. fisherman, Alaska, 1987—. Founding pres. Anchorage Waterways Coun., 1985. Democrat. Roman Catholic. Avocations: outdoor sports, team sports, photography, running. Office: PO Box 110640 Juneau AK 99811-0640

NORDLUND, WILLIAM CHALMERS, lawyer; b. Chgo., Aug. 29, 1954; s. Donald E. and Jane H. (Houston) N.; m. Elizabeth Apell, Oct. 1, 1983; children: William Chalmers Jr., Scott Donald. BA, Vanderbilt U., 1976; JD, Duke U., 1979; MM, Northwestern U., 1990. Bar: Ill. 1979, Md. 1991, Mich. 1992. Assoc. Winston & Strawn, Chgo., 1979-87, ptnr., 1987-90; atty. Constellation Holdings, Inc., 1990-91; v.p., sec., gen. counsel The Oxford Energy Co., Dearborn, Mich., 1991-92, sr. v.p., sec., gen counsel, 1992-93; gen. counsel Panda Energy Corp., Dallas, 1993-94, v.p. and gen. counsel, 1994-95; v.p., gen. counsel Panda Energy Internat., Inc., Dallas, 1995—. Bd. dirs. Orch. of Ill., Chgo., 1983-85; bd. dirs., sec. Literacy Vols. of Am.-Ill., Chgo., 1985-88, treas., 1988-90. Mem. Gleneagles C.C. Avocations: golf, tennis, skiing. Office: Panda Energy Internat Inc 4100 Spring Valley Rd Ste 1001 Dallas TX 75244-3646

NORDMAN, CHRISTER ERIC, chemistry educator; b. Helsinki, Finland, Jan. 23, 1925; came to U.S., 1948, naturalized, 1960; s. Eric Johan and Gertrud (Nordgren) N.; m. Barbara Lorraine Neal, Nov. 28, 1952 (div. 1993); children: Christina, Aleta, Eric, Carl; m. Outi Marttila, Dec. 28, 1994. Dipl. Ing., Finnish Inst. Tech., Helsinki, 1949; Ph.D., U. Minn., 1953. Research asso. Inst. Cancer Research, Phila., 1953-55; mem. faculty U. Mich., Ann Arbor, 1955—; prof. chemistry U. Mich., 1964-95; prof. emeritus, 1995—. Mem. U.S. Nat. Com. Crystallography, 1970-72. Served with Finnish Army, 1943-44. NIH spl. fellow, 1971-72. Fellow AAAS; mem. Am. Chem. Soc., Am. Phys. Soc., Am. Crystallographic Assn., Finnish Soc. Scis. and Letters. Home: 2200 Fuller Rd Apt 207B Ann Arbor MI 48105-2309 Office: Univ Mich Dept Chemistry Ann Arbor MI 48109

NORDMAN, RICHARD DENNIS, chemical company executive; b. Iowa, Sept. 30, 1946; s. Victor and Dorothy Nordman; m. Patricia Lynn Boehnke, Aug. 27, 1966; children: Sarah, Matthew, Angela. BSBA, Iowa State U., 1968. CPA, Ill. Mgr. Arthur Andersen & Co., Chgo., 1968-74; treas. Lawter Internat., Inc., Northbrook, Ill., 1974-80, v.p. fin., 1980-83, exec. v.p., 1983-86, pres., COO, 1986-96, bd. dirs., 1982. Trustee Cornerstone Found. Luth. Social Svcs. of Ill. Mem. AICPA, Ill. Soc. CPAs, Chgo. Sunday Evening Club (trustee), Econ. Club, Exec. Club. Avocations: golf, tennis, flying. Office: Lawter Internat Inc 990 Skokie Blvd Northbrook IL 60062-4005

NORDQUIST, SANDRALEE RAHN, lay worker; b. Chgo., Dec. 5, 1940; d. Herbert Henry and Elinor Gertrude (Duben) Rahn; m. George Leczewski, Oct. 13, 1962 (div. Dec. 1968); 1 child, Peter George (dec.); m. David Arthur Nordquist, July 19, 1969; children: Kerilinn D., Sharianne R. AA, Harper Coll., 1982; BS in English, Elmhurst (Ill.) Coll., 1985, BS in Theology, 1988; postgrad., Northestern Ill. U., Chgo., Drake U. Cert. tchr. English, history, learning disordered, behaviorally disordered, Ill. Tchr. English, gen. music and spl. edn. Foreman H.S., Chgo., 1990—; tchr. English summer sch. Luther H.S., Chgo., 1990, 92-94; feature writer Daily Herald, Paddock Publs., 1991—; tchr. sci. summer sch. Weber H.S., Chgo., 1995. Columnist (newspaper) Pulitzer Pubs. Notebook, 1986-90. Leader Girl Scouts U.S., Chgo. and Elk Grove, 1968-70, 77-81; v.p. Dist. 59 Orch. Assn., Elk Grove Village, Ill., 1985-87; pres. Sch. Dist. 59 Project 444, Elk Grove Village, 1981; confirmation tchr. Evang. Luth. Ch. of the Holy Spirit, Elk Grove, Ill., 1990-91, guild pres., adv. trinity preaching, 1990-91, leader adult Bible study, 1991-93; lector, greeter, actress Trinity Luth. Ch., Roselle, Ill., 1992—, also Drama Guild. Mem. Nat. Coun. Tchrs. of English, Ill. Assn. Tchrs. of English, Sigma Tau Delta. Home: 639 Sycamore Dr Elk Grove Village IL 60007-4624 Office: Foreman High Sch 3235 N Leclaire Ave Chicago IL 60641-4238

NORDQVIST, ERIK ASKBO, shipping company executive; b. Copenhagen, Aug. 8, 1943; s. Joergen and Lissie (Moeller) A.; m. Kirsten Vibeke Kenholt, Sept. 17, 1970; children: Ken-Martin, Alexander. Student, Danish Comml. Coll. Commerce, London, 1963-64, U. S.C., London, 1964-65. Vice pres. Import Center W.S., L.A., 1964-65; mgr. Denning Freight Forwarders Ltd., Toronto, Ont., Can., 1965-66; sales dir. overseas Samson Transp. Co., Copenhagen, 1967-68; mng. dir., pres. Seair AS, Copenhagen, 1969-71, Nordbird Group, Vedbaek, Denmark, 1971—, Nordbird AS, 1971—; chmn. European Steamship Line, Vedbaek, 1995—, European Airline Sys., Vedbaek, 1995—; also Nordbird Oil, Nordbird Fin., Copenhagen, Nordbird Internat. Financing Ltd., Toronto, Ont.; v.p. N. Sea Products Inc., High Point, N.C., 1980—; bd. dirs. Fino Travel, Odense, Denmark, Annex Furniture Galleries, European Broadcast Comm., Vedbaek, On Holding Ltd., Gibraltar, Olsen & Nordqvist Holding, Holbaek, Denmark, pres., 1986—, NQ-Byg Aps, Holbaek, Auto Dan-Am., Holbaek, Autotel Internat., Roskilde, On Holding APS, Vedbaek Dansk-Fransk Osters Aps, 3 Danish Open, U.S., Gt. Britain, Japan,, Tins and Cans, Denmark; chmn. European Broadcast Comm., Charlottenlund, Denmark, London, European Aid Found., Vedbeak, Denmark, Lac, Albanien; cons. Frederikshavns. Skibsvaerf AS, Copenhagen Cmty. Chmn. European Broadcast Comm., Copenhagen and London, 1992—, European Aid Found., Copenhagen and N.Y.C.; del. Internat. Red Cross, Copenhagen, 1994—. Recipient Devel. honor for shipping City of Le Havre, France, 1971. Mem. Det Udenrigspolitiske Selskab, Funen Soc. (founder, past pres.). Conservative. Lutheran. Office: 35 Flintemarken, 2950 Vedbaek Denmark

NORDSTROM, BRUCE A., department store executive; b. 1933; married. BA, U. Wash., 1956. With Nordstrom, Inc., Seattle, 1956—, v.p., 1964-70, pres., 1970-75, chmn., 1975-77, co-chmn., 1977—, dir. Office: Nordstrom Inc 1501 5th Ave Seattle WA 98101-1603*

NORDSTROM, JOHN N., department store executive; b. 1937; married. BA, U. Wash., 1958. With Nordstrom, Inc., Seattle, 1958—, v.p., 1965-70, exec. v.p., 1970-75, pres., 1975-77, co-chmn., 1977—, dir.; bd. dirs. Fed. Res. Bank San Francisco. Office: Nordstrom Inc 1501 5th Ave Seattle WA 98101-1603*

NOREK, FRANCES THERESE, lawyer; b. Chgo., Mar. 9, 1947; d. Michael S. and Viola C. (Harbecke) N.; m. John E. Flavin, Aug. 31, 1968 (div.); 1 child, John Michael. B.A., Loyola U., Chgo., 1969, J.D., 1973. Bar: Ill. 1973, U.S. Dist. Ct. (no. dist.) Ill. 1973, U.S. Ct. Appeals (7th cir.) 1974. Assoc. Alter, Weiss, Whitesel & Laff, Chgo., 1973-74; asst. states atty. Cook County, Chgo., 1974-86; assoc. Clausen, Miller, Gorman, Caffrey & Witous P.C., 1986—; mem. trial practice faculty Loyola U. Sch. Law, Chgo., 1980—; judge, evaluator mock trial competitions, Chgo., 1978—; lectr. in field. Recipient Emil Gumpert award Am. Coll. Trial Lawyers, 1982. Mem. Chgo. Bar Assn. (instr. fed. trial bar adv. program young lawyer's sect. 1983-84). Office: Clausen Miller Gorman Caffrey & Witous PC 10 S La Salle St Chicago IL 60603-1002

NOREK, JOAN I., lawyer; b. Chgo., Jan. 26, 1945; d. Michael Stephen and Viola Catherine (Harbecke) N. BA in Chemistry, U. Ill., 1968; JD, DePaul U., 1975. Bar: Ill. 1975, U.S. Dist. Ct. (no. dist.) Ill. 1976, U.S. Ct. Appeals (7th cir.) 1976; registered patent atty. Assoc. Willian Brinks et al, Chgo., 1975-80; pvt. practice Chgo., 1980—. Mem. Chgo. Intellectual Property Law Assn. (bd. mgrs. 1989-91), Chgo. Bar Assn., Am. Chem. Soc. Roman Catholic. Avocations: sailboat racing, dog obedience training, gardening. Home: 2722 N Pine Grove Ave Chicago IL 60614-6145 Office: 180 LaSalle St Chicago IL 60601

NORELL, MARK ALLEN, paleontology educator; b. St. Paul, July 26, 1957; s. Albert Donald Norell and Helen Louise Soltau; m. Vivian Pan, Nov. 1, 1991. BS, Long Beach State U., 1980; MS, San Diego State U., 1983; PhD, Yale U., 1988. Assoc. curator Am. Mus., N.Y.C., 1989-96, 1994-95; adj. assoc. prof. dept. biology Yale U., New Haven, 1991—. Author: All You Need to Know About Dinosaurs, 1991, Discovering Dinosaurs, 1995. Fellow Willi Hennig Soc., Explorers Club; mem. Soc. Vertebrate Paleontology (Romer prize 1987). Office: Am Mus Natural History 79th At Ctrl Park West New York NY 10024-5192

NOREM, RICHARD FREDERICK, SR., musician, music educator; b. Joliet, Ill., June 28, 1931; s. Oscar Lewis and Mabel Vera (Meyer) N.; m. Sally Lou Jarvis, July 24, 1954; 1 son, Richard Frederick II. Mus.B., U. Rochester, 1953, Mus.M., 1958; postgrad., Guildhall Sch., London, 1974. Instr. Joliet Musical Coll., Ill., 1951-53; tchr. Rochester Pub. Schs., N.Y., 1956-57; mem. faculty La. State U., Baton Rouge, 1957-95; prof., asst. dean music La. State U., 1969-84; prof. emeritus La. State U., Baton Rouge, 1995; dir., sec.-treas. Bank Commerce, 1983—; bd. dirs., sec.-treas. NBC Fin. Corp., 1988—. Mem. Baton Rouge Symphony Orch., 1957—, Timm Woodwind Quintet, 1957-95. With USMC Band, 1953-56. Mem. Am. Legion (past post comdr.), Rolls-Royce Owners Club (sec.-treas. So. Delta region), Starlighters Club, La. State U. Faculty Club, Baton Rouge Model R.R. Club, Rotary. Republican. Episcopalian. Home: 4821 Sweetbriar St Baton Rouge LA 70808-8660 Office: La State U Sch Music Baton Rouge LA 70803 *I have been blessed by the divine creator with an artistic talent in music to which I have dedicated my life. Early during my performing career I knew I must share with others the knowledge I had obtained in music; consequently my goals have been to train and educate the hundreds of music students I have taught during my teaching career. I have also tried to continue to bring beauty to our world in my own way as an active performing musician.*

NOREN-IACOVINO, MARY-JO PATRICIA, insurance company executive; b. N.Y.C., Feb. 20, 1951; d. James Pierce and Grace Virginia (Keating) Keelty; m. Louis T. Iacovino, Sept. 23, 1989. Student, CUNY, 1971-72. Asst. v.p. Huntoon, Paige & Co., Inc., N.Y.C., 1972-79; v.p. Merrill Lynch Capital Mkts., N.Y.C., 1979-85, Security Pacific Merchant Bank, N.Y.C., 1985-89, Oxford Resources Corp., Woodbury, N.Y., 1989-90; securities products coord. Equitable Life, N.Y.C., 1990-94. Mem. Oratorio Soc. N.Y. (bd. dirs., mktg. dir. 1993), Women's Life Underwriters Coun., Nat. Assn. Life Underwriters. Avocations: choral singing, photography, travel. Home: 17 Park Ave # 9A New York NY 10016-4306 Office: The Equitable Fl 32 1221 Ave of the Americas New York NY 10020-1088

NORFOLK, WILLIAM RAY, lawyer; b. Huron, S.D., Mar. 15, 1941; s. James W. and Helen F. (Thompson) N.; m. Marilyn E. Meadors; children: Stephanie G., Allison T., Meredith H. BA, Miami U., Oxford, Ohio, 1963; student, U. London, 1963-64; LLB, Duke U., 1967. Bar: N.Y. 1968, U.S. Dist. Ct. (so. and ea. dists.) N.Y. 1969, U.S. Ct. Appeals (2d cir.) 1969, U.S. Ct. Appeals (9th cir.) 1977, U.S. Ct. Appeals (5th cir.) 1979, U.S. Ct. Appeals (3d and 11th cirs.) 1981, U.S. Dist. Ct. (ea. dist.) Mich. 1986, U.S. Ct. Appeals (6th and 8th cirs.) 1986, U.S. Ct. Appeals (Fed. cir.) 1990, U.S. Ct. Internat. Trade 1990, U.S. Dist. Ct. (we. dist.) Mich. 1992. Assoc. Sullivan & Cromwell, N.Y.C., 1967-74, ptnr., 1974—. Trustee N.Y. Meth. Hosp. Mem. ABA, N.Y. State Bar Assn., Am. Soc. Internat. Law. Office: Sullivan & Cromwell 125 Broad St New York NY 10004-2400

NORGARD, MICHAEL VINCENT, microbiology educator, researcher; b. Glenridge, N.J., Oct. 5, 1951; s. Bernard Raymond and Marion C. (Testa) N.; m. Gabriella Rosella Lombardo, July 18, 1976; 1 child, Gina Gabriella. AB, Rutgers U., 1973; PhD, U. Medicine and Dentistry, N.J., 1977. Postdoctoral fellow Roche Inst. Molecular Biology, Nutley, N.J., 1977-79; asst. prof. U. Tex. Southwestern Med. Sch., Dallas, 1979-86, assoc. prof., 1986-91, prof., 1991—, vice chmn. microbiology, 1994—; cons. U.S. Dept. Justice, Washington, 1986-92; mem. study sect. on bacteriology and mycology NIH, Bethesda, Md., 1990-94, chmn., 1994, panelist Internat. Sexually Transmitted Diseases Diagnostics Network, 1990—; panelist Congenital Syphillis Policies Ctrs. for Disease Control, Atlanta, 1987, Trepenol Vaccines, WHO, Birmingham, Eng., 1989. Mem. editl. bd. Jour. Sexually Transmitted Diseases, 1988—, Jour. Infection and Immunity, 1993—; contbr. articles to profl. publs., including Infection and Immunity, Jour. Infectious Diseases, Current Opinion Infectious Diseases, 1989—. Grantee NIH, 1980—, Robert A. Welch Found., 1982—, Austin, Tex., 1982—, Serex Internat., Van Nuys, Calif., 1983, 86, 89, Dallas Biomed. Corp., 1988-89, Tex. Higher Edn. Coordinating Bd., Austin, 1990. Fellow Infectious Diseases Soc. Am.; mem. AAAS, Am. Venereal Disease Assn., Am. Soc. Microbiology, Tex. Infectious Diseases Soc. Roman Catholic. Achievements include U.S. patents for monoclonal antibodies against Treponema, methods for Diagnosing Syphilis, cloning of the 47-KDa antigen of Treponema pallidum; first to develop monoclonal antibodies against the syphilis bacterium; discoverer of membrane lipoproteins in T pallidum. Office: U Tex Southwestern Med Ctr Dept Microbiology 5323 Harry Hines Blvd Dallas TX 75235-9048

NORGLE, CHARLES RONALD, SR., federal judge; b. Mar. 3, 1937. BBA, Northwestern U., Evanston, Ill., 1964; JD, John Marshall Law Sch., Chgo., 1969. Asst. state's atty. DuPage County, Ill., 1969-71, dep. pub. defender, 1971-73, assoc. judge, 1973-77, 78-81, cir. judge, 1977-78, 81-84; judge U.S. Dist. Ct. (no. dist.) Ill., Chgo., 1984—; mem. exec. com. No. Dist. Ill.; mem. 7th Cir. Jud. Coun., 7th Cir. Jud. Conf. planning com., subcom. grant requests Fed. Defender Orgn., Fed. Defender Svcs. Com. Mem. ABA, Fed. Bar Assn., Ill. Bar Assn., DuPage Bar Assn., Nat. Attys. Assn., DuPage Assn. Women Attys., Chgo. Legal Club. Office: US Dist Ct 219 S Dearborn St Ste 1703 Chicago IL 60604-1706

NORGREN, C. NEIL, retired manufacturing company executive; b. Silt, Colo., Aug. 23, 1923; s. Carl August and Juliet (Lien) N.; m. Carolyn Sutherland, Apr. 12, 1980; children by previous marriage: Jeraldine Leigh, Carol Ann, John Carl, David Laurence. Student, U. Colo., 1941-43. With C.A. Norgren Co. (mfrs. pneumatic products), Englewood, Colo., 1938-84; asst. gen. mgr. C.A. Norgren Co. (mfrs. pneumatic products), 1947-53, v.p., 1953-55, exec. v.p., 1955-62, pres., 1962-84, also dir.; chmn., chief exec. officer Butler Fixture Co., Denver, 1984-91; dir. United Bank of Denver (mem. exec. com. 1957-90). Bd. dirs. Bus. and Industry Polit. Action Com., 1967-89, Carl A. Norgren Found., 1955-90, Unitog Co., 1971-84; pres. Met. Denver chpt. Jr. Acheivement, 1954-56, nat. exec. com. 1956-62; bd. dirs. Denver Mus. Natural History, 1st v.p., 1983-88, pres., 1988-91; pres. C. Neil and Carolyn S. Norgren Found., 1990—; bd. dirs. U. Colo. Found., 1961-68, 81—, vice chmn., 1985-87, chmn., 1987-90, chmn. exec. com., 1990-92; Colo. divsn. exec. com. Am. Cancer Soc., 1961-67. Staff sgt. USAAF, 1942-46. Mem. NAM (bd. dirs. 1966-87, regional v.p. 1966-71, divsn. v.p. 1972-78, exec. com. 1966-78), Nat. Fluid Power Assn., Nat. Coun. Profit Sharing Industries (past chmn. exec. com.), Nat. Western Stock Show Assn. (former bd. dirs.), Inst. Dirs. London, Met. Denver Execs. Club (co-founder, past pres.), Athletic Club, Pinehurst Country Club, Air Force Acad. Golf Club (Colorado Springs), Met. Club, Greencroft Club, Flatirons Club, Beta Theta Pi. Home: 350 Barracks Hl Charlottesville VA 22901-8845

NORGREN, WILLIAM ANDREW, religious denomination administrator; b. Frostburg, Md., May 5, 1927; s. William Andrew and Martha Elizabeth Leona (Richardson) N. BA, Coll. William and Mary, 1948; STB, now STM, Gen. Theol. Sem., N.Y.C., 1953; LittB, Oxford (Eng.) U., 1959; DD (hon.), Gen. Theol. Sem., N.Y.C., 1984, Berkeley Div. Sch. at Yale, 1995. Ordained to ministry Episcopal Ch., 1953. Chaplain Christ Ch. Cathedral, Oxford, 1955-59; exec. dir. Commn. on Faith and Order Nat. Coun. Chs. of Christ in U.S.A., N.Y.C., 1959-71; mem. gen. bd. Nat. Coun. Chs. in Christ in U.S.A., N.Y.C., 1979-95; pastoral asst. Trinity Ch., N.Y.C., 1972-74; assoc. ecumenical officer Episcopal Ch., N.Y.C., 1975-79, ecumenical officer, 1979-94, theol. cons., 1995—; observer 2d Vatican Coun., Roman Cath. Ch., Vatican City, 1963-65; mem. assemblies World Co. Chs., various cities, 1961, 68, 83, 91. Editor: Living Room Dialogues, 1965, Implications of the Gospel, 1988, Toward Full Communion and Concordat of Agreement, 1991; compiler: What Can We Share, 1985. Fellow Gen. Theol. Sem., 1953-55. Democrat. Avocations: art, music, theatre, walking. Office: Episcopal Church Ctr 815 2nd Ave New York NY 10017-4503

NORICK, RONALD J., mayor of Oklahoma City; b. Oklahoma City, Aug. 5, 1941; m. Carolyn Marshall, July 28, 1961; children: Allyson, Lance. BS in Mgmt., Oklahoma City U., 1964, LHD (hon.), 1990. Pres. Norick Bros., Inc., 1981-92; mayor City of Oklahoma City, Oklahoma City, 1987—; gen. ptnr. Norick Investment Inc.; former chmn. bd. Norick Software, Inc. Trustee Community Ch. of Redeemer; mem. Ctrl. Okla. Transp. and Parking Authority, Oklahoma City Water Utilities Trust, Myriad Gardens Authority; bd. dirs. Okla. State Fair; mem. McGee Creek Authority; bd. dirs. Oklahoma City Philharm.; mem. exec. com. Oklahoma City U., Allied Arts Found. Mem. Nat. League Cities, U.S. Conf. Mayors, Okla. Mcpl. League, Oklahoma City C. of C. (bd. dirs.), South Oklahoma City C. of C. (bd. dirs.). Avocations: golf, fishing, boating. Office: Office of Mayor City Hall 200 N Walker Ave Oklahoma City OK 73102-2247*

NORIEGA, DOROTHY LORRAINE, nursing educator; b. San Bernardino, Calif., Jan. 9, 1927; d. Emmett C. and Dagmar D. (Nelson) Hert; m. William E. Noriega; children: Robert, Lynda, Merridee. AA, San Bernardino Valley Coll., 1961; BS, Loma Linda U., 1968; MS, Calif. State U., L.A., 1972. Staff nurse psychiatry Patton (Calif.) State Hosp., 1961-62, unit supr., 1962-64, supr. nurse psychiatry, 1964-66, dir. psychiatric edn., 1966-68; cons. mental health State of Calif., Sacramento, 1968-76; coord. nursing Patton State Hosp., 1976-79, dir. nursing, 1979-81; dir. nursing Lanternon Behavioral Ctr., Pomona, Calif., 1981-87; instr. psychiatric nursing San Bernardino (Calif.) Valley Coll., 1987—; v.p. adv. bd. Mental Health Soc., San Bernardino, 1980-92; mem. adv. bd. U.A.W., San Bernardino, 1989-90; vol. RSVP, Ojai, Calif., 1990—. Col. ARC, 1993; bd. dirs. Vis. Nurses Assn., Riverside, Calif., 1979; vol. tchr. Am. Cancer Soc., 1980. Democrat. Mem. LDS Ch. Avocations: golf, computers, geneaology, reading. Home: 304 Topa Topa Dr Ojai CA 93023-3232

NORIEGA, RUDY JORGE, hospital administrator; b. Havana, Cuba, Apr. 23, 1937; s. Rodolfo and Iris (Santini) N.; came to U.S., 1961; naturalized, 1966; BS, Masonic U., 1960; m. Rosa E. Del Castillo, Jan. 2, 1960; children: Rudy A., George. Acct., Continental Can Co., Havana, Cuba, 1961, Am. Fgn. Ins. Assn., N.Y.C., 1961-62, North Miami Gen. Hosp., Miami, Fla., 1962-64; asst. controller Jackson Meml. Hosp., Miami, 1964-65; asst. adminstr. Plantation (Fla.) Gen. Hosp., 1965-72, adminstr., trustee, 1972-80; v.p., trustee Internat. Hosp., Miami, 1980-83; exec. v.p., chief operating officer Gen. Health L.P., Miami, 1983—; sr. v.p. Ornda So. Fla., 1993—; pres., chmn. Golden Glades Gen. Hosp., 1991—; mem. sch. bldg. com. U. Miami Law Sch., 1989—; bd. dirs. Kendall Hosp., 1989—; coord. health needs for Pope John Paul II's U.S. Visit, 1987. Mem. jud. nominating commn. 3rd dist. ct. appeals. Mem. Am. Coll. Hosp. Adminstrs., jud. nominating commn. Fla. Supreme Ct., 1992—, So. Fla. Hosp. Assn. (pres. 1979-80), Broward County Hosp. Assn. (pres. 1978-79), Fla. League Hosps. (pres. 1974-75), Fedn. Am. Hosps. (dir. 1973-74), Hosp. Fin. Mgmt. Assn. (dir. 1971-72), Plantation C. of C. (pres. 1978-79), Kiwanis (v.p. 1978-79). Office: Ornda So Fla Miami FL 33152

NORINS, ARTHUR LEONARD, physician, educator; b. Chgo., Dec. 2, 1928; s. Russell Joseph and Elsie (Lindemann) N.; m. Mona Lisa Wetzer, Sept. 12, 1954; children: Catherine, Nan, Jane, Arthur. B.S. in Chem. Engring, Northwestern U., 1951, M.S. in Physiology, 1953, M.D., 1955. Diplomate: Am. Bd. Dermatology; subcert. in dermatopathology. Intern U. Mich., Ann Arbor, 1955-56; resident in dermatology Northwestern U., Chgo., 1956-59; asst. prof. Stanford U., 1961-64; prof., chmn. dept. dermatology, prof. pathology Ind. U. Sch. Medicine, Indpls., 1964-93, prof. emeritus, 1993—; mem. staff Riley Children's Hosp., Univ. Hosp., Wishard Hosp.; cons. VA Hosp. Contbr. articles to profl. jours. Capt. M.C. U.S. Army, 1959-61. Recipient Pres.' award Ind. U., 1979. Fellow ACP; mem. Am. Acad. Dermatology (bd. dirs.), Am. Dermatol. Assn., Soc. Pediatric Dermatology (founder, past pres.), Am. Soc. Dermatopathology, Am. Soc. Photobiology (founder), Soc. Investigative Dermatology. Home: 1234 Kirkham Ln Indianapolis IN 46260-1637 Office: 550 University Blvd Ste 3240 Indianapolis IN 46202-5270

NORINS, LESLIE CARL, publisher; b. Balt., Mar. 23, 1937; s. Abe and Patricia N.; m. Ann Rainey Hammatt, Nov. 19, 1994. AB, Johns Hopkins U., Balt., 1958; MD, Duke U., 1962; PhD, U. Melbourne, Australia, 1966. M.D., N.C. Lab. dir. Ctrs. for Disease Control, Atlanta, 1966-72; pres. Am. Health Cons., Atlanta, 1972-87, Global Success Corp., Naples, Fla., 1990—; cons. World Health Orgn., Geneva, 1970, NIH, Bethesda, Md., 1972, Pharmaceutical Mfrs., N.J. and N.Y., 1972-76; bd. dirs. Newsletter Publishers Assoc. Contbr. articles to sci. jours. Recipient Best Med. Student Rsch. award Borden Found., 1962; student of Sir MacFarlane Burnet, Nobel Laureate. Fellow Infectious Disease Soc. of Am.; Nat. Press Club (Washington). Home: 4301 Gulfshore Blvd # 1404 Naples FL 33940 Office: Global Success Corp 851 5th Ave N Ste 301 Naples FL 33940

NORKUS, MICHAEL, management consultant; b. Stuttgart, W. Ger., July 4, 1946; came to U.S. 1973; s. Hans and Gisela (Fritz) N.; m. Andrea G. Gluck, June 13, 1975; 1 child, Tyler David. MBA, Harvard U., 1975; PhD, U. Hamburg, W.Ger., 1973; Law Diplome, U. Paris, 1971. V.p., dir. Boston Cons. Group, 1975-86; pres., founder Alliance Cons. Group, Cambridge, Mass., 1986—. Author: Market Dominance and Anti-Trust Law, 1976. Lt. W. German Navy, 1966-68. Office: Alliance Cons Group One Kendall Sq Bldg 200 Cambridge MA 02139*

NORLAND, DONALD RICHARD, retired foreign service officer; b. Laurens, Iowa, June 14, 1924; s. Norman and Aletta (Brunsvold) N.; m. Patricia Bamman, Dec. 13, 1952; children: Richard Boyce, David, Patricia D. Student, Iowa State Tchrs. Coll., 1941-43, N.W. Mo. State Tchrs. Coll., 1943-44; BA, U. Minn., 1948, MS, 1950; postgrad., U. Mich., 1951-52, Grenoble (France) U., 1948-49. Instr. history and polit. sci. U. No. Iowa, 1949-51; teaching fellow U. Mich., 1951-52; with Fgn. Svc., U.S. Dept. State, 1952-81; posts include Rabat, Morocco, 1952-56, Washington, 1956-58, Abidjan, Ivory Coast, 1958-60; mem. NATO del., Paris, 1961-63, NATO delegation, The Hague, The Netherlands, 1964-69; dep. chief mission Conakry, Guinea, 1970-72; U.S. Dept. State fellow Stanford (Calif.) U., 1969-70; dep. dir. Office Mil. Assistance and Sales, Bur. Politico-Mil. Affairs, Dept. State, Washington, 1972-73, chief polit. officers counseling br. Office Pers., 1973-75; dep. dir. Office Mgmt. Ops., 1975-76; amb. to Botswana, Lesotho and Swaziland Gaborone, Botswana, 1976-79; amb. to Chad, 1979-81; ret. Fgn. Svc., U.S. Dept. State, 1981; lectr. African affairs; internat. cons., specialist econ. devel.; chmn. African studies Fgn. Svc. Inst. of U.S. Dept. of State, Washington, 1987-89; program dir. Ctr. for Internat. Pvt. Enterprise affiliate U.S. C. of C., Washington, 1990-91; sr. cons. World Space, Inc., 1995, sr. policy advisor, 1996—. Bd. dirs. Calvert New Africa Fund, 1995. Lt. (j.g.) USNR, 1943-46. Mem. Am. Fgn. Svc. Assn. (v.p. for retirees 1993-95, sec. 1995—, mem. editl. bd. Fgn. Svc. Jour. 1992-95). Home: 4000 Cathedral Ave NW Apt 138B Washington DC 20016-5249

NORLANDER, JOHN ALLEN, hotel executive; b. Chgo., Nov. 19, 1930; s. Everett C. and Anna (Hall) N.; m. Diana A. Dahl, June 29, 1957; children: Lisa D., Erik D., Krist D., Britt H. Student, Carleton Coll., 1948-50; BS in Hotel Adminstrn., Cornell U., 1953; PhD (hon.), Johnson and Wales U., 1991. Sales mgr. Hilton Hotels, Chgo., 1956-59; nat. sales mgr. Hilton Hotels, Washington, 1959-60; exec. asst. mgr. Hilton Hotels, Chgo., 1960-64; gen. mgr. Hilton Hotels, St. Paul, 1965-68, Washington, 1968-70, Beverly Hills, Calif., 1970-75; exec. v.p. Radisson Hotel Corp., 1975-83, pres., 1984-95; pres., CEO Carlson Hospitality Worldwide, Mpls., 1995—; bd. dirs. Radamer Point Venture, Moscow, Diamond Cruise, Helsinki, Finland. Bd. dirs. Ednl. Inst., Lansing, Mich., Mpls. Conv. Bur. With USN, 1953-56, Korea. Recipient cert. of merit Calif. Hotel Assn., 1975. Mem. Am. Hotel Mgrs. Assn. (cert.), Chaine des Rotisseurs (chevallier). Avocations: oil painting, tennis.

NORMAN, ALBERT GEORGE, JR., lawyer; b. Birmingham, Ala., May 29, 1929; s. Albert G. and Ila Mae (Carroll) N.; m. Catherine Marshall DeShazo, Sept. 3, 1955; children: Catherine Marshall, Albert George III. BA, Auburn U., 1953; LLB, Emory U., 1958; MA, U. N.C., 1960. Bar: Ga. 1957. Assoc. Moise, Post & Gardner, Atlanta, 1958-60, ptnr., 1960-62; ptnr. Hansell & Post, Atlanta, 1962-86, Long, Aldridge & Norman, Atlanta, 1986—; dir. Atlanta Gas Light Co. Served with USAF, 1946-49. Mem. ABA, Ga. Bar Assn., Atlanta Bar Assn., Lawyers Club Atlanta (pres. 1973-74), Am. Law Inst., Am. Judicature Soc. (dir. 1975-78), Old War Horse Lawyers Club, (pres. 1991-92), Cherokee Town and Country Club. Episcopalian.

NORMAN, ANTHONY WESTCOTT, biochemistry educator; b. Ames, Iowa, Jan. 19, 1938; s. A. Geoffrey and Marian Ester (Foote) N.; children—Thea C., Jacqueline E., Derek P.G. M.S., U. Wis., 1960, Ph.D., 1963. From asst. prof. to prof. dept. biochemistry U. Calif., Riverside, 1963—, chmn. dept., 1975-80, prof. biomedical scis., 1986—, divisional dean biomed. scis., 1986-91; asst. dean UCLA Sch. Medicine, 1986-91. Recipient Ernst Oppenheimer award Endocrine Soc., 1977; Prix Andre Lichwitz award French Govt., 1981; Fulbright fellow, 1970. Mem. AAAS, Am. Inst. Nutrition (Mead Johnson award 1977, Osborne-Mendel award 1989), Am. Chem. Soc., Am. Soc. Biol. Chemists, Am. Soc. Bone & Mineral Rsch. (Wilham Newman award 1995). Home: 7225 Lenox Ave Riverside CA 92504-4922 Office: U of Calif-Riverside Dept of Biochemistry Riverside CA 92521

NORMAN, ARNOLD MCCALLUM, JR., engineer; b. Little Rock, May 1, 1940; s. Arnold McCallum and Ann Carolyn (Gibson) N.; m. Sylvia Burton, July 1, 1962 (div. 1967); m. Marisha Irene Malin, June 7, 1969; children: Frank Lee, Paul James. BS in Physics, Ga. Inst. Tech., 1962. Test engr. Rocketdyne div. Rockwell Internat., Canoga Park, Calif., 1962-64, engr. in charge of various programs, 1964-75, engr. in charge, project engr. large chem. lasers, 1975-85, project engr. space sta. propulsion system, 1985-87, project engr. nat. launch system health mgmt. systems, 1987-92, project engr. kinetic energy weapons, 1993-94; project engr. advanced propulsion systems Rockwell Internat., Canoga Park, Calif., 1994-95, sr. engring. specialist, 1995—; mem. ops. com. health mgmt. ctr. U. Cin., 1988-94; mem. program com. Ann. Internat. Conf. on Engring. Applications of Artificial Intelligence, 1988-90; presenter in field. Mem. editorial bd. Jour. Applied Intelligence, 1990-94; author numerous papers in field. Fellow AIAA (assoc., sect. chair sr. adv. com. 1991-93, San Fernando Valley sect., chmn. 1989-90, sys. effectiveness & safety com. 1995—), Inst. Advancement Engring; mem. Tau Beta Pi. Home: 20238 Mobile St Canoga Park CA 91306-4241 Office: Rockwell Internat Rocketdyne divsn 6633 Canoga Ave Canoga Park CA 91303-2703

NORMAN, CHARLES HENRY, broadcasting executive; b. St. Louis, June 13, 1920; s. Charles Henry and Grace Vincent (Francis) N. BS, U. So. Calif., L.A., 1942. Announcer WIL, KSTL Radio Stas., St. Louis, 1948-55; owner Norman Broadcasting Co., St. Louis, 1961—. Lt. USN, 1943-45. Mem. St. Louis Ambassadros, Phi Kappa Phi. Episcopalian. Office: Portland Towers 275 Union Blvd Ste 1315 Saint Louis MO 63108-1236

NORMAN, COLIN ARTHUR, astrophysics educator; b. Melbourne, Australia, May 3, 1948; came to U.S., 1984; s. Howard Arthur Norman and Jean Olice (Macgregor) Downing; m. Wen Shen, June 2, 1988; children: Alexandra Jean, Arthur Shen, Victoria Amelia. BE with honours, U. Melbourne, 1969; DPhil, Oxford U., 1973. Rsch. fellow Magdalen Coll., Oxford (Eng.) U., 1973-77, U. Calif., Berkeley, 1975-77; asst. prof. U. Leiden (Netherlands), 1977-84; prof. physics and astronomy Johns Hopkins U., Balt., 1984—, head acad. affairs div. Space Telescope Sci. Inst., 1987-91, head Hubble Fellow program Space Telescope Sci. Inst., 1991—; sr. rsch. fellow Inst. Astronomy, Cambridge, Eng., 1981-84, European So. Obs., Munich, 1983-84; vis. prof. U. Paris, 1983; bd. dirs. Norman Bros. Pty. Ltd., Melbourne; trustee Norman Family Trusts, Melbourne. Editor: Stellar Populations, 1987, Quasar Absorption Lines, 1988, Massive Stars and Star Formations, 1991; contbr. articles to astrophysics jours. Rhodes scholar, 1970-73. Fellow Royal Astron. Soc.; mem. Am. Phys. Soc., Am. Astron. Soc., Amnesty Internat., Greenpeace, Johns Hopkins Club, Hamilton St. Club. Office: Johns Hopkins U Dept Physics and Astronomy Baltimore MD 21218

NORMAN, DONALD ARTHUR, cognitive scientist; b. N.Y.C., Dec. 25, 1935; s. Noah N. and Miriam F. N.; m. Martha Karpati (div.); children—Cynthia, Michael; m. Julie Jacobsen; 1 child, Eric. BSEE, MIT, 1957; MSEE, U. Pa., 1959, PhD in Psychology, 1962; degree in psychology (hon.), U. Padua, Italy, 1995. Lectr. Harvard U., 1962-66; Prof. dept. psychology U. Calif.-San Diego, La Jolla, 1966-92, prof. emeritus, 1992—, prof., chair dept. cognitive sci., 1988-92, chair dept.psychology, 1974-78, dir. cognitive sci. program, 1977-88, dir. Inst. for Cognitive Sci., 1981-89; Apple fellow Apple Computer Inc., Cupertino, Calif., 1993-95, v.p. advanced tech., 1993—; mem. sci. adv. bd. Naval Pers. Rsch. Ctr., San Diego, 1982-86; cons. to industry on human computer interaction and user-centered design. Author: Learning and Memory, 1982, Human Information Processing, 2d edit., 1977, User Centered System Design, 1986, The Psychology of Everyday Things, 1988, The Design of Everyday Things, 1989, Turn Signals Are the Facial Expressions of Automobiles, 1992, Things That Make Us Smart, 1993; editor: Perspectives on Cognitive Science, 1981, Exploration in Cognition, 1975, Cognitive Sci. Jour., 1981-85; series editor Cognitive Sci. Series Lawrence Earlbaum Assoc., 1979—. Recipient Excellence in Rsch. award U. Calif., 1984. Fellow Am. Psychol. Soc., Am. Acad. Arts and Scis.; mem. Am. Assn. Arts and Scis., Am. Assn. for Artificial Intelligence, Assn. for Computational Machinery, Cognitive Sci. Soc. (chmn. founding mem.). Office: Apple Computer Inc MS 301-4D 1 Infinite Loop Cupertino CA 95014-2083

NORMAN, DUDLEY KENT, hospital administrator, nurse; b. Cleve., July 27, 1949; s. George R. and Coral L. (Henrickson) N.; m. Martha Alice; children: David, Nicholas. BS in Edn., MEd, Kent State U., 1976; BS in Nursing, Case Western Res. U., 1976; MS, MSN, Tex. Women's U., 1981; EdD, U. Houston, 1990. RN; cert. nursing home adminstr. Tchr. Beachwood City Schs., Cleve., 1972-74; clin. nurse Univ. Hosp., Cleve., 1976-78; asst. adminstr. Parkland Hosp., Dallas, 1979-83, St. Lukes Hosp./Tex. Heart Inst., Tex. Children's Hosp., Houston, 1983-84; asst. dean U. Tex. Med. Sch., Houston, 1984-85; adminstr. U. Tex. Mental Scis. Inst., Houston, 1985-87; asst. adminstr. U. Tex.-Harris County Psychiat. Ctr., Houston, 1987-90; adminstr. U. Tex. Med. Br., Galveston, 1990—; cons. St. Lukes Hosp., N.Y.C., 1980; dir. nurse tng. Bd. Nurse Examiners Approved Program, Dallas, 1979-81. Recipient Chemistry Scholar prize Lubrizol Found., Cleve., 1971, Cushing Robb prize Case Western Res. U., Cleve., 1976; named One of Outstanding Young Men of Am., U.S. Jaycees, 1978. Fellow Am. Coll. Health Care Execs.; mem. ANA, Assn. for Study of Higher Edn., Healthcare Fin. Mgmt. Assn., Sigma Theta Tau. Methodist. Office: U Tex Med Br Galveston TX 77550

NORMAN, E. GLADYS, business computer educator, consultant; b. Oklahoma City, June 13, 1933; d. Joseph Eldon and Mildred Lou (Truitt) Biggs; m. Joseph R.R. Radeck, Mar. 1, 1953 (div. Aug. 1962); children: Jody Matti, Ray Norman, Warren Norman (dec. May 1993), Dana Norman; m. Leslie P. Norman, Aug. 26, 1963 (dec. Feb. 1994); 1 child, Elayne Pearce. Student, Fresno (Calif.) State Coll., 1951-52, UCLA, 1956-59, Linfield Coll., 1986-95. Math. aid U.S. Naval Weapons Ctr., China Lake, Calif., 1952-56, computing systems specialist, 1957-68; systems programmer Oreg. Motor Vehicles Dept., Salem, 1968-69; instr. in data processing, dir. Computer Programming Ctr., Salem, 1969-72; instr. in data processing Merritt-Davis Bus. Coll., Salem, 1972-73; sr. programmer, analyst Teledyne Wah Chang, Albany, Oreg., 1973-79; sr. systems analyst Oreg. Dept. Vets. Affairs, Albany, 1979-80; instr. in bus. computers Linn-Benton Community Coll., Albany, 1980-95; ret., 1995; computer cons. for LBCC Ret. Sr. Vol. Program, 1995—; presenter computer software seminars State of Oreg., 1991-93, Oreg. Credit Assoc. Conf., 1991, Oreg. Regional Users Group Conf., 1992; computer tchr. Linn-Benton C.C., 1996; computer cons. Oremet Titanium, 1996; computer cons. in field. Mem. Data Processing Mgmt. Assn. (bd. dirs. 1977-84, 89-95, region sect. 1995—, assoc. v.p. 1988, Diamond Individual Performance award 1985). Democrat. Avocations: drawing, painting, sewing.

NORMAN, GEOFFREY ROBERT, financial executive; b. Orpington, Kent, Eng., Jan. 31, 1944; came to U.S., 1968, naturalized, 1974; s. Leonard Robert and Minnie Rose (Carter) N.; m. Christina Norman, June 8, 1968; children—Catarina, Camilla. B.A., St. Catharine's Coll., Cambridge, Eng., 1966, M.A., 1968. Corp. auditor Gen. Electric Co., Schenectady, 1971-74, comptroller GE Española, Bilbao, Spain, 1974-78, cons. corp. fin., Fairfield, Conn., 1978-81, mgr. fin., Bridgeport, Conn., 1981-83; v.p., treas. Gen. Electric Fin. Services, Inc. and Gen. Electric Capital Corp., N.Y.C., 1983-85, Stamford, Conn., 1985-88; exec. v.p. GE Investments, 1988—. State scholar U.K. Govt., 1962, Open Exhbn. scholar St. Catharine's Coll., 1962. Office: GE Investments 3003 Summer St Stamford CT 06905-4316

NORMAN, GREGORY JOHN, professional golfer; b. Mt. Isa, Australia, Feb. 10, 1955; m. Laura Norman; children: Morgan-Leigh, Gregory. Profl. golfer, 1976—. Winner Martini Internat., 1977, 79, 81, French Open, 1980, Australian Open, 1980, 85, 87, Dunlop Masters, 1981, 82, Hong Kong Open, 1981, Australian Masters 1981, 83, 84, 87, 89, 90 State Express Classic, 1982, Benson and Hedges, 1982, Canadian Open, 1984, 92, Kemper Open, 1984, Las Vegas Invitational, 1986, Kemper Open, 1986, British Open, 1986, 93, European Open, 1986, Suntory World Match, 1986, Queensland Open, 1986, New South Wales Open, 1985, 86, 88, Australian Tournament Players Championship, 1988, 89, Heritage Classic, 1988, Italian Open, 1988, Doral Ryder Open, 1990, 93, Memorial Tournament, 1990, Tournament Players Championship, 1994, Johnnie Walker Asian Classic, 1994, winner Vardon trophy, 1989, 90, 94; recipient Arnold Palmer award for leading money winner, 1995, Byron Nelson trophy for the lowest scoring average, 1995; ranked #1 by Sony; named PGA Player of Yr., 1995, PGA Tour Player of Yr., 1995. Leading Money Winner PGA Tour 1986, 90. Address: Great White Shark Enterprises Inc PO Box 1189 Hobe Sound FL 33475-1189

NORMAN, JACK LEE, church administrator, consultant; b. Lancaster, Ohio, Aug. 5, 1938; s. Clearence Herbert and Jeanette Belle (Bennett) N.; m. Boneda Mae Coppock, June 30, 1957; children: Anthony Lee, Becky Lynn Norman Hux. Student, Circleville Bible Coll., Olivet U. Ordained min. Ch. of Christ, 1961. Pastor Chs. of Christ in Christian Union, Chillicothe, Ohio, 1959-62, 65-90, Winchester, Ohio, 1962-65; dist. supt. Chs. of Christ in Christian Union, Circleville, Ohio, 1990—; trustee Chs. of Christ in Christian Union, mem. dist. bd., mem. ch. ext. bd., mem. bd. exam. and ordination, mem. Evang. Christian Youth Bd. Trustee Circleville Bible Coll. Sgt. USNG, 1956-59. Avocations: fishing, boating, classic cars. Office: Ch of Christ in Christian Union PO Box 30 Circleville OH 43113-0030

NORMAN, JESSYE, soprano; b. Augusta, Ga., Sept. 15, 1945; d. Silas Sr. and Janie (King) N. B.M. cum laude, Howard U., 1967; postgrad., Peabody Conservatory, 1967; M.Mus., U. Mich., 1968; MusD (hon.), U. South, 1984, Boston Conservatory, 1984, U. Mich., 1987, U. Edinburgh, 1989, Cambridge U., 1989. Debut, Deutsche Oper, Berlin, 1969, Italy, 1970; appeared: in operas Die Walküre, Idomeneo, L'Africaine, Marriage of Figaro, Aida, Don Giovanni, Tannhauser, Gotterdammerung, Ariadne auf Naxos, Les Troyens, Dido and Aeneas, Oedipus Rex, Hérodiade, Les Contes d'Hoffmann; debut in operas, La Scala, Milan, Italy, 1972, Salzburg Festival, 1977, U.S. debut, Hollywood Bowl, 1972, appeared with, Tanglewood Festival, Mass., also Edinburgh (Scotland) Festival, debut, Covent Garden, 1972; appeared in 1st Great Performers recital, Lincoln Center, N.Y.C., 1973—; other guest performances include, L.A. Philharm. Orch., Boston Symphony Orch., Am. Symphony Orch., Chgo. Symphony Orch., San Francisco Symphony Orch., Cleve. Orch., Detroit Symphony, N.Y. Philharm. Orch., London Symphony Orch., London Philharm. Orch., BBC Orch., Israel Philharm. Orch., Orchestre de Paris, Nat. Symphony Orch., English Chamber Orch., Royal Philharm., London Phila. Orch., Milw. Symphony Orch., Stockholm Philharm. Orch., Vienna Philharm. Orch., Berlin Philharm. Orch.; tours, Europe, S. Am., Australia, numerous recs., Columbia, EMI, Philips Records; PBS TV spcls. include Kathleen Battle and Jessye Norman Sing Spirituals, 1991, Concert at Avery Fisher Hall, 1994. Recipient 1st prize Bavarian Radio Corp. Internat. Music Competition, 1968, Grand Prix du Disque, Acad. du Disque Francais, 1973, 76, 77, 82, 84, Deutsche Schallplatten, Preis, 1975, 81, Alumni award U. Mich., 1982, Outstanding Musician of Yr. award Musical Am., 1982, Grand Prix du Disque Academie Charles Cros, 1983, Commandeur de l'Ordre des Arts et des Lettres, France, 1984, Grammy awards, 1980, 82, 85, numerous other awards; named hon. life mem. Girl Scouts U.S., 1987. Mem. Royal Acad. Music (hon.), Alpha Kappa Alpha, Gamma Sigma Sigma, Sigma Alpha Iota, Pi Kappa Lambda. Club: Friday Morning Music (Washington). Office: care Shaw Concerts Inc 1900 Broadway New York NY 10023-7004

NORMAN, JOHN BARSTOW, JR., designer, educator; b. Paloa, Kans., Feb. 5, 1940; s. John B. and Ruby Maxine (Johnson) N.; m. Roberta Jeanne Martin, June 6, 1967; children: John Barstow III, Elizabeth Jeanne. BFA, U. Kans., 1962, MFA, 1966. Designer and illustrator Advt. Design, Kansas City, Mo., 1962-64; asst. instr. U. Kans., Lawrence, 1964-66; art dir. Hallmark Cards, Inc., Kansas City, Mo., 1966-69; instr. dept. art U. Denver, 1969-73, asst. prof., 1973-78, assoc. prof., 1978—, Disting. prof., 1980; sr. designer Mo. Coun. Arts and Humanities, 1966-67; cons. designer Rocky Mountain Bank Note Corp., Denver, 1971—, Signage Identity System, U. Dever; bd. dirs. communications U. Denver; tech. cons. Denver Art Mus., 1974—, designed exhbns., 1974-75; adv., cons. Jefferson County (Colo.) Sch., System, 1976—; chmn. Design and Sculpture Exhbn., Colo. Celebration of the Arts, 1975-76. One man shows include: Gallery Cortina, Aspen, Colo., 1983; commd. works include: Jedda, Saudi Arabia, Synegistics Corp., Denver; represented in permanent collections Pasadena Ctr. for the Arts, N.Y. Art Dirs. Club, Calif. State U./Fiber Collection, Pasadena (Calif.) Ctr. for the Arts, 1984, N.Y. Art Dirs. Club, 1985 Midland Art Coun./Fiber Collection, 1985, Geologic Soc. Am.; represented in traveling exhbns. L.A. Art Dirs. Show and N.Y. Art Dirs. Show, U.S., Europe, Japan, 1985; feaured in Denver Post, 1984, Post Electric City Mag., 1984, Rocky Mt. News, 1984, Douglas County Press, 1984, Mile High Cable Vision, 1985, Sta. KWGN-TV, 1985, Les Krantz's Am. Artists, 1988, Illustrated Survey of Leading Contemporaries, 1988, U.S. Surface Design Jour., 1988; co-work represented in film collection Mus. Modern Art, N.Y.C.; selected fashion show designs displayed to Sister City dels., Denver, 1987. Co-recipient Silver Medal award N.Y. Internat. Film and Video Competition, 1976, Design awards Coun. Advancement and Support of Edn., 1969, 71, 73, 76, Honor Mention award L.A. Art Dirs. Club, 1984, Honor Mention award N.Y. Art Dirs. Club, 1984, Native Am. Wearable Art Competition, 1985, 5th pl. Nat. Wind Sail Am. Banners Competition, Midland, Mich., 1985, also awards for surface designs in Colo. Ctr. for the Arts Wearable Art Competition, 1984-85, Foothills Art Gallery Nat. Wearable Art Competition, 1984-85, Fashion Group of Denver Competition, 1984-85. Mem. Art Dirs. Club Denver (Gold medals 1974-82, Best of Show Gold medal 1983, Honor Mention award, 1984, 3 Gold medals 1989), Univ. Art Dirs. Assn. Home: PO Box 302 751 Willow Lake Dr Franktown CO 80116 Office: U Denver Sch Art 2121 E Asbury Ave Denver CO 80210-4303

NORMAN, JOHN EDWARD, petroleum landman; b. Denver, May 22, 1922; s. John Edward and Ella (Warren) N.; m. Hope Sabin, Sept. 5, 1946; children—J. Thomas, Gerould W., Nancy E., Susan G., Douglas E. BSBA, U. Denver, 1949, MBA, 1972. Clk., bookkeeper Capitol Life Ins. Co., Denver, 1940-42, 45-46; salesman Security Life and Accident Co., Denver, 1947; bookkeeper Central Bank and Trust Co., Denver, 1947-50; automobile salesman H.A. Hennies, Denver, 1950; petroleum landman Continental Oil Co. (name changed to Conoco Inc. 1979), Denver, 1950-85; ind. petroleum landman, 1985; ind. investor 1985—. Lectr. pub. lands Colo. Sch. Mines, 1968-85; lectr. mineral titles and landmen's role in oil industry Casper Coll., 1969-71. Mem. Casper Mcpl. Band Commn., 1965-71, mem. band, 1961-71, mgr., 1968-71; former musician, bd. dirs. Casper Civic Symphony; former bd. dirs. Jefferson Symphony, performing mem., 1972-75. Served with AUS, World War II. Mem. Am. Assn. Petroleum Landmen (dir. at large, chmn. publs. for regional dir.), Wyo. Assn. Petroleum Landmen (pres.), Denver Assn. Petroleum Landmen, Rocky Mountain Oil and Gas Assn. (pub. lands com. 1981-85), Rocky Mountain Petroleum Pioneers. Episcopalian (mem. choir, vestryman, past dir. acolytes). Club: Elks. Home and Office: 2710 S Jay St Denver CO 80227-3856

NORMAN, LALANDER STADIG, insurance company executive; b. Binford, N.D., Apr. 10, 1912; s. John and Corinne (Stadig) N.; m. Garnet Johnston, Nov. 8, 1941; children: Eric John, Martha Mary Norman Neely, Carol Jean Norman Wellborn, Shirley Ann Norman Cook. A.B., U. Mich., 1935, M.B.A., 1937. Actuarial asst. Central Life Ins. Co. of Ill., Chgo., 1937-40; mgr. Eastern dept. Central Life Ins. Co. of Ill., 1940-41; actuary Mich. Life Ins. Co., Detroit, 1941-43; asst. actuary Guarantee Mut. Life Co., Omaha, 1946-49; asso. actuary Am. United Life Ins. Co., Indpls., 1949; actuary Am. United Life Ins. Co., 1950-77, dir., 1959-77, v.p., 1962-69, sr. v.p., 1969-77; ret., 1977; bd. mgrs. AUL Fund B, 1969-84, chmn., 1973-84; actuary Ind. Dept. Ins., 1977-79. Bd. dirs. Cypress Village Assn., 1981, 83-85. Served with USNR, 1943-46. Recipient Navy Commendation award, 1946, Theta Xi Distinguished Service award, 1958. Fellow Soc. Actuaries; mem. Am. Acad. Actuaries, Indpls. Actuarial Club (past pres.), Woodland Country Club (Carmel), Sugarmill Woods Golf and Racquet Club, So. Woods Golf Club, Phi Beta Kappa, Theta Xi (regional dir. 1953-59), Phi Kappa Phi, Beta Gamma Sigma. Republican. Home: Sugarmill Woods 21 Graytwig Ct W Homosassa FL 34446-4727 Office: 1 American Sq Indianapolis IN 46282-0001

NORMAN, MARSHA, playwright; b. Louisville, Sept. 21, 1947; d. Billie Lee and Bertha Mae (Conley) Williams; m. Michael Norman (div. 1974); m. Dann C. Byck Jr., 1978 (div.); m. Timothy Dykman; 2 children: Angus, Katherine. B.A., Agnes Scott Coll., 1969; M.A.T., U. Louisville, 1971. Author: (plays) Getting Out, 1977 (John Gassner New Playwrights medallion, Outer Critics Circle award 1979, George Oppenheimer-Newsday award 1979), Third and Oak, 1978, Circus Valentine, 1979, The Holdup, 1980, 'Night, Mother, 1982 (Susan Smith Blackburn prize 1982, Tony award nomination for best play 1983, Pulitzer prize for Drama 1983, Elizabeth Hull-Kate Warriner award Dramatists Guild 1983), Traveler in the Dark, 1984, Sarah and Abraham, 1987, D. Boone, 1992; (book of musical, lyrics) The Secret Garden, 1991 (Tony award for best book of musical 1991, Tony award nominee for best original score 1991, Drama Desk award for best book of musical 1991; Loving Daniel Boone (play) 1992, Trudy Blue (play), 1995, The Red Shoes (book and lyrics), 1992; (screenplay) 'Night, Mother, 1986; (teleplays) It's the Willingness, 1978, In Trouble at Fifteen, 1980, The Laundromat, 1985, Third and Oak: The Pool Hall, 1989, Face of a Stranger, 1991; (novel) The Fortune Teller, 1987; (collection) Four Plays by Marsha Norman, 1988. NEA grantee, 1978-79, Rockefeller playwright-in-residence grantee, 1979-80, Am. Acad. and Inst. for Arts and Letters grantee; recipient Lit. Lion award N.Y. Pub. Libr., 1986. Office: Jack Tantleff 375 Greenwich St Ste 700 New York NY 10013-2338

NORMAN, MARY MARSHALL, counselor, therapist; b. Auburn, N.Y., Jan. 10, 1937; d. Anthony John and Zita Norman. BS cum laude, LeMoyne Coll., 1958; MA, Marquette, U., 1960; EdD, Pa. State U., 1971. Cert. Alcoholism Counselor. Tchr., St. Cecilia's Elem. Sch., Theinsville, Wis., 1959-60; vocat. counselor Marquette U., Milw., 1959-60; dir. testing and counseling U. Rochester (N.Y.), 1960-62; dir. testing and counseling, dean women, asso. dean coll., asst. dean students, dir. student activities, asst. prof. psychology Corning (N.Y.) C.C., 1962-68; rsch. asst. Center for Study Higher Edn., Pa. State U., University Park, 1969-71; dean faculty South Campus, C.C. Allegheny County, West Mifflin, Pa., 1971-72, exec. dean, coll. v.p., 1972-82; pres. Orange County C.C., 1982-90; sr. counselor The Horton Family Program, 1990—. cons. Boricua Coll., N.Y.C., 1976-77; reader NSF, 1977-78; mem. govtl. commn. com. Am. Assn. Cmty. and Jr. Colls., 1976-79, bd. dirs., 1982—; mem. and chmn. various middle state accreditation teams. Bd. dirs. Orange County United Way; bd. dirs. Orange County Alcoholism and Drug Abuse Coun., 1993—. Mem. Am. Assn. Higher Edn., Nat. Assn. Women Deans Counselors, Am. Assn. Women in Community and Jr. Colls. (charter, Woman of Yr. 1981), Pa. Assn. Two-Yr. Colls., Pa. Assn. Acad. Deans, Pitts. Council Women Execs. (charter), Am. Council on Edn. (Pa. rep. identification women for adminstrn. 1978—), Pa. Council on Higher Edn., Orange County C. of C., Gamma Pi Epsilon. Contbr. articles to profl. jours. Home: 8 Crabapple Ln Middletown NY 10940-1006 Office: 406 E Main St Middletown NY 10940

NORMAN, PHILIP SIDNEY, physician; b. Pittsburg, Kans., Aug. 4, 1924; s. P. Sidney and Mildred A. (Lawyer) N.; m. Marion Birmingham, Apr. 15, 1955; children: Margaret Reynolds, Meredith Andrew, Helen Elizabeth. A.B., Kans. State Coll., 1947; M.D. cum laude, Washington U., St. Louis, 1951. Intern Barnes Hosp., St. Louis, 1951-52; resident Vanderbilt U. Hosp., Nashville, 1952-54; fellow Rockefeller Inst., 1954-56; instr. medicine Johns Hopkins U. Sch. Medicine, Balt., 1956-59; asst. prof. Johns Hopkins U. Sch. Medicine, 1959-64, assoc. prof., 1964-75, prof., 1975—, chief allergy and immunology div., 1971-91. Editor Jour. of Allergy and Clin. Immunology, 1993—; contbr. chpt. to books, articles to profl. jours. Served with USAAF, 1943-46; Served with USPHS, 1954-56. Fellow Am. Acad. Allergy (pres. 1975); mem. Am. Fedn. Clin. Research, Am. Assn. Immunologists, Am. Soc. Clin. Investigation, Am. Assn. Physicians, N.Y. Acad. Scis., Soc. Exptl. Biology and Medicine, Am. Thoracic Soc., Am. Clin. and Climatol. Assn., Johns Hopkins Med. Soc., Alpha Omega Alpha. Episcopalian. Home: 13500 Manor Rd Baldwin MD 21013-9775 Office: Johns Hopkins U Asthma and Allergy Ctr 5501 Hopkins Bayview Cir Baltimore MD 21224-6821

NORMAN, RALPH LOUIS, physicist, consultant; b. Kingston, Tenn., Mar. 25, 1933; s. Walter Hugh and Helen Irene (Smith) N.; m. Agnes Irene Pickel, Sept. 5, 1964; children: Mark Alan, Max Alvin. B.S., U. Tenn., 1959; LL.B., Blackstone Sch. Law, 1967, J.D., 1971; certificate, Indsl. Coll. Armed Forces, 1969; M.A. in Pub. Adminstrn, U. Okla., 1971; D.Sci. (hon.), Apollo Research Inst., 1976. Engr. Chrysler Corp. Missile Div., Huntsville, Ala., 1959-60; physicist Army Rocket & Guided Missile Agy., Redstone Arsenal, Ala., 1960-61; asst. project mgr. Army Missile Command, Redstone Arsenal, 1961-62; project mgr. Army Missile Command, 1962-89, ret., 1989; cons. to several def. constractors, 1989—; faculty Athens (Ala.) Coll., 1970-71, Calhoun Jr. Coll., Decatur, Ala., 1971-74, 85-90, U. Montevallo, Ala., 1973-74, U. Ala. at Huntsville, 1976-77, Columbia (Mo.) Coll., 1977-79; cons. firm Bishop and Sexton, 1973—, Athens (Ala.) State Coll.; reviewer NSF, 1974-76; FAA examiner. Contbr. articles profl. jours. Served with USN, 1951-55. Recipient Dept. Def. commendations, 1961, 65, Dept. Army commendation, 1972. Mem. N.Y. Acad. Scis., Assn. U.S. Army. Home: 13889 Dupree Worthey Rd Harvest AL 35749-7321 *I strive to make the knowledge gained through my research benefit all mankind.*

NORMAN, RICHARD ARTHUR, humanities educator; b. Columbus, Ohio, July 11, 1915; s. Norman Oscar and Marie (Falter) Kuhnheim. BA, George Washington U., 1951; MA, Columbia U., 1952, PhD, 1957. Instr. Columbia U., N.Y.C., 1952-57; asst. prof. English Barnard Coll., 1957-64, asso. prof., 1964-72, prof., 1972-81, spl. lectr., 1981-85, prof. emeritus, 1985—; instr. grad. div. Hunter Coll., 1960-62; Speech cons. CBS News, 1971-85; reader Talking Books Am. Found. for Blind, 1973-80. Radio announcer, producer, actor, 1934-50; commentator for chamber music concert; broadcast, from Library of Congress, Washington, 1948-50; Author: (with George W. Hibbitt) A Guide to Speech Training, 1964; radio series The Wonder of Words, 1962. Vice pres. Axe-Houghton Found., now emeritus. Served to capt. USAAF, 1942-45. Home: 9 Branchville Rd Ridgefield CT 06877-5012

NORMAN, RONALD, church officer; b. Watertown, Wis., Mar. 1, 1945; m. Sandra Lang; children: Corey, Chanda, Cherie. Student, Carroll Coll.; BA, Sioux Falls Coll., 1968; MA, N.Am. Bapt. Sem., 1972, postgrad. Ordained pastor Bapt. Ch., 1972. Student pastor United Ch. of Christ, Valley Springs, S.D., 1971-72, 1st Presbyn. Ch., Bridgewater, S.D., 1970-71, St. Paul's Presbyn. Ch., Emergy, S.D., 1970-71; dir. church edn. and youth Bismarck (N.D.) Bapt. Ch., 1972-74, sr. pastor, 1974-79; sr. pastor Village Green Bapt. Ch., Glen Ellyn, Ill., 1980-82; dir. growth dept. Nat. Am. Bapt. Ch. Ext., 1982-86; sr. pastor 1st Bapt. Ch., Elk Grove, Calif., 1986—; moderator Nat. Am. Bapt. Coun. Office: North Am Baptist Con 1 S 210 Summit Ave Villa Park IL 60181

NORMAN, STEPHEN PECKHAM, financial services company executive; b. Norwich, Conn., May 20, 1942; s. Richard Leonard and Mary Ellen (Carr) N.; m. Jacqueline Mary Batten, June 29, 1968; children—Adrian Gates, Hilary Batten, Philip Douglas, Matthew Jeremy Mitchell. B.A., Yale U., 1964; J.D., U. Pa., 1967. Bar: Conn. 1967, N.Y. 1972. Atty. Am. Express Co., N.Y.C., 1970-78, v.p. corp. office, 1978-82, sec., 1982—; Mem. bd. editors Corp. Governance. Served to sgt. U.S. Army, 1968-70; Vietnam. Mem. Am. Soc. Corp. Secs. (past chmn.), Conn. Bar Assn., N.Y. Bar Assn., U.S. Working Com. Group 30. Republican. Episcopalian. Club: Am. Yacht (Rye). Home: 6 Highland Park Pl Rye NY 10580-1736 Office: Am Express Co World Fin Ctr 200 Vesey St New York NY 10281-1009

NORMAN, WILLIAM STANLEY, travel and tourism executive; b. Roper, N.C., Apr. 27, 1938; s. James Colbitt and Josephine Cleo (Woods) N.; m. Elizabeth Patricia Patterson, May 31, 1969; children: Lisa Renée, William Stanley II. BS, West Va. Wesleyan U., 1960; MA, Am. U., 1967; exec. program, Stanford U., 1976. Math. tchr. Washington High Sch., Norfolk, 1961; commd. USN, 1962; advanced through grades to comdr., 1973; naval flight officer Airborne Early Warning Squadron Eleven, 1962-65; asst. combat info. ctr. officer U.S.S. Constellation, 1965; staff officer air weapons systems analysis Office Chief Naval Ops., Pentagon, Washington, 1965-66; history and fgn. affairs instr. U.S. Naval Acad., 1967-69; social aide The White House, 1967-69; carrier div. staff officer SE Asia, 1969-70, spl. asst. to Chief Naval Ops. for Minority Affairs, 1970-72, asst. to Chief Naval Ops. for Spl. Projects, 1972-73; dir. corp. action Cummins Engine Co. Inc., Columbus, Ind., 1973-74, exec. dir. corp. responsibility, 1974-76; exec. mktg. mgr., 1976-77; exec. dir. distbn. mktg. Cummins Engine Co. Inc., Columbus, Ind., 1977-78; v.p. eastern divsn., 1978-79; v.p. sales and mktg. Amtrak, Washington, 1979-81, group v.p., 1981-84, exec. v.p., 1984-94; pres., CEO Travel Industry Assn. of Am., Washington, 1994—; bd. dirs. CPC Internat., Englewood Cliffs, N.J., Logistics Mgmt. Inst., McLean, Va. Bd. dirs. USN Meml. Found., Washington, 1980—; bd. visitors Am. U. Kogod Sch. of Bus. Capt. USNR. Mem. Travel Industry Assn. Am. (bd. dirs. 1980—, chmn. bd. 1987-89, chmn. bd. dirs. of found. 1990-92), UN Assn. U.S. (bd. dirs. 1983—, bd. govs. 1985—), Coun. on Fgn. Rels., Inst. Cert. Travel. Agts., Bretton Woods Com., Travel and Tourism Govt. Affairs Coun. (bd. dirs. 1988—). Democrat. Episcopalian. Avocations: golf, tennis, jogging, walking, cycling. Home: 1308 Timberly Ln Mc Lean VA 22102-2504 Office: Travel Industry Assn of Am 1100 New York Ave Ste 450 Washington DC 20005-3934

NORMAND, ROBERT, lawyer; b. Montreal, Que., Can., Sept. 24, 1936; s. Lucien and Eva (Rochon) N.; m. Madeleine Scott, Sept. 16, 1961; children: Eric, Yves, Genevieve. BA, U. Montreal, 1956; LLL, U. Sherbrooke, Que., 1960; diploma, Inst. d'etudes politiques, Paris, 1962. Bar: Que. 1960. Legal adviser Nat. Assembly, Quebec City, 1962-67, law clk., 1967-71; asst. dep. min. justice Que. Govt., Quebec City, 1970-71, dep. min. justice, 1971-77, dep. min. intergovtl. affairs, 1977-82, dep. min. fin., 1982-87; pres., pub. Le Soleil (Hollinger), Quebec City, 1987-93; v.p. corp. affairs UniMedia Inc., 1993-94, dep. min. internat. affairs, 1994—; sec. Study Com. on Expropriation 1965-67; guest prof. legis. law faculty Laval U., Ottawa U., 1971; pres.

Que. Police Inst., 1974; chmn. Com. Supervising Olympic Security, 1974-76; chmn. Uniform Law Conf. Can.; dir. Caisse de Dèpot et Placement du Québec, 1982-87; v.p. Can. del. Diplomatic Conf. on travel contracts, Brussels, 1970; pres. Can. del. at convs. Internat. Inst. French Lang. law, 1974, 76. V.p. Hosp. du Saint-Sacrement, Quebec City, 1988-94; vice chmn. Inst. Rsch. on Pub. Policy, Montreal, 1988-94; pres. Que. Symphony Orch., Quebec City, 1989-92; consul gen. Sweden, Quebec City, 1989-94; co-pres. United Way Campaign Greater Quebec Region, 1989, hon. chmn. Telethon for Cerebral Palsy, 1990; mem. Citizens Forum, Spicer Commn., 1990-91. Capt. Can. Army, 1954-60. Named Queen's Counsel, 1971; recipient Pub. Adminstrn. award of excellence Nat. Sch. Pub. Adminstrn. Alumni, Quebec City, 1986. Mem. Investment Dealers Assn. Can. (dir. 1989-94), Que. Garrison Club (dir. 1991—), Profl. Liability Ins. of Que. Bar (dir. 1991-94), Que. Bar (supervisory com. 1988-93), Can. Bar Assn., la Commanderie de Bordeaux. Roman Catholic. Avocations: fishing, hunting. Home: 2750 de L'Anse, Sainte-Foy, PQ Canada G1W 2G5 Office: Dept Internal Affairs, 525 boul René-Lévesque est, Quebec, PQ Canada G1R 5R9

NORMAND, ROBERT, utility industry executive; b. Montreal, Que., Can., Jan. 9, 1940; s. Albert and Germaine (Levesque) N.; m. Pauline Ross, July 14, 1962; children—Patrice, Isabelle. Bus. cert., U. Montreal, 1966. Chartered acct., Can. External auditor Richter Usher Vineberg, Montreal, 1962-65, Coopers & Lybrand, Montreal, 1966-67; chief acct. Tioxide of Can., Tracy, 1967-68; comptroller Scott Lasalle Ltd., Montreal, 1969-71; v.p. Gaz Metropolitain Inc., Montreal, 1972—; bd. dirs. Daubois Inc., Montreal, Fonds Investments REA, TQM Pipeline, Vt. Gas. Roman Catholic. Avocation: tennis. Home: 177 Grande Cote, Rosemere, PQ Canada J7A 1H5

NORMANDEAU, ANDRE GABRIEL, criminologist, educator; b. Montreal, Que., Can., May 4, 1942; s. Gabriel E. and Laurette D. (Sauve) N.; m. Pierrette La Pointe, Aug. 14, 1965; children: Alain, Louis, Jean. M.A. in Criminology, U. Pa., 1965, Ph.D. in Sociology, 1968. Asst. prof. criminology U. Montreal, 1968-71, assoc. prof., 1971-76, prof., 1976—, chmn. dept. criminology, 1970-80, dir. Internat. Ctr. Comparative Criminology, 1983-89, dir. Rsch. Inst. on Police, 1990—. Author: Public Attitudes and Crime, 1970, The Measurement of Crime, 1975, Patterns of Robbery, 1980, Crimes of Violence, 1985, A Vision of the Police, 1990, Crime Prevention, 1993, Justice and Minorities, 1995, Community Policing, 1996. Woodrow Wilson fellow, 1964-68. Mem. Internat. Soc. Criminology, Am. Soc. Criminology, Am. Sociol. Assn., Can. Criminal Justice Assn. Roman Catholic. Home: 3150 Ave Kent, Montreal, PQ Canada H3S 1N1 Office: Dept Criminology U Montreal, Montreal, PQ Canada H3C 3J7 *Happiness is achieved by working for it, not by waiting for it to come to you.*

NORMENT, ERIC STUART, newspaper editor; b. Butler, Pa., July 26, 1956; s. Hillyer Gavin and Reva Lucille (Shepherd) N.; m. Ann Hobin, Aug. 22, 1987; chldren: Timothy Hobin, Peter John, Laura Mary. BA, U. Chgo., 1979; MS, Northwestern U., Evanston, Ill., 1980. Reporter Paddock Publs., Arlington Heights, Ill., 1980-83; asst. night editor Cape Cod Times, Hyannis, Mass., 1983; copy editor The Boston Herald, 1983-84, copy desk chief news, 1984-88, features prodn. editor, 1987-88, asst. Sunday editor, 1988-94, Sunday editor, 1994—; instr. journalism Northeastern U., Boston, 1984. Recipient Peter Lisagor Pub. Svc. award Chgo. Headline Club, 1981, Edn. Reporting award Ill. Press Assn., 1981. Office: Boston Herald 1 Herald St Boston MA 02118-2200

NORQUIST, JOHN OLOF, mayor; b. Princeton, N.J., Oct. 22, 1949; s. Ernest O. and Jeannette (Nelson) N.; m. Susan R. Mudd, Dec. 1986; 1 child, Benjamin Edward. Student, Augustana Coll., Rock Island, Ill., 1967-69; BS, U. Wis., 1971, MPA, 1988. Assemblyman Wis. State Assembly, Madison, 1974-82, co-chmn. state joint com. fin., 1980-81; mem. Wis. State Senate, 82-88, asst. majority leader, 1984-85, 87; mayor City of Milw., 1988—. Sgt. USAR, 1971-77. Mem. Nat. League of Cities, Wis. Alliance of Cities. Democrat. Presbyterian. Avocation: map collecting. Office: Office of Mayor City Hall Rm 201 200 E Wells St Milwaukee WI 53202-3515*

NORRBY, KLAS CARL VILHELM, pathology educator; b. Shanghai, China, Jan. 8, 1937; s. Åke Vilhelm and Ingrid Maria (Wedblad) N.; m. Ulla Margareta Hjort, June 17, 1961; children: Katarina, Cecilia, Jacob. MB, Göteborg (Sweden) U., 1959, lic. in medicine, 1964, MD, 1970, PhD, 1970. Asst. prof. pathology Göteborg U., 1967-71, prof. pathology, regal chair, 1985—; sr. lectr. in pathology Linköping U., 1972-84, chmn. Inst. Med. Microbiology and Pathology, 1980-84; vis. prof. in cell biology Harvard Med. Sch., Boston, 1989-90. Author over 200 articles to profl. jours. Sub-lt. Royal Swedish Navy Med. Corps, 1972-86. Fellow European Study Group for Cell Proliferation, European Histamine Rsch. Soc., N.Y. Acad. Sci. Avocations: hiking, sailing, skiing, classical music. Office: Sahlgrenska U Hosp, Dept Pathology, S-413 45 Göteborg Sweden

NORRED, WILLIAM PRESTON, JR., pharmacologist, educator; b. Tallassee, Ala., July 11, 1945; s. William Preston and Halley May (Ingram) N.; m. Carol Joyce Nelson, Sept. 13, 1969; children: Amy, Leigh, Richard. BA, Emory U., 1966; BS in Pharm., U. Ga., 1969, PhD, 1971. Rsch. pharmacologist Agrl. Rsch. Ctr. USDA, Athens, Ga., 1971-81, supervisory pharmacologist, 1984—; adj. asst. prof. U. Ga., Athens, 1976-84, assoc. prof., 1984—. Author: (with others) Diagnosis of Mycotoxicoses, 1986; contbr. more than 75 articles to profl. jours. Mem. Am. Soc. for Pharmacology and Exptl. Therapeutics, Ga. Acad. Sci., Soc. Toxicology, Sigma Xi, Phi Sigma, Rho Chi, Phi Kappa Phi. Avocations: golf, woodworking, fishing. Office: USDA/ARS Russell Rsch Ctr 950 College Station Rd Athens GA 30605-2720

NORRELL, MARY PATRICIA, nursing educator; b. Seymour, Ind., Jan. 3; d. William C. and Mary Elizabeth (Elkins) Ulrey; m. Robert Gerald Norrell, Aug. 17, 1974; children: Shannan, Richard, Trisha. BSN, Ball State U., 1971; postgrad., Ind. U. Cert. neonatal resuscitation, inpatient obstetrics. Team leader Mt. Sinai Med. Ctr., Miami Beach, Fla., 1971-73; charge nurse Jackson County Schneck Meml. Hosp., Seymour, 1971, 73-74; nurse Camp Matoaka, Oakland, Maine, 1973; master instr. Ivy Tech. State Coll., Columbus, Ind., 1974—; item writer Nat. Coun. Licensure Exam. for Practical Nurses, 1992. Mem. Assn. of Women's Health, Obstetric and Neonatal Nurses, Ind. Soc. for Healthcare Edn. and Tng. Home: 572 Shawnee Ct Seymour IN 47274-1956

NORRGARD, KRISTIN ANN, magazine publisher; b. London, June 19, 1957; came to U.S., 1959; d. John Thomas and Barbara Ann (Erikson) N. BA, William Smith Coll., 1979. Account mgr. The Media Book, N.Y.C., 1979-80; dir. advt. Ad Forum mag., N.Y.C., 1980-83; nat. account mgr. Ladies' Home Jour., N.Y.C., 1983-85; dir. advt. Savvy Woman mag., N.Y.C., 1985-86, pub., 1986-90, v.p., 1988-90; assoc. pub. Inc. Mag., N.Y.C., 1990-92; pub. Working Woman Mag., Avon, Colo., 1993-94; exec. v.p. sales and mktg. Eagle River Comms., Avon, 1995—. Active Jr. League of Greenwich, Conn., 1979-80, Jr. League of N.Y.C., 1980-87, Fountain House, N.Y.C. Mem. Advt. Women N.Y.C., Ad Club N.Y. Republican. Congregationalist. Avocations: skiing, swimming, windsurfing, traveling, cycling. Office: PO Box 3600 Avon CO 81620

NORRID, HENRY GAIL, osteopath, surgeon, researcher; b. Amarillo, Tex., June 4, 1940; s. Henry Horatio and Johnnie Belle (Combs, Cummins) N.; m. Andreia Maybeth Hudson, Jan. 29, 1966 (dec. 1988); children: Joshua Andrew, Noah Adam; m. Cheryll Diane Payne, Mar. 19, 1989; stepchildren: Kim Sheri Payne, Matthew Dominic Payne. AA, Amarillo Coll., 1963; BA, U. Tex., 1966; MS, West Tex. State U., 1967; DO, Kirksville Coll. Osteo. Medicine, 1973. Diplomate Bd. Osteo. Physicians and Surgeons, Nat. Bd. Examiners Osteo. Physicians and Surgeons; cert. basic sci. tchr. Iowa, Tex., Colo. Intern Interboro Gen. Hosp., Bklyn., 1973-74; attending physician dept. gen. practice Osteo. Hosp. and Clinic N.Y., N.Y.C., 1974-77; gen. practice medicine specializing in osteo., Amarillo, Tex., 1978—; emergency care physician Amarillo Emergency Receiving Ctr. Amarillo Hosp. Dist., Tex., 1978-79, Ready Care Emergency Center, Arlington and Bedford, Tex., 1990-92; emergency room physician St. Anthony Hosp., Amarillo, Tex., 1992; emeritus mem. consulting staff physician dept. family practice Northwest Tex. Hosp., Amarillo, 1995; emergency/trauma physician Tex. EM Care, 1995—; mem. mass casualty nat. disaster response team ARC, 1995; contract staff physician Tex. Tech Univ. Sch. Medicine and Health Scis. Ctr., med. dept. and infirmary Tex. Dept. Corrections, Tex. Dept. Criminal Justice; med. cons. rehab. medicine vocat. rehab. divsn Tex. Rehab. Commn., Plano; cattleman, ranch owner, Van Zandt County, Tex.; lectr. osteo. prins. and practice, The Osteo. Hosp. and Clinic N.Y., 1974-77, mem. credentials com., 1975-76; mem. exec. com. Southwest Osteo. Hosp., Amarillo, 1983-84, chief of staff, 1984-85; sec. dept. family practice Northwest Tex. Hosp., Amarillo, 1981-82, mem. credentials com., 1984-85, joint practice com. dept. family practice, 1986-87; mem. orgnl. com. for devel. of dept. osteo. prins. and practices, chmn. N.Y.C. group N.Y. Coll. Osteo. Med., 1977; mem. North Tex. Amputee Support Group, Dallas. Contbr. articles to Tex. Jour. Sci., other publs. Scout physician Llano Estecato council Boy Scouts Am., Texas, 1978-85. Served to E-4 U.S. Army, 1956-63. Recipient William M. Giltner Meml. Fund award 1972, Humanitarian award Am. Cath. Conf., 1979, Century award Boy Scouts Am., 1982; Maxwell D. Warmer Meml. scholar 1973; scholar Kirksville Coll. Osteo. Medicine, 1970, Tex. Legislature, 1969-73, Pfizer, 1973; named to Eminent Soc. Border Legionaires, 11th Armored Cavalry Regiment, Germany, 1958. Mem. Am. Coll. Gen. Practitioners, Tex. Osteo. Med. Assn. (pres. dist. I, mem. ho. of dels. 1981-82, 95), Sons of Am. Revolution, The Sons of Republic of Tex., Am. Congress Rehab. Medicine, Am. Osteo. Assn., World Future Soc. (profl.), Gen. Soc. War of 1812, Tex. & Southwest Cattle Raisers Assn., N.Y. Acad. Scis., Ex-Student's Assn. of The Univ. Tex. (life), 11th Armored Cavalry Regiment Assn., 36th (Tex.) Inf. Divsn. Assn. (life), Baron of the Magna Charta (Sommerset chpt. 1994—), Masons, Am. Legion, Trinity Fellowship, Beta Beta Beta, Sigma Sigma Phi (pres. 1972), Alpha Phi Omega, Psi Sigma Alpha, Theta Psi, Theta Psi Clowns (1969-73). Avocations: astronomy, short wave listening, camping, fishing, anthropology. Office: 1422 S Tyler St Ste 102 Amarillo TX 79101-4238

NORRIE, K. PETER, manufacturing executive; b. Madison, Wis., Mar. 7, 1939; s. Kenneth Peter and Clara Frances (Storey) N.; m. Susan Kelliher, Sept. 6, 1960 (dec. 1975); children: Peter Clark, David Doherty, Charles Kelliher; m. Betty Buzard, Oct. 14, 1978 (div. Apr. 1989). BCE, Gonzaga U., 1961; MBA, Harvard U., 1964. Estimator H. Halvorsen Contractors, Spokane, Wash., 1961-62; gen. mgr. Boise (Idaho) Cascade Corp., 1964-70, mgr. gen. sales, 1970-72, v.p., 1972-76, sr. v.p., gen. mgr. paper group, 1976-89; chmn. bd. dirs. Specialty Paperboard, Inc., 1989—; pres. Parma Labs., Inc., 1993—. Trustee UCLA Found. With USMCR, 1956-62. Recipient Disting. Alumni Merit award Gonzaga U., 1987. Republican. Roman Catholic. Avocation: golf.

NORRIS, ALAN EUGENE, federal judge; b. Columbus, Ohio, Aug. 15, 1935; s. J. Russell and Dorothy A. (Shrader) N.; m. Nancy Jean Myers, Apr. 15, 1962 (dec. Jan. 1986); children: Tom Edward Jackson, Tracy Elaine; m. Carol Lynn Spohn, Nov. 10, 1990. BA, Otterbein Coll., 1957, HLD (hon.), 1991; cert., U. Paris, 1956; LLB, NYU, 1960; LLM, U. Va., 1986. Bar: Ohio 1960, U.S. Dist. Ct. (so. dist) Ohio 1962, U.S. Dist. Ct. (no. dist) Ohio 1964. Law clk. to judge Ohio Supreme Ct., Columbus, 1960-61; assoc. Vorys, Sater, Seymour & Pease, Columbus, 1961-62; ptnr. Metz, Bailey, Norris & Spicer, Westerville, Ohio, 1962-80; judge Ohio Ct. Appeals (10th dist.), Columbus, 1981-86, U.S. Ct. Appeals (6th cir.), Columbus, 1986—. Contbr. articles to profl. jours. Mem. Ohio Ho. of Reps., Columbus, 1967-80. Named Outstanding Young Man, Westerville Jaycees, 1971; recipient Legislator of Yr. award Ohio Acad. Trial Lawyers, Columbus, 1972. Mem. ABA, Am. Judicature Soc., Inst. Jud. Adminstrn., Ohio Bar Assn., Columbus Bar Assn. Republican. Methodist. Lodge: Masons (master 1966-67). Office: US Ct Appeals 328 US Courthouse 85 Marconi Blvd Columbus OH 43215-2823

NORRIS, ALBERT STANLEY, psychiatrist, educator; b. Sudbury, Ont., Can., July 14, 1926; s. William and Mary (Zell) N.; m. Dorothy James, Sept. 2, 1950; children: Barbara Ellen, Robert Edward, Kimberly Ann. M.D., U. Western Ont., 1951. Intern Ottawa (Ont.) Civic Hosp., 1951-52; resident in psychiatry U. Iowa, Psychopathic Hosp., Iowa City, 1953-55, Boston City Hosp., 1955-56; practice medicine Kingston, Ont., Can., 1956-57; instr. Queen's U., Kingston, 1956-57; asst. prof. psychiatry U. Iowa, 1957-62, asso. prof., 1962-64, 1965-66, prof., 1966-72; asso. prof. U. Oreg., 1964-65; prof. So. Ill. U. Sch. Medicine, Springfield, 1972-84, chmn. dept. psychiatry, 1972-82; prof. emeritus, 1984—; practice medicine specializing in psychiatry Cedar Rapids, Iowa, 1984—; vis. prof. U. Auckland, N.Z., U. Otago, New Zealand, U. Liverpool. Contbr. chpts. to books, articles to med. jours. Fellow Am. Psychiat. Soc. (life); mem. AMA, Am. Psychopath. Assn., Soc. Biol. Psychiatry, Can. Psychiat. Soc., Am. Soc. Psychosomatic Ob-Gyn, Royal Soc. Medicine. Republican. Presbyterian. Home: 5 Penfro Dr Iowa City IA 52246-4927 Office: 1730 1st Ave NE Ste 133 Cedar Rapids IA 52402-5433 *A life is only fulfilled by a quest, a vision of the future and a commitment to a greater value than one's self. A flickering candle is poor light, unless there is no other.*

NORRIS, ALFRED LLOYD, theological seminary president, clergyman; b. Bogalusa, La., Feb. 6, 1938; s. Leslie Henry Peter and Adele Theresa (Washington) N.; m. Mackie Lyvonne Harper, Sept. 9, 1961; children: Alfred Lloyd II, Angela Renee. BA, Dillard U., 1960; MDiv, Gammon Theol. Sem., Atlanta, 1964, DD (hon.), 1976; DD (hon.), Centenary Coll., 1989; LLD, Dillard U., 1989. Ordained ministry United Meth. Ch., 1963. Pastor Haven United Meth. Ch., New Orleans, 1963-66, Peck United Meth. Ch., New Orleans, 1966-68, First Street United Meth. Ch., New Orleans, 1972-74, Mt. Zion United Meth. Ch., New Orleans, 1980-85; dist. supt. New Orleans dist. United Meth. Ch., New Orleans, 1974-80; dir. recruitment Gammon Theol. Sem., 1968-72, pres., 1985—; now bishop of New Mexico United Methodist Church, Albuquerque, N.Mex.; mem. Am. Preaching Mission, 1967; mem. bd. publs. United Meth. Pub. House, Nashville, 1980—; bd. dirs. Gulfside Assembly, Waveland, Miss., 1975—; mem. La. Conf. Bd. Higher Edn. and Campus Ministry; chmn. bd. ordained ministry La. Ann. Conf., 1980-88; guest preacher Liberia, West Africa, 1988. Trustee Centenary Coll., Shreveport, La., 1979—; mem. exec. com. NAACP, New Orleans, 1980-85; bd. dirs. New Orleans Urban League, 1981-84, Wesley Homes, Inc., Atlanta, 1986—; mem. exec. com. Met. Area Com., New Orleans, 1983-85; chmn. bd. dirs. Lafon Home for Elderly, New Orleans, 1983-85. Crusade scholar, 1961-63. Mem. Assn. United Meth. Theol. Schs. (sec. 1986-88), Adminstrv. Deans' Coun. (v.p. 1986—), Masons, Sigma Pi Phi, Theta Phi. Democrat. Avocations: reading, spectator sports.

NORRIS, ANDREA SPAULDING, art museum director; b. Apr. 2, 1945; d. Edwin Baker and Mary Gretchen (Brendle) Spaulding. BA, Wellesley Coll., 1967; MA, NYU, 1969, PhD, 1977. Intern dept. western European arts Met. Mus. Art, N.Y.C., 1970, 72; rsch. and editorial asst. Inst. Fine Arts NYU, 1971, lectr. Washington Sq. Coll., 1976-77; lectr. Queens Coll. CUNY, 1973-74; asst. to dir. Art Gallery Yale U., New Haven, 1977-80, lectr. art history, 1979-80; chief curator Archer M. Huntington Art Gallery, Austin, Tex., 1980-88; lectr. art history Dept. Art U. Tex., Austin, 1984-88; dir. Spencer Mus. Art U. Kans., Lawrence, 1988—. Co-author: (catalogue) Medals and Plaquettes from the Molinari Collection at Bowdoin College, 1976; author: (exhbn. catalogues) Jackson Pollock: New-Found Works, 1978; exhbn. The Sforza Court: Milan in the Renaissance 1450-1535, 1988-89. Mem. Renaissance Soc. Am., Coll. Art Assn., Assn. Art Mus. Dirs., Phi Beta Kappa. Office: Spencer Mus Art U Kans Lawrence KS 66045

NORRIS, CHARLES HEAD, lawyer, financial executive; b. Boston, Sept. 14, 1940; s. Charles Head and Martha Marie N.; B.A., U. Pa., 1963, J.D., 1968; M.A., U. Wash., 1965; m. Diana D. Strawbridge, July 27, 1974 (div. 1994); 1 dau., Margaret Dorrance. Bar: Pa. 1968. Mem. firm Morgan, Lewis & Bockius, Phila., 1968-77; pres., chief exec. Artemis Corp., 1978-79; chmn. bd., chief exec., 1979-91; chmn. exec. com., vice chmn. bd. Remington Rand Corp., 1979-81; ptnr. Artemis Energy Co., 1980-92; chmn., chief exec. Norris Investment Co., 1992—; trustee mgj. stockholders' voting trust Campbell Soup Co., 1987-90; bd. dirs. SBSF Funds, Inc., 1988-91, del. trust, 1987-91. Bd. dirs. Asprey & Co. Ltd.; mem. Harvard U. Bd. Overseas Com. to Visit the Libr., 1989—; mem. Pa. Commn. Crime and Delinquency, 1980-84; mem. Thouron Award Selection Com., 1985-90; mem. Pa. Electoral Coll., 1980; mem. West Pikeland Twp. Suprs., 1969-72; mem. bd. visitors Carnegie Mellon U. Sch. Urban and Pub. Affairs, 1988-90; corp. mem. Belmont Hill Sch., 1990—. Officer USAF, 1959. Mem. ABA, Pa. Bar Assn., Am. Econ. Assn. Clubs: Phila., Seminole Golf, Knickerbocker, Union League, Vicmead Hunt, Everglades (bd. dirs. 1986-91); Sunningdale Golf (Eng.); The Country (Brookline). Office: PO Box 112 Boston MA 02117

NORRIS, CHUCK (CARLOS RAY), actor; b. Ryan, Okla., Mar. 10, 1940; m. Dianne Norris (div.); children: Mike, Eric. Appeared in films The Wrecking Crew, 1969, Return of the Dragon, 1972, Breaker, Breaker, 1976, Good Guys Wear Black, 1977, Force of One, 1978, The Octagon, 1979, An Eye for an Eye, 1980, Silent Rage, 1981, Forced Vengeance, 1981, Lone Wolf McQuade, 1982, Missing in Action, 1984, Missing in Action II-The Beginning, 1985, Code of Silence, 1985, (co-screenwriter) Invasion, U.S.A., 1985, Delta Force, 1986, Firewalker, 1986, (co-screenwriter) Braddock: Missing in Action III, 1987, Hero and the Terror, 1988, Delta Force 2: Operation Stranglehold, 1990, The Hitman, 1991, (co-exec. prodr.) Sidekicks, 1993, Top Dog, 1994; TV series Walker: Texas Ranger, 1993—; author: (with Joe Hyams) The Secret of Inner Strength: My Story, 1988; host: The Ultimate Stuntman: A Tribute to Dar Robinson. Profl. world middleweight karate champion, 1968-74. Office: 144 S Beverly Dr Penthouse Beverly Hills CA 90212*

NORRIS, CURTIS BIRD, writer, journalist; b. Quincy, Mass., July 14, 1927; s. Lowell Ames and Helen (Curtis) N.; m. Eileen Patricia Schindler, Mar. 23, 1959; children: Katharine Eileen, Helen Carolyn, Suzanne Elizabeth. AB, Middlebury Coll., 1951; postgrad., Bridgewater (Mass.) State Coll., 1986-95. Free-lance writer, 1945—; writer Sikorsky Aircraft Co., Stratford, Conn., 1957-59, N.Am. Aviation, Downey, Calif., 1959-61; editor Hughes Aircraft Co., Fullerton, Calif., 1961-62, Whitman (Mass.) News, 1962-65; sci. writer U. Vt., 1965-66; editor Wareham (Mass.) Courier, 1966-69; med. sci. editor Brown U., Providence, 1969-77; dir. pub. affairs Stonehill Coll., North Easton, Mass., 1977-83; staff columnist Quincy (Mass.) Patriot Ledger, 1982—; news dir. Bridgewater State Coll., 1985-87; indsl. rels. dir. Morgan Meml. Goodwill Industries, Boston, 1987-89; instr. Stonehill Coll., North Easton, 1991—; lectr., feature writer Boston Sunday Herald-Traveler, 1963-76, Yankee mag., 1963—; staff investigative reporter Globe Communications, Montreal, Can., 1973—; bd. dirs. pub. rels. programs Composite Tech. Alloys Co., Attleboro, Mass., 1975—; coord. Ea. Writers Conf., Salem, Mass., 1982; cons. pub. rels., 1983—; instr. Stonehill Coll., 1991. Author: Seldom Heard Tales of New England, 1964, American Holocaust, 1975, Phantom P. 40, 1981, Little Known Mysteries of New England, 1992, Ghosts I Have Known, 1993, The Boston Bogeyman, 1995, The Man Who Talked to Trees, 1995; assoc. editor: Stonehill Alumni News, 1977-81; editor: Stonehill Rev., 1977-83; originator (TV programs) Health Call, Science Call, Providence; prodr.: (cable TV program) Seldom Heard Tales of New Eng., 1986-88; represented in anthologies including Yankees Under Steam, 1970, Mysterious New England, 1971, Danger, Disaster and Horrid Deeds, 1974, Best Detective Cases, 1975-77, True Police Yearbook, 1975, 77, Startling Detective Yearbook, 1975-77, The World Wars Remembered, 1979, Best of Old Farmers Almanac, 1991; author manuscripts in Norris Collection, Brown U.; contbr. numerous stories to mags., TV Unsolved Mysteries, 1989. Chmn. publicity Wareham chpt. Am. Cancer Soc., 1966, cmty. chmn., 19678-69; assoc. mem. Federated Ea. Indian League; bd. dirs. Opera New Eng. of Greater Brookton. With USAAF, 1945-57; maj. Mass. N.G. Recipient Grand award Coun. Advancement and Support of Edn., 1976-77, Philippine Liberation medal Philippine Govt., 1994. Mem. New Eng. Press Assn., Am. Defenders of Bataan and Corregidor, Am. Med. Writers Assn., Assn. Am. Med. Colls., Mystery Writers Am., State Def. Force Assn. of U.S., Ret. Officers Assn., U.S. Coast Guard Aux. Flotilla 1108, Kappa Delta Rho. Unitarian. Home: 166 E Main St Norton MA 02766-2310 *Life can be like a jaunt thru a candy store, full of tasty morsels for the creative and adventurous to grasp. Always observe nobless obligeand the ten commandments - you will be rewarded severalfold. My most useful knowledge? High school latin. Regrets? Unable to return to Bataan or to visit English roots.*

NORRIS, DARELL FOREST, insurance company executive; b. Pontiac, Mich., Oct. 19, 1928; s. Forest Ellis and Mabel Marie (Smith) N.; m. Thordis Marie Johansen, Aug. 21, 1955; children: Dara Lee, Jennifer, Lisa, Nancy. BS, U. Kans., 1950. CLU, chartered fin. cons. Reporter, sports staff Kansas City Star, Mo., 1950-51; pilot TWA, 1955-56; div. agy. mgr. Merced region Farmers Group, Inc., Calif., 1959, sales rep., Colorado Springs region, 1962, regional agy. mgr., Aurora, Ill., 1964, regional sales mgr., Santa Ana, Calif., 1966, mgmt. tng. program staff, dir. agys., L.A., 1969, regional mgr., Austin, Tex., 1971, v.p. sales, L.A., 1973, v.p. field ops. midwestern zone, 1976, v.p. field ops., western zone, 1979—; pres. Farmers New World Mgmt. Co., 1977-81, v.p. staff ops., 1981-85, sr. v.p. life co. ops. and staff support svcs., 1985-90, farmers cons., 1990-93; gen. ins. cons., 1993—; bd. dirs. Northridge Hosp. Med. Found. Chmn. bd. deacons First Baptist Ch., Granada Hills, Calif., 1977-89; sustaining mem. Rep. Nat. Com. Capt. USAF, 1951-55. Mem. Am. Soc. CLUs, Chartered Fin. Cons. (San Fernando Valley chpt.), Ins. Edn. Assn. (trustee 1982-84). Office: Farmers Ins Group Cos 11633 Porter Valley Dr Northridge CA 91326-1413

NORRIS, DENNIS E., religious organization executive. Dir. Am. Baptist Chs. Cleve. Region.

NORRIS, DOLORES JUNE, elementary school educator; b. Belmore, N.Y., Feb. 10, 1938; d. Abe and Doris Cyril (Stahl) Wanser; m. William Dean Norris, June 11, 1960; children: William Dean II, Ronald Wayne, Darla Cyrille. BS in Elem. Edn., So. Nazarene U., 1959; MS in Computer Edn., Nova U., 1988, EdS in Computer Applications, 1990. Cert. elem. edn. and computer sci. tchr., Fla. Tchr. 4th and 5th grades Ruskin (Fla.) Elem. Sch., 1959-61; tchr. 5th grade Emerson Elem. Sch., Kansas City, Kans., 1961-63; tchr. 1st grade Hickman Mills, Mo., 1964-65; tchr. 3d and 4th grades Lake Mary Elem. Sch., Sanford, Fla., 1968-72; tchr. 1st grade St. Charles Cath. Sch., Port Charlotte, Fla., 1976-77; primary tchr. Meadow Park Elem. Sch., Port Charlotte, 1977-89; computer specialist Vineland Elem. Sch., Rotanda West, Fla., 1989-90; computer specialist Myakka River Elem. Sch., Port Charlotte, 1990—, tech. trainer, 1995—; reading coun. Charlotte County Schs., Port Charlotte, 1987—, rep., 1989-90, in-svc. com. 1990-93; program planner Meadow Park Elem. Sch., 1988-89; program planner Myakka River Elem. Sch. 1991-93. Mem. Rotary, Punta Gorda, Fla., 1982-86; co-dir. teens Touring Puppet Group, Punta Gorda, 1982-86; puppet co-dir. NOW Teens, Punta Gorda, 1976-80. Mem. Fla. Assn. Computers in Edn. Avocations: piano, swimming, travel. Home: 1171 Richter St Port Charlotte FL 33952

NORRIS, EDWIN L., lawyer; b. Columbus, Ohio, Oct. 6, 1946. BA, Duke U., 1968; JD, Yale U., 1972; LLM, NYU, 1978. Bar: N.Y. 1973, U.S. Tax Ct. 1979, Calif. 1987. Ptnr. Sidley & Austin, L.A. Mem. ABA (mem. fgn. activities on U.S. taxpayers com. sect. taxation 1984—), State Bar Calif. (mem. tax sect.), L.A. County Bar Assn. Office: Sidley & Austin 555 W 5th St Fl 40 Los Angeles CA 90013-1010*

NORRIS, FLOYD HAMILTON, financial journalist; b. L.A., Sept. 6, 1947; s. Floyd H. and Martha Leota (Buntin) N.; m. Mary Christine Bockelmann, Oct. 5, 1984; 1 child, John Buntin. Student, U. Calif., Irvine, 1965-68; MBA, Columbia U., 1982. Reporter Coll. Press Svc., Washington, 1969-70, Manchester (N.H.) Am., 1970-72, Concord (N.H.) Monitor, 1972-74, UPI, Vt. and Ala., 1974-77; press sec. Sen. John Durkin, Washington, 1977-78; fin. writer AP, N.Y.C., 1978-81; columnist Barron's, N.Y.C., 1982-88; fin. columnist N.Y. Times, N.Y.C., 1988—. Office: N Y Times 229 W 43rd St New York NY 10036-3913

NORRIS, FRANKLIN GRAY, surgeon; b. Washington, June 30, 1923; s. Franklin Gray and Ellie Narcissus (Story) N.; m. Sara Kathryn Green, Aug. 12, 1945; children: Gloria Norris Sales, F. Gray III. BS, Duke U., 1947; MD, Harvard U., 1951. Resident, Peter Bent Brigham Hosp., Boston, 1951-54, Bowman Gray Sch. Medicine, 1954-57; practice medicine specializing in thoracic and cardiovascular surgery, 1957—; prof. anatomy and physiology, Valencia C.C., Orlando, Fla., 1995—; pres. Norris Assocs., Orlando, 1985—; mem. staff Brevard Meml. Hosp., Melbourne, Fla., Waterman Meml. Hosp., Eustis, Fla., West Orange Meml. Hosp., Winter Garden, Fla., Orlando Regional Med. Ctr., Fla. Hosp., Lucerne Hosp., Arnold Palmer Children Hosp., Princeton, Fla. Hosp. N.E. and South (all Orlando). Bd. dirs. Orange County Cancer Soc., 1958-64, Ctrl. Fla. Respiratory Disease Assn., 1958-65. Served to capt. USAAF, 1943-45. Decorated Air medal with 3 oak leaf clusters. Diplomate Am. Bd. Surgery, Am. Bd. Thoracic and Cardiovasc. Surgery, Am. Bd. Gen. Vascular Surgery. Mem. Fla. Heart Assn. (dir. 1958—), Orange County Med. Soc. (exec. com. 1964-75, pres. 1971-75), Cen. Fla. Hosp. Assn. (bd. dirs., 1980-85), ACS, Soc. Thoracic Surgeons, So.

Thoracic Surg. Assn., Am. Coll. Chest Physicians, Fla. Soc. Thoracic Surgeons (pres. 1981-82), Am. Coll. Cardiology, So. Assn. Vascular Surgeons, Fla. Vascular Soc., Phi Kappa Psi. Presbyterian (elder). Clubs: Citrus, Orlando Country. Home: 1801 Bimini Dr Orlando FL 32806-1515 Office: Norris Assocs 1801 Bimini Dr Orlando FL 32806-1515

NORRIS, GENIE M., senior government official; b. N.Y.C., July 15, 1951; d. Eugene and Peggy (Carter) Martell; m. Larry Specht, Apr. 22, 1982; children: Amanda Michele, Joshua Albert, Rachel Elizabeth. Adminstr. Senator Patrick Moynihan, N.Y.C., 1976; exec. asst. U.S. Senate, Washington, 1982-86; dep. field dir. Carter/Mondale Presdl. Campaign, Washington, 1979; dep. dir. Dem. Nat. Com., Washington, 1980-81; dir., sr. assoc. Francis Assocs., Ltd., Washington, Germany, 1981-82; exec. asst. Senator Patrick Moynihan, Washington, 1982-86; guest lectr. USIA, Washington, 1987-90; mgr. Amb. Residence, Bonn, Germany, 1987-90; sr. assoc. FMR Group, Washington, 1990; dep. exec. dir. Dem. Congl. Campaign Com., Washington, 1990-91, exec. dir., 1991-94; dep. asst. sec. for ops. Dept. of State, Washington, 1995—; com. rep. Dem. Nat. Com. South Africa, 1980, Dem. Congl. Campaign Com., Republic of China, 1992; Peace Corp. transistion team leader Pres. Transition Team, Washington, 1992-93; South Africa elections obs. UN, 1994. With U.S. Army, 1975-78. Democrat. Roman Catholic. Avocations: art history, 1st edition books, horseback riding, music, antiques. Home: 1630 Davidson Rd Mc Lean VA 22101-4306

NORRIS, GEOFFREY, geology educator, consultant; b. Romford, Essex, Eng., Aug. 6, 1937; came to Can., 1964; s. Alfred Frederick Henry and Winifred Lucy (Camps) N.; m. Anne Frances Facer, Sept. 20, 1958; children—Grant, Theresa, Brett, Sonia. B.A., Cambridge U., Eng., 1959, M.A., 1962, Ph.D., 1964. Sci. officer N.Z. Geol. Survey, Lower Hutt, 1961-64; postdoctoral fellow McMaster U. Hamilton, Ont., Can., 1965; rsch. scientist Pan Am. Petroleum, Tulsa, Okla., 1965-67; prof. U. Toronto, Ont., Can., 1967—, chmn. dept. geology, 1980-90; rsch. assoc. Royal Ont. Mus., Toronto, 1967—; A.V. Humboldt fellow Cologne U., W.Ger., 1976; Ptnr. Austin and Cumming Exploration, Calgary, Alta., Can., 1980-87; vis. scientist Fla. Marine Research Lab., St. Petersburg, 1986, Fla. Mus. Natural History, U. Fla., Gainesville, 1994. Contbr. articles to profl. jours. Pres. White Light Hospice Found., Toronto, 1987—; dir. Metro Toronto Residents Action Com. for Rail Safety, 1980-95. Recipient numerous operating, equipment and travel grants, Nat. Scis. and Engring. Research Council of Can., 1967—. Fellow Am. Assn. Stratigraphic Palynologists (pres. 1972), Royal Soc. Can. (sec. divsn. earth, ocean and atmospheric scis. 1990-92, dir. 1993—), Geol. Assn. Can. (councilor 1987-90), Geol. Soc. Am.; mem. Can. Assn. Palynologists (pres. 1982), Internat. Commn. Palynology (sec.-treas. 1975-80), Internat. Union Geol. Scis. (Can. nat. com. 1990—). Home: 12 Astley Ave, Toronto, ON Canada M4W 3B4 Office: U Toronto, Dept Geology, Toronto, ON Canada M5S 3B1

NORRIS, GERALD LEE, dean; b. Effingham, Ill., Feb. 2, 1940; s. Howard C. and Phyllis C. (Koester) N.; m. Ruth E. Norris, Aug. 13, 1961 (div. 1980); 1 child, Heather Raye; m. Joye Kaye Hall, Jan. 1, 1981; 1 child, Jackson Clay. BS in Edn., Ea. Ill. U., 1962, MS in Edn., 1967; EdD, Ill. State U., 1976. Art tchr. Robinson (Ill.) Cmty. Schs., 1962-67; art tchr. univ. high sch. Ill. State U., Normal, 1967-73, prin., asst. prin., 1973-79; dean coll. edn., prof. Western N.Mex. U., Silver City, 1979-86; prof. sch. adminstrn. U. Ctrl. Ark., Conway, 1986-87; dean coll. profl. studies Bemidji (Minn.) State U., 1987—; CEO Norris Enterprises, Bemidji, 1980—. Mem. cabinet United Way, Bemidji, 1993—. Grantee U.S. Office Edn., 1988-91. Mem. Bemidji Cmty. Arts Coun. (bd. dirs. 1988—), Rotary (pres. Sunrise of Bemidji chpt. 1994—). Avocation: antique automobiles. Office: Bemidji State U Dean Coll Profl Studies 1500 Birchmont Dr NE Bemidji MN 56601-2600

NORRIS, H. THOMAS, pathologist, academic administrator; b. Johnson City, Tenn., Nov. 24, 1934; s. Herbert Thomas and Ruth M. (Church) N.; m. Patricia Henry, June 19, 1956; children: Ruth Eileen, Margaret Ann, Edward Robert. BS with honors, Wash. State U., 1956; MD, U. So. Calif., 1959. Diplomate Am. Bd. Anatomic and Clin. Pathology. Resident pathology Mallory Inst. Pathology, Boston, 1960-62, 64-65; instr. Tufts U. Sch. Medicine, Boston, 1964-66; fellow Harvard Med. Sch., Cambridge, Mass., 1966-67; from asst. prof. to prof. U. Wash. Sch. Med., 1967-83; prof., chmn. East Carolina U. Sch. Medicine, Greenville, N.C., 1983—; asst. pathologist Mallory Inst. Pathology, Boston, 1965-66; asst. chief lab svc. VA Hosp., Seattle, 1967-74; dir. hosp. pathology U. Hosp., Seattle, 1974-83; chief pathology Pitt County Meml. Hosp., Greenville, 1983—. Editor: Contemporary Issues in Surgical Pathology, 1983, Pathology of the Colon, Small Intestine and Anus, 1991; contbr. articles to profl. jours. Bd. dirs. Am. Cancer Soc., Greenville, 1984—. Capt. USAR, 1962-64. Recipient Cert. Outstanding Achievement with Honorarium U.S. Army Sci. Conf., West Point, N.Y., 1964. Fellow ACP, Am. Soc. Clin. Pathologists, Coll. Am. Pathologists, Am. Pathology Found.; mem. AAAS, AMA, Am. Gastroent. Assn., Internat. Acad. Pathology, U.S. and Can. Acad. Pathology, Am. Assn. Pathologists, Arthur Purdy Stout Soc. Surg. Pathologists, Acad. Clin. Lab. Physicians and Scientists, Assn. Pathology Chmn., Am. Men and Women Sci., N.Y. Acad. Scis., Mass. Med. Soc., N.C. Med. Assn., N.C. Soc. Pathologists, Pitt County Med. Soc., Gastrointestinal Pathology Club (charter), Alpha Omega Alpha, Sigma Xi. Office: East Carolina U Sch Medicine Dept Pathology Lab Medicine Greenville NC 27858-4354

NORRIS, JAMES ARNOLD, government executive; b. Fargo, N.D., May 26, 1937; s. Cedric Leon and Gladys Louise (Arnold) N.; m. Catherine Anne Wright, Mar. 2, 1963; children: Suzanne, Erica, James. SB, MIT, 1959, SM, 1965; PhD, U. Calif., 1963. Economist Agy. Internat. Devel., Tunis, Tunisia, 1966-71, Jakarta, Indonesia, 1971-76, Cairo, 1976-80; dir. Bangladesh-India office Agy. Internat. Devel., Washington, 1980-82; mission dir. Agy. Internat. Devel., Dhaka, Bangladesh, 1982-84, Islamabad, Pakistan, 1988-92, Moscow, 1992—; counselor to agy. Agy. Internat. Devel., Washington, 1984-85, dep. adminstr. Asia Near East, 1985-88. Recipient Presdl. Meritorious Svc. award President U.S., 1984, 87, Presdl. Disting. Svc. award President U.S., 1989. Home: Psc 77 Aid APO AE 09721

NORRIS, JAMES HAROLD, lawyer; b. New Kensington, Pa., Sept. 18, 1953; s. J. Harold and Eleanore Rose (Arch) N.; m. Ann Marie Annase, Nov. 25, 1988; children: Ryan, Scott, Nicholas. BA, Washington Jefferson Coll., 1975; JD, Duquesne U., 1978. Bar: Pa. 1978, U.S. Dist. Ct. (we. dist.) Pa. 1978, U.S. Ct. Appeals (3d cir.) 1994. Assoc. Ruffin Hazlett Snyder Brown & Stabile, Pitts., 1979-83; ptnr. Eckert Seamans Cherin & Mellott, Pitts., 1983—, vice chmn. litigation dept., 1995. Mem. Allegheny County Bar Assn., Pa. Bar Assn. (chmn. adminstrv. law sect. 1992-94, sect. del., sports, entertainment and art law com., spl. achievement award 1993). Home: 2545 Country Side Ln Wexford PA 15090-7941 Office: Eckert Seamans Cherin & Mellott 600 Grant St Pittsburgh PA 15219-2702

NORRIS, JAMES RUFUS, JR., chemist, educator; b. Anderson, S.C., Dec. 29, 1941; s. James Rufus and Julia Lee (Walker) N.; m. Carol Anne Poetzsch, Dec. 28, 1963; children: Sharon Adele, David James. BS, U. N.C., 1963; PhD, Washington U., St. Louis, 1968. Postdoctoral appointee Argonne (Ill.) Nat. Lab., 1968-71, asst. chemist, 1971-74, chemist, 1974-79, photosynthesis group leader, 1979-95, sr. chemist, 1991-95; prof. dept. chemistry U. Chgo., 1995—; prof. chemistry U. Chgo., 1984—; chmn. internat. organizing com. 7th Internat. Conf. on Photochemical Conversion and Storage of Solar Energy, Northwestern U., Evanston, Ill., 1988. Coeditor: Photochemical Energy Conversion, 1989; mem. editorial bd. Applied Magnetic Resonance Jour., 1989—. Recipient Disting. Peformance award U. Chgo., 1977, 2 R&D 100 awards R&D mag., 1988, E.O. Lawrence Meml. award Dept. of Energy, 1990, Rumford Premium AAAS, 1992, Humboldt Rsch. award for Sr. Scientists, 1992, Zavoisky award Am. Acad. Arts and Scis., 1994. Mem. Am. Chem. Soc., Biophysical Soc. Achievements include discovery that the primary donor of photosynthesis is a dimeric special pair of chlorophyll molecules. Office: U Chgo Dept Chemistry 5735 S Ellis Ave Chicago IL 60637-1403

NORRIS, JOHN, school system administrator; b. Springfield, Ill., Jan. 19, 1940. BS, Loyola U., Chgo., 1962; MS, St. Mary's Coll., Winona, Minn., 1968; PhD, U. Md., 1975. Tchr. St. Michael's, Chgo., 1962-65; tchr., adminstr. Notre Dame H.S., Niles, Ill., 1965-70; with Archdiocese of Chgo., 1970-78, Diocese of Saginaw, 1978-89; supt. schs., dir. child-youth ministry Archdiocese of Milw., 1989—. Office: Office Schs Child and Youth Ministries PO Box 07912 Milwaukee WI 53207-0912

NORRIS, JOHN ANTHONY, health sciences executive, lawyer, educator; b. Buffalo, Dec. 27, 1946; s. Joseph D. and Maria L. (Suite) N.; m. Kathleen E. Mullen, July 13, 1969; children: Patricia Marie, John Anthony II, Joseph Mullen, Mary Kathleen, Elizabeth Mary. BA, U. Rochester, 1968; JD, MBA with honors, Cornell U., 1973; cert., Harvard U. Sch. Govt., 1986. Bar: Mass. 1973. Assoc. Peabody, Brown, Boston, 1973-75; assoc. Powers Hall, Boston, 1975-76, ptnr., mem. exec. com., 1976-80, v.p., dir., 1979-80, chmn. adminstrv. com., 1976-79, chmn. hiring com., 1979-80; chmn. bd., pres., chief exec. officer, founder Norris & Norris, Boston, 1980-85; dep. commr. and chief operating officer FDA, Washington, 1985-88, chmn. action planning and cap coms., 1985-88, chmn. reye syndrome com., 1985-87, chmn. trade legis. com., 1987-88; corporate exec. v.p. Hill & Knowlton, Inc., N.Y.C., 1988-93; worldwide dir. Health Scis. Cons. Group., 1988-93, chmn. health scis. policy coun., 1989-93; chmn. bd., pres., CEO, founder John A. Norris, Esq., P.C., Boston, 1993—; pres., CEO Nat. Pharm. Coun., Reston, Va., 1995-96; mem. faculty Tufts Dental Sch., 1974-79, Boston Coll. Law Sch., 1976-80, Boston U. Law Sch., 1979-83, Harvard U. Pub. Health Sch., 1988—; mem. bd. editors FDA Drug Bull. and FDA Consumer Report, 1985-88; bd. dirs. Summit Tech., Inc., Cytologics, Inc., Horus Therapeutics Inc., Nat. Applied Scis. Founder, faculty editor-in-chief Am. Jour. Law and Medicine, 1973-81, emeritus 1981—; editor-in-chief Cornell Internat. Law Jour., 1971-73; reviewer New Eng. Jour. Medicine Law-Medicine Notes, 1980-81; assoc. editor Medicolegal News, 1973-75. Mem. U.S. Del. to Japan (chmn.), Austria, Saudi Arabia, 1987, mem., chmn. Finland, Denmark, Italy, 1986; chmn. Mass. Statuatory Adv. Com. on Regulation of Clin. Labs., 1977-83; chmn. Boston Alumni and Scholarship Com., U. Rochester, 1979-85; mem. trustees coun. U. Rochester, 1979-85; mem. exec. com. Cornell Law Sch. Assn., 1982-85; mem. Mass. Gov.'s Blue Ribbon Task Force on DON, 1979-80, bd. trustees Jordan Hosp., 1978-80, mem. exec. com., 1979-80, chmn., chief exec. officer search com., 1980; chmn. Joseph D. Norris, Esq. Health Law and Pub. Policy Fund., 1979—; chmn. bd. Boston Holiday Project, 1981-83; mem. U.S. Pres. Chernobyl Task Force, 1986, vice-chmn. health affects sub.-com.; mem. U.S. Intra-Govtl. AIDS Task Force, 1987; mem. IOM Drug Devel. Forum, 1986-88, co-chmn. end points sub-com., 1987-88, Fed. Pain Commn., 1984-85. With U.S. Army, 1972-73. Fed. Comprehensive Health Planning fellow, 1970-73; recipient Kansas City Hon. Key award, 1988, Nat. Health Fraud Conf. award, 1988, TOYL award, 1982, FDA Award of Merit, 1987, 88, PHS award, 1987, HHS Sec. award, 1988. Mem. ABA (vice chmn. medicine and law com. 1977-80), Mass. Bar Assn., Am. Soc. Hosp. Attys., Nat. Health Lawyers, Am. Soc. Law and Medicine (1st v.p. 1975-80, chmn. bd. 1981-84, life mem. award 1981), Soc. Computer Applications to Med. Care (bd. dirs. 1984-85), Internat. Coun. for Global Health Progress (bd. dirs. 1989-95), Phi Kappa Phi. Home: 531 W Washington St Hanson MA 02341-1067 also: 2209 Burgee Ct Reston VA 22091

NORRIS, JOHN HART, lawyer; b. New Bedford, Mass., Aug. 4, 1942; s. Edwin Arter and Harriet Joan (Winter) N.; m. Anne Kiley Monaghan, June 10, 1967; children: Kiley Anne, Amy O'Shea. BA, Ind. U., 1964; JD, U. Mich., 1967. Bar: Mich. 1968, U.S. Ct. Mil. Appeals 1969, U.S. Supreme Ct. 1974, U.S. Ct. Claims 1975, U.S. Tax Ct. 1979. Assoc., then ptnr. Monaghan, Campbell, LoPrete, McDonald and Norris, 1970-83; of counsel Dickinson, Wright, Moon, Van Dusen & Freeman, 1983-84, ptnr.1985—; natural gas law counsel to claims mediator Columbia Gas Transmission Corp.; chpt. 11 bankruptcy proceedings in Wilmington, Del. Bankruptcy Ct., 1992—; bd. dirs. Prime Securities Corp., Ray M. Whyte Co., Ward-Williston Drilling Co. Mem. Rep. State Fin. Com.; founder, co-chmn. Rep. majority club; bd. trustees Boys and Girls Clubs of Southeastern Mich., 1979—, Mich. Wildlife Habitat Found., Mercy Coll., Detroit, Detroit Hist. Soc., 1984—; bd. trustees, bd. dirs. African Wildlife Found.; trustee and 1st vice chmn. Salk Inst. With M.I., U.S. Army, 1968-70. Recipient numerous civic and non-profit assn. awards. Fellow Mich. State Bar Found.; mem. ABA (litigation and natural resources sects.), Mich. Oil and Gas Assn. (legal and legis. com.), State Bar Mich. (chmn. environ. law sect. 1982-83, probate and trust law sect., energy conservation task force, oil and gas com.), Oakland County Bar Assn., Detroit Bar Assn. (pub. adv. com.), Am. Arbitration Assn., Fin. and Estate Planning Council of Detroit, Def. Orientation Conf. Assn., Detroit Zool. Soc., Blue Key Nat. Hon. Fraternity, Phi Delta Phi. Roman Catholic. Clubs: Bloomfield Hills Country; Thomas M. Cooley, Detroit Athletic, Economic (Detroit); Hundred, Prismatic, Turtle Lake, Yondotega. Contbr. articles to profl jours. Home: 1325 Buckingham Ave Birmingham MI 48009-5881 Office: Dickinson Wright 525 N Woodward Ave Bloomfield Hills MI 48304-2971

NORRIS, JOHN WINDSOR, JR., manufacturing company executive; b. Marshalltown, Iowa, Feb. 10, 1936; s. John Windsor Norris and Mary Merrill Margerin; m. Terry Reibsamen, Dec. 26, 1956; children: John Windsor III, Julie, Jeffrey. B.S. in Bus. Adminstrn, M.I.T., 1960. With Lennox Industries Inc., Dallas, 1960—, sr. v.p., 1975-77; pres. Lennox Industries Inc., 1977-80, past pres., chief exec. officer, 1980—, dir.; past pres., chief exec. officer Lennox Internat., Dallas, now chmn. bd., CEO; dir. Central Life Assurance Co., Des Moines. Chmn. parents div., mem. ann. gifts council Tex. Christian U. Mem. ARI (dir. at large, vice chmn. cert. programs and policy com., vice chmn. communications com.), GAMA (chmn. furnace div. 1978-79, chmn. bd. 1980). Club: Bent Tree Country (Dallas). Office: Lennox Industries Inc 2100 Lake Park Blvd Richardson TX 75080-2254*

NORRIS, KATHERINE CECELIA, mechanical engineer; b. Syracuse, N.Y., Nov. 7, 1943; d. James Dalton and Bertha Genevieve (Bourque) N.; children: Mary Rose Courtney. BSME, Duke U., 1966; MSME, Mass. Inst. Tech., 1967. Registered profl. engr. Vt., N.Y. Jr. engr. through staff engr. IBM Corp., Hopewell Junction, N.Y., 1967-76; staff engr. IBM Corp., Essex Junction, Vt., 1976-78, project engr., 1978-80, devel. engr., 1980-88, adv. engr., 1988—; project mgr., Sematech, Austin, Tex., 1992-93. Contbr. articles to profl. jours. Awards chair Vt. Engr. Week Com., 1994, 95; vol. Milton Family Com. Ctr., Milton, Vt., 1992; production staff vol. Cmty. Newspaper, Milton, 1990-94; canvasser United Way, 1985-91. Recipient fellowship Nat. Sci. Found., 1966-67. Mem. ASME, NSPE, Soc. Women Engrs. (sr. life; bd. dirs. 1990-92, chair sch. com. 1993-96), Phi Beta Kappa, Tau Beta Pi. Achievements include development of physical model for thermal fatigue of solder interconnections, construction of a ceramic module with internal glass plane, deep UV photolithography process. Home: 406 Route 7 North Milton VT 05468 Office: IBM Corp Microelectronics Div 1000 River St Essex Junction VT 05452

NORRIS, KATHY HORAN, school counselor; b. Perryton, Tex., Jan. 31, 1944; d. Shirley Coppoc and Margaret Z. (George) Horan; m. Kenneth L. Haralson, July 3, 1965 (dec. May 1983); children: Dale Kirk, Dana; m. Vernon Lee Norris, Apr. 5, 1984. BS in Elem. Edn., Hardin-Simmons U., 1966; MEd, Wayland Bapt. U., 1986. Cert. sch. counselor, Tex.; lic. profl. counselor, Tex. Elem. tchr. Lubbock (Tex.) Ind. Sch. Dist., 1966-69, Colorado Springs County Sch. Dist., 1969-73; elem. tchr. Plainview (Tex.) Ind. Sch. Dist., 1974-85, 87-89, counselor, 1989-92; grad. asst. Wayland Bapt. U., Plainview, 1985-86; owner, operator The Tchr. Store, Plainview, 1986-87; sch. counselor College Hill Elem. Sch., Plainview, 1992—; asst. prof. Wayland Bapt. U., 1989-94; mem. adv. coun. College Hill Sch., Plainview, 1993—; ind. cons. on tchr. expectations and student achievement, Plainview, 1989—; mkem. sch. collaboration initiative Region 17 Sci. Ctr., Lubbock, 1994—; presenter in field. Contbr. 1st grade math. textbook Riverside Pub. Co., 1985; author curriculum materials in field. Mem. choir First Bapt. Ch., Plainview, 1994—. Mem. Tex. Counseling Assn., Assn. Tex. Profl. Educators (bldg. rep. 1975-85), Plainview Counseling Assn. (pres. 1990-91, 94-95). Republican. Avocations: sewing, gardening, yard work, reading. Office: College Hill Elem Sch 707 Canyon St Plainview TX 79072-6756

NORRIS, KENNETH L., accountant; b. Hartville, Ohio, Jan. 9, 1939; s. William J. and Thelma A. (Bennett) N.; m. M. Sue Weathers, June 17, 1957 (div. Mar. 1963); 1 child, W. Gregory; m. Ursel I. Simon, July 4, 1969. BSBA, U. Fla., 1961; MBA, Brenau Coll., 1989. CPA, Ga. Audit mgr. Arthur Andersen and Co., Atlanta, 1961-69; treas. Buck Creek Industries, Inc., Atlanta, 1969-81; v.p. fin. So. Aggregates Co., Atlanta and Augusta, Ga., 1982-84, Beaulieu of Am., Inc., Dalton, Ga., 1985—. Mem. Am. Inst. CPA's, Ga. Soc. CPA's, Nat. Assn. of Accts. Avocation: golf. Home: 1235 Covie Dr Dalton GA 30720-2524*

NORRIS, LAWRENCE GEOFFREY, lawyer; b. Centralia, Ill., June 4, 1926; s. Patrick Iranaeus and Julia Catherine (Lordan) N.; m. Lauretta Shore, Feb. 7, 1953; children: Deborah, Lawrence, David, Steven; m. Barbara H. DeKorte, Sept. 28, 1979. BSEE, U. Ill., 1947; MSEE, Northeastern U., 1962; JD, Boston Coll., 1953. Bar: Mass. 1953, Va. 1968, D.C. 1988. Div. patent counsel GE Co., 1962-69; assoc. patent counsel, sr. corp. atty. Polaroid Corp., 1969-80; v.p., corp. counsel Energy Conversion Devices, Inc., Troy, Mich., 1980-87; ptnr. Rothwell, Figg, Ernst & Kurz, Washington, 1987—. Served with U.S. Army, 1944-46. Mem. ABA, Am. Patent Law Assn., Assn. Corp. Patent Counsel. Club: Fides Soc. Boston Coll. Office: Rothwell Figg Ernst & Kurz Columbia Sq 555 13th St NW Washington DC 20004-1109

NORRIS, LOIS ANN, elementary school educator; b. Detroit, May 13, 1937; d. Joseph Peter and Marguerite Iola (Gourley) Giroux; m. Max Norris, Feb. 9, 1962 (div. 1981); children: John Henry, Jeanne Marie, Joseph Peter. BS in Social Sci., Ea. Mich. U., 1960, MA, 1960; cert. adminstr., Calif. State U., Bakersfield, 1983. Kindergarten tchr. Norwalk-LaMirada Unified Sch. Dist., 1960-62; tchr. various grades Rialto Unified Sch. Dist., 1962-66; kindergarten tchr. Inyokern (Calif.) Sch., 1969-82; 1st grade tchr. Vieweg Basic Sch, 1982-92, kindergarten tchr., 1992-96; retired, 1996; head tchr. Sierra Sands Elem. Summer Sch.; adminstrv. intern Sierra Sands Adult Sch., master tchr., head tchr., counselor. Ofcl. scorekeeper, team mother, snack bar coord. China Lake Little League; team mother, statistician Indian Wells Valley Youth Football; bd. mem. PTA; pres. Sch. Site Coun.; treas. Inyokern Parents Club; run coord. City of Hope; timekeeper, coord. Jr. Olympics; mem. planning com. Sunshine Festival; active Burros Booster Club. Recipient Hon. Svc. award PTA, 1994. Mem. Desert Area Tchrs. Assn., Assn. Calif. Sch. Adminstrs., Inyokern C. of C. (sec.), Am. Motorcycle Assn., NRA, Bakersfield Coll. Diamond Club. Republican. LDS Ch. Avocations: swimming, physical fitness, music, American history. Home: PO Box 163 201 N Brown Rd Inyokern CA 93527 Office: Sierra Sands Unified Sch 113 W Felspar Ave Ridgecrest CA 93555-3520

NORRIS, LOUISE, religious organization executive. Nat. supr. Women's Dept. of the Ch. of God in Christ Internat. Office: Women's Dept of the Ch of God in Christ Internat 360 Colorado Ave Bridgeport CT 06605-1746

NORRIS, MARTIN JOSEPH, lawyer; b. N.Y.C., Mar. 23, 1907; s. Louis and Esther (Wohlgemuth) Knaris; m. Helen Stella Hecht, June 5, 1930; 1 child, Barbara. LL.B., Bklyn. Law Sch., 1930. Bar: N.Y. 1932. Pvt. practice law N.Y.C., 1932-35; atty. U.S. Shipping Bd. Bur., Dept. Commerce, Washington, 1935-36, U.S. Maritime Commn., Washington and N.Y.C., 1936-42, War Shipping Adminstrn., N.Y.C., 1945-50; admiralty trial atty. admiralty and shipping sect. Dept. Justice, N.Y.C., 1950-56; adminstrv. law judge U.S. Coast Guard, N.Y.C., 1956-70; lectr. Sch. for World Trade, N.Y.C., Practicing Law Inst., N.Y.C., Lawyers Sq. Club, N.Y.C., U.S. Merchant Marine Acad., N.Y. State Maritime Coll.; cons. maritime law, shipping. Author: Your Boat and the Law, 1965, The Law of Seamen, 3 vols., 4th edit., 1985, The Law of Maritime Personal Injuries, 2 vols., 4th edit., 1990, The Law of Salvage, 1990; contbr. articles in field to legal jours. Served to capt. U.S. Army, 1942-45. Mem. Am. Soc. Writers on Legal Subjects. Jewish.

NORRIS, MELVIN, lawyer; b. Cambridge, Mass., Aug. 17, 1931. A.B., Northeastern U., Boston, 1954; J.D., Boston Coll., 1959. Bar: Mass. 1959, U.S. Supreme Ct. 1965. Atty. FTC, Boston, 1960-62; individual practice law Boston, 1962-76; ptnr. Norris, Kozody, Krasnoo & Fong, Boston, 1976-90, Norris, Kozody & Fong, Boston, 1991—. Bd. editors Mass. Lawyers Weekly, 1984-93. Vice chmn. Newton (Mass.) Crime Commn., 1966-67; mem. Newton Bldg. Code Revision Com., 1972-73; chmn. bd. dirs., pres. Waterville Estates Assn., Campton, N.H., 1992-94. With USCG, 1954-56. Mem. Fed. Bar Assn. (pres. Boston chpt. 1977-78, v.p. 1st circuit 1978—, exec. com. 1982-83), Mass. Bar Assn. Address: 18 Tremont St Boston MA 02108-2301

NORRIS, RICHARD ANTHONY, accountant; b. Birmingham, Eng., July 6, 1943; s. Albert Edward and Audrey (Rowley) N.; m. Geri M., Jan. 20, 1947; 1 child, Karen Louise. BA, U. Leeds, York, Eng., 1966. Chartered acct., Can. Auditor Price Waterhouse & Co., Bristol, Eng., 1966-70; mgr. Price Waterhouse & Co., Montreal, Que., Can., 1970-78; from mgr. corp. acctg. to controller Can. Pacific Enterprises, Montreal and Calgary, Alta., Can., 1978-85; v.p. fin. U.S. Ops. Laidlaw Waste Systems Inc., North Richland Hills, Tex., 1986—. Home: 2401 Hillside Ct Southlake TX 76092-8793

NORRIS, RICHARD PATRICK, museum director, history educator; b. Galveston, Tex., May 21, 1944; s. William Gerard and Iris Elsa (Allington) N.; m. Therese Louise Aalid, July 26, 1974; children: William Gerard, John Patrick. BA, Ohio State U., 1966; MA, SUNY, Binghamton, 1968; PhD, U. Minn., 1976. Instr. U. Minn., Mpls., 1970-76; lectr. U. Md., Europe/Asia, 1976-78; dir. Chippewa Valley Mus., Eau Claire, Wis., 1978-80, Kalamazoo Valley Mus., 1985—; curator of history Mus. Sci. & Hist., Fort Worth, 1980-85; lectr. Tex. Christian U., Fort Worth, 1981-85; cons. Am. Assn. Mus., Washington, 1979—, NEH, 1989; grant reviewer Inst. Mus. Svcs., Washington, 1984—, Mich. Coun. Humanities, Lansing, 1985—; adj. prof. Western Mich. U., Kalamazoo, 1986—. Author: History by Design, 1984; book reviewer Mus. News, History News; contbr. articles to profl. jours. Dir. Downtown Kalamazoo Inc., 1995—, dir. at large Arts Coun. Greater Kalamazoo, 1987-93; chmn. internat. com. Ft. Worth 150 Com., 1984. 1st lt. U.S. Army, 1968-70. Mem. Am. Assn. Mus., Am. Assn. State and Local Hist., Internat. Coun. Mus., Midwest Mus. Conf., Tex. Assn. Mus., Rotary (dir. Kalamazoo club 1991-93). Democrat. Roman Catholic. Office: Kalamazoo Valley Museum PO Box 4070 PO Box 4070 230 N Rose St Kalamazoo MI 49003-4070

NORRIS, ROBERT MATHESON, geologist; b. Los Angeles, Apr. 24, 1921; s. Robert DeWitt and Jessie (Matheson) N.; m. Virginia Grace Oakley, Jan. 5, 1952; children—Donald Oakley, James Matheson, Elizabeth Anne. A.B., UCLA, 1943, M.A., 1949; Ph.D. Scripps Inst. Oceanography, U. Calif., San Diego, 1951. Teaching asst. UCLA, 1946-49; asso. marine geology Scripps Inst. Oceanography, 1951-52; mem. faculty U. Calif., Santa Barbara, 1952—; prof. geology U. Calif., 1968-86, prof. emeritus, 1986—; also dir. Channel Islands Field Sta., 1970-75. Contbr. articles profl. jours. Served with USNR, 1944-46. Fulbright scholar, 1961-62. Mem. Geol. Soc. Am., Geol. Soc. N.Z., Nat. Assn. Geology Tchrs. (pres. 1988-89), Am. Assn. Petroleum Geologists, Soc. Econ. Paleontologists and Mineralogists, Sigma Xi, Phi Kappa Sigma, Phi Delta Kappa. Congregationalist. Address: 4424 Nueces Dr Santa Barbara CA 93110-2006

NORRIS, ROBERT WHEELER, lawyer, military officer; b. Birmingham, Ala., May 22, 1932; s. Hubert Lee and Georgia Irene (Parker) N.; m. Martha Katherine Cummins, Feb. 19, 1955; children—Lisha Katherine Norris Utt, Nathan Robert. B.A. in Bus. Adminstrn., U. Ala., 1954, LL.B., 1955; LL.M., George Washington U., 1979; postgrad., Air Command & Staff Coll., 1968, Nat. War Coll., 1975. Commd. 2d lt. USAF, advanced through grades to maj. gen.; dep. judge advocate gen. USAF, Washington, 1983-85, judge advocate gen., 1985-88; gen. counsel Ala. Bar Assn., Montgomery, 1988-95; ptnr. London & Yancey, Birmingham, Ala., 1995—. Decorated D.S.M., Legion of Merit, Meritorious Svc. medal. Mem. ABA. Methodist. Office: London & Yancey 2001 Park Pl Ste 1000 Birmingham AL 35203

NORRIS, STEPHEN LESLIE, merchant banking, tax and finance executive; b. Mobile, Ala., Apr. 3, 1950; s. Thomas G. and Jean (Branyon) N.; m. Frances McMurtray, Oct. 8, 1981; 1 child, Christopher Edward. BS, Ala. U., 1972, JD, 1975; LLM in Taxation, NYU, 1976. Bar: Ala. 1975, D.C. 1976. Fellow Yale Law Sch., New Haven, Conn., 1977; tax atty. Cohen and Uretz, Washington, 1978-81; v.p. corp. officer Marriott Corp., Washington, 1981-86; mng. dir. The Carlyle Group, 1986-94; founder, pres. The Appian Group, 1995; asst. prof. Georgetown U. Law Sch., Washington, 1983; prof. law Am. U., Washington, 1983-86. Named one of Outstanding Young Men

Am., 1983. Mem. ABA (real estate com.), D.C. Bar. Club: Athletic (N.Y.C.), Univ. (Washington). *

NORRIS, THOMAS CLAYTON, paper company executive; b. York, Pa., May 9, 1938; m. Joan G. Wachob, Mar. 24, 1962; children: Robert, Richard, Mary Catherine. B.A., Gettysburg Coll., 1960. Chmn., pres., chief exec. officer P.H. Glatfelter Co., Spring Grove, Pa., 1980—. Home: 330 Rhonda Dr York PA 17404-6117 Office: P H Glatfelter Co 228 S Main St Spring Grove PA 17362-1000*

NORRIS, WILLIAM ALBERT, federal judge; b. Turtle Creek, Pa., Aug. 30, 1927; s. George and Florence (Clive) N.; m. Merry Wright, Nov. 23, 1974; children: Barbara, Donald, Kim, Alison; m. Jane Jelenko. Student, U. Wis., 1945; B.A., Princeton U., 1951; J.D., Stanford U., 1954. Bar: Calif. and D.C. 1955. Assoc. firm Northcutt Ely, Washington, 1954-55; law clk. to Justice William O. Douglas U.S. Supreme Ct., Washington, 1955-56; sr. mem. firm Tuttle & Taylor, Inc., L.A., 1956-80; judge U.S. Ct. Appeals (9th cir.), L.A., 1980-94, sr. judge, 1994—; spl. counsel Pres.' Kennedy's Com. on Airlines Controversy, 1961; mem., v.p. Calif. State Bd. Edn., 1961-67. Trustee Calif. State Colls., 1967-72; pres. L.A. Bd. Police Commrs., 1973-74; Democratic nominee for atty. gen. State of Calif., 1974; founding pres. bd. trustees Mus. Contemporary Art, L.A., 1979—; trustee Craft and Folk Art Mus., 1979—. With USN, 1945-47. Home: 1473 Oriole Dr West Hollywood CA 90069-1155 Office: US Ct Appeals 9th Cir 312 N Spring St Los Angeles CA 90012-4701*

NORROD, JAMES DOUGLAS, computer subsystems company executive; b. Detroit, Feb. 18, 1948; s. Charles Douglas and Bonnie Gene (Phillips) N.; m. Vickie Carolyn Newsom, Aug. 23, 1969; children: Heather Victoria, April Elizabeth. BS cum laude, Oakland U., Rochester, Mich., 1970; MBA, U. Detroit, 1975. Sales rep. IBM Corp., Detroit, 1970-77, mktg. mgr., 1977-80; v.p. Auto-trol Tech. Corp., Denver, 1980-86; pres., chief exec. officer CGX Corp., Acton, Mass., 1986-87, Adage, Inc. (acquired by Telebit Corp.), Billerica, Mass., 1987—. Republican. Home: 161 Ember Ln Carlisle MA 01741-1309 also: Telebit Corp. 1 Executive Dr Chelmsford MA 01824-2558*

NORSKOG, EUGENIA FOLK, elementary education educator; b. Staunton, Va., Mar. 23, 1937; d. Ernest and Edna Virginia (Jordan) Folk; m. Russell Carl Norskog, Nov. 25, 1967; children: Cynthia, Carl, Roberta, Eric. BA, King Coll., 1958; MEd, George Mason U., 1977. Cert. tchr., Va. Tchr. elem. Bristol (Va.) Pub. Schs., 1958-61, 62-65, Staunton (Va.) Pub. Schs., 1961-62, Fairfax (Va.) County Pub. Schs., 1965-68; with Project 100, 000, USAFI, 1966-68; project 100,000 USAF, Fort Ord, Calif., 1969; tchr. elem. Monterey (Calif.) Peninsula Sch. Div., 1970-71, Prince William County Schs., Manassas, Va., 1972—; Va. rehab. sch. Prince William County, Richmond, Va., 1979-82. V.p. Fauquier Gymnastics, Warrenton, Va., 1982-83, pres., 1983-85; coach, bd. dirs., referee Warrenton Soccer Assn., 1980-88; soccer referee Piedmont Referee Assn., Manassas, 1990-95. Mem. NEA, Va. Edn. Assn. Prince William Edn. Assn. (bd. dirs. 1974-77). Home: 7160 Airlie Rd RR 8 Box 398 Warrenton VA 22186-9448

NORSWORTHY, LAMAR, petroleum company executive; b. 1946. With Holly Corp., Dallas, 1967—, pres., 1971-75, treas., from 1975, now chmn., pres.; chmn., pres. Navajo Refining Co., Artesia, N.Mex., 1982—. Office: Holly Corp 100 Crescent Ct Ste 1600 Dallas TX 75201-1884 also: Navajo Refining Co 501 E Main St Artesia NM 88210-9606*

NORTH, ANITA, secondary education educator; b. Chgo., Apr. 21, 1963; d. William Denson and Carol (Linden) N. BA, Ind. U., 1985; MS in Edn., Northwestern U., 1987. Cert. tchr., Ill. High sch. social studies and English tchr. Lake Park High Sch., Roselle, Ill., 1987-89; high sch. social studies tchr. West Leyden High Sch., Northlake, Ill., 1989—; exch. program coord. West Leyden High Sch., 1989—, head coach boys' tennis team, 1989—, asst. coach girls' tennis team, 1994—, asst. speech coach, 1992-93. Humanities fellow Nat. Coun. Humanities, 1995; recipient Fern Fine Tchg. award West Leyden H.S., 1992. Mem. AAUW, Nat. Coun. for Social Studies, Ill. Coun. for Social Studies, Orgn. Am. Historians, Ill. Tennis Coaches Assn., Phi Delta Kappa. Christian. Avocations: wilderness backpacking, tennis, orienteering, gardening, antique books and maps.

NORTH, DANIEL WARNER, consulting analyst; b. N.Y.C., Mar. 12, 1941; s. James Dennis and Margaret P. North; m. Diane M. Tarantino, Nov. 26, 1978 (div. May 27, 1993); 1 child, Evan Armstrong; m. Cheryl Jeanne Bonham, May 27, 1993. BS, Yale U., 1962; MS, Stanford U., 1964, PhD, 1970. Analyst SRI Internat., Menlo Park, Calif., 1967-74, asst. dir. decision analysis dept., 1974-77; sr., v.p. Decision Focus Inc., Mountain View, Calif., 1977—; consulting prof. Dept. of Eng.-Econ. Sys., Stanford U., 1977—; mem. sci. adv. bd. EPA, Washington, 1978—, gov.'s sci. adv. panel Calif. Propostion 65, 1987-89, Nuc. Waste Tech. Review Bd., 1989-94. Mem. Soc. Risk Analysis, (pres. 1991-92), Inst. Ops. Rsch. Mgmt. Sci., Sigma Xi. Office: Decision Focus Inc 650 Castro St Ste 300 Mountain View CA 94041-2057

NORTH, DORIS GRIFFIN, physician, educator; b. Washington, Nov. 30, 1916; d. Edward Lawrence and Ruth Gladys (Spray) Griffin; m. Victor North, Nov. 2, 1940 (dec. 1984); children: James, Daniel, Frederick. BA, U. Kans., 1938, MT, 1939; MD, Kans. U., 1947. Med. tech. Ralph G. Ball, M.D., Manhattan, Kans., 1939-40, St. Francis Hosp., Pitts., 1940-41, John Minor, M.D., Washington, 1941-43; intern Wesly Hosp., Wichita, Kans., 1947-48; resident in pediat. and internal medicine Sedgwick Hosp., Wichita, 1948-49; pvt. practice family physician Wichita, Kans., 1951-96; clin. asst. prof. medicine Kans. State U. Sch. Medicine, Wichita, 1974-96. Mem. AMA, Am. Acad. Family Practice, Kans. Med. Soc., Med. Soc. Sedgwick County, Phi Beta Kappa, Alpha Omega Alpha. Home: 1000 S Woodlawn St Apt 408 Wichita KS 67218-3641 Office: 1148 S Hillside St Wichita KS 67211-4005

NORTH, DOUGLASS CECIL, economist, educator; b. Cambridge, Mass., Nov. 5, 1920; s. Henry Emerson and Edith (Saitta) N.; m. Elisabeth Willard Case, Sept. 28, 1972; children by previous marriage: Douglass Alan, Christopher, Malcolm Peter. B.A., U. Calif., Berkeley, 1942, Ph.D., 1952; D Rer. Pol. (hon.), U. of Cologne, Federal Republic of Germany, 1988, U. Zurich, Switzerland, 1993, Stockholm Sch. of Econs., Sweden, 1994, Prague Sch. Econs., 1995. Asst. prof. econs. U. Wash., 1950-56, assoc. prof., 1957-60, prof., 1960-83, prof. emeritus, 1983—, chmn. dept., 1967-79; dir. Inst. Econ. Research, 1960-66, Nat. Bur. Econ. Research, 1967-87; Luce prof. law and liberty, prof. econs. Washington U., St. Louis, 1983—; Pitt prof. Am. history and instns. Cambridge U., 1981-82; fellow Ctr. for Advanced Study on Behavioral Scis., 1987-88. Author: The Economic Growth of the U.S. 1790-1860, 1961, Growth and Welfare in the American Past, 1966, (with L. Davis) Institutional Change and American Economic Growth, 1971, (with R. Miller) The Economics of Public Issues, 1971, 74, 76, 78, 80, (with R. Thomas) The Rise of the Western World, 1973, Structure and Change in Economic History, 1981, Institutions, Institutional Change and Economic Performance, 1990. Guggenheim fellow, 1972-73; grantee Social Sci. Rsch. Coun., 1962, Rockefeller Found., 1960-63, Ford Found., 1961, 66, NSF, 1967-73, Bradley Found., 1986—. Recipient Nobel Prize in Economic Science, Nobel Foundation, 1993. Fellow Am. Acad. Arts and Scis.; mem. Am. Econ. Assn., Econ. History Assn. Office: Washington U Dept Econs Campus Box 1208 Saint Louis MO 63130-1208

NORTH, HAROLD LEBRON, JR., lawyer; b. Chattanooga, Feb. 17, 1944; s. Harold L. and Frances E. (Starr) N.; m. Teresa L. Hampton, Aug. 29, 1981; children: Harold L. III, Grant Gibson. BA, U. Tenn., 1977; JD, Memphis State U., 1980. Bar: Tenn. 1980, U.S. Dist. Ct. (ea. dist.) Tenn. 1980, U.S. Ct. Appeals (6th cir.) 1984, U.S. Supreme Ct. 1990, D.C. 1991, U.S. Dist. Ct. D.C. 1991, U.S. Ct. Appeals (D.C. cir.) 1992. Assoc. Tanner, Jahn, Atchley, Bridges & Jahn, Chattanooga, from 1980; ptnr. Tanner, Jahn, Anderson, Bridges & Jahn, Chattanooga, Ray & North, P.C., Chattanooga, until 1990, Shumacker & Thompson, P.C., Chattanooga, 1990—. Bd. dirs. Chattanooga Big Bros.-Big Sisters, 1994—, Scenic Land Sch., Chattanooga, 1993-94; bd. dirs. Chattanooga Area Crime Stoppers, Inc., 1984-93, chmn., 1989-90; grad. Leadership Chattanooga, 1988-89; grad. leadership tng. program Chattanooga Resource Found., 1992; mem. Tenn. Rep. Exec. Com., 1990—; chmn. Hamilton County Rep. Party, 1989-91; mem. Hamilton County Election Commn., Chattanooga, 1988-89. Mem. ABA, ATLA, Tenn. Bar Assn., Chattanooga Bar Assn. (chmn. bankruptcy and comml. law sect. 1993-94), D.C. Bar Assn., Tenn. Trial Lawyers Assn., Am. Bankruptcy Inst. Presbyterian. Avocations: golf, hunting, water sports. Home: 16 Fairhills Dr Chattanooga TN 37405-4325 Office: Shumacker & Thompson PC First Tennessee Bldg 5th Fl Chattanooga TN 37402

NORTH, HELEN FLORENCE, classicist, educator; b. Utica, N.Y.; d. James H. and Catherine (Debbold) N. A.B., Cornell U., 1942, M.A., 1943, Ph.D., 1945; LL.D. (hon.), Rosary Coll., 1982; D.Litt. (hon.), Trinity Coll., Dublin, 1984; L.H.D. (hon.), La Salle U., 1985, Yale U., 1986. Instr. classical lang. Rosary Coll., River Forest, Ill., 1946-48; mem. faculty Swarthmore Coll., 1948-91, prof. classics, 1961-91, chmn. dept., 1959-91, emerita, 1991—, Centennial prof. classics, 1966-73, 78-91, Kenan prof., 1973-78; vis. asst. prof. Cornell U., summer 1952—; vis. assoc. prof. Barnard Coll., 1954-55; vis. prof. LaSalle Coll., Phila., 1965, Am. Sch. Classical Studies, Athens, 1975, 87; Blegen disting. vis. rsch. prof. Vassar Coll., 1979. Author: Sophrosyne: Self-Knowledge and Self-Restraint in Greek Literature, 1966, From Myth to Icon: Reflections of Greek Ethical Doctrine in Literature and Art, 1979; translator: John Milton's Second Defense of the English People, 1966; editor: Interpretations of Plato: A Swarthmore Symposium, 1977; co-editor: Of Eloquence, 1970; editor: Jour. History of Ideas; mem. editorial bd.: Catalogus Translationum et Commentariorum, 1979—. Bd. dirs. Am. Coun. Learned Socs., 1977-85; chmn. bd. trustees LaSalle U., 1991-93; trustee King's Coll., Am. Acad. in Rome; chmn. com. on Classical Sch. Recipient Harbison prize Danforth Found., 1969; named Distinguished Daughter of Pa., 1989, del. of Am. Philological Assn. to Am. Coun. Learned Studies, 1991-95 ; grantee Am. Council Learned Socs., 1943-45, 73, fellow, 1971-72, 87-88; Mary Isabel Sibley fellow Phi Beta Kappa Found., 1945-46, Ford Fund Advancement Edn. fellow, also Fulbright fellow Rome, 1953-54; grantee Danforth Found., 1962, Lindbach Found., 1966; fellow AAUW, 1963-64; NEH sr. fellow, 1967-68; NEH Coll. Tchrs. fellow, 1983-84; Martin classical lectr. Oberlin Coll., 1972; Guggenheim fellow, 1958-59,75-76. Mem. Am. Philol. Assn. (dir. 1968—, pres. 1976—, Charles J. Goodwin award of merit 1969), Classical Assn. Atlantic States, Catholic Commn. Intellectual and Cultural Affairs (chmn. 1968-69), Am. Acad. Arts and Scis., Am. Philos. Soc., Soc. Religion Higher Edn., Phi Beta Kappa (mem. bd. vis. scholars 1975-76, senate 1991—), Phi Kappa Phi. Home: 604 Ogden Ave Swarthmore PA 19081-1131

NORTH, MARJORIE MARY, columnist; b. Mt. Clemens, Mich., Oct. 21, 1945; d. Robert Haller and Hilla Beryl (Willard) Wright; m. William B. Hirons; children: Laura, Christina, Angela. Student, Wayne State U., 1963-65. Features editor Elizabeth City (N.C.) Daily Advance, 1966-69; news/mng. editor Brandon (Fla.) News, 1977-78; city editor Leesburg (Fla.) Daily Comml., 1978-79; metro editor Sarasota (Fla.) Herald Tribune, 1979-80, Fla. West editor, 1980-85, daily columnist, 1985—. Author: Sarasota: A City For All Seasons, 1994, (play) With the Best Intentions, 1994. Recipient Layout, Creativity and Overall Publ. awards Fla. Press Assn., numerous comty. awards and citations; winner Fla. shorts competition Fla. Studio Theater New Play Festival, 1994; Paul Harris fellow, 1994. Avocations: sailing, tennis, entertaining, theater. Office: Sarasota Herald-Tribune PO Box 1719 Sarasota FL 34230-1719

NORTH, PHIL RECORD, retired banker; b. Fort Worth, July 6, 1918; s. James M. and Lottie R. North; m. Janis Harris, July 28, 1944; children: Phillip Kevin (dec.), Kerry Lawrence, Mairin Kathleen, Deirdre Aine. A.B., U. Notre Dame, 1939. With Fort Worth Star Telegram, 1937-62, exec. editor, 1956-62, asst. gen. mgr., 1959-62; v.p. Carter Publs., Inc., 1949-62; with Tandy Corp., Fort Worth, 1966-82; chief exec. officer Tandy Corp., 1978-81, pres., 1978-81, chmn. bd., 1978-82; chmn. bd. 1st City Nat. Bank, Ft. Worth, 1982-86; chmn. bd. dirs. JMJ Fin. Corp., Ft. Worth, CXE, inc., Plano, Tex., Haeco II, Inc., Hillsboro, Ohio; bd. dirs. Del Norte Tech., Euless, Tex. Served to maj. AUS, 1940-46. Decorated Bronze Star. Mem. Ft. Worth Club, River Crest Club, Shady Oaks Club, Rockport Country Club, Rockport Yacht Club, Corpus Christi Yacht Club. Roman Catholic.

NORTH, ROBERT CARVER, political science educator; b. Walton, N.Y., Nov. 17, 1914; s. Arthur W. and Irene (Davenport) N.; m. Dorothy Anderson, Mar. 12, 1977; children by previous marriage: Woesha Kristina, Mary Davenport, Elizabeth Katrynka, Robert Cloud, Renya Catarina. A.B., Union Coll., 1936; M.A., Stanford U., 1948, Ph.D., 1957. Tchr. English, History Milford (Conn.) Sch., 1939-42; research asst. Hoover Instn., Stanford, Calif., 1948-50, research assoc., 1950-57; assoc. prof. polit. sci. Stanford (Calif.) U., 1957-62, prof., 1962-85, prof. emeritus, 1985—. Author: Revolt in San Marcos, 1941 (Commonwealth Gold medal), Moscow and Chinese Communists, 1952, The World That Could Be, 1976, (with Nazli Choucri) Nations in Conflict, 1975, War, Peace, Survival, 1990, (with Nazli Choucri and Susumu Yamakage) The Challenge of Japan: Before World War II and After, 1992. Served to capt. USAAF, 1942-46. Mem. Am. Polit. Sci. Assn. (Conflicts Processes Sect. Lifetime Achievement award 1993), Internat. Studies Assn. (pres. 1970-71), Internat. Peace-Sci. Assn., Explorers Club. Democrat. Unitarian. Office: Stanford U Dept Polit Sci Stanford CA 94305

NORTH, ROBERT JOHN, biologist; b. Bathurst, Australia, Aug. 22, 1935; s. Herbert John North and Loraine (Grace) Lamrock. BS, Sydney U., Australia, 1958; PhD, Nat. U., Canberra, Australia, 1967; DSc (hon.), SUNY, 1992. Vis. investigator Trudeau Inst., Saranac Lake, N.Y., 1967-70; assoc. mem. Trudeau Inst., 1970-74, mem., 1974-76, dir., 1976—. Mem. editorial bd. Jour. Exptl. Medicine, Infection and Immunity, Cancer Immunology and Immunotherapy; contbr. articles on immunity to infections and cancer to profl. jours. Recipient Friedrich Sasse sci. prize, 1984, rsch. award Soc. of Leukocyte Biology, 1990; grantee NIH, Am. Cancer Soc. Mem. Am. Assn. Immunologists, Reticuloendothelial Soc. (pres. 1983), Transplantation Soc., AAAS, Am. Soc. Microbiologists. Avocation: classical music. Office: Trudeau Inst Inc PO Box 59 Saranac Lake NY 12983-0059

NORTH, WARREN JAMES, government official; b. Winchester, Ill., Apr. 28, 1922; s. Clyde James and Lucille Adele (Bishop) N.; m. Mary Strother; children—James Warren, Mary Kay, Susan Lee, Diane. B.S. in Engring, Purdue U., 1947; M.S., Case Inst. Tech., 1954, Princeton, 1956. Engr. and test pilot NACA, Cleve., 1947-55; asst. chief aerodynamics br. NACA, 1955-59; chief manned satellites NASA, Washington, 1959-62; chief flight crew support div. NASA (Manned Spacecraft Center), Houston, 1962-71; asst. dir. space shuttle NASA (Flight Ops. Directorate), 1972-85; pres. Spalding Edn. Found., Glendale, Ariz., 1986—. Contbr. articles to profl. jours. Served with USAAF, 1943-45. Recipient DeFlorez tng. award, 1966; NASA award for exceptional service, 1968, 69. Mem. Am. Inst. Aero. and Astronautics (asso. fellow 1955), Tau Beta Pi, Pi Tau Sigma. Club: Mason. Home: 6933 W Kimberly Way Glendale AZ 85308-5757 Office: Spalding Edn Found 5930 W Greenway Rd Ste 4 Glendale AZ 85306-3296

NORTH, WHEELER JAMES, marine ecologist, educator; b. San Francisco, Jan. 2, 1922; s. Wheeler Orrin and Florence Julia (Ross) N.; m. Barbara Alice Best, Apr. 25, 1964; children: Hannah Catherine, Wheeler Orrin. BS in Engring, Calif. Inst. Tech., 1944, BS in Biology, 1949; MS in Oceanography, U. Calif. at San Diego, 1953; Ph.D., 1953. NSF postdoctoral fellow Cambridge (Eng.) U.; Electronics engr. U.S. Navy Electronics Lab., Point Loma, Calif., 1947-48; asst. research biologist Scripps Inst. Oceanography, U. Calif. at San Diego, 1953, Rockefeller postdoctoral fellow, 1955-56; asst. research biologist Inst. Marine Resources Scripps Inst. Oceanography, 1956-63; assoc. prof. Calif. Inst. Tech., Pasadena, 1963-70; prof. Calif. Inst. Tech., 1970-92, prof. emeritus, 1992—; Cons. marine biology U.S. Govt., State of Calif., San Francisco, Los Angeles, San Diego, numerous industries, 1957—; Phi Beta Kappa vis. scholar, 1973-74; mem. Calif. Adv. Commn., 1972-73, Nav. and Ocean Devel. Commn., 1973-76; dir. Marine Biol. Cons. Contbr. articles to profl. jours. Recipient NOGI award Underwater Soc. Am., 1975. Mem. Am. Littoral Soc. (James Duggan award), AAAS, Am. Soc. Limnology and Oceanography, Am. Soc. Zoology, Soc. Gen. Physiology, Calif. Acad. Sci., Fish Protective Assn. (dir.), N.Y. Acad. Sci., Am. Geophys. Union, Smithsonian Instn., Am. San Diego museums, Marine Tech. Soc., Western Soc. Naturalists, Calif. Soc. Profl. Engrs., Am. Zoomalac Soc., Internat. Oceanographic Found., Sigma Xi. Home: 205 Carnation Ave Apt 5 Corona Del Mar CA 92625-2807 Office: Calif Inst Tech Div Engring and Applied Sci Pasadena CA 91125

NORTH, WILLIAM HAVEN, foreign service officer; b. Summit, N.J., Aug. 17, 1926; s. Eric M. and Gladys (Haven) N.; m. Jeanne Foote, Sept. 2, 1950; children: Jeannette Haven, William Ashby, Charles Eric. B.A. with high distinction and honors in History, Wesleyan U., Middletown, Conn., 1949; M.A. In History, Columbia, 1951. Program officer ICA, Ethiopia, 1953-57; then dep. chief program div. ICA (African-European Regional Office), Washington; asst. dir. for program Lagos, Nigeria, AID, until 1965; dir. Ctrl. and Western African affairs AID, Washington, 1966-70, U.S. AID mission to Ghana, 1970-76; dep. asst. adminstr. Africa Bur. AID, 1976-82, spl. asst. Office of the Adminstr., 1982-83, assoc. asst. adminstr. Ctr. Devel. Info. and Evaluation, 1983-89, ret.; pvt. cons. Internat. Devel. for World Bank, 1989—, UN Devel. Program USAID, 1989—; coord. Evaluation of Global Environ. Facility, 1993; fellow Ctr. for Internat. Affairs, Harvard U., 1965-66; chmn. experts group on evaluation Devel. Assistance Commn., OECD, 1985-88; vice-chmn. editl. bd. Fgn. Svc. Jour., 1983-86; mem. adv. panel on evaluation Inter-Am. Devel. Bank, 1993-94; prin. evaluator Internat. Fin. Corp., 1994-95, U.S. AID Africa Program. Served with AUS, 1944-46. Recipient Meritorious Svc. award for exemplary achievement in pub. adminstrn., W.A. Jump Honor cert., Superior Honor award for Nigerian Relief Adminstrn., Equal Employment Opportunity award, Disting. Honor award AID, Presdl. Meritorious Svc. medal, Adminstrs. Career Svc. award. Mem. Soc. for Internat. Devel., African Studies Assn., Assn. Diplomatic Studies and Tng., Am. Evaluation Assn., Applachian Mountain Club. Methodist. Home and Office: Internat Development 6748 Brigadoon Dr Bethesda MD 20817-5436

NORTHCUTT, CLARENCE DEWEY, lawyer; b. Guin, Ala., July 7, 1916; s. Walter G. and Nancy E. (Homer) N.; m. Ruth Eleanor Storms, May 25, 1941; children: Gayle Marie (Mrs. John J. Young), John E. A.B., U. Okla., 1939, LL.B., 1938. Bar: Okla. 1938. Pvt. practice Ponca City, 1938—; Mem. bd. visitors U. Okla. Served with AUS, 1941-46. Decorated Bronze Star, Air medal with oak leaf cluster., Order St. John of Jerusalem; named Outstanding Citizen of Ponca City, 1982. Fellow Am. Coll. Trial Lawyers, Am. Coll. Trust and Estate Attys., Am. Bar Found.; mem. Acad. Univ. Fellows, Internat. Soc. Barristers, Am. Bd. Advocacy, Internat. Acad. Trial Lawyers, Okla. Bar Assn. (pres. 1975, bd. govs.), Ponca City C. of C. (past pres.). Democrat. Baptist. Clubs: Mason, Kiwanian. Home: 132 Whitworth Ave Ponca City OK 74601-3438 Office: PO Box 1669 Ponca City OK 74602-1669

NORTHCUTT, KATHRYN ANN, elementary school and gifted-talented educator, reading recovery educator; b. Ft. Worth, Nov. 11, 1953; d. Lawrence William and Eva Jo (McCormick) Lloyd; m. Frank E. Northcutt, Aug. 28, 1980; 1 child, Matthew Adam. Student, North Tex. State U., 1972-75; BS in Edn., U. Tex., Tyler, 1980, MEd, 1986. Cert. elem. educator, music educator, supr. K-8; cert. curriculum and instrn. supr. Tchr. grade 1 Longview (Tex.) Ind. Sch. Dist., Longview, 1980-87, tchr. gifted and talented reading, 1990-92, tchr. 3d grade, 1992-93, tchr. 4th grade, 1993-95, reading recovery tchr., 1995—; tchr. 1st grade Pine Tree Ind. Sch. Dist., 1987-90. Mem. Gregg County Hist. Soc.; pres. Longview Opera Guild. Mem. ASCD, Nat. Coun. Tchrs. Math., Assn. Tex. Profl. Educators, Reading Recovery Coun. N.Am., Jr. League of Longview (sustaining), Phi Beta Kappa, Sigma Alpha Iota. Home: 5 Latonia Ct Longview TX 75605-1537 Office: Longview Ind Sch Dist PO Box 3268 Longview TX 75606

NORTHEN, CHARLES SWIFT, III, banker; b. Birmingham, Ala., Jan. 25, 1937; s. Charles Swift and Jennie Hood (Hunt) S.; m. Margaret Carson Robinson, Dec. 27, 1959 (div. 1972); children—Margaret Allen, Charles Swift IV, Bryce Robinson,; m. Betty Jean Taylor, Oct. 3, 1981. B.A. cum laude, Vanderbilt U., 1959, M.A., 1961. Chartered fin. analyst. Mem. staff trust dept. Birmingham Trust Nat. Bank, 1960-64; with First Ala. Bank Birmingham, 1964-80, sr. v.p., trust officer, 1975-80; sr. v.p., trust officer Central Bank of South, Birmingham, 1981-85; exec. v.p. 1st Ala. Bancshares, 1985—, Corp. Investment Officer, 1993-95; mng. dir. Sterne, Agee & Leach, Inc., Birmingham, 1995—; lectr. So. Trust Sch., Birmingham So. Coll.; pres. First Ala. Investments Inc.; dir. Hubbard Press, Findlay, Ohio. Bd. dirs. United Presbyn. Found., N.Y.C., 1977—; mem. Birmingham Com. Fgn. Relations, 1970—. Mem. Ala. Security Dealers Assn. (pres.), Ala. Soc. Fin. Analysts (pres.), Inst. Chartered Fin. Analysts, Newcomen Soc., SAR. Presbyterian. Clubs: Mountain Brook, The Club. Lodge: Kiwanis. Home: 3024 N Woodridge Rd Birmingham AL 35223-2748 Office: 1901 6th Ave N Ste 2100 Birmingham AL 35203

NORTHINGTON, DAVID KNIGHT, III, research center director, botanist, educator. BA in Biology, U. Tex., 1967, PhD in Systematic Botany, 1971. Prof. Texas Tech U., 1971-84; exec. dir. Nat. Wildflower Rsch. Ctr., Austin, Tex., 1984—; vis. assoc. prof. Southwest Tex. State U., 1985—; adj prof. dept. botany U. Tex., 1984—; curator E.L. Reed Herbarium Tex. Tech. U.; dir. Tex. Tech. Ctr., Junction. Co-author 3 sci. books; contbr. numerous articles to profl. jours., mags., newspapers, newsletters. Mem. Am. Assn. Bot. Gardens and Arboreta, Am. Soc. Plant Taxonomists, Nature Conservancy (bd. dirs. Tex. chpt.). Office: Nat Wildflower Rsch Ctr 4801 La Crosse Ave Austin TX 78739

NORTHRIP, ROBERT EARL, lawyer; b. Sleeper, Mo., May 8, 1939; s. Novel and Jessie (Burch) N.; m. Linda Kay Francis, June 15, 1968; children: Robert E. Jr., William F., Darryl F., David F. BA, Southwest Mo. State, 1960; MA, U. N.C., 1965; JD, U. Mo., 1968. Bar: Mo. 1968, U.S. Dist. Ct. (we. dist.) Mo. 1968, U.S. Ct. Appeals (10th cir.) 1976, U.S. Ct. Appeals (8th cir.) 1980, U.S. Ct. Appeals (9th cir.) 1983, U.S. Ct. Appeals (3d cir.) 1987, U.S. Supreme Ct. 1978. Ptnr. Shook, Hardy & Bacon, Kansas City, Mo., 1968—. Active Nelson Art Gallery, Soc. of Fellows, Kans. City, Mo. 1st lt. US Army, 1963-65. Mem. ABA, Mo. Bar Assn., Lawyers Assn. Kansas City, Mo. Orgn. Def. Lawyers, Kansas City Met. Bar Assn., U. Mo. Alumni Assn. (past pres. Kansas City chpt.), Nat. Soc. Arts and Letters. Republican. Avocations: baseball, football. Office: Shook Hardy & Bacon 1200 Main St Kansas City MO 64105-2100

NORTHROP, CARL WOODEN, lawyer; b. Princeton, N.J., Sept. 30, 1950; s. M. Starr and Margaret Leigh (Wooden) N.; m. Michaelanne Provencher, July 21, 1972; children: Lisa Erin, Kristen Elizabeth. BBA, U. Mich., 1972; JD, Georgetown U., 1976. Assoc. Norm Jorgensen Law Office, Washington, 1976-78; ptnr. Jorgensen, Johnson & Northrop, Washington, 1978-81; ptnr. Kadison, Pfaelzer, Woodard, Quinn & Rossi, Washington, 1981-85, mng. ptnr., 1985-87; ptnr. Bryan Cave, Washington, 1987-96, Paul, Hastings, Janofsky & Walker, 1996—. Editor Georgetown U. Law Jour., 1975-76. Mem. Fed. Communications Bar Assn. Office: Paul Hastings Janofsky & Walker/10th Flr 1299 Pennsylvania Ave NW Washington DC 20004

NORTHROP, EDWARD SKOTTOWE, federal judge; b. Chevy Chase, Md., June 12, 1911; s. Claudian Bellinger and Eleanor Smythe (Grimke) N.; m. Barbara Middleton Burdette, Apr. 22, 1939; children: Edward M., St. Julien (Mrs. Kevin Butler), Peter. LL.B., George Washington U., 1937. Bar: Md. 1937. Village mgr. Chevy Chase, Md., 1934-41; pvt. practice Rockville, Md., Washington, D.C., 1937-61; mem. Md. Senate, 1954-61, chmn. fin. com., joint com. taxation fiscal affairs, majority leader, 1959-61; judge U.S. Dist. Ct. Md., Balt., 1961—; chief judge U.S. Dist. Ct. of Md., Balt., 1970-81; mem. Met. Chief Judges Conf., 1970-81; mem. Jud. Conf. Com. on Adminstrn. of Probation System, 1973-79, Adv. Corrections Council U.S., 1976—, Jud. Panel on Multidist. Litigation, 1979—; judge U.S. Fgn. Intelligence Surveillance Ct. of Rev., 1985—. Trustee Woodberry Forest Sch.; founder Washington Met. Area Coun. Govts. & Mass Transp. Agy. Served to comdr. USNR, 1941-45. Decorated Army commendation medal, Navy commendation medal; recipient Profl. Achievement award George Washington U., 1975, Disting. Citizen award State of Md., 1981, Spl. Merit citation Am. Judicature Soc., 1982. Mem. ABA, Md. Bar Assn. (Disting. Svc. award 1982), D.C. Bar Assn., Montgomery County Bar Assn., Barristers, Washington Ctr. Met. Studies. Democrat. Episcopalian. Club: Chevy Chase (Md.). Lodge: Rotary. Office: US Dist Ct 101 W Lombard St Baltimore MD 21201-2626

NORTHROP, MARY RUTH, mental retardation nurse; b. Washington, June 5, 1919; d. William Arthur and Emma Aurelia (Kaech) N. Diploma in nursing, Georgetown U., 1951, BS in Nursing cum laude, 1952; MS, U. Md., 1958; MA in Anthropology, U. Va., 1970. RN, Va. Asst. dir. nursing U. Md. Hosp., Balt., 1958-60; dir. nursing Georgetown U. Hosp., Washington,

1961; nursing rep. ARC, Pa., 1962; regional dir. nursing ARC, New Eng. and N.Y., 1963-68; pediatric nursing cons. Va. Dept. Health, Richmond, 1971-84; clin. nursing specialist Va. Dept. Mental Health and Mental Retardation, Petersburg, Va., 1988—; adj. asst./assoc. prof. U. Md. Sch. Nursing, Balt., 1958-60. Nursing fellow rsch. HEW, U. Md., Bethesda, 1957-68, nursing fellow anthropology U. Va., 1968-70; recipient Recognition Georgetown U. Alumni Assn., Richmond, 1987. Mem. ANA, Va. Nursing Assn., DAR (chpt. regent 1983-86, dist. treas. 1992-95), Mensa, Sigma Theta Tau. Republican. Roman Catholic. Avocations: genealogy, reading, travel. Home: 300 W Franklin St # 401E Richmond VA 23220-4904 Office: Southside Va Tng Ctr PO Box 4110 Petersburg VA 23803-0110

NORTHROP, STUART JOHNSTON, manufacturing company executive; b. New Haven, Oct. 22, 1925; s. Filmer Stuart Cuchow and Christine (Johnston) N.; divorced; children: Christine Daniell, Richard Rockwell Stafford. B.A. in Physics, Yale U., 1948. Indsl. engr. U.S. Rubber Co., Naugatuck, Conn., 1948-51; head indsl. engring. dept. Am. Cyanamid Co., Wallingford, Conn., 1951-54; mfg. mgr. Linear, Inc., Phila., 1954-57; mgr. quality control and mfg. Westinghouse Electric Co., Pitts., 1957-58; mfg. supt. SKF Industries, Phila., 1958-61; v.p. mfg. Am. Meter Co., Phila., 1961-69; founder, v.p., gen. mgr. water resources div. Singer Co., Phila.; pres., dir. Buffalo Meter Co., Four Layne Cos.; dir. Gen. Filter Co., 1969-72; chmn., CEO Huffy Corp., Dayton, Ohio, 1972-85, chmn. exec. com., 1985-94; bd. dirs. Lukens, Inc., Coatesville, Pa., Union Corp., N.Y.C., Wolverine Worldwide, Rockford, Mich., DSLT, Inc., St. Clair, Mich., Elbit Sys. Am., Ft. Worth. County fin. chmn. George Bush Presdl. campaign, 1980; presdl. appointee Pres.'s Commn. on Ams. Outdoors, 1985-86; chmn. nat. hwy. safety adv. com. Dept. Transp., 1986—; founder, dir. emeritus Recreation Roundtable, Washington. Served with USAAF, 1944-45. Named Chief Exec. Officer of Yr. for leisure industry Wall Street Transcript, 1980. Mem. Del. Valley Investors (past pres.), Interlocutors, Elihu, Am. Bus. Conf. (founding), Fin. Commn. of Funds Am. Future, Boulders Club (Scottsdale), KOA Soc., Delta Kappa Epsilon. Home: 7474 E Boulders Pky Unit 4 Scottsdale AZ 85262-1247 Office: Huffy Corp 7701 Byers Rd Miamisburg OH 45342-3657

NORTHRUP, HERBERT ROOF, economist, business executive; b. Irvington, N.J., Mar. 6, 1918; m. Eleanor Pearson, June 3, 1944; children: James Pearson, Nancy Warren, Jonathan Peter, David Oliver, Philip Wilson. A.B., Duke U., 1939; A.M., Harvard U., 1941, Ph.D., 1942. Instr. econs. Cornell U., 1942-43; sr. hearing officer Nat. War Labor Bd., 1943-45; asst. prof. econs. Columbia U., 1945-49; labor economist Nat. Indsl. Conf. Bd., 1949-52; indsl. relations cons. Ebasco Services, 1952-55; v.p. indsl. relations Penn-Texas Corp., N.Y.C., 1955-58; employee relations mgr. Gen. Electric Co., 1958-61; prof. industry Wharton Sch., U. Pa., Phila., 1961-88; prof. emeritus Wharton Sch. U. Pa., Phila., 1988—; chmn. dept. industry Wharton Sch., U. Pa., 1964-69, dir. indsl. research unit, 1964-88, chmn. Labor Relations Council, 1968-85; cons. and expert witness on manpower, pers. and labor rels. problems for many cos.; arbitrator in labor rels. disputes. Author: Organized Labor and the Negro, 1944, Unionization of Professional Engineers and Chemists, 1946, Economics of Labor Relations, 1950, 9th edit., 1981, Government and Labor, 1963, Readings in Labor Economics, 1963, Boulwarism: Labor Policies of General Electric Company, 1964, Negro and Employment Opportunity, 1965, Hours of Labor, 1965, Compulsory Arbitration and Government Intervention in Labor Disputes, 1966, Restrictive Labor Practices in Supermarket Industry, 1967, Negro in the Automobile Industry, 1968, Negro in the Aerospace Industry, 1968, Negro in the Rubber Tire Industry, 1969, Negro in Paper Industry, 1969, Negro in the Tobacco Industry, 1970, Negro Employment in Basic Industry, 1970, Negro Employment in Southern Industry, 1970, Negro Employment in Land and Air Transport, 1971, Impact of Government Manpower Programs, 1975, Open Shop Construction, 1975, The Impact of OSHA, 1978, Objective Selection of Supervisors, 1978, Black and Other Minority Participation in the All-Volunteer Navy and Marine Corps, 1979, Manpower in the Retail Pharmacy Industry, 1979, The Impact of the ATT-EEO Consent Decree, 1979, Multinational Collective Bargaining Attempts, 1979, Multinational Union Organizations in the Manufacturing Industries, 1980, Employee Relations and Regulations in the 80s, 1982, Internat. Transport Workers' Federation and Flag of Convenience Shipping, 1983, Open Shop Construction Revisited, 1984, Personnel Policies for Engineers and Scientists, 1985, Doublebreasted Operations and Pre-Hire Agreements in Construction: The Facts and the Law, 1987, The Federal Government as Employer: The Federal Labor Relations Authority and the PATCO Challenge, 1988, The Changing Role of Women in Research and Development, 1988, Government Protection of Employees in Mergers and Acquisitions, 1989, The Railway Labor Act, 1990, Union Corporate Campaigns and Inside Games as a Strike Form, 1994, also over 300 articles in field. Mem. Am. Econ. Assn., Indsl. Relations Research Assn., Am. Arbitration Assn., Phi Beta Kappa. Clubs: Harvard (N.Y.C.); Harvard-Radcliffe (Phila.); University (Washington), Faculty (U. Pa.). Home and Office: 205 Avon Rd Haverford PA 19041-1612

NORTHUP, JOHN DAVID, management consultant, inventor; b. Toledo, Sept. 8, 1910; s. Charles S. and Alice Delia (Bachelder) N.; m. Ruth Bender, Jan. 15, 1937; children: John David, Mary Elizabeth, Nancy Ross (Mrs. H.T. Lehrkind). B.S., MIT, 1932. With Owens-Ill. Glass Co., 1933-74; mgr. Owens-Ill. Glass Co., Clarion, Pa., 1943-46, Charleston, W.Va., 1946-47; gen. purchasing agt. glass container div. Owens-Ill. Glass Co., 1947-49, gen. mgr. corrugated package ops., 1949-53, dir. engring., 1953-55, v.p. adminstrv. div., 1956-61, v.p., gen. mgr. Closure div., 1961-72, v.p. charge glass container mfg., 1972-74; ind. inventor, mgmt. cons., 1974—; chmn. closure com. Glass Container Mfrs. Inst., 1966-69; tech. adviser on poison prevention packaging FDA, 1971-72. Mem. Inverness Club, Beta Theta Pi. Republican. Home: 2460 Underhill Rd Toledo OH 43615-2332

NORTON, ANDRE ALICE, author; b. Cleve., Sept. 17, 1912; d. Adalbert and Bertha Stemm N. Librarian Cleve. Public Library, until 1951. Author: 125 books including The Sword is Drawn (Dutch Gov. award 1946) 1944, Sword in Sheath (Ohioana Juevenile award Honor Book 1950) 1949, Starhunter (Hugo award nomination World Sci. Fiction Convention 1962) 1961, Witch World (Hugo award nomination World Sci Fiction Convention 1964) 1963, Night of Masks (Boy's Club of Am. Certificate of Merit 1965) 1964; series include Swords Trilogy, Star Ka'at Sci. Fiction Series, Witch World Fantasy Series. Recipient Invisible Little Man award Westercon XVI, 1963, Phoenix award 1976, Gandalf Master Fantasy award World Sci. Fiction Convention, 1977, Andre Norton award Women Writers of Sci. Fiction, 1978, Balrog Fantasy award 1979, Ohioana award, 1980, Fritz Leiber award, 1983, E.E. Smith award, 1983, Nebula Grand Master award Sci. Fiction Writers of Am., 1984, Jules Verne award, 1984, Second Stage Lensman award, 1987; named to Ohio Hall of Fame, 1981. Mem. Sci. Fiction Writers Am.

NORTON, AUGUSTUS RICHARD, political science educator; b. Bklyn., Sept. 2, 1946; m. Deanna Lampros, Dec. 27, 1969; 1 child, A. Timothy. BA in Polit. Sci. magna cum laude, U. Miami, Fla., 1974, MA in Polit. Sci., 1974; PhD in Polit. Sci., U. Chgo., 1984. Commd. 2d lt. U.S. Army, 1967, advanced through grades to col., 1990, ret., 1993; prof. polit. sci., dept. social scis. U.S. Mil. Acad., West Point, N.Y., 1981-93; prof. internat. rels. Boston U., 1993—; dir. Civil Soc. in Mid. East program NYU, 1992-94. Author: Amal and the Shi'a: Struggle for the Soul of Lebanon, 1987; co-author: International Terrorism: An Annotated Bibliography and Research Guide, 1980, UN Peacekeepers: Soldiers with a Difference, 1990, Political Tides in the Arab World, 1992; contbr., sr. editor: Studies in Nuclear Terrorism, 1979, The International Relations of the PLO, 1989, Touring Nam: The Vietnam War Reader, 1989; editor: Civil Society in the Middle East, vol. I, 1995, vol II, 1996; mem. editl. bd. Ethics and Internat. Affairs, 1990, Current History, 1992—. Sr. rsch. fellow Internat. Peace Acad., 1990-92, Woodrow Wilson Nat. fellow, 1990-93; Fulbright rsch. prof., Norway, 1989; grantee NEH summer 1986, MacArthur Found., 1989-90, Ford Found., 1991—, Rockefeller Found., 1993-94. Fellow Inter-Univ. Seminar on Armed Forces and Soc. (assoc. chmn., regional rep. N.E. region 1982—); mem. Am. Polit. Sci. Assn., Coun. Fgn. Rels., Internat. Inst. Strategic Studies, Mid. East Studies Assn., Am. Rsch. Ctr. Egypt, Columbia Univ. Seminar on Middle East, Mid. East Inst. Columbia U., Conf. Group on Mid. East (cofounder), Phi Kappa Phi, Pi Sigma Alpha. Office: Dept Internat Rels Boston U 152 Bay State Rd Boston MA 02215-1501

NORTON, DAVID C., federal judge; b. Washington, July 25, 1946; s. Charles Edward and Louise Helen (Le Feber) N.; m. Dee Holmes, June 16, 1973; children: Phoebe Elizabeth, Christine Baron. BA in History, U. of the South, 1968; JD, U. S.C., 1975. Assoc. Holmes & Thomson, Charleston, S.C., 1975-77, 80-82, ptnr., 1982-90; dep. solicitor 9th Jud. Ct., Charleston, 1977-80; U.S. Dist. judge Charleston, 1990—. With USN, 1969-72. Mem. Fed. Judges Assn., Charleston County Bar Assn. (sec.-treas. 1983-90), S.C. Def. Trial Attys. Assn. (exec. com. 1988-90), S.C. Bar Assn. (Ho. Dels. 1986-90). Episcopalian. Avocations: boating, racquet ball. Office: Hollings Judicial Ctr PO Box 835 Broad & Meeting Sts 3rd Fl Charleston SC 29402-0835

NORTON, DAVID JERRY, mechanical research engineer; b. Manhattan, Kans., Oct. 23, 1940; married; 1 child, Kristin. BS, MS, Tex. A&M U., 1963; PhD, Purdue U., 1968. Sr. rsch. engr. Jet Propulsion Lab., 1968-70; from asst. prof. to prof. aerospace engring. Tex. A&M Rsch. Ctr., Houston, 1970—; asst. dir. Tex. Engring. Exptl. Station Tex. A&M U., 1981-86, v.p. rsch. Houston Advanced Rsch. Ctr., 1986—; bd. dirs. Space Found. Fellow AIAA; mem. ASME, Am. Soc. Engring. Edn., Sigma Xi. Office: Houston Advanced Rsch Ctr 4800 Research Forest Dr Bldg I The Woodlands TX 77381*

NORTON, DELMAR LYNN, candy company executive, video executive; b. Vernal, Utah, Sept. 6, 1944; s. La Mar and Velma (Hullinger) N.; m. Connie Jean Bryan, Mar. 10, 1967; children: Bryan Lynn, Christopher Max, Wendy, Nicholas Delmar. Student, U. Utah, 1962-63, Famous Artists Sch., 1966-69. Nat. sales mgr. Maxfield Candy Co., Salt Lake City, 1965-72; sec.-treas. Ice Cream & Candy Shops, Salt Lake City, 1972-73; pres., gen. mgr. Ostlers' Candy Co., Salt Lake City, 1973—; chmn. bd. Nat. Mktg. Co., Salt Lake City, 1974—; pres., gen. mgr. Rent-A-Flick, Inc., Salt Lake City.; v.p. Redi-Therm Insulation, Inc., Salt Lake City, 1991-94; nat. sales mgr. Uphill Down U.S.A., 1994—. Mem. Ch. Jesus Christ of Latter-Day Saints (missionary). Home: 4240 S 1650 E Salt Lake City UT 84124-2556 Office: PO Box 71470 Salt Lake City UT 84171

NORTON, DONN H., insurance company executive; b. 1942. BBA, Nichols Coll., 1066. CPA. Acct. Arthur Young & Co., 1966-70; pres. Bellemend Devel. Corp., 1970—; from sr. v.p. to exec. v.p. Chubb Corp., Warren, NJ. with USN, 1959-62. Office: Chubb Corp PO Box 1615 15 Mountain View Rd Warren NJ 07061-1615 Office: Bellmead Development Corp 4 Becker Farm Rd Roseland NJ 07068-1734*

NORTON, DOUGLAS RAY, auditor general; b. Portales, N.Mex., Mar. 23, 1933; s. Clayton G. and Lillian W. (Powers) N.; m. Wanda Jones, May 23, 1951 (div. July 1979); children: Debbie Norton Goodman, Vicki Norton Hulet, Denise Norton Jolley; m. Patricia M. Zins, July 21, 1982. BS, U. Ariz., 1963. CPA, Ariz. Staff acct., audit supr. Ernst & Ernst, Tucson, Ariz., 1963-67; ptnr. Baker, Price & Norton, Prescott, Ariz., 1968-75, Lester Witte & Co., Prescott, Ariz., 1975-76; auditor gen. State of Ariz., Phoenix, 1976—; mem. auditing standards adv. coun. Office of U.S. Comptr. Gen.; mem. Profl. Adv. Bd. Sch. Acctg. Ariz. State U., Tempe; mem. acctg. bd. advisors U. Ariz. Pres. Prescott Bd. Edn., 1976. Served with U.S. Army, 1953-55. Mem. AICPA, Ariz. Soc. CPAs, Nat. Assn. State Auditors, Comptrollers and Treasurers (pres. 1993-94), Nat. State Auditors Assn. (pres. 1982-83), Nat. Intergovtl. Audit Forum, Lions (pres. Prescott chpt. 1973-74). Home: PO Box 1251 Phoenix AZ 85001-1251 Office: Office Ariz Auditor Gen 2910 N 44th St Ste 410 Phoenix AZ 85018-7256

NORTON, DUNBAR SUTTON, economic developer; b. Hoquiam, Wash., Jan. 30, 1926; s. Percy Dunbar and Anna Fedelia (Sutton) N.; m. Kathleen Margaret Mullarky, Dec. 21, 1948 (dec. Apr. 1994); children: Priscilla K., Rebecca C., Jennifer A., Douglas S.; m. Mary Ethel Wolff, May 25, 1996. Student, U. Oreg., 1946-48; diploma, U.S. Army Command & Gen. Staff, 1964. Commd. 2d lt. U.S. Army, 1948, advanced through grades to lt. col., ret., 1974; dir. econ. devel. dept. Yuma (Ariz.) County C. of C., 1974-83; exec. v.p. Lakin Enterprises, Yuma, 1983-87; owner Norton Cons., Yuma, 1987—; corp. mem. Greater Yuma Econ. Devel. Corp., 1984—, vice chmn., 1993-95. Mem. Yuma County Indsl. Devel. Authority, 1984-90, 92—, pres. 1992—; chmn. fundraising com. Yuma Cross Park Coun., 1984-88, sec. 1988-90, v.p. 1990-92, bd. dirs. 1982-96; bd. dirs. Yuma Leadership, Inc., 1978-88, Yuma Youth Leadership, 1990-93; chmn. devel. com. Yuma County Airport Authority, 1985-92, v.p. 1992—; vice chmn. Yuma Main St. Bd., 1988-90, Yuma County Geog. Info. Sys. Task Force, 1991-95, Yuma Kids Voting, 1990-91, bd. dirs. Ariz. Partnership Air Transp., 1990-96, v.p. 1993-95; bd. dirs. Yuma County Civic Trusteeship, 1993-95; chmn. The Southwest Inst., 1995—, What's Best for Our Kids, 1995-96. Decorated Legion of merit with oak leaf cluster, Bronze Star. Mem. Ariz. Assn. for Econ. Devel. (bd. dirs. 1975-82, pres. 1982-83, Developer of Yr. 1977), Yuma Execs. Assn. (sec.-treas., exec. dir. 1987—). Republican. Episcopalian. Avocations: golf, swimming, singing. Home: 12267 E Del Norte Yuma AZ 85367-7356 Office: 11411 S Fortuna Rd Ste 205 Yuma AZ 85367-7827

NORTON, ELEANOR HOLMES, congresswoman, lawyer, educator; b. Washington, June 13, 1937; d. Coleman and Vela (Lynch) Holmes; m. Edward W. Norton (div.); children: Katherine Felicia, John Holmes. BA, Antioch Coll., 1960; MA in Am. Studies, Yale U., 1963, LLB, 1964. Bar: Pa., 1965, U.S. Supreme Ct., 1968. Law clk. to Judge A. Leon Higgonbotham Fed. Dist. Ct., 1964-65; asst. legal dir. ACLU, 1965-70; exec. asst. to mayor City of N.Y., 1971-74; chmn. N.Y.C. Commn. on Human Rights, 1970-77, EEOC, Washington, 1977-81; sr. fellow Urban Inst., Washington, 1981-82; prof. law Georgetown U., Washington, 1982—; mem. 100th-104th Congresses from D.C. dist., 1990—; lead Dem. mem. D.C. subcom., water resources and environ. subcom., pub. bldgs. and econ. devel. subcom. Office: 1424 Longworth HOB Washington DC 20515 also: Georgetown U Law Ctr 600 New Jersey Ave NW Washington DC 20001-2075

NORTON, ELIZABETH WYCHGEL, lawyer; b. Cleve., Mar. 25, 1933; d. James Nicolas and Ruth Elizabeth (Cannell) Wychgel; m. Henry Wacks Norton Jr., July 16, 1954 (div. 1971); children: James, Henry, Peter, Fred; m. James Cory Ferguson, Dec. 14, 1985 (div. Apr. 1988). BA in Math., Wellesley Coll., 1954; JD cum laude, U. Minn., 1974. Bar: Minn. 1974. Summer intern Minn. Atty. Gen.'s Office, St. Paul, 1972; with U.S. Dept. Treasury, St. Paul, 1973; assoc. Gray, Plant, Mooty, Mooty & Bennett, P.A., Mpls., 1974-79, prin., 1980-94, of counsel, 1995—; mem. Minn. Lawyers Bd. Profl. Responsibility, 1984-89; mem. U. Minn. Law Sch. Bd. Visitors, 1987-92. trustee YWCA, Mpls., 1979-84, 89-91, co-chmn. deferred giving com., 1980-81, chmn. by-laws com., bd. dirs., 1976-77, lectr.; treas. Minn. Women's Campaign Fund, 1985, guarantor, 1982-83, budget and fin. com. bd. dirs., 1984-87; trustee Ripley Meml. Found., 1980-84; treas. Jones-Harrison Home, 1967, bd. dirs., 1962-69, 2d v.p., chmn. fin., 1968-69; mem. Sen. David Durenberger's Women's Network, 1983-88. Durant scholar. Fellow Am. Bar Found.; mem. ABA (mediation task force family law sect. 1983-84), Minn. Bar Assn. (human rights com. family law sect., task force uniform marital property act 1984-85), Minn. Bar Found. (dir. 1991-94), Hennepin County Bar Assn. (pres. 1987-88, chmn. task force on pub. edn. 1984, chmn., mem. exec. com. family law sect. 1979-94), Minn. Inst. Legal Edn., Minn. Women's Lawyers (exec. com.), U. Minn. Law Sch. Alumni Assn. (dir. 1975-81, exec. com. 1981-83), Wellesley Club, Phi Beta Kappa. Home: 4980 Dockside Dr Apt 204 Fort Myers FL 33919-4657 Office: Gray Plant Mooty Mooty & Bennett 33 S 6th St Ste 3400 Minneapolis MN 55402-3705

NORTON, EUNICE, pianist; b. Mpls., June 30, 1908; d. Willis I. and Charlotte (O'Brien) N.; m. Bernard Lewis, May 4, 1934; 1 child, Norton Lewis. Student, U. Minn., 1922-24, Tobias Matthay Pianoforte Sch., London, 1924-31, Artur Schabel Master Piano Classes, Ger., 1931-33, Arthur Schabel Master Piano Classes, Italy, 1933; MusD (hon.), Wooster Coll., 1977. vis. prof. piano Carnegie Mellon U.; lectr. U. Pitts., Cath. U. Am.; lectr., condr. master piano classes univs.; condr. pvt. master classes, Pitts., N.Y.C., Vt.; dir. Peacham (Vt.) Piano Festivals; founder, musical dir. Pitts. New Friends of Music, Pitts. Concert Artists. Concert pianist in U.S. and Europe, 1927—; soloist with numerous symphony orchs., including N.Y. Philharm., Boston, Phila., Pitts., Mpls., London, Berlin symphony orchs., also orchs. in Leipzig, Germany, Vienna, Austria, Birmingham, Eng., Manchester, Eng.; chamber musician with Budapest, Juilliard and Griller string quartets, Am. Chember Orch.; recorded Well Tempered Clarier (J.S. Bach); performed Beethoven's entire piano sonatas, Carlow Coll., Pitts., 1983, U. Pitts., 1988, recorded ltd. edit., 1988; recorded 4 one-hour illustrated lectrs. on video Teaching of Arthur Schnabel, U. Pitts., 1987, video The Teaching of Tobias Matthay, 1995; her complete piano repertoire produced on CD's (over 150 works from Bach through Stravinsky including 48 preludes and fugues of Well Tempered Clavier and Beethoven's 32 sonatas), 1995. Recipient Bach prize, 1927; recipient Chappell Gold medal Chappell Piano Co., London, 1928. Mem. Am. Matthay Piano Assn. (founder mem.), Sigma Alpha Iota (hon.). Club: Tuesday Musical (hon.) (Pitts.). Home: 5863 Marlborough Ave Pittsburgh PA 15217-1415 *I am convinced that music is not an ornament but an essential part of life. It is a serious activity. I live with the principle of uncompromising adherence to musical values without regard for popular approval and economic gain.*

NORTON, FLOYD LIGON, IV, lawyer; b. Shreveport, La., Oct. 23, 1950; s. Floyd Ligon III and Grace Louise (Julian) N.; m. Kathleen Fair Patterson, Nov. 24, 1979; children: Caroline, Elizabeth. BA with honors, U. Va., 1972, JD, 1975. Bar: Va. 1975, D.C. 1975. Assoc. Reid & Priest, Washington, 1975-83, ptnr., 1983-95; ptnr. Morgan Lewis & Bockius, 1995—. Mem. ABA, Fed. Energy Bar Assn. Episcopalian. Home: 4107 Bradley Ln Bethesda MD 20815-5236 Office: Morgan Lewis & Bockius 1800 M St NW Washington DC 20036

NORTON, GALE A., state attorney general; b. Wichita, Mar. 11, 1954; d. Dale Bentsen and Anna Jacqueline (Lansdowne) N.; m. John Goethe Hughes, Mar. 26, 1990. BA, U. Denver, 1975, JD, 1978. Bar: Colo. 1978, U.S. Supreme Ct. 1981. Jud. clk. Colo. Ct. of Appeals, Denver, 1978-79; sr. atty. Mountain States Legal Found., Denver, 1979-83; nat. fellow Hoover Instn. Stanford (Calif.) U., 1983-84; asst. to dep. sec. U.S. Dept. of Agr., Washington, 1984-85; assoc. solicitor U.S. Dept. of Interior, Washington, 1985-87; pvt. practice law Denver, 1987-90; atty. gen. State of Colo., Denver, 1991—; Murdock fellow Polit. Economy Rsch. Ctr., Bozeman, Mont., 1984; sr. fellow Ind. Inst., Golden, Colo., 1988-90; policy analyst Pres. Coun. on Environ. Quality, Washington, 1985-88; lectr. U. Denver Law Sch., 1989; transp. law program dir. U. Denver, 1978-79. Contbr. chpts. to books, articles to profl. jours. Participant Rep. Leadership Program, Colo., 1988, Colo. Leadership Forum, 1989; past chair Nat. Assn. Attys. Gen. Environ. Com.; co-chair Nat. Policy Forum Environ. Coun.; candidate for 1996 election to U.S. Senate, 1995—. Named Young Career Woman Bus. and Profl. Wome, 1981, Young Lawyer of Yr., 1991. Mem. Federalist Soc., Colo. Women's Forum, Order of St. Ives. Republican. Methodist. Avocation: skiing. Office: Colo Dept of Law 1525 Sherman St Fl 5 Denver CO 80203-1714

NORTON, GERALD PATRICK, lawyer; b. West Roxbury, Mass., Jan. 25, 1940; s. Thomas W. and Genevieve (Sweeny) N.; m. Judith C. Ralphs, Apr. 24, 1965 (dec. Oct. 1969); children: Jeremy, Elizabeth; m. Amanda B. Pedersen, Sept. 25, 1971; 1 child, Adam. AB magna cum laude, Princeton U., 1961; LLB magna cum laude, Columbia U., 1964. Bar: N.Y. 1964, D.C. 1966. Law clk. to judge U.S. Ct. Appeals (2d cir.), N.Y.C., 1964-65; assoc. Covington & Burling, Washington, 1965-73; asst. to solicitor gen. Dept. Justice, Washington, 1973-75; dep. gen. counsel FTC, Washington, 1975-79; ptnr. Pepper Hamilton & Scheetz, Washington, 1979-92, Harkins Cunningham, Washington, 1992—; mediator U.S. Dist. Ct. for D.C.; lectr. various seminars. Mng. and research editor Columbia U. Law Rev., 1963-64; contbr. articles to profl. jours. Bd. dirs. Washington Lawyer Com. for Civil Rights & Urban Affairs, 1984—; 1st v.p., bd. dirs. Washington Met. Planning and Housing Assn., 1969-70; vol. atty. ACLU, Washington. Recipient Arthur E. Flemming award Jaycees of Nat. Capital Area, 1979; named Grad. of Yr., Province I Phi Delta Phi, 1964. Mem. Nat. Assn. Atty.'s Gen., D.C. Bar (spl. com. on profl. responsibility for govt. employees, legal ethics com. 1989-95, com. on rev. of profl. conduct 1995—), D.C. Cir. Jud. Conf. (mem. com. on admissions and grievances 1988-94), Supreme Ct. Moot Ct. (mem. panel). Democrat. Office: Harkins Cunningham 1300 19th St NW Washington DC 20036-1609

NORTON, GLYN PETER, French literature educator; b. Exeter, Devonshire, Eng., May 22, 1941; s. Trevor Thomas and Betty (Marshall) N.; m. Victoria Josefina Perez, Oct. 28, 1966; children—Alexandra, Leslie. A.B., U. Mich., 1963, A.M., 1965, Ph.D., 1968. Asst. prof. Dartmouth Coll., Hanover, N.H., 1968-71; prof. French lit. Pa. State U., University Park, 1971-88; prof. French lit., chmn. dept. romance langs, dir. Ctr. for Fgn. Langs., Lits. and Cultures Williams Coll., Williamstown, Mass., 1988-93, Willcox B. and Harriet M. Adsit prof. Internat. Studies, 1993—. Author: Montaigne and the Introspective Mind, 1975; The Ideology and Language of Translation in Renaissance France, 1984; editor: The Cambridge History of Literary Criticism, vol. III; contbr. articles to ednl. jours. NEH fellow, 1973-74, Guggenheim fellow, 1986-87; Am. Council of Learned Socs. grantee, 1980-81, 85; recipient medal City of Melun, France, 1985. Fellow Camargo Found., mem. MLA, Renaissance Soc. Am., Soc. Franç aise des Seiziemistes. Avocations: music; gardening; traveling. Office: Williams Coll Dept Romance Langs Weston Hall Williamstown MA 01267

NORTON, HUGH STANTON, economist, educator; b. Delta, Colo., Sept. 18, 1921; s. Cecil A. and Olive S. (Stanton) N.; m. Miriam Jarmon, Dec. 19, 1949 (dec. 1983); children: Pamela, John; m. Mary Jo Roberts. A.B., George Washington U., 1947, Ph.D., 1956. Johnson prof. econs. U. S.C., Columbia, 1968—; disting. prof. emeritus U. S.C., 1988—; cons. anti-trust and transp. econs. to indsl. firms. Author: The Role of the Economist in Government Policy Making, 1969, The World of the Economist, 1973, 2d edit., 1977, The Employment Act and the Council of Economic Advisers 1946-76, 1977, The Quest for Economic Stability: Roosevelt to Reagan, rev. edit., 1990. Served with Signal Corps AUS, 1942-45. Club: Cosmos (Washington). Home: 3335 Overcreek Rd Columbia SC 29206-5145

NORTON, JAMES J., union official; b. Boston, June 9, 1930; s. Patrick P. and Annie (Flaherty) N.; m. Patricia A. Tuley, Sept. 19, 1953; children: James, Ann Marie, Robert, Thomas, Donald, David, Brian. Treas. Boston Photo Engravers Union, 1957-60, pres., 1960-62; internat. rep. Graphic Arts Union, Boston, 1962-78; sec. treas. Graphic Arts Union, Washington, 1979-83; rec. and fin. sec. Graphic Communications Internat. Union, 1983-85, pres., 1983—; exec. coun. AFL-CIO, Union Labor Life Ins. Co.; bd. govs. ARC. Coach Peewee-Bantum level Dorchester Youth Hockey Program, Boston, 1958-79; coach Midget level Fairfax (Va.) Hockey Program, 1980-81; exec. bd. mem. ARC. Mem. AFL-CIO (exec. coun.), Montclair C. of C. Roman Catholic. Lodge: K.C. Office: Graphic Comms Internat Union 1900 L St NW Washington DC 20036-5001

NORTON, JODY (JOHN DOUGLAS NORTON), English language educator; b. Princeton, N.J., Nov. 13, 1943; s. Paul Foote and Alison Edmunds (Stuart) N.; m. Alexandra Holt Morey, Aug. 20, 1977; children: Joselle, Jackson, Tayo. BA, U. Mass., Amherst, 1966; MA, U. Calif., Berkeley, 1981, PhD, 1988. Vis. asst. prof. Rice U., Houston, 1988-89, Albion (Mich.) Coll., 1989-94; lectr. Ea. Mich. U., Ypsilanti, 1994—. Contbr. articles to profl. jours. Fellow U. Calif., 1979-80, 80-81, 84-85, 87-88, Yale U., 1966-67; faculty rsch. grantee Albion Coll., 1992, 93, 94. Mem. MLA, Midwest MLA, Soc. for Critical Exch., Popular Culture Assn., Phi Beta Kappa, Phi Kappa Phi. Avocations: tennis, mountain climbing, camping, playing electric bass, blues and country western music. Home: 415 Ventura Ct Ann Arbor MI 48103-4319 Office: Eastern Mich U Dept English Lang & Lit Ypsilanti MI 48197

NORTON, JUDY, actress; b. Santa Monica, Calif., Jan. 29; d. Harry Vincent and Constance (Glazebrook) Norton; m. Randy Apostle, Apr. 8, 1991. Participated in 2 world skydiving records. Appeared in film Hotel, 1966; actress repertory co. The Stable Players, 1969-71, Cinderella, 1981, Annie Get Your Gun, 1983, I Ought to Be in Pictures, 1983, Perfect Pitch, 1984, Spring at Marino, 1984, Times of Your Life, 1985, Social Security (Stage West, Calgary, Can.), 1987, Sound of Music, 1989, Alive & Kicking, 1989, Move Over, Mrs. Markham (Stage West, Can.), 1991, Weekend Comedy (Stage West, Can.), 1991, Volstead Blues (Souris Valley Theatre, Can.), 1993, Ranchers & Rustlers (Can.), 1994; TV movies include The Homecoming, 1971, Valentine, 1978, Valentine's Day-A Love Story, 1982, A Day of Thanks, 1982appeared in TV series The Waltons, 1972-81, also Circus of the Stars, 1983, 84; TV movie A Walton Thanksgiving, 1993, A Walton Wedding, 1995; TV guest appearances in The Love Boat, 1981, Trial by Jury, 1989; co-writer Knaughty Knights, 1992, Ranchers And Rustlers,

1992; co-dir., co-writer Laura & Johnny Were Lovers, 1992, Hot Summer Nights, 1992, Gillian's Island, 1992, Murder on the Prairie Express, 1993, Mugs and Molls, 1993, I Dream of Jimmy, 1993, Rock N Roll Candidate, 1993, Star Trax, 1993, There's No Life Like It, 1993, He Shoots, She Scores, 1994, Of Course, Elvis Will Be Here, 1994, Monster High Reunion, 1994, Don't Touch That Dial, 1994, Ranchers and Rustlers II, 1994, Captain Vancouver & The Land Pirates, 1995, Philip Harlow, 1995, Phantom of the Theatre, 1995, Fantasy Island, 1995, Crystal's Palace, 1995, Super Heroes in Retirement Land, 1996. Mem. AFTRA, SAG, Actors Equity, Can. Actors Equity.

NORTON, KENNETH HOWARD, professional football player; b. Jacksonville, Ill., Sept. 29, 1966; s. Ken Norton. Student, UCLA. Linebacker Dallas Cowboys, 1988-93, San Francisco 49ers, 1994—. Selected to Pro Bowl, 1991-95; played in Super Bowls XXVII-XXIX, 1992-94. Office: San Francisco 49ers 4949 Centennial Blvd Santa Clara CA 95054-1229*

NORTON, MARY BETH, history educator, author; b. Ann Arbor, Mich., Mar. 25, 1943; d. Clark Frederic and Mary Elizabeth (Lunny) N. BA, U. Mich., 1964; MA, Harvard U., 1965, PhD, 1969; DHL (hon.), Siena Coll., 1983, Marymount Manhattan Coll., 1984, De Pauw U., 1989; DLitt (hon.), Ill. Wesleyan U., 1992. Asst. prof. history U. Conn., Storrs, 1969-71; from asst. prof. to prof. Cornell U., Ithaca, N.Y., 1971-87, Mary Donlon Alger prof. Am. history, 1987—. Author: The British-Americans: The Loyalist Exiles in England, 1774-1789, 1972, Liberty's Daughters: The Revolutionary Experience of American Women, 1750-1800, 1980 (Berkshire prize for Best Book Woman Historian 1980), Founding Mothers and Fathers: Gendered Power and the Forming of American Society, 1996; co-author: A People and A Nation, 1982, 4th rev. edit., 1994; editor: AHA Guide to Historical Literature, 3d rev. edit., 1995; co-editor: Women of America: A History, 1979, To Toil the Livelong Day: America's Women at Work, 1790-1980, 1987, Major Problems in American Women's History, 1989, 2nd rev. edit., 1995; contbr. articles to profl. jours. Trustee Cornell U., 1973-75, 83-88; mem. Nat. Coun. Humanities, Washington, 1979-84. Woodrow Wilson Found. fellow, 1964-65, NEH fellow, 1974-75, Shelby Cullom Davis Ctr. fellow Princeton U., 1977-78, Rockefeller Found. fellow, 1986-87, Soc. for Humanities fellow Cornell U., 1989-90, John Simon Guggenheim Meml. Found. fellow, 1993-94. Fellow Soc. Am. Historians (exec. bd. 1974-87, Allan Nevins prize 1970); mem. Am. Hist. Assn. (v.p. for rsch. 1985-87) Orgn. Am. Historians (exec. bd. 1983-86), Berkshire Conf. Women Historians (pres. 1983-85). Democrat. Methodist. Office: Cornell U Dept History Ithaca NY 14853

NORTON, NATHANIEL GOODWIN, marketing executive; b. Chgo., Jan. 7, 1948; s. Wilbur H. and Eva (Geneen) N.; m. Ariel Taylor, Nov. 15, 1980 (div. July 1987). BA, U. N.C., 1969. Mktg. mgr. Canteen Corp., Chgo., 1971-74; sr. v.p. Mathieu, Gerfen & Bresner, N.Y.C., 1974-83; pres., ptnr. Rand Pub. Rels., N.Y.C., 1983-89; ind. marketing cons. North Hampton, N.H., 1989—.

NORTON, NORMAN JAMES, exploration geologist; b. Du Quoin, Ill., Apr. 26, 1933; s. James Harlan Norton and Helen Jane (Riley) Norton Rosen; m. Bettie Jean Greer, July 7, 1955; children—Matthew James, Jane Alison. B.S., So. Ill. U., 1958; M.S., U. Minn., 1960, Ph.D., 1963. Successively, asst., assoc., then full prof. biology Hope Coll., Holland, Mich., 1964-74; prof., chmn. dept. biology Ball State U., Munice, Ind., 1974-78, acting v.p. acad. affairs, 1978-79; acting dean Coll. Arts and Scis. Ball State U., 1979-81; provost, v.p. acad. affairs Ind. U. Pa., 1981-83; cons. geologist Gulf Oil Corp., Houston, 1970-83; sr. staff geologist Gulf Oil Exploration and Prodn. Co., Houston, 1983-85; biostratigrapher, stratigraphic services, exploration Chevron Overseas Petroleum Inc., San Ramon, Calif., 1985-91; supr. biostratigraphy sect. Chevron U.S.A., Inc., Houston, 1991—; acting divsn. geologist Chevron U.S.A. Inc., Houston, 1993-95, divsn. geologist, 1995—. Contbr. articles to profl. jours. Served with USAF, 1952-56. Recipient Outstanding Tchr. Educator award Sr. Class of Hope Coll., 1969, acad. citation for disting. achievement Mich. Acad. Scis., Art and Letters, 1969, Outstanding Achievement award Chevron Overseas Petroleum Inc., 1990. Mem. Am. Assn. Stratigraphic Palynologists (Disting. Svc. award 1978, chmn. bd. trustees found., archives com. 1970—, constrn. revision com.). Home: 4419 St Michaels Ct Sugar Land TX 77479-2989 Office: CUSA PO Box 1635 Houston TX 77251-1635

NORTON, PAUL ALLEN, insurance executive; b. Ardmore, S.D., Sept. 10, 1913; s. Albert James and Leota (Clute) N.; m. Ruth Stephens Richards, July 4, 1941; children: Richard Allen, Carolyn Ruth (Mrs. Robert Padgette). A.B. magna cum laude, Chadron State Coll., 1935, LLH (hon.), 1987; M.B.A. with distinction, Harvard U., 1937; LL.D., Bethany Coll., 1973. Mgr. N.Y. Life Ins. Co., Worcester, Mass., 1938-41, Boston, 1941-43; mgr. N.Y. Life Ins. Co., Phila., 1944-47; asst. supt. agys. N.Y. Life Ins. Co., 1947; mgr. N.Y. Life Ins. Co., Houston, 1948-49; supt. agys. N.Y. Life Ins. Co., N.Y., 1947; mgr. N.Y. Life Ins. Co., Houston, 1948-49; supt. agys. N.Y. Life Ins. Co., N.Y.C., 1950; v.p. charge group sales N.Y. Life Ins. Co., 1951, agy. v.p., 1952, field v.p., 1952, regional v.p., 1953, v.p., 1954-59, v.p. in charge sales mgmt., 1959-62, v.p. in charge mktg., 1962-64, sr. v.p. in charge mktg., 1964-69, exec. v.p., 1969-73. Contbr. articles to profl. pubs. Hon. chmn. Greater N.Y. council Boy Scouts Am. Mem. Life Ins. Agy. Mgmt. Assn. (past pres.), Nat. Assn. Life Underwriters (v.p. Worcester chpt. 1940-41), Exec. Assn. (pres. Worcester chpt. 1939-41), Am. Soc. C.L.U.s (dir.). Clubs: Harvard, Economic (N.Y.C.); Am. Yacht (Rye, N.Y.). Home: 20 Church St Greenwich CT 06830-5631

NORTON, PETER BOWES, publishing company executive; b. London, May 4, 1929; came to U.S., 1969; s. James Peter and Margaret (Bowes) N.; m. Heather Pearch, Jan. 16, 1954; children: Jan Heather, Fiona Mary. Student, S.E. Essex Tech. Coll., 1942-45, Royal Naval Colls., 1949-54. Commd. officer Royal Navy, 1945, advanced through grades to lt., 1954, ret., 1960; pers. officer United Dominions Trust, London, 1960-63; jr. exec. to mng. dir. Ency. Britannica, London, 1963-68, mng. dir., 1968-69; v.p. internat. div. Ency. Britannica, Chgo., 1969-70; pres. Ency. Britannica Can., 1970-73, Ency. Britannica U.S.A., Chgo., 1974-85; pres. Ency. Britannica Inc., 1986-93, pres., CEO, 1993-95; also bd. dirs. Ency. Britannica Inc., Chgo.; bd. dirs. Ency. Universalis (Paris); chmn. bd. dirs. Ency. Britannica Ednl. Corp., Chgo., 1988-95. Bd. dirs. William Benton Found., 1986-95. Fellow Chartered Inst. Secs. (Eng.), Chartered Inst. Adminstrs. U.K., Chartered Inst. Dirs. U.K.; mem. Japan Am. Soc. Chgo., Inc., Chgo. Club. Mem. Ch. of Eng. Clubs: Royal Automobile (London); Chgo., Carlton. Avocations: tennis, reading. Home: 180 E Pearson St Apt 3401 Chicago IL 60611-2125

NORTON, PETER J., publishing executive. Chmn. of the bd. Merriam-Webster Inc., Springfield, Mass. Office: Merriam Webster Inc 47 Federal St Springfield MA 01105-3805

NORTON, ROBERT HOWARD, entertainer, musical arranger, author; b. N.Y.C., July 19, 1946; s. Howard R. and Lena (Triano) N.; m. Eileen Williams, Sept. 29, 1966 (div. 1976); children: Brian, Lelania. Student, Broward C.C., Ft. Lauderdale, Fla., 1970-75; community antenna TV engr. cert., Nat. Cable TV Inst., 1976. Rec. session artist Motown and various other recording labels, 1964—; entertainer various concerts, 1964—; systems technician Selkirk Communications, Ft. Lauderdale, Fla., 1979-81; cable TV engr. Gen. Instrument Corp., Hatboro, Pa., 1981-84; entertainer (with Leilani Chandler) The Sophisticats, Ft. Pierce, Fla., 1984—; owner, author, software writer Norton Music, Ft. Pierce, Fla., 1990—. Author: The Artist's and Entertainer's Tax Bible, 1990, Entertainer's Guide to Cruising, 1991; writer mus. software 135 User Styles, 1991, Band-in-a-Box Supercharger, 1993, 3 Band-in-a-Box Fake Disks, 1994—, 5 Band-in-a-Box User Style Disks, 1993—; writer software 475 Gen. MIDI Sequences, 1993—; composer numerous songs; arranger of more than 300 songs. Home and Office: Norton Music PO Box 13149 Fort Pierce FL 34979-3149

NORTON, ROBERT LEO, SR., mechanical engineering educator, researcher; b. Boston, May 5, 1939; s. Harry Joseph and Kathryn (Warren) N.; m. Nancy Auclair, Feb. 27, 1960; children: Robert L., Jr., MaryKay, Thomas J. AS in Mechanical Engring. cum laude, Northeastern U., 1962, BS in Indsl. Tech. summa cum laude, 1967; MS in Engring. Design, Tufts U., 1970. Registered profl. engr., Mass. Engr. Polaroid Corp., Cambridge, Mass., 1959-66, sr. engr., Waltham, 1979-81; project engr. Jet Spray Cooler, Inc., Waltham, Mass., 1966-69; bio-med. engr. Tufts surg. rsch. dept. N.E. Med. Ctr. Hosps., Boston, 1969-71; rsch. assoc. Tufts surg. svc. Boston City Hosp., 1971-74; lectr. bio-med. engring. Franklin Inst., Boston, 1973-76; instr. dept. surgery, Tufts U., Boston, 1970-82, asst. prof. engring. design, Medford, 1974-79; prof. mech. engring. Worcester Poly. Inst., Mass., 1981—; pres. Norton Assocs., Norfolk, Worcester, 1970—. Patentee (13) in field; contbr. articles to profl. jours; author engring. textbooks including Design of Machinery: An Introduction to the Synthesis and Analysis of Mechanisms and Machines, 1992, internat. edit., 1992, Korean translation, 1995, Machine Design: An Integrated Approach, 1996, internat. edit., 1996, others; reviewer IFTOMM Jour. Mechanism and Machine Theory; presenter in field. Mem. ASME (reviewer Jour. Mechanisms, Transmission, and Automation in Design), Am. Soc. Engring. Edn. (program chmn. computers in edn. divsn. 1985-86, sec. computers in edn. divsn. 1986-87, pres. computers in edn. divsn. 1988-90, reviewer Jour. Prism, J.F. Curtis award 1984, Merle Miller award 1987, 92), Pi Tau Sigma, Sigma Xi. Democrat. Avocations: sailing, computers. Office: Worcester Poly Inst Dept Mechanical Engring 100 Institute Rd Worcester MA 01609-2247

NORTON, ROBERT R., JR., food products executive; b. 1946. BS, Mo. Western State Coll., 1966; MBA, N.W. Mo. State U., 1968. Sec., treas. Dugdale Packing Co., St. Joseph, Mo., 1966-86; with BeefAmerica Operating Co., Inc., Omaha, 1986—, pres., 1988—. Office: Beef Am 14748 W Center Rd Ste 201 Omaha NE 68144*

NORTON, STEPHEN ALLEN, geological sciences educator; b. Newton, Mass., May 21, 1940; m. Anne Peer, Apr. 25, 1970; children: David S., Lisa A., Stephen A. B.A., Princeton U., 1962; M.A., Harvard U., 1963, Ph.D., 1967. Prof. geol. scis. U. Maine, Orono, 1978—; chmn. dept. U. Maine-Orono, 1978-82, 93-96, dean arts and scis., 1984-86. Fellow Geol. Soc. Am.; mem. Am. Soc. Limnology and Oceanography, Sigma Xi. Office: U Maine Dept Geol Scis Boardman Hall Orono ME 04469-5711

NORTON, WILLIAM ALAN, lawyer; b. Garretsville, Ohio, Apr. 26, 1951; s. Hugh Delbert and Tommie (Leet) N.; m. Denise Ann Johnson, May 2, 1991; children: Rachel Johnson, Sara Meagan, William Tucker. AA, U. Fla., 1972, BS, 1973, JD, 1976. Bar: Fla. 1977, U.S. Dist. Ct. (so. and mid. dist.) Fla. 1995. Assoc. Law Office of David Paul Horan, Key West, Fla., 1978-79; asst. pub. defender 16th Jud. Cir., Monroe County, Fla., 1979-81, 1st Jud. Cir., Ft. Walton Beach, Fla., 1981-85; assoc. Jones & Foster, P.A., West Palm Beach, Fla., 1985-88, Montgomery Searcy & Denney, West Palm Beach, 1988-89, Searcy Denney Scarola Barnhart & Shipley, P.A., 1989-93; atty./shareholder Searcy Denney Scarola Barnhart & Shipley, P.A., West Palm Beach, 1989—, shareholder, 1993; lectr. in civil trial and securities litigation. Bd. dirs. Ctr. for Children in Crisis, West Palm Beach, 1994—. Mem. Fla. Bar Assn. (cert. civil trial litigation), Pub. Investors Arbitration Bar Assn., Palm Beach County Bar Assn., Acad. Fla. Trial Lawyers. Home: 8152 Needles Dr Palm Beach Gardens FL 33418 Office: Searcy Denney Scarola et al 2139 Palm Beach Lakes Blvd West Palm Beach FL 33409

NORVELL, PATSY, artist; b. Greenville, S.C., July 13, 1942; d. Wendell Norvell and Margaret Marie (Schaefer) Nichols; m. Robert Rahway Zakanitch, May 2, 1982; 1 child, Amelia Zakanitch Norvell. BA, Bennington Coll., 1964; studied with David Smith, Bolton Landing, N.Y., 1964; MA, CUNY-Hunter Coll., 1970. Asst. instr. Colo. Springs (Colo.) Fine Arts Ctr., 1967; instr. dept. art Rutgers U., Newark, 1969-70, Montclair (N.J.) State Coll., 1970-74; assoc. in sculpture Columbia U., N.Y.C., 1977; instr. pvt. studio seminar, N.Y.C, 1973-74; adj. lectr. in sculpture SUNY, Queens, 1978-79; adj. asst. prof. dept. art Hunter Coll., N.Y.C., 1979-81, vis. asst. prof., 1982-83; vis. artist N.Y. Exptl. Glass Workshop, 1980, 84; cons. sculpture panel N.Y. State Creative Artist Pub. Svc., 1980, 81; panelist sculpture fellowship N.J. State Coun. Arts, 1983, gen. svc. adminstrn. NEH, 1984, Hunter's Point Selection Com., 1987; presenter numerous seminars. One woman shows include A.I.R. Gallery, N.Y.C., 1973, 75, 78, 80, 82, 87, 91, LaGrangeville, N.Y., 1977, Vassar College & Barrett Ho., Poughkeepsie, N.Y., 1979, Avery Fisher Hall, Lincoln Ctr., N.Y.C., 1980, Sidney James Gallery, N.Y.C., 1982, Norton Gallery of Art, West Palm Beach, Fla., 1983, Matthew Hamilton Gallery, Phila., 1984; exhibited in group shows at 117 Prince St, N.Y.C., 1972, Kent (Ohio) State Galleries, 1972, Alonzo Gallery, N.Y.C., 1972, Newark Mus., 1973, Nancy Hoffmann Gallery, N.Y.C., 73, Erotic Art Gallery, N.Y.C., 1973, Indpls. Mus. Art, Cin., 1974, Taft Mus., Cin., 1974, Central Hall Gallery, Port Washington, N.Y., 1975, 77, Skidmore Coll., Saratoga Springs, N.Y., 1975, Fine Arts Bldg., N.Y.C., 1976, Webb and Parsons, Bedford Village, N.Y., 1976, Hurlbutt Gallery, Greenwich, Conn., 1977, County Mus. Fine Arts, Roslyn, N.Y., 1977, Whitney Downtown Mus., N.Y.C., 1978, 79, Robert Freidus Gallery, N.Y.C., 1978, Ginza Kaigaken, Tokyo, 1978, Battery Park Landfill, N.Y.C., 1978, Thorpe Intermedia Gallery, Sparkill, N.Y., 1979, Perkins Ctr. Arts, Moorestown, N.J., 1979, McKintosch/Drysdale Galleryn Washington, 1980, Danforth (Mass.) Mus., 1981, Berkshire (Mass.) Mus., 1981-82, Women's Hall of Fame, Seneca Falls, N.Y., 1981, U. Houston, 1981, Sidney Janis Gallery, N.Y.C., 1982, Norton Gallery Art, West Palm Beach, Fla., 1983, High Mus. Art, Atlanta, 1983, Nat. Gallery Art, Washington, 1984, Palladium, N.Y.C., 1985, Tanabaum Gallery, N.Y.C., Contemporary Arts Ctr., Cin., 1986, Lowe Art Mus., Coral Gables, Fla., 1987, Max Protetch Gallery, N.Y.C., 1987, Toledo Mus. Art, 1988, Fort Wayne (Ind.) Mus. Art, 1988, The Home Saving Tower, L.A., 1989, Md. Coll. Art and Design, 1989, Bernice Steinbaum Gallery, 1989-93, Noyes Mus., Oceanville, N.J., 1990, Art Mus., Southampton, N.Y., 1991, Midtown-Payson Gallery, 1992, Willow Gallery, N.Y.C., 1993, Steinbaum-Krauss Gallery, N.Y.C., 1993, others; commd. works include glass, mirror, railing, and stone sculptures for Nicholas Recital Hall, Douglass Coll., New Brunswick, N.H., 1981-82, Bridgeport (Conn.) Fed. Bldg. and Courthouse, 1983-85, Battery Park City Authority, N.Y.C., 1983-86, 4600 East-West Hwy, Bethesda, Md., 1984-88, Bellevue Hosp., 1986, Home Savings Am. Tower, L.A., 1987-88, 14th St. Union Sq. Local Devel. Corp., 1988—, Beverly and Cortelyou Subway Stas., M.T.A., N.Y., 1992-96; represented in permanent collections including Jim Henson Apt., N.Y.C., Brown's Residence, Bethesda, Md., Steinbaum Residence, L.I., N.Y., Bill and Norma Roth Collection, Winterhaven, Fla. Recipient Spl. Recognition award Art Commn. N.Y.C., 1993; Nat. Endowment for Arts artist fellow, 1976-77Patlock/Krasner Artist fellow, 1995; artist residency grantee Art Awareness, Lexington, N.Y., 1995. Home: 78 Greene St New York NY 10012-5100

NORVILLE, DEBORAH, news correspondent; b. Aug. 8, 1958; m. Karl Wellner; 2 children: Karl Nikolai, Kyle Maximilian. BJ, U. Ga., 1979. Reporter Sta. WAGA-TV, Atlanta, 1978-79, anchor, reporter, 1979-81; anchor, reporter Sta. WMAQ-TV, Chgo., 1982-86; anchor NBC News, N.Y.C., 1987-89; news anchor Today Show, NBC, N.Y.C., 1989, co-anchor, 1990-92; corr. Street Stories, CBS, N.Y.C., 1992-94; co-anchor America Tonight, CBS, N.Y.C., 1994; anchor Inside Edition, King World Prodns., 1994—; contbg. editor McCall's, N.Y.C. Bd. dirs. Greater N.Y. coun. Girl Scouts U.S. Recipient Outstanding Young Alumni award Sch. Journalism, U. Ga., Emmy award, 1985-86, 89; named Person of Yr., Chgo. Broadcast Advt. Club, 1989, Anchor of Yr. 2000, Washington Journalism Rev., 1989. Mem. Soc. Profl. Journalists. Office: Inside Edition 402 E 76th St New York NY 10021-3104

NORWOOD, BERNARD, economist; b. Boston, Nov. 21, 1922; s. Hyman and Rose (Fink) N.; m. Janet Lippe, June 25, 1943; children: Stephen Harlan, Peter Carlton. BA, Boston U., 1947; MA, Fletcher Sch. Law and Diplomacy, 1948, PhD, 1957. Internat. economist State Dept., 1949-58; joined U.S. Fgn. Svc., 1955; 1st. sec. U.S. mission to European Communities, Brussels, Belgium, 1958-62; asst. chief comml. policy and treaties divsn. Dept. State, 1962; chmn. trade staff com. Office Spl. Rep. for Trade Negotiations, Exec. Office Pres., 1963-67; assigned The Nat. War Coll., 1967-68; advisor divsn. internat. fin. bd. govs. Fed. Res. Sys., 1968-75; prin. assoc., sr. cons. Nathan Assocs., Inc., 1975-94; mem. U.S. del. to negotiations and confs. GATT, Geneva, 1953-67. Served with AUS, 1943-46. Home and Office: 5610 Wisconsin Ave 21D Chevy Chase MD 20815-4415

NORWOOD, CAROLE GENE, middle school educator; b. Odessa, Tex., Feb. 27, 1943; d. Perry Eugene and Jeffie Lynn (Stephens) Knowles; m. James Ralph Norwood, Aug. 4, 1973. BA, U. Tex., 1966; MA, U. North Tex., 1975; cert. ESL, Our Lady of the Lake U., San Antonio, 1988. Cert. Sec. Edn. English, Spanish, ESL. Student intern Dept. of the Interior, Washington, 1962; receptionist Senate Chambers, Austin, Tex., 1965; English instr. Universidade Mackenzie, Sao Paulo, Brazil, 1966-67, Uniao Cultural Brasil-Estados Unidos, Sao Paulo, 1966-67; tchr. Terrell (Tex.) Jr. Sr. High Sch., 1967-68, Agnew Jr. High Sch., Mesquite, Tex., 1968-70; teaching asst. U. North Tex. Denton, Tex., 1970-71; sec. to pres. The Village Bank, Dallas, 1971-72; tchr. Plano (Tex.) High Sch., 1972-74; ESL adult edn. tchr. Dallas, 1972-73; tchr., yearbook sponsor Brentwood Middle Sch., San Antonio, 1975-90; instructional specialist Gus Garcia Jr. High Sch., San Antonio, 1990—, interdisciplinary team leader, 1992-93, 96—; yearbook and newspaper sponsor, Agnew Jr. High Sch., 1969-70. Contbr. articles to profl. jours. Mem. World Wildlife Fund, Audubon Soc., Nat. Wildlife Fedn., Nature Conservancy, San Antonio Museum Assn., San Antonio Zoological Soc., Los Padrinos (Mission Rd. Devel. Ctr.); U.I.L. coach 1976-87, 92-93. Named Outstanding Young Woman of Am., 1972. Mem. AAUE, NEA, ADCD, Nat. Coun. Tchrs. of English, San Antonio Area Coun. Tchrs. English, Tex. State Tchrs. Assn., Edgewood Classroom Tchrs. Assn. (faculty rep. 1991-94), Longhorn Singers Alumni Assn., Tex. Exes Alumni Assn., Delta Kappa Gamma (chpt. pres. 1990-92, San Antonio coord. coun. chair 1995—, state program com. mem. 1995—). Presbyterian. Office: Edgewood Ind Sch Dist Gus Garcia Jr School 3306 Ruiz San Antonio TX 78228

NORWOOD, CAROLYN VIRGINIA, business educator; b. Florence, S.C., Dec. 11; d. James Henry and Mildred (Jones) N. BS, N.C. A&T State U., 1956; MA, Columbia U., 1959; postgrad., Seton Hall U., Temple U.; cert. scholarly distinction, Nat. Acad. Paralegal Studies, 1991. Instr. Gibbs. Jr. Coll., St. Petersburg, Fla., Fayetteville State Coll., N.C.; asst. prof. Community Coll. Phila.; prof. Essex County Coll., Newark, 1968—; cons. Mercer County Coll., Trenton, N.J.; mem. assessment team Mid.-States Commn., Phila., 1980—. Co-author: Alphabetic Indexing, 1989. Recipient Eddy award Gregg/McGraw-Hill Co., N.Y.C., 1986, Who's Who in N.J. Bus. Edn. award N.J. Dept. Edn. Divsn. Vocat. Edn., 1990, Cert. of Recognition of Outstanding and Dedicated Svc., Mid. States Assn. Colls. and Schs., Commn. on Higher Edn., 1994; profiled in NBEA Yearbook chpt. on Leadership in Bus. Edn., 1993; doctoral fellow Temple U., Phila., 1977-78. Mem. AAUW, NAFE, NAACP, Nat. Bus. Edn. Assn. (bd. dirs. 1982-85), Ea. Bus. Edn. Assn. (pres. 1986-87, membership dir. 1976-85, Educator of the Yr. 1994), Nat. Coun. Negro Women, N.J. Bus. Edn. Assn., Alpha Kappa Alpha, Phi Delta Kappa, Delta Pi Epsilon. Avocations: bowling, photography. Office: Essex County Coll 303 University Ave Newark NJ 07102-1719

NORWOOD, CHARLES W., JR., congressman; b. Valdosta, Ga., July 27, 1942; m. Gloria Norwood; 2 children. BS, Ga. So. U., 1964; DDS, Georgetown U., 1967. Pvt. practice Augusta, Ga., 1969—; owner Norwood Tree Nursery, 1984—; mem. 104th Congress from 10th Ga. dist., 1995—. Capt. U.S. Army, 1967-69, Vietnam. Decorated Combat Medic badge, Bronze Star for Meritorious Svc., Bronze Star for Meritorious Achievement. Mem. Ga. Dental Assn. Republican. Methodist. Office: US Ho of Reps 1707 Longworth Washington DC 20515

NORWOOD, DEBORAH ANNE, law librarian; b. Honolulu, Nov. 12, 1950; d. Alfred Freeman and Helen G. (Papsch) N.; 1 child, Nicholas. BA, U. Wash., 1972; JD, Willamette U., 1974; M in Law Librarianship, U. Wash., 1979. Bar: Wash., U.S. Dist. Ct. (we. dist.) 1975, U.S. Ct. Appeals (9th cir.) 1980. Ptnr. Evans and Norwood, Seattle, 1975-79; law librarian U.S. Courts Library, Seattle, 1980-89; state law librarian Wash. State Law Libr., Olympia, 1989—, reporter of decisions, 1994—. Mem. ALA, Am. Assn. Law Librs. (chmn. state, ct. and county spl. interest section 1995-96). Office: Wash State Law Libr PO Box 40751 Temple of Justice Olympia WA 98504-0751

NORWOOD, JANET LIPPE, economist; b. Newark, Dec. 11, 1923; d. M. Turner and Thelma (Levinson) Lippe; m. Bernard Norwood, June 25, 1943; children—Stephen Harlan, Peter Carlton. BA, Douglass Coll., 1945; MA, Tufts U., 1946; PhD, Fletcher Sch. Law and Diplomacy, 1949; LLD (hon.), Fla. Internat. U., 1979; LL.D. (hon.), Carnegie Mellon U., 1984. Instr. Wellesley Coll., 1948-49; economist William L. Clayton Ctr., Tufts U., 1953-58; with Bur. Labor Stats., U.S. Dept. Labor, Washington, 1963-91; dep. commr., then acting commr. Bur. Labor Stats. Dept. Labor, Washington, 1975-79, commr. labor stats., 1979-92; sr. fellow The Urban Inst., Washington, 1992—; dir. Republic Nat. Bank, Consortium for Internat. Earth Scis. Info. Network, chair adv. coun. unemployment compensation, 1993-96; mem. com. on nat. stats. NAS. Author papers, reports in field. Recipient Disting. Achievement award Dept. Labor, 1972, Spl. Commendation award, 1977, Philip Arnow award, 1979, Elmer Staats award, 1982, Pub. Svc. award, 1984; named to Hall Disting. Alumni, Rutgers U., 1987; recipient Presdl. Disting. Exec. rank, 1988. Fellow AAAS, Am. Statis. Assn. (pres. 1989), Royal Statis. Soc., Nat. Assn. Bus. Economists; mem. Am. Econ. Assn., Indsl. Rels. Rsch. Assn., Women's Caucus in Stats., Com. Status Women Econs. Profession, Internat. Statis. Inst., Internat. Assn. Ofcls. Stats., Nat. Acad. Pub. Adminstrn., Nat. Inst. Statis. Sci. (bd. trustees); mem. Cosmos Club (pres. 1995-96), Douglas Coll. Soc. Disting. Achievement. Home: Apt PH 21-D 5610 Wisconsin Ave Chevy Chase MD 20815-4415 Office: The Urban Inst 2100 M St NW Washington DC 20037

NORWOOD, SAMUEL WILKINS, III, diversified financial services company executive; b. Chgo., Apr. 6, 1941; s. Samuel Wilkins and Miriam Lois (Cary) N.; m. Julianne Parker Jones, Jun. 15, 1962 (div. Sept. 1981); children: Samuel Parker, Elizabeth Cary. Student, Vanderbilt U., 1959-61; BA, Tulane U., 1964; MBA, U. Chgo., 1965. Supr. spl. studies Allied Corp., N.Y.C., 1965-67; mgr. analysis and planning ITT Semiconductors Corp., West Palm Beach, Fla., 1967-69; dir. fin. planning Fuqua Industries, Atlanta, 1969-73, v.p. planning, 1976-81, v.p. corp devel., exec. asst. to chmn., 1981-89; pres., CEO, dir. Vista Resources, Inc., Atlanta, 1991—; cons., Atlanta, 1973-76. Founder N. Atlanta Mediation Ctr., 1972. Mem. Planning Execs. Inst. (bd. dirs. 1979-85, chmn. 1984-85, pres. Atlanta chpt. 1976-77), The Planning Forum (bd. dirs. 1985-87), Atlanta Yacht Club (bd. govs. 1984-87, commodore 1989), Allatoona Canoe and Sailing Club (commodore 1988-89), Assn. for Corp. Growth, Soc. Internat. Bus. Fellows, Ctr. for Puppetry Arts (bd. dirs.). Avocations: competitive sailing, skiing. Home: 42 Camden Rd NE Atlanta GA 30309-1508 Office: Vista Resources Inc Ste 5000 1201 W Peachtree St NW Atlanta GA 30309-3400

NOSANOW, BARBARA SHISSLER, art association administrator; b. Roanoke, Va.; d. Willis Morton and Kathryn Sabin (Bradford) Johnson; m. John Lewis Shissler Jr., July 28, 1957 (dec. May 1972); children: John Lewis Shissler III, Ada Holland Shissler; m. Lewis Harold Nosanow, Oct. 15, 1973. AB, Smith Coll., 1957; MA, Case Western Res. U., 1958. Asst. mng. editor Jour. Aesthetics and Art Criticism, Cleve. Mus. Art, 1958-63; dir. publs. and rsch. Mpls. Inst. Arts, 1963-72; dir. U. Minn. Gallery, Mpls., 1972-76; dir. exhbns. and edn. Nat. Archives, Washington, 1976-79; curator of edn. Smithsonian Instn., Washington, 1979-82; asst. dir. Nat. Mus. Am. Art, Smithsonian Instn., 1982-88; dir. Portland (Maine) Mus. Art, 1988-93, Art Spaces, 1993—. past mem. various rev. panels NEH, Washington. Bd. dirs. Md. Com. for Humanities, Balt., 1980-83. Mem. Internat. Women's Forum (Maine Women's Forum divsn.). Avocation: travel. Office: Art Spaces 23 Wildwood Cir Portland ME 04103

NOSEK, LAURA J., health facility administrator; b. Cleve.; d. LeRoy VanPelt and Florence Isabel (Acker) John; m. Frank Joseph Nosek, Sept. 9, 1961; children: Karin Beth, Kevin Bruce. Diploma in nursing, Grace New Haven Sch. Nursing, 1958; BSN, Case We. Res. U., 1961, MSN, 1981, PhD, 1986. RN, Vt. Adminstrv. nurse clin. U. Hosps. Cleve., dir. nursing mgmt. svcs.; asst. clin. prof. nursing Case Western Res. U., Cleve.; assoc. v.p. nursing and patient svcs. Med. Ctr. Hosp. Vt., Burlington, 1990-93, v.p. nursing and patient svcs., 1993-94; assoc. hosp. dir., nurse exec. Edward Hines Jr. V.A. Hosp., Hines, Ill., 1995—; adj. assoc. prof. nursing U. Vt., Loyola U., Chgo., 1996—; cons. Mt. Sinai Med. Ctr., N.Y.C. Contbr. articles to profl. jours. Mem. ANA, AONE, Nat. Commn. on Edn., NLN, Am. Nurses Found., Vt. Nurses Assn. (past pres.), Vt. Orgn. Nurse Execs. (past pres.), Sigma Theta Tau (Info. Resources Tech. award). Office: Edward Hines Jr VA Hosp PO Box 5000/118 Hines IL 60141

NOSTA, JOHN JAMES, advertising agency executive; b. Perth Amboy, N.J., Aug. 20, 1959; s. John Terrence and Rose (Cygan) N. BA, Boston U.,

1982. Sr. v.p. for creative and strategic devel. Lyons Lavey Nickel Swift Inc., N.Y.C., 1990—; bd. dirs. Acad. Pharms., Inc., Chgo.; lectr. sci., medicine and philosophy; guest lectr. CNN-TV, 1990, Sta. WOR, 1994. Contbr. articles to profl. jours. Pres. First Aid Squad, Perth Amboy Fire Dept., 1991-92. Recipient award N.J. Art Dirs., 1987, 88, spl. distinction award Rx Club, 1991, 92, 93, 94, In-Awe award for creative excellence, 1993. Home: 2025 Broadway Apt 21-H New York NY 10023 Office: Lyons Lavey Nickel Swift 488 Madison Ave New York NY 10022

NOSTRAND, HOWARD LEE, language and literature educator; b. N.Y.C., Nov. 16, 1910; s. Elijah H. and Ida Josephine (Maeder) N.; m. Frances Anne Levering, June 23, 1933 (div. Aug. 1967); children: David L., Richard L., Robert M.; m. Frances Helen Brewer, Aug. 9, 1967. BA, Amherst Coll., 1932; MA, Harvard U., 1933; D, l'Université de Paris, 1934. Tchr. U. Buffalo, 1934-36, U.S. Naval Acad., 1936-38, Brown U., 1938-39; prof. romance langs. U. Wash., Seattle, 1939-81, chmn. dept., 1939-64, prof. emeritus, 1981—; vis. prof. Coll. de France, 1975, Simon Fraser U., 1982.; Fulbright lectr., France, 1970-71; cons. Am. Coun. on Teaching Fgn. Langs., 1982, chair Nat. Commn. on Ethnography, 1974-80; Am. Assn. of Tchr. of French (pres.1960-62); Nat. Commn. Profl. Stds., 1986—; mem. Nat. Commn. on Profiency, 1986-93, mem., chair Nat. Commn. on Telematics, 1990-92; co-chair Nat. Commn. on Cultural Competence, 1992—; mem. Nat. Commn. Student Stds., 1993—; cons. Ednl. Testing Svc., 1988—. Author: Le Theatre Antique, 1934, Mission of the University, 1944, The Cultural Attaché, 1947, Research on Language Teaching...International Bibliography, 1962, 2d edit., 1965, The University and Human Understanding, 1963, Film-Recital of French Poems and Cultural Commentary, 1964, Background Data for the Teaching of French, 1967; (with others) La France en mutation, 1979, Savoir vivre en français, 1988, Databases: Our Third Technical Revolution, 1991, Acquiring Cross-Cultural Competence, 1996; contbr. articles to profl. jours. Bd. mem. Seattle Nantes Sister City Assn., 1980-90, pres., 1987-89; bd. mem. U.S. Com. for a Cmty. Democracies, 1983-92, hon. chair, Seattle, 1986-92. Guggenheim fellow, 1953-54; named Order of Sun Peru, 1947, French Govt. Palmes Académiques, 1950, Chevalier, Legion d'Honneur, 1962, Officer, 1994; recipient Pro Lingua award Wash. Assn. Fgn. Lang. Tchrs., 1977, award for leadership N.E. Conf. on Teaching Fgn. Langs., 1978, Nelson Brooks award Am. Coun. Teaching Fgn. Langs., 1980, Outstanding Pub. Svc. award U. Wash. Alumni, 1980, award for vision and leadership Vols. of Bonjour Seattle Festival, 1979-80. Mem. Assn. pour la recherche interculturelle (hon.). Democrat. Unitarian. Home: U Washington 18550 29th Ave NE Seattle WA 98155-4137

NOTARBARTOLO, ALBERT, artist; b. N.Y.C., Jan. 12, 1934; s. Leopold and Elvira (Caputo) N.; m. Valerie Cervelli, June 1, 1962. Student (scholar), Nat. Acad. Fine Arts, 1950; apprentice to mural painter, Ignacio LaRussa, 1951-53. Tchr., 1967—. Represented in permanent collections, Smithsonian Instn., Washington, Mus. Modern Art, N.Y.C.; one-man shows include Hemisphere Gallery of Time-Life Inc., 1973, U. P.R., 1966, David Gavin Gallery, Millerton, N.Y., 1993; exhibited group shows, Tate Gallery, London, 1965, Corcoran Gallery Art, Washington, 1968, Del. Art Mus., Wilmington, 1970, Mus. Modern Art, N.Y.C., 1971, 74, 76, Nat. Gallery Art, Washington, 1976, Smithsonian Instn., Washington, 1976, Santa Barbara (Calif.) Mus. Art, 1976, Taft Mus., Cin., Bell Gallery, Greenwich, Conn., 1977, Huntsville (Ala.) Mus. Art, 1978, Hokin Gallery, Palm Beach, Fla., 1982. Served with AUS, 1957-59. Recipient Nat. Community Art Competition award HUD, 1973; U.S. Bicentennial Flag Competition award, A Flag for the Moon, 1976. Mem. Nat. Soc. Lit. and the Arts. Home: 99 Battery Pl Apt 27H New York NY 10280-1329 *When I turned thirteen my Aunt Rosa Pucci gave me a gift—a small packet of reproductions of Raphael's paintings. On the overleaf she inscribed, "Art does affect the lives of men; it moves to ecstasy, thus giving colour and movement to what be otherwise a rather grey and trivial affair." The intonation of this phrase today makes me believe that an act of art echoes on, invoking a continuing music, a vitality for the future while all else turns into the dust of history.*

NOTARI, PAUL CELESTIN, communications executive; b. Chgo., Sept. 8, 1926; s. Peter and Mae Rose (Luvisi) N.; m. Marlene Fineman, Feb. 21, 1969; children: Cathy Notari Davidson, Kenneth, Sharon Notari Westover, Mindy Nielsen, Debbie McGrath. B.S. in Physics, DePaul U., 1952; M.S. in Comml. Sci., Rollins Coll., 1968. Mgr. publs. and tng. Motorola Inc., Chgo., 1952-65; supr., publs. engr. Martin Co., Orlando, Fla., 1966-67; dir. communications Bus. Equipment Mfrs. Assn., N.Y.C., 1967-70; dir. publs., pub. jour. Am. Water Works Assn., Denver, 1971-79; mgr. tech. info. Solar Energy Research Inst., Denver, 1979-91; pres. SciTech Communications, Inc., Denver, 1992—; lectr. bus. communications Northwestern U. Served with USNR, 1944-46. Mem. Assn. Computer Programmers and Analysts (founding pres. 1970-73), Soc. Tech. Writers and Pubs. (chmn. chpt. 1965-66), Am. Solar Energy Soc. (nat. chmn. 1990-91). Office: SciTech Comm Inc 1000 S Monaco Pky Ste 77 Denver CO 80224-1603 *In this complex world we live in, a nation lives or dies by its technological achievements, made possible by a steady flow of information between scientists, engineers, technicians and producers. I believe I have made a significant contribution on this behalf.*

NOTARIS, MARY, lawyer; b. Bklyn., Aug. 20, 1962; d. Antonio Frank and Marie Nancy (Ruggiero) N.; children: Jaime Marie Defelice-Notaris, Jason Stephen Defelice-Notaris. BA in English, Northeastern U., 1988; JD, Franklin Pierce, 1991. Bar: Maine 1992, N.H. 1993, Mass. 1993. Store mgr. Party Supreme, Billenca, Mass., 1980-94; law clk. Sheehan, Phinney, Bass & Green, Manchester, N.H., 1990; jud. law clk. U.S. Dist. Ct. N.H., Concord, 1990-91, Superior Ct. N.H., Manchester, 1991-92; of counsel Trianta Fillou & Guerin, Cambridge, Mass., 1992-94; pres. Mary Notaris, Atty. at Law PC, Salem, N.H., 1994—; bd. dirs. N.H. Aids Found., Manchester. Mem. Exch. Club Salem (sec. 1994—). Office: 14 Stiles Rd Ste 101 Salem NH 03079-2883

NOTARO, MICHAEL R., data processing and computer service executive; b. Chgo., Nov. 1, 1914; s. Anthony and Felicia (Franzese) N.; m. Irene Hapsude, May 5, 1936 (dec.); children: Michael R., Phyllis Ann; m. Ruth Bostrom, Mar. 10, 1984. Student, Northwestern U. Sch. Commerce, 1930-36, Chgo. Law Sch., 1930-32; LL.D., DePaul U. dir. St. Paul Fed. Savs. Bank. Bd. dirs. Cath. Charities of Archdiocese of Chgo., Boys Clubs Chgo., Loyola U.; trustee De Paul U. Decorated knight Malta, knight St. Gregory, Knight comdr. Order Merit Italy). Roman Catholic (lay trustee). Clubs: Union League, Mid-Am., Tavern, Chgo. Athletic Assn. (Chgo.); Butterfield Country (Hinsdale, Ill.). Home & Office: 1400 Bonnie Brae River Forest IL 60305-1202

NOTEBAERT, RICHARD C., telecommunications industry executive; b. 1947; married. With Wisconsin Bell, 1969-83; v.p. marketing and operations Ameritech, Chicago, 1983-86; pres. Ameritech Mobile Comm., 1986-89, Indiana Bell Telephone Co., 1989-92; pres. Ameritech Services, 1992-93, pres., COO, 1993-94; chmn., pres., CEO Ameritech Corp., Chicago, 1994—. Office: Ameritech Corp 30 S Wacker Dr Chicago IL 60606-7402

NOTHERN, MARJORIE CAROL, nursing administrator; b. Bonners Ferry, Idaho, June 23, 1936; d. Carl John and Ione Faye (Hobson) Frank; m. Abbott Burton Squire, Dec. 15, 1956 (div. Aug. 5, 1972); m. William Thomas Nothern, Aug. 5, 1972. Diploma, Deaconess Hosp. Sch. Nursing, Spokane, Wash., 1956; BA, Stephens Coll., Columbia, Mo., 1981; MBA, Golden Gate U., San Francisco, 1987. Relief head nurse Deaconess Hosp., Spokane, Wash., 1956-57; staff nurse Kadlec Meth. Hosp., Richland, Wash., 1957-58, Southern Pacific Hosp., San Francisco, 1958-59; relief evening supr. The Gen. Hosp., Eureka, Calif., 1959-60; med. office nurse Ely & Davis, Eureka, Calif., 1960-66; head nurse Redbud Cmty. Hosp., Clear Lake, Calif., 1968-72, dir. nurses, 1972-77; supr. Hosp. Nursing Kaiser Found. Hosp., Martinez, Calif., 1977-78; dir. med. ctr. nursing Kaiser Permanente Med. Ctr., Richmond, Calif., 1978-80; asst. hosp. administr. Kaiser Found. Hosp., Hayward, Calif., 1980-94; assoc. M2, Inc., San Francisco, 1996—. Mem. health sci. adv. commn. Ohlone Coll., Fremont, Calif., 1980-94; mem. med. aux. and nursing adv. com. Chabot Coll., Hayward, Calif., 1980-94; mem. Grad. Coll. Nursing adv. bd. San Francisco State U., 1986—. Recipient Leadership award Sigma Theta Tau, Alpha Gamma, San Jose State U., 1990. Mem. ANA-Calif., Orgn. Nurse Execs.-Calif., East Bay Orgn. Nurse Execs., Assistance League Diablo Valley, Blackhawk Country Club, Blackhawk Bus. Women, Blackhawk Garden Club, Sigma Theta Tau., Alpha Gamma, Nu Xi. Republican. Avocations: philately, gardening. Office: 363 Jacaranda Dr Danville CA 94506-2124

NOTHMANN, GERHARD ADOLF, retired engineering executive, research engineer; b. Berlin, Germany, Dec. 9, 1921; came to U.S., 1939, naturalized, 1944; s. Rudolf and Margarete (Caro) N.; m. Charlotte Braude, June 21, 1943; children—Joyce Anne, Ruth Ellen, Barbara Fay. B.S. in Mech. Engring, Purdue U., 1942, M.S. in Mech. Engring, 1942; Ph.D., Cornell U., 1948. Tchr. machine design and kinematics Cornell U., 1942-44, 46-48, instr., 1942-44, 46-48, asst. prof., 1948; engr. for design spl. bindery R. R. Donnelley & Sons, 1946-47; research engr. Armour Research Found., Ill. Inst. Tech., Chgo., 1948-59; successively asst. supr., asst. chmn., chmn., mgr. dept. mech. engring. research Armour Research Found., Ill. Inst. Tech., 1952-59; dir. creative and devel. engring. Miehle div. Miehle-Goss-Dexter, Inc., 1959-62, dir. research and devel., 1962-64, dir. engring., 1964-67, dir. tech. research, 1967-68; dir. engring. Robertson Photo-Mechanix, Inc., 1968-69, v.p. engring., 1969-71; chief engr. duplicators Addressograph Multigraph Corp., 1971-77; dir. engring. Visual Graphics Corp., Tamarac, Fla., 1977-79; prin. engr. Xerox Corp., Pasadena, Calif., 1979-89, ret., 1989; chmn. mechanics colloquim Ill. Inst. Tech., 1953-54; mem. adv. com. Graphic Arts Tech. Found. Author: Nonimpact Printing, 1989. Pres. bd. dirs. Wilmette United Fund, 1963; mem. Wilmette Sch. Bd., 1968-74; pres. Pasadena Jewish Temple and Ctr., 1989-91. With USNR, 1944-46. Named one of six outstanding young men in Chgo. area. Chgo. Jr. Assn. Commerce and Industry, 1954. Mem. ASME, Am. Soc. Engring. Edn., Tech. Assn. for Graphic Arts, Jewish Geneal. Soc. of L.A., Sigma Xi, Tau Beta Pi, Pi Tau Sigma. Home: 3760 Edgeview Dr Pasadena CA 91107-1309

NOTHMANN, RUDOLF S., legal researcher; b. Hamburg, Fed. Republic of Germany, Feb. 4, 1907; came to U.S., 1941, naturalized, 1943; s. Nathan and Henrietta G. (Heymann) N. Referendar, U. Hamburg, 1929, PhD in Law, 1932; postgrad. U. Liverpool Law Sch. (Eng.), 1931-32. Law clk. Hamburg Cts., 1929-31, 32-33; export, legal adviser, adviser ocean marine ins. various firms, Ger., Eng., Sweden, Calif., 1933-43, 46-47; instr. fgn. exchange, fgn. trade Extension div. UCLA, 1947-48, vis. assoc. prof. UCLA, 1951; asst. prof. econs. Whittier Coll., 1948-50, assoc. prof., 1950-51; contract work U.S. Air Force, U.S. Navy, 1953-59; contract negotiator space projects, space and missile systems orgn. USAF, L.A., 1959-77; pvt. researcher in internat. comml. law, Pacific Palisades, Calif., 1977—; pres. Hanseatic Devel. Corp., Pacific Palisades, Calif., 1989—. With U.S. Army, 1943-45; ETO. Recipient Gold Tape award Air Force Systems Command, 1970. Mem. Internat. Bar Assn. (vice chmn. internat. sales and related comml. trans. com. 1977-82), Am. Econ. Assn., Calif. Bar Assn. (internat. law sect.), Am. Soc. Internat. Law, Uebersee Club (Hamburg, Germany). Author: The Insurance Certificate in International Ocean Marine Insurance Law and Foreign Trade, 1932; The Oldest Corporation in the World: Six Hundred Years of Economic Evolution, 1949. Home: PO Box 32 Pacific Palisades CA 90272-0032

NOTKIN, LEONARD SHELDON, architect; b. N.Y.C., Apr. 1, 1931; s. Murry and Evelyn (Mofshatz) N.; m. Ann Mathilda Stefanko, Nov. 24, 1956; children: Jennifer, Mead. BArch, U. Pa., 1954. Registered architect, N.Y., Mass., Ohio, Pa., Nat. Coun. Archtl. Registration Bds. Architect, Percival Goodman (Architect), N.Y.C., 1956-58; Architect Bloch and Hesse (Architects), N.Y.C., 1958-59, Resnick and Green (Architects), N.Y.C., 1959-60; architect, prin., v.p. The Architects Collaborative, Inc., Cambridge, Mass., 1960-95; chief design critic Boston Archtl. Center, 1964-69; mem. Lexington (Mass.) Design Adv. Com., 1970-73, chmn., 1972; profl. studio critic Harvard Grad. Sch. Design, 1974-76; pres. Boston Design Assocs., Inc., Waltham, Mass., 1995—. Major recent works include Intermediate Sch. 137, Bronx, N.Y., 1976, Visual Arts Instructional Facility SUNY, Purchase, 1976, Lahey Clinic Med. Ctr., Burlington, Mass., 1976—, W. Penn Hosp., Pitts., 1977, St. Francis/St. George Hosp., Cin., 1978, Blue Cross/Blue Shield of Conn. Hdqrs., North Haven, Temple U. Hosp., Phila., composite hosp. Loring AFB, Linestone, Maine, Med. Facilities, Fort Drum, N.Y., Health Care Internat. Ltd., Glasgow, Scotland, Intensive Care Hosp. and Hotel, Univ. Ky. Cancer Rsch. Ctr., Children's Hosp. Med. Ctr. Rsch. Lab., Cin., new main entrance, lobby and admissions facilities Hosp. of U. Pa., Phila., Childrens Hosp., Kuwait, 1996, Health Facilities, Algiers, Algeria, 1996. Served with U.S. Army, 1954-56. Recipient Design award for IBM Hdqrs., Gaithersburg, Md. Progressive Architecture mag., 1964; 1st pl. award for Worcester (Mass.) Community Center AIA, 1966; Design award for Worcester Found. Exptl. Biology bldg. Mass. chpt. AIA, 1968; Design award NIH Research Lab., Bethesda, Md. GSA, 1972; Best Bldg. of Yr. award for Norwalk (Conn.) High Sch. Assn. for Better Community Design, 1972; Honor award Conn. Soc. Architects AIA, 1974. Mem. AIA, Mass. State Assn. Architects, Boston Soc. Architects (dir. 1976-79, spl. design citation 1993). Office: Boston Design Assocs Inc 393 Totten Pond Rd Waltham MA 02159

NOTO, LUCIO R., gas and oil industry executive; b. 1939. With Mobil Corp., 1962—; pres. Mobil Saudi Arabia, 1981-85, chmn., 1985-86; v.p. planning and econs. Mobil Corp./Mobil Oil Corp., 1986-88, CFO, 1989-93, pres., 1993—, chmn. bd., CEO, COO, 1994—. Office: Mobil Corp 3225 Gallows Rd Fairfax VA 22031-4872*

NOTOPOULOS, ALEXANDER ANASTASIOS, JR., lawyer; b. Altoona, Pa., Jan. 29, 1953; s. Alexander Anastasios Sr. and Christine (Economou) N.; m. Alexis J. Anderson, Aug. 4, 1984. BA, Amherst Coll., 1974; JD, Harvard U., 1977. Bar: Mass. 1978, U.S. Dist. Ct. Mass. 1979. Law clk. to judge U.S. Ct. Appeals (3d cir.), Phila., 1977-78; assoc. Sullivan & Worcester, Boston, 1978-85, ptnr., 1985—. Home: 96 Shornecliffe Rd Newton MA 02158-2421 Office: Sullivan & Worcester One Post Office Sq Boston MA 02109

NOTTAY, BALDEV KAUR, microbiologist; b. Nairobi, Kenya, East Africa, Jan. 15, 1936; d. Santa Singh and Swaran (Kaur) N. B.S. with honors, U. Bombay, 1960; M.Sc., U. Bombay, 1964. Research student Polio Research Unit, Haffkine Inst., Bombay, India, 1962-63; assoc. head poliovirus research Virology Dept., Med. Research Lab., Nairobi, 1964-71; vis. assoc. viral reagents Ctrs. Disease Control, Atlanta, 1972-74, vis. assoc. enteric virology br., 1974-78, research microbiologist molecular biology section, respiratory and enterovirus br., div. viral and rickettsial diseases, 1978—. Contbr. articles to profl. jours. Home: 5574 Wylstream St Norcross GA 30093-4153 Office: 1600 Clifton Rd NE Atlanta GA 30329-4018

NOTTINGHAM, EDWARD WILLIS, JR., federal judge; b. Denver, Jan. 9, 1948; s. Edward Willis and Willie Newton (Gullett) N.; m. Cheryl Ann Card, June 6, 1970 (div. Feb. 1981); children: Amelia Charlene, Edward Willis III; m. Janis Ellen Chapman, Aug. 18, 1984; 1 child, Spencer Chapman. AB, Cornell U., 1969; JD, U. Colo., 1972. Bar: Colo. 1972, U.S. Dist. Ct. Colo. 1972, U.S. Ct. Appeals (10th cir.) 1973. Law clk. to presiding judge U.S. Dist. Ct. Colo., Denver, 1972-73; assoc. Sherman & Howard, Denver, 1973-76, 78-80, ptnr., 1980-87; ptnr. Beckner & Nottingham, Grand Junction, Colo., 1987-89; asst. U.S. atty. U.S. Dept. Justice, Denver, 1976-78; U.S. dist. judge Dist. of Colo., Denver, 1989—. Bd. dirs. Beaver Creek Met. Dist., Avon, Colo., 1980-88, Justice Info. Ctr., Denver, 1985-87, 21st Jud. Dist. Victim Compensation Fund, Grand Junction, Colo., 1987-89. Mem. ABA, Colo. Bar Assn. (chmn. criminal law sect. 1983-85, chmn. ethics com. 1988-89), Order of Coif, Denver Athletic Club, Delta Sigma Rho, Tau Kappa Alpha. Episcopalian. Office: US Dist Ct 1929 Stout St Denver CO 80294-2900

NOTTINGHAM, ROBINSON KENDALL, life insurance company executive; b. Balt., Apr. 4, 1938; s. Robinson Jr. and Juliet (Moore) N.; m. Elizabeth LeViness, Aug. 26, 1960; children: Robinson Kendall Jr., Charles Denmead. BA in Polit. Sci., Johns Hopkins U., 1959; postgrad., Johns Hopkins U., Washington, 1965. With Am. Internat. Group, Inc., Hong Kong and Bangkok, 1968-71; chief exec. officer for Japan and Korea Am. Internat. Group, Inc., Tokyo, 1986-89; mng. dir. Hanover Ins. Co., Universal Ins. Co., Bangkok, 1971-73, Am. Internat. Ins. Co., Lagos, Nigeria, 1973-75; regional pres. African div. Am. Internat. Underwriters, N.Y.C., 1975-78, Middle Ea. div., 1978-83, European div., 1983-86; chmn., bd. dirs., CEO Am. Life Ins. Co., Wilmington, Del., 1989—; bd. dirs. AIG Overseas Fin. (Japan) Inc., Tokyo, Am. Home Assurance Co., N.Y.C., AIU Ins. Co., N.Y.C. Pres. USO Coun., Tokyo, 1987-89; mem. world bd. govs. USO, Washington, 1987—; mem. adv. coun. Johns Hopkins U. Sch. Advanced Internat. Studies, Washington, 1984—, Reischauer Ctr. Japan Studies, Washington, 1986—. Served to lt. comdr. USNR, 1960-68. Mem. Princeton Club (N.Y.C.), Short Hills Club (N.J.), Bay Head Yacht Club (N.J.), Baltusrol Club (Springfield, N.J.), Chevy Chase (Md.) Club, Delta Phi. Republican. Episcopalian. Avocation: sailing. Home: 393 Charlton Ave South Orange NJ 07079-2405 Office: Am Life Ins Co 1 Alico Plz Wilmington DE 19899

NOTTINGHAM, WILLIAM JESSE, church mission executive, minister; b. Sharon, Pa., Nov. 22, 1927; s. Jess William and Alice May (Green) N.; m. Patricia Clutts, Feb. 1, 1949; children: Theodore Jess, Deborah Joan Selke, Nancy Alice, Gregory Philip. BA, Bethany Coll., W.Va., 1949, DD (hon.), 1987; BD, Union Theol. Sem., N.Y.C., 1953; PhD, Columbia U., 1962; DD (hon.), Christian Theol. Sem., Indpls., 1984. Ordained to ministry Christian Ch. (Disciples of Christ), Oct. 21, 1945. Pastor Ch. of Christ, Canoe Camp and Covington, Pa., 1949-50; field worker Ch. of the Master, N.Y.C., 1950-53; assoc. min. Nat. City Christian Ch., Washington, 1954-58; fraternal worker Coun. on Christian Unity, France, 1958-65; with CIMADE and Centre de Glay; with youth dept. World Coun. of Chs., Geneva, 1965-68; exec. sec. for Latin Am. and Caribbean Divsn. Overseas Ministries, Christian Ch. (Disciples of Christ and United Ch. Christ), Indpls., 1968-76, exec. sec. East Asia and Pacific, 1976-83, pres., 1984-94; affiliate prof. mission Christian Theol. Sem., 1995—. Author: Chriatian Faith and Secular Action: An Introduction to the Life and Thought of Jacques Maritain, 1968, The Practice and Preaching of Liberation, 1986, The Social Ethics of Martin Bucer, 1491-1551; translator: God's Underground, 1970, Prayer at the Heart of Life, 1975, Materialist Approaches to the Bible, 1985, Madeleine Barot, 1991. Fulbright scholar, Strasbourg, France, 1953-54. Mem. Nat. Coun. Chs. of Christ in USA (gen. bd.), Assn. Disciples for Theol. Discussion, Christians Associated for Relations with Eastern Europe. Democrat.

NOTZ, JOHN KRANZ, JR., arbitrator and mediator, retired lawyer; b. Chgo., Jan. 5, 1932; s. John Kranz and Elinor (Trostel) N.; m. Janis Wellin, Apr. 23, 1966; children: Jane Elinor, John Wellin. BA, Williams Coll., 1953; JD, Northwestern U., 1956. Bar: Ill. 1956, Fla. 1957, Wis. 1989, U.S. Supreme Ct. 1960. Assoc. 1st Nat. Bank Chgo., 1954, 1956; from assoc. to ptnr. Gardner, Carton & Douglas, Chgo., 1960-95, of counsel, 1990-95; ret., 1996; arbitrator, mediator CPR Inst. for Dispute Resolution, Am. Arbitration Assn., Nat. Assn. Securities Dealers, Nat. Futures Assn., N.Y. Stock Exch., Am. Stock Exch. Contbr. numerous articles to profl. jours. Sec. State Corp. Acts Adv. Com., 1982-95, chmn., 1987-89; bd. dirs., pres. Chgo. Lit. Club; bd. dirs. Ill. Inst. Continuing Legal Edn., 1980-91, chmn., 1990-91; bd. dirs., treas. Inspired Ptnrs.; bd. trustees Graceland Cemetery, Beloit Coll. 1st lt. USAF, 1957-60. Recipient Svc. award Northwestern U., 1978. Fellow Am. Bar Found., Ill. Bar Found.; mem. Am. Law Inst., Ill. State Bar Assn., Chgo. Bar Assn., Fla. Bar Assn., Wis. State Bar, Law and Legal Clubs City Chgo., Racquet Club Chgo., John Evans Club (Northwestern U. bd. dirs.), Lake Geneva Country Club, Mid-Day Club (Chgo., bd. trustees), Literary and Caxton Clubs (Chgo., bd. dirs.). Office: c/o Gardner Carton & Douglas 3300 Quaker Tower 321 N Clark St Chicago IL 60610-4714

NOVA, CRAIG, writer; b. Los Angeles, July 5, 1945; s. Karl and Elizabeth (Sinclair) N.; m. Christina Barnes, July 2, 1977; children: Abigail, Tate. B.A., U. Calif.-Berkeley, 1967; M.F.A., Columbia U., 1969. Author: Turkey Hash, 1972, The Geek, 1975, Incandescence, 1978, The Good Son, 1982, The Congressman's Daughter, 1986, Tornado Alley, 1989, Trombone, 1992, The Book of Dreams, 1994. Recipient Harper-Saxton prize Harper and Row, Pubs., 1972; recipient award in lit. Am. Acad. and Inst. Arts and Letters; Guggenheim Found. fellow, 1977; fellow Nat. Endowment for Arts, 1973, Nat. Endowment for Arts, 1975, Creative Artists Pub. Service, 1976; NEA fellow, 1985; story included in Best Am. Short Stories, 1987.

NOVACEK, JAY MCKINLEY, professional football player; b. Martin, S.D., Oct. 24, 1962. BS in Indsl. Edn., U. Wyoming, 1986. With St. Louis Cardinals, 1985-87, Phoenix Cardinals (formerly St. Louis Cardinals), 1988-89; tight end Dallas Cowboys, 1990—; player Pro Bowl, 1991-93, Super Bowl XXVII, 1992, XXVIII, 1993. Office: Dallas Cowboys 1 Cowboys Pky Irving TX 75063-4945

NOVACEK, MICHAEL JOHN, curator, museum administrator; b. Evanston, Ill., June 3, 1948; s. Albin John and June Shirley (White) N.; m. Vera Ellen Novacek, June 19, 1971; 1 child, Julie. BA in Zoology, UCLA, 1971; MA in Biology, San Diego State U., 1973; PhD in Paleontology with honors, U. Calif., Berkeley, 1978. Lectr. dept. zoology San Diego State U., 1976-77, asst. prof., 1977-79, assoc. prof., 1979-82; asst. curator dept. vertebrate paleontology Am. Mus. Natural History, N.Y.C., 1983-85, chmn., 1983-89, assoc. curator, 1985-89, curator, 1989—, v.p., dean sci., 1989—; v.p., provost sci., 1994—; adj. prof. San Diego State U., 1982—; panel mem. systematic biology program NSF, 1986-90, mem. bioadv. com., 1992—; adj. prof. dept. biology CUNY, 1987—; chmn. biospherics com. Yale U., New Haven, 1993—; expedition leader, Wyo., Mex., Chile, Mongolia; lectr. in field. Editor: Extinction and Phylogeny, 1992, Mammal Phylogeny, 1993; contbr. over 100 articles to profl. jours. Grantee Nat. Geog. Soc., 1985-86, 88-90, Eppley Found., 1986-88, NSF, 1989-95, Sloan Found., 1990, Internat. Rsch. and Exch. Bd.; Nat. Needs postdoctoral fellow NSF, 1979-80. Fellow Explorer's Club; mem. AAAS (bd. dirs. 1995—), Soc. Study Evolution, Soc. Systematic Biologists (pres. 1992-93), Systematics Agenda 2000 (co-chair 1992—). Avocations: music, climbing, cycling, skiing, art. Office: Am Mus Natural History Central Park West at 79th New York NY 10024

NOVACK, ALVIN JOHN, physician; b. Red Lodge, Mont., Mar. 11, 1925; s. John and Anna Geraldine (Maddio) N.; m. Betty P. Novack, Jan. 10, 1952; children—Vance, Deborah, Michelle, Mitchel, Craig, Brad, Mary Ellen, Garth. M.D., U. Wash., 1952. Intern Harper Hosp., Detroit, 1952; resident in surgery Harper Hosp., 1953; resident in otolaryngology Johns Hopkins U., 1954-57; resident in surgery Columbia-Presbyn. Med. Center, N.Y.C., 1957-60; fellow head and neck surgery Columbia-Presbyn. Med. Center, 1957-60; dir. head and neck surgery Swedish Hosp., Seattle, 1960-91; dir. otolaryngology Children's Orthopedic Hosp., Seattle, 1965-78; ret., 1991. Contbr. articles to med. jours. Served to lt. AUS, 1940-43. Nat. Cancer Inst. fellow, 1957-60. Fellow A.C.S.; mem. AMA, Am. Acad. Otolaryngology and Head and Neck Surgery, Soc. Head and Neck Surgeons, North Pacific Surg. Assn., Pacific Coast Surg. Assn., Seattle Surg. Soc.

NOVACKY, ANTON JAN, plant pathologist, educator; b. Bratislava, Czechoslovakia, June 3, 1933; came to U.S., 1968; s. Jan Martin and Katarina (Fischer) N.; m. Dorothy Edit Hyross, June 28, 1958; children: Andrea Novacky Congdon, Thomas Martin. Student, Charles U., Prague, Czechoslovakia; BS, Comenius U., Bratislava, 1955, MS, 1956; PhD, Czechoslovak Acad. Sci., Prague, 1965. Postgrad. fellow U. Moscow, Russia, 1964; postdoctoral fellow U. Ky., Lexington, 1966-69; postdoctoral rsch. assoc. U. Mo., Columbia, 1969-70, asst. prof., 1970-74, assoc. prof., 1974-82, prof., 1982—; rsch. phytopathologist Inst. Exptl. Phytopathology and Entomology, Bratislava, Czechoslovakia, 1962-68. Author: (with R.N. Goodman) The Hypersensitive Reaction in Plants to Pathogens, 1994; speaker various seminars and meeting presentations; contbr. articles to profl. jours. Grantee NSF, 1986-89, 1978-82, USDA, 1978-83, 93-95, MSMC, 1986-89; fellow Japanese Soc. for Promotion of Sci. Rsch., 1984; recipient German Academic Exch. award, 1976, Alexander von Humboldt Sr. U.S. Scientist, 1983. Mem. AAAS, Am. Phytopathol. Soc. (fellow 1986, chair 1984-85), Am. Soc. Plant Physiologists, Sigma Xi. Roman Catholic. Home: 311 Crown Pt Columbia MO 65203-2202 Office: U Mo Agriculture Bldg 3-18 Columbia MO 65211

NOVAK, ALFRED, retired biology educator; b. Chgo., Jan. 28, 1915; s. Phillip and Celia (Kaplan) N.; m. Helen Ascher, Feb. 19, 1944 (dec. Oct. 20, 1985); children—Paul, Gregory, David. A.A., U. Chgo., 1934, B.S., 1936; M.S., 1941; M.Ed., Chgo. Tchrs. Coll., 1940; Ph.D., Mich. State U., 1950. Mem. faculty Mich. State U., 1945-61, asso. prof. biology, 1951-55, prof., 1955-61; sci. coordinator, prof. emeritus biology Stephens Coll., Columbia, Mo., 1961-80; prof. biology div. U. Mo., Columbia, 1980-81; cons., writer Biol. Sci. Curriculum Study, Boulder, Colo., 1960-61; cons. sci. curriculum, facilities planning for colls. and univs., 1955—; heart damage research U. Bologna (Italy) Med. Sch., 1972; bd. dirs. Allied Health Programs. Adv. biology editor, writer: Ency. Americana, 1959-69. Served with USAAF, 1941-44. Recipient Favilli medal Istituto di Patologia Generale, Bologna,

1972; Guggenheim fellow Cambridge (Eng.) U., 1957-58; NIH fellow Cal. Inst. Tech., 1950. Mem. Am. Assn. Gen. Liberal Edn. (past pres.), Nat. Assn. Biology Tchrs., AAAS. Discovered cold pack treatment for mumps orchitis, 1945. Home: 4954 W 60th Ter Mission KS 66205-3079 *I have lived through two major wars, the 1929 depression, the turbulent 60's, distressing inflation of the 70's and rejuvenation in the early 80's. I am dismayed with bureaucratic waste, the decay in character, honesty & morality. I am also appalled by the ineptitude of the U.S. judicial system. There are too many laws and too many corrupt lawyers. Our freedoms are being eroded, yet democracy is still the greatest hope of the world.*

NOVAK, BARBARA, art history educator; b. N.Y.C.; d. Joseph and Sadie (Kaufman) N.; m. Brian O'Doherty, July 5, 1960. B.A., Barnard Coll., 1951; M.A., Radcliffe Coll., 1953, Ph.D., 1957. TV instr. Mus. Fine Arts, Boston, 1957-58; mem. faculty Barnard Coll., Columbia U., N.Y.C., 1958—; prof. art history Barnard Coll., Columbia U., 1970—, Helen G. Altschul prof., 1984—; adv. council Archives of Am. Art, NAD. Author: American Painting of the 19th Century, 1969, Nature and Culture, 1980, The Thyssen-Bornemisza Collection 19th Century American Painting, 1986, Alice's Neck, 1987, The Ape and the Whale, 1995, (play) The Ape and the Whale: Darwin and Melville in Their Own Words, 1987 (performed at Symphony Space 1987), Dreams and Shadows: Thomas H. Hotchkiss in 19th Century Italy, 1993; co-editor: Next to Nature, 1980; mem. editorial bd. Am. Art Jour. Commr. Nat. Portrait Gallery; trustee N.Y. Hist. Soc. Fulbright fellow Belgium, 1953-54; Guggenheim fellow, 1974; Nat. Book Critics nominee, 1980; Los Angeles Times Book Award nominee, 1980; Am. Book Award paperback nominee, 1981. Fellow Soc. Am. Historians, Phila. Atheneum; mem. Soc. Am. Historians, Am. Antiquarian Soc., Coll. Art Assn. (dir. 1974-77), N.Y. Hist. Soc. (trustee), PEN. Office: Barnard Coll Art History Dept 606 W 120th St New York NY 10027-5706

NOVAK, DAVID, Judaic studies educator, rabbi; b. Chgo., Aug. 19, 1941; s. Syd and Sylvia (Wien) N.; m. Melva Ziman, July 3, 1963; children: Marianne, Jacob George. AB in Classics and Ancient History, U. Chgo., 1961; M in Hebrew Lit., Jewish Theol. Sem. Am., 1964; PhD, Georgetown U., 1971. Ordained rabbi, 1966. Rabbi Shaare Tikvah Congregation, 1966-69; dir. Jewish chaplaincy St. Elizabeth's Hosp., 1966-69; rabbi Emanuel Synagogue, Oklahoma City, 1969-72, Beth Tfiloh Congregation, Balt., 1972-77, Congregation Beth El, Norfolk, Va., 1977-81, Congregation Darchay Noam, Far Rockaway, N.Y., 1981-89; Edgar M. Bronfman prof. modern Judaic studies U. Va., Charlottesville, 1989—; lectr. philosophy Oklahoma City U., 1969-72, New Sch. for Social Rsch., 1982-84; lectr. Jewish studies Balt. Hebrew Coll., 1972-77; adj. asst. prof. philosophy Old Dominion U., 1977-81; vis. assoc. prof. Talmud Jewish Theol. Sem. Am., 1986-88; adj. assoc. prof. Baruch Coll., CUNY, 1984-88, adj. prof., 1989; founder, v.p., coord. panel Halakhic Inquiry Union Traditional Judaism/Inst. Traditional Judaism; disting. vis. prof. religion and corp. ethics Drew U., 1995. Contbg. editor Sh'ma, First Things. Sec.-treas. Inst. on Religion and Pub. Life. Essay winner Hyman G. Enelow prize Jewish Theol. Sem. Am., 1975; recipient Rabbi Jacob B. Augus award Jewish Theol. Sem. Am., 1984; Woodrow Wilson Internat. Ctr. for Scholars fellow, 1992-93. Fellow Acad. for Jewish Philosophy; mem. Am. Theol. Soc., Assn. for Jewish Studies, Am. Acad. Religion, Jewish Law Assn., Leo Baeck Inst. Home: 5311 Cutshaw Ave Richmond VA 23226-1105 Office: U Va Dept Religious Studies Cocke Hall Charlottesville VA 22903-3281

NOVAK, EDWARD FRANK, lawyer; b. Berwyn, Ill., Sept. 25, 1947; s. Edward F. and Myrtle L. (Weese) N.; 1 child, Jay P. BA, Knox Coll., 1969; JD, DePaul U., 1976. Bar: Ill. 1976, Ariz. 1979, D.C. 1985. Assoc. Coffield, Ungaretti & Harris, Chgo., 1976-79, Jordan Green, P.C., Phoenix, 1979-81; assoc. Lewis and Roca, Phoenix, 1981-83, ptnr., 1983—. Sgt. U.S. Army, 1969-72, Vietnam. Mem. State Bar Ariz. (vice chmn. criminal justice sect. 1985, chmn. 1986-88). Office: Lewis and Roca 40 N Central Ave Ste 1900 Phoenix AZ 85004-4424*

NOVAK, HARRY R., manufacturing company executive; b. Chgo., Sept. 30, 1951; s. Edward M. and Rose (Loncar) N.; m. Shawn Sternquist, Sept. 7, 1975; children: Andrea, Jacob, Bethany. BS in Econs., MacMurray Coll., Jacksonville, Ill., 1973; MBA in Fin., DePaul U., 1977. Ops. mgr. to v.p., regional mgr. Heller Fin. Inc., Chgo., 1974-87; v.p. Golenberg & Assocs., Cleve., 1987-88; sr. v.p., CFO Gibson-Homans Co., Twinsburg, Ohio, 1988—. Congregation pres. First Luth. Ch., Strongsville, Ohio, 1987-92; founder Strongsville Area Youth Group, 1992; mem. Strongsville Choral Boosters, 1991-94. Mem. Cleve. Growth Assn. Avocations: chess, golf, pocket billards, computers. Office: Gibson-Homans Co 1755 Enterprise Pky Twinsburg OH 44087-2203

NOVAK, JOSEPH DONALD, science educator, knowlege studies specialist; b. Mpls., Dec. 2, 1930; s. Joseph Daniel and Anna (Podany) N.; m. Joan Owen, July 18, 1953; children: Joseph Mark, Barbara Joan, William John. BS, U. Minn., 1952, MA, 1954, PhD, 1958. Teaching asst. U. Minn., Mpls., 1952-56, instr., 1956-57; asst. prof. Kans. State Tchrs. Coll., 1957-59; asst. prof. Purdue U., West Lafayette, Ind., 1959-62, assoc. prof., 1962-67; prof. Cornell U., Ithaca, N.Y., 1967-95, prof. emeritus, 1995—; knowledge constrn. and orgn. cons. to Procter & Gamble and other cos.; cons. to over 300 schs. and colls., 1975—; vis. fellow Harvard U., 1965-66; disting. vis. prof. U. N.C., Wilmington, 1980, U. Western Fla., 1987-88; vis. prof. U. South Fla., 1995. Author: Learning How to Learn, 1984, in 10 langs. 1984-96, Educational Psychology: A Cognitive View, 1978, A Theory of Education, 1977, 15 others; contbr. over 100 articles to profl. jours. Fellow Tozer Found., Lydia Anderson, 1955-56; research assoc. Harvard U., 1965-66; Fulbright-Hayes Sr. Scholar, Australia, 1980. Fellow AAAS (sec. sect. Q); mem. APA, Am. Inst. Biol. Scis., Nat. Sci. Tchrs. Assn., Nat. Assn. Rsch. in Sci. Teaching (Outstanding Contbns. Sci. Teaching Through Rsch. award 1990), Nat. Assn. Biology Tchrs., Assn. for Edn. of Tchrs. of Sci., Am. Ednl. Rsch. Assn., Sigma Xi. Avocations: hiking; swimming; dancing; music. Home: 1403 Slaterville Rd Ithaca NY 14850-6207 Office: Cornell U Dept Edn Kennedy Hall Ithaca NY 14853

NOVAK, JULIE COWAN, nursing educator, researcher, clinician; b. Peoria, Ill., Oct. 2, 1950; m. Robert E. Novak, 1972; children: Andrew, Christopher, Nicholas. BS in Nursing, U. Iowa, 1972, MA in Nursing of Children, 1976; D.N.Sc., U. San Diego, 1989. RN, Va., Calif. Charge nurse surg. and med. ICU U. Iowa Hosp. and Clinics, 1972-73; instr. med. sur. nursing St. Luke's Sch. Nursing, Cedar Rapids, Iowa, 1973-74; instr. family and cmty. health U. Iowa Coll. of Nursing, 1974-75; perinatal nurse clinician U. Iowa Hosps., 1976-77; pediatric nurse practitioner Chicano Cmty. Health Ctr., 1978-80; lectr., asst. prof. child health nursing and physical assesstment San Diego State U., 1977-79; child health nurse practitioner program coord. U. Calif., San Diego, 1978-82; pediatric nurse practitioner San Diego City Schs., 1980-82; coord. infant spl. care ctr. follow-up program U. Calif., San Diego, 1982-83, assoc. clin. prof. intercampus grad. studies, 1983-90, dir. health promotion divsn. cmty. and family medicine, 1985-90; assoc. clin. prof. dept. cmty. family medicine U. Calif. Divsn. Health Care Sci., San Diego, 1990-94; assoc. prof. San Diego State U. Sch. Nursing, 1990-94, Calif. Nursing Students Assn. faculty advisor, 1992-94; pediatric nurse practitioner Naval Hosp., 1990-92, Comp. Health Clinic, 1990-94; prof., dir. Master's in Primary Care/Family Nurse Practitioner, Pediatric Nurse Practitioner, Women's Health Practitioner programs U. Va. Schs., Charlottesville, 1994—; cons. child health San Diego State U. Child Study Ctr.; mem. accident prevention com. Am. Acad. Pediats.; mem. adv. bd. Albemarle County Sch Health, 1995—, Camp Holiday Trails, 1995—. Contbr. numerous articles to profl. jours. and book chpts. to 7 texts; co-author: Ingall's & Salerno's Maternal Child Nursing, 1995, Mosby Year Book; mem. editl. bd. Jour. Perinatal and Neonatal Nursing, 1986-93, Children's Nurse, 1982-88, ; mem. editl. bd., reviewer Jour. Pediatric Health Care, 1987-93; speaker in field. Chair Ann. Refugee Clothing Drive, East San Diego, ESL Program, Car Seat Roundup U. Calif., San Diego, 1983-85; mem. telethon March of Dimes; mem. steering com. Healthy Mothers/ Healthy Babies Coalition; chair ways and means com. Benchley-Weinberger Elem. Sch. PTA, 1985-87, pres., 1988-90; v.p., pres. Friends Jamul Schs. Found.; co-chair teen outreach program Jr. League San Diego, 1987-88, chair, 1989-90, bd. dirs., 1990-92; educator presch. health San Carlos Meth. Ch.; mem. Head Start Policy Coun., 1992-94, San Diego County Dropout Prevention Roundtable, 1991-93, Western Albemarle H.S. Planning Team, 1994—. Recipient Svc. award Benchley-Weinberger Elem. Sch. PTA, 1988, Hon. Youth Svc. award Calif. Congress Parents and Tchrs., Loretta C. Ford Award for excellence as an nurse practitioner in edn. U. Colo., 1990, March of Dimes Svc. commendation, 1983, Project Hope Svc. commendation, 1983,Hon. Svc. award Calif. Congress of Parents, Tchrs. & Students, 1988, Doctoral Student fellowship U. San Diego, 1986, and numerous others. Mem. ANA, Nat. Assn. Pediat. Nurse Practioners Assoc. (chpt. pres., program com., coord. legis. field, nat. cert. chair 1992—), Calif. Nurse Assn., Pi Lamda Theta, Sigma Theta Tau (mem. nominations com. 1990-91, pres. elect Gamma Gamma chpt. 1993-94, Beta Kappa 1995—, Media award, 1992). Home: 2415 Harmony Dr Charlottesville VA 22901-8990

NOVAK, KIM (MARILYN NOVAK), actress; b. Chgo., Feb. 13, 1933; d. Joseph A. and Blanche (Kral) N.; m. Richard Johnson, April 1965 (div.); m. Robert Malloy, Jan. 1977. Student, Wright Jr. College, Chgo.; A.A., Los Angeles City College, 1958. appeared in: (films) The French Line, 1953, Pushover, 1954, Phffft, 1954, Five Against the House, 1955, Son of Sinbad, 1955, Picnic, 1955, The Man with the Golden Arm, 1956, The Eddie Duchin Story, 1956, Jeanne Eagles, 1957, Pal Joey, 1958, Vertigo, 1958, Bell, Book and Candle, 1958, Middle of the Night, 1959, Strangers When We Meet, 1960, Pépé, 1960, Boys' Night Out, 1962, The Notorious Landlady, 1962, Of Human Bondage, 1964, Kiss Me Stupid, 1964, The Amorous Adventures of Moll Flanders, 1965, The Legend of Lylah Clare, 1968, The Great Bank Robbery, 1969, Tales That Witness Madness, 1973, The White Buffalo, 1977, Just a Gigolo, 1979, The Mirror Crack'd, 1980, Liebestraum, 1991; (TV movies) Third Girl from the Left, 1974, Satan's Triangle, 1975, Malibu, 1983. Named one of 10 most popular movie stars by Box-Office mag. 1956, All-Am. Favorite 1961, Brussels World Fair poll as favorite all-time actress in world 1958. Office: William Morris Agency 151 El Camino Dr Beverly Hills CA 90212*

NOVAK, MICHAEL (JOHN), religion educator, author, editor; b. Johnstown, Pa., Sept. 9, 1933; s. Michael John and Irene (Sakmar) N.; m. Karen Ruth Laub, June 29, 1963; children: Richard, Tanya, Jana. AB summa cum laude, Stonehill Coll., North Easton, Mass., 1956; BT cum laude, Gregorian U., Rome, 1958; MA, Harvard U., 1966; LLD, Keuka (N.Y.) Coll., 1970, Stonehill Coll., Mass., 1977, Thomas More Coll., 1992; LHD, Davis and Elkins (W.Va.) Coll., 1971, LeMoyne (N.Y.) Coll., 1976, Sacred Heart U., 1977, Muhlenberg Coll., 1979, D'Youville Coll., 1981, Boston U., 1981, New Eng. Coll., 1983, Rivier Coll., 1984, Marquette U., 1987; D en Ciencias Sociales, U. Francisco Marroquin, Guatemala, 1993; Jacksonville U., 1994; HHD, Saint Xavier U., 1995. Teaching fellow Harvard U., 1961-63; asst. prof. Stanford U., 1965-68; assoc. prof. philosophy and religious studies State U. N.Y., Old Westbury, 1968-71; assoc. dir. humanities Rockefeller Found., N.Y.C., 1973-75; provost Disciplines Coll., SUNY, Old Westbury, 1969-71; vis. prof. Jan. session Carleton Coll., Northfield, Minn., 1970, Immaculate Heart Coll., Hollywood, Calif., 1971; vis. prof. U. Calif., Santa Barbara, 1972, Riverside, 1975; Ledden-Watson disting. prof. religion Syracuse U., 1977-79; journalist nat. elections Newsday, 1972; writer in residence The Washington Star, 1976, syndicated columnist, 1976-80, 84-89; columnist Forbes Mag., 1989—; resident scholar in religion and public policy Am. Enterprise Inst., Washington, 1978—, George Frederick Jewett chair pub. policy research, 1983—, dir. social and polit. studies, 1987—; chmn. working seminar on family and Am. welfare policy Ind., 1986; faculty U. Notre Dame, Ind., 1986-87, vis. W. Harold and Martha Welch Prof. Am. Studies, 1987, 88; judge Nat. Book awards, 1971, DuPont Broadcast Journalism awards, 1971-80; speechwriter nat. polit. campaigns, 1970, 72; mem. Bd. Internat. Broadcasting, 1983—; mem. Presdl. Task Force Project Econ. Justice, 1985-87, Council Scholars Library of Congress, 1986—; mem. monitoring panel UNESCO, 1984; vice chmn. Lay Commn. Cath. Social Teaching and U.S. Economy, 1984-86; U.S. Ambassador to Experts Meeting on Human Contacts of the Conf. On Security and Cooperation in Europe, Bern, Switzerland, 1986; U.S. rep. to human rights commn. UN, 1981-83; hon. prof. U. Cuyo, Argentina, 1992. Author: novel The Tiber was Silver, 1961, A New Generation, 1964, The Experience of Marriage, 1964, The Open Church, 1964, Belief and Unbelief, 1965, 3d edit., 1994, A Time to Build, 1967, A Theology for Radical Politics, 1969, American Philosophy and the Future, 1968, Story in Politics, 1970, (with Brown and Herschel) Vietnam: Crisis of Conscience, 1967; Politics: Realism & Imagination, 1971, Ascent of the Mountain, Flight of the Dove, 1971, A Book of Elements, 1972, All the Catholic People, 1971, novel Naked I Leave, 1970, The Experience of Nothingness, 1970, The Rise of the Unmeltable Ethnics, 1972, Choosing Our King, 1974, The Joy of Sports, 1976, The Guns of Lattimer, 1978, The American Vision, 1978, Rethinking Human Rights I and II, 1981, 82, The Spirit of Democratic Capitalism, 1982, Confession of a Catholic, 1983, Moral Clarity in the Nuclear Age, 1983, Freedom with Justice, 1984, Human Rights and the New Realism, 1986, Will It Liberate? Questions About Liberation Theology, 1986, Character and Crime, 1986, The New Consensus on Family and Welfare, 1987, Taking Glasnost Seriously: Toward an Open Soviet Union, 1988, Free Persons and the Common Good, 1989, This Hemisphere of Liberty, 1990, The Spirit of Democratic Capitalism, 1991 (Anthony Fisher award 1992), Choosing Presidents, 1992, The Catholic Ethic and the Spirit of Capitalism, 1993, Awakening from Nihilism, Joy of Sports, rev. 1995; Belief and Unbelief, rev, 1995; Business as a Calling, 1996; To Empower People, anniv. ed, 1995; numerous other articles and books transl. into all maj. langs.; assoc. editor Commonweal mag., 1966-69; contbg. editor Christian Century, 1967-80, Christianind Crisis, 1968-76, Jour. Ecumenical Studies, 1967—, This World, 1982-89, First Things, 1990—; religion editor Nat. Rev., 1979-86; founder, pub. Crisis, 1982—, editor-in-chief, 1993—. Decorated K.M.G., Soverign Mil. Order of Malta, 1987; Kent fellow, 1961—; fellow Hastings Inst., 1970-76; named Most Influential Prof. Sr. Class Stanford U., 1967, 68; Man of Yr. Johnstown, Pa., 1978; recipient Faith and Freedom award Religious Heritage Am., 1978, HIAS Liberty award, 1981, Friend of Freedom award, 1981; Newman Alumni award CCNY, 1984; George Washington Honor medal, 1984; award of Excellence, Religion in Media, 8th annual Angel Awards, 1985, Ellis Island Honor medal, 1986, Anthony Fisher award, 1992, Wilhelm Weber Prize, 1993, Templeton Progress in Religion prize, 1994; Internat. prize Inst. World Capitalism, 1994; diploma as vis. prof. U. Francisco Marroquin, 1985; named acad. corr. mem. from U.S., Argentina Nat. Acad. Scis., Morals & Politics, 1985, others. Mem. Soc. Religion in Higher Edn. (ctrl. com. 1970-73), Am. Acad. Religion (prog. dir. 1968-72), Coun. Fgn. Rels., Cath. Theol. Soc., Soc. Christian Ethics, Inst. Religion and Democracy (dir. 1981—), Nat. Ctr. Urban and Ethnic Affairs (dir. 1982-86). Office: Am Enterprise Inst 1150 17th St NW Washington DC 20036-4603 *Many persons have found a certain emptiness at the heart of human life —an experience of nothingness. Hidden in it, implicit in it, are prior commitments to honesty, courage, freedom, community. To increase the frequency of such acts in our lives is to grow, and to feel them diminish is to wither.*

NOVAK, RAYMOND FRANCIS, research institute director, pharmacology educator; b. St. Louis, July 26, 1946; s. Joseph Raymond and Margaret A. (Cerutti) N.; m. Frances C. Holy, Apr. 12, 1969; children: Jennifer, Jessica, Janelle, Joanna. BS in Chemistry, U. Mo., St. Louis, 1968; PhD in Phys. Chemistry, Case Western Res. U., 1973. Assoc. in pharmacology Northwestern U. Med. Sch., Chgo., 1976-77, asst. prof. pharmacology, 1977-81, assoc. prof., 1981-86, prof., 1986-88; prof. pharmacology Wayne State U. Sch. Medicine, Detroit, 1988—; dir. Inst. Chem. Toxicology Wayne State U., Detroit, 1988—, dir. NIEHS Ctr. in Molecular and Cellular Toxicology with Human Application, 1994—; mem. toxicology study sect. NIH, Bethesda, Md., 1984-88; adj. sci. Inhalation Toxicology Rsch. Inst., Lovelace Biomed. and Environ. Rsch. Inst., 1991—. Assoc. editor Toxicol. Applied Pharmacology, 1992—; editor Drug Metabolism and Disposition, 1994—; mem. editorial bd. Jour. Toxicology and Environ. Health, 1987-92, In Vivo, 1986—, Toxic Substances Jour., 1993—; mem. bd. pub. trustees Am. Soc. Pharmacology and Experimental Therapeutics, 1994—; contbr. articles to profl. jours. Recipient Disting. Alumni award U. Mo., St. Louis, 1988; grantee Nat. Inst. Environ. Health Sci., 1979—, Gen. Medicine sect. NIH, 1979—. Mem. Am. Soc. for Biochem. and Molecular Biology, Soc. Toxicology, Am. Assn. for Cancer Rsch., Am. Soc. for Pharmacology and Exptl. Therapeutics (bd. publ. trustees 1994—), Am. Soc. Hematology, Am. Chem. Soc., Biophys. Soc., Internat. Soc. for Study Xenobiotics. Office: Wayne State U Inst Chem Toxicology 2727 2nd Ave Rm 4000 Detroit MI 48201-2654

NOVAK, ROBERT DAVID SANDERS, newspaper columnist, television commentator; b. Joliet, Ill., Feb. 26, 1931; s. Maurice Pall and Jane Anne (Sanders) N.; m. Geraldine Williams, Nov. 10, 1962; children: Zelda, Alexander. AB, U. Ill., 1952; LLD (hon.), Kenyon Coll., 1987. Reporter Joliet (Ill.) Herald-News, 1947-51, Champaign-Urbana (Ill.) Courier, 1951-52, AP, Omaha, Lincoln, Nebr., Indpls. and Washington, 1954-58, Wall St. Jour., Washington, 1958-63; syndicated columnist N.Y. Herald-Tribune, Washington, 1963-66; commentator Corinthian Broadcasting, Washington, 1963-65, Metromedia, Washington, 1966-76, RKO-Features, Washington, 1976-78; syndicated columnist Chgo. Sun-Times, Washington, 1966—; commentator Cable News Network, Washington, 1980—, Nat. Empowerment TV, 1993—; pub. Evans-Novak Polit. Report, Washington, 1967—, Evans-Novak Tax Report, Washington, 1985-92, Evans-Novak Japan Report, Washington, 1989-92; roving editor Readers Digest, 1979—. Author: The Agony of the GOP, 1965, (with Rowland Evans) Lyndon B. Johnson: The Exercise of Power, 1967, Nixon In The White House, 1971, The Reagan Revolution, 1981. Trustee Bullis Sch., Potomac, Md., 1987—, Phillips Found., 1991—. 1st lt. U.S. Army, 1952-54. Recipient ACE award Cable Broadcasting Industry, 1990. Mem. Soc. Profl. Journalists, Washington Gridiron Club, Nat. Press Club, Army and Navy Club. Home: 801 Pennsylvania Ave NW Washington DC 20004-2615 Office: Ste 1312 1750 Pennsylvania Ave NW Washington DC 20006-4502

NOVAK, TERRY LEE, public adminstration educator; b. Chamberlain, S.D., Sept. 1, 1940; s. Warren F. and Elaine M. N.; m. Barbara Hosea, Aug. 29, 1981; 1 child, David. B.Sc., S.D. State U., 1962; postgrad. (Rotary fellow), U. Paris, 1962-63; M.P.A., Colo. U., 1965, Ph.D., 1970. Asst. city mgr. City of Anchorage, 1966-68; city mgr. City of Hopkins, Minn., 1968-74, City of Columbia, Mo., 1974-78, City of Spokane, Wash., 1978-91; v.p. bus. and fin. Ea. Wash. U., Cheney, 1991-92, prof. public adminstrn., 1992—, dir. grad. program pub. administrn., 1994—; dir. Spokane Joint Ctr. for Higher Edn., 1995—; asst. adj. prof. U. Mo., Columbia, 1975, 77; adj. instr. Gonzaga U., Spokane, 1986-88; mem. nat. adv. coun. on environ. policy and tech. EPA. Author: Special Assessment Financing in American Cities, 1970; contbr. articles to profl. jours. Mem. Internat. City Mgrs. Assn. (Acad. Profl. Devel.), Am. Soc. Public Adminstrn. Episcopalian. Office: N 665 Riverpoint Blvd Spokane WA 99202

NOVAK, VICTOR ANTHONY, semi-retired manufacturing company executive; b. Antigo, Wis., Mar. 23, 1930; s. Joseph F. and Mary C. (Jirovec) N.; m. Marcella A. Tessmer, Nov. 3, 1951; children: Deborah, Mark, Jeffrey, Lori. Cert. in Mgmt., Marquette U., 1980. Mgr. repairshop Novak's Machineshop, Antigo, 1947-52; model maker AC Spark Plug co., Oakcreek, Wis., 1952-66; supr. experimental div. Oster Corp., Glendale, Wis., 1966-72; gen. foreman toolroom Square D Co., Milw., 1972-82, mgr. tool engring., 1982-89; sr. mfg. engr. Square D Co., Milw., Wis., 1993—; tchr. Milw. Area Tech. Coll., 1973—. Avocations: golf, bowling, fishing, skiing. Home: 6705 N Braeburn Ln Milwaukee WI 53209-3327 Office: Square D Co 4080 N 1st St Milwaukee WI 53212-1239

NOVAK, WILLIAM ARNOLD, author, lecturer; b. Toronto, Ont., Can., Aug. 1, 1948; s. George Joseph and Esther (Brill) N.; m. Linda Mali Manaly, June 19, 1977; children: Ben, Jesse, Lev. BA, York U., Toronto, 1969; MA, Brandeis U., 1973. Editor Reponse mag., 1969-74; exec. editor Moment mag., 1976-78; editor New Traditions mag., 1984-86. Author: High Culture: Marijuana in the Lives of Americans, 1980, The Great American Man Shortage, 1983; co-author: (with Moshe Waldoks) The Big Book of Jewish Humor, 1981, (with Lee Iacocca) Iacocca: An Autobiography, 1984, (with Sydney Biddle Barrows) Mayflower Madam, 1986, (with Herb Schmertz) Goodbye to the Low Profile, 1986, (with Tip O'Neill) Man of the House, 1987, (with Nancy Reagan) My Turn, 1989, (with Moshe Waldoks) The Big Book of New American Humor, 1990, (with Oliver North) Under Fire, 1991, (with Magic Johnson) My Life, 1992. Jewish. Office: care Axelrod Agy 54 Church St Lenox MA 01240-2554

NOVAKOV, GEORGE JOHN, JR., gifted and talented educator; b. New Orleans, Apr. 1, 1945; s. George John Novakov Sr. and Gloria (Edwards) Frost; m. Ann Marie Mariano, Dec. 27, 1969; children: Jay, Jaime. BA, U. New Orleans, 1967, MEd, 1970, postgrad., 1985; postgrad., Tulane U., Loyola U., 1985. Tchr. New Orleans Pub. Schs., 1967—, adminstrv. asst. Edna Karr Magnet Sch., 1994—; grant writer asst. New Orleans Pub. Libr., 1987-89. Author: (play) The Christmas Caper, 1980. Ind. Study Humanities fellow, 1991. Mem. La. Assn. of Computer Using Educators (assoc. editor newsletter, 1992), Greater New Orleans Coun. of Tchrs. of English. Democrat. Roman Catholic. Avocations: opera, science fiction, computers. Home: 7340 Edward St New Orleans LA 70126-2012 Office: Edna Karr Magnet Sch 3332 Huntlee Dr New Orleans LA 70131-7046

NOVALES, RONALD RICHARDS, zoologist, educator; b. San Francisco, Apr. 24, 1928; s. William Henry and Dorothy (Richards) N.; m. Barbara Jean Martin, Dec. 19, 1953; children: Nancy Ann, Mary Elizabeth. B.A., U. Calif., Berkeley, 1950, M.A., 1953, Ph.D., 1958; postgrad., U. Calif., Los Angeles, 1951-52. Asst. prof. biol. scis. Northwestern U., Evanston, Ill., 1958-64; assoc. prof. Northwestern U., 1964-70, prof., 1970-80, prof. neurobiology and physiology, 1981-93, emeritus prof. neurobiology and physiology, 1993—; cons. A.J. Nystrom Co., 1969. Mem. editorial bd.: The American Zoologist, 1969-73; Contbr.: articles to profl. jours. Ency. Brit. Book of Year. Served with U.S. Army, 1953-55. NSF research grantee, 1959-73, 75-78. Fellow AAAS. Unitarian. Home: 2008 Mcdaniel Ave Evanston IL 60201-2125 *Remember not to "die on the barbed wire" of all the conflicting demands of your work. It is possible for you to cut through the individual strands and to make a successful rush for the enemy's trench.*

NOVALES-LI, PHILIPP, neuropharmacologist; b. Manila, Philippines, May 27, 1962; s. Angelita Tobillo de Novales-Li. DMSc, PhD, Gifu U. Sch. Medicine, Japan, 1989; DPhil, U. Oxford, U.K., 1993. Rsch. fellow U. Oxford, U.K., 1990-94; fellow U. So. Calif. Sch. Medicine, L.A., 1994, project mgr., 1995; pres. St. Hugh's Coll. MCR, U. Oxford, 1991, exec. officer, 1992, pharmacology tutor, 1993; cons. Novales-Li Rsch., Ltd., 1994. Columnist Manila Bull., 1994-95; contbr. articles to sci. jours. Monbusho Rsch. scholar Ministry Edn. & Culture, Tokyo, 1986-89; recipient Outstanding Youth award City of Manila, 1979, ORS award CVCP, London, 1989-92. Mem. Internat. Brain Rsch. Orgn., World Fedn. Mental Health, European Neuroscis. Assn., Oxford Union Soc., Gridiron Club, Oxford Soc. (hon. sec. So. Calif. 1995), Phi Kappa Phi, Phi Epsilon, Phi Sigma (Acad. Excellence in Biol. award 1984). Home: 1201 Orosa St, Manila 1000, The Philippines Office: U Oxford, Dept Pharmacology, Oxford OX1 3QT, England also: U So Calif Sch Medicine 1540 Alcazar St CHP 205 Los Angeles CA 90033

NOVAS, JOSEPH, JR., advertising agency executive; b. Bueu, Pontevedra, Spain, Sept. 21, 1921; came to U.S., 1928; s. Joseph and Josephine (Regueira) N.; m. Carmen Ramos, Feb. 9, 1989; children by previous marriage: Stephen, Robert, Paul, Patricia. A.B., Brown U., 1946; postgrad., Columbia U., 1948-49. Asst. advt. mgr. Colegate-Palmolive, Jersey City, 1946-49; internat. advt. mgr. The Gillette Co., Boston, 1949-53; founder, pres. Laradiotel, C.A., Havana, Caracas, Mexico, San Juan, N.Y.C., 1953-58; founder Telefilms, C.A., Venezuela, 1955; founder, pres. Novas-Criswell Advt., Caracas, Mexico City, Madrid, Bogota, Sao Paulo, San Juan, Buenos Aires, 1958-74; chmn. and mem. exec. com. Leo Burnett Co., Inc., Spain, Portugal, 1974-77; sr. v.p. Leo Burnett Co., Inc., Chgo., 1977-83, also bd. dirs.; chmn. Leo Burnett Europe/ME Ltd., London, 1983-86; cons. CMQ-TV, Havana, Cuba, 1953-54, Channel 2, Caracas, Venezuela, 1951-58, Heinz Co., Europe, 1985-87, Leo Burnett, 1986—; lectr. Caracas Central U., Caracas Andres Bello U., Mich. State U., Ohio U., Eastern Ill. U., McGill U., Montreal, Can. Served to lt. (j.g.) USN, 1942-46. Named Advt. Man of Yr., Venezuela. Mem. Internat. Advt. Assn. (world pres. 1974-76), Sales and Mktg. Execs. (pres. Venezuela chpt. 1962-64), Las Brisas Club (Marbella, Spain), Broken Sound Club (Boca Raton). *Frankness, forthrightness—always with the cards on the table. You lose some but you win most, and you always look in the mirror with pride and self respect.*

NOVATNEY, JOHN F., JR., lawyer; b. Cleve., May 26, 1930. AB, Brown U., 1952; LLB, U. Va., 1955. Bar: Ohio 1959. Ptnr. Baker & Hostetler, Cleve. Office: Baker & Hostetler 3200 Nat City Ctr 1900 E 9th St Cleveland OH 44114-3485*

NOVECOSKY, PETER WILFRED, abbot; b. Humboldt, Sask., Can., Apr. 27, 1945; s. Martin Benedict and Elizabeth (Suchan) N. BA, St. John's U.,

1966, MST, 1970. Abbot St. Peter's Abbey, Muenster, Sask., 1970—. Roman Catholic.

NOVELLO, ANTONIA COELLO, United Nations official, former U.S. surgeon general; b. Fajardo, P.R., Aug. 23, 1944; d. Antonio and Ana D. (Flores) Coello; m. Joseph R. Novello, May 30, 1970. BS, U. P.R., Rio Piedras, 1965; MD, U. P.R., San Juan, 1970; MPH, Johns Hopkins Sch. Hygiene, 1982; DSc (hon.), Med. Coll. Ohio, 1990, U. Ctrl. Caribe, Cayey, P.R., 1990, Lehigh U., 1992, Hood Coll., 1992, U. Notre Dame, Ind., 1991, N.Y. Med. Coll., 1992, U. Mass., 1992, Fla. Internat. U., 1992, Cath. U., 1993, Washington Coll., 1993, St. Mary's Coll., 1993, Ea. Va. Med. Sch., 1993, Ctrl. Conn. State U., 1993, Georgetown U., 1993, U. Mich., 1994, Mt. Sinai Sch. Medicine, 1995. Diplomate Am. Bd. Pediatrics. Intern in pediatrics U. Mich. Med. Ctr., Ann Arbor, 1970-71, resident in pediatrics, 1971-73, pediatric nephrology fellow, 1973-74; pediatric nephrology fellow Georgetown U. Hosp., Washington, 1974-75; project officer Nat. Inst. Arthritis, Metabolism and Digestive Diseases NIH, Bethesda, Md., 1978-79, staff physician, 1979-80; exec. sec. gen. medicine B study sect., div. of rsch. grants NIH, Bethesda, 1981-86; dep. dir. Nat. Inst. Child Health & Human Devel., NIH, Bethesda, 1986-90; surgeon gen. HHS, Washington, 1990-93; spl. rep. for health and nutrition UNICEF, N.Y.C., 1993—; clin. prof. pediatrics Georgetown U. Hosp., Washington, 1986, 89, Uniformed Svcs. U. of Health Scis., 1989; adj. prof. pediatrics and communicable diseases U. Mich. Med. Sch., 1993; adj. prof. internat. health Sch. Hygiene and Pub. Health, Johns Hopkins U., Balt.; mem. Georgetown Med. Ctr. Interdepartmental Rsch. Group, 1984—; legis. fellow U.S. Senate Com. on Labor and Human Resources, Washington, 1982-83; mem. Com. on Rsch. in Pediatric Nephrology, Washington, 1981—; participant grants assoc. program seminars Nat. Inst. Arthritis, Diabetes and Digestive and Kidney Diseases, NIH, Bethesda, 1980-81; pediatric cons. Adolescent Medicine Svc., Psychiat. Inst., Washington, 1979-83; nephrology cons. Met. Washington Renal Dialysis Ctr. affiliate Georgetown U. Hosp., Washington, 1975-78; phys. diagnosis class instr. U. Mich. Med. Ctr., Ann Arbor, 1973-74; chair Sec.'s Work Group on Pediatric HIV Infection and Diseases, DHHS, 1988; cons. WHO, Geneva, 1989; mem. Johns Hopkins Soc. Scholars, 1991. Contbr. numerous articles to profl. jours. and chpts. to books in field; mem. editorial bd. Internat. Jour Artificial Organs, Jour. Mexican Nephrology. Served to capt. USPHS, 1978—. Recipient Intern of Yr. award U. Mich. Dept. Pediatrics, 1971, Woman of Yr. award Disting. Grads. Pub. Sch. Systems, San Juan, 1980, PHS Commendation medal HHS, 1983, PHS Citation award HHS, 1984, Cert. of Recognition, Divsn. Rsch. Grants, NIH, 1985, PHS Outstanding medal HHS, 1988, PHS Unit Commendation, 1988, PHS Surgeon Gen.'s Exemplary Svc. medal, 1989, PHS Outstanding Unit citation, 1989, DHHS Asst. Sec. for Health Cert. of Commendation, 1989, Surgeon Gen. Medallion award, 1990, Alumni award U. Mich. Med. Ctr., 1991, Elizabeth Blackwell award, 1991, Woodrow Wilson award for disting. govt. svc., 1991, Congl. Hispanic Caucus medal, 1991, Order of Mil. Med. Merit, 1992, Washington Times Freedom award, 1992, Charles C. Shepard Sci. award, 1992, Golden Plate award, 1992, Elizabeth Ann Seton award, 1992, Ellis Island Congl. Medal of Honor, 1993, Legion of Merit medal, 1993, Athena award Alumnae Coun., 1993, Nat. Citation award Mortar Bd., 1993, Disting. Pub. Svc. award, 1993, Healthy Am. Fitness Leaders award, 1994, Pub. Leadership Edn. Network Mentor award, 1994, Disting. Svc. award Nat. Coun. Cath. Women, 1995, James E. Van Zandt Citizenship award, 1995, Ronald McDonald Children's Charities Excellence award, 1995; named Health Leader of Yr., COA, 1992; inductee Nat. Women's Hall of Fame, 1994. Fellow Am. Acad. Pediatrics (Excellence Pub. Svc. award 1993); mem. AMA (Nathan Davis award 1993, Meritorious Svc. award 1993), Internat. Soc. Nephrology, Am. Soc. Nephrology, Latin Am. Soc. Nephrology, Soc. for Pediatric Rsch., Pediatric Soc., Assn. Mil. Surgeons U.S., Am. Soc. Pediatric Nephrology, Pan Am. Med. and Dental Soc. (pres.-elect, sec. 1984), D.C. Med. Soc. (assoc.), Johns Hopkins U. Soc. Scholars, Alpha Omega Alpha. Avocation: collecting antique furniture. Home: 1315 31st St NW Washington DC 20007-3334 Office: UNICEF 3 UN Plz Rm 634 New York NY 10017-4414

NOVELLO, DON, writer, comedian, actor; b. Ashtabula, Ohio, Jan. 1, 1943; s. A.J. and Eleanor (Finnerty) N. BA, U. Dayton, 1964. Writer, performer TV show Smothers Brothers Show, 1975; author novel The Lazlo Letters, 1977; writer, performer TV show Saturday Night Live, 1978-80; performer feature film Gilda Live, 1979; writer, performer rec. Live At St. Douglas Convent, 1980; producer TV series SCTV, 1982; author novel The Blade, 1985; performer TV spl. Father Guido Sarducci Goes To College, 1985; writer, performer rec. Breakfast in Heaven, 1986; performer feature film Head Office, 1986; performer TV spl. The Vatican Inquirer, 1987; performer feature film Tucker, 1988, N.Y. Stories, 1989, Godfather III, 1990, La Pastorela, 1991. Author: (children's mus.) Full Moon Over Tutti, 1992, (novel) Citizen Lazlo, 1992; contbr. articles to Rolling Stone, Playboy, Washington Post, Mother Jones, Spy mag.; performer feature film Casper, 1995, One Night Stand, 1995, Jack, 1996, Touch, 1996. Founder The People's Cath. Ch. Mem. AFTRA, Writers Guild Am., Screen Actors Guild. Club: Cavalier's. Office: PO Box 245 Fairfax CA 94978

NOVELLY, PAUL A., petrochemical and refining company executive; b. 1941; married. With Shell Oil Co., St. Louis, 1962-68; with Apex Oil Co., Inc., St. Louis, 1968—; vice-chmn. dir. Clark Oil & Refining Co., St. Louis. Office: Apex Oil Corp 8182 Maryland Ave Saint Louis MO 63105*

NOVETZKE, SALLY JOHNSON, former ambassador; b. Stillwater, Minn., Jan. 12, 1932; married; 4 children. Student, Carlton Coll., 1950-52; HHD (hon.), Mt. Mercy Coll., 1991. Amb. to Malta, Am. Embassy, Valletta, 1989-93. Past mem., legis. rep. Nat. Coun. on Vocat. Edn.; past mem. adv. coun. for career edn., past mem. planning coun. Kirkwood C.C.; bd. dirs., life trustee Cedar Rapids (Iowa) Cmty. Theater; bd. dirs. James Baker III Pub. Policy Inst., Rice U.; trustee Shattuck-St. Mary's Sch., Faribault, Minn., Mt. Mercy Coll., Cedar Rapids; vice chmn., life trustee, mem. exec. com. Hoover Presdl. Libr., 1982-85; state chmn. Iowa Rep. Com., 1985-87; chmn. Linn County Rep. Com., 1980-83; mem. adv. bd. Iowa Fedn. Rep. Women, 1987-89; vice chmn. campaign adv. bd. Nat. Fedn. Rep. Women, 1987-89; co-chmn. V.P. Bush Inauguration, 1980; Iowa co-chmn. George Bush for Pres., 1988; bd. dirs. Greater Cedar Rapids Found., also chmn. grants com.; mem. Coun. Am. Ambs.; bd. dirs. Ambs. Forum; mem. nat. bd. New Designs for Two Yr. Insts. Higher Edn. Decorated dame Order of Knights of Malta; recipient Disting. Alumnus award Stillwater High Sch., 1991; Disting. Alumni award for outstanding achievement Carleton Coll., 1994. Home: 4747 Mount Vernon Rd SE Cedar Rapids IA 52403-3941

NOVICH, BRUCE ERIC, materials engineer; b. Phila., Mar. 15, 1957; s. Samuel David and Vivian Rose Novich; m. Susan S. Novich, Sept. 5, 1982; children: Scott, Spencer, Corey. BA, Colgate U., 1979; BSChemE, MIT, 1980, MS in Geology, 1982, MSCE, 1982, ScD in Materials Processing, 1984. V.p. R & D and engring. Ceramics Process System, Milford, Mass., 1984-95; mgr. advanced tech. PPG Industries, Pitts., Pa., 1995—. Contbr. over 50 articles to profl. jours. Achievements include 15 patents in ceramics, composites and electronic packaging. Office: PPG Industries 201 Zeta Dr Pittsburgh PA 15238

NOVICK, ANDREW CARL, urologist; b. Montreal, Apr. 5, 1948; came to U.S., 1974; s. David and Rose (Ortenberg) N.; m. Thelma Silver, June 29, 1969 (div. Dec. 1983); 1 child, Lorne J.; m. Linda Friedman, May 24, 1992; children: Rachel H., Eric D. BSc, McGill U., Montreal, 1968, MD, CM, 1972. Diplomate Am. Bd. Urology. Resident in surgery Royal Victoria Hosp., Montreal, 1972-74; resident in urology Cleve. Clinic Found., 1974-77, staff dept. urology, 1977—, head sect. renal transplant, 1977—, chmn. dept. urology, 1985—, chmn. Organ Transplant Ctr., 1985—; trustee Am. Bd. Urology. Editor: Vascular Problems in Urology, 1982, Stewart's Operative Urology, 1989, Renal Vascular Disease, 1995; contbr. over 400 articles to profl. jours. Fellow ACS, Med. Coun. Can.; mem. Am. Urol. Assn., Am. Assn. Genito-Urinary Surgeons, Clin. Soc. Genito-Urinary Surgeons. Home: 22325 Canterbury Ln Cleveland OH 44122-3901 Office: Cleve Clinic Found 9500 Euclid Ave Cleveland OH 44195-0001

NOVICK, JULIUS LERNER, theater critic, educator; b. N.Y.C., Jan. 31, 1939; s. Solomon Joseph and Ethel (Lerner) N.; m. Phyllis Belle Spaeth, May 27, 1983; 1 child, Ilana. B.A., Harvard U., 1960; D.F.A., Yale U., 1966. Theatre critic WNDT-TV, Channel 13, N.Y.C., 1968-70; asst. prof. English NYU, N.Y.C., 1969-72; assoc. prof. lit. SUNY-Purchase, 1972-80, prof., 1980—; theatre critic The Village Voice, N.Y.C., 1958-89, The N.Y. Observer, N.Y.C., 1987-91, Newsday, N.Y.C., 1992-94, The Threepenny Rev., Berkeley, Calif., 1994—; vis. lectr. drama div. Juilliard Sch., N.Y.C., 1968-71; dramaturg The Acting Co., N.Y.C., 1971-73; vis. critic Dartmouth Summer Repertory Co., Hanover, N.H., 1976, 79, 80, 82, 83, 84; master critic Nat. Critics Inst., Waterford, Conn., 1971—. Author: Beyond Broadway, 1968. Fulbright scholar, 1960-61; Woodrow Wilson fellow, 1961-62; Guggenheim fellow, 1977; recipient George Jean Nathan award for dramatic criticism, 1981-82. Mem. Drama Desk, Am.Soc. for Theatre Rsch., Am. Theatre Critics Assn. (adv. coun.). Jewish.

NOVICK, MARVIN, investment company executive, former automotive supplier executive, accountant; b. N.Y.C., July 16, 1931; s. Joseph and Anna Novick; m. Margaret A. Blau, Apr. 9, 1960; children: Jeffrey, Stuart, Barry. BBA, CCNY, 1952; MBA, NYU, 1955, postgrad., 1955-58. CPA, N.Y., Mich., La., N.C. Sr. v.p. Mich. Blue Cross/Blue Shield, Detroit, 1961-70; v.p., dir. fin. Meadowbrook Ins., Southfield, Mich., 1970-72; ptnr. Touche Ross and Co., Detroit, 1972-84; vice chmn. Dura Corp., Southfield, 1984-87, Wesnovtek Corp., Birmingham, Mich., 1987-91; pres. R&M Resources Inc., Birmingham, 1991—; advisor Meadowbrook Ins. Group, Southfield, Mich., 1995—. Chmn. Oak Park-Huntington Woods-Pleasant Ridge (Mich.) Dem. Orgn., 1970-72, 18th Dem. Congl. Dist., 1972-74; trustee Mich. Assn. for Emotional Children, 1965—, also past pres.; trustee Providence Hosp., Southfield, 1975-83, also past chmn., trustee bldg. bd., 1982-89; trustee Oak Park (Mich.) Bd. Edn., 1964-71, also past pres.; trustee Temple Beth El, Birmingham, Mich., 1968—, also past pres.; trustee, vice chmn. Union of Am. Hebrew Congregation, 1981—; chmn. fin. com., fin. sec. World for Prog. Judaism-Internat., 1985—; chmn. pers. com. Jewish Welfare Found., 1987-91, assoc. chmn. cultural and edn. fedn. com., 1984—, chmn. subcom. Israel and Overseas Com., 1988—; mem. com. Jewish Agy. in Israel, 1987—; vice chmn. fin. com., trustee Sinai Hosp., 1988-92, mem. audit com., 1995—; trustee fin. com. Mich. Cancer Found., 1992—; trustee Mariners Inn, 1996—; bd. dirs. B'nai B'rith Centennial Lodge, 1970-79, past v.p.; trustee, mem. exec. com. Rose Hill Ctr., Inc., 1992—; mem. com. Hillel Ctr., U. Mich.; mem. various coms. Jewish Welfare Fedn. Recipient Honor and Service cert. Oak Park Bd. Edn., 1972, Past Pres. award Mich. Assn. Emotionally Disturbed Children, 1986; named one of Outstanding Young Men of Am., Outstanding Am. Found., 1968. Mem. Am. Inst. CPA's, Mich. Assn. CPA's, N.Y. State Assn. CPA's. Home: 12820 Burton St Oak Park MI 48237-1679

NOVICK, NELSON LEE, dermatologist, internist, writer; b. Bklyn., June 27, 1949; s. Benjamin and Vivian (Meltzer) N.; m. Meryl Sohnis, June 20, 1971; children: Yonatan, Yoel, Ariel, Daniel, Avraham. BA in Biology magna cum laude, Bklyn. Coll., 1971; MD, Mt. Sinai Sch. Medicine, 1975. Diplomate Am. Bd. Internal Medicine, Am. Bd. Dermatology, Am. Bd. Med. Examiners. Resident in internal medicine Mt. Sinai Med. Ctr., N.Y.C., 1975-78, assoc. attending, 1980—, postgrad. preceptee, 1980-83, outpatient dept. clinic chief, dermatology svc., 1983; resident Skin and Cancer Unit NYU Med. Ctr., N.Y.C., 1978-80; assoc. clin. prof. Mt. Sinai Sch. Medicine, N.Y.C., 1980—; cons. Westwood-Squibb Skin Care Info. Ctr., Vaseline Intensive Care Rsch., Bausch & Lomb, Schering-Plough, Sandoz Internat., Procter & Gamble, Lever-2000, Inst. for Med. Info. Author: Saving Face, Skin Care for Teens, Super Skin, Baby Skin, You Can Do Something About Your Allergies, You Can Look Younger at Any Age, Diseases of the Mucus Membranes, (novel) In the Path of the Wolf; co-author: The External Ear; reviewer Annals Internal Medicine, Jour. Am. Acad. Dermatology, Jour. Dermatol. Surgery and Oncology, Internat. Jour. Dermatology; editl. advisor Exec. Health's Good Health Report, Snyder Comm., Your Baby Wallboard Program; former med. editor Current Podiatric Medicine, Jour. Am. Analgesia Soc.; contbr. articles to profl. publs. Regent's Coll. scholar, 1971, Max and Leah Strauss Fund scholar, 1971, Grand St. Found. scholar, 1971. Fellow ACP (direct election), Am. Acad. Dermatology, Am. Soc. Dermatol. Surgery, Am. Acad. Cosmetic Surgery, Skin Cancer Found. (hon.); mem. AMA, AAAS, Soc. Investigative Dermatology, Skin Phototrauma Found., Internat. Soc. for Androgenic Disorders, Skin Cancer Found. (charter), N.Y. Acad. Scis., N.Y. County Med. Soc., Am. Soc. Dermatologic Surgery, Am. Analgesia Soc. (past bd. dirs.), Nature Conservancy, Audubon Soc., Nat. Geog. Found., N.Y. Zool. Soc., Am. Mus. Natural History, Smithsonian Instn., Nat. Wildlife Fedn., The Wilderness Soc., Author's Guild, Author's League Am., Phi Beta Kappa. Jewish. Office: 328 E 75th St New York NY 10021-3305 *The true measure of a person's success in life is not how much he accomplished, but how much of his God-given potential he has used.*

NOVICK, PETER, historian, educator; b. Jersey City, July 26, 1934; s. Michael and Esther (Liebman) N.; m. Carroll Ott, July 10, 1957 (div. 1962); m. Joan Kroll, May 24, 1964; 1 child, Michael. BS, Columbia U., 1957, PhD, 1965. Asst. prof. U. Calif., Santa Barbara, 1965-66; asst. prof. history U. Chgo., 1966-69, assoc. prof., 1969-87, prof., 1987—; lectr. Rutgers U., New Brunswick, N.J., 1961-62, Columbia U., N.Y.C., 1961-65. Author: The Resistance vs. Vichy: The Purge of Collaborators in Liberated France, 1969 (Clark M. Ansley award Columbia U. Press 1969), That Noble Dream: The "Objectivity Question" and the American Historical Profession, 1988 (Albert J. Beveridge prize Am. Hist. Assn. 1989). With U.S. Army, 1953-55. French Govt. fellow, 1960-61, William Bayard Cutting travelling fellow, 1962-63, NEH fellow, 1990-91, Ctr. for Advanced Study in Behavioral Scis. fellow, 1991-92. Mem. Am. Hist. Assn. Home: 5000 S Cornell Ave Chicago IL 60615-3041 Office: U Chgo Dept History 1126 E 59th St Chicago IL 60637-1580

NOVICK, ROBERT, physicist, educator; b. N.Y.C., May 3, 1923; s. Abraham and Carolyn (Weisberg) N.; m. Bernice Lehrman, July 2, 1947; children: Beth, Amy, Peter. M.E., Stevens Inst. Tech., 1944, M.S., 1949; Ph.D., Columbia, 1955. Microwave engr. Wheeler Lab., Inc., Great Neck, L.I., N.Y., 1946-47; instr. physics Columbia U., 1952-54, research assoc., 1954-57, assoc. prof. physics, dir. radiation lab., 1960-62, prof., co-dir. Astrophysics Lab., 1968-77, 86-92, dir. Astrophysics Lab., 1977-86, prof., 1977-93, prof. of physics emeritus, 1993—, chmn. dept. physics, 1983-88; asst. prof. physics U. Ill., Urbana, 1957-59, assoc. prof., 1959-60; Cons to labs., research insts.; chmn. subpanel on atomic and molecular physics Nat. Acad. Sci., 1964-65; mem. NASA Commn. on Sci. Uses of Space Sta., 1984-86. Recipient Exceptional Sci. Achievement medal NASA, 1980, Honor award Stevens Inst. Tech., 1989; A.P. Sloan fellow, 1958-70. Fellow Am. Phys. Soc., IEEE, AAAS; mem. Am. Astron. Soc. (sec.-treas. high energy astrophysics sect. 1975-78), Internat. Astron. Union. Research, publs. on atomic physics, atomic collisions, quantum electronics, atomic frequency standards, nuclear spins and moments, X-ray astronomy. Home: 366 W 245th St Bronx NY 10471-3902 Office: Dep Physics Columbia Univ 538 W 120th St New York NY 10027-6601

NOVICK, SHELDON M., author, lawyer; b. N.Y.C., June 19, 1941; s. Irving and Ruth (Rosenblatt) N.; m. Carolyn M. Clinton; 1 child, Michael Clinton; 1 child by previous marriage: Melia Bensussen. BA, Antioch Coll., 1963; JD, Washington U., 1977. Adminstr. Center for Biology of Natural Systems, Washington U., St. Louis, 1966-69; assoc. editor Environment mag., St. Louis, 1964-69; editor Environment mag., 1969-77, pub., 1972-74; assoc. firm Milgrim Thomajan Jacobs & Lee, N.Y.C., 1977-78; regional counsel U.S. EPA, Phila., 1978-86; staff atty. Environ. Law Inst., 1986-87; scholar in residence Vt. Law Sch., 1987—. Author: The Careless Atom, 1969, The Electric War, 1976, Law of Environmental Protection, 1987, Honorable Justice: The Life of Oliver Wendell Holmes, 1989, Henry Dames: The Young Master, 1996; editor: (with Dorothy Cottrell) Our World in Peril, 1971, The Collected Works of Justice Holmes, Vols. I-III, 1995. Town agt., grand juror Strafford Twp., 1988-96; pres. South Strafford Cafe, Inc., 1994—; mem. Vt. Water Resources Bd., 1988-92. Home: PO Box 259 South Strafford VT 05070-0259

NOVINGER, CATHY BLACKBURN, utility company executive; b. Portsmouth, Ohio, Apr. 7, 1949; s. Donald E. and Leona (Collingsworth) Blackburn; m. Robert L. Novinger, June 8, 1968; 1 child, Travis Andrew. Diploma, Portsmouth Bus. coll., 1968; cert. sec., U. S.C., 1977; student, Limestone Coll., 1980-81, Edison Electric Inst., 1984. Adminstrv. asst. to pres. S.C. Electric and Gas Co., Columbia, 1979-81, exec. asst. to pres., 1981-82, v.p. corp. services, 1982-83, v.p., group exec. adminstrn., 1983, sr. v.p. adminstrn. and mktg., 1984-88; sr. vp. administn. govt. and public affairs SCANA Corp., 1988—; sem. instr. U. S.C., Columbia, 1982—. Bd. dirs. Nat. Soc. Prevent Blindness, Columbia, pres., 1986; adv. bd. Salvation Army, Columbia, 1986—; personel relations com. Edison Electric Inst.; bd. dirs. Jr. Achievement, Columbia, 1981—; bd. dirs. exec. com. Community Relations Council, Columbia, 1984—. Recipient Tribute to Women in Industry award YWCA, 1982; Ind. Bus. Women award, 1984; named Career Woman of Yr., Nat. Fedn. Bus. and Profl. Women, 1983; named to Tribute to Women in Industry Acad., YWCA, 1987. Mem. SE Electric Exchange (employee relations com.). Republican. Baptist. Avocations: tennis, cooking, reading. Office: SCANA Corp 1426 Main St Box 764 Columbia SC 29202*

NOVINSKA, DEIRDRE ANN, special education educator; b. West Plains, Mo., Nov. 24, 1960; d. Delbert Bruce and Genevieve Mae (Diels) Wells; m. James Joseph Novinska, Aug. 20, 1983; children: Megan Ann, Justin James. BS, U. Wis., Eau Claire, 1982, MS, 1983; MS in Edn. Adminstrn., U. Wis., Superior, 1996. Lic. speech-lang. pathologist, Wis. Speech/lang. therapist Wauzeka (Wis.) Pub. Sch., 1983-84, Iowa-Grant Pub. Schs., Livingston, Wis., 1984-85; speech/lang. therapist Medford Area (Wis.) Pub. Schs., 1985-92, speech/lang. therapist, early edn. coord., 1992-94, spl. edn. coord., early edn. coord., 1994—; speech/lang. pathologist Taylor County (Wis.) Birth-3 Program, 1992-93. Bd. dirs. Parent Resource Ctr., Medford, 1994—, Black River Industries, Medford, 1994—; co-chair Early Childhood Coun., Medford, 1992—. Mem. Am. Speech/Lang. Assn., Coun. for Exceptional Children, Wis. Speech Hearing Assn., Jaycettes, Optimists. Avocations: skiing, reading, collecting, walking. Office: Medford Pub Schs 1015 W Broadway Ave Medford WI 54451-1311

NOVITCH, MARK, physician, educator, retired pharmaceutical executive; b. New London, Conn., Apr. 23, 1932; s. Charles Weinger and Mary (Margolick) N.; m. Katherine Louise Henderson, Oct. 9, 1971; 1 dau., Julia Drummond. A.B., Yale U., 1954; M.D., N.Y. Med. Coll., 1958. Intern, asst. resident in medicine Boston City Hosp., 1958-60; rsch. fellow Harvard Med. Sch., 1960-62, asst. in medicine, 1962-64, instr. medicine, 1964-67; mem. med. staff Peter Bent Brigham Hosp., Boston, 1962-67; asst. physician Univ. Health Svcs., Harvard U., 1961-67; asst. to dep. asst. sec. for health and sci. affairs HEW, Washington, 1967-71; dep. assoc. commr. for med. affairs FDA, Washington, 1971-78; assoc. commr. for health affairs FDA, 1978-81; dep. commr. food and drugs HHS, 1981-85; corp. v.p. The Upjohn Co., Kalamazoo, 1985-86, sr. v.p. sci. adminstrn., 1986-88, exec. v.p., 1989-90, vice-chmn. bd. dirs., 1991-93; prof. health scis. George Washington U., Washington, 1994—; bd. dirs. Biomed. Svcs. Bd. ARC, Guidant Corp. Calypte Biomed., Inc., Neurogen Corp., Osiris Therapeutics, Inc., Alteon, Inc., Challenger Ctr. for Space Sci. Edn.; trustee and past pres. U.S. Pharmacopeial Conv. Inc. Trustee Coun. for Excellence in Govt. USPHS fellow, 1960-62; Brookings Instn. fed. exec. fellow, 1970-71. Mem. AMA, Mass. Med. Soc., Am. Pub. Health Assn., Am. Soc. Clin. Pharmacology and Therapeutics, Nat. Acad. Social Ins. Home: 3558 Albemarle St NW Washington DC 20008-4214

NOVITZ, CHARLES RICHARD, television executive; b. Chgo., Oct. 25, 1934; m. Eve Krzyzanowski, Feb. 11, 1988; 1 child, Alexandra Maris. BS in Journalism, U. Ill., Champaign-Urbana, 1956; MS, Columbia U., 1960; MPA, NYU, 1971. Reporter, writer, editor City News Bur., Chgo., 1956-57, UPI, Chgo., 1957-59; editor, writer, field producer NBC News, N.Y.C. and Chgo., 1959-60; with ABC News, 1960-79; mgr. ABC News (TV network syndication), 1973-79; mng. dir. Ind. TV News Assn., N.Y.C., 1979-81; producer, exec. NBC News, N.Y.C., 1982-85, 87; assoc. Rowan & Blewitt, Inc./Exec. TV Workshop, N.Y.C., 1985-95; pres. NovaNews Comm. Cons., N.Y.C., 1994—; on-air talent Money Call News, 1988; freelance TV producer, cable and pub. TV series, 1985—; adj. instr. LIU, 1967-69, NYU, 1969-70; asst. adj. prof. Lehman Coll., 1970-71; adj. prof., producer interactive televised course CUNY, 1972-75. Mem. Broadcast Pioneers, Radio TV News Dirs. Assn., Alumni Assn. Columbia Grad. Sch. Journalism (pres. 1979, Deadline Club (N.Y.C.; pres. 1969), Soc. Profl. Journalists-Sigma Delta Chi (pres. 1981-82). Office: 160 W End Ave Apt 29D New York NY 10023-5616

NOVOGROD, NANCY ELLEN, editor; b. N.Y.C., Jan. 30, 1949; d. Max and Hilda (Kirschbaum) Gerstein; m. John Campner Novogrod, Nov. 7, 1976; children: James Campner, Caroline Anne. AB, Mt. Holyoke Coll., 1971. Sec. fiction dept. The New Yorker, N.Y.C., 1971-73, reader, 1973-76; asst. editor Clarkson N. Potter, Inc., N.Y.C., 1977-78, assoc. editor, 1978-80, editor, 1980-83, sr. editor, 1984-86, exec. editor, 1987; sr. editor HG (formerly House and Garden mag.), N.Y.C., 1987-88, editor-in-chief, 1988-93; editor-in-chief Travel & Leisure, N.Y.C., 1993—. Bd. dirs. N.Y. Bot. Garden, 1991, Mount Holyoke Coll., 1992—. Office: Travel & Leisure 1120 Avenue Of The Americas New York NY 10036-6700

NOVOTNEY, DONALD FRANCIS, superintendent of schools; b. Streator, Ill., July 10, 1947; s. Andrew Stephen and Irene Marie (Lux) Novotney; m. Jane Francis Loeffelholz, June 3, 1973; children: Nicole, Tara, Thomas, Michael, Theresa. BA, Loras Coll., 1969; MST, U. Wis., Platteville, 1973; MS, U. Dayton, 1985. Cert. tchr., Wis.; cert. tchr. and adminstr., Ohio. Prin. Holy Ghost Sch., Dickeyville, Wis., 1969-75, St. John Sch., Green Bay, Wis., 1975-76, Beaver Dam (Wis.) Cath. Schs., 1976-83; coord. Jordan Cath. Schs., Rock Island, Wis., 1983-85; supt. schs. Diocese of Fargo, N.D., 1985-86, Diocese of La Crosse, Wis., 1987—. Mem. Nat. Cath. Edn. Assn. (del. to nat. congress for cath. schs.). Republican. Roman Catholic. Avocations: athletics, travel. Home: 3314 33rd St La Crosse WI 54601 Office: Diocese of La Crosse 3710 East Ave La Crosse WI 54601

NOVOTNY, DAVID JOSEPH, lawyer; b. Melrose Park, Ill., Oct. 3, 1953; s. Joseph F. and Dorothy E. (Erickson) N.; m. Gladys Ruth Korynecky, May 1, 1982. BSc, DePaul U., 1975, JD, 1978. Bar: Ill. 1978, U.S. Dist. Ct. (no. dist.), Ill. 1978, U.S. Ct. Appeals (7th cir.) 1985, U.S. Dist. Ct. (no. dist.), Ind. 1995. Law clk. to justice Ill. Appellate Ct., Chgo., 1978-80; assoc. Rooks, Pitts & Poust, Chgo., 1980-83; assoc. Peterson, Ross, Schloerb & Seidel (now Peterson & Ross), Chgo., 1983-88, ptnr., 1988—; arbitrator Am. Arbitration Assn., 1987—, Cir. Ct. Cook County Ct.-Annexed Arbritration, 1990—. Exec. editor DePaul Law Rev., 1978. Mem. ABA, Ill. State Bar Assn., 7th Cir. Bar Assn., Soc. Trial Lawyers, Asia-Pacific Lawyers Assn., Lawyer-Pilots Bar Assn., Legal Club Chgo. Office: Peterson & Ross 200 E Randolph St Ste 7300 Chicago IL 60601-6436

NOVOTNY, DONALD WAYNE, electrical engineering educator; b. Chgo., Dec. 15, 1934; s. Adolph and Margaret Novotny; m. Louise J. Eenigenburg, June 26, 1954; children: Donna Jo Kopp, Cynthia Mason. BEE, Ill. Inst. Tech., 1956, MS, 1957; PhD, U. Wis., 1961. Registered profl. engr., Wis. Instr. Ill. Inst. Tech., 1957-58; mem. faculty U. Wis., Madison, 1958—, prof. elec. engring., 1969—, chmn. dept. elec. and computer engring., 1976-80, Grainger prof. power electronics, 1990—; vis. prof. Mont. State U., 1966, Eindhoven (The Netherlands) Tech. U., 1974, Tech. U. Louvain, Belgium, 1986; Fulbright lectr. Tech. U. Ghent, Belgium, 1981; dir. Wis. Elec. Machines and Power Electronics Consortium, 1981—; assoc. dir. Univ.-Industry Rsch. Program, 1982-93; chmn. elec. engring. program Nat. Technol. U., 1989—; cons. to industry. Author: Introductory Electromechanics, 1965, Vector Control and Dynamics of AC Drives, 1996; also rsch. papers; assoc. editor: Electric Machines and Power Systems, 1976—. Recipient Kiekhofer tchg. award U. Wis., 1964, Benjamin Smith Reynolds tchg. award, 1984, Holdridge tchg. award, 1995; Outstanding paper award Engring. Inst. Can., 1966; fellow GE, 1956, Ford Found., 1960; grantee numerous industries and govt. agys. Fellow IEEE (prize paper awards 1983, 84, 86, 87, 90, 91, 93, 94); mem. Am. Soc. Engring. Edn., Sigma Xi, Tau Beta Pi, Eta Kappa Nu. Congregationalist. Lodge: Rotary. Home: 1421 E Skyline Dr Madison WI 53705-1132 Office: U Wis Dept Elec and Computer Engring 1415 Johnson Dr Madison WI 53706-1607

NOVY, MILES JOSEPH, obstetrician/gynecologist, educator; b. Berlin, Germany, Nov. 23, 1937; s. Joseph Miloslav and Helena (Lukowski) N.; m. Katherine Stephens, Dec. 20, 1978 (div.); children: Milena, Julia. BA, Yale U., 1959; MD, Harvard U., 1963. Diplomate Am. Bd. Obstetrics and Gynecology. Fellow dept ob/gyn Harvard U., Boston, 1969-70; asst. prof. dept. ob/gyn Oreg. Health Scis. U., Portland, 1970-72; assoc. prof. Oreg. Health Scis. U., 1972-78, asst. chmn. ob/gyn., 1986-88, co-dir. reprodn./endocrine infertility svc., 1984-88, dir. div. reproductive endocrine fertility div., 1988—, prof. ob/gyn., 1978—; assoc. scientist reproductive biology behavior Oreg. Reg. Primate Rsch. Ctr., Beaverton, 1970-72; scientist, now sr. scientist Oreg. Reg. Primate Rsch. Ctr., 1972—; cons. Kaiser Permanente, Portland, 1980—; lectr. in field. Contbr. articles to profl. jours., chpts. to books; inventor in field. Lt. comdr., USPHS, 1965-68. NIH Merit awardee, 1989; recipient Outstanding Movie award, Am. Fertility Soc., 1989. Fellow Am. Coll. Obstetricians and Gynecologists (Hoechst award 1969); mem. Am. Fertility Soc. (postgrad. prog. com. 1990—), Yale U. Alumni Assn. (del. 1988-90), Am. Physiol. Soc., Soc. for Gynecologic Investigation, AMA, Am. Gynecology and Obstetrical Soc., Soc. of Reproductive Surgeons, Pacific Coast Ob/Gyn Soc. (Meml. Found. award 1974). Avocations: tennis, scuba diving, skiing. Home: 3107 SW Nottingham Dr Portland OR 97201-1611 Office: Oregon Regional Primate Ctr 505 NW 185th Ave Beaverton OR 97006*

NOWACKI, JAMES NELSON, lawyer; b. Columbus, Ohio, Sept. 12, 1947; s. Louis James and Betty Jane (Nelson) N.; m. Catherine Ann Holden, Aug. 1, 1970; children: Carrie, Anastasia, Emma. AB, Princeton U., 1969; JD, Yale U., 1973. Bar: Ill. 1973, N.Y. 1982, U.S. dist. Ct. (no. dist.) Ill. 1973, U.S. Ct. Appeals (7th cir.) 1978, U.S. Ct. Appeals (6th cir.) 1987, U.S. Supremem Ct. 1992. Assoc. Isham, Lincoln & Beale, Chgo., 1976-80; ptnr. Kirkland & Ellis, Chgo., 1980—. Mem. Winnetka Sch. Bd. Dist. 36, Ill. 1983-91, bd. pres., 1989-91. Harlan Fiske Stone prize Yale U., 1972. Mem. ABA (forum com. on constrn. industry, litigation sect.), Mid-Am. Club, Skokie Country Club. Home: 708 Prospect Ave Winnetka IL 60093-2320 Office: Kirkland & Ellis 200 E Randolph St Chicago IL 60601-6436

NOWAK, JACQUELYN LOUISE, administrative officer, realtor, consultant; b. Harrisburg, Pa., Sept. 2, 1937; d. John Henry and Irene Louise (Clark) Snyder; children: Andrew Alfred, IV, Deirdre Anne. Student, Pa. State U., 1973-74; BA, Lycoming Coll., 1975. Editorial writer Patriot News Co., Harrisburg, Pa., 1957-58; dir. West Shore Sr. Citizens Ctr., New Cumberland, Pa., 1969-72; exec. dir. Cumberland County Office Aging, Carlisle, Pa., 1972-80; bur. dir. Bur. Advocacy, Pa. Dept. Aging, Harrisburg, 1980-88; exec. asst. to Pa. Senator John D. Hopper, Senate Com. on Aging and Youth, 1989; owner D&J Prodns., Art and Handcrafted Teddy Bears 1986, Ted E. Bear's Emporium, Harrisburg, 1988-92; assoc. Century 21 Piscioneri Realty, Inc., Camp Hill, Pa.; spl. projects coord. Pa. div. Am. Trauma Soc., 1991-93; adminstr. Country Meadows of West Shore II. Mechanicsburg, Pa., 1993-94; admininstrv. officer Am. Trama Soc., 1994—; recorder Pa. Gov's. Coun. Aging Cen. Region, 1972-74; chmn. pub. rels., 1973-74; mem. state planning com. Pa. State Conf. Aging, 1974, panelist, 1975-78; mem. state bd. Pa. Coun. Homemakers-Home Health Aide Svcs., 1972-80, v.p., 1975, chmn. ann. meeting, 1973-75; sr. citizens subcom. chmn. Pa. Atty. Gens. Commn. to Prevent Shoplifting, 1983; mem. adv. com. Tri-County Ret. Sr. Vol. Program, 1972-74; bd. dirs. Coun. Human Svcs. Cumberland, Dauphin, and Perry Counties, 1973-74; mem. svc. com. Family and Children's Svc. Harrisburg, 1970-74, mem. policy com., 1973-74, bd. dirs. Cumberland County unit Am. Cancer Soc., 1964-76, state del., 1964-66, chmn. county pub. rels., 1965-66, cancer crusade chmn., 1964. Recipient Herman Melitzer award, Pa. Conf. Aging, 1978; named Woman of the Yr. Sta. WIOO Radio, Carlisle, Pa., 1979. Mem. Nat. Assn. Area Ags. on Aging (bd. dir. 1975-80, pres. 1976-77; sec. 1978-79), Nat. Soc. Decorative Painters (bd. dirs. Penns Woods painters chpt. 1995—), Pa. Watercolor Soc., Harrisburg Art Assn., Mechanicsburg Art Ctr. (pres. 1987-90, bd. dirs. 1984-95), Gerontol Soc. Am., Am. Trauma Soc. (Pa. div. state bd. 1985-88), Older Women's League (founder chpt.), Lycoming Coll. Alumni Assn. (exec. bd. 1987-89), Pa. Fedn. of Women's Club (div. chmn. 1972-76), Torch Club (pres. 1987-88, 2d v.p. 1985-86), Zonta Internat. (sec. 1986-89). Home: 15 Paddock Ln Camp Hill PA 17011-1268

NOWAK, JAN ZDZISLAW, writer, consultant; b. Warsaw, Poland, May 15, 1913; came to U.S., 1977; s. Waclaw Adam and Elisabeth (Piotrowski) Jezioranski; m. Jadwiga Zaleski, Sept. 7, 1944. M.S., U. Poznan, Poland, 1936; Doctorate honoris causa, U. Poznan. Sr. researcher U. Poznan, 1937-39; emissary Polish resistance movement, 1941-45; editor BBC, London, 1947-51; dir. Polish Service Radio Free Europe, Munich, Fed. Republic of Germany, 1951-76; nat. dir. Polish Am. Congress, Washington, 1979—; cons. Nat. Security Coun., 1979-92. Author: Courier from Warsaw, 1982, War on Airways, 1985, Poland From Afar, 1988; contbr. articles to mags. Served to maj. Polish Army, 1939-45. Decorated Virtuti Militari; decorated Cross of Valour, King's medal for Courage, Order of White Eagle, Poland, gt. ribbon Polonia Restituta, Comdrs. Cross of Merit with star (Poland). Roman Catholic. Home: 3815 Forest Grove Dr Annandale VA 22003-1959

NOWAK, JOHN E., law educator; b. Chgo., Jan. 2, 1947; s. George Edward and Evelyn (Bucci) N.; m. Judith Johnson, June 1, 1968; children: John Edwin, Jeffrey Edward. AB, Marquette U., 1968; JD, U. Ill., 1971. Law clk. Supreme Ct. of Ill., Chgo., 1971-72; asst. prof. U. Ill., Urbana, 1972-75, assoc. prof., 1975-87, law prof., 1978—, grad. coll. faculty, 1982—, Baum Prof. Law, 1993—; chmn. Constl. Law Sch. Sect.; faculty rep. Big Ten Intercollegiate Conf., Schaumburg, Ill., 1981—; vis. prof. law U. Mich., Ann Arbor, 1985; Lee Disting. vis. prof. Coll. William and Mary, 1993. Coauthor: Constitutional Law, 4th edit. 1991, Treatise on Constitutional Law, 1986, 2nd edit., 1992, Story's Commentaries on the Constitution, 1987. Scholar-in-Residence, U. of Ariz., Tucson, 1985, 87. Mem. Assn. of Am. Law Schs. (chm. constl. law sect., accreditation com. 1980-88), Nat. Collegiate Athletic Assn. (mem. infractions com. 1987—), Am. Law Inst., Am. Bar Assn., Ill. Bar Assn., Order of the Coif (Triennial Book award com.). Roman Catholic. Home: 1701 Mayfair Rd Champaign IL 61821-5522 Office: U Ill Coll Law 504 E Pennsylvania Ave Champaign IL 61820-6909

NOWAK, JOHN MICHAEL, air force officer; b. Grand Rapids, Mich., Dec. 17, 1941; s. John F. and Dorothy F. (Smigiel) N.; m. Maureen K. Henry, Apr. 20, 1963; children: Kimberly, Susan, John, Michael, Lynn. BA in Sociology and Polit. Sci., Aquinas Coll., Mich., 1963; M in Mgmt., U. So.Calif., 1973. Commd. 2d lt. U.S. Air Force, 1963, advanced through grades to lt. gen., 1993; dir. maintenance Ogden Air Logistics Ctr., Hill AFB, Utah, 1984-86; dep. chief staff for maintenance Air Force Logistics Command, Wright-Patterson AFB, Ohio, 1986-89; dep. chief staff for logistics and engring. Hdqrs. Mil. Airlift Command, Scott AFB, Ill., 1989-92; dep. chief staff for logistics Hdqrs. Air Mobility Command, Scott AFB, 1992; dir. of supply Hdqrs. U.S. Air Force, Washington, 1992-93, dep. chief for logistics, 1993-1995; pres., ceo Logtec, Fairborn, OH, 1995—. Decorated DSM, Legion of Merit, Bronze Star medal, Meritorious Svc. medal with 3 oak leaf clusters, Air Force Commendation medal. Avocations: golf, reading. Office: Logtec 2900 Presidential Dr Fairborn OH 45324*

NOWAK, NANCY STEIN, judge; b. Des Moines, Sept. 17, 1952; d. Russell D. and Christine (Evanoka) Stein; m. Raymond A. Nowak, May 26, 1973. BA, Drake Univ., Iowa, 1974, MA, 1976; JD, George Washington Univ., D.C., 1980. Bar: D.C. 1980, Iowa 1982, Tex. 1986. Briefing atty. Judge Jamie Boyd, 1983-84, Judge Edward Prado, 1984-87; asst. U.S. atty., 1987-88, asst. U.S. trustee, 1988-89; magistrate judge U.S. Dist. Ct. (Tex. we. dist.), 5th circuit, San Antonio, 1989—. Office: US Courthouse 655 E Durango Blvd San Antonio TX 78206-1102

NOWAK, ROBERT MICHAEL, chemist; b. South Milwaukee, Wis., Oct. 28, 1930; s. Casimer M. and Anita Marie (Anderson) N.; m. Susan Lora Boyd, Oct. 12, 1957; children: Karen Sue Nowak Sapsford, Janet Lynn Nowak McMorris. Student, U. Wis., Racine, 1949-51; BS, U. Wis., Madison, 1953; PhD, U. Ill., 1956. Rsch. chemist Phys. Rsch. Lab., Dow Chem. Co., Midland, Mich., 1956-64, from group leader to asst. lab dir., 1964-72; dir. rsch. and devel. plastics dept. Dow Chem. Co., Midland, 1972-73, dir. rsch. and devel. Olefin and Styrene plastics depts., 1973-78, dir. rsch. and devel. plastics dept., 1978-83, dir. cen. rsch., 1983-90, chief scientist, dir. cen. rsch. and devel., 1990-94; pres., CEO Mich. Molecular Inst., Midland, 1994—. Contbr. articles to profl. jours.; patentee organic reaction mechanisms and reinforced plastics. Mem. NAE, AIChE, Am. Chem. Soc., Soc. Chem. Industry, Coun. for Chem. Rsch. Office: MI Molecular Inst 1910 W St Andrews Rd Midland MI 48640

NOWELL, GLENNA GREELY, librarian, consultant; b. Gardiner, Maine, Apr. 15, 1937; d. Bion Mellon and Faith Louise (Hutchings) Greely; m. Dana Richard Nowell, Sept. 1, 1956 (div. 1971); children: Dana A., Mark R., Dean E. BA in English, U. Maine, 1986. Dir. Gardiner Pub. Libr., 1974—; bd. dirs. Gardiner Bd. Trade: mem. Maine Libr. Commn., 1980-88, Gov.'s Commn. Employment of Handicapped, 1978-81; mem. adv. bd. Gardiner Savs. Bank, 1986—; trustee J. Walter Robinson Welfare Trust, 1986—. Creator, editor Who Reads What publ., 1988—. Mem. Gardiner Econ. Devel. Com., 1989—; interim city mgr. City of Gardiner, 1991; bd. dirs. Kennebec Valley Mental Health, 1995—. Recipient Hugh Hefner 1st Amendment award Playboy Found., 1987, Outstanding Libr. award Maine Libr. Assn., 1993, Cmty. Svc. award Kennebec Valley C. of C., 1993. Mem. Rotary (pres. Gardiner chpt. 1993-94). Office: Gardiner Pub Libr 152 Water St Gardiner ME 04345-2195

NOWELL, PETER CAREY, pathologist, educator; b. Phila., Feb. 8, 1928; s. Foster and Margaret (Matlack) N.; m. Helen Worst, Sept. 9, 1950; children: Sharon, Timothy, Karen, Kristin, Michael. B.A., Wesleyan U., Middletown, Conn., 1948; M.D., U. Pa., 1952. Intern Phila. Gen. Hosp., 1952-53; resident pathology Presbyn. Hosp., Phila., 1953-54; med.-teaching, research specializing in cancer Phila., 1956—; from instr. to prof. pathology Sch. Medicine U. Pa., 1956—, chmn. dept. pathology, 1967-73; dir. (Cancer Center), 1973-75. Served to lt., M.C. USNR, 1954-56. Recipient Research Career award USPHS, 1964-67, Parke-Davis award, 1965, Lindback Disting. Teaching award, 1967, Passano award, 1984, Rous-Whipple award Am. Assn. Pathology, 1986, de Villers award Leukemia Soc. Am., 1987, Mott prize GM Cancer Rsch. Found., 1989, 3M award, FASEB, 1993. Home: 345 Mt Alverno Rd Media PA 19063-5313 Office: U Pa Sch Medicine Dept Pathology and Lab Medicine Philadelphia PA 19104-6082

NOWICK, ARTHUR STANLEY, metallurgy and materials science educator; b. N.Y.C., Aug. 29, 1923; s. Hyman and Clara (Sperling) N.; m. Joan Franzblau, Oct. 30, 1949; children: Jonathan, Steven, Alan, James. A.B., Bklyn. Coll., 1943; A.M., Columbia U., 1948, Ph.D., 1950. Physicist NACA, Cleve., 1944-46; instr. U. Chgo., 1949-51; asst. prof., then assoc. prof. metallurgy Yale U., 1951-57; mgr. metallurgy research IBM Corp Research Center, Yorktown Heights, N.Y., 1957-66; prof. metallurgy Columbia U., 1966-90, Henry Marion Howe prof. metallurgy and materials sci., 1990—; A. Frank Golick lectr. U. Mo., 1970; vis. prof. Technion, Haifa, Israel, 1973; co-chmn. Internat. Conf. Internal Friction, 1961, 69 (medal 1989); cons. in field. Author: Crystal Properties Via Group Theory, 1995; co-author: Anelastic Relaxation in Crystalline Solids, 1972; co-editor: Diffusion in Solids, 1975, Diffusion in Crystalline Solids, 1984; contbr. articles to profl. jours. Named David Turnbull lecturer Materials Rsch. Soc., 1994. Fellow AIME, Am. Phys. Soc.; mem. Materials Rsch. Soc. (Turnbull lectr. 1994), Sigma Xi (pres. Kappa chpt. 1983-85). Office: 1144 Mudd Bldg Columbia U New York NY 10027

NOWICKI, GEORGE LUCIAN, retired chemical company executive; b. Rutherford, N.J., Dec. 4, 1926; s. Justin Nowicki; m. Mary Elisabeth Baker, Aug. 30, 1947; children: Barbara, Peter, Paul, James. BSChemE, CCNY, 1949; MSChemE, NYU, 1956. Registered profl. engr., N.Y., Pa. Chemist Ideal Toy Co., N.Y.C., 1949; chem. engr. Bklyn. Union Gas Co., 1949-50, Sonotone Corp., Elmsford, N.Y., 1950-52; dept. head Burroughs Wellcome Co., Tuckahoe, N.Y., 1952-70; v.p. mfg. Quaker Chem. Corp., Conshohocken, Pa., 1970-79, v.p. domestic ops., 1984-89; ret. Quaker Chem. Corp., Conshohocken, 1989; pres. Selby Batersby Co., Phila., 1979-81; mng. dir. Quaker Chem. Holland BV, Uithoorn, The Netherlands, 1981-84; chmn. bd. Overdale Corp., Alsip, Ill., 1987-89, Quaker Chem. Can. Ltd., Toronto, 1985-89. Pres. Ctrl. Sch. Dist. 7, Hartsdale, N.Y., 1960-69, Westchester County Sch. Bds. Assn., White Plains, N.Y., 1965; bd. dirs. Suburban Gen. Hosp., Norristown, Pa., 1986; mem. governing bd. Vt. Common Cause, 1993—; bd. dirs. Martha Canfield Libr., Arlington, Vt., 1994—; counselor Svc. Corps Ret. Execs., 1993-95. Mem. Am. Inst. Chem. Engrs., Mfrs. Assn. Del. Valley (bd. dirs. 1987-89). Avocations: swimming, skiing, video photography, stamps. Home: RR 1 Box 1809 Arlington VT 05250-9716

NOWLAN, DANIEL RALPH, engineering executive; b. Hammond, Ind., Feb. 23, 1947; s. Kenneth Edwin and Patricia Jane (Prendergast) N.; m. Sharon Louise Greichunos, Sept. 7, 1968; children: Daniel Ralph Jr., Kevin Anthony, Cynthia Ann. BSEE, Purdue U., 1969, MSEE, 1969. Engr./scientist McDonnell Douglas Astronautics Co, Santa Monica, Calif., 1969-75; engring. mgr. McDonnell Douglas Aerospace-West, Huntington Beach, Calif., 1975—; tax preparer Tax Corp. of Am., Montrose, Calif., 1975-76; cons. in field. Eucharistic minister to convalescent homes St. Vincent De Paul Soc., Huntington Beach, 1993—; youth soccer coach Am. Youth Soccer Orgn., Westminster and Huntington Beach, 1975-82; bldg. fund dr. capt. St. Vincent De Paul Cath. Ch., Huntington Beach, 1979, 82. Recipient Popular Sci. Achievement award L.A. and Orange County Engring. Coun., 1993, Space Frontier award, 1994, Engring. Project Achievement award, 1994. Mem. AIAA (sr.), IEEE, Phi Kappa Theta, Tau Beta Pi, Eta Kappa Nu, Phi Eta Sigma. Roman Catholic. Avocations: arranging music for piano and keyboard, study of modern physics, study of philosophy. Home: 15931 Diamond St Westminster CA 92683-7203 Office: McDonnell Douglas Aerospace 5301 Bolsa Ave Huntington Beach CA 92647-2048

NOWLAN, GEORGE JOSEPH See DAVIS, DANNY

NOWLIN, JAMES ROBERTSON, federal judge; b. San Antonio, Nov. 21, 1937; s. William Forney and Jeannette (Robertson) N. B.A., Trinity U., 1959, M.A., 1962; J.D., U. Tex., Austin, 1963. Bar: Tex. 1963, Colo. 1993, U.S. Dist. Ct. D.C. 1966, U.S. Ct. Claims 1969, U.S. Supreme Ct. 1969, U.S. Dist. Ct. (we. dist.) Tex. 1971. Assoc. Kelso, Locke, & King, San Antonio, 1963-65; assoc. Kelso, Locke & Lepick, San Antonio, 1966-69; legal counsel U.S. Senate, Washington, 1965-66; propr. Law Offices James R. Nowlin, San Antonio, 1969-81; mem. Tex. Ho. of Reps., Austin, 1967-71, 73-81; judge U.S. Dist. Ct. (we. dist.) Tex., Austin, 1981—; instr. Am. govt. and history San Antonio Coll., 1964-65, 71-73. Served to capt. U.S. Army, 1959-60, USAR, 1960-68. Life fellow State Bar Found; mem. ABA, Travis County Bar Assn., San Antonio Bar Assn. Republican. Presbyterian. Avocations: pilot; skiing; hiking; jogging. Office: US Courthouse 200 W 8th St Austin TX 78701-2333

NOYCE, PHILLIP, film director; b. Griffith, New South Wales, Austalia, Apr. 27, 1950; films include: (dir., writer): Backroads, 1977 (also prodr.), Newsfront, 1979, Heatwave, 1983; (dir.): Shadows of the Peacock, 1987 (in U.S. as Echoes of Paradise, 1989), Dead Calm, 1989, Blind Fury, 1990, Patriot Games, 1992, Sliver, 1993, Clear and Present Danger, 1994; television work includes (as dir.): The Dismissal, 1983, The Cowra Breakout, 1985, The Hitchhiker (The Curse), 1986, Nightmare Cafe (pilot), 1992. Office: ICM 8942 Wilshire Blvd Beverly Hills CA 90211-1934

NOYES, H(ENRY) PIERRE, physicist; b. Paris, Dec. 10, 1923; s. William Albert and Katharine Haworth (Macy) N.; m. Mary Wilson, Dec. 20, 1947; children—David Brian, Alan Guinn, Katharine Hope. B.A., Harvard U., 1943; Ph.D., U. Calif., Berkeley, 1950. Physicist MIT, 1943-44, U. Calif., Berkeley, 1949-50; Fulbright fellow U. Birmingham, Eng., 1950-51; asst. prof. U. Rochester, N.Y., 1951-55; group leader Lawrence Livermore Lab., 1955-62; Leverhulme lectr. U. Liverpool, Eng., 1957-58; adminstrv. head theory sect. Stanford Linear Accelerator Center, 1962-69; asso. prof. Stanford U., 1962-67, prof., 1967—; vis. scholar Center Advanced Study Behavioral Scis., Stanford, 1968-69; cons. in field. Author papers in field. Chmn. Com. for Direct Attack on Legality of Vietnam War, 1969-72; mem. steering com. Faculty Political Action Group, Stanford U., 1970-72; mem. policy com. U.S. People's Com. on Iran, 1977-79. Served with USNR, 1944-46. Fellow NSF, 1962; Fellow Nat. Humanities Faculty, 1970; recipient Alexander von Humboldt U.S. Sr. Scientist award, 1979. Mem. Alternative Natural Philosophy Assn. (pres. 1979-87, 1st alternative natural philosopher award 1989), Am. Phys. Soc., AAAS, Sigma Xi. *What success I may have had has come because I have tried to bring together my physics and politics and family to serve the people. I aim to achieve a unified materialist philosophy that might help others to greater success than my own. I sum up this philosophy as "fixed past - uncertain future".*

NOYES, JUDITH GIBSON, library director; b. N.Y.C., Apr. 19, 1941; d. Charles II and Alice (Klauss) Gibson; m. Paul V. Noyes, June 1, 1991; children from previous marriage: Andrea Elizabeth Green, Michael Charles Green. BA, Carleton Coll., 1962; MLS, U. Western Ont., London, Can., 1972. Librarian edn. U. New Brunswick, 1972-86; libr. Can. Inst. Sci. and Tech. Info., Ottawa, Ont., Can., 1975-86; univ. librarian Colgate U., Hamilton, N.Y., 1986—; mem. OCLC Adv. Com. on Coll. and Univ. Librs., 1991-94; pres. bd. trustees Ctrl. N.Y. Libr. Resources Coun., 1992-96. Mem. ALA, Am. Coll. and Rsch. Librs. (nominating com. 1988-89, 92-93, legis. com. coll. libr. sect. liaison 1989-91, chair task force on intellectual freedom, 1992-94), Internat. Standards Orgn. (tech. com. 46, 1981-89). Office: Colgate U Everett Needham Case Libr 13 Oak Dr Hamilton NY 13346-1338

NOYES, RICHARD HALL, bookseller; b. Evanston, Ill., Feb. 12, 1930; s. George Frederick and Dorothy (Hall) N.; m. Judith Claire Mitchell, Oct. 10, 1953; children—Catherine, Stephanie, Matthew. B.A., Wesleyan U., 1952. Tng. program, elementary-high sch. salesman Rand McNally & Co., Colo., Utah, Idaho, Wyo., 1955-59; founder, owner, mgr. The Chinook Bookshop, Colorado Springs, Colo., 1959—. Contbr. to A Manual on Bookselling, 1974, The Business of Book Publishing, 1984; contbr. articles to newspapers and trade jours. Co-chmn. Colo. Media Coalition, 1974—; bd. dirs. Colorado Springs Fine Arts Ctr., 1977-81, Citizens Goals for Colorado Springs, 1976-88; trustee Fountain Valley Sch., 1979-81; vice chmn. Colorado Springs Charter Rev. Commn., 1991-92. Served with AUS, 1952-54. Recipient Intellectual Freedom award Mountain Plains Librs. Assn., 1977, Disting. Svc. award U. Colo., 1980, Recognition award Pikes Peak Arts Coun., 1989, Charles S. Haslam award, 1990), Entrepreneur of Yr. award U. Colo., 1992. Mem. Am. Booksellers Assn. (pres., dir.). Home: 1601 Constellation Dr Colorado Springs CO 80906-1609 Office: The Chinook Bookshop Inc 210 N Tejon St Colorado Springs CO 80903-1314

NOYES, RICHARD MACY, physical chemist, educator; b. Champaign, Ill., Apr. 6, 1919; s. William Albert and Katharine Haworth (Macy) N.; m. Winninette Arnold, July 12, 1946 (dec. Mar. 1972); m. Patricia Jean Harris, Jan. 26, 1973. A.B. summa cum laude, Harvard U., 1939; Ph.D., Calif. Inst. Tech., 1942. Research assoc. rocket propellants Calif. Inst. Tech., 1942-46; mem. faculty Columbia U., 1946-58, assoc. prof., 1954-58; Guggenheim fellow, vis. prof. U. Leeds, Eng., 1955-56; prof. chemistry U. Oreg., 1958—, head dept., 1963-68, 75-78, ret., 1984—. Editorial adv. com.: Chem. Revs, 1967-69; editorial adv. com.: Jour. Phys. Chemistry, 1973-80; assoc. editor: Internat. Jour. Chem. Kinetics, 1972-82, Jour. Phys. Chemistry, 1980-82; Contbr. to profl. jours. Fulbright fellow; Victoria U. Wellington, New Zealand, 1964; NSF sr. postdoctoral fellow Max Planck Inst. für Physikalische Chemie, Göttingen, Fed. Republic Germany, 1965; sr. Am. scientist awardee Alexander von Humboldt Found., 1978-79. Fellow Am. Phys. Soc.; mem. NAS, Am. Acad. Arts and Scis., Am. Chem. Soc. (chmn. div. phys. chemistry 1961-62, exec. com. div. 1960-75, mem. coun. 1960-75, chmn. Oreg. sect. 1967-68, com. on nominations and elections 1962-68, com. on publs. 1969-72), Chem. Soc. (London), Wilderness Soc., ACLU, Hungarian Acad. Scis. (hon.), Sierra Club (past chmn. Atlantic and Pacific N.W. chpts., N.W. regional v.p. 1973-74), Phi Beta Kappa, Sigma Xi. Achievements include research mechanisms chemical reactions, developing general theories, intrepretation physical properties chemicals. Home: 2014 Elk Ave Eugene OR 97403-1734 Office: U of Oregon Dept Chemistry Eugene OR 97403 *When I was young, I wanted to be an "explorer" I am fortunate to have a job in which I can make discoveries as exciting as those of the explorers who first sailed uncharted seas. Then I can try to convey the excitement to another generation. As an avocation, I try to influence government policies toward our least developed lands. It is a gratifying mix of satisfying curiousity and serving society.*

NOYES, ROBERT EDWIN, publisher, writer; b. N.Y.C., June 22, 1925; s. Clarence A. and Edith (LaDomus) N.; m. Janet Brown, Mar. 24, 1952 (div. June 1963); children—Keith, Steven, Mark, Geoffrey; m. Mariel Jones, July 24, 1964; children—Rebecca, Robert. B.S. in Chem. Engring, Northwestern U., 1945. Chem. engr. Am. Cyanamid Co., Pearl River, N.Y., 1947; sales exec. Titanium Pigment Corp., N.Y.C., 1948-55; market research mgr. U.S. Indsl. Chem. Co., N.Y.C., 1956-58; sales mgr. atomic energy Curtiss Wright Export, N.Y.C., 1958-60; founder, pres., chmn. bd. Noyes Data Corp., Park Ridge, N.J., 1960—; pub. Noyes Press, Noyes Publs., Park Ridge, 1961—. Author numerous books in fields of internat. fin., devel., tech. Served to lt. (j.g.) USNR, 1945-47. Mem. Am. Chem. Soc., Am. Inst. Chem. Engrs., Indian Harbor Yacht Club (Conn.), N.Y. Yacht Club. Episcopalian. Office: 224 West Saddle River Rd Saddle River NJ 07458

NOYES, RONALD TACIE, agricultural engineering educator; b. Leedey, Okla., Jan. 4, 1937; s. Johnnie Lyle and Anna Madeline (Allen) N.; m. Zona Gail McMillen, Apr. 16, 1960; children: Cynthia Gail, Ronald Scott, David Eric. BS in Agrl. Engring., Okla. State U., 1961, MS in Agrl. Engring., 1964; postgrad., Purdue U., 1966-68, U. Okla., 1988-96. Profl. engr., Ind., Okla. Asst. prof. Purdue U., West Lafayette, Ind., 1964-68; chief engr. Beard Industries, Inc., Frankfort, Ind., 1968-81, v.p. engring., 1981-85; assoc. prof. Okla. State U., Stillwater, 1985-88, prof., 1988—; cons. Ronald T. Noyes, Profl. Agrl. Engr., Stillwater, 1988—. Co-author: Designing Pesticide and Fertilizer Containment Facilities, 1991, revised edit., 1995; contbr. chpts. to books. 1st lt. U.S. Army, 1961-63. Recipient Disting. Svc. award U.S. Dept. Agr., 1992, Outstanding Ext. Faculty award Okla. State U., 1991. Fellow Am. Soc. Agrl. Engrs.; mem. Aircraft Owners & Pilots Assn., Nat. Agrl. Aviation Assn. (assoc.). Achievements include 6 patents in field; developed new aeration management procedure for controlling insects in stored grain that reduces chemical use, manifolded phosphine fumigation process for grain tanks and silos that reduces chemical use. Home: 1116 Westwood Dr Stillwater OK 74074-1116 Office: Oklahoma St Univ Biosyss & Agrl Engring Dept 224 Ag Hall Stillwater OK 74078-6041

NOYES, WARD DAVID, hematologist, medical educator; b. Schenectady, N.Y., Aug. 25, 1927; s. Ward and Marion (French) N.; m. Nancy Adair, Aug. 10, 1973; children: Patricia, Ward David, Jeffrey, Katherine, John, Elizabeth, Layne. BA, U. Rochester, 1949, MD, 1953. Intern King County Hosp., Seattle, 1953-54, resident, 1954-56; instr. medicine U. Wash., Seattle, 1959-61, asst. prof., 1961-65, assoc. prof., 1965-68; assoc. prof. Sch. Medicine, U. Fla., Gainesville, 1968-70, prof., 1970—, chief hematology, 1968—; cons. in hematology WHO, 1974-75, 78. Contbr. articles to profl. jours. With USAAF, 1946-47. USPHS fellow, 1956-69. Mem. Fla. Med. Assn., Alachua County Med. Soc., Am. Fedn. Clin. Rsch., Am. Soc. Hematology, Internat. Soc. Hematology, So. Soc. Clin. Investigation, Alpha Omega Alpha. Rsch. in iron metabolism. Address: 11006 SW 89th St Gainesville FL 32608-6298

NOZERO, ELIZABETH CATHERINE, lawyer; b. Detroit, June 13, 1953; d. Peter J. and Pauline R. (Reeves) N.; m. Stephen A. Catalano, May 23, 1981 (div. May 1993); 1 child: Alexandra L. BA in history, U. Calif., 1975; JD, U. San Diego, 1978. Bar: Calif. 1979, Nev. 1980. Counsel State Industrial Ins. System, Las Vegas, 1980-81; sr. legal counsel Reynolds Elec. & Engring. CO., Las Vegas, 1981-85; asst. gen. counsel U. Nev., Las Vegas, 1985-89; v.p., gen. counsel Harrah's Casino Hotels, Las Vegas, 1989-95; sr. legal counsel Sierra Health Svcs., Inc., 1996—; mem. exec. bd. Nev. Bar Assn. Fee Dispute com. 1982-88, Nev. Law Found., 1980-88. Chairperson S. Nev. Area Health Edn. Ctr., Las Vegas, 1990-94; former chair Nev. Adv. Com. U.S. Commn. on Civil Rights, Nev., 1989-94; gov.'s com. Infrastructive Financing, 1994-95. Recipient Woman of Achievement award Las Vegas C. of C., 1992, Silver State Citizen award Nev. Atty. Gen., 1992. Mem. Nev. Gaming Attys. (v.p. 1994-95), Nev. Resort Assn. (chairperson, regulations com. 1993-95). Office: Sierra Health Svcs Inc PO Box 15645 2724 N Tenaya Way Las Vegas NV 89114-5645

NOZICK, ROBERT, philosophy educator, author; b. Bklyn., Nov. 16, 1938; s. Max and Sophie (Cohen) N.; m. Barbara Fierer, Aug. 15, 1959 (div. 1981); children: Emily, David; m. Gjertrud Schnackenberg, Oct. 5, 1987. A.B., Columbia U., 1959; A.M., Princeton U., 1961, Ph.D., 1963; A.M. (hon.), Harvard U., 1969; DHL (hon.), Knox Coll., 1983. Asst. dir. Social Sci. Research Council Summer Inst., 1962; instr. philosophy Princeton U., 1962-63, asst. prof., 1964-65; Fulbright scholar Oxford (Eng.) U., 1963-64; asst. prof. philosophy Harvard U., Cambridge, Mass., 1965-67; prof. Harvard U., 1969—, chmn. dept., 1981-84, Arthur Kingsley Porter prof., 1985—, sr. fellow Soc. Fellows; assoc. prof. Rockefeller U., 1967-69. Author: Anarchy, State, and Utopia, 1974 (Nat. Book award 1975), Philosophical Explanations, 1981 (Ralph Waldo Emerson award 1982), The Examined Life, 1989, The Nature of Rationality, 1993; mem. bd. editors Philosophy and Pub. Affairs; contbr. articles to profl. jours. Fellow Ctr. Advanced Study Behavioral Scis., 1971-72, Rockefeller Found. humanities fellow, 1979-80, NEH fellow, 1987-88, Guggenheim fellow, 1996-97. Mem. Am. Philos.

Assn., Am. Acad. Arts and Scis., Council of Scholars, Library of Congress, Phi Beta Kappa. Office: Harvard U Emerson Hall Cambridge MA 02138

NTLOLA, PETER MAKHWENKWE, translator, retired; b. Phillipstown, Cape, South Africa, July 7, 1908; s. Fanteni and Sarah Notsitsa (Bonani) N.; m. Constance Nomalanga Siningwa, July 7, 1949 (dec. Mar. 1976). pub. serials on Man's Footprints on the Moon in state-sponsored monthly, 1963-76; columnist to 3 African monthly periodicals. Journalist, editor, reporter, proofreader, photographer, layout artist 5 books translated from English, 1966-86. Home: PO Box 77396, Mamelodi West 0101, South Africa

NUBER, PHILIP WILLIAM, air force officer; b. Bozeman, Mont., Sept. 27, 1939; s. Carl Philip and Harriet Catherine (Shane) N.; m. Maureen Jill Pepper, Mar. 24 1962; children: Greg, Jennifer. BS, Mont. State U., 1962. Commd. 2d lt. USAF, 1962, advanced through grades to major gen., 1992; ops. officer 354th Tactical Fighter Squadron, Davis-Monthan AFB, Ariz., 1975-78; chief officer assignments Hdqrs. Tactical Air Command/DP, Langley AFB, Va., 1978-80; comdr. 425th Tactical Fighter Tng. Squadron, Williams AFB, Ariz., 1980-82; dep. comdr., then comdr. 833d Combat Support Group, Holloman AFB, N.Mex., 1982-84; vice comdr., then wing comdr. 343d Tactical Fighter Wing, Eielson AFB, Alaska, 1984-88; dep. dir. for ops. Air Forces/X00, Washington, 1988-89; dep. comdr. Joint Task Force, USS LaSalle, Mid. East, 1989; dir. internat. programs Hdqrs. USAF/PRI, Washington, 1989-91; asst. dep. undersec. for internat. affairs SAF/IA, Washington, 1991-92; chief Joint U.S. Military Mission for Aid to Turkey, 1992; ret., 1996. Home: 4780 Command Ln Andrews AFB MD 20335-5568 Office: HQ DMA 8613 Lee Hwy # Dma Fairfax VA 22031-2130

NUCCI, LEO, baritone; b. nr. Bologna, Italy, 1942. Studied with, Guiseppe Marchesi, Ottaviano Bizzarri. Mem. chorus La Scala, Milan, Italy, 1969-75. Debut as Figaro in The Barber of Seville at Spoleto, 1967, Covent Garden, London, 1987, San Francisco, 1987; appeared in La Boheme, La Fenice, Venice, Italy, 1975, as Rodrigo in Don Carlo, La Scala, Milan, as Belcore in L'Elisir d'amore, as Francesco Foscari in I due Foscari, as Miller in Luisa Miller, Covent Garden, 1978, as Renato in Un Ballo in Maschera, Met. Opera, N.Y., 1980, Paris Opera, 1981, La Scala, 1987, Barber of Seville Met. Opera, 1984, Falstaff, London, Adriana Levouvreur, San Francisco Opera, 1985, La Traviata, Met. Opera, 1985, Don Carlo, 1986, Madame Butterfly, 1986, Aida, 1986, Rigoletto, Hamburg, Barcelona, Spain, 1987, Il Trovatore, Lyric Opera Chgo., 1987, Met. Opera, 1987; The Force of Destiny, Lyric Opera Chgo., 1988, Macbeth, Marseille, 1988, Il Trovatore and Barber of Seville, Met. Opera, 1988, Rigoletto, Met. Opera, 1989, Un Ballo in Maschera, Salzburg Festival, 1989, Rigoletto, Houston Grand Opera, 1990, Elisir d'Amore, Vienna State Opera, 1990, Rigoletto and Simone Boccanegra, Vienna, Rigoletto Lyric Opera Chgo., 1990, Rigoletto in Bologna, Italy and Munich, 1990, Luisa Miller, Ballo in Maschera Met. Opera, 1991; Otello Chgo. Symphony; Rigoletto Rome Opera, Verona Festival, Covent Garden, 1991, Simon Boccanegra in Santiago, Chile, Trovatore in Torino, Rigoletto in Venice, 1992; opera recs. include La Rondine, Le Villi, Andrea Chenier, The Barber of Seville, Don Pasquale, Tosca, Turco in Italia, Ernani, Aida, Falstaff, Don Carlo, Macbeth, 1987, Un Ballo in Maschera, Simone Boccanegra, Otello, Rigoletto, bel canto arias Il Viaggio a Reims, Idomeneo, Elisir d'Amore, Simon Boccanegra Popular Italian Songs, Gianni Schicchi, Italian Songs, Bel Canto Arias from Puritani, Pirata, Beatrice di Tenda, Guglielmo Tell, Poliuto, Duca d'Alba, Don Sebastiano, Favorita; films include: Macbeth, 1987. Office: care Allied Artists Agency, 42 Montpellier Square, London SW7 152, England

NUCCIARONE, A. PATRICK, lawyer; b. Denville, N.J., Aug. 29, 1947; s. H. Joseph and Alice Marie (McGuirk) N. BA, U. So. Calif., 1969; JD, George Washington U., 1973. Bar: N.J. 1973, N.Y. 1981, Vt. 1984, U.S. Dist. Ct. N.J. 1973, U.S. Dist. Ct. (no. dist.) Ohio 1986, U.S. Ct. Appeals (3d cir.) 1976, U.S. Supreme Ct. 1995. Com. staff asst. U.S. House of Reps., Washington, 1971-72; staff asst. Exec. Office of Pres. of U.S., Washington, 1972-73; asst. U.S. Atty. Office of U.S. Atty., Newark, 1974-83, chief environ. sect., 1978-83; spl. asst. Atty. Gen. Office of Atty. Gen., Montpelier, Vt., 1984; ptnr. Hannoch Weisman, Roseland, N.J., 1984-91, Dechert, Price & Rhoads, Princeton, N.J., 1991-95; co-chmn. N.J. Hazardous Task Force, Trenton, 1978-83; supr. Rutgers U. Environ. Law Clinic, Newark, 1978-83; mem. Environ. Expn. Adv. Bd., Trenton, 1985-90; chmn. ann. seminar on impacts of environ. law bus. trans. Practicing Law Inst., 1986-92; mem. faculty NYU Summer Inst. on Environ. Law, 1991-94. Contbr. articles to profl. jours. Recipient Outstanding Service award U.S. Dept. Justice, Washington, 1980, Spl. Achievement awards U.S. Dept. Justice, 1978, 79, Presdl. Citation for Excellent Performance Exec. Office of Pres., Washington, 1973. Mem. ABA (vice chmn. sect. on natural resources, energy and environ. law 1987-93), N.J. State Bar Assn. (bd. dirs. environ. law sect. 1985-89), Monmouth County Bar Assn. Avocations: flying, sailing, skiing, hiking. Office: 321 Broad St Red Bank NJ 07701

NUCHIA, SAMUEL M., protective services official, lawyer; b. Beaumont, Tex.; m. Elizabeth Nuchia; 3 children. Student, U. Houston, 1964-67; BS in Criminal Justice and Polit. Sci., Abilene Christian Coll., 1974; JD with honors, South Tex. Coll. Law, 1983; grad. in mgmt., FBI Nat. Acad. Bar: Tex. Asst. U.S. atty. for So. Dist. Tex., U.S. Dept. Justice, Houston, 1987-92; patrol officer Houston Police Dept., 1967-71, detective sgt. robbery div., 1971-76, lt. N.W. patrol and recruiting divsns., 1976-80, capt. internal affairs and criminal intelligence divsns., 1980-85, dep. chief West Patrol and Legal Svcs. Burs., 1985-87, gen. counsel, 1987, chief police, 1992—; former corp. security cons., also cons., expert witness for numerous law firms. Contbr. articles to law enforcement publs. Mem. Tex. Bar Assn., Houston Bar Assn., Internat. Assn. Chiefs Police, Houston Police Officers Assn., FBI Nat. Acad. (assoc.), Rotary. Office: Police Department 61 Riesner St Houston TX 77002*

NUCKOLLS, JOHN HOPKINS, physicist, researcher; b. Chgo., Nov. 17, 1930; s. Asa Hopkins and Helen (Gates) N.; m. Ruth Munsterman, Apr. 21, 1952 (div. 1983); children—Helen Marie, Robert David; m. Amelia Aphrodite Liaskas, July 29, 1983. B.S., Wheaton Coll., 1953; M.A., Columbia U., 1955; D.Sc. (hon), Fla. Inst. Tech., 1977. Physicist U. Calif., Lawrence Livermore Nat. Lab., 1955—, assoc. leader thermonuclear design div., 1965-80, assoc. leader laser fusion program, 1975-83, div. leader, 1980-83, assoc. dir. physics, 1983-88, dir., 1988-94, assoc. dir. at large, 1994—. Recipient E.O. Lawrence award AEC, 1969, Fusion Leadership award Fusion Power Assocs., 1983, Edward Teller medal Internat. Workshop Laser Interaction and Related Plasma Phenomena, 1991, Disting. Assoc. award U.S. Dept. Energy, 1996. Fellow AAAS, Am. Phys. Soc. (J.C. Maxwell prize 1981); mem. NAE. Office: Lawrence Livermore Nat Lab PO Box 808 Livermore CA 94551-0808

NUCKOLLS, LEONARD ARNOLD, retired hospital administrator; b. Park City, Utah, Feb. 22, 1917; s. Harry Leonard and Mabel Hill (Ganson) N.; m. Rachel A. Beckner, Apr. 18, 1942; children: Rachel Nuckolls Conine, Peter Leonard. AB, Pueblo Jr. Coll., 1938; BA, U. Colo., 1940. Commd. U.S. Army, 1942, advanced through grades to lt. col., 1962; adj. gen. 2d Army Div., Ft. Hood, Tex., 1960-62; ret., 1962; acct. Colo. State Hosp., Pueblo, 1963-64; caseworker N.Mex. Dept. Pub. Welfare, Clovis, 1964-66; unit coord. N.Mex. Dept. Hosps. and Instns., Las Vegas State Hosp., 1966-69; hosp. adminstr. Las Vegas Med. Ctr., 1969-76; adminstr. Vista Sandia Hosp., Albuquerque, 1980-83. Vol. Internat. Exec. Svc. Corp. Mem. Ret. Officers Assn., Mensa, Rotary. Home: 810 Faldas De La Sierra Santa Fe NM 87501-1252

NUCKOLS, FRANK JOSEPH, psychiatrist; b. Akron, Ohio, Apr. 7, 1926; s. William Alexander Jr. and Jean (Harrison) N.; m. Jane Fleetwood McIntosh, June 16, 1948; children: Claud Alexander, John Andrew. BA, U. Louisville, 1946; MD, U. Ala., 1951. Diplomate Am. Bd. Psychiatry and Neurology. Intern Holy Name Jesus Hosp., Gadsden, Ala., 1951; ward physician Ala. State Hosp., Tuscaloosa, 1951-52; resident U. Louisville, USPHS Hosp., Lexington, Ky., 1953-56; mem. faculty dept. psychiatry U. Ala. Med. Ctr., Birmingham, 1958-68, dir. tng. psychiat. residents, 1964-68, head div. community psychiatry, 1964-68, head continuing psychiat. edn. for physicians, 1964-68; chief psychiat. staff in-patient svc. U. Hosp., Birmingham, 1966-68; dir. tng. Hill Crest Hosp., Birmingham, 1975-79; pvt. practice Birmingham, 1968-93; cons. Ala. Div. Disability Determinations, Birmingham, 1993—; staff Med. Ctr. East Hosp., Birmingham, Bapt. Med. Ctr. Montclair, Birmingham; cons. staff St. Vincent's Hosp., Birmingham, Lloyd Noland Hosp., Birmingham, South Highland Hosp., Birmingham; vis. faculty, mem. interuniv. forum in cmty. psychiatry Harvard U., Boston, 1963-66; vis. faculty Baylor U. Med. Sch., Houston, 1967-71. Ensign USNR, 1941-43; sr. surgeon USPHS, 1956—. Fellow Am. Psychiat. Assn. (life), So. Psychiat. Assn.; mem. Med. Assn. Ala., So. Med. Assn., Jefferson County Mental Health Assn. (v.p. 1960), Jefferson County Med. Soc., Mental Health Assn. State Ala. (chmn. profl. adv. com. 1961), Nat. Assn. Disability Examiners, Phi Beta Pi, Tau Kappa Epsilon. Home and Office: 3741 River Oaks Cir Birmingham AL 35223-2117

NUDELMAN, PHILLIP M., insurance company executive. V.p. Geriatric Health Corp., Seattle, 1968-1973; pres., ceo Group Health Coop of Puget Sound, Seattle, 1973—. Office: Group Health Coop of Puget Sound 521 Wall St Seattle WA 98121-1524*

NUERNBERG, WILLIAM RICHARD, lawyer; b. Pitts., July 7, 1946; s. William W. and Frances (Hubler) N. BA cum laude, Denison U., 1968; JD cum laude, U. Mich., 1971. Bar: Pa. 1971, U.S. Dist.Ct. (we. dist.) Pa. 1971, Fla. 1995. Ptnr. Eckert Seamans Cherin & Mellott, Miami, 1981—. Pitt fellow U. Pitts. Sch. Bus., 1987-88. Mem. ABA, Pa. Bar Assn., Fla. Bar Assn., Rivers Club. Office: Eckert Seamans Cherin & Mellott 701 Brickell Ave 18th Fl Miami FL 33131

NUESSE, CELESTINE JOSEPH, retired university official; b. Sevastopol, Wis., Nov. 25, 1913; s. George and Salome Helen (Martens) N.; m. Margaret O'Donoghue, 1969. B.E., Central State Tchrs. Coll., Stevens Point, Wis., 1934; M.A., Northwestern U., 1937; Ph.D., Cath. U. Am., 1944, L.H.D., 1982; LL.D., Merrimack Coll., 1960. Tchr. social studies Pub. High Sch., Antigo, Wis., 1934-40; instr. sociology Coll. St. Catherine, St. Paul, 1943, Marquette U., 1943-45; instr. Cath. U. Am., Washington, 1945-48, asst. prof., 1948-52, assoc. prof., 1952-64, prof., 1964-81, prof. emeritus, 1981—, dean Sch. Social Sci., 1952-61, exec. v.p., 1967-81, provost, 1968-79, provost emeritus, 1981—; Spl. rep. in Germany, Nat. Cath. Welfare Conf., 1950-51; mem. U.S. Nat. Commn. for UNESCO, 1950-56, 63-69, exec. com., 1954-56; mem. gov. bd. UNESCO Youth Inst., Munich, Germany, 1955-59; mem. U.S. Bd. Fgn. Scholarships, 1954-58, chmn., 1956-58; mem. D.C. Commr.'s Council Human Relations, 1958-64, D.C. Commn. on Postsecondary Edn., 1975-80. Author: The Social Thought of American Catholics, 1634-1829, 1945, The Catholic University of America: A Centennial History, 1990; co-author, co-editor: The Sociology of the Parish, 1951; staff editor New Cath. Ency., 1963-66, chmn. editl. bd. supplements, 1973-79; contbr. articles to profl. jours. Mem. Am. Cath. Hist. Assn., Am. Cath. Sociol. Soc. (pres. 1954), Am. Sociol. Assn., Cath. Assn. Internat. Peace (pres. 1954-56), Cath. Commn. Intellectual and Cultural Affairs, Inst. Internat. Sociologie, Internat. Conf. on Sociology of Religion (past v.p.), Nat. Cath. Ednl. Assn., Cath. Interracial Council Washington (pres. 1962-66), Phi Beta Kappa (hon.), Alpha Kappa Delta, Pi Gamma Mu, Sigma Tau Delta, Phi Sigma Epsilon. Club: Cosmos (Washington). Lodge: KC. Home: 8108 River Crescent Dr Annapolis MD 21401-8414

NUGENT, CHARLES ARTER, physician; b. Denver, Nov. 18, 1924; s. Charles Arter and Florence (Cohn) N.; m. Margaret Flint, Aug. 30, 1950; children—Stephen, Sara, Daniel. Student, U. Chgo., 1941-43, Ill. Inst. Tech., 1943, U. Minn., 1944, U. S.D., 1945-46; M.D., Yale U., 1951. Intern, asst. resident New Haven Hosp., 1951-53; resident Salt Lake County Gen. Hosp., Salt Lake City, 1954-56; mem. faculty U. Utah Coll. Medicine, 1956-67, assoc. prof. medicine, 1965-67; prof. dept. internal medicine U. Hawaii Med. Sch., 1967-70; prof. sect. endocrinology dept. internal medicine U. Ariz. Coll. Medicine, Tucson, 1970—. Contbr. articles to profl. jours. Served with U.S. Army, 1943-46, 53. James Hudson Brown Meml. fellow, 1949-50. Mem. AAUP, Endocrine Soc., Western Assn. Physicians, Physicians Forum, Am. Soc. Clinical Investigators. Home: 3242 E 5th St Tucson AZ 85716-4902 Office: 1501 N Campbell Ave Tucson AZ 85724-0001

NUGENT, CONSTANCE MARIE JULIE, health facility administrator; b. Lewiston, Maine, July 3, 1933; d. Joseph E.W. Sr. and Beatrice M.J. (Levasseur) Lessard; m. John Thomas Nugent Sr., Jan. 2, 1954 (dec. Feb. 27, 1982); children: John Thomas Jr., Michael Joseph. Diploma in nursing, Maine Gen. Hosp., 1953; BA, St. Joseph's Coll., Windham, Maine, 1974; family nurse practitioner cert., U. Maine Sch. of Nursing, 1976; M in Health Svc. Adminstrn., St. Joseph's Coll., Windham, Maine, 1995. RNNP, Maine, Calif., Ariz. Staff nurse med. surg., peds., gyn. Maine Med. Ctr., Portland, 1953-57; staff nurse ob-gyn. Mercy Hosp., Portland, Maine, 1957-59; emergency rm. nurse Huntington Meml. Hosp., Pasadena, Calif., 1959-63; supr. critical care unit Osteopathic Hosp. of Maine, Portland, 1963-69; clin. instr. sch. nursing Mercy Hosp., Portland, 1969; supr. ICU Dallas (Tex.) Osteopathic Hosp., 1970; adminstr. Nat. Med. Care of Portland, 1970-80; dir. nursing svcs. Lassen Cmty. Hosp., Susanville, Calif., 1980-87, Hospice of Monterey Peninsula, Carmel Valley, Calif., 1987; adminstr. Ukiah (Calif.) Convalescent Hosp., 1988—; cons. Office of Alcohol Drug Abuse Prevention, Augusta, Maine, 1975-77; mem. adv. com. Home Health Care, Portland, 1974-76, adv. coun. Bur. of Elderly, Portland, 1975-80, Provider Health Forum, Susanville, 1983-87. Sec. Lassen County Mental Health Bd., Susanville, 1980-81; co-facilitator Diabetic Clinic, Susanville, 1983-87; vice-chair Lassen County Health Human Svcs. Bd., Susanville, 1985-87. Mem. Bus. and Profl. Women (treas., v.p. 1990-94), Calif. Assn. Health Facilities, Coun. of Long Term Care Nurses of Calif. (pres. Redwood Empire chpt. 1989-92). Republican. Roman Catholic. Avocations: photography, travel, golf, reading. Office: Ukiah Convalescent Hosp 1349 S Dora St Ukiah CA 95482-6512

NUGENT, DANIEL EUGENE, business executive; b. Chgo., Dec. 18, 1927; s. Daniel Edward and Pearl A. (Trieger) N.; m. Bonnie Lynn Weidman, July 1, 1950; children: Cynthia Lynn, Mark Alan, Dale Alan. BSME, Northwestern U., 1951. With U.S. Gypsum Co., Chgo., 1951-71, dir. corp. devel., to 1971; pres. Am. Louver Co., Chgo., 1971-72; v.p. ops. ITT Corp., Cleve., 1972-74; exec. v.p. ITT Corp., St. Paul, 1974-75; v.p., ops. Pentair, Inc., St. Paul, 1974-75, pres., COO, 1975-81, pres., CEO, 1981-86, chmn., CEO, 1986-92, chmn. exec. com., 1992—; chmn. nominating com., dir. Pentair, Inc.; bd. dirs., audit, exec., compensation and corp. governance coms. Apogee Enterprises, Inc. Vice-chmn. local planning commn., 1968-72; co-chmn. Wellspring, 1989-92; trustee Harper Coll., Palatine, 1970-73; mem. adv. commn. McCormick Engring. and Kelloggg Schs. at Northwestern U., MBA Sch. of St. Thomas U., St. Paul; mem. exec. com. Indian Head coun. Boy Scouts Am. With AUS, 1946-47. Mem. North Oaks Golf Club, Mpls. Club. Republican. Presbyterian.

NUGENT, JANE KAY, utility executive; b. Detroit, Aug. 31, 1925; d. Albert A. and Celia (Betzing) Kay; m. Robert L. Nugent, Apr.3, 1991. BS, U. Detroit, 1948; MA, Wayne State U., 1952; MBA, U. Mich., 1963. Sr. personnel interviewer employment Detroit Edison Co., 1948-60, personnel coord. for women, 1960-65, office employment adminstr., 1965-70, gen. employment adminstr., 1970-71, dir. personnel svcs., 1971-72, mgr. employee rels., 1972-77, asst. v.p. employee rels., 1977-78, v.p. employee rels., 1978-82, v.p. adminstrn., 1982-90, ret., 1990; bd. dirs. First Am. Bank-SE Mich., 1986-90, Bon Secours of Mich. Healthcare System, Inc., 1984-93, Detroit Exec. Svc. Corp., 1990—; tchr. U. Detroit Evening Coll. Bus. and Adminstrn., 1963-75; seminar leader div. mgmt. edn. U. Mich., 1968-74, Waterloo Mgmt. Edn. Centre, 1972-77. Mem. Mich. Employment Security Adv. Coun., 1967-81; chmn. bd. dirs. Detroit Inst. Commerce, 1976-79; exec. bd. NCCJ, 1980-91, nat. trustee, 1984-88; bd. dirs. Childrens Home Detroit, 1991—, 1st v.p. 1994-96, pres. 1996—. Recipient Alumni Tower award U. Detroit, 1967, Headliner award Women Wayne State U., 1970, Wayne State U. Alumni Achievement award, 1974, Career Achievement award Profl. Panhellenic Assn., 1973, Bus. Achievement award Assn. Bus. Deans, 1989; named one of Top Ten Working Women of Detroit, 1970, Alumnus of Yr., U. Detroit, 1981, Woman of Yr. Am. Lung Assn., 1991, Sr. Profl. in Human Resources Soc. Human Resource Mgmt.; cert. Adminstrv. Mgr. Am. Mgmt. Soc.; inducted in Mich. Women's Hall of Fame, 1988. Mem. Internat. Assn. Personnel Women (pres. 1969-70), Women's Econ. Club (v.p. 1971-72, pres. 1972-73), Am. Soc. Employees (bd. dirs. 1979-90), Personnel Women Detroit (pres. 1960-61), U. Detroit Alumni Assn. (pres. 1964-66), Phi Gamma Nu (nat. v.p. 1955-57), Boys and Girls Club S.E. Mich. (pres. 1987-89), Econ. Club Detroit (v.p. 1981-90), Internat. Womens Forum.

NUGENT, JOHNNY WESLEY, tractor company executive, state senator; b. Cleve., July 18, 1939; s. Carl Howard and Velma (Holland) N.; m. Nancy Carol Whiteford, Dec. 16, 1960; 1 child, Suzette. Grad. high sch., Aurora, Ind. Owner, mgr. Nugent Tractor Sales, Lawrenceburg, Ind., 1960—; mem. Ind. Senate, Indpls., 1978—; bd. dirs. 1st Nat. Bank Aurora. Commr. Dearborn County, Lawrenceburg, 1966-74. With USAR, 1957-64. Republican. Baptist. Office: State Senate State Capital Indianapolis IN 46204

NUGENT, LORI S., lawyer; b. Peoria, Ill., Apr. 24, 1962; d. Walter Leonard and Margery (Frost) Meyer; m. Shane Vincent Nugent, June 14, 1986; 1 child, Justine Nicole. BA in Polit. Sci. cum laude, Knox Coll., 1984; JD, Northwestern U., Chgo., 1987. Bar: Ill. 1987, U.S. Dist. Ct. (no. dist.) Ill. 1988, U.S. Ct. Appeals (7th cir.) 1995. Assoc. Peterson & Ross, Chgo., 1987-94; assoc. Blatt, Hammesfahr & Eaton, Chgo., 1994, ptnr., 1994—. Co-author: Punitive Damages: A Guide to the Insurability of Punitive Damages in the United States and Its Territories, 1988, Punitive Damages: A State-by-State Guide to Law and Practice, 1991, Japanese edit., 1995; contbr. articles to law jours. Mem. Def. Rsch. Inst. Office: Blatt Hammesfahr & Eaton 333 W Wacker Dr Ste 1900 Chicago IL 60606-1226

NUGENT, MARY KATHERINE, elementary education educator; b. Terre Haute, Ind., Aug. 15, 1953; d. Thomas Patrick and Jeanne (Butts) N. BS, Ind. State U., Terre Haute, 1975, MS, 1978. Cert. in elem. edn., spl. edn., Ind. Tchr. 6th grade Cloverdale (Ind.) Sch. Corp., 1976-79; tchr. 4th-6th grades Glenwood Sch., Richardson, Tex., 1986-88; tchr. intermediate mentally handicapped class Meadows Elem. Sch., Terre Haute, 1988-89, tchr. 5th grade, 1989-90, tchr. 4th grade, 1990-93; tchr. 6th grade lang. arts and reading Woodrow Wilson Mid. Sch., Terre Haute, 1993—; mem. steering com. Tchr. Applying Whole Lang., Terre Haute, 1989-91. Avocations: reading, gardening, computers. Office: Vigo County Sch Corp 961 Lafayette Ave Terre Haute IN 47804-2929

NUGENT, NELLE, theater, film and television producer; b. Jersey City, May 24, 1939; d. John Patrick and Evelyn Adelaide (Stern) N.; m. Donald G. Baker, June 6, 1960 (div. 1962); m. Benjamin Janney, June 22, 1969 (div. Apr., 1980); m. Jolyon Fox Stern, Apr. 7, 1982; 1 child, Alexandra Fox Stern. BS, Skidmore Coll., 1960, DHL (hon.), 1981. Chmn. bd. McCann & Nugent, Prodns. Inc. (mgmt. and prodn. co.), N.Y.C., 1976-86; pres. Foxboro Prodns., Inc., N.Y.C., 1985-94; pres., CEO Foxboro Entertainment, 1990-94; pres. The Foxboro Co., Inc.; co-prin. Golden Fox Films, Inc. Stage mgr. various off-Broadway shows, 1960-64; prodn. asst.: Broadways plays Any Wednesday, 1963-64, Dylan, 1964, Ben Franklin in Paris, 1964-65; stage mgr. Broadway shows, 1964-68; prodn. supr., then gen. mgr., 1969-76, assoc. mng. dir. Nederlander Corp., operating theaters and producing plays in, N.Y.C. and on tour, 1970-76; prodr.: Dracula, 1977 (Tony award), The Elephant Man, 1978 (Tony award, Drama Critics award), Morning's at Seven, 1980 (Tony award), Home, 1980 (Tony nomination), Amadeus, 1981 (Tony award); also produced: Rose and Piaf, 1980, The Life and Adventures of Nicholas Nickleby, 1981 (Tony award, Drama Critics award), The Dresser (Tony award nominee), 1981, Mass Appeal, 1981; The Lady & The Clarinet, 1982; The Glass Menagerie (revival), 1983; Painting Churches (Obie award), 1983; Total Abandon, 1983; All's Well That End's Well, 1983 (Tony nominee); Pilobolus Dance Company, 1983; Pacific Overtures (revival), 1984; Much Ado about Nothing/Cyrano de Bergerac (repertory) (Tony award nominees), 1984; Leader of the Pack (Tony award nominee), 1985, The Life and Adventures of Nicholas Nickleby (revival) (Tony award nominee), 1986; prodr.: TV spls.; Morning's At Seven, Piaf; Pilobolus; producer A Fighting Choice, Walt Disney Prodns., 1986, Phoenix Entertainment Group, 1986-88, A Conspiracy of Love, CBS, 1987, The Final Verdict, TNT, 1990 (Cable Ace award nominee Best Picture); exec. prodr. (TV pilot) Morning Maggie, 1987, Dick Clark Prodns., 1988-90, (feature film) Student Body, 1993, (Showtime) In the Presence of Mine Enemies, 1995. Mem. Am. Women's Econ. Devel. Corp. (bd. dirs.). Office: Foxboro Co Inc 133 E 58th St Ste 301 New York NY 10022-1236

NUGENT, ROBERT J., JR., fast food company executive; b. 1942. BBA, U. Cin., 1964. loan officer Citizens Savs., 1964-67; asst. v.p. Gem City Savs., 1967-69; v.p. Ponderosa System Inc., 1969-78, Ky. Fried Chicken, 1978-79; v.p. Foodmaker Inc., San Diego, from 1979, exec. v.p. ops., mktg., 1985-95; CEO, pres. Foodmaker Inc., 1995—. Office: Foodmaker Inc 9330 Balboa Ave San Diego CA 92113*

NUGENT, THEODORE ANTHONY, musician; b. Detroit, Dec. 13, 1948; s. Warren Henry and Marion Dorothy (Johnson) N.; divorced; children: Sasha Emma, Theodore Tobias. Ed., Oakland Community Coll., Detroit. Also profl. off-road racer, 1981—. Guitarist, 1958—, mem. group, Amboy Dukes, 1965, solo artist, 1965—; recs. include: (with Amboy Dukes) Ted Nugent and the Amboy Dukes, 1968, Journey to the Center of the Mind, 1968, Marriage on the Rocks, 1970, Survival of the Fittest, 1974, Call of the Wild, 1974, Tooth, Fang, and Claw, 1975; (solo albums) Ted Nugent, 1975, Free for All, 1976, Cat Scratch Fever, 1977, Double Live Gonzo, 1977, Weekend Warriors, 1978, State of Shock, 1979, Scream Dream, 1980, Great Gonzos/The Best of, 1981, Intensities in Ten Cities, 1981, Penetrator, 1984, Little Miss Dangerous, 1986, If You Can't Lick 'Em...Lick 'Em, 1988; (with Damn Yankees) Damn Yankees, 1990, Don't Tread, 1992. Mem. ASCAP, Nat. Rifle Assn. (life), Ducks Unlimited (life sponsor), Nat. Trappers Assn., Mich. Bowhunters, Safari Club Internat. Address: PO Box 15108 Ann Arbor MI 48106-5108 also: Sony Music Entertainment Inc. 550 Madison Ave New York NY 10022-3211

NUGTEREN, CORNELIUS, air force officer; b. Colton, S.D., Feb. 7, 1928; s. Adrian Joe and Marie Johanna N.; m. Liane Albrecht, Sept. 22, 1956; children: Cecile, Aneli. B.A., Central Coll., Pella, Iowa, 1951. Commd. 2d lt. USAF, 1953, advanced through grades to maj. gen., 1980; advisor Vietnam Air Force, 1970-71, served in Germany, 1971-77; vice comdr. (Air Logistics Center), Utah, 1977-79; comdr. (Aerospace Rescue and Recovery Service), Scott AFB, Ill., 1979-81; chief (Joint U.S. Mil. Aid Group), Greece, 1981-82; comdr. Air Logistics Ctr., Robins AFB, Ga, 1983-88, ret.; cons. for def. industries Warner Robins, Ga., 1988—; v.p. Chem. Tech. Internat., Warner Robins; 1988—. Decorated D.S.M., Legion of Merit, Bronze Star, Superior Service medal; recipient USAF EEO award, 1979. Mem. Air Force Assn., Order Daedalians, Internat. Order Hansen, Order of the Sword. Office: 114 Holly Dr Warner Robins GA 31088-6615 *Service to one's country is not just a job...it's a calling. Integrity to and within the institution to which you belong is an absolute necessity. Loyalty to peers and subordinates is equally important as loyalty to your superiors. Attitude toward life, humankind and profession is key determinant to success. Goals should be set high enough so as to be unattainable. Standard of conduct must always include duty, honor, country.*

NULAND, SHERWIN, surgeon, author; b. N.Y.C., Dec. 8, 1930; s. Meyer and Violet (Lutsky) N.; m. Sarah Peterson, May 29, 1977; children: Victoria Jane, Andrew Meyer, William Peterson, Amelia Rose. BA, NYU, 1951; MD, Yale U., 1955. Surgeon Yale-New Haven Hosp. (Conn.), 1962-91; clin. prof. surgery Yale Sch. Medicine, New Haven, 1962—. Author: The Origins of Anesthesia, 1983, Doctors: The Biography of Medicine, 1988, Medicine: The Art of Healing, 1991, The Face of Mercy, 1993, How We Die: Reflections on Life's Final Chapter, 1994 (Nat. Book award for non-fiction 1994, Pulitzer prize finalist 1995). Pres. med. com. Jewish Home Aged, New Haven, 1985-87; v.p. Conn. Hospice, New Haven, 1978-80. Fellow ACS; mem. New Eng. Surg. Soc., Assocs. of Yale Med. Sch. Libr. (chmn. 1982-94), Yale-China Assn. (chmn. med. 1988-93). Democrat. Jewish. Avocation: tennis. Home: 29 Old Hartford Tpke Hamden CT 06517-3523 Office: PO Box 6356 Hamden CT 06517-0356

NULL, JACK ELTON, schools superintendent; b. New Haven, Ind., May 22, 1938; s. Clifford Lewis and Violet Alice (Shuler) N.; 1 child, Richard Lance; m. Bonnie Bermes Ottenweller, Dec. 2, 1995. BS in Bus. Mgmt., Ind. U., 1960; MA in Elem. Edn., Ball State U., 1963; EdD in Ednl. Adminstrn., Ariz. State U., 1974. Cert. elem. edn. tchr., prin., bus. mgr., supt., Ariz. Adminstrv. asst. to dir. of purchasing Cummins Engine Co., Columbus, Ind., 1960-61; tchr. Randolph Cen. Schs., Winchester, Ind., 1963; tchr., coach East Allen County Schs., New Haven, 1963-66; from prin. to adminstrv. asst. to prin. Wilson Sch. Dist. 6, Phoenix, 1966-73; acting supt., exec. asst. Washington Sch. Dist. 7, Phoenix, 1973-79; supt. Fowler Sch. Dist. 45, Phoenix, 1979—; supt.'s chmn. Westside IMPACT, Phoenix, Tolleson,

Avondale, Goodyear and Litchfield, Ariz., 1988-92; All Ariz. Supt., 1992-93. Football ofcl. PAC-10, Big Sky, Ariz. C.C. Athletic Conf., Ariz. Interscholastic Assn., 1966-95, basketball ofcl., 1963-85; clock operator NFL, Phoenix, 1987—; vice chmn. West Phoenix Cactus League Baseball Coalition, 1991-93, Ariz. Edn. Revorm Com., 1993—. Sgt. USAFR, 1961-66. Named Football Ofcl. Yr. ACCAC, 1990, 94. Mem. Am. Assn. Sch. Adminstrs., Ariz. Sch. Adminstrs. Inc. (charter; chmn. lgeis. com. 1992—, bd. dirs. supts. divsn. 1993—, pres. 1995-96, exec. bd. 1994—), Maricopa County Supt. Assn. (treas. 1970-71, pres. 1971-72), Greater Phoenix Supts. Assn. Democrat. Congregationalist. Avocations: investments, sports.

NULL, PAUL BRYAN, minister; b. Oakland, Calif., May 7, 1944; s. Carleton Elliot and Dorothy Irene (Bryan) N.; m. Renee Yvonne Howell, Aug. 23, 1969; children: Bryan Joseph, Kara Renee. BS, Western Bapt. Coll., 1973; MDiv, Western Conservative Bapt. Sem., 1979; DMin, Trinity Theol. Sem., 1994. Ordained to ministry Bapt. Ch., 1982. Asst. pastor Bethel Bapt. Ch., Aumsville, Oreg., 1972-74, sr. pastor, 1974-87; sr. pastor The Calvary Congregation, Stockton, Calif., 1987-94; pastor Sierra Comty. Ch., South Lake Tahoe, Calif., 1994—; trustee Conservative Bapt. Assn. of Oreg., 1982-85, mem. Ch. extension com., 1975-85. Radio show commentator Food for Thought, 1987. Panel mem. Presdl. Anti-Drug Campaign, 1984. Served with U.S. Army, 1965-67. Named Outstanding Young Man Am., 1979. Mem. Conservative Bapt. Assn. of Am., No. Calif. Conservative Bapt. Assn. (pres. 1992-93), Delta Epsilon Chi. Avocations: weight training, aerobics, writing, hiking, cross-country skiing. Home: 1399 Iroquois Circle South Lake Tahoe CA 96150 Office: Sierra Comty Ch 1165 Sierra Blvd South Lake Tahoe CA 96150

NULTON, WILLIAM CLEMENTS, lawyer; b. Pittsburg, Kans., Feb. 22, 1931; s. Perley Edgar and Mary Celia (Anderson) N.; m. Vicki Smith, Aug. 20, 1956; children: Carnie, Erica. BA, Kans. U., 1953, LLB with honors, 1958; postgrad., NYU, 1953-54. Bar: Kans. 1958, Mo. 1959. Sr. atty. Great Lakes Pipe Line Co., Kansas City, Mo., 1958-66, asst. sec., 1961-66; assoc. Blackwell, Sanders, Matheny, Weary & Lombardi, Kansas City, 1966-68, ptnr., 1968-81; assoc. Shughart Thomson & Kilroy, Kansas City, 1981-83, ptnr., 1983-94. Contbr. articles to profl. jours. Bd. dirs. Corinth Hills Home Assn., Shawnee Mission, 1974-76; pres. Beta Theta Pi Kansas City Alumni Assn., 1977; mem. Elder Village United Presbyn. Ch., Prairie Village, Kans., 1976—, trustee, 1992-94; bd. dirs. Kansas City Civil Rights Consortium, 1993—, Marillac Acad., 1994—; mem. Kans. adv. com. U.S. Civil Rights Commn., 1994—; mem. Shawnee Mission Unified Bd. Edn., 1969-73, v.p., 1973; pres. Corinth Elem. Bd. Edn., Johnson County, Kans., 1969; chmn. Full Employment Task Group on Employment Disabled, Kansas City, 1987. Summerfield scholar Kans. U., 1949-53, Root-Tilden scholar NYU, 1953-54. Mem. ABA (mgmt. chmn. labor and employment law sect., com. on arbitration and collective bargaining 1989-92), Am. Acad. Hosp. Attys. (co-chmn. task group on bylaws for small rural hosps. 1992—), Mo. Bar Assn. (chmn. labor law com. 1982), Nat. Health Lawyers Assn. (co-chmn. task group on alternative dispute resolution in health care field 1990—), Phi Beta Kappa. Republican. Home: 7908 El Monte St Shawnee Mission KS 66208-5047

NUNES, GEOFFREY, lawyer, corporate executive; b. N.Y.C., July 7, 1930; s. Kenneth Neville and Helen (Landsberg) N.; m. Clare Harwood, Sept. 13, 1958; children: Geoffrey Jr., John Kenneth, Margaret Hamilton Nunes Rogers. AB, Princeton U., 1952; LLB, Harvard U., 1957. Bar: N.Y. 1957, N.J. 1968, Mass. 1978. Assoc. atty. Breed Abbott & Morgan, N.Y.C., 1957-61, Shea & Gould, N.Y.C., 1961-66; v.p., gen. counsel Lenox, Inc., Princeton, N.J., 1966-76; sr. v.p., gen. consel Millipore Corp., Bedford, Mass., 1976—; bd. dirs. Reebok Internat., Stoughton, Mass., Scottish Widows Internat. Mut. Found. Trustee, bd. dirs. DeCordova Mus., Lincoln, Mass., Boston Biomed. Rsch. Inst., 1992; bd. overseers New Eng. Conservatory, 1996. Office: Millipore Corp 80 Ashby Rd Bedford MA 01730-2237

NUNEZ-LAWTON, MIGUEL G., international finance specialist; b. Havana, Cuba, Feb. 8, 1949; came to U.S., 1964; s. Miguel Nunez-Portuondo and Silvia Lawton-Alfonso. BBA, Georgetown U., 1971, postgrad. in Econs., 1973. Asst. treas. Deltec Securities Corp., N.Y.C., 1971; debt specialist internat. econs. dept. World Bank, Washington, 1973—; UNCTAD chief tech. adviser Bureau of the Treasury, Manila, Philippines, 1989-90. Bd. dirs., treas. Friends of Art Mus. of the Americas, OAS, Washington, 1988-90; bd. dirs. Friends of Peru, 1991—; panel mem. The Lawrenceville Sch., 1992. Roman Catholic. Avocations: art collecting, genealogy. Home: 2844 Wisconsin Ave NW Apt 510 Washington DC 20007-4720 Office: World Bank 1818 H St NW Washington DC 20433-0001

NUNEZ-PORTUONDO, RICARDO, investment company executive; b. N.Y.C., June 9, 1933; s. Emilio and Maria (Garcia) N-P.; m. Dolores Maldonado, Sept. 7, 1963; children—Ricardo Jose, Emilio Manuel, Eduardo Javier. LL.D., U. Havana, Cuba; postdoctoral in law, U. Fla., 1975. Bar: Cuba, Fla. Editor Latin Am. div. USIA, Miami, Fla., 1961-71; editor Latin Am. div. USIA, Washington, 1961-71; nat. dir. Cuban Refugee Program, Washington, 1975-77; pres. Cultural Pub., Inc., Miami, 1994—, Central Investment Trust, Coral Gables, Fla., 1977—; chmn. bd. Interstate Bank of Commerce, Miami, 1986-88; v.p. Century 21, Coral Gables, 1989—. Author: A Critique on the Linowitz Report, 1975, Cuba: La Otra Imagen, 1994, Un Procer Cubano, 1994, Cuban Refugee Program, The Early Years, 1995. dir. Nat. Hispanic Scholarship Fund, San Francisco, 1978—; dir. COSSMHO, Washington, 1980—; trustee emeritus Fla. Internat. U., 1984—; pres. Mercy Hosp. Found., Miami, 1985—; bd. dirs. ARC, Greater Miami. Recipient numerous awards for civic contbns. including day named in honor Ricardo Nunez Day, Miami, 1975. Mem. Cuban Lawyers Assn., Cuban Acad. History, Metro. Club, Lyford Cay Club, Ocean Reef Club, Key Biscayne Yacht Club, Big Five Club, 200 Club. Republican. Roman Catholic. Home: 675 Solano Prado Miami FL 33156-2373 Office: PO Box 141720 Coral Gables FL 33114-1720

NUNIS, DOYCE BLACKMAN, JR., historian, educator; b. Cedartown, Ga., May 30, 1924; s. Doyce Blackman and Winnie Ethel (Morris) N. B.A., U. Calif., Los Angeles, 1947; M.S., U. So. Calif., 1950, M.Ed., 1952, Ph.D., 1958. Lectr. U. So. Calif., 1951-56; instr. El Camino Coll., 1956-59; asst. prof. edn. and history UCLA, 1959-65; assoc. prof. history U. So. Calif., 1965-68, prof., 1968-89, emeritus, 1989—; asst. research historian U. Calif., Los Angeles, 1959-63; asso. U. Calif., 1963-65, lectr., 1960-61, asst. prof. edn. and history, 1961-64, asso. prof., 1964-65. Author: Andrew Sublette, Rocky Mountain Prince, 1960, Josiah Belden, 1841 California Overland Pioneer, 1962, The Golden Frontier: The Recollections of Herman Francis Rinehart, 1851-69, 1962, The California Diary of Faxon Dean Atherton, 1836-39, 1964, Letters of a Young Miner, 1964, The Journal of James H. Bull, 1965, The Trials of Isaac Graham, 1967, The Medical Journey of Pierre Garnier in California, 1851, 1967, Past is Prologue, 1968, Hudson's Bay Company's First Fur Brigade to the Sacramento Valley, 1968, Sketches of a Journey on Two Oceans by H.J.A. Alric, 1850-1867, 1971, San Francisco 1856 Vigilance Committee: Three Views, 1971, The Drawings of Ignatio Tirsh, Los Angeles and Its Environs in the 20th Century, A Bibliography, 1973, A History of American Political Thought, 2 vols, 1975, The Mexican War in Baja California, 1977, Henry Hoyt's A Frontier Doctor, 1979, Los Angeles from the Days of the Old Pueblo, 1981, The 1769 Transit of Venus, 1982, The Missionary Letters of Jacob Baegert, 1982, Men, Medicine and Water, 1982, Southern California Historical Anthology, 1984, George Coe's Frontier Fighter, 1984, Life of Tom Horn, 1987, A Guide to the History of California, 1989, Great Doctors of Medicine, 1990, The Bidwell-Bartleson Party, 1991, The Life of Tom Horn Revisited, 1992, Southern California's Spanish Heritage, 1992, Southern California Local History, A Gathering of W.W. Robinson's Writings, 1993, From Mexican Days to the Gold Rush, 1993, Tales of Mexican California, 1994, Women in the Life of Southern California, 1996, Hispanic California Revisited, 1996, The Presidio of San Francisco under Spain and Mexico, 1775-1848, 1996; editor So. Calif. Quar., 1962—; contbr. articles to profl. jours. Trustee Mission Santa Barbara Archives-Libr., 1970—, pres., 1972—. Decorated Denemerenti, Papal medal, 1984; recipient Distinction award Calif. Com. for Promotion of History, 1985, Merit award Calif. Conf. Hist. Socs., 1986, Franciscan Hist. award, 1990, Disting. Emeritus award U. So. Calif., 1993, Knight Comdr. of St. Gregory, 1993, Order of Isabella the Cath. (Spanish Govt.), 1995, Oscar Lewis award Book Club of Calip, 1996; Henry E. Huntington Libr. grantee-in-aide, 1960, Am. Philos. Soc. grantee, 1969; Guggenheim fellow, 1963-64. Fellow Calif. Hist. Soc. (trustee 1987-93, v.p. 1989-93, Henry R. Wagner award 1988), Hist. Soc. So. Calif.; mem. Am. Antiquarian Soc., Am. Hist. Assn., Orgn. Am. Historians, Western Hist. Assn., Zamorano Club, L.A. Corral Westerners, Phi Alpha Theta, Pi Sigma Alpha. Home: 4426 Cromwell Ave Los Angeles CA 90027-1250

NUNIS, RICHARD A., amusement parks executive; b. Cedartown, Ga., May 30, 1932; s. Doyce Blackman and Winnie E. (Morris) N.; m. Mary Nunis; 1 child from previous marriage, Richard Dean. B.S. in Edn, U. So. Calif., 1954. With The Walt Disney Co., 1955—; dir. ops. Disneyland, Calif., 1961-68; chmn. park ops. com. Disneyland, 1968-74; corp. v.p. Disneyland Ops. (Disneyland, Walt Disney World, Tokyo Disneyland), 1968-91, Walt Disney World, Orlando, Fla., 1971—; exec. v.p., then pres. Walt Disney Attractions and Disneyland Internat., 1972-91; chmn. Walt Disney Attractions, 1991—; mem. exec. com. Walt Disney Co.; adv. bd. Travel and Tourism, U.S. Dept. of Commerce; Recreation Roundtable; bd. dirs. Suntrust, Orlando, Fla. Exec. adv. bd. dirs. Give the Kids the World; bd. dirs. Fla. Progress Bd., Econ. Devel. commn. Mid-Fla. Inc., U. Ctrl. Fla. Found., Inc., Fla. Coun. of 100 Bd., United Arts of Ctrl. Fla., Enterprise Fla. Inc.; mem. adv. bd. In Roads/Ctrl. Fla. Inc.; mem. Fla. Transp. Commn. Named First Acad. All-Am. U. So. Calif., 1952, Richard L. McLaughlin Fla. Econ. Devel. Vol. of Yr., 1995. Mem. Fla. Isleworth Golf and Country Club. Republican. Avocations: sports, fishing, golf. Office: Walt Disney Attractions Inc PO Box 10000 Lake Buena Vista FL 32830-1000 *Do the best job you can with the job you are given to do. Those who look over the hill never climb the mountain.*

NUNLEY, MALINDA VAUGHN, retired elementary school educator; d. William D. and Callie (Ross) Vaughn; m. Harry H. Nunley, Dec. 24, 1940 (dec.); chidlren: Jerry Michael, Sally Coleen. BS in Edn., Mid. Tenn. State U., 1961; MEd in Psychology, Middle Tenn. State U., 1972; postgrad., U. Tenn., Chattanooga, 1974-80, Mid. Tenn. State U. Cert. art tchr., spl. edn. tchr., guidance counselor and cons., individual testing and diagnostics in spl. edn. Tenn. Tchr. Panama Canal Co, Balboa, Panama Canal Zone, 1954-56; adult tchr. U.S. Army, Ft. Davis, Panama Canal Zone, 1956-60; elem. tchr. Ancon Elem. Panama Canal Zone Sch., Tenn., 1961-64; tchr. South Pitts. High Sch., 1964-66, Normal Park Elem. Sch., Chattanooga, Tenn., 1966-71; spl. edn. tchr. Griffith Creek Elem. Sch., Tenn., 1971-83; ret. Tenn.; tutor, substitute tchr., speaker to groups, Tenn., 1994—; homebound tchr. for alcohol and drug abuse adolescents, 1989-90; spl. speaker to class groups 4th-7th, 1993-94. Mem. NEA, Tenn. Edn. Assn., Marion County Tchrs. Assn., Tenn. Ret. Tchrs. Assn., Chattanooga Edn. Assn. (past faculty rep.). Home: 6555 Highway 27 Chattanooga TN 37405-7288

NUNN, CHARLES BURGESS, religious organization executive; b. Richmond, Va., May 1, 1931; s. Charles Burgess Sr. and Virginia Atkinson (Goode) N.; m. Helen Agnes Parker, Sept. 1, 1957; children: Patsy Virginia, Catherine Louise, Stephen Charles, Stewart Gavin. BA in Econs., Randolph Macon Coll., 1953; BD, Southwestern Bapt. Theol. Sem., 1959, MD, 1969; DD, Pitts. Theol. Sem., 1979. Ordained to Gospel ministry, 1954. Pastor Warwick Rd. Bapt. Chapel, Richmond, Va., 1952-53, Garrett's Bluff Bapt. Ch., Arthur City, Tex., 1954-56, Plymouth Haven Bapt. Ch., Alexandria, Va., 1959-68, First Bapt. Ch., Bluefield, W.Va., 1968-77; exec. dir. missions Richmond (Va.) Bapt. Assn., 1977—; trustee Bluefield (W.Va.) Coll., 1972-82, U. Richmond, Va., 1989-93; first v.p. Va. Bapt. Gen. Bd., Richmond, 1974-75; dir. Home Mission Bd., So. Bapt. Conv., Atlanta, 1976-84. Author: (children's book) Following Jesus, 1968. Commr. Bluefield (W.Va.) Urban Renewal Authority, 1971-74; chmn. Bluefield (W.Va.) Beautification Commn., 1972-73; pres. North Chamberlayne Civic Assn., Richmond, 1989-91. Recipient Disting. Svc. award City of Bluefield, 1970, Disting. Alumnus award Alumni Soc. Randolph Macon, Ashland, Va., 1992, Vol. Missions award Richmond Regional Devel. Coun. of the Fgn. Mission Bd., So. Bapt. Conv., 1995. Mem. Richmond Rotary Club (bd. dirs. 1990-92), Omicron Delta Kappa. Avocations: traveling, fishing, photography, baseball. Office: Richmond Bapt Assn 3111 Moss Side Ave Richmond VA 23222

NUNN, GRADY HARRISON, political science educator emeritus; b. Arlington, Tex., Apr. 12, 1918; s. William Roy and Floy Brooke (Dugan) N.; m. Ann Torrey Welsh, June 15, 1951 (dec. 1980); 1 child, Therese von Hohoff.; m. Virginia Cotton Chivington, Dec. 18, 1982. B.A., U. Okla., 1939, M.A., 1941; Ph.D. (Penfield fellow), N.Y.U., 1961. Instr. N.Y.U., 1946-49; from instr. to asso. prof. U. Ala., Tuscaloosa, 1949-65; prof., chmn. dept. polit. sci. U. Ala., Birmingham, 1969-83, prof. emeritus, 1983—; vis. asst. prof. Ind. U., 1960-61; asst. prof., assoc. prof. U. Pitts. at Ahmadu Bello U., Nigeria, 1964-68; assoc. prof. U. Pitts., 1968, Auburn U., 1968-69; Bd. dirs. Unitarian Universalist Service Com., 1978-84, v.p., 1981-82. Assoc. editor: Background on World Politics, 1957-62; Contbr. to: Readings in Government in American Society, 1949, Federalism in the Commonwealth, 1963, The Politics and Administration of Nigerian Government, 1965; editorial bd.: Jour. of Politics, 1971-74. Served to capt., F.A. AUS, 1942-46. Ford Found. Fgn. Area fellow, 1956-57. Mem. Am. Polit. Sci. Assn., So. Polit. Sci. Assn. (exec. council 1974-77), Royal African Soc., AAUP (pres. Ala. conf.), Phi Beta Kappa, Pi Sigma Alpha, Phi Eta Sigma, Alpha Tau Omega, Omicron Delta Kappa. Unitarian. Home: 1152 52nd St S Birmingham AL 35222-3925

NUNN, KENNETH LEE, lawyer; b. Louisville, Mar. 22, 1940; s. Richard and Grace (Lynch) N.; m. Leah K. Blades, Aug. 19, 1962; children: Vicky A., David L. BS in Bus., Ind. U., 1964, JD, 1967. Bar: Ind. 1967, U.S. Dist. Ct. (so. dist.) Ind. 1967, U.S. Ct. Appeals (7th cir.) 1974, U.S. Supreme Ct. 1974. Ptnr. Nunn, Kelley & Greene, Bloomington, Ind. Office: Nunn Kelley & Greene 123 S College Ave Bloomington IN 47404-5166

NUNN, ROBERT WARNE, lawyer; b. Salem, Oreg., Sept. 20, 1950; s. Warne Harry and Delores (Netz) N.; m. Kandis Brewer; 1 child, Hayley Elisabeth. Student, U. Vienna, Austria, 1971; BS, Willamette U., 1972; MS in Acctg., Northeastern U., Boston, 1973; JD, U. Oreg., 1976. Bar: Oreg 1976, U.S. Dist. Ct. Oreg. 1977, U.S. Ct. Appeals (9th cir.) 1977, U.S. Supreme Ct. 1982, Wash. 1986. Ptnr. Schwabe, Williamson &, Wyatt, Portland, Oreg., 1976-92; ptnr., chmn. corp. dept. Preston, Gates & Ellis, Portland, 1992-96; founder, mng. ptnr. Nunn & Motschenbacher LLP, Portland, 1996—. Mem. exec. com. Am. Leadership Forum, 1988-94, sr. fellow, 1988—; bd. mgrs. Multnomah Metro Br. YMCA, Portland, 1983-86, chmn., 1984-85; pres. Oreg. divsn. Am. Cancer Soc., Portland, 1986-87, bd. dirs., 1982-88; trustee Marylhurst Coll., Oreg., 1985-91, Willamette U., 1991—; trustee World Affairs Coun. Oreg., 1991—, pres., 1995-96; bd. dirs. United Way of Columbia-Willamette, Portland, 1984-87. Am. Leadership fellow, 1987; named Order of Red Sword Am. Cancer Soc., 1985. Mem. ABA, Oreg. Bar Assn. (CPA joint com., past chmn. legal assts. and legal investigators com., cert. subcom., fee arbitration panel), Internat. Bar Assn., Nat. Assn. Bond Lawyers (vice-chmn. mcpl. utility obligations com.), Pacific N.W. Internat. Trade Assn., Portland C. of C. (chmn. internat. trade com.), Univ. Club, Multhnomah Athletic Club (Portland). Republican. Lutheran. Avocations: computers, skiing, sailing. Home: 10910 SW 29th Ct Portland OR 97219-7585

NUNN, SAMUEL (SAM NUNN), senator; b. Perry, Ga., Sept. 8, 1938; s. Samuel Augustus and Elizabeth (Cannon) N.; m. Colleen O'Brien, Sept. 25, 1965; children: Michelle, Brian. Student, Ga. Tech. Coll., 1956-59; A.B., LL.B., Emory U., 1962. Bar: Ga. 1962. Legal counsel armed services com. U.S. Ho. Reps., 1963; mem. firm Nunn, Geiger & Rampey, Perry, Ga., 1964-73; mem. Ga. Ho. Reps., 1968-72; U.S. senator from Ga., 1972-96; ranking Dem. mem. Armed Services Com.; mem. Govtl. Affairs Com., Small Bus. Com., Senate Dem. Steering and Coordination Com.; ranking Dem. Permanent Subcom. on Investigations of Govt. Affairs; farmer, Perry, 1964—. Office: US Senate 303 Dirksen Senate Bldg Washington DC 20510

NUNN, TREVOR ROBERT, director; b. Ipswich, Eng., Jan. 14, 1940; s. Robert Alexander and Dorothy May (Piper) N.; m. Janet Suzman, 1969 (div. 1985); 1 child; m. Sharon Lee Hill, 1986 (div. 1991); 2 children; m. Imogen Stubbs, 1994; 2 children. Student, Ipswich Coll., Downing Coll., Cambridge, Eng.; LLD, U. Warwick, 1982; MA (hon.), U. Newcastle-upon-Tyne, 1982. Trainee dir. Belgrade Theatre, Coventry; assoc. dir. Royal Shakespeare Co., Warwickshire, Eng., 1964-68, artistic dir., 1968-78, joint artistic dir., 1978-86, chief exec., 1968-86, dir. emeritus, 1986—; artistic dir. designate Royal Nat. Theatre, London; artistic dir. designate Royal Nat. Theatre. Dir. plays including Tango, 1965, The Revenger's Tragedy, 1965, 69, The Taming of the Shrew, The Relapse, The Winter's Tale, 1969, Hamlet, 1970, Henry VIII, 1970, Roman Season: Antony and Cleopatra, Coriolanus, Julius Caesar, Titus Andronicus, 1970, Macbeth, 1974, 76, Hedda Gabler (own version) 1975, Romeo and Juliet, 1976, Comedy of Errors, 1976, The Alchemist, 1977, As You Like It, 1977, Every Good Boy Deserves Favour, 1977, Three Sisters, 1978, The Merry Wives of Windsor, 1979, Once in a Lifetime, 1979 (Evening Standard Best Dir. award), Juno and the Paycock, 1980, The Life and Adventures of Nicholas Nickleby (with John Caird), 1980 (Tony Best Dir. award 1981, Evening Standard Best Dir. award), touring revival, 1985, Cats, 1981 (Best Dir. Tony award 1982), All's Well That Ends Well, 1981, Henry IV (parts I and II), 1981, 82, Peter Pan (with John Caird), 1982, Starlight Express, 1984, Les Miserables (with John Caird), 1985 (Tony award for best dir. 1987), Fair Maid of the West, 1986, Chess, 1986, Aspects of Love, 1989, Othello, 1989, The Baker's Wife, 1989, Timon of Athens, 1991 (Evening Standard Best Dir. award, Best Dir. Critics' Cir. award), The Blue Angel, 1991, Measure for Measure, 1991, Heartbreak House, 1992, Arcadia, 1993, Sunset Boulevard, 1993 (Tony nominee - Direction of a Musical, 1995); (opera) Idomeneo, 1982, Porgy and Bess, 1986, revived 1987,92, Cosi Fan Tutte, 1991, Peter Grimes, 1992, Katya Kabanova, 1994; TV shows Include: Anthony and Cleopatra, 1975, Comedy of Errors, 1976, Every Good Boy Deserves Favour, 1978, Three Sisters, 1978, Macbeth, 1978, Great Hamlets, 1983, Othello, 1990, Porgy and Bess, 1993; writer, dir. Shakespeare Workshops Word of Mouth, 1979, films Hedda, Lady Jane, 1985, Twelfth Night, 1996; author: British Theatre Design, 1989. Recipient London Theatre Critics Best Dir. award, 1969; Soc. Film and TV Arts award, 1975, Ivor Novello award for best Brit. Musical, 1976; numerous others. Office: Homevale Ltd, Gloucester Mansions 3d Fl, Cambridge Circus London WC2H 8HD, England

NUNNALLY, DOLORES BURNS, retired physical education educator; b. Strong, Ark., Jan. 2, 1932; d. Marion Saunders Burns and Emma Jo (Burns) Baca; m. Curtis Jerome Nunnally, Apr. 16, 1954; 1 child, Jo Lynn Nunnally Blair. BSE, Ark. State Tchrs. Coll., 1953; MSE, State Coll. Ark., 1964; EdD, U. Sarasota, 1981. Phys. edn. tchr. El Dorado (Ark.) Pub. Schs., 1953-72; real estate salesman Continental Real Estate, Downers Grove, Ill., 1972-74; phys. edn. instr. Triton Coll., River Grove, Ill., 1973-74; substitute tchr. DuPage and Kane County Schs., Ill., 1972-74; phys. edn. tchr. Wheeling (Ill.) Sch. Dist. 21, 1974-91; tennis coach El Dorado Pub. Schs., 1953-73; tennis pro El Dorado Racquet Club, City of El Dorado, summers 1965-72. Contbr. articles to profl. jours. Pres. Ark. Sq. Dance Fedn., Little Rock, 1971-72, Progressive Sunday Sch., El Dorado, 1994—. Recipient All Star Coaches Clinic award Ark. H.S. Coaches Assn., 1971. Mem. NEA, AAHPERD (pres. 1969-70, State Honor award 1972), Ark. Assn. Health, Phys. Edn., Recreation and Dance (life), Ill. Assn. Health, Phys. Edn., Recreation and Dance (Quarter Century award 1981, Svc. award 1991), U.S. Tennis Assn., Order Eastern Star, Delta Phi Kappa. Methodist. Avocations: league tennis, swimming. Home: PO Box 641 1415 Huttig Hwy Strong AR 71765

NUNNELLEY, CAROL FISHBURNE, editor newspaper; m. William A. Nunnelley; 1 child, Meg. BA, Samford U.; postgrad., U. Ky. Reporter The Birmingham (Ala.) News, city editor, mng. editor. Recipient reporting and writing awards Ala. Soc. Profl. Journalists, Ala. Press Assn., Ala. Associated Press, Journalist of the Yr. award Troy State U., Achievement award Birmingham Emancipation Assn. Mem. Soc. Profl. Journalists, Leadership Birmingham, The Women's Network. Office: The Birmingham News 2200 4th Ave North Birmingham AL 35203

NUNNELLY, WALTER SANDELS, III, corporate executive; b. Union City, Tenn., Sept. 13, 1943; s. Walter Sandels II and Betty Jane (Cox) N.; m. Sarah Anne Chaffin, June 23, 1984. BA, Vanderbilt U., 1966. Customer svc. rep. Robert Orr/SYSCO, Nashville, 1969-71, nat. accounts exec., 1971-77, nat. accounts dir., 1978-81, v.p. mktg., 1982-85, v.p. sales, 1985-87, exec. v.p., 1987-95; pres. SYSCO, Little Rock, 1995—. Pres. Cockrill Bend Bus. Coun., Nashville, 1990. With USAF, 1967-69. Mem. Tenn. Hotel and Motel Assn. (bd. dirs. 1982-90), Nashville City Club, Masons. Methodist. Avocations: reading, snow skiing, hunting, farming. Home: 159 N Berwick Ln Franklin TN 37064-7132 Office: SYSCO PO Box 194060 Little Rock AR 72219

NUNZ, GREGORY JOSEPH, program manager, aerospace engineer, educator; b. Batavia, N.Y., May 28, 1934; s. Sylvester Joseph and Elizabeth Marie (Loesell) N.; m. Georgia Monyea Costas, Mar. 30, 1958; children: Karen, John, Rebecca, Deirdre, Jaimie, Marta. BSChemE, Cooper Union, 1955; postgrad., U. So. Calif., Calif. State U.; MS in Applied Math., Columbia Pacific U., 1991, PhD in Mgmt. Sci., 1993. Adv. design staff, propulsion mgr. U.K. project Rocketdyne div. Rockwell, Canoga Park, Calif., 1955-65; mem. tech. staff Aerospace Corp., El Segundo, Calif., 1965-70; mem. tech. staff propulsion div. Jet Propulsion Lab., Pasadena, Calif., 1970-72; chief. monoprop. engring. Bell Aerospace Corp., Buffalo, N.Y., 1972-74; group supr. comb. devices Jet Propulsion Lab., Pasadena, 1974-76; asst. div. leader, program mgr. internat. HDR geothermal energy program, project mgr. space-related projects Los Alamos (N.Mex.) Nat. Lab., 1977—; assoc. prof. electronics L.A. Pierce Coll., Woodland Hills, Calif., 1961-72; instr. No. N.Mex. C. C., Los Alamos, 1978-80, div. head scis., 1980-92; adj. prof. math. U. N.Mex., Los Alamos, 1980—; sr. mgmt. rep. Excel Telecommunications, Inc., 1995—. Author: Electronics Lab Manual I, 1964, Electronics in Our World, 1972; co-author: Electronics Mathematics, vol. I, II, 1967; contbg. author Prentice-Hall Textbook of Cosmetology, 1975, Alternative Energy Sources VII, 1987; contbr. articles to profl. jours.; inventor smallest catalytic liquid N2H4 rocket thrustor, co-inventor first monoprop/biprop bimodal rocket engine, tech. advisor internat. multi-prize winning documentary film One With the Earth. Mem. Aerial Phenomena Research Orgn., L.A., 1975. Fellow AIAA (assoc.); mem. Tech. Mktg. Soc. Am., Math. Assn. Am., ARISTA, Shrine Club, Masons, Ballut Abyad Temple. Avocations: travel, archaeology, fgn. langs., golf. Office: Los Alamos Nat Lab PO Box 1663 MS D460 Los Alamos NM 87545

NURCOMBE, BARRY, director psychiatry, educator; b. Brisbane, Queensland, Australia, Jan. 11, 1933; came to U.S., 1976; s. Arthur Cyril and Alice Ursula (O'Gorman) N.; m. Alison Carson Thatcher, Dec. 7, 1956; children: Victor, Stephen, Lisa. MB, BS, U. Queensland, Brisbane, 1956; DPM, U. Melbourne, Victoria, Australia, 1959, MD, 1973. Diplomate Am. Bd. Psychiatry and Neurology. Med. dir. Australia Div. Youth Welfare & Guidance, Brisbane, 1960-67; assoc. prof. child psychiatry U. New South Wales, Sydney, Australia, 1967-76; dir. child psychiatry, prof. U. Vt., Burlington, 1976-84; prof. psychiatry and human behavior Brown U., Providence, 1984-89; dir. child and adolescent psychiatry, prof. Med. Sch. Vanderbilt U., Nashville, 1989—. Author: Children of the Dispossessed, 1976, The Clinical Process in Psychiatry, 1986, Child Mental Health and the Law, 1994. Capt. Australian Army, 1956-70, Res. Fellow Am. Psychiat. Assn., Am. Coll. Psychiatrists, Am. Acad. Child and Adolescent Psychiatry. Avocations: cinema, tennis, cricket, reading. Home: 110 Lynwood Ter Nashville TN 37205-2912 Office: Vanderbilt U Dept Child Psychiatry 1601 23rd Ave S Nashville TN 37212-3133

NURENBERG, DAVID, oil company executive; b. N.Y.C., Mar. 25, 1939; s. Abraham S. and Katherine G. N.; m. Brenda G. Schwait, Sept. 1963; children—Jill Suzanne, Brian Michael. B.S. in Marine Engring, U.S. Mcht. Marine Acad., 1960; M.S. in Indsl. Mgmt, Columbia U., 1963, Ph.D. in Mgmt. Sci, 1965. With Exxon Corp., 1963-67; employee relations mgr. Esso Pappas, Athens, Greece, 1968-72; labor relations and compensation mgr. Esso Europe, London, 1972-77; corp. sec. Esso Eastern Inc., Houston, 1977-82; mgr. exec. compensation Exxon Corp., N.Y.C., 1982-90; mgr. compensation and exec. programs Exxon Corp., Irving, Tex., 1990—; mem. coun. exec. compensation Conf. Bd., past chmn.; adj. prof. Union Inst. Mem. Am. Compensation Assn. (bd. dirs., chmn., exec. comp. coun., bd. steering com.). Office: Exxon Corp 5959 Las Colinas Blvd Irving TX 75039-2298

NURHUSSEIN, MOHAMMED ALAMIN, internist, geriatrician, educator; b. Adwa, Ethiopia, Apr. 4, 1942; came to U.S., 1972; s. Hagos and Teberih (Yusuf) N.; m. Zahra Said, June 10, 1972; children: Nadia, Siham, Safy. BS, Haile Selasie Mil. Acad., Harar, Ethiopia, 1961; MD, Zagreb (Yugoslavia) U., 1968. Intern, resident, then fellow Bklyn.-Cumberland Med. ctr., 1972-

77; emergency rm. physician Cumberland Hosp., Bklyn., 1977-79; attending physician in medicine Kings County Hosp. Ctr., Bklyn., 1979—; faculty practice medicine, geriatrics SUNY Univ. Hosp., Bklyn., 1983—; instr., then asst. prof. SUNY Health Sci. Ctr., bklyn., 1979—; med. cons., dir. drug abuse treatment Coney Island Hosp., Bklyn., 1982-84; adv. bd. Bklyn. Alzheimer's Disease Assistance Ctr., 1992—. Fellow ACP; mem. Am. Geriatric Soc., Am. Lung Assn., N.Y. Acad. Scis., Amnesty Internat., Physicians for Human Rights. Democrat. Moslem. Office: SUNY Health Sci Ctr 450 Clarkson Ave Brooklyn NY 11203-2012

NURKIN, HARRY ABRAHAM, hospital administrator; b. Durham, N.C., Feb. 15, 1944; s. Leo and Nell Margaret (Webster) N.; m. Anne Jarleth Van Meter, Nov. 18, 1967; children—Matthew Harry, Bradley Kabat, Scott Webster, Patrick Christopher, Alexander Jeffrey. B.A., Duke U., 1966, M.H.A., 1968; Ph.D., U. Ala., 1983. Asst. dir. Meml. Mission Hosp., Asheville, N.C., 1971-74; assoc. adminstr., chief ops. officer U. Ala. Hosps., Birmingham, 1974-81; pres., chief exec. officer Carolinas Med. Ctr., Charlotte, N.C., 1981—, Charlotte Mecklenburg Hosp. Authority, 1983—. Bd. dirs. ARC, Charlotte, 1985, Arts and Sci. Council, Charlotte, 1985, Charlotte Symphony, 1984, Health Svcs. Found.; mem. bd. visitors Davidson Coll., N.C., 1983—, U. N.C., Charlotte, 1982—. Fellow Am. Coll. Hosp. Adminstrs.; mem. Am. Hosp. Assn., N.C. Hosp. Assn. (bd. trustees), United Way (div. chair 1990). Home: 3022 Chaucer Dr Charlotte NC 28210-4810 Office: Carolinas Med Ctr PO Box 32861 Charlotte NC 28232*

NURNBERGER, JOHN I., JR., psychiatrist, educator; b. N.Y.C., July 18, 1946; married; 3 children. BS in Psychology magna cum laude, Fordham U., 1968; MD, Ind. U., 1975, PhD, 1983. Diplomate Am. Bd. Psychiatry and Neurology. Resident in psychiatry Columbia Presbyn. Med. Ctr., N.Y.C., 1975-78, med. officer sect. psychogenetics, 1977-78; sr. staff fellow, outpatient clinic adminstr. sect. psychogenetics NIH, Bethesda, Md., 1978-83, staff psychiatrist, chief NIMH Outpatients Clinic, 1983-86, acting chief sect. clin. genetics, 1986; prof. psychiatry, dir. Inst. Psychiatric Rsch., rsch. coord. dept. psychiatry Ind. U. Med. Ctr., Indpls., 1986—; prof. med. neurobiology Ind. U. Grad. Sch., Indpls., 1987—; clin. cons. Cold Spring VA Hosp., 1986—; cons., lectr. in field. Editor-in-chief: Psychiatric Genetics; field editor: Neuropsychiatric Genetics; contbr. articles to profl. jours. NSF fellow, 1968; recipient NAMI Exemplary Psychiatrist award Nat. Alliance Mentally Ill, 1992, 94. Fellow Am. Psychiatric Assn., Am. Psychpathological Assn.; mem. AAAS, Am. Soc. Human Genetics, Internat. Soc. Psychiatric Genetics (bd. dirs.), Am. Coll. Neuropsychopharmacology, Soc. Light Treatment and Biol. Rhythms, Soc. Neursci., Assn. Rsch. in Nervous and Mental Disease, Soc. Biol. Psychiatry, Sigma Xi. Office: Ind U Sch Medicine Psychiatric Rsch Inst 791 Union Dr Indianapolis IN 46202-4887

NUROCK, ROBERT JAY, investment analysis company executive; b. Phila., May 25, 1937; s. Abe and Sid (Smokler) N.; m. Doris L. Whitliff, Oct. 19, 1974 (div.); m. 2d, Bridget A. McManus, June 16, 1984; children: Megan, Andrew. BA, Pa. State U., 1958. Owner, pres. Md. Brake Alignment Service, Balt., 1959-67; v.p. investor support Merrill Lynch & Co., Inc., N.Y.C., 1967-79; 1st v.p. market strategy Butcher & Singer, Inc., Phila., 1979-82; pres., market strategist Investor's Analysis, Inc., 1982—; lectr. various ednl. and fin. orgns., 1973—. Panelist program Wall St. Week, Pub. Broadcasting System TV, 1970-89; author, pub. Bob Nurock's Advisory, Santa Fe, 1979—; contbg. editor The Hume Moneyletter, Atlanta, 1982—; creator E$P-Elves $hortterm Predictor, EMI-Elves Market Index, TMI-Tech. Market Index. Bd. dirs. Tredyffrin/Easttown Edn. Found., Wharton Esherick Mus., Paoli, 1989—, Penna. Trust Co. Mem. Market Technicians Assn. (chartered market technician, v.p. 1977-78), N.Y. Soc. Security Analysis, Assn. for Investment Mgmt. and Rsch., Analysts Club (pres. 1979), Rolls Royce Owners Club (dir. Keystone region). Office: PO Box 460 Santa Fe NM 87504-0460

NUSBACHER, GLORIA WEINBERG, lawyer; b. N.Y.C., July 22, 1951; d. Murray and Doris (Togman) Weinberg; m. Burton Nusbacher, Aug. 4, 1974; 1 child, Shoshana. BA, Barnard Coll., 1972; JD, Columbia U., 1975. Bar: N.Y. 1976. Assoc. Hughes Hubbard & Reed, N.Y.C., 1975-83, counsel, 1983-91, ptnr., 1991—; atty. specializing in exec. compensation and employee benefits; lectr. in field. Contbr. articles to profl. jours. Troop leader, leader trainer Girl Scouts USA. Mem. ABA (employee benefits and exec. compensation com. 1987—, fed. regulation securities com., subcom. employee benefits and exec. compensation 1983—, task force exec. compensation 1983—, task force exec. compensation, chmn. subcom. fed. and state securities laws of com. employee benefits and exec. compensation 1994—, task force sect. 16 1992-94), Phi Beta Kappa. Office: Hughes Hubbard & Reed 1 Battery Park Plz New York NY 10004-1405

NUSIM, STANLEY HERBERT, chemical engineer, consultant; b. N.Y.C., Oct. 2, 1935; s. Seymour and Ranna T. (Weiner) N.; m. Marcia Anne Borsig, Feb. 21, 1960; children: David Mark, Jill Wendi. BSChemE, CCNY, 1957; MSChemE, N.Y. U., 1960, PhD, 1967. Rsch. engr. Battelle Meml. Inst., Columbus, Ohio, 1956; researcher, chem. engring. rsch. and devel. Merck Rsch. Labs. Div., Rahway, N.J., 1957-68; sect. mgr. Merck Rsch. Labs. Div., Rahway, 1968-70; tech. svcs. mgr. Merck Chem. Mfg. Div., Rahway, 1970-73, mfg. mgr., 1973-80; dir. subsidiary projects Merck Internat. Div., Rahway, 1981-82, exec. dir. Latin Am., Far East, Near East ops., 1982-88; exec. dir. licensee, Latin Am., Far East, Asia ops. Merck Pharm. Mfg. Div., Rahway, 1989-92; exec. dir. licensee ops. worldwide Merck mfg. divsn. Merck & Co. Inc., Whitehouse Station, N.J., 1992-94; pres. S.H. Nusim Assocs., Inc., Hollywood, Fla., 1994—; v.p. mfg. Therics, Inc., N.Y.C., 1994—; adv. bd. CCNY Sch. Engring., 1982—. Author: Kinetic Studies on C4 Hydrocarbon Systems, 1967. V.p. men's club Temple Beth Shalom, Livingston, N.J., 1975-78; rep. to bd. edn. Livingston Home and Sch. Assn., 1982-83; bd. govs. Turnberry Isle Yacht and Racquet Club, Aventura, Fla., 1992-94. Mem. Am. Inst. Chem. Engrs. (bd. dir. N. Jersey sect. 1968-71, scholarship award 1955), Am. Chem. Soc., Tau Beta Pi, Garden State Yacht Club (bd. govs. 1987-88). Achievements include U.S. and foreign patents on the continuous manufacture of halogenated acetone, development of "clean room" concepts for pharmachemical manufacturing, development of sophisticated training techniques for sterile pharmaceutical manufacturing. Home: Apt 4L 19355 Turnberry Way Aventura FL 33180 Office: SH Nusim Assocs 686 N Dixie Hwy Hollywood FL 33020-3906 also: Therics Inc 99 Hudson St New York NY 10013

NUSINOVICH, GREGORY SEMEON, physicist, researcher; b. Berdichev, Russia, July 18, 1946; came to U.S., 1991; s. Semeon and Esther (Burdo) N.; m. Yelena Naydich, July 2, 1968; children: Maria, Liza, Paulina. MSc, Gorky (Russia) State U., 1968, PhD, 1975. Rsch. scientist Radiophys. Rsch. Inst., Gorky, 1968-77; sr. rsch. scientist, group leader Inst. Applied Physics, Acad. Scis. of Russia, Gorky, 1977-90; sr. rsch. scientist Inst. for Plasma Rsch., U. Md., College Park, 1991—; mem. sci. coun. on phys. electronics Acad. Scis. Russia, 1981-90; cons. Phys. Scis., Inc., Alexandria, Va., 1991-93, Sci. Applications Internat. Corp., McLean, Va., 1991-93, Omega-P, New Haven, Conn., 1995—. Co-editor: Gyrotron, 1981, Gyrotrons, 1989; contbr. chpts. to books. Mem. IEEE (sr.), Am. Phys. Soc. Achievements include development of the nonlinear theory of relativistic gyrodevices and the gyrotron producing 100 KW power at the frequency of 500 GHZ. Office: University of Maryland Inst for Plasma Rsch College Park MD 20742

NUSS, ELDON PAUL, casket manufacturer; b. Sumner, Iowa, Apr. 24, 1933; s. Paul John and Helen (Nolting) N.; m. Carolyn Ann Krug, June 6, 1959; children—Susan Elizabeth, Laurie Ann. Student, Grinnell Coll., 1950; B.S. with highest honors, U. Iowa, 1954; student, Harvard, 1971. With Arthur Young & Co. (C.P.A.'s), 1957-68; prin. Arthur Young & Co. (C.P.A.'s), Houston, 1967-68; v.p. Marathon Mfg. Co., Houston, 1969-71; exec. v.p., dir. Marathon Mfg. Co., 1972-75; pres., chief exec. officer PMI Industries, Houston, 1975-91; pres., chief exec. officer The York Group, Houston, 1991—, chmn., CEO. Served with USNR, 1955-57. Mem. Assn. for Corporate Growth, AICPA. Lutheran (council 1966-67). Club: Lakeside Country. Home: 327 Knipp Forest St Houston TX 77024-5030 Office: 9430 Old Katy Rd Houston TX 77055-6368

NUSSBAUM, A(DOLF) EDWARD, mathematician, educator; b. Rheydt, Fed. Republic Germany, Jan. 10, 1925; came to U.S., 1947; s. Karl and Franziska (Scheye) N.; m. Anne Ebbin, Sept. 1, 1957; children: Karl, Franziska. MA, Columbia U., 1950, PhD, 1957. Mem. staff electronic computer project Inst. Advanced Study, Princeton, N.J., 1952-53; mem. Inst. Advanced Study, 1962-63; instr. math U. Conn., Storrs, 1953-55; asst. prof. Rensselaer Poly. Inst., Troy, N.Y., 1957-58; vis. scholar Stanford U., Calif., 1967-68; asst. prof., then assoc. prof. Washington U., St. Louis, 1958-66, prof., 1966-95, prof. emeritus, 1995—. Contbr. articles to profl. jours. Grantee NSF, 1960-79. Mem. Am. Math. Soc. Home: 8050 Watkins Dr Saint Louis MO 63105-2517 Office: Washington U Dept Math Saint Louis MO 63130

NUSSBAUM, BERNARD J., lawyer; b. Berlin, Mar. 11, 1931; came to U.S., 1936; s. William and Lotte (Frankfurther) N.; m. Jean Beverly Enzer, Sept. 4, 1956; children—Charles, Peter, Andrew. A.B., Knox Coll., 1948-52; J.D., U. Chgo., 1955. Assoc. Proskauer Rose Goetz & Mendelsohn, N.Y.C., 1955-56; assoc. Sonnenschein Nath & Rosenthal, Chgo., 1959-65, sr. ptnr., 1965—; master bencher Am. Inns of Ct., 1986—; appointed to com. on civility 7th cir. U.S. Ct. Appeals, 1989-92. Editor U. Chgo. Law Rev., 1954-55; mem. nat. adv. bd. BNA Civil Trial Man., 1985—; contbr. articles to profl. jours. Mem. vis. com. U. Chgo. Law Sch., 1977-83. Served to capt. U.S. Army, 1956-59. Fellow Am. Bar Found., Ill. Bar Found. (charter); mem. ABA, Chgo. Bar Assn. (chmn. com. on fed. civil procedure 1968-69, mem. com. on judiciary 1970-76), Ill. Bar Assn. (council Antitrust sect. 1971-73, assembly del. 1972-80), U. Chgo. Law Sch. Nat. Alumni Assn. (pres. 1981-83), Law Club Chgo., Legal Club Chgo. Avocations: skiing; cycling. Office: Sonnenschein Nath & Rosenthal 8000 Sears Tower 233 S Wacker Dr Chicago IL 60606-6306

NUSSBAUM, HOWARD JAY, lawyer; b. N.Y.C., Dec. 17, 1951; s. Norman and Ruth (Rand) N.; children: Martin Garrett, Daniel Todd. BA, SUNY, Binghamton, 1972; JD, Boston Coll., 1976. Bar: Fla. 1977, U.S. Dist. Ct. (so. dist. trial and bankruptcy bar) Fla. 1977, U.S. Ct. Appeals (5th and 11th cirs.) 1981. Mng. atty. Legal Aid. Svc., Ft. Lauderdale, Fla., 1976-88; ptnr. Weinstein, Zimmerman & Nussbaum, P.A., Tamarac, Fla., 1988-92; pres. Howard J. Nussbaum, P.A., 1993—; chmn. Legal Aid com. North Broward Bar Assn., Pompano Beach, Fla., 1986-87; cons. Police Acad. of Broward County, Ft. Lauderdale, 1985-87. Author: Florida Landlord/Tenant Law and the Fair Housing Act, 1989. Legis. advisor Fla. Senate Majority Leader Peter Weinstein, Broward County, 1990—; gen. coun. Registered Apt. Mgrs. Assn. South Fla., 1993—, Jetlease Finance Corp., Ft. Lauderdale, Fla., 1992—, Wynmoor Community Coun., 1993—. Regents scholar N.Y. State, 1968-72, Presdl. scholar Boston Coll. Law Sch., 1973-76. Mem. ABA (litigation sect.), ATLA, Acad. Fla. Trial Lawyers, Broward Bar Assn., Justice Lodge J.C.C. Avocations: softball, tennis, swimming. Office: Howard J Nussbaum PA 100 W Cypress Creek Rd Ste 805 Fort Lauderdale FL 33309-2181

NUSSBAUM, KAREN, federal agency administrator; b. Chgo., Apr. 25, 1950; d. Myron G. and Annette (Brenner) N.; m. Ira Arlook; children: Gene, Jack, Eleanor. BA, Goddard Coll., 1973. Exec. dir. 9 to 5 Nat. Assn. of Working Women, 1973-93; pres. dist. 925 Svc. Employees Internat. Union, 1975-93; dir. Women's Bur. U.S. Dept. Labor, Washington, 1993—. Co-author: Solutions for the New Work Force: Policies for a New Social Contract, 9 to 5: The Working Woman's Guide to Office Survival. Named to Ohio Women's Hall of Fame, 1984. Office: Dept of Labor Women's Bur 200 Constitution Ave NW Washington DC 20210-0001

NUSSBAUM, LEO LESTER, retired college president, consultant; b. Berne, Ind., June 27, 1918; s. Samuel D. and Margaret (Mazelin) N.; m. Janet Nell Gladfelter, Nov. 25, 1942; children: Felicity Ann, Luther James, Margaret Sue. BS, Ball State U., 1942, MA, 1949; PhD, Northwestern U., 1952; Postgrad., U. Mich., 1963. Tchr. Monmouth High Sch., Decatur, Ind., 1946-48; dean men, asst. prof. bus. Huntington Coll., (Ind.), 1948-51; dean coll. liberal arts, assoc. prof. edn. and psychology U. Dubuque, (Iowa), 1952-60; dean coll., prof. edn. and psychology Austin Coll., 1960-67; dean coll., prof. psychology Coe Coll., 1967-70, pres., 1970-82, pres. emeritus, 1982—; dir. Acad. Sr. Profls. Eckerd Coll., 1983-87; dir. PEL-ASPEC Project, 1988-95; coord. faculty ASPEC Colleagues, St. Petersburg, 1992—; cons. pvt. practice St. Petersburg, Fla., 1982—; Fulbright lectr. U. Mysore (India), 1958-59; cons., evaluator So. Assn. Colls. and Schs., Atlanta, 1963-67, North Cen. Assn. Colls. and Schs., 1959-60, 67-82, dir. I.E. Industries and Iowa Electric Light and Power Co., Cedar Rapids, 1982-91, dir. emeritus, 1991-92. Contbr. articles to scholastic and profl. jours. and periodicals. Bd. dirs. Cedar Rapids Symphony, 1968-70; mem. cabinet Cedar Rapids United Way, 1980-82; elder Presbyn. Ch., moderator Presbytery of S.W. Fla., 1989. Sgt. U.S. Army, 1942-46. Recipient Disting. Alumnus award Ball State U., 1976, Alumni Merit award Northwestern U., 1977. Mem. Assn. Colls. Midwest (chmn. 1975-77), Iowa Assn. Ind. Colls. and Univs. (chmn. 1976-77), Danforth Assocs., Rotary (Cedar Rapids, pres. 1975-76), Phi Delta Kappa, Blue Key, Pi Gamma Mu. Home: # 336 6909 9th St Saint Petersburg FL 33705-6207

NUSSBAUM, MARTHA CRAVEN, philosophy and classics educator; b. N.Y.C., May 6, 1947; d. George and Betty (Warren) Craven; m. Alan Jeffrey Nussbaum, Aug., 1969 (div. 1987); 1 child, Rachel Emily. BA, NYU, 1969; MA, Harvard U., 1971, PhD, 1975; LHD (hon.), Kalamazoo Coll., 1988, Grinnell Coll., 1993. Asst. prof. philosophy and classics Harvard U., Cambridge, 1975-80, assoc. prof., 1980-83; vis. prof. philosophy, Greek and Latin Wellesley (Mass.) Coll., 1983-84; assoc. prof. philosophy and classics Brown U., Providence, R.I., 1984-85, prof. philosophy, classics and comparative lit., 1985-87, David Benedict prof. philosophy, classics and comparative lit., 1987-89, prof., 1989-95; prof. law and ethics U. Chgo., 1995—; rsch. advisor World Inst. Devel. Econs. Rsch., Helsinki, Finland, 1986-93; vis. prof. law U. Chgo., 1994. Author: Aristotle's De Motu Animalium, 1978, The Fragility of Goodness, 1986, Loe's Knowledge, 1990, The Therapy of Desire, 1994, Poetic Justice: The Literary Imagination and Public Life, 1996; editor: Language and Logos, 1983; (with A. Rorty) Essays on Aristotle's De Anima, 1992, (with A. Sen) The Quality of Life, 1993, (with J. Brunschwig) Passions and Perceptions, 1993, (with J. Glover) Women, Culture and Development, 1995. Soc. Fellows Harvard U. jr. fellow, 1972-75, Humanities fellow Princeton U., 1977-78, Guggenheim Found. fellow, 1983, NIH fellow, vis. fellow All Souls Coll., Oxford, Eng., 1986-87; recipient Brandeis Creative Arts award, 1990, Spielvogel-Diamondstein award, 1991; Gifford lectr. U. Edinburgh, 1993. Fellow Am. Acad. Arts and Scis. (membership com. 1991-93, coun. 1992—), Am. Philos. Soc.; mem. Am. Philos. Assn. (exec. com. Ea. divsn. 1985-87, chair com. internat. coop., ex-officio mem. nat. bd. 1989-92, chair com. on status of women 1994—), Am. Philol. Assn., PEN. Office: U Chicago The Law Sch 1111 E 60th St Chicago IL 60637

NUSSBAUM, PAUL EUGENE, journalist; b. Upland, Ind., Aug. 30, 1952; s. Elmer N. and Ruth Ellen (Shugart) N.; m. Debra Stone, Oct. 31, 1987; children: Molly Elizabeth, Matthew Connor. Student, Taylor U., 1970-71; BS, Ball State U., 1974. Reporter Muncie (Ind.) Star, 1973-74, Indpls. Star, 1974, Anchorage Times, 1975-76; staff writer Anchorage Daily News, 1976-78, metro editor, 1978-80; staff writer L.A. Times, 1980-82; staff writer Phila. Inquirer, 1982-91, dep. fgn. editor, 1991-94; mng. editor Phila. Inquirer Mag., 1994—. Recipient Best Editorial award Alaska Press Club, 1978, Best News Story award Sigma Delta Chi, 1984, Best Mag. Story, Sigma Delta Chi Soc. of Profl. Journalists, 1991, 1st Pl. news reporting award Pa. AP Mng. Editors, 1985. Methodist. Office: Phila Inquirer 400 N Broad St Philadelphia PA 19130-4015

NUSSBAUM, V. M., JR., former mayor; b. Ft. Wayne, Ind., June 25, 1919; m. Terry O'Hayer, 1943; 9 children. Student, Holy Cross Coll., Univ. Pa., Harvard Univ. City councilman Greensboro, N.C., 1973-81; mayor City of Greensboro, Greensboro, 1987-93; founder, pres. So. Food Svc. Inc., 1954, So. Foods, 1960. Gen. chmn. united fund drive United Way, 1971, pres., 1972; former pres. United Arts Coun., Boy Scouts Am., Gen. Greene Coun. Lt. comdr. USN. Recipient Nat. Greene award Greensboro C. of C., 1983, Citizen of Yr. award, 1993; named N.C. Entrepreneur of Yr., 1995. Home: 9 Saint Augustine Sq Greensboro NC 27408-3834

NUSSBAUMER, GERHARD KARL, metals company executive; b. Linz, Austria, Mar. 25, 1959; came to U.S., 1987; s. Franz and Stefanie (Hinternberger) N. MBA, U. Vienna, 1982. Jr. auditor Price Waterhouse, Vienna, 1983-85; corp. staff contr. Oesterreichische Industrieholding AG, Vienna, 1985-87; v.p. fin. Voest-Alpine Internat. Corp., N.Y.C., 1987-92, pres., 1993—; bd. dirs. Voest-Alpine Internat. Corp., N.Y.C., Voest-Alpine Svcs. and Technologies, Pitts., Voest-Alpine Tubular Corp., Houston, Voest-Alpine M.C.E. Corp., Berlin, Voest-Alpine Steel Products Corp., N.Y.C. Mem. U.S. Austrian C. of C., Am. Mgmt. Assn. Avocations: theatre, constitutional law, history, tennis, skiing. Office: Voest-Alpine Internat Corp 60 E 42nd St New York NY 10165

NUSSDORF, BERNARD, wholesale distribution executive. CEO Quality King Distributors. Office: Quality King Distribution 2060 9th Ave Ronkonkoma NY 11779-6253*

NUSSENBAUM, SIEGFRIED FRED, chemistry educator; b. Vienna, Austria, Nov. 21, 1919; came to U.S., 1939; s. Marcus and Susan Sara (Rothenberg) N.; m. Celia Womark, Feb. 20, 1951; children: Deborah M., Evelyn R. BS in Chemistry, U. Calif., Berkeley, 1941, MS in Food Tech., 1948, PhD in Comparative Biochemistry, 1951. Analytical chemist Panam. Engring. Co., Berkeley, 1942-43; asst. chief chemist Manganese Ore Co., Las Vegas, 1943-45; rsch. assoc. U. Calif., Berkeley, 1951-52; dir. master clin. lab. sci. program U. Calif., San Francisco, 1969-87; from instr. to prof. Calif. State U., Sacramento, 1952-90, chair dept. chemistry, 1958-65; cons. biochemist Sacramento County Hosp., 1958-70; lectr. U. Calif. Davis Med. Ctr., 1970-93, guest lectr., 1993—. Author: Organic Chem-Principles and Applications, 1963; contbr. articles to profl. jours. Sgt. U.S. Army, 1945-47. Fellow AAAS; mem. Am. Chem. Soc., Am. Assn. Clin. Chemistry (Outstanding Contbn. in Edn. award no. sect. 1991), Nat. Acad. Clin. Biochemistry. Achievements include research in pectic enzymes, mechanism of amylopectin formation and differentiation from amylose, phenotyping of lipemias. Home: 2900 Latham Dr Sacramento CA 95864-5644

NUSSLE, JAMES ALLEN, congressman; b. Des Moines, June 27, 1960; s. Mark S. and Lorna Kay (Fisher) N.; m. Leslie J. Harbison, Aug. 23, 1986. BA, Luther Coll., Decorah, Iowa, 1983; JD, Drake U., 1985. Bar: Iowa 1985. Pvt. practice law Manchester, Iowa, 1986; states atty. Delaware County Atty., Manchester, 1986-90; mem. 102nd-104th Congresses from 2d Iowa dist., Washington, 1991—; mem. house ways and means com., budget com. 102nd-104th Congresses from 2d Iowa dist. Lutheran. Avocation: guitar. *

NUTE, DONALD E., JR., philosophy educator; b. Maysville, Ky., Aug. 12, 1947; s. Donald E. Sr. and Virginia (Boyd) N.; m. Jane Greifenkamp, Aug. 17, 1968; 1 child, Achsa Lynn. BA, U. Ky., 1969; PhD, Ind. U., 1974. Assoc. instr. Ind. U., Bloomington, 1970-71; asst. prof. U. Ga., Athens, 1973-78, assoc. prof., 1978-83, prof. philosophy, 1983—, dir. MS in artificial intelligence program, 1987—, head dept. philosophy, 1989—, dir. artificial intelligence ctr., 1994—; vis. prof. U. Tubingen, Germany, 1985; pres. AI Assocs., Athens, 1987—; rsch. assoc. U. Antwerp, Belgium, 1989. Author: Topics in Conditional Logic, 1980, Essential Formal Semantics, 1981; co-author: Prolog Programming in Depth, 1988. Mem. Am. Philos. Assn., Am. Assn. Artificial Intelligence, So. Soc. for Philosophy and Psychology, Assn. for Symbolic Logic, Soc. for Exact Philosophy, Phi Beta Kappa. Office: U Ga Dept Philosophy Athens GA 30602

NUTTALL, RICHARD NORRIS, state agency administrator; b. Hamilton, Ont., Can., Feb. 7, 1940; s. James William and Margaret Gay (Walsh) N.; m. Ethel Jane Pickering, July 9, 1977; children: Andrew Richard, John Patrick. BSA, U. Toronto, 1961; MPA, Harvard U., 1964; MB, BS, U. London, Eng., 1974. Cert. Coll. Family Physicians Can., Mgmt. Cons. Zone dir. Health and Welfare Can., Prince Rupert, B.C., 1977-79; regional dir. Health and Welfare Can., Edmonton, Alta., 1980-82; pres. Rutland Consulting Group, Ltd., Vancouver, B.C., 1982-87, Richmond Assocs. Internat., Vancouver, 1988-90; med. health officer Govt. N.W. Ters., Yellowknife, B.C., 1990-93, Regina Health Dist., 1993—. Mem. Can. Pub. Health Assn. (bd. dirs. 1991-93), Rotary Club North Regina. Office: Regina Health Dist, 1910 McIntyre St, Regina, SK Canada S4P 2R3

NUTTER, FRANKLIN WINSTON, lawyer; b. Charleston, W.Va., Apr. 17, 1946; s. Frank Hamilton and Marie Agnes (Pyles) N.; m. Linda Jean Davis, Sept. 2, 1972; children: Alycia Marie, Aaron Davis. BBA in Econs., U. Cin., 1968; JD, Georgetown U., 1974. Bar: D.C., Va., U.S. Dist. Ct. (no. dist.) Va., U.S. Ct. Appeals (9th and D.C. cirs.), U.S. Supreme Ct. 1993. Gen. counsel Nat. Flood Ins. Assn., Washington, 1975-78; gen. counsel Reins. Assn. Am., Washington, 1978-81, pres., 1981-84, 91—; pres. Alliance Am. Insurers, Schaumburg, Ill., 1984-91, Property Loss Research Bur., Schaumburg, 1984-91; bd. overseers Inst. Civil Justice subs. Rand Corp.; chair Natural Disaster Coalition. Bd. dirs. Advs. for Hwy. and Auto Safety; trustee Nat. Commn. Against Drunk Driving. Lt. (j.g.) USN, 1968-72. Mem. ABA (torts and injury practice sect., past chmn. internat. ins. law, excess and surplus lines and reins. com., coun. tort and ins. practice sect.), Va. Bar Assn., Ins. Inst. Hwy. Safety (bd. dirs.), Workers' Compensation Rsch. Inst., Industry Sector Adv. Coun. on Svcs. Home: 8458 Portland Pl Mc Lean VA 22102-1708 Office: 1301 Pennsylvania Ave NW Washington DC 20004-1701

NUTTER, WALLACE LEE, paper manufacturing executive; b. 1944. BA, U. Washington, 1967; grad. advanced mgmt. program, Harvard U., 1987. Ops. asst. N.W. timber div. ITT Rayonier Inc., Stamford, Conn., 1967-69, contract logging foreman, 1969-70, contract logging supt., 1970-71, mgr. log sales and purchases, 1971-78, mgr. wood resources sales and procurement, 1978-80, regional dir. forest and wood products N.W. regional ops., 1980-82, dir. timber and wood products N.W., 1982-84, dir. forest products ops., 1984-85, v.p. forest and wood products ops., from 1985, v.p. pulp mfg.; exec. v.p. Rayonier (no longer divsn. of ITT), Stamford, Conn., 1987—. Office: Rayonier 1177 Summer St Stamford CT 06905-5522

NUTTER, ZOE DELL LANTIS, retired public relations executive; b. Yamhill, Oreg., June 14, 1915; d. Arthur Lee Lantis and Olive Adelaide (Reed) Lantis-Hilton; m. Richard S. West, Apr. 30, 1941 (div. Nov. 1964); m. Ervin John Nutter, Dec. 30, 1965. Assoc. in Bus., Santa Ana Jr. Coll., 1944. Cert. gen. secondary sch. tchr., Calif.; FAA cert. lic. commercial, instrument, single/multi engine land airplanes pilot. Promoter World's Fair & Comml. Airlines Golden Gate Internat. Expn., San Francisco, 1937-39; pirate theme girl, official hostess Treasure Island's World Fair, San Francisco, 1939-40; prin. dancer San Francisco Ballet, 1937-41; artist, 1941-45; program dir. Glenn County High Sch., Willows, Calif., 1952-58; pub. rels. Monarch Piper Aviation Co., Monterey, Calif., 1963-65; pilot, pub. rels. Elano Corp., Xenia, Ohio, 1968-85; bd. dirs. Nat. Aviation Hall of Fame, Dayton, Ohio, pres., chmn., 1989-92, bd. trustees, 1976—, chmn. bd. nominations, 1992—; bd. trustees Ford's Theatre, Washington, Treasure Island Mus., San Francisco; charter mem. Friends of First Ladies, Smithsonian, Washington, 1990-93. Assoc. editor KYH mag. of Shikar Safari Internat., 1985-87; contbg. columnist Scripps Howard San Francisco News, 1938. Bd. dirs. Cin. May Festival, 1976-80; cen. com. Glenn County Rep. Party, Willows, 1960-64; state cen. com. Rep. Party, 1962-64; adv. bd. Women's Air & Space Mus., Dayton, 1987-94. Warrant officer, Civil Air Patrol, 1967-69. Recipient Civic Contbn. Honor award Big Brothers/Big Sisters, 1991, John Collier Nat. award Camp Fire Girls & Boys, 1988, Tambourine award Salvation Army, 1982, State of Ohio Gov.'s award for Volunteerism, 1992; named Most Photographed Girl in World, News Burs. & Clipping Svcs., 1938-39. Fellow Pres.'s Club U., Ohio State U., Wright State U.; mem. 99's Internat. Women Pilots Orgn. (life, hospitality chmn. 1968), Monterey Bay Chapter 99's (mem. chmn. 1964-65), Walnut Grove Country Club, Lost Tree Country Club, Windstar County Club (Naples, Fla.), Rotary (Paul Harris fellow 1987), Old Port Yacht Club, Shikar Safari Internat. (host com. 1976). Avocations: flying, horseback riding, hunting, shooting, fashion. Home: 986 Trebein Rd Xenia OH 45385-9534

NUTTING, GEORGE OGDEN, newspaper publisher; b. Washington, Oct. 21, 1935; s. George Kegley and Margaret Lawson (Ogden) N.; m. Betty S. Woods; children—William Ogden, Robert McLain. B.A., Williams Coll., 1956. With Martinsburg (W.Va.) Jour., 1956, Wheeling (W.Va.) News Register, 1957; with Ogden Newspapers, Inc., Wheeling, 1958—; pres., gen. mgr. Ogden Newspapers, Inc., 1970—; chmn. bd. United Nat. Bank North, Wheeling; bd. dirs. Stone & Thomas, United Bankshares. Bd. dirs. Bethany Coll.; mem. Wheeling Park Commn., Linsly Sch., Ohio Valley Indsl. and Bus. Devel. Corp., W.Va. U. Found. Mem. So. Newspaper Pubs. Assn.

Republican. Episcopalian. Office: Wheeling News-Register 1500 Main St Wheeling WV 26003-2826

NUTTING, PAUL A., medical educator, medical science administrator; b. Aug. 24, 1944; m. Kaia M. Gallagher; children: Paul James, Kaia Elise. AB in Psychology, Cornell U., 1966; MD, U. Kans., 1970; MSPH, U. Colo., 1988. Diplomate Am. Bd. Family Practice, Am. Bd. Preventive Medicine. Intern in pediat. U. Pitts., 1970-71; resident in preventive medicine U. Ariz., 1973-75; clin. dir. Santa Rosa (Ariz.) Clinic Indian Health Svc., 1971-72, maternal and child health officer Sells (Ariz.) Svc. Unit, 1972-73; med. rsch. office Office of R&D Indian Health Svc., Tucson, 1973-77, assoc. dir. rsch. Office of R&D, 1977-83; sr. scholar-in-residence Inst. Medicine-NAS, Washington, 1983-84; dir. Office of Primary Care Studies Health Resources and Svcs. Adminstrn., DHHS, Rockville, Md., 1984-86; resident in family medicine Mercy Med. Ctr., Denver, 1986-88; dir. rsch. Indian Health Svc., Tucson, 1989-90; dir. divsn. primary care and dep. dir. Ctr. for Gen. Health Svcs. Rsch., DHHS, Rockville, 1990-93; dir. Ambulatory Sentinel Practice Network, Denver, 1993—; prof. family medicine dept. family medicine U. Colo. Health Scis. Ctr., 1993—; rsch. assoc. prof. dept. family and cmty. medicine U. Ariz., 1981-87, 88-90; clin. assoc. prof. dept. cmty. and family medicine Georgetown U. Sch. Medicine, 1983-86; mem. subcom. on cardiovascular disease Sec.'s Task Force on Black and Minority Health, 1984-85; mem. interagy. com. on infant mortality USHPS, 1990-93, chair rsch. subcom., clin. preventive svcs. steering com., 1991-93, nat. steering com. primary care-substance abuse linkage initiative, 1991-93; chairperson Workshop on Early Detection of Prostate Cancer, Nat. Cancer Inst., Bethesda, Md., 1993; cons. in field. Author: (with L.A. Green) From Research to Policy to Practice: Closing the Loop in Clinical Policy Development in Primary Care, 1994; editor: Community-Oriented Primary Care: From Principle to Practice, 1987, co-editor: Primary Care Research: Theory and Methods, 1991; mem. editl. bd. Jour. Cmty. Health, 1981-84, Jour. Family Practice, 1990—, Am. Family Physician, 1990—, Jour. Rural Health, 1994—; contbr. chpts. to books and articles to profl. jours. Capt. USPHS, 1982. Recipient Cert. appreciation Nat. Indian Health Bd., 1982, Modern Medicine award for disting. achievement, 1993. Mem. APHA (sect. in med. care, epidemiology, internat. health), Inst. Medicine-NAS, Am. Acad. Family Physicians (liaison mem. com. on rsch. 1993—), Am. Acad. Pediat. (mem. steering com. pediat. rsch. in office settings 1993—), N.Am. Primary Care Rsch. Group (bd. dirs. 1994—, chair com. on bldg. capacity for rsch. in family practice 1994—), Soc. for Epidemiologic Rsch., Soc. Tchrs. Family Medicine. Office: Ambulatory Sentinel Practice Network 1650 Pierce St Denver CO 80214

NUTTING, WALLACE HALL, army officer; b. Newton, Mass., June 3, 1928; s. Gerry B. and Ethel M. (Hall) N.; m. Jane Anne Walker, June 17, 1950; children: Elizabeth J., John T., Katherine A., Sally W. BS, U.S. Mil. Acad., 1950; MA in Internat. Affairs, George Washington U., 1963; postgrad., Naval War Coll., 1963, Nat. War Coll., 1968. Commd. cavalry officer U.S. Army, 1950, advanced through grades to gen.; asst. dir. plans Dept. Army, Washington, 1968-70; dep. dir. plans Dept. Army, 1973-74; comdr. 11th Armored Cavalry Regiment, Vietnam, 1970-71; dep. comdr. ops. 1st brigade 5th Inf. Div., Vietnam, 1971; Army mem. chmn.'s staff group Orgn. Joint Chiefs of Staff, Washington, 1971-73; comdg. gen. 1st Inf. div. forward, Fed. Republic Germany, 1974-75; dir. strategy plans and policy Dept. Army, 1975-77; comdg. gen. 3d Armored div., Fed. Republic Germany, 1977-79; comdr. in chief U.S. So. Command, Quarry Heights, Panama, 1979-83; comdr.-in chief U.S. Readiness Command, dir. Joint Deployment Agy., MacDill AFB, Fla., 1983-85; assoc. fellow Ctr. for Internat. Affairs, Harvard U., 1986; sr. fellow Inst. Higher Def. Studies, Nat. Def. U., Washington, 1986—. Mem. exec. bd., Panama Canal Council, Boy Scouts Am., 1979-83; mem. Gulf Ridge council, Boy Scouts Am., 1983-85. Decorated Defense D.S.M. with oak leaf cluster, Silver Star, Legion of Merit with 2 oak leaf clusters, Soldier's medal, Bronze Star with oak leaf cluster, Air medal (7), Purple Heart with oak leaf cluster, Army Commendation medal with oak leaf cluster, Presdl. Unit citation, Korean Svc. medal with 5 stars, Vietnam Svc. medal with 4 stars, U.N. Svc. medal, JCS Identification badge, Gen. staff Identification badge, Vietnamese Cross of Gallantry with palm and silver star, Brazilian Order Mil. Merit, Order Mil. Merit Dominican Republic, Cross of Venezuelan Armed Forces, Mil. Star Armed Forces Chile, Cross Armed Force Republic of Honduras, Order Mil. Merit in grade grand officer (Argentina), Order Mil. Merit (Panama), Vietnamese Campaign medal; recipient Silver Beaver award. Mem. U.S. Armor Assn., Assn. U.S. Army. Congregationalist. Home: PO Box 96 Biddeford Pool ME 04006-0096 Office: Dept of Army Gen Officer Mgmt Office Washington DC 20310

NUTWELL, ROBERT MICHAEL, naval officer; b. Takoma Park, Md., Nov. 10, 1944; s. George Perrie Jr. and Iras Jane (Burroughs) N.; m. Lynn Greenley, June 22, 1967; children: Brian Mills, Kevin Scott. BSME, U.S. Naval Acad., 1966; MS in Ops. Rsch., U.S. Naval Postgrad. Sch., 1972. Commd. ensign USN, 1966, advanced through grades to rear adm., 1996; naval aviator Naval Air Tng. Command, various places, 1966-67; pilot Attack Squadron 215, Lemoore, Calif., 1968-70, Attack Squadron 25, Lemoore, 1973-76; pilot, comdg. officer Attach Squadon 105, Jacksonville, Fla., 1978-80; exec. officer USS Nimitz, Norfolk, Va., 1984-86; comdg. officer USS Trenton, Norfolk, 1988-90, USS George Washington, Norfolk, 1990-93; dep. dir. plans and policy U.S. European Command, Stuttgart, Germany, 1993-95; comdr. Carrier Group Three, Alameda, Calif., 1995—. Contbr. articles to profl. proceedings. Decorated D.S.S.M., Legion of Merit, Air medal; recipient John Paul Jones award for Leadership, 1993. Mem. Am. Soc. Quality Control, Assn. Naval Aviation, Ops. Rsch. Soc. Am., U.S. Naval Inst. Avocations: reading, jogging. Home: 100 Alameda Rd Alameda CA 94501 Office: Comdr Carrier Group Three Unit 25059 FPO AP 96601-4303

NUTZLE, FUTZIE (BRUCE JOHN KLEINSMITH), artist, author, cartoonist; b. Lakewood, Ohio, Feb. 21, 1942; s. Adrian Ralph and Naomi Irene (Rupert) Kleinsmith; children: Adrian David, Arielle Justine and Tess Alexandra (twins). Represented by The Pope Gallery, Santa Cruz, Calif. Author: Modern Loafer, Thames and Hudson, 1981, (autobiography) Futzie Nutzle, 1983, Earthquake, 1989, Run the World: 50 Cents Chronicle Books, 1991; illustrator: The Armies Encamped Beyond Unfinished Avenues (Morton Marcus), 1977, Box of Nothing, 1982, The Duke of Chemical Birds (Howard McCord), 1989, Book of Solutions, 1990, Fact and Friction, 1990, Managing for the 90s, 1992, Soundbites for Success, 1994; feature cartoonist Rolling Stone, N.Y.C., 1975-80, The Japan Times, Tokyo and L.A., 1986—, The Prague Post, Czechoslovakia, 1991—; contbr. exhbns. include Inaugural, 1966, Cupola, 1967, Rolling Renaissance, San Francisco, 1968, 100 Acres, O.K. Harris 1971, N.Y.C., San Francisco Mus. Art, 1972, Indpls. and Cin. Mus. Art, 1975, Leica, L.A., 1978, Santa Barbara Mus. Annex, Calif., 1978, Swope, Santa Monica, West Beach Cafe, Venice, Calif., 1985, Les Oranges, Santa Monica, Correspondence Sch., 1970-78, 1st Ann. Art-A-Thon, N.Y.C., 1985, Am. Epiphany with Phillip Hefferton, 1986, Polit. Cartoon Show, Braunstein, San Francisco, Komsomolskaya Pravda, 1988, retrospective Eloise Packard Smith, 1990, exemplary contemporary, Cowell, U. Calif. Santa Cruz, 1991, Silicon Graphics Inc., Computer Graphics for NAB, Las Vegas, 1993, Prague Eco-Fair, 1991; represented in pvt. and pub. collections (complete archives) Spl. Collections, McHenry Libr., U. Calif., Santa Cruz, Mus. Modern Art, N.Y.C., San Francisco Mus. Modern Art, Oakland Mus., San Francisco Mus. Cartoon Art, Whitney Mus. Am. Art, N.Y.C. regular contbr. The Japan Times. Ltd., Tokyo. Address: PO Box 325 Aromas CA 95004-0325

NUZUM, JOHN M., JR., banker; b. Milw., Dec. 22, 1939; s. John M. and Helen (Ollis) N.; m. Margaret Bolway, Feb. 25, 1967; children: Kimberly, Courtney, Leah, Jonathan. AB, Princeton U., 1962; MBA, U. Pa., 1964. Sr. v.p. Chase Manhattan Bank, N.Y.C., 1965—. Project Reach Youth, Bklyn., 1977—, Park Slope Family Ctr., Bklyn., 1984-95. Mem. Montauk Club (bd. dirs. 1985-94), Heights Casino Club, Princeton Club. Office: Chase Manhattan Bank 1 Chase Manhattan Plz New York NY 10081-1000

NUZUM, ROBERT WESTON, lawyer; b. Evanston, Ill., Dec. 11, 1952; s. John Weston and Janet Marie (Talbot) N.; m. Julia Ann Abadie, Sept. 16, 1983. BS in Fin., La. State U., 1974, JD, 1977; LLM in Taxation, N.Y.U., 1978. Bar: La. 1977, D.C. 1979. Assoc. Office Chief Counsel, Washington, 1978-81, Jones, Walker, Waechter, Poitevent, Carrere & Denegre, New Orleans, 1981-85; ptnr. Jones, Walker, Waechter, Potevent, Carrere & Denegre, New Orleans, 1985-88, Deutsch, Kerrigan & Stiles, New Orleans, 1988-89, Phelps & Dunbar and predecessor firm, New Orleans, 1989—; adj. instr. Tulane U., New Orleans, 1984—. Editor La. Law Rev., 1977; contbr. articles to profl. jours. Wallace scholar N.Y.U., 1978. Mem. La. Bar Assn. (program chmn. tax sect. 1992-93, sec.-treas. 1993-94, vice-chmn. 1994-95, chmn. 1995—), Tulane Tax Inst. (planning com. 1993—), Order of Coif. Republican. Roman Catholic. Avocations: golf, reading, fishing. Office: Phelps Dunbar LLP 400 Poydras St New Orleans LA 70130-3245

NUZZO, SALVATORE JOSEPH, defense, electronics company executive; b. Norwalk, Conn., Aug. 6, 1931; s. Rocco and Angelina (Renzull) N.; m. Lucille Cocco, Oct. 3, 1953; children: James, David, Thomas, Dana. B.S. in Elec. Engring, Yale U., 1953; M.S. in Bus, Columbia U., 1974. With Hazeltine Corp., Greenlawn, N.Y., 1953-88, v.p. govt. products and mktg., 1969-73, v.p. govt. products div., 1973-74, sr. v.p. ops., 1974-76, exec. v.p., chief oper. officer, 1976, pres., chief oper. officer, 1977-88, chief exec. officer, 1980-87, chmn., 1986-88, ret., 1988; chmn., Technautics Corp., Cleve., 1991-94; chmn. Marine Mech. Corp., Cleve., 1994—; bd. dirs. Avnet Inc., Datron Inc.; chmn. SL Industries. Fellow Poly. Inst. N.Y. Mem. Yale Sci. and Engring. Assn. (former pres.). Home: 118 St Mellions Dr Pinehurst NC 28374 also: 1101 Waterfront on Ocean 800 Ocean Dr Juno Beach FL 33408

NWA, WILLIA L., special education educator; b. Cleve., July 20; d. Thurman and Josephine (Deadwyler); m. Umoh U. Nwa, Sept. 4, 1971; children: Idara Umoh, Jakitoro Deadwyler, Ayama Nseabasi, Ifiok Odudu, Uko Obong. Student, Cleve. Inst. Music, 1965-66; BS, Ohio State U., 1971; MS, U. Akron, 1975, PhD, 1992. Cert. elem. and secondary edn. tchr., spl. edn. tchr., spl. edn. supr., Ohio. Pianist/organist 7th Ave Community Bapt. Ch., Columbus, Ohio, 1970-71; educator N.E. Local Schs., Springfield, Ohio, 1971-74; supr. U. Akron, Ohio, 1989; educator Canton (Ohio) City Schs., 1975—; presenter, instr. 13th, 14th, and 15th ann. internat. confs. critical thinking and ednl. reform Sonoma State U., Rohnert Park, Calif., 1993-95, 7th Internat. Conf. Career Devel. and Transition, Albuquerque, 1993, 41st Ann. Conf. Connecting Edn./Collaboration, Toledo, 1993, 8th Internat. Conf. Collaboration/Cooperation in Edn., Lewis & Clark Coll., Portland, Oreg., 1994, 4th Internat. Conf.: Mental Retardation and Devel. Disabilities, Arlington Heights, Ill., 1994. Co-author: (grant) Reading for Survival, 1988; author: The Extent of Participation in Extracurricular Activities with Exceptional Children, 1992. Mem. Bapt. Student Union, Ohio State U., Columbus, 1969-71, mem. choir, 1969-71; pianist, organist Freedom Bapt. Ch., Canton, 1994—. Recipient Impact II award Ohio Dept. Edn., 1995; named Outstanding Educator, Pi Lambda Theta, 1995; Charles S. Seelback scholar Forest City Foundaries, Cleve., 1966, Alice A. White scholar Ohio State U., 1970, univ. scholar U. Akron, 1989; Kurdziel Found. grantee, 1995. Mem. ASCD, NEA, Am. Edn. Rsch. Assn., Nat. Alliance of Black Sch. Educators, Coun. Exceptional Children (exec. com., Outstanding Contbn. in Edn. recognition 1993), Ohio Edn. Assn., East Ctrl. Ohio Edn. Assn., Canton Profl. Educators Assn., Leila Green Alliance of Black Sch. Educators, Deaconess Bd., Missionary Soc., Kappa Delta Pi (presenter 38th biennial convocation Memphis 1992), Pi Lambda Theta (presenter Great Lakes region II profl. conf. Beechwood, Ohio 1994). Avocations: bowling, reading, playing piano/organ, travel. Office: Canton City Schs 521 Tuscarawas St W Canton OH 44702-2019

NWAGBARA, CHIBU ISAAC, industrial designer, consultant; b. Umuahia, Abia, Nigeria, Apr. 24, 1957; s. Marcus and Catherine (Onyemairo) N.; m. Audrey Denis Rainey, July 5, 1985; children: Obinna Alex, Amara Joy. BS, No. Ill. U., 1984, MS, 1986; MS, Purdue U., 1990, PhD, 1993. Cert. indsl. technologist. Tech. mgr. 3M Internat., Lagos, Nigeria, 1977-80; founder, pres. ChiMarc Assocs., DeKalb, Ill., 1981-84; rsch. asst. No. Ill. U., DeKalb, Ill., 1985-86; assoc. editor Purdue U., West Lafayette, Ind., 1987-89, rsch. assoc., 1990-91, grad. lectr., 1990-93; cons. Arthur Andersen & Co., St. Charles, Ill., 1993-95; program mgr. Allen-Bradley Co., Milw., 1995—; cons. Arnett Clinic, Lafayette, 1992—, Chimarc Assocs., DeKalb, 1986—, GoldMark Ltd., Lagos, 1985—. Coord. community outreach program Purdue U. Afro-Am. Studies and Rsch. Ctr., West Lafayette, 1990-91; coach Am. Youth Soccer Orgn., West Lafayette, 1987-90. Named one of Outstanding Young Men of Am., 1989, Men of Achievement, 1994. Mem. Inst. Indsl. Engrs., Am. Soc. for Quality Control, Am. Edn. Rsch. Assn., Nat. Assn. Indsl. Tech., Nat. Soc. for Performance and Instrn. Methodist. Avocations: enjoys travel, reading, meeting people, music, sports. Home: 6826 W Obikoba Circle Mequon WI 53092 Office: Allen-Bradley Co Inc 1201 S Second St Milwaukee WI 53204

NWOFOR, AMBROSE ONYEGBULE, vocational assessment evaluator; b. Amandugba, Nigeria, Dec. 7, 1947; came to the U.S., 1975; s. Wewe Ogbuihe and Nwanyi-Ihuoma (Olujie) N.; m. Clara Chinyere, June 14, 1975; children: Chiugo, Chiedoziem, Uzonna, Nnanaka, Ozioma. Diploma in elec. engring., Inst. Mgmt. & Tech. Engring., Enugu, Nigeria, 1973; BS in Electronics, Norfolk State U., 1977; MS in Ind. Tech., Ea. Mich. U., 1978; MEd in Ednl. Adminstrn., Ariz. State U., 1980. Electronic engr. Geoservices (Nigeria) Ltd., Nigeria, 1973-74, Taylor Electronics, Ariz., 1979-80; internat. svcs. engr. Dowell Schlumberger Overseas, Brazil, 1981-82; engring. lab. dir. U. Port Harcourt, Nigeria, 1982-83; sr. rsch. fellow, computer cons. Fed. U. Tech., Nigeria, 1983-89; pvt. specialist N.Y., 1989-91; elec. vocat. tchr. N.Y. Bd. Edn., 1991-93, vocat. assessment evaluator, 1993—; H.S. bd. mem. Amandugba Tech. Sch., Nigeria, 1984-88; pvt. vocat. assessment cons., 1989—. Inventor in field. Active Amandugba (Nigeria) Alms, 1973—, Amandugba (Nigeria) Dynamic Front, 1987—; chmn. Amandugba (Nigeria) Water Project, 1982-89; pres. Amandugba Fed. Union, Inc., 1992—. Mem. IEEE, Am. Vocat. Assn., Soc. Mfg. Engrs., Nat. Tech. Assn., Sci. Assn. Nigeria, N.Y. State Occupl. Assn. Roman Catholic. Avocation: video recording. Home: 702 Sturgis Pl Baltimore MD 21208

NYBERG, DONALD ARVID, oil company executive; b. Ridgewood, N.J., Aug. 23, 1951; s. Arvid H. and Rita T. (Tenwick) N.; m. Susan Radis, Feb. 16, 1985; children: Matthew D., Ryan T. BA, St. Lawrence U., 1973; MBA, Harvard U., 1975. Mgr. marine ops. Standard Oil, L.A., 1982-83; mgr. ops. planning Standard Oil, Cleve., 1984-85, dir. strategic studies, 1986; divsn. mgr. Brit. Petroleum, Ltd., London, 1987-88; v.p., gen. mgr. U.S. gas bus. BP Exploration, Houston, 1989, v.p., gen. mgr. tech., 1990; v.p. BP Exploration, Anchorage, 1991-94; pres., CEO BP Pipelines, Anchorage, 1991—; pres. Marya Resources, 1995; v.p. MAPCO Inc., 1996. Mem. adv. bd. Providence Hosp. Anchorage. Avocations: running, weight lifting, reading. Office: MAPCO Inc Tulsa OK 74101-0645

NYBERG, STANLEY ERIC, cognitive scientist; b. Boston, Jan. 30, 1948; s. Leroy Milton and Anna Maria (Olson) N. PhD, SUNY, Stony Brook, 1975; M of Pub. and Pvt. Mgmt., Yale U., 1984. Postdoctoral fellowship U. Calif., Berkeley, 1975-76; asst. prof. North Pk. Coll., Chgo., 1976-79, Barnard Coll., Columbia U., N.Y.C., 1979-82; systems mgmt. Interactive Data Corp., Lexington, Mass., 1984-88, Dept. of Revenue, Commonwealth of Mass., Boston, 1988—; bd. dirs. Children's Home of Cromwell, Conn. Co-author: Human Memory: An Introduction to Research and Theory, 1982. Bd. dirs. Decade Fund, Yale U. Sch. Mgmt., 1986—; mem. ch. coun. Luth. Ch. of Redeemer, Woburn, Mass., 1989—; v.p. West Roxbury Rugby Football Club, 1984-87, L Street Running Club, South Boston, 1993. Fellow Am. Psychol. Soc.; mem. Soc. for Applied Rsch. in Memory and Cognition, Eastern Psychol. Assn., Midwestern Psychol. Assn. Home: PO Box 1849 GMF Boston MA 02205

NYCE, ROBERT EUGENE, state legislator, tax accountant; b. Allentown, Pa., Oct. 14, 1946; s. Preston Nyce and Flora Louise (Beck) Jones; m. Maria Irene Datta, Oct. 3, 1970; 1 child, Jennifer. BA in Acctg., Moravian Coll. Tax acct. Lehigh Portland Cement Co., 1970-72; mgr. credit, taxes & ins. Frick Co., 1973-75; sr. tax acct. Bethlehem Steel Corp., 1975-85; asst. v.p., tax dir. Chrysler First, Inc., 1985-90; mem. Ho. of Reps. Commonwealth of Pa., Harrisburg, 1990—; mem. edn. com., mem. spl. sub-com. Ho. Reps. 37, higher edn. and basic edn. subcoms., fin. com., chmn. spl. task force on local tax reform, 1995-96, game & fish, policy com., Gov.'s motor carrier adv. bd., 1991-92, 93-94, 95-96. Mem. Northampton (Pa.) Sch. Bd., 1984-90, pres., 1987-89, v.p., 1986-87; mem. Bethlehem Area Vo-Tech Joint Com., 1984-90, chmn., 1986-87, vice chmn., 1985-86, 88-89; mem. East Allen Twp. Mcpl. Authority, 1979-84, former chmn.; endorsed Rep. candidate auditor gen. of Pa., 1996. Mem. Masons, Lehigh Consistory, Rajan Temple, Star Grange, Am. Legion, State Belt C. of C., East Bath Rod & Gun Club. Republican. Lutheran. Avocations: fishing, tennis, skiing, cars. Home: 7416 Carol Ln Northampton PA 18067-9074 Office: House PO Box 202020 House PO Box 147 Main Capitol Bldg Harrisburg PA 17120-0028

NYCKLEMOE, GLENN WINSTON, bishop; b. Fergus Falls, Minn., Dec. 8, 1936; s. Melvin and Bertha (Sumstad) N.; m. Ann Elizabeth Olson, May 28, 1960; children: Peter Glenn, John Winston, Daniel Thomas. BA, St. Olaf Coll., 1958; MDiv, Luther Theol. Sem., St. Paul, 1962; D of Ministry, Luth. Sch. Theology, Chgo., 1977. Ordained to ministry Am. Luth. Ch., 1962. Assoc. pastor Our Savior's Luth. Ch., Valley City, N.D., 1962-64; assoc. pastor Our Savior's Luth. Ch., Milw., 1964-67, co-pastor, 1967-73; sr. pastor Our Savior's Luth. Ch., Beloit, Wis., 1973-82, St. Olaf Luth. Ch., Austin, Minn., 1982-88; bishop Southeastern Minn. Synod, Evang. Luth. Ch. in Am., Rochester, 1988—; bd. dirs. Luth. Social Svcs. of Minn., Mpls., Bd. of Social Ministries, St. Paul, Minn. Coun. Chs., Mpls. Mem. bd. regents St. Olaf Coll., Northfield, Minn., 1988—. Avocations: skiing, trap shooting, golf. Office: SE Minn Synod Evang Luth Ch Am Assist Heights Box 4900 Rochester MN 55903

NYCUM, SUSAN HUBBELL, lawyer. B.A., Ohio Wesleyan U., 1956; J.D., Duquesne U., 1960; postgrad., Stanford U. Bar: Pa. 1962, U.S. Supreme Ct. 1967, Calif. 1974. Sole practice law Pitts., 1962-65; designer, adminstr. legal research system U. Pitts., Aspen Systems Corp., Pitts., 1965-68; mgr. ops. Computer Ctr., Carnegie Mellon U., Pitts., 1968-69; dir. computer facility Computer Ctr., Stanford U., Calif., 1969-72, Stanford Law and Computer fellow, 1972-73; cons. in computers and law, 1973-74; sr. assoc. MacLeod, Fuller, Muir & Godwin, Los Altos, Los Angeles and London, 1974-75; ptnr. Chickering & Gregory, San Francisco, 1975-80; ptnr.-in-charge high tech. group Gaston Snow & Ely Bartlett, Boston, NYC, Phoenix, San Francisco, Calif., 1980-86; mng. ptnr. Palo Alto office Kadison, Pfaelzer, Woodard, Quinn & Rossi, Los Angeles, Washington, Newport Beach, Palo Alto, Calif., 1986-87; sr. ptnr. Baker & McKenzie, Palo Alto, 1987—; trustee EDUCOM, 1978-81; mem. adv. com. for high tech. Ariz. State U. Law Sch., Santa Clara U. Law Sch., Stanford Law Sch., U. So. Calif. Law Ctr., law sch. Harvard U., U. Calif.; U.S. State Dept. del. OECD Conf. on Nat. Vulnerabilities, Spain, 1981; invited speaker Telecom, Geneva, 1983; lectr. N.Y. Law Jour., 1975—, Law & Bus., 1975—, Practicing Law Inst., 1975—; chmn. Office of Tech. Assessment Task Force on Nat. Info. Systems, 1979-80. Author:(with Bigelow) Your Computer and the Law, 1975, (with Bosworth) Legal Protection for Software, 1985, (with Collins and Gilbert) Women Leading, 1987; contbr. monographs, articles to profl. publs. Mem. Town of Portola Valley Open Space Acquisition Com., Calif., 1977; mem. Jr. League of Palo Alto, chmn. evening div., 1975-76. NSF and Dept. Justice grantee for studies on computer abuse, 1972—. Mem. ABA (sect. on sci. and tech. chmn. 1979-80, chmn. elect 1978-79), Internat. Bar Assn. (U.S. mem. computer com. of corps. sect.), Assn. Computing Machinery (mem. at large of council 1976-80, nat. lectr. 1977—, chmn. standing com. on legal issues 1975—, blue ribbon com. on rationalization of internat. proprietary rights protection on info. processing devel. in the '90s, 1990—), Computer Law Assn. (v.p. 1983-85, pres. 1986—, bd. dirs. 1975—), Calif. State Bar Assn. (founder first chmn. econs. of law sect., vice chmn. law and computers com.), Nat. Conf. Lawyers and Scientists (rep. ABA), Strategic Forum on Intellectual Property Issues in Software of NAS. Home: 35 Granada Ct Portola Valley CA 94028 Office: Baker & McKenzie PO Box 60309 Palo Alto CA 94306*

NYDICK, DAVID, school superintendent; b. N.Y.C., Feb. 10, 1929; s. Irving and Minnie (Bilibom) N.; m. Gilda Pivnick, June 14, 1953; children: Leslie Ruth, Jay Scott. BA, NYU, 1950, MA, 1952, profl. Diploma, 1960, postgrad., 1960—. Tchr. pub. schs., Great Neck, N.Y., 1954-60; prin. asst. supt. Princeton Pub. Schs., N.J., 1961-65; asst. supt. Jericho Pub. Schs., N.Y., 1965-68, supt., 1968-84; exec. dir. Guide Dog Found., Smithtown, N.Y., 1984-89; supt. Syosset (N.Y.) Pub. Schs., 1989-90, Bethpage (N.Y.) Pub. Schs., 1991—; assoc. prof. L.I. U., 1975—, Hofstra U., 1976—, Pace U., 1978—; asst. prof. Bklyn. Coll., 1979—; arbitrator Am. Arbitration Assn., Better Bus. Bur., Nat. Assn. Securities Dealers, N.Y. Stock Exchange, various N.Y. state agys. Syndicated columnist UPI, Copley News, DANY News, 1962—. Pres., East Plains Mental Health Ctr., 1964—. Served with U.S. Army, 1952-54. Recipient Edn. Achievement award NCCJ, 1975. Mem. N.Y.U. Alumni Assn. (pres. 1971-72), Am. Assn. Sch. Adminstrs., Ednl. Writers Assn., Overseas Press Club, Nat. Press Club, Masons. Home and Office: 22 Lesley Dr Syosset NY 11791-5222

NYDLE, NANCY EVE, clinical nursing educator, critical care nurse; b. Ottumwa, Iowa, Sept. 23, 1946; d. Francis Vernon and Luana Elizabeth (Walker) N. RN diploma, St. Joseph Hosp. Sch. Nursing, Ottumwa, 1968; BSN, Graceland Coll. CCRN, RN, Iowa; cert. BLS, ACLS. Staff nurse St. Francis Hosp., Waterloo, Iowa, 1968-69, head nurse CCU, 1969-71; staff nurse ICU Mt. Zion Hosp., San Francisco, 1971-76, supr. ICU, 1976-79, staff devel. ICU, 1979-80, day shift charge RN ICU, 1980-82; supr. ICU Lake Havasu Regional Hosp., Lake Havasu City, Ariz., 1982-85; staff nurse MICU U. Iowa Hosps. and Clinics, Iowa City, 1985-86; staff nurse ICU Ottumwa Regional Health Ctr., 1986—; clin. nursing instr. Indian Hills C.C., Ottumwa, 1989-95; adj. faculty Mohave C.C., Lake Havasu City, 1983-84; mem. Indian Hills C.C. faculty senate, Ottumwa, 1992-95, sec.-treas., 1993-94. Mem. AACN. Democrat. Home and Office: 227 E Main St Agency IA 52530-0193

NYE, DANIEL WILLIAM, elementary school educator; b. Harrisburg, Pa., Apr. 14, 1942; s. Daniel J. and Clarice L. (Stonesifer) N.; m. Carol A. Stewart, Aug. 10, 1968; 1 child, Michael S. BS in Health Edn., West Chester (Pa.) U., 1964; MEd in Elem. Edn., Towson (Md.) U., 1970. Cert. tchr., Md. Tchr. phys. edn. elem. sch. Harford County Pub. Schs., Bel Air, Md., 1964-72, 74—, tchr. phys. edn. mid. sch., 1972-73; rep. United Rep. Life Ins. Co., Harrisburg, Pa., 1981-85. Mem. AAHPERD, NEA, Md. State Tchrs. Assn., Harford County Edn. Assn., Md. chpt. AAHPERD. Republican. Avocations: avid golfer, antique car collector and restorer, stamp collector. Home: 1119 Carrs Mill Rd Bel Air MD 21014-2414 Office: Harford County Pub Schs 45 E Gordon St Bel Air MD 21014

NYE, EDWIN PACKARD, mechanical engineering educator; b. Atkinson, N.H., Jan. 29, 1920; s. Eben W. and Gertrude Florence (Dunn) N.; m. Persephone Fern Drumheller, Aug. 12, 1944; children: David Edwin, Sarah Leone, Benjamin Alfred. BS with high honor, U. N.H., 1941; ScM, Harvard U., 1947. Registered profl. engr., Pa., Conn. Service engr. Bailey Meter Co., Cleve., 1941-42; instr. mech. engring. U. N.H., 1942-44; project engr. NACA, 1944-46; from instr. to assoc. prof. mech. engring. Pa. State U., 1947-59; Hallden prof. Trinity Coll., Hartford, Conn., 1959-83; chmn. dept. engring. Trinity Coll., 1960-70, dean of faculty, 1970-79; pres. Charter Oak Coll., 1989; sec. Univ. Research Inst. Conn., 1964-68, pres., 1968-71, chmn., 1971-74; bd. dir. Hallden Machine Co.; chmn. coll. work Episcopal Diocese Conn., 1960-64. Co-author: Steam Power Plants, 1952, Power Plants, 1956, Thermal Engineering, 1959. Mem. bd. edn., Bloomfield, Conn., 1961-65; mem. State Bd. Acad. Awards, 1974-94, dean faculty, 1979-83; corporator Hartford Pub. Libr., 1978-82. Mem. ASME, Am. Soc. Engring. Edn., Conn. Acad. Sci. and Engring., Phi Kappa Phi, Pi Tau Sigma. Home: Bug Hill Rd Ashfield MA 01330

NYE, ERIC WILLIAM, English language and literature educator; b. Omaha, July 31, 1952; s. William Frank and Mary Roberta (Lueder) N.; m. Carol Denison Frost, Dec. 21, 1980; children: Charles William, Ellen Mary. BA, St. Olaf Coll., 1974; MA, U. Chgo., 1976, PhD, 1983; postgrad., Queens' Coll., Cambridge, England, 1979-82. Tutor in coll. writing com. U. Chgo., 1976-79, tchg. intern, 1978; tutor Am. lit. Cambridge (Eng.) U., 1979-82; asst. prof. English U. Wyo., Laramie, 1983-89, assoc. prof., 1989—; v.p., bd. dirs. Plainview Tel. Co., Nebr.; hon. vis. fellow U. Edinburgh (Scotland) Inst. for Advanced Studies in the Humanities, 1987; guest lectr. NEH summer Inst., Laramie, Wyo., 1985, Carlyle Soc. of Edinburgh, 1987, Wordsworth summer Conf., Grasmere, Eng., 1988, cons. NEH. Contbr. articles and reviews to profl. jours. Mem. Am. Friends of Cambridge U., Gen. Soc. Mayflower Descendants; elected mem. Wyo. Coun. for Humanities, 1992-96, mem. exec. com., 1993-94; mem. adv. bd. Wyo. Ctr. for the Book, 1995—. Named Nat. Merit Scholar St. Olaf Coll., 1970-74; recipient Grad. Fellowship, Rotary Found., 1979-80, grant Am. Coun. of Learned Socs., 1988, Disting. Alumnus award, Lincoln (Neb.) E. High Sch., 1986. Mem. MLA (del. assembly 1991-93), Assn. for Documentary Editing, Bibliog. Soc. London, Assn. for Computers and the Humanities, Assn. for Lit.

and Linguistic Computing, Coleridge Soc. (life), Friends of Dove Cottage (life), Charles Lamb Soc., Carlyle Soc., Rsch. Soc. for Victorian Periodicals, The Victorians Inst., Gen. Soc. Mayflower Descs., The Tennyson Soc., Penn Club (London), Queens Coll. Club (Cambridge) Phi Beta Kappa (pres., v.p., sec. Wyo. chpt. 1988—). Home: 1495 Apache Dr Laramie WY 82070-6966 Office: U Wyo Dept English PO Box 3353 Laramie WY 82071-3353

NYE, ERLE ALLEN, utilities executive, lawyer; b. Ft. Worth, June 23, 1937; s. Ira Benjamen N.; m. Alice Ann Grove, June 5, 1959; children: Elizabeth Nye Janzen, Pamela Nye Schneider, Erle Allen Jr., Edward Kyle, Johnson Scott. BEE, Tex. A&M U., 1959; JD, So. Meth. U., 1965. With Dallas Power & Light Co., 1960-75, v.p., 1975-80; exec. v.p. Tex. Utilities Co., Dallas, 1980-87, pres., 1987—, CEO, 1995—; pres. Chaco Energy Co., Dallas, 1994-96, CEO, 1996—; pres. Tex. Utilities Mining Co., Dallas, 1982-96, CEO, 1996—; CEO Tex. Utilities Svcs., Inc., Dallas, 1982—; chmn. bd., CEO Tex. Utilities Electric Co., Dallas, 1987—; CEO Basic Resources Inc., Dallas, 1994—, Chaco Energy Co., Dallas, 1994—, TU Svcs., 1982—, Tex. Utilities Commn., Dallas, 1995—; pres. Tex. Utilities Fuel Co., 1982—; chmn. Tex. Utilities Australia Pty., Ltd., 1996—. Bd. dirs. Dallas Bar Found., 1980-83, Dallas Cen. Bus. Plan Com., 1980-83, Inroads/Dallas-Ft. Worth Inc., 1984-88, trustee Baylor Dental Coll., Dallas, 1985-94; mem. Dallas Together Forum, 1989—, Dallas Com. Fgn. Rels., 1991—, Bd. of Boys & Girls Clubs of Am., 1991—; The Dallas Found., 1994—; The Science Pl., Dallas, 1995—; The Salvation Army's Dallas County Adv. Bd., 1995—. Mem. ABA, Dallas Bar Assn., Tex. State Bar Assn., Dallas C. of C. (bd. dirs. 1991-95, vice chmn. 1992-95). Methodist. Clubs: Engineers (pres. 1982-83), Northwood (Dallas). Home: 6924 Desco Dallas TX 75225-1716 Office: Texas Utilities Company 41st Floor 1601 Bryan Street Dallas TX 75201-3411

NYE, GENE WARREN, art educator; b. Sacramento, July 3, 1939; s. Charles Frederick and Dorthy Dell Nye; m. Alena Mae Nye, Sept. 20, 1974; children: Dirk, Ronni, Anthony, Timothy. AA, American River Coll., Sacramento, 1962; AB, Sacramento State U., 1964; cert. Secondary Art Tchr., U. Calif., Berkeley, 1966. Printer Roseville (Calif.) Press Tribune, 1957-60; typographer Oakland (Calif.) Tribune, 1960-65; tchr. art Long Beach (Calif.) Unified Sch. Dist., 1965-67; tchr., chair art dept. Woodland (Calif.) Unified Sch. Dist., 1967—; freelance artist Wildcat Art, Sacramento, 1985—; cons. N.Mex. Ctrl. Coun. Student Activities, 1991; workshop presenter. Author: (workbook set and video) Posters Made EZ, 1990. Mem. task force Constn. Revision of CADA, L.A., 1988-89. Named to Calif. Assn. Dirs. of Activities Hall of Fame, 1992. Mem. NEA (life), Calif. Tchrs. Assn., Woodland Edn. Assn. (v.p. 1971-72), Calif. Art Edn. Assn., Nat. Art Edn. Assn., Calif. League Mid. Schs., U. Calif.-Berkeley Alumni Assn. (life). Home: 2200 Eastern Ave Sacramento CA 95864-0805 Office: Lee Jr HS 520 West St Woodland CA 95695-3705

NYE, JOHN CALVIN, agricultural engineer, educator; b. Anthony, Kans., Mar. 24, 1945; s. Paul Everet and Alice Anna (Schmidt) N.; m. Gloria Tara Giese, Dec. 8, 1974; 1 child, Jaffe. BS in Agrl. Engring., Kans. State U., 1968; MS in Agrl. Engring., Purdue U., 1970, PhD, 1971. Registered profl. engr., La., Ind., Del. Asst. prof. Purdue U., West Lafayette, Ind., 1971-73, assoc. prof., then prof., 1975-84; chief agrl. permit team region V U.S. EPA, Chgo., 1974-75; prof., head agrl. engring. dept. La. State U., Baton Rouge, 1984-91; dean Coll. of Agrl. Scis. U. Del., Newark, 1991—; chair joint coun. food and agrl. sci. USDA; bd. dirs. Accreditation Bd. Engring. and Tech., Delmarva Poultry Industries, Inc. Bd. dirs. La. Sci. and Engring. Fair, Baton Rouge, 1986-91. 1st lt. U.S. Army, 1971. Recipient Disting. Svc. award La. Acad. Sci., 1990, Professionalism award La. Engring. Found., 1990. Mem. NSPE, Am. Soc. Engring. Educators, Am. Soc. Agrl. Engrs. Home: 204 Wilson Rd Newark DE 19711-3629 Office: U Del Coll Agrl Scis 133 Townsend Hall Newark DE 19717-1303

NYE, JOSEPH BENJAMIN HARDING, government executive; b. Boston, June 17, 1965; s. Joseph Samuel and Mary (Harding) N.; m. Jennifer M. Pyle, Oct. 23, 1993. BA, Harvard U., 1987; MBA, Harvard Bus. Sch., Boston, 1992. Fin. analyst Paine Webber, Inc., N.Y.C., Tokyo, 1987-89; analyst controller's office Ford Motor Co., Dearborn, Mich., 1989-92; assoc. Mercer Mgmt. Cons., Lexington, Mass., 1992-93; exec. sec. U.S. Treas. Dept., Washington, 1993—. Office: US Treasury Dept 1500 Pennsylvania Ave NW Washington DC 20220

NYE, THOMAS RUSSELL, retired drafting, reproduction and surveying company executive; b. Arlington, Mass., July 16, 1928; s. Russell Van Buren and Sibyl (Partridge) N.; m. Patricia Bentley, Dec. 14, 1951; children; Bradford V. B., Debra Nye Moran. AB, Brown U., 1950; MBA, Harvard U., 1952. Salesman Russell Nye Co., Inc., Boston, 1951-52; assignment dir., sr. assoc. Bruce Payne & Assocs., N.Y.C., 1953-59; with Keuffel & Esser Co., Morristown, N.J., 1959-84, exec. v.p., 1970, pres., 1970-82, chief exec. officer, 1971-82; bd. dirs. J.K. Adams Co., Inc.; arbitrator N.Y. Stock Exch., Nat. Assn. Securities Dealers. Author articles. Bd. dirs. United Way, Madison, N.J., 1968-73, Madison YMCA, 1970-72; mem. corp. United Way Morris County, 1973-91; mem. adv. bd. R & D Coun. N.J., 1980-88, Morristown Meml. Hosp. Corp., 1985-91. Lt. USAF, 1952-53. Mem. Assn. Reproduction Materials Mfrs. (pres. 1978, bd. dirs.), Am. Mgmt. Assn., NAM, Internat. Assn. Blueprinters and Allied Industries, Am. Congress Mapping and Surveying, Soc. Advancement Mgmt., Lake Sunapee Country Club, Boca Grande Club, Morris County Golf Club. Baptist. Home: PO Box 936 The Seasons New London NH 03257

NYE, W. MARCUS W., lawyer; b. N.Y.C., Aug. 3, 1945; s. Walter R. and Nora (McLaren) N.; m. Eva Johnson; children: Robbie, Stephanie, Philip, Jennifer. BA, Harvard U., 1967; JD, U. Idaho, 1974. Bar: Idaho 1974, U.S. Dist. Ct. Idaho 1974, U.S. Ct. Appeals (9th cir.) 1980. Ptnr. Racine, Olson, Nye, Cooper & Budge, Pocatello, Idaho, 1974—; vis. prof. law U. Idaho, Moscow, 1984; adj. prof. Coll. Engring. IDaho State U., 1993—. Recipient Alumni Svc. award U. Idaho, 1988. Fellow ABA (mem. ho. dels. 1988—, state chmn. ho. of dels. 1991—), Am. Bar Found. (stat. chmn. 1992—); mem. Am. Bd. Trial Advs., Am. Coll. Trial Lawyers, Idaho Bar Assn. (commr. 1985—, pres. bd. commrs. 1987-88), Idaho Def. Counsel Assn. (pres. 1982), Idaho State Centennial Found. (commr. 1985-90), 6th Dist. Bar Assn. (pres. 1982). Home: 173 S 15th Ave Pocatello ID 83201-4056 Office: Racine Olson Nye Cooper & Budge PO Box 1391 Pocatello ID 83204-1391

NYENHUIS, JACOB EUGENE, college official; b. Mille Lacs County, Minn., Mar. 25, 1935; s. Egbert Peter and Rosa (Walburg) N.; m. Leona Mae Van Duyn, June 6, 1956; children: Karen Joy, Kathy Jean, Lorna Jane, Sarah Van Duyn. AB in Greek, Calvin Coll., 1956; AM in Classics, Stanford U., 1961, PhD in Classics, 1963. Asst. in classical langs. Calvin Coll., Grand Rapids, Mich., 1957-59; acting instr. Stanford (Calif.) U., 1962; from asst. prof. to prof. Wayne State U., Detroit, 1962-75, dir. honors program, 1964-75, chmn. Greek and Latin dept., 1965-75; prof. classics, dean for humanities Hope Coll., Holland, Mich., 1975-78, dean for arts and humanities, 1978-84, provost, 1984—; cons. Mich. Dept. Edn., Lansing, 1971-72, Gustavus Adolphus Coll., St. Peter, Minn., 1974, Northwestern Coll., Orange City, Iowa, 1983, Whitworth Coll., Spokane, Wash., 1987, The Daedalus Project, 1988; reviewer NEH, Washington, 1986-87, Lilly Endowment, Indpls., 1987-89, U.S. Dept. Edn., 1993; vis. assoc. prof. U. Calif., Santa Barbara, 1967-68, Ohio State U., Columbus, 1972; vis. rsch. prof. Am. Sch. Classical Studies, Athens, Greece, 1973-74, also mem. mng. com.; panelist NEH, 1991; vis. scholar Green Coll. Oxford U., 1989. Co-author: Latin Via Ovid, 1977, rev. edit., 1982; editor: Petronius: Cena Trimalchionis, 1970, Plautus: Amphitruo, 1970; articles in field. Elder Christian Reformed Ch., Palo Alto, Calif., 1960-62; elder, clk. Christian Reformed Ch., Grosse Pointe, Mich., 1964-67; elder, clk. Christian Reformed Ch., Holland, Mich., 1976-85, v.p., 1988-91, mem. exec. com., 1994-95; chmn. human rels. coun. Open Housing Com., Grosse Pointe, 1971-73. Mem. Am. Philol. Assn., Danforth Assocs. (chmn. regional com. 1975-77), Mich. Coun. for Humanities (bd. dirs., 1976-84, 88-92, chmn. 1980-82, Disting. Svc. award 1984), Nat. Fedn. State Humanities Couns. (pres. 1979-84), Gt. Lakes Colls. Assn. (bd. dirs. 1991-93), Coun. on Undergrad. Rsch. (councilor-at-large 1993—). Democrat. Avocations: photography, carpentry, cross-country skiing. Home: 51 E 8th St Ste 200 Holland MI 49423-3501 Office: Hope Coll Office of the Provost 141 E 12th St PO Box 9000 Holland MI 49422-9000

NYERE, ROBERT ALAN, banker; b. Aberdeen, Wash., July 19, 1917; s. George Louis and Augusta (Draheim) N.; m. Jeanne Fortier, Nov. 8, 1941; children: Sharon L. Nyere Olson, Barbara J. Nyere Slevin. B.A., U. Wash., 1939; M.B.A., Harvard U., 1941; grad., Stonier Sch. Banking, Rutgers U., 1951. With First Nat. Bank of Boston, 1941-79, asst. mgr., mgr., asst. v.p., 1948-58, v.p., 1958-69, sr. v.p., 1969-79; former dir. Mastercard Internat. Corp., FNBC Acceptance Corp., 1st La. Acceptance Corp., Boston Trust & Savs., Ltd.; cons., dir. Credit Card Services Corp., Springfield, Va., 1981-83; mem. Sr. Corps Ret. Execs., SBA, 1980-85. Served from ensign to lt. USNR, 1942-46. Fellow U. Ky., 1995. Mem. Algonquin Club, U. Ky. Faculty Club, The Lexington Club, Masons (32 deg.), Shriners, Alpha Kappa Psi. Episcopalian. Home: 4922 Hartland Pky Lexington KY 40515-1109

NYERGES, ALEXANDER LEE, museum director; b. Rochester, N.Y., Feb. 27, 1957; s. Sandor Elek and Lena (Angeline) N.; 1 child, Robert Angeline. BA, George Washington U., 1979, MA, 1981. Intern The Octagon, Washington, 1976-79; archeol. asst. Smithsonian Instn., Washington, 1977, curatorial intern Nat. Mus. Am. History, 1978-79; adminstrv. asst. George Washington U., Washington, 1979-81; exec. dir. DeLand Mus. Art, Fla., 1981-85, Miss. Mus. Art, Jackson, 1985-92; dir. Dayton (Ohio) Art Inst., 1992—; grants panel Nat. Endowment for the Arts, 1988—; field surveyor Inst. Mus. Svcs., Washington, 1985-88, nat. review panel, 1990-92; treas., bd. dirs. Volusia County Arts Coun., Daytona Beach, Fla., 1983-85. Contbr. articles to profl. jours. Bd. dirs. West Volusia Hist. Soc., 1984-85; pres. Miss. Inst. Arts and Letters, 1987-88; trustee Cultural Arts Ctr., DeLand, 1984-85, Miami Valley Cultural Alliance, 1993—, Intermus. Conservation Lab., 1993—, Montgomery county arts and culture district, 1994—. U.S. Dept. Edn. scholar, 1973. Mem. DeLand Area C. of C. (bd. dirs., tourist adv. com. 1984-85), Assn. Art Mus. Dirs., Am. Assn. Mus. (SE regional rep. to non-print media com. 1983-85, nat. legis. com. 1986-93), Miss. Mus. Assn., Assn. Art Mus. Dirs., Southeastern Mus. Conf. (bd. dirs. 1991-92), Fla. Mus. Assn., Fla. Art Mus. Dirs. Assn., Cultural Roundtable (pres. 1993—), Ohio Mus. Assn. (trustee 1993—), Phi Beta Kappa. Presbyterian. Avocations: restoring old houses, gardening, music, writing, sports. Home: 1719 Auburn Ave Dayton OH 45406 Office: Dayton Art Inst 456 Belmonte Park N Dayton OH 45405-4700

NYERGES, GEORGE LADISLAUS, lawyer; b. Cleve., Aug. 27, 1925; s. Constantine L. and Irene (Schneider) N.; m. Joanne Mayo, Aug. 2, 1958; children: James George, Susan Joanne. BS, Case Western Reserve U., 1946; LLB, Cleveland-Marshall Law Sch., 1951, LLM, 1956; JD, Cleve. State U., 1969. Bar: Ohio 1951, U.S. Dist. Ct. (no. dist.) Ohio 1954, U.S. Ct. Appeals (6th cir.) 1985, U.S. Supreme Ct. 1991. Lawyer, sole practice Cleve., 1951—; lectr. legal and med. ethics Cuyahoga C.C., Cleve., 1989; cons. to various religious groups, 1985—. Mem. Magyar Club of Cleve., 1952—, sec., 1954-57, pres. 1958; mem. "Night in Budapest Com." in Cleve., 1958-65, Vermilion (Ohio) Yacht Club, 1973—, sec., 1974-76; coach girls baseball Summer Recreational Jr. Girls Baseball, Westlake, Ohio, 1980, coach boys football Fall Recreational Jr. Boys Football, Westlake, 1980-82; former precinct committeeman Dem. Party, Westlake, 1990. Recipient Cert., Am. Judicature Soc., 1961, Plaque Am. Arbitration Assn., 1970, Cert. of Appreciation, Cleve. Bar Assn., 1987-88. Mem. ABA, Ohio State Bar Assn. (Cert. of Appreciation 1991), Fed. Bar Assn., Phi Gamma Delta Alumni Group. Democrat. Presbyterian. Avocations: former comdr., including lesser chairs and charter mem. of Rocky River Power Squadron. Home: 1999 Dover Center Rd Westlake OH 44145 Office: United Office Bldg 2012 W 25th St Ste 803 Cleveland OH 44113-4131

NYGAARD, RICHARD LOWELL, federal judge; b. 1940. BS cum laude, U. So. Calif., 1969; JD, U. Mich. Mem. Orton, Nygaard & Dunlevy, 1972-81; judge Ct. Common Pleas, 6th Dist. Pa., Erie, 1981-88, U.S. Ct. Appeals (3d cir.) Pa., Erie, 1988—. Councilman Erie County, 1977-81. With USNR, 1958-64. Mem. ABA, Pa. Bar Assn., Erie County Bar Assn. Office: US Ct Appeals 3d Cir 500 First Nat Bank Bldg 717 State St Erie PA 16501-1341

NYGARD, HOLGER OLOF, English and folklore educator; b. Vasa, Finland, Feb. 24, 1921; came to U.S., 1953, naturalized, 1958; s. Victor N. and Maria (Bergman) Nygard; m. Margaret C. Rodger, Oct. 11, 1944; Jennifer K., Stephen V., Kerstin M., Karl Erik. B.A., U. B.C., Vancouver, 1944; M.A., U. Calif.-Berkeley, 1949, Ph.D., 1955. Instr. U. B.C., 1945-47; asst. prof. U. Kans., Lawrence, 1953-57; assoc. prof. U. Tenn., Knoxville, 1957-60; prof. English Duke U., Durham, N.C., 1960-90, prof. emeritus, 1990—. Author: (Chgo. Folklore prize 1959) The Ballad of Heer Halewijn, 1958. Fellow Am. Council Learned Socs., 1952; Guggenheim fellow, 1966; fellow Inst. Advanced Studies Humanities, U. Edinburgh, Scotland, 1979; NEH fellow, 1980. Mem. Am. folklore Soc., MLA. Home: 4015 Cole Mill Rd Durham NC 27712-2907

NYHAN, WILLIAM LEO, pediatrician, educator; b. Boston, Mar. 13, 1926; s. W. Leo and Mary (Cleary) N.; m. Christine Murphy, Nov. 20, 1948; children: Christopher, Abigail. Student, Harvard U., 1943-45; M.D., Columbia U., 1949; M.S., U. Ill., 1956, Ph.D., 1958; hon. doctorate, Tokushima U., Japan, 1981. Intern Yale U.-Grace-New Haven Hosp., 1949-50, resident, 1950-51, 53-55; asst. prof. pediatrics Johns Hopkins U., 1958-61, assoc. prof., 1961-63; prof. pediatrics, biochemistry U. Miami, 1963-69, chmn. dept. pediatrics, 1963-69; prof. U. Calif., San Diego, 1969—; chmn. dept. pediatrics U. Calif., 1969-86; mem. FDA adv. com. on Teratogenic Effects of Certain Drugs, 1964-70; mem. pediatric panel AMA Council on Drugs, 1964-70; mem. Nat. Adv. Child Health and Human Devel. Council, 1967-71; mem. research adv. com. Calif. Dept. Mental Hygiene, 1969-72; mem. med. and sci. adv. com. Leukemia Soc. Am., Inc., 1968-72; mem. basic adv. com. Nat. Found. March of Dimes, 1973-81; mem. Basil O'Connor Starter grants com., 1973-93; mem. clin. cancer program project rev. com. Nat. Cancer Inst., 1977-81; vis. prof. extraordinario U. del Salvador (Argentina), 1982. Author: (with E. Edelson) The Heredity Factor, Genes, Chromosomes and You, 1976,Genetic & Malformation Syndromes in Clinical Medicine, 1976, Abnormalities in Amino Acid Metabolism in Clinical Medicine, 1984, Diagnostic Recognition of Genetic Disease, 1987; editor: Amino Acid Metabolism and Genetic Variation, 1967, Heritable Disorders of Amino Acid Metabolism, 1974; mem. editorial bd. Jour. Pediatrics, 1964-78, King Faisal Hosp. Med. Jour., 1981-85, Western Jour. Medicine, 1974-86, Annals of Saudi Medicine, 1985-87, mem. editorial com. Ann. Rev. Nutrition, 1982-86; mem. editorial staff Med. and Pediatric Oncology, 1975-83. Served with U.S. Navy, 1944-46; U.S. Army, 1951-53. Nat. Found. Infantile Paralysis fellow, 1955-58; recipient Commemorative medallion Columbia U. Coll. Physicians and Surgeons, 1967. Mem. AAAS, Am. Fedn. Clin. Rsch., Am. Chem. Soc., Soc. Pediatric Rsch. (pres. 1970-71), Am. Assn. Cancer Rsch., Am. Soc. Pharmacology and Exptl. Therapeutics, Western Soc. Pediatric Rsch. (pres. 1976-77), N.Y. Acad. Sci., Am. Acad. Pediatrics (Borden award 1980), Am. Pediatric Soc., Am. Inst. Biol. Scis., Soc. Exptl. Biology and Medicine, Am. Soc. Clin. Investigation, Am. Soc. Human Genetics (dir. 1978-81), Inst. Investigaciones Citologicas (Spain, corr.), Biochem. Soc., Société Française de Pediatrie (corr.), South African Human Genetics (hon.), Sigma Xi, Alpha Omega Alpha. Office: U Calif San Diego Dept Pediatrics # 0609A La Jolla CA 92093

NYHART, ELDON HOWARD, employee benefits consultant, lawyer; b. Lafayette, Ind., Jan. 17, 1927; s. Howard E. and Mabel (Keller) N.; m. Frieda Ernie, Apr. 12, 1971; children: Maria, Malott, Sallie, Eldon Jr. AB cum laude, Princeton U., 1948; JD, Ind. U., 1952. Exec. v.p. The Nyhart Co., Inc., Indpls., 1953-55, pres., chief exec. officer, 1955-60, chief exec. officer, 1960-91, chmn. bd. dirs., 1991—; lectr. Purdue U., Lafayette; tchr. Ind. U. Grad. Sch. Bus., Bloomington, dir. Midwest Pension Conf. Contbr. articles to profl. jour. Life trustee Indpls. Mus. Art, bd. govs., 1990—; bd. dirs. Ind. Swiss Found., pres. 1991—, Ind. State Symphony Soc., 1990—, Eiteljorg Mus., 1990, Contemporary Art Soc., 1991—, Friends of Herron Gallery, 1990—; del. White House Conf. on Aging. Mem. ABA, Internat. Bar Assn., Ind. Bar Assn., Assn. Pvt. Pension and Welfare Plans, trustee 1987-91, Am. Judicature Soc., Am. Pension Conf., Woodstock Club, Chgo. Racquet Club, Univ. Club (Indpls.), Princeton Club (N.Y.). Episcopalian. Home: 7468 Lions Head Dr Apt D Indianapolis IN 46260-3457 Office: Nyhart Co Inc 3515 N Washington Blvd Indianapolis IN 46205-3718

NYHART, ELDON HOWARD, JR., biopharmaceuticist, biomedical engineer; b. Indpls., Nov. 19, 1955; s. Eldon H. Nyhart and Jane (Eaglesfield) Darlington; m. Deborah Elaine Fortune, Sept. 7, 1991. BS in Biomed. Engring., Vanderbilt U., 1978; PhD in Biopharmaceutics, Purdue U., 1984. Rsch. asst. Indpls. Ctr. for Advanced Rsch., Fortune-Fry Lab., 1978; rsch. asst./tchg. asst. dept. industrial and physical pharmacy Purdue U., West Lafayette, Ind., 1979-84; sr. scientist Eli Lilly and Co., Indpls., 1984—. Contbr. articles to profl. jours. Mem. Ind. Mus. Art, Indpls., 1992; amb. People to People Program, Washington, 1972. Recipient David Ross fellowship Purdue U., 1981-83. Mem. Am. Assn. Pharm. Scientists, Rho Chi, Alpha Tau Omega (pres. 1974), Univ. Club Indpls., Woodstock Country Club. Avocations: market timing, soccer. Home: 40 E Ash St Zionsville IN 46077 Office: Eli Lilly and Co Lilly Clinic 1001 W 10th St Indianapolis IN 46202

NYHUS, LLOYD MILTON, surgeon, educator; b. Mt. Vernon, Wash., June 24, 1923; s. Lewis Guttorm and Mary (Shervem) N.; m. Margaret Goldie Sheldon, Nov. 25, 1949; children: Sheila Margaret, Leif Torger. B.S., Pacific Luth. Coll., 1945; M.D., Med. Coll. Ala., 1947; Honoris Doctoris Causa, Aristotelian U., Thessalonika, Greece, 1968, Uppsala U., Sweden, 1974, U. Chihuahua, Mex., 1975, Jagallonian U., Cracow, Poland, 1980, U. Gama Filho, Rio de Janeiro, 1983, U. Louis Pasteur, Strasbourg, France, 1984, U. Athens, 1989. Diplomate Am. Bd. Surgery (chmn. 1974-76). Intern King County Hosp., Seattle, 1947-48; resident in surgery King County Hosp., 1948-55; practice medicine specializing in surgery Seattle, 1956-67, Chgo., 1967—; instr. surgery U. Wash., Seattle, 1954-56; asst. prof. U. Wash., 1956-59, assoc. prof., 1959-64, prof., 1964-67; Warren H. Cole prof., head dept. surgery U. Ill. Coll. Medicine, 1967-89, emeritus head, 1989—, prof. emeritus, 1993; emeritus surgeon-in-chief U. Ill. Hosp.; sr. cons. surgeon Cook County, West Side VA, Hines (Ill.) VA hosps.; cons. to Surgeon Gen. NIH, 1965-69. Author: Surgery of the Stomach and Duodenum, 1962, 4th edit., 1986, named changed to Surgery of the Esophagus, Stomach and Small Intenstine, 5th edit., 1995, Hernia, 1964, 2d edit., 1978, 3d edit., 1989, 4th edit., 1995, Abdominal Pain: A Guide to Rapid Diagnosis, 1969, 95, Manual of Surgical Therapeutics, 1969, latest rev. edit., 1996, Mastery of Surgery, 1984, 2d edit., 1992, Surgery Ann., 1970-95, Treatment of Shock, 1970, 2d rev. edit., 1986, Surgery of the Small Intestine, 1987; editor-in-chief Rev. of Surgery, 1967-77, Current Surgery, 1978-90, emeritus editor, 1991—; assoc. editor Quar. Rev. Surgery, 1958-61; editl. bd. Am. Jour. Digestive Diseases, 1961-67, Scandinavian Jour. Gastroenterology, 1966—, Am. Surgeon, 1967-89, Jour. Surg. Oncology, 1969—, Archives of Surgery, 1977-86, World Jour. Surgery; contbr. articles to profl. jours. Served to lt. M.C. USNR, 1943-46, 50-52. Decorated Order of Merit (Poland); postdoctoral fellow USPHS, 1952-53; recipient M. Shipley award So. Surg. Assn., 1967, Rovsing medal Danish Surg. Soc., 1973; Disting. Faculty award U. Ill Coll. Medicine, 1983, Disting. Alumnus award Med. Coll. Ala., 1984, Disting. Alumnus award U. Wash., 1993; Guggenheim fellow, 1955-56. Fellow ACS (1st v.p. 1987-88), Assn. Surgeons Gt. Brit. and Ireland (hon.), Royal Coll. Surgeons Eng. (hon.), Royal Coll. Surgeons Ireland (hon.), Royal Coll. Surgeons Edinburgh (hon.), Royal Coll. Physicians and Surgeons Glasgow (hon.); mem. Am. Gastroent. Assn., Am. Physiol. Soc., Pacific Coast Surg. Assn., Am. Surg. Assn. (recorder 1976-81, 1st v.p. 1989-90), Western Surg. Assn., Ctrl. Soc. Clin. Rsch., Chgo. Surg. Soc. (pres. 1974), Ctrl. Surg. Assn. (pres. 1984), Seattle Surg. Soc., St. Paul Surg. Soc. (hon.), Kansas City Surg. Soc. (hon.), Inst. Medicine Chgo., Internat. Soc. Surgery (pres. U.S. sect. 1986-88, pres. 34th World Congress 1991, internat. pres. 1991-93), Internat. Soc. Surgery Found. (sec. treas. 1992—), Collegium Internat. Chirurgiae Digestivae (pres III world congress Chgo. 1974, internat. pres. 1978-84), Soc. for Surgery Alimentary Tract (sec. 1969-73, pres. 1974), Soc. Clin. Surgery, Soc. Surg. Chmn., Soc. U. Surgeons (pres. 1967), Duetschen Gesellschaft für Chirurgie (corr.), Polish Assn. Surgeons (hon.), L'Academie de Chirurgie (France) (corr.), Swiss Surg. Soc. (hon.), Brazilian Coll. Surgeons (hon.), Surg. Biology Club, Warren H. Cole Soc. (pres. 1981), Japan Surg. Soc. (hon.), Assn. Gen. Surgeons of Mex. (hon.), Columbian Surg. Soc. (hon.), Internat. Fedn. Surg. Colls. (hon. treas. 1992—), Sigma Xi, Alpha Omega Alpha, Phi Beta Phi. Home: 310 Maple Row Winnetka IL 60093-1036 Office: M/C 958 840 S Wood St Chicago IL 60612-7317

NYIRJESY, ISTVAN, obstetrician, gynecologist; b. Budapest, Hungary, Nov. 14, 1929; came to U.S., 1954, naturalized, 1960; s. Sandor D. and Margit (Bertalan) N.; m. Michelle Shoepp, June 16, 1956; children—Francis, Paul, Christine. M.D., Catholic U. Louvain, Belgium, 1955. Diplomate: Am. Bd. Ob-Gyn. Intern Cath. U. Louvain and Little Co. Mary Hosp., Evergeen Park, Ill., 1954-55; resident in gynecology obstetrics, 1960-63; chief obstetrical research Nat. Naval Med. Center, Bethesda, Md., 1966-68; ret., 1968; practice medicine specializing in Ob-Gyn Bethesda, 1968—; clin. prof. Ob-Gyn Georgetown U., 1968—; cons. NIH, 1974—, FDA, 1977-88. Lit. editor Breast Disease: contbr. articles to med. jours.; author: Prevention and Detection of Gynecologic and Breast Cancer, 1994. Pres., Internat. Found. for Gynecol. Cancer Detection and Prevention, 1993—. Officer M.C. USN, 1956-68; advanced through grades to comdr. Recipient Sword of Hope pin Am. Cancer Soc., 1973, Vicennial medal Georgetown U., 1988. Fellow ACOG (Host award 1964), Internat. Coll. Surgeons; mem. Montgomery County (Md.) Med. Soc. (chmn. profl. edn. com. 1971-72), Gynecol. Soc. Study of Breast Disease (past pres.), Assn. Profs. Ob-Gyn., Am. Fertility Soc., Washington Gynecol. Soc. (v.p. 1993-94, 1st v.p. 1994-95, pres.-elect). Office: 5301 Westbard Cir Ste 5 Bethesda MD 20816-1425

NYKROG, PER, French literature educator; b. Copenhagen, Nov. 1, 1925; came to U.S., 1979; s. Kai S. Nathanson and Karen E. (Olsen) Nykrog; m. Vibeke H. Rasmussen, 1951 (dec. 1977); children: Thomas, Jakob; m. Usha Saksena Nilsson, Jan. 2, 1981. Grad., U. Copenhagen, 1952; PhD, U. Aarhus, Denmark, 1957. Asst. prof. U. Aarhus, 1953-57, prof., 1957-79; prof. French lang. and lit. Harvard U., Cambridge, Mass., 1979—. Author: Les Fabliaux, 1957, La Pensée de Balzac, 1965, L'Amour et la Rose, 1986, La Recherche du Don perdu, 1987, Chrétien de Troyes romancier discutable, 1995. Mem. Royal Soc. Scis. Denmark. Home: 243 Concord Ave Cambridge MA 02138-1360 Office: Harvard U Dept Romance Langs Boylston Hall Cambridge MA 02138

NYKVIST, SVEN VILHEM, cinematographer; b. Moheda, Sweden, Dec. 3, 1922; s. Gustaf Nathanael and Gerda Emilia (Nilson) N.; 1 son, Carl-Gustaf. Student, Stockholm Photog. Sch.; hon. doctorate, Am. Film Inst., 1991. Asst. cameraman Stockholm, 1941-44; co-owner film prodn. co. Josephson-Nykvist, Stockholm. Dir. photography over 100 feature films, including 22 films directed by Ingmar Bergman, 1945—; cinematographer: (films) Sawdust and Tinsel, 1953, The Virgin Spring, 1960, Winter Light, 1962, Karin Mansdotter, The Silence, 1963, Loving Couples, 1964, Persona, 1966, Hour of the Wolf, 1968, One Day in the Life of Ivan Denisovich, 1971, The Dove, 1973, Cries and Whispers, 1973, Scenes from a Marriage, 1973, Black Moon, 1975, The Magic Flute, 1975, Face to Face, 1976, The Tenant, 1976, The Serpent's Egg, 1977, Autumn Sonata, 1978, King of the Gypsies, 1978, Pretty Baby, 1978, Hurricane, 1979, Starting Over, 1979, Willie and Phil, 1980, The Postman Always Rings Twice, 1981, Cannery Row, 1982, Fanny and Alexander, 1983, Star 80, 1983, Swann in Love, 1984, Agnes of God, 1985, Dream Lover, 1986, The Sacrifice, 1986, The Unbearable Lightness of Being, 1988 (nominated Oscar award), Brothers, 1988, segment of film New York Stories, 1988-89, Crimes and Misdemeanors, 1989, Sleepless in Seattle, 1992, Him, 1993, Gilbert Grape, 1993, Him, 1993, Night Before Christmas, 1993, Kirsten Laviansdatter, 1994; (TV) Bergman, 1995; dir. film The Vine Bridge, 1965; dir., cinematographer The Ox, 1991, Charlie, 1992; dir. With Honors, 1993; author: Resan Till Lambarene. Recipient Acad. award Am. Acad. Motion Picture Arts and Scis. for Cries and Whispers, 1974, for Fanny and Alexander, 1984, Caesar French Acad. award, Swedish Acad. award, nominee for best fgn. film for the Ox, 1991, Doctorate Am. Film Inst., 1991. Mem. Swedish Film Acad., Am. Soc. Cinematographers (Life Achievement award 1996), Svenska Teaterforbundet. Office: care Milton Forman 433 N Palm Dr Beverly Hills CA 90210

NYLANDER, JANE LOUISE, museum director; b. Cleve., Jan. 27, 1938; d. James Merritt and Jeannette (Crosby) Cayford; m. Daniel Harris Giffen, Nov. 30, 1963 (div. 1970); children: Sarah Louise, Thomas Harris; m. Richard Conrad Nylander, July 8, 1972: 1 child, Timothy Frost. AB, Brown U., 1959; MA, U. Del., 1961; postgrad., Attingham (Eng.) Summer Sch., 1970; PhD (hon.), New England Coll., 1994. Curator Hist. Soc. York (Pa.) County, 1961-62, N.H. Hist. Soc., Concord, 1962-69; instr. New England Coll., Henniker, N.H., 1964-65, Monadnock Community Coll., Peterborough, N.H., 1966-69; curator of textiles and ceramics Old Sturbridge (Mass.) Village, 1969-85; adj. assoc. prof. Boston U., 1978-85; sr. curator Old Sturbridge Vill., 1985-86; dir. Strawbery Banke Mus., Portsmouth, N.H.,

1986-92, Soc. Preservation New England Antiquities, Boston, 1992-93; pres. Soc. for Preservation of New Eng. Antiquities, 1993—; adj. asst. prof. U. N.H., Durham, 1987-92; adj. prof. art history and Am. studies Boston U., 1993—; trustee Worcester (Mass.) Hist. Mus., 1978-84, Hist. Deerfield (Mass.), Inc., 1981-94, Hist. Mass. Inc., 1991-93, Decorative Arts Trust, 1991—, Portsmouth Athenaeum, 1988-90, Japan Soc. N.H., 1988-92; mem. adv. bd. Concord (Mass.) Mus., 1986-94, Wentworth-Coolidge Commn., 1991—, John Nicholas Brown Ctr. for Am. Studies, Providence, 1995—; mem. adv. bd. dept. Am. decorative arts Mus. Fine Arts, Boston, 1971—; mem. coun. Colonial Soc. Mass., 1993—; cons. in field. Author: Fabrics for Historic Buildings, 4th edit., 1990, Our Own Snug Fireside: Images of the New England Home 1760-1860, 1993, paperback edit., 1994; mem. editorial bd. Hist. New Hampshire; 1993—; contbr. numerous articles to profl. jours. Mem. adv. bd. New Eng. Heritage Ctr., 1993—; active State House Adv. Com., Boston, 1984-85, Gov.'s Coun. for Wentworth Coolidge Mansion, Concord, 1964-66; mem. Com. for Preservation of N.H. State Flags, 1989-92; mem. H.F. duPont award com. Winterthur Mus., 1993—, Mt. Vernon adv. com. for 1999, 1996—, collections com. N.J. Hist. Soc., 1996—. Recipient Charles F. Montgomery Prize Decorative Arts Soc., 1985. Mem. Am. Antiquarian Soc., Am. Assn. for State and Local History, Nat. Trust Hist. Preservation, Royal Oak Assn., Portsmouth Athenaeum, New Eng. Mus. Assn., Trustees of Reservations, Soc. Winterthur Fellows, Hist. Mass., Soc. Preservation of N.H. Forests, N.H. Audubon Soc., N.H. Humanities Coun., New Eng. Hist. Genealogical Soc., Hist. Houses Trust NSW, Costume Soc. Am. (bd. dirs. 1977-83), Dublin Seminar, Nat. Soc. Colonial Dames in N.H. (bd. dirs. 1967-73), Colonial Soc. of Mass., The Garden Conservancy, N.H. Hist. Soc., Friends of Hist. Deerfield, Nat. Soc. The Colonial Dames in Mass. (courtesy), Brown Club N.H. (trustee 1988-93). Episcopalian. Home: 17 Franklin St Portsmouth NH 03801-4501 Office: Soc Preservation New England Antiquities 141 Cambridge St Boston MA 02114-2702

NYMAN, CARL JOHN, JR., university dean and official; b. New Orleans, Oct. 21, 1924; s. Carl John Sr. and Dorothy (Kraft) N.; m. Betty Spiegelberg, July 15, 1950; children: Gail Katherine, John Victor, Nancy Kraft. B.S., Tulane U., 1944, M.S., 1945; Ph.D., U. Ill., 1948. Jr. technologist Shell Oil Co., Wilmington, Cal., 1944; instr. chemistry U. Ill., 1948, Wash. State U., Pullman, 1948-50; asst. prof. Wash. State U., 1950-55, assoc. prof., 1955-61, prof., 1961-88, prof. emeritus, 1988—, vice provost for rsch., 1981-86, acting dean grad. sch., 1968-69; dean, 1969-87; dean and vice provost emeritus for rsch. grad. sch. Wash. State U., 1988—; vis. asst. prof. Tulane U., summer, 1950, adj. prof., 1986-87; vis. fellow Cornell U., 1959-60, Imperial Coll. Sci. and Tech., 1966-67; vis. fellow Swiss Fed. Inst. Tech., Zurich, 1973; chmn. Acad. Coun. Ctr. Grad. Study, Richland, Wash., 1968-70, N.W. Assn. Colls. and Univs. for Sci., 1969; mem. Gov.'s Adv. Coun. on Nuclear Energy, 1968-70, Washington State High Tech. Coord. Bd., 1984-86. Author: (with G. B. King and J. A. Weyh) Problems for General Chemistry and Qualitative Analysis, 4th edit., 1980, (with R. E. Hamm) Chemical Equilibrium, 1967, (with W. E. Newton) Procs. of the 1st Internat. Conf. Nitrogen Fixation; contbr. articles to profl. jours. Mem. Am. Chem. Soc. (chmn. Wash.-Idaho border sect. 1961-62), AAAS, Sigma Xi, Phi Lambda Upsilon, Alpha Chi Sigma, Omicron Delta Kappa. Home: East 1419 Cambridge Ln Spokane WA 99203

NYMAN, GEORGIANNA BEATRICE, painter; b. Arlington, Mass., June 11, 1930; d. Daniel Eugene Nyman and Irene Krans (Müller) Lombardi; m. David Aronson, June 10, 1956; children: Judith, Benjamin, Abigail. Diploma, Boston Mus. Sch. Art., 1952, student, 1952-54; postgrad., Longy Sch. Music, Cambridge, Mass., 1965-73. Portraits displayed in Brookline (Mass.) Hosp., Inst. Critical Care Medicine, U. Pitts., McClosky Inst. Voice Therapy, Boston, U.S. Supreme Ct., Washington, New Eng. Sch. of Law, Boston, 1991, Milton (Mass.) Acad., Boston Acad. Music; group exhbns. include Shore Studio Gallery, Boston, 1960,61, Lee Nordness Gallery, N.Y.C., 1963, Copley Soc., Boston, 1980, Nat. Acad. Design, N.Y.C., 1990; solo exhbns. include Nancy Lincoln Gallery, Brookline, 1990; represented in permanent collections Rose Art Mus., Brandeis U., U. Pitts. Sch. Medicine; commd. portraits include Justice Sandra Day O'Connor, Mr. and Mrs. Pieh--headmaster Milton Acad., 1992, Justice Harry A. Blackmun, 1993, Julie Harris Am. actress, 1994, Hon. James R. Lawton, 1994, Richard Conrad, opera singer, dir. Boston Acad. Music, 1994, Justice Clarence Thomas, 1995, David Leisner, 1995. Jurist Art and Mental Illness--An Itinerary Boston U., 1989; active in LeMoyne Found., Fla., 1989. Recipient Boit prize, 1951, cert. of merit NAD, 1992; Kate Morse fellow Boston Mus. Fine Arts, 1953. Mem. Women's Indsl. Inst. (life), Mass. Soc. Mayflower Descendants. Avocations: music, vocal recitals. Home and Studio: 137 Brimstone Ln Sudbury MA 01776-3203 also: RR 2, Cornwall, PE Canada C0A 1H0

NYMAN, MICHAEL LAWRENCE, composer; b. London, Eng., Mar. 23, 1944; s. Mark and Jeanette N.; m. Aet Toome, May 16, 1970; 2 children. Attended, King's Coll., London, 1964-67; B.Mus., Royal Acad. of Music, 1965; attended, Conservatoire and Folklore Inst., Bucharest, 1965-66. Music critic Spectator, New Statesman, The Listener, 1968-78; founder Michael Nyman Band, 1977. Music dir., composer, performer: (film scores) 1-100, 1977, A Walk Through H, 1977, Tom Philips, 1977, Vertical Features Remake, 1978, The Falls, 1980, Brimstone and Treacle, 1982, Frozen Music, 1983, Nelly's Version, 1983, The Draughtsman's Contract, 1983, The Cold Room, 1984, L'ange frenetique, 1985, A Zed and Two Noughts, 1985, Ballet Mechanique, 1986, The Disputation, 1986, Photographic Exhibits, 1987, Drowning By Numbers, 1988, La Traversee de Paris, 1989, The Cook, the Thief, His Wife, Her Lover, 1989, Monsieur, 1989, Prospero's Books, 1991, Les enfants volants, 1991, Le Mari de la Coiffeuse, 1991, The Piano, 1993; musical performer, composer: (theatre) The Masterwork/Award-Winning Fishknife, 1979, , (ballets) Portraits in Reflection, 1985, And Do They Do, 1986, (dance works) The Fall of Icarus, 1989, Garden Party, 1990; composer: (ballets) A Broken Set of Rules, 1984, Touch the Earth, 1987, (dance works) Miniatures, 1989, (operas) The Man Who Mistook His Wife for a Hat, 1986, La Princesse de Milan, 1991, Letters, Riddles and Writs, 1992, (TV spls.) Act of God, 1980, The Man Who Mistook His Wife for a Hat, 1987, Fairly Secret Army Series 2, 1987, Dancing in Numbers, 1988, Touch the Earth, 1988, Out of the Ruins, 1989, Death in the Seine, 1989, Men of Steel, 1990, Letters, Riddles and Writs, 1991, The Final Score, 1992, The Fall of Icarus, 1992; author: (music criticism) Experimental Music: Cage and Beyond, 1975; recs. include The Convertibility of Lute Strings, 1993, For John Cage, 1993, Goodbye Frankie, Goodbye Benny, 1993. Office: Gorfaine Schwartz Agency 3301 Barham Blvd Ste 201 Los Angeles CA 90068-1477

NYMANN, P. L., lawyer; b. Clermont, Iowa, May 18, 1924; s. Jens Christian and Minnie Amalia (Osmundson) N.; m. Charmaine Ann Petersen, Dec. 2, 1951 (div. 1979); children: Michel, Candace, Kimberly, Christopher, Jon (dec.); m. Anne Barrett McDermott, Feb. 15, 1992. BA, U. Iowa, 1949, JD, 1951. Bar: Iowa 1951. Assoc. Louis S. Goldberg, Sioux City, Iowa, 1951-57; ptnr. Goldberg, Nymann & Probasco, Sioux City, 1957-64; v.p., gen. counsel IBP, Inc., Dakota City, Nebr., 1964-72; pvt. practice Sioux City, 1972-74, 83-87; ptnr. Jacobs, Gaul, Nymann & Green, Sioux City, 1974-83, Nymann & Kohl, Sioux City, 1987—. Chmn., Civil Svc. Commn., 1977-79; bd. dirs. United Way Siouxland, 1979-85. With AUS, 1943-46. Mem. ABA, Iowa Bar Assn., Am. Arbitration Assn., Rotary Club. Republican. Avocations: travel, boating, music. Home: PO Box 1760 Lake Ozark MO 65049-1760 Office: Nymann & Kohl 383390 Orpheum Electric Sioux City IA 51101

NYQUIST, JOHN DAVIS, retired radio manufacturing company executive; b. Peoria, Ill., May 28, 1918; s. Eliud and Linnea (Widen) N.; m. Alice Schmidt, June 5, 1942; 1 child, Sarah Lynn. B.S. in Mech. Engring, U. Ill., 1941. With Collins Radio Co., Cedar Rapids, Iowa, 1941—; v.p., gen. mgr. Iowa region Collins Radio Co., Cedar Rapids, 1965-69; v.p. operations Collins Radio Co., 1969-70, sr. v.p., 1970-73, also dir.; ret., 1973; cons. Rockwell-Collins; dir. Norwest Bank Iowa N.A. (formerly Peoples Bank & Trust Co.), Cedar Rapids. Bd. dirs. Am. Cancer Soc., YMCA, St. Lukes Hosp. Recipient award for outstanding achievement Am. Inst. Indsl. Engrs., 1966, Indsl. Engring. award, 1969, Coll. Engring. Alumni Honor award, 1977; both U. Ill.). Mem. Iowa Mfrs. Assn., Am. Mgmt. Assn., Am. Inst. Indsl. Engrs., IEEE, Cedar Rapids C. of C. (dir.). Club: Cedar Rapids Country. Home: 3279 Jordans Grove Rd Springville IA 52336-9786

NYQUIST, THOMAS EUGENE, consulting business executive, mayor; b. Froid, Mont., June 20, 1931; s. Richard Theodore and Lydia (Baker) N.; m. Corinne Elaine Johnson, Dec. 22, 1956; children: Jonathan Eugene, Lynn Marie Nyquist Bergstrausser. BA, Macalester Coll., 1956; MA, U. Mont., 1958; PhD, Northwestern U., 1966. Prof. SUNY, New Paltz, 1968-76; adminstr. cen. div. SUNY, Albany, 1976-90; pres. Nyquist Assocs., New Paltz, N.Y., 1991—; mem. adv. bd. George Washington's Hdqrs., Newburgh, N.Y., 1980-92; acad. dir. N.Y. Edn. Dept., Kenya, 1982; head del. House of Peace and Friendship/Village of New Paltz delegation, St. Petersburg, Russia, 1992. Author: (monograph) Urban Africans in South Africa, 1977, (book) African Middle Class Elite, 1983. Mem. Ulster County Legislature, 1976-79; dep. mayor Village of New Paltz, 1983-87, mayor, 1987—; chmn. New Paltz Centennial Com., 1986-87; bd. dirs. Ulster Region Credit Union, Kingston, N.Y., 1976-87, Partnership in Svc. Learning, 1985—, Ulster Performing Arts Ctr., 1978-82, Friends of Cuttington Coll., Liberia, 1994—; treas. Lower Hudson Conf., 1988, 89-90, 91-92. With U.S. Army, 1952-54. Fellow SUNY, South Africa, 1975; Ford Found. grantee, 1986. Mem. African Studies Assn., N.Y. African Studies Assn. (exec. bd. dirs. 1973—, co-editor newsletter 1974—), Am. Polit. Sci. Assn. Democrat. Avocations: hiking, cross county skiing. Home: 62 S Chestnut St New Paltz NY 12561-1936 Office: Office of Mayor Village Hall 25 Plattekill Ave New Paltz NY 12561-1918 also: Nyquist Assocs 62 S Chestnut St New Paltz NY 12561

NYREN, NEIL SEBASTIAN, publisher, editor; b. Boston, June 13, 1948; s. Karl Edwin and Dorothy Elizabeth (Smith) N.; m. Lois Miriam Sharfman, Oct. 11, 1970; 1 child, Alexander. B.A., Brandeis U. Editor Random House Pubs., N.Y.C., 1974-77, Arbor House Pubs., N.Y.C., 1977-78; exec. editor Atheneum Pubs., N.Y.C., 1978-84; sr. editor G.P. Putnam's Sons Pub., N.Y.C., 1984-86, editor-in-chief, 1986—, pub., 1989—. Democrat. Jewish. Office: G P Putnam's Sons 200 Madison Ave New York NY 10016-3903

NYROP, DONALD WILLIAM, airline executive; b. Elgin, Nebr., Apr. 1, 1912; s. William A. and Nellie (Wylie) N.; m. Grace Cary, Apr. 19, 1941; children: Nancy, William, Karen, Kathryn. A.B., Doane Coll., 1934; LL.B., George Washington U., 1939. Bar: D.C. 1938. Atty. Gen. Counsel's Office, CAA, Washington, 1939-41; exec. officer to chmn. CAB, 1942, chmn., 1952; rep. U.S. airlines; mem. ofcl. U.S. delegations Internat. Civil Aviation Orgn. Assemblies, 1946, 47; dep. adminstr. for ops. CAA, 1948-50, adminstr., 1950-51; chmn. CAB, 1951-52; pres. Northwest Airlines, Inc., 1954-78. Served with Air Transport Command USAAF, 1942-46. Decorated Legion of Merit. Clubs: Minneapolis, Minnesota. Home: 4505 Golf Ter Minneapolis MN 55424-1510

NYSTRAND, RAPHAEL OWENS, university dean, educator; b. Maryville, Mo., Nov. 6, 1937; s. Phillip Owens and Emily (Martin) M.; m. Suzanne Rose Duval, Apr. 1, 1961; children: Kathryn Lee, Kristin Sue. B.A., Cornell Coll., 1959; M.A.T., Johns Hopkins U., 1960; Ph.D., Northwestern U., 1966. Tchr. Lyons Twp. High Sch., La Grange, Ill., 1960-64; research assoc. Research Council of Great Cities Program for Sch. Improvement, Chgo., 1965-66; asst. prof. Coll. Edn., Ohio State U., Columbus, 1967-69, assoc. prof., 1969-71, prof., chmn. dept., 1972-78; dean Sch. Edn., U. Louisville, 1978—, prof., 1978—; sec. edn. and humanities cabinet Commonwealth of Ky., 1984 (on leave); postdoctoral fellow U. Chgo., 1966-67, vis. lectr., 1967; vis. prof. U. Victoria, B.C., Can., 1977; cons. various sch. dists., state agys.; v.p. Holmes Group, 1990—; mem. Nat. Policy Bd. for Edn. Adminstrn., 1991-93, Nat. Coun. Accreditation tchr. Edn. State Partnership Bd., 1994—. Co-author: The Organization and Control of American Schools, 6th edit., 1990, Introduction to Educational Administration, 6th edit., 1983; co-editor: Educational Administration: The Developing Decades, 1977, Strategies for Educational Change, 1981. Trustee Columbus Met. Sch., 1974-78, Fairmount Fund, 1980—, Louisville Youth Choir, 1983-85, Louisville Art Gallery, 1985-87, Wesley Comty. House, 1986-90, Stage One, 1989-91, Ky. Derby Festival, 1990-92; adv. bd. Inst. Creative Learning, Inc., Louisville, 1980-90, Jr. League Louisville, 1984-87, Gov.'s Sch. for Arts, 1986-87; mem. Ky. Edn. Profl. Stds. Bd., 1993—. Mem. Am. Ednl. Rsch. Assn., Nat. Soc. Study Edn., Phi Delta Kappa. Methodist. Home: 3015 Springcrest Dr Louisville KY 40241-2755 Office: U Louisville Belknap Campus Louisville KY 40292

NYSTROM, JOHN WARREN, geographer, educator; b. Worcester, Mass., Nov. 22, 1913; s. John Walfred and Hulda Alfreda (Sundstrom) N.; m. Anne Hildegarde Carlson, Aug. 6, 1938; children—Jon Alfred, David Alan, Karen Elizabeth. A.B., Clark U., 1936, A.M., 1937, Ph.D., 1942. Instr. R.I. Coll. Edn., 1937-40, asst. prof. geography, 1940-43; asst. prof. U. Pitts., 1943-45, asso. prof., 1945, prof., dept. head, 1947-53; head fgn. policy dept. U.S. C. of C., 1953-62, adminstrv. coordinator, 1956-62; partner firm Allen, Murden & Nystrom (internat. relations), Washington, 1962-64; mem. sr. staff Brookings Instn., 1964-66; exec. dir. Assn. Am. Geographers, Washington, 1966-79; prof. George Washington U., 1973-79; prof. geography U. Miami, 1980, Fla. Atlantic U., 1981—; exec. dir. Pitts. regional Inter-Am. Center, 1943-45, Fgn. Policy Assn. Pitts., 1945-53; cons. Dept. State, 1976-84; chmn. U.S. Nat. Com. Internat. Geog. Union; chmn. U.S. del. Internat. Geographic Congress, Stockholm, Sweden, 1960, London, 1964, New Delhi, 1968, Budapest, 1971, Montreal, 1972, Moscow, 1976, Tokyo, 1980; mem. geography commn. NRC; chmn. Conf. of Secs., Am. Council Learned Socs., 1973-75; U.S. rep. Pan Am. Inst. Geography and History, 1973-77, ofcl. del., Panama, 1973, Quito, Ecuador, 1977; mem. U.S. Nat. Commn. for UNESCO, 1979-85. Author: A Geographic Study-Netherlands Information, 1942, Beyond Our Borders, 1954, Within Our Borders, 1957, Within The Americas, 1957, The Common Market, 1962, Alliance for Progress, 1966, The Common Market, 1976. Trustee Clark U. Mem. Nat. Council Geog. Edn., Assn. Am. Geographers, Am. Geog. Soc., AAUP, Sigma Xi. Club: Cosmos. Home: 783 SW 3rd St Boca Raton FL 33486-4607

NYTKO, EDWARD C., printing company executive; b. Chgo., Feb. 20, 1943; s. Edward Frank and Helen Nytko; m. Deborah Harriet Nytko, Nov. 21, 1980; children: Jeffrey Daniel, Christopher Edward. BBA in Mktg., U. Tex., 1965; MBA in Fin., Loyola U., Chgo., 1969. Mgmt. trainee W.F. Hall Printing Co., Chgo., 1965-67, group v.p. Gravure, 1980-81, pres., chief operating officer, 1981, pres., chief exec. officer, 1982-85; pres., chief exec. officer Ringier Am. (fomerly Krueger Ringier Inc., W.F. Hall Printing Co.), Itasca, Ill., 1985—. Mem. Gravure Assn. Am. (bd. dirs. 1987—). Office: Ringier Am 1 Pierce Pl Itasca IL 60143-1253*

NZEYIMANA, NOAH, bishop. Bishop Free Meth. Ch. N.Am., Winona Lake, Ind., 1987—. Office: Free Meth Ch N Am PO Box 535002 Indianapolis IN 46253-5002

OAK, CLAIRE MORISSET, artist, educator; b. St. Georges, Quebec, Can., May 31, 1921; came to U.S., 1945; d. Louis and Bernadette (Coulombe) Morisset; m. Alan Ben Oak, July 2, 1947. Student, Ecole des Beaux Arts, 1938-42, Parsons Sch. Design, N.Y.C., 1945, Art Students League, N.Y.C., 1945-46. Staff artist Henry Morgan & R. Simpson, Montreal, 1942-45; artist illustrator W.B. Golovin Advt. Agy., N.Y.C., 1947-49; freelance illustrator Arnold Constable & Advt. Agy., N.Y.C., 1948-50, Le Jardin des Modes, Paris, 1950-51, May & Co., L.A., 1956, Katten & Marengo Advt., Stockton, Calif., 1962-84; pvt. practice illustrator, designer San Joaquin Valley, Calif., 1984-92; art instr. San Joaquin Delta Coll., Stockton, 1973—; owner Fashion Illustrator's Workshop, N.Y.C., 1953-54; instr. Bauder Coll., Sacramento, 1975-76; painting workshop leader Lodi Art Ctr., 1991—; watercolor workshop leader D'Pharr Painting Adventures, Virginia City, Nev., 1992; ongoing watercolor workshop Galerie Iona, Stockton, Calif., 1993—. Named S.B. Anthony Woman of Achievement in the Arts, U. Pacific, 1982. Mem. Stockton Art League, Lodi Art Ctr., Ctrl. Calif. Art League, The League of Carmichael Artists, Delta Watercolor Soc. (bd. mem. 1988—). Avocations: outdoor painting, drawing from a model. Home: 2140 Waudman Ave Stockton CA 95209-1755 *You are a success in the visual arts if you teach others how to see.*

OAKAR, MARY ROSE, former congresswoman; b. Cleve., Mar. 5, 1940; d. Joseph M. and Margaret Mary (Ellison) O. BA in English, Speech and Drama, Ursuline Coll., Cleve., 1962, LHD (hon.); MA in Fine Arts, John Carroll U., Cleve., 1966; LLD (hon.), Ashland U., 1978, Ursuline Coll., 1984, St. Mary's Notre Dame, 1989, Baldwin Wallace Coll., 1988; LHD (hon.), Trinity Coll., 1987. Instr. English and drama Lourdes Acad., Cleve., 1963-70; asst. prof. English, speech and drama Cuyahoga Community Coll., Cleve., 1968-75; mem. Cleve. City Council from 8th Ward, 1973-76; mem. 95th-102nd Congresses from 20th Dist. Ohio, 1977-92, mem. Pepper Commn. on Long Term Health Care; chair subcom. internat. devel., fin., trade and monetary policy; chair task force on social security, elderly, women; chair subcom. on personnel and police, mem. banking, fin. and urban affairs com., select com. on aging, post office and civil service com., com. on house adminstrn., also numerous subcoms.; apptd. to Sec. Conf. to Establish Nat. Action Plan on Breast Cancer, 1994, by Pres. Clinton to bd. dirs. Bldrs., For Peace, 1994, to policy to White House Conf. on Aging. Founder, vol.-dir. Near West Side Civic Arts Center, Cleve., 1970; ward leader Cuyahoga County Democratic Party, 1972-76; mem. Ohio Dem. Central Com. from 20th Dist., 1974; trustee Fedn. Community Planning, Cleve., Health and Planning Commn. Cleve., Community Info. Service Cleve., Cleve. Soc. Crippled Children, Public Services Occupational Group Adv. Com., Cuyahoga Community Coll., Cleve. Ballet, Cleve. YWCA. Recipient Outstanding Service awards OEO, 1973-78, Community Service award Am. Indian Center, Cleve., 1973, Community Service award Nationalities Service Center, 1974, Community Service award Club San Lorenzo, Cleve., 1976, Cuyahoga County Dem. Woman of Yr., 1977, Ursuline Coll. Alumna of Yr. award, 1977, awards Irish Nat. Caucus, awards West Side Community Mental Health Center, awards Am. Lebanese League, awards Cleve. Fedn. Am.-Syrian Lebanese Clubs, Breast Cancer Awareness award Nat. Women's Health Resource Ctr., 1989, 1st lay recipient Barbara Bohen-Pfeiffer award Italian-Am. Found. Cancer Rsch., 1989, Disting. Svc. award Am. Cancer Soc., 1989, Myrl H. Shoemaker award Ohio Dem. Party, 1992, Philip Hart award Consumer Fedn. Am., 1987; cert. appreciation City of Cleve.; Woman of Yr. award Cuyahoga County Women's Polit. Caucus, 1983; decorated Knight of Order of St. Ladislaus of Hungary, Women in Aerospace Outstanding Ach. award, Black Focus Woman of the Decade award. Office: 2621 Lorain Ave Cleveland OH 44113-3414

OAKES, JAMES L., federal judge; b. Springfield, Ill., Feb. 21, 1924; m. Evelena S. Kenworthy, Dec. 29, 1973; one son, two daus. by previous marriage. AB, Harvard U., 1945, LLB, 1947; LLD, New Eng. Coll., 1976, Suffolk U., 1980; LLD (hon.), Vt. Law Sch., 1995. Bar: Calif. 1949, Vt. 1950. Pvt. practice Brattleboro, Vt.; spl. counsel Vt. Pub. Service Commn., 1959-60; counsel Vt. Statutory Revision Commn., 1957-60; mem. Vt. Senate, 1961-65; atty. gen. Vt., 1967-69, U.S. dist. judge, 1970-71; U.S. cir. judge 2d Cir. Ct. Appeals, Brattleboro, 1971—; chief judge 2d Circuit Ct. Appeals, 1989-92; adj. faculty Duke U. Law Sch., 1985—, Iowa U. Coll. Law, 1993—. Office: US Ct Appeals PO Box 696 Brattleboro VT 05302-0696

OAKES, JOHN BERTRAM, writer, editor; b. Elkins Park, Pa., Apr. 23, 1913; s. George Washington Ochs Oakes and Bertie (Gans) Ochs; m. Margery C. Hartman, Oct. 24, 1945; children: Andra N., Alison H., Cynthia J., John G. H. A.B. magna cum laude, Princeton U., 1934; A.B., A.M. (Rhodes scholar), Queen's Coll., Oxford, 1936; LL.D. (hon.), U. Hartford, 1960; L.H.D. (hon.), Chatham Coll., 1969; Litt.D. (hon.), CUNY, 1976. Reporter Trenton (N.J.) State Gazette, Trenton Times, 1936-37; polit. reporter Washington Post, 1938-41; editor Rev. of the Week, Sunday N.Y. Times, 1946-49; mem. editorial bd. N.Y. Times, 1949-76; columnist on conservation environ., 1951-61, editor of edit. page, 1961-76; originator Op.-Ed. page N.Y. Times, 1970, contbg. columnist, 1977-90. Author: The Edge of Freedom, 1961; contbr.: Essays Today, 1955, Foundations of Freedom, 1958, Tomorrow's American, 1977, On the Vineyard, 1980, The March to War, 1991, Cast a Cold Eye, 1991. Mem. adv. bd. Nat. Parks Dept. Interior, 1955-62; Pres.'s Commn. White House Fellows, 1964-69; founding trustee Natural Resources Def. Coun., 1970—; adv. coun. U.S. Bur. Land Mgmt., 1980-81; mem. N.Y. State Commn. on Future of Adirondacks, 1989-90; past trustee Nat. Parks Conservation Assn., Fisk U., Chatham Coll., N.Y. Found., Sierra Club, Wilderness Soc., Nature Conservancy, Washington Journalism Ctr., Temple Emanu-El. Decorated Bronze Star, Order Brit. Empire, Croix de Guerre, Medaille de Reconnaissance (France); recipient Columbia-Catherwood award for disting. journalism, 1961, Dept. Interior Conservation award 1963, George Polk Meml. award, 1965, Silurian Soc. award, 1969, Woodrow Wilson award Princeton U., 1970, Audubon medal Nat. Audubon Soc., 1976, UN Environ. award, 1982, Lawrenceville Sch. medal, 1994, other. Mem. Am. Philos. Soc., Coun. Fgn. Rels., Phi Beta Kappa, Century Assn. (N.Y.C.), Cosmos Club (Washington, D.C.). Jewish. Home: 1120 5th Ave New York NY 10128-0144

OAKES, LESTER CORNELIUS, retired electrical engineer, consultant; b. Knoxville, Oct. 11, 1923; s. Charles Vaughn and Maude Cornelia (Harrison) O.; m. Kathleen Clark, Dec. 27, 1947; children: Michael, Richard, Cynthia, Melissa. B.S. in E.E., U. Tenn., 1949, M.S., 1962. Registered profl. engr., Tenn. Engr. Fairchild Engring. and Aircraft, Oak Ridge, 1949-51; engr. I&C div. Oak Ridge Nat. Lab., 1951-68, dept. head I&C div., 1968—, asst. dir. I&C div., 1971-90; cons. Oak Ridge Nat. Lab., electric Power Rsch. Inst., Nuclear Regulatory Commn., 1990—. Contbr. articles to profl. jours.; patentee in field. Served with USAF, 1943-46. Martin Marietta Corp. fellow. Fellow IEEE. Presbyterian. Home: 710 Pleasant Hill Rd Maryville TN 37803-7337

OAKES, MARIA SPACHNER, nurse; b. Cinn., Mar. 27, 1947; d. A. William and Roberta Mae (Linville) Stephens; m. John Cullwell Oakes, Nov. 27, 1976; children: John Cullwell II, Laura Suzann. Diploma Sch. Nursing, King's Daughters' Hosp., 1968. Cert. med./surg. nurse. Staff nurse Ohio State U. Hosp., Columbus, Lawrence County, Ironton; head nurse, neonatal intensive care King's Daughters' Med. Ctr., Ashland, Ky., staff nurse; staff nurse neonatal IC, Huntington Hosp. Behavioral Medicine. Bd. dirs. Am. Cancer Soc.; deacon bd. sessions, pres. Women's Assn. First Presbyn. Ch.; v.p. West Ironton Parent-Tchr. Group; pres. Kingsbury Parents for Better Schs.; past pres. Kings Daus. Hosp. Sch. Nursing Alumni Assn.; mem. strategic planning com. Ironton City Sch. Dist., Acad. Boosers Assn., H.S. Band Boosters mem., band nurse. Mem. ANA, Ky. Nurses Assn. (state offices nursing practice comm., legis. com., state nominating com., nurse practice commn., past pres., v.p., treas. Dist. 4, former v.p., program chmn., seminar planner, continuing edn. coord., current v.p. Dist. 4, mem. ad hoc com. health care reform). Home: 2210 N 3rd Ave Ironton OH 45638-1068

OAKES, MELVIN ERVIN LOUIS, physics educator; b. Vicksburg, Miss., May 11, 1936; married, 1963; three children. Student, Fla. State U., 1958-64, PhD in Plasma Physics, 1964. Physicist USAR Guided Missile Agy., Redstone Arsenal, 1960; asst. in physics Fla. State U., Tallahassee, 1958-60, 60-64; asst. prof. physics U. Ga., Athens, 1964, rsch. assoc., 1964-65, from asst. prof. to assoc. prof., 1965-70; prof. of physics U. Tex., Austin, 1975—. Mem. Am. Phys. Soc., Am. Assn. Physics Tchrs. Achievements include rsch. on electromagnetic interaction with plasmas, plasma waves and radio frequency heating. Office: U Tex Dept Physics Austin TX 78712-1081

OAKES, ROBERT JAMES, physics educator; b. Mpls., Jan. 21, 1936; s. Sherman E. and Josephine J. (Olson) O.; children: Cindy L., Lisa A. B.S., U. Minn., 1957, M.S., 1959, Ph.D., 1962. NSF fellow Stanford U., 1962-64; asst. prof. physics, 1964-68; assoc. prof. physics Northwestern U., 1968-70, prof. physics, 1970-76, prof. physics and astronomy, 1976—; vis. staff mem. Los Alamos Sci. Lab., 1971—; vis. scientist Fermi Nat. Accelerator Lab., 1975—; faculty assoc. Argonne Nab. Lab., 1982—; U.S. scientist NSF-Yugoslav joint program, 1982—; panelist Nat. Rsch. Coun., 1990—. A.P. Sloan fellow 1965-68; Air Force Office Sci. Rsch. grantee, 1969-71, NSF grantee 1971, Dept. Energy grantee, 1987; named Fulbright-Hays Disting. prof. U. Sarajevo, Yugoslavia, 1979-80; recipient Natural Sci. prize China, 1993. Fellow Am. Phys. Soc., AAAS; mem. N.Y. Acad. Sci., Ill. Acad. Sci., Physics Club (Chgo.), Sigma Xi, Tau Beta Pi. Club: Physics (Chgo.). Office: Northwestern U Dept Physics 633 Clark St Evanston IL 60208-0001

OAKES, THOMAS WYATT, environmental engineer; b. Danville, Va., June 14, 1950; s. Wyatt Johnson and Relia (Sceacre) O.; m. Terry Lynn Jenkins, June 15, 1974; 1 child, Travis Wyatt. BS in Nuclear Engring., Va. Polytechnic U., 1973, MS in Nuclear Engring., 1975; MS in Environ. Engring., U. Tenn., 1981. Health physics asst. Va. Polytechnic U., Blacksburg, 1972-74; radiation engr. Babcock and Wilcox Co., Lynchburg, Va., 1974-75; dept. mgr. Oak Ridge (Tenn.) Nat. Lab., 1975-78, environ. mgr., 1978-85; corp. environ. coord. Martin Marietta, Oak Ridge, 1985-87; asst. v.p. Sci. Applications Internat. Corp., Oak Ridge, 1987-90; environ. mmgr. Westinghouse Environ. and Geotech. Svcs., Knoxville, Tenn., 1990-91; mgr. S.E. region environ. svcs. ATEC & Assocs., Inc., Marietta, Ga., 1991-93; asst. environ. svcs. Scitek, Fort Campbell, Ky., 1993—. Contbr. over 107 articles to scholarly and profl. jours. Recipient Spl. Recognition award Union Carbide Corp., 1980, Best Paper award Nat. Safety Coun., 1982, Tech. Publs. award Soc. Tech. Communications, 1987. Mem. AAAS, Am. Indsl. Hygiene Assn., N.Y. Acad. Scis., Health Physics Soc. (sec.-treas. environ. sect. 1984-85), Am. Naval Soc., Am. Soc. for Quality Control. Office: Scitek PO Box 527 Fort Campbell KY 42223

OAKES, TIMOTHY WAYNE, tobacco import-export company executive; b. Chatham, Va., Nov. 27, 1938; s. John Averett and Edna Cora (Bolling) O.; m. Nancy Osborn Bunn, Mar. 19, 1965; children—Elizabeth, John. BA in Psychology, U. Va., 1961. With Imperial Tobacco Co., Ltd., 1961-68; asst. dir. internat. leaf purchase Philip Morris, Inc., Richmond, Va., 1968-75; with Dibrell Bros., Inc., Danville, Va., 1975—, sr. v.p., 1982—; also bd. dirs. Dimon Inc. (formerly Dibrell Bros. Inc.), Danville, Va.; bd. dirs. Carolina Leaf Tobacco Co., Greenville, N.C. Mem. Leaf Tobacco Exporter's Assn. (pres. 1981-83, chmn. exec. com. Raleigh sect. 1984—), Tobacco Mchts. Assn. (chmn. Princeton, N.J. chpt. 1988—). Republican. Episcopalian. Avocations: golf, snow skiing. Home: 388 Hawthorne Dr Danville VA 24541-3516 Office: Dimon Inc 512 Bridge St Danville VA 24541-1406*

OAKES, WALTER JERRY, pediatric neurosurgeon; b. De Soto, Mo., July 10, 1946; s. Marvin Melton and Mildred Florene (Link) O.; m. Linda Helen Maas (div. Jan. 1985); 1 child, Kathleen Suzanne; m. Jean Evans, Dec. 1988; children: Matthew Marvin, Peter Clifford. BA in Chemistry, U. Mo., 1968; MD, Duke U., 1972. Diplomate Am. Bd. Neurol. Surgeons. Neurosurgery resident Duke U., Durham, N.C., 1972-78, asst. prof. neurosurgery, 1979-90, assoc. prof. neurosurgery, 1991—, asst. prof. pediatrics, 1981-92; assoc. prof. pediatrics Duke U., 1992; pediatric neurosurgery resident U. Toronto Hosp. for Sick Children, Ont., Can., July-Dec., 1975; registrar pediatric neurosurgery U. London Hosp. for Sick Children, Eng., Sept., 1978-Feb., 1979; prof. neurosurgery and pediatrics U. Ala. Birmingham, 1992—. Fellow ACS. Office: Children's Hosp of Ala 1600 7th Ave S Ste 400 Birmingham AL 35233-1711

OAKEY, JOHN MARTIN, JR., lawyer; b. Roanoke, Va., Jan. 29, 1935; s. John Martin and Mildred Hunter (Urquhart) O.; m. Jean Lindsey, May 7, 1966; children: John M. III, Daniel L., Christopher K. BA, U. Va., 1957, LLB, 1963. Law clk. U.S. Dist. Ct. (ea. dist.) Va., Richmond, 1963-64; assoc. McGuire, Woods & Battle, Richmond, 1964-69, ptnr., 1969-87; ptnr. McGuire, Woods, Battle & Boothe, Richmond, 1987—; mem. 4th Cir. Jud. Conf., Richmond, 1976—; chmn. Bar Com. on Unprofl. Conduct, 1977, Com. on Rules of Evidence, 1984-85. Chmn. Richmond Bd. Housing Appeals, 1975; pres. Richmond Tennis Patrons Assn., 1979. Served to lt. USN, 1958-61. Fellow Am. Coll. Trial Lawyers; mem. Va. Bar Assn., Richmond Bar Assn., Va. Assn. Def. Attys. (pres. 1994-95), Def. Rsch. Inst., Boyd Graves Conf. (chair 1991-94), Bull and Bear Club, Westwood Club, Phi Beta Kappa, Omicron Delta Kappa. Episcopalian. Avocations: tennis, travel. Home: 11 Roslyn Rd Richmond VA 23226-1609 Office: McGuire Woods Battle & Boothe 1 James Ctr Richmond VA 23219

OAKLEY, ANDREW ARTHUR, journalist; b. Chgo., Oct. 22, 1958; s. Arthur George and Dolores Margarite (Hernandez) O.; m. Suzanna Pinter, Sept. 7, 1985; 1 child, Glen Matthias. BS in Journalism, Northwestern U., 1980, MS, 1981. Reporter Woodstock (Ill.) Daily Sentinel, 1980-81; police reporter Herald-Palladium, St. Joseph, Mich., 1981-82; city hall reporter Daily Herald, Arlington Heights, Ill., 1982-84; instr. journalism Oakton C.C., Des Plaines, Ill., 1984-85; features editor North Shore Mag., Winnetka, Ill., 1985-86; news editor City and State, Chgo., 1986-93; journalism editor P.O. Publ. Co., Port Murray, N.J., 1993—; lectr. Northwestern U., Evanston, Ill., 1990-96; columnist Daily Herald, Arlington Heights, Ill., 1995-96. Author: Eighty-Eight, 1988, Issues Confronting City and State Governments, 1992, Beginning Journalism Packet, 1994; cons. editor P.O. Pub. Co., Skokie, Ill., 1988-92. Lifetime mem. N Club, 1980—; commr. Skokie Human rels. Commn., 1987-94; co-chmn. Skokie Centennial Events Com., 1987-88. Mem. No. Ill. Newspaper Assn. (Pub. Affairs Reporting award 1983), Ill. Press Assn. (Edn. Reporting award 1983), Suburban Press Club Chgo. (Investigative Series award 1984), Soc. Profl. Journalists (Peter Lisagor award 1984), Investigative Reporters and Editors, Chgo. Headline Club, Assn. for Edn. in Journalism and Mass Comm., Medill Alumni Assn., Evanston Running Club. Methodist. Avocations: distance running, weight lifting, writing, Spanish language. Office: P O Publishing Co Box 7 Port Murray NJ 07865-0007

OAKLEY, BILL, television producer; m. Rachel Pulido, Jan. 27, 1991. AB in History, Harvard U., 1988. Co-writer Lampoon parodies USA Today, Time, also others.; co-writer Spy, Nat. Lampoon, America's Most Wanted. Writer The Simpsons, from 1992, also story editor, supervising prodr., now exec. prodr. (Emmy award 1995). Office: care Fox Publicity PO Box 900 Beverly Hills CA 90213

OAKLEY, CAROLYN LE, state legislator, small business owner; b. Portland, Oreg., June 28, 1942; d. George Thomas and Ruth Alveta Victoria (Engberg) Penketh; m. Donald Keith Oakley, June 27, 1965; children: Christine, Michelle. BS in Edn., Oreg. State U., 1965. Educator Linn County (Oreg.) Schs., 1965-76; owner Linn County Tractor, 1965-90; mem. Oreg. Legis. Assembly, Salem, 1989—, asst. majority leader, 1993—, majority whip, 1994; mem. exec. bd. Oreg. Retail Coun., 1987-90. Chmn. Linn County Rep. Ctrl. Com., 1982-84; chmn. bd. dirs. North Albany Svc. Dist., 1988-90; chair Salvation Army, Linn and Benton Counties, 1987—; vice chmn. bd. trustees Linn-Benton C.C. Found., 1987—; pres. Women for Agr., Linn and Benton Counties, 1984-86; mem. STRIDE Leadership Round Table, 1991—; state chair Am. Legis. Exch. Coun., 1991-96; nat. bd. dirs., exec. com., nat. sec.; mem. Edn. Commn. of the States, 1991—, com. policies and priorities, 1993—; mem. Leadership Coun. on State Rules in Higher Edn., 1995—; mem. nat. policy bd. Danforth Found., 1995—; state dir., Women in Govt., 1996; state dir., Nat. Order Women Legislators, 1993—; hon. mem. Linn-Benton Compact Bd., 1993—; active Linn County Criminal Justice Coun., 1994—. Named Woman of Yr. Albany chpt. Beta Sigma Phi, 1970. Mem. Nat Conf. State Legislators (chmn. edn. com. 1992—), Albany C. of C. (bd. dirs. 1986-93), Linn County Rep. women (legis. chmn. 1982-91). Republican. Methodist. Avocations: gardening, camping. Home: 3197 NW Crest Loop Albany OR 97321-9627 Office: Oreg Legis Assembly State Capital Salem OR 97310

OAKLEY, DAVID STERLING, physics educator, consultant; b. Denver, Apr. 2, 1958; s. Gary Addison and JoAnn (Winans) O.; m. Barbara JoAnn Quinn, Apr. 5, 1986; children: David Addison, Andrew Timothy, Madeleine. BA, Colo. U., 1981; MA, Tex. U., 1985, PhD, 1987. Rsch. assoc. Colo. U., Boulder, 1987-89; asst. prof. Lewis and Clark Coll., Portland, Oreg., 1989-93; assoc. prof. Colo. Christian U., Lakewood, 1993—; dir. rsch. Safe Air Monitoring Systems, Inc., Denver, 1989—. Contbr. articles to profl. jours. Youth counselor Young Life, Austin, Tex., 1981-87; mem. So. Utah Wilderness Alliance, Salt Lake City, 1986—, Oreg. Rivers Coun., Portland, 1992—. Mem. Am. Phys. Soc. Presbyterian. Achievements include patent in method for detecting hydrogen containing compounds, detection of natural gas and household radon; research in correlation between solar neutrino flux and solar magnetic fields, in nuclear structure, role of space-time in Christian theology and how modern physics changes this role. Office: Colo Christian Univ 180 S Garrison St Lakewood CO 80226

OAKLEY, DEBORAH JANE, researcher, educator; b. Detroit, Jan. 31, 1937; d. George F. and Kathryn (Willson) Hacker; m. Bruce Oakley, June 16, 1958; children: Ingrid Andrea, Brian Benjamin. BA, Swarthmore Coll., 1958; MA, Brown U., 1960; MPH, U. Mich., 1969, PhD, 1977. Dir. teenage and adult programs YWCA, Providence, 1959-63; editorial asst. Stockholm U., 1963-64; rsch. investigator, lectr. dept. population planning U. Mich., 1971-77; asst. prof. community health programs U. Mich., Ann Arbor, 1977-79, asst. prof. nursing rsch., 1979-81, assoc. prof., 1981-89, prof., 1989—, interim dir. Ctr. Nursing Rsch., 1988-90; prin. investigator NIH-funded Rsch. grants on family planning and women's health, mem. nat. adv. com. nursing rsch., 1993—; co-chair Mich. Initiative for Women's Health, 1993—. Author: (with Leslie Corsa) Population Planning, 1979; contbr. articles to profl. jours. Bd. dirs. Planned Parenthood Fedn. Am., 1975-80. Recipient Margaret Sanger award Washtenaw County Planned Parenthood, 1975; Outstanding Young Woman of Ann Arbor award by Jaycees, 1970, Dist. Faculty award, Mich. Assn. Gov. Bds., 1992. Mem. Am. Pub. Health Assn. (chmn. population sect. council), Internat. Union Sci. Study Population, Midwest Nursing Rsch. Soc., Population Assn. Am., Nat. Family Planning and Reproductive Health Assn. (nat. comms.), Delta Omega, Sigma Theta Tau (hon.). Democrat. Home: 5200 S Lake Dr Chelsea MI 48118-9481 Office: U Mich Sch Nursing Ann Arbor MI 48109-0482

OAKLEY, DIANE, insurance executive, benefit consultant; b. Teaneck, N.J., Dec. 27, 1953; d. Geard Joseph and Joan B. (Peterson) O.; m. John J. McCabe Jr., June 8, 1986. BS, Fairfield U., 1975; MBA, Fordham U., 1984. Actuarial asst. TIAA-CREF, N.Y.C., 1975-79, benefit plan counselor, 1979-82, adv. officer, 1982-85; branch mgr., 2nd v.p. TIAA-CREF, Bethesda, Md., 1985-89, v.p., assns. & govt. rels., 1989-95, v.p., 1995—. Mem. Am. Assn. Higher Edn., Am. Assn. Women in C.C.'s, Nat. Assn. Women in Edn., Washington EE Benefits Forum, Working in Employee Benefits. Roman Catholic. Home: 7823 White Cliff Ter Rockville MD 20855-2222 Office: TIAA-CREF 601 13th St NW Ste 1100N Washington DC 20005-3807

OAKLEY, FRANCIS CHRISTOPHER, history educator, former college president; b. Liverpool, Eng., Oct. 6, 1931; came to U.S., 1957, naturalized, 1968; s. Joseph Vincent and Siobean (NiCurean) O.; m. Claire-Ann Lamenzo, Aug. 9, 1958; children: Deirdre, Christopher, Timothy, Brian. BA, Corpus Christi Coll., Oxford U., 1953, MA, 1957; postgrad., Pontifical Inst. Medieval Studies, Toronto, 1953-55; MA, Yale U., 1958, PhD, 1960; LLD, Amherst Coll., 1986; Wesleyan U., 1989; LHD, Northwestern U., 1990, North Adams State Coll., 1993, Bowdoin Coll., 1993; LittD, Williams Coll., 1994. Mem. faculty Yale U., 1959-61; Mem. faculty Williams Coll., Williamstown, Mass., 1961—, prof. history, 1970—, dean faculty, 1977-84, Edward Dorr Griffin prof. history of ideas, 1984-85, 94—, pres., 1985-94, pres. emeritus, 1994—; hon. fellow Corpus Christi Coll., Univ. Oxford, 1991—; vis. lectr. Bennington (Vt.) Coll., 1967; mem. Inst. Advanced Study Princeton, 1981-82; assoc. Nat. Humanities Ctr., 1991; guest scholar Woodrow Wilson Internat. Ctr. for Scholars, 1994; chair bd. dirs. Am. Coun. Learned Socs., 1993—; trustee Sterling and Francine Clark Art Inst., 1985—, MassMoCA Found., 1995—, Willamstown Art Conservation Ctr., 1995—; mem. MassMoCA Cultural Devel. Commn., 1988—. Author: The Political Thought of Pierre d'Ailly: The Voluntarist Tradition, 1964, Kingship and the Gods: The Western Apostasy, 1968, Council over Pope?, Towards a Provisional Ecclesiology, 1969, Medieval Experience: Foundations of Western Cultural Singularity, 1974, rev. England edit., The Crucial Centuries, 1979, Spanish edit., 1980, 95, Medieval Acad. edit., 1988, 93, The Western Church in the Later Middle Ages, 1979, rev. edit., 1985, 88, 91, Natural Law, Conciliarism and Consent in the Late Middle Ages, 1984, Omnipotence, Covenant and Order: An Excursion in the History of Ideas, 1984, Community of Learning: The American College and the Liberal Arts Tradition, 1992, Scholarship and Teaching: A Matter of Mutual Support, 1996; editor: (with Daniel O'Connoer) Creation: The Impact of an Idea, 1969; contbr. articles to profl. jours. Lt. Brit. Army, 1955-57. Goldsmith's Co. London fellow, 1953-55, Social Sci. Rsch. Coun. fellow, 1963, Am. Coun. Learned Socs. fellow, 1965, 69-70, Weil Inst. fellow, 1965, Folger Shakespeare Libr. fellow, 1974, NEH fellow, 1976, 81-82. Fellow Medieval Acad. Am.; mem. Am. Hist. Assn., Am. Cath. Hist. Assn., Am. Ch. History Soc., New Eng. Medieval Conf., Am. Coun. Learned Socs. (chair bd. dirs. 1993—), The Century Assn. Democrat. Roman Catholic. Office: Williams Coll Oakley Ctr for Humanities and Social Scis Williamstown MA 01267

OAKLEY, GARY WILLIAM, travel incentive executive; b. Norfolk, Va., Dec. 29, 1942; s. Francis and Mabel (Waters) O.; m. Suzy Bridge Oakley, Apr. 3, 1982; div. 1980; children Gary W. Jr., Sara W. BA in Econs., Amherst Coll., 1960-64; MBA in Mktg., U. Pa., 1968. Assoc. N.W. Ayer & Sons, Inc., Phila., 1968-70; group. prodn. mgr. Lever Bros., Inc., N.Y.C., 1970-73; mktg. dir. Am. Can Co., Greenwich, Conn., 1973-78; cons., chmn., CEO The Saugatuck Group, Westport, Conn., 1980-93; chmn., CEO The Saugatuck Travel Co., Westport, Conn., 1987-93, Media Mktg. Svcs., Atlanta, 1994—. Mem. Country Club New Canaan, Edgartown (Mass.) Yacht Club, The Mornings Club (Vero Beach, Fla.). Home: 243 White Oak Shade Rd New Canaan CT 06840-6833

OAKLEY, GODFREY PORTER, JR., health facility administrator, medical educator; b. Greenville, N.C., June 1, 1940; s. Godfrey Porter and Carrie O.; m. Mary Ann Bryant, Sept. 2, 1961; children: Martha Gray, Susan Herndon, Robert Bryant. Student, Duke U., 1958-61; MD, Bowman Gray Sch. of Medicine, 1965; MS in Preventive Medicine, U. Washington, 1972. Diplomate Am. Bd. Pediatrics, Nat. Bd. Med. Examiners, Am. Bd. Preventive Medicine, Am. Bd. Med. Genetics. Intern in straight pediatrics Cleve. Met. Gen. Hosp., 1965-66, resident in pediatrics, 1966-68; sr. fellow in teratology and human embryology U. Washington Sch. of Medicine, Ctrl. Lab. Human Embryology, Dept. of Pediatrics, Seattle, 1970-72; sr. fellow U. Washington Sch. Pub. Health and Community Medicine, Seattle, 1971-72; EIS officer leukemia sect. Ctrs. Disease Control and Prevention (CDC), Atlanta, 1968-70, chief etiology studies sect., bur. epidemiology, cancer and birth defects, 1972-81; chief birth defects br., choronic diseases divisn. Nat. Ctr. Environ. Health, Ctrs. Disease Control and Prevention, Atlanta, 1981-85, dir. divsn. birth defects and devel. disabilities, 1985—; clin. asst. prof. pediatrics divsn. med. genetics Emory U., Atlanta, 1968-70, 72—, clin. asst. prof. gynecology-obstetrics divsn. med. genetics, 1981—; mem. visiting med. staff Grady Meml. Hosp., Atlanta, 1974—; med. adv. bd. Ctrs. Disease Control & Prevention (CDC); mem. task force on predictors of hereditary desease or congenital defects NIH Consensus Conf., 1979; mem. genetics coordinating com. NIH/CDC; mem. adv. com. biometric and epidemiological methodology FDA/CDC; cons. bur. med. svcs. FDA; mem. Chronic Diseases Surveillance Working Group; mem. patient registry com. Cystic Fibrosis Found., med. adv. coun., 1978—; mem. drug experience coordinating com. Dept. Health, Edn. and Welfare; mem. genetics com. Ga. Dept. Human Resources, 1980—; ex-officio mem. genetic diseases rev. and adv. com. Health Svcs. Adminstrn., 1981; mem. master community health program, interdisciplinary faculty com., curriculum com. Emory U.; mem. working group on heart disease epidemiology Nat. Heart, Lung and Blood Insts., 1978; mem. ad hoc com. on Alpha-fetoprotein Pub. Health Svc.; mem. profl. adv. coun. Spina Bifida Assn. Am., 1981—; mem. WHO EURO-China Consultation, Beijing, China, 1983; lectr. in field. Mem. editorial bd. Pediatric & Perinatal Epidemiology, 1987-89; contbr. articles to profl. jours., chpts. to books. Nancy Lybrook Lasater scholar 1961-67; recipient Physician's Recognition award AMA, 1973-76, Outstanding Svc. medal Pub. Health Svc., 1981, Meritorious Svc. award, 1988, Spl. Recognition award, 1993, President's Excellence award Spina Bifida Assn. Am., 1988-89, Disting. Alumnus award U. Washington Sch. Pub. Health, 1990. Mem. Am. Acad. Pediatrics (past com. drugs/CDC liaison, com. genetics 1990, exec. com. 1990—, CDC rep. Ga. chpt. 1993), Am. Soc. Human Genetics, Am. Coll. Epidemiology, Am. Coll. Med. Genetics, Atlanta Genetics Soc., Greater Atlanta Pediatric Soc., Atlanta Obstetrical and Gynecological Soc. (assoc.), Soc. Epidemiologic Rsch., Soc. Pediatric Rsch., Teratology Soc. (pres. elect 1983-84, pres. 1984-85, editorial bd. Teratology 1978-83, edn. com. 1988), Internat. Clearinghouse Birth Defects Monitoring Systems (chmn. 1981-82, vice chmn. 1982-83, chmn. 1983-84), Alpha Omega Alpha. Home: 2224 Kodiak Dr NE Atlanta GA 30345-4152 Office: CDC NCEH BDDD 4770 Buford Hwy NE # F34 Atlanta GA 30341-3724*

OAKLEY, JOHN BILYEU, law educator, lawyer, judicial consultant; b. San Francisco, June 18, 1947; s. Samuel Heywood and Elsie-Maye (Bilyeu) O.; m. Fredericka Barvitz, May 25, 1969; children: Adèle, Antonia. BA, U. Calif., Berkeley, 1969; JD, Yale U., 1972. Bar: Calif. 1972, U.S. Dist. Ct. (no. dist.) Calif. 1974, U.S. Dist. Ct. (ctrl. and ea. dists.) Calif. 1975, U.S. Supreme Ct. 1977, U.S. Ct. Appeals (5th cir.) 1979, U.S. Ct. Appeals (9th cir.) 1992. Rsch. atty. chief justice Donald R. Wright Supreme Ct. of Calif., 1972-73, sr. rsch. atty. chief justice Donald R. Wright, 1974-75; sr. law clk. chief judge M. Joseph Blumenfeld U.S. Dist. Ct. Conn., Hartford, 1973-74; acting prof. law U. Calif., Davis, 1975-79, prof. law, 1979—; reporter Speedy Trial Planning Group, U.S. Dist. Ct., Sacramento, 1977-82, Civil Justice Reform Act Adv. Group, 1991-94, U.S. Jud. Conf. Com. on Fed.-State Jurisdiction, 1991-96, Western Regional Conf. on State-Fed. Jud. Relationships, 1992-93; scholar-in-residence, sr. trial atty. Civil Rights Divsn., U.S. Dept. Justice, Washington, 1979-80; vis. scholar U. Coll., Oxford (Eng.) U., 1982-83; apptd. counsel death penalty appeal Supreme Ct. Calif., 1984-96; cons. Calif. Jud. Coun. Commn. on the Future of the Cts., 1992-93. Co-author: Law Clerks and the Judicial Process, 1980, An Introduction to the Anglo-American Legal System, 1980, 2nd edit., 1988, Civil Procedure, 1991; contbr.: Restructuring Justice, 1990. Pub. mem. New Motor Vehicle Bd. Calif., Sacramento, 1976-82; bd. dirs. Fallen Leaf Lake (Calif.) Mutual Water Co., 1980-82, 94—; western regional assoc., field assoc. Duke U. Primate Ctr., 1986-91. With U.S. Merchant Marine, 1969, Vietnam. Nat. Merit scholar, 1964. Mem. Am. Law Inst. (reporter project on the fed. jud. code 1995—), Assn. Am. Law Schs. (chair sect. on civil procedure 1979-80, 96—), Phi Beta Kappa. Avocations: aviation, photography, railroads, rugby, running. Office: Sch Law Univ Calif Davis CA 95616

OAKLEY, MARY ANN BRYANT, lawyer; b. Buckhannon, W.Va., June 22, 1940; d. Hubert Herndon and Mary F. (Deeds) Bryant; m. Godfrey P. Oakley, Jr., Sept. 2, 1961; children: Martha, Susan, Robert. AB, Duke U., 1962; MA, Emory U., 1970, JD, 1974. Tchr., Winston-Salem/Forsyth County Schs., N.C., 1961-65; assoc. Margie Pitts Hames, Atlanta, 1974-80; ptnr. Stagg Hoy & Oakley, Atlanta, 1980-83, Oakley & Bonner, Atlanta, 1984-90; pvt. practice, 1990—; adj. prof. trial practice Ga. State U., 1986-95; adj. prof. pretrial practice Emory U. Law Sch., 1991, 95—; bd. dirs. Nat. Employment Lawyers Assn., 1989-94; founding coodr. NELA, Ga.; mem. Ga. Supreme Ct. Commn. on Racial and Ethnic Bias. Contbr. articles to law jours. Notes and Comments editor Emory Law Jour., 1973-74. Author: Elizabeth Cady Stanton, 1972; Bd. dirs. Atlanta Met. YWCA, 1975-79, 1st v.p., 1978-79; mem. Leadership Atlanta, 1979; bd. dirs. Ga. chpt. ACLU, 1981-83; trustee Unitarian Universalist Congregation Atlanta, 1977-80, pres., 1979-80, mem. Unitarian Universalist Commn. Appraisal, 1980-85; bd. dirs. Unitarian Universalist Service Com., 1984-90, v.p., 1986-88, pres. 1988-90. Nat. Merit scholar, 1958. Mem. ABA, Am. Judicature Soc., State Bar Ga. (chmn. individual rights sect. 1979-81), Atlanta Bar Assn., Lawyers Club Atlanta, No. Dist. Bar Council, 1982-86, Ga. Assn. Women Lawyers, Ga. State Bar Disciplinary Bd. (investigative panel 1985-88, chmn., 1987-88), Gate City Bar Assn., Ga. Legal Svcs. Program Bd., LWV, Phi Beta Kappa, Order of Coif. Home: 2224 Kodiak Dr NE Atlanta GA 30345-4152 Office: 315 W Ponce De Leon Ave Ste 721 Decatur GA 30030-2441

OAKLEY, PHYLLIS ELLIOTT, diplomat; b. Omaha, Nov. 23, 1934; d. Thomas Myron Elliott and Elsa (Kerkow) Elliott Garabedian; m. Robert Bigger Oakley, June 8, 1958; children: Mary Oakley Kress, Thomas Elliott. B.A., Northwestern U., 1956; M.A., Fletcher Sch. Law and Diplomacy, 1957. Commd. fgn. svc. officer Dept. State, 1957-58, 74—, asst. cultural affairs officer, Kinshasa, Zaire, 1979-82, desk officer, Afghanistan, 1982-85, Pearson Exchange officer Senator Mathias, 1985-86; dep. spokesman, 1986-86, AID Afghan Humanitarian Assistance program, Islamabad, 1989-91, dep. asst. sec. INR Bur., 1991-93, sr. dep. PRM, 1993-94, asst. sec. PRM, 1994—. Mem. Coun. Fgn. Rels., Cosmos Club, Phi Beta Kappa. Office: Dept of State Bur Population Refugees & Migration 2201 C St NW Washington DC 20520-5824

OAKLEY, ROBERT LOUIS, law librarian, educator; b. N.Y.C., Nov. 6, 1945; s. Bert Tuttle Oakley and Allese (Duffin) Vestigo; m. Madeleine Cohen, Aug. 13, 1971; children: Esther Shulamit, Daniel Isaac-Meir. BA, Cornell U., 1968; MLS, Syracuse U., 1972; JD, Cornell U., 1976. Bar: N.Y. 1977, U.S. Dist. Ct. (no. dist.) N.Y. 1977. Assoc. dir. law libr. Cornell U., Ithaca, N.Y., 1976-79; dir. law libr., assoc. prof. Boston U. Law, 1979-82; dir. law libr., assoc. prof. Georgetown U., Washington, 1982-87, dir. law libr., prof., 1987—; AALL Washington Affairs Rep., 1989—. Contbr. articles to profl. jours. Mem. Libr. of Congress, mem. Network Adv. Com., 1986-92, 95—; adv. nat. commn. on Preservation and Access, 1988-94; mem. AALL Exec. Bd., 1991-94; bd. dirs. Montgomery County (Md.) Pub. Librs., 1988-92. Mem. ABA, ALA, Assn. Am. Law Schs., Libr. of Congress Fgn. Law Classification Adv. Com. Avocations: photography, music, personal computers, amateur radio. Office: Georgetown U Law Ctr 111 G St NW Washington DC 20001-1417

OAKLEY, TRACY L., lawyer; b. Mattoon, Ill., Sept. 6, 1963; s. Max L. and Sharon L. (Freeman) O.; m. Linda M. Tylka, June 30, 1984; children: Jacob, Melissa, Lucs, Tracy, Caroline. BS, U. So. Miss., 1986; JD, U. Miss., 1989. Bar: La. 1989, U.S. Dist. Ct. (ea., mid. and we. dists.) La. 1989, U.S. Ct. Appeals (5th cir.) 1990, Ill. 1991. Assoc. Onebane, Donohoe, Barnard, Torian, Lafayette, La., 1989-92; ptnr. Wilkerson & Oakley, Ruston, La., 1992—. Republican. Roman Catholic. Avocations: hunting, fishing. Office: Law Offices of Tracy Oakley 609 N Vienna Ruston LA 71270

OAKS, B. ANN, plant physiologist, educator; b. Winnipeg, Man., Can., June 4, 1929; d. H.A. and Bernice (Farlinger) O. BA with honors, U. Toronto, Ont., Can., 1951; MA, U. Sask., Can., 1954, PhD, 1959. Alexander von Humbolt assoc. Rsch. Inst. for Dairying, Freising, Fed. Republic Germany, 1958-60; rsch. assoc. Purdue U., West Lafayette, Ind., 1960-64, Oak Ridge (Tenn.) Nat. Lab., 1964-65; asst. prof. biology McMaster U., Hamilton, Ont., 1965-68, assoc. prof., 1968-74, prof., 1974-89; prof. emeritus McMaster U., Hamilton, 1989—; prof. U. Guelph, Ont., 1989—; vis. prof. Wash. State U., 1979-80, U. Nancy, France, 1980, Chiba U., Japan, 1984; adj. prof. U. Guelph, 1987-89; affiliated scientist NRC Lab., Saskatoon, Sask., 1988-92. Assoc. editor Biochemistry and Cell Biology, 1988-90; mem. editl. bd. Plant Physiology, 1970-89, Jour. Plant Physiology, 1984-95, Physiologia Plantarium, 1995—, Plant and Cell Physiology, 1989-93; contbg. author various books; contbr. articles to profl. jours. Rsch. grantee in field. Fellow Royal Soc. Can.; mem. Can. Soc. Plant Physiologists (treas. 1974-76, Gold medal 1989), Am. Soc. Plant Physiologists. Avocations: skiing, hiking, naturalist, writing letters to members of parliament. Office: U Guelph, Dept Botany, Guelph, ON Canada N1G 2W1

OAKS, DALLIN HARRIS, lawyer, church official; b. Provo, Utah, Aug. 12, 1932; s. Lloyd E. and Stella (Harris) O.; m. June Dixon, June 24, 1952; children: Sharmon, Cheri Lyn, Lloyd D., Dallin D., TruAnn, Jenny June. BA with high honors, Brigham Young U., 1954, LLD (hon.), 1980; JD cum laude, U. Chgo., 1957; LLD (hon.), Pepperdine U., 1982, So. Utah U., 1991. Bar: Ill. 1957, Utah 1971. Law clk. to Chief Justice Earl Warren U.S. Supreme Ct., 1957-58; with firm Kirkland, Ellis, Hodson, Chaffetz & Masters, Chgo., 1958-61; mem. faculty U. Chgo. Law Sch., 1961-71, assoc. dean and acting dean, 1962, prof., 1964-71, mem. vis. com., 1971-74; pres. Brigham Young U., Provo, Utah, 1971-80; also prof. law J. Reuben Clark Law Sch., 1974-80; justice Utah Supreme Ct., 1981-84; mem. Coun. of Twelve Apostles Ch. Jesus Christ of Latter Day Sts., 1984—; legal counsel Bill of Rights com. Ill. Constl. Conv., 1970. Author: (with G.G. Bogert) Cases on Trusts, 1967, 78, (with W. Lehman) A Criminal Justice System and The Indigent, 1968, The Criminal Justice Act in the Federal District Courts, 1969, (with M. Hill) Carthage Conspiracy, 1975, Trust Doctrines in Church Controversies, 1984, Pure in Heart, 1988, The Lord's Way, 1991; editor: The Wall Between Church and State, 1963. Mem. Wilson coun. Woodrow Wilson Internat. Ctr. for Scholars, 1973-80; trustee Intermountain Health Care Inc., 1975-80; mem. adv. com. Nat. Inst. Law Enforcement and Criminal Justice, 1974-76; bd. dirs. Notre Dame Ctr. for Constl. Studies, 1977-80, Rockford Inst., 1980—; bd. dirs. Pub. Broadcasting Svc., 1977-85, chmn., 1980-85; bd. dirs. Polynesian Cultural Ctr., 1987-96, chmn., 1988-96. Fellow Am. Bar Found. (exec. dir. 1970-71); mem. Am. Assn. Pres. Ind. Colls. and Univs. (pres. 1975-78, dir. 1971-78), Order of Coif. Mem. Ch. of Jesus Christ of Latter-day Saints (regional rep. 1974-80; past 1st counselor Chgo. South Stake). Address: 47 E South Temple Salt Lake City UT 84150

OAKS, MAURICE DAVID, retired pharmaceutical company executive; b. Everett, Pa., Jan. 22, 1934; s. Jacob Garvin and Hannah Alma (Young) O.; m. Judith Ann Rayne; 1 child, Kimberly. BS in Biology, Franklin and Marshall Coll., 1956. Sales rep. Squibb Pharm., Salisbury and Balt., Md., 1959-69; div. sales mgr. Squibb Pharm., Columbus, Ohio, 1969-71; product mgr. Squibb Pharm., Princeton, N.J., 1971-76, group product dir. antibiotics, cardiovasculars, and insulin, 1976-78, dir. product planning, U.S., 1979-80, v.p. world wide mktg. devel., 1980-82, v.p. mktg. svcs., 1983-85, pres. Princeton Pharm. Products, 1985-89; exec. v.p. Squibb Pharm. Group U.S., Princeton, N.J., 1989-90; v.p. worldwide ops. planning Bristol-Myers Squibb Pharms. Ops., Princeton, 1990-92; bd. dirs. Nat. Pharm. Coun., McLean, Va., 1985-90, mem. exec. com., 1988-90; bd. dirs., mem. audit com. Penn Engring. Mfg., Danboro, Pa. Mem. coun. Franklin and Marshall Coll. Commn. on Found. and Corp. Support, Lancaster, Pa., 1987-90, ann. fund class capt., 1991-96; mem., pres. Mid-Atlantic regional adv. coun. Franklin and Marshall Coll.; bd. dirs. Surf's Edge Condo Assn., Ocean City, Md.,

1995—; active YMCA, Doylestown, Pa. With U.S. Army, 1956-58. Republican. Methodist. Avocations: tennis, golf, bicycling.

OATES, ADAM R., professional hockey player; b. Weston, Ont., Can., Aug. 27, 1962. Attended, Rensselaer Polytech. Inst., 1985. With Detroit Red Wings, 1985-89, St. Louis Blues, 1989-92, Boston Bruins, 1992—; player NHL All-Star Game, 1991-94. Named NCAA All-American, 1984-85; named to Sporting News All-Star Team, 1990-91. Office: Boston Bruins 1 Fleet Ctr Ste 250 Boston MA 02114-1310*

OATES, BART STEVEN, professional football player; b. Mesa, Ariz., Dec. 16, 1958; m. Michelle Oats. BA in Acctg., Brigham Young U.; JD, Seton Hall U. Bar: N.J. 1990. With Phila. Stars, USFL, 1983-85, N.Y. Giants, 1985-94, San Francisco 49ers, 1994-94; assoc. Ribis, Graham & Curtin, Morristown, N.J.; Player Super Bowl XXI, 1986, XXV, 1990, XXVIV, 1994. Named USFL All-Star Team Ctr. by Sporting News, 1983. Played in Pro Bowl, 1990-91, 93.

OATES, CARL EVERETTE, lawyer; b. Harlingen, Tex., Apr. 8, 1931; s. Joseph William and Grace (Watson) O.; m. Eileen N. Hudnall; children: Carl William, Gregory Carl Hudnall, Patricia O. Chase, Matthew Noble Hudnall. BS, U.S. Naval Acad., 1955; LLB, So. Meth. U., 1962. Bar: Tex. 1962, D.C. 1977, Nebr. 1985. Assoc. Akin, Gump, Strauss, Hauer & Feld, Dallas, 1962-64, ptnr., 1965-91. Asst. atty. gen. State of Texas, 1992-94, spl. coun., Tex. Dept. Banking, 1994-95, prin. Carl E. Oates, P.C. Chmn. bd. trustees S.W. Mus. Sci. and Tech., Dallas; v.p. S.W. Sci. Mus. Found., Dallas; bd. dirs. Kiwanis Wesley Dental Ctr., Inc., Dallas; pres. Wesley Dental Found., Dallas. Served to lt. USN, 1955-59. Mem. ABA, D.C. Bar Assn., Tex. Bar Assn., Dallas Bar Assn., Nebr. Bar Assn., Barristers, Northwood Club, Delta Theta Phi. Office: 1030 One Energy Sq 4925 Greenville Ave Dallas TX 75206

OATES, JAMES G., advertising executive; b. Kenton, Ohio, Apr. 2, 1943; m. Sue Ann Minter; 2 children. BS, Ohio State U. Trainee Leo Burnett USA, Chgo., 1966-68, asst. acct. exec., 1968-69, acct. exec., 1969-73, acct. supv., 1973-74, v.p., 1974-77, acct. supv. GM Olds acct., 1977-80, mgmt. dir. Philip Morris account, 1980-84, sr. v.p., 1984-86, exec. v.p., 1986-90, vice chmn., dir. client svcs., 1990-92, chmn., bd. dirs., mem. exec. com., 1992—, group pres. Asia/Pacific, 1993—; bd. dirs. The Advt. Coun. mem. MBA adv. bd. Ohio State U.; Kellogg Adv. Bd.; active Chgo. Crime Commn. Mem. Am. Assn. Advt. Agys. (bd. govs. Chgo. chpt.). Office: Leo Burnett Co Inc 35 W Wacker Dr Chicago IL 60601*

OATES, JOHN ALEXANDER, JR., medical educator; b. Fayetteville, N.C., Apr. 23, 1932; s. John Alexander and Isabelle (Crowder) O.; m. Meredith Stringfield, June 12, 1956; children: David Alexander, Christine Larkin, James Caldwell. BS magna cum laude, Wake Forest Coll., 1953; MD, Bowman Gray Sch. Medicine, 1956. Intern, then asst. resident medicine N.Y. Hosp.-Cornell U. Med. Center, N.Y.C., 1956-58, 61-62; clin. assoc., then sr. investigator Nat. Heart Inst., 1958-63; mem. faculty Vanderbilt U. Sch. Medicine, 1963—, prof. medicine and pharmacology, 1969—, Werthan prof. investigative medicine, 1974-84, chmn. dept. medicine, 1983—; mem. drug research bd. Nat. Acad. Scis.-NRC, 1967-71; chmn. pharmacology and toxicology tng. com. Nat. Inst. Gen. Med. Scis., 1969-70; mem . adv. coun. Nat. Heart, Lung and Blood Inst., 1985-89. Fellow ACP, Am. Acad. Arts & Scis.; mem. Am. Fedn. Clin. Rsch. (pres. 1970-71), Am. Soc. Clin. Investigation (v.p. 1976-77), Assn. Am. Physicians (pres. 1981-82), Am. Soc. Pharmacology and Exptl. Therapeutics (chmn. exec. com. divsn. clin. pharmacology 1967-69), Inst. of Medicine. Participated in discovery antihypertensive effect of methyldopa, elucidation of a number of interactions between drugs in man; research on the biochemistry and pathophysiology of eicosanoids. Home: 6440 Brownlee Dr Nashville TN 37205-3162 Office: Vanderbilt U Med Ctr 1611 21st Ave S Nashville TN 37212-3103

OATES, JOHN FRANCIS, classics educator; b. Holyoke, Mass., Aug. 7, 1934; s. William Adrian and Lilian (Woods) O.; m. Rosemary Walsh, June 27, 1957; children: Elizabeth, Emily, John Francis, Sarah. B.A., Yale U., 1956, M.A., 1958, Ph.D., 1960; postgrad. (Fulbright fellow), Am. Sch. Classical Studies in Athens, Greece, 1956-57. Instr. classics Yale U., 1960-63, asst. prof., 1963-67; asso. prof. ancient history Duke U., 1967-71, prof., 1971—, chmn. dept. classical studies, 1971-80, chmn. Humanities Council, 1975-80, dir. database of documentary papyri, 1982—, dir. papyrus catalog project, 1992-95; Hon. research asst., Morse fellow Univ. Coll. London (Eng.), 1965-66; vis. prof. Smith Coll., Northampton, Mass., 1967, 68; mem. mng. com. Intercollegiate Center Classical Studies in Rome, Italy, 1972-77, Am. Sch. Classical Studies in Athens, 1973—, mem. com. on coms., 1975-77; mem. Council for Internat. Exchange of Scholars, 1974-77; v.p., trustee Triangle Univs. Center for Advanced Study, Inc., 1975-90; trustee Nat. Humanities Center, 1977-90, trustee emeritus, 1990—; adv. council Sch. Classical Studies, Am. Acad. in Rome, 1976—; dir. summer seminar Nat. Endowment Humanities, 1978; dir. Nat. Fedn. State Humanities Councils, 1980-83; mem. N.C. Humanities Com., 1977-83, chmn. 1980-82. Author: The Status Designatin, 1963 (with A.E. Samuel and C.B. Welles) Yale Papri in the Beinecke Library, 1967, (with W.H. Willis and R.S. Bagnall) A Check-list of Papyrological Editions, 4th edit., 1992, (with Willis) Duke Data Bank of Documentary Paprus Archive, 1996, The Basilikos Grammateus, 1995; mem. adv. bd. Greek, Roman and Byzantine Studies, 1977—, Humanities Report, 1981-83. Am. Council Learned Socs. fellow, 1973-74. Mem. Am. Philol. Assn. (chmn. com. computer activities 1974-75, dir. 1975-78, mem. nominating com. 1980-83), Archaeol. Inst. Am., Am. Hist. Assn., Am. Soc. Papyrologists (v.p. 1971-73, pres. 1976-80, dir.), Assn. Internationale de Papyrologues, Classical Assn. Middle West and South (v.p. 1972-74, pres. So. sect. 1974-76). Home: 2416 Alpine Rd Durham NC 27707-3818 Office: Dept of Classical Studies Duke U Durham NC 27708-0103

OATES, JOHNNY LANE, professional baseball team manager; b. Sylva, N.C., Jan. 21, 1946. BS in Health and Phys. Edn., Va. Tech. U. Player minor league team Chgo. White Sox, 1967; player minor league team Balt. Orioles, 1967-71, player, 1970, 72, mgr. minor league team, 1988, coach, 1989-91, mgr., 1991-94; player Atlanta Braves, 1973-75, Phila. Phillies, 1975-76, L.A. Dodgers, 1977-79; player N.Y. Yankees, 1980, minor league coach, 1981-83; coach Chgo. Cubs, 1984-87; mgr. Texas Rangers, 1995—. Named Internat. League Mgr. of Yr., 1988. Office: The Ballpark in Arlington 1000 Ballpark Way Arlington TX 76011*

OATES, JOYCE CAROL, author; b. Lockport, N.Y., June 16, 1938; d. Frederic James and Caroline (Bush) O.; m. Raymond Joseph Smith, Jan. 23, 1961. BA, Syracuse U., 1960; MA, U. Wis., 1961. Instr. English U. Detroit, 1961-65, asst. prof., 1965-67; prof. English U. Windsor, Ont., Can., 1967-87; writer-in-residence Princeton (N.J.) U., 1978-81, prof., 1987—. Author: (short story collections) By the North Gate, 1963, Upon the Sweeping Flood, 1966, The Wheel of Love, 1970, Marriages and Infidelities, 1972, The Hungry Ghosts, 1974, The Goddess and Other Women, 1974, Where Are You Going, Where Have You Been?: Stories of Young America, 1974, The Poisoned Kiss and Other Stories From the Portuguese, 1975, The Seduction and Other Stories, 1975, Crossing the Border, 1976, Night-Side, 1977, All the Good People I've Left Behind, 1978, The Lamb of Abyssalia, 1980, A Sentimental Education: Stories, 1981, Last Days: Stories, 1984, Wild Nights, 1985, Raven's Wing: Stories, 1986, The Assignation, 1988, Heat: And Other Stories, 1991, Where is Here?, 1992, Haunted: Tales of the Grotesque, 1994, Will You Always Love Me? and Other Stories, 1995; (novels) With Shuddering Fall, 1964, A Garden of Earthly Delights, 1967 (Nat. Book award nomination 1968), Expensive People, 1967 (Nat. Book award nomination 1969), them, 1969 (Nat. Book award for fiction 1970), Wonderland, 1971, Do With Me What You Will, 1973, The Assassins, 1975, Childwold, 1976, The Triumph of the Spider Monkey, 1976, Son of the Morning, 1978, Unholy Loves, 1979, Cybele, 1979, Bellefleur, 1980 (L.A. Times Book award nomination 1980), A Sentimental Education, 1981, Angel of Light, 1981, A Bloodsmoor Romance, 1982, Mysteries of Winterthorn, 1984, Solstice, 1985, Marya, 1986, You Must Remember This, 1987, (as Rosamond Smith) The Lives of the Twins, 1987, American Appetites, 1989, (as Rosamond Smith) Soul-Mate, 1989, Because It Is Bitter, and Because It Is My Heart, 1990, (as Rosamond Smith) Nemesis, 1990, I Lock My Door Upon Myself, 1990, The Rise of Life on Earth, 1991, Black Water, 1992, (as Rosamond Smith) Snake Eyes, 1992, Foxfire: Confessions of a Girl Gang, 1993, What I Lived For, 1994 (PEN/Faulkner award nomination 1995); (poetry collections) Women in Love, 1968, Expensive People, 1968, Anonymous Sins, 1969, Love and Its Derangements, 1970, Angel Fire, 1973, Dreaming America, 1973, The Fabulous Beasts, 1975, Season of Peril, 1977, Women Whose Lives are Food, Men Whose Lives are Money: Poems, 1978, The Stepfather, 1978, Celestial Timepiece, 1981, Invisible Women: New and Selected Poems, 1970-1972, 1982, Luxury of Sin, 1983, The Time Traveller, 1987; (plays) The Sweet Enemy, 1965, Sunday Dinner, 1970, Ontological Proof of My Existence, 1970, Miracle Play, 1974, Three Plays, 1980, Daisy, 1980, Presque Isle, 1984, Triumph of the Spider Monkey, 1985, In Darkest America, 1990, I Stand Before You Naked, 1990, The Perfectionist and Other Plays, 1995; (essays) The Edge of Impossibility, 1972, The Hostile Sun: The Poetry of D.H. Lawrence, 1973, New Heaven, New Earth, 1974, Contraries: Essays, 1981, The Profane Art, 1984, On Boxing, 1987, (Woman) Writer: Occasions and Opportunities, 1988; editor, compiler: Scenes from American Life: Contemporary Short Fiction, 1973, (with Shannon Ravenel) Best American Short Stories of 1979, 1979, Night Walks, 1982, First Person Singular: Writer's on Their Craft, 1983, (with Boyd Litzinger) Story: Fictions Past and Present, 1985, (with Daniel Halpern) Reading and Fights, 1988, The Oxford Book of American Short Stories, 1992, The Sophisticated Cat: An Anthology, 1992; editor (with Raymond Smith) Ontario Rev.; contbr. to nat. mags. including N.Y. Times Book Rev., Mich. Quarterly Rev., Mademoiselle, Vogue, North Am. Rev., Hudson Rev., Paris Rev., Grand Street, Atlantic, Poetry, Esquire. Recipient O. Henry award, 1967, 73, Rosenthal award Nat. Inst. Arts and Letters, 1968, O. Henry Spl. award continuing achievement, 1970, 86, Award of Merit Lotos Club, 1975, St. Louis Lit. award, 198, Rea award for the Short Story, 1990, Alan Swallow award for fiction, 1990, Nobel Prize in Lit. nomination, 1993; Guggenheim fellow, 1967-68, Nat. Endowment for the Arts grantee, 1966, 68. Mem. Am. Acad. and Inst. Arts and Letters. Office: c/o John Hawkins 71 W 23rd St Ste 1600 New York NY 10010*

OATES, SHERRY CHARLENE, portraitist; b. Houston, Sept. 11, 1946; d. Charles Emil and Berniece Faye (Lohse) O. Student, North Tex. State U., 1965-66; student under Martin Kellogg; BA in English, Health and Phys. Edn., Houston Bapt. U., 1968. Cert. art tchr., Tex. Tchr. Jackson Jr. High Sch., Houston, 1968-69, Percy Priest Sch., Nashville, 1969-70, Franklin (Tenn.) High Sch., 1970-84; freelance illustrator Bapt. Sunday Sch. Bd., Nashville, 1978-85, United Meth. Pub. House, Nashville, 1980-85; portraitist in oils, owner Portraits, Ltd., Nashville, 1984—. Portraits include corp. leaders, educators, politicians, hist. and equestrian subjects, society figures and children; participated in various exhbns. at Bapt. Sunday Sch. Bd. and All State and Ctr. South Exhibits at the Parthenon. Recipient 3d place in graphics Ctrl. South Exhbn. at The Parthenon-Tenn. Art League, 1986. Mem. Tenn. Art League. Republican. Baptist. Avocations: antiques, photography. Studio: 816 Kirkwood Ave Nashville TN 37204-2602

OATES, STEPHEN BAERY, history educator; b. Pampa, Tex., Jan. 5, 1936; s. Steve Theodore and Florence (Baer) O.; divorced; children: Gregory Allen, Stephanie; m. Marie Phillips. B.A. magna cum laude, U. Tex., 1958, M.A., 1960, Ph.D., 1968; Litt.D. (hon.), Lincoln Coll., 1981. Prof. history U. Mass., Amherst, 1971—; now also Paul Murray Kendall prof. biography U. Mass., adj. prof. English, 1980—. Author: Confederate Cavalry West of the River, 1961, Rip Ford's Texas, 1963, Republic of Texas, 1968, Visions of Glory, 1970, To Purge This Land With Blood: A Biography of John Brown, 1970, Portrait of America, 2 vols., 1973, rev. edits., 1976, 83, 86, 90, 94, The Fires of Jubilee: Nat Turner's Fierce Rebellion, 1975, With Malice Toward None: The Life of Abraham Lincoln (Christopher award for outstanding lit., Barondess/Lincoln award N.Y. Civil War Round Table 1977), Our Fiery Trial: Abraham Lincoln, John Brown, and the Civil War Era, 1979, Let the Trumpet Sound: The Life of Martin Luther King, Jr., 1982 (Christopher award, Robert F. Kennedy Meml. Book award), Abraham Lincoln, The Man Behind the Myths, 1984, Biography as High Adventure: Life Writers Speak on Their Art, 1986, William Faulkner: The Man and the Artist, 1987, A Woman of Valor: Clara Barton and the Civil War, 1994; contbr. articles and essays to periodicals; lectr. Recipient Chancellor's medal for outstanding scholarship U. Mass., 1976, Disting. Teaching award, 1981, Faculty fellowship award, 1981; Presdl. Writers award, 1985; Master Tchr. award U. Hartford, 1985; Silver Medal award Case Council for Advance and Support of Edn., Prof. of Yr., 1986, 87, Kidger award New Eng. History Tchrs. Assn., Nevins-Freeman award Chgo. Civil War Round Table, 1993; Guggenheim fellow, 1972; sr. summer fellow NEH, 1978. Fellow Tex. State Hist. Assn.; mem. Tex. Inst. Letters, Soc. Am. Historians, Am. Antiquarian Soc., Phi Beta Kappa. Office: U Mass Dept History Amherst MA 01003

OATES, THOMAS R., university executive; married; 4 children. BA in English and Philosophy, St. Louis U., 1964, MA in English, 1970; postgrad., Am. Film Inst. Ctr., Beverly Hills, Calif., 1971; PhD in Am. Lit., St. Louis U., 1979. Coord., dir. program assts. and counselors upward bound pgm. Webster Coll., 1970-71, dir. media/journalism degree program, 1974-81, coord. MA program in media comms., 1975-81; chair, assoc. prof. dept. journalism St. Michael's Coll., 1981-85; campus dean U. Wis. Ctr., Richland Center, 1985-89; dir. U.S. ops. and acad. programs Coop. Assn. of States for Scholarships, Georgetown U., Washington, 1989-94; pres. Spalding U., Louisville, 1994—; mem. media adv. com. Mo. State Coun. of Arts, 1973-77; mem. planning commn. State Dept. of Higher Edn., Baton Rouge, 1979-80; mem., rep. Mo.'s ind. colls. and univs. Cen. Ednl. Network Mo., 1979-81; mem. adv. bd. Tri-State Bilingual Tng. Program, St. Michael's Coll., 1981-83; mem. Vt. Cath. Press Assn. Bd., 1984-85; mem., appointed chair Internat. Edn. Coun., U. Wis. Sys., 1987-88, designer, author Ctr. of Excellence project, 1988; mem. acad. staff adv. bd., U. Wis. Ctr. Sys., 1987-89, chair acad. staff grievance com., 1988; mem. 9-person state commn. to develop criteria for legal evaluations of devel. projects reviewed under Act 250 environ. law, Vt., 1984-85; presenter on internat. ednl. regional and nat. meetings of various orgns. Author, designer: (slide-tape program on history of early French and English explorers in mid-west) Old Land, New Land, 1985; author, designer: (book) Images, Values, and Development in Chittenden County, 1984; prodr.: (documentary photographic study on 5 rural Alaskan comtys.) Images of Continuity, Images of Change, 1977; prodr., dir.: (16mm documentary film) The Faces of British Honduras, 1974. Grantee Mo. Coun. on Arts, 1972, 76, NEH, 1975, U. Alaska, 1978, Mo. Coun. on Humanities, 1979, Vt. Coun. on Humanities, 1981, IBM, 1982, U. Wis. Ext., 1988, Wis. Coun. for Humanities, 1989, Orgn. for Petroleum Exporting Countries, 1992, C.C.'s for Internat. Devel., 1992. Office: Spalding U Office pres 851 S 4th St Louisville KY 40203

OATES, WILLIAM ARMSTRONG, JR., investment company executive; b. Pitts., July 27, 1942; s. Wiliiam Armstrong and Margaret (Nichols) O.; m. Elizabeth Dick Macy, Sept. 7, 1968; children: Elizabeth N., Katherine M., Emily E.A. BA, Colby Coll., 1965; MBA, Harvard U., 1972. Asst. treas. Morgan Guaranty Trust, N.Y.C., 1966-70; trustee, dir. Northeast Investors Trust, Boston, 1972—; pres. Northeast Investors Growth Fund, Boston, 1980—; ptnr. Guild, Monrad & Oates, Inc., 1984—; dir. Horn Corp., Ayer, Mass., Furman Lumber Co., Boston, Clifford Inc., Bethel, Vt. Pres. bd. trustees Groton (Mass.) Sch., 1979; trustee, treas. Roxbury Latin Sch., West Roxbury, Mass., 1975—. Served to 2d lt. Army N.G., 1966-70. Republican. Episcopalian. Clubs: Harvard (Boston); Brookline Country (Brookline, Mass.); Somerset (Boston). Home: 201 Village Ave Dedham MA 02026-4230 Office: Guild, Monrad & Oates Inc 50 Congress St Boston MA 02109-4002

OATHOUT, BRENDA HALM, auditor; b. Tecumseh, Nebr., Aug. 16, 1960; d. William W. and H. Lenore (Bentzinger) B.; m. Randall L. Oathout, Sept. 26, 1992. BSBA, U. Nebr., Omaha, 1983. Clk. Boardwalk Hardware, Omaha, 1976-8l; claims auditor Physicians Mut. Ins. Co., Omaha, 198l-87; auditor LaHood & Assocs., Overland Park, Kans., 1987-89; advanced auditor Physicians Mut. Ins. Co., Omaha, 1989-92, sr. auditor, 1992—. Republican. Methodist.

OATWAY, FRANCIS CARLYLE, corporate executive; b. Bermuda, Nov. 29, 1936; s. Charles Y. and Josephine (McLellan) O.; m. Ann Thomason; children—Stephen F., Karen E., Andrew C., Christopher M. BSBA, Boston Coll., 1960. C.P.A., Mass., N.Y., others. With Deloitte Haskins & Sells, N.Y.C., 1960-80, ptnr., 1970-80; v.p. taxation Continental Group, Inc., Stamford, Conn., 1980-81, v.p. treasury and taxation, 1981-82, v.p. fin., 1982-83, v.p., chief fin. officer, 1983; exec. v.p., pres., dir. Continental Forest Industries, Inc., Stamford, Conn., 1984-85; pres. Hargro Assocs., Stamford, Conn., 1985—; pres., CEO, dir. Hargro Enterprises, Inc., Stamford, 1985—; chmn., bd. dirs. Hargro Packaging, Boyertown, Pa., 1985—; chmn., CEO, bd. dirs. NER Data Products, Glassboro, N.J., 1985—; pres., bd. dirs. Covent Ins. Co. Ltd., Hamilton, Bermuda, 1980-85; chmn. bd., mng. dir. CCC Finanz A.G., Zug, Switzerland, 1980-85; mng. dir. Continental Group Overseas Fin. N.V., Curacao, Netherlands Antilles, 9181-85; bd. dirs. Hansa Reins Co. Am., Tarrytown, N.Y., chmn. bd. Apple Syndicate Corp., Westport, Conn., 1983-85. Contbg. editor: Federal Income Taxation of Banks and Financial Institutions, 1968, Professional Responsibility in Federal Tax Practice, 1970; contbr. articles to fin. jours. Trustee Convent of Sacred Heart, Greenwich, Conn., 1979-83; mem. acctg. adv. bd. Columbia U. Grad. Sch. Bus., N.Y.C., 1982-86; mem. exec. com. Boston Coll. Wall St. Coun., 1989—; trustee Conn. Pub. Expenditure Coun., Inc., Hartford, 1984-85; mem. pres.'s adv. bd. Weston Sch. Theology, Cambridge, 1993—. Roman Catholic. Clubs: Union League (N.Y.C.); Landmark (Stamford); Country of New Canaan (Conn.). Office: Hargro Assocs One Landmark Sq Stamford CT 06901

OBAIDAT, MOHAMMAD SALAMEH, electrical and computer engineering educator; b. Kofrsoum, Irbid, Jordan, Dec. 22, 1952; came to U.S., 1981; s. Salameh Mohammad and Wardeh Ahmed Obaidat; m. Balqies I. Sadoun, June 1, 1988. BS in Elec. Engring., Aleppo U., Syria, 1975; MS in Elec. and Computer Engring., Ohio State U., 1982, PhD in Elec. and Computer Engring., 1986. Chief engr. video dept. Jordan TV, Amman, 1975-81; grad. rsch. asst. elec. engring. Ohio State U., 1981-86; asst. prof. elec. engring. U. Sci. and Tech., Irbid, 1986-89; asst. prof., dir. computer engring. rsch. lab. U. Mo., Columbia, 1989-92; assoc. prof. elec. engring. CUNY, 1992—; vis. rschr. Ohio State U., 1987; organizer, prin. instr. workshop Jordan U. Sci. and Tech., 1989; instr. engr.-in-tng. course U. Mo., Truman, 1990; reviewer IEEE Trans. Sys. Man and Cybernetics, Computers and Elec. Engring. Jour., Info. Scis. Jour., Simulation Jour., Internat. Jour. in Computer Simulation, IEEE Transactions Instrumentation & Measurement Conf. on Distributed Computing Systems; presenter numerous seminars. Mem. editl. bd. IEEE Transactions on Instrumentation and Measurement, ACM Applied Computing Rev.; assoc. editor Modeling and Simulation, 1991, 92, IEEE Trans. Sys. Man, Cybernetics, SCS Simulation Jour., Jour. Computers & Elec. Engring.; guest editor Simulation Jour., 1993, 95; contbr. numerous articles to profl. jours. Grantee Gerhard Cibis Inc., 1992, Mo. Rsch. Asst. Act and TransSoft 32 Ltd., 1991-93, Intel Corp., 1991, Tex. Instruments, 1991, U. Mo. at Columbia, 1991, Motorola, 1990, 95, U. Mo. at Columbia/U. Mo. at Kans. City Engring., 1990, ODA, 1989, U. Mo., 1991, CUNY, 1992-94, Nat. Security Agy., 1995. Mem. IEEE (sr. admission and advancement com. 1991-92, com. Kansas City sect. ednl. activities 1990-92, ACM dist. vis. lectr., tutorial chair IPCCC conf. 1993-95, program chair internat. conf. electronics, circuits & sys., program chair 1996 internat. Phoenix conf. on computers and comms., disting. spkr. 1994—), IEEE Computer Soc. (chmn. Kansas City chpt. 1991-92, co-founder, CSAB evaluator, vice chmn. 1990-91, recognition certs., reviewer jours., transactions, participant, organizer numerous confs.), Soc. for Computer Simulation (chair numerous conf. sessions and tracks, presenter numerous seminars), Assn. for Computing Machinery (chair numerous confs., sessions and tracks).

O'BANNON, ED, professional basketball player; b. Aug. 14, 1972; 1 child, Aaron. Grad., UCLA. Forward N.J. Nets, 1995—. Recipient John Wooden award as Nat. Player of Yr., Chevrolet/CBS, Most Outstanding Player in Final Four, Player of Yr. USBWA; named to 1st Team All-Am., AP. Office: NJ Nets 405 Murray Hill Pkwy East Rutherford NJ 07073

O'BANNON, FRANK LEWIS, state official, lawyer; b. Louisville, Jan. 30, 1930; s. Robert Pressley and Rosella Faith (Dropsey) O'B.; m. Judith Mae Asmus, Aug. 18, 1957; children: Polly, Jennifer, Jonathan. AB, Ind. U., 1952, JD, 1957. Ind. 1957. Pvt. practice Corydon; ptnr. Hays, O'Bannon & Funk, Corydon, 1966-80, O'Bannon, Funk & Simpson, Corydon, 1980-94, Funk, Simpson, Thompson & Byrd, Corydon, 1995—; mem. Ind. Senate, Corydon, 1970-89, minority floor leader, 1979-89, asst. minority floor leader, 1972-76; lt. gov. State of Ind., Corydon, 1989—; chmn., dir. O'Bannon Pub. Co., Inc. Served with USAF, 1952-54. Mem. Ind. Dem. Editorial Assn. (pres. 1961), Am. Judicature Soc., Am. Bar Assn., Ind. Bar Assn. Democrat. Methodist. Office: Lt Govs Office 333 State House Indianapolis IN 46204

OBASEKI, LOVETTE I., consulting company executive, systems analyst; b. July 4, 1953; d. Samson O. Amba A. (Okai) O. BS, Fla. A&M U., 1979, MEd, 1984; diploma in systems analysis, NYU, 1989; cert. in CNE, Touro Coll., 1995; cert. in small bus. program, Baruch Coll., 1995. cert. Novell netware engr. Supr. systems adminstrn. Buccellati Ltd., N.Y.C.; systems mgr. JCCA, N.Y.C., 1988-95; cons. Binam Cons. Svcs., 1995—. Active numerous ch. groups. Recipient Honors awards Fla. A&M U. Mem. NAFE, NOW, AAUW, Assn. Sys. Mgmt. (bd. dirs. 1989—, v.p. 1992-93, Excellence in Sys. Mgmt. award 1994, Outstanding Svc. award 1992-93, Appreciation cert. 1990-91, Honors award), Data Processing Mgmt. Assn., Am. Mgmt. Assn., DAV Comdrs. Club (Bronze Leader 1995). Democrat. Address: PO Box 901026 Far Rockaway NY 11690-1026

OBEAR, FREDERICK WOODS, academic administrator; b. Malden, Mass., June 9, 1935; s. William Fred and Dorothea Louise (Woods) O.; m. Patricia A. Draper, Aug. 30, 1959 (dec. Dec. 1993); children: Jeffrey Allan, Deborah Anne, James Frederick. BS with high honors, U. Mass., Lowell, 1956, LHD, 1985; PhD, U. N.H., 1961. Mem. faculty dept. chemistry Oakland U., Rochester, Mich., 1960-81, prof., 1979-81, v.p. for acad. affairs, provost, 1970-81; chancellor U. Tenn., Chattanooga, 1981—; mem. nat. addv. panel Nat. Commn. on Higher Edn. Issues, 1981; mem. pres. commn. NCAA, 1991-94. Trustee Marygrove Coll., 1973-79. Am. Council Edn. fellow, 1967-68. Mem. AAAS, Am. Assn. State Colls. and Univs. (bd. dirs. 1992—, chair 1995), Am. Chem. Soc., Am. Assn. Higher Edn., Sigma Xi. Roman Catholic. Office: U Tenn Office of Chancellor 615 Mccallie Ave Chattanooga TN 37403-2504

OBENBERGER, THOMAS E., lawyer; b. Milwaukee, Wis., Nov. 29, 1942. AB, Marquette U., 1965, JD, 1967. Bar: Wis. 1967. Law clk. to Hon. E. Harold Hallows Wis. Supreme Ct., 1967-68; mem. Michael, Best & Friedrich, Milw. Mem. editorial bd. Marquette Law Rev., 1966-67. Mem. ABA. Office: Michael Best & Friedrich 100 E Wisconsin Ave Milwaukee WI 53202-4108*

OBENDORF, SHARON KAY, fiber science educator; b. Lewis, Kans., Nov. 25, 1939; d. Emery H. and Pauline (Mahan) Randel; m. Ralph L. Obendorf, Mar. 11, 1967; children: Michael, Kevin. BS, Kans. State U., 1962; MS, U. Ill., 1963, Cornell U., 1974; PhD, Cornell U., 1976. Instr. textiles and clothing Washington State U., Pullman, 1963-65; lab. technician U. Calif., Davis, 1965-66; asst. prof. textiles and clothing Cornell U., Ithaca, N.Y., 1966-71, lectr. design and environ. analysis, 1971, grad. rsch. asst. in chemistry, 1973-75, postdoctorate assoc. in biochemistry, 1975-78, assoc. prof. design and environ. analysis, 1978-85, prof. textiles and apparel, 1985—, chair dept., 1985-95; vis. asst. Inst. Cancer Rsch., Phial., 1972-73. Contbr. articles to profl. jours. Mem. ASTM, Internat. Textiles and Apparel Assn., Am. Chem. Soc., Am. Assn. Textile Chemists and Colorists, Am. Home Econs. Assn. (Manufactured Fiber award 1986), Fiber Soc. (lectr. 1985-86). Home: 24 Dart Dr Ithaca NY 14850-1111 Office: Cornell Univ 288 Van Rensselaer Hall Ithaca NY 14853-4401

OBER, DOUGLAS GARY, investment company executive; b. Balt., Apr. 15, 1946; s. Richard Francis and Caroline Fischer (Gary) O.; m. Rosina Bigham Huppman, July 17, 1971 (div. June 1986); children: Kenneth Houghton, Patrick Macgill; m. Francesmarie Kleinfelter, Aug. 2, 1986; children: William McDonald, Carlin DeLancey. BS in Engring., Princeton U., 1968; cert., U.S. Naval Test Pilot Sch., Patuxent River, Md., 1970; postgrad., Harvard U., 1971-72; M in Fin., Loyola Coll., Balt., 1979; cert., U. Pa., Phila., 1989. Chartered fin. analyst. Test project engr. U.S. Naval Air Test Ctr., Patuxent River, 1968-71; credit analyst First Nat. Bank of Md., Balt., 1972-78, v.p., 1978-80; securities analyst The Adams Express Co., Balt., 1980-86, exec. v.p., 1986-88, also bd. dirs., vice chmn., chief exec. officer, 1990-91, chmn., chief exec. officer, bd. dirs., 1991—; exec. v.p. Petroleum & Resources Corp., Balt., 1986-89, vice chmn., 1989-91, chmn., chief exec. officer, bd. dirs., 1991—; bd. govs. Investment Co. Inst., 1993—. Trustee Mary Byrd Wyman Meml. Assn., Balt. Mem. Princeton Alumni Assn. of

Md. (bd. dir. 1989—), N.Y. Soc. Security Analysts, Balt. Security Analysts Soc., Md. Club, Elkridge Club, Sky Club. Republican. Episcopalian. Avocations: skiing, sailing, model trains. Home: 1915 Old Court Rd Ruxton MD 21204-1851 Office: Adams Express Co 7 St Paul St Baltimore MD 21202-1626

OBER, ERIC W., broadcasting executive. BA, Yale U.; Woodrow Wilson Fellow, Columbia U. With CBS, 1966—; newswriter, producer, exec. producer, asst. news dir., WCBS-TV N.Y.C.; news dir., WCAU-TV, Phila.; news dir. WBBM-TV, Chgo.; v.p. news CBS TV stations, 1981-82; v.p., station mgr. WCBS-TV; v.p., gen. mgr. WBBM-TV Chgo., 1983-84; v.p. pub. affairs broadcasts CBS News, 1984-87; pres. CBS TV Stations, from 1987; now pres. CBS News Div. Served with U.S. Army. Office: CBS Inc 524 W 57th St New York NY 10019-2902

OBER, JOSIAH, history educator; b. Brunswick, Maine, Feb. 27, 1953; s. Nathaniel and Patricia Wilder (Stride) O. B.A., U. Minn., 1975, M.A., 1977; Ph.D., U. Mich., 1980. Asst. prof. history Mont. State U., Bozeman, 1980-84, assoc. prof., 1984-88, prof., 1988-90; prof. classics, Princeton U., 1990—; chmn. Dept. Classics, 1994—; vis. prof. U. Mich., Ann Arbor, 1986-87; sr. rsch. assoc. Am. Sch., Classical Studies, Athens, 1981, 83, 85, 88; vis. lectr. Archeol. Inst. Am., 1984-87; Martin Classical lctr. Oberlin Coll., 1994; Magie chair in Classics, 1994—; bd. dirs Princeton U. Press. Author: Fortress Attica, 1985, Mass and Elite in Democratic Athens, 1989, The Athenian Revolution, 1996. Contbr. articles to profl. jours. Grantee Am. Council Learned Socs., 1981, 89, NEH, 1981, 89, 96, Nat. Humanities Center N.C., 1983-84, Ctr. Hellenic Studies, 1989-90, Guggenheim Found., 1996. Mem. Archaeol. Inst. Am., Am. Philol. Assn. (bd. dirs.), Am. Sch. Classical Studies. Home: 55 Aiken Ave Princeton NJ 08540-5257 Office: Princeton U Dept Classics Princeton NJ 08544

OBER, RICHARD FRANCIS, JR., lawyer, banker; b. Balt., Dec. 12, 1943; s. Richard Francis and Caroline Fisher (Gary) O.; m. Carol Laycock Munger, Aug. 25, 1973; children: Julia Keyser, Margaret Delancey. A.B. cum laude, Princeton U., 1965; LL.B., Yale U., 1968. Bar: Md. 1968, Pa. 1970, N.J. 1977. Law clk. to chief judge Md. Ct. Apls., Annapolis, 1968; assoc. Ballard, Spahr, Andrews & Ingersoll, Phila., 1969-75; gen. counsel UJB Fin. Corp. Princeton, N.J., 1975—, sec., 1978—, sr. v.p., 1982-88, exec. v.p., 1988—; bd. dirs., sec. United Jersey Credit Life Ins. Co., UJB Credit Corp., N.J. Spl. Olympics; sec. United Jersey Bank, United Jersey Leasing Co., United Jersey Venture Capital, Inc.; fire commr. South Brunswick (N.J.) Fire Dist. 3, 1981-85; Republican county committeeman, 1975—; v.p. Republican Assn. Princeton; Princeton Day Sch., trustee, 1986-92, treas., 1988-92, vice chmn., 1990-92; trustee Yale Law Sch. Assn. N.J. Mem. ABA, Bank Corp. Counsel Com. (chmn. 1979-80), N.J. Bar Assn. (mem. gen. coun. 1982-85, 93-94, mem. exec. com. banking law sect. 1979-94, sec. sect. 1980-81, vice chmn. 1981-82, chmn. 1984-85), N.J. Corp. Counsel Assn. (exec. com. 1980—, 2d v.p. 1982-85, pres. 1985-86, chmn. banking and fin. instns. com. 1984-85), Am. Bankers Assn. (exec. com. bank counsel unit 1990—, vice chmn. 1993—, chmn. 1994-95), N.J. Bankers Assn. (chmn. bank lawyers coun. 1993-94), N.J. Bus. and Industry Assn. (legal affairs com.), Pa. Bankers Assn. (Legal Affairs com.), Phila. Bar Assn., Assn. Corp. Counsel Am., Princeton Bar Assn., Bankers Roundtable, Lawyers Coun. Episcopalian. Club: Bedens Brook (Princeton).

OBER, RUSSELL JOHN, JR., lawyer; b. Pitts., June 26, 1948; s. Russell J. and Marion C. (Hampson) O.; m. Kathleen A. Stein, Apr. 8, 1972; children: Lauren Elizabeth, Russell John III. BA, U. Pitts., 1970, JD, 1973. Bar: Pa. 1973, U.S. Dist. Ct. (we. dist.) Pa. 1973, U.S. Tax Ct. 1982, U.S. Ct. Appeals (4th cir.) 1976, U.S. Ct. Appeals (3d cir.) 1979, U.S. Ct. Appeals (D.C. cir.) 1985, U.S. Ct. Appeals (2d cir.), 1990, U.S. Ct. Appeals (7th cir.) 1993, U.S. Supreme Ct. 1976. Asst. dist. atty. Allegheny County, Pitts., 1973-75; ptnr. Wallace Chapas & Ober, Pitts., 1975-80, Rose, Schmidt, Hasley & DiSalle, Pitts., 1980-92, Meyer, Unkovic & Scott, Pitts., 1992—. Bd. dirs. Parent and Child Guidance Ctr., Pitts., 1983-90, treas., 1985-86, pres., 1986-88; bd. mgmt. South Hills Area YMCA, 1989-91; mem. Mt. Lebanon Traffic Commn., 1976-81; bd. dirs. Whale's Tale Youth Family Counseling Ctr., 1990-95. Mem. ABA (discovery com. litigation sect. 1982-88, ho. of dels. young lawyers div. 1982-83), Pa. Bar Assn. (ho. of dels. 1983—), Allegheny County Bar Assn. (chmn. young lawyers sect. 1983, bd. govs. 1984, fin. com. 1984-88, mem. coun. civil litigation sect. 1991-93), Nat. Bd. Trial Advocacy (diplomate), Acad. Lawyers Allegheny County (fellow 1983—, bd. govs. 1988-90) U. Pitts. Law Alumni Assn. (bd. govs. 1984-89, v.p. 1985-87, pres. 1987-88), Rivers Club, Chartiers Country Club. Home: 393 Parker Dr Pittsburgh PA 15216-1323 Office: Meyer Unkovic & Scott 1300 Oliver Bldg Pittsburgh PA 15222

OBER, STUART ALAN, investment consultant, book publisher; b. N.Y.C., Oct. 2, 1946; s. Paul and Gertrude E. (Stollerman) O.; m. Joanne Michaels, Sept. 20, 1981 (div. July 27, 1995); 1 child Erik Kenneth. BA, Wesleyan U., Middletown, Conn., 1968; postgrad., U. Sorbonne, Paris, 1970, CUNY, 1976-77. Pres., editor-in-chief, chmn. bd. Beekman Pubs. Inc., N.Y.C., 1972—; investment cons., 1972—; investment cons., expert witness Loeb, Rhoades & Co., 1976-77; div. dir. tax investment dept. Josephthal & Co., Inc., 1977; mgr. tax investment dept. Bruns, Nordeman, Rea & Co., 1978-80; pres. Ober Tax Investment Cons., 1980—, Securities Investigations, Inc., 1981—; sr. v.p. Cash Franchise Mgmt., Inc., 1988-89. Author: Everybody's Guide to Tax Shelters; editor-in-chief: Ober Income Letter, 1983-88; pub.: Tax Shelter Blue Book, 1983—. Bd. dirs., pres. Woodstock Playhouse Assn., 1985-87; trustee Maverick Concerts, 1986—; chmn. Woodstock Arts and Cultural Com., 1988. Mem. Inst. Cert. Fin. Planners (fin. standards product bd. 1986—, treas. 1988—, bd. dirs.). Office: PO Box 888 Woodstock NY 12498-0888

OBERDANK, LAWRENCE MARK, lawyer, arbitrator; b. Cleve., Nov. 1, 1935; s. Leonard John and Mary (Pavelich) O.; m. Arlene C. Baldini, Aug. 25, 1962; 1 child, Karen A. BA, Western Res. U., 1958, JD, 1965. Bar: Ohio 1965, U.S. Dist. Ct. (no. dist.) Ohio 1966, U.S. Ct. Appeals (6th cir.) 1968, U.S. Supreme Ct. 1970. Assoc. Law Offices Mortimer Riemer, Cleve., 1965-69; ptnr. Riemer and Oberdank, Cleve., 1969-76; prin. Lawrence M. Oberdank Co., L.P.A., Cleve., 1976—; arbitrator Ohio Employment Rels. Bd., 1985-89, Cleve. Civil Svc. Commn., 1983—, FMHA, 1989—; chmn. mandatory arbitration panel Ct. Common Pleas; mem. Nat. Mediation Bd., 1986—; instr. indsl. rels. law Cleve. State U., 1982-85; instr. labor rels. Cuyahoga C.C., 1983; arbitrator/mediator U.S. Dist. Ct. (no. dist.) Ohio, ea. divsn. fee dispute panel Cleve. Bar Assn.; mem. securities arbitration panel Am. Stock Exch., N.Y. Stock Exch., 1995—. Lt. USNR, 1958-62. Mem. ABA (labor and employment sect., labor arbitration, law collective bargaining agreements, alternate dispute resolution sect., fed. ct. annexed/connected programs com.), Am. Arbitration Assn. (securities arbitrator, nat. labor panel 1973—, comml. arbitration panel, nat. panel of employment arbitrators), Nat. Assn. Securities Dealers, Inc., Bar Assn. Greater Cleve. (labor law com.), Cuyahoga County Bar Assn., Fed. Bar Assn., Am. Judicature Soc., Internat. Soc. Labor Law and Social Legislation, Ohio State Bar Assn. (chmn. labor law sect. 1970-73), Indsl. Rels. Rsch. Assn., Pub. Sector Labor Rels. Assn., Soc. Profls. in Dispute Resolution (bd. dirs. Southwest Ohio chpt.), Masons, Phi Gamma Delta. Roman Catholic. Avocations: golf, Civil War history. Home: 8051 Lakeview Ct N Royalton OH 44133-1214 Office: Corporate Plaza I Ste 100 6450 Rockside Woods Blvd S Cleveland OH 44131

OBERDORFER, LOUIS F., federal judge; b. Birmingham, Ala., Feb. 21, 1919; s. A. Leo and Stella Maud (Falk) O.; m. Elizabeth Weil, July 31, 1941; children: John Louis, Kathryn Lee, Thomas Lee, William L. A.B., Dartmouth, 1939; LL.B., Yale, 1946. Bar: Ala. bar 1946, D.C. bar 1949. Law clk. to Justice Hugo L. Black, 1946-47; pvt. practice, 1947-51; mem. firm Wilmer, Cutler, & Pickering (and predecessors), 1951-61, 65-77; asst. atty. gen. tax div. Dept. of Justice, 1961-65; judge, now sr. judge U.S. Dist. Ct. (D.C. dist.), 1977—; vis. lectr. Yale Law Sch., 1966-71; adv. com. Fed. Rules Civil Procedure, 1962-84; co-chmn. lawyers com. Civil Rights Under Law, 1967-69; adj. prof. law Georgetown U., Washington, 1993—. Editor-in-chief Yale Law Jour., 1941. Served to capt. AUS, 1941-46. Mem. ABA, D.C. Bar Assn. (bd. govs. 1972-77, pres. 1977), Ala. Bar Assns., Am. Law Inst., Yale Law Sch. Assn. (pres. 1971-73). Office: US Dist Ct US Courthouse 3d and Constitution Ave NW Washington DC 20001

OBERG, LARRY REYNOLD, librarian; b. Midvale, Idaho; s. Gustav Wilhelm and Esther Marie (Watkins) O.; m. Marilyn Ann Gow, Jan. 1, 1964 (div. 1985); 1 child, Marc Aurelien. AB in Anthropology, U. Calif., Berkeley, 1977, MLS, 1978. Reference librarian Stanford (Calif.) U., 1979-80, U. Calif., Berkeley, 1981-82; dir. library Lewis-Clark State Coll., Lewiston, Idaho, 1984-86, Albion (Mich.) Coll., 1986-92; univ. libr. Willamette U., Salem, Oreg., 1993—. Author: Human Services in Postrevolutionary Cuba, 1985 (named a Choice Outstanding Acad. Book, Choice Editors 1984-85); mem. editl. bd. College and Research Libraries; mem. adv. bd. Jour. Info. Ethics; contbr. articles to profl. jours. Mem. Am. Library Assn., Oreg. Library Assn., Phi Beta Kappa. Democrat. Office: Willamette U Mark O Hatfield Libr 900 State St Salem OR 97301

OBERG, ROGER WINSTON, management educator; b. Mpls., Oct. 5, 1919; s. Ezra Nathaniel and Adele Erika Wilhelmina (Boquist) O.; m. Pansy Jane Sherrill, June 29, 1957; children: Sherrill Katherine, Roger Winston, Keith Eric, Elizabeth Jane. Student, North Park Coll., 1937-38; B.B.A. with distinction, U. Minn., 1941; M.B.A., Ohio State U., 1947; Ph.D., M.I.T., 1955. Mgmt. trainee Sears Roebuck & Co., 1941-43; grad. asst. Ohio State U., 1946-47, M.I.T., 1947-50; human relations research analyst Prudential Ins. Co., Newark, 1950-51; personnel specialist Esso Research & Engring. Co., Linden, N.J., 1952-57; assoc. prof. mgmt. Mich. State U., 1957-65, prof. mgmt., 1965-86, prof. emeritus, 1986—; vis. prof. Leeds U., Eng., 1959, U. Rio Grande do Sul, Brazil, 1959-61, Stanford U., 1964, North European Mgmt. Inst., Norway, 1974-76; World Bank cons. to Bangladesh univs., 1985. Served to 2d lt. USAAF, 1943-46, PTO. Recipient Forensic medal U. Minn., 1941, Lit. Rev. prize, 1941. Mem. Beta Gamma Sigma, Delta Sigma Rho. Mem. Evangelical Covenant Ch. Clubs: University (Mich. State U.), Scandinavian Am. Home: 1585 Hillside Dr Okemos MI 48864-2319

OBERHELMAN, HARRY ALVIN, JR., surgeon, educator; b. Chgo., Nov. 15, 1923; s. Harry Alvin and Beatrice (Babel) O.; m. Betty Jane Porter, June 12, 1946; children: Harry Alvin III, James I., Robert P., Thomas L., Nancy L. Student, Yale U., 1942-43; B.S., U. Chgo., 1946, M.D., 1947. Diplomate: Am. Bd. Surgery. Intern U. Chgo. Clinics, 1947-48, resident in surgery, 1948-51, 52-57; asst. prof., then assoc. prof. surgery U. Chgo. Sch. Medicine, 1957-60; mem. faculty Stanford (Calif.) Sch. Medicine, 1960—, prof. surgery, 1964-95, prof. emeritus, 1995—; mem. div. licensing Calif. Bd. Med. Quality Assurance, 1970-82. Author papers in field. Served with USAF, 1951-53. Mem. AMA, Calif. Med. Assn., Soc. Univ. Surgeons, Am., Western, Pacific Coast surg. assns., Soc. Alimentary Tract, Halsted Soc., Fedn. State Med. Bds. U.S. (bd. dirs. 1979-82). Home: 668 Cabrillo St Stanford CA 94305-8404

OBERHUBER, KONRAD JOHANNES, art museum curator, educator; b. Linz/Donau, Austria, Mar. 31, 1935. Ph.D., U. Vienna, Austria, 1959, Dozent, 1971. Asst. U. Vienna; delegated as research fellow to Austrian Inst. in Rome, 1959-61; asst., then curator Albertina, Vienna, 1961-71; research curator Nat. Gallery Art, Washington, 1971-74; guest lectr. Fogg Art Mus., Harvard U., Cambridge, Mass., spring 1974; curator of drawings, prof. fine arts Fogg Art Mus., Harvard U., 1974-85, Ian Woodner curator of drawings, prof. fine arts, 1985-87; dir. Graphische Sammlung Albertina, Vienna, 1987—; T.A.O. prof. U. Vienna, 1991; Italian Ministry of Culture scholar, Rome, winter 1958; asst. prof. Smith Coll., 1964-65; Kress fellow Harvard Center for Renaissance Studies, Florence, Italy, 1965-66; guest prof. Cambridge (Eng.) U., 1968. Author: Raphael, Die Zeichnungen, 1983, Poussin, The Early Years in Rome, 1988; contbr. articles to profl. jours. fellow Inst. Advanced Study Princeton, N.J., 1974-75; Nat. Endowment Humanities grantee, 1979-80; Gerda Henkel Stiftung grantee, 1983-84. Office: Graphische Sammlung Albertina, Augustinerstrasse 1, A-1010 Vienna Austria

OBERLANDER, CORNELIA HAHN, landscape architect; b. Muelheim-Ruhr, Germany, June 20, 1924; arrived in U.S., 1939; d. Franz and Lotte Beate (Jastrow) H.; m. H. Peter Oberlander, Jan. 2, 1953; children: Judith A., Timothy A., Wendy E. BA, Smith Coll., 1944; B of Landscape Architecture, Harvard U., 1947; LLD (hon.), U. British Columbia, 1991. guest prof. U. B.C. Dept. Landscape Architecture, 1992; lectr. for guided tour Renaissance Gardens of No. Italy, Smith Coll. Alumni Assn., 1988; mem. adv. com. on design Nat. Capital Commn., 1975-82; mem. adv. panel, co-founder Children's Play Resource Centre, Vancouver, 1978—; lectr. in field. Prin. works include Cathedral Place, Vancouver, B.C., 1991-93, New Pub. Library, 1992—, Asian Inst., U. B.C., 1993—, Thunderbird Housing, U. B.C., 1992—, Chan Shun Performing Arts Centre, 1992—, Kwantlen Coll., 1991—, Cariboo Coll., 1991—, N.W. Territories Legis. Bldg., 1991—, UN Peacekeeping Meml., 1990—, Ritsumeikan U. B.C. Ho., 1990—, Ottawa City Hall, 1989—, Environ. Sci. Bd., Ward Environ. Garden, Trent U., 1989—, Canadian Chancery, Washington D.C., 1983-89. Recipient medal Smith Coll., 1982, Regional Honor award and Nat. Merit award Christopher Phillips Landcape Architects, Inc., 1992, Cathedral Place, 1983-88, Nat. Gallery of Can., Ottawa, Ontario, Can. Chancery Am. Assn. of Nurserymen, 1990, Grand award for L'Ambassade du Can., Landscape Contractors Assn., 1989, Can. Architect award of Excellence, Matsuzaki Wright Architects, Inc., 1989, Amenity award City of Vancouver for Robson Square, 1986, Citation award Can. Soc. of Architects for Chancery & Nat. Gallery, 1990. Fellow Am. Soc. Landscape Architects, Can. Soc. Landscape Architects (pres. 1986-87, pres. elect. 1985-86, chair environ. com. 1987-88, Internat. Citation award 1991, Nat. and Regional Citation award 1989); mem. Order of Can., Royal Can. Acad. Arts. Home: 1372 Acadia Rd, Vancouver, BC Canada V6T 1P6

OBERLANDER, HERBERT, insect physiologist, educator; b. Manchester, N.H., Oct. 2, 1939 s. Solomon and Minnie (Shapiro) O.; m. Barbara Judith Marks, June 12, 1962; children: Jonathan, Beth. BA cum laude in Zoology, U. Conn., 1961; PhD in Biology, Western Res. U., 1965. Postdoctoral fellow U. Zurich (Switzerland), 1965-66; asst. prof. Brandeis U., Waltham, Mass., 1966-71; rsch. physiologist USDA, Agrl. Rsch. Svc., Gainesville, Fla., 1971-76, rsch. leader, physiology unit, insect attractants lab., 1976-84, lab. dir. insect attractants, behavior and basic biology rsch. lab., Gainesville, 1984—; prof. entomology U. Fla., Gainesville, 1979—. NSF fellow, 1961-65; NIH fellow, 1965-66; NSF Research grantee, 1966-71, 83; grantee U.S.-Israel BARD, 1989-93. Fellow Entomol. Soc. Am. (Founders' Meml. award 1995); mem. Tissue Culture Assn., Entomol. Soc. Am. (Founders Award, 1995), Phi Beta Kappa, Sigma Xi, Phi Kappa Phi. Contbr. chpts. to books, articles to profl. jours. Office: USDA Insect Attractant Behav Lab PO Box 14565 1700 SW 23rd Dr Gainesville FL 32604-2565

OBERLANDER, RONALD Y., paper manufacturing company executive. Past exec. v.p. Abitibi-Price Inc., Toronto, Ont., Can., now pres. and CEO. *

OBERLIES, JOHN WILLIAM, physician organization executive; b. Rochester, N.Y., June 9, 1939; s. Hubert H. and Martha (Voght) O.; m. Mary Theresa Sundholm, Sept. 29, 1962; children: Katie, Daniel. BCE, Villanova U., 1961; MBA, U. Rochester, 1978. From surveyor to purchasing agt. Rochester Gas & Electric Co., 1959-79, gen. mgr., 1979-82, v.p., 1982-87, sr. v.p., 1988-90; chief ops. officer Le Chase Constrn., Inc., Rochester, 1990-95; COO Rochester Individual Practice Assn. Inc., 1995—; bd. dirs. Transmation, Inc. Trustee Aquinas Inst., Rochester, 1986-93; bd. dirs. Cath. Charities, Rochester, 1984-85; chmn. bd. Preferred Care, Inc., Rochester, 1986-90; mem. Diocesan Pastoral Coun., Health Futures of Rochester Commn.; bd. dirs. Rochester Area Found., 1984-85, Highland Hosp.; chmn. nominations com. United Way, Rochester; mem. Rochester Housing Partnership Commn. With U.S. Army, 1961-62. Mem. Rochester C. of C. (chmn. polit. action com. 1987). Republican. Avocation: fishing. Home: 242 Shoreham Dr Rochester NY 14618-4112 Office: Rochester Individual Practice Assn Inc 2000 Winton Rd S Rochester NY 14618

OBERLY, CHARLES MONROE, III, lawyer, former attorney general; b. Wilmington, Del., Nov. 9, 1946; s. Charles M. and Prudence Elizabeth (Curry) O.; children: Kimberly, Michael and Kristi-Lyn (twins). AA, Wesley Coll., 1966; BAA, Pa. State U., 1968; JD, U. Va., 1971. Bar: Del. Clk. U.S. Dist. Ct., 1971-72; assoc. Morris James Hitchens & Williams, Wilmington, Del., 1972-75; dep. atty. gen. Del. Dept. Justice, 1974-82, state prosecutor, 1976-78; atty. gen. State of Del., Wilmington, 1982-96; individual practice law, 1996—; instr. U. Del. Mem. Phi Beta Kappa, Phi Kappa Phi. Democrat. Lutheran. Office: Office of Atty Gen Justice Dept 820 N French St Wilmington DE 19801-3509

OBERMAN, MICHAEL STEWART, lawyer; b. Bklyn., May 21, 1947; s. Hyman Martin and Gertrude O.; m. Sharon Land, Oct. 8, 1975; 1 child, Abigail Land. AB, Columbia U., 1969; JD, Harvard U., 1972. Bar: N.Y. 1973, U.S. Dist. Ct. (so. and ea. dists.) N.Y. 1973, U.S. Ct. Appeals (2d cir.) 1973, U.S. Supreme Ct. 1976, Calif. 1981, U.S. Dist. Ct. (no. dist.) Calif. 1981, U.S. Ct. Appeals (9th cir.) 1981, U.S. Dist. Ct. (so. and cen. dists.) Calif. 1982, U.S. Ct. Appeals (5th cir.) 1989, D.C. 1992, U.S. Ct. Appeals (7th cir.) 1993. Law clk. to Hon. Milton Pollack U.S. Dist. Ct. (so. dist.) N.Y., 1972-73; assoc. Kramer, Levin, Naftalis & Frankel, N.Y.C., 1973-79; ptnr. Kramer, Levin, Naftalis, Nessen, Kamin & Frankel, N.Y.C., 1980—. Contbr. articles to profl. jours. Recipient Nathan Burkan prize ASCAP, 1973. Mem. N.Y. State Bar Assn. (mem. ho. of dels. 1989-91, exec. com. comml. and fed. litigation sect.). Office: Kramer Levin Naftalis & Frankel 919 3rd Ave New York NY 10022

OBERMAN, SHELDON ARNOLD, writer, educator; b. Winnipeg, Manitoba, Canada, May 20, 1949; s. Allan and Dorothy (Stein) O.; m. Lee Anne Block, Sept. 8, 1973 (div. Mar. 9, 1990); children: Adam, Mira; m. Lisa Ann Dveris, Sept. 2, 1990; 1 child: Jesse. BA in English, U. Winnipeg, Man., Can., 1972; BA in English with honors, U. Jerusalem, Israel, 1973; teaching cert., U. Man., Winnipeg, Can., 1974. tchr. W. C. Millar Collegiate, Altona, Man., Can., 1975-76, Joseph Wolinsky Collegiate, Winnipeg, Man., Can., 1976-95. Author: The Folk Festival Book, 1983, Lion in the Lake: A French English Alphabet Book, 1988, Julie Gerond and the Polka Dot Pony, 1988, TV Sal and the Game Show From Outer Space, 1993, This Business With Elijah, 1993, The Always Prayer Shawl, 1994, The White Stone in the Castle Wall, 1995; co-editor: A Mirror of a People: The Canadian Jewish Experience in Poetry and Prose, 1985. Nat. Jewish Book award Jewish Book Coun., 1995, Sydney Taylor award, 1995, Best Book of the Yr. A Child's Mag., 1994, Pick of the List award Am. Bookseller, 1994, Can. Author Short Story award Canadian Author's Assn., 1987; Bliss Carmen Poetry prize Banff Sch. of Fine Arts, 1980; various writer and film maker grants. Avocations: public address, acting, collage sculptor, canoeing. Home: 822 Dorchester Ave, Winnipeg, MB Canada R3M 0R7

OBERMAN, STEVEN, lawyer; b. St. Louis, Sept. 21, 1955; s. Albert and Marian (Kleg) O.; m. Evelyn Ann Simpson, Aug. 27, 1977; children: Rachael Diane, Benjamin Scott. BA in Psychology, Auburn U., 1977; JD, U. Tenn., 1980. Bar: Tenn. 1980, Tenn. Supreme Ct. 1980, Tenn. Criminal Ct. Appeals 1980, U.S. Dist. Ct. (ea. dist.) Tenn. 1980, U.S. Ct. Appeals (4th cir.) 1981, U.S. Ct. Appeals (6th cir.) 1983, U.S. Supreme Ct. 1985. Law clk. Daniel, Duncan & Claiborne, Knoxville, Tenn., 1978-80; assoc. Daniel, Claiborne & Lewallen, Knoxville, Tenn., 1980-82; ptnr. Daniel, Claiborne, Oberman & Buuck, Knoxville, 1983-85, Daniel & Oberman, Knoxville, 1986—; pres., Project First Offender, Knoxville, 1983-86;bd. dirs. Fed. Defender Svcs. Eastern Tenn., Inc., v.p. 1994-95; guest instr. U. Tenn. 1988-90; guest lectr. U. Tenn. Law Sch., 1982-88; guest instr. U. Tenn. Grad. Sch. Criminal Justice Program, 1983, 84; guest speaker Ct. Clk's Meeting, Cambridge, Eng., 1984; instr. legal clinic , trial advocacy program U. Tenn., 1987-88; adj. prof. U. Tenn. Law Sch., 1993— (Forrest W. Lacey award for outstanding faculty contbn. to U. Tenn. Coll. Law Moot Ct. Program, 1993-94; coach U. Tenn. Law Sch. Nat. Trial Team, 1991—; spl. judge Criminal Divsn. Knox County Gen. Sessions Court; founding mem. Nat. Coll. for DUI Def.; speaker in field. Author: D.U.I.: The Crime and Consequences in Tennessee, 1991, supplemented annually; co-author: D.W.I. Means Defend With Ingenuity, 1987; contbr. legal articles on drunk driving to profl. jours. Bd. dirs. Knoxville Legal Aid Soc., Inc., 1986-88 (pres. 1990), Arnstein Jewish Community Ctr., 1987-91, pres. 1990; bd. dirs. Knoxville Racquet Club, 1991-93, pres. 1992-93. Col. Aide de Camp Tenn. Gov.'s Staff, 1983, Moot Ct. Bd. Spl. Svc. award, 1995-96. Mem. ABA, ATLA, Nat. Assn. Criminal Def. Lawyers (co-chair DUI advocacy com. 1995-96), Tenn. Assn. Criminal Def. Lawyers (bd. dirs. 1983-89), Knoxville Bar ASsn. Jewish. Office: Daniel & Oberman 550 W Main St Ste 950 Knoxville TN 37902-2567

OBERMANN, RICHARD MICHAEL, governmental technology and policy analyst; b. May 21, 1949; s. Baird J. and Phyllis L. (Weber) O. BS of Engring. in Aerospace and Mech. Scis. cum laude, Princeton U., 1971, PhD in Engring., Aerospace and Mech. Scis., 1977; MS of Engring. in Astronautics and Aeros., Stanford U., 1972; postgrad., Va. Poly. Inst. and State U., Am. U. With MITRE Corp., McLean, Va., 1977-88, engr. transp. systems analysis, transp. energy analysis, telecommunications, project leader, mem. tech. staff in communications and system design; sr. staff officer aeros. and space engring. bd. NRC, Washington, 1988-90, study dir. and analyst technol. and policy issues; mem. profl. staff for space subcom. U.S. Ho. of Reps. Com. on Sci., Space and Tech., Washington, 1990-95; minority staff dir., space subcom. U.S. House of Reps. Com. on Sci., Washington, 1995—. Author tech. papers and presentations. Fellow AIAA (assoc.), Brit. Interplanetary Soc.; mem. N.Y. Acad. Scis., IEEE, Internat. Inst. Communications, Japan-Am. Soc., Asia Soc., Am. Astronaut. Soc. (v.p.), Nat. Space Club, Pacific Telecommunications Coun., Women in Aerospace (bd. dirs.). Avocations: Japanese, Chinese and Spanish langs., sports, trumpet.

OBERNAUER, MARNE, corporate executive; b. Pitts., Mar. 6, 1919; s. Arthur H. and Anna (Somerman) O.; m. Joan Strassburger, Aug. 1, 1941; children: Marne Jr., Wendy Damon. Grad., Cornell U., 1941. Chmn. exec. com. Devon Group, Inc., Stamford, Conn.; chmn. Beverage Distbrs. Corp. and BDH Inc., Aurora, Colo.; pres. Doric Securities Co.; bus. cons., pvt. investor. Pres., bd. dirs. The Obernauer Found., Inc. Served to lt. USNR, 1942-45. Mem. Hillcrest Country Club (L.A.), Concordia Club (Pitts.), Century Country Club (Purchase, N.Y.), Banyan Golf Club (Palm Beach, Fla.). Office: Devon Group Inc 281 Tresser Blvd #501 Stamford CT 06901-3227

OBERNAUER, MARNE, JR., business executive; b. Lakehurst, N.J., July 1, 1943; s. Marne and Joan Carolyn (Strassburger) O.; m. Marion Fleck Gislason, Aug. 22, 1976 (dec. Jan. 1996); children: Matthew Gene, Michael Sidney. BA, Yale U., 1965; MBA, Harvard U., 1972. With First Nat. City Bank (Citibank, N.A.), N.Y.C., 1965-70, Donaldson, Lufkin & Jenrette, N.Y.C., 1972-74; with Devon Group, Inc., N.Y.C. and Stamford, Conn., 1974—, pres., 1978, chief exec. officer, 1980—, chmn. bd., 1986—; bd. dirs. Devon Group Inc., Beverage Distbrs. Corp. Trustee Trinity Sch., The Obernauer Found., Inc.; bd. dirs. Com. for Responsible Fed. Budget, Assocs. of Harvard Bus. Sch. Mem. Am. Bus. Conf. (bd. dirs., vice chmn.), Yale Club of N.Y.C. Office: Devon Group Inc 450 Park Ave New York NY 10022-2605

OBERNDORF, MEYERA E., mayor; m. Roger L. Oberndorf; children: Marcie, Heide. BS in Elem. Edn., Old Dominion U., 1964. Broadcaster Sta. WNIS, Norfolk, Va.; mem. city coun. City of Virginia Beach, Va., 1976—, vice-mayor, 1986, mayor, 1988—. Mem. exec. bd. Tidewater coun. Boys Scouts Am.; bd. dirs. Virginia Beach Pub. Libr., 1966-76, chmn. bd., 1967-76. Mem. AAUW, U.S. Conf. Mayors, Va. Mcpl. League (exec. bd.), Nat. League Cities (vice-chmn.), Princess Anne Women's Club. Jewish. Home: 5404 Challedon Dr Virginia Beach VA 23462-4112 Office: Office of the Mayor Municipal Ctr City Hall Bldg Virginia Beach VA 23456*

OBERNE, SHARON BROWN, elementary education educator; b. Lakeland, Fla., Sept. 2, 1955; d. Morris C. and Amy (Beecroft) Brown; m. Ronald Allan Oberne, Mar. 29, 1980; children: Laura, Aaron, Kelley. AA in Pre-tchg., Hillsborough C.C., Tampa, Fla., 1975; BA in Elem. Edn., U. South Fla., 1976, cert., 1980, AA in Acctg., 1980. Cert. tchr. K-8. 3rd grade tchr. Zolfo Springs Elem., Wauchula, Fla., 1976-77, 2nd grade tchr., 1977-79; 1st grade tchr. Westgate Christian Sch., Tampa, Fla., 1979-80; 5th grade tchr. Pasoc Elem., Dade City, Fla., 1980-81; 3rd grade tchr. San Antonio Elem., Dade City, 1981-86; temporary reading tchr. Chesterfield Heights Elem., Norfolk, Va., 1986-87; 2nd grade tchr. Ocean View Elem., Norfolk, 1987—; dir. Ocean View Writing Club, Norfolk, 1992—. Author: Pink Monkey, 1994, Space Traveler, 1995, Daisy Dolphin (Spelling in Context). Pres. USS Guam's Wife's Club, Norfolk Naval Base, 1990-91; amb. of goodwill USS Guam, 1990-91; founder AmeriKids of Ocean View, Norfolk, 1991-93; liaison Adopt-A-Sch. Program, Norfolk, 1991—. Recipient Good Neighbor award NEA, 1994. Mem. Norfolk Reading Coun., Nat. Autism Soc.,

CHADD. Avocations: writing, reading, swimming, walking. Home: 8243 Briarwood Cir Norfolk VA 23518-2862

OBERREIT, WALTER WILLIAM, lawyer; b. Paterson, N.J., Oct. 7, 1928; s. William and Gertrud (Limpert) O.; m. Anne-Marie Gohier, July 6, 1955; children: Stephan, Alexis, Jerome. BA, U. Mich., 1951; diploma, U. Paris Inst. Polit. Studies, 1955; JD, Yale U., 1958. Bar: N.Y. Assoc. Cleary, Gottlieb, Steen & Hamilton, N.Y.C., 1958-62, Paris, 1962-66; assoc. Cleary, Gottlieb, Steen & Hamilton, Brussels, 1966-67, ptnr., 1967—. Contbr. articles to profl. jours., chpts. to books. Lt. (j.g.) USN, 1953-55. Mem. ABA, Assn. of Bar of City of N.Y. (co-chmn. com. on rels. with European Bars 1981—), Am. Arbitration Assn., Ctr. European Policy Studies, Inst. Royal Rels. Internat., Union Internat. Des Avocats. Clubs: Cercle Royal Gaulois, Cercle Nations, Am. Common Market (Brussels). Avocations: sailing, tennis, skiing. Home: Ave Geo Bernier 7, 1050 Brussels Belgium Office: Cleary Gottlieb Steen & Hamilton, rue de la Loi 23, 1040 Brussels Belgium

O'BERRY, CARL GERALD, air force officer, electrical engineer; b. Lansing, Mich., Apr. 11, 1936; s. Gerald Ray and Edith Lenore (Watson) O'B.; m. Charlene Marice Bussche, June 21, 1958; children: Brian, Eileen, Kevin, Bradley, Kathleen. BSEE, N.Mex. State U., 1972; MS in Systems Mgmt., Air Force Inst. Tech., 1977. Commd. 2d lt. USAF, 1961, advanced through grades to lt. gen., 1993; comdr. 2019 Communications Squadron, Griffiss AFB, N.Y., 1974-76; project engr. Rome Air Devel. Ctr., Griffiss AFB, 1978-81; asst. dep. chief of staff requirements Air Force Systems Command, Andrews AFB, Md., 1982-84; comdr. Rome Air Devel. Ctr., Griffiss AFB, 1984-86; joint program mgr. WWMCCS info. system Hdqrs. USAF, Washington, 1986-88; dir. command, control and communications U.S. European Command, Stuttgart, Fed. Republic Germany, 1988-90; dir. command control systems and logistics U.S. Space Command, Peterson AFB, Colo., 1990-92; command control comm. and computers DCS, HQ USAF, Washington, 1992-95; v.p., dir. strategic planning Motorola Govt. & Space Tech. Group, Scottsdale, Ariz., 1995—; v.p. Motorola, Inc. Mem. Air Force Assn., Armed Forces Communications-Electronics Assn., Soc. Logistics Engrs. Roman Catholic.

O'BERRY, PHILLIP AARON, veterinarian; b. Tampa, Fla., Feb. 1, 1933; s. Luther Lee and Marjorie Mae (Mahlum) O'B.; m. Terri Martin, July 31, 1960; children: Kelly, Eric, Holly, Danny, Andy, Toby, Michael Asefa. BS in Agr., U. Fla., 1955; DVM, Auburn U., 1960; PhD, Iowa State U., 1967. With Agrl. Rsch. Svc. USDA, 1956—; asst. to dir. vet. scis. rsch. div. USDA, Beltsville, Md., 1967-72; asst. dir. Nat. Animal Disease Ctr., Ames, Iowa, 1972-73, dir., 1973-88, nat. tech. transfer coord., 1988—; prin. scientist Office Agr. Biotech., USDA, 1988-90; adj. prof. Coll. Vet. Medicine, Iowa State U., 1973—; mem. expert panel livestock infertility FAO; sci. adv. com. Pan Am. Zoonosis Ctr., Buenos Aires; mem. Fed. Coun. Sci. and Tech.; mem. com. animal health, world food and nutrition study NRC; cons. Govt. of Italy, USDA; mem. nat needs grad. fellowship rev. panel USDA, 1989-91, cons. agr. biotech. rsch. adv. com.; mem. sci. adv. bd. Biotech. R&D Corp., 1992—, sci. review bd. Am. Jour. Vet. Rsch., 1990-92; mem. USDA Patent Review Com., 1988—. Author 27 research publs. Recipient Cert. of Merit, Agrl. Rsch. Svc., 1972, 84, Alumni Merit award Iowa State Club of Chgo., 1982, Cert. Appreciation, 1988, Tech. Transfer award 1989, USDA Disting. Alumnus award Auburn U., 1991; named Hon. Diplomate Am. Coll. of Vet. Microbiologists, 1995. Mem. APHA, AVMA, AAAS, Nat. Assn. Fed. Vets., Iowa Vet. Med. Assn., N.Y. Acad. Scis., Conf. Rsch. Workers Animal Diseases, Am. Soc. Microbiology, Am. Assn. Lab. Animal Sci., U.s. Animal Health Assn., Am. Assn. Bovine Practitioners, Livestock Cons. Inst., Sigma Xi, Phi Zeta, Phi Kappa Phi, Gamma Sigma Delta (Alumni award Merit 1976), Alpha Zeta, Spades, Blue Key. Democrat. Home: 3319 Woodland St Ames IA 50014-3550 Office: Nat Soil Tilth Lab Rm 114 Ames IA 50011

OBERSTAR, JAMES L., congressman; b. Chisholm, Minn., Sept. 10, 1934; s. Louis and Mary (Grillo) O.; m. Jo Garlick, Oct. 12, 1963 (dec. July 1991); children: Thomas Edward, Katherine Noelle, Anne-Therese, Monica Rose; m. Jean Kurth, Nov. 1993; stepchildren: Corinne Quinlan Kurth, Charles Burke Kurth, Jr. B.A. summa cum laude, St. Thomas Coll., 1956; postgrad. in French, Laval U., Que., Can.; M.S. in Govt. (scholar), Coll. Europe, Bruges, Belgium, 1957; postgrad. in govt, Georgetown U. Adminstrv. asst. Congressman John A. Blatnik, 1963-74; adminstr. Pub. Works Com. U.S. Ho. of Reps., 1971-74; mem. 94th-104th Congresses from 8th Minn. Dist., 1975—; ranking minority mem. transp. and infrastructure subcom. on aviation. Mem. Am. Polit. Sci. Assn. Office: US Ho of Reps 2366 Rayburn HOB Washington DC 20515-2308*

OBERSTEIN, MARYDALE, geriatric specialist; b. Red Wing, Minn., Dec. 30; d. Dale Robert and Jean Ebba-Marie (Holmquist) Johnson; children: Kirk Robert, Mark Paul, MaryJean. Student, U. Oreg., 1961-62, Portland State U., 1962-64, Long Beach State U., 1974-76. Cert. geriatric specialist, Calif. Florist, owner Sunshine Flowers, Santa Ana, Calif., 1982—; pvt. duty nurse Aides in Action, Costa Mesa, Calif., 1985-87; owner, activity dir., adminstr. Lovelight Christian Home for the Elderly, Santa Ana, 1987—; activity dir. Bristol Care Nursing Home, Santa Ana, 1985-88; evangelist, speaker radio show Sta. KPRZ-FM, Anaheim, Calif., 1985-88; adminstr. Leisure Lodge Resort Care for Elderly in Lake Forest, Lake Forest; nursing home activist in reforming laws to eliminate bad homes, 1984-90; founder, tchr. hugging classes/laughter therapy terminally ill patients, 1987—; founder healing and touch therapy laughter Therapy, 1991-93; bd. dirs. Performing Arts Ctr.; speaker for enlightenment and healing. Author (rewrite) Title 22 Nursing Home Reform Law, Little Hoover Commn.; model, actress and voiceovers. Bd. dirs. Orange County Coun. on Aging, 1984—; chairperson Helping Hands, 1985—, Pat Robertson Com., 1988, George Bush Presdl. Campaign, Orange County, 1988; bd. dirs., v.p. Women Aglow Orange County, 1985—; evanglist, pub. spkr., v.p. Women Aglow Huntington Beach; active with laughter therapy and hugging classes for terminally ill. Recipient Carnation Silver Bowl, Carnation Svc. Co., 1984-85, Gold medal Pres. Clinton; named Woman of Yr., Kiwanis, 1985, ABI, 1990, Am. Biog. Soc., Woman of Decade; honored AM L.A. TV Show, Lt. Gov. McCarthy, 1984. Mem. Calif. Assn. Residential Care Homes, Orange County Epilepsy Soc. (bd. dirs. 1986—), Calif. Assn. Long Term Facilities. Home: 2722 S Diamond St Santa Ana CA 92704-6013

OBERT, CHARLES FRANK, banker; b. Cleve., Apr. 28, 1937; s. Carl William and Irene Frances (Urban) O.; m. Linda Marie Thoss, June 3, 1961; children—Lisa Marie, Charles David. Student, Ohio State U., 1955-57. With Ameritrust Corp., Cleve., 1958—, sr. v.p. affiliate bank div., 1975-80, sr. v.p. corp. service div., 1980-87, sr. v.p. br. adminstrn., 1987-92, mgmt. cons., 1993—; pres. Acoustical Cleaning Systems Inc. Mem. Solon (Ohio) Recreation Commn., 1978-94, Solon Bd. Edn., 1986-94. Mem. Am. Inst. Banking, Am. Bankers Assn., Ohio Bankers Assn., Bank Adminstrn. Inst., Internat. Assn. Laryngectomees, Cleve. Hearing and Speech Ctr., Greater Cleve. Growth Assn., Solon C. of C. Home and Office: 8270 Pebble Creek Ct Chagrin Falls OH 44023-4866

OBERT, PAUL RICHARD, manufacturing company executive, lawyer; b. Pitts., Aug. 24, 1928; s. Edgar F. and Elizabeth T. (Buchele) O. B.S., Georgetown U., 1950; J.D., U. Pitts., 1953. Bar: Pa. 1954, D.C. 1956, Ohio 1972, Ill. 1974, U.S. Supreme Ct. 1970. Sole practice Pitts., 1954-60; asst. counsel H.K. Porter Co., Inc., Pitts., 1960-62, sec., gen. counsel, 1962-71; sec., gen. counsel Addressograph-Multigraph Corp., Cleve., 1972-74; v.p. law Marshall Field & Co., Chgo., 1974-82, sec., 1976-82; v.p., gen. counsel, sec. CF Industries, Inc., Long Grove, Ill., 1982—, also officer, dir. various subs. Served to lt. col. USAF. Mem. ABA (corp. gen. counsel com.), Pa. Bar Assn., Allegheny County Bar Assn., Ill. Bar Assn., Chgo. Bar Assn., Am. Soc. Corp. Secs., Am. Retail Fedn. (bd. dirs. 1977-80), Georgetown U. Alumni Assn. (bd. govs.), Pitts. Athletic Assn., Univ. Club (Chgo.), Delta Theta Phi. Office: CF Industries Inc 1 Salem Lake Dr Long Grove IL 60047-8401

OBEY, DAVID ROSS, congressman; b. Okmulgee, Okla., Oct. 3, 1938; s. Orville John and Mary Jane (Chellis) O.; m. Joan Therese Lepinski, June 9, 1962; children: Craig David, Douglas David. BS in Polit. Sci, U. Wis., 1960, MA, 1962. Mem. Wis. Gen. Assembly, 1963-69, asst. minority leader, 1967-69; mem. 91st-104th Congresses from 7th Wis. dist., 1969—; ranking minority mem. appropriations com., ranking minority mem. labor, HHS and edn. subcom., mem. joint econ. com.; mem. adminstrv. com. Wis. Dem. Com., 1960-62. Named Edn. Legislator of Yr., Rural div. NEA, 1968; recipient Legislative Leadership award Eagelton Inst. Politics, 1964, award of merit Nat. Council Sr. Citizens, 1976, citation for legis. statesmanship Council Exceptional Children, 1976. Office: US Ho of Reps 2462 Rayburn HOB Washington DC 20515*

OBIORA, CHRIS SUNNY, architect; b. Lagos, Nigeria, Sept. 2, 1954; came to U.S., 1978; s. Patrick M. and Virginia E. Obiora. Diploma, Christ the King Coll., Onitsha, Anambra, 1974; student, Tex. A&M U., 1986, Coll. Profl. Mgmt., Lintas, Lagos, 1992. Accounts clk. Lintas, Ltd., Lagos, 1976-78, media accounts clk., 1977-78; with San Jacinto Jr. Coll., Houston, Tex., 1980-81; The Wacherhit Corp., Coral Gables, Fla., 1980-84; gen. merchant Joncod Overseas Ltd., Lagos, 1974—; world trade strategist Joncod Overseas Ltd., Houston, 1987—; retail trader Star Liquor Store, Hempstead, Tex., 1987—; coord. Jancod/Bexpharm, Houston, 1987-88; cost acct. Jancod Overseas Ltd., Houston, 1980—; founder, pres. Joncod Internat., Inc., 1987—; founder, com. group head Star Liquor Store, Hempstead, 1987—. Active ARC, 1967-70, numerous charitable activities, Lagos, 1970-74. Recipient Professionalism Cert. AMA, 1994, Meritorious Svc. award AIA Students, 1985, Recognition award Nat. Fire Protection Assn., 1986. Fellow The Highlanders Club (svcs. prof. 1993—), Nat. Shrine; mem. Assn. Corp. Tech. Computer Profls., Instr. of Profl. Mgmt. and Adminstrn., Internat. Assn. of Account Practitioners, Constrn. Specs. Inst. Avocations: table and lawn tennis, photography, swimming. Office: Joncod Overseas Ltd PO Box 87483 Houston TX 77287-7483

OBLAK, JOHN BYRON, academic administrator; b. Little Falls, N.Y., June 1, 1942; s. Henry John Oblak and Lillian Ann (Walrath) Farber; m. Janiece Bacon, Nov. 12, 1966; children: Jeb, Jonathan, Jolynn, Jessica. BS in Speech Edn., State U. Coll. Arts & Scis., Geneseo, N.Y., 1964; MA in Speech/Theatre, U. Nebr., 1966; PhD in Theatre History, U. Kans., 1971. Tech. dir. U. Nebr., Lincoln, 1964-66; asst. instr. speech/theatre U. Kans., Lawrence, 1966-69; asst. prof. speech Ind. State U., Terre Haute, 1969-79, asst. dean student life, 1970-73, acting dir. theatre/acad. chmn., 1973-75, asst. dean summer and evening sessions, 1975-76, asst. dean acad. services and spl. programs, 1976-79; dir. summer sessions and continuing edn. Ithaca (N.Y.) Coll., 1979-80, assoc. dean summer sessions and continuing edn., 1980-82, dean sch. humanities and scis., assoc. prof., 1982-88, v.p. student affairs and campus life, 1988—; adminstrv. advisor to All-Univ. Ct. Appeals Ind. State U., mem. non-acad. com. Univ. Student Affairs, chmn. search com. for chmn. speech dept., adminstrv. advisor to interfraternity student ct., mem. univ. housing com.; mem. personnel tng. and devel. com. Ithaca Coll., calendar com., chmn. Greek Life Rev. Com. Author: Bringing Broadway to Maine: The History of Lakewood--1900-1969, 1971; contbr. articles to profl. jours. Committeman Cub Scouts Am., Ithaca, 1979-80, den leader, 1980-82; committeeman Boy Scouts Am., Ithaca, 1981-85, Dems., 1990-93; chmn. publicity com., bd. dirs. Hangar Theatre, Ithaca, 1980-83; mem. allocations bd. United Way, Ithaca, 1979-82, chmn. Ithaca Coll. United Way fund raising campaign, 1981-83, campaign solicitor, Terre Haute, 1976-79; trustee Village of Lansing, N.Y., 1981-85; bd. dirs. Community Theatre Terre Haute, 1976-79, Cayuga Chamber Orch., 1988-90; adv. bd. Tompkins County Tourism Devel., 1991-94; chair Tompkins County United Way Campaign, 1993; pres. bd. Tompkins County United Way, 1993-94. Mem. Am. Assn. Higher Edn., Tompkins County C. of C. (bd. dirs. 1985-88). Democrat. Roman Catholic. Home: 34 Highgate Cir Ithaca NY 14850-1484 Office: Ithaca Coll VP Student Affairs & Campus Life Ithaca NY 14850

O'BLOCK, ROBERT PAUL, management consultant; b. Pitts., Mar. 9, 1943; s. Paul Joseph and Mary Elizabeth (Galicic) O'B.; m. Megan Marie. BSME, Purdue U., 1965; MBA, Harvard U., 1967. Rsch. and teaching fellow in fin., econs. and urban mgmt., Harvard U., 1967-70; assoc. in real estate mgmt. and fin. McKinsey & Co., Inc., Boston, 1969-78, prin., 1979-84, dir., 1984—; gen. and mng. ptnr. Freeport Center, Clearfield, Utah, 1971—; vis. lectr. urban econs. Yale Law Sch., Princeton U.; cons. Mass., N.J. housing fin. agys., Rockefeller Assn., HUD, 1968-76; chmn. mgmt. com. Snowbird Lodge (Utah), 1974-86. Mem. nat. adv. bd. Snowbird Arts Inst., 1977-83; mem. budget com. N.Y. Pub. Libr., 1977-79; mem. adv. bd. Internat. Tennis Hall of Fame, 1986-89, bd. dirs., 1989-95; mem. bd. overseers Boston Symphony Orch., 1988—, vice-chmn. bd. overseers, 1992-95, chmn., 1995—; mem. bd. trustees U.S. Ski Ednl. Found., 1989—. Rsch. fellow Harvard U., 1967. Roman Catholic. Clubs: River (N.Y.C.), Devon Yacht, Maidstone (East Hampton, N.Y.), Nat. Golf Links Am. (Southampton, N.Y.), Alta (Salt Lake City), The Country Club (Brookline, Mass.). Contbr. articles to profl. jours. Office: McKinsey & Co Inc 75 Park Pl 3d fl Boston MA 02116

OBLOY, LEONARD GERARD, priest; b. Cleve., Sept. 1, 1951; s. Henry Joseph and Ruth Elsie (Walter) O. AB, Borromeo Coll. of Ohio, 1973; MDiv, St. Mary's Seminary, 1977; SSL, Pontifical Biblical Inst., Rome, 1983, postgrad., 1984. Ordained priest Roman Cath. Ch., 1977. Assoc. pastor St. Helen Parish, Newbury, Ohio, 1977-80, St. Rose of Lima Parish, Cleve., 1984-88; adj. prof. St. Mary's Sem., Cleve., 1984-88; vice rector, asst. prof. sacred scripture and computer sci. Mt. St. Mary's Sem., Emmitsburg, Md., 1988—; mem. curriculum com. Cath. Distance U., Paeonian Springs, Va., 1986—, dean grad. divsn., 1995; guest lectr. Our Lady of Holy Cross Coll., New Orleans, 1988—; lectr. in field. Author, narrator pub. TV series And God Said, Witness; author various pamphlets/audio casettes for Cath. Distance U. Mem. IEEE Computer Soc., N.Y. Acad. Scis., Cath. Bibl. Fedn., Cath. Distance U., Corp. for Pub. Broadcasting, nat. Cath. Edn. Assn., Sacred Congregation for Doctrine of Faith, Vatican Radio, Eternal Word TV Network. Avocations: computers, audio engineering, audio recording, auto mechanics. Home and Office: Mt St Mary's Sem Emmitsburg MD 21727

OBNINSKY, VICTOR PETER, lawyer; b. San Rafael, Calif., Oct. 12, 1944; s. Peter Victor and Anne Bartholdi (Donston) O.; m. Clara Alice Bechtel, June 8, 1969; children: Mari, Warren. BA, Columbia U., 1966; JD, U. Calif., Hastings, 1969. Bar: Calif. 1970. Sole practice, Novato, Calif., 1970—; arbitrator Marin County Superior Ct., San Rafael, 1979—; superior ct. judge pro tem, 1979—; lectr. real estate and partnership law. Author: The Russians in Early California, 1966. Bd. dirs. Calif. Young Reps., 1968-69, Richardson Bay San. Dist., 1974-75, Marin County Legal Aid Soc., 1976-78; baseball coach Little League, Babe Ruth League, 1970-84; mem. nat. panel consumer arbitrators Better Bus. Bur., 1974-88; leader Boy Scouts Am., 1970-84; permanent sec. Phillips Acad. Class of 1962, 1987—; mem. Phillips Acad. Alumni Council, 1991-95; bd. community advisors Buck Ctr. for Rsch. on Aging. Mem. ABA, State Bar Calif., Marin County Bar Assn. (bd. dirs. 1985-91, treas. 1987-88, pres.-elect 1989, pres. 1990), Phi Delta Phi, Phi Gamma Delta. Republican. Russian Orthodox. Office: 2 Commercial Blvd Apt 103 Novato CA 94949-6121 *An all-out intellectual attempt to understand baseball thoroughly may give sufficient insight to understand oneself; the so-called "designated hitter" rule should be abolished immediately.*

OBOLENSKY, IVAN, investment banker, foundation consultant, writer, publisher; b. London, May 15, 1925; s. Serge and Alice (Astor) O. (parents Am. citizens); m. Claire McGinnis, 1949 (div. 1956); children—Marina Ava, Ivan Serge, David; m. Mary Elizabeth Morris, 1959; 1 child, Serge. AB, Yale U., 1947. Pres. Hotel Investments, Inc., N.Y.C., 1950-58; v.p., treas. Serge Obolensky Assocs., 1952-75; Ivan Obolensky Inc. and Astor books, pubs. Ivan Obolensky Inc., pubs., 1956-65; dir. Silver Bear Inc., Atlanta; ptnr. A.T. Brod & Co., investment bankers, Dominick & Dominick Inc., investment bankers, 1965-70, Middendorf Colgate, investment bankers, 1970-73; v.p. C.B. Richard, Ellis/Moseley Hallgarten, investment bankers, 1974-81, Sterling Grace & Co., investment bankers, N.Y.C., 1982-87; sr. v.p. Jesup, Josephthal & Co., investment bankers, N.Y.C., 1987-90; gen. ptnr. Astor Capital Mgmt. Assocs., 1980—; v.p. Capital Mgmt. Assocs., N.Y.C., 1990—; v.p. Shields & Co., N.Y.C., 1990—; bd. dirs. Gold Canyon Resources, 1996—; cons. and lectr. in field. Author: Rogues' March, 1956; contbr. to Nihon Keizai Shimbun, Tokyo, on precious metals, 1985—, program com. N.Y. Soc. of Security Analysts for pub., oil and gas; contbr. articles to profl. publs. Bd. dirs. Police Athletic League, N.Y.C., 1975-85, exec. com., 1980-85, U.S.O., 1987—, Audubon Canyon Ranch, Calif., 1989—, Tolstoy Found., 1994—, Soldiers', Sailors' and Airmen's Club, 1976—, pres., 1987—, Russian Nobility Assn. in Am., 1990—, treas., 1991—, Musicians Emergency Fund, 1985-93, pres., 1987-92, Children's Blood Found., N.Y. Hosp., 1952—, pres., 1981-95, pres. emeritus, 1995—; pres., dir. Josephine Lawrence Hopkins Found., 1971—; pres. Whitemarsh Found., 1980-90. Lt. (j.g.) USNR, 1943-45, ret., 1980. Published works by James Agee: A Death in the Family and Tad Mosel: All the Way Home, which received Pulitzer prizes, 2 Caldecott awards. Mem. Am. Legion, Mil. Order Loyal Legion U.S. (sr. vice-comdr. 1955, comdr. 1967-70), St. Elmo Soc., Met. Mus. Art (life), Knickerbocker Club, N.Y. Yacht Club, New Eng. Soc. N.Y., St. Georges Soc. N.Y., The Navy League, West Point Soc., Army and Navy Club, Explorers Club, Masons (Holland #8 master 1981, dist. dep. grand master 1st Manhattan 1983-84, grand treas. 1994-96). Office: Shields & Co 71 Broadway New York NY 10006-2601

OBOLENSKY, MARILYN WALL (MRS. SERGE OBOLENSKY), metals company executive; b. Detroit, Aug. 13, 1929; d. Albert Fraser and Christine (Frischkorn) Wall; m. Serge Obolensky, June 3, 1971. Student, Duschesne Jr. Coll., 1947. Chmn. bd. Wall-Colmondy Corp., Detroit, 1959-61, exec. sec., 1961—; chmn. bd. Wall-Gases Inc., Morrisville, Pa., 1959-61; pres. Serge Obolensky Assocs. Bd. dirs. Heart and Lung Assn. N.Y.C., 1963—. Republican. Roman Catholic. Clubs: Bathing Corp. (Southampton, N.Y.), Southampton. Home: New York NY Address: 45 Preston Pl Grosse Pointe MI 48236-3035

OBOMSAWIN, ALANIS, director, producer; b. Lebanon, N.H., Aug. 31, 1932; arrived in Can., 1933; d. Herman and Maria (Benedict) O.; 1 child Kisos. Dir., prodr. numerous filmstrips, 2 multimedia packages, 2 vignettes, 6 half hour 16mm films for ednl. TV; dir. 17 documentaries, short fiction film for children about racism; author, composer album Bush Lady, 1988. Chair bd. dirs. Native Women's Shelter Montreal; mem. Can. Coun.'s Native Adv. Com. Recipient several prizes for her films. Mem. Order of Can. Office: care Nat Film Bd CAN, CP 6100 Succ A, Montreal, PQ Canada H3C 3H5

O'BOYLE, ROBERT L., landscape architect; b. Alma, Mich., Oct. 26, 1935; s. Frederick and Ella (Keefer) O'B.; m. Kay Louise Wells, Dec. 18, 1954; children—Robert M., Brian P., Cathleen S., Andrew F. B.A., Alma Coll., 1958; B.S. in Landscape Architecture, Mich. State U., 1960. Registered landscape architect, Mich. Landscape designer Jane Smith Assocs., Lansing, Mich., 1959-61; park planner State of Mich., Lansing, 1961-62; landscape architect Light's Landscape, Richland, Mich., 1962-64; pres. O'Boyle, Cowell, Blalock & Assocs., Inc., Kalamazoo, 1964—; mem. Bd. Licensing and Registration, State of Mich., 1970-76. Contbr. articles to profl. jours. Bd. dirs. Kalamazoo Nature Ctr., 1971-76, Kalamazoo County Parks Commn., 1974-78; bd. dirs. Kalamazoo Flower Fest, Inc., 1983-89, pres., 1987-88; Parchment Downtown Devel. Authority, 1991—. Fellow Am. Soc. Landscape Architects (trustee Mich. chpt., v.p. 1991-92, award 1980, 89); Kalamazoo County C. of C. (chair transp. com. 1993-95), Rotary (editorian 1985—). Methodist. Avocations: sailing; photography; wood working. Home: 311 E Thomas Ave Kalamazoo MI 49004-1446 Office: O'Boyle Cowell Blalock & Assocs 521 S Riverview Dr Kalamazoo MI 49004-1230

OBRAMS, GUNTA IRIS, research administrator; b. Düsseldorf, Germany, Sept. 2, 1953; came to U.S., 1961; d. Robert and Olga (Baltins) O.; m. Malcolm DeWitt Patterson, Dec. 22, 1975; 1 child, Andrew McDougal Patterson. BS in Biology cum laude, Rensselaer Poly. Inst., 1977; MD, Union U., Albany, N.Y., 1977; MPH, Johns Hopkins U., 1982, PhD, 1988. Resident in obstetrics and gynecology Ea. Va. Grad. Sch. Medicine, Norfolk, 1977-78; community physician Southampton Meml. Hosp., Franklin, Va., 1978-81; resident in gen. preventive medicine sch. hygiene and pub. health Johns Hopkins U., Balt., 1981-84, project dir., 1983-85, med. dir., 1985-86; med. officer divsn. cancer etiology Nat. Cancer Inst., Bethesda, Md., 1986-89, dep. chief, 1989-90, chief, 1990—. Editor: (with M. Potter): The Epidemiology and Biology of Multiple Myeloma, 1991; contbr. articles to profl. jours. With USPHS, 1987—. Recipient Nat. Cancer Inst. Nat. Rsch. Svc. award, 1981, Rsch. Career award Nat. Inst. Occupational Safety & Health; scholar Am. Med. Women's Assn., 1977. Mem. Phi Beta Kappa, Delta Omega, Alpha Omega Alpha. Office: National Cancer Institute 6130 Executive Blvd Ste 535 Bethesda MD 20892

O'BRIAN, BONNIE JEAN, library services supervisor; b. Great Bend, Kans., Oct. 19, 1940; d. Claude Marion and Mildred Geraldine (Schmaider) Baker; m. Patrick Gilbert Gibson (div.); 1 child, Debra Kathleen; m. John Robinson O'Brian, Nov. 2, 1968. BS, UCLA, 1961; MS, Calif. State U., Northridge, 1977; Credential in Libr. Media Svcs., Calif. State U., Long Beach, 1978. Libr. L.A. Unified Sch. Dist., Northridge, 1978-84; supr. chpt. 2 L.A. Unified Sch. Dist., L.A., 1984, coord. field libr., 1984-87, supr. libr. svcs., 1987—; asst. prof. libr. sci. Calif. State U., L.A.; condr. workshops in field. Recipient N.W. Valley Parent Tchr. Student award 1978, San Fernando Valley Reading Assn. Myrtle Shirley Reading Motivation award 1986. Mem. ALA, Am. Assn. Sch. Librs., Calif. Sch. Libr. Assn. (pres.), So. Calif. Coun. on Lit. for Children and Young People, White House Conf. on Libr. and Info. Svcs. Republican. Office: Los Angeles Unifed Sch Dist 1320 W 3rd St Los Angeles CA 90017-1410

O'BRIAN, JACK, journalist; b. Buffalo, Aug. 16, 1921; s. Charles Joseph and Josephine Loretto (Kelleher) O'B.; m. Yvonne Johnston, Jan. 15, 1947; children—Bridget Mary, Kate Mary. D.Litt. (hon.), Niagara U., Niagara Falls, N.Y., 1966, St. Joseph's Coll., Wyndham, Maine, 1975, St. John's U., N.Y.C., 1978, Canisius Coll., Buffalo, 1979. With Buffalo Times, 1939, N.Y. World-Telegram, 1939-40, Buffalo News, 1940, Buffalo Courier-Express, 1940-43; drama critic, daily N.Y. columnist, movie and music critic Broadway columnist AP, 1943-49; columnist N.Y. Jour.-Am., 1949-67, Voice of Broadway, King Features Syndicate, N.Y.C., 1967—; host daily radio show Critics Circle, WOR, N.Y.C.; Bicentennial lectr. history of Am. theatre Columbia U., 1976; lectr. Fordham U., Caldwell Coll., Harvard Univ. Club, N.Y. U., New Sch. Social Research. (nominated for Pulitzer prize 1942, 61-62); Author: The Great Godfrey, 1953; Contbr. articles to popular mags. Bd. dirs. Damon Runyon-Walter Winchell Fund for Cancer Research. Named One of the Five Most Influential U.S. TV Critics, Ford Found.; recipient Christophers award, 1955, Deems Taylor award ASCAP, 1974, 76, 79, 81, United Jewish Appeal award, 1955, Am. Legion award, 1958, Nat. Catholic War Vets. award, 1972, Morality in Media award, 1971, 73, World Mercy Fund award, 1975, George M. Cohan award Cath. Actors Guild, 1977, Theater award L.I. U., 1982; media sect. Buffalo Conv. Ctr. named in his honor, 1991. Mem. Cath. Actors Guild (nat. pres. 1978—). Home: 225 E 73rd St New York NY 10021-3654 Office: Sta WOR 1440 Broadway New York NY 10018 also: King Features Syndicate 235 E 45th St New York NY 10017-3305

O'BRIEN, ALBERT JAMES, management consultant; b. St. Louis, Oct. 30, 1914; s. James Daniel and Lydia Helena (Dreher) O'B.; m. Ruth Virginia Foster, Mar. 26, 1938 (dec. Jan. 1991); children: Denis James, James Douglas, Douglas Alan; m. Nancy Johnson Schuessler, Oct. 30, 1994. A.B., Washington U., St. Louis, 1935, A.M., 1940; LL.B., Mo. Inst. Law and Accountancy, 1944. Banking trainee, asst. mgr. indsl. service dept. First Nat. Bank, St. Louis, 1935-42; spl. asst. to gen. mgr. Atlas Powder Co., Weldon Springs, Mo., 1942-44; personnel mgr. prodn., mgr. prodn. staff dept. Ralston Purina Co., 1944-57, sec., 1957-59, v.p. finance, sec., 1959-61, exec. v.p., 1961-68, pres., 1968-69, vice chmn. bd., 1969-71; chmn. exec. com. R. Rowland & Co., St. Louis, 1972-74; bus. mgmt. cons., 1974—; chmn. bd. Union Bank of Ill., Union Ill. Co., State Bank of Jersyville, Ill. Mem. adv. bd. Salvation Army; bd. dirs. Met. YMCA, Boy Scouts Am., United Way Greater St. Louis; investment trustee St. Louis Pub. Sch. Retirement System; bd. dirs. Coll. of Ozarks. Mem. Mo. Athletic Club (St. Louis). Presbyterian. Home: 5 Doubletree Ln Saint Louis MO 63131-3908

O'BRIEN, AMY JOY, electrical engineer; b. Smithtown, N.Y., June 22, 1964; d. Morgan Leo and Dorothea Helen (Carelli) O'B. BSEE, U. Del., 1987; MSEE, Loyola Coll., Balt., 1991. Rsch. asst. U. Del., Newark, 1987; cons. engr. Henry Adams, Inc., Balt., 1987-89; software design engr. Tex. Instruments, Inc., Hunt Valley, Md., 1989-90; elec. engr. Ques Tech, Inc., Falls Church, Va., 1990-91, Naval Rsch. Lab., Washington, 1991—; bd. dirs., chair project rev. Vol. for Med. Engring., Balt., 1988-92. Mem. IEEE. Roman Catholic. Office: Naval Rsch Lab Code 5344 4555 Overlook Ave SW Washington DC 20375-5336

O'BRIEN, ANNMARIE, education educator; b. N.Y.C., Nov. 10, 1949; d. Hugh and Margaret (Doherty) O'B.; m. William James McGinty, Dec. 30, 1976; children: Michael Hugh, Liam Patrick. BS in Elem. Edn., Boston U., 1971; MS in Early Childhood Edn., Queens Coll., 1976; EdD in Ednl. Leadership, Portland State U., 1994. Tchr. St. Gerard Majella Elem. Sch., Hollis, N.Y., 1972-76, Lower Kuskokwim Sch. Dist., Bethel, Alaska, 1977-85; child sexual abuse prevention coord. Resource Ctr. for Parents and Children, Fairbanks, Alaska, 1986; grad. asst., project evaluator Portland (Oreg.) State U., 1989-92, student tchr. supr., 1992; prof. edn., rsch. assoc. Inst. Social and Econ. Rsch. U. Alaska, Anchorage, 1993—. Author: A Child Abuse Prevention Training Manual for Educators, 1976; co-author: The Academy for Future Educators Guidebook, 1992. Recipient scholarship Portland State U., 1991. Mem. AAUW, Kappa Delta Pi. Office: U Alaska Anchorage 3211 Providence Dr Anchorage AK 99508-4614

O'BRIEN, CHARLES H., lawyer, retired state supreme court chief justice; b. Orange, N.J., July 30, 1920; s. Herbert Rodgers and Agnes Sidman (Montanya) O'B.; m. Anna Belle Clement, Nov. 9, 1966; children: Merry Diane, Steven Shawn (dec.), Heather Lynn. LLB, Cumberland U., 1947. Rep. Tenn. Legislature, Memphis, 1963-65, senator, 1965-67; assoc. judge Tenn. Ct. Criminal Appeals, Crossville, 1970-87; assoc. justice Tenn. Supreme Ct., 1987-94, chief justice, 1994-95; ret., 1995; pvt. practice, Crossville, 1995—. Bd. dirs. Lake Tansi Village Property Owners Assn., 1984-89, chmn., 1989. With U.S. Army, 1938-45, ETO, 1950, UN Command, Tokyo. Decorated Bronze Star, Purple Heart with oak leaf cluster. Fellow Tenn. Bar Found.; mem. ABA, Tenn. Bar Assn., Cumberland County Bar Assn., Am. Legion, Lake Tansi Village Chowder and Marching Soc. (pres.). Democrat. Avocation: outdoor activities.

O'BRIEN, CHARLES P., psychiatrist, educator. BA, Tulane U., 1960, MS, 1964, MD, 1966, PhD in Neurophysiology, 1964. Resident in internal medicine Mass. Gen. Hosp., 1964-65; neurologist, psychiatrist Tulane U., 1965-67, Nat. Hosp. Nervous Disorders, 1967-68; psychiatrist U. Pa., Phila., 1968-69, from instr. to asst. prof. to assoc. prof., 1969-78, prof. psychiatry, 1978—, vice chmn., 1986—; tchg. asst. neurophysiology Tulane Med. Sch., 1965-66, instr., 1966-67; vis. prof. Sch. Medicine Hahnemann U., 1980; Pfizer vis.prof. Albert Einstein Coll. Medicine, 1990. Fellow APA, Am. Coll. Neuropsychopharmacology; mem. Psychiat. Rsch. Soc., Am. Acad. Neurol., Soc. Psychotherapy Rsch., Am. Psychosomatic Soc., Group for Advancement Psychiatry, Soc. Behavioral Medicine, Soc. Neurosci., Assn. Rsch. Nervous and Mental Dis. (pres. 1989-90). Office: U Pa VA Med Ctr 3900 Chestnut St Philadelphia PA 19104

O'BRIEN, CONAN, writer, performer, talk show host; b. Brookline, Mass., Apr. 18, 1963. BA Am. Hist., Lit., Harvard U., 1981-85. staff mem. The Harvard Lampoon, 1981-85 (pres. 1983, 84). Stage appearances with: The Groundlings (L.A.) 1985-87; writer, performer The Happy Happy Good Show (L.A., Chgo.) 1988; writer (TV) Not Necessarily the News (HBO) 1985-87, Saturday Night Live, 1988-91 (NBC, Emmy Outstanding Writing in Comedy series 1989), Lookwell (NBC) 1991; writer, prodr. The Simpsons (Fox) 1991-93, The Wilton North Report (syndicated) 1987, Late Night with Conan O'Brien (NBC) 1993—. Office: Late Night with Conan O'Brien NBC 30 Rockefeller Plz New York NY 10112

O'BRIEN, DANIEL DION, track and field athlete, Olympic athlete; b. Portland, Oreg., July 18, 1966. Student, U. Idaho, 1989. Track and field athlete Reebock Racing Club; pub. personality Reebok. Winner Decathlon World Championship, 1991, 93; ranked No.1 in Decathlon Track & Field News, 1991. Office: USA Track and Field Press Info Dept PO Box 120 Indianapolis IN 46204

O'BRIEN, DANIEL WILLIAM, lawyer, corporation executive; b. St. Paul, Jan. 6, 1926; s. Daniel W. and Kathryn (Zenk) O'B.; m. Sarah Ward Stoltze, June 20, 1952; children: Bridget Ann, Daniel William, Kevin Charles, Timothy John. Student, U. Dubuque, 1943, Ill. State U., 1944; B.S.L., U. Minn., 1948, LL.B., 1949. Bar: Minn. 1949. Practice in St. Paul, 1950—; partner Randall, Smith & Blomquist, 1955-65; of counsel Doherty, Rumble & Butler, 1965—; pres. F.H. Stoltze Land & Lumber Co., 1964—, Maple Island, Inc., 1968—; dir. Villaume Industries, Inc., Evercolor Corp. Served to ensign USNR, 1943-46. Mem. Minn., Ramsey County bar assns., World Pres's. Orgn., Chief Execs. Orgn. Home: 4734 Bouleau Rd White Bear Lk MN 55110-3355 Office: Ste 105 2497 Seventh Ave E North Saint Paul MN 55109

O'BRIEN, DARCY, English educator, writer; b. Los Angeles, July 16, 1939; s. George and Marguerite (Churchill) O'B.; m. Ruth Ellen Berke, Aug. 26, 1961 (div. 1968); 1 child, Molly; m. Suzanne Beesley, Feb. 27, 1987. A.B., Princeton U., 1961; postgrad., Cambridge (Eng.) U., 1963-64; M.A., U. Calif., Berkeley, 1963, Ph.D., 1965. Asst. prof. English Pomona Coll., Claremont, Calif., 1965-70, assoc. prof., 1970-75, prof., 1975-78; prof. English U. Tulsa, 1978—. Author: The Conscience of James Joyce, 1968, W.R. Rodgers, 1971, Patrick Kavanagh, 1975, A Way of Life, Like Any Other (Ernest Hemingway Found. award 1978), Moment By Moment, 1978, The Silver Spooner, 1981, Two of a Kind, 1985, Murder in Little Egypt, 1989, Margaret in Hollywood, 1991, A Dark and Bloody Ground, 1993, Power to Hurt, 1996. Woodrow Wilson fellow, 1961-62; U. Ill. Ctr. for Advanced Study fellow, 1969-70; Mellon Found. fellow, 1973-74; Guggenheim fellow, 1978-79. Mem. PEN, James Joyce Soc., Internat. Assn. Crime Writers, Authors Guild, Am. Irish Hist. Soc., Screen Writers Guild. Office: U Tulsa Dept English 600 S College Ave Tulsa OK 74104-3126

O'BRIEN, DAVID A., lawyer; b. Sioux City, Iowa, Aug. 30, 1958; s. John T. and Doris K. (Reisch) O'B. BA, George Washington U., 1981; JD, U. Iowa, 1984. Bar: Iowa 1985, U.S. Dist. Ct. (no. dist.) Iowa 1985, Nebr. 1990, U.S. Dist. Ct. Nebr. 1990. Legis. asst. Nat. Transp. Safety Bd., Washington, 1978-81; assoc. O'Brien, Galvin & Kuehl, Sioux City, 1985-88; ptnr. O'Brien, Galvin Moeller & Neary, Sioux City, 1989-94; chair Wage Appeals Bd. & Bd. of Svc. Contract Appeals U.S. Dept. Labor, Washington, 1994-96, acting dir. Office Adminstrv. Appeals, 1995-96, chair adminstrv. review bd., 1996—. Dem. candidate for Congress, 6th dist. of Iowa, Sioux City, 1988; chmn. Woodbury County Dem. Party, Sioux City, 1992-94, chair Iowa campaign Clinton for Pres., Des Moines, 1992; bd. dirs. Mid-Step Svcs. Inc., Sioux City, 1986-91, Mo. River Hist. Devel., Sioux City, 1989-94. Mem. Nat. Assn. Trial Lawyers, Iowa Trial Lawyers Assn. (bd. govs. 1991-94). Roman Catholic. Avocations: sports, politics. Office: O'Brien Galvin Moeller & Neary PO Box 3223 922 Douglas St Sioux City IA 51101-1026

O'BRIEN, DAVID MICHAEL, law educator; b. Rock Springs, Wyo., Aug. 30, 1951; s. Ralph Rockwell and Lucile O'Brien; m. Claudine M. Mendelovitz, Dec. 17, 1982; children: Benjamin, Sara, Talia. BA, U. Calif., Santa Barbara, 1973, MA, 1974, PhD, 1977. Fulbright lectr. Oxford (Eng.) U., 1987-88; lectr. U. Calif., Santa Barbara, 1976-77; asst. prof. U. Puget Sound, Tacoma, Wash., 1977-79; prof. law U. Va., Charlottesville, 1979—; Fulbright rschr., Tokyo, Kyoto, Japan, 1993-94; jud. fellow U.S. Supreme Ct., Washington, 1982-83; vis. postdoctoral fellow Russell Sage Found., N.Y.C., 1981-82; lectr. USIA, Burma, Japan, France, 1994-95. Author: Supreme Court Watch, 1991—, Constitutional Law and Politics, 2 vols., 2d edit., 1995, Storm Center: The Supreme Court in American Politics, 4th edit., 1996, To Dream of Dreams: Constitutional Politics in Postwar Japan, 1996; editor: Views from the Bench, 1985. Rappatour, jud. selection 20th Century Fund Task Force, N.Y., 1986-87. Tom C. Clark Jud. Fellow, Jud. Fellows Commn., Washington, 1983. Mem. ABA (Silver Gavel award 1987), Am. Judicature Soc., Am. Polit. Sci. Assn., Supreme Ct. Hist. Soc. (editl. bd. 1982—), Internat. Polit. Sci. Assn. Democrat. Avocations: painting, travel. Home: Rt 12 Box 64A Charlottesville VA 22901 Office: U Va 232 Dabell Hall Charlottesville VA 22901

O'BRIEN, DAVID PETER, oil company executive; b. Montreal, Que., Can., Sept. 9, 1941; s. John Lewis and Ethel (Cox) O'B.; m. Gail Baxter Corneil, June 1, 1968; children: Tara, Matthew, Shaun. B.A. with honors in Econs., Loyola Coll., Montreal, 1962; B.C.L., McGill U., 1965. Assoc. and ptnr. Ogilvy, Renault, Montreal, 1967-77; v.p., gen. counsel Petro-Can., Calgary, Alta., 1977-81; sr. v.p. Petro-Can., Calgary, 1982-85, sr. v.p. fin. and planning, 1982-85, exec. v.p., 1985-89; pres., chief exec. officer Noverco Inc., Montreal, 1989; chmn. bd., pres., chief exec. officer PanCan. Petroleum Ltd., Calgary, Alta., Can., 1990-94; pres., COO Can. Pacific Ltd., Montreal, 1995-96; chmn., pres., CEO Can. Pacific Ltd., Calgary, 1996—; bd. dirs. United Westburne Inc., Can. Pacific Ltd., Can. Pacific Enterprises Ltd., Can. Pacific Securities Ltd., Can. Pacific Securities (Ont.) Ltd., Marathon Realty Co. Ltd., Fording Coal Ltd., Laidlaw Inc.; chmn. bd. dirs. PanCan. Petroleum Ltd. Mem. Quebec Bar Assn., Bus. Coun. on Nat. Issues, Glencoe Club, Calgary Petroleum Club, Calgary Golf and Country Club. Home: 906 Riverdale Ave SW, Calgary, AB Canada T2S 0Y6 Office: Can Pacific Ltd, PO Box 2850, Calgary, AB Canada T2P-2S5*

O'BRIEN, DONAL CLARE, JR., lawyer; b. N.Y.C., May 16, 1934; s. Donal Clare and Constance (Boody) O'B.; m. Katharine Louise Slight, June 20, 1956; children: Donal Clare III, Constance Nancy O'Brien Ashforth, Katharine Louise O'Brien Rohn, Caroline Clare. BA, Williams Coll., 1956; LLB, U. Va., 1959. Bar: N.Y. 1961. Assoc. Milbank, Tweed, Hadley & McCloy, N.Y.C., 1959-67, ptnr, 1967-83, 91—; chief legal counsel Rockefeller Family & Assoc., N.Y.C., 1968-91; pres., CEO Rockefeller Trust Co., N.Y.C., 1986-91; bd. dirs. Greenacre Found., N.Y.C., Quebec Labrador Found., Ipswich, Mass., Nat. Audubon Soc., N.Y.C., chmn. emeritus. Chmn. bd. dirs. Atlantic Salmon Fedn., N.Y.C.; trustee N.Am. Wildlife Found., Wendell Gilley Mus., Southwest Harbor, Maine, Waterfowl Rsch. Found., N.Y.C., Am. Bird Conservancy, Washington, The JDR 3d Fund, N.Y.C., Trust for Mut. Understanding, Winthrop Rockefeller Charitable Trust, Little Rock; mem. coun. Rockefeller U.; commr. State of Conn. Bd. Fisheries and Game, 1971-72; mem. Coun. on Environ. Quality, Conn., 1971-76, 91—. Mem. Century Assn. Anglers Club of N.Y. Home: 436 Trinity Pass Rd New Canaan CT 06840-2530 Office: Milbank Tweed Hadley & McCloy 1 Chase Manhattan Plz New York NY 10005-1401

O'BRIEN, DONALD EUGENE, federal judge; b. Marcus, Iowa, Sept. 30, 1923; s. Michael John and Myrtle A. (Toomey) O'B.; m. Ruth Mahon, Apr. 15, 1950; children: Teresa, Brien, John, Shuivaun. LL.B., Creighton U., 1948. Bar: Iowa bar 1948, U.S. Supreme Ct. bar 1963. Asst. city atty. Sioux City, Iowa, 1949-53; county atty. Woodbury County, Iowa, 1955-58; mcpl. judge Sioux City, Iowa, 1959-60; U.S. atty. No. Iowa, 1961-67; pvt. practice law Sioux City, 1967-78, U.S. Dist. judge, 1978—; chief judge U.S. Dist. Ct. (no. dist.) Iowa, Sioux City, 1985-92, sr. judge, 1992—; rep. 8th cir. dist. ct. judges to Jud. Conf. U.S., 1990—. Served with USAAF, 1943-45. Decorated D.F.C., air medals. Mem. Woodbury County Bar Assn., Iowa State Bar Assn. Roman Catholic. Office: US Dist Ct PO Box 267 Sioux City IA 51102-0267

O'BRIEN, EDMUND J., Canadian provincial official; b. Montreal, Can., Sept. 21, 1925. Sales and advt. rep. Imperial Tobacco Co. CAn., 1948-51; supr. fin. divsn. Canadair Ltd., 1951-56, chief econ. analyst internat. mktg. divsn., 1956-65; sec./treas., dir. Unica Rsch. Co. Ltd., Montreal, pres., 1965-69; dir. adminstrn. Internat. Devel. Rsch. Ctr., 1970; dir. transp. Newfoundland, 1973-87; cons., 1987—; mem. Nat. Transp. Agy., Ottawa, Ont., Can., 1988, 93—; sec. Can. Transp. Rsch. Forum, 1987—. With Royal Can. Artillery, 1943-45. Office: Nat Transp Agy, Ottawa, ON Canada K1A 0N9

O'BRIEN, EDWARD IGNATIUS, lawyer, private investor; b. N.Y.C., Sept. 15, 1928; s. Edward I. and Marguerite (Malone) O'B.; m. Margaret M. Feeney, June 29, 1957; children: Edward Ignatius III, Margaret Mary, Thomas Gerard, John Joseph. AB, Fordham U., 1950; LLB, St. John's U., 1954; grad., Advanced Mgmt. Program, Cornell U., 1965. Bar: N.Y. 1954. With firm Hale, Kay & Brennan, N.Y.C., 1954-55; with Bache & Co., Inc., N.Y.C., 1955-74, gen. counsel, 1960, gen. ptnr., 1964, sec., 1968, v.p., 1965-68, sr. v.p., mem. exec. com., 1969, exec. v.p., 1969, chmn. exec. com., 1971-74; pres. Securities Industry Assn., 1974-93; retired, 1993; bd. dirs. 8 corps.; lectr. Am. Law Inst., Practising Law Inst., Am. Mgmt. Assn.; exch. ofcl. Am. Stock Exch., 1972; mem. adv. bd., mem. exec. com. Securities Regulation Inst., U. Calif., 1975—. Mem. Cardinal's com. Laity Cath. Archdiocese N.Y., mem. Cardinal's com. for edn.; chmn. Fordham U. Coun., 1971-73; bd. dirs. 3 non-profit orgns.; chmn. corp. devel. com. Fordham U.; trustee, chmn. bd. trustees Fordham Prep. Sch., 1975-77, Capt. USAR. Mem. Assn. of Bar of City of N.Y., N.Y. State Bar Assn., Am. Arbitration Assn., Am. Soc. Internat. Law, Guild Cath. Lawyers, Securites Industry Assn. (chmn. publicly owned firms com. 1972), Nat. Assn. Securities Dealers (dist. com. 1973-74), City Midday Club, Shenorock Shore Club (Rye, N.Y.), Town Club (Scarsdale, N.Y.), Met. Club (Washington). Home and Office: 12 Woods Ln Scarsdale NY 10583-6408

O'BRIEN, ELMER JOHN, librarian, educator; b. Kemmerer, Wyo., Apr. 8, 1932; s. Ernest and Emily Catherine (Reinhart) O'B.; m. Betty Alice Peterson, July 2, 1966. A.B., Birmingham So. Coll., 1954; Th.M., Iliff Sch. Theology, 1957; M.A., U. Denver, 1961. Ordained to ministry Methodist Ch., 1957; pastor Meth. Ch., Pagosa Springs, Colo., 1957-60; circulation-reference librarian Boston U. Sch. Theology, Boston, 1961-65; asst. librarian Garrett-Evang. Theol. Sem., Evanston, Ill., 1965-69; librarian, prof. United Theol. Sem., Dayton, Ohio, 1969-96, prof. emeritus, 1996—; abstractor Am. Bibliog. Center, 1969-73; dir. Ctr. for Evang. United Brethren Heritage, 1979-96; chmn. div. exec. com. Dayton-Miami Valley Libr. Consortium, 1983-84; rsch. assoc. Am. Antiquarian Soc., 1990. Author: Bibliography of Festschriften in Religion Published Since 1960, 1972, Religion Index Two: Festschriften, 1960-69; contbg. author: Communication and Change in American Religious History, 1993; pub. Meth. Revs. Index, 1818-1985, 1989-91. Recipient theol. and scholarship award Assn. Theol. Schs. in U.S. and Can., 1990-91; Assn. Theol. Schs. in U.S. and Can. library staff devel. grantee, 1976-77, United Meth. Ch. Bd. Higher Edn. and Ministry research grantee, 1984-85. Mem. ALA, Acad. Libr. Assn. Ohio, Am. Theol. Libr. Assn. (head bur. personnel and placement 1969-73, dir. 1973-76, v.p. 1977-78, pres. 1978-79), Am. Antiquarian Soc. (rsch. assoc. 1990), Delta Sigma Phi, Omicron Delta Kappa, Eta Sigma Phi, Kappa Phi Kappa. Club: Torch Internat. (v.p. Dayton club 1981-82, pres. 1982-83). Home: Apt 281 4840 Thunderbird Dr Boulder CO 80303

O'BRIEN, FRANCIS ANTHONY, lawyer; b. Albany, N.Y., Sept. 23, 1936; s. Francis Joseph and Helen Marie (Smith) O'B.; m. Maryanne Delia Mahoney, May 2, 1964; children—John, Dennis, Kathleen, Eileen. AB, Hamilton Coll., 1958; LLB, Cornell U., 1961. Bar: N.Y. 1962, D.C. 1968. Trial atty. FTC, Washington, 1962-68; assoc. Howrey & Simon, Washington, 1968-70, ptnr., 1971-86; prin. Francis A. O'Brien & Assocs., Washington. Alumni trustee Hamilton Coll., Clinton, N.Y., 1980-84; mem. Chesterbrook Woods Citizen Assn., McLean, Va., 1976—. Mem. ABA, Fed. Bar Assn., N.Y. Bar Assn., D.C. Bar Assn. Roman Catholic. Avocations: basketball; soccer; Civil War history. Home: 1600 Forest Ln Mc Lean VA 22101-3314 Office: Francis A O'Brien & Assocs 1150 Connecticut Ave NW Ste 900 Washington DC 20036-4104

O'BRIEN, FRANK B., manufacturing executive; b. Evanston, Ill., Dec. 5, 1946; s. Frank B. and Barbara (Greene) O'B.; m. Karen Eby, Oct. 12, 1974; children: Frank B. IV, Caroline Ann, Mary Karen, Margaret Greene, John Patrick, William Thomas. BSBA, Ohio State U., 1972. CPA, Ohio. Acct. Ernst & Whinney, Cleve., 1973-80; asst. to v.p. fin. The N.Am. Coal Corp., Cleve., 1980-82, mgr. corp. planning, 1982-87; v.p. corp. devel. NACCO Industries, Inc., Cleve., 1987-93, sr. v.p. corp. devel., chief fin. officer, 1994—; chmn. corp. planning coun. Mfrs.' Alliance for Productivity and Innovation, Washington, 1987—. Bd. dirs. The Guidance Ctr., Boy Scouts of Am., Boys Hope, 1993; founder Children's Little Theater Endowment Fund, Cleve., 1987—. Sgt. U.S. Army, 1968-71. Mem. Assn. for Corp. Growth, Mayfield Country Club, Cleve. Playhouse Club, Pine Lake Trout Club. Republican. Roman Catholic. Office: NACCO Industries Inc 5875 Landerbrook Dr Mayfield Heights OH 44124-4017

O'BRIEN, GEOFFREY PAUL, editor; b. N.Y.C., May 4, 1948; s. Joseph Aloysius and Margaret Dorothy (Owens) O'B.; m. Carly Francis O'Brien, Mar. 18, 1977; 1 child, Heather. Student, Yale U., 1966-67, SUNY, Stony Brook, 1968-70. Editor Reader's Catalog, N.Y.C., 1987-91; exec. editor Libr. of Am., N.Y.C., 1992—. Author: Hardboiled America, 1981, Dream Time, 1988, A Book of Maps, 1989, The Phantom Empire, 1993, The Hudson Mystery, 1994, Floating City: Selected Poems 1978-95, 1996; contbr. poetry, essays and revs. to profl. jours.; contbg. writer The Village Voice, 1982-90; editor: Frogpond, 1980-81; co-editor: Montemora, 1974-76. Recipient Writing award Whiting Found., 1988. Office: Libr of Am 14 E 60th St New York NY 10022-1006

O'BRIEN, GEORGE DENNIS, retired university president; b. Chicago, Ill., Feb. 21, 1931; s. George Francis and Helen (Fehlandt) O'B.; m. Judith Alyce Johnson, June 21, 1958; children: Elizabeth Belle, Juliana Helen, Victoria Alyce. AB in English, Yale, 1952; PhD in Philosophy, U. Chgo., 1961. Tchr. humanities, Carnegie rsch. fellow U. Chgo., 1956-57; successively instr., asst. prof., asst. dean coll. Princeton (N.J.) U., 1958-65; on leave in Athens, Greece, 1963-64; spl. honors seminars LaSalle Coll., spring 1963, fall 1964, spring 1965; assoc. prof. philosophy Middlebury (Vt.) Coll., 1965-71, prof., 1971-76, dean of men, 1965-67, dean of coll., 1967-74, dean faculty, 1975-76; pres. Bucknell U., 1976-84, U. Rochester, N.Y., 1984-94; ret., 1994; dir. Salzburg Seminar in Am. Studies. Author: Hegel on Reason in History, 1975, God and the New Haven Railway, 1986, What to Expect from College, 1991; contbr. articles to profl. jours. Trustee LaSalle Coll., Phila., 1965—; bd. dirs. Union Theol. Sem., 1985-90, Rsch. Librs. Group, 1994—; v.p. Commonweal Found., 1994—. Fellow Am. Coun. Learned Socs., London, 1971-72. Mem. Am. Philos. Assn., Phi Beta Kappa. Home: RR 3 Box 510 Middlebury VT 05753-8728

O'BRIEN, GEORGE DONOGHUE, JR., engineering consultant company executive; b. Detroit, Feb. 4, 1938; s. George Donoghue and Margaret (Foley) O'B.; m. Elise Maria Montilla, May 28, 1961; children: George III, Caroline, Kevin, Roseleen. BS, US Naval Acad., 1960; PhD, Naval Postgrad. Sch., 1970. Commd. ensign USN, 1960, advanced through grades to capt., 1982, naval aviator, test pilot, 1961-75, comdg. officer Attack Squadron 35, 1977-78, comdr. officer nuclear powered aircraft carrier, 1986-89, ret., 1989; pres., ceo Cygna Group, Oakland, Calif., 1990-92; chmn. infrastructure group ICF Kaiser Engrs., Oakland, 1991—. Chmn. Alameda County Bus. Devel. Com., Oakland, 1991-92. Decorated Legion of Merit, others. Mem. Bohemian Club San Francisco, St. Francis Yacht Club. Roman Catholic. Avocations: reading, running, sailing. Home: 1216 Paru St Alameda CA 94501-4038 Office: ICF Kaiser Engrs 1800 Harrison St Oakland CA 94612-3429

O'BRIEN, GERALD JAMES, utilities executive; b. St. Paul, May 1, 1923; s. Dewey Joseph and Henrietta Elizabeth O'B.; m. Patricia Margaret McCorison, Feb. 23, 1946; children: Kathleen, Thomas, John, Andrew. Student, St. Thomas Coll., 1940-41, 45-46; B.C.S., Drake U., 1948. Staff acct. Haskins & Sells, Mpls., 1948-50; with Donovan Cos., Inc., St. Paul, 1950-81; sec., asst. treas. Donovan Cos., Inc., 1977-81; utility rate cons., 1981-84; dir. Alumbaugh Coal Co., Donovan Constrn. Co., So. Tier Gas Corp., Gas Distbrs. Info. Service. Served with U.S. Army, 1942-45. Decorated Purple Heart. Address: 13313 W Meeker Blvd Sun City West AZ 85375-3808

O'BRIEN, HELEN ANDERSON, health services administrator; b. Worcester, Mass., Apr. 19, 1934; d. Albert and Mary Ellen (Connor) Anderson; m. Charles Gerald O'Brien, Jan. 24, 1955 (div. Apr. 1977); children: Mark, Karen O'Brien Tomko. Diploma in nursing, Mass. Gen. Hosp., Boston, 1956; BSN, Western Conn. State U., 1977; MPH with acad. honors, Yale U., 1979. RN, N.Y., Ohio, Mass., Conn. Nurse, charge nurse various locations, 1960-64; chmn. publicity and community edn. Wausau (Wis.) Hosp., 1966-69; adminstrv. resident Danbury (Conn.) Health Dept., 1978; health svcs. cons., Darien, 1979; pres., CEO, Stratford (Conn.) Vis. Nurse Assn., Inc., 1980—; presenter in field. Bd. dirs. Women's Leadership Coun., Bridgeport (Conn.) Regional Bus. Coun., 1995—; active Needs of Elderly Commn., Stratford, 1980-87; founder Hospice Program Greater Bridgeport, Conn., 1981—; vol. domestic violence and rape counselor YWCA, Bridgeport, 1990—. Fellow Yale U., 1977-79. Mem. APHA, Am. Mgmt. Assn., Conn. Pub. Health Assn. (bd. dirs. 1980-86), Yale Hosp. Adminstrv. Alumni Assn., Nat. League for Nursing, Assn. Yale Alumni in Pub. Health. Avocations: reading, painting, classic cars. Home: 129 Gallows Hill Rd Redding CT 06896-1408 Office: Stratford Vis Nurse Assn 88 Ryders Ln Stratford CT 06497-1666

O'BRIEN, J. WILLARD, lawyer, educator; b. N.Y.C., Oct. 19, 1930; s. J. Willard and Anna C. (Carroll) O.'B.; m. Peggy J. O'Brien. B.S., Fordham U., 1952, J.D., 1957. Bar: N.Y. 1957. Assoc. Cahill, Gordon, Reindel & Ohl, N.Y.C., 1957-62; asst. prof. law Syracuse U. Coll. Law, 1962-65; prof. law Villanova (Pa.) U. Sch. Law, 1965—, dean, 1972-83, dir. Connelly Inst. Law and Morality, 1983-95; mem. Pa. Fed. Jud. Nominating Commn., 1977-80, vice chmn., 1978-80; mem. Pa. Law and Justice Inst., 1972-73, chmn. exec. com., 1973-75, pres., 1975-77. Editor-in-chief Fordham Law Rev, 1956-57. Bd. dirs. Nat. Inst. on Holocaust, 1984-85; bd. dirs. Phila. Coordinating Council on the Holocaust, 1983—. Served with USAF, 1952-54; Served with N.Y. Air N.G., 1954-58. Mem. ABA, N.Y. State Bar Assn., Pa. Bar Assn., Canon Law Soc. Am. Roman Catholic.

O'BRIEN, JACK GEORGE, artistic director; b. Saginaw, Mich., June 18, 1939; s. J. George and Evelyn (MacArthur Martens) O'B. A.B., U. Mich., 1961, M.A., 1962. Asst. dir. APA Repertory Theatre, N.Y.C., 1963-67; asso. dir. APA Repertory Theatre, 1967-69; worked with San Diego Nat. Shakespeare Festival, 1969-82, A.C.T., 1970-80, Loretto Hilton, 1975, Ahmanson, Los Angeles, 1978-80, San Francisco Opera, Houston Grand Opera, Washington Opera Soc., N.Y.C. Opera. Lyricist: Broadway prodn. The Selling of the President, 1972; dir.: on Broadway Porgy and Bess (Tony award nominee 1977), Most Happy Fella, Street Scene, Two Shakespearean Actors, 1993, Damn Yankees, 1994, Hapgood, 1994, others; artistic dir.: Old Globe Theatre, San Diego, 1981. Mem. Actors' Equity, Am. Soc. Composers and Performers, Soc. Stage Dirs. and Choreographers, Dirs. Guild Am.

O'BRIEN, JAMES ALOYSIUS, foreign language educator; b. Cin., Apr. 7, 1936; s. James Aloysius and Frieda (Schirmer) O'B.; m. Rumi Matsumoto, Aug. 26,1961. B.A., St. Joseph's Coll., 1958; M.A., U. Cin., 1960; Ph.D., Ind. U., 1969. Instr. English St. Joseph's Coll., Rensselaer, Ind., 1960-62; asst. prof. Japanese U. Wis.-Madison, 1968-74, assoc. prof., 1974-81, chmn. East Asis langs. and lit., 1979-80, 82-85, prof. Japanese, 1981—. Author: Dazai Osamu, 1975, Akutagawa and Dazai: Instances of Literary Adaptation, 1988; translator: Selected Stories and Sketches (Dazai Osamu), 1983, Three Works (Muro Saisei), 1985, Crackling Mountain and Other Stories (Dazai Osamu), 1989. Ford Found fellow, 1965-66; Fulbright-Hays and NDEA fellow, 1966-68; Social Sci. Research Council fellow, 1973-74; Japan Found. fellow, 1977-78. Mem. Assn. Asian Studies, Assn. Tchrs. of Japanese (exec. com. 1981-84, dir. devel. 1981-83, pres. 1984-90). Home: 2533 Branch St Middleton WI 53562-2812 Office: U Wis Dept East Asian Langs & Lit 1220 Linden Dr Madison WI 53706-1525

O'BRIEN, JAMES FREEMAN, lawyer; b. Waltham, Mass., Jan. 23, 1951; s. John Smith and Miriam Anna (Cary) O'B.; m. Norma Jo Greenberg, Feb. 19, 1977 (div. Jan. 1989); 1 stepchild, Nicholas S. Elfner. BA, U. Pa., 1973; JD, Northeastern U., 1978. Bar: Mass., U.S. Dist. Ct. Mass., U.S. Ct. Appeals (1st cir.). Law clk. to the justices Mass. Superior Ct., 1978-79; assoc. Dane, Howe & Brown, Boston, 1979-80, Lawson & Wayne, Boston, 1981-84, Dane & Greenberg, Concord, Mass., 1985-88; ptnr. Dane & Greenberg, Concord, 1988, Dane & O'Brien, Concord, 1988-93; pvt. practice law Concord, 1993—; advisor Harvard Trial Adv. Workshop, Cambridge, Mass., 1992—; atty. judge Harvard Ames Moot Ct., Cambridge, 1992—. Actor, dir. numerous amateur and profl. stage plays, 1958—; contbr. articles to profl. jours. Sec., mem. Pub. Ceremonies and Celebrations Com., Concord, 1993—. Named Best Dir., New England Theatre Conf., Brandeis, 1985, 91. Mem. Mass. Bar Assn., Ctrl. Middlesex Bar Assn., Concord Lodge of Elks, Concord Ind. Battery, Frank J. Murray Inn Ct. Avocations: theater, music. Office: Ste 100 30 Monument Sq Concord MA 01742

O'BRIEN, JAMES JEROME, construction management consultant; b. Phila., Oct. 20, 1929; s. Sylvester Jerome and Emma Belle Filer (Fulforth) O'B.; m. Carmen Hiester, June 10, 1952 (div. Aug. 1, 1984); children: Jessica Susan, Michael, David; m. Rita F. Gibson, Nov. 1, 1984. BCE, Cornell U., 1952; postgrad., U. Houston, 1957-58. Registered profl. engr., N.Y., N.J., Pa., Ga., Conn., Maine. Project engr. Rohm & Haas, Phila. and Tex., 1955-59, RCA Corp., Moorestown, N.J., Greenland and Alaska, 1959-62; cons. Mauchly Assocs., Fort Washington, Pa., 1962-65; founding ptnr., exec. v.p. Meridian Engring. Co., Phila., 1965-68; pres. MDC Systems, Cherry Hill, 1968-72; ptnr. James J. O'Brien P.E., Cherry Hill, 1972-77; pres. O'Brien-Kreitzberg & Assocs., N.Y.C., Pennsauken, San Francisco, 1977-80, chief exec. officer, 1980-89, chmn. bd. dirs., 1989-93, vice chmn., 1993—. Author:

CPM in Construction Management-Scheduling by the Critical Path Method, 1965, CPM in Construction Management-Project Management with CPM, 4th edit., 1993, Management Information Systems-Concepts, Techniques and Applications, 1970, Management with Computers, 1972, Construction Inspection Handbook, 1974, 3d edit., 1989, Value Analysis in Design and Construction, 1976, Construction Delay-Risks, Rsponsibilities and Litigation, 1976, Preconstruction Estimating: Budget to Bid, 1994, Construction Documentation, 3d edit., 1995; co-author: Construction Management: A Professional Approach, 1974; editor: Recollections (L.D. Miles), 1987; author, editor: Scheduling Handbook, 1969, Contractor's Management Handbook, 1971, 2d edit., 1990, Standard Handbook of Heavy Construction, 3d edit., 1996; contbr. articles to profl. jours. Lt. 1952-55, USN. Recipient Profl. Mgr. award N.Y. chpt. Soc. Advancement Mgmt., 1969. Fellow ASCE (Constrn. Mgmt. award 1976, v.p. 1985, pres. South Jersey br. 1985, Disting. Engr. South Jersey br. 1986, pres. N.J. sect. 1987-89, mem. com. on quality in civil engring. profession 1990—), Project mgmt. Inst. (sec. 1971, v.p. 1972, pres. 1973, chmn. bd. 1974-75, award for contbn. to project mgmt. 1983, Fellow award 1989), Constrn. Mgmt. Assn. Am. (bd. dirs. 1990-92, Fellow award 1993, Constrn. Mgr. of Yr. award N.Y.-N.J. chpt. 1994), Cornell Soc. Engrs. (dean's adv. com. sch. civil and environ. engring. 1986-87); mem. Am. Inst. Indsl. Engrs. (sr.), Am. Assn. Cost Engring., Soc. Am. Value Engrs. (cert. value specialist, v.p. N.E. region 1986-87, Fallon Value-in-Life award 1993), Miles Value Found. (bd. dirs. 1987-90, trustee 1990—), Soc. Advancement Mgmt. (v.p. CPM divsn. 1970), Tau Beta Pi, Chi Epsilon. Home: 2 Linden Ave Riverton NJ 08077-1124 Office: 4350 Haddonfield Rd Pennsauken NJ 08109-3377

O'BRIEN, JAMES PHILLIP, lawyer; b. Monmouth, Ill., Jan. 6, 1949; s. John Matthew and Roberta Helen (Cavanaugh) O'B.; m. Laurene Reason, Aug. 30, 1969 (div. 1980); m. Lynn Florsheim, Sept. 5, 1987. BA, Western Ill. U., 1971; JD, U. Ill., 1974. Bar: Ill. 1974. Asst. atty. gen. State Ill., Springfield, 1974-75; jud. clerk Ill. Appellate Ct., Springfield, 1975-76; assoc. Graham & Graham, Springfield, 1976-81; corp. counsel Am. Hosp. Assn., Chgo., 1981-84; ptnr., co-chmn. health care dept. Katten, Muchin & Zavis, Chgo., 1984—; task force med. malpractice reform legislation Am. Hosp. Assn., 1983-84, tax adv. com., 1987-91, tax reporting and compliance com., 1990-91; spkr. in field. Contbr. numerous articles to profl. jours. Recipient cert. recognition Ill. Dept. Children and Family Svcs., 1981; Edward Arthur Mellinger Found. scholar, Western Ill. U. 1971. Mem. Nat. Health Lawyers Assn., Am. Soc. Hosp. Attys., Am. Acad. Hosp. Attys., Am. Arbitration Assn. (Task Force Health Care Dispute Resolution 1982-84). Office: Katten Muchin & Zavis 525 W Monroe St Ste 1600 Chicago IL 60661-3629

O'BRIEN, JOHN CONWAY, economist, educator, writer; b. Hamilton, Lanarkshire, Scotland; s. Patrick and Mary (Hunt) O'B.; m. Jane Estelle Judd, Sept. 16, 1966; children: Kellie Marie, Kerry Patrick, Tracy Anne, Kristen Noël. B.Com., U. London, 1952, cert. in German lang., 1954; tchr.'s cert., Scottish Edn. Dept., 1954; AM, U. Notre Dame, 1959, PhD, 1961. Tchr. Scottish High Schs., Lanarkshire, 1952-56; instr. U. B.C., Can., 1961-62; asst. prof. U. Sask., Can., 1962-63, U. Dayton, Ohio, 1963-64; assoc. prof. Wilfrid Laurier U., Ont., Can., 1964-65; from asst. to full prof. Econs. and Ethics Calif. State U., Fresno, 1965—; vis. prof. U. Pitts., 1969-70, U. Hawaii, Manoa, 1984; keynote speaker Wageningen Agrl. U., The Netherlands, 1987; presenter papers 5th, 6th, 10th World Congress of Economists, Tokyo, 1977, Mexico City, 1980, Moscow, 1992; presenter Schmoller Symposium, Heilbronn am Neckar, Fed. Republic Germany, 1988, paper The China Confucius Found. and "2540" Conf., Beijing, 1989, 6th Internat. Conf. on Cultural Econs., Univ. Umeå, Sweden, 1990, Internat. Soc. Intercommunication New Ideas, Sorbonne, Paris, 1990, European Assn. for Evolutionary Polit. Economy, Vienna, Austria, 1991; active rsch. U. Göttingen, Fed. Republic Germany, 1987; acad. cons. Cath. Inst. Social Ethics, Oxford; presenter in field. Author: Karl Marx: The Social Theorist, 1981, The Economist in Search of Values, 1982, Beyond Marxism, 1985, The Social Economist Hankers After Values, 1992; editor: Internat. Rev. Econs. and Ethics, Internat. Jour. Social Econs., Ethical Values and Social Econs., 1981, Selected Topics in Social Econs., 1982, Festschrift in honor of George Rohrlich, 3 vols., 1984, Social Economics: A Pot=Pourri, 1985, The Social Economist on Nuclear Arms: Crime and Prisons, Health Care, 1986, Festschrift in honor of Anghel N. Rugina, Parts I and II, 1987, Gustav von Schmoller: Social Economist, 1989, The Eternal Path to Communism, 1990, (with Z. Wenxian) Essays from the People's Republic of China, 1991, Festschrift in Honor of John E. Elliott, Parts I and II, 1992, Communism Now and Then, 1993, The Evils of Soviet Communism, 1994, Ruminations on the USSR, 1994, The Future Without Marx, 1995; translator econ. articles from French and German into English; contbr. numerous articles to profl. jours. With British Royal Army Service Corps, 1939-46, ETO, NATOUSA, prisoner of war, Germany. Recipient GE Corp. award Stanford U., 1966, Ludwig Mai Svc. award Assn. for Social Econs., Washington, 1994; named Disting. Fellow of Internat. Soc. for Intercomm. of New Ideas, Paris, 1990. Fellow Internat. Inst. Social Econs. (mem. coun., program dir. 3d World Cong. Social Econs. Fresno Calif. 1983, keynote spkr. 4th conf. Toronto 1986), Internat. Soc. for Intercomm. New Ideas (disting.); mem. Assn. social Econs. (dir. west region 1977—, pres.-elect 1988-89, program dir. conf. 1989, pres. 1990, presdl. address Washington 1990), Western Econ. Assn. (organizer, presenter 1977-95), History Econs. Soc., Soc. Reduction Human Labor (exec. com.), European Assn. Evolutionary Polit. Econs. Roman Catholic. Avocations: jogging, collecting miniature paintings, soccer, tennis, photography. Home: 2733 W Fir Ave Fresno CA 93711-0315 Office: Calif State U Econs And Ethics Dept Fresno CA 93740

O'BRIEN, JOHN F., insurance company executive. Pres., CEO First Allmerica Fin. Life Ins. Co., Worcester, Mass., 1989—; also bd. dirs. State Mut. Life Assurance Co. Am., Worcester, Mass.; pres. Allmerica Fin. Life Ins. and Annuity Co., Worcester, 1989—; pres., CEO Allmerica Property & Casualty Co., Inc., Worcester, 1992—; also bd. dirs. Citizens Corp.; pres., CEO Citizens Corp., Worcester, 1992—, Allmerica Fin. Corp., Worcester, Mass., 1995—; chmn. The Hanover Ins. Co., Worcester; pres., dir., CEO Allmerica Property & Casualty Cos., Inc., First Allmerica Life Ins. Co.; pres., CEO, chmn. bd. Citizens Corp; pres., chmn. bd. Allmerica Fin. Life Ins. and Annuity Co.; chmn. bd. Hanover Ins. Co., Citizens Ins. Co. Am.; bd. dirs. Am. Coun. Life Ins., Cabot Corp.; trustee Worcester Poly. Inst.; vis. com. bd. overseers Harvard Coll., 1990—, com. on univ. resources, 1990—, com. on mng. acad. resources, 1990—. Mem. Am. Coun. Life Ins. (bd. dirs. 1992—), Life Ins. Assn. Mass. (bd. dirs. 1989—), Harvard Alumni Assn. (exec. com. 1991—, past pres.). Office: Allmerica Fin 440 Lincoln St Worcester MA 01653-0002

O'BRIEN, JOHN FEIGHAN, investment banker; b. Cleve., Aug. 8, 1936; s. Francis John and Ann (Feighan) O'B.; m. Regina Quaid Harahan, June 27, 1959 (div. 1976); children: Regina, Victoria, Julie, John Jr.; m. Marilyn E. Schreiner. BS, Georgetown U., 1958. Salesman Appliance Mart, Cleve., 1958-59, ptnr., 1960-66; investment broker McDonald & Co. Investments, Cleve., 1966-71, ptnr., 1971-83, exec. v.p., 1983-88, mng. dir., 1988-91, sr. mng. dir., 1993—. Bd. dirs. Hitchcock House, Cleve., 1978-89; chmn. Alcoholism Svcs. of Cleve., 1989-92, Alcohol and Drug-Addiction Svcs. Bd. of Cuyahoga County, 1992—; trustee St. Edward H.S., Lakewood, Ohio, chmn. capital campaign, 1993-95. Mem. Leadership Cleve., Greater Cleve. Growth Assn., Georgetown U. Alumni Assn. (alumni bd. senator), Westwood Country Club, Cleve. Yacht Club, Catawba Island Club. Home: 1031 Brook Ln Cleveland OH 44116-2184 Office: McDonald & Co Investments 800 Superior Ave E Ste 2100 Cleveland OH 44114-2601

O'BRIEN, JOHN GERALD, chemical company executive; b. Newark, Nov. 9, 1938; s. John J. and Elizabeth O'B.; B.S. in Chemistry, Seton Hall U., 1960; m. Judith A. O'Brien, Oct. 14, 1967; children—Jacqueline, Margaret, John. Quality control chemist Stepan Chem. Co., 1960-64, research chemist, 1965-70, asst. plant mgr., 1971-73, gen. mgr. Maywood (N.J.) dept., 1974—. Mem. Am. Chem. Soc., Essential Oil Assn. Home: 11 Evelyn Rd Roseland NJ 07068-1416 Office: 100 W Hunter Ave Maywood NJ 07607-1006

O'BRIEN, JOHN M., newspaper publishing company executive; b. North Bergen, N.J., 1942. BA, Fairleigh Dickinson U., 1970. Sr. v.p. fin. and human resources The New York Times, now exec. v.p., dep. gen. mgr. Office: New York Times Co 229 W 43rd St New York NY 10036-3913

O'BRIEN, JOHN THOMAS, illustrator, cartoonist; b. Phila., Nov. 18, 1953; s. John Thomas and Esther Anne (Carideo) O'B: 1 child, Terase. BFA, Phila. Coll. Art, 1975. lifeguard North Wildwood (N.J.) Beach Patrol, 1970—, lt., 1986—. Author and illustrator: Sam and Spot, 1995, The Idle Wizards, 1995; illustrator: Six Creepy sheep, 1992, Daffy Down Dillies, 1992, Funny You Should Ask, 1992, What His Father Did, 1992, Brother Billy Bronto's Bygone Blues Band, 1992, Fast Freddie Frog, 1993, The Twelve Days of Christmas, 1993, This Is Baseball, 1993, Six Snowy Sheep, 1994, The Saracen and Leon Garfield, 1994, Tyranosaurus Tex, 1994, others; illustrator: The Saracen Maid; (mag. covers) Highlights for Children, The New Yorker, Global Fin.; cartoonist (mags.) Omini, Worth, Electronic Engring. Times; (newspaper) The Washington Post, The N.Y. Times, The Village Voice. Banjo profl. various dixieland bands. Recipient Pewter Plate awards Highlights for Children. Mem. U.S. Lifeguard Assn., Soc. Children's Book Writers and Illustrators, Cartoonist Assn. Avocations: running, crossword puzzles, bagpipes, piano. Office: 178 A Willow Turn Mount Laurel NJ 08054

O'BRIEN, JOHN WILFRID, economist, emeritus university president, educator; b. Toronto, Ont., Can., Aug. 4, 1931; s. Wilfred Edmond and Audrey (Swain) O'B.; m. Joyce Helen Bennett, Aug. 4, 1956; children—Margaret Anne, Catherine Audrey. B.A., McGill U., 1953, M.A., 1955, Ph.D., 1962, LL.D., 1976; postgrad., Inst. Polit. Studies, Paris, France, 1954; D.C.L., Bishop's U., 1976. Lectr. econs. Sir George Williams U., Montreal, 1954-57; asst. prof. Sir George Williams U., 1957-61, assoc. prof., 1961-63, asst. dean U., 1961-63, dean arts, 1963-68, vice prin. acad., 1968-69, prof., 1995-96, prin., vice chancellor, pres., 1969-74; rector, vice chancellor, pres. Concordia U., Montreal, 1974-84; rector emeritus Concordia U., 1984—; mem. Provincial Ednl. TV Com., Dept. Edn. Que., 1962-66, dep. chmn., 1965-66, mem. tchr. tng. planning com., 1964-66; mem. Gauthier Ad Hoc Com., Univ. Operating Budgets, 1965-68, Council Univs., 1969-76; pres. Conf. Rectors and Prins. Que. Univs., 1974-77; mem. council Assn. Commonwealth Univs., 1975-78; bd. dirs. Assn. Univs. and Colls., Can., 1977-79; mem. Conseil Consultatif sur l'Immigration, Que. Gov., 1977-79, Corp. Higher Edn. Forum, 1983-84; bd. govs. YMCA, 1969-89, Vanier Coll., 1975-79, Fraser-Hickson Inst., 1975—, pres. 1989-92, Que. div. Can. Mental Health Assn., 1977-79, Montreal World Film Festival, 1985—; sec., treas. Cinematheque Can., 1988—, World Film Fest. Found., 1989—; exec. mem. Alliance Que., 1989—; chmn. Alliance Que., 1990-91, 92—; hon. mem. Corp. Higher Edn. Forum, 1984—; hon. v.p. Que. Provincial council Boy Scouts Can., 1974-90; hon. councillor Montreal Mus. Fine Arts, 1969—. Author: Canadian Money and Banking, 1964, (with G. Lermer) 2d edit., 1969. Office: 1455 de Maisonneuve Blvd, Montreal, PQ Canada H3G 1M8

O'BRIEN, JOHN WILLIAM, JR., investment management company executive; b. Bronx, N.Y., Jan. 1, 1937; s. John William and Ruth Catherine (Timon) O'B.; BS, MIT, 1958; M.S., UCLA, 1964; m. Jane Bower Nippert, Feb. 2, 1963; children: Christine, Andrea, Michael, John William III, Kevin Robert. Sr. assoc. Planning Research Corp., Los Angeles, 1962-67; dir. fin. systems group Synergetic Scis., Inc., Tarzana, Calif., 1967-70; dir. analytical services div. James H. Oliphant & Co., Los Angeles, 1970-72; chmn. bd., chief exec. officer, pres. O'Brien Assocs., Inc., Santa Monica, Calif., 1972-75; v.p. A.G. Becker Inc., 1975-81; chmn., chief exec. officer Leland O'Brien Rubinstein Assos., 1981—. Served to 1st lt. USAF, 1958-62. Recipient Graham and Dodd award Fin. Analysts Fedn., 1970; named Businessman of Yr. Fortune Mag., 1987. Mem. Delta Upsilon. Home: 332 Piazza Lido Newport Beach CA 92663-4646 Office: Leland O'Brien Rubinstein Assocs 523 W 6th St Ste 220 Los Angeles CA 90014-1228

O'BRIEN, JOSEPH PATRICK, JR., printing company executive; b. Haverhill, Mass., May 25, 1940; s. Joseph P. and Helen M. (Atwood) O'B.; m. Gail E. Harris, May 19, 1962 (div. Apr. 1981); children: Michael, Pamela, Matthew, Amy; m. Phyllis L. Corso, July 12, 1981; children: Alicia, Jack. B.S.B.A., Northeastern U., Boston, 1963. CPA, N.J. Auditor Ernst & Ernst, N.Y.C., 1962-65; acctg. mgr. Austenal div. Howmet Corp., Dover, N.J., 1965-68, controller Alloy div., 1969-71, budget dir., 1972-75; controller Pechiney Ugine Kuhlmann Co., Greenwich, 1976-80; v.p. fin. Howmet Corp., Greenwich, 1980-93, Hart Holding and Reeves Industries, Darien, Conn., 1993-94; pres. Technicom, Inc., Norwalk, Conn., 1995—. Trustee King and Low-Heywood Thomas Schs. Mem. AICPA, Nat. Assn. Accts., Fin. Execs. Inst., Nat. Assn. Bus. Economists. Home and Office: 324 Main Ave S600 Norwalk CT 06851

O'BRIEN, KATHLEEN ANNE, special education educator; b. Toledo, Jan. 18, 1952; d. Robert Eugene and Livia Josephine (Marini) O'B. BS of Edn., Bowling Green State U., 1974; MEd, U. Tex., 1981. Cert. elem. edn., mental retardation, visually impaired, physically impaired, early childhood and adminstrn. and supervision. Tchr. pre-sch. handicapped Okeechobee (Fla.) Sch. Bd., 1974-76; tchr. visually impaired Manatee County Sch. Sys., Bradenton, Fla., 1981-82; tchr. varying exceptionalities Sarasota (Fla.) County Sch. Sys., 1976-80, tchr. presch. handicapped, 1982—; selected mem. steering com. Tchr. of Visually Handicapped for State of Fla., Tallahassee, 1978-80; selected mem. Validation Team for State Career Ladder Exam., Tallahassee, 1987; guest lectr. U. South Fla., Sarasota, 1979; presenter conf. for visually impaired presch. children, Tampa, Fla., 1984. Mem. adv. bd. Prevention of Blindness, Sarasota, 1978-81; bd. dirs. Planned Parenthood, Sarasota, 1983-84, United Cerebral Palsy, Sarasota, 1984-94; dir. Jr. League, Sarasota, 1993—. Mem. Fla. Developmental Disabilities (bd. dirs. 1989—, planning coun./gov. appointment), Fla. Assn. for Edn. and Rehab. (pres.-elect, pres. 1988—), State of Fla. Pilot Women Svc. Orgn. (Woman of Yr. 1990). Home: 107 Whispering Sands Cir Sarasota FL 34242-1624

O'BRIEN, KEITH THOMAS, engineering researcher and educator; b. Woking, Eng., Feb. 7, 1949; came to U.S., 1979; s. Thomas F. and Emily W. (Crabbe) O'B.; m. Kay K. Persaud, 1973; children: Siobhan K., Meghan M. BS in Engring., London U., 1971; MS, Leeds U., 1972, PhD, 1974. Enseigant Algerian Inst., Boumerdas, 1976-79; prof. Stevens Inst., Hoboken, N.J., 1979-81; sr. rsch. engr. Celanese, Summit, N.J., 1979-81, 1981-83, staff engr., 1983-85; staff engr. Celanese, Chatham, N.J., 1985-87; devel. assoc. Hoechst Celanese, Chatham, N.J., 1987-88; prof. N.J. Inst. Tech., Newark, 1988-92; mgr. R&D Johnson & Johnson Vision Products, 1992—. Patentee in field; editor: Computer Modeling, 1992; contbr. over 200 articles to profl. jours. Rsch. fellow Bradford U., 1974-76. Fellow Inst. Mechanical Engrs., Soc. Plastics Engrs. Episcopalian. Avocations: sailing, skiing, scuba diving, game fishing. Home: 7575 Hollyridge Rd Jacksonville FL 32256-7146 Office: Vistakon 5985 Richard St Jacksonville FL 32256

O'BRIEN, KENNETH ROBERT, life insurance company executive; b. Bklyn., June 18, 1937; s. Emmett Robert and Anna (Kelly) O'B.; m. Eileen M. Halligan, July 1, 1961; children: Joan Marie, Margaret Mary, Kathy Ann. B.S. in Bus. Adminstrn, Coll. Holy Cross, Worcester, Mass., 1959. With N.Y. Life Ins. Co., N.Y.C., 1962—; 2d v.p. N.Y. Life Ins. Co., 1973-77, v.p. investments, 1977-82, sr. v.p. pensions, 1982-87, sr. v.p. individual products, 1987-89, exec. v.p., 1989-91; chief exec. officer Aurora Nat. Life Assurance Co., L.A., 1991—; founder, pres., CEO O'Brien Asset Mgmt., Inc., 1993—. Served to 1st lt. USAF, 1959-62. Mem. Nat. Consumer Fin. Assn., Fin. Forum, N.Y. Soc. Security Analysts. Home: 165 Loines Ave E Merrick NY 11566-3211

O'BRIEN, KEVIN J., lawyer; b. N.Y.C., Mar. 12, 1934; s. George and Kathleen (Fox) O'B.; m. Winifred Gallagher, Aug. 23, 1958; children: Karen A., Kevin J., Susan M. BS, Fordham U., 1959; LLB, Columbia U., 1962. Bar: N.Y. 1962, U.S. Ct. Appeals (2d cir.) 1971, U.S. Dist. Ct. (so. dist.) N.Y. 1972, U.S. Tax Ct. 1972. Law clk. to presiding justice U.S. Ct. Appeals (2d. cir.), N.Y.C., 1962-63; assoc. Paul, Weiss, Rifkind, Wharton & Garrison, N.Y.C., 1963-70, ptnr., 1970—. Contbr. articles to profl. jours. Trustee Convent of Sacred Heart, Greenwich, Conn., 1979-82; mem. Cardinal's Com. of Laity, N.Y.C., 1986—. Served with USN, 1952-55. Mem. ABA, N.Y. State Bar Assn. (exec. com. sect. 1979-83), Assn. of Bar of City of N.Y. Office: Paul Weiss Rifkind Wharton & Garrison 1285 Avenue Of The Americas New York NY 10019-6028

O'BRIEN, L. DOUGLAS, banking executive; b. Mineola, N.Y., Mar. 27, 1939; s. Leonard D. and Melda B. (Anderson) O'B.; m. Mary Jo McIntyre, Feb. 27, 1965 (div. May 1979); m. Ellen Mary Downs, June 8, 1979; children: Karin D., Kenneth D., Kristine D., Kimberly D., Kevin D. BA, Rutgers U., 1964. Cadet trainee Consol. Edison, N.Y.C., 1964; v.p. Bankers Trust Co., N.Y.C., 1965-77; sr. v.p. Midlantic Banks Inc., Edison, N.J., 1977-82; sr. exec. v.p. Nat. Westminster Bank U.S.A., N.Y.C., 1982-89; pres., chief exec. officer Nat. Westminster Bank N.J., Jersey City, 1990-92; sr. exec. v.p., dir. Nat. Westminster Bancorp., 1990-92; pres., CEO Bank of Ireland First Holdings Inc./First N.H. Bank, Manchester, 1992—; trustee N.H. Bank, Manchester, 1992—; trustee N.J. Partnership, Princeton, 1990-92; bd. dirs. N.J. State C. of C.; chmn. N.H. Bankers Assn.; vice chmn. Bus. and Industry Assn.; bd. dirs. Currier Gallery of Art, N.H. Pub. TV, N.H. Charitable Found., Optima Health, Greater Manchester C. of C. Trustee Stevens Inst. Tech., Hoboken, N.J., 1990—; bd. dirs. UNICEF, N.Y.C., 1987-88, Boy Scouts Am., N.Y.C., 1986-90. Sgt. U.S. Army, 1959-61. Recipient Norman Feldman award Goodwill Industries of N.J., 1990, Gimble award MS Care Ctr. Comprehensive, Holy Dame Hosp., 1990, Silver Beaver award Boy Scouts Am., 1990, Bus. Industry Expo Leadership award Middlesex County Regional C. of C., 1991. Mem. N.J. Bankers Assn. (exec. com. 1990-92), Westchester County Assn. (bd. dirs. 1987-90), Consumer Bankers Assn. Republican. Roman Catholic. Avocations: music, sports, tennis, golf, theatre. Office: Bank Ireland 1st Holdings/1st NH Bank 1000 Elm St Manchester NH 03101

O'BRIEN, MARGARET HOFFMAN, educational administrator; b. Melrose, Mass., Aug. 22, 1947; d. John Francis and Margaret Mary (Colbert) Hoffman; m. Edward Lee O'Brien, June 13, 1970 (div. Sept. 1988); children: John Hoffman, Elizabeth Lee; m. Michael Ellis-Tolaydo, Mar. 9, 1991. AB, Trinity Coll., Washington, 1969; LHD (hon.), Trinity Coll., 1994; MA, Cath. U., 1971; LHD (hon.), Georgetown U., 1991; PhD, Am. U., 1993. English tchr. D.C. Pub. Schs., Washington, 1969-73; edn. coord. Street Law, Georgetown Law Ctr., Washington, 1973-75; owner, mgr. Man in the Green Hat Restaurant, Washington, 1976-81; head of edn. Folger Shakespeare Libr., Washington, 1981-94; dir. Teaching Shakespeare Inst., Washington, 1983-94; v.p. edn. Corp. for Pub. Broadcasting, Washington, 1994—; mem. faculty Prince of Wales Shakespeare Sch., Stratford on Avon, Eng., 1993; edn. dir. Fairfax (Va.) Family Theatre, 1988-93, Md. Shakespeare Festival, St. Mary's City, 1988-91; head of faculty Atlantic Shakespeare Inst., Wroxton, U.K., 1985-90. Gen. editor: Shakespeare Set Free, 1993-95. Bd. dirs. Edmund Burke Sch., Washington, 1993—, Capitol Hill Day Sch., 1994—, Fillmore Arts Ctr., Washington, 1991-93, Capitol Hill Arts Workshop, Washington, 1989-91, Horizons Theatre, 1991, Janice F. Delaney Found., 1991—; site visitor U.S. Dept. Edn., Washington, 1990; mem. nat. adv. bd. Orlando Shakespeare Festival, 1990-93. Mem. Shakespeare Assn. Am., Nat. Coun. Tchrs. English. Office: Corp for Pub Broadcasting 901 E St NW Washington DC 20004-2037

O'BRIEN, MARGARET JOSEPHINE, retired community health nurse; b. N.Y.C., Dec. 5, 1918; d. John J. and Nellie (Coyle) O'B. BS, St.John's U., 1954, MS, 1962; MPH, Columbia U., 1964. With Health Dept., City of New York, 1943-81, assoc. dir. Bur. Pub. Health Nursing, dir. Pub. Health Nursing Svc., asst. commr. pub. health nursing; retired. Contbr. articles to profl. jours. Recipient Outstanding Alumnus of Columbia U. Sch. of Pub. Health award, 1994. Mem. ANA, APHA, NLN, N.Y. State Nurses Assn., N.Y.C. Pub. Health Assn. Home: 11055 72nd Rd Forest Hills NY 11375-5472

O'BRIEN, MARK STEPHEN, pediatric neurosurgeon; b. West New York, N.J., Jan. 2, 1933; s. Mark Peter and Hannah (Dempsey) O'B.; m. Mary Morris Johnson, June 3, 1961 (div.); children: David, Derek, Marcia; m. Karen-Marie Sampson, June 1, 1984; children: Blythe, Blake, Lauren-Blair, Connor. A.B. cum laude, Seton Hall U., 1955; M.D., St. Louis U., 1959. Intern St. John's Hosp., St. Louis, 1959-60; resident in surgery St. John's Hosp., 1960; resident in neurology Charity Hosp., New Orleans, 1962-63; resident in neurosurgery St. Vincent's Hosp., N.Y.C., 1963-64; resident in surgery St. Vincent's Hosp., 1965; sr. resident, chief resident Cin. Children's Hosp., U. Cin., 1965-68, research fellow in neurosurgery, 1966-67, 67-68; NIH spl. fellow in neuroradiology Albert Einstein Coll. Medicine, N.Y.C., 1968-69; mem. faculty dept. surgery Emory U. Sch. Medicine, Atlanta, 1969—; prof. surgery, assoc. prof. pediatrics Emory U. Sch. Medicine, 1979—; chief neurosurgery Henrietta Egleston Hosp. for Children, Atlanta, 1971—; trustee Elaine Clark Center for Exceptional Children; mem. med. adv. bd. Nat. Found., March of Dimes; trustee Henrietta Egleston Hosp. for Children; mem. profl. adv. panel Spina Bifida Assn. Am. Editorial bd. Pediatric Neurosurgery; contbr. chpts. to books, articles to med. jours. Served with USNR, 1960-62. Mem. Am. Assn. Neurol. Surgeons, Soc. Neurol. Surgeons, Congress Neurol. Surgeons, Internat. Soc. Pediatric Neurosurgery, Greater Atlanta Pediatric Soc., Med. Soc. Atlanta, AMA, ACS, Ga. Neurosurg. Soc., Am. Acad. Pediatrics, Am. Soc. Pediatric Neurosurgery, Pediatric Oncology Group, Am. Bd. Pediatric Neurol. Surgery (sec.), Acad. Pediatric Neurosurgeons. Home: 82 Huntington Rd Atlanta GA 30309 Office: 1900 Century Blvd NE Ste 4 Atlanta GA 30345-3304

O'BRIEN, MARY DEVON, communications executive, consultant; b. Buenos Aires, Argentina, Feb. 13, 1944; came to U.S., 1949, naturalized, 1962; d. George Earle and Margaret Frances (Richards) Owen; m. Gordon Covert O'Brien, Feb. 16, 1962 (div. Aug. 1982); children: Christopher Covert, Devon Elizabeth; m. Christopher Gerard Smith, May 28, 1983. BA, Rutgers U., 1975, MBA, 1976. Project mgmt. cert., 1989. Contr. manpower Def. Comm. divsn. ITT, Nutley, N.J., 1977-80, adminstr. program, 1977-78, mgr. cost, schedule control, 1978-79, voice processing project, 1979-80; mgr. project Avionics divsn. ITT, Nutley, 1980-81, sr. mgr. projects, 1981-93, cons. strategic planning, 1983-95; pres. Anamex, Inc., 1995—; bd. trustees South Mountain Counseling Ctr., 1987—, chmn. bd. trustees, 1994—; bd. dirs. N.J. Eye Inst.; session leader Internet Conf., Florence, Italy, 1992; session moderator, panel mem. MES Conf., Cairo, Egypt, 1993, speaker, session leader Calgary, 1994, keynote speaker New Zealand, 1995; lectr. in field. Author: Pace: System Manual, 1979, Voices, 1982; contbr. articles to profl. jours. and Maplewood Community calendar. Chmn. Citizens Budget Adv. Com., Maplewood, N.J., 1984-87, chmn. recreation, libr., pub. svcs., 1982-83, 94—, chmn. pub. safety, emergency svcs., 1983-84, chmn. schs. and edn., 1984-85; bd. trustees United Way Essex and West Hudson Community Svc. Coun., 1988—; first v.p. Maplewood Civic Assn., 1987-89, pres., 1989-91, sec. 1993-94, bd. dirs., officer, 1984—; chmn. Maple Leaf Svc. award Com., 1987-89, 94—, Community Svc. Coun. of Oranges and Maplewood Homelessness, Affordable Housing, Shelter Com., 1988—; chmn. speaker's bur. United Way, 1989-93; v.p. mktg. United Way Community Svc. Coun. of Oranges and Maplewood, 1990-93, v.p. 1994; mem. Maplewood Zoning Bd. of Adjustment, 1983—; officer, mem. exec. bd. N.J. Project Mgmt. Inst., 1985—, pres., 1987-88, v.p. adminstrn., 1994—, pres., 1995—; bd. dirs. Performance Mgmt. Assn.; chmn. Charter Com.; chmn. Internat. Project Mgmt. Inst. Jour. and Membership survey, 1986-87, mktg. com., 1986-89, long range planning and steering com., 1987—; bd. dirs., vice chmn. Coun. Chpt. Pres. Interaction Com., 1986-90, chmn., 1991—, pres. Internat. Project Mgmt. Inst., 1991, chmn., 1992, v.p. Region II, 1989-90; adv. bd. Project Mgmt. Jour., 1987-90, N.J. PMI Ednl., 1987—; liaison officer; apptd. fellow Leadership N.J., 1993—, Internat. Project Mgmt. Inst. and Performance Mgmt. Assocs.; mem. MCA/N.J. Blood Bank Drive; chmn. Maplewood Community Calendar, 1990—; trustee community svc. coun. and edn. program United Way Essex and West Hudson, 1988—, also, chmn. leadership div., chmn. speakers bur., 1991— and mem. communications com., v.p. mktg. community svc. coun., Oranges and Maplewood, 1991-93. Recipient Spl. commendation for Community Svc. Twp. Maplewood, 1987; First Place award Anti-Shoplifting Program for Distributive Edn. Club Am., 1981, N.J. Fedn. of Women's Clubs, 1981, 82, Retail Mchts. Assn., 1981, 82; Commendation and Merit awards Air Force Inst. Tech., 1981; Pres.'s Safety award ITT, 1983; State award 1st Pl. N.J. Fedn. of Women's Clubs Garden Show, 1982, Outstanding Pres. award Internat. Project Mgmt. Inst., 1988, Outstanding Svc. and Contbrn. award 1986-87; Cert. Spl. Merit award N.J. Fedn. of Women's Clubs, 1982, Disting. Contbn. award United Way, 1990, Pursuit of Exellence Cost Savings Achievement award ITT Avionics, 1990, Meritorious Svc. Recognition award Internat. Project Mgmt. Inst., 1989-90, Maple Leaf award for outstanding community svc., 1992, Phoebe and Benjamin Shackelford award United Way, 1992, U.S. Ho. Reps. citation, 1992, N.H. Gen. Assembly Senate resolution for Community Leadership and Svc., 1992, resolution of Appreciation Township of Maplewood; N.J. Leadership fellow, 1993, awarded fellow of Internat. Project Mgmt. Inst., 1995. Mem. Internat. Platform Speakers Assn., Grand Jury Assn., Telecommunications Group and Aerospace Industries Assn., Women's CarNat. Security Indsl. Assn., Assn. for Info. and

Image Mgmt., Internat. Project Mgmt. Inst. (liaison officerpres. 1991—), Performance Mgmt. Assn, ITT Mgmt. Assn., NAFE, Rutger's Grad. Sch. Bus. Mgmt. Alumni Assn., Maplewood LWV (chair women and family issues com., bd. dirs.), Maplewood Women's Evening Membership Div. (pres. 1980-82), Lions (Maplewood dir. 1992-95, program chmn. 1991-92, treas. 1994-95, N.J. dist. 16E zone chmn. 1992-93, cabinet sec. internat. dist., region chmn. 1993-94, trustee Eye Bank N.J., internat. dist. 16-E cabinet sec. 1994-95). Home: 594 Valley St Maplewood NJ 07040-2616 Office: 21 Madison Plz Ste 152 Madison NJ 07940-2354

O'BRIEN, SISTER MAUREEN, school system administrator; b. Manchester, England, Dec. 3, 1939. BEd (equivalent), U. Durham, Eng., 1960; BA, U. Pacific, 1969; diploma in secondary sch. adminstrn., Manchester Poly., Eng., 1978. Joined Daus. of Cross of Liège, 1962. Tchr. St. Ambrose Secondary Sch., Rawtenstall, Calif., Eng., 1960-62, St. Philomena's Collegiate Sch., Carshalton, Eng., 1962-67; tchr. St. Bernard Sch., Tracy, Calif., 1969-76, vice prin., 1972-76; vice prin. Holy Cross Coll., Bury, Eng., 1976-84; prin. St. Bernard Sch., 1985-93; supt. schs. Roman Cath. Diocese of Stockton, Calif., 1993—. Office: Office Supt Schs PO Box 4237 Stockton CA 95204-0237

O'BRIEN, MAURICE JAMES, business executive; b. Chgo., Aug. 30, 1925; m. Frances McDonald; children—Marynell, James M., Paula, Elizabeth, William, Martha, Timothy, John, Joe, Peter, Clare, Catherine, Jane. B.S., Northwestern U., 1947, J.D., 1949; LL.D., Coll. Great Falls, Mont., 1967. Asst. to pres. Robinson Bros. & Co., Chgo., 1950—; founder, pres. Chgo. Coke Co., (changed to Bulk Chems. Co., then Luria Bros., subs. Ogden & Co., N.Y.), 1951-61; v.p. sales Marblehead Lime Co., Chgo., subs. Gen. Dynamics Corp., St. Louis, 1961, pres., 1966-84, chmn., chief exec. officer, 1984-88, ret.; pres., chief exec. officer Arnel, Inc., Winnetka, Ill., 1988—; chmn. bd. subsidiaries Darlington Brick & Clay Products Co., Pa., Powell & Minnock Brick Works, Inc., Albany, N.Y.; dir. 1st Nat. Bank, Evanston, chmn. exec. com., 1970-85; dir. Pepper Constrn. Co., Chgo.; former dir. Advance Ross Corp., Chgo., Laidlaw Industries, Hinsdale, Ill., Miller Co., Chgo., Asbestos Corp., Ltd. Bd. dirs. former chmn. bd. St. Francis Hosp., Evanston. Served with U.S. Army, 1943-45. Recipient Merit award Northwestern U., 1968. Mem. Ill. Mfrs. Assn. (chmn. bd.), NAM (former dir.), Nat. Lime Assn. (chmn., merit award 1967). Clubs: John Henry Wigmore (former dir., past pres.) (Northwestern U. Sch. Law); Chgo., University (Chgo.); Econ., Bob O'Link Golf, Glen View, Riomar Golf Club (Vero Beach, Fla.). Home and Office: 33 Meadowview Dr Northfield IL 60093-3547

O'BRIEN, NANCY PATRICIA, librarian, educator; b. Galesburg, Ill., Mar. 17, 1955; d. Leo Frederick O'Brien and Yvonne Blanche (Uhlmann) O'Brien Tabb; 1 child, Nicole Pamela. AB in English, U. Ill., 1976, MS in LS, 1977. Vis. instr. U. Ill., Urbana, 1977-78, asst. prof. libr. adminstrn., 1978-84, assoc. prof., 1984-91, prof., 1991—, serials bibliographer, 1977-78, social sci. bibliographer collection devel. div., 1979-81, project dir. Title II-C grant, 1987-88, acting libr. and info. sci. libr., 1989-90, head Edn. and Social Sci. Libr., 1994—, edn. subject specialist, 1981—; discussion leader Ill. White House Conf. on Libr. and Info. svcs., 1990; mem. nat. adv. bd. Office Ednl. Rsch. and Improvement, U.S. Dept. Edn., 1989-91; grant proposal reviewer NEH, 1991; mem. adv. bd. Ctr. for Children's Books, 1992—; cons. Ark. Coll., 1989; chmn. rev. team Instrnl. Materials Ctr., U. Wis., Madison, 1989; presenter in field. Author: Test Construction: A Bibliography of Resources, 1988, (with Emily Fabiano) Core List of Books and Journals in Education, 1991; co-editor Media/Microforms column Series Rev., 1979-82; mem. editl. bd. Bull. Bibliography, 1982-90; asst. editor Libr. Hi Tech., 1983-85; editor EBSS Newsletter, 1990-91; contbr. articles to profl. jours., chpts. to books. Mem. ALA (Whitney-Carnegie grantee 1990-91), Am. Ednl. Rsch. Assn. (spl. interest group on libr. resources and info. tech.), Assn. Coll. and Rsch. Librs. (access policy guidelines task force 1990—, vice chmn., chmn.-elect edn. and behavioral scis. sect. 1993—, chmn. 1994-95), Libr. Adminstrn. and Mgmt. Assn. (edn. and tng. com. pub. rels. sect. 1990-95), Resources and Tech. Svcs. Divsn.(micropub. com. 1982-85, chmn. 1983-85, cons. 1985-87). Office: U Ill Edn & Social Sci Libr 100 Main Libr 1408 W Gregory Dr Urbana IL 61801-3607

O'BRIEN, ORIN YNEZ, musician, educator; b. Hollywood, Calif., June 7, 1935; s. George Joseph and Marguerite Graham (Churchill) O'Brien. Studied double bass with Frederick Zimmermann and Milton Kestenbaum; diploma, The Juilliard Sch., 1957. Former double bassist N.Y.C. Ballet Orch., Saidenberg Little Symphony, Am. Symphony, 1956-66; double bassist N.Y. Philharm., N.Y.C., 1966—; former mem. faculty YMHA Sch. Music, 1967-71; mem. faculty Manhattan Sch. Music, N.Y.C., 1969—, Mannes Coll. Music, N.Y.C., 1988—, The Julliard Sch., N.Y.C., 1990—; co-chair double bass dept., 1992—; participant numerous chamber music festivals, including Marlboro; featured in 1st performances of Gunther Schuller Quartet for 4 double basses; artist for GM, CBS and RCA Recording cos. Mem. Am. Fedn. Musicians, Internat. Soc. Bassists. Avocations: reading, writing, cooking.

O'BRIEN, PATRICK MICHAEL, library administrator; b. Newport, R.I., Mar. 17, 1943; s. Joseph Xavier and Loretta (DeCotis) O'B.; m. Roberta Luther, Nov. 27, 1977; children—Megan MacRae, Brendan Watters. B.A. in Eng. Lit., Merrimack Coll., North Andover, Mass., 1964; M.L.S., U. R.I., Kingston, 1965; M.B.A., Case Western Res. U., Cleve., 1983. Reference libr. Newsweek mag., N.Y.C., 1965-72; asst. dir. rsch. FIND/SVP, N.Y.C., 1972-74; head cen. libr., cultural ctr. Chgo. Pub. Libr., 1974-79; dir. Cuyahoga County Pub. Libr., Cleve., 1979-84; dir. librs. Dallas Pub. Libr., 1984-92; dir. Alexandria (Va.) Libr., 1992—. Mem. editorial bd. Handel's Nat. Directory for Performing Arts; contbr. articles to profl. jours. Participant, alumnus Leadership Dallas Program, 1984-85, Leadership Cleve. Program, 1981; mem. nat. adv. com. to Libr. of Congress; mem. adv. coun. Tex. State Libr., Libr. Svcs. and Constrn. Act, 1986-89; co-chair, del. selection com. Tex. Conf. on Librs. and Info. Svcs.; mem. com. Goals for Dallas, 1985; mem. exec. bd. univ. librs. So. Meth. U., 1985—; bd. dirs. Urban Community Sch., Cleve., 1982-84, Mus. African-Am. Life and Culture, 1985-86; mem. client data base com. Dallas Assn. Svcs. to Homeless, 1988-90; mem. Latchkey Children's Task Force, 1985-90. Recipient Servant as Leader award City of Dallas, 1989, Disting. Alumnus award U. R.I. Grad. Sch. Libr. and Info. Studies, 1990. Mem. ALA (coun. mem. 1987-95), Am. Libr. Trustee Assn. (bd. dirs.), Pub. Libr. Assn. (pres. 1985-86), Pub. Libr. Systems Sect (pres. 1983), Tex. Libr. Assn. (legis com. 1986-92), Tex. Women's Univ. Sch. Libr. and Info. Studies Vis. Com., Tex. Ctr. for Book Dallas Pub. Libr., Cleve. Area Met. Libr. Systems (pres. bd. 1980), Chgo. Libr. Club (pres. 1978), D.C. Libr. Assn., Va. Pub. Libr. Dirs. Assn. (bd. dirs. 1994—), Va. Libr. Assn., Online Computer Libr. Ctr. (bd. trustees 1992—), The White House Conf. on Librs. and Info. Svcs. (del. 1991), Pub. Lib. Adminstrs. N.Tex. (pres. 1990-91), Dallas 40, Rotary of Alexandria (bd. dirs. 1996—), Beta Gamma Sigma. Office: Alexandria Libr 717 Queen St Alexandria VA 22314-2420

O'BRIEN, PATRICK WILLIAM, lawyer; b. Chgo., Dec. 5, 1927; s. Maurice Edward and Ellen (Fitzgerald) O'B.; m. Deborah Bissell, July 2, 1955; children: Kathleen, Mariellen, Patrick, James, Patricia. BS in Mech. Engring., Northwestern U., 1947, JD, 1950. Bar: Ill. 1951, U.S. Dist. Ct. (no. dist.) Ill. 1954, U.S. Dist. Ct. (so. dist.)Ill. 1956, U.S. Ct. Appeals (7th cir.) 1955, U.S. Ct. Appeals (8th cir.) 1972, U.S. Supreme Ct. 1970. Assoc. Bell, Boyd, Marshall & Lloyd, Chgo., 1950-51; assoc. Mayer, Brown & Platt, Chgo., 1953-62, ptnr., 1962-94, sr. counsel, 1995—. Served to capt. USAF, 1951-53. Fellow Am. Coll. Trial Lawyers; mem. ABA, Ill. Bar Assn., Chgo. Bar Assn. Republican. Roman Catholic. Clubs: Chgo., Mid-Day, University, Westmoreland Country, Cliff Dwellers, Dairymen's Country. Home: 1119 Judson Ave Evanston IL 60202-1314 Office: Mayer Brown & Platt 190 S La Salle St Chicago IL 60603-3441

O'BRIEN, PAUL CHARLES, telephone company executive; b. N.Y.C., May 12, 1939; s. Charles Edward and Clare Mary (Becker) O'B.; m. Marie P. Moane, Dec. 30, 1961; children: Carolyn M., Deirdre M., Barbara M., Erin M. BEE, Manhattan Coll., 1960; MBA, NYU, 1968. Supervising engr. N.Y. Telephone Co., N.Y.C., 1964-67, div. engr., 1967-72, gen. staff supr., 1972-75, gen. planning engr., 1975-77, asst. v.p., 1977-83, pres. N.Y. New Eng. Exchange Enterprises, 1973-85, v.p. customer service, 1985-86; now chmn. exec. com., pres., CEO NYNEX, Boston, 1987—, also dir.; bd. dirs. N.Y. New Eng. Exchange Systems Mktg. Co., N.Y.C., N.Y. New Eng. Exhange Info. Resources Co., Lynn, Mass., N.Y. New Eng. Exchange Service Co., White Plains, N.Y. Bd. dirs. YMCA, N.Y.C., 1986, Greater Boston Adult Literacy Fund, 1988, Jobs for Mass., Boston, 1988; assoc. chmn. United Way Ea. New Eng., 1988. Capt. USAF, 1961-64. Mem. AFCA, IEEE. Roman Catholic. Avocations: golf, musical shows. Office: O'Brien Group 1 International Pl Fl 30 Boston MA 02110*

O'BRIEN, PAUL HERBERT, surgeon; b. Evanston, Ill., Sept. 12, 1930; s. Maurice Edward and Nellie (Fitzgerald) O'B.; m. Ann Hope Miller, Aug. 28, 1965; children—Jennifer, Paul Edward. B.S., Northwestern U., 1950, M.D., 1954. Diplomate: Am. Bd. Surgery. Intern Northwestern U. Hosp., Chgo., 1954-55; asst. prof. surgery Northwestern U. Hosp., 1967-69; resident in surgery Cook County Hosp., Chgo., 1957-62; sr. resident Meml. Sloan Kettering Inst. Cancer and Allied Diseases, N.Y.C., 1962-65; also USPHS sr. fellow; assoc. prof. Med. U. S.C., Charleston, 1970-72, prof., 1972—, Am. Cancer Soc. clin. prof. oncology, 1974-79; chief Gold Surgery. Contbr. articles to profl. jours. Served to capt. AUS, 1955-57. Recipient career devel. award Schweppe Found. Mem. A.C.S., Soc. Surg. Oncology, Am. Cancer Soc. (past pres. profl. edn. com.), AMA, Halsted Soc., AAUP, Chgo. Surg. Soc. Anglo Catholic. Home: 1467 Burningtree Rd Charleston SC 29412-2602 Office: 171 Ashley Ave Charleston SC 29425-0001

O'BRIEN, RAYMOND VINCENT, JR., banker; b. Bronx, N.Y., Sept. 23, 1927; s. Raymond Vincent and Blanche (Harper) O'B.; m. Theresa Sweeney, Mar. 29, 1952 (dec. June 1981); children: Susan, Raymond, Christopher, Sean, Carol, Nancy Meisenzahl; m. Ellen Boyle, July 24, 1982. A.B., Fordham U., 1951, J.D., 1958; postgrad., Advanced Mgmt. Program, Harvard U., 1969. With Chase Manhattan Bank (N.A.), N.Y.C., 1953-74; chief exec. officer, chmn. bd. Emigrant Savs. Bank, N.Y.C., 1978-92; dir. Emigrant Savs. Bank, 1974—; bd. dirs. Emigrant Savs. Bank, Internat. Shipholding Corp. Trustee Fordham U., 1979-92; chmn. bd. trustees Regis High Sch., 1988-92; past chmn. Community Bankers Assn., N.Y., Nat. Assn. Community Bankers. Served with AUS, 1946-47, 51-53. Mem. N.Y. State Bar Assn., Guild Cath. Lawyers, Sky Club, Econ. Club, Navesink Country Club (Middletown, N.J.), Sawgrass Country Club (Ponte Vedra, Fla.), Plantation Country Club (Ponte Vedra), Knights of Malta, Friendly Sons St. Patrick. Republican. Roman Catholic. Home: 102 Lands End Ponte Vedra Beach FL 32082-3906

O'BRIEN, RICHARD DESMOND, university administrator, neurobiologist; b. Sydenham, Eng., May 29, 1929; came to U.S., 1960, naturalized, 1966; s. Joseph Andrew and Louise (Stevens) O'B.; m. Ann Margaret Thom, Mar. 16, 1961; 1 child, Ian Richard; m. Susan Krauss Whitbourne, Sept. 19, 1981, 1 child, Jennifer Louise. B.Sc., Reading (Eng.) U., 1950; Ph.D. in Chemistry, U. Western Ont., Can., 1954, B.A. in Arts, 1956. Soil specialist Ont. Agrl. Coll., Guelph, 1950-51; chemist Pesticide Research Inst., London, Can., 1954-60; faculty Cornell U., 1960-78, prof. entomology, 1964-78, prof. neurobiology, 1965-78, chmn. dept. biochemistry, 1964-65, chmn. sect. neurobiology and behavior, 1965-70, dir. div. biol. scis., 1970-78, Richard J. Schwartz prof. biology and soc., 1977-78; provost U. Rochester (N.Y.), 1978-84; exec. vice chancellor, provost U. Mass., Amherst, 1984-91, chancellor, 1991—; NRC fellow Babraham, Cambridge, Eng., 1956-57; vis. assoc. prof. U. Wis., 1958-59; cons. Melpar Inc., 1960-65, Am. Cyanamid Co., 1960-69; dir. Lincoln First Bank, 1978-84. Author: Toxic Phosphorus Esters, 1960, (with L.S. Wolfe) Radiation, Radioactivity and Insects, 1964, Insecticides, Action and Metabolism, 1967, (with I. Yamamoto) Biochemical Toxicology of Insecticides, 1970, (with E.O. Wilson, others) Life on Earth, 1973, The Receptors, A Comprehensive Treatise, vol. I, 1979; also articles.; Founding editor: Pesticide Biochemistry and Physiology, 1971. Trustee Center for Govtl. Research, 1979-84, vice-chmn., 1980-84; trustee Rochester Mus. and Sci. Center, 1979-84, Donald Guthrie Found. Med. Research, Sayre, Pa., 1977-84; pres. Rochester Area Colls., 1982-84; bd. dirs. Five Colls. Inc., 1990—. Guggenheim fellow Naples, Italy, 1967-68. Fellow AAAS; mem. Am. Chem. Soc. (Internat. award pesticide chemistry 1971), Internat. Brain Rsch. Orgn., Phi Beta Kappa, Sigma Xi. Office: U Mass Office of Chancellor Amherst MA 01003

O'BRIEN, RICHARD FRANCIS, advertising agency executive; b. Everett, Mass., Aug. 3, 1942; s. James Raymond and Gertrude Lucille O'B.; m. Clare Lynch, Apr. 7, 1973; children: Catherine Lynch, Miles Edward. A.B. magna cum laude, Boston Coll., 1964; M.A., Ind. U., 1965; M.B.A., Columbia U., 1967. With Grey Advt. Inc., N.Y.C., 1967-83; v.p., mgmt. supr. Grey Advt. Inc., 1973-77, sr. v.p., mgmt. rep., 1977-80, exec. v.p., mgmt. rep., 1980-83; exec. v.p., mgmt. dir. Dancer Fitzgerald Sample, Inc. (name changed to Saatchi & Saatchi Advt.), N.Y.C., 1983-88; vice chmn. Dancer Fitzgerald Sample, Inc. (became Saatchi & Saatchi Advt.), N.Y.C., 1988—; bd. dirs. Saatchi & Saatchi Advt. Worldwide, 1989—. Bd. dirs. Spl. Olympics Internat., 1983—. Office: Saatchi & Saatchi Advt 375 Hudson St New York NY 10014-3658

O'BRIEN, RICHARD L(EE), academic administrator, physician, cell biologist; b. Shenandoah, Iowa, Aug. 30, 1934; s. Thomas Lee O'B. and Grace Ellen (Sims) Parish; m. Joan Frances Gurney, June 29, 1957; children: Sheila Marie, Kathleen Therese, Michael James, Patrick Kevin. M.S. in Physiology, Creighton U., 1958, M.D., 1960. Diplomate: Nat. Bd. Med. Examiners. Intern and resident Columbia med. div. Bellevue Hosp., N.Y.C., 1960-62; postdoctoral fellow in biochemistry Inst. for Enzyme Research, U. Wis., 1962-64; asst. prof. to prof. pathology Sch. Medicine, U. So. Calif., Los Angeles, 1966-82, dep. dir. Cancer Ctr., 1975-80, dir. research and edn. Cancer Ctr., 1980-81; dir. Cancer Ctr. Sch. Medicine, U. So. Calif., 1981-82; dean Sch. Medicine Creighton U., Omaha, 1982-92; acting v.p. health scis. Creighton U., 1984-85, v.p. health scis., 1985—; vis. prof. molecular biology U. Geneva, 1973-74; cons. in field; mem. cancer control research grants rev. com. NIH, Nat. Cancer Inst.; mem. Cancer Ctr. Support grant rev. com. Nat. Cancer Inst., 1984-88, chmn. 1987-88; co-chmn. United Way/CHAD Pacesetter campaign, 1988, 94. Contbr. articles; editor various profl. jours. Served to capt. U.S. Army, 1964-66. Spl. fellow Nat. Cancer Inst., 1967-69; Combined Health Agys. Drive—Health Citizen of Yr., 1986. Mem. ACP, Am. Assn. Pathologists, Am. Assn. Cancer Rsch., Am. Assn. Cancer Edn., AAAS, Am. Assn. Cancer Insts. (dir. 1982-83), Assn. Am. Med. Colls. (chmn. MCAT evaluation panel 1987-88, liaison com. on med. edn., 1988-93, co-chmn, 1989-93, adv. panel Strategic Planning Health Care Reform 1992—), Assn. Acad. Health Ctrs. (long-range planning com. 1986, nominating com. 1987, 96, Task Force Health Care Delivery 1992, mem. task force on leadership and instl. values 1993—), Am. Cancer Soc. (adv. com. Inst. rsch. Grants 1977-80 Outstanding Leadership award, dir. Calif. div. 1980-82, dir. Nebr. divsn. 1992-96), Am. Hosp. Assn. (com. on med. edn. 1986-89), Alpha Omega Alpha. Home: 142 N Elmwood Rd Omaha NE 68132-3452 Office: Creighton Univ VP Health Sci California at 24th Omaha NE 68178

O'BRIEN, ROBERT BROWNELL, JR., investment banker, consultant, savings bank executive, yacht broker, performing company executive; b. N.Y.C., Sept. 6, 1934; s. Robert Brownell and Eloise (Boles) O'B.; m. Sarah Lager, Nov. 28, 1958; children: Robert Brownell III, William Stuart, Jennifer. BA, Lehigh U., 1957; postgrad., NYU, Am. Inst. Banking. Asst. treas., credit officer, br. locations officer Bankers Trust Co., N.Y.C., 1957-63; v.p., dir. bus. devel. George A. Murray Co., gen. contractors, N.Y.C., 1964; also v.p. Bowery Savs. Bank, 1964-69; dir., chief exec. officer Fed. Savs. & Loan Ins. Corp., Washington, 1969-71; chmn. exec. com. Fed. Home Loan Bank Bd., 1969-71; v.p. Bowery Savs. Bank, N.Y.C., 1972; exec. v.p. First Fed. Savs. & Loan Assn., N.Y.C., 1973-75; chmn., chief exec. officer Carteret Savs. Bank, Morristown, 1975-91, also bd. dirs.; mng. dir. Printon Kane Group Inc., Short Hills, N.J., 1991-94; dir., former chief exec. officer Govs. Bank Corp., West Palm Beach, 1992—; bd. dirs. Fed. Home Loan Bank N.Y., Govs. Bank Corp.; vice chmn. 1st Mortgage Capital Corp., Vero Beach, Fla.; chmn. Neighborhood Housing Svcs. Am., 1972-91; vice chmn., bd dirs. U.S. League Savs. Instns., Washington, O'Brien Yacht Sales. Contbr. articles to trade mags. Trustee Trinity Pawling Sch., Palm Beach County Housing Partnership, Lehigh U.; chmn. Housing Opportunities Found.; trustee, past chmn. Cmty. Found. of N.J., 1987—; vice chmn., bd. dirs. Dalt Found.; chmn. adv. bd. Palm Beach Maritime Mus., Peanut Island, Fla.; active Nat. Commn. on Neighborhoods; past chmn., exec. dir. N.J. State Opera. Mem. Nat. Coun. Savs. Instns. (past chmn.), Essex County Savs. and Loan League (past chmn.), N.J. Savs. League (past chmn.), N.J. Hist. Soc. (past chmn.), Greater Newark C. of C. (bd. dirs.), N.J. C. of C. (bd. dirs.), Union League Club, Delray Beach Yacht Club (past commodore), New York Yacht Club, Morris County Golf Club, Somerset Hills Golf Club, Palm Beach Yacht Club, Bay Head Yacht Club (past commodore). Republican. Episcopalian. Home: 12 Banyan Rd Gulf Stream FL 33483-7425 Office: 1400 Centrepark Blvd Ste 909 West Palm Beach FL 33401-7412

O'BRIEN, ROBERT JOHN, JR., public relations executive, former government official, air force officer; b. Wheeling, W. Va., Apr. 16, 1935; s. Robert John and Martha Virginia (Hunter) O'B.; m. Margaret Eugenia Schultz. B.S. in Journalism, Northwestern U., 1957; M.A. in Journalism, U. Wis., 1970; grad., Indsl. Coll. Armed Forces, 1977. Comnd. officer U.S. Air Force, 1957, advanced through grades to col.; dir. pub. affairs N. Am. Air Def. Command, Colorado Springs, Colo., 1977-80, Air Force Systems Command, Camp Springs, Md., 1980-82; dir. def. info. Office Sec. Def., Washington, 1982-83, dep. asst. sec. def., 1983-86; dir. pub. rels., Washington McDonnell Douglas Corp., Arlington, Va., 1986—. Decorated D.S.M., Legion of Merit, Bronze Star, Air medal, Medal of Honor (Republic Vietnam). Mem. Air Force Assn., Pub. Rels. Soc. Am., Aviation/Space Writers Assn., U.S. Space Found., Ret. Officers Assn., U.S. C. of C. (pub. affairs com.), Hidden Creek Country Club (Reston, Va.), Nat. Aviation Club, Nat. Press Club. Republican. Methodist. Avocations: golf; stamp collecting; model railroading. Home: 13804 Leighfield St Chantilly VA 22021-2503

O'BRIEN, ROBERT KENNETH, insurance company executive; b. Worcester, Mass., Dec. 8, 1934; s. Robert Ivor O'Brien and Arline Mary (Lanois) Knight; m. Barbara Ann Hickey, Dec. 28, 1957; children: Kevin Robert, Brendan Robert. BS in Edn., Worcester State Coll., 1958. CLU. Group underwriter State Mut. of Am., Worcester, 1958-74, v.p. group underwriting, 1974-86, v.p. bus. unit, 1987, v.p. reins., 1988-90; pres. Health Reins. Mgmt., Inc., Salem, Mass., 1990—; v.p., bd. dirs. Bibliomania, Inc., West Yarmouth, Mass, 1982-87. Pres. Westboro PTA, 1965; chmn. Young Reps. Conv., Mass., 1960. Mem. Health Ins. Assn. Am., Life Office Mgmt. Assn., Am. Soc. CLUs, Self-Ins. Inst. Am., Am. Arbitration Assn. Avocations: boating, fishing, scuba diving, flying, golf. Office: Health Reinsurance Mgmt Inc 27 Congress St Salem MA 01970-5575

O'BRIEN, ROBERT S., state official; b. Seattle, Sept. 14, 1918; s. Edward R. and Maude (Ransom) O'B.; m. Kathryn E. Arvan, Oct. 18, 1941 (dec. June 1984). Student public schs. With Kaiser Co., 1938-46; restaurant owner, 1946-50; treas. Grant County, Wash., 1950-65, State of Wash., 1965-89; chmn. Wash. State Fin. Com., 1965-89, Wash. Public Deposit Protection Commn., 1969-89, Wash. Public Employees Retirement Bd., 1969-77, Law Enforcement Officers and Firefighters Retirement System, 1971-77, Wash. State Investment Bd., 1981-89; retired, 1989; mem. Wash. Data Processing Adv. Bd., 1967-73; Gov.'s Exec. Mgmt. and Fiscal Affairs Com., 1978-80, Gov.'s Cabinet Com. on Tax Alternatives, 1978-80; trustee Wash. Tchr.'s Retirement System, 1965-89; bd. dirs. Centennial Bank, Olympia, Wash. Recipient Leadership award Joint Council County and City Employees-Fedn. State Employees, 1970, Eagles Leadership award, 1967. Mem. Nat. Assn. State Auditors, Comptrollers and Treasurers (pres. 1977), Nat. Assn. Mcpl. Fin. Officers, Nat. Assn. State Treasurers, Western State Treasurers Assn. (pres. 1970), Wash. County Treas. Assn. (pres. 1955-56), Wash. Assn. Elected County Ofcls. (pres. 1955-58), Olympia Area C. of C., Soap Lake C. of C. (pres. 1948). Democrat. Clubs: Elks (hon. life); Moose, Eagles, Lions, Olympia Yacht, Olympia Country and Golf; Empire (Spokane); Wash. Athletic (Seattle). Address: 3613 Plummer St SE Olympia WA 98501-2126

O'BRIEN, ROBERT THOMAS, investment company executive; b. Phila., Oct. 7, 1941; s. James Francis Sr. and Mildred Anita (Gomez); m. Aurora Carol Forsthoffer, Nov. 7, 1964; 1 child, Michael Joseph. Cert., N.Y. Inst. Fin., 1963; BS, St. Joseph's U., 1971. Securities trader Brown Bros. Harriman, Phila., 1964-69, portfolio mgr., 1969-77, investment officer, 1977-80, asst. mgr., investment adv., 1980-83; v.p. Newbold's Asset Mgmt., Phila., 1983-85, sr. v.p., 1985-93, also bd. dirs., 1990-93; mng. dir. W.H. Newbold's Son & Co., Phila., 1993—. Bd. dirs. Cath. Philopatrian Literary Inst., 1973-76, Mary J. Drexel Home, 1992—, treas. 1992—; mem. fin. and investment com. Neumann Coll., 1990—. Served with USAF and Pa. Air N.G., 1960-67. Mem. Phila. Securities Assn., Air Force Assn. (life), Confederate Air Force (life, wing fin. officer 1992). Republican. Roman Catholic. Clubs: Racquet of Phila., Sailing Assn. (commodore 1980-82); Lewes Yacht, Miles River Yacht, Avalon Yacht, Eastport Yacht, Aronimink Golf, Idle Hour Tennis. Avocations: tennis, squash, sailing, golf. Home: 665 Dodds Ln Gladwyne PA 19035-1514 Office: WH Newbold's Son & Co 1500 Walnut St Philadelphia PA 19102-3523

O'BRIEN, STEPHEN JAMES, geneticist; b. Rochester, N.Y., Sept. 30, 1944; s. Bernard Carroll and Kathryn Marie O'Brien; m. Diane Louise Rockhill, Nov. 28, 1968; children: Mary Kirsten, Meghan Rockhill. BS, St. Francis Coll., Loretto, Pa., 1966; PhD, Cornell U., 1971. Postdoctoral fellow genetics-biochemistry Gerontology Rsch. Ctr., Balt., 1971-72; NIH postdoctoral fellow Nat. Cancer Inst., NIH, Bethesda, Md., 1972-73; staff fellow Lab. Viral Carcinogenesis, Nat. Cancer Inst., NIH, Bethesda, 1973-78; rsch. geneticist Lab. Viral Carcinogenesis, Nat. Cancer Inst., NIH, Frederick, Md., 1978-80; chief sect. of genetics Lab. Viral Carcinogenesis, Nat. Cancer Inst., NIH, Frederick, 1980—, acting chief, 1983-85, chief, 1986—; zoology and botany tchg. asst. St. Francis Coll., 1965-66; gen. genetics lab. instr. and lectr. Cornell U., 1966-71, biology and soc. tchg. asst., 1969-71, human genetics discussion leader, 1970-71; adj. prof. genetics George Washington U., 1974—; adj. grad. advisor dept. biology Am. U., 1979—, Hood Coll., 1982—; adj. prof. dept. zoology U. Md., 1982—, dept. biology Johns Hopkins U., 1982—; faculty affiliate dept. pathology Colo. State U., 1994—; affiliate prof. dept. biology George Mason U., 1994—; apptd. rsch. fellow Smithsonian Instn., Washington, 1982—; bd. trustees Am. Type Culture Assn., Rockville, Md., 1983—; apptd. exec. bd. Am. Type Culture Collection, Rockville, 1984—, sec.-treas. bd. trustees, 1987— ; founder, co-dir. New Opportunities in Animal Health Scis., Ctr. for Wildlife Scis., Smithsonian Instn., 1985—; mem. cat specialist group Internat. Union for Conservation of Nature, Geneva, 1985—, mem. captive breeding specialist group species survival commn., 1986—; lectr. in field. Editor Isozyme Bulletin, 1975-78, Genetic Maps, 1980—; exec. editor Jour. Heredity, Am. Genetics Assn., 1987—; assoc. editor Genomics, 1987-91, Mammalian Genome, 1990—, Molecular Phylogenetics and Evolution, 1990—; guest editor Current Biology, 1993; jour. adv. bd. Cosmos, 1994; contbr. numerous articles to profl. jours. Mem. AAAS, Genetics Soc. Am., Am. Soc. Naturalists, Tissue Culture Assn., Am. Genetics Assn. (bd. dirs. 1984—, chmn. long range planning com. 1985—), Am. Assn. Zool. Pks. and Aquariums (advisor spl. survival plan-cheetah 1986—), N.Y. Acad. Sci., Cosmos Club. Achievements include research in molecular genetics, developmental and cell biology, genetics of oncology, viral oncology, immunology and reproductive physiology, molecular evolution, paleontology, cytology, populations genetics.

O'BRIEN, THOMAS FRANCIS, manufacturing company executive; b. Cambridge, Mass., Mar. 28, 1938; s. Thomas Francis and Ann (Deneen) O'B.; m. Elizabeth A. Coppinger, Sept. 3, 1960; children: Nancy Ann, Thomas F., Lisa Jean. B.S., Boston Coll., 1960; M.B.A., Boston U., 1965. Analyst Nat. Shawmut Bank Boston, 1964; fin. analyst Gen. Foods Corp., N.Y.C., 1965-66; asst. controller Hewitt Robins (Litton) Conn., Stamford, 1966-67; sec.-treas. controller Electra Motors (Litton) Calif., Anaheim, 1967-69; v.p., controller Power Transmission div. (Litton) Conn., Hartford, 1969-71, A-T-O, Inc., Willoughby, Ohio, 1971-74; v.p. Recreation Group, 1974-80; pres. Rawlings Sporting Goods, 1974-80; pres. men's and children's apparel group Kellwood Co., Chesterfield, Mo., 1980-83; sr. v.p. adminstrn. Sunmark Cos., St. Louis, 1983-90; pres., chief exec. officer Sumark Capital

Corp., 1990—; bd. dirs. Sunmark Capital Corp., St. Louis, Dunmon Corp., St. Louis, Diagraph Corp., St. Louis, Overland Aviations Systems, Inc., St. Louis, ABC, Birmingham, Ala., Assn. Corp. Growth, St. Louis; chmn. bd. L-H Rsch., Tustin, Calif.; chmn. bd. Pub. Safety Equipment, Inc., St. Louis; mem. faculty Westchester C.C., 1966-67. Bd. dirs. Cen. St. Louis County chpt. Am. Cancer Soc., 1977-80. Served with AUS, 1960-63. Fellow Boston U., 1965. Home: 2821 Stonington Pl Saint Louis MO 63131-3417 Office: Sunmark Capital Corp 510 Maryville College Dr Saint Louis MO 63141-5801

O'BRIEN, THOMAS GEORGE, III, lawyer; b. N.Y.C., Aug. 26, 1942; s. Thomas George Jr.and Margaret Patricia (Arctander) O'B.; m. Alison Marie Rich, Aug. 26, 1967; children: Christian Arctander, Kylin Stafford. AB magna cum laude, U. Notre Dame, 1964; LLB, Yale U., 1967. Bar: N.Y. 1967, Fla. 1988. Assoc. Carter, Ledyard & Milburn, N.Y.C., 1971-78; assoc. gen. counsel Frank B. Hall & Co. Inc., Briarcliff Manor, N.Y., 1978-79, v.p., sec., gen. counsel, 1979-86; exec. v.p., sec., gen. counsel CenTrust Savs. Bank, Miami, 1986-87; of counsel Steel Hector & Davis, Miami, 1987-88, ptnr., West Palm Beach, Fla., 1988—; Author: Florida Law of Corporations and Business Organizations, 1990, 92-95. Trustee Bus. Vols. for Arts, Miami, 1986-88, Fla. Repertory Theatre, West Palm Beach, 1989-91, chmn., 1990-91; mem. vestry Episcopal Ch. Bethesda-by-the-Sea, 1991-94, sr. warden, 1992-94; bd. dirs. Bus. Devel. Bd. Palm Beach County, 1991—, sec., 1992-93, chmn., 1993-94; bd. dirs. Palm Beach Fellowship Christians and Jews, 1993—, Directions 21st Century, 1995—. Lt. USNR, 1967-71, Vietnam. Mem. ABA (com. on legal opinions 1992—), N.Y. State Bar Assn., Fla. Bar (mem. corps./securities law com. 1988—, vice-chmn. 1989-90, chmn. 1990-91, chmn. com. on opinion standards 1988—, exec. coun. bus. law sect. 1989-93), Am. Soc. Corp. Secs. (sec. N.Y. regional group 1984-86), Govs. Club, PGA Nat. Club (Palm Beach Gardens). Home: 81 Sandbourn Ln Palm Beach Gardens FL 33418-8085 Office: 1900 Phillips Point W 777 S Flagler Dr West Palm Beach FL 33401-6198

O'BRIEN, THOMAS HENRY, bank holding company executive; b. Pitts., Jan. 16, 1937; s. J. Vick and Georgia (Bower) O'B.; m. Maureen Sheedy; children—Thomas Henry, Lauren C., Timothy B. BS in Commerce, U. Notre Dame, 1958; MBA, Harvard U., 1962. With Pitts. Nat. Bank, 1962—, v.p., 1967-73, sr. v.p., 1973-80, exec. v.p., 1980-83, vice chmn., 1983-84; pres., bd. dirs., chief exec. officer PNC Fin. Corp., 1984—; also chmn. PNC Fin. Corp., Pitts., 1988—; bd. dirs. Hilb, Rogal & Hamilton Co., Aristech Chem. Corp., Bell Atlantic Corp., Pvt. Export Funding Corp., Fed. Adv. Council, Internat. Monetary Conf. Bd. dirs. United Way Southwest Pa., Pitts. Symphony Soc., Children's Hosp., Pitts., Allegheny Trails council Boy Scouts Am., Pitts. Allegheny Conf. Community Devel., U. Pitts., World Affairs Council Pitts., Carnegie Inst. Res. City Bankers. Named Man of Yr. in fin. Vectors, Pitts., 1985. Mem. Assn. Res. City Bankers, Pa. Bankers Assn. Roman Catholic. Clubs: Duquesne, Allegheny (bd. dirs.), Pitts. Field, Rolling Rock, Laurel Valley Golf. Avocation: golf. Office: PNC Fin Corp 5th Ave & Wood St Pittsburgh PA 15265 also: Pitts Pirates 600 Stadium Cir Pittsburgh PA 15212-5731*

O'BRIEN, THOMAS IGNATIUS, lawyer; b. Troy, N.Y., Dec. 24, 1925; s. Timothy F. and Catherine M. (McCarthy) O'B.; m. Barbara Lasher; children: Kathleen, Stephanie, Alicia. BAE, Rensselaer Poly. Inst., 1946; LLB, JD, Georgetown U., 1951. Bar: N.Y. 1951, U.S. Ct. Appeals (3d cir.) 1968, U.S. Dist. Ct. N.Y. (so. dist.) 1973, U.S. Ct. Appeals (9th cir.) 1973, U.S. Ct. Appeals (2d cir.) 1975, U.S. Ct. Appeals (fed. cir.) 1982, Conn. 1988. Patent examiner U.S. Patent Office, Washington, 1946-51; patent atty. North Am. Phillips, Irvington, N.Y., 1951, Pollard, Johnston, Smythe & Robertson, N.Y.C., 1952-54; patent atty. Union Carbide Corp., Danbury, Conn., 1954-90, chief patents counsel, 1969-90; counsel Morgan & Finnegan, N.Y.C., 1991—. Mem. ABA (chmn. coms.), Am. Intellectual Property Law Assn. (bd. dirs. 1986-89), Pacific Indsl. Property Assn. (pres.), Assn. Corp. Patent Counsel (pres.), Chem. Mfrs. Assn., Internat. Patent and Trademark Assn., Intellectual Property Orgn. (bd. dirs.), Assn. Bar City N.Y. Home: 58 Stonehenge Dr New Canaan CT 06840-3524 Office: Morgan & Finnegan 345 Park Ave New York NY 10154-0004

O'BRIEN, THOMAS JOSEPH, bishop; b. Indpls., Nov. 29, 1935. Grad., St. Meinrad Coll. Sem. Ordained priest Roman Catholic Ch., 1961. Bishop of Phoenix, 1982—. Office: 400 E Monroe St Phoenix AZ 85004-2336*

O'BRIEN, TIMOTHY ANDREW, writer, journalist, lawyer; b. N.Y.C., July 11, 1943; s. Timothy Andrew and Hildegarde J. (Schenkel) O'B.; m. Maria de Guadalupe Margarita Moreno, Jan. 15, 1971; children: Theresa Marie, Tim A. B.A. in Communications, Mich. State U., 1967; M.A. in Polit. Sci., U. Md., 1972; postgrad., Tulane U. Law Sch., 1974-75; J.D., Loyola U., New Orleans, 1976. Bar: La. 1976, D.C. 1977, U.S. Supreme Ct 1981. News writer, reporter, anchorman WKBD-TV, Detroit, 1968-69, WTOP-TV, Washington, 1969-72, WDSU-TV, New Orleans, 1972-74, WVUE-TV, New Orleans, 1974-77; law corr. ABC News, Washington, 1977—. Contbr. articles to profl. jours. Bd. govs. Woodward Acad., College Park, Ga. Recipient AP award for outstanding reporting of extraordinary event, 1976, New Orleans Press Club award for non-spot news reporting, 1976, Emmy award for documentary on D.C., 1969, ABA awards of merit, 1979 (2), 80, 85, Gavel award for documentary, 1980, Nat. award for human rights reporting Women in Comm., 1981, Disting. Alumnus award Mich. State U., 1996. Mem. Am. Law Inst., Radio-TV Corrs. Assn. Washington, Am. Judicature Soc. (bd. dirs. 1991—), Sigma Delta Chi, Pi Sigma Alpha, Phi Kappa Phi. Office: ABC News Washington Bur 1717 Desales St NW Washington DC 20036-4401

O'BRIEN, TIMOTHY JAMES, lawyer; b. Detroit, Nov. 4, 1945; m. Hyon Baek, Jan. 31, 1970; children: Jean, Jane. AB, Yale U., 1967; JD, Harvard U., 1976. Bar: N.Y. 1977, U.S. Dist. Ct. (so., ea. and we. dists.) N.Y. 1978. Assoc. Cleary, Gottlieb, Steen & Hamilton, N.Y.C., 1976-80; ptnr. Coudert Bros., N.Y.C., 1980—; lectr. symposium on internat. investment Southwestern Law Found., 1995. Mem. Harvard Law Rev., 1975-76. Assoc. dir., vol. Peace Corps, Republic of Korea, 1967-73. Mem. ABA (co-chmn. conf. on Korea-U.S. trade and investment 1990-92), Assn. of Bar of City of N.Y. (internat. law com., Asian affairs com. 1989-94). Office: Coudert Bros 1114 Avenue of the Americas New York NY 10036-7703

O'BRIEN, WALTER FENTON, mechanical engineering educator; b. Roanoke, Va., Feb. 4, 1937; s. Walter Fenton and Lorraine Estelle (Doolin) O'B.; m. Nancy Brooks, Mar. 20, 1959; children: Julia, Kelly. BSME, Va. Poly. Inst. & State U., 1960; MSME, Purdue U., 1961; PhD in Mech. Engring., Va. Poly. Inst. & State U., 1968. Registered profl. engr., Va. Engring. specialist Aerospace Rsch. Corp., Roanoke, 1961-64; instr. in mech. engring. Va. Poly. Inst. & State U., Blacksburg, 1964-67; mgr. new products Litton Industries, Blacksburg, 1967-70; asst. prof. mech. engring. Va. Poly. Inst. & State U., Blacksburg, 1970-72, assoc. prof. mech. engring., 1972-78, prof. mech. engring., 1978-85, J. Bernard Jones prof. mech. engring., 1985—, assoc. dean rsch. and grad studies coll. engring., 1990-93, head dept. mech. engring., 1993—; cons. to various cos. and govt., 1970—; vis. scientist aeropropulsion lab. USAF, Wright AFB, Ohio, 1987-88; lectr. NATO, Boston, Munich, Paris, 1992. Contbr. over 60 articles to profl. jours. Bd. dirs. Va. Mus. Transp., Roanoke, 1985-92. Fellow ASME (chmn. internat. gas turbine inst. 1983-89, v.p. 1994-97); assoc. fellow AIAA. Achievements include work in propulsion engineering and turbine compressors. Avocations: golf, antique automobiles, model building. Home: 1602 Carlson Dr Blacksburg VA 24060-5553 Office: Mech Engring Dept 100 S Randolph Hall Va Tech Blacksburg VA 24061

O'BRIEN, WILLIAM J., lawyer. BS, Holy Cross Coll., 1965; LLB, Yale U., 1969. Bar: N.Y. 1970, Mich. 1985. Former dep. gen. coun. Chrysler Corp., Highland Park, Mich., now v.p., gen. counsel, sec. Office: Chrysler Corp 12000 Chrysler Dr Highland Park MI 48288-0001

O'BRIEN, WILLIAM JAMES, II, lawyer; b. Schenectady, Oct. 23, 1940; s. William V. and Dorothy T. O'B.; m. Shannon M. Collins, July 8, 1967; children—Shannon A., Ashley T., William J. A.B., Williams Coll., 1963; J.D., Northwestern U., 1966. Bar: Ill. 1966, N.Y. 1970, U.S. Dist. Ct. (no. dist.) Ill. 1967, U.S. Dist. Ct. (so. dist.) N.Y. 1971, U.S. Ct. Appeals (2d cir.) 1971, U.S. Ct. Appeals (7th cir.) 1968, U.S. Supreme Ct. 1971. Clk. to judge Appellate Ct. Ill., 1966-67; assoc. Peterson, Lowry, Rall, Barber & Ross, Chgo., 1967-69; assoc. Rogers & Wells, N.Y.C., 1969-73; assoc. Gould & Wilkie, N.Y.C., 1973-74, ptnr., 1974; successively staff counsel, sr. counsel, sr. lead counsel, asst. to gen. counsel ITT, N.Y.C., 1974-82, sr. group counsel, dep. dir. legal ops. internat. and worldwide, 1982-83, exec. asst. to pres. ITT Telecom., exec. v.p. ITT Corp., 1983-85; counsel Seyfarth, Shaw, N.Y.C., 1986-90; capital ptnr. Keck, Mahin & Cate, Washington, 1990—. Mem. ABA, N.Y. State Bar Assn; pres., Lakeside Partners Ltd., 1995. Home/Office: Lakeside Ptnrs Ltd 3378 Lakeside View Dr Falls Church VA 22041 Office: Keck Mahin & Cate 3378 Lakeside View Dr Falls Church VA 22041-2447*

O'BRIEN, WILLIAM JEROME, II, lawyer; b. Darby, Pa., Oct. 22, 1954; s. Richard James O'Brien and Margaret (McGill) Hahn. BA in Econ. and Polit. Sci., Merrimack Coll., 1976; JD, Del. Law Sch., 1981. Bar: Pa. 1982, U.S. Dist. Ct. (ea. dist.) Pa. 1983, U.S. Supreme Ct. 1986. Law clk. Commonwealth Ct. of Pa., Harrisburg, 1982-83; assoc. Philips, Curtin and DiGiacomo, Phila., 1983-86, O'Brien & Assocs. PC, Phila., 1986—; bd. dirs. New Manayunk Corp., Phila, counselor, 1987—. Bd. dirs. North Light Inc., 1986-94, sec., 1988-90, pres., 1990-92; bd. dirs. Manayunk Cmty. Ctr. for Arts, 1988-90, chmn. Chaminouix Mansion, 1989—, chmn., 1991—; spl. asst. to U.S. Senator H. John Heinz, 1976-78; Rep. candidate for Phila. City Coun., 1991. Mem. Phila. Bar Assn., Pa. Bar Assn., Del. Law Sch. Alumni Assn. (sec. 1985-87), Bus. Assn. Manayunk (bd. dirs. 1987-89), Union League. Republican. Roman Catholic. Club: Racquet (Phila.) (committeeman 1985-87). Avocations: squash, court tennis, scuba, golf. Office: O'Brien & Assocs PC 4322 Main St Philadelphia PA 19127-1421

O'BRIEN, WILLIAM JOHN, ecology researcher; b. Summit, N.J., Nov. 30, 1942; m. Mavion Meier, 1964; children: Connor, Shay, Lia. BA, Gettysburg Coll., 1965; postgrad., Cornell U., 1965-69; PhD, Mich. State U., 1970. sch. rsch. assoc. Ctr. Northern Studies, 1977; disting. lectr. Kans. Acad. Sci., 1990. From asst. prof. to prof. aquatic ecology U. Kans., Lawrence, 1971—; chair dept. sys. & ecology U. Kans., 1991—, rsch. scientist ecosystem ctr. Marine Biol. Lab., 1986—. Grantee NSF, 1975—. Mem. Am. Soc. Limnology & Oceanography, Ecol. Soc. Am., Internat. Assn. Theoretical and Applied Limnology, Am. Fisheries Soc., Animal Behavioral Soc. Office: Univ Kansas Kansas Ecological Reserves Lawrence KS 66045-2106 Office: U Kans Dept Biology 6010 Haworth Lawrence KS 66045*

O'BRIEN, WILLIAM JOSEPH, materials engineer, educator, consultant; b. N.Y.C., July 25, 1940; s. William P. O'Brien; divorced; children: Anne Marie, Matthew. BS, CCNY, 1958; MS, NYU, 1962; PhD, U. Mich., 1967. Assoc. dir. rsch. J.F. Jelenko Inc., N.Y.C., 1956-61; from asst. to assoc. prof. Marquette U., Milw., 1961-67; mech. engr., dir. Biomaterials Rsch. Ctr., Milw., 1967-70; prof. biologic and materials scis. U. Mich., Ann Arbor, 1970—, dir. Biomaterials Rsch. Ctr., 1994—; cons. WHO, N.Y.C., 1967-70, Johnson & Johnson, Inc., New Brunswick, N.J., 1970-83; chmn. rsch. com. Sch. Dentistry U. Mich., 1987-91. Editor: (book) Dental Materials, 1989; inventor Magnesia Ceramic, 1985. Recipient UN Cert., 1967, Disting. Contbn. award Mexican Prosthodontics Soc., 1991. Mem. Materials Rsch. Soc., Acad. Dental Materials, Adhesion Soc., Dental Materials Group (pres. 1985). Office: U Mich Biomaterials Rsch Ctr 1011 N University Ave Ann Arbor MI 48109-1078

O'BRIEN, WILLIAM K., accounting firm executive; b. 1945. With Coopers & Lybrand, 1967—, ptnr., 1975—, dep. chmn., 1991—. Office: Coopers & Lybrand 1251 Avenue Of The Americas New York NY 10020-1104*

OBRIG, ALICE MARIE, nursing educator; b. Bklyn., Apr. 1, 1939; d. Gordon A. and Virginia (Morgan) O.; BSN, Cornell U., 1961; MS, Boston U., 1964; CNM, John Hopkins U., 1968; EdD, Tchrs. Coll., Columbia U., 1987. Asst. head nurse N.Y. Hosp., N.Y.C., 1961-62; pub. health nurse N.Y.C. Vis. Nurses, 1962-63; instr. Russell Sage Coll., Troy, N.Y., 1964-67, Yale U., New Haven, 1969-72; asst. prof. Fairfield U., Conn., 1973—; cons. and lectr. in field.; contbr. chpt. to book. Mem. APHA, Am. Coll. Nurse Midwives, Nat. League for Nursing, Conn. Pub. Health Assn., Cornell U.-N.Y. Hosp. SON Alumnae Assn. (sec.), Sigma Theta Tau, Delta Kappa Gamma (mem. nominating com., alpha kappa state). Episcopalian. Home: 50 Lafayette Pl Greenwich CT 06830-5405 Office: Fairfield U N Benson Rd Fairfield CT 06430

O'BRYAN, WILLIAM HALL, insurance executive; b. Tulia, Tex., June 15, 1919; s. Barnett and Goldie (Hall) O'B.; m. Marjorie Mae Lewis, Apr. 14, 1962; children: Richard L., Clelie S. Student, Internat. Bus. Coll., El Paso, Tex., 1936-37, Hills Bus. U., Oklahoma City, 1937, Tulsa Law Sch., 1939. With Okla. Compensation Rating Bur., Oklahoma City, 1937; underwriter, v.p. Tri State Ins. Co., Tulsa, 1937-61; pres. Occidental Fire & Casualty Co., Denver, 1961-72; founder, owner Am. Underwriters, Denver, 1972-74; pres., chmn. bd. Prime Ins. Corp., 1973-74, exec. v.p., 1976-77; v.p. Asso. Internat. Mgmt., 1974-75; conservator Equity Educators Assurance Co., Denver, 1974-75; spl. dep. Colo. ins. commr. acting as receiver Equity Educators Assurance Co., 1975-77; receiver Mfrs. & Wholesalers Indemnity Exchange, 1975-77; pres. Mo. Profl. Liability Ins. Assn., Jefferson City, Mo., 1977-86; pres. subs. Providers Ins., 1981-86; dep. receiver Profl. Mut. Ins. Co., Kansas City, Mo., 1987—, Protective Casualty Ins. Co., Kansas City, Mo., 1991—. Capt. AUS, 1942-46. Episcopalian. Home: 5404 S Fulton Ct Englewood CO 80111-3660

O'BRYAN, WILLIAM MONTEITH, lawyer; b. Manning, S.C., Apr. 27, 1912; s. Samuel Oliver and Frances (Davis) O'B.; m. Jeane Barrett, Nov. 22, 1942; 1 dau., Donna. Student, U. Miami, Fla., 1931-32; LL.B., U. Fla., 1937. Bar: Fla. bar 1937. Practice in Miami, 1937-50, in Ft.Lauderdale, 1950—; partner firm Fleming, O'Bryan & Fleming (and predecessor), 1950—; Regional v.p. Def. Research Inst., 1963-65. Served to lt. USNR, 1942-45. Fellow Am. Coll. Trial Lawyers, Internat. Acad. Trial Lawyers; mem. Internat. Assn. Ins. Counsel (exec. com. 1964-67), Sigma Chi. Presbyn. Clubs: Mason (Shriner), Rotarian (pres. Ft. Lauderdale 1954-55). Home: 707 NE 26th Ave Fort Lauderdale FL 33304-3613 Office: 1415 E Sunrise Blvd Fort Lauderdale FL 33304-2339

O'BRYON, JAMES FREDRICK, defense executive; b. Schenectady, N.Y., Oct. 1, 1941; s. Frederick Stanley and Elizabeth Mary (Leppo) O'B.; m. Margaret Adina Bell, Oct. 23, 1965; children: Daniel, Douglas, Cris, Kera. BS in Math., King's Coll., Briarcliff, N.Y., 1964; MSA in Ops. Rsch., George Washington U., 1973; SM Through Elec. Engring. Dept., MIT, 1975. Mathematician Ballistics Rsch. Lab. Aberdeen (Md.) Proving Ground, 1966-74, asst. to dir. Ballistics Rsch. Lab., 1975-76, ops. rsch. analyst smart munitions group Ballistics Rsch. Lab., 1976-79, chmn. red-on-blue working group Joint Tech. Coord. Group, 1979-85, chief combat survivability and tech. U.S. Army Materiel Systems Analysis Activity, 1985-86; asst. dep. undersec. def. Office Sec. Def., Washington, 1986-88, dir. live-fire testing, 1988-95, dep. dir. operational test and evaluation, 1995—; dir. Joint Live Fire Program, Washington, 1986—; mem. Conventional Systems Com., Washington, 1987—. Co-author: (manual) Red-on-Blue Weapons, Effects, 1983; contbr. over 50 articles to profl. jours. Active edn. coun. MIT, Cambridge, 1980—; trustee King's Coll., Briarcliff Manor, N.Y., 1988—. With U.S. Army, 1964-66. Named Outstanding Young Man in Am., Jaycees, 1970, Disting. Lectr., Def. Systems Mgmt. Coll., 1988. Fellow Ctr. Advanced Engring. Study MIT; mem. Am. Def. Preparedness Assn. (chmn. test and evaluation divsn.), Internat. Test and Evaluation Assn., Assn. Governing Bds. of Univs. and Colls., Sigma Xi. Home: 1608 S Tollgate Rd Bel Air MD 21015-5825 Office: The Pentagon Rm 1C730 DOT&E OSD Washington DC 20301-0001

O'BRYON, LINDA ELIZABETH, television station executive; b. Washington, Sept. 1, 1949; d. Walter Mason Ormes and Iva Genevieve (Batrus) Ranney; m. Dennis Michael O'Bryon, Sept. 8, 1973; 1 child, Jennifer Elizabeth. BA in Journalism cum laude, U. Miami, Coral Gables, Fla. News reporter Sta. KCPX, Salt Lake City, 1971-73; documentary and pub. affairs producer Sta. WPLG-TV, Miami, Fla., 1974-76; producer, reporter, anchor, news dir. then v.p. for news and pub. affairs, exec. editor, sr. v.p. The Nightly Business Report Sta. WPBT-TV (PBS), Miami, 1976—. Recipient award Fla. Bar, Tallahassee, 1977, 2 awards Ohio State U., 1976, 79, local Emmy award So. Fla. chpt. Nat. Acad. TV Arts and Scis., 1978, award Corp. for Pub. Broadcasting, 1978, Econ. Understanding award Amos Tuck Sch. Bus. Dartmouth Coll., Hanover, N.H., 1980, award Fla. AP, 1981, 1st prize Nat. Assn. Rea Hors, 1986, Bus. News Luminary award Bus. journalism Rev., 1990, Am. Women in Radio and TV award, 1995. Mem. Nat. Acad. TV Arts and Scis. (former So. Fla. bd. dirs.), Radio-TV News Dirs. Assn., Sigma Delta Chi. Republican. Roman Catholic. Avocations: aerobics, tennis, golf. Office: Sta WPBT 14901 NE 20th Ave Miami FL 33181-1121

OBRZUT, TED, lawyer; b. Hatfield, Eng., May 26, 1949; came to U.S., 1956; naturalized, 1961; s. Stanley Jan Obrzut and Christel Maria (Achenbach) Obrzut Wenzel; m. Rochelle Marie Lindsey, Sept. 24, 1983. Student Columbia U., 1967-69; B.A., U. Calif.-Santa Barbara, 1969-71; LL.B., UCLA, 1974. Bar: Calif. 1974, N.Y., 1990. Assoc., O'Melveny and Myers, Los Angeles, 1974-82; ptnr. Lillick, McHose and Charles, Los Angeles, 1982-87; ptnr. Milbank Tweed Hadley & McCloy, L.A., 1987—. Mem. Calif. State Bar Assn. (uniform comml. code com. 1980-83), ABA, (com. commercial fin. services), Order of the Coif, Phi Beta Kappa. Office: Milbank Tweed Hadley & McCloy 601 S Figueroa St Los Angeles CA 90017-5704

OBST, LYNDA ROSEN, film company executive, producer, screenwriter; b. N.Y.C., Apr. 14, 1950; d. Robert A. and Claire (Shenker) Rosen; m. David Obst (div.); 1 child, Oliver. BA, Pomona Coll., 1972; degree in philosophy, Columbia U., 1974. Editor Rolling Stone History of 60's, N.Y.C., 1974-76, New York Times mag., N.Y.C., 1976-79; exec. Polygram Pictures, Los Angeles, 1979-81, Geffen Films, Los Angeles, 1981-83; co-producer Paramount Pictures, Los Angeles, 1983-85, Disney Pictures, Los Angeles, 1986—. assoc. prodr. Flashdance, 1983; co-prodr. Adventures in Babysitting, 1987, Heartbreak Hotel, 1988; prodr. The Fisher King, 1991, This is My Life, 1992; exec. prodr. Sleepless in Seattle, 1993, Bad Girls, 1994; contbr. articles to mags. Mem. Writers Guild Am. Office: Lynda Obst Prodns care 20th Century Fox 10201 W Pico Blvd Los Angeles CA 90064-2606

O'BYRNE, PAUL J., bishop; b. Calgary, Alta., Can., Dec. 21, 1922. Ordained priest Roman Catholic Ch., 1948; bishop of Calgary, 1968—.

O'CALLAGHAN, JERRY ALEXANDER, government official; b. Klamath Falls, Oreg., Feb. 23, 1922; s. Jeremiah Patrick and Marie Jane (Alexander) O'C.; m. Florence Marie Sheehan, Aug. 6, 1949; children—Jane Mary, Susan Margaret. B.S. with honors, U. Oreg., 1943, M.A. with honors, 1947; Ph.D., Stanford, 1951. Acting instr. history Stanford, 1951-52, U. Wyo., 1952-53; oil editor Tribune-Herald, Casper, Wyo., 1953-55; acting asst. prof. U. Wyo., 1955-56; legis. asst. to Senator Joseph O'Mahoney (Wyo.), 1956-60; exec. asst. to Senator Joseph Hickey(Wyo.), 1961; asst. dir. lands and minerals mgmt. Bur. Land Mgmt., Dept. Interior, 1961-62, asst. dir. plans and legislation, 1962-64, chief legislation and office coop. relations, 1964-69, chief div. coop. relations, 1969-80, chief hist. studies, 1980-82, historian emeritus, 1982—. Author: Disposition of the Public Domain in Oregon, 1960, America 200—The Legacy of Our Lands, 1976. Bd. govs. St. Columba's Episc. Nursery Sch., 1959-71; vestryman Episc. Ch., 1964-68, outreach leader, 1985-90; lay ministry St. Columba's, 1990—. With AUS, 1943-46. Mem. Soc. of Forest History, Fed. Profl. Assn. (pres. 1972), Fossils, Phi Kappa Psi. Home: 5607 Chesterbrook Rd Bethesda MD 20816-1301

O'CALLAGHAN, ROBERT PATRICK, lawyer; b. Mpls., Aug. 8, 1924; s. Robert Desmond and Claire Marie (Moe) O'C.; married Albina Julie Sepich, June 4, 1949; children: Michael, Edward, Catherine, Diana, Robert, Daniel. BA, Drake U., 1949; JD, U. Denver, 1951. Bar: Colo. 1951, U.S. Dist. Ct. Colo. 1956, U.S. Tax Ct. 1971, U.S. Ct. Appeals (10th cir.) 1978. Pvt. practice law Denver, 1952-53, Rangely, Colo., 1953-63; real estate broker Grand Junction, Colo., 1963-65; ptnr. Bellinger, Faricy, Tursi & O'Callaghan, Pueblo, Colo., 1965-73; pvt. practice law Pueblo, 1973-76; ptnr. Lattimer, O'Callaghan & Ware P.C., Pueblo, 1978-81; of counsel Quiet & Dice, Denver, 1981-83; pvt. practice law Pueblo, 1983—; atty. Town of Rangely, 1953-63; bd. atty. Pueblo Bd. Realtors, 1971-82; instr. real estate U. Colo., 1968-79; sr. cert. valuer Internat. Real Estate Inst. Pres. Homes for Sr. Citizens Inc., Pueblo, 1978-80; pres. Mt. Carmel Credit Union, 1972-74; adv. bd. dirs. Pueblo Salvation Army, 1987-91. With USNR, 1943-46. Mem. ABA, Colo. Bar Assn., Pueblo County Bar Assn., Nat. Network Estate Planning Attys., B.P.O., Elks (exalter ruler Rangley Lodge No. 1907). Republican. Roman Catholic. Avocation: photography. Address: Union Depot 132 W B St Ste 230 Pueblo CO 81003-3402

OCAMPO, RAYMOND L., JR., data processing executive. Sr. v.p., gen. counsel, corp. sec. Oracle Corp., Redwood, Calif. Office: Oracle Corp 500 Oracle Pkwy Redwood CA 94065

OCASIO-MELENDEZ, MARCIAL ENRIQUE, history educator; b. San Juan, P.R., Aug. 22, 1942; s. Manuel C. and Amparo (Melendez) Ocasio; m. Mimi Rivera, Apr. 15, 1973 (div. 1976). BA, U. P.R., 1964, MA, 1977; PhD, Mich. State U., 1988. Tchr. sci. P.R. Dept. Edn., San Juan, 1966-67; tchr. sci., history Nyack (N.Y.) Schs., 1967-71; tchr. sci. Robinson Prep. Sch., Condado, P.R., 1971-72; instr., asst. prof. P.R. Jr. Coll., Rio Piedras, 1972-80; teaching asst. Mich. State U., E. Lansing, 1979-83; instr. history Caribbean U., Bayamon, P.R., 1983-85; instr. Inter Am. U., Bayamon, 1985-87, U. P.R., Rio Piedras, 1983-87; vis. asst. prof. Mich. State U., E. Lansing, 1987-88; asst. prof. history U. Mich., Flint, 1988-91; assoc. prof. history U. P.R., Rio Piedras, 1991—, dir. grad. program history, 1991-93, assoc. dean acad. affairs Coll. Humanities, 1993-95, dir. internat. studies, 1995—; bd. dirs. Spanish Speaking Info. Ctr., Flint; lectr. Universidad del Valle, Cali, Universidad de Los Andes, Bogota, Universidad Pedagogica Nacional, Tunja, U. del Norte Barranquilla, Colombia; dir. Rockefeller Found. Caribbean 2000 Project, U. P.R., 1994-95, Urban Preservation Project of Rio Piedras, P.R., 1994-95; mem. editorial bd. Caribbean Review, 1994—. Author: Rio Piedras Notas, 1985. Geogratia e Historia Am. Latina, 1966; Fulbright scholar (Colombia) 1989, 90; NEH fellow, 1973, 78-79, 91. Mem. U.S. Nexus, Social Sci. Studies Assn., Coun. L.Am. History, Am. Hist. Assn., L.Am. Studies Assn., Sociedad Historiadores de P.R., Sociedad Puertorriqueña de Historiadores (pres. 1995—), P.R. Assn. Historians (pres. 1995—), Joint Border Rsch. Inst., Assn. Caribbean Historians, Hispanic Coun. on Internat. Rels., Phi Alpha Theta. Office: Univ PR History Dept PO Box 23350 San Juan PR 00931-3350

OCCHIATO, MICHAEL ANTHONY, city official; b. Pueblo, Colo.; s. Joseph Michael and Joan Occhiato; m. Peggy Ann Stefonowicz, June 27, 1964 (div. Sept. 1983); children: Michael, James, Jennifer; m. Patsy Gay Payne, June 2, 1984; children: Kim Carr, Jerry Don Webb. BBA, U. Denver, 1961; MBA, U. Colo., 1984; postgrad., U. So. Colo. Sales mgr. Tivoli Brewing co., Denver, 1965-67, acting brewmaster, prodn. control mgr., 1967-68, plant mgr., 1968-69; adminstrv. mgr. King Resources Co., Denver, 1969-70; ops. mgr. Canners Inc., Pepsi-Cola Bottling Co., Pueblo, 1970-76; pres. Pepsi-Cola Bottling Co., Pueblo, 1978-82; gen. mgr. Pepsi-Cola Bottling Group div. PepsiCo., Pueblo, 1982, area v.p., 1982-83; ind. cons. Pueblo, 1983—; v.p. Colo. Soft Drink Assn., 1978, pres., 1979; regional dir. Pepsi Cola Mgmt. Inst. divsn. Pepsi Co., 1979-82; pres. Ethnic Foods Internat. dba Taco Rancho, Pueblo; chmn. Weifang (China) Sister City Del., 1991—; bd. dirs. HMO So. Colo. Health Plan, 1988-93; rancher, 1976—. V.p. Colo. Soft Drink Assn., 1979-80; pres., 1980-81; mem. coun. City of Pueblo, 1978-93, pres., 1986, 87, 90, 91; mem. bd. health, 1978-80, regional planning commn., 1980-81, Pueblo Action Inc., 1978-80, Pueblo Planning and Zoning Commn., 1985; chmn. Pueblo Area Coun. Govts., 1980-82; mem. Pueblo Econ. Devel. Corp., 1983-91; chmn. fundraising Pueblo chpt. Am. Heart Assn., 1983—; bd. dirs. El Pueblo Boys Ranch, 1971-73; del. 1st World Conf. Local Elected Orcls. to 1st UN Internat. Coun. for Local Environ. Initiative; active Earth Wise Pueblo, 1991. Lt. USN, 1961-65. Mem. So. Colo. Emergency Med. Technicians Assn. (pres. 1975), Am. Saler Assn., Am. Quarter Horse Assn., Colo. Cattle Assn., Pueblo C. of C., Rotary, Pi Kappa Alpha (v.p. 1960). Home and Office: 11 Harrogate Ter Pueblo CO 81001-1723

OCHBERG, FRANK MARTIN, psychiatrist, health science facility administrator, author; b. N.Y.C., Feb. 7, 1940; s. Gerald Frank and Belle (Solomon) O.; m. Lynn Jeffie Wescott, July 1, 1962; children: Billie Jennifer, Jesse Frank, Abigail Kathryn. A.B., Harvard U., 1961; M.D., Johns

Hopkins U., 1965; postgrad. in psychiatry, Stanford U., 1966-69. Diplomate: Am. Bd. Psychiatry and Neurology. Intern USPHS Hosp., San Francisco, 1965-66; resident in psychiatry Stanford (Calif.) U. Med. Ctr., 1966-69; with NIMH, 1969-79, dir. div. mental health service programs, 1973-76; dir. Mich. Dept. Mental Health, 1979-81; pres. Victimization Research and Tng. Inst., 1981—; Med. dir. St. Lawrence Mental Health Center, Lansing, 1981-84; med. dir. Dimondale Stress Reduction Ctr., 1983-85; clin. prof. psychiatry and behavioral medicine, adj. prof. criminal justice, adj. prof. journalism, Mich. State U., East Lansing, 1979—; psychiat. adviser FBI, 1977—, U.S. Secret Service, 1978—. Co-editor: Violence and the Struggle for Existence, 1970, The Victim of Terrorism, 1982; editor: Post Traumatic Therapy and Victims of Violence, 1988. Fellow Am. Psychiat. Assn. (past chmn. coun. on nat. affairs 1979-87); mem. Internat. Soc. for Traumatic Stress Studies (founding bd. dirs.). Address: 4211 Okemos Rd Ste 6 Okemos MI 48864-3287

OCHELTREE, RICHARD LAWRENCE, lawyer, retired forest products company executive; b. Springfield, Ill., Oct. 9, 1931; s. Chalmer Myerly and Helen Margaret (Camm) O.; m. Ann Maureen Washburn, Apr. 11, 1958; children: Kirstin Ann, Lorraine Page, Tracy Lynn. A.B., Harvard U., 1953, LL.B., 1958. Bar: Calif. 1959. Sec., gen. counsel Am. Forest Products Corp./Bendix Forest Products Corp., San Francisco, 1961-81; v.p. adminstrn., sec., gen. counsel Am. Forest Products Co., 1981-87. Served with USAF, 1953-55. Mem. Am., San Francisco bar assns. Home: 1446 Floribunda Ave Apt 102 Burlingame CA 94010-3810

OCHILTREE, NED A., JR., retired metals manufacturing executive; b. Omaha, Dec. 23, 1919; s. Ned A. and Garnett (Briggs) O.; m. Isabel Hayden, Oct. 25, 1946; 1 child, Judith Ann Ochiltree Herseth. B.S., Purdue U., 1942. Research engr. Gen. Motors Research Labs., 1942-47; with Ceco Industries, Inc., Oakbrook, Ill., 1947-86; exec. v.p. mfg. Ceco Industries, Inc., 1964-70, exec. v.p. sales and prodn., 1970-71, pres., 1971-80, chief exec. officer, 1976-84, chmn. bd., 1979-86, chmn. exec. com., 1986-87, also bd. dirs., 1984-86; also bd. dirs. The Ceco Corp. Mem. Oak Park Country Club, University Club (Chgo.), DuPage Club. Home: 153 Pheasant Hollow Dr Burr Ridge IL 60521

OCHMANEK, DAVID ALAN, defense analyst; b. Oak Park, Ill., Apr. 10, 1951; s. Edwin Joseph and Phyllis Jean (Straass) O.; m. Barbara Jane Larson, June 16, 1973; children: James Edwin, Anne Skaaden. BS in Internat. Affairs, Polit. Sci., USAF Acad., 1973; MPA in Pub. Affairs and Internat. Rels., Princeton U., 1980. Fgn. svc. officer U.S. Dept. State, 1980-85; profl. staff The Rand Corp., 1985-93, 95—; dep. asst. sec. of def. for strategy Washington, 1993-95; def. analyst The RAND Corp., Washington, 1995—. Author: (with Edward L. Warner III) Next Moves: An Arms Control Agenda for the 1990's, 1989, (with Christopher Bowie et al) The New Calculus, 1993; contbr. articles to profl. jours., chpts. to books. Capt. USAF, 1973-78. Lutheran. Office: The RAND Corp 2100 M St NW Washington DC 20037

OCHOA, ERNESTO A., television station executive; b. Holguin, Cuba, Nov. 7, 1958; came to U.S., 1991; s. Mario and Magda (Perez) O.; m. Marina Kouvina, Dec. 2, 1982; children: Tony, Kevin, Daniel. MA in Philosophy, U. Moscow, 1983. Prof. philosophy Matanzas (Cuba) U., 1983-84; editor, rschr. Ctr. Studies of Am., Havana, Cuba, 1984-89; reporter Latin Press, Toronto, Ont., Can., 1991, Noticias del Mundo, N.Y.C., 1992; wrriter Sta. WNJU-TV, N.Y.C., 1992-93, series prodr., 1993-95, mng. editor, 1996&; mem. adv. bd. L.Am. Inst., N.Y.C., 1995—. Author: Balseros, 1994 (Letras de Oro award 1994); translator: American Judiciary System, 1987; editor Cuba en el Mes, 1989; contbr. articles to various publs. Mem. L.Am. Writers Assn. Office: Sta WNJU-TV 47 Industrial Ave Teterboro NJ 07608

OCHOA, MANUEL, JR., oncologist; b. N.Y.C., Apr. 22, 1930; s. Manuel and Maria (Diaz) O.; m. Suzanne Ellen Recca, Sept. 1, 1956; children: Elizabeth, Suzanne Elise. AB, Columbia Coll., 1951; MD, Columbia U., 1955. Diplomate Am. Bd. Internal Medicine; lic. physician, N.Y., Mass. Asst. in medicine U. Rochester (N.Y.) Med. Sch., 1958-61; instr. medicine, assoc., asst. prof. Columbia U., N.Y.C., 1964-68; attending physician Kettering Cancer Ctr., N.Y.C., 1973—; investigator Marine Biol. Lab., Woods Hole, Mass., 1965; assoc. prof. clin. medicine Cornell U., N.Y.C., 1982-96, prof., 1996—; cons. Harlem Hosp. Ctr., N.Y.C., 1966-68, Kingston (N.Y.) Hosp., 1970-85; vis. prof. U. Hawaii, Honolulu, 1971, U. Mex., Mexico City, 1979. Contbr. articles to profl. jours. Capt. USAF, 1956-58, ETO. Fellow Lalor Found., 1965. Fellow ACP, ACS. Republican. Roman Catholic. Achievements include discovering genetic code and protein synthesis in cancer cells, cancer chemotherapy. Home: 82 E Middle Patent Rd Bedford NY 10506 Office: Meml Sloan Kettering Inst 1271 York Ave New York NY 10021

OCHS, CAROL REBECCA, philosophy and religion educator, writer; b. N.Y.C., May 7, 1939; d. Herman and Clara Florence (Michaels) Blumenthal; m. Michael Ochs, Sept. 27, 1959; children: Elisabeth Amy, Miriam Adina. BA, CUNY, 1960, MA, 1964; PhD, Brandeis U., 1968. Philosophy lectr. CUNY, 1964-65; from asst. prof. to prof. philosophy Simmons Coll., Boston, 1967-92, prof. emerita, 1992—; adj. faculty Grad. Sch., Union Inst., Cin., 1992—, Hebrew Union Coll.-Jewish Inst. Religion, N.Y.C., 1992—; cons. Inst. for Svc. to Higher Edn., Chestnut Hill, Mass., 1972, St. Mary's Coll., South Bend, Ind., 1980; scholar-in-residence Hollins Coll., Roanoke, Va., 1987, Temple Beth El, Rochester, N.Y., 1990; mem. selection com. Kent Postdoctoral Fellowships, Bunting Inst., Radcliffe Coll.; lectr. in field. Author: Behind the Sex of God: Toward a New Consciousness Transcending Matriarchy and Patriarchy, 1977, Women and Spirituality, 1983, An Ascent to Joy: Transforming Deadness of Spirit, 1989, The Noah Paradox: Time as Burden, Time as Blessing, 1991, Song of the Self: Biblical Spirituality and Human Holiness, 1994; contbr. articles to profl. jours. Mem. Jewish-Cath. Dialogue, Boston, 1989-93; mem. Cath.-Jewish com. Archdiocese of Boston, 1989-93. Fellow NEH, 1976, 88, Nat. Humanities Inst., U. Chgo., 1978-79, Danforth Found., 1981-86, Coolidge Rsch., Colloquium, 1985, Resource Theologian, 1995-96. Fellow Soc. for Values in Higher Edn. (bd. dirs. 1982-88, chair ctrl. com. 1985-87), Assn. for Religion and Intellectual Life (mem. editl. bd. 1986—).

OCHS, MICHAEL, editor, librarian, music educator; b. Cologne, Germany, Feb. 1, 1937; came to U.S., 1939, naturalized, 1945; s. Isaac Julius and Claire (Baum) O.; m. Carol Rebecca Blumenthal, Sept. 27, 1959; children—Elisabeth Amy, Miriam Adina. B.A., CCNY, 1958; M.S., Columbia U., 1963; A.M., NYU, 1964; D.A., Simmons Coll., 1975. Cataloguer CCNY, 1963-65, lectr. in music, 1964; music libr. Brandeis U., Waltham, Mass., 1965-68; creative arts libr. Brandeis U., Waltham, 1968-74; asst. prof. libr. sci. Simmons Coll., Boston, 1974-78; libr. Eda Kuhn Loeb Music Libr., Harvard U., Cambridge, Mass., 1978-88; Richard F. French libr. Eda Kuhn Loeb Music Libr., Harvard U., Cambridge, 1988-92; lectr. music Harvard U., Cambridge, Mass., 1978-81, sr. lectr. music, 1981-92, also libr. cons., 1977-78; music editor W. W. Norton and Co., N.Y.C., 1992—; libr. cons. Biblioteca Berenson, Florence, Italy, 1983, Columbia U., 1987; project dir. U.S. Répertoire International des Sources Musicales Manuscript Inventory Ctr. at Harvard U., NEH, Cambridge, Mass., 1985-88. Editor Notes, Jour. Music Libr. Assn., 1987-92, Music Librarianship in America, 1991; contbr. articles to profl. jours., 1976—. Mem. Internat. Assn. Music Librs. (pres. rsch. librs. br. 1987-90), Music Libr. Assn. (chmn. New Eng. chpt. 1968-69, chmn. com. on bibliog. description 1971-73, chmn. music libr. adminstrn. com. 1975-76, chmn. fin. com. 1976-78, bd. dirs. 1976-78, chmn. publs. com. 1983-87, pres. 1993-95). Office: W W Norton and Co 500 5th Ave New York NY 10110

OCHS, ROBERT DAVID, history educator; b. Bloomington, Ill., Mar. 27, 1915; s. Herman Solomon and Fannie Leah (Livingston) O. A.B., Ill. Wesleyan U., 1936; M.A., U. Ill., 1937, Ph.D., 1939; M.A., Oxford U., Eng., 1964. Research dir. Anti-Defamation League, 1939-41; mem. faculty U. S.C., 1946—, prof. history, 1957-76, disting. prof. emeritus, 1976—, chmn. dept., 1960-74; acting dean U. S.C. (Coll. Arts and Sci.), 1970-71; asso. editor U. S.C. Press, 1950-53; vis. prof. Merton Coll., Oxford U., 1964; Mem. S.C. Archives Commn., 1960-74. U.S. cons.: History of The 20th Century, 1967. Bd. dirs. Columbia Music Festival Assn., 1957-64, 77-85, v.p., 1961-62, pres., 1962-63; dir. Columbia Lyric Opera, Columbia Mus. Art, 1966-69, 74-77, McKissick Mus., 1991-96. Maj. AUS, 1941-46; lt. col. Mem. Am. Hist. Assn., So. Hist. Assn. (exec. council 1973-76), S.C. Hist. Assn. (editor 1947-55, pres. 1956-57), Am. Studies Assn., Orgn. Am. Historians, Southeastern Am. Studies Assn. (pres. 1960-61), Omicron Delta Kappa. Home: 100 Sunset Blvd Apt 401 West Columbia SC 29169-7565

OCHS, SIDNEY, neurophysiology educator; b. Fall River, Mass., June 30, 1924; s. Nathan and Rose (Kniaz) O.; m. Bess Ratner; children—Rachel F., Raymond S. Susan B. Ph.D., U. Chgo., 1952. Research assoc. Ill. Neuropsychiat. Inst., Chgo., 1952-54; research fellow Calif. Inst. Tech., Pasadena, 1954-56; asst. prof. dept. physiology U. Tex. Med. Br., Galveston, 1956-58; assoc. prof. dept. physiology Ind. U., Indpls., 1958-61; prof. Ind. U., 1961-94, prof. emeritus, 1994—. Author: Elements of Neurophysiology, 1965; Axoplasmic Transport and Its Relation to Other Nerve Functions, 1982; founding editor, editor-in-chief Jour. Neurobiology, 1969-76; assoc. editor Jour. Neurobiology, 1977-86. Served with U.S. Army, 1943-45. Mem. Internat. Brain Rsch. Orgn., Am. Physiol. Soc., Soc. Neurosci., Am. Soc. Neurochemistry, Peripheral Nerve Soc. Democrat. Jewish. Office: Ind U Med Ctr Dept Physiology/Biophys 635 Barnhill Dr Indianapolis IN 46202-5126

OCHS, WALTER J., civil engineer, drainage adviser; b. Springfield, Minn., May 20, 1934; s. Walter Minrod and Cleo (Schultz) O.; m. Connie Mae Strate, Sept. 15, 1956; children: Julie, Brian. BS in Agrl. Engring., South Dakota U., 1957. Registered profl. civil engr., Mich. Engr. in training USDA, Soil Conservation Svc., Watertown, S.D., 1957-58; project engr. USDA, Soil Conservation Svc., Britton, S.D., 1958-61; area engr. USDA, Soil Conservation Svc., Sioux Falls, S.D., 1961-63; asst. state conservation engr. USDA, Soil Conservation Svc., East Lansing, S.D., 1963-66, state conservation engr., 1966-69; asst. state conservationist USDA, Soil Conservation Svc., Saint Paul, Minn., 1969-71; nat. drainage engr. USDA, Soil Conservation Svc., Washington, 1971-86; drainage adviser World Bank, Washington, 1986—; bd. dirs. Internat. Inst. for Land Reclamation and Improvement Postgrad Land Drainage Course, The Netherlands; cons. for over 25 countries; mem. Internat. Commn. Irrigation and Drainage. Contbr. to profl. jours. Named Federal Engr. Of The Year, Nat. Soc. Profl. Engrs., 1982; recipient Outstanding Alumnus award South Dakota State Univ., 1977, Outstanding Contributions award Corrugated Plastic Tubing Assn., 1981. Fellow Am. Soc. Agrl. Engrs., 1991; Mem. Am. Soc. Civil Engrs. (chmn. drainage com. 1975-76). Home: 6731 Fern Ln Annandale VA 22003-1903 Office: The World Bank 1818 H St NW Washington DC 20433-0001

OCHSNER, JOHN LOCKWOOD, thoracic-cardiovascular surgeon; b. Madison, Wis., Feb. 10, 1927; s. Edward William Alton and Isabel (Lockwood) O.; m. Mary Lou Hannon, Mar. 20, 1954; children: John L., Joby Hannon, Katherine Lockwood, Frank Hannon. MD, Tulane U., 1952. Diplomate Am. Bd. Thoracic Surgery (chmn.), Am. Bd. Surgery, Am. Bd. Vascular Surgery. Intern Univ. Mich. Hosp., Ann Arbor, 1952-53, resident, 1953-54; resident Baylor U. Affilliated Hosp., Houston, 1956-58, 1958-59; chief surg. resident Tex. Children's Hosp., 1959-60; instr. Baylor U., Houston, 1960-61; mem. staff Ochsner Clinic, New Orleans, 1961-66, chmn. dept. surgery, 1966-87, chmn. emeritus dept surgery, 1987—; clin. asst. prof. Tulane U., New Orleans, 1961-65, clin. assoc. prof., 1965-70, clin. prof., 1970—. Author: (with others) Coronary Artery Surgery, 1978. Pres. Tennis Patrons Assn. New Orleans, 1972; image amb. City of New Orleans, 1982; bd. dirs. Internat. Trade Mart, New Orleans, 1983. Capt. USAF, 1954-56. Recipient award Life Mag., 1961, Golden Plate Acad. Achievement award, 1962, medal of honor, Ecuador, 1981. Mem. Internat. Soc. Cardiovascular Surgery (pres. N.Am. chpt. 1983-84, internat. pres. 1989-91), Am. Assn. Thoracic Surgery (sec. 1979-83, pres. 1992-93), New Orleans Surg. Soc. (pres. 1977-78), So. Surg. Assn. (pres. 1991), So. Assn. for Vascular Surgery (pres. 1983), Boston Club, La. Club, New Orleans Country Club, City Club, Alpha Omega Alpha. Republican. Home: 84 Audubon Blvd New Orleans LA 70118-5540 Office: Ochsner Clinic & Hosp 1514 Jefferson Hwy New Orleans LA 70121-2429*

OCKERBLOOM, RICHARD C., newspaper executive; b. Medford, Mass., Dec. 19, 1929; s. Carl F. and Helen C. (Haraden) O.; m. Anne Joan Torpey, Sept. 17, 1955; children: Catherine, Carl, Gail, Mark, John, Peter. BSBA, Northeastern U., 1952; D Pub. Svc. (hon.), Westfield State Coll., 1989; LLD (hon.), Northeastern U., 1995. With Boston Globe, 1948—, salesman, 1955-63, asst. nat. advt. mgr., 1963-70, nat. advt. mgr., 1970-72, asst. advt. dir., 1972-73, advt. dir., 1973-77, v.p. mktg. and sales, 1977-81, exec. v.p., 1981—, gen. mgr., chief operating officer, 1984-86, pres., chief operating officer, 1986-93, vice chmn., 1993-94; ret.; retired; chmn. bd. Met. Sunday Newspapers. Bd. dirs. Greater Boston Conv. and Visitors Bur., Winchester Hosp., United Way Mass. Bay; trustee Northeastern U.; adv. bd. U. Mass., Boston. With U.S. Army, 1952-54. Mem. Algonquin Club (pres.), WInchester Country Club, Phi Kappa Phi. Nat. Honor Soc. Home: 80 Arlington St Winchester MA 01890-3735

OCKERMAN, HERBERT W., agricultural studies educator; b. Chaplin, Ky., Jan. 16, 1932; m. Frances Ockerman (dec.). BS with Distingtion, U. Ky., 1954, MS, 1958; PhD, N.C. State U., 1962; postgrad., Air Univ., 1964-70, Ohio State U., 1974, 83, 87. Asst. prof. Ohio State U., Columbus, 1961-66, assoc. prof., 1966-71, prof., 1971—; former mem. Inst. Nutrition and Food Tech.; judge regional and state h.s. sci. fairs, 1965—, Ham Contest, Ky. State Fair, Sausage and Ham Contest, Ohio Meat Processing Groups; cons. various food companies, 1975—, Am. Meat Inst., 1977-88, USDA, 1977-88, CRC Press, Inc., 1988—; bd. examiners U. Calcutta, 1987-88; examiner U. Mysore, India, 1990—; expert witness, various firms, 1992—, UN expert 95; presenter in field. Author: China Today: Contemporary Animal Husbandry (book award 1992), Quality Control of Post-Mortem Muscle Tissue, 1969, 14th rev. edit., 1986; contbr. chpts. to books, abstracts and articles to profl. jours, conf. proceedings. Comdr, USAF, 1955-58. Fisher Packing scholar; named Highest Individual in Beef Grading, Kansas City Meat Judging Contest, 1952; recipient Cert. of Appreciation, Ohio Assn. Meat Processors, 1987-91, Profl. Devel. award Cahill faculty, commendation for internat. work in agr. Ohio Ho. of Reps., badge of merit for svc. to agr. Polish Govt., plaque Argentina Nat. Meat Bd., animal sci. award Roussel UCALF, France, U. Assiuit, Egypt, silver platter Nat. Meat Bd., Sec. Agr., Livestock and Fishery, Argentina, Svc. award Coun. Grad. Students, Pomerance Tchg. award, Outstanding Alumni award U. Ky., also named to Hall of Disting. Alumni, 1995, award for outstanding ednl. achievements Argentine Soc. Agr., Coop. award vet. faculty U. Cordoba, Svc. award Panoma Legis. Br., Brazil; veterinary faculty U. Cordoba, Spain, 1982, 94, Nat. Chung-Hsing U., 1982, 95, Vet. Mus. Ciechanowcu, Poland. Mem. NAS, NCR, ASTM, Am. Meat Sci. Assn., Am. Soc. Animal Sci. (rsch. award 1987), Reciprocal Meat Conf., European Meeting of Meat Rsch. Workers, Polish Vet. Soc. (hon.), Inst. Food Technologists (nat. and OVS chpts.), Can. Meat Sci. Assn., Internat. Congress Meat Sci. and Tech., Rsch. in Basic Sci., Phi Beta Delta (treas. 1987, pres. 1991, internat. scholar award 1991, internat. faculty award 1991, Presdl. medallion award), Gamma Sigma Delta (rsch. award 1977, internat. award of merit 1988), Sigma Xi (outstanding advisor in coll. award 1995). Office: Ohio State U Meat Lab Animal Sci 2029 Fyffe Rd Columbus OH 43210-1007

OCKERSE, THOMAS, graphic design educator; b. Dutch Bandung, Java, Apr. 12, 1940; came to U.S., 1957, naturalized, 1964; s. Willem Fedor Pieter and Louise Johanna (Tideman) O.; m. Susan Carol Florence, Aug. 31, 1963; children: Kirsten Ingred, Eerin Irene, Tara Manisses. B.F.A., Ohio State U., 1963; M.F.A., Yale U., 1965. Sr. designer Fogleman Assos., Morristown, N.J., 1965-67; asst. prof. Ind. U., Bloomington, 1967-71; prof. graphic design R.I. Sch. Design, Providence, 1971—; head graphic design dept. R.I. Sch. Design, 1973-93, program head grad. studies in graphic design, 1976—; ptnr., prin. Ockerse Ltd. (design cons.); ptnr. Humanity Found. Inc.; mem. adv. bd. Visible Lang.; adj. faculty Jan van Eyck Acad., Maastricht, Netherlands, 1992—. Artist, poet, freelance graphic designer, Providence, 1972—; author: SP-VII, 1968, Stamps-To, 1968, The A-Z Book, 1969, T.O.P., 1970, TV Documentracing, 1974, Son of Fury, 1974, Time, 1974, 26 Poems 1, 1975, Word and Image Equations, 1975, Fact of Fiction, 1976, Stamps-USA, 1975, Graphic Design Education: An Exposition, 1977, Space Window, 1977, Semiotics and Graphic Design Education, Chance/Choice, 1988, Spirals, 1993. Recipient Edn. award Am. Ctr. for Design, 1991; faculty rsch. grantee Ind. U., 1969, RISD, 1992, Scottish Internat. Trust grantee for edn. and art, 1972. Mem. Am. Inst. Graphic Arts (v.p. 1980-85, chmn. edn. com.), Indsl. Design Soc. Am., Semiotic Soc. Am., Am. Ctr. for Design, Theosophical Soc. (pres. Blavatsky br. 1957-67, 89—), Sigma Chi. Home: 37 Woodbury St Providence RI 02906-3509 Office: RI Sch Design Graphic Design Dept 2 College St Providence RI 02903-2717

OCKUN, ROBERT J., manufacturing executive. Sr. v.p., reinsurance divsn., no. am. Montell Inc. (formerly Himont Inc.), Wilmington, Del. Office: Montell Inc. Box 15439 2801 Centerville Rd Wilmington DE 19850*

O'CONNELL, ANTHONY J., bishop; b. Lisheen, County Clare, Ireland, May 10, 1938. Ed., Mt. St. Joseph Coll., Cork, Ireland; Mungret Coll., Mangret Coll., Limerick, Ireland; ed., St. Louis. Ordained priest Roman Cath. Ch., 1963. Bishop Diocese of Knoxville, 1988—. Office: Bishop of Knoxville 805 Northshore Dr Knoxville TN 37919

O'CONNELL, BRIAN, community organizer, public administrator, writer, educator; b. Worcester, Mass., Jan. 23, 1930; s. Thomas J. and Mary (Carroll) O'C.; m. Ann C. Brown, July 11, 1953; children: Todd, Tracey, Matthew. B.A., Tufts Coll., 1953; postgrad., Maxwell Sch. Citizenship and Pub. Adminstrn., 1953-54; also numerous hon. degrees. Field rep. Am. Heart Assn., Pa., 1954-56; exec. dir. Am. Heart Assn., Md., 1956-61, Calif., 1961-66; exec. dir. Nat. Assn. Mental Health, 1966-78, dir. emeritus, 1978—; pres. Nat. Council on Philanthropy, 1978-80; exec. dir. Coalition of Nat. Vol. Orgns., 1978-80; pres. Ind. Sector, 1980-95, founding pres., 1980—; prof. pub. svc. Tufts U., Medford, Mass., 1995—; mem. U.S. Pres.'s Com. Employment of Handicapped, 1966-68; chmn. Liaison Group Mental Health, 1969-72. Author: Effective Leadership in Voluntary Organizations, 1976, Finding Values That Work: The Search for Fulfillment, 1977, America's Voluntary Spirit, A Book of Readings, 1983, The Board Members Book, 1985, Philanthropy in Action, 1987, Our Organization, 1987, Volunteers in Action, 1989, People Power: Service Advocacy, Empowerment, 1994, Board Overboard, 1995. Mem. Alumni Coun. Tufts U., 1970-80, trustee, 1988—, chmn. pres. search com., 1992; trustee Points of Light Found., 1989-95; bd. dirs. Hogg Found., 1990-95; chmn. organizing com., co-chmn., chmn. exec. com. Civicus: World Alliance for Citizen Participation, 1992-95; bd. dirs. E.M. Kaufman Found., 1994—. Recipient outstanding agy. prof. award United Way Am., 1979, Lincoln Filene Citizenship award, 1985, John W. Gardner Leadership award, 1994, Gold Key award, 1994, Chmns. award, NSFBE, 1994. Fellow Am. Pub. Health Assn., Nat. Acad. Pub. Adminstrn. (trustee 1993—), Nat. Com. Patients' Rights (chmn. 1975-77). Home: 50 Chase St Chatham MA 02633-2404 Office: Lincoln Filene Ctr Tufts U Medford MA 02155

O'CONNELL, BRIAN JAMES, priest, former university president; b. Hartford, Conn., Aug. 21, 1940; s. Jerry and Mary (Moloney) O'C. AB, Mary Immaculate Sem., 1964, MDiv, 1968; MA, St. John's U., Jamaica, N.Y., 1970; PhD, Ohio State U., 1974. Ordained priest Roman Cath. Ch., 1968. Social studies tchr. St. John's Prep. Sch., Bklyn., 1968-70; lectr. sociology St. John's U., Jamaica, 1970-71, asst. prof. sociology, 1974-79, assoc. prof., 1979-87, assoc. dean arts and scis., 1987-88, also bd. dirs., 1989—; exec. v.p. Niagara U., N.Y., 1988-89, pres., 1989-95. Author: Blacks in White Collar Jobs, 1979; also articles. Cons. Bklyn. Ecumenical Coops., 1981-88. Mem. Niagara Falls C. of C. (bd. dirs. 1989—).

O'CONNELL, SISTER COLMAN, college president, nun. BA in English, Speech, Coll. St. Benedict, St. Joseph, Minn., 1950; MFA in Theater, English, Cath. U., 1954; PhD in Higher Edn. Adminstrn., U. Mich., 1979; student, Northwestern U., Birmingham U., Stratford, Eng., Denver U., Stanford U., Sophia U., Tokyo. Entered Order of St. Benedict. Tchr. English Pierz (Minn.) Meml. High Sch., 1950-53, Cathedral High Sch., St. Cloud, Minn., 1950-53; chairperson theater and dance dept. then prof. theater Coll. of St. Benedict, St. Joseph, 1954-74, dir. alumnae, parent relations, ann. fund, 1974-77, dir. planning, 1979-84, exec. v.p., 1984-86, pres., 1986-96; cons. Augsburg Coll., Mpls., 1983-85, Assn. Cath. Coll. and Univs., 1982, Minn. Pvt. Coll. Council, 1982, SW (Minn.) State U., Marshall, 1980-82, Wilmar (Minn.) Community Coll., 1980-82, Worthington (Minn.) Community Coll., 1980-82, U. Minn., Morris, 1980-82; bd. dirs. Minn. Publ Radio. Chair bd. dirs. Minn. Pvt. Coll. Coun., 1991-92; bd. dirs. St. Cloud Cmty. Found., 1991-94. Mem. Nat. Assn. Ind. Colls. and Univs. (bd. dirs. 1993), St. Cloud Area C. of C. (bd. dirs. 1987-90). Office: Coll Saint Benedict 37 College Ave S Saint Joseph MN 56374-2001

O'CONNELL, DANIEL CRAIG, psychology educator; b. Sand Springs, Okla., May 20, 1928; s. John Albert and Letitia Rutherford (McGinnis) O'C. B.A., St. Louis U., 1951, Ph.L., 1952, M.A., 1953, S.T.L., 1960; Ph.D., U. Ill., 1963. Joined Soc. of Jesus, 1945; asst. prof. psychology St. Louis U., 1964-66, asso. prof., 1966-72, prof., 1972-80, trustee, 1973-78, pres., 1974-78; prof. psychology Loyola U., Chgo., 1980-89; prof. psychology Georgetown U., Washington, 1990—, chmn., 1991-96; vis. prof. U. Melbourne, Australia, 1972, U. Kans., 1978-79, Georgetown U., 1986; Humboldt fellow Psychol. Inst. Free U. Berlin, 1968; sr. Fulbright lectr. Kassel U., W. Ger., 1979-80. Author: Critical Essays on Language Use and Psychology, 1988; contbr. articles to profl. jours. Recipient Nancy McNeir Ring award for outstanding teaching St. Louis U., 1969; NSF fellow, 1961, 63, 65, 68; Humboldt Found. grantee, 1973; Humboldt fellow Tech. U. of Berlin, 1987. Fellow Am., Mo. psychol. assns., Am. Psychol. Soc.; mem. Midwestern, Southwestern, Eastern psychol. assns., Psychologists Interested in Religious Issues, Psychonomic Soc., Soc. for Scientific Study of Religion, N.Y., Mo. acads. sci., AAUP, AAAS, Phi Beta Kappa. Home and Office: Georgetown U Dept Psychology 37th & O Sts NW Washington DC 20057 *Were it over, it would have been more than my expected share already. The challenge of learning to serve others has moved it along at a quick pace, and I am grateful that I have always received more than I've been able to give in return—from the Lord and from many good people.*

O'CONNELL, DANIEL JAMES, lawyer; b. Evergreen Park, Ill., Aug. 14, 1954; s. Edmund J. and Kathryn J. (Hanna) O'C.; m. Nancy L. Eichler, March 21, 1992; children: Kelly Jacklyn, Kirby Kathryn. BS, Millikin U., 1976; JD, IIT, 1980; postgrad., DePaul U., 1981. Bar: Ill. 1980, U.S. Dist. Ct. (no. dist.) Ill. 1980, U.S. Dist. Ct. Ariz. 1989. Ins. regulatory counsel Kemper Group, Long Grove, Ill., 1980-81, environ. claims counsel, 1981-82; sr. home office claim counsel Zurich Ins. Cos., Schaumburg, Ill., 1982-83; assoc. Clausen, Miller, Gorman et al, Chgo., 1983-86; ptnr. environ. toxic tort litigation O'Connell & Moroney, P.C., Chgo., 1986-90; ptnr. toxic tort litigation Burditt, Bowles & Radzius, Chgo., 1990-91; ptnr. Daniel J. O'Connell & Assocs., P.C., Elgin, 1991—. James S. Kemper Found. scholar, 1972-76. Mem. ABA, Ill. Bar Assn., Chgo. Bar Assn. (Cert. of Appreciation 1984), Def. Rsch. Inst. Home: 177 Macintosh Ct Glen Ellyn IL 60137-6478

O'CONNELL, DANIEL S., private investments and management buyouts; b. N.Y.C., Feb. 7, 1954; s. Daniel R. and Josephine (Morris) O'C.; m. Gloria Perri, Nov. 26, 1976; children: Carly, Evan, Jared, Jamie, Colin. AB, Brown U., 1976; M in Pub. and Pvt. Mgmt., Yale U., 1980. Assoc. Dillon, Read & Co., Inc., N.Y.C., 1980-82; assoc. The First Boston Corp., N.Y.C., 1982-84, v.p., 1984-87, pres., 1986-88, mng. dir., 1987-88; also bd. dirs. First Boston LBO, Inc., N.Y.C.; founding ptnr., chief exec. officer Vestar Capital Ptnrs., Inc., N.Y.C., 1988—; bd. dirs. Prestone Products Corp., Danbury, Conn., La Petite Acad., Inc., Kansas City, Mo., Anvil Knitwear, Inc., N.Y.C., Russell-Stanley Corp., Red Bank, N.J., Super D Drugs, Inc., Memphis, Pyramid Comms., Inc., Medford, Mass., Cabot Safety Corp., Boston, Alvey Sys., Inc., St. Louis. Roman Catholic. Club: Field (Greenwich, Conn.). Avocation: athletics. Home: 16 Rock Ridge Ave Greenwich CT 06831-4401 Office: Vestar Capital Ptnrs Inc 245 Park Ave New York NY 10167

O'CONNELL, DENNIS E., lawyer; b. Mo., 1944. BA, U. Notre Dame, 1966; JD, St. Louis U., 1969. Bar: Mo. 1969, U.S. Ct. Military Appeals. With Bryan Cave, St. Louis. Mem. ABA, Bar Assn. Met. St. Louis, Mo. Orgn. Defense Lawyers, Delta Theta Phi. Address: Bryan Cave 211 N Broadway Saint Louis MO 63102-2733

O'CONNELL, EDWARD JAMES, JR., psychology educator, computer applications and data analysis consultant; b. Sterling, Ill., Aug. 15, 1932; s. Edward James and Elizabeth E. (Clapham) O.; m. Pamelia Canon Floyd, Aug. 21, 1959; children—Edward James III, John Matthew. B.S. in Psychology, Ill. Inst. Tech., 1958; M.A. in Psychology, Northwestern U., 1961, Ph.D. in Psychology, 1962. NSF postdoctoral fellow Carnegie Inst. Tech., Pitts., 1962-63; asst. prof. psychology Carnegie Inst. Tech., 1963-65;

psychology faculty Syracuse (N.Y.) U., N.Y., 1965-93; prof. Syracuse (N.Y.) U., 1975-93, prof. emeritus, 1993—; cons. Rand Corp., Santa Monica, Calif., 1962-64, Abt Assocs., Boston, 1970-73, Marcy Psychiat. Hosp., N.Y., 1979-82. Served to cpl. U.S. Army, 1952-54. NSF predoctoral fellow, 1959-62: NSF postdoctoral fellow, 1962-63; Northwestern U. predoctoral fellow, 1958-59. Mem. Am. Psychol. Assn., Assn. Computing Machinery, Sigma Xi. Democrat. Avocations: billiards; computer programming. Home: 508 Halsted Rd Cashiers NC 28717 Address: PO Box 570 Cashiers NC 28717-0570

O'CONNELL, EDWARD JOSEPH, III, financial executive, accountant; b. Evergreen Park, Ill., Aug. 9, 1952; s. Edward Joseph Jr. and Mary Jane O'C.; m. Mary M. Witt, May 30, 1976; children: Kelly, Edward IV, Molly, Kevin. BBA, U. Notre Dame, 1974. CPA, Ill. Mem. audit staff Coopers and Lybrand, Chgo., 1974-78, audit mgr., 1978-81; controller Union Spl. Corp., Chgo., 1981-83, v.p., treas., 1983-85, v.p., chief fin. officer, 1985-89, exec. v.p. fin. and adminstrn., chief. fin. officer, 1989-91; sr. v.p. fin., chief fin. officer GenDerm Corp., Lincolnshire, Ill., 1991-95; COO Keck, Mahin & Cate, Chgo., 1995—. Mem. Am. Inst. CPA's, Ill. Soc. CPA's, Fin. Execs. Inst., Machinery and Allied Products Inst. (fin. council II). Roman Catholic. Club: Notre Dame of Chgo. (bd. govs. 1984-86). Avocations: rugby, running, reading, golf. Home: 10420 Lamon Ave Oak Lawn IL 60453-4743 Office: Keck Mahin & Cate 77 W Wacker Dr Chicago IL 60601

O'CONNELL, FRANCIS JOSEPH, lawyer, arbitrator; b. Ft. Edward, N.Y., Mar. 19, 1913; s. Daniel Patrick and Mary (Bowe) O'C.; m. Adelaide M. Nagro, Sept. 27, 1937; children: Chris, Mary Gaynor Lavonas. AB, Columbia U., 1934; JD, Fordham U., 1938; SJD summa cum laude, Bklyn. Law Sch., 1945. Bar: N.Y. 1938, U.S. Dist. Ct. (so. dist.) N.Y. 1942, U.S. Tax Ct. 1941. Counsel and asst. to chmn. exec. com. for labor law and litigation Allied Chem. Corp., N.Y.C., 1942-70; ptnr. Bill & O'Connell and predecessor, Garden City, N.Y., 1970-76; pvt. practice Garden City, N.Y., 1976-85, Cutchogue, N.Y., 1985—; arbitrator, fact-finder, mediator Fed. Mediation and Conciliation Svc., 1970—, N.Y. State Mediation Bd., Am. Arbitration Assn., N.Y. State, Nassau and Suffolk County pub. employment rels. bds., 1970—; adminstrv. law judge N.Y. State Dept. Health, 1979—; instr. labor law and labor rels. Cornell U.; U.S. del. ILO, Geneva, 1948, 59, 69, 72. Author: Labor Law and the First Line Supervisor, 1945, Restrictive Work Practices, 1967, National Emergency Strikes, 1968. Trustee Village of Garden City, 1948-50; mem. bd. edn. Diocese of Rockville Centre (N.Y.), 1972-80; pres. various civic orgns., 1942—. Mem. ABA (labor and internat. law sects.), N.Y. State Bar Assn. (labor com.), Bar Assn. Nassau County (labor and arbitration coms., former chmn. arbitration andlabor law coms.), Mfg. Chemists Assn. (chmn. indsl. rels. com.), U.S. C. of C. (indsl. rels. com.), Southold Indian Mus. (bd. dirs.). Republican. Roman Catholic. Office: PO Box 819 Cutchogue NY 11935-0819

O'CONNELL, FRANCIS V(INCENT), textile printing company executive; b. Norwich, Conn., July 8, 1903; s. Thomas Francis and Isabelle (Gelino) O.'C.; LL.B., Blackstone Coll. Law, 1932, J.D., 1940, LL.M., 1942; m. Marie Louise Lemoine, Nov. 7, 1940. Textile screen printer U.S. Finishing Co. Norwich, 1921-30; foreman Ahern Textile Print Co., Norwich, 1930-36; pres., owner Hand Craft Textile Print Co., Plainfield, Conn., 1936—. Roman Catholic. Home: 25 14th St Norwich CT 06360-2823 Office: Bishop's Crossing Plainfield CT 06374

O'CONNELL, G. M., communications executive; b. Stamford, Conn., 1962. BA in English and History, Middlebury (Conn.) Coll., 1983. House painter Middlebury, 1983; mktg. exec. Productivity Inc., 1984; product mgr. Comp-U-Mall, CUC Internat., 1985-87; founder, ptnr. Modem Media, Westport, Conn., 1987—. Avocation: fishing. Office: Modem Media 228 Saugatuck Ave Westport CT 06880*

O'CONNELL, GEORGE EDWARD, state official; b. Springfield, Mass., Feb. 20, 1940; s. George Edward and Delia Marie (Harper) O'C.; m. Joan Marie Cermak, Aug. 24, 1974; 1 child, George William. BA, U. Notre Dame, 1961, MA, 1966; MA, Niagara U., 1969; PhD, U. Minn., 1974. Dir. labor and urban affairs, asst. prof. indsl. rels. U. Minn., Mpls., 1974-78; dir., assoc. prof. Labor Edn. Ctr. U. Conn., Storrs, 1978-84, ext. prof. labor edn., 1985-87; asst. commr. Minn. Dept. Labor and Industry, St. Paul, 1981-82; dep. commr. of labor N.Y. State Dept. Labor, Albany, 1987-95, dir. labor-mgmt. affairs, 1995—; pres. OHRD, Inc., Hebron, Conn., 1986-87; exec. bd. dirs. OSHA State Plan Assn., 1989-90; v.p., pres. Nat. Assn. Govtl. Labor Ofcls., Washington, 1990-92; exec. bd. dirs. Nat. Apprenticeship Program, Washington, 1991-93; chair exec. com. N.Y. Labor Legacy Project, Troy, N.Y., 1989-96; exec. bd. Gov.'s Excelsior award, Albany, 1991-95. Contbr. articles to profl. jours. Recipient Disting. Svc. Commendation as Pres. Nat. Assn. Govtl. Labor Ofcls., 1994. Mem. Am. Sociol. Assn. (nat. cert. orgnl. analysis 1991—), Indsl. Rels. Rsch. Assn., Svc. Employees Internat. Union. Office: NY State Dept Labor Bldg 12 State Office Bldg Campus Albany NY 12240

O'CONNELL, HAROLD PATRICK, JR., banker; b. Chgo., Sept. 11, 1933; s. Harold P. and Charlotte Anne (Woodward) O'C.; m. Geraldine Taylor McLaughlin, 1979; children: Alexandra T. Close, Geraldine S. Kuchman, Peter B. McLaughlin Jr. AB, Dartmouth Coll., 1955; JD, U. Mich., 1958. V.p. Continental Ill. Nat. Bank and Trust Co., Chgo., 1958-83, No. Trust Co., Chgo., 1983-86; dir. Terra Mus. of Am. Art, Chgo., 1987-92; chmn. exec. com. Mid-Am. Nat. Bank, 1989-92, pres., CEO, dir., 1992-93, chmn. bd., 1993—. Trustee Better Govt. Assn. Chgo., 1974—, pres., 1979-83; governing mem. Chgo. Symphony Orchestra, 1979—; sustaining fellow Art Inst. Chgo., 1982—; bd. dirs. Rehab. Inst. Chgo., 1980—. Mem. Chgo. Club, Racquet Club, Econ. Club, Casino Club (pres. 1988-91), Onwentsia Club (Lake Forest, Ill.), Shoreacres (Lake Bluff, Ill.), Old Elm Club (Highland Park, Ill.), Cypress Point Club (Pebble Beach, Calif.). Home: 435 Thorne Ln Lake Forest IL 60045-2343 Office: Mid-Am Nat Bank of Chgo 130 E Randolph St Chicago IL 60601

O'CONNELL, HENRY FRANCIS, lawyer; b. Boston, Jan. 4, 1922; s. Henry F. and Anna (Cunning) O'C. BA, Boston Coll., 1943, JD, 1948. Bar: Mass. 1948, U.S. Supreme Ct. 1956. House counsel electronics div. Am. Machine & Foundry Co., Boston, 1951-54; sole practice Boston, 1954-60; assoc. Glynn & Dempsey, Boston, 1960-70, Avery, Dooley, Post & Avery, Boston, 1970-88; asst. atty. gen. mcpl. affairs State of Mass., Boston, 1969-88; mcpl. cons. State of Mass., Winthrop, 1989—. Mem. Winthrop Bd. of Selectmen, 1958-64, 68-72, chmn., 1960-61, 68-69, 71-72; mem. Winthrop Improvement and Hist. Assn. Lt. USCGR, WWII, ret. capt. Mem. VFW (life), Internat. Platform Assn., Mass. Bar Assn., Nat. Boating Fedn. (life, past pres.), Mass. Selectmen's Assn. (life), Mass. Boating and Yachts Club Assn. (life, past commodore), Pleasant Park Yacht Club (Winthrop, Mass.), Port Norfolk Yacht Club (hon. life mem.), Res. Officers Assn. (life), Ret. Officers Assn. (life), Winthrop Hist. and Improvement Assn., Commodore Club Am. (life), KC (hon., life), Elks, Am. Legion (life), Winthrop Yacht Club (past commodore, life). Home and Office: 20 Belcher St Winthrop MA 02152-3014

O'CONNELL, HUGH MELLEN, JR., architect, retired; b. Oak Park, Ill., Nov. 29, 1929; s. Hugh M. and Helen Mae (Evans) O'C.; m. Frances Ann Small, Apr. 13, 1957; children—Patricia Lynn, Susan Marie, Jeanette Maureen. Designer, John Mackel. Student mech. engring., Purdue U., 1948-50; B.S. in Archtl. Engring, U. Ill., 1953. Registered architect, Ariz., Calif., La., Nev., Nat. Council Archtl. Registration Bds. Structural engr. Los Angeles, 1955-57; architect Harnish & Morgan & Causey, Ontario, Calif., 1957-63; self-employed architect Ventura, Calif., 1963-69; architect Andrews/O'Connell, Ventura, 1970-78; dir. engring. div. Naval Constrn. Bn. Center, Port Hueneme, Calif., 1978-91; supervisory architect Naval Constrn. Bn. Center, Port Hueneme, 1991-93; ret., 1993; mem. tech. adv. com. Ventura Coll., 1965-78; sec. Oxnard Citizens' Adv. Com., 1969-79, v.p., 1970-72, pres., 1972—; chmn. Oxnard Beautification Com., 1969, 74, Oxnard Cmty. Block Grant adv. com., 1975-76; mem. Oxnard Planning Commn., 1976-86, vice chmn., 1978-79, chmn., 1980-81. Mem. Oxnard Art-in-Pub. Places Commn., 1988—. Served with AUS, 1953-55. Mem. AIA (emeritus, pres. Ventura chpt. 1973), Am. Concrete Inst., Soc. Am. Registered Architects (Design award 1968, dir. 1970), Am. Legion, Soc. for Preservation and Encouragement of Barbershop Quartet Singing in Am. (chpt. pres. 1979, chpt. sec. 1980-83), Acad. Model Aeros. (#9190 1948—), Alpha Rho Chi. Presbyterian (elder 1963, deacon 1967). Lodges: Kiwanis (pres. 1969, div. sec. 1974-75), Elks. Home and Office: 520 Ivywood Dr Oxnard CA 93030-3527

O'CONNELL, JAMES JOSEPH, port official; b. Lockport, Ill., Feb. 7, 1933; m. Phyllis Ann Berard, Aug. 1, 1953; children: Lynn, Kathryn, Julie. BSBA, Lewis U., 1958. lic. pvt. pilot FAA. Recorder Will County, Joliet, Ill., 1976-88; dir., treas., corp. sec., v.p. Joliet Regional Port Dist., 1972-96; dir. Des Plaines Valley Enterprise Zone, Joliet. Precinct committeeman Will County, Joliet, 1962-72, exec. cen. committeeman, 1965-70, dir. Will County Young Reps., Joliet, 1984, sec. Will County Econ. Affairs Commn., Joliet; candidate for U.S. Congress, 1994. With U.S. Army, 1953-54, Korea. Mem. Ill. Assn. Port Dists. (sec., treas. 1982—), Ill. Jaycees (senate pres. 1972-73, named to Hall of Fame 1993), Joliet Flying Club (sec.), K.C., Joliet Exch. Club, Three Rivers Mfg. Assn. (pub. affairs com.), Joliet Columbian Club (pres.), Am. Legion (life, former post officer), VFW (life), others. Roman Catholic. Office: 1009 Western Ave Joliet IL 60435-6801

O'CONNELL, KATHLEEN LECLEAR, nursing educator; b. Steubenville, Ohio, Jan. 28, 1952; d. E. Robert and Irene (Ciancetta) LeClear; m. Thomas Barry O'Connell, July 1, 1970; children: Christopher Thomas, Ryan Thomas. ADN, Purdue U., 1978, BSN, 1986; MSN, Ind. U., 1988; post-grad., Ball State U., Ind. U. Staff and charge nurse critical care unit Parkview Meml. Hosp., Ft. Wayne, Ind., 1978-84, patient care mgr. critical care unit, 1984-86; assoc. faculty Ind. U.-Purdue U., Ft. Wayne, 1986-89, asst. prof. nursing, 1990-95, assoc. prof. nursing, 1996—; nurse cons. Assn. for Retarded Citizens, Ft. Wayne, 1988—; nurse reviewer Lincoln Nat. Corp., Ft. Wayne, 1989-90; cons. Assn. for Retarded Citizens, Ft. Wayne, 1998—; nurse reviewer Lincoln Nat. Corp., Ft. Wayne, 1989-90. Contbr. articles to profl. jours. Vol. nurse practitioner Matthew 25 Health Clinic, Ft. Wayne, 1988—; bd. dirs Whitley County chpt. Am. Cancer Soc., Columbia City, Ind., 1991—, pres., 1994—, mem. state bd., med. dir. Region 3, 1994—. Mem. ISNA (publs. com. 1994—), Sigma Theta Tau (Alpha chpt. 1988—). Roman Catholic. Office: Ind U Purdue U Ft Wayne 2101 E Coliseum Blvd Fort Wayne IN 46805-1445

O'CONNELL, KENNETH JOHN, state justice; b. Bayfield, Wis., Dec. 8, 1909; s. Daniel W. and Kathryn B. (Smith) O'C.; m. Evelyn L. Wachsmuth, June 2, 1938; children: Daniel, Thomas; m. Esther Erickson, July 3, 1964. LL.B., U. Wis., 1933, S.J.D., 1934; LL.D. (hon.), Williamette U., 1983. Bar: Wis. 1933, Oreg. 1944. Assisted preparation Restatement of Law of Property, Am. Law Inst.; asst. atty. Wis. Tax Commn., 1934; pvt. practice law Eugene, Oreg., 1944-47; mem. Oreg. Supreme Ct., 1958-77, chief justice, 1970-76; asst. prof. law U. Oreg. Law Sch., 1935-40, asso. prof., 1940-44, prof., 1947-58; Mem. faculty N.Y. U. Law Sch. Appellate Judges Seminar, 1966, 67; Disting. vis. prof. law U. Oreg., 1977; vis. prof. law Willamette U. Sch. Law, 1977-79, adj. prof., 1981-85; Chmn. Oreg. Statute Revision Council, 1950-54; mem. 2d Triennial Coif Award Com., 1965, Oreg. Jud. Reform Commn., 1971—; vice chmn. Constl. Revision Com., Oreg., 1961-63; mem. exec. com. Conf. Chief Justices.; Chmn. Oreg. Rhodes Scholarship Selection Com., 1969—; elector N.Y.U. Hall of Fame for Great Ams. Author article, monographs legal topics. Recipient Oreg. State Bar award of merit, 1953, Disting. Service award U. Oreg., 1967, Herbert Harley award Am. Judicature Soc., 1976, Cert. Distinction award U. Wis., 1983, E.B. McNaughton award ACLU, 1984, Legal Citizen of Yr., Oreg. Law Related Edn. Project, 1984, Disting. Service award U. Oreg. Law Sch., 1985. Center Advanced Study Behavioral Scis., 1965-66. Mem. Oreg. Jud. Council, Oreg. State Bar, Order of Coif, Omicron Delta Tau, Phi Delta Phi. Home: 3393 Country Club Rd S Salem OR 97302-9710

O'CONNELL, KEVIN, lawyer; b. Boston, Sept. 4, 1933; s. Michael Frederick and Kathryn Agnes (Kelley) O'C.; m. Mary Adams, July 14, 1990; children: Tiffany W., Elizabeth H., Dana A., Liesel E. A.B., Harvard, 1955, J.D., 1960. Bar: Calif. 1961. Assoc. firm O'Melveny & Myers, L.A., 1960-63; asst. U.S. atty. criminal div. Cen. Dist. Calif., L.A., 1963-65; staff counsel Gov. Calif. Commn. to Investigate Watts Riot, L.A., 1965-66; ptnr. Tuttle & Taylor, L.A., 1966-70, Coleman & O'Connell, L.A., 1971-75; pvt. practice law L.A., 1975-78; of counsel firm Simon & Sheridan, L.A., 1978-89; ptnr. Manatt, Phelps & Phillips, L.A., 1989—. Bd. editors: Harvard Law Rev, 1958-60. Mem. Los Angeles County (Calif.) Democratic Central Com., 1973-74. Served to lt. USMCR, 1955-57. Mem. Am. Law Inst. Home: 426 N Mccadden Pl Los Angeles CA 90004-1026 Office: Manatt Phelps & Phillips Trident Ctr E Tower 11355 W Olympic Blvd Los Angeles CA 90064-1614

O'CONNELL, KEVIN GEORGE, priest, foreign missionary, former college president; b. Boston, May 22, 1938; s. George Lawrence and Mary Margaret (Cohan) O'C. BA, Boston Coll., 1962, MA, 1963; PhD, Harvard U., 1968; MDiv, Weston Sch. Theology, Cambridge, Mass., 1969. Joined S.J., 1956; ordained priest Roman Cath. Ch., 1969. Asst. prof. Old Testament Weston Sch. Theology, Cambridge, 1971-77, dir. field edn., 1972-75, assoc. prof. Old Testament, 1977-80; assoc. prof., chmn. dept. religious studies John Carroll U., Cleve., 1981-87; pres., prof. Le Moyne Coll., Syracuse, N.Y., 1988-93; provincial asst. for capital devel. Soc. of Jesus of New Eng., Boston, 1994-96; fgn. missionary and pastor for English-speaking Caths. Amman, Jordan, 1996—; vis. prof. O.T., Woodstock Coll., Balt., 1969-70; vis. prof. theology U. San Francisco, 1970; William K. Warren Disting. vis. prof. Roman Cath. studies U. Tulsa, 1987; sabbatical John Carroll U., University Heights, Ohio, 1993-94; chmn. bd. Joint Archeol. Expdn. to Tell el-Hesi, Israel, 1982—. Author: The Theodotionic Revision of the Book of Exodus, 1972; editor: The Tell el-Hesi Field Manual, 1980, Tell el-Hesi: Modern Military Trenching and Muslim Cemetery, 1985, Tell el-Hesi: The Persian Period (Stratum V), 1989, Tell el-Hesi: The Site and the Expedition, 1989, Tell el-Hesi: The Muslim Cemetery in Fields V and VI/IX (Stratum II), 1993; mem. editorial adv. bd. Bible Rev., 1987—. Bd. dirs. Hiawatha coun. Boy Scouts Am., 1988-93, Syracuse Opera, 1991-94; trustee Albright Inst. Archeol. Rsch., Jerusalem, Israel, 1982—; trustee Am. Schs. Oriental Rsch., Balt., 1983-96, vice chmn., 1993-96; trustee Boston Coll., 1988-96, Loyola U. Chgo., 1990-96, U. Scranton, 1992-96. Kent fellow Danforth Found., 1965-67; Am. Coun. Learned Socs. study fellow, 1970-71, grantee, 1980-81; Grauel Faculty fellow John Carroll U., 1986-87. Mem. Cath. Bibl. Assn., Soc. Bibl. Lit., Internat. Fedn. Cath. Univs. (trustee, v.p., mem. coun. 1988-94). Office: The Jesuit Ctr, PO Box 212074, Amman Jordan

O'CONNELL, KEVIN PATRICK, insurance company executive; b. Albany, N.Y., Feb. 15, 1950; s. Matthew F. and Ellen M. (Tracy) O'C.; m. Christine M. Roman, May 29, 1971; 1 child, Bridget K. BA, U. Notre Dame, 1972. CLU, ChFC. Tchr. Notre Dame H.S., Elmira, N.Y., 1972-76; salesman, agt. Northwestern Mut. Life, Elmira, 1976-80; exec. officer Swan & Sons Morss Co. Inc., Elmira, 1980—. Co-editor: LUTC Business Course Text, 1994. Treas., bd. dirs. Salvation Army, Elmira, 1983-89; Chemung-Schuyler chpt. ARC, Elmira, 1986-91; chmn. bd. dirs. Cath. Charities, Inc., Elmira, 1993-94. Mem. Twin Tier Life Underwriters (chmn. bd. dirs. 1980, Life Underwriter of Yr. award 1981). Office: Swan & Sons Morss Co Inc 309 E Water St Elmira NY 14901-3402

O'CONNELL, LAWRENCE B., lawyer; b. Corpus Christi, Tex., July 18, 1947; s. Lawrence M. and Isabelle Susan (Strawbridge) O.; m. Carolyn Janet Rush, Sept.24, 1967; children: Suzanne Michelle, Elizabeth Danielle, Jason Lawrence. BA, Purdue U., 1970; JD, Ind. U., Indpls., 1975. Bar: Ind. 1975, U.S. Dist. Ct. (no. and so. dists.) Ind. 1975. Chief investigator Consumer Protection Div. Office of the Ind. Atty. Gen., Indpls., 1974-75; dep. atty. gen. Office of the Ind. Atty. Gen., Indpls., 1975; assoc. Schultz, Ewan & Burns Law Firm, Lafayette, Ind., 1975-79; ptnr. Schultz, Ewan, Burns & O'Connell, Lafayette, 1979-82, Gothard, Poelstra & O'Connell, Lafayette, 1982-86, Profl. Assn. Gothard & O'Connell, Lafayette, 1987-93; pvt. practice, 1994—; atty. Tippecanoe County, Lafayette, 1983-95. Edn. cons. Ind. U., 1973-75; treas. Ind. Young Rep. Fedn. 1976-77, chmn. 1977-79; Hoosier Assoc. Ind. Reps., 1980—. Recipient Sagamore of the Wabash citation, Gov. Otis R. Bowen, M.D., Ind. 1978, Gov. Robert D. Orr, Ind. 1980. Mem. ABA, Ind. Bar Assn., Tippecanoe County Bar Assn. (treas. 1976-77), Columbia Club (Indpls.), Ind. Soc. of Chgo., Ind. Mcpl. Lawyers Assn. (bd. dirs. 1989-95, pres. 1994-95). Office: Lawrence B O'Connell Esq # 558 223 Main St Lafayette IN 47901-1261

O'CONNELL, MARY ANN, state senator, business owner; b. Albuquerque, Aug. 3, 1934; d. James Aubrey and Dorothy Nell (Batsel) Gray; m. Robert Emmett O'Connell, Feb. 21, 1977; children: Jeffery Crampton, Gray Crampton. Student, U. N.Mex., Internat. Coun. Shopping Ctrs. Exec. dir. Blvd. Shopping Ctr., Las Vegas, Nev., 1968-76, Citizen Pvt. Enterprise, Las Vegas, 1976; media supr. Southwest Advt., Las Vegas, 1977—; owner, operator Meadows Inn, Las Vegas, 1985—, 3 Christian bookstores, Las Vegas, 1985—; state senator Nev. Senate, 1985—; chmn. govtl. affairs; vice chmn. commerce and labor; mem. taxation com.; vice chmn. Legis. Commn., 1985-86, 95-96; mem., 1987-88, 91-93; commr. Edn. Commn. States; rep. Nat. Conf. State Legislators; past vice chair State Mental Hygiene & Mental Retardation Adv. Bd. Pres. explorer div. Boulder Dam Area coun. Boy Scouts Am., Las Vegas, 1979-80, former mem. exec. bd.; mem. adv. bd. Boy Scouts Am.; pres., bd. dirs. Citizens Pvt. Enterprise, Las Vegas, 1982-84, Secret Witness, Las Vegas, 1081-82; vice chmn. Gov.'s Mental Health-Mental Retardation, Nev., 1983—; past mem. community adv. bd. Care Unit Hosp., Las Vegas; past mem. adv. bd. Kidney Found., Milligan Coll., Charter Hosp.; tchr. Young Adult Sunday Sch. Recipient Commendation award Mayor O. Grayson, Las Vegas, 1975, Outstanding Citizenship award Bd. Realtors, 1975, Silver Beaver award Boy Scouts Am., 1980, Free Enterprise award Greater Las Vegas C. of C., Federated Employers Assn., Downtwon Breakfast Exch., 1988, Award of Excellence for Women in Politics, 1989, Legislator of Yr. award Bldg. and Trades, 1991, Legislator of Yr. award Nat. ASA Trade Assn., 1991, 94, Guardian of Liberty award Nev. Coalition of Conservative Citizens, 1991, Internat. Maxi Awards Promotional Excellence; named Legislator of Yr., Nev. Retail Assn., 1992. Mem. Retail Mchts. Assn. (former pres., bd. dirs.), Taxpayers Assn. (bd. dirs.), Greater Las Vegas C. of C. (past pres., bd. dirs., Woman of Achievement Politics women's coun. 1988). Republican. Mem. Christian Ch. Avocations: china painting, reading. Home: 7225 Montecito Cir Las Vegas NV 89120-3118 Office: Nev Legislature Senate 401 S Carson St Carson City NV 89701-4747

O'CONNELL, MAURICE DANIEL, lawyer; b. Ticonderoga, N.Y., Nov. 9, 1929; s. Maurice Daniel and Leila (Geraghty) O'C.; m. Joan MacLure Landers, Aug. 2, 1952; children: Mark M., David L., Ann M., Leila K., Ellen A. Grad., Phillips Exeter Acad., 1946; A.B., Williams Coll., 1950; LL.B., Cornell U., 1956. Bar: Ohio 1956. Since practiced in Toledo; assoc. Williams, Eversman & Black, 1956-60; ptnr. Robison, Curphey & O'Connell, 1961-95, of counsel, 1996—; spl. hearing officer in conscientious objector cases U.S. Dept. Justice, 1966-68; mem. complaint rev. bd. Bd. Commrs. on Grievance and Discipline of Supreme Ct. Ohio, 1987. Mem. Ottawa Hills Bd. Edn., 1963-66, pres., 1967-69; former trustee Toledo Soc. for Handicapped; past trustee Woodlawn Cemetery; past trustee Toledo Hearing and Speech Center, Easter Seal Soc.; mem. alumni council Phillips Exeter Acad. Served to 1st lt. USMCR, 1950-53. Fellow Ohio State Bar Found.; mem. NW Ohio Alumni Assn. of Williams Coll. (past pres.), ABA, Ohio Bar Assn., Toledo Bar Assn. (chmn. grievance com. 1971-74), Kappa Alpha, Phi Delta Phi. Club: Toledo. Home: 3922 W Bancroft St Toledo OH 43606-2533 Office: Four SeaGate 9th Fl Toledo OH 43604

O'CONNELL, NEIL JAMES, priest, academic administrator; b. Buffalo, N.Y., May 21, 1937; s. Cornelius James and Marie Katherine (Schneider) O'C. BA, St. Bonaventure U., 1960; STB, Cath. U., Washington, 1964; MA, Siena Coll., 1967; PhD, U. Ga., 1970. Ordained priest Roman Cath. Ch., 1964. Instr. history and sociology St. Francis Coll., Rye Beach, N.H., 1965-67; asst. prof. history Prairie View (Tex.) A&M Coll., 1970-71; asst. assoc. prof. history Fisk U., Nashville, 1971-80, chmn. history, 1975-80, dir. div. fine arts and humanities, 1976-79; acad. dean Erie Community Coll., City Campus, Buffalo, 1980-86; dean faculty and instrn. Elizabeth Seton Coll., Yonkers, N.Y., 1986-89; dean Elizabeth Seton Sch. Assoc. Degree Studies of Iona Coll., Yonkers, N.Y., 1989-90; pres. St. Bonaventure U., St. Bonaventure, N.Y., 1990—. Contbr. articles to jours. in field. Trustee Archbishop Walsh High Sch., Olean, N.Y., 1990—, Bishop Timon High Sch., Buffalo, Trocaire Coll., Buffalo; bd. dirs. Econ. Devel. Zone, Olean, YMCA, Olean, 1990—; chair bd. dirs. Coll. Consortium for Internat. Studies. Mem. Olean C. of C. (bd. dirs. 1990—), Rotary, Phi Beta Kappa, Phi Kappa Phi, Phi Delta Kappa, Phi Beta Sigma. Democrat. Avocations: walking, theater, music. Home: Saint Bonaventure U Saint Bonaventure NY 14778 Office: Saint Bonaventure U Office of Pres Saint Bonaventure NY 14778 *Teaching/learning is an act of worship wherein we encounter divine wisdom. Faculty and students who engage in this act are responding to a vocation to be the ministers of this worship.*

O'CONNELL, PAUL EDMUND, publisher; b. Cambridge, Mass., Dec. 15, 1924; s. William Henry and Catherine O'C.; m. Phyllis B. Borgeson, July 18, 1970; children—Eileen Lucy, Brian Paul, Philip Bartlett, Douglas John, Donald Paul, Lori Ann, Stephanie Elizabeth, Kirsten Lynn. A.B., Harvard U., 1949. Salesman Am. Tobacco Co., 1949-50; sales rep. dept. coll. texts Prentice-Hall Co., 1950-58, editor, 1958-62, exec. editor, asst. v.p., 1963-68; chmn. Winthrop Pubs. Inc. subs. Prentice Hall Co., Cambridge, Mass., 1969-81; cons., 1981-82; sr. acquisition editor Bobbs-Merrill Ednl. Pubs., 1983-84; sr. editor Dorsey Press, 1985-88, Lexington Books, 1988-91; pub. cons., 1991—. Served with AC U.S. Army, 1943-47. Decorated Purple Heart. Mem. Am. Sociol. Assn., Am. Pyschol. Assn. Home: 60 Pleasant St #221 Arlington MA 02174

O'CONNELL, PHILIP RAYMOND, retired lawyer, paper company executive; b. N.Y.C., June 2, 1928; s. Michael Joseph and Ann (Blaney) O'C.; m. Joyce McCabe, July 6, 1957; children: Michael, Kathleen, Jennifer, David. AB, Manhattan Coll., 1949; LLB, Columbia U., 1956; grad., Advanced Mgmt. Program, Harvard U., 1967. Bar: N.Y. 1956, U.S. Supreme Ct. 1961, Conn. 1988. Assoc. Dewey, Ballantine, Bushby, Palmer & Wood, N.Y.C., 1956-61, 62-64; gen. counsel, sec. Laurentide Finance Corp., San Francisco, 1961-62; gen. counsel Wallace-Murray Corp., 1964-66, div. mgr., 1966-70; pres., chief exec. officer, dir. Universal Papertech Corp., Hatfield, Pa., 1970-71; sec. Champion Internat. Corp., Stamford, Conn., 1972-90, v.p., 1979-81, sr. v.p., 1981-90; mem. legal adv. com. N.Y. Stock Exch., 1985-88, corp. governance subcom., legal adv. com., 1985-94; chmn. lawyers steering com. corp. governance task force The Bus. Roundtable, 1981-87, mem., 1981-94. Mem. Champion Internat. Found., 1979-90; mem. bd. visitors Fairfield Univ. Sch. Bus., 1981-93, chmn., 1983-93; bd. dirs. Kearney-Nat. Corp., 1975-78. With USNR, 1951-54. Mem. ABA, Am. Soc. Corp. Secs. (chmn. 1988-89).

O'CONNELL, ROBERT FRANCIS, physics educator; b. Athlone, Ireland, Apr. 22, 1933; came to U.S., 1958; s. William and Catherine (O'Reilly) O'C.; m. Josephine Molly Buckley, Aug. 3, 1963; children: Adrienne Molly, Fiona Catherine, Eimear Kathleen. BSc, Nat. U. Ireland, Galway, 1953, DSc, 1975; PhD, U. Notre Dame, 1962. Telecommunications engr. Dept. Posts and Telegraphs, Dublin, Ireland, 1954-58; scholar Inst. Advanced Studies, Dublin, 1962-63; systems analyst IBM, Dublin, 1963-64; sr. rsch. assoc. Inst. Space Studies, N.Y.C., 1966-68; asst. prof. physics La. State U., Baton Rouge, 1964-66, assoc. prof., 1966-69, prof., 1969-86, Boyd prof., 1986—. Editor for theoretical physics Hadronic Jour.; bd. mem. Phys. Rev. A; contbr. articles to profl. jours. Named Disting. Rsch. Master, La. State U., 1975; NAS-NRC fellow, 1966-68, Sci. Rsch. Coun. (Eng.) sr. vis. fellow, 1976. Fellow Am. Phys. Soc.; mem. Am. Astron. Soc., Internat. Astronomy Union, Internat. Soc. Gen. Relativity and Gravitation. Republican. Roman Catholic. Avocation: tennis. Home: 522 Bancroft Way Baton Rouge LA 70808-4807 Office: La State Univ Dept Physics and Astronomy Baton Rouge LA 70803-4001

O'CONNELL, ROBERT JOHN, insurance company executive; b. N.Y.C., May 16, 1943; m. Claire M. Costantini; children: Kristin, Jared. BA, Fordham U., 1965; MA, U. Pa., 1966. With N.Y. Life Ins. Co., N.Y.C., 1970-89, v.p., 1983-86, sr. v.p., 1986-89; sr. v.p. group mgmt. divsn. AIG, 1989-91; pres., CEO AIG Life Ins. Cos., 1991—; also bd. dirs. A.I. Life; mem. adv. com. to Cato Inst. project on Social Security Privatization. Mem. Am. Internat. Life Assn. N.Y., AIG Life Ins. Co., AIG Equity Sales Corp., Delam Life Ins. Co., State Dept. Fin. Svcs. Corps Mission to Czechoslovakia. Mem. Am. Coun. Life Ins. Home: 3040 North St Fairfield CT 06430-1624

O'CONNELL, WILLIAM EDWARD, JR., finance educator; b. N.Y.C., Sept. 16, 1937; s. William Edward and Helen Margaret (Brazel) O'C.; m.

Janet Elinor Shields, Aug. 15, 1965; children: William Edward III, Cathleen Anne. AB, Manhattan Coll., 1959; MBA, Columbia U., 1961; D in Bus. Adminstrn. with honors, Ind. U., 1967; JD, Coll. William & Mary, 1974. Fin. analyst Pfizer, Inc., N.Y.C., 1962-64; asst. prof. U. Conn., Storrs, 1967-69; Morris prof. banking U. Va., Charlottesville, 1988; Chessie prof. bus. Coll. William and Mary, Williamsburg, Va., 1969—; mem. faculty Va. Bankers Sch., Chrlottesville, 1975—, Stonier Grad. Sch. Banking, Newark, 1977—, Bank Adminstrn. Inst., Madison, Wis., 1978—; dir. Citizens & Farmers Bank. Author: Asset & Liability Management, 1979, Advanced Financial Planning, 1984, Financial Planning for Credit Unions, 1989, Strategic Financial Management for Commercial Banks, 1993. Mem. Am. Fin. Assn., Fin. Mgmt. Assn., Beta Gamma Sigma, Omicron Delta Epsilon. Roman Catholic. Home: 102 Overlook Dr Williamsburg VA 23185-4434 Office: Coll William & Mary Sch Bus Williamsburg VA 23187-8795

O'CONNELL, WILLIAM RAYMOND, JR., educational consultant; b. Richmond, Va., Jan. 4, 1933; s. William Raymond and Mary Helen (Wenenger) O'C.; m. Peggy Annette Tucker, June 29, 1957; 1 child, William Raymond III. BMusEd, Richmond Profl. Inst., 1955; MA, Columbia U., 1962, EdD, 1969. Asst. to provost Richmond (Va.) Profl. Inst., 1955-57, dean of men, 1957-59, dean of students, dean of men, 1959-61; asst. to provost, dir. student info. ctr. Tchrs. Coll. Columbia U., N.Y.C., 1962-65, rsch. asst. inst. of higher edn. Tchrs. Coll., 1965-66; rsch. assoc. So. Regional Edn. Bd., Atlanta, 1966-69, dir. spl. programs, 1969-73, project dir., undergrad. edn. reform, 1973-79; dir. curriculum and faculty devel. Assn. Am. Colls., Washington, 1979-80, v.p. for programs, 1980-82, v.p., 1982-85; pres. New Eng. Coll., Henniker, N.H., 1985-95; cons. Coun. for Advancement Small Colls., 1975; mem. adv. com. project on instnl. renewal through improvement of teaching Soc. for Values in Higher Edn., 1975-78; mem., evaluator N.H. Postsecondary Edn. Commn., 1987-95, vice chmn., 1990-92, chmn., 1992-94; evaluator Nat. Ctr. for Rsch. to Improve Postsecondary Teaching and Learning, 1987-90, New Eng. Assn. Schs. and Colls., 1988, 91; mem. higher edn. rev. panel awards for pioneering achievements in higher edn. Charles A Dana Found., 1988, 89. Author, editor articles in field. Pres. Richmond Cmty. Amb. Project, 1958-60, bd. dirs., 1960-61; bd. dirs. Alumni Assn. Acad. divsn. Va. Commonwealth U., 1970-73; trustee Atlanta Boys Choir, Inc., 1978-79, chmn. fundraising com., 1976-77; trustee Atlanta Coun. for Internat. Visitors, 1973-76, 78-79; pres. UN Assn., Atlanta, 1976, 77; mem. steering com. Nat. Coun. chpt. and divsn. pres. UN Assn. U.S., 1977-79, nat. coun., 1980-90; mem. steering com. Leadership Concord, 1992-95, chmn., 1994-95. Named Community Amb. to Sweden Community Amb. Project of the Experiment in Internat. Living, 1956. Fellow Royal Soc. of the Arts (U.K.); mem. Am. Assn. Higher Edn., Newcomen Soc. U.S., N.H. Coun. on World Affairs (bd. dirs. 1993-95), Greater Concord C. of C. (bd. dirs. 1989-93), Phi Delta Kappa. Methodist. Avocations: antiques, travel.

O'CONNER, LORETTA RAE, former court reporter; b. Denver, Dec. 23, 1958; d. Ronald Lee and Norma Jareene (Warner) Barkdoll; m. George Ellis Bentley, Dec. 31, 1976 (div. 1979); m. Donald Hugh O'Conner, Feb. 3, 1987; children: Justin Lee, Brandon Craig. AS, Denver Acad. Ct. Reporting, 1983; BA summa cum laude, Regis U., 1992; postgrad., U. Colo., 1992-96. Cert. registered profl. reporter. Ct. reporter Denver, 1983-87; dist. ct. reporter Judicial Dept., State of Colo., Pueblo, 1987-91; ct. reporter Pueblo, 1991-93; student atty. Pueblo County Legal Svcs. Chief justice Student Govt. Ct., U. So. Colo., Pueblo, 1992; trained facilitator Kettering Found., Pub. Policy Inst., Dayton, Ohio, 1992; sec. So. Colo. Registered Interpretors for Deaf, Pueblo, 1991. President's scholar U. So. Colo., 1991-92, Alumni Assn. scholar, 1991-92; grantee Kettering Found., 1992; Colo. Legislature grantee and scholar Regis U., 1992; Colo. Legislature grantee U. Colo. Sch. Law, 1993-95, Dean's scholar, Dazzo Scholar, King scholar U. Colo. Sch. Law, 1993-96. Mem. ATLA, ABA, Nat. Ct. Reporters Assn., Colo. Trial Lawyers Assn., Colo. Bar Assn., Colo. Womens Bar Assn., Colo. Ct. Reporters Assn., Boulder Bar Assn., Phi Delta Phi (clk. 1994-95). Avocations: women's studies, political activism. Home: 1911 N Santa Fe Dr Pueblo CO 81003

O'CONNOR, BETTY LOU, service executive; b. Phoenix, Oct. 29, 1927; d. Georg Eliot and Tillie Edith (Miller) Miller; m. William Spoeri O'Connor, Oct. 10, 1948 (dec. Feb. 1994); children: Thomas W., William K., Kelli Anne. Student, U. So. Calif., 1946-48, Calif. State U., Los Angeles, 1949-50. V.p. O'Connor Food Svcs., Inc., Jack in the Box Restaurants, Granada Hills, Calif., 1983-93; pres. O'Connor Food Svcs., Inc., Granada Hills, Calif., 1994—, Western Restaurant Mgmt. Co., Granada Hills, 1986—; mem. adv. bd. Bank of Granada Hills. Recipient Frannie award Foodmaker, Inc., Northridge, Calif., 1984, First Rate award, 1992. Mem. Jack in the Box Franchisee Assn., Spurs Hon. (sec. U. So. Calif. 1947-48), Associated Women Students (sec. U. So. Calif. 1946-47), Gamma Alpha Chi (v.p. 1947-48), Chi Omega. Republican. Roman Catholic. Avocation: sewing. Office: Western Restaurant Mgmt Co 17545 Chatsworth St Granada Hills CA 91344-5720

O'CONNOR, CARROLL, actor, writer, producer; b. N.Y.C., Aug. 2, 1924; s. Edward Joseph and Elise Patricia (O'Connor) O'C.; m. Nancy Fields, July 28, 1951; 1 son, Hugh (dec.). B.A., Nat. U. Ireland, 1952; M.A., U. Mont., 1956, L.H.D. (hon.), 1985. Actor, Dublin, Cork, Limerick, Galway, London, Paris, Edinburgh, 1950-54; appeared in: Ulysses in Nightown, 1958, The Big Knife, 1959, Brothers, 1983, Home Front, 1984; TV appearance in The Sacco and Vanzetti Story, 1960; TV guest appearances on Armstrong Circle Theater; films include: Fever in the Blood, 1961, By Love Possessed, 1961, Lad a Dog, 1961, Lonely Are the Brave, 1962, Cleopatra, 1963, Not With My Wife, You Don't, 1966, Warning Shot, 1967, What Did You Do In The War Daddy?, 1968, Marlowe, 1969, Death of a Gunfighter, 1969, Kelly's Heroes, 1970, Doctors' Wives, 1971, Law and Disorder; TV film Brass, 1985; star TV series: All in the Family, 1971-79, Archie Bunker's Place, 1979-83, (also co-exec. producer) In The Heat of the Night, 1987-94; star TV spls. including: The Funny Papers, 1972, Of Thee I Sing, 1972, The Carroll O'Connor Special, 1973, The Last Hurrah, 1973. Recipient Emmy award for best actor, 1973, 77, 78, 79, 89; recipient George Foster Peabody award for broadcasting excellence, 1980; named to Hall of Fame Acad. TV Arts and Scis., 1990. Mem. The Players, Sigma Phi Epsilon. Office: Lionel Larner Ltd 119 W 57th St New York NY 10019 *Everyone should rid himself of the illusion that his fulfillments are of much interest to anyone else.*

O'CONNOR, CHARLES ALOYSIUS, III, lawyer; b. Providence, Apr. 7, 1942; s. Charles Aloysius Jr. and Mary Catherine (McGinn) O'C.; m. Wendy Law-Yone, Oct. 11, 1980; children: Charles Aloysius IV, Elisabeth. AB cum laude in Eng., Harvard U., 1964; JD, Georgetown U., 1967, MA, 1985. Bar: D.C. 1969. Assoc. Sellers, Conner & Cuneo, Washington, 1970-74; ptnr. McKenna & Cuneo, L.L.P., Washington, 1974—, chmn. environ. dept., 1980—; adj. prof. Georgetown U., Washington, 1973-77; lectr. Cath. U. Am., Washington, 1975-77. Author: (with others) Consumer Product Safety Law, 1977, Pesticide Regulat Handbook, 1983, 2d rev. edit. 1991, TSCA Handbook, 1987, 2d rev. edit. 1991. Lt. USNR, 1967-69. Mem. ABA, Bar Assn. D.C., Univ. Club. Office: McKenna & Cuneo LLP 1575 I St NW Washington DC 20005-1105

O'CONNOR, CHARLES P., lawyer; b. Boston, Sept. 29, 1940; m. Mary Linda Hogan; children: Jennifer, Amy, Austin, Catherine. Bachelors degree, Holy Cross Coll., Worcester, Mass., 1963; LLB, Boston Coll., 1966. Bar: Mass. 1966, D.C. 1968, U.S. Supreme Ct. 1974. Atty., gen. counsel's office NLRB, Washington, 1966-67; assoc. Morgan, Lewis & Bockius, Washington, 1968-71, ptnr., 1971—; gen. counsel Major League Baseball Player Rels. Com., N.Y.C., 1989-94. Contbr. numerous articles on labor and employment law to law jours. spl. counsel elections com. U.S. Ho. of Reps., Washington, 1968-69. Mem. ABA, D.C. Bar Assn., Belle Haven Country Club, N.Y. Athletic Club. Home: 6121 Vernon Ter Alexandria VA 22307-1152 Office: Morgan Lewis & Bockius 1800 M St NW Ste 800 Washington DC 20036-5802

O'CONNOR, DANIEL WILLIAM, retired religious studies and classical languages educator; b. Jersey City, Mar. 17, 1925; s. Daniel William and Emma Pauline (Ritz) O'C.; m. Carolyn Lockwood, June 26, 1954; children—Kathlyn Forssell Beal, Daniel William III. B.A., Dartmouth Coll., 1945; M.A., Columbia U., 1956, Ph.D., 1960; M.Div., Union Theol. Sem., 1950. Ordained to ministry United Ch. of Christ, 1950. Mem. exec. com., bd. home missions Congl. Chs., 1946-51; pastor Paramus Congl. Ch., N.J., 1950-55; assoc. sec. Student Christian Movement YMCA, N.Y., 1947-48; exec. sec. Earl Hall Columbia U., N.Y.C., 1948-50; tutor asst., dept. N.T. Union Theol. Sem., N.Y.C., 1958-59; successively asst. prof., assoc. prof., prof. religious studies and classical langs. St. Lawrence U., Canton, N.Y., 1959-67, dir. summer session, 1966, assoc. dean coll., 1967-68, Charles A. Dana prof. religious studies and classical langs., 1967-89, chmn. dept. religious studies and classical langs., 1974-89, Charles A. Dana emeritus prof., 1989—. Author: Peter in Rome, 1969; contbr. articles to Ency. Britannica and profl. jours., also revs. Trustee Silver Bay Assn. YMCA, N.Y., 1978-86, 86-92, Lit. Vols. Am., St. Lawrence County, N.Y., 1991-94; bd. dirs. U.S. Power Squadron, St. Lawrence Squadron, N.Y., 1972-75. With USNR, 1943-45. Grantee Lilly Found., Columbia U., 1969-70, Mellon Found., Am. Schs. Oriental Research, Jerusalem, 1979. Mem. AAUP, Am. Assn. Ret. Persons, Adirondack Mountain Club, Rotary (pres. Canton Club 1972-73, Rotary Found. scholarship selection com. dist. 7040 1983-87, dist. gov. 1987-88, dist. 7040 ext. com. 1988-89, youth exch. com. dist. 7040 1990-93, lit. com. 1991-93). Home: 3 Hillside Cir Canton NY 13617-1409

O'CONNOR, DONALD THOMAS, lawyer; b. Lackawana, N.Y., Apr. 14, 1935; s. Thomas Joseph and Edna Mabel (Thomas) O'C.; children: Kevin M., David T., Donna M., Cheryl L. Grad., U. Buffalo, 1957; LLB, Boston Coll., 1966. Bar: Mass., Pa. Asst. pers. supr. Continental Can Co., Tonawanda, N.Y., 1957-62; pers. supr. Continental Can Co., Natick, Mass., 1962-65; asst. div. mgr. labor rels. Weyerhaeuser Co., Fitchburg, Mass., 1956-66; field atty. NLRB, Pitts., 1966-67; assoc. Berkman, Ruslander, Pohl, Lieber & Engel, Pitts., 1967-71; ptnr. Randolph & O'Connor, P.C., Pitts., 1971-74; ptnr. Buchanan Ingersoll, P.C., Pitts., 1974—, chmn. labor sect., 1984-88, co-chmn. labor sect., 1988-90; speaker in field. Contbr. articles to profl. jours. Solicitor Twp. of Penn Hills, Pa., 1971. Mem. ABA, Pa. Bar Assn., Allegheny County Bar Assn. (chmn. labor sect. 1971-73), St. Thomas More Soc. (treas. 1970-72), Rivers Club, Alcoma Golf Club (Penn Hills). Republican. Avocations: golf, sailing, water skiing, reading, dancing. Home: 1414 Towne Square Dr Allison Park PA 15101-1951 Office: Buchanan Ingersoll One Oxford Ctr 301 Grant St 20th Flr Pittsburgh PA 15219-1410

O'CONNOR, DORIS JULIA, non-profit fundraiser, consultant; b. N.Y.C. Apr. 30, 1930; d. Joseph D. and Mary (Longinotti) Bisagni; m. Gerard T. O'Connor, Oct. 8, 1950 (div. Dec. 1972); 1 dau., Kim C. BA cum laude in Econs., U. Houston, 1975. Adminstrv. asst. Shell Cos. Found., Inc., N.Y.C., 1966-71, asst. sec., Houston, 1971-73, sec., 1973-76, sr. v.p., dir., mem. exec. com., 1976-93; prin. Doris O'Connor & Co., 1993—; adj. prof. bus. adminstrn. U. Houston, 1994—. Corp. assoc. United Way of Am., Washington, 1976-93; corp. advisor Bus. Com. of Arts, N.Y.C., 1976-91; del. Bus. Com. of Arts, Houston, 1982-87; dir. Ind. Sector, Washington, 1981-89, vice chmn., 1983-87; mem. contbns. coun. Conf. Bd., N.Y.C., 1976-93; advisor Coun. of Better Bus. Burs., Washington, 1975—, vice chmn., 1983-87; commr. adv. commn. on work based learning Dept. Labor, 1991-93; mem. Houston/Harris County Arts Task Force, 1991-93, Houston Ind. Sch. Dist. Task Force, 1991-93; bd. trustees Houston Grand Opera, Houston Symphony Orch., Houston Symphony Soc., Soc. Performing Arts, Cultural Arts Coun., Greater Houston Coalition Edn. Execellence, 1993—; mem. adv. bd. Ctr. for Edn. Rice U., The Houston Zool. Soc., 1993—. Mem. Nat. Soc. Fundraising Execs. (Houston com. on fgn. rels. 1993—), Omicron Delta Epsilon. Club: Pla. (bd. govs. 1987-89).

O'CONNOR, EARL EUGENE, federal judge; b. Paola, Kans., Oct. 6, 1922; s. Nelson and Mayme (Scheetz) O'C.; m. Florence M. Landis, Nov. 3, 1951 (dec. May 1962); children: Nelson, Clayton; m. Jean A. Timmons, May 24, 1963; 1 dau., Gayle. B.S., U. Kans., 1947, LL.B., 1950. Bar: Kans. 1950. Practiced in Mission, Kans., 1950-51; asst. county atty. Johnson County, Kans., 1951-53; probate and juvenile judge, 1953-55; dist. judge 10th Jud. Dist., Olathe, Kans., 1955-65; justice Kans. Supreme Ct., 1965-71; judge U.S. Dist. Ct., Dist. of Kans., Kansas City, 1971—, chief judge, 1981-92; mem. Jud. Conf. U.S., 1988-91. Served with AUS, World War II, ETO. Mem. ABA, Nat. Conf. Fed. Trial Judges, Kans. Bar Assn., Phi Alpha Delta. Office: US Courthouse 500 State Ave Kansas City KS 66101-2403

O'CONNOR, EDWARD CORNELIUS, army officer; b. Middlesex County, Mass., June 22, 1931; s. Edward Denis and Gladys Marie (Devine) O'C.; m. Charlotte Hubble, June 1, 1958. A.B., Boston Coll., 1952; M.S., U. N.C., 1966; M.S. George Washington U., 1979. Commd. 2d lt. U.S. Army, 1952, advanced through grades to maj. gen., 1981; asst. for NATO Affairs, Office of Sec. Def., 1970-72; sec. Joint Staff, Vietnam, 1972; chief staff Joint Mil. Commn., Vietnam, 1973; arty. comdr. 1st Armored Div., Europe, 1973-74; Fed. Exec. fellow Brookings Inst., Washington, 1975-76; chief Army Initiatives Group, Army Staff, Pentagon, 1976-77; dep. dir. ops. Nat. Mil. Command Center, Joint Chiefs of Staff, Washington, 1977-78; asst. div. comdr. (maneuver) 1st Armored Div., Europe, 1978-79; chief nuclear activities SHAPE, Belgium, 1979-82; dir. ops., readiness and mobilization ODCSOPS, Dept. Army, 1982-83; comdg. gen. Security Affairs Command Army Material Command, 1983-86; chief exec. officer, pres. Global Mktg. Corp. (doing bus. as GMA Internat., Inc.), 1986—; chmn. Contraves, Inc., Pitts., 1992—; mem. policy working group U.S. State Dept. Def. Trade Adv. Group, Washington, 1994—; internat. lectr. in field. Author: Performance Appraisal, 1966. Chmn. Harvard U. Grad. Sch. rels. com. Decorated D.S.M., Legion of Merit with 3 oak leaf clusters, Bronze Star, Air medal with 6 oak leaf clusters, Army Commendation medal with V device and 7 oak leaf clusters, Def. Meritorious Service medal, Def. Superior Service medal, Joint Service Commendation with oak leaf cluster, Identification Badges of Sec. Def. Office, Joint Chiefs of Staff and Army Gen. Staff. Mem. Harvard U. Alumni Assn. (bd. dirs. 1989-93). Address: 10202 Eagle Landing Ct Burke VA 22015-2524

O'CONNOR, EDWARD GEARING, lawyer; b. Pitts., May 5, 1940; s. Timothy R. and Irene B. (Gearing) O'C.; m. Janet M. Showalter, June 17, 1972; children: Mark G., Susan M. BA, Duquesne U., 1962, JD, 1965. Bar: Pa. 1965, U.S. Dist. Ct. (we. dist.) Pa. 1965, U.S. Ct. Appeals (3d cir.) 1968, U.S. Supreme Ct. 1976. Assoc. Eckert, Seamans, Cherin & Mellott, Pitts., 1965-72, ptnr., 1973—; mem. adv. com. on appellate ct. rules Supreme Ct. Pa., 1986-92. Editor Duquesne U. Law Rev., 1964-65. Chmn. Hampton (Pa.) Twp. Planning Commn., 1986-87; bd. dirs. Pa. Health Choice Plan, St. Francis Health Sys., Duquesne U.; trustee Noble J. Dick Edn. Fund, 1989—. Recipient Disting. Alumni award Duquesne U. Law Rev., 1985, Disting. Law Alumni award Duquesne U. Sch. Law, 1991, Disting. Svc. award Hampton Twp., 1991, McAnurlty Svc. award Duquesne U., 1992; named Century Club Disting. Alumni, Duquesne U., 1985. Fellow Am. Bar Found., Pa. Bar Found.; mem. Pa. Bar Assn. (ho. of dels. 1985-90), Acad. Trial Lawyers Allegheny County (bd. govs. 1986-89), Duquesne U. Alumni Assn. (pres. 1980-82, 88-90, bd. govs. 1982-90, bd. dirs. 1988-89), Duquesne Club, Pitts. Athletic Assn. Republican. Roman Catholic. Home: 4288 Green Glade Ct Allison Park PA 15101-1202 Office: Eckert Seamans Cherin & Mellott 600 Grant St Ste 42D Pittsburgh PA 15219-2703

O'CONNOR, FRANCINE MARIE, magazine editor; b. Springfield, Mass., Apr. 8, 1930; d. Wallace Harold and Celestine Margaret (Morrison) Provost; m. John Francis O'Connor, Dec. 27, 1951 (dec. Feb. 1992); children—Margaret Anne McGlynn, Kathryn Mary Boswell, Timothy John. Grad. high sch., Springfield. Editorial asst. Liguori Publs., Mo., 1975-76, assoc. editor, 1976-79, mng. editor, 1979-93; assoc. editor Parish Edn. Products, Mo., 1993—. Author: ABC's of Faith series, including The Stories of Jesus, 1982, The ABC's of the Rosary, 1984, The ABC's of the Mass, 1989, The ABC's of the Sacraments, 1989, The ABC's of the Old Testament, 1989, The ABC's of Prayer, 1989, Lessons of Love, 1991 (hon. mention Cath. Press Assn. 1992), God and You: Friends Forever, 1993, The ABC's of Christmas, 1994, The ABC's of Our Church, 1996, Forming Children in the Faith, 1996. Religious edn. coord. Sts. Peter and Paul Roman Cath. Ch., St. Louis, 1978—. Mem. Cath. Press Assn. Avocations: bird watching, crossword puzzles. Home: 157 Crest Manor Dr House Springs MO 63051-1477 Office: Liguorian 1 Liguori Dr Liguori MO 63057-9998

O'CONNOR, FRANCIS X., financial executive; b. Bklyn., May 7, 1929; s. Richard B. and Mary (McCafferty) O'C.; m. Leona A. Windorf, June 30, 1951; children: Francis X., Edward K., Brendan T., Richard B. III, A. Bruce, Marianne, Margaret, Leona. BS, St. Peter's Coll., 1951. CPA, N.Y., N.J. Audit mgr. Coopers & Lybrand, N.Y.C., 1951-65; controller Ward Foods, Inc., N.Y.C., 1965-66, v.p. fin., CFO, 1966-72, also bd. dirs., 1968-73; v.p. fin., CFO UMC Industries, Inc., N.Y.C., 1973-76; v.p. fin. and corp. devel., CFO SKF Industries, Inc., King of Prussia, Pa., 1976-87; v.p. corp. fin. Moore & Schley Securities Corp., Morristown, N.J., 1987-89; mng. dir. Sterling Manhattan Corp. Investment Bankers, N.Y.C., 1989-93; adv. bd. Boyden Cons. Corp. Mem. AICPA, AIM, N.Y. State Soc. CPAs. Fin. Excs. Inst., Nat. Conf. on Power Transmission (trustee), Machinery and Allied Products Inst. Fin. Coun., St. Peter's Coll. Alumni Assn. (trustee, past pres. Monmouth chpt.), Navy League U.S., Spring Lake Golf Club, (past pres., trustee), Seaview Country Club (N.J.), Green Gables Club (past pres.), Reserve Golf Club (Ft. Pierce, Fla.). Clubs: Spring Lake Golf and Country (pres., trustee); Seaview Country (Absecon, N.J.); Green Gables; Reserve Golf (Ft. Pierce, Fla.). Home: 2355 NE Ocean Blvd Stuart FL 34996-2945 Office: Boyden Cons Group Morristown NJ 07960

O'CONNOR, GAYLE MCCORMICK, law librarian; b. Rome, N.Y., July 8, 1956; d. John Joseph and Barbara Jane (Molyneaux) McC. Head libr. Bolling, Walter & Gawthrop, Sacramento, 1987-88, Weintraub, Genshlea & Sproul, Sacramento, 1988-93, Brobeck, Phleger & Harrison, San Diego, 1993-96; legal cons., author, 1996—; instr. law Lincoln U., Sacramento. Contbr. articles to profl. jours. Mem. ABA, No. Calif. Assn. Law Librs., So. Calif. Assn. Law Librs., Am. Assn. Law Librs., Spl. Librs. Assn. Avocations: bodybuilding, skiing.

O'CONNOR, SISTER GEORGE AQUIN (MARGARET M. O'CONNOR), college president, sociology educator; b. Astoria, N.Y., Mar. 5, 1921; d. George M. and Joana T. (Loughlin) O'C. B.A., Hunter Coll., 1943; M.A., Catholic U. Am., 1947; Ph.D. (NIMH fellow), NYU, 1964; LL.D. Manhattan Coll., 1983. Mem. faculty St. Joseph's Coll., Bklyn., 1946—; prof. sociology and anthropology St. Joseph's Coll., 1966—, chmn. social sci. dept., 1966-69, pres., 1969—; Fellow African Studies Assn., Am. Anthrop. Assn.; Bklyn. C. of C. (dir. 1973—), Alpha Kappa Delta, Delta Epsilon Sigma. Author: The Status and Role of West African Women: A Study in Cultural Change, 1964. Office: Saint Joseph's Coll Office of Pres 245 Clinton Ave Brooklyn NY 11205-3602

O'CONNOR, G(EORGE) RICHARD, ophthalmologist; b. Cin., Oct. 8, 1928; s. George Leo and Sylvia Johanna (Voss) O'C. AB, Harvard U., 1950; MD, Columbia U., 1954. Resident in ophthalmology Columbia-Presbyn. Med. Center, N.Y.C., 1957-60; research fellow Inst. Biochemistry, U. Uppsala, Sweden, 1960-61, State Serum Inst., Copenhagen, 1961-62; asst. prof. ophthalmology U. Calif., San Francisco, 1962-68; prof. U. Calif., 1972-84; dir. Francis I. Proctor Found. for Research in Ophthalmology, 1970-84; mem. Nat. Adv. Eye Council NIH, 1974-78. Author: (with G. Smolin) Ocular Immunology, 1981; asso. editor: Am. Jour. Ophthalmology, 1976-81. Served with USPHS, 1955-57. Recipient Janeway prize Coll. of Physicians and Surgeons, Columbia U., 1954; Doyne medal Oxford U., 1984; NIH grantee, 1962-84. Mem. Am. Bd. Ophthalmology (examiner), Assn. for Rsch. in Vision and Ophthalmology (trustee 1979-83, pres. 1982-83, Weisenfeld award 1990), AMA, Am. Ophthal. Soc., Calif. Med. Assn., Frederic C. Cordes Eye Soc., Pan Am. Ophthal. Assn. Republican. Presbyterian. Club: Faculty. Home: 22 Wray Ave Sausalito CA 94965-1831 Office: U Calif Med Ctr 315-S San Francisco CA 94143

O'CONNOR, HAROLD J., retired wildlife research administrator. Dir. Patuxent Environ. Sci. Ctr., Laurel, Md.; now ret., 1995. Office: Patuxent Environ Sci Ctr Laurel MD 20708-4039

O'CONNOR, JAMES ARTHUR, theatre educator; b. Buffalo, Nov. 24, 1937; s.Bernard and Elsie (Thoman) O'C.; children: Anita, Lisa. BS, SUNY, 1960; MA, U. N.Mex., 1963; MFA, Pa. State U., 1969. Assoc. prof. art N.Mex. Inst. Tech., 1963-70; prof. theatre Purdue U., West Lafayette, Ind., 1978—, chair theatre divsn., 1986—, dir. theatre, 1987—; stage dir. Repertory Theatre St. Louis, 1980-95, Stage West, Springfield, Mass., 1983, Alley Theatre, Houston, 1984, Walnut St. Theatre, Phila., 1995, others. Recipient Cleve. Critics Cir. award for Direction; nominated Joseph Jefferson award for Direction. Mem. Univ./Resident Theatre Assn. (v.p. 1986-92, pres. 1992—). Office: Purdue U 1376 Stewart Ctr West Lafayette IN 47907-1376

O'CONNOR, JAMES JOHN, utility company executive; b. Chgo., Mar. 15, 1937; s. Fred James and Helen Elizabeth O'Connor; m. Ellen Louise Lawlor, Nov. 24, 1960; children: Fred, John (dec.), James, Helen Elizabeth. BS, Holy Cross Coll., 1958; MBA, Harvard U., 1960; JD, Georgetown U., 1963. Bar: Ill. 1963. With Commonwealth Edison Co., Chgo., 1963—, asst. to chmn. exec. com., 1964-65, comml. mgr., 1966, asst. v.p., 1967-70, v.p., 1970-73, exec. v.p., 1973-77, pres., 1977-87, chmn., 1980—; CEO, also bd. dirs.; chmn., CEO Unicom Corp., 1994—; bd. dirs. Corning, Inc., Chgo. Bd. of Trade, Tribune Co., United Air Lines, Scotsman Industries, Am. Nat. Can., 1st Chgo. NBD Corp., 1st Nat. Bank Chgo.; past chmn. Nuc. Power Oversight Com., Edison Electric Inst., bd. dirs.; chmn. Advanced Reactor Corp. Mem. The Bus. Coun.; bd. dirs. Assocs. Harvard U. Grad. Sch. Bus. Adminstrn., Lyric Opera, Helen Brach Found.; bd. dirs., trustee Mus. Sci. and Industry; past chmn. Met. Savs. Bond Campaign; trustee Northwestern U.; bd. dirs., past chmn. Chgo. Urban League, Chicagoland C. of C.; past chmn. bd. trustees Field Mus. Natural History; life trustee Adler Planetarium; mem. exec. bd. Chgo. area Coun. Boy Scouts Am.; chmn. Cardinal Bernardin's Big Shoulders Fund; exec. v.p. The Hundred Club Cook County; dir., past pres. Cath. Charities; past chmn., hon. dir. Am. Cancer Soc., Chgo. Conv. and Tourism Bur. With USAF, 1960-63. Mem. ABA, Ill. Bar Assn., Chgo. Bar Assn., Chgo. Assn. Commerce and Industry (bd. dirs., chmn.), Ill. Bus. Roundtable, Chicagoland C. of C. (dir., past chmn.). Home: 1500 Lake Shore Dr 5C Chicago IL 60610 Office: Commonwealth Edison Co PO Box 767 1 1st Nat Plz Chicago IL 60690-0767

O'CONNOR, JENNIFER, public administrator; b. Somerville, Mass., Feb. 12, 1966; m. Paul J. Meyer, Nov. 13, 1993. BA in Govt. magna cum laude, Harvard U., 1987; MPA, Columbia U., 1992. Dep. press sec., econ. devel. assoc. Office of Manhattan Borough Pres Ruth Messinger, N.Y.C., 1990-92; budget specialist, N.E. regional polit. dir. Presdl. Transition Office, Little Rock, 1992-93; dep. dir. Office of Mgmt. and Adminstrn. The White House, Washington, 1993, spl. asst. to Pres. for Cabinet affairs, 1993-95, spl. asst. to Pres. Office Dep. Chief of Staff, 1995—; field. dir. N.Y. primary campaign, polit. dir. N.J. primary campaign, dep. mgr. at Dem. Nat. Conv., state dir. Vt. gen. election campaign Clinton for Pres./Clinton-Gore '92, 1992. Democrat. Roman Catholic. Office: Office of Chief of Staff 1600 Pennsylvania Ave NW Washington DC 20500-0001

O'CONNOR, JOHN CHRISTOPHER, JR., consulting petroleum engineer; b. New Orleans, Feb. 13, 1920; s. John Christopher and Adelaide Pauline (Estopinal) O'C.; m. Olivia Hortense Cazayoux, Dec. 27, 1944; children: Maureen Judith, Karen Inez, Rebecca Frances, Denise Olivia. BS in Petroleum Engring., La. State U., 1941. Registered petroleum engr., La., Tex. Petroleum engr. The Calif. Co., La., Gulf of Mex., Okla., Colo., Wyo. and Utah, 1946-56; v.p. ops. Continental Shelf Drilling Corp., New Orleans, 1956-59; consulting petroleum engr. New Orleans, 1959—. Eucharistic min. St. Edward the Confessor Cath. Ch.; mem. U.S. Com. for Battle of Normandy Mus. With Corps Engrs., U.S. Army, 1941-46, CBI and ETO. Mem. NSPE, Soc. Petroleum Engrs., Am. Petroleum Inst., Am. Assn. Drilling Engrs., La. Engring. Soc., Knights of Columbus, Holy Name Soc., Equestrian Order of Holy Sepulchre of Jerusalem (Knight of Holy Sepulchre), Sovereign Mil. Order of Malta (Knight of Order of Malta), St. Vincent de Paul Soc., China-Burma-India Vets. Assn., Burma Star Assn., Am. Legion, Ret. Officers Assn., Serra Club New Orleans, Petroleum Club New Orleans, Plimsoll Club, Internat. House Club. Republican.

O'CONNOR, JOHN DENNIS, academic administrator; b. Chgo., Mar. 20, 1942; married, 1964; 3 children. B.S., Loyola U, Chgo., 1963; M.S., DePaul U., 1966; Ph.D., Northwestern U., 1968. NIH fellow Mich. State U., East Lansing, 1968-70; asst. prof. biology UCLA, 1969-74, assoc. prof., 1974-77, prof. biology, 1977-81, chmn. biology, 1979-81, dean, life scis., 1981-87; vice chancellor for research, dean of grad. sch., prof. biology U. N.C.; prof. biology U. N.C., Chapel Hill, 1988-91; chancellor, prof. biology U. Pitts., 1991-96; provost Smithsonian Instn., Washington, 96—; vis. prof. U. Nijmegen, Netherlands, 1975-76, Monash U., 1977. Fellow AAAS; mem. Am. Soc. Zoology, Soc. Devel. Biology, Am. Soc. Molecular Biology and Biochemistry, Bus. Higher Edn. (vice chair 1994-96, chair 1996—). Office:

Smithsonian Instn Office of Provost 1000 Jefferson Dr SW Washington DC 20560

O'CONNOR, JOHN JAY, III, lawyer; b. San Francisco, Jan. 10, 1930; s. John Jay and Sally (Flynn) O'C.; m. Sandra Day, Dec. 20, 1952; children: Scott, Brian, Jay. AB, Stanford U., 1951, LLB, 1953. Bar: Calif. 1953, Ariz. 1957, D.C. 1981. Mem. Fennemore, Craig, von Ammon & Udall, Phoenix, 1957-81, Miller & Chevalier, Washington, 1982-88; ptnr. Bryan Cave, Washington and Phoenix, 1988—; judge pro-tem Superior Ct. State of Ariz., 1979-81. Chmn. Ariz. Crippled Children's Services, 1968; Chmn. planning and zoning commn. Town of Paradise Valley, 1967; Chmn. Maricopa County Young Republicans, 1960, Ariz. Young Rep. League, 1962; bd. dirs. Ariz. Tax Research Assn., 1966-81; chmn. bd. dirs. Maricopa County Gen. Hosp., 1967-70; exec. com. bd. visitors Stanford Law Sch., 1976-80; pres. Stanford Law Fund, 1980-82; mem. nat. council Salk Inst. Biol. Studies, San Diego, 1977-90; pres. Phoenix-Scottsdale United Way, 1977-79; bd. dirs. World Affairs Council of Phoenix, 1970-81, Legal Aid Soc. Phoenix, Maricopa County Mental Health Assn.; trustee Meridian House Internat., Washington, 1982-88; mem. policy devel. com. Phoenix Community Service Fund, 1978; mem. exec. com. Valley Leadership, 1979-81; bd. dirs. Trusteeship for St. Luke's Hosp., 1979-81; mem. adv. com. Nat. Postal Mus., Washington, 1992—. Served to 1st lt. AUS, 1954-57. Mem. ABA, Stanford Assocs., Paradise Rotary (pres. 1977-78), Paradise Valley Country Club, Ariz. Club (pres. 1979-81), Valley Field Riding and Polo Club, Stanford Club of Phoenix (pres.), Iron Springs Club (pres. 1974-76), Bohemian Club, Met. Club, Alfalfa Club, Alibi Club, Ariz. Acad. Delta Upsilon, Phi Delta Phi. Office: Bryan Cave 700 13th St NW Washington DC 20005-3960

O'CONNOR, JOHN JOSEPH CARDINAL, archbishop, former naval officer; b. Phila., Jan. 15, 1920; s. Thomas Joseph and Dorothy Magdalene (Gomple) O'C. M.A., St. Charles Coll., 1949, Catholic U. Am., 1954; Ph.D., Georgetown U., 1970; D.R.E., Villanova (Pa.) U., 1976. Ordained priest Roman Cath. Ch., 1945, elevated to monsignor, 1966, consecrated bishop, 1979, created cardinal, 1985; served in Chaplain Corps U.S. Navy, 1952, advanced through grades to rear adm.; assigned to Atlantic and Pacific fleets U.S. Navy, Okinawa and Vietnam; sr. chaplain U.S. Naval Acad.; chief of chaplains U.S. Navy, Washington; aux. bishop, vicar gen. Mil. Vicariate, 1979-83; apptd. bishop of Scranton Pa., 1983-84; archbishop Archdiocese of N.Y., 1984—; Exec. bd. Nat. USO, Georgetown Center Strategic and Internat. Studies, Marine Corps Found. Author: Principles and Problems of Naval Leadership, 1958, A Chaplain Looks at Vietnam, 1969, In Defense of Life, 1981, (with Edward I. Koch) His Eminence and Hizzoner: A Candid Exchange, 1989, (with Elie Wiesel) A Journey of Faith, 1990. Decorated DMS, Legion of Merit (3), Meritorious Service medal. Mem. Am. Polit. Sci. Assn. Office: Archdiocese NY 452 Madison Ave New York NY 10022

O'CONNOR, JOHN MORRIS, III, philosophy educator; b. Evanston, Ill., Sept. 21, 1937; s. John Morris and Clare Evelyn (Merrick) O'C.; m. Mary Bittner, Dec. 31, 1960 (div.); 1 dau., Emily; m. Miranda E. P. Ind, Aug. 14, 1971 (div.); 1 dau., Amanda. Student, Georgetown U., 1955-56; B.A., Cornell U., 1959; M.A., Harvard U., 1962, Ph.D., 1965. Instr. Vassar Coll., 1964-66, asst. prof. philosophy, 1966-68; asst. prof. Case Western Res. U., Cleve., 1968-70, assoc. prof., 1970-77; exec. sec. Am. Philos. Assn. U. Del., Newark, 1977-84, assoc. prof., 1977-83; asst. dir. for programs Nat. Humanities Ctr., Research Triangle Park, N.C., 1983-87; dean Sch. Humanities William Paterson Coll., Wayne, N.J., 1987-91, dean Sch. Humanities, Mgmt. and Social Scis., 1991-92, coord. spl. projects Office of Provost, 1992-93, prof. philosophy, 1992—. Contbr. articles to profl. jours.; editor: (with others) Introductory Philosophy, 1967, Modern Materialism, 1969, Moral Problems in Medicine, 1976. Woodrow Wilson nat. fellow, 1959-60. Office: William Paterson Coll Dept Philosophy Wayne NJ 07470

O'CONNOR, JOHN T., civil engineering educator; b. N.Y.C., Feb. 11, 1933; married, 1966; 2 children. BCE, Cooper Union, 1955; MSCE, N.J. Inst. Tech., 1958; EngD, Johns Hopkins U., 1961. Sanitary engr. Elson T. Killam Sanit & Hydraulic Consulting Engrs., 1955-56; civil engr. George A. Fuller Constrn. Co., N.Y., 1956-57; sanitary engr. Parsons, Brinckerhoff, Quade & Douglas, 1957; from asst. assoc. prof. sanitary engr. U. Ill., Urbana-Champaign, 1961-69, prof. civil engring., 1969-75; prof. civil engring. U. Mo., Columbia, 1975-92, chmn. dept., 1975-89; chief Ill. State Water Survey, 1992—. Mem. ASCE, Am. Chem. Soc., Am. Water Works Assn., Am. Soc. Limnology and Oceanography, Water Environment Fedn. Achievements include research on drinking water treatment processes; removal of microorganisms, organic substances, iron and manganese radionuclides; wastewater treatment and disinfection; solid and hazardous waste site remediation. Address: 2118 Robert Dr Champaign IL 61821-6535

O'CONNOR, JOSEPH A., JR., lawyer; b. N.Y.C., Aug. 12, 1937; s. Joseph A. and Louise G. (Lucht) O'C.; children: Joseph A. III, Edward W. BA, Yale U., 1959; LLB, Columbia U., 1962. Bar: N.Y. 1963, U.S. Supreme Ct. 1968, Pa. 1973, Fla. 1978. Assoc. Davis, Polk & Wardwell, N.Y.C., 1963-72; ptnr. Morgan, Lewis & Bockius, Phila., 1972—. Mem. ABA, N.Y. State Bar Assn., Pa. Bar Assn., Fla. Bar Assn., Phila. Bar Assn., Assn. of Bar of City of N.Y. Roman Catholic. Club: Racquet (Phila.). Office: Morgan Lewis & Bockius LLP 2000 One Logan Sq Philadelphia PA 19103

O'CONNOR, KARL WILLIAM, lawyer; b. Washington, Aug. 1, 1931; s. Hector and Lucile (Johnson) O'C.; m. Sylvia Gasbarri, Mar. 23, 1951 (dec.); m. Judith Ann Byers, July 22, 1972 (div. 1983); m. Eleanor Celler, Aug. 3, 1984 (div. 1986); m. Alma Hepner, Jan. 1, 1987 (div. 1996); children: Blair, Frances, Brian, Brendan. BA, U. Va., 1952, JD, 1958. Bar: Va. 1958, D.C. 1959, Am. Samoa 1976, Calif. 1977, Oreg. 1993. Law clk. U.S. Dist. Ct. Va., Abingdon, 1958-59; practice law Washington, 1959-61; trial atty. U.S. Dept. Justice, Washington, 1961-65; dep. dir. Men's Job Corps OEO, Washington, 1965-67; mem. civil rights div. Dept. of Justice, chief criminal sect., prin. dep. asst. atty. gen., 1967-75, spl. counsel for intelligence coordination, 1975; v.p., counsel Assn. of Motion Picture and Television Producers, Hollywood, Calif., 1975-76; assoc. justice Am. Samoa, 1976, chief justice, 1977-78; sr. trial atty. GSA Task Force, Dept. Justice, 1978-81; insp. gen. CSA, 1981-82; spl. counsel Merit Systems Protection Bd., Washington, 1983-86; U.S. atty. for Guam and the No. Marianas, 1986-89, ret.; pvt. practice Medford, Oreg., 1989—; Am. counsel O'Reilly Vernier Ltd., Hong Kong, 1992-93; ptnr. O'Connor & Vernier, Medford, Oreg., 1993-94; pvt. practice Medford, 1994—. Served with USMC, 1952-55. Mem. Oreg. Bar Assn., D.C. Bar Assn., Va. Bar Assn., Calif. Bar Assn., Am. Samoa Bar Assn., Phi Alpha Delta, Sigma Nu. Home: Box 112 4804 Dark Hollow Rd Medford OR 97501-0008 Office: 916 W 10th St Medford OR 97501-3018

O'CONNOR, KAY, state legislator; b. Everett, Wash., Nov. 28, 1941; d. Ernest S. and Dena (Lampers) Wells; m. Arthur J. O'Connor, Sept. 1, 1959; 6 children. Diploma, Lathrop H.S., Fairbanks, Alaska, 1959. Office mgr. Blaylock Chemicals, Bucyrus, Kans., 1981-84; store mgr. Copies Plus, Olathe, Kans., 1984-86; acct. Advance Concrete Inc., Spring Hill, Kans., 1986-92; mem. Kansas Ho. of Reps., 1993—; bd. dirs. Hometel Ltd.; author sch. voucher legis. for State of Kans., 1994, 95, 96. Republican. Roman Catholic. Avocations: choir dir., statue renovations, spkr. on sch. vouchers. Home: 1101 N Curtis St Olathe KS 66061-2709 Office: PO Box 2232 Olathe KS 66051-2232

O'CONNOR, KEVIN JOHN, psychologist; b. Jersey City, N.J., July 18, 1954; s. John Lanning and Marilyn (Reynolds) O'C.; m. Ryan Michael, Matthew Benham. BA, U. Mich., 1975; PhD, U. Toledo, 1981. Clin. psychologist Blythedale Children's Hosp., Valhalla, N.Y., 1980-83; dir. Psychol. Svcs. Walworth Barbour Am. Internat. Sch., Kfar Shmaryahu, Israel, 1983-84; adjunct asst. prof. Dept. Psychology Iona Coll., New Rochelle, N.Y., 1984; clin. psychologist Northern Westchester Guidance Clinic, Mt. Kisco, N.Y., 1985; exec. dir., newsletter editor Assn. for Play Therapy, Fresno, Calif., 1982—; consulting psychologist Fresno (Calif.) Treatment Ctr., 1986-87, Diagnostic Sch. for Neurologically Handicapped Children, Fresno, Calif., 1986-90; adjunct faculty Pacific Grad. Sch. of Psychology, Palo Alto, Calif., 1987—, Calif. Sch. Profl. Psychology, Berkeley, Calif., 1988-89; prof. Calif. Sch. Profl. Psychology, Fresno, 1985—. Contbr. numerous presentations in field. Named Psychologist of Yr. San Joaquin Psychol. Assn., 1994. Mem. APA, Assn. for Play Therapy, Mental Health Assn. Greater Fresno, San Joaquin Psychol. Assn., Western Psychol. Assn., Coun. for Nat. Register of Health Svc. Providers in Psychology. Democrat. Avocations: travel, art, ceramics. Office: Calif Sch Profl Psych 5130 M St Fresno CA 93721

O'CONNOR, KIM CLAIRE, chemical engineering and biotechnology educator; b. N.Y.C., Nov. 18, 1960; d. Gerard Timothy and Doris Julia (Bisagni) O'C. BS magna cum laude, Rice U., Houston, 1982; PhD, Calif. Inst. Tech., Pasadena, 1987. Postdoctoral rsch. fellow chemistry dept. Calif. Inst. Tech., Pasadena, 1987-88; postdoctoral rsch. fellow chem. engring., biochemistry, molecular biology, and cell biology depts. Northwestern U., Evanston, Ill., 1988-90; asst. prof. chem. engring. Tulane U., New Orleans, 1990-96, assoc. prof. chem. engring., 1996—, faculty molecular and cellular biology grad. program, Newcomb fellow, 1991—; mem. steering com. molecular and cellular biology grad. program Tulane U., 1993—; mem. Tulane Cancer Ctr., 1994—; cons. in field. Reviewer of profl. jours. Mem. Am. Inst. Chem. Engrs., Am. Soc. Engring. Edn., European Soc. Animal Cell Tech., Soc. In Vitro Biology, Assn. for Women in Sci., Sigma Xi, Tau Beta Pi, Phi Lambda Upsilon. Achievements include interdisciplinary research in engineering, animal- and microbial-cell culture, genetics, and protein chemistry; specifically research in enzyme structure and function with immobilization and protein engineering, oxygenation and cell metabolism of animal cells in bioreactors, bioseparation of DNA fragments with HPLC, and large-scale production of recombinant protein. Office: Tulane U Dept Chem Engring Lindy Boggs Ctr Rm 300 New Orleans LA 70118

O'CONNOR, LAWRENCE JOSEPH, JR., energy consultant; b. Tulsa, Dec. 29, 1914; s. Lawrence Joseph and Bess (Yarbrough) O'C. Student, Tulsa U., 1932-33; A.B., Rice U., 1936; M.B.A., Harvard U., 1938. With Haskins & Sells (C.P.A.s), Houston, 1938-45; v.p., treas. Goldston Oil Corp., Houston, 1945-58; oil and gas cons. Houston, 1958-59; asst. dir. Office Oil and Gas, Dept. Interior, 1959-60, adminstr. oil import adminstrn., 1960-61; commr. Fed. Power Commn., 1961-71; v.p. Standard Oil Co. (Ohio), Washington, 1971-74; energy cons. Houston, 1975—. Roman Catholic. Clubs: Congressional Country, Houston Country. Home: 846 Augusta Dr Houston TX 77057-2014 Office: PO Box 130505 Houston TX 77219-0505

O'CONNOR, MARY SCRANTON, public relations executive; b. New Haven, May 9, 1942; d. James T. and Mary E. (Scranton) O'C. BA, Manhattanville Coll., 1964. Women's editor Hartford Times, Conn., 1964-68; pub. rels. account exec. Wilson, Haight & Welch, Hartford, 1968-72, v.p., dir. pub. rels., 1972-75; pub. rels. cons. O'Connor/PR, Farmington, Conn., 1975-76; v.p. pub. rels. Lowengard & Brotherhood, Hartford, 1976-78, pres., 1978-83; pres. Harland, O'Connor, Tine & White, Hartford, 1983-84; v.p. communications Conn. Mut. Life Ins. Co., Hartford, 1984-88; pres. Bradford Advt., Inc., Old Saybrook, Conn., 1988-90; prin. Strategic Communications, Old Lyme, Conn., 1990-95; dir. com. and pub. rels. N.E. region Kaiser Permanente, Farmington, 1995—; instr. pub. rels. mgmt. Manchester Community Coll., 1975. Bd. dirs. Child and Family Svcs., Inc., Hartford, 1980-89, Better Bus. Bur., 1980-83, Criminal Justice Edn. Ctr., 1981; trustee The Mark Twain House, Hartford, 1994—. Recipient Woman of Yr. award YWCA, 1980. Mem. Pub. Rels. Soc. Am. (Merit award 1992), Greater Hartford C. of C. (bd. dirs. 1983-86). Office: Kaiser Permanente 76 Batterson Park Rd Farmington CT 06034-4011

O'CONNOR, NEAL WILLIAM, former advertising agency executive; b. Milw., Aug. 25, 1925; s. Arthur J. and Helen (Radell) O'C.; m. Nancy K. Turner, July 8, 1950; children: Robert W., Thomas N., David J. B.S. cum laude, Syracuse U., 1949. With N.W. Ayer Inc., N.Y.C., 1949-80; v.p., mgr. N.Y. service N.W. Ayer Inc., 1962-65, pres., 1965-73, chmn. bd., 1973-76, chief exec. officer, 1966-76, chmn. exec. com., 1976-80; Past dir. Advt. Council; past. chmn. Am. Assn. Advt. Agys.; past pres. Consumer Research Inst. Pres. Found. for Aviation WWI, 1980—; past chmn. and pres. League of WWI Aviation Historians. With inf. AUS, 1943-45, ETO. Decorated Bronze Star, Combat Inf. badge. Mem. Beta Theta Pi, Alpha Delta Sigma. Clubs: Pretty Brook Tennis, Wings (N.Y.C.). Home: 10 Constitution Hl E Princeton NJ 08540-6749 Office: PO Box 212 Princeton NJ 08542-0212

O'CONNOR, PAUL DANIEL, lawyer; b. Paterson, N.J., Nov. 24, 1936; s. Paul Daniel and Anne Marie Christopher O'C.; children: Steven Paul, Sheryl Lynn, Laura Ann. B.S. in Engring, U.S. Naval Acad., 1959; LL.B., U. Va., 1965. Bar: N.Y. 1965, Calif. 1996. Assoc. firm Winthrop, Stimson, Putnam & Roberts, N.Y.C., 1965-72; partner Winthrop, Stimson, Putnam & Roberts, 1972-80; sr. v.p., gen. counsel Singer Co., Stamford, Conn., 1980-86; chief exec. officer Citation Builders, 1986-95; trustee Valley Trusts, San Ramon, Calif., 1986—. 1st lt. USAF, 1959-62. Mem. Assn. of Bar of City of N.Y., Bar Assn. of San Francisco, Am. Horse Shows Assn., Fairfield County Hunt Club. Home: 1150 Lombard StUnit 22 San Francisco CA 94109 Office: Valley Trusts 3170 Crow Canyon Pl Ste 270 San Ramon CA 94583-1347

O'CONNOR, R. D., health care executive. BS Psychology, Sociology, U. So. Miss., 1960, MS Adminstrv. Personnel, 1961, PhD Mgmt., Orgnl. Communication, 1983. Asst. dean student affairs Holmes Jr. Coll., Goodman, Mo., 1961-64; spl. counselor vocat. rehab. divsn. Dept. Edn., Jackson, Mo., 1964-65; asst. adminstr. Hinds Gen. Hosp., Jackson, Mo., 1965-68; adminstr. Rankin Gen. Hosp., Brandon, Mo., 1968-76; v.p. Human Resources/ Mktg. Delta Mgmt. Systems, Metairie, La., 1976-79; asst. to exec. dir. Baptist Med. Ctr., Jacksonville, Fla., 1979-82; pres. RiverGroup Riverside Hosp., Rivercorp Inc., Riverside Found., Jacksonville, Fla., 1982-87; owner O'Connor & Assocs., Jacksonville, Fla., 1987-91; pres. Fla. 1st: Managed Health Care, Winter Haven, Orlando & Tampa, Fla., 1991-94; v.p. quality Mid Florida Med. Svcs. Inc., Winter Haven, Fla., 1994—; instr. U. So. Miss., Hattiesburg, Ms.; tchr., lectr. various univs., C.C.s, military acads.; grad. faculty coord. Webster U. Contbr. articles to profl. jours. Commr. Cleary Heights Sewer Dist., 1978-79; pres'. selective task force Induction Procedures, 1969; chmn. personnel com. San Jose Baptist Ch., 1981-86, strategic planning com., 1986-87; gov's. com. Statewide Planning Vocat. Rehab., 1968; bd. dirs. Rankin County C. of C., 1970-73, exec. com., chmn. health affairs com., 1970-72, chmn. highway com. 1970-74, fin. com. 1971-73), Family Blood Assurance Program, 1972-77, v.p. 1977, Vol. Action Coun., 1973-76, United Givers Fund, 1973-76. With Air Nat. Guard, Med. Svc. Corps., ret. Fellow Am. Coll. Healthcare Execs.; mem. Fla. Hosp. Assn. (com. chmn. 1984), Greater Jacksonville Area Hosp. Coun. (chmn. 1985), Jackson-Vicksburg Hosp. Coun. (chmn. 1974), Nat. Assn. Mental Health (bd. dirs. 1973-74), Miss. Assn. Mental Health (pres. 1972-74), Miss. Hosp. Assn. (bd. dirs .1973-76, exec. devel. com. 1972-75, mgmt. engring. adminstrv. bd. 1973, fin. com. 1972-74, chmn. nominating com. 1971, coord. divsn. profl. practice 1970). Home: 2 Casarena Ct Winter Haven FL 33881-1290

O'CONNOR, RALPH STURGES, investment company executive; b. Pasadena, Calif., Aug. 27, 1926; s. Thomas Ireland and Edith Masury (Sturges) O'C.; m. Alice Maconda Brown, Apr. 28, 1950; children—George Rufus, Thomas Ireland III, Nancy Isabel, John Herman. B.A., Johns Hopkins, 1951. With Highland Resources, Inc., Houston, 1951-87, exec. v.p., 1961-64; pres. Highland Resources, Inc., 1964-87; pres., chief exec. officer Ralph S. O'Connor and Assocs., 1987—; chmn. bd. Arnaud's Restaurant, New Orleans, PanEnergy. Trustee emeritus Rice U., Houston Oldfields Sch., Glencoe, Md., Nat. Found. Advancement in the Arts. With USAAF, 1943-46. Mem. NAS (Pres.'s Circle), Am. Assn. Petroleum Landmen, All Am. Wildcatters. Clubs: Bayou (Houston), Ramada (Houston), River Oaks Country (Houston). Home: 5627 Indian Cir Houston TX 77056-1006 Office: Ralph S O'Connor & Assocs 1001 Fannin St Ste 622 Houston TX 77002-6707

O'CONNOR, RICHARD DENNIS, lawyer; b. Worcester, Mass., Oct. 22, 1937. BS, Coll. of Holy Cross, 1959; LLB, Georgetown U., 1964. Bar: Conn. 1964, U.S. Dist. Ct. Conn. 1964, U.S. Ct. Appeals (2d cir.) 1969, U.S. Dist. Ct. D.C. 1971, U.S. Supreme Ct. 1973, U.S. Ct. Appeals (D.C. cir.) 1974, Mass. 1985, U.S. Dist. Ct. Mass. 1985. Law clk. to hon. judge Clarie U.S. Dist. Ct. Conn., Hartford, 1964-65; prin., founding ptnr. Siegel, O'Connor, Schiff & Zangari, P.C., Hartford, 1965—; spkr. on labor issues, Conn., 1985-90; arbitrator Am. Arbitration Assn., Conn., 1985—; mem. Magistrate Reappointment Rev. Com., Conn.; arbitrator panel Gov.'s State Bd. of Edn., Conn., 1987—. Lt. USN, 1959-61. Mem. ABA (labor and employment law internat. labor law com. mgmt. co-chmn. 1992-95), ATLA, Conn. Bar Assn., Mass. Bar Assn., Fed. Bar Coun., Am. Assn. Hosp. Attys., Conn. Sch. Attys.' Coun. Office: Siegel OConnor Schiff & Zangari PC 370 Asylum St Hartford CT 06103-2003

O'CONNOR, RICHARD DONALD, advertising company executive; b. Nyack, N.Y., Dec. 29, 1931; s. James Patrick and Sophi Kathryn (Hensel) O'C.; m. Lucille Hartigan, Jan. 25, 1958 (div. 1986); children: Richard D., Kathryn Helen, Timothy Joseph, Meghan Mary, John Patrick; m. Katherine M. Unger, Apr. 7, 1989. BA, U. Mich., 1954. With Campbell-Ewald Co., Detroit, 1956—; exec. v.p., chief operating officer Lintas: Campbell-Ewald Co., Detroit, 1975-76, pres., 1976-79, vice chmn., chief exec. officer, 1979-82; chief exec. officer, vice chmn. Marschalk/Campbell-Ewald Worldwide, 1982-86, chmn., chief exec. officer, 1984-85; chmn., chief exec. officer Lintas: Campbell-Ewald Co., N.Y.C. and Warren, Mich., 1985—; bd. dirs. Lintas: Worldwide. Trustee Walsh Coll., Troy, Mich., 1976-77, Northwood U., Menninger Found.; promotion chmn. United Found. Torch Drive, 1976; adv. com. Mich. Cancer Found., 1976-77; past trustee Detroit Country Day Sch.; active Boys Clubs N.Y., Boys Clubs Am., past trustee; adv. bd. Eton Acad.; dir. Boys and Girls Clubs Southeastern Mich. Recipient Robert E. Healy award Interpub. Group Cos., 1974. Mem. Adcraft Club Detroit (past pres.), Am. Assn. Advt. Agys. (bd. dirs.), Am. Advt. Fedn. (bd. dirs. 1987—, chmn. 94-95), Advt. Coun. (bd. dirs. 1987-91), Advt. Ednl. Found. (bd. dirs.), Advt. Club of N.Y. (v.p. 1985-86, pres. 1987-89, chmn. 1989-91), Am. Ireland Fund (bd. dirs. 1985—), U.S. Space Found. (dir.), U. Mich. Alumni Assn., Bloomfield Hills Country Club, Detroit Athletic Club, Econ. Club Detroit (dir.), Grosse Pointe Club, Hundred Club, The Old Club (Mich.), Links, Friars Club. *. Republican. Roman Catholic.

O'CONNOR, ROD, chemist, inventor; b. Cape Girardeau, Mo., July 4, 1934; s. Jay H. and Flora (Winters) O'C.; m. Shirley Ann Sander, Aug. 7, 1955; children: Mark Alan, Kara Ann, Shanna Suzanne, Timothy Patrick. BS, S.E. Mo. State Coll., 1955; PhD, U. Calif., Berkeley, 1958. Asst. prof. chemistry U. Omaha, 1958-60, Mont. State Coll., 1960-63; assoc. prof. chemistry Mont. State U., Bozeman, 1963-66; assoc. prof., coordinator gen. chemistry Kent (Ohio) State U., 1966-67; prof., dir. 1st year chemistry U. Ariz., Tucson, 1968-72; staff assoc. Adv. Council on Coll. Chemistry Stanford (Calif.) U., 1967-68; vis. prof. Wash. State U., Pullman, 1972-73; prof. chemistry Tex. A&M, College Station, 1973-86; pres. Texas ROMEC Inc., College Station, 1983—; cons. insect venoms Hollister-Stier Labs., Spokane, Wash., 1963-67; lab. separates editor W.H. Freeman Co., 1968-78; ednl. cons. TUCARA-4 Media Resources, Inc., 1971-74; mem. Coll. Chemistry Cons. Service; vis. scientist, tour lectr. Am. Chem. Soc., 1970—. Author: (with T. Moeller) Ions in Aqueous Systems, 1972, Fundamentals of Chemistry, 1981, (with C. Mickey and A. Hassell) Solving Problems in Chemistry, 1981, (with L. Peck and K. Irgolic) Fundamentals of Chemistry in The Laboratory, 1981, (with T.E. Taylor and P. Glenn) Toward Success in College, 1981; films Laboratory Safety, 1971; Contbr. articles to profl. jours.; patentee in field. Recipient nat. teaching award Mfg. Chemists Assn., 1978; 4 regional teaching awards. Fellow AAAS, Am. Inst. Chemists; mem. Internat. Soc. Toxinology, Am. Chem. Soc., Sigma Xi. Office: Texas ROMEC Inc 1300 Angelina Cir College Station TX 77840-4855 *Only those who truly care can ever be hurt ... or know real joy.*

O'CONNOR, RUTH SUSAN, physician, educator; b. Augusta, Ga., Apr. 23, 1952; d. Henry and Margaret Adeline (Schneider) Wynstra; m. Thomas Joseph O'Connor, Apr. 23, 1977; children: Samuel, Grace, Anna, Rhoda, Daniel. Student, Wheaton Coll., 1970-73; MD, Med. Coll. Wis., 1977; cert. family practice, Caraway Meth. Med. Ctr., 1980. Diplomate Am. Bd. Family Practice. Intern Carraway Meth. Med. Ctr., Birmingham, Ala., 1977-78, resident in family practice, 1978-80; fellow family practice Caraway Meth. Med. Ctr., Birmingham, Ala., 1980-81, instr. family practice, 1981-85; pvt. practice Greenville, Ill., 1986-88; instr. family practice Sch. Medicine So. Ill. U., Belleville, 1986-88; staff physician Student Health Ctr. Purdue U., West Lafayette, Ind., 1989—; instr. family medicine Ind. U., Indpls., 1989—; clin. asst. prof. family medicine. Recipient Achievement citation Am. Women's Med. Soc., 1977. Mem. Christian Med. Soc. Baptist. Avocation: caring for children. Home: 714 Kossuth St Lafayette IN 47905-1447 Office: Purdue U 1826 Student Health Ctr West Lafayette IN 47907

O'CONNOR, SANDRA DAY, United States supreme court justice; b. El Paso, Tex., Mar. 26, 1930; d. Harry A. and Ada Mae (Wilkey) Day; m. John Jay O'Connor, III, Dec. 1952; children: Scott, Brian, Jay. AB in Econs. with great distinction, Stanford U., 1950, LLB, 1952. Bar: Calif. Dep. county atty. San Mateo, Calif., 1952-53; civil atty. Q.M. Market Ctr., Frankfurt am Main, Fed. Republic of Germany, 1954-57; pvt. practice Phoenix, 1958-65; asst. atty. gen. State of Ariz., 1965-69; Ariz. state senator, 1969-75, chmn. com. on state, county and mcpl. affairs, 1972-73, majority leader, 1973-74; judge Maricopa County Superior Ct., 1975-79, Ariz. Ct. Appeals, 1979-81; assoc. justice U.S. Supreme Ct., 1981—; referee juvenile ct., 1962-64; chmn. vis. bd. Maricopa County Juvenile Detention Home, 1963-64; mem. Maricopa County Bd. Adjustments and Appeals, 1963-64, Anglo-Am. Legal Exchange, 1980, Maricopa County Superior Ct. Judges Tng. and Edn. Com., Maricopa Ct. Study Com.; chmn. com. to reorganize lower cts. Ariz. Supreme Ct., 1974-75; faculty Robert A. Taft Inst. Govt.; vice chmn. Select Law Enforcement Rev. Commn., 1979-80. Mem. bd. editors Stanford (Calif.) U. Law Rev. Mem. Ariz. Pers. Commn., 1968-69, Nat. Def. Adv. Com. on Women in Svcs., 1974-76; trustee Heard Mus., Phoenix, 1968-74, 76-81, pres., 1980-81; mem. adv. bd. Phoenix Salvation Army, 1975-81; trustee Stanford U., 1976-81, Phoenix County Day Sch.; mem. citizens adv. bd. Blood Svcs., 1975-77; nat. bd. dirs. Smithsonian Assocs., 1981—; past Rep. dist. chmn.; bd. dirs. Phoenix Cmty. Coun., Ariz. Acad., 1969-75, Jr. Achievement Ariz., 1975-79, Blue Cross/Blue Shield Ariz., 1975-79, Channel 8, 1975-79, Phoenix Hist. Soc., 1974-78, Maricopa County YMCA, 1978-81, Golden Gate Settlement. Recipient Ann. award NCCJ, 1975, Disting. Achievement award Ariz. State U., 1980; named Woman of Yr., Phoenix Advt. Club, 1972. Lodge: Soroptimists. Office: US Supreme Ct Supreme Ct Bldg 1 First St NE Washington DC 20543

O'CONNOR, SHEILA ANNE, freelance writer; b. Paisley, Scotland, Jan. 20, 1960; came to the U.S., 1988; d. Brian Aubrey Witham and Margaret Kirk (Reid) Davies; m. Frank Donal O'Connor, Aug. 9, 1986; children: David Michael, Andrew James, Christine Charlotte. BA in French and German, Strathclyde U., 1980, postgrad. diploma in office studies, 1981, MBA, 1992. Office asst. BBC, London, 1982-83; asst. to mng. dir. Unimatic Engrs. Ltd., London, 1983-84; freelance word processing operator London, 1984-88; staff asst. Internat. Monetary Fund, Washington, 1988-95; prin. Internat. Media Assn., Washington, 1988—. Contbr. numerous articles to various publs. Mem. Am. Mktg. Assn., Bay Area Travel Writers Assn., Calif. Writers Club. Avocations: animals, travel. Home and Office: 2531 39th Ave San Francisco CA 94116-2752

O'CONNOR, SINEAD, singer, songwriter; b. Dublin, Dec. 8, 1966; 1 child, Jake. Albums include The Lion and The Cobra, 1987, I Do Not Want What I Haven't Got (Grammy award for Best Alternative Performance), 1990, My Special Child, 1991, Am I Not Your Girl?, 1992, Universal Mother, 1994. Office: Chysalis Records 810 7th Ave Frnt 4 New York NY 10019-5818

O'CONNOR, THOMAS EDWARD, petroleum geologist, world bank officer; b. Boston, Dec. 16, 1936; s. John Stephen and Lucille (Arnold) O'C.; m. Jeannette Canuel, June 30, 1962 (dec. Mar. 1976); children: Kevin Patrick, David Andrew, Shelley Elizabeth; m. Mofida Banawi, Apr. 28, 1977; children: Tammer Thomas, Amr Adel Hammouda. BSc, Stanford U., 1958; MSc., U. Colo., 1961. Geologist Amoco Prodn. West, Denver, 1963-67, Amoco Netherlands, Utrecht, 1968-69, Amoco Europe, London, 1969-74; chief geologist Gulf of Suez Petroleum Co., Cairo, 1974-79; geol. mgr. Amoco Africa, Mid East, Houston, 1979-80; v.p. Aminoil, Houston, 1980-84; prin. petroleum engr. The World Bank, Washington, 1985—. Presenter numerous sci. confs., seminars, workshops in U.S. and abroad, 1976—. Lt. USNR, 1960-63. Mem. AAAS, Am. Assn. Petroleum Geologists (cert. petroleum geologist), Geol. Soc. Am., Houston Geol. Soc. Moslem. Home: 3637 Winfield Ln NW Washington DC 20007-2350 Office: The World Bank 1818 H St NW Washington DC 20433-0001

OCVIRK, OTTO GEORGE, artist; b. Detroit, Nov. 13, 1922; s. Joseph and Louise (Ekle) O.; m. Betty Josephine Lebie, June 11, 1949; children: Robert Joseph, Thomas Frederick, Carol Louise. B.F.A., State U. Iowa, 1949, M.F.A., 1950. Advt. artist apprentice Bass-Luckoff Advt. Agy., Detroit,

1941; engring. draftsman Curtiss-Wright Aircraft Corp., Buffalo, 1942; faculty Bowling Green (Ohio) State U., 1950—, assoc. prof., 1960-65, prof. art, 1965-85, prof. emeritus, 1985—. Exhibited in group shows at, Denver Mus. Art, 1949, 50, 53, Detroit Inst. Art, 71948, 49, 50, 53, 56, Dayton (Ohio) Art Inst., 1950, 51, 56, Ohio State U., 1953, Walker Art Center, Mpls., 1948, 49, Library of Congress, Washington, 1949, Bklyn. Mus., 1949, Joslyn Mus., Omaha, 1949, Colorado Springs Fine Arts Center, 1949; represented in permanent collections, Detroit Inst. Arts, Dayton Art Inst., Friends of Am. Art, Grand Rapids, Mich., State U. Iowa, Iowa City, Bowling Green State U.; (Recipient 24 nat., regional juried art exhbn. awards 1947-57, others.); Author: (with R. Stinson, P. Wigg, R. Bone and David Cayton) Art Fundamentals—Theory and Practice, 1960-94, 7th edit., 1994. Scoutmaster Toledo Area council Boy Scouts Am., 1960-63, asst. scoutmaster, 1963-74, dist. commr., 1978-80. Served with AUS, 1943-46. Recipient Silver Beaver award Boy Scouts Am., 1976, Magnifico award Medici Circle, Bowling Green State U., 1987. Mem. Internat. Sculpture Center Washington, Coll. Art Assn. Am., Delta Phi Delta (hon.). Methodist. Home and Office: 231 Haskins Rd Bowling Green OH 43402-2206 *"Freedom for expression" keys creative thought into a productive whole.*

ODA, TAKUZO, biochemist, educator; b. Shinichicho, Japan, Oct. 20, 1923; s. Ryoichi and Misu Oda; M.D., Okayama U., 1947, Ph.D., 1953; m. Kazue Matsui, Dec. 8, 1946; children: Mariko, Yumiko. Intern, Okayama U. Hosp., 1947-48, mem. faculty, 1949—, prof. biochemistry, 1965—, dir. Cancer Inst., from 1969; dean Okayama U. Med. Sch., 1985-87; prof. Okayama U. Sci., 1989—; pres. and prof. Niimi Women's Coll., 1993—; postdoctoral trainee Inst. Enzyme Research, U. Wis., Madison, 1960-62. Fellow Rockefeller Found., 1959-60, grantee, 1964; USPHS grantee, 1963-68. Mem. Japanese Soc. Electron Microscopy (Seto prize 1966), Japanese Soc. Biochemistry, Am. Soc. Cell Biology, Japanese Soc. Cancer, Japan Soc. Human Genetics, Japanese Soc. Histochemistry, Japanese Soc. Virology, Am. Soc. Microbiology. Author: Biochemistry of Biological Membranes, 1969, Mitochondria, Handbook of Cytology; editor, writer: Cell Biology series, 1979—; chief editor Acta Medica Okayama, 1975-85 . Home: 216-38 Maruyama, Okayama 703, Japan Office: Niimi Women's Coll, 1263-2 Nishikata, Niimi City Okayama 718, Japan

ODA, YOSHIO, physician, internist; b. Papaaloa, Hawaii, Jan. 14, 1933; s. Hakuai and Usako (Yamamoto) O.; AB, Cornell U., 1955; MD, U. Chgo., 1959. Diplomate Am. Bd. Internal Medicine. Intern U. Chgo. Clinics, 1959-60; resident in pathology U. Chgo., 1960-62, Queen's Hosp., Hawaii, 1962-63, Long Beach (Calif.) VA Hosp., 1963-65; resident in allergy, immunology U. Colo. Med. Center, 1966-67; pvt. practice, L.A., 1965-66; pvt. practice internal medicine, allergy and immunology, Honolulu, 1970—; asst. clin. prof. medicine U. Hawaii, Honolulu, 1970—. Maj., AUS, 1968-70. Mem. ACP, Am. Acad. Allergy. Office: Piikoi Med Bldg 1024 Piikoi St Honolulu HI 96814-1925

O'DAIR, BARBARA, editor. Editor US mag., N.Y.C. Office: US mag 1290 Ave of the Americas New York NY 10104*

O'DAY, ANITA BELLE COLTON, entertainer, singer; b. Chgo., Oct. 18, 1919; d. James and Gladys (Gill) C. Student, Chgo. public schs. Singer and entertainer various Chgo. Music Clubs, 1939-41; singer with Gene Krupa's Orch., 1941-45, Stan Kenton Orch., 1944, Woody Herman Orch., 1945, Benny Goodman Orch., 1959; singing tours in U.S. and abroad, 1947—; rec. artist Polygram, Capitol, Emily Records, Verve, GNP Crescendo, Columbia, London, Signature, DRG, Pablo; million-seller songs include Let Me Off Uptown, 1941, And Her Tears Flowed Like Wine, 1944, Boogie Blues, 1945; appeared in films Gene Krupa Stody, 1959, Jazz on a Summer's Day, 1960, Zigzag, 1970, Outfit, 1974; TV shows 60 Minutes, 1980; Tonight Show, Dick Cavett Show, Today Show, Big Band Bash, CBS Sunday Morning, CNN Showbiz Today, others. Author: High Times, Hard Times, 1981, rev. edit., 1989; performed 50 yr. anniversary concert Carnegie Hall, 1985, Avery Fisher Hall, 1989, Tanglewood, 1990, Town Hall, 1993, Rainbow and Stars, 1995, currently touring worldwide; albums include Drummer Man, Kenton Era, Anita, Anita Sings The Most, Pick Yourself Up, Lady is a Tramp, An Evening with Anita O'Day, At Mr. Kelly's, Swings Cole Porter, Travelin' Light, All the Sad Young Men, Waiter Make Mine Blues, With the Three Sounds, I Told Ya I Love Ya Now Get Out, Uptown, My Ship, Live in Tokyo, Anita Sings the Winners, Incomparable, Anita 1975, Live at Mingos, Anita O'Day/The Big Band Sessions, Swings Rodgers and Hart, Time for Two, Tea for Two, In a Mellowtone, At Vine St. Live, Mello'Day, Live at the City, Angel Eyes, The Night Has a Thousand Eyes, The Rules of the Road, Jazz Masters, others. Mem. AFTRA, Screen Actors Guild, BMI. Office: 1824 Vista Del Mar Ave Los Angeles CA 90028-5208 *From the time I was twelve or thirteen, my life was music. I never thought about being on top. I only wanted to be a part of the scene.*

O'DAY, DENIS MICHAEL, ophthalmologist, educator; b. Melbourne, Victoria, Australia, Dec. 10, 1935; came to U.S., 1967; s. Kevin John and Bernadette John (Hay) O'D.; m. Ann Georgina Despard, May 28, 1966; children: Luke Gerard, Simon Patrick, Edward Daniel. Diploma, Xavier Coll., 1953; MBBS, Melbourne U., 1960. Diplomate Am. Bd. Ophthalmology. Intern St. Vincent's Hosp./U. Melbourne, 1961; resident in internal medicine St. Vincent's Hosp., 1962-64, chief resident dept. medicine, 1964, clin. asst. medicine, 1965-66; 3d asst., mem. asst. Royal Victoria Eye & Ear Hosp., Melbourne, 1967-70; resident in ophthalmology U. Calif., San Francisco, 1970; Wellcome rsch. fellow in corneal disease Inst. Opthalmology, London, 1970-72; asst. prof. ophthalmology Vanderbilt U. Sch. Medicine, Nashville, 1972-74, assoc. prof. ophthalmology, 1974-77; prof. ophthalmology, now chmn. Vanderbilt U. Sch. Medicine, 1977; cons. ophthalmologist Royal Commonwealth Soc. of Blind, Nigeria, 1972; cons. VA Hosp., 1973-74, active staff, 74; mem. active staff Nashville Gen. Hosp., 1974, Park View Hosp., 1980, Vanderbilt Hosp., 1972; mem. cons. staff St. Thomas Hosp.; bd. dirs. Am. Bd. Ophthalmology, Phila., 1988—; proctor lectr. U. Calif., San Francisco, 1993; co-med. dir. Lions Eye Bank and Sight Svc., 1973-86, med. dir. 1986—; bd. dirs. Lions Eye Bank Mid. Tenn., 1987—; ad-hoc mem. NIH Visual Sci. Study Sect., 1977. Author: Management of Functional Impairment due to Cataract, 1993; contbr. numerous articles, abstracts to profl. publs., chpts. to books. Chair ethics com. Cath. Pub. Policy Commn., Nashville, 1991—. Joyn Hayden rsch. fellow, 1965; recipent Felton Bequest and Potter Found. awards, 1967, recognition award Alcon Rsch. Inst., 1983, Sr. Sci. Investigator award Rsch. to Prevent Blindness, 1987, Health Profl. of Yr. award Tenn. chpt. Assn. for Edn. and Rehab. of Blind and Visually Impaired, 1990. Fellow ACS, Royal Australia Coll. Physicians, Royal Soc. Medicine, Am. Acad. Ophthalmology (sec. quality of care com. 1993—, Honor award for Ednl. Contbns. 1981-85, dir. clin. alert program, pub. health com. 1985-88); mem. AMA, AAUP, Am. Ophthalmol. Soc., Assn. for Rsch. in Vision and Ophthalmology, Nashville Acad. Medicine, Nashville Acad. Ophthalmology (v.p. 1980-81), Oxford Ophthalmol. Soc., Royal Australasian Coll. Physicians, Tenn. Acad. Medicine, Tenn. Acad. Ophthalmology. Roman Catholic. Avocation: sailing. Office: Vanderbilt U Med Ctr East Dept Ophthal and Vis Scis Nashville TN 37232*

O'DAY, PAUL THOMAS, trade association executive; b. May 2, 1935; s. James Thomas and Jeannette Irene (Deschenes) O'D.; m. Nancy Frances Eitler, June 16, 1962; children: Kathleen, Maureen, Michael, Ellen. B.A., Am. Internat. Coll., Springfield, Mass., 1958; J.D., Georgetown U., 1963; MPA, Am. U., 1967. Bar: D.C. 1964, U.S. Supreme Ct. 1974. Patent examiner U.S. Patent Office, Washington, 1959-62; exec. sec. panel high-speed ground transp., auto. air poll. Dept. Commerce, Washington, 1965-66, staff asst. to sec., 1967-69, exec. asst. to sec., 1969-71, dep. dir. bur. domestic commerce, 1972-74; dep. dir. Nat. Bus. Coun. for Consumer Affairs, Washington, 1971-72; cons. to Gen. Counsel GE, Fairfield, Conn., 1974-75; asst. trade rep. Exec. Office of the Pres., Washington, 1975-77; dep. asst. sec. U.S. Dept. Commerce, Washington, 1978-84; pres. Am. Fiber Mfrs. Assn., Washington, 1984—; chmn. Fiber Econs. Bur., 1984—; pres. Eisenhower World Affairs Inst., 1993—. Corporator Am. Internat. Coll., 1974—; mem. governing coun. Shakespeare Theater Guild, 1989—. Recipient Constl. Law award Georgetown U. Law Ctr., 1962; Alumni award Am. Internat. Coll., 1970; Pres.'s Meritorious Exec. award., 1984; Nat. Inst. Pub. Affairs fellow Princeton U., 1964. Mem. World Econ. Forum, AAAS, Am. Chem. Soc., Cosmos Club, Jefferson Islands Club (bd. dirs. 1993—), Federal City Club. Home: 8261 Private Ln Annandale VA 22003-4471 Office: Am Fiber Mfrs Assn 1150 17th St NW Washington DC 20036-4603

O'DAY, ROYAL LEWIS, former banker; b. Avon, N.Y., Apr. 28, 1913; s. Roy Lyday and Winifred (Heath) O'D.; m. Elizabeth M. Fearon, Oct. 12, 1952; children: Margaret (Mrs. Thomas W. Wright), Patti (Mrs. Warner Blow), Timothy N. BS, Syracuse U., 1936. With Gen. Motors Acceptance Corp., 1936-42; sr. v.p. Mchts. Nat. Bank & Trust Co., Syracuse, N.Y., 1942-61; exec. v.p. Marine Midland Bank—Central, Syracuse, 1961-68; pres. Marine Midland Bank—Central, 1968-71, chmn. bd., 1971-76, chief exec. officer, 1973-76, cons., 1976—; bd. dirs. Syracuse Chiefs Baseball Club. Bd. dirs. Syracuse Rsch. Corp.; past pres. Met. Devel. Assn., Syracuse, Syracuse Rep. Citizens Com.; past chmn. bd. trustees, now trustee Syracuse U.; past chmn. bd. N.Y. divsn. Am. Cancer Soc.; trustee Crouse Irving Meml. Hosp., Syracuse. Lt. USNR, WWII. Named Outstanding Man in Syracuse Area in Bus. and Fin. Syracuse Herald Jour., 1963; recipient Torch of Liberty award Anti-Defamation League of B'nai B'rith, 1974. Mem. Nat. Alumni Assn. Syracuse U. (pres. 1965-69), Automobile Club Syracuse (dir., vice chmn.) Hosp. Svcs. Assn. Cen. N.Y. (dir.), Greater Syracuse C. of C. (past pres.), Masons (33 deg., Shriner, Jester), Onondaga Golf and Country Club (Fayetteville, N.Y.), Royal Poinciana Golf Club (Naples, Fla.), Phi Gamma Delta. Mem. Dewitt Community Ch. (finance com.). Clubs: Mason (Fayetteville, N.Y.) (33 deg., Shriner, Jester), Onondaga Golf and Country (Fayetteville, N.Y.), Royal Poinciana Golf (Naples, Fla.). Home: 714 Scott Ave Syracuse NY 13224-2160 Office: 360 S Warren St Syracuse NY 13202-2017

ODDEN, ALLAN ROBERT, education educator; b. Duluth, Minn., Sept. 16, 1943; s. Robert Norman and Mabel Eleanor (Bjornnes) O.; m. Eleanor Ann Rubottom, May 28, 1966; children: Sarina, Robert. BS, Brown U., 1965; MDiv, Union Theol. Sem., 1969; MA, Columbia U., 1971, PhD, 1975. Tchr. N.Y.C. Pub. Schs., 1967-72; rsch. assoc. Teachers' Coll. Columbia U., N.Y.C., 1972-75; dir. policy Edn. Commn. of the States, Denver, 1975-84; prof. U. So. Calif., L.A., 1984-93, U. Wis., Madison, 1993—; rsch. dir. Sch. Fin. Commns. Conn., 1974-75, S.D., 1975-76, Mo. 1975-76, 93, 94, N.Y., 1978-81, N.J., 1991-92; dir. finance ctr. Consortium for Policy Rsch. in Edn.; cons. Nat. Govs. Assn., Nat. Conf. State Legislatures, U.S. Sec. Edn., U.S. Senate, U.S. Dept. Edn. and many state legislatures and govs. Author: Education Leadership for America's Schools, 1995; co-author: School Finance: A Policy Perspective, 1992; editor: Education Policy Implementation, 1991, Rethinking School Finance, 1992; contbr. articles to profl. jours., chpts. to books. Mem. L.A. Chamber Edn. and Human Resources Commn., 1986, Gov.'s Sch. Fin. Commn., Calif., 1987, Calif. Assessment Policy Com., Gov.'s Edn. Task Force, Wis., 1996, Carnegie Corp. Task Force on Edn. in the Early Years, 1994. Grantee Dept. Edn., Spencer Found., Ford Found., Mellon Found., Carnegie Corp., Pew Charitable Trusts. Mem. Am. Ednl. Rsch. Assn., Am. Ednl. Fin. Assn. (pres. 1979-80), Nat. Tax Assn., Politics of Edn. Assn., Nat. Soc. for Study of Edn. Democrat. Avocations: Lionel train collector, youth soccer and baseball coach. Home: 3128 Oxford Rd Madison WI 53705-2224 Office: U Wis Sch Edn Wis Ctr Edn Rsch 1025 W Johnson St # 753E Madison WI 53706-1706

ODDIS, JOSEPH ANTHONY, social services administrator; b. Greensburg, Pa., Nov. 5, 1928; s. Giacinto and Felicetta (D'Amico) O.; m. Jeanne Trevena, July 10, 1954; children—Joseph Michael, Marie Thersa. B.S., Duquesne U., 1950; D.Sc. (hon.), Mass. Coll. Pharmacy, 1975, Phila. Coll. Pharmacy and Sci., 1975, Albany Coll. Pharmacy, Union U., 1976, Duquesne U., 1989, Mercer U., 1995; LHD (hon.), L.I. U., 1991. Staff pharmacist Mercy Hosp., Pitts., 1950-51; asst. chief pharmacist Mercy Hosp., 1953-54; chief pharmacist Western Pa. Hosp., Pitts., 1954-56; staff rep. hosp. pharmacy Am. Hosp. Assn., Chgo., 1956-60; dir. div. hosp. pharmacy Am. Pharm., Washington, 1960-62; exec. v.p. Am. Soc. Health-System Pharmacists, Washington, 1960—; pres. Am. Soc. Hosp. Pharmacists Research and Edn. Found., 1986—. Active Boy Scouts Am., Camp Fire Girls; Sec. Am. Soc. Health-System Pharmacists Research and Edn. Found., 1970-86. Served with AUS, 1951-53. Recipient 1st cert. Honor award Duquesne U. Sch. Pharmacy, 1969, named Outstanding Alumnus, 1978; recipient Harvey A.K. Whitney award Am. Soc. Hosp. Pharmacists, 1970, Julius Sturmer Meml. Lecture award Rho Chi soc. Phila., 1971, Howard C. Newton Lecture award 1977, Samuel Melendy Lecture award, 1978, Hugo H. Schaefer award, 1983, Reed and Alice Henninger Lecture award, 1984, Donald E. Francke medal, 1986, Remington medal award, 1990. Fellow AAAS; mem. Am. Pharm. Assn., Am. Soc. Hosp. Pharmacists, Am. Inst. History Pharmacy, Internat. Pharm. Fedn. (pres. hosp. pharmacy sect. 1977-81, v.p. 1984-86, pres. 1986-90), Drug Info. Assn., Am. Soc. Assn. Execs., Can. Soc. Hosp. Pharmacists (hon.), Soc. Hosp. Pharmacists Australia (hon.), Pharm. Soc. Gt. Britain (hon.), Pharm. Soc. Nigeria (hon.), Nat. Coun. Patient Info. and Edn. (sec. 1982-85), Israel Pharm. Soc. (hon.), Rho Chi, Kappa Psi (hon.), Duquesne U. Century Club (charter). Home: 6509 Rockhurst Rd Bethesda MD 20817-1661 Office: Am Soc Health-System Pharmacists 7272 Wisconsin Ave Bethesda MD 20814-3410

O'DEA, DENNIS MICHAEL, lawyer; b. Lowell, Mass., Nov. 1, 1946; s. James Lawrence and Carol Frances (Gibbons) O'D.; children: Emily C., Dennis C., Daniel P.; m. Mary Gail Frawley. BA in Govt., U. Notre Dame, 1968; JD magna cum laude, U. Mich., 1972. Bar: Mass. 1972, D.C. 1980, Ill. 1981, N.Y. 1994. Assoc. Goodwin, Procter & Hoar, Boston, 1972-74, Fine & Ambrogne, Boston, 1974-77; assoc. prof. Syracuse U. Coll. Law, 1977-78; vis. assoc. prof. Nat. Law Ctr., George Washington U., 1978-80; ptnr. Keck, Mahin & Cate, N.Y.C., 1980—. Mem. Order of the Coif (Mich.), Chgo. Literary Club (pres. 1993). Presbyterian. Home: 75 N Broadway Nyack NY 10960-2624 Office: Keck Mahin & Cate 220 E 42nd St Fl 16 New York NY 10017-5806

ODEGAARD, CHARLES EDWIN, history educator; b. Chicago Heights, Ill., Jan. 10, 1911; s. Charles Alfred and Mary (Cord) O.; m. Elizabeth Jane Ketchum, Apr. 12, 1941 (dec. 1980); 1 child, Mary Ann Quarton. AB, Dartmouth Coll., 1932; M.A., Harvard U., 1933, Ph.D., 1937; L.H.D., Lawrence Coll., 1951; LL.D., Miami U., Oxford, Ohio,, 1955, U. B.C., Can., 1959, Gonzaga U., 1962, UCLA, 1962, Seattle U., 1965, U. Mich., 1969; Litt.D., U. Puget Sound, 1963. Asst. in history Radcliffe Coll., 1935-37; from instr. to prof. U. Ill., 1937-48; exec. dir. Am. Council Learned Soc., Washington, 1948-52; prof. history, dean Coll. Lit. Sci. and Arts U. Mich., Ann Arbor, 1952-58; pres. U. Wash., Seattle, 1958-73; pres. emeritus, prof. higher edn. U. Wash., 1974—, prof. biomed. history, 1975—; mem. U.S. Nat. Commn. UNESCO, 1949-55, advisor U.S. del. 5th Gen. Conf., Florence, Italy, 1950; chmn. Commn. Human Resources and Advanced Tng., 1949-53, pres. Internat. Council of Philosophy and Humanistic Studies, 1959-65; mem. adv. com. cultural info. USIA, 1955-62, Western Interstate Com. on Higher Edn., 1959-70, Citizens Com. on Grad. Med. Edn., 1963-66, Nat. Adv. Health Counci USPHS, 1964-68, Nat. Adv. Health Manpower, 1965-67, NEH, 1966-72, Study Commn. Pharmacy, 1973-75; mem. Macy Study Commn. on Acad. Psychiatry, 1978-79. Author: Fideles and Vassi in the Carolingian Empire, 1945; Minorities in Medicine, 1977, Area Health Education Centers, 1979, Dear Doctor: A Personal Letter to a Physician, 1986; contbr. articles on mediaeval history and higher edn. to profl. jours. bd. regents Uniformed U. Health Scis., 1973-80; chmn. Wash. State Bd. Continuing Legal Edn., 1976-79. Served from lt. (j.g.) to lt. comdr. USNR, 1942-46. Recipient Medal of Merit State of Wash., 1989. Mem. Am. Coun. on Edn. (dir., chmn. 1962-63), Am. Hist. Assn., NAS, Medieval Acad. Am., Tchrs. Ins. and Annuity Assn. (dir. 1963-69, trustee 1970-86, coll. retirement equity fund 1970-86), Inst. Medicine, Phi Beta Kappa, Phi Eta Sigma, Beta Theta Pi, Seattle Yacht Club, Univ. Club (Seattle), Cosmos Club (Washington), Bohemian Club (San Francisco), Rotary. Office: U Wash 222 Miller Hall Box 353600 Seattle WA 98195-3600

O'DELL, CHARLES ROBERT, astronomer, educator; b. Hamilton County, Ill., Mar. 16, 1937; s. Herman and Madge (Allen) O'D.; children: Cynthia Dianne Rogers, Nicholle Ann Schreiber. Student, U. Ill., 1957; B.S. in Edn, Ill. State U., 1959; Ph.D., U. Wis., 1962. Carnegie fellow Mt. Wilson and Palomar Obs., Pasadena, Calif., 1962-63; asst. prof. U. Calif., at Berkeley, 1963-64; faculty U. Chgo., 1964-72, prof. astronomy, 1967-72, chmn. dept., 1967-72; dir. Yerkes Obs., Williams Bay, Wis., 1966-72; cons. Marshall Space Flight Center, Huntsville, Ala., 1968-70; project scientist Hubble Space Telescope, Marshall Space Flight Center, 1972-83, assoc. dir. sci., 1976-80, asso. dir. astronomy, 1972-76, 80-82; prof. space physics and astronomy Rice U., Houston, 1982-92, Buchanan prof. astrophysics, 1992—; mem. astronomy missions bd. NASA, 1967-70, space telescope Sci. Working Group NASA, 1983-91, presdl. adv. com. on space program, 1968-69, inter Halley watch steering group, 1981-89; astronomy adv. panel NSF, 1968-71, chmn., 1969-71; U.S. scientist Copernicus Astron. Ctr., Warsaw, Poland, 1972-78; team leader Hubble Space Telescope, 1989-95; lectr. U. Coll., London, 1970, U. Moscow, 1971. Mem. adv. com. Physics Today, 1986-92. Trustee Adler Planetarium, Chgo., 1967-75. Recipient Gold medal Order of Merit Polish Govt., 1977, Alumni Achievement award Ill. State U., 1981, Pub. Svc. Medal award NASA, 1991, Humboldt prize, 1996. Fellow AAAS; mem. Am. Astron. Soc. (treas. 1988-96), Internat. Astron. Union, Internat. Aerobatic Club, Astron. Soc. Pacific, Soaring Soc. Am., U.S. Sailplane Aerobatics Team (pilot 1985, 87, 89, 93), Sailplane Aerobatics Assn. (pres. 1987-90), Internat. Astron. Union (chief U.S. del. 1973). Office: Rice U MS108 Po Box 1892 Houston TX 77251-1892

O'DELL, EDWARD THOMAS, JR., lawyer; b. Lowell, Mass., Nov. 26, 1935; s. Edward Thomas and Helen Louise (Shaw) O'D.; m. Kerstin Lilly Sjoholm, Mar. 18, 1962; children: Edward Thomas III, Brian Patrick, Christine Marie. BA, Brown U., 1957; JD, U. Chgo., 1960. Bar: N.Y. 1961, Mass. 1968, U.S. Dist. Ct. Mass. 1968, U.S. Ct. Appeals (1st cir.) 1968. Ptnr. Goodwin, Procter and Hoar, Boston, 1966—. Trustee Gov. Dummer Acad., Byfield, Mass, 1982-87. Mem. ABA, Mass. Bar Assn., Internat. Bar Assn. (sec. 1986-88, chmn. investment cos. com. 1994—). Home: 96 Wildwood Rd Andover MA 01810-5126 Office: Goodwin Procter & Hoar Exchange Pl Boston MA 02109

ODELL, FRANK HAROLD, banker; b. Hobart, N.Y., May 17, 1922; s. Harold E. and Naomi (Cole) O.; m. Elizabeth J. Hetherington, Dec. 29, 1946; children: Thomas A., Nancy E., Susan. AB, U. Ala., 1943; MBA, Harvard U., 1949; postgrad., Stonier Grad. Sch. Banking, Rutgers U., 1958. With State Bank of Albany, N.Y., 1949-71; v.p. State Bank of Albany, 1963-69, sr. v.p. in charge bank's loan portfolio, 1969-71; exec. v.p. Norstar Bancorp Inc., Albany, 1971-72; also vice chmn. Norstar Bancorp Inc.; chmn., chief exec. officer Norstar Bank of Upstate N.Y., 1972-87, also bd. dirs. Bd. dirss. YMCA, Saratoga Performing Arts Ctr.; bd. dirs. Albany Inst. History and Art, Robert Morris Assn., Capital Region Tech. Devel. Council, Mayor's Downtown Adv. Com., N.Y. State Banking Bd., Albany Med. Ctr., Albany chpt. ARC, United Way, Russell Sage Coll., Sta. WMHT-TV. Capt. C.E., AUS, 1943. Mem. Harvard Club (N.Y.C.), Harvard Club of Naples (pres.), Fort Orange Club (past pres.), Club Pelican Bay, Forum Club of Collier County, Moorings Country Club, Masons. Republican. Presbyterian.

ODELL, HERBERT, lawyer; b. Phila., Oct. 20, 1937; s. Samuel and Selma (Kramer) O.; m. Valerie Odell; children: Wesley, Jonathan, James, Sarah, Samuel. BS in Econs., U. Pa., 1959; LLB magna cum laude, U. Miami, 1962; LLM, Harvard U., 1963. Bar: Fla. 1963, Pa. 1968. Trial atty. tax div. U.S. Dept. Justice, Washington, 1963-65; assoc. Walton, Lantaff, Schroeder, Carson & Wahl, Miami, Fla., 1965-67; from assoc. to ptnr. Morgan, Lewis & Bockius, Phila., 1967-89; ptnr. Zapruder & Odell, Washington, 1989—; adj. prof. U. Miami, Villanova U.; lectr. various tax insts. Contbr. articles to profl. jours. Ford fellow, 1962-63. Mem. ABA, Fla. Bar Assn., Pa. Bar Assn., Phila. Bar Assn., Chester County Bar Assn., Phi Kappa Phi, Omicron Delta Kappa, Beta Alpha Psi. Clubs: Harvard, U. Pa. Avocations: sailing, running, tennis, scuba diving. Office: Zapruder & Odell 401 City Ave Ste 415 Bala Cynwyd PA 19004

O'DELL, JAMES E., newspaper publishing executive. V.p. ops. and techs. Chgo. Tribune. Office: Chgo Tribune 435 N Michigan Ave Chicago IL 60611-4001

O'DELL, LYNN MARIE LUEGGE (MRS. NORMAN D. O'DELL), librarian; b. Berwyn, Ill., Feb. 24, 1938; d. George Emil and Helen Marie (Pesek) Luegge; student Lyons Twp. Jr. Coll., La Grange, Ill., 1957; student No. Ill. U., Elgin Community Coll., U. Ill., Coll. of DuPage; m. Norman D. O'Dell, Dec. 14, 1957; children—Jeffrey, Jerry. Sec., Martin Co., Chgo., 1957-59; dir. Carol Stream (Ill.) Pub. Library, 1964—; chmn. automation governing com. DuPage Library System, v.p., 1982-85, pres. exec. com. adminstrv. librarians, 1985-86, chair automation search com., 1991-92. Named Woman of Yr., Wheaton Bus. and Profl. Woman's Club, 1968. Mem. ALA, Ill. Library Assn., Library Adminstrs. Conf. No. Ill. Lutheran. Home: 182 Yuma Ln Carol Stream IL 60188-1917 Office: 616 Hiawatha Dr Carol Stream IL 60188-1616

ODELL, MARY JANE, former state official; b. Algona, Iowa, July 28, 1923; d. Eugene and Madge (Lewis) Neville; m. Garry Chinn, 1945 (dec.); 1 child, Brad; m. Jonn Odell Mar. 3, 1967 (dec.); 1 child, Chris; m. Ralph Sigler, Nov. 22, 1987. B.A., U. Iowa, 1945; hon. doctorate, Simpson Coll., 1982. Host public affairs TV programs Des Moines and Chgo., 1953-79; with Iowa Public Broadcasting Network, 1975-79, host Assignment Iowa, 1975-78, host Mary Jane Odell Program, 1975-79; sec. of state State of Iowa, 1980-87; ret., 1987—; tchr. grad. classes in communications Roosevelt U., Chgo., Drake U., Des Moines. Chmn. Iowa Easter Seals campaign, 1979-83; mem. Midwest Com. Future Options; bd. dirs. Iowa Shares; mem. exec. bd. Iowa Peace Inst., 1985-92. Recipient Emmy award, 1972, 75; George Washington Carver award, 1978; named to Iowa Women's Hall of Fame, 1979. Republican. Address: Apt 206 6129 Meadow Crest Dr Johnston IA 50131

ODELL, PATRICK LOWRY, mathematics educator; b. Watonga, Okla., Nov. 29, 1930; s. Max Vernon and Pamela (Massey) O.; m. Norma Lou Maddox, Aug. 16, 1958 (dec. May, 1980); children: James M., David L., Michael R.L., Julie K., Patricia L., Deborah L.; m. Dovalee Dorsett, Aug. 3, 1985. BS, U. Tex., 1952; postgrad., UCLA, 1953-54; MS, Okla. State U., 1958, PhD, 1962. Mathematician White Sands (N.Mex.) Proving Grounds, 1952-53, Kaman Nuclear, Albuquerque, 1958-59, U.S. Naval Nuclear Ordnance Evaluation Unit, 1959-62, Ling-Temco Vought Aeros., 1962; asst. prof. math. U. Tex., Austin, 1962-66; prof., chmn. dept. math. Tex. Technol. U., Lubbock, 1966-71, coordinator insts., dir. rsch., Coll. Arts and Sci., 1971-72; prof math. scis. and environ. scis. U. Tex., Dallas, 1972-88, prof. emeritus, 1988—, exec. dean grad. studies and rsch., 1972-75; prof. math. sci. Baylor U., Waco, Tex., 1988—; assoc. dir. Tex. Ctr. for Rsch., Austin, 1964-66; rsch. scientist Def. Rsch. Lab., 1963-65; cons. math statistician, 1962—. Capt. USAF, 1953-57. Fellow Tex. Acad. Sci. (Disting. Tex. Scientist award 1994), Am. Statis. Assn.; mem. Soc. Indsl. and Applied Math. Home: 3200 Windsor Ave Waco TX 76708-3113

ODELL, STUART IRWIN, lawyer; b. Phila., Jan. 1, 1940; s. P. Samuel and Selma Odell; m. Andrea L. Villegas; children: Stuart Irwin Jr., Benjamin Eaton, Manuela, Sebastian Patricio. BS in Econ., U. Pa., 1961; LLB cum laude, U. Miami, 1964; LLM in Tax, NYU, 1965. Bar: Fla. 1965, Pa. 1966, N.Y. 1982. Assoc., Morgan, Lewis & Bockius, 1966-70, ptnr. 1970-88; ptnr. Dewey Ballantine, 1988—; lectr. law NYU, 1965-66, adj. prof. law, 1966-80; adj. lectr. Temple U. Law Sch., 1972. Recipient Harry J. Ruddick award NYU. Mem. ABA, N.Y. State Bar Assn., Fla. Bar Assn., Assn. of Bar of City of N.Y., Univ. Assoc. editor U. Miami Law Rev., 1963-64. Office: Dewey Ballantine 1301 Avenue Of The Americas New York NY 10019-6022

ODELL, WILLIAM DOUGLAS, physician, scientist, educator; b. Oakland, Calif., June 11, 1929; s. Ernest A. and Emma L. (Mayer) O.; m. Margaret F. Reilly, Aug. 19, 1950; children: Michael, Timothy, John D., Debbie, Charles. AB, U. Calif., Berkeley, 1952; MD, MS in Physiology, U. Chgo., 1956; PhD in Biochemistry and Physiology, George Washington U., 1965. Intern, resident, chief resident in medicine U. Wash., 1956-60, postdoctoral fellow in endocrinology and metabolism, 1957-58; sr. investigator Nat. Cancer Inst., Bethesda, Md., 1960-65; chief endocrine service NICHD, 1965-66; chief endocrinology Harbor-UCLA Med. Center, Torrance, Calif., 1966-72; chmn. dept. medicine Harbor-UCLA Med. Center, 1972-79; vis. prof. medicine Auckland Sch. Medicine, New Zealand, 1979-80; prof. medicine and physiology, chmn. dept. medicine U. Utah Sch. Medicine, Salt Lake City, 1980—. Mem. editorial bds. med. jours.; author 6 books in field; contbr. over 300 artilces to med. jours. Served with USPHS, 1960-66. Recipient Disting. Svc. award U. Chgo., 1973, Pharmacia award for outstanding contbns. to clin. chemistry, 1977, Gov.'s award State of Utah Sci. and Tech., 1988, also rsch. awards, Mastership award ACP, 1987. Mem. Am. Soc. Clin. Investigation, Am. Physiol. Soc., Assn. Am. PHysicians, Am. Soc. Andrology (pres.), Endocrine Soc. (v.p. Robert Williams award 1991),

Soc. Study of Reprodn. (bd. dirs.), Pacific Coast Fertility Soc. (pres.), Western Assn. Physicians (pres.), Western Soc. Clin. Rsch. (Mayo Soley award), Soc. Pediatric Rsch., Alpha Omega Alpha. Office: U of Utah Med Ctr 50 N Medical Dr Salt Lake City UT 84132-0001

O'DELL, WILLIAM FRANCIS, retired business executive, author; b. Detroit, Jan. 24, 1909; s. Frank Trevor and Garnett (Aikman) O'C.; m. Bess Baer, June 10, 1933 (dec. July 1986); m. Helen M. Porter, May 16, 1987; children: Peggy, David. B.S., U. Ill., 1930. With Penton Pub. Co., 1933-37; v.p. Ross Fed. Research Corp., 1937-44; mng. dir. Statis Research Co., 1944-45; pres. Market Facts, Inc., 1946-64, chmn., 1964-74; pres. ROC Internat., 1961-64; mem. census adv. bd. Dept. Commerce, 1963-73; prof. mktg. McIntire Sch. Commerce U. Va., 1965-78; vis. prof. Chinese U. of Hong Kong, 1969. Author: Marketing Decision, 1968, Marketing Decision Making, 1976, 4th edit., 1988, How to Make Lifetime Friends—With Peers and Parents, 1978, Twelve Families—An American Experience, 1981, Effective Business Decision Making and the Educated Guess, 1991; mem. editorial rev. bd. Jour. Mktg, 1964-73. Recipient Leader in Mktg. award, 1970, Jour. Mktg. Research editorial award, 1979; William F. O'Dell professorship in commerce named in his honor U. Va., 1983. Mem. Am. Mktg. Assn. (pres. 1960-61), Colonnade Club (Charlottesville), Univ. Club of Ft. Myers, Rotary, Delta Upsilon, Beta Gamma Sigma. Home: 5707 Junonia Ct Fort Myers FL 33908-1667

ODEN, JOHN TINSLEY, mechanical engineering educator, consultant; b. Alexandria, La., Dec. 25, 1936; s. John James and Sara Elizabeth (Lyles) O.; m. Barbara Clare Smith, Mar. 19, 1965; children: John Walker, Elizabeth Lee. BS, La. State U., 1959; MS, Okla. State U., 1960, PhD, 1962; doctorate in sci. (hon.), Tech. U. Lisbon, Portugal, 1986. Registered profl. engr., Tex., La. Teaching asst. La. State U., Baton Rouge, 1959; asst. prof. Okla. State U., Stillwater, 1961-63; sr. structures engr. Gen. Dynamics, Fort Worth, 1963-64; prof., head dept. engrng. mechanics U. Ala., Huntsville, 1964-73; prof. U. Tex., Austin, 1973—; Carol and Henry Groppe prof. engrng. U. Tex.; Ernest and Virginia Cockrell chair in engrng. U. Tex., Austin, 1987-93, Cockrell Family Regents prof. engrng. 2, 1993—; prof. Coope U. Fed., Brazil, 1974; dir. Tex. Inst. Computational Mechanics, Austin, 1974-93, Tex. Inst. Computational and Applied Math., Austin, 1993—; Sci. Rsch. Coun. vis. scholar Brunel U., Eng., 1981; mem. com. on computational mechanics NRC; chmn. U.S. Nat. Com. on Theoretical and Applied Mechanics, 1992-94. Author, editor 45 books; contbr. numerous articles to profl. jours. Decorated chevalier Ordre des Palms Academique (France); recipient rsch. award Southeastern Conf. on Theoretical and Applied Mechanics, 1978, Lohmann medal Okla. State U., 1991, Computational Mechanics medal Japan Soc. Med. Engrs., 1993. Fellow ASCE (Outstanding Svc. award 1968, Walter Huber rsch. award 1973, Theodore von Karman medal 1992), ASME (Worcester Reed Warner medal 1990), NAE, Soc. Engrng. Sci. (pres. 1978, Eringen medal 1991), Am. Acad. Mechanics (pres. 1990-94, Disting. Svc. medal 1995); mem. Soc. Indsl. and Applied Math., Internat. Assn. Computational Mechanics (pres. 1990-94, Congress-Gauss-Newton medal 1994), U.S. Assn. Computational Mechanics (pres. 1990-92, John Von Neumann medal 1993), Soc. Natural Philosophy, Nat. Acad. Engrng. Mex. Home: 7403 W Rim Dr Austin TX 78731-2044 Office: ASE-EM Dept U Tex WRW Bldg 305A Austin TX 78712

ODEN, ROBERT RUDOLPH, surgeon; b. Chgo., Dec. 2, 1922; s. Rudolph J.E. and Olga H. (Wahlquist) O.; m. Nancy Clow; children: Louise, Boyd, Beach, Lisbeth. BS, U. Ill., 1943; MD, Northwestern U., 1947, MS in Anatomy, 1947. Intern Augustana Hosp., Chgo., 1947-48, resident in surgery, 1948-49; resident in orthopaedics Hines Vets. Hosp., Chgo., 1949-51; resident in children's orthopaedics Shriner's Hosp., 1953-54; pvt. practice Chgo., 1954-57, Aspen, Colo., 1957—; clin. assoc. prof. in orthopaedics U. Colo.; orthopaedic surgeon U.S. Olympic Com., 1960, 72, 76, 80. Assoc. editor: Clin. Orthopaedics and Related Rsch. Trustee U.S. Ski Ednl. Found., 1967-82, Aspen Valley Hosp., 1978-86; founder Aspen Orthopaedic and Sports Medicine Pub. Found., 1985, Aspen Inst. for Theol. Futures, 1978, Great Tchrs. and Preachers Series Christ Episc. Ch., 1989; mem. organizing com. Aspen World Cup, 1976-92; founder, trustee Pitkin County Bank, 1983—; founder Aspen Pitkin Employee Housing, 1975. Recipient Blegan award for most outstanding svc. to U.S. skiing, 1985, Halsted award U.S. Ski Assn., 1987, inducted into Aspen Hall of Fame, 1996. Mem. Am. Acad. Orthopaedic Surgeons, ACS, Internat. Coll. Surgeons, Western Orthopaedic Assn., SICOT, Am. Assn. Bone & Joint Surgeons, Rocky Mountain Traumatologic Soc., Canadian Orthopaedic Assn., Am. Orthopaedic Soc. for Sports Medicine, Internat. Ski Safety Soc., ACL Study Group, Internat. Soc. Knee, Internat. Knee Inst., Phi Beta Kappa. Home: PO Box 660 Aspen CO 81612-0660 Office: 100 E Main St Aspen CO 81611-1778

ODEN, WILLIAM BRYANT, bishop, educator; b. McAllen, Tex., Aug. 3, 1935; s. Charles Alva and Evea (Bryant) O.; m. Marilyn Brown, July 12, 1957; children: Danna Lee Oden Bowen, William Dirk, Valerie Lyn, Charles Bryant. BA, Okla. State U., 1958; MDiv, Harvard U., 1961, postgrad., 1974; ThD, Boston U., 1964; DD (hon.), Oklahoma City U., 1980; LHD (hon.), Centenary Coll., 1990. Ordained to ministry Meth. Ch., 1961. Pastor Aldersgate United Meth. Ch., Oklahoma City, 1963-69, St. Stephen's United Meth. Ch., Norman, Okla., 1969-76, Crown Heights United Meth. Ch., Oklahoma City, 1976-83; prof. Phillips Grad. Sem., Enid, 1976-88; pastor 1st United Meth. Ch., Enid, 1983-88; bishop United Meth. Ch., Baton Rouge, 1988—; assigned to La. area; pres. SCJ Coll. of Bishops, 1989-90; del. Gen. Conf., 1976, 80, 84, 88; chmn. Okla. Del. to Gen. and Jurisdictional Confs., 1984, 88; Jackson lectr. Perkins Sch. Theology, So. Meth. U., 1975, Wilson lectr. SCJ Bishop's Week, 1989; co-chair World Meth.-Anglican Dialogue, 1991—; bd. dirs. Wesley Works Project. Author: Oklahoma Methodism in the Twentieth Century, 1968, Liturgy as Life Journey, 1976, Wordeed: Evangelism in Biblical and Wesleyan Perspective, 1978; contbr.: Send Me: The Iteneracy in Crisis, 1991. Trustee Oklahoma City U., 1980-88, Southwestern U., Winfield, Kans., 1983-88, Centenary Coll., 1988—, Dillard U., 1988—. Mem. Am. Acad. Homiletics. Avocations: writing, reading biographies, mountain climbing, backpacking. Home: 7344 Woodstock Dr Baton Rouge LA 70809-1136 Office: La United Meth Hdqrs 527 North Blvd Baton Rouge LA 70802-5720

ODENWELLER, ROBERT PAUL, philatelist, association executive, airline pilot; b. Colon, C.Z., Sept. 19, 1938; s. Charles Joseph and Robina Katharine (Watson, O.; m. Jane Blackstone Rawlings, June 24, 1965; 1 stepchild, Joy McCorriston; 1 child, Liesl Hasbrouck. BS U.S. Air Force Acad., 1960. Commd. USAF, 1956, advanced through grades to capt., 1963, resigned, 1956-66; mem. Collectors Club, Inc., N.Y.C., 1964—, gov. 1969—, program chmn., 1970-80, mem. editl. bd., 1975—, sec. 1979-82, v.p., 1983-86, pres. 1987-90, trustee, 1992—; trustee, vice chmn. then chmn. expert com. Philatelic Found., N.Y.C., 1970—. Author: The FIP Guide to Exhibiting and Judging Traditional and Postal History Exhibits, 1993; author, Editor: Philatelic Vocabulary in Five Languages, 1978 (Vermeil medal 1979); editor: Opinions VI, 1992 (Gold medal); contbr. articles to profl. pubs. Recipient Grand Prix d' Honneur, Zeapex Orgn., 1980; selected to sign Roll of Disting. Philatelists, Brit. Philatelic Fedn., 1991, Alfred Lichtenstein Meml. award Collectors Club, N.Y., 1993, TWA Flight Ops. Meritorious Achievement award, 1995, award of Excellence, 1995. Fellow Royal Philatelic Soc. London, Royal Philatelic Soc. N.Z.; mem. Fedn. Internationale de Philatelie (pres. commn. traditional philately 1978-96; Grand Prix d' Honneur 1980), Am. Philatelic Soc. (bd. dirs. 1981-84, 89-90, named Champion of Champions 1973), Assn. Internationale Des Experts Philateliques (expert 1980—, bd. dirs. 1987—), Fedn. New Zealand Philatelic Socs., Grand Prix Club Internat. (sec., treas. 1980-89, bd. dirs. 1989-92, 94—, v.p. 1994—), Soc. Australasian Specialists (pres. 1969-72), U.S. Chess Fedn. Republican. Episcopalian. Avocations: stamp collecting; photography; languages; chess; bridge. Home: Chalon Round Top Rd Bernardsville NJ 07924 Office: Collector's Club 22 E 35th St New York NY 10016-3806

ODER, BROECK NEWTON, school emergency management consultant; b. Highland Park, Ill., Apr. 20, 1953; s. Bruce Newton and Mary Louise (Roe) O.; m. Jolene Marie Peragine, June 28, 1975 (dec. June 1979). BA in History, U. San Diego, 1974, MA in History, 1975; postgrad., U. N.Mex., 1976-79. Life C.C. teaching credential, Calif. Rsch. asst. to pres. U. San Diego, 1975; grad. asst. U. N.Mex., Albuquerque, 1976-79; tchr. history, chmn. dept. Santa Catalina Sch., Monterey, Calif., 1979—, asst. dean students, 1981-83, dir. ind. study, 1981-95, dean students, 1983-91, dir. emergency planning, 1986—, dean campus affairs, 1991-94, dir. security, 1994—; mem. disaster preparedness coun. Monterey County Office Edn., 1988—; chair Diocesan Sch. Emergency Preparedness Coun., 1991—. Mem. bd. of tchrs. The Concord Rev.; contbr. articles to profl. publs. Participant Jail and Bail, Am. Cancer Soc., Monterey, 1988, 89; reviewer sch. emergency plans, Monterey, 1989—. Recipient award of merit San Diego Hist. Soc., 1975, Outstanding Tchr. award U. Chgo., 1985, Outstanding Young Educator award Monterey Peninsula Jaycees, 1988, resolution of commendation Calif. Senate Rules Com., 1988, cert. of commendation Calif. Gov.'s Office Emergency Svcs., 1991, nat. cert. of achievement Fed. Emergency Mgmt. Agy., 1991. Mem. ACLU, NRA (life), Congress Racial Equality, Am. Hist. Assn., Orgn. Am. Historians, Nat. Coun. on History Edn., Soc. for History Edn., Second Amendment Found., Individual Rights Found., Phi Alpha Theta. Avocations: reading, sports, target shooting. Office: Santa Catalina Sch 1500 Mark Thomas Dr Monterey CA 93940-5238

ODER, FREDERIC CARL EMIL, retired aerospace company executive, consultant; b. Los Angeles, Oct. 23, 1919; s. Emil and Katherine Ellis (Pierce) O.; m. Dorothy Gene Brumfield, July 2, 1941; children—Frederic E., Barbara Oder Debes, Richard W. B.S., Calif. Inst. Tech., 1940, M.S., 1941; Ph.D., UCLA, 1952. Commd. 2d lt. U.S. Army Air Force, 1941; advanced through grades to col. U.S. Air Force, 1960; ret., 1960; asst. dir. and program mgr. for research and engrng. Apparatus and Optical div. Eastman Kodak Co., Rochester, N.Y., 1960-66; with Lockheed Missiles & Space Co., Sunnyvale, Calif., 1966-91; v.p., asst. gen. mgr. div. space systems Lockheed Missiles & Space Co., 1972-73, v.p., gen. mgr. div. space systems, 1973-84, exec. v.p., 1984-85; cons., 1985-91; mem. Def. Intelligence Agy. Sci. Adv. Com., 1972-76, assoc. mem., 1976-78; mem. Air Force Studies Bd., Assembly Engrng., NRC, 1975-79, Def. Sci. Bd. Summer Study, 1975, Rev. Panel, 1979, Space Applications Bd., 1985-88. Contbr. articles to profl. publs. Decorated Legion of Merit. Fellow AIAA; mem. NAE, Masons, Sigma Xi. Episcopalian. Home: 400 San Domingo Way Los Altos CA 94022-2143

ODER, KENNETH WILLIAM, lawyer; b. Newport News, Va., July 9, 1947; s. Thomas William and Joy Reletta (McNeil) O.; m. Lucinda Ann Fox, July 20, 1969; children: Joshua, Devon, Chelsea. BA, U. Va., 1969, JD, 1975. Bar: Calif. 1975, U.S. Dist. Ct. (cen. dist.) Calif. 1975, U.S. Dist. Ct. (so. and no. dists.) Calif. 1977, U.S. Ct. Appeals (9th cir.) 1977, D.C. 1979. Assoc. Latham & Watkins, Los Angeles, 1975-77, 79-82, ptnr., 1982-94; assoc. Latham & Watkins, Washington, 1978-79; exec. v.p. Safeway Inc., Oakland, 1994—. Exec. editor U. Va. Law Rev., 1973-74. Coach San Marino Little League, Calif., 1983—, Am. Youth Soccer Orgn., Rosemeade, Calif., 1984—. Mem. Calif. Bar Assn. (employment law sect.), Los Angeles County Bar Assn., D.C. Bar Assn. Republican. Methodist. Avocations: jogging, hiking, fishing. Office: Safeway Inc 201 4th St Oakland CA 94660*

ODERMATT, ROBERT ALLEN, architect; b. Oakland, Calif., Jan. 3, 1938; s. Clifford Allen and Margaret Louise (Budge) O.; m. Diana Birtwistle, June 9, 1960; children: Kristin Ann, Kyle David. BArch, U. Calif., Berkeley, 1960. Registered architect, Calif., Oreg., Nev., Colo., Hawaii; cert. Nat. Coun. Archtl. Registration Bds. Draftsman Anderson Simonds Dusel Campini, Oakland, 1960-61; architect James R. Lucas, Orinda, Calif., 1961-62, ROMA Architects, San Francisco, 1962-76; architect, pres. ROMA Architects, 1976-84; prin. ROMA Design Group, San Francisco, 1962-92; pres. The Odermatt Group, Orinda, Calif., 1992—; prin. speaker Internat. Conf. on Rebuilding Cities, Pitts., 1988; mem. U.S. Design in Am. Program, Sofia, Bulgaria, Armenian Disaster Assn. Team, 1989; prin. State of Calif. Bay Area Facilities Plan, 1992; princ. Greece Resort Privatization Program, 1993. Prin. designer Grand Canyon Nat. Park, 1977, Yosemite Nat. Park, 1987; prin. planner hotel complex Westin Hotel, Vail, Colo., 1982, Kaanapali Resort, 1987, Las Montanas Resort, San Diego; master plan U. Calif., Berkeley, 1988, Kohanaiki and Mauna Lani resorts, 1989, Calif. State Strategic Real Estate Plan, 1992, Greek Resort/Marina Privatization Program, 1993, Tektronix Strategic Plan, 1994, United Labs, Manila Master Plan, 1995, State of Calif. Reorganization Plan. Mem. Oakland Mayor's Com. on High Density Housing, 1982, Oakland Gen. Plan Congress, 1994, waterfront plan adv. com. City of Oakland, 1996; prin. charge Am. Embassy, Bahrain. Fellow AIA (dir. East Bay chpt. 1969-71, pres. 1980-81, dir. Calif. coun. 1979-81, Disting. Svc. award 1991, nat. dir. 1983-86, nat. v.p. 1986-87, chair AIA internat. steering com. 1993-94, graphic stds. adv. com. 1991-92, U. Calif. archtl. review commn. 1992-96, exec. com. Coll. Fellows 1996—). Office: The Odermatt Group 39 Drury Ln Berkeley CA 94705

ODGERS, RICHARD WILLIAM, lawyer; b. Detroit, Dec. 31, 1936; s. Richard Stanley and Elsie Maude (Trevarthen) O.; m. Gail C. Bassett, Aug. 29, 1959; children: Thomas R., Andrew B. AB, U. Mich., 1959, JD, 1961. Bar: Calif. 1962. Assoc. Pillsbury, Madison & Sutro, San Francisco, 1961-69, ptnr., 1969-87; exec. v.p., gen. counsel, sec. external affairs Pacific Telesis Group, 1987—. Mem. steering com. Calif. Minorty Coun. Program; exec. com. Legal Cmty. Against Violence; dir., sec./treas. Van Loben Sels Charitable Found. Served with USNR. Fellow Am. Bar Found., Am. Judicature Soc., Am. Coll. Trial Lawyers; mem. ABA, Am. Law Inst., Legal Aid Soc. San Francisco (bd. dirs., v.p.), NAACP (legal def. fund steering com.). Office: Pacific Telesis Group 130 Kearny St Ste 3700 San Francisco CA 94108-4818

ODIER, PIERRE ANDRE, educator, writer, photographer, artist; b. Lausanne, Switzerland, May 24, 1940; came to U.S., 1959; s. Leon Odier and Gretha (Vesper) Hough; m. Mary Ellen Patton, Apr. 2, 1967 (div. Apr. 1984); children: Yvette, Debbi. BA, U. Puget Sound, 1967; MFA, Calif. State U., L.A., 1974; postgrad., UCLA, 1976-83. Cert. tchr., Calif. Owner restaurant The End, Tacoma, Wash., 1961-64; owner gallery Place des Arts, Tacoma, 1964-65; interpeter Weyerhauser Corp., Tacoma, 1964; chairperson dept. fine arts Hoover H.S., Glendale, Calif., 1967—. Author: The Rock, A History of Alcatraz, 1983, Lummis Inside his Habitat, 1977 (State Hist. Soc. award 1981), A Discovery of Age, Students Look at Aging Process, 1992. Editor: Nat. Photographers Assn. quar., 1980-84. Served with U.S. Army, 1959-62. Recipient Tchr. of Yr. award Parent Tchrs. Student Assn., Glendale, Calif., 1979, Tchr. of Yr. award Glendale C. of C., 1983, Hon. Tchr. award Puiching Sch. China, 1994. Mem. Glendale Tchrs. Assn. (contract negotiator 1977), Nat. Photography Instrs. Assn. (chmn. election com., pres. 1980-85, chairperson conv. 1982), China Exploration and Rsch. Soc. (v.p., editor newsletter, expedition leader China, Mongolia, Siberia, Russia, U.S.A. 1994), NEA. Democrat. Lutheran. Club: Adventurers (1st v.p.), Explorers N.Y. Home: 1255 Hill Dr Los Angeles CA 90041-1610 Office: Hoover High Sch 651 Glenwood Rd Glendale CA 91202

ODLAND, GERALD CLARK, association executive; b. Bellefonte, Pa., July 26, 1946; s. Martin Luther and Ethel Gladys (Wentzel) O.; m. Dianne Marlo DePue, May 29, 1969; children—Brian Martin, Kevin Michael. BS, U. Md., 1973, MS, 1976. Dir. services, computer mgr. Entomol. Soc. Am., College Park, Md., 1972-85; dep. exec. dir. Assn. for Childhood Edn. Internat., Wheaton, Md., 1985-91, exec. dir., 1991—. Editor: Directory of North American Entomologists, 1979; contbr. articles to profl. jours. Served as sgt. U.S. Army, 1967-70, Vietnam. Mem. Entomol. Soc. Am., Am. Soc. Assn. Execs. Republican. Lutheran. Avocations: hunting, fishing, boating, woodworking. Home: 13715 Oster Farm Rd West Friendship MD 21794 Office: Assn Childhood Edn Internat 11501 Georgia Ave Ste 315 Silver Spring MD 20902-1954

ODLE, ROBERT CHARLES, JR., lawyer; b. Port Huron, Mich., Feb. 15, 1944; s. Robert Charles and Elizabeth Dagmar (Lassen) O.; m. Lydia Ann Karpinol, Aug. 2, 1969. B.A., Wayne State U., Detroit, 1966; J.D., Detroit Coll. Law, 1969, LLD (hon.), 1992. Staff asst. to pres. of U.S., 1969-71; dir. adminstrn. Com. Re-election of President, 1971-73; dep. asst. sec. HUD, 1973-76; Washington corp. affairs rep. Internat. Paper Co., 1976-81; asst. sect. Dept. Energy, 1981-85; ptnr. Weil, Gotshal & Manges, 1985—. Mem. Mich. Bar Assn., D.C. Bar Assn., Delta Theta Phi. Republican. Roman Catholic. Club: University (Washington). Home: 219 S Lee St Alexandria VA 22314-3307 Office: Weil Gotshal & Manges 1615 L St NW Washington DC 20036-5610

ODLIN, RICHARD BINGHAM, retired banker; b. Olympia, Wash., Nov. 22, 1934; s. Reno and Edith Mary (Murphy) O.; m. 1963 (div. 1969); children: Julia Eleanor Odlin Lord, Tracy Edith; m. Barbara Ellen Button, Aug. 8, 1985. AB, Whitman Coll., 1957. With Wells Fargo Bank, San Francisco, 1957-63; various positions to sr. v.p., sec. Puget Sound Nat. Bank, Tacoma, Wash., 1963-92; pres. New Tacoma Parking Corp., 1969-91. Bd. dirs. Tacoma-Pierce County chpt. ARC, 1964-69, vice chmn., 1969; active Wash. State Hist. Soc., treas., 1971-92. Mem. Am. Contract Bridge League (life master), Tacoma Country and Golf Club, Tacoma Lawn Tennis Club, Columbia Tower Club (Seattle), Tacoma Club, Balboa Club (Mazatlan, Mex.), Kappa Sigma. Republican. Avocations: duplicate bridge, opera, old time radio. Home: 507 N 3d St Apt 301-A Tacoma WA 98403-2753

O'DOHERTY, BRIAN, writer, filmmaker; b. Ballaghadereen, County Roscommon, Ireland; came to U.S., 1957; m. Barbara Novak, 1960. M.D., Univ. Coll. Dublin, Nat. U. Ireland, 1952, D.P.H. with honors, 1955; MS in Hygiene, Harvard U., 1958; TV host programs Mus. Fine Arts, Boston, 1958-61; art critic N.Y. Times, 1961-64; vis. prof. Berkeley U., 1967; dir. visual arts Nat. Endowment for Arts, 1969-76, dir. media arts, 1976-94; dir. Millennium Project, 1994—; art and architecture critic Today Program, 1971-76; adj. prof. Barnard Coll., 1969—. Author: Object and Idea: A New York Art Journal 1961-67, 1967; editor: Museums in Crisis, 1972, American Masters, The Voice and the Myth, 1973 2d. revised edit., 1988, Inside the White Cube, 1986, The Strange Case of Mlle. P, 1992. Contbr. articles to profl. jours. Smith-Mundt fellow; recipient Mpls. Citizens award, 1961; Emmy nominations; Eire Soc. Gold medal for contbns. to Culture, 1963; Mather award, 1964; Grand Prix Montreal Internat. Festival of Arts Film award, 1982; Sagittarius award London, 1993. Mem. Am. Irish Historical Soc. (bd. dirs.), N.Y., Irish Mus. of Modern Art (bd. dirs.), Dublin, Coll. Art Assn. (life mem.). Office: NEA 1100 Pennsylvania Ave NW Washington DC 20004-2501

ODOM, WILLIAM E., automobile finance company executive; b. 1936; married. Student, U. S.C., U.S. Naval Acad., Wayne State U. With Ford Motor Credit Co., 1966—, dist. mgr. diversified financing ops., 1966-69, field ops. mgr., then mng. credit officer, then mgr. and sr. loan officer field ops. & real estate financing activities, 1969-79, ops. mgr. leasing truck & tractor financing, 1979-80, v.p. leasing truck and tractor financing ops., 1980-83, v.p. eastern U.S. and Canadian ops., 1983-85, exec. v.p. N. Am. automotive financing ops., 1985-86, past pres., 1986—, now chmn., chief exec. officer, bd. dirs. Office: Ford Motor Credit Co American Rd Dearborn MI 48121*

ODOM, WILLIAM ELDRIDGE, army officer, educator; b. Cookeville, Tenn., June 23, 1932; s. John Albert and Callie Frances (Everhart) O.; m. Anne Weld Curtis, June 9, 1962; 1 child, Mark Weld. BS, U.S. Mil. Acad., 1954; MA, Columbia U., 1962, PhD, 1970; DSc (hon.), Middlebury Coll., 1987. Commd. 2nd lt. U.S. Army, 1954, advanced through grades to lt. gen., 1984; mem. U.S. Mil. Liaison Mission to Soviet Forces, Germany, 1964-66; from asst. prof. to assoc. prof. govt. U.S. Mil. Acad., West Point, 1966-69, 74-76; asst. Army attache U.S. embassy, Moscow, 1972-74; nat. security staff mem. White House, 1977-81; asst. chief of staff for intelligence Dept. Army, Washington, 1981-85; dir. Nat. Security Agy., Fort Meade, Md., 1985-88; dir. nat. security studies Hudson Inst., 1988—; adj. prof. pol. sci. Yale U., 1989—. Author: The Soviet Volunteers, 1973, On Internal War, 1992, Trial After Triumph, 1992, America's Military Revolution, 1993, (with Robert Dujarric) Commonwealth or Empire? Russia, Central Asia and The Transcaucasus, 1995; contbr. articles to profl. jours. Trustee Middlebury Coll. Bd., 1987—. Decorated Def. Disting. medal with oak leaf cluster, DSM with oak leaf cluster, Legion of Merit, Nat. Security medal, Nat. Intelligence Disting. Svc. medal; grand cross Order of Merit with Star (Fed. Republic Germany); Order Nat. Security Merit (Republic of Korea), officer Nat. Order of Merit (France). Mem. Coun. on Fgn. Rels., Am. Assn. for Advancement of Slavic Studies, Internat. Inst. for Strategic Studies, Am. Polit. Sci. Assn., Acad. Polit. Sci. Conglist. Office: Hudson Inst 1015 18th St NW Ste 200 Washington DC 20036-5203

ODOMS, DAVE, collegiate athletic coach. Head coach-basketball Wake Forest U., Winston-Salem, N.C. Office: Wake Forest U PO Box 7265 Winston Salem NC 27109*

O'DONNELL, CHRIS, actor; b. Winetka, Ill., 1970. Actor: (films) Men Don't Leave, 1990, Fried Green Tomatoes, 1991, Scent of a Woman, 1992 (Golden Globe award nomination best supporting actor 1992), School Ties, 1992, The Three Musketeers, 1993, Blue Sky, 1994, Circle of Friends, 1995, Mad Love, 1995, Batman Forever, 1995. Office: CAA 9830 Wilshire Blvd Beverly Hills CA 90212*

O'DONNELL, EDWARD FRANCIS, JR., lawyer; b. Waterbury, Conn., May 13, 1950; s. Edward Francis and Dorothy Patricia (Breheny) O'D.; m. Jayne Ann DeSantis, Dec. 29, 1972; children: Ryan Anderson, Brooke Stires. BA, St. Anselm Coll., Manchester, N.H., 1972; JD, U. Conn., 1977. Bar: S.C. 1978, Conn. 1977, U.S. Dist. Ct. S.C. 1978, U.S. Dist. Ct. Conn. 1980, U.S. Ct. Appeals (1st and 2d cirs.) 1980. Assoc. Ogeltree, Deakins, Nash, Smoak & Stewart, Greenville, S.C., 1977-79; ptnr. Siegel, O'Connor, Schiff & Zangari, Hartford, Conn., 1979—. Contbr. articles to profl. jours. Mem. ABA, Conn. Bar Assn., S.C. Bar Assn., Hartford Bar Assn., Wampanoag Country Club, Phi Alpha Theta. Roman Catholic. Office: Siegel O'Connor Schiff & Zangari 370 Asylum St Hartford CT 06103-2025

O'DONNELL, EDWARD JOSEPH, bishop, former editor; b. St. Louis, July 4, 1931; s. Edward Joseph and Ruth Mary (Carr) O'D. Student, Cardinal Glennon Coll., 1949-53; postgrad., Kenrick Sem., 1953-57. Ordained priest Roman Cath. Ch., 1957, consecrated bishop, 1984; asso. pastor in 5 St. Louis parishes, 1957-77; pastor St. Peter's Ch., Kirkwood, Mo., 1977-81; assoc. dir. Archdiocesan Commn. on Human Rights, 1962-70; dir. Archdiocesan Radio-TV Office, 1966-68, Archdiocesan Vocation Council, 1965; editor St. Louis Rev., 1968-81; vicar-gen. Archdiocese of St. Louis, 1981-84, aux. bishop, 1984-94; bishop Diocese of Lafayette, Lafayette, LA, 1994—; bd. dirs. Nat. Cath. Conf. for Interracial Justice, 1980-85, NAACP, 1964-66, Urban League St. Louis, 1962-68; chmn. Interfaith Clergy Coun. Greater St. Louis, 1963-67. Named to Golden Dozen Internat. Soc. Weekly Newspaper Editors, 1970, 77. Mem. Cath. Press Assn., Nat. Assn. TV Arts and Scis. Office: PO Box 3387 Lafayette LA 70502-3387

O'DONNELL, EUGENE J., department stores executive; b. 1946. BA, U. Vt.; MBA, Dartmouth Coll. V.p. Hills Dept. Stores Inc., 1981-85, sr. v.p., gen. merchandise mgr., from 1985, now exec. v.p. Office: Hills Dept Stores Inc 15 Dan Rd Canton MA 02021-2847

O'DONNELL, F. SCOTT, banker; b. Brownsville, Pa., Sept. 20, 1940; s. Francis Horner and Rebecca (Warren) O'D.; m. Ann Bukmir, Dec. 30, 1976. BA, Grove City (Pa.) Coll., 1962; postgrad., U. Wis. Grad. Sch. Banking, 1970, Internat. Sch. Banking, U. Colo., 1972. Nat. bank examiner Comptroller of Currency, Cleve., 1965-71; supt. of banks State of Ohio, Columbus, 1975-77; sr. v.p. First Nat. Bank, Steubenville, Ohio, 1971-75; exec. v.p. Heritage Bancorp, Steubenville, 1977-80; v.p. Society Corp., Cleve., 1980-86, sr. v.p., 1986—; mem. state banking bd. Div. of Banks, Columbus, 1979-85, govt. affairs com. Ohio Bankers Assn., 1982-84; special asst. Tax Commr. State of Ohio, 1996. Served with USCG, 1963-69. Mem. Columbus Athletic Club, Univ. Club, Elks. Avocations: golfing, antiques. Home: 31830 Lake Rd Avon Lake OH 44012-2022 Office: Dept Taxation 22nd floor 30 East Broad St Columbus OH 43215

O'DONNELL, G. DANIEL, lawyer; b. Scranton, Pa., 1951. BA summa cum laude, U. Notre Dame, 1973; JD, U. Pa., 1976. Bar: Pa. 1976. Ptnr., chmn. bus. dept. Dechert Price & Rhoads, Phila. Mem. Order of Coif. Home: 102 West Chestnut Hill Ave Philadelphia PA 19118 Office: Dechert Price & Rhoads 4000 Bell Atlantic 1717 Arch St Philadelphia PA 19103-2713

O'DONNELL, JAMES FRANCIS, health science administrator; b. Cleve., July 22, 1928; s. John Michael and Mary Louise (Hayes) O'D.; m. Winifred Locke, Sept. 10, 1955; children—Anne Catherine, Patrick John, Mary Elizabeth. B.S. in Biology, St. Louis U., 1949; Ph.D. in Biochemistry, U. Chgo., 1957. Asst., then. assoc. prof. biol. chemistry and exptl. medicine Coll. Medicine, U. Cin., 1957-68; grants assoc., div. research grants NIH, Bethesda, Md., 1968-69; program dir. population and reprodn. grants br. Ctr. for Population Research, Nat. Inst. Child Health and Human Devel.,

NIH, 1969-71; asst. dir. div. research resources NIH, Bethesda, 1971-76, dep. dir. div. research resources, 1976-90, acting dir. div. research resources, 1981-82, dir. Office of Extramural Programs, Office of the Dir., 1990—. Served with U.S. Army, 1950-52. Home: 11601 Bunnell Ct S Rockville MD 20854-3603 Office: NIH Rm 6182 6701 Rockledge Dr Bethesda MD 20892-7910

O'DONNELL, JOHN LOGAN, lawyer; b. Chgo., Mar. 6, 1914; s. William Joseph and Elizabeth (McLogan) O'D.; m. Mary Ellen Sipe, Sept. 2, 1939 (dec. Dec. 29, 1979); 1 son, John Logan; m. Michele G. Fischer, May 9, 1981. B.A., Williams Coll., 1934; J.D., Northwestern U., 1937. Bar: Ill. 1937, N.Y. 1943, D.C. 1977. Asso. firm Defrees, Buckingham, Jones and Hoffman, Chgo., 1937-38; staff atty. Office Gen. Counsel, SEC, 1938-41; instr. Cath. U. Law Sch., 1938-41; assoc. Cravath, Swaine & Moore, N.Y.C., 1941-52; ptnr. Olwine, Connelly, Chase, O'Donnell & Weyher, N.Y.C., 1952-91, of counsel, 1991; of counsel Aron, Twomey, Hoppe & Gallanty, N.Y.C., 1991—. Bd. dirs. Near East Found., 1968-84. Fellow Am. Coll. Trial Lawyers; mem. Assn. Bar City N.Y., Am., Fed., bar assns., Beta Theta Pi, Phi Delta Phi. Roman Catholic. Clubs: Union, Univ., Williams, (N.Y.C.). Avocations: piano, sports. Home: 181 E 73rd St New York NY 10021-3549 Office: Aron Twomey Hoppe & Gallanty 757 3rd Ave New York NY 10017-2013

O'DONNELL, KEVIN, retired metal working company executive; b. Cleve., June 9, 1925; s. Charles Richard and Ella (Kilbane) O'D.; m. Ellen Blydenburgh, Aug. 16, 1965; children: Kevin, Susan, Michael, John, Maura, Neil, Megan, Hugh. AB, Kenyon Coll., Gambier, Ohio, 1947, PhD in Law (hon.), 1980; MBA, Harvard U., 1947; PhD in Econs. (hon.), Pusan (Korea) Nat. U., 1970; Ph.D. in Humanities (hon.), Ohio Wesleyan U., 1972. Gen. sales mgr. Steel Improvement & Forge Co., Cleve., 1947-60; mgmt. cons. Booz, Allen and Hamilton, Cleve., 1960-62; gen. mgr., dir. Atlas Alloys-Rio Algom Corp., Cleve., 1963-66; dir. Peace Corps, Seoul, 1966-70; dir. adminstrn. and fin., then dep. acting dir. Peace Corps, 1970-71; assoc. dir. internat. ops. ACTION, 1971-72; exec. v.p. SIFCO Industries, Inc., Cleve., 1972-75; pres., chief oper. officer SIFCO Industries, Inc., 1976-83, pres., chief exec. officer, 1983-89, chief exec. officer, 1989-90, chmn., exec. comm., 1990-94; bd. dirs. Nat. Machinery, Tiffin, Ohio, Lamson and Sessions, R.P.M. Inc., Medina, Ohio. Trustee Alcohol Svcs. Cleve., 1993—, Cleve. Coun. World Affairs, Nat. Peace Corps Assn.; mem. Coun. Fgn. Rels., N.Y.C., Washington Inst. Fgn. Affairs, Cleve. Com. Fgn. Rels., chmn., 1979-82; chmn. CCWA, 1982-89; pres. Guest House, Inc., 1990-92. Decorated Order Civil Merit (Republic of Korea). mem. Harvard Bus. Sch. Club Cleve., Harvard Bus. Sch. Alumni Assn. (dir. Boston 1991-94), First Friday Club, 50 Club, Union Club, Pepper Pike Country Club, Westwood Country Club, Army-Navy Club (Washington), Knights of Malta (master knight). Republican. Roman Catholic. Avocations: golf, reading.

O'DONNELL, LAURENCE GERARD, editorial consultant; b. Bklyn., June 30, 1935; s. Thomas Edward and Dorothy (Clark) O'D.; m. Joan M. Coniglio, Jan. 9, 1960; children: Christopher, Carolyn, Jeffrey, Anthony. AB, Holy Cross Coll., 1957. Reporter Wall Street Jour., N.Y.C., 1958-66, chief Detroit Bur., 1966-74, asst. mng. editor, N.Y.C., 1974-77, mng. editor, 1977-83; assoc. editor Dow Jones & Co., Inc., N.Y.C., 1983-90; cons. Dow Jones & Co., Inc., 1991—; pres. Dow Jones Newspaper Fund, 1988-93; bd. dirs. Dow Jones Newspaper Fund, Inter Am. Press Assn.; vis. lectr. Queens Coll./CUNY, 1992—. Trustee Holy Cross Coll., 1982-90; mem. journalism adv. bd. Queens Coll./CUNY, 1989—; juror Pulitzer Prize, 1982, 83. Mem. Am. Soc. Newspaper Editors. Office: Dow Jones Newspaper Fund PO Box 300 Princeton NJ 08543-0300

O'DONNELL, LAWRENCE, III, lawyer; b. Houston, Dec. 14, 1957; s. Lawrence Jr. and Annell (Haggart) O'D.; m. Dare Boswell, May 22, 1981; children: Linley, Lawrence IV. BS in Archtl. Engring., U. Tex., 1980; JD cum laude, U. Houston, 1983. Bar: Tex. 1983. Assoc. Wood, Campbell, Moody & Gibbs, Houston, 1983-84; ptnr. Campbell & Riggs, Houston, 1984-91; dep. gen. counsel and corp. sec. Baker Hughes Inc., Houston, 1991-94; v.p., gen. counsel Baker Hughes Oilfield Ops., Houston, 1993-95; v.p., gen. counsel, corp. sec. Baker Hughes Inc., Houston, 1995—. Trustee Houston Police Activities League. Mem. ABA, Tex. State Bar (corp. law com. of bus. law), Houston Bar Assn., am. Corp. counsel Assn., Am. Soc. Corp. Sec., Tex. Bus. Law Found., Houston Bar Assn., Am. Soc. Civil Engrs., Order of Barons, Phi Delta Phi. Avocations: golf, tennis, sailing, skiing. Office: Baker Hughes Inc 3900 Essex Ln Ste 1200 Houston TX 77027-5112

O'DONNELL, LAWRENCE FRANCIS, JR., author; b. Boston, Nov. 7, 1951; s. Lawrence Frances and Frances Marie (Buckley) O'D.; m. Kathryn Hunter Harrold; 1 child, Elizabeth Buckley Harrold. AB, Harvard U., 1976. Writer self-employed, Boston and N.Y.C., 1976-84, 84-87; sr. advisor Senator Daniel Patrick Moynihan, Washington, 1988-92; chief of staff U.S. Senate Com. on Environment and Pub. Works, Washington, 1992-93, U.S. Senate Com. on Fin., Washington, 1993-95. Author: Deadly Force, 1983; assoc. producer: A Case of Deadly Force, 1986. Mem. Writers Guild of Am. Home: 434 11th St Santa Monica CA 90402 Office: 1505 4th St Ste 215 Santa Monica CA 90401

O'DONNELL, MARTIN J., lawyer; b. Boston, Dec. 19, 1936; s. Michael Vincent and Ann Theresa O'Donnell; m. Louise Jaskiel, May 14, 1966; children: Christopher M., Elisabeth L., Leah K. BS, MIT, 1961; JD, Boston Coll. Law, 1964. Bar: Mass. 1964, U.S. Ct. Appeals (1st cir.) 1966, U.S. Ct. Appeals (fed. cir.) 1977, U.S. Supreme Ct. 1984. Assoc. Kenway, Jenney & Hildreth, Boston, 1964-67; assoc., then ptnr. Cesari & McKenna, Boston, 1967—; adj. faculty New Eng. Sch. of Law, Boston, 1974-84; lectr. Mass. Continuing Legal Edn., Boston, 1975—. Mem. vis. com. on humanities MIT, 1993—, chmn. Boston region ednl. coun., 1981—. Mem. IEEE, Boston Patent Law Assn. (pres. 1978-79), Assn. for Computing Machinery. Avocations: language, curling.

O'DONNELL, PIERCE HENRY, lawyer; b. Troy, N.Y., Mar. 5, 1947; s. Harry J. and Mary (Kane) O'D.; m. Dawn Donley, Mar. 17, 1995; children: Meghan Maureen, Brendan Casey, Courtney Dawn. BA, Georgetown U., 1969, JD, 1972; LLM, Yale U., 1975. Bar: D.C. 1973, U.S. Supreme Ct. 1975, Calif. 1978. Law clk. to Justice Byron R. White U.S. Supreme Ct.; law clk. to Judge Shirley M. Jufstedler U.S. Dist. Ct. (9th cir.); assoc. Williams & Connolly, Washington, 1975-78; ptnr. Beardsley, Hufstedler & Kemble, L.A., 1978-81, Hufstedler, Miller, Carlson & Beardsley, L.A., 1981-82, O'Donnell & Gordon, L.A., 1982-88, Kaye, Scholer, Fierman, Hays & Handler, L.A., 1988-95, O'Donnell, Reeves & Shaeffer, LLP, L.A., 1996—; exec. asst. U.S. Sec. Edn., 1979; spl. counsel Commn. Jud. Performance, San Francisco, 1979; chmn. Nat. Media, Inc., 1984-92. Co-author: Fatal Subtraction: The Inside Story of Buchwald v Paramount, 1992; contbr. articles to profl. jours. Chmn. Friends of Calif. Tech. YMCA, 1983-84, Verduga-San Rafael Urban Mountain Park Fund, 1980-84; bd. dirs. Friends of Altadena Libr., 1979-81, Pasadena-Foothill Urban League; bd. dirs. Foothill Family Svc., 1979-85, chmn., 1984-85; bd. dirs. Interfaith Ctr. To Reverse Arms Law, 1984-90, pres., 1987-88. Mem. PEN, NAACP, Am. Law Inst., Econ. Round Table L.A., Sierra Club, Bel Air Country Club, Gridiron Club (Georgetown U.). Roman Catholic. Home: 405 Linda Vista Ave Pasadena CA 91105 Office: O'Donnell Reeves et al 633 W 5th St Ste 1700 Los Angeles CA 90071

O'DONNELL, RICHARD WALTER, lawyer, accountant, brokerage company executive; b. Newark, Oct. 17, 1945; s. James Richard and Alice (Drep) O'D. BA, Rutgers U., 1967, MBA in Fin., 1969, MBA in Acctg., 1972, JD, 1985. Bar: N.J. 1985; CPA, N.J. Fin. analyst Allied Chem. Corp., Morristown, N.J., 1969-72; sr. audit mgr. Peat, Marwick, Mitchell & Co., Newark, 1972-80; asst. controller Crane Co., N.Y.C., 1980-81, controller, 1981-83; treas. Lehman Bros. Kuhn Loeb, Inc., N.Y.C., 1983-84; sr. v.p. Shearson Lehman Bros., Inc., N.Y.C., 1984-85; mng. dir. Kidder, Peabody & Co., Inc., N.Y.C., 1985—. Mem. AICPA, N.J. Soc. CPAs (chmn. community svcs. com. 1978-80), Nat. Assn. Accts., N.J. Bar Assn., Wayne C. of C. (treas. 1979-80), Beta Gamma Sigma. Home: 12 Perrin Dr Wayne NJ 07470-4034 Office: Kidder Peabody & Co Inc 10 Hanover Sq New York NY 10005-3516*

O'DONNELL, ROBERT MICHAEL, electrical engineering executive; b. Lynn, Mass., Aug. 31, 1941; s. Michael Cornelius and Katherine (Niland) O'D.; m. Margaret Ann Connell, Aug. 20, 1968 (div. 1978); children: Michael, Meghan; m. Janice Elaine Nickerson, Aug. 1, 1983; children: Brian, Andrew. BS in Physics, MIT, 1963; MS in Physics, U. Pa., 1964, PhD in Physics, 1970. Mem. tech. staff MITRE Corp., Beford, Mass., 1969-73, MIT Lincoln Lab., Lexington, Mass., 1973-83; mgr. systems engring. RCA, Moorestown, N.J., 1983-86; v.p., chief scientist ISC Def. and Space Group, Lancaster, Pa., 1986-88; sr. staff MIT Lincoln Lab., Lexington, Mass., 1988—. Contbr. numerous articles to profl. jours. Mem. IEEE (sr., vice-chmn. radar panel 1983-84, chmn. 1985-86). Mem. United Ch. Christ. Avocations: amateur radio, classical music. Office: MIT Lincoln Lab 244 Wood St Lexington MA 02173-6426

O'DONNELL, ROSIE, comedienne, actress; b. Commack, N.Y., 1962; 1 son: Parker Jaren. Attended, Dickinson Coll., Boston Univ. Appearances include (TV series) Gimme A Break, 1986-87, Stand By Your Man, 1992, Women Aloud, 1992, Stand-up Spotlight, VH-1 (American Comedy award nomination best female performer in a TV special 1994, Cable ACE award nomination best entertainment host 1994); (film) A League of Their Own, 1992, Sleepless in Seattle, 1993 (American Comedy award nomination best supporting female in a motion picture 1994), Another Stakeout, 1993 (American Comedy award nomination best actress in a motion picture 1994), Car 54, Where Are You?, 1994, The Flintstones, 1994, Exit to Eden, 1994; (theatre) Grease (Broadway prodn.), 1994. Office: Internat Creative Mgmt 8942 Wilshire Blvd Beverly Hills CA 90211-1934

O'DONNELL, SCOTT RICHARD, aviation administrator; b. Pitts., Sept. 27, 1950; s. Robert Thomas and Corinne Ann (Phelps) O'D.; m. Patricia Lea Donnelly, Sept. 1, 1978; children: Ronald, Michael, Daniel. BA, Geneva Coll., 1972. Cert. secondary edn. teaching. Tchr. Montour High Sch., McKees Rocks, Pa., 1973-74; project adminstr. Allegheny County Law Dept., Pitts., 1974-76; adminstrv. asst. Allegheny County Police Dept., Pitts., 1976-77; exec. asst. Allegheny County Commr., Pitts., 1977-80; dir. adminstrn. Allegheny County, Pitts., 1980-88, dir. aviation, 1988-94, dir. property assessment appeals, 1994; v.p. airports Lockheed Air Terminals (now Airport Group Internat.), 1994—. Chmn. Higher Edn. Bldg. Authority, Pitts., 1983-90; dir. Allegheny West Authority, Pitts., 1988-94; mem. Mediate, Moon Twp., Pa., 1991-94. Recipient Disting. Alumni award Geneva Coll., Beaver Falls, Pa., 1988, Disting. Svc. award FAA, Jamaica, N.Y., 1992; named Man of Yr. in Law and Govt., Vectors, Pitts., 1992. Mem. Am. Soc. Pub. Adminstrn. (past pres., exec. bd.), Airport Area C. of C. (exec. bd. 1988-94), Airport Coun. Internat., Am. Assn. Airport Execs. Democrat. Presbyterian. Avocation: golf. Home: 20241 Ruston Rd Woodland Hills CA 91364-5642 Office: PO Box 7229 Burbank CA 91510-7229

O'DONNELL, TERRENCE, lawyer; b. N.Y.C., Mar. 3, 1944; s. Emmett and Lorraine (Muller) O'Donnell; m. Margaret Lynne Kidder; children: Stephanie T., Erin K., Victoria L. BS, U.S. Air Force Acad., 1966; JD, Georgetown Law Sch., 1971. Bar: D.C. 1971, U.S. Ct. Appeals (D.C. cir.) 1978, U.S. Ct. Appeals (4th cir.) 1987, U.S. Dist. Ct. Md. 1986, U.S. Ct. Mil. Appeals 1990. Commd. 2d lt. USAF, 1966, advanced through grades to capt.; various positions USAF, Washington and Republic of Vietnam, 1966-72; resigned USAF, 1972; spl. asst. Pres. of U.S., The White House, Washington, 1972-77; appointments sec. Pres. Ford, Washington, 1974-77; assoc. Williams & Connolly, Washington, 1977-82, ptnr., 1982-89; gen. counsel Dept. Def., Washington, 1989-92; ptnr. Williams and Connolly, Washington, 1992—; Presdl. appointee to bd. visitors U.S. Air Force Acad., Colorado Springs, 1982-87, chmn., 1985-86; U.S. corr. and rep. UN Program to Prevent Crime, Washington and N.Y.C., 1977-81; bd. dirs. IGI Inc. Trustee Gerald R. Ford Found., Grand Rapids, Mich., 1987—; mem. Adminstrv. Conf. U.S., 1991-92; mem. claims ct. adv. com., mem. code com. U.S. Ct. Mil. Appeals, 1993—; bd. dirs. Falcon Found., 1988—. Decorated Bronze star; recipient Disting. Pub. Svc. medal Dept. of Def., 1992, Disting. Svc. award U.S. Atty. Gen., 1992. Mem. ABA, D.C. Bar Assn., Fed. Bar Assn., Bar of U.S. Supreme Ct., Bar of U.S. Ct. Appeals, Bar of U.S. Dist. Ct. of Md., Bar of Mil. Ct. Appeals, Bar Fed. Ct. Claims. Home: 5133 Yuma St NW Washington DC 20016-4336 Office: Williams and Connolly 725 12th St NW Washington DC 20005-3901

O'DONNELL, THOMAS FRANCIS, vascular surgeon; b. Providence, R.I., Sept. 7, 1941; s. Thomas Francis and Mary Jo O'Donnell; m. Carolyn Eva Rogean, Aug. 28, 1965; children: Thomas F. III, Hugh Jackson. AB, Harvard Coll., 1963; MD, Tufts U., 1967. Vascular fellow St. Thomas Hosp., London, 1974-75, Mass. Gen. Hosp., Boston, 1975; vascular surgeon, chief vascular surgery New Eng. Med. Ctr., Boston, chmn. dept. surgery; Andrews profl surgery Tufts U. Sch. Medicine; Kinmouth meml. lectr. Vascular Soc. of Great Britain and Ireland, 1989. Author numerous book chpts. on vascular surgery; reviewer jour. publs. Coach Wellesley Youth Work, Wellesley Youth Hockey, 1977-80. Lt. comdr. USN, 1969-71. Fellow Royal Soc. Medicine; mem. Soc. Vascular Surgery (head membership com.), Internat. Vascular Soc. (N.Am. chpt.), N.E. Soc. for Vascular Surgery (pres. 1994). Roman Catholic. Avocations: tennis, golf. Home: 49 Cliff Rd Wellesley MA 02181-3025 Office: New Eng Med Ctr 750 Washington St Boston MA 02111-1533

O'DONNELL, THOMAS LAWRENCE PATRICK, lawyer; b. Taunton, Mass., Aug. 12, 1926; s. Patrick Francis and Ellen Balfe (Brady) O'D.; m. Carol Hodgdon, Feb. 16, 1952; children—Ellen, Thomas, Janet Gael, Christopher Hodgdon. A.B. magna cum laude, Harvard U., 1947, LL.B., 1949. Bar: Mass. 1950. Assoc. Ropes & Gray, Boston, 1949-52, 54-61, ptnr., 1962—, chmn., 1984-90; dir. Rath & Strong, Inc. Trustee, Trustees of Reservations, 1970—, chmn. bd., 1975-76; bd. dirs. Mass. Land Conservation Trust, 1975—, chmn. bd., 1986—; bd. dirs. Mass. Taxpayers Found., 1972—, chmn. bd., 1977-79, 93-95, mem. exec. com., 1976—; bd. dirs. Boston Mcpl. Rsch. Bur., 1965—, chmn. bd., 1967-72; mem. pub. pension task force Mass. Bus. Roundtable, 1983-86; bd. dirs., sec. Jobs for Mass., Inc., 1981-83; moderator Town of Hingham, 1967—; del. Rep. Nat. Conv., 1972, all Rep. State convs., 1960-94; dir. Rep. Club of Mass., 1974—; overseer Harvard U., 1986-92; bd. dirs. United Way Mass. Bay, 1987—, mem. exec. com. 1993—. Lt. USNR, 1944-45, 52-54. Recipient Cushing award Labor Guild of Archdiocese Boston, 1973; Pub. Servant award Sons of Italy, Hingham, 1978; mem. Knights of Malta, 1983—. Fellow Am. Bar Found.; mem. ABA, Mass. Bar Assn., Boston Bar Assn., Am. Arbitration Assn., New England Legal Found. (Mass. adv. coun. 1980—), Indsl. Rels. Rsch. Assn. (pres. Boston chpt. 1980), Harvard Alumni Assn. (bd. dirs. 1978-81; 1st marshal class of 1947). Roman Catholic. Clubs: Harvard of Boston (bd. govs. 1985-91), Union of Boston; Hingham Yacht, Comml. Home: 7 South Ln Hingham MA 02043-2446 Office: Ropes & Gray 1 International Pl Boston MA 02110-2600

O'DONNELL, THOMAS MICHAEL, brokerage firm executive; b. Cleve., Apr. 9, 1936; s. John Michael and Mary L. (Hayes) O'D.; m. Nancy A. Dugan, Feb. 4, 1961; children—Christopher, Colleen, Julie. BBA, U. Notre Dame, 1959; MBA, U. Pa., 1960. Cert. Chartered Fin. Analyst. Fin. analyst Saunders Stiver & Co., Cleve., 1960-65; rsch. dir. McDonald & Co., Cleve., 1965-66, exec. v.p. corp. fin., 1967-83, gen. ptnr., 1968-83; pres. McDonald & Co. Investments, Inc./McDonald & Co. Securities, Cleve., 1984-88; chmn., chief exec. officer McDonald & Co. Securities, Cleve., 1988—; bd. dirs. Seaway Food Town; mem. regional firms adv. com. N.Y. Stock Exch., 1986-92, chmn., 1991-92; dir. C.I.D. Venture Funds. Author: The Why and How of Mergers, 1968. Trustee Cath. Charities, Cleve.; bd. dirs. Greater Cleve. Growth Assn., Inroads Northeast Ohio, PlayHouse Square Found.; adv. bd. Salvation Army; bd. regents St. Ignatius High Sch., Cleve.; steering com. Leadership Cleve. Mem. Cleve. Soc. Security Analysts (cert.), Securities Industry Assn. (dir. 1988-94, chmn. 1993), Union Club, Westwood Country Club, 50 Club Cleve., Pepper Pike Club, Double Eagle Club. Roman Catholic. Avocation: golf. Home: 1325 Timber Lea Ct Cleveland OH 44145-2648 Office: McDonald & Co Securities Inc 800 Superior Ave E Ste 2100 Cleveland OH 44114-2601

O'DONNELL, VICTORIA J., communication educator; b. Greensburg, Pa., Feb. 12, 1938; d. Victor C. and Helen A. (Detar) O'D.; children from previous marriage: Christopher O'Donnell Stupp, Browning William Stupp; m. Paul M. Monaco, Apr. 9, 1993. BA, Pa. State U., 1959, MA, 1961, PhD, 1968. Asst. prof. comm. Midwestern State U., Wichita Falls, Tex., 1965-67; prof. dept. chair comm. U. No. Tex., Denton, 1967-89; prof., dept. chair comms. Ore. State U., Corvallis, 1989-91; prof. comm., basic course dir. Mont. State U., Bozeman, 1991-93, prof. comm., dir. honors program, 1993—; prof. Am. Inst. Fgn. Studies, London, 1988; cons. Arco Oil & Gas, Dallas, 1983-86, Federal Emergency Mgrs. Agy., Salt Lake City, 1986; speechwriter Sen. Mae Yih, Salem, Ore., 1989-91; steering com. Ore. Alliance Film & TV Educators, 1990-91. Author: Introduction to Public Communication, 1992, 2d edit., 1993; co-author: Persuasion, 1982, Propaganda and Persuasion, 1986, 2d edit., 1992; producer: (video) Women, War and Work, 1994. Bd. dirs. Friends of the Family, Denton, 1987-89, Bozeman Film Festival, 1991—; del. Tex. Dem. Convention, Denton, 1976. Grantee Mont. Com. or the Humanities, 1993, Oreg. Coun. for the Humanities, 1991, NEH, 1977. Mem. Nat. Collegiate Honors Coun., Speech Comm. Assn., Internat. Comm. Assn., Univ. Film & Video Assn. (nom. com. 1995, 96, conf. v.p. 1989-91, bd. dirs. 1978-80), Western States Comm. Assn. Home: 290 Low Bench Rd Gallatin Gateway MT 59730-9741 Office: Univ Honors Program Mont State U Bozeman MT 59717

O'DONNELL, WILLIAM JAMES, engineering executive; b. Pitts., June 19, 1935; s. William James and Elizabeth (Rau) O'D.; m. Joanne Mary Kusen, Jan. 31, 1959; children—Suzanne, Janice, William, Thomas, Kerry, Amy. B.S.M.E., Carnegie Inst. Tech., 1957; M.S.M.E., U. Pitts., 1959, Ph.D., 1962. Jr. engr. Westinghouse Research Lab., 1957-58, asso. engr., 1958; with Westinghouse Bettis Atomic Power Lab., West Mifflin, Pa., 1961-70, adv. engr., 1966-70; pres., chmn. bd. O'Donnell & Assos., Inc., Pitts., 1970—. Contbr. numerous articles on engring. and mechanics to profl. jours.; holder patents on processes and devices. Served with C.E. AUS, 1963-64. Recipient Machinery's Achievement award as outstanding mech. designer, 1957, Pi Tau Sigma Gold medal for achievements in engring., 1967, Pressure Vessel and Piping award Am . Soc. of Mechanical Engineers, 1994. Fellow ASME (nat. award for outstanding contbn. to engring. profession 1973, internat. award for best publ. in pressure vessels and poping 1988, Engr. of Yr. award 1988, Pressure Vessel and Piping medal 1994); mem. NSPE, AAAS, ASTM, Soc. Exptl. Mechanics, Am. Nuclear Soc., Am. Soc. Metals Internat., The Minerals, Metals and Materials Soc., Sigma Xi. Home: 3611 Maplevue Dr Bethel Park PA 15102-1423 Office: O'Donnell Consulting Engrs 3611 Maplevue Dr Bethel Park PA 15102-1423

O'DONOHUE, WALTER JOHN, JR., medical educator; b. Washington, Sept. 23, 1934; s. Walter John and Mavis Leota (Terry) O'D.; m. Cynthia Ann Halminitoller, Aug. 10, 1957 (div. 1978); 1 child, Diane Louise; m. Maria Theresa Sauer, Nov. 27, 1978; children: Walter John III, Mary Theresa. BA, Va. Mil. Inst., 1957; MD, Med. Coll. Va., 1961. Diplomate Am. Bd. Internal Medicine, Am. Bd. Pulmonary Medicine. Resident internal medicine Med. Coll. Va., Richmond, 1961-63, 65-66, chief med. resident, 1966-67, cardio-pulmonary fellow, 1967-69, asst. prof. medicine, 1968-73, assoc. prof., 1973-77; prof. Creighton U., Omaha, Nebr., 1977—, chief pulmonary medicine div., 1977—, chmn. dept. medicine, 1985—. Editor: Current Advances in Respiratory Care, 1984, Long-term Oxygen Therapy: Scientific Basis and Clinical Application, 1995; contbr. over 100 articles to med. jours., chpts. to books. Served to capt. M.C., U.S. Army, 1963-65. Fellow ACP, Am. Coll. Chest PHysicians (regent 1986-88, gov. for Nebr. 1982-88); mem. AMA (CPT adv. com. 1992—), Am. Lung Assn. (bd. dirs. 1981-87), Nebr. Lung Assn. (bd. dirs., pres. 1979-81), Am. Assn. Respiratory Care (chmn. bd. med. advisors 1986-87), Assn. Profs. Medicine, Nat. Assn. Med. Dirs. on Respiratory Care (pres. 1995-97). Republican. Roman Catholic. Avocations: hunting, fishing. Home: 12773 Izard St Omaha NE 68154-1243 Office: Creighton U Sch Medicine 601 N 30th St Omaha NE 68131-2137

O'DONOVAN, LEO JEREMIAH, university president, theologian, priest; b. N.Y.C., Apr. 24, 1934; s. Leo J. Jr. O'D. AB, Georgetown U., 1956; Licentiate in Philosophy, Fordham U., 1961; STB, Woodstock Coll., 1966, Licentiate in Sacred Theology, 1967; ThD, U. Münster, Fed. Republic Germany, 1971. Joined S.J., 1957, ordained priest Roman Cath. Ch., 1966. Instr. philosophy Loyola Coll., Balt., 1961-63; asst. prof. Woodstock (Md.) Coll., 1971-74; assoc. prof. Weston Sch. Theology, Cambridge, Mass., 1974-81, prof., 1981-89; pres. Georgetown U., Washington, 1989—; provincial asst. formation Md. Province S.J., Balt., 1985-88; cons. Nat. Conf. Cath. Bishops, Washington, 1986-89; vis. fellow Woodstock Theol. Ctr.; bd. dirs. The Riggs Nat. Bank. Co-editor: The Society of Jesus and Higher Education in America, 1965; (author preface) Faithful Witness: Foundations of Theology for Today's Church, 1989; assoc. editor Jour. Am. Acad. Religion, 1985-89; mem. adv. bd. America mag., 1985-89; contbr. numerous articles to America, Washington Post, Theol. Studies, Communio, Cross Currents. Bd. dirs. U. Detroit Mercy, 1986—; vice chair Consortium of Univs. of Washington Met. Area, 1993-94, chair, 1994—, trustee, 1989—; mem. campaign for communities com. Local Initiatives Support Corp., 1993—; mem. exec. com. Fed. City Coun., 1993-95; bd. dirs. Nat. Assn. Ind. Colls. and Univs., 1991-94, Consortium on Financing Higher Edn., 1990—; active Bus.-Higher Edn. Forum, 1989—, Nat. Coun. on Arts, 1994—. Fulbright scholar Fulbright Found., U. Lyon, France, 1956-57; Danforth fellow Danforth Found., 1956-71; Assn. Theol. Schs. grantee on teaching, 1978-79. Fellow Soc. for Values in Higher Edn.; mem. Assn. of Jesuit Colls. and Univs. (fed. rels. com. 1994—), Assn. Cath. Colls. and Univs. (bd. dirs. 1994—), Boston Theol. Soc., University Club. Office: Georgetown U Office of President 37th O St NW Washington DC 20057

O'DOR, RON, physiologist, marine biology educator; b. Kansas City, Mo., Sept. 20, 1944; s. Claude Marvin O'Dor and Opal LaMoyne (Sears) Mathes; m. Janet Ruth Spiller, Dec. 30, 1967; children: Matthew Arnold, Stephen Roderick. AA, El Camino Coll., 1965; AB, U. Calif., Berkeley, 1967; PhD, U. B.C., 1971. From asst. prof. to prof. Dalhousie U., Halifax, N.S., 1973—; dir. Aquatron Lab., Halifax, 1986-93; summer scientist Laboratoire Arago, Banyuls-sur-Mer, France, 1979-85; vis. scientist Pacific Biol. Sta., Nanaimo, B.C., 1980, U. Papua New Guinea, Motupore Island, 1989-91, Port Elizabeth Mus., South Africa, 1994; vis. prof. U. B.C., Vancouver, 1986-87; sessional prof. Bamfield (B.C.) Marine Sta., 1987; cons. UN, Rome, 1987—; adv. space stas. Can. Space Agy., Ottawa, 1992—; mem. mgmt. com. Ocean Prodn. Enhancement Network, Halifax, 1993-95. Author, editor: Cephalopod Fishery Biology, 1993, Physiology of Cephalopod Molluscs, 1994; contbg. author Cephalopod Life Cycles, Vol. I, 1983, Vol. II, 1987; contbr. articles and revs. to profl. jours. Scholar Med. Rsch. Coun. Can., 1968; fellow MRC, Cambridge U., Eng., 1971-73, Stazione Zoologica, Naples, Italy, 1971-73; recipient Hon. Mention Rolex Awards Enterprise, 1987. Mem. Can. Soc. Zoologists (councillor 1989-92), Can. Fedn. Biological Socs.,Am. Soc. Zoologists, Am. Soc. Gravitational and Space Biology, Cephalopod Internat. Adv. coun. (councillor, pres. 1988-91), Phi Beta Kappa. Achievements include co-development of acoustic pressure transducer/transmitters and radio-linked tracking systems for monitoring cephalopod bioenergetics in nature; co-organization of projects in the Azores, South Africa and Papua New Guinea to monitor squid and nautilus, first international cephalopod research conference in Japan, investigation for Aquatic Research Facility for Space Shuttle. Home: 1181 South Park St, Halifax, NS Canada B3H 2W9 Office: Dalhousie University, Biology Dept, Halifax, NS Canada B3H 4J1

O'DORISIO, THOMAS MICHAEL, internal medicine educator, researcher; b. Denver, May 29, 1943; s. Angelo Benedict and Olga Ester (Zarlengo) O'D.; m. M. Sue Wedemeyer; children: Joel, Rachelle, Nathan. BS, Regis Coll., 1965; MS in Anatomy, Creighton U., 1967, MD, 1971. Diplomate Am. Bd. Internal Medicine, Nat. Bd. Med. Examiners. Intern Creighton U., Omaha, 1971-72; resident Ohio State U., Columbus, 1972-74, fellow, 1974-77, asst. prof., 1977-79, assoc. prof., 1979-84, asst. program dir. clin. research ctr., 1984—, prof. medicine, 1984—, prof. physiology, 1985—, prof. pathology, 1993—, prof. human nutrition, 1993—, dir. div. endocrinology, diabetes and metabolism, 1989—; chmn. human subjects rev. bd. Ohio State U., 1987-89. Recipient Prof. of Yr. award Ohio State U. Class of 1983, tchg. awards from sr. class of 1981, 82, 84, 85, 89, 90, Alumni Tchg. award, 1995; grantee NIH, 1987—, Nat. Cancer Inst., 1974-77, 91, 92. Fellow Am. Assn. Clin. Endocrinology; mem. ACP, Am. Fedn. Clin. Rsch., Am. Gastroenterology Assn., Ctrl. Soc. Clin. Rsch., Endocrinology Soc. Democrat. Roman Catholic. Club: St. Thomas Moore (Newman Ctr.). Avocation: golf, skiing. Office: Ohio State U Hosp 1581 Dodd Dr Columbus OH 43210-1228

O'DOWD, DONALD DAVY, retired university administrator; b. Manchester, N.H., Jan. 23, 1927; s. Hugh Davy and Laura (Morin) O'D.; m.

Janet Louise Fithian, Aug. 23, 1953; children: Daniel D., Diane K., James E., John M. BA summa cum laude, Dartmouth Coll., 1951; postgrad. (Fulbright fellow), U. Edinburgh, Scotland, 1951-52; MA, Harvard U., 1955, PhD, 1957. Instr., asst. prof. psychology, dean freshmen Wesleyan U., Middletown, Conn., 1955-60; assoc. prof., prof. of psychology, dean Univ. Oakland Univ., Rochester, Mich., 1960-65, provost, 1965-70; pres. Oakland U., Rochester, Mich., 1970-80; exec. vice chancellor SUNY, Albany, 1980-84; pres. U. of Alaska Statewide System, 1984-90. Chmn. U.S. Arctic Rsch. Commn.; sr. cons. Assn. Governing Bds. of Univs. and Colls. Carnegie Corp. fellow, 1965-66. Mem. Am. Psychol. Assn., AAAS, Phi Beta Kappa, Sigma Xi. Home and Office: 1550 La Vista Del Oceano Santa Barbara CA 93109-1739

O'DRISCOLL, CORNELIUS JOSEPH, lawyer; b. Skibbereen, Ireland, Mar. 19, 1936; came to U.S., 1951; s. Cornelius and catherine O'D.; m. Beverly Elizabeth Brotemarkle, Feb. 4, 1972; children: Cara Suzanne, Catherine Elise. BS, Boston Coll., 1957; LLB, Suffolk U., 1965; postgrad., George Washington U., 1966-67. Bar: Mass. 1965, U.S. Dist. Ct. D.C. 1967, U.S. Dist. Ct. Md. 1968, Ariz. 1969, U.S. Dist. Ct. Ariz. 1969, U.S. Ct. Appeals (9th cir.) 1969, U.S. Supreme Ct. Atty. pvt. practice, Boston, 1965-66, U.S. Govt., Washington, 1966-67; atty. pvt. practice, Washington, 1967-69, Phoenix, 1969—; judge pro tem Phoenix Mcpl. Ct., 1993—. Bd. dirs. Crossroads, Inc., Phoenix, 1993-94, Family Svc. Agy., 1994—, Ctr. for New Directions, 1993-94. Fellow Ariz. Bar Found.; mem. Mass. Bar Assn., D.C. Bar Assn., State Bar Ariz., KC (Grand Knight). Office: 4630 N 7th St Ste 109 Phoenix AZ 85014-3807

O'DRISCOLL, PERRY R., archbishop. Archbishop of Ontario The Anglican Ch. Can.

ODRON, EDWARD ANDREW, supermarket executive; b. Chgo., Mar. 28, 1938; s. Edward John and Emily Mary (Rakicky) O.; m. Mary Jean Howe; children: Edward Russell, Scott Andrew. BS, Drake U., 1960. Produce buyer Atlantic and Pacific Tea Co., Chgo., 1960-65, Lucky Stores, Milan, Ill., 1965-71; produce buyer, merchandiser Lucky Stores, Annandale, Va., 1971-74, grocery buyer, merchandiser, 1974-76, dist. mgr., 1976-77; v.p., produce specialist Lucky Stores, Milan, 1977-85; corp. v.p., produce specialist Lucky Stores, Dublin, Calif., 1985-86; v.p. produce and svc. deli/bakery sales and merchandising Lucky Stores, San Leandro, Calif., 1986—; bd. dirs. 5-a-Day Produce for Better Health. Mem. United Fresh and Vegetable Assn. (retail merchandising bd. 1985-87, chmn. retail merchandising bd. 1986-87), Produce Mktg. Assn. (bd. dirs. 1989-92), San Joaquin Kennel Club (pres. 1994—). Avocation: showing purebred dogs. Home: 10367 Capewood Ln Stockton CA 95212-9447 Office: Lucky Stores Inc 1701 Marina Blvd San Leandro CA 94577-4230

ODUM, EUGENE PLEASANTS, ecologist, educator; b. Lake Sunapee, N.H., Sept. 17, 1913; s. Howard Washington and Anna Louise (Kranz) O.; m. Martha Ann Huff, Nov. 18, 1940; 1 child, William Eugene. A.B., U. N.C., 1934, A.M., 1936; Ph.D., U. Ill., 1939; hon. degree, Hofstra U., 1980, Ferum Coll., 1986, U. N.C., Ashville, 1990. Instr. Western Res. U., Cleve., 1936-37; resident biologist Edmund Niles Huyck Preserve, Rensselaerville, N.Y., 1939-40; instr., asst. prof., assoc. prof., prof. U. Ga., Athens, 1940-58, Alumni Found. disting. prof. zoology, 1957-85, prof. emeritus, 1985—, Callaway prof. ecology, 1973-85, prof. emeritus, 1985—, dir. Inst. Ecology, 1960-65, dir. emeritus Inst. Ecology, 1985—; instr. in charge marine ecology tng. program Marine Biol. Lab., Woods Hole, Mass., 1957-61; cons. and lectr. in field. Author: Fundamentals of Ecology, 3d edit., 1971, Ecology, 1963, 3d edit., 1989; co-author: Birds of Georgia, 1945, (with H.H. Brimley) A North Carolina Naturalist, 1949, Basic Ecology, 1983; contbr. articles to profl. jours. Recipient Michael award U. Ga., 1945, Internat. award L'Institut de la Vie, Paris, 1975, Tyler Ecology award, Educator of Yr. award Nat. Wildlife Fedn., 1977, Crafoord prize Royal Swedish Acad., 1987, Disting. Alumni Svc. award U. N.C., U. Ill., Theodore Roosevelt Disting. Svc. award, 1991; named Scientist of Yr., State of Ga., 1968, Conservationist of Yr., 1976, NSF sr. postdoctoral fellow, 1958-59. Fellow AAAS, Am. Acad. Arts and Scis., Am. Ornithologists Union; mem. Nat. Acad. Sci., Ecol. Soc. Am. (pres. 1964-65, Mercer award 1956, Eminent Ecologist's award 1975), Am. Inst. Biol. Scis. (Disting. Service award 1978), Estuarine Rsch. Fedn., Internat. Soc. Ecol. Econs., Am. Naturalist Soc., Sigma Xi (exec. com. 1965-67), Phi Sigma, Phi Kappa Phi. Home: Beech Creek Rd Athens GA 30606

OEFFINGER, JOHN CLAYTON, research foundation executive, educator; b. Ft. Sill, Okla., Oct. 30, 1952; s. Jack Clayton and Sally Josephine (Lehman) O.; m. Kathryn Gayle Pourteau, May ll, 1975; 1 child, John Clayton II. BA, Tex. A&M U., 1976, postgrad. in pol. sci., 1976-77. Mgr. congl. campaign T. Chet Edwards, Duncanville, Tex., 1977-78; congl. campaign asst. Congressman James Mattox, Dallas, 1978, dist. rep., 1979-80, mgr. congl. campaign, 1980, dist. rep., 1980-81; dir. office of grants mgmt. Baylor U. Med. Ctr., Dallas, 1981-82; v.p. Baylor U. Med. Ctr. Found., Dallas, 1982; founder, v.p. Baylor U. Rsch. Found., Dallas, 1982-88; also bd. dirs. Baylor Research Found., Dallas; pres., sec., treas., bd. dir., CEO Tex. Hosp. Edn. and Rsch. Found., Austin, Tex., 1988—; sr. v.p., edn. & info. technologist Tex. Hosp. Assn., 1995—; co-chmn., co-founder Internat. Informatics Access, Dallas, 1986-87; internat. cons. UN Indsl. Devel. Orgn., 1987—; cons. Pan Am. Health Orgn., Washington, 1986-88; editorial adv. bd. Telematics & Informatics, Pergamon Press, 1988—; adv. bd. MEDNET Telecommunication Project Health Sci. Ctr. Tex. Tech. U., 1989-93; startup Ed Venture Learning Network for Health Care Systems, 1994; bd. dirs. Tex. Higher Edn. Coord. Bd., Health Profls. Edn. Adv. Bd. Founding mem., bd. dirs. MSC Enrichment Fund, 1979-84; campaign coord. dist. 7 Dallas Area Rapid Transit Bond Election, Dallas, 1984, councilman John Evans, 1985, 87, Opportunity Dallas, fall 1987. Grantee Apple Corp., 1984-94; named one of Outstanding Young Men of Am. U.S. Jaycees, 1993. Mem. AAAS, Nat. Coun. Univ. Rsch. Adminstrs., Tex. Tech. Transfer Assn. (bd. dirs. 1987), Dallas C. of C. (internat. com. 1986-87), Internat. Info. Access. Democrat. Roman Catholic. Lodge: Rotary (dir. internat. svc. Fair Park club Dallas 1987-88). Avocations: golf, computer communications, southern historical collector. Office: Tex Hosp Edn & Rsch Found PO Box 15587 Austin TX 78761-5587

OEHLER, RICHARD WILLIAM, lawyer; b. N.Y.C., Nov. 24, 1950; s. John Montgomery and Florence Mae (Jahn) O.; m. Linda Tyson. BA, Dartmouth Coll., 1972; JD, Harvard U., 1976. Bar: Calif. 1976, Wash. 1987, D.C. 1988, U.S. Dist. Ct. (no. dist.) Calif. 1976, U.S. Dist. Ct. Wash. 1987, U.S. Claims Ct. 1979, U.S. Ct. Appeals (fed. cir.) 1982, U.S. Ct. Appeals (9th cir.) 1976. Assoc. Pillsbury, Madison & Sutro, San Francisco, 1976-78; trial atty. U.S. Dept. Justice, Washington, 1978-87; of counsel Perkins Coie, Seattle, 1987-90, ptnr., 1990—. Mem. ABA, Nat. Contract Mgmt. Assn. (Spl. Achievement award 1990-92), Wash. State Bar Assn. Office: Perkins Coie 1201 3rd Ave Fl 40 Seattle WA 98101-3000

OEHLERT, WILLIAM HERBERT, JR., cardiologist, administrator, educator; b. Murphysboro, Ill., Sept. 11, 1942; s. William Hebert Sr. and Geneva Mae (Roberts) O.; m. L. Keith Brown, Mar. 14, 1976; children: Emily Jane, Amanda Elizabeth. BA, So. Ill. U., 1967; MD, Washington U., St. Louis, 1967. Diplomate Nat. Bd. Med. Examiners, Am. Bd. Internal Medicine, Am. Bd. Cardiovascular Disease, North Am. Soc. Pacing and Electrophysiology. Intern Union Meml. Hosp., Balt., 1967-68, resident, 1968-69; resident U. Iowa, Iowa City, 1969-70, cardiology fellow, 1970-72; asst. prof. medicine, dir. coronary care units U. Okla. Health Sci. Ctr., Oklahoma City, 1972-74, asst. clin. prof. medicine, 1974-82, assoc. clin. prof. medicine, 1982-88, clin. prof. medicine, 1988—; chmn. dept. cardiology Bapt. Med. Ctr., 1992-95; pvt. practice Oklahoma City, 1993—; med. dir. cardiovascular svcs. Bapt. Med. Ctr., 1993-95; pres. Cardiovascular Clinic, Oklahoma City, 1987-91, chmn. exec. com., 1987-91; pres. med. dir. Cardiovascular Imaging Svcs. Corp., Oklahoma City, 1987-92; v.p. Plaza Med. Group, 1992-93; CEO W.H. Oehlert, MD, P.C., 1993—. Author: Arrhythmias, 1973, Cardiovascular Drugs, 1976; contbr. articles to profl. jours. Fellow Am. Heart Assn. (nat. program com. 1979-82, pres. Okla. affiliate 1985-86, bd. dirs. 1974-88, ACLS nat. affiliate faculty 1987-90), Am. Coll. Cardiology; mem. AMA, ACP, Nat. Assn. Residents and Interns, Am. Soc. Internal Medicine, Am. Coll. Physician Execs., Okla. County Med. Assn. (chmn. quality of care com. 1990-91), Okla. State Med. Assn., Okla. City Clin. Soc., Okla. Cardiac Soc. (pres. 1978-79), Osler Soc., Soc. Nuclear Medicine, Wilderness Med. Soc., Stewart Wolf Soc., Phi Eta Sigma, Phi Kappa Phi. Home and Office: 3017 Rock Ridge Pl Oklahoma City OK 73120-5713

OEHME, FREDERICK WOLFGANG, medical researcher and educator; b. Leipzig, Germany, Oct. 14, 1933; came to U.S., 1934; s. Friedrich Oswald and Frieda Betha (Wohlgamuth) O.; m. Nancy Beth MacAdam, Aug. 6, 1960 (div. June 1981); children: Stephen Frederick, Susan Lynn, Deborah Ann, Heidi Beth; m. Pamela Sheryl Ford, Oct. 2, 1981; 1 child, April Virginia. BS in Biol. Scis., Cornell U., 1957, DVM, 1958; MS in Toxicology and Medicine, Kans. State U., 1962; DMV in Pathology, Justus Liebig U., Giessen, Germany, 1964; PhD in Toxicology, U. Mo., 1969. Diplomate Am. Bd. Toxicology, Am. Bd. Vet. Toxicology, Acad. Toxicological Scis. Resident intern, Large Animal and Ambulatory Clinic Cornell U., 1957-58; gen. practice vet. medicine, 1958-59; from asst. to assoc. prof. medicine Coll. Vet. Medicine Kans. State U., 1959-66, 69-73, dir. comparative toxicology labs., 1969—, prof. toxicology, medicine and physiology Coll. Vet. Medicine, 1974—; postdoctoral research fellow in toxicology, NIH U. Mo., 1966-69; cons. FDA, Washington, Ctr. for Vet. Medicine, Rockville, Md., Animal Care com. U. Kans., Lawrence, 1969-76, Syntex Corp., Palo Alto, Calif., 1976-77; mem. sci. adv. panel on PBB Gov.'s Office, State of Mich., 1976-77, Coun. for Agrl. Sci. and Tech. Task Force on Toxicity, Toxicology and Environ. Hazard, 1976-83; cons., mem. adv. group on pesticides EPA, Cin., 1977—; expert state and fed. witness; advisor WHO, Geneva; presenter more than 550 papers to profl. meetings; numerous other activities. Author over 650 books and articles on toxicology and vet. medicine; editor, pub. Vet. Toxicology, 1970-76, Vet. and Human Toxicology, 1977—; assoc. editor Toxicology Letters; mem. editl. bd. Am. Jour. Vet. Rsch., 1975-83, Toxicology, 1979-85, Clin. Toxicology, Jour. Toxicologie Medicale, Toxicology and Indsl. Health, Poisindex, Jour. Analytical Toxicology, Companion Animal Practice; reviewer Toxicology and Applied Pharmacology, Jour. Agrl. and Food Chemistry, Spectroscopy, numerous others. Mem. council Luth. Ch. Am., sr. choir, numerous coms., adv. council Cub Scouts Am., Eagle Scouts, mgr., coach Little League Baseball; council rep., treas. area council, various coms. PTA; mem. Manhattan Civic Theatre; bd. trustees Manhattan Marlin Swim Team; dir. meet Little Apple Invitational Swim Meet, 1984. Recipient Disting. Grad. Faculty award Kans. State U., 1977-79, Dir.'s Letter of Commendation, FDA, 1983, Kenneth P. DuBois award Midwest Soc. Toxicology, 1991, Kenneth F. Lampe award Am. Acad. Clin. Toxicology, 1993, John Doull award Ctrl. States Soc. Toxicology, 1994, medal Azabu U., 1994, Silver award Aristotelian U., 1995, others; project fellow Morris Animal Found., 1967-69. Fellow Am. Acad. Clin. Toxicology (charter, past pres., numerous coms.), Am. Acad. Vet. and Comparative Toxicology (past sec.-treas., numerous coms.); mem. Soc. Toxicology (past pres., numerous coms.), World Fedn. Clin. Toxicology Ctrs. and Poison Control Ctrs. (past pres.), Soc. Toxicologic Pathologists, N.Y. Acad. Scis., Am. Vet. Med. Assn. (com. on environmentology 1971-73, adv. com. council on biol. and therapeutic agts. 1971-74, various others), Nat. Ctr. Toxicological Rsch. (vet. toxicology rep. sci. adv. bd.), Nat. Rsch. Coun. (subcom. on organic contaminants in drinking water, safe drinking water com., adv. ctr. on toxicology assembly life scis. 1976-77, panel on toxicology marine bd., assembly of engring. 1976-79, com. on vet. med. scis. assembly life scis. 1976-78), Nat. Ctr. for Toxicological Rsch. (grad. edn. subcom., sci. adv. bd. 1974-77), Cornell U. Athletic Assn, Omega Tau Sigma, Phi Zeta, Sigma Xi, numerous others. Republican. Clubs: Cornell U. Crew; Manhattan Square Dance. Avocations: hist. readings, sci. writings, nature tours and walks, travel. Home: 148 S Dartmouth Dr Manhattan KS 66502 Office: Comparative Toxicology Labs Kans State U Manhattan KS 66506

OEHME, REINHARD, physicist, educator; b. Wiesbaden, Germany, Jan. 26, 1928; came to U.S., 1956; s. Reinhold and Katharina (Kraus) O.; m. Mafalda Pisani, Nov. 5, 1952. Dr. rer. nat., U. Goettingen, Germany, 1951; Diplom Physiker, U. Frankfurt am Main, Germany, 1948. Asst. Max Planck Inst. Physics, Goettingen, 1949-53; research asso. Fermi Inst. Nuclear Studies, U. Chgo., 1954-56; mem. faculty dept. physics and Fermi Inst., 1958—, prof. physics, 1964—; mem. Inst. Advanced Studies, Princeton, 1956-58; vis. prof. Inst. de Física Teórica, São Paulo, Brazil, 1952-53, U. Md., 1957, U. Vienna, Austria, 1961, Imperial Coll., London, Eng., 1963-64, U. Karlsruhe, Fed. Republic Germany, 1974, 75, 77, U. Tokyo, 1976, 88; vis. scientist Internat. Centre Theoretical Physics, Miramare-Trieste, Italy, Brookhaven Nat. Lab., Lawrence Radiation Lab., U. Calif., Berkeley, CERN, Geneva, Switzerland, Max Planck Inst., Munich, Fed. Republic Germany, Rsch. Inst. for Fundamental Physics, Kyoto (Japan) U. Author articles in field, chpts. in books. Guggenheim fellow, 1963-64; recipient Humboldt award, 1974, Japan Soc. for Promotion of Sci. Fellowship awards, 1976, 88. Fellow Am. Phys. Soc. Office: Univ of Chicago Enrico Fermi Inst 5640 S Ellis Ave Chicago IL 60637-1433

OEHME, WOLFGANG WALTER, landscape architect; b. Chemnitz, Germany, May 18, 1930; came to the U.S., 1957; s. Walter Gustav and Elisabeth Elsa (Neumann) O.; 1 child, Roland. Degree in horticulture, Bitterfeld Trade Sch., 1950; degree in landscape architecture, U. Berlin, 1954. Exch. student Waterer & Sons Nurseries, Bagshot, United Kingdom, 1954-56; landscape architect Baltimore County Planning, Towson, Md., 1958-65, The Rouse Co., Columbia, Md., 1965-66; asst. prof. U. Pa., Phila., 1962-64, U. Ga., Athens, 1965; pvt. practice Balt., 1965-74; CEO Oehme, Van Sweden and Assocs., Inc., Washington, 1974—. Co-author: Bold Romantic Gardens, 1990, Gardening with Water, 1995, Process Architecture, 1996. Fellow Am. Soc. Landscape Architects; mem. Perennial Plant Assn. (Disting. Svc. 1988), Garden Writers Assn. (Quill and Trowel award 1991). Home: 511 A W Joppa Rd Baltimore MD 21204 Office: 800 G St SE Washington DC 20003-2816

OEHMLER, GEORGE COURTLAND, corporate executive; b. Pitts., May 6, 1926; s. Rudolph Christian and Virgia Sylvia (Stark) O.; B.S. in Indsl. Engring, Pa. State U., 1950; m. Martha Jane Swagler, July 3, 1954; children—Wendy Lynn, Christy Ann, Geoffrey Colin. Indsl. engr. Allegheny Ludlum Steel Corp., Pitts., 1953-54, salesman, 1954-60, mgr. export sales, 1960-67, mgr. flat rolled products, 1967-68, asst. to chmn., 1968-73, v.p. internat., 1973-75, v.p. internat. Allegheny Internat., Inc., Pitts., 1975-81, v.p. public and internat. affairs, 1981-86; pres., chief operating officer World Affairs Council, Pitts., 1987—; dir. Mathews Internat. Corp., 1982—; Mem. exec. bd. Pa. State U. Alumni Council, 1976-82; bd. dirs. United Way Allegheny County, 1982-84, Pitts. Ballet, 1982-89, Pitts. Pub. Theater, 1986-95, Mendelssohn Choir of Pitts., 1987—. With U.S. Army, 1944-46, 51-52. Mem. Am. Iron and Steel Inst., Assn. Iron and Steel Engrs., Machinery and Allied Products Inst. (internat. and pub. affairs councils), World Affairs Council Pitts. (chmn. 1980-82, dir.), Pitts. Council for Internat. Visitors (dir. 1975-87, pres. 1976-78), Greater Pitts. C. of C. Republican. Presbyterian. Clubs: Duquesne, Longue Vue (gov. 1982-84). Home: 321 Braddsley Dr Pittsburgh PA 15235-5302 Office: World Affairs Coun Pitts 400 Oliver Ave Pittsburgh PA 15219-1807

OELBAUM, HAROLD, lawyer, corporate executive; b. Bklyn., Jan. 9, 1931; s. Max and Betty (Molomet) O.; m. Nancy Rothkopf, June 28, 1968; children—Louise, Andrew, Jennifer. A.B., Franklin and Marshall Coll., 1952; J.D., Harvard, 1955; LL.M., N.Y. U., 1959. Bar: N.Y. 1955, Mass. 1960. Atty. Hellerstein & Rosier, Esqs., N.Y.C., 1955-59; gen. atty. Raytheon Co., Lexington, Mass., 1959-68; sr. atty. Revlon, Inc., N.Y.C., 1968-72; pres., dir., mem. exec. com. Kane-Miller Corp., Tarrytown, N.Y., 1972—. Home: 77 Chestnut Rd Bedford Corners NY 10549 Office: Kane-Miller Corp 555 White Plains Rd Tarrytown NY 10591-5109

OELGESCHLAGER, GUENTHER KARL, publisher; b. Jersey City, Apr. 19, 1934; s. Herman Wilhelm and Frieda Johanna (Onken) O.; m. Jacqueline L. Braley, July 16, 1962; children: Stacey, Lauren, Amy. BA cum laude, Princeton U., 1958; postgrad., Columbia U., 1959. Nat. sales mgr. Harper & Row Pubs., N.Y.C., 1959-67; dir. coll. div. F.A. Praeger Co., N.Y.C., 1968; v.p., gen. mgr. D.C. Heath & Co., Lexington, Mass., 1969-72; pres., dir. Ballinger Pub. Co., Cambridge, Mass., 1973-78; v.p., dir. J.B. Lippincott Co., Phila., 1973-78; pres. Oelgeschlager, Gunn & Hain, Pubs., Inc., Cambridge, 1979—; pres., bd. dirs. Falcon Software Inc., Wentworth, N.H. With U.S. Army, 1954-56. Mem. Software Pubs. Assn. Democrat. Episcopalian. Home: 245 Merriam St Weston MA 02193-1350

OELMAN, ROBERT SCHANTZ, retired manufacturing executive; b. Dayton, Ohio, June 9, 1909; s. William Walter and Edith (Schantz) O.; m. Mary Coolidge, Oct. 17, 1936; children: Bradford Coolidge, Robert Schantz, Jr., Kathryn Peirce, Martha Forrer. A.B. summa cum laude, Dartmouth Coll., 1931, M.A., 1963, LL.D. (hon.), 1981; postgrad., U. Vienna, 1931-32; H.H.D. (hon.), U. Dayton, 1959; LL.D. (hon.), Miami U., Oxford, Ohio, 1960, Wright State U., 1976; L.H.D. (hon.), Wilmington Coll. (Ohio), 1965. With NCR Corp., Dayton, 1933-80; asst. to pres. NCR Corp., 1942-45, v.p., 1946-50, exec. v.p., 1950-57, pres., 1957-62, chmn., pres., 1962-64, chmn., 1962-74, chmn. exec. com., 1974-80, dir., 1948-80; ret., 1980; former dir. Koppers Co., Inc., Pitts., Winters Nat. Bank & Trust Co., Dayton, Citibank and Citicorp, N.Y.C., Ford Motor Co., Detroit., Ohio Bell Telephone, Cleve., Procter & Gamble, Cin. Trustee Dartmouth Coll., 1961-76; Mem. Bus. Council, 1965—; chmn. bd. trustees Wright State U., 1961-76; bd. dirs. Miami Conservancy, 1967-79, pres., 1975-79; chmn. Air Force Mus. Found., Dayton, 1970-80; trustee C.F. Kettering Med. Center, 1971-80; ind. dir. tournament policy bd. PGA Tour, Ponte Vedra, Fla., 1974-83, chmn., 1978-83. Mem. Country Club of Fla., Ocean Club of Fla., Augusta Nat. Club (Ga.), Delray Beach Yacht Club. Clubs: Country of Fla., Ocean of Fla., Augusta (Ga.), Delray Beach Yacht.

OEMLER, AUGUSTUS, JR., astronomy educator; b. Savannah, Ga., Aug. 15, 1945; s. Augustus and Isabelle Redding (Clarke) O.; children: W. Clarke, Bryan S. AB, Princeton U., 1969; MS, Calif. Inst. Tech., 1970, PhD, 1974. Postdoctoral assoc. Kitt Peak Nat. Obs., Tucson, 1974-75; instr. astronomy Yale U., New Haven, 1975-77, asst. prof., 1977-79, assoc. prof., 1979-83, prof., 1983-96, chmn. dept., 1988-96; dir. obs. Carnegie Instn. Washington, Pasadena, Calif., 1996—. Contbr. articles to profl. jours. Alfred P. Sloan fellow, 1978-80. Mem. Am. Astronom. Soc., Internat. Astronom. Union. Republican. Roman Catholic. Home: 88 Mulberry Farms Rd Guilford CT 06437-3215 Office: Carnegie Obs 813 Santa Barbara St Pasadena CA 91101

OERTEL, GOETZ K. H., physicist, professional association administrator; b. Stuhm, Germany, Aug. 24, 1934; came to U.S., 1957; s. Egon F.K. and Margarete W. (Wittek) O.; m. Brigitte Beckmann, June 17, 1960; children: Ines M.H. Oertel Downing, Carsten K.R. Abitur, Robert Mayer, Heilbronn, Fed. Republic Germany, 1953; vordiplom, U. Kiel, Fed. Republic Germany, 1956; PhD, U. Md., 1963. Aerospace engr. Langley Ctr. NASA, Hampton, Va., 1963-68; chief solar physics NASA, Washington, 1968-75; analyst Office of Mgmt. and Budget, Washington, 1974-75; head astronomy div. NSF, Washington, 1975; dir. def. and civilian nuclear waste programs U.S. Dept. Energy, Washington, 1975-83; acting mgr. sav. river ops. office Aiken, S.C., 1983-84; dep. mgr. ops. office Albuquerque, 1984-85; dep. asst. sec. EH Washington, 1985-86; pres. Assn. Univs. for Rsch. in Astronomy, Inc. (AURA, Inc.), Washington, 1986—, also bd. dirs.; cons. Los Alamos Lab., N.Mex., 1987-92, Westinghouse Electric, 1988—; bd. dirs. AURA, Inc., Inst. for Sci. and Soc., Ellensburg, Wash., IUE Corp., Inst. for Info., George Mason U., Nat. Rsch. Coun., U.S. Com. for CODATA, 1993—. Patentee in field. Fulbright grantee, 1957. Fellow AAAS; mem. Am. Phys. Soc., Am. Astron. Soc., Internat. Astron. Union, N.Y. Acad. Scis., Internat. U. Exch., Inc. (bd. dirs.), Cosmos Club, Sigma Xi. Lutheran. Avocations: fitness, chess, computing. Home: 9609 Windcroft Way Potomac MD 20854-2864 Office: Assn Univs for Rsch in Astronomy Ste 701 1625 Massachusetts Ave NW Washington DC 20036-2212

OESTERLE, DALE ARTHUR, law educator; b. West Lafayette, Ind., Oct. 25, 1950; s. Eric Clark and Germaine Dora (Seelye) O.; m. Patricia Marie Pessemier, May 6,1972; children: Helen, Ann, William. BA, U. Mich., 1972, M in Pub. Policy, 1974, JD, 1975. Bar: N.Y., Va. Law clk. to Robert R. Merhige, Jr. U.S. Dist. Ct., Richmond, Va., 1975-76; assoc. Hunton & Williams, Richmond, 1976-79; prof. law Cornell U., Ithaca, N.Y., 1979-92; Monfort prof. comml. law U. Colo., Boulder, 1992—. Author: Mergers, Acquisitions and Reorganizations, 1991; contbr. articles to profl. jours. Sir William Henry Cooper fellow U. Auckland, New Zealand, 1992. Office: Univ Colo Law Sch Campus Box 401 Boulder CO 80309

OESTERLE, ERIC ADAM, lawyer; b. Lafayette, Ind., Dec. 2, 1948; s. Eric Clark and Germaine Dora (Seelye) O.; m. Carolyn Anne Scherer, Sept. 16, 1973; children: Adam Clark, Allison Margaret. BS, U. Mich., 1970, JD, 1973. Bar: Ill. 1973, U.S. Dist. Ct. (no. dist.) Ill. 1973, U.S. Ct. Appeals (7th cir.) 1987, U.S. Supreme Ct. 1986. Assoc. Sonnenschein, Carlin, Nath & Rosenthal, Chgo., 1973-80; ptnr. Sonnenschein Nath & Rosenthal, Chgo., 1980—. Mem. ABA, Ill. Bar Assn., Chgo. Bar Assn. Home: 645 Lake Rd Glen Ellyn IL 60137-4249 Office: Sonnenschein Nath & Rosenthal 8000 Sears Tower 233 S Wacker Dr Chicago IL 60606-6306

OESTERREICHER, JAMES E., department stores executive; b. 1941. B.S., Mich. State U., 1964. With J. C. Penney Co. Inc., 1964—; pres. Western Region J. C. Penney Co. Inc., 1987-88, exec. v.p., 1988-94; vice chm., CEO J.C. Penny Co. Inc., 1994—. Office: J C Penney Co Inc 6501 Legacy Dr Plano TX 75024-3612

OESTMANN, MARY JANE, retired radiation specialist; b. Chgo., May 22, 1924; d. Charles Edward and Harriet Evelyn (Stoltenberg) O. BA in Math, Chemistry with honors, Denison U., 1946; MS, U. Wis., 1948, PhD, 1954; DSc., Denison U., 1975. Research chemist Inst. for Atom Energy, Oslo, 1954-55; vis. scientist AB Atom Energy, Stockholm, 1955-56; vis. prof. chem. dept. U. Iowa, Iowa City, 1957; sr. scientist Battelle Meml. Inst., Columbus, Ohio, 1957-61; assoc. chemist Argonne (Ill.) Nat. Lab, 1961-71; environ. project mgr. U.S. AEC, Washington, 1971-75; sr. radiation specialist U.S. Nuclear Regulatory Commn., Glen Ellyn, Ill., 1975-87. Contbr. numerous articles to scientific jours. Mem. planning and zoning commn. Town of Burlington. Recipient Internat. Women's Yr. award Nuclear Regulatory Commn., 1975. Fellow Am. Inst. Chemists, Am. Nuclear Soc. (bd. dirs. 1983-86); mem. Am. Chem. Soc., Inst. Environ. Scis. (sr. mem.), Health Physics Soc. (sec.-treas. Midwest chpt. 1978, exec. com. 1983-86), N.Y. Acad. Scis., Wis. Acad. Scis., Arts and Letters, Sigma Xi, Phi Beta Kappa, Sigma Delta Epsilon, Iota Sigma Pi. Clubs: Burlington (Wis.) Women's Club, Browns Lake Yacht (Burlington, adv. com.). Home: 2520 Cedar Dr Burlington WI 53105-9174

OESTREICH, CHARLES HENRY, college president emeritus; b. Columbus, Ohio, June 8, 1932; s. Henry F. and Martha (Schwartz) O.; m. Rhoda J. Haseley, Aug. 26, 1957; children: Martha, Mary, David. BS, Capital U., 1954; MS, Ohio U., 1956, PhD, 1961; LLD, Capital U., 1986. Instr. chemistry Va. Military Inst., 1956-57; instr. Capital U., Columbus, 1960-62; asst. prof. chemistry Capital U., 1962-64, asso. prof. chemistry, 1965-69; acad. dean Tex. Luth. Coll., Seguin, 1969-76; interim pres. Tex. Luth. Coll., 1976-77, pres., 1977-94; area rep. Evang. Luth. Ch. Found., New Braunfels, Tex., 1994—; postdoctoral research fellow Vanderbilt U., 1965-66. Bd. dirs. Mid-Tex. Symphony. Mem. Seguin Rotary Club (past prs.). Home: 2269 S Abbey Loop New Braunfels TX 78130-8965

OETTER, BRUCE CHRISTIAN, lawyer; b. St. Louis, June 25, 1949; s. Donald L. and Joana (D'Arancha) O.; m. Rebecca P. Cullinane, May 20, 1973; 1 child, Ethan R. AB magna cum laude, Brown U., 1971; JD, Washington U., St. Louis, 1976. Bar: Mo. 1976. Assoc. Bryan, Cave, McPheeters & McRoberts, St. Louis, 1976-84, ptnr., 1985—. Mem. ABA, Mo. Bar Assn., Bar Assn. Met. St. Louis, Mo. Athletic Club, Phi Beta Kappa. Avocations: tennis, squash. Office: Bryan Cave 211 N Broadway Saint Louis MO 63102-2733*

OETTGEN, HERBERT FRIEDRICH, physician; b. Cologne, Germany, Nov. 22, 1923; came to U.S., 1958; s. Peter and Minna (Kaul) O.; m. Trudi Hesberg, Feb. 16, 1957; children: Hans Christoph, Joerg Peter, Anne Barbara. MD, U. Cologne, 1951. Diplomate Bd. Internal Medicine, Fed. Republic of Germany. Resident in pathology City Hosp., Cologne, 1952-54, resident in medicine, 1955-58; fellow Meml. Sloan-Kettering Cancer Ctr., N.Y.C., 1958-62, assoc. to assoc. mem., 1963-69, mem., 1972—, attending physician, 1971—; prof. medicine Cornell U. Med. Coll., N.Y.C., 1972—; assoc. dir. Cancer Rsch. Inst., N.Y.C., 1985—. Author over 350 pubs. in hematology, cancer rsch., immunology and clin. oncology. Recipient award for cancer rsch. Wilhelm Warner Found., Hamburg, Fed. Republic Germany, 1970, Lisec-Artz award for cancer rsch. Friedrich Wilhelm U., Bonn, Fed. Republic of Germany, 1982. Presbyterian. Avocations: violin, woodworking. Home: 48 Overlook Dr New Canaan CT 06840-6825 Office: Meml Sloan-Kettering Cancer Ctr 1275 York Ave New York NY 10021-6007

OETTINGER, ANTHONY GERVIN, mathematician, educator; b. Nuremberg, Germany, Mar. 29, 1929; came to U.S., 1941, naturalized, 1947; s. Albert and Marguerite (Bing) O.; m. Marilyn Tanner, June 20, 1954; children: Douglas, Marjorie. A.B., Harvard U., 1951, Ph.D., 1954; Henry fellow, U. Cambridge, Eng., 1951-52; Litt.D. (hon.), U. Pitts., 1984. Mem. faculty Harvard, 1955—, asso. prof. applied math., 1960-63, prof. linguistics, 1963-75, Gordon McKay prof. applied math., 1963—, chmn. program on info. resources policy, 1972—, mem. faculty of govt., 1973—, prof. info. resources policy, 1975—; mem. command control comm. and intelligence bd. Dept. Navy, 1978-83; mem. sci. adv. group Def. Comm. Agy., 1979-90; chmn. bd. visitors Joint Mil. Intelligence Coll., 1994—; chmn., dir. Ctrl. Intelligence Advanced Tech. Panel, 1995—; cons. Arthur D. Little, Inc., 1956-80, Office Sci. and Tech., Exec. Office of Pres., 1960-73, Bellcomm, Inc., 1963-68, Sys. Devel. Corp., 1965-68, Nat. Security Coun., Exec. Office of Pres., 1975-81, Pres.'s Fgn. Intelligence Adv. Bd., 1981-90; chmn. computer Sci. and Engring. Bd., Nat. Acad. Scis., 1968-73; mem. Mass. Cmty. Antenna TV Commn., 1972-79, chmn., 1975-79; mem. rsch. adv. bd. Com. for Econ. Devel., 1975-79; trustee Babbage Inst., 1991—; panel mem. Naval Studies Bd. NAS/NRC, 1993-95. Author: A Study for the Design of an Automatic Dictionary, 1954, Automatic Language Translation: Lexical and Technical Aspects, 1960, Run Computer Run: The Mythology of Educational Innovation, 1969, High and Low Politics: Information Resources for the 80s, 1977, Behind the Telephone Debates, 1988, Mastering the Changing Information World, 1993; editor: Proc. of a Symposium on Digital Computers and Their Applications, 1962. Fellow Am. Acad. Arts and Scis., AAAS, IEEE, Assn. Computing Machinery (mem. coun. 1961-68, chmn. com. U.S. Govt. Rels. 1964-66, editor computational linguistics sect. Commn. 1964-66, pres. 1966-68); mem. Soc. Indsl. and Applied Math. (mem. coun. 1963-67), Coun. on Fgn. Rels., Phi Beta Kappa, Sigma Xi. Clubs: Cosmos (Washington); Harvard (N.Y.C.). Home: 65 Elizabeth Rd Belmont MA 02178-3819 Office: Harvard U Program Info Resources Policy 200 Aiken Cambridge MA 02138-2901

OETTINGER, FRANK FREDERIC, retired electronics executive, researcher; b. N.Y.C., Aug. 6, 1940; s. Frank B. and Elizabeth (Leimer) O.; m. Kathleen Linda Johnson, Aug. 24, 1963; children: Meredith L., Melanie B., Megan M. BEE, Pratt Inst., 1963; MEE, NYU, 1966; postgrad., Columbia U., 1966-67. Electronics engr. U.S. Naval Applied Sci. Lab., N.Y.C., 1963-67; project leader Nat. Bur. Standards, Gaithersburg, MD, 1967-73, sect. chief, 1973-80, dep. div. chief, 1980-85; div. chief Nat. Inst. Standards & Tech. (formerly Nat. Bur. Standards), Gaithersburg, Md., 1985-95; ret., 1995. Contbr. articles to profl. jours.; author 15 standards in semiconductor metrology. Deacon Roman Cath. Ch. Recipient Silver medal Dept. Commerce, 1976, E.B. Rosa award Nat. Inst. Standards & Tech., 1990. Fellow IEEE; mem. Eta Kappa Nu. Office: Nat Inst Standards & Tech Semiconductor Elec Dv Gaithersburg MD 20899

OETTINGER, JULIAN ALAN, lawyer, pharmacy company executive. BS, U. Ill., 1961; JD, Northwestern U., 1964. Bar: Ill. 1964. Atty. SEC, 1964-67; atty. Walgreen Co., Deerfield, Ill., 1967-72, sr. atty., 1972-78, dir. law, 1978-89, v.p., gen. counsel, corp. sec., 1989—. Office: Walgreen Co 200 Wilmot Rd Deerfield IL 60015-4620

O'FARRELL, MARK THEODORE, religious organization administrator; b. Milw., Apr. 13, 1948; s. Theodore Wolfred and Ernestine (Shelhammer) O.; m. Phillis Gilley, Sept. 18, 1948; children: Gwen, Kevin. BA, Columbia Bible Coll., 1970; DD, Toccan Falls Coll., 1996. Asst. pastor 1st Alliance Ch., Macon, Ga., 1970-71; sr. pastor 1st Alliance Ch., Port Charlotte, Fla., 1981-86, Belle Glade (Fla.) Alliance Ch., 1971-81; asst. to dist. supt., ext. dir. Southeastern Dist. of Christian and Missionary Alliance, Orlando, Fla., 1986-93, dist. supt., 1993—. Recipient Spiritual Aims award Kiwanis. Home: Christian & Missionary Alliance Southeastern District 2450 Donaldson Dr Orlando FL 32812 Office: PO Box 720430 Orlando FL 32872-0430

OFFENBERGER, ALLAN ANTHONY, electrical engineering educator; b. Wadena, Sask., Can., Aug. 11, 1938; s. Ivy Viola (Hagglund) O.; m. Margaret Elizabeth Patterson, Apr. 12, 1963; children: Brian, Gary. BS, U. B.C., 1962, MS, 1963; PhD, MIT, 1968. Asst. prof. U. Alta., Edmonton, Can., 1968-70, assoc. prof., 1970-75, prof., 1975-95, prof. emeritus, 1996—; cons. Lawrence Livermore (Calif.) Nat. Lab., 1993—; vis. prof. U.K. Atomic Energy Agy., Abingdon, Oxon, Eng., 1975-76; project dir. Laser Fusion Project, Edmonton, 1984-91; mem. strategic adv. com. Nat. Fusion Program, Atomic Energy of Can. Ltd., Chalk River, Ont., 1987—; vis. prof. U. Oxford, U.K., 1992. Mem. editorial bd. Laser and Particle Beams, 1987—; contbr. over 100 sci. articles on lasers and plasma physics. Killam Rsch. fellow Can. Coun., 1980-82. SERC rsch. fellow, Eng., 1992. Mem. Can. Assn. Physicists (exec. officer, v.p. elect 1987-88, pres. 1989-90), Am. Phys. Soc., Sigma Xi. Home: 412 Lessard Dr, Edmonton, AB Canada T6M 1A7 Office: Dept Elec Engring, U Alta, Edmonton, AB Canada T6G 2G7

OFFER, DANIEL, psychiatrist; b. Berlin, Germany, Dec. 24, 1930; married; 3 children. Grad., U. Chgo., 1957. Intern Ill. Research and Ednl. Hosps., Chgo., 1957-58; resident Inst. Psychosomatics and Psychiat. Research and Tng. Michael Reese Hosp., Chgo., 1958-61; psychiatrist Chgo. Inst. Psychoanalysis, 1963-68; career investigator Nat. Inst. Mental Health, Psychosomatic and Psychiat. Inst., Michael Reese Hosp., 1961-64; asst. dir. Inst. Psychosomatics and Psychiat. Research and Tng., Chgo., 1961-64; assoc. dir. Inst. Psychosomatics and Psychiat. Research and Tng., 1965-74, co-dir., 1974-76, acting chmn., 1976-77, chmn., 1977-87; dir. Ctr. for Study of Adolescence, 1987-90; assoc. prof. psychiatry U. Chgo., 1969-73, prof., 1973-90, prof. psychiatry Northwestern U., 1991—; fellow Center for Advanced Studies in Behavioral Scis., Stanford, 1973-74. Author: Normality: Theoretical and Clinical Concepts of Mental Health, 1966, rev. edit., 1973, new edit., 1984, The Psychological World of the Teen-ager, 1969, From Teenage to Young Manhood: A Psychological Study, 1975, Psychological World of the Juvenile Delinquent, 1979, The Adolescent: A Psychological Self Portrait 1981, Patterns of Adolescent Self-Image, 1984, The Leader, 1985, The Teenage World, 1988, The Diversity of Normal Behavior, 1991, Adolescent Suicide and Homicide, 1994; also numerous articles.; editor in chief Jour. Youth and Adolescence. Served with Israeli Army. Fellow Chgo. Inst. Medicine, Am. Soc. Adolescent Psychiatry (pres. 1972-73, Schonfeld Meml. award for rsch. 1985, John P. Hill Meml. award 1990). Office: Northwestern U Med Sch Dept Psychiatry & Behavioral Scis 303 E Ohio St Chicago IL 60611-3015

OFFER, STUART JAY, lawyer; b. Seattle, June 2, 1943; m. Judith Spitzer, Aug. 29, 1970; children: Rebecca, Kathryn. BA, U. Wash., 1964; LLB, Columbia U., 1967. Bar: D.C. 1968, U.S. Tax Ct. 1968, Calif. 1972. Atty., advisor U.S. Tax Ct., Washington, 1967-68; assoc. Morrison & Foerster, LLP, San Francisco, 1972-76; ptnr. Morrison & Foerster, San Francisco, 1976—. Mem. San Francisco Dir.'s Adv. Com. 1985. Served as capt. U.S. Army, 1968-72. Mem. ABA (chmn. taxation sect., corp. tax com. 1991-92, coun. dir. 1995—), Internat. Fiscal Assn., Am. Coll. Tax Counsel. Office: Morrison & Foerster LLP 345 California St San Francisco CA 94104-2635

OFFERMAN, JOSE ANTONIO DONO, professional baseball player; b. San Pedor de Macoris, Dominican Republic, Nov. 8, 1968. Student, Colegio Biblico Cristiano, Dominican Republic. Shortstop L.A. Dodgers, 1990—. Selected to N.L All-Star Team, 1995. Office: LA Dodgers 1000 Elysian Park Ave Los Angeles CA 90012*

OFFHOLTER, JEAN MARY, management consultant; b. Berkeley, Calif., Sept. 14, 1932; d. Clarence Ballard Hills and Frances Desire (Ramsay) Hanna; divorced; children: Cheryl Diane McKibbin, Sally Lynn Hillman. BA, San Jose State Coll., 1954. Tech. exec. U.S. Gen. Svcs. Adminstrn., San Francisco, 1966-70; inventory mgmt. specialist U.S. Gen. Svcs. Adminstrn., Washington, 1971-75, supervisory inventory mgmt. specialist, 1975-76, spl. asst., regional commr., 1977-78, dir. retail svcs. div., 1979-83; dir. supply and contracting divs. U.S. Gen. Svcs. Adminstrn., Kansas City, Mo., 1984-86; ret., 1986; cons. in procurement tng. and course devel. Washington, 1986—. Avocations: reading fiction and non-fiction. Home: 11566 Rolling Green Ct # 200 Reston VA 22091-2243

OFFIT, MORRIS WOLF, investment management executive; b. Balt., Jan. 22, 1937; s. Michael and Rhea (Wolf) O.; m. Nancy Silverman, Nov. 26, 1959; children: Ned S., Daniel W. BA in History, Johns Hopkins U., 1957; MBA in Fin., U. Pa., 1959. V.p. investment dept. Mercantile Safe Deposit and Trust, Balt., 1960-68; gen. ptnr. Salomon Bros. Inc., N.Y.C., 1970-80; pres. Julius Baer Securities, N.Y.C., 1980-82, Offit Assocs. Inc., N.Y.C., 1983—; now ceo Offit Assoc. Inc., N.Y.C.; bd. dirs. Merc. Bancshares Corp., Balt. Chmn. bd. trustees Johns Hopkins U.; mem. adv. coun. Sch. Advanced Internat. Studies, Washington; trustee Jewish Mus., former chmn.; trustee Union Theol. Sem., Jewish Theol. Sem. Mem. Coun. Fgn. Rels. Office: Offitbank 520 Madison Ave New York NY 10022-4213*

OFFIT, SIDNEY, writer, educator; b. Balt., Oct. 13, 1928; s. Barney and Lillian (Cohen) O.; m. Avodah Crindell Komito, Aug. 8, 1952; children: Kenneth, Michael Robert. B.A., Johns Hopkins U., 1950. Editorial staff Mercury Publs., N.Y.C., 1952-53, Macfadden Publs., N.Y.C., 1953-54; contbg. editor Baseball mag., Washington, 1955-58; mem. faculty N.Y. U., 1964—, adj. prof. creative writing, 1977—; asso. editor Intellectual Digest, 1970-72, sr. editor, 1972-74; lectr. creative writing New Sch. Social Research, 1965—; curator George Polk Awards for Journalism, 1977—; mem. nat. bd. Nat. Book Com., 1973-75; commentator Channel 5 TV, N.Y.C., 1975-85, Channel 11 TV, 1992. Author: He Had it Made, 1959, The Other Side of the Street, 1962, Soupbone, 1963, Topsy Turvey, 1965, the Adventure of Homer Fink, 1966, The Boy Who Made a Million, 1968; short stories Not All the Girls Have Million Dollar Smiles, 1971; Only a Girl Like You, 1972, What Kind of Guy Do You Think I Am?, 1977, Memoir of the Bookie's Son, 1995; series sports books for boys, 1961-65, also essays, revs., short stories; book editor: Politics Today, 1978-80. Mem. selection com. Dist. Sch. Bd., N.Y.C., 1968; Mem. exec. bd. Lexington Democratic Club, 1957-60, N.Y. Dem. County Com., 1966—; chmn. 19th Precinct Community Council of N.Y.C., 1964-80. Recipient Disting. Alumni award Valley Forge Mil. Acad., 1961, Otty Community Svc. award, 1975, Teaching Excellence award NYU, 1981, commendation for achievment as teacher, scholar, communicator N.Y. State Legislature, 1983, proclamation for contbns. to city, N.Y.C. Coun., 1983, Police Athletic League citation for svc. to children of N.Y.C., 1991, Honors Convocation award Marymount Manhattan Coll., 1994, Detlev W. Bronk award Johns Hopkins Alumni Assn., 1994. Mem. Tudor and Stuart Club, Authors Guild Found. (pres. 1993—), Authors Guild (coun. 1970-77, 79—, v.p. 1993-95), Authors League (nat. coun. 1976-79), Am. Ctr. PEN (exec. com. 1969-88, 89—, v.p. 1970-74, internat. del. 1971, 72, 74). Clubs: Century Assn. (N.Y.C.), Coffee House (N.Y.C.). Home: 23 E 69th St New York NY 10021-4919 *I have been guided by a strong devotion to my family and friends and moderate ambition. In both these priorities I have been influenced by my parents. With my writing I have tried to fulfill my own needs, and for the most I have been satisfied by the reception. I do not aspire to fame or great fortune, and this leaves me free to enjoy the sharing of experiences with my friends and family. I consider myself a lucky man and this keeps me grateful to whatever forces there are that contrive man's fortune.*

OFFNER, ERIC DELMONTE, lawyer; b. Vienna, Austria, June 23, 1928; came to U.S., 1941, naturalized, 1949; s. Sigmund J. and Kathe (Delmonte) O.; m. Julie Cousins, 1955 (dec. 1959); m. Barbara Ann Shotton, July 2, 1961; 1 son, Gary Douglas; m. Carol Sue Marcus, Jan. 12, 1980 (dec. 1983). B.B.A., CCNY, 1949; LL.B. in Internat. Affairs, Cornell U., 1952. Bar: N.Y. 1952. Assoc. Langner, Parry, Card & Langner, N.Y.C., 1952-57; ptnr. Haseltine, Lake, Waters & Offner, N.Y.C., 1957-77; sr. ptnr. Offner & Kuhn, 1978-83; pvt. practice N.Y.C., 1983—; instr. George Washington U. Law Sch., Cornell U. Law Sch.; spl. prof. law Hofstra Law Sch., 1974-92, Cornell Law Sch., 1979. Author: International Trademark Protection, 1964, Japanese edit., 1977, International Trademark Service, Vols. I-III 1970, Vol. IV, 1972, Vol. V., 1973, Vol. VI, 1976, Vol. VII, 1981, Vols. I-VII, 2d edit., 1981, Legal Training Course on Trademarks, 1982; editor in chief: Cornell Law Forum, 1950-51; mem. editorial bd.: Trademark Reporter, 1961-64, 69-72; book reviewer Jour. Humanism and Ethical Religion; contbr. articles to profl. jours. V.p. Riverdale Mental Health Clinic, N.Y.C., 1966-67; pres. Riverdale Mental Health Assn., 1967-69, Ethical Culture Soc., Riverdale-Yonkers, 1964-67, Ethical Cultural Retirement Ctr., 1975-94; trustee Am. Ethical Union, 1967-73, Internat. Alliance of Holistic Lawyers; bd. dirs. Fit Kids. Mem. N.Y. Patent Law Assn. (assoc. editor Bull. 1961-66, gov. 1973-76), ABA, City N.Y. Bar Assn. (sec. 1962-64), U.S. Trademark Assn., World Peace Through Law (charter), Trademark Soc. Washington (charter), Inst. Trade Mark Agts. (London), Australian Patent Inst., Internat. Assn. Protection Indsl. Property, Nat. Coun. Patent Law Assn., Internat. Patent, Trademark Assn., Internat. Alliance of Holistic Lawyers, Phi Alpha Delta. Home: 20 Joy Dr New Hyde Park NY 11040-1109 *Do unto others so as to elicit the best in them and thereby the best in yourself.*

OFFNER, HEBE ZONCHELLO, special education educator; b. Easton, Pa., Dec. 30, 1924; d. Costantino and Mercedes (Luppi) Zonchello; m. Harry G. Offner, June 15, 1953; children: Lawrence, James, Kenneth. Student, Ohio State U., 1943-47; BA in French, Calif. State U., Northridge, 1970; postgrad., Calif. State U., L.A., 1974, Calif. State U., Carson, 1993. Cert. elem. tchr., spl. edn. of severely handicapped tchr., Calif. Tchr., spl. edn. tchr. Glendale (Calif.) Unified Sch. Dist., 1983-84; spl. edn. tchr. of mentally handicapped and autistic Los Angeles County Office of Edn., Downey, Calif., 1985—. Mem. Alliance for the Mentally Ill. Home: 7924 Loma Verde Ave Canoga Park CA 91304-5130

OFFUTT, DREW GRIFFITH, physical education educator; b. Bethesda, Md., May 9, 1969; s. Ralph Worthington Jr. and Suzanne Clements (Griffith) O. AA in Phys. Edn., Montgomery Jr. Coll., Rockville, Md., 1992; BS in Kinesiology, Phys. Edn., U. Md., 1996. Supr. dept. intramurals Montgomery Coll., Rockville, 1992; head coach boys basketball St. Johns H.S., Washington, 1992—; head coach, dir. camp Laurel, Laurel, Maine, 1993—; personal trainer Sport & Health Assocs., Rockville, 1993—; tutor U. Md., College Park, 1992—, tchr. fitness/wellness dept., 1994—; head coach freshman baseball, asst. varsity coach baseball Potomac Sch., McLean, Va., 1995. Mem. AAPERD, Md. Alliance Phys. Edn., Recreation and Dance, World Wildlife. Roman Catholic. Avocations: baseball, camping, weight training, writing, reading biographies. Home: 16705 Bethayres Rd Derwood MD 20855-2024

OFFUTT, GERALD M., lawyer; b. New Haven, Conn., Sept. 20, 1950. AB, Harvard U., 1973, JD, 1976. Bar: Ill. 1976. Ptnr. McDermott, Will & Emery, Chgo. Mem. ABA, Chgo. Bar Assn., Cook County Bar Assn., Nat. Bar Assn. Address: 2679 Saint Paul St Denver CO 80205-4829*

O'FLAHERTY, PAUL BENEDICT, lawyer; b. Chgo., Feb. 11, 1925; s. Benedict Joseph and Margaret Celestine (Harrington) O'F.; m. Catherine Margaret Bigley, Feb. 13, 1954; children: Paul, Michael, Kathleen, Ann, Neil. JD cum laude, Loyola U., Chgo., 1949. Bar: Ill. 1949, U.S. Dist. Ct. (no. dist.) Ill. 1949, U.S. Ct. Appeals (7th cir.) 1956, U.S. Supreme Ct. 1959. Ptnr. Madden, Meccia, O'Flaherty & Freeman, Chgo., 1949-56; ptnr. Groble, O'Flaherty & Hayes, Chgo., 1956-63, Schiff Hardin & Waite, Chgo., 1963—; mem. adj. faculty Loyola U., 1959-65. Author: (with others) Illinois Estate Administration, 1983; contbr. articles to profl. jours. Bd. advisors Cath. Charities, Chgo., 1979-92; trustee Clarke Coll., Dubuque, Iowa, 1982—. Served to 2d lt. U.S. Army, 1943-46. Fellow Am. Coll. Trust and Estate Counsel; mem. ABA, Ill. Bar Assn. (past chmn. fed. taxation sect. council), Chgo. Bar Assn. (past chmn. trust law com.), Chgo. Estate Planning Council. Clubs: Union League, Metropolitan (Chgo.). Office: Schiff Hardin & Waite 7200 Sears Tower Chicago IL 60606

O'FLAHERTY, TERRENCE, journalist; b. What Cheer, Iowa, July 15, 1917; s. Leo J. and Lelia (Thomas) O'F. B.A., U. Calif. at Berkeley, 1939. Hist. researcher Metro-Goldwyn-Mayer Studios, 1940-42; columnist San Francisco Chronicle, 1949-86; writer nationally syndicated TV column, 1960-86; mem. bd. Peabody Awards for Radio and TV, 1952-84. Host: TV program PM West, San Francisco, 1961-62; created The Terrence O'Flaherty TV Collection for UCLA TV Archives and Theater Arts Library, 1987; author: Masterpiece Theatre: A Celebration, 1995; contbr. articles to McCalls, Reader's Digest, TV Guide. Served as lt. USNR, 1942-46. Recipient Gov.'s award (Emmy) NATAS, 1988. Mem. Beta Theta Pi. Subject of UCLA oral history program. Home and Office: 4 Whiting St San Francisco CA 94133-2419

O'FLARITY, JAMES P., lawyer; b. Yazoo City, Miss., Oct. 15, 1923; s. James P. and Jessie E. (Marshall) O'F.; m. Betty Reichman, Apr. 9, 1955; children: Michael J., Deborah J. O'Flarity James, Steven M., Pamela G. BS, Millsaps Coll., 1950; postgrad., Miss. Coll. Sch. Law, 1948, 53-54; J.D., U. Fla., 1965. Bar: Miss. 1954, Fla. 1966, U.S. Dist. Ct. (so. dist.) Miss. 1954, U.S. Ct. Mil. Appeals 1957, U.S. Dist. Ct. (so. and mid. dists.) Fla. 1966, U.S. Dist. Ct. (no. dist.) Fla. 1967, U.S. Ct. Appeals (5th cir.) 1957, U.S. Ct. Appeals (11th cir.) 1981, U.S. Supreme Ct. 1957; state ct. cert. arbitrator. Assoc. law firm Cone, Owen, Wagner, Nugent & Johnson, West Palm Beach, Fla., 1966-69; sole practice law West Palm Beach, 1969—; mem. Supreme Ct. Matrimonial Law Commn. Fla., 1982-85; ABA observer family ct. proc. Nat. Jud. Coll., 1983; mem. U. Fla. Law Ctr. Coun., 1972—, mem. legal edn. com., 1973, chmn. membership and fin. com., 1977-78; lectr. on marital and family law; leader del. for legal exchange on family law to Ministry of Justice, Peoples Republic of China, 1984. Contbr. articles to profl. publs. Mem. U. Fla. Pres.'s Council; mem. U.S Rep. Senatorial Inner Circle, 1988—; col. La. Gov.'s Staff, 1982—. With USAAF, 1942-45. Decorated Air medal with five oak leaf clusters. Fellow Royal Geog. Soc. (life), Am. Bar Found. (life), Roscoe Pound-Am. Trial Lawyers Found. (life), Am. Acad. Matrimonial Lawyers (nat. pres. 1985-86, nat. bd. of govs. 1977-88, founding pres. Fla. chpt. 1976-80, bd. mgrs. Fla chpt. 1976—, hon. permanent pres. emeritus 1982—), Internat. Acad. Matrimonial Lawyers (convenor, founder), Trusler Soc., Fla. Bar Found. (life, exec. dir. screening com. 1976, chmn. projects com. 1976-77, asst. sec. 1973-79, dir. 1977-81); mem. Internat. Soc. Family Law, Internat. Bar Assn. (assoc.), Am. Law Inst. (consultative group law of family dissolution 1990—, Nat. Conf. Bar Pres'. 1991), ABA (chmn. coms. 1973-75, 78-81, 82-83, editor Family Law Newsletter 1975-77, mem. council family law sect. 1976-85, vice-chmn. sect. 1981-82, chmn. sect. 1983-84, mem. conf. sect. chairmen 1982-85, mem. adv. bd. jour. 1978-80), Assn. Trial Lawyers Am. (Fla. State committeeman 1973-75, 1st chmn. family law sect. 1971-72, 72-73), Fla. Supreme Ct. Hist. Soc., Fla. Council Bar Assn. Presidents (life mem.), U. Fla. Law Ctr. Assn. (life), Acad Fla. Trial Lawyers (dir. 1974-77, coll. diplomates 1977), Fla. Bar (exec. council 1973-84, sec.-treas. family law sect. 1973-74, chmn. family law sect. 1974-75, 75-76, guest editor spl. issue jour. 1978, chmn. jour. and news editorial bd. 1978-79, mem. bd. legal specialization and edn. 1982-91, 92-95, jud. nominating procedures com. 1992-93, Family Law Rules com. 1992-95), Palm Beach County Bar Assn. (cir. ct. civil adv. com. 1981, mem. cir. ct. juvenile domestic rels. adv. com. 1971-80, 81-83, adv. com. chmn. 1974-78), Solicitor's Family Law Assn. (Eng.), Gov.'s Club of Palm Beach (founder, life, gov's. coun.), Explorers Club (life, vice chmn. South Fla. chpt. 1990-95), Circumnavigators Club, Travelers Century Club (life), Phi Alpha Delta (life), Sigma Delta Kappa. Home: 908 Country Club Dr No Palm Beach FL 33408-3714 Office: 215 5th St Ste 108 West Palm Beach FL 33401-4026

O'FLINN, PETER RUSSELL, lawyer; b. Bklyn., Jan. 8, 1953; s. Russell William and Mary (Tavoulareas) O'F.; m. Kathleen Tracy, May 28, 1981; children: Peter Andrew, Michael Christopher. BA, Colgate U., 1974; JD, Columbia U., 1977. Bar: N.Y. 1978. Assoc. Dewey, Ballantine, Bushby, Palmer & Wood, N.Y.C., 1977-81; assoc. LeBoeuf, Lamb, Leiby & MacRae, N.Y.C., 1982-85, ptnr., 1986—. *

OFNER, J(AMES) ALAN, management consultant; b. East Orange, N.J., Mar. 23, 1922. Student, Newark U., 1941; B.A., Antioch Coll., 1949. Trainee, L. Bamberger & Co., Newark, 1941; asst. dept. mgr. Carson Pierie Scott Co., Chgo., 1949; sr. personnel rep. Argonne (Ill.) Nat. Lab., 1950-55; mgmt. cons. McKinsey & Co., Chgo. and San Francisco, 1955-60; mgr. orgn. planning J.C. Penney Co., Inc., N.Y.C., 1960-65; dir. orgn. devel. J.C. Penney Co., Inc., 1965-74, div. v.p., 1974-82, dir. corp. personnel planning, 1976-82; pres. Mng. Change, Inc., 1981—. Served with USAAF, 1941-44. Mem. Exec. Forum Group, Strategic Leadership Forum, Human Resources Planning Soc., World Future Soc., Nat. Retail Fedn., Inst. Mgmt. Cons., N.C. Citizens for Bus. and Industry, Soc. for Human Resource Mgmt., Princeton Club. Office: Mng Change Inc PO Box 98387 Raleigh NC 27624-8387

OFTE, DONALD, environmental executive, former management consultant; b. N.Y.C., Aug. 23, 1929; s. Sverre and Ingeborg Ofte; m. Margaret Mae McHenney, July 23, 1955; children: Marc Christian, Nancy Carolyn Ofte Appleby, Kirk Donald Jr. BA in Chemistry, Dana Coll., 1952; postgrad. study metall. engring., Ohio State U., 1958-60. Jr. chemist Inst. Atomic Research, Ames, Iowa, 1952-53; sr. research chemist Monsanto Research Corp., Miamisburg, Ohio, 1958-66; ops. engr. AEC, Miamisburg, 1966-69; br. chief, div. dir. ops. office AEC, Albuquerque, 1969-73; mgr. Pinellas area office AEC, Largo, Fla., 1973-79; mgr. Rocky Flats area office Dept. Energy, Golden, Colo., 1979-82; asst. mgr. devel. and prodn. Dept. Energy, Albuquerque, 1982-83, dep. mgr. ops. office, 1983-84; prin. dep. asst. sec. Dept. Energy Defense Programs, Washington, 1984-87; mgr. ops. office Dept. Energy, Idaho Falls, Idaho, 1987-89; mgmt. cons. Idaho Falls, 1989-92; v.p. govt. ops. United Engrs. and Constructors, Denver, 1992-93; v.p. Adv. Scis., Inc., Albuquerque, 1993-94; pres. FERMCO, Cin., 1994-96; v.p. Fluor-Daniel, Inc., 1994—; affiliate prof. Idaho State U., 1990-92; bd. dirs. Denver Fed. Exec. Bd., 1979-82. Author: (with others) Plutonium 1960, 1965, Physiochemical; contbr. articles to profl. jours. on metallurgy and ceramics. Campaign chmn. United Way Pinellas, St. Petersburg, Fla., 1978; bd. dirs. Bonneville County United Way, Idaho Rsch. Found.; mem. adv. bd. Teton Peaks Council Boy Scouts of Am., 1987-92, Eastern Idaho Tech. Coll.; chmn. Excellence in Edn. Fund Com., 1990-92; vice chmn., bd. dirs. Rio Grande Ch. ARC, Albuquerque, 1982-84. Served to lt. (j.g.) USN, 1953-57. Recipient citation AEC for Apollo 12 SNAP 27 Radioisotope Generator, 1969, High Quality Performance award AEC, 1968, Group Achievement award NASA, 1972; Meritorious Svc. award Dept. Energy, 1985, Disting. Career Svc. award, 1989. Mem. Am. Chem. Soc., Am. Nuclear Soc., Am. Soc. Metals, Nat. Contract Mgmt. Assn., Am. Soc. Pub. Adminstrs., Suncoast Archeol. Soc., Idaho Falls C. of C. (bd. dirs., cmty. svc. award 1990), Rotary Internat. Avocations: reading, bridge, hiking, gardening, golf. Home: 1129 Salamanca NW Albuquerque NM 87107 Office: Fermco PO Box 538704 Cincinnati OH 45253-8704

OGAN, RUSSELL GRIFFITH, business executive, retired air force officer; b. Reading, Pa., Nov. 20, 1923; s. Russell John and Edna Gwendlyn (Griffith) O.; m. Gloria Mae Withers, Oct. 30, 1943; children: Susan Ann (Mrs. Greg Gunn), Russell Lee. Student, Wyomissing Polytech. Inst., 1942, Air Command Staff Coll., 1948, Nat. War Coll., 1963. Enlisted as pvt. U.S. Army, 1942; advanced through grades to brig. gen. USAF, 1970; fighter squadron comdr. Dover AFB, Del., 1951; dir. combat operations (11th Air Div.), Ladd AFB, Alaska, 1951-53; dir. (Combat Operations Center), Hamilton AFB, Calif., 1953-56; with (Hdqrs. Air Def. Command), Ent AFB, Colo., 1956-60; dir. (Aerospace Def. Systems Office, Air Force Ballistic Missile Div.), 1960-62; from dep. dir. plans to comdr. Sector Operation Ctr. NATO, Germany, 1963-66; dep. dir. personnel data and records (USAF Mil. Personnel Center), Randolph AFB, Tex., 1966-68; comdr. 71st Missile Warning Wing, then vice comdr. (14th Aerospace Force), Ent AFB, Colo., 1968-71; dep. dir. personnel programs Hdqrs. USAF, Washington, 1971-72; dir. Prisoner of War and Missing in Action Affairs, Office Sec. Def., Washington, 1972-74; former pres. Vacation Interval Mktg.; real estate broker Fishermen's Village, Punta Gorda, Fla. Decorated D.S.M., Legion of Merit with bronze oak leaf cluster, Air medal with 1 silver and 1 bronze oak leaf cluster. Mem. Daedalians, T.R.O.A., Venice Golf and Country Club. Home: 528 Cheval Dr Venice FL 34292-4605

OGATA, KATSUHIKO, engineering educator; b. Tokyo, Jan. 6, 1925; came to U.S., 1952; s. Fukuhei and Teruko (Yasaki) O.; m. Asako Nakamura, Sept. 6, 1961; 1 son, Takahiko. B.S., U. Tokyo, 1947; M.S., U. Ill., 1953; Ph.D., U. Calif., Berkeley, 1956. Research asst. Sci. Research Inst., Tokyo, 1948-51; fuel engr. Nippon Steel Tube Co., Tokyo, 1951-52; mem. faculty U. Minn., 1956—, prof. mech. engring., 1961—; prof. elec. engring. Yokohama Nat. U., 1960-61, 64-65, 68-69. Author: State Space Analysis of Control Systems, 1967, Modern Control Engineering, 1970, 2d edit., 1990, 3d edit., 1996, Dynamic Programming, 1973, Ingenieria de Control Moderna, 1974, 2d edit., 1990, Metody Przestrzeni Stanow w Teorii Sterowania, 1974, System Dynamics, 1978, 2d edit., 1992, Engenharia de Controle Moderno, 1982, 2d edit., 1993, Teknik Kontrol Automatik, 1985, Discrete-Time Control Systems, 1986, 2d edit., 1995, Gendai Seigyo Riron, 1986, Dinamica de Sistemas, 1987, Solving Control Engineering Problems with MATLAB, 1994, Gendai Seigyo Kogaku, 1994, Designing Linear Control Systems with MATLAB, 1994. Recipient Outstanding Adv. award Inst. of Tech., U.

Minn., 1981. Fellow ASME; mem. Sigma Xi, Pi Tau Sigma. Office: U Minn Dept Mech Engring Minneapolis MN 55455

OGAWA, HIDEMICHI, anesthesiologist, researcher; b. Asahikawa, Hokkaido, Japan, Nov. 14, 1932; s. Taizui and Toyoko (Hata) O.; m. Hisako Mizushina, Mar. 15, 1935; children: Hideaki, Toshiaki, Masaaki. MD, Sapporo Med. U., 1957, PhD, 1962. Diplomate Japan Soc. Anesthesiology; cert. anesthesiologist, Min. Health and Welfare, Japan. Asst. Sapporo (Japan) Med. U., 1962, asst. prof., 1962-65, assoc. prof., 1965-73; dir. dept. anesthesiology Kushiro (Japan) City Hosp., 1973-76; prof., chmn. dept. anesthesiology Asahikawa (Japan) Med. Coll., 1976-82, prof., chmn. dept. anesthesiology and critical care medicine, 1992—; vis. prof. Nanjing (China) Coll. of TCM, 1991—, Sun Yat-Sen U. of Med. Scis., Guang Zhou, China, 1993—, The Fourth Mil. U., Xian, China, 1993—, Tian Jin U. Medicine, China, 1994—; hon. prof. China-Japan Friendship Hosp., Beijing, 1992—; hon. cons. U. Wash., Seattle, 1992—. Editor Clin. Pharmacology and Therapy, 1992—, The Clin. Report, 1992—, Japanese Jour. Oriental Medicine, 1993—. Hon. pres. Aging Soc. Devel. Found., Sapporo, 1990—; mem. spl. com. Coun. of Propulsion for Devel. of Acute Care, Asahikawa, Japan, 1992—; spl. lectr. Hokkaido Coll. of High Tech., Eniwa, Japan, 1992—. Recipient Hokkaido Gov.'s prize for Med. Scis., 1985, prize for med. advancement Hokkaido Med. Assn./Hokkaido Gov., 1985; Cleve. Clin. Found. fellow, 1969-71. Fellow Internat. Coll. Surgeons; mem. Am. Assn. Advancement of Med. Instrumentation, Am. Soc. Artificial Internal Organs (assoc.), N.Y. Acad. Scis. Avocations: art appreciation, gardening, horticulture, photography, golf. Home: Midorigaoka 2-3-3, Idaishukusha E-25, Asahikawa, Hokkaido 078, Japan Office: Asahikawa Med Coll Dept Anes and Critical Care Medicine, Nishikagura 4-5 3-11, Hokkaido 078, Japan

OGAWA, MAKIO, physician; b. Otsu, Shiga, Japan, Jan. 22, 1940; s. Takeo and Yasuko (Sugata) O.; m. Mary-Jane Trevithick, June 21, 1969; children: Terry, Lesley. MD, Osaka U. Med. Sch., Japan, 1964; PhD, Toronto U., Can., 1973. Diplomate Am. Bd. Internal Medicine, Am. Bd. Hematology. Rotating intern U.S. Naval Hosp., Yokosuka, Japan, 1964-65; resident in Medicine Osaka U. Hosp., 1965-66; resident in Medicine Dartmouth Med. Sch. Affiliated Hosp., Hanover, N.H., 1966-68, fellow in Hematology, 1968-70; asst. prof. medicine Med. U. S.C., Charleston, 1973-77, assoc. prof., 1977-80, prof., 1980—, dir. div. exptl. hematology, 1984—; ACOS for R and D Va. Med. Ctr., Charleston, 1993—. Recipient W.S. Middleton award Dept. Vets. Affairs, 1989, William Dameshek prize Am. Soc. Hematology, 1991, Behring-Kitasato award in immunology, 1994; Leukemia Soc. Am. scholar, 1975-80; med. investigator Dept. Vets Affairs, 1980-85, 87-92. Mem. So. Soc. Clin. Investigation, Am. Soc. Clin. Investigation, Internat. Soc. Exptl. Hematology (pres. 1989-90), Assn. Am. Physicians. Office: VA Med Ctr 109 Bee St Charleston SC 29401-5703

OGBUOKIRI, JUSTINA ENUMA, pharmacist, educator; b. Orlu, Imo, Nigeria, Dec. 28, 1949; came to the U.S., 1970; d. Edmund and Patricia (Ubozoh) Ezie; m. Chukwuma Godwin Ogbuokiri, Sept. 5, 1970; children: Uchenna, Obianuju, Kelechi, Ginika, Emeka. BSc in Pharmacy, U. Cin., 1975, D in Pharmacy, 1977. Registered pharmacist, Ohio. Asst. prof. hosp. pharmacy tech. U. Cin. (Ohio)-Raymond Walters Coll. Br., 1977-79; assoc. prof. pharmacology Coll. Medicine, U. Nigeria, Enugu, 1993—; postdoctoral Takemi fellow dept. population/internat. health Harvard Sch. Pub. Health, Boston, 1994—; cons. Nat. Malaria Tech. Com., Fed. Ministry Health, Lagos, Nigeria, 1987—, Nat. Essential Drugs Programme, Fed. Ministry Health, Lagos, 1990—; bd. dirs. Majane Specialist Hosp., Aba, Nigeria. Contbr. articles to profl. jours. Cmty. woman leader Nachi (Enugu-Nigeria) Health Coop., 1991-94. Named Woman of the Yr. Diocese of Orlu, Nigeria, 1993; fellow West African Pharm. Fedn., Lagos, 1993. Mem. AAAS, ECOWEMN (founder, exec. dir., researcher), ACCP, Enugu Lioness Club (charter pres. 1984-87). Roman Catholic. Avocations: sewing, writing, gourmet cooking, travel, computers. Office: Harvard Sch Pub Health 665 Huntington Ave Boston MA 02115

OGBURN, CHARLTON, writer; b. Atlanta, Mar. 15, 1911; s. Charlton and Dorothy (Stevens) O.; m. Mary C. Aldis, June 6, 1945 (div. 1951); 1 child, William O. Aldis; m. Vera Weidman, Feb. 24, 1951; children: Nyssa, Holly. S.B. cum laude, Harvard, 1932; grad., Nat. War Coll., 1952. Writer Alfred P. Sloan Found., 1937-39; book reviewer Book-of-the-Month Club, 1940-41; with Div. Southeast Asian Affairs, Dept. of State, 1946-50, polit. adviser, acting U.S. rep. com. good offices on Indonesia UN Security Council, 1947-48, policy planning adviser Bur. Far Eastern Affairs, 1952-54, chief div. research for Near East, South Asia and Africa, 1954-57. Author: The White Falcon, 1955, The Bridge, 1957, Big Caesar, 1958, The Marauders, 1959, U.S. Army, 1960, The Gold of the River Sea, 1965, The Winter Beach, 1966, The Forging of Our Continent, 1968, The Continent in Our Hands, 1971, Winespring Mountain, 1973, The Southern Appalachians: A Wilderness Quest, 1975, The Adventure of Birds, 1976, Railroads: The Great American Adventure (Nat. Geog. Soc.), 1977, The Mysterious William Shakespeare: the Myth and the Reality, 1984, 2d edit., 1992, The Man Who Was Shakespeare, 1995; contbr. to mags. Served to capt. AUS, 1941-46, India-Burma. Recipient John Burroughs medal, 1967, Indonesian Order of Svc. medal, 1995. Home: 403 Hancock St Beaufort SC 29902-4717

OGBURN, HUGH BELL, chemical engineer, consultant; b. Lexington, Va., July 13, 1923; s. Sihon Cicero Jr. and Bettie Mae (Bell) O.; m. Anne Wotherspoon, Mar. 2, 1946 (div.); children: Margaret Mathews Berenson, Scott A.; m. Nancy Wrenn Petersen, Sept. 5, 1974. B.S., Princeton U., 1944, M.S., 1947, Ph.D., 1954. Sect. dir. research and devel. dept. Atlantic Refining Co., Phila., 1950-61; mgr. process engring. M.W. Kellogg Co., N.Y.C., London, 1961-67; dir. research and engring. Union Carbide Corp., N.Y.C., 1967-69; dir. new bus. devel. Weyerhaeuser Co., Tacoma, 1969-72; pres. H.B. Ogburn Assoc., Greenwich, Conn. and Honolulu, 1971—; v.p., dir. Incontrade Inc., Stamford, Conn., 1973-78; v.p. Pacific Resources Inc., Honolulu, 1978-83; chmn. Pacific Oasis, Los Angeles, 1983-85; dir. Danmore Corp., Planning Research Corp.; cons. AEC; prof. chem. engring. Drexel U., Phila., 1951-61. Contbr. articles to profl. jours.; patentee in field. Pres. bd. trustees Woman's Hosp., Phila., 1954-62, Kapiolani Women's and Children's Med. Ctr., 1980-90; mem. adv. bd. Princeton U., 1960-70. Served to lt. j.g. USNR, 1942-46, PTO. Mem. Am. Inst. Chem. Engrs., Am. Chem. Soc., Research Engrs. Soc., Phi Beta Kappa, Sigma Xi, Tau Beta Pi. Republican. Presbyterian. Clubs: Pacific (Honolulu); Greenwich Field (Conn.); Merion Cricket (Haverford, Pa.); Princeton (N.Y.C.). Home and Office: 4340 Pahoa Ave Apt 16 A Honolulu HI 96816-5032

OGBURN, WAYNE LEE, health science facility administrator; b. Tulsa, July 23, 1947; s. Luther Calveston and LaDessa Malvina (Bohrer) O.; m. Kay McAdoo, Dec. 27, 1969 (div. July 1984); children: Vicki Elizabeth, Donna Marie; m. Cherry Lynn Manuel Roberts, Feb. 1, 1986; 1 child, Jared Brandon Roberts. BA, Tex. A&M U., 1970; MS, Trinity U., 1972. Adminstrv. resident St. Paul Hosp., Dallas, 1973; asst. adminstr. Tarrant County Hosp. Dist., Ft. Worth, 1973-75, assoc. adminstr., 1975, acting dep. adminstr., 1976; adminstr. Caney Valley Meml. Hosp., Wharton, Tex., 1976-79; v.p. Hendrick Med. Ctr., Abilene, 1979-88, Hendrick Med. Devel. Corp., Abilene, 1979-88, Western Hosp. Affiliates, Inc., Abilene, 1985-88; sr. v.p. Dallas County Hosp. Dist., Parkland Meml Hosp, Dallas, 1988-91; CEO Titus County Meml. Hosp., Mt. Pleasant, Tex., 1991-95, Brazos Valley Med. and Surg. Ctrs., College Station, Tex., 1995—; commr. Houston/Galveston Area Hosp. System Agy., Houston, 1976-79; bd. mem. Group One, Inc., 1989-91; mem. Tex. State Bd. Vocat. Nurse Examiners, 1987-91, sec.-treas. 1988-89. Loaned exec. Abilene United Way, 1980-81, com. mem., 1986-87. Served with U.S. Army, 1970-71. Fellow Am. Coll. Healthcare Exec. (regents adv. coun. 1993-95); mem. Am. Hosp. Assn. (alt. del. regional policy bd. dirs. 1996—), Tex. Hosp. Assn. (bd. dirs. 1995—, divsn. sec. 1980-81), N.W. Tex. Hosp. Assn. (bd. dirs. 1985-88, pres. 1987-88), Wharton C. of C. (chmn. com. 1977), Mt. Pleasant C. of C. (bd. dirs. 1992—). Methodist. Avocations: antique autos, photography. Home: 5000 Crystal Dowas Ct College Station TX 77845 Office: Brazos Valley Med Ctr 1604 Rock Prairie Rd College Station TX 77845

OGDEN, ALFRED, lawyer; b. Bklyn., Oct. 14, 1909; s. Alfred Trecartin and Sophronia (Wisner) O.; m. Mary Fell Jordan, June 25, 1938; 1 child, Alfred Trecartin II. Grad., Phillips Acad., 1928; B.A., Yale, 1932; LL.B., Harvard, 1935. Bar: N.Y. 1936. Since practiced N.Y.C.; partner Alexander & Green, 1955-75; of counsel firm Morgan, Lewis & Bockius, 1979-80, c/o Reboul, MacMurray, Hewitt, Maynard & Kristol, 1980—; Pres., dir. C. Tennant, Sons & Co., N.Y.C., 1952-54. Trustee Fay Sch., Southborough, Mass., 1950-70, Population Reference Bur., 1963-68, Daniel and Florence Guggenheim Found., 1972—, Lavenberg Found., 1986—; trustee Mystic Seaport Mus., Mystic, Conn., 1959—, chmn., 1982-83, chmn. emeritus, 1983—; bd. mgrs., bd. overseers Meml. Sloan Kettering Cancer Ctr., 1959—; trustee, exec. com. Robert Coll., Istanbul, Turkey, 1952-73, chmn., 1955-63; bd. dirs., v.p. English Speaking Union U.S., 1950-92, acting pres., 1983-84; bd. dirs., mem. exec. com. Winston Churchill Meml. Fund., 1966—; trustee Planned Parenthood N.Y.C., 1977-83; bd. dirs. Children's Mus. Manhattan, 1985-87. Served to lt. col. Gen. Staff Corps AUS, 1942-46. Decorated Legion of Merit. Mem. ABA, Internat. Law Assn., Soc. Colonial Wars, Pilgrims of U.S., Coun. on Fgn. Rels., Century Assn., Yale Club (N.Y.C.), Wadawanuck Club (Stonington, Conn.), Cosmopolitan Club, Thursday Evening Club. Home: 150 E 73rd St New York NY 10021-4362 Also: PO Box 214 Stonington CT 06378-0214 Office: 10th Fl 45 Rockefeller Plz Fl 10 New York NY 10111-1099 *There is nothing permanent except change.*

OGDEN, ANITA BUSHEY, nursing educator; b. Malone, N.Y., May 23, 1938; d. John Richard and Eleanor Miriam (Wright) Bushey; m. William Alan Ogden, Dec. 27, 1972. Nursing diploma, N.Y. Med. Coll., 1959; BSN, Columbia U., 1962; MS in Adult Health, SUNY, Buffalo, 1968; PhD, Cornell U., 1984. Faculty Flower-Fifth Ave. Sch. Nursing, N.Y.C., 1959-62, Meth. Hosp., Bklyn. Sch. Nursing, N.Y.C., 1962-66, Hartwick Coll., Oneonta, N.Y., 1968-73; faculty, chair divsn. nursing edn. Corning (N.Y.) C.C., 1973-89; faculty Alfed U., Alfed Station, N.Y., 1984-88; prof., dir. nurse edn. Elmira (N.Y.) Coll., 1989—; clin. staff nurse various orgns., 1959—; cons. curriculum devel., 1978—. Mem. adv. coun. Alfed U., Alfed Station, 1984-87; mem. bd. dirs. Cmty. Health Svcs. for Elderly, Elmira, 1992—; nursing cons. St. Kitts/Nevis U.S. Aid Ptnrs. Ams., 1986-87. Mem. ANA (various offices), N.Y. State Nurses Assn. (various offices), Internat. Resources Instructional Svcs. (faculty 1990—), Nat. League for Nursing (regional bd. dirs. 1973—, ednl. cons. 1982—), LWV (regional coord.), Order Ea. Star (various offices), Delta Kappa Gamma (scholarship award 1981, 83), Delta Kappa Gamma (pres., bd. dirs. 1970), Sigma Theta Tau. Republican. Avocations: bicycling, hand crafts, cats. Home: 104 Fairview Ave Painted Post NY 14870-1215

OGDEN, DANIEL MILLER, JR., government official, educator; b. Clarksburg, W.Va., Apr. 28, 1922; s. Daniel Miller and Mary (Maphis) O.; m. Valeria Juan Munson, Dec. 28, 1946; children: Janeth Lee Martin, Patricia Jo Hunter, Daniel Munson. BA in Polit. Sci., Wash. State U., 1944; MA, U. Chgo., 1947, PhD, 1949. From instr. to assoc. prof. Wash. State U., Pullman, 1949-61; staff asst. resources program U.S. Dept. Interior, 1961-64; asst. dir. U.S. Bur. Outdoor Recreation, 1964-67; dir. budget U.S. Dept. Interior, Washington, 1967-68; dean Coll. Humanities and Social Scis. Colo. State U., Ft. Collins, 1968-76; disting. vis. prof. Lewis and Clark Coll. and Portland (Oreg.) State U., 1977-78; dir. Office of Power Mktg. Coordination U.S. Dept. Energy, 1978-84; mgr. Pub. Power Coun., Portland, Oreg., 1984-88, ret., 1988; mem. profl. staff com. interstate and fgn. commerce U.S. Senate, 1956-57; spll. asst. to chmn. Dem. Nat. Com., 1960-61; lectr. Mgmt. Devel. Ctrs., U.S. Office Pers. Mgmt., 1966—. Co-author: Electing the President, rev. edit., 1968, American National Government, 7th edit., 1970, American State and Local Government, 5th edit., 1972, Washington Politics, 1960, How National Policy is Made, 2d edit., 1995. Committeeman Wash. Dem. Ctrl. Com., 1952-56; chmn. Whitman County Dem. Ctrl. Com., 1958-60; chmn. 49th Legis. Dist. Dem. Com., 1990-94; chmn. Clark County Dem. Ctrl. com., 1994—. With inf. U.S. Army, 1943-46. Mem. Phi Beta Kappa, Phi Kappa Phi, Pi Sigma Alpha, Sigma Delta Chi. Mem. Unitarian Ch. Home: 3118 NE Royal Oak Dr Vancouver WA 98662-7435

OGDEN, DAVID WILLIAM, lawyer; b. Washington, Nov. 12, 1953; s. Horace Greeley and Elaine Celia (Condrell) O.; m. Wannett Smith, 1988; children: Jonathan Smith, Elaine Smith. BA summa cum laude, U. Pa., 1976; JD magna cum laude, Harvard U., 1981. Bar: D.C. 1983, Va. 1986, U.S. Dist. Ct. D.C. 1984, U.S. Dist. Ct. (ea. dist.) Va. 1988, U.S. Ct. Appeals (D.C. cir.) 1984, U.S. Ct. Appeals (4th cir.) 1986, U.S. Ct. Appeals (1st cir. 1989), U.S. Ct. Appeals (10th cir.) 1991, U.S. Supreme Ct. 1987. Law clk. to presiding judge U.S. Dist. Ct. (so. dist.) N.Y., N.Y.C., 1981-82; law clk. to assoc. justice Harry A. Blackmun U.S. Supreme Ct., Washington, 1982-83; assoc. atty. Ennis, Friedman, Bersoff & Ewing, Washington, 1983-85; atty., ptnr. Ennis, Friedman & Bersoff, Washington, 1986-88, Jenner & Block, Washington, 1988-94; legal counsel, dep. gen. counsel U.S. DOD, Washington, 1994-95; assoc. dep. atty. gen. U.S. Dept. Justice, Washington, 1995—; adj. prof. law Georgetown U. Law Ctr., 1992-95. Mem. ABA, D.C. Bar Assn. Democrat. Office: US Dept Justice 10th St & Constitution Ave Washington DC 20530

OGDEN, DAYTON, executive search consultant. CEO Spencer Stuart & Assocs., Stamford, Conn. Office: SpencerStuart & Assocs Fin Centre 695 E Main St Stamford CT 06901-2112

OGDEN, JOHN HAMILTON, lawyer; b. Newport News, Va., Sept. 14, 1951; s. Donald Thomas and Bernice (Hamilton) O.; m. Mary Lynne Vogel, May 11, 1973; children: Amy Elizabeth, Christopher Michael, Andrew David. AB, Villanova U., 1973; JD, Fordham U., 1977. Bar: N.J. 1977, U.S. Dist. Ct. N.J. 1977, U.S. Ct. Internat. Trade 1990. Sr. buyer Consol. Edison of N.Y., N.Y.C., 1973-77; contract mgr. Jersey Cen. Power & Light, Morristown, N.J., 1977-80; atty. Foster Wheeler Corp., Livingston, N.J., 1980-83; gen. counsel Werner & Pfleiderer Corp., Ramsey, N.J., 1983—; corp. sec. Werner & Pfleiderer Corp., Ramsey, 1989—; asst. sec., counsel Krupp USA Fin. Svcs. Inc., Ramsey, 1993—. Mem. Am. Corp. Counsel Assn. (chair 1990-91, small law dept. subcom., chmn. small law dept. com. 1991-92, bd. dirs. 1991—, sec. bd. dirs. 1994— chmn. edn. bd. com. 1992—, exec. com. 1992—, chair coun. nat. coms. 1994, sec. 1995, treas. 1996), N.J. Corp. Counsel Assn. (bd. dirs. 1992—, v.p., sec. 1992-93, pres. 1994-95, past pres., editor, contbr. Small Law Department Practitioners Desk Manual, 1993), N.J. Corp. Counsel Assn. Office: Werner & Pfleiderer Corp 663 E Crescent Ave Ramsey NJ 07446-1220

OGDEN, LOUANN MARIE, dietitian, consultant; b. Enid, Okla., Dec. 16, 1952; d. Raymond Michael Schiltz and Donna Mae Stuever; m. Wendell Edwin Ogden, Jan. 5, 1979; 1 child, Gregory Jacob Jeremiah. BS in Home Econs., Okla. State U., 1974, MS, 1977. Registered dietitian; lic. dietitian, Tex. Dietetic intern Ind. U. Med. Ctr., Indpls., 1974; therapeutic dietitian-clin. svcs. and trayline ops. Bapt. Med. Ctr. Okla., Oklahoma City, 1975-76; grad. teaching asst. lower and upper level food preparation Okla. State U., Stillwater, 1976-77, teaching assoc. lower and upper level food preparation, 1977; chief clin. dietitian adminstrv. and clin. coordination Borgess Hosp., Kalamazoo, 1978; dietary cons. nutrition program Iowa Commn. on Aging, Des Moines, 1979-80; asst. food svc. dir., adminstrv. dietitian Timberlawn Psych. Hosp., Dallas, 1980-92; rep. group one purchasing program, mem. student tng. program Zale Lipshy U. Hosp., Dallas, 1992-93, food svc. cons., 1993—. Mem. Am. Dietetic Assn., Am. Soc. Hosp. Food Svc. Adminstrn. (nat. nominating com. 1990-91, Disting. Health Care Food Svc. Adminstr. 1992, North ctrl. Tex. chpt.: corr. sec. 1985-86, comms. chair 1986-87, rec. sec. 1987-89, pres.-elect 1989-90, pres. 1990-91, nominating com. chair, health care food svc. week com. chair 1991-92, Outstanding Mem. award 1992), Tex. Dietetic Assn., Dallas Dietetic Assn. Democrat. Roman Catholic. Avocations: photography, traveling. Home and Office: 3302 Oxford Dr Rowlett TX 75088-5936

OGDEN, MAUREEN BLACK, retired state legislator; b. Vancouver, B.C., Nov. 1, 1928; came to U.S., 1930; d. William Moore and Margaret Hunter (Leitch) Black; m. Robert Moore Ogden, June 23, 1956; children: Thomas, Henry, Peter. BA, Smith Coll., 1950; MA, Columbia U., 1963; M in City and Regional Planning, Rutgers U., 1977. Researcher, staff asst. Ford Found., N.Y.C., 1951-56; staff assoc. Fgn. Policy Assn., N.Y.C., 1956-58; mem. Millburn (N.J.) Twp. Com., 1976-81; mayor Twp. of Millburn, N.J., 1979-81; mem. N.J. Gen. Assembly, Trenton, 1982—; chmn. Assembly Environment Com., N.J. Gen. Assembly; chmn. Energy and Pub. Utilities Com., Coun. State Govts., 1991-92; mem. adv. bd. Sch. Policy and Planning, Rutgers U., New Brunswick, N.J., 1992—. Author: Natural Resources Inventory, Township of Millburn, 1974. Bd. govs. N.J. Hist. Soc., Newark, 1990—; trustee N.J. chpt. The Nature Conservancy; hon. trustee Paper Mill Playhouse, Millburn, 1990—; former trustee St. Barnabas Med. Ctr., Livingston, N.J.; former pres. N.J. Drug Abuse Adv. Coun. Recipient citation Nat. Assn. State Outdoors Recreation Liaison Officers, 1987, cert. appreciation John F. Kennedy Ctr. for the Performing Arts, The Alliance for Art Edn., 1987, disting. svc. award Art Educators N.J., 1987, ann. environ. quality award EPA Region II, 1988, citation Humane Soc. U.S., 1989, award N.J. Hist. Sites Coun., 1989, N.J. Sch. Conservation, 1990, pres.'s award The Nature Conservancy, 1995, pub. policy award Nat. Trust for Hist. Preservation, 1995. Republican. Episcopalian. Home: 59 Lakeview Ave Short Hills NJ 07078-2240

OGDEN, PEGGY A., personnel director; b. N.Y.C., Mar. 21, 1932; d. Stephen Arnold and Margaret (Stern) O. BA with honors, Brown U., 1953; MA, Trinity Coll., Hartford, Conn., 1955. Asst. dir. YMCA Counseling Svc., Hartford, 1953-55; employment interviewer R.H. Macy & Co., N.Y.C., 1955; asst. pers. dir. Inst. Internat. Edn., N.Y.C., 1956-59; pers. advisor Girl Scouts U.S.A., N.Y.C., 1959-61; store and pers. mgr. Ohrbachs, Inc., N.Y.C., 1961-74; dir. pers. N.Y.C. Tech. Coll. CUNY, Bkyn., 1974—; arbitrator Better Bus. Bur., N.Y.C., 1988—; cons. Girl Scout Coun. N.Y., N.Y.C., 1988-89. Mem APA, Am. Assn. U. Adminstrs., Women in Human Resources, N.Y. Pers. Mgmt. Assn. Home: 1100 Park Ave New York NY 10128-1202 Office: NYC Tech Coll 300 Jay St Brooklyn NY 11201-2902

OGDEN, PETER JAMES, investment banker; b. Rochdale, Lancashire, Eng., May 26, 1947; s. James Platt and Frances (Simmonds) O.; m. Catherine Rose Blincoe, Aug. 22, 1970; children—Tiffany, Cameron, Edward. B.S., U. Durham, Eng., 1968, Ph.D., 1971; M.B.A., Harvard U., 1973. Mng. dir. Merrill Lynch Capital Market, London, 1975-80; mng. dir. Morgan Stanley Internat., London, 1980-87, adv. dir., 1987—; chmn. Computacenter Ltd., 1981—, also bd. dirs.; mng. dir. MC & Cie Ltd. Home: 10 Upper Phillimore Gardens, London W8 7HA, England Office: Computacenter Ltd, 93-101 Blackfriars Rd, London SE1 8HW, England

OGDEN, VALERIA JUAN, management consultant, state representative; b. Okanogan, Wash., Feb. 11, 1924; d. Ivan Bodwell and Pearle (Wilson) Munson; m. Daniel Miller Ogden Jr., Dec. 28, 1946; children: Janeth Lee Ogden Martin, Patricia Jo Ogden Hunter, Daniel Munson Ogden. BA magna cum laude, Wash. State U., 1946. Exec. dir. Potomac Coun. Camp Fire, Washington, 1964-68, Ft. Collins (Colo.) United Way, 1969-73, Designing Tomorrow Today, Ft. Collins, 1973-74, Poudre Valley Community Edn. Assn., Ft. Collins, 1977-78; pres. Valeria M. Ogden, Inc., Kensington, Md., 1978-81; nat. field cons. Camp Fire, Inc., Kansas City, Mo., 1980-81; exec. dir. Nat. Capital Area YWCA, Washington, 1981-84, Clark County YWCA, Vancouver, Wash., 1985-89; pvt. practice mgmt. cons. Vancouver, 1989—; mem. Wash. Ho. of Reps., 1991—; mem. adj. faculty pub. adminstrn. program Lewis and Clark Coll., Portland (Oreg.) State U., 1979-94; mem. Pvt. Industry Coun., Vancouver, 1986-95; mem. regional Svcs. Network Bd., 1993—. Author: Camp Fire Membership, 1980. County vice chmn. Larimer County Dems., Ft. Collins, 1974-75; mem. precinct com. Clark County Dems., Vancouver, 1986-88; mem. Wash. State Coun. Vol. Action, Olympia, 1986-90; treas. Mortar Bd. Nat. Found., Vancouver, 1987—; bd. dirs. Clark County Coun. for Homeless, Vancouver, 1989—, chmn., 1994; bd. dirs. Wash. Wildlife and Recreation Coalition, 1995—, Human Svcs. Coun., 1996—. Named Citizen of Yr. Ft. Collins Bd. of Realtors, 1975; recipient Gulick award Camp Fire Inc., 1956, Alumna Achievement award Wash. State U. Alumni Assn., 1988. Mem. Internat. Assn. Vol. Adminstrs. (pres. Boulder 1989-90), Nat. Assn. YWCA Exec. Dirs. (nat. bd. nominating com. 1988-90), Sci. and Society Assn. (bd. dirs. 1993—), Women in Action, Philanthropic and Ednl. Orgn., Phi Beta Kappa. Democrat. Avocation: hiking, travel. Home: 3118 NE Royal Oak Dr Vancouver WA 98662-7435 Office: John L O'Brien Bldg Rm 342 State Ave NE Olympia WA 98504-1134

OGDON, WILBUR, composer, music educator; b. Redlands, Calif., Apr. 19, 1921; s. Alfred Benjamin and Ethel (Brooks) O.; m. Beverly Jean Porter, Aug. 22, 1958; children—Bethany, Benjamin, Erica. MusB, U. Wis., 1942; MA, Hamline U., 1947; postgrad., U. Calif., Berkeley, 1949-50; pvt. composition studies with René Leibowitz, Paris, 1952-53; composition studies; Ph.D., Ind. U., 1955. Asst. prof. U. Tex., 1947-50; prof. Coll. St. Catherine, St. Paul, 1955-56; assoc. prof. Ill. Wesleyan U., 1956-65; dir. music Pacifica Found., KPFA, Berkeley, Calif., 1962-64; coordinator music programming U. Ill., 1965-66; prof. music U. Calif., San Diego, 1966-91, chmn. dept. music, 1966-71, research fellow Project for Music Expt., 1973-74. Author: (with Krenek and Stewart) Horizons Circled, 1974; mem. editorial bd. Perspective of New Music; composer: Three Sea Choruses, 1960-62, String Quartet, 1960, By the Isar, 1969, Un Tombeau de Cocteau, I, 1964, II, 1972, III, 1975, Sappho, The Awakening (chamber opera), 1976-80, Capriccio and Five Comments for Orch, 1980, Images, A Winter's Calendar (Soprano, piano and 3 winds), 1980, Six Small Trios for trumpet, marimba and piano, 1982, Five Preludes for violin and piano, 1982, Summer Images and Reflections, 1984-85, Five Preludes for Violin and Chamber Orchestra, 1985, Two Serenades for Wind Quintet, 1987, 90-94, Two Sea Chanteys for soprano, baritone and percussion, 1987-88, Seven Piano Pieces, 1987, 7 pieces and a Capriccio for violin and piano, 1988-89, Four D.H. Lawrence Songs for Soprano and Chamber Ensemble, 1989, 13 Expressions for solo violin and chamber ensemble, 1993, others. Bd. dirs. San Diego Opera Inc., 1967-70, La Jolla Civic Orch. and Chorus Assn., 1967-72, 80-82; hon. dir. N.C. Gov.'s Bd. Music, 1964—. Served with AUS, 1942-46. Nat. Endowment of Arts fellow, 1975. Mem. Anton Webern Soc. (charter), Music Execs. Calif., Calif. Profl. Music Tchrs. Assn. (hon.). Home: 452 15th St Del Mar CA 92014-2521 Office: U Calif at San Diego Dept Music La Jolla CA 92037 *As years pass, one becomes increasingly aware of an indebtedness to others: to those who taught, encouraged, tolerated and even sacrificed. That increasing sense of indebtedness serves to sustain one's own efforts to teach and encourage.*

OGG, GEORGE WESLEY, retired foreign service officer; b. Washington, June 13, 1932; s. William Raymond and Carrie (Blair) O.; m. Frances Zabilsky, Sept. 17, 1954; children: David Stuart, Carolyn Ogg Tripp. A.B., Colgate U., N.Y., 1954; M.A., George Washington U., Washington, 1970; postgrad., U. Md., College Park, 1968-69, Nat. Def. Coll., Can., 1977-78. Chief econ. sect. U.S. Embassy, San Jose, Costa Rica, 1974-77; chief commodities and developing countries div. Dept. of State, 1978-80; dep. dir. Office Canadian Affairs, Dept. of State, 1980-82; consul gen. U.S. Consulate Gen., Vancouver, B.C., Can., 1982-86; prof. internat. rels. Nat. Defense U., Washington, 1986-91. Served to 1st lt. USAF, 1954-57. Recipient Superior Honor award U.S. Dept. State, 1974, Meritorious Honor award, 1980. Avocations: tennis, photography.

OGG, JAMES ELVIS, microbiologist, educator; b. Centralia, Ill., Dec. 24, 1924; s. James and Amelia (Glammeyer) O.; m. Betty Jane Ackerson, Dec. 27, 1948; children—James George, Susan Kay. B.S., U. Ill., 1949; Ph.D., Cornell U., 1956. Bacteriologist Biol. Labs., Ft. Detrick, Md., 1950-53; cons. Biol. Labs., 1953-56, med. bacteriologist, 1956-58; prof. microbiology Colo. State U., Ft. Collins, 1958-85, prof. emeritus, 1985—; asst. dean Grad. Sch., 1965-66, head dept. microbiology, 1967-77; dir. Advanced Sci. Edn. Program div. grad. edn. in sci. NSF, Washington, 1966-67; Fulbright-Hays sr. lectr. in microbiology, Nepal, 1976-77, 81; acad. adminstrn. advisor Inst. Agr. and Animal Sci., Tribhuvan U., Nepal, 1988-91; cons. NASA, 1968-69, NSF, 1968-73, Martin Marietta Corp., 1970-76; cons.-evaluator North Central Assn. Colls. and Secondary Schs., 1974-89; cons. Consortium for Internat. Devel., 1990—, Winrock Internat. Inst. for Agrl. Devel., 1992—. Contbr. articles to profl. jours. Served with AUS, 1943-46, 50-51. Fellow AAAS, Am. Acad. Microbiology; mem. Am. Soc. Microbiology (chmn. pub. service and adult edn. com. 1975-80). Home: 1442 Ivy St Fort Collins CO 80525-2348

OGG, ROBERT DANFORTH, corporate executive; b. Gardiner, Maine, June 10, 1918; s. James and Eleanor B. (Danforth) O.; m. Nancy Foote, Oct. 21, 1978; children by previous marriage: Richard Aasgaard, Robert Danforth, James Erling. Student U. Calif., Berkeley, Stanford U. Utilities engr. State of Calif., 1946-48; gen. mgr. Danforth Anchors, Berkeley, 1948-51, pres., chief exec. officer, 1951-59; mng. dir. Danforth div. The Eastern Co., 1959-79, dir., 1972-80; dir. Hodgdon Bros., East Boothbay, Maine, 1961-65; pres. Brewers Boatyard, West Southport, Maine, 1963-65; v.p. Henry R. Hinckley Co., Manset, Maine, 1974-79; pres. Ogg Oceans Systems, 1980—; chmn. Alpha Ocean Systems, 1983—. Author: Anchors & Anchorin (8 editions); contbr. chpts. to books, articles to profl. jours.; patentee in field;

inventor The Danforth Anchor, Inertial Altimeter, Digital Depth Sounder, others. Mem. adv. com. U. Calif. Rsch. Expeditions Program, 1979, co-chmn., 1983—; trustee U. Calif.-Berkeley Found., 1981, exec. com., 1983—, chmn. audit com., 1984-89, fellow, 1990, lifetime emeritus trustee: advisor Lawrence Hall Sci.; founder, sr. warden St. Ann's Episcopal Ch., Windham, Maine, 1976-79; life fellow U. Calif., Berkeley; contbr. to ABC and BBC documentaries on Pearl Harbor. With USN Intelligence, 1941-46. Recipient Wheeler Oak meritorious award U. Calif., 1987. Fellow Explorers Club (life), Calif. Acad. Scis. (life); mem. Navy League (founder Marin coun.), Soc. Naval Architects & Marine Engrs., Am. Soc. Naval Engrs., Am. Boat & Yacht Coun., Boating Writers Internat., Am. Geophys. Union, IEEE, Chancflors Cir. U. Calif., Sports Adv. Coun. U. Calif., Bodega Marine Lab., U.S. Naval Inst., R.G. Sproul Assocs., Tail Hook Assocs., Woodshole Assocs., Bunckle Microsurgical Found. (bd. dirs. 1994—), Sierra Club, U. Calif.-Berkeley Alumni Assn., Engring. Alumni Assn., N.Y. Yacht Club, Pacific Union Club, Elks Club, Bear Backers Club, U. Calif. Berkeley Chancellor's Circle Club, U. Calif. San Francisco Heritage Club. Address: 11490 Franz Valley Rd Calistoga CA 94515-9549

OGG, WILSON REID, lawyer, poet, retired judge, lyricist, curator, publisher, educator, philosopher, social scientist, parapsychologist; b. Alhambra, Calif., Feb. 26, 1928; s. James Brooks and Mary (Wilson) O. Student Pasadena Jr. Coll., 1946; A.B., U. Calif. at Berkeley, 1949, J.D., 1952; Cultural D in Philosophy of Law, World Univ. Roundtable, 1983. Bar: Calif. Assoc. trust Dept. Wells Fargo Bank, San Francisco, 1954-55; pvt. practice law, Berkeley, 1955—; adminstrv. law judge, 1974-93; real estate broker, cons., 1974—; curator-in-residence Pinebrook, 1964—; owner Pinebrook Press, Berkeley, Calif., 1988—; rsch. atty., legal editor dept. of continuing edn. of bar U. Calif. Extension, 1958-63; psychology instr. 25th Sta. Hosp., Taegu, Korea, 1954; English instr. Taegu English Lang. Inst., Taegu, 1954. Trustee World U., 1976-80; dir. admissions Internat. Soc. for Phil. Enquiry, 1981-84; dep. dir. gen. Internat. Biographical Centre, Eng., 1986—; dep. gov. Am. Biographical Inst. Research Assn., 1986—. Served with AUS, 1952-54. Cert. community coll. instr. Mem. VFW, AAAS, ABA, State Bar Calif., San Francisco Bar Assn., Am. Arbitration Assn. (nat. panel arbitrators), World Future Soc. (profl. mem.), Calif. Soc. Psychical Study (pres., chmn. bd. 1963-65), Internat. Soc. Unified Sci., Internat. Soc. Poets, (life), Internat. Platform Assn., Amnesty Internat., Am. Civil Liberties Union, Intertel, Internat. Soc. Individual Liberty, Triple Nine Soc., Wisdom Soc., Inst. Noetic Scis., Men's Inner Circle of Achievement, Truman Libr. Inst. (hon.), Am. Legion, Faculty Club (U. Calif.), City Commons Club (Berkeley), Commonwealth Club of Calif., Town Hall Club of Calif., Marines Meml. Club, Masons, Shriners, Elks. Unitarian. Contbr. numerous articles profl. jours; contbr. poetry to various mags. including American Poetry Anthology Vol. VI Number 5, Hearts on Fire: A Treasury of Poems on Love, Vol. IV, 1987, New Voices in American Poetry, 1987, The Best Poems of the 90's, Distinguished Poets of America, The Poetry of Life A Treasury of Moments Am. Poetry Anthology, Vol. VII, 1988, Nat. Libr. Poets, 1992, Disting. Poets Of Am., 1993, The Best Modern Writer of 1994, Parnassus of World Poets, 1994, 95, 96, Best Poems of 1995. Home: Pinebrook 8 Bret Harte Way Berkeley CA 94708-1611 Office: 1104 Keith Ave Berkeley CA 94705-1607 also: 14895 E 14th St Ste 240 San Leandro CA 94578 also: 39229 Liberty St # C-4 Fremont CA 94538

OGIDA, MIKIO, history of religion educator; b. Akita, Japan, Jan. 20, 1938; s. Shigeji and Kiyono (Sato) O.; m. Noriko Yamamoto, May 3, 1966; 1 child, Satoshi. BD, Doshisha U., Kyoto, Japan, 1961; S.T.M., Doshisha U., 1963; ThM, Harvard U., 1969. Assoc. minister Heian Ch., United Ch. of Christ in Japan, Kyoto, 1963-66; lectr. Kobe Jogakuin U., Nishinomiya, Hyogo, Japan, 1969-72; assoc. prof. Kobe Jogakuin U., 1972-81, prof., 1981—, dean students, 1989-93. Author: Religions of the World, 1981. Mem. Japan Soc. Christian Studies, Soc. Hist. Studies Christianity Japan, Classical Soc. Japan. Avocation: igo, skiing. Home: 4 11 1 108 Makami cho, Takatuki shi Osaka, Japan Office: Kobe Jogakuin U. 4 1 Okadayama, Nishinomiya Hyogo, Japan

OGIER, WALTER THOMAS, retired physics educator; b. Pasadena, Calif., June 18, 1925; s. Walter Williams and Aileen Vera (Polhamus) O.; m. Mayrene Miriam Gorton, June 27, 1954; children: Walter Charles, Margaret Miriam, Thomas Earl, Kathryn Aileen. B.S., Calif. Inst. Tech., 1947, Ph.D. in Physics, 1953. Research fellow Calif. Inst. Tech., 1953; instr. U. Calif. at Riverside, 1954-55, asst. prof. physics, 1955-60; asst. prof. physics Pomona Coll., Claremont, Calif., 1960-62, assoc. prof., 1962-67, prof. physics, 1967-89, prof. emeritus, 1989—, chmn. dept., 1972-89. Contbr. articles on metals, liquid helium, X-rays and proton produced X-rays to profl. jours. Served with USNR, 1944-46. NSF Sci. Faculty fellow, 1966-67. Mem. Am. Phys. Soc., Am. Assn. Physics Tchrs. (pres. So. Calif. sect. 1967-69), Tau Beta Pi. Home: 8555 San Gabriel Rd Atascadero CA 93422-4928

OGILVIE, DONALD GORDON, bankers association executive; b. N.Y.C., Apr. 7, 1943; s. John B. and Ann (Stephens) O.; m. Fan Staunton, Apr. 18, 1966; children: Jennifer B., Adam C. B.A., Yale U., 1965; M.B.A., Stanford U., 1967. Systems analyst Dept. of Def., Washington, 1967-68; pres., dir. ICF Inc., Washington, 1969-73; dep. assoc. dir. Office of Mgmt. and Budget, Washington, 1973-74, assoc. dir., 1974-76; assoc. dean Yale U., New Haven, 1977-80; v.p. Celanese Corp., N.Y.C., 1980-85; exec. v.p. Am. Bankers Assn., Washington, 1985—; dir. Colonial Bancorp, 1979-85, MacDermid Corp., 1986—, Marine Spill Response Corp., 1991—. Bd. dirs. N.Y.C. Ballet, 1981-88, Hospiec Edn. and Rsch., New Haven, 1978-81; mem. adv. bd. Yale Sch. Orgn. and Mgmt., 1992-94. Home: 1425 34th St NW Washington DC 20007-2804 Office: Am Bankers Assn 1120 Connecticut Ave NW Washington DC 20036-3902

OGILVIE, KELVIN KENNETH, university president, chemistry educator; b. Windsor, N.S., Can., Nov. 6, 1942; s. Carl Melbourn and Mabel Adelia (Wile) O.; m. Emma Roleen, May 7, 1964; children: Kristine, Kevin. B.Sc. with honors, Acadia U., 1964, D.Sc. honoris causa, 1983; Ph.D., Northwestern U., 1968; D.Sc. honoris causa, U. N.B., Can., 1991. Assoc. prof. U. Man., Winnipeg, 1968-74; prof. chemistry McGill U., Montreal, 1974-88, Can. Pacific prof. biotech., 1984-87; bd. dirs. Sci. Adv. Bd., Biologicals, Toronto, Ont., 1979-84; dir. Office of Biotech. McGill U., 1984-87; v.p. acad. affairs, prof. chemistry Acadia U., Wolfville, N.S., 1987-93, pres., vice-chancellor, 1993—; bd. dirs. Royal Pharm. Corp., Toronto; invited lectr. on biotech. Tianjin, People's Republic of China, 1985; Snider lectr. U. Toronto, 1991; Gwen Leslie Meml. lectr., 1991; mem. Nat. Adv. Bd. Sci. and Tech., 1994—; chair selection com. Indsl. Postgrad. Scholarship program NSERCC, 1994; mem. Coun. N.S. U. Pres. 1993—; mem. Coun. of Applied Sci. and Tech. for N.S., 1988-93; mem. Nat. Biotech. Adv. Com., 1988—; mem. Fisher (Can.) Biotech. Adv. Ctr., 1989-92; mem. sci. adv. bd. Allelix Biopharms., 1991-93; bd. dirs. Hyal Pharm. Corp.; chair adv. bd. NRC Inst. for Marine Bioscis., 1990-93; mem. steering com. on biotech. labor Can., 1990-92; chair Atlantic regional com. Prime Min.'s Awards for Tchg. Excellence in Sci., Tech. and Math., 1993—; chair regional planning forum for a pharm. industry, Atlantic, Can., 1993. Mem. editorial bd. Nucleosides and Nucleotides, 1981-92; contbr. over 150 articles to profl. jours.; holder 14 patents. Bd. dirs. Plant Biotech. Inst., 1987-90. Hon. col. Can. Air Force, 1995. Decorated Knight of Malta, 1985, Order of Can., 1991, Hon. Col. 14th Air Maintenance Squadron, Can. Air Force, 1995—; recipient Commemorative medal for 125th Anniversary of Confedn. Can., 1992, Buck-Whitney medal, 1983, Manning Prin. award,1 992; named to McLean's Honor Roll of Canadians Who Made a Difference, 1988; E.W.R. Steacie Meml. fellow, 1982-84; named Hon. Col. Can. Air Force, 1995. Fellow Chem. Inst. Can.; mem. Am. Chem. Soc., Ordre des Chemists of Que., Assn. Canadienne Française pour l'Advancement des Scis., Assn. Univs. and Colls. Can. (standing com. on rsch. 1993—). Achievements include inventing of BIOLF-62 (ganciclovir), antiviral drug used worldwide; developed general synthesis of RNA; developed original 'gene machine'; developer complete chemical synthesis of large RNA molecules. Home: PO Box 307, Canning, NS Canada B0P 1H0 Office: Acadia U, Office of Pres, Wolfville, NS Canada B0P 1X0

OGILVIE, RICHARD IAN, clinical pharmacologist; b. Sudbury, Ont., Can., Oct. 9, 1936; s. Patrick Ian and Gena Hilda (Olson) O.; m. Ernestine Tahedl, Oct. 9, 1965; children—Degen Elisabeth, Lars Ian. M.D., U. Toronto, 1960. Intern Toronto (Ont.) Gen. Hosp., 1960-61; resident Montreal Gen. and Univ. Alta. hosps., 1962-66; fellow in clin. pharmacology McGill U., Montreal, 1966-68; asst. prof. medicine, pharmacology and therapeutics McGill U., 1968-73, assoc. prof., 1973-78, prof., 1978-83, chmn. dept. pharmacology and therapeutics, 1978-83; clin. pharmacologist Montreal Gen. Hosp., 1968-83, dir. div. clin. pharmacology, 1976-83; prof. medicine and pharmacology U. Toronto, 1983—; dir. div. cardiology Toronto Western Hosp., 1983-88, div. clin. pharmacology, 1983-91; mem. pharm. grants com. Med. Research Coun. Can., 1977-82, chmn. 1980-82; mem. med. adv. com. Que. Heart Found., 1976-82, chmn. 1977-81. Editor Hypertension Canada, 1989—. Bd. dirs. PMAC Health Care Found., 1986-92; hon. sec.-treas. Banting Research Found., 1984-87, chmn. grant rev. com., 1985-86. Decorated knight comdr. Sovereign Mil. Order St. John of Jerusalem, Knights of Malta, 1987, nat. chmn., recipient prize in med. ethics, 1988—, sci. advisor to the prior, 1987—, Knight Grand Cross, 1990; jury mem. Can. Prix Galien, 1994—; grantee Can. Kidney Found., J.C. Edwards Found., Med. Rsch. Coun., Que. Heart Found., Can. Found. Advancement Therapeutics, Conseil de la recherche en sante du Que. Fellow ACP, Royal Coll. Physicians of Can.; mem. Can. Soc. Clin. Investigation (coun. 1977-80), Can. Hypertension Soc. (bd. dirs. 1979-81, 89—, v.p. 1991-92, pres. 1992-93), Can. Found. Advancement Clin. Pharmacology (dir. 1978-86), Canadian Soc. for Clin. Pharmacology (pres. 1979-82, Sr. Investigator award 1993), Internat. Union Pharmacology (coun. mem. clin. pharmacology sect. 1981-84, chmn. 1984-87), Pharm. Soc. Can., Can. Cardiovascular Soc., Am. Soc. Pharmacology and Exptl. Therapeutics, Am. Soc. Clin. Pharm., Am. Fedn. Clin. Rsch., Toronto Hypertension Soc. (pres. 1988—). Home: 79 Collard Dr, King City, ON Canada L7B 1E4 Office: Toronto Hosp Western Div, 399 Bathurst St, Toronto, ON Canada M5T 2S8

OGILVIE, T(HOMAS) FRANCIS, engineer, educator; b. Atlantic City, Sept. 26, 1929; s. Thomas Fleisher and Frances Augusta (Wilson) O.; m. Joan Husselton, Sept. 11, 1950; children: Nancy Louise, Mary Beth, Kenneth Stuart. B.A. in Physics, Cornell U., 1950; M.Sc. in Aero. Engring., U. Md., 1957; Ph.D. in Engring. Sci., U. Calif., Berkeley, 1960. Physicist, David Taylor Model Basin, Dept. Navy, Bethesda, Md., 1951-62, 64-67; liaison scientist Office of Naval Research, London, 1962-63; asso. prof. naval architecture and marine engring. U. Mich., Ann Arbor, 1967-70; prof. fluid mechanics U. Mich., 1970-81, chmn. dept. naval architecture and marine engring., 1973-81; prof. ocean engring. MIT, Cambridge, 1982-96, prof. emeritus, 1996—, head dept., 1996—; vis. prof. naval architecture Osaka (Japan) U., 1976; vis. prof. math. U. Manchester, Eng., 1976. Contbr. articles to profl. jours. Mem. Soc. Naval Architects and Marine Engrs. (coun. 1977-82, exec. com. 1978-80, 83-84), Sigma Xi, Phi Beta Kappa. Home: 110 Gray St Arlington MA 02174-6337 Office: MIT Dept Ocean Engring Cambridge MA 02139

OGILVY, DAVID MACKENZIE, advertising executive; b. West Horsley, Eng., June 23, 1911; s. Francis John Longley and Dorothy (Fairfield) O.; m. Herta Lans, July 6, 1973; 1 son, David Fairfield. Ed., Fettes Coll., Edinburgh, 1924-29, Christ Church, Oxford U., 1929-31. Asso. dir. Audience Research Inst., Princeton, 1939-42; with Brit. Security Coordination, 1942-44; 2d sec. Brit. embassy, Washington, 1944-45; founder, later chmn. Ogilvy & Mather (advt. agy.), N.Y.C., 1948-73; chmn. bd. Ogilvy & Mather (advt. agy.), 1961-75; chmn. WPP Group, London, 1988-92, consultant, 1992—. Author: Confessions of an Advertising Man, 1963, Blood, Brains and Beer, 1978, Ogilvy on Advertising, 1983, The Unpublished David Ogilvy, 1988. Chmn. pub. participation com. Lincoln Center, 1959; trustee Colby Coll., 1963-69; bd. dirs. N.Y. Philharmonic, 1957-67; chmn. United Negro Coll. Fund, 1968; mem. of honor World Wildlife Fund Internat. Decorated comdr. Order Brit. Empire; recipient Parlin award Am. Mktg. Assn., 1972; elected to Advt. Hall of Fame, 1977, officier de L'Ordre des Arts et des Lettres, 1990. Office: Chateau De Touffou, 86300 Bonnes France

OGLE, WALTER L., insurance company executive. Exec. v.p. Nations Bank of Ga., NA. Office: 123 N Wacker Dr Ste 100 Chicago IL 60606

OGLESBY, BEVERLY CLAYTON, kindergarten educator; b. Jacksonville, Fla., Mar. 11, 1950; d. Willie Edward Clayton and Venetta (Preston) Singleton; m. Eugene Oglesby, June 23, 1974; children: Venetta, Erin. BS, Fla. Meml. Coll., 1971; MEd, U. North Fla., 1982. Cert. tchr., Fla. 3d grade tchr. S. Bryan Jennings Elem. Sch., Orange Park, Fla., 1971-75, kindergarten tchr., 1975-77, 83-90, 1993-94, 2d grade tchr., 1977-82, 1st grade tchr., 1982-83, devel. 1st grade tchr., 1990-92, devel. 2d grade tchr., 1992-93, devel. kindergarten tchr., 1994—; kindergarten team leader S. Bryan Jennings Elem. Sch. 1975-90; mem. instrnl. material coun. Clay County Schs., Green Cove Springs, Fla., 1989, devel. dist. com. 1990-92; presenter Clay County Whole Lang. Clay County Reading Coun., Orange Park, 1988-89, So. Early Childhood Assn. and Early Childhood Assn. of Fla. Confs. SACS com. mem. Forest Hill Elem. Sch., Jacksonville, 1973; SECA rep. State of Fla.; mem. PTA bd. Oceanway Jr. High Sch., Jacksonville, 1980. Named S. Bryan Jenning Elem. Sch. Tchr. of Yr., 1989-90. Mem. Early Childhood Assn. Fla. (past pres. 1973-91, pres. 1992-93, SECA rep. 1995—), So. Early Childhood Assn. (chair membership com. 1993-95), Nat. Assn. for Edn. Young Children, Assn. Childhood Edn. Internat., North Fla. Assn. Young Children (pres. 1986-87), Phi Delta Kappa. Avocations: reading and collecting children's books, walking. Home: 3138 Rhone Dr Jacksonville FL 32208-2465

OGLESBY, CINDY SUE, accountant; b. Dumas, Tex., Oct. 15, 1963; d. Lawrence Ray Morris and Sue Ellen Shockley; m. James Thomas Oglesby, Jr., Dec. 30, 1984; 1 child, Kathlyna Sue Morris. BBA in Acctg., U. Tex., Tyler, 1988, MBA, 1992. CPA Tex.; CMA. Bookkeeper, office mgr. Mr. "C" Food Store, Dallas, 1982-84; staff acct., accts. payable clk. Lehigh Press, Inc., Dallas, 1984-86; quality control statistician Manpower, Inc. (Trane, Inc.), Tyler, 1986-87; staff acct. Dr.'s Meml. Hosp., Tyler, 1987-89; profit planning acct. Tyler Pipe Industries, Inc., 1989-90, profit planning supr., 1990—. Leader Camp Fire Boys and Girls, Tyler, 1991-94. Mem. AICPA, Tex. Soc. CPAs, Inst. Mgmt. Accts. (dir. newsletter 1991-92, v.p. adminstrn. 1992-93, chpt. pres. 1993-94, dir. CMA programs 1994-95). Avocations: reading, sewing, camping. Home: 10804 County Road 212 Tyler TX 75707-9516 Office: Tyler Pipe Industries Inc PO Box 2027 Tyler TX 75710-2027

OGLESBY, SABERT, JR., retired research institute administrator; b. Birmingham, Ala., May 14, 1921; s. Sabert Sr. and Myrtle (Dunn) O.; m. Carolyn Vance, Mar. 4, 1944; 1 child, Donald Thomas. B.S.E.E., Auburn U., 1943; M.S.E.E., Purdue U., 1951. Registered profl. engr., Ala. Research engr. So. Research Inst., Birmingham, 1946-48; various positions So. Research Inst., 1951-80, pres., 1980-87, pres. emeritus, 1987—; instr. Purdue U., West Lafayette, Ind., 1948-51. Author: Heat Pump Application; Electrostatic Precipitation. Mem. exec. bd. Birmingham Music Club, 1982—. 1st lt. Signal Corps, U.S. Army, 1943-46. Named to Ala. Engring. Hall of Fame, 1989. Mem. Internat. com. on Electrostatic Precipitation (steering com. 1978-85), Kiwanis (bd. dirs. 1982-83, 85-86), Vestavia Country Club, Sigma Xi, Tau Beta Pi, Eta Kappa Nu. Republican. Presbyterian. Avocations: golf; gem cutting; music. Home: 1348 Panorama Dr Birmingham AL 35216-3013

OGLIARUSO, MICHAEL ANTHONY, chemist, educator; b. Bklyn., Aug. 10, 1938; s. Andrea and Anna (Bianco) O.; m. Basila Gallo, Apr. 2, 1961; 1 child, Michael Dana. B.S., Poly. Inst. Bklyn., 1960, Ph.D., 1965. Postdoctoral research assoc. UCLA, 1965-67; asst. prof. chemistry Va. Poly. Inst. and State U., Blacksburg, 1967-72; assoc. prof. Va. Poly. Inst. and State U., 1972-78, prof., 1978-95, assoc. dean Coll. Arts and Scis., 1984-95; ret. Coll. Arts and Scis. Contbr. articles to profl. jours. Served with C.E. U.S. Army, 1960-61. Mem. Am. Chem. Soc., Va. Acad. Sci., Sigma Xi, Phi Lambda Upsilon. Office: Va Poly Inst and State U Dept Chemistry Davidson Hall Blacksburg VA 24061 *I have been fortunate to be associated with the most personally rewarding profession available today, the professional education of young men and women. This career is best suited to persons who wish to remain young in spirit, since regardless of your age you are always surrounded with students who are between 18 and 22 years old. This is the best way I know to remain spiritually young.*

OGNIBENE, ANDRE J(OHN), physician, army officer, educator; b. N.Y.C., Nov. 18, 1931; s. Morris S. and Josephine C. (Macaluso) O.; m. Margaret A. Haug, Apr. 21, 1957; children: Judy, Andrea, Adrienne, Marc, Eric. B.A. cum laude, Columbia U., 1952; M.D., NYU, 1956. Diplomate Am. Bd. Internal Medicine, Am. Bd. Geriatrics, Am. Bd. Med. Mgmt. Intern in medicine Bellevue Hosp., N.Y.C., 1956-57; resident in medicine Bellevue Hosp., 1957-59; commd. capt. U.S. Army M.C., 1957, advanced through grades to brig. gen., 1978; resident in medicine Manhattan VA Hosp., N.Y.C. and chief resident in medicine, 1959-60; chief med. service U.S. Army Hosp., Nurnburg, Germany, 1961-62; chief dept. medicine U.S. Army Hosp., 1962-64; fellow in cardiology Walter Reed Gen. Hosp., Washington, 1964-65; asst. in cardiology Walter Reed Gen. Hosp., 1965-66, asst. chief dept. medicine, 1969-72; chief dept. medicine, chief profl. services U.S. Army Hosp., Ft. Meade, Md., 1966-68; cons. in medicine Hdqrs. U.S. Army, Vietnam, 1969; asst. chief Dept. of Medicine Walter Reed Army Med. Ctr., 1970-72; chief dept. medicine Brooke Army Med. Center, Ft. Sam Houston, Tex., 1972-76; dir. med. edn. Brooke Army Med. Center, 1976-78, dep. comdr. and chief profl. services, 1976-78, comdr., 1978-81; hosp. dir. San Antonio State Chest Hosp., 1981-85; program dir. internal medicine Canton, Ohio, 1985-95; assoc. dean for med. edn., med. dir. Timken Mercy Med. Ctr., Canton, 1995—; prof. medicine N.E. Ohio U., Rootstown, 1985—; chmn. dept. medicine N.E. Ohio U., 1989—; instr. medicine NYU, 1960; assoc. clin. prof. Georgetown U., 1970-72; clin. prof. U. Tex. Health Sci. Center, San Antonio, 1973-85, mem. postgrad. adv. com., 1977-78; mem. Instl. Rev. Bd., 1981-85; pres. Bexar Met. unit Am. Cancer Soc., 1984; dir. Eisenhower Nat. Bank; bd. dirs. Cancer Therapy and Research Ctr.; chmn. South Tex. Epilepsy Found., 1985. Contbr. articles to med. publs. and chpts. to books; editor, prin. author Internal Medicine in Vietnam, vol. II, 1982; editor-in-chief: Internal Medicine in Vietnam, vol. I, 1977. Bd. govs. S.W. Cancer Therapy Inst., 1982-85; bd. trustees Regina Health Ctr., 1992—. Decorated Disting. Service medal, Legion of Merit, Meritorious Service medal, Army Commendation medal. Fellow ACP (laureate, master tchr.), Am. Coll. Physician Execs.; mem. N.Y. Acad. Scis., Am. Fedn. Clin. Rsch., Bexar County Med. Soc., Stark County Med. Soc., Assn. Profs. Medicine, Alpha Omega Alpha. Home: 1409 Harbor Dr NW Canton OH 44708-3098 Office: 2600 6th St SW Canton OH 44710-1702 *Compassion must remain the universal prescription in medical practice. Technology can provide no solutions in the absence of humanity.*

OGNIBENE, EDWARD JOHN, mechanical engineer; b. Aug. 27, 1965; s. Peter Edward and Dorothy May (Gasdaska) O.; m. Donna Lee Paul, Dec. 14, 1991; children: Ariana JoAnn, Corinne Elizabeth. B. Engring. in Mech. Engring., SUNY, Stony Brook, 1989; MS in Mech. Engring., MIT, 1991, PhD, 1995. Engring. asst., intern Baker Engring., Inc., Elmsford, N.Y., summer 1988; rsch. intern Schlumberger-Doll Rsch., Ridgefield, Conn., summer 1989; rsch. asst. MIT, Cambridge, 1989-91, 92-95, postdoctoral assoc., 1995; mech. engr. United Technologies, Norden Sys., Norwalk, Conn., 1991-92; rsch. engr./cons. Praxair Inc., Tarrytown, N.Y., 1992; R&D engr. SatCon Tech. Corp., Cambridge, Mass., 1995—. Recipient Grumman Corp. Award for Scholastic Excellence, 1988. Mem. ASME, Sigma Xi, Tau Beta Pi. Achievements include patent pending on steam generating dynamometer. Avocations: chess, cycling, hiking, photography, sailing. Home: 19 Marion Rd Belmont MA 02178

O'GORMAN, JAMES FRANCIS, art educator, writer; b. St. Louis, Sept. 19, 1933; s. Paul Joseph and Dorothy Frances (Hogan) O'G.; m. Jean Baer, Feb. 9, 1957 (div. 1987); children—Christopher, Harold, Michael (dec.), Samuel. B.Arch., Washington U., St. Louis, 1956; M. Arch., U. Ill., 1960; Ph.D., Harvard U., 1966. Grace Slack McNeil prof. Am. art Wellesley Coll., Mass., 1975—. Author: H.H. Richardson and His Office: Selected Drawings, 1973; This Other Gloucester, 1976; H.H. Richardson. Architectural Forms for an American Society, 1987; ThreeAmerican Architects: Richardson, Sullivan, and Wright, 1865-1915, 1991; (with others) The Architecture of Frank Furness, 1974; editor, translator: Paul Frankl, Principles of Architectural History, 1968. Phila. Athenaeum fellow, 1985. Office: Wellesley Coll Dept Art 106 Central St Wellesley MA 02181-8209

O'GORMAN, KATHLEEN, newspaper editor. Education editor Detroit Free Press. Office: Detroit Free Press 321 W Lafayette Blvd Detroit MI 48226-2705

O'GORMAN, PETER JOSEPH, retail company executive; b. Surbiton, Surrey, Eng., May 25, 1938; came to U.S., 1981; s. Peter and Noreen (O'Gorman) McCormack; m. Rosemary Anne Underhill, July 20, 1974; 1 child, Ruth. B in Nautical Sci., Nellists Nautical Coll., Gt. Britain, 1959; M in Nautical Sci., Auckland U., New Zealand, 1963. Cert. master mariner. Supermarket mgr., later sr. v.p. devel. Tesco Stores Ltd., London, 1964-81; pres. Doody Co., Columbus, Ohio, 1981-83; sr. v.p. devel. and mktg. Great Atlantic and Pacific Tea Co., Montvale, N.J., 1983-90, exec. v.p. real estate, store devel. and mktg., 1990—. Bd. dirs. Bergen County (N.J.) United Way; mem. food industry steering com. ECR; mem. svcs. com., trustee food industry FICAH. Office: Gt Atlantic & Pacific Tea Co Inc 2 Paragon Dr Montvale NJ 07645-1718

O'GORMAN, TARA ANN, elementary education educator; b. Yonkers, N.Y., July 22, 1965; d. John T. O'Gorman and Josephine M. (Corneila) O'G. BA in Communication Arts, Iona Coll., 1987, MS in Multicultural Edn., 1994. Cert. tchr., N.Y. Presch. asst. head tchr. Bright Horizons, Yonkers, N.Y., 1991-93, summer reading program specialist, 1992-93; 2nd grade tchr. St. Ann Sch., Bronx, N.Y., 1993—; acad. cons., Yonkers, 1990—. Recipient Partial Tuition scholarship N.Y. State Archdiocese, 1993-94. Mem. Phi Delta Kappa. Roman Catholic. Avocations: reading, acting, music, crafting, tennis. Office: Saint Ann Sch 3511 Bainbridge Ave Bronx NY 10467-1401

OGRA, PEARAY L., physician, educator; b. Srinagar, Kashmir, India, Mar. 19, 1939; came to U.S., 1961, naturalized, 1969; s. Govinda Kaul and Gunvati (Daftari) O.; m. Kathleen Marie Ogra; children: Sanjay, Monica. MB, Christian Med. Coll., Ludhiana, India, 1961. Intern Binghamton (N.Y.) Gen. Hosp., 1962-63; resident U. Chgo., 1963-64; resident N.Y. U.-Bellevue Med Center, 1964-66, fellow infectious diseases, 1966-68; asst. prof. pediatrics SUNY, Buffalo, 1968-71; assoc. prof. pediatrics and microbiology SUNY, 1972-74, prof., 1974-91; John Sealy disting. chair and prof., chmn. dept. pediatrics U. Tex. Med. Br., Galveston, 1991—; dir. div. virology Children's Hosp. Buffalo, 1969-81, chief dept. infectious diseases, 1970-91; dir. Clin. Labs. Children's Hosp., 1985-90; mem. study sect. NIH, 1979-85, maternal child health com., 1987-91; mem., chmn. bd. Internat. Pediat. Rsch. Found., Inc., 1984-89, respiratory diseases steering com. WHO. Recipient E. Mead Johnson award for Pediatric Research Am. Acad. Pediatrics, 1978; Kalhana award Kashmir Sci. Culture and Soc., 1984; Stockton Kimball award SUNY, 1985; Buswell fellow, 1968-71. Fellow Royal Soc. Medicine, Assn. Am. Physicians, Am. Acad. Pediatrics, Am. Acad. Microbiology; mem. Am. Soc. Clin. Investigation, Soc. Pediatric Rsch., Infectious Disease Soc. Am., Soc. Exptl. Biology and Medicine, Am. Assn. Immunologists, Am. Soc. Microbiology, AAAS, Am. Fedn. Clin. Rsch., Reticuloendothelial Soc., Am. Soc. Virology. Home: 6919 Williams Galveston TX 77551

O'GRADY, BEVERLY TROXLER, investment executive, counselor; b. Greensboro, N.C., Nov. 26, 1941; d. Robert Andrew and Beverly Beam (Barrier) Troxler; m. Robert Edward O'Grady, Aug. 6, 1966. BA, St. Mary's Coll., 1963; MA, Columbia U., 1965. Exec. v.p. Wilkinson & Hottinger Inc., N.Y.C., 1973-94, Helvetia Capital Corp., N.Y.C., 1987-94; pres. Wilkinson O'Grady & Co., Inc., N.Y.C., 1994—; mem. adv. bd. Charles Schwab Fin., San Francisco, 1991-93. Active Women's Nat. Rep. Club, N.Y.C., 1991-94. Mem. Assn. Investment Mgrs., N.Y. Soc. Security Analysts, Women's Bond Club (pres. 1992-94), Univ. Club. Roman Catholic. Office: Wilkinson O'Grady & Co Inc 520 Madison Ave New York NY 10022-4213

O'GRADY, DENNIS JOSEPH, lawyer; b. Hoboken, N.J., Nov. 16, 1943; s. Joseph A. and Eileen (Broderick) O'Grady; m. Mary Anne Amoruso, Sept. 9, 1966 (div. Apr. 1984); 1 child, Kara Anne. AB, Seton Hall Coll., 1965; MA, U. So. Calif., 1969; JD, Rutgers U., 1973. Bar: N.J. 1973, U.S. Ct. Appeals (3d cir.) 1975, U.S. Dist. Ct. N.J. Ptnr. Riker, Danzig, Scherer, Hyland & Perretti, Newark, Trenton and Morristown, N.J., 1974—; adj. asst. prof. of bus. law St. Peter's Coll., Jersey City, 1973—. Mem. ABA (bus./bankruptcy sect.), N.Y. State Bar Assn. (debtor/creditor sect.), Fed. Bar Assn., Am. Bankruptcy Inst. Democrat. Roman Catholic. Office: Riker Danzig Scherer Hyland & Perretti 1 Speedwell Ave Morristown NJ 07960-6845

O'GRADY, JOHN JOSEPH, III, lawyer; b. N.Y.C., Mar. 21, 1933; s. John Joseph and Terese (O'Rourke) O'G.; m. Mary E. McHugh, June 28, 1958; children—Glennon, Ellen, Carol, Paul. A.B., Holy Cross Coll., 1954; J.D., Harvard U., 1957. Bar: N.Y. 1958. Assoc. Cadwalader, Wickersham & Taft, N.Y.C., 1958-66, ptnr., 1966—. Mem. ABA, N.Y. State Bar Assn. Office: Cadwalader Wickersham & Taft 100 Maiden Ln New York NY 10038-4818

O'GRADY, MARY J., editor, foundation consultant; b. Chgo., Sept. 25, 1951; d. Valentine Michael and Lillian Mary (Quinlan) O'G. Student, St. Mary's Coll., Rome, Italy, 1970-71; BFA, Manhattanville Coll., 1973. Assoc. editor Magnum Photos, N.Y.C., 1973-76; asst. picture editor Modern Photography Mag., N.Y.C., 1976-78; freelance photographer N.Y.C., 1978-80; sr. producer Trans-Atlantic Enterprises, N.Y.C., L.A., 1981-82; dir. pub. info. World Wildlife Fund, Washington, 1983-84; sr. analyst Mead Data Cen., Washington, 1985-87; editor photos U.S. News and World Report, Washington, 1987-90; program dir. Sacharuna Found., 1990-92; adminstr. Roland Films, 1991-92; assoc. dir. AIDS Control and Prevention Project Family Health Internat., 1994—; cons. Time, Inc., N.Y.C., 1981, Exxon Corp., N.Y.C., 1981-82, U.S. News and World Report, Washington, 1987, The German Marshall Fund of U.S., Conservation Internat., Washington, 1992, W. Alton Jones Found., 1993-94. Asst. editor: The Family of Woman, 1978; producer (TV shows) A Conversation With..., 1982, The Helen Gurley Brown Show, 1982, Outrageous Opinions, 1982; photo editor America's Best Colleges, 1989, 90, Great Vacation Drives, 1989. Recipient Editorial Excellence award Natural Resources Coun. Am., 1984. Mem. Soc. Environ. Journalists, Worldwide Women in Environment and Devel., Status and Trends of HIV/AIDS Epidemics in Africa Working Group.

O'GRADY, THOMAS B., Canadian provincial official; m. Betty O'Grady. Commr. Can. Police Cmty. Recipient Police Exemplary Svc. medal, The Can. 125 medal. Mem. Can. Chiefs of Police Assn. (v.p.), Ont. Pub. Svc. Quarter Century Club (pres.), Order of St. John of Jerusalem (officer). Office: 777 Memorial Ave, Orillia, ON Canada L3V 7V3

OGREAN, DAVID WILLIAM, sports executive; b. New Haven, Feb. 7, 1953; s. Richard Berton and Dorothy (Nystrom) O.; m. Maryellen Harvey, Aug. 10 1974; children: Matthew David, Tracy Erin, Dana Marie. BA in English cum laude, U Conn., 1974; MS in Film, Boston U., 1978. Asa S. Bushnell intern Ea. Coll. Athletic Conf., Centervill, Mass., 1977-78; pub. rels. dir. Amateur Hockey Assn. U.S., Colorado Springs, Colo., 1978-80; mng. editor Am. Hockey and Arena mag., 1979-80; communications rep. ESPN, Inc., Bristol, Conn., 1980-83, program mgr., 1983-88; asst. exec. dir. for TV Coll. Football Assn., Boulder, Colo., 1988-90; dir. of broadcasting U.S. Olympic Com., Colorado Springs, 1990-93; exec. dir. USA Hockey, Colorado Springs, 1993—; pres. Colorado Spring's Sports Corp., 1996—. Mem. Country Club Colo. Office: US Olympic Com 1750 E Boulder St Colorado Springs CO 80909-5724

OGREN, CARROLL WOODROW, retired hospital administrator; b. Mpls., Mar. 22, 1927; s. Peter L. and Mabel (Wohleen) O.; m. Patricia Ann Sweeney. B.A., U. Minn., 1952; M.Hosp. Adminstrn., Washington U., St. Louis, 1958. Asst. adminstr. Washoe Med. Center, Reno, 1958-59; adminstr. Washoe Med. Center, 1959-80, Jean Hannah Clark Rehab. Center, Las Vegas, Nev., 1980-92. Served with USNR, 1944-46, 50-54, PTO. Mem. Am. Coll. Hosp. Adminstrs., Am. Hosp. Assn. (nat. com. state hosp. assn. 1967—), Nev. Hosp. Assn. (pres. 1961-62, sec. 1961-62). Club: Gourmet Toastmasters (Reno) (pres. 1960). Home: 5860 Via Manigua Las Vegas NV 89120-2348

OGREN, ROBERT EDWARD, biologist, educator; b. Jamestown, N.Y., Feb. 9, 1922; s. David Paul and Mary Gladys (Ahlstrom) O.; m. Jean Blose Jackson, Aug. 28, 1948; children: Paul Robert, Philip Edward. B.A., Wheaton Coll., 1947; M.S., Northwestern U., 1948; Ph.D., U. Ill., 1953. Asst. prof. biology Ursinus Coll., Collegeville, Pa., 1953-57, Dickinson Coll., Carlisle, Pa., 1957-63; mem. faculty Wilkes Coll., Wilkes-Barre, Pa., 1963—, prof. biology, 1981-86, prof. emeritus, 1986—. Contbr. articles to profl. lit. Bd. dirs. Northeastern Pa. chpt. Am. Heart Assn., 1971-88; chmn. bd. Northeastern Pa. chpt. Am. HeartAssn., 1973-76; bd. dirs. Wyo. Valley West Sch. Dis., 1973-79, pres., 1979. Served with AUS, 1943-46. Recipient Frank B. Shepela Meml. Vol. award Northeastern Pa. Heart Assn., 1977; NSF grantee, 1960, 63, 65. Fellow AAAS; mem. Am. Soc. Zoologists, Am. Soc. Parasitologists, Am. Micros. Soc., Soc. Protzoologists, Electron Micros. Soc. Am., Wyo. Commemorative Assn., Pa. Acad. Sci. (editor procs. 1961-62 Darbaker award 1989), Soc. Systematic Zoology, N.Y. Acad. Sci., Helminthological Soc. Washington, AAUP, Ecol. Soc. Am., Nat. Audubon Soc., Western N.Y. Geneol. Soc., Wyo. Hist. and Geol. Soc., Sigma Xi (chpt. pres. 1981-82). Republican. Presbyterian. Home: 88 Lathrop St Wilkes Barre PA 18704-4811 Office: Wilkes Univ Dept Biology S Franklin St Wilkes Barre PA 18701-1201 *To be involved as a citizen in some aspect of community life. To use academe as an opportunity to prepare scholarly works for publication advancing knowledge in your discipline. To work beyond your limitations. To recognize opportunities and use them for making progress. To be positive, honest, creative and persevering. To enjoy the fruits of your labor and the freedom of expression and movement in our great land.*

OGREN, WILLIAM LEWIS, physiologist, educator; b. Ashland, Wis., Oct. 8, 1938; m. Carolyn Schottland, June 24, 1967; children: Jason, Aaron, Susan. BS, U. Wis., 1961; PhD, Wayne State U., 1965. Research chemist Parker Rust Proof Co., Detroit, 1961-62; plant physiologist U.S. Dept. Agr., Urbana, Ill., 1965-79, research leader, 1979—; asst. prof. U. Ill., Urbana, 1966-72, assoc. prof., 1972-77, prof., 1977—. Recipient von Humboldt award Alexander von Humboldt Found., 1990. Fellow Crop Sci. Soc. Am. (Rsch. award 1979), Am. Acad. Arts and Scis., Am. Soc. Agronomy; mem. AAAS, NAS, Am. Soc. Plant Physiologists (sec. 1987-89, pres. 1990-91, Kettering award 1986), Am. Soc. for Biochemistry and Molecular Biology, Japanese Soc. Plant Physiologists. Office: USDA 1201 W Gregory Dr Urbana IL 61801-3838

OGUL, MORRIS SAMUEL, political science educator, consultant; b. Detroit, Apr. 15, 1931; s. Jack and Sarah (Zimmerman) O.; m. Eleanor Simon, Aug. 26, 1954. B.A., Wayne State U., 1952; M.A., U. Mich., 1953, Ph.D., 1958. Instr. polit. sci. U. Pitts., 1957-59, asst. prof., 1959-64, assoc. prof., 1964-67, prof., 1967—; cons. U.S. Ho. of Reps., 1973, 83, U.S. Office Personnel Mgmt., Washington, 1975—, U.S. Senate, 1977. Author: (with William J. Keefe) American Legislative Process, 1964, 7th edit., 1989, 8th edit., 1993, Congress Oversees the Bureaucracy, 1976. Carnegie Corp. research grantee, 1965-68. Mem. Am. Polit. Sci. Assn., Midwest Polit. Sci. Assn. (council 1982-84), Pa. Polit. Sci. Assn. Democrat. Home: 1500 Cochran Rd Apt 814 Pittsburgh PA 15243-1068 Office: U Pitts Dept Polit Sci 4n25 Forbes Quadrangle Pittsburgh PA 15260-7454

OH, JOHN KIE-CHIANG, political science educator, university official; b. Seoul, Korea, Nov. 1, 1930; came to U.S., 1954, naturalized, 1971; s. Sung-Jun and Duk-Cho (Kim) O.; m. Bonnie Cho, Sept. 5, 1959; children: Jane J., Marie J., James J. B.S., Marquette U., 1957; postgrad., Columbia U., 1957-58; Ph.D., Georgetown U., 1962. Asst. prof. St. Thomas Coll., St. Paul, 1962-66; assoc. prof. polit. sci. Marquette U., Milw., 1967-71, prof., chmn., 1971-77, dean grad. sch., 1977-85; acad. v.p. Cath. U. Am., Washington, 1985-89, prof. politics dept., 1990—. Author: Korea: Democracy on Trial, 1968, (with Peter Cheng et. al.) Emerging Roles of Asian Nations in the 1980's, 1979, Democratization and Economic Development in Korea, 1990; contbr. articles to profl. jours. Chmn. scholarship com. World Affairs Council, 1976-78; mem. Wis. Gov.'s Commn. for UN, Madison, 1971-74; chmn. Korean Studies com., Assn. Asian Studies, 1975-76. Grantee Hill Found., 1963, Relm Found., 1968, Social Sci. Rsch Coun., 1973, Am. Coun. Learned Socs., 1973. Mem. Am. Polit. Sci. Assn., Assn. Asian Studies, Internat. Polit. Sci. Assn., Midwest Conf. Assn. Affairs (pres. 1970-71, nat. chmn. China-Japan-Korea-The Philippines-Thailand sect.) Fulbright Hays Program, Assn. Cath. Colls. and Univs. (bd. dirs. 1983-87). Roman Catholic. Home: 8807 Maxwell Dr Potomac MD 20854-3123 Office: Cath U Am Politics Dept Washington DC 20064

OH, KEYTACK HENRY, industrial engineering educator; b. Hamduk, Korea, Mar. 16, 1938; s. DalPyong and Kee-Sook (Yang) O.; m. Youngsim Lee, Sept. 15, 1967; children: Jeanne, Susan. BS, Hanyang U., Seoul, Korea, 1962; MS, Okla. State U., 1966; PhD, The Ohio State U., 1974. Supr. East Gate Telephone Exch., Seoul, Korea, 1958-61; ops. rschr. Western Elec. Co., Oklahoma City, 1966-68; MIS staff mem. Western Elec. Co., Columbus, Ohio, 1968-72; logistics engr. Ross Labs., Columbus, Ohio, 1972-75; asst. prof. U. Mo./St. Louis Grad. Engring. Ctr., Rolla, 1975-82; assoc. prof. U. Toledo, 1982—; pres. Oh Enterprises Corp., Toledo, 1995—. Author: Computers and Industrial Engineering, 1994, Productivity and Quality Research Frontiers, 1995. Chmn. bd. dirs. Korean Sch., Toledo, 1995. Recipient presdl. fellowship Okla. State U., 1965. Mem. Inst. Indsl. Engrs. (pres. Toledo chpt. 1984), Am. Soc. for Engring. Edn., Anthony Wayne Toastmasters (pres. 1994), Toastmasters Internat. (area gov. 1995, divsn. gov. 1996), Korean Assn. of Greater Toledo (pres. 1996—). Republican. Presbyterian. Avocations: tennis, golf. Home: 2817 Westchester Rd Toledo OH 43615 Office: U Toledo Toledo OH 43606

OH, SE-KYUNG, immunochemist; b. Seoul, South Korea, Jan. 11, 1943; came to U.S., 1966; s. Bang-Whan and Pong-Ho (Park) O. BS, Seoul Nat. U., 1965; M in Nutritional Sci., Cornell U., 1968; PhD, U. Ga., 1972. Postdoctoral fellow Scripps Clinic and Rsch. Found., La Jolla, Calif., 1972-74; vis. scientist Cornell U., Ithaca, N.Y., 1974-76, NIA, NIH, Balt., 1974-76; lectr. Harvard Med. Sch., Boston, 1976-79; asst. prof. Sch. Medicine Boston U., 1979-84, assoc. prof., 1984-92, adj. prof. biochemistry, 1992—; staff scientist Ciba-Corning Diagnostics Corp., Walpole, Mass., 1992—. Editor Jour. Nutritional Biochemistry, 1990—. NIH grantee, 1979-86. Mem. Am. Assn. Immunologists, Am. Assn. Cancer Rsch., Korean Scientists and Engring. Assn. (mem. coun. 1990-93), Boston Cancer Rsch. Assn. (pres. 1992-93). Presbyterian. Achievements include patent and patent pending in field. Office: Ciba-Corning Diagnostics 333 Coney St East Walpole MA 02032

OH, TAI KEUN, business educator; b. Seoul, Korea, Mar. 25, 1934; s. Chin Young and Eui Kyung (Yun) O.; came to U.S., 1958, naturalized, 1969; B.A., Seijo U., 1957; M.A., No. Ill. U., 1961; M.L.S., U. Wis., 1965, Ph.D., 1970; m. Gretchen Brenneke, Dec. 26, 1964; children: Erica, Elizabeth, Emily. Asst. prof. mgmt. Roosevelt U., Chgo., 1969-73; assoc. prof. Calif. State U., Fullerton, 1973-76, prof. mgmt., 1976—; vis. prof. U. Hawaii, 1983-84, 86; advisor Pacific Asian Mgmt. Inst., U. Hawaii; internat. referee Asia-Pacific Jour. of Mgmt., 1990—; cons. Calty Design Research, Inc. subs. Toyota Motor Corp. The Employers Group; seminar leader and speaker. Named Outstanding Prof., Sch. Bus. Adminstrn. and Econs., Calif. State U., Fullerton, 1976, 78. NSF grantee, 1968-69, recipient Exceptional Merit Service award Calif. State U., 1984, Meritorious Performance and Profl. Promise award Calif. State U., 1987. Mem. Acad. Mgmt., Indsl. Relations Research Assn., Acad. Internat. Bus. Editorial bd. Acad. Mgmt. Rev., 1978-81; contbg. author: Ency. Profl. Mgmt., 1978, Handbook of Management 1985; contbr. articles to profl. jours. Home: 2044 E Eucalyptus Ln Brea CA 92621-5911 Office: Calif State U Fullerton CA 92634

OH, WILLIAM, physician; b. The Philippines, May 22, 1931; came to U.S., 1958, naturalized, 1970; s. Bun Kun and Chay Suat (Lim) O.; m. Mary Oh, June 4, 1960; children—Kenneth Albert, Kerstin Amy. M.D., U. Santo Tomas, Phillipines, 1958; M.A. (hon.), Brown U., 1974. Diplomate Am. Bd. Pediatrics, Am. Bd. Neonatal Perinatal Medicine. Intern Deaconess Hosp., Milw., 1958-59; resident in pediatrics Michael Reese Hosp., Chgo., 1959-63; fellow in neonatology Kavolinska Inst., Stockholm, 1963-65; dir. neonatology Michael Reese Hosp., Chgo., 1965-69; dir. neonatology, assoc. prof. pediatrics UCLA, 1969-73, prof., 1973-74; prof. pediatrics and obstetrics Brown U., Providence, 1974-88, Sylvia Hassenfeld prof. pediatrics, chmn. dept., 1989—; pediatrician-in-chief Women and Infants Hosp. of R.I., Providence, 1974—, R.I. Hosp.; prof., chmn. dept. pediatrics Brown U., 1989—; mem. NIH study sect. on human embryology and devel., chmn., 1985—; mem. pediatric test com. Bd. Med. Exam., 1985-89; mem. sub-bd. of neonatal-perinatal medicine Am. Bd. Pediatrics, 1982-88; chair com. on Fetus and Newborn, Am. Acad. Pediatrics; mem. Nat. Adv. Coun. for Child Health, 1995—. Author book in field; contbr. chpts. to books, numerous articles to profl. jours.; editor profl. jour. Adv. com. Nat. Found. of March of Dimes. NIH grantee. Mem. Am. Pediatric Soc., Am. Acad. Pediatrics (fetus and newborn com. 1986—), Soc. Pediatric Research, Perinatal Research Soc. (pres. 1981), Am. Inst. Nutrition, Fedn. Am. Socs. Exptl. Biology. Roman Catholic. Club: University. Home: 24 Robbins Dr Barrington RI 02806-2612 Office: 101 Dudley St Providence RI 02905-2401

O'HAGAN, JAMES JOSEPH, lawyer; b. Chgo., Dec. 29, 1936; s. Francis James and Florence Agnes (Dowgialo) O'H.; m. Suzanne Elizabeth Wiegand, June 28, 1958; children: Timothy, Karen, Peggy, Kevin. B in Commerce, De Paul U., 1958, JD, 1962. Law clk. Querrey & Harrow, Chgo., 1958-62, assoc., 1963-67, ptnr., 1968—, chmn. mgmt., 1985—; lawyer Chgo. Claim Mgrs. Assn., Chgo., 1992-93. Bd. dirs. Park Ridge (Ill.) Fine Arts Soc., 1984—, pres., 1992-94. Mem. ABA, Ill. Bar Assn. Chgo. Bar Assn. (mediator mediation program), Internat. Assn. Def. Coun., Trial Lawyers Club. Roman Catholic. Avocations: golf, tennis, physical conditioning, painting, reading. Office: Querrey & Harrow 180 N Stetson Ave Chicago IL 60601-6710

O'HAIR, JOHN D., lawyer, county prosecuting attorney; b. Detroit, Sept. 29, 1929; s. Walter R. and Willis W. (Watts) O.; m. Barbara Stanton, Jan. 15, 1966; 1 child: John Dennis. B.A., DePauw U., 1951; J.D., Detroit Coll. Law, 1954. Bar: Mich. 1954. Asst. corp. counsel City of Detroit, 1957-65; judge Common Pleas Ct., Detroit, 1965-68; judge Wayne County Cir. Ct., 1968-83; Wayne County pros. atty., 1983—; Wayne County corp. counsel, 1983—; mem. Mich. Jud. Tenure Commn., 1977-82. Trustee, Detroit Coll. Law, 1982—. Served with Intelligence Corps, U.S. Army, 1955-56. Mem. ABA, Mich. Bar Assn. Democrat. Presbyterian. Office: 1441 St Antoine 12th fl F Murphy Hall of Justice Detroit MI 48226*

OHALA, JOHN JEROME, linguistics educator; b. Chgo., July 19, 1941; s. Stanley Andreas and Grace Marie (Mack) O.; m. Manjari Agrawal, Nov. 24, 1969. AB, U. Notre Dame, 1963; postgrad., U. Iowa, 1963-64; MA, UCLA, 1966, PhD, 1969; PhD (hon.), U. Copenhagen, 1992. Asst. prof. dept. linguistics U. Calif., Berkeley, 1970-72, assoc. prof., 1972-77, prof., 1977—; vis. lektor Inst. Phonetics, Copenhagen U., 1973; vis. prof. dept. linguistics UCLA, 1981; vis. prof. dept. hearing and speech sci. U. Md., College Park, 1982; vis. prof. dept. linguistics U. Alta., Edmonton, Can., 1991-92; pres. Permanent Coun. Internat. Conf. Spoken Lang. Processing, 1992—; chair Internat. Confs. Spoken Lang. Processing, Banff, 1992; mem. Permanent Coun. Internat. Congress of Phonetic Scis., 1995—. Author, co-editor: Experimental Phonology, 1986, Sound Symbolism; author, guest co-editor vol. 3 Phonology Yearbook, 1986; N.Am. editor Phonetica, 1985—, Speech Commn., 1993—, Education Speech Sci. and Phoentics Pergamon Ency. of Lang. and Linguistics; Subject of Restschrift in Lang. and Speech, vol. 35, 1992. Grantee NSF, 1975-80, post doctoral fellow, 1969-70; grantee Harry Frank Guggenheim Found., 1981-82; sr. Fulbright lectureship Inst. Phonetics, Copenhagen U., 1985. Fellow Acoustical Soc. Am.; mem. Linguistic Soc. Am., N.Y. Acad. Scis., Internat. Phonetic Assn. (coun. 1985—, pres. 1995—), European Speech Comm. Assn. Democrat. Avocations: collecting rare books, bookbinding, photography. Home: 1149 Hillview Rd Berkeley CA 94708-1705 Office: Univ of Calif Dept Linguistics Berkeley CA 94720

O'HALLORAN, THOMAS ALPHONSUS, JR., physicist, educator; b. Bklyn., Apr. 13, 1931; s. Thomas Alphonsus Sr. and Nora (Sheehan) O'H.; m. Barbara Joyce Hug, June 4, 1954; children: Theresa Joyce, Maureen Ann, Kevin Thomas, Patrick Joseph. Student, San Jose State U., 1948-50; BS in Physics & Math., Oreg. State U., 1953, MS in Physics, 1954; PhD, U. Calif., Berkeley, 1963. Rsch. asst. Lawrence Berkeley Lab., U. Calif., 1963-64; rsch. fellow Harvard U., Cambridge, Mass., 1964-66; asst. prof. physics U. Ill., Urbana, 1966-68, assoc. prof., 1968-70, prof., 1970-93, prof. emeritus, 1993—; vis. scholar U. Utah, Salt Lake City, 1990-93, rsch. prof. physics, 1993—; mem. program adv. com. Argonne Nat. Lab., Lemont, Ill., Fermi Lab., Batavia, Ill., Brookhaven Nat. Lab., Upton, L.I.; vis. scientist Lawrence Berkeley Lab., U. Calif., 1979-80. Contbr. numerous articles on elem. particle physics to profl. jours. Lt. USN, 1954-58. Guggenheim fellow, 1979-80. Fellow Am. Phys. Soc. Home: 4614 Ledgemont Dr Salt Lake City UT 84124-4735 Office: U Utah Physics Dept 201 Jfb Salt Lake City UT 84112

OHANIAN, KREKOR See CONNORS, MIKE

OHANIAN, MIHRAN JACOB, engineering educator; b. Istanbul, Turkey, Aug. 7, 1933; came to U.S., 1956, naturalized, 1967; s. Mark and Mary Catherine (Sayabalian) O.; m. Sandra Jean Blair, Apr. 22, 1962; children: Heather Jean Allen, Holly Lynn. B.S.E.E. with high honors, Robert Coll. Engring. Sch., Istanbul, 1956; M.E.E., Rensselaer Poly. Inst., 1960, Ph.D. in Nuclear Engring. and Sci., 1963. Lectr. nuclear engring. Rensselaer Poly. Inst., 1963, instr., 1958-62; asst. prof. nuclear engring. U. Fla., Gainesville, 1964-67, assoc. prof., 1967-70, prof., 1970—, chmn. dept., 1969-79, assoc. dir. Engring. and Indsl. Expt. Sta., 1977—, assoc. dean for research, 1979-90, assoc. dean for adminstrn. and planning, 1990-91, assoc. dean for rsch. and adminstrn., 1991—; sabbatical leave Inst. Energy Analysis, Oak Ridge, 1976-77; on assignment Inst. Energy Analysis, 1977-78; cons. Fla. Power Corp., Batelle Meml. Inst., Fla. Nuclear Assos., Oak Ridge Nat. Lab., Inst. Energy Analysis, Argonne Nat. Lab., Savannah River Lab., U. Va., Tex. Higher Edn. Bd., NSF; U. Fla. rep. U.S. Nuc. Energy Inst., 1972—, mem. adv. council, 1972-80; U. Fla. rep. to Oak Ridge Assoc. Univs., 1972-76; mem. engring. accreditation commn. Accreditation Bd. Engring. and Tech., 1984-88; mem. rev. com. Reactor Analysis and Safety div. Argonne Nat. Lab, 1982-88, chmn. 1986-87, mem. rev. com. Reactor Engring. div., 1992—; mem. adv. com. Consol. Fuel Reprocessing Program Oak Ridge Nat. Lab., 1982-88; mem. com. on univ. research reactors Energy Engring. Bd., NRC, 1986-88; mem. U.S. Dept. Energy's Adv. Com. on Nuclear Facility Safety (ACNFS), 1988-90; bd. dirs., chmn. Fla. Inst. Phosphate Rsch., 1990—. Contbr. articles to profl. jours. Trustee Fla. Defenders of the Environment, 1969-71, treas., 1969-70, mem., 1969—. Recipient valor medal Am. Legion, 1966, Disting. Faculty award Fla. Blue Key, 1984; Alumnus fellow Rensselaer Poly. Inst., 1994. Fellow AAAS, Am. Nuclear Soc. (v.p., pres.-elect 1989-90, pres. 1990-91, bd. dirs. 1974-77, 84-93, vice chmn., chmn. edn. divsn. 1975-76, exec. com. nuclear fuel cycle divsn. 1978-81, mem. profl. devel. and accreditation com., chmn. tech. program of internat. conf. Washington, 1980, mem. nominating com., 1980-81, 87-88, chmn., 1991-92, exec. com., 1986-92, Exceptional Svc. award 1980, adv. editor Nuclear Sci. and Engring. Jour. 1989—), Engrs.'s Coun. Profl. Devel. (dir. 1976-78), Am. Assn. Engring. Socs. (awards com. 1985-86, bd. dirs. 1990-91, exec. com. 1990-95, sec.-treas., 1992, chair-elect 1993, chair 1994, chair nominating com. 1995, chair awards com. 1996), Am. Soc. Engring. Edn. (adv. com. Ford Found. Resident Fellow Program 1971-79, sec.-treas. nuclear engring. divsn. 1981-82, vice-chmn. 1982-83, chmn. 1983-84, projects bd. 1981-87, chmn. awards com. 1985-87; mem. Nat. Audubon Soc. (pres. 1965-66), Sigma Xi, Tau Beta Pi (eminent engr.), Alpha Nu Sigma (pres. 1981-83), Eta Kappa Nu, Phi Kappa Phi, Rotary (Paul Harris fellow. Presbyterian. Home: 315 NW 28th St Gainesville FL 32607-2565

OHANNESSIAN, GRISELDA JACKSON, publishing executive; b. N.Y.C., Feb. 5, 1927; d. Schuyler Brinckerhoff and Katharine Savage (Townsend) Jackson; m. Garo Ohannessian, May 5, 1955 (dec.); children: Ani Maria, Lucia Victoria, Mary Margaret. BA, Barnard Coll., 1949; MA, Columbia U., 1951. Asst. to prodn. mgr. Scribners Pub. Co., N.Y.C., 1951-53; music and movie reviewer Al Nida, Beirut, Lebanon, 1955-56; promotion and prodn. mgr. New Directions Pub., N.Y.C., 1956-60, publicity dir., gen. asst., 1972-83, v.p., trustee, 1983-93, mng. dir., trustee, 1994—. Democrat. Episcopalian. Avocations: piano playing, reading, attending concerts. Office: New Directions Pub Co 80 8th Ave New York NY 10011-5126

O'HARA, ALFRED PECK, lawyer; b. Patterson, N.Y., Apr. 27, 1919; s. Peter and Anna L. (Peck) O'H.; m. Muriel A. Sandberg, Aug. 30, 1940 (dec.); children: Jane Ann O'Hara Toth, Margaret Kathleen O'Hara Duff, Peter James, John Edward; m. 2d Thelma deVries (div.); m. 3d Martha Stein, June 22, 1984. B.A., Syracuse U., 1940; LL.B., Fordham U., 1942. Bar: N.Y. bar 1942, U.S. Supreme Ct 1956. Sec. to U.S. Dist. Ct., 1942-43; partner firm McLaughlin & Stickles, 1946-52; asst. U.S. atty., chief civil div. So. Dist. N.Y., 1953-56; cons. to atty. gen. N.Y. State, 1956; sr. ptnr. firm Rogers Hoge & Hills, N.Y.C., 1958-86; of counsel Kelley, Drye & Warren, N.Y.C., 1986—; counsel U.S. Trademark Assn., 1967-70; pres., chmn. bd. Bacardi Corp., 1976-87; bd. dirs. Guiding Eyes for the Blind, chmn., 1994—. Mem. ABA, NAM (bd. dirs. 1978-90), N.Y. State Bar Assn., Assn. Bar City N.Y., Fed Bar Coun., Am. Law Inst. (life), Internat. Patent adn Trademark Assn., Quaker Hill Club, Key Biscayne Yacht Club. Home: RR 4 Box 55 Birch Hill Rd Patterson NY 12563 Office: Kelley Drye & Warren 101 Park Ave New York NY 10178

O'HARA, CATHERINE, actress, comedienne; b. Toronto, Mar. 4, 1954; m. Bo Welch, 1992. Actress, writer with Second City, Toronto, 1974; co-founder of SCTV, 1976 (Emmy award); films include After Hours, 1985, Heartburn, 1986, Beetlejuice, 1988, Dick Tracy, 1990, Betsy's Wedding, 1990, Home Alone, 1990, Little Vegas, 1990, There Goes The Neighborhood, 1992, Home Alone II: Lost In New York, 1992, The Nightmare Before Christmas, 1993 (voice), The Paper, 1994, Wyatt Earp, 1994, A Simple Twist of Fate, 1994, Tall Tale, 1995; TV, SCTV, Comic Relief, Dream On (dir.); co-writer SCTV, Cinemax, 1984, Really Weird Tales, HBO, 1986. Office: care ICM 8942 Wilshire Blvd Beverly Hills CA 90211-1934*

O'HARA, JAMES THOMAS, lawyer; b. Hazleton, Pa., Oct. 11, 1936; s. Thomas James and Bridget Helen (Campbell) O'H.; m. Kathleen M. Shane, Aug. 3, 1963; children: Colleen, Michael, Brian. BS in Acctg., Kings Coll., 1958; LLB, Cath. U., 1962; LLM, Georgetown U., 1967. Bar: D.C. 1962. Ptnr. Casey, Tyre et al, N.Y.C., 1969-73, Jones, Day, Reavis & Pogue, Washington, 1973—; adj. prof. tax Georgetown U., Washington, 1976—; bd. advisers Corp. Taxation. Contbr. articles to profl. jours. Served with USAR, 1959. Fellow Am. Bar Found.; mem. ABA (chmn. subcom. tax sect. 1982-86), Am. Coll. Tax Counsel. Democrat. Roman Catholic. Clubs: Metropolitan (Washington); Union (Cleve.). Home: 1610 44th St NW Washington DC 20007-2025 Office: Jones Day Reavis & Pogue 1450 G St NW Ste 600 Washington DC 20005-2001

O'HARA, ROBERT SYDNEY, JR., lawyer; b. Englewood, N.J., Apr. 26, 1939; s. Robert Sydney and Katharine (Drayton) O'H.; m. Elizabeth Crocker, June 17, 1961; children—Jennifer, Isabelle; m. 2d Bonnie Durkin, July 19, 1975. A.B., Princeton U., 1960; J.D., U. Pa., 1963. Bar: N.Y. 1964. Mem., Amer. Bar Assn. Ptnr. firm Milbank, Tweed, Hadley & McCloy, N.Y.C., 1965—. Served to capt. AUS 1963-65. Office: Milbank Tweed Hadley & McCloy 1 Chase Manhattan Plz New York NY 10005-1401*

O'HARA, THOMAS EDWIN, professional administrator executive; b. Springfield, Mo., July 28, 1915; s. Robert John and Olga Florence (Lindberg) O'H.; m. Eleanor McLennan Urquhart, May 6, 1950; children: Thomas Edwin, Robert Andrew, Shelley Janette. AB, Wayne State U., 1938. Accountant Nash-Kelvinator Corp., 1938-39, Gen. Electric Co., 1938-41, Ernst & Ernst, 1941-42; dir. payrolls Detroit Bd. Edn., 1942-58; chmn. bd. trustees Nat. Assn. Investment Clubs, Madison Heights, Mich., 1951—; treas. Sunshine Fifty, Inc., 1969-77; vice chmn. H.W. Rickel & Co., 1971-76; dir. N.Y. Stock Exch., 1973-75; mem. adv. com. individual investors, 1988—; dir. Investment Edn. Inst., 1962—; chmn. NAIC Growth Fund, Inc., 1990—. Bd. dirs. William Tyndale Coll.; chmn. N.Y. Stock Exch. Individual Investors Adv. Com., 1987-89; mem. U.S. Securities and Exch. Commn. Consumers Affairs Adv. Com. and Compensation Practices Com. With USAAF, 1942-45. Recipient Disting. Service award in investment edn., 1969, Disting. Alumni award Wayne State U. Sch. Bus. Adminstrn., 1987, Roalman award Nat. Investor Rels. Inst., 1987. Mem. World Fedn. Investment Clubs (dir., chmn. 1985-90), Arab Frat., Gamma Beta Phi. Presbyn. Home: 367 Sycamore Ct Bloomfield Hills MI 48302-1173 Office: National Assoc of Investors Corp 711 W 13 Madison Heights MI 48071

O'HARA, THOMAS PATRICK, managing editor; b. Phila., July 15, 1947; s. Hugh James and Agatha Mary (Gilroy) O'H.; m. Juliet Munro, 1970 (div. 1974); m. Pamela Smith, Oct. 8, 1977; children: Rachel Kathleen, Patrick Graham. BA in English, Rutgers South Jersey, 1972; MA in Communications, U. Fla., 1974. Sports reporter Gainesville SUN, 1972-74; reporter Orlando (Fla.) Sentinel, 1974-76, Daytona Beach (Fla.) News Jour., 1976-78; various editing and reporting positions Miami (Fla.) Herald, 1978-86, city editor Palm Beach ed., 1985-86; asst. met. editor Palm Beach Post, West Palm Beach, Fla., 1986-87; met. editor Palm Beach Post, West Palm Beach, 1987-88, asst. mng. editor, 1988-89, mng. editor, 1989—. Sgt. USAF, 1969-

71. Home: 107 Seabreeze Ave Delray Beach FL 33483-7017 Office: Palm Beach Post PO Box 24700 2751 Dixie Hwy West Palm Beach FL 33416-4700

O'HARE, DEAN RAYMOND, insurance company executive; b. Jersey City, June 21, 1942; s. Francis and Ann O'H.; m. Kathleen T. Walliser, Dec. 2, 1967; Dean, Jason. BS, NYU, 1963; MBA, Pace U., 1968. Trainee Chubb Corp., N.Y.C., 1963-64, tax advisor, 1964-67, asst. v.p., mgr. corp. fin. devel., 1968-72, sr. v.p., mgr. corp. fin. devel. dept., from 1979, chief fin. officer, 1979-94, pres., 1986-88, chmn., chief exec. officer, 1988—; chmn. Chubb Life Ins. Co. N.H., 1981—; chmn., pres. Fed. Ins. Co., 1988—, Vigilant Ins. Co., 1988—; chmn., dir. Bellemead Devel. Corp., 1973—; chmn. Colonial Life Ins. Co. Am., 1980—, Chubb Life Ins. Co. Am., 1980—; bd. dirs. Chubb Ins. Co. Can., Fed. Ins. Co., Vigilant Ins. Co. Dir. Coalition Svc. Industries, The N.J. Partnership; trustee com. for econ. devel., WDC. Mem. Am. Inst. Assn. (chmn. bd. dirs. 1991), Urban Land Inst., The Links Club (N.Y.C.), India House, Hanover Square Club, Halifax Club (Daytona Beach, Fla.), India House Club, Hanover Square Club. Home: 370 Lake Rd Far Hills NJ 07931-2314 Office: Chubb Corp PO Box 1615 15 Mountain View Rd Warren NJ 07061 also: Alliance Assurance Co Ltd 15 Mountainview Rd Warren NJ 07059-6711*

O'HARE, JAMES RAYMOND, energy company executive; b. Evergreen Park, Ill., July 20, 1938; s. Raymond Clarence and Helen (Nickel) O'H.; m. Nan Jane Raleigh, Sept. 18, 1965; children: Joan, Daniel, Colleen, Patrick. B.S., Marquette U., 1960; M.B.A., U. Calif. at Los Angeles, 1961. C.P.A., Ind., Ill., Ky., Calif., Tex. Mgr. Peat, Marwick, Mitchell & Co., Chgo., 1961-68, South Bend, Ind., 1968-69; controller Essex Internat., Inc., Fort Wayne, Ind., 1969-76, Am. Air Filter Co., Inc., Louisville, 1976-80; fin. v.p. and treas. Petrolane Inc., Long Beach, Calif., 1980-85; treas. Tex. Eastern Corp., Houston, 1985-87, v.p., treas., 1987-88; sr. v.p. fin. and adminstrn. Texas Eastern Gas Pipeline Co., Houston, 1988-89; v.p., CFO Enclean Inc., Houston, 1991-93; fin. cons., 1993—. Served with USNR, 1962-68. Mem. AICPA, Evans Scholars, Fin. Execs. Inst., The Woodlands Country Club, Beta Gamma Sigma.

O'HARE, JEAN ANN, lawyer; b. St. Louis, July 26, 1950; d. Eugene and Henrietta (Greenblatt) O'H. BS cum laude, U. Conn., 1972; MA magna cum laude, Fairfield U., 1976; JD, Fordham U., 1979. Bar: N.Y. 1980, Conn. 1980, U.S. Dist. Ct. (ea., so. and no. dists.) N.Y. 1980. Assoc. Weil Gotshal & Manges, N.Y.C., 1979-82, Emmet Marvin & Martin, N.Y.C., 1982-83; atty. sole practice N.Y.C., 1983-86; atty. Crane Co., N.Y.C., 1986-88; corp. counsel Pfizer Inc., N.Y.C., 1988—. Vol. N.Y. chpt. Am. Heart Assn., N.Y.C., 1990; bd. dirs. United Neighbors East Midtown Manhattan, 1991—. Mem. ABA (litigation sect., tort and ins. practice sect., vice chair 1993—), Corp. Bar (co-chair N.Y.C. com. 1988-90), Internat. Assn. Defense Counsel, Product Liability Adv. Coun. Office: Pfizer Inc 235 E 42nd St New York NY 10017-5703

O'HARE, JOHN MITCHELL, lawyer; b. Oak Park, Ill., Apr. 9, 1946; s. John Mitchell Jr. and Doris Margaret (Lundblad) O'h.; m. Carole Beth Silver, Jan. 6, 1985; children: Rachele Olia, Suzanna Dee. AB, U. Ill., 1967, MS in Fin., 1969; JD, Harvard U., 1971. Bar: Ill. 1971, U.S. Dist. Ct. (no. dist.) Ill. 1971. Assoc. Sidley & Austin, Chgo., 1971-76, ptnr., 1977-85, 88—; resident ptnr. Sidley & Austin, Singapore, 1985-88. Mem. ABA, Chgo. Bar Assn., Phi Beta Kappa. Office: Sidley & Austin 1 First Nat Plz Chicago IL 60603

O'HARE, JOSEPH ALOYSIUS, academic administrator, priest; b. N.Y.C., Feb. 12, 1931; s. Joseph Aloysius and Marie Angela (Enright) O'H. AB, Berchmans Coll, Cebu City, Philippines, 1954, MA, 1955; STL, Woodstock Coll., Md., 1962; PhD, Fordham U., 1968; DHL (hon.), Fairfield U., 1980, Rockhurst Coll., Kansas City, Mo., 1984, Ateneo de Manila U., 1990, CUNY, 1991, Coll. of St. Rose, Albany, N.Y., 1995; DLitt (hon.), Coll. of New Rochelle, 1984. Joined S.J., 1948, ordained priest Roman Cath. Ch., 1961. Instr. Ateneo de Manila U., 1955-58, prof. philosophy, 1968-72; assoc. editor Am. Mag., N.Y.C., 1972-75, editor-in-chief, 1975-84; pres. Fordham U., Bronx, N.Y., 1984—. Author weekly column Of Many Things (Best Original Column award Cath. Press Assn. 1976, 78, 81, 84). Chmn. N.Y.C. Campaign Fin. Bd. Office: Fordham U Office of Pres New York NY 10458

O'HARE, LINDA PARSONS, management consultant; b. Robinson, Ill., Nov. 30, 1947; d. William Wayne and Silvetta (Simmons) Parsons; m. John M. O'Hare, Oct. 5, 1968 (div. May 1983). BS, U. Ill., 1965-68, 72; M in Mgmt., Northwestern U., 1984. Various positions Harvard U., Cambridge, Mass., 1968-71; mgr. employment dept. Leo Burnett Co., Inc., Chgo., 1972-75; various positions Booz, Allen & Hamilton, Inc., Chgo., 1975-81; pres. The Bridge Orgn., Inc., Chgo., 1981—, also bd. dirs.; bd. dirs. All Am. Bank Chgo.; former mem. adv. bd. human resources devel. Northeastern Ill. U., Chgo., 1980-93; mem. Kellogg Alumni Adv. Bd., 1989—. Steering com. Kellogg Alumni Club Cmty. Svcs. Project, Chgo., 1986-95; gov. bd. Ill. Coun. on Econ. Edn., 1992—. Mem. Inst. Mgmt. Cons. (bd. dirs., v.p. 1986-91), Chgo. Fin. Exch. (bd. dirs., sec. 1988-89, v.p. 1990-91, pres. 1991-92), Nat. Assn. Women Bus. Owners (bd. dirs. 1981-84), Chgo. Health Execs. Forum, Univ. Club Chgo. (bd. dirs. 1993—), Execs. Club Chgo. (bd. dirs. 1993—), Econ. Club Chgo., Chgo. Network, Wis. Arabian Horse Assn. Avocation: Arabian horses. Home: N1212 Academy Rd Lake Geneva WI 53147 Office: Bridge Orgn Inc 33 N Dearborn St Chicago IL 60602-3102

O'HARE, PATRICK K., lawyer; b. N.Y.C., Dec. 1, 1946. BA, Brown U., 1968; JD, Stanford U., 1971. Bar: D.C. 1973. Ptnr. McDermott, Will & Emery, Washington. Mem. Am. Acad. Hosp. Attys., Nat. Assn. Coll. & Univ. Attys. Office: McDermott Will & Emery 1850 K St NW Washington DC 20006-2213*

O'HARE, SANDRA FERNANDEZ, secondary education educator; b. N.Y.C., Mar. 19, 1941; d. Ricardo Enrique and Rosario de Los Angeles (Arenas) Fernandez; m. S. James O'Hare, Oct. 12, 1963; children: James, Richard, Michael, Christopher. BA, Marymount Coll., 1962; MA, U. San Francisco, 1980. Cert. elem. and coll. tchr.; bilingual and lang. devel. specialist. Instr. adult edn. Guam, 1964-66, Spanish Speaking Ctr., Harrisburg, Pa., 1977-79; tchr. Colegio Salesiano, Rota, Spain, 1973, 84, Alisal Sch. Dist., Salinas, Calif., 1979-81, Liberty Sch., Petaluma, Calif., 1981-85, Cinnabar Sch., Petaluma, 1985—; instr. Chapman U., 1994—; also summer migrant edn. programs Cinnabar Sch., Petaluma, 1990, 91; instr. Santa Rosa (Calif.) Jr. Coll., 1982-83; mem. math. curriculum com. Sonoma County Office Edn., Santa Rosa, 1988; mem. Summer Sci. Connections Inst., Sonoma State U., 1994, Redwood Empire Math. Acad., summer 1995; mem. Sonoma County Math Project, 1995-96; summer '96 NEH stipend to Harvard U. Translator: Isabel la Catolica, 1962. Mem. Asian relief com. ARC, Harrisburg, 1975, Boy Scouts Am., Petaluma, 1983, Mechanicsburg, Pa., 1974, Monterey, Calif., 1971. Sarah D. Barder fellow Johns Hopkins U., 1990. Mem. NEA, AAUW (chair edn. founds. com. 1985-86), Calif. Assn. Bilingual Educators, Cinnabar Tchrs. Assn., Club Hispano-Americano Petaluma (pres. 1987-89). Roman Catholic. Avocation: travel. Home: 1289 Glenwood Dr Petaluma CA 94954-4326

OHASHI, SHOICHI, business administration educator; b. Seto, Aichi, Japan, Mar. 7, 1932; s. Mitsuo and Yoshie Ohashi; m. Kimiko Ohashi, Nov. 20, 1957; Reisaku. MBA, Kobe (Japan) U., 1957, DBA, 1967. Acad. asst. Kansai U., Suita, Japan, 1957-60, lectr., 1960-63, assoc. prof., 1963-70, prof. bus. adminstrn., 1970—, vice dean students div., 1972-74, vice dean faculty commerce, 1977-78, dean faculty commerce, 1979-80, dean vocat. div., 1982-86, acad. v.p., 1986-92, dean of entrance divsn., 1993—; lectr. Osaka U. Fgn. Studies, 1968-74, Kobe U., 1971, Ritsumeikan U., Kyoto, Japan, 1971-73, Kwanseigakuin U., Nishinomiya, Japan, 1979-80, 94—. Author: Theories on Works Community, 1966, Theory of Business Administration, 1992; couthor: Workers' Participation, 1979; co-editor: Information Society Business, 1988, Business Administration, 1991, Lexicon of Business Administration, 1994, An Inquiry into the Japanese Management, 1996. Researcher com. Rsch. Fund Commn. Japan Ministry Edn., 1987-89. Mem. Japan Soc. Bus. Adminstrn. (internat. com. 19880-83, exec. com. 1983-89, 92—), Assn. for Comparative Study of Mgmt. (pres. 1994-96), Soc. for the History of Mgmt. Theories (exec. com. 1993—). Home: 2-13-16 Tsukimiyama, Takarazuka Hyogo665, Japan Office: Kansai U, 3-3-35 Yamate-cho, Suita Osaka564, Japan

OHAYON, MAURICE M., research center administrator, psychiatrist; b. Casablanca, Morocco, June 22, 1948; arrived in Can., 1990; MD, U. Aix Marseille II, France, 1979, Cert. d'Etudes Spéciales Psychiatry, 1980, D in Computer Scis., 1992. Resident in psychiatry and neurology C.H.U. Marseille, 1975-77; hosp. psychiatrist France, 1980-90; sci. dir. Rsch. Ctr. Fernand Seguin, Montreal, Que., Can., 1990-92; dir. rsch. ctr. Inst. Philippe Pinel, Montreal, 1992—; rsch. coord. U. Montreal, 1992—; assoc. prof. U. Que. Trois-Rivières, 1993—; sci. conseiller Ctr. Hos. Vinatier, France, 1994—; vis. clin. scientist St. Mary's Hosp., London, 1995—; cons. prof. psychiatry Stanford U., 1995—. Author: Intelligence Artificielle et Psychiatrie, 1989, Apprentissage, Adaptation et Réadaptation: Etat de la Recherche, 1995. Mem. APHA, Can. Psychol. Assn., N.Y. Acad. Scis., Coll. Médecins. Home: 2933 Ave Soissons, Montreal, PQ Canada H3S 1W1 Office: Ctr Rsch Philippe Pinel, 10905 Henri Bourassa E, Montreal, PQ Canada H1C 1H1

OHE, SHUZO, chemical engineer, educator; b. Tokyo, Mar. 31, 1938; s. Kunio and Chizu (Tabata) O.; m. Nobuko Motegi, Oct. 31, 1975; 1 child, Kenzo. BS, Sci. U. Tokyo, 1962; D of Engring., Tokyo Met. U., 1971. Chem. engr. Ishikawajima-Harima Heavy Indsl. Co. Ltd., Tokyo, 1962-65, reseracher, then rsch. mgr., 1966-80; assoc. prof. Tokai U., Tokyo, 1980-82; prof. chem. engring. Tokai U., 1982-91, Sci. U. of Tokyo, 1991—; vis. researcher Fractionation Rsch., Inc., South Pasadena, Calif., 1973; cons. Chiyoda Engring. Co. Ltd., 1986-89, NKK, Tokyo, 1988—, Sibata Scientific Tech. Ltd., Siber Instrument Co. Ltd. Inventor angle tray distillation tower; author, editor: Computer-Aided Data Book of Vapor Pressure, 1976, Vapor-Liquid Equilibrium Data, 1988, Vapor-Liquid Equilibrium Data at High Pressure, 1990, Vapor-Liquid Equilibrium Data-Salt Effect, 1991; author: Chemical Engineering Design By P.C., 1985. Mem. AAAS, AIChE, Kanagawa Micon Club (pres. 1988—), Japan Info. Ctr. Sci. and Tech., Japan Soc. Chem. Engring., N.Y. Acad. Scis. Avocation: golf. Office: Sci Univ Tokyo, 1-3 Kagurazaka Shinjuku-ku, Tokyo 162, Japan

O'HEARN, JAMES FRANCIS, chemical company executive; b. Fall River, Mass., Nov. 5, 1935; s. Francis Henry and Eileen Eleanor (James) O'H.; m. Sabrina Sieley Hu, Dec. 31, 1966; children: Kevin, Claudine. BS in Edn., Bridgewater Coll., 1960; student, Sofia U., 1962-63. Tchr. Freetown (Mass.) Elem. Sch., 1960-62, Dept. Def., Tokyo, 1962-63; regional mgr. Reynolds Metals Co., Hong Kong, L.A., 1963-69; regional mgr. Uniroyal Chems., Hong Kong, Singapore, 1969-76, Akron, Ohio, 1976-77; dir. mktg. Uniroyal Chems., Brussels, 1977-80; pres. Premier Chem. Co., Taipei, Taiwan, 1980—; dir. USA-ROC Econ. Coun., Taipei, 1991—, chmn. chem. group, 1986—. Mem. Petrochem. Ind. Assn. Taipei (dir. 1981-86), Am. Club in China (pres. 1993-94), Am. C. of C. (pres. 1991, 92), Am. Univ. Club (dir. 1992—). Republican. Roman Catholic. Avocations: golf, tennis, aerobics, mountain climbing. Home: 229 Chung Shan N Rd Sec 7, Taipei Taiwan Office: Premier Chem Co Ltd, 205 Tun Hwa N Rd Ste 704, Taipei Taiwan

O'HEARN, ROBERT RAYMOND, stage designer; b. Elkhart, Ind., July 19, 1921; s. Robert Raymond, Sr. and Ella May (Stoldt) O'H. B.A., Ind. U., 1939-43; student, Art Students League, 1943-45. Designer Brattle Theatre, Cambridge, Mass., 1948-52; prof. stage design, chmn. design dept. Sch. Music Ind. U., 1989—; instr. Studio and Forum Scenic Design, 1968-88. Stage designer: Broadway shows The Relapse, 1950, Loves Labor's Lost, 1953, Othello, Festival, 1955, The Apple Cart, Child of Fortune, 1956; asst. designer: Broadway shows Kismet, 1953, Pajama Game, 1955, My Fair Lady, 1956, West Side Story, 1958; designer: for film A Clerical Error, 1955; designer prodns. Central City Opera House, 1959-63, Opera Soc. Washington, 1958-61, L'Elisir D'Amore at Met. Opera House, 1960, Die Meistersinger, 1962, Aida, 1963; stage designer: As You Like It, Stratford, Conn., 1961, Troilus and Cressida, Stratford, 1961, Kiss Me Kate, Los Angles Civic Light Opera, 1964, N.Y.C. Center, 1965, Samson and Delila, Met. Opera, 1964, La Sylphide, Am. Ballet Theatre, 1964, Italian Symphony, 1971, Adam Cochrane, Broadway, 1964, Pique Dame, Met. Opera, 1965, La Ventana, 1966, Die Frau Ohne Schatten, 1966, Porgy and Bess, Vienna Volksoper, 1965, Bregenzer Festspiele, 1971, Otello, Boston Opera, also Hamburg State Opera, 1967, Hansel and Gretel, Met. Opera, 1967, Nutcracker Ballet, San Francisco Ballet, 1967, L.A. Ballet, 1979, La Traviata, Santa Fe Opera, 1968, Rosalinda, L.A. Civic Light Opera, 1968, Der Rosenkavalier, Met. Opera, 1969, Tallis Fantasia, N.Y.C. Ballet, 1969, Boris Godunov (unproduced), Met. Opera, 1970, Parsifal, Met. Opera, 1970, Porgy and Bess, Bregenz Festspiel, Austria, 1971, Falstaff, Marriage of Figaro, Gianni Schicci, Central City Opera House, 1972, Barber of Seville, 1973, The Enchanted, Kennedy Center, 1973, The Mind with the Dirty Man, Los Angeles, 1973, Midsummer Night's Dream, Central City Opera, 1974, Coppelia, Ballet West, 1974, Carmen, Strasbourg, 1974, The Pearl Fishers, Miami Opera, 1974, N.Y.C. Opera, 1980, Don Pasquale, Miami Opera, 1976, Scipio Africanus, Central City Opera, 1975, Swan Lake, Strasbourg, 1975, Marriage of Figaro, Met. Opera, 1975, Die Meistersinger, Karlsruhe, Germany, 1975, Girl of the Golden West, Houston Opera, 1976, N.Y.C. Opera, 1977, Vienna Staatsoper, 1976, Boris Godunov, Strasbourg, 1976, Der Rosenkavelier, Karlsruhe, 1976, Don Quixote, Ballet West, 1977, Die Meistersinger, Chgo. Lyric Opera, 1977, Adriana Lecouvreur, Miami Opera, 1978, La Boheme, 1978, Coppelia, Pacific N.W. Dance, Seattle, 1978, Andrea Chenier, N.Y.C. Opera, 1978, Der Rosenkavelier, Can. Opera Co., Toronto, 1978, Taming of the Shrew, Pa. State U., 1980, Die Fledermaus, Miami Opera, 1980, Tosca, Miami Opera, 1981, West Side Story, Bregenz Festspiel, Austria, 1981, Mich. Opera Theatre, 1985; Pique Dame, San Francisco Opera, 1982, La Traviata, Miami Opera, 1982, Of Mice and Men, Miami Opera, 1982, Carousel, Annie Get Your Gun, Miami Opera, 1984, Lucia di Lammermoor, 1984, L'Italiana in Algeri, 1985, Porgy and Bess, Met. Opera, 1985, West Side Story, Mich. Opera Theatre, 1985, Aida, Don Giovanni, Opera Colo., 1986, My Fair Lady, Mich. Opera Theatre, 1986, Samson and Delilah, Manon Lescaut Opera Colo., 1987, Annie Get Your Gun, Paper Mill Playhouse, 1987, Peter Grimes, Ind. U., 1987, Madama Butterfly, N.J. State Opera, 1990. Mem. vis. com. Costume Inst., Met. Museum. Mem. United Scenic Artists. Home: 2604 E 2nd St Bloomington IN 47401-5351

O'HEARNE, JOHN JOSEPH, psychiatrist; b. Memphis, Feb. 5, 1922; s. John Joseph and Norma Rose (Ford) O'H.; children: Patricia Ann, Marilyn Eileen, John Stephen, Brian Donal. BS, Rhodes Coll., Memphis, 1944; MD, U. Tenn., 1945; MS in Psychiatry, U. Colo., 1951. Diplomate Am. Bd. Psychiatry and Neurology. Intern Denver Gen. Hosp., 1945-46; fellow U. Colo., Denver, 1948-51, instr., 1949-52; instr. U. Denver, 1951; clin. dir. psychiatry Kansas City (Mo.) Gen. Hosp. and Psychiat. Receiving Ctr., 1952-56; pvt. practice medicine specializing in psychiatry Kansas City, 1956—; adj. prof. sociology U. Mo., Kansas City, 1986—, Ctrl. Bapt. Theol. Sem., Kansas City, Kans.; mem. faculty Western Mo. Sch. for Ministry (Episc.); mem. staff St. Luke's Hosp.; cons. Lifewise, Kansas City, 1984—; clin. prof. psychiatry U. Kans., 1972—, U. Mo., Kansas City, 1974—; pres. Transactional Analysis Inst., Kansas City, 1974—. Co-author: Practical Transactional Analysis in Management, 1977; contbr. articles to profl. jours. Priest Episcopal Ch.; coun. Friends of Art Nelson-Atkins Mus. Art, 1991—. Capt. AUS, 1942-45, 46-48. Recipient Bronze medal NASTAR, 1984. Fellow Am. Psychiat. Assn. (life), Am. Group Psychotherapy Assn. (disting., dir. 1970-78, pres. 1974-78)), Internat. Assn. Group Psychotherapy, Am. Orthopsychiat. Assn. (life); mem. Am. Psychiat. Assn. (pres. Western Mo. dist. br. 1960-61, 64-65), Mo. State Med. Assn. (chmn. mental health com. 1960-62, physicians rehab. com. 1979-89, chmn. 1987-88, chmn. impaired physicians' com. 1987-88), Jackson County Med. Soc. (chmn. mental health com. 1959-66, mem., family life com. 1989-90, mem., legal com. 1990-92, patient-physicians rels. com. 1992), Internat. Transactional Analysis Assn. (trustee 1972-83), Internat. Wine and Food Soc. of London (chmn. wine com. Kansas City chpt. 1989, dinner chmn. 1992, sec. 1993), Carriage Club. Republican. Episcopalian. Avocations: photography, wine, travel, herb gardening, skiing. Office: 4706 Broadway St Ste 103 Kansas City MO 64112-1961

O'HERN, DANIEL JOSEPH, state supreme court justice; b. Red Bank, N.J., May 23, 1930; s. J. Henry and Eugenia A. (Sansone) O'H.; m. Barbara Ronan, Aug. 8, 1959; children: Daniel J., Eileen, James, John, Molly. AB, Fordham Coll., 1951; LLB, Harvard U., 1957. Bar: N.J. 1958. Clk. U.S. Supreme Ct., Washington, 1957-58; assoc. Abramoff, Apy & O'Hern, Red Bank, N.J., 1966-78; commr. N.J. Dept. Environ. Protection, 1978-79; counsel to Gov. N.J. Trenton; justice N.J. Supreme Ct., Trenton, 1981—; former mem. adv. com. profl. ethics N.J. Supreme Ct. Past trustee Legal Aid Soc. Monmouth County, (N.J.); mayor Borough of Red Bank, 1969-78, councilman, 1962-69. Served as lt. (j.g.) USNR, 1951-54. Fellow Am. Bar Found.; mem. ABA, N.J. Bar Assn., Monmouth County Bar Assn., Harvard Law Sch. Assn. N.J. (past pres.). Office: NJ Supreme Ct 151 Bodman Pl Red Bank NJ 07701*

O'HERN, ELIZABETH MOOT, microbiologist, writer; b. Richmondville, N.Y., Sept. 1, 1913; s. Carl Melvin and Margaret Esther (Dibble) Moot; B.A., U. Calif., Berkeley, 1945, M.A., 1947; Ph.D. (grad. fellow), U. Wash., 1956; m. William J. O'Hern, Jan. 4, 1952. Instr. SUNY, Bklyn., 1957-62; asst. prof. George Washington U., Washington, 1962-65; prin. investigator rsch. Bionetics Rsch. Lab., Kensington, Md., 1965-67; adminstr. rsch. grants in microbiology, genetics and anesthesiology NIH, Nat. Inst. Gen. Med. Scis., Bethesda, Md., 1968-75, spl. asst. to dir., 1975-77, adminstr. spl. programs, 1977-86, also programs adminstr. Mem. bd. examiners in basic scis. Commn. on Licensure to Practice Healing Arts in D.C., 1974-75; panel mem. Washington Area Office, U.S. Civil Svc. Commn., 1977-86; program cons. U. Calif., 1990. Fellow Am. Acad. Microbiology; mem. AAUW (pres. Washington br. 1967-69, trustee edn. found. 1976-81), AAAS, Am. Inst. Biol. Sci., Am. Public Health Assn., Am. Soc Cell Biology, Am. Soc. Microbiology (chmn. status of women in the profession 1975-78), Am. Soc. Tropical Medicine and Hygiene, Med. Mycology Soc. Am., Mycol. Soc. Am., N.Y. Acad. Sci., Wash. Acad. Sci., Assn. Women in Sci., Astron. Soc. Pacific, Planetary Soc., Grad. Women in Sci. (nat. sec. 1974-77, chpt. pres. 1979-80), Sigma Xi. Author: Profiles of Pioneer Women Scientists. Contbr. articles to profl. publs. Home: 522 Russell Ave Gaithersburg MD 20877

O'HERN, JANE SUSAN, psychologist, educator; b. Winthrop, Mass., Mar. 21, 1933; d. Joseph Francis and Mona (Garvey) O'H. BS, Boston U., 1954, EdD, 1962; MA, Mich. State U., 1956. Instr. Mercyhurst Coll., 1954-55, Hofstra Coll., 1956-57, State Coll., Salem and Boston, 1957-60; asst. prof. Boston U., 1962-67, assoc. prof., 1967-75, prof. edn. and psychiat. (psychology), 1975-95, prof. emeritus, 1995—, chmn. dept. counseling psychology, 1972-75, 88-89, dir. mental health edn. program, 1975-81, dir. internat. edn., 1978-81, asst. v.p. internat. edn., 1981; pres. ASSIST Internat., Inc., 1989—; adv. bd. Internat. Study Cons., 1994—. Contbr. articles to profl. jours. Trustee Boston Ctr. Modern Psychoanalytic Studies, 1980-92. Recipient grants U.S. Office Edn., NIMH, Dept. of Def. Mem. Assn. Counselor Edn. and Suprs., Am. Counseling Assn., North Atlantic Assn. Counselor Edn. and Supervision (past pres.), Mass. Psychol. Assn., Am. Psychol. Assn., Mortar Bd., Pi Lamda Theta, Sigma Kappa, Phi Delta Kappa, Phi Beta Delta. Home: 111 Perkins St Apt 287 Boston MA 02130-4324

OHGA, NORIO, electronics executive; b. Numazu, Japan, Jan. 29, 1930; m. Midori Ohga. Grad., Tokyo Nat. U. Fine Arts and Music, 1953, Kunst U., Berlin, 1957. Cons., advisor Tokyo Tsushin Kogyo (later Sony Corp.), 1953-59; gen. mgr. tape recorder divsn., product planning divsn., indsl. design divsn. Sony Corp., Tokyo, 1959, bd. dirs., 1964-72, mng. dir., 1972-76, dep. pres., 1976-82, pres., chief oper. officer, 1982-89, pres., chief exec. officer, 1989—; sr. mng. dir. CBS/Sony Group, Inc., 1968-70, pres., 1970-80, chmn., 1980-91; chmn. Sony Corp. Am., 1988—, Sony Software Corp., 1991—. Decorated Medal of Honor with Blue Ribbon by J.M. the Emperor of Japan, 1988, Cmdrs. Cross First Class of the Order of Merit of the Rep. of Austria, 1987. Mem. Tokyo C. of C. and Industry (vice chmn.). Office: Sony Corp, 7-35 Kitashinagawa 6-chome, Shinagawa-ku Tokyo 141, Japan Office: Sony Corp Am 550 Madison Ave New York NY 10022*

OHIA, SUNDAY EDET, pharmacologist; b. Kano, Nigeria, Nov. 18, 1956; came to U.S., 1988; s. Joseph Nduka and Rose Atim (Bassey) O.; m. Ekanem Offiong, Sept. 10, 1983; children: Odochi, Uchechukwu. BSc, U. Ibadan, Nigeria, 1978; MSc, U. Glasgow, Scotlant, 1981; PhD, U. Glasgow, U.K., 1986. Grad. asst. U. Ibadan, 1978-82; grad. demonstrator U. Glasgow, 1982-86; rsch. fellow Meml. U. Nfld., Can., 1986-88; rsch. assoc. U. Louisville, 1988-91; asst. prof. pharm. scis. Creighton U., Omaha, 1991—, asst. prof. pharmacology, 1991—, chmn. pharm. scis., 1992—, assoc. prof., 1995. Contbr. articles to profl. jours. U. Louisville travel awardee, 1989-91; Rsch. Starter grantee Pharm. Mfg. Found., 1991; recipient John C. Kenefick Faculty Devel. award, 1991. Mem. AACP, AAAS, Soc. Neuroscis., N.Y. Acad. Scis., Am. Soc. Pharmacology and Exptl. Therapeutics (Young Scientist Travel award 1991), Assn. Rsch. in Vision and Ophthalmology, Sigma Xi, Phi Beta Delta, Rho Chi, Phi Lambda Sigma. Office: Creighton Univ Dept Pharmaceutical Scis Omaha NE 68178

OHINOUYE, TSUNEO, automobile manufacturing executive; b. Tokyo, Mar. 13, 1932; came to U.S., 1977; s. Tatsuo and Haru (Ito) O.; m. Tomie Murate, Oct. 23, 1958; children: Mariko Itoh, Yuko Ohinouye. B Mech. Engring., Kyoto (Japan) U., 1954; M Automobile Engring., Cranfield Inst. Tech., Bedford, Eng., 1964. Mgr. engine design Mitsubishi Heavy Industries, Kyoto, 1955-77; pres. Mitsubishi Motors Corp. Svcs., Southfield, Mich., 1977-80; chief coord. vehicle devel. passenger car ctr. Mitsubishi Motors Corp., Okazaki, Japan, 1980-85; corp. chief engr. export product planning Mitsubishi Motors Corp., Tokyo, 1985-87; pres. Mitsubishi Motors Am., Southfield, 1987-91; pres., CEO Diamond-Star Motors (subs. Mitsubishi Motors Corp.), Normal, Ill., 1991-95; chmn., CEO Mitsubishi Motor Mfg. of Am., Inc., Normal, 1995—. UN fellow Cranfield Inst. Tech. Mem. Bloomington C. of C. (bd. dirs. 1993—). Office: Mitsubishi Motor Mfg America Inc US Rte 150 Normal IL 61761-8099

OHIRA, KAZUTO, theatre company executive, writer; b. Hiroshima, Japan, Jan. 5, 1933; s. Kitaro and Ryo (Sugimoto) O.; m. Evelyn Lanham, Sept. 3, 1964. BA, Waseda U., Tokyo, 1956. Theatre mgr. Toho's La Brea Theatre, L.A., 1961-63; gen. mgr. Toho Cinema, N.Y.C., 1963-64; publicity mgr. Towa Co., Ltd., Tokyo, 1965-69; rep., dir., mgr. Toho Internat. Inc., N.Y.C., 1969, chief exec. officer, 1988—; pres. Internat. Cultural Prodn. Inc., N.Y.C. Producer (dance performance and drama) Yasuko Nagamine's Musume Dojoji, 1982, Mandara, 1985, (drama) Yukio Ninagawa's Media, 1987, Takarazuka Show at Radio City Music Hall, N.Y., 1989, KanashibetsU: Furano Group at La Mama, Takarazuka Dance Concert at Joyce Theater, 1992, Sotoba Komachi, Yasuko Nagamine and Co., Beauty of Tokyo, Met. Tokyo, City Ctr., N.Y., 1993; author: Broadway parts I and II, 1982, 2d edit., 1987, Broadway, Broadway, 1987, Performing Arts of New York, 1989, Haiku Collection: Though The Travel is Short, The Charms of Broadway, 1994, Broadway Criticism, 1995. Bd. dirs. House Found. Meredith Monk, N.Y. Symphony Ensemble, Saeko Ichinohe Dance Co. Recipient 2d Fumiko Yamaji Cultural award, 1985. Mem. UNESCO, Internat. Theatre Critics Assn., Internat. Theatre Inst. Japan, N.Y. Waseda Univ. Alumni Assn. (hon. dir.), Players Club. Avocation: golf. Home: Island House 555 Main St Apt 1204S New York NY 10044-0123 Office: ICP Inc 235 W 48th St Apt 33B New York NY 10036-1431

OHL, RONALD EDWARD, academic administrator; b. Warren, Ohio, May 30, 1936; s. Howard Edward and Ella May (Van Auker) O.; m. Joan Ann Elizabeth Eschenbach, June 29, 1974. BA, Amherst Coll., 1958; MA, Columbia U., 1961; M in Divinity, Union Theol. Sem., N.Y.C., 1964; PhD, U. Pa., 1980. Ordained minister Congregationalist Ch., 1964. Counselor to grad. students Columbia U., N.Y.C., 1960-62; asst. dean students, asst. prof. history Elmhurst (Ill.) Coll., 1964-67; spl. asst. to dean of men Temple U., Phila., 1967-68; assoc. dean coll., dean student affairs, instr. in edn. Colo. Coll., Colorado Springs, 1968-74; with Fairleigh Dickinson U., Rutherford, N.J., 1975-83, successively acting v.p. for external relations, asst. to pres., acting chmn. and cons. relations div. univ. resources and pub. affairs; pres. Salem (W.Va.)-Teikyo U., 1983—, trustee, 1989—, also bd. dirs.; bd. dirs. One Valley Bank, Clarksburg. Contbr. articles to profl. jours. Bd. dirs. Sta. WNPB-TV, 1992—. Recipient Edward Poole Lay Traveling fellowship award Amherst Coll., 1958-59, Young Am. Artists' Dirs. award U.S. Embassy, Rome, 1959-60; Rockefeller Bros. Fund fellow, 1961-62; named Research Asst., U. Pa., 1967-68. Mem. W.Va. Assn. Ind. Colls. (pres. 1985-89), North Ctrl. Assn. Colls. and Schs. (cons.-evaluator 1987—), W.Va. Found. for Ind. Colls. (acad. vice chmn. 1992-94), Clarksburg C. of C. (bd. dirs. 1985-91, 93-96), Univ. Club, W.Va. Christopher Quincentenary Commn., Rotary. Avocations: reading, writing, aviation, skiing, backpacking. Home: 63 Terrace Ave Salem WV 26426-1124

OHLKE, CLARENCE CARL, public affairs consultant; b. Kansas City, Mo., Feb. 16, 1916; s. William Erdman and Amanda (Rubin) O.; m. Frances Woodley Nicholson, Oct. 9, 1954; children: Daniel N., Carl E., Amanda A. A.A., Kansas City Jr. Coll., 1935; B.S., U. Mo., 1940. Personnel examiner, rsch. asst. to city mgr. Mcpl. Govt., city of Kansas City, 1940-41; personnel specialist WPB, Washington, 1942; dir. civilian personnel Chief Naval Operations, Washington, 1946-47; successively personnel specialist, asst. dir. community ops., dir. contracts br., prodn. div. AEC, Washington, 1947-58, spl. asst. to chmn. and commr., 1959-61; asst. dir. operations div. contracts AEC, 1961, asst. to asst. gen. mgr. ops., 1962-63, dir. Office Econ. Impact and Conversion, 1964-66; spl. asst. to dir., head congl. and pub. affairs, govt. and pub. programs dir. NSF, Washington, 1966-73; cons., dir. Center Urban Research and Environ. Studies Drexel U., 1973-75; cons. pub. affairs, 1976—. Served to lt. USNR, 1942-46. Recipient Disting. Service award NSF, 1973; resolution of commendation Pres.' Nat. Sci. Bd., 1973. Mem. AAAS (public understanding of sci. com. 1977-80). Home: Bear Branch Farms 7380 Ira Sears Rd Adamstown MD 21710-8501

OHLMEYER, DONALD WINFRED, JR., film and television producer; b. New Orleans, Feb. 3, 1945; s. Donald W. and Eva Claire (Bivens) O.; m. Adrian Perry, Feb. 11, 1978; 1 son, Kemper Perry; children by previous marriage: Justin Drew, Christopher Brett, Todd Bivens. BA in Communications, U. Notre Dame, 1967. Pres. Roadblock Prodns., 1977—; chmn. bd., chief exec. officer Ohlmeyer Communications, Los Angeles, 1982—. Assoc. dir. ABC Sports, N.Y.C., 1967-70, dir., 1971-72, producer, 1972-77; dir. Olympic Games, 1972, Walt Disney World's 4th of July Spectacular; producer, dir. Summer and Winter Olympics, 1976; producer Monday Night Football, 1972-76; exec. producer NBC Sports, N.Y.C., 1977-82; exec. producer: 1980 Olympic Games, Crime of Innocence, Under Siege, Bluffing It, Right to Die; exec. producer: (movies) Special Bulletin, The Golden Moment: An Olympic Love Story; producer Battle of the Network Stars. Recipient 11 Emmy awards 1975-83, Cine Golden Eagle award, 1979, Miami Film Festival award 1979. Mem. Dirs. Guild Am., Acad. TV Arts and Scis. Clubs: Bel-Air (Calif.); Deepdale (N.Y.); Outrigger Canoe, Waialae Country (Honolulu). Office: NBC 3000 W Alameda Ave Burbank CA 91523-0001*

OHLSON, DOUGLAS DEAN, artist; b. Cherokee, Iowa, Nov. 18, 1936; s. Lloyd E. and Effie O. (Johnson) O. B.A., U. Minn., 1961. Prof. art Hunter Coll., N.Y.C., 1964—. One man shows include Fischbach Gallery, N.Y.C., 1964, 66-70, 72, Susan Caldwell Gallery, N.Y.C., 1974, 76, 77, 79, 81, 82, 83, Portland (Oreg.) Ctr. for Visual Arts, 1977, Ruth Siegel Gallery, N.Y.C., 1985, 87, Andre Zarre Gallery, N.Y.C., 1985, 90, 92, 93, 95, Gallery 99, Miami, Fla., 1986, Nina Freudenheim Gallery, Buffalo, 1986, Jaffe Gallery, Miami, 1989; group shows include Mus. Modern Art, N.Y.C., 1968, Tate Gallery, London, 1969, Whitney Mus., N.Y.C., 1969, 71, Corcoran Gallery, Washington, 1972, 73, UCLA, 1975; represented in permanent collections Met. Mus. Art, N.Y.C., Nat. Gallery Art, Washington, Am. Fedn. Art, Mus. Modern Art, Frankfurt, Fed. Republic Germany, Mus. Contemporary Art, Helsinki, Mpls. Inst. Art, Dallas Mus., Bklyn. Mus., Born in Iowa: The Homecoming, 1986-87; invitational Am. Acad. Arts and Letters, 1992, 94. Served with USMC, 1955-58. Guggenheim fellow, 1968; Creative Artists Public Service grantee, 1974; Nat. Endowment for Arts grantee, 1976. Home and Studio: 35 Bond St New York NY 10012-2426

OHLWILER, CLIFFORD ROBERT, civil engineer; b. Cottonwood, Ariz.z, Sept. 16, 1954; s. Robert Earl and Delores Ann Ohlwiler; m. Cindy Ann Shore, Aug. 2, 1975; children: Paul Sandor, Trista Kay. BS in Civil Engring. Tech., No. Ariz. U., 1976. Registered profl. engr., Calif. Lab. supr. Engrs. Testing Lab., Phoenix, 1976-77; mgr. quality control TPAC div. Tanner Cos., Etiwanda, Calif., 1977-80; tech. svcs. engr. Transit Mixed Concrete Co., Azusa, Calif., 1980-91; engring. mgr. Utility Vault Co., Inc., Fontana, Calif., 1991—. Cub scout leader Boy Scouts Am., Pomona, Calif., 1985-86, Fontana, 1986-87. Mem. ASCE, Internat. Conf. Bldg. Ofcls., Am. Concrete Inst. (bd. dirs. So. Calif. chpt.). Avocation: camping. Office: Utility Vault Co Inc 10650 Hemlock Ave Fontana CA 92337-7296

OHM, HERBERT WILLIS, agronomy educator; b. Albert Lea, Minn., Jan. 28, 1945; s. Wilhelm Carl and Lena Ann (Finkbeiner) O.; m. Judy Ann Chrisinger, Aug. 8, 1964; children: Cari Lynn, David William. BS in Agrl. Edn., U. Minn., St. Paul, 1967; MS in Plant Breeding, N.D. State U., 1969; PhD in Plant Genetics and Breeding, Purdue U., 1972. Cert. agronomist. Asst. prof. Purdue U., West Lafayette, Ind., 1972-77, assoc. prof. agronomy, 1977-83, prof., 1983—; team leader Interdisciplinary Wheat and Oat Genetics and Breeding Program, West Lafayette, 1980—, Interdisciplinary Purdue/AID Devel. Program, Burkina Faso, West Africa, 1983-85; mgr. hard red winter wheat rsch. Pioneer Hi-Bred Internat., Inc., Hutchinson, Kans., 1980. Contbr. book chpts. Recipient Soils and Crops Merit award Ind. Crop Improvement Assn., 1988, Merit award Orgn. of African Unity, 1989, Meritorious Svc. award Sci., Tech. and Rsch. Commn., 1989, Agronomic Acheivement award American Soc. of Agronomy, 1994. Fellow Am. Soc. Agronomy (Agronomic Achievement award), Crop Sci. Soc. Am. (chmn. divsn. 1991); mem. Am. Oat Workers Conf. (chmn.), Nat. Oat Improvement Coun. (chmn.), Coun. Agrl. Sci. and Tech., Am. Registry Cert. Profls. in Agrl. Crops and Soils (cert.). Avocations: woodworking, music. Office: Purdue U Dept Agronomy Lilly Hall Life Scis West Lafayette IN 47907-7899

OHMAN, DIANA J., state official, former school system administrator; b. Sheridan, Wyo., Oct. 3, 1950; d. Arden and Doris Marie (Carstens) Mahin. AA, Casper Coll., 1970; BA, U. Wyo., 1972, MEd, 1977, postgrad., 1979—. Tchr. kindergarten Natrona County Sch. Dist., Casper, Wyo., 1971-72; tchr. rural sch. K-8 Campbell County Sch. Dist., Gillette, Wyo., 1972-80, rural prin. K-8, 1980-82, prin. K-6, 1982-84, assoc. dir. instrn., 1984-87; dir. K-12 Goshen County Migrant Program, Torrington, Wyo., 1988-89; prin. K-2 Goshen County Sch. Dist., Torrington, Wyo., 1987-90; state supt. pub. instrn. State of Wyo., Cheyenne, 1991-94, secretary of state, 1995—; chmn. Campbell County Mental Health Task Force, 1986-87; mem. Legis. Task Force on Edn. of Handicapped 3-5 Yr. Olds, 1988-89. State Committeewoman Wyo. Rep. Party, 1985-88. Recipient Wyo. Elem. Prin. of Yr. award, 1990; named Campbell County Tchr. of Yr. 1980, Campbell County Profl. Bus. Woman of Yr. 1984, Outstanding Young Woman in Am., 1983. Mem. Coun. of Chief of State Sch. Officers (Washington chpt.), Internat. Reading Assn., Wyo. Assn. of Sch. Adminstrs., Kappa Delta Pi, Phi Kappa Phi, Phi Delta Kappa. Republican. Lutheran. Office: Sec State Office State Capitol Cheyenne WY 82002-0020*

OHNAMI, MASATERU, mechanical engineering educator; b. Kyoto, Japan, Apr. 6, 1931; s. Eijiro and Hisae O.; m. Hiroko Ohnami, Oct. 10, 1959; 1 child, Masahiro. B in Engring., Ritsumeikan U., Kyoto, Japan, 1954; D in Engring., Kyoto U., 1960; D Internat. Rels. (honoris causa), Am. U., Washington, 1995. Asst. prof. Kyoto U., 1955-61; assoc. prof. Ritsumeikan U., Kyoto, 1961-67, prof., 1967—, dean acad. affairs, 1978-80, dean faculty sci. & engring., 1988-90, pres., 1991—; vis. rsch. prof. Columbia U., N.Y.C., 1963-64; mng. dir. Japan Assn. Pvt. Colls. and Univs., Tokyo, 1991—; dir. Japanese Univ. Accreditation Assn., Tokyo, 1992—; mem. Sci. Coun., Ministry Edn., 1984-86, 89-91, Univ. Formation Coun., 1995—, Univ. Coun. Ministry Edn., 1995—. Author: Plasticity and High Temperature Strength of Materials, 1988, Fracture and Society, 1992. Mem. Deutscher Verband für Materialforschung and prüfung e.V. (hon. 1992—), soc. of Materials Sci. Japan (bd. dirs. 1971-74, 81-84, 85-88, Prize 1971), Japanese Soc. for Strength and Fracture of Materials (bd. dirs. 1984—), Sci. Coun. Japan (material rsch. liaison com. 1988-94), Engring. Acad. Japan. Avocations: oil painting, reading. Home: 8-10 Hyugacho, Takatsuki Osaka 569, Japan Office: Ritsumeikan Univ, 56-1 Tojiin Kitamachi Kita, Kyoto 603, Japan

OHNO, SUSUMU, research scientist; b. Seoul, Korea, Feb. 1, 1928; came to U.S., 1953; s. Kenichi and Toshiko (Saito) O.; m. Midori Aoyama, Jan. 7, 1951; children: Azusa, Yukali, Takeshi. DVM, Tokyo U. Agr. and Tech., 1949; PhD, Hokkaido U., 1956, DSc, 1961; DSc, U. Pa., 1984; HHD (hon.), Kwansei Gakuin U., 1983. Rsch. staff pathology Tokyo U., 1950-53; rsch. assoc. City of Hope, Duarte, Calif., 1953-66, chmn. biology, 1966-81, disting. scientist, 1981-95, emeritus, 1996—; vis. prof. Albert Einstein Med. Sch., Bronx, N.Y., 1969, Basel Inst. for Immunology, Switzerland, 1976; prof. at large Tohoku U., Japan, 1987—; bd. dirs. Beckman Rsch. Inst., Duarte, Calif. Author monographs. Recipient Kihara prize Genetic Soc. Japan, Tokyo, 1983. Fellow AAAS (Amory prize 1981); mem. NAS, Royal Danish Acad. Scis. and Letters (fgn.). Avocations: horsemanship, dressage, fishing, musical transformation of gene DNA sequences. Office: Beckman Rsch Inst City of Hope 1450 Duarte Rd Duarte CA 91010-3011

O'HOLLAREN, PAUL JOSEPH, former international fraternity administrator; b. Portland, Oreg., Dec. 24, 1927; s. Charles Edward and Helen Henrietta (McHugh) O'H.; m. Patricia Marie Foley, June 27, 1953; children: Mark T., Kevin J., Brian T., Patrick S., Kelly P. JD, Northwestern Coll. of Law, 1954. Bar: Oreg., 1954. Atty. Oreg. State Bar, 1954-83; mem. supreme coun. Moose Internat., Inc., Mooseheart, Ill., 1968-79; supreme gov. Loyal Order of Moose, Mooseheart, Ill., 1978-79, dir. gen., 1984-94, retired, 1994; chmn. exec. bd. Moose Internat., Inc., 1994—. Bd. dirs. Ill. Math. and Sci. Acad., Aurora. With U.S. Army, 1945-46. Named Jr. First Citizen, U.S. Jr. C. of C., Portland, 1959; recipient Oreg. State Bar award of Merit, 1979. Mem. Multnomah Athletic Club, Loyal Order of Moose. Republican. Roman Catholic. Avocation: golf. Office: 1850 Benjamin Franklin Plz 1 SW Columbia St Portland OR 97258-2002

O'HORGAN, THOMAS FOSTER, composer, director; b. Chgo., May 3, 1924. BA, MA, DePaul U. Chgo. Debut performance in Fallout; off-Broadway revue, 1959; directing debut with prodn. The Maids, 1964; dir.: Hair (Tony award nominee 1968), Lenny (Drama Desk award 1971), Jesus Christ Super Star, Inner City, Six from La Mama, The Hessian Corporal, Futz (Obie award 1967, Drama Desk award 1968), Tom Paine (Drama Desk award 1968), Massachusetts Trust, Dude, The Leaf People, Sergeant Pepper's Lonely Hearts Club Band on the Road, Capitol Cakewalk, 1990, The Architect and The Emperor of Abyssinia; composer: music for numerous prodns. including Open Season at Second City Senator Joe (also dir.), 1989, The Body Builder's Book of Love, 1990; music for films including Futz, 1969, Alex in Wonderland, 1970, Rhinocerous, 1974; performer in: film All Men Are Apes, 1965. Recipient Creative Arts award Brandeis U., 1968. Office: care Dirs Guild Am 110 W 57th St New York NY 10019-3319

OHRENSTEIN, ROMAN ABRAHAM, economics educator, economist, rabbi; b. Slomniki, Poland, June 12, 1920; came to U.S., 1951, naturalized, 1957; s. Joseph Barukh and Gena (Fiefkopf) O.; m. Ruth Silberstein, Aug. 30, 1953; children: Gena Ann, Ilana Rose. M.A. in Econs., U. Munich, 1948, Ph.D. cum laude in Econs., 1949, postgrad. in medicine, 1949-51; M.H.L., Jewish Theol. Sem. Am., 1955; postgrad., Columbia U., 1963-64. Ordained rabbi, 1955. Rabbi Auburn, N.Y., 1955-57, Pittsfield, Mass., 1957-60, Atlanta, 1960-62, N.Y.C., 1962-66; prof. econs. Nassau Coll., SUNY-Garden City, 1964—, chmn. econs. dept., 1976-78, 82-84, campus chaplain, 1970—; chaplain Nassau County Civic Preparedness, N.Y., 1965—; prof. econs. Am. Coll. Jerusalem, 1968-73, mem. Coll. Council, 1967-73; vis. prof. U. Newcastle, Australia, 1985, vis. rsch. prof., 1989; past chaplain Kiwanis, Police Dept. Cayuga County, N.Y., 1955-57, Mt. Sinai Hosp., N.Y.C., 1963-64; nat. dir. Jewish Rights Council; mem. Council of Orgns., U.S.A., 1978-85; mem. spl. com. on Jewish law Rabbinical Assembly, 1971; condr. seminars U. Queensland, Sydney U., Nat. Univ., all Australia, 1989, Sorbonne, Paris, 1990; lectr., guest speaker on radio, TV, Jewish civic and profl. orgns. Author: (series) Economic Thought in Talmudic Literature, 1968, 70, 83, 86, 87, 89, 91-93, 96, Inventories During Business Fluctuations, 1973, Inventory Control as an Economic Shock Absorber, 1975, Economic Analysis in Talmudic Literature, 1992; mem. editl. adv. bd. Internat. Rev. Econs. and Ethics; contbr. articles to profl. jours. Mem. nat. exec. comm. Am. Profs. for Peace in the Mid. East, 1971-73; mem. adv. bd. Am. Acad. Alliance for Israel, 1995—. Recipient 1st Faculty Disting. Achievement award Nassau Coll., SUNY, 1992, 95; SUNY fellow, 1968, 70. Mem. Nat. Assn. Jewish Chaplains, Rabbinical Assembly N.Y. Bd. Rabbis, Am. Econ. Assn., History of Econs. Soc., Assn. Social Econs., Learned Soc., N.Y. Acad. Scis., Internat. Soc. for Intercommunication New Ideas, Literati Club (Eng.). Home: 28-74 208th St Bayside NY 11360-2421 Office: Nassau Coll Dept Econ Stewart Ave Garden City NY 11530 *I kept my faith in God coupled with loyalty to tradition, sharpened my mind while maintaining discipline of the heart; tenacity in the face of adversity, turning stumbling blocks into stepping stones while never losing sight of life's supreme purpose: to leave the world a little better than I found it.*

OHRN, NILS YNGVE, chemistry and physics educator; b. Avesta, Sweden, June 11, 1934; came to U.S., 1966; s. Nils E. and Gerda M. (Akerlund) O.; m. Ann M.M. Thorsell, Aug. 24, 1957; children: Elisabeth, Maria. M.S., Uppsala U., 1958, Ph.D., 1963, F.D., 1966. Research assoc. Uppsala (Sweden) U., 1963-66; assoc. prof. U. Fla., Gainesville, 1966-70, prof. chemistry and physics, 1971—, assoc. dir. Quantum Theory Project, 1976-77, dir. Quantum Theory Project, 1983—, chmn. dept. chemistry, 1977-83. Editor: Internat. Jour. Quantum Chemistry, 1970—. Fulbright grantee Com. for Internat. Exchange of Scholars, Washington, 1961-63; recipient Bicentennial Gold medal King of Sweden, 1980; Fla. Acad. Scis. medal, 1984. Fellow Am. Phys. Soc., Chaire Francqui Interuniversitaires Belgium; mem. Am. Chem. Soc., Royal Acad. Scis. Sweden (fgn.), Finnish Acad. Scis. (fgn.), Royal Danish Acad. Scis. (fgn.), Sigma Xi, Phi Beta Kappa. Home: 1823 NW 11th Rd Gainesville FL 32605-5323 Office: U Fla Quantum Theory Project 362 Williamson Hall Gainesville FL 32611-2085

OHSOL, ERNEST OSBORNE, consulting chemical engineer; b. Washington, May 28, 1916; s. Johann Gottfried and Klara Elizabeth (Karpowitz) O.; m. Mary Rosamond Montgomery, June 15, 1940 (div. Jan. 4, 1977); children: Frederick M., Richard B., Barbara Alison Allen, Elizabeth Anne Gustafson; m. Barbara I. Handy, Mar. 24, 1977. Student, Fed. Polytech. Inst., Zurich, Switzerland, 1934-35; B.S., Coll. City N.Y., 1936; Sc.D., Mass. Inst. Tech., 1939. Registered profl. engr., N.J. Devel. engr. Standard Oil Devel. Co., Linden, N.J., 1939-50; mgr. process devel. chem. div. Gen. Elec. Co., Pittsfield, Mass., 1950-52; dir. research and devel. Pitts. Coke and Chem. Co., 1953-60; v.p. Haveg Industries, Inc. (plastics), Wilmington, Del., 1960-65, Chem. Constrn. Corp., N.Y.C., 1965-67, Escambia Chem. Co., N.Y.C., 1967; dir. chem. engring. dept. Am. Cyanamid Co. (central research div.), Stamford, Conn., 1967-72; cons. chem. engr. Plainfield, N.J., 1973; chief process engr. Eastern group Jacobs Engring. Co., Mountainside, N.J., 1973-75; corp. mgr. European fluid processing Selas Corp. Am., Munich, W. Ger., 1975-78; coordinator C.H. Dexter div. Dexter Corp., Windsor Locks, Conn., 1978-80; cons. Scallop Corp., Houston, Shell Nigerian Oil Co., Aramco, Tek-Rap, Petromin Shell, EnviroKinetics; chmn. emeritus Unipure Corp., 1993—; adj. prof. Grad. Sch., Stevens Inst. Tech., 1946-50. Patentee in field. Naumburg fellow CCNY, 1934-35; Arthur D. Little fellow Mass. Inst. Tech., 1937-38. Fellow Am. Inst. Chem. Engrs. (dir. 1973); mem. Am. Chem. Soc., Chemists Club N.Y.C., Sigma Xi. Episcopalian (vestryman 1963-65). Home and Office: 711 Hyannis Port North Crosby TX 77532-5515

OHTSU, MASAKAZU, electronics executive; b. Osaka, Japan, Dec. 17, 1937; m. Yoshiko Asano, Feb. 4, 1962; children: Masashi, Ben. BE, Doshisha U., Kyoto, Japan, 1962. With Itochu Corp., 1962—; sr. v.p., gen. mgr. Aerospace & Electronics Divsn. Itochu Internat., Inc., N.Y.C., 1988—; chmn. DX Comm., Inc., Hawthorn, N.Y., 1988—, VueScan, Inc., Deerfield Beach, Fla., 1994—, Telerent Leasing Corp., Raleigh, N.C., 1989—. Office: Itochu Internat Inc 335 Madison Ave New York NY 10017-4605

OHYAMA, HEIICHIRO, music educator, violist, conductor; b. Kyoto, Japan, July 31, 1947; came to U.S., 1970; s. Heishiro and Sumi (Ohara) O.; 1 child, Shinichiro Allen Ohyama. Assocs. degree, Guildhall Sch. Music and Drama, London, 1970. Instr. N.C. Sch. Arts, Winston-Salem, 1972-73; prof. music U. Calif., Santa Barbara, 1973—; prin. violist L.A. Philharm., 1979-91, asst. condr., 1987-90; music dir. Santa Barbara Chamber Orch., 1983—, Crossroads Chamber Orch., Santa Monica, Calif., 1981-93, Cayuga Chamber Orch., 1993—; music dir., condr. Japan Am. Symphony Orch., 1991—; artistic dir. La Jolla (Calif.) Chamber Music Festival, 1986—; condr. Round Top Music Festival, 1983—, N.W. Chamber Orch., 1985-87; vis. lectr. Ind. U., Bloomington, 1972-73; artistic dir. Santa Fe Chamber Music Festival, 1992—. Appearances at Marlboro Music Festival, Vt., 1972-76, Santa Fe Chamber Music Festival, 1977-85, Round Top Music Festival, Tex., 1983—, La Jolla (Calif.) Chamber Music Summer Fest., 1986—; various recordings. Recipient award Young Concert Artist N.Y., 1974, Calif. Artists Mgmt., 1991. Avocations: diving, kendo, photography. Home: 1823 Mira Vista Ave Santa Barbara CA 93103-2025

OIKAWA, HIROSHI, materials science educator; b. Sakhalin, Japan, Oct. 15, 1933; s. Torao and Tomi (Kumagai) O.; m. Ayako Otomo, May 4, 1963; children: Makoto, Junko. BE, Tohoku U., Sendai, Japan, 1956, ME, 1958, D in Engring., 1961. Instr. Tohoku U., Sendai, 1961-63, lectr., 1963-64, assoc. prof., 1964-82; rsch. fellow U. Fla., Gainesville, 1966-68; prof. Tohoku U., Sendai, 1982—, councilor, 1993-95, dean faculty engring., 1995—. Co-editor: Metals Handbooks, 1990, Metals Databook, 1993. Mem. Engring. Acad. of Japan, Japan Inst. Metals (bd. dirs. 1992-94, 96—, bd. dirs. Tohoku chpt. 1991-93, pres. 1996—), Iron and Steel Inst. of Japan (bd. dirs. 1990-92), Japan Inst. Light Metals (bd. dirs. 1989-95), Minerals, Metals and Materials Soc., ASM Internat., Inst. Materials. Office: Tohoku U, Dept Materials Sci Faculty Engring, Sendai 980-77, Japan

OISHI, SATOSHI, architectural and engineering executive; b. Japan, Jan. 19, 1927; came to U.S., 1932, naturalized, 1954; s. Mitsuhei and Yei O.; m. Jeanette Corrine Allard, July 2, 1960; 1 dau., Michelle Yuki. B.S. in Civil Engring. with high honors, U. Conn., 1949. With Edwards & Kelcey, Inc., Newark and Livingston, N.J., 1949—, chief structural engr., assoc., 1958-65, ptnr., 1965—; pres., chief exec. officer Edwards & Kelcey, Inc., Livingston, 1987-90, chmn. bd., 1990-94, chmn. emeritus, 1995-95, sr. cons., 1995—. Prin. works include rehab. of Manhattan Bridge, 1979-83, also transit tunnels and sta. designs, Washington, Atlanta, Balt., Buffalo, bridges in N.J., N.Y., Conn., Minn., New Eng.; investigator bridges and structures/failures. Chmn. Berkeley Heights (N.J.) Planning and Zoning Bd., 1974, Fritz Medal Bd., 1990-91, Hoover Medal Bd., 1995—; trustee Summit Unitarian Ch.; mem. Engring. Found Bd.; co-chair Journalism Award Com.; mem. alumni award and engring. adv. com. U. Conn.; mem. adv. coun. Al Dorman Honors Coll., N.J. Inst. Tech. Fellow ASCE (v.p. zone 1, dir. dist. 1, past pres. met. sect., Harland Bartolomew award 1992, Citizen Engrs. award 1992), N.Y. Assn. Cons. Engrs. (bd. dirs.), Am. Cons. Engrs. Coun.; mem. AIA (emeritus), Soc. Mil. Engrs. (sr. exec. com.), Internat. Assn. Bridge and Structural Engring., Japan Soc., RPA N.J. Com., Sigma Xi, Chi Epsilon (hon.), Tau Beta Pi. Unitarian. Home: 67 River Rd Berkeley Heights NJ 07922-1006 Office: Edwards & Kelcey PO Box 1936 299 Madison Ave Morristown NJ 07962-1936

OJALVO, MORRIS, civil engineer, educator; b. N.Y.C., Mar. 4, 1924; s. Nissim and (Fanny) O.; m. Anita Bedein, Dec. 26, 1948; children—Lynne, Joseph, Howard, Isobel. B.C.E., Rensselear Poly. Inst., Troy, N.Y., 1944, M.C.E., 1952; Ph.D., Lehigh U., Bethlehem, Pa., 1960; J.D., Ohio State U., Columbus, 1978. Bar: Ohio bar 1979. Draftsman Am. Bridge Co., Elmira, N.Y., 1946-47; tutor civil engring. CCNY, 1947-49; instr. Rensselear Poly. Inst., 1949-51; asst. prof. Princeton U., 1951-58; research instr. Lehigh U., 1958-60; mem. faculty Ohio State U., 1960—, prof. civil engring., 1964-82, prof. emeritus, 1982—; vis. prof. U. Tex.-Austin, 1982-83. Author: Thin-Walled Bars With Open Profiles, 1990; contbr. papers in field. Served with USNR, 1944-46. Mem. ASCE, Structural Stability Research Council. Patentee warp restraining device. Home: 2258 Wickliffe Rd Columbus OH 43221-1832 Office: Hitchcock Hall Ohio State Univ Columbus OH 43210

OJEMANN, GEORGE A., neurosurgeon, medical association executive; b. Iowa City, Feb. 25, 1935. MD, U. Iowa, 1959. Diplomate Am. Bd. Neurol. Surgery (dir. 1987, chmn. 1992). Intern in neurosurgery King County Hosp., Seattle, 1959-60; resident in neurosurgery U. Wash. Hosps., Seattle, 1960-64; attending neurosurgeon U. Hosp., Seattle, 1966—; prof. neurosurgery U. Wash., Seattle, 1979—. Author: (with William Calvin): Inside the Brain, Conversations with Neil's Brain. Office: U Wash Dept Neurol Surgery PO Box 356-470 Seattle WA 98195

OJEMANN, ROBERT GERDES, neurosurgeon; b. Iowa City, May 5, 1931; s. Ralph H. and Freda (Metzger) O.; m. Jean Munson; children: David, James, Michael, John. BA, U. Iowa, 1951, MD, 1955. Diplomate Am. Bd. Neurol. Surgery (mem. 1987-93, chmn. 1982-83). Intern Cin. Gen. Hosp., 1955-56; resident in gen. surgery Baylor U. Coll. Medicine, Houston, 1956-57; resident in neurosurgery Mass. Gen. Hosp., Boston, 1957-61, mem. staff, 1961—, also vis. neurosurgeon, chmn. staff assocs., 1977-79, mem. exec. com., 1981-84; mem. staff Harvard Med. Sch., Boston, 1961—, now prof. surgery. Co-author: Operative Microneurosurgery, 1985, Surgical Management of Cerebrovascular Disease, 1983, 3d edit., 1995; contbr. chpts. to books, numerous articles to profl. pubs. Deacon Trinitarian Congl. Ch., Wayland, Mass., 1984-87, 93-96. Recipient Disting. Alumni award U. Iowa, 1992. Mem. Congress Neurol. Surgeons (pres. 1975-76, honored guest 1992), Am. Acad. Neurol. Surgery (pres. 1989-90, Best Resident Rsch. Paper award 1960), Am. Assn. Neurol. Surgeons (pres. 1986-87), Soc. Neurol. Surgeons (pres. 1990-91), RRC Neurol. Surgery, Harvard Club (Boston). Avocations: landscaping, carpentry, hiking, tennis, stamp collecting. Office: Mass Gen Hosp 32 Fruit St Boston MA 02114-2620

OJIMA, IWAO, chemistry educator; b. Yokohama, Japan, June 5, 1945; came to U.S., 1983; s. Masaharu and Sumiko (Takatsuki) O.; m. Yoko Ogino, Apr. 24, 1971. BS, U. Tokyo, 1968, MS, 1970, PhD in Organic Chemistry, 1973. Rsch. fellow Sagami Inst. for Chem. Rsch., Japan, 1970-76, sr. rsch. fellow, group leader, 1976-83; assoc. prof. chemistry SUNY, Stony Brook, 1983-84, prof., 1984-91, leading prof., 1991-95, disting. prof., 1995—; lectr. Tokyo Inst. Tech., 1978-79, 83, Tokyo U. Agr. and Tech., 1983; prin. investigator NSF, 1983—, N.Y. Sci. Tech. Found., 1985—, NIH, 1986—, ACS prof. 1987—; vis. prof. U. Claude Bernard, Lyon, France I, 1989; mem. adv. com., NIH, 1988—, NSF, 1992, DUE, 1992; mem. editl. adv. bd. Elsevier Pubs., Lausanne, Switzerland, 1986-95; cons. Nippon Steel Corp., Yokohama, 1989—, Rhone-Poulenc Rorer, Vitry, France, 1991—, Ajinomoto Co., Inc., Kawasaki, 1995—. Editor: Catalytic Asymmetric Synthesis, 1993, Taxane Anticancer Agents, 1994; contbr. numerous articles to profl. jours.; numerous patents in field. Named fellow J.S. Guggenheim Meml. Found., 1995-97. Mem. AAAS, Am. Chem. Soc. (editl. adv. bd. 1995—, A.C. Cope Scholar award 1994), Chem. Soc. Japan (progress award 1976), N.Y. Acad. Scis., Sigma Xi. Achievements include research in homogenous catalysis of transition metal complexes; asymmetric synthesis; organic synthesis by means of organometallic reagents; peptides and peptide mimetics; beta-lactam chemistry; organo flourine chemistry, medicinal chemistry especially in regard to enzyme inhibitors and taxane anticancer agents. Home: 6 Ivy League Ln Stony Brook NY 11790 Office: State U New York Dept Chemistry Stony Brook NY 11794-3400

OKA, TAKESHI, physicist, chemist, astronomer, educator; b. Tokyo, June 10, 1932; arrived in Can., 1963, naturalized, 1973; s. Shumpei and Chiyoko O.; m. Keiko Nukui, Oct. 24, 1960; children: Ritsuko, Noriko, Kentaro, Yujiro. B.Sc., U. Tokyo, 1955, Ph.D., 1960. Research asso. U. Tokyo, 1960-63; fellow NRC Can., Ottawa, Ont., 1963-65; asst. NRC Can., 1965-68, asso., 1968-71, sr. research physicist, 1971-80; prof. U. Chgo., 1981—; Robert A. Millikan disting. prof., 1989—. Mem. editorial bd. Chem. Physics, 1972—, Jour. Molecular Spectroscopy, 1973—, Jour. Chem. Physics, 1975-77. Recipient Steacie prize, 1972; Earle K. Plyler prize, 1982. Fellow Royal Soc. Can., Royal Soc. London, Am. Phys. Soc., Optical Soc. Am., Am. Acad. Scis. and Arts; mem. Am. Astron. Soc. Office: U Chgo Dept Chemistry Astronomy & Astrophysics Chicago IL 60637

OKADA, RONALD MASAKI, insurance agent; b. Tokyo, Oct. 23, 1941; s. Robert M. Okada and Betty (Nakai) Chung; m. Barbara Moo Ching Lau, May 1, 1971; 1 child, Evie Michi. BBA, U. Hawaii, 1964. CLU; ChFC; CFP, Coll. for Fin. Planning. Ops. supr. Cen. Pacific Bank, Honolulu, 1964-68; mgmt. trainee Bank of Hawaii, Honolulu, 1968-70; life ins. agt. Conn. Mut. Life, Honolulu, 1970—. Chmn. bd. dirs. Hawaii Bapt. Found., Honolulu, 1993—; exec. bd. dirs. Hawaii Bapt. Conv., Honolulu, 1977-80; deacon, tchrs., various coms., Sunday Sch. dir. Mililani Bapt. Ch., Mililani Town, Hawaii, 1975—. Mem. Hawaii Assn. Life Underwriters (pres. 1994-95, Life Ins. Profl. of Yr. runner-up 1984), Nat. Assn. Life Underwriters (nat. sales achievement award, nat. quality award, Million Dollar Round Table), Am. Soc. CLU's and ChFC's (com. chmn. 1984-87, 91-92), West Honolulu Assn. Life Underwriters (bd. dirs. 1982-87), Hawaii Estate Planning Coun., Assn. Health Ins. Agts. Office: Conn Mut Life 1600 Kapiolani Blvd Ste 1130 Honolulu HI 96814-3804

OKADA, RYOZO, medical educator, clinician and researcher; b. Kiryu, Gummaken, Japan, July 20, 1931; s. Kenji and Sachi (Ishihara) O.; m. Shigeko Shindo, May 25, 1958; children: Kyoko, Taro. MD, Tokyo U., 1956, PhD, 1961. Intern then resident; asst. Sch. Med. Tokyo U., 1962-63; research fellow Hektoen Inst. Cook County Hosp., Chgo., 1963-66; attending physician Yoikuin Hosp., Tokyo, 1966-68; assoc. prof. Sch. Med. Juntendo U., Tokyo, 1968-83, prof., 1983—, dir. cardiovascular lab., 1985—; cons. Migita Hosp., Tokyo, 1968—; councilor Cardiovascular Inst. Roppongi, Tokyo, 1990—, Indsl. Medicine Found., 1995—. Contbr. articles to med.

jours. and books. Active group study specific intractable diseases Met. Office of Tokyo, 1972—, cardiomyopathies Ministry of Health and Welfare, Japan, 1974—, occupational diseases Ministry of Labor, Japan, 1987—; bd. dirs. Shirane Kaizen Sch., Gumma, Japan. Fellow Am. Geriatrics Soc., Coun. Prevention Heart Disease, Japanese Circulation Soc. (councilor), Japanese Angiology Soc., Japanese Geriatrics Soc.; mem. Japanese Soc. Medicine. Avocation: travel. Home: 53 Asahigoaka, Kanagawa-ku, Yokohama 221, Japan Office: Juntendo U Sch Medicine, 2-1-1 Hongo, Bunkyoku, Tokyo 113, Japan

OKADA, TAKUYA, food service and retail executive; b. Sept. 19, 1925; m. Yasuko Okada. Student, Waseda U., Japan, 1948. Pres. Diamond City K.K.; chmn. Jusco Co. Ltd., N.Y.C.; bd. dirs. Laura Ashley Holdings, Plc, U.K. Office: Jusco USA Inc 525 Madison Ave Fl 24 New York NY 10022-4301*

OKAMURA, ARTHUR, artist, educator, writer; b. Long Beach, Calif., Feb. 24, 1932; s. Frank Akira and Yuki O.; m. Elizabeth Tuomi, Aug. 7, 1953 (div.); children: Beth, Jonathan, Jane, Ethan; m. Kitty Wong, 1991. Student, Art Inst. of Chgo., 1950-54, U. Chgo., 1951, 52, 57, art seminar Yale, 1954. Faculty Central YMCA Coll., Chgo., 1956, 57, Evanston Art Center, 1956-57, Art Inst. Chgo., North Shore Art League, Winnetka, Ill., Acad. Art, San Francisco, 1957, Calif. Sch. Fine Arts, 1958, Ox Bow Summer Art Sch., Saugatuck, Mich.; faculty Calif. Coll. Arts and Crafts, 1958-59, prof. arts, 1966—; instr. watercolor painting, 1987; dir. San Francisco Studio Art, 1958; tchr. watercolor workshops, Bali, Indonesia, 1989, 92; lectr. in field. Author: (with Robert Creeley) 1, 2, 3, 4, 5, 6, 7, 8, 9, 0, 1971, (with Joel Weishaus) Ox-Herding, 1971, (with Robert Bly) Basho, 1972, Ten Poems by Issa, 1992, (with Steve Kowit) Passionate Journey, 1984, Magic Rabbit, 1995; one-man shows include Charles Feingarten Galleries, Chgo., 1956, 58, 59, San Francisco, 1957, Santa Barbara Mus. Art, 1958, Oakland Mus. Art, 1959, Legion Honor, San Francisco, 1961, Dallas, 1962, La Jolla (Calif.) Mus., 1963, U. Utah, 1964, San Francisco Mus. Art, 1968, Hanssen Gallery, 1968, 71, Ruth Braunstein, San Francisco, 1981, 82, 84, 86-88, 90, 94; exhibited in group shows including Pa. Acad. Fine Art, U. Chgo., U. Wash., U. Ill., Art Inst. Chgo., L.A. County Mus., Am. Fedn. Art, Denver Mus., NAD, De Young Mus., San Francisco, Knoedler Gallery, N.Y.C., Feingarten Galleries, Whitney Mus. Art, others; retrospective at Bolinas Mus. and Claudia Chapline Galleries, Stinson Beach, Calif., 1995; represented in permanent collections including Art Inst. Chgo., Borg-Warner Collections, Chgo., Whitney Mus. Art, N.Y.C., Santa Barbara Mus. Art, San Francisco Mus. Art, Ill. State Normal, Corcoran Mus., Nat. Collection Fine Arts, Smithsonian Instn., 1968, many others. Served as pvt. AUS, 1955-56. Recipient 1st prize religious art U. Chgo., 1953; Ryerson travelling fellow, 1954; Martin Cahn award contemporary Am. paintings Art Inst. Chgo., 1957; purchase award U. Ill., 1959; purchase award Nat. Soc. Arts and Letters, N.Y.C., 1960; Neysa McMein purchase award Whitney Mus. Art, 1960; Schwabacher-Frey award 79th Ann. of San Francisco Mus. Art, 1960. Mem. Commonweal (bd. dirs. 1993-94). Home: 210 Kale Rd Bolinas CA 94924 Office: Calif Coll Arts and Crafts 5212 Broadway Oakland CA 94618-1426

OKAY, JOHN LOUIS, information scientist; b. Emmett, Mich., Mar. 27, 1942; s. Stanley John and Mildred Isabell (Little) O.; m. Judith Ann Gerlach, Aug. 22, 1964; children: Stephen, Christopher, Douglas. BS in Agr., Mich. State U., 1964, MS in Agrl. Econs., 1967, PhD in Resource Econs., 1974. Agrl. economist U.S. Soil Conservation Svc., East Lansing, Mich., 1967-73; program analyst U.S. Soil Conservation Svc., Washington, Mich., 1974-83; dir. info. systems U.S. Soil Conservation Svc., Washington, 1983-85; assoc. dir. info. systems USDA, Washington, 1985-91, dir. info. systems, 1991-95; dep. commr. Fed. Telecom. Svc., GSA, Falls Church, Va., 1995—. Recipient Meritorious Exec. award Pres. of U.S., 1989. Mem. Armed Forces Comms. and Electronics Assn. (bd. dirs. 1994—), Sr. Execs. Assn. (bd. dirs. 1989—, vice chair 1994—). Office: Fed Telecom Svc GSA 7799 Leesburg Pike Ste 210 Falls Church VA 22043

OKE, JOHN BEVERLEY, astronomy educator; b. Sault Ste. Marie, Ont., Can., Mar. 23, 1928; s. Charles Clare and Lyla Jane (Partushek) O.; m. Nancy Sparling, Aug. 20, 1955; children—Christopher, Kevin, Jennifer, Valerie. B.A., U. Toronto, 1949, M.A., 1950; Ph.D., Princeton U., 1953. Lectr. U. Toronto, 1953-55, asst. prof., 1955-58; asst. prof. Calif. Inst. Tech., Pasadena, 1958-61, assoc. prof., 1961-64, prof., 1964-92; assoc. dir. Hale Observatories, 1970-78; vis. Dominion Astrophysical Observatory, 1992—. Mem. Astron. Soc. of the Pacific, Am. Astronomical Soc. (councillor 1969-72), Internat. Astronomical Union. Office: Dominion Astrophysical Obs, 5071 W Saanich Rd, Victoria, BC Canada V8X 4M6

O'KEEFE, DANIEL P., lawyer; b. Superior, Wis., 1952. BA cum laude, Coll. St. Thomas, 1974; JD magna cum laude, William Mitchell Coll. Law, 1978. Bar: Minn. 1978. Law clerk U.S. Dist. Ct., Minn., 1978; ptnr. Dorsey & Whitney, Mpls., E.W. Blanch & Co., Bloomington; adj. prof. William Mitchell Coll. Law. Exec. editor William Mitchell Law Review, 1977-78. Office: E. W. Blanch & Co. 3500 W 80th St Ste 600 Bloomington MN 55431*

O'KEEFE, EDWARD FRANKLIN, lawyer; b. S.I., N.Y., June 9, 1937; s. Francis Franklin and Bertha (Hall) O'K.; m. Toni Lynne McGohan; children: Kira Kathleen, Douglas Franklin, Andrew Franklin, Alison Elizabeth, Theadore William, Nigel Francis. A.B., U. N.C., 1959; J.D., U. Denver, 1961. Bar: Colo. 1962. Law clk. Colo. Supreme Ct., Denver, 1962-63; assoc. gen. counsel Hamilton Mgmt. Corp., Denver, 1966-69; sec. Hamilton Mgmt. Corp., 1968-76, v.p. legal, gen. counsel, 1969-76; now mng. ptnr. Moye, Giles O'Keefe, Vermeire & Gorrell, Denver; assoc. gen. counsel, sec. ITT Variable Annuity Ins. Co., Denver, 1969, v.p. legal, gen. counsel, 1969-70; sec. Hamilton Funds Inc., Denver, 1968-76. Served with USNR, 1963-66. Mem. Nat. Assn. Security Dealers (dist. conduct com., chmn. 1976), Colo. Assn. Corporate Counsel (pres. 1974-75). Home: 6300 Montview Blvd Denver CO 80207-3947 Office: Moye Giles O'Keefe Vermeire 1225 17th St Fl 29 Denver CO 80202-5534

O'KEEFE, GERALD FRANCIS, bishop, retired; b. St. Paul, Mar. 30, 1918; s. Francis Patrick and Lucille Mary (McDonald) O'K. Student, St. Paul Sem., 1938-44; B.A., Coll. St. Thomas, 1945; LLD (hon.), St. Ambrose Coll., 1967, Loras Coll., 1967; LHD, Marycrest Coll., 1967. Ordained priest Roman Cath. Ch., 1944. Asst. St. Paul Cathedral, 1944, rector, 1961-67; chancellor Archdiocese of St. Paul, 1945-61, aux. bishop, 1961-67, vicar gen., 1962-67; bishop Diocese of Davenport, Iowa, 1967-93; ret., 1993; instr. St. Thomas Acad., St. Paul, 1944-45. Home: 2706 Gaines St Davenport IA 52804-1914

O'KEEFE, JAMES WILLIAM, JR., investment manager and banker; b. Troy, N.Y., Oct. 23, 1948; s. James William and Antoinnette (Shannon) O'K.; m. Ann Palmer Ghiglione, June 4, 1977; 1 child, Courtney Anne. BA, Georgetown U., 1970; MBA, Harvard U., 1972. Mng. dir. Morgan Stanley & Co. Inc., N.Y.C., 1972-87, Kidder, Peabody & Co. Inc., N.Y.C., 1987-92; CEO Aetna Realty Investors, Inc., 1993—; bd. dirs. Fishers Island Devel. Co. Mem. bd. advisors Georgetown Univ. Coll., NYU Real Estate Inst. Mem. Urban Land Inst., Nat. Assn. Real Estate Investment Trusts, Nat. Realty Com., Pension Real Estate Assn., Nat. Assn. of Real Estate Investment Mgrs., N.Y. Athletic Club, Fishers Island Club. Avocation: golf. Home: 1088 Park Ave New York NY 10128-1132 Office: Aetna Realty Investors Inc 242 Trumbull St Hartford CT 06103-1212

O'KEEFE, JOHN DAVID, investment specialist; b. N.Y.C., Nov. 16, 1941; s. Timothy J. and Agnes V. (Timlin) O.; m. Stefanie Carreau Keegan, Jan. 28, 1978; children: Douglas G., Hillary C., John M., Meredith B. BBA, Iona Coll., 1963; MBA, L.I. U., 1968. Analyst L.I. Lighting Co., Mineola, N.Y., 1965-69, Pershing and Co., N.Y.C., 1969-72; mng. dir. Kidder, Peabody and Co., Inc., N.Y.C., 1972-89; v.p. Smith Barney, N.Y.C., 1989—. Bd. dirs. Heisman Found. Sgt. USMC, 1963-65. Fellow Fin. Analysts Fedn.; mem. N.Y. Soc. Security Analysts, Securities Industry Assn. Republican. Club: Down Town Athletic (gov. 1986, 88, chmn. Heisman Trophy com. 1987, 88). Home: 31 Linden Tree Rd Wilton CT 06897-1613 Office: Smith Barney 1 Village Sq Westport CT 06880-3211

O'KEEFE, JOSEPH THOMAS, bishop; b. N.Y.C., Mar. 12, 1919. Ed. Cathedral Coll., N.Y.C., St. Joseph's Sem., Yonkers, N.Y., Cath. U., Washington. Ordained Roman Catholic priest, 1948; ordained titular bishop of Tre Taverse and aux. bishop of N.Y., 1982-87; apptd. and installed bishop of Syracuse, 1987. Office: PO Box 511 240 E Onondaga St Syracuse NY 13202-2608*

O'KEEFE, KATHLEEN MARY, state government official; b. Butte, Mont., Mar. 25, 1933; d. Hugh I. and Kathleen Mary (Harris) O'Keefe; B.A. in Communications, St. Mary Coll., Xavier, Kans., 1954; m. Nick B. Baker, Sept. 18, 1954 (div. 1970); children—Patrick, Susan, Michael, Cynthia, Hugh, Mardeen. Profl. singer, mem. Kathie Baker Quartet, 1962-72; research cons. Wash. Ho. of Reps., Olympia, 1972-73; info. officer Wash. Employment Security Commn., Seattle, 1973-81, dir. public affairs, 1981-90, video dir., 1990-95, ret., 1995; freelance writer, composer, producer, 1973—. Founder, pres. bd. Eden, Inc., visual and performing arts, 1975—; public relations chmn. Nat. Women's Democratic Conv., Seattle, 1979, Wash. Dem. Women, 1976-85; bd. dirs., composer, prodr., dir. N.Y. Film Festival, 1979; Dem. candidate Wash. State Senate, 1968. Recipient Silver medal Seattle Creative Awards Show for composing, directing and producing Rent A Kid, TV pub. svc. spot, 1979. Mem. Wash. Press Women. Democrat. Roman Catholic. Author: Job Finding In the Nineties, The Third Alternative, handbook on TV prodn., (children) So You Want to be President, 1995; composer numerous songs, also writer, dir., producer Job Service spots, Immigration & Naturalization Svc. spots, U.S. Dept. Labor spots, Dept. VA spots. Home: 4426 147th Pl NE # 12 Bellevue WA 98007-3162

O'KEEFE, KEVIN, public relations executive. BA, Washington Coll.; MA, U. Ill. Joined Adams Sandler, 1976; pres. The Sandler Group, 1986-89, Adams Group, 1989-90, Adams Sandler, A Shandwick Co., 1990-95; mng. dir. Shandwick USA (formerly Adams Sandler, A Shandwick Co.), 1995—. Office: Shandwick USA 1629 Thames St Baltimore MD 21231-3430*

O'KEEFE, MICHAEL DANIEL, lawyer; b. St. Louis, Jan. 3, 1938; s. Daniel Michael and Hanoria (Moriarty) O'K.; m. Bonnie Bowdern, July 11, 1964; children: Collen Coyne, Daniel Michael. AB, St. Louis U., 1961, LLB, 1961; postgrad., George Washington U., 1963. Bar: Mo. 1961, U.S. Ct. Appeals (8th cir.) 1961, U.S. Dist. Ct. (ea. dist.) Mo. 1961, Ill. 1975, U.S. Dist. Ct. (so. dist.) Ill. 1975, U.S. Ct. Appeals (5th and 7th cirs.) 1983, (10th cir.) 1995. Asst. atty. U.S. Ct. Appeals, St. Louis, 1962-63, 64-65; pvt. practice St. Louis, 1964-67; ptnr. Lucas, Murphy & O'Keefe, St. Louis, 1967-74, Thompson & Mitchell, St. Louis, 1974—; adj. prof. trial practice Sch. of Law, St. Louis U., 1992—. Editor: American Maritime Cases, 1985—. Active Port Commn., St. Louis; trustee St. Louis U. Capt. USAF, 1962-64. Fellow Am. Coll. Trial Lawyers; mem. Internat. Assn. Def. Counsel, Fedn. Ins. and Corp. Counsel, Maritime Law Assn., USAZ, Nat. Assn. Railroad Trial Counsel, Am. Law Inst. Democrat. Roman Catholic. Avocations: reading, tennis, fencing, archaeology, microbiology. Home: 372 Walton Row Saint Louis MO 63108-1909 Office: Thompson Coburn Ste 3300 1 Mercantile Ctr Saint Louis MO 63101-1643

O'KEEFE, ROBERT, insurance executive. Office mgr. Mercer Williamm Inc, Detroit. Office: Mercer Williamm Inc 400 Rennissance Ctr Detroit MI 48243

O'KEEFE, ROBERT JAMES, retired banker; b. Boston, Dec. 30, 1926; s. James J. and Irene (Egan) O'K.; m. Mary U. Hughes, Oct. 12, 1951 (dec.); children—Mary F., Robert James; m. Simone A. Charbonneau, Apr. 3, 1976. A.B., Boston Coll., 1951; grad., Advanced Mgmt. Program, Harvard, 1968. Mem. staff Mass. Inst. Tech., Cambridge, 1951-55; cons. Arthur D. Little, Inc., Cambridge, 1955-58; with Chase Manhattan Bank, N.Y.C., 1958-79, v.p., 1964-69, sr. v.p., 1969-79; sr. v.p. Am. Security Bank, Washington, 1979-89; exec. v.p. MNC Info. Svcs., Balt., 1989-90, ret. Trustee Boston Coll., 1974-82, trustee assoc., 1982-86; mem. computer sci. and engring. bd. Nat. Acad. Sci., 1971-73. Served with AUS, 1945-46. Recipient Alumni medal Boston Coll., 1970. Mem. Boston Coll. Alumni Assn. (pres. 1973-74), Country Club at Jacaranda West, Am. Legion, KC. Home: 944 S Doral Ln Venice FL 34293

O'KEEFE, THOMAS JOSEPH, metallurgical engineer; b. St. Louis, Oct. 2, 1935; s. Thomas and Hazel (Howard) O'K.; m. Jane Gilmartin, Aug. 31, 1957; children—Thomas, Kathleen, Matthew, Daniel, Margaret, Robert. B.S., Mo. Sch. Mines, 1958; Ph.D., U. Mo., Rolla, 1965. Process control engr. Dow Metal Products Co., Madison, Ill., 1959-61; mem. faculty U. Mo., Rolla, 1965—, prof. metall. engring., 1972—, Curators prof. metall. engring., 1985-86, Curators Disting. prof., 1986—; rsch. technologist NASA, Houston, summer 1965; rsch. metall. engr. Ames (Iowa) Lab., 1966-67; rsch. metall. engr., cons. Cominco Ltd., Trail, B.C., Can., 1970-71. Recipient Alumni Merit award U. Mo., Rolla, 1971, Outstanding Tchg. award, 1979, Silver medal paper award AESF, 1994; Jefferson-Smurfit fellow, 1984-85; named Disting. Hydrometallurgy lectr. U. B.C., 1992. Mem. AIME (dir. 1976-77, 79-81, EMD lectr. 1991), Testing Materials Soc., The Metall. Soc., Sigma Xi, Alpha Sigma Mu, Tau Beta Pi, Phi Kappa Theta (dir. 1965-77, cert. commendation 1970, pres. citation 1986). Home: 905 Southview Dr Rolla MO 65401-4720 Office: Material Research Center Univ Mo Rolla MO 65401

O'KEEFE, THOMAS MICHAEL, foundation executive; b. St. Cloud, Minn., Mar. 25, 1940; s. Thomas William and Genevieve B. (McCormick) O'K.; m. Kathleen Marie Gnifkowski, Aug. 20, 1966; children: Steven Michael, Ann Catherine. Student, Marquette U., 1961-65, BS, 1965; MS in Nuclear Physics, U. Pitts., 1968; DHL, Hamline U., 1989. Dir. edn. planning HEW, Washington, 1969-70, dep. asst. sec., 1977-80; v.p. Carnegie Found. for Advancement of Teaching, Washington, 1980-83; pres. Consortium for Advancement Pvt. Higher Edn., Washington, 1983-89; exec. v.p. McKnight Found., Mpls., 1989—; dir. Washington internships in edn. George Washington U., 1970-73; dir. policy analysis and evaluation U. Ill., Chgo., 1973-74, assoc. v.p. acad. affairs, 1974-77; head U.S. del. to Orgn. Econ. Coop. and Devel., 1979, 80; mem. Carnegie Forum on Edn. and the Economy, 1985-88; mem. N.J. Commn. on Ind. Higher Edn., 1986-88; mem. task force on ind. higher edn. Edn. Commn. States, 1987-89; cons. in field. Contbg. editor and contbr. articles on fed. edn. programs, acad. policies, internships, and nuclear physics Change mag., 1985—; bd. dirs. Editl. Projects in Edn., 1984-93. Bd. dirs. The Edn. Resources Inst., Boston, 1987-94, Minn. Coun. on Founds., 1994—; trustee Buena Vista Coll., Storm Lake, Iowa, 1984-90; mem. Coun. on Fgn. Rels., 1995—. Mem. Minn. Club St. Paul, Mpls. Club. Democrat. Office: McKnight Found 121 S 8th St Ste 600 Minneapolis MN 55402-2825

O'KEEFE, VINCENT THOMAS, clergyman, educational administrator; b. Jersey City, Jan. 10, 1920; s. James and Sarah (Allen) O'K. A.B., Georgetown U., 1943; M.A., Woodstock Coll., 1945, Ph.L., 1944; Th.L., St. Albert de Louvain, Belgium, 1951; student, Muenster (Germany) U., 1951-52; S.T.D., Gregorian U., Rome, 1954. Ordained priest Roman Cath. Ch., 1950. Instr. Latin and math. Regis High Sch., N.Y.C., 1944-47; assoc. prof. fundamental theology Woodstock Coll., 1954-60; acad. v.p. Fordham U., Bronx, N.Y., 1960-62; exec. v.p. Fordham U., 1962-63, pres., 1963-65, rector Jesuit community, 1984-88; gen. asst. to superior gen. Soc. of Jesus, Rome, 1965-83; v.p. spl. projects Jesuit Conf. Soc. of Jesus, 1988-90; superior, writer provincial residence Soc. of Jesus, Bronx, 1990-94; superior Am. House, N.Y.C., 1994—; mem. regents exams. and scholarship center N.Y. State Dept. Edn.; pres., dir., mem. exec. com. Council Higher Ednl. Instns. of N.Y.C. Author: The History and Meaning of Ex Attrito Fit Contritus, 1957; Contbr. articles to religious publs., also book reviews. Dir. N.Y. World's Fair, 1964-65; Corp. Bd. mgrs. New York Bot. Garden; dir., mem. bd. Center Intercultural Formation, Cuernavaca, Mexico; trustee Fordham U. Fellow Royal Soc. Encouragement Arts Mfrs. and Commerce (London); mem. Council Higher Edn. City N.Y., Religion Council Cath. Secondary Schs. Archdiocese of N.Y., Cath. Bibl. Assn., Cath. Theol. Assn. Am., Religion Ednl. Assn., NEA, Jesuit Ednl. Assn., Nat. Cath. Edn. Assn., Internat. Assn. Univs., Soc. Cath. Coll. Tchrs. Sacred Doctrine, Phi Beta Kappa. Office: 106 W 56th St New York NY 10019-3803

O'KEHIE, COLLINS EMEKA, lawyer, consultant; b. Aba, Nigeria, Apr. 4, 1952; came to U.S., 1976; s. Simon A. and Elizabeth Jane (Oledibe) O.; m. Justina Amuche Nnadi, Aug. 6, 1983; children: Pamela, Collins Emeka Jr., Stanley, Charles. Assoc. in Bus., Ellsworth Coll., 1977; BS, U. Tex., Richardson, 1979; MBA, N. Tex. State U., 1981; JD, Tex. So. U., 1984. Bar: Tex. 1985, U.S. Ct. Appeals (5th cir.) 1986, U.S. Dist. Ct. (so. dist.) Tex. 1987, Internat. Ct. of Trade 1990, U.S. Ct. Appeals (fed. cir.) 1990, U.S. Supreme Ct. 1992. Ptnr. Gregg, O'Kehie & Cashin, Houston, 1985-90; prin. O'Kehie & Assocs., Houston, 1990—; legal cons. various cos. and law firms in Eng., France, Belgium, Holland, Nigeria, 1985—. Mem. ABA, Tex. Bar Assn., Tex. Trial Lawyers Assn, Coll. of State Bar Tex., Assn. Trial Lawyers Am., Internat. Bar Assn., MBA Execs. Assn., Chartered Ins. Inst. London, Internat. Bar Assn., Internat. Platform Assn., Phi Delta Phi. Roman Catholic. Avocations: tennis, jogging. Office: O'Kehie and Assocs 1300 Main St Ste 1930 Houston TX 77002-6814 *In my life I have found that one should use an opportunity to help less fortunate people and that the reward comes from sources other than the recipients.*

O'KELLEY, WILLIAM CLARK, federal judge; b. Atlanta, Jan. 2, 1930; s. Ezra Clark and Theo (Johnson) O'K.; m. Ernestine Allen, Mar. 28, 1953; children: Virginia Leigh O'Kelley Wood, William Clark Jr. AB, Emory U., 1951, LLB, 1953. Bar: Ga. 1952. Pvt. practice Atlanta, 1957-59; asst. U.S. atty. No. Dist. Ga., 1959-61; partner law firm O'Kelley, Hopkins & Van Gerpen, Atlanta, 1961-70; U.S. dist. judge No. Dist. Ga., Atlanta, 1970—, chief judge, 1988-94; mem. com. on adminstrn. of criminal law Jud. Conf. U.S., 1979-85, exec. com., 1983-84, subcom. on jury trials in complex criminal cases, 1981-82, dist. judge rep. 11th cir., 1981-84, mem. adv. com. of fed. rules of criminal procedure, 1984-87; bd. dirs. Fed. Jud. Ctr., 1987-91, adv. com. history program, 1989—, com. on orientation of newly appointed dist. judges, 1985-88; mem. Com. Jud. Resources, 1989-94; mem. Jud. Coun. 11th Cir., 1990—, exec. com., 1990—; mem. Fgn. Intelligence Surveillance Ct., 1980-87; corp. sec., dir. Gwinnett Bank & Trust Co., Norcross, Ga., 1967-70. Mem. exec. com., gen. counsel Ga. Republican Com., 1968-70; mem. fin. com. Northwest Ga. Girl Scout Coun., 1958-70; trustee Emory U., 1991—. Served as 1st lt. USAF, 1953-57; capt. USAFR. Mem. Ga. State Bar, Atlanta Bar Assn., Dist. Judges Assn. 5th Cir. (sec.-treas. 1976-77, v.p. 1977-78, pres. 1978-80), Lawyers Club Atlanta, Kiwanis (past pres.), Atlanta Athletic Club, Sigma Chi, Phi Delta Phi, Omicron Delta Kappa. Baptist. Home: 550 Ridgecrest Dr Norcross GA 30071-2158 Office: US Dist Ct 1942 US Courthouse 75 Spring St SW Atlanta GA 30303-3361

O'KELLY, BERNARD, university dean; b. Winnipeg, Man., Can., Aug. 10, 1926; came to U.S., 1954; s. Bartholomew Bernard and Cora (Beadle) O'K.; m. Marcia Herz Levin, Feb. 2, 1957; children: Christopher D.B. (dec.), Elizabeth S., Peter B.J. Student, U. Man., 1942-44; BA, Coll. de l'Immaculée Conception, Montreal, 1950, LPh, 1950; M.A., Harvard U., 1955, Ph.D., 1960. Lectr. classics St. Paul's Coll., U. Man., 1950-52; lectr. French and English Loyola Coll., Montreal, 1952-54; instr., then asst. prof. Ohio State U., 1957-66; research assoc. Yale U., 1964-65; prof. English, dean Coll. Arts and Scis., U. N.D., 1966—; Vice pres. Council Colls. Arts and Scis., 1972-73, pres., 1973-74; bd. dirs. Am. Conf. Acad. Deans, 1975—, sec.-treas., 1976-94; pres., chmn. exec. com. Fedn. Pub. Programs in the Humanities, 1977-79; mem. adv. panel U.S. Army, 1980-82; bd. dirs. Assn. Am. Colls., 1984-87. Editor: The Renaissance Image of Man and the World, 1966; (with C.A.L. Jarrott) John Colet's Commentary on I Corinthians, 1985. Hart scholar classics U. Man., 1944; Dexter travelling fellow Harvard, 1956; research grantee Am. Philos. Soc. Mem. MLA, AAUP, Nat. Council Tchrs. English, Renaissance Soc. Am., Assn. for Canadian Studies in U.S. Office: U ND PO Box 8038 Grand Forks ND 58202-8038

OKERLUND, ARLENE NAYLOR, university official; b. Emmitsburg, Md., Oct. 13, 1938; d. George Wilbur and Ruth Opal (Sensenbaugh) Naylor; m. Michael Dennis Okerlund, June 6, 1959 (div. Apr. 1983); 1 dau., Linda Susan. B.A., U. Md., 1960; Ph.D., U. Calif.-San Diego, 1969. Instr. sci. Mercy Hosp. Nursing Sch., Balt., 1959-63; prof. English San Jose State U., Calif., 1969-80, 94—, dean humanities and arts, 1980-86, acad. v.p., 1986-93; cons. Ednl. Testing Service, Berkeley, Calif., 1976-80. Editor: San Jose Studies, 1975-80; contbr. articles on the humanities to profl. jours. Bd. dirs. World Forum Silicon Valley, Am. Beethoven Soc. Grantee NEH, 1979; grantee San Jose State U., 1971-72. Mem. Philol. Assn. Pacific Coast (sec.-treas. 1975-78), MLA (del. to assembly, west coast rep. 1976-77), Internat. Coun. Fine Arts Deans, Calif. Coun. Fine Arts Deans (pres. 1984-86), Am. Beethoven Soc. (bd. dirs.). Democrat. Office: San Jose State U Dept English Washington Sq San Jose CA 95192

OKEZIE, B. ONUMA, food scientist, nutritionist, educator; b. Obizi, Imo, Nigeria, Mar. 31, 1936; came to U.S., 1962; s. Chief Anyanwu and Lolo Ihuoma (Ogbediya) O.; m. Monique Chika Offurum, Sept. 4, 1971; children: Uchechi, Okezie II, Ihuoma, Oluchi. BS, U. Calif., Davis, 1966, MS, 1966; PhD, Cornell U., 1975. Cert. nutrition specialist. Sci. officer Ministry of Animal Health, Enugu, Biafra, 1967-68; advisor on nutrition Rehab. Commn., Okigwe, Biafra, 1968-70; rsch. fellow U. Ife, Ile-Ife, Nigeria, 1970; exec. advisor on nutrition Internat. Union for Child Welfare, Geneva, 1970-71; teaching and rsch. asst. Cornell U., Ithaca, N.Y., 1971-74, rsch. assoc., 1974; asst. prof. Howard U., Washington, 1975; assoc. prof. food sci. & nutrition Ala. A&M U., Huntsville, 1975-82, prof., 1982—, dir. internat. programs, 1979—; spl. asst. to pres. Ala. A&M U., 1988-90; trustee S.E. Cons. for Internat. Devel., Washington, 1980—, vice chair bd. trustees, 1992-93, chair-elect, 1993-94, chair, 1995-96; bd. dirs. USAID-Peanut-CRSP, Washington, 1982—; chair Assn. Dirs. Internat. Agr. Progs. 1992—; pres. Aries Enterprises, Inc., Huntsville, 1983—; disting. lectr. Berger Found. Cornell U., Ithaca, N.Y., 1993. Author: International Dimensions in Human Ecology, 1975, Effective Participation in Technical Assistance Programs, 1982; contbr. articles to profl. jours. NSF fellow, 1959-60, U.S. AID sci. fellow, 1962-66. Mem. Am. Dietetic Assn., Am. Coll. Nutrition, Inst. Food Technologists (chair-elect internat. divsn., 1991-92, chair 1992-93, div. com. chair of two coms., 1990-93, mem. IFT awards com., 1993-95), Assn. Nigerians in North Ala. (pres. 1994-96), Am. Assn. Cereal Chemists, Am. Chem. Soc., So. Assn. Agr. Scientists, Ala. Acad. Sci., Ala. Coun. for Internat. Programs (exec. com.), Assn. Internat. Edn. Adminstrn., North Ala. Internat. Trade Assn., Huntsville C. of C. (small bus. com. 1985-87), Alpha Zeta. Avocations: tennis, jogging, photography. Home: 561 Hurricane Rd New Market AL 35761-8204 Office: Ala A&M U Office of Internat Programs Normal AL 35762

OKHAMAFE, IMAFEDIA, English literature and philosophy educator; b. Otuo, Nigeria; s. Obokhe and Olayemi (Bello) O. Double PhD, Purdue U., 1984. Prof. philosophy and English U. Nebr., Omaha, 1993—. Office: U Nebr Annex 39 Omaha NE 68182-0208 also: U Nebr English Dept Omaha NE 68182-0175

OKI, BRIAN MASAO, software engineer; b. Inglewood, Calif., Oct. 17, 1958; s. Masao and Chiyoe (Yata) O. BS summa cum laude, U. Calif., Irvine, 1980; MS, MIT, 1983, PhD, 1988. Mem. rsch. staff Xerox Palo Alto (Calif.) Rsch. Ctr., 1988-92; sr. mem. tech. staff Teknekron Software Systems, Inc., Palo Alto, 1992-94; sr. tech. staff Oracle Corp., Redwood Shores, Calif., 1994-96; staff engineer, software Sun Microsystems, Inc., Menlo Park, Calif., 1996—. Mem. IEEE, Assn. Computing Machinery, Phi Beta Kappa, Sigma Xi. Avocations: competitive ballroom dancing, golf. Home: 493 Mill River Ln San Jose CA 95134-2420 Office: Sun Soft Inc 2550 Garcia Ave Mountain View CA 94043

OKIISHI, THEODORE HISAO, mechanical engineering educator; b. Honolulu, Jan. 15, 1939; s. Clifford Muneo and Dorothy Asako (Tokushima) O.; m. Rae Wiemers, May 28, 1963; children: Christopher Gene, John Clifford, Mark William, Kenneth Edward. Student, U. Hawaii, 1956-57; BS, Iowa State U., 1960, MS, 1963, PhD, 1965. Registered profl. engr., Iowa, Ohio. From asst. prof. to assoc. dean coll. engring. Iowa State U., Ames, 1967—; cons. on fluid dynamics. Contbr. articles to profl. jours. Served to capt. C.E., U.S. Army, 1965-67. Decorated Joint Services Commendation award; named Outstanding Prof., Iowa State U. student sect. ASME, 1983, Mech. Engring. Dept. Prof. of Yr., Iowa State U., 1977, 86, 90; recipient award for research NASA, 1975; Ralph R. Teetor award Soc. Automotive Engrs., 1976, Engring. Coll. Superior Teaching award Iowa State U., 1987, Cardinal Key Iowa State U., 1991. Fellow ASME (Melville medal 1989); mem. AIAA, Sigma Xi. Republican. Mem. Ch. of Jesus Christ of Latter-day Saints. Club: Osborn Research. Home: 2940 Monroe Dr Ames IA 50010-4362 Office: Iowa State U 104 Marston Hall Ames IA 50011

OKINAGA, LAWRENCE SHOJI, lawyer; b. Honolulu, July 7, 1941; s. Shohei and Hatsu (Kakimoto) O.; m. Carolyn Hisako Uesugi, Nov. 26, 1966; children: Carrie, Caryn, Laurie. BA, U. Hawaii, 1963; JD, Georgetown U., 1972. Bar: Hawaii 1972, U.S. Dist. Ct. Hawaii 1972, U.S. Ct. Appeals (9th cir.) 1976. Administrv. asst. to Congressman Spark Matsunaga, Honolulu, 1964, 1965-69; law clk. to chief judge U.S. Dist. Ct. Hawaii, Honolulu, 1972-73; assoc. Carlsmith, Ball, Wichman Murray and Ichiki, Honolulu, 1973-76, ptnr., 1976—; mem. Gov.'s Citizens Adv. Com. Coastal Zone Mgmt., 1974-79; sec. Hawaii Bicentennial Corp., 1975-77, chmn., 1985-87, vice chmn., mem. Jud. Selection Commn., State of Hawaii, 1979-87, vice chmn., 1986; mem. consumer adv. coun. Fed. Res. Bd., 1984-86; chmn. State of Hawaii Judicial Conduct Commn., 1991-94; apptd. mem. Fed. Savings and Loan Adv. Council, Washington, 1988-89; mem. nat. adv. coun. U.S. Small Bus. Adminstrn., 1994—; mem. adv. coun. on small bus. and agr. Fed. Reserve Bank of San Francisco, 1995—. Bd. dirs. Moiliili Community Ctr., Honolulu, 1965-68, 1973-86; bd. visitors Georgetown U. Law Ctr., 1993—; trustee Kuakini Med. Ctr., 1984-88, 89-96. Served to capt. USAFR, 1964-72, 1974-76. Mem. ABA (house of delegates 1991-94, mem. standing com. on judicial selection tenure and compensation, 1993—), Hawaii Bar Assn. (sec., bd. dirs. 1981), Am. Judicature Soc. (v.p. 1990-92, bd. dirs. 1986—, sec. 1993-95, treas. 1995—), Georgetown U. Law Alumni Assn. (bd. dirs. 1986-91), Omicron Delta Kappa. Office: Carlsmith Ball Wichman Case & Ichiki PO Box 656 Honolulu HI 96809-0656

OKITA, GEORGE TORAO, pharmacologist educator; b. Seattle, Jan. 18, 1922; s. Kazuo and Fusao (Muguruma) O.; m. Fujiko Shimizu, Nov. 29, 1958; children: Ronald Hajime, Sharon Mariko, Glenn Torao. Student, U. Cin., 1943-44; BA, Ohio State U., 1948; PhD, U. Chgo., 1951. Rsch. asst., rsch. assoc., instr., then asst. prof. U. Chgo., 1949-63; assoc. prof. Northwestern U., 1963-66, prof. pharmacology, 1966-90, prof. emeritus, 1990—, acting chmn. dept., 1968-70, 76-77. Contbr. articles to profl. jours.; Asst. editor: Jour. Pharmacology and Exptl. Therapeutics, 1965-68. Served with AUS, 1944-46. NIH Postdoctoral fellow, 1952. Mem. AAAS, AAUP, Am. Soc. Pharmacology and Exptl. Therapeutics, Internat. Soc. Biochem. Pharmacology, Am. Heart Assn., Cardiac Muscle Soc., Sigma Xi. Achievements include research in med. field. Home: 8619 Vineyard Ridge Pl San Jose CA 95135-2153

OKO, ANDREW JAN, art gallery director, curator; b. London, Sept. 7, 1946; arrived in Can., 1948; s. Jan Kazimierz and Julia Helena (Suska) O.; m. Helen Marie Blanc, Dec. 21, 1972; children: Sonya Celeste, Michelle Kathleen. BA, U. Calgary, 1968; MA, U. Toronto, 1972. Preparator Glenbow Mus., Calgary, Alta., 1972-73, curatorial asst., 1973-74, asst. curator, 1974-77; curator Art Gallery of Hamilton, Ont., 1977-86; dir. MacKenzie Art Gallery, Regina, Sask., 1986—. Author: Country Pleasures: The Angling Art of Jack Cowin, 1984, (with others) Art Gallery Handbook 1982; author/curator: (exhbn. catalogue) The Frontier Art of R.B. Nevitt, 1974, T.R. MacDonald 1908-1978, 1980, The Society of Canadian Painter-Etchers and Engravers in Retrospect, 1981, The Prints of Carl Schaefer, 1983, Canada in the Nineteenth Century: The Bert and Barbara Stitt Family Collection, 1984, Jan Gerrit Wyers 1888-1973, 1989. Mem. Can. Mus. Assn., Can. Art Mus. Dirs.' Orgn., Sask. Arts Alliance (pres. 1991-93), Rotary. Avocations: flyfishing, swimming, music.

O'KON, JAMES ALEXANDER, engineering company executive; b. N.Y.C., Aug. 8, 1937; s. A.C. and Rita (McGaugh) O'K.; m. Carol Ann Smith, 1988; children: Sean Fitzgerald, Katherine Shannon. BCE, Ga. Inst. Tech., 1961; MCE, NYU, 1970. Registered profl. engr., Tenn., N.Y., Mo., Conn., Ill., Fla., Tex., Miss., Calif., Ga., Mass., La. N.J., S.C., Ala., Ky., Va., N.C., Kans., Colo. Hwy. engr. Ga. Hwy. Dept., Atlanta, 1960-62; structural engr. Robert & Co., Atlanta, 1962-64; project coord. So. Design, Spartanburg, S.C., 1964-67; project engr. Crawford-Russell, Stamford, Conn., 1967-68, Farkas Barron Ptnr., N.Y.C., 1968-69; v.p. Lev Zetlin Assocs., N.Y.C., Atlanta, 1969-77; pres. O'Kon and Co. (formerly Lev Zetlin Assocs.), Atlanta, 1977—; bd. dirs. Superior Demolition Co, Atlanta, Friends of Mexico; chmn. bd. Five Star Travel, Inc. Author: Floating Factory to Produce Precast Concrete Components, 1973, Energy Conservation Noise and Vibration Control in Construction of Offshore Power Plants, 1975, Guidelines for Failure Investigation, 1989, Methodology For The Life Prediction of Buildings, 1989. Author: Floating Factory to Produce Precast Concrete Components, 1973, Energy Conservation Noise and Vibration Control in Construction of Offshore Power Plants, 1975, Guidelines for Failure Investigation, 1989, Methodology for the Life Prediction of Buildings, 1989, Methods to Reduce Errors Due to Dependency on Computers, 1994, Bridge From the Past, 1995. Recipient Grand award Builder's Mag., 1983, Archtl. Excellence award Am. Inst. Steel Constructors, 1984, Engring. Excellence award Am. Consulting Engrs. Coun. Ga., 1983, 88, Grand Award for Engring. Excellence, 1988, 89, 91, 92, 93. Fellow Internat. Biog. Assn., World Lit. Acad.; mem. ASCE (chmn., com. to develop quidelines for failure investigation, vice-chmn. tech. coun. forensic engring.), Am. Inst. Archaeology, Ga. Tech. Bldg. Rsch. Ctr., Bldg. Futures Coun., Soc. Am. Mil. Engrs., Smithsonian Inst., Atlanta Preservation Soc. (mem. Preservation Profls. Group), Am. Arbitration Assn. (panel of arbitrators), Friends of Mex. (v.p.). Democrat. Roman Catholic. Home: 26104 Plantation Dr NE Atlanta GA 30324-2959 Office: O'Kon & Co Inc 1349 W Peachtree St # 1200 Atlanta GA 30309

OKOSHI, SUMIYE, artist; b. Seattle; d. Masanari and Riyoko (Fukuda) Ushiyama; m. George Mukai, Mar. 21, 1976. Grad. Rikkyo Jogakuin U., Futabakai; postgrad., Seattle U., Henry Fry Mus. Modern Art, Seattle, 1957-59. One-woman shows include Gallery Internat., N.Y.C., 1970, Miami Mus. Modern Art, 1972, NAS, Washington, Galerie Saison, Tokyo, 1982, St. Peter's Ch. Living Room Gallery, N.Y.C., 1987, Viridian Gallery, N.Y.C., 1987, 92, 96, Port Washington Pub. Libr., 1989, NAS, Washington, 1991-92; exhibited in group shows Met. Mus. Art, N.Y.C., 1977, World Trade Center, N.Y.C., 1979, Tokyo Nat. Mus., 1979, Pace U. Gallery, Briarcliff, N.Y., 1981, Joslyn Center Arts, Torrance, Calif., Newark Mus., 1983, Bergen Mus. Art and Scis., 1983, Am. Acad. Arts and Scis., 1984, Nassau C.C., 1985-86, Port Washington Pub. Library, L.I., N.Y., 1985, Hudson River Mus., 1985, NAWA Ann. Javits Fed. Bldg., 1986, São Paulo and N.Y. Culture Exchange, 1988, Hyndai Gallery, Pusan, Korea, 1988; represented in permanent collection at Steve Hasegawa Bank of Alaska, Kaplan Fund., N.Y., Mr. & Mrs. K. Yoshikawa, N.Y., Mr. & Mrs. Haruo Yoshida, Conn., Nobart Pub. Co. Inc., The Mitsui & Co., N.Y., Hotel Nikko, Atlanta, Bank of Nagoya, N.Y., Palace Hotel, Guam Island, 1991, Port Washington (N.Y.) Pub. Libr., 1989, Lowe Gallery-U. Miami, Miami Mus. of Modern Art, Nat. Women's Edn. Ctr., Saitama-ken, Japan, NAS, Washington, 1992, Hammond Mus., N. Salem, N.Y., 1993, The Jane Voorhees Zimmerli Art Mus., N.J., 1994, Permanent Collection NAWA. Mem. Japanese Artists Assn. N.Y., Nat. Women Artists Assn. (Belle Cramer award, Ziuta and Joseph Fund. award, Ralph Mayer Meml. award), Nat. Mus. Women in the Arts (charter mem. 1994). Episcopalian. Office: 55 Bethune St # 226G New York NY 10014-1703

OKRENT, DANIEL, magazine editor, writer; b. Detroit, Apr. 2, 1948; s. Harry and Gizella (Adler) O.; m. Cynthia Jayne Boyer, June 23, 1969 (div. Aug. 1977); m. Rebecca kathryn Lazear, Aug. 28, 1977. BA, U. Mich., 1969; DHL, North Adams (Mass.) State Coll, 1988. Editor Alfred A. Knopf, Inc., N.Y.C., 1969-73; editorial dir. Grossman Pubs., Inc., N.Y.C., 1973-76; editor-in-chief Harcourt Brace Jovanovich, N.Y.C., 1976-77; pres. Hilltown Press, Inc., Worthington, Mass., 1978-91, Tex. Monthly Press, Inc., Austin, 1978-83; editor New Eng. Monthly, Northampton, Mass., 1983-89; asst. mng. editor Life mag., N.Y.C., 1991-92, mng. editor, 1992—; columnist Esquire mag., N.Y.C., 1985-89. Author: Nine Innings, 1985, The Way We Were: New England Then and Now, 1989; co-author: Baseball Anecdotes, 1989; co-editor: The Ultimate Baseball Book, 1979. Mem. Am. Soc. Mag. Editors (bd. dirs. 1987-89), Cuttyhunk Yacht Club, Century Assn. Jewish. Office: Time Inc 1271 6th Ave New York NY 10020

OKRENT, DAVID, engineering educator; b. Passaic, N.J., Apr. 19, 1922; s. Abram and Gussie (Pearlman) O.; m. Rita Gilda Holtzman, Feb. 1, 1948; children—Neil, Nina, Jocelyne. M.E., Stevens Inst. Tech., 1943; M.A., Harvard, 1948, Ph.D. in Physics, 1951. Mech. engr. NACA, Cleve., 1943-46; sr. physicist Argonne (Ill.) Nat. Lab., 1951-71; regents lectr. UCLA, 1968, prof. engring., 1971-91, prof. emeritus, rsch. prof., 1991—; vis. prof. U. Wash., Seattle, 1963, U. Ariz., Tucson, 1970-71; Isaac Taylor chair Technion, 1977-78. Author: Fast Reactor Cross Sections, 1960, Computing Methods in Reactor Physics, 1968, Reactivity Coefficients in Large Fast Power Reactors, 1970, Nuclear Reactor Safety, 1981; contbr. articles to profl. jours. Mem. adv. com. on reactor safeguards AEC, 1963-87, also chmn., 1966; sci. sec. to sec. gen. of Geneva Conf., 1958; mem. U.S. del. to all Geneva Atoms for Peace Confs. Guggenheim fellow, 1961-62, 77-78; recipient Disting. Appointment award Argonne Univs. Assn., 1970, Disting. Service award U.S. Nuclear Regulatory Commn., 1985. Fellow Am. Phys. Soc., Am. Nuclear Soc. (Tommy Thompson award 1980, Glenn Seaborg medal 1987), Nat. Acad. Engring. Home: 439 Veteran Ave Los Angeles CA 90024-1956

OKSAS, JOAN KAY, economist, educator; b. Chgo., Feb. 21, 1927; d. John Joseph and Antoinette (Pestinick) Kazanauskas; m. Casimir G. Oksas, Nov. 3, 1956; children: Stephen, Mary. BS, Northwestern U., 1944; MS in Edn., Chgo. State U., 1975, Northern Ill. U., 1981; EdD, Loyola U., Chgo., 1986. From instr. to assoc. prof. Chgo. State U., 1976-89, prof., 1989-93; ret., 1993; chair dept. libr. sci. and communication Chgo. State U., 1986-88; judge Am. Film and Video Festival, N.Y., Chgo., 1980-93, Chicagoland History Fairs, 1986—; mem. vis. com. North Ctrl. Assn. Accreditation, Chgo., 1980-93; cons. Adopt-a-Sch. program, 1984; bd. dirs. Mut. Fedn. Savs. and Loan, Chgo. Contbr. articles, revs. to profl. jours. Recipient Faculty Excellence award Chgo. State U., 1991. Mem. Ill. Libr. Assn., Phi Delta Kappa, Delta Kappa Gamma (Ill. Gamma Alpha chpt.) (bd. dirs. 1982—, pres. 1986-88). Republican. Roman Catholic.

OKUI, KAZUMITSU, biology educator; b. Ohta, Japan, July 8, 1933; s. Sadajiroh and Ume (Tanaka) O.; m. Mizue Aoki Okui, May 6, 1961; children: Teiichiroh, Ari. B Agr., Tokyo U. Agr., 1962, M Agr., 1964, D Agr., 1967. Lectr. biology Denki-Tsushin U., Tokyo, 1968-70; lectr. biology Kitasato U., Sagamihara, Japan, 1970-73, asst. prof. biology, 1973-82, prof. ethology, 1982—, dean Ednl. Ctr. of Liberal Arts and Sci., 1995—, councilor, 1995—; v.p. Internat. Centre of Wild Silkworm, 1990—; vis. rsch. prof. Waikato U., New Zealand, 1991; mem. book rev. com. Yomiuri Shimbun, Tokyo, 1981-85, Sankei Shimbun, Tokyo, 1990—. Author: Entomology, 1976, Ethology, 1976, General Zoology, 1984, General Zoology, 1985, General Entomology, 1992, Human Ethology, 1992, Essay of Insects, 1993, Textbook For Ethology, 1994. Mem. Internat. Soc. Wild Silkworm (sec. 1988—, v.p. 1990—), Japan Cosmo-Biol. Soc. (councilor 1987-89), Japan Wild Silkworm Soc. (v.p. 1994—), Sci. Coun. of Japan (mem. rsch. com. 1994—). Home: 972-7 Yumoto-machi, Kanagawa-ken 250-03, Japan Office: Ednl Ctr Liberal Arts/Sci, 1-15-1 Kitasato, Sagamihara, Kanagawa 228, Japan

O'KUINGHTTONS, CAMILO OCTAVIO, mechanical engineer; b. San Felipe, Chile, May 4, 1935; came to U.S., 1974; s. Camilo Octavio and Lola Maria (Bunout) O'K.; m. Ingrid Gisela Kroneberg, Sept. 16, 1960 (div. July 1975); 1 child, Camilo Octavio; m. Andrea Jean Neuman, Aug. 31, 1978; 1 child, Ryan Lee. BSME, Chilean Mil. Sch., Santiago, 1954; MSME, Mil. Poly. Acad., Santiago, 1965. With Chilean Army, 1953-67; design engr. Famae, Santiago, 1965-67; pvt. practice Santiago, 1967-74; head metall. dept. U. Concepcion, Chile, 1969-74; prof. Cath. U., Santiago, 1969; head engring. dept. Intricast, Santa Rosa, Calif., 1974-79; sr. design engr. Fairchild Stratus, Manhattan Beach, Calif., 1979-81; head engring. dept. Chromalloy S.A., Mexicali, Mex., 1981-83; pres., CEO ECO-Energy Engring., Carson City, Nev., 1981—; advisor, registered contract cons. office project svcs. UN Devel. Programme; cons. bd. City of Concepcion, 1970-74; cons. in field; part-time prof. Western Nev. C.C. Author: Physical Metallurgy, 1972. Founder first continuing edn. program for adults, Chile. Decorated Minerva medal, Malta Cross (Chile). Mem. ASHRAE, Am. Solar Assn., Solar Energy Internat., Nat. Bus. Assn., Found. Earth Resources Scis. and Tech. (v.p. 1994), Sierra Club, Audubon. Avocations: three day eventing, running, sailing, hiking. Home and Office: Eco-Energy Engring 2239 Lakeshore Dr Carson City NV 89704-9215

OKULITCH, VLADIMIR JOSEPH, geologist, university administrator; b. St. Petersburg, Russia, June 18, 1906; came to Can., 1927, naturalized, 1932; s. Joseph Konstantin and Alexandra Andrea (Drozhilov) Okulitch-Oksha; m. Susanne Kouhar, Jan. 19, 1934 (dec. 1968); children—Andrew, Peter. B.Sc. in Geol. Engring., U. B.C., Vancouver, Can., 1931, M.Sc., 1932; Ph.D. in Geology, McGill U., Montreal, Can., 1934; D.Sc. (hon.), U. B.C., Vancouver, 1973. Research fellow Harvard U., Cambridge, Mass., 1934-36; asst. prof. U. Toronto, Ont., Can., 1936-44; asst. prof. U. B.C., Vancouver, B.C., Can., 1944-46, assoc. prof., 1946-49, prof., 1949-64, head dept. geology, 1959-64, dean faculty sci., 1963-71; Mem. Can. Nat. Adv. Com. Research in Geol. Scis., 1958-61; Nat. Adv. Com. Astronomy, 1965—. Author: North American Pleospongia, 1943; (with Delaubenfels) Archaeocyatha and Porifera, Treatise on Invertebrate Palaeontology, 1955. Contbr. numerous articles to sci. jours. Fellow Royal Soc. Can., Geol. Soc. Am. (vice chmn. Cordilleran sect., research grants 1940, 41, 46, 55), Paleontological Soc. (v.p. 1954-55), Geol. Assn. Can.; mem. Royal Astron. Soc. Can. Club: Faculty (Vancouver). Avocations: photography; amateur astronomy.

OKULSKI, JOHN ALLEN, principal; b. Mineola, N.Y., July 28, 1944; s. John Joseph and Rose (Zebrowski) O.; m. Martina Carol Schoneboom, July 16, 1966; children: Richard, Peter, John. BS, Rutgers U., 1966; MS, C.W. Post Coll., 1972; postgrad., Hofstra U., 1975-76, Queens Coll., 1973. Social studies tchr. Long Beach (N.Y.) Jr. H.S., 1966-67, Lynbrook (N.Y.) H.S., 1967-69, Herricks H.S., New Hyde Park, N.Y., 1969-72; guidance counselor Herricks Jr. H.S., 1972-75; dept. chmn. sec. sch. guidance Herricks pub. schs., 1975-78; asst. prin. Herricks H.S., 1978-87; prin. Bay Shore (N.Y.) H.S., 1987-92, Garden City (N.Y.) H.S., 1992—. Cubmaster Boy Scouts Am., New Hyde Park, 1975-83; v.p. New Hyde Park Little League, 1978-83. Recipient Outstanding Achievement award Garden City C. of C., 1995. Mem. L.I. Pers. and Guidance Assn. (officer), Mid. States Accreditation Assn. (adv. com. N.Y. chpt.), Garden City C. of C. (Outstanding Achievement award 1995). Presbyterian. Home: 1505 Washington Ave New Hyde Park NY 11040-4332 Office: Garden City High Sch 170 Rockaway Ave Garden City NY 11530-1430

OKUMA, ALBERT AKIRA, JR., architect; b. Cleve., Feb. 10, 1946; s. Albert Akira Sr. and Reiko (Suwa) O.; m. Janice Shirley Bono, July 17, 1971; children: Reiko Dawn, Benjamin Scott. BS in Archtl. Engring, Calif. Poly. State U., San Luis Obispo, 1970, BArch, 1975; ednl. facility planning cert., U. Calif., Riverside, 1990. Lic. architect, Calif., Mont., Ariz., Ill., Nev., N.Mex., Oreg., Maine; cert. Nat. Coun. Archtl. Bds. Architect USN, Point Mugu, Calif., 1975-76; designer Wilson Stroh Wilson Architects, Santa Paula, Calif., 1976-79; architect, project mgr. W.J. Kulwiec AIA & Assocs., Camarillo, Calif., 1979-83, Wilson & Conrad Architects, Ojai, Calif., 1983-84, Dziak, Immel & Lauterbach Services Inc., Oxnard, Calif., 1984-85; ptnr. Conrad & Okuma Architects, Oxnard, 1985—; commr. Calif. Bd. Archtl. Examiners, 1985—, City of San Buenaventura Hist. Preservation Commn., 1990-94, chmn., 1991-93, City of San Buenaventura Planning Commn., 1994—, City of San Buenaventura Design Rev. Com., 1994—, vice chair 1994—; peer reviewer Am. Cons. Engrs. Coun., 1987—; lectr. U. Calif. Ext., Riverside, 1991—. Prin. works include Hobson Bros. Bldg. (reconstrn. and preservation), Ventura, Calif., (Design for Excellence award 1991, Historic Bldg. of Yr. award 1992, Archtl. Rev. Design award 1993), Oxnard (Calif.) Main Post Office Renovation (Design for Excellence award 1994). Mem. Spiritual Assembly Baha'is of Ventura, Calif., 1978—, treas., 1978-79, 84, 86-88, chmn., 1992-93; treas.'s rep. Nat. Spiritual Assembly Baha'is U.S., Wilmette, Ill., 1981-91, mem. dist. tchg. com., 1992-93; treas. Parents and Advs. for Gifted Edn., 1988-89; chmn. Ventura Unified Sch. Dist. Citizens Budget Adv. Com., 1990, 91, 92; mem. City of San Buenaventura specific plan citizens com., 1990-93, multicultural/cmty. heritage task force of the cultural arts plan com., 1991-92, strategic planning citizens adv. com., 1992-93. 1st lt. U.S. Army, 1971-73. Mem. AIA (chpt. bd. dirs. 1976-79, 81—, chpt. sec. 1981, v.p. 1982, pres. 1983, Intern Devel. Program Outstanding Firm award 1993), Am. Planning Assn., Internat. Conf. Bldg. Ofcls., Nat. Trust for Hist. Preservation, Calif. Preservation Found., Constrn. Specifications Inst., Design Methods Group, Coalition for Adequate Sch. Housing, Coun. Ednl. Facility Planners Internat., Structural Engrs. Assn. So. Calif. (affiliate), Ventura County Econ. Devel. Assn., Calif. Polytech. State U. Alumni Assn. (life), Toastmasters Internat. Office: Conrad & Okuma Architects 167 Lambert St Oxnard CA 93030-1044 *Personal philosophy: Live a life of service to others while keeping a global perspective on life and maintaining a clear vision of one's future goals. This service must be balanced among our own faith, family, and career.*

OKUN, DANIEL ALEXANDER, environmental engineering educator; b. N.Y.C., June 19, 1917; s. William Howard and Leah (Seligman) O.; m. Elizabeth Griffin, Jan. 14, 1946; children: Michael Griffin, Tema Jon. BS, Cooper Union, 1937; MS, Calif. Inst. Tech., 1938; ScD, Harvard U., 1948. Registered profl. engr., N.C., N.Y. With USPHS, 1940-42; tchg. fellow Harvard, 1946-48; with Malcolm Pirnie (cons. environ. engrs.), N.Y.C., 1948-52; assoc. prof. dept. environ. scis. and engring. U. N.C. at Chapel Hill, 1952-55, prof., 1955-73, Kenan prof., 1973-82, Kenan prof. emeritus, 1982—, head dept. environ. scis. and engring., 1955-73; bd. dirs. Water Resources Research Inst., 1965-84, chmn. faculty, 1970-73; vis. prof. Tech. U. Delft, 1960-61, Univ. Coll., London, 1966-67, 73-75, Tianjin U., 1981; editor environ. scis. series Acad. Press, 1968-75; cons. to industry, cons. engrs., govtl. agys. World Bank, WHO, UNDP, with spl. svc. in Switzerland, Israel, Jordan, Peru, Egypt, Colombia, Brazil, Venezuela, Thailand, Indonesia, Kenya, Zambia, Tunisia, Australia, Taiwan, Bangladesh, Argentina, Chile, Jamaica, Turkey, Finland, Eng., Morocco, China; mem. environ. coun. Rohm & Haas Co., Inc., 1985-92; chmn. expert panel on N.Y.C. water supply EPA, 1992-93. Author: (with Gordon M. Fair and John C. Geyer) Water and Wastewater Engineering, 2 vols., 1966-68, Elements of Water Supply and Wastewater Disposal, 1971; (with George Ponghis) Community Wastewater Collection and Disposal, 1975; Regionalization of Water Management—A Revolution in England and Wales, 1977; editor: (with M.B. Pescod) Water Supply and Wastewater Disposal in Developing Countries, 1971; (with C.R. Schulz) Surface Water Treatment for Communities in Developing Countries, 1984; contbr. to publs. in field. Chmn. Chapel Hill Fellowship for Sch. Integration, 1961-63; mem. adv. bd. Ackland Meml. Art Mus., 1973-78; bd. dirs. Warrren Regional Planning Corp., 1971-77, Inter-Faith Coun. Housing Corp., 1975-83, N.C. Water Quality Coun., 1975-77; mem. adv. com. for med. rsch. Pan Am. Health Orgn., 1976-79; chmn. Washington Met. Area Water Supply Study Com., 1976-80, NAS-NRC; mem. bd. sci. and tech. for internat. devel. NRC, 1978-81, vice chmn. environ. studies bd., 1980-83, chmn. water sci. and tech. bd., 1991-94; mem. com. on human rights NAS, 1988-94; pres. Chapel Hill chpt. N.C. Civil Liberties Union, 1991-93. Maj. AUS, 1942-46. Recipient Harrison Prescott Eddy medal for research Water Pollution Control Fedn., 1950, Gordon Maskew Fair award Am. Acad. Environ. Engrs., 1973, Thomas Jefferson award U. N.C. at Chapel Hill, 1973, Gordon Y. Billard award N.Y. Acad. Scis., 1975, 1st Thomas R. Camp Meml. lectr. Boston Soc. Environ. Engrs., Gordon Maskew Fair medal Water Pollution Control Fedn., 1978, First Allen Hazen lectr. New England Water Works Assn., 1990, Donald R. Boyd award Assn. Met. Water Agys., 1993; Friendship medal Inst. Water Engrs. and Scientists (Gt. Britain), 1984; NSF fellow, 1960-61; Fed. Water Pollution Control Adminstrn. fellow, 1966-67; Fulbright-Hayes lectr., 1973-74. Mem. NAE, AAUP (pres. U. N.C. chpt. 1963-64), ASCE (hon., chmn. environ. engring. divsn. 1967-68, 1st Simon W. Freese award 1977), Am. Water Works Assn. (hon., N.C. Fuller award 1983, Best Paper award ednl. divsn. 1985, Abel Wollman award of Excellence 1991), Inst. Medicine, Water Environ. Fedn. (hon., chmn. rsch. com. 1961-66, dir.-at-large 1969-72), Am. Acad. Environ. Engring. (pres. 1969-70, hon. diplomate, Kappe lectr. 1995), Assn. Environ. Engring. Profs. (Founders' award 1994), N.C. Pub. Health Assn. (Jarrett award 1994), Order of Golden Fleece), Sigma Xi (pres. U. N.C. chpt. 1968-69). Home: 900 Linden Rd Chapel Hill NC 27514-9162

OKUN, HERBERT STUART, ambassador, international executive; b. N.Y.C., Nov. 27, 1930; s. Irving and Ida Muriel (Levine) O.; m. Lorraine Joan Price, Dec. 5, 1954 (div. 1985); children: Jennifer, Elizabeth, Alexandra; m. Enid Curtis Bok Schoettle, Dec. 27, 1990. AB with gt. distinction, Stanford U., 1951; postgrad., Syracuse U., 1951-52, Princeton U., 1952; Hochschule fuer Politische, Wissenschaft, Munich, Fed. Republic of Germany, 1956-57; MPA, Harvard U., 1959. Mem. U.S. Fgn. Service, 1955-91; vice consul U.S. Fgn. Service, Munich, Fed. Republic Germany, 1955-57; with bur. intelligence & research Office of Soviet Union Affairs, Dept. State, 1959-61, alt. dir., 1971-73; 2d sec. Am. embassy U.S. Fgn. Service, Moscow, 1961-63; consul, prin. officer U.S. Fgn. Service, Belo Horizonte, Brazil, 1964-65; 1st sec., prin. officer embassy U.S. Fgn. Service, Brasilia, Brazil, 1965-66, counsellor embassy, prin. officer, 1967-68; assigned Naval War Coll. U.S. Fgn. Svc., 1968-69; spl. asst. to Sec. of State U.S. Fgn. Service, 1969-71, dep. chmn. U.S. Del., U.S.-USSR Talks on Prevention Incidents at Sea, 1971-72; spl. asst. for internat. affairs to comdr.-in-chief NATO So. Command, Naples, Italy, 1973-74; minister-counsellor, dep. chief mission Am. Embassy, Lisbon, Portugal, 1975-78; dep. chmn. U.S. del. SALT, Geneva, 1978-79, U.S. del. to trilateral U.S.-U.K.-USSR Talks on comprehensive test ban treaty, Geneva, 1979-80; ambassador to German Democratic Republic East Berlin, 1980-83; ambassador-in-residence Aspen Inst., Washington, 1983-85; ambassador, dep. permanent rep. of U.S. to the UN N.Y.C., 1985-89; rep. of U.S. to 40th, 41st, 42d and 43d sessions of Gen. Assembly of UN, to UN Security Coun., 1985-89, to 29th and 30th sessions of Com. on Peaceful Uses of Outer Space, 1986, 87, to Disarmament Commn. of UN, 1985-89, to Commn. Human Rights, to 27th and 29th session of com. on program and coordination of Econ. and Social Coun., 1987, 89; amb. in residence Carnegie Corp. of N.Y., 1989-90; mem. UN sec. Gen's. Expert Group on Enhancing UN Structure for Drug Abuse Control, 1990; exec. dir. Fin. Svcs. Vol. Corps, N.Y.C., 1990—; vis. lectr. Yale Law Sch., New Haven, 1991—; spl. adviser to the personal envoy of the sec. gen. UN, Yugoslavia and Nagorno-Karabakh, 1991-92; spl. adv., dep. co-chmn. Internat. Conf. on former Yugoslavia, 1992-93; U.S. mem. UN Internat. Narcotics Control Bd., Vienna, Austria, 1992—; adv. bd. Chazen Inst. Internat. Bus. Grad. Sch. Bus., Columbia U.; bd. The European Inst.; mem. bd. dirs. World Rehab. Fund; mem. adv. bd. Minority Rights Group U.S.A.; spl. advisor Carnegie Commn. on Preventing Deadly Conflict. Commr. U.S.-Poland Action Commn; mem. Internat. Coun., Found. Inter-Ethnic Rels., The Hague, The Netherlands, 1995—, mem. Adv. Com., Human Rights Watch, N.Y., 1995—, mem. Internat. Adv. Coun., Internat. Com. Red Cross, Geneva, 1996—. Served with AUS, 1952-54. Recipient Meritorious Honor award Dept. of State, 1972, Superior Honor award Dept. of State, 1980, Presdl. Meritorious Svc. award, 1983. Mem. Am. Fgn. Svc. Assn., Coun. Fgn. Rels., Am. Fgn. Policy (nat. com.), Am. Acad. Diplomacy, Washington Inst. Fgn. Affairs, Phi Beta Kappa. Home: 1133 Park Ave Apt 16E New York NY 10128-1246 Office: Fin Svcs Vol Corps 425 Lexington Ave New York NY 10017-3903

OKUN, JANICE, food editor; b. Buffalo, Dec. 3, 1932; d. Abraham I. and Berta Okun; m. Randolph J. Seidenberg Jr., Jan. 2, 1955; children: Jane Seidenberg-Lenk, Robert J. Seidenberg. BS, Cornell U., 1954. TV host WBEW-TV, Buffalo, 1954-55; asst. dir. Dairy Coun. of Niagara Frontier, Buffalo, 1962-79; food editor, restaurant critic Buffalo News, 1979—. Editor (with Eleanor Ostman): The Best Places to Eat in America, 1987. Mem. Assn. Food Journalists (pres. 1985, 86, v.p. 1974—). Office: Buffalo News 1 News Plz Buffalo NY 14203-2930

OKUNIEFF, PAUL, radiation oncologist, physician; b. Chgo., Mar. 8, 1957; s. Michael and Beverly Okunieff; m. Debra Trione, Sept. 7, 1989. SB in Elec. Engring. & Biology, MIT, 1978; MD, Harvard U., 1982. Diplomate Nat. Bd. Med. Examiners; cert. in therapeutic radiology Am. Bd. Radiology. Intern in medicine Beth Israel Hosp., Boston, 1982-83; resident in radiation oncology Mass. Gen. Hosp., Boston, 1983-86, fellow in radiation oncology, 1986-87, asst. prof. radiation oncology, 1987-93; chief dept. radiation oncology NIH, Bethesda, Md., 1993—; instr. in radiation medicine Harvard Med. Sch., Boston, 1987, asst. prof. radiation oncology, 1988-93; asst. radiation therapist Waltham (Mass.) Hosp. Med. Ctr., 1989-93, Mt. Auburn Hosp., Cambridge, Mass., 1989-93; assoc. radiation oncologist Univ. Hosp., Boston, 1990-93, co-dir. dept. radiation therapy, 1990-93; chief radiation neuro-oncology Mass. Gen. Hosp., Boston, 1991-93; chief radiation oncology br. Nat. Cancer Inst., Bethesda, 1993—; invited lectr. various med. schs., congresses & confs. Contbr. over 50 articles to profl. jours., also chpts. to books. Recipient Essay award IEEE, 1978, Young Oncologist Essay award Am. Radium Soc., 1987, travel award Am. Coll. Radiology, 1987, Young Investigator travel award VIth Internat. Meeting on Chem. Modifiers of Cancer Treatment, 1988, Basic Sci. travel grant ASTRO Ann. Meeting, 1989, USNC/UICC travel grant UICC Meeting, Hamburg, Germany, 1990, Melvin H. Knisely award Internat. Soc. Oxygen, 1991; grantee/fellow Am. Cancer Soc., 1985-86, 86-87, 89-92, Mass. Gen. Hosp., 1986, NIH, 1988-93. Office: NCI-Radiation Oncology Branch Bldg 10 B3B69 9000 Rockville Pike Bethesda MD 20892

OKUSANYA, OLUBUKANLA TEJUMOLA, ecologist; b. Ikenne-Remo, Ogun, Nigeria, Aug. 22, 1941; s. Samuel Tayo and Esther Oyeyinka (Bolorunde) O.; m. Iretiola Hope Titilola Omoleye, Sept. 25, 1971; children: Tolulope, Omotayo, Ibukunolu, Olugbenga. BS, U. Ibadan, 1966; MS, U. North Wales, 1970; PhD, U. Lancaster, 1976; MI Biol., Inst. Biology, London, 1971; FLS, Linnean Soc., London, 1977. Tchr. Ijebu-Ode Grammar Sch., Nigeria, 1966-68; asst. prof. U. Lagos, Nigeria, 1971-83, assoc. prof., 1983-85, prof., 1985-92, head of botany dept., 1984-85, dean, Sch. Postgrad. Studies, 1986-90; vis. rsch. prof. Ohio U., Athens, 1985, U. Agr., Abeokuta, Nigeria, 1990-91; adj. lectr. Ocean County Coll., Toms River, N.J., 1992-94; cons. Ministry of Sci. and Tech., Lagos, 1989-92. Editorial bd. Nigerian Jour. of Botany, 1993; contbr. articles to profl. jours. Pres. Lagos chpt. Lancaster U. Grad. Assn., 1990-92; commr. Civil Svc., Ogun State, Abeokuta, Nigeria, 1978-80. Recipient commonwealth scholarship Assn. Commonwealth U., London, 1968, 74, commonwealth travel fellowship, 1991. Mem. Botanical Soc. Nigeria (coun. mem. 1986-92), Ecol. Soc. Nigeria (coun. mem. 1989-94), Nigerian Inst. Biology (v.p. 1990-94). Anglican. Achievements include identification of some tropical legumes for growing in saline areas to increase land productivity; salt stress alleviation by mineral nutrients in halophytes is species specific; contrary to exptl. nom. in germination studies, it is necessary to state not only the date of seed collection, but also very important to state prevailing environ. factors - especially temperature and soil characteristics at time of seed prodn. and collection. Home: 869 Astoria Dr Toms River NJ 08753

OKUYAMA, SHINICHI, physician; b. Yamagata, Japan, Dec. 4, 1935; s. Kinzo Okuyama and Asayo Hasegawa; m. Masako Fujii, Dec. 4, 1966 (dec.); children: Yuriko, Izumi, Takashi, Jun; m. Junko Hsun Chen, Mar. 21, 1983; children: Midori, Shaw. MD, Tohoku (Japan) U., 1961, PhD, 1966. Intern Saiseikan Hosp., Yamagata, 1961-62; resident in radiology Tohoku U. Research Inst., Sendai, Japan, 1962-66; research assoc. Tohoku U. Inst. Tb, Leprosy and Cancer, 1966-73, assoc. prof. radiology, 1974-80; dir. radiology Tohoku Rosai Hosp., Sendai, 1980—. Author: Diagnostic Bone Scintigraphy, 1974, Compton Radiography, 1979, Induction of Cancer Redifferentiation, 1983, Evolution of Cancer, 1990, Origin of Reed-Sternberg cell in Hodgkin's Disease, 1991, Evolution of Human Diseases, 1991, Morphogenesis of Reed-Sternberg Cells, 1994. Recipient Compton Tomography-Radiotherapy Planning award Japanese Ministry of Edn., 1980. Mem. AAAS, Japanese Soc. Radiology, Japanese Soc. Nuclear Medicine, Japanese Soc. Reticuloendothelial Systems, Japanese Soc. Internal Medicine, N.Y. Acad. Scis. Achievements include reinforcing aerosol cisplatin for radiotherapy of laryngeal cancer, pasting chemotherapy for radiotherapy of uterine, rectal, penile and esophageal cancer, antibiotic pasting for putrefactive cancers, reduced perfusion of the cerebral basal ganglia for micro-aspiration pneumonia. Home: Kamo 4-4-5, Izumi-ku, Sendai 981-31, Japan Office: Tohoku Rosai Hosp, Dainohara 4-3-21, Aoba-ku Sendai 981, Japan

OKWUMABUA, BENJAMIN NKEM, corporate executive; b. Issele-Uku, Nigeria, June 20, 1939; came to U.S., 1963; naturalized, 1978; s. Daniel Ikeduba and Nwaonogwu Emily O.; m. Constance Lee, Mar. 16, 1968; children: Benjamin Nkem, Oblamaka Patricia, Richard Ikeduba, Daniel Ikeduba. BS, Cen. State U., 1967; MBA, Mich. State U., 1969, M in Labor and Indsl. Relations, 1971, PhD, 1974. Prof. Saginaw (Mich.) Valley State Univ., 1971-75, dept. chmn., 1971-75; sales mgr. Oldsmobile div. Gen. Motors Corp., Buffalo, 1975-78; pres., chief exec. officer AFRO-LECON, Inc., Jamestown, N.Y., 1978-89, Watson Industries, Inc., Jamestown, N.Y., 1989—; N.Y. state del. White House Conf. Small Bus. Mem. gov.'s adv. council on minority bus. devel. State of N.Y., council on western N.Y. econ. devel.; pres. African-Am. Coalition, Jamestown. Researcher in field. Mem. Acad. Mgmt., Am. Mgmt. Assn., Am. Mktg. Assn., Indsl. Relations Research Assn., Beta Gammas Sigma, Sigma Iota. Democrat. Baptist. Lodge: Rotary. Home: 505 Chautauqua Ave Jamestown NY 14701-7615 Office: Watson Industries Inc 335 Harrison St Jamestown NY 14701-6903

OLAFSON, FREDERICK ARLAN, philosophy educator; b. Winnipeg, Man., Can., Sept. 1, 1924; s. Kristinn K. and Fredericka (Björnson) O.; m. Allie Lewis, June 20, 1952 (dec.); children—Peter Niel, Christopher Arlan, Thomas Andrew. A.B., Harvard U., 1947, M.A., 1948, Ph.D., 1951. Instr. philosophy and gen. edn. Harvard U., 1952-54; asst. prof. philosophy, then assoc. prof. Vassar Coll., 1954-60; assoc. prof. Johns Hopkins U., 1960-64; prof. edn. and philosophy Harvard Grad. Sch. Edn., 1964-71; prof. philosophy U. Calif., San Diego, 1971-91, chmn. dept., 1973-76, assoc. dean grad. studies and research, 1980-85. Author: Principles and Persons, 1967, Ethics and Twentieth Century Thought, 1973, The Dialectic of Action, 1979, Heidegger and the Philosophy of the Mind, 1987, What Is A Human Being?, 1995. Served to lt. (j.g.) USNR, 1943-46. Mem. Nat. Acad. Edn. Home: 6081 Avida Chamnez La Jolla CA 92037-7404

OLAGUNJU, AMOS OMOTAYO, computer science educator, consultant; b. Igosun, Kwara, Nigeria, Nov. 27, 1954; came to U.S., 1980; s. Solomon Atoyebi and Ruth Ebun (Adegoke) O.; 1 child, Amanda. EdD, U. N.C., Greensboro, 1987; PhD, Kensington U., 1990. Mgmt. info. system dir. Barber-Scotia Coll., Concord, N.C., 1981-82; lectr. N.C. A&T State U., Greensboro, 1982-87, asst. prof., 1987-90; mem. tech. staff Bell Communications Rsch., Piscataway, N.J., 1986-90; vis. prof. Mich. State U., East Lansing, 1990-91; coord. acad. computing, assoc. prof. Del. State U., 1991-92, prof., chair dept. math. and computer sci., 1992—; cons. NSF, Washington, 1991-93, ETS, Princeton, N.J. Author: Scientific and Engineering Applications of Fortran, 1991; contbr. articles to Software Metrics, Automatic Indexing, Perfect Hashing, Number Theory. Pres. Ahmadu Bello Assn. Computer Univ. Students, Zaria, Nigeria, 1976, Orgn. United Africans, Concord, N.C., 1982. Recipient Queen's Grad. award Queen's Univ., Kingston, Ont., 1979; named Outstanding Young Man of Am., 1989. Mem. Assn. for Modelling and Simulation in Enterprises (program chair 1989-90, editor), Assn. for Computing Machinery (reviewer), N.C. Acad. Scis. (program chair 1991—), N.Y. Acad. Scis. Achievements include invention of the Bell Communication Rsch. Software Daily Software Report and Analysis Measurement Sytem and Generic Adminstrative Quantitative Decision Support System. Home: 121 Red Oak Dr Dover DE 19904

OLAH, GEORGE ANDREW, chemist, educator; b. Budapest, Hungary, May 22, 1927; came to U.S., 1964, naturalized, 1970; s. Julius and Magda (Krasznai) O.; m. Judith Agnes Lengyel, July 9, 1949; children: George John, Ronald Peter. PhD, Tech. U. Budapest, 1949, D honoris causa, 1989; DSc honoris causa, U. Durham, 1988, U. Munich, 1990, U. Crete, Greece, 1994, U. Szeged, Hungary, 1995, U. Veszprem, Hungary, 1995, Case Western Res. U., 1995, U. So. Calif., 1995, U. Montpellier, 1996. Mem. faculty Tech. U. Budapest, 1949-54; assoc. dir. Cen. Chem. Rsch. Inst., Hungarian Acad. Scis., 1954-56; rsch. scientist Dow Chem. Can. Ltd., 1957-64, Dow Chem. Co., Framingham, Mass., 1964-65; prof. chemistry Case-Western Res. U., Cleve., 1965-69, C.F. Mabery prof. rsch., 1969-77; Donald P. and Katherine B. Loker disting. prof. chemistry, dir. Hydrocarbon Rsch. Inst., U. So. Calif., L.A., 1977—; vis. prof. chemistry Ohio State U., 1963, U. Heidelberg, Germany, 1965, U. Colo., 1969, Swiss Fed. Inst. Tech., 1972, U. Munich, 1973, U. London, 1973-79, L. Pasteur U., Strasbourg, 1974, U. Paris, 1981; hon. vis. lectr. U. London, 1981; cons. to industry. Author: Friedel-Crafts Reactions, Vols. I-IV, 1963-64; (with P. Schleyer) Carbonium Ions, Vols. I-V, 1969-76, Friedel-Crafts Chemistry, 1973, Carbocations and Electrophilic Reactions, 1973, Halonium Ions, 1975; (with G.K.S. Prakash and J. Somer) Superacids, 1984; (with Prakash, R.E. Williams, L.D. Field and K. Wade) Hypercarbon Chemistry, 1987; (with R. Malthotra and S.C. Narang) Nitration, 1989, Cage Hydrocarbons, 1990; (with Wade and Williams) Electron Deficient Boron and Carbon Clusters, 1991; (with Chambers and Prakash) Synthetic Fluorine Chemistry, 1992; (with Molnar) Hydrocarbon Chemistry, 1995; also chpts. in books, numerous papers in field; patentee in field. Recipient Leo Hendrik Baekeland award N.J. sect. Am. Chem. Soc., 1966, Morley medal Cleve. sect., 1970, Alexander von Humboldt Sr. U.S. Scientist award, 1979, Pioneer of Chemistry award Am. Inst. Chemists, 1993, Mendeleev medal Russian Acad. Scis., 1992, Nobel prize in Chemistry, 1994, Kapitsa medal Russian Acad. Scis., 1995. Recipient Leo Hendrik Baekeland award N.J. sect. Am. Chem. Soc., 1966, Morley medal Cleve. sect., 1970, Cotton medal Tex. A&M sect., 1996, Alexander von Humboldt Sr. U.S. Scientist award, 1979, Pioneer of Chemistry award Am. Inst. Chemists, 1993, Mendellev medal Russian Acad. Scis., 1992, Nobel Prize in Chemistry, 1994, Kapitsa medal Russian Acad. Scis., 1995. Home: 2252 Gloaming Way Beverly Hills CA 90210-1717 Office: U So Calif Labor Hydrocarbon Rsch Inst Los Angeles CA 90007 *America still is offering a new home and nearly unlimited possibilities to the newcomer who is willing to work hard for it. It is also where the "main action" in science and technology remains.*

OLAJUWON, HAKEEM ABDUL, professional basketball player; b. Lagos, Nigeria, Jan. 21, 1963; s. Salaam and Abike O. Student, U. Houston, 1980-84. With Houston Rockets, 1984—. Named to Sporting News All-Am. First Team, 1984, NBA All-Rookie Team, 1985, All-Star team, 1985-90, 92-94, All-NBA First Team, 1987-89, 93-94, NBA All-Defensive First Team, 1987-88, 90, 93-94; named MVP 1993-94, NBA Defensive Player of Yr., 1993-94, mem. NBA championship team, 1994-95; named MVP NBA finals, 1994-95; recipient award IBM, 1993. Office: Houston Rockets The Summit Ten Greenway Pl E Houston TX 77046-3865*

OLANDER, RAY GUNNAR, retired lawyer; b. Buhl, Minn., May 15, 1926; s. Olof Gunnar and Margaret Esther (Meisner) O.; m. Audrey Joan Greenlaw, Aug. 1, 1959; children: Paul Robert, Mary Beth. BEE, U. Minn., 1949, BBA, 1949; JD cum laude, Harvard U., 1959. Bar: Minn. 1959, Wis. 1962, U.S. Patent Office 1968. Elec. engr. M. A. Hanna Co., Hibbing, Minn., 1950-56; assoc. Leonard, Street & Deinard, Mpls., 1959-61; comml. atty. Bucyrus-Erie Co., South Milwaukee, Wis., 1961-70, dir. contracts, 1970-76, v.p. comml., 1976-88, gen. atty., 1978-80, corp. sec., 1978-88, gen. counsel, 1980-88; vice chmn., dir. Bucyrus-Erie Co., South Milwaukee, 1988-92; ret. Bd. dirs. Ballet Found. Milw., Inc., 1978-92, Pub. Expenditure Rsch. Found., Inc., Madison, Wis., 1978-94, Pub. Expenditure Survey Wis., Madison, 1978-82. With USN, 1944-46. Mem. ABA, Wis. Bar Assn., Wis. Intellectual Property Law Assn., Am. Soc. Corp. Secs., Inc., Am. Corp. Counsel Assn., VFW, Harvard Club (N.Y.C.), Harvard of Wis. Club, Bonita Bay Club. Republican. Roman Catholic. Home: 3708 Woodlake Dr Bonita Springs FL 33923-8605 *Strive for success in whatever you endeavor in every honorable way. Respect the dignity and rights of all persons with whom you come in contact, irrespective of their station in life. Recognize you own shortcomings and allow for those of others.*

OLANITORI, SANDRA JOYCE, women's health nurse; b. South Norfolk, Va., June 1, 1950; d. Floyd L. and Dorothy M. (Corbett) Brown; m. Peter A. Olanitori; children: Adetola, Peter A. AS in Nursing, Norfolk (Va.) State Coll., 1975, BS, 1979; MS, Old Dominion U., Norfolk, 1985. Cert. CPR instr., neonatal resucitation program instr. Respiratory intensive care tech Norfolk Gen. Hosp., 1977-78, staff nurse, 1978-79, charge nurse, 1979-81, head nurse newborn nursery, 1981-90; adminstr., supr. Sentara Bayside Hosp., 1991-92; nurse mgr. newborn nursery Norfolk Community Hosp., 1992—. Mem. ANA (cert. nursing adminstr.), Va. Nurses Assn., Va. Pub. Health Assn., Nat. Perinatal Assn., Va. Perinatal Assn. (pres.), Action for Prevention, Chi Eta Phi. Home: 901 Harbour North Dr Chesapeake VA 23320-6516

O'LAUGHLIN, SISTER JEANNE, university administrator; b. Detroit, May 4, 1929. Pres. Barry U., Miami. Office: Barry U Office of the President 11300 NE 2nd Ave Miami FL 33161-6695

OLAYAN, SULIMAN SALEH, corporate executive; b. Onaiza, Saudi Arabia, Nov. 5, 1918; s. Saleh and Heya (Al Ghanem) O.; student public schs., Bahrain Islands; m. Mary Perdikis, Feb. 22, 1974; children: Khaled, Hayat, Hutham, Lubna. Rsch. specialist Arabian Am. Oil Co., 1937-47; founder and chmn. The Olayan Group, Saudi Arabia, 1947—, which includes Olayan Investments Co. Establishment Ltd., Olayan Europe Ltd., Olayan Devel. Corp., Ltd., Olayan Europe Ltd., Olayan Am. Corp., Crescent Holding GmbH, Competrol Real Estate Ltd., Competrol Establishment, Olayan Financing Co., Olayan Saudi Holding Co., Saudi Arabian Oil Co., Supreme Coun. (mem., 1989—); chmn. bd. The Saudi Brit. Bank, Riyadh, Saudi Arabia, 1977-89; adv. bd. Am. Internat. Group, 1982—; mem. internat. coun. J.P. Morgan & Co. Inc. N.Y., 1979-90; internat. councillor, mem. adv. bd. Ctr. for Strategic and Internat. Studies, Washington, 1977-95; bd. dirs. CS First Boston, Inc., 1988-95. Decorated Knight Comdr. of Brit. Empire, 1987, comdr. 1st class Royal Order of the Polar Star (Sweden), 1988; recipient Great Cross of the Order of Merit, Spain, 1984, Medal of Honor, Madrid C. of C., 1985. Mem. internat. adv. coun. SRI Internat., Menlo Park, Calif., 1965—. Alumnus Mem. The Rockefeller U. Coun., N.Y.C., 1978—; trustee Am. U. of Beirut, 1979-84; co-chmn. U.S.-Saudi Arabian Businessmen's Dialogue under the U.S.-Saudi Arabian Joint Commn. on Econ. Cooperation, 1980-92; Mem. Internat. Coun. Inst. Europeen de Adminstrn. des Affaires (INSEAD), Internat. Indsl. Conf., San Francisco (participant, internat. chmn. 1985), Inst. for Internat. Econs., Washington (bd. dirs.), The Conf. Bd. of N.Y. (sr. mem., internat. counselor), Royal Inst. Internat. Affairs, 1979-91, London, Riyadh Handicapped Children Assn. (vice chmn., 1983-88). Islam. Clubs: Equestrian (Riyadh), Knickerbocker, N.Y. Athletic (N.Y.C.), Pacific-Union and Bohemian (San Francisco), Royal Automobile (London). Office: The Olayan Group, PO Box 8772, Riyadh 11492, Saudi Arabia

OLBERMANN, KEITH, sportscaster; b. Jan. 27, 1959. BS in Comm. Arts, Cornell U., 1979. Sports reporter UPI Radio, N.Y.C., 1979-80, RKO Radio, N.Y.C., 1980-82, WNEW-AM, N.Y.C., 1980-83; nat. sports reporter, anchor CNN, N.Y.C., 1981-84, WCVB-TV, Boston, 1984; weeknight sports anchor, reporter KTLA-TV, L.A., 1985-88; sports commentator KNX-AM, L.A., 1996-91; sports anchor, host The Keith Olbermann Show KCBS-TV, L.A., 1988-91; weekend co-host ESPN Sports Radio, 1992-93; co-anchor, co-host SportsCenter ESPN, Bristol, Conn., 1992—; co-anchor SportsNight ESPN2, 1993-94. Recipient 11 Golden Mike awards Best Sportscaster, 1985, 86, 87, 88, 89, 90, Best Sportscast Calif. Radio and TV News Assn., 1985-91, Cable Ace award Best Sportscaster Nat. Acad. Cable Programming, 1995; voted Calif. A.P. Sportscaster of Yr., 1985, 87, 89. Office: ESPN Inc Comms Dept ESPN Plz Bristol CT 06010

OLCOTT, JOHN WHITING, aviation executive; b. Orange, N.J., Oct. 20, 1936; s. Egbert Whiting and Marion Richmond (Braillard) O.; m. Hope Bennett Phillips, May 14, 1966 (div. Feb. 1987); children: David Whiting, Bradley Phllips, Carter Howell; m. Isobel Waxman Ritter, Nov. 25, 1989. BS in Aero. Engring., Princeton U., 1960, MS in Aero. Engring., 1964; MBA in Gen. Mgmt., Rutgers U., 1970. V.p. Linden (N.J.) Flight Svc., 1960-66; flight rsch. specialist Princeton (N.J.) U., 1966-68; v.p. corp. devel., sr. cons. Aero. Rsch. Assocs. Princeton, Inc., 1968-74; v.p., group pub., editorial dir. McGraw-Hill Aviation Week Group, Rye Brook, N.Y., 1973-92; pres. Nat. Bus. Aircraft Assn., Inc., 1992—; mem. rsch. engring. and devel. adv. com. FAA, 1990-96; mem. bd. govs. Flight Safety Found., 1992—. Crew chief, mem. New Vernon (N.J.) Vol. First Aid Squad, 1974-92; bd. dirs. Aviation Rsch. and Edn. Found., Washington, 1988-92; mem. bd. visitors Aircraft Owner anbd Pilots Assn. Air Safety Found., Frederick, Md., 1988-93; trustee Embry-Riddle Aero. U., Daytona Beach, Fla., 1988-93, 95—; chmn. panel on gen. aviation and commuter tech. NASA, Washington, 1974-86; chmn. panel gen. aviation safety FAA, Washington, 1983-88. Recipient Meritorious Svc. award Flight Safety Found., 1983, Dir.'s award FAA Ctral Region, 1984, Commendation cert. FAA, 1984, Gill Robb Wilson award Embry-Riddle Aero. U., 1986, Journalism award Helicopter Assn. Internat., 1990. Republican. Presbyterian. Office: NBAA 1200 18th St NW Washington DC 20036-2506 also: 3808 N Richmond St Arlington VA 22207

OLCOTT, WILLIAM ALFRED, magazine editor; b. Bklyn., June 29, 1931; s. W. Alfred and Margaret Mary (Carr) O.; m. Anne Maria Gorman, Sept. 7, 1963; children: Christopher, James, Katharine, William, Terence. B.A. in Philosophy, Mary Immaculate Sem. and Coll., Northampton, Pa., 1956; postgrad., Columbia U. Reporter, writer AP, 1960-66; with McGraw-Hill Publs. Co., 1966-80, 81-84, chmn. editorial bd., 1976-77, editor in chief 26 Plus mag., 1973-77, editor in chief Nat. Petroleum News mag., 1977-81, editor in chief Office Adminstrn. and Automation mag., 1984; editor in chief Fund Raising Mgmt. mag., Garden City, N.Y., 1985—; publs. exec. editor Hoke Communications, Garden City, 1989—. Mem. adv. com. Garden City Bd. Edn., N.Y., 1976—; prin. religious edn. home program St. Joseph's Roman Cath. Ch., Garden City, 1976—, mem. pastoral coun., 1990-94. Recipient Jesse H. Neal Editorial Achievement award Am. Bus. Press, 1974, 80, Golden Mike award Nat. Religious Broadcasters, 1989. Home: 70 Greensboro Rd Hanover NH 03755-3101 Office: 224 7th St Garden City NY 11530-5747

OLD, BRUCE SCOTT, chemical and metallurgical engineer; b. Norfolk, Va., Oct. 21, 1913; s. Edward H.H. and Eugenia (Smith) O.; m. Katharine G. Day, Oct. 7, 1939; children: Edward H., Randolph B., Lansing G., Ashlee Virginia, Barbara Stuart. B.S., U. N.C., 1935; Sc.D., M.I.T., 1938. Research engr. devel. and research dept. Bethlehem Steel Corp., 1938-41; with Arthur D. Little, Inc., Cambridge, Mass., 1946-78; v.p. Arthur D. Little, Inc., 1950-60, sr. v.p., 1960-78; pres. Bruce S. Old Assos., Inc., 1979—; pres., chmn. Cambridge Corp., 1952-53; pres. Nuclear Metals, Inc., 1954-57; dir. Mass. Investors Trust and 13 other mut. funds in MFS group, 1973-85; chief metallurgy and materials br., div. research AEC, 1947-49; mem. Sci. Adv. Com. to Pres., 1952-56. Co-author: The Game of Singles in Tennis, 1962, Stroke Production in the Game of Tennis, 1971, The Game of Doubles in Tennis, 1956, Tennis Tactics, 1983; Contbr. articles to profl. publs.; patentee in field. Corporator Deaconess Hosp., Boston. Served to comdr. USNR, 1941-46. Fellow AAAS, Am Soc. Metals, Am. Inst. Chemists; mem. N.Y. Acad. Scis., Nat. Acad. Engring., Wianno (Mass.) Club, Sigma Xi, Tau Beta Pi. Address: PO Box 635 150 West St Osterville MA 02655-2242

OLD, LLOYD JOHN, cancer biologist; b. San Francisco, Sept. 23, 1933; s. John H. and Edna A. (Marks) O.;. BA, U. Calif., Berkeley, 1955; MD, U. Calif., San Francisco, 1958; MD (hon.), Karolinska Inst., 1994, U. Lausanne, Switzerland, 1995. Rsch. fellow Sloan-Kettering Inst. Cancer Rsch., N.Y.C., 1958-59, rsch. assoc., 1959-60, assoc., 1960-64, assoc. mem., 1964-67, mem., 1967—; rsch. assoc. biology Sloan-Kettering div. grad. sch. Med. Scis., Cornell U., N.Y.C., 1960-62, asst. prof. biology, 1962-66, assoc. prof. biology, 1966-69, prof. biology, 1969-81, prof. immunology, 1981—; acting assoc. dir. research planning Sloan-Kettering Inst. Cancer Rsch., N.Y.C., 1972, v.p., assoc. dir., 1973-76, v.p., assoc. dir. for sci. devel., 1976-83; assoc. dir. for research Meml. Sloan-Kettering Cancer Ctr. and Meml. Hosp., N.Y.C., 1973-83, William E. Snee Chair cancer immunology, 1983—; Harvey Soc. lectr., 1972, G.H.A. Clowes Meml. lectr., 1980; assoc. med. dir. N.Y. Cancer Rsch. Inst. Inc., 1970; med. dir. Cancer Rsch. Inst., Inc., 1971-74, dir. sci. adv. coun., 1974—; vis. prof. clin. investigation GM Cancer Rsch. Found., Dana-Farber Cancer Inst.; vis. prof. pathology Harvard U., 1986; fgn. adj. prof. med. faculty Karolinska Inst., 1994—; cons. in field. Adv. editor: Jour. Exptl. Medicine, 1971-76, 90—; Progress in Surface and Membrane Sci., 1972-74; assoc. editor: Virology, 1972-74; editl. adv. bd.: Cancer Rsch., 1967-70, Cancer, 1968-71, Recent Results in Cancer Rsch., 1972, editl. bd. Immunobiology, 1987—. Contbr. articles to profl. jours. Sci. dir., mem. Emeritus Sci. Com., Ludwig Inst. Cancer Rsch., 1971-86, chmn. sci. com. 1988—, bd. dirs. 1989—, CEO, 1995, dir. N.Y. unit, 1990; mem. rsch. coun. Pub. Health Rsch. Inst. City N.Y., 1977-80, bd. dirs., 1979-89, vice chmn. exec. com. 1984-89; adv. bd. biology div. N.Y. Hall of Sci., 1985—; mem. med. and sci. adv. bd., trustee Leukemia Soc. Am. Inc., 1970-73; mem. sci. adv. bd. Jane Coffin Childs Meml. Fund for Med. Rsch., 1970-75. Recipient Roche award, 1957; Alfred P. Sloan award cancer research, 1962, Lucy Wortham James award James Ewing Soc., 1970, Louis Gross award, 1972, Founders Tumor Immunology award Cancer Research Inst., 1975, Rabbi Shai Shacknai Meml. award, 1976; Research Recognition award Noble Found., 1978; Robert Roesler de Villiers award, 1981; N.Y. Acad. Medicine medal, 1985, Robert Koch prize, 1990. Mem. NAS, AAAS, N.Y. Acad. Scis., Harvey Soc., Am. Acad. Arts and Scis., Am. Assn. Cancer Research (bd. dirs. 1980-83), Am. Assn. Immunologists, Inst. Medicine of Nat. Acad. Scis., Phi Beta Kappa, Sigma Xi, Alpha Omega Alpha. Office: Ludwig Inst Cancer Rsch 1345 Avenue Of The Americas New York NY 10105

OLDEN, KENNETH, science administrator, researcher; b. Parrottsville, Tenn., July 22, 1938; s. Mack L. and Augusta (Christmas) O.; m. Sandra L. White; children: Rosalind, Kenneth, Stephen, Heather. BS, Knoxville Coll., 1960; MS, U. Mich., 1964; PhD, Temple U., 1970. Rsch. fellow, physiology instr. Harvard U., Cambridge, Mass., 1970-74; sr. staff fellow NIH, Nat. Cancer Inst., Bethesda, Md., 1974-77, biochemistry expert, 1977-78, rsch. biologist, 1978-79; assoc. dir. rsch. Howard U. Med. Sch. Cancer Ctr., Washington, 1979-82, dep. dir., 1982-85, dir., 1985-91; dir. Nat. Inst. Environ. Health Scis. and Nat. Toxicology Program NIH, Rsch. Triangle Park, N.C., 1991—. Author numerous books; assoc. editor Cancer Rsch., 1990—, Jour. Nat. Cancer Inst., 1990—, Molecular Biology of the Cell, 1991-93, Environ. Health Perspectives, 1992—; contbr. articles to profl. jours. Mem. awards bd. Gen. Motors Cancer Rsch. Found., Detroit, 1992—. Porter Devel. Postdoctoral fellow Am. Physiol. Soc., 1970, Postdoctoral fellow NIH, 1970-73, Macy Faculty fellow Macy Found., 1973-74. Mem. Am. Soc. Cell Biology, Am. Soc. Biol. Chemistry, So. Biol. Response Modifiers, Metastasis Rsch. Soc., Inst. Medicine, Internat. Soc. Study Comparative Oncology. Baptist. Avocations: tennis, hiking, cycling, cooking. Home: 19 Quail Ridge Rd Durham NC 27705-1870 Office: Nat Inst Environ Health Scis & Nat Toxicology Prog PO Box 12233 Research Triangle Park NC 27709-2233

OLDENBURG, CLAES THURE, artist; b. Stockholm, Sweden, Jan. 28, 1929; s. Gosta and Sigrid Elisabeth (Lindforss) O.; m. Patricia Joan Muschinski, Apr. 13, 1960 (div. Apr. 1970); m. Coosje van Bruggen, July 22, 1977. B.A., Yale, 1951; student, Art Inst., Chgo., 1952-54. One-man shows include Reuben Gallery, N.Y.C., 1960, Green Gallery, N.Y.C., 1962, Sidney Janis Gallery, N.Y.C., 1964-70, Galerie Ileana Sonnabend, Paris, 1964, Robert Fraser Gallery, London, 1966, Moderna Museet, Stockholm, 1966, 77, Mus. Contemporary Art, Chgo., 1967, 77, Irving Blum Gallery, Los Angeles, 1968, Mus. Modern Art, N.Y.C., 1969, U. Calif. at Los Angeles Art Gallery, 1970, Stedelijk Mus., Amsterdam, 1970, 77, Tate Gallery, London, 1970, Nelson-Atkins Mus., Kansas City, 1972, Art Inst. Chgo., 1973, Leo Castelli Gallery, N.Y.C., 1974, 76, 80, 90, Kunstmus., Basel, 1992, Margo Leavin Gallery, Los Angeles, 1975, 76, 78, 88, Art Gallery of Toronto, Ont., 1976, Centre Georges Pompidou Musée National d'Art Moderne, Paris, 1977, Kröller-Muller Mus., 1979, Mus. Ludwig, Cologne, 1979, Wave Hill, Bronx, N.Y., 1984, Pace Gallery, 1992, 94, Nat. Gallery of Art, Washington, 1995, Mus. Contemporary Art, L.A., 1995, Solomon R. Guggenheim Mus., N.Y.C., 1995, Kunst und Ausstellungshalle der Bundersrepublik Deutschland, Bonn, 1995; group shows include Martha Jackson Gallery, N.Y.C., 1960, 61, Dallas Mus. Contemporary Art, 1961, 62, Sidney Janis Gallery, N.Y.C., 1962, 64, Inst. Contemporary Arts, London, 1963, Art Inst. Chgo., 1962, 63, Allen Art Mus. Oberlin (Ohio) Coll., 1963, Mus. Modern Art, N.Y.C., 1963, 88, 90, 91, Washington Gallery Modern Art, 1963, Am. Pavilion, Venice, 1964, Moderna Museet, Stockholm, 1964, Gulbenkian Found. Tate Gallery, London, 1964, Rochester (N.Y.) Meml. Mus., 1964-65, Worcester (Mass.) Mus., 1965, Met. Mus. Art, N.Y.C., 1969, Walker Art Center, 1975, others, numerous commd. works, rep. permanent collections at, Guggenheim Mus., N.Y.C., Mus. Modern Art, Albright-Knox Art Gallery, Buffalo, Centre Georges Pompidou, Stedelijk Mus., Tate Gallery, Mus. Ludwig, Moderna Museet, Rose Art Mus. Brandeis U., Waltham, Mass., Oberlin Coll., Nat. Gallery Art, Canberra, Art Gallery Ont., Toronto, Art Inst. Chgo., Hirshorn Gallery and Sculpture Garden, Whitney Mus. Modern Art, N.Y.C., Mus. Contemporary Art, L.A., many others; Numerous outdoor works in corporate and private collections. (Recipient Creative Arts citation Brandeis U. 1971, Sculpture award Am. Ann., Chgo. Art Inst. 1976, medal AIA 1977, Wilhelm Lehmbruck Sculpture award 1981); author: Store Days, 1967, Proposals for Monuments and Buildings, 1969, Notes in Hand, 1971, Raw Notes, 1973, Multiples in Retrospect, 1991, Claes Oldenburg Coosje van Bruggen: Large Scale Projects. Recipient Sculpture award Brandeis U., 1971, Skowhegan Sculpture medal, 1972, Wilhelm Lehmbruck Sculpture award, 1981, Wolf Prize in Arts, 1989, Jack I. and Lillian Poses medal Brandeis U., 1993, Lifetime Achievement award Contemporary Sculpture Internat. Sculpture Ctr., 1994. Mem. Am. Acad. & Inst. Arts & Letters. Office: care Pace Gallery 32 E 57th St New York NY 10022-2513*

OLDENBURG, RICHARD ERIK, auction house executive; b. Stockholm, Sept. 21, 1933; came to U.S., 1936, naturalized, 1959; s. Gösta and Sigrid Elisabeth (Lindforss) O.; m. Harriet Lisa Turnure, Dec. 17, 1960. A.B., Harvard U., 1954. Mgr. design dept. Doubleday & Co., Inc., N.Y.C., 1958-61; mng. editor trade div. Macmillan Co., Inc., N.Y.C., 1961-69; dir. publs. Mus. Modern Art, N.Y.C., 1969-72, dir., 1972-94, dir. emeritus, hon. trustee, 1995—; chmn. Sotheby's N.Am., N.Y.C., 1995—. Served with AUS, 1956-58. Home: 447 E 57th St New York NY 10022-3064 Office: Sotheby's Inc 1134 York Ave New York NY 10021-4806

OLDER, RICHARD SAMUEL, elementary school music educator; b. Cuba, N.Y., Aug. 10, 1947; s. Laurence Charles and Ann Nell (Reese) O.; m.

Harriet Karangelan, June 24, 1972 (div. Mar. 28, 1978); m. Helen Mary DiOrio, Nov. 8, 1986; 1 child, Michelle Ann. B in Music Edn., Westminster Choir Coll., 1971. Cert. tchr. of music, N.J. Tchr. 8th grade vocal and gen. music Columbia Jr. H.S., Berkeley Heights, N.J., 1971-81; tchr. vocal and gen. music Woodruff and Mountain Park elem. schs., Berkeley Heights, 1981-88, Woodruff and T.P. Hughes schs., Berkeley Heights, 1988—. Recipient 20 Yrs. of Svc. award PTA Woodruff Sch., 1990. Mem. N.J. Edn. Assn. (local rep. 1986-87), Foxhollow Golf Club. Republican. Presbyterian. Avocations: golf, bowling, swimming, piano, guitar. Home: 43 River Bend Rd Berkeley Heights NJ 07922-1812 Office: Woodruff Elem Sch Briarwod W Berkeley Heights NJ 07922

OLDERSHAW, LOUIS FREDERICK, lawyer; b. New Britain, Conn., Aug. 30, 1917; s. Louis A. and Annie Louise (Bold) O.; m. Virginia Wakelin, Nov. 30, 1940; children: Peter W., Robert J., David L. A.B., Dartmouth Coll., 1939; LL.B., Yale U., 1942. Bar: Mass. 1946, Fed. 1947. Mem. legal staff Army Ordnance Dist., Springfield, Mass., 1942-43; with firm Lyon, Green, Whitmore, Doran & Brooks, Holyoke, Mass., 1947-49; partner firm Davenport, Millane & Oldershaw, Holyoke, 1949-64; treas. Nat. Blank Book Co., Inc., Holyoke, 1964-65; pres. Nat. Blank Book Co., Inc., 1965-78, chmn. bd., 1978-83; group v.p., dir. Dennison Mfg. Co., Framingham, Mass., 1967-82; counsel Bulkley, Richardson & Gelinas, Springfield, Mass., 1983—. Mem. editorial bd.: Yale Law Jour, 1941-42. Trustee Mt. Holyoke Coll., 1966-76, Greater Holyoke YMCA; bd. dirs. Holyoke Community Coll. Found., The Ctr. Redevel. Corp subs. Mt. Holyoke Coll., South Hadley, Mass., Sta. WGBY-TV. Lt. USNR, 1943-47. Republican. Mem. United Ch. Christ. Clubs: Longmeadow (Mass.) Country; Mill Reef (Antigua). Lodge: Rotary. Home: 1 Brookwood Rd Holyoke MA 01040-9510 Office: Baybank Tower 1500 Main St Ste 2700 Springfield MA 01115-0001

OLDFATHER, CHARLES EUGENE, lawyer; b. Brady, Nebr., Oct. 7, 1927; s. Harold and Marcia (Hazlett) O.; m. Diane C. Harris, June 15, 1957; children: David H., Jane Oldfather Light. Student, U. Colo., 1945, Kearney (Nebr.) State Tchrs. Coll., 1946-48, U. Cal. at Berkeley, 1949; A.B., U. Nebr., 1950; J.D. with distinction, U. Mich., 1953. Bar: Nebr. bar 1953. Since practiced in Lincoln; asso. Cline, Williams, Wright & Johnson, 1953-58; partner Cline, Williams, Wright, Johnson & Oldfather, 1958-80, of counsel, 1980—. Bd. editors: U. Mich Law Rev, 1952-53. Past pres. Family Svc. Assn., Lincoln, Nebr. State Hist. Soc. Found.; trustee U. Nebr. Found. Served with Adj. Gen. Divsn. AUS, 1946-48. Mem. Am., Nebr., Lincoln bar assns., Lincoln C. of C. (past dir.), Phi Kappa Psi, Phi Delta Phi. Republican. Presbyn. Club: Lincoln Country. Home: 6719 Old Cheney Rd Lincoln NE 68516-3561 Office: 1900 Firstier Bank Bldg Lincoln NE 68508

OLDFIELD, EDWARD CHARLES, JR., retired naval officer, communications company executive; b. Hampton, Va., July 21, 1919; s. Edward Charles and Alice Toomer (Parrish) O.; m. Lucy Garnett Jordan, Apr. 19, 1941; children: Edward Charles III, William Marshall, Henry Jordan. BS in Commerce, U. Va., 1940; MBA with distinction, Harvard U., 1950; grad., Naval War Coll., 1956. Commd. ensign USN, 1942, advanced through grades to capt., 1962, served in ships of Atlantic and Pacific fleets and major naval installations, 1942-70; dep. comdr. Def. Indsl. Supply Ctr., Phila., 1966-68; comdg. officer Naval Supply Ctr., Newport, R.I., 1968-70; dir. U.S. Naval Audit Svc., S.E. U.S., 1970-71; ret. USN, 1971; asst. to pres. Tele-Cable Corp., Norfolk, Va., 1971-73; treas. TeleCable Corp., Norfolk, 1973-74, v.p. corp. devel., 1974-83; v.p., asst. to chmn. Landmark Communications Inc., Norfolk, 1983-88; ret., 1988. Mem. dean's adv. com., bd. dirs. ctr. for econ. edn., lectr. Old Dominion U. Sch. Bus. and Pub. Adminstrn., Norfolk, 1985-88. Baker scholar Harvard U., 1950. Mem. Tower Club-So. Cable TV Assn., Alpha Kappa Psi, Beta Gamma Sigma, Kappa Alpha, Harbor Club (Norfolk, bd. dirs. 1980-86, pres. 1986-88), Norfolk Yacht and County Club. Republican. Roman Catholic. Home: 4301 Lookout Rd Virginia Beach VA 23455-1520

OLDHAM, BILL W., mathematics educator; b. Paris, Tex., Oct. 30, 1934; s. H.H. and Margaret Irene (McDowna) O.; m. Monda Underwood, Jan. 30, 1954; children: Clifford, Brent, Bill. BA in Math., Abilene Christian U., 1956; MS in Math., U. Ark., 1963; EdD in Math. Edn., U. No. Colo., 1972. Tchr. math. Mcpl. Sch., Ft. Summer, N.Mex., 1956-61; prof. math. Harding U., Searcy, Ark., 1961—. Mem. Math. Assn. Am., Nat. Coun. Tchrs. Math., Am. Coun. Tchrs. Math., Phi Delta Kappa. Ch. of Christ. Home: 1403 W Arch Ave Searcy AR 72143-5105 Office: Harding Univ PO Box 764 Searcy AR 72149-1001

OLDHAM, CHARLES HERBERT GEOFFREY, science advisor; b. Harden, Yorkshire, Eng., Feb. 17, 1929; s. Herbert Cecil and Evelyn Selina (Brooke) O.; m. Brenda Mildred Raven, Sept. 1, 1951; children: David Charles (dec.), Jon Geoffrey, Janice Kathryn, Keith Andrew. BSc, U. Reading, Eng., 1950, BSc with spl. honours, 1951; MA in Physics, U. Toronto, Ont., Can., 1952, PhD in Physics, 1954. Geophyicist Standard Oil Co. Calif., La Habra, 1954-57; sr. geophysicist Standard Oil Co. Calif., San Francisco, 1957-60; fellow Inst. Current World Affairs, Hong Kong, 1960-66; dep. dir. Sci. Policy Rsch. Unit, Sussex, Eng., 1966-80, dir., 1980-92; sci. advisor Internat. Devel. Rsch. Ctr., Ottawa, Ont., Can., 1992—; chmn. adv. com. on sci. and tech. for devel. UN, N.Y.C., 1990-92; U.K. del. UN Commn. Sci. and Tech. for Devel., 1992—; chmn. Gender Working Group, Ottawa, 1993-95. Sci. editor World Devel., 1975-90; contbr. articles on sci. policy and Chinese Sci. to profl. jours. Decorated comdr. Order Brit. Empire, 1990. Fellow Royal Soc. Arts, Manufactures and Commerce; mem. Lewes Golf Club. Avocations: golf, long distance train travel, swimming, hiking, theatre. Home: 35 Murray St Apt 502, Ottawa, ON Canada K1N 9M5 Office: Internat Devel Rsch Ctr, PO Box 8500, Ottawa, ON Canada K1G 3H9

OLDHAM, CHRISTOPHER RUSSELL, wine company executive; b. Basingstoke, U.K., Sept. 18, 1946; came to U.S., 1986; s. Henry Russell Oldham and Esme Grace (Craufurd) Anderson; m. Elizabeth Jacoba Graham, Jan. 9, 1971 (div. 1978); children: Justin, Mark; m. Janet Patricia Gough, Dec. 9, 1978; children: Carro, Nicholas. Student, Rugby Sch., U.K., 1965, Madrid U., 1967, London Bus. Sch., 1972. Mgmt. exec. Guthrie & Co. (U.K.) Ltd., London and Singapore, 1973-74; mktg. dir. Guthrie & Co. (U.K.) Ltd., London, 1974-75; mng. dir. William Armes & Son, Sudbury, U.K., 1975-76; chmn. Transmarine Air Holdings Ltd., Luton, U.K., 1976-80; pres., owner S.C.E.A. Du Chateau De Lacaze, Gabarret, France, 1980-87; corp. devel. dir. Chateaux Shippers Ltd., London, 1984—; pres. Wine Link Inc., San Diego, 1987—, 1990—; cons. Transmarine Holdings Ltd., London, 1980—. Author: Armagnac and Eaux-De-Vie, 1986; author, editor (bi-monthly pub.) Wine Line, 1990—; contbr. articles to profl. jours. Hist. rsch. Societe Borda, Pau, France, 1981-87; mem. Worshipful Co. of Glaziers, City of London, Liveryman. Capt. U.K. Cavalry, 1967-71. Recipient Freedom of City of London by Lord Mayor of London, 1975. Mem. British Inst. of Mgmt., Confrerie Cadets de Gascogne, Cavalry Club London, Fairbanks Ranch Country Club, Southwestern Yacht Club (San Diego). Avocations: sailing, wine collecting, golf, computing, literature. Office: Chateaux Shippers Group 12526 High Bluff Dr Ste 300 San Diego CA 92130-2067

OLDHAM, DALE RALPH, life insurance company executive, actuary; b. Topeka, May 31, 1943; s. Ralph W. and Anna Marie (Minch) O.; m. Marilyn D. Morris, June 5, 1965; children: Kent D., Kevin L. BS magna cum laude, Washburn U., 1965; AM, U. Mich., 1967. Asst. actuary Nat. Res. Life, Topeka, Kans., 1967-72, assoc. actuary, 1972-74, v.p., assoc. actuary, 1974-76, v.p., chief actuary, 1976-84; also bd. dirs.; sr. v.p. adminstrn. Security Benefit Group, Topeka, 1984-88, sr. v.p. affiliated products, services, 1988-89; pres., COO, Savers Life Ins. Co. Am., 1989-90, pres., CEO, chmn. bd., 1990-94, pres., CEO 1994—. Bd. dirs., treas. United Way Greater Topeka, 1988-89; mem. adv. council Unified Sch. Dist., Topeka, 1981-84; trustee Meml. Hosp. Corp. Topeka, 1984-89, chmn., 1989; mem. adv. bd. Ctr. Ins. Edn., 1987-89. Fellow Soc. Actuaries; mem. Am. Acad. Actuaries, Kansas City Actuaries Club (pres. 1980-81), Adminstrv. Mgmt. Soc. (bd. dirs. 1975-82, 84—, pres. 1981-82, Merit award 1980, Diamond Merit award 1987), Topeka Geneal. Soc. (pres. 1988-89). Republican. Lodge: Kiwanis (Topeka pres. 1980). Home: 12414 Wedd St Overland Park KS 66213-1841 Office: Savers Life Ins Co Am 9300 W 110th St Overland Park KS 66210-1403

OLDHAM, DARIUS DUDLEY, lawyer; b. Beaumont, Tex., July 6, 1941; s. Darius Saran and Mary Francis (Carraway) O.; m. Judy J. White, Jan. 23, 1965; children: Steven, Michael. BA, U. Tex., Austin, 1964; JD, U. Tex., 1966. Bar: Tex. 1966, U.S. Dist. Ct. (so., no., ea. and we. dists.) Tex. 1966, U.S. Supreme Ct. 1974, U.S. Ct. Appeals (5th and 11th cirs.) 1968. Assoc. Fulbright & Jaworski, Houston, 1966-74, ptnr., 1974—, mem. policy com., 1980—; mem. faculty grad. litigation program U. Houston; lectr. on corp. def. ins. and product liability. Mem. bd. editors Aviation Litigation Reporter, Personal Injury Def. Reporter; country corr. Internat. Ins. Law Rev.; contbr. articles to profl. jours. Mem. Nat. Jud. Coll. Coun. for the Future; bd. dirs., former sec.-treas. FIC Found., 1979-87; past bd. dirs. Houston Pops Orch.; mem. liberal arts adv. coun. U. Tex. Fellow Am. Coll. Trial Lawyers, Tex. Bar Found. (life), Am. Bar Found. (life), Houston Bar Found. (life), Am. Bd. Trial Advs.; mem. ABA (vice chmn. aviation com. tips sect. 1980-82, chmn. aviation com. litigation sect. 1982-84, vice chmn. econs. law practice com. 1985-86, mem. coun. tort and ins. practice sect. 1988-91, vice chair 1991-92, chair-elect 1992-93, chmn. ann. meeting program com. 1987, chmn. professionalism com. 1990-91, fin. com. 1986-93, chmn. long range planning com. 1991-92, chair tort and ins. practice sect. 1994-95, presdl. emissary 1993-95), Tex. Bar Assn. (liaison law schs. and law students com. 1983-86, PEER com. 1979-82, chmn. liaison fed. jud. com. 1989-90, pattern jury charges Vol. IV com. 1988-92), Tex. Young Lawyers Assn. (bd. dirs., chmn.), Fed. Ins. and Corp. Counsel (exec. v.p., pres.-elect 1988-89, pres. 1989-90, chmn. bd. 1990-91, exec. com. 1988-91, coord. com. 1984-87, sec.-treas. 1987-88), Tex. Assn. Def. Counsel, Maritime Law Assn. U.S., Am. Counsel Assn. (bd. dirs. 1982-83, 89-94), Def. Rsch. Inst. (chmn. aerospace com. 1984-87, vice chmn. 1983-84, Presdl. Achievement award 1987, bd. dirs. 1989-92, exec. com. 1991-92), Lawyers for Civil Justice (bd. dirs. 1988-92, 95—, exec. com. 1990-92, 95—, pres. elect 1996), River Oaks Country Club, Houston Ctr. Club, Sigma Chi, Phi Delta Phi. Office: Fulbright & Jaworski 51st Fl 1301 Mckinney St Fl 51 Houston TX 77010

OLDHAM, ELAINE DOROTHEA, retired elementary and middle school educator; b. Coalinga, Calif., June 29, 1931; d. Claude Smith Oldham and Dorothy Elaine (Hill) Wilkins. AB in History, U. Calif., Berkeley, 1953; MS in Sch. Adminstrn., Calif. State U., Hayward, 1976; postgrad. U. Calif., Berkeley, Harvard U., Mills Coll. Tchr. Piedmont Unified Sch. Dist., Calif., 1956-94, ret., 1994. Pres., bd. dirs. Camron-Stanford House Preservation Assn., 1979-86, adminstrv. v.p., bd. dirs., 1976-79, 86—; mem. various civic and community support groups; bd. dirs. Anne Martin Children's Ctr., Lincoln Child Ctr., Acacia br. Children's Hosp. Med. Ctr., No. Light Sch. Aux., East Bay League II of San Francisco Symphony, Piedmont Hist. Soc. (bd. dirs.), Mem. Am. Assn. Museums, Am. Assn. Mus. Trustees, Internat. Council Museums, Inst. Internat. Edn., Am. Assn. State and Local History, Am. Decorative Arts Forum, Oakland Mus. Assn. (women's bd.), DAR (vice regent, Outstanding Tchr. Am. History award), Colonial Dames Am., Magna Charta Dames, Daus. of Confederacy (bd. dirs.), Huguenot Soc. (bd. dirs.), Plantagenent Soc., Order of Washington, Colonial Order of Crown, Americans of Royal Descent, Order St. George and Descs. of Knights of Garter, San Francisco Antiques Show (com. mem.), U. Calif. Alumni Assn. (co-chmn. and chmn. of 10th and 25th yr. class reunion coms.), Internat. Churchill Soc., English Speaking Union, Pacific Mus. Soc., Prytanean Alumnae Assn. (bd. dirs.), Phi Delta Kappa, Delta Kappa Gamma. Republican. Episcopalian. Clubs: Harvard (San Francisco), Bellevue.

OLDHAM, JOE, editor; b. Bklyn., Aug. 1, 1943. B.S., NYU, 1965. Editor Car Model OLR Pub., North Arlington, N.J., 1966-68; assoc. editor Automobile Internat. Johnston Internat. Publs., N.Y.C., 1968-70; spl. projects editor Magnum-Royal Publs., N.Y.C., 1970-72; book devel editor Hearst Corp., N.Y.C., 1972-77; editor Motor Mag. Hearst Corp., 1977-81, exec. editor Popular Mechanics, 1981-85, editor-in-chief Popular Mechanics, 1985—; contbr. numerous articles to various mags. Recipient cert. of appreciation Nat. Inst. for Automotive Service Excellence, 1976; recipient cert. of appreciation Automotive Service Councils, 1979, cert. of appreciation Northwood Inst., 1981, cert. of appreciation Automotive Hall of Fame, 1981. Mem. Internat. Motor Press Assn. (pres. 1973-74, 81-82), Am. Soc. Mag. Editors, Soc. Profl. Journalists, Am. Auto Racing Writers and Broadcasting Assn. Club: Detroit Press. Office: Popular Mechanics The Hearst Corp 224 W 57th St New York NY 10019-3212*

OLDHAM, JOHN MICHAEL, physician, psychiatrist, educator; b. Muskogee, Okla., Sept. 6, 1940; s. Henry Newland and Alice Gray (Ewton) O.; m. Karen Joan Pacella, Apr. 24, 1971; children: Madeleine Marie, Michael Clark. BS in Engring., Duke U., 1962; MS in Neuroendocrinology, Baylor U., 1966, MD, 1967. Licensed physician N.Y., N.J., Tex.; diplomate in psychiat. Am. Bd. Psychiatry and Neurology. Intern pediatrics St. Luke's Hosp., N.Y.C., 1967-68; resident psychiat. Columbia U. Dept. Psychiat., N.Y.S. Psychiatric Inst., N.Y.C., 1968-70, chief resident in psychiat., 1970-71; auditor Washington Psychoanalytic Inst., 1971-72; candidate Columbia Psychoanalytic Ctr., N.Y.C., 1969-77; dir. psychiatric emergency svcs. Roosevelt Hosp., N.Y.C., 1973-74, dir. residency tng. dept. psychiat., 1974-77; dir. short term diagnostic and treatment unit N.Y. Hosp. Westchester Divsn., White Plains, N.Y., 1977-80; dir. divsn. acute treatment svcs. N.Y. Hosp. Westchester Divsn., White Plains, 1980-84; dept. dir. N.Y. State Psychiatric Inst., N.Y.C., 1984-89, acting dir., 1989-90, dir., 1990—; assoc. chmn. dept. psychiatry Columbia U. Coll. Physicians & Surgeons, N.Y.C., 1986—; chief med. officer N.Y. State Office Mental Health, Albany, 1989—; instr. clin. psychiat. Columbia U. Coll. Physicians & Surgeons, 1974-76, assoc. clin. psychiat., 1976-77, lectr. psychiat., 1977-84, assoc. prof. clin. psychiat., 1984-88, prof. clin. psychiat., 1988—; asst. prof. psychiat. Cornell U. Med. Coll., N.Y.C., 1977-83, assoc. prof. clin. psychiat., 1983-84; attending staff dept. psychiat. Roosevelt Hosp., N.Y.C., 1973-77; assoc. attending psychiat., N.Y. Hosp., 1977-84, Presbyn Hosp., N.Y.C., 1984-88, attending psychiat., 1988—; tng., supervising psychoanalyst Columbia Psychoanalytic Ctr., N.Y.C., 1983—; coord. med. student edn., Cornell U. Med. Coll. Dept. Psychiat., Westchester Divsn., White Plains, N.Y., 1977-84; coord. clin. clerkships in psychiat. Roosevelt Hosp., Columbia U. Coll. Physicians & Surgeons, N.Y.C., 1974-77; mem. acad. adv. com. Pfizer vis. professorship program in psychiat., 1990-92; mem. Sandoz Clozaril nat. adv. bd; spl. adv. bd. Freedom From Fear, Inc.; examiner Am. Bd. Psychiatry and Neurology; chmn. acute divisin rsch. group, Westchester Divsn., N.Y. Hosp., 1981-84, co-project dir. borderline rsch. group, 1982-84, co-prin. investigator familial transmission DSM III personality disorders, 1982-84; prin. investigator personality disorders in bulimia, N.Y.S. Psychiatric Inst., 1985-90, structured DSM III assessment psychoanalytic patients, Columbia Psychoanalytic Ctr., 1986-91; co-prin. investigator validity DSM III R personality disorders, N.Y. State Psychiatric Inst., 1987—. Author: (with L.B. Morris) The Personality Self-Portrait, 1990; contbg. editor Jour. Personality Disorders; sect. editor Psychiatry; mem. editl. adv. bd. Am. Psychiat. Press, Inc.; mem. exec. editl. bd. Psychiat. Quar.; reviewer Psychiat. Svcs., Jour. of Neuropsychiatry; contbr. numerous articles to profl. jours.; more than 100 presentations in field. Recipient John J. Weber prize Excellence in Psychoanalytic Rsch. Columbia Psychoanalytic Ctr., 1990. Fellow Am. Coll. Psychiatrists, Am. Psychiat. Assn. (chmn. com. psychoanalytic liaison N.Y. County dist. br. 1986-87, pres. 1989-90, com. rsch. psychiat. treatment 1987-93, coun. rsch., steering com. practice guidelines, chmn. sci. program com. 1992-95, cons. 1991-92, 95-96), Am. Psychopath. Assn., N.Y. Acad. Medicine;mem. Am. Psychoanalytic Assn. (cert.), Assn. Facility Dirs. (N.Y. State Office Mental Health, coun. ethics), Assn. Psychoanalytic Medicine (pres. 1989-91), Internat. Psychoanalytical Assn., N.Y. Acad. Sci., N.Y. State Med. Soc., Assn. Rsch. Personality Disorders (bd. dirs.). Office: NY State Psychiatric Inst 722 W 168th St New York NY 10032-2603

OLDHAM, MAXINE JERNIGAN, real estate broker; b. Whittier, Calif., Oct. 13, 1923; d. John K. and Lela Hessie (Mears) Jernigan; m. Laurance Montgomery Oldham, Oct. 28, 1941; 1 child, John Laurence. AA, San Diego City Coll., 1973; student Western State U. Law, San Diego, 1976-77, LaSalle U., 1977-78; grad. Realtors Inst., Sacramento, 1978. Mgr. Edin Harig Realty, LaMesa, Calif., 1966-70; tchr. Bd. Edn., San Diego, 1959-66; mgr. Julia Cave Real Estate, San Diego, 1970-73; salesman Computer Realty, San Diego, 1973-74; owner Shelter Island Realty, San Diego, 1974—. Author: Jernigan History, 1982, Mears Geneology, 1985, Fustons of Colonial America, 1988, Sissoms. Mem. Civil Svc. Commn., San Diego, 1957-58. Recipient Outstanding Speaker award Dale Carnegie. Mem. Nat. Assn. Realtors, Calif. Assn. Realtors, San Diego Bd. Realtors, San Diego Apt. Assn., Internationale des Professions Immobilieres (internat. platform speaker), DAR (vice regent Linares chpt.), Colonial Dames 17th Century, Internat. Fedn. Univ. Women. Republican. Roman Catholic. Avocations: music, theater, painting, geneology, continuing edn. Home: 3348 Lowell St San Diego CA 92106-1713 Office: Shelter Island Realty 2810 Lytton St San Diego CA 92110-4810

OLDMAN, GARY, actor; b. London, Mar. 21, 1958; m. Lesley Manville (div.); 1 child, Alfred; m. Uma Thurman (div.). BA, Rose Buford Coll. Speech and Drama, 1979. Appearances include (TV movies) Remembrance, 1982, Meantime, 1984, Honest, Decent and True, 1985, Fallen Angels: Dead End for Delia, 1993 (Cable Ace award, Actor in a Dramatic Series); (video) Since I Don't Have You by Guns n' Roses, 1994; (film) Sid and Nancy, 1986, Prick Up Your Ears, 1987 (Brit. Acad. Film and TV Arts nomination 1988), Track 29, 1988, We Think the World of You, 1988, Criminal Law, 1988, Paris by Night, 1989, Chattahoochee, 1990, State of Grace, 1990, Rosencrantz and Guildenstern Are Dead, 1991, JFK, 1991, Bram Stoker's Dracula, 1992, True Romance, 1993, Romeo is Bleeding, 1994, The Professional, 1994, Immortal Beloved, 1994, Murder in the First, 1995, The Scarlet Letter, 1995; (theatre) Massacre at Paris, 1980, Chinchilla, 1980, Desperado Corner, 1980, A Waste of Time, 1980, Summit Conference, 1982, Rat in the Skull, 1984, The Pope's Wedding, 1984 (Drama Mag. Best Actor award 1985, Fringe Best Newcomer award 1985-86), The War Plays, 1985, The Desert Air, 1985, Women Beware Women, 1986, Real Dreams, 1986, Serious Money, 1987. Office: c/o Douglas J Urbanski Douglas Mgmt Inc 8446 1/2 Melrose Pl Los Angeles CA 90069-5308*

OLDS, ELIZABETH, dancer; b. Mpls.. Attended, SouthWest Ballet Ctr., Nat. Acad. of Arts, Ill., Royal Winnipeg (Man., Can.) Ballet Sch. Dancer Royal Winnipeg Ballet, 1982-85, soloist, 1985-89, prin. dancer, 1989—; various guest performances in U.S. and Can. Dance performances include Nuages, Symphony in D, Four Last Songs, Romeo & Juliet, Adagio Hammerklavier, Three Pieces, Giselle, Fall River Legend, Rodeo, Dark Elegies, Deuce Coupe, The Nutcracker, Tarantella, Apollo, Scotch Symphony, Roses, There is a Time, Lilac Garden, The Sleeping Beauty, Gâité Parisienne, many others. Master of ceremonies Western Can. Summer Games, 1990, Access Awareness Week, 1991; chairperson Easter Seals Campaign, 1994. Avocations: pottery, gardening. Office: Royal Winnipeg Ballet, 380 Graham Ave, Winnipeg, MB Canada R3C 4K2

OLDS, JOHN THEODORE, banker; b. N.Y.C., Dec. 24, 1943; s. Richard J. and Barbara (Moses) O.; m. Candace Rose; children: Richard W., Samantha. Grad., Hill Sch., 1961; BA, U. Pa., 1965. With Morgan Guaranty Trust Co. N.Y., N.Y.C.; now mng. dir. J.P. Morgan & Co., N.Y.C. Mem. Univ. Club, Bedford Golf and Tennis Club, Mid-Ocean Club. Episcopalian. Home: 7 Plateau Ln Bedford NY 10506-1339 Office: Morgan Guaranty Trust Co 9 West 57th St New York NY 10005-2807

OLDSHUE, JAMES Y., chemical engineering consultant; b. Chgo., Apr. 18, 1925; s. James and Louise (Young) O.; m. Betty Ann Wiersema, June 14, 1947; children: Paul, Richard, Robert. B.S. in Chem. Engring., Ill. Inst. Tech., 1947, M.S., 1949, Ph.D. in Chem. Engring., 1951. Registered engr., N.Y. With Mixing Equipment Co., Rochester, N.Y., 1950-92, dir. research, 1960-63, tech. dir., 1963-70, v.p. mixing tech., 1970-92; pres. Oldshue Techs. Internat., Inc., Fairport, N.Y., 1992—; adj. prof. chem. engring. Beijing Inst. Chem. Tech., 1992—. Author: Fluid Mixing Technology, 1983; contbr. chpts. and articles to books and jours. Chmn. budget com. Internat. div. YMCA; bd. dirs. Rochester YMCA. Served with AUS, 1945-47. Recipient 1st Disting. Svc. award N.E. YMCA Internat. Com., 1979, J.E. Purkyne medal Czech Republic Acad. Sci.; named Rochester Engr. of Yr., 1980. Fellow AIChE (pres. 1979, treas. 1983-89, chmn. internat. activities com. 1989-92, Founders award 1981, Eminent Chem. Engr. award 1983, Svc. to Soc. award 1989); mem. NAE, Am. Assn. Engring. Socs. (chmn. 1985, K.A. Roe award 1987), Am. Chem. Soc., Internat. Platform Assn., World Congress Chem. Engrs. (v.p. 1986, pres. 1994—), N.Am. Mixing Forum (chmn. 1990-93, Mixing Achievement rsch. award 1992), Interam. Confedn. Chem. Engrs. (sec. gen. 1991-93, v.p. 1993-95, pres. 1995-96), Victor Marquez award 1983), Rochester Engring. Soc. (pres. 1992-93). Mem. Reformed Ch. in Am. (gen. program coun.). Achievements include design and scale-up procedures in field of fluid mixing. Home: 141 Tyringham Rd Rochester NY 14617-2522 Office: 811 Ayrault Rd Fairport NY 14450-8964

OLDSON, WILLIAM ORVILLE, history educator; b. Hampton, Va., Jan. 23, 1940; s. James Orville and Kathryn Francis (Zephir) O.; m. Judith Ann Kinsinger, June 11, 1967; children: Scott Ryan, Darren Randall. BA magna cum laude, Spring Hill Coll., Mobile, Ala., 1965; MA, Ind. U., 1966, PhD, 1970. Mem. Soc. of Jesus, 1959-65. Asst. prof. dept. history Fla. State U., Tallahassee, 1969-74; assoc. prof. history Fla. State U., 1974-79, assoc. chmn. undergrad. affairs, 1973-75, 83-84, dir. hist. adminstrn. and pub. history prog., 1987—, prof. history, 1979—, dir. history computer programs and rsch., 1993—, assoc. chmn. grad. affairs, 1994; dir. grievances and arbitration United Faculty of Fla., 1978-80, chief negotiator, 1980-81; dir. Social Sci. Interdisciplinary Program, Fla. State U., Panama City campus, 1986-90; charter mem. Pres.'s Coun. for Excellence in Coll. Tchg., 1990; assoc. dir. Holocaust Study Summer Inst. for Secondary Sch. Tchrs., 1996—. Author: The Historical and Nationalistic Thought of Nicolae Iorga, 1973, A Providential Anti-Semitism: Nationalism and Polity in Nineteenth Century Romania, 1991; author numerous hist. manuals. Recipient Outstanding Tchr. award Phi Eta Sigma, 1990, John Frederick Lewis award Am. Philos. Soc., 1991, Univ. Tchg. award, 1988, 95; NDEA fellow, 1966-67; Russian and East European Inst. fellow Ind. U., 1965-66; Fulbright fellow, 1967-68, Internat. Rsch. and Exch. Bd. fellow, 1973; Loyola U. of New Orleans honors fellow, Romanian State fellow, 1967-68; Holocaust Ednl. Found. fellow, 1994, 96; Inst. on the Holocaust and Jewish Civilization fellow Northwestern U., 1996; Coun. Rsch. and Creativity Planning grantee, 1994-95; Wolfson Found. grantee, 1995; Louis E. and Patrice J. Wolfson Found. grantee, 1995; Wolfson Family Found. grantee, 1996. Mem. Sigma Pi Sigma, Delta Tau Kappa, Phi Alpha Theta (Prof. of Yr. 1988). Democrat. Roman Catholic. Home: 1116 Sandhurst Dr Tallahassee FL 32312-2530 Office: Fla State U History Dept Tallahassee FL 32306-2029

OLEARCHYK, ANDREW S., cardiothoracic surgeon, educator; b. Peremyshl, Ukraine, Dec. 3, 1935; s. Simon and Anna (Kravéts) O.; m. Renata M. Sharan, June 26, 1971; children: Christina N., Roman A., Adrian S. Grad., Med. Acad., Warsaw, Poland, 1961; med. edn. grad., U. Pa., 1970. Diplomate Am. Bd. Surgery, Am. Bd. Thoracic Surgery. Chief div. anesthesiology, asst. dept. surgery Provincial Hosp., Kielce, Poland, 1963-66; resident in gen. surgery Geisinger Med. Ctr., Danville, Pa., 1968-73; resident in thoracic, cardiac surgery Allegheny Gen. Hosp., Pitts., 1980-82; pvt. practice medicine specializing in cardiac, thoracic and vascular surgery Phila. and Camden, N.J., 1982—. Contbr. articles to med. jours., also 7 monographs. Achievements include grafting of the internal thoracic to coronary arteries without touching the atherosclerotic ascending aorta, on cardiopulmonary bypass with a beating, warm and vented heart and bradycardia induced by beta-blocker; design of double occlusion clamps for the ascending aorta, Olearchyk R Triple Ringed Cannula Spring Clip to secure vein grafts over blunted cannulas in coronary artery bypass surgery; demonstration of safety of simultaneous use of fluothane and curare as gen. anesthesia; intro. of endarterectomy and external prosthetic grafting of ascending and transverse aorta under hypothermic circulatory arrest; pioneering promotion of grafting of the left anterior descending coronary artery sys. during resection of cardiac aneurysms, and of diffusely diseased coronary arteries with the internal thoracic artery; first to combine insertion of the inferior vena cava filter with iliofemoral venous thrombectomy; combined right femoral and iliac retroperitoneal surgical approach to remove retained intraaortal balloon device; applied a technique for early antegrade flow from an axillary to main graft during replacement of the ascending aorta in proximal aortic dissection. Address: 129 Walt Whitman Blvd Cherry Hill NJ 08003-3746

O'LEARY, DANIEL FRANCIS, university dean; b. Boston, Apr. 17, 1923; s. Dennis Joseph and Catherine Mary (O'Connell) O'L. BA, Oblate Coll., 1950; EdM, U. Buffalo, 1953, EdD, 1956. Tchr. gen. sci., biology Bishop Fallon High Sch., Buffalo, 1951-62, asst. prin., 1962-65; dir. edn. Oblate Fathers, Washington, 1963-68; prin. Bishop Fallon High Sch., Buffalo, 1968-74; dir. spl. programs Niagara U. (N.Y.), 1974-77, dean spl. programs, 1977-81, prof. edn., 1982—, dean edn. and continuing studies, 1982-88, prof., dean Coll. Edn., 1988—; adj. prof. Mt. St. Joseph's Tchrs. Coll., Buffalo, 1956-64, edn. evaluator reading clinic, 1956-64. Asst. dir. family life dept. Diocese of Buffalo, 1953-64. Mem. AAIP, ASCD, ATE, Am. Assn. Sch. Adminstrs., Nat. Coun. for Adminstrn. Tech. Edn., N.Y. State Assn. Tchr. Educators,

Am. Assn. Colls. for Tchr. Edn., Phi Delta Kappa. Roman Catholic. Office: Niagara U Dept Edn Niagara University NY 14109

O'LEARY, DANIEL VINCENT, JR., lawyer; b. Bklyn., May 26, 1942; s. Daniel Vincent and Mary (Maxwell) O'L.; m. Marilyn Irene Gavigan, June 1, 1968; children: Daniel, Katherine, Molly, James. AB cum laude, Georgetown U., 1963; LLB, Yale U., 1966. Bar: Ill. 1967. Assoc. Wilson & Mc Ilvaine, Chgo., 1967-75, ptnr., 1975-1987; ptnr. Peterson & Ross, Chgo., 1987-94, Schwartz & Freeman, Chgo., 1994-95; of counsel Davidson, Goldstein, Mandell & Menkes, Chgo., 1995—; bd. dirs. Atlantic Charter Ins. Co.; pres., bd. dirs. Jim's Cayman Co., Ltd. Lt. comdr. USNR, ret. Mem. Kenilworth Sailing Club (commodore 1985-87). Roman Catholic. Avocations: fishing, scuba diving. Office: Davidson Goldstein Mandell & Menkes 303 W Madison Ste 1900 Chicago IL 60606

O'LEARY, DAVID MICHAEL, priest, educator; b. Lynn, Mass., Mar. 11, 1958; s. Edward William and Kathryn O'L. BA, St. John's Sem., Boston, 1981, MDiv, 1984; MEd, Boston Coll., 1986; STL, Weston Sch. of Theology, 1990. Ordained priest Roman Catholic Ch., 1986; cert. alcohol counselor. Deacon intern Immaculate Conception Parish, Malden, Mass., 1984-86; parochial vicar Immaculate Conception Parish, Everett, Mass., 1986-91, St. Augustine's Parish, South Boston, 1991-93; priest St. Theresa's Ch., North Reading, Mass., 1993-95; prof. St. Mary's Sem. and U., Balt., 1995—; spl. edn. tchr., 1977-81, coll. dir. St. John's spl. edn. program, 1980-81, rschr., writer, film editor Office Religious Edn., Boston diocese, Brighton, Mass., 1981-82; group therpy leader, case worker Brigham and Women's Hosp., Kenmore Sq. De-Tox, 1982-83; substance abuse counselor St. John/ St. Hugh Parish, Roxbury, Mass., 1983-84; lectr. Pro-Life Archdiocese of Boston, 1986—, Basic Tchr. and Intermediate Tchr Trainer and Cert., 1987; vis. lectr. coll. level, 1991, 92; cons. in counseling. Contbr. articles to religious and other pubs. Counselor Camp Fatima Exceptional Citizens Week, 1978-90, asst. resident dir., 1991, resident dir., 1992; founding mem. Everett Ltd. Equity Coop. Project, 1988; mem. steering com., synthesizer and co-editor report to Nat. Conf. Cath. Bishops on Women's Pastoral, 1989; active mem. South Boston Pastoral Com., 1991; mem. Instn. Rev. Bd. Human Subjects Com., U. Mass., 1992; founder spiritual support group for AIDS victims and families, 1992. Mem. KC (life). Democrat. Avocation: long distance running. Home and Office: St Mary's Sem and U 5400 Roland Ave Baltimore MD 21210

O'LEARY, DENIS JOSEPH, retired physician, insurance company executive; b. Ireland, Feb. 5, 1924; came to U.S., 1949, naturalized, 1954; s. Joseph and Mary Christine (Dennis) O'L.; m. Audrey Mary Ryan, Nov. 26, 1952; children: Michael, Brian, Denis, Kevin. MD, Nat. U. Ireland, Cork, 1947. Intern St. Michael's Hosp., Toronto, Ont., Can., 1947-48; resident St. Michael's Hosp., 1948-49, St. Vincent's Hosp., N.Y.C., 1949-50, Triboro Hosp., Jamaica, N.Y., 1950-51; with N.Y. Life Ins. Co., N.Y.C., 1952-88; med. dir. employees' health N.Y. Life Ins. Co., 1961-70, v.p., 1970-82, sr. v.p., 1982-88; asst. attending physician Bellevue Hosp., N.Y.C., 1955-69; assoc. attending physician Bellevue Hosp., 1969-77, attending physician, 1977-84, sr. attending physician, 1984-87; instr. medicine, Columbia U., 1958-63, assoc. in medicine, 1963-68; asst. prof. clin. medicine NYU, 1968-86; sec. N.Y. Lung Assn., 1962-67, 69-71, v.p., 1967-69, dir., 1961-86, pres.-elect, 1983, pres., 1985-86. Bd. dirs. Nat. Council on Alcoholism, N.Y.C., 1979-86, pres., 1984-86. Served as capt. M.C. AUS, 1953-55. Fellow Am. Coll. Chest Physicians, Am. Occupational Med. Assn., Am. Pub. Health Assn.; mem. AMA, N.Y. State, New York County med. socs., Am. Thoracic Assn., Soc. Alumni Bellevue Hosp., N.Y. Occupational Med. Assn. (exec. com. 1967—, pres. 1973-74). Club: Scarsdale (N.Y.) Golf (gov. 1981-84), Rancho Bernardo Golf.

O'LEARY, DENNIS JOSEPH, lawyer; b. Phila., Jan. 11, 1941; s. Joseph P. and Catherine (Brannigan) O'L.; married; children: Dennis J., Terrance P., Patricia M., Maryann M. BS, Villanova U., 1963; JD, Temple U., 1972. Bar: Pa. 1972. Ptnr. White and Williams, Phila., 1972—. Mem. Pa. Bar Assn., Phila. Bar Assn., Defense Rsch. Inst., Pa. Defense Inst. Roman Catholic. Avocations: photography, travel, fishing, gardening. Office: White & Williams 1650 Market St Philadelphia PA 19103-7301

O'LEARY, DENNIS PATRICK, biophysicist; b. Dec. 24, 1939; married, 1964; 2 children. BS, U. Chgo., 1962; PhD, U. Iowa, 1969. Asst. prof. surg. and anatomy UCLA, 1971-74; rsch. assoc. prof. otolaryngology and pharmacology U. Pitts., 1974-78, assoc. prof. otolaryngology and physiology, 1978-84; prof. depts. otolaryngology, physiology, biophysics U. So. Calif., 1984—; USPHS rsch. fellow UCLA, 1969-70. Mem. AAAS, Inst. Medicine-Nat. acad. Sci., Am. Physiol. Soc., Soc. Neurosci., Internat. Brain Rsch. Orgn. Office: U So Calif Parkview Med Bldg C103 1420 San Pablo St Los Angeles CA 90033

O'LEARY, DENNIS SOPHIAN, medical organization executive; b. Kansas City, Mo., Jan. 28, 1938; s. Theodore Morgan and Emily (Sophian) O'L.; m. Margaret Rose Wiedman, Mar. 29, 1980; children: Margaret Rose, Theodore Morgan. BA, Harvard U., 1960; MD, Cornell U., 1964. Diplomate Am. Bd. Internal Medicine, Am. Bd. Hematology. Intern U. Minn. Hosp., Mpls., 1964-65, resident, 1965-66; resident Strong Meml. Hosp., Rochester, N.Y., 1966-68; asst. prof. medicine and pathology George Washington U. Med. Ctr., Washington, 1971-73, assoc. prof., 1973-80, prof. medicine, 1980-86, assoc. dean grad. med. edn., 1973-77, dean clin. affairs, 1977-86; pres. Joint Commn. on Accreditation Healthcare Orgns., Chgo., 1986—; med. dir. George Washington U. Hosp., 1974-85, v.p. Univ. Health Plan, 1977-85; pres. D.C. Med. Soc., 1983. Chmn. editorial bd. Med. Staff News, 1985-86; contbr. articles to profl. jours. Founding mem. Nat. Capital Area Health Care Coalition, Washington, 1982; trustee James S. Brady Found., Washington, 1982-87; bd. dirs. D.C. Polit. Action Com., 1982-84. Maj. U.S. Army, 1968-71. Recipient Community Service award D.C. Med. Soc., 1981, Key to the City, Mayor of Kansas City, Mo., 1982. Fellow Am. Coll. Physician Execs.; mem. ACP, AMA (resolution commendation 1981), Am. Soc. Internal Medicine, Soc. Med. Adminstrs., Am. Hosp. Assn. (del. 1984-86, resolution commendation 1981), Internat. Club (Chgo.). Avocation: tennis.

O'LEARY, EDWARD CORNELIUS, bishop; b. Bangor, Maine, Aug. 21, 1920; s. Cornelius J. and Annabel (McManus) O'L. B.A., Holy Cross Coll., Worcester, Mass., 1942; S.T.L., St. Paul's U. Sem., Ottawa, Can., 1946. Ordained priest Roman Cath. Ch., 1946, named monsignor, 1954, consecrated bishop, 1971; vice-chancellor, then chancellor of Diocese of Portland, Maine; diocesan consultor, pro-synodal judge of diocese, pres. priests senate, mem. finance com. of diocese, also dir. Commodity Service Corp., 1969-75; titular bishop of Moglaena, aux. bishop Portland, 1971-74; bishop Roman Cath. Diocese Portland, 1974-89, bishop emeritus, 1989—; mem. Maine Office Religious Coop., from 1973. Mem. Nat. Conf. Cath. Bishops. Address: 307 Congress St Portland ME 04101-3638

O'LEARY, HAZEL R., federal official, former power company executive, lawyer; b. Newport News, Va., May 17, 1937; d. Russell E. and Hazel (Palleman) Reid; m. John F. O'Leary, Apr. 23, 1980 (dec.); 1 child, Carl G. Rollins. BA, Fisk U., Nashville, 1959; JD, Rutgers U., Newark, 1966. Bar: N.J. 1967, D.C. 1985; cert. fin. planner. V.p., gen. counsel O'Leary Assocs., Inc., Washington, 1981-89; exec. v.p. corp. affairs No. States Power Co., Mpls., 1989-93, pres., 1993; sec. U.S. Dept. Energy, Washington, 1993—. Mem. Phi Beta Kappa. Office: US Dept Energy Office Sec 1000 Independence Ave SW Washington DC 20585-0001

O'LEARY, JAMES JOHN, economist; b. Manchester, Conn., May 7, 1914; s. James Henry and Helen Agnes (Hogan) O'L.; m. Rita Marie Phelps, May 31, 1941; children: James Phelps, Martha Ellen, Paul Howard, Mark Evans. B.A., Wesleyan U., 1936, M.A., 1937; Ph.D., Duke, 1941. Instr. econs. Wesleyan U., 1939-42, asst. prof., 1943-46, instr. air navigation U.S. Naval Flight Preparatory Sch., 1943-44; cons. Conn. Gen. Life Ins. Co., 1945-46; assoc. prof. econs. Duke, 1946-47; dir. investment research, economist Life Ins. Assn. Am., 1947-59, v.p., dir. econ. research, economist, 1959-67; chmn., chief economist Lionel D. Edie & Co., 1967-69; exec. v.p., economist U.S. Trust Co. of N.Y., 1969-70, vice chmn., 1970-80, econ. cons., 1980-91; bd. dirs. Bowery Savs. Bank, Guardian Life Ins. Co. Am., Atlantic Mut. Ins. Co.; dir. rsch. Com. on Pub. Debt Policy, 1946-47; mem. com. on rsch. in fin. Nat. Bur. Econ. Rsch.; alt. mem. nat. com. vol. credit restraint program Fed. Res. Bd., 1951-52. Author: Stagnation or Healthy Growth? The Challenge to the United States Economy in the Nineties, 1992; contbr. articles to profl. publs. Bd. dirs. Student Loan Mktg. Assn., Fed. Nat. Mortgage Assn., Kennecott/Copper Co., GAF/Corp., Excelsior Income Shares; mem. adv. com. Grad. Sch. Bus. NYU; trustee Wesleyan U.; bd. dirs. Nat. Bur. Econ. Rsch., chmn., 1976-80; trustee St. Joseph Coll. Recipient Silver Anniversary Sports Illustrated All Am. award, 1961, Disting. Alumnus award Wesleyan U., 1965, William Butler award for excellence in econs., 1985. Mem. Am., So. econ. assns., Am. Finance Assn., Am. Statis. Assn., Phi Beta Kappa, Pi Gamma Mu, Alpha Chi Rho. Club: University (N.Y.C.). Home: 8 Crooked Mile Rd Westport CT 06880-1123

O'LEARY, JOSEPH EVANS, lawyer; b. Newton, Mass., Sept. 17, 1945; s. Cornelius Joseph and Dorothy Mary (Evans) O'L.; m. Carolyn Brady, Aug. 16, 1969; children: Caryn, Kevin, David, Catherine. AB, Boston Coll., 1967, JD, 1970; LLM, Georgetown U., 1974. Bar: Mass. 1970, Ill. 1974, N.Y. 1979. Assoc. Seyfarth, Shaw, Fairweather & Geraldson, Chgo., 1974-78; ptnr. Seyfarth, Shaw, Fairweather & Geraldson, N.Y.C., 1978-82; of counsel Choate, Hall & Stewart, Boston, 1982-83, ptnr., 1983—. Lt. USN, 1971-74. Mem. ABA, Mass. Bar Assn., Boston Bar Assn. Home: 5 Penobscot St Medfield MA 02052-3008 Office: Choate Hall & Stewart Exchange Pl Boston MA 02109

O'LEARY, MARION HUGH, chemistry educator; b. Quincy, Ill., Mar. 24, 1941; s. J. Gilbert and Ruth Elizabeth (Kerr) O'L.; m. Sandra E. Eisemann, Sept. 5, 1964 (div. 1979); children—Catherine, Randall, Jessica; m. Elizabeth M. Kean, Jan. 24, 1981. B.S., U. Ill., 1963; Ph.D., MIT, 1966. Asst. prof. U. Wis., Madison, 1967-73, assoc. prof., 1973-78; prof. chemistry and biochemistry Coll. Letters and Scis. and Coll. Agrl. and Life Scis., Madison, 1978-89; prof. and head dept. biochemistry U. Nebr., Lincoln, 1989—; cons. Institut Pertanian Bogor, Indonesia, 1983-84; vis. prof. Universitas Andalas, Padang, Indonesia, 1984-85, Australian Nat. U., 1982-83. Author: Contemporary Organic Chemistry, 1976. Editor: Isotope Effects on Enzyme-Catalyzed Reactions, 1977. Contbr. articles to sci. publs. Grantee, NSF, U.S. Dept. Agr., Dept. Energy, NIH; Guggenheim Found. fellow, 1982-83; Sloan Found. fellow, 1972-74. Fellow AAAS; mem. Am. Chem. Soc., Am. Soc. Biochemists and Molecular Biologists, Am. Soc. Plant Physiologists. Home: 8333 Horseshoe Dr Lincoln NE 68516-3926 Office: U Nebraska Dept Biochemistry Lincoln NE 68583-0664

O'LEARY, PAUL GERARD, investment executive; b. Boston, June 22, 1935; s. Gerard Paul and Marie Agnes (Hennessey) O'L.; m. Elizabeth Jane Pollins, Oct. 14, 1961; children: Paul Hennessey, William Gerard, Mary Elizabeth, James Daniel. AB cum laude, Harvard U., 1956; MBA, U. Pa., 1958. Alumni dir. Wharton Grad. Sch., U. Pa., Phila., 1958-60; asst. sec. Empire Trust Co., N.Y.C., 1960-65; sr. investment analyst Blyth & Co., Inc., N.Y.C., 1965-70; v.p. William D. Witter, Inc., N.Y.C., 1970-76, also bd. dirs.; v.p. portfolio mgmt. Prudential Investment Corp., Newark, 1977—; instr. fin. U. Pa., 1957-60. V.p. Prudential Found., Newark, 1986—. Mem. Inst. Chartered Fin. Analysts, Am. Nuclear Insurers (chmn. investment com. West Hartford, Conn. 1989—), Assn. Ins. & Fin. Analysts (pres. 1973-74), Ins. Inst. for Hwy. Safety (investment com. 1983—), N.Y. Property Ins. Assn. (investment com. 1994—), N.Y. Soc. Security Analysts, Harvard Club of N.J. (pres. 1983-84), Boston Latin Sch. Alumni Assn., Indian Trail Club (Franklin Lakes, N.J.), Upper Ridgewood Tennis Club. Roman Catholic. Avocations: tennis, squash, philately, cartography, history. Home: 719 Belmont Rd Ridgewood NJ 07450-1300 Office: Prudential Investment Corp Gateway Ctr Two Newark NJ 07102

O'LEARY, ROSEMARY, law educator; b. Kansas City, Mo., Jan. 26, 1955; d. Franklin Hayes and Mary Jane (Kelly) O'L; m. Larry Dale Schroeder; 1 child, Meghan Schroeder O'Leary. BA, U. Kans., 1978, JD, 1981, MPA, 1982; PhD, Syracuse U., 1988. Bar: Kans. 1981. Gov.'s fellow Office of Gov., Topeka, 1981-82; asst. gen. counsel kans. Corp. Com., Topeka, 1982-83; dir. policy, lawyer Kans. Dept. Health and Environment, Topeka, 1983-85; asst. prof. Ind. u., Bloomington, 1988-90; assoc. prof. Ind. U., Bloomington, 1994—; asst. prof. Syracuse (N.Y.) U., 1990-94. Author: Environmental Change: Federal Courts and the EPA, 1993, Public Administration and the Law, 2d edit., 1996; contbr. more than 50 articles to profl. jours. Bd. govs. U. Kans. Sch. Law, Lawrence, 1980-82, devel. bd., 1981-85; bd. dirs. League Women Voters Syracuse, 1986-88; vol. Habitat for Humanity, Mex., 1990; cons. NSF, 1990; panel mem. Nat. Acad. Scis., Washington, 1990—. Recipient Outstanding Rsch. award Lily Found., 1992. Mem. ABA (editorial bd. Natural Resources and Environment jour. 1989-95, Award for Excellence 1981), ASPA (exec. com. law and environ. sects., chair environment sect., Rsch. award 1991), Am. Polit. Sci. Assn. (nat. chair pub. adminstrn. sect., exec. com. sect. publ.), Acad. Mgmt., Law and Soc. Assn., Assn. Pub. Policy Analysis and Mgmt. Avocations: kayaking, hiking, swimming, canoeing. Office: Ind U SPEA 410J Bloomington IN 47405

O'LEARY, TERESA, controller; b. N.Y.C., Jan. 21, 1960; d. Donald James and Frances W. (McGowan) O'L. BS, N.Y. Inst. Tech., 1981; JD, N.Y. Law Sch., 1994. Lic. fin. and ops. prin. Sr. compliance examiner Nat. Assn. Securities Dealers, N.Y.C., 1982-85; asst. v.p., sr. compliance officer Ryan, Beck & Co., West Orange, N.J., 1985-89; v.p., contr. Chapdelaine & Co., N.Y.C., 1989—. Avocations: boating, travel. Office: Chapdelaine & Co 80 Maiden Ln New York NY 10038-4811

O'LEARY, THOMAS HOWARD, resources executive; b. N.Y.C., Mar. 19, 1934; s. Arthur J. and Eleanor (Howard) O'L.; m. Cheryl L. Westrum; children: Mark, Timothy, Thomas, Denis, Daniel, Mary Frances. A.B., Holy Cross Coll., 1954; postgrad., U. Pa., 1959-61. Asst. cashier First Nat. City Bank, N.Y.C., 1961-65; asst. to chmn. finance com. Mo. Pacific R.R. Co., 1966-70, v.p. finance, 1971-76, dir., 1972-82, chmn. finance com., 1976-82; treas. Mo. Pacific Corp., St. Louis, 1968-71; v.p. finance Mo. Pacific Corp., 1971-72, exec. v.p., 1972-74, dir., 1972-82, pres., 1974-82; chmn. bd., CEO Mississippi River Transmission Corp., 1974-82; vice chmn. Burlington No., Inc., Seattle, 1982-89; chmn., CEO Burlington Resources, 1989—; bd. dirs. BF Goodrich, Kroger Co. Served to capt. USMC, 1954-58. Mem. Blind Brook Club (N.Y.C.), Chgo. Club. Office: Burlington Resources Inc 999 3rd Ave Ste 2810 Seattle WA 98104-4001

O'LEARY, THOMAS MICHAEL, lawyer; b. N.Y.C., Aug. 16, 1948; s. James and Julia Ann (Conolly) O'L.; m. Luise Ann Williams, Jan. 13, 1978; 1 child, Richard Meridith. BA, CUNY, 1974; JD, Seattle U Sch. of Law (formerly U. Puget Sound Law Sch.), 1977. Bar: Wash. 1977, U.S. Ct. Mil. Appeals 1978, U.S. Supreme Ct. 1983, U.S. Ct. Appeals (9th cir.). Dep. pros. atty. Pierce County, Tacoma, 1978; commd. 1st lt. U.S. Army, 1978, advanced through grades to capt., 1978; chief trial counsel Office of Staff Judge Adv., Fort Polk, La., 1978-79, trial def. counsel trial def. svc., 1979-81; chief legal advisor Office Insp. Gen., Heidelberg, Fed. Republic of Germany, 1981-82; sr. def. counsel Trial Def. Svc., Giessen, Germany, 1982-84; asst. chief adminstrv. law U.S. Army Armor Ctr., Fort Knox, Ky., 1984-85, chief adminstrv law, 1985, chief legal asst., 1985-86; sr. trial atty. Immigration and Naturalization Svc., Phoenix, 1987; sector counsel, spl. asst. U.S. atty., U.S. Border Patrol, Tucson, 1987-90; enforcement counsel U.S. Immigration and Naturalization Svc., Tucson, 1990-95, asst. dist. counsel Phoenix litigation, 1995—. Decorated Purple Heart, Cross of Gallantry (Vietnam). Mem. ABA, ATLA, Judge Advs. Assn., Wash. State Bar Assn., Pierce County Bar Assn. Home: 9080 E 25th St Tucson AZ 85710-8675 Office: US Border Patrol Sector Hdqrs 1970 W Ajo Way Tucson AZ 85713-5605

OLEJAR, PAUL DUNCAN, former information science administrator; b. Hazelton, Pa., Sept. 13, 1906; s. George and Anna (Danco) O.; m. Ann Ruth Dillard, Jan. 6, 1933 (dec. Oct. 1978); 1 child, Peter; m. Martha S. Ross, Sept. 8, 1979. AB, Dickinson Coll., 1928. Dir. edn. W.Va. Conservation Commn., 1936-41; coordinator U.S. Fish and Wildlife Service, 1941-42; chief press and radio Bur. Reclamation, Dept. Interior, 1946-47; editor Plant Industry Sta. AGRI, 1948-51; chmn. spl. reports Agrl. Research Adminstrn., 1951-56; dir. tech. info. Edgewood Arsenal, Md., 1956-63; chief, tech. info. plans and programs Army Research Office, Washington, 1963-64; chmn. chem. info. unit NSF, Washington, 1965-70; dir. drug info. program Sch. Pharmacy, U. N.C., Chapel Hill, 1970-73, ret., 1973. Author: West Virginia Units in Conservation, 1939, Rockets in Early American Wars, 1946, A Taste of Red Onion, 1981, Sentinel at the Crossroads, 1991; editor: Computer-Based Information Systems in the Practice of Pharmacy, 1971; newspaper columnist, editor AP, Pa. and W.Va.; editor Hanover Record-Herald, Pa. Served with AUS, 1942-46. Decorated Army Commendation medal. Mem. Ravens Claw, Mil. Order of The World Wars (lt. col.), Masons (32 degree), Theta Chi, Omicron Delta Kappa. Methodist. Home: 724 Port Malabar Blvd NE Palm Bay FL 32905-4409 also: 407 Russell Ave # 111 Gaithersburg MD 20877

OLEKSIW, DANIEL PHILIP, former foreign service officer, consultant; b. Wilkes Barre, Pa., Feb. 5, 1921; s. Rev. Michael Nicholas and Maria Helena (von Kotzko) O.; m. Elizabeth Louise Hyatt, Aug. 21, 1948 (dec. 1990); children: Barbara Anne, Daniel Hyatt. BA, Pa. State U., 1940; student, Duke U.; postgrad., U. Mo., Princeton U., 1941-42; grad., Nat. War Coll., 1962. Reporter, editor small newspapers Mo. and Mich.; advt. copywriter Cleve.; info. specialist Civilian Prodn. Adminstrn., Washington, 1946; dep. chief press br. pub. rels. USAF Hdqrs., Washington, 1947, 48; pub. advt. newspapers Arlington and Alexandria, Va., 1948, 49; pub. rels. officer U.S. Mission for Aid to Turkey, 1949-50; attache Am. embassy, USIS, Ankara, 1951; press attache Am. embassy, Cairo, 1952-55; 1st sec. Am. embassy, dep. pub. affairs officer USIS, Tehran, 1956-58; consul, pub. affairs officer consulate gen. Bombay, 1958-61; program coord. Africa USIA, 1962-63, dep. area dir. Africa, 1963-64, dir. media content, 1964-65; spl. asst. to permanent rep. U.S. mission to UN, 1966; area dir. for East Asia and Pacific USIA, 1966-70; minister-counselor pub. affairs Am. Embassy, New Delhi, 1970-73; dir. USIS, India; sr. faculty adviser Nat. War Coll., 1973; insp. gen. USIA, Washington, 1973-78; dir. ednl. programming Middle East Svcs., Inc., Washington, 1979-80; dir. Washington Export Info., Inc., 1980-89; program evaluation cons. Bur. Cultural and Ednl. Affairs, USIA, 1984-85; dir. Dan Oleksiw & Assocs., Washington; cons. program evaluator Brit.-Am. Project Johns Hopkins U. Sch. Advanced Internat. Studies, 1986-95, Royal Inst. Internat. Affairs, Coun. for Internat. Devel. on Mercy Fund programs in Burkina Faso, Eselen Inst. San Francisco, 1988, U.S. Bus Leadership Exchange Program, USSR, 1988, Washington, 1987, Fgn. Svc. Inst., Dept. State, 1989-90. 2d lt. inf. AUS, 1942-45. Recipient Disting. Service award USIA, 1966. Roman Catholic. Home: 8100 Conn Ave #707 Chevy Chase MD 20815-2814

OLENDER, JACK HARVEY, lawyer; b. McKeesport, Pa., Sept. 8, 1935; m. Lovell Olender. BA, U. Pitts., 1957, JD, 1960; LLM, George Washington U., 1961. Bar: D.C. 1961, U.S. Supreme Ct. 1965, Md. 1966, Pa. 1985. Pvt. practice Washington, 1961-79; prin. Jack H. Olender & Assocs., P.C., Washington, 1979—. Contbr. articles to profl. jours. Active World Peace through Law, Washington. Named to Hall of Fame Nat. Assn. Black Women Attys., 1987. Mem. Am. Bd. Profl. Liability Attys., Am. Coll. Trial Lawyers, Assn. Trial Lawyers Am., Inner Circle Advocates, Nat. Bd. Trial Advocates, Internat. Acad. Trial Lawyers. Office: Jack H Olender & Assocs PC 888 17th St NW 4th fl Washington DC 20006

OLER, WESLEY MARION, III, physician, educator; b. N.Y.C., Mar. 8, 1918; s. Wesley Marion Jr. and Imogene (Rubel) O.; m. Virginia Carolyn Craemer, Dec. 8, 1951; children: Helen Louise (dec.), Wesley Marion IV, Stephen Scott. Grad., Phillips Andover Acad., 1936; AB, Yale U., 1940; MD, Columbia U., 1943. Intern Bellevue Hosp., N.Y.C., 1944; resident Bellevue Hosp., 1948-50; fellow Hosp. U. Pa., 1951; practice medicine specializing in internal medicine Washington, 1952-93; mem. emeritus staff, vice chmn. dept. medicine Washington Hosp. Ctr., 1962-64; v.p. med. bd. Washington Hosp. Center, 1971-72, trustee, 1973-81, emeritus, 1994; clin. prof. medicine emeritus Med. Sch. Georgetown U. Contbr. articles on old musical instruments to jours. Founder, past pres. Washington Recorder Soc.; bd. dirs. Am. Recorder Soc. Maj. M.C. U.S. Army (paratroops), 1944-47. Fellow ACP (gov. 1980-84); mem. SAR, Mensa, Osler Soc. Washington (past pres.), Met. Club, Cosmos Club, Chevy Chase Club. Republican. Episcopalian. Home: Apt 612N 8101 Connecticut Ave Chevy Chase MD 20815-2805

OLERUD, JOHN GARRETT, professional baseball player; b. Seattle, Aug. 5, 1968; s. John E. Olerud. Student, Washington State U. With Toronto Blue Jays, 1989—; mem. Am. League All-Star Team, 1993. winner A.L batting title, 1993. Office: Toronto Blue Jays, 1 Blue Jay Way Ste 3200, Toronto, ON Canada MJV 1J1*

OLES, PAUL STEVENSON (STEVE OLES), architect, perspectivist, educator; b. San Antonio, Sept. 26, 1936; s. Paul Stevenson Sr. and Suda (Willis) O.; m. Carole Simmons, Oct. 11, 1963 (div. 1991); children: Brian Thomas, Julia Oles Carr; m. Susan Thompson, Sept. 26, 1992. BArch, Tex. Tech U., 1960; MArch, Yale U., 1963. Registered architect, Mass. Draftsman The Architects Collaborative, Cambridge, Mass., 1963-65, Cambridge Seven Assocs., Cambridge, 1965-67; architect MIT, Cambridge, 1968-70; prin. architect Interface Architects, Newton, Mass., 1971—; vis. faculty RISD, Providence, 1974-79; lectr. architecture Harvard Grad. Sch. Design, Cambridge, 1984-88, vis. scholar, 1989-91. Author: Architectural Illustration, 1979, Drawing the Future, 1988. Mem. vestry Episcopalian Ch., 1995—. Named Loeb fellow Harvard Grad. Sch. Design, 1982. Fellow AIA (inst. honor 1983, fellow 1989), Boston Soc. Architects, Am. Soc. Archtl. Perspectivists (founder, pres. 1986-90, bd. dirs. 1993—, Hugh Ferriss Meml. prize 1996). Democrat. Avocations: music, painting, photography. Office: Interface Architects 1 Gateway Ctr Ste 501A Newton MA 02158-2802

OLES, STUART GREGORY, lawyer; b. Seattle, Dec. 15, 1924; s. Floyd and Helen Louise (La Violette) O.; B.S. magna cum laude, U. Wash., 1947, J.D., 1948; m. Ilse Hanewald, Feb. 12, 1954; children: Douglas, Karl, Stephen. Admitted to Wash. bar, 1949, U.S. Supreme Ct. bar, 1960; dep. pros. atty. King County (Wash.), 1949, chief civil dept., 1949-50; gen. practice law, Seattle, 1950-95; sr. partner firm Oles, Morrison & Rinker and predecessor, 1955-90, of counsel, 1991-95. Author: A View From the Rock, 1994. Chmn. Seattle Community Concert Assn., 1955; pres. Friends Seattle Pub. Library, 1956; mem. Wash. Pub. Disclosure Commn., 1973-75; trustee Ch. Div. Sch. of Pacific, Berkeley, Calif., 1974-75; mem. bd. curators Wash. State Hist. Soc., 1983; former mem. Seattle Symphony Bd.; pres. King County Ct. House Rep. Club, 1950, U. Wash. Young Rep. Club, 1947; Wash. conv. floor leader Taft, 1952, Goldwater, 1964; Wash. chmn. Citizens for Goldwater, 1964; chmn. King County Rep. convs., 1966, 68, 76, 84, 86, 88, 90, 92, 96, Wash. State Rep. Conv., 1980. Served with USMCR, 1943-45. Mem. ABA (past regional vice chmn. pub. contract law sect.), Wash. Bar Assn., Order of Coif, Scabbard and Blade, Am. Legion, Kapoho Beach Club (pres.), Am. Highland Cattle Assn. (v.p. and dir.), Phi Beta Kappa, Phi Alpha Delta. Episcopalian (vestryman, lay-reader), Rainier Club, Seattle Yacht Club. Home: 22715 SE 43d Ct Issaquah WA 98029 Office: Oles Morrison & Rinker 701 5th Ave Ste 3300 Seattle WA 98104-7016

OLESEN, DOUGLAS EUGENE, research institute executive; b. Tonasket, Wash., Jan. 12, 1939; s. Magnus and Esther Rae (Myers) O.; m. Michaele Ann Engdahl, Nov. 18, 1964; children: Douglas Eugene, Stephen Christian. B.S., U. Wash., 1962, M.S., 1963, postgrad., 1965-67, Ph.D., 1972. Research engr. space research div. Boeing Aircraft Co., Seattle, 1963-64; with Battelle Meml. Inst., Pacific NW Labs., Richland, Wash., 1967-84, mgr. water resources systems sect., water and land resources dept., 1970-71, mgr. dept., 1971-75, dep. dir. research labs., 1975, dir. research, 1975-79, v.p. inst., dir. NW div., 1979-84; exec. v.p., chief operating officer Battelle Meml. Inst., Columbus, Ohio, 1984-87, pres., chief exec. officer, 1987—. Patentee process and system for treating waste water. Trustees Capital Univ., Columbus Mus. of Art, Riverside Hosp., INROADS/Columbus Inc., Franklin County United Way; bd. dirs. Ohio State U. Found. Mem. Ohio C. of C. (trustee). Office: Battelle Meml Inst 505 King Ave Columbus OH 43201-2696*

OLESKIEWICZ, FRANCIS STANLEY, retired insurance executive; b. Chicopee, Mass., Jan. 2, 1928; s. Francis and Agata (Gniady) O.; m. Ruth M. Ventrice, June 16, 1951; children—Francis H., Laurie. B.S., Am. Internat. Coll., Springfield, Mass., 1953; LL.B, Western New Eng. Coll., 1961. Bar: Mass. 1962. With Ins. Co. N.Am., Boston, 1953-67; property mgr. Employers-Comml. Union, Boston, 1967-69; pres., chmn. Lexington Ins. Co., Boston, 1969-86; v.p. Am. Internat. Group, N.Y.C., 1979-86; retired, 1986; limited sole practice law Framingham, Mass., 1986—; ins. arbitrator; chmn. bd. Risk Specialists Cos., Inc., Boston; vice chmn. Starr Assocs., N.Y.C., C.V. Starr & Co., Inc., Calif.; bd. dirs. Audubon Ins. Co., Baton Rouge, Union Atlantique d'Assurances S.A., Brussels; bd. trustees, mem.

devel. com. We. New England Coll., Springfield, Mass., 1987—. Served as pfc. USMC, 1946-47, PTO. Mem. Mass. Bar Assn. (vol. law speaker, 1988—), Marine Corps League, Amvets, Am. Legion, Alpha Chi. Home: 19 Hickory Hill Ln Framingham MA 01701-6113 also: 3328 Providence Plantation Ln Charlotte NC 28270-3719

OLESON, RAY JEROME, computer service company executive; b. Windom, Minn., June 20, 1944; s. Ray Jerome and Evah Oleson; m. Kathleen Ruth Johnson, July 2, 1966; children: Michelle Dawn, Carrie Elisabeth. BS in Math., Mankato State U., 1966; MS in Applied Stats., Villanova U., 1970. Mgr., dir. Sperry Univac, Egan, Minn., 1966-77; v.p. Computer Scis. Corp., Moorestown, N.J., 1977-84; from v.p. mktg. to pres. Systems and Applied Scis. Corp., Vienna, Va., 1984-87; pres. systems devel. and implementation div. CACI, Inc., Arlington, Va., 1987-90; pres., COO CACI, Inc., Arlington, 1990—. Mem. Armed Forces Electronic and Comm. Assn. (pres. Phila. chpt. 1980-82), River Bend Country Club. Democrat. Lutheran. Avocations: golf, bridge, home computing. Home: 1312 Tulip Poplar Ln Vienna VA 22182-1340 Office: CACI 1100 N Glebe Rd Arlington VA 22201-4798

OLEXY, JEAN SHOFRANKO, English educator; b. Plymouth, Pa., Oct. 23, 1938; d. John Andrew and Elizabeth (Lawrence) Shofranko; m. Joseph P. Olexy Jr., Oct. 29, 1960; children: Lysbeth Olexy Kilcullen, Joseph P. Olexy III, Douglas L. Olexy. BA in English, Wilkes U., Wilkes-Barre, Pa., 1960; MEd in Teaching and Curriculum, Pa. State U., Harrisburg, 1992. Secondary English tchr. Wilkes-Barre (Pa.) City Schs., 1960-61, Brick Township Sch. Dist., Brick Town, N.J., 1964-66, Upper Merion Area Sch. Dist., King of Prussia, Pa., 1968—; lectr., cons. dept. fgn. langs. Safarik U., Slovak Republic, 1992; mem. strategic plan steering com. Ctrl. Montgomery County Area Vocat. Tech. Ctr., Norristown, Pa., 1995-96, bd. dirs., 1996—; curriculum cons. Evang. Lyceum, Slovakia, 1992, Bratislava, 1996—. Mem. Balch Inst. for Ethnic Studies, Phila., 1982-93; mem. N.E. Pa. Slovak Heritage Soc., Wilkes-Barre, Pa., 1982-94; sec. Valley Forge-Exch. Club, King of Prussia, Pa., 1985-89; bd. dirs. Francisvale Home for Smaller Animals, Wayne, Pa., 1987-88. Named Outstanding Educator of Yr. Beta Pi Chpt. Delta Kappa Gamma, King of Prussia, Pa., 1988; Nat. Faculty Acad. fellow Pa. State U., 1993. Mem. NEA, ASCD, Nat. Coun. Tchrs. English, Pa. Edn. Assn., N.E. Pa. Slovak Heritage Soc., Upper Merion Edn. Assn., Delta Kappa Gamma (pres. Beta Pi chpt. 1994-96). Lutheran. Avocations: music, reading, gardening, genealogy research, handcrafts. Home: 382 Maiden Ln Kng Of Prussa PA 19406-1803 Office: Upper Merion Area Sch Dist Crossfield Rd King Of Prussia PA 19406

OLGUIN, VICTOR HUGO, school counselor, educator; b. Mexico City, July 28, 1941; came to U.S., 1967; s. Arnulfo and Columba (Rodriguez) O.; m. Vivian Karen Hogue, Apr. 21, 1967; 1 child, Nikolas Alejandro. Student, North Seattle C.C., 1970-72; BA in Psychology, U. Wash., 1974; MEd in Guidance and Counseling, City U., Bellevue, Wash., 1994. Cert. sch. counselor, Wash. Lang. instr. Berlitz Sch. Langs., Seattle, 1974-75; instr., interpreter, tech. translator Boeing Aircraft Co., Seattle, 1975; human rels. assoc., spl. edn./vocat. edn. tchr., advisor Seattle Sch. Dist., 1975—. Rep. evening students adv. bd. U. Wash., Seattle, 1978. Sgt. Mexican Army, 1960-61. Mem. ACA, APA, NEA, Wash. Edn. Assn., Seattle Edn. Assn., U. Wash. Alumni Assn., City U. Alumni Assn. Avocations: landscaping, athletic equipment design and construction, painting, reading. Office: Seattle Sch Dist 815 4th Ave Seattle WA 98104-1603

OLI, MADAN KUMAR, wildlife ecologist; b. Pokhari, Terathum, Nepal, May 27, 1961; s. Bishnu P. and Laxmi K. (Thapaliya) O.; m. Monika Oli; 1 child, Muna Oli. Diploma in sci., Tribhuvan U., Kathmandu, Nepal, 1983, MS, 1986; MPhil, U. Edinburgh, Scotland, 1992. Field biologist Red Panda Project, WWF-U.S., Nepal, 1987; co-investigator Nar-Phu Valley Project, WWF, Nepal, 1987; rsch. officer Annapurna CA Project, Nepal, 1988-92; prin. investigator Snow Leopard project WWF-U.S., Nepal, 1990-92; rsch. asst. Miss. State U., 1993-95; grad. asst. Auburn (Ala.) U., 1995—; rsch. dir. Wildland Rsch. Nepal program San Francisco State U., 1987. Contbr. articled to sci. jours. Recipient Young Scientist award UNESCO, South and Ctrl. Asia, 1988, 90, Tech. Coop. Tng. award Brit. Coun., Eng., 1989. Mem. Internat. Union for Conservation of Nature and Natural Resources (World Conservation Union, species surival commn., cat specialist group), Am. Soc. Mammalogists, Internat. Assn. Bear Rsch. & Mgmt., Internat. Snow Leopard Trust, Wildlife Soc., Smithsonian Assocs., Wildlife Conservation Soc., Sigma Xi. Home: 900 Linden Apt 6 Auburn AL 36830 Office: Dept Zoology and Wildlife Auburn U Auburn AL 36849-5414

OLIAN, JOANNE CONSTANCE, curator, art historian; b. N.Y.C., d. Richard Edward and Dorothy (Singer) Wahrman; m. Howard Olian; children: Jane Wendy, Patricia Ann. Student, Syracuse U.; BA, Hofstra U., 1969; MA, NYU/Inst. Fine Arts, 1972. Grad. internship Met. Mus., N.Y.C., 1973; asst. curator Mus. of City of N.Y., 1974, curator costume collection, 1975-91; cons. curator Costume Collection, 1992—; lectr. Parsons Sch. Design; vis. lectr. Musée des Arts Decoratifs, Paris, summer 1983, 84, 85. Author: The House of Worth: The Gilded Age, 1860-1918, 1982; editor: Authentic French Fashions of the Twenties, 1990, Everyday Fashions of the Forties, 1992, Children's Fashions from Mode Illustre 1860-1912, 1994; contbr. articles to profl. jours., chpts. to books. Mem. Internat. Council Mus. (costume com.), Costume Soc. Am. (dir. 1976-79, 83-86), Fashion Group (bd. dirs. 1985-86), Centre Internat. d'Etude des Textiles Anciens. Club: Cosmopolitan (N.Y.C.). Home: Shepherds Ln Port Washington NY 11050 Office: Shepherds Ln Sands Point NY 11050

OLIAN, ROBERT MARTIN, lawyer; b. Cleve., June 14, 1953; s. Robert Meade and Doris Isa (Hessing) O.; m. Terri Ellen Ruther, Aug. 10, 1980; children: Andrew Zachary, Alix Michelle, Joshua Brett. AB, Harvard U., 1973, JD, M in Pub. Policy, 1977. Bar: Ill. 1977, U.S. Dist. Ct. (no. dist.) Ill. 1977, U.S. Ct. Appeals (7th cir.) 1983, U.S. Dist. Ct. (no dist. trial bar) Ill. 1992, U.S. Dist. Ct. (we. dist.) Mich. 1994. Assoc. Sidley & Austin, Chgo., 1977-84, ptnr., 1985—. Editor: Illinois Environmental Law Handbook, 1988. Panel atty. Chgo. Vol. Legal Svcs., Chgo., 1983—; mem. regional strategic planning/mktg. com. Alexian Bros. Ill., Inc., Elk Grove, 1985-88; trustee North Shore Congregation Israel, 1990—, sec., 1995—. Mem. ABA, Chgo. Bar Assn., Ill. Assn. Environ. Profls. (bd. dirs. 1984-85), Standard Club, Harvard Club (Chgo.). Jewish. Home: 85 Oakmont Rd Highland Park IL 60035-4111 Office: Sidley & Austin 1 First Nat Plz Chicago IL 60603

OLIANSKY, JOEL, author, director; b. N.Y.C., Oct. 11, 1935; s. Albert and Florence (Shaw) O.; children: Ingrid, Adam. M.F.A., Yale, 1962; B.A., Hofstra U., Hempstead, N.Y., 1959. Playwright-in-residence Yale, 1962-64; co-founder Hartford Stage Co., 1963; writer Universal Studios, 1974—. Author: Shame, Shame on the Johnson Boys!, 1966; writer, dir.: The Competition, 1980, The Silence at Bethany, 1987, Birds, 1988. Recipient Emmy award, 1971, Humanitas prize, 1975, Writers Guild award 1975. *I have, I think, used less than 1 percent of my talent. If I have achieved anything, it is because others have used even less of theirs.*

OLICK, ARTHUR SEYMOUR, lawyer; b. N.Y.C., June 15, 1931; s. Jack and Anita (Babsky) O.; m. Selma Ada Kaufman, June 27, 1954; children: Robert Scott, Karen Leslie. B.A., Yale U., 1952, LL.B., J.D., 1955. Bar: N.Y. 1956. Asst. instr. polit sci. Yale U., New Haven, Conn., 1953-55; instr. polit. sci.-bus. law U. Ga., 1955-57; assoc. atty. Casey, Lane & Mittendorf, N.Y.C., 1957-62; asst. U.S. atty. So. Dist. N.Y., 1962-68; chief civil div., 1965-68; partner Otterbourg, Steindler, Houston & Rosen, N.Y.C., 1968-71, Kreindler, Relkin, Olick & Goldberg, N.Y.C., 1971-74; officer, dir. Anderson, Kill Olick & Oshinsky, P.C. and predecessor firms, N.Y.C., 1974—; ptnr. Anderson, Kill, Olick & Oshinsky and predecessor firms, Washington, 1979—; ptnr. Anderson, Kill, Olick & Oshinsky, Phila., 1990—, Newark, 1991—, San Francisco, 1992—, Phila., 1994—, Phoenix, 1994—, New Haven, Conn., 1994—; lectr. Practicing Law Inst., N.Y.C., 1965—, Bklyn. Bar Assn., Comml. Law League, Nat. Jud. Coll.; lectr., CLE instr. Fordham Law Sch.; candidate N.Y. State Supreme Ct., 1971; counsel Tarrytown (N.Y.) Urban Renewal Agy., 1968-73, 75-77; town atty., Greenburgh, N.Y., 1974; spl. counsel, Town of New Castle, N.Y., 1979—; village atty., Tarrytown, N.Y., 1968-73, 75-77, Dobbs Ferry, N.Y., 1975-77, North Tarrytown, N.Y., 1978-81; dir. Westechester County (N.Y.) Legal Aid Soc., 1976-79. Pres. Hartsdale (N.Y.) Bd. Edn., 1968-72; bd. dirs. Westchester County Mcpl. Planning Fedn., 1976-78, Circle in the Sq. Theater, 1978—; trustee Calhoun Sch., N.Y.C., 1973-80. Served with U.S. Army, 1955-57. Fellow Am. Bankruptcy Coll.; mem. ABA (bus. bankruptcy com., chmn. sect. subcom., ad hoc com. on partnerships in bankruptcy), Am. Bar Found., N.Y. State Bar Assn., Assn. of Bar of City of N.Y. (com. on profl. reposnibility), Fed. Bar Coun., Am. Arbitration Assn. (nat. panel arbitrators), Am. Law Inst., Bklyn. Soc. for Prevention Cruelty to Children (bd. dirs. 1994—), Yale Club, Merchants Club (N.Y.C.), Nat. Lawyers Club (Washington), Rockefeller Ctr. Club, Phi Beta Kappa. Home: 300 E 54th St New York NY 10022-5018 also: Lake Oscawana 7 Wildwood Ln Putnam Valley NY 10579 Office: 1251 Avenue Of The Americas New York NY 10020-1104 also: 2000 Pennsylvania Ave NW Washington DC 20006-1812

OLICK, PHILIP STEWART, lawyer; b. N.Y.C., Oct. 2, 1936; s. Jack and Anita (Babsky) O.; m. Alice D. Chait, Mar. 25, 1961; children: Jonathan A., Jeffrey K., Diana M. B.A., Columbia U., 1957; LL.B., NYU, 1960. Bar: N.Y. 1961, Mo. 1966. Ptnr. Benjamin, Galton, Robbins & Flato, N.Y.C., 1961-65; gen. counsel, v.p., sec. Nat. Bellas Hess, Inc., Kansas City, Mo., 1965-69; dir. Nat. Bellas Hess, Inc., 1970-76; ptnr. Burke & Burke, N.Y.C., 1970-73, Townley & Updike, 1973-89, Moses & Singer, 1989—; bd. arbitrators N.Y. Stock Exch. Bd. dirs. Univ. Glee Club N.Y.C.; bd. dirs.; counsel Found. Interventional Cardiology, Inc., N.Y.C. With AUS, 1960-61. Mem. N.Y. Bar Assn., Assn. of Bar of City of N.Y., Univ. Club (N.Y.C.), Columbia Club. Home: 941 Park Ave New York NY 10028-0318 Office: 1301 Avenue Of The Americas New York NY 10019-6022 also: 4 Rosebud Ln East Quogue NY 11942-3627

OLIENSIS, SHELDON, lawyer; b. Phila., Mar. 19, 1922. AB with honors, U. Pa., 1943; LLB magna cum laude, Harvard U., 1948. Bar: N.Y. State 1949. With Kaye Scholer Fierman Hays & Handler, N.Y.C., 1960—; chair N.Y.C. Conflicts of Interest Bd., 1990—. Pres.: Harvard Law Rev., 1948. Trustee Harvard Law Sch. Assn., 1973-77, 1st v.p., 1980-82, pres., 1982-84, trustee, N.Y.C., 1962-65, v.p., 1972-73, pres., 1978-79; nat. chmn. Harvard Law Sch. Fund, 1973-75; mem. Harvard U. overseers com. to visit law sch., 1981-87; spl. master appellate divsn. 1st dept. N.Y. State Supreme Ct., 1983-89, 91—; bd. dirs. Legal Aid Soc., 1969-88, pres., 1973-75; vice chmn. N.Y.C. Cultural Coun., 1968-75; bd. dirs. Cultural Coun. Found., 1968-88, pres., 1968-72, v.p., 1972-82; bd. dirs. Park Assn. N.Y.C., Inc., 1963-73, exec. com., 1967-73, pres., 1965-67; bd. dirs. Gateway Sch., N.Y.C., 1968-83, chmn. bd. trustees, 1968-70; dir. officer Wiltwyck Sch. for Boys, Inc., 1951-71; bd. dirs. East Harlem Tutorial Program, 1972-80, Fund for Modern Cts., 1979-91, N.Y. Lawyers for Pub. Interest, 1980-85, 91-94; bd. dirs. Vols. of Legal Svc. Inc., 1984—, pres., 1984-87, trustee Lawyers' Com. for Civil Rights Under Law, 1978-91. Fellow Am. Coll. Trial Lawyers; mem. N.Y. State Bar Assn., N.Y. County Lawyers Assn., Assn. of Bar of City of N.Y. (exec. com. 1961-65, v.p. 1974-75, 86-87, pres. 1988-90, chmn. com. state legis. 1959-61, com. revision of constn. and by-laws 1965-66, com. electric power and environ. 1971-74, com. on grievances 1975-78, com. on access to legal svcs. 1982-87, com. on fee disputes and conciliation 1987-89, nominating com. 1991, task force on N.Y. state constn. conv. 1994—). Office: Kaye Scholer Fierman et al 425 Park Ave New York NY 10022-3506

OLIKER, DAVID WILLIAM, healthcare management administrator; b. Elkins, W.Va., Mar. 29, 1948; married; 3 children. BA in Sociology and Anthropology, East Carolina U., 1970; MA in Social Anthropology, Am. U., 1973; Cert. in Healthcare Adminstrn., George Washington U., 1977. Health svcs. specialist United Mine Workers Am. Health and Retirement Funds, 1976-78; health planner Health Sys. Agy. Western Md., Cumberland, 1978-79; ops. mgr. Md.-Individual Practice Assn., Inc., Rockville, 1979-81; project dir. N.Y. Health Maintenance Plan, Inc., N.Y.C., 1981-82; pres., CEO MVP Health Plan, Schenectady, N.Y., 1982—. Mem. APHA, Am. Managed Care and Review Assn., N.Y. State HMO Conf. (bd. dirs.), Nat. Managed Care Inc. (bd. dirs.). Office: MVP Health Plan 111 Liberty St Schenectady NY 12305-1892

OLIKER, VLADIMIR, mathematician, educator; b. Ulianovsk, Russia, Oct. 7, 1945; came to U.S. 1975, naturalized 1980; s. Yosef and Sonia (Bakelman) O.; m. Elena Matis, Mar. 20, 1969; children—Olga, Aviva, Josef Matis. M.S., Leningrad U., Russia, 1967; Ph.D., Leningrad U., 1971. Sr. researcher Hydrometeorological Inst., Leningrad, Russia, 1970-72; group leader Dept. Transportation, 1972-74; vis. prof. Temple U., Phila., 1975-77; assoc. prof. to prof. U. Iowa, Iowa City, 1977-80, 80-84; prof. math. Emory U., Atlanta, 1984—; vis. mem. Math Scis. Research Inst., Berkeley, Calif., 1983; vis. prof. U. Florence, Italy, 1983, Technische U., Berlin, 1982, U. Heidelberg, Fed. Republic Germany, 1981. Contbr. articles to profl. jours. Jewish. Home: 1565 Adelia Pl NE Atlanta GA 30329-3805 Office: Emory U Dept Math and Computer Sci Atlanta GA 30322

OLIN, KEN, actor; b. Evanston, Ill., July 30, 1955; m. Patricia Wettig, 1982; children: Clifford, Roxanne. Student, Putney Sch., Vt.; degree in English Lit., U. Pa.; studies with Warren Robertson, Stella Adler. Actor: (TV movies) Women at West Point, 1979, Flight 90: Disaster on the Potomac, 1984, There Must be a Pony, 1986, Tonight's the Night, 1987, A Stoning in Fulham County, 1988, Goodnight Sweet Wife: A Murder in Boston, 1990, Telling Secrets, 1993, Nothing But the Truth, 1995; (TV series) Bay City Blues, 1983, Hill Street Blues, 1984-85, Falcon Crest, 1985-86, thirtysomething, 1987-91; (films) Ghost Story, 1981, Queen's Logic, 1991; dir. TV films: The Broken Cord, 1992, Doing Time On Maple Drive, 1992, White Fang 2: Myth of the White Wolf, 1994. Avocations: spending time with family, basketball, baseball, distance running, weightlifting. *

OLIN, KENT OLIVER, banker; b. Chgo., July 27, 1930; s. Oliver Arthur and Beatrice Louise (Thompson) O.; m. Marilyn Louise Wood, May 27, 1956. BS in Econs., Ripon Coll., 1955. Dist. sales rep. Speed Queen Corp., Ripon, Wis., 1955-57; v.p. United Bank, Denver, 1957-71; exec. v.p., pres. Bank One Boulder (formerly Affiliated First Nat. Bank), Boulder, Colo., 1971-74; pres., CEO Bank One Colorado Springs, Colorado Springs, 1974-86; pres., CEO Bank One Colo. (formerly Affiliated Bankshares of Colo.), Denver, 1986-91, vice chmn. bd., 1992-94, also bd. dirs. Trustee Colo. Coll., Colorado Springs, 1983-89, Falcon Found., Colorado Springs, 1983—, El Pomar Found., Colorado Springs, 1992—, Colorado Springs Fine Arts Ctr., 1992-95; sec.-treas. Air Force Acad. Found., Colorado Springs, 1988; bd. dirs. Rocky Mountain Arthritis Found., Denver, 1989-94, Goodwill Industries, Colorado Springs, 1994. Staff sgt. USAF, 1950-54. Mem. Broadmoor Golf Club (dir. 1975-88, 93—). Office: El Pomar Found 10 Lake Cir Colorado Springs CO 80906-4201

OLIN, LENA MARIA JONNA, actress; b. Stockholm, Mar. 22, 1955; d. Britta Alice Holmberg; 1 child, August. Actress Royal Dramatic Theatre, Stockholm, Bklyn. Acad. Music; performances include (theater) The Alchemist, Paradisbarnen, Juno and the Peacock, Gross and Klein, Servitore Di Due Padrone, Restoration, King Lear, Nattvarden, Summer, A Dream Play, The Master and Margerita, Miss Julie; (films) The Adventures of Picasso, 1978, Karleken, 1980, Fanny and Alexander, 1982, Grasanklingar, 1982, After the Rehersal, 1984, Friends, 1987, The Unbearable Lightness of Being, 1988, Enemies, A Love Story, 1989, Havana, 1990, Mr. Jones, 1993, Romeo is Bleeding, 1994.

OLIN, ROBERT FLOYD, mathematics educator and reseacher; b. Evanston, Ill., Oct. 8, 1948; s. Floyd Thomas and Anne Elanor (Knutson) O.; m. Linda Renee King, Aug. 23, 1969; children: Kristopher Robert, Susan Michelle. BSc, Ottawa U., 1970; PhD, Ind. U., 1975. Asst. prof. math. Va. Poly. Inst. and State U., Blacksburg, 1975-80, assoc. prof., 1980-87, prof., 1987—, dept. head, 1994—; vis. assoc. prof. Ind. U., Bloomington, 1985; rschr. NSF, 1975-94, grad. chmn., 1993-94; chmn. rsch. commn., 1993-94. Co-author: A Functional Calculus for Subnormal Operators II, 1977, Subnormal Operators, and Representations of Bounded Analytic Functions and Other Uniform Algebras, 1985. Pres. Southwestern Va. Soccer Assn., Blacksburg, 1989-90; tchr. Sunday Sch. Blacksburg Bapt. Ch., 1983—; treas. Margaret Beeks PTA, 1993-95; chmn. steering com. Southeastern Analysis Meeting, 1984—. Named Hon. Faculty Mem., Sichuan U., Chengdu, China, 1988; recipient cert. Math. Edn. Devel. Ctr., Ind. U., Bloomington, 1976. Mem. N.Y. Acad. Scis., Va. Acad. Scis., Am. Math. Soc., Math. Assn. Am., Nat. Coun. Tchrs. Math., Coun. Undergrad Rsch., Am. Assn. Higher Edn., Sigma Xi, Pi Mu Epsilon. Avocations: racquetball, cooking, computers, soccer. Home: 707 Draper Rd SW Blacksburg VA 24060-4654 Office: Va Poly Inst and State U Math Dept Blacksburg VA 24061

OLIN, WILLIAM HAROLD, orthodontist, educator; b. Menominee, Mich., Mar. 7, 1924; s. Harold H. and Lillian (Hallgren) O.; m. Bertha Spitters, May 6, 1950; children—William Harold, Paul Scott, Jon Edward. D.D.S., Marquette U., 1947; M.S., U. Iowa, 1948. Asst. prof. orthodontics Univ. Hosps., U. Iowa, Iowa City, 1948, assoc. prof., 1963-70, prof., 1970-93; prof. emeritus, 1995; chmn. bd. Hills Bank, Iowa. Author: Cleft Lip and Palate Rehabilitation, 1960; contbr. articles on treatment of craniofacial deformities to profl. jours. Served to capt. U.S. Army, 1952-54. Mem. Angle Orthodontic Soc. Midwest (pres. 1982), Midwest Orthodontic Soc. (pres. 1968-69), Iowa Orthodontic Soc. (pres. 1959), Am. Cleft Palate Assn. (pres. 1970), Am. Acad. for Sports Dentistry (bd. dirs., sec./treas. 1989—). Republican. Methodist. Club: Univ. Athletic (bd. dirs.) (Iowa City). Lodge: Rotary (pres. Iowa City). Avocations: coins, antique music boxes, sports, travel, political memorabilia. Home: 426 Mahaska Dr Iowa City IA 52246-1610 Office: University Hospitals Iowa City IA 52242

OLINGER, CARLA D(RAGAN), medical advertising executive; b. Cin., Oct. 8, 1947; d. Carl Edward and Selene Ethel (Neal) Dragan; m. Chauncey Greene Olinger, Jr., May 30, 1981. B.A., Douglass Coll., 1975. Mgr. info. retrieval services Frank J. Corbett, Inc., N.Y.C., 1976-77; editor, proofreader, prodn. asst. Rolf W. Rosenthal, Inc., N.Y.C., 1977-78, copywriter, 1978-80, copy supr., 1980-82, v.p. copy dept., 1982-83; v.p., group copy supr., adminstrv. copy supr. Rolf W. Rosenthal, Inc., div. Ogilvy & Mather, 1984-89, v.p., assoc. creative dir. RWR Advt., 1989; v.p., copy supr. Barnum & Souza, N.Y.C., 1990-92; v.p., copy supr. Botto, Roessner, Horne & Messinger, Ketchum Comm., N.Y.C., 1992-95, Lyons Lavey Nickel Swift, N.Y.C., 1995—. Editor: Antimicrobial Prescribing (Harold Neu), 1979. Mem. Ch. Club N.Y., St. George's Soc. N.Y. Office: Lyons Lavey Nickel Swift 488 Madison Ave New York NY 10022

OLINGER, GLENN SLOCUM, entrepreneur, consultant, investor; b. New Castle, Ind., May 3, 1929; s. Glenn Arthur and Eva Lillian (Slocum) O.; m. Phyllis Lucille Roper, July 6, 1949 (div. Oct. 1981); children: Deborah Sue, Glenn Alan, Craig William, Gwen Gay; m. Diana Sue Hurst, Oct. 2, 1972. B.S., U. Chattanooga, 1952; M.B.A., Northwestern U., 1955. Various sales and gen. mgmt. positions Gen. Electric, Louisville, 1955-75; pres. Speed Queen Corp., Ripon, Wis, 1975-79; gen. mgr. Major Appliance Internat. div. Gen. Electric, Louisville, 1979-82; pres. Kitchen Aid Inc., Troy, Ohio, 1982-87; v.p. Whirlpool Corp., Benton Harbor, Mich., 1986-87; v.p. MII Inc., pres. Lundia Div., 1987-91; pres. Olinger Enterprises, Inc., 1991—. Trustee Ripon Coll., 1976-79; trustee Dayton Art Inst., 1984-85. Served with USN, 1946-49, 52-53. Northwestern U. scholar, 1954. Mem. Am. Mktg. Assn., Am. Mgmt. Assn., Mfrs. Agts. Nat. Assn., Jacksonville C. of C., Mensa, Masons, Rotary. Republican. Presbyterian. Avocations: golf; tennis; travel; reading. Home: 12 Westgate Cir Jacksonville IL 62650-2643 Office: Olinger Enterprises Inc PO Box 947 Jacksonville IL 62651-0947 *Welcome change! Advocate, instigate and implement change. Without change everything dies. And always remember that the law of supply and demand has never been repealed.*

OLINGER, GORDON NORDELL, surgeon; b. Denver, 1942. MD, U. Rochester, 1968. Intern UCLA, 1968-69, resident, 1969-70, 72-74; resident in surgery NIH Clinic, Bethesda, Md., 1970-72; with Milw. County Med. Complex; prof., chmn. Med. Coll. Wis. Mem. ACS, STS, SUS. Office: Acad Faculty 8700 W Wisconsin Ave Milwaukee WI 53226-3512

OLINGER, SHEFF DANIEL, neurologist, educator; b. Olinger, Va., Oct. 23, 1930; s. Sheff Daniel and Ada Sue O.; m. Norma Lanier, June 25, 1953; children: Nancy, Sheff D. III, Amy. BS, Va. Mil. Inst., 1949; MD, U. Va., 1953. Diplomate Am. Bd. Psychiatry and Neurology. Intern Tripler Army Hosp., Honolulu, 1953-54; resident in neurology U. Mich., Ann Arbor, 1956-59, clin. instr., 1958-59; instr. Southwestern Med. Sch., Dallas, 1960-82, assoc. prof. neurology, 1982—; pvt. practice in neurology Dallas, 1959-72; dir. dept. neurology Baylor U. Med. Ctr., Dallas, 1972-90, dir. stroke unit and EEG dept., 1972-90; cons. Presbyn. Hosp., Dallas, 1960—, Parkland Hosp., Dallas, 1960—, Timberlawn Psychiatric Hosp., 1960-90, also U.S. Dept. Labor, Dallas Mil. Entrance Processing Sta. Contbr. articles to profl. jours. Fellow Am. Acad. Neurology; mem. AMA, Tex. Med. Assn., Tex. Neurol. Soc. (founding pres. 1975), Dallas County Med. Soc., Dallas So. Clin. Soc. Home: 3564 Colgate Ave Dallas TX 75225-5009

OLINS, ROBERT ABBOT, communications research executive; b. Cambridge, Mass., Sept. 25, 1942; s. Harry and Janice Olins; m. Irma Westrich, June 16, 1967; 1 son, Matthew Abbott. Student, Hobart Coll., 1961-62, San Francisco Art Inst., 1962; BA, U. Mass., 1967; postgrad., U. Tampa, 1968; MA, U. Mo., 1969, PhD, 1972. With Marsteller, 1972, N.W. Ayer, 1972, Post, Keys & Gardner, Chgo., 1973; with Young & Rubicam, Chgo., 1973-76, mng. dir. communications research div., 1976-77; pres., chief exec. officer, subs. Communications Research Inc., Chgo., 1978—; owner, chmn. Communications Research Inc., 1979—; pres., chief exec. officer Insights, Chgo., 1976—. Contbr. articles to profl. jours. Recipient Chgo./4 award for creative excellence, 1974; overall winner Chgo. Mackinac race, 1981; Am. Assn. Advt. Agys. grantee, 1968-71. Mem. Am. Mktg. Assn., Lake Michigan Yachting Assn., U.S. Yacht Racing Union, Chgo. Yacht Club (chmn. membership, bd. dirs.), Skyline Club. Avocations: skiing, sailing. Office: Communications Rsch Inc 233 E Wacker Dr Apt 2105 Chicago IL 60601-5110

OLIPHANT, BETTY, ballet school director; b. London, Eng., Aug. 5, 1918. Studied classical ballet under Tamara Karsavina and Laurent Novikoff; student, Queen's and St. Mary's Colls.; LLD (hon.), Queen's U., 1978, Brock U., 1978, U. Toronto., 1980; DLitt, York U., 1992. Prin. dancer and arranger Prince & Emile Littler Prodns., London, 1936-46; dance arranger Howard & Wyndham, London, 1936-46; tchr. ballet London, 1936-40; dancer, dance arranger and ballet mistress Blue Pencils Concert Party, Eng., 1944-46; tchr. ballet Oliphant Sch., Toronto, Can., 1948-59; ballet mistress Nat. Ballet of Can., Toronto, 1951-62; prin. and dir. Nat. Ballet Sch., 1959; asso. artistic dir. Nat. Ballet of Can., 1969-75, artistic dir., 1975-89; founder Nat. Ballet Sch., 1991—; founder reorganized Ballet Sch. of Royal Swedish Opera, 1967, Royal Danish Theatre, 1978; mem. jury Internat. Ballet Competition, Moscow, 1977-81, III Internat. Ballet Competition, Jackson, MIss., 1986. Contbr. articles on dance and teaching to profl. publs. Decorated officer Order of Can., 1972, Companion Order of Can., 1985; recipient Centennial medal, 1967, Molson prize, 1978, Diplome d'Honneur Can. Conf. Arts, 1982, Lifetime Achievement award, Toronto Arts Awards Found., 1989, Order of Napoleon, France, 1990, Commemorative medal 125th Anniversary Can., 1992; fellow Ont. Inst. for Studies in Edn., 1985. Fellow Imperial Soc. Tchrs. of Dancing (examiner), Ont. Inst. Studies in Edn., 1985; mem. Can. Dance Tchrs. Assn. (founder, past pres.), Internat. Soc. of Tchrs. of Dancing, Can. Assn. Profl. Dance Orgns. (founding mem.). Office: Nat Ballet Sch, 105 Maitland St, Toronto, ON Canada M4Y 1E4

OLIPHANT, CHARLES ROMIG, physician; b. Waukegan, Ill., Sept. 10, 1917; s. Charles L. and Mary (Goss) R.; student St. Louis U., 1936-40; m. Claire E. Canavan, Nov. 7, 1942; children: James R., Cathy Rose, Mary G., William D. Student, St. Louis U., 1936-40, MD, 1943; postgrad. Naval Med. Sch., 1946. Intern, Nat. Naval Med. Ctr., Bethesda, Md., 1943; pvt. practice medicine and surgery, San Diego, 1947—; pres., CEO Midway Med. Enterprises; former chief staff Balboa Hosp., Doctors Hosp., Cabrillo Med. Ctr.; chief staff emeritus Sharp Cabrillo Hosp.; mem. staff Mercy Hosp., Children's Hosp., Paradise Valley Hosp., Sharp Meml. Hosp.; sec. Sharp Sr. Health Care, S.D.; mem. exec. bd., program chmn. San Diego Power Squadron, 1985-93, 95. Charter mem. Am. Bd. Family Practice. Served with M.C., USN, 1943-47. Recipient Golden Staff award Sharp Cabrillo Hosp. Med. Staff, 1990. Fellow Am. Geriatrics Soc. (emeritus), Am. Acad. Family Practice, Am. Assn. Abdominal Surgeons; mem. AMA, Calif. Med. Assn., Am. Acad. Family Physicians (past pres. San Diego chpt., del. Calif. chpt.), San Diego Med. Soc., Public Health League, Navy League, San Diego Power Squadron (past comdr.), SAR. Clubs: San Diego Yacht, Cameron Highlanders. Home: 4310 Trias St San Diego CA 92103-1127

OLIPHANT, JODIE JENKINS, secondary school consultant; b. Huntsville, Tex., May 1, 1945; d. Lewis George and Mydusta (McGuire) Jenkins; m. Lou Cal Oliphant, Nov. 8, 1963; children: Rosalind, Patrick, Liranda, Ashley. BS, Tex. So. U., 1970; MEd, Prairie View A&M U., 1972. Cert. sch. adminstr. Tchr. bus. Houston Ind. Sch. Dist., 1970-79, sch. counselor, 1979-85, sch. cons., 1985—; chmn., bd. dirs. Oliphant Found., Houston; co-owner FOLKTALES African Am. Bookstore, Austin. Co-author 7th grade typewriting curriculum, 1979. Vol. Voter Registration Campaign, Houston, 1979, 80, 83, United Negro Coll. Fund, 1983, Girl Scouts U.S., Houston, 1986-94, Jesse Jackson for Pres. Campaign, Houston, 1988, Ann Richards for Gov. Campaign, Houston, 1990; del. State Dem. Conv., Houston, 1988; mem. Brentwood Bapt. Ch., Houston, Dowling Mid. Sch. PTA Bd., 1990-91. Recipient Cert. of Appreciation Mayor of Houston, 1979. Mem. Nat. Coun. Negro Women (exec. bd. Dorothy I. Heights sect. 1979-80, Svc. award 1977, Human Rels. award 1979, Community Svc. award 1991), Nat. Women of Achievement (v.p. Galena Pk. Metroplex chpt. 1991, pres. 1995, Golden Apple Ednl. Svc. award 1993), Eta Phi Beta (past. pres. and cons. Xi chpt., exec. bd. 1973—, nat. fin. sec. 1986-90), Alpha Kappa Alpha (exec. bd. Alpha Kappa Omega chpt. 1979-82, 87), Phi Delta Kappa, Top Ladies of Distinction, Inc. Avocations: travel, reading, modeling. Office: Houston Ind Sch Dist 3830 Richmond Ave Houston TX 77027-5864

OLIPHANT, PATRICK, cartoonist; b. Adelaide, Australia, July 24, 1935; came to U.S., 1964; s. Donald K. and Grace L. (Price) O.; children: Laura, Grant, Susan. L.H.D. (hon.), Dartmouth Coll., 1981. Copyboy, press artist Adelaide Advertiser, 1953-55, editorial cartoonist, 1955-64; world tour to study cartooning techniques, 1959; editorial cartoonist Denver Post, 1964-75, Washington Star, 1975-81, L.A. Times Syndicate, 1965-80, Universal Press Syndicate, 1980—; represented by Susan Conway Gallery, Washington. Author: The Oliphant Book, 1969, Four More Years, 1973, An Informal Gathering, 1978, Oliphant! A Cartoon Collection, 1980, The Jellybean Society, 1981, Ban this Book, 1982, But Seriously Folks, 1983, The Year of Living Perilously, 1984, Make My Day, 1985, Between a Rock and a Hard Place, 1986, Up to There in Alligators, 1987, Nothing Basically Wrong, 1988, What Those People Need Is a Puppy, 1989, Fashions for the New World Order, 1991, Just Say No, 1992, Why do I Feel Uneasy?, 1993, Waiting for the Other Shoe to Drop, 1994, Off to the Revolution, 1995. Recipient 2d Place award as funniest cartoonist Internat. Fedn. Free Journalists in Fleet St., London, 1958, Profl. Journalism award Sigma Delta Chi, 1966, Pulitzer prize for editl. cartooning, 1967, Cartoonist of Yr. award Nat. Cartoonist Soc., 1968, 72, Best in Bus. award Washington Journalism Rev., 1985, 87, Premio Satira Politica award Forte de Marmi, 1992, Thomas Nast award, 1992. Office: Universal Press Syndicate 4900 Main St Fl 9 Kansas City MO 64112-2630 also: care Susan Conway Gallery 1214 30th St NW Washington DC 20007-3401

OLITSKI, JULES, artist; b. Snovsk, USSR, Mar. 27, 1922; came to U.S., 1923, naturalized, 1943; s. Jevel and Anna (Zarnitsky) Demikovsky; m. Gladys Katz, 1944 (div. 1951); 1 dau., Eve; m. Andrea Hill Pearce, Jan. 21, 1956 (div. 1974); 1 dau., Lauren; m. Kristina Gorby, Feb. 29, 1980. Student, Academie de la Grande Chaumiere, Paris, 1949-50; BA, NYU, 1952, MA, 1954; postgrad., Beaux Arts Inst., N.Y.C., 1940-42, Nat. Acad. Design, N.Y.C., 1940-42, Ednl. Alliance, N.Y.C., 1947, Zadkine Sch. Sculpture, Paris, 1949. Assoc. prof. art SUNY, New Paltz, N.Y., 1954-55; curator Art Edn. Gallery, NYU, 1955-56; chmn. fine arts div. C.W. Post Coll. L.I. U., Greenvale, N.Y., 1956-63; tchr. Bennington Coll., 1963-67. Exhibited in many one-man shows including Galerie Huit, Paris, 1951, Iolas Gallery, N.Y.C., 1958, French & Co., N.Y.C., 1959-61, Poindexter Gallery, N.Y.C., 1961-68, Bennington (Vt.) Coll., 1962, Kasmin, Ltd., London, 1964-75, 89, Galerie Lawrence, Paris, 1964, David Mirvish Gallery, Toronto, Ont., Can., 1964-78, Nicholas Wilder, L.A., 1966, Corcoran Gallery, Washington, 1967, 74, Am. Pavillion, Venice Biennale Art Exhbn., 1966, 88, Andre Emmerich Gallery, N.Y.C., 1966-95, Zurich, Switzerland, 1973-78, Met. Mus. Art, N.Y.C., 1969, Inst. Contemporary Art, U. Pa., 1968, 86, Lawrence Rubin Gallery, N.Y.C., 1969, 71, 72, 73, Knoedler Contemporary Art, 1973-77, 79, 81, 83, 85, 87, Dart Gallery, Chgo., 1975, FIAL, Paris, 1976, Berlinische Galerie, 1977, Downstairs Gallery, Edmonton, Can., 1980, 82, Janus Gallery, L.A., 1981, Gallery One, Toronto, 1980-90, Yares Gallery, Scottsdale, Ariz., 1986-89, Galerie Wentzel, Hamburg and Cologne, Fed. Republic Germany, 1975, 77, 81, 89, Mus. Fine Arts, Boston, 1973, 77, Whitney Mus. Am. Art, 1973, Galleria Dell'Ariete, Italy, 1974, Corcoran Gallery Art, 1974-76, Waddington Gallery, London, 1975, Galerie Templon, Paris, 1984-85, Hirshhorn Mus., Washington, 1977, Edmonton (Alta., Can.) Art Gallery, 1979, Martha White Gallery, Louisville, 1982, Harcus/Krakow Gallery, Boston, 1978, 81, 82, Harcus Gallery, Boston, 1984, 86, Meredith Long, Houston, 1981, 82, 87, 90, (retrospective) Fondation du Chateau de Jau, Perpignon, France, 1984, La Musee de Valence, France, 1985, Hokin Gallery, Palm Beach, Fla., 1988, Associated Am. Artists, N.Y.C., 1989, (retrospective) Buschlen/Mowatt Gallery, Vancouver, B.C., Can., 1990, Salander-O'Reilly Galleries, N.Y.C., 1990, 92, 94, Gallery Camino Real, Boca Raton, Fla., 1987, 88, 90, 92, 94, 95, 96, Thorne-Sagendorf Art Gallery, Keene, N.H., 1993, Long Fine Arts, N.Y.C., 1994, 95, U. Miami, Coral Gables, Fla., 1994, C.S. Schulte Gallery, Milburn, N.J., 1995; exhibited in many group shows including Carnegie Internat., Pitts., 1961, 1965, Washington Gallery Modern Art, 1963, Los Angeles County Mus., 1964, Fogg Art Mus. Harvard, 1965, Pasadena Art Mus., 1965, Mus. Basel, Switzerland, 1965, 74, Whitney Mus. Am. Art, 1972, 73, Musée d'Art Contemporain, Montreal, 1973, Hirshhorn Mus., 1974, Corcoran Gallery Art, 1975, Everson Mus. Art, Syracuse, N.Y., 1976, Bass Mus., Miami, Am. Embassy, Madrid, 1984, Ft. Worth Art Mus., Mus. Art, Ft. Lauderdale, 1986, Joseloff Gallery, Hartford, Conn., 1994, Galerie Piltzer, Paris, 1994, N.Y. Studio Sch., N.Y., 1996; represented in permanent collections including Mus. Modern Art, N.Y.C., Art Inst. Chgo., Whitney Mus., Corcoran Art Gallery, Nat. Gallery Can., Met. Mus. Art, N.Y.C., Bklyn. Mus., Hirshhorn Mus., Washington, Everson Mus. Art, Syracuse, N.Y., Mus. Fine Arts, Boston, Norman MacKensie Art Gallery, Regina, Can., also pvt. collections; subject book Jules Olitski by Kenworth Moffett, 1981, Nat. Acad. Design, N.Y., 1993. Recipient 2d prize Carnegie Internat. 1961, 1st prize Corcoran Biennial, Washington, 1967, Award for Distinction in the Arts Univ Union, U. S.C., 1975, The Milton and Sally Avery Disting. Professorship, Bard Coll., 1987; named Assoc. Nat. Academician Nat. Acad. of Design, 1993. Fellow AAAS, Nat. Acad. Arts and Scis. Office: PO Box 440 Marlboro VT 05344-0440

OLIVA, LAWRENCE JAY, academic administrator, history educator; b. Walden, N.Y., Sept. 23, 1933; s. Lawrence Joseph and Catherine (Mooney) O.; m. Mary Ellen Nolan, June 3, 1961; children: Lawrence Jay, Edward Nolan. BA, Manhattan Coll., 1955; MA, Syracuse U., 1957, PhD, 1960; postgrad., U. Paris, 1959; DHL (hon.), Manhattan Coll., 1987; LLD (hon.), St. Thomas Aquinas Coll., 1988; DHL (hon.), Hebrew Union Coll., 1992; DLitt, Univ. Coll., Dublin, 1993; PhD, Tel Aviv U., 1994. Prof. history NYU, 1969—, assoc. dean, 1969-70; vice dean N000, 1970-71; dean faculty NYU, 1971-72, dep. vice chancellor, 1970-75, v.p. acad. planning and services, 1975-77, v.p. acad. affairs, 1977-80, provost, exec. v.p. acad. affairs, 1980-83, chancellor, exec. v.p., 1983-91, pres., 1991—. Author: Misalliance: A Study of French Policy in Russia during the Seven Years' War, 1964, Russia in the Era of Peter the Great, 1969; editor: Russia and the West from Peter to Kruschev, 1965, Peter the Great, 1970, Catherine the Great, 1971; contbr. article and revs. to profl. lit. Trustee Inst. Internat. Edn.; active Onassis Found., UN Assn. of N.Y. Adv. Coun., N.Y.C. Partnership, Assn. for Better N.Y., Am. Mus. Immigration; bd. dirs. Chatham House, Royal Inst. Internat. Affairs, Am. Bd. Dirs. Coun. for U.S. and Italy Nat. Collegiate Athletic Assn., Pres.'s Commn., N.Y. State Commn. on Nat. and Cmty. Svc.; adv. bd. U. Athletic Assn., Pres.'s Coun. Fribourg fellow, 1959; recipient Medal of Sorbonne, U. Paris, 1992, Man in Edn. award Italian Welfare League, Ellis Island medal of honor. Mem. Am. Coun. Edn., Assn. Colls. and Univs. of State of N.Y., Irish-Am. Cultural Inst., Soc. Fellows NYU, Phi Beta Kappa, Phi Gamma Delta. Home: 33 Washington Sq W New York NY 10011-9154 Office: NYU 70 Washington Sq S New York NY 10012-1019

OLIVA, TERENCE ANTHONY, marketing educator; b. Rochester, N.Y., Feb. 21, 1943; s. Anthony J. and Teresa (Savasta) O.; children: Mark, Andrea. BA in Math. and Art, St. Mary's Coll., Calif., 1964; MBA with distinction, Fresno State U., 1971; PhD, U. Ala., 1974. Assoc. prof. mgmt. La. State U., Baton Rouge, 1974-82; vis. assoc. mktg. Columbia U., N.Y.C., 1982-83; assoc. prof., mktg. Rutgers U., Newark, 1983-88; vis. assoc. prof. Wharton Sch., U. Pa., Phila., 1985-87, assoc. prof., 1989-90; prof. Temple U., 1990—; mem. editl. bd. Org. Sci., 1993—. Author: Production Mgmt., 1981, editor, 1983; reviewer Behavioral. Sci., 1978—, Jour. Mktg., 1987—, Jour. Consumer Rsch., 1988—; assoc. editor Mgmt. Sci. Dept. Tech., 1989-91; editl. bd. mem. Org. Sci.; contbr. articles to profl. jours. Capt. USAF, 1965-69, Vietnam. Decorated Bronze Star; recipient Andrisani/Frank Undergrad Teaching award. Mem. Am. Mktg. Assn., Inst. for Mgmt. Sci. Avocation: restoring old Victorian homes. Office: Temple U Sch Bus Dept Mktg Philadelphia PA 19122 *Swimming upstream is often very productive. Just be prepared to jump obstacles and have a hard head.*

OLIVE, ALICIA NORMA JOHNSON, retired elementary school educator; b. Phila., Mar. 25, 1922; d. Emmett McCoy and Anna Johnson; m. John Mancheon Olive, Dec. 14, 1942; children: Alicia Carlma and Edna Clarisse. BA, Howard U., 1942; MA, George Washington U., 1977. English and reading tchr. Miller Jr. H.S., Washington, 1961-62, Evans Jr. H.S., Washington, 1962-64, MacFarland Jr. H.S., Washington, 1964-66; English, reading and spl. edn. tchr. Rabaut Jr. H.S., Washington, 1966-76, English tchr., 1981-84, chmn. English dept., 1970-76; curriculum writer Langdon Elem. Sch., Washington, 1976-81; reading tchr. Episcopal Ctr. for Children, Washington, 1987-93; ret., 1993; cons., demonstrator D.C. Pub. Schs. Sys., 1976-84, evaluator of tchr.'s programs, 1976-81. Author handbooks: Meeting Ind. Needs Daily, 1970, Rabaut Reading Bulletins 1-12, 1975; editor curriculum materials; contbr. articles to profl. publs. Vestry mem. St. George's Ch., Washington, 1992—, pres. Parish Guild, 1975, pres. Sunday Sch. Tchrs., 1973, sec./pres. Women of Ch., 1976. Grantee D.C. Pub. Schs. Sys., 1984. Mem. D.C. Tchrs. Retiree Orgn., Internat. Reading Assn., Nat. Coun. English Tchrs., D.C. Coun. English Tchrs. Democrat. Episcopalian. Avocations: writing fiction and educational articles.

OLIVE, DAVID MICHAEL, magazine writer, magazine editor; b. Toronto, Ont., Canada, Nov. 9, 1957; s. Harold Leslie and Alison Linton (Black) O.; m. Margaret Anne O'Reilly, Feb. 13, 1982 (div. June 1992). B of Applied Arts in Journalism, Ryerson Polytech. U., 1979. Copy editor Toronto Life Mag., 1979-81; assoc. editor Can. Bus. Mag., Toronto, 1981-84; sr. writer Report on Bus. Mag., Toronto, 1984-87, Toronto Life Mag., 1988-90; editorial writer The Globe and Mail, Toronto, 1990-91; editor Report on Bus. Mag., 1991—; dir. Can. Ctr. for Ethics and Corp. Policy, 1988-91, Jessie's Ctr. for Teenagers, 1994—; pres. Jessie's Ctr. Non-Profit Homes Corp., 1994—; pres. Nat. Mag. Awards Found., 1988-90. Author: Just Rewards: The Case for Ethical Reform in Business, 1987, White Knights and Poison Pills: A Cynic's Dictionary of Business Jargon, 1990, Political Babble: The 1,000 Dumbest Things Ever Said by Politicians, 1992, Gender Babble: The Dumbest Things Men Ever Said About Women, 1993, Canadian Political Babble: A Cynic's Dictionary of Political Jargon, 1993, More Political Babble: The Dumbest Things Ever Said by Politicians, 1996. Recipient Nat. Mag. awards Silver, 1987, Gold, 1988, Nat. Bus. Writing awards, 1983, 85, Nat. Journalism award, 1983. Mem. Can. Soc. Mag. Editors. Office: The Globe and Mail, 444 Front St W, Toronto, ON Canada M5V 2S9

OLIVEIRA, ELMAR, violinist; b. Waterbury, Conn., June 28, 1950. Student, Hartt Coll. Music, Hartford, Conn., Manhattan Sch. Music; studied with Raphael Bronstein, Ariana Bronne, John Oliveira; MusD (hon.), Manhattan Sch. Music, 1985. Prof. violin Manhattan Sch. Music, N.Y.C., 1990-91; vis. prof. Harper Coll., Binghamton, N.Y.; guest artist Chamber Music Soc. Lincoln Ctr., N.Y.C., 1994-95. Debut with Hartford Symphony Orch.; appeared on nat. TV as soloist with Young People's Concert series of N.Y. Philharmonic; N.Y.C. debut in Town Hall, 1973; appeared in recitals at Alice Tully Hall, 1976, 77; appeared with orchs. of Atlanta, Balt., Chgo., Cin., Cleve., Dallas, Minn., Phila., Pitts., St. Louis, Denver, Portland (Oreg.), also appeared with Nat. Symphony, L.A. Chamber Orch., L.A. Philharmonic Orch., Boston Symphony Orch., Milw. Orch., Ton Halle Orch., Zurich, London Philharmonic Orch., Gewand Haus Orch., Leipzig, Casals Festival Orch., and in Europe, Far East, S. Am.; appeared TV CBS Sunday Morning, Good Morning Am.; appeared with Madeira Bach Festival, 1980; Carnegie Hall debut, 1979; honored by Pres. Carter, 1978; recs. include Elmar Oliveira; cs. for CBS, Angel, EMI, MMG, RCA, Delos, IMP, VOX Unique, Elan. Winner 1st prize G.B. Dealey-Dallas News award, 1975, 1st Naumberg Internat. Violin Competition, 1975, Gold medal in violin Tchaikovsky Internat. Competition, 1978, Avery Fisher prize, 1983. Office: care Shaw Concerts Inc 1900 Broadway 2nd fl New York NY 10023

OLIVEIRA, MARY JOYCE, middle school education educator; b. Oakland, Calif., Feb. 16, 1954; d. Joseph and Vivian (Perry) O. BA, U. Calif., Berkeley, 1978; student, Holy Names Coll., Oakland, 1992; grad. in math., Calif. State U., Hayward, 1994. Cert. tchr., Calif.; cert. single subject math. credential, Hawaii. Recreation specialist Oakland Parks and Recreation, 1977-89; substitute tchr. Diocese of Oakland, 1989-90; tutor Oakland Pub. Schs., 1991; substitute tchr. Alameda (Calif.) Unified Sch. Dist., 1991—, Piedmont (Calif.) Unified Sch. Dist., 1993-96; tchr. summer program Wood Mid. Sch., Alameda, 1993, 96, Chipman Mid. Sch., Alameda, 1994, Encinal H.S., Alameda, 1995; math. tutor Calif. State U., Hayward, 1996—. Creator children's sock toys Oliveira Originals, 1985. Vol. in art therapy oncology ward Children's Hosp., Oakland, 1985; vol. Berkeley Unified Sch. Dist., 1990-91. Mem. Nat. Coun. Tchrs. Math., Calif. Math. Coun., Math. Assn. Am. Avocations: swimming, weight lifting, reading, arts and crafts. Home: 3903 Mera St Oakland CA 94601-4222

OLIVELLA, BARRY JAMES, financial executive; b. Can., 1947. BA, York U., Toronto, Ont., Can., 1968. Chartered acct., Ont. Ptnr. Arthur Young Clarkson Gordon and Woods Gordon (name now Ernst & Young), Toronto, 1968-87; v.p. fin. Bombardier Inc., Montreal, Que., Can., 1987-89, v.p. planning and acquisitions, 1989-93, v.p. acquisitions and strategic alliances, 1993—; bd. dirs. Nova Bus Inc. Pres. Uxbridge (Ont.) C. of C., 1986-87. Mem. Inst. Chartered Accts. Ont. and Can., Nat. Club (Toronto). Office: Bombardier Inc Ste 2900, 800 Rene-Levesque Blvd W, Montreal, PQ Canada H3B 1Y8

OLIVER, ALEXANDER R., management consultant; b. Liverpool, Eng., Jan. 25, 1944; came to U.S., 1968; s. Cecil B. and Eileen F. O.; m. Lorraine S. Cooper, June 14, 1983. BA, Cambridge (Eng.) U., 1965; MBA, Stanford U., 1970. Mktg. cons. The J. Walter Thompson Co. Ltd., London, 1965-68; mgmt. cons. Boston Cons. Group, London and Boston, 1970-74; sr. v.p. M. Lowenstein & Sons Inc., N.Y.C., 1974-78; ptnr. Booz, Allen & Hamilton Inc., N.Y.C., 1980-84; chmn. Oliver, Wyman & Co. Inc., N.Y.C., 1984—. Harkness fellow Commonwealth Fund of N.Y., 1968-70. Home: 1016 5th Ave New York NY 10028-0132 Office: Oliver Wyman & Co 666 5th Ave 16th Floor New York NY 10103-0001*

OLIVER, DANIEL, foundation fellow, lawyer; b. N.Y.C., Apr. 10, 1939; s. Andrew and Ruth (Blake) O.; m. Anna Louise Vietor, Sept. 16, 1967; children: Anna Louise, Andrew II, Daniel Jr., Susan F., Peter A. AB, Harvard U., 1964; LLB, Fordham U., 1967. Bar: N.Y. 1967. Assoc. Hawkins, Delafield & Wood, N.Y.C., 1967-70; editorial asst. Nat. Rev. mag., N.Y.C., 1970-71, exec. editor, 1973-76; assoc. Alexander & Green, N.Y.C., 1971-73, 76-79; pvt. cons., 1980-81; gen. counsel U.S. Dept. Edn., Washington, 1981-83, USDA, Washington, 1983-86; chmn. FTC, Washington, 1986-89; disting. fellow The Heritage Found., Washington, 1989-91, Citizens for a Sound Economy Found., Washington, 1991-93; sr. fellow The Heritage Found., Washington, 1993-96; assoc. Preferred Health Systems, Bethesda, Md., 1996—; coun. Adminstrv. Conf. U.S., 1983-89. Vestryman Christ Ch., Greenwich, Conn. 1972-75, St. Andrews Ch., Edgartown, Mass., 1985-87, Ch. of Ascension and St. Agnes, 1991—. Mem. Federalist Soc. Law Pub. Policy Studies (v.p. 1984, 86), Phila. Soc. (pres. 1991-92), Mont Pelerin Soc. Republican. Office: Preferred Health Systems 7500 Old Georgetown RdSte 900 Bethesda MD 70814*

OLIVER, DIANE FRANCES, publisher, writer; b. N.Y.C., Feb. 7, 1935; m. Ben Martin Oliver, Sept. 3, 1960 (div. 1973). BA, Syracuse U., 1955. Reporter Millinery Rsch. mag., N.Y.C., 1956-58; with N.Y.C. Bur., London Daily Mail and London Daily Sketch, 1964-69; editor The Celebrity Bull., Celebrity Svc. Inc., N.Y.C., 1971-78; pub. The Celebrity Bull., pres., owner Celebrity Svc. Ltd., London, 1978—; former publicist Lake Lucerne (N.Y.) Playhouse, Bklyn. Acad. Music, Statler Hilton Hotel, N.Y.C. Author: Older Woman/Younger Man, 1975; columnist Palm Beach Social Pictorial mag., 1981-85. Avocations: music, ballet, films, theater, travel. Home: 44 Lennox Gardens, London SW1X 0DJ, England Office: Celebrity Svc Ltd, 93/97 Regent St, London W1R 7TA, England

OLIVER, EDWARD CARL, state senator, retired investment executive; b. St. Paul, May 31, 1930; s. Charles Edmund and Esther Marie (Bjugstad) O.; m. Charlotte Severson, Sept. 15, 1956; children—Charles E., Andrew T., Peter A. B.A., U. Minn., 1955. Sales rep. Armstrong Cork Co., N.Y.C., 1955; registered rep. Piper, Jaffray & Hopwood, Mpls., 1958; mgr. Mut. Funds, Inc. subs. Dayton's, Mpls., 1964; mgr. NWNL Mgmt. Corp. subs. Northwestern Nat. Life Ins. Co., Mpls., 1968-72, v.p., 1972-81, pres., dir., 1981-90; mem. Minn. Senate, 1992—; arbitrator, Nat. Assn. Securities Dealers, 1988—; bd. dirs. Minn. World Trade Ctr. Corp. Commr. Great Lakes Commn., 1993—. Served to sgt. USAF, 1951-52. Mem. Internat. Assn. Fin. Planners (past pres. Twin City chpt., mem. nat. governing com.), Psi Upsilon. Presbyterian (elder). Club: Mpls. Athletic. Home: 20230 Cottagewood Rd Deephaven MN 55331-9300 Office: Washington Sq Securities Inc 100 Washington Ave S Ste 1639 Minneapolis MN 55401-2154

OLIVER, ELIZABETH KIMBALL, writer, historian; b. Saginaw, Mich., May 21, 1918; d. Chester Benjamin and Margaret Eva (Allison) Kimball; m. James Arthur Oliver, May 3, 1941 (div. July 1967); children: Patricia Allison, Dexter Kimball. BA, U. Mich., 1940. Tchr. Dexter (Mich.) High Sch., 1940-41; libr. Sherman (Conn.) Libr. Assn., 1966-75; pres. Sherman (Conn.) Libr. Assn., 1983-84; writer, historian, 1976—; reporter Sherman Sentinel, 1965-70; editor newsletter Sherman Hist. Soc., 1977-78; columnist Citizen News, Fairfield County, Conn., 1981-83; guest columnist Mandarin News. Author: History of Staff Wives-AMNH, 1961, Background and History of the Palisades Nature Association, 1964, History and Architecture of Grace United Methodist Church, 1990, Legacy to St. Augustine, 1993. Vol. N.Y. Hist. Soc., N.Y.C., 1961-65; treas. Coburn Cemetery Assn., Sherman, 1976-82; historian Greenbrook-Palisades Nature Assn., Tenafly, N.J., 1962-64, Wesley Manor/Wesley Village Retirement Cmty., 1995—; mem. St. Augustine Hist. Soc., Naromi Land Trust (life), Cedar Key Hist. Soc. Mem. AAUW, Friends of Libr. (life), Inst. Am. Indian Studies, Marjorie Kinnan Rawlings Co. (charter), St. Augustine Woman's Club (cert. of appreciation 1990), Sherman Hist. Soc., Mandarin Hist. Soc. Republican. Congregationalist. Avocations: sacred choral music, research, reading, piano and dulcimer playing, botany. Home: 1500 Bishop Estates Rd Apt 12 B Jacksonville FL 32259-4250 *There are four words which I endeavor to live up to im my work, my personal contacts and every day life. They are the guideposts which I use in all I do: love, courage, integrity and steadfastness.*

OLIVER, EUGENE ALEX, speech and language pathologist; b. East Palatka, Fla., Apr. 18, 1938; s. John T. and Ida (McBride) O.; m. Barbara Ann Gainer, Apr. 20, 1963; 1 child, Zulika Bonita. BA, Fla. A&M Univ., 1962; MA (equiv.), Southern Conn. State Univ., 1983; cert. advanced studies (equiv.), Fairfield Univ., 1989. Cert. speech and language pathology, Conn., lic. speech pathologist, Conn. Speech and lang. pathologist Florence (S.C.) Pub. Schs., 1962-63, Baltimore Pub. Schs., 1963-66, Imperial County Supt.'s Office, El Centro, Calif., 1967-69, Danbury (Conn.) Pub. Schs., 1969-80, Albuquerque Pub. Schs., 1980-81, Monzano H.S., Albuquerque, 1980-81; speech and lang. pathologist & coord. Cuba (N.Mex.) Pub. Schs., 1981-84; speech and lang. pathologist Waterbury (Conn.) Pub. Schs., 1985—; specialist comm. disorders on H.S. level Crosby H.S., Waterbury, 1986—, specialist Wilson Learning Ctr., Waterbury, 1985—. Founding mem. Black Congress, New Milford Conn., 1969; cons. Kwanzaa Celebrations, Conn., 1993; mem. Greater Bridgeport, Conn. chpt. NAACP, 1994—. Recipient Spl. Recognition, speech dept. Waterbury Pub. Sch., 1993, Wilson Learning Ctr., 1991. Mem. NEA, Conn. Speech Lang. Hearing Assn., Conn. Edn. Assn., Waterbury Tchrs. Assn. Avocations: tennis, horseback riding, archery, swimming, writing. Home: 3 Rolling Ridge Rd Monroe CT 06468-2660 Office: Waterbury Pub Schs 236 Grand St Waterbury CT 06702-1930

OLIVER, G(EORGE) BENJAMIN, educational administrator, philosophy educator; b. Mpls., Sept. 17, 1938; s. Clarence P. and Cecile (Worley) O.; m. Paula Rae Foust, Sept. 15, 1963; children: Paul Benjamin, Rebecca Lee. B.A. with honors, U. Tex., 1960; M.Div., Union Theol. Sem., N.Y.C., 1963; M.A., Northwestern U., 1966, Ph.D., 1967. Lectr. Northwestern U., Evanston, Ill., 1966-67; asst. prof. Hobart & William Smith Coll., Geneva, N.Y., 1967-71, chmn. dept. philosphy, 1969-77, assoc. prof., 1971-77; prof., 1977; dean Southwestern U., Georgetown, Tex., 1977-89, provost, 1986-89; pres. Hiram (Ohio) Coll., 1989—; chmn. Coun. of Acad. Deans and V.P.s of Tex., 1987-88. Contbr. articles to profl. jours. Trustee John Cabot Univ., Rome, 1989—, Grand River Acad., Austinburg, Ohio, 1991—, Northeast Ohio Coun. Higher Edn., 1991—, Ohio Found. Ind. Colls., 1989—, Assn. Ind. Colls. and Univ. of Ohio, 1993—, Am. Coun. Edn. Commn. Govtl. Rels., 1994—; chmn., bd. trustees, East Central Coll. Consortium, 1993-95. Rockefeller Found. fellow, 1960-61, Internat. fellow Columbia U., 1962-63; research grantee NEH, 1973-74. Mem. AAUP, Am. Coun. Edn. (mem. commn. on govtl. rels.), Soc. for Values in Higher Edn., Assn. Indep. Coll. and Univ. of Ohio (treas. 1993-94), East Ctrl. Colls. Consortium (chair, bd. trustees, 1993-95), Ohio Found. Ind. Colls. (exec. com. 1994—), Am. Assn. Higher Edn., Interat. Assn. U. Pres. Episcopalian. Office: Hiram Coll Office of Pres Hiram OH 44234

OLIVER, HARRY MAYNARD, JR., retired brokerage house executive; b. Kansas City, Mo., Jan. 21, 1921; s. Harry Maynard and Marie (Curtin) O. BA, Williams Coll., 1943. Pres. M.A. Gesner & Co., Marsh & McLennan Co., Chgo., 1947-88. Chmn. Chgo. Commn. for Sr. Citizens, 1960-69; mem. Chgo. Bd. Edn., 1966-69; pres. Vol. Agys. Chgo., 1956-86; mem. vis. com. Sch. Edn. and div. of social scis., U. Chgo.; pres., bd. dirs. Benton House Settlement, 1953-58; bd. dirs. Adult Edn. Council Greater Chgo., Nat. Fedn. Settlements and Community Centers, 1961-67; trustee Old Peoples Home Chgo., Pub. Sch. Tchrs. Pension and Retirement Fund Chgo., 1966-69, George M. Pullman Ednl. Found., Field Mus. Natural History, 1971-75. Served to lt. (j.g.) USNR, World War II. Mem. Chgo. Club, Racquet Club, Commonwealth Club, Tavern Club, Onwentsia Club (Lake Forest, Ill.), Chi Psi. Home: 1948 N Lincoln Ave Chicago IL 60614-5476 also: PO Box 1319 Big Pine Key FL 33043 also: New Richmond PO Box 100 Fennville MI 49408

OLIVER, JACK ERTLE, geophysicist; b. Massillon, Ohio, Sept. 26, 1923; s. Chester L. and Marie (Ertle) O.; m. Gertrude van der Hoeven, Apr. 16, 1964; children: Cornelia Oliver, Amy Oliver. AB, Columbia U., 1947, MA, 1950, PhD, 1953; DSci (hon.), Hamilton Coll., 1988. Rsch. asst., then rsch. assoc. Columbia, 1947-55, mem. faculty, 1955-73, prof. geology, 1961-71, chmn. dept., 1969-71, adj. prof., 1971-73; Irving Porter Church prof. engring. dept. geol. scis. Cornell U., 1971-93, prof. emeritus, 1993—, chmn. dept., 1971-81; chmn. exec. com. COCORP; terrestrial physicist USAF Cambridge (Mass.) Rsch. Labs., 1951; dir. Inst. for Study of the Continents, 1981-88; cons. AEC, 1969-72, ACDA, 1962-74, USAF Tech. Applications Ctr., 1959-65; mem. Polar Rsch. Com., 1959-71, also nat. commn. uppermantle program, 1963-71; mem. panel solid earth problems NAS, 1962; mem. adv. com. U.S. Coast and Geodetic Survey, 1962-66, on seismology, 1960-72, chmn., 1966-70; mem. Geophysics Rsch. Bd., 1969-70; U.S. coord. 2d U.S.-Japan Earthquake Prediction Conf., Palisades, 1966; earth sci. panel NSF, 1962-65; mem. USAF Sci. Adv. Bd., 1960-63, 64-69; mem. geophysics adv. panel Office Sci. Rsch., USAF, 1961-74, chmn., 1966-68; U.S. del. Test Ban Conf., Geneva, Switzerland, 1958-59; intergovtl. meeting seismology and earthquake engring., mem. exec. com. IASPEI, 1968-71; mem. governing com. Internat. Seismol. Summary Commn., 1963-67, 75-76; mem. exec. com. UNESCO, Paris, France, 1964, U.S.-Japan Earthquake Prediction Conf., Tokyo, 1964; mem. UNESCO Joint Com. on Seismology and Earthquake Engring., 1965-71; chmn. exec. com. Office Earth Scis., NRC, 1976-79, Internat. Seismol. Centre, 1976-78; mem. U.S. Geodynamics Com., 1979-87, chmn., 1984-87; mem. Geol. Scis. Bd., Assembly of Math. and Phys. Scis., NRC, 1981-84; Cabot Disting. vis. scholar U. Houston, 1985-86; commn. on phys. scis., math. and resources NRC, 1987-90, commn. on geoscis., environ. and resources, 1990—. Served with USNR, 1943-46. Recipient Hedberg award Inst. for Study of Earth and Man, So. Meth. U., 1990. Fellow Am. Geophys. Union (pres. seismology sect. 1964-68, Walter H. Bucher medal 1981), Geol. Soc. Am. (coun. 1970-73, v.p. 1986, pres. 1987, Woollard medal 1990), Geol. Soc. London (hon.); mem. AAAS (chmn. geol. geog. sect. 1993), NAS, Seismol. Soc. Am. (pres. 1964-65, bd. dirs. 1961-70, 72-76, Eighth medal 1984), Soc. Exploration Geophysicists (Virgil Kauffman Gold medal 1983), European Union Geoscis. (hon. fgn. fellow), Sigma Xi. Home: 125 Cayuga Park Rd Ithaca NY 14850-1405

OLIVER, JAMES JOHN, lawyer; b. Norristown, Pa., Feb. 18, 1944; s. James Adam and Geraldine M. (Bartlett) O.; m. Judy M. Oliver; children: Justin J., Christine P. BA, St. Mary's U., Halifax, Nova Scotia, 1967; LLB, Dalhousie U., Halifax, Nova Scotia, 1970; postgrad., Harvard U., 1982. Bar: Pa. 1972, U.S. Dist. Ct. Pa. 1973, U.S. Ct. Appeals (3rd cir. 1973). Atty. Nationwide Ins. Co., Phila., 1970-73, Wright, Manning, Kinkead & Oliver, Norristown, Pa., 1974-90; ptnr. Murphy & Oliver, P.C., Norristown, Pa., 1990—. Author/listed in Contemporary Poets of America, 1980, New Voices in American Poetry, 1983. Vice-chmn. East Norristown Bd. Suprs., 1974-79; pres. Am. Cancer Soc., Norristown, 1974-82; chmn. ARC, Norristown, 1975-76; sec., treas. Child Devel. Found., 1974—; bd. advisor Gwynedd Mercy Coll., 1984-86; dir. Montgomery County Higher Edn. Authority, 1993—. Recipient Spl. Recognition award Montgomery County Assn. for Retarded Citizens, 1993, Individual award of Excellence, 1994, Award for Excellence, Am. Cancer Soc., 1994. Mem. Am. Arbitration Assn. (panel of arbitrators), Montgomery County Bar Assn. (mem. ins. com., med. legal com., trial com.), Pa. Bar Assn. (mem. torts com., med. legal com., trial com.), ABA, Pa. Trial Lawyers Assn., Assn. Trial Lawyers of Am., Tail Twisters/Lions Club. Avocations: sailing, hiking. Office: Murphy & Oliver 43 E Marshall St Norristown PA 19401-4818

OLIVER, JOHN PRESTON, chemistry educator, academic administrator; b. Klamath Falls, Oreg., Aug. 7, 1934; s. Robert Preston and Agnes May (McCornack) O.; m. Elizabeth Ann Shaw, Aug. 12, 1956; children: Karen Sue Oliver Vernon, Roy John, Gordon Preston. BA, U. Oreg., 1956; PhD, U. Wash., 1959. Asst. prof. chemistry Wayne State U., Detroit, 1959-64, assoc. prof., 1964-67, prof., 1967—, assoc. dean R&D, Coll. Liberal Arts, 1987-91, acting dean, 1991-92, interim dean Coll. Sci., 1992-93, dep. v.p. for acad. affairs, 1996—; chmn. organizing com. XIV Internat. Conf. on Organometallic Chemistry. Mem. Ferndale (Mich.) Bd. Edn., 1984-88. Mem. Am. Chem. Soc., Detroit sect. Am. Chem. Soc., Sigma Xi. Office: Wayne State Univ Rm 4101 FAB Detroit MI 48202-3489

OLIVER, JOHN THOMASON, JR., commercial bank executive; b. Birmingham, Ala., Apr. 19, 1929; s. John Thomason and Sara (Crumpton) O.; m. Barbara Bankhead, Nov. 4, 1952; children: Melissa, Beth, Rebecca, John III, Will. BS, U. Ala., 1949, LLB, 1952; cert. in banking, La. State U., 1962. V.p. 1st Nat. Bank, Jasper, Ala., 1955-59, pres., CEO, 1959-89, chmn., CEO, 1989-95, chmn., 1995—; pres. Bankhead Found., Jasper, 1987—; bd. dirs., mem. exec. com. Synovus Fin. Corp., 1993—, vice chair 1995—. Pres. Jasper Area C. of C., 1960-67, United Appeal, Jasper, 1961; trustee U. Ala. System, Tuscaloosa, 1971—, pres. pro-tempore bd. trustees, 1985-87; trustee Ala. Dept. Archives and History, Montgomery, 1990—, Walker Coll., Jasper. 1st lt. JAGC, U.S. Army, 1952-54. Episcopalian. Office: First Commercial Bancshares 200 18th St W Jasper AL 35501-5363

OLIVER, JOHN WILLIAM POSEGATE, minister; b. Vincennes, Ind., Apr. 9, 1935; s. Dwight L. and Elizabeth (Posegate) O.; m. Cristina Shepard Hope, Oct. 19, 1968; children: John William Posegate Jr., Sloan Christian Shepard. BA, Wheaton Coll., 1956; BD, Fuller Theol. Sem., 1959; ThM, So. Bapt. Theol. Sem., 1963; DD, Western Sem., 1996. Ordained to ministry Presbyn. Ch. in Am., 1962. Asst. pastor Covenant Presbyn. Ch., Hammond, Ind., 1964-66, Trinity Presbyn. Ch., Montgomery, Ala., 1966-69; pastor 1st Presbyn. Ch., Augusta, Ga., 1969—; moderator Cen. Ga. Presbytery, Presbyn. Ch. in Am., 1976. Founder, trustee Westminster Schs., Augusta, 1972—; chmn. clergy Augusta United Way Campaign, 1974; mem. exec. bd. clergy staff Univ. Hosp., Augusta, 1975-76; mem. bd. commrs. Augusta Housing Authority, vice-chmn., 1976-93; trustee, chmn. bd. Columbia Internat. U., 1978—; mem. ministerial adv. bd. Reformed Theol. Sem., 1978-85, 89-93; bd. dirs. Mission to the World, Presbyn. Ch. in Am., 1984-89, 92-96; dir. Bailey Manor Retirement Ctr., Clinton, S.C., 1992—. Mem. Evang. Theol. Soc., Nassau Club of Princeton, Augusta Country Club. Home: 3205 Huxley Dr Augusta GA 30909-3128 Office: 642 Telfair St Augusta GA 30901-2325

OLIVER, JOSEPH J., consumer products company executive. With R J Reynolds Foods, Winston-Salem, N.C., 1978-79; ceo Ken J. Pezrow Corp., Ramsey, N.J., 1979—. Office: Ken J Pezrow Corp 535 E Crescent Ave Ramsey NJ 07446-1219*

OLIVER, MARY, poet; b. Maple Heights, Ohio, Sept. 10, 1935; d. Edward William and Helen Mary (Vlasak) O. Student, Ohio State U., 1955-56, Vassar Coll., 1956-57. Chmn. writing dept. Fine Arts Work Ctr., Provincetown, 1972-73, mem. writing com., 1984; Banister poet in residence Sweet Briar Coll., 1991-95; William Blackburn vis. prof. creative writing Duke U., 1995; Catharine Osborn Foster prof. Bennington Coll., 1996—. Author: No Voyage and Other Poems, 1963, enlarged edit., 1965, The River Styx, Ohio, 1972, The Night Traveler, 1978, Twelve Moons, 1979, American Primitive, 1983, Dream Work, 1986, House of Light, 1990, new and Selected Poems, 1992, A Poetry Handbook, 1994, White Pine, 1994, Blue Pastures, 1995; contbr. to Yale U. Rev., Kenyon Rev., Poetry, Atlantic, Harvard mag., others. Recipient Shelley Meml. award, 1970, Alice Fay di Castagnola award, 1973; Cleve. Arts prize for lits., 1979; Achievement award Am. Acad. and Inst. Arts and Letters, 1983; Pulitzer prize for poetry, 1984; Christopher award, 1991, L.L. Winship award, 1991, Nat. Book award, 1992; Nat. Endowment fellow, 1972-73; Guggenheim fellow, 1980-81. Mem. PEN, Authors Guild. Home: care Molly Malone Cook Lit Agy PO Box 338 Provincetown MA 02657

OLIVER, MARY LOU, school nurse; b. New Haven, Nov. 29, 1943; d. Ralph F. and Margaret E. (Good) Deucker; m. Bruce L. Oliver, Aug. 28, 1965 (div. Nov. 1989); children: Todd, Colleen. BSN, U. Cin., 1965. RN, Ohio, N.Y. Staff nurse Cleve. Clinic, 1965; staff nurse U. Wash. Hosp., Seattle, 1965-66, asst. head nurse, 1966-68; pub. health nurse Delaware County Pub. Health Dept., Chester, Pa., 1969-70; sch. nurse Shenendehowa Ctrl. Schs., Clifton Park, N.Y., 1980—; mem. mentor program Shenendehowa Ctrl. Schs., 1988—, mem. crisis intervention team, 1989—, mem. shared decision-making team, 1991—; active preceptor program RN/BS program SUNY Utica/Rome, Albany, 1988-94; coord. asthma program Am. Lung Assn., 1990-92; presenter in field. Contbr. Shenendehowa Manual, 1984, 94, The Communicator, 1990, 91. Sch. coord. Shenendehowa PTA, 1978-80; tchr. children's ch., missions chairperson Jonesville Meth. Ch., Clifton Park, 1986—; vol. CAPTAIN, Clifton Park, 1990-92; coordinating mem. Shenendehowa Meth. Singles Group, Clifton Park, 1992—. Recipient PTA Life Membership award Karigon PTSA, 1988, Sch. Nurse of Yr., State of N.Y., 1994. Mem. Nat. Assn. Sch. Nurses, N.Y. State Assn. Sch. Nurses (zone rep. bd. dirs. 1986-94, policy and resolutions chairperson 1994—, conf. chairperson 1994, pres.-elect 1995-96), Capital Zone Sch. Nurse Assn. (coord., newsletter editor 1990—). Methodist. Avocations: country line dancing, rollerblading, cross-country skiing, cross-stitch. Home: 29 Green Meadow Dr Clifton Park NY 12065-1836 Office: Shenendehowa High Sch 970 Rt 146 Clifton Park NY 12065

OLIVER, MARY WILHELMINA, law librarian, educator; b. Cumberland, Md., May 4, 1919; d. John Arlington and Sophia (Lear) O. AB, Western Md. Coll., 1940; BS in Library Sci, Drexel Inst. Tech., 1943; JD, U. N.C., 1951. Bar: N.C. 1951. Asst. circulation librarian N.J. Coll. Women, 1943-45; asst. in law library U. Va., 1945-47; asst. reference, social sci. librarian Drake U., 1947-49; tech. asst. Inst. Govt., U. N.C., Chapel Hill, 1951-52, asst. law librarian, 1952-55, asst. prof. law, law librarian, 1955-59, assoc. prof. law, law librarian, 1959-69, prof. law, law librarian, 1969-84, prof. law and law librarian emeritus, 1984—. Mem. ABA, N.C. Bar Assn., Am. Assn. Law Librs. (pres. 1972-73, Marion Gould Gallagher Disting. Svc. award 1992), Assn. Am. Law Schs. (exec. com. 1979-81), Law Alumni Assn. U. N.C., Order of Coif. Home: 157 Carol Woods Chapel Hill NC 27514 Office: U NC Law Libr Van Hecke Wettach Hall # 064A Chapel Hill NC 27514

OLIVER, ROBERT BRUCE, retired investment company executive; b. Brockton, Mass., Aug. 1, 1931; s. Stanley Thomas and Helen (Sabine) O.; m. Sylvia E. Bell, Feb. 17, 1954; children: Susan Pamela, Robert Bruce. A.B., Harvard U., 1953; postgrad., Bus. Sch., 1971, Boston U. Law Sch., 1955-57; M.A., Mich. State U., 1958. Ret. chmn., pres., chief exec. officer John Hancock Income Securities Trust, Boston, 1989; ret. chmn., pres. chief exec. officer John Hancock Investors Trust, John Hancock Bond Trust, John Hancock Growth Trust, John Hancock Tax Exempt Cash Mgmt. Trust, John Hancock Govt. Securities Trust, John Hancock Tax Exempt Income Trust, John Hancock Cash Mgmt. Trust, John Hancock Spl. Equities Trust, John Hancock Global Trust, John Hancock World Trust, John Hancock High Income Trust, John Hancock Tax Exempt Series Trust; chmn., dir. John Hancock Distbrs.; vice chmn., chief exec. officer John Hancock Advisers, Inc.; chmn., mng. dir. John Hancock Advisers Internat. Ltd. 1st lt. USMCR, 1953-55. Mem. Marine Corps League, Club at Pelican Bay. Home: 6619 Trident Way Naples FL 33963-8243

OLIVER, ROBERT WARNER, economics educator; b. L.A., Oct. 26, 1922; s. Ernest Warner and Elnore May (McConnell) O.; m. Darlene Hubbard, July 1, 1946 (dec. Mar. 1987); children: Lesley Joanne Oliver McClelland, Stewart Warner; m. Jean Tupman Smock, July 15, 1989. AB, U. So. Calif., 1943, AM, 1948; AM, Princeton U., 1950, PhD, 1958. Teaching asst. U. So. Calif., 1946-47; instr. Princeton U., 1947-50, Pomona Coll., L.A., Calif., 1950-52; asst. prof. U. So. Calif., Los Angeles, 1952-56; economist Stanford Research Inst., South Pasadena, Calif., 1956-59; mem. faculty dept. econs. Calif. Inst. Tech., 1959-88, prof. econs., 1973-88, prof. emeritus, 1988—; urban economist World Bank, Washington, 1970-71; cons. Brookings Instn., 1961, OECD, Paris, 1979; vis. prof. U. So. Calif., 1985; vis. scholar Pembrook Coll., Cambridge U., Eng., 1989-90. Author: An Economic Survey of Pasadena, 1959, International Economic Cooperation and the World Bank, 1975, reissued with a new intro, 1996, Bretton Woods: A Retrospective Essay, 1985, Oral History Project: The World Bank, 1986; contbg. author: Ency. of Econs., 1981, 984, George Woods and the World Bank, 1995. Mem. Human Rels. Com. City of Pasadena, 1964-65, Planning Commn., 1972-75, 91-95; bd. dirs. Pasadena City Coun., 1965-69; mem. Utilities Adv. Commn., 1984-88, Strategic Planning Com., 1985; pres. Pasadena Beautiful Found., 1972-74; bd. dirs. Pasadena Minority History Found., 1984—, Jackie Robinson Meml. Found., 1994—, UN Assn., Pasadena chpt., 1996—; trustee Pasadena Hist. Soc., 1992-94. Lt. (j.g.) USN, 1942-46. Social Sci. rsch. fellow London Sch. Econs., 1954-55; Rockefeller Found. fellow, 1974, 91; Danforth assoc., 1981; recipient Outstanding Teaching award, 1982, Master of the Student Houses, 1987; Hon. Alumnus, 1987—. Mem. Am. Econs. Assn., Royal Econs. Assn., Phi Beta Kappa, Phi Kappa Phi, Delta Tau Delta. Democrat. Methodist. Club: Athenaeum. Home: 3197 San Pasqual St Pasadena CA 91107-5330 Office: 1201 E California Blvd Pasadena CA 91125-0001 *The world is so full of beauty, natural and manmade, that human intelligence should seek to comprehend and enjoy it. Observation and reflection which lead to understanding are more important than performance, and the most important performance is service to others. The greatest human virtue is love, which is why family is important. If there be a God, I believe He works His will amongst civilized men through love, and He manifests His works through beauty.*

OLIVER, RONALD, medical technologist; b. New Orleans, July 16, 1949; s. Wilbert and Everlina (Theard) O.; m. Ora Grant, July 12, 1995; children: Nannette Marie, Joseph Byron. Diploma in bus. adminstrn., Meadows-Draughon Coll., New Orleans, 1972; AS in Environ. Health Tech., Delgado C.C., New Orleans, 1976; BS in Biology Edn., So. U., 1980, BS in Chemistry Edn., 1983; MA in Hosp. Adminstrn., Southwest U., La., 1986; PhD in Hosp. Adminstrn., Southwest U., 1987; cert., Charity Hosp. Sch. Nuclear Med, 1986; PhD in Pub. Health, Columbia State U., La., 1992; PhD in Health Adminstrn., Kennedy-Western U., 1993; PhD in Environ. Engring., Kensington U., Glendale, Calif., 1994; PhD in Electrophysiology, Summit U., New Orleans, 1995. Med. technologist, med. technologist supr. Charity Hosp., New Orleans, 1969-93; mem. faculty Pacific Western U., 1993—. Author 6 books, including A Primer in Electrocardiography with Technical and Some Evaluative Values, 1991, 2d edit., 1995; also articles. Author 6 books, including A Primer in Electrocardiography with Technical and Some Evaluative Values, 1991; also articles. Recipient Outstanding Svc. award Charity Hosp., 1972, acknowledgement letter Nobel Found., 1992, cert. of acknowledgement Coll. Am. Pathologists, 1981, Am. Assn. Profl. Cons.; candidate Pulitzer Prize, 1995. Mem. AAUP, Am. Med. Technologists, Am. Coll. Healthcare Execs. (cert. of acknowledgment) , Nat. Soc. for Cardiovascular and Pulmonary Technologists, La. Environ. Health Assn., Profl. and Tech. Cons. Assn., Am. Assn. for Clin. Chemistry (cert. of acknowledgment). Methodist. Achievements include over 30 copyrights in the field of electrophysiology in Library of Congress; patentee in field, 1 reg. U.S. Dept. Commerce. Home: 5131 Bundy Rd Apt K33 New Orleans LA 70127-5319

OLIVER, RUFUS W., III, lawyer; b. Port Sulphur, La., Aug. 13, 1947. BA with high honors, U. Tex., 1969, JD with high honors, 1972. Bar: Tex. 1972. Ptnr. Baker & Botts LLP, Houston. Mem. ABA (chmn. antitrust sect. subcom. fuel and energy inds. 1989), State Bar Tex. (coun. mem. antitrust and bus. litigation sect. 1990—), Houston Bar Assn. (chmn, antitrust and trade regulation sect. 1990-92). Office: Baker & Botts 1 Shell Plz 910 Louisiana St Houston TX 77002*

OLIVER, SAMUEL WILLIAM, JR., lawyer; b. Birmingham, Ala., Apr. 18, 1935; s. Samuel William and Sarah Pugh (Coker) O.; m. Anne Holman Marshall, Aug. 26, 1961; children: Sarah Bradley Oliver Crow, Samuel William III, Margaret Nelson Oliver Little. BS, U. Ala., 1959, JD, 1962. Bar: Ala. 1962, U.S. Dist. Ct. (no. dist.) Ala. 1963. Law clk. Supreme Ct. Ala., Montgomery, 1962-63, U.S. Dist. Ct. (no. dist.) Ala., Birmingham, 1963; assoc. Burr & Forman (formerly Thomas, Taliaferro, Forman, Burr), Birmingham, 1964-65, ptnr., 1966—, also chmn. bus./corp. law sect., 1990-93; dir. Metalplate Galvanizing Inc., Birmingham; mem. panel arbitrators commercial Am. Arbitration Assn., Atlanta and Nashville, 1981—. Chmn. bd. govs. The Relay House, Birmingham, 1985-89; mem. Leadership Birmingham, 1990; mem. adv. bd. Jr. League Birmingham, 1975-77; bd. dirs. Jr. Achievement Greater Birmingham, Inc., 1975—; sr. warden St. Stephen's Episcopal Ch., Birmingham, 1979; mem. diocese coun. Episcopal Diocese Ala., Birmingham, 1981-85; chmn. bd. trustees Highlands Day Sch. Found., Inc., Birmingham, 1980-81; bd. dirs. Ala. Kidney Found., Birmingham, 1990-94. With U.S. Army, 1956-58. Mem. ABA (bus. law sect. 1965—, negotiated acquisitions com. 1990—, task force on joint venture and asset purchase agreements 1994—, sect. internat. law and practice), Internat. Bar Assn. (corp. law sect.), Birmingham Bar Assn., Country Club Birmingham, Summit Club (bd. govs.), Monday Morning Quarterback Club, Rotary Club. Episcopalian. Avocations: fishing, golf, investments.

OLIVER, SANDRA KAY, nursing researcher; b. Orangeburg, S.C., Oct. 20, 1945; d. John Walthall and Miriam (Garrick) O.; m. R. Wayne Matthews, Dec. 28, 1977; children: Joseph Lenear Oliver Matthews, Miriam Elizabeth Oliver Matthews. BSN, U. Tex. Med. Br., 1967; MA, U. Iowa, 1971, PhD, 1981. Cert. CCRN, CNS. Staff nurse U. Iowa Hosp. and Clinic, Iowa City, 1971-81; asst. prof. U. Iowa, Iowa City, 1971-81, U. S.C., Columbia, 1981-82; assoc. prof. S.C. State Coll., Orangeburg, 1983-84, Tex. Woman's U., Dallas, 1984-86; asst. prof. Tex. A&M Health Sci. Ctr., Temple, 1990—; Temple site MSN coord. Tex. A&M at Corpus Christi, 1992—; rsch. assoc. Scott and White Meml. Hosp., Temple, 1986—. Contbr. articles to profl. jours. Pres. Agens Waddson chpt. DAR, Belton, Tex., 1992—; lay leader 1st United Meth. Ch., Temple, 1993—; adult leader Tigertown 4H, Belton, 1987—; dist. commr. Heart of Tex. Coun. Boy Scouts Am., Waco, 1992-94. Mem. Tex. League for Nursing (pres. 1993-95), Tex. Nurses Assn. (govt. affairs com. 1993-95, pres. dist. VII 1991-93), Sigma Theta Tau (Excellence in Rsch. award Epsilon Theta chpt. 1995), Pi Lambda Theta, Phi Delta Kappa. Democrat. United Methodist. Office: Scott and White Meml Hosp 2401 S 31st St Temple TX 76508-0001

OLIVER, STEPHANIE STOKES, magazine editor; b. Seattle; m. Reginald Oliver; 1 child, Anique. BA in Journalism cum laude, Howard U., 1974. Former fashion & beauty merchandising editor Glamour Mag.; editor contemporary living sect. Essence Mag., N.Y.C., 1978-80, sr. editor, 1980-84; West Coast editor Essence Mag., Seattle, 1984-85; editor of mag. Essence Mag., N.Y.C., 1986-94; editor-in-chief Heart & Soul Mag., N.Y.C., 1994—; keynote and panel spkr. Recipient Outstanding Alumnae award Howard U., 1986. Mem. Am. Soc. Mag. Editors (sec. bd. dirs.), Nat. Assn. Black Journalists, Fashion Group Internat., Black Women in Pub., Women's Media Group, Women in Comm., Inc. Office: Heart & Soul 733 3rd Ave Fl 15 New York NY 10017-3204

OLIVER, STEVEN WILES, banker; b. Los Angeles, May 27, 1947; s. Frank Wiles and Hazel Gloria (Patton) O.; m. Susan Elizabeth Peace, Nov. 27, 1971; children: Andrew Wells, Elizabeth Patton, Laura Rice. AB cum laude, Claremont Men's Coll., 1969; JD, Vanderbilt U., 1972. Officer Citibank, N.A., S.E. Asia, 1972-79; mng. dir. Lazard Asia Ltd., Hong Kong, 1980-88, Lazard Freres & Co. Ltd., London, 1988-90; gen. ptnr. Lazard Frères & Co., N.Y.C., 1988-94; mng. dir. Lazard Frères K.K., Tokyo, 1990-95; founding ptnr. Lazard Asia Ltd., Singapore, Singapore, 1995; non-exec. dir. Lazard Bros. & Co. Ltd., London, 1989. Mem. president's coun. The Asia Soc. Mem. Tokyo Lawn Tennis Club, Tokyo Am. Club, Hong Kong Country Club, Penang Club, Leland Country Club. Presbyterian. Office: Lazard Freres & Co 30 Rockefeller Plz New York NY 10020 also: Lazard Asia Ltd. #22-20 UOB Plz II 80 Raffles, Singapore 048624, Singapore

OLIVER, THOMAS K., JR., pediatrician; b. Hobart Mills, Calif., Dec. 21, 1925; married, 1949; two children. MD, Harvard U., 1949. Diplomate Am. Bd. Pediats. Pediats. instr. Med. Coll. Cornell U., N.Y.C., 1953-55; from asst. to assoc. prof. Ohio State U., N.Y.C., 1955-63; from assoc. prof. to prof. pediats. U. Wash., Stockholm, 1963-70; prof. pediats., chmn. dept. Sch. Med. U. Pitts., 1970-87; v.p. Am. Bd. Pediats., 1987—; prof. pediatrics Duke U., U. N.C.; spl. fellow neonatal physiol. Karolinska Inst., Sweden, 1960-61; med. dir. Children's Hosp., Pitts., 1971-78. Cons. editor Monographs Neonatology, 1975—; co-editor Seminars Perinatology, 1975-85. Mem. Soc. Pediat. Rsch., Am. Pediat. Soc., Assn. Am. Med. Colls., Am. Acad. Pediat., Inst. Med. Rsch. *

OLIVER, THORNAL GOODLOE, health care executive; b. Memphis, Aug. 26, 1934; s. John Oliver and Evelyn Doris (Goodloe) Mitchell; m. Pauline Reid, Oct. 1, 1959. B.S., Tenn. State U., Nashville, 1956; M.H.A., Washington U., St. Louis, 1973. Cert. nursing home adminstr., Mo. Asst. dir., King Meml. Hosp., Kansas City, Mo., 1973-75; evening mgr. Truman Med. Ctr., Kansas City, Mo., 1975-77; asst. adminstr. Mid-Am. Radiation Ctr. U. Kans. Coll. Health Sci., Kansas City, Kans., 1977-81; dir. CHS, Inc., Leawood, Kans., 1981-82; adminstr. Poplar Bluff Hosp., Mo., 1982-83; adminstr. The Benjamin F. Lee Health Ctr., Wilberforce, Ohio, 1983-86; asst. clin. prof. Dept. Community Medicine, Wright State U., Dayton, 1986-89; asst. patent adminstr. Munson Army Hosp., Ft. Leavenworth, Kans., 1987—; cons. Urban Health Assocs., Nashville, 1986-87, others. Contbr. articles to profl. jours. Served with U.S. Army, 1957-59, USAR, 1959-63. Fellow Am. Coll. Hosp. Adminstrs.; mem. Am. Hosp. Assn., Nat. Assn. Health Services Execs., Am. Med. Record Assn., Mo. League of Nursing Home Adminstrs. Home: 10641 N Grand Ave Kansas City MO 64155-1655 Office: Munson Army Hosp Fort Leavenworth KS 66027

OLIVER, WILLIAM ALBERT, JR., paleontologist; b. Columbus, Ohio, June 26, 1926; s. William Albert and Mary-Maud (Thompson) O.; m. Johanna L. Kramer, Sept. 1, 1948 (dec.); children: Robert A., James A. B.S., U. Ill., 1948; M.A., Cornell U., 1950, Ph.D., 1952. Instr., then asst. prof. geology Brown U., Providence, 1952-57; research geologist-paleontology U.S. Geol. Survey, Washington, 1957-93, emeritus scientist, 1993—; mem. U.S. Nat. Com. on Geology, 1975-79, chmn., 1978-79; U.S. rep. Internat. Subcommn. on Devonian Stratigraphy, 1973-92; chmn., 1984-89; rsch. assoc. dept. paleobiology U.S. Nat. Mus. Natural History-Smithsonian Instn., Washington, 1993—. Contbr. articles to profl. jours. Fellow AAAS (coun. 1971-73), Geol. Soc. Am.; mem. Paleontol. Soc. (councilor 1964-69, 73-76, editor Jour. 1964-69, pres. 1974-75), Paleontol. Assn. Soc. (London), Palaeontol. Rsch. Inst. (trustee 1976-89, pres. 1984-86, Harris award, 1994), Am. Geol. Inst. (dir. 1974-77, v.p. 1975-76, pres. 1976-77), Internat. Assn. for Study of Fossil Cnidaria (coun. 1971-88, pres. 1983-88), Internat. Palaeontological Assn. (sec. gen. 1984-89). Home: 4203 McCain Ct. Kensington MD 20895-1321 Office: Natural Hist Bldg MRC137 Smithsonian Inst E-305 Washington DC 20560

OLIVER, WILLIAM EDWARD, JR., mental health nurse; b. Providence, Apr. 22, 1945; s. William E. and Lillian E. (Keeling) O.; m. Jane S. Oliver, May 23, 1970; children: Lydia J., Lynnette K. BS in Psychology, Howard U., 1973; AAS in Nursing, U. D.C. cert. substance abuse nurse, behavior modification. Psychiat. technician Sibley Meml. Hosp., Washington, 1965-68; dir. resident svcs. Overbrook Children's Ctr., Falls Church, Va., 1967-68; nursing asst. Psychiat. Inst. Washington, D.C., 1968-72; team leader, counselor Dominion Psychiat. Treatment Ctr., Falls Church, 1974-77; ins. agt. Mut. Life Ins. Co., Washington, 1977-81, United Ins. Co. Am., Washington, 1981-83; RN Leland Meml. Hosp., Washington, 1988-89, Approtech Agy., Washington, 1989, J and E Agy., Washington, 1989—; counselor Comprehensive Alcohol and Drug Abuse Ctr., Washington, 1986-90; psychiat. nurse, team leader St. Elizabeth Hosp., Washington, 1991—; mem. libr. staff, student asst. U. D.C., Washington, 1984-87. With U.S. Army, 1964-67. Mem. D.C. Nurses' Assn., Psy-Chi.

OLIVER, WILLIAM JOHN, pediatrician, educator; b. Blackshear, Ga., Mar. 30, 1925; s. John Wesley and Katherine (Schalwig) O.; m. Marguerite Bertoni, May 28, 1949; children: Ralph Scott, Catherine, Susan. Student, Ga. Southwestern Coll., 1942-43, Mercer U., 1943-44; MD cum laude, U. Mich., 1948. Diplomate Am. Bd. Pediatrics (examiner), Subsplty. Bd. Pediatric Nephrology. Intern, resident U. Mich. Med. Center, 1948-53, dir. pediatric labs., 1959-67; pvt. practice medicine specializing in pediatrics Ann Arbor, Mich., 1953—; instr. dept. pediatrics U. Mich., 1953-56, asst. prof., 1956-61, assoc. prof., 1961-65, prof., 1965, chmn. dept. pediatrics, 1967-79; chief pediatric service Wayne County Hosp., 1958-61; co-chmn. task force on recent advances of coordinating com. on continuing edn. and recertification Am. Bd. Pediats. and Am. Acad. Pediats., 1977-80; mem. task force for pediatric rev. edn. program, 1980-88; mem. com. program for renewal certification in pediat. Am. Bd. Pediat., 1989-91, mem. exam writing com. for cert. pediatric nephrology, 1989—, PRCP pilot test com., 1993—; mem. rev. and question writing com. for pediat. in Rev. Am. Acad. Pediat., 1991—; cons. U. Riyadh, Saudi Arabia, 1980, Rsch. Rev. Com. on Pediat., 1989; ednl. cons. dept. pediat. Stanford U. Hosps., 1991—; mem. self-assessment program for Pediat. in Rev., 1990—; investigator adaptation primative So. Ams. Indians, 1976—, African Pygmies, 1987—. Mem. editl. bd. IRCS Jour. Med. Sci., 1975-90. Pres. Mich. Kidney Disease Found., 1969, Washtenaw County br. Mich. Childrens Aid Soc., 1964; trustee Ann Arbor Hands-On Mus., 1983-88; pres. bd. trustees Perry Nursery Sch., Ann Arbor, 1989-90. With USNR, 1950-52. Fellow Am. Acad. Pediatrics (chmn. com. med. edn. 1974-80, chmn. council on pediatric edn. 1975-80, chmn. task force oversight of pediatric rev. and edn. program 1984-88, Clifford G. Grulee award 1979); mem. Soc. Pediatric Research, Midwest Soc. Pediatric Research (pres. 1968), Am. Soc. Nephrology, Assn. Med. Sch. Pediatric Dept. Chairmen (mem. council 1977-79), Soc. for Exptl. Biology and Medicine, Am. Pediatric Soc., Alpha Omega Alpha, Gamma Sigma Epsilon. Home: 2892 Bay Ridge Dr Ann Arbor MI 48103-1704

OLIVERO, GARY, insurance company executive, financial planner; b. Newark, Oct. 1, 1949; s. Anthony and Anna Maria (Borra) O.; m. Nancilee E. Yannetta, May 25, 1952; children: Jason Matthew, Eric John, Stephanie Anne. Student, U. Mo., 1967-69. ChFC, CLU. Sales rep. METLIFE, Somerville, N.J., 1972-75, sales mgr., 1975-77; tng. mgr. METLIFE, N.Y.C., 1977-79; dist. sales mgr. METLIFE, Rutherford, N.J., 1979-83; territorial dir. annunity mktg. METLIFE, Tampa, Fla., 1991-92; nat. dir. variable products METLIFE, N.Y.C., 1992-94; regional sales mgr. ea. Pa. METLIFE, Allentown, Pa., 1994-95; regional v.p.L.I. METLIFE, Melville, N.Y., 1995—; gen. agt. Life of Va., Tampa, 1983-87; regional dir. recruiting Century 21 Ins. Svcs., Tampa, 1987-91. Author: (tng. guide) Annuity Resource Guide, 1991, (tng. video) Seminar Marketing to Seniors, 1992; co-author: (tng. video) Variable Life Markets, 1991. Councilman Borough of Bound Brook, N.J., 1974-75; county coord. U.S. Senator Frank Lautenberg, Somerset, N.J., 1983; bd. mem. Urban League, Jersey City, 1979-83; advisor campaign funding Tampa Bay Performing Arts, 1984-86; corp. fund raising solicitor United Way, Tampa, 1986-88; com. chmn. troop 11 Boy Scouts Am., Valrico, Fla., 1986-88. With U.S. Army, 1969-72. Named Keyman of Yr. Somerville Jaycees, 1975. Mem. Am. Soc. CLUs, Gen. Agts. Mgrs. Assn. (v.p. 1984-88). Avocations: photography, camping, cooking, racquetball, trap shooting. Home: 2005 Meadow Crest Way Virginia Beach VA 23456-1254 Office: Metlife 135 Pinelawn Rd Ste 220 Melville NY 11747

OLIVER-SIMON, GLORIA CRAIG, human resources manager, advisor, lawyer; b. Chester, Pa., Sept. 19, 1947; d. Jesse Harper and Lavinia Craig

Cuff; m. James Russell Norwood, Sept. 1970 (div.); 1 child, James Russell Jr.; m. Joseph M. Simon, Jan. 1993. BS, U. Md., 1987; JD, Am. U., 1990, MS, 1992. Bar: Pa. 1991, U.S. Ct. Appeals (fed. cir.) 1994. Pers. specialist VA Med. Ctr., Phila., 1974-80; pers./human resources specialist VA Ctrl. Office, Washington, 1980-90, human resources mgr., 1990—; mem. VA Work Group on Minority Initiatives, 1990, 93—; VA coord., rep. Coun. for Excellence in Govts. Spkrs. Bur. Project, 1991-92, Pub. Employees Roundtable for Pub. Svc. Recognition Week, 1991-92; subcom. chair Student Employee Programs, Office of Pers. Mgmt. Work Group, 1993; coord. VA Caring and Courtesy Campaign Focus Group, 1993; mem. VA Veterans Health Adminstrn. Nursing Shortage Task Group, 1987, 93, VA Work Group on the Nat. and Cmty. Svc. Program, 1993-94, 95—, Veterans Health Adminstrn. Healthcare Reform Work Group on Customer Svc., 1993-94; VA's Nat. Com. on Employment of Disabled Vets. and People with Disabilities, 1992—; VA Office Human Resources Mgmt. coord. Pres.'s Com. on Employment of Persons with Disabilities/Dept. of Def. Student Employment Initiative, 1994—; VA Office of Human Resources Mgmt. steering com. 1994—; active mem. Dept. of Energy Student Employment Task Group, 1994—. Mem. ABA, Fed. Bar Assn., Nat. Bar Assn., Fed. Cir. Bar Assn., Phi Delta Phi, U. Md. Alumni Assn. (mentor program), Am. U. Alumni Assn. (Black chpt., alumni admissions com.), AKA Sorority Inc., DAV Aux. (fed. unit 1). Avocations: reading, traveling. Home: 809 Braeburn Dr Fort Washington MD 20744-6022 Office: Dept Vets Affairs 810 Vermont Ave NW Washington DC 20420

OLIVER-WARREN, MARY ELIZABETH, retired library science educator; b. Hamlet, N.C., Feb. 23, 1924; d. Washington and Carolyn Belle (Middlebrooks) Terry; m. David Oliver, 1947 (div. 1971); children: Donald D., Carolyn L.; m. Arthur Warren, Sept. 14, 1990. BS, Bluefield State U., 1948; MS, South Conn. State U., 1958; student, U. Conn., 1977. Cert. tchr., adminstr. and supr., Conn. Media specialist Hartford (Conn.) Pub. Schs., 1952-86; with So. Conn. State U., New Haven, 1972—, asst. prof. Sch. Libr. Sci. and Instructional Tech., 1987-95, ret., 1995; mem. dept. curriculum com. So. Conn. State U., 1987-95, adj. prof., 1995—. Author: My Golden Moments, 1988, The Elementary School Media Center, 1990, Text Book Elementary School Media Center, 1991, I Must Fight Alone, 1991, (textbook) I Must Fight Alone, 1994. Mem. ALA, Conn. Ednl. Media Assn., Black Librs. Network N.J. Inc., Assn. Ret. Tchrs. Conn., Black and Hispanic Consortium, So. Conn. State U. Women's Assn., Cicuso Club (v.p.), Friends Club (v.p.) Delta Kappa Gamma. Avocations: reading, music, piano, walking. Home: 6 Freeman Rd Somerset NJ 08873-2925 Office: So Conn State U 501 Crescent St New Haven CT 06515-1330

OLIVETO, FRANK LOUIS, recreation consultant; b. Bellaire, Ohio, Oct. 9, 1956; s. Donald Albert and Patricia Edna (Pezdriz) O.; m. Ann Marie Mongelli, Mar. 13, 1982; children: Leah Marie, Hannah Emily. BS, Pa. State U., 1980. Intern, then asst. dir. recreation Kiawah Island Resort, Charleston, S.C., 1980; dir. recreation Seabrook Island Resort, Charleston, 1981-85, Innisbrook Resort, Tampa, Fla., 1985-88; pres., owner Recreation Mgmt. Assn., Tampa, 1988—. Contbr. articles to mags. Elder, home group leader In the Name of Jesus World Outreach Ctr., Odessa, Fla., 1989. Mem. Resort and Comml. Recreation Assn. (founding mem., pres. 1983, exec. dir. 1988—), Fla. Recreation and Park Assn., Nat. Recreation and Park Assn. Republican. Avocations: travel, public speaking, racquetball, photography. Home: 6850 Larchmont Ave New Port Richey FL 34653-5921 Office: Recreation Mgmt Assn PO Box 215 New Port Richey FL 34656-0215

OLKERIIL, LORENZA, English educator; b. Koror, Palau, Oct. 10, 1948; d. Ngiratewid and Modekngei Olkeriil; children: Kevin O. Chin, Renee Chin. BA in Elem. Edn., U. Guam, 1982; MA in Instnl. Tech. in Edn., San Jose State U., 1989. Classroom tchr. Ministry of Edn., Koror, 1972-76, 78—, curriculum specialist, 1976-78, edn. trainer, 1988—, coord. bilingual program, 1988—; chair English dept. Palau High Sch.; tng. dir. Peace Corp, Palau, summer 1987; GED instr., Palauan lang. instr. Micronesian Coll., Koror; cons. to pvt. sch., Koror. Speaker Ngiwal State Legis., Koror, 1992; mem. Ngiwal State Constitution, 1983. San Jose State U. fellow, 1987. Mem. Didil Belau (pres. 1992-93), Ngaraboes (treas.-sec. 1980—). Avocations: farming, fishing, softball, weaving, dancing. Home: PO Box 966 Palau PW 96940-0843 Office: PO Box 159 Palau PW 96940-0159

OLKINETZKY, SAM, artist, retired museum director and educator; b. N.Y.C., Nov. 22, 1919; s. Isidor and Jennie O.; m. Sammie Lee Sturdevant, Dec. 20, 1959; children: Jov Shan, Tova Shana. B.A., Bklyn. Coll., 1942; postgrad., Inst. Fine Arts, N.Y. U., 1946-47. Asst. prof. art and humanities Okla. A&M U., Stillwater, 1947-57; vis. asst. prof. art U. Okla., Norman, 1957-58; assoc. prof. art Mus. of Art, 1959—; dir. Mus. Art U. Okla., Norman, 1959-83; vis. prof. art and humanities U. Ark., Fayetteville, 1962-63, 67-68, Langston (Okla.) U., 1969-70; art cons. Kerr-McGee Industries, Inc.; advisor State of Okla. Visual Arts; mem. State Art Collection Com.; Mem. Norman Arts and Humanities Council. One-man exhbns. include Arts Place II, Okla. Art Ctr., Firehouse Art Ctr., Norman, 1989; other exhbns. include Mus. Non-Objective Art, N.Y.C., Mus. Modern Art, N.Y.C.; 50-yr. Retrospective Exhbn., 1942-92, Norick Art Ctr., Oklahoma City, 1992; represented in permanent collections Philbrook Art Ctr., Tulsa, Okla. Art Ctr., Mus. Art. U. Okla. Served with USAAF, 1942-45. Recipient Gov.'s Art award, 1981. Mem. Okla. Museums Assn. (pres. 1978-79), Internat. Council Museums, Mountain-Plains Museums Assn., Am. Assn. Museums, Art Mus. Assn.

OLLEMAN, ROGER DEAN, industry consultant, former metallurgical engineering educator; b. Cornelia, Ga., Nov. 25, 1923; s. Faye Erlando and Esther (Perkins) O.; m. Elizabeth Ann Deutsch, May 24, 1947; children—Esther Jean, Ruth Ellen, Mark Charles. B.S. in Mech. Engring. U. Wash., 1948; M.S. in Metall. Engring, Carnegie Inst. Tech., 1950; Ph.D., U. Pitts., 1955. Group leader Westinghouse Research Labs., Pitts., 1950-55; asst. br. head, dept. metall. research Kaiser Aluminum & Chem. Corp., Spokane, Wash., 1955-59; mem. faculty dept. mech. and metall. engring. Oreg. State U., Corvallis, 1959-76, now courtesy prof.; pres. Accident and Failure Investigations, Inc., 1974—; cons. to industry, also Lawrence Radiation Lab., 1965-66, U.S. Bur. Mines Metallurgy Research Ctr., Albany, 1962-72. Bd. dirs. Benton Assn. Retarded Children. Served with AUS, 1944-46. Recipient Lloyd Carter award outstanding teaching Sch. Engring., Oreg. State U., 1962. Mem. ASTM (Templin award 1953), ASME (past sec. nonferrous subcom. boiler and pressure vessle code), Am. Soc. Engring. Edn., Am. Soc. Metals Internat., Am. Inst. Mining, Metall. and Petroleum Engrs., Sigma Xi, Tau Beta Pi, Pi Tau Sigma. Home: 1005 NW 30th St Corvallis OR 97330-4441

OLLER, WILLIAM MAXWELL, retired energy company executive, retired naval officer; b. Lancaster, Pa., Apr. 7, 1924; s. John Secrist and Mabel Margaret (Coffman) O.; m. Doris Seitz Greenleaf, June 15, 1946; children: Arthur G., J. Richard. BS, U.S. Naval Acad., 1946; MBA, George Washington U., 1960. Commd. ensign U.S. Navy, 1946, advanced through grades to rear adm., 1972; svc. in Samoa, Philippines and Italy; exec. officer Naval Supply Ctr., Newport, R.I., 1966-67, Ships Parts Control Ctr., Mechanicsberg, Pa., 1970-72; comdr. Def. Fuel Supply Ctr., Alexandria, Va., 1972-76; comdg. officer Naval Supply Ctr., Norfolk, Va., 1976-77; gen. mgr. corp. supply and distbn. Champlin Petroleum Co., Houston, 1977-79, Ft. Worth, 1979-81; sr. v.p. Petroleum Ops. and Support Svcs., Inc., New Orleans, 1981-82, pres., 1982-84; spl. asst. to pres., chief exec. officer Kaneb Svcs., Inc., Houston, 1984-85; exec. v.p. Tex. Ea. Products Pipeline Co., Houston, 1986-90; pres. Maxwell Woodworks Inc., Sugar Land, Tex., 1991—. Pres. Am. Leadership Forum, Houston, 1986. Decorated Legion of Merit with gold star, Meritorious Svc. medal with gold star, Joint Svc. Commendation medal. Mem. Sugar Creek Country Club (Sugar Land, Tex.), Army Navy Country Club (Arlington, Va.). Home: 46847 Grissom St Sterling VA 20165

OLLEY, ROBERT EDWARD, economist, educator; b. Vendun, Que., Can., Apr. 16, 1933; s. Edwin Henry and Elizabeth (Reed) O.; m. Shirley Ann Dahl, Jan. 19, 1957; children—Elizabeth Anne, George Steven, Susan Catherine, Maureen Carolyn. B.A., Carleton U., Can., 1960; M.A., Queen's U., Can., 1961, Ph.D. in Econs., 1969. Vis. asst. prof. Queen's U., Kingston, Ont., Can., 1967-68; asst. prof. econs. U. Sask., Saskatoon, Can., 1963-67, 68-69, assoc. prof., 1969-71, 73-75, prof., 1975-93, prof. emeritus, 1993—; pres. Gen. Econs. Ltd., 1993—; dir. rsch. Royal Commn. on Consumer Problems and Inflation, 1967-68; econ. advisor Bell Can., Montreal, Que., 1971-73, 78-79, Can. Telecom. Carriers Assn., 1978-85, Sask. Power Corp., 1980-83; econ. advisor AT&T, 1980-90, Waste Mgmt., Inc., 1990-92, SaskTel, 1989-93; chmn. adv. com. on consumer stds. Stds. Coun. Can., 1992-93; Can. rep. to ISO/COPOLCO, Geneva, 1992-93. Author, editor: Consumer Product Testing, 1979; Consumer Product Testing II, 1981; Consumer Credit in Canada, 1966; Economics of the Public Firm: Regulation, Rates, Costs, Productivity Analysis, 1983, Total Factor Productivity of Canadian Telecommunications, 1984; Consumer Reps. Conf. Procs., 1st-4th, 1982-91. Bd. dirs. Can. Found. for Econ. Edn., 1974-82, Can. Gen. Standards Bd., 1977-81. Recipient Her Magesty The Queen silver Jubilee medal, 1977, Can.'s Jean P Carriere Exptl. Contbr. Vol. Standardization award, 1995. Mem. Royal Econ. History Soc., Royal Econs. Assn., Econ. History Assn., Am. Econ. Assn., Can. Econ. Assn., Consumers Assn. Can. (v.p. 1967-75, chmn. 1975-77), Can. Stds. Assn. (dir., mem. exec. com. 1971-93, vice chmn. 1985-87, chmn. 1987-89, Award of Merit 1995), Consumer's Assn. Found. Can. (v.p. 1989-95), Can. Comms. Rsch. Ctr. (dir. 1992—), Internat. Telecom. Soc. (bd. dirs. 1986—), Shaw Guild. Home and office: PO Box 1040, 374 Queen St, Niagara on the Lake, ON Canada L0S 1J0

OLLINGER, W. JAMES, lawyer; b. Kittanning, Pa., Apr. 5, 1943; s. William James and Margaret Elizabeth (Reid) O.; m. Susan Louise Gerspacher, Oct. 20, 1979; children: Mary Rebecca, David James. BA, Capital U., Columbus, Ohio, 1966; JD, Case Western Res. U., 1968. Bar: Ohio 1968, U.S. Dist. Ct. (no. dist.) Ohio 1971. Ptnr. Baker & Hostetler, Cleve., 1968—; bd. dirs. Parts Assocs., Inc., Cleve., 1975—. Mem. Bentleyville (Ohio) Village Coun., 1990-93. Mem. Wembley Club, Order of Coif, Phi Delta Phi. Office: Baker & Hostetler 3200 Nat City Ctr 1900 E 9th St Cleveland OH 44114-3401

OLLWERTHER, WILLIAM RAYMOND, newspaper editor; b. Neptune, N.J., Jan. 1, 1950; S. William Frederick and Daphne Marie (Hawkins) O.; m. Arlene Judith Newman; children: Geoffrey Vaughan, Alyssa Irene. BA, Princeton U., 1971; MS, Northwestern U., 1972. Reporter Asbury Park (N.J.) Press, 1972-76, bur. chief, 1977-78, night suburban editor, 1979-82, asst. to editor, 1982-84; asst. mng. editor Asbury Park (N. J.) Press, Neptune, 1985-87, exec. editor, 1988—, v.p. news, 1994—; adj. prof. Rutgers U., New Brunswick, N.J., 1988. Editor: The Shore Catch, 1987. Commr. Ocean County Cultural & Heritage Commn., Toms River, N.J., 1977-78. Mem. Am. Soc. Newspaper Editors. Unitarian. Office: Asbury Park Press PO Box 1550 3601 Hwy 66 Neptune NJ 07754-1550

OLMER, LIONEL HERBERT, lawyer; b. New Haven, Nov. 11, 1934; s. Abraham and Gertrude (Jacobs) O.; m. Jody R. Westby, 1992; children from a previous marriage: Stuart A., Sally A. BA, U. Conn., 1956; JD, Am. U., 1963; postgrad., Nat. War Coll., 1972-73. Bar: Conn. 1963, D.C. 1975. Commd. ensign U.S. Navy, advanced through grades to capt., 1977; sea duty and shore assignments in Japan, Philippines, Hawaii, and the Atlantic; staff of chief of naval ops., 1969-72; staff exec. Pres.'s Fgn. Intelligence Adv. Bd., 1973-77; ret., 1977; dir. internat. programs Motorola Corp., Washington, 1977-81; undersec. internat. trade U.S. Dept. Commerce, Washington, 1981-85; ptnr. Paul, Weiss, Rifkind, Wharton & Garrison, Washington, 1985—; bd. dirs. Dresser Industries. Bd. dirs. Internat. Rescue Com., 1980-85. Mem. Conn. Bar Assn., Fed. Bar Assn. Home: 1615 L St NW # 1300 Washington DC 20036-5610 Office: Paul Weiss Rifkind Wharton & Garrison 1615 L St NW Ste 1300 Washington DC 20036-5610*

OLMOS, EDWARD JAMES, actor; b. L.A., Feb. 24, 1947; m. Kaija Keel; m. Lorraine Bracco, Jan. 28, 1994; 2 children. AA in Sociology, East Los Angeles City Coll.; postgrad., Calif. State U., Los Angeles. Performed in exptl. theater, Los Angeles; actor (play) Zoot Suit (Tony nominee, Los Angeles Drama Critics Circle award, Theatre World award), Broadway and Los Angeles, 1978-80; actor, producer film The Ballad of Gregorio Cortez, 1982, Triumph of the Spirit, 1989; actor, co-producer film Stand and Deliver, 1988 (nominee best actor Acad. Awards 1988); actor films Wolfen, 1981, Zoot Suit, 1981, Blade Runner, 1982, (also assoc. prodr., composer, music adapter) The Ballad of Gregorio Cortez, 1983, Saving Grace, 1986 (also prodr.) Stand and Deliver, 1988, Triumph of the Spirit, 1989, Talent for the Game, 1991, (also dir., prodr.) American Me, 1992, A Million to Juan, 1994, My Family, 1995; TV series Miami Vice, 1984-89 (Emmy award for best supporting actor in drama series 1985, Golden Globe award 1986), TV miniseries The Fortunate Pilgrim, 1988, Menendez: A Killing in Beverly Hills, 1994; prodr., dir. TV documentary Lives in Hazard, 1994, The Limbig Region, 1995, (TV miniseries) Dead Man's Walk, 1995, Teh Burning Season, 1995, Mirage, 1995, Slave of Dreams, 1995, Roosters, 1995. Address: Olmos Productions Sunset Gower Studios 1438 N Gower St Box9 Los Angeles CA 90028

OLMSTEAD, CECIL JAY, lawyer; b. Jacksonville, Fla., Oct. 15, 1920; s. Cecil Jay Sr. and Bessie (Irby) O.; m. Frances Hughes; children: Cecil Jay III, Frank Hughes, Jane Olmstead Murphy, Amy Olmstead Vanecek. B.A., U. Ga., 1950, LL.B., 1951; Sterling Grad. fellow, Yale Law Sch., 1951-52; LL.D. (hon.), U. Hull, Eng., 1978. Bar: Ga. 1950, U.S. Supreme Ct 1964, D.C. 1978. Asst. to legal adviser Dept. State, counsel Mut. Security Agy., counsel Hoover Commn. on Orgn. Exec. Br. of Govt., 1952-55; prof. N.Y. U. Sch. Law, 1953-61; dir. Inter-Am. Law Inst., 1958-61, adj. prof. law, 1961-69; atty. Texaco, Inc., N.Y.C., 1961-62; asst. to chmn. bd. Texaco, Inc., 1962-70, v.p., asst. to chmn. bd., 1970, v.p., asst. to pres., 1970-71, v.p., asst. to chief exec. officer, 1971-73, exec. dept., v.p., 1973-80; mem. firm Steptoe & Johnson, Washington, 1980—; Wang Disting. vis. prof. St. Johns U., 1987-90; mem. adv. panel on internat. law to sec. state; adv. com. law of sea State Dept.; also adv. com. transnat. enterprise; U.S. del. UN Com. on Law of Sea, 1972-73; U.S. del. UN Conf. on Law of Sea, 1974-76; Eisenhower lectr. Nat. War Coll., 1973; mem. U.S. del. UN Conf. on Code of Conduct for Trans-nat. Corps., ann. 1984-90; mem. World Bank's panel of conciliatiors of the Internat. Ctr. for Settlement of Investment Disputes, 1988-95; vis. fellow All Souls Coll., Oxford U., 1988; vis. scholar Yale Law Sch., 1990-91. With USAF, 1943-46. Recipient Gold medal City of Brussels (Belgium, 1973, Gold medal City of Paris (France), 1984; named Commdr. Brit. Empire (hon.), 1990. Mem. Internat. Law Assn. (pres. Am. br. 1966-73, pres. 1972-75, vice chmn. exec. council 1975-86, chmn. exec. council, 1986-88, patron 1989), Am. Law Inst. (assoc. reporter Restatement of the Fgn. Relations Law of the U.S., 2d edit. 1964 adviser, 3d edit.), Council on Fgn. Relations, Washington Inst. Fgn. Affairs, Nat. Fgn. Trade Council (dir.), Am. Council on Germany (hon. dir.), Council on Ocean Law (dir.); Phi Beta Kappa. Clubs: Knickerbocker, Yale (N.Y.C.); Fairfield County Hunt (Westport); 1925 F Street, Cosmos (Washington). Home: 4 Sprucewood Ln Westport CT 06880-4021 Office: 1330 Connecticut Ave NW Washington DC 20036-1704

OLMSTEAD, CLARENCE WALTER, JR., lawyer; b. Alexandria, Va., Jan. 24, 1943; s. Clarence Walter and Rhea Nancy (Donnelly) O.; m, Kathleen Frances Heenan, Sept. 7, 1973; children: Nicholas Heenan, Jonathan Heenan, Caitlin Heenan. AB, Stanford U., 1965; LLB, Columbia U., 1968. Bar: N.Y. 1970, U.S. Dist. Ct. (so. and ea. dists.) N.Y. 1970, U.S. Ct. Appeals (2d cir.) 1970, U.S. Supreme Ct. 1986. Law clk. to presiding judge U.S. Dist. Ct. (we. dist.) Wis., 1968-69; assoc. Shearman & Sterling, N.Y.C., 1969-76, ptnr., 1976—. Bd. dirs. West Side Montessori Sch., N.Y.C., 1983-89, pres., 1985-87; mem. sch. com. Cathedral Sch., N.Y.C., 1992—; trustee North Country Sch. Camp Treetops, 1992—. Mem. ABA, N.Y. State Bar Assn., Assn. Bar City of N.Y., Phi Beta Kappa. Home: 470 W End Ave New York NY 10024-4933 Office: Shearman & Sterling 153 E 53rd St New York NY 10022-4602*

OLMSTEAD, FRANCIS HENRY, JR., plastics industry executive; b. Corning, N.Y., June 21, 1938; s. Francis Henry and Josephine (Andolino) O.; BS, Detroit U., 1960; M.S., Purdue U., 1962; postgrad. program for mgmt. devel. Harvard, 1976; m. Mary Helen Nelson, Sept. 2, 1961; children: Kathleen, Ann, John. Foreman, Corning Glass Works, 1962, sect. foreman, 1963-64, dept. foreman, 1965-66, prodn. supt., 1967-69, plant mgr., 1970-71, mgr. mktg., 1972-73, gen. sales and mktg. mgr., 1973-75, bus. mgr. lighting products, 1976-79, bus. mgr. TV products, 1979-80, v.p., gen. mgr. TV products, 1981—, gen. mgr. elec. products div., 1982-83 ; exec. v.p. N.Am. Philips Lighting Corp., Bloomfield, N.J., 1984-86, exec. v.p., gen. mgr., Somerset, N.J., 1986-88; pres., chief operating officer Anchor Advanced Products, Inc., Morristown, Tenn., 1988-90, chmn., pres., chief exec. officer, 1990—; instr. bus. adminstrn. Elmira Coll., 1972-73; vis. lectr. Purdue U., 1973. Mem. exec. bd. Steuben area council Boy Scouts Am., 1975—, v.p. fin., 1977-79, coun. pres., 1979-84, bd. dirs. N.E. region, 1984-88, pres. N.J. Area, 1985-88, pres., bd. dirs. South region Boy Scouts Am., 1988-91, v.p. S.E. region, 1991-93, pres. Southeast region, 1993-95, nat. bd. dirs., 1993—, nat. commr., 1995—; mem. dean's adv. coun. Krannert Sch. Purdue U., Coll. Engring. U. Detroit.; bd. dirs. Knoxville Symphony, 1994—; Served to capt. U.S. Army, 1961-62. Recipient Silver Beaver award, Silver Antelope award, St. George Catholic award, Boy Scouts Am., Disting. Alumni award Purdue U. Mem. ASME, Am. Soc. Plastics Engrs., Am. Brush Mfg. Assn., Cosmetics, Toiletry and Fragrance Assn., Corning C. of C., Krannert Sch. Alumni Assn. Purdue U. (pres.), Corning Country Club, Cherokee Country Club, Tau Beta Pi, Pi Tau Sigma. Republican. Roman Catholic. Home: 7328 Misty Meadow Pl Knoxville TN 37919-7219 Office: Anchor Advanced Products 1111 Northshore Dr NW Ste N-600 Knoxville TN 37919-4005

OLMSTEAD, LAURENCE DANIEL, journalist; b. Bronx, N.Y., July 31, 1957; s. John Napoleon and Miriam Priscilla (Randolph) O.; m. Michele Renee Chandler, May 29, 1983; 1 child, Nyasha Chandler. Student, George Washington U., 1974-78. Reporter Balt. Evening Sun, 1978-80; successively copy editor, asst. city editor, city desk reporter Detroit Free Press, 1980-84, Africa corr., 1985-88, dep. city editor, 1989-90, city editor, 1991—. Recipient citation Overseas Press Club, 1988. Mem. Nat. Assn. Black Journalists (Internat. Reporting award 1986, 88). Avocation: tennis. Office: Detroit Free Press 321 W Lafayette Blvd Detroit MI 48226-2705

OLMSTEAD, MARJORIE ANN, physics educator; b. Glen Ridge, N.J., Aug. 18, 1958; d. Blair E. and Elizabeth (Dempwolf) O. BA in Physics, Swarthmore Coll., 1979; MA in Physics, U. Calif., Berkeley, 1982, PhD, 1985. With rsch. staff Palo Alto (Calif.) Research Ctr. Xerox Corp., 1985-86; asst. prof. physics U. Calif., Berkeley, 1986-90; asst. prof. physics U. Wash., Seattle, 1991-93, assoc. prof., 1993—; prin. investigator materials sci. divsn. Lawrence Berkeley Lab., 1988-93; mem. exec. com. Stanford (Calif.) Synchotron Radiation Lab., 1986-90, chmn., 1988-89; mem. exec. com. Advanced Light Source, Berkeley, 1995—. Contbr. articles to profl. jours. Named Presdl. Young Investigator, Nat. Sci. Found., 1987; recipient Devel. awards IBM, 1986, 87. Peter Mark Memorial award, Am. Vacuum Soc., 1994. Fellow Am. Vacuum Soc. (exec. com. elec. materials divsn. 1994—, Peter Mark Meml. award 1994); mem. Am. Assn. Physics Tchrs., Am. Phys. Soc. (Maria Goeppart-Mayer award 1996), Materials Rsch. Soc., Assn. Women in Sci., Phi Beta Kappa, Sigma Xi. Office: Univ Washington Dept Physics PO Box 351560 Seattle WA 98195-1560

OLMSTEAD, WILLIAM EDWARD, mathematics educator; b. San Antonio, June 2, 1936; s. William Harold and Gwendolyn (Littlefield) O.; m. Adele Cross, Aug. 14, 1957 (div. 1967); children: William Harold, Randell Edward. BS, Rice U., 1959; MS, Northwestern U., 1962, PhD, 1963. Mem. research staff S.W. Research Inst., San Antonio, 1959-60; Sloan Found. postdoctoral fellow Johns Hopkins, 1963-64; prof. applied math. Northwestern U., Evanston, Ill., 1964—, chmn. dept. engring. scis. and applied math., 1991-93; vis. mem. Courant Inst. Math. Scis., NYU, 1967-68; faculty visitor Univ. Coll. London, Eng., 1973, Calif. Inst. Tech., 1987, 90. Contbr. articles to profl. jours. Named Technol. Inst. Tchr. of Yr., 1980; recipient Award for Tchg. Excellence, Northwestern Alumni Assn., 1993; appointed Charles Deering McCormick prof., 1994. Mem. Am. Acad. Mechanics, Am. Math. Soc., Am. Phys. Soc., Soc. Indsl. and Applied Math., Am. Contract Bridge League (silver life master), John Evans Club, Sigma Xi, Tau Beta Pi, Sigma Tau. Episcopalian. Home: 141 Lockerbie Ln Wilmette IL 60091-2947 Office: Northwestern U Dept Engring Scis and Applied Math Evanston IL 60208

OLMSTED, AUDREY JUNE, communications educator; b. Sioux Falls, S.D., June 5, 1940; d. Leslie Thomas and Dorothy Lucille (Else) Perryman; m. Richard Raymond Olmsted; 1 child, Quenby Anne. BA, U. No. Iowa, 1961, MA, 1963; PhD, Ind. U., 1971. Comm. instr. Boston U., 1964-71, acting chair comm., 1972-73, asst. prof. comm., 1971-74; debate coach R.I. Coll., Providence, 1978-92, asst. prof. comm., 1987—, internat. student advisor, 1980—; text editor Prentice-Hall Pub., 1986-88. Recipient Faculty award R.I. Coll. Alumni Assn., 1987. Mem. Nat. Assn. Fgn. Student Advisors, Internat. Comm. Assn. Democrat. Office: RI Coll Dept Comm 600 Mount Pleasant Ave Providence RI 02908-1924

OLMSTED, JERAULD LOCKWOOD, telephone company executive; b. Des Moines, Aug. 26, 1938; s. George Hamden and Virginia (Camp) O.; m. Mary Karen Autenrieth, June 20, 1962 (div. Dec. 1986); children: Scott H., Victoria L., Jerauld; m. Gisele A. Child, June 17, 1988. B.S., Iowa State U., 1961; M.B.A., George Washington U., 1979; Cert. mgmt. accountant. Vice-pres. First Nat. Bank of Washington, 1969; v.p., dir. Intermediate Credit Corp., 1969-73; v.p., dir. Internat. Gen. Industries, Inc., 1974-79, pres., dir., 1980-82; pres., dir. IB Credit Corp., 1982-85, N.Am. Communications, Inc., Bethesda, Md., 1985—; sr. v.p., dir. Internat. Bank, 1978-85. Bd. govs. Iowa State U. Found., 1980—; chmn. corporate adv. bd. div. arts and humanities U. Md., 1982—; sec.-treas. George Olmsted Found., 1970—. Served with U.S. Army, 1961-63. Decorated Knight of Malta, Order of St. John. Mem. Fin. Execs. Inst., Mensa, Soc. Cincinnati, Beta Alpha Psi., Beta Gamma Sigma. Republican. Episcopalian. Clubs: Metropolitan, City, Georgetown (Washington). Home & Office: 7735 Arrowood Ct Bethesda MD 20817-2821

OLMSTED, RONALD DAVID, foundation executive, consultant; b. Portland, Oreg., June 27, 1937; s. Clifford Wolford and Ruth Emily (Driesner) O.; m. Susan Mary Spare, Dec. 27, 1961 (div. June 1972); 1 child, Craig William. Student, Lewis and Clark Coll., 1955-57, U. So. Calif., L.A., 1959-62. V.p., exec. dir. L.A. Ctr. for Internat. Visitors, 1961-67; assoc. dir. devel. U. Chgo., 1967-71; v.p. devel. and pub. affairs Northwestern Meml. Hosp., Chgo., 1971-79; dir. devel. Marimed Found., Honolulu, 1989-93; exec. dir. Alzheimer's Assn., Honolulu, 1995-96; cons. on health, edn. and human svc. orgns., Ill., Mich., Oreg., Hawaii, 1979—; mem. Honolulu Mayor's Com. on People with Disabilities, 1995-96. Contbr. articles on African travels and African affair to profl. pubis. Co-founder, treas. Civil Found. of Chelsea, Mich., 1982-83; treas. Chelsea Area C. of C., 1981-83; trustee Harris Sch., Chgo., 1972-73, Ogden Dunes (Ind.) Town Bd.; bd. dirs. United Way Porter County, Ind., 1969-71; mem. L.A. Com. on Fgn. Rels., 1965-69; bd. dirs. Am. Friends of Africa, 1965-68, Nat. Coun. for Cmty. Svcs. to Internat. Visitors, 1965-67; mem. exec. com. L.A. Mayor's Coun. for Internat. Visitors and Sister Cities, 1964-68; vice chmn. Greater L.A. Com. Internat. Student Svcs., 1966; mem. Honolulu Mayor's Com. on People with Disablities, 1995—. Recipient Koa Anvil award Pub. Rels. Soc. Am.-Honolulu, 1992, multiple awards Assn. Am. Colls., 1975-79, multiple MacEachern awards Am. Acad. Hosp. Pub. Rels., 1974-79, multiple awards Nat. Assn. for Hosp. Devel., 1975-79. Mem. Nat. Soc. Fund Raising Execs. Presbyterian. Avocations: cooking, gardening, sailing, wines. Home and Office: 469 Ena Rd Apt 1506 Honolulu HI 96815-1710

OLNEY, JAMES, English language educator; b. Marathon, Iowa, July 12, 1933; s. Norris G. and Doris B. (Hawk) L.; 1 child, Nathan. B.A., U. Iowa, 1955; M.A., Columbia U., 1958, Ph.D., 1963. Asst. prof. Drake U., Des Moines, 1963-67; Fulbright lectr. Cuttington Coll., Liberia, 1967-69; prof. English N.C. Central U., Durham, 1970-83; Voorhies prof. English La. State U., Baton Rouge, 1983—; vis. prof. Northwestern U., 1974, Amherst Coll., 1978-79. Author: Metaphors of Self, 1972, Tell Me Africa, 1973, the Rhizome & the Flower, 1980, The Language(s) of Poetry, 1993; editor: Autobiography, 1988; editor So. Rev., 1983—. Fellow NEH, 1975-76, Guggenheim Found., 1980-81, Nat. Humanities Ctr., Research Triangle Park, N.C., 1980-81. Mem. MLA (exec. council 1983-87). Home: 1744 Pollard Pky Baton Rouge LA 70808-8854 Office: La State U Southern Review 43 Allen Hall Baton Rouge LA 70803

OLNEY, PETER BUTLER, JR., retired management consulting firm executive; b. N.Y.C., Nov. 29, 1924; s. Peter Butler and Amy (Cruger) O.; m. Elinor Ann Bowman, Sept. 10, 1949; children: Peter B., Ann B., Stephen R. AB, Harvard U., 1949; MA, Boston U., 1951. Cert. mgmt. cons. Credit investigator Shawmut Bank, Boston, 1949-51; tchr. social studies Cohasset (Mass.) Sch., 1951-53; mgmt. trainee Corn Exch. Bank, N.Y.C., 1953-55; job analyst Allied Chem., N.Y.C., 1955-56; pers. adminstr. Avco Corp., Lawrence, Mass., 1956-58; dir. pers. Avco Corp., Cin., 1958-61; dir. human resources United Shoe Corp., Beverly, Mass., 1961-64; mgmt. cons. Frank C.

Brown Co., Boston, 1964-66; founder, pres. of mgmt. cons. corp. Olney Assocs., Inc., Boston, 1966-89. Author: (periodical) Meeting the Challenge of Comparable Worth, 1987. Pres. West Andover PTA, Andover, Mass., 1963; bd. dirs. Unitarian Universalist Ch., Andover, 1964-70, Interfaith Counseling, Andover, 1986-93. Named one of Top 100 Cons. Firms in U.S. by Inst. Mgmt. Cons., 1987. Mem. North Andover Country Club (bd. dirs. 1970-74). Democrat. Avocations: traveling, water color painting. Home: 18 Royal Crest Dr Apt 10 North Andover MA 01845-6454

OLNEY, ROBERT C., diversified products manufacturing executive; b. Bklyn., Aug. 19, 1926; s. Herbert Mason and Martha L. (Otten) O.; m. Wanda G. Olney, July 17, 1948 (dec. 1988); children: Robert C. Jr., Thomas J., Douglas P.; m. Ann Waters Bell, Mar. 14, 1992. BA in Econs., Cornell U., 1946. With Chem. Bank, N.Y.C., 1946-48; various mgmt. positions 3M Co., from 1948; v.p., gen. mgr. 3M-Nat. Adv. Co., Bedford Pk., Ill., 1976-80; chmn., mng. dir. 3M UK plc, Bracknell, Eng., 1980-86; dir. Yale-Valor plc, Chiswick, London, Eng., 1986-91; chmn. Nutone Inc., Cin., 1987-91; bd. dirs. Revere Holdings Inc., Balt., Merton Assocs. Ltd. Mem. Hinsdale (Ill.) Golf Club, Worshipful Co. of Upholders (London), Royal Automobile Club (London). Avocation: skiing. Home: PO Box 223 Montchanin DE 19710 also: Oatlands Park, 32 Lakeside Grange, Weybridge Surrey KT139ZE, England KT139ZE also: PO Box 1764 Avon CO 81620-1764

OLOFSON, ROY LEONARD, retail executive; b. Kenmore, N.Y., Jan. 13, 1939; s. Eric Leonard and Karin (Smith) O.; m. Lillian Dimich, Apr. 28, 1962; children—Eric Leonard, Erin Diane, Roy Andrew. B.S., UCLA, 1965; A.M.P., Harvard U., 1980. C.P.A., Calif. Mgr. Price Waterhouse, Los Angeles, 1965-70; v.p., Carter, Hawley, Hale Stores, Inc., Los Angeles, 1970-82; CEO Fedco, Inc., Santa Fe Springs, Calif., 1982—; pres., dir. Fedco Credit Corp., Santa Fe Springs, 1983—. Served with USMC, 1956-59. Mem. Am. Inst. C.P.A.s, Calif. Soc. C.P.A.s. Clubs: Jonathan (Los Angeles), Los Angeles Athletic. Office: Federal Employees Distrg Co 9300 Santa Fe Springs Rd Santa Fe Springs CA 90670-2621

OLOFSON, TOM WILLIAM, electronics executive; b. Oak Park, Ill., Oct. 10, 1941; s. Ragnar V. and Ingrid E. Olofson; BBA, U. Pitts., 1963; m. Jeanne Hamilton, Aug. 20, 1960; children: Christopher, Scott. Various mgmt. positions Bell Telephone Co. of Pa., Pitts., 1963-67; sales mgr. Xerox Corp., Detroit, 1967-68, nat. account mgr., Rochester, N.Y., 1968, mgr. govt. planning, Rochester, 1969, mgr. Kansas City (Mo.) br., 1969-74; corp. v.p. health products group Marion Labs., Inc., Kansas City, Mo., 1974-78, sr. v.p., mem. Office Pres., 1978-80; exec. v.p., dir. Electronic Realty Assocs., Inc., 1980-83; chmn. bd., CEO Emblem Graphic Systems, Inc., 1983-88, Electronic Processing, Inc., 1988—; dir. DemoGraFX, Wordenglass & Electricity, Inc., Elinco Internat., Access Industries, Inc., Saztec Internat., Capital Ptnrs. Bd. visitors U. Pitts. Joseph M. Katz Grad. Sch. Bus.; past trustee Barstow Sch.; past chmn. bd. trustees Village United Presbyn. Ch.; bd. dirs. Mid. Am. Immunotherapy and Surg. Research Found., Inc. Mem. Omicron Delta Kappa, Sigma Chi. Republican. Presbyterian. Club: Kansas City. Office: Electronic Processing Inc 501 Kansas Ave Kansas City KS 66105-1309

O'LOUGHLIN, JOHN KIRBY, retired insurance executive; b. Bklyn., Mar. 31, 1929; s. John Francis and Anne (Kirby) O'L.; m. Janet R. Tag, July 5, 1952; children: Robert K., Steven M., Patricia A., John A. BA in Econs., St. Lawrence U., Canton, N.Y., 1951. State agt. Royal Globe Ins. Group, 1953-58; with Allstate Ins. Co., 1958—, mktg. v.p., group v.p., then exec. v.p., 1972—; pres. Allstate Life Ins. Co., 1977—; chmn. bd. Allstate Ins. Co. and Life Co. Can., 1976—, sr. exec. v.p., chief planning officer, 1980-90; ret.; bd. dirs. all cos. in Allstate Ins. Group and Allstate Enterprises, Inc.; former pres. Allstate Enterprises, Inc.; pres., CEO JKO Cons. Ltd., Lake Forest, Ill., Royal Links Ventures Ltd. Trustee St. Lawrence U., U.S. MArine Staff and Command Coll. Found. Bd.; bd. dirs. Marine Corps Assn., Am. Ireland Fund, USMC Scholarship Found. Inc., Coun. on Ind. Colls.; past chmn. No. Suburban Chgo. United Way; elder 1st United Presbyn. Ch., Lake Forest, Ill. Capt. USMCR, 1951-53. Mem. Sales and Mktg. Execs. Internat. (bd. dirs., past chmn., pres.), Marine Corps Assn. (bd. dirs.), Met. Club (Chgo.), Knollwood Club, Whispering Woods Golf Club, Pinehurst Country Club, Lahinch Club, Country Club of N.C. Office: JKO Cons Ltd 133 E Laurel Ave Lake Forest IL 60045-1205

OLPIN, OWEN, lawyer; b. July 10, 1934; m. Jan Cummings. BS with honors, Brigham Young U., 1955; JD, Columbia U., 1958. Bar: U.S. Supreme Ct. 1973. Assoc. O'Melveny & Myers, Los Angeles, 1958-66, ptnr., 1966-69, 76—, now consulting counsel; adj. prof. Loyola U., Los Angeles, 1967-69; prof. law U. Utah, Salt Lake City, 1970-76, Farr presdl. endowed chair, 1973-76; Baker vis. prof. law U. Tex., Austin, 1969-70; lectr. in field. Contbr. articles to profl. jours. Bd. dirs. Environ. Law Inst., Sierra Club Legal Def. Fund; sr. conf. fellow Adminstrv. Conf. U.S., past pub. mem., past chmn. com. interagy. coordination. Mem. ABA (adminstrv. law and natural resources sects., coun. adminstrv. law sect.), Calif. Bar Assn., D.C. Bar Assn., L.A. County Bar Assn., Am. Law Inst. Office: O'Melveny & Myers 400 S Hope St Los Angeles CA 90071-2801*

OLPIN, ROBERT SPENCER, art history educator; b. Palo Alto, Calif., Aug. 30, 1940; s. Ralph Smith and Ethel Lucille (Harman) O.; m. Mary Florence Catharine Reynolds, Aug. 24, 1963; children: Mary Courtney, Cristin Lee, Catharine Elizabeth, Carrie Jean. BS, U. Utah, 1963; AM, Boston U., 1965, PhD, 1971. Lectr. art history Boston U., 1965-67; asst. prof. U. Utah, Salt Lake City, 1967-72, assoc. prof., 1972-76, prof., 1976—, chmn. dept., 1975-82, dir. art history program, 1968-76, 83-84, dean Coll. Fine Arts, 1987—; cons. curator Am. and English art Utah Mus. Fine Arts, 1973—. Grantee U. Utah, 1972, 85, Utah Mus. Fine Arts, 1975, Utah Bicentennial Commn., 1975, Ford Found., 1975, Utah Endowment for Humanities, 1984, 85, Quinney Found., 1986, U. Utah, 1987, State Utah, 1989, Christensen Found., 1993, Eccles Found, 1994, 95; trustee Pioneer State Theatre Found., 1988—; vice chair Utah Arts Coun., 1993-95, chair, 1995—, Utah Sci. Ctr. Authority, 1995—. Mem. NASULGC (commn. on the arts, 1989-93), Utah Arts Coun., Utah Sci. Authority, Archives Am. Art Smithsonian Instn., Coll. Art Assn. Am., Utah Acad. Scis. Arts Letters, Assn. Historians Am. Art, Internat. Coun. Fine Arts Deans, Phi Kappa Phi, Sigma Nu. Republican. Mormon. Author: Alexander Helwig Wyant, 1836-92, 1968, Mainstreams/Reflections-American/Utah Architecture, 1973, American Painting Around 1850, 1976, Art-Life of Utah, 1977, Dictionary of Utah Art, 1980, A Retrospective of Utah Art, 1981, Waldo Midgley: Birds, Animals, People, Things, 1984, A Basket of Chips, 1985, The Works of Alexander Helwig Wyant, 1986, Salt Lake County Fine Arts Collection, 1987, Signs and Symbols...Utah Art, 1988, J.A.F. Everett, 1989, George Dibble, 1989, Utah Art, 1991; contbd. articles to profl. jours. including Utah, State of the Arts, 1993, Utah History Ency., 1994, Garland's Dutch Art Ency., 1996, Macmillan's Dictionary of Art, 1996. Home: 887 Woodshire Ave Salt Lake City UT 84107-7639 Office: U Utah Coll Fine Arts 250 Art & Architecture Ctr Salt Lake City UT 84112 *Personal philosophy: Not to reduce what I think about life to a motto.*

OLSCAMP, PAUL JAMES, academic administrator; b. Montreal, Que., Can., Aug. 29, 1937; s. James J. and Luella M. (Brush) O.; m. Ruth I. Pratt, Dec. 2, 1978; children by previous marriage: Rebecca Ann, Adam James. BA, U. Western Ont., 1958, MA, 1960; PhD, U. Rochester, 1962. Instr. Ohio State U., Columbus, 1962, asst. prof., 1963-66, assoc. prof., 1966-69, assoc. dean humanities, 1969; dean faculties, prof. philosophy Roosevelt U., Chgo., 1970-71, v.p. acad. affairs, 1971-72; prof. philosophy Syracuse (N.Y.) U., 1972-75, exec. asst. to chancellor, 1972, vice chancellor student programs, 1972-75; pres. Western Wash. U., Bellingham, 1975-82, Bowling Green (Ohio) State U., 1982—; Grad. fellow in humanities U. Western Ont., 1959. Author: Descartes: The Discourse, Optics, Geometry and Meteorology, 1965, The Moral Philosophy of George Berkeley, 1970, An Introduction to Philosophy, 1971, Malebranche: The Search After Truth, 1980; contbr. articles to profl. jours. Mem. Nat. Coun. on the Humanities, 1988-92, NCAA Pres.'s Commn., 1989-91; bd. dirs., treas. Inter-Am. Univ. Coun. for Econ. and Social Devel. 1991—. Recipient Mackintosh Pub. Speaking and Lecturing award U. Western Ont., 1959-60, Alfred J. Wright award Ohio State U., 1970; Grad. fellow in humanities U. Western Ont., 1959, Grad. Studies fellow U. Rochester, 1960, 61-62; Danforth Found. assoc., 1966—. Mem. Am. Assn. State Colls. and Univs. (mem. com. undergrad. edn. 1982-90, com. confs. and profl. devel. 1989-92), Am. Philos. Assn. Office: Bowling Green State U McFall Ctr Bowling Green OH 43403

OLSCHWANG, ALAN PAUL, lawyer; b. Chgo., Jan. 30, 1942; s. Morton James and Ida (Ginsberg) O.; m. Barbara Claire Miller, Aug. 22, 1965; children: Elliot, Deborah, Jeffrey. B.S., U. Ill., 1963, J.D., 1966. Bar: Ill. 1966, N.Y. 1984, Calif. 1992. Law clk. Ill. Supreme Ct., Bloomington, 1966-67; assoc. Sidley & Austin, and predecessor, Chgo., 1967-73; with Montgomery Ward & Co., Inc., Chgo., 1973-81, assoc. gen. counsel, asst. sec., 1979-81; ptnr. Seki, Jarvis & Lynch, Chgo., 1981-84, dir., mem. exec. com.; exec. v.p., gen. counsel, sec. Mitsubishi Electric Am., Inc., N.Y.C., 1983-91, Cypress, Calif., 1991—. Mem. ABA, Am. Corp. Counsel Assn., Calif. Bar Assn., Ill. Bar Assn., Chgo. Bar Assn., N.Y. State Bar Assn., Bar Assn. of City of N.Y., Am. Arbitration Assn. (panel arbitrators). Office: Mitsubishi Electric Am 5665 Plaza Dr Cypress CA 90630-5023

OLSEN, ALFRED JON, lawyer; b. Phoenix, Oct. 5, 1940; s. William Hans and Vera (Bearden) O.; m. Susan K. Smith, Apr. 15, 1979. B.A. in History, U. Ariz., 1962; MS in Acctg., Ariz. State U., 1964; J.D., Northwestern U., 1966. Bar: Ariz. 1966, Ill. 1966; C.P.A., Ariz., Ill. cert. tax specialist. Acct. Arthur Young & Co., C.P.A.s, Chgo., 1966-68; dir. firm Ehmann, Olsen & Lane (P.C.), Phoenix, 1969-76; dir. Streich, Lang, Weeks & Cardon (P.C.), Phoenix, 1977-78; v.p. Olsen-Smith, Ltd., Phoenix, 1978—. Bd. editors: Jour. Agrl. Law and Taxation, 1978-82, Practical Real Estate Lawyer, 1983-95. Mem. Phoenix adv. bd. Salvation Army., 1973-81. Fellow Am. Coll. Trust and Estate Counsel, Am. Coll. Tax Counsel; mem. State Bar Ariz. (chmn. tax sect. 1977-78), ABA (chmn. com. on agr., sect. taxation 1976-78, chmn. CLE com. sect. taxation 1982-84), Am. Law Inst. (chmn. tax planning for agr. 1973-84), Cen. Ariz. Estate Planning Coun. (pres. 1972-73), Nat. Cattlemen's Assn. (tax com. 1979-88), Internat. Acad. Estate and Trust Law (exec. coun. 1994—), Sigma Nu Internat. (pres. 1986-88). Office: 3300 Virginia Financial Pla 301 E Virginia Ave Phoenix AZ 85004-1215

OLSEN, ARTHUR MARTIN, physician, educator; b. Chgo., Aug. 29, 1909; s. Martin I. and Aagot (Rovelstad) O.; m. Yelena Pavlinova, Sept. 16, 1936; children: Margaret Ann (Mrs. Frank A. Jost), David Martin, Karen Yelena (Mrs. Dori Kanellos), Mary Elizabeth. AB, Dartmouth Coll., 1930; MD, U. Chgo., 1935; MS, U. Minn., 1938. Diplomate Am. Bd. Internal Medicine. Intern Cook County Hosp., Chgo., 1935-36; fellow in medicine, resident Mayo Found., U. Minn., 1936-40, from instr. to prof. medicine, 1950-57, prof., 1957—; cons. medicine Mayo Clinic, Rochester, Minn., 1940-76, chmn. divsn. thoracic diseases, 1968-71. Author numerous publs. on diseases of the lungs and esophagus. Mem. nat. heart and lung adv. coun. NIH, 1970-71; trustee Mayo Found., 1961-68, mem. subsplty. bd. pulmonary diseases, 1958—, chmn., 1961-63. Recipient Alexander B. Vishnevski medal Inst. Surgery, Moscow, 1966, Andres Bello medal Govt. of Venezuela, 1987, Disting. Alumnus award Rush Med. Coll., U. Chgo., 1989. Fellow ACP, Am. Coll. Chest Physicians (master, regent 1955—, chmn. 1959-66, pres. 1970, Disting. Fellow award 1978, dir. internat. activities 1976-83, cons. internat. activities 1983-85); mem. AMA (Billings gold meadl for exhibit on esophagitis 1955), Am. Soc. Gastrointestinal Endoscopy (pres. 1962-63), Minn. Respiratory Health Assn. (pres. 1964-68), Minn. Med. Assn., Am. Assn. Thoracic Surgery, Am. Thoracic Soc., Minn. Thoracic Soc. (pres. 1952), Am. Bronchoesophagol. Assn. (pres. 1969-70, Chevalier Jackson award 1973), Internat. Bronchoesophagol. Soc. (pres. 1979-81), Minn. Soc. Internal Medicine, Brit. Thoracic Soc. (hon.), Nat. Acad. Medicine of Buenos Aires (hon.), Portuguese Soc. Respiratory Pathology (corr.), Sigma Xi, Alpha Omega Alpha. Episcopalian. Home: 211 2nd St NW Apt 2002 Rochester MN 55901-3101 Office: Mayo Clinic Rochester MN 55901

OLSEN, BARBARA ANN, mathematics educator; b. Ann Arbor, Mich., Sept. 25, 1949; d. Bruce Christian and Jean Bernice (Tuin) O. BS, Mich. State U., 1971; MEd, Wayne State U., 1976. Secondary edn. tchr. Math. tchr. Lake Shore Pub. Schs., St. Clair Shores, Mich., 1971—; chmn. math. curriculum com. Lake Shore Pub. Schs., 1988-92, mem. mfg. acad. curriculum com., 1993—, faculty coun. Nat. Honor Soc., 1987—, sr. class advisor, 1995—. Recipient Citation of merit for Outstanding Professionalism in Influencing The Lives of Students, Northwood Inst., Midland, Mich., 1990. Mem. Nat. Coun. Tchrs. of Math., Mich. Coun. Tchrs. Math. Avocations: boating, reading.

OLSEN, CLIFFORD WAYNE, consultant, retired physical chemist; b. Placerville, Calif., Jan. 15, 1936; s. Christian William and Elsie May (Bishop) O.; m. Margaret Clara Gobel, June 16, 1962 (div. 1986); children: Anne Katherine Olsen Cordes, Charlotte Marie; m. Nancy Mayhew Kruger, July 21, 1990 (div. 1994). AA, Grant Tech. Coll., Sacramento, 1955; BA, U. Calif.-Davis, 1957, PhD, 1962. Physicist, project leader, program leader, task leader Lawrence Livermore Nat. Lab., Calif., 1962-93; ret., 1993, lab. assoc., 1993-95; mem. Containment Evaluation Panel, U.S. Dept. Energy, 1984—, mem. Cadre for Joint Nuclear Verification Tests, 1988; organizer, editor procs. for 2nd through 7th Symposiums on Containment of Underground Nuclear Detonations, 1983-93. Contbr. articles to profl. jours. Mem. bd. convocators Calif. Luth. U., 1976-78. Recipient Chevalier Degree, Order of DeMolay, 1953, Eagle Scout, 1952. Mem. AAAS, Am. Radio Relay League, Seismol. Soc. Am., Livermore Amateur Radio Klub (pres. 1994-96), Sigma Xi, Alpha Gamma Sigma (life), Gamma Alpha (U. Calif.-Davis chpt. pres. 1960-61). Democrat. Lutheran. Avocations: photography, amateur radio, music, cooking.

OLSEN, DAVID ALEXANDER, insurance executive; b. Bklyn., Nov. 29, 1937; s. Alexander and Meile (Anderson) O.; m. Roberta Ruth Garverick, May 11, 1963; children: Bradford, Amy. BA, Bowdoin Coll., 1959. With marine dept. Gt. Am. Ins. Co., N.Y.C. and Chgo., 1959-62; acct. exec. Johnson & Higgins, San Francisco, 1966-71; v.p., mgr. marine dept. Johnson & Higgins, Chgo., 1971-78, exec. v.p. Ill. br., 1978-79; br. mgr., exec. v.p. Johnson & Higgins, Houston, 1979-80, chmn., bd. dirs. Tex. br., 1980-85; exec. v.p. Johnson & Higgins, N.Y.C., 1985-87, pres., COO, 1987-93, CEO, 1990—, chmn., 1991—; trustee, exec. com. Am. Inst. Chartered Property Casualty Underwriters, Ins. Inst. Am., Coll. of Ins., N.Y.C., 1994—, U.S. Coun. Internat. Bus., N.Y.C., 1995. Vice-chmn. South St. Seaport Mus., N.Y.C.; v.p. bd. overseers Bowdoin Coll., Brunswick, Maine; bd. dirs. United Way, N.Y.C., N.Y.C. Partnership; bd. dirs. corp. congress N.Y. Pub. Libr.; co-chmn. Corp. Coun. The N.Y. Botanical Garden. 1st lt. U.S. Army, 1960-62. Mem. India House (bd. dirs.), River Club, Econ. Club N.Y., Psi Upsilan. Republican. Avocations: art, photography, antiques, scuba diving, tennis, skiing. Home: 1120 Park Ave New York NY 10128-1242 Office: Johnson & Higgins 125 Broad St New York NY 10004-2400

OLSEN, DONALD EMMANUEL, architect, educator; b. Mpls., July 23, 1919; s. Clarence Edward and Thea (Scharnell) O.; m. Helen Karen Ohlson, Apr. 2, 1944; 1 child, Alan Edward. B.Arch., U. Minn., 1942; M. Arch., Harvard U., 1946; postgrad. in civic design, U. Liverpool, Eng., 1953; postgrad. in philosophy of sci., London Sch. Econs., 1962-63, 68. Registered architect, Calif. Archtl. designer Saarinen, Swanson & Saarinen, Bloomfield Hills, Mich., 1946; project mgr. Skidmore, Owings & Merrill, San Francisco, 1948; designer, draughtsman Wurster, Bernardi & Emmons, San Francisco, 1949-51; pvt. practice architecture Berkeley, Calif., 1954—; prof. architecture U. Calif.-Berkeley, 1954-90, prof. emeritus, 1990—; guest prof. various univs., lectr. in field, U.S., Eng., Germany, Denmark; nominator Carnegie Grant Personality Assessment and Research Creativity Study Architects, 1959; profl. adviser City of San Francisco, 1961-62; juror, critic, evaluator various programs, projects. Contbr. articles, chpts. to profl. publs.; subject of numerous profl. publs. Numerous exhibits throughout U.S., Europe; prin. works include numerous design commns. Recipient awards, including nat. awards of Excellence Archtl. Record, Houses of 1966; scholar Harvard U., Cambridge, Mass., 1945-46; A. W. Wheelwright fellow Harvard U., 1953. Fellow AIA (2 nat. honor awards 1970, 8 various regional, local Honor, Excellence and Merit awards 1967-89); mem. Brit. Soc. for Philosophy of Sci., Soc. for Philosophy and Tech., Open Soc. and Its Friends. Avocations: study of philosophy; travel and travel photography; opera. Home: 771 San Diego Rd Berkeley CA 94707-2025 Office: Donald E Olsen & Assocs Architects 771 San Diego Rd Berkeley CA 94707-2025

OLSEN, DOUGLAS H., superintendent. Supt. Southfield Christian Schs., Mich. Recipient Blue Ribbon award, 1990-91. Office: Southfield Christian Sch 28650 Lahser Rd Southfield MI 48034-2020

OLSEN, EDWARD GUSTAVE, education educator emeritus; b. Portland, Oreg., Mar. 26, 1908; s. Gustav Adolph and Emma Maria (Bush) O.; m. Faith Theresa Elliott, June 25, 1931 (dec. died 1947); children: Marvin Elliott, Marcia Evelyn; m. Pauline Marie Walsh, Sept. 11, 1948; 1 son, Douglas Walsh. AB, Pacific U., Forest Grove, Oreg., 1930; BD, Union Theol. Sem., N.Y.C., 1933; AM, Columbia U., 1932, EdD, 1937. Instr., acting chmn. dept. edn. Colgate U., 1935-41; assoc. prof., dir. sch. edn. Russell Sage Coll., 1941-45; dir. sch. and community relations Wash. State Office of Pub. Instrn., 1945-50; assoc. prof. ednl. adminstrn. U. Tex., 1950-51; edn. dir. NCCJ, Chgo. region, 1951-66; prof. edn. Calif. State U. at Hayward, 1966-73, emeritus, 1973—; formerly vis. prof. Ga. Tchrs. Coll., U. Wash., William and Mary, Western Wash. Coll. Edn., U. Maine, Wash. State U., Stanford; cons. Phila. Teachers Workshop; dir. Kitsap County Teachers' Workshop; dir. workshop on community resources U. Tex., Mont. State U.; dir. workshop on human relations Northwestern U., Nat. Coll. Edn., U. Oreg., Roosevelt U., U. Chgo., Pacific U., Pacific Lutheran U.; dir. Curry County (Oreg.) Ednl. Service Dist. Prin. author: School and Community; co-author: Life Centering Education; compiler: School and Community Programs; compiler, editor: The School and Community Reader; editor: The Modern Community School; editor, prin. author: Then Till Now: A Social History of the Brookings-Harbor Community; contbr. numerous articles to profl. jours. Exec. sec. Wash. State Coordinating Council for UNESCO; pres. Park Ridge Council Human Relations. Recipient Thomas H. Wright award City of Chgo., 1957; Distinguished Service award Nat. Community Edn. Assn., 1969; Fulbright scholar U. Coll. Rhodesia and Nyasaland, 1958. Mem. NEA (life), Oreg. Community Edn. Assn. (life membership award 1987), Nat. Community Edn. Assn. (life mem. award 1977), Blue Key, Kappa Delta Pi, Phi Delta Kappa. Unitarian. Lodge: Rotary. Home: 317 Memory Ln Brookings OR 97415-9031 *The goal of education should be to improve the quality of human living, both as individuals and in group life on this planet. The school curriculum must be centered in the enduring life concerns of human kind, oriented to the future yet ever aware of the relevant past in relation to present human needs.*

OLSEN, EDWARD JOHN, geologist, educator; b. Chgo., Nov. 23, 1927; s. Edward John and Elizabeth (Bornemann) O.; children—Andrea, Erick-a. A.B., U. Chgo., 1951, M.S., 1955, Ph.D., 1959. Geologist Geol. Survey Can., 1953, U.S. Geol. Survey, 1954—, Canadian Johns-Manville Co., Ltd., 1956, 57, 59; asst. prof. Case Inst. Tech., also Western Res. U., 1959-60; curator mineralogy Field Mus. Natural History, 1960-91, chmn. dept. geology, 1974-78; research assoc. prof. dept. geophys. scis. U. Chgo., 1977—; adj. prof. U. Ill., Chgo. Circle, 1970-91. Assoc. editor Geochim. et Cosmochim. Acta., 1985-91. Fellow Mineral. Soc. Am.; mem. Mineral. Assn. Can., Geochem. Soc., Meteoritical Soc. Spl. research stability relations of minerals in earth's mantle and meteorites. Office: U Chgo Dept Geophys Sci Chicago IL 60637

OLSEN, FRANCES ELISABETH, law educator, theorist; b. Chgo., Feb. 4, 1945; d. Holger and Ruth Mathilda (Pfeifer) O.; m. Harold Irving Porter, June 8, 1984. Cert., Roskilde (Denmark) Højskole, 1967; BA, Goddard Coll., 1968; JD, U. Colo., 1971; SJD, Harvard U., 1984. Bar: Colo. 1972, U.S. Dist. Ct. Colo. 1972. Law clk. hon. Arraj U.S. Dist. Ct. Colo., Denver, 1972; lawyer Am. Indian Movement, Wounded Knee, S.D., 1973; pvt. practice Denver, 1973-74; law prof. U. Puget Sound, Tacoma, Wash., 1975-79, St. John's U., Jamaica, N.Y., 1982-83, UCLA, 1984—; vis. fellow New Coll., Oxford, Eng., 1987; vis. prof. U. Mich., Ann Arbor, 1988, Harvard U., Cambridge, Mass., 1990-91, Humboldt U., Berlin, 1995; Fulbright prof. U. Frankfurt, Germany, 1991-92. Co-author: Cases and Materials on Family Law: Legal Concepts and Changing Human Relationships, 1994; editor: Feminist Legal Theory I: Foundations and Outlooks, 1995, Feminist Legal Theory II: Positioning Feminist Theory Within the Law, 1995; contbr. articles to law revs. Named Outstanding Alumnus U. Colo., 1989. Mem. Am. Assn. Law Schs. (chair jurisprudence sect. 1987-88, chair women in law tchg. sect. 1995-96), European Conf. Critical Legal Studies, Conf. Critical Legal Studies. Avocations: wind-surfing, bicycling, mountain climbing. Office: UCLA Sch Law 405 Hilgard Ave Los Angeles CA 90095

OLSEN, GORDON, retired lawyer; b. Pitts., July 5, 1927; s. ALvin Gordon and Alma (Wollbrandt) O.; m. Nancy Smith, Dec. 26, 1955; children: Lars Andrew, Lisa Olsen Lerch (dec.). Student, Duquesne U., 1947-48; B.A., Pa. State U., 1951; LL.B., Fordham U., 1957; student, Ariz. State U., 1986. Bar: Ariz. 1958. Sr. asst. furniture buyer Macy's, N.Y.C., 1953-54; practice law Phoenix, until 1986, ret.; law clk. to justice Ariz. Supreme Ct., 1957-58; assoc. Lewis & Roca, 1958-63, ptnr., 1963-86. Bd. dirs. Family Svc. Phoenix, 1962-68, pres., 1966-67; bd. dirs. Ariz. Assn. for Health and Welfare, 1967-70, 1st v.p., 1967-68; bd. dirs. Community Coun., 1969-75; commr. LEAP Commn., Phoenix Community Action Agy., 1971-75, chmn., 1972-73; mem. plan steering com. Comprehensive Health Planning Coun., 1973-75; mem. CETA Manpower Adv. Coun., 1974-76, chmn., 1974-75, vice chmn., 1975-76; bd. dirs. Planned Parenthood Cent. and No. Ariz., 1975-81, pres., 1977-78; pres. Trinity Luth. Ch. of Maricopa County, 1989-91. Seaman 1st cl. USNR, 1945-46; 1st lt. USAF, 1951-53. Home: 232 W Frier Dr Phoenix AZ 85021-7233

OLSEN, HANS PETER, lawyer; b. Detroit, May 21, 1940; s. Hans Peter and Paula M. (Olsen) O.; m. Elizabeth Ann Gayton, Sept. 14, 1968; children: Hans Peter, Heidi Susanne, Stephanie Elizabeth. BA, Mich. State U., 1962; JD, Georgetown U., 1965; LLM, NYU, 1966. Bar: Mich. 1967, Pa. 1969, R.I. 1974. Law clk. firm Monaghan, McCrone, Campbell & Crawmer, Detroit, 1964; law clk. U.S. Ct. of Claims, Fed. Appellate Ct., Washington, 1966-68; assoc. firm Pepper, Hamilton & Scheetz, Phila., 1968-72; ptnr. firm Hinckley, Allen, & Snyder, Providence, 1972—; adv. planning com. U. R.I. Fed. Taxation Inst.; continuing legal edn. adv. bd., tax symposium adv. bd. Bryant Coll.; mem. Gov.'s State Task Force, R.I. Pub. Expenditure Coun.; cons. Bur. Nat. Affairs; liaison Bar Assn. and North Atlantic region IRS; tax adminstrs. adv. com. R.I.; lectr. tax insts. and other profl. groups N.Y., L.A., Phila., Boston, R.I. Contbr. numerous articles on taxation to legal jours. Fellow Am. Bar Found.; mem. ABA (sect. taxation, exempt orgns. com., subcom. healthcare, corp.-shareholders rels. com., partnerships com.), R.I. Bar Assn. (sect. taxation, sec.-treas. 1977-80, liaison with CPAs, specialization com., mem. various comms.), Providence C. of C., R.I. C. of C. (chmn. com. on bus. taxes and public spending, mem., past chmn. legis. action council), Mich. State Bar, Pa. State Bar. Home: 274 Olney St Providence RI 02906-2305 Office: 1500 Fleet Ctr Providence RI 02903

OLSEN, HAROLD FREMONT, lawyer; b. Davenport, Wash., Oct. 17, 1920; s. Oscar E. and Dorothy (Sprowls) O.; m. Jeanne L. Rounds, Aug. 30, 1942; children: Eric O., Ronald R., Margaret Ruth. B.A., Wash. State U., 1942; LL.B., Harvard U., 1948. Bar: Wash. 1948, U.S. Ct. Claims 1970, U.S. Supreme Ct. 1982; C.P.A., Wash. Instr. Oxford Bus. Sch., Cambridge, Mass., 1946-47; examiner Wash. State Dept. Pub. Utilities, 1948; with firm Perkins Coie (and predecessors), Seattle, 1949—, ptnr., 1954-88, of counsel, 1989—; bd. dirs. Exotic Metals Forming Co.; dir. Barker Ranch, Inc.; trustee Exec. Svcs. Corp. of Wash. Bd. dirs. Northwest Hosp. Found., Northwest Hosp., 1980-90; trustee Wash. State U. Found., chmn. 1986-88; mem. adv. coun. Wash. State U. Sch. Bus. and Econs., 1978-90; trustee, mem. exec. com., pres. Mus. of Flight, 1991-92, chmn., 1993; trustee Horizon House. Served to Major USAF, 1942-45, NATOUSA, Middle East, ETO. Decorated Silver Star. Mem. ABA, Wash. Bar Assn., Seattle Bar Assn., Aircraft Industry Assn. (chmn. legal com. 1957), Nat. Contract Mgmt. Assn., Alumni Assn. Wash. State U. (pres. 1956), Mcpl. League Seattle and King County, Seattle C. of C., Internat. Law Soc., Am. Judicature Assn., Phi Beta Kappa, Phi Kappa Phi, Tau Kappa Epsilon, Rainier Club, Seattle Golf Club (pres. 1986-87), Sr. N.W. Golf Assn. Congregationalist. Home: 8875 Overlake Dr W Medina WA 98039-5347 Office: 1201 3rd Ave Ste 4500 Seattle WA 98101-3000

OLSEN, HARRIS LELAND, real estate and international business executive, educator; b. Rochester, N.H., Dec. 8, 1947; s. Harries Edwin and Eva Alma (Turmelle) O.; m. Mimi Kwi Sun Yi, Mar. 15, 1953; children: Garin Lee, Gavin Yi, Sook Ja. AS, SUNY, Albany, 1983, BS, 1988; MA in Polit. Sci., U. Hawaii, 1990; PhD in Internat. Bus. Adminstrn., Kennedy Western U., Idaho, 1993. Enlisted USN, 1967, advanced through grades to; served in various nuclear power capacities USN, Conn., 1971-76, Hawaii, 1976-87; ret. USN, 1987; v.p. Waiono Land Corp., Honolulu, 1981-92, dir., 1993-95; v.p. Asian Pacific Electricity, Honolulu, 1988-89, Kapano Land Assocs.,

Honolulu, 1988-92, 94-95, MLY Networks, Inc., Honolulu, 1989—, THO Consultants Cor., 1991—, Clarix Internat. Corp., 1994; staff cons. Mariner-Icemakers, Honolulu, 1982-84, Transpacific Energy Corp., Honolulu, 1982-84; dir. Asian Pacific Devel. Bank, 1983; sr. cons. Western Rsch. Assocs., Honolulu, 1984-87, 94-95; quality assurance cons. Asian Pacific, Inc., Hoholulu, 1987-88; instr., lectr. Asian history and culture U. Chaminade in Honolulu, 1991; nuclear reactor plant specialist Pearl Harbor Emergency Recall Team, 1991-95; instr. nuclear reactor theory Pearl Harbor, Hawaii, 1992-95; v.p. Schwartz, inc., 1992—; cons. Waiono/Kapano Devel. Co., 1993; bd. dirs., sec. Pacific Internat. Engring. Corp., 1994-95; Keiretsu sec. Global Ocean Cons., Inc. and Assocs., 1994-95; joint venture Premier Fisheries Pty. Ltd., Papua New Guinea, 1995; cons. BFD Devel. Group, 1995—; co-drafter Nat. Tuna Industry Devel. Plan for Papua New Guinea, 1995; quality analyst, Pearl Harbor, 1995; rep. for Min. for Fisheries, Papua New Guinea, Bi-lateral Fisheries Access Rights Japan and Papua New Guinea, 1996—; U.S. del. to 4th World Tuna Conf., Manila, 1995; apptd. rep. Abau Electorate, Papua New Guinea Timber Sales, 1995—. Inventor, alternate power supply system; contbr. articles to profl. publs. Head coach USN Men's Softball, Honolulu, 1978-79; pres. Pearl Harbor (Hawaii) Welfare and Recreation Com., 1983-84; mem. Bishop Mus. Rep. Senatorial Inner Cir. Named Alumnus of Yr., Kennedy Western U., 1993. Mem. ASCD, AAAS, Internat. Fedn. Profl. and Tech. Engrs., Am. Polit. Sci. Assn., Semiotic Soc. Am., N.Y. Acad. Scis., Toronto Semiotics Cir., USCG Aux., Am. Legion, Fleet Res. Assn., Internat. Platform Assn., Navy League, U.S. Naval Inst., UN Assn., U.S. Submarine Vets., Honolulu Acad. Arts, U. Hawaii Founders Assn., U. Hawaii Coll. Arts and Sci. Found., Delta Epsilon Sigma. Republican. Buddhist. Avocations: chess, philosophy. Home: #56 94-1025 Anania Cir Apt 56 Mililani HI 96789-2045 Office: Schwartz Inc 1149 Bethel St Ste 314 Honolulu HI 96813-2210

OLSEN, JACK, writer; b. Indpls., June 7, 1925; s. Rudolph O. and Florence (Drecksage) O.; m. Su Peterson, 1966; children: John Robert, Susan Joyce, Jonathan Rhoades, Julia Crispin, Evan Pierce, Barrie Elizabeth, Emily Sara Peterson, Harper Alexander Peterson. Student, U. Pa., 1946-47. Newspaper reporter San Diego Union Tribune, 1947-48, San Diego Jour., 1949-50, Washington Daily News, 1950- 51; TV news editor and broadcaster sta. WMAL-TV, Washington, 1950-51; newspaper reporter New Orleans Item, 1952-53, Chgo. Sun-Times, 1954-55; corr. Time mag., 1956-58, Midwest chief, 1959-59. Author: The Mad World of Bridge, 1960, (pseudonym Jonathan Rhoades) Over the Fence is Out, 1961, The Climb up to Hell, 1962, (with Charles Goren) Bridge Is My Game, 1965, Black is Best: The Riddle of Cassius Clay, 1967, The Black Athlete: A Shameful Story, 1968, Silence on Monte Sole, 1968, Night of the Grizzlies, 1969, The Bridge at Chappaquiddick, 1970, Aphrodite: Desperate Mission, 1970, Slaughter the Animals, Poison the Earth, 1971, The Girls in the Office, 1971, The Girls on the Campus, 1972, Sweet Street, 1973, The Man with the Candy, 1974, Alphabet Jackson, 1974, Massy's Game, 1976, The Secret of Fire Five, 1977, Night Watch, 1979, Missing Persons, 1981, Have You Seen My Son?, 1982, Son: A Psychopath and His Victims, 1983, Give a Boy a Gun, 1985, Cold Kill, 1987, Doc: The Rape of the Town of Lovell, 1990, Predator, 1991, The Misbegotten Son, 1993, Charmer: A Ladies Man and His Victims, 1994, Salt of the Earth, 1996; work included in numerous anthologies. Served with OSS AUS, 1943-44. Recipient Edgar award Mystery Writers Am., Page One award Chgo. Newspaper Guild; Nat. Headliners award; Wash. Gov.'s award; citations U. Ind., Columbia U.

OLSEN, KENNETH HAROLD, geophysicist, astrophysicist; b. Ogden, Utah, Feb. 20, 1930; s. Harold Reuben and Rose (Hill) O.; m. Barbara Ann Parson, June 15, 1955; children: Susan L., Steven K., Christopher P., Richard Scott. BS, Idaho State Coll., 1952; MS, Calif. Inst. Tech., 1954, PhD, 1957. Grad. rsch. asst. Calif. Inst. Tech., Mt. Wilson and Palomar Obs., Pasadena, 1952-57; staff member, group leader Los Alamos (N.Mex.) Nat. Lab., 1957-89; lab. assoc. Los Alamos Nat. Lab., 1989—; geophys. cons. GCS Internat., Lynnwood, Wash., 1989—; vis. rsch. fellow Applied Seismol. Group, Swedish Nat. Def. Inst., Stockholm, Sweden, 1983; sr. vis. scientist fellow Norwegian Seismic Array, Oslo, Norway, 1983; vis. scholar Geophysics Program, Univ. Wash., Seattle, 1989-91. Author, editor: Continental Rifts: Evolution, Structure, Tectonics, 1995; contbr. articles to profl. jours. Mem. Am. Geophys. Union, Geol. Soc. Am., Seismol. Soc. Am., Royal Astron. Soc. Home: 1029 187th Pl SW Lynnwood WA 98036

OLSEN, KENNETH HARRY, manufacturing company executive; b. Bridgeport, Conn., Feb. 20, 1926; s. Oswald and Svea (Nordling) O.; m. Eeva-Liisa Aulikki Valve, Dec. 12, 1950. B.S. in Elec. Engring, MIT, 1950, M.S., 1952. Elec. engr. Lincoln Lab., MIT, 1950-57; founder Digital Equipment Corp., Maynard, Mass., 1957, pres. emeritus; bd. dirs. Polaroid Corp., Ford Motor Co. Patentee magnetic devices. Mem. Pres.'s Sci. Adv. Com., 1971-73; trustee, v.p. Joslin Diabetes Found.; mem. corp. Wentworth Inst., Boston, MIT, Cambridge; trustee Gordon Coll., Wenham, Mass. Served with USNR, 1944-46. Named Young Elec. Engr. of Year Eta Kappa Nu, 1960; recipient of Nat. Medal of Tech., Nat. Sci. Found., 1993. Mem. Nat. Acad. Engring. Office: Digital Equipment Corp 40 Old Bolton Rd Stow MA 01775-1215*

OLSEN, KURT, investment company executive, adviser; b. Astoria, Oreg., Nov. 2, 1924; s. Matt J. and Irene (Lindholm) O.; m. Lois Helen Giberson, Mar. 23, 1947; children: Kurt F., Eric J., Mark C. BS, U. Oreg., 1949. RR mgr. and ptnr. Foster & Marshall, Eugene, Oreg., 1948-61; mgr., v.p., dir. Harris, Upham Inc., Portland, Oreg., 1961-70; v.p., dir. Foster & Marshall Inc., Portland, 1971-76; pres. Alpen Securities, Inc., Portland, 1977—. Mem. adv. bd. Columbia Pacific coun. Boy Scouts Am., mem. nat. coun., 1966-73; bd. dirs. United Way Columbia and Willamette, 1973-77, Oreg. Law Found., 1986-89. With USNR, 1944-46. Mem. Nat. Assn. Securities Dealers (chmn. dist. 1 1967), Investment Bankers Assn. Am. (bd. govs. 1968-70), Sigma Alpha Epsilon, Rotary. Home: 1127 SW Myrtle Dr Portland OR 97201-2270 Office: Alpen Securities Inc 1425 Yeon Bldg Portland OR 97204

OLSEN, MERLIN JAY, sports analyst, former professional football player, actor; b. Logan, Utah, Sept. 15, 1940; s. Lynn Jay and Merle (Barrus) O.; m. Susan Wakley, Mar. 30, 1962; children: Kelly Lynn, Jill Catherine, Nathan Merlin. B.S. in Fin., Utah State U., 1962, M.S. in Econs, 1970. Profl. football player Los Angeles Rams, 1962-76; with Allied Chem. Corp., 1962-67; motivational cons. Liggett & Myers, 1971-72, Consol. Cigar, 1972-73; pub. relations exec. Combined Communications Corp., 1972-73; owner Merlin Olsen Porsche Audi, 1969—; TV spokesman Florists' Transworld Delivery. Sports analyst, NBC, 1977-93; numerous other TV performances; regular in: Little House on the Prairie; star: TV series Father Murphy, 1981, Fathers & Sons (NBC-TV), Aaron's Way; co-host Children's Miracle Network Telethon, 1983—, TV movies: A Fire in the Sky, The Golden Moment, An Olympic Love Story, Time Bomb; TV Specials: The Juggler of Notre Dame, 1982, (host, narrator) Lifequest, 1987-89, The Sleeping Beauty, 1987, The Nutcracker, 1990, Fantastic Facts, 1991-92; co-producer: films include: All Pro, Mitchell, Something Big, One More Train to Rob, The Undefeated. Grand marshall 94th Tournament of Roses Parade; v.p. So. Calif. Multiple Sclerosis Soc. Recipient Numerous football awards including MVP (Maxwell Trophy), 1974, Coll. Football Hall of Fame, 1980; named to Pro Football of Fame, 1982, NFL-AFL Quarter Century Team. Mem. Sigma Chi, Phi Kappa Phi.

OLSEN, REX NORMAN, trade association executive; b. Hazeltown, Idaho, Apr. 9, 1925; s. Adolph Lars and Pearl (Robbins) O. B.J., B.A. in English, U. Mo., 1950. Editor Clissold Pub. Co., Chgo., 1950-54; copy editor Am. Peoples Ency., Chgo., 1955; asst. editor Am. Hosp. Assn., Chgo., 1956-59; mng. editor Am. Hosp. Assn., 1959-64, dir. jours. div., 1964-69, dir. publs. bur., 1969-75, exec. editor, asso. pub., 1975-79; v.p., treas. Am. Hosp. Pub., Inc., 1980-85; pres. Words Ltd., 1985—. Served with USNR, 1943-46. Mem. Am. Pub. Health Assn., Am. Med. Writers Assn., Soc. Nat. Assn. Pubs. (sec. 1975-76, 2d v.p. 1976-77, 1st v.p. 1977-78, pres. 1978-79), Chgo. Bus. Publs. Assn. (dir. 1974-78, 4th v.p. 1978-79), Sigma Delta Chi. Home and Office: 3845 N Alta Vista Ter Chicago IL 60613-2907

OLSEN, RICHARD GALEN, biomedical engineer, researcher; b. Colorado Springs, Colo., Aug. 10, 1945; s. Floyd Edwin and Ruth Elizabeth (Robinson) O.; m. Karen Fidler Brubaker, June 17, 1973; children: Kathryn Elizabeth, Nickolas Robert. BSEE, U. Mo., Rolla, 1968; MS, U. Utah, 1970, PhD, 1975. Registered profl. engr., Fla. Engr. Bendix Corp., Kansas City, Mo., 1968-69; elec. engr. Naval Aerospace Med. Rsch. Lab., Pensacola, Fla., 1975-79, chief engring. systems div., 1979-82, head bioengring. divsn., 1982-94; head bioengring. dept. Naval Med. Rsch. Inst. Detachment, Brooks AFB, Tex., 1994—; tech. cons. Armstrong Lab., USAF, 1991—, German Ministry of Def., Munster, 1994, Naval Surface Warfare Ctr., Dahlgren, Va., 1989-95, Naval Sea Sys. Command, Arlington, Va., 1989-91. Contbr. articles to profl. jours. and books. With U.S. Army, 1970-72. Recipient NDEA fellowship U. Utah, 1969, Fred A. Hitchcock award Aerospace Physiologist Soc. of Aerospace Med., 1987; named Engr. of the Yr., N.W. Fla. Engrs. Coun., 1991. Mem. IEEE (sr., chmn. Pensacola sect. 1982-83, radio frequency and microwave measuring methods com. 1982—, nonionizing radiation hazards com. 1983—, SCC-28 com., Cert. of Appreciation 1983), Bioelectromagnetics Soc. (charter, editl. bd. 1990—), Aerospace Med. Assn. (editl. cons. 1986—), Rotary (bd. dirs. Suburban West 1980-81), Sigma Xi, Eta Kappa Nu, Tau Beta Pi, Phi Kappa Phi. Republican. Adventist. Achievements include conducting the first shipboard measurements of specific absorption rate (SAR) and of electromagnetic pulse (EMP) induced body current, obtaining the first evidence of reduced RF heating in wrists and ankles from wearing conductive gloves and socks; patents in RF coil for hypothermia resuscitation, RF dosimetry system and RF warming of submerged extremities. Home: 1503 N Baylen St Pensacola FL 32501-2101 Office: Naval Med Rsch Inst Detach 8308 Hawks Rd Brooks AFB TX 78235-5423 *Live an ordinary life except in attainment.*

OLSEN, RICHARD W., advertising executive; b. Flushing, N.Y., Jan. 27, 1952; s. Harold William and Hilda (Flanner) O.; m. Patricia Lynn Richards, Apr. 22, 1978; children: Lindsay Hunt, Caroline Wallace. BA History, Bethany Coll., 1974. Acct. exec. SSC&B Lintas, N.Y.C., 1975-77, Marschalk Co., N.Y.C., 1977-79; sr. v.p. mgmt. supr. Saatchi & Saatchi, N.Y.C., 1979-90; sr. v.p. mgmt. rep. Bozell Inc., N.Y.C., 1990-92; exec. v.p. gen. mgr. Cliff Freeman and Ptnrs., N.Y.C., 1992—. Republican. Avocations: sailing, golf. Home: 35 Christie Hill Rd Darien CT 06820-3726 Office: Cliff Freeman and Partners 375 Hudson St New York NY 10014-3658

OLSEN, ROBERT ARTHUR, finance educator; b. Pittsfield, Mass., June 30, 1943; s. Arthur Anton and Virginia O.; BBA, U. Mass., 1966, MBA, 1967; PhD, U. Oreg., 1974; m. Maureen . Joan Carmell, Aug. 21, 1965. Security analyst Am. Inst. Counselors, 1967-68; rsch. assoc. Center for Capital Market Rsch., U. Oreg., 1972-74; asst. prof. fin. U. Mass., 1974-75; prof. fin., chmn. dept. fin. & mktg. Calif. State U., Chico, 1975—; cons. bus. feasibility studies for Fin. Svc. Industry, Calif. State U., Chico, Endowment Fund, U.S. Forest Svc. Stonier Banking fellow, 1971-72; Nat. Assn. Mut. Savs. Banks fellow, 1975-76; scholar Stanford U., 1986, rsch. fellow Decision Research, Inc., 1986, 95, 96. Recipient Research award Calif. State U.-Chico, 1983, 86, 96, Profl. Achievement award, 1985. Mem. Am. Fin. Assn., Fin. Execs. Inst., Western Fin. Assn. (Trefftzs award 1974), Southwestern Fin. Assn., Fin. Mgmt. Assn., Eastern Fin. Assn., Sierra Club. Contbr. articles to profl. jours. Office: Calif State U Sch Bus Chico CA 95929

OLSEN, ROBERT JOHN, savings and loan association executive; b. N.Y.C., July 8, 1928; s. Christian Marinius and Agnes Geraldine (Jensen) O.; m. Eleanor Marion Peters, June 19, 1981; 1 child, Philip John. BS, Strayer Coll., 1956. Supervisory agt. Fed. Home Loan Bank Bd., N.Y.C., 1956-65; pres., dir. Keystone Savs. & Loan Assn., Asbury Park, N.J., 1965-82; chmn. bd., pres. Rapid Money Svcs., Inc., Deal, N.J., 1977-82, Elmora Savs. and Loan Assn., Elizabeth, N.J., 1982-88; pres. Ramsey (N.J.) Savs. and Loan Assn., 1988-90; pres., mng. agt. Resolution Trust Corp., 1990—; also bd. dirs. Ramsey (N.J.) Savs. and Loan Assn.; pres. 2d Century Corp., Asbury Park, 1980-82; dir. Central Corp. of Savs. & Loans, Newark, 1976-82, Fed. Home Loan Bank N.Y., 1974-77. Councilman, Borough of Oceanport, N.J., 1971-73, 77-80, pres., 1979; police commr. Oceanport, N.J., 1972-80; v.p. Econ. Devel. Corp., Asbury Park, N.J., 1972-81, Oceanport, N.J., 1974-77; mem. Zoning Bd. of Adjustment, Oceanport, 1969-70; mem. Citizens Adv. Coun., Oceanport, 1975-76; dir. Monmouth and Ocean Devel. Coun., Eatontown, N.J., 1974-82; trustee Savs. and Loan Found. of Washington, 1978-82; chmn. N.J. Electronic Funds Transfer Com., 1971-82; mem. Monmouth County Fair Housing Task Force, 1980-82, Monmouth County Vocat. Sch. Bd., 1981-83; pres. Paulinskill Lake Assn., 1987-90, chpt. 56 Heart Assn., Morristown, N.J., 1989. Served with USMC, 1946-48, 1950-56. Mem. N.J. Savs. League (pres. chpt. 1966-67), U.S. Savs. League (vice chmn. com. on internal ops., chmn. ATM com.), Nat. Assn. Review Appraisers and Mortgage Underwriters, Fin. Mgrs. Soc. (adv. coun.), Nat. Assn. Savs. and Loan Suprs., Nat. Soc. Fin. Examiners, Monmouth County, Eastern Union County Realtors Assn., Sussex County Realtors Assn., Internat. Union Bldg. Socs. and Savs. Assns., Navy League, Assn. U.S. Army., World Trade Club (N.Y.C.), Channel Club (Monmouth Beach, N.J.), Provost Marshals Guild Club (Ft. Monmouth, N.J.), Wheelman's Club (Asbury Park). Home: 23 Homestead Dr W Long Branch NJ 07764 Office: Resolution Trust Corp 10 Waterview Blvd Parsippany NJ 07054-1286

OLSEN, T. FRED, timing instruments manufacturing company executive. Chmn., chief exec. officer Timex Group Ltd., Waterbury, Conn. Office: Timex Group Ltd PO Box 310 Middlebury CT 06722-0310*

OLSEN, THOMAS RICHARD, SR., air force officer; b. Houston, June 28, 1934; s. Oscar Leonard and Catherine (Byers) O.; m. Dorothy Kendrick Taylor, July 7, 1956; children: Thomas Richard Jr., Lisa Kendrick Olsen Wesolick. BSME, Tex. A&M U., 1956; MS in Internat. Affairs, George Washington U., 1968. Mech. engr. Tex. Gas Corp., Houston, 1956; commd. 2d lt. USAF, 1957, advanced through grades to maj. gen., 1986; pilot trainee Greenville AFB, Miss., 1957-58; fighter pilot 326 FIS/526 FIS, U.S. and Fed. Republic Germany, 1958-65, 614 TFS/615 TFS, England AFB, La., 615 TFS, Phan Rang AB, Vietnam, 1966-67; instr. U.S. Naval Amphibious Sch., Coronado, Calif., 1968-71; fighter pilot 391 TFS, Mt. Home AFB, Idaho, 1971-72; squadron ops. officer, squadron comdr. 391 TFS, Mt. Home AFB, 1972-74; chief rated officer Mgmt. Hdqrs. AFMPC, Randolph AFB, Tex., 1975-78; chief of staff Hdqrs. 9th Air Force, Shaw AFB, S.C., 1978-79; dep. comdr. Hdqrs. 314th Air Div., Seoul, Republic of Korea, 1979-81; dir. ops. Hdqrs. 5th Air Force, Yokota AFB, Japan, 1981-82; wing comdr. 51 TFW, Osan AB, Republic of Korea, 1982-83; dep. dir. ops. Hdqrs. Pacific Command, Camp Smith, Hawaii, 1983-85; asst. chief of staff ops. Hdqrs. AFCENT, NATO, Brunssum, The Netherlands, 1985-87; dep. comdr., chief of staff Hdqrs. 4 ATAF, NATO, Heidelberg, Fed. Republic Germany, 1987-89; vice comdr. Hdqrs. 9th Air Force, Shaw AFB, S.C., 1989-91; dep. comdr. U.S. Cen. Command Air Forces (Desert Shield/Desert Storm), Riyadh, Saudi Arabia, 1990-91; ret., 1991. Mem. Optimist Club, Coronado, 1969-71. Mem. Air Force Assn., Ret. Officers Assn., Daedalians, Kiwanis, Rotary. Presbyterian. Home: 1006 Golfcrest Rd Sumter SC 29154-6179

OLSEN, TILLIE, author; b. Omaha, Nebr., Jan. 14, 1912; d. Samuel and Ida (Beber) Lerner; m. Jack Olsen; children: Karla, Julie, Kathie, Laurie. LittD (hon.), U. Nebr., 1979, Knox Coll., 1982, Hobart and William Smith Coll., 1984, Clark U., 1985, Albright Coll., 1986, Wooster Coll., 1991, Mills Coll., 1995. Writer-in-residence Amherst Coll., 1969-70; vis. faculty Stanford U., 1972; Writer-in-residence, vis. faculty English M.I.T., 1973-74, U. Mass., Boston, 1974; internat. vis. scholar Norway, 1980; Hill prof. U. Minn., spring 1986; writer-in-residence Kenyon Coll., 1987—; Regents lectr. U. Calif. at San Diego, 1977—, UCLA, 1987; commencement spkr. English dept. U. Calif., Berkeley, 1983, Hobart and William Smith Coll., 1984 Bennington Coll., 1986. Author: Tell Me A Riddle, 1961 (title story received First prize O'Henry award 1961), Rebecca Harding Davis: Life in the Iron Mills, 1972, Yonnondio: From the Thirties, 1974, Silences, 1978, The Word Made Flesh, 1984; editor: Mother to Daughter, Daughter to Mother, 1984; Preface Mothers and Daughters, That Special Quality: A Exploration in Photographs, 1989; short fiction published in over 200 anthologies; books translated in 11 langs. Recipient Am. Acad. and Nat. Inst. of Arts and Letters award, 1975, Ministry to Women award Unitarian Universalist Fedn., 1980, Brit. Post Office and B.P.W. award, 1980, Mari Sandoz award Nebr. Libr. Assn., 1991, REA award Dungannon Found., 1994, Disting. Achievement award Western Lit. Assn., 1996; Grantee Ford Found., 1959, NEA, 1968; Stanford Univ. Creative Writing fellow, 1962-64, Guggenheim fellow, 1975-76, Bunting Inst. Radcliffe Coll. fellow, 1985; Tillie Olsen Day designated in San Francisco, 1981. Mem. Authors Guild, PEN, Writers Union. Home: 1435 Laguna St Apt 6 San Francisco CA 94115-3742

OLSHEN, RICHARD A., statistician, educator; b. Portland, Oreg., May 17, 1942; s. A.C. and Dorothy (Olds) O.; m. Susan Abroff, 1979. AB, U. Calif., Berkeley, 1963; PhD, Yale U., 1966. Rsch. staff statistician, lectr. Yale U., New Haven, 1966-67; asst. prof. of statistics Stanford (Calif.) U., 1967-72; assoc. prof. of statistics and math. U. Mich., Ann Arbor, 1972-75; assoc. prof. of math. U. Calif., San Diego, 1975-77, prof. of math., 1977-89, dir. lab. for math. and statistics, 1982-89; prof. of biostatistics Sch. Medicine Stanford U., 1989—, prof. by courtesy dept. statis., 1990—, prof. by courtesy dept. elec. engring., 1995—. Office: Stanford U Sch Medicine Hrp Bldg Stanford CA 94305

OLSHIN, SAMUEL E., architect. BA in Design of the Environment, U. Pa., 1982, MArch, 1986. Registered architect, Pa. Arch. Atkin, Olshin, Lawson-Bell & Assocs., Phila., 1986—; juror Temple U., U. Pa., Drexel U., Bryn Mawr Coll., Villanova U., Phila. Coll. Textiles and Sci.; asst. prof. U. Pa., fall 1988; lectr. Bryn Mawr Coll., 1990—. Prin. works include Jaffe History of Art Bldg. at U. Pa., Hitchings Residence (Merit award Cedar Shake and Shingle Bur. 1989, 1st prize Sympathetic Additions category Nat. Trust Hist. Preservation 1990), Mitchell Residence (Merit award Builder Mag. 1991), Historic Kesher Israel Synagogue renovation, Pensacola St. Beach Pavilion, Seaside, Fla.; one man shows include AIA, Phila., 1995. Phila. Chpt. scholar Victorian Soc., summer 1991. Office: Atkin Olshin Lawson-Bell & Assocs Archs 125 S 9th St Ste 900 Philadelphia PA 19107-5122

OLSHWANGER, RON, photojournalist. Freelance photographer St. Louis Post-Dispatch. Recipient Pulitzer prize for spot news photography, 1989. Office: Saint Louis Post-Dispatch Dept of Photography 900 N Tucker Blvd Saint Louis MO 63101-1069*

OLSON, ANN MARTIN, language education specialist; b. N.Y.C., Apr. 3, 1933; d. Arthur Francis and Jane Frances (Ryan) Martin; m. Peter Byrne Olson, Feb. 11, 1967; children: Sven Martin, Katrin Ann, Gunnar Byrne. Superior degree, Sorbonne, Paris, 1954; BA, Coll. New Rochelle, 1955; MS in Edn., SUNY, Oswego, 1993. Cert. tchr. French, N.Y.; cert. ESOL tchr., N.Y. Tchr. French Scarsdale (N.Y.) Pub. Schs., 1959-67; instrnl. specialist Bilingual/ESL Assistance Ctr., Syracuse, N.Y., 1987—; coord. multi-cultural assessment conf., Binghamton, 1994; coord., presenter Colloquium on Bilingual Exceptional Students, 1993, 94. Editor (student anthology) Visions and Voices, 1988-95. Mem. Concord Coalition, Washington, 1994, Social Justice Com., Fayetteville, N.Y., 1994; active area French club. Recipient Cert. of Recognition divsn. bilingual edn. N.Y. State Dept. Edn., Albany, 1992, Cert. of Appreciation, Hispanic Task Force N.Y. State Assembly, Albany, 1993. Mem. Tchrs. of English to Speakers of Other Langs. (workshop presenter 1994), N.Y. State Tchrs. of English to Speakers of Other Langs. (workshop presenter 1994). Avocations: bridge, reading, bicycling, swimming, cooking. Home: 309 Elm St Fayetteville NY 13066-1413

OLSON, BARBARA FORD, physician; b. Iowa City, June 15, 1935; d. Leonard A. and Anne (Swanson) Ford; m. Robert Eric Olson, March 21, 1959 (div. 1973); children: Katherine Gee, Eric Ford, Julie Marie. BA, Gustavus Adolphus Coll., 1956; MD, U. Minn., 1960. Diplomate Am. Bd. Family Practice (cert. added qualifications geriatric medicine). Intern St. Paul-Ramsy Med. Ctr., 1960-61; resident in anesthesiology U. Hosp. Cleve., 1961-62, U. Minn. Hosp., Mpls., 1962-63; pvt. practice anesthesiology St. Johns Hosp. and Devine Redeemer Hosp., St. Paul, 1963-67, Mercy Hosp., Coon Rapids, Minn., 1967-74; staff physician Oak Terrace Nursing Home, Minnetonka, Minn., 1974-88; med. dir. nursing home care unit VA Med. Ctr., St. Cloud, Minn., 1988—. Pres., bd. dirs. Alpha Epsilon Iota Med. Found., Mpls., 1980-86. Mem. Minn. Med. Assn., Minn. Women Physicians (pres. 1981-82), Minn. Nursing Home Med. Dirs. Home: PO Box 7306 Saint Cloud MN 56302-7306 Office: VA Med Ctr 4801 8th St N Saint Cloud MN 56303-2014

OLSON, BOB MOODY, marketing executive; b. Memphis, June 18, 1934; s. Nels Antone and June Esther (Hogan) O.; m. Sandra Holmes, Oct. 2, 1956; children: Jeffrey, Sandra Leigh, Karen Louise. AB in Econs., Princeton (N.J.) U., 1955; postgrad., U. Va., 1974; MBA in Bus., Fordham U., 1977. With IBM Corp., 1955-80, industry dir. ins., 1969-74; account exec. IBM Corp., N.Y.C., 1974-80; sr. v.p. sales and mktg. div. ITT World Communications, Inc., N.Y.C., 1980-83; v.p. sales and mktg. div. Siemens/Databit, Hauppauge, N.Y., 1983-85, Amdahl Communications, Richardson, Tex., 1985-86; v.p. U.S. div. Gandalf Techs., Inc., Nepean, Ont., Can., 1986-88; sr. dir. Motorola Info. Systems Group, King of Prussia, Pa., 1988—. Capt. USAF, 1956-59. Mem. Charter Club (bd. govs. 1968-85), Princeton Club of N.Y. Republican. Avocations: tennis, golf. Home: 222 Nevin Ln Lower Gwynedd PA 19002-2033 Office: Motorola ISG 660 Am Ave Ste 105 King Of Prussia PA 19406

OLSON, BONNIE WAGGONER-BRETERNITZ (MRS. O. DONALD OLSON), civic worker; b. North Platte, Nebr.; d. Floyd Emil and Edith (Waggoner) Breternitz; AB, U. Chgo., 1947; m. O. Donald Olson, May 17, 1944; children: Pamela Lynne, Douglas Donald. Dep. clk. Dist. Ct., Lincoln County, Nebr., 1940-42; advt. researcher Burke & Assoc., Chgo., 1942; contbg. newspaper columnist Chgo. Herald-Am., 1943; social worker A.R.C., Chgo., 1942-44, Sacramento, Calif., 1944, Amarillo, Tex., 1945; exec. sec. Econometrica, Cowles Commn. for Rsch. in Econs., Chgo., 1945-47; interior designer, antique dealer. Col.; participant Chgo. Maternity Ctr. Fund Drive, 1953, Chgo. Coun. on Fgn. Rels., 1948-54; mem. Colo. Springs Community Council, 1956-58, chmn. children's div., 1956-58, mem. exec. bd., 1956-58, mem. budget com., 1957-58; mem. Colorado Springs Charter Assn., 1956-60, mem. exec. bd., 1957-59, sec., 1958; chmn. El Paso County PTA, Protective Svcs. for Children, 1959-61; chmn. women's div. fund drive ARC, 1961; mem. League Women Voters, 1957—, mem. state children's law com., 1961-63; chmn. ad hoc com. El Paso County Citizens' Com. for Nat. Probation and Parole Survey, Juvenile Ct. Procedures and Detention, 1957-61; mem. children's adv. com. Colo. Child Welfare Dept., 1959-63, chmn., 1961; del. White House Conf. on Children and Youth, 1960, 70; sec. Citizens Ad Hoc Com. for Comprehensive Mental Health Clinic for Pikes Peak Region, 1966—; mem. Colorado Springs Human Rels. Commn., 1968-71; sustaining mem. Symphony Guild, 1970-72, Fine Arts Ctr., 1957—; mem. Pikes Peak Mental Health Ctr., 1964-67 (bd. dirs.); Colo. observer White House Conf. on Aging, 1981, Colo. Gov.'s Conf. on Aging, 1981, Dist. Atty.'s Child Abuse Task Force, 1986; panelist career planning documentary film Not Just a Job, Radcliffe Coll. Career Svcs., 1990; counselor Health Info. Needs of Elders (Mass. Shine Program), 1992—. Recipient Lane Bryant Ann. Nat. Awards citation, 1971; alumni citation for pub. service U. Chgo., 1961. Mem. Am. Acad. Polit. and Social Sci., Nat. Trust Historic Preservation, Women's Ednl. Soc. Colo. Coll. (life), Council on Religion and Internat. Affairs. Episcopalian. Clubs: Quadranglar, University (Chgo.). Home: PO Box 1324 Duxbury MA 02331-1324

OLSON, CAL OLIVER, golf architect; b. Grindstone, S.D., Oct. 18, 1939; s. Harold John and Maxine Lorraine (Knutson) O.; m. Paula Lavon Hancock, Dec. 27, 1971. BSCE, Calif. Poly., Pomona, 1974. Prin. Peridian Group, Irvine, Calif., 1966-78; v.p. L.D. King Engring., Ontario, Calif., 1978-79; prin. Cal Olson Golf Architect, Costa Mesa, Calif., 1979—. Author: Turftgrass Science, 1983. Mem. ASCE, Am. Soc. Landscape Architects. Republican. Lutheran. Avocation: golf. Office: Cal Olson Golf Architect 3070 Bristol St Ste 460 Costa Mesa CA 92626-3070

OLSON, CAROL LEA, lithographer, educator, photographer; b. Anderson, Ind., June 10, 1929; d. Daniel Ackerman and Marguerite Louise Olson. AB, Anderson Coll., 1952; MA, Ball State U., 1976. Pasteup artist Warner Press, Inc., Anderson, 1952-53, apprentice lithographer stripper, 1953-57, journeyman, 1957-63, lithographic dot etcher, color corrector, 1959-73, prepres coord. art dept., 1973-81, prepres tech. specialist, 1981-83, color film assembler, 1983-96; part-time photography instr. Anderson Univ.; tchr. photography Anderson Fine Arts Ctr., 1976-79; instr. photography, photographics Anderson U., 1979—; mag. photographer Bd. Christian Edn. of Ch. of God, Anderson, 1973-86; freelance photographer. One person show Anderson U., 1979; exhibited in group shows Anderson U., 1980-93, Purdue U., 1982. Instr. 1st aide ARC, Anderson, 1969-79; sec. volleyball Anderson Sunday Sch. Athletic Assn., 1973—. Recipient Hon. mention, Ann Arbor, Mich., 1977, Anderson Fine Arts Ctr., 1977, 78, 83, 1st Pl.,

1983, Hon. Mention, 1983, 2d Pl., 1988, Hon. Mention, 1988, 93, Best of Show, 1983, 91, 92, Best Nature Catagory Anderson Fine Arts Ctr., 1994. Mem. AAUW, Associated Photographer Internat., Nat. Inst. Exploration, Profl. Photographers Am. Mem. Ch. of God. Avocations: camping, travel, canoeing. Home: 2604 E 6th St Anderson IN 46012-3725

OLSON, CATHERINA, state legislator, farmer; b. Rock Rapids, Iowa, Oct. 24, 1928; d. Corneluis and Cornelia (Bakker) Gaalswyk; m. Robert R. Olson, Nov. 13, 1948; children: Cynthia, Shirley, Roberta, Kent, Amy. Student, Luther Coll., Mankato State U. Bd. mem. PTA Minn. State, 1968-84; mem. Trimont Sch. Bd., Minn., 1976-86; bd. mem. Edn. Coop. Svc. Unit, Mankato, Minn., 1980-86; commr. Region 9 Devel. Commn., 1982-86; rep. Minn. State Govt., St. Paul, 1986-94; vice chair Edn. Com. in House, St. Paul, 1986-94; asst. maj. leader Minn. House of Reps., 1992-94; ret., 1994; cons., lobbyist Minn. Rural Edn. Assn.; bd. dirs. Southeastern Minn. Initiative Fund, Heron Lake Environ. Learning Ctr. Avocations: golf, fishing, family activities. Home: RR 2 Box 115 Sherburn MN 56171-9747 Office: Minn State Office Rm 523 Saint Paul MN 55155-1606

OLSON, CHARLES ERIC, economist; b. Wausau, Wis., June 2, 1942; s. Roland Anthony and Lois (Erickson) O.; student U. Wis., Marathon County, 1960-62; B.B.A. with honors, U. Wis., Madison, 1964, M.S., 1966, Ph.D. (Vilias fellow), 1968; m. Pamela Ann Templin, July 1, 1967 (div. Oct. 1973), children—Sonja Anne, Erika Christine; m. 2d, Carole Emily Collesian, Dec. 1, 1973 (div. Oct. 1990); children—Cora Elizabeth, Sarah Emily; m. 3d, Jeanne Esther Katz, Apr. 14, 1991. Instr., U. Wis., Madison, 1966-68; asst. prof. U. Md., College Park, 1968-71, assoc. prof. bus. adminstrn., 1971-76; sr. economist H. Zinder & Assos., Washington, 1976—, v.p., 1977-79, sr. v.p., 1979—; pres. Olson & Co., Inc., 1980-86, pres. H. Zinder and Assocs., 1986—; cons. Devel. Adv. Service, atty. gens. N.C., Minn., Ky., Mass., Va. U.S. Postal Rate Commn., Dept. Def., numerous electric and gas utlities in U.S. and Can. Testified numerous pub. utility rate cases, before Senate Subcom. on Inter-govtl. Relations; mem. advisory com. research and devel. and energy conservation Fed. Power Commn., 1973-74, vice chmn. rate design task force, 1976—. Mem. Prince Georges County (Md.) Citizens Airpark Advisory Com., 1970-71. Inst. Pub. Utilities grantee, 1967-68; U. Md. grantee, 1970, 76. Mem. Transp. and Pub. Utilities Group, Beta Gamma Sigma. Author: Cost Considerations for Efficient Electricity Supply, 1970. Contbr. chpts. to books, articles to profl. jours. Home: 10822 Alloway Dr Rockville MD 20854-1503 Office: 1828 L St NW Washington DC 20036-5118

OLSON, CLARENCE ELMER, JR., newspaper editor; b. Edgerton, Wis., July 1, 1927; s. C. Elmer and Helen (Turnbull) O.; m. Arielle North, Sept. 4, 1954; children: Randall Jack, Christina North, Jens Sterling Elmer. B.S., U. Wis., 1950. News editor Edgerton Reporter, 1953; photographer, writer Madison (Wis.) Capital Times, 1953-59; writer St. Louis Post-Dispatch Pictures mag., 1959-65, asst. editor, 1965-68; asst. mng. editor Careers Today mag., Delmar, Calif., 1968-69; book editor St. Louis Post-Dispatch, 1969-91, ret., 1991. Served with USNR, 1945-46. Home: 236 N Elm Ave Saint Louis MO 63119-2420

OLSON, CLIFFORD LARRY, management consultant, entrepreneur; b. Karlstad, Minn., Oct. 11, 1946; s. Wallace B. and Lucille I (Pederson) O.; m. B.A. Blue Blodgett, March 18, 1967; children: Derek, Erin. B in Chemical Engring., U. Minn., 1969, B in Physics, 1969; MBA, U. Chgo., 1972; Licence en Sciences Economiques, U. de Louvain, Brussels, 1972. CPA, Cert. mgmt. cons. Project engr. Procter & Gamble, Chgo., 1969-71; engagement mgr. McKinsey & Co., Chgo., 1972-75; ptnr., midwest regional dir. mgmt. consulting Peat, Marwick, Mitchell, St. Louis, 1976-87; chmn. Casson Industries Inc., Mpls., 1987—; bd. dirs. Castlerock Group, Inc., Chevron, Inc. Mem. AICPA, Inst. Mgmt. Cons., Union League Club Chgo., Tavern Club, Interlachen Country Club. Episcopalian. Avocations: skiing, carpentry. Office: 5804 Schaefer Rd Minneapolis MN 55436-1116

OLSON, CLINTON LOUIS, foreign service officer, former ambassador; b. S.D., Mar. 31, 1916; s. William H. and Allie (Sparling) O.; m. Ethel Hoover, June 14, 1943; children: Merilee, Peter, David, Steven. B.S., Stanford U., 1939, M.B.A., 1941. Petroleum engr. with Robert S. Lytle, 1939-40; partner Chino Homes, Inc. (realtors), 1946- 47; pres. EXIM of Calif., 1946-48; with U.S. Fgn. Service, 1948-75; 2d sec. U.S. legation, Vienna, Austria, 1948-52; consul. French West Indies, 1953-55; budget examiner State Dept., 1956; exec. dir. bur. Inter-Am. Affairs, 1957-59; assigned Nat. War Coll., 1959-60; counselor of embassy London, Eng., 1960-62; counselor econ. affairs Am. embassy, Vienna, 1962-66; charge d'affaires, minister-counselor Am. embassy, Lagos, Nigeria, 1966-70; sr. fgn. service insp., 1970-72; U.S. ambassador to Sierra Leone, 1972-75; internat. cons., 1975—. Served to lt. col., ordnance AUS, 1941-46, Russia, Iran. Fellow Explorers Club; mem. Fgn. Service Assn., Theta Xi. Clubs: Rolling Rock (Ligonier, Pa.); Ross Mountain (Pa.); Mill Reef (Antigua, W.I.). Home: Ross Mountain Club New Florence PA 15944

OLSON, DALE C., public relations executive; b. Fargo, N.D., Feb. 20, 1934; s. Arthur Edwin and Edith (Weight) Olson Neubauer. Sr. v.p., prin., pres. motion picture divsn. Rogers and Cowan, Inc., Beverly Hills, Calif., 1967-85; prin. Dale C. Olson & Assocs., Beverly Hills, 1985—; cons. Filmex, L.A., 1972-83; U.S. del. Manila Film Festival, 1982-83. Editor L.A. edit. Theatre ann. Best Plays, 1963-67. V.p. Diamond Cir. City of Hope, Duarte, Calif., 1980-83; mem. adv. bd. Calif. Mus. Sci. and Industry, L.A., 1975-81; mem. bd. govs. Film Industry Workshops, Inc., 1965-80; pres. Hollywood Press Club, 1963-66; assoc. Los Angeles County Art Mus., 1981-83. Recipient Golden Key, Pub. Rels. News, 1982, Les Mason and pub. svc. awards Publicists Guild. Mem. NATAS, Acad. Motion Picture Arts and Scis. (chmn. pub. rels. coordinating com. 1982—), Actors Fund Am. (chmn. Western coun. 1991, trustee 1992), Pres.'s Club, Thalians. Lutheran. Office: 6310 San Vicente Blvd Ste 340 Los Angeles CA 90048-5426

OLSON, DAVID HENRY, aircraft manufacturing company executive; b. Milw., Sept. 19, 1933; s. Henry John and Evelyn Bertha (Bergstrom) O.; m. Kathryn Townsend Snow, Sept. 4, 1965; children—Henry David, Andrew Alan, Kathryn Perry, David Charles. AB, UCLA, 1955; LLB, U. Calif., Berkeley, 1958. Bar: Calif. 1959, U.S. Dist. Ct. (so. dist.) Calif. 1959, U.S. Ct. Mil. Appeals 1959, U.S. Ct. Appeals (9th cir.) 1967, U.S. Supreme Ct. 1968. Trial atty. Transit Casualty Co., Los Angeles, 1961-64, Republic Indemnity Co., Los Angeles, 1964-65, Veatch, Carlson, Dorsey & Quimby, Los Angeles, 1965-67; asst. sec. Northrop Guimman Corp., Los Angeles, 1967-72; sec. Northrop Guimman Corp., 1973-76, div. gen. counsel, 1976-88, sr. corp. counsel, 1988—; mem. Am. Soc. Corp. Secs., 1969-85, Am. Bd. Trial Advs., 1965-72. Capt. JAGC, USAF, 1959-61. Mem. L.A. Bar Assn., Am. Bd. Trial Advocates, Sigma Alpha Epsilon, Phi Delta Phi. Unitarian. Home: 415 Avondale Ave Los Angeles CA 90049-4801 Office: 1840 Century Park E Los Angeles CA 90067-2101

OLSON, DAVID JOHN, political science educator; b. Brantford, N.D., May 18, 1941; s. Lloyd and Alice Ingrid (Black) O.; m. Sandra Jean Crabb, June 11, 1966; 1 dau., Maia Kari. B.A., Concordia Coll., Moorhead, Minn., 1963; Rockefeller fellow Union Theol. Sem, N.Y.C., 1963-64; M.A. (Brookings Instn. predoctoral research fellow 1968-69), U. Wis., Madison, 1966, Ph.D. (univ. fellow 1967), 1971. Community planner Madison Redvel. Authority, 1965-66; lectr. U. Wis., 1966-67; from lectr. to asso. prof. polit. sci. Ind. U., Bloomington, 1969-76; prof. polit. sci. U. Wash., Seattle, 1976—; chmn. dept. U. Wash., 1983-88, Harry Bridges endowed chairlabor studies, 1992-94; bd. dirs. Harry Bridges Inst.; dir.Ctr. Labor Studies U. Wash., 1992-94; Disting. lectr. in labor studies San Francisco State U., 1994; vis. prof. U. Bergen, 1987, Harvard U., 1988-89, U. Hawaii, 1989, U. Calif., Berkeley, 1996. Co-author: Governing the United States, 1978, Commission Politics, 1977, To Keep the Republic, 1975, Black Politics, 1971; co-editor: Theft of the City, 1974. Recipient Disting. Teaching award Ind. U., 1973, faculty fellow, 1973. Mem. Am. Polit. Sci. Assn., Western Polit. Sci. Assn. (v.p. 1984, pres. 1985), Midwest Polit. Sci. Assn., So. Polit. Sci. Assn. Democrat. Lutheran. Home: 6512 E Green Lake Way N Seattle WA 98103-5418 Office: Univ Wash Dept Polit Sci Seattle WA 98195

OLSON, DAVID R., lawyer; b. Mpls., May 21, 1938; s. Russell M. and Lenore E. (Goulet) O.; m. m. Judith A., Sept. 23, 1966; children: Mary, Stephen, Kathleen, Jennifer, Kristin. BBA, U. Minn., 1960, JD, 1963. Bar: Wis. 1963. Assoc. Michael, Best & Frederich, Milw., 1963-70, ptnr., 1970—. Mem. bd. editors U. Minn.Law Review 1962-63. Mem. ABA, Milw. Bar Assn. (pres. 1991-92). Roman Catholic. Avocations: tennis, landscaping, history. Office: Michael Best & Friedrich 100 E Wisconsin Ave Ste 3300 Milwaukee WI 53202-4108*

OLSON, DONALD ERNEST, retired physician; b. Portland, Oreg., June 22, 1921; s. Ernest S. and Edith (Swanman) O.; m. Alice Curtis Bergh, July 7, 1951; children—Julie Rene, Reid Martin, Kathy Ruth, Marc Ernest. B.A., Reed Coll., 1943; M.S., U. Oreg., 1947, M.D., 1947, Ph.D., 1948. Diplomate: Am. Bd. Internal Medicine (chmn. subsplty. pulmonary disease 1968-70; mem. bd. 1972-79). Intern U. Hosps., Madison, Wis., 1948-49; resident U. Hosps., 1949-51; research fellow dept. medicine U. Wis., 1952-53; staff physician VA Hosp., Madison, 1952-53, Portland Clinic, 1955-92; mem. staff VA Hosp., Portland; assoc. clin. prof. medicine U. Oreg., now clin. prof. medicine emeritus. Served with M.C., AUS, 1953-55. Fellow ACP (master 1992); mem. Am., Oreg. thoracic socs., Am. Coll. Chest Physicians, North Pacific Soc. Internal Medicine, Am., Ore. med. assns., Am. Clin. and Climatol. Assn., Multnomah County Med. Soc., Phi Beta Kappa, Alpha Omega Alpha. Home: 8375 SW Crestwood Ln Portland OR 97225-2227

OLSON, DONALD RICHARD, mechanical engineering educator; b. Sargent, Nebr., Dec. 26, 1917; s. Harry T. and Gyneth E. (Wittemyer) O.; m. Nancy Walker Benton, June 17, 1944; children: Walter H., Sally, Timothy W. B.S., Oreg. State U., 1942; M.Engring., Yale U., 1944, D.Engring., 1951. Profl. engr., Conn. Asst. prof., asso. prof. mech. engring. Yale U., New Haven, 1951-62; prof. mech. engring. Pa. State U., University Park, 1962-83; prof. emeritus Pa. State U., 1983—; head underwater power plants Applied Research Lab., 1962-72, head dept. mech. engring., 1972-83; mem. engring. accreditation commn., 1979-82. Contbr. tech. papers in field to publs. Mem. ASME, Soc. Automotive Engrs. (dir. 1968-71), Sigma Xi. Home: 621 Glenn Rd State College PA 16803-3475

OLSON, FERRON ALLRED, metallurgist, educator; b. Tooele, Utah, July 2, 1921; s. John Ernest and Harriet Cynthia (Allred) O.; m. Donna Lee Jefferies, Feb. 1, 1944; children: Kandace, Randall, Paul, Jeffery, Richard. BS, U. Utah, 1953, PhD, 1956. Ordained bishop LDS Ch., 1962. Research chemist Shell Devel. Co., Emeryville, Calif., 1956-61; assoc. research prof. U. Utah, Salt Lake City, 1961-63, assoc. prof., 1963-68, chmn. dept mining, metall. and fuels engring., 1966-74, prof. dept. metallurgy and metall. engring., 1968—; cons. U.S. Bur. Mines, Salt Lake City, 1973-77, Ctr. for Investigation Mining and Metallurgy, Santiago, Chile, 1978; dir. U. Utah Minerals Inst., 1980-91. Author: Collection of Short Stories, 1985, (novel) Harriet Cynthia Allred Olson, 1995; contbr. articles to profl. jours. Del. State Rep. Conv., Salt Lake City, 1964; bishop, 1962-68, 76-82, missionary, 1988. With U.S. Army, 1943-46, PTO. Named Fulbright-Hayes lectr., Yugoslavia, 1974-75, Disting. prof. Fulbright-Hayes, Yugoslavia, 1980, Outstanding Metallurgy Instr., U. Utah, 1979-80, 88-89, Disting. Speaker U. Belgrade-Bor, Yugoslavia, 1974. Mem. Am. Inst. Mining, Metall. and Petroleum Engrs. (chmn. Utah chpt. 1978-79), Am. Soc. Engring. Edn. (chmn. Minerals div. 1972-73), Fulbright Alumni Assn., Am. Bd. Engring. and Tech. (bd. dirs. 1975-82). Republican. Achievements include research on explosives ignition and decomposition; surface properties of thoria, silica gels, silicon monoxide in ultra high vacuum; kinetics of leaching of Chrysocolla, Malachite and Bornite; electrowinning of gold; nodulation of copper during electrodeposition. Home: 1862 Herbert Ave Salt Lake City UT 84108-1832 Office: U Utah Dept Metallurgy 412 Browning Building Bldg Salt Lake City UT 84112-1118

OLSON, FRANK ALBERT, car rental company executive; b. San Francisco, July 19, 1932; s. Alfred and Edith Mary (Hazeldine) O.; m. Sarah Jean Blakely, Oct. 19, 1957; children—Kimberly, Blake, Christopher. AA, City Coll. San Francisco, 1961. V.p. and gen. mgr. Barrett Transp. Inc., San Francisco, 1950-64; v.p., gen. mgr. Valcar Co. subs. Hertz Corp., San Francisco, 1964-68; mgr. N.Y. zone Hertz Corp., N.Y.C., 1968-69, v.p., mgr. eastern region, v.p., gen. mgr. rent-a-car div., exec. v.p. rent-a-car div., gen. mgr., also bd. dirs., 1973-77, pres., chief exec. officer, 1977-80, chmn. bd., 1980, also dir., chief exec. officer, from 1982; chmn., chief exec. officer Allegis Corp., 1987; pres., chief exec. officer United Airlines, 1987; chmn., chief exec. officer Hertz Corp., Park Ridge, N.J., 1987—; bd. dirs. Becton Dickinson & Co., Cooper Industries, Commonwealth Edison, Found. Health Corp. Bd. dirs. World Travel & Tourism Coun., (mem. exec. com.). Mem. Am. Assn. Sovereign Mil. Order of Malta, Olympic Club (Calif.), Pine Valley Golf Club (N.J.), Royal and Ancient St. Andrews (Scotland), Arcola Country Club (Paramus, N.J.), Metropolitan Club (N.Y.C.). Republican. Roman Catholic. Office: Hertz Corp 225 Brae Blvd Park Ridge NJ 07656-1870*

OLSON, FRANK L., electrical power industry executive. With Crisp County Power Commission, Cordele, Ga., 1964-91; pres., gen. manager Municipal Electric Auth of Ga., Atlanta, 1992—. Office: Municipal Electric Auth of Ga 1470 Riveredge Pky NW Atlanta GA 30328-4640*

OLSON, FREDERICK IRVING, retired history educator; b. Milw., May 30, 1916; s. Frank and Clara (Hansen) O.; m. Jane Marian Correll, June 8, 1946; children: David Frederick, Donald Frank, Roger Alan. B.A. magna cum laude, Harvard U., 1938, M.A. (George W. Dillaway fellow 1938-39), 1939, Ph.D. in History, 1952. Mem. faculty U. Wis., Milw., 1946-85, prof. history, 1956-85, chmn. com. on univ. future, 1959-60, chmn. dept. history, 1960-62, 67-70, assoc. dean Coll. Letters and Sci., 1971-76, acting dean Sch. Library Sci., 1977-79; exec. dir. Milw. Humanities Program, 1979-84; vis. prof. history U. Wis.-Madison, summer 1957; assoc. dean U. Wis. extension, Mil., 1960-68; dir. Ridge Stone Fin. Svcs., Brookfield, 1995—. Author: (with Harry H. Anderson) Milwaukee: At the Gathering of the Waters, 1981, 2d edit., 1984, (with Frank Cassell and J. Martin Klotsche) The University of Wisconsin-Milwaukee: A Historical Profile, 1885-92, 1992, (with James Correll Olson) Dear Jane: A Soldier's Letters from Africa and the Middle East, 1942-45, 1994; contbr. articles and book revs. to profl. jours. Trustee Milw. Pub. Mus., 1951-52; bd. dirs. Milw. County Hist. Soc., 1947-85, 95—, pres., 1953-57, 72-75; bd. curators State Hist. Soc. Wis., 1961-91; mem. Milw. Landmarks Commn., 1964-71, Milw. County Landmarks Commn., 1976—, chmn., 1976-82; mem. rev. bd. Wis. Hist. Preservation, 1978-89; bd. dirs. Wis. Heritages, Inc., 1983-93, pres., 1989-90; bd. dirs. Wauwatosa Hist. Soc., 1984-96. With AUS, 1942-45. Mem. Orgn. Am. Historians, Wis. Acad. Scis., Arts and Letters, Lincoln Group (Boston), North Hills Country Club (Waukesha, Wis.), Phi Beta Kappa, Phi Alpha Theta, Phi Kappa Phi. Lutheran. Home: 2437 N 90th St Milwaukee WI 53226-1803

OLSON, GARY ROBERT, banker; b. Milw., May 9, 1946; s. Ward Louis and Mary Jane (Brown) O.; m. Mia Kristina Sohn, Feb. 26, 1972; children: Kristin Anne, Brian Ward. Student, Loyola U., Rome, 1966-67; AB, Marquette U., 1968; M Internat. Mgmt., Am. Grad. Sch. Internat. Mgmt., Glendale, Ariz., 1973. Instr. Sogang Jesuit U., Seoul, 1968-70, Hankuk U. Fgn. Studies, Seoul, 1971-72; grad. asst. Am. Grad. Sch. Internat. Mgmt., 1972; credit analyst Chase Manhattan Bank, N.A., N.Y.C. and Tokyo, 1973-75; asst. treas. Chase Manhattan Bank, N.A., N.Y.C., 1975-77; 2d v.p. Chase Manhattan Bank, N.A., Madrid, 1977, Paris, 1977-80; v.p., mgr. Regional Banking Office Chase Manhattan Bank, N.A., Chgo., 1980-83; v.p., regional mgr. Case Nat. Corp. Svcs., San Francisco, 1983-87; sr. v.p. Chase Bank Ariz., Phoenix, 1987-90; v.p. Bklyn. and S.I. commercial mgr. Chase Manhattan Bank, N.A., Bklyn., 1990-93; v.p. Chase Manhattan Bank, N.A., Melville, L.I., 1993—. Advisor English program USIS, Seoul, 1969; alumni domestic counselor Am. Grad. Sch. Internat. Mgmt. Marquette U., 1990—; vol. Spl. Olympics, Phoenix, 1988-89; fund drive capt. Phoenix Econ. Growth Corp., 1988; trustee, bd. dirs. Variety Pre-schooler's workshop, 1994—; bd. bd.dirs. L.I. cpht. Robert Morris Assocs., 1994—, chmn., 1995—; mem. devel. com. Hecksher Mus., Huntington, N.Y., 1995—. Mem. Robert Morris Assocs. (assoc.), Econ. Club Phoenix, World Trade Club. Republican. Roman Catholic. Avocations: reading, skiing, swimming, golf. Office: Chase Manhattan Bank NA 135 Pinelawn Rd Melville NY 11747-3133

OLSON, GREGORY BRUCE, materials science and engineering educator, academic director; b. Bklyn., Apr. 10, 1947; s. Oscar Gustav Fritz and Elizabeth Rose (Dorner) O.; m. Jane Ellen Black, May 10, 1980; 1 child, Elise Marie. BS, MS in Materials Sci. and Engring., MIT, 1970, ScD in Materials Sci. and Engring., 1974. Rsch. assoc. dept. materials sci. and engring. MIT, Cambridge, 1974-79, prin. rsch. assoc., 1979-85, sr. rsch. assoc., 1985-88; prof. materials sci. and engring. Northwestern U., Evanston, Ill., 1988—; cons. Army Materials Tech. Lab., Watertown, Mass., 1975-88, Lawrence Livermore (Calif.) Nat. Lab., 1983-89; Jacob Kurtz Exchange Scientist Technion-Israel Inst. Tech., 1979; SERC vis. prof. U. Cambridge, 1992; now assoc. chmn. dept. materials sci. and engring. Northwestern U., dir. materials rsch. ctr.-steel rsch. group, 1985—. Editor: Innovative UHS Steel Technology, 1990, Martensite, 1992; contbr. over 135 papers and articles to jours., encyclopedias and symposia, inventor hydrogen-res. UHS steel, stainless bearing steel. Fellow AMAX Found., 1972-74; named N.Mex. Disting. lectr. in Materials, 1983; recipient Creativity Extension award NSF, 1983-85; Wallenberg grantee Jacob Wallenberg Found., Sweden, 1993, Technology Recognition award NASA, 1994. Fellow ASM (chmn. phase transformation com. 1987-90, Boston chpt. Sauveur meml. lectr. 1986), ASM Internat.; mem. AAAS, Materials Rsch. Soc., Internat. Com. Martensitic Transformation, Internat. Conf. Martensitic Transformation (co-chmn. 1992), TMS-AIME (student affairs com.), ISS-AIME (M.R. Tenenbaum award 1993). Lutheran. Avocations: sports cars, jazz trumpet. Office: Northwestern U Dept Materials Sci and Engring 2225 N Campus Dr Evanston IL 60208-3108

OLSON, HARRY ANDREW, JR., communications consultant; b. Nashwauk, Minn., Jan. 8, 1923; s. Harry Arnold and Elizabeth C. (Wigen) O.; m. Dorothy M. Kuntz July 25, 1946 (div. 1978); children: Dana, Sarah, Cara, Christopher, Eric, Todd. B.S., U. Minn., 1948; LL.B., St. Paul Coll. Law, 1950. Bar: Minn. 1950. Investment analyst Investors Diversified, Mpls., 1954-57; dir. investment div. Investors Diversified, 1958-61; pres., dir. Am. Plan, Mpls., 1961-66; v.p. investments Fireman's Fund, San Francisco, 1966-67, Fund Am., 1967-69; v.p. corp. devel. Am. Express Co., N.Y.C., 1969-72; sr. v.p. corp. personnel Am. Express Co., 1974-78, sr. v.p. investment planning and adminstrn., 1978-80, sr. v.p. fin. analysis and investor relations, 1980-81; pres. dir. Am. Express Investment Mgmt. Co., 1972-74; pres. Partnership for Neighborhood Safety, 1982-83; v.p. Nat. Exec. Svc. Corps, N.Y.C., 1983-87, nat. coord. affiliates network, 1990-91; adminstr. Diocese of the Armenian Ch. of Am., N.Y.C., 1992-94; comm. cons. ELF Techs., Mercer Island, Wash., 1994—. Founder, pres. Found. Disadvantaged Youth; bd. dirs. Andrew Glover Youth Program. Unitarian. Office: 505 Court St Apt 5R Brooklyn NY 11231-3951 Office: ELF Techs Inc 9423 SE 36th St Mercer Island WA 98040-3702

OLSON, HERBERT THEODORE, trade association executive; b. Bridgeport, Conn., Feb. 9, 1929; s. Herbert Theodore and Inez Evelyn (Lindahl) O.; children: Christina, Victoria; m. Kathleen A. Harrison, Dec. 27, 1988. Student Heidelberg Coll., 1947-49; A.B., Ohio U., 1951, postgrad., 1951-52. Asst. to dean of men Ohio U., Athens, 1951-52; with Union Carbide Corp., 1952-71, mgr. employee relations, coordinator pub. affairs, N.Y.C., 1969-71; exec. v.p. Am. Assn. for Aging, Washington, 1971-75; dir. spl. projects Am. Health Care Assn., Washington, 1975-79; pres. Promotional Products Assn. Internat., Irving, Tex., 1979-96, pres. emeritus 1996—; adv. bd. Allied Bank. Mem. long-term care for elderly research rev. and adv. com. Dept. Health, 1972-77; mem. Longterm Care grant rev. com. HEW, 1972-77; mem. planning commn. City of Torrance, Calif., 1962-64, city councilman, 1964-67; mem. nat. exploring com., vice chmn. nat. events com., ann. meetings com., mem.-at-large nat. council Boy Scouts Am.; chmn. Gov's Operation Leegit; treas. U.S. Found. for Internat. Scouting, 1988—, chmn. audit com. 1984-87; adv. bd. Irving Hosp.; bd. dirs. Irving Cancer Soc. Served with USAR. Lord Baden Powell fellow, 1986; recipient Disting. Eagle award Boy Scouts Am., 1974, Silver Beaver award, 1968; named Person of Yr. in Promotional Products UN Counselor MAg, 1995, Hall of Fame Promotional Products Assn. Can. Mem. Meeting Planners Internat. (charter), Am. Soc. Assn. Execs., U.S. C. of C., Washington Soc. Assn. Execs., Nat. Assn. Exhibit Mgrs., Small Bus. Legal Council (chmn. bd. 1993-95), Dallas Ft. Worth Soc. Assn. Execs. (v.p. 1985-87), Irving C. of C. (past bd. dirs.), Am. Advt. Fedn., Tex. Soc. Assn. Execs. Lutheran. Club: Las Colinas Country. Lodges: Rotary (past bd. dirs.), Masons, Shriners. Home: 2910 Pacific Ct Irving TX 75062-4624 Office: 3125 Skyway Cir N Irving TX 75038-3541

OLSON, HILDING HAROLD, surgeon, educator; b. Burlington, Wash., Apr. 30, 1916; s. Adolph and Gerda (Gerdin) O.; m. Donna D. Anderson, Aug. 14, 1943; children: Sheila K. Richardson, Susan L. LeClerq, Daniel L. BS, U. Wash., 1939; MD, U. Oreg., 1943. Diplomate Am. Bd. Surgery. Intern King County Hosp., Seattle, 1944-45, resident, 1945-51, attending surgeon, 1951—; clin. prof. surgery U. Wash., Seattle, 1964-87, emeritus, 1987—; mem. staff Providence Med. Ctr., Harborview Med. Ctr., Swedish Hosp. Med. Ctr., Univ. Hosp.; teaching fellow Dept. Anatomy, U. Oreg., 1940-43; dir. surgical clerkship program U. Wash. Dept. Surgery, 1954-73; dir. residency program Providence Med. Ctr., U. Wash. Dept. Surgery, 1976-87. Author: A Retrospective View of Northwest Medicine: The Early History of the Department of Surgery and the Health Sciences of the University of Washington, 1989; co-author: Saddlebags to Scanners: The First 100 Years of Medicine in Washington State, 1989; contbr. numerous articles to profl. jours. Served with U.S. Army, 1941-43, 46. Recipient Outstanding Tchr. award U. Wash. Sch. Medicine, 1958, 68, 85. Fellow Am. Coll. Surgeons; mem. AMA, Western Surg. Assn., Pacific Coast Surg. Assn. (pres. 1982-83), North Pacific Surg. Assn., Seattle Surg. Soc. (pres. 1975), Internat. Soc. Surgeons, King County Med. Assn., Pan Pacific Surg. Assn. Avocations: piano, pipe organ. Home and Office: 401 100th Ave NE Apt 317 Bellevue WA 98004-5456

OLSON, JAMES CLIFTON, historian, university president; b. Bradgate, Iowa, Jan. 23, 1917; s. Arthur Edwin and Abbie (Anderson) O.; m. Vera Blanche Farrington, June 6, 1941; children: Elizabeth, Sarah Margaret. AB, Morningside Coll., 1938, LLD, 1968; MA, U. Nebr., 1939, PhD, 1942, LittD, 1980; LittD, Chonnam Nat. U., Korea, 1978. Instr. Northwest Mo. State Tchrs. Coll., summers 1940-42; dir. Nebr. State Hist. Soc., 1946-56; lectr. U. Omaha, 1947-50; lectr. U. Nebr., 1946-54, part-time assoc. prof., 1954-56, prof., chmn. dept. history, 1956-65, Bennett S. and Dorothy Martin prof. history, 1962-65; dean Grad. Coll., univ. research adminstr., 1966-68, vice chancellor, 1968; chancellor U. Mo.-Kansas City, 1968-76; interim pres. U. Mo. System, 1976-77, pres., 1977-84, pres. emeritus, 1984—; OAS prof. Am. history El Colegio de Mexico, Mexico City, 1962; vis. prof. U. Colo., summer 1965; commr. N. Cen. Assn. Colls. and Schs.; bd. dirs. Uhlmann Co. Author: J. Sterling Morton, 1942, The Nebraska Story, 1951, History of Nebraska, 1955, (with Vera Farrington Olson) Nebraska is My Home, 1956, This is Nebraska, 1960, Red Cloud and the Sioux Problem, 1965, paper edit., 1975, 79, (with Vera Farrington Olson) The University of Missouri: An Illustrated History, 1988, Serving the University of Missouri: A Memoir of Campus and System Administration, 1993; contbg. author: The Army Air Forces in World War II, 1951, 53; editor: Nebraska History, 1946-56; contbr. articles to profl. jours., encys. Bd. dirs. Harry S. Truman Libr. Inst., Mid-Am. Arts Alliance; chmn. Mo. Arts Coun.; trustee Midwest Rsch. Inst., Kansas City. Mem. Am. Assn. State and Local History, Coun. Basic Edn., Am. Hist. Assn., Orgn. Am. Historians, State Hist. Soc. Mo. (exec. com.), Nebr. State Hist. Soc., We. Hist. Assn., Cosmos Club, Phi Beta Kappa, Omicron Delta Kappa, Phi Kappa Phi, Pi Gamma Mu.

OLSON, JAMES RICHARD, transportation company executive; b. Alexandria, Minn., Mar. 11, 1941; s. Orie D. and Theresa Marie (Erickson) O.; m. Ronna Lee, Feb. 1, 1969 (dec.); 1 child, Trevor James. BS, N.D. State U., 1963; LLD, U. Minn., 1966; MBA, Harvard U., 1968. Asst. to v.p. finance Cargill Inc., Mpls., 1968-69; with Graco Inc., Mpls., 1969-75; v.p. finance Graco Inc., 1972-75; exec. v.p finance Ponderosa System, Inc., Dayton, Ohio, 1975-77; v.p. planning Pillsbury Co., Mpls., 1977-79; v.p. restaurant group Pillsbury Co., 1979-80; group v.p.-restaurants The Carlson Cos., Inc., Mpls., 1981-83; exec. v.p., chief fin. and adminstrv. officer Schneider Nat., Inc., 1983-87, pres. van group, 1987-92, pres. transp. sector, 1992—; mem. corp. bd. dirs. Curative Rehab. Ctr.; mem. bd. dirs The Ground Round, Inc. Mem. Financial Execs. Inst., Citizens League Mpls.-St. Paul, Harvard Bus. Sch. Club Minn. (past pres.). Lutheran. Home: 2512 Riverside Dr Green Bay WI 54301-1950 Office: PO Box 2545 Green Bay WI 54306-2545

OLSON, JAMES ROBERT, consulting engineer; b. Columbus, Nebr., Nov. 23, 1940; s. Robert August and Jean Elizabeth O.; 1 child, Eric Robert. Student, U.S. Naval Acad., 1962; BA, U. Nebr., 1965; MA, Cen. Mich. U., 1977; diploma Nat. Def. U., 1981. Commd. ensign USN, 1965, advanced through grades to comdr., 1980; svc. in S.W. Pacific, Philippines and Vietnam; designated Space Systems Ops. Subspecialist, 1982; ret., 1983; sr. systems engr. G.E. Space Systems Div., Valley Forge, Pa., 1983-92; mem. faculty Def. Intelligence Sch., 1970-71; mem. Naval Insp. Gen. Staff, 1982. Decorated Bronze Star with combat V, Air medal (5), Republic of Vietnam Cross of Gallantry, numerous others. Mem. NRA, Inst. Navigation, Fla. Gulf Coast R.R. Mus., Rlwy. and Locomotive Hist. Soc. (life), Colo. R.R. Hist. Found. (life), Am. Swedish Hist. Found., VASA Order of Am., Phi Alpha Theta, Army-Navy Country Club (Washington). Methodist. Home: 1311 Lambeth Cir Venice FL 34292-1642

OLSON, JAMES WILLIAM PARK, architect; b. St. Louis, Oct. 6, 1940; s. James William Park; s. Louis Garfield and Gladys Helen (Schuh) O.; m. Katherine Fovargue, June 11, 1971; children: Park, Reed. BArch, U. Wash., 1963. Registered architect, Wash., Oreg., Calif., Ill. Ptnr. Olson/Sundberg Architects, Seattle, 1985—; assoc. architect New Seattle Art Mus., 1991. Prin. works include Pike and Virginia Bldg. (AIA Honor award 1980), Seattle's Best Coffee Retail Locations (AIA Honor award 1984), Hauberg Residence Complex, 1992, Olympic Block Bldg. (Outstanding Merit award Wash. Trust Hist. Preservation 1986), numerous residences nationwide. Bd. dirs. On The Bds., Ctr. Contemporary Art, Seattle, 1982-86, Artist Trust, Seattle, 1986-90, U. Wash. Henry Art Gallery, Seattle, 1986-92, Seattle Art Mus.; active Allied Arts. Recipient Best Architect award Seattle Mag., 1985. Fellow AIA; mem. IFRAA, NEA (juror). Avocation: art. Work published in numerous mags, jours., including The AD 100 Architects, N.Y. Times, Archtl. Digest, Archtl. Record, Global Architecture and others. Office: Olson/Sundberg Architects 108 1st Ave S Fl 4 Seattle WA 98104-2502

OLSON, JARLE, clergy member, Church administrator. Exec. dir. World Missions of the Church of the Lutheran Brethren of America, Fergus Falls, Minn. Office: Ch Luth Brethren Am PO Box 655 Fergus Falls MN 56538-0655

OLSON, JOHN MARSHALL, lawyer; b. Milw., Feb. 16, 1949; s. John Robert and Helen (Linder) O.; m. Lynde Bradley Uihlein, Jan. 6, 1973 (div. Dec. 1986); children: Sarah Lynde, John Uihlein. BA summa cum laude, Princeton U., 1971; postgrad., Oxford (Eng.) U., 1971-72; JD, Yale U., 1976. Bar: Wis. 1976, U.S. Dist. Ct. (ea. dist.) Wis. 1981, U.S. Ct. Appeals (7th cir.) 1981. Assoc. Whyte & Hirschboeck, S.C., Milw., 1976-82, ptnr., 1982-89; ptnr. Foley & Lardner, Milw., 1989—; bd. dirs. Banner Welder, Inc., Germantown, Wis., Phoenix Products Co., Inc., Milw., Schroeder-Manatee Ranch, Inc., Sarasota, Fla. Contbr. articles to profl. jours. Trustee David Uihlein Racing Mus. Found., Cedarburg, Wis., 1978, Univ. Sch. Milw., 1979-85, Lakeland Coll., Sheboygan, Wis., 1984-86; bd. dirs. AWARE Inc., Ft. Atkinson, Wis., 1991—, Tympanuchus Soc., Milw., 1992—. Mem. State Bar Wis. (chmn. bus. law sect. 1992-93), Univ. Club. Milw., Coleman Lake Club (bd. dirs., Goodman, Wis.), Milw. Club., Milw. Country Club. Avocations: grouse hunting, fly fishing, tennis. Office: Foley & Lardner 777 E Wisconsin Ave Milwaukee WI 53202-5367

OLSON, JOHN MICHAEL, lawyer; b. Grafton, N.D., Feb. 9, 1947; s. Clifford Inguold and Alice M. (Schwandt) O.; children: Dana Michel, Kirsten Lee. BA, Concordia Coll., Moorhead, Minn., 1969; JD, U. N.D., 1972. Bar: N.D. 1972. Asst. atty. gen. N.D. Atty. Gen.'s Office, Bismarck, 1972-74; state's atty. Burleigh County, Bismarck, 1974-82; pvt. practice Bismarck, 1983-91; mem. 49th dist. N.D. Senate, Bismarck, 1983-91, minority leader, 1987-91; ptnr. Olson Cichy Bismarck, Bismarck, 1994—, Olson Cichy Attys., Bismarck, 1994—. Recipient Disting. Svc. award N.D. Peace Officers Assn., 1981, Outstanding Bismarcker award Bismarck Jaycees, 1981. Mem. N.D. Bar Assn. Republican. Lutheran. Office: 115 N 4th St Bismarck ND 58501

OLSON, JUDY MAE, geography, cartography educator, consultant; b. Waupaca, Wis., May 15, 1944; d. Leonard A. and Hilma R. (Johnson) O. B.S., Wis. State U., Stevens Point, 1966, M.S., U. Wis., Madison, 1968, Ph.D., 1970. Asst. prof. U. Ga., Athens, 1970-74; asso. prof. Boston U., 1974-83; prof. geography Mich. State U., East Lansing, 1983—, chair dept. 1989-94; vis. asst. prof. U. Minn., Mpls., 1973, vis. assoc. prof., 1981; cons. U.S. Bur. Census, Washington, 1975, U.S. Army Engr. Topog. Labs., Washington, 1983, U.S. Dept. Transp., Boston, 1980. Editor: The Am. Cartographer, 1977-82; U.S. Nat. Report to ICA, 1984; co-editor Geography's Inner Worlds, 1992; contbr. articles to profl. jours. Recipient Presdl. citation Am. Congress Surveying and Mapping, 1979, 80, 84, 85; AAG hon., 1990. Fellow Am. Congress Surveying and Mapping (dir. 1976-79, 81-82); mem. Am. Cartographic Assn. (pres. 1981-82), Assn. Am. Geographers councillor 1990-93, sec. 1991-93, pres. 1995-96), U.S. Nat. Com. for ICA (chmn. 1985-88), Internat. Cartographers Assn. (v.p. 1992—). Office: Mich State Univ 315 Natural Sci Bldg East Lansing MI 48824

OLSON, KAREN L., emergency nurse; b. Wichita, Kans., Oct. 16, 1945; d. James E. and W. Maxine (Sage) Kealiher; m. Manfred Robert Olson, Oct. 8, 1989; 1 child, Mark A. Campbell. ADN, Mohave C.C., Kingman, Ariz., 1984; BSN, U. Phoenix, 1993. Cert. pub. health nurse, cert. in health care mkt.; BLS instr., ACLS, PALS. Emergency nurse Tri-City Med. Ctr., Oceanside, Calif. Named Nurse of the Yr., Hosp. Couns. of San Diego, 1994. Mem. Nat. League Nursing, Emergency Nurses Assn., Calif. Nurses Assn. Avocations: swimming, horseback riding, sailing, scuba. Office: Tri-City Medical Ctr 4002 Vista Way Oceanside CA 92056-4506

OLSON, KAY MELCHISEDECH, magazine editor; b. Mpls., Nov. 16, 1948; d. John William and Carol Louise (Born) Melchisedech; m. John Addison Olson, Sept. 5, 1970 (div. 1988); children: Jennifer Marie, Nathan John. BA, U. Minn., 1971. News editor New Hope-Plymouth Post, Crystal, Minn., 1971-73; features editor Sun Newspapers, Bloomington, Minn., 1973-75; with pub. rels. dept. Nat. Car Rental, Bloomington, Minn., 1975-77; free-lance pub. rels. profl. Mpls., 1977-82; mag. editor Miller Pub., Minnetonka, Minn., 1982-90; exec. editor Flower & Garden mag., Workbasket mag. Easy-Does-It Needework & Crafts mag. KC Pub. Inc., Kansas City, Mo., 1990—. Mem. Garden Writers Assn. Am. Roman Catholic. Avocation: fiction writing. Home: 4726 W 78th Ter Shawnee Mission KS 66208-4413 Office: KC Pub Inc 700 W 47th St Ste 310 Kansas City MO 64112-1805

OLSON, KEITH WALDEMAR, history educator; b. Poughkeepsie, N.Y., Aug. 4, 1931; s. Ernest Waldemar and Elin Ingeborg (Rehnstrom) O.; m. Marilyn Joyce Wittschen, Sept. 10, 1955; children—Paula, Judy. B.A., SUNY-Albany, 1957, M.A., 1959; Ph.D., U. Wis., 1964. Mem. history faculty Syracuse U., N.Y., 1963-66; mem. history faculty U. Md., College Park, 1966—; prof. history U. Md.; Fulbright prof. U. Tampere, Finland, 1986-87, U. Oulu, 1993, U. Jyväskylä, 1994. Author: The G.I. Bill, the Veterans and the Colleges, 1974; Biography of a Progressive: Franklin K. Lane, 1979. Pres. Am. Scandinavian Found., Washington, 1977-79. Served with U.S. Army, 1952-54. U.S. Office Edn. grantee, 1965-66; U. Md. grantee, 1971, 76, 78. Mem. Am. Hist. Assn., Orgn. Am. Historians, Wis. Hist. Soc., Swedish Am. Hist. Soc., Finnish Hist. Soc., Soc. Historians of Am. Fgn. Rels., Cen. Study of Presidency. Unitarian. Home: 10746 Kinloch Rd Silver Spring MD 20903-1226 Office: Dept History U Md College Park MD 20742

OLSON, KENNETH HARVEY, computer company executive; b. Souris, N.D., May 7, 1927; s. Oscar L. and Clara (Haugen) O.; m. Darlene R. Gronseth, Aug. 19, 1950 (div. 1987); children: Kenneth David, Martha C., Marie K. BA, Concordia Coll., Moorhead, Minn., 1950; MS, U. N.D., 1953; postgrad., U. Minn., 1955. Instr. math. U. N.D., Grand Forks, 1952-54; programming supr. Convair, San Diego, 1955-59; mgr. software Control Data Corp., Mpls., 1959-61, project mgr., 1961-62; sales mgr. Control Data Corp., San Diego, 1962-70; v.p. Automated Med. Analysts, San Diego, 1970-90; pres., dir. Focus 010 Group, San Diego, 1975—; pres., dir. Health Care Svcs. Corp., San Diego, 1971-74, H.C.S. Corp., San Diego, 1972-75; v.p., trustee Calif. Prepaid Health Plan Coun., 1971-74; trustee HMO Assn. Am., 1974-75; bd. dirs. Touch Techs., Inc., San Diego. Editor: Approximations for the 1604 Computer, 1960; contbr. papers to Computer Applications, 1957-61. Pres. Lemon Grove (Calif.) Luth. Ch., 1957-59; treas. St. Luke's Luth. Ch., La Mesa, Calif., 1992-93; founder San Diego Nat. Bank, 1980, mem. bus. adv. com., 1981-85. Named Subcontractor of Yr., Small Bus. Assn. and SAI Corp., 1985; day proclaimed in his honor Mayor of San Diego, 1986; recipient Pres.'s award for disting. svc. Concordia Coll., 1991. Mem. Assn. for Computing Machinery, Sons of Norway. Republican. Avocations: photography, travel, classical concerts.

OLSON, LEROY CALVIN, retired educational administration educator; b. Kane, Pa., Mar. 7, 1926; s. Vernon Reinhold and Gertrude Viola (Hutchins) O.; m. Miriam Marie Vogler, June 19, 1954; children—David Lee, Thomas Edward, Steven Andrew. B.S., Clarion State Coll., 1949; M.Ed., Pa. State Coll., 1950; Ed.D., Pa. State U., 1962; postgrad., U. Del., 1964-65. Tchr.-counselor Boiling Springs (Pa.) High Sch., 1950-52, Gordon Jr. High Sch., Coatesville, Pa., 1952-54; guidance dir. Cen. Dauphin Sch. Dist., Harrisburg, Pa., 1954-57; coordinator pupil personnel services, asst. supt. for instrn. and personnel, acting supt. Alfred I. duPont Sch. Dist., Wilmington, Del., 1957-65; prof. ednl. adminstrn. Temple U., Phila., 1965-92, prof. emeritus, 1992—; cons. to schs. bds. and dists., also Nat., Wis., Pa. sch. bds. assns. Contbr. articles to profl. jours. Trustee Luth. Ch., 1963-66, chmn. bd., 1976-78, chmn. various coms., discussion groups. Served with USNR, 1944-46, PTO. Recipient Disting. Alumni award Clarion State Coll., 1972. Mem. Am. Personnel and Guidance Assn., AAUP, Am. Assn. Sch. Personnel Adminstrs., Assn. Supervision and Curriculum Devel., Council Profs. Instrn. Supervision, Nat. Staff Devel. Council, Am. Legion, Phi Delta Kappa, Phi Kappa Phi. Republican. Home: 231 Prospect Dr Wilmington DE 19803-5331 *God's gift of life is a marvelous thing. My attempt to make the best use of that gift is to try to live an integrated and balanced life. This means that active attention must be paid to the physical, social, spiritual, and recreational aspects as well as to the work or career dimension. It also means we must share that gift through loving and caring about others.*

OLSON, LUTE, university athletic coach; b. Mayville, N.D., Sept. 22, 1934; s. Albert E. and Alinda E. (Halvorson) O.; m. Roberta R. Russell, Nov. 27, 1953; children: Vicki, Jodi, Gregory, Christi, Steven. B.A., Augsburg Coll., Mpls., 1956; M.A., Chapman Coll., Orange, Calif., 1964. Cert. counselor. Head basketball coach Mahonomen High Sch., Minn., 1956-57, Two Harbors High Sch., Minn., 1957-61; dean of boys Baseline Jr. High Sch., Boulder, Colo., 1961-62; head basketball coach Loara High Sch., Anaheim, Calif., 1962-64, Marine High Sch., Huntington Beach, Calif., 1964-69, Long Beach City Coll., Calif., 1969-73, Long Beach State U., 1973-74, U. Iowa, Iowa City, 1974-83; head basketball coach U. Ariz. Wildcats, 1983—, head coach NCAA Divsn. 1A basketball, ranked #10, 1992, head coach NCAA Tournament winner West Region, semifinalist (overall), 1994. Author: Passing Game Offense, 1980, Multiple Zone Attack, 1981, Pressure Defense, 1981, Match-up Zone, 1983. Crusade chmn. Am. Cancer Soc., Iowa, 1982. Named Coach of Yr. Orange League, 1964; named Coach of Yr. Sunset League, 1968, Coach of Yr. Met. Conf. Calif., 1970-71, Coach of Yr. PCAA, 1974, Coach of Yr. Big Ten Conf., 1979, 80. Mem. Nat. Assn. Basketball Coaches (Coach of Yr. 1980). Lutheran. Office: U Ariz Mckale Ctr Tucson AZ 85721*

OLSON, LYNN, sculptor, painter, writer; b. Chgo., Mar. 23, 1952; s. Ellen (Nelson) Olson. instr. direct cement sculpture workshops Montoya Art Studios, West Palm Beach, Fla., 1988-89, Alta. Sculptors Assn., Edmonton, Can., 1990, Mendocino (Calif.) Art Ctr., 1992-93, Sierra Nev. Coll. at Lake Tahoe, Incline Village, 1993, Lighthouse Art Ctr., Crescent City, Calif., 1990-96, Elisabet Ney Sculpture Conservatory, Austin, Tex., 1995, Tarrant County Jr. Coll., Ft. Worth, 1995. Prin. works include Good Shepherd, Ch. Good Shepherd, Albion, Ind., Kneeling Figure, Manta Ray. World of Concrete, Addison, Ill., Rose, Carter Meml., Chesterton, Ind., Redwood Tree, Lighthouse Art Ctr., Crescent Cuty, Calif., George Bartholomew Meml., Bellefontaine, Ohio, Color Concerto, Purdue U., Hammond, Ind., Continuity III, Tower East, Shaker Heights, Ohio, Aluma Beam, Aluma Corp., Toronto; author, pub.: Sculpting with Cement, 1981-95; contbr. over 50 articles to mags. Mem. Am. Concrete Inst. (com. 124 concrete aesthetics). Home and Office: Steelstone 4607 Claussen Ln Valparaiso IN 46383

OLSON, MARIAN EDNA, nursing consultant, social psychologist; b. Newman Grove, Nebr., July 20, 1923; d. Edward and Ethel Thelma (Hougland) Olson; diploma U. Nebr., 1944, BS in Nursing, 1953; MA, State U. Iowa, 1961, MA in Psychology, 1962; PhD in Psychology, UCLA, 1966. Staff nurse, supr. U. Tex. Med. Br., Galveston, 1944-49; with U. Iowa, Iowa City, 1949-59, supr. 1953-55, asst. dir. 1955-59; asst. prof. nursing UCLA, 1965-67; prof. nursing U. Hawaii, 1967-70, 78-82; dir. nursing Wilcox Hosp. and Health Center, Lihue, 1970-77; chmn. Hawaii Bd. Nursing, 1974-80; prof. nursing No. Mich. U., 1984-88; cons., ind. nursing svcs. adminstr. practice & curriculum, 1988—. Bd. trustees Bay de Noc C.C., 1988—. Mem. Am. Nurses Assn. (mem. nat. accreditation bd. continuing edn. 1975-78), Nat. League Nursing, Am. Hosp. Assn., Am. Public Health Assn., LWV. Democrat. Roman Catholic. Home and Office: 6223 County 513 T Rd Rapid River MI 49878-9595

OLSON, MARIAN KATHERINE, emergency management executive, consultant, publisher, information broker; b. Tulsa, Oct. 15, 1933; d. Sherwood Joseph and Katherine M. (Miller) Lahman; m. Ronald Keith Olson, Oct 27, 1956, (dec. May 1991). BA in Polit. Sci., U. Colo., 1954, MA in Elem. Edn., 1962; EdD in Ednl. Adminstrn., U. Tulsa, 1969. Tchr. public schs., Wyo., Colo., Mont., 1958-67; teaching fellow, adj. instr. edn. U. Tulsa, 1968-69; asst. prof. edn. Eastern Mont. State Coll., 1970; program assoc. research adminstrn. Mont. State U., 1970-75; on leave with Energy Policy Office of White House, then with Fed. Energy Adminstrn., 1973-74; with Dept. Energy, and predecessor, 1975—, program analyst, 1975-79, chief planning and environ. compliance br., 1979-83; regional dir. Region VIII Fed. Emergency Mgmt. Agy., 1987-93; exec. dir., Search and Rescue Dogs of the U.S., 1993—; pres. Western Healthclaims, Inc., Golden, Co.; pres. Marian Olson Assocs., Bannack Pub. Co.; mem. Colo. Nat. Hazards Mitigation Coun., Colo. Urban Search and Rescue Task Force. Contbr. articles in field. Grantee Okla. Consortium Higher Edn., 1969, NIMH, 1974. Mem. Am. Soc. for Info. Sci., Am. Assn. Budget and Program Analysis, Assn. of Contingency Planners, Internat. Assn. Ind. Pubs., Assn. of Contingency Planners, Nat. Inst. Urban Search and Rescue (bd. dirs.), Nat. Assn. for Search and Rescue, Colo. Search and Rescue, Search and Rescue Dogs of U.S., Colo. Emergency Mgmt. Assn., Front Range Rescue Dogs, Colo. State Fire Chiefs Assn., Kappa Delta Pi, Phi Alpha Theta, Kappa Alpha Theta. Republican. Home: 203 Iowa Dr Golden CO 80403-1337 Office: Western Healthclaims Inc 203 Iowa Dr Ste B Golden CO 80403-1337

OLSON, NORMAN FREDRICK, food science educator; b. Edmund, Wis., Feb. 8, 1931; s. Irving M. and Elva B. (Rhinerson) O.; m. Darlene Mary Thorson, Dec. 28, 1957; children: Kristin A., Eric R. BS, U. Wis., 1953, MS, 1957, PhD, 1959. Asst. prof. U. Wis.-Madison, 1959-63, assoc. prof., 1963-69, prof., 1969—, dir. Walter V. Price Cheese Research Inst., 1976-93; dir. Ctr. Dairy Research, 1986-93; disting. prof. U. Wis., 1993—. Author: Semi-soft Cheeses; inventor enzyme microencapsulation; assoc. editor Jour. Dairy Sci., 1996—. Lt. U.S. Army, 1953-55. Fellow Inst. Food Technologists (Macy award 1986); mem. Am. Dairy Sci. Assn. (v.p. 1984-85, pres. 1985-86, Pfizer award 1971, Dairy Rsch. Inc. award 1978, Borden Found. award 1988), Inst. Food Technologists. Democrat. Lutheran. Avocation: cross-country skiing. Home: 114 Green Lake Pass Madison WI 53705-4755 Office: U Wis Dept Food Sci Babcock Hall Madison WI 53706

OLSON, PATRICIA JOANNE, artist, educator; b. Chgo., Aug. 22, 1927; d. Fred William and Fern Leslie (Shaffer) Kohler; m. Paul J. Olson, Jan. 21, 1950 (dec. July 1968); adopted children: Paulette, Dominic; stepchildren: Cindy, Katie, Larry, Daniel. BA, Northeastern Ill. U., 1976; MA, Loyola U., 1981. Advt. art dir. Chas. A. Stevens Dept. Store, Chgo., 1950-55; art dir. McCann, Erickson Advt. Agy., Chgo., 1955-57; pres. Olson Studio, Chgo., 1957-75; dept. chair, mem. faculty Chgo. Acad. Fine Art, 1974-78; exhibiting artist Chicago and Santa Barbara, Calif., 1981—; instr. Old Town Triangle Art Ctr., Chgo., 1978—, Bernard Horwich Ctr., Chgo., 1982-86, Art Inst. Chgo., 1987; prof. Columbia Coll., Chgo., 1978—; panelist Chgo. Cultural Ctr.; spkr., demonstrator Skokie Cultural Ctr., 1992, Joliet Art Ctr., 1992; guest spkr. AAUW, Evanston, Ill., 1991, Columbia Coll. Humanities, Chgo., 1992. Author: Women of Different Sizes, 1981; contbr. poetry to mags.; one woman shows include Artemesia Gallery, 1985, Highland Park H.S., 1987, One Ill. Ctr., 1987, Gallery 6000, 1988, Countryside Gallery of New Work, 1991, Old Town Triangle Gallery, 1991, Loyola U. Gallery, 1991; exhibited in group shows New Horizons, Art Inst. Gallery, 1975, 90, Beverly Art Ctr., 1978, 79, 82, 87, 89, 90, Beacon St. Gallery, 1984, 89, Art Inst. Chgo., 1984, Galex 19 Internat., Galesburg, Ill., 1985, Suburban Art League, 1986, Natalini Gallery, 1987, Societe des Pastellistes de France, 1987, Campanile Gallery, 1987, Artemsia Gallery, 1987, Delora Cultural Ctr., 1988, Alexandrian Mus., 1988, Gallery Genesis, 1988, 89, Adler Cultural Ctr., 1989, Post Rd. Gallery, 1989, Evanston Co-op Gallery, 1990, Pilsen Gallery, 1991, Old Town Triangle Gallery, 1991, Loyola U. Gallery, 1991, Chgo. Soc. Artists, 1992, R.H. Love Gallery, 1992, Chgo. Cultural Ctr., 1992, Wood St. Gallery, 1994, North Lakeside Cultural Ctr., 1994, State of Ill. Bldg. Chgo. Sr. Citizen Art Network (award), others. Hostess Rogers Park (Ill.) Hist. Soc., 1993. Named to Sr. Hall of Fame, Mayor Daley, Chgo., 1991, Womens Mus., Washington. Mem. Chgo. Soc. Artists, Chgo. Womens Caucus for Art (curator 1989-90), North Lakeside Cultural Ctr. (mem. art adv. bd. 1990—), Am. Jewish Art Club (juror, curator, speaker 1991), Wizo (juror 1989), Sr. Citizens Art Network. Democrat. Avocations: writing poetry, theatre, photography, hiking, reading. Home: 1955 W Morse Ave Chicago IL 60626-3111

OLSON, PAUL RICHARD, Spanish literature educator, editor; b. Rockford, Ill., Nov. 2, 1925; s. Oscar Wilhelm and Jenny Ingeborg (Taube) O.; m. Phyllis Elizabeth Edwards, Jan. 10, 1953; children: Thomas Jeremy, John Stephen, Carl Philip, Paul Andrew. A.B., U. Ill., 1948, A.M., 1950; Ph.D., Harvard U., 1959. Instr. Dartmouth Coll., Hanover, N.H., 1956-59, asst. prof., 1959-61; asst. prof. modern Spanish lit. Johns Hopkins U., Balt., 1961-63, assoc. prof., 1963-67, prof., 1967-91, prof. emeritus, 1991—. Author: Circle of Paradox, 1967, Unamuno: Niebla, 1984, Unamuno and the Primacy of Language, 1989; editor: Unamuno: Como se hace una novela, 1977; gen. editor: Modern Lang. Notes, 1983-86. Guggenheim Found. fellow, 1964; Fulbright grantee, 1964-65; Am. Council Learned Socs. grantee, 1969. Mem. MLA, Acad. Lit. Studies, Asociacion Internacional Hispanistas.

OLSON, PAUL S., nuclear engineer; b. Cambridge, Mass., May 2, 1933; s. Charles Louis and Mary Agnis (Navin) O.; m. Elaine Marylyn Selvitella, Nov. 25, 1956; children: Cheryl McCarthy, Christine Baginski, Karen Barbarick. BSChemE, Northeastern U., 1957; MS Nuclear Engring., U. Cin., 1962. Registered prof. engr. Calif. Commd. 2d lt. Rockwell, 1952; advanced through ranks to col. U.S. Army, 1978, retired, 1985; engr. GE, Cin., 1958-62, Rocckwell, Canoga Park, Calif., 1962—. Bd. dirs. Univ. Mo. NE, Rolla, 1994-97, St. Anthony Home for Troubled Youngsters, Canoga Park, 1983-89. Fellow ASTM (chmn. 1958—, Merit award 1983); mem. K.C. (Grand Knight 1980—, Merit award 1985), Tau Beta Pi, Sigma Xi. Democrat. Roman Catholic. Avocation: outdoor activities. Home: 18649 Tulsa St Northridge CA 91326 Office: Rockwell 6633 Canoga Ave Canoga Park CA 91304

OLSON, PHILLIP DAVID LEROY, agriculturist, chemist; b. Anchorage, Feb. 3, 1940; s. Marvin Willard and Bernadette (McName) O.; m. Deborah Andreé Butler, Apr. 10, 1982; children from a previous marriage: Jamie Kay, Samuel Phillip, Jill Andre. BS, U. Idaho, 1963; MS, Oreg. State U., 1972. Technician U. Calif., Riverside, 1963-65; rsch. staff Oreg. State U., Corvallis, 1965-75; r & d mgr. Hoechst-Roussel Agri-Vet Co., Somerville, N.J., 1975-91; pres. Profl. Agrl. Cons., Hayden Lake, Idaho, 1991—; rsch. and devel. cons., investigator Atochem NA, Bryan, Tex., 1991—, Dupont, Wilmington, Del., 1991—, Ciba-Geigy, Greensboro, N.C., 1991—, BASF, Research Triangle Park, N.C., 1991, ISK-Bioscis., Fresno, Calif., 1992—, Rhone-Plulenc, Durham, N.C., 1992—, Sandoz Agro, Inc., Des Plaines, Ill., 1992—, Zeneca, Inc., Richmond, Calif., 1992—, Stewart AG, Macon, Mo., 1995—; cons. in field rsch. and devel. Mem. Soc. Quality Assurance, Pacific Regional Quality Assurance Soc., Elks. Avocations: reading, fishing, RC model building, rose gardening. Office: Profl Agricultural Cons RR 3 Box 125 Hayden Lake ID 83835-8304

OLSON, PHILLIP ROGER, naval officer; b. Elmhurst, Ill., June 23, 1939; s. Willard Clarence and Carol (Schulz) O.; m. Marsha Andrea Lippert, July 10, 1966; children: Christine Carole, Phillip Roger Jr. B in Naval Sci., U.S. Naval Acad.; M in Physics, Naval Postgrad. Sch. Commd. ens. USN, 1991-96, advanced through grades to rear adm., 1991—; instr. ship material readiness group USN, Idaho Falls, 1978-81; commdg. officer USS Pharris (FF 1094) USN, Norfolk, Va., 1981-82; commdg. officer USS Mississippi (CGN 40) &, Norfolk, 1983-86; sr. instr. ship material readiness group &, Newport, R.I., 1986-87; dep. dir. ops. Joint Staff &, Washington, 1987-88, dep. dir. strategy & policy Joint Staff, 1988-89; comdr. logistics group two &, Norfolk, 1989-90; comdr. cruiser-destroyer group one &, San Diego, 1990-92; pres. bd. inspection & survey &, Norfolk, 1992-96. Decorated Legion of Merit (3). Mem. Surface Navy Assn. Lutheran. Avocations: golf, tennis. Office: Bd of Inspection & Survey 2600 Tarawa Ct Ste 250 Norfolk VA 23521-3235

OLSON, RENÉE ALICIA, magazine editor; b. Evanston, Ill., Jan. 15, 1962; d. Samuel Paul and Barbara Mae (Mulligan) Mizerack. BA in Journalism, Ind. U., 1984; AB in Spanish, U. Ill., 1987, MS in Libr. Sci., 1987. Head reference svcs. Reading (Mass.) Pub. Libr., 1987-94; news and features editor Sch. Libr. Jour., N.Y.C., 1994—. Editor: New Eng. Librs. newsletter of New Eng. Libr. Assn., 1990-94, Bay State Libr. newsletter of Mass. Libr. Assn., 1989-90; contbr. articles to profl. jours. Visitor guide Bklyn. Bot. Garden, 1995—. Mem. ALA, Ednl. Press Assn. Avocation: travel. Office: Sch Libr Jour 245 W 17th St New York NY 10011

OLSON, RICHARD DAVID, psychology educator; b. Reading, Pa., Oct. 10, 1944; s. Milton Stuart and Sarah Ellen (Moyer) O.; m. M. Gayle Augustine, Aug. 26, 1967. B.A., U. Redlands, 1966; M.S., St. Louis U., 1968, Ph.D., 1970. Lic. psychologist, La. Asst. prof. psychology U. New Orleans, 1970-74, assoc. prof., chmn. dept. psychology, 1974-79, prof., chmn. dept., 1979-81, assoc. dean Grad. Sch., 1981-82, dean, 1982-88, vice chancellor, 1984-88, rsch. prof., 1988—; chmn. dept. psychology, 1995—; cons. psychologist, New Orleans, 1973—; pres. Statis. Cons. of New Orleans, 1977-82. Editor: Learning in the Classroom, 1971, The Comma After Love, The Selected Poems of Raeburn Miller, 1994; contbr. articles to profl. jours. Grantee HEW, 1976-81. Fellow APA, Am. Psychol. Soc.; mem. Soc. for Neuroscis., Animal Behavior Soc., Am. Statis. Assn. Home: 103 Doubloon Dr Slidell LA 70461-2715 Office: U New Orleans Dept Psychology Lake Front New Orleans LA 70148

OLSON, RICHARD DEAN, researcher, pharmacology educator; b. Rupert, Idaho, June 22, 1949; s. Emerson J. and Thelma Maxine (Short) O.; m. Carol Ann Dyba, Jan. 5, 1974; children: Stephan Jay, David Richard, Jonathan Philip. BS, Coll. Idaho, 1971; postgrad., Idaho State U., 1972-74; PhD, Vanderbilt U., 1978. Instr. Vanderbilt U., Nashville, 1980-81, asst. prof., 1982, head pediatric clin. pharmacology unit, 1982; asst. prof. U. S. Ala., Mobile, 1982-83; acting asst. prof. U. Wash., Seattle, 1984-85, research assoc. prof., 1985-95; v.p. Olson, Wong and Walsh Labs., Inc., Lindenhurst, Ill., 1987-90; pres. Olson, Mushlin and Walsh Labs., Birmingham, Ala., 1990—; chief cardiovascular pharmacology rsch. VA Med. Ctr., Boise, Idaho, 1984—; hon. dir. cardiovascular rsch. lab. Capital Inst. Medicine Beijing, People's Republic of China, 1986; investigator Am. Heart Assn., Nashville, 1981, NIH, Mobile, 1982; bd. dirs. Idaho affiliate Am. Heart Assn.; pres. JB Internat. Inc., Boise, 1990; sr. cons. Longwood Cons. Group, Boston, 1990—; adj. assoc. prof. U. So. Ala., Mobile, 1995—; cardiovascular sect. head Mountain States Med. Rsch. Inst., Boise, Idaho, 1995—. Contbr. articles to profl. jours. Pres. Fellowship Crusade for Christ, Inc., Nampa, Idaho, 1986—. Grantee Am. Heart Assn., 1981, 83, 84, 86, 88, Am. Fedn. Aging Research, Inc., Boise, 1985; VA Merit Review grantee, 1985, 88, 91; NIH trainee, 1975-78; NIH New Investigator 1982; fellow, Am. Fedn. Aging Research, Inc. 1985—, NIH U. Colo., Denver, 1978-80. Mem. AAAS, N.Y. Acad. Scis., Am. Soc. Pharmacology and Exptl. Therapeutics, Am. Heart Assn., Am. Fedn. for Clin. Research, Sigma Xi. Avocations: camping, radio-controlled model airplanes. Home: 605 Crocus Ct Nampa ID 83651-6549 Office: VA Med Ctr # 151 500 W Fort St Boise ID 83702-4501

OLSON, RICHARD EARL, lawyer, state legislator; b. Elmhurst, Ill., Apr. 24, 1953; s. Earl Leroy and Helen (Wanamaker) O.; m. Patricia Michelle McKinney, May 16, 1976; children: Shelley, Rachel, Eric. BA, U. Miss., Oxford, 1975; Jd, So. Meth. U., 1978. Bar: N.Mex. 1978. Ptnr. Hinkle, Cox, Eaton, Coffield & Hensley, Roswell, N.Mex., 1978—; mem.

N.Mex. Ho. of Reps., 1989-95, mem. various coms.; bd. trustees Eastern N.Mex. Med. Ctr., 1995—. Mem. Roswell City Coun., 1986-88, chmn. sts. and alleys com., mem. various other coms.; past chmn. pastor-parish rels. com. 1st United Meth. Ch., Roswell; bd. dirs. Roswell Econ. Forum, Roswell Mus. and Art Ctr. Found., city coun. liaison; bd. dirs. Assurance Home, 1980—, former v.p.; mem. N.Mex. 1st, former bd. dirs. Mem. ABA, Am. Legis. Exec. Coun. (civil justice task force), Def. Rsch. Inst., Noon Optimist Club, Order of Coif, Phi Kappa Phi. Republican. Home: 5003 Thunderbird Ln Roswell NM 88201-9386 Office: Hinkle Cox Eaton Coffield & Hensley PO Box 10 Roswell NM 88202-0010

OLSON, ROBERT EDWARD, coal mining executive; b. Phila., Aug. 5, 1927; s. Oscar E. and Marie B. (Kilgallon) O.; m. Jean Emilie Wadsworth, Dec. 31, 1955; children: Grace Olson Carmichael, Nancy Olson Ashcraft, Karen Olson Culbertson. Student U. Richmond, 1945, Duke, 1945-46, U. Pa., 1946; BS in Mining Engring., Pa. State U., 1952. Registered profl. engr., Pa., W.Va. Indsl. engr. Island Creek Coal Co., Holden, W.Va., 1952-55; dir., treas., sr. assoc. Coal Standards, Inc., mgmt. cons., Charleston, W.Va., 1955-61; v.p. adminstrn. Rochester & Pitts. Coal Co., Indiana, Pa., 1961-81; pres., chief operating officer, Valley Camp Coal Co., Oil City, Pa., 1981-86, vice chmn., dir., mem. exec. com., 1986-88, ret., 1988; past pres., dir. Kanawha and Hocking Coal & Coke Co., Kelley's Creek and Northwestern R.R. Co., Valley Camp Coal Sales Co.; pres., chief exec. officer Gt. Lakes Coal & Dock Co.; chmn., dir. Donaldson Mine Co., Elm Grove Coal Co., Shrewsbury Coal Co., Helen Mining Co., Valley Camp of Utah Inc.; chmn., CEO Pa. and W.Va. Supply Co.; bd. dirs. Strickland Constrn. Co. Bd. dirs. United Way of Venango County, 1983-88; pres. bd. trustees Venango County Community Area Found., 1988-94, former dir.; mem. Ind. County C. of C. 1973-81, pres. 1976-77; mem. vestry Christ Episc. Ch., Oil City, 1989-92. With USN, 1945-47. Mem. Wanango Country Club, Univ. Club, Franklin Club, Rotary Internat., Theta Delta Chi, Sigma Phi Sigma. Home: 8 Glenwood Dr Oil City PA 16301-2104

OLSON, ROBERT EUGENE, physician, biochemist, educator; b. Minn., Jan. 23, 1919; s. Ralph William and Minnie (Holtin) O.; m. Catherine Silvoso, Oct. 21, 1944; children: Barbara Lynn, Robert E., Mark Alan, Mary Ellen, Carol Louise. A.B., Gustavus Adolphus Coll., 1938; Ph.D., St. Louis U., 1944; M.D., Harvard, 1951; M.D. (hon.), Chiang Mai U., Thailand, 1983. Diplomate: Nat. Bd. Med. Examiners, Am. Bd. Nutrition (pres. 1962-63). Postgrad. research asst. biochemistry St. Louis U. Sch. Medicine, 1938-43, asst. biochemistry, 1943-44, Alice A. Doisy prof. biochemistry, chmn. dept. biochemistry, 1965-82, asso. prof. medicine, 1966-72, prof. medicine, 1972-82; vis. prof. (sabbatical) dept. biochemistry U. Freiburg, Breisgau, West Germany, 1970-71; also Hoffman-La Roche Co., Basel, Switzerland, 1970-71; instr. biochemistry and nutrition Harvard Sch. Pub. Health, 1946-47; research fellow Nutrition Found., 1947-49; research fellow Am. Heart Assn., 1949-51, established investigator, 1951-52; house officer Peter Bent Brigham Hosp., Boston, 1951-52; prof., head dept. biochemistry and nutrition Grad. Sch. Pub. Health U. Pitts.; lectr. medicine Sch. Medicine, 1952-65; mem. panel malnutrition Japan-U.S. Med. Scis. Program, 1965-69; dir. Nutrition Clinic, Falk Clinic, 1953-65; mem. sr. staff Presbyn. Hosp., dir. metabolic unit, 1960-65; mem. staff St. Louis U. Hosp., 1965-81; prof. biochemistry, prof. medicine, assoc. dean acad. affairs U. Pitts. Sch. Medicine, 1982-84; prof. medicine, prof. pharm. scis. SUNY-Stony Brook, 1984-90, prof. emeritus, 1990-94; prof. pediatrics U. South Fla., Tampa, 1994—; cons. Mercy Hosp., U. Pitts. Med. Center; assoc. in medicine St. Margaret's Meml. Hosp., Pitts., dir. metabolic unit, 1954-60; cons. div. research grants USPHS, 1954-69, 72-76; dir. Anemia and Malnutrition Center, Chiang Mai, Thailand, 1967-77; vis. scholar dept. biochemistry Oxford (Eng.) U., 1961-62; vis. prof. dept. biochemistry U. Freiburg, West Germany, 1970-71; mem. food and nutrition bd. NRC, 1977-83; mem. adv. council Nat. Inst. Arthritis, Diabetes, Digestive and Kidney Diseases, 1981-85; William A. Noyes lectr. U. Ill., Urbana, 1980. Assoc. editor Nutrition Revs., 1954-56, editor, 1978-88; assoc. editor Am. Jour. Medicine, 1956-65, Circulation Rsch., 1956-76, Am. Heart Jour., 1958-65, Am. Jour. Clin. Nutrition, 1960-66, Methods in Med. Rsch., 1963-70, Biochem. Medicine, 1967-90, Molecular and Cellular Cardiology, 1967-78; assoc. editor Ann. Rev. Nutrition, 1979-84, editor, 1984-94; co-editor: Vitamins and Hormones, 1975-81. Bd. dirs. Nat. Nutrition Consortium, 1977-81, Am. Council on Sci. and Health, 1984-91. Served as lt. (j.g.) USNR, 1944-46. Recipient Fulbright award, 1961-62; Guggenheim Found. award, 1961-62, 70-71; McCollum award, 1965; Joseph Goldberger award, 1974; Atwater Meml. lectr., 1978; Geiger Meml. lectr., 1979, William A. Noyes lectr. U. Ill., 1980, H. Brooks James lectr. N.C. State U., 1981, Virginia Beal lectr. U. Mass., 1990. Fellow ACP, Am. Pub. Health Assn. (chmn. food and nutrition sect. 1960-61), Am. Inst. Nutrition (Pres. 1981-82), Assn. Am. Physicians; mem. AAAS (sec. med. scis. N. sect. 1965-67), Am. Assn. Cancer Research, Am. Heart Assn., AMA (mem. council food and nutrition 1959-67, vice chmn. 1962-67), Royal Soc. Health (London), N.Y. Acad. Scis., Am. Fedn. Clin. Research, Am. Soc. Clin. Investigation, Boyleston Med. Soc., Am. Chem. Soc. (pres. biochemistry group Pitts. sect. 1960-61), Am. Soc. Biol. Chemists, Soc. Exptl. Biology and Medicine, Am. Soc. Clin. Nutrition (pres. 1961-62, McCollum award 1965), Assn. Med. Sch. Depts. Biochemistry (pres. 1979-80), Pa., St. Louis, Allegheny County med. socs., Am. Soc. Study Liver Diseases, Phi Beta Kappa, Sigma Xi, Phi Lambda Upsilon, Alpha Omega Alpha, Alpha Sigma Nu. Clubs: Cosmos (Washington), Countryside Country Club (Tampa). Home: 2673 Camille Dr Palm Harbor FL 34684-2217 Office: U South Fla Dept Pediatrics 1 Davis Blvd Ste 307 Tampa FL 33606-3422

OLSON, ROBERT GOODWIN, philosophy educator; b. Mpls., May 8, 1924; s. Goodwin Carl and Mary Helen (Hutchins) O. B.A., U. Minn., 1943; Docteur (French Govt. scholar 1951), U. Paris, 1953; Ph.D., U. Mich., 1957. Staff editor Grolier Soc., N.Y.C., 1946-48; historian Office Mil. Govt., Berlin, Germany, 1948-49; asst. prof. philosophy Ripon (Wis.) Coll., 1953-56; instr. philosophy U. Mich., 1956-58; asst. prof. Columbia U., 1958-61; asso. prof., chmn. dept. philosophy Rutgers U., 1961-65, prof., chmn. dept. philosophy, 1965-69; prof., chmn. dept. philosophy L.I. U., Bklyn., 1969—. Author: An Introduction to Existentialism, 1962, The Morality of Self-Interest, 1965, A Short Introduction to Philosophy, 1967, Meaning and Argument, 1969, Ethics: A Short Introduction, 1977; Contbr. articles to profl. jours. Served with USAAF, 1943-46. Mem. Am., L.I. philos. assns., AAUP, United Fedn. Coll. Tchrs. Home: 2 Cornelia St New York NY 10014-5668 Office: Long Island U Dept Philosophy Bklyn Ctr Brooklyn NY 11201

OLSON, ROBERT GRANT, lawyer; b. Ft. Dodge, Iowa, Mar. 29, 1952; s. Grant L. and R. June (Pohlmann) O.; m. Cynthia Lynn Murray, Sept. 7, 1978; children: Brendon, Elisabeth, Jeffrey, Daniel. BS, Iowa State U., 1973; JD, U. Iowa, 1976. Bar: Mo., 1976, Ill. 1977. Ptnr. Thompson & Mitchell, St. Louis, 1976-92, Riezman & Blitz, P.C., St. Louis, 1992—. Editor Jour. Corp. Law, 1975-76. Vol. Gephardt for Pres. Campaign, 1988, Carnahan for Lt. Gov. Campaign, 1988, Carnahan for Gov. Campaign, 1992. Mem. ABA, Mo. Bar Assn., Ill. Bar Assn., Met. St. Louis Bar Assn., Downtown St. Louis Lions Club (pres. 1990-91). Home: 424 E Jackson Rd Saint Louis MO 63119-4128 Office: Riezman & Blitz PC 120 S Central Ave Saint Louis MO 63105-1705

OLSON, ROBERT HOWARD, lawyer; b. Indpls., July 6, 1944; s. Robert Howard and Jacquline (Wells) O.; m. Diane Carol Thorsen, Aug. 13, 1966; children: Jeffrey, Christopher. BA in Govt. summa cum laude, Ind. U., 1966; JD cum laude, Harvard U., 1969. Bar: U.S. Dist. Ct. (no. dist.) Ohio 1970, U.S. Dist. Ct. (no. Dist.) Ind. 1970, U.S. Dist. Ct. (so. Dist.) Ohio 1971, U.S. Supreme Ct. 1973, Ariz. 1985. Assoc. Squire, Sanders & Dempsey, Cleve., 1969, 70-71, 76-81, ptnr., 1981—, ptnr., Phoenix, 1985—; sr. law clk. U.S. Dist. Ct., No. Dist. Ind. 1969-70; chief civil rights div. Ohio Atty. Gen.'s Office, Columbus, 1971-73, chief consumer protection, 1973-75, chief counsel, 1975, 1st asst. (chief of staff), 1975-76; instr. Law Sch., Ohio State U., Columbus, 1974; mem. Cen. Phoenix com. to advise city council and mayor, 1987-89; bd. dirs., sec. Orpheum Theater Found., 1989-90, pres., 1990—; bd. dirs. The Ariz. Ctr. for Law in the Pub. Interest, 1988—, mem. exec. com., 1990—, treas. 1992-93, v.p., 1993-94; mem. Ariz. Ctr. for Disability Law, 1994—, treas. 1994-95; mem. Valley Leadership Class XIV. Author monograph on financing infrastructure, 1983; also law rev. articles on civil rights, consumer protection. Bd. dirs. 1st Unitarian Ch. Phoenix, v.p., 1987-89; bd. dirs. 1st Unitarian Ch. Found., 1987-93, pres., 1990-93. Mem. Ariz. State Bar Assn., Phi Beta Kappa. Democrat. Home: 5201 E Paradise Dr Scottsdale AZ 85254-4746 Office: Squire Sanders & Dempsey 40 N Central Ave Ste 2700 Phoenix AZ 85004-4424

OLSON, ROBERT LEONARD, retired insurance company executive; b. Auburn, Mass., Aug. 11, 1930; s. Henry Leroy and Marie Albertina (Holquist) O.; m. Muriel E. Storms, Mar. 22, 1958; children: Cynthia L., Mark W., Keith E. AAS, Becker Jr. Coll., 1956; BBA, Clark U., 1958; grad. exec. program, Dartmouth Coll., 1986. Supr. payroll and expense acctg. State Mut. Life Assurance Co. Am., Worcester, 1958-66, asst. mgr. budget fiscal planning, 1966-68; mgr. cost acctg. State Mut. Life Assurance Co. Am., Worcester, Mass., 1968-72, asst. contr., 1972-75, asst. v.p., 1975-82, 2d v.p. fin. planning and reporting, 1982-85, v.p. fin. planning and reporting, 1985-87, v.p., contr., 1987-90, also bd. dirs. Asst. treas. Mass. affiliate Am. Heart Assn., 1982-90, mem. budget, fin. and audit com., 1983-90; treas. Auburn Dist. Nursing Assn., 1972—. Mem. Inst. Mgmt. Accts., Fin. Execs. Inst., Bus. Planning Bd., Am. Mgmt. Assn. (cert. mgmt. course 1982). Avocations: antique and classic cars. Home: 7 Ridgewood Dr Auburn MA 01501-2316 Office: State Mut Life Assurance Co 440 Lincoln St Worcester MA 01653-0002

OLSON, ROBERTA JEANNE MARIE, art historian, author, educator; b. Shawano, Wis., June 1, 1947; d. Robert Bernard Olson and Emma Pauline (Dallmann) Hoops; m. Alexander Buchanan Vance Johnson, June 15, 1980; 1 child, Allegra Alexandra Olson Johnson. BA, St. Olaf Coll., 1969; MA, U. Iowa, 1971; MFA, Princeton U., 1973, PhD, 1976. Preceptor Princeton (N.J.) U., 1972-74; contbg. editor Arts Mag., N.Y.C., 1973-75; art news editor The Soho Weekly News, N.Y.C., 1976-78; asst. prof., assoc. prof. Wheaton Coll., Norton, Mass., 1975-88, prof., 1988—, chmn. art dept., 1987-89, 92-93; A. Howard Meneely chair Wheaton Coll., 1990-92; cons. Smithsonian Instn., Washington, 1984-86; bd. dirs. The Drawing Soc., N.Y.C., 1989-94, The Friends of Art; bd. advisers Halley's Comet Soc., 1986—; mem. vis. com. drawing and print dept. Met. Mus. Art, 1993—. Author: Italian Nineteenth Century Drawings and Watercolors: An Album, 1976, Italian Drawings 1780-1890, 1980 (N.Y. Times Best Art Book award 1981, Whole Earth Book award), Fire and Ice: A History of Comets in Art, 1985, Italian Renaissance Sculpture, 1992, French edit., 1993, Ottocento: Romanticism and Revolution in 19th Century Italian Painting, 1993; contbr. articles to profl. jours., including Burlington Mag., Art Bull., Master Drawings, Jour. History of Astronomy, Artibus et Historiae, Sci. Am., Mitteilungen des Kunsthistorischen Insts. in Florenz, Arte Cristiana, Gazette des Beaux-Arts, Antologia di Belle Arti, Astronomy and Astrophysics (qtrly.), Art Jour., Studies in History of Art; contbr. articles to art exhbn. catalogs, including Six Centuries of Sculptors Drawings, The Drawing Ctr., N.Y.C., 1981, Disegni di Tommaso Minardi, 2 vols., 1982, Old Master Drawings from the Mus. Art RISD, 1983; guest curator Art Mus. Princeton U., 1974, Nat. Gallery Art, 1980, N.Y. Hist. Soc., 1990. Fellow Samuel H. Kress Found., 1973-74, Whiting Found. for Humanities, 1974-75, NEH, 1982-83; grantee NEH, 1987-88, Am. Philos. Soc., 1989, Am. Coun. Learned Socs., 1990-91, Getty sr. rsch. grantee, 1994-95, Samuel H. Kress Found., 1996. Mem. Coll. Art Assn. Am., Am. Assn. Univ. Profs. Italian, Drawing Soc., Phi Beta Kappa (pres. 1980-82, Kappa chpt.). Avocations: running, squash, collecting. Home: 35 Howard St Norton MA 02766 Office: Wheaton Coll Watson Hall Norton MA 02766

OLSON, RONALD DALE, grain company executive; b. Ft. Dodge, Iowa, Oct. 22, 1947; s. Albert Dale and Gladys Marie (Peters) O.; m. Lynn Diane Rustwick, Nov. 22, 1969; children: Jenna, Jill. BS in Agr. Bus., Iowa State U., 1969, MS in Econs., 1971. Instr. econs. Iowa State U., Ames, 1969-71; various merchandising and mgmt. positions Continental Grain Co., Portland, Oreg., San Francisco, Fairmont, Minn. and Mpls.; regional mgr., v.p. N.W. region Continental Grain Co., 1971-90; pres. Atwood-Kellogg Co., Mpls., 1990-95; v.p. Gen. Mills, Mpls., 1996—; bd. dirs. Mpls. Grain Exchange, chmn. bd., 1985-87. Mem. ch. council Mt. Olivet Luth. Ch., Mpls., 1975—. Avocations: sports; music; woodworking. Home: 3510 Beard Curve Minneapolis MN 55431-2724 Office: Gen Mills Inc Commerce Sta 680 Grain Exchange Minneapolis MN 55415

OLSON, RUE EILEEN, librarian; b. Chgo., Nov. 1, 1928; d. Paul H. and Martha M. (Fick) Meyers; m. Richard L. Olson, July 18, 1964; children: Catherine, Karen. Student Herzl Coll., 1946-48, Northwestern U., 1948-50, Ill. State U., 1960-64, Middle Mgmt. Inst. Spl. Librs. Assn., 1985-87. Acct. Ill. Farm Supply Co., Chgo., 1948-59; asst. libr. Ill. Agrl. Assn., Bloomington, 1960-66, libr., 1966-86, dir. libr. svcs., 1986—; bd. dirs. Corn Belt Libr. System, 1989-94, sec., 1991—. Mem. area Com. Nat. Libr. Week, 1971, area steering com., 1972; mem. steering com. Illinet/OCLC, 1985-87; mem. adv. council of librs. Grad. Sch. Libr. Sci. U. Ill., 1976-79; mem. Ill. State Libr. Adv. Com. for Interlibr. Cooperation, 1979-80; del. Ill. White House Conf. on Libr. and Info. Svcs., 1978; coordinator Vita Income Tax Assistance, Bloomington, Ill., 1986-89, preparer 1978—. Mem. Am., Ill., McLean County (pres. 1970-71) Libr. Assns., Spl. Librs. Assn. (pres. Ill. chpt. 1977-78, first to be named Disting. Mem. food, agr. and nutrition div. 1989), Ill. OCLC Users Group (treas. 1988-90, bd. dirs. 1991-92), Internat. Assn. Agrl. Librs. and Documentalists, Am. Soc. Info. Sci., Am. Mgmt. Assn., USAIN, Mended Hearts, Inc. (sec. Ill. chpt. 250 1994-95, v.p. 1995—, newsletter editor, 1994—), Zonta (pres. 1987-89), Bloomington Club. Office: Ill Agrl Assn 1701 N Towanda Ave Bloomington IL 61701

OLSON, RUSSELL L., pension fund administrator; b. Elizabeth, N.J., Jan. 3, 1933; s. Harold B. and Edythe M. (Roberts) O.; m. Jeanette A. Sanderson, Aug. 9, 1958; children: Tracy, Stephen, Heather. BA, Rutgers U., 1954; MBA, Harvard U., 1971. Trainee Eastman Kodak Co., Rochester, N.Y., 1954-56, with pub. rels. dept., 1957-69, coordinator internt. info. svcs., 1964-69, treas. staff, 1971-74; adminstrv. asst. pension investments Eastman Kodak Co., Rochester, 1974-82, dir. pension investments worldwide, 1982—. With USAF, 1954-56. Presbyterian. Office: Eastman Kodak Co 343 State St Rochester NY 14650-0001

OLSON, SIGMUND LARS, corporate finance executive; b. Green Bay, Wis., Feb. 7, 1935; s. Edwin Louis and Marjorie Magdelene (Miller) O.; m. Diana Lynn Armentrout, Mar. 15, 1961 (div. 1974); children: Eric L., Lafe S., Britta C., Gunnar A.; m. Linda Marie Larson, Sept. 25, 1976. BS, Calif. State U., Long Beach, 1963; MBA, U. Iowa, 1964. With fin. staff Ford Motor Co., Detroit, 1964-69; with mgmt. staff Mattel, Inc., Los Angeles, 1969-72, Allen Group, Los Angeles, 1972-77; dir. planning Internat. Harvester Co., Chgo., 1977-78, dir. fin. German div., Düsseldorf, 1978-79, v.p. fin. European div., Paris, 1979-82, asst. controller, Chgo., 1982-84, asst. treas., 1984-85; v.p. treas. Ecolab, Inc., St. Paul, 1985-86, v.p., controller, 1986-88, sr. v.p. fin., 1988-90; CFO Henkel-Ecolab Joint Venture, Dusseldorf, Fed. Republic Germany, 1990-94; v.p. fin. Internat. Ecolab., Inc., St. Paul, 1995—. Bd. dirs. YMCA, St. Paul, 1986-90, chmn., 1989-90. Served to cpl. USMA, 1957-60. Mem. Fin. Execs. Inst., Planning Execs. Inst., Am. Mgmt. Assn., Nat. Assn. Corp. Treas. Lutheran. Club: PGA Nat. (Fla.). Avocations: sailing, reading, skiing, investments. Office: Ecolab Inc 370 Wabasha St Saint Paul MN 55102-1306

OLSON, STANLEY WILLIAM, physician, educator, medical school dean; b. Chgo., Feb. 10, 1914; s. David William and Agnes (Nelson) O.; m. Lorraine Caroline Lofdahl, June 26, 1936; children: Patricia Ann, Richard David, Robert Dean. BS, Wheaton Coll., 1934, LLD (hon.), 1956; MD, U. Ill., 1938; MS in Medicine (fellow), U. Minn., 1943; ScD, U. Akron, 1979, N.E Ohio U., 1985, Morehouse Sch. Medicine. Diplomate: Am. Bd. Internal Medicine. Intern Cook County Hosp., Chgo., 1938-40; asst. dir. Mayo Found., from 1947; cons. medicine Mayo Clinic, 1947—; instr. medicine grad. sch. U. Minn., 1947-50; dean and prof. coll. medicine, med. dir. Rsch. and Ednl. Hosp. U. Ill., 1950-53; dean and prof. Coll. Medicine Baylor U., Tex. Med. Ctr., Houston, 1953-66; prof. medicine Vanderbilt U.; clin. prof. medicine Meharry Med. Coll., 1966-68; dir. Tenn. Mid-South Regional Med. Program, 1967-68; dir. Div. Regional Med. Programs Svc. USPHS, 1968-70; pres. S.W. Found. for Rsch. and Edn., San Antonio, 1970-73; provost Coll. Medicine N.E. Ohio U., 1973-79, cons. med. edn. Morehouse Coll. Medicine, 1980-81; dean Morehouse Sch. Medicine, Atlanta, 1985-87; past chmn. med. bd., chief staff Ben Taub Hosp., Jefferson Davis Hosp., Houston; nat. adv. council for health research facilities NIH, 1963-68; rev. panel constrn. med. schs. USPHS, 1964-65; spl. cons. div. Regional Med. Programs NIH, 1966-68; med. cons. bd. trustees. SUNY, 1949; cons. to Hoover Commn., 1954; mem. bd. trustees. Wheaton Coll., Ill., 1953-68. Contbr. articles to profl. jours. Capt., M.C. AUS, 1943-46. Mem. AMA, Houston Philos. Soc. (pres. 1962-63), Tex. Philos. Soc., Assn. Am. Med. Colls., Alumni Assn. Mayo Found., Sigma Xi, Alpha Kappa Kappa, Alpha Omega Alpha. Baptist. Home: 5901 Churchview Dr Unit 25 Rockford IL 61107

OLSON, STEPHEN M(ICHAEL), lawyer; b. Jamestown, N.Y., May 4, 1948; s. Charles R. and Marilyn (Dietzel) O.; m. Linda C. Hanson, Aug. 24, 1968; children: Kevin, Darren. AB cum laude, Princeton U., 1970; JD, U. Chgo., 1973. Bar: Pa. 1973, U.S. Dist. Ct. (we. dist.) Pa. 1973, U.S. Ct. Appeals (3d cir.) 1975, U.S. Ct. Appeals (1st and D.C. cirs.) 1986, U.S. Ct. Appeals (7th cir. and 8th cir. 1988), U.S. Supreme Ct. 1986. Assoc. Kirkpatrick & Lockhart, Pitts., 1973-81, ptnr., 1981—. Mem. bd. editors Health-Span. Vice chair bd. trustees Chatham Coll.; bd. dirs. Competitive Employment Opportunities. Mem. ABA (rwy./airline labor law com.), Pa. Bar Assn., Allegheny County Bar Assn., Princeton Alumni Assn. West Pa., Duquesne Club, Edgeworth Club. Avocations: photography, music, tennis. Office: Kirkpatrick & Lockhart 1500 Oliver Building Bldg Pittsburgh PA 15222-2312

OLSON, THEODORE ALEXANDER, former environmental biology educator; b. Oakes, N.D., Sept. 12, 1904; s. Henry Martin and Anna R. (Anderson) O.; m. Grace Myrtle Lundberg, Jan. 5, 1929; children—Theodore A., R. Thomas, Robert C. B.S., U. Minn., 1926; M.A., Harvard, 1938, Ph.D., 1958. Econ. entomologist U. Wis., 1926; instr. entomology U. Minn., 1926-28; prof. environmental biology Sch. Pub. Health, 1938-73, prof. emeritus, 1973—; biologist Minn. Dept. Health, 1928-38; Cons. health depts., Minn., N.Y., Wash.; Cons. health depts. Ohio River Valley Sanitation Commn., WHO, Norwegian Inst. Water Research, NIH; participant internat. study rodent control, Europe, Mid East, Pacific WHO, 1965, Internat. Conf., Munich, 1966. Author 1 book and over 100 profl. publs. Served from 1st lt to lt. col. San. Corps AUS, 1942-46. Rockefeller fellow, 1947; WHO fellow Caribbean, 1955; USPHS fellow N. Europe, 1962. Mem. AAAS, Am. Pub. Health Assn. (sect. vice chmn., chmn. lab. sect., governing council 1960-70), Am. Soc. Limnology and Oceanography, Am. Micros. Soc., Entomol. Soc. Am., State and Territorial Lab. Dirs. Assn., Sigma Xi, Internat. Assn. Great Lakes Research (dir., pres. 1968—). Clubs: University Minnesota, Harvard. Research on basic limnology of Lake Superior. Home: 4752 16th Ave S Minneapolis MN 55407-3607

OLSON, THEODORE BEVRY, lawyer; b. Chgo., Sept. 11, 1940; 2 children. B.A., U. Pacific, 1962; LL.B., U. Calif.-Berkeley, 1965. Bar: Calif. 1965, D.C. 1982. Assoc. Gibson, Dunn & Crutcher, Los Angeles, 1972-81, 84—, ptnr., 1972-81; asst. atty. gen. Dept. Justice, Washington, 1981—. Mem. Calif. Commn. on Uniform State Laws, 1972-74; del. Republican Nat. Conv., 1976, 80. Mem. ABA, L.A. County Bar Assn. Office: Gibson Dunn & Crutcher 1050 Connecticut Ave NW Ste 90 Washington DC 20036-5303

OLSON, THOMAS FRANCIS, II, communications company executive; b. Chgo., July 31, 1948; s. Thomas Francis and Nora Theresa (Shaw) O.; m. Maureen Eunice Walsh, July 28, 1972; children: Amy Michelle, Danielle Renee. B in Bus. Mktg., Western Ill. U., 1970. Sales exec. Sta. WQAD-TV, Moline, Ill., 1970-73; computer salesman Honeywell, Inc., Springfield, Ill., 1973; project mgr. Olson Bros. and Sons Constrn. Co., Chgo., 1973-75; sales exec. Katz Communications, Chgo., 1975-77, sales team mgr., 1977-81; v.p., nat. sales mgr. Katz Communications, N.Y.C., 1981-83, v.p., gen. sales mgr., 1983-84, div. pres., 1984-90, exec. v.p. TV group, 1991-92; pres. Katz TV Group, N.Y.C., 1992—; pres. chief exec. officer Katz Media Group, Inc., 1994—. Mem. Nat. Assn. Broadcasters, TV Bur. Advt., Sta. Reps. Assn. (pres.). Roman Catholic. Avocations: running, skiing, hiking, sailing, scuba diving. Office: Katz Media Grp Inc 125 W 55th St New York NY 10019

OLSON, WALTER GILBERT, lawyer; b. Stanton, Nebr., Feb. 2, 1924; s. O.E. Olson and Mabel A. Asplin; m. Gloria Helen Bennett, June 26, 1949; children: Clifford Warner, Karen Rae Olson. BS, U. Calif., Berkeley, 1947, JD, 1949. Bar: Calif. 1950, U.S. Dist. Ct. (no. dist.) Calif. 1950, U.S. Tax Ct. 1950, U.S. Ct. Appeals (9th cir.) 1950. Assoc. Orrick, Herrington and Sutcliffe (formerly Orrick, Dahlquist, Herrington and Sutcliffe), San Francisco, 1949-54, ptnr., 1954-88, of counsel, 1989—; bd. dirs. Alltel Corp., Little Rock, 1988-94; mem. Commn. to Revise Calif. Corp. Securities Law, 1967-69, Securities Regulatory Reform Panel, 1978-80; mem. corp. security adv. com. Calif. Commr. of Corps, 1975—. Editor-in-chief Calif. Law Review, 1948-49. Bd. dirs. Internat. Ho., Berkeley, 1981-86. With U.S. Army, 1943-46, ETO. Fellow Am. Bar Found.; mem. ABA (trust divsn. nat. conf. of lawyers and reps. of Am. Bankers Assn.), Calif. Bar Assn. (chmn. corps com. 1975-76, exec. com. bus. law sect. 1977-78), San Francisco Bar Assn., U. Calif. Alumni Assn., Boalt Hall Alumni Assn. (bd. dirs. 1982-90, sec. 1985, v.p. 1987, pres. 1988), Order of Coif, Menlo Country Club (Woodside, Calif.), Pacific-Union Club. Office: Orrick Herrington & Sutcliffe 400 Sansome St San Francisco CA 94111-3308

OLSON, WALTER JUSTUS, JR., management consultant; b. Paterson, N.J., July 27, 1941; s. Walter Justus and Viola (Trautvetter) O. BS, BA, Brown U., 1964; MBA, Columbia U., 1967. CPA, Va. Design engr. Rockwell Internat., Inc., Downey, Calif., 1964-65; mgmt. officer CIA, Washington, 1969-73; sr. cons. Booz, Allen and Hamilton, Inc., Washington, 1973-78; corp. planning coordinator Washington Gas Light Co., Washington, 1978-82; prin. Walter J. Olson and Assoc., McLean, Va., 1982-83; dep. asst. sec. for export adminstrn. U.S. Dept. Commerce, Washington, 1983-86; prin. Walter J. Olson & Assoc., Washington, 1986—. Vice-chmn. fin. com. Fairfax County (Va.) Reps., 1982-83. Served to 1st lt., USAF, 1967-69. Mem. AICPA, D.C. Inst. CPAs, Strategic Leadership Forum (pres. Washington chpt. 1990-91). Republican. Episcopalian. Home: 7348 Dartford Dr Mc Lean VA 22102-7348 Office: 1815 H St NW Ste 600 Washington DC 20006-3604

OLSON, WALTER THEODORE, research scientist, consultant; b. Royal Oak, Mich., July 4, 1917; s. Oscar Thomas and Edith Margaret (Ketcham) O.; m. Ruth Elisabeth Barker, Oct. 28, 1943; 1 child, David Paul. AB, DePauw U., 1939; MS, Case Inst. Tech., 1940, PhD, 1942. Instr. Case Inst. Tech., 1941-42; research scientist Lewis Research Center, NASA, Cleve., 1942-45; chief combustion br. Lewis Research Center, NASA, 1945-50, chief chemistry and energy conversion research div., 1950-63, asst. dir., 1963-72, dir. tech. utilization and public affairs, 1972-81, disting. research assoc., 1981-82; pvt. cons., 1981—; mem. numerous govt. adv. coms. Editor: (with W.R. Hawthorne) Design and Performance of Gas Turbine Power Plants, 1960; editorial bd.: Combustion and Flame, 1955-65; contbr. articles to profl. jours. Dir. Build Up Greater Cleve. Program, 1981-91; vice chmn. United Appeal Greater Cleve., 1965-73; chmn. legis. affairs Ohio Assn. Gifted Children, 1969-76; trustee Blue Cross N.E., Ohio, 1972-84, N.E. Ohio Transit Coalition, 1992—; mem. industry adv. com. Coll. Engrs., Cleve. State U., 1975-85, chmn., 1975-76; mem. Ohio Pub. Works Commn., 1988-89. Recipient Career Service award Greater Cleve. Growth Assn., 1972, Exceptional Contbns. award NASA, 1981, Excellence award Am. Soc. Assn. Execs., 1987. Fellow AIAA (dir. 1969-75, Disting. Svc. award Cleve.-Akron sect. 1966, 75, Exceptional Svc. award 1981, other awards), AAAS; mem. Combustion Inst. (dir. 1954—), Am. Chem. Soc., Sigma Xi, Phi Gamma Delta. Methodist. Clubs: Cosmos (Washington); City (Cleve.). Patentee in field. Home and Office: 18960 Coffinberry Blvd Cleveland OH 44126-1602

OLSON, WILLIAM CLINTON, international affairs educator, author, lecturer; b. Denver, Aug. 19, 1920; s. Albert Merrill and Frances (Murray) O.; m. Mary Elizabeth Matthews, Aug. 16, 1943; children: Jon Eric, Peter Murray, Elizabeth Ann. AB, U. Denver, 1942; PhD, Yale U., 1953; DHL (hon.), U. Denver, 1992. Staff officer Social Sci. Found., Denver, 1947-49; chmn. com. on internat. rels. Pomona Coll., 1953-61; sr. mem. St. Antonys Coll., Oxford (Eng.) U., 1959-60; assoc. dean sch. internat. affairs Columbia U., 1965-67; assoc. dir. for social scis. Rockefeller Found., N.Y.C., 1967-79; prof. Sch. Internat. Service, Am. U., Washington, 1979-90, prof. emeritus, 1990—, dean, 1979-86; vis. rsch. fellow Royal Inst. Internat. Affairs, London, 1986-87; dir. The Bellagio Study and Conf. Ctr. of The Rockefeller Found., Villa Serbelloni, Italy, 1970-79; prof. Grad. Inst. Internat. Studies, Geneva, 1976-78; life fellow Clare Hall, Cambridge; cons. to vice chancellor U. Colombo, Sri Lanka, 1983; lectr. Johns Hopkins U., Washington, 1961-65, Bologna, 1973-75. Author, editor: The Theory and Practice of International Relations, 1960, 9th edit., 1994; contbr.: International Relations: British and American Perspectives, 1985, The Aberystwth Papers, 1972,

Jahrbuch des offentlichen Rechts der gegenwart, 1972, 74, 78, 80, Internat. Affairs, 1976, 91; co-author: Internat. Relations Then and Now: Origins and Trends in Interpretation, 1991. Trustee Experiment in Internat. Living, 1959-65, Social Sci. Found. U. Denver, 1967-76, 80-92, 94—; co-founder Am. Friends Wilton Park, Inc., 1986. Recipient Disting. Alumnus award Grad. Sch. Internat. Studies, Denver, 1986; received medal and named Hon. Ancien, NATO Def. Coll., 1989. Mem. Coun. Fgn. Rels., Washington Inst. Fgn. Affairs, Internat. Studies Assn. (nat. pres. 1968-69), British Internat. Studies Assn., Cosmos Club (Washington), Phi Beta Kappa (pres. Gamma of Calif. 1957-58), Sigma Iota Rho (founder).

OLSON, WILLIAM HENRY, neurology educator, administrator; b. Haxtun, Colo., Sept. 2, 1936; s. William Henry and Burdene (Anderson) O.; m. Shirley Gorden, July 24, 1967; children: Erik, Marnie. B.A., Wesleyan U., 1959; M.D., Harvard U., 1963. Diplomate: Am. Bd. Psychiatry and Neurology. Intern Beth Israel Hosp., Boston, 1963-65; resident Children's Hosp. Med. Ctr., Boston, 1965-67; staff assoc. NIH, Bethesda, Md., 1969-70; asst. prof. neurology and anatomy Vanderbilt U., Nashville, 1970-73, assoc. prof. neurology and anatomy, 1973-75; prof., chmn. dept. adult neurology U. N.D., Fargo, 1975-80; chmn., prof. dept. neurology U. Louisville, 1980—. Co-author: Practical Neurology and the Primary Care Physician, 1981, Symptom Oriented Neurology, 1994. Fulbright scholar Tubingen, Germany, 1958-59. Fellow Am. Acad. Neurology; mem. Phi Beta Kappa. Home: 331 Zorn Ave # 1 Louisville KY 40206-1542 Office: Dept Neurology Univ Louisville Louisville KY 40292

OLSON, WILLIAM JEFFREY, lawyer; b. Paterson, N.J., Oct. 23, 1949; s. Walter Justus and Viola Patricia (Trautvetter) O.; m. Janet Elaine Bollen, May 22, 1976; children: Robert J., Joanne C. AB, Brown U., 1971; JD, U. Richmond, 1976. Bar: Va. 1976, D.C. 1976, U.S. Ct. Claims 1976, U.S. Ct. Appeals (4th and D.C. cirs.) 1976, U.S. Supreme Ct. 1982. Assoc. Jackson & Campbell, Washington, 1976-79; ptnr. Gilman, Olson & Pangia, Washington, 1980-92; prin. William J. Olson PC, McLean, Va. and Washington, 1992—; sec., treas. bd. dirs. Victims Assistance Legal Orgn., Virginia Beach, Va., 1979—; presdl. transition team leader Legal Svcs. Corp., Washington, 1980; chmn. and bd. dirs. Nat. Legal Svcs. Corp., 1981-82; mem. Pres.'s Export Coun. Subcom. on Export Adminstrn., Washington, 1982-84; spl. counsel bd. govs. U.S. Postal Svc., Washington, 1984-86. Author: Tuition Tax Credits and Alternatives, 1978; co-author: Debating National Health Policy, 1977. Trustee Davis Meml. Goodwill Industries, Washington, 1980-86, 88-93; chmn. Fairfax County Rep. Com., Fairfax, Va., 1980-82; mem. Rep. State Ctrl. Com., Richmond, Va., 1982-86. Mem. Va. Bar Assn., Assn. Trial Lawyers Am., Va. Trial Lawyers Assn., Christian Legal Soc. Republican. Baptist. Avocation: gardening. Office: 8180 Greensboro Dr Ste 1070 Mc Lean VA 22102-3823

OLSON-HELLERUD, LINDA KATHRYN, elementary school educator; b. Wisconsin Rapids, Wis., Aug. 26, 1947; d. Samuel Ellsworth and Lillian (Dvorak) Olson; m. H. A. Hellerud, 1979; BS, U. Wis.-Stevens Point, 1969, teaching cert., 1970, MST, 1972; postgrad. U. Wis. at Madison, 1969-70; MS, U. Wis. Whitewater, 1975; EdS, U. Wis.-Stout, 1978; cert. k-12 reading tchr. and specialist. Clk., Univ. Counseling Ctr., U. Wis., Stevens Point, 1965-69; elementary sch. tchr., Wisconsin Rapids, 1970-76, sch. counselor, 1976-79, dist. elem. guidance dir., 1979-82, elem. and reading tchr., 1982—, also cons.; advocate Moravian Ch. Sunday sch. Mem. NEA, Wisconsin Rapids Edn. Assn., Internat. Reading Assn., Wis. Reading Assn., Ctrl. Wis. Reading Assn., Wis. State Hist. Soc., Wood County Hist. Soc., Wood County Literacy Coun. (cons.). Mem. United Ch. of Christ.Avocations: gardening, piano. Home: 120 11th St N Wisconsin Rapids WI 54494-4548 Office: Howe Elem Sch Wisconsin Rapids WI 54494

OLSSON, ANN-MARGRET See ANN-MARGRET

OLSSON, BJÖRN ESKIL, railroad supply company executive; b. Kristianstad, Sweden, Oct. 7, 1945; came to U.S., 1990; m. Cecilia Lindblad, July 6, 1968; children: Fredrik, Karin, Eva. M Bus. and Adminstrn., U. Lund, Sweden, 1968. Internal auditor Kockums Mek. Verkstad, Malmö, Sweden, 1969-71, mgr. acctg., 1971-74; v.p. fin. and adminstrn. Kockums Industri, Söderhamn, Sweden, 1974-76, Linden Alimak, Skellefteå, Sweden, 1976-81, Sonessons, Malmö, 1981-82; pres. Sab-Nife, Malmö, 1982-87; v.p. corp. devel. Investment AB Cardo, Malmö, 1987-90; pres., CEO Harmon Industries Inc., Blue Springs, Mo., 1990—; bd. dirs. Deve Schindler, Stockholm, Green & Co., Malmö; mem. adv. bd. Ctrl. Mo. State U. Bus. Sch., Warrensburg, 1991—. Staff sgt. Swedish Army, 1964-65. Avocations: golf, skiing. Office: Harmon Industries Inc 1300 NW Jefferson Ct Blue Springs MO 64015-7265*

OLSSON, CARL ALFRED, urologist; b. Boston, Nov. 29, 1938; s. Charles Rudolph and Ruth Marion (Bostrom) O.; m. Mary DeVore, Nov. 4, 1962; children: Ingrid, Leif Eric. Grad., Bowdoin Coll., 1959; MD, Boston U., 1963. Diplomate Am. Bd. Urology (trustee 1988-94, pres. 1993-94). Asst. prof. urology Boston U. Sch. Medicine, 1971-72, assoc. prof., 1972-74, prof., chmn. dept., 1974-80; dir. urology dept. Boston City Hosp., 1974-77; chief urology dept. Boston VA Med. Ctr., 1971-75; urologist-in-chief Univ. Hosp., Boston, 1971-80; John K. Lattimer prof., chmn. dept. urology Coll. Phys. and Surgs., Columbia U., N.Y.C., 1980—; dir. Squier Urol. Clinic, urology service Presbyn. Hosp., N.Y.C.; lectr. surgery Tufts U. Sch. Medicine. Bd. dirs. New England Interhosp. Organ Bank, 1976-79; mem. working cadre Nat. Prostate Cancer Project, Nat. Cancer Inst., 1979-84; mem. adv. coun. Nat. Inst. Diabetes, Digestive Disease and Kidney. Editl. bd. Jour. Prostate, World Jour. Urology, Jour. Urodynamics and Neurourology, Jour. Urology; asst. editor Jour. Urology, 1978-89; contbr. chpts. to books, articles to med. jours. Recipient Disting. Alumnus award Boston U., 1985. Fellow ACS; mem. Am. Urol. Assn. (coord. continuing med. edn. New Eng. sect. 1977-80, del. rsch. com., Gold Cystoscope award 1979, Grayson-Carroll award 1971, 73), Boston Surg. Soc. (exec. com. 1976-80), Am. Assn. Clin. Urologists, Am. Surg. Assn., Am. Assn. Genitourinary Surgeons, Clin. Soc. Genitourinary Surgeons, Transplantation Soc., Soc. Urologic Oncology (pres. 1993), Soc. Univ. Urologists (pres. 1990), N.Y. Sect. Am. Urol. Assn., Am. Fertility Soc., AMA, Assn. Acad. Surgery, Am. Soc. Artificial Internal Organs, Am. Soc. Transplant Surgeons, Assn. Med. Colls., Can. Urol. Assn., Societe Internationale d'Urologie, Internat. Urodynamics Soc., Mass. Med. Soc., Soc. Govt. Urologists, Australasian Urol. Soc. (hon.), New Eng. Handicapped Sportsmen's Assn. (exec. com. 1977-81), U.S. Yacht Racing Union, Yacht Racing Union L.I. Sound Club, N.Y. Yacht Club, Cottage Park Yacht Club, Larchmont Yacht Club, Storm Trysail Club, Alpha Omega Alpha. Episcopalian. Home: 18 Elm Ave Larchmont NY 10538-3649 Office: Columbia-Presbyn Hosp P&S Box 44 630 W 168th St New York NY 10032-3702

OLSSON, NILS WILLIAM, former association executive; b. Seattle, June 11, 1909; s. Nils A. and Mathilda (Lejkell) O.; m. Dagmar T. Gavert, June 15, 1940; children: Karna B., Nils G. and Pehr C. (twins). Student, North Park Coll., Chgo., Northwestern U., U. Minn., 1929-34; A.M., U. Chgo., 1938, Ph.D., 1949; Ph.D., U. Uppsala, Sweden, 1968; LHD, North Park Coll., Chgo., 1990. Admissions counselor, instr. Swedish North Park Coll., 1937-39; asst. Scandinavian U. Chgo., 1939-42, instr., 1945-50, asst. prof., 1950; mem. U.S. diplomatic service, 1950-67; 2d sec., pub. affairs officer Am. legation, Reykjavik, Iceland, 1950-52; attache, pub. affairs officer Am. embassy, Stockholm, Sweden, 1952-55; 1st. sec., consul Am. embassy, 1955-57; pub. affairs adviser Dept. State, 1957-59; chief Am. sponsored schs. abroad, 1959-62; 1st sec. Am. embassy, Oslo, Norway, 1962-64; counselor for polit. affairs Am. embassy, 1964-66; diplomat in residence Ind. U., 1966-67; dir. Am. Swedish Inst., Mpls., 1967-73; exec. dir. Swedish Council of Am., 1973-84. Author: Swedish Passenger Arrivals in New York 1820-1850, 1967, Swedish Passenger Arrivals in U.S. Ports (except New York) 1820-1850, 1979, Tracing Your Swedish Ancestry, 1974, (with Erik Wiken) Swedish Passenger Arrivals in the U.S. 1820-1850, 1995; editor: A Pioneer in Northwest America, 1841-1858, vol. I, 1950, vol. II, 1959, Veckobladet, 1934-35; editor, pub.: Swedish American Genealogist, 1981—; editor: A Swedish City Directory of Boston 1881, 1986; contbr. to hist. and ednl. jours. Mem. bd. Evang. Covenant Hist. Commn., Chgo., 1958; asst. naval attache Am. legation, Stockholm, 1943-45. Served from lt. (j.g.) to lt. comdr. USNR, 1942-45. Decorated knight Order Vasa 1st class, knight comdr. Order North Star, Sweden; recipient Swedish Pioneer Centennial medal, 1948; King Carl XVI Gustaf Bicentennial Gold medal, Carl Sandburg medal Swedish Pioneer Hist. Soc., 1982, Charlotta medal Emigrant Inst. Växjö, Sweden; named Swedish Am. of Yr. Stockholm, 1969; recipient Hans Mattsson Plaque, Önnestad, Sweden, 1992; Victor Örnberg prize, Sweden, 1994. Fellow Geneal. Soc. (Finland), Geneal. Soc. (Sweden), Am. Soc. Genealogists; mem. Wermländska Sällskapet Stockholm (hon.), Nat. Geneal Soc., Carl Johan Soc. Sweden, Swedish-Am. Hist. Soc. (exec. sec. 1949-50, 57-68, pres. 1986-88), Royal Acad. Belles Lettres, History and Antiquities (Sweden, fgn. corr.), Pro Fide et Christianismo (Sweden, hon.), Royal Soc. Pub. Manuscripts Dealing with Scandinavian History (Sweden, fgn.). Clubs: Skylight (Mpls.); Grolier (N.Y.C.); Cosmos (Washington); Explorers (Central Fla.); Univ. (Winter Park, Fla.). Lodge: Rotary. Home: Winter Park Gardens Apt # G-21 700 Melrose Ave Winter Park FL 32789

OLSTAD, ROGER GALE, science educator; b. Mpls., Jan. 16, 1934; s. Arnold William and Myra (Stroschein) O.; m. Constance Elizabeth Jackson, Aug. 20, 1955; children: Karen Louise, Kenneth Bradley. B.S., U. Minn., 1955, M.A., 1959, Ph.D., 1963. Instr., U. Minn., Mpls., 1956-63; asst. prof. U. Ill., Urbana, 1963-64; mem. faculty U. Wash., Seattle, 1964—; asso. prof. sci. edn. U. Wash., 1967-71, prof., 1971—, asso. dean grad. studies Coll. Edn., 1971-95; prof. emeritus, 1995—. Fellow AAAS; mem. NSTA (bd. dirs.) Wash. Sci. Tchrs. Assn. (pres. 1973-74), Nat. Assn. Rsch. Sci. Teaching (pres. 1977-78, bd. dirs.), N.W. Sci. Assn. (chmn. 1966-68), Assn. Edn. Tchrs. in Sci. (regional pres. 1966-68, pres. 1991-92), Nat. Assn. Biology Tchrs., Biol. Scis. Curriculum Study (chmn., bd. dirs. 1989-94), U. Wash. Faculty Club, Phi Delta Kappa. Home: 20143 53rd Ave NE Seattle WA 98155-1801 Office: U Wash Coll Edn Seattle WA 98195

OLSTEN, STUART, personnel services company executive; s. William O. Exec. v.p. Olsten Corp., Westbury, N.Y. Office: Olsten Corp 1 Merrick Ave Westbury NY 11590-6601*

OLSTOWSKI, FRANCISZEK, chemical engineer, consultant; b. N.Y.C., Apr. 23, 1927; s. Franciszek and Marguerite (Stewart) O.; A.A., Monmouth Coll., 1950; BSCE, Tex. A&M U., 1954; m. Rosemary Sole, May 19, 1952; children: Marguerita Antonina, Anna Rosa, Franciszek, Anton, Henryk Alexander. Research and devel. engr. Dow Chem. Co., Freeport, Tex., 1954-56, project leader, 1956-65, sr. research engr., 1965-72, research specialist, 1972-79, research leader, 1979-87; dir. Tech. Cons. Services, Freeport, 1987—. Lectr. phys. scis. elementary and intermediate schs., Freeport, 1961-85. Vice chmn. Freeport Traffic Commn., 1974-76, chmn., 1976-79, vice-chmn. 1987-89, chmn., 1989-92. With USNR, 1944-46. Fellow Am. Inst. Chemist; mem. AAAS, Am. Chem. Soc., Electrochem. Soc. (sec. treas. South Tex. sect. 1963-64, vice chmn. 1964-65, chmn. 1965-67, councillor 1967-70), N.Y. Acad. Sci, Velasco Cemetery Assn. (sec.-treas. 1992-95). Patentee in synthesis of fluorocarbons, natural graphite products, electrolytic prodn. magnesium metal and polyurethane tech.

OLSZEWSKI, EDWARD JOHN, art history educator; b. Detroit, Jan. 7, 1937; s. John Peter and Mary Catherine (Kaminski) O.; m. I. Monica Foltarz (dec.). BS, U. Detroit, 1958, MS, 1962; PhD, U. Ill., 1964, U. Minn., 1974. Rsch. assoc. prof. U. South Fla., Tampa, 1964-65; rsch. chemist Archer Daniels Midland, Mpls., 1965-68; asst. prof. art history Case Western Res. U., Cleve., 1971-77, assoc. prof., 1977-89, prof., 1989—. Author: Art of Painting, 1977, Draftsman's eye, 1981, Drawings in Midwestern collections, 1996. Fellow NEH, 1979, Fulbright-Hays fellow, 1980, fellow Gladys Kriebl Delmas Found., 1986. Mem. Coll. Art Assn., Midwest Art History Soc. (pres. 1981-84), Renaissance Soc. Am. Avocation: travel. Office: Case Western Reserve U University Cir Cleveland OH 44106

OLSZEWSKI, SHARON ANN, adult education educator; b. Wausau, Wis., Nov. 20, 1956; d. Florian Edward and Elizabeth (Grochmal) O.; Romatowski; m. Robert Adam Olszewski, Aug. 12, 1978; children: Elissa Beth, Andrew Robert, Adam Michael. BS, U. Wis., La Crosse, 1978; MA, Marian Coll., 1993. Cert. tchr., sch. adminstr., Wis. Elem. sch. instr. pvt. sch. Mosinee, Wis., 1979-81, 86-93; comty. edn. coord., adult comty. edn. instr. North Cen. Tech. Coll., Wausau, 1993—, ESL adult edn. instr., 1994—; Asian-Am. tutor The Neighbor's Pl., Wausau, 1993—; mem. strategic planning com. Mosinee Sch. Dist., 1994, Alcohol and Other Drugs com., 1992; organizer, supr. Coll. Camp '94, Mosinee, 1994-95; chief instr. Shorei Kempo Larate, Yin Yang Do Assn., 1985—. Leader Am. Spirit Wis. 4-H, Wausau, 1994-95, mem. cultural arts com., 1994—. Mem. AAUW, ASCD, Am. Assn. Cmty. Coll. Women, Assn. Wis. Sch. Adminstrs., Delta Epsilon Sigma, Kappa Delta Pi. Democrat. Avocations: bicycling, youth and adult karate, softball, baseball. Home: 1438 Old Highway 51 Mosinee WI 54455-8512

OLTMAN, C. DWIGHT, conductor, educator; b. Imperial, Nebr., May 27, 1936; s. George L. and Lois Beryl (Wine) O.; m. Shirley Jean Studebaker, May 30, 1966; children—Michelle Leigh, Nicole Alicia. B.S., McPherson Coll., 1958; M.Mus., Wichita State U., 1963; postgrad., U. Cin., 1967-70; student, Nadia Boulanger, Paris, 1960, Pierre Monteux, 1963. Asst. prof. music Manchester Coll., North Manchester, Ind., 1963-67; prof. of conducting, music dir. symphony orch. and Bach Festival Baldwin-Wallace Coll., Berea, Ohio, 1970—; music dir. Ohio Chamber Orch., Cleve., 1972-92, laureate conductor, 1992—; music dir., prin. condr. Cleve. Ballet, 1976—; music dir. Cullowhee Music Festival, N.C., 1977-79; guest conductor Europe, Can., U.S.A. Mem. Am. Symphony Orch. League, Conductor's Guild. Democrat. Avocations: reading; walking; theater; spectator sports. Home and Office: 21631 Cedar Branch Trl Strongsville OH 44136-1287

OLTZ, RICHARD JOHN, publishing executive, minister; b. Duluth, Minn., Sept. 20, 1945; s. Donald F. and Helen J. (Richardson) O.; m. Mary Jane Willman, June 1969; children: Shawn Richard, Jennifer Marie. Student, Olivet Coll., 1963-64; pastorial ministries, Berean Coll., 1980-83, counseling, 1984. Sr. pastor First Missionary Ch., Bad Axe, Mich., 1985-87; exec. dir. Bethel Pub., Elkhart, Ind., 1987—; sr. pastor Grace Chapel, N. Liberty, Ind., 1990—; pastor Oslo Missionary Ch., Elkhart, 1995. Mem. Christian Booksellers Assn., Anabaptist Pubs., Christian Mgmt. Assn., Evang. Christian Pubs. Assn., Am. Assn. Christian Counselors. Office: Bethel Pub Co 1819 S Main St Elkhart IN 46516-4212 *No matter how successful life may appear to be, no matter what you may have accomplished, God must get all the glory or you will have labored in vain.*

OLUYITAN, EMMANUEL FUNSO, university public relations director; b. Efon-Alaye, Nigeria, July 25, 1944. BA cum laude in Polit. Sci., Bowie (Md.) State U., 1972; MPA in Policy Analysis and Journalism, Ind. U., 1975, EdD in Instructional Tech., 1980. News reporter Nigerian Nat. Press, Lagos, 1964-65; music libr., news translator, news reporter Nigerian Broadcasting Corp., 1965-69; pub. info. coord. Aerospace Rsch. Ctr., Sch. Pub./Environ. Affairs, Ind. U., Bloomington, 1973-75; victim assistance officer Indpls. Police Dept., 1975-76; prin. lectr. Nigerian TV Authority, Lagos, 1978-81; assoc. prof. dept. edn. Ahmadu Bello U., Zaria, Nigeria, 1981-88, asst. dean postgrad. studies, 1985-88, head instructional tech. divsn., 1983-88; program officer Nat. Assn. for Equal Opportunity in Higher Edn., Washington, 1988-93; dir. Office of Pub. Rels. and Pubs. Lincoln University, Pa., 1993—; staff writer Office of Pub. Info., Bowie State U., 1973; vice chmn. bd. Adventures in Health, Edn. and Agrl. Devel., Inc., Rockville, Md., 1993—; bd. dirs. Anthony J. Cebrun Journalism Ctr., Nashville; founder, pres. Global Linkage Enterprises. Photographer, fgn. news editor Ebony Tree, 1970-72; editor: African Insight, 1973, Nigeria Audio-Visual Newsletter, 1982-86, Nigeria Audio-Visual Jour., 1982-86, Global Vision, 1988-93, Update, 1988-93; assoc. editor Black Excellence, 1988-93; editor-in-chief Weekly Calendar, 1993—, LU Newsletter, 1993—, The Lincoln Lion, 1993—, The Lincoln-Jour., 1993—; contbr. articles to profl. jours., newspapers; contbr. photographs to books, jours.; prodr. numerous ednl. materials (videos, slides, pictures). Recipient Dir. Gen.'s Commendation, Nigerian TV Authority, 1987, Fed. Govt. of Nigeria's Postgrad. award, 1977-80, Award of Accomplishment and Worthiness, Indpls. Police Dept., 1976, Contr.'s Citation, Nigerian Broadcasting Corp., 1967. Mem. Assn. of Nigerians Against Corruption (founder), Nigerian Assn. for Ednl. Media and Tech., Internat. Assn. Black Profls. in Internat. Affairs, Assn. of Ednl. Comm. and Tech., Oxford Rotary Club (pres. 1996—). Avocations: tennis, ping-pong, photography, travel. Office: Lincoln Univ Office of Pub Rels PO Box 179 Lincoln University PA 19352

OLVER, JOHN WALTER, congressman; b. Honesdale, Pa., Sept. 3, 1936; s. Helen Fulleborn Olver; m. Rose Alice Richardson, Sept. 12, 1959; children: Martha, Jane. BS, Rensselaer Poly. Inst., 1955; MS, Tufts U., 1956; PhD, MIT, 1961. Asst. prof. chemistry, U. Mass., Amherst, 1962-68; mem. Mass. Ho. of Reps., Boston, 1969-72, Mass. Senate, 1973-91; mem. 101st-104th Congresses from 1st Mass. dist., 1991—, mem. com. on budget and sci. Contbr. articles to profl. jours. Democrat. Avocations: hiking; gardening; tennis. Office: US Ho of Reps 1027 Longworth HOB Washington DC 20515-2101

OLVER, MICHAEL LYNN, lawyer; b. Seattle, June 22, 1950; s. Manley Deforest and Geraldine (Robinson) O.; m. Wendy Kay, July 6, 1974; children: Erin, Christina. BA, U. Wash., 1972; JD, Calif. Western Sch. of Law, 1976. Assoc. Robbins, Merrick & Kraft, Seattle, 1976-77; lawyer, sole practitioner Michael L. Olver, Seattle, 1977-80; ptnr., pres. Merrick & Olver, P.S., Seattle, 1980—; bd. dirs. Found. for Handicapped, Seattle, 1988-93; commr. pro tem Ex part Dept. King County Superior Ct., Seattle, 1992—. Author: Wills and Trusts for the Disabled, 1989, Living Trusts--Pros and Cons, 1992, Special Needs Trusts After OBRA '93, 1994, Bascomb's Rogue, 1994, others; editor Calif. Western Internat. Law Jour., 1975-76. Chmn. Ann. Cath. Appeal, Assumption Parish, Seattle, 1989-90. Mem. Nat. Acad. Elder Law Attys. (dir. Wash. chpt. 1994—), Wash. State Trial Lawyers Assn. Office: Merrick & Olver PS 9222 Lake City Way NE Seattle WA 98115-3268

OLWIN, JOHN HURST, surgeon; b. Robinson, Ill., May 28, 1907; s. Charles Hurst and Etta (Campbell) O.; m. Betty Smothers, Apr. 17, 1943; children: Holly Corinne, Barbara Hurst. BA, U. Ill., 1929; MD, U. Chgo., 1934. Diplomate: Am. Bd. Surgery. Intern Presbyn. Hosp., Chgo., 1935-36, surg. resident, 1937-39; practice in Chgo., 1938—; clin. prof. surgery Rush Med. Coll., 1942—; attending surgeon Presbyn.-St. Luke's Hosp., Chgo., Rush North Shore Med. Ctr.; clin. prof. surgery U. Ill. Coll. Medicine, 1959-71; chmn., dir. TEI Analytical Inc., 1970—; bd. dirs. Wm. Blair Mut. Funds Inc. Contbr. more than 170 articles to profl. jours. Bd. dirs. Vascular Disease Rsch. Found., 1963—. Lt. col. M.C., AUS, 1940-46. Decorated Bronze Star. Mem. AMA, Chgo., Western, Central surg. assns., Soc. Vascular Surgery (recorder 1960-66), Internat. Cardiovascular Soc., Internat. Surg. Soc. Episcopalian (warden). Home: 1508 Hinman Ave Evanston IL 60201-4664 Office: 9631 Gross Point Rd Skokie IL 60076-1264

OLYPHANT, DAVID, cultural, educational association executive; b. N.Y.C., Feb. 3, 1936; s. John Kensett Olyphant and Adele (Hammond) Emery; m. Pamela Moore, Apr. 27, 1962 (div. Aug. 1988); children: Hillary, Fanny, David K., Elgin, Flora; m. Tatyana Doughty, Oct. 22, 1988. BA, Harvard U., 1958. V.p. Citibank, N.Y.C., 1959-75; ptnr. Harold Denton Assocs., Princeton, N.J., 1975-76; owner/operator Cluaran Farm, Pittstown, N.J., 1976-87; exec. dir., sec. The English Speaking Union US, N.Y.C., 1987-93; dir. Plays For Living, Inc., N.Y.C.; pres. 164 East 72 Corp.; treas./sec. Am. Trust for The British Libr., 1992—. Fellow Met. Mus. Art (life), NAD (life); mem. St. Andrew's Soc. (life), Harvard Club of N.Y., Porcellan Club (Cambridge, Mass.), The Pilgrims of the U.S. Republican. Presbyterian. Office: The English-Speaking Union US 16 E 69th St New York NY 10021-4906

O'MAHONEY, ROBERT M., lawyer; b. Indpls., Jan. 4, 1925; s. Joseph Francis and Evelyn (O'Connor) O'M.; m. Mary C. Mitchell, Sept. 12, 1953; children: Terrance M., Patrick J., Mary E., Susan M., Sharon A. B.S., Purdue U., 1948; J.D., Georgetown U., 1954. Bar: D.C. 1954, Ind. 1954, U.S. Supreme Ct. 1959. Assoc. Ross McCord, Ice and Miller, Indpls., 1954-55; dep. atty. gen. Ind., 1954-59; gen. counsel Def. Air Transp. Adminstrn., 1959; dep. asst. gen. counsel for transp. Dept. Commerce, 1959-66; adviser to dep. asst. sec. state for transp. and communications, 1966-67; asst. gen. counsel Fed. Hwy. Adminstrn., 1968-69; commr. transp. and telecommunications service GSA, 1969-73; transp. cons. EPA, 1973; atty. Fed. Power Commn., Washington, 1973-77, Fed. Energy Regulatory Commn., Washington, 1977-80; sales assoc. Shannon & Luchs, Potomac, Md., 1980-83, Merrill Lynch Realty, Potomac, Md., 1983-85, Long & Foster Realtors, Rockville, Md., 1985-86. Co-author: Great Lakes Pilotage Act, 1960. Served with USAAF, 1943-45; Served with USAF, 1950-52. Decorated Air medal with oak leaf cluster. Mem. Phi Alpha Delta. Republican. Roman Catholic.

O'MALLEY, BERT WILLIAM, cell biologist, educator, physician; b. Pitts., Dec. 19, 1936; s. Bert Alloysius O'M.; m. Sally Ann Johnson; children: Sally Ann, Bert A., Rebecca, Erin K. BS, U. Pitts., 1959, MD summa cum laude, 1963; DSc (hon.), N.Y. Med. Coll., 1979, Nat. U. Ireland, 1985; MD (hon.), Karolinska Inst., Stockholm, 1984. Intern, resident Duke U., Durham, N.C., 1963-65; clin. assoc. Nat. Cancer Inst., NIH, Bethesda, Md., 1965-67, head molecular biology sect., endocrine br., 1967-69; Lucius Birch prof., dir. Reproductive Biology Ctr. Vanderbilt U. Sch. Medicine, Nashville, 1969-73; Tom Thompson prof., chmn. dept. cell biology Baylor Coll. Medicine, Houston, 1973—, Disting. Svc. prof., 1985, dir. Baylor Ctr. for Reproductive Biology, 1973—; mem. endocrine study sect., NIH, 1970-73, chmn., 1973-74; chmn. CETUS-UCLA Symposium on Gene Expression, 1982; con., mem. coun. rsch. and clin. investigation awards Am. Cancer Soc., 1985-87. Author: (with A.R. Means) Receptors for Reproductive Hormones, 1973, (with L. Birnbaumer) Hormone Action, vols. I and II, 1977, vol. III, 1978, (with A.M. Gotto) The Role of Receptors in Biology and Medicine, 1986; co-author: Methods in Enzymology: Hormone Action: Calmodulin and Calcium-Binding Proteins, 1983, Mechanism of Steriod Hormone Regulation of Gene Transcription, 1994; editor: Gene Regulation: UCLA Symposium on Molecular Cellular Biology, 1982; contbg. author to over 400 publs. Lt. comdr. USPHS, 1965-69. Recipient Ernst Oppenheimer award Am. Endocrine Soc., 1975, Gregory Pincus medal, 1975, Lila Gruber Cancer award, 1977, Disting. Achievement in Modern Medicine award, 1978, Borden award Assn. Am. Med. Colls., 1978, Dickson prize for Basic Med. Rsch., 1979, Philip S. Hench award U. Pitts., 1981, Axel Munthe Reproductive Biology award, Capri, Italy, 1982, Bicentennial Medallion of Distincton U. Pitts., 1987. Mem. AAAS, NAS, Inst. Med. NAS, Am. Soc. Biol. Chemists, Endocrine Soc. (pres. 1985, Fred Conrad Koch medal 1988), Am. Soc. Clin. Investigation, Am. Inst. Chemists, Fedn. Clin. Rsch., Harvey Soc., Alpha Epsilon Delta, Phi Beta Kappa, Alpha Omega Alpha. Democrat. Roman Catholic. Office: Baylor Coll Medicine Dept Neuroscience One Baylor Pla Houston TX 77030-3411

O'MALLEY, CARLON MARTIN, judge; b. Phila., Sept. 7, 1929; s. Carlon Martin and Lucy (Bol) O'M.; m. Mary Catherine Lyons, Aug. 17, 1957; children: Carlon Martin III, Kathleen B. O'Malley Aikman, Harry Tighe, John Todd, Cara M. B.A., Pa. State U., 1951; LL.B., Temple U., 1954. Bar: Pa. 1955, Fla. 1973, U.S. Supreme Ct. 1973. Practiced law, 1957-61; asst. U.S. atty. for Middle Dist. Pa., Dept. Justice, 1961-69, U.S. atty., 1979-82; ptnr. O'Malley & Teets, 1970-72, O'Malley, Jordan & Mullaney (and predecessor firms), 1976-79; pvt. practice Pa. and Fla., 1972-79, 82-87; judge Ct. Common Pleas of Lackawanna County (45th Judicial Dist.), 1987—; dir. pub. safety City of Scranton, 1983-86; lectr. Lackawanna Jr. Coll., 1982-86. Editorial bd.: Temple Law Rev, 1952-53. Pres. Lackawanna County (Pa.) unit Am. Cancer Soc., 1966-67; bd. dirs. Pa. Cancer Soc., 1967-68, Lackawanna county chpt. ARC, 1967-69; mem. solicitation team, govtl. divsn. Lackawanna United Fund, 1963-68, B.P.O.E. Judiciary Com., 1985-89, 94-95, justice grand forum B.P.O.E., 1995—; chmn. profl. divsn. Greater Scranton (Pa.) YMCA Membership Drives; trustee Everhart Mus., Scranton, 1987—; justice Grand Forum Elks, 1991, chief justice, 1992-93. Pilot USAF, 1955-57, Pa. N.G., 1957-59. Mem. Am. Judges Assn., Nat. Assn. Former U.S. Attys., Pa. Bar Assn., Lackawanna County Bar Assn., Fla. Bar Assn., Country Club of Scranton, Elks (pres. Pa. chpt. 1978-79), K.C., Phi Kappa (pres.), Delta Theta Phi (pres.). Democrat. Office: Judges Chambers Lackawanna County Courthouse Scranton PA 18503

O'MALLEY, EDWARD, physician, consultant; b. Hudson, N.Y., May 30, 1926; s. Thomas Patrick and Helen Mary (Cornell) O. BS, St. John's U., Bklyn., N.Y., 1949; MS, Loyola U., Chgo., 1952, PhD, 1954; MD, SUNY, Bklyn., 1958. Psychiat. cons. dept. of corrections N.Y.C., 1962-68; psychiatrist Cath. Charities, N.Y.C., 1963-68; dir. of mental health Suffolk County Govt., Hauppauge, N.Y., 1968-70; commr. of mental health Orange County, Goshen, N.Y., 1970-72; dir. drug abuse services State of N.Y., Bronx, 1972-78; lic. sch. psychiatrist N.Y.C. Bd. of Edn., 1962-82; chief psychiatry services VA, Huntington, W.Va., 1982-86; med. cons. State of Calif., San Diego, 1986—, psychiat. cons. dept. of corrections, 1987—; asst. prof. psychiatry N.J. Med. Sch., Newark, 1975—; examiner Am. Bd. of Psychiatry and Neurology, Los Angeles, 1980; assoc. prof. psychiatry U. Calif., San Diego, 1980—; prof. psychiatry Marshall U. Sch. of Medicine, Huntington, 1982-86; dir. com. on sea cadets Navy League, San Diego, 1987—; cons. HHS, Social Security Adminstrn., Office of Hearings and Appeals, 1989—. Contbr. articles to profl. jours. Bd. dirs. Suffolk Community Council, Hauppauge, 1968-70, United Fund of Long Island, Huntington, 1968-70. Served to capt. USN, 1978-81. Scholar N. Y. State Coll., 1946-49, SUNY Joseph Collins Med. Sch., 1955-58; Teaching and Research fellow Loyola U., 1952-54. Fellow Am. Psychiat. Assn.; mem. San Diego Psychiat. Soc., Soc. of Med. Cons. to the Armed Forces, Soc. of Mil. Surgeons of U.S.A., N.Y. Celtic Med. Soc., Union Am. Physicians and Dentists (steward 1990—), State Employed Physicians Assn. (bd. dirs. 1993—). Roman Catholic. Home: 3711 Alcott St San Diego CA 92106-1212

O'MALLEY, JAMES TERENCE, lawyer; b. Omaha, Nov. 24, 1950; s. John Austin and Mayme Bernice (Zentner) O'M.; m. Colleen L. Kizer, May 22, 1972; children: Erin C., Michael B., James P. BA magna cum laude, U. Notre Dame, 1972; JD, Stanford U., 1975. Bar: Calif. 1975. Ptnr. Gray, Cary, Ames & Frye, San Diego, 1975-87, of counsel, 1987-91, ptnr., 1991—; vice chmn., exec. v.p., gen. counsel Noble Broadcast Group, Inc., San Diego, 1987-91. Bd. dirs. Children's Mus., San Diego, 1986-87, Am. Ireland Fund. Mem. Am. Judicature Soc., San Diego Taxpayers Assn. (pres. 1986-87), Order of Coif. Avocation: jogging, music. Office: Gray Cary Ware & Freidenrich PC 401 B St San Diego CA 92101-4223

O'MALLEY, JOHN DANIEL, law educator, banker; b. Chgo., Dec. 18, 1926; s. William D. and Paula A. (Skaugh) O'M.; m. Caroline Tyler Taylor, July 12, 1958; children: John Daniel, Taylor John. Grad., St. Thomas Mil. Acad., 1945; B.S., Loyola U., Chgo., 1950, M.A., 1952, J.D., 1953; grad., U.S. Army Intelligence Sch., 1962, Command & Gen. Staff Coll., 1965. Bar: Ill. 1953, Mich. 1954, U.S. Supreme Ct. 1962. Asst. prof. law Loyola U., 1953-59, asso. prof., 1959-65; formerly spl. counsel and bond claims mgr. Fed. Ins. Co.; prof. law Loyola U. Grad. Sch. Bus., 1965—, chmn. dept. law, 1968-86; trust officer, v.p. First Nat. Bank Highland Park (Ill.), Marina City Bank, Chgo., Hyde Park Bank & Trust Co., 1970-75; exec. v.p. Harris Bank Winnetka, Ill., 1975-95. Author: Subrogation Against Banks on Forged Checks, 1967, Common Check Frauds and the Uniform Commercial Code, 1969; Contbr. articles to profl. jours. and law revs. Served to maj. AUS, 1945-47, 61-62. Decorated Army Commendation medal; knight grand officer Papal Order of Holy Sepulchre, knight with star Constantinian Order of St. George (Italy), knight Order of St. Maurice and St. Lazarus (Italy). Mem. ABA, Chgo., Ill., Mich. bar assns., Chgo. Crime Commn., French Nat. Hon. Soc., Am., Chgo. bus. law assns., Mil. Govt. Assn. Home: 1040 Chestnut Ave Wilmette IL 60091-1732 Office: Loyola U 820 N Michigan Ave Chicago IL 60611-2103

O'MALLEY, JOHN PATRICK, dean; b. Hoosick Falls, N.Y., Nov. 27, 1928; s. Thomas Joseph and Mary Margaret (Mulvihill) O.'M.; m. Margaret Parlin, June 24, 1989. BA, Villanova U., 1950; MA, PhD, Cath. U., 1969. Tchr. Archbishop Carroll High Sch., Washington, 1954-68; prin. Archibishop Carroll High Sch., Washington, 1987-89; asst. prof. Cath. U., Washington, 1968-69; asst. prof. Merrimack Coll., North Andover, Mass., 1969-74, dean humanities, 1976-78; chair edn. dept. Emmanuel Coll., Boston, 1974-76; dean coll. arts and scis. Villanova (Pa.) U., 1978-84; provost St. Thomas U., Miami, Fla., 1985-86; assoc. prof. Widener U., Chester, Pa., 1990—. Editor: Non-Fiction, Books I and II, 1968. Mem. Assn. Tchr. Edn., Middle Atlantic States Philosophy of Edn. Soc., ASCD, Assn. Ind. Liberal Arts Colls. for Tchr. Edn. Home: 64 Crestline Rd Wayne PA 19087-2669 Office: Widener U 1 University Pl Chester PA 19013

O'MALLEY, JOSEPH JAMES, lawyer; b. Wilkes-Barre, Pa., Oct. 24, 1923; s. Edward Leo and Mary Catherine (Moran) O'M.; m. Helen Alberta Hyde, Mar. 21, 1952 (div. Jan. 1979); children: Patricia, Katherine, Sharon, Edward, Joseph James; m. Theresa Hernandez, Jan. 20, 1979 (div. Dec. 1995); 1 child, James Christopher. B.A., U. Scranton, 1946; J.D., Georgetown U., 1956. Bar: D.C. 1956, Calif., 1977, U.S. Supreme Ct. 1967. Sr. trial atty. antitrust div. Dept. Justice, Washington, 1957-65; assoc. chief counsel Comptroller of Currency, Washington, 1965-68; asst. dir. FTC, Washington, 1968-76; ptnr. Paul, Hastings, Janofsky & Walker, Los Angeles, 1976-94; pvt. practice Glendale, Calif., 1994—; guest lectr. Georgetown U., 1966-68. Mem. ABA, L.A. County Bar Assn. (exec. com. antitrust sect. 1990—), KC (grand knight 1963-64, state dep. 1971). Office: Law Offices Joseph O'Malley Ste 950 801 N Brand Blvd Glendale CA 91203

O'MALLEY, KATHLEEN M., federal judge; b. 1956. AB magna cum laude, Kenyon Coll., 1979; JD, Case Western Reserve, 1982. Law clk. to Hon. Nathaniel R. Jones U.S. Ct. of Appeals, 6th circuit, 1982-83; with Jones, Day, Reavis & Pogue, Cleve., 1983-84, Porter, Wright, Morris & Arthur, Cleve., 1985-91; chief counsel, first asst. atty. gen., chief of staff Office of Atty. Gen., Columbus, 1991-94; district judge U.S. Dist. Ct. (Ohio no. dist.), 6th circuit, Cleve., 1994—. Mem. Am. Bar Assn., Fed. Bar Assn., Ohio State Bar Assn., Cleve. Bar Assn. Office: US Courthouse 201 Superior Ave E Ste 135 Cleveland OH 44114-1201

O'MALLEY, KEVIN FRANCIS, lawyer, writer, educator; b. St. Louis, May 12, 1947; s. Peter Francis and Dorothy Margaret (Cradick) O'M.; m. Dena Hengen, Apr.2, 1971; children: Kevin Brendan, Ryan Michael. AB, St. Louis U., 1970, JD, 1973. Bar: Mo. 1973, U.S. Ct. Appeals D.C. 1974, U.S. Ct. Appeals (8th cir.) 1979, Ill. 1993. Trial lawyer U.S. Dept. Justice, Washington, 1973-74, Los Angeles, 1974-77, Phoenix, 1977-78; asst. U.S. atty. U.S. Dept. Justice, St. Louis, 1978-83; adj. prof. law St. Louis U., 1979—. Author: (with Devitt, Blackmar, O'Malley) Federal Jury Practice and Instruction, 1990, 92; contbr. articles to law books and jours. Community amb. Expt. in Internat. Living, Prague, Czechoslovakia, 1968; bd. dirs. St. Louis-Galway (Ireland) Sister Cities. Capt. U.S. Army, 1973. Recipient Atty. Gen.'s Disting. Service award U.S. Dept. Justice, 1977, John J. Dwyer Meml. Scholarship award, 1967-70. Mem. ABA (chmn. govt. litigation counsel com. 1982-86, chmn. jud. com. 1986-87, chmn. com. on ind. and small firms, chmn. trial practice com. 1991-94, health care litigation 1994—), Am. Law Inst., Met. Bar Assn. St. Louis (chmn. criminal law sect.), Nat. Inst. Trial Advocacy, Mo. Athletic Club. Roman Catholic. Office: 10 S Brentwood Blvd Ste 102 Saint Louis MO 63105-1694

O'MALLEY, MARJORIE GLAUBACH, health care executive; b. Orange, N.J., Apr. 28, 1950; d. Robert M. and Joanne (Weil) Glaubach; m. Charles A. O'Malley III, Dec. 27, 1969; children: Gregory, Ashley. BA in Econs., U. Pa., 1969. With Old Stone Bank, Providence, 1970-75, v.p., 1975-76; sr. v.p., treas. Old Stone Bank and Old Stone Corp., Providence, 1976-80; dir. corp. fin. Conn. Gen. Corp., Hartford, 1980-81; 2d v.p., dept. head mktg. pensions Cigna Corp., Hartford, 1981-85, v.p. fin. employee benefit group, 1985-89; v.p. corp. acctg. and planning Cigna Corp., 1989-90; v.p., contr. employee benefits div. Cigna Corp., Hartford, 1990-92, pres. Rx Prime, 1993-95; pres. Strategic Healthcare Cons., Avon, Conn., 1995—. Mem. health Planning Coun. R.I., 1976-79, Statewide Planning Coun. R.I., 1978; mem. bd. Health Sys. Agy.-North Cen. Conn., Hartford, 1980. Mem. Life Ins. Mktg. and Rsch. Assn. (chmn. group and pension com. 1989), New Eng. Econ. Project (bd. mem. 1976-79, treas. 1978-79). Home: 23 Henley Way Avon CT 06001-4067 Office: Strategic Healthcare Cons Cigna Corp Avon CT 06001

O'MALLEY, PATRICIA, critical care nurse; b. Boston, May 13, 1955; d. Peter and Catherine (Dwyer) O'M. BSN, Coll. Mt. St. Joseph, Cin., 1977; MS, Ohio State U., 1984, postgrad., 1990—. Cert. critical care nurse. Primary nurse critical care unit Miami Valley Hosp., Dayton, Ohio, nurse educator, clin. nurse specialist, cons.; adj. faculty Wright State U., Dayton. Contbr. articles to profl. jours., textbooks. Recipient honors Dayton Area Heart Assn., Ohio Ho. of Reps., 1994, Ohio Dept. Health, 1996. Mem. AACN (bd. dirs. Dayton-Miami Valley), Soc. Critical Care Medicine, Sigma Theta Tau. Office: Miami Valley Hosp 1 Wyoming St Dayton OH 45409-2722

O'MALLEY, PETER, professional baseball club executive; b. N.Y.C., Dec. 12, 1937; s. Walter F. and Kay (Hanson) O'M.; m. Annette Zacho, July 10, 1971; children: Katherine, Kevin, Brian. B.S. in Econs, U. Pa., 1960. Dir. Dodgertown, Vero Beach, Fla., 1962-64; pres., gen. mgr. Spokane Baseball Club, 1965-66; v.p. Los Angeles Dodgers Baseball Club, 1967-68, exec. v.p., from 1968; pres. Los Angeles Dodgers, Inc., 1970—, also bd. dirs.; bd. dirs. Tidings newspaper. Bd. dirs. L.A. Police Meml. Found., L.A. World Affairs Coun., Jackie Robinson Found., L.A.-Gungzhou (Republic of China) Sister City Assn., Amateur Athletic Found.; pres. Little League Found.; active L.A. County Bd. Govs., Music Ctr., So. Calif. Com. for the Olympic Games. Mem. Korean-Am. C. of C. of L.A. Office: LA Dodgers 1000 Elysian Park Ave Los Angeles CA 90012-1112

O'MALLEY, ROBERT EDMUND, JR., mathematics educator; b. Rochester, N.H., May 23, 1939; s. Robert E. and Jeanette A. (Dubois) O'M.; m. Candace G. Hinz, Aug. 31, 1968; children: Patrick, Timothy, Daniel. B.S. in Elec. Engring., U. N.H., 1960, M.S., 1961; Ph.D., Stanford U., 1966. Mathematician Bell Labs., Gen. Electric Research Co., RCA, summers 1961-63; asst. prof. U. N.C., Chapel Hill, 1965-66; vis. mem. Courant Inst., NYU, 1966-67; research mem. Math. Research Ctr., Madison, Wis., 1967-68; asst. prof., assoc. prof. NYU, N.Y.C., 1968-73; prof. math. U. Ariz., Tucson, 1973-81, chmn. applied math. program, 1976-81; prof. math. Rensselaer Poly. Inst., Troy, N.Y., 1981-90, chmn. dept. math. scis., 1981-84, Ford Found. prof., 1989-90; prof., chair applied math. U. Wash., Seattle, 1990-93, prof., 1993—; sr. vis. fellow U. Edinburgh, (Scotland), 1971-72; guest prof. Tech. U. Vienna, 1987-88; vis. Univ. Lyon 1 and Univ. of Cambridge, 1994-95. Author: Introduction to Singular Perturbations, 1974; editor: Asymptotic Methods and Singular Perturbations, 1976, Singular Perturbation Methods for Ordinary Differential Equations, 1991, ICIAM 91 procs.; contbr. numerous articles to profl. jours. Mem. Soc. for Indsl. and Applied Math. (pres. 1991-92), Am. Math. Soc. Roman Catholic. Home: 3415 W Laurelhurst Dr NE Seattle WA 98105-5345 Office: U Wash Dept Applied Math FS # 20 Seattle WA 98195

O'MALLEY, SEAN, bishop; b. Lakewood, Ohio, June 29, 1944. Ed., St. Fidelis Sem., Herman, Pa., Capuchin Coll. and Cath. U., Washington. Ordained priest Roman Cath. Ch., 1970. Espiscopal vicar of priests serving Spanish speakin Washington archdiocese, 1978-84; exec. dir. Spanish Cath. Ctr., Washington, from 1973; bishop Roman Cath. Ch., St. Thomas, V.I., 1985-92, Fall River, NH, 1992—. Office: Bishop of Fall River PO Box 2577 47 Underwood St Fall River MA 02722*

O'MALLEY, SUSAN, professional basketball team executive. Degree in Bus. and Finance, Mt. St. Mary's, 1983. Dir. advt. Washington Bullets, 1986-87, dir. mktg., 1987-88, exec. v.p., 1988-91, pres., 1991-95; pres. Washington Capitals, 1995—. Avocations: tennis, vacations. Office: Washington Bullets USAir Arena Landover MD 20785*

O'MALLEY, THOMAS D., diversified company executive; b. N.Y.C., 1941. Grad., Manhattan Coll., 1963. Vice chmn., dir. Salomon, Inc. (formerly Phibro-Salomon, Inc.), N.Y.C.; former chmn., chief exec. officer, pres. Phibro Energy Inc., Greenwich, Conn.; chmn. Argus Investments (formerly Argus Resources), Stamford, Conn., from 1987; now chmn., chief exec. officer Tosco Corp., Conn. Office: Tosco Corp Hdqrs 72 Cummings Point Rd Stamford CT 06902-7919*

O'MALLEY, THOMAS PATRICK, academic administrator; b. Milton, Mass., Mar. 1, 1930; s. Austin and Ann Marie (Feeney) O'M. BA, Boston Coll., 1951; MA, Fordham U., 1953; STL, Coll. St.-Albert de Louvain, 1962; LittD, U. Nijmegen, 1967; LLD (hon.), John Carroll U., 1988. Entered Soc. of Jesus, 1952. Instr. classics Coll. of Holy Cross, Worcester, Mass., 1956-58; asst. prof., chmn. dept. classics Boston Coll., 1967-69, assoc. prof., chmn. dept. theology, 1969-73; dean Boston Coll. (Coll. Arts and Scis.), 1973-80; pres. John Carroll U., Cleve., 1980-88; vis. prof. Cath. Inst. W. Africa, 1988-89; assoc. editor AMERICA, N.Y.C., 1989-90; rector Jesuit Com. Fairfield U., 1990-91; pres. Loyola Marymount U., L.A., 1991—. Author: Tertullian and the Bible, 1967. Trustee Boston Theol. Inst., 1969-73, Fairfield U., 1971-82, 89-91, John Carroll U., 1976-88, Xavier U., 1980-86, U. Detroit, 1982-88, Boston Coll. H.S., 1986-88, Boys Hope, 1986-88, Loyola Marymount U., 1991—. Mem. AAUP, Soc. Bibl. Lit., N.Am. Patristic Soc.

OMAN, HENRY, retired electrical engineer, engineering executive; b. Portland, Oreg., Aug. 29, 1918; s. Paul L. and Mary (Levonen) O.; m. Winifred Eleanor Potter, June 17, 1944 (dec. Nov. 1950); m. Earlene Mary Boot, Sept. 11, 1954; children: Mary Janet, Eleanor Eva, Eric Paul. BSEE, Oreg. State U., 1940, MSEE, 1951. Registered profl. engr., Wash. Application engr. Allis Chalmers Mfg. Co., Milw., 1940-48; rsch. engr. Boeing Co., Seattle, 1948-63, engring. mgr., 1963-91. Author: Energy Systems Engineering Handbook, 1986; contbr. more than 50 articles to profl. jours. Mem. team that restarted amateur radio communication to the outside world from the People's Republic of China, 1981. Recipient prize paper award Am. Inst. Elec. Engrs., 1964. Fellow IEEE (founder power electronics systems confs., 1970—, v.p. Aerospace and Electronics Systems Soc. 1984-88, Harry Mimno award 1989, editor-in-chief, 1995), AIAA (assoc.); mem. AAAS (bd. dir. Pacific divsn. 1992—). Republican. Methodist. Achievements include development of concepts for solar power satellite which generates power in geo-synchronous orbit 24 hours per day and beams it to the Earth surface with a microwave beam; research in simple battery-powered electric bicycles for low-cost, pollution-free transportation in developing nations. Home: 19221 Normandy Park Dr SW Seattle WA 98166-4129

OMAN, RALPH, lawyer; b. Huntington, N.Y., July 1, 1940; s. Henry Ferdinand and Annamarie (Retelsdorf) O.; m. Anne K. Henehan, Oct. 21, 1967; children: Tabitha Russell, Caroline Adams, Charlotte Ericsson. Diploma, Sorbonne U., Paris, 1961; BA, Hamilton Coll., 1962; LLD, Georgetown U., 1973. Bar: D.C. 1973, U.S. Dist. Ct. Md. 1973, U.S. Ct. Appeals (4th cir.) 1974, U.S. Supreme Ct. 1977. Law clk. to U.S. Dist. Ct. judge U.S. Dist. Ct. Md., Balt., 1973-74; trial atty U.S. Dept. Justice, Washington, 1974-75; chief minority counsel patents, trademarks and copyrights subcom. U.S. Senate, Washington, 1975-77; legis. dir. Senator Charles Mathias, Washington, 1977-78; minority counsel judiciary com. U.S. Senate, Washington, 1978-81, chief counsel, staff dir. criminal law subcom., 1981-82, chief counsel patents, copyrights and trademarks subcom., 1982-85; register of copyrights U.S. Copyright Office, Washington, 1985-94; adj. prof. copyright law George Washington U.; speaker in field. Contbr. numerous articles to profl. jours. Served to lt. USN, 1965-70, Vietnam. Mem. ABA, Fed. Bar Assn. (pres. Capitol Hill chpt.). Episcopalian. Home: 1110 E Capitol St NE Washington DC 20002-6225 Office: Dechert Price and Rhoads Ste 500 1500 K St NW Washington DC 20005

OMAN, RICHARD GEORGE, museum curator; b. Salt Lake City, Oct. 15, 1945; s. Dorse Miles and Margaret (Call) O.; m. Susan Staker, May 31, 1970 (div. 1983); children: Sarah Elizabeth, Nathan Bryan, Bevin Marie; m. Pamela Fillmore, Oct. 4, 1984; children: Emily Anne, Lisa Meleana. AA, Big Bend Community Coll., 1965; BA in History, Brigham Young U., 1970; BA in Art History, U. Wash., 1971, postgrad., 1971-75. Dir. audio-visual sect. Seattle Art Mus., 1973-75; mgr. mus. sect., hist. dept. Ch. of Jesus Christ of Latter-day Saints, Salt Lake City, 1975-86; curator acquisitions Mus. Ch. History and Art, Salt Lake City, 1986—; high priest missionary to Quebec and Ontario, 1965-67; v.p., Import Broker, Salt Lake City, 1984—; instr. Brigham Young U., Provo, 1979; cons., Utah State Hist. Soc., Salt Lake City, 1980—, Utah Endowment for Humanities, Salt Lake City, 1981; bd. dirs., Utah Children's Mus., Salt Lake City, 1981-83. Contbg. author: Aarts and Inspiration, 1980, Utah Folk Art, 1980, Encyclopedia of Mormonism, 1992, Mormon Americana, 1995, Encyclopedia of Utah, 1995; co-author: Images of Faith: Art of the Latter-day Saints, 1995; contbr. articles to numerous publs. Asst. commr., Salt Lake City area Boy Scouts Am., 1979-82; chmn. Cen. City Parks Com., Salt Lake City, 1980-83; cons. L.D.S. Hosp. Found., Salt Lake City, 1984; cons., judge, Dixie Coll. Ann. Art Exhbn., St. George, Utah, 1987-89, Springville (Utah) Mus. Art; cons. art mus., Brigham Young U., 1984-87; mem. sesquicentennial com., Mormon Ch., Salt Lake City, 1980. Mem. Utah Mus. Assn. (pres. 1979-81), Am. Assn. State and Local History, Am. Assn. Mus., Mormon History Assn. Republican. Mormon. Avocations: skiing, camping, gardening, sailing, gourmet cooking. Home: 3266 Bonview Dr Salt Lake City UT 84109-3704 Office: Mus Ch History and Art 45 N West Temple Salt Lake City UT 84150

OMAN, RICHARD HEER, lawyer; b. Columbus, Ohio, Jan. 4, 1926; s. B. R. Oman and Marguerite H. (Oman) Andrews; m. Jane Ellen Wert, Oct. 5, 1963; children: Sarah M., David W. B.A., Ohio State U., 1948, J.D., 1951. Bar: Ohio 1951. Atty. Ohio Nat. Bank, Columbus, 1951-55; partner firm Isaac, Postlewaite, O'Brien & Oman, Columbus, 1955-71; dir. Columbus Found., 1955-77, counsel, 1955—; partner firm Porter, Wright, Morris and Arthur (and predecessor firm), Columbus, 1972-89; of counsel Vorys, Sater, Seymour and Pease, Columbus, 1990; ptnr. Vorys, Sater, Seymour and Pease, 1991—. Mem. Columbus Airport Commn., 1960-64; trustee Reinberger Found., Cleve., 1980—, Columbus Acad., 1981-87, Grant Hosp., 1978-86, Harding Hosp., 1978-86; sr. warden Trinity Epsic. Ch., 1985-88. Fellow Ohio State Bar Found.; mem. ABA, Am. Coll. Trust and Estate Counsel, Ohio State Bar Assn. (past mem. bd. govs. probate and trust law sect.), Columbus Bar Assn., Columbus Club, Rocky Fork Hunt and Country Club, Nantucket (Mass.) Yacht Club, Kit Kat Club. Republican. Episcopalian. Office: Vorys Sater Seymour & Pease PO Box 1008 52 E Gay St Columbus OH 43216

OMAR, AMEENAH E.P., college dean; b. Laurel, Miss., Apr. 3, 1941; d. Denothras (Pickens) Pierce; m. Abdul Aziz Omar, Apr. 28, 1979 (dec.); children: Lakisha, Cheryl. BA in English, U. Detroit, MA in Curriculum Devel., EdS; EdD candidate, Wayne State U. Human resource specialist, personnel specialist U.S. Women Army Corps, 1965-70; tchr. Detroit Pub. Sch., 1972-77; mid. sch. tchr., spl. asst. to supt. Highland Pk. (Mich.) Pub. Schs., 1977-86; dir. coll. placement coop. edn. Highland Park Community Coll., 1986-88, dean student svcs.; sec. H.P. Bldg. Authority. Vice chairperson City of Highland Park Planning Commn.; mem. Highland Park Mothers Club, Parent Adv. Coun. for Gifted and Talented, Highland Park Caucus Club; bd. dirs. Reggie McKenzie Found.; mem. Ferris Sch. PTA; sec. Highland Park Bus. Authority; councilwoman Highland Park, 1996—. Recipient Outstanding Svc. to PTA award, 1978, Svc. Beyond Duty award Highland Park Sch. Dist., 1980, Outstanding Svc. award Black History Celebration, 1980, Outstanding Svc. award Mich. Week Celebration, 1980-85, Outstanding Svc. to Class awrd, 1986, Spirit of Detroit award, 1993, Achievement award Black Men Inc., 1993, Outstanding Leadership award City of Highland Park, 1994, Enstooled Queen Mother Village of Akwakrom, Ghana, 1994; named Outstanding Recruiter in State of Mich., 1970. Mem. Mich. Assn. Collegiate Registrars and Admissions Officers, Mich. Coun. Coll. Placement Officers, United Negro Coll. Fund (grad. landmark edn. forum, forum celebration 50th anniversary), Coun. Coll. Placement Officers, C.C. Employment Network, Coop. Edn. Assn., Nat. Assn. Sch. Execs., Nat. Alliance Black Sch. Educators, Alpha Kappa Alpha (outstanding soror Lambda Pi Omega chpt. 1994), Phi Delta Kappa. Home: 30 Farrand Park Highland Park MI 48203-3350 Office: Highland Pk C of C Glendale and Third Aves Highland Park MI 48203

O'MARA, JOHN ALOYSIUS, bishop; b. Buffalo, Nov. 17, 1924; s. John Aloysius and Anna Theresa (Schenck) O'M. Student, St. Augustine's Sem., Toronto, Ont., Can., 1944-51; J.C.L., St. Thomas U., Rome, 1953. Ordained priest Roman Catholic Ch., 1951; mem. chancery Archdiocese of Toronto, 1953-69; pres., rector St. Augustine's Sem., Toronto, 1969-75; pastor St. Lawrence Parish, Scarboro, Ont., 1975-76; bishop Diocese of Thunder Bay, Ont., 1976-94, Diocese of St. Catharines, Ont., 1994—; St. Catharines, 1994—; pres. Ont. Conf. Cath. Bishops, 1986-92. Bd. dirs. Ont. Hosp. Assn., 1961-65, Cath. Ch. Extension Soc. Can.; mem. Ont. Hosp. Services Commn., 1964-69. Named hon. prelate of Papal Household with title monsignor, 1954. Address: 122 Riverdale Rd, Saint Catharines, ON Canada L2R 4C2

O'MARA, ROBERT EDMUND GEORGE, radiologist, educator; b. Flushing, N.Y., Dec. 8, 1933; s. George Harold and Leonora (Potter) O'M.; m. Brenda Mae Millard, Feb. 15, 1964; children—Robert, Susan, Bridget. B.S., U. Rochester, 1955; M.D., Albany Coll. Medicine, 1959. Diplomate: Am. Bd. Radiology, Am. Bd. Nuclear Medicine (sec. 1982—, chmn. 1983-84). Resident in radiology St. Vincent's Hosp., N.Y.C., 1963-66; fellow in nuclear medicine Upstate Med. Center SUNY, Syracuse, 1966-67; instr. radiology Upstate Med. Center SUNY, 1967-68, asst. prof. radiology, 1968-71; asso. prof. radiology, dir. nuclear medicine U. Ariz., Tucson, 1971-74; prof., dir. nuclear medicine U. Ariz., 1974-75; prof. radiology, chief div. nuclear medicine U. Rochester Sch. Medicine and Dentistry, 1975—; acting chmn. dept. radiology U. of Rochester, 1987-88, chmn. dept. radiology, 1988-93; med. dir. nuclear medicine tech. program Rochester Inst. Tech., 1976-92. Contbr. articles to med. jours. Pres. Clover Hills Assn., Rochester, N.Y., 1978-79; pres. Fruchtendler Parent Tchr. Assn., Tucson, 1974-75. Served with M.C. USAF, 1960-62. Fellow Am. Coll. Radiology (councillor 1983-89), Am. Coll. Nuclear Physicians (pres. 1980, trustee 1972-80), N.Y. State Radiol. Soc. (pres. 1989-90); mem. Soc. Nuclear Medicine (trustee 1978-82, v.p. 1985-86, Gold medal for sci. exhibit 1977), Radiol. Soc. N.Am., Assn. Univ. Radiologists. Office: 601 Elmwood Ave Rochester NY 14642-0001

O'MARA, THOMAS PATRICK, manufacturing company executive; b. St. Catharine's, Ont., Can., Jan. 17, 1937; s. Joseph Thomas and Rosanna Patricia (Riordan) O'M.; m. Nancy Irene Rosevear, Aug. 10, 1968; children: Patricia Catharine, Tracy Irene, Sara Megan. B.S., Allegheny Coll., 1958; M.S., Carnegie Inst. Tech., 1960. Mktg. analyst U.S. Steel Corp., Pitts., 1960-65; dir. info. systems AMPCO Pitts. (formerly Screw & Bolt Corp.), Pitts., 1965-68; v.p., gen. mgr. Toy div. Samsonite Corp., Denver, 1968-73; regional mgr. Mountain Zone, Hertz Corp., Denver, 1973-75; asst. to chmn. Allen Group, Melville, N.Y., 1975-76; group exec. v.p. fin. and adminstrn. Bell & Howell Co., Chgo., 1976-77; corp. controller Bell & Howell Co., 1977-78, corp. v.p., 1978-85, pres. visual communications, 1978-85; pres., chief operating officer, dir. Bridge Product Inc., Northbrook, Ill., 1985-87; chmn., chief exec. officer Micro Metl Corp., Indpls., 1987-91; chmn. Omara Ptnrs., 1992—; bd. dirs. Loyola U. Press; trustee Barat Coll., 1994—. Mem. Lake Forest H.S. Bd., 1989-96, pres. 1993-96. With USAR, 1961-66. Mem. Econs. Club Chgo., Newcomen Soc. U.S., Sigma Alpha Epsilon, Knollwood Club. Home: 1350 Inverleith Rd Lake Forest IL 60045-1540

O'MEALLIE, KITTY, artist; b. Bennettsville, S.C., Oct. 24, 1916; d. Earle and Rosa Estelle (Bethea) Chamness; m. John Ryan O'Meallie, June 27, 1939 (dec. Apr. 26, 1974); children—Sue Ryan, Kathryn Bethea; m. Lee Harnie Johnson, Aug. 21, 1976. BFA Tulane U., 1937; postgrad., 1954-59. One-woman shows include Masur Mus., Monroe, La., 1979, Marlboro County Mus. of S.C., 1975, Meridian Mus. Art, Miss., 1981, 85; exhibited in group shows at New Orleans Mus. Art, Contemporary Art Ctr., Meadows Mus., Cushing Gallery, SE Ctr. of Contemporary Art, Art 80, Art Expo West, Art Expo 81. Represented in permanent collections New Orleans Mus. Art, Tulane U. Pan-Am. Life Ctr., Masur Mus. Art, Meridian Mus. Art. Nat. officer Newcomb Coll. Alumnae Assn., 1964-66; lectr. exhibitor for many charitable orgns. Recipient award WYES-TV, 1979, Hon. Invitational New Orleans Women's Caucus, 1986, numerous awards and prizes in competitive exhibitions; grant St. Charles Ave. Presbyn. Ch., New Orleans, 1995-96. Mem. Womens Caucus for Art, New Orleans Womens Caucus for Art, Chi Omega Alumnae Assn. (pres. mothers' club 1964), Town and Country Garden Guild (pres. 1970, 1986). Avocations: bird-watching; bridge. Home and Office: 211 Fairway Dr New Orleans LA 70124-1018

O'MEARA, DAVID COLLOW, retired banker; b. Cin., Apr. 21, 1929; s. Joseph Gibson (Jr.) and Jean (Collow) O'M.; m. Marnell Jackson; children: Shawn Kathleen, Scott Matthew, Patrick Michael. B.A., U. Ariz., 1951. Sr. v.p. Security Pacific Nat. Bank, Los Angeles, 1955-84. Served with USMC, 1951-53. Home: 541 Calle De La Paz Escondido CA 92029-7949

O'MEARA, JOHN CORBETT, federal judge; b. Hillsdale, Mich., Nov. 4, 1933; s. John Richard and Karolyn Louise (Corbett) O'M.; m. Penelope Reingier Appel, June 9, 1962 (div. Feb. 1975); children: Meghan Appel, John Richard, Corbett Edge, Patrick Fitzpatrick, Tighe Roberts; m. Julia Donovan Darlow, Sept. 20, 1975; 1 child, Gillian Darlow. AB, U. Notre Dame, 1955; LLB, Harvard U., 1962. Bar: Mich. 1962. Assoc. Dickinson, Wright, Moon, Van Dusen & Freeman, Detroit, 1962-70; mem. faculty U. Detroit, 1965-70; ptnr. Dickinson, Wright, Moon, Van Dusen & Freeman, Detroit, 1970-94, head of labor group, 1985-94; judge U.S. Dist. Ct., Detroit, 1994—; bd. dirs. Mich. Opera Theatre, Detroit. Contr. articles to profl. jours. Fin. chmn. Dem. Party Mich., 1968-70; chmn. U.S. Cts. Com. State Bar Mich., 1984-94. Lt. USN, 1955-59. Fellow Am. Coll. Trial Lawyers,

Am. Bar Found.; mem. ABA, U.S. Supreme Court Bar, Am. Judicature Soc., Mich. State Bar Assn., 6th Cir. Court Appeals Bar (life mem., 6th Cir. Jud. Conf. 1986). Office: US Dist Ct 231 W Lafayette Blvd Detroit MI 48226-2719

O'MEARA, ONORATO TIMOTHY, academic administrator, mathematician; b. Cape Town, Republic of South Africa, Jan. 29, 1928; came to U.S., 1957; s. Daniel and Fiorina (Allorto) O'M.; m. Jean T. Fadden, Sept. 12, 1953; children—Maria, Timothy, Jean, Kathleen, Eileen. B.Sc., U. Cape Town, 1947, M.Sc., 1948; Ph.D., Princeton U., 1953; LLD (hon.), U. Notre Dame, 1987. Asst. lectr. U. Natal, Republic South Africa, 1949; lectr. U. Otago, New Zealand, 1954-56; mem. Inst. for Advanced Study, Princeton, N.J., 1957-58, 62; asst. prof. Princeton, 1958-62; prof. math. U. Notre Dame, Ind., 1962-76; chmn. dept. U. Notre Dame, 1965-66, 68-72, Kenna prof. math., 1976—, provost, 1978—; vis. prof. Calif. Inst. Tech., 1968; Gauss prof. Göttingen Acad. Sci., 1978; mem. adv. panel math. scis. NSF, 1974-77, cons., 1960—. Author: Introduction to Quadratic Forms, 1963, 71, 73, Lectures on Linear Groups, 1974, 2d edit., 1977, 3d edit., 1988, Russian translation, 1976, Symplectic Groups, 1978, 82, Russian translation, 1979, The Classical Groups and K-Theory (with A.J. Hahn), 1989; contbr. articles on arithmetic theory of quadratic forms and isomorphism theory of linear groups to Am. and European profl. jours. Mem. Cath. Commn. Intellectual and Cultural Affairs, 1962—; bd. govs., trustee U. Notre Dame Australia, 1990—. Recipient Marianist award U. Dayton, 1988; Alfred P. Sloan fellow, 1960-63. Mem. Am. Math. Soc., Am. Acad. Arts and Scis., Collegium (bd. dirs. 1992—). Roman Catholic. Home: 1227 E Irvington Ave South Bend IN 46614-1417 Office: U Notre Dame Office of Provost Notre Dame IN 46556

O'MEARA, PATRICK O., political science educator; b. Cape Town, South Africa, Jan. 7, 1938; came to U.S., 1964.; s. Daniel and Fiorina (Allorto) O'M. B.A., U. Capetown, 1960; M.A., Ind. U., 1966, Ph.D., 1970. Dep. dir. African studies program, asst. prof. polit. sci. Ind. U., Bloomington, 1970-72, dir. African studies program, 1972—, assoc. prof. polit. sci. and pub. and environ. affairs, 1972-81, prof. polit. sci. and pub. and environ. affairs, 1981—, dean office of internat. programs, 1993—; cons. in field. Author: Rhodesia: Racial Conflict or Coexistance?, 1975; editor: (with Gwendolen M. Carter) Southern Africa in Crisis, 1977, African Independence: The First Twenty-Five Years, 1985, Southern Africa: The Continuing Crisis, 1979, International Politics in Southern Africa, 1982 (with Phyllis M. Martin) Africa, 1977, 2d edit. 1986, 3d edit. 1995, (with C.R. Halisi and Brian Winchester) Revolutions of the Late Twentieth Century, 1991; contbr. articles to profl. jours., book chpts. Mem. African Studies Assn., Pi Alpha Alpha. Roman Catholic. Office: Ind U Woodburn Hall # 211 Bloomington IN 47405

O'MEARA, SARA, foundation administrator; b. Knoxville, Tenn., Sept. 9; m. Robert O'Meara (dec.); children: John Hopkins, Charles Hopkins (dec.); m. Robert Sigholtz, Nov. 1986; stepchildren: Taryn, Whitney. Chmn., CEO, co-founder Childhelp USA/Internat., Hollywood, Calif., 1960—; bd. dirs. Internat. Alliance of Child Abuse and Neglect, Children to Children, Inc. Past pres., sustaining mem. Spastic Children's League; past recording sec. Assistance League of Calif. Recipient Outstanding Achievement award YWCA, 1986, Internat. Collaboration to Prevent Child Abuse awarded by HRH Queen of England, 1989, Living Legacy award Women's Internat. Ctr., 1989, Kiwanis World Svc. medal, 1991, Family Circle award Family Circle Mag., 1992, Chancellor's Founders award U. Calif., 1993, Outstanding Woman from Tenn. award Nat. Mus. Women in Arts, 1993, Nat. Caring award Nat. Caring Inst., 1993, Hubert Humphrey award Touchdown Club, 1994 and numerous others. Mem. World Fund of Successful Women. Office: Childhelp USA Inc 1345 El Centro Hollywood CA 90028

O'MEARA, THOMAS FRANKLIN, priest, educator; b. Des Moines, May 15, 1935; s. Joseph Matthew and Frances Claire (Rock) O'M. MA, Aquinas Inst, Dubuque, Iowa, 1963; PhD, U. Munich, Germany, 1967. Ordained priest Roman Cath. Ch., 1962. Assoc. prof. Aquinas Inst. of Theology, Dubuque, Iowa, 1967-69; prof. U. Notre Dame, South Bend, Ind., 1981-84, William K. Warren prof. of theology, 1985—. Author 14 books, including: Romantic Idealism and Roman Catholicism, 1983, Theology of Ministry, 1985, Church and Culture, 1991, Thomas Aquinas: Theologian, 1996. Mem. Catholic Theol. Soc. Am. (pres. 1980). Office: U Notre Dame Dept Of Theology Notre Dame IN 46556

O'MELIA, CHARLES RICHARD, environmental engineering educator; b. N.Y.C., Nov. 1, 1934; s. Charles James and Anne Frances (Dobbin) O'M.; m. Mary Elizabeth Curley, Oct. 27, 1956; children: Kathleen Marie, Mary Margaret, Charles James, Anne Marie, John Thomas, Michael Joseph. BCE, Manhattan Coll., 1955; M San. Engring., U. Mich., 1956, PhD in San. Engring., 1963. Registered profl. engr., Ga. Asst. engr. Hazen & Sawyer Engrs., N.Y.C., 1956-67; teaching fellow, rsch. asst. U. Mich., 1957-61; asst. prof. san. engring. Ga. Inst. Tech., Atlanta, 1961-64; postdoctoral fellow Harvard U., Cambridge, Mass., 1964-65, lectr., 1965-66; assoc. prof. environ. scis. and engring. U. N.C., Chapel Hill, 1966-70, prof., 1970-80, dep. chmn. dept., 1977-80; prof. Johns Hopkins U., Balt., 1980—, chmn. dept. geography and environ. engring., 1990—; vis. scientist Swiss Fed. Inst. Tech., summer 1971; vis. scholar Woods Hole Oceanographic Inst., summer 1975; vis. prof. Calif. Inst. Tech., Pasadena, 1973-74; guest prof. Eidgenössische Anstalt für Wasserversorgung Abwasserreinigung und Gewässerschutz, Zurich, Switzerland, 1988-89; mem. engring and urban health scis. study sec. EPA, 1970-72, com. on rsch. needs in water supply, pollution control processes peer rev. panel, 1980—, sci. adv. bd., 1981-89; mem. program com. Water Pollution Control Fedn., 1980-86, chmn. rsch. symposium subcom., 1980-85; chmn. waste disposal com. Marine Scis. Coun. N.C., 1970-72; dep. chmn. Gordon Rsch. Confs., Environ. Scis.: Water, 1976, chmn. 1984; mem. com. on non-phosphorus detergent builders Internat. Joint Commn., 1976-83; cons. Monsanto Chem. Co., Union Carbide Corp., Office Gov. Puerto Rico, EPA, others. Contbr. numerous articles to profl. jours, chpts. to books. Recipient Best Lectr. award Environ. Engring Students U. N.C., 1969-70, 71-71, Pergammon Press Publs. award Internat. Assn. on Water Pollution Rsch. and Control, 1988. Mem. NAE (co-chmn. safe drinking water com., subcom. on particulate contaminants 1976, com. on water treatment chemicals 1983-85, wastewater mgmt. in coastal zones com. 1989—), ASCE (Simon W. Freese lectr. 1985, rsch. award 1969), Am. Acad. Environ. Engrs. (cert.), Am. Chem. Soc. (assoc. editor Environ. Sci. and Tech. 1975-83, chmn. water program environ. chemistry div. 1970-72), Am. Soc. Limnology and Oceanography, Am. Water Works Assn. (Publs. award 1965, 85, Best Paper award rsch. div. 1989, A.P. Black award 1990), Water Environment Fedn. (Gordon Maskew Fair medal 1993), AAAS, Assn. Environ. Engring. Profs. (Disting Faculty award 1972, Engring Sci. award 1975, CH2M-Hill award 1988, Outstanding Publ. award 1989, 91, bd. dirs. 1977-80, 88—, v.p. 1978-79, pres. 1979-80), Sigma Xi, Chi Epsilon. Roman Catholic. Office: Johns Hopkins U 34th And Charles St Baltimore MD 21218*

OMENN, GILBERT STANLEY, university dean, physician; b. Chester, Pa., Aug. 30, 1941; s. Leonard and Leah (Miller) O.; m. Martha Darling; children: Rachel Andrea, Jason Montgomery, David Matthew. AB, Princeton U., 1961; MD, Harvard U., 1965; PhD in Genetics, U. Wash., 1972. Intern Mass. Gen. Hosp., Boston, 1965-66; asst. resident in medicine Mass. Gen. Hosp., 1966-67; research assoc. NIH, Bethesda, Md., 1967-69; fellow U. Wash., 1969-71, asst. prof. medicine, 1971-74, assoc. prof., 1974-79, investigator Howard Hughes Med. Inst., 1976-77, prof., 1979—, prof. environ. health, 1981—, chmn. dept., 1981-83, dean Sch. Pub. Health and Community Medicine, 1982—; bd. dirs. Rohm & Haas Co., Amgen, BioTechniques Labs. Inc., Immune Response Corp., Clean Sites, Inc., Population Svcs. Internat., Pacific N.W. Pollution Prevention Rsch. Ctr.; White House fellow/spl. asst. to chmn. AEC, 1973-74; assoc. dir. Office Sci. and Tech. Policy, The White House, 1977-80; assoc. dir. human resources Office Mgmt. and Budget, 1980-81; vis. sr. fellow Wilson Sch. Pub. and Internat. Affairs, Princeton U., 1981; sci. and pub. policy fellow Brookings Instn., Washington, 1981-82; cons. govt. agys., Lifetime Cable Network; mem. Nat. Com. on the Environment, environ. adv. com. Rohm & Haas, Rene Dubos Ctr. for Human Environments, AFL-CIO Workplace Health Fund., Electric Power Rsch. Inst., Carnegie Commn. Task Force on Sci. and Tech. in Jud. and Regulatory Decision Making, adv. com. to dir., Ctrs. Disease Control, 1992—, adv. com. Critical Technologies Inst., RAND; mem. Pres.'s Coun., U. Calif., 1992—. Co-author: Clearing the Air, Reforming the Clean Air Act, 1981. Editor: (with others) Genetics, Environment and Behavior: Implications for Educational Policy, 1972; Genetic Control of Environmental Pollutants, 1984; Genetic Variability in Responses to Chemical Exposure, 1984, Environmental Biotechnology: Reducing Risks from Environmental Chemicals through Biotechnology, 1988, Biotechnology in Biodegradation, 1990, Biotechnology and Human Genetic Predisposition to Disease, 1990, Annual Review of Public Health, 1991, 92, 93, 94, Clinics in Geriatric Medicine, 1992; assoc. editor Cancer Rsch., Cancer Epidemiology, Biomarkers and Prevention, Environ. Rsch., Am. Jour. Med. Genetics, Am. Jour. Preventive Medicine; contbr. articles on cancer prevention, human biochem. genetics, prenatal diagnosis of inherited disorders, susceptibility to environ. agts., clin. medicine and health policy to profl. publs. Mem. President's Council on Spinal Cord Injury; mem. Nat. Cancer Adv. Bd., Nat. Heart, Lung and Blood Adv. Council, Wash. State Gov.'s Commn. on Social and Health Services, Ctr. for Excellence in Govt.; chmn. awards panel Gen. Motors Cancer Research Found., 1985-86; chmn. bd. Environ. Studies and Toxicology, Nat. Rsch. Coun., 1988-91; mem. Bd. Health Promotion and Disease Prevention, Inst. Medicine; mem. adv. com. Woodrow Wilson Sch., Princeton U., 1978-84; bd. dirs. Inst. for Sci. in Society; trustee Pacific Sci. Ctr., Fred Hutchinson Cancer Research Ctr., Seattle Symphony Orch., Seattle Youth Symphony Orch., Seattle Chamber Music Festival, Santa Fe Chamber Music Festival; mem. Citizens for a Hunger-Free Washington; chmn. rules com. Democratic Conv., King County, Wash., 1972. Served with USPHS, 1967-69. Recipient Research Career Devel. award USPHS, 1972; White House fellow, 1973-74. Fellow ACP, AAAS, Nat. Acad. Social Ins., Western Assn. Physicians, Hastings Ctr., Collegium Ramazzini; mem. Inst. Medicine of NAS, White House Fellows Assn., Am. Soc. Human Genetics, Western Soc. Clin. Rsch. Jewish. Home: 5100 NE 55th St Seattle WA 98105-2821 Office: U Wash Dean Sch Pub Health Box 357230 Seattle WA 98195-7230

OMENS, SHERWOOD, cinematographer. Prodr.: (documentary) Somebody Waiting, 1971 (Academy award nomination best documentary short subject 1971); cinematographer: (TV movies) Ishi, the Last of His Tribe, 1978, The Man in the Santa Claus Suit, 1979, Stone, 1979, Madame X, 1981, The Facts of Life Goes to Paris, 1982, Fire on the Mountain, 1982, Policewoman Centerfold, 1983, Grace Kelly, 1983, The Red Light Sting, 1984, Why Me?, 1984, An Early Frost, 1985 (Emmy award outstanding cinematography 1986), Blade in Hong Kong, 1985, Evergreen, 1984 (Emmy award nomination outstanding cinematography 1985), I Saw What You Did, 1987 (Emmy award outstanding cinematography 1988), (TV series) Magnum P.I., 1981 (Emmy award nomination outstanding cinematography 1982), Alfred Hitchcock Presents ("Road Hog"), 1985 (Emmy award nomination outstanding cinematography 1986), (TV pilots) Lime Street, 1985, Heart of the City, 1986 (Emmy award outstanding cinematography 1987), (films) History of the World, Part I, 1981, Coming to America, 1988, Harlem Nights, 1989, Boomerang, 1992. Office: 6647 Morella Ave North Hollywood CA 91606-1629

OMER, GEORGE ELBERT, JR., orthopedic surgeon, hand surgeon, educator; b. Kansas City, Kans., Dec. 23, 1922; s. George Elbert and Edith May (Hines) O.; m. Wendie Vilven, Nov. 6, 1949; children: George Eric, Michael Lee. B.A., Ft. Hays State U., 1944; M.D., Kans. U., 1950; M.Sc. in Orthopaedic Surgery, Baylor U., 1955. Diplomate Am. Bd. Orthopaedic Surgery, 1959, re-cert. orthopaedics and hand surgery, 1983 (bd. dirs. 1983-92, pres. 1987-88), cert. surgery of the hand, 1989. Commd. 1st lt. U.S. Army, 1949; advanced through grades to col., 1967; ret. U.S. Army, 1970; rotating intern Bethany Hosp., Kansas City, 1950-51; resident in orthopaedic surgery Brooke Gen. Hosp., San Antonio, 1952-55, William Beaumont Gen. Hosp., El Paso, Tex., 1955-56; chief surgery Irwin Army Hosp., Ft. Riley, Kans., 1957-59; cons. in orthopaedic surgery 8th Army Korea, 1959-60; asst. chief orthopaedic surgery, chief hand surgeon Fitzsimons Army Med. Center, Denver, 1960-63; dir. orthopaedic residency tng. Armed Forces Inst. Pathology, Washington, 1963-65; chief orthopaedic surgery and chief Army Hand Surg. Center, Brooke Army Med. Center, 1965-70; cons. in orthopaedic and hand surgery Surgeon Gen. Army, 1967-70; prof. orthopaedics, surgery, and anatomy, chmn. dept. orthopaedic surgery, chief div. hand surgery U. N.Mex., 1970-90, med. dir. phys. therapy, 1972-90, acting asst. dean grad. edn. Sch. Medicine, 1980-81; mem. active staff U. N.Mex. Hosp., Albuquerque, chief of med. staff, 1984-86; cons. staff other Albuquerque hosps.; cons. orthopedic surgery USPHS, 1966-85, U.S. Army, 1970-92, USAF, 1970-78, VA, 1970—; cons. Carrier Tingley Hosp. for Crippled Children, 1970—, interim med. dir., 1970-72, 86-87, mem. bd. advisors, 1972—, chair, 1994-96. Mem. bd. editors Clin. Orthopaedics, 1973-90, Jour. AMA, 1973-74, Jour. Hand Surgery, 1976-81; trustee Jour. Bone and Joint Surgery, 1993—, sec., 1993—; contbr. more than 200 articles to profl. jours., numerous chpts. to books. Decorated Legion of Merit, Army Commendation medal with 2 oak leaf clusters; recipient Alumni Achievement award Ft. Hays State U., 1973, Recognition plaque Am. Soc. Surgery Hand, 1989, Recognition plaque N.Mex. Orthopaedic Assn., 1991; recognized with Endowed Professorship U. N.Mex. Sch. Medicine, 1995. Fellow ACS, Am. Orthopaedic Assn. (pres. 1988-89, exec. dir. 1989-93), Am. Acad. Orthopaedic Surgeons, Assn. Orthopaedic Chmn., N.Mex. Orthopaedic Assn. (pres. 1979-81), La. Orthopaedic Assn. (hon.), Korean Orthopaedic Assn. (hon.), Peru Orthopaedic Soc. (hon.), Caribbean Hand Soc., Am. Soc. Surgery Hand (pres. 1978-79), Am. Assn. Surgery of Trauma, Assn. Bone and Joint Surgeons, Assn. Mil. Surgeons U.S., Riordan Hand Soc. (pres. 1967-68), Sunderland Soc. (pres. 1981-83), Soc. Mil. Orthopaedic Surgeons, Brazilian Hand Soc. (hon.), S.Am. Hand Soc. (hon.), Groupe D'Etude de la Main, Brit. Hand Soc., Venezuela Hand Soc. (hon.), South African Hand Soc. (hon.), Western Orthopaedic Assn. (pres. 1981-82), AAAS, Russell A. Hibbs Soc. (pres. 1977-78), 38th Parallel Med. Soc. (Korea) (sec. 1959-60); mem. AMA, Phi Kappa Phi, Phi Sigma, Alpha Omega Alpha, Phi Beta Pi. Home: 316 Big Horn Ridge Rd NE Sandia Heights Albuquerque NM 87122 Office: U N Mex Dept Orthopaedic Surgery 2211 Lomas Blvd NE Albuquerque NM 87106-2745

OMER, ROBERT WENDELL, hospital administrator; b. Salt Lake City, Feb. 10, 1948; s. Wayne Albert and Melva Bernice (Thunell) O.; m. Deborah Jackson, May 4, 1972;children: Melinda, Carmen, Creighton, Preston, Allison. BS in Biology, U. Utah, 1972; MHA, Washington U., St. Louis, 1975. V.p. St. Luke's Hosp., Cedar Rapids, Iowa, 1974-80; asst. adminstr. Franciscan Med. Ctr., Rock Island, Ill., 1980-82, Latter Day Saints Hosp., Salt Lake City, 1982-85; asst. adminstr. Clarkson Hosp., Omaha, 1985-93, v.p., COO, 1993—; bd. dirs. ARC, Heartland chpt. Omaha; bd. dirs. Nebr. Scanning Svcs. Lt. col. USAR, 1972. Fellow Am. Coll. of Healthcare Execs. 1975; mem. Nebr. Hosp. Assn., Omaha C. of C. (leadership Omaha award 1978), Omaha Healthcare Execs. Group (pres. 1989-90), Rotary (bd. dirs. 1990). Republican. Mem. LDS Ch. Avocations: jogging, history, cycling, backpacking, racquetball. Home: 14111 Cedar Cir Omaha NE 68144-2120

OMINSKY, ALAN JAY, lawyer, medical educator; b. Phila., Apr. 7, 1938; s. Benjamin B. and Ida S. (Snydman) O.; m. Marlene Lachman, Nov. 1, 1992; 1 child, Sara. BA, U. Pa., Phila., 1958, MD, 1962, JD, 1988. Bar: Pa. 1989, U.S. Supreme Ct. 1994; cert. Am. Bd. Anesthesiology, Am. Bd. Psychiatry. Assoc. prof. anesthesiology U. Pa., Phila., 1972-88, assoc. prof. psychiatry, 1975-88; assoc. Bernstein Silver & Agins, Phila., 1989—. Mem. ABA, Pa. Bar Assn., Phila. Bar Assn. (chiar medicolegal com. 1993-95, mem. sr. lawyers, state civil, and computer users coms.), Assn. Trial Lawyers Am., Pa. Trial Lawyers Assn., Phil. Trial Lawyers Assn., Am. Soc. Anesthesiologists, Am. Psychiat. Soc., Lawyers Club Phila., Phi Beta Kappa. Home: 233 S 6th St Apt 701 Philadelphia PA 19106-3751 Office: Bernstein Silver & Agins 1600 Market St Philadelphia PA 19103-7240

OMINSKY, HARRIS, lawyer; b. Phila., Sept. 14, 1932; s. Joseph and Lillian (Herman) O.; m. Rosalyn Rita Rutenberg, June 4, 1961; children—Michelle, David. B.S. in Econs., U. Pa., 1953, LL.B., 1956. Bar: Pa. 1956. Ptnr. Ominsky & Ominsky, Phila., 1958-64; ptnr. Blank, Rome, Comisky & McCauley, Phila., 1964—, mem. mgmt. com., 1981-84, 88-92, co-chmn. real estate dept., 1988-93; lectr. Law Sch., Temple U., Phila., 1969-71, lectr. Real Estate Inst., 1996—. Contbr. numerous articles to profl. jours. Pres. bd. Phila. Singing City Choir, 1984-88; chmn. zoning com. Merion Civic Assn., Pa., 1984-91. Fellow Am. Bar Found.; mem. ABA (Harrison Tweep spl. merit award 1988), Pa. Bar Assn. (ho. of dels. 1984—), Pa. Bar Inst. (bd. dirs. 1981—, exec. com. 1986-93, v.p. 1988-89, pres. 1989-90, lectr., planner 1969—), Phila. Bar Assn. (chmn. real estate taxes subcom. 1984-85, real property sect. 1991-92, Leon J. Obermayer Edn. award 1989), Am. Coll. Real Estate Lawyers (chmn. publs. com. 1987-91, bd. govs. 1993-95), Order of Coif. Home: 526 Baird Rd Merion Station PA 19066-1302 Office: Blank Rome Comisky & McCauley 4 Penn Center Plz Philadelphia PA 19103-2521

OMMAYA, AYUB KHAN, neurosurgeon; b. Pakistan, Apr. 14, 1930; came to U.S., 1961, naturalized, 1968; s. Sultan Nadir and Ida (Counil) Khan; children: David, Alexander, Shana, Aisha, Iman, Sinan. M.D., U. Punjab, Pakistan, 1953; M.A., Oxford U., Eng., 1956. Diplomate Am. Bd. Neurological Surgery. Intern Mayo Hosp., Lahore, Pakistan, 1953-54; resident in neurosurgery Radcliffe Infirmary, Oxford, Eng., 1954-61; vis. scientist NIH, Bethesda, Md., 1963-63, assoc. neurosurgeon, 1963-68, head sect. applied rsch., 1968-74, chief neurosurgery, 1974-79; clin. prof. George Washington U. Med. Sch., 1970—; cons. VA Armed Forces Radiobiology Rsch. Inst.; chmn. Inter-Agy. Com. for Protection Human Rsch. Subjects of Fed. Coordinating Coun. for Sci., Engring. and Tech., NAS; chmn. biomechanics adv. com. com. Nat. Hwy. Traffic Safety Adminstrn.; mem. adv. com. Nat. Ctr. Injury Control & Prevention, Atlanta; inaugural Lewin Meml. lectr. U. Cambridge, Eng., 1983; mem. adv. coun. CDC; Shively lectr. Am. Assn. Auto. Medicine, 1988; Ibn-Sina lectr. Islamic Med. Assn. N.Am. Contbr. articles to profl. jours.; inventor, patentee spinal fluid flow driven artificial organs for diabetes and degenerative diseases of the nervous system. Pres. Found. for Fundamental and Applied Neurosci., Bethesda; v.p., dir. rsch. Cyborgan, Inc., Bethesda. Recipient J. W. Kirkdaldy prize Oxford U., 1956, Lifetime Achievement award Internat. Coll. Surgeons, 1996; recipient Sitara-i-Imtiaz for Achievements in Neurosurgery Govt. Pakistan, 1981; Hunterian prof. Royal Coll. Surgeons, 1968; Rhodes scholar, 1954-60. Fellow ACS, Third World Acad. Scis. (assoc., med. scis. com.), Royal Coll. Surgeons Eng.; mem. ASME (exec. affiliate), Soc. for Neurosci., Am. Assn. Neurol. Surgeons, Rsch. Soc. Neurosurgeons, Brit. Soc. Neurol. Surgeons, Am. Assn. Pakistani Physicians (pres.), Internat. Brain Rsch. Orgn. (life), Pan-Am. Med. Assn. Home: 8901 Burning Tree Rd Bethesda MD 20817-3007 Office: 8006 Glenbrook Rd Bethesda MD 20814-2608 *My research on how consciousness is disrupted and restored after brain injuries is serving as a paradigm for my current investigations into the mind-body problem. In this work my scientific training as well as experiential work in both Eastern and Western modes are useful.*

OMMODT, DONALD HENRY, dairy company executive; b. Flom, Minn., July 7, 1931; s. Henry and Mabel B. (Kvidt) O.; m. Evelyn Mavis Blilie, June 15, 1957; children—Linette, Kevin, Lee, Jodi. Student, Interstate Bus. Coll., Fargo, N.D. Acct. Farmers State Bank, Waubun, Minn., 1950-53; chief acct. Cass-Clay Creamery, Inc., Fargo, 1953-61, office mgr., 1961-65, gen. mgr., 1965-83, pres., 1983—. Pres. Messiah Luth. Ch., Fargo, 1976-78; mem. Minn. Dairy Task Force Com., 1988-90; bd. dirs. Communicating for Agr., Fergus Falls, Minn., 1977-80, Blue Cross of N.D., Fargo, 1971-88. Recipient Builder of the Valley award Minn. Red River Valley Devel. Assn., 1991, N.D. Milky Way award, 1993. Mem. N.D. Dairy Industries Assn. (bd. dirs., past pres.), Am. Dairy Assn. (bd. dirs. N.D. 1970-80), N.D. Dairy Product Promotion Commn. (bd. dirs. 1970-80), Messiah Found. Christian Communications (pres. 1987—), Moorhead C. of C. Office: Cass-Clay Creamery Inc 1220 Main Ave # 2947 Fargo ND 58103-8201

OMOLE, GABRIEL GBOLABO, international venture capitalist; b. Akungba-Akoko, Nigeria, Mar. 15, 1940; came to U.S., 1975; s. Amos Akindele and Victoria Ola (Olutu) O.; children: Juliana Olufunke, Esther Oluremi, Christiana Oluseun, George Abayomi. PhD, D MSc. Chmn. Gay Omole & Co., Ltd., Lagos, Nigeria, 1968—, Akoko Indsl. Devel. Ltd., 1973—, Akoko Mktg. & Investment Ltd., 1973—, Johngay Enterprises, Ltd., Accra, Ghana, 1977—, Gayom Travel & Tours, Ltd., 1977—, Unifood Industries Nigeria Ltd., 1979—, Unity Village Complex, 1979—, 1st Akoko Internat. Corp., N.Y.C., 1978—, UCM Services Corp., N.Y.C., 1979—, The Akoko Group, Ltd., London, 1983—, Gay Omole Internat. Ltd., London, 1983—, Gay Omole Investment Ltd., Brunei Internat. Investors (West Africa) Ltd.; pres., CEO Mastercard Internat. Svcs. Ltd., 1996—; mng. dir. Galleria Tourist Devel. Property Co. Ltd., Lagos, 1993—, Galleria Transp. Systems Ltd., Lagos, 1993, Combined Billionaires Network Svcs. Ltd., 1996—, Direct Resources Internat. Ltd., 1996—, Galleria City Devel. Ltd., 1996—; Co-founder Brunei Resources (West Africa) Ltd., 1990—; pres., co-founder African Continental Corp., Miami, Fla.; dir.-gen. IBB World Leaders Gallery, Gay Omole Petroleum. Chmn. bd. dirs. Akoko Specialist Hosp., N.Y.C.; trustee, chmn., Gay Omole Found., Lagos, 1979—; founder Unity Ch. Mission, 1976, chmn. devel. fund, 1979—. Mem. Am. Mgmt. Assn., Akungba Devel. Union, Am. Mgmt. Internat., Assn. Venture Founders, Akure C. of C., N.Y.C. C. of C., Nigerian-Am. C. of C., Nigerian-ASEAN C. of C., Nigerian-South Africa C. of C., N.Y. Acad. Scis., Nat. Geo. Soc., London Inst. Dirs., U.S. C. of C. Home: PO Box 74147 Victoria Island, Lagos Nigeria also: PO Box 4447, Garki Abuya Nigeria

O'MORCHOE, CHARLES CHRISTOPHER CREAGH, administrator, anatomical sciences educator; b. Quetta, India, May 7, 1931; came to U.S., 1968; s. Nial Francis C. and Jessie Elizabeth (Joly) O'M.; m. Patricia Jean Richardson, Sept. 15, 1955; children: Charles Eric Creagh, David James Creagh. B.A., Trinity Coll., Dublin (Ireland) U., 1953, M.B., B.Ch., B.A.O., 1955, M.A., 1959, M.D., 1961, Ph.D., 1969, Sc.D., 1981. Resident Halifax Gen. Hosp., U.K., 1955-57; lectr. in anatomy Sch. Medicine Trinity Coll., Dublin (Ireland) U., 1957-61, 63-65, lectr. in physiology, 1966-67, assoc. prof. in physiology, 1967-68; instr. in anatomy Harvard Med. Sch., Boston, 1962-63; vis. prof. physiology U. Md. Sch. Medicine, Balt., 1961-62, assoc. prof. anatomy, 1968-71, prof. anatomy, 1971-74; chmn. anatomy bd. State of Md., 1971-73; prof., chmn. dept. anatomy Stritch Sch. Medicine Loyola U., Maywood, Ill., 1974-84; dean Coll. Medicine, U. Ill., Urbana-Champaign, 1984—, prof. anat. scis. and surgery, 1984—; WHO cons., vis. prof. physiology Jaipur, India, 1967, S.M.S. Med. Coll., U. Rajasthan, vis. prof. anatomy, 1971. Assoc. editor: Anatomical Record, 1978—, Am. Jour. Anatomy, 1987-91; contbr. articles to profl. jours. Elected fellow Trinity Coll., Dublin U., 1966; named faculty mem. of yr. Loyola U., Chgo., 1982. Mem. AMA, Am. Soc. Nephrology, N.Am. Soc. Lymphology (v.p. 1982-84, pres. 1984-86, sec. 1993—, Cecil K. Drinker award 1992), Am. Assn. Anatomy Chairmen (emeritus), Am. Assn. Anatomists (dir. placement svc. 1981-91), Internat. Soc. Lymphology (exec. com. 1987—, pres. 1993-95), Ill. State Med. Soc., Champaign County Med. Soc., Alpha Omega Alpha. Mem. Church of Ireland. Home: 2709 Holcomb Dr Urbana IL 61801-7724 Office: U Ill Coll Medicine 190 Med Scis Bldg 506 S Mathews Ave Urbana IL 61801-3618

O'MORE, ELOISE PITTS, designer; b. Fayetteville, Tenn., June 7, 1911; d. William Woodruff and Josephine Martin (Diemer) Pitts; student Ward-Conley Art Sch., 1928-30, Ward-Belmont Coll., 1930-32; Baccalaureat d'Art Decoratif, Le College Feminin, Paris, 1937; m. James Robert Muratta, Oct. 4, 1929; 1 child, Donna Maria; m. Rory O'More, IV, Dec. 26, 1940; 1 child, Rory V. Self-employed designer and muralist, 1938-60; dir. design Stoddards Office Designs, Nashville, 1960-66; partner Mitchell & O'More, designers, Nashville, 1966-69; founder, dir. O'More Sch. of Design, Franklin, Tenn., 1970—; executed historic murals 3d Nat. Bank, Nashville, 1963, First Franklin Fed., 1964, First Nat. Bank, Centerville, 1972, United Am. Bank, Nashville, 1972, Harpeth Nat. Bank, Franklin; lectr. design and decoration for various schs., clubs and bus. orgns. Mem. Heritage Found. Franklin; mem. Cheekwood Fine Arts Center, Nashville; mem. Nashville Hist. Commn. Mem. Interior Design Educators Council, Am. Soc. Interior Designers, Nat. Trust Historic Preservation, Williamson County Hist. Soc., Societe des Arts, Alliance Francaise. Roman Catholic. Office: O'More Sch of Design PO Box 908 Franklin TN 37065-0908

OMORI, MORIO, lawyer; b. Maui, Hawaii, Oct. 15, 1921; m. Rachel T. Tanaka, June 29, 1946; children: Sharyn, Colleen. BE, U. Hawaii, 1942, 5th yr. cert., 1943; LLB, U. Colo., 1954. Bar: Hawaii 1955, U.S. Dist. Ct. Hawaii 1955, U.S. Supreme Ct. 1959. Law clk. to chief justice Supreme Ct. Hawaii, Honolulu, 1954-55, dep. atty. gen., 1955-56, spl. dep. atty. gen., 1956-68; pvt. practice law, 1957—; gen. counsel Pacific Savs. & Loan, Honolulu, 1968-76, chmn. bd., 1972-76; gen. counsel Halekulani Corp., Honolulu, 1985—, bd. dirs., 1985—; bd. dirs. Mitsui Real Estate Sales, Inc. Campaign coord. for U.S. Senator Daniel Inouye, Hawaii, 1959, 62, state rep., 1959-70. With U.S. Army, 1944-46, ETO. Mem. ABA, Hawaii Bar Assn., 442d Vets. Club, Phi Delta Phi. Avocations: golf, landscaping, travel. Home: 1031 Waiiki St Honolulu HI 96821-1234

OMURA, GEORGE ADOLF, medical oncologist; b. N.Y.C., Apr. 30, 1938; s. Bunji K. and Martha (Pilger) O.; m. Emily Fowler, Dec. 27, 1962; children: June Ellen, Susan, Ann, George Fowler. B.A. magna cum laude, Columbia U., 1958; M.D., Cornell U., 1962. Intern Bellevue Hosp., N.Y.C., resident, 1965-67; fellow Meml. Sloan Kettering Cancer Ctr., N.Y.C., 1967-70; asst. prof. medicine U. Ala., Birmingham, 1970-73, assoc. prof. medicine, 1973-78, prof. medicine, 1978-95, prof. emeritus, medicine, 1995—, prof. ob-gyn., 1991-95; v.p. clin. devel. BioCryst Pharmaceuticals, Inc., Birmingham, 1995—; prof. emeritus, ob-gyn U. Ala., Birmingham, 1996—, mid. dir., 1996—; cons. Nat. Cancer Inst., 1975—; chmn. Southeastern Cancer Study Group, 1983-87; cons. to FDA, 1994-95. Contbr. articles to profl. jours. Served with USNR, 1963-65. Am. Cancer Soc. jr. faculty clin. fellow, 1971-74. Fellow A.C.P.; mem. Gynecol. Oncology Group (co-prin. investigator for Ala. 1988, prin. investigator cancer and leukemia Group B for Ala. 1986), Am. Soc. Clin. Oncology, Am. Soc. Hematology, Am. Assn. Cancer Research, Phi Beta Kappa, Alpha Omega Alpha. Home: 3621 Crestside Rd Birmingham AL 35223-1514 Office: Ste B 2190 Parkway Lake Dr Birmingham AL 35244

OMURA, JAMES MATSUMOTO, journalist, editor, publisher; b. Bainbridge Island, Washington, Nov. 27, 1912; m. Karen Haruko; children: Gregg Kiyoshi, Wayne Stanley. English lang. editor New Japanese Am. News, L.A., 1933-34, New World Daily, San Francisco, 1934-36; columnist Passing Show Japanese Am. News, San Francisco, 1938-40; founder Nisei mag. Current Life, San Francisco, 1940-42; English lang. editor, pub. rels. dir. The Rocky Shimpo, Denver, 1944, 47; columnist Plain Speaking Hokubei Mainichi, San Francisco, 1984-88; writer and speaker in field; speaker in protest over eviction/detention of Japanese people before Tolan Congl. Com., San Francisco, 1942. Recipient Cert. of Honor award Status of Liberty/Ellis Island Centennial Commn., 1983, Bicentennial Recognition, Smithsonian Instn., 1988, Lifetime Achievement award Asian Am. Journalists Assn., 1989, Internat. Order of Merit, 1990; inducted Maison Internat. Des Intellectuals (France); honored as Ethnic Benefactor Nat. Coun. Redress/Reparation, 1992, Fighting Spirit award, 1994. Mem. Grand Coun. World Parliament of Chivalry (Sidney, Australia)(life, 20th Century Award of Achievement 1993), World Biographical Hall of Fame. Address: 1455 S Irving St Denver CO 80219-3916

OMURA, JIMMY KAZUHIRO, electrical engineer; b. San Jose, Calif., Sept. 8, 1940; s. Shomatsu and Shizuko Dorothy (Takesaka) O.; divorced; children: Daniel, Dawn. B.S., MIT, 1963, M.S., 1963; Ph.D. (NSF fellow 1963-66), Stanford U., 1966. Research engr. Stanford Research Inst., 1966-69; mem. faculty UCLA, 1969-85; founder, chmn. bd. Cylink Corp., Sunnyvale, Calif., 1983—; cons. to industry and govt. Co-author: Principles of Digital Communication and Coding, 1979, Spread Spectrum Communications Handbook, 1994; contbr. articles to profl. jours. NSF grantee, 1970-78. Fellow IEEE (info. theory group). Office: Cylink Corp 910 Hermosa Ct Sunnyvale CA 94086-4103

OMURA, YOSHIAKI, physician, educator; b. Tomari, Toyama-ken, Japan, Mar. 28, 1934; came to U.S., 1959, naturalized, 1979; s. Tsunejiro and Minako (Uozu) O.; m. Rose Ninon Alexander, Sept. 8, 1962 (separated); children: Alexander Kenji, Vivienne Midori, Richard Itsuma; assoc. degree in elec. engring. and pre-med., Nihon U., 1952-54; BSc in Applied Physics, Waseda U., 1957; MD, Yokohama City U., 1958, postgrad. exptl. physics, Columbia U., 1960-63; ScD (Med.), Coll. Physicians and Surgeons, Columbia U., 1965. Diplomate Am. Acad. Pain Mgmt. Rotating intern Tokyo U. Hosp., 1958, Norwalk (Conn.) Hosp., 1959; rsch. fellow cardiovascular surgery Columbia U., N.Y.C., 1960, resident physician in surgery, Francis Delafield Hosp., Cancer Inst., Columbia U., 1961-65; asst. prof. pharmacology and instr. surgery N.Y. Med. Coll., 1966-72; vis. prof. U. Paris, summers 1973-77; Maitre de recherche, Disting. Fgn. Scientist program of INSERM, Govt. of France, 1977; rsch. cons. orthopedic surgery Columbia U., 1965-66; part-time emergency rm. physician Englewood Hosp., 1965-66; rsch. cons. pharmacology dept. N.Y. Down State Med. Center, SUNY, 1966; co-founder, cons. Lincoln Hosp. Acupuncture Drug Detoxification Program, 1973-74; chmn. Columbia U. Affiliation and Cmty. Medicine com., Community Bd., Francis Delafield Hosp., 1974-75; vis. rsch. prof. dept. elec. engring., Manhattan Coll., 1962—; chmn. Sci. Div., Children's Art & Sci. Workshops, N.Y.C., 1971-92; dir. Med. Rsch., Heart Disease Rsch. Found., Bklyn., 1972—; adj. prof. dept. pharmacology Chgo. Med. Sch., 1982-93; adj. prof. physiology Sch. Med., Showa U., Tokyo, 1988—; attending physician Dept. Neurosci., L.I. Coll. Hosp., 1980-88; cons. New York Pain Center, 1988-92; prof. dept. non-orthodox medicine Ukrainian Nat. Med. U., Kiev, 1993—; v.p. Internat. Kirlian Rsch. Assn., 1981—; mem. N.Y. State Bd. Medicine, 1984—; mem. alumni council Coll. Phys. and Surg. Columbia U., 1986—; founder, editor-in-chief Acupuncture & Electro-Therapeutics Rsch. Internat. Jour., 1974—. Mem. editorial bd. Alternative Medicine, 1985—, Scandinavian Jour. Acupuncture and Electrotherapy, 1987—, Functional Neurology, 1988—; editorial cons. Jour. Electrocardiology, 1980-86; mem. NIH Rsch. Grant Evaluation Com., 1994—. Columbia U. rsch. fellow, 1960; Am. Cancer Soc. Inst. grantee, 1961-63; John Polacek Found. grantee, 1966-72; NIH grantee, 1967-72; Heart Disease Rsch. Found. grantee, 1972—; recipient: Acupuncture Scientist of the Year award, Internat. Congress of Chinese Medicine, 1989, Qi Gong Scientist of Yr. award Int. Congress of Chinese Medicine & Qi Gong, 1990, granted 4 U.S. patents and 3 Japanese patentsothers. Fellow Internat. Coll. Acupuncture and Electro-Therapeutics (pres. 1980—); mem. N.Y. Cardiol. Soc. (fellow), Am. Coll. Angiology (fellow), Am. Coll. Acupuncture (fellow), N.Y. Acad. Sci., Japan Bi-Digital O-Ring Test Assn. (hon. pres. 1986—), Japan Bi-Digital O-Ring Test Med. Soc. (hon. pres. 1990—), Am. Soc. Artificial Internal Organs, N.Y. Japanese Med. Soc. (pres. 1963-73), others. Author 6 books, also chpts. in books; contbr. over 160 articles to profl. jours. Home: 800 Riverside Dr Apt 8-I New York NY 10032-7416

ONAK, THOMAS PHILIP, chemistry educator; b. Omaha, July 30, 1932; s. Louis Albert and Louise Marie (Penner) O.; m. Sharon Colleen Neal, June 18, 1954. BA, Calif. State U., San Diego, 1954; PhD, U. Calif., Berkeley, 1957. Research chemist Olin Mathieson Chem. Corp., Pasadena, Calif., 1957-59; asst. prof. Calif. State U., Los Angeles, 1959-63, assoc. prof., 1963-66, prof. chemistry, 1966—. Author: Organoborane Chemistry, 1975; Contbr. articles to profl. jours., chpts. to books. Recipient Rsch. Career award NIH, 1973-78, Nat. award Am. Chem. Soc., 1990, Outstanding Prof. award Calif. State U., System, 1993-94; named Calif. Prof. of Yr. Carnegie Found. and Coun. for the Advancement and Support of Edn., 1995; Fulbright Rsch. fellow U. Cambridge, Eng., 1965-66. Home: PO Box 1477 South Pasadena CA 91031-1477 Office: Calif State U Dept Chemistry 5151 State U Dr Los Angeles CA 90032

ONA-SARINO, MILAGROS FELIX, physician, pathologist; b. Manila, May 8, 1940; came to U.S., 1965, naturalized, 1983; d. Venancio Vale Ona and Fidela Torres Felix; m. Edgardo Formantes Sarino, June 11, 1966; children: Edith Melanie, Edgar Michael, Edenn Michele. AA, U. Santo Tomas, Manila, 1959, MD meritissimus cum laude 1964. Diplomate Am. Bd. Pathology; med. licensure N.Y., N.J., W.Va. Rotating intern N.Y. Infirmary, pediatrics, Roosevelt Hosp., N.Y.C., 1965-66; resident in anatomic and clin. pathology Lenox Hill Hosp., N.Y.C., 1966-71, asst. adj. pathologist, 1972-74; assoc. pathologist St. Francis Med. Ctr., Trenton, N.J., 1974-84, Hamilton Hosp., N.J., 1974-84; pathologist, chief pathology and lab. medicine svc. Louis A. Johnson VA Med. Ctr., Clarksburg, W.Va., 1984—; clin. instr. pathology Columbia U. Coll. Physicians and Surgeons, N.Y.C., 1973-85; clin. assoc. prof. pathology, W.Va. U. Sch. Medicine. Fellow Am. Soc. Clin. Pathologists, Coll. of Am. Pathologists; mem. Internat. Acad. Pathology, N.Y. Acad. Scis. (life). Office: Louis A Johnson VA Med Ctr Dept Pathology Clarksburg WV 26301

ONDETTI, MIGUEL ANGEL, chemist, consultant; b. Buenos Aires, Argentina, May 14, 1930; came to U.S., 1960, naturalized, 1971; s. Emilio Pablo and Sara Cecilia (Cerutti) O.; m. Josephine Elizabeth Garcia, June 6, 1958; children: Giselle Christine, Gabriel Alexander. Licensiate in Chemistry, U. Buenos Aires, 1955, D.Sc., 1957. Prof. chemistry Inst. Tchrs., Buenos Aires, 1957-60; instr. organic chemistry U. Buenos Aires, 1957-60; rsch. scientist Squibb Inst. Med. Rsch., Buenos Aires, 1957-60; rsch. investigator Squibb Inst. Med. Rsch., Princeton, N.J., 1960-66; rsch. supr. Squibb Inst. Med. Rsch., 1966-73, sect. head, 1973-76, dir. biol. chemistry, 1976-79; assoc. dir. Squibb Inst., 1980-82, v.p. rsch. cardiopulmonary disease, 1982-86, sr. v.p. cardiovascular rsch., 1987-91; pharm. cons., 1991—; ad-hoc cons., sculptor NIH; mem. adv. com. dept. chemistry Princeton U., 1982-86. Patentee in field (115); contbr. articles to sci. jours. Served with Argentine Army, 1950-51. Recipient Thomas Alva Edison Patent award R&D Coun. N.J., 1983, Ciba award for hypertension rsch. Am. Heart Assn., 1983, Perkins medal Soc. Chemistry Industry, 1991, Warren Alpert Found. award, 1991; scholar Brit. Coun., 1960, Squibb, 1956. Mem. AAAS, Am. Chem. Soc. (Alfred Burger award 1981, Creative Invention award 1992, Perkin medal 1992), Am. Soc. Biol. Chemists. Home: 79 Hemlock Cir Princeton NJ 08540-5405

ONDRICEK, MIROSLAV, cinematographer. Cinematographer: (films) If..., 1969, Slaughterhouse Five, 1971, Taking Off, 1971, O Lucky Man!, 1973, Hair, 1979, Ragtime, 1981 (Academy award nomination best cinematography 1981), The World According to Garp, 1982, Silkwood, 1983, The Divine Emma, 1983, Amadeus, 1984 (Academy award nomination best cinematography 1984), Heaven Help Us, 1985, F/X, 1986, Big Shots, 1987, Funny Farm, 1988, Valmont, 1989, Awakenings, 1990, A League of Their Own, 1992. Office: The Gersh Agency 232 N Canon Dr Beverly Hills CA 90210-5302

O'NEAL, BOB H., utilities company executive; b. 1934. BBA, East Tex. State U., 1955. With Stewart & Stevenson Power Inc., Denver, 1978-81, pres.; with Stewart & Stevenson Svcs. Inc., 1964—, v.p., from 1981, now pres., also bd. dirs. Office: Stewart & Stevenson Svcs Inc Box 1637 2707 N Loop W 8th Fl Houston TX 77251*

O'NEAL, DALE, JR., lawyer; b. Ft. Worth, Nov. 6, 1957; s. Dale O. and Delora (Neal) O'N.; m. Teresa Thompson, June 28, 1986. BBA, U. Tex., 1980; JD, South Tex. Coll., 1983. Bar: Tex. 1983, U.S. Dist. Ct. (no. dist.) Tex. 1988. Pvt. practice Ft. Worth, 1983—; adj. prof. family law U. Tex.; mem. State Bar Tex. Com. for Family Law Revisions, 1994-95. Author: Divorce: Understanding and Preparing for Trial, 1987, Security Agreements for Divorce Collateralization, 1989; asst. editor Tex. Young Lawyers Assn., mem. editl. bd., 1985-86; contbr. articles to profl. jours., convs., and seminars. Mem. Am. Acad. Matrimonial Lawyers, Tex. Young Lawyers Assn. (coun. mem. 1985-86, mem. family law com. 1989), Masons. Avocation: hunting. Office: PO Box 225 Fort Worth TX 76101-0225

O'NEAL, EDGAR CARL, psychology educator; b. St. Louis, Apr. 30, 1939; s. Clarence Edgar O'Neal and Alyce (Mullins) Redwine; m. Ellen Rose Luther, Aug. 31, 1963; children—Colleen Ruth, Patrick Blaine. B.A., Duke U., 1961; M.Div., Drew U., 1964; M.A., U. Mo., 1968, Ph.D., 1969. Ordained to ministry United Meth. Ch., 1964. Minister Community Meth. Ch., Cold Spring Harbor, N.Y., 1962-65; NIMH fellow U. Mo., Columbia, 1966-69; asst. prof., assoc. prof. psychology Tulane U., New Orleans, 1969-76, chmn. dept. psychology, 1978-84, prof. psychology, 1977—. Editor: Perspectives on Aggression, 1976; mem. editl. bd. Jour. Personality and Social Psychology, 1991—, Jour. Non-verbal Behaviour, 1991-94, Aggressive Behavior, 1995—; contbr. articles to profl. jours. Fellow APA (coun. 1982-85); mem. Sigma Xi, Sigma Chi. Democrat. Home: 7219 Oneil Dr Harahan LA 70123-4844 Office: Tulane U Dept Psychology 2007 Stern Hall New Orleans LA 70118

O'NEAL, EDWIN A., geologist, geophysicist, petroleum engineer; b. Gulfport, Miss., Jan. 5, 1929; s. Aurelius Pericles and Eula Lee (Walker) O'N.; m. Nelle Gray Fulton, Feb. 10, 1952 (dec. Dec. 25, 1994); children: David Edwin, Kerry Christian. BS in Petroleum Geology, Miss. State U., 1952; MS in Geology, Tulane U., 1973. Geophysicist Western Geophysical Co., Shreveport, La., 1954-56; asst. dist. geologist Ark. Fuel Oil Corp., Shreveport, 1956-59; mgr. exploration and prodn. Whitaker Oil Co., Carthage, Tex., 1959-64; geologist Internat. Helium Inc., Longview, Tex., 1964-66, Robbins Drilling Co., Longview, 1966-67; prof., dean engring. and indsl. tech. Delgado C.C., New Orleans, 1967-88; geologist, resource evaluation Minerals Mgmt. Svc., New Orleans, 1988-96. 1st lt. Army Artillery, 1952-54, Korea. Mem. Am. Assn. Petroleum Geologists, Soc. Petroleum Engrs. Avocations: lapidary, camping. Home: 4942 Friar Tuck Dr New Orleans LA 70128

O'NEAL, HANK, entertainment producer, business owner; b. Kilgore, Tex., June 5, 1940; s. Harold Lee and Sarah (Christian) O'N.; m. Shelley M. Shier, May 14, 1985. BA, Syracuse U., 1962. With CIA, Washington and N.Y.C., 1963-76; exec. v.p. Hammond Music Enterprises, N.Y.C., 1980-83; pres., owner Chiaroscuro Records Co./Downtown Sound recording studio, N.Y.C., 1970-80, 85—; exec. v.p. HOSS, Inc., N.Y.C., 1983—; instr., dept. head New Sch. for Social Rsch., N.Y.C., 1970-92; bd. dirs. Composer's and Choreographer's Theater, N.Y.C.; pres. SOS Prodns., Wilkes Barre, Pa., 1987—. Author: Eddie Condon Scrapbook of Jazz, 1973, A Vision Shared, 1976, Berenice Abbott-American Photographer, 1982, Djuna Barnes 1978-81, 1990, Charlie Parker/The Funky Blues Date, 1995; author/photographer: The Floating Jazz Festival, 1985, The Ghosts of Harlem, 1996; photographer: (books) Allegra Kent's Water Beauty Book, 1976, All the King's Men, 1990; producer, cover photographer/designer numerous record albums, 1967—. Capt. U.S. Army, 1963-67. Recipient various awards and prizes for books. Mem. Phi Gamma Delta. Home: Glenside Box 101 River Rd Thornhurst PA 18424 Office: Chiaroscuro Records 830 Broadway New York NY 10003-4827

O'NEAL, LESLIE CORNELIUS, professional football player; b. Pulaski County, Alaska, May 7, 1964. Student, Okla. State U. Defensive end San Diego Chargers, 1986—. Named to Sporting News Coll. All-Am. 1st Team, 1984-85; selected to Pro Bowl, 1989, 90, 92-94. Holder of NFL rookie-season record for most sacks, 1986. Office: San Diego Chargers Jack Murphy Stadium San Diego CA 92160*

O'NEAL, MICHAEL RALPH, state legislator, lawyer; b. Kansas City, Mo., Jan. 16, 1951; s. Ralph D. and Margaret E. (McEuen) O'N.; m. Tammy E. Miller, Dec. 30, 1978 (div.); children: Haley Anne, Austin Michael. BA in English, U. Kans., 1973, JD, 1976. Bar: Kans. 1976, U.S. Dist. Ct. Kans. 1976, U.S. Ct. Appeals (10th cir.) 1979. Intern Legis. Counsel State of Kans., Topeka, 1975-76; assoc. Hodge, Reynolds, Smith, Peirce & Forker, Hutchinson, Kans., 1976-77; ptnr. Reynolds, Peirce, Forker, Suter, O'Neal & Myers, Hutchinson, 1980-88, Gilliland & Hayes, P.A., Hutchinson, 1988—; mem. Kans. Ho. of Reps.; chmn. jud. com., 1984, 93—; minority whip Kans. Ho. of Reps., 1991-92, majority whip, 1995—; instr. Hutchinson C.C., 1977-88. Vice chmn. Rep. Ctrl. Com., Reno County, Kans., 1982-86; bd. dirs. Rento County Mental Health Assn., Hutchinson, 1984-89, YMCA, 1984-86, Crime Stoppers (ex-officio), Hutchinson; chmn. adv. bd. dirs. Wesley Towers Retirement Cmty., 1984-96; mem. Kans. Travel and Tourism Commn., 1990-94; bd. govs. U. Kans. Law Sch., 1991—. Recipient Leadership award Kans. C. of C. and Industry, 1985; named one of Outstanding Young Men Am., 1986. Mem. ABA, ATLA, Nat. Conf. State Legislatures (criminal justice com.), Kans. Assn. Def. Counsel, Def. Rsch. Inst., Kans. Bar Assn. (prospective legis. com., Outstanding Svc. award), Hutchinson C. of C. (ex-officio bd. dirs., Leadership award 1984), Am. Coun. Young Polit. Leaders (del. to Atlantic conf. biennial assembly), Kans. Jud. Coun., Commn. on Uniform State Laws. Avocations: basketball, tennis, golf. Home: 8 Windemere Ct Hutchinson KS 67502-2020 Office: Gilliland & Hayes PA 335 N Washington St Ste 2977 Hutchinson KS 67501-4863

O'NEAL, MICHAEL SCOTT, SR., lawyer; b. Jacksonville, Fla., Dec. 22, 1948; s. Jack Edwin and Lucille (Colvin) O'N.; m. Barbara Louise Hardie, Jan. 30, 1971 (div. Sept. 1974); 1 child, Jennifer Erin; m. Helen Margaret Joost, Mar. 18, 1985; children: Mary Helen, Angela Marie, Michael Scott O'Neal Jr. AA, Fla. Jr. Coll., 1975; BA in Econs. summa cum laude, U. No. Fla., 1977; JD cum laude, U. Fla., 1979. Bar: Fla. 1980, U.S. Dist. Ct. (mid. dist.) Fla. 1980, U.S. Dist. Ct. (no. dist.) Fla. 1981, U.S. Ct. Appeals (5th and 11th cirs.) 1981, U.S. Supreme Ct. 1986. Assoc. Howell, Liles, Braddock & Milton, Jacksonville, Fla., 1980-83; ptnr. Commander, Legler, Werber, Dawes, Sadler & Howell, Jacksonville, 1983-91, Foley & Lardner, Jacksonville, 1991-93, Howell O'Neal & Johnson, Jacksonville, 1993—; pro bono atty. Legal Aid Soc., Jacksonville, 1980—; practicing atty. Lawyers Reference, Jacksonville, 1980—; pres. N.E. Fla. Med. Malpractice Claims Coun., 1996. Pres. Julington Landing Homeowners Assn., Jacksonville, 1980-83. Served to staff sgt. USAF, 1968-74. Mem. ABA, Jacksonville Bar Assn., Fed. Bar Assn., Assn. Trial Lawyers Am., Fla. Def. Lawyers Assn., Jacksonville Assn. Def. Counsel (treas. 1996), Internat. Assn. Def. Counsel. Republican. Methodist. Clubs: University, San Jose Country (Jacksonville). Avocations: golf, music. Home: 1299 Norwich Rd Jacksonville FL 32207-7525 Office: Howell O'Neal & Johnson 200 N Laura St Ste 1100 Jacksonville FL 32202-3500

O'NEAL, RYAN (PATRICK RYAN O'NEAL), actor; b. Los Angeles, Apr. 20, 1941; s. Charles and Patricia (Callaghan) O'N.; m. Joanna Moore, Apr. 1963 (div. Feb. 1967); children: Tatum Beatrice, Griffin Patrick; m. Leigh Taylor-Young, Feb. 1967; 1 child, Patrick; 1 child (with Farrah Fawcett), Redmond James Fawcett. Grad. high sch. Appeared in several TV series in early 1960s including Dobie Gillis, Two Faces West, Perry Mason, Gen. Electric Theatre, The Virginian, This Is the Life, The Untouchables, My Three Sons, Bachelor Father, June Allyson Show, Empire, Peyton Place, 1964-69; actor: (films) The Big Bounce, 1969, The Games, 1970, Love Story, 1970 (David of Donatello award), The Wild Rovers, 1971, What's Up, Doc?, 1972, The Thief Who Came to Dinner, 1973, Paper Moon, 1973, Barry Lyndon, 1975, Nickelodeon, 1976, A Bridge Too Far, 1977, Oliver's Story, 1978, The Main Event, 1979, The Driver, 1978, So Fine, 1981, Partners, 1982, Irreconcilable Differences, 1984, Green Ice, The Fever Pitch, 1984, Tough Guys Don't Dance, 1987, Chances Are, 1989, (TV movies) Love, Hate, Love, 1971, Small Sacrifices, 1989; (TV series) Empire, 1962-63, Peyton Place, 1964-69, Good Sports, 1991. *

O'NEAL, SHAQUILLE RASHAUN, professional basketball player; b. Newark, Mar. 6, 1972; s. Philip A. Harrison and Lucille O'Neal. Student, La. State U. Center Orlando Magic, 1992-96, L.A. Lakers, 1996—. Appeared in movie Blue Chips, 1994, Kazaam, 1996. Named to Sporting News All-American first team, 1990-91; recipient Rookie of the Yr. award NBA, 1993; mem. NBA All-Star team, 1993, 94, Dream Team II, 1994; first pick overall, 1992 draft. Office: LA Lakers PO Box 10 Inglewood CA 90306*

O'NEAL, TATUM, actress; b. Nov. 5, 1963; d. Ryan and Joanna (Moore) O'N.; m. John McEnroe, Aug. 1, 1986; 3 children: Kevin, Sean, Emily. Ed., pvt. schs. and tutors. Appearences include (films) Paper Moon, 1973 (Acad. award for best supporting actress), The Bad News Bears, 1976, Nickelodeon, 1976, International Velvet, 1978, Little Darlings, 1979, Circle of Two, 1981, Certain Fury, 1985, Little Noises, 1992; (TV movies) Woman on the Run: The Lawrencia Bambenek Story, 1993.

O'NEAL, TIMOTHY D., church administrator. Dir. of computer and info. svcs. Ch. of God. Office: Church of God PO Box 2430 Cleveland TN 37320-2430

O'NEAL, VICKI LYNN, elementary education educator; b. Joplin, Mo., Feb. 20, 1950; d. Alven Rush Hall and Betty June (Cochran) Berry; m. Larry Dean O'Neal, June 17, 1977; children: Valerie Renee, Natalie Michelle. BS in Elem. Edn., Mo. So. Coll., 1972; MS in Edn., Pittsburg State U., 1979. Tchr. elem. Lincoln Elem. Sch., Baxter Springs, Kans., 1972—. Elder First Presbyn. Ch., Baxter Springs, 1989-91, 92-94. Grantee Southeast Kans. Ednl. Found., 1993-94, 94-95; named Educator of Yr. Baxter Springs C. of C., 1994. Mem. BT-PEO (corr. sec. 1994-96), Girl Scouts U.S.A. (leader/co-leader 1986-94, Green Angel 1992), Kans. Chpt. PEO Sisterhood, Beta Sigma Phi (scholarship co-chair 1993-95). Avocations: travel, walking, reading. Home: 18 Gaineswood Dr # A Baxter Springs KS 66713-2245 Office: Lincoln Elem Sch 801 Lincoln Ave Baxter Springs KS 66713-2429

O'NEIL, CHARLOTTE COOPER, environmental education administrator; b. Chgo., Sept. 21, 1949; d. Adolph H. and Charlotte Waters (Edman) Cooper; m. William Randolph O'Neil, Nov. 18, 1972; children; Sean, Megan. BA in Polit. Sci., Okla. State U., 1969; BS in Edn., U. Tenn., 1988. Cert. tchr., Tenn. Intern Senator Charles H. Percy, Washington, 1969; state treas., state hdqrs. office mgr. Jed Johnson for U.S. Senate, Okla., 1972; mem. acct. staff Pacific Architects & Engrs., Barrow, Alaska, 1973; tchr. social studies Jefferson Jr. High Sch., Oak Ridge, Tenn., 1988; edn. specialist Sci. Applications Internat. Corp., Oak Ridge, Tenn., 1988-94, mgr. environ. edn. and info. tech. sect., 1994-95, mgr. comm. edn. and pub. info. sect., 1995—; edn. and tng. strategies com. U.S. DOT/FHWA/ITS Edn., 1995—. Author: Science, Society and America's Nuclear Waste, 1992, Technical Career Opportunities in High-Level Waste Management, 1993, The Environmental History of the Tonawanda Site, 1994, FAA Community Involvement Training: Better Decisions Through Consensus, 1996; contbr. articles to profl. jours. Publicity chair, mem. steering com. Am. Mus. Sci. & Energy Tribute to Tech. Mem. ASCD, AAUW, Triangle Coalition, Tenn. Geography Alliance, Nat. Coun. for Social Studies (culture, sci. and tech. com., sci. and society com., sec.-treas. 1991—), Earthwatch, Internat. Alliance for High-Level Radioactive Waste Mgmt., Golden Key, Atomic City Aquatic Club (chair constl. rev. com. 1991—). Office: Sci Applications Internat PO Box 2502 Oak Ridge TN 37831-2502

O'NEIL, CHLOE ANN, state legislator; m. John G.A. O'Neil (dec.); children: Beth Ann Rice, John A.S. BS in Psychology, SUNY, Potsdam, 1967, MS in Edn. Tchr. Hermon-DeKalb Ctr. Sch.; tchr. SUNY, Canton, N.Y., Potsdam; elem. tchr. Parishville (N.Y.)-Hopkinton Ctrl. Sch.; mem. N.Y. State Assembly, 1993—. Past mem. St. Mary's Sch. Bd. Edn.; active St. Michael's Ch. in Parishville, N.Y. Mem. N.Y. State United Tchrs. Home: Cassidy Rd Hopkinton NY 12940 Office: NY State Assembly State Capitol Albany NY 12224*

O'NEIL, DANIEL JOSEPH, science research executive, university consultant; b. Boston, June 5, 1942; s. Daniel Joseph and Grace Veronica (Francis) O'N.; m. Elizabeth Noone, Nov. 14, 1964; children: Elizabeth Grace, Daniel Joseph, Dara Veronica. BA, Northeastern U., 1964; MS, So. Conn. State U., 1967; PhD, U. Dublin, 1972. Sr. rsch. chemist Raybestos-Manhattan Advanced Rsch. Lab., Stratford, Conn., 1964-67; unit leader Hitco Materials Sci. Ctr., Gardena, Calif., 1967-68; tech. dir. Euroglas Ltd., Middlesex, Eng., 1970-72, Kildare, Ireland, 1970-72; founding faculty mem., dir. external liaison and coop. edn., lectr. polymer sci. U. Limerick, Ireland, 1972-75; chief exec. European Rsch. Inst. Ireland, Limerick, 1981-83; sr. rsch. scientist Ga. Tech. Rsch. Inst., Atlanta, 1975-78, prin. rsch. scientist, 1978-91, dir. energy and materials sci. lab., 1988-90, group dir. office of dir., 1990-91; v.p. and dean grad. coll. U. Okla., Norman, 1991-93, prof. chemistry, 1991-93; pres., dir. Sarkeys Energy Ctr. Univ. Okla. Rsch. Corp., Norman, 1992-93; founder, mng. dir. Okla. Energy Rsch. Ctr., Atlanta, 1992-93; chmn., pres. CRADA Corp., Atlanta, 1993, pres., 1993—; bd. dirs. U. Okla. Rsch. Corp., Okla. Ctr. for Advancement of Sci. and Tech., Okla. Exptl. Program Stim. Comp. Res.; mem. adv. bd. Gov.'s Energy Coun.; mem. Okla. Higher Edn. State Regents Coun. on Rsch. and Grad. Edn., 1991-93; panelist bd. on sci. and tech. for internat. devel. NAS/NRC, Washington, 1978-79, 86-87; cons. EEC, Brussels, 1982, 87, 89, U.S. rep., 1989; mem. nat. policy rev. panel U.S. Dept. Energy, Washington, 1986; witness, cons. energy R & D com. U.S. Senate, Washington, 1986-88; reviewer small bus. innovation rsch. program U.S. Dept. Energy, Washington, 1988-90; active Israel Tech. Project Com., Atlanta Jewish Fedn., Jewish Agy for Israel, 1990-91; rep., lectr. Fedn. Arab. Sci. Rsch. Coun., Arab Bur. Edn. for Gulf States, 1987. Author, co-author of 100 reports and publs. including University Strategic Planning, 1993, High Flux Materials Treatment, 1990, USDOE Solar Thermal Tech., 1989, Energy from Biomass and Wastes XIII, 1989, Internat. Conf. Pyrolysis/Gasification, 1989, Energy Initiative and Competitive Strategies, 1991, Research Innovation and the University, 1992, University Research and Economic Development, 1992. Pres. U. Okla. Res. Corp, 1982-83, bd. dirs., 1992-93; mng. dir. Okla. Energy Res. Ctr., 1992-93; expert evaluator NBS Office Energy-Related Inventions, Gaithersburg, Md., 1978-86; adv. bd. dirs. tech. utilization USDOC Office Minority Bus. Enterprises, Washington, 1977-86; U.S. del. U.S.-Brazil energy workshop U.S. Dept. State, Washington and Brazil, 1980; active Okla. Higher Edn. State Regents Coun. on Rsch. and Grad. Edn., 1991-93; Okla. Ctr. Advancement of Sci. and Tech., 1991-94; mem. Team Ireland com. Atlanta Olympics, 1995-96; mem. White House Conf. Trade and Investment, Ireland, 1995—; mem. No. Ireland and Border Countries Trade and Investment Coun., Inc., 1995—. Fellow Am. Inst. Chemists; mem. AAAS, Com. Grad. Rsch., Oak Ridge Associated Univs., Univ. Rsch. Assn., Midwest Assn. Grad. Schs., Nat. Assn. State Univs. and Land Grant Colls., Nat. Coun. Univ. Rsch. Adminstrs., Am. Chem. Soc., Assn. Big Eight Univs., Biomass Energy Rsch. Assn. (bd. dirs. 1990—), Coun. on Rsch., Edn. and Tech., Ga. Acad. Sci. (councillor 1990-91), Ga. Inst. Chemistry (pres. 1988-90), Assn. Western U.

(bd. dirs. 1991-93), Univ. Okla. Assn., Trinity Coll. Dublin Alumni Assn., Japan-Okla. Soc., Internat. Club of Atlanta (founder), Petroleum Club of Okla., Husky Club Northeastern U., Sigma Xi. Office: CRADA Corp Atlanta HQ 2660 Goodfellows Rd Tucker GA 30084-2702

O'NEIL, JAMES PETER, financial printing company executive; b. Bloomfield, N.J., Dec. 8, 1944; s. John F. and Mary (Kane) O'N.; m. Jo Anne Elizabeth Schweitzer, Oct. 10, 1970; children: Pamela, James, Kathleen. BBA, Seton Hall U., 1966. CPA, N.J. Ptnr. J.H. Cohn and Co., N.Y.C., 1968-84; v.p. fin. Bowne and Co., Inc., N.Y.C., 1984-94, exec. v.p., COO, 1994—. Sgt. U.S. Army, 1966-68. Decorated twice Bronze Star with Valor. Office: Bowne & Co Inc 345 Hudson St New York NY 10014-4502

O'NEIL, J(AMES) PETER, elementary education educator, computer software designer; b. Rockville Center, N.Y., Apr. 2, 1946; s. Clement Lee and Frances Rita (Theis) O'N.; m. Carol Ann Sypniewski, June 8, 1968; children: Kelly Ann, Thomas Joseph. BA in Psychology, Loyola U., Chgo., 1968; M in Sci. Edn., Webster Coll., St. Louis, 1972. Cert. elem. tchr. K-8, Mo., elem. tchr. K-8, Wis., dir. instruction, Wis. Tchr., student tchr. Sacred Heart Sch., Florissant, Mo., 1968-73; tchr. sci. Waunakee (Wis.) Mid. Sch., 1973—, chmn. K-8 sci. dept., chmn. K-12 dept., 1984-92; dir. Waukakee Summer Sci. Program, 1975-91; designer sci. curriculum computer CD-ROM programs Sci. Curriculum Assistance Program and Elem. Sci. Curriculum Assistance Program, 1990—. Editor: Science Scope, 1989—; contbr. over 30 activities and articles to profl. jours. Group worker settlement houses Chgo., St. Louis; mem. Parish Coun.; dir. Waunakee Area Edn. Found. Named Master Tchr. NSF, Waunakee, 1986—; recipient Tchr. of Yr. award Waunakee, 1984, 90, 92, Kohl Found. award, 1992, Mid. Sch. Tchr. of Yr. award Wis., 1992-93. Mem. Nat. Sci. Tchrs. Assn., Wis. Soc. Sci. Tchrs., Wis. Elementary Sci. Tchrs., NEA, Wis. Ednl. Assn. Roman Catholic. Avocations: computers, sports, writing, jogging. Home: 119 Simon Crestway Waunakee WI 53597-1721 Office: Waunakee Mid Sch 1001 South St Waunakee WI 53597-1651

O'NEIL, JILL ALANE, computer analyst, computer security advisor; b. Irvington, N.J., Sept. 10, 1954; d. Roger Allen and Nancy Jean (Chapman) Remington; m. James Francis O'Neil, Jan. 17, 1954; children: Kelly Michelle, Rebecca Alane, Jessica Nicole. AAS in Computer Sci., Union County Tech. Inst., 1974, BS in Computer Sci., 1979. Programmer asst. Exxon Corp., Florham Park, N.J., 1974, programmer, 1974-76, programmer analyst, 1976-81; project leader fin. systems Exxon Rsch. and Engring., Florham Park, 1981-85; systems analyst Exxon Rsch. and Engring., Annandale, N.J., 1985-88, Unix systems adminstr., 1988—, computer security advisor, 1993—. Active Bethlehem Twp. PTA, 1986—. Mem. Computer Security Inst., Soc. Computer and Info. Protection, Cray User's Group. Avocations: needlework, crafts, gardening, reading. Office: Exxon Rsch and Engring Co RR 22 Annandale NJ 08801

O'NEIL, JOHN, artist; b. Kansas City, Mo., June 16, 1915; s. Michael and Emma (Harms) O'N. BFA, U. Okla., 1936, MFA, 1939; student, Taos Sch. Art, 1942, U. Florence, Italy, 1951. Dir. U. Okla. Sch. Art, 1951-65; chmn. dept. fine arts Rice U., Houston, 1965-70; dir. Sewall Art Gallery, 1972-77, Joseph and Joanna Nazro prof. art and art history, 1979-81; vis. lectr. NYU, U. Mich., U. Mass., l'Accademia di Belle Arti, Rome, Moana Olu Coll., Hawaii. One-man show, Mus. Art, U. Okla., Sask. (Can.) Art Centers, Seattle Art Mus., M-59 Galleries, Copenhagen, Denmark, Los Robles Galleries, Calif., La. Gallery, Houston, Philbrook Art Ctr., Tulsa, Firehouse Art Ctr., Norman, Okla.; works exhibited, Carnegie Inst., Artists West of Mississippi at Colorado Springs, Denver Art Mus., San Francisco Mus., Art Inst. of Chgo., U. Ill., Dallas Mus., Cin. Mus., Sadeer Gallery, Kuwait, Kauffman Galleries, Houston, Graham Gallery, Houston, Wierzbowski Gallery, Houston, N.Y. World's Fair, Pickard Gallery, Oklahoma City, U.S. Art Expo, San Francisco; rep. collections, Philbrook Art Center, U. Mich., Denver Art Mus., Dallas Mus., Am. Arts., Kansas City, Chgo., others. Recipient 30 painting and graphics awards. Painting fellow Huntington Hartford Found., MacDowell Colony, Montalvo Assn. Mem. Coll. Art Assn., Southwestern, Mid-Am. art confs., Delta Phi Delta. Home: 1701 Hermann Dr Apt 901 Houston TX 77004-7326

O'NEIL, JOHN JOSEPH, lawyer; b. Detroit, July 20, 1943; s. John J. and Dora J. (Collins) O'N.; children: Meghan, Kathryn. BA, Trinity Coll., 1965; LLB, U. Va., 1968. Bar: N.Y. 1969, U.S. Ct. Appeals (2d cir.) 1969, Fla. 1979, D.C. 1982. Assoc. Jackson & Nash, N.Y.C., 1968-71; assoc. Paul, Weiss, Rifkind, Wharton & Garrison, N.Y.C., 1971-77, ptnr., 1977—. Fellow Am. Coll. Trusts and Estates Counsel; mem. ABA (com. on spl. problems of aged), N.Y. State Bar Assn. (com. on taxation, trusts and estates sect.), Assn. Bar City N.Y. (com. on trusts and estates), Pi Gamma Mu. Office: Paul Weiss Rifkind Wharton & Garrison 1285 Avenue Of The Americas New York NY 10019-6028

O'NEIL, JOHN P(ATRICK), athletic footwear company executive; b. Malden, Mass., 1921; s. Jeremiah James and Elizabeth Agnes (McMahon) O'N.; m. nancy Hodgkins, Dec. 21, 1944; children: John W., Michael P., Martha E., Timothy P. B.S., Tufts U., 1943. Vice pres. prodn. Granite State div. Converse Inc., Berlin, N.H., 1946-66; v.p. mfg. Converse Rubber Co., Malden, Mass., 1966-70; v.p. ops. Converse Rubber Co., Wilmington, Mass., 1970-73, exec. v.p., 1974; pres. Converse Inc., Wilmington, 1974-87, vice chmn., 1987—; dir. Footwear Industries Am., Washington; chmn. Athletic Footwear Council, North Palm Beach, Fla., 1981-90; trustee Mass. Bank for Savs., Reading, 1982-87. Bd. overseers for athletics, Tufts Univ. 1st lt. U.S. Army, 1943-46. Named Businessman of Yr. Dr. I. Fund Found., N.Y.C., 1982. Mem. Internat. Athletic Footwear and Apparel Mfg. Assn. (pres.), Rubber and Plastics Footwear Mfg. Assn. (pres.), Internat. Athletic Footwear Assn. (pres. worldwide). Roman Catholic. Clubs: Lanam (Andover, Mass.); Meadow Brook Golf (Reading, Mass.) (bd. dirs. 1980-86), Country Club of New Seabury (Mass.), Mariner Sands Country (Stuart, Fla.); Tufts of Boston. Office: Converse Inc 1 Fordham Rd North Reading MA 01864-2619

O'NEIL, JOSEPH FRANCIS, association executive; b. Chicopee, Mass., Oct. 3, 1934; s. Joseph Francis and Mary Agnes (Sheehan) O'N.; m. Carol Marie Quindlen, June 12, 1975; 1 child, Anne Lyons. B.A., Holy Cross Coll., 1956; M.S. in Theology, St. Mary's U., Balt., 1960; M.S. in Journalism, Columbia U., 1965. Mem. editorial staff Cath. Observer, Springfield, Mass., 1961-64; asst. editor Cath. Observer, 1965-69, editor, 1969-74; editor Child Devel. Asso. Consortium, Washington, 1975-77; asst. exec. sec. Am. Council Independent Labs., Washington, 1977-80; exec. dir. Am. Council Independent Labs., 1981—. Chmn. Bus. Coalition for Fair Competition, 1983-90; sec., treas. Bus. Coalition for Fair Competition, 1990-92; chmn., cons. coun. Nat. Inst. Bldg. Scis., 1992-93; bd. dirs. Small Bus. Legis. Coun. Mem. Am. Nat. Standards Inst. (bd. dirs.), Assn. Chief Execs. Coun. Home: 1712 N Jefferson St Arlington VA 22205-2817 Office: Am Coun Ind Labs 1629 K St NW Washington DC 20006-1602

O'NEIL, KATHLEEN JOAN, home healthcare administrator; b. Chgo., June 3, 1945; d. John Howard and Evelyn M. (Peterson) Venable; m. Margaret, Andrew, Victoria. BSN, Northwestern U., 1981; MBA, Ill. Benedictine Coll., 1986. V.p. Home Care Med. Svcs., LaGrange, Ill., 1982-84; dir. transitional patient care svcs. Hinsdale (Ill.) Hosp., 1984-89; v.p. EHS Home Health Care, Oakbrook, Ill., 1989-94; pres., CEO Vineyard Nursing Assn., Oak Bluffs, Mass., 1994—; bd. dirs. St. Thomas Hospice, Hinsdale, 1987-94; mem. Congl. Subcom. on Aging, 1988; presenter in field. Leader Girl Scouts Am., Stickney, Ill., 1972-76; pres. Sch. Bd., Stickney, 1976-79; bd. mem. Am. Cancer Soc., 1983-87. Scholar in clin. excellence Northwestern U., Chgo., 1981; Fed. grantee, 1994. Mem. Nat. Assn. Home Care, Ill. Hosp. Assn. (steering com. 1993-94), Ill. Home Care Coun. (chair state legis. 1993-94), Sigma Theta Tau. Avocation: sailing. Office: Vineyard Nursing Assn Linton Ave Oak Bluffs MA 02557

O'NEIL, LEO E., bishop; b. Holyoke, Mass., Jan. 31, 1928. Ed. Mary-knoll Sem., St. Anselm's Coll., Manchester, N.H., Grand Sem., Montreal, Que., Can. Ordained Roman Cath. priest, 1955; ordained titular bishop of Bencenna and aux. bishop of Springfield (Mass.), 1980-89, co-adjutor bishop Manchester, N.H., 1989-90, bishop, diocese of Manchester, 1990—. Office: Bishop of Manchester 657 N River Rd Manchester NH 03104*

O'NEIL, MARY AGNES, health science facility administrator; b. Bridgeport, Conn., Sept. 26, 1926. Diploma in nursing, St. Vincent's Hosp., Bridgeport, 1947; BS, St. Joseph's Coll., Emmitsburg, Md., 1952; MS in Nursing Services Adminstrn., Boston Coll., 1960; LLD (hon.), Sacred Heart U., Bridgeport, 1974. Nurse St. Vincent's Hosp., 1947-48, dir. nursing, 1961-63, assoc. adminstr., 1969, adminstr., 1969-74, chmn. bd. dirs., 1969-76, coordinator constrn., in-residence chmn. bd. dirs., 1973—; 3d directress Sisters of Charity Sem., Emmitsburg, 1949-54; supr. nursing services Carney Hosp., Boston, 1954-57, dir. nursing svcs., 1957-60, adminstrv. asst. patient care svcs., 1960-61, asst. to pres., 1981-83; assoc. adminstr. St. Mary's Hosp., Troy, N.Y., 1963, adminstr., 1963-69, pres., chief exec. officer, chmn. bd. dirs., ex-officio lay adv. bd., 1976—; sr. v.p., chmn. bd. dirs. Good Samaritan Hosp., Pottsville, Pa., 1983-86, chmn. bd. dirs., v.p. corp. affairs, 1986, chmn. corp. reorgn., chmn. bd. dirs., bd. liaison, 1986—; acting bd. chair Sisters of Charity Hosp., Buffalo, N.Y., 1991-92; mem. Upper Hudson subarea council, mem. project rev. com. Health Systems Agy. of Northeastern N.Y.; mem. regional bd. Nat. Comml. Bank and Trust Co., N.Y., 1979; bishop's rep., mem. legis. com. N.Y. State Council Cath. Hosps., 1980; rep. governing bd. Iroquois Hosp. Consortium, Inc., N.Y., 1980; mem. Green Island Bridge Task Force Com., Troy, 1981; mem. Northeast Province Health Commn., 1987, Devel. Corp. Good Samaritan Hosp., Pottsville, Pa., 1989-90, chmn. bd. dirs., 1983-90; provincial health councillor Dau. of Charity Northeast Province De Paul Provincial House, Albany, N.Y., 1990-93, provincial asst., 1991-93; acting bd. chairperson Sisters of Charity Hosp., Buffalo, N.Y., 1991-92; bd. dirs. Carney Hosp., Boston, St. Vincent's Med. Ctr., Bridgeport, Conn., Sisters of Charity Hosp., Buffalo, N.Y., Dau. of Charity of St. Vincent de Paul, Northeast Province, Inc.; sec. regional corp. DCNHS-NE, bd. dirs., treas., Daus. of Charity Nat. Health System; bd. dirs. St. Mary's Hosp., Troy, N.Y., chair, 1993-94; chair Our Lady Lourdes Meml. Hosp., Binghamton, N.Y, 1993-94; chair Seton Health Sys., Inc., Troy, N.Y., 1994—. V.p. Greater Bridgeport C. of C., 1975; mem. mayor's human rights commn. City of Troy, 1976; bd. dirs. Northeastern/Southeastern Shared Services of Daus. of Charity, 1977, treas. Eastern Coop. Services, 1980, chmn. investment com., 1981, mem. health adv. commn. N.E. Province, 1986; v.p. govtl. relations City of Troy, 1978; hon. chmn. Upper Hudson area chpt. Am. Diabetes Assn., Inc., 1978-79; bd. dirs. Blue Cross of Northeastern N.Y., 1977; bd. dirs. Lourdes Hosp., Binghamton, N.Y., 1985, chmn. evaluation com., 1987; mem. adv. bd. Jr. League, Troy, 1979; mem. St. Mary's Hosp. Found. Bd., 1981; provincial asst. Daus. of Charity, Buffalo, 1991. Recipient Cmty. Svcs. award City of Troy, 1968, Leadership and Svc. cert. Conn. Hosp. Assn., 1973, Cmty. Svc. and Accomplishment award Sta. WICC-FM, 1975, Cmty. Svc. award Sta. WNAB-FM, 1975, Key to City of Bridgeport, 1975, Caritase award Seton Health Sys. Found., 1995; named one of Outstanding Women of State of Conn., Gov. Ella Grasso, 1976; Sister Mary Agnes Day proclaimed by City of Bridgeport, 1976, by City of Troy, 1981. Fellow Am. Coll. Hosp. Adminstrs.; mem. Hosp. Assn. Northeastern N.Y. (mem. program com. 1978, chmn. bylaws com. 1979). Democrat. Avocations: music, walking, swimming. Home: Sacred Heart Sisters' Residence 76 Adams Ave Cohoes NY 12047-3502 Office: Seton Health Sys 1300 Massachusetts Ave Troy NY 12180-1628

O'NEIL, MICHAEL JOSEPH, opinion survey executive, marketing consultant; b. Springfield, Mass., June 22, 1951; s. James Francis and Mary Helen (Apolis) O'N.; m. Catherine Mary Zirkel, Sept. 10, 1983; children: Heather Rose, Sean Michael, Ryan Joseph. BA, Brown U., 1974, MA, 1975; PhD, Northwestern U., 1977. Mem. faculty U. Ill., Chgo., 1977; mem. faculty U. Mich., Ann Arbor, 1977-79, postdoctoral fellow Survey Rsch. Ctr., Inst. Social Rsch., 1977-79; dir. Pub. Opinion Rsch. Ctr. Ariz. State U., Tempe, 1979-81; pres. O'Neil Assocs., Tempe, 1981—; reviewer grant proposals NSF, Washington, 1977—; mem. mktg. com. Phoenix Art Mus., 1992—; mem. bd. dirs. Phoenix Children's Hosp. Found., 1993—. Manuscript reviewer Social Problems, 1977—, Pub. Opinion Quar., 1977—, Urban Affairs Quar., 1977—, Jour. Ofcl. Statistics, 1990—, Sociological Methods and Rsch., 1993; contbr. articles to profl. jours. Chmn. Tempe Union High Sch. Dist. Bus. Edn. adv. com., 1986-88; mem. mktg. com. Mesa Assn. Retarded Citizens, 1985-87; bd. dirs. East Valley Camelback Hosp., Mesa, 1985-90, v.p., 1988-90; active Valley Leadership, Class X, Ariz. Acad., Maricopa County Citizens' Jud. Adv. Coun.; mem. Phoenix Pride Commn., 1991-94. Mem. Am. Mktg. Assn., Am. Assn. Pub. Opinion Rsch., Alumni Assn. Brown U. (bd. dirs. 1985-90), Brown U. Club of Phoenix (pres. 1984—), Phoenix City Club (bd. dirs. 1987-93, pres. 1990-91), East Valley Partnership (mem. bd. dirs. 1993—), Phi Beta Kappa. Democrat. Avocation: tennis. Home: 418 E Erie Dr Tempe AZ 85282-3711 Office: O'Neil Assocs 412 E Southern Ave Tempe AZ 85282-5212

O'NEIL, ROBERT MARCHANT, university administrator, law educator; b. Boston, Oct. 16, 1934; s. Walter George and Isabel Sophia (Marchant) O'N.; m. Karen Elizabeth Elson, June 18, 1967; children—Elizabeth, Peter, David, Benjamin. A.B., Harvard U., 1956, A.M., 1957, LL.B., 1961; LL.D., Beloit Coll., 1985, Ind. U., 1987. Bar: Mass. 1962. Law clk. to justice U.S. Supreme Ct., 1962-63; acting assoc. prof. law U. Calif.-Berkeley, 1963-66, prof., 1966-67, 1969-72; exec. asst. to pres., prof. law SUNY-Buffalo, 1967-69; provost, prof. law U. Cin., 1972-73, exec. v.p., prof. law, 1973-75; v.p., prof. law Ind. U., Bloomington, 1975-80; pres. U. Wis. System, 1980-85; prof. law U. Wis.-Madison, 1980-85; prof. law U. Va., Charlottesville, 1985—, pres., 1985-90; gen. counsel. AAUP, 1970-72, 91-92. Author: Civil Liberties: Case Studies and the Law, 1965, Free Speech: Responsible Communication Under Law, 2d edit., 1972, The Price of Dependency: Civil Liberties in the Welfare State, 1970, No Heroes, No Villians, 1972, The Courts, Government and Higher Education, 1972, Discriminating Against Discrimination, 1976, Handbook of the Law of Public Employment, 1978, 2d rev. edit., 1993, Classrooms in the Crossfire, 1981; co-author: A Guide to Debate, 1964, The Judiciary and vietnam, 1972, Civil Liberties Today, 1974. Trustee Tchrs. Ins. and Annuity Assn.; bd. dirs. Commonwealth Fund, James River Corp., Sta. WVPT Pub. TV. Home: 1839 Westview Rd Charlottesville VA 22903-1632 Office: Thomas Jefferson Ctr 400 Peter Jefferson Pl Charlottesville VA 22911-8691

O'NEIL, THOMAS MICHAEL, physicist, educator; b. Hibbing, Minn., Sept. 2, 1940; married; 1 child. BS, Calif. State U., Long Beach, 1962; MS, U. Calif., San Diego, 1964, PhD in Physics, 1965. Rsch. physicist Gen. Atomic, 1965-67; prof. physics U. Calif., San Diego, 1967—; mem. adv. bd. Inst. Fusion Studies, 1980-83, Inst. Theoretical Physics, 1983-86. Assoc. editor Physics Review Letters, 1979-83; correspondent Comments Plasma Physics & Controlled Fusion, 1980-84. Alfred P. Sloan fellow, 1971; recipient Alumni Disting. Tchg. award UCSD, 1996. Fellow Am. Phys. Soc. (Plasma Physics Rsch. award 1991). Achievements include research in theoretical plasma physics with emphasis on nonlinear effects in plasmas and on non-neutral plasmas. Office: Univ of California Dept of Physics 9500 Gilman Dr La Jolla CA 92093-5003

O'NEIL, WAYNE, linguist, educator; b. Kenosha, Wis., Dec. 22, 1931; s. L.J. and Kathryn (Obermeyer) O'N.; married; children: Scott Leslie, Patrick Sean, Elizabeth Erla. AB, U. Wis., 1955, AM, 1956, PhD, 1960; AM (hon.), Harvard U., 1965. Asst. prof. linguistics and lit. U. Oreg., 1961-65; prof. linguistics and edn. Harvard U., 1965-68, lectr. edn., 1968-72, vis. prof. edn., 1978-86; prof. linguistics and humanities MIT, 1968—, chmn. lit. faculty, 1969-75, chmn. linguistics program, 1986—, head dept. linguistics and philosophy, 1989—; lectr. bilingualism Wheelock Coll., Boston, 1991—; lectr. Beijing Normal U., 1980, Beijing and Shanghai Fgn. Lang. Insts., 1981; lectr. linguistics Shandong (China) U., 1982-83, prof., 1984—; prof. Summer Inst. on Lang. Change, NEH, 1978; vis. prof. Tsuda Coll., Tokyo, 1983. Mem. editorial group Radical Teacher, 1975—; author: (in Chinese) English Transformational Grammar, 1981, Linguistics and Applied Linguistics, 1983, (with S.J. Keyser) Rule Generalization and Optionality in Language Change, 1985, (with S. Flynn) Linguistic Theory in Second Language Acquisition, 1988; contbr. articles to profl. jours. Mem. steering com. Resist, 1967—, Peoples Coalition for Peace and Justice, 1970-72; co-founder, mem. Linguistics for Nicaragua, 1985—. With U.S. Army, 1952-54. Fulbright fellow in Iceland, 1961; Am. Council Learned Socs. study fellow M.I.T., 1964-65. Mem. AAAS, Linguistic Soc. Am., Nat. Coun. Tchrs. English, Native Am. Langs. Inst., Soc. Pidgin and Creole Linguistics. Office: MIT Dept Linguistics and Philosophy Cambridge MA 02139

O'NEIL, WILLIAM FRANCIS, academic administrator; b. Worcester, Mass., Mar. 26, 1936; s. John J. and Mary A. (Trahant) O'N.; m. Mary Elizabeth Dillon, Aug. 22, 1959; children: Kathleen, Mary Elizabeth. BS, Boston U., 1960; MEd, Worcester State Coll., 1963; diploma, U. Conn., 1970; EdD, Wayne State U., 1972. Tchr. Worcester Pub. Schs., 1960-68, community sch. dir., 1968-73; assoc. prof., dir. community edn. devel. ctr. Worcester State Coll., 1973-75, dir. community svc., 1975-77, dean grad. and continuing edn., 1977-83, exec. v.p., 1983-85; exec. v.p. Mass. Coll. Art, Boston, 1985-86, acting pres., 1986-87, pres., 1987—. Contbr. articles to profl. jours. Mem. Worcester Dem. City Com., Ward I Dem. Com., 1980—; pres., trustee Worcester Pub. Libr., 1977-82; mem. Mass. Bd. Libr. Commrs., 1984-89. Recipient citation Mass. Ho. of Reps., 1977, key City of Worcester, 1982; Mott fellow Charles Stewart Mott Found., 1971. Mem. Mass. Pub. Colls. and Univs. Pres. and Chancellors Assn. (chair 1991-92), Assn. Ind. Colls. Art and Design (bd. dirs.), Mass. Cmty. Edn. Assn. (life; bd. dirs. 1972-77), Mass. State Colls. Pres. Assn. (chair 1992-93), Profl. Arts Consortium (v.p. Boston, pres. 1993-94), Emerald Club. Roman Catholic. Office: Mass Coll Art Office Pres 621 Huntington Ave Boston MA 02115-5801

O'NEIL BIDWELL, KATHARINE THOMAS, fine arts association executive, performing arts executive; b. Dayton, Ohio, Mar. 23, 1937; d. Charles Allen and Margaret Stoddard (Talbott) Thomas; children: Margaret, Stephen, Thomas; m. J. Truman Bidwell. B.A., Sarah Lawrence Coll., Bronxville, N.Y., 1959. Mng. dir. Met. Opera Assn., 1977-86, v.p., 1979-86; first v.p. Met. Opera Guild, N.Y.C., 1978-79, pres., chief exec. officer, 1979-86; dir. spl. projects Lincoln Ctr., N.Y.C., 1986—; dir. Norlin Corp. Bd. dirs. Lincoln Ctr. for Performing Arts, N.Y.C., Assn. of Mentally Ill Children, 1975-76, Valerie Bettis Sch. of Theater/Dance, 1976-79, Salisbury Sch., Conn., 1982-84; trustee Sarah Lawrence Coll., 1977-86; Westminster Choir Coll., 1986-91, Greenwall Found., 1986, Vol. Cons. Group, 1986. Mem. Assn. Sarah Lawrence Coll. (pres. 1975-77). Republican. Episcopalian. Home: 455 E 57th St New York NY 10022-3065 Office: Lincoln Center 70 Lincoln Center Plz New York NY 10023-6548*

O'NEILL, ALBERT CLARENCE, JR., lawyer; b. Gainesville, Fla., Nov. 25, 1939; s. Albert Clarence and Sue Virginia (Henry) O'N.; m. Vanda Marie Nigels, Apr. 26, 1969; 1 child, Heather Marie. B.A. with high honors, U. Fla., 1962; LL.B. magna cum laude, Harvard U., 1965. Bar: Fla. bar 1965. Law clk. to judge U.S. Dist. Ct. (mid. dist.) Fla., Jacksonville, 1965-66; assoc. Fowler, White, Collins, Gillen, Humkey & Trenam, Tampa, Fla., 1966-69; ptnr. Trenam, Simmons, Kemker, Scharf & Barkin, Tampa, 1970-77; mem. firm Trenam, Kemker, Scharf, Barkin, Frye, O'Neill & Mullis (P.A.), Tampa, 1977—, also bd. dirs.; vis. lectr. law Stetson Law Sch., 1970-73. Exec. editor: Harvard Law Rev, 1964-65; contbr. articles to profl. jours. Bd. dirs. Fla. Gulf Coast Symphony, Inc., 1975-86, U. Fla. Found., Inc., 1976-84, Fla. Orch., 1988-95. Mem. ABA (chmn. tax sect. 1992-93), Am. Law Inst., Am. Coll. Tax Counsel, Am. Bar Retirement Assn., Fla. Bar (chmn. tax sect. 1975-76), Phi Beta Kappa. Office: Trenam Kemker Scharf Barkin Frye O'Neill & Mullis 2800 Barnett Plz Tampa FL 33602

O'NEILL, ALICE JANE, lawyer; b. Houston, May 14, 1951; d. Edward John Sr. and Martha Elisabeth (Alford) O'N. BA in Polit. Sci., U. St. Thomas, Houston, 1972, MBA, 1982; MEd in Ednl. Psychology, Tex. A&M U., 1974; JD, South Tex. Coll. Law, 1992. Bar: Tex. 1993, U.S. Dist. Ct. (so. dist.) Tex. 1993, U.S. Dist. Ct. Ariz. 1994. Therapist, supr. Family Svc. Ctr., Houston, 1978-81; personnel coord. Guest Quarters Hotel, Houston, 1981-84; therapist in pvt. practice Houston, 1984-90; law clk. Abraham Watkins Nichols Ballard & Friend, Houston, 1991-93; contract atty. Nelson & Zeidman, Houston, 1994, O'Quinn Kerensky McAninich & Laminanck, Houston, 1994; assoc. Rosen & Newey, Houston, 1994—; mem. adv. bd. Juvenile Justice, Houston, Harris County Detention Ctr., Houston, 1986-93. Mem. ABA, Houston Bar Assn., Assn. for Women Attys., Houston Young Lawyers Assn. Republican. Methodist. Avocations: tennis, dogs, reading, travel. Home: 403 Euclid St Houston TX 77009-7222 Office: Rosen & Newey 440 Louisiana St Ste 1800 Houston TX 77002-1636

O'NEILL, BEVERLY LEWIS, mayor, former college president; b. Long Beach, Calif., Sept. 8, 1930; d. Clarence John and Flossie Rachel (Nicholson) Lewis; m. William F. O'Neill, Dec. 21, 1952. AA, Long Beach City Coll., 1950; BA, Calif. State U., Long Beach, 1952, MA, 1956; EdD, U. So. Calif., 1977. Elem. tchr. Long Beach Unified Sch. Dist., 1952-57; instr., counsellor Compton (Calif.) Coll., 1957-60; curriculum supr. Little Lake Sch. Dist., Santa Fe Springs, Calif., 1960-62; women's advisor, campus dean Long Beach City Coll., 1962-71, dir. Continuing Edn. Ctr. for Women, 1969-75, dean student affairs, 1971-77, v.p. student svcs., 1977-88, supt.-pres., 1988—, exec. dir. Found., 1983—; mayor City of Long Beach, Calif. Advisor Jr. League, Long Beach, 1976—, Nat. Coun. on Alcoholism, Long Beach, 1979—, Assistance League, Long Beach, 1982—; bd. dirs. NCCJ, Long Beach, 1976—, Meml. Hosp. Found., Long Beach, 1984-92, Met. YMCA, Long Beach, 1986-92, United Way, Long Beach, 1986-92. Named Woman of Yr., Long Beach Human Rels. Commn., 1976, to Hall of Fame, Long Beach City Coll., 1977, Disting. Alumni of Yr., Calif. State U., Long Beach, 1985, Long Beach Woman of Yr. Rick Rackers, 1987, Assistance League Aux., 1987; recipient Hannah Solomon award Nat. Coun. Jewish Women, 1984, Outstanding Colleague award Long Beach City Coll., 1985, NCCJ Humanitarian award, 1991, Woman of Excellence award YWCA, 1990, Community Svc. award Community Svcs. Devel. Corp., 1991, Citizen of Yr. award Exch. Club, 1992, Pacific Regional CEO award Assn. Community Coll. Trustees, 1992. Mem. Assn. Calif. Community Coll. Adminstrs. (pres. 1988-90, Harry Buttimer award 1991), Calif. Community Colls. Chief Exec. Officers Assn., Rotary, Soroptomists (Women Helping Women award 1981, Hall of Fame award 1984). Democrat. Office: Office of the Mayor 333 W Ocean Blvd Long Beach CA 90802

O'NEILL, BRIAN, research organization administrator; b. Bristol, Eng., Sept. 20, 1940; s. Raymond and Phyllis Mary (Marshall) O'N.; m. Alayne O'Neill, Aug. 31, 1969 (div. Sept. 1987); children: Allison Sarah, Stuart Douglas, Leslie Alexandra; m. Karen O'Neill, Feb. 20, 1988. BSc in Math. and Stats., Bath. U. Tech., 1965. Cons. in stats. and ops. research Unilever Ltd., London, 1965-66; research assoc. Tech. Ops. Inc., Ft. Belvoir, Va., 1966-67; mgr. applied math. dept. Wolf Research & Devel. Corp., Riverdale, Md., 1967-69; v.p., sr. v.p., exec. v.p. Ins. Inst. for Hwy. Safety, Washington, 1969-85, pres., 1985—; v.p., sr. v.p., exec. v.p. Hwy. Loss Data Inst., Washington, 1969-85, pres., 1985—; witness at numerous fed. and state hearings on hwy. safety and transp. Contbr. numerous articles to profl. jours.; also presentations at profl. confs. Mem. Am. Pub. Health Internat. Com. on Alcohol Drugs and Traffic Safety, Royal Statis. Soc., Soc. Automotive Engrs. Office: Ins Inst for Hwy Safety 1005 N Glebe Rd Ste 800 Arlington VA 22201-4751

O'NEILL, BRIAN BORU, lawyer; b. Hancock, Mich., June 7, 1947; s. Brian Boru and Jean Anette (Rimpela) O'N.; m. Ruth Bohan Sept. 18, 1991; children: Brian Boru, Maggie Byrne, Phelan Boru, Ariel Margaret. B.S., U.S. Mil. Acad., 1969; J.D. magna cum laude U. Mich., 1974. Bar: Mich. 1974, U.S. Ct. Mil. Appeals 1975, U.S. Ct. Appeals (6th cir.) 1975, Minn. 1977, U.S. Dist. Ct. Minn. 1977, U.S. Ct. Appeals (8th cir.) 1977. U.S. Ct. Claims, 1981, U.S. Supreme Ct. 1981, U.S. Ct. Appeals (fed. cir.) 1983, U.S. Ct. Appeals (7th cir.) 1985, U.S. Ct. Appeals (10th cir.) 1986, U.S. Ct. Appeals (9th cir.) 1990. Asst. to gen. counsel Dept. Army, Washington, 1974-77; assoc., ptnr. Faegre & Benson, Mpls., 1977—; mem. com. vis. Mich. Law Sch., 1994—; counsel Defenders of Wildlife, Washington, 1977—, also bd. dirs; counsel Sierra Club, Audubon Soc. Mng. editor Mich. Law Rev., 1973-74; contbr. articles to law jours. Served to capt. U.S. Army, 1969-77. Named Environmentalist of Yr., Sierra Club North Star, 1982; recipient William Douglas award Sierra Club, 1985, Trial Lawyer of the Yr. award Trial Lawyers for Public Justice, 1995. Fellow Am. Coll. Trial Lawyers; mem. Order Coif. Clubs: Mpls. Golf, Mpls. Athletic. Office: Faegre & Benson 2200 Norwest Tower 90 S 7th St Minneapolis MN 55402-3903

O'NEILL, BRIAN DENNIS, lawyer; b. Phila., Feb. 21, 1946; s. Harry William and Margaret Elizabeth (Miller) O'N.; m. Bonnie Anne Ryan, Aug. 17, 1968; children: Aimee Kathleen, Catherine Margaret. BA, Fla. State U., 1968, JD, 1971. Bar: Fla. 1971, D.C. 1975, U.S. Ct. Appeals (D.C. cir.) 1978, U.S. Ct. Appeals (5th and 11th cirs.) 1981, U.S. Ct. Appeals (10th cir.) 1985. Trial atty. Fed. Power Commn., Washington, 1972-75; assoc. Farmer, Shibley, McGuinn & Flood, Washington, 1975-80; ptnr. LeBoeuf, Lamb, Greene & MacRae, Washington, 1980—; lectr. in field. Editorial bd. Energy Law Jour., Washington, 1983-84; contbr. articles to profl. jours. Bd. dirs. Immaculata Coll., Rockville, Md., 1989-91; bd. advisors Acad. of the Holy

Cross, Kensington, Md., 1994—; bd. visitors Fla. State U. Coll. of Law, 1994—. 2d lt. USAF, 1971-72. Mem. Fla. Bar Assn. (pub. utilities com. 1985-90), Fed. Energy Bar Assn. (chmn. coms. 1983-84), Montgomery Village Golf Club (Gaithersburg, Md.) (bd. dirs. 1984-88), Congl. Country Club (Bethesda, Md.), Phi Alpha Delta. Democrat. Roman Catholic. Office: LeBoeuf Lamb Green & MacRae 1875 Connecticut Ave NW Washington DC 20009-5728

O'NEILL, BRIAN FRANCIS, professional hockey executive; b. Montreal, Que., Can., Jan. 29, 1929; s. Stafford John and Jean (Ferry) O'N.; m. Jean Yates, Aug. 20, 1955; children: Sean, Darcy, Nancy, Patrick, Sandra. B.A., Loyola Coll., Montreal, 1949; B.Com., McGill U., Montreal, 1951. Publisher Wallace Pub. Co., Montreal, 1953-62; bus. mgr. Fin. Times Can., Montreal, 1961-66; with Nat. Hockey League, Montreal, 1966—; now exec. v.p. Nat. Hockey League. Bd. dirs., past pres. St. Mary's Hosp., Montreal; bd. dirs. St. Mary's Hosp. Found., Loyola Coll. Found., Que. Student Intra Exchange Program; pres. Loyola High Sch. Found. Mem. Montreal Amateur Athletic Assn. Roman Catholic. *

O'NEILL, CATHERINE R., emergency nurse, nurse manager; b. Lexington, Va., Oct. 11, 1946; d. Donald Franklin Sr. and Virginia Hazel (Birch) Ruth; m. John Joseph O'Neill Jr., Aug. 16, 1969; children: John Joseph III, Catherine Ann. Diploma, Church Home and Hosp., Balt., 1968; BS in Bus. Adminstrn., U. Balt., 1993. Cert. emergency nurse, trauma nurse core course, pediatric advanced life support, emergency nurse pediatric course, ACLS, EMT, haz-mat. Staff nurse Church Home and Hosp., 1968-70; intravenous therapy staff nurse Franklin Sq. Hosp., 1970-71; charge nurse in emergency rm. Mercy Med. Ctr., 1972-90; nurse mgr. emergency dept. Homewood Hosp. Ctr., 1990-91, North Arundel Hosp., 1991—. Co-author: White Paper on Over Crowding in ERs, ENA Legislative Manual. Mem. Am. Trauma Soc., Orgn. Nurse Execs., Emergency Nurses Assn. Home: 2402 Charlton Ct Monkton MD 21111-1914

O'NEILL, CHARLES KELLY, marketing executive, former advertising agency executive; b. Springfield, Mo., Apr. 2, 1933; s. Charles Chester and Frances (Kelly) O'N.; m. Kyoko Hirano, June 2, 1981. B.J., U. Mo., 1955. With Galvin-Farris-Alvine, Kansas City, Mo., 1957-58; copy chief Galvin-Farris-Alvine, 1958; with Potts-Woodbury, Inc., Kansas City, 1958-61; chief time buyer Potts-Woodbury, Inc., 1960-61; with Gardner Advt. Co., St. Louis, 1962-88; assoc. media dir. Gardner Advt. Co., 1964-65, media dir., 1965-69, v.p., 1966-76, corp. media dir., dir. co., 1969-88, sr. v.p., 1976-78, pres., 1978-88; gen. mgr. Advanswers div., 1971-72; pres. Advanswers Media/Programming, Inc., 1973-78, chmn., 1978-88; v.p. Wells, Rich, Greene, N.Y.C., 1974-88; exec. v.p. Wells, Rich, Greene, 1979-88, dir., 1978-88; vice chmn. WRG-USA, 1981-88; chmn. O'Neill Mktg., Honolulu, 1988—; exec. v.p. Kyoko O'Neill, Inc., 1993—; dir. Colony Surf Ltd., Honolulu, 1990-94, chmn., bd. dirs., 1994. Bd. dirs. Waialae Iki Ridge Cmty. Assn., Honolulu, 1991—, 1st v.p., 1993-94. Lt. (j.g.) USN, 1955-57. Mem. St. Louis Advt. Club (gov. 1981-83), Outrigger Canoe Club (Honolulu), N.Y. Athletic Club, St. Louis Club, St. Louis Racquet Club, The Bridge (Navy League of the U.S.-Honolulu), Labrador Retriever Club of Hawaii, Sigma Chi, Alpha Delta Sigma. Episcopalian. Home: 1594 Hoaaina St Honolulu HI 96821-1345

O'NEILL, DANIEL JOSEPH, lawyer; b. N.Y.C., Apr. 15, 1937; s. Daniel and Catherine (Early) O'N.; m. June Marie Kelly, July 9, 1960; children—Daniel J., Kerry Marie, Elizabeth Ann, William, Brian, Peter. A.B., Coll. of the Holy Cross, Worcester, Mass., 1959; J.D., Fordham U. Sch. Law, 1962. Bar: N.Y. 1962. Asst. staff judge advocate 52d Fighter Wing, USAF, Westhampton Beach, NY, 1963-65; assoc. Chadbourne, Parke, Whiteside & Wolff, N.Y.C., 1965-72; ptnr. Chadbourne & Parke LLP, N.Y.C., 1972—. Served to capt. USAF, 1963-65. Mem. ABA. Democrat. Roman Catholic. Avocations: fishing; golf. Home: 118 Hilton Ave Garden City NY 11530-3000 Office: Chadbourne & Parke LLP 30 Rockefeller Plz New York NY 10112

O'NEILL, DONALD EDMUND, health science executive; b. Port Angeles, Wash., Feb. 10, 1926; s. Edward I. and Christine (Williamson) O'N.; m. Violet Elizabeth Oman, June 12, 1948; children: Shelly O'Neill Lane, Erin O'Neill Kennedy, Shawn O'Neill Hoffman. B.S., U. Wash., 1949. With G.D. Searle & Co., 1950-71, regional sales dir., 1962-64, dir. med. service, 1964-68, dir. mktg., 1968-71; with Warner-Lambert Co., 1971—, v.p., 1974-77, exec. v.p. pharm. group, 1977, exec. v.p.; chmn. Internat. profl. group, 1974-76; pres. Parke-Davis & Co., 1976-78; pres., exec. dir. Warner-Lambert/Parke Davis Research Div., 1978, pres. Health Care Group, 1978-81; pres. Parke-Davis Group, 1981, Health Techs. Group, 1982-86, Internat. Ops., 1986-89; exec. v.p., chmn. internat. ops. Warner-Lambert Co, 1989-91; ret., 1991; bd. dirs. Fujisawa U.S.A., N.J. Resources, Alliance Pharm. Immunogen Co., Fuisz Techs., Cytogen, M.D.L. Info. Sys., Targeted Genetics. Served with USAF, 1944-46. Mem. John's Island and Bent Pine Golf Clubs, Morris County Golf Club, Elk River Country Club.

O'NEILL, EDWARD, actor; b. Youngstown, Ohio, Apr. 12, 1946; s. Edward Phillip and Ruth Ann (Quinlan) O'N.; m. Cathy Rusoff, Feb., 1986. Student, Ohio State U., Youngstown State U. Appearances include (theatre) Knockout (Broadway debut), 1979, Androcles and the Lion, 1986, Lakeboat, 1983, Elm Circle, 1984, Of Mice and Men, 1984; (films) Cruising, 1980, Dogs of War, 1981, Disorganized Crime, 1989, K-9, 1989, Sibling Rivalry, 1990, The Adventures of Ford Fairlane, 1990, Dutch, 1991, Wayne's World, 1992, Blue Chips, 1993, Little Giants, 1994; (TV episodes) Miami Vice, Spencer for Hire; (TV series) Married...with Children, 1987—; (TV movies) The Day the Women Got Even, 1980, Farrell for the People, 1982, When your Lover Leaves, 1983, Popeye Doyle, 1986, A Winner never Quits, 1986, Right to Die, 1987, The Wherabouts of Jenny, 1991. Avocations: handball, history, literature. Office: ICM 8942 Wilshire Blvd Beverly Hills CA 90211*

O'NEILL, ELIZABETH STERLING, trade association administrator; b. N.Y.C., May 30, 1938; d. Theodore and Pauline (Green) Sterling: m. W.B. Smith, June 18, 1968 (div. Aug., 1978); 1 child, Elizabeth S. Kroese; m. Francis James O'Neill, May 19, 1984. BA, Cornell U., 1958; postgrad. studies, Northwestern U., 1959-60. Social sec. Perle Mesta Ambassador Luxembourg, N.Y.C.; spl. asst. Vivian Beaumont Allen, philanthropist, N.Y.C.; rep. Prentice-Hall Pub. Co., Eastern Europe; exec. dir. New Canaan (Conn.) C. of C., 1986—; speaker various orgns. including Lions Club, Exchange Club, Kiwanis, Rotary, Poinsettia Club; apptd. Commn. Small Bus. State of Conn., 1996. Pres. Newcomers, New Canaan, Conn.; pub. rels. rep. Girl Scouts of U.S., Fairfield County; bd. dirs. Young Women's Rep. Club; mem. Gov. Weicker's Com. for Curriculum Reform; mem. community bd. Waveny Care Ctr., New Canaan; apptd. mem. Gov. John Roland's Commn. on Small Bus., Conn., 1996—. Recipient Service awards New Canaan YMCA, N.Y. ASPCA, certs. of appreciation New Canaan Lions Club, President Bush. Mem. AAUW (bd. dirs. New Canaan chpt.), Kiwanis. Christian Scientist. Avocations: tennis, horses, travel. Home: Indian Waters Dr New Canaan CT 06840 Office: New Canaan C of C 111 Elm St New Canaan CT 06840-5419

O'NEILL, EUGENE FRANCIS, communications engineer; b. N.Y.C., July 2, 1918; s. John J. and Agnes (Willmeyer) O'N.; m. Kathryn M. Walls, Oct. 24, 1942; children—Kathryn Anne, Kevin, Jane A., Andrew Thomas. B.S. in Elec. Engring, Columbia U., 1940, M.S., 1941; D.Sc. (hon.), Bates Coll.; D.Engring. (hon.), Politecnico di Milano; D.Sc. (hon.), St. John's U., N.Y.C. With Bell Telephone Labs., Holmdel, N.J., until 1983, engaged in radar devel., 1941-45, coaxial and submarine cable and microwave radio relay, 1945-56, headed devel. of speech interpolation terminals which doubled capacity submarine telephone cables, 1956-60, dir. Telstar satellite projects, 1960-66, exec. dir. network projects, 1966-83. Pulitzer prize; scholar Columbia, 1936-40. Fellow IEEE; mem. Nat. Acad. Engring., Sigma Xi, Tau Beta Pi. Home: 17 Dellwood Ct Middletown NJ 07748-3010

O'NEILL, EUGENE MILTON, mergers and acquisitions consultant; b. Richmond, Calif., Nov. 4, 1925; s. John Milton and Vivian Elda (Vogel) O'N.; m. Jane Prigmore; children: Karen, Kay, Mary. B.S. in Bus. and Pub. Adminstrn., Washington U., St. Louis, 1949. CPA, Mo. Acct., Jeff K. Stone & Co., St. Louis, 1948-52; controller Campbell Holton & Co. (div. Gen. Grocer Co.), Bloomington, Ill., 1953-54; pres. Campbell Holton & Co. (div. Gen. Grocer Co.), 1955-57; v.p. Gen. Grocer Co., St. Louis, 1957-60, pres., 1960-74, chmn. bd., pres., 1974-83. Sec., trustee Food Industry Crusade Against Hunger. With Army Air Corp., 1943-45. Mem. Nat. Wholesale Am. Grocers Assn. (past chmn.). Home: 8 Deacon Dr Saint Louis MO 63131-4803

O'NEILL, FRANCIS XAVIER, III, marketing executive; b. Hampton, Va., June 25, 1953; s. Francis Xavier Jr. and Elizabeth Theresa (Javorsky) O'N. Student, U. Md., 1974; BA in History cum laude, So. Conn. State U., 1980. Clk. FBI, Washington, N.Y.C., 1975-78; rsch. analyst McGavren Guild Radio, N.Y.C., 1981; rsch. mgr. McGavren Guild Radio, 1982, rsch. dir., 1982-84; v.p. mktg. rsch. div. Interep, 1984-90; mgr. mktg. devel. The Arbitron Co., N.Y.C., 1990-93, cons. mktg. comm. and joint ventures, 1994-95; dir. sports rsch. CBS TV Network, 1995—. Author (booklets) Radio's Got Rhythm, 1984, Flying to Succeed: Frequent Business Air Travelers, 1988, The Vital Link: Adults 35-54 in American Society, 1988, On The Air: American Team Sports and the Media, 1989, Seasonal Listening Trends, 1991, Frequent Moviegoers, 1994, Reaching The Non-Prescription Drug Consumer, 1994. Campaigner Francis O'Neill Jr. for State Rep., Conn., 1980-92. Avocations: writing, music, biking, tennis. Home: 47 Valley Shore Dr Guilford CT 06437-2151 Office: 51 West 52nd St New York NY 10019

O'NEILL, FRANK, airport executive. Exec. v.p., gen. mgr. Vancouver (B.C., Can.) Internat. Airport. Office: Vancouver Internat Airpt Authrty, Airport Postal Outlet, PO Box 23750, Richmond, BC Canada V7B 1Y7*

O'NEILL, HARRY WILLIAM, survey research company executive; b. Atlantic City, Jan. 30, 1929; s. Harry William and Marian Elizabeth (Kuhl) O'N.; m. Carmel Gullo, Sept. 21, 1952; children: Sharon Ruth, Randal Bruce. B.A., Colgate U., 1950; M.S., Pa. State U., 1951. Lic. practicing psychologist, N.J. Research analyst Prudential Ins. Co., Newark, 1957-62; with Opinion Research Corp., Princeton, N.J., 1962-87; sr. v.p. Opinion Research Corp., 1970-73, exec. v.p., 1973-80, pres., 1980-85, vice chmn., 1985-87; vice chmn. Roper Starch Worldwide, N.Y.C., 1988—; mem. coadj. faculty Rutgers U., 1959-64; vis. lectr. Woodrow Wilson Sch., Princeton U., 1980-82;. Editor Marketing Research: A Magazine of Management & Applications, 1988-93. Pres. Nat. Coun. Pub. Polls, 1984-94, trustee, 1994—; bd. dirs. Roper Ctr. for Pub. Opinion Rsch., 1984-94, chmn., 1994—; bd. dirs. Coun. Am. Survey Rsch. Orgns., 1981-83, chmn., 1982-83; vice chmn. Rsch. Industry Coalition, 1993-94, chmn., 1994-95; mem. Highland Park (N.J.) Human Rights Commn., 1973-77; bd. dirs. Del-Raritan Lung Assn., 1974-88, v.p., 1977-82, chmn., 1982-84; fin. chmn. Highland Park Rep. Orgn., 1977-89. Served with USAF, 1951-54. Recipient Maroon citation Colgate U., 1975. Mem. Am. Psychol. Assn., Ea. Psychol. Assn., Am. Assn. Pub. Opinion Rsch., Assn. Consumer Rsch., Am. Mktg. Assn., Market Rsch. Coun., Highland Park Rep. Club, Masons, Elks. Presbyterian. Office: Roper Starch Worldwide 205 E 42nd St New York NY 10017-5706

O'NEILL, JAMES ANTHONY, JR., pediatric surgeon, educator; b. N.Y.C., Dec. 7, 1933; m. Susan Pokorny; childen: James Anthony III, Elizabeth, Kathryn S. BS, Georgetown U., 1955; MD, Yale U., 1959. Diplomate Am. Bd. Surgery (bd. dirs. 1981-87, sr. 1988—), Am. Bd. Thoracic Surgery; lic. surgeon, Ohio, La., Tenn., Pa.; cert. instr. advanced trauma life support. Intern Vanderbilt U. Hosp., 1959-60, asst. resident, 1960-64, resident, instr. surgery, 1964-65; chief burn study divsn. U.S.A. Surgl Rsch. Unit Brooke Army Med. Ctr., 1965-67; resident, USPHS fellow in pediatric oncology Columbus Children's Hosp., 1967-69; instr. pediatric surgery Coll. Medicine Ohio State U., 1967-69; asst. prof. surgery and pediatrics, chief pediatric surg. svc. Sch. Medicine La. State U., 1969-70, assoc. prof. surgery, chief sect. pediatric surgery, 1970-71; prof. surgery, chmn. dept. pediatric surgery Sch. Medicine Vanderbilt U., 1971-81, chief med. staff Med. Ctr., 1976-77; prof. pediatric surgery Sch. Medicine U. Pa., Phila., 1981-95, C.E. Koop prof. pediatric surgery, 1988-95; surgeon-in-chief Children's Hosp. Phila., 1981-95; chmn. Vanderbilt U. Med. Ctr., Nashville, 1995—; site visitor residency rev. com. for surgery AMA; mem. trauma care subcom. med. adv. com. Phila. Emergency Med. Svcs. Coun.; surg. cons. U.S. Army Inst. Surg. Rsch., Ft. Sam Houston, Tex. Mem. editorial bd. Jour. Burn Care and Rehab., Jour. Enteral and Parenteral Nutrition, Jour. Surg. Rsch., Pediatrics, 1984—, Pediatric Emergency Care, 1984—, Pediatric Surgery, Pediatric Surgery Internat., 1988; mem. assoc. editorial bd. Jour. Pediatric Surgery; editorial cons. Jour. Trauma, 1983—, Jour Vascular Surgery, 1992; contbr. 250 articles to med. jours. Mem. med. adv. bd. Hope Found.; mem. adv. bd. James Whitcomb Riley Rsch. Found., 1986-89; mem. standards com. State Pa. Found. for Trauma Care. Fellow Am. Acad. Pediatrics (surg., pediatric trauma care coord. Pa. chpt., sect. on oncology-hematology chmn. surg. sect. program com. 1975-77, adv. com. postgrad. edn. 1979-81, exec. com. surg. sect. 1977-80, chmn. 1980-81); mem. ACS (founding, cancer liason physician, Met. Phila. chpt., exec. com. trauma com. 1975-77, adv. coun. pediatric surgery 1977-83, 86-88, 90—, postgrad. edn. com. 1979-82, continuing edn. com. 1981-88, nominating com. 1986, regental ad hoc com. on legis issues in trauma in emergency med. svcs. 1987—, bd. govs. 1990—, com. to study fiscal affairs coll. 1992-93, subcom. on burns, spl. soc. gov. from. AM. Pediatric Surg. Assn. 1992—, coun. on acad. surgery 1993—, v.p. Phila chpt. 1993-94), Am. Assn. for Surgery Trauma, Am. Trauma Soc. (bd. dirs. 1974-78), Am. Burn Assn., Am. Pediatric Surg. Assn. (sec. 1976-79, chmn. edn. com. 1984-87, pres.-elect 1987-88, pres. 1988-89, manpower, trauma and issues and ethics coms.), Am. Surg. Assn., Assn. for Acad. Surgery (membership com. 1973-74), Soc. for Surgery Alimentary Tract, Soc. Univ. Surgeons (edn. com. 1974-75), Assn. Program Dirs. in Surgery (steering com. 1990-94), Internat. Soc. for Burn Injuries, Internat. Soc. Parenatal Nutrition, Brit. Assn. Pediatric Surgeons, S.E. Surg. Congress (program com. 1979-82), So. Gut Club, So. Soc. for Pediatric Rsch., So. Surg. Assn., Tenn. Med. Assn. (del. 1976, 77), Tenn. Pediatric Soc., New Orleans Surg. Soc., Phila. Acad. Surgery, Phila Peduatric Soc., Coll. Physicians Phila. (coun. 1988-91), Portland Surg. Soc. (hon.), Nashville Surg. Soc., Davidson County Med. Assn., James D. Rives Surg. Soc., Halsted Soc. (bd. govs. 1986-89), Alpha Omega Alpha. Office: Vanderbilt Univ Med Ctr Dept of Surgery T 2116 MCN Nashville TN 37232

O'NEILL, JOHN H., JR., lawyer; b. Bainbridge, Md., Oct. 20, 1946; s. John Hardin and Lois May (Schnepfe) O'N.; m. Vivian Lidwina Gemelli, Nov. 29, 1969; children: Eric Michael, David Christopher, Sean Timothy, Daniel Ryan. BS with distinction Naval Engring., U.S. Naval Acad., Annapolis, Md., 1968; Nuclear Power Tng., U.S. Navy, Bainbridge, 1969; JD, Yale U., 1976. Bar: Md. 1976, D.C. 1977, U.S. Supreme Ct., U.S. Dist. Ct. D.C.; lic. to supervise operation, maintenance naval nuclear propulsion power plants AEC. Officer nuclear submarines USN, 1968-73; ptnr. Shaw, Pittman, Potts & Trowbridge, Washington, 1976—; gen. counsel various nuclear industry cos.; cons. in field to fgn. govs. Mem. ABA, Internat. Bar Assn., Internat. Nuclear Law Assn. Republican. Roman Catholic. Avocations: squash, tennis, skiing. Office: Shaw Pittman Potts & Trowbridge 2300 N St NW Washington DC 20037-1122

O'NEILL, JOHN JOSEPH, speech educator; b. De Pere, Wis., Dec. 6, 1920; s. John Joseph and Elizabeth (Murray) O'N.; m. Dorothy Jane Arnold, Dec. 28, 1943; children—Katherine, Thomas, John, Philip. B.S., Ohio State U., 1947, Ph.D., 1951. From instr. to assoc. prof. speech Ohio State U., 1949-59; prof. speech U. Ill. at Champaign, 1959-91, prof. emeritus, 1991—; prof. audiology U. Ill. Coll. Medicine, Chgo., 1965-79, head speech and hearing sci. dept., 1973-79; research assoc. U.S. Naval Sch. Aviation Medicine, summers 1953, 54; cons. in field. Co-author: Visual Communication, 1961, 81;, Hard of Hearing, 1964, Applied Audiometry, 1966. Pres. Columbus Hearing Soc., 1956-58; Bd. dirs. Champaign County Assn. Crippled-United Cerebral Palsy, 1961-63. Served with inf. AUS, 1942-46. Decorated Purple Heart, Bronze Star with oak leaf cluster; recipient Disting. Alumhnus award dept. speech Ohio State U., 1969, recipient honors, 1979. Fellow Am. Speech and Hearing Assn. (pres. 1969), Ohio Psychol. Assn.; mem. Am. Bd. Examiners Speech Pathology and Audiology (pres. 1967-68), Acad. Rehabilitative Audiology (pres. 1969). Home: 1203 W University Ave Champaign IL 61821-3224

O'NEILL, JOHN JOSEPH, JR., business consultant, former chemical company executive; b. N.Y.C., Sept. 13, 1919; s. John Joseph and Margaret (Patterson) O'N.; m. Irene Ray, Apr. 18, 1940; children—Anne, Mary (Mrs. George Schuler). B.S. in Chem. Engring, Mo. Sch. Mines, 1940, Chem. Engr., 1951. Research engr. Western Cartridge Co., 1940-49; with Olin Industries, Inc., 1949-60, dir. prodn. explosives operations, energy div., 1959-60; with Olin Mathieson Chem. Corp., 1960-71, asst. to pres., 1963-64, staff v.p. planning, 1964-65, v.p. comml. devel., chems. group, 1965-67, corporate v.p. plastics, 1967-70, corporate v.p. product diverification, 1970-71; cons., 1971-72; exec. v.p., chief operating officer Kleer-Vu Inc., N.Y.C., 1972-76; v.p. planning and devel. Vertac Consol., 1976-77; pres., chief exec. officer Vertac, Inc., 1977-78, cons., 1979-80, vice chmn. bd., chief oper. officer, 1980-81; cons., 1981—; pres. Jonco, Inc., 1986-89. Contbr. articles to profl. jours.; patentee explosives, chemicals, ordnance items. Emeritus trustee St. Mary-of-Woods Coll., Terre Haute, Ind. Fellow Am. Inst. Chemists; mem. Am. Inst. Chem. Engring. Club: Chemists (N.Y.C.). Home and Office: 7 Castlewood Ln PO Box 429 Pinehurst NC 28374-0429

O'NEILL, JOHN ROBERT, airline executive; b. Bronxville, N.Y., Feb. 13, 1937; s. John R. and Hazel (Edwards) O'N.; m. Laura M. Bellmer, May 25, 1962; children: Amy, Wendy. B.A., Hamilton Coll., 1958. Various positions in scheduling Eastern Airlines, Miami, Fla., 1961-71, dir. schedule planning, 1971-74, systems dir. schedule planning, 1974-75, dir. current schedules, 1975-80, dir. schedules, 1980-81, v.p. schedules, 1981-87; v.p. scheduling TWA Airlines, 1987—. Mem. Phi Beta Kappa. Presbyterian. Office: TWA Airlines 515 N 6th St Saint Louis MO 63101-1842

O'NEILL, JOHN T., toy company executive; b. N.Y.C., Oct. 25, 1944; s. John and Rhoda (Dillon) O'N; m. Lois E. McGarry, Oct. 8, 1966; children: John, Margaret, Gregory, Brian. BS in Acctg., Providence Coll., 1962-66. Acct. Arthur Andersen & Co., Providence, 1966-67; ptnr. Peat Marwick, KPMG, Providence, 1970-84; mng. ptnr. Peat Marwick KPMG, 1984-87; sr. v.p. fin. Hasbro, Inc., Pawtucket, R.I., 1987-88; sr. v.p., chief fin. officer Hasbro, Inc., 1988-89, exec. v.p., chief fin. officer, 1990—; mem. pres. coun. Providence Coll.; bd. dirs., past pres. Jr. Achievement R.I.; pres., bd. dirs. Galaxy Funds. Trustee Women and Infants Hosp. R.I., Providence; treas., bd. dirs. R.I. Philharmonic Orch., Providence, C. of C.; chmn. Catholic Charity Fund, Providence. Capt. Med. Svc. Corps, U.S. Army, 1967-70. Decorated Bronze Star. Mem. AICPA, R.I. CPA Soc., Inst. Mgmt. Accts., Fin. Execs. Inst., Warwick Country Club, Hope Club, Dunes Club, Bonita Bay Club, Univ. Club. Avocations: golf, outdoors, art. Office: Hasbro Inc 200 Narragansett Park Dr Pawtucket RI 02862-0200

O'NEILL, JUNE ELLENOFF, economist; b. N.Y.C., June 14, 1934; d. Louis and Matilda (Liebstein) Ellenoff; m. Sam Cohn, 1955 (div. 1961); 1 child, Peter; m. David Michael O'Neill, Dec. 24, 1964; 1 child, Amy. BA, Sarah Lawrence Coll., Bronxville, N.Y., 1955; PhD, Columbia U., 1970. Econs. instr. Temple U., Phila., 1965-68; rsch. assoc. Brookings Instn., Washington, 1968-71; sr. economist Pres.'s Coun. Econ. Advisors, Washington, 1971-76; chief human resources budget Congl. Budget Office, Washington, 1976-79; sr. rsch. assoc. The Urban Inst., Washington, 1979-86; dir. Office Policy and Rsch. U.S. Commn. Civil Rights, Washington, 1986-87; prof. econs. and fin., dir. Ctr. for Study Bus. and Govt. Baruch Coll., CUNY, 1987-95; dir. Congl. Budget Office U.S. Congress, Washington, 1995—; mem. Nat. Adv. Com., The Poverty Inst., U. Wis., 1988-95. Contbr. articles to profl. jours. Rsch. grantee, U.S. Dept. Labor, NICHD, Dept. Health & Human Svcs., others. Mem. Am. Econs. Assn. (past bd. dirs. com. on status of women). Republican. Jewish. Home: 420 Riverside Dr New York NY 10025-7773 Office: Congressional Budget Ofc Ford HOB US Congress Washington DC 20515

O'NEILL, LAWRENCE DANIEL, lawyer, consultant, entrepreneur; b. Granite City, Ill., May 16, 1946; s. Lawrence Frederick and Dorthy Lee (Breckenridge) O'N.; m. Feena MacLaverty, Oct. 28, 1989; children: Oisin Miceal, Lorcan Shane, Jaishri Erin, Tara Breckenridge. Student U. Mo., 1964-66; BA, U. Md., 1970; postgrad. Georgetown U., 1970; JD, U. Balt., 1975. Bar: Md. 1975, D.C. 1978, U.S. Supreme Ct. 1980, U.S. Ct. Claims 1982. Cryptologist/linguist Nat. Security Agy., Fort Meade, Md., 1966-70; fgn. svc. officer U.S. Info. Agy., Washington, New Delhi (India), 1970-73; budget officer U.S. Consumer Product Safety Commn., Washington, 1973-75; asst. to dir. then dir. policy White House Office Telecommunication Policy, 1975-78; assoc. chief counsel Nat. Telecommunications and Info. Adminstrn., U.S. Dept. Commerce, 1978-81; chmn., chief exec. Technology Analysis Group, Washington, 1981-87; Washington counsel Fenwick, Stone, Davis & West, Palo Alto, Calif., 1982-86; ptnr. Winston & Strawn, Washington, 1986-88, counsel, 1988-92; sec. gen. Internat. Soc. Aero. Telecommunications, Paris, 1988-91; ptnr. O'Neill & Co., Internat. Legal Advisers, Dublin and Paris; chmn. Pan Am Tech. Policy Forum, Miami, Fla., 1982—; bd. dirs. Teleport Internat., Washington, 1984-90; bd. dirs. In-Flight Phone Europe, Dublin, Virtual Comm. Internat. Ltd., Dublin, Internat. Groupware Assn. S.A., Nice, France; chmn. Stentor Comm. PLC, Dublin. Author: The Telecommunications Revolution, 1981, Five Top Technologies 1984-1995, 1982. Contbr. chpt. to Media Privacy, 1984. Mem. legis. adv. bd. Md. Senate, 1983-84. Sgt. U.S. Army, 1966-70. Mem. ABA (mem. coun. 1984—), AAAS, Md. Bar Assn., D.C. Bar Assn., Nat. Conf. Lawyers and Scientists. Democrat. Roman Catholic. Lodge: Order of Hibernians. Home: Le Bailliage, 12 Rue du Dr Rochefort, Chatou France also: Killadreenan Grange, Newcastle County, Wicklow Ireland Office: Internat Soc Aero Telecommunications, 112 Ave Charles de Gaulle, 92522 Neuilly sur Seine France

O'NEILL, MICHAEL FOY, business educator; b. Milw., Apr. 16, 1943; s. Edward James and Marcellian (Wesley) O'N.; m. Karen Lynn Shoots, June 13, 1968; children: Kristine, Brenna. BBA, Ohio State U., 1966; PhD in Bus. Adminstrn., U. Oreg., 1978. Cons. Robert E. Miller and Assocs., San Francisco, 1969-73; mem. faculty Calif. State U., Chico, 1971-73, 1980—, U. Oreg., Eugene, 1974-77, U. Ariz., Tucson, 1977-79; pres. Decision Sci. Inst., Atlanta, 1986-87, v.p., 1985-86. Contbr. articles to profl. jours. Served with U.S. Army, 1962-68. Recipient Dean's Research award Calif. State U., Chico, 1981. Avocations: golf, fly fishing. Home: 2819 North Ave Chico CA 95926-0916 Office: Calif State U Dept Fin and Mktg Chico CA 95926

O'NEILL, MICHAEL JAMES, editor, author; b. Detroit, Nov. 19, 1922; s. Michael J. and Ellen Mary (Dacey) O'N.; B.A., U. Detroit, 1946, L.H.D. (hon.), 1977; postgrad. Fordham U., 1946-47; m. Mary Jane Kilcoyne, May 31, 1948; children: Michael, Maureen, Kevin, Kathryn. Writer Standard News Assn., N.Y.C., 1946-47; with UPI, 1947-56; Washington corr. N.Y. Daily News, 1956-66, asst. mng. editor, 1966-68, mng. editor, 1968-74, exec. editor, 1974-75, editor, 1975-82, v.p., 1971-79, exec. v.p., 1979-82, also dir.; freelance writer, lectr., 1983—. Mem. Nat. Adv. Coun. Health Professions Edn., 1967-71. Served with U.S. Army, 1943-45; ETO. Decorated Bronze Star. Recipient Nat. Affairs Reporting award Nat. Headliner's, 1956. Mem. Overseas Writers (pres. 1965), Am. Soc. Newspaper Editors (pres. 1981-82), Council Fgn. Relations. Club: Century (N.Y.C.). Author: (with L. Tanzer) The Kennedy Circle, 1961; China Today, 1976, Terrorist Spectaculars: Should TV Coverage Be Curbed, 1986, The Roar of the Crowd, How TV and People Power are Changing the World, 1993. Address: 23 Cayuga Rd Scarsdale NY 10583-6941

O'NEILL, PATRICK HENRY, consulting mining engineer; b. Cordova, Alaska, Aug. 11, 1915; s. Harry I. and Florence (Leahy) O'N.; m. Sandra Dorris, Dec. 5, 1967; children: Kevin Reddy, Erin Dorris, Patrick Henry, Timothy Hazleton, Frederick Leahy. B.S., B.Min.E., U. Alaska, 1941, E.M., 1953, D.Sc. (hon.), 1976. Engr. and supt. U.S. Smelting Refining & Mining Co., Fairbanks, Alaska, 1939-41, 46-53; chief engr. Compañia Minera Choco Pacifico, Colombia, 1953-54; v.p. South Am. Gold & Platinum Co., N.Y.C., 1954-57; exec. v.p. Internat. Mining Corp. (formerly SAG&P Co.), 1957-70; chmn. Frontino Gold Mines Ltd., London, 1958-76; pres. S.Am. Placers, Bolivia, 1960-76; chmn. Pato Consol. Gold Dredging Ltd., Can., 1961-76, Consol. Purchasing and Designing, San Francisco, 1961-77; pres. Internat. Mining Corp., 1970-76; sr. v.p. Rosario Resources Corp., N.Y.C., 1977-80; exec. v.p. Rosario Resources Corp., 1981-82; mining cons., 1982—; bd. dirs. Zemex Corp., Toronto, Ont. Chmn. bd. trustees Joslin Diabetes Ctr., Boston, 1981-94. Served to maj. USAAF, 1941-46. Mem. Mining and Metall. Soc. Am., Am. Inst. Mining, Metall. and Petroleum Engrs., Can. Inst. Mining and Metallurgy, Arctic Inst., NAM (gov., chmn. 1972-73), Pioneers of Alaska, Instn. Mining and Metallurgy London, Am. Geog. Soc. (councilor), Ireland-U.S. Coun. for Commerce and Industry (dir.), Explorers Club, Chemists Club, Wings Club, Met. Club (N.Y.C.), Darien Country Club, Woodway Country Club. Home and Office: 42 Dunning Rd New Canaan CT 06840-4008

O'NEILL, PAUL ANDREW, professional baseball player; b. Columbus, Ohio, Feb. 25, 1963. BS, Otterbein Coll. With Cin. Reds, 1985-92; outfielder N.Y. Yankees, 1993—. Recipient Am. League Batting Champion, 1994; named to Am. League All-Star Team, 1994, Nat. League All-Star Team, 1991. Mem. World Series Champions. Office: New York Yankees Yankee Stadium E 161 St and River Ave Bronx NY 10451

O'NEILL, PAUL HENRY, aluminum company executive; b. St. Louis, Dec. 4, 1935; s. John Paul and Gaynald Elsie (Irvin) O'N.; m. Nancy Jo Wolfe, Sept. 4, 1955; children: Patricia, Margaret, Julie, Paul Henry. AB, Fresno State Coll., 1960; Haynes Found. fellow, Claremont Grad. Sch., 1960-61; postgrad., George Washington U., 1962-65; MPA, Ind. U., 1966; hon. degree, Clarkson U., 1993. Site engr. Morrison-Knudsen, Inc., Anchorage, 1955-57; systems analyst VA, Washington, 1961-66; budget examiner Bur. of Budget, Washington, 1967-69; chief human resources program div. U.S. Govt. Office of Mgmt. and Budget, Washington, 1969-70; asst. dir. U.S. Govt. Office of Mgmt. and Budget, 1971-72, assoc. dir., 1973-74, dep. dir., 1974-77; v.p. Internat. Paper Co., N.Y.C., 1977-81, sr. v.p., 1981-85, pres., dir., 1985-87; chmn., CEO Aluminum Co. Am., Pitts., 1987—, also bd. dirs.; bd. dirs. Rand Corp.; chmn. Pres.'s Edn. Policy Adv. Com., 1989-92. Bd. dirs. Gerald R. Ford Found., 1981—; dir. Manpower Demonstration Rsch. Corp., 1981—; trustee Am. Enterprise Inst.. H. John Heinz III Ctr. for Sci., Econs. and the Environment. Recipient Nat. Inst. Pub. Affairs Career Edn. award, 1965, William A. Jump Meritorious award, 1971; Fellow Nat. Inst. Pub. Affairs, 1966. Mem. Bus. Coun., Bus. Roundtable (policy com.), Hudson Inst. (mem. edn. policy com.), Nat. Acad. Social Ins. (founding mem.), Inst. Internat. Econs. (bd. dirs.), Inst. Rsch. on Econs. of Taxation, Internat. Primary Aluminum Inst. (former chmn.), Mgmt. Exec. Soc. Methodist. Office: Alumninum Co Am 425 6th Ave 31st Fl Pittsburgh PA 15219-1850

O'NEILL, PHILIP DANIEL, JR., lawyer, educator; b. Boston, Sept. 19, 1951; s. Philip Daniel Sr. and Alice Maureen (Driscoll) O'N.; m. Lisa G. Arrowood, June 25, 1983; children: Alexander Edwin, Sean Matthew, Madeleine Clarice. BA, Hamilton Coll., 1973; JD cum laude, Boston Coll., 1977. Bar: Mass. 1977, N.Y. 1985, R.I. 1988. Assoc. Hale and Dorr, Boston, 1977-83, ptnr., 1983-87; ptnr. Edwards & Angell, Boston, 1987—; adj. rsch. fellow John F. Kennedy Sch. Govt., Ctr. for Sci. and Internat. Affairs Harvard U., 1983-86; adj. prof. law Boston U., 1992; cons. Arms Control and Disarmament Agy. U.S. Dept. Def., 1983-84; guest lectr., commentator Boston Coll. Law Sch., Harvard U. Bus. Sch., Kennedy Sch. Govt., 1985, Boston U. Law Sch., 1990-91, Harvard Law Sch., 1994-95; internat. and domestic comml. arbitrator Am. Arbiration Assn., Hong Kong Ctr. for Internat. Arbitration, N.Am. Free Trade Agreement, Internat. C. of C. Ct. Arbitration Paris, Inter-Am. Comml. Arbitration Commn., Japanese Comml. Arbitration Assn., Cairo Regional Ctr., Euro-Arab C. of C., World Intellectual Property Orgn.; panelist in internat. and domestic legal programs. Contbr. chpts. to books and articles to profl. jours. Fellow Chartered Inst. Arbitrators (Eng.); mem. ABA, Internat. Law Assn. (chmn. am. br. arbitration com. 1985-89, rep. internat. arbitration com. 1989—), Mass. Bar Assn., Boston Bar Assn. (chmn. internat. law sect. 1994-96, past chmn. internat. litigation and arbitration com.), Am. Soc. Internat. Law. Home: 11 Blackburnian Rd Lincoln MA 01773-4317 Office: Edwards & Angell 101 Federal St Boston MA 02110-1800

O'NEILL, RICHARD PAUL, federal agency administrator; b. Balt., Nov. 19, 1943; m. Nichole Rose O'Neill; children: Shannon, Colin. BS in Chem. Engring., U. Md., MBA in Ops. Rsch., Math., PhD in Ops. Rsch., Math. Asst. prof. U. Md., Coll. Park, 1969-73, La. State U., Baton Rouge, 1973-78; dir. oil and gas analysis Energy Info. Adminstrn., Washington, 1978-86; dir. pipeline and producer regulation Fed. Energy Regulatory Commn., Washington, 1986-88, chief economist, dir. office of econ. policy, 1988—. Office: Dept Energy Econ Policy 888 1st St NE Washington DC 20426

O'NEILL, ROBERT CHARLES, consultant, inventor; b. Buffalo, Dec. 3, 1923; s. Albert T. and Helen (Lynch) O'N.; m. Agnes Balischak; 1 dau., Eileen Anne. BS in Chemistry, Rensselaer Poly. Inst., 1945; PhD in Organic Chemistry, Mass. Inst. Tech., 1950. Sr. chemist Merck & Co., Inc., Rahway, N.J., 1950-56, marketing devel. specialist, 1956-58; v.p. Stauffer Pharms. div. Stauffer Chem. Co., N.Y.C., 1958-61; v.p., dir. R & D Cooper Labs., Inc., 1961-70, exec. v.p., 1970-76, gen. mgr., 1975-76, pres., 1976-77, also dir.; cons., inventor, 1977—. Contbr. articles to profl. jours. Served with USNR, 1943-46. Mem. Am. Chem. Soc., Chemists Club N.Y. Patentee in field. Home: 10 Whitlaw Close Chappaqua NY 10514-1008

O'NEILL, ROBERT EDWARD, business journal editor; b. N.Y.C., Aug. 30, 1925; s. Joseph Michael and Ethel Agnes (Seymour) O'N.; m. Phyllis Ann Schreck, Apr. 19, 1952; children: Keith, Kathy, Kim, Karen. B.A. in Journalism, Syracuse (N.Y.) U., 1950. Reporter Southeasterner, Long Island, N.Y., 1950-51; rep. Bklyn. Daily, 1952; asso. editor Progressive Grocer, N.Y.C., 1952-62; sr. editor Progressive Grocer, 1962-69, exec. editor, 1970-86; editor in chief Monitor mag., Stamford, Conn., 1986-92; editorial dir. Progressive Grocer; dir. Sopro Foods, Inc. Contbg. author/editor: Foodtown Study, 1954, Super Valu Study, 1957, Dillon Study, 1959, Colonial Study, 1961, Outstanding New Super Markets, 1961, Consumer Dynamics, 1963, A & P Study, 1970, Merchandising in Action, 1972, Consumer Behavior Study, 1976, Brand Power Study, 1977. Served with USN, 1944-47. Mem. Am. Bus. Press (editorial com. 1974-75, co-winner, Jesse H. Neal award 1961, 66, 74, 89, 90, Points of Light award 1991), Glacier Hills Assn. (pres. 1964-66), Sigma Delta Chi. Club: Overseas Press. Home: 67 Moraine Rd Morris Plains NJ 07950-2752 Office: O'Neill Assocs 67 Moraine Rd Morris Plains NJ 07950

O'NEILL, RUSSELL RICHARD, engineering educator; b. Chgo., June 6, 1916; s. Dennis Alysious and Florence Agnes (Mathurin) O'N.; m. Margaret Bock, Dec. 15, 1939; children: Richard A., John R.; m. Sallie Boyd, June 30, 1967. BSME, U. Calif., Berkeley, MSME, 1940; PhD, UCLA, 1956. Registered profl. engr., Calif. Design engr. Dowell, Inc., Midland, Mich., 1940-41; design engr. Dow Chem. Co., Midland, 1941-44, Airesearch Mfg. Co., Los Angeles, 1944-46; lectr. engring. UCLA, 1946-56, prof. engring., 1956, asst. dean engring., 1956-61, assoc. dean, 1961-73, acting dean, 1965-66, dean, 1974-83, dean emeritus, 1983—; staff engr. NAS-NRC, 1954; dir. Data Design Labs., 1977-86, dir. emeritus, 1986—; mem. engring. task force Space Era Edn. Study Fla. Bd. Control, 1963; mem. regional Export Expansion Coun. Dept. Commerce, 1960-66, Los Angeles Mayor's Space Adv. Com., 1964-69; mem. Maritime Transp. Rsch. Bd., 1974-81; bd. advisers Naval Postgrad. Sch., 1976-84; mem. Nat. Nuclear Accreditation Bd., 1983-88; mem. accrediting bd. Dept. Energy, 1992—. Trustee West Coast U., 1981-90; bd. dirs. Western region United Way, 1982-90. Mem. NAE, Am. Soc. Engring. Edn., Sigma Xi, Tau Beta Pi. Home: 15430 Longbow Dr Sherman Oaks CA 91403-4910 Office: 405 Hilgard Ave Los Angeles CA 90095-1600

O'NEILL, SALLIE BOYD, education educator, business owner, sculptor; b. Ft. Lauderdale, Fla., Feb. 17, 1926; d. Howard Prindle and Sarah Frances (Clark) Boyd; AA, Stephens Coll., 1945; m. Roger H. Noden, July 8, 1945; children: Stephanie Ann Ballard, Ross Hopkins Noden; m. Russell R. O'Neill, June 30, 1967. Course coord. UCLA Extension, 1960-72, specialist continuing edn. dept. human devel., acad. appointment, 1972-83; pres. Learning Adventures, Inc., 1985-86; v.p., CFO The Learning Network, Inc., 1985-86; ednl. cons., 1986—; sculptor, 1987—. Bd. dirs. Everywoman's Village, Sherman Oaks, Calif., 1988—, v.p. 1993-95. Mem. Women in Bus. (v.p., bd. dirs. 1976-77, 86-87), Golden State Sculpture Assn., UCLA Assn. Acad. Women. Democrat. Home and Studio: 15430 Longbow Dr Sherman Oaks CA 91403-4910

O'NEILL, SHEILA, principal. Prin. Cor Jesu Acad., St. Louis. Recipient Blue Ribbon award U.S. Dept. Edn., 1990-91. Office: Cor Jesu Acad 10230 Gravois Rd Saint Louis MO 63123-4030

O'NEILL, THOMAS NEWMAN, JR., federal judge; b. Hanover, Pa., July 6, 1928; s. Thomas Newman and Emma (Cornpropst) O'N.; m. Jeanne M. Corr., Feb. 4, 1961; children: Caroline Jeanne, Thomas Newman, III, Ellen Gitt. A.B. magna cum laude, Catholic U. Am., 1950; LL.B. magna cum laude, U. Pa., 1953; postgrad. (Fulbright grantee), London Sch. Econs., 1955-56. Bar: Pa. 1954, U.S. Supreme Ct. 1959. Law clk. to Judge Herbert F. Goodrich U.S. Ct. Appeals (3d cir.), 1953-54; to Justice Harold H. Burton U.S. Supreme Ct., 1954-55; assoc. firm Montgomery, McCracken, Walker & Rhoads, Phila., 1956-63; ptnr. Montgomery, McCracken, Walker & Rhoads, 1963-83; judge U.S. Dist. Ct. (ea. dist.) Pa., 1983—; counsel 1st and 2d Pa. Legis. Reapportionment Commns., 1971, 81; lectr. U. Pa. Law Sch., 1973. Articles editor: U. Pa. Law Rev. 1952-53. Former trustee Lawyers Com. for Civil Rights Under Law; former mem. Gov.'s Trial Ct. Nominating Commn. for Phila. County; former mem. bd. overseers U. Pa. Mus. Fellow Am. Coll. Trial Lawyers; mem. Am. Law Inst. (life), Phila. Bar Assn. (chancellor 1976), Pa. Bar Assn. (gov. 1978-81), U. Pa. Law Alumni Soc. (pres. 1976-77), Pa. Conf. County Bar Officers (pres. 1981-82), Am. Inn of Ct. (founding chmn. U. Pa.), Order of Coif (pres. U. Pa. chpt. 1971-73), Merion Cricket Club, Edgemere Club, Broadacres Trouting Assn., Phi Beta Kappa, Phi Eta Sigma. Office: US Dist Ct 14613 US Courthouse 601 Market St Philadelphia PA 19106-1510

O'NEILL, TIMOTHY, federal agency administrator; m. Virginia O'Neill; children: Elizabeth Porter, John Timothy Jr., David Elliott. Degree in fgn. svc. magna cum laude, Georgetown U., 1976; JD, Harvard U., 1980. Legis. dir. U.S. Senator John Heinz of Pa., Washington; dep. dir. congl. affairs U.S. AID, Washington; sr. legis. mgr. for internat. affairs U.S. Dept. Treasury, Washington; dir. congl. affairs Fed. Housing Fin. Bd., Washington, dir., 1995—; ptnr. O'Connor & Hannan, Washington. Office: Fed Housing Fin Bd 1777 F St NW Washington DC 20006

O'NEILL, WALTER JOHN HUGH, university director, consultant; b. Freeport, N.Y., May 31, 1962; s. John Hugh and Mary Adele (Crawford) O'N. BS, SUNY, Binghamton, 1986. Counselor aid fin. aid SUNY, Binghampton, 1983-86; dir. fin. aid SUNY, Old Westbury, 1987-91; adminstr. fin. aid Columbia U., N.Y., 1986-87; dir. fin. aid Chgo. State U., 1991-92, Ill. Inst. Tech., Chgo., 1992—; enrollment, aid cons. O'Neill Cons., Freeport, N.Y., 1987-89, Chgo., 1993—. Active Chgo. Alternative Policing Strategy, 1994—. Named one of Outstanding Young Men of Am., 1986-87. Mem. Nat. Assn. Student Fin. Aid Adminstrs., Ill. Assn. Student Fin. Aid Adminstrs. Roman Catholic. Home: 3101 S Wabash Ave Apt 508 Chicago IL 60616-3859 Office: Ill Inst Tech 3300 S Federal St Rm 212 Chicago IL 60616-3732

O'NEILL, WILLIAM LAWRENCE, history educator; b. Big Rapids, Mich., Apr. 18, 1935; s. John Patrick and Helen Elizabeth (Marsh) O'N.; m. Elizabeth Carol Knollmueller, Aug. 20, 1960; children: Cassandra Leigh, Catherine Lorraine. A.B., U. Mich., 1957; M.A., U. Calif., Berkeley, 1958, Ph.D., 1963. Asst. prof. history U. Colo., 1964-66; asst. prof. U. Wis., 1966-69, asso. prof., 1969-71; prof. Rutgers U., New Brunswick, N.J., 1971—; vis. asst. prof. U. Pitts., 1963-64; vis. asso. prof. U. Pa., 1969-70. Author: Divorce in the Progressive Era, 1967, Everyone Was Brave: The Rise and Fall of Feminism in America, 1969, rev. and repub. as: Feminism in America: A History, 1989, Coming Apart: An Informal History of America in the 1960's, 1971, The Last Romantic: A Life of Max Eastman, 1978, 2d edit., 1991, A Better World: The Great Schism: Stalinism and the American Intellectuals, 1982, repub. as: A Better World: Stalinism and the American Intellectuals, 1989, American High: The Years of Confidence, 1945-60, 1986, A Democracy at War: America's Fight at Home and Abroad in World War II, 1993. Nat. Endowment Humanities fellow, 1979-80. Mem. Am. Hist. Assn. Office: Rutgers U Dept History New Brunswick NJ 08903

O'NEILL, WILLIAM PATRICK, lawyer; b. Joplin, Mo., Sept. 14, 1951; s. Fred Charles and Dorothy Isabel (Snyder) O'N.; m. Mary Louise Richardson, June 17, 1989. BA, U. Kans., 1973; JD, U. Mich., 1976. Bar: Ill. 1976, U.S. Dist. Ct. (no. dist.) Ill. 1976, U.S. Dist. Ct. D.C. 1982. Assoc. Kirkland & Ellis, Chgo., 1976-81, Sidley & Austin, Chgo., 1982-85, Skadden, Arps, Slate, Meagher & Flom, N.Y.C., 1986-87; assoc. Crowell & Moring, Washington, 1987-88, ptnr., 1988—; gen. counsel Ill. Common Cause, Chgo., 1979-81. Editor, author: (with others) Successfully Acquiring A U.S. Business, 1990; editorial chmn. Antitrust Law Jour., 1984-89. Mem. University Club of Chgo. Office: Crowell & Moring 1001 Pennsylvania Ave NW Washington DC 20004-2505

ONEK, JOSEPH NATHAN, lawyer; b. N.Y.C., Jan. 9, 1942; s. Jacob J. and Doris (Aaronson) O.; m. Margot Debra Piore, June 29, 1963; children: David, Matthew. A.B. magna cum laude, Harvard Coll., 1962; M.A., London Sch. Econs., 1964; LL.B. magna cum laude, Yale Law Sch., 1967. Bar: D.C. 1968. Law clk. to chief judge David L. Bazelon, U.S. Ct. Appeals (D.C. cir.), 1967-68; law clk. Justice William J. Brennan, U.S. Supreme Ct., 1968-69; staff Senate Adminstrv. Practice and Procedure Subcom., Senate Labor and Pub. Welfare Commn., 1969-71; dir., atty. Ctr. for Law and Social Policy, 1971-76; adj. prof. U. Md. Law Sch., Health Care Law, 1976-77; dir. health policy analysis Carter-Mondale Transition Planning Group, 1976-77; assoc. dir. for health and human resources Domestic Policy Staff, White House, 1977-79; dep. counsel to Pres., White House, 1979-81; ptnr. Onek, Klein & Farr, Washington, 1981-91; ptnr. Crowell & Moring, 1991—; presdl. appointee to D.C. Jud. Nominating Com., 1994—. Marshall scholar, 1962. Mem. ABA, Phi Beta Kappa. Home: 3723 Ingomar St NW Washington DC 20015-1819 Office: Crowell & Moring 1001 Pennsylvania Ave NW Washington DC 20004-2505

ONESTI, SILVIO JOSEPH, psychiatrist; b. San Francisco, Jan. 3, 1926; s. Silvio Joseph and Johanna (Kristoffy) O.; m. Jean Thomas, May 12, 1956; children: Sally Joanna, Stephen Thomas. BS, Stanford U., 1947; MD, McGill U., 1951. Diplomate Am. Bd. Psychiatry and Neurology. Instr. pediatrics Yale Med. Sch., New Haven, 1956-58; career tchr. psychiatry NIMH, Harvard Med. Sch., Beth Israel Hosp., Boston, 1963-65; head child psychiatry unit Beth Israel Hosp., Boston, 1965-73; dir. child and adolescent psychiatry McLean Hosp., Belmont, Mass., 1973-91; dir. Hall-Mercer Ctr. for children and adolescents McLean Hosp., Belmont, 1973-91; dir child and adolescent psychiat. tng., 1973-92; dir. clin. svcs. McLean Hosp., Belmont, 1981-83; asst. prof. psychiatry Harvard Med. Sch., Boston, 1969—; faculty Boston Psychoanalytic Soc. and Inst. Inc., Boston, 1971-81. Contbr. articles to profl. jours. With USN, 1944-46. Fellow Am. Psychiat. Assn., Am. Acad. Child and Adolescent Psychiatry, Am. Coll. Psychiatrists; mem. Group for Advancement of Psychiatry (fellow 1959-61, bd. dirs. 1987-89), Boston Psychoanalytic Soc. and Inst. Inc., Mass. Med. Soc., Alpha Omega Alpha. Home: 4 Gray Gdns W Cambridge MA 02138-2312 Office: McLean Hosp 115 Mill St Belmont MA 02178-1041

ONG, CHEE-MUN, engineering educator; b. Ipoh, Perak, Malaysia, Nov. 23, 1944; came to U.S., 1978; s. Chin-Kok Ong and Say-Choo Yeoh; m. Penelope Li-Lok, July 17, 1971; children: Yi-Ping, Yi-Ching, Chiew-Jen. BE with honors, U. Malaya, 1967; MS, Purdue U., 1968, PhD, 1974. Registered profl. engr. Ind., Eng. Plant engr. Guinness Brewery, Malaysia, 1967; asst. lectr. U. Malaysia, 1968-73, lectr., 1976-78; rsch. asst. Purdue U., West Lafayette, Ind., 1973-74, vis. asst. prof., 1975-76, asst. prof., 1978-81, assoc. prof., 1981-85, prof., 1985—; cons. SIMTECH, West Lafayette, 1978-85, L.A. Water and Power Co., 1986-88. Contbr. articles to jours. in field. Fulbright-Hayes scholar, 1967-68; UNESCO fellow, 1969-70. Fellow Inst. Elec. Engrs. (U.K.); mem. IEEE (sr.). Avocations: gardening, fishing, reading. Office: Purdue U Dept Elec Engring 1285 Elec Engring Bldg West Lafayette IN 47907

ONG, JOHN DOYLE, lawyer; b. Uhrichsville, Ohio, Sept. 29, 1933; s. Louis Brosee and Mary Ellen (Liggett) O.; m. Mary Lee Schupp, July 20, 1957; children: John Francis Harlan, Richard Penn Blackburn, Mary Katherine Caine. BA, Ohio State U., 1954, MA, 1954; LLB, Harvard, 1957; LHD, Kent State U., 1982. Bar: Ohio 1958. Asst. counsel B.F. Goodrich Co., Akron, 1961-66, group v.p., 1972-73, exec. v.p., 1973-74, vice chmn., 1974-75, pres., dir., 1975-77, pres., chief operating officer, dir., 1978-79, chmn. bd., pres., chief exec. officer, 1979-84, chmn. bd., chief exec. officer, 1984—; asst. to pres. Internat. B.F. Goodrich Co., Akron, 1966-69, v.p., 1969-70, pres., 1970-72; bd. dirs. Cooper Industries, Ameritech Corp., The Kroger Co., Asarco, Inc., Geon Co., TRW, Inc. V.p. exploring Great Trail coun. Boy Scouts Am., 1974-77; bd.d irs. Nat. Alliance of Bus., 1981-84; trustee Mus. Arts Assn., Cleve., Bexley Hall Sem., 1974-81, Case Western Res. U., 1980-92, Kenyon Coll., 1983-85, Hudson (Ohio) Libr. and Hist. Soc., pres., 1971-72, Western Res. Acad., Hudson, 1975-95, pres. bd. trustees, 1977-95; nat. trustee Nat. Symphony Orch., 1975-83, John S. and James L. Knight Found., 1995—; mem. bus. adv. com. Transp. Ctr. Northwestern U., 1975-78, Carnegie-Mellon U. Grad. Sch. Indsl. Adminstrn., 1978-83; trustee U. Chgo., 1991—; chmn. Ohio Bus. Roundtable, 1994—. Mem. Ohio Bar Assn. (bd. govs. corp. counsel sect. 1962-74, chmn. 1970), Rubber Mfrs. Assn. (bd. dirs. 1974-84), Chem. Mfrs. Assn. (bd. dirs. 1988-91, 94—), Conf. Bd., Bus. Roundtable (chmn. 1992-94), Bus. Coun., Portage Country Club, Union Club, Links, Union League, Ottawa Shooting Club, Met. Club, Rolling Rock Club, Castalia Trout Club, Phi Beta Kappa, Phi Alpha Theta. Episcopalian. Home: 230 Aurora St Hudson OH 44236-2941 Office: The B F Goodrich Co 3925 Embassy Pky Akron OH 44333-1799

ONG, MICHAEL KING, mathematician, educator, banker; b. Manila, Philippines, Dec. 16, 1955; s. Sanchez and Remedios (King) O. BS in Physics cum laude, U. Philippines, 1978; MA in Physics, SUNY, Stony Brook, 1979, MS in Applied Math., 1981, PhD in Applied Math., 1984. Asst. prof. Bowdoin Coll., Brunswick, Maine, 1984-91; sr. mathematician, fin. analyst Chgo. Rsch. & Trading Group Ltd., 1990-92; v.p., sr. rsch. analyst First Chgo. Corp., 1993-94, head market risk analysis unit, 1994—, 1st v.p., head corp. rsch. unit, 1996—; adj. prof. fin. markets and trading program Stuart Sch. Bus. Ill. Inst. Tech., 1990—. Mem. editl. bd. Jour. Fin. Regulation & Compliance; contbr. articles to profl. jours. Mem. Am. Fin. Assn., Am. Math. Soc., Math. Assn. Am., Soc. Indsl. and Applied Math., Consortium for Math. and Its Applications, Am. Phys. Soc., Phi Kappa Phi. Avocations: writing, singing, traveling, painting. Home: 2650 N Lakeview Ave Apt 4106 Chicago IL 60614-1833 Office: First Chgo NBD Corp 1 First Nat Plz Chicago IL 60670-0690

ONG, WALTER JACKSON, priest, English educator, author; b. Kansas City, Mo., Nov. 30, 1912; s. Walter Jackson and Blanche Eugenia (Mense) O. AB, Rockhurst Coll., 1933; PhL, St. Louis U., 1940, AM, 1941, STL, 1948; PhD, Harvard U., 1955; various hon. degrees. Joined S.J., Roman Cath. Ch., 1935, ordained priest, 1946. Newspaper, comml. positions until, 1935; instr. English and French Regis Coll., Denver, 1941-43; asst. English St. Louis U., 1944-47, instr., 1953-54, asst. prof., 1954-57, assoc. prof., 1957-59; prof., 1959—, prof. humanities in psychiatry Sch. Medicine, 1970—, Univ. prof. humanities, 1981—, prof. emeritus, 1984—; mem. Fulbright nat. selection com., France, 1957-58, chmn., 1958; regional asso. Am. Coun. Learned Socs., 1957-66; mem. White House Task Force on Edn., 1966-67, Nat. Coun. on Humanities, 1968-74, vice chmn., 1971-74; co-chmn. adv. com. on sci., tech. and human values NEH, 1974-78; mem. Rockefeller Found. Commn. on Humanities, 1978-80; vis. prof. U. Calif., 1960; Terry lectr., Yale, 1963-64; vis. lectr. U. Poitiers, 1962; Berg prof. English N.Y. U., 1966-67; McDonald lectr. McGill U., 1967-68; Willett vis. prof. humanities U. Chgo., 1968-69; nat. Phi Beta Kappa vis. scholar, 1969-70; Lincoln lectr. Central and West Africa, 1973-74; Messenger lectr. Cornell U., 1979-80; Alexander lectr. U. Toronto, 1981; vis. prof. comparative lit. Washington U., 1983-84; Wolfson Coll. lectr. Oxford U., 1985. Author: Frontiers in American Catholicism, 1957, Ramus, Method, and the Decay of Dialogue, 1958, Ramus and Talon Inventory, 1958, Am. Cath. Crossroads, 1959, The Barbarian Within, 1962, In the Human Grain, 1967, The Presence of the Word, 1967, Rhetoric, Romance and Technology, 1971, Why Talk?, 1973, Interfaces of the Word, 1977, Fighting for Life: Contest, Sexuality, and Consciousness, 1981, Orality and Literacy, 1982, Hopkins, the Self and God, 1986, Faith and Contexts, 3 vols., 1992-95; co-author, editor: Darwin's Vision and Christian Perspectives, 1960, Knowledge and the Future of Man, 1968; editor: Petrus Ramus and Audomarus Talaeus, Collectaneae praefationes epistolae, orationes, 1969, Petrus Ramus, Scholae in liberales artes, 1970; co-editor, translator: Logic (John Milton), 1982; mem. editl. bd. Studies in English Literature, 1962—; editl. adv. bd. Philosophy and Rhetoric, 1967—, The English Literary Renaissance, 1969—, Manuscripta, 1957—, others; contbr. articles, chpts. to learned and popular publs. Mem. adv. bd. John Simon Guggenheim Meml. Found., 1962-84; trustee Nat. Humanities Faculty, 1968-76, chmn., 1974-76. Decorated chevalier l'Ordre des Palmes Académiques (France); Guggenheim fellow, 1949-50, 51-52; fellow Ctr. Advanced Studies, Wesleyan U., Middletown, Conn., 1961-62; fellow Sch. Letters, Ind. U., 1965—; fellow Ctr. for Advanced Study in Behavioral Scis., Stanford, 1973-74. Fellow Am. Acad. Arts and Scis.; mem. AAUP, MLA (pres. 1978), Renaissance Soc. Am. (adv. coun. 1957-59), Modern Humanities Rsch. Assn., Nat. Coun. Tchrs. English, Cambridge Bibliog. Soc. (Eng.), Catholic Commn. Intellectual and Cultural Affairs (exec. com. 1962-63), Milton Soc. of Am. (pres. 1967), Phi Beta Kappa, Alpha Sigma Nu. Office: Saint Louis University Sch Medicine Saint Louis MO 63103

ONGERT, STEVEN WALTER, lawyer, mediator; b. Palm Springs, Calif., Aug. 9, 1945; m. Kathy D. Dean, July 4, 1991. BA, Hastings (Nebr.) Coll., 1972; JD, South Tex. Coll. Law, 1988. Bar: Tex. 1989, U.S. Dist. Ct. (so. dist.) Tex. 1990. Assoc. Bill De La Garza & Assocs., Houston, 1988-90; ptnr. Dean & Ongert, P.C., Houston, 1990—. Sgt. USAF, 1965-69. Mem. ABA, Houston Bar Assn., Galveston Family Law Bar Assn. (pres. 1993, 94), Assn. Trial Lawyers Am., Tex. Assn. Mediators, Coll. State Bar Tex. Avocations: fishing, collecting antiques. Office: Ste 220 1020 Bay Area Blvd Houston TX 77058-2631

ONGMAN, JOHN WILL, lawyer; b. Chgo., July 19, 1951; s. John Warner and Helen Will (Dunbar) O.; m. Joanne Patricia Sawicki, Oct. 17, 1981. BS, Purdue U., 1972; MS, U. Ill., 1973; JD, Northwestern U., 1976. Bar: Ill. 1976, D.C. 1984, N.Y. 1990. Law clk. to Hon. Walter J. Cummings U.S. Ct. Appeals 7th cir., Chgo., 1976-77; assoc. Sidley & Austin, Chgo. and Washington, 1977-83; ptnr. Pepper, Hamilton & Scheetz, Washington, 1983—. Contbr. numerous articles to law jours. Mem. University Club of Chgo., Metropolitan Club of Washington. Office: Pepper Hamilton & Scheetz 1300 19th St NW Washington DC 20036-1609

ONKEN, GEORGE MARCELLUS, lawyer; b. Bklyn., Aug. 15, 1914; s. William Henry and Lillian Charlotte (Dawe) O.; m. Mildred Ann Tausch, Dec. 13, 1958; children: Jane Elizabeth, Nancy Catherine. AB, Princeton U., 1936; LLB, Columbia U., 1948; LLM, NYU, 1952. Bar: N.Y. 1949. Asst. to pres. Welsbach Engring. and Mgmt. Corp., Phila., 1939-43; mem. legal staff L.I. R.R., 1949-78, gen. counsel, 1963-78, v.p., 1966-78, sec., 1968-78. Bd. dirs. Orphan Asylum Soc., Bklyn., 1958—, YMCA Greater N.Y., 1963-80, Pop Warner Little League, 1976-78; bd. mgrs. Pa. R.R. br. YMCA, N.Y.C., 1957-80, chmn., 1967-80; trustee Bklyn. YWCA, 1976-92. Lt. (j.g.) USNR, 1943-46. Recipient Man of Year award YMCA, 1977; Outstanding Svc. award Bklyn. Chpt. ARC Greater N.Y., 1994. Mem. Newcomen Soc. N.Am. Republican. Episcopalian (vestry 1958-64, 76-85). Clubs: Union League (N.Y.C.), Univ. (N.Y.C.), Church (N.Y.C.); Rembrandt (Bklyn.), Heights Casino (Bklyn.), Ihpetonga (Bklyn.). Home: 215 Adams St Brooklyn NY 11201-2856

ONO, CHERYL EIKO, senior controls engineer; b. Chgo., Feb. 26, 1965; d. Mitsuo and Sachiye (Ikeda) O. BS, Eastern Ill. U., 1987, MS, 1988. Grad. asst. Eastern Ill. U., Charleston, 1987-88; intern GE Co., Mattoon, Ill., 1988, mfg./quality engr., 1988-92; controls engr. GE Co., Ravenna, Ohio, 1992-94; advanced process engr. GE Co., Nela Park, Cleve., 1994-95, sr. controls engr., 1995—. Mem. Am. Soc. Quality Engrs., Epsilon Pi Tau. Avocations: camping, aerobics, biking. Office: GE Lighting 1975 Noble Rd Cleveland OH 44112-1719

ONO, MASATOSHI, tire manufacturing executive; b. 1937. BS in Elec. Engring., Kumamoto U., 1959. With Bridgestone Tire Co. (now Bridgestone Corp.), 1959-87, dir., 1987-90, v.p., plant mgr. Kurume Plant, 1990; exec. v.p. mfg. and tech. Bridgestone/Firestone, Inc., 1991-93, CEO, 1993—. Office: Bridgestone Firestone Inc 50 Century Blvd Nashville TN 37214-3672*

ONOFRIO, BURTON M., neurosurgeon; b. New Milford, Conn., Jan. 1, 1933. MD, Cornell U., 1957. Diplomate Am. Bd. Neurol. Surgery. Intern N.Y. Hosp. Med. Ctr., N.Y.C., 1957, resident, 1958; fellow Mayo Clinic, Rochester, N.Y., 1960-64; neurol. surgeon St. Mary's Hosp., Rochester, Minn.; faculty neurosurg. dept. Mass. Gen. Hosp., Boston; cons. neurosurgeon Mayo Clinic, Rochester, Minn. Mem. AMA, Coll. Neurol. Surgeons, Minn. Neurol. Surgery Soc. Office: Mayo Clinic 200 1st St SW # E-6B Rochester MN 55905-0001 Office: Mayo Clinic E-68 200 First St SW Rochester MN 55905-0001

ONONYE, DANIEL CHUKA, social scientist; b. Aba, Mo., June 30, 1948; s. Daniel Okonai and Paulina N. (Ayuno) O.; m. Debbie S. Ononye, Sept. 3, 1977 (div. 1983); m. Kate Okonji Egoye, Dec. 6, 1984; 1 child, Ray E. BS,

Huntington (Ind.) Coll., 1977; MA, Ball State U., 1979. Mgr. Huntington Meml. Hosp., 1978-79; sr. adminstrv. officer U. Portharcourt, Nigeria, 1979-82; personnel officer Anambra State Coll. Edn. Nigeria Registry Dept., Awka, 1983-85; pres. Super Nig Ltd., Portharcourt, 1985-87, Astros of St. Louis Internat. Inc., 1988—, Green Eagle Corp. of Dallas, Ft. Worth, 1991—. Mem. Nigerian Inst. Mgmt. (assoc.), Inst. Mgmt. Cons. (assoc.), Internat. Club (pres. 1975-76), Grand Lodge of Amroc. Avocations: music, dancing.

ONORATO, NICHOLAS LOUIS, program director, economist; b. South Barre, Mass., Feb. 24, 1925; s. Charles and Amalia (Tartaglia) O.; m. Elizabeth Louise Settergren, July 19, 1947; children: Gary, Deborah, Nicholas, Jeffrey, Glenn, Charles, Lisa. B.S. in Pub. Relations, Boston U., 1951; M.A. in Econs, Clark U., 1952, Ph.D., 1959. Mem. faculty Becker Jr. Coll., Worcester, Mass., 1952-54; prof. econs. Worcester Poly. Inst., 1955-68, chmn. dept. econs., govt., bus., 1968-74, dir. Sch. Indsl. Mgmt., 1972—; prof. emeritus Worcester (Mass.) Poly Inst., 1994; vis. prof. Clark U., Worcester, 1964-66; fin. cons. Coz Chem. Co., Northbridge, Mass., 1959-95. Contbr. to newspapers and mags. Trustee Bay State Savs. Bank, Worcester. Served with USNR, 1943-46. Mem. Am. Finance Assn., Am. Econ. Assn., Am. Accounting Assn., Phi Kappa Theta. Club: Torch (pres. Worcester 1967, 87, 95). Home: 39 Knollwood Dr Shrewsbury MA 01545-3329 Office: Institute Rd Worcester MA 01609

ONSAGER, JEROME ANDREW, research entomologist; b. Northwood, N.D., Apr. 8, 1936; s. Alfred and Anne Marie (Kielbauch) O.; m. Bette Lynn Stanton, Aug. 16, 1958. B.S., N.D. State U., 1958, M.S., 1960, Ph.D., 1963. Research entomologist USDA Agrl. Research Service, Bozeman, Mont., 1963—. Contbr. articles on biology, ecology, population dynamics of rangeland grasshoppers to profl. jours. Fellow NSF, 1960. Mem. Entomol. Soc. Am., Entomol. Soc. Can., Orthopterist Soc., Sigma Xi, Alpha Zeta. Lutheran. Avocations: fishing; big game hunting; equestrian activities. Home: 4141 Blackwood Rd Bozeman MT 59715-9130 Office: USDA ARS Rangeland Insect Lab Bozeman MT 59717

ONSLOW FORD, GORDON MAX, painter; b. Wendover, Buckinghamshire, Eng., Dec. 26, 1912; came to U.S., 1947, naturalized, 1952; s. Max and Maud Elizabeth (Woollerton) Onslow Ford; m. Jacqueline Marie Johnson, May 5, 1941. Grad., Royal Naval Coll., Dartmouth, Eng., 1929; grad., Royal Naval Coll., Greenwich, Eng., 1930. Mem. Surrealist Group, Paris, London, N.Y.C., 1938-43. One-man shows include New Sch. for Social Rsch., N.Y.C., 1940, Nierendorf Gallery, N.Y.C., 1946, San Francisco Mus. Art, 1948, M.H. DeYoung Mus., San Francisco, 1962, San Francisco Mus., 1951, 59, 70, Oakland (Calif.) Mus., 1977, Art Gallery Greater Victoria, B.C., 1971, Samy Kinge Gallery, Paris, 1985; group shows: Paris, 1983, London, 1940, N.Y.C., 1943, L.A. County Mus., 1950, 61, 70, 87, Newport Harbor Mus., 1986, Mus. Rath, Geneva, 1987, Centro Atlantico De Arte Moderno, Gran Canaica, Spain, 1989, Laguna Art Mus., 1990, U. Calif.-Berkeley Art Mus., 1990, Pepperdine U. Art Mus., 1992, Harcourt Gallery, San Francisco, 1993, Pavillion Gallery, Munich, 1993, Brochier Gallery, Munich, 1993, Mus. Bochum, Ger., 1994, Museo de Arte Contemporáneo, Santiago, Chile, 1995, Kunsthaus foram, Bonn, Germany, 1996; permanent collections: San Francisco Mus. Modern Art, Tate Gallery, London, M.H. deYoung Mus., Oakland Mus., Guggenheim Mus., N.Y.C., Whitney Mus. Modern Art, N.Y.C., Denver Mus., Fogg Mus., U. Mass., U. Calif.-Davis, L.A. County Mus. Art, Chgo. Art Inst.; author: Toward A New Subject in Painting, 1947, Painting in the Instant, 1964, Creation, 1978, Yves Tanguy and Automatism, 1983, Insights, 1991, Ecomorphology, 1993.

ONSTEAD, RANDALL, consumer goods company executive. Pres. Randall's Food & Drug Inc., Houston, 1976—. Office: Randall's Food & Drug Inc 3663 Briarpark Dr Houston TX 77042-5229*

ONSTEAD, ROBERT R., consumer goods company executive; b. 1931. Student, North Tex. State Tchrs. Coll., 1952-54. With IBM Co., Dallas, 1954-55, Randall's Super Valu, Houston, 1955-57; v.p. Randall's #1, Inc., Houston, 1957-64, pres., 1964-66; pres. & COO Randall's Food Markets, Inc., Houston, 1966-1996, now chmn. bd., CEO, pres., 1996—. With USAF, 1951-52. Office: Randalls Food Markets Inc 3663 Briarpark Dr Houston TX 77042-5229*

ONTIVEROS, STEVEN, professional baseball player; b. Tularosa, N.Mex., Mar. 5, 1961. Student, U. Mich. With Seattle Mariners, 1983; pitcher Oakland (Calif.) A's, 1985-88, 94—; with Phila. Phillies, 1989-90. Selected to A.L. All-Star Team, 1995. Office: Oakland A Oakland Coliseum 7000 Coliseum Way Oakland CA 94621-1918*

ONTJES, DAVID AINSWORTH, medicine and pharmacology educator; b. Lyons, Kans., July 19, 1937; s. Max S. and Elizabeth (Ainsworth) O.; m. Sherri James, Aug. 27, 1960; children: Linden F., Sarah E., Ethan A., Jason A. B.A., U. Kans., 1959; M.A., Oxford U., 1961; M.D., Harvard U., 1964. Am. Bd. Internal Medicine, sub-board endocrinology. Intern, resident Boston City Hosp., 1964-66; research assoc. NIH, Besthesda, Md., 1966-69; asst. prof. dept. medicine and pharmacology U. N.C., Chapel Hill, 1969-72, assoc. prof., 1972-76, prof., 1976—, Eunice Bernhardt Disting. prof., 1982—. Contbr. articles in field to profl. jours. Served with USPHS, 1966-69. Rhodes scholar Oxford U., 1959-61; USPHS grantee Nat. Insts. Arthritis and Metabolic Diseases, NIH, 1969-82; recipient Basic Sci. Teaching award U. N.C., 1978. Fellow ACP; mem. Endocrine Soc., Am. Soc. Clin. Investigation, Am. Soc. Pharmacology and Exptl. Therapeutics, Assn. Profs. Medicine. Republican. Presbyterian. Office: U NC Sch Medicine Dept Medicine Chapel Hill NC 27599-7527

ONTOLCHIK, ROBERT GEORGE, insurance company executive; b. Cleve., Oct. 24, 1941; s. George Jr. and Bertha (Zelez) O.; m. Beverly J. Hamilton, Sept. 30, 1972; 1 child, Robert W. AAS in Mktg., Monroe Coll., Rochester, N.Y., 1972; Exec. Diploma, Syracuse Grad. Sch. Sales, 1986; Exec. Tng. Cert., Coll. of Ins., 1992. CLU. Sales rep. Liberty Mut. Ins. Group, Cleve., 1964; N.W. regional sales mgr. Liberty Mut. Ins. Group, Pitts., 1964—. Bd. dirs. Mothers Against Drunk Drivers, Pitts., 1993—; mem. county com. Rep. Party, Upper St. Clair, Pa., 1984—, treas., 1986—. Mem. CLU Soc. Avocations: golf, family activities. Home: 656 Tuscany Dr Uppr Saint Clair PA 15241-2027 Office: Liberty Mut Ins Group One PPG Pl Ste 2700 Pittsburgh PA 15222

ONUCHIC, JÓSE NELSON, biophysics educator, electrical engineer; came to U.S., 1990; BS in Elec. Engring., U. Sao Paulo, Brazil, 1980, BS in Physics, 1981, MS in Applied Physics, 1982; PhD in Chemistry, Calif. Inst. Tech., 1987. Asst. prof. physics Inst. Physics and Chemistry Sao Carlos U. Sao Paulo, Brazil, 1987-90; asst. prof. physics U. Calif. San Diego, 1990-92, assoc. prof. physics, 1992-95, prof. of physics, 1995—. Contbr. articles to profl. jours. Recipient Engring. Inst. prize, Sao Paulo, 1980, Internat. Ctr. for Theoretical Physics Prof. Werner Heisenberg prize, Trieste, Italy, 1988; elected assoc. mem. Acad. Scis. Estado de Sao Paulo, 1991; named Beckman Young Investigator, 1992. Office: Univ Calif at San Diego Dept Physics La Jolla CA 92093 Office: U Calif San Diego Dept Physics 9500 Gilman Dr La Jolla CA 92093-0219

ONUFRAK, JOSEPH J., lawyer; b. N.Y.C., June 13, 1949; s. Joseph and Helen Marie (Heiman) O.; m. Joanne Miserendino, Aug. 21, 1975 (div. 1981); m. Lorraine Wolz, June 3, 1990; children: Kimberly Anne Gutowski, Raymond W. Gutowski. AB, Iona Coll., 1970; AM, U. Md., 1973; M Phil., Columbia U., 1977; JD, Rutgers U., 1978. Bar: N.J. 1978, U.S. Dist. Ct. N.J. 1978, N.Y. 1979, U.S. Dist. Ct. (so. dist.) N.Y. 1979. Assoc. Trubin Sillcocks, N.Y.C., 1978-79, Weil Gotshal & Manges, N.Y.C., 1979-82, Simpson Thacher & Bartlett, N.Y.C., 1982-87; counsel Donovan Leisure Newton & Irvine, N.Y.C., 1987-88, ptnr., 1988—; instr. in field. Author Construction Financing, 1983; Editor Rutgers Law Review, 1977, 78. Chmn. N.Y. Coun. Adoptable Children 1980-90; vice chmn. Encore Community Ctr., 1990—; bd. adv. trustees Iona Coll., 1987—. Rsch. fellow Columbia U., 1974-75. Mem. N.Y. State Bar Assn., Assn. Bar City N.Y. Democrat. Avocations: sailing, show-jumping, equestrianship. Home: 315 E 58th St New York NY 10022-2024 Office: Donovan Leisure Newton & Irvine 30 Rockefeller Plz New York NY 10112

ONUFROCK, RICHARD SHADE, pharmacist, researcher; b. Colorado Springs, Colo., July 5, 1934; s. Frank and Mildred Joy (Overstreet) O.; m. Karen Faye Larson, June 15, 1958 (div. 1980); children: Richard Alan (dec.), Amy Mildred. BS in Pharmacy, U. Colo., 1961; diploma, Famous Artists Schs., 1963. Registered pharmacist, Colo., Ariz., South Africa. Pharmacist Aley Drug Co., Colorado Springs, 1961-75, St. Joseph Hosp., Denver, 1976-77, Navajo Nation Health Found., Ganado, Ariz., 1977-81, Kearny (Ariz.) Kennecott-Samaritan Hosp., 1984-85, NIH, Warren G. Magnuson Clin. Ctr., Bethesda, Md., 1988—; dir. pharmacy, chief pharmacist Tintswalo Hosp., South Africa, 1981-84; pharmacist, chief pharmacist Miami (Ariz.)-Inspiration Hosp., 1985-88; instr. Coll. of Ganado, 1979-80; asst. in textbook revision and illustration U. Colo., 1961; cons. Heritage Health Care Ctr., Globe, Ariz., 1988. Illustrator Pharmacy for Nurses, 1961, Colo. Jour. of Pharmacy, 1962-64; illustrations exhibited Colo. Springs Fine Art Ctr., 1964-66, Gilpin County Art Assn., Central City, Colo., 1968-74, 1st Nat. Space Art Show, Denver, 1969. dem. precinct committeeman, 1974-76; den leader Boy Scouts Am., com. mem., 1975-76; fireman, lt. Ganado Vol. Fire Dept., 1977-81; compassionate med. missionary Nazarene Ch., Tintswalo Hosp. Gazankulu, South Africa, 1981-84;bd. dirs. Friends of Libr., Kearny, 1985-87; active Grace Episcopal Ch. Mem. Am. Pharm. Assn., Am. Soc. Hosp. Pharmacists, Washington Met. Soc. Hosp. Pharmacists, Phi Delta Chi, Delta Sigma Phi. Avocations: traveling, bicycling, hiking, skiing, computers. Home: 4831 36th St NW Apt 202 Washington DC 20008-4917 Office: NIH Clin Ctr 9000 Rockville Pike Bethesda MD 20892-0001

ONWUKA, UME NDEMBUIKE, rail transportation executive, tax accountant; b. Amangwu, Ohafia, Nigeria, May 3, 1951; came to U.S., 1982; s. Ukpai and Orie (Ukpong) O.; m. Orie R. Onwuka, Apr. 8, 1988; children: Nanna, Nenna, Ume. BSc, Troy State U., 1985; MBA, Averett Coll., 1991. CPA, Va. Adminstrv. supr. McDermott Internat., Lagos, Nigeria, 1974-81; tax acct. Norfolk So. Corp., Roanoke, Va., 1986-93, internal auditor, 1993—; adj. faculty Averett Coll., Roanoke, 1991—. Mem. AICPA, Va. Inst. CPAs. Avocations: racquetball, tennis, golf, soccer. Home: 2706 Byron Dr Roanoke VA 24019-3306

ONYEJEKWE, CHIKE ONYEKACHI, physician, medical director; b. Ubaha-Okigwe, Nigeria, June 8, 1960; came to U.S., 1978; s. Eleweke and Agbara Caroline (Eloagu) O; 1 child, Chike I. BS in biology, Western Ky. U., 1981, BS in chem., 1981; MD, Howard U., 1986. Diplomate Am. Bd. Internal Medicine, Nat. Bd. Medical Examiners. Medical officer D.C. Gen. Hosp., Washington, 1989—; chief resident Howard Medical Svc. D.C. Gen. Hosp., Washington, 1989-90; medical officer Malcom Grow Hosp., Washington, 1989-90, Andrews Airforce Base, Washington, 1990; emergency room physician Oakland (Md.) Gen. Hosp., 1991; medical dir. Prime Medical Corp., Landover, Md., 1992—; pres., CEO Chydok Internat. Corp., Landover, Md., 1993—. Mem. Am. Soc. Internal Medicine, Nat. Medical Assn., Southern Medical Assn., Grand Lodge. Avocations: football, photography, reading, running. Office: Chykod Internat Corp PO Box 5334 Capitol Heights MD 20791

OOLIE, SAM, investment company executive; b. N.Y.C., Aug. 11, 1936; s. Bernadt S. and Rose (Moyel) O.; m. Marjorie R. Oolie, Dec. 3, 1961; children: Janis, Caroline, Tara. BS in Metallurgy, MIT, 1958; MBA, Harvard U., 1961. Chmn. Food Concepts, Inc., Rutherford, N.J., 1962-85; pres. CFC Venture Capital Corp., Fairfield, N.J., 1984-90; chmn. Oolie Enterprises, Upper Saddle River, N.J., 1985—; vice chmn. Am. Mobile, Inc., Secaucus, N.J., 1986-89; chmn. The Nostalgia Network, N.Y.C., 1987-90, New Thermal Corp., Keasbey, N.J., 1991-95; chmn., CEO NoFire Tech., Inc., Upper Saddle River, N.J., 1995—; bd. dirs. Avesis, Inc., Phoenix, Comverse Tech., N.Y.C., Noise Cancellation Tech., Stamford, Conn. Mem. exec. com. State of N.J.-Israel Commn., 1989—; commr. Essex County Improvement Authority, 1987-88; trustee Coun. Jewish Fedns., 1986—; bd. govs. Haifa U., 1986-90, 93—; trustee Garden State Cancer Ctr., 1989—, Beth Israel Med. Ctr., 1990—, Assn. Reform Zionists Am., 1990—, Am. Joint Distbn. Com., 1990—; pres. United Jewish Fedn. Met. West N.J., 1988-90; vice chmn. United Jewish Appeal, 1986—; chmn. Beth Israel Health Care Found., 1993-96. Recipient Gates of Jerusalem award Boys Town of Jerusalem, 1990, Israel 40th Ann. medal State of Israel Bonds, 1988. Mem. World Bus. Coun., Harvard Club of N.Y., Greenbrook Country Club. Avocations: golf, numismatics. Office: 21 Industrial Ave Upper Saddle River NJ 07458-2301

OOMMEN, GEORGE, architect, painter, athletic facilities planning consultant, educator; b. Munnar, India, Feb. 27, 1942; came to U.S., 1968; s. George and Achy (Abraham) O.; m. Laurie Jeanne; children—Mia, Christie, Sarah. B.Arch., Delhi U., 1964; M. Arch. in Urban Design, Harvard U., 1970. Registered architect, planner. Prin., Khanna, Oommen, Jain, New Delhi, India, 1964-65, George Oommen & Assocs., Mepral, Kerala, India, 1964-67; archtl. designer Ewing Miller Assocs., Terre Haute, Ind., 1967-68; project planner Harvard U., Cambridge, Mass., 1970-72, planning officer, 1972-79, spl. asst. to v.p. adminstrn., 1979-84, critic Grad. Sch. Design, 1973-74, faculty Grad. Sch. Design and Continuing Edn., 1983—, sr. property devel. officer Planning Group, 1984—; faculty Boston Archtl. Ctr., 1970-73, Babson Exec. Edn. Program, 1985-86; cons. infield. Author: Program for Athletic Facilities, 1975; urban designer various jours., Eng., Greece, Italy, India, Japan, U.S.A.; creator first outdoor fine tuned track McCurdy Track, Harvard U., 1984. Exec. council Harvard/Radcliffe Child Care Council, Cambridge, 1974; mem. Gov.'s Task Force Commonwealth of Mass., 1975; athletic cons. Long Island U., Franklin & Marshall Coll., Drew U., Babson Coll., Western Mont. Sports Medicine & Fitness Ctr., DePaul U., Assumption Coll., St. Marks Sch., Mansfield U., The Nutrasweet Co., Hamline U., Adelphi U. Exhbns. include Wellbridge Ctr., Boston, 1994, Harvard Club of Boston, 1994, Dru Arstark, N.Y.C., 1994, Kresge Gallery, Boston, 1994, Rocco's Charles St. South, Boston, 1994. Recipient award of distinction for exhibit Internat. Conf. Architects, India, 1964, Cert. of Merit, Winthrop Housing Design Competition, Boston, 1975, Athletic Bus. Facility of Merit Award, 1987, 88 89, 90, Preservation Honor award Nat. Trust Hist. Preservation, 1987; John D. Rockefeller III Found. grantee, 1969. Mem. AIA (assoc.), Am. Inst. Cert. Planners, Am. Planning Assn., Am. Inst. Planners, Boston Soc. Architects, Mass. State Assn. Architects, Indian Inst. Architects (assoc.). Clubs: Harvard (Boston); Harvard Varsity (hon.) (Cambridge). Office: Harvard Planning Group 912 Holyoke Ctr 1350 Massachusetts Ave Cambridge MA 02138-3846

OOMS, VAN DOORN, economist; b. Chgo., Oct. 29, 1934; s. Casper William and Ruth P. (Miller) O.; m. Theodora J. Parfit, June 17, 1961; children: Katrina, Alex, Tamara. BA summa cum laude, Amherst Coll., 1956, LHD (hon.), 1981; BA with 1st class honors, Oxford (Eng.) U., 1958, MA, 1962; M.A., Yale U., 1960, Ph.D., 1965. Lectr. Yale U., 1962, asst. prof. econs., to 1968; assoc. prof. Swarthmore Coll., 1968, prof., to, 1978; chief economist U.S. Senate Budget Com., Washington, 1977-78; asst. dir. for econ. policy U.S. Office Mgmt. and Budget, Washington, 1978-81; chief economist U.S. House Budget Com., Washington, 1981-91, exec. dir. for policy, 1989-91; sr. v.p., dir. rsch. Com. for Econ. Devel., Washington, 1991—. Rhodes scholar, Oxford U., 1958; Ford Found. Dissertation fellow Yale U., 1965. Office: 2000 L St NW Ste 700 Washington DC 20036-4907

OORT, ABRAHAM HANS, meteorologist, researcher, educator; b. Leiden, The Netherlands, Sept. 2, 1934; came to U.S., 1961; s. Jan Hendrik and Johanna Maria (Graadt Van Roggen) O.; m. Bineke Pel, May 20, 1961; children: Pieter Jan, Michiel, Sonya. MS, MIT, 1963; PhD in Meteorology, U. Utrecht, The Netherlands, 1964. Rsch. meteorologist Koninklyk Nederlands Meteorologisch Instituut, De Bilt, The Netherlands, 1964-66; rsch. meteorologist Geophysical Fluid Dynamics Lab/NOAA, Washington, 1966-68; rsch. meteorologist Geophysical Fluid Dynamics Lab/NOAA, Princeton, N.J., 1968-77, sr. rsch. meteorologist, 1977—; prof. dept. geological and geophysical scis., Princeton U., 1971—. Author: Physics of Climate, 1992; contbr. monographs in field. 2nd lt. Netherlands Air Force, 1959-61. NATO sci. fellow MIT, Cambridge, 1961-63; 10th Victor P. Starr Meml. lectr. MIT, 1988; recipient Gold medal U.S. Dept. Commerce, Washington, 1979. Fellow N.Y. Acad. Scis., Am. Meteorol. Soc. (Jule G. Charney award 1993), Royal Meteorol. Soc.; mem. Am. Geophys. Union. Democrat. Avocations: sculpture, shiatsu, meditation. Office: Princeton U NOAA Box 308 Princeton NJ 08542

OPALA, MARIAN P(ETER), state supreme court justice; b. Lódz, Poland, Jan. 20, 1921. BSB in Econs., Oklahoma City U., 1957, JD, 1953, LLD, 1981; LLM, NYU, 1968; HHD, Okla. Christian U. Sci. & Arts, 1981. Bar: Okla. 1953, U.S. Supreme Ct. 1970. Asst. county atty. Oklahoma County, 1953-56; practiced law Oklahoma City, 1956-60, 65-67; referee Okla. Supreme Ct., Oklahoma City, 1960-65; prof. law Oklahoma City U. Sch. Law, 1965-69; asst. to presiding justice Supreme Ct. Okla., 1967-68; adminstrv. dir. Cts. Okla., 1968-77; presiding judge Okla. State Indsl. Ct., 1977-78; judge Workers Compensation Ct., 1978; justice Okla. Supreme Ct., 1978—, chief justice, 1991-93; adj. prof. law Okla. City U., 1962—, U. Okla. Coll. Law, 1969—; prof. law U. Tulsa Law Sch., 1982—; mem. permanent faculty Am. Acad. Jud. Edn., 1970—; mem. NYU Inst. Jud. Adminstrn.; mem. faculty Nat. Jud. Coll., U. Nev., 1975—; chmn. Nat. Conf. State Ct. Adminstrs., 1976-77; mem. Nat. Conf. Commrs. on Uniform State Laws, 1982—. Co-author: Oklahoma Court Rules for Perfecting a Civil Appeal, 1969. Mem. Adminstrn. Conf. U.S., 1993-95. Recipient Herbert Harley award Am. Judicature Soc., 1977, Disting. Alumni award Oklahoma City U., 1979, Americanism medal Nat. Soc. DAR, 1984, ABA/Am. Law Inst. Harrison Tweed Spl. Merit award, 1987, Humanitarian award NCCJ, 1991, Jour. Record award, 1995. Mem. AbA (edn. com. appellate judges conf. 1984-93), Okla. Bar Assn. (Earl Sneed Continuying Legal Edn. award 1988), Okla. County Bar Assn., Am. Soc. Legal History, Oklahoma City Title Lawyers Assn., Am. Judicature Soc. (bd. dirs. 1988-92), Am. Law Inst. (elected), Order of Coif, Phi Delta Phi (Oklahoma City Alumni award). Office: Okla Supreme Ct State Capitol Rm 238 Oklahoma City OK 73105

OPARA, EMMANUEL CHUKWUEMEKA, biochemistry educator; b. Lagos, Nigeria, July 4, 1951; came to U.S., 1984; s. Eugene Uba and Caroline (Adanma) O.; m. Clarice Adaku Njemanze, Mar. 28, 1980; children: Ogechi, Chiedu, Chukwuka, Ikenna. BS with honors, U. Nigeria, 1976; MS, U. Surrey, Eng., 1980; PhD, U. London, 1983. Assoc. Royal Coll. of Pathologists. Inspecting officer Food and Drug Adminstrn., Lagos, 1977-78; clin. biochemist Epsom (Eng.) Hosp. Labs., 1978-81; teaching asst. Chelsea Coll., London, 1981-83; rsch. fellow Mayo Clinic, Rochester, Minn., 1984-86; vis. fellow NIH, Bethesda, Md., 1986-88; rsch. assoc. Duke U. Med. Ctr., Durham, N.C., 1988-89; asst. prof. Duke U. Med. Ctr., 1989—. Contbr. articles to numerous scientific and med. jours. Com. chairperson Holy Cross Ch., Durham, 1992. WHO fellow, Geneva, 1984; Fogarty Internat. fellow, Bethesda, 1986; recipient Cystic Fibrosis Found. grant, 1990, Am. Diabetes Assn. grant, 1993. Mem. Am. Fedn. for Clin. Rsch., Am. Diabetes Assn., Am. Pancreatic Assn., Assn. Clin. Biochemists (U.K.), Biochemistry Soc. Democrat. Roman Catholic. Avocations: tennis, walking, current affairs, reading, television. Home: 2 Scarsdale Pl Durham NC 27707-5526 Office: Duke U Med Ctr Dept of Surgery PO Box 3065 Durham NC 27710

OPARIL, SUZANNE, cardiologist, educator, researcher; b. Elmira, N.Y., Apr. 10, 1941; d. Stanley and Anna (Penkova) O. AB, Cornell U., 1961; MD, Columbia U., 1965. Diplomate Am. Bd. Internal Medicine. Intern in medicine Presbyn. Hosp., N.Y.C., 1965-66; sr. asst. resident in medicine Mass. Gen. Hosp., Boston, 1967-68, clin. and rsch. fellow in medicine, cardiac unit, 1968-71; asst. prof. medicine Med. Sch., U. Chgo., 1971-75, assoc. prof., 1975-77; assoc. prof. dept. medicine U. Ala., Birmingham, 1977-81, asst. prof. physiology and biophysics, 1980-81, assoc. prof., 1981—, prof. medicine, 1981—, dir. vascular biology and hypertension program, 1985—; mem. vis. faculty Nat. High Blood Pressure Edn. Program, 1974—, Joint Nat. Com. on Detection, Evaluation and Treatment High Blood Pressure, 1991; mem. bd. sci. advisors Sterling Drug, Inc., 1988-91; lectr. in field; Selkurt lectr. Ind. U. Sch. Medicine, 1994; hon. prof. Peking Union Med. Coll., 1994. Author books on hypertension; editor Am. Jour. Med. Scis., 1984-94; assoc. editor Hypertension, 1979-83, mem. editl. bd., 1984—; assoc. editor Am. Jour. Physiology-Renal, 1989-91; mem. editl. bd. Jour. Hypertensioin, 1989—; contbr. over 300 articles to profl. jours., chpts. to books. Recipient Young Investigator award Internat. Soc. Hypertension, 1979, ann. award Med. Coll. Pa., 1984; fellow Am. Coll. Cardiology, 1992. Fellow Am. Coll. Cardiology; mem. Inst. Medicine of NAS (corr. com. on human rights 1992, chmn. com. advise Dept. Def. 1993 Breast Cancer Rsch. Program), AAAS, Endocrine Soc., Inter-Am. Soc. Hypertension, Am. Soc. Hypertension (pub. policy com. 1990—, sci. program com. 1990-92), Assn. for Women in Sci., Am. Heart Assn. (coun. for high blood pressure rsch., 1973—, exec. com. 1985-90, vice chmn. 1986, coun. on basic scis. 1978—, mem.-at-large, exec. com. 1979-81, mem.-at-large bd. dirs. 1992, chmn. Louis B. Katz Prize com. 1984-86, chmn., 1988-90, chmn. budget com. 1990-91, v.p. Ala. affiliate 1986-87, pres.-elect Ala. affiliate 1987-88, 93-94, pres. Ala. affiliate 1988-89, nat. pres.-elect 1993-94, nat. pres. 1994—, Lewis K. Dahl Meml. Lectr. 1993), Am. Physiol. Soc. (clin. physiology adv. com. 1992—), Am. Soc. for Clin. Investigation (sec.-treas. 1983-86), Soc. Exptl. Biology and Medicine (councillor 1993—), So. Soc. for Clin. Investigation (Founder's award 1995), Assn. Am. Physicians, Am. Fedn. for Clin. Rsch. (midwest councillor 1974-75, nat. councillor 1975-78, sec.-treas. 1978-80, pres. 1981-82), Phi Beta Kappa, Sigma Xi, Alpha Omega Alpha (mem. nat. bd. dirs., dir.-at-large 1991, treas. 1993). Avocations: horseback riding, tennis, hiking, travel. Office: U Ala Sch Medicine 1034 Zeigler Research Bldg Birmingham AL 35294*

OPDYCKE, LEONARD EMERSON, retired secondary education educator, publisher; b. Boston, May 22, 1929; s. Leonard and Frances (Prescott) O.; m. Susan Wolcott, 1951 (div.); children: Susan, Deborah, Margot; m. Jeanne Bernhard, 1963 (div.); children: Sarah, Frances; m. Sandra S. Auchincloss, 1976. BA, Harvard U., 1951; MA, U. Rochester, 1965. Tchr. Southfield Sch., Shreveport, L.A., 1952-53, Dedham (Mass.) Country Day, Harley Sch., Rochester, N.Y., 1956-64; dir. Poughkeepsie (N.Y.) Day Sch., 1965-72; chair English dept. Rhinebeck (N.Y.) High Sch., 1974-77; adj. prof. Marist Coll., Poughkeepsie, N.Y., 1977-84, 93-95. Editor, pub. WWI Aero, 1961—; pub. Skyways, 1987—. Mem. Phi Beta Kappa. Avocations: building aircraft, linguistics, education. Home and Office: 15 Crescent Rd Poughkeepsie NY 12601

OPEL, JOHN R., business machines company executive; b. Kansas City, Mo., Jan. 5, 1925; s. Norman J. and Esther (Roberts) O.; m. Julia Carole Stout, Dec. 28, 1953; children: Robert, Nancy, Julia, Mary, John. AB, Westminster Coll., 1948; MBA, U. Chgo., 1949. With IBM Corp., Armonk, N.Y., 1949—, salesman, various mgmt. positions, 1949-66, v.p., 1966-68, mem. mgmt. com., 1967, v.p. corp. finance and planning, 1968-69, sr. v.p. finance and planning, 1969-72, group exec. data processing group, 1972-74, dir., 1972-94, pres., 1974-83, chief exec. officer, 1981-85, chmn., 1983-86, chmn. exec. com., 1986-93, ret. chmn., 1993. Trustee, Westminster Coll. Served with U.S. Army, 1943-45. Mem. Bus. Coun., Coun. on Fgn. Rels. Office: IBM Corp 590 Madison Ave New York NY 10022

OPEL, WILLIAM, medical association administrator. Exec. dir. Huntington Med. Rsch. Inst., Pasadena, Calif. Office: Huntington Med Rsch Inst 734 Fairmount Ave Pasadena CA 91105

OPELA, MARIAN MEADE, principal, consultant; b. Sharon, Conn., July 5, 1941; d. Jerry Roselle and Ruth Bean (Wills) Meade; m. H. Terry Opela, July 1, 1967; children: Stephen, Glenn, H. Kevin. BA, Middlebury Coll., 1962; MEd, SUNY, Buffalo, 1968; postgrad., Coll. of St. Rose, 1993—. Cert. tchr. social studies, N.Y.; cert. SAS. Tchr. Cheektowaga (N.Y.) Ctrl. High Sch., 1963-67; nursery sch. dir. Magic Dragon Pre-Sch., Stockport, N.Y., 1979-81; tchr. Acad. of the Holy Names, Albany, N.Y., 1981-84; tchr. Ichabod Crane Ctrl. Sch., Valatie, 1984-94, strategic planning coord., 1991-94; asst. prin. Ravena (N.Y.)-Coeymans-Selkirk Mid. Sch., 1994—, summer sch. prin., 1996; cons. N.Y. State Edn. Dept., Albany, 1990, 92, 94. Lay leader, speaker North Chatham (N.Y.) Meth. Ch., 1990—; del. Columbia County Environ. Mgmt. Coun., Hudson, N.Y., 1984-92; candidate for Kinderhook Town Bd., 1991. Mem. N.Y. State Coun. for Social Studies, Kinderhook Rep. Club, Nat. Campers and Hikers Assn. (exec. bd. 1968-93, Nat. plaque 1980), Delta Kappa Gamma, Phi Delta Kappa. Avocations: camping, hiking, reading, mentoring. Home: 309 Rt 28 B Valatie NY 12184-9782

OPHULS, MARCEL, film director and producer; b. Frankfurt, Germany, Nov. 1, 1927; came to U.S., 1947, naturalized, 1950; s. Max and Hilda (Wall) Oppenheimer; m. Regine Ackermann, Aug. 21, 1956; children: Catherine Julie, Danielle, Jeanne Dorothee. Student, Occidental Coll., Los Angeles,

1946-49; Licencie es Letters, U. Paris, 1950; DArts (hon.), Columbia Coll., Chgo., 1983. Asst. dir. films France, 1951-56; tchr. film Princeton U., 1973-74, also sr. vis. fellow council humanities and mem. adv. council sociology dept. Program dir. TV and radio plays, Sudwestfunk, Fed. Republic of Germany, 1956-60; dir. feature films, Paris, 1961-65; producer, dir. documentary films, 1966—; dir.: (sketch) Love at Twenty, 1961, (films) including Banana Peel, 1963, Fire at Will, 1964, Munich, or Peace in Our Time, 1966, The Sorrow and The Pity, 1971, America Revisited, 1972, A Sense of Loss, 1972, The Memory of Justice, 1976, Kortner Geschichten, 1980, Yorktown, The Sense of A Battle, 1982, Hotel Terminus: The Life and Times of Klaus Barbie, 1988 (Acad. award best documentary feature 1989), November Days, 1990; The Troubles We've Seen, 1993, contbg. editor Am. Film. Served with AUS, 1946-47. Decorated knight of arts and letters French Ministry Culture; recipient film and TV awards including Best Documentary award, 1988, award Brit. Acad., 1972, 88, Best Documentary French Authors' Soc., 1994, Achievement award Acad. of Motion Pictures, 1995; MacArthur fellow, 1991. Mem. German Acad. Arts, French Authors Guild, French Dirs. Guild, Am. Acad. Arts and Scis. Address: 10 Rue Ernest Deloison, Neuilly sur Seine France *I believe that individuals shape history, but are also shaped by it.*

OPIE, WILLIAM ROBERT, retired metallurgical engineer; b. Butte, Mont., Apr. 3, 1920; s. Ellison Stuart and Myrtle (Williams) O.; m. Constance E. Kickuth, Oct. 14, 1944; children: Lyde Margaret, Guy William. B.S., Mont. Sch. Mines, 1942, M.E. (hon.), 1965; Sc.D., MIT, 1949; student, Advanced Mgmt. Program, Harvard U., 1967; Sc.D. (hon.), Mont. Coll. Mineral Sci. and Tech., 1980. Foundry metallurgist Wright Aero Corp., Paterson, N.J., 1942-45; research asso. MIT, Cambridge, 1946-48; research metallurgist Am. Smelting and Refining, Perth Amboy, N.J., 1948-50; research supr. Nat. Lead Co., Sayreville, N.J., 1950-60; pres. Amax Base Metals Research & Devel., Inc., Carteret, N.J., 1960-85; cons., 1985—. Contbr. articles to profl. jours. Served with U.S. Navy, 1945-46. Fellow AIME, Am. Soc. Metals; mem. Nat. Acad. Engring. Patentee in field. Home: 119 Crawfords Corner Rd Holmdel NJ 07733-1947

OPITZ, JOHN MARIUS, clinical geneticist, pediatrician; b. Hamburg, Germany, Aug. 15, 1935; came to U.S., 1950, naturalized, 1957; s. Friedrich and Erica Maria (Quadt) O.; m. Susan O. Lewin; children: Leigh, Teresa, John, Chrisanthi, Emma. BA, State U. Iowa, 1956, MD, 1959; DSc (hon.), Mont. State U., 1983; MD (hon.), U. Kiel, Germany, 1986. Diplomate Am. Bd. Pediatrics, Am. Bd. Med. Genetics. Intern, State U. Iowa Hosp., 1959-60, resident in pediatrics, 1960-61; resident and chief resident in pediatrics U. Wis. Hosp., Madison, 1961-62; fellow in pediatrics and med. genetics U. Wis., 1962-64, asst. prof. med. genetics and pediatrics, 1964-69, assoc. prof., 1969-72, prof., 1972-79; dir. Wis. Clin. Genetics Ctr., 1974-79; clin. prof. med. genetics and pediatrics U. Wash., Seattle, 1979—; adj. prof. medicine, biology, history and philosophy, vet. rsch. and vet. sci. Mont. State U., Bozeman, 1979-94, McKay lectr., 1992, Univ. prof. med. humanities MSU, Bozeman, 1994—; adj. prof. pediatrics, med. genetics U. Wis., Madison, 1979—, Class of 1947 Disting. prof., U. of Wis., 1992; coordinator Shodair Mont. Regional Genetic Svcs. Program, Helena, 1979-82; chmn. dept. med. genetics Shodair Children's Hosp., Helena, 1983-94; dir. Found. Devel. and Med. Genetics, Helena, Mont.; Farber lectr. Soc. Pediatric Pathology, 1987; Joseph Garfunkel lectr. So. Ill. U., Springfield, 1987, McKay lectr. Mont. State U., 1992; Warren Wheeler vis. prof. Columbus (Ohio) Children's Hospital, 1987; Bea Fowlow lectr. in med. genet. U. Calgary, 1996. Editor, author 13 books; founder, editor in chief Am. Jour. Med. Genetics, 1977—; mng. editor European Jour. Pediatrics, 1977-85; contbr. numerous articles on clin. genetics. Chair Mont. Com. for Humanities, 1991. Recipient Pool of Bethesda award for excellence in mental retardation rsch. Bethesda Luth. Home, 1988, Med. Alumni Citation U. Wis., 1989, Col. Harlan Sanders Lifetime Achievement award for work in the field of genetic scis. March of Dimes, Purkinje medal Czech Soc. Medicine, Mendel medal Czech Soc. Med. Genetics, 1996. Fellow AAAS, Am. Coll. Med. Genetics (founder); mem. German Acad. Scientists Leopoldina, Am. Soc. Human Genetics, Am. Pediatric Soc., Soc. Pediatric Rsch., Am. Bd. Med. Genetics, Birth Defects Clin. Genetic Soc., Am. Inst. Biol. Scis., Am. Soc. Zoologists, Teratology Soc., Genetic Soc. Am., European Soc. Human Genetics, Soc. Study Social Biology, Am. Acad. Pediatrics, German Soc. Pediatrics (hon.), Western Soc. Pediatrics Rsch. (emeritus), Italian Soc. Med. Genetics (hon.), Israel Soc. Genetics (hon.), Russian Soc. Med. Genetics (hon.), So. Africa Soc. Med. Genetics (hon.), Japanese Soc. Human Genetics (hon.), Sigma Xi. Democrat. Roman Catholic. Home: 2180 Lime Kiln St Helena MT 59601-5871 Office: FRB Ste 229 100 Neill Ave Helena MT 59601

OPLINGER, KATHRYN RUTH, computer specialist; b. Wadsworth, Ohio, Apr. 18, 1951; d. Herman Carl and Blanche Ruth (White) Simshauser; m. Douglas E. Oplinger, July 26, 1986; children: Raymond, Karla, Kathleen, Laura Dawn. Student, Washington Coll., 1969-71, Kennesaw (Ga.) State Coll., 1988-89. Pres., chief exec. officer Dawn Enterprises, Inc., CMAS, Tiller Stewart & Co. LLC, Atlanta, 1981—; cons. mgmt. info. systems Procter & Gamble, Atlanta, 1989—, Arthur Andersen, USA, Peat Marwick, Guam, others; software expert, programmer Novell Network & Acctg.; spokesperson, designer Saks Fifth Ave, nationwide, 1981-86. Firestone Found. scholar, 1969. Mem. NAFE, Am. Bus. Women's Assn., Lions Internat. (pres. Woodstock, Ga. chpt. 1986-87). Republican. Methodist. Avocations: golf, whitewater rafting, hiking. Office: Dawn Enterprises c/o CMAS Tiller Stewart & Co LLC 780 Johnson Ferry Rd NE Ste 325 Atlanta GA 30342-1434

OPOTOWSKY, MAURICE LEON, newspaper editor; b. New Orleans, Dec. 13, 1931; s. Sol and Fannie (Latter) O.; m. Madeleine Duhamel, Feb. 28, 1959 (dec.); children: Didier Sol Duhamel, Joelle Duhamel, Arielle Duhamel (dec.); m. Bonnie Feibleman, May 4, 1991. Student, Tulane U., 1949-51; B.A. cum laude, Williams Coll., 1953. Reporter Berkshire Eagle, Pittsfield, Mass., 1951-53; pub. Sea Coast Echo, Bay St. Louis, Miss., 1953-54; reporter U.P.I., 1956-62; feature editor Newsday, Ronkonkoma, N.Y., 1962-64; Suffolk day editor Newsday, 1964-65, Nassau night editor, 1965-67, nat. editor, 1967-70, Suffolk editor, 1970-72; dir. L.I. Mag., 1972; day editor Press-Enterprise, Riverside, Calif., 1973-84, mng. editor features/adminstrn., 1984-87, sr. mng. editor, 1987-92, mng. editor, 1992—; chief N.Y. State Syndicate Service, 1961-74; mem. Calif. Freedom of Info. Exec. Com., sec., 1979-80, treas., 1980-81, v.p., 1981-82, pres., 1982-83. Trustee Harbor Country Day Sch., 1970-72; bd. dirs. Calif. Newspaper Editor Conf. Bd., 1978-83; mem. Smithtown (N.Y.) Hunt, 1970-73, West Hills Hunt, 1976-80, Santa Fe Hunt, Whip, 1985—; co-chmn. Calif. Bench-Bar Media Com.; mem. adv. coun. dept. comm. Calif. State U., Fullerton, 1995—. Served with AUS, 1954-56. Mem. AP News Execs. Calif. (chmn. 1986-87), Calif. 1st Amendment Coalition (pres., treas.), Calif. Soc. Newspaper Editors (bd. dirs., vice chmn. steering com. 1983), AP Mng. Editors Assn., Am. Soc. Newspaper Editors. Office: Press Enterprise Co 3512 14th St Riverside CA 92501-3814

OPOTOWSKY, STUART BERGER, holding company executive; b. N.Y.C., Feb. 23, 1935; s. Rubin S. and Rebecca (Sapolin) O.; m. Enid Berk, June 27, 1959 (div. Apr. 1972); children: Peter, Catherine; m. Barbara Berger, Aug. 3, 1972; 1 child, Sasha. BBA, Wayne State U., 1957, LLB, 1962. Bar: Mich. 1963, Calif. 1965, N.Y. 1972; CPA, Mich. Gen. tax counsel Norton Simon Inc., N.Y.C., 1964-76; ptnr. Phillips Nizer Benjamin Krim & Ballon, N.Y.C., 1976-80; gen. tax counsel The Penn Cen. Corp., N.Y.C., 1980-82; ptnr. Feit & Ahrens, N.Y.C., 1982-87; v.p. tax Loews Corp., N.Y.C., 1987—; adj. prof. law NYU, N.Y.C., 1975-85. Mem. ABA, N.Y. State Bar Assn. Office: Loews Corp 1 Park Ave New York NY 10016-5802

OPPEDAHL, JOHN FREDRICK, newspaper editor; b. Duluth, Minn., Nov. 9, 1944; s. Walter H. and Lucille (Hole) O.; m. Alison Owen, 1975 (div. 1983); m. Gillian Coyro, Feb. 14, 1987; 1 child, Max. B.A., U. Calif., Berkeley, 1967; M.S., Columbia U., 1968. Reporter San Francisco Examiner, 1967; reporter, asst. city editor Detroit Free Press, 1968-75, city editor, 1975-80, exec. city editor, 1981, exec. news editor, 1981-82, asst. mng. editor, 1983; nat. editor Dallas Times Herald, 1983-85, asst. mng. editor, 1985-87; mng. editor/news L.A. Herald Examiner, 1987-89; mng. editor Ariz. Republic, Phoenix, 1989-93; exec. editor Phoenix Newspapers, 1993-95; pub., CEO Phoenix Newspapers, Inc., 1996—. Trustee Walter Cronkite Sch. Journalism and Telecomm., Ariz. State U.; bd. dirs. Found. for Am. Comms., Downtown Phoenix Partnership, Valley of the Sun United Way, 1996; mem. Greater Phoenix Leadership. Mem. Am. Soc. Newspaper Editors, AP Mng. Editors. Office: Phoenix Newspapers Inc 120 E Van Buren St Phoenix AZ 85004-2227

OPPEDAHL, PHILLIP EDWARD, computer company executive; b. Renwick, Iowa, Sept. 17, 1935; s. Edward and Isadore Hannah (Gangstead) O.; B.S. in Naval Sci., Navy Postgrad. Sch., 1963, M.S. in Nuclear Physics, 1971; M.S. in Systems Mgmt., U. S.C., 1978; m. Sharon Elaine Ree, Aug. 3, 1957 (dec. Aug. 1989); children: Gary Lynn, Tamra Sue, Sue Ann, Lisa Kay. Commd. ensign U.S. Navy, 1956, advanced through grades to capt., 1977; with Airborne Early Warning Squadron, 1957-59, Anti-Submarine Squadron, 1959-65; asst. navigator USS Coral Sea, 1965-67; basic jet flight instr., 1967-69; student Armed Forces Staff Coll., 1971; test group dir. Def. Nuclear Agy., 1972-74; weapons officer USS Oriskany, 1974-76; program mgr. for armament Naval Air Systems Command, Washington, 1977-79; test dir. Def. Nuclear Agy., Kirtland AFB, N.Mex., 1979-82, dep. comdr. Def. Nuclear Agy., 1982-83; pres., chief exec. officer Am. Systems, Albuquerque, 1983—; dir., bd. dirs. BASIS Internat., 1991—. Pres., bd. dirs. Casa Esperanza, 1990-92. Decorated Disting. Service medal. Mem. Naval Inst., Am. Nuclear Soc., Aircraft Owners and Pilots Assn., Assn. Naval Aviation Navy League. Lutheran. Author: Energy Loss of High Energy Electrons in Beryllium, 1971; Understanding Contractor Motivation and Incentive Contracts, 1977. Home: 11200 Montgomery NE # 8-11-8 Albuquerque NM 87111 *Personal philosophy: The remainder of my life is dedicated to giving back to the universe the life, love and energy that the universe has given me.*

OPPEL, RICHARD ALFRED, newspaper executive; b. Newark, Jan. 30, 1943; s. Alfred William and Jane Genevieve (Owen) O.; m. Carol Freeman Van Aken, Apr. 1, 1967; children: Richard Alfred, Shelby Reid. B.A. in Polit. Sci., U. South Fla. Reporter Tampa Tribune, Fla., 1963-65; newsman, corr., chief bur. AP, Tallahassee, Tampa, Miami and Detroit, 1965-76; assoc. editor Detroit Free Press, 1976-77; exec. editor, v.p. Tallahassee Democrat, 1977-78; v.p. Charlotte (N.C.) Observer, 1978-93; editor Charlotte News, 1985-87; chief Washington bur. Knight-Ridder Newspapers, Washington, 1993—. Pres. N.C. First Amendment Found. Served with USMCR, 1960-65. Recipient Disting. Alumni award U. South Fla.; named Editor of Yr. Nat. Press Found., 1987, Ralph McGill Lectr. U. Ga., 1992. Mem. N.C. Press Assn. (pres. 1992-93), Am. Soc. Newspaper Editors. Episcopalian. Avocations: long distance running, hunting, fishing. Office: Knight-Ridder 529 14th St NW Washington DC 20045-1000

OPPENHEIM, ALAN VICTOR, electrical engineering educator; b. N.Y.C., Nov. 11, 1937; s. Sydney and Dorothy (Arenz) O.; m. Phyllis Arnold, June 20, 1964; children: Justine Ruth, Jason Philip. S.B., MIT, 1961, S.M., 1961, Sc.D., 1964; D (hon.), Tel Aviv U., 1995. Asst. prof. dept. elec. engring. MIT, 1964-69, assoc. prof. dept. elec. engring. and computer scis., 1969-76, prof. dept. elec. engring. and computer sci., 1976-90, Disting. prof. elec. engring., 1990—; staff scientist Lincoln Lab., 1967-69, assoc. head data systems div., 1978-80; cons. Lincoln Lab., Atlantic Aerospace Inc., Sanders Assocs., Inc. Co-author: Digital Signal Processing, 1975, Signals and Systems, 1983, Discrete-Time Signal Processing, 1989, others; editor: Applications of Digital Signal Processing, 1978, (with others) Advanced Topics in Signal Processing, 1988; contbr. articles to profl. jours. Guggenheim fellow, 1972-73. Fellow IEEE (Edn. medal 1988, other awards); mem. Nat. Acad. Engring., Sigma Xi, Eta Kappa Nu, Tau Beta Pi. Office: MIT Dept Electric Engring & Computer Sci 50 Vassar St Cambridge MA 02139-4309

OPPENHEIM, ANTONI KAZIMIERZ, mechanical engineer; b. Warsaw, Poland, Aug. 11, 1915; came to U.S., 1948, naturalized, 1954; s. Tadeusz and Zuzanna (Zuckerwar) O.; m. Lavinia Stephens, July 18, 1945; 1 dau., Terry Ann. Diploma in Engring., Warsaw Inst. Tech., London, 1943; PhD in Engring., U. London, 1945; diploma of Imperial Coll., 1945; DSc, U. London, 1976; Dr. Honoris Causa, U. Poitiers, France, 1981, Tech. U., Warsaw, 1989. Registered profl. engr., Calif. Research asst. City and Guilds Coll., 1942-48, lectr., 1946-48; asst. prof. mech. engring. Stanford U., 1948-50; faculty U. Calif. at Berkeley, 1950—, prof. mech. engring., 1958-86, Miller prof., 1961-62, prof. emeritus, 1986—; vis. prof. Sorbonne, Paris, 1960-61, U. Poitiers, France, 1973, 80; staff cons. Shell Devel. Co., 1952-60. Editor-in-chief: Acta Astronautica, 1974-79; contbr. articles to profl. jours., also monographs. Chmn. Heat Transfer and Fluid Mechanics Inst., 1958; IAA Com. on Gasdynamics of Explosions, 1968—; organizer Internat. Colloquia on Gas Dynamics of Explosions and Reactive Systems, 1967, 69, 71, 73, 75, 77, 79, 81, 83; mem. NASA, adv. com. fluid mechanics, 1963-69. Fellow Imperial Coll., 1995; recipient Water Arbitration prize Inst. Mech. Engrs., 1948, Numa Manson medal Inst. for Dynamics of Explosions and Reactive Sys., 1981, Dionizy Smolenski medal Polish Acad. Scis., 1987, Alfred C. Egerton medal The Combustion Inst., 1988, citation U. Calif., Berkeley, 1988. Recipient Water Arbitration prize Inst. Mech. Engrs., 1948, Numa Manson medal Inst. for Dynamics of Explosions and Reactive Sys., 1981, Dionizy Smolenski medal Polish Acad. Scis., 1987, Alfred C. Egerton medal The Combustion Inst., 1988, citation U. Calif., Berkeley, 1988. Spl. research compressible fluid flow, gas turbines and internal combustion engines, heat transfer, combustion, detonation and blast waves. Home: 54 Norwood Ave Kensington CA 94707-1119

OPPENHEIM, DAVID JEROME, musician, educational administrator; b. Detroit, Apr. 13, 1922; s. Louis and Julia (Nurko) O.; m. Judy Holliday, 1948; 1 child, Jonathan; m. Ellen Adler, Apr. 14, 1957; children: Sara, Thomas; m. Pat Jaffe, June 13, 1987. Student, Julliard Sch. Music, 1939-40; MusB, U. Rochester, 1943. Dir. Masterworld div. Columbia Records, N.Y.C., 1950-59; producer, dir., writer network news CBS-TV, N.Y.C., 1962-68; exec. producer Pub. Broadcasting Lab., N.Y.C., 1968-69; dean Tisch Sch. of the Arts NYU, N.Y.C., 1969-92, dean emeritus, 1992—; adv. com. Sta. WNCN; mem. Tony awards com., 1983-88. Clarinet soloist Casals Festival, Prades, France, 1955, San Juan, P.R., 1959, recs. include Budapest Quartet, Brahms Clarinet Quintet, Opus 115 and Mozart Clarinet Quintet in A Maj., (Stravinsky conducting) L'Histoire du Soldat, Octet, Septet, Bernstein Sonata, Leonard Bernstein, piano (dedicated to David Oppenheim), (with Julliard Quartet) Copland Sextet, (with New Music Quartet) Douglas Moore Quintet; co-producer (play) Saul Bellow's Last Analysis on Broadway, 1962; producer documentary films on Stravinsky and Casals, CBS News. Bd. dirs. emeritus Film Soc. Lincoln Center, Inc., Town Hall Found.; bd. dirs. Am. Stefan Wolpe Soc.; bd. advisors New Sch. Concerts. With AUS, World War II, ETO. Recipient Prix Italia Radiotelevisione Italiana, 1964. Mem. Nat. Soc. Lit. and Arts, Internat. Council Fine Arts Deans, N.Y. State Arts Deans, Town Hall Found., Soc. of Fellows (charter), Am. Fedn. Arts (film program). Avocations: camping, reading, gardening, hiking.

OPPENHEIM, IRWIN, chemical physicist, educator; b. Boston, June 30, 1929; s. James L. and Rose (Rosenberg) O.; m. Bernice Buresh, May 18, 1974; 1 child, Joshua Buresh. A.B. summa cum laude, Harvard U., 1949; postgrad., Calif. Inst. Tech., 1949-51; Ph.D., Yale, 1956. Physicist Nat. Bur. Standards, Washington, 1953-60; chief theoretical physics Gen. Dynamics/Convair, San Diego, 1960-61; assoc. prof. chemistry MIT, Cambridge, 1961-65; prof. MIT, 1965—; lectr. physics U. Md., 1953-60; vis. assoc. prof. physics U. Leiden, 1955-56, Lorentz prof., 1983; vis. prof. Weizmann Inst. Sci., 1958-59, U. Calif., San Diego, 1966-67; Van der Waals prof. U. Amsterdam, 1966-67. Author: (with J.G. Kirkwood) Chemical Thermodynamics, 1961; editor: Phys. Rev. E, 1992—. Fellow Am. Phys. Soc., Am. Acad. Arts and Scis., Washington Acad. Sci.; mem. Phi Beta Kappa, Sigma Xi. Research in quantum statis. mechanics, statis. mechanics of transport processes, thermodynamics. Home: 140 Upland Rd Cambridge MA 02140-3623 Office: MIT 77 Massachusetts Ave #6-221 Cambridge MA 02139-4301

OPPENHEIMER, FRANZ MARTIN, lawyer; b. Mainz, Germany, Sept. 7, 1919; s. Arnold and Johanna (Mayer) O.; m. Margaret Spencer Foote, June 17, 1944; children: Martin Foote, Roxana Foote, Edward Arnold. B.S., U. Chgo., 1942; student, U. Grenoble, France, 1938-39; LL.B. cum laude (note editor Law Jour. 1945), Yale U., 1945. Bar: N.Y. 1946, D.C. 1955. Rsch. asst. com. human devel. U. Chgo., 1942-43; law clk. to Judge Swan, U.S. Circuit Ct. of Appeals, N.Y., 1945-46; assoc. atty. Chadbourne, Wallace, Parke & Whiteside, N.Y.C., 1946-47; atty. IBRD, Washington, 1947-57; individual practice law, 1958-59; ptnr. firm Leva, Hawes, Symington, Martin & Oppenheimer, 1959-83, Fort & Schlefer, Washington, 1984-94; pvt. practice Washington, 1995-96; sr. of counsel Swidler & Berlin, Washington, 1996—. Contbr. articles to profl. jours. Bd. dirs. Internat. Student House; founding mem. Company of Christian Jews; hon. trustee Com. 100 on Fed. City, Washington. Decorated officer's cross Order of Merit (Fed. Republic Germany), chevalier Nat. Order of Merit (France). Mem. ABA, Fed. Bar Assn., Am. Soc. Internat. Law (treas. 1964-76), Coun. Fgn. Rels., Yale Club, Century Assn. (N.Y.), City Tavern, Met. Club (Washington). Episcopalian. Home: 3248 O St NW Washington DC 20007-2847 Office: 3000 K St NW Ste 300 Washington DC 20007-5116

OPPENHEIMER, JACK HANS, internist, scientist, educator; b. Egelsbach, Hesse, Germany, Sept. 14, 1927; came to U.S., 1937; s. Julius and Elsa (Reis) O.; m. Ann Ehrlich, Dec. 20, 1953; children: Mark, Lawrence, Adele Oppenheimer Brown. BA, Princeton U., 1949; MD, Columbia U., 1953. Diplomate Am. Bd. Internal Medicine. Intern Boston City Hosp., 1953-54; fellow Sloan Kettering Inst., N.Y.C., 1954-55, Columbia Presbyn. Hosp., N.Y.C., 1959-60; resident Duke U., 1957-59; asst. prof. to prof. medicine Albert Einstein Coll. Medicine, Bronx, N.Y., 1964-76; prof. medicine U. Minn., Mpls., 1976—, Cecil J. Watson prof., dir. divsn. endocrinology, 1986—; staff physician Montefiore Hosp. Med. Ctr., Bronx, 1960-76. Contbr. over 200 articles to profl. jours.; editor 2 books. Capt. U.S. Army, 1955-57. Fellow ACP; mem. Endocrine Soc. (coun. 1974-78, Astwood award 1978), Am. Thyroid Assn. (pres. 1985-86, Van Meter award 1965, Parke-Davis award 1984), Am. Soc. Clin. Investigation, Assn. Am. Physicians. Home: 4100 Kerry Ct Hopkins MN 55345-1825 Office: U Minn 520 Delaware St SE Minneapolis MN 55455-0356

OPPENHEIMER, JERRY L., lawyer; b. Birmingham, Ala., Feb. 22, 1937; s. Jerome H. and Mina (Loveman) O.; m. Joan H. Chadwick-Collins, Feb. 23, 1963; children: Julia Cole, James Chadwick. BS, U. N.C., 1958; LLB, U. Va., 1961. Bar: D.C. 1961, Va. 1961. Assoc. Covington & Burling, Washington, 1961-69; atty., advisor U.S. Treasury Dept., Washington, 1969-70, assoc. tax legis. counsel, 1970-71, dep. tax legis. counsel, 1971-73; ptnr. Mayer, Brown & Platt, Washington, 1973—. Home: 4655 Garfield St NW Washington DC 20007-1026 Office: Mayer Brown & Platt 2000 Pennsylvania Ave NW Washington DC 20006-1812

OPPENHEIMER, MARTIN J., lawyer; b. Apr. 11, 1933; s. Julius and Sylvia (Haas) O.; m. Suzanne Rosenhirsch, July 3, 1958; children: Marcy, Evan, Joshua, Alexandra. BS with honors, U. Pa., 1953; LLB, Yale U., 1956. Assoc. Hays, Sklar & Hertzberg, Mendes & Mount; ptnr. Proskauer Rose Goetz & Mendelsohn, N.Y.C., 1958—. Contbr. articles to profl. jours. Chmn. City Ctr. of Music and Drama, Lincoln Ctr., N.Y., 1984—; vice chmn. N.Y.C. Opera, 1985—; bd. dir. 92nd St. YWCA, N.Y., 1985—, Lincoln Ctr. for Performing Arts, 1987—. Fulbright scholar Goethe U., Frankfurt, Fed. Republic Germany, 1956-57. Home: 400 Claflin Ave Mamaroneck NY 10543-3906 Office: Proskauer Rose et al 1585 Broadway New York NY 10036-8200

OPPENHEIMER, MAX, JR., foreign language educator, consultant; b. N.Y.C., July 27, 1917; s. Max and Louise (Pourfuerst) O.; m. Christine Backus, Oct. 14, 1942; children: Edmund Max, Carolyn Christine Oppenheimer Burns. Bachelier ès Lettres, U. Paris, 1935; BA cum laude, NYU, 1941; MA, UCLA, 1942; PhD, U. So. Calif., 1947. Instr. fgn. langs. San Diego State Coll., 1947-49; asst. prof. Romance langs. Washington U., St. Louis, 1949-51; assoc. prof. modern langs. Fla. State U., Tallahassee, 1958-61; prof., chmn. dept. Russian U. Iowa, Iowa City, 1961-67; prof. SUNY, Fredonia, 1967-76, prof. emeritus, 1976—, chmn. dept. fgn. langs., 1967-74; prof. English Yunnan Normal U., Kunming, Peoples Republic of China, 1985-86; intelligence officer CIA, 1956-58. Author: Outline of Russian Grammar, 1962; translator: Theory of Molecular Excitons (Davydov), 1962, Theory of Ship Waves and Wave Resistance (Kostyukov), 1968, The Fake Astrologer (Calderón de la Barca), 1976, 94, The Lady Simpleton (Lope de Vega), 1976, Don Juan (Tirso de Molina), 1976, Swim First and Last, 1981; contbr. articles to scholarly and profl. jours. Active YMCA, 1936—. Served to lt. col., MI, AUS, 1942-46, lt. col. Res., ret. Decorated Bronze Star; Fla. State U. grantee, 1961, Office Naval Rsch. grantee, 1965, SUNY grantee, 1973. Mem. MLA, Am. Soc. Geolinguistics (pres. 1975-76), Am. Soc. Dowsers, Ariz. Soc. for Profl. Hypnosis, Dobro Slovo, Am. Mensa Ltd., Elks, Phi Beta Kappa, Sigma Delta Pi, Pi Delta Phi (nat. pres. 1946-51), Alpha Mu Gamma. Avocation: swimming. Home: 10963 Coggins Sun City AZ 85351 *When you speak, always say what you think, not what you think you should say for the sake of expediency. Steadfastly, stubbornly, cling to your ideals, principles and beliefs, but be flexible enough to change whenever changing them reflects wisdom, not weakness or compromise. Avoid ego trips or being awed by your own alleged accomplishments.*

OPPENHEIMER, MICHAEL, physicist; b. Bklyn., Feb. 28, 1946; s. Harry and Shirley (Meyer) O.; m. Leonie Haimson, Dec. 31, 1986; 1 child, Chloe. S.B., MIT, 1966; Ph.D., U. Chgo., 1970. Research fellow Harvard Coll., 1971-73; lectr. astronomy Harvard U., 1973-81; physicist Harvard-Smithsonian Center for Astrophysics, Harvard U., 1973-81, Environ. Def. Fund, N.Y.C.; 1981—; mem. panel on atmospheric effects of aviation NRC, 1995—; chmn. adv. panel on global warming Am. Mus. Natural History, 1990-93; mem. environ. adv. com. to N.Y. Gov. Cuomo, 1991-94. Author: Dead Heat: The Race Against the Greenhouse Effect, 1990; contbr. articles to profl. jours. Union Carbide fellow, 1969-70; A.F. Morrison fellow, 1979; Guggenheim fellow, 1978-79. Mem. AAAS, Am. Phys. Soc., Am. Geophys. Union, Am. Meteorol. Soc. Office: Environ Def Fund 257 Park Ave S New York NY 10010-7304

OPPENHEIMER, PAUL EUGENE, English comparative literature educator, poet, author; b. N.Y.C., May 1, 1939; s. Fred R. Oppenheimer and Gertrude Samuels; children: Julie Sarah, Ben. BA, Princeton U., 1961; MA, Columbia U., 1963, PhD, 1970. Lectr. Hunter Coll. CUNY, N.Y.C., 1964-67, lectr., poet-in-residence City Coll., 1967-70, from asst. prof. to assoc. prof. City Coll., 1970-84, prof. City Coll., 1984—; exch. prof., dir. CUNY student exch. program Sorbonne nouvelle, Paris, 1984-85; exch. prof. U. North London, Eng., 1989-90, Univ. Coll. London, 1993, German Dept., 1993, 95; Fulbright prof. U. Osnabrück, Germany, 1993-94. Author: Before a Battle and Other Poems, 1967, The Birth of the Modern Mind: Self, Consciousness, and the Invention of the Sonnet, 1989, Beyond the Furies, New Poems, 1985; author, translator: Till Eulenspiegel: His Adventures, 1972, 91, 95, Evil and the Demonic: A New Theory of Monstrous Behavior, 1996. Woodrow Wilson fellow, 1961-62, Alfred Hodder fellow, 1969-70, Fulbright sr. fellow, Germany, 1993-94. Mem. Dante Soc. Am. Home: 50 W 67th St New York NY 10023-6227 Office: CCNY Dept English and Comparative Lit NAC 138 St and Convent Ave New York NY 10031

OPPENHEIMER, STEVEN BERNARD, biology educator; b. Bklyn., Mar. 23, 1944; s. Hugo and Irma (Schellenberg) O.; m. Carolyn Roberta Weisenberg, May 23, 1971; 1 child, Mark. BS magna cum laude, Bklyn. Coll., 1965; PhD, Johns Hopkins U., 1969. Am. Cancer Soc. postdoctoral fellow U. Calif., San Diego, 1969-71; asst. prof. biology Calif. State U., Northridge, 1971-74, assoc. prof., 1974-77, prof., 1977—, dir. Sch. Sci. and Math. Ctr. for Cancer and Devel. Biology; panel mem. NSF, Washington, 1985, NIH, 1987, 94; cons. Northridge Hosp., 1984-92. Author: introduction to Embryonic Development, 1980, 3d rev. edit., 1989, Cancer Biological and Clinical Introduction, 1982, 2d rev. edit., 1985, 3d rev. edit., 1995, Cancer Prevention Guidebook, 1984, 2d rev. edit., 1991, Atlas of Embryonic Development, 1984; editor Cancer, Longevity Letter, 1984-85; editor Jour. of Student Rsch. Abstracts, 1995—; writer (film) Cancer Prevention, A Way of Life, 1986; contbr. articles to profl. jours. Recipient Disting. Prof. award Calif. State U., 1977, Statewide Outstanding Prof. award Bd. Trustees of 19 Campuses, 1984, Excellence in Sci. Edn. award Calif. Sci. Tchrs. Assn., 1988; grantee Nat. Cancer Inst., 1972-84, NSF, 1981—, NICHHD, 1986-88, NIH, 1993—, Joseph Drown Found., 1988—, NASA, 1988-95, Urban Cmty. Svc. Program, 1992-95, Eisenhower Program, 1990, others; Exxon fellow, 1982, Thomas Eckstrom Trust fellow, 1982—. Fellow AAAS; mem. Am. Soc. Zoologists (nat. program chmn., devel. biology and nat. membership chmn. 198-85), Am. Soc. Cell Biology, Soc. Devel. Biology, Am. Cancer Soc. (bd. dirs. San Fernando Valley chpt. 1985-89, Pub. Edn. award 1985, grantee 1977-86), Sigma Xi (Disting. Rsch. award 1984), Phi Kappa Phi. Home: 8933 Darby Ave Northridge CA 91325-2706 Office: Calif State U Dept Biology 18111 Nordhoff St Northridge CA 91330-8303

OPPENHEIMER, SUZI, state senator; b. N.Y.C., Dec. 13, 1934; d. Alfred Elihu Rosenhirsch and Blanche (Schoen) O.; m. Martin J. Oppenheimer, July 3, 1960; children: Marcy, Evan, Josh, Alexandra. BA in Econs., Conn. Coll. for Women, 1956; MBA, Columbia U., 1958. Security analyst McDonnell & Co., N.Y.C., 1958-60, L.F. Rothschild Co., N.Y.C., 1960-63; mayor Village of Mamaroneck, N.Y., 1977-85; mem. N.Y. State Senate, Albany, 1985—; ranking mem. transp. com., mem. fin., edn., environ. conservation, consumer protection and drugs com., chmn. Senate Dem. Task Force on Women's Issues, treas. Legis. Women's Caucus, pres. Senate Club. Former pres. Mamaroneck LWV, Westchester County Mcpl. Ofcls. Assn., Westchester Mcpl. Planning Fedn. Recipient Humanitarian Svc. award Am. Jewish Com., 1988, Legis. Leadership award Young Adult Inst., 1988, Legis. award Westchester Irish Com., 1988, Hon. Svc. award Vis. Nurses Svcs., 1989, Humanitarian Svc. award Project Family, 1990, Meritorious Svc. award N.Y. State Assn. Counties, 1990, Friend of Edn. award N.Y. State United Tchrs., 1991; honoree Windward Sch. Ann. Dinner, 1992; named Legislator of Yr., N.Y. State Women's Press Club. Democrat. Jewish. Dist Office: 16 School St Rye NY 10580

OPPENHEIMER-NICOLAU, SIOBHAN, think tank executive; married; 5 children. MD, Goucher Coll. Supr. internat. svcs. Fuller, Smith and Ross Advt., N.Y.C., 1952-56; asst. to commr. N.Y.C. Cmty. Devel. Agy., 1966-68; program office divsn. nat. affairs Ford Found., N.Y.C., 1968-81; cons. to pres. Hallmark Corp., Kansas City, Mo., 1989-91; cons. to ct. apptd. spl. master The Buck Trust, Marin County, Calif., 1992; cons. to chmn. and pres. Enterprise Found., Columbia, Md., 1981—; with Univision TV Network, Miami, 1992; pres., founder Hispanic Policy Devel. Project, N.Y.C., Washington, 1982—; cons. Levi-Straus Found., Marin County, 1990, U.S. Dept. Labor, 1995, Acad. for Ednl. Devel., N.Y.C., 1993—, The Ewing Marion Kauffman Found., Kansas City; cmty. spokesperson for TV network GEMS Internat. TV, Miami, 1992—; dir. annual seminar Aspen Inst., 1987—; bd. dirs. Edn. Pub. Co., Ewing Marion Kauffman Found., other cos. Contbr. articles to profl. jours. Bd. dirs. Hispanic Women's Project; trustee First Nations' Fin. Inst., Mus. of the Am. Indian; pres., bd. dirs. Internat. Inst. for the Arts. Mem. Women's Prison Assn. (trustee). Home: 36 E 22nd St 9th Fl New York NY 10010 Office: 125 East 10th St New York NY 10003

OPPENLANDER, ROBERT, retired airline executive; b. N.Y.C., May 20, 1923; s. Robert and Lillian (Ahrens) O.; m. Jessie I. Major, Sept. 30, 1950; children: Kris Oppenlander Austin, Robert Kirk, Tenley. B.S., MIT, 1944; M.B.A., Harvard U., 1948. With Metals & Controls Corp., Attleboro, Mass., 1948-53; prin. Cresap, McCormick & Paget, N.Y.C., 1953-58; comptroller, treas. Delta Air Lines, Inc., Atlanta, 1958-88; v.p. fin. Delta Air Lines, Inc., 1964-67, sr. v.p. fin., treas., 1967-78, sr. v.p. fin., 1978-83, vice chmn. bd., chief fin. officer, 1983-88, ret., 1988, also adv. dir. Served to lt. USNR, 1944-46. Club: Capital City. Home: 3944 Powers Ferry Rd NW Atlanta GA 30342-4026

OPPERMAN, DWIGHT DARWIN, publishing company executive; b. Perry, Iowa, June 26, 1923; s. John H. and Zoa L. Opperman; m. Jeanice Wifvat, Apr. 22, 1942 (dec.); children: Vance K., Fane W. JD, Drake U., 1951. Bar: Iowa 1951, U.S. Supreme Ct. 1976, U.S Ct. Internat. Trade, 1988. Editor, asst. editorial counsel West Pub. Co., St. Paul, Minn., 1951-64, mgr. reporters and digest depts., 1964-65; v.p. West Pub. Co., 1965-68, pres., 1968-93, CEO, 1978—, chmn., 1993—; dir. Inst. Judicial Adminstrn. V.p., trustee Supreme Ct. Hist. Soc.; dir. Inst. Jud. Adminstrn.; bd. govs., mem. nat. task force Drake U., Des Moines; dir. Minn. D.A.R.E. Inc.; dir. Brennan Ctr. for Justice, Nat. Legal Ctr. for Pub. Interest. Recipient Herbert Harley award Am. Judicature Soc., 1984, Justice award, 1992, 1st George Wickersham Founder's award Friends of Law Libr. of Congress, 1993. Fellow Am. Bar Found.; mem. ABA, Fed. Bar Assn., Am. Judicature Soc., Am. Law Inst., Drake U. Nat. Alumni Assn. (disting. svc. award 1974, Centennial award 1981, Outstanding Alumni award 1988), Minn. Club (pres. 1975-76). Office: West Pub Co 610 Opperman Dr Eagan MN 55123-1340

OPPERMANN, JOSEPH KAY, architect; b. Galveston, Tex., Apr. 15, 1949; s. Gustav John and Katherine (Shuberg) O.; m. Langdon Edmunds, Oct. 24, 1987; children: Joseph Sjöberg, Frances Edmunds. BA in Liberal Arts, U. Tex., 1971, BArch, 1975, MArch, 1975, cert. in mus. conservation, 1986. Registered architect, N.C., S.C., Ga., Ky., La., D.C. Grants mgr. Tex. Hist. Commn., Austin, 1976-79, dir. tech. svcs., 1979-81, dep. state hist. preservation officer, 1981-87; prin. C. Phillips & Co., Winston-Salem, N.C., 1987; pres. Phillips & Oppermann, P.A., Winston-Salem, 1988—; mem. hist. Am. bldgs. survey team Winedale Inst., 1975; architect mem. nat. register adv. com. N.C. Dept. Cultural Resources; lectr. in field. Contbr. articles to profl. publs. Architect mem. task group to prepare mandatory growth plan City of Austin, 1986; architect mem. rev. panel for hist. facade grants City of Winston-Salem, 1990-91; bd. advisors Hist. Preservation Found. N.C.; bd. advisors grad. archtl. program in hist. preservation Tex. A&M U., 1986-87; bd. dirs. Preservation Action, 1984-87; bd. dirs. Nat. Conf. State Hist. Preservations Officers, 1984-86, chmn. grants appropriations com.; pres. Tex. chpt. Soc. Archtl. Historians, 1980-82. Recipient Tower award for Outstanding Restoration, 1992, 93, 94. Mem. AIA (mem. hist. resources com. N.C. chpt.), Assn. for Preservation Tech., Soc. Archtl. Historians (pres. Tex. chpt. 1980-82), Am. Inst. Conservation of Hist. and Artistic Works, Vernacular Archtl. Forum. Office: Phillips & Oppermann PA 1134 Burke St # A Winston Salem NC 27101-2415

OPPMANN, ANDREW JAMES, newspaper editor; b. Hopkinsville, Ky., Apr. 3, 1963; s. Patrick George Oppmann and Elizabeth Anne (Freeman) Peace; m. Emily Elise Wey, Oct. 8, 1988. BA in Journalism, U. Ky., 1985. Staff writer The Orange County Register, Santa Ana, Calif., 1985-86; copy editor, staff writer Lexington (Ky.) Herald-Leader, 1986-87, bur. chief, asst. metro editor, 1988-91; urban affairs writer The Knoxville (Tenn.) News-Sentinel, 1987-88; asst. city editor The Houston Post, 1991-92, dep. met. editor, 1992, asst. to mng. editor, 1992, met. editor, 1992-94; Ky. editor The Cin. (Ohio) Enquirer, Covington; supervising editor The Ky. Enquirer, Covington, 1994—. Bd. vis. U. Ky. Sch. Journalism, 1994—. Fellow U. Ky., 1984. Office: The Ky Enquirer 309 Garrard St Covington KY 41011-1737

OPRE, THOMAS EDWARD, magazine editor, film company executive, corporate travel company executive; b. Evansville, Ind., Nov. 6, 1943; s. William Jennings and Ruth (Strouss) O.; children: Thomas Andrew, William Hartley. A.B. in Journalism, Ind. U., 1965. Writer sports and outdoors Decatur (Ill.) Herald and Rev., 1965-66; outdoor editor Detroit Free Press, 1966-90; field editor Midwest div. Field and Stream mag., 1971-81; editorial dir. Gt. Lakes Sportsman mag., 1972-75; editor-at-large and sports vehicles editor Outdoor Life mag., 1981-93; pres. Tom Opre Prodns., 1967—; pres. TOP Safaris, Inc., 1986—. Author numerous articles in outdoor and travel fields. Recipient James Henshall award Am. Fish Tackle Mfrs. Assn., 1969, Teddy award Internat. Outdoor Travel Film Festival, 1973, Environ. award EPA, 1977, Nat. Writer's award Safari Club Internat., 1977, Deep Woods Writing award OWAA, 1977, Conservation Service award Ducks Unltd., 1977; World Wildlife Found. award, 1981; named to Internat. Fishing Hall of Fame, 1968, Conservation Communicator of Yr., 1985. Mem. Outdoor Writers Assn. Am. (past dir., pres., v.p., chmn. bd.), Assn. Gt. Lakes Outdoor Writers (past dir., chmn. bd., pres., v.p.), Mich. Outdoor Writers Assn. (v.p., pres., chmn. bd. dirs.), Alpha Tau Omega. Home and Office: PO Box 156 Northville MI 48167-0156

O'QUINN, APRIL GALE, physician, educator; b. Columbia, Miss., Apr. 21, 1936; d. R.V. and Anna Pauline (Cook) O'Q.; diploma Scott and White Hosp. Sch. Nursing, 1965; A.A., Temple Jr. Coll., 1965; B.S. with honors, Baylor U., 1968; M.D., U. Tex. Med. Br., 1971. Intern, U. Tex. Med. Br., Galveston, 1971-72, resident ob-gyn., 1972-75; fellow in oncology M.D. Anderson Hosp., Houston, Tex., 1976-78; practice medicine specializing in ob-gyn., Galveston, 1978-81; asst. prof. dept. ob-gyn. U. Tex. Med. Br., Galveston, 1975-81; practice medicine specializing in ob-gyn, New Orleans, 1981—; mem. staff John Sealy Hosp., St. Mary's Hosp., Galveston, Tulane Med. Center, New Orleans Charity Hosp., So. Baptist Hosp. and Touro Infirmary, New Orleans; assoc. prof., dir. div. gynecol. oncology dept. ob-gyn Tulane U. Sch. Medicine, New Orleans, 1981-85, prof., 1985-89, prof., chair dept. ob.-gyn., 1989—. Diplomate Am. Bd. Ob-Gyn. Fellow Willard R. Cooke Obstet. and Gynecol. Soc., Am. Coll. Ob-Gyn.; mem. Soc. Gynecologic Oncologists, Western Assn. Gynecol. Oncologists, Tex. Assn. Obstetricians and Gynecologists, Houston Gynecol. and Obstetrical Soc., Tex. Med. Assn., Galveston County Med. Soc., Felix Rutledge Soc. Republican. Baptist. Home: 5100 Bancroft Dr New Orleans LA 70122-2801 Office: Tulane U Sch Medicine Ob Gyn Dept New Orleans LA 70112

O'QUINN, JOHN M., lawyer; b. 1941. JD magna cum laude, U. Houston, 1967. Bar: Tex. 1967, U.S. Dist. Ct. (so. and ea. dists.) Tex., U.S. Ct. Appeals (5th cir.) 1971, U.S. Supreme Ct. 1972. Founding ptnr. O'Quinn, Kerensky, McAninch & Laminack, Houston, 1981—; mem. adv. com. Tex. State Supreme Ct., 1984-94; trustee U. Houston Law Found., 1985—. Regent U. Houston, 1993—. Honored by Nat. Law Jour. as one of 100 Most Influential Lawyers in U.S., 1994; named as mem. to Inner Circle of Advocates. Am. Trial Lawyers Assn., Tex. Trial Lawyers Assn. (dir.), Houston Trial Lawyers Assn. (dir.), State Bar Tex., U. Houston Law Alumni Assn. (pres. 1978). Office: O'Quinn Kerensky McAninch & Laminack PC 2300 Lyric Centre 440 Louisiana Houston TX 77002*

ORAEFO, JOHNNY NDUBUISI, geologist, corporation executive, consultant; b. Jos, Plateau, Nigeria, June 26, 1945; s. George Madubike and Comfort O. (Onwuamaegbu) O.; m. Comfort Chinwe Onyekaba, July 9, 1976; children: Adaora, Ebeleann, Oge, Obi, Amy. AB, U. N.C., 1982; Cert. profl. geologist, N.C. Dir. Flamingo Imports Exports, Inc., Raleigh, N.C., 1984—; pres., co-owner African Supermarkets and Gift Shop, Raleigh, 1987—; pres. B.J. Internat., 1994—; dir. African Safari Stores, 1995—; cons. Internat. Trades, Raleigh, 1984—. Pres. Nigerian Student Assn. of U.S.A., Raleigh, 1981. Recipient cert. Merit Internat. Traders Assn., 1982. Mem. Am. Assn. Petroleum Geologists, Soc. Econ. Paleontologists Mineralogists, Dip. Computer Electronics Tech., Travel Internat. Club. Mem. Christian Ch. Avocations: tennis; travel; singing; ping-pong; reading. Home: 1802 Cantwell Ct Raleigh NC 27610-1010

ORAM, ROBERT W., library administrator; b. Warsaw, Ind., June 11, 1922; s. George Harry and Lottie Mae (Gresso) O.; m. Virginia White, June 16, 1949; 1 child, Richard W. B.A., U. Toledo, 1949; M.S. in Library Adminstrn., U. Ill., 1950. Asst. to librarian U. Mo.-Columbia, 1950-56; circulation librarian U. Ill.-Urbana, 1956-67, dir. pub. service, 1968-71, assoc. univ. librarian, 1971-79, acting univ. librarian, 1975-76; dir. Central Univ. Libraries So. Meth. U., Dallas, 1979-89, dir. emeritus, 1989; mem. adv. com. Ill. State Library, Springfield, 1975-79. Contbr. articles to profl. jours. Exec. sec. Friends of So. Meth. U. Librs., 1980-89; former mem. bd. dirs. Urbana Free Libr., Lincoln Trails Libr. Sys., Champaign, Ill.; trustee Friends Austin (Tex.) Pub. Libr., 1994—. Mem. ALA (life, pub. com. 1975-79), Friends of Libraries U.S.A. (exec. bd. 1980-86), Ill. Library Assn. (treas. 1972-73),. Democrat. Avocations: reading; music. Home: 8410 Lone Mesa Austin TX 78759-8025

ORAN, GERALDINE ANN, assistant principal; b. Burleson, Tex., June 27, 1938; d. Clyde Lloyd and Ruth (Baxley) Renfro; m. Francis Larry Oran, Dec. 18, 1960; children: Angelique Michelle, Jeremy Lloyd. AS summa cum laude, Roane State Community Coll., Harriman, Tenn., 1976; BS summa cum laude, U. Tenn., 1978, MS summa cum laude, 1990. IBM instr., office mgr. Kelsey-Jenney Bus. Coll., San Diego, 1958-61; exec. sec. Bendix Corp., San Diego, 1961-62; ednl. adminstr. South Harriman Bapt. Ch., 1964-74; tchr. Midtown Elem., Harriman, 1979-89; adminstrv. intern, prin. preparation program Danforth Found. Leadership 21, 1989; asst. prin. Cherokee Mid. Sch., Kingston, Tenn., 1990—. Mem., sec., treas., pres. PTA and PTO, Harriman, 1967-81; active Cancer, Heart Fund and March of Dimes, Harriman, 1979—; dir. vacation Bible sch. South Harriman Bapt. Ch., 1983-86, tchr. women's Bible sch., 1965—; club sponsor Tenn. Just Say No to Drugs Team, Roane County, 1985-87; mem. Task Force on Mid. Schs., Tenn. Dept. Edn., 1990; selection com. Tenn. Mid. Sch. Tchr. of Yr., 1992. Named Tchr. of Yr., Roane County, 1987. Mem. ASCD, NEA (del. rep. 1985-86), Tenn. Assn. Supervision and Curriculum Devel., Tenn. Assn. Middle Schs., Nat. Assn. of Secondary Sch. Prins., Tenn Edn. Assn. (del. rep. 1984-86, Outstanding Svc. award 1985-86), Roane County Edn. Assn. (membership chair 1984-85, pres. 1985-86), Roane County Adminstrs. Assn. (pres. 1993), Gamma Phi Beta, Kappa Delta Pi, Phi Kappa Phi, Delta Kappa Gamma. Baptist. Avocations: reading, painting, crafts, sculpting, walking. Home: PO Box 917 Harriman TN 37748-0917 Office: Cherokee Mid Sch Paint Rock Ferry Rd Kingston TN 37763-2914

ORAV, HELLE REISSAR, retired dentist; b. Tartu, Estonia, July 10, 1925; came to U.S., 1949, naturalized, 1954; d. Johan and Adele Johanna (Minski) Reissar; m. Arnold Orav, May 30, 1952; children: Ilmar Erik, Hillar Thomas. Student Friedrich Alexander U., Erlangen, West Germany, 1946-49; DDS, NYU, 1952. Practice dentistry, N.Y.C., 1952, 60, 62, 68, Valencia, Venezuela, 1953-68. Counselor, Red Cross, Valencia, 1954-55; past mem. Rotary Ladies Republican. Lutheran. Clubs: Country of Maracaibo (Venezuela); Palm Beach Polo and Country (Fla.); Korp Filiae Patriae (N.Y.C.). Avocations: Pre-Colombian art, bridge, travel, swimming, reading. Address: 44 Cocoanut Row Palm Beach FL 33480-4005

ORBACH, JERRY, actor, singer; b. N.Y.C., Oct. 20, 1935; s. Leon and Emily (Olexy) O.; m. Marta Curro, June 21, 1958 (div. 1975); children: Anthony Nicholas, Christopher Ben; m. Elaine Cancilla, Oct. 7, 1979. Student, U. Ill., 1952-53, Northwestern U., 1953-55; studied acting with, Herbert Berghof, Mira Rostova, Lee Strasberg, N.Y.C.; studied singing with, Hazel Schweppe, N.Y.C. Actor various films, on and off-Broadway prodns., 1956—. Profl. stage debut: Room Service, 1952; resident actor: Show Case Theatre, Evanston, Ill., summers 1953-54; N.Y.C. stage debut: Three Penny Opera, 1955; actor: (stage) Chicago, 3 Penny Opera, The Fantasticks, Carnival, Scuba Duba, Promises Promises, The Rose Tattoo, 6 Rums Riv Vu, The King and I, Guys and Dolls, The Student Prince, Annie Get Your Gun, The Trouble With People ... And Other Things, 42d Street, 1980; (films) Cop Hater, 1958, Mad Dog Coll, 1961, John Goldfarb Please Come Home, 1965, The Gang That Couldn't Shoot Straight, 1971, A Fan's Notes, 1974, Sentinel, 1977, The Prince of the City, 1982, Brewster's Millions, 1985, F/X, 1986, The Image Maker, 1986, Dirty Dancin', 1987, Someone to Watch Over Me, 1988, Crimes and Misdemeanors, 1989, Last Exit to Brooklyn, 1990, Out for Justice, 1991, Toy Soldiers, 1991, Delusion, 1991, Delirious, 1991, Beauty and the Beast, 1991 (voice only), Straight Talk, 1992, Universal Soldier, 1992, Mr. Saturday Night, 1992, The Cemetary Club, 1993; (TV episodes) including Love American Style, Murder She Wrote; (TV series) The Law and Harry McGraw, 1987-88, Law and Order, 1992—; (TV movies) An Invasion of Privacy, 1983, Out on a Limb, 1987, Love Among Thieves, 1987, In Defense of a Married Man, 1990, Broadway Bound, 1992, Quiet Killer, 1992; (TV miniseries) Dream West, 1986. Recipient New March of Dimes Horizon award, 1961, award of merit Actors Fund, 1961, Tony award Antoinette Perry Com., 1968. Mem. AFTRA, Screen Actors Guild, Actors Equity Assn. Club: Lone Star Boat. Avocations: poker, pool, golf, tennis. Office: Artists Group 10100 Santa Monica Blvd Ste 2490 Los Angeles CA 90067*

ORBACH, RAYMOND LEE, physicist, educator; b. Los Angeles, July 12, 1934; s. Morris Albert and Mary Ruth (Miller) O.; m. Eva Hannah Spiegler, Aug. 26, 1956; children: David Miller, Deborah Hedwig, Thomas Randolph. BS, Calif. Inst. Tech., 1956; PhD, U. Calif., Berkeley, 1960. NSF postdoctoral fellow Oxford U., 1960-61; asst. prof. applied physics Harvard U., 1961-63; prof. physics UCLA, 1963-92, asst. vice chancellor acad. change and curriculum devel., 1970-72, chmn. acad. senate L.A. divsn., 1976-77, provost Coll. Letters and Sci., 1982-92; chancellor U. Calif., Riverside, 1992—; mem. physics adv. panel NSF, 1970-73; mem. vis. com. Brookhaven Nat. Lab., 1970-74; mem. materials rsch. lab. adv. panel NSF, 1974-77; mem. Nat. Commn. on Rsch., 1978-80; chmn. 16th Internat. Conf. on Low Temperature Physics, 1981; Joliot Curie prof. Ecole Superieure de la Physique et Chimie Industrielle de la Ville de Paris, 1982, chmn. Gordon Rsch. Conf. on Fractals, 1986; Lorentz prof. U. Leiden, Netherlands, 1987; Raymond and Beverly Sackler lectr. Tel Aviv U., 1989; faculty rsch. lectr. UCLA, 1990; Andrew Lawson lectr. U. Calif., Riverside, 1992; mem. external rev. com. Nat. High Magnetic Fields Lab., 1994—. Author: (with A.A. Manenkov) SpinLattice Relaxation in Ionic Solids, 1966; Div. assoc. editor Phys. Rev. Letters, 1980-83, Jour. Low Temperature Physics, 1980-90, Phys. Rev., 1983—; contbr. articles to profl. jours. Alfred P. Sloan Found. fellow, 1963-67; NSF sr. postdoctoral fellow Imperial Coll., 1967-68; Guggenheim fellow Tel Aviv U., 1973-74. Fellow Am. Phys. Soc. (chmn. nominations com. 1981-82, counselor-at-large 1987-91, chmn. divsn. condensed matter 1990-91); mem. AAAS (chairperson steering group physics sect.), NSF (mem. rsch. adv. com. divsn. materials 1992-93), Phys. Soc. (London), Univ. Rsch. Assn. (chair coun. pres. 1993), Sigma Xi, Phi Beta Kappa, Tau Beta Pi. Home: 4171 Watkins Dr Riverside CA 92507-4738 Office: U Calif Riverside Chancellor's Office Riverside CA 92521-0101

ORBACZ, LINDA ANN, physical education educator; b. Schenectady, N.Y., June 29, 1948; d. Victor and Genevieve (Stempkowski) O. AAS, Ulster C.C., Stone Ridge, N.Y., 1969; BS, So. Ill. U., 1972; MA, George Washington U., 1982. Cert. permanent tchr., N.Y. Tchr., coach Ellenville (N.Y.) Ctrl. Sch., 1972-73, New Fairfield (Conn.) Sch., 1973-75, Middletown (N.Y.) City Sch., 1975-84, Liberty (N.Y.) Ctrl. Sch., 1984-86; dir. athletics, phys. edn. tchr., coach Newburgh (N.Y.) Enlarged City Sch., 1986—; alumni adv. Ulster County C.C., Stone Ridge, 1981—. Softball, soccer and basketball coach, Newburgh, 1987-92, softball, field hockey, basketball and cheerleading coach Ellenville, Middletown, New Fairfield, Liberty, 1972-86. Recipient Presdl. Sports award Sports Fitness, Washington, 1988, 94. Mem. Am. Alliance Health, Phys. Edn., Recreation and Dance, N.Y. State Alliance Health, Phys. Edn., Recreation and Dance. Avocations: nautilus weight tng., phys. conditioning, in-line skating, skiing, aerobic exercise. Office: Gardnertown Fundamental Magnet Sch 6 Plattekill Tpke Newburgh NY 12550-1708

ORBAN, EDMOND HENRY, political science educator; b. Heron, Liege, Belgium, Apr. 25, 1925; emigrated to Can., 1961; s. Edmond and Maria (Jamar) O.; m. Anne Marie Anciaux, May 10, 1955; children: Margaret, Christine, Yvon, Francois, Benoit. Ph.D. in Polit. Sci., U. Louvain, Belgium, 1967. Asst. adminstr. Province of Kasaï Govt. of Belgium, 1951-59, adminstr. Province of Kasaï, 1961; prof. polit. sci. U. Montreal, Que., Can., 1961—. Author: La Presidence moderne, 1974, Le Conseil legislatif, 1967, Le Conseil nordique, 1978; author-editor: Mecanismes constitutionnels, 1982, Dynamique de la Centralisation dans l'Etat Fédéral, 1984, Le Systeme politique des Etats-Unis, 1987, Federalism and Supreme Courts, 1991, Federalism, 1992, Systéme Politique Américain, 1994. Served as info.-commando Belgium Army, 1950-51. Decorated Medal of the Resistance, 1945, chevalier de l'Ordre de la Couronne (Belgium), 3 other decorations. Roman Catholic. Home: 337 Lac des chats, Saint-Sauveur, PQ Canada J0R 1R1 Office: U Montreal Dept Sci Politique, 2900 Boul Edouard Montpetit, Montreal, PQ Canada H3C 3J7

ORBAN, KURT, foreign trade company executive; b. S.I., N.Y., Aug. 6, 1916; s. Kurt and Gertrude (Astfalck) Orbanowski; children: Robert Arnold, Robin Ann, Kurt-Matthew, Jonathan; m. 2d, Ann Norris, Oct. 1986. Grad. steel fgn. trade course, Stahlunion-Export GmbH, Duesseldorf, Germany, 1938. Fgn. trade corr. Stahlunion, Dusseldorf, 1938; rep. Stahlunion, Bulgaria, 1939-40; steel export trader Steel Union Sheet Piling Co., N.Y.C., 1941; v.p. North River Steel Co., N.Y.C., 1941; chmn., pres. Kurt Orban Co., Inc., Wayne, N.J., from 1946; now sr. ptnr. Kurt Orban Ptnrs. Mem. field hockey games com. U.S. Olympic Com., 1948-61; playing mgr. U.S. Field Hockey Team., London, Eng., 1948, playing coach, Melbourne, Australia, 1956; U.S. rep. Bur. Internat. Hockey Fedn., Brussels, 1954-62. Served to 1st lt. USAAF, 1943-45. Field Hockey Assn. Am. named its cup for each yrs. men's team competition for him. Mem. Am. Inst. Imported Steel (pres. 1966-68, 78-80, bd. dirs. N.Y.C.), Am. Exporters and Importers Assn. (pres. 1972-73, bd. dirs.), West Coast Metal Importers Assn. (bd. dirs.), Wire Assn. Internat. Climbed Mt. Shasta, Calif. (14, 203') and Mt. Kilimanjaro (20, 103'), 1987. Avocation: sr. tennis, skiing, photography, languages. Address: 450 Kings Rd Brisbane CA 94005-1650

ORBEN, JACK RICHARD, investment company executive; b. Bklyn., June 16, 1938; s. Stanley Souza and Helena Emily (Hall) O.; A.A., Valley Forge, 1956; B.A., Tufts U., 1960; m. Patricia Wells, Dec. 17, 1960; children—Stacey Souza, Stephanie Anne, Bradford Richard. Sales mgr. nat. accounts N.Y. Telephone Co., 1960-66; founder, exec. v.p. Facts, Inc., 1966-69; with Oben Assocs., Inc., N.Y.C., 1970—, pres., 1979—; chmn. CEO Associated Family Svcs., Inc., Econ. Analysts, Inc., Starwood Corp.; chmn. Fiduciary Counsel, Inc., Estate Mgmt. Co., Seward, Groves, Richard & Wells; bd. dirs. Vintage Holdings, Vintage Funds, Unified Advisers, Inc., Vintage Advisors. Chmn. White Plains Charter Revision Commn.; mem. Fin. Com. City of White Plains; past pres. White Plains Child Day Care Assn., Thomas Slater Ctr.; past chmn., bd. dirs. YMCA of Cen. and No. Westchester. Served with N.G., 1960-66. Clubs: Larchmont Yacht, N.Y. Yacht, City Midday, Union League, Windemere Island, University, Down Town Assn. Home: 177 Soundview Ave White Plains NY 10606-3825 Office: The AFS Group 40 Wall St New York NY 10005

ORBEN, ROBERT, editor, writer; b. N.Y.C., Mar. 4, 1927; s. Walter August and Marie (Neweceral) O.; m. Jean Louise Connelly, July 25, 1945. Humor and speech writer for entertainment personalities, bus. execs., politicians, 1946—; writer Jack Paar Show, N.Y.C., 1962-63, Red Skelton Hour, Hollywood, Calif., 1964-70; editor Orben's Current Comedy, Wilmington, Del., 1971-89; cons. to Vice Pres. Gerald R. Ford, Washington, 1974; speechwriter Pres. Gerald R. Ford, Washington, 1974-75; spl. asst. to pres., dir. White House speechwriting dept., Washington, 1976-77; speaker on uses of humor in communication, 1977—. Author: 2500 Jokes to Start 'Em Laughing, 1979, 2100 Laughs for All Occasions, 1983, 2400 Jokes to Brighten Your Speeches, 1984, 2000 Sure-Fire Jokes for Speakers, 1986; numerous other books of humor for performers and public speakers. Recipient World Humor award Workshop Libr. on World Humor, 1992; Literary fellow Acad. Magical Arts, 1996. Mem. Writers Guild Am. Unitarian. Club: Nat. Press (Washington). Avocations: travel, theater. Home: # 205 E 3709 S George Mason Dr Falls Church VA 22041-3760 *I have spent most of my lifetime creating laughter and consider it a lifetime well spent. Laughter is one of the glories of the human experience. It warms, amuses, instructs, and opens emotional doors. For me, laughter has been a living and a living as well.*

ORCE, KENNETH W., lawyer; b. Yonkers, N.Y., Apr. 3, 1943; s. Edmund John and Helen (Mulcahy) O.; m. Helene Mary Sparti, Aug. 20, 1966; children: Kenneth W., Kimberley J., Brian C. B.S. with honors, Manhattan Coll., 1965; LL.B. cum laude, Harvard U., 1968. Bar: N.Y. 1969. Assoc. Cahill Gordon & Reindel, N.Y.C., 1968-76, ptnr. 1976—; bd. dirs. La. Land and Exploration Co. Mem. ABA, Assn. Bar City N.Y., Down Town Assn. (N.Y.C.), Scarsdale (N.Y.) Golf Club, Met. Opera Club. Editor: Harvard Law Rev. 1966-68. Home: 220 Highland Rd Scarsdale NY 10583-1227 Office: Cahill Gordon & Reindel 80 Pine St New York NY 10005-1702

ORCHARD, HENRY JOHN, electrical engineer; b. Oldbury, Eng., May 7, 1922; came to U.S., 1961, naturalized, 1973; s. Richard John and Lucy Matilda O.; m. Irene Dorothy Wise, Sept. 13, 1947; 1 child, Richard John; m. Marietta Eugenie Gayet, Aug. 2, 1971. B.Sc., U. London, 1946, M.Sc., 1951. Prin. sci. officer Brit. Post Office, London, 1947-61; sr. staff GTE Lenkurt Inc., San Carlos, Calif., 1961-70; mem. faculty UCLA, 1970—, prof. elec. engring., 1970-91, prof. emeritus, 1991—, vice chmn. dept., 1982-91. Author. Fellow IEEE (Best Paper award group circuit theory 1968). Republican. Patentee in field. Home: 828 19th St Unit E Santa Monica CA 90403 Office: UCLA Elec Engring Dept Los Angeles CA 90095-1594

ORCHARD, ROBERT JOHN, theater producer, educator; b. Maplewood, N.J., Dec. 3, 1946; s. Robert Orchard and Beatrice (Gould) Todd; m. Pamela Marcy Pritchard, Sept. 6, 1969; children: Christopher, Katherine. Student, The Lawrence Acad., 1965; BA, Middlebury Coll., 1969; MFA, Yale U., 1972. Gen. mgr. Peterborough (N.H.) Players, 1967-70; asst. mng. dir. Yale Repertory Theatre, 1971-72, artistic adminstr., 1972-73; instr. Yale Sch. Drama, 1972-73; mng. dir. Yale Repertory Theatre and Sch. Drama, 1973-79, Am. Repertory Theatre, Cambridge, Mass., 1979—; assoc. prof., co-chmn. Theatre Adminstrn. Tng. Program Yale Sch. Drama, 1975-79; mng., dir. Loeb Drama Ctr., Inst. for Advanced Theatre Tng. Harvard U., 1979—. Bd. dirs. Theatre Comms. Group; pres. bd. Mass. Cultural Edn. Collaborative; former bd. dirs. Am. Arts Alliance, Peterborough Players, Cambridge Multi-Cultural Arts Ctrs.; former exec. com. League of Residents Theatres; chmn. NEA, Profl. Theatre Cos. Panel. Office: Am Repertory Theatre 64 Brattle St Cambridge MA 02138-3443

ORCUTT, JOHN ARTHUR, geophysicist; b. Holyoke, Colo., Aug. 29, 1943; married, 1967; 2 children. BS, U.S. Naval Acad., 1966; MSc, U. Liverpool, 1968; PhD in Earth Scis., U. Calif., San Diego, 1976. Rsch.

geophysicist Scripps Inst. Oceanography, La Jolla, Calif., 1977—, assoc. prof., 1982-84, prof. geophysics, 1984—, dir. geophysics & planetary physics divsn., 1984—. Recipient Newcomb Cleveland prize AAAS, 1980, Maurice Ewing award Am. Geophys. Union, 1994. Mem. Am. Geophys. Union (Maurice Ewing award 1994), Soc. Exploration Geophysicists. Office: U Calif Inst Geophys & Planetary Physics 9500 Gilman Dr La Jolla CA 92093

ORD, LINDA BANKS, artist; b. Provo, Utah, May 24, 1947; d. Willis Merrill and Phyllis (Clark) Banks; m. Kenneth Stephen Ord, Sept. 3, 1971; children: Jason, Justin, Kristin. BS, Brigham Young U., 1970; BFA, U. Mich., 1987; MA, Wayne State U., 1990. Asst. prof. Sch. Art U. Mich., Ann Arbor, 1994—; juror Southeastern Mich. Scholastic Art Award Competition, Pontiac, 1992, Scarab Club Watercolor Exhbn., Detroit, 1991, Women in Art Nat. Exhbn., Farmington Hills, Mich., 1991, U. Mich. Alumni Exhbn., 1989-90. One-woman shows Atrium Gallery, Mich., 1990, 91; group shows include Am. Coll., Bryn Mawr, Pa., Riverside (Calif.) Art Mus., Kirkpatrick Mus., Oklahoma City, Montgomery (Ala.) Mus. Fine Arts, Columbus (Ga.) Mus., Brigham Young U., Provo, Utah, Kresge Art Mus., Lansing, Mich., U. Mich., Ann Arbor, Detroit Inst. Arts, Kirkpatrick Ctr. Mus. Complex, Oklahoma City, 1994, Riverside (Calif.) Art Mus., 1995, San Bernadino County Mus., Redlands, Calif., 1996; works in many pvt. and pub. collections including Kelly Svcs., Troy, Mich., FHP Internat., Fountain Valley, Calif., Swords Into Plowshares Gallery, Detroit; work included in book The Artistic Touch, 1995. Chairperson nat. giving fund Sch. Art, U. Mich., 1993; Sch. Art rep. Coun. Alumni Socs., U. Mich., 1992—. Recipient 1st Pl. award Swords Into Plowshares Internat. Exhbn., Detroit, 1989, Silver award Ga. Watercolor Soc. Internat. Exhbn., 1991, Pres.'s award Watercolor Okla. Nat. Exhbn., Oklahoma City, 1992, Flint Jour. award Buckham Gallery Nat. Exhbn., 1993, Ochs Meml. award N.E. Watercolor Soc. Nat. Exhbn., Goshen, N.Y., 1993, Color Q award Ga. Watercolor Soc., 1994, St. Cuthberts award Tex. Watercolor Soc., 1996, many state and nat. painting awards. Mem. U. Mich. Alumni Assn. (bd. dirs. 1992—, Sch. Art rep.), U. Mich. Sch. Art Alumni Soc. (bd. dirs. 1989-91, pres.), Mich. Watercolor Soc. (chairperson 1992-93, bd. dirs. adv. 1993-94). Avocations: music, theatre, tennis, golf, reading.

ORDAL, CASPAR REUBEN, business executive; b. Martell, Wis., May 5, 1922; s. Zakarias John and Sina Carlovna (Wulfsberg) O.; m. Ann Elizabeth Brady, June 7, 1947; Christopher Rolf, Peter Stuart. B.S., Harvard Coll., 1946; M.P.A., Harvard U., 1947. Supr. central indsl. relations staff Ford Motor Co., Dearborn, Mich., 1947-53; dir. orgn. planning and mgmt. devel. Colgate-Palmolive Co., N.Y.C., 1953-65; v.p., gen. mgr. New Holland div. Sperry Rand Corp., (Pa.), 1965-76; corp. v.p. personnel Norton Simon Inc., N.Y.C., 1976-78; sr. v.p. adminstrn. Max Factor & Co., Hollywood, Calif., 1978-85. Served to 1st lt. USAAF, 1943-46. Mem. Personnel Round Table (chmn. 1983-84), Am. Mgmt. Assn. (Adv. council 1977-82), Phi Beta Kappa. Republican. Lutheran. Club: Lancaster (Pa.) Country.

ORDEN, TED, gasoline service stations executive; b. 1920. With Thrifty Oil Co., Inc., Downey, Calif., 1959—, now pres., also bd. dirs. Office: Thrifty Oil Co Inc 10000 Lakewood Blvd Downey CA 90240-4020*

ORDIN, ANDREA SHERIDAN, lawyer; m. Robert Ordin; 1 child, Maria; stepchildren: Allison, Richard. AB, UCLA, 1962, LLB, 1965. Bar: Calif. 1966. Dep. atty. gen. Calif., 1965-72; So. Calif. legal counsel Fair Employment Practices Commn., 1972-73; asst. dist. atty. Los Angeles County, 1975-77; U.S. atty. Central Dist. Calif. Los Angeles, 1977-81; adj. prof. UCLA Law Sch., 1982; chief asst. atty. gen. Calif. L.A., 1983-90; ptnr. Morgan, Lewis & Bockius, L.A., 1993—. Mem. Los Angeles County Bar Assn. (past pres., past exec. dir.). Office: Morgan Lewis & Bockius 801 S Grand Ave Fl 22 Los Angeles CA 90017-4613

ORDOVER, ABRAHAM PHILIP, lawyer, mediator; b. Far Rockaway, N.Y., Jan. 18, 1937; s. Joseph and Bertha (Fromberg) O.; m. Carol M. Ordover, Mar. 23, 1961; children: Andrew Charles, Thomas Edward. BA magna cum laude, Syracuse U., 1958; JD, Yale U., 1961. Bar: N.Y. 1961, U.S. Dist. Ct. (so. and ea. dists.) N.Y., U.S. Ct. Appeals (2d cir.), U.S. Supreme Ct. Assoc. Cahill, Gordon & Reindel, N.Y.C., 1961-71; prof. law Hofstra U., Hempstead, N.Y., 1971-81; L.Q.C. Lamar prof. law Emory U., Atlanta, 1981-91; CEO Resolution Resources Corp., Atlanta, 1991—; mediator and arbitrator; vis. prof. Cornell U., Ithaca, N.Y., 1977; vis. lectr. Tel Aviv U., 1989, Am. Law Inst.; team leader nat. program Nat. Inst. Trial Advocacy, Boulder, Colo., 1980, 82, 84, 86, 89, tchr. program Cambridge, Mass., 1979-84, 88, adv. program Gainesville, Fla., 1978-79, northeast regional dir., 1977-81; team leader SE regional program, 1983; team leader Atlanta Bar Trial Tech. Program, 1981-91; lectr. in field. Author: Argument to the Jury, 1982, Problems and Cases in Trial Advocacy, 1983, Advanced Materials in Trial Advocacy, 1988, Alternatives to Litigation, 1993, Cases and Materials in Evidence, 1993, Art of Negotiation, 1994; producer ednl. films; contbr. articles to profl. jours. Bd. dirs. Atlanta Legal Aid Soc., 1984-91, 7 Stages Theatre, 1991—. Recipient Gumpert award Am. Coll. Trial Lawyers, 1984, 85, Jacobsen award Roscoe Pound Am. Trial Lawyer Found., 1986. Mem. ABA, N.Y. State Bar Assn., Assn. Am. Law Schs. (chair litigation sect.), Atlanta Lawyers Club, Am. Law Inst. Avocation: photography.

ORDWAY, FREDERICK IRA, III, educator, consultant, researcher, author; b. N.Y.C., Apr. 4, 1927; s. Frederick Ira and Frances Antoinette (Wright) O.; m. Maria Victoria Arenas, Apr. 13, 1950; children: Frederick Ira IV, Albert James, Aliette Marisol. S.B., Harvard, 1949; postgrad., U. Alger, 1950, U. Paris, France, 1950-51, 53-54, U. Barcelona, Spain, 1953, U. Innsbruck, Austria, 1954, Air U., 1952-63, Alexander Hamilton Bus. Inst., 1952-58, Indsl. Coll. Armed Forces, 1953, 63; DSc (hon.), U. Ala., 1992. Various geol., engring. positions Mene Grande Oil Co., San Tome, Venezuela, 1949-50, Orinoco Mining Co., Cerro Bolivar, Venezuela, 1950, Reaction Motors, Inc., Lake Denmark, N.J., 1951-53; with guided missiles div. Republic Aviation Corp., 1954-55; pres. Gen. Astronautics Research Corp., Huntsville, Ala., 1955-59, 65-66; v.p. Nat. Research & Devel. Corp., Atlanta, 1957-59; asst. to dir. Saturn Systems Office, Army Ballistic Missile Agy., Huntsville, 1959-60; chief space information systems br. George C. Marshall Space Flight Center NASA, 1960-64; prof. sci. and tech. applications Sch. Grad. Studies and Research, U. Ala. Research Inst., 1967-73; cons. Sci. and Tech. Policy Office, NSF, 1974-75, Ops. Analysis div. Gen. Research Corp., 1974-75; asst. to adminstr. ERDA, 1975-77; Dept. Energy, 1977-80, dir. spl. projects, 1981-94; aerospace cons., 1994—; also participant internat. energy devel. program Office of Asst. Sec. Internat. Affairs, Dept. Energy, 1978-79; cons. to industry, Ency. Britannica, Am. Coll. Dictionary of English Lang., M.G.M. film 2001: A Space Odyssey, 1965-66, Paramount Picture Corp., The Adventurers , 1968-69; internat. lectr. space flight and energy programs. Author: (with C.C. Adams) Space Flight, 1958, (with Ronald C. Wakeford) International Missile and Spacecraft Guide, 1960, Annotated Bibliography of Space Science and Technology, 1962, (with J.P. Gardner, M.R. Sharpe, Jr.) Basic Astronautics: An Introduction to Space Science, Engineering and Medicine, 1962, (with Adams, Wernher von Braun) Careers in Astronautics and Rocketry, 1962, (with Gardner, Sharpe, R.C. Wakeford) Applied Astronautics: An Introduction to Space Flight, 1963, (with Wakeford) Conquering the Sun's Empire, 1963, Life in Other Solar Systems, 1965, (with Roger A. MacGowan) Intelligence in the Universe, 1966, (with W. von Braun) History of Rocketry and Space Travel, 1966, 1969, 75, L'Histoire Mondiale de l'Astronautique, 1968, 70, Rockets Red Glare, 1976, (with C.C. Adams, M.R. Sharpe) Dividends from Space, 1972, Pictorial Guide to Planet Earth, 1975, (with W. von Braun) New Worlds, 1979, (with M.R. Sharpe) The Rocket Team, 1979, (with F.C. Durant and R.C. Seamans) Between Sputnik and the Shuttle, 1981, (with E.M. Emme) Science Fiction and Space Futures, 1982, (with von Braun, Dave Dooling) Space Travel: A History, 1985, (with Ernst Stuhlinger) Wernher von Braun: Aufbrach in den Weltraum, 1992, Wernher von Braun: Crusader for Space (2 vols.), 1994, (with Randy Liebermann) Blueprint for Space, 1992; editor: Advances in Space Science and Technology, vols. I-XII, 2 supplements, 1959-72, (with R.M.L. Baker, N.W. Makemson) Introduction to Astrodynamics, 1960, (with others) From Peenemünde to Outer Space, 1962, Astronautical Engineering and Science, 1963; mem. editorial bd.: (with others) IX Internat. Astronautical Congress procs., 2 vols, 1959, Xth Congress procs., 2 vols, 1960; guest editor: Acta Astronautica, 1985, 94, History of Rocketry and Astronautics, Vol. IX, 1989; contbr. (with others) numerous articles to profl. jours., U.S. and fgn. encys., chpts. to books, sects. to others; organizer Blueprint for Space exhbn., 1991-95, U.S. Space and Rocket Ctr., IBM Gallery of Sci. and Art, NASA Vis. Ctr., Houston, Spaceport USA, Cape Canaveral, Fla., Nat. Air and Space Mus., Washington, Va. Air and Space Ctr., Hampton and numerous others. Served with USNR, 1945. Recipient (with W. von Braun) diplôme d'honneur French Commn. d'Histoire, Arts et Letters, Paris, 1969; commended for contbns. to U.S. Space and Rocket Ctr., Ala. Space Sci. Exhibit. Fellow AAAS, AIAA (history com. 1975—, internat. activities com. 1980-89, Pendray award 1974, Hermann Oberth award 1977), Brit. Interplanetary Soc.; mem. Internat. Acad. Astronautics (history of astronautics com. 1983—, chmn. 1989, space activities and soc. com. 1986—, peer rev. com. 1985—, co-recipient Luigi Napolitano Lit. award 1992), Am. Astron. Soc. (Emme award 1994), Brit. Interplanetary Soc., Nat. Space Soc. (bd. dirs. 1986—, mem. publs. com. 1987-88, nominating com. 1990-92), Royal Soc. Arts, Mfrs. and Commerce, Eurasian Acad. Scis., Cosmos Club (bd. mgmt. 1986-91), v.p. 1988-90), Harvard Club N.Y. Home: 2401 N Taylor St Arlington VA 22207

ORDWAY, JOHN DANTON, retired pension administrator, lawyer, accountant; b. Mpls., Mar. 19, 1928; s. John Dunreath Ordway and Inez Adelaide (Stahl) Larson; m. Mary E. Bateman, June 16, 1951(div. 1978); 1 child, David. BBA, Am. U., 1963, JD, 1965. Bar: U.S. Dist. Ct. D.C. 1966; CPA, Minn. Dir. ins. Nat. Automobile Dealers Assn., Washington, 1957-69; v.p. Edward H. Friend and Co., Washington, 1969-74; exec. v.p. and CEO Pension Bds. United Ch. of Christ, N.Y.C., 1974-96. Alt. mem. Planning Bd., Stamford, Conn., 1982-86. With U.S. Army, 1946-47. Mem. AICPAs. Republican. Mem. United Ch. of Christ. Club: Westwood Country (Vienna, Va.); Quail Run Golf Club (Naples, Fla.). Lodge: Kena Temple. Home: 206 Woodshire Ln Naples FL 33942

OREAR, JAY, physics educator, researcher; b. Chgo., Nov. 6, 1925; s. Leslie and Edna (Tragnitz) O.; m. Jeanne Bliven, Mar. 10, 1951; children—Scott, Robin, Wendy; m. Virginia Watts, Sept. 6, 1974. Ph.B., U. Chgo., 1944, Ph.D., 1953. Research assoc. U. Chgo., 1953-54; instr. to asst. prof. Columbia U., N.Y.C., 1954-58; assoc. prof. Cornell U., Ithaca, N.Y., 1958-64, prof. physics, nuclear studies, 1964—; Chmn. Fedn. Am. Scientists, 1967-68. Author: Nuclear Physics, 1951, Fundamental Physics, 1961, Programmed Manual, 1963, Statistics for Physicists, 1958, 82, Physics, 1979. Served with USNR, 1944-46. Fellow AAAS, Am. Phys. Soc. (editor Forum Newsletter 1972-74); mem. Phi Beta Kappa, Sigma Xi. Office: Cornell U Newman Lab Ithaca NY 14853 *"Whatever you do, or dream you can, begin it. Boldness has genius, power and magic in it. Begin it now." J. W. Goethe "To sin by silence when they shouldprotest makes cowards of men." Abe Lincoln "Neither those who know, nor those who know they do not know make mistakes. Those who do not know and think that they know are disgraceful and mischievous." Plato.*

OREFFICE, PAUL FAUSTO, retired chemical company executive; b. Venice, Italy, Nov. 29, 1927; came to U.S., 1945, naturalized, 1951; s. Max and Elena (Friedenberg) O.; children: Laura Emma, Andrew T. B.S. in Chem. Engring., Purdue U., 1949. With Dow Chem. Co., various internat. locations, 1953-92; assigned to Switzerland, Italy, Brazil and Spain, to 1969; pres. Dow Chem. Latin Am., Coral Gables, Fla., 1966-70; corporate fin. v.p. Dow Chem. Co., Midland, Mich., 1970-75, pres. Dow Chem. U.S.A., 1975-78, pres., CEO, 1978-86, chmn., pres., CEO, 1986-87, chmn. bd., 1987-92; ret., 1992; bd. dirs. Morgan Stanley Group Inc., Inc., CIGNA Corp., No. Telecom Ltd., Coca Cola Co. Chmn. bd. trustees Am. Enterprise Inst.; trustee Morehouse Coll.; bd. govs. Nat. Parkinson Found.; chmn. bd. overseers Inst. Civil Justice; mem. sr. adv. bd. Arthritis Found. Decorated Encomienda del Merito Civil Spain, 1966. Mem. Chem. Mfrs. Assn., Bus. Coun. (mem. adv. com. for trade policy and negotiations). Home: 2630 Barcelona Fort Lauderdale FL 33301

O'REGAN, RICHARD ARTHUR, editor, retired foreign correspondent; b. Boston, July 15, 1919; s. Arthur R. and Amelia H. (Egbers) O'R.; m. Elizabeth A. Hill, Mar. 23, 1946; children—John K., Michael L. Student, Temple U., 1940-41, Vienna U., Austria, 1953-54. With London Daily Mail and London Daily Sketch, 1938-39; reporter, night city editor Phila. Bull., 1939-43; writer Russian-German war specialist UPI, 1943-45; fgn. corr. AP, 1945-84; assigned AP, London, Paris, Germany, 1945-50; chief bur. AP, Vienna, 1950-55, Germany, 1956-66, London, 1966-77; dir. gen. for AP, Europe, Africa and Middle East, 1977-84; mng. dir., editor-in-chief Oriole Internat. Publs., Geneva, 1987—; bd. dirs. A.P. Ltd. Co-author: International Geneva (ann.). Mem. Assn. Am. Corrs. in London (pres. 1969). Clubs: Overseas Press (N.Y.C.); Press (Frankfurt, Germany) (past pres.); London Press, London Directors. Home: 33 Chemin de Grange Canal, 1208 Geneva Switzerland

O'REILLY, ANTHONY JOHN FRANCIS, food company executive; b. Dublin, Ireland, May 7, 1936; s. John Patrick and Aileen (O'Connor) O'R.; m. Susan Cameron, May 5, 1962 (div.); children: Susan, Cameron, Justine, Gavin, Caroline, Tony; m. Chryss Goulandris, Sept. 14, 1991. Student, Belvedere Coll., Dublin, Univ. Coll., Dublin, Wharton Bus. Sch. Overseas, 1965; B.C.L.; D.C.L. (hon.), Ind. State U.; Ph.D. in Agrl. Mktg, U. Bradford, Eng.; LL.D. (hon.), Wheeling Coll., 1974, Trinity Coll., Dublin, 1978, Allegheny Coll., 1983, De Paul U., Chgo., 1988; D in Bus. Studies (hon.), Rollins Coll., 1978; D in Civil Law honoris causa, Ind. State U., 1980; DBA (hon.), Boston Coll., 1985; D in Econ. Sci. (hon.), Nat. U. Ireland, 1989. Indsl. cons. Weston Evans, 1958-62; personal asst. to chmn. Suttons Ltd., Cork, Ireland, 1960-62; lectr. dept. applied psychology Univ. Coll., Cork, 1960-62; dir. Robert McCowen & Sons Ltd., Tralee, Ireland, 1961-62; mng. dir. An Bord Bainne/Irish Dairy Bd., 1962-66; dir. Agrl. Credit Corp. Ltd., 1965-66, Nitrigin Eireann Teoranta, 1965-66; mng. dir., chief exec. officer Comhlucht Siuicre Eireann Teo. (Irish Sugar Co.) and Erin Foods Ltd., Dublin, 1966-69; joint mng. dir. Heinz-Erin Ltd., 1967-70; mng. dir. H.J. Heinz Co. Ltd., Eng., 1969-71; sr. v.p. N.Am. and Pacific H.J. Heinz Co., 1971-72; exec. v.p., chief operating officer H.J. Heinz Co., Pitts., 1972-73, pres., chief operating officer, 1973-79, pres., chief exec. officer, 1979—, also chmn., 1978—, also bd. dirs.; chmn. Fitzwilton Plc.,Independent Newspapers Plc., Atlantic Resources, Dublin, Am. Ireland Fund.; ptnr. Cawley Sheerin Wynne and Co., solicitors, Dublin; bd. dirs. Bankers Trust N.Y. Corp., Bankers Trust N.Y. Corp., Washington Post Co., London Tablet Found. Inc., Starkist Foods Inc., Ore-Ida Foods Inc. Author: Prospect, 1962, Developing Creative Management, 1970, The Conservative Consumer, 1971, Food for Thought, 1972. Bd. govs. Hugh O'Brian Found., L.A.; mem. counc. Rockefeller U., N.Y.C.; bd. dirs. Assocs. Grad. Sch. Bus. Adminstrn. of Harvard U., Cambridge, Mass.; sr. bd. dirs. The Conf. Bd.; trustee U. Pitts., Com. for Econ. Devel.; mem. Nat. Com. Whitney Mus. Am. Art. Named Hon. Officer Order of Australia, 1988. Fellow Brit. Inst. Mgmt., Royal Soc. Arts; mem. Inst. Dirs., Inc., Law Soc. Ireland (treas.), Grocery Mfrs. Am. (sec., bd. dirs.), Am. Irish Found., Internat. Life Scis. Inst. Nutrition Found. (chmn., chief exec. officer council), Irish Mgmt. Inst. (council), Exec. Council Fgn. Diplomats (bd. dirs.). Clubs: St. Stephens Green, Kildare St., University (Dublin); Annabels, Les Ambassadeurs, Marks (London); Union League, The Links, The Bd. Room (N.Y.C.); Duquesne, Allegheny, Pitts. Golf, Fox Chapel Golf, Pitts. Press, Pitts. Golf (Pitts.); Rolling Rock (Ligonier) (bd. govs.); Lyford Cay (Bahamas). Office: H J Heinz Co PO Box 57 600 Grant St Pittsburgh PA 15219-2857 also: Mobil Corp 150 E 42nd St New York NY 10017-5612*

O'REILLY, CHARLES TERRANCE, university dean; b. Chgo., May 30, 1921; s. William Patrick and Ann Elizabeth (Madden) O'R.; m. Rosella Catherine Neilland, June 4, 1955; children—Terrance, Gregory, Kevin, Joan Bridget, Kathleen Ann. B.A., Loyola U., Chgo., 1942, M.S.W., 1948; postgrad., U. Cattolica, Milan, Italy, 1949-50; Ph.D., U. Notre Dame, 1954. Instr. DePaul U., Chgo., 1948-49; asst. in psychology U. Cattolica, 1949-50; caseworker Cath. Charities, N.Y.C., 1953-54; exec. dir. Family Service, Long Branch, N.J., 1954-55; asst. prof. Loyola U., 1955-59; vis. lectr. Ensiss Sch. Social Work, Milan, 1959-60; asso. prof. U. Wis.-Milw., 1961-64; prof., asso. dir. U. Wis. Sch. Social Work, Madison, 1965-68; dean social welfare, v.p. acad. affairs SUNY-Albany, 1969-76; dean social work Loyola U., Chgo., 1976-92, dean emeritus, sr. prof., 1994—; vis. prof. sch. social work SS Maria Asunta, Rome, 1992-93. Author: OAA Profile, 1961, People of Inner Core North, 1965, Men in Jail, 1968; contbr. articles to profl. jours. Pres. Community Action Commn. Dane County, Wis., 1967-68; bd. dirs. Council Community Services, Albany, Family and Children's Service, Albany; mem. adv. bd. Safer Found.; vice chmn. Ill. Pub. Aid Citizens Council. Served with AUS, 1942-46, 51-52. Fulbright scholar, 1949-50; fellow, 1959-60. Mem. AAUP, Nat. Assn. Social Workers. Roman Catholic. Home: 4073 Bunker Ln Wilmette IL 60091-1001 Office: Sch Social Work Loyola Univ Chicago IL 60611

O'REILLY, FRANCES LOUISE, academic administrator; b. Great Falls, Mont., Feb. 20, 1947; d. Francis Joseph and Bernadine Madeline (DeRose) O'R. BA in Sociology and English, Carroll Coll., 1969; MBA, U. Mont., 1977. Head Start tchr. Rocky Mountain Devel. Coun., Helena, Mont., 1969, social svc. dir. Head Start, 1970-76; rsch. asst. U. Mont., Missoula, 1976, teaching asst., 1976-77; broker, owner Manning & O'Reilly Realty Inc., Great Falls, 1977-81; dir. residence hall Carroll Coll., Helena, 1981—; dir. residential life Carroll Coll., 1992—, coord. residential life, 1991-92, adj. faculty mem. dept. bus. acctg. & econs., 1982-86, dept. communications, 1991—, dir. summer programs, 1983—, mem. adv. bd. student affairs com., 1983—; social work cons. Office Children Devel. Region #8, Denver, 1970-76; supr. social work practicums Head Start Rocky Mountain Devel. Coun., 1970-76. Vol. Diabetes Found., Helena, 1993-94, various polit. campaigns, Helena, 1993-94. Mem. Mont. Assn. Student Affairs, Beta Gamma Sigma. Avocations: reading, symphony, yoga, aerobics, theater. Office: Carroll Coll Box 64 OConnell Hall Helena MT 59625

O'REILLY, JAMES THOMAS, lawyer, educator, author; b. N.Y.C., Nov. 15, 1947; s. Matthew Richard and Regina (Casey) O'R.; children: Jean, Ann. BA cum laude, Boston Coll., 1969; JD, U. Va., 1974. Bar: Va. 1974, Ohio, 1974, U.S. Supreme Ct. 1979, U.S. Ct. Appeals (6th cir.) 1980. Atty. Procter & Gamble Co., Cin., 1974-76, counsel, 1976-79, sr. counsel for food, drug and product safety, 1979-85, corp. counsel, 1985-93, assoc. gen. counsel, 1993—; adj. prof. in adminstrv. law U. Cin., 1980—; cons. Adminstrv. Conf. U.S., 1981-82, 89-90, Congl. Office of Compliance, 1995—; arbitrator State Employee Relations Bd.; mem. Ohio Bishops Adv. Council, Mayor's Infrastructure Commn, Cin. Environ. Adv. Coun. Author: Federal Information Disclosure, 1977, Food and Drug Administration Regulatory Manual, 1979, Unions' Rights to Company Information, 1980, Federal Regulation of the Chemical Industry, 1980, Administrative Rulemaking, 1983, Ohio Public Employee Collective Bargaining, 1984, Protecting Workplace Secrets, 1985, Emergency Response to Chemical Accidents, 1986, Product Defects and Hazards, 1987, Toxic Torts Strategy Deskbook, 1989; Protecting Trade Secrets Under SARA, 1988, Complying With Canada's New Labeling Law, 1989, Solid Waste Mgmt., 1991, Ohio Products Liability Handbook, 1991, Toxic Torts Guide, 1992, ABA Product Liability Resource Manual, 1993, RCRA and Superfund Practice Guide, 1993, Clean Air Permits manual, 1994, United States Environmental Liabilities, 1994, Elder Safety, 1995, Environmental and Workplace Safety for University and Hospital Managers, 1996; contbr. articles to profl. jours.; editorial bd. Food and Drug Cosmetic Law Jour. Mem. Hamilton County Dem. Central Com. Served with U.S. Army, 1970-72. Mem. Food and Drug Law Inst. (chair program com.), ABA (chmn. AD law sect.), Fed. Bar Assn., Leadership Cin. Democrat. Roman Catholic. Office: Procter & Gamble Co PO Box 599 Cincinnati OH 45201-0599

O'REILLY, RICHARD BROOKS, journalist; b. Kansas City, Mo., Feb. 19, 1941; s. Charles Alfred and Wilma Faye (Brooks) O'R.; m. Anne Pustmeuller, June 27, 1964 (div. 1978); children—Kathleen Marie, Randall Charles; m. Joan Marlene Sweeney, Jan. 1, 1981. B.A., U. Denver, 1966. Reporter Washington Park Times, Denver, 1963-64; mng. editor Aurora Advocate, Colo., 1964; police reporter Rocky Mountain News, Denver, 1964-66, night rewrite reporter, 1966, city hall reporter, 1966-67, statehouse reporter, 1967-68, investigative reporter, 1971-74; minority affairs reporter Denver Post, 1968-70; freelance writer St. Georges, Grenada, 1970; investigative reporter Orange County edition Los Angeles Times, 1974-78, chief county bur., 1978, asst. met. editor, 1978-80, environ. reporter, 1980-84, computer columnist, syndicated columnist, 1983—, coord. tech. resources, 1984-89, dir. editorial computer analysis, 1989—; adj. prof. journalism U. So. Calif., 1990-92; mem. electronic filing adv. com. Calif. Sec. of State, 1995. Named Colo. Journalist of Yr., Sigma Delta Chi, 1972; recipient Pub. Svc. award U.S. Justice Dept., 1973, McWilliams award Denver Press Club, 1974, Investigative Reporting award Orange Country Press Club, 1977, 95, Los Angeles Times, 1977, Nat. Journalism award Soc. Profl. Engrs., 1983, Clean Air award Am. Lung Assn., 1985. Democrat. Avocations: flying; sailing; camping. Office: Los Angeles Times Times Mirror Sq Los Angeles CA 90012

O'REILLY, THOMAS EUGENE, human resources consultant; b. Wichita, Kans., Sept. 7, 1932; s. Eugene William and Florence Irene (Gustner) O'R.; m. Lorraine Bryant, Feb. 9, 1957; children: Thomas Jr., Patricia, Susan, Gregory, Pamela. BA, Iona Coll., 1954; MBA, NYU, 1958. Mem. human resources staff Chase Manhattan Bank, N.Y.C., 1957-69; dir. employee rels. Chase Manhattan Bank, 1969-71, mgr. internat. personnel, 1971-75, dir. internal staffing, 1976-77, dir. mgmt. resources, 1978-80; dir. exec. resources Chase Manhattan Bank, N.Y.C., 1980-87; v.p., sr. cons. Lee Hecht Harrison, Inc., N.Y.C., 1988-93. Spl. agt. counter-intelligence corps, U.S. Army, 1954-57. Mem. Nat. Fgn. Trade Coun., Exec. Issues Forum. Republican. Roman Catholic. Home and Office: 6200 E Cielo Run Cave Creek AZ 85331-7645

O'REILLY, TIMOTHY PATRICK, lawyer; b. San Lorenzo, Calif., Sept. 12, 1945; s. Thomas Marvin and Florence Ann (Ohlman) O'R.; m. Susan Ann Marshall, July 18, 1969; children: T. Patrick Jr., Sean M., Colleen K. BS, Ohio State U., 1967; JD, NYU, 1971. Bar: Pa. 1971, U.S. Dist. Ct. (ea. dist.) Pa. 1971, U.S. Dist. Ct. (mid. dist.) Pa. 1972, U.S. Ct. Appeals (3d cir.) 1977, U.S. Supreme Ct. 1988. Ptnr. Morgan, Lewis & Bockius, Phila., 1978—. Editor: Developing Labor Law, 1989; contbr. articles to profl. jours. V.p. Chester Valley Bd. Govs., Malvern, Pa., 1980-85; bd. dirs. Notre Dame Acad. and Devon Preparatory Sch. Mem. ABA (chmn. com. on devel. of the law under the Nat. Labor Relations Act., editor-in-chief The Developing Labor Law jour.), Pa. Bar Assn., Phila. Bar Assn., Ohio State U. Alumni Assn. Avocation: golf. Home: 1127 Cymry Dr Berwyn PA 19312-2056 Office: Morgan Lewis & Bockius 2000 One Logan Sq Philadelphia PA 19103

O'REILLY, VINCENT M., accounting firm executive; b. 1937. BS, Boston Coll., 1959; MBA, U Pa., 1961. With Coopers & Lybrand, N.Y.C., 1961—, dep. chmn., 1988—. Office: Coopers & Lybrand 1251 Avenue Of The Americas New York NY 10020-1104*

OREL, HAROLD, literary critic, educator; b. Boston, Mar. 31, 1926; s. Saul and Sarah (Wicker) O.; m. Charlyn Hawkins, May 25, 1951; children: Sara Elinor, Timothy Ralston. BA cum laude, U. N.H., 1948; MA, U. Mich., 1949, PhD, 1952; postgrad., Harvard U., 1949. Teaching fellow U. Mich., 1948-52; instr. dept. English, U. Md., 1952-54, 55-56; overseas program U. Md., Germany, Austria, Eng., 1954-55; tech. editor Applied Physics Lab., Johns Hopkins U., Balt., 1953-56; flight propulsion lab. dept. Gen. Electric Co., Cin., 1957; asso. prof. U. Kans., Lawrence, 1957-63; prof. U. Kans., 1963-74, Disting. prof. English, 1974—, asst. dean faculties and research adminstrn., 1964-67; cons. to various univ. presses, scholarly jours., Can. Coun. Arts, Nat. Endowment of Humanities, Midwest Rsch. Inst., 1958—; lectr., Japan, 1974, 88, India, 1985. Author: Thomas Hardy's Epic-Drama: A Study of The Dynasts, 1963, The Development of William Butler Yeats, 1885-1900, 1968, English Romantic Poets and the Enlightenment: Nine Essays on a Literary Relationship in Studies in Voltaire and the Eighteenth Century, vol. CIII, 1973, The Final Years of Thomas Hardy, 1912-1928, 1976, Victorian Literary Critics, 1984, The Literary Achievement of Rebecca West, 1985, The Victorian Short Story: Development and Triumph of a Literary Genre, 1986, The Unknown Thomas Hardy: Lesser-Known Aspects of Hardy's Life and Career, 1987, A Kipling Chronology, 1990, Popular Fiction in England, 1914-1918, 1992, The Historical Novel from Scott to Sabatini, 1995; contbg. author: Thomas Hardy and the Modern World, 1974, The Genius of Thomas Hardy, 1976, Budmouth Essays on Thomas Hardy, 1976, Twilight of Dawn: Studies in English Literature in Transition, 1987; contbr. numerous articles on English lit. history and criticism to various mags.; editor: The World of Victorian Humor, 1961, Six Essays in Nineteenth-Century English Literature and Thought, 1962, Thomas Hardy's Personal Writings: Prefaces, Literary Opinions, Reminiscences, 1966, British Poetry 1880-1920: Edwardian Voices, 1969, The Nineteenth-Century Writer and his Audience, 1969, Irish History and Culture, 1976, The Dynasts

(Thomas Hardy), 1978, The Scottish World, 1981, Rudyard Kipling: Interviews and Recollections, 2 vols., 1983, Victorian Short Stories: An Anthology, 1987, Critical Essays on Rudyard Kipling, 1989, Victorian Short Stories 2: The Trials of Love, 1990, Sir Arthur Conan Doyle: Interviews and Recollections, 1991, Critical Essays on Sir Arthur Conan Doyle, 1992, Gilbert and Sullivan: Interviews and Recollections, 1994, Critical Essays on Thomas Hardy's Poetry, 1995; delivered orations Thomas Hardy ceremonies, Westminster Abbey, 1978, 90. With USN, 1944-46. Recipient Higuchi Endowment Rsch. Achievement award, 1990; grantee Am. Coun. Learned Socs., 1966, NEH, 1975, Am. Philos. Soc., 1964, 80. Fellow Royal Soc. Literature; mem. Thomas Hardy Soc. (v.p. 1968—), Am. Com. on Irish Studies (v.p. 1967-70, pres. 1970-72). Unitarian. Home: 713 Schwarz Rd Lawrence KS 66049-4507 Office: U Kans Dept English Lawrence KS 66045

OREM, HENRY PHILIP, retired chemist, chemical engineer, consultant; b. Campbellsburg, Ky., Feb. 28, 1910; s. Mal Lee and Alice (Green) O.; m. Lydia C. Orem (dec. Feb. 1988). BS in Indsl. Chemistry, U. Ky., 1932, MS, 1934; postgrad., Pa. State U., 1934-36. Grad. asst. phys. chemistry U. Ky., 1933; grad. rsch. scholar Pa. State Coll., 1934-37; with rsch. dept. Calco Chem. Co. subs. Am. Cyanamid Co., Bound Brook, N.J., 1937-39; plant rschr./process developer Am. Cyanamid Co., Bound Brook, 1939-42; asst. chief chemist Azo Dye and Intermediate divsn. Am. Cyanamid Co., Bound Brook, N.J., 1942-46; departmental chemist Azo Dye and Intermediate divsn. Am. Cyanamid Co., Bound Brook, 1947, tech. supt., 1947-50; rsch. chemist Sloss Sheffield Steel and Iron Co. (now U.S. Pipe and Foundry Co. subs. Jim Walter Co.), Birmingham, Ala., 1950-52, rsch. ehcm. engr., 1952-65, group leader, 1965-75, ret., 1975; cons. Jim Walter Resources, Inc., Arichem, Inc. (now subs. Jim Walter Resources, Inc.). Contbr. articles to various publs. Fellow Am. Inst. Chemists (profl. accredited chemist); mem. AIChE (life, 1st sec. N.J. sect. 1949-50, chmn. 1963, treas. Ala. sect. 1971, 72), Am. Chem. Soc. (emeritus life, sec.-treas. Raritan Valley group N.J. sect. 1948, chmn. 1950, sec. Ala. sect. 1956-57), NRA (life), Nat. Muzzle Loading Rifle Assn. (life, contbr. and reviewer articles Muzzle Blasts, technical advisor muzzle blasts, powder and ballistics), U.S. Revolver Assn. (life), Ala. Gun Collectors Assn. (life), Magic City Gun Club (life), Va. Gun Collectors Assn. (life), Kate Carpenter Muzzleloaders Inc., Stonewall Rifle and Pistol Club (Churchville, Va.), Shenandale Gun Club (Buffalo Gap, Va.), Homestead Shooting Club (Hot Springs, Va.), Va. Muzzle Loading Rifle Assn., Va. State Rifle and Revolver Assn., Ft. Lewis Hunting Club (life), Am. Def. Preparedness Assn., Sigma Xi. Achievements include 22 patents in field (U.S. and Can.), numerous publs. in chemistry and ballistics. Home: HCR 02 Box 259 Warm Springs VA 24484-9508

OREN, BRUCE CLIFFORD, newspaper editor, artist; b. Mineola, N.Y., Aug. 31, 1952; s. Ralph and Bernice (Lands) O.; 1 child, Adam Nathaniel; m. Angela Malone Williams, Mar. 4, 1990. Student, U. Md., College Park, 1970-74. Archtl. sculptor Universal Restoration Inc., Washington, 1974-76; tech. illustrator Tex. Instruments, Stafford, Tex., 1976-77; graphic artist Houston Chronicle, 1977-79, photo editor, 1979-86, artist, 1986—; artist L.A. Times Syndicate, 1987-91. Recipient Bronze medal Soc. Newspaper Design, 1992. Jewish. Office: 801 Texas St Houston TX 77002-2906

OREN, JOHN BIRDSELL, retired coast guard officer; b. Madison, Wis., Dec. 27, 1909; s. Arthur Baker and Lucile Grace (Comfort) O.; m. Harriet Virginia Prentis, Feb. 9, 1934; children—Virginia Joan (Mrs. Luther Warren Strickler II), John Edward. B.S., USCG Acad., 1933; M.S. in Marine Engring, MIT, 1942. Commd. ensign USCG, 1933, advanced through grades to rear adm., 1964; chief engring. div. (11th Coast Guard Dist.), 1957-59, (12th Coast Guard Dist.), 1960-61; dep. chief (Office Engring.), Washington, 1962-63; chief Office of Engring. (Office Engring.), 1964-68; now ret.; Mem. Mcht. Marine Council, 1964—; chmn. ship structures com. Transp. Dept., 1964—; exec. dir. Maritime Transp. Research Bd., Nat. Acad. Scis., 1968—; mem. nat. adv. bd. Am. Security Council. Recipient Legion of Merit. Mem. Soc. Am. Mil. Engrs. (pres. 1966, Acad. of Fellows), Am. Soc. Naval Engrs. (pres. 1965), Internat. Inst. Welding (vice chmn. Am. coun. 1964), Ret. Officers Assn. (bd. dirs. 1978), Pan Am. Inst. Naval Engring., Masons. Republican. Episcopalian. Home: 6521 Old Dominion Dr #221 Mc Lean VA 22101

ORENSTEIN, JANIE ELIZABETH, educational association administrator; b. Winston-Salem, N.C., Mar. 3, 1961; d. William Ralph and Mary Elizabeth (Brantley) Mauney; m. Gary Stephen Catarina, Sept. 10, 1983 (div. Oct. 1991); m. Alan Jay Orenstein, Feb. 13, 1993; children: Sara, Becky. Student, Westchester (N.Y.) C.C., 1985-87. Cert. YMCA sch. age child care dir., Child Devel. Assn. Tchg. asst. The Cottage Sch., Pleasantville, N.Y., 1984-87; program dir. Broward YMCA, Ft. Lauderdale, Fla., 1989—; south teen cluster co. dir. YMCA of USA, Ft. Lauderdale, 1994—; advisor, coach Spl. Olympics, Ft. Lauderdale, 1992—; presenter Fla. Sch. Age Childcare Coalition, Orlando, Fla., 1992; assessing schoolage quality advisor Wellsley (Mass.) Coll., 1993—, Childcare Connection, North Lauderdale, 1994—; com. mem. Broward County Schs., Ft. Lauderdale, 1993—. Co-mem. United Way, 1989; vol. Safe Place, 1994. Recipient Good Samaritan award Coral Springs Handicapped Com., Coral Springs, Fla., 1990. Mem. Coun. for Exceptional Children. Democrat. Episcopalian. Avocations: youth coaching, soccer, dance, theater. Home: 1225 NW 111th Ave Coral Springs FL 33071-6443 Office: YMCA 7718 Wiles Rd Coral Springs FL 33067-2075

ORENSTEIN, (IAN) MICHAEL, philatelic dealer, columnist; b. Bklyn., Jan. 6, 1939; s. Harry and Myra (Klein) O.; m. Linda Turer, June 28, 1964; 1 child, Paul David. BS, Clemson U., 1960; postgrad., U. Calif., Berkeley, 1960-61. Career regional mgr. Minkus Stamp & Pub. Co., Calif., 1964-70; mgr. stamp div. Superior Stamp & Coin Co., Inc., Beverly Hills, Calif., 1970-90; dir. stamp divsn. Superior Galleries, Beverly Hills, Calif., 1991-94; dir. space memorabelia Superior Stamp and Coin. Co., Inc., Beverly Hills, Calif., 1992-94; dir. stamp and space divsn. Superior Stamp & Coin an A-Mark Co., Beverly Hills, 1994—; stamp columnist L.A. Times, 1965-93; bd. Adelphi U. N.Y. Inst. Philatelic and Numismatic Studies, 1978-81. Author: Stamp Collecting Is Fun, 1990; philatelic advisor/creator The Video Guide To Stamp Collecting, 1988. With AUS, 1962-64. Mem. Am. Stamp Dealers Assn., C.Z. Study Group, German Philatelic Soc., Confederate Stamp Alliance, Am. Philatelic Soc. (writers unit 1975-80, 89-93), Internat. Fedn. Stamp Dealers, Internat. Soc. Appraisers: Stamps, Space Memorabilia. Republican. Avocation: fishing. Office: Superior Stamp & Coin An A-Mark Co 9478 W Olympic Blvd Beverly Hills CA 90212-4246

ORENSTEIN, WALTER A., health facility administrator; b. N.Y.C., Mar. 5, 1948; m. Diane Rauzin; children: Eleza Tema, Evan William. BS, CCNY, 1968; MD, Albert Einstein Coll. Medicine, 1972. Intern U. Calif., San Francisco, 1972-73, resident in pediat., 1973-74; EIS officer divsn. immunization Ctr. for Disease Control, Atlanta, 1974-76, med. epidemiologist divsn. immunization, 1976-77, 80-82; resident pediat. Childrens Hosp. L.A., 1977-78; fellow infectious diseases U. So. Calif. Med. Sch., 1978-80; resident preventive medicine Ctrs. Disease Control, Atlanta, 1980-82, chief surveillance and investigations sect., 1982-88, dir. divsn. immunization, 1988-93; dir. nat. immunization program Ctrs. for Disease Control and Prevention, Atlanta, 1993—; cons. smallpox eradication program WHO, Uttar Pradesh, India, 1974-75; med. adv. bd. Ctrs. Disease Control, Atlanta, 1981-84, nat. vaccine adv. com., 1988—, adv. commn. on childhood vaccines, 1989—; clin. assoc. prof. dept. cmty. health Emory U. Sch. Medicine, 1985; adj. prof. The Rollins Sch. Pub. Health, 1992—; cons. and presenter in field. Editor Pediat. Infectious Disease Jour., 1987; contbr. articles to profl. jours. Asst. surgeon gen. USPHS, 1995. Fellow Am. Acad. Pediat. (liaison mem., com. on infectious diseases 1989—), Infectious Diseases Soc. Am., Pediat. Infectious Diseases Soc.; mem. APHA, Am. Epidemiological Soc., Soc. for Epidemiologic Rsch., Coun. the Pediat. Infectious Diseases Soc. Home: 50 Battle Ridge Dr Atlanta GA 30342-2451 Office: Nat Immunization Program Mailstop EO5 Atlanta GA 30333

ORESKES, IRWIN, biochemistry educator; b. Chgo., June 30, 1926; s. Herman and Clara (Rubenstein) O.; m. Susan E. Nagin, June 18, 1949; children: Michael, Daniel, Naomi, Rebecca. B.S. in Chemistry, CCNY, 1949; M.A. in Phys. Chemistry, Bklyn. Coll., 1956; Ph.D. in Biochemistry, CUNY, 1969. Cert. clin. lab. dir. N.Y.C., N.Y. State. Chemist Tech. Tape Co., Bronx, N.Y., 1949; technician NYU Sch. Medicine, 1950-51; phys. chemist Kingsbrook Jewish Med. Ctr., 1951-56; research fellow Poly. Inst., N.Y., 1957-58; research assoc. Mt. Sinai Hosp., N.Y., 1959-68, dir. arthritis lab., 1961-90; rsch. asst. prof. Mt. Sinai Sch. Medicine, 1969-74, rsch. assoc. prof., 1974-91; assoc. prof. Hunter Coll. Sch. Health Scis., CUNY, 1970-74, prof., 1974—, dean, 1977-80; mem. doctoral faculty in biochemistry Grad. Center, CUNY, 1970—; vis. prof. Johns Hopkins U. Sch. Health Services, 1976-77; cons to diagnostic reagent and instrument mfrs., 1953—; mem. Internat. Sci. Council, Albert Einstein Research Inst., Buenos Aires, Argentina, 1969-79; mem. bd. examiners for clin. labs. N.Y.C. Dept. Health, 1973-75; sr. cons. Biotech. Rev. Assocs., 1983—. Co-editor: Rheumatology for the Health Care Professional, 1991; contbr. numerous articles to profl. jours. Served with U.S. Army, 1944-46. Nat. Inst. Arthritis and Metabolic Diseases grantee, 1961-69; Arthritis Found. grantee, 1961-65, 69, 72; Lupus Found. grantee, 1975-76; CUNY Found. grantee, 1982-83. Mem. Am. Chem. Soc., Am. Coll. Rheumatology, AAAS, N.Y. Acad. Scis., Am. Assn. Immunologists, Am. Assn. Clin. Chemistry, Harvey Soc., Nat. Acad. Clin. Biochemistry, Acad. Clin. Lab. Physicians and Scientists, Clin. Immunology Soc., Sigma Xi, Phi Lambda Upsilon. Home: 670 W End Ave New York NY 10025-7313 Office: Hunter Coll Sch Health Sci 425 E 25th St New York NY 10010-2547 *I have always tried to live and work by the idea that strength is not harshness, caring is not sentimentality, and honesty is not vulnerability.*

ORESKES, SUSAN, private school educator; b. N.Y.C., May 24, 1930; d. Morris and Sarah (Rudner) Nagin; m. Irwin Oreskes, June 19, 1949; children: Michael, Daniel, Naomi, Rebecca. BA, Queens Coll., 1952; dance student, Eddie Torres Sch., Manhattan, N.Y., 1984-90. Organizer Strycker's Bay Neighborhood Coun., N.Y.C., 1961-75; dir. weekly column cmty. newspaper Enlightenment Press, N.Y.C., 1975-85; assoc. tchr. Riverside Ch. Weekday Sch., N.Y.C., 1985-95. Organizer, v.p. F.D.R.-Woodrow Wilson Polit. Club, Manhattan, 1961-71; organizer Hey Brother Coffee House, 1968—. Democrat. Jewish. Avocations: music, dance, travel with husband. Home: 670 W End Ave New York NY 10025-7313

ORESMAN, DONALD, entertainment and publishing company executive, corporate lawyer; b. 1925. BA, Oberlin Coll., 1946; LLB, Columbia U., 1957. Ptnr. Simpson, Thacher & Bartlet, N.Y.C., 1957-83; exec. v.p., sec., gen. counsel, chief adminstrv. officer Paramount Communications Inc., N.Y.C., 1983—, also bd. dirs., mem. exec. com. Office: Paramount Comm Inc 15 Columbus Cir New York NY 10023-7706

ORESTANO-JAMES, LORI ESTER, middle school educator; b. Hollywood, Fla., Oct. 11, 1963; d. Arthur Jacob and Ruth Virginia (Moncine) Budoff; m. Bill James, Aug. 16, 1987. MusB in Music Edn., Ithaca Coll., 1986; MS in Edn., SUNY, New Paltz, 1990. Cert. music edn. k-12, N.Y.S., cert. elem. edn., N.Y.S. Tchr. music, vocal, gen. Monticello (N.Y.) Ctrl. Sch., 1985—; dir. theatre, jr. high vocal dir. Monticello Ctrl. Sch., 1986—; advisor Monticello Middle Sch. Builders Club, 1989—. Sec., mem. com. Town of Thompson Rep. Com., 1987—; county chair fashion show Com. to Elect Ben Gilman Congressman, 1994; bd. dirs. Sullivan County Branch Big Bros./Big Sisters, 1987-93; regional pres. Orange, Rockland, Sullivan County Regional Bd. Am. Heart Assn., 1986—. Recipient Deans award for Excellence in Tchg., SUNY; named Vol. of Yr. Am. Heart Assn., 1989, Top 10 Finalist Tchr. of Yr. State Edn. Dept., 1992, Sullivan County Woman of Yr. by Sullivan County Dem., 1993. Mem. N.Y. State Theatre Educators Assn., Sullivan County Music Educators Assn. (corr. sec. 1986—), Bus. and Profl. Women, Music Educators Nat. Conf., N.Y. State Music Educators Assn., Sullivan County Dramatic Workshop, Monticello Elks Ladies Aux., Monticello Hadassah (chair publicity 1992—), Monticello Kiwanis Club (hon.), Mu Phi Epsilon. Jewish. Avocation: theatre. Office: Monticello Middle Sch St John St Monticello NY 12701

ORFIELD, MYRON WILLARD, JR., state legislator, educator; b. Mpls., July 27, 1961. BA summa cum laude, U. Minn., 1983; grad., Princeton U., 1983-84; JD, U. Chgo., 1987. Bar: Minn. 1988. Law clk. Judge Gerald W. Heaney, U.S. Ct. Appeals, 8th Cir., 1987-88; rsch. assoc. Ctr. for Studies in Criminal Justice, U. Chgo., 1988-89; assoc. Faegre & Benson, 1989; asst. atty. gen. Minn. Atty. Gen.'s Office, 1989—; Bradley fellow Ctr. for Studies in Criminal Justice, U. Chgo., 1990-91; rep. Minn. Ho. of Reps. Dist. 60B, Mpls., 1991—; adj. prof. law U. Minn., 1991—, Hamline U., 1991—; prin. Met. Area Project, Mpls. Contbr. articles to profl. jours. Office: 521 State Office Bldg Saint Paul MN 55155

ORGAN, JOSEPH B., lawyer; b. Oak Park, Ill., Oct. 28, 1951. BA, Rollins Coll., 1974; JD, Northwestern U., 1977; LLM Taxation, NYU, 1983. Bar: Ill. 1977. Ptnr. Mayer Brown & Platt, Chgo. Office: Mayer Brown & Platt 190 S La Salle St Chicago IL 60603-3410*

ORGANSKI, ABRAMO FIMO KENNETH, political scientist, educator; b. Rome, May 17, 1923; came to U.S., 1939, naturalized, 1944; s. Menasce and Anna (Feinstein) O.; m. Katherine Davis Fox, May 29, 1947 (dec. Feb. 1973); children: Eric Fox, Elizabeth Anna; m. Patricia Joan Bard, June 14, 1986. BA, NYU, 1947, MA, 1948, PhD, 1951; student, Ginnasio Liceo Torquato Tasso, Rome, 1933-38. From asst. prof. to prof. polit. sci. Bklyn. Coll., CUNY, 1952-64; prof. polit. sci. U. Mich., Ann Arbor, 1965—, James Orin Murfin prof. polit. sci., 1985-87, sr. scientist, program dir. Ctr. Polit. Sci., Inst. Social Research, 1969—; adj. prof. polit. sci. Grad. Sch. Pub. Adminstrn. NYU, 1960; vis. assoc. prof. pub. law and govt. Columbia U., N.Y.C., 1961-62; vis. prof. Fletcher Sch. Law and Diplomacy, 1963-66, Dartmouth Coll., 1963-64, U. Pa., 1983, U. Catania, 1975, 77, U. Florence, Italy, 1990, U. Turin, Italy, 1991; sr. cons., bd. dirs. Policon Corp., 1982—, Decision Insights, 1991—; lectr., cons. to various pvt. and govlt. instns., U.S. and abroad, 1960—, European Inst., Florence, 1993; vis. scholar The Hoover Instn., Stanford U., 1991, 92, 93; vis. scholar in residence Agnelli Found., 1991. Author: World Politics, 1958, 68, (with Katherine Organski) Population and World Power, 1961, Stages of Political Development, 1965, (with Jacek Kugler) The War Ledger, 1980, (with Kugler, Y. Cohen and T. Johnson) Births, Deaths and Taxes: The Political and Demographic Transition, 1984, The 36 Billion Dollar Bargain: Strategy and Politics in U.S. Assistance to Israel, 1990; bd. editors: Affari Sociali Internazionali, Comparative Politics, International Interactions. Served with U.S. Army, 1943-45. Decorated Cavaliere della Republic Italy; recipient Disting. Faculty Achievement award U. Mich., 1983; Social Sci. Rsch. Coun. fellow, 1976, Fulbright fellow, 1977. Mem. Am. Polit. Sci. Assn. (coun. 1969, Lifetime Achievement award conflict processes sect., 1992), Internat. Polit. Sci. Assn. Avocations: skiing, tennis. Home: 460 Hillspur Rd Ann Arbor MI 48105-1049 Office: U Mich Ctr Polit Studies Inst Social Rsch Ann Arbor MI 48106-1248

ORGEBIN-CRIST, MARIE-CLAIRE, biology educator; b. Vannes, France, Mar. 20, 1936. License Natural Scis., License Biology, Sorbonne, U. Paris, 1957; D. Scis., Lyons U., France, 1961. Stagiaire dept. biochemistry faculty medicine Paris, France, 1957-58; stagiaire Centre Nat. de la Recherche Scientifique, Paris, 1958-60, attachee de recherche, 1960-62; research assoc. Population Council (Med. Div.), N.Y.C., 1962-63; research assoc. dept. ob/gyn Vanderbilt Sch. Medicine, 1963-64, research instr., 1964-66, asst. prof., 1966-70, assoc. prof., 1970-73, Lucius E. Burch prof. reproductive biology, 1973—, prof. dept. anatomy, 1975—; dir. Vanderbilt Sch. Medicine (Center Reproductive Biology Research.), 1973—; Editor-in-Chief Jour. Andrology, 1983-89. Recipient Career Devel. award NIH, 1968-73, NIH Merit award, 1986, Disting. Andrologist award Am. Soc. Andrology, 1990; Fogarty Internat. sr. fellow, 1977. Mem. Am. Assn. Anatomists, Am. Soc. Cell Biology, Am. Soc. Andrology (v.p. 1994-95, pres. 1995-96), Internat. Com. on Andrology, Endocrine Soc., Soc. for Study Fertility (Eng.), Soc. for Study Reprodn., N.Y. Acad. Scis. Office: Vanderbilt U Sch Med Ctr Reproductive Biology Rsch Rm D-2303 MCN Nashville TN 37232

ORIANI, RICHARD ANTHONY, metallurgical engineering educator; b. El Salvador, July 19, 1920; came to U.S., 1929, naturalized, 1943; s. Americo and Berta (Siguenza) O.; m. Constance Amelia Gordon, June 26, 1949; children—Margaret, Steven, Julia, Amelia. B. Chem.Engring, CCNY, 1943; M.S., Stevens Inst. Tech., 1946; M.A., Princeton U., 1948, Ph.D., 1949. Lab. asst. CCNY, 1943; chemist Bakelite Corp., Bloomfield, N.J., 1943-46; instr. physics Miss Fine's Finishing Sch., Princeton, N.J., 1946-47; research asso. Gen. Electric Corp. Research Lab., Schenectady, 1949-59; asst. dir. U.S. Steel Corp. Research Lab., Monroeville, Pa., 1959-80; prof. U. Minn., Mpls., 1980-89, dir. Corrosion Rsch. Ctr., 1980-87, prof. and dir. emeritus, 1989—; cons. in field. Contbr. chpts. to books, articles to profl. jours. Founder, mem. Foxwood Civic Assn., Monroeville, 1959-80; founder, v.p. Monroeville Public Library, 1960-80. Recipient Alexander von Humboldt Sr. Scientist award, 1984, W.R. Whitney award, 1987. Fellow Am. Soc. for Metals, Am. Inst. Chemists, N.Y. Acad. Scis., Nat. Assn. Corrosion Engrs., Electrochem. Soc.; mem. AAAS, Am. Phys. Soc., Am. Inst. Metall. Engrs. Republican. Home: 4623 Humboldt Ave S Minneapolis MN 55409-2264 Office: U Minn 112 Amundson Hall 221 Church St SE Minneapolis MN 55455-0152

ORIANS, GORDON HOWELL, biology educator; b. Eau Claire, Wis., July 10, 1932; s. Howard Lester and Marion Meta (Senty) O.; m. Elizabeth Ann Newton, June 25, 1955; children: Carlyn Elizabeth, Kristin Jean, Colin Mark. BS, U. Wis., 1954; PhD, U. Calif., Berkeley, 1960. Asst. prof. zoology U. Wash., Seattle, 1960-64, assoc. prof., 1964-68, prof., 1968-95, prof. emeritus, 1995—; active Wash. State Ecol. Commn., Olympia, 1970-75, ecology adv. com. EPA, Washington, 1974-79; assembly life scis. NAS/NRC, Washington, 1977-83, environ. studies and toxicology bd., 1991—. Author: Some Adaptations of Marsh Nesting Blackbirds, 1980, Blackbirds of the Americas, 1985, Life: The Science of Biology, 1995; editor: Convergent Evolution in Warm Deserts, 1968. 1st lt. U.S. Army, 1955-56. Mem. AAAS, NAS, Am. Inst. Biol. Scis. (Disting. Svc. award 1994), Am. Ornithologists Union (Brewster award 1976), Am. Soc. Naturalists, Animal Behavior Soc., Royal Netherlands Acad. Arts and Scis., Orgn. for Tropical Studies (pres. 1988-94), Ecol. Soc. Am. (v.p. 1975-76, pres. 1995-96). Avocations: hiking, opera. Office: U Wash Dept Zoology Box 351800 Seattle WA 98195

ORIHEL, THOMAS CHARLES, parasitology educator, research scientist; b. Akron, Ohio, Feb. 10, 1929; s. Joseph Andrew and Mary Susannah (Barno) O.; m. Dorothy Lila Williams, Dec. 27, 1952; children—Timothy Stewart, Charles Theodore, Susan Ethra, Adrianne Louise. B.S., U. Akron, 1950; M.S., U. Wash., 1952; Ph.D., Tulane U., 1959. Sr. scientist Tulane Delta Primate Ctr., Covington, La., 1963-85; prof. parasitology Tulane Med. Ctr., New Orleans, 1972—; William Vincent prof. tropical diseases Tulane Med. Ctr., 1982—; dir. Tulane U. Internat. Collaboration Infectious Diseases Rsch. Program, New Orleans, 1976-89; cons. NIH, Bethesda, Md., 1973-77; mem. expert panel WHO, Geneva, 1973-83; mem. U.S.-Japan Cooperative Med. Sci. Program, Bethesda, 1974-78; external examiner U. Queensland, Australia, U. Guelph, Ont., Can., U. Claude Bernard, Lyon, France, U. Malaya, Kuala Lumpur, Malaysia. Author books on subject of medical parasitology, 1976, 81, 84, 90, 94, 95; contbr. articles to Am. and internat. jours. Served to 1st lt. Med. Service Corps, U.S. Army, 1953-56, Korea. Mem. Am. Soc. Tropical Medicine and Hygiene (councilor 1975-78), Royal Soc. Tropical Medicine and Hygiene, Am. Soc. Microbiology, Southwestern Assn. Parasitologists (v.p. 1972-73), Am. Soc. Parasitologists, Sigma Xi. Avocations: gardening; woodworking. Home: 115 Bertel Dr Covington LA 70433-4815 Office: Tulane Med Ctr Dept Tropical Medicine 1430 Tulane Ave New Orleans LA 70112-2699

ORING, STUART AUGUST, visual information specialist, writer/photographer; b. Bronx, N.Y., Aug. 28, 1932; s. Irving and Helen Flora (Greenhut) O.; m. Mary Carolyn Barth, Aug. 22, 1957; children: Carlene Marie Oring, Sheri Alyce Oring. AAS, Rochester Inst. Tech., 1957; BFA, R.I. Tech., 1959; MA, Am. U., 1970. Photo lab asst. Nat. Geographic, Washington, summer 1957; photography asst. I.J. Becker, Studio Assocs. and Art Green Inc., N.Y.C., 1959-61; freelance photographer pvt. practice, Washington, 1961; indsl. photographer Vitro Corp., Rockville, Md., 1962-64; health photographer Nat. Ctr. Radiol. Health, Rockville, Md., 1964-67; visual info. specialist ARS Info. div. USDA, Washington, 1967-69; audio visual specialist Nat. AV Ctr., Washington, 1969-71; photojournalist Office of Econ. Opportunity, Washington, 1971-74; visual info. specialist ASCS, U.S. Dept. Agr., Washington, 1974-94; ret., 1994; mgr., owner ISIS Visual Comms.; photography tchr. Prince George's C.C., Largo, Md., 1975—; guest lectr. U. Md. Balt. County, Towson, Corcoran Gallery of Art, Washington; program spkr. Conf. Internat. Soc. Psychopathology of Expression. Author, editor and pub.: (textbook/gallery text) Understanding Pictures-A Teacher's Planning Guide, 1994, Understanding Pictures-Theories, Exercises and Procedures, 1990, rev. 1992, rev. 1995; contbr. numerous articles to profl. jours.; photos published in books, mags., brochures, pamphlets. Pub. rels. Calvert County Humane Soc., 1990. Photographer with U.S. Army, 1952-55. Recipient Cert. Recognition award Eastman Kodak Co., 1973, Nat. Ctr. Radiol. Health, Rockville, Md., 1965. Mem. Soc. Photographic Edn., Am. Soc. Psychopathology of Expression, Inst. for Psychol. Study of Arts (program spkr. internat. conf.). Avocations: chess, swimming, classical music, oriental philosophy, art. Home and Office: 2570 Redbud Ln Owings MD 20736-4308

ORITSKY, MIMI, artist, educator; b. Reading, Pa., Aug. 14, 1950; d. Herbert and Marcia (Sarna) O. Student, Phila. Coll. Art, 1968-70; BFA, Md. Inst. Coll. Art, 1975; MFA, U. Pa., 1979. Artist, supr. subway mural projects Crisis Intervention Network, Phila., 1978-83; instr. painting U. Arts, Phila., 1984, 89-93, Abington Art Ctr., Jenkintown, Pa., 1989—, Main Line Art Ctr., Haverford, Pa., 1993—. One-woman shows include Gross McCleaf Gallery, 1980-82, Callowhill Art Gallery, Reading, Pa., Amos Eno Gallery, N.Y.C., 1986, 89, 91, 94, 96, Hahnemann U. Gallery, Phila.,1 988, Kaufmann Gallery, Shippensburg, Pa., 1989, Kimberton (Pa.) Gallery, 1990, Rittenhouse Galleries, Phila., 1992-94; group exhbns. include Current Representational Painting in Phila., 1980, Gross McCleaf Gallery, 1980-82. Recipient Purchase award Pa. Coun. Arts/Beaver Coll., 1983, Reading Pub. Mus., 1984; fellow Artists for Environment Found., 1980, Millay Colony for Arts, 1983. Mem. Coll. Art Assn.

ORKAND, DONALD SAUL, management consultant; b. N.Y.C., Mar. 2, 1936; s. Harold and Sylvia (Wagner) O.; children: Dara Sue, Katarina Day. BS summa cum laude, NYU, 1956, MBA, 1957, PhD, 1963. Statistician, Western Electric Co., N.Y.C., 1956-58; group v.p. Ops. Rsch., Inc., Silver Spring, Md., 1960-69; pres. Ops. Rsch. Industries, Ltd., Ottawa, Ont., Can., 1968-69; pres., CEO The Orkand Corp., Tysons Corner, Va., 1970—; bd. dirs. U. Md. Found., Inc., College Park, 1993—. Contbr. articles to profl. jours. Bd. visitors coll. of bus. and mgmt. U. Md., College Park, 1985—; trustee Suburban Hosp., 1994—. 1st lt. Ordnance Corps, USAR, 1958-60. Mem. Am. Econs. Assn., Am. Statis. Assn., Ops. Rsch. Soc. Am. Republican. Jewish. Avocations: reading, theater, travel, exercise. Office: The Orkand Corp 7799 Leesburg Pike Tysons Corner VA 22043

ORKAND, RICHARD KENNETH, neurobiologist, researcher, educator; b. N.Y.C., Apr. 23, 1936. BS, Columbia U., 1956; PhD, U. Utah, 1961; MA, U. Pa., 1974. Fellow U. Coll. London, 1961-64, Harvard U., Boston, 1964-66; asst. prof. U. Utah, Salt Lake City, 1966-68; prof. UCLA, 1968-74; prof., chmn. U. Pa., Phila., 1974-86; dir. Inst. Neurobiology U. P.R., San Juan, 1986—; Benjamin Meaker prof. U. Bristol, 1993; adj. prof. biology Calif. Poly. U., San Luis Obispo, 1993—; exec. dir. Caribbean Neurosci. Found., 1987—; mem. adv. coun. Conservation Trust of P.R., 1990-94; councilor AAAS, Caribbean, 1990-95. Co-author: Introduction to Nervous Systems, 1977; contbr. over 80 articles to profl. jours. Mem. com. Dem. Party, Phila., 1981. Fellow AAAS. Achievements include research in studies of physiology of neuroglia and neuron-glia interaction. Office: U PR Inst Neurobiology 201 Calle Blvd Del Vly San Juan PR 00901-1123

ORKIN, LOUIS RICHARD, physician, educator; b. N.Y.C., Dec. 23, 1915; s. Samuel David and Rebecca (Rish) O.; m. Florence Fine, Mar. 5, 1938; 1 dau., Rita. B.A., U. Wis., 1937; M.D., N.Y. U., 1941; AAS in Marine Tech., Kingsborough Coll., 1992. Intern Bellevue Hosp., N.Y.C., 1942; resident anesthesiology Bellevue Hosp., 1946-48; practice medicine specializing in anesthesiology Bronx, N.Y., 1946—; dir. anesthesiology Backus Hosp., Norwich, Conn., 1948-50; asst. prof. anesthesiology N.Y. U. Coll. Medicine, 1950-55; prof., chmn. dept. anesthesiology Albert Einstein Coll. Medicine, 1955-82, Disting. univ. prof., 1982-86, dist. univ. prof. emeritus, 1986—; vis. prof. depts. bioengring., anesthesiology U. Calif., San Diego, 1971; Cons. VA, USPHS, USN; mem. com. anesthesiology Nat. Acad. Scis., 1964-69; mem. com. anesthetic drugs FDA, Dept. Health, Edn. and Welfare, 1970—. Author: Patient in Shock, 1965, Physiology of Obstetrical Anesthesia, 1969; Contbr. articles to profl. jours. Vice pres., trustee Wood Library Mus. Served to capt. M.C. AUS, 1942-45. Decorated Bronze Star. Fellow Am. Coll. Chest Physicians, N.Y. Acad. Sci., N.Y. Acad. Medicine, Am. Coll. Anesthesiology (past chmn. bd. govs.); mem. N.Y. State Soc.

Anesthesiologists (past pres.). Home: 11 Stuyvesant Oval New York NY 10009-2001 Office: Albert Einstein Coll Medicine Dept Anesthesiology Bronx NY 10461

ORLAND, FRANK, oral microbiologist, educator; b. Little Falls, N.Y., Jan. 23, 1917; s. Michael and Rose (Dorner) O.; m. Phyllis Therese Mrazek, May 8, 1943; children: Frank R., Carl P., June Rose, Ralph M. AA, U. Chgo., 1937, SM, 1945, PhD, 1949; BS, U. Ill., 1939, DDS, 1941. Diplomate Am. Bd. Med. Microbiology. With U. Chgo., 1941—; intern Zoller Meml. Dental Clinic, U. Chgo., 1941-42; Zoller fellow, asst. in dental surgery U. Chgo., 1942-49, instr., asst. prof., assoc. prof., prof. dental sci., 1949-88, prof. emeritus, 1988—, from instr. to assoc. prof. microbiology, 1950-58, rsch. assoc. prof., 1958-64; dir. Zoller Meml. Dental Clinic, 1954-66; prof. Fishbein Ctr. for Study History Sci. and Medicine, 1980-88, prof. emeritus, 1988—; attending dentist Country Home for Convalescent Children; past cons. Nat. Inst. Dental Rsch., NIH, Bethesda, Md.; mem. panel on dental drugs The Nat. Formulary; past chmn. dental adv. bd. Med. Heritage Soc. Author: The First Fifty-Year History of the International Association for Dental Research, 1973, Microbiology in Clinical Dentistry, 1982, William John Gies-His Contributions to the Advancement of Dentistry, 1992; editor: Jour. Dental Rsch., 1958-69, (Centennial brochure) Loyola U. Sch. Dentistry, 1983; editor, contbr. Microbiology in Clinical Dentistry, 1982; writer, prodr. 50th anniversary booklet Zoller Meml. Dental Clinic U. Chgo., 1987; contbr. articles to profl. jours. Past chmn. adv. coun. Forest Park (Ill.) Bd. Edn.; mem. Forest Park Citizens Com. for Better Schs.; past pres. Garfield Sch. PTA, 1953-55; chairperson heritage com. Bicentennial Commn. on Forest Park, 1983-85; editor Chronicles of Forest Park, 1976—. Recipient Rsch. Essay award Chgo. Dental Soc., 1955, Cook County Sheriff Medal of Honor award, 1993; named Citizen of Yr., Forest Park, 1989. Fellow AAAS, Inst. Medicine Chgo. (chmn. com. publ. comm.), Am. Acad. Microbiology (William J. Gies award 1994), Am. Coll. Dentists; mem. ADA (past chmn. coun. dental therapeutics), Internat. Assn. Dental Rsch. (pres. 1971-72, past councilor Chgo. sect., past chmn. program com., past chmn. com. on history), Am. Assn. Dental Schs. (past chmn. conf. oral microbiology past chmn. com. on advanced edn.), Am. Assn. Dental Editors (William Gies Editl. award 1968), Ill. State Dental Soc. (chmn. com on history), Fedn. dentaire Internat. (Commn. on History Rsch.), Am. Acad. History Dentistry (pres. 1976-77, Hayden-Harris award 1980), Hist. Soc. Forest Park (pres.), Soc. Med. History Chgo. (past pres.), Chgo. Lit. Club, Sigma Xi. Home: 519 Jackson Blvd Forest Park IL 60130-1807 Office: 521 Jackson Blvd Forest Park IL 60130-1807

ORLANDO, CARL, medical research and development executive; b. Palermo, Italy, Sept. 26, 1915; came to U.S., 1928; s. Peter and Maria (Bongiorno) O.; m. Ann Bovè, May 29, 1943; children: Ann Marie, Francine, Patricia, Charleen, Joan. BS, Columbia U., 1941; postgrad., Rochester U., 1943. Chief photo optics U.S. Army Elec. Commd., Ft. Monmouth, N.J., 1945-75; cons. pvt. practice, New Shrewsbury, N.J., 1975-79; v.p. rsch. & devel. Analytical R&D Inc., Eatontown, N.J., 1979-88; cons. rsch. & devel. Engrng. Devel. Co., Tinton Falls, N.J., 1986-88; pres., rsch. & devel. dir. Sens-O-Tech Indsutries Inc., Eatontown, N.J., 1988—; chmn. bd. dirs. Sens-O-Tech Industries, 1988-92. Contbr. articles to profl. jours. Bd. dirs. Monmouth Regional High Sch., Tinton Falls, 1974; com. mem. Tinton Falls Environ. Unit, 1984; chmn. Entertainment Activities St. Dorothaas Ch., Eatontown, 1983. With USN, 1945. Recipient Monetary Suggestion award Signal Corp. Engrng. Lab., 1948. Mem. Soc. Photographic Scientist & Engrs. (sr. mem.), Soc. Imaging Sci. & Tech., Elks, Battle Ground Country Club. Republican. Roman Catholic. Achievements include over 20 patents in various fields including non-invasive heart and breathing alarm monitors, moving target indicator, photographic reproduction in 0.2 second, one step photographic technic, image stabilization system, perk-type automatic drip coffee maker, military tactical image interpretation facility, production and reconstruction of holograms, device for intensifying photoelectrostatic images, bandwidth compression of photographic images, Natinol photographic high speed shutter. Home and Office: 47 Willow Rd Tinton Falls NY 07724-3135

ORLANDO, DANIELLE, opera company administrator. Artistic adminstr. Opera Co. of Phila., until 1994; voice coach The Curtis Inst. of Music, Phila., 1995—. Office: The Curtis Inst of Music 1726 Locust St Philadelphia PA 19103

ORLANDO, GEORGE (JOSEPH), union executive; b. N.Y.C., Nov. 27, 1944; s. Joseph and Anita O.; m. Joan Perrotta, Nov. 5, 1967; children: Gregory, Valerie, Dana, Christopher, Lauren. B.A. in Polit. Sci., St. John's U., Bklyn., 1966. Adminstrv. asst. Distillery, Wine and Allied Workers Internat., Englewood, N.J., 1966-67; internat. v.p. Distillery, Wine and Allied Workers Internat., 1968-74, gen. sec.-treas., 1974-85, gen. pres., 1985-95; trustee Distillery, Wine and Allied Workers Internat. Social Security fund, 1974, chmn. bd. trustees, 1985; trustee pension fund; mem. exec. bd. dept. food and allied svc. trades AFL-CIO, 1975; pres. Wine, Liquor & Distillery Workers Union Local 1D, 1985—; internat. v.p. United Food & Comml. Workers Internat. Union (bd. dirs. Distillery, Wine & Allied Workers Divsn. 1995—). Office: Distillery Wine & Allied Workers Divsn UFCW 66 Grand Ave PO Box 567 Englewood NJ 07631

ORLEN, JOEL, professional society administrator; b. Holyoke, Mass., Aug. 1, 1924; s. Barnet and Fannie (Fuchs) O.; m. Yana Sorra Edmundson, Nov. 24, 1963; 1 stepson, Charles. BA, U. Chgo., 1950, MA, 1952. Fgn. svc. officer U.S. Dept. State, Washington, 1952-56; fgn. affairs officer AEC, Washington, 1956-58; officer NAS, Washington, 1958-63; asst. dir. Desert Rsch. Inst., Reno, 1963-65; exec. officer, provost MIT, Cambridge, 1965-80; v.p. Sci. Mus. Minn., St. Paul, 1980-86; exec. officer Am. Acad. Arts and Letters, Cambridge, 1986—; dir. Mounds Park Acad., St. Paul, 1983-86; cons. MIT, 1980-82; exec. sec. Mass. Tech. Devel. Corp., Boston, 1978-80; advisor U.S. del. to UN, N.Y.C. and Geneva, 1952-63. Contbr. chpts. to several books. Staff sgt. U.S. Army, 1943-46, ETO. Home: 130 Mt Auburn St Cambridge MA 02138-5757 Office: Am Acad Arts and Scis 136 Irving St Cambridge MA 02138-1929

ORLIK, PETER BLYTHE, media educator, author, musician; b. Hancock, Mich., Sept. 30, 1944; s. Harry Victor and Ruth Estelle (Blythe) O.; m. Christina Grace Bear, Aug. 18, 1967; children: Darcy Anne, Blaine Truen. BA with distinction, Wayne State U., 1965, MA, 1966, PhD, 1968. Copywriter Robin Prodns., Huntington Woods, Mich., 1962-63; announcer Sta. WQRS-FM, Detroit, 1963; copywriter Campbell-Ewald Advt., Detroit, 1965; asst. music dir. Sta. WDET-FM, Detroit, 1965-66; instr. Wayne State U., Detroit, 1966-69; from asst. prof. to assoc. prof. to prof. Cen. Mich. U., Mt. Pleasant, Mich., 1969—; univ. Merit prof. Cen. Mich. U., Mt. Pleasant, 1988, 92, also founder, head dept. Broadcast and Cinematic Arts, 1969-79, chmn. dept., 1996—; freelance copywriter Mt. Pleasant, 1979—; profl. clarinetist various Mich. ensembles, Detroit, Saginaw, 1965—; asst. dir. creative svcs. Sta. WXYZ-TV, Detroit, 1982; coord. prior learning assessment external degree program Ctrl. Mich. U., 1978-85; cons. various univs., 1980—; judge Thomas Jefferson Broadcast Awards, Dept. Def., 1994. Author: Broadcast/Cable Copywriting, 1978, 5th edit., 1994, Mass Media Description and Performance, 1979, Critiquing Radio and Television Content, 1988, The Electronic Media: An Introduction to the Profession, 1992, Electronic Media Criticism, 1994; mem. editl. bd. Media Mgmt. Rev.; contbr. articles to profl. jours. Lectr., liturgical clarinet soloist, eucharistic minister Sacred Heart Parish, Mt. Pleasant, 1969—, mem. religious edn. bd., 1978-84; adjudicator various H.S. speech and drama competitions, Mich., 1971-80; vice chmn. Zoning Bd. Appeals, Mt. Pleasant, 1974-78, 89-91, chmn., 1978-82, 91—; mem. faculty adv. com. Mus. Broadcast Comms. Named one of Outstanding Young Men Am. Nat. Jaycees, 1979; Nat. Assn. TV Program Execs. Faculty fellow, 1982. Mem. Broadcast Edn. Assn. (chmn. courses and curricula divsn. 1974-76, 80-82, bd. dirs. 1989-93, chmn. faculty internship com. 1990-91, chmn. nat. scholarship com. 1991—), Assn. for Edn. in Journalism and Mass Comms., Nat. Assn. TV Program Execs., Alpha Epsilon Rho (nat. v.p. profl. alumni rels. 1976-77, legis. coord. 1979-82), Phi Kappa Phi. Avocation: writing half-time show scripts for college and profl. football games. Home: 613 Kane St Mount Pleasant MI 48858-1949 Office: Cen Mich U 343 Moore Hall Mount Pleasant MI 48859

ORLIN, JAMES BERGER, mathematician, management scientist, educator; b. Buffalo, Apr. 19, 1953; s. Albert Norman and Roslyn Louise (Berger) O.; m. Donna Lynn Hogan, Jan. 3, 1982; children: Jennifer Robin, Benjamin Aaron, Caroline Anne. BA, U. Pa., 1974; MS, Caltech, 1976; MMath, U. Waterloo, Ont., Can., 1976; PhD, Stanford U., 1981. Asst. prof. MIT, Cambridge, Mass., 1979-83, assoc. prof., 1983-87, prof., 1987—; vis. prof. Erasmus U., Rotterdam, The Netherlands, 1984-85; vis. sci. Collaborative Rsch. Inc., Waltham, Mass., 1992-93, Whitehead Inst., 1993-96. Coauthor: Network Flows: Theory, Algorithms and Applications, 1993; assoc. editor Networks, 1992—; contbr. over 50 articles to profl. jours. Fulbright Rsch. grantee, 1984-85, UPS fellow, 1991-94; recipient Presdl. Young Investigator award NSF, 1985-90. Mem. Informs (co-recipient Lanchester prize 1993), Assn. Computing Machinery, Math. Programming Soc., Soc. Indsl. and Applied Math. Home: 10 Taft Dr Winchester MA 01890-3748 Office: MIT E53-357 77 Massachusetts Ave # E53-357 Cambridge MA 02139-4301

ORLOFF, CHET, cultural organization administrator; b. Bellingham, Wash., Feb. 22, 1949; s. Monford A. and Janice (Diamond) O.; m. Wendy Lynn Lee, Sept. 20, 1970; children: Callman Labe, Hannah Katya, Michele Alison. BA, Boston U., 1971; MA, U. Oreg., 1978; postgrad., Portland State U. Tchr. Peace Corps, Afghanistan, 1972-75; asst. dir. Oreg. Hist. Soc., Portland, 1975-86, dir., 1991—; dir. Ninth Cir. Hist. Soc., Pasadena, Calif., 1987-91. Editor: Western Legal History, 1987-91, Law for the Elephant, 1992; sr. editor: Oreg. Hist. Quar.; contbr. articles to profl. jours. Commr. Met. Arts Commn., Portland, 1981-84, Portland Planning Commn., 1989-92. Mem. Phi Alpha Theta. Avocations: reading, tennis. Office: Oregon Historical Society 1200 SW Park Ave Portland OR 97205-2441

ORLOFF, NEIL, lawyer; b. Chgo., May 9, 1943; s. Benjamin R. and Annette (Grabow) O.; m. Jan Krigbaum, Oct. 9, 1971 (div. 1979); m. Gudrun Mirin, Oct. 2, 1992. BS, MIT, 1964; MBA, Harvard U., 1966; JD, Columbia U., 1969. Bar: D.C. 1969, N.Y. 1975, Calif. 1989, Utah 1993. Ops. officer World Bank, Washington, 1969-71; dir. regional liaison staff EPA, Washington, 1971-73; legal counsel Pres.'s Council on Environ. Quality, Washington, 1973-75; prof. dept. environ. engrng. Cornell U., Ithaca, N.Y., 1975-88, sch. law UCLA, 1992; dir. Ctr. for Environ. Research, 1984-87, Am. Ecology Corp., 1986-88; of counsel Morgan, Lewis & Bockius, N.Y.C., 1986-87; ptnr. Irell & Manella, Los Angeles, 1986-92, Parsons, Behle & Latimer, Salt Lake City, 1992—; vice chmn. bd. dirs. S.W. Research and Info. Ctr., Albuquerque, 1975-84; vice chmn. air quality commn. ABA, Chgo., 1983-92, co-chmn. intensive course in environ. law ABA, 1994—. Author: The Environmental Impact Statement Process, 1978, The National Environmental Policy Act, 1980, Air Pollution-Cases and Materials, 1980, Community Right-to-Know Handbook, 1988; mem. editorial bd. Natural Resources and Environment, 1984-87. Adviser Internat. Joint Com. Can., 1979-81; governing bd. N.Y. Sea Grant Inst., 1984-87; vice chmn. City of Ithaca Environ. Commn., 1976-77; adviser N.Y. Dept. Environ. Conservation, 1984-87.

ORLOWSKA-WARREN, LENORE ALEXANDRIA, art educator; b. Detroit, May 22, 1951; d. William Leonard and Aloisa Clara (Hrapkiewicz) Orlowski; m. Donald Edward Warren, May 11, 1990. AA, Henry Ford C.C., 1972; BS in Art Edn., Wayne State U., 1974, M Spl. Edn., 1978. Tchr. arts and crafts Detroit Pub. Schs., 1974—; cons. Arts Detroit Cmty. Plan. Contbr. to Sch. Arts Mag. Mem. LWV, Cranbrook Acad. Art, Art Inst. Chgo. Mem. Nat. Art Edn. Assn. (electronic gallery coord. 1992—), Mich. Art Edn. Assn., Am. Craft Coun., Detroit Artist Market, Detroit Inst. Arts-Founders Soc., Dearborn Cmty. Arts Coun. Avocations: fiber art, travel, colonial gardening, reading colonial history and biographies. Home: 10 Berwick Ln Dearborn MI 48120-1102

ORLOWSKY, MARTIN L., retail company executive; b. N.Y.C., Dec. 7, 1941; s. Solomon and Sylvia (Levine) O.; m. Carolyn Louise Brady, Mar. 25, 1973; children—Daniel, Keith, Matthew. B.A., Long Island U., N.Y.C., 1963. Media planner Compton Advertising, N.Y.C., 1968-69; media planner Young & Rubicam Inc., N.Y.C., 1969-71; v.p. media Grey Advertising, N.Y.C., 1971-76; sr. v.p., media and mktg. services Needham, Harper & Steers, N.Y.C., 1976-77; media dir. R.J. Reynolds Tobacco Co., Winston-Salem, N.C., 1977-80, dir. mktg. services, 1980-82, v.p. brand mktg., 1982-84, sr. v.p. mktg., 1984-85, exec. v.p., 1986; pres. Grocery div. Nabisco Brands, U.S.A., Parsippany, N.J., 1986—, Planters and Life Savers div. Nabisco Brands, U.S.A., Parsippany, N.J., 1987—, DKM Holdings, 1988-90; sr. v.p. mktg. Lorillard Tobacco Co., N.Y.C., 1990-92, exec. v.p. mktg. and sales, 1992-95, pres., 1995—. Vol., Peace Corps, Bolivia, 1963-65. Served to sgt. U.S. Army, 1966-68. Avocations: fishing; tennis. Home: 15 Manette Rd Morristown NJ 07960-6345

ORMAN, LEONARD ARNOLD, lawyer; b. Balt., June 15, 1930; s. Samuel and Bertie (Adler) O.; m. Barbara Gold, June 9, 1978; children: Richard Harold, Robert Barton. AB summa cum laude, U. Md., 1952, JD, 1955. Bar: Md. 1955, U.S. Ct. Appeals (4th cir.) 1956, U.S. Dist. Ct. Md. 1955, Ct. Appeals Md. 1955, U.S. Supreme Ct. 1977, U.S. Ct. Claims 1990, D.C. Ct. Appeals 1987; cert. civil trial advocate by Nat. Bd. Trial Advocacy. Law clk. Hon. Frederick W. Brune, Chief Judge Md. Ct. of Appeals, 1955-56; mem. dept. legis. reference Md. Legislature, 1957-58; mem. Gov.'s Commn. to Revise Criminal Code, 1958-59; pvt. practice law Balt., 1956—; lectr. trial tactics. Mem. editorial bd.: Md. Law Rev, 1953-55; Contbr. articles to profl. jours. Pres. Young Dems. 2d Dist., Balt., 1960-63. With AUS, 1948-49; lt. col. USAF Res. ret. Rosco Pound Found. fellow, trustee. Mem. Md. State Bar Assn. (various coms.), Balt. City Bar Assn. (various coms.), Nat. Coll. Trial Advocacy (trustee), Assn. Trial Lawyers Am. (numerous coms./offices, including nat. committeeman 1976-80, bd. govs. 1985—, exec. com. 1988-90, chmn. orgn. rev. com., home office and budget com., orgn. and home office com., election com., key man com., past mem. steering com., past mem. publ. com., past mem. ednl. adv. group 1989-90, co-chair Hall of Fame com., past vice-chair ABA-ATLA liaison com., M Club, co-chair conv. site planning com., co-chairpolit. insight com., long-range planning com., auth-hwy. adv. com., toy safety conf., med. malpractice adv. com., product liability adv. com., co-chair home office capital improvements adv. com., co-chmn. conv. planning com. Washington), Md. Trial Lawyers Assn. (bd. govs., pres. 1984-85), Order of Coif, Masons. Home: 2 Celadon Rd Owings Mills MD 21117-3010 Office: 5 Light St Ste 1100 Baltimore MD 21202-1224

ORME, ANTONY RONALD, geography educator; b. Weston-Super-Mare, Somerset, Eng., May 28, 1936; came to U.S., 1968; s. Ronald Albert and Anne (Parry) O.; m. Amalie Jo Brown, Nov. 18, 1984; children: Mark Antony, Kevin Ronald, Devon Anne. B.A. with 1st class honors, U. Birmingham, 1957, Ph.D., 1961. Lectr. Univ. Coll., Dublin, Ireland, 1960-68; mem. faculty UCLA, 1968—, prof. geography, 1973—, dean social scis., 1977-83; cons. geomorphology various orgns., throughout U.S., 1968—. Editor-in-chief Phys. Geography; mem. editorial bd. Catena, Springer-Verlag, Berlin, U. Calif. Press. Recipient Award of Merit Am. Inst. Planners, 1975; recipient Outstanding Service award USAF, 1977-80. Mem. Geol. Soc. Am., Assn. Am. Geographers, Assn. Geography Tchrs. Ireland (pres. 1964-68), Inst. Brit. Geographers, Internat. Geog. Union. Home: 5128 Del Moreno Dr Woodland Hills CA 91364-2426 Office: UCLA Dept Geography Los Angeles CA 90095-1524

ORME, MELISSA EMILY, mechanical engineering educator; b. Glendale, Calif., Mar. 12, 1961; d. Myrl Eugene and Geraldine Irene (Schmuck) O.; m. Vasilis Zissis Marmarelis, Mar. 12, 1989. BS, U. So. Calif., L.A., 1984, MS, 1985, PhD, 1989. Rsch. asst. prof. U. So. Calif., 1990-93; asst. prof. U. Calif., Irvine, 1993—; panel reviewer NSF, Arlington, Va., 1993—; cons. MPM Corp., Boston, 1993—. Contbr. articles to profl. jours. Recipient Young Investigator award NSF, 1994, Arch T. Colwell Merit award SAE, 1994. Mem. AAUW, AIAA, ASME, Am. Phys. Soc., Minerals, Metals and Materials Soc. Achievements include 4 U.S. patents. Office: U Calif Irvine CA 92717-3975

ORMES, JONATHAN FAIRFIELD, astrophysicist, science administrator, researcher; b. Colorado Springs, Colo., July 18, 1939; s. Robert Manly and Suzanne (Viertel) O.; m. Karen Lee Minnick, Dec. 26, 1960 (div.); 1 child, Laurie Kylee; m. Janet Carolyn Dahl, Sept. 12, 1964; children: Marina, Nicholas. BS, Stanford U., 1961; PhD, U. Minn., 1967. NRC assoc. Goddard Space Flight Ctr., NASA, Greenbelt, Md., 1967-69, astrophysicist, 1969, head cosmic radiations br., 1981-82, head nuclear astrophysics br., 1983-87, assoc. chief lab. for high energy astrophysics, 1987-90, chief lab. for high energy astrophysics, 1990—; acting head high energy physics NASA hdqrs., Washington, 1982-83, mem. high energy astrophysics mgmt. ops. working group, 1975-83, mem. cosmic ray program working group, 1984-91; mem. com. on space and solar physics, com. on cosmic ray physics Nat. Acad. Sci., Washington, 1991-94. Editor: Essays in Space Science, 1987; assoc. editor astrophysics Phys. Rev. Letters, 1991-93; contbr. Astrophysics Jour., Phys. Rev. Letters, Astronomy and Astrophysics. Trustee Paint Br. Unitarian Universalist Ch., Adelphi, Md., 1987-88, chair bd. trustees, 1989, numerous positions, 1972-91. Fellow Am. Phys. Soc. (various div. offices); mem. Internat. Astron. Union, Am. Astron. Soc. (sec.-treas. High Energy Astrophysics div. 1985-87), Am. Geophys. Union. Achievements include discovery of unusual isotopic abundance of Ne in galactic cosmic rays; research on high energy spectra of cosmic rays, on anti-protons in galactic cosmic rays. Office: NASA Code 660 Goddard Space Flight Ctr Greenbelt MD 20771

ORMSBY, ERIC LINN, library administrator, researcher; b. Atlanta, Oct. 16, 1941; s. Robert and Virginia (Haire) O.; m. Dorothy Louise Hoffmann, July 22, 1967; children: Daniel Paul, Charles Martin. BA summa cum laude, U. Pa., 1971; MA, Princeton U., 1973, PhD, 1981; MLS, Rutgers U., 1978. Near East bibliographer libr. Princeton U., N.J., 1975-77; Near East curator libr. Princeton U., 1977-83; libr. dir. Cath. U. Am., Washington, 1983-86, McGill U., Montreal, Can., 1986—; assoc. prof. Inst. Islamic Studies McGill U., 1986—; cons. NYU, 1981-82; mem. libr. com. Mid. East Inst., Washington, 1985—, Al Akhawayn U., Morocco, 1994-95, Saudi Arabian Monetary Agy., Riyadh, 1995—; chmn. continuing edn. com. Washington Consortium, 1983-86; mem. bd. Ctr. Rsch. Librs., 1989-95. Author: Theodicy in Islamic Thought, 1984 (Choice Mag. award 1984), Bavarian Shrine and Other Poems, 1990 (QSPELL award for poetry 1991), (poems) Coastlines, 1992, (with others) Handlist of Arabic Manuscripts, 1986; editor: Moses Maimonides and His Time, 1989; contbr. articles and book revs. to profl. jours., poetry to various mags., including New Republic, New Yorker, Grant St., Shenandoah, So. Rev. and Chelsea. Instr. Princeton Adult Sch., 1978-80. DAAD fellow German Acad. Exch., 1973-74; recipient Ingram Merrill award, 1993. Mem. Middle East Librs. Assn. (v.p. 1981-82, pres. 1982-83), Hoelderlin Gesellschaft, Can. Assn. Rsch. Librs. (v.p. 1988-89), Can. Libr. Assn., Assn. pour l'Avancement des Scis. et des Techniques de la Documentation, Conseil des recteurs et des principaux des univs. du Québec, Sous-Comité des Bibliotheques (pres. 1989-91). Roman Catholic. Avocations: natural history, writing, cooking, photography. Office: McGill U Librs, 3459 McTavish St, Montreal, PQ Canada H3A 1Y1

ORNAUER, RICHARD LEWIS, retired educational association administrator; b. Bklyn., Oct. 19, 1922; s. Edwin L. and Emma (Handler) O.; m. Jane Robb, May 15, 1955 (div. Jan. 7, 1976); children: David S., Michael J., SaraJo; m. J. Rexene Ashford, Nov. 24, 1985. BJ, U. Mo., 1947. Wire editor Coastal Georgian, Brunswick, Ga., 1947-48; reporter copyreader, night editor, city editor Nassau Daily Rev.-Star, Rockville Centre, N.Y., 1948-53; city editor L.I. Press, Jamaica, N.Y., 1953-71; asst. commr. Nassau County Dept. Social Services, Mineola, 1971-74; pub. health info. program officer Nassau County Dept. Health, Mineola, 1974-87; adminstr. Bur. Epidemiology, 1979-84; dir. communications N.Y. State Sch. Bds. Assn., Albany, 1987-89; instr. Queens Coll., Flushing, N.Y., 1955-59; instr., mentor 55/Alive mature driving program AARP, Dover, Del., 1994—; asst. state coord. Kent County, Del., 1996—; mem. exec. bd. Hofstra U. Sch. Bd. Forum, 1969-87; chmn. Merrick Planning Com., 1959-61; mem. publs. com. N.Y. State Sch. Bds. Assn., 1961-64, cons. to com., 1980-81, mem. BOCES com., 1971-74; vice chmn. State Sch. Bd. Leaders Com., 1975-79, cons. to com., 1980, bd. dirs., 1979-87, v.p., 1981, 84, 85, 86, 87, mem. exec. com., 1981-87, cons. to disting. service com., 1984, 85; cons. cities com., 1986, cons. grants com., 1987; del. L.I. Ednl. Conf. Bd., 1967-86; trustee Merrick Bd. Edn., 1962-87, pres., 1966-71; trustee Bd. Coop. Ednl. Services Nassau County, 1967-87, v.p., 1967-71, pres., 1971-87; mem. exec. com. Nassau-Suffolk Sch. Bds. Assn., 1962-87, v.p., 1974-77, pres., 1977-79; mem. exec. com. Merrick Citizens Com. for Pub. Schs., 1959-87; mem. fed. relations network 4th Congl. dist. Nat. Sch. Bds. Assn., 1973-87, study com. on career edn., 1976-78, sub-chmn. for N.E. region presdl. task force on edn. of handicapped children, 1977-78, presdl. task force on critical viewing of TV by children, 1979-80; del. Northeast Region, Nat. Sch. Bds. Assn., 1980-87, vice chmn., 1985-87, chmn., 1987; adv. com. N.Y. State Senate Standing Com. on Civil Service and Pensions, 1978-79; mem. Instructional Service Television Com. WLIW-TV/Channel 21, pres., 1973-82; mem. Com. for Better Schs. of Merrick, 1975-87, Hist. Soc. Merricks, 1976-88; bd. dirs. L.I. Coalition Fair Broadcasting, 1979-82; mem. commr.'s adv. council N.Y. State Edn. Dept., 1980-87; mem. City of Dover Pub. Safety Issues Implementation Studies Commn., 1993—; comms. officer Dover AFB Mus., 1995—. Mem. citizens addv. com. Dover Met. Planning Orgn., 1993—, chmn. 1995—; del. Planned Parenthood, United Way; ptnr. Spl. Olympics, Medic Alert Internat. With AUS, 1942-45, PTO. Recipient citations N.Y. State Police Conf., 1949, citations Rockville Centre Police Benevolent Assn., 1953, citations Nassau Div. Am. Cancer Soc., 1961, citations Nassau Am. Legion, 1963, citations Nassau Library System, 1964, citations Firemen's Assn. of Nassau County, 1964, citations Nassau County Scholastic Press Assn., 1965, citations United Fund of L.I., 1970, citations Kiwanis Clubs Internat., 1971, citations Jewish War Vets., 1972, citations WLIW-TV, 1982; Educator of Yr. award Hofstra U. chpt. Phi Delta Kappa, 1973; Educator of Yr. award Assn. for the Help of Retarded Children, Nassau County chpt., 1977; Disting. Service award Nassau-Suffolk Sch. Bds. Assn., 1979, 87, Spl. Merit award Nassau-Suffolk Sch. Bds. Assn., 1987; named Educator of Yr. U.S. Congress, 1987, County of Nassau, 1987, Town of Hempstead (N.Y.), 1987, Merrick Bd. Edn., 1987, various depts. Nassau County Bd. Coop. Ednl. Services, 1987, Merrick Sch. Dist. Faculty Assn., 1987; named Man of Yr. L.I. Spl. Edn. Adminstrs. Assn., 1979, Man of Yr. Merrick C. of C., 1980, Man of Yr. N.Y. State Legislature, 1980, 87, Man of Yr. Nassau-L.I. dist. N.Y. State Congress Parents and Tchrs., 1980. Mem. Nat. Sch. Pub. Rels. Assn. (exec. com. N.Y. State chpt., Capital Dist. chpt.), Edn. Writers Assn., Am. Newspaper Guild, Nat. Congress Parents and Tchrs. (life), N.Y. State Congress Paand Tchrs. (life), N.Y. State Pub. Health Assn., Assn. Emotionally Handicapped Children, Assn. to Help Retarded Children, Assn. Children With Learning Abilities, N.Am. Assn. Environ. Edn., N.Y. Citizens Com. Pub. Schs., Nat. Soc. Autistic Children, Am. Assn. Career Edn., Ad Hoc Planning Com. Mobilized Community Resources, L.I. Sch.-Community Relations Assn., N.Y. Civil Svc. Employees Assn., N.Y. State Outdoor Edn. Assn., Nat. Parks and Conservation Assn., Nat. Arbor Day Found., Conf. Sch. Bds. Assn. Communicators, Am. Assn. Retired Persons (Greater Dover area chpt., bd. dirs. 1995—), Ednl. Press Assn. Am., U. Mo. Alumni Assn., Boise State U. Alumni Assn., Albany Inst. History and Art (charter mem.), N.Y. State Mus. Assocs., Smithsonian Inst. Assocs., Libr. Congress Assocs. (charter), U.S. Holocaust Meml. Mus. Assocs. (charter), Newtonville Neighborhood Assn., Mifflin Rd. Neighborhood Assn. (gov. rels. chmn., exec. com.), Deerfield Civ. Assn., Consumer Union Assocs., Common Cause, Nat. Com. to Preserve Social Security and Medicare, Soc. Profl. Journalists, Sigma Delta Chi (life, Empire State chpt.), Alpha Epsilon Pi (life). Jewish. Home: 17 Mifflin Rd Dover DE 19904-3316

ORNDUFF, ROBERT, botany educator; b. Portland, Oreg., June 13, 1932; s. Robert and Kathryn (Davis) O. B.A., Reed Coll., 1953; M.Sc., U. Wash., 1956; Ph.D., U. Calif.-Berkeley, 1961. Asst. prof. Reed Coll., 1962, Duke U., 1963; asst. prof. botany U. Calif., Berkeley, 1963-66, assoc. prof., 1966-69, prof., 1969-93, prof. emeritus, 1993—, dir. Jepson Herbarium, 1968-83, dir. Univ. Herbarium, 1975-83, exec. dir. Miller Inst. for Basic Research in Sci., 1984-87, chmn. dept. botany, 1986-89. Dir. Stanley Smith Hort. Trust, 1992—. Fellow AAAS, Calif. Acad. Scis.; mem. Calif. Native Plant Soc. (pres. 1972-73), Am. Soc. Plant Taxonomists (pres. 1975). Home: 490 Arlington Ave Berkeley CA 94707-1609 Office: Dept Integrative Biology U Calif Berkeley CA 94720-3140

ORNITZ, RICHARD MARTIN, lawyer, business executive; b. Annapolis, Md., July 4, 1945; s. Martin Nathaniel and Beatrice Cynthia (Swick) O.; m. Margareth Adams, June 15, 1971 (div. Apr. 1977); m. Janet Alma Steen, Dec. 5, 1981; children—Alexandra, Zachary, Darren, Erik, Nicholas. B.S. in Metall. Engrng., Cornell U., 1967; J.D., NYU, 1970; grad. sr. exec. program, MIT, 1985. Bar: N.Y. 1971, U.S. Dist. Ct. (ea. dist.) 1972, U.S. Supreme Ct. 1984. Assoc. Cravath, Swaine & Moore, N.Y.C., 1972-77; v.p., gen. counsel, sec. Degussa Corp., Teterboro, N.J. 1977-90, mem. mgmt. com., 1987-90; of counsel, Hughes, Hubbard & Reed, N.Y.C., 1985-92; dir. Degussa Corp. subs., 1980-92; ptnr. Stroock, Stroock & Lavan, 1991-95, Coudert Bros., 1996—; dir. Metal Products Internat., Inc., Greenwich, Conn;

speaker Risk Ins. Mgmt. Soc., 1984, 85, 86, IBA, 1986, ACCA, 1986, European Co. Lawyers Assn., 1986; Swiss Co. Lawyers Assn., 1987; Norwegian Co. Lawyers Assn., 1988; mem. pvt. law adv. com. Office of Legal Adv. U.S. Dept. State, adv. bd. Nat. Inst. Preventive Maintenance, adv. bd. corp. counsel Am. Arbitration Assn. Assoc. editor Ann. Survey of Law, NYU, 1970. Fin. com. Conn. Spl. Olympics; bd. dirs. Old Greenwich Civic Assn. Served to 1st lt. U.S. Army, 1970-72. Mem. ABA (chmn. European law sect., human relations and labor law, 1987-90), N.Y. State Bar Assn., Internat. Bar Assn., Am. Corp. Counsel Assn. (chmn. of internat. sect. com., 1986-90) European Am. Gen. Counsels Group (chmn. 1986-87), N.J. Gen. Counsels Group, Cornell Soc. Engrs. Republican. Jewish. Clubs: Old Greenwich Republican (Conn.), Innis Arden, Rocky Point. Home: 18 Meadowbank Rd Old Greenwich CT 06870-2312 Office: Stroock Stroock & Lavan 7 Hanover Sq New York NY 10004-2616

ORNSTEIN, DONALD SAMUEL, mathematician, educator; b. N.Y.C., July 30, 1934; s. Harry and Rose (Wisner) O.; m. Shari Richman, Dec. 20, 1964; children—David, Kara, Ethan. Student, Swarthmore Coll., 1950-52; Ph.D., U. Chgo., 1957. Fellow Inst. for Advanced Study, Princeton, N.J., 1955-57; faculty U. Wis., Madison, 1958-60; faculty Stanford (Calif.) U., 1959—, prof. math., 1966—; faculty Hebrew U., Jerusalem, 1975-76. Author: Ergodic Theory Randomness and Dynamical Systems, 1974. Recipient Bocher prize Am. Math. Soc., 1974. Mem. NAS, Am. Acad. Arts and Sci. Jewish. Office: Dept Math Stanford U Stanford CA 94305

ORNSTEIN, NORMAN JAY, political scientist; b. Grand Rapids, Minn., Oct. 14, 1948; s. Joseph and Dorothy (Latz) O.; m. Judith Linda Harris, May 29, 1977; children—Matthew, Daniel. BA, U. Minn., 1967; MA, U. Mich., 1968, PhD, 1972. Asst. prof. Johns Hopkins U., Bologna, Italy, 1971-72; prof. Cath. U. Am., Washington, 1972-84; staff mem., staff dir. Senate Com. on Com. System, Washington, 1976-77; fellow Ctr. for Advanced Study in Behavioral Scis., Palo Alto, Calif., 1979-80; resident scholar Am. Enterprise Inst., Washington, 1980—; co-dir. Renewing Congress Project, Washington, 1992—, Times Mirror-Gallup Study: The People, the Press and Politics, 1987-90, Times Mirror Ctr. for People and Press (now Pew Rsch. Ctr.), 1991—; columnist Roll Call newspaper, 1993—; polit. editor Lawmakers program Sta. WETA-TV, Washington, 1980-84; cons. CBS News Election Unit, N.Y.C., 1982—; commentator, cons. MacNeil/Leher News Hour, Washington and N.Y.C., 1983—; moderator Calif. Congl. Report, Sta. KCET-TV, L.A., 1983. Author: Interest Groups Lobbying and Policy, 1978; (with others) The New Congress, 1981, Vital Statistics on Congress, 1995-96, Debt and Taxes, 1994; writer, editor, co-host: (TV series) Congress: We the People, 1984 (cert. of merit 1985). Fortieth Anniversary Fulbright Disting. fellow, 1986-87. Mem. Coun. on Fgn. Rels., Am. Polit. Sci. Assn. (coun. 1984-86, Congl. fellow 1969-70), Nat. Commn. Pub. Svc. (bd. dirs., Volcker commn. 1987-90), Phi Beta Kappa (vis. scholar 1986-87). Jewish. Home: 5818 Surrey St Bethesda MD 20815-5419 Office: Am Enterprise Inst 1150 17th St NW Washington DC 20036-4603

ORNSTEIN-GALICIA, JACOB LEONARD (JACK ORNSTEIN-GALICIA), foreign language educator, linguist, author; b. Cleve., Aug. 12, 1915; s. Joseph and Bertha (Schwartz) Ornstein; m. Janet Ann Eaton, Dec. 25, 1962 (div. Nov. 1977); 1 child, Dena Hayden. BS in Edn., Ohio State U., 1936, MA, 1937; PhD, U. Wis., 1940. Cert. tchr., Ohio. Instr. Spanish and Portuguese U. Wis., Madison, 1940-41; asst. prof. Washington U., St. Louis, 1941-42; intelligence officer Office Strategic Svcs., Washington, North Africa and Italy, 1942-45; assoc. prof. Waldorf Coll., Forest City, Iowa, 1947-49, N.Mex. State U., Las Cruces, 1949-51; intelligence officer, sci. linguist CIA, Washington, 1951-68; prof. linguistics and langs. U. Tex., El Paso, 1968—, now emeritus prof.; lectr. Sch. Langs. and Linguistics, Georgetown U., Washington, 1964-68; cons. U.S. Office Edn., Washington, 1968-74, S.W. Coop. Ednl. Lab., Albuquerque, 1970, Ednl. Testing Svc., Princeton, N.J., 1974; reader proposals NSF, Washington, 1975—; faculty mem. U. Ctr. for Lifelong Learning, 1992—, prof. continuing edn. U. Tex., El Paso, 1993—. Author: Slavic and East European Studies: Their Development in the Western hemisphere, 1957, A Sociolinguistic Study of Mexican-American and Anglo Students in a Border University, 1975, Sociolinguistic Foundations of Language Assessment, 1983; also articles; co-author: Elements of Russian, 1964, Programmed Instruction and Educational Technology in the Language Teaching Field, 1971, The New ABC's of Language and Linguistics, 1977, A Problem-Solving Model for Integrating Science and Language in Bilingual-Bicultural Education, 1983; editor: Repetición de amores (Luis de Lucena), 1954, Form and Function in Chicano English: New Insights, 1984, rev. edit., 1988; co-editor: Studies in Language and Linguistics, 1969-70, Studies in Language and Linguistics II, 1970-71, College English and the Mexican-American, 1976, Problems of Standard vs. Non-Standard: Dimensions of Foreign Language Teaching, 1977, Problems in Applied Educational Sociolinguistics: Readings on Language and Cultural Problems of U.S. Ethnic Groups, 1978, Bilingualism and Bilingual Education: New Readings and Insights, 1979, Sociolinguistic Studies in Language Contact: Methods and Cases, 1979, Problems of Loyalty and Accomodation Among Minority Languages and Dialects, 1980, Social and Educational Issues in Bilingualism and Biculturalism, 1981, Politics and Society in the Southwest: Ethnicity and Chicano Pluralism, 1982, Chicano English: An Ethnic Contact Dialect, 1985, Mexican-American Language: Usage, Attitudes, Maintenance, Instruction and Policy, 1986, Chicano Speech in the Bilingual Classroom, 1988, Research Issues and Problems in U.S. Spanish, 1988, Mexican-American Spanish in its Societal and Cultural Context, 1989, Jewish Farmer in America, The Unknown Chronicle, 1992. Adviser Armadillo, Disabled Students' Orgn., U. Tex., El Paso, 1969-81; organizer Town and Gown forum, El Paso, 1975-85. Recipient A. G. Solalinde award U. Wis., 1938, Outstanding Alumnus award Ohio State U. Stadium Scholarship Alumni Assn., 1989. Mem. MLA, Linguistic Soc. Am., Am. Assn. Tchrs. Spanish and Portuguese, Assn. Lingistica y Filologia de America Latina Linguistica. Home: 315 W Schuster Ave Apt 4 El Paso TX 79902-3434 Office: U Tex Dept Langs and Linguistics University and Hawthorne El Paso TX 79968

ORNSTON, DARIUS GRAY, JR., psychiatrist; b. Phila., Sept. 13, 1934; s. Darius Gray and Marie Elizabeth (Wallace) O. BA, U. Pa., 1955, MD, 1959. Intern U. Mich., 1959-60; resident Yale U., New Haven, 1960-62, chief resident, 1963, fellow dept. student mental hygiene, 1964, psychiatrist dept. student mental hygiene, 1964-72; assoc. clin. prof. Yale U., New Haven, S.C., 1972-86; pvt. practice psychiatry New Haven, 1964-85, Greenville, S.C., 1986—; mem. dept. psychiatry Greenville (S.C.) Hosp., 1986—, chmn. dept. psychiatry, 1990-94; clin. prof. U. S.C., Columbia, 1988—, Med. U. S.C., Charleston, 1988—. Editor: Translating Freud, 1993.

O'RORKE, JAMES FRANCIS, JR., lawyer; b. N.Y.C., Dec. 4, 1936; s. James Francis and Helen (Weber) O'R.; m. Carla Phelps, Aug. 6, 1964. A.B., Princeton U., 1958; J.D., Yale U., 1961. Bar: N.Y. 1962. Assoc. Davies, Hardy & Schenck, 1962-69; ptnr. Davies, Hardy, Ives & Lawther, 1969-72, Skadden, Arps, Slate, Meagher & Flom, N.Y.C., 1972—; dir. Clinipad Corp.; mem. adv. bd. Chgo. Title Ins. Co. N.Y. Trustee Mus. Am. Indian-Heye Found., 1977-80. Mem. ABA, N.Y. State Bar Assn., Assn. Bar City N.Y., Am. Coll. Real Estate Lawyers, Princeton Club N.Y.C. Office: Skadden Arps Slate Meagher & Flom 919 3rd Ave New York NY 10022

O'ROURKE, C. LARRY, lawyer; b. Colusa, Calif., Dec. 10, 1937; s. James Harold and Elizabeth Janice (Jenkins) O'R.; m. Joy Marie Phillips, May 22, 1965; children: Ryan, Paula. BSEE, Stanford U., 1959, MBA, 1961; JD, George Washington U., 1972. Bar: Va. 1971, D.C. 1974, U.S. Ct. Appeals (fed. cir.) 1973, U.S. Patent and Trademark Office 1971, U.S. Supreme Ct. Patent atty. Westinghouse Elec., Washington, 1969-70, Pitts., 1970-73; assoc. Finnegan, Henderson, Farabow, Garrett & Dunner, Washington, 1974-79, ptnr., 1979—; dir. Zest Inc., Md., 1988, chmn. bd. dirs., 1990-95. Mem. ABA, Am. Intellectual Property Law Assn. Democrat. Presbyterian. Office: Finnegan Henderson Farabow Garrett & Dunner 1300 I St NW Ste 700 Washington DC 20005-3314

O'ROURKE, DENNIS, lawyer; b. Whiteclay, Nebr., Oct. 31, 1914; s. Frank L. and Jerene (Rebbeck) O'R.; m. Ruth Rouss, Jan. 21, 1940; children: Susan, Kathleen, Brian, Dennis, Ruth, Dolores. A.B. cum laude, Nebr. Tchrs. Coll., 1935; J.D. with distinction, George Washington U., 1939; LLD (hon.), Chadron State Coll., 1993. Bar: D.C. 1939, U.S. Supreme Ct 1945, Colo. 1946. Typist, auditor GAO, Washington, 1935-39; lawyer solicitor's office U.S. Dept. Agr., Washington, 1939-45; chief basic commodity div. U.S. Dept. Agr., 1945; gen. counsel Group Health Assn., Washington, 1943, Holly Sugar Corp., Colorado Springs, Colo., 1945; v.p. Holly Sugar Corp., Colorado Springs, 1953-63, pres., 1963-67, chmn. bd., 1967-69, dir., 1983-88; vice chmn. bd., mem. exec. com. Holly Sugar Corp. (merged with Imperial Sugar Co.), Colorado Springs, 1986-88; v.p., gen. counsel Holly Oil Co., 1955-63; sr. ptnr. Rouss & O'Rourke, Colorado Springs and Washington; U.S. counsel Union Nacional de Productores de Azucar, Mexico, 1970-82; pres. Man Exec., Inc., Colorado Springs and Washington; chmn. examining com. 1st Nat. Bank Colorado Springs, 1983-84. Contbr. articles financial and bus. jours. Bd. dirs. Colo. Pub. Expenditure Coun., vice chmn., exec. com., 1968-76; dir. Nat. C. of C. of the U.S., 1968-70; trustee, pres. Colorado Springs Fine Arts Center, 1961-62, 68-71, 73, chmn. adv. com., 1981-84, hon. trustee, 1988; founder, 1st chmn. Colo. Com. (now Coun.) on Arts and Humanities, 1963; Mem. Bus. and Industry Adv. Com. OECD, Paris, France, 1969-71; adviser U.S. dels. Internat. Sugar Confs., Geneva, 1965, Mexico City, 1959; chmn. Colorado Springs-El Paso County Citizens' Task Force on Local Govt. Reorgn., 1976-77. Mem. Am. Soc. Sugar Beet Technologists, Internat. Soc. Sugar Cane Technologists, Fed. Bar Assn., Colo. Bar Assn., El Paso County Bar Assn, Order of Coif, Cheyenne Mountain Country Club, El Paso Club, Garden of Gods Club, Sugar Club, Met. Club (Washington), Rotary, Phi Delta Phi. Home: 8 Heather Dr Broadmoor Colorado Springs CO 80906 Office: PO Box 572 Colorado Springs CO 80901-0572

O'ROURKE, J. TRACY, manufacturing company executive; b. Columbia, S.C., Mar. 14, 1935; s. James Tracy and Georgia Adella (Bridges) O'R.; m. Lou Ann Turner, Mar. 19, 1954; 1 son, James Tracy. BSME, Auburn U., 1956. Teflon specialist duPont Co., Wilmington, Del., 1957-62; pres., chief exec. officer LNP Corp., Malvern, Pa., 1962-72; v.p. Carborundum, Niagara Falls, N.Y., 1972-76; exec. v.p. Chemetron, Chgo., 1976-78; sr. v.p. Allen Bradley Co. subs. Rockwell Internat. Corp., Milw., 1978-81, pres., chief oper. officer, 1981-86, also chief exec. officer, dir., 1986-90; chmn., chief exec. officer Varian Assocs., Palo Alto, Calif., 1990—. Served as 1st lt. USAF, 1957-59. Office: Varian Assocs PO Box 10800 3050 Hansen Way Palo Alto CA 94304-1000*

O'ROURKE, JAMES LOUIS, lawyer; b. Bridgeport, Conn., July 5, 1958; s. James G. and Margaret Elizabeth (Fesco) O'R.; m. Margaret C. DiCicco, Sept. 18, 1994. BS, U. Bridgeport, 1984, JD, 1987. Bar: Conn. 1988, U.S. Dist. Ct. Conn. 1989, Mashantucket Pequot Tribal Bar 1995. Pvt. practice Stratford, Conn., 1987—. With USN, 1976-79. Mem. ABA, Assn. Am. Trial Lawyers Assn., Conn. Trial Lawyers Assn., Conn. Bar Assn., Greater Bridgeport Bar Assn. Roman Catholic. Avocations: boating, cycling, swimming, golf. Office: 2526 Main St Stratford CT 06497

O'ROURKE, P. J. (PATRICK JAKE O'ROURKE), writer, humorist; b. Toledo, Ohio, Nov. 14, 1947; s. Clifford Bronson and Delphine (Loy) O'R. BA, Miami U. of Ohio, 1969; MA, Johns Hopkins U., 1970. Writer Nat. Lampoon mag., from 1973, former prin. editor; freelance writer, wrote screenplays, 1980s; writer Rolling Stone mag., 1981—, now fgn. affairs desk chief. Author: Modern Manners: An Etiquette Book for Rude People, 1983, The Bachelor Home Companion: A Practical Guide to Keeping House Like a Pig, 1987, Republican Party Reptile, 1987, Holidays in Hell, 1988, Parliament of Whores: A Lone Humorist Attempts to Explain the U.S. Government, 1991, Give War a Chance: Eyewitness Accounts of Mankind's Struggle Against Tyranny, Injustice and Alcohol-Free Beer, 192, All the Trouble in the World: The Lighter Side of Overpopulation, Famine, Ecological Disaster, Ethnic Hatred, Plague and Poverty, 1994, Age and Guile Beat Youth, Innocence and a Bad Haircut, 1995. Office: care Rolling Stone 1290 Avenue Of The Americas New York NY 10104

O'ROURKE, RICHARD LYNN, lawyer; b. Bklyn., Nov. 27, 1949; s. Joseph and Loretta (Casey) O'R.; m. Renee Marie Kupiec, July 17, 1971; children: Shannon, Kathleen. BA, SUNY, Geneseo, 1971; MA, Bowling Green State U., 1972; JD, Pace U. Sch. Law, 1981. Bar: N.Y. 1982, U.S. Ct. Appeals (10th cir.) 1983, U.S. Ct. Appeals (2d cir.) 1994, U.S. Dist. Ct. (all dists.) N.Y. 1982. Dir. career planning Pace U., Pleasantville, N.Y., 1977-81; assoc. Keane & Beane P.C., White Plains, N.Y., 1981-86, ptnr., v.p., 1986—. Judge Village of Brewster, N.Y., 1992—; pres. Brewster Edn. Found., 1992-94; town atty. Southeast Brewster, 1986-89, chmn. zoning bd. appeals, 1986-88; adv. bd. Jr. Achievement West, White Plains, 1977-82. Mem. Putnam County Magistrates Assn. (v.p. 1994—). Avocations: golf, history. Office: Keane & Beane One N Broadway White Plains NY 10601

O'ROURKE, THOMAS DENIS, civil engineer, educator; b. Pitts., July 31, 1948; s. Lawrence Robert and Adel Mildred (Moloski) O'R.; m. Patricia Ann Lane, Aug. 12, 1978; B.S.C.E., Cornell U., Ithaca, N.Y., 1970; M.S.C.E., U. Ill., 1973, Ph.D., 1975. Soils engr. Dames & Moore, N.Y.C., 1970; research asst. U. Ill., Urbana, 1970-75, asst. prof., 1975-78; asst. prof. Cornell U., 1978-80, assoc. prof., 1981-87, prof, 1987—. Elected to Nat. Acad. Engring., 1993. Mem. ASCE (pres. Ithaca sect. 1981-82, Collingwood prize 1983, Huber prize 1988, C. Martin Duke award 1995), ASME, ASTM (C.A. Hogentogler award 1976), Earthquake Engring. Research Inst., Internat. Soc. Engring. Geology, Internat. Soc. Rock Mechanics, U.S. Nat. Com. on Tunnelling Tech. (chmn. 1987-88). Home: 10 Twin Glens Rd Ithaca NY 14850-1041 Office: Cornell U Sch Civil Environ Engring 265 Hollister Hall Ithaca NY 14853-3501

O'ROURKE, WILLIAM ANDREW, English language educator, author; b. Chgo., Dec. 4, 1945; s. William Andrew and Elizabeth (Kompare) O'R.; m. Marion Teresa Ghilarducci, July 9, 1986; 1 child, Joseph Ghilarducci. B.A., U. Mo. at Kansas City, 1968; M.F.A., Columbia U., 1970. Instr. journalism Kean Coll., Union, N.J., 1973; asst. prof. English Rutgers U., 1975-78, Mount Holyoke Coll., 1978-81; asst. prof. English U. Notre Dame, Ind., 1981-87, assoc. prof., 1987-94, prof., 1994—; writer-in-residence Thurber House, Columbus, Ohio, fall 1984. Author: The Harrisburg 7 and the New Catholic Left, 1972, The Meekness of Isaac, 1974, Idle Hands, 1981, Criminal Tendencies, 1987, Signs of the Literary Times: Essays, Reviews, Profiles 1970-92, 1993, Notts, 1996; editor: On the Job, 1977. Fine Arts Work Ctr. fellow, Provincetown, Mass., 1970-72; recipient Creative Artists Pub. Svc. award N.Y. State Coun. on Arts, 1975; Nat. Endowment for Arts creative writing fellow, 1981-82, 90-91. Mem. Nat. Emergency Civil Liberties Com. (nat. coun.), Authors Guild, PEN Am. Ctr., Nat. Book Critics Cir. Office: U Notre Dame Dept English Notre Dame IN 46556

OROZ, PEDRO ANGEL, mining company executive; b. Calatayud, Zaragoza, Spain, July 15, 1934; s. Pedro and Lucia (Julvez) O.; m. Maria Pilar Cortes, Mar. 8, 1965; children: Lucia Jesus, Jose Pablo. B in Bus., Bus. Sch., Zaragoza, 1954. CPA. Asst. controller Warship Bldg. Co., Cartagena, Spain, 1958-62; fin. mgr. Pegaso Truck Bldg., Madrid, 1962-70; internal audit mgr. Civil Shipbldg., Madrid, 1970-78; control and fin. dir. Ram Diary Products, Madrid, 1978-83; asst. corp. controller Nat. Industry Inst., Madrid, 1983-89; planning and control dir. Hunosa Ming Co., Oviedo/Madrid, 1989-95, Bazan Warship Bldg. Co., Madrid, 1995—. 2d lt., 1954-55, Spain. Mem. Internat. Inst. Fin. Execs., Mgmt. Ctr. Europe. Avocations: bicycling, golf. Home: Julian Romea 21-9 C, Madrid 28003, Spain Office: Bazan Warship Bldg Co, Paseo Castella na 55-5 plta, Madrid 28046, Spain

OROZCO, LUZMARÍA, language educator; b. Mexico City, Nov. 3, 1933; came to U.S., 1953; BA in French and English, Marycrest Coll., Davenport, Iowa, 1956; MA in English, Marquette U., 1958; PhD in Comparative Lit., U. Minn., 1973. Chair humanities div. Marycrest Coll., 1975-78, prof. English and Spanish; humanities rep. human rights commn. Palmer Sch. Chiropracters, 1979—; official translator Latin Am. affairs Diocese of Davenport, 1978; vis. prof. St. Agnes Coll., Md., 1978, St. Jerome Coll., Waterloo, Ontario, Canada, 1976, Yale U., New Haven, Conn., 1986-87; cons., participant Iowa Program in Humanities, 1975-79; translator, cons. testing program on bilingual edn. U. Iowa, 1978. Editor of publs. Sister of Humility of Mary, 1960-85; contbr. numerous poems to competitions. Danforth Instn. grantee, 1967-69, Fulbright grantee, 1970-72; recipient award for teaching excellence and campus leadership Sears-Roebuck and Found. for Ind. Higher Edn., 1990. Mem. MLA, Popular Culture Assn., Spanish-Speaking Commn., Chaparral Poetry Assn. Roman Catholic. Avocations: tennis, swimming, fighting illiteracy. Home: 1607 W 12th St Davenport IA 52804-4034 Office: Marycrest Coll Dept English Davenport IA 52804

OROZCO, RAYMOND E., fire protective services official; b. Chgo., Dec. 17, 1933; m. Patricia King; children: Linda Orozco Stinson, Raymond II, Maripat Orozco Lannin, Michael. Cert. in firefighting and fire instrn. State of Ill. Br. chief Chgo. Fire Dept., 1970-80, dep. dist. chief, 1980-81, exec. asst. to fire commr., 1981-82, dist. chief, 1982-86, asst. dep. fire commr., 1986-88, dep. fire commr., 1988-89, fire commr., 1989—. With USN, 1953-57. Office: Fire Department City Hall Rm 105 121 N La Salle St Chicago IL 60602-1202

ORPHANIDES, NORA CHARLOTTE, ballet educator; b. N.Y.C., June 4, 1951; d. M.T. and Mary Elsie (Tilly) Feffer; m. James Mark Orphanides, July 1, 1972; children: Mark, Elaine, Jennine. BA, CUNY, 1973; student, Joffrey Ballet Sch., N.Y.C., 1970-75; postgrad., Princeton Ballet Sch., 1976-86. Cert. speech and hearing handicapped tchr. Sr. sales assoc. Met. Mus. Art, N.Y.C., 1970-86; membership asst. Patrons Lounge, M.M.A., N.Y.C., 1987—; mem. faculty Princeton (N.J.) Ballet Sch., 1983—, trustee emeritus, 1992—. Mem. cast Princeton Ballet ann. Nutcracker, 1985-90, now Am. Repertory Ballet Co., 1993—; appeared in Romeo & Juliet, 1995-96. Fundraising gala chmn. Princeton Ballet, 1985, 86, 91-92, chmn. spl. events, 1987—, trustee, 1986—, chmn. Nutcracker benefit, 1990—, Dracula benefit, 1991; vol. libr. Plainsboro (N.J.) Free Libr., 1985; program solicitation chmn. to benefit Princeton Med. Ctr., 1988, T-shirt chmn. benefit, 1990-91, 96, publicity chmn. ann. June Fete, 1992; mem. worship and arts commn. Nassau Presbyn. Ch., 1989, 90, dinner chmn. Bach Music Festival, 1989, Cambridge Singers, 1990; vol. Nat. Hdqrs. Recording for the Blind, 1991-93; trustee Princeton Youth Fund, 1991-92; dinner chmn. Nassau Ch. Music Festival, 1992, Handel Festival, Nassau Ch., 1993, Princeton Chamber Symphony, 1993; vol. Cmty. Park Sch. Libr., 1992-93; hon. chmn. Princeton Ballet Gala, 1993; chmn. Christmas Boutique, Princeton Med. Ctr., 1993; trustee, Princeton Med. Ctr. Auxilary Bd., 1992—, pres.-elect, trustee 1995—. Democrat. Avocations: piano, aerobics, skiing, swimming, tennis. Home: 35 Brearly Rd Princeton NJ 08540-6767 Office: 301 N Harrison St Princeton NJ 08540

ORR, BOBBY (ROBERT GORDON ORR), former hockey player; b. Parry Sound, Ont., Can., Mar. 20, 1948; m. Peggy Orr; children: Darren, Brent. With Boston Bruins, 1966-76; with Chgo. Black Hawks, 1976-77, asst. coach, 1976-77; spokesman Nabisco Brands, Inc., N.Y.C., Bay Banks, Inc., Boston; asst. to the pres. Pandick New Eng.; host Hockey Legends program CBC; bd. dirs. numerous cos. Winner Calder Meml. trophy, 1967, Art Ross trophy, 1970, 75, James Norris Meml. trophy, 1968-75, Hart Meml. trophy, 1970-72, 2 Conn Smythe trophies, Lou Marsh trophy, 1970; named Male Athlete of Yr., Can. CP Poll, 1970, Athlete of Yr., Sport Mag. and Sports Illustrated, Most Valuable Player, Can. Cup, 1976. Address: 647 Summer St Boston MA 02210-2189*

ORR, BOBETTE KAY, diplomat; b. Oak Park, Ill., Oct. 28, 1941; d. Robert Jay and Neta (Hoobler) Pottle; m. William Rucker Orr, Oct. 11, 1974; step children: Bridgette, Brietta, Alyson, William Jr. BA in Econs., Conn. Coll. for Women, 1963; student auditor Internat. Econs., London Sch. of Econs., 1964; postgrad. studies in Econs., George Washington U., 1964-65. Rsch. asst. C. of C. USA, Washington, 1965-66; country desk officer for Scandanavia U.S. Dept. Commerce, Washington, 1966-69, country desk officer for France, 1970-72, 79-81, country desk officer for Belgium, Netherlands, Luxembourg, 1974-77, country desk officer for Japan, 1981-82; mkt. rsch. officer United States Trade Ctr., Stockholm, 1973; trade promotion officer United States Trade Ctr., London, 1977-78; asst. comml. attache Am. Embassy, Paris, 1982-87; comml. attache Am. Consulate Gen., Auckland, New Zealand, 1988-92; consul gen. Am. Consulate, Edinburgh, Scotland, 1992-95; comml. counselor Am. Embassy, London, 1995—; mem. bd. dirs. U.S. Dept. Commerce Fed. Credit Union, Washington, D.C., 1972-77, pres., 1976-77, mem. supervisory com., 1979-81; equal employment opportunity counselor for Greater Washington Met. Area, 1972-75; mem. affirmative action com. for DIBA/Commerce Dept., 1972-73; detailed to Dept. Commerce Office of Protocol to assist during U.S.-USSR trade negotiations, Sept.-Oct. 1972, Poland, Nov. 1972; selected by President's Commn. on Exec. Interchange as candidate for placement in bus./govt. pers. exchange program, 1979; mission dir. for USDOC's Concrete Constrn. Techniques Seminar Mission to Hong Kong, Singapore, Malaysia, 1980; detailed to Office of Dir. Fgn. Comml. Svc. to participate in Assessment Ctrs. in Washington and Miami as evaluator of candidates for careers in Fgn. Comml. Svc., 1981. Author: (with others) 10 pamphlet series, on free enterprise, The Power of Choice, 1966; contbr. to Bus. Am., 1966-81, Overseas Bus. Reports 1966-76 (Dept. Commerce publs.); also studies on markets in various countries. Commerce dept. rep. for Combined Fed. Campaign, 1969-70, Savings Bond Campaign, 1971. Mem. Am. Women's Club of Edinburgh, (hon. pres.), The English Speaking Union, Grampian-Houston Assn. Avocations: skiing, jogging, bicycle riding. Home: PO Box 63 Great Falls VA 22066 Office: Am Embassy, 24 Grosvenor Sq, London England W1A 1AE

ORR, CAROL WALLACE, book publishing executive; b. Newton, Mass., Dec. 17, 1933; d. Barton Stuart Wallace and Mary (Blanthorne) Stigler; children: Brett Amanda, Ross Wallace. Student, Boston U., 1951-53; BA, Douglass Coll., 1966. Successively permissions mgr., paperback editor, reprint editor, asst. to assoc. dir. Princeton (N.J.) U. Press, 1966-75, exec. asst. to dir. then asst. dir., 1975-78; dir. U. Tenn. Press., Knoxville, 1978-91; aerobics instr., freelance editor, 1992—. Mem. editorial bd. Book Rsch. Quar., 1988-92; contbr. articles to Scholarly Pub. jour., 1974-86. Recipient Book Woman award Women's Nat. Book Assn., 1987, Disting. Career award Needham (Mass.) H.S., 1995. Mem. Assn. Am. Univ. Presses (pres. 1987-88), Internat. Assn. Scholarly Pubs. (sec.-gen. 1980-83), Women in Scholarly Pub. (first pres. 1980-81), AAUP Lang. Task Force (chair 1989-91), AAUP Golden Fluke Award Com. (chair 1984-91), Phi Beta Kappa, Phi Kappa Phi. Avocations: jogging, aerobics, gardening, travel, music.

ORR, DANIEL, educator, economist; b. N.Y.C., May 13, 1933; s. Robert Connell and Lillian (Nagle) O.; m. Mary Lee Hayes, Oct. 12, 1957; children—Rebecca, Matthew, Sara. A.B., Oberlin Coll., 1954; Ph.D., Princeton, 1960. Ops. analyst Procter & Gamble Co., 1956-58; instr. econs. Princeton U., 1959-60; asst. prof. econs. Amherst Coll., 1960-61, Grad. Sch. Bus., U. Chgo., 1961-65; mem. faculty U. Calif. at San Diego, 1965-78, chmn. econs. dept., 1969-72; prof. econs., cons. in field; prof., head dept. econs. Va. Poly. Inst. and State U., 1978-89; prof. econs. U. Ill., Champaign-Urbana, 1989—, dept. head, 1989-94; vis. prof. U. Nottingham, Eng., 1972, U. Calif., 1988, U. Warsaw, 1992. Author: Cash Management and the Demand for Money, 1970, Property, Markets and Government Intervention, 1976. Trustee Oberlin (Ohio) Coll., 1993—. Served with AUS, 1958. Mem. Am. Econ. Assn., Crystal Downs Country Club. Home: 515 S Willis Ave Champaign IL 61821-3917 Office: U Ill 330 Commerce Bldg W 1206 S 6th St Champaign IL 61820-6915

ORR, DAVID E., electronics executive; b. Pitts., Sept. 10, 1951; s. Lewis E. and Betty (Bauer) O.; m. Kathleen Ann Engist, Mar. 23, 1979; children: Michael, Kristen. BS in Indsl. Engring., Gannon U., 1973; MBA, U. Chgo., 1986. Bus. rels. mgr. GTE Svc. Corp., Indpls., 1982-83; engring. and constrn. dir. GTE Wis., Madison, 1983-85; mktg. dir. Rockwell Internat., Richardson, Tex., 1985-89; v.p. mktg. and sales network transmission systems Rockwell Internat., Richardson, 1989-90, v.p., gen. mgr., 1990-92; pres., CEO, Alcatel Network Systems Inc., Dallas, 1992—. Mem. IEEE, Inst. Indsl. Engrs. Avocations: golf, biking. Office: Alcatel Network Systems Inc PO Box 833802 1225 Alma Rd Richardson TX 75081*

ORR, FRANKLIN MATTES, JR., petroleum engineering educator; b. Baytown, Tex., Dec. 27, 1946; s. Franklin Mattes and Selwyn Sage (Huddleston) O.; m. Susan Packard, Aug. 30, 1970; children: David, Katherine. BSChemE, Stanford U., 1969; PhDChemE, U. Minn., 1976. Asst. to dir. Office Fed. Activities EPA, Washington, 1970-72; research engr. Shell Devel. Co., Houston, 1976-78; sr. engr. N.Mex. Petroleum Recovery Research Ctr., Socorro, 1978-84; assoc. prof. petroleum engring. Stanford (Calif.) U., 1985-87, prof., 1987—, interim dean Sch. Earth Scis., 1994-95, dean Sch. Earth Scis., 1995—. Contbr. articles to profl. jours. Bd. dirs. Wolf Trap Found. for the Performing Arts, 1988-94, Monterey Bay

Aquarium Rsch. Inst., 1987—; chair sci. adv. com. David and Lucile Packard Found. Fellowships for Sci. and Engring. With USPHS, 1970-72. Mem. Soc. Petroleum Engrs. (named Distin. Lectr. 1988-89, Disting. Achievement award for petroleum engring. faculty 1993), AIChE, AAAS, Soc. Indsl. and Applied Math. Office: Stanford U Sch Earth Scis Mitchell Bldg Rm 101 Stanford CA 94305

ORR, J. SCOTT, newspaper correspondent. Coor., wash. bur. The Star-Ledger, Newark, N.J.

ORR, JAMES F., III, insurance company executive; b. Mpls., 1943. BA, Villanova U., 1962; MA, Boston U., 1969. With New Eng. Mchts. Bank, Boston, 1965-67, Bache & Co., N.Y.C., 1967-69; ptnr. Cardinal Mgmt. Co., Boston, 1969-75; exec. v.p., treas. Conn. Bank and Trust Corp., 1975-86; with UNUM, 1986—, formerly pres., COO; chmn. bd., CEO UNUM Corp.; also pres., chmn., CEO UNUM Life Ins. Co. (subs.). Office: UNUM Corp 2211 Congress St Portland ME 04122-0002*

ORR, JIM (JAMES D. ORR), columnist, writer; b. Buffalo, Feb. 7, 1960; s. David James and Doris Kathleen (Wolos) O.; m. JoEllen Black, June 4, 1994. B in Journalism, Ind. U. of Pa., 1982, M in Comm., 1987. Station mgr. Sta. WIUP-TV, Ind., Pa., 1983-84; sports writer, news writer Ind. (Pa.) Gazette, 1984-88; edn. reporter Stuart (Fla.) News, 1988-89; staff writer, columnist Gannett Rochester (N.Y.) Newspapers, 1989—. Columnist Orrdinary People, 1994—. Moderator polit. debate Edu-Cable Corp., Greece, N.Y., 1993. Recipient Agrl. Writing 1st Place award Penn-Ag Industries, 1985, 2d place Keystone State Press award Pa. Newspaper Pub. Assn., 1987. Home: 1035 Edgemere Dr Rochester NY 14612-1503 Office: Gannett Rochester Newspapers 55 Exchange Blvd Rochester NY 14614-2001

ORR, JOEL NATHANIEL, computer graphics consultant; b. Bklyn., June 19, 1947; s. Martin J. and Esther B. Filler; m. Gail Naomi Smith, June 15, 1973; children—David, Anne, John, Thomas, Stephen, Shir. Ph.D. in Math., SUNY, 1972. Editor, translator Israel Program Sci. Translations, Jerusalem, 1967-68; tech. writer, editor then analyst Compat, Westbury, N.Y., 1969-72; system mgr. Met. Nashville, 1973-74; pres. Jerusalem Systems; pub. Computer Graphics newsletter; pres., prin. cons. Orr Assocs. Inc., Great Falls, Va., 1975—; mem. seminar faculty, lab. computer graphics and spatial analysis Harvard U., 1979—; dir. CAD-CAM Inst., 1982—. Author: Computer Graphics Extravaganza, 1977; co-editor: The CAD/CAM Handbook, 1985, The CIM Handbook, 1986, Thoughts on Engineering Automation, 1994; contbg. editor: Windows Sources, 1992—, NextWorld; contbr. articles to profl. jours.; contbr. editor: Harvard Newsletter on Computer Graphics, 1979-80, Computer Graphics Today, 1984—, Computer Graphics World, 1985—; series editor McGraw-Hill, 1989—; host Computer Talk. Exec. dir. Virtual Worlds Soc., 1992—; chmn. bd. Xanadu Operating Co., 1992-94; bd. dirs. Macscitech, Virtus Corp., Ithaca Software Corp., COB Agorics, Inc., 1993—. With Israeli Army, 1964-67. Named Disting. Fellow, Autodesk Inc., 1990; recipient Orthogonal medal N.C. State U., 1991. Mem. IEEE, Assn. Computing Machinery, Nat. Computer Graphics Assn. (pres. 1988-89, directory editor, interim pres. 1990), Urban and Regional Info. Systems Assn., Am. Congress Surveying and Mapping Land Info. Inst. (pres.), Inst. Modernization Land Data System, League for Engring. Automation Productivity (founder), Soc. Mfg. Engrs., Soc. Mfg. Engrs./Computers and Automated Systems Assn. Jewish. Office: Orr Assocs Inc 261 Marsh Island Dr Chesapeake VA 23320

ORR, JOSEPH NEWTON, recreational guide, outdoor educator; b. San Francisco, Oct. 25, 1954; s. James Neewah and Verna Louise (Butler) O. BA in Spanish, Sul Ross State U., 1981. Cert. swiftwater rescue technician; cert. wilderness first responder; cert. advanced open water SCUBA diver; cert. Utah river guide, Grand Canyon river guide. Instr. astronomy lab. Sul Ross State U., Alpine, Tex., 1972-75; svc. sta. attendent, store clerk Nat. Park Concessions, Big Bend Nat. Park, 1975-78; surveyor's aide Gila Nat. Forest U.S. Dept. Agriculture, N. Mex., 1979; instr. English as a foreign lang. Centro Universitario de Idiomas, Mexico City, 1981; English and Spanish tutor Ctr. Student Devel. Sul Ross State U., 1980-81, 82-83; instr. English as a fgn. lang. Intensive Summer Lang. Tng. Inst., 1980-83; ednl. cons. Chihuahuan Desert Rsch. Inst., Alpine, Tex., 1983; editor The Skyline (student newspaper) Sul Ross State U., 1984; interpreter, translator, guide Dr. John M. Miller, Mex., 1980-85; waiter Kangaroo Court Rest., San Antonio, 1981-82, 84-86; guide Far Flung Adventures, U.S., Mexico, Belize, Guatemala, Honduras, 1986—. Active Am. Mus. Natural History, Four Corners Sch. Outdoor Edn., Canyonlands Field Inst., Crow Canyon Archeol. Ctr., Grand Canyon River Guides, Mus. No. Ariz., Friends of Lowell Obs., Grand Canyon Trust, others. Mem. Nat. Geog. Soc., Archaeol. conservancy, Archaeol. Inst. Am., Astron. Soc. of Pacific, Planetary Soc., Internat. Dark Sky Assn., Beta Beta Beta. Democrat. Avocations: astronomy, archaeology. Home: 223 N Guadalupe # 429 Santa Fe NM 87501

ORR, L. GLENN, JR., banker; b. Charlotte, N.C., Apr. 28, 1940; s. Laney G. and Mildred Rice O.; m. Ruthlee Phillips, June 15, 1962; children: Mildred Ruth, Laney G., Virginia DeArmon. AB, Wofford Coll., 1962; MBA, U. S.C., 1963; PhD (hon.) Pembroke (N.C.) State U., 1993. V.p. Wachovia Bank & Trust Co., Winston-Salem, N.C., 1965-72; pres. Community Bank, Greenville, S.C., 1972-73, Forsyth Bank & Trust, Winston-Salem, 1973-82; sr. exec. v.p. So. Nat. Bank, Winston-Salem, 1982-83, vice-chmn., Lumberton, N.C., 1983—; chmn., CEO So. Nat. Bank N.C., 1985—; chmn., pres., CEO So. Nat. Corp., 1990—; chmn. So. Nat. Bank S.C., 1990—; mem. Charlotte br. Fed. Res. Bd. of Richmond, Va., Econ. Devel. N.C. Deacon, supt. Sunday sch. Knollwood Baptist Ch., 1965; div. head United Fund, 1966; adv. bd. treas. Salvation Army, 1965; mem. adv. bd. Boys' Club, 1970, Amos Cottage, 1973; bd. dirs. Goodwill Industries, 1975, Forsyth Country Day Sch., 1975, 79, Sch. Pastoral Care, 1979, Winston-Salem Industries for the Blind, 1980-81, Industries for the Blind, Carolina Civic Ctr. Lumberton, Brennen Children's Hosp., Old Salem, Inc.; trustee Wake Forest U., 1982-83, 88—, vice chmn. bd. trustees 1985-86; bd. trustees U. N.C., Greensboro, 1993—; bd. dirs. Lineberger Cancer Research Ctr. U. N.C., Chapel Hill, 1985—, Alumni Bd. Wofford Coll., 1981-85; Winston-Salem Nat. Little League, 1979, chmn. fin. com., 1979-80; mem. long range planning com. United Way, 1982-83; bd. dirs., mem. fin. com. Better Bus. Bur., 1979; chmn. bd. dirs. Goodwill Industries, 1979; mem. endowment com. Converse Coll., 1972. Served to 1st lt. U.S. Army, 1963-65. Mem. C. of C. (dir. 1965), N.C. Bankers Assn. (group chmn. 1979, pres. 1987), Am. Bankers Assn., Kappa Alpha. Republican. Baptist. Lodge: Rotary. Office: Orr Management 110 S Stratford Rd Winston Salem NC 27104*

ORR, PARKER MURRAY, former lawyer; b. Cleve., Mar. 29, 1927; s. Stanley Lutz and Katherine (Murray) O.; m. Joan Luttrell, June 8, 1946; children: Kathleen Orr Guzowski, Parker Murray, Louise Orr Black, Kevin J. B.A., Western Res. U., 1948, LL.B., 1950. Bar: Ohio 1950. Atty. Leckie, McCreary, Schlitz, Hinslea & Petersilge, Cleve., 1950-51; owner Orr Constrn. Co., Cleve., 1951-57; assoc. firm Baker & Hostetler, Cleve., 1957-67, ptnr., 1967-88; ret. Chmn. City of Willoughby Hills Planning Commn., Ohio, 1964-78. Mem. ABA, Ohio Bar Assn., Greater Cleve. Bar Assn. Republican. Club: Mayfield Country (Cleve.). Home: 37801 Rogers Rd Willoughby OH 44094-9485 Office: Baker & Hostetler 3200 National City Ctr Cleveland OH 44114

ORR, RICHARD TUTTLE, journalist; b. Springfield, Ill., Feb. 19, 1915; s. Thomas Edward and Anna Maude (Tuttle) O.; m. Lois Marie Hollesen, June 3, 1939. B.S. in Journalism, U. Ill., 1937. Reporter City News Bur., Chgo., 1941-42; reporter Chgo. Tribune, 1941-49, farm editor, 1949-83, editorial writer, 1961-72, rural affairs writer, 1983—. Served with USAF, 1943-46. Recipient Edward Scott Beck award Chgo. Tribune, 1962, Oscar in Agr. award DeKalb Agrl. Research Inc., 1969, Pfizer Agr. Communications award Pfizer Genetics Inc., 1969, Champion Media award Dartmouth Coll., 1982, Hall of Fame award Saddle and Sirloin Club, 1972. Mem. Nat. Assn. Agrl. Journalists (pres. 1958, J.S. Russell Meml. award 1965, Nat. Farm Features award 1977, 79, Nat. Farm Column award 1981), Chgo. Press Club (pres. 1966), Chgo. Press Vets. Assn. (chmn. 1968). Republican. Methodist. Avocations: photography; watercolor painting; jazz records; western Americana. Home: 2933 N Sheridan Rd Apt 809 Chicago IL 60657-5938 Office: Chgo Tribune PO Box 25340 Chicago IL 60625-0340

ORR, SAN WATTERSON, JR., lawyer; b. Madison, Wis., Sept. 22, 1941; s. San Watterson and Eleanor Augusta (Schalk) O.; m. Joanne Marie Ruby, June 26, 1965; children: San Watterson III, Nancy Chapman. BBA, U. Wis., 1963, JD, 1966. Bar: Wis. 1966; CPA, Wis. Sec., tres., bd. dirs. Yawkey Lumber Co., Wausau, Wis., 1971—; chmn. exec. com. Wausau Paper Mills Co., 1977—, chmn. bd., 1989—; pres. Woodson Fudiciary Corp., Wilmington, Del., 1979—, also bd. dirs.; pres. Forewood, Inc., Wausau, 1979—, also bd. dirs.; chmn. Marathon Electric Mfg. Corp., Wausau, 1982—, also bd. dirs.; chmn. Mosinee (Wis.) Paper Corp., 1987—, also bd. dirs.; dir. M&I First Am. Bank, Wausau, 1988—, Marshall & Ilsley Corp., 1994—; bd. dirs. Wausau Ins. Cos., M&I Marshall & Ilsley Bank, Milw., MDU Resources Group, Inc., Bismark, N.D. Editor: U. Wis. Law Rev., 1962-63. Bd. dirs. The Aytchmonde Woodson Found., Inc., Wausau, 1966—, The Leigh Yawkey Woodson Art Mus., Inc., Wausau, 1981—, Wis. Taxpayers Alliance, Madison, 1983—, Competitive Wis., Inc., Milw., 1989—, U. Wis. Found., Madison, 1991—; dir. Wis. Policy Rsch. Inst., Milw., 1995—; mem. bd. regents U. Wis. Sys., Madison, 1993—; v.p., bd. dirs. Wausau YMCA Found., 1979—; bd. dirs. U. Wis. Hosp. and Clinics Authority, 1995—; trustee U. Wis. Hosp. and Clinics, 1980—, chair, 1993—. Mem. Wis. Bar Assn., Am. Law Inst., Wausau Club. Office: Yawkey Lumber Co 500 3rd St Ste 602 Wausau WI 54403-4857

ORR, STANLEY CHI-HUNG, financial executive; b. Shanghai, China, May 19, 1946; s. Chiu-Lai and Chiu-Chun (Ma) O.; children: Simon K., Edmund K., Norman K. Grad., Hong Kong Bapt. Coll., 1966; M in Econs., Chu Hoi Coll., Hong Kong, 1973; post grad., East Anglia U, Eng., 1975; MBA, Bradford U., Eng., 1977, West Coast U., L.A., 1980. CPA, Calif.; CMA, Eng.; notary pub. Chief acct. Cordial Knitting Factory Ltd., Hong Kong, 1966-69, mgr., 1969-71; chief acct. for Asia Mark Holding Co. Ltd., Hong Kong, 1971-74; chief fin. officer Knits-Cord Ltd., Montebello, Calif., 1977—; broker Dept. of Real Estate, 1992—. Treas., sec. World Univs. Svc., Hong Kong, 1965-66. Mem. AICPA, Chinese-Am. CPA Soc. (chmn., pres. 1991), Calif. Soc. CPAs. Republican. Office: Knits-Cord Ltd 1600 Date St Montebello CA 90640-6371

ORR, STEVEN R., health facility administrator; b. 1947. Undergrad. degree, Macalester Coll.; M in Hosp. Adminstrn., U. Minn., 1973. Tchr., coord. master's degree program in hosp. adminstrn. U. Minn., 1974-76; v.p. corp. planning, v.p. managed and affiliated hosp. divsn. Fairfield Community Hosps., Mpls., 1976-81; COO Mid-Atlantic Health Group, 1981-83; adminstr. Monmouth Med. Ctr. Mid-Atlantic Health Group, Long Branch, N.J., 1981-83; ptnr., cons. Peat, Marwick, Main & Co., Mpls., 1984-88; pres., CEO Lutheran Health Systems, Fargo, N.D., 1988—. Office: Luth Health System PO Box 6200 Fargo ND 58106-6200*

ORR, SUSAN PACKARD, foundation administrator. Pres. Packard Found., Los Altos, Calif. Office: The Packard Foundation 300 2nd St Ste 200 Los Altos CA 94022-3621

ORR, TERRENCE S., dancer; b. Berkeley, Calif., Mar. 12, 1943; m. Cynthia Gregory (div.); m. Marianna Tcherkassky. Student, San Francisco Ballet Sch. With San Francisco Ballet, 1959-65; with Am. Ballet Theatre, N.Y.C., 1965—, soloist, 1967-72, rehearsal asst., 1970-73, prin. dancer, 1972-78, assoc. ballet master, 1973-78, ballet master, 1978—; Mounted prodns. for the Royal Winnipeg Ballet, The National Ballet of Mexico, Teatro alla Scala in Millan, National ballet de Nancy in France, Teatro Colon in Buenos Aires, Pittsburgh Ballet Theatre, Boston Ballet, Ballet West, Dance theatre of Harlem, New York City Ballet, the Cleveland/San jose Ballet, the San Francisco Ballet and Ballet Arizona. Repertoire includes (with San Francisco Ballet) The Nutcracker, Fantasma, Divertissement d'Auber, Jeu des Cartes, Con Amore, (with Am. Ballet Theatre) Billy the Kid, Coppelia, La Fille Mal Gardee, Petrouchka, The River, Rodeo, Don Quixote, (leading roles) At Midnight, Dark Elegies, Fancy Free, Graduation Ball, Harbinger, Variations for Four, Pulcinella Variations, Brahms Quintet, Schubertiade, Mendelssohn Symphony, Polyandrion, (featured roles) Giselle, Swan Lake, La Sylphide, Gartenfest, Ontogeny; prodr., dir. Gala Performance, 1984, 86; stage prodns. La Sylphide, Rodeo, Fancy Free, Graduation Ball, Etudes, Billy the Kid, Fall River Legend, Giselle. Office: care Am Ballet Theatre 890 Broadway New York NY 10003-1211

ORR, T(HOMAS) J(EROME) (JERRY ORR), airport terminal executive; b. Charlotte, N.C., Feb. 25, 1941; m. Marcia Mincey; 3 children. BS in Civil Engring., N.C. State U., 1962. Registered profl. engr., N.C. Pvt. practice land surveyor Charlotte, 1962-75; with Charlotte/Douglas Internat. Airport, 1975—, asst. mgr. airport ops., until 1989, aviation dir., 1989—. Mem. pers. com. Park Rd. Bapt. Ch.; chmn. employees campaign United Way of Ctrl. Carolinas, 1990; active Neighborhood Task Force, Charlotte's Cities in Schs. Program. Recipient Outstanding Support award N.C. Air Nat. Guard, 1989, Spirit award Charlotte-Mecklenburg Spirit Sq. Ctr. for Arts, 1990, Design award Precast/Prestressed Concrete Inst. Jour., 1990, Continuing Contbg. award N.C. Dept. Transp., 1990. Mem. Am. Assn. Airport Execs., N.C. Airports Assn. (past pres.), Airport Operators Coun. Internat., Charlotte Chamber Aviation Com., Airport Adv. Com. Office: Charlotte/Douglas Internat Airport PO Box 19066 Charlotte NC 28219-9066*

ORR-CAHALL, CHRISTINA, art gallery director, art historian; b. Wilkes-Barre, Pa., June 12, 1947; d. William R.A. and Anona (Snyder) Boben; m. Richard Cahall. BA magna cum laude, Mt. Holyoke Coll., 1969; MA, Yale U., 1974, MPhil, 1975, PhD, 1979. Curator of collections Norton Gallery Art, West Palm Beach, Fla., 1975-77; asst. prof. Calif. Poly. State U., San Luis Obispo, 1978-81, Disting. prof., 1981; dir. art div., chief curator Oakland (Calif.) Mus., 1981-88; chief exec. officer Corcoran Gallery Art, Washington, 1988-90; dir. Norton Mus. Art, West Palm Beach, 1990—. Author: Addison Mizner: Architect of Dreams and Realities, 1974, 2d printing, 1993, Gordon Cook, 1987, Claude Monet: Am Impression, 1993; editor: The Art of California, 1984, The American Collection at the Norton Museum of Art, 1995. Office: Norton Gallery of Art 1451 S Olive Ave West Palm Beach FL 33401-7162

ORREGO-SALAS, JUAN ANTONIO, composer, retired music educator; b. Santiago, Chile, Jan. 18, 1919; came to U.S., 1961; s. Fernando M. and Filomena E. (Salas) Orrego-S.; m. Carmen Benavente, Apr. 17, 1943; children: Juan Cristian, Francisca, Juan Felipe, Juan Miguel, Juan Matias. Bachillerato, Liceo AlemÁn, Santiago, 1938; MusM, State U., 1942; MusD, Conservatorio Nacional de Música, Santiago, 1942; architect diploma, Cath. U. Chile, 1943; postgrad., Columbia U., 1944-45, Princeton U., 1945-46; MusD, U. Chile, Santiago, 1953; D Honoris Causa, Cath. U., Santiago, 1973. Condr. Cath. U. Choir, Santiago, 1938-57; prof. composition and musicology U. Chile, Santiago, 1942-61; editor Revista Musical Chilena, 1949-53; music critic El Mercurio, Santiago, 1950-61; dir. Instituto de Extension Musical, 1957-59; founder, chmn. dept. music Cath. U., Santiago, 1959-61; prof. music, dir. Latin Am. Music Center, Sch. Music, Ind. U., Bloomington, 1961-87, now prof. emeritus; chmn. composition dept. Latin Am. Music Center, Sch. Music, Ind. U., 1975-79; mem. Contemporary Music Panel, NEA, Washington, 1978-80. Composer Canciones Castellanas, 1948, Concertos for piano and orch., 1950, 85, Sextet, 1954, 5 symphonies, 1949, 54, 61, 66, 95, string quartets, 1957, 95, The Tumbler's Prayer Ballet, 1960, Sonata a Quattro, 1986, Missa, 1968, The Days of God, 1976, The Celestial City, 1992, Concerto for violin and orch., 1983, Riley's Merriment, 1986, Partita, 1988, (operas) The Dawn of the Poor King, 1952, Widows, 1990, (cantata) The Heavenly City, 1992, others, inluding chamber music, ballet, choral and solo instrumental music; contbr. articles to profl. jours. and encys. Mem. Frei Found. 5th Centennial of Discovery Commn., 1992. Served with Army of Chile, 1938. Recipient Olga Cohen prize Cohen Found., 1955, 58, Biennial Chilean Music Festival awards, 1948, 50, 54, 58, 60, InterAm. Mistral Cultural prize OAS, 1987, de National Prize Chilean Gov't., 1992; fellow Rockefeller Found., 1944, Guggenheim Found., 1945, 54; grantee Nat. Endowment for the Arts, 1975, 87. Mem. Am. Soc. Univ. Composers, Latin Am. Studies Assn., Interam. Music Council, Nat. Acad. Art (Chile), Broadcast Music Inc. Roman Catholic. Avocations: gardening, water coloring. Home: 490 Serena Ln Bloomington IN 47401-9226

ORRICK, WILLIAM HORSLEY, JR., federal judge; b. San Francisco, Oct. 10, 1915; s. William Horsley and Mary (Downey) O.; m. Marion Naffziger, Dec. 5, 1947; children: Mary-Louise, Marion, William Horsley III. Grad., Hotchkiss Sch., 1933; B.A., Yale, 1937; LL.B., U. Calif.-Berkeley, 1941. Bar: Calif. 1941. Partner Orrick, Dahlquist, Herrington & Sutcliffe, San Francisco, 1941-61; asst. atty. gen. civil div. Dept Justice, 1961-62, antitrust div., 1963-65; dep. under sec. state for adminstrn. Dept. State, 1962-63; practice law San Francisco, 1965-74; former partner firm Orrick, Herrington, Rowley & Sutcliffe; U.S. dist. judge No. Dist. Calif., 1974—. Past pres. San Francisco Opera Assn., Trustee, World Affairs Council; former trustee San Francisco Law Library, San Francisco Found., Children's Hosp. San Francisco, Grace Cathedral Corp. Served to capt. M.I. AUS, 1942-46. Recipient Alumnus of Yr. award Boalt Hall Alumni Assn., U. Calif., 1980. Fellow Am. Bar Found.; mem. Bar Assn. San Francisco (past trustee, treas.). Office: US Dist Ct PO Box 36060 450 Golden Gate Ave San Francisco CA 94102

ORRMONT, ARTHUR, writer, editor; b. Albany, N.Y., July 3, 1922; m. Lora Orenstein, Oct. 6, 1956 (div. 1965); m. Leonie Rosenstiel, Aug. 22, 1995. Student, U. Ala., 1941, U. Mich., 1942-45, Cornell U., 1945; BA, U. Mich., 1945. Editl. dept. head Farrar, Straus & Co., N.Y.C., 1945-51; sr. editor Popular Libr., N.Y.C., 1951-55; exec. editor Fawcett Books, N.Y.C., 1955-57; pres., editl. dir. Author Aid Assocs., N.Y.C., 1967—; v.p. Rsch. Assocs. Internat., N.Y.C., 1980—; lectr. creative writing CCNY, 1966, Columbia U., 1967. Author: Love Cults and Faith-Healers, 1961, (with Capt. Marion Aten) Last Train Over Rostov Bridge, 1962, Brit. edit., 1962, Indestructible Commodore Matthew Perry, 1962, Japanese edit., 1963, Amazing Alexander Hamilton, 1964, Portuguese edit., 1965, Chinese Gordon: Hero of Khartoum, 1966, Fighter Against Slavery: Jehudi Ashmun, 1966, Mr. Lincoln's Master Spy: Lafayette Baker, 1966, Diplomat in Warpaint: Chief Alexander Gillivray of the Creeks, 1967, Richard Burton, 1969, Brit. edit., 1969, James Buchanan Eads: The Man Who Mastered the Mississippi, 1970, (with Fr. Joseph Lauro) Action Priest, 1970, French edit., 1970, Requiem for War: The Life of Wilfred Owen, 1972; editor: (with Leonie Rosenstiel) Literary Agents of North America, 1984, 5th edit., 1995; editor Nat. Hall of Fame Biography series, 1970-72. With U.S. Army, 1942. Recipient Avery Hopwood award for short story U. Mich., 1943, 44, 45. Office: Author Aid Assocs 340 E 52nd St New York NY 10022-6728

ORSATTI, ALFRED KENDALL, organization executive; b. Los Angeles, Jan. 31, 1932; s. Alfredo and Margaret (Hayes) O.; m. Patricia Decker, Sept. 11, 1960; children: Scott, Christopher, Sean. B.S., U. So. Calif., 1956. Assoc. prodr., v.p. Sabre Prodns., L.A., 1957-58; assoc. prodr. Ror Vic Prodns., L.A., 1958-59; bus. rep. AFTRA, L.A., 1960-61; Hollywood exec., sec. SAG, L.A., 1961-81, nat. exec. dir., 1981—; trustee Pension Welfare Plan SAG, 1971—; del. Los Angeles County Fedn. Labor, Los Angeles, Hollywood Film Council, Los Angeles; v.p., mem. exec. Calif. Fedn. Labor; v.p. Calif. Theatrical Fedn.; chmn. arts, entertainment and media com. dept. profl. employees AFL-CIO. Mem. Mayor's Film Devel. Com., Los Angeles. Mem. Hollywood C. of C. (bd. dirs.), Actors and Artists Am. Assn. (1st v.p.). Office: SAG 5757 Wilshire Blvd Los Angeles CA 90036

ORSBON, RICHARD ANTHONY, lawyer; b. North Wilkesboro, N.C., Sept. 23, 1947; s. Richard Chapman and Ruby Estelle (Wyatt) O.; m. Susan Cowan Shivers, June 13, 1970; children: Sarah Hollingsworth, Wyatt Benjamin, David Allison. BA Disting. mil. grad. ROTC, Davidson Coll., 1969; JD, Vanderbilt U., 1972; honor grad. Officers Basic Course, U.S. Army, 1972. Bar: N.C. 1972, U.S. Dist. Ct. (we. dist.) N.C., 1972; cert. specialist in probate and fiduciary law. Assoc. Kennedy, Covington, Lobdell & Hickman, Charlotte, N.C., 1972-75; assoc. Parker, Poe et al, Charlotte, 1975-77, ptnr. 1978—; lectr. on estate planning, probate. Assoc. editor, contbr. Vanderbilt Law Rev., 1971-72. Pres. ECO, Inc., Charlotte, 1982—; bd. dirs. Charlotte United Way, 1983—; mem. planning bd. Queens Coll. Estate Planning Day, 1978—, chmn., 1991; active Myers Park United Meth. Ch., chmn. adminstrv. bd., 1994—; trustee Davidson Coll., 1990-91, Camp Tekoa, Hendersonville, N.C.; mem. YMCA basketball com., Dem. precinct chmn., 1980-86; mem. Dem. state exec. com., 1980; bd. dirs. law explorer program Boy Scouts Am., Charlotte, 1976-78; bd. vis. Johnson C. Smith Univ., 1986-89. 1st lt. U.S. Army, 1972-73. Named Outstanding Vol., Charlotte Observer/United Way, 1984; Patrick Wilson Merit scholar Vanderbilt U. Law Sch., 1969-72. Mem. ABA (real property probate sect.), N.C. State Bar (cert. specialist estate planning and probate, 1987), N.C. Bar Assn. (probate and fiduciary law sect., author, speaker 1987-92), N.C. Bar Assn. Coll. of Advocacy, Mecklenburg County Bar Assn. (law day com., vol. lawyers program, bd. dirs., chmn. 1988-89, grievance com. 1987-88), Deans Assn. of Vanderbilt U. Law Sch. (bd. dirs.), Davidson Coll. Alumni Assn. (bd. dirs. 1983, class alumni sec. 1986—, pres.-elect 1989-90, pres. 1990-91, bd. dirs. Wildcat Club 1989—, pres. 1993—), Charlotte Estate Planning Coun. (exec. com., 1992—, sec. 1994—), Foxcroft Swim and Racquet Club (pres. 1986-87, bd. dirs. 1985-88), Omicron Delta Kappa. Home: 2819 Rothwood Dr Charlotte NC 28211-2623 Office: Parker Poe Thompson 2600 Charlotte Plz Charlotte NC 28244

ORSER, EARL HERBERT, insurance company executive; b. Toronto, Ont., Can., July 5, 1928; s. Frank Herbert and Ethel Marjorie (Cox) O.; m. Marion Queenie Ellis, Aug. 4, 1951; children: Darlene, Barbara, Beverley, Nancy. B in Comm., U. Toronto, 1950, Chartered Acct., 1953. bd. dirs. DMR, Inc., London, Ont.; chmn. bd. dirs. SPAR Aerospace Ltd., Inter-Provincial Pipe Line Ltd. With Clarkson Gordon, 1950-61, ptnr., 1958-61; treas. Anthes Imperial Ltd., 1961-63, v.p. fin., 1963-68, also bd. dirs.; sr. v.p. Molson Industries Ltd., 1968-70, also bd. dirs.; v.p. fin. Air Can., Montreal, Que., 1970-73; with T. Eaton Co. Ltd., Toronto, 1973-77, pres., CEO, 1975-77; exec. v.p., COO London Life Ins. Co. subs. Lonvest Corp., Ont., 1978-80; pres. London Life Ins. Co. subs. London Ins. Group, 1980-81, COO, 1980-81, CEO, 1981-89, chmn. bd. dirs.; Mem. univ. coll. com. U. Toronto, Ont., Can., Geneva Assn., Brit.-N.Am. Com. Mem. London Club (Ont.), Granite Club, St. James' of Montreal Club, Toronto Club, Nat. Toronto Rosedale Golf Club, London Hunt and Country Club. Mem. Can. Life and Health Ins. Assn. (chmn. 1987-88), London Club (Ont.), Granite Club, St. James' of Montreal Club, Toronto Club, Nat. Toronto Rosedale Golf Club, London Hunt and Country Club. Office: London Life Ins Co, 255 Dufferin Ave, London, ON Canada N6A 4K1*

ORSILLO, JAMES EDWARD, computer systems engineer, company executive; b. Elmira, N.Y., Oct. 30, 1939; s. Giacomo and Irene (Heppy) O.; 1 child, June Lynne. BEE, RCA Insts., 1962; BS in Elec. Engring. and Math., Ind. Inst. Tech., 1964; MS, Rensselear Poly., 1968; BS in Nuclear Engring., Capital Radio Electronic Inst., 1974. Communications engr. Bell Telephone Labs., Holmdel, N.J., 1962-63; video engr. Westinghouse, Elmira, N.Y., 1965-66; computer engr. GE, Pittsfield, Mass., 1966-67; systems specialist Control Data Corp., Mpls., 1968-70; software specialist Computer Sci. Corp., Morristown, N.Y., 1970-72; prin. cons. Computer Cons. Assocs., Elmira, 1972-78; pres. ORTHSTAR, Inc., Elmira, 1974—; owner, pres. Shadowstand Properties, Inc. (FKA O-K Properties), Elmira, 1984—, Thundering Hooves Stables, Elmira, 1985—. Mem. IEEE, Am. Nuclear Soc., Soc. Indsl. and Applied Math., Am. Helicopter Soc., Army Aviation Assn. Am., Internat. Flying Engrs., USAF Assn., U.S. Naval League, U.S. Polo Assn. Republican. Achievements include invention of Integrated Data Acquisition System (IDAS), of Thread Algebra used in simulation development, of Extended Sentient Non-linear Ensemble (ESNE). Office: ORTHSTAR Inc PO Box 3430 1864 W Water St Elmira NY 14905-0430

ORSINI, ERIC ANDREW, army official; b. Lodi, N.J., Jan. 7, 1918; s. Serafino and Valentina Lena (Dinino) O.; m. Mildred Jean Andre, Feb. 8, 1947; children: Donna Jean, Debra Jane. BS, GED, Fort Knox, Ky., 1948; student, Def. Sys. Mgmt. Coll., Ft. Belvoir, Va., 1978, Harvard U., 1982, George Washington U., 1986. Registered mech. engr. Commd. 2d lt. armor U.S. Army, 1943, advanced through grades to col., 1965; ret., 1971; appt. dep. asst. sec. for logistics U. S. Army, 1971—. Developer policy guidance mil. identification symbology technologies LOGMARS, 1982; policy developer mil. ordnance/maintenance policies and procedures. Decorated Purple Heart, Silver Star, Bronze Star, Legion of Merit; named to Ordnance Hall of Fame, 1991; recipient Presdl. Meritorious Exec. award, 1991, 94. Avocations: golf, fishing. Office: Office Asst Sec Army Installations Logistics 110 Army The Pentagon Washington DC 20310-0110

ORSINI, MYRNA J., sculptor, educator; b. Spokane, Wash., Apr. 19, 1943; d. William Joseph Finch and Barbara Jean (Hilby) Hickenbottom; m. Donald Wayne Lundquist, Mar. 31, 1962 (div. Mar. 1987); children: Laurie Jeanine Winter, Stephanie Lynne Lundquist. BA, U. Puget Sound, 1969,

MA, 1974; postgrad., U. Ga., 1987. Tchr. Tacoma (Wash.) Pub. Schs., 1969-78; owner, pres. Contemporary Print Collectors, Lakewood, Wash., 1978-81, Orsini Studio, Tacoma, 1985—. Sculptor: works include Vartai symbolic gate for Ctrl. Europas Park, Vilnius, Lithuania, 1994; Menat steel and neon corp. commn. completed in Tacoma, Wash. 1995. Chair Supt.'s Supervisory Com., Tacoma, 1978-79; lobbyist Citizens for Fair Sch. Funding, Seattle, 1979; art chair Women's Pres. Coun., Tacoma, 1987-88; founder, bd. dirs. Monarch Contemporary Art Ctr., Wash. Recipient 1st pl. sculpture award Pleinair Symposium Com., Ukraine, 1992, Peron Symposium Com., Kiev, Ukraine, 1993; recognized 1st Am. sculptor to exhibit work in Ukraine, 1993; prin. works include seven monumental sculptures worldwide. Mem. N.W. Stone Sculptors Assn. (coun. leader 1989—), Pacific Gallery Artists, Internat. Sculpture Ctr., Tacoma City Club. Avocations: reading, sailing, biking. Office: Orsini Studio 4411 N 7th St Tacoma WA 98406-3507

ORSINI, PAUL VINCENT, music educator; b. Albany, N.Y., Oct. 4, 1955; s. Paul Vincent and Lucia (Rutolo) O.; m. Yvette Louise Kirk, Apr. 11, 1987. MusB in Music Edn., SUNY, Potsdam, 1977; MusM in Performance, Syracuse U., 1979. Cert. K-12 music tchr., N.Y. Musician Mirage, 1978-79; entertainer The Carmen Canavo Show, Tampa, Fla., 1979-83; freelance entertainer Albany, N.Y., 1983-86; substitute tchr. Suburban Coun. Schs., Albany, 1983-86; tchr. Corinth (N.Y.) Sch. Dist., 1986-87, Shenendehowa Sch. Dist., Clifton Park, N.Y., 1987—; band leader High Society big band, Clifton Park, 1988-91. Advisor Shenendehowa Crisis Intervention Team, Clifton Park, 1988-93; faculty rep., exec. bd. Friends of Music of Shenendehowa, Clifton Park, 1993; active Shenendehowa Partnership Team, 1995—. Mem. Albany Musicians Assn., Internat. Trumpet Guild, N.Y. State Congress of Parents and Tchrs. (hon. life mem.). Avocations: fishing, sports, travel, reading, jazz. Home: 2 Fenimore Dr Clifton Park NY 12065-7436

ORSZAG, STEVEN ALAN, applied mathematician, educator; b. N.Y.C., Feb. 27, 1943; s. Joseph and Rose (Siegel) O.; m. Reba Karp, June 21, 1964; children—J. Michael, Peter Richard, Jonathan Marc. B.S., M.I.T., 1962; postgrad. (Henry fellow), St. John's Coll., Cambridge (Eng.) U., 1962-63; Ph.D., Princeton U., 1966. Mem. Inst. Advanced Study, Princeton, N.J., 1966-67; prof. applied math. M.I.T., 1967-84; prof. applied and computational math. Princeton U., 1984—, dir., 1990-92, Hamrick prof. engring., 1989—; cons. in field. Author: Studies in Applied Mathematics, 1976, Numerical Analysis of Spectral Methods, 1977, Advanced Mathematical Methods for Scientists and Engineers, 1978; editor: Springer Series in Computational Physics, 1977—, AIP Lecture Series Computational Physics, 1993—, Jour. Sci. Computing, 1986—; numerous research publs. in field. A.P. Sloan Found. fellow, 1970-74, Guggenheim fellow, 1989-90. Fellow Am. Inst. Physics (Otto Laporte award 1991), AIAA (Fluid and Plasmadynamics award, 1986), Soc. Indsl. and Applied Math., Soc. Engring. Sci. (G.I. Taylor medal, 1995). Office: 206 Fluid Dynamics Rsch Ctr Princeton NJ 08544

ORTENBERG, ELISABETH CLAIBORNE See **CLAIBORNE, LIZ**

ORTENZIO, ROBERT A., health/medical products executive. Pres., COO Continetal Med. Systems, Inc., Mechanicsburg, Pa., 17055. Office: Continental Med Systems Inc 600 Wilson Ln PO Box 715 Mechanicsburg PA 17055*

ORTENZIO, ROCCO ANTHONY, health care executive; b. Steelton, Pa., Nov. 28, 1932; s. Rocco and Minnie O.; m. Nancy Miller, Jan. 29, 1955; children—John, Robert, Martin. B.S., West Chester U., 1955; postgrad. in phys. therapy U. Pa., 1955-56. Pvt. practice phys. therapy, Harrisburg, Pa., 1957-69; founder, pres., chief exec. officer Rehab. Corp., Harrisburg, 1969-77, Pa. Health Corp., Mechanicsburg, 1977-79, Rehab. Hosp. Service Corp., Mechanicsburg and Camp Hill, Pa., 1979-85; pres. chief exec. officer Continental Med. Systems, Inc., Mechanicsburg, 1986—; bd. dirs. Continental Med. Systems, Inc., PNC, N.A., AMSCO Internat., Quorum Health Group, Inc. Mem. World Pres.'s Orgn. Republican. Roman Catholic. Home: 3428 Lisburn Rd Mechanicsburg PA 17055-6714 Office: Continental Med Systems Inc PO Box 715 Mechanicsburg PA 17055-0715

ORTH, DAVID NELSON, physician, educator; b. East Orange, N.J., Mar. 5, 1933; s. John Joseph and Marjorie Adelaide (Wauters) O.; m. Linda Diana D'Errico, June 9, 1979; children by previous marriage: John Randall (dec.), Jennifer Stewart, Julie Thomas. Sc.B. in Chemistry, Brown U., 1954; M.D., Vanderbilt U., 1962. Intern, Osler med. service Johns Hopkins Hosp., Balt., 1962-63; fellow in medicine Johns Hopkins Hosp., 1962-65; asst. resident John Hopkins Hosp., 1963-65; mem. faculty dept. medicine Vanderbilt U. Sch. Medicine, Nashville, 1965—; prof. Vanderbilt U. Sch. Medicine, 1975—, joint dir. endocrinology div. dept. medicine, 1968-81, dir. cancer research and treatment ctr., 1972-77, dir. div. endocrinology, 1984—; scholar-in-residence Rockefeller Found. Bellagio (Italy) Study and Conf. Ctr., 1989; vis. scientist Vollum Inst. for Advanced Biomed. Rsch., Oreg. Health Scis. U., Portland, 1993-94. Contbr. numerous articles in field of endocrinology to med. jours. Served with U.S. Navy, 1954-57. John and Mary R. Markle scholar, 1968-73; Howard Hughes Med. Inst. investigator, 1969-75. Mem. AAUP, AAAS, ACP, Assn. Am. Physicians, Am. Soc. Clin. Investigation, Endocrine Soc. (sec.-treas. 1989-94), N.Y. Acad. Scis., Am. Fedn. Clin. Rsch., So. Soc. Clin. Investigation. Office: Vanderbilt U Med Ctr North 715 A MRB II Nashville TN 37232-6303

ORTH-AIKMUS, GAIL MARIE, police chief; b. Kansas City, Dec. 31, 1956; d. Ben Roy and Janet Ferrell (Buckner) O.; m. Frank Henry Aikmus Jr., Oct. 5, 1980 (div. Oct. 1990); 1 child, Brian Russell. Cert. law enforcement officer, Mo.; cert. drug canine handler; cert. vanner. Patrol officer Parkville (Mo.) Police Dept., 1977-78; deputy Platte County Sheriff, Platte City, Mo., 1978-79; patrol officer, sgt., lt. Pleasant Valley (Mo.) Police Dept., 1979-85, police chief, 1985-95; police chief Avondale (Mo) Police Dept., 1995-96; dep. sheriff Clay County Police Dept., Liberty, Mo., 1996—; bd. dirs. Clay County Investigative, pres. bd. dirs., 1991-93; guest spkr. Clay County Mcpl. Judges Conf.; testified before House Com. with Mo. Ho. of Reps., 1994. Appeared in fraud investigation on ABC 20/20 mag., 1980. Named Officer of Yr. Vets. Fgn. Wars Aux., Kansas City, 1991; recipient Key to Manor Pleasant Valley Manor, 1990, Puppy Trucker award Heart of Am. Van Club, 1994, Lifesaving award ribbon, 1996, Unit citation ribbon, 1996. Mem. Mo. Police Chief's Assn., Mo. Peace Officer's Assn., Kansas City Police Chief's Assn., Kansas City Major Case Squad, Kansas City Women in Law Enforcement, Nat. Assn. Chief's of Police, NRA, Weimaraner Club Am., Weimaraner Club Greater Kansas City (pres. 1991—), World Wide Race Fans. Avocations: hunting, dog training, dogs shows, camping, crafts. Home: 8405 Kaill Rd Pleasant Vly MO 64068-9007 Office: Clay County Sheriffs Liberty MO 64068

ORTHWEIN, WILLIAM COE, mechanical engineer; b. Toledo, Jan. 27, 1924; s. William Edward and Millie Minerva (Coe) O.; m. Helen Virginia Poindexter, Feb. 1, 1948; children—Karla Frances, Adele Diana, Maria Theresa. B.S., M.I.T., 1946; M.S., U. Mich., 1951, Ph.D., 1959. Registered profl. engr., Ill., Ind., Ky. Aerophysicist Gen. Dynamics Co., Ft. Worth, 1951-52; research asso. U. Mich., 1952-59; adv. engr. IBM Corp., Owego, N.Y., 1959-61; dir. computer centers U. Okla., Norman, 1961-63; research scientist Ames Lab., NASA, Moffett Field, Calif., 1963-65; mem. faculty So. Ill. U., Carbondale, 1965—; prof. engring. So. Ill. U., 1967—; cons. in field. Author: Clutches and Brakes, 1986, Machine Component Design, 1990; papers, revs., books in field. Pres. Jackson County (Ill.) Taxpayers Assn., 1976. Served with AUS, 1943-46. Mem. ASME (Outstanding Svc. award 1972), Am. Gear Mfrs. Assn., Am. Acad. Mechanis, Soc. Automotive Engrs., Ill. Acad. Sci., Ill. Soc. Profl. Engrs. (chmn. salary and employment com. 1974, chmn. ad hoc com. continuing edn. 1975), NRA, Aircraft Owners and Pilots Assn., Sigma Xi. Mem. LDS Ch. Home: 879 Springer Ridge Rd Carbondale IL 62901 Office: So Ill U Dept Engring Carbondale IL 62901 *Success in engineering is, I believe, contingent upon one's ability to see the world as it really is, to quickly gain insight enough to detect fundamental parameters that determine behavior of the system, to conduct a straightforward check of one's analysis, and to simply synthesize a means of modifying and/or controlling the parameters to obtain the desired results. These ingredients apply to both physical mechanisms and to human organizations—only the means of implementation differ.*

ORTINO, HECTOR RUBEN, chemical company executive; b. Buenos Aires, July 23, 1942; came to U.S., 1983; s. Miguel and Maria Julia (Moauro) O.; m. Beatriz Monica Mayantz, Dec. 14, 1972; children: Nicolas Martin, Gabriela Andrea. B in Acctg. and Adminstrn., Buenos Aires U., 1971. Mng. dir. Ferro Argentina, Buenos Aires, 1976-81, also bd. dirs.; mng. dir. Ferro Mexicana, Mexico City, 1982-83, also bd. dirs.; asst. to v.p. fin. Ferro Corp., Cleve., 1983-84, v.p. fin., 1984—, chief fin. officer, 1987-93, exec. v.p., chief fin.-adminstrv. officer, 1993—. Mem. Fin. Exec. Inst. Roman Catholic. Clubs: Cleve. Skating, Cleve. Athletic. Avocations: tennis, swimming, hunting. Home: 32100 Meadow Lark Way Pepper Pike OH 44124-5523 Office: Ferro Corp 1000 Lakeside Ave E Cleveland OH 44114-1117*

ORTIQUE, REVIUS OLIVER, JR., city official; b. New Orleans, June 14, 1924; s. Revius Oliver and Lillie Edith (Long) O.; m. Miriam Marie Victorianne, Dec. 29, 1947; children—Rhesa Marie (Mrs. Alden J. McDonald). AB, Dillard U., 1947; MA, Ind. U., 1949; JD, So. U., 1956; LLD (hon.), Campbell Coll., 1960; LHD (hon.), Ithaca Coll., 1971; LLD (hon.), Ind. U., 1983, Morris Brown Coll., 1992, Loyola U. South, 1993. Bar: La. 1956, U.S. Dist. Ct 1956, Eastern Dist. La 1956, U.S. Fifth Circuit Ct. of Appeals 1956, U.S. Supreme Ct 1956. Practiced in New Orleans, 1956-79; judge Civil Dist. Ct. for Orleans Parish, 1979-92; assoc. justice La. Supreme Ct., 1993-94; chmn. New Orleans Aviation Bd., 1994—; lectr. labor law Dillard U., 1950-52, U. West Indies, 1986-94; formerly assoc. gen. counsel Cmty. Improvement Agy.; gen. counsel 8th Dist. A.M.E. Ch.; mem. Fed. Hosp. Coun., 1966, Pres.'s Commn. on Campus Unrest, 1970, Bd. Legal Svcs. Corp., 1975-83; chief judge civil cts. Orleans Parish, 1986-87; spkr. in field. Contbr. articles to profl. jours. Former pres. Met. Area Com.; former mem. Bd. City Trusts, New Orleans, New Orleans Legal Assistance Corp. Bd., Ad Hoc Com. for Devel. of Ctrl. Bus. Dist. City of New Orleans; bd. dirs. Cmty. Rels. Coun., Am. Lung Assn.; trustee Antioch Coll. Law, New Orleans chpt. Operation PUSH, 1981—; pres. Louis A. Martinet Soc., 1959; active World's Fair, New Orleans, 1984, Civil Rights Movement, 1960-79; bd. dirs., mem. exec. com. Nat. Sr. Citizens Law Ctr., L.A., 1970-76, Criminal Justice Coordinating Com., UN Assn. New Orleans, 1980—; former mem. exec. bd. Nat. Bar Found.; mem. exec. com. econ. Devel. Coun. Greater New Orleans; past chmn. Health Edn. Authority of La.; trustee, mem. exec. com. Dillard U.; former mem. bd. mgmt. Flint Goodridge Hosp.; mem. adv. bd. League Women Voters Greater New Orleans; mem. men's adv. bd. YWCA; trustee AME Ch., aldo connectional trustee; chancellor N.O. Fedn. Chs.; bd. dirs. Nat. Legal Aid and Defender Assn.; bd. trustees Civil Justice Found.; served on over 50 bds., commns. 1st lt. AUS, 1943-47, PTO. Recipient Arthur von Briesen medal Disting. Svcs. Disadvantaged Ams. NLADA, 1971, Weiss award NCCJ, 1975, Brotherhood award NCCJ, 1976, Nat. Black Achievement award, 1979, Poor People's Banner award, 1979, William H. Hastie award, 1983, Outstanding Citizen award Kiwanis of Pontchartrain, 1986, Civil Justice award, 1989, Daniel E. Byrd award NAACP, 1991, A.P. Tureaud Meml. medal La. State NAACP, 1993; Revius O. Ortique Jr. Law Libr. named in his honor, Lafayette, La., 1988; named Outstanding Young Man Nat. Urban League, 1958, Outstanding Person in La. Inst. Human Understanding, 1976, Citizen of Yr. Shreveport, 1993. Mem. ABA (del., Legal Svcs. program, Nat. adv. coun., 1964-71, jud. divsn.), Nat. Bar Assn. (pres. 1965-66, exec. bd., Raymond Pace Alexander award, jud. coun. 1987, William Hastie award 1982, Gertrude E. Rush award 1991), La. State Bar Assn. (former mem. ho. of dels., Lifetime Achievement award 1986), Nat. Legal Aid and Defender Assn. (past pres., mem. exec. bd.), La. District Judges Assn., Am. Judicature Soc. (bd. dirs. 1975-79), Civil Justice Found. (trustee), Louis A. Martinet Legal Soc., World Peace Through Law (charter mem.), Blue Key Honor Soc., Phi Delta Kappa, Alpha Kappa Delta. Home: 10 Park Island Dr New Orleans LA 70122-1229 Office: New Orleans Aviation Bd PO Box 20007 New Orleans LA 70141-0007 *In 1989 the National Black Law Journal in cooperation with the UCLA Law Center published: Struggle: A Power Reserved to the People, which was distributed nationwide in commemoration of Black History month, the State of Louisiana thru the office of the Secretary of State has permanently installed a life size portrait of Justice Ortique in the gallery of the State Archives the Law Day Celebration on college campuses, 1992. "With little or no effort on our part, life unfolds with opportunities and rewards, except that we permit our frailties to enslave our ambitions. I am grateful that there are only horizons."*

ORTIZ, ANGEL VICENTE, church administrator; b. L.A., Nov. 9, 1956; s. Benjamin and Petra (Santiago) O.; m. Michele Annette Gaunt, May 5, 1979; children: Angela Nicole, Michael David. BS in Bibl. Studies, Ft. Wayne (Ind.) Bible Coll., 1982. Ordained to ministry Christian and Missionary Alliance, 1987. Pastor, ch. planter Christian and Missionary Alliance, Chula Vista, Calif., 1983-90; supt. Spanish western dist. Christian and Missionary Alliance, Escondido, Calif., 1991—, also nat. conf. speaker, evangelist. Republican. Avocations: camping, woodworking, refinishing, travel, teaching. Home: 334 Springtree Pl Escondido CA 92026-1417

ORTIZ, BEVERLY RUTH, ethnographic consultant; b. L.A., Feb. 5, 1956; d. Joseph Antonio and Beverly Rae (Miller) O. BS, U. Calif., Davis, 1974; postgrad. U. Calif., Berkeley, 1993—. Dist. historian Plumas Nat. Forest, Greenville, Calif., 1976; park technician Yosemite Nat. Park, Wawona, Calif., summers 1978-81; naturalist Bay Regional Park Dist., Oakland, Calif., 1980—; ethnographic cons. Walnut Creek, Calif., 1986—; cons. Mount Diablo State Park, Walnut Creek, 1990-93, Healdsburg (Calif.) Mus., 1989, Sonoma State U. Acad. Found., Inc., Calif., 1993-95. Author: It Will Live Forever, 1991; contbr. articles to profl. jours. Pres., bd. mem. Miwok Archeol. Preserve of Marin, 1985-89; chair, commr. Walnut Creek Park and Recreation Commn., 1988-92; founder, bd. dirs., pres. Friends of Creeks in Urban Settings, Walnut Creek, 1984—; mem. adv. com. Oyate, Berkeley, 1990—; mem. Citizens Task Force on Creeks Restoration and Trails Master Plan, 1992-93, Contra Costa County Urban Creeks Task Force, 1986-88, Drainage Area 46 Task Force, 1986-87, Walnut Creek in the Yr. 2000 Subcom. on Open Space and Recreation, 1986. Recipient Cert. of Achievement and Profl. Merit East Bay Regional Parks, 1988. Mem. Phi Kappa Phi. Avocations: writing, hiking, basketry. Address: Coyote Hills Regional Park 8000 Patterson Ranch Rd Fremont CA 94555-3502

ORTIZ, DANIEL ROY, law educator; b. Pitts., Aug. 29, 1956; s. Daniel S. and Retha Lois (Vinson) O. BA, Yale U., 1978, JD, 1983; MPhil, Oxford (England) U., 1980. Bar: Va. 1988. Asst. prof. sch. law U. Va., Charlottesville, 1985-90, prof., 1990—; vis. prof. law ctr. U. So. Calif., L.A., 1991, 94-96. Office: U Va Sch Law 580 Massie Rd Charlottesville VA 22903-1738

ORTIZ, FRANCIS VINCENT, JR., retired ambassador; b. Santa Fe, Mar. 14, 1926; s. Francis Vincent and Margaret Mary (Delgado) O.; m. Dolores Duke, May 2, 1953; children: Christina, Francis, Stephen, James. BS, Georgetown U., 1950, postgrad., 1951-53; postgrad., U. Madrid, Spain, 1950, Am. U. Beirut, Lebanon, 1952; MS, George Washington U., 1967; LLD (hon.), U. N.Mex., 1986. Joined U.S. Fgn. Service, 1951; asst. officer charge Egyptian affairs State Dept., 1951-53; 3d sec. embassy Addis Ababa, Ethiopia, 1953-55; 2d sec. Am. embassy, Mexico City, 1955-57; spl. asst. to ops. coordinator Office Undersec. State, 1957-60, staff asst. to asst. sec. interam. affairs, 1960-61; spl. asst. Am. ambassador to Mexico, 1961-63; officer charge Spanish affairs State Dept., 1963-66; assigned Nat. War Coll., 1966; chief polit. sect. Am. embassy, Lima, Peru, 1967-70; dep. chief of mission Am. embassy, Montevideo, Uruguay, 1970-72; charge' d'affairs Am. embassy, 1973; country dir. for Argentina, Uruguay and Paraguay, 1973-75; dep. exec. sec. Dept. State, 1973-77; ambassador to Barbados and Grenada, spl. rep. to Antigua, Dominica, St. Christopher-Nevis-Anguilla, St. Lucia & St. Vin, 1977-79; U.S. ambassador to Guatemala, 1979-80; spl. advisor for polit. affairs U.S. So. Command, Panama, 1980-81; U.S. ambassador to Peru, 1981-83, to Argentina, 1983-86; diplomat-in-residence U. N.Mex., Santa Fe, 1986-88; spl. asst. to under sec. of state for mgmt., 1988-90, ret., 1990. With USAAF, 1944-46. Decorated Air medal; Knight of Malta; recipient Honor award Dept. State, 1952, Superior Service award, 1964, Unit Superior Service award, 1973, Meritorious Civilian Svc. award U.S. Sec. of Def. 1981; Orden del Quetzal (Guatemala), 1980; Gran Cruz Merito Civil award (Spain), 1980; Gran Cruz Orden de Mayo (Argentina), 1991; U.S., Mexican Presdl. Chamizal Commemorative medals, 1964. Mem. Am. Fgn. Service Assn., Sigma Chi. Roman Catholic.

ORTIZ, KATHLEEN LUCILLE, travel consultant; b. Las Vegas, N.Mex., Feb. 8, 1942; d. Arthur L. and Anna (Lopez) O. BA, Loretto Hghts. Coll., 1963; MA, Georgetown U., 1966; cert. tchg., Highlands U., 1980; cert. travel, ABQ Travel Sch., 1984. Mgr. Montezuma Sq., Las Vegas, 1966-70; office mgr. Arts Food Market, Las Vegas, 1971-75; tchr. Robertson H.S., Las Vegas, 1976-80; registered rep. IDS Fin. Svcs., N.Mex., 1980-84; travel cons. VIP Travel & Tours, Albuquerque, 1985-86, New Horizons Travel, Albuquerque, 1986-87, All World Travel, Albuquerque, 1987-90, Premium Travel Svcs., Albuquerque, 1990-91; travel cons., group tours Going Places Travel, Albuquerque, 1991—. Contbr. 100 articles to newspapers. Founding mem. Citizens Com. for Hist. Preservation, Las Vegas, 1977-79; fund raiser St. Anthony's Hosp., Las Vegas, 1969-75. Mem. LWV (numerous positions), Internat. Airlines Travel Agent Network, Airlines Reporting Corp. Agent, Georgetown Club of N.Mex. (bd. dirs. at large 1991-94). Avocations: tennis, langs., photography, writing. Home: 7600 Adele Pl NE Albuquerque NM 87109-5362 Office: Going Places Travel 6400 Uptown Blvd NE Ste 429E Albuquerque NM 87110-4203

ORTIZ, PAULINA PATRICIA, banker, research analyst; b. Panama City, Panama; came to U.S., 1964; d. Felix Alejandro Córdova and Esther (Burke) Blackburn; m. Philip Ortiz (dec. 1985); 1 child, Vanessa D. Grad. in bus. adminstrn., Excelsior Coll., Jamaica, 1962; student, Staten Island C.C., 1977-80, Bklyn. Coll., 1994, Pace U., 1980-85. Cert. data processor and computer programmer. Sec. Dr. Carlos Ibanez, Balboa, Panama, 1964; claims examiner Associated Hosp. Svcs. Greater N.Y., N.Y.C., 1965-66; comptometer operator Lerner Shops Exec. Office, N.Y.C., 1966-69; interect clk. examiner Citibank, N.A., N.Y.C., 1969-70, investigator, corr. clk., 1970-72, claims examiner, 1973, svc. asst., 1973-76, ombudsperson, 1976-79, counselor, 1979-84, customer svc. rep. for S.Am. and Carribean, 1984-86, rsch. investigator, 1986-93, rsch. analyst, 1993—. Former mem. East Bklyn. Chs. for devel. of Nehemiah Housing Project, 1984; mem. fin. com. Our Lady of Charity, former mem. alter guild, mem. ushers com., bd. trustees, sec. parish coun. on fund raiser com., v.p. and pres. Pastor's Aid Soc., 1986; campaign worker Howard Golden for Bklyn. Borough Pres., Congressman Adolphus Towns, 1986, Dist. Leader DaCosta Headley, 1994, Assemblyman Ed Griffith, 1988; candidate Sch. Bd. Dist. # 19, 1989; chairperson Linden Plz. Leaseholders, 1990-92; co-writer bylaws New Linden Plz. Tenants Assn., 1991-92, active, 1992—; charter mem. Day of Independence Com. of Panamanians in N.Y., 1993—; counselor St. Paul's Ch., 1994; active Divino Niño Jesus, 1994. Recipient Appreciation cert. as charter mem. Dem. Sen. task force Dem. Senatorial Campaign Com., 1994, Appreciation cert. Pres. Bill Clinton for support of Dem. Nat. Com., 1994, Outstanding Cmty. Svc. award Sen. Ada L. Smith, 1994, Third Degree, Grand Lady Carmela Rodriguez, 1993, Merit cert. Fourth Degree Georgiana Evans, Faithful Navigator, Ladies of Grace, 1993, Women's History Month Spl. Recognition award Congressman Adolphus Towns, 1989, Mother of Yr. award Jr. Daus. Ct. 229, 1990, Partner in Edn. award Adopt-a-Class Program N.Y. Bd. Edn., 1992-93, Hon. Trustee cert. Am. Indian Relief Coun., 1994, Citizenship cert. Boys Town, 1994, Silver Leader of Yr. cert. DAV Comdrs. Club, 1994. Mem. Urban Bankers Coalition, Knights of Peter Claver & Ladies' Aux. Ct. (vice grand lady of ct. 229 in Bklyn. 1984, grand lady of ct. 229 in Bklyn. 1985, 86, 87, co-founder chpt. 33, established ct. 333 in Queens, N.Y., area dep. N.Y.C.). Avocations: dancing, cooking, mentoring, opera.

ORTIZ, RAPHAEL MONTAÑEZ, performance artist, educator; b. Bklyn., Jan. 30, 1934; s. Joseph H. and Eusabia (Velazquez) O. BS, Pratt Inst., 1964, MFA, 1964; MEd, Columbia U., 1974, EdD, 1982. Instr. grad. art faculty Tchr. Coll. Columbia U., N.Y.C., 1967; instr. art NYU, N.Y.C., 1968; adj. prof. art Fordham U., N.Y.C., 1971, C. W. Post Coll., L.I., N.Y., 1971; adj. prof. art Livingston Coll. Rutgers U., New Brunswick, N.J., 1971, assoc. prof. art Livingston Coll., 1972; assoc. prof. grad. and undergrad. faculty Mason Gross Sch. Arts Rutgers U., 1972, prof. I Mason Gross Sch. Arts, 1991—; lectr., panelist Sch. of Visual Arts 4th Ann. Nat. Conf. on Edn. of Artist, 1990, Internat. Exposition: Art Miami Art and Tech., 1995; panelist, moderator The Artist in Multiculturalism and Art History, Alternative Mus., Soho, N.Y.C., 1992, numerous others; The Robert Flaherty seminar spkr. Its All Digital, Wells Coll., Aurora, N.Y., 1993, The Mus. of Modern Art panelist the Artist as Activist, 1993, Cleve. Ctr. for Contemporary Art panelist: Performance is Dead Long Live Performance, 1994; presenter in field. Numerous one-man performances including Piano Destruction concert, BBC, London, 1966, Mother Father, Mercury Theater, London, 1966, Paper Bag and Piano Destruction concert, Fordham U., N.Y.C., 1967, Ecce Homo Gallery, N.Y.C., 1967, Piano Destruction concert, Bitter End Cafe, N.Y.C., 1967, Piano Destruction concert, Johnny Carson Show, 1968, Riverside Ch., N.Y.C., 1968, Theater Ritual, Middle Atlantic States regional meeting Am. Theater Assn., Temple U., Phila., 1970, Crossing, Mime Theater, N.Y.C., 1976, physio-psycho-alchemy San Francisco Art Inst., 1982, UCLA, 1985, Twin Palms Gallery, San Francisco, 1985, Museo del Barrio, N.Y.C., 1988, Piano Destruction duet Hommage to Huelsenback, Conz Archival Gallery, Verona, Italy, 1986, Atelier Sommering, Ko, 1990, Antiteatro U. P.R., Cleve. Ctr. Contemporary Art Performance-Installation, 1994, Snug Harbor Cultural Ctr., Performance-Installation, S.I., N.Y., 1995; co-exec. dir. and participant in Art and the Invisible Reality Internat. Symposium, Munich, 1988; organizer, participant Internat. Symposium of Art and the Invisible-Reality, U.S.A., Franklin-Furnace Mus., N.Y.C., Rutgers U., New Brunswick, N.J., 1989, Vision Quest Gallery Rem, Vienna, Austria, 1988, Vision Quest II Bloomfield Coll., N.J., 1989, Piano Destruction concert Hommage to Huelsenback, Soul Release project, Alternative Mus., N.Y.C., 1989, Exhbn. Kölnischer Kunstverein, Köln, computer-laser-video, Köln, Fed. Republic Germany, Soul Release-Ritual Kunst Müller Köln, 1989, Soul Release project Piano Sacrifice concert, Atelier Eva Ohlaw Bildskulpturenaktionmusik, Köln, 1990, Decade Show Dance Theater Workshop, N.Y.C., performance-ritual sponsored by the New Mus., N.Y.C., The Mus. of Contemporary Hispanic Art, N.Y.C., The Harlem Mus. of Contemporary Art, N.Y.C., 1990, Alternative Mus., Soho, N.Y.C., 1992, Mus. Modernerkunst, Stiftung Ludwig, 1992, performance-installation, Vienna, 1992, I.S.D.N. Video Conf. interactive audience participation between Kôlin and Kassel Germany, The Electronic Cafe Gallery at Documenta, Kassel, 1993, Grand Prix, Regime Lomabdia, Prix Lago Maggiore XIV Festival Internat. de la video et des arts electroniques, Dance Number 22, computer-laser-video, Locarno, Switzerland, 1993, Cleve. Ctr. Contemporary Art, 1994, Museo del Barrio, N.Y.C., 1994, Whitney Biennial: Whitney Mus. of Am. Art, N.Y.C., 1995; one-person sculpture exhbn. Fordham U., N.Y.C., 1967, Museo del Barrio, N.Y.C., 1988, Francesco Conz Archival Gallery, Verona, Italy, 1986, DiMaggio Mus., Milan, Italy, 1989, Ateliér Sommering, Kô, 1990, (sculpture with text) Galerie David, Bielefeld, Germany, 1992, works Children of Treblinka in Memorium, Archaological Find No. 3, Estacion Plaza de Armas, Seville, Spain, 1992, Kunsthalle, Kôlin, 1993, Mus. Modern Art, N.Y.C., 1993, Johnson Mus. at Cornell U., Ithaca, N.Y., 1993, Whitney Mus. Am. Art, N.Y.C., 1993; group shows include Whitney Mus. Am. Art, N.Y.C., 1965, 95, The Object Transformed, sculpture, Mus. Modern Art, N.Y.C., 1966, Franklin Furnace Mus., N.Y.C.; participated in Internat. Destruction in Art Symposium, London, 1966, Finch Coll. Mus. Art Destruction in Art Symposium Sculpture, 1968, sculpture, Everson Mus. Art, Syracuse, N.Y., 1973, sculpture, Chgo. Mus. Comtemporary Art, 1979, Ancient Roots New Visions, sculpture, Palacio de Mineria Mus., Mexico City, 1980, Rutgers Computer Art Group, Walters Gallery, Rutgers U., 1982, computer animation, Paul Robeson Gallery, Rutgers U., 1983, computer art, The Salem Syndrome, Tamasulo Gallery, N.J., 1985, computer graphics and sound, computer-laser-video, Bonnefanten Mus., Maastricht, Holland, 1986, computer-laser-video, De-Haag, Fed. Republic Germany, 1986, computer-laser-video Bridge Game, Mülheim Mus., Fed. Republic Germany, 1986, computer-laser-video, Berlin Internat. Video and Film Festival, Coll. of Art, Gwent, Wales, Eng., 1986, 87, computer-laser-video Techno-Bop 87, The Kitchen, N.Y.C., El Museo del Barrio, 1995; numerous one-man exhbns. including Rene Gallery Video Installation, Music Reconstruction, Amsterdam, Holland, 1988, computer-laser-video, Museo del Barrio, N.Y.C, 1988, Infermental 9, Internat., Video Mag., Dance No. 6, 1989, computer-laser-video, Barcelona Biennale, Spain, 1989, Beograd, Yugoslavia, 1989, Kriens Videodrom, Switzerland, 1989, computer-laser-video, Vienna, Austria, 1990, computer-laser-video, The Internat. Berlin Video and Film Festival, Berlin, 1990, computer-laser-video, Leningrad, Riga-Cine Fantom, USSR, 1990, Video Presentation Series I and II Median Werk Statt, Vienna, 1991, computer-laser-video, Stadtisches Kunstmus., Bonn, 1990, Median Operative, Juried Internat. Video Festival, Berlin, 1992, 6th Juried Internat. Video and TV Festival Montbeliard, France, 1992, Videonale 5 Juried Internat. Video Festival, Bonn, 1993, Video Arco 93 Juried Internat. Video Festival, Madrid, 1993, Mus. Modern Art, Video

Works of Latin Am. Artists, Filmreferet Forum Stadpark, Graz, Austria, 1994, Berlin Internat. Film and Video Festival, 1994, Associazione Italiana Cinema d'Essai, 1995, Cinema Video Bienniale, De Lyon, France, 1996, Video Installation Performance, Trinity Video/Inter Access/V-Tape, Toronto, Canada, 1996; represented in mus. collections: sculpture Mattress de-structed by the artist, Mus. Modern Art, 1963, sculpture Disassembled Sofa, Whitney Mus. Am. Art, 1964, sculpture Shoe Construct-Destruct, Memorial to Buchenwald Holocaust Victims, Menil Mus., Houston, 1965, sculpture Disassembled Upholstered Chair, Chrysler Mus., Va., 1965, sculpture Disassembled Sofa, Everson Mus., Syracuse, N.Y., 1972, sculpture Feather Pyramids Museo del Barrio, 1982, computer-laser-video, Museo del Barrio, 1985, computer-laser-video, Everson Mus., Syracuse, N.Y., 1985, computer-laser-video, Friedricheshof Mus., Zurndorf, Austria, 1986, computer-laser-video, Mus. Modern Art, Brussels, 1987, Piano Destruction Fragments, Museo del Barrio, N.Y.C., 1988, Ludwig Mus., Cologne, Fed. Republic Germany, 1988, Centre Georges Pompidou, Paris, 1989, Stadishces Kunst Mus., Bonn, Germany, 1990, Neuer Belriner Kunstverein, Berlin, 1994. Recipient Cert. of Outstanding Achievement in Multicultural Edn., N.J. Dept. Higher Edn., 1993. Mem. Mus. Computer Art (founder, pres. 1984), Hispanic Assn. Higher Edn. (N.J.), Art Educators N.J., Coll. Art Assn., Assn. Rsch. and Enlightenment. Office: Mason Gross Sch Vis Arts New St & Livingston Ave New Brunswick NJ 08904

ORTIZ, SOLOMON P., congressman; b. Robstown, Tex., June 3, 1937; children: Yvette, Solomon P. Student, Del Mar Coll., Corpus Christi, Tex.; cert., Inst. Applied Sci., Chgo.; student, Nat. Sheriff's Tng. Inst., Los Angeles. Constable Neuces County, Tex., 1965-68, commr., 1969-76, sheriff, 1977-82; mem. 98th-104th Congresses from 27th Tex. dist., Washington, D.C., 1983—; mem. armed svcs. com., military installations and facilities subcom., readiness subcom., mcht. marine and fisheries com., subcoms.-environ. & natural resources, oceanography, Gulf of Mex., outer continental shelf, mcht. marine. Served with U.S. Army, 1960-62. Named Man of Yr., Internat. Order Foresters, 1981. Mem. Nat. Sheriff's Assn., Sheriff's Assn. Tex. Office: US Ho Reps 2136 Rayburn Bldg Washington DC 20515-0005*

ORTIZ-BUTTON, OLGA, social worker; b. Chgo., July 12, 1953; d. Luis Antonio and Pura (Acevedo) Ortiz; m. Dennis Vesley, Aug. 11, 1973 (div. 1976); m. Randall Russell Button, Nov. 3, 1984 (div. Oct. 1993); children: Joshua, Jordan, Elijah. BA, U. Ill., 1975; MSW, Western Mich. U., 1981. Cert. social worker, sch. social worker. Social svcs. dir. Champaign County Nursing Home, Urbana, Ill., 1976; social svcs. and activity dir. Lawton (Mich.) Nursing Home, 1977; job developer Southwestern Mich. Indian Ctr., Watervliet, 1977-78; staff asst. New Directions Alcohol Treatment Ctr., Kalamazoo, 1978; counselor, instr. Alcohol Hwy. Safety, Kalamazoo, 1978-79; clin. social worker Mecosta County Community Mental Health, Big Rapids, Mich., 1981-84; program dir. substance abuse Sr. Svcs., Inc., Kalamazoo, 1984-85; sch. social worker Martin (Mich.) Pub. Schs., 1985-96; owner, therapist Plainwell (Mich.) Counseling Ctr., 1989—; S.W. cons. Med. Pers. Pool, 1993-94, G.L. Network Mktg., 1993—. Vol. social worker Hospice-Wings of Hope, Plainwell, 1984-85, mem. CQI bd., 1993—; supporter Students Against Aparteid South Africa, Kalamazoo, 1979-81; mem. World Vision and Countertop Ptnr., 1984—; sponsor, vol. People for Ethical Treatment of Animals, 1986-91; vol. helper Sparkies for Awana Club Ch., 1989-95; consortium mem. Mich. Post Adoption Svc. System, 1994—. NIMH Rural Mental Health grantee, 1979-81. Mem. NASW, Mich. Assn. Sch. Social Workers, Am. Assn. Christian Counselors. Avocations: jogging, plants, cross country skiing. Office: Plainwell Counseling Ctr 211 E Bannister St Ste K Plainwell MI 49080-1372

ORTLEPP, BRUNO, marine navigation educator, master mariner; b. Nortorf, Germany, Apr. 3, 1935; s. Carl and Emilie (Strambovski) O. 1 mate fgn. going, Fachhochschule Hamburg, 1958; master fgn. going, N.S. Nautical Inst., Halifax, Can., 1976; teacher diploma, N.S. Tchrs. Coll., Truro, 1984. O.s., a.b. various cos., Germany, 1951-56; 3rd officer German East Africa Line, Hamburg, 1958-60; from 2d officer to chief officer to master Irving Oil Ltd., Saint John, N.B., Can., 1960-76; chief officer Sanko Marine, Tokyo, Japan, 1976-81; marine educator, dept. edn. N.S. Nautical Inst., Halifax, 1982-92. Author: Canadian Maritimes Sailing Aids, Vol. I, Tidal Streams for Bay of Fundy, 1965, 89, Vol. II, Tidal Streams for the River St. Lawrence, 1966, Vol. III, Distance Tables, 1966, 88, Vol. IV, Natural Squat, 1983, 89, Vol. V, The Deviascope, 1990; contbr. articles to profl. jours. Mem. AAAS, FIBA, Nautical Inst. London. Home: Friedrichstrasse 19, 99894 Friedrichroda Thuringia, Germany Office: care Capt Walter S Franke, 12 Sycamore Ct, Lower Sackville, NS Canada B4C 1G1

ORTLIEB, ROBERT EUGENE, sculptor; b. San Diego, July 4, 1925; s. William Martin and Ruth Lina (Powers) O.; m. Donna Lynn Forman, Dec. 28, 1976. B.F.A., U. So. Calif., 1950, M.F.A., 1951. Instr. sculpture Riverside (Calif.) Art Center and Mus., 1960-85, Village Ctr. for the Arts, Palm Springs, Calif., 1966-90, U. So. Calif., Idyllwild Arts Found., 1964-76, Palos Verdes Community Arts Assn., 1970—, Instituto Professionale Stato Industria Artigianato, Marmo, Carrara, Italy, 1972; mem. art juries. Sculptor stone, plexiglas, wood, terra cotta, bronze, exhbns. in over 100 museums, galleries, including, Creative Galleries, N.Y.C., Cin. Art Mus., Denver Art Mus., Dallas Mus. Fine Arts, Oakland (Calif.) Art Mus., Santa Barbara (Calif.) Mus. Art, San Diego Fine Arts Gallery, Pasadena (Calif.) Art Mus., Los Angeles County Mus., San Francisco Mus. Art, Palm Springs Desert Mus.; represented in permanent collections, including, Met. Mus., N.Y.C., Achenbach Found. Graphic Arts Calif. Palace Legion Honor, San Francisco, Riverside Art Mus., Laguna Beach Art Mus., U. So. Calif., U. Calif. Riverside, Loma Linda (Calif.) U., Lawson Products, Inc., Chgo., City of Costa Mesa (Calif.) Community Center; represented by Miranda Galleries, Laguna Beach, Calif., Gallery La Jolla, Calif. Recipient numerous awards. Address: 11111 Jerry Ln Garden Grove CA 92640-3320 *To create a totality of expression, sensitivity to dynamics and a comprehensive aliveness is indispensable to the nature of my work. In a broader sense, sculpture is life, disciplined, balancing on a knife edge between the emotional and intellectual forces. Art is like a religion, requiring a spiritual equilibrium from physical to etheric.*

ORTLIP, MARY KRUEGER, artist; b. Scranton, Pa.; d. John A. and Ida Mae (Phillips) Smale; m. Emmanuel Krueger, June, 1940 (dec. Nov. 1979); children: Diane, Keith; m. Paul D. Ortlip, June 26, 1981. Student, New Sch. Social Rsch., N.Y.C., 1957-59, Margarita Madrigal Langs., N.Y.C., Montclair (N.J.) Art Mus. Sch., 1978-79; Nomina Accademico Conferita, Accademia Italia, Italy, 1986; DFA (hon.), Houghton Coll., 1988. Dancer, dance instr. Fleischer Dance Studio, Scranton, Pa., 1934-38. One-woman shows include Curzon Gallery of Boca Raton, Fla. and London, 1986-93, Galerie Les Amis des Arts, Aix-en-Provence, France, 1987; group exhbns.: Salmagundi Club, N.Y.C., 1980, James Hunt Barker Galleries, Nantucket, Mass. and N.Y.C., 1983, Salon Internationale Musée Parc Rochteau à Revin, France, 1985, 90, Accademia Italia, Milan, 1986, many others in Europe and Am.; permanent collections Musée de parc Rocheteau, Revin, France, Pinacothèque Arduinna, Charleville-Meziéres, France. Named Invité d'Honneur, Le Salon des Nations a Retenu L'oeuvre, Paris, 1983, Artist of the Year, La Cote des Arts, France, 1986; recipient La Medaille d'Or, Du 13ème Salon Internationale al du Parc Rocheau au Revin, France, 1985, Medaille d' Honneur Ville de Marseille, France, 1987, Targo D'Oro, Accademia Italia Premio D'Italia, 1986; Trophy Arts Internationale Exposition de Peinture Marseille, Plaquette d' Honneur, Palais des Arts, 1987, Grand Prix Salon de Automne Club Internationale, 1987, Connaissance de Notre Europa Ardennes Eifel, Revin, France, 1990. Mem. Nat. Mus. Women in Arts, Accademia Italia (charter), Instituo D'Art Contemporanea Di Milano, Nat. Soc. Arts and Letters, Gov.'s Club, Salmagundi Club. Home (winter): Apt 703 2917 S Ocean Blvd #703 Highland Bch FL 33487-1876 Home (summer): 588 Summit Ave Hackensack NJ 07601 Office: The Curzon Gallery 501 E Camino Real Boca Raton FL 33432-6127

ORTLIP, PAUL DANIEL, artist; b. Englewood, N.J., May 21, 1926; s. Henry Willard and Aimee (Eschner) O.; m. Mary Louise Krueger, June 1981; children from previous marriage: Carol, Kathleen, Sharon (dec.), Danielle (dec.), Michelle. Diploma, Houghton Acad., 1944; student, Art Students League, 1947-49; diploma, Acad. la Grande Chaumiere, Paris, 1950; DFA (hon.), Houghton Coll., 1988. Tchr. Fairleigh Dickinson U., Teaneck, N.J., 1956-68; artist in residence, curator Fairleigh Dickinson U., Rutherford, N.J., 1968-72; official USN artist on assignment, Cuban missile crisis, Fla., 1963, Gemini 5 Recovery, Atlantic Ocean, 1965, Vietnam, 1967, Apollo 12 recovery, Pacific Ocean, 1969, Apollo 17 recovery, Pacific Ocean, 1972, Internat. Naval Rev., N.Y. harbor, 1976, USCG Sta., Key West, Fla., 1985; mem. USN Art Coop. and Liason Com. Exhbns. include Salonde L'Art Libre, Paris, 1950, Nat. Acad. Design, 1952, Allied Artists of Am., N.Y.C., Acad. Sci., Rundell Gallery, Rochester, N.Y., Monclair Art Mus., Hist. Mus, Lima, Ohio, Butler Art Inst., Youngstown, Ohio, Fine Arts Gallery, San Diego, State Capitol Bldg., Sacramento, Calif., Capitol Mus., Olympia, Wash., Mus. Gt. Plains, Lawton, Okla., Witte Meml. Mus., San Antonio, Nimitz Meml. Mus., Fredericksberg, Tex., Pentagon Collection of Fine Arts, James Hunt Barker Galleries, Palm Beach, Fla., Nantucket, Mass, N.Y.C., Smithsonian Inst., Gallerie Vollem Breuse, Biarritz, France, Galerie Mouffe, Paris, Guggenheim Gallery, London, Wickersham Gallery, N.Y.C., Soc. Illustrators, N.Y.C.; retrospective exhbn. Bergen Community Mus., Paramus, N.J. 1970, The Curzon Gallery, 1987, 88, 89, 93, Ardennes et de l'Eifel, Charleville Mézières, France, June-Sept. 1990; represented permanent collections including Salmagundi Club N.Y.C., Houghton (N.Y.) Coll., Portrait Meml. J.F. Kennedy Library, Fairleigh-Dickinson U., Nat. Air and Space Mus., Smithsonian Inst., Intrepid Sea-Air Space Mus., N.Y.C., Hist. Mural Visitors Ctr., Palisades Interstate Pk., Ft. Lee, N.J., Vets. Med. Ctr., East Orange, N.J., USN Exhbn. Ctr., Washington Navy Yard, Am. Coll. Clin. Pharmacology, N.Y.C., N.J. U. Dentistry & Medicine, Newark, Bergen County Ct. House, Hackensack, N.J., Dickinson Coll., Carlisle, Pa., George Washingtogn Meml Pk., Paramus, N.J., Marietta (Ohio) Coll., Mcpl. Bldg., Ft. Lee, N.J., Navy League U.S., Arlington, Va., Nat. Archives and Records Adminstrn., Washington, (mural) Pub. Libr., Fort Lee, N.J. Served to sgt. U.S. Army, 1944-47, ETO, PTO, 1946-47. Recipient 1st prize Am. Artists Profl. League State Exhibit N.J. chpt., Paramus, 1960, 1st prize U.S. Armed Forces Exhibit Far East, Seoul, Korea, Tokyo, 1946, Franklin Williams award, Salmagundi Club, N.Y., 1967, Outstanding Achievement award for oil painting, USN, 1968, Artist of Yr. award, Hudson Artists, Jersey City (N.J.) Mus., 1970, Statue of Victory World Culture prize, Academia Italia, Parma, 1982, Men of Achievement medal Cambridge, Eng., 1990, Connaissance de Notre Europe Gold medal Charleville-Mézières, France, 1990. Mem. Allied Artists Am. (art coop. and liaison com. with USN), Nat. Soc. Mural Painters, Nat. Soc. Arts and Letters, Bergen County Artists Guild (pres. 1960-62), Am. Portrait Soc., Artists Fellowship, Inc., U.S. Coast Guard Art Program, Art Students League N.Y. (life), Navy League U.S., VFW (life), Am. Legion. Clubs: Salmagundi (N.Y.C.) (art chmn. 1979-81); Gov.'s of the Palm Beaches (Fla.). Home: 2917 S Ocean Blvd # 703 Highland Beach FL 33487-1876 Office: care The Curzon Gallery 501 E Camino Real Boca Raton FL 33432-6127

ORTLOFF, GEORGE CHRISTIAN, SR. (CHRIS ORTLOFF), journalist, state legislator; b. Lake Placid, N.Y., Sept. 20, 1947; s. Carl Jacob and Lillian Grace (Travis) O.; m. Ruth Mary Hart, Jan. 28, 1978; children: George Christian Jr., Jonathan Hart. BS, Rensselaer Poly. Inst., 1969; MA, U. Mich., 1975. Reporter, producer Sta. WUOM-FM, Ann Arbor, Mich., 1973-75; reporter Nat. Pub. Radio, 1973-75, Adirondack Daily Enterprise, Saranac Lake, N.Y., 1976-77, Sta. WNBZ-Am, Saranac Lake, 1975-77; pub. rels. dir. Ctr. for Music, Drama and Art, Lake Placid, 1975-76; pres. Macromedia, Inc., Lake Placid, 1976-82; anchor, mng. editor Sta. WPTZ-TV, Plattsburgh, N.Y., 1981-85; mem. N.Y. State Assembly, Albany, 1986—, ranking minority mem. Legis. Commn. on Sci. and Tech., 1987—, chmn. Rep. program com., 1993—; mem. health care reform task force Am. Legis. Exch. Coun., 1994—. Author: Lake Placid, The Olympic Years: 1932-80, 1976, A Lady in the Lake, 1985; reporter, producer (TV news series) "Special Segment", 1981-85 (N.Y. State Broadcasters Best Series award 1982, 83, 84, 85), (TV documentary) "A Time to Choose", 1985 (N.Y. State Broadcasters Best award 1986). Chief ceremonies 1980 Olympic Winter Games, Lake Placid, 1978-80; field asst. to congressman, David O'B. Martin, Plattsburgh, 1981; chmn. Clinton County Rep. Com., 1995—; committeeman Essex County Rep. Com., 1980-81; trustee Lake Placid Village, 1977-81; lay reader Episcopal Ch., Lake Placid and Plattsburgh, 1976-92. Mem. VFW, AMVETS, Am. Legion, North Country Vietnam Vets. Assn., Elks, Kiwanis (pres. Lake Placid 1980-81). Avocations: skiing, piano, trumpet, painting, woodworking. Home: 23 Morrison Ave Plattsburgh NY 12901-1417 Office: NY State Assembly 450 Legislative Office Bldg Albany NY 12248

ORTMAN, ELDON E., entomologist, educator; b. Marion, S.D., Aug. 11, 1934; s. Emil and Kathryn (Tieszen) O.; m. Margene Adrian, June 27, 1957; children—Karen, Connie, Nancy. A.B., Tabor Coll., 1956; M.S., Kansas State U., 1957, Ph.D., 1963. Research entomologist USDA, No. Grain Insects Research Lab., Brookings, S.D., 1961-68; dir., leader investigations USDA, No. Grain Insects Research Lab., 1968-72; asst. prof. entomology S.D. State U., Brookings, 1961-63; asso. prof. S.D. State U., 1963-68, prof., 1968-72; asst. Entomology Research Div. Office, Beltsville, Md., 1971; prof. entomology Purdue U., West Lafayette, Ind., 1972-89; head dept. entomology Purdue U., 1972-89; assoc. dir. Ind. Agrl. Rsch. Programs, 1989—. Fellow AAAS; mem. Entomol. Soc. Am., Phi Kappa Phi, Gamma Sigma Delta, Sigma Xi. Research in plant resistance to insects and pest mgmt. Home: 3805 Capilano Dr West Lafayette IN 47906-8870 Office: Purdue U Agrl Rsch AGAD West Lafayette IN 47907

ORTMAN, GEORGE EARL, artist; b. Oakland, Calif., Oct. 17, 1926; s. William Thomas and Anna Katherine (Noll) O.; m. Conni Whidden, Aug. 5, 1960 (dec.); 1 stepson, Roger Graham Whidden. Student, Calif. Coll. Arts and Crafts, 1947-49, Atelier Stanley William Hayter, 1949, Acad. Andre L'Hote, Paris, 1949-50, Hans Hoffman Sch. Art, 1949-50. Instr. painting and drawing NYU, 1962-65; co-chmn. fine arts Sch. Visual Arts N.Y.C., 1963-65; artist-in-residence Princeton U., 1966-69, Honolulu Acad. Art, 1969; head painting dept. Cranbrook Acad. Art, Bloomfield Hills, Mich., 1970-92. One-man exhbns. include Tanager Gallery, 1954, Wittenborn Gallery, 1955, Stable Gallery, 1957, 60, Howard Wise Gallery, 1962, 63, 64, 66, 69, Gimpel-Weitzenhoffer Gallery, 1972 (all N.Y.C.), Swetzoff Gallery, Boston, 1961-62, Fairleigh Dickinson U., 1962, Mirvish Gallery, Toronto, Can., 1964, Walker Art Center, Mpls., 1965, Milw. Art Center, 1966, Dallas Mus. Art, 1966, Portland Mus. Art, 1966, Akron Inst. Art, 1966, U. Chgo., 1967, Princeton U. Art Mus., 1967, Honolulu Acad. Art, 1969, Reed Coll., 1970, Cranbrook Acad. Art, 1970, 92, Indpls. Mus. Art, 1971, J.L. Hudson Gallery, Detroit, 1971, Gimpel-Weitzenhoffer, N.Y.C., 1972, 73, Gertrude Kasle Gallery, Detroit, 1976, Lee Hoffman Gallery, Detroit, 1977, Flint (Mich.) Mus. Art, 1977; other one-man exhbns. include Cranbrook Mus. Art, 1982; exhibited numerous group shows including Whitney Mus. Am. Art Annual, 1962, 63, 64, 65, 67, 73, Carnegie Internat., Pitts., 1964, 67, 70, Jewish Mus., N.Y.C., 1964, Corcoran Mus., Washington, 1964, others; represented permanent collections, Walker Art Center, Mpls., Mus. Modern Art, Whitney Mus. Am. Art, (both N.Y.C.), Guggenheim Mus., N.Y.C., Albright-Knox Mus., Buffalo, NYU, Christian Theol. Sem., Indpls., Indpls. Mus. Art, Cleve. Mus. Art, Mus. Am. Art, Washington, Honolulu Acad. Art, Newark Mus. Art, Container Corp. Am., Chgo. Ind. U. Music Bldg., Wausau (Wis.) Hosp. Center, Unitarian Ch., Princeton, Mfr. Hanover Trust Bldg., Albert Kahn & Assos., Detroit, Renaissance Center, Detroit, Mich. State Univ. Performing Arts Ctr., East Lansing, Detroit Inst. Arts. Guggenheim fellow, 1965-66; Ford Found. grantee, 1966; One of five Am. artists selected for 1965 Japanese Bi-ann.; recipient Gov. N.J.'s Purchase award 2d ann. exhbn. art, 1967; Best of Show Religion in Art Exhbn., Birmingham, Ala., 1966. Mem. Nat. Acad. of Design. Office: Tim Hill Gallery 163 Townsend St Birmingham MI 48009-6001

ORTNER, DONALD J., biological anthropologist, educator; b. Stoneham, Mass., Aug. 23, 1938; s. A.W. and Marie B. (Schweizer) O.; m. Joyce E. Walker, April 9, 1960; children: Donald J. Ortner Jr., Allison A. May, Karen L. Ortner. BA, Columbia Union Coll., 1960; MA, Syracuse U., 1967; PhD, U. Kans., 1970; DSc (hon.), U. Bradford, England, 1995. Asst. curator Smithsonian Instn., Washington, 1969-71, assoc. curator, 1971-76, curator, 1976—, chmn. anthropology, 1988-92; acting dir. Nat. Mus. Natural History, Washington, 1994-96; vis. prof. U. Bradford, 1988—; mem. editl. bd. Jour. Paleopathology, 1988—, Internat. Jour. Osteoarch., 1990—. Author: (book) Identification of Pathological Conditions in Human Skeletal Remain, 1981; editor: How Humans Adapt, 1983; co-editor: Human Paleopathology, 1991. Mem. Am. Assn. Phys. Anthropology (mem. exec. com. 1987-90), Internat. Skeletal Soc., Paleopathology Assn. Office: Smithsonian Inst Nat Mus Natural History 10th & Constitution Ave NW Washington DC 20560

ORTNER, EVERETT HOWARD, magazine editor, writer; b. Lowell, Mass., Aug. 25, 1919; s. Herman and Anne (Ehrenhaus) O.; m. Evelyn Francis Gelbman, Jan. 1, 1953. B.A., U. Ark., 1939. Editor Popular Publs., N.Y.C., 1946-52; assoc. editor Popular Sci., N.Y.C., 1953-56, copy chief, 1956-70, group editor, 1970-76, mng. editor, 1976-80, editor, 1980-85. Pres. Brownstone Revival Com. N.Y., 1968-76, chmn., 1986—; founder, pres. Back to the City, Inc., N.Y.C., 1974-83, chmn. bd., 1983—; v.p. L.I. Hist. Soc., Bklyn., 1979-83. Lt. U.S. Army, 1942-46, ETO. Recipient Cinderella award Bklyn. Union Gas Co., 1978, Honor citation Borough Pres. Bklyn., 1983, Disting. Citizen award City Louisville, 1979, Quality of Life award Kings County Hosp. Ctr., Bklyn., 1976, Spirit of Life award N.Y. Congl. Home, 1994. Mem. Overseas Press Club, Montauk Club, Ft. Hamilton Officers Club.

ORTOLANO, LEONARD, civil engineering educator, water resources planner; b. Bklyn., Sept. 26, 1941; s. Salvatore Thomas and Anna (Salerno) O. B.S. in Civil Engring., Poly. Inst. Bklyn., 1963; M.S. in Engring., Harvard U., 1966, Ph.D., 1969. Sanitary engr. USPHS, Denver, 1963-65; research scientist Ctr. for the Environment and Man, Hartford, Conn., 1969-70; prof. civil engring. Stanford U., Calif., 1970—, dir. program on urban studies, 1980—; vis. prof. Inst. Ricerca sulle Acqua, Rome, 1979, South China Environ. Inst. Sci., Guanzhou, 1987, Ecole Nat. des Ponts et Chaussées, Paris, 1987-88; vis. scholar Kyoto (Japan) U., 1992; vis. lectr. Nat. Sci. Coun. China, 1991. Author: Environmental Planning and Decision Making, 1984 (Chinese edit. 1989); co-author: Implementing Environmental Policy in China, 1995. Resources for the Future Natural Resources fellow, 1968-69; Fulbright-Hays grantee, 1979, 87. Mem. ASCE, Internat. Water Resources Assn., Internat. Assn. for Impact Assessment. Office: Stanford Univ Dept Civil Engring Stanford CA 94305

ORTOLANO, RALPH J., engineering consultant; b. Phila., Apr. 12, 1931. BS in Marine Engring., U.S. Mcht. Marine Acad., 1954; MBA, Santa Clara U., 1969. Registered profl. engr., Calif. Engring. watch officer USN, 1954-56; sr. design engr. marine divsn. Westinghouse, Lester, Pa., 1956-64, Sunnyvale, Calif., 1964-69; mgr. project engring. corp. cost recovery dept. Litton Ship Systems, Inc., L.A., 1969-72; consulting engr., scientist So. Calif. Edison Co., Rosemead, Calif., 1972-92, chief cons., 1993—; formed Turbine RESCUE, 1984. Contbr. more than 100 articles to profl. jours.; holder 21 U.S. patents in field. Recipient William R. Gould award SCE, 1992. Mem. ASME (past dir. ASME-SCAC power chpt., past chmn. steam turbine com., past chmn. power divsn., mem. exec. com., co-chmn. steam turbine course 1984—, George Westinghouse Gold medal 1991).

ORTON, COLIN GEORGE, medical physicist; b. London, Essex, England, June 4, 1938; came to U.S., 1966; s. Frederick G. and Audrey V. (Sewell) O.; m. Barbara G. Scholes, July 25, 1964; children: Nigel, Susanne, Philip. BS in Physics with honors, Bristol U., 1959; MS in Radiation Physics, London U., 1961, PhD in Radiation Physics, 1965; MA (hon.), Brown U., 1976. ABR, ABMP. Instr. London U. St. Barts' Hosp., 1961-66; assoc. prof. NYU Med. Ctr., 1966-75, Brown U., R.I., 1975-81; prof., chief physicist Wayne State U., Harper Hosp., Detroit, 1981—; dir., grad program, Wayne State U., 1981—. Author: Radiation Physics Review Books I, 1971, II, 1978; editor: Electron Treatment Planning, 1978, Progress in Medical Physics I, 1982, II, 1985, Radiation Dosimetry, 1986. Marie Curie Gold Medal, Health Physics Soc., 1987. Fellow Am. Assn. Physicists in Am. (pres. 1981, William D. Coolidge award 1993), Am. Coll. Med. Physics (chmn. 1985), Inst. Physics London, Internat. Orgn. for Med. Physics (sec. gen. 1988-94, v.p. 1994—), Am. Coll. Radiology. Avocations: golf, badminton, tennis, running, squash. Home: 8 Lakeside Ct Grosse Pointe MI 48230-1906 Office: Harper Hosp 3990 John R St Detroit MI 48201-2018

ORTON, GEORGE FREDERICK, aerospace engineer; b. Flushing, N.Y., Aug. 8, 1941; s. Harry and Evelyn (Brostrom) O.; m. Susan K., Dec. 21, 1962; children: Karen, Kevin, Kristen. BS in Aeron. Engring., U. Md., 1964; MS in Engring. Mechanics, St. Louis U., 1971. Engr. propulsion McDonnell Douglas, St. Louis, 1964-73, sr. engr. propulsion, 1973-77, unit chief propulsion, 1977-81, sect. chief propulsion, 1981-86, br. chief nat. aerospace plane, 1986-90, staff dir. nat. aerospace plane, 1990-92, dir. space programs, 1992-93, program mgr. Hypersonics Ctr. Excellence, 1993—. Contbr. articles to profl. jours. Advisor Explorer Post 9005, St. Louis, 1980-87; sci. advisor University City (Mo.) Schs. Fellow AIAA (assoc., mem. liquid propulsion tech. com. 1980-84, 91-95, Best Paper award 1986), St. Louis Head Injury Assn. Methodist. Achievements include patent for propellant acquisition device for zero-g engine starts, patent for propellant resupply system, NASA technology cash award for work on shuttle auxiliary propulsion. Office: McDonnell Douglas Corp Mailcode 1067250 PO Box 516 Saint Louis MO 63166

ORTON, STEWART, retail company executive, merchant; b. Cin., Nov. 19, 1915; s. Henry S. and Helen (Block) O.; m. Hanni Stern, Nov. 16, 1946; children: Judith, John. B.A., U. Mich., 1937. With Shillito's Dept. Store, Cin., 1937-57; v.p., gen. mdse. mgr. Shillito's Dept. Store, 1954-57; pres. J.N. Adam & Co. (dept. store), Buffalo, 1957-60; v.p. parent co. Asso. Dry Goods Corp., N.Y.C., 1957-60; exec. v.p. Boston Store, Milw., 1960-63; v.p. Federated Dept. Stores, Cin., 1963; exec. v.p. Foley's, Houston, 1964-68, pres., 1968-78, chmn., chief exec. officer, 1979-82; exec. v.p. Federated Dept. Stores Inc. Found., 1982-88. Campaign chmn. Houston United Fund, 1968, pres., 1969; trustee U. Houston Found., Mus. Fine Arts, Houston, 1980-88; bd. dirs. Alley Theatre, Consumer Credit Conseling Svc., 1988—, chmn., 1990-92; bd. dirs. St. Joseph Hosp. Found., chmn., 1978-80; bd. dirs. Houston Com. for Pvt. Sector Initiatives, co-chmn., 1981-86; bd. dirs., v.p. Communities in Schs., 1986—; pres. Houston Econ. Devel. Coun., 1984-85; bd. dirs. Houston Symphony Orch., 1988—, chmn., 1990-91. Maj. Q.M.C., AUS, 1942-45. Mem. Houston C. of C. (dir., vice chmn. 1979-80, chmn. 1981-82). Clubs: Forum of Houston (pres. 1983, chmn. 1984); Plaza. Home: 3711 San Felipe St Apt 11J Houston TX 77027-4040 Office: 2360 Citicorp Ctr 1200 Smith St Houston TX 77002

ORTON, WILLIAM H. (BILL ORTON), congressman, lawyer; b. North Ogden, Utah, Sept. 22, 1948. BS, Brigham Young U., 1973, JD, 1979. Adj. prof. Portland (Oreg.) State U./Portland C.C., 1974-76, Brigham Young. U., Provo, Utah, 1984-85; tax auditor IRS, 1976-77; corp. counsel WI Forest Products, Inc., Portland, Oreg., 1980-81; of counsel Merritt & Tenney, Atlanta, 1986-90; tax atty. pvt. practice, Utah, 1986-90, Washington, 1986-90; atty., 1980-90; mem. 102d-104th Congresses from 3f Utah dist., 1990—; mem. budget com., mem. banking and fin. svcs. com. Democrat. Mormon. Office: US Ho of Reps 440 Cannon HOB Washington DC 20515-4403

ORTTUNG, WILLIAM HERBERT, chemistry educator; b. Phila., June 16, 1934; s. Elmer Herbert and Rosalind Orttung; married; children: Robert W., Mark. H. SB, MIT, 1956; PhD, U. Calif., Berkeley, 1961. Asst. prof. chemistry Stanford (Calif.) U., 1960-63; asst. prof. chemistry U. Calif., Riverside, 1963-69, assoc. prof., 1969-79, prof., 1979-94; emeritus prof., 1994—. Mem. AAAS, Am. Chem. Soc., Am. Phys. Soc.

ORULLIAN, B. LARAE, bank executive; b. Salt Lake City, May 15, 1933; d. Alma and Bessie (Bacon) O.; cert. Am. Inst. Banking, 1961, 63, 67; grad. Nat. Real Estate Banking Sch., Ohio State U., 1969-71. With Tracy Collins Trust Co., Salt Lake City, 1951-54, Union Nat. Bank, Denver, 1954-57; exec. sec. Guaranty Bank, Denver, 1957-64, asst. cashier, 1964-67, asst. v.p., 1967-70, v.p., 1970-75, exec. v.p., 1975-77, also bd. dirs.; chair, CEO, dir. The Women's Bank N.A., Denver, 1989—, Colo. Bus. Bankshares, Inc., 1980—; vice chmn. Colo. Bus. Bank Littleton; chmn. bd., dir. Colo. Blue Cross/Blue Shield; bd. dirs. Rocky Mountain Life Ins. Co., Pro-Card, Inc., Holladay (Utah) Bank; chmn. bd. dirs. Frontier Airlines. Treas. Girl Scouts U.S.A., 1981-87, 1st. nat. v.p., chair exec. com., 1987-90, nat. pres., 1990—; bd. dirs., chair Rocky Mountain Health Care Corp.; bd. dirs. Ams. Clean Water Found., Denver Improvement Assn.; bd. dirs. Commn. Savings in Am. Recipient Woman Who Made a Difference award Internat. Women's Forum, 1994; named to Colo. Women Hall of Fame, 1988, Colo. Entrepreneur of Yr., Inc. Mag. and Arthur Young and Co., 1989, Woman of the Yr., YWCA, 1989, EMC Lion Club (citizen of the year, 1995). Mem. Bus. and Profl. Women Colo. (3d Century award 1977), Colo. State Ethics Bd., Denver C. of C., Am. Inst. Banking, Am. Bankers Assn. (adv. bd. edn. found.), Nat. Assn. Bank Women, Internat. Women's Forum (Woman Who

Makes a Difference award 1994), Com. of 200. Republican. Mormon. Home: 10 S Ammons St Lakewood CO 80226-1331

ORUMA, FRANCIS OBATARE, mechanical engineering educator, consultant; b. Jimeta-Yola, Nigeria, Nov. 28, 1948; s. Chief W.O. Oruma and Margaret A. Abramita; m. roseline Taino Cookey, Aug. 5, 1978; children: Frenka, Essee, Alima, Erthel. BSME, Ind. Tech., Ft. Wayne, 1977; PhD in Mech. Engring., N.C. State U., Raleigh, 1984; MBA, Ashland (Ohio) U., 1990. Mech. engr. ITT, Raleigh, 1978-80; cons. Raleigh, 1984-86; assoc. prof. mech. engring., dir. PC-CAD Ohio No. U., Ada, 1988—, Leroy H. Lylte Disting. chair in mech. engring., 1990-91, 93—; vis. prof. U. Okla., Norman, 1987. Trustee Food Bank/Artspace, Lima, Ohio, 1993—, Allen-Lima Econ. Devel. Consortium, Vet.'s Meml. Conv. and Civic Ctr. of Lima/Allen County. Mem. ASME (faculty advisor 1992—), Bradfield Lions, Masons, Rotary Club (trustee 1993-95, v.p. 1994-95), Cavalier Club of Lima (pres. 1994-95). Home: 3307 Roundtree St Lima OH 45805-4021 Office: Ohio No U Ada OH 45810

ORVICK, GEORGE MYRON, church denomination executive, minister; b. Hanlontown, Iowa, Jan. 9, 1929; s. George and Mabel Olina (Mandsager) O.; m. Ruth Elaine Hoel, Aug. 25, 1951; children: Daniel, Emily, Mark, Kirsten. AA, Bethany Luth. Coll., Mankato, Minn., 1948, candidate of theology, 1953; BA, Northwestern Coll., Watertown, Wis., 1950. Ordained to ministry Evang. Luth. Synod, 1953. Pastor Our Saviour Luth. Ch., Amherst Junction, Wis., 1953-54, Holy Cross Luth. Ch., Madison, Wis., 1954-86; cir. visitor Evang. Luth. Synod, Mankato, 1964-69, pres., 1970-76, 1980—. Author: Our Great Heritage, 1966; columnist: The Luth. Sentinel, 1982—. Home: 1117 Lori Ln Mankato MN 56001-4728 Office: Evang Luth Synod 447 N Division St Mankato MN 56001-6138

ORVILLE, RICHARD EDMONDS, atmospheric science educator; b. Long Beach, Calif., July 28, 1936; s. Howard Thomas and Lillian (Duvall) O.; m. Barbara Isabel Pierce, Jan. 25, 1964; children—Richard Edmonds (dec.), John Keith. AB, Princeton U., 1958; MS, U. Ariz., 1963, PhD in Meteorology, 1966. Mfg. mgr. Procter & Gamble Co., 1959-60; rsch. asst. physics Johns Hopkins U., 1960-61; rsch. asst. meteorology U. Ariz., 1961-64; rsch. assoc. Westinghouse Electrical Corp., 1964-66; sr. rsch. scientist Westinghouse Electric Corp., Pitts., 1966-68; assoc. prof. atmospheric sci. SUNY, Albany, 1968-81; prof. SUNY, 1981-91, chmn. dept. atmospheric sci., 1983-88, trustee univ. corp. for atmospheric research, 1984-90; rsch. scientist Coop. Inst. for Applied Meteorol. Studies, dept. meteoroly Tex. A&M U., College Station, 1991-93, dir. Coop. Inst. for Applied Meteorol. Studies, dept. meteorology, 1993—; bd. dirs. Thunderstorm Analysis Ctr., SUNY, Albany, assoc. program dir. NSF, Washington, 1970-71; vis. sr. scientist Nat. Center Atmospheric Research, Boulder, Colo., 1976; vis. scientist Swiss Inst. Tech., Zurich, 1967, 69, 70; vis. prof. U. Wis., Madison, 1979. Contbr. articles to profl. jours. Mem. environ. adv. com. City of Niskayuna, N.Y., 1972-74. Served to 2d lt. U.S. Army, 1958-59. Research grantee Office Naval Research, 1967-69, NSF, 1968—, USAF, 1977-82, NASA, 1979-89, Electric Power Research Inst., 1983-90; recipient Sackler medal for Geophysics, Tel Aviv U., 1987, First Suomi Lecture U. Wis., 1989. Fellow Am. Meteorol. Soc. (chmn. publs. Commn. 1985-92, Charles Franklin Brooks award 1994), Am. Geophys. Union (atmospheric sci. sect., pres. 1988-90); mem. AAAS, Royal Meteorol. Soc., Am. Soc. Physics Tchrs., Optical Soc., Sigma Xi. Office: Texas A&M Univ Dept Meteorlogy 1204 Eller O & M Bldg College Station TX 77843-3150

ORWOLL, GREGG S. K., lawyer; b. Austin, Minn., Mar. 23, 1926; s. Gilbert M. and Kleonora (Kleven) O.; m. Laverne M. Flentie, Sept. 15, 1951; children: Kimball G., Kent A., Vikki A., Tristen A., Erik G. BS, Northwestern U., 1950; JD, U. Minn., 1953. Bar: Minn. 1953, U.S. Supreme Ct. 1973. Assoc. Dorsey & Whitney, Mpls., 1953-59, ptnr., 1959-60; assoc. counsel Mayo Clinic, Rochester, Minn., 1960-63, gen. counsel, 1963-87, sr. legal counsel, 1987-91, sr. counsel, 1991-92; gen. counsel, dir. Rochester Airport Co., 1962-84, v.p., 1981-84; gen. counsel Mayo Med. Svcs., Ltd., 1972-90; bd. dirs., sec. and gen. counsel Mayo Found. for Med. Edn. and Rsch., 1984-90; gen. counsel Mid-Am. Orthopaedic Assn., 1984—, Minn. Orthopaedic Soc., 1985—; asst. sec./sec. Mayo Found., Rochester, 1972-91; bd. dirs. Charter House, 1986-90; dir. Travelure Motel Corp., 1968-86, sec., 1968-83, v.p., 1983-86; dir., v.p. Echo Too Ent., Inc.; dir., v.p. Oberhamer Inc.; bd. dirs. Am. Decal and Mfg. Co., 1989-93, sec., 1992-93; adj. prof. William Mitchell Coll. Law, 1978-84. Contbr. articles and chpts. to legal and medico-legal publs.; bd. editors HealthSpan, 1984-93; editorial bd. Minn. Law Rev., 1952-53. Trustee Minn. Coun. on Founds., 1977-82, Mayo Found., 1982-86; trustee William Mitchell Coll. Law, 1982-88, 89—, mem. exec. com. 1990—; bd. visitors U. Minn. Law Sch., 1974-76, 85-91; mem. U. Minn. Regent Candidate Adv. Coun., 1988—, Minn. State Compensation Coun., 1991, 91-95. With USAF, 1944-45. Recipient Outstanding Svc. medal U.S. Govt., 1991. Mem. ABA, AMA (affiliate), Am. Corp. Counsel Assn., Minn. Soc. Hosp. Attys. (bd. dirs. 1981-86), Minn. State Bar Assn. (chmn. legal/med. com. 1977-81), Olmsted County Bar Assn. (v.p., pres. 1977-79), Rochester C. of C., U. Minn. Law Alumni Assn. (bd. dirs. 1973-76, 85-91), Rochester U. Club (pres. 1977), The Doctors Mayo Soc., Mid Am. Ortho. Assn. (hon.), Mayo Alumni Assn. (hon.), Phi Delta Phi, Phi Delta Theta. Republican. Home: 2233 Fifth Ave NE Rochester MN 55906-4017 Office: Mayo Clinic 200 1st St SW Rochester MN 55905-0001

ORWOLL, MARK PETER, magazine editor; b. Lynwood, Calif., Dec. 3, 1953; s. Sylfest Peter Jr. and Frances Patricia (Giffin) O.; m. Kathleen F. Fox, Aug. 6, 1983; children: Caitlin, Gillian, Rory. BA in Journalism, San Diego State U., 1978, MA in English, 1985. Reporter Star-News, Chula Vista, Calif., 1978-79; staff writer The Reader, San Diego, 1979-81; features editor Woman's World, Englewood, N.J., 1981; bus. editor American Salon, N.Y.C., 1981-83; editor Transfer, San Francisco, 1983-84; sr. editor USAir Mag., N.Y.C., 1985-87; mng. editor Travel & Leisure, N.Y.C., 1987—; lectr. Rice U. Pub. Program, Houston, 1994, Seabourn Cruise Line, India-Singapore, 1994; spkr. Am. Soc. Journalists and Authors, N.Y.C., 1991, New Sch. Social Rsch., N.Y.C., 1992. Ky. col. Hon. Order Ky. Cols., Frankfort, 1995. Mem. Am. Soc. Mag. Editors, 1990—. Office: Travel & Leisure 1120 Avenue of the Americas New York NY 10036

ORWOLL, ROBERT ARVID, chemistry educator; b. Mpls., Aug. 28, 1940; s. Arvid Lyder and Agnes Gertrude (Christiansen) O.; m. Betty Lou Magers, Feb. 24, 1972; children: Katherine Sonja, Karen Elizabeth. BA, St. Olaf Coll., Northfield, Minn., 1962; PhD, Stanford U., 1967. Postdoctoral fellow Dartmouth Coll., Hanover, N.H., 1966-67, rsch. instr., 1967-68; postdoctoral fellow U. Conn., Storrs, 1968-69; asst. prof. Coll. William and Mary, Williamsburg, Va., 1969-72, assoc. prof., 1972-82, prof., 1982, dir. applied sci., 1988-92, chair dept. of chemistry, 1995—. Bd. dirs. Williamsburg Hospice, 1989-94; bd. dirs. Wesley Found., 1974-84, 95—, treas., 1976-80. Recipient Alumni fellow teaching award Soc. Alumni William and Mary, 1985. Methodist. Home: 202 Buford Rd Williamsburg VA 23188-1509 Office: Coll William & Mary Dept Chemistry Williamsburg VA 23187

ORY, MARCIA GAIL, social science researcher; b. Dallas, Feb. 8, 1950; d. Marvin Gilbert and Esther (Levine) O.; m. Raymond James Carroll, Aug. 13, 1972. BA magna cum laude, U. Tex., 1971; MA, Ind. U., 1972; PhD, Purdue U., 1976; MPH, Johns Hopkins U., 1981. Rsch. asst. prof. U. N.C., Chapel Hill, 1976-77; from adj. asst. prof. to assoc. prof. sch. pub. health U. N.C., 1978-88; rsch. fellow U. Minn., Mpls., 1977-78; asst. prof. Sch. Pub. Health U. Ala., Bham, 1978-80; program dir. biosocial aging and health Nat. Inst. on Aging, Bethesda, Md., 1981-86; chief social sci. rsch. on aging Nat. Inst. on Aging, Bethesda, 1987—. Contbr. articles, editor vols. profl. jours. Mem. several nat. task forces on aging and health issues. Recipient Dept. of Health and Human Svcs. award, 1984, 85, 88, Am. Men and Women of Sci., 1989-90, Nat. Inst. of Health Dir.'s award, 1995; named Disting. Alumna by Purdue U. Fellow Gerontol. Soc. Am.; mem. APHA (gov. coun. 1986-88, program chmn. 1986, chmn.-elect 1989-91, chmn. 1992-93), Am. Sociol. Assn. (regional reporter 1984—, program com. 1986, nominations com. 1987, councilor-at-large 1992-93), Soc. Behavioral Medicine (program chmn. pub. health track 1988-89, program com. 1991-92), Phi Kappa Phi, Omicron Nu. Avocations: biking, birding, travel. Office: Nat Inst Aging Gateway Bldg Ste 533 7201 Wisconsin Ave # 9205 Bethesda MD 20892-9205

ORYSHKEVICH, ROMAN SVIATOSLAV, physician, physiatrist, dentist, educator; b. Olesko, Ukraine, Aug. 5, 1928; came to U.S., 1955, naturalized, 1960; s. Simeon and Caroline (Deneszczuk) O.; m. Oksana Lishchynsky, June 16, 1962; children: Marta, Mark, Alexandra. DDS, Ruperto-Carola U., Heidelberg, Ger., 1952, MD, 1953, PhD cum laude, 1955. Cert. Am. Assn. Electromygraphy and Electrodiagnosis, 1964; diplomate Am. Bd. Phys. Medicine and Rehab., 1966, Am. Bd. Electrodiagnostic Medicine, 1989. Research fellow in cancer Esptl. Cancer Inst., Rupert-Charles U., 1953-55; rotating intern Coney Island Hosp., Bklyn., 1955-56; resident in diagnostic radiology NYU Bellevue Med. Ctr.-Univ. Hosp., 1956-57; resident, fellow in phys. medicine and rehab. Western Res. U. Highland View Hosp., Cleve., 1958-60; orthopedic surgery Met. Gen. Hosp., Cleve., 1959; asst. chief rehab. medicine service VA West Side Med. Ctr., Chgo., 1961-74, acting chief, 1974-75, chief, 1975—; dir., coord. edn. U. Ill. Integrated Residency Program, Phys. Medicine & Rehab, 1974-89; clin. instr. U. Ill., 1962-65, asst. clin. prof., 1965-70, asst. prof., 1970-75, assoc. clin. prof., 1975-94, clin. prof., 1994—. Author, editor: Who and What in U.W.M.M., 1978; contbr. articles to profl. jours; splty. cons. in phys. medicine and rehab. to editorial bd. Chgo. Med. Jours., 1978-89. Founder, pres. Ukrainian World Med. Mus., Chgo., 1977; founder, 1st pres. Am. Mus. Phys. Medicine and Rehab., 1980-91. Fellow AAUP, Am. Acad. Phys. Medicine and Rehab.; mem. Assn. Acad. Physiatrists, Am. Assn. Electromyography and Electrodiagnosis, Ill. Soc. Phys. Medicine and Rehab. (pres., dir. 1979-80), Ukrainian Med. Assn. N.Am. (dir., pres. chpt. 1977-79, fin. mgr. 17th med. conv. and congress Chgo. 1977, adminstr. and conv. chmn. 1979), World Fedn. Ukrainian Med. Assns. (co-founder and 1st exec. sec. research and sci. 1977-79), Internat. Rehab. Medicine Assn., Rehab. Internat. U.S.A., Nat. Assn. VA Physicians, AAAS, Assn. Med. Rehab. Dirs. and Coordinators, Nat. Rehab. Assn., Nat. Assn. Disability Examiners, Am. Med. Writers Assn., Biofeedback Research Soc. Am., Chgo. Soc. Phys. Medicine and Rehab. (pres., founder 1978-79), Ill. Rehab. Assn., Ukrainian Acad. Med. Scis. (founder, pres. 1979-80), Gerontol. Soc., Internat. Soc. Electrophysiol. Kinesiology, Internat. Soc. Prosthetics and Orthotics, Fedn. Am. Scientists. Ukrainian Catholic. Major research interests: prosthetics, amputations, normal and pathological gaits, bracing-orthotics, strokes, rehabilitation. Home: 1819 N 78th Ct Chicago IL 60635-3502 Office: 820 S Damen Ave Chicago IL 60612-3728

ORZECHOWSKI, ALICE LOUISE, accountant; b. Washington, Jan. 14, 1952; d. Casimir T. and Frances (Zemaites) O.; m. Scott Mitchell Hoyman Jr. BS in Econs., U. Md., 1973, BS in Acctg., 1976; MS in Adminstrn. and Mgmt., Hood Coll., 1983. CPA, Md.; cert. mgmt. acct. Mgr. Gen. Bus. Svcs., Rockville, Md., 1972-78, Ross Assocs., Alexandria, Va., 1978-87; owner Alice L. Orzechowski, CPA, Cert. Mgmt. Acct., Frederick, Md., 1987—; adj. faculty Frederick (Md.) C.C., 1990-92, Montgomery Coll., Rockville, Md., 1992-96; spkr. in field. Named Outstanding Young Marylander, Md. Jaycees, 1991. Mem. AICPA, Am. Women's Soc. CPAs, Md. Assn. CPAs, Nat. Assn. Accts., Nat. Assn. Tax Pracittioners, Downtowne Frederick Toastmasters (pres. 1991, Toastmaster of Yr. 1990), Frederick C. of C. (chair small bus. coun. 1990-91, dir. 1992—, Entrepreneur of Yr. 1992). Office: 529 N Market St Frederick MD 21701-5242

OSBALDESTON, GORDON FRANCIS, business educator, former government official; b. Hamilton, Ont., Can., Apr. 29, 1930; s. John Edward and Margaret (Hanley) O.; m. Geraldine Keller, Oct. 3, 1953; children—Stephen, David, Robert, Catherine. B.Commerce, U. Toronto, Ont., Can., 1952; M.B.A., U. Western Ont., London, 1953, LL.D., 1984; LL.D., York U., Toronto, 1984, Dalhousie U., Halifax, N.S., 1985, Carleton U., Ottawa, Ont., Can., 1987. Fgn. service officer Dept. Trade and Commerce, Ottawa, 1953-54; vice consul, asst. trade commr. Dept. Trade and Commerce, Sao Paula, Brazil, 1954-57, Chgo., 1957-60; consul, trade commr. Dept. Trade and Commerce, Los Angeles, 1960-64; asst. dir., personnel trade commr. service Dept. Trade and Commerce, Ottawa, 1964-66, asst. dir. ops. trade commr. service, 1966-67, exec. dir. trade commr. service, 1967-68; asst. dep. minister Dept. Consumer and Corp. Affairs, Ottawa, 1968-70, dep. minister, 1972-73; dep. sec. Treasury Bd. Secretariat, Ottawa, 1970-72, sec., 1973-76; dep. minister Dept. Industry, Trade and Commerce, Ottawa, 1976-78; sec. Ministry of State for Econ. Devel., Ottawa, 1978-82; undersec. of state Dept. External Affairs, Ottawa, 1982; clk. privy council, sec. to cabinet Privy Council Office, Ottawa, 1982-86; mem. Queen's Privy Coun. for Can., 1986; prof. emeritus Western Bus. Sch. U. Western Ont., 1986—; bd. dirs. Molson Cos., Ltd., DuPont of Can. Inc., Nat. Bank of Can., Bell Can., Ellis Don Can., NatCan Trust Co. Author: Keeping Deputy Ministers Accountable, 1989, Organizing to Govern, 1990. Decorated officer Order of Can.; recipient Outstanding Achievment award Can. Govt., 1981, Vanier medal Inst. Pub. Adminstrn., 1990. Mem. Psi Upsilon. Roman Catholic. Avocations: philately; golf. Home: 1353 Corley Dr N, 1353 Corley Dr N, London, ON Canada N6G 4L4 Office: U Western Ont Sch Bus, London, ON Canada N6A 3K7

OSBERG, TIMOTHY M., psychologist, educator, researcher; b. Buffalo, Aug. 11, 1955; s. John Carlton and Adeline Rose (Weichsel) O.; m. Debra A. Morreale, July 14, 1990; children: John Peter, Erika Evelyn. BA, SUNY, Buffalo, 1977, MA, 1980, PhD, 1982. Lic. psychologist, N.Y. Intern VA Med. Ctr., Buffalo, 1981-82; from asst. prof. to prof. Niagara U., N.Y., 1982—; pvt. practice Niagara Falls, N.Y., 1985—; psychologist Optifast Weight Loss Program, Niagara Falls, 1989-92; editorial bd. Jour. Personality and Social Psychology, 1988-92, Teaching of Psychology, 1991—, Jour. Correctional Edn., 1993—; instr. Attica Correctional Facility, 1980—; presenter in field. Contbr. articles to profl. jours. Vol. group leader prerelease program Attica (N.Y.) Correctional Facility, 1984-90, exec. com. Psychol. Assn. Western N.Y., Buffalo, 1982-87. Recipient Feldman-Cohen Meml. award SUNY, Buffalo, 1977. Fellow APA; mem. Am. Psychol. Soc., Eastern Psychol. Assn., Soc. for Personality Assessment, Assn. Advancement Behavior Therapy, Phi Beta Kappa. Democrat. Roman Catholic. Avocations: spectator sports, running, golf, tennis. Home: 2652 David Dr Niagara Falls NY 14304-4619 Office: Niagara U Dept Psychology Niagara University NY 14109

OSBORN, DAVID LEE, engineer; b. Muscatine, Iowa, Feb. 10, 1953; s. Donald Dean and Emogene Faye (Strausbaugh) O.; m. Frances Marie Barnes, Apr. 11, 1981 (div. Feb. 1994); 1 child, Meredith Leigh. BSME, U. Iowa, 1978. Mech. engr. Stanley Cons., Muscatine, Iowa, 1978-82; gen. engr. Hdqrs. U.S. Army Armament, Munitions & Chem. Commd., Rock Island, Ill., 1982-89, Rock Island Arsenal, 1989—. Recipient Fed. Energy Mgmt. award Dept. Energy, 1993. Mem. Assn. Energy Engrs. Achievements include development of nationally recognized energy conservation program, development of over 13 million dollars in conservation projects including hydroelectric, lighting and heat/cooling system projects. Avocations: landscaping, home designs, golf, skiing, billiards. Office: Rock Island Arsenal Attn SIORI-PWE Rock Island IL 61299-5000

OSBORN, DONALD ROBERT, lawyer; b. N.Y.C., Oct. 9, 1929; s. Robert W. and Ruth C. (Compton) O.; m. Marcia Lontz, June 4, 1955; children: David, Judith, Robert; m. Marie A. Johnson, Sept. 11, 1986. BA, Cornell U., 1951; LLB, Columbia U., 1957. Bar: N.Y. 1957, U.S. Tax Ct. 1958, U.S. Ct. Claims 1961, U.S. Ct. Appeals (2d cir.) 1974, U.S. Ct. Appeals (8th cir.) 1974, U.S. Dist. Ct. (so. and ea. dists.) N.Y. 1975, U.S. Supreme Ct. 1975. Assoc. Sullivan & Cromwell, N.Y.C., 1957-64, ptnr., 1964—. Trustee Hamilton Coll., 1978-88, Mus. of Broadcasting, 1975-80; trustee, treas. Kirkland Coll., 1969-78; mem. coun. White Burkett Miller Ctr. Pub. Affairs, 1976-82; bd. dirs., pres. Stevens Kingsley Found., 1967—; sec., treas. Dunlevy Milbank Found., 1974—; bd. dirs. Spanel Found., 1978-88, CBS, Inc., 1975-80. Served with USN, 1951-54. Mem. ABA, N.Y. State Bar Assn., Assn. of Bar of City of N.Y., Am. Bar Found., Scarsdale Golf Club, India House, World Trade Ctr. Club (N.Y.C.), Regency Whist Club, Country Club of the Rockies. Presbyterian. Home: 1049 Park Ave New York NY 10128-1061 Office: Sullivan & Cromwell 125 Broad St New York NY 10004-2400

OSBORN, FREDERICK HENRY, III, foundation administrator; b. Phila., Dec. 31, 1946; s. Frederick Henry Osborn Jr. and Anne de Witt (Pell) O.; m. Anne Hampton de Peyster Todd, July 10, 1971; children: Frederick Henry IV, Elisabeth Van Cortlandt, Graham Livingston. Student in Econs., Princeton U., 1964-66; BA in Bus. Adminstrn., Colby Coll., 1971; postgrad., Nat. Planned Giving Inst., 1987, Philanthropy Tax Inst., 1988. Registered investment advisor. Pres. Call-Us, Inc., Edgartown, Mass., 1969-72; exec. v.p. Hall Labs., Boston, 1972-74; fin. officer Episcopal Diocese Mass., Boston, 1972-76; diocesan adminstr. Episcopal Diocese Maine, Portland, 1976-80; dir. adminstrn. Episcopal Diocese Conn., Hartford, 1980-86; dir. of devel. and planned giving Nat. Episcopal Ch., N.Y.C., 1987-94; dir. of devel. programs Episcopal Ch. Found., N.Y.C., 1995—; bd. dirs. Living Music, Inc., Ulysses Co., William O. Benson Co., FAN Trusts, Oslands, Inc., Boscobel Restoration, Inc., Garrison Sta. Plz., Inc., Garrison Landing Assn., Covenant Svcs., Inc.; prin. Cat Rock Counsel, Garrison, N.Y., 1990—. Co-author: Planned Giving for the Episcopal Parish, 1989. Bd. dirs. The Giraffe Project, chmn. 1989-93, Alice Desmond & Hamilton Fish Libr., Harvest with Heart; chmn. bd. dirs. Hudson Highlands Land Trust; v.-chair., bd. dirs. Scenic Hudson, Berkeley Divinity Sch. Yale U., Nature Conservancy (lower Hudson chpt. chair 1994—); trustee Tabor Acad., Cathedral Ch. St. John the Divine; chair devel. com. Soc. Promoting Christian Knowledge, chair Hudson Highlands Music Festival; With U.S. Army, 1966-68, Vietnam. Mem. Nat. Assn. Fund Raising Execs., Nat. Planned Giving Assn., Nat. Environ. Leadership Coun., Planned Giving Group Greater N.Y., Social Investment Forum, Coun. Econ. Priorities, Social Venture Network, Century Assn., St. Andrews Soc. of N.Y., Highlands Country Club, N.Y. Yacht Club, Portland Yacht Club, Dauntless Club, Garrison Yacht Club, Princeton Club (N.Y.), Internat. Platform Assn. Avocations: sailing, music, photography. Home: PO Box 347 Cat Rock Rd Garrison NY 10524-0347 Office: Episcopal Ch Found Rm 400 815 2d Ave New York NY 10017-4563

OSBORN, GUY A., food products company executive; b. 1936. BSBA, Northwestern U., 1958. Group mktg. mgr. Pillsbury Co., Mpls., 1958-65; with Universal Foods Corp., Milw., 1971—, dir. mktg., 1971-73, v.p. spl. products, 1973-78, group v.p., 1978-82, exec. v.p., 1982-84, past pres., chief operating officer, 1984-88, chief exec. officer, 1988—, also chmn. bd., dir. Office: Universal Foods Corp 433 E Michigan St Milwaukee WI 53202-5104*

OSBORN, JOHN EDWARD, lawyer, former government official, writer; b. Davenport, Iowa, Sept. 4, 1957; s. Edward Richard and Patricia Anne (O'Donovan) O.; m. Deborah Lynn Powell, Aug. 11, 1984; 1 child, Delaney Powell. Student, Coll. William and Mary, 1975-76; BA, U. Iowa, 1979; postgrad., Georgetown U., 1980; JD, U. Va., 1983; postgrad. Wadham Coll., Oxford U., 1987; MIPP, Johns Hopkins U., 1992; postgrad. Wharton Sch., U. Pa., 1994-95. Bar: Mass. 1985. Law clk. to Hon. Albert V. Bryan U.S. Ct. Appeals (4th cir.), Alexandria, Va., 1983-84; assoc. Hale and Dorr, Boston, 1984-88, Dechert Price & Rhoads, Phila., 1988-89; spl. asst. to legal adviser U.S. Dept. State, Washington, 1989-92; sr. counsel DuPont Merck Pharm. Co., Wilmington, Del., 1992-94, assoc. gen. counsel, 1994-96, v.p., assoc. gen. counsel, asst. sec., 1996—; legal cons. Amnesty Internat. USA, 1987-88; vis. scholar East European studies, Woodrow Wilson Internat. Ctr. for Scholars Smithsonian Instn., Washington, 1991, assoc. scholar Fgn. Policy Rsch. Inst., Phila., 1992—. Contbr. articles to profl. jours., newspapers and periodicals; articles editor: Va. Jour. Internat. Law, 1982-83. Mem. Hist. Commn., Hull, Mass., 1988; mem. U. Va. Law Sch. Bus. Advisory Coun., Charlottesville, mem. nat. steering com. U. Iowa Endowment 2000 Campaign, Iowa City; mem. steering com., town chmn., rsch. aide, speechwriter George Bush for Pres. Com., 1979-80, 87-88, mem. Del. Rep. State Comm., 1995—, mem bd. del. to Republican Nat. Conv., 1996, mem., bd. dirs. Del. Ctr. for the Contemporary Arts, 1995—, ACLU Del., 1996—. Mem. ABA (bus law, internat. law and practice sects.), Am. Corp. Counsel Assn., The Atlantic Coun. of the U.S., Mortar Board, Phi Beta Kappa, Phi Delta Phi, Omicron Delta Kappa, Omicron Delta Epsilon, Sigma Delta Chi. Republican. Roman Catholic. Clubs: Capitol Hill, DuPont Country. Home: 236 Stone Row Yorklyn DE 19736-0324 Office: 974 Centre Rd Wilmington DE 19807-2802

OSBORN, JOHN SIMCOE, JR., lawyer; b. Louisville, Jan. 14, 1926; s. John S. and Ruby (Pinnell) O.; m. Mary Jo Fishback, Sept. 6, 1947; children—Robert, John, Donna. LL.B., U. Louisville, 1949. Bar: Ky. 1949, U.S. Dist. Ct. (ea. and we. dists.) Ky. 1952. Exec. v.p., gen. counsel Louisville Title Ins. Co., 1954-72; ptnr. Tarrant Combs & Bullitt (name changed to Wyatt Tarrant & Combs 1980), Louisville, 1972—; chmn. bd. Beargrass Corp. Served to capt. JAGC, U.S. Army, 1952-54. Fellow Am. Bar Found.; mem. Ky. Bar Assn., Louisville Bar Assn., ABA, Am. Land Title Assn., Am. Coll. Real Estate Lawyers. Democrat. Presbyterian. Lodge: Rotary (Louisville). Office: Wyatt Tarrant & Combs 2800 Citizens Plz Louisville KY 40202

OSBORN, JUNE ELAINE, pediatrician, microbiologist, educator; b. Endicott, N.Y., May 28, 1937; d. Leslie A. and Dora W. (Wright) O.; divorced; children: Philip I. Levy, Ellen D. and Laura A. Levy (twins). BA, Oberlin (Ohio) Coll., 1957; MD, Western Res. U., 1961; DSc (hon.), U. Med. Dental Sch. N.J., 1990; DMS (hon.), Yale U., 1992; DSc (hon.), Emory U., 1993, Oberlin Coll., 1993; LHD (hon.), Med. Coll. Pa., 1994; DSc (hon.), Rutgers U., 1994. Intern, then resident in pediatrics Harvard U. Hosp., 1961-64; postdoctoral fellow Johns Hopkins, 1964-65, U. Pitts., 1965-66; mem. faculty, prof. med. microbiology and pediat. U. Wis. Med. Sch., Madison, Wis., 1966-84; prof. pediat. and microbiology U. Wis. Med. Sch., 1975-84, assoc. dean Grad. Sch., 1975-84; dean Sch. Pub. Health U. Mich., 1984-93; prof. epidemiology, pediat. and communicable diseases U. Mich., Sch. Pub. Health and Med. Sch., 1984—; mem. rev. panel viral vaccine efficacy FDA, 1973-79, mem. vaccines and related biol. products adv. com., 1981-85; mem. exptl. virology study sect. Divsn. Rsch. Grants, NIH, 1975-79; mem. med. affairs com. Yale U. Coun., 1981-86; chmn. life scis. associateships rev. panel NRC, 1981-84; mem. U.S. Army Med. R&D Adv. Com., 1983-85; chmn. working group on AIDS and the Nation's Blood Supply, NHLBI, 1984-89; chmn. WHO Planning Group on AIDS and the Internat. Blood Supply, 1985-86. Contbr. articles to med. jours. Mem. task force on AIDS, Inst. of Medicine, 1986; mem. com. Robert Wood Johnson Found. Health Svcs. Program, 1986-91; mem. nat. adv. com. on health of pub. program Pew and Rockefeller Founds.; mem. health promotion and disease prevention bd. IOM, 1987-90, Global Commn. on AIDS, WHO, 1988-92; chmn. Nat. Commn. on AIDS, 1989-93; trustee Kaiser Found., 1990—; trustee Case Western Res. U., Cleve., 1993—; mem. coun. Inst. Medicine, 1995—; mem. Nat. Vaccine Adv. Cte., HHS, 1995—. Grantee NIH, 1969, 72, 74-75, Nat. Multiple Sclerosis Soc., 1971; Scientific Freedom and Responsibility Award AAAS, 1994. Fellow Am. Acad. Arts and Scis., Am. Acad. Pediat., Am. Acad. Microbiology, Infectious Diseases Soc. Am.; mem. Am. Assn. Immunologists, Soc. Pediat. Rsch., Inst. Medicine. Office: U Mich Dept Epidemiology Sch Pub Health Ann Arbor MI 48109

OSBORN, LESLIE ANDREWARTHA, psychiatrist; b. Warrnambool, Victoria, Australia, Aug. 10, 1906; came to U.S., 1931, naturalized, 1938; s. Andrew Rule and Annie (Delbridge) O.; m. Dora Wright, June 12, 1931 (dec.); children: Anne L. Osborn Krueger Henderson, June E.; m. Gwen F. Arnold, Aug. 13, 1960 (dec. Mar. 12, 1976); m. Corinne H. Kirchmaier, June 7, 1985. Student, Wesley Coll., Melbourne, 1920-23; M.B., B.S., Melbourne Med. Sch., 1929; M.D., U. Buffalo, 1945. Diplomate: Am. Bd. Psychiatry and Neurology, 1944. Intern Melbourne Gen. Hosp., 1930-31; postgrad. Post Grad. Hosp., N.Y.C., 1934; in chest diseases Trudeau Sch. Tb, Saranac Lake, 1937; in neurology and psychiatry Columbia U., 1940; gen. practice medicine, physician Endicott-Johnson Med. Dept., Binghamton, N.Y., 1932-38; asst. physician Willard (N.Y.) State Hosp., 1938-41; psychiatrist Meyer Meml. Hosp.; assoc. psychiatry U. Buffalo, 1941-45; attending psychiatrist, dir. psychiatry Edward J. Meyer Meml. Hosp., psychiat. service, 1946-49; prof. psychiatry U. Buffalo Sch. Medicine, 1946, acting dir. dept. psychiatry, 1946-49, head dept., 1949-50; dir. Wis. Psychiat. Inst.; prof. psychiatry U. Wis. Med. Sch., 1950-60; dir. div. mental hygiene Wis. Dept. Pub. Welfare, 1950-60; dir. Walworth County Family Counseling Center, 1960; prof. psychiatry dept. neurology and psychiatry U. Nebr., 1960-66; dir. Swanson Clinic for Multiply Handicapped Children, Nebr. Psychiat. Inst., Omaha, 1960-64; med. dir. Winnebago County Mental Health Clinic, Rockford, Ill., 1966; dir. Mental Health Services, Tompkins County, 1967-68; pvt. practice psychiatry Seneca Falls, N.Y., 1968-74, Scottsdale, Ariz., 1974—. Author: Psychiatry and Medicine, 1952, Prognosis, A Guide to the Study and Practice of Clinical Medicine, 1966, Foundation Learning and Innumeracy, 1977, King of the Hill: Chess for Children: 1981, Preventing War: A Doctor's Trilogy: Vol. 1 Living in a Changed World, 1994. Fellow Am. Psychiat. Assn. (life). Presbyterian. Address: 4800 N 68th St Unit 110 Scottsdale AZ 85251-1142 *Within 200 years a changed medical approach brought the Health Age. World War I troubled my childhood and another holocaust was coming as I began my practice. Homo sapiens was now the main cause* *of mortality and morbidity, and war spread like pestilence. The work of a country doctor began the control of pestilence; I have tried to apply the powerful principle he discovered to contribute to ultimate control of War. "Human history becomes more and more a race between education and catastrophe" (H. G. Wells). My 50-plus years of research have sought clues to the sense in which education may avert impending catastrophe. "Living in a Changed World" proposes a redesign of educating at all levels and prevention of schooling, personality and social problems leading ultimately to control and prevention of aggression.*

OSBORN, MARVIN GRIFFING, JR., educational consultant; b. Baton Rouge, Sept. 7, 1922; s. Marvin Griffing and Mamie (Hester) O.; m. Sarah Fleming, Aug. 3, 1945; children: Jane Fleming, Charles Porter. BA, La. State U., 1942, MA, 1946; LLD, St. Xavier U., 1971; DHum, Phillips U., 1977. Pub. relations counsel La. State U., 1945-47, acting dir. bur. pub. service, 1947; assoc. prof., chmn. dept. journalism and dir. pub. relations Howard Coll. (now Frank Samford U.), 1947-49; dir. pub. relations, lectr. journalism Miss. State Coll. (now Miss. State U.), 1949-53; dir. information Washington U., 1953-58, pub. relations adviser, 1955-58, dir. Devel. Funds, 1958-61; cons. coll. and univ. adminstrn., 1961—, including Drake, Duke, Phillips, Tampa, Tex. Christian univs., Atlantic Christian Coll. (now Barton Coll.), Bethany (W.Va.), Eckerd, Loretto Heights, St. Xavier U., Tenn. Wesleyan, Webster U., Hendrix, Mercy (Detroit), Bethel (Tenn.), McMurry U., St. Scholastica, Coker Coll., Christian Ch. Found., Nat. Meth. Found. Christian Higher Edn., Lexington Theol. Sem., Memphis Theol. Sem., Nat. Benevolent Assn. Christian Ch., Sisters of Loretto; interim pres. St. Xavier Coll., now St. Xavier U., 1968-69; mem. planning com. Conf. for Advancement Understanding and Support Higher Edn., White Sulphur Springs, W.Va., 1958; mem. exec. com. program and arrangements com. Gen. Assembly Christian Ch., 1977, 87-89. Bd. dirs. St. Louis Heart Assn., 1969-75, Fla. Christian Ctr., 1986-88; trustee Nat. City Christian Ch. Corp., 1981-85; mem. Christian Ch., bd. dirs., exec. com., sec. divsn. of higher edn., 1973-77, mem. panel to study fin. procedures of Christian Ch. (Disciples of Christ), 1987-89, Cypress Village Devel. Coun., Jacksonville, Fla., 1992—, chmn., 1995-96. Served from lt. to capt. 28th Inf. Divsn. AUS, 1942-45, ETO. Recipient Harry T. Ice award Christian Ch. Found., 1991. Mem. Am. Coll. Pub. Rels. Assn. (v.p. dists. 1951-52, v.p. membership 1952-53, sec.-treas. 1953-55, pres. 1959-60), Nat. Benevolent Assn. (amb. 1992—), Soc. Profl. Journalists, Omicron Delta Kappa, Sigma Chi. Home: 13655 Myrica Ct Jacksonville FL 32224-6626 also: PO Box 1639 Cashiers NC 28717-1639

OSBORN, MARY JANE MERTEN, biochemist; b. Colorado Springs, Colo., Sept. 24, 1927; d. Arthur John and Vivien Naomi (Morgan) Merten; m. Ralph Kenneth Osborn, Oct. 26, 1950. B.A., U. Calif., Berkeley, 1948; Ph.D., U. Wash., 1958. Postdoctoral fellow, dept. microbiology N.Y. U. Sch. Medicine, N.Y.C., 1959-61; instr. N.Y. U. Sch. Medicine, 1961-62, asst. prof., 1962-63; asst. prof. dept. molecular biology Albert Einstein Coll. Medicine, Bronx, N.Y., 1963-66; asso. prof. Albert Einstein Coll. Medicine, 1966-68; prof. dept. microbiology U. Conn. Health Center, Farmington, 1968—; dept. head U. Conn. Health Center, 1980—; mem. bd. sci. counselors Nat. Heart, Lung and Blood Inst., 1975-79; mem. Nat. Sci. Bd., 1980-86; adv. coun. Nat. Inst. Gen. Med. Sci., 1983-86, divsn. rsch. grants NIH, 1989-94, chair, 1992-94; trustee Biosci. Info. Systems, 1986-91; mem. German Am. Acad. Coun., 1994—; mem. space scis. bd. NRC, 1994—, chair com. space biology and medicine, 1994—. Assoc. editor Jour. Biol. Chemistry, 1978-80; contbr. articles in field of biochemistry and molecular biology to profl. jours. Mem. rsch. com. Am. Heart Assn., 1972-77, chair, 1976-77. NIH fellow, 1959-61; NIH grantee, 1962—; NSF grantee, 1965-68; Am. Heart Assn. grantee, 1968-71. Fellow Am. Acad. Arts and Scis. (coun. 1988-91), NAS (coun. 1990-93, com. sci. engring. and pub. policy 1993—); mem. Am. Chem. Soc. (chmn. divsn. biol. chemistry 1975-76), Am. Fedn. Soc. Exptl. Biology (pres. 1982-83), Am. Soc. Biol. Chemists (pres. 1981-82), Am. Soc. Microbiology. Democrat. Office: U Conn Health Ctr Dept Microbiology Farmington CT 06030

OSBORN, NANCY JO, insurance producer, small business owner; b. Springfield, Ill., Oct. 2, 1950; d. Elmer Charles Jr. and Edna Virginia (Lowe) Forcade; m. Scott Alan Guetterman, Mar. 1, 1969 (div. May 1978); children: Stephanie Ann Bertelsmann, Marsha Lynn.; m. Daniel Francis Osborn, Oct. 13, 1990; 1 chld, Caitlin Elizabeth. Grad. high sch., St. Teresa's Acad., East St. Louis, Ill. Lic. ins. producer. Clk., typist Forcade Ins. Agy., Granite City, Ill., 1972-80, casualty agt., 1980-82, property & casualty ins. agt., 1982—, life & health agt., 1984—, owner, chief exec. officer, 1986—; corp. sec. A-Age Elec. Contractors, Inc., Washington Pk., Ill., 1990—; dir. Kaskaskaia Indsl. Devel. Corp., 1992—; dir. Kaskaskia Indsl. Devel. Corp., Redbud, Ill., 1990—. Pres. Collinsville (Ill.) Jaycees, 1987-88, state dir., 1989-90; publicity chmn. Collinsville Italian Fest, 1992—. Named Outstanding Local Pres., Gateway Region Jaycees, 1987-88, #8 State Dir. of Yr., Ill. Jr. C. of C., 1989-90, Outstanding State Chmn. of 1st Quarter, 1990, Outstanding Membership Devel. State Chmn., 1990-91, Outstanding State Chmn. of Yr., 1990-91, Henry Giessenbier fellow, 1995. Mem. Nat. Model R.R. Assn., U.S. Jr. C. of C. (alumni mem.). Roman Catholic. Avocations: golf, quilting, oil painting, model railroading, Miss Illinois pageant training. Office: Forcade Ins Agy 1822 State St Granite City IL 62040-4619

OSBORN, RONALD EDWIN, minister, church history educator; b. Chgo., Sept. 5, 1917; s. George Edwin and Alma Edith (Lanterman) O.; m. Naomi Elizabeth Jackson, Sept. 10, 1940 (dec.); 1 dau., Virginia Elizabeth (dec.); m. Nola L. Neill, Aug. 29, 1986. Student, Lynchburg Coll., 1934-35, Union Theol. Sem. in Va., 1936; A.B., Philips U., 1938, M.A., 1939, B.D., 1942, Litt. D., 1969; postgrad., U. Okla., 1940-41; Ph.D., U. Oreg., 1955; D.D., Bethany Coll., 1989. Ordained to ministry Christian Ch. (Disciples of Christ), 1940. Min. Christian Ch., Lahoma, Okla., 1936-38, 1st Christian Ch., Geary, Okla., 1938-42, First Christian Ch., Jonesboro, Ark., 1942-43; editor youth publs. Christian Bd. Publ., St. Louis, 1943-45; prof. ch. history Northwest Christian Coll., Eugene, Oreg., 1946-50; min . Ch. of Christ, Creswell, Oreg., 1946-50; assoc. prof. ch. history Christian Theol. Sem. (formerly Butler U. Sch. Religion), Indpls., 1950-53, prof., 1953-73, dean, 1959-70; dir. ecumenical study Council Christian Unity, Disciples Christ, Indpls., 1954-57; vis. prof. ch. history and ecumenics Union Theol. Sem., Manila, Philippines, 1965; vis. prof. ch. history Sch. Theology, Claremont, Calif., 1970-71; prof. Sch. Theology, 1973-82; lectr. Grad. Sch. Ecumenical Studies, Chateau de Bossey, Switzerland, 1954-55; Del. World Conf. on Faith and Order, 1952, 63, 4th Assembly World Council Chs., Sweden, 1968; pres. Internat. Conv. Christian Chs., 1967-68; 1st moderator Christian Ch. (Disciples of Christ), 1968; staff Assembly World Council Chs., Evanston, Ill., 1954. Author: Toward the Christian Church, 1964, A Church for These Times, 1965, In Christ's Place, 1967, Experiment in Liberty, 1978, The Faith We Affirm, 1979, The Education of Ministers for the Coming Age, 1987, Creative Disarray: Models of Ministry in a Changing America, 1991; editor: Seeking God's Peace in a Nuclear Age, 1985, symposium The Reformation of Tradition, 1963, Encounter (formerly Shane Quar.), 1952-63. Mem. Disciples of Christ Hist. Soc. (trustee emeritus, past pres.), Am. Hist. Assn., Am. Soc. Ch. History, ACLU, Phi Kappa Phi, Theta Phi. Home: 85647 Bradbury Ln Eugene OR 97405-9683 *"A person who doesn't think is a slave; a person who won't imagine is a prisoner." — Daniel Dyer from "Imagine the world without imagination," Cleve. Plain Dealer, Jan. 3, 1986.*

OSBORN, TERRY WAYNE, biochemist, executive; b. Roswell, N.Mex., May 17, 1943; s. Woodrow Edward and Wilma Marie (Meador) O. AA, Ventura Coll., 1967; BS, U. Calif., Riverside, 1969; PhD, U. Calif.-Riverside, 1975; MBA, Pepperdine U., 1981. Research scientist McGaw Labs., Irvine, Calif., 1976, research scientist-project leader, 1976, research scientist, project team leader, 1976-77, group leader, sr. research scientist, 1978-79, mgr. clin. research, 1979-81, mktg. product mgr., 1981-82, mktg. group product mgr., 1982-83, dir. mktg., 1983-84; mktg. dir. IVAC Corp., San Diego, 1984-87; v.p. sales/mktg., officer Nichols Inst., Calif., 1987-89, v.p., asst. to chmn., 1990-91; v.p., gen. mgr. regional labs. Nichols Inst., 1991-93; pres., CEO Health Advance Inst., 1993—; 010 dirs. Med. Mktg. Assn., Peoria Med. Rsch. Corp.; mem. chemistry faculty Riverside City Coll., 1974-76, San Bernardino Valley Coll., 1974-76; asst. prof. clin. pharmacology U. Ill. Coll. Medicine. Served with U.S. Army, 1962-65. Recipient Agnes M. Toland Meml. Trust award, 1966; recipient Ventura Emblem Club award, 1967; Environ. Sci. fellow, 1970-73; Dean's Spl. fellow, 1974-75. Mem. Am. Chem. Soc., Am. Oil Chemists Soc., Med. Mktg. Assn. (bd. dirs.), Inst. Food Technologists, U.S. Ski Assn., One Mile Soc., Sigma Xi, Chi Gamma Iota, Alpha Gamma Sigma. Club: Tyrolean Ski (pres. 1972-73). Office: PO Box 1466 1 Illini Dr Peoria IL 61655-1466 *Nothing would be done at all if a man waited till he could do it so well that no one could find fault with it.*

OSBORN, WILLIAM A., trust company executive. Chmn. bd. dirs. No. Trust Corp., Chgo. Office: No Trust Corp 50 S La Salle St Chicago IL 60675*

OSBORN, WILLIAM GEORGE, savings and loan executive; b. Alton, Ill., Dec. 9, 1925; s. Ralph A. and Pauline J. (Horn) O.; m. Hilda M. Alexander, Aug. 12, 1950; children: Barbara K., David A., Robert W., James A. B.S. in Math., Shurtleff Coll., 1947; certificate, Grad. Sch. Savs. and Loan, Ind. U., 1946-48; A.M. in Econs., St. Louis U., 1962. With Germania Fed. Savs. and Loan Assn., Alton, 1946-90; exec. officer Germania Fed. Savs. and Loan Assn., 1955-86, pres., 1964-86, chmn., 1981-86, chmn. trust com., 1982-86; pres. Fin. Service Assocs., Ft. Lauderdale, Fla., 1986—; pres. Germania Fin. Corp., 1970-86; owner Fin. Guidance, Alton, 1951—; mem. Opportunities Unltd., 1954-58; instr. Am. Savs. and Loan Inst.; bd. dirs. Nat. Coun. Savs. Instns., Washington, 1984-86. Author: Savings and Loan Operating Policies Manual, 1960, Economic Factors Influencing Savings and Loan Interest Rates, 1962. Pres. Alton Wood River Community Chest, 1959; bd. dirs. Piasa Bird coun. Boy Scouts Am., 1961-88, Mississippi Valley Jr. Achievement, Alton Area United Fund, 1961-63; founder, bd. dirs., treas. New Piasa Chautauqua Ch. Assembly, 1982-86; treas. Lewis and Clark Community Coll. Found., 1976-86; bd. dirs., sec. Riverbend Civic Progress, 1984-86. Served to lt. (j.g.) USNR, 1943-46, 50-51. Mem. Nat. Assn. Bus. Economists, Nat. Economists Club, St. Louis Economists Club, Am. Inst. Mgmt. Presbyterian (elder). Clubs: Masons (Alton); Shriners; Lockhaven Country (Alton); Chautauqua (Ill.) Yacht.

OSBORNE, BURL, newspaper publisher, editor; b. Jenkins, Ky., June 25, 1937; s. Oliver and Juanita (Smallwood) O.; m. Betty S. Wilder, Feb. 14, 1974; 1 son, Burl Jonathan. Student, U. Ky., 1955-57; B.A. in Journalism, Marshall U., 1960; M.B.A., L.I. U. Sch. Bus., 1984; A.M.P., Harvard Bus. Sch., 1984. Reporter Ashland (Ky.) Daily Ind., 1957-58; reporter, editor Sta. WHTN-TV, Huntington, W.Va., 1958-60; corr. AP, Bluefield, W.Va., 1960-62; statehouse corr. AP, Charleston, W.Va., 1963-64; corr. AP, Spokane, Wash., 1964-67; news editor AP, Denver, 1967-70; chief of bur. AP, Ky., 1970-72, Ohio, 1972-74; asst. chief of bur. AP, Washington, 1974-76; mng. editor AP, N.Y.C., 1977-80; exec. editor Dallas Morning News, 1980-83, v.p., 1981, sr. v.p., editor, 1983-84, pres., editor, 1985-90, pub., editor, 1991—; bd. dirs., pres. publ. divsn. A.H. Belo Corp., AP; bd. dirs. Pulitzer Prize, 1986-95, co-chair, 1994-95; bd. mem. adv. com. Nieman Found., Harvard U.; mem. journalism adv. com. Knight Found. Named Newspaper Exec. of Yr., Nat. Press Found., 1992; inducted to Ky. Journalism Hall of Fame, 1994. Mem. Orgn. Profl. Journalists, Am. Soc. Newspaper Editors (bd. dirs. 1982-91, pres. 1990-91), Am. Newspaper Pubs. Assn., Am. Press Inst. (chmn. 1988-93), Tex. Daily Newspaper Assn. (bd. dirs. 1982-92, pres. 1993), So. Newspaper Pub. Assn. (bd. dirs. 1995—). Home: 7609 Southwestern Blvd Dallas TX 75225-7927 Office: Dallas Morning News AH Belo Corp PO Box 655237 Dallas TX 75265-5237

OSBORNE, CHARLES WILLIAM (BILL OSBORNE), transportation executive; b. Dungannon, Va., Nov. 9, 1942; s. David Doyle and Lula Cordelia (Gillenwater) O.; m. Sandra Jean Elliot, Oct. 6, 1968; children: Jennifer, Michael, William. BS, Va. Tech., 1965; MA, West Ga. Coll., 1975. Mktg. planner Union Oil Co., Schaumburg, Ill., 1974-75, mgr. mktg. planning, 1981-82, mgr. purchasing, 1983-84, divsn. mktg. mgr., 1984-86; gen. mgr. mktg. Union Oil Co., Schaumburg, 1986-89; dist. sales mgr. Union Oil Co., Atlanta, 1975-78, mgr. divsn. svc., 1978-81; v.p. mktg. Uno-Ven Co., Arlington Heights, Ill., 1989-93; pres., CEO, bd. dirs. Nat. Auto/Truckstops, Inc., Nashville, 1992—; spl. asst. to chmn. U.S. Internat. Trade Commn., Washington, 1982-83. Bd. dirs. N.W. Comty. Hosp., Arlington Heights, 1989-94; active bus. adv. bd. Roosevelt U., Arlington Heights, 1989-94. 1st lt. U.S. Army, 1966-68. Mem. Am. Trucking Assn., Nat. Assn. Truckstop Operators, Petroleum Marketers Assn. Am., Petroleum Marketers Edn. Found. (bd. dirs.), Soc. Ind. Gasoline Marketers. Avocations: golf, racquetball, reading. Home: 6201 Belle Rive Dr Brentwood TN 37027-5613 Office: National Auto/Truckstops Inc 3100 W End Ave Ste 200 PO Box 76 Nashville TN 37202

OSBORNE, DEE S., banker; b. Winters, Tex., Dec. 14, 1930; s. M.S. and Lillie (Hambright) O.; m. Patricia Anne Seeley; children: Cynthia Anne Osborne Beckham, Shelley Elizabeth Osborne Allen. BBA, West Tex. State U., 1952; LLB, U. Tex., 1955. Bar: Tex. 1955. Assoc. Price, Veltmann & Skelton, Houston, 1957-63; v.p., treas. South Coast Life Ins. Co., Houston, 1963-66; exec. v.p. fin. Quintana Petroleum Corp., Houston, 1966-78; co-chmn. bd. Cullen Ctr. Bank & Trust Co., 1969-78; chmn. bd. Cullen Savs. Assn., 1972-78, Cullen Ctr., Inc., 1974-78, Cullen Bankers, Inc., 1975-78; vice chmn. bd. Citizens Nat. Bank-Dallas, 1973-77; co-chmn., pres. Finial Investment Corp., Houston, 1978—; pres., dir. internat. Bank of Fin., Cayman Island, B.W.I., 1977—, also bd. dirs.; chief exec. officer, pres. Magnesium Internat. Corp., Ltd.; chmn. Uniteg Investment Co.; bd. dirs. Seagull Energy Corp., EnCap/Tenneco Joint Venture, Bogan Aerotech, Inc., EOTT Energy Corp., Jacintoport Terminal Co., Legacy Trust Co. Trustee Scott and White Meml. Hosp., Vivian L. Smith Found., Sherwood and Brindley Found., Temple, Tex., Ralph A. Johnston Found. Endowment; mem. adv. com. U. Houston System; fin. com. St. Luke's Meth. Ch.; mem. devel. bd. U. Tex. Health Sci. Ctr., Houston; mem. tech. investment and licensing com. Pres. Adv. Coun. Houston Advanced Rsch. Ctr. With U.S. Army, 1955-57. Mem. Tex. Bar Assn., Houston Bar Assn., Houston Country Club, Coronado Club (bd. dirs.). Home: 3860 Olympia Dr Houston TX 77019-3032 Office: 6800 Texas Commerce Tower Houston TX 77002

OSBORNE, GEORGE DELANO, performing arts company director; b. Ft. Worth, Aug. 25, 1938; s. Hugh and Eula Catherine (Trent) O.; children from previous marriage: David Warren, Hugh Philip, George Douglas. B in Mus, Oklahoma City U., 1960; M in Mus, Ind. U., 1964; postgrad. in Arts Mgmt., Hartford Grad. Ctr., 1978. Mem. faculty Tex. Tech. U., Lubbock, 1962-64, S.W. Mo. State U., Springfield, 1964-66, Memphis State U., 1966-76, W.Va. U., Morgantown, 1976-78; gen. dir. Memphis Opera, Morgantown, 1971-76, Hartford (Conn.) Chamber Orch., Morgantown, 1978-79, Conn. Opera, Hartford, 1979—, Hartford Chamber Orch., 1979-88, Hartford Ballet, 1982-88; dir. opera prodns. Hartt Sch. Music, U. Hartford, 1993—. Mem. Hartford Cultural Affairs Commn., 1980. Fulbright scholar, Rome, 1960; Am. Leadership Forum fellow, 1986-87. Mem. Cen. Opera Svc. (regional dir.), Nat. Opera Assn. Home: 26 River View Avon CT 06001 Office: Conn Opera Assn 226 Farmington Ave Hartford CT 06105-3501

OSBORNE, HAROLD WAYNE, sociology educator, consultant; b. Eldorado, Ark., Sept. 5, 1930; s. Carl Clinton and Mary Eunice (Peace) O.; m. Alice June Williams, Feb. 15, 1953; children—Michael, Van, Samuel. B.A. in History, Ouachita Bapt. Coll., 1952; M.A. in Sociology, La. State U., 1956, Ph.D. in Sociology, 1959. Research assoc. dept. rural sociology La. State U., 1954-56; social sci. analyst USDA, Baton Rouge, 1956-58; asst. prof. sociology Baylor U., Waco, 1958-60; assoc. prof. Baylor U., 1960-63, prof., 1963—, dir. grad. studies dept. sociology, 1963-87, chair dept. sociology, anthropology, social work and gerontology, 1988—; cons. in field; dir. workshops on crime and delinquency. Co-editor: Research Methods: Issues and Insights, 1971, Sociology: A Pragmatic Approach, 1996; co-author: Sociology: A Pragmatic Approach, 1981; assoc. editor for sociology Social Sci. Quar., 1965-75. Bd. dirs. Mclennan County Mental Health Assn., Tex., 1970-80. Served with inf. U.S. Army, 1952-54. Named Outstanding Baylor Prof., Baylor U., 1976, Master Tchr., 1993. Mem. Am. Sociol. Assn., Southwestern Sociol. Assn. (v.p. 1985-87, pres. 1987-88), Southwestern Social Sci. Assn., Population Assn. Am., Population Reference Bur., Am. Social Health Assn. (bd. dirs. Southwestern region). Democrat. Baptist. Home: 2717 Braemar St Waco TX 76710-2118 Office: Baylor U Dept Sociology Waco TX 76798

OSBORNE, HARRY ALAN, orthodontist; b. Youngstown, Ohio, Mar. 9, 1934; s. Kenneth L. and Marguerite (Filmer) O.; m. Carol June Williams, June 30, 1956 (dec. 1989); children: Elizabeth Ann, J. Scott, Linda J., Robert K.; m. Linda Sue Leister Simmons, May 9, 1993; stepchildren: William A. Simmons, John S. Simmons, Susan Jane Simmons. Student, Westminster Coll., New Wilmington, Pa., 1952-55; DDS, U. Pitts., 1959; MS, Northwestern U., 1962. Diplomate Am. Bd. Orthodontics. Intern Youngstown Hosp. Assn., 1959; practice dentistry specializing in orthodontics Canton, Ohio, 1964—. Supt. adv. com. North Canton Sch. Dist., 1960-87; mem. adv. com. Soc. Bank, Canton, 1962-89; chmn. bldg. com. Faith United Meth. Ch., 1975-80; chmn. cmty bd. YMCA, North Canton, 1986-96, charter mem. Heritage Club; v.p. Hills and Dales Homeowners Assn., 1993-96; mem. Christ Presbyn. Ch., Canton, Ohio. Recipient Disting. Service award, Jaycees, 1968. Mem. ADA, Am. Assn. Orthodontists, Coll. of Diplomates of Am. Bd. Orthodontists (charter), Gt. Lakes Orthodontic Assn., Ohio Dental Assn., Cleve. Orthodontic Soc. (pres. 1983), Stark County Dental Soc. (pres. 1975-76), World Fedn. Orthodontists, Internat. Coll. Dentists, Shady Hollow Country Club (Massillion, Ohio) (bd. dirs. 1984-85, 87—), Brookside Country Club. Republican. Avocation: golf. Home: 2410 Strathmore Dr NW Canton OH 44708-1364 Office: 1021 Schneider St SE Canton OH 44720-3857

OSBORNE, JAMES ALFRED, religious organization administrator; b. Toledo, July 3, 1927; s. Alfred James and Gladys Irene (Gaugh) O.; m. Ruth Glenrose Campbell, Nov. 26, 1945; 1 child, Constance Jean (Mrs. Donald William Canning). Grad., Salvation Army Coll., 1947; student, U. Chattanooga, 1954-55; D of Pub. Svc. (hon.), Gordon Coll., 1991. Corps officer Salvation Army, Magness, Nashville, 1947, Southside, Memphis, 1948, Owensboro, Ky., 1949-54; comdg. officer Salvation Army, Chattanooga, 1954-61; city comdr. Salvation Army, Miami, Fla., 1961-65; divisional sec. Ky.-Tenn. Div. Salvation Army, 1965-68, gen. sec. N.C. and S.C. Div., 1968-70, pub. rels. sec. 15 so. states, D.C. and Mex., 1970-71, divisional comdr. Md. and No. W.Va. Div., 1971-73; divisional comdr. Nat. Capital and Virginias Div. Salvation Army, Washington, 1973-78; divisional comdr. Fla. Div. Salvation Army, 1978-80, chief sec. Western Ter., 1980-84; nat. chief sec. Salvation Army, Verona, N.J., 1984-86; territorial comdr. so. states Salvation Army, Atlanta, 1986-89; nat. comdr., Republic of Marshall Islands, Guam, P.R., Virgin Islands Salvation Army USA, 1989-93; chmn. Salvation Army Nat. Planning and Devel. Commn., 1974-76, 84-86; exec. bd. Vision Interfaith Satellite Network, Nat. Assn. Evangelicals, Christian Children's Fund Inc.; chmn. bd. Christian Mgmt. Assn., 1993-94; exec. com. religious alliance Against Pornography; rep. Salvation Army to numerous orgns. Bd. dirs. Nat. Law Ctr. for Children and Families; sec. Tenn. Conf. on Social Welfare, 1959, v.p., 1960; pres. Fla. Conf. on Social Welfare, 1965; pres. Ky. Welfare Assn., 1970. Mem. Chattanooga Pastors Assn. (pres. 1958), Va. and W. Va. Welfare Confs., Rotary.

OSBORNE, JAMES WILLIAM, radiation biologist; b. Pana, Ill., Jan. 17, 1928; s. Samuel Frederick and Ruby Clascena (Irel) O.; m. Marilyn Corrine Shaw, July 1, 1950; children—Walter, David. B.S., U. Ill., Champaign-Urbana, 1949, M.S., 1951, Ph.D., 1955. Research asst. dept. physics U. Ill., 1949-51; research asso. Control Systems Lab., 1951-55; asst. prof. Radiation Research Lab., U. Iowa, 1955-61, assoc. prof., 1961-67, prof., 1967—, dir. lab., 1978-93; dir. grad. program radiation biology U. Iowa, 1978—. Served with USAAF, 1946-47. Mem. Am. Soc. Therapeutic Radiology and Oncology, Radiation Rsch. Soc., Am. Physiol. Soc., Cell Kinetics Soc., Soc. Exptl. Biology and Medicine, Am. Assn. for Cancer Rsch., Sigma Xi. Methodist. Research, publs. on biol. effects of radiation and kinetics of cell populations. Home: 815 14th Ave Coralville IA 52241-1742 Office: Radiation Research Lab 77 Med Labs U Iowa Iowa City IA 52242

OSBORNE, JOHN WALTER, historian, educator, author; b. Bklyn., Aug. 19, 1927; s. Douglas Walter and Gertrude Ann (Purcell) O.; m. Frances Patricia Hannon, Aug. 2, 1958; 1 son, David. B.A., Rutgers U., 1957, M.A. (Louis Bevier fellow), 1959, Ph.D., 1961. Asst. prof. history Kean Coll. of N.J., 1961-63, N.J. Inst. Tech., 1963-64; asst. prof. Rutgers U., New Brunswick, N.J., 1964-66; assoc. prof. Rutgers U., 1966-69, prof., 1969-93, prof. emeritus, 1993—. Author: William Cobbett-His Thought and His Times, 1966, The Silent Revolution: The Industrial Revolution in England as a Source of Cultural Change, 1970, John Cartwright, 1972; co-author: Cobbett in His Times, 1990; editor: Jour. of Rutgers U. Libraries, 1975-80; co-editor: A Grammar of the English Language, 1983; contbr. articles to profl. jours. Recipient Henry Browne award for disting. teaching Rutgers U., 1988; Am. Philos. Soc. grantee, 1966, 75. Home: 16 Townwoods Rd Ivoryton CT 06442-1271

OSBORNE, MARY POPE, writer; b. Ft. Sill, Okla., May 20, 1949; d. William Perkins and Barnette (Dickens) Pope; m. William R. Osborne, May 16, 1976. BA in Religion, U. N.C., 1971. Author: Run, Run, As Fast As You Can, 1982, Love Always, Blue, 1983, Best Wishes, Joe Brady, 1984, Mo to the Rescue, 1985, Last One Home, 1986, Beauty and the Beast, 1987, Favorite Greek Myths, 1988, American Tall Tales, 1990, The Many Lives of Benjamin Franklin, 1990, Moon Horse, 1991, George Washington, Leader of a New Nation, 1991, Spider Kane Mystery Series, 1992, 93, Magic Tree House Series, 1992-95, Haunted Waters, 1994, Molly and the Prince, 1994. Recipient Disting. Alumna award U. N.C., Chapel Hill, 1994. Mem. PEN, Authors Guild (pres. 1993—, dir. found.), Authors League Fund (bd. dirs.), Author's Registry (founder). Office: Brandt & Brandt Lit Agy 1501 Broadway Ste 2310 New York NY 10036-5601

OSBORNE, PAUL DOUGLAS, hospital administrator; b. Blackwater, Va., Apr. 29, 1943; s. Paul James and Addie Mae (Bledsoe) O.; m. Susan Henry, Apr. 23, 1966; children: Karen D. Bennett, Amy Lynn. BA, Lynchburg Coll., 1965; MHA, Ga. State U., 1971. Health planner Ctrl. Va. Health Planning Coun., Lynchburg, Va., 1971-72; assoc. adminstr. N.E. Ga. Reg. Med. Ctr., Gainesville, Ga., 1972-76; adminstr. Mary Black Meml. Hosp., Spartanburg, S.C., 1976-80; v.p. Spartanburg (S.C.) Regional Med. Ctr., 1980-90; dep. supt. Ctrl. State Hosp., Milledgeville, Ga., 1990—. Bd. dirs. United Way Ctrl. Ga., 1993—, Regional Girl Scout Coun., 1987-90, Salvation Army, 1986-88; sr. warden St. Christopher's Episc. Ch., Spartanburg, 1983. Capt. U.S. Army, 1966-69, Vietnam. Fellow Am. Coll. Healthcare Execs., Milledgeville Country Club, Rotary. Avocations: tennis, photography. Home: 218 Pine Knoll Ln SE Eatonton GA 31024 Office: Ctrl St Hosp Dept Supt Milledgeville GA 31062

OSBORNE, RICHARD DE JONGH, mining and metals company executive; b. Bronxville, N.Y., Mar. 19, 1934; s. Stanley de Jongh and M. Elizabeth (Ide) O.; m. Cheryl Anne Archibald, Dec. 14, 1957; children: Leslie Coleman, Lindsay Vogel, Nicholas de J., Stanley De J. A.B. in Econs., Princeton U., 1956. With Cuno Engring. Corp., Meriden, Conn., 1956-60; fin., planning and mktg. exec. IBM Corp., Armonk, N.Y., 1960-69; investment adviser Sherman M. Fairchild, N.Y.C., 1969-70; exec. v.p. fin. and bus. devel., dir. Fairchild Camera & Instrument Corp., Mountain View, Calif., 1970-74; v.p. fin. ASARCO Inc. (formerly Am. Smelting & Refining Co.), N.Y.C., 1975-77, exec. v.p., 1977-81, pres., 1982-85, chmn., pres., chief exec. officer, 1985—, also bd. dirs.; bd. dirs. Schering-Plough Corp., B.F. Goodrich, The Tinker Found.; chmn. Copper Devel. Assn. Mem. Nat. Mining Assn., Ams. Soc., Coun. Fgn. Rels. (bd. dirs.), Am. Australian Assn. (bd. dirs.), Internat. Copper Assn. (bd. dirs.), Down Town Assn., Econs. Club, City Midday Club, Sakonnet Golf Club. Home: 40 E 94th St Apt 32B New York NY 10128-0759 Office: Asarco Inc 180 Maiden Ln New York NY 10038-4925

OSBORNE, RICHARD HAZELET, anthropology and medical genetics educator; b. Kennecott, Alaska, June 18, 1920; s. Clarence Edward and Margaret Jerenne (Hazelet) O.; m. Barbara White, Oct. 14, 1944; children: Susan, Richard, David; m. Barbara Teachman, Sept. 1, 1970. Student, U. Alaska, 1939-41; BS, BA, U. Wash., 1949; postgrad., Harvard U., 1949-50; PhD (Viking Fund Pre-doctoral fellow, Spl. fellow Inst. for Study Human Variation), Columbia, 1956; hon. doctor odontology, U. Oulu, Finland, 1994. Research asso. Columbia U., 1953-58; asst. Sloan-Kettering Inst., N.Y.C., 1958-60; asso. Sloan-Kettering Inst., 1960-62, asso. mem., head sect. human genetics, 1962-64; prof. anthropology and med. genetics U. Wis., Madison, 1964-86, prof. emeritus, 1986—; asso. prof. preventive medicine Cornell Med. Coll., 1962-64; clin. geneticist Meml. Hosp. for Cancer, N.Y.C., 1963-65; vis. scientist Forsyth Dental Center, Boston, 1969-71; cons. human genetics Newington (Conn.) Childrens Hosp., 1971-73; Mem. com. on epidemiology and vets. follow-up studies NRC, 1969-73; mem. perinatal research com. Nat. Inst. Neurol. Diseases and Stroke, NIH, 1970-72; mem. cultural anthropology fellowship and rev. NIMH, 1969-73. Author: Genetic Basis of Morphological Variation, 1959, Biological and Social Meaning of Race, 1971; Editor: Social Biology, 1961-77, 81—; contbr. articles to profl. jours.

Served to maj. USAAF, 1942-46. Decorated D.F.C., Air medal with 3 oak leaf clusters.; Named Health Research Council Career Scientist City N.Y., 1962-64. Fellow Explorers Club; Mem. Am. Assn. Phys. Anthropology (exec. com. 1965-67, v.p. 1968-70), Am. Soc. for Human Genetics (dir. 1960-61, 67-69), Behavior Genetics Assn. (pres. pro-tem 1970-71), Soc. for Study Social Biology (dir. 1981-83, 86—), Pioneers of Alaska (life), Sigma Xi. Office: PO Box 2349 Port Angeles WA 98362-0303

OSBORNE, RICHARD JAY, electric utility company executive; b. N.Y.C., Feb. 16, 1951; s. Victor and Evelyn Celia (Sweetbaum) O. B.A., Tufts U., 1973; M.B.A., U. N.C., 1975. Fin. analyst Duke Power Co., Charlotte, N.C., 1975-78, sr. fin. analyst, 1978-80, mgr. fin. rels., 1980-81, mgr. treasury activities, 1981, treas., 1981-88, v.p. fin., CFO, 1988-94, sr. v.p., CFO, 1994—. Pres. Charlotte Jewish Fedn. Mem. Fin. Execs. Inst., Edison Electric Inst. (fin. & regulatory sect.), Found. for the Carolinas (chmn. investment com.), N.C. Coun. Edn. (chair). Democrat. Jewish. Office: Duke Power Co 422 S Church St Charlotte NC 28242-0001

OSBORNE, STANLEY DE JONGH, investment banker; b. San Jose, Costa Rica, Mar. 27, 1905; m. Elizabeth Ide, Oct. 28, 1929 (dec. Sept. 1984); children: Mary Ide (Mrs. John Witherbee), Richard de Jongh, Cynthia Adams (Mrs. Richard M. Hoskin). Student, Phillips Acad., Andover, Mass., 1918-22; AB cum laude, Harvard U., 1926, postgrad. bus. sch., 1926-27. Dir. publicity Harvard Athletic Assn., 1927-28; with Old Colony Corp., Boston, 1928-29; asst. to pres. Atlantic Coast Fisheries Co., 1929-30, treas., 1930-36, 39-43, sec., 1932-42, v.p., 1936-43; spl. asst. to rubber dir. Washington, 1942-43; v.p. Eastern Airlines, Inc., 1944-50; fin. v.p. Mathieson Chem. Corp., Balt., 1950-54; exec. v.p. Olin Mathieson Chem. Corp., 1954-57, pres., chmn. dir., 1957-64; gen. ptnr. Lazard Freres & Co., N.Y.C., 1963-69, ltd. ptnr., 1970—; chmn. Pvt. Investment Corp. for Asia, Singapore, 1980-85. Spl. asst. to Pres., Am. Olympic Team, Gen. Douglas McArthur, Amsterdam, 1928; spl. adviser to Pres. John F. Kennedy, 1963-64; mem. Pres.'s Adv. Com. Supersonic Transport, 1964-67; spl. cons. to adminstr. NASA, 1966-68; bd. govs. Soc. N.Y. Hosp.-Cornell Med. Ctr., N.Y.C., 1957—, pres., 1975-80, chmn., 1980-85, hon. chmn., 1986—. Mem. Harvard Club, Brook Club, River Club. Episcopalian. Home: 1 E End Ave New York NY 10021-1102 Office: Lazard Freres & Co 30 Rockefeller Plz New York NY 10020

OSBORNE, TOM, college football coach; b. Feb. 23, 1937; m. Nancy Tederman; children: Mike, Ann, Susie. B.A., Hastings Coll., 1959; M.A., U. Nebr., 1963, Ph.D. in Ednl. Psychology, 1965. Flankerback Washington Redskins, NFL, 1959-61, San Francisco 49ers, NFL, 1961-62; asst. football coach U. Nebr., 1962-73, head football coach, 1973—; coach team U. Nebr. (Cotton Bowl), 1974, U. Nebr. (Sugar Bowl), 1971, U. Nebr. (Astro-Bluebonnet Bowl), 1976, U. Nebr. (Liberty Bowl), 1977, U. Nebr. (Sun Bowl), 1980, U. Nebr. (Orange Bowl), 1979, 83, 84, 89, 92-95. Served in U.S. Army. Named Big Eight Coach of Yr., 1975, 78, 80; named Bobby Dodds Nat. Coach of Yr., 1978. Coached team to NCAA Divsn. IA Nat. Championship, 1994. Office: care Nebr Sports Info 116 South Stadium Lincoln NE 68588*

OSBORNE-POPP, GLENNA JEAN, health services administrator; b. East Rainelle, W.Va., Jan. 5, 1945; d. B.J. and Jean Ann (Haranac) Osborne; m. Thomas Joseph Ferrante Jr., June 11, 1966 (div. Nov. 1987); 1 child, Thomas Joseph Osborne; m. Brian Mark Popp, Aug. 13, 1988. BA cum laude, U. Tampa, 1966; MA, Fairleigh Dickinson U., 1982; cert., Kean Coll., 1983. Cert. English, speech, dramatic arts tchr., prin./supr.; cert. nursing child assessment feeding scale and nursing child assessment tchg. scale, 1996. Tchr. Raritan High Sch., Hazlet, N.J., 1966; tchr. Keyport (N.J.) Pub. Schs., 1968-86, coord. elem. reading and lang. arts, 1980-84, supr. curriculum and instrn., 1984-86; prin. Weston Sch., Manville, N.J., 1986-88, The Bartle Sch., Highland Park, N.J., 1988-91, Orange Ave. Sch., Cranford, N.J., 1991-92; dir. The Open Door Youth Shelter, Binghamton, N.Y., 1992-94; child protective investigator supr. Dept. Health and Rehab. Svcs., Orlando, Fla., 1994-95; program supr. Children's Home Soc., Sanford, Fla., 1995; clin. supr. Healthy Families-Orange, Orlando, Fla., 1995—; regional trainer Individualized Lang. Arts, Weehawken, N.J., 1976-86; cons. McDougal/Little Pubs., Evanston, Ill., 1982-83; adv. bd. Women's Residential Ctr., Orlando, 1996, Ctr. for Drug-Free Living, Orlando, 1996. Contbr. chpt. to: A Resource Guide of Differentiated Learning Experiences for Gifted Elementary Students, 1981. Sunday sch. tchr. Reformed Ch., Keyport, 1975-80, supt. Sunday sch., 1982-84. Mem. Order Ea. Star (Tampa, Fla.), Phi Delta Kappa. Republican. Methodist. Avocation: writing. Office: Healthy Families 6231 S Texas Ave Orlando FL 32805

OSBOURN, GORDON CECIL, materials scientist; b. Kansas City, Mo., Aug. 13, 1954; 2 children. BS, U. Mo., 1974, MS, 1975; PhD in Physics, Calif. Inst. Tech., 1979. Tech. staff Sandia Nat. Labs., 1979-83, divsn. supr., 1983—. Recipient E.O. Lawrence award Dept. Energy, 1985; Internat. prize For New Materials Am. Physical Soc., 1993. Fellow Am. Physical Soc. Home: 5851 Lost Dutchman Ave NE Albuquerque NM 87111-5902 Office: Sandia Nat Labs MS 1423 Albuquerque NM 87185-1423

OSBOURNE, OZZY (JOHN OSBOURNE), vocalist; b. Birmingham, Eng., Dec. 3, 1948. Vocalist Black Sabbath band, 1969-78, solo career, 1978—. Albums include Blizzard of Ozz, 1980, Diary of a Madman, 1981, Bark at the Moon, 1983, The Ultimate Sin, 1986, No Rest for the Wicked, 1989, Just Say Ozzy, 1990 (EP), No More Tears, 1991, Live & Loud, 1993, (with Black Sabbath) Black Sabbath, 1969, Paranoid, 1970, Master of Reality, 1971, Sabotage, 1975, Technical Ecstasy, 1976, Never Say Die, 1978; singles: So Tired, 1984, (with Black Sabbath) Paranoid, 1970. Grammy award, Best Heavy Metal Performance 1994 for "I Don't Want to Change the World".

OSBURN, CHARLES BENJAMIN, librarian, university dean; b. Pitts., May 25, 1939; s. C. Benjamin and Lydia (Harmon) O.; divorced; 1 child, Christopher Bart; m. Sharon Tuffendsam, June 12, 1987; 1 stepchild, Bradley Alan Tuffendsam. B.A., Grove City Coll., 1961; M.A., Pa. State U., 1963; M.S., U. N.C., 1971; Ph.D., U. Mich., 1978. Instr. French Pa. State U., University Park, 1963-66; asst. prof. U. Wis.-Whitewater, 1966-69; humanities bibliographer U. N.C., Chapel Hill, 1969-74; asst. dir. libraries SUNY-Buffalo, 1974-76; asst. univ. librarian Northwestern U., Evanston, 1976-80; dean, univ. librarian U. Cin., 1980-86; dean libraries U. Ala., Tuscaloosa, 1986—; prof. library sci. U. Ala., 1986—; bd. dirs. Ctr. for Research Libraries, Chgo., SOLINET, Atlanta, Assn. Rsch. Librs., 1987-93; mem. rsch. libr. adv. counc. to Online Computer Library Ctr., Dublin, Ohio. Author: Academic Research and Library Resources: Changing Patterns in America, 1979 (award ALA 1980); compiler: Research and Reference Guide to French Studies, 2d edit., 1981; mem. editorial bd. Literary Research: A Journal of Scholarly Method and Technique, 1986—; co-editor: (with R. W. Atkinson) Collection Management: A New Treatise, 2 vols., 1991. Mem. ALA, MLA, Assn. Rsch. Librs., Phi Sigma Iota, Beta Phi Mu. Office: University of Alabama Library Office of the Librarian Tuscaloosa AL 35487

OSBURN, ELLA KATHERINE, elementary education educator; b. Waycross, Ga., Nov. 25, 1961; d. William Daniel and Mabelle Irene (Tatum) O. BS in Home and Consumer Econs., Freed-Hardeman Coll., Henderson, Tenn., 1984, MEd in Curriculum and Instrn., 1992. Cert. in elem. edn. K-8, Ga. Tchr. 1st grade South Ga. Christian Acad., Albany, 1986-88; substitute tchr. Gwinnett County Schs., Lawrenceville, Ga., 1988-89; childcare worker The Children's Home, Valdosta, Ga., 1989-90; sec. Ga. Christian, Valdosta, 1990-91; tchr. 1st grade S.W. Elem.-Hancock County Schs., 1994-96. Author: (curriculum guide) Log of Intervention and Curriculum Guides for Reading Difficulties, 1991-92. Mem. NEA, Ga. Assn. Educators, Smithsonian Inst. Mem. Ch. of Christ. Avocations: collecting and saving pennies, travel, collecting antiques, playing putt-putt golf. Home: PO Box 575 Hoschton GA 30548

OSBURNE, LEANNE CHRISTY, financial consultant; b. New Castle, Pa., May 2, 1936; d. Leon Roosevelt and Anna Mae (Milsom) Christy; children: John Christy Lind, Patrick James. Student, Jacksonville U., 1953-64, postgrad., 1979, 90; MS in Fin. Svcs., Am. Coll., 1979, MS in Mgmt., 1990. CLU, ChFC; registered securities rep., registered securities prin. Claims examiner, agent Prudential Ins. Co., Jacksonville, Fla., 1953-66; v.p. H.M. Harrell Assocs.-Gulf Life Ins. Co., Jacksonville, 1967-74; prodn. mgr. Travelers Ins. Co., Jacksonville, 1974-82; mktg. officer USF&G Corp., Balt., 1982-92; owner cons. practice Jacksonville, 1993—; owner Annuity Mktg. Inst., Jacksonville, 1992—; mem. pres.'s cabinet USF&G Corp., Balt., 1986-92; bd. dirs. Stelko Corp., Sarasota, Fla.; mem. ins. adv. com. Fla. C.C., Jacksonville, 1975-82. Author: Executive Personal Power, 1990, Annuities, 1992. Recipient Eve award Bus. Woman of Yr., Fla. Pub. Co., 1978, Ins. Exec. of Yr. award Fla. C.C. of Jacksonville and CLU Chpt., 1979. Mem. N.E. Fla. Estate Planning Coun. (bd. dirs. 1979-83), Women's Life Underwriters Conf. (nat. bd. dirs. 1981-83), Jacksonville Assn. Life Underwriters (pres. 1981-82), Jacksonville chpt. CLU and ChFC (pres. 1980-81, Heritage Heubner award 1979), Jacksonville Women's Network (founding bd. dirs. 1979), Torch Club Internat. (pres. Jacksonville chpt. 1982, pres. Balt. chpt. 1988), Bull Snort Forum (treas. 1975-82), Mensa (pres. Jacksonville chpt. 1969-79). Unitarian. Avocations: fibre arts, sports cars. Home: # 1043 7701 Baymeadows Cir W Apt 1043 Jacksonville FL 32256-7782

OSBY, LARISSA GEISS, artist; b. Artemowsk, Russia, June 7, 1928; came to U.S., 1951, naturalized, 1958; d. Andrew Frank and Valentine G. (Pogoreloff) Geiss; m. Howard M. Osby, June 7, 1952; children: Erik Andrew, Karin Marian. Student, U. Goettingen (Germany), 1947, 48, 49, Acad. Art, 1949-50, U. Munich, 1949-50; postgrad., U. Goettingen, Germany, 1951. BA in Philosophy U. Goettingen, Germany, 1950, MA in Philosophy, 1951; rsch. asst., translator, med. illustrator U. Pitts. Med. Sch., 1952-53; art instr. Pitts. Ctr. for Arts, 1961-64, 88-90; pvt. art tchr. Pitts., 1961-64; adv. artist Pitts. Bd. Edn., 1964-66; instr. anatomy, drawing and painting High Sch. for Creative and Performing Arts, Pitts., 1984—. One woman shows at, AAP Gallery, Pitts., 1960, Pitts. Plan for Art Gallery, 1961, 63, 65, 68, 71, 79, Carnegie Inst., Pitts., 1972, Pa. State U., 1973, Duquesne U., Pitts., 1980, Pitts. Ctr. for Arts, 1983, St. Vincent Coll., 1983, others; exhibited in group shows at, Butler Inst., Youngstown, Ohio, 1958, 59, 79, 86, Chautauqua Nat. Anns., 1964, 73, St. Paul Art Center, 1963, Marietta Coll., 1968, Walker Art Center, Mpls., 67, William Penn Meml. Mus., Harrisburg, Pa., 1971, also museums in Germany, France, Scotland, numerous others; represented in permanent collections at, Carnegie Inst., U. Pitts., Pitts. Bd. Edn., Am. Cancer Soc., Alcoa, U.S. Steel, Westinghouse, Koppers Co., others; commns. include, Koppers Co., First Fed. Savings & Loan Assn., Pitts., U.S. Steelworkers Am., others. Recipient Citation as Woman of Distinction, Gov. Pa., 1972; named Artists of Yr., Pitts. Ctr. for Arts, 1983, award Women in Art, 1995, 96, 20 Jury awards, others. Mem. Abstract Group Pitts. (pres. 1964-65), Associated Artists Pitts. (bd. dirs. 1965-68, 80-83), Pitts. Ctr. for Arts, Concept Gallery. Democrat. Address: 4218 Maple Ln Allison Park PA 15101-3017

OSBY, ROBERT EDWARD, protective services official; b. San Diego, Oct. 29, 1937; s. Jesse William and Susie Lillian (Campbell) O.; m. Clydette Deloris Mullen, Apr. 11, 1961; children: Daryl Lawrence, Gayle Lorraine. AA in Fire Sci., San Diego Jr. Coll., 1970; BA in Mgmt., Redlands U., 1985. Recreation leader San Diego Parks and Recreation Dept., 1955-58; postal carrier U.S. Postal Service, San Diego, 1958-59; fire fighter San Diego Fire Dept., 1959-67, fire engr., 1967-71, fire capt., 1971-76, fire bn. chief, 1976-79; fire chief Inglewood (Calif.) Fire Dept., 1979-84, San Jose (Calif.) Fire Dept., 1985—. Served to 2d lt. Calif. NG, 1960-65. Mem. Calif. Met. Fire Chiefs (chmn. 1987—), Internat. Assn. Black Firefighters (regional dir. 1974-77), Brothers United (pres. 1972-75). Democrat. Avocations: fishing, jogging, landscaping. Home: 28203 Engelmann Oak Trl Escondido CA 92026-6960 Office: San Diego Fire Dept 1010 2nd Ave Ste 400 San Diego CA 92101-4903*

O'SCANNLAIN, DIARMUID FIONNTAIN, judge; b. N.Y.C., Mar. 28, 1937; s. Sean Leo and Moira (Hegarty) O'S.; m. Maura Nolan, Sept. 7, 1963; children: Sean, Jane, Brendan, Kevin, Megan, Christopher, Anne, Kate. BA, St. John's U., 1957; JD, Harvard U., 1963; LLM, U. Va., 1992. Bar: Oreg. 1965, N.Y. 1964. Tax atty. Standard Oil Co. (N.J.), N.Y.C., 1963-65; assoc. Davies, Biggs, Strayer, Stoel & Boley, Portland, Oreg., 1965-69; dep. atty. gen. Oreg., 1969-71; public utility commr. of Oreg., 1971-73; dir. Oreg. Dept. Environ. Quality, 1973-74; sr. ptnr. Ragen, Roberts, O'Scannlain, Robertson & Neill, Portland, 1978-86; judge, U.S. Ct. Appeals (9th cir.), San Francisco, 1986—, mem. exec. com., 1988-89, 1993-94, mem. Jud. Coun. 9th Cir., 1991-93; mem. U.S. Judicial Conf. Com. on Automation and Tech., 1990—; cons. Office of Pres.-Elect and mem. Dept. Energy Transition Team (Reagan transition), Washington, 1980-81; chmn. com. adminstrv. law Oreg. State Bar, 1980-81. Mem. council of legal advisers Rep. Nat. Com., 1981-83; mem. Rep. Nat. Com., 1983-86, chmn. Oreg. Rep. Party, 1983-86; del. Rep. Nat. Convs., 1976, 80, chmn. Oreg. del., 1984; Rep. nominee U.S. Ho. of Reps., First Congl. Dist., 1974; team leader Energy Task Force, Pres.'s Pvt. Sector Survey on Cost Control, 1982-83, trustee Jesuit High Sch.; mem. bd. visitors U. Oreg. Law Sch., 1988—; mem. citizens adv. bd. Providence Hosp., 1986-92. Maj. USAR, 1955-78. Mem. Fed. Bar Assn., ABA (sec. Apellate Judges Conf. 1989-90, exec. com. 1990—, chmn.-elect 1994—), Arlington Club, Multnomah Club. Roman Catholic. Office: US Ct Appeals 313 Pioneer Courthouse 555 SW Yamhill St Portland OR 97204-1336*

OSCARSON, KATHLEEN DALE, writing assessment coordinator, educator; b. Hollywood, Calif., Sept. 16, 1928; d. Chauncey Dale and Hermine Marie Rulison; m. David Knowles Leslie, June 16, 1957 (div. Aug. 1970); m. William Randolph Oscarson, Apr. 27, 1974. AB, UCLA, 1950, MA, 1952; Cert. Advanced Study, Harvard U., 1965; Diplomé Elementaire, Le Cordon Bleu U. Paris, 1972. Gen. secondary life credential, Calif. Cons. Advanced Placement English Calif. Dept. Edn., Sacramento, 1968-70; reader Calif. Assessment Program, Sacramento, 1989—; instr. individual study U. Calif. Extension, Berkeley, 1979-92; reader, leader Ednl. Testing Svc., Princeton, N.J. and Emeryville, Calif., 1967—; reader San Jose (Calif.) State U., 1991—; tchr. English, counselor Palo Alto (Calif.) Unified Sch. Dist., 1954-90, H.S. writing assessment coord., 1987—; adj. lectr. English Santa Clara (Calif.) U., 1990-91; commr. Curriculum Study Commn., San Francisco Bay Area, 1978—; chair tchrs. English Spring Asilomar Conf., Pacific Grove, Calif., 1992, Asilomar 44, Pacific Grove, 1994; presenter Conf. on English Leadership, Chgo., 1996. Mem. lang. arts assessment adv. com. Calif. State Dept. Edn., Sacramento, 1975-90; mem.-at-large exec. bd. Ctrl. Calif. Coun. Tchrs. English, Bay Area, 1969-71; mem. Medallion Soc. San Francisco Opera, 1984—; mem. ann. summer event com., membership com. Internat. Diplomacy Coun. Mem. MLA, Nat. Coun. Tchrs. English (group leader conf. San Francisco), Calif. Assn. Tchrs. English, Internat. Diplomacy Coun. San Francisco (membership and events coms. 1996), Harvard Club San Francisco, Christopher Marlowe Soc. Avocations: cuisine, voice, writing. Home: 230 Durazno Way Portola Valley CA 94028

OSEGUERA, PALMA MARIE, marine corps officer, reservist; b. Kansas City, Mo., Dec. 29, 1946; d. Joseph Edmund and Palma Louise (Utke) O'Donnell; m. Alfonso Oseguera, Jan. 1, 1977; stepchildren: Kristie M. Daniels, Michelle L. Russell, Lori A. Kelley. BA in Phys. Edn., Marycrest Coll., 1969. Commd. 2d lt. USMC, 1969, advanced through grades to col., 1991; asst. marine corps exch. officer Hdqs. and Hdqs. Squadron, Marine Corps Air Sta., Beaufort, S.C., 1969-71; classified material control officer Hdqs. and Svcs. Battalion, Camp S.D. Butler, Okinawa, 1971-73; adminstrv. officer, asst. marine corps exch. officer Marine Corps Air Sta., El, Toro, Santa Ana, Calif., 1973-76; marine corps exch. officer Marine Corps Air Sta., Yuma, Ariz., 1976-77; asst. marine corps exch. officer Hdqrs. and Support Bat., Marine Corps Devel. & Edn. Command, Quantico, Va., 1977-79; marine corps exch. officer Hqrs. Marine Corps, Washington, 1979-80; adminstrv. officer Marine Air Base Squadon 46, Marine Air Group 46, Marine Corps Air Sta., Santa Ana, 1981-83, Hdqs. and Maintanence Squadron 46, Marine Air Group 46, Marine Corps Air Sta., Santa Ana, 1983-85, Mobilization Tng. Unit Calif. 53, Landing Force Tng. Command, Pacific, San Diego, 1985-89, 3d Civil Affairs Group, L.A., 1989; dep. asst. chief of staff G-1 I Marine Expeditionary Force, Individual Mobilization Augumentaee Detachment, Camp Pendleton, Calif., 1990-91; assoc. mem. Mobilization Tng. Unit Del. 01, Del., 1992-94; adminstrn. officer Mobilization Tng. Unit, CA-53, EWTG Pac, NAB, Coronado, San Diego, 1994-96; exch. officer MWRSPT ACT IMA Det MCB, Camp Pendleton, Calif., 1996—. Mem. choir St. Elizabeth Seaton, Woodbridge, Va., 1978-80, St. Patricks, Arroyo Grande, Calif., 1990—; vol. Hospice, San Luis Obispo, 1995—; mem. Los Osos (Calif.) veteran's events com. Mem. AAUW (past libr.), Marine Corps Assn., Marine Corps Res. Officer Assn., Marine Corps Aviation Assn. (12 dist. dir. 1987), Women in Mil. Svc. for Am. Republican. Roman Catholic. Avocations: skiing, jogging, reading, pet care/sitting. Home: 728 Scenic Cir Arroyo Grande CA 93420-1617

OSENTON, THOMAS GEORGE, publisher; b. Boston, Apr. 9, 1953; s. George Thomas and Helen (Curran) O.; m. Mary Ellen Dalzell, Aug. 16, 1975; children: Curran Lynn, Matthew. BA, U. New Hampshire, 1976. Pub. relations dir. USA Hockey, Colorado Springs, Colo., 1976-78; exec. dir. Blue Line Club Wis., Madison, 1978-81; writer WCVB-TV Ch.5 ABC Affil., Boston, 1981-82; dir. olympic pub. ABC TV Network, N.Y.; dir. mktg. ABC Pub., N.Y., 1983-86; pub. Sports Mktg. News, Conn., 1986-88; pub. Am. Artist Billboard Publs. Inc., N.Y.C., 1988-89; pres., chief exec. officer Sporting News Pub. Co., St. Louis, 1989-93; pres. Courier New Media, Lowell, Mass., 1993—; chmn. Altered States, Inc., N.Y.C. Avocation: golf. Home: 7 Reimer Rd Westport CT 06880-2733 Office: 165 Jackson St Lowell MA 01852-2131

OSEPCHUK, JOHN MOSES, engineering physicist, consultant; b. Peabody, Mass., Feb. 11, 1927; s. Moses Nicholas and Mary (Sukoff) O.; m. Shirley Greenwood Small; children: Jonathan Greenwood, Lauren Ann, Janet Miriam. AB, Harvard U., 1949, AM, 1950, PhD, 1957. Devel. engr. power tube div. Raytheon, Waltham, Mass., 1950-56, liaison engr. at CSF, 1956-57; devel. engr. microwave and power tube div. Raytheon Co., Burlington, Mass., 1957-62; prin. rsch. engr. rsch. div. Raytheon Co., Waltham, 1964-74; cons. scientist Raytheon Co., Lexington, Mass., 1974-95; chief microwave engr. Sage Labs., Natick, Mass., 1962-64; cons. in microwave heating and microwave safety Full Spectrum Cons., Concord, Mass., 1995—; mem. accredited standards com. C95 Am. Nat. Standards Inst., N.Y.C., 1968—. Editor: Biological Effects of Electromagnetic Radiation, 1983; contbr. over 80 articles to profl. jours.; patentee in field. Clk. Park St. Ch., Boston, 1958-65, trustee, 1965-72; mem. Rep. Town Com., Concord, Mass., 1974—. With U.S. Army, 1945-46. Fellow IEEE (chmn. com. on man and radiation, exec. sec. stds. coord. com. 1991-95, chmn. stds. coord. com. 1995—), Internat. Microwave Power Inst. (pres. 1992-95), Am. Sci. Affiliation; mem. Microwave Soc. of IEEE (nat. lectureship 1977-78), Electromagnetic Energy Policy Alliance (advisor to bd. dirs.), Bioelectromagnetics Soc., Sigma Xi, Phi Beta Kappa. Republican. Congregationalist. Avocations: tennis, music, tree work, writing. Home: 248 Deacon Haynes Rd Concord MA 01742-4712 Office: Full Spectrum Cons 248 Deacon Haynes Rd Concord MA 01742

OSGOOD, CHARLES, news broadcaster, journalist; b. N.Y.C., Jan. 8, 1933; s. Charles Osgood and Mary F. (Wilson) Wood; m. Jean Crafton, Dec. 5, 1973; children: Kathleen, Winston, Anne Elizabeth, Emily Jean, James Edward. B.S., Fordham U., 1954; L.H.D. (hon.), St. Bonaventure U., 1977; PhD (hon.), Fordham U.; LLD, St. John's U. Program dir. Sta. WGMS, Washington, until 1963; gen. mgr. Sta. WHCT, Hartford, Conn., 1963-64; reporter ABC Radio News, 1964-67; anchorman Sta. WCBS, 1967-72; corr. television and radio CBS, N.Y.C., 1972—; host CBS Sunday Morning, 1994—. Author: Nothing Could Be Finer Than A Crisis That Is Minor in the Morning, 1979, There's Nothing That I Wouldn't Do If You Would Be My POSSLQ, 1981, Osgood on Speaking, 1988, The Osgood Files, 1991. Mem. AFTRA. Office: CBS Radio Network 524 W 57th St New York NY 10019-2902

OSGOOD, FRANK WILLIAM, urban and economic planner; b. Williamston, Mich., Sept. 3, 1931; s. Earle Victor and Blanche Mae (Eberly) O.; children: Ann Marie, Frank William Jr. BS, Mich. State U., 1953; M in City Planning, Ga. Inst. Tech., 1960. Prin. planner Tulsa Met. Area Plnning Commn., 1958-60; sr. assoc. Hammer & Co. Assocs., Washington, 1960-64; econ. cons. Marvin Springer & Assocs., Dallas, 1964-65; sr. assoc. Gladstone Assocs., Washington, 1965-67; prof. urban planning Iowa State U., Ames, 1967-73; pres. Frank Osgood Assoc./Osgood Urban Rsch., Dallas, 1973-84; dir. mktg. studies MPSI Americas Inc., Tulsa, 1984-85, Comarc Systems/Roulac & Co., San Francisco, 1985-86; pres. Osgood Urban Rsch., Millbrae, Calif., 1986-95; freelance writer Millbrae, Calif., 1994-95; VISTA vol. coord. Chrysalis, Santa Monica, Calif., 1995-96; pres. Osgood Urban Rsch., L.A., 1996—; adj. prof. U. Tulsa, 1974-76; lectr. U. Tex., Dallas, 1979, U. Tex., Arlington, 1983. Author: Control Land Uses Near Airports, 1960, Planning Small Business, 1967, Continuous Renewal Cities, 1970; contbr. articles to profl. jours. Chmn. awards Cub Scouts Am., Ames, 1971-73; deacon Calvary Presbyn. Ch., San Francisco, 1987-90. 1st lt. USAF, 1954-56. Recipient Community Leaders and Noteworthy Americans award 1976. Mem. Am. Planning Assn. (peninsula liaison 1987-89, dir. pro-tem 1990 No. Calif. sect., edn. coord. 1991-92, Calif., dir. N. Cen. Tex. sect., Tex. chpt. 1983), Am. Inst. Planners (v.p. Okla. chpt. 1975-77), Okla. Soc. Planning Cons. (sec., treas. 1976-79), Urban Land Inst., Le Club. Republican. Presbyterian. Home: Ter Trousdale 11400 National Blvd Los Angeles CA 90064

OSGOOD, RICHARD MAGEE, JR., applied physics and electrical engineering educator, research administrator; b. Kansas City, Mo., Dec. 28, 1943; s. Richard Magee and Mary Neff (Russell) O.; m. Alice Rose Dyson, June 25, 1966; children—Richard Magee, III, Nathaniel David, Jennifer Anne. B.S. in Engring., U.S. Mil. Acad., 1965; M.S. in Physics, Ohio State U., 1968; Ph.D., MIT, 1973. Rsch. assoc. dept. physics MIT, Cambridge, 1969-72, mem. rsch. staff Lincoln Lab., 1973-80, project leader Lincoln Lab., 1980-81; assoc. prof. applied physics and elec. engring. Columbia U., N.Y.C., 1981-82, prof., 1982-91, Higgins prof., 1989—, dir., 1984-90; bd. dirs. Microelectronics Scis. Labs.; mem. Army Sci. and Tech. Basic Energy Scis. Adv. Com. Materials Rsch. Coun.-Advanced Rsch. Projects Agy.; cons. Los Alamos Nat. Lab. Editor: Laser Diagnostics and Photochemical Processing of Semiconductor Devices, 1983; assoc. editor: Applied Physics; contbr. articles to profl. jours.; patentee in field. Served to capt. USAF, 1965-69. Recipient Samuel Burka award USAF Avionics Lab., 1968, Leos Travelling Lectr. award, 1986-87, Disting. Travelling Lectr. APS, R.W. Wood Prize, 1991, Optical Soc. Am.; John Simon Guggenheim fellowship, 1989. Fellow IEEE, Optical Soc. Am. (R.W. Wood award, 1991); mem. Am. Chem. Soc., Materials Rsch. Soc. (councillor 1983-86), Optical Device Assn. (Japanese hon. lectr. 1990), Am. Phys. Soc. (travelling lectureship 1992). Home: 345 Quaker Rd Chappaqua NY 10514-2615 Office: Columbia U Radiation Laboratory New York NY 10027

OSGOOD, ROBERT MANSFIELD, lawyer; b. Elmira, N.Y., Jan. 27, 1942; s. Roland Lorenzo and Isabelle (Mansfield) O.; m. Janice Deakin, 1992; children: Christopher, Elisabeth, Abigail. BA, Syracuse U., 1963, JD, 1968; postgrad. diploma in EC law, Kings Coll., London, 1994. Bar: N.Y. 1968, U.S. Dist. Ct. (no. dist.) N.Y. 1969, U.S. Dist. Ct. (so. dist.) N.Y. 1970, U.S. Ct. Appeals (2d cir.) 1971, U.S. Dist. Ct. (ea. dist.) N.Y. 1974, U.S. Ct. Appeals (D.C. cir.) 1976, U.S. Supreme Ct. 1977. Ptnr. Sullivan & Cromwell, N.Y.C. and London, 1968—. Fellow Am. Coll. Trial Lawyers; mem. Am. Law Inst. Office: Sullivan & Cromwell 125 Broad St New York NY 10004-2400 also: 9A Ironmonger Ln, London EC2V 8EY, England

O'SHAUGHNESSY, ELLEN CASSELS, writer; b. Columbia, S.C., Oct. 1, 1937; d. Melvin O. and Grace Ellen (Cassels) Hemphill; m. John H. Sloan (dec.); children: John H., Anne H.; m. John F. O'Shaughnessy, Dec. 8, 1979 (div. Mar. 1990). BA, Internat. Coll., L.A., 1977; MA in Counseling Psychology, Fielding Inst., Santa Barbara, Calif., 1980. Tchr.'s aide, art instr. Monterey Peninsula (Calif.) Unified Sch. Dist., 1968-74; tchr. adult sch. Pacific Grove (Calif.) Unified Sch. Dist., 1974-82, spl. edn. coms., 1984-85; substitute tchr. Monterey County Office Edn., Salinas, Calif., 1983-84; owner, writer, pub. Synthesis, Pacific Grove, Calif., 1984—. Author: Teaching Art to Children, 1974, Synthesis, 1981, You Love to Cook Book, 1983, I Could Ride on the Carousel Longer, 1989, Somebody Called Me A Retard Today...And My Heart Felt Sad, 1992, Walker & Co., N.Y.C. Episcopalian. Home: PO Box 51063 Pacific Grove CA 93950-6063

O'SHAUGHNESSY, GARY WILLIAM, military officer; b. N.Y.C., Feb. 6, 1939; s. William Eugene and Anne Elizibeth O'Shaughnessy; m. Diane Gertrude Gavin, May 8, 1971; children: Kim Gavin, Karen Anne. BA in English, Fordham U., 1960; MEd, Manhattan Coll., 1970. Commd. 2d lt. USAF, 1960, advanced through grades to maj. gen., 1989; adminstrv. officer Air Flight Test Ctr., Edwards AFB, Calif., 1960-62; student Communication Intelligence Officer Course, Goodfellow AFB, Tex., 1962-63; dir. ops. 6923RSM and OL, Vietnam, 1963; intelligence officer 6922ESG, Clark AB, P.I., 1963-65, Nat. Security Agy., Ft. Meade, Md., 1965-67; instr., comdt. of cadets Manhattan Coll., N.Y.C., 1967-70; intelligence officer Pacific Security Region, Wheeler AFB, Hawaii, 1970-72; asst. ops. officer 6921ESW, Misawa AB, Japan, 1972; intelligence officer USAF Security Svc., San Antonio, 1972-

73; rep. to air staff Nat. Security Agy., Ft. Meade, 1974-77; comdr. 6903ESS, Korea, 1977-78, Electronic Security Command Units in Pacific, Hickam AFB, Hawaii, 1979-82, Electronic Security Command Units in Europe, Ramstein AB, Germany, 1982-85; assoc. dep. dir. for ops. Nat. Security Agy., Ft. Meade, 1985-87; dep. chief of staff, intelligence Hdqrs. U.S. Forces in Europe, Ramstein AB, Germany, 1987-88; dir. intelligence Hdqrs. U.S. European Command, Stuttgart-Vaihingen, Germany, 1988-89; comdr. Air Force Intelligence Command, San Antonio, 1989-93. Contbr. articles to profl. jours. Decorated Def. Superior Svc. medal, Legion of Merit, Bronze Star, Meritorious Svc. medal, Joint Svc. Commendation medal. Mem. Air Force Assn., USAF Security Svc./Electronic Security Command Assn. (pres. Potomac chpt.), Armed Force Comm. and Electronics Assn., Nat. Mil. Intelligence Assn., Assn. Old Crows, World Affairs Coun. Avocations: reading, carpentry, tennis, exercise. Home: 17808 Stoneridge Dr North Potomac MD 20878-1020 Office: Oracle Govt Corp 3 Bethesda Metro Ctr Bethesda MD 20814-5330

O'SHAUGHNESSY, JAMES PATRICK, lawyer; b. Rochester, N.Y., Mar. 3, 1947; s. John Andrew and Margaret May (Yaxley) O'S.; m. Terry Lee Wood. BS cum laude, Rensselaer Poly. Inst., 1972; JD, Georgetown U., 1977. Bar: Va. 1977, Ohio 1979, Wis. 1987. Assoc. Squire, Sanders & Dempsey, Cleve., 1978-81; ptnr. Hughes & Cassidy, Sumas, Wash., 1981-84; patent counsel Kimberly-Clark Corp., Neenah, Wis., 1984-85; ptnr. Foley & Lardner, Milw., 1986-96; v.p., chief intellectual property counsel Rockwell Internat. Corp., Seal Beach, Calif., 1996—; founder Innovatech Co., 1996—; mem. adv. bd. Licensing Econs. Rev.; frequent lectr., chmn. seminars to legal and bus. groups. Contbr. articles to chpts. to profl. publs. Bd. dirs. Skylight Opera Theatre, 1991-92. With USN, 1964-68. Mem. CPR Inst. for Dispute Resolution (mediation/arbitration panel), Lic. Execs. Soc., Am. Intellectual Property Law Assn., Disabled Am. Vets., Tau Beta Pi, Alpha Sigma Mu. Home: 3367 Crownview Rd Rancho Palos Verdes CA 90274 Office: Rockwell Internat Corp 2201 Seal Beach Blvd Seal Beach CA 90740-8250

O'SHAUGHNESSY, JOSEPH A., restaurant company executive. Sr. exec. v.p. Friendly Ice Cream Corp., Wilbraham, Mass., 1957—. Office: Friendly Ice Cream Corp 1855 Boston Rd Wilbraham MA 01095-1002

O'SHEA, CATHERINE LARGE, marketing and public relations consultant; b. Asheville, N.C., Feb. 27, 1944; d. Edwin Kirk Jr. and Mary Mitchell (Westall) Large; m. Roger Dean Lower, Dec. 19, 1970 (dec. Sept. 1977); children: Thaddeus Kirk Lower and David Alexander Lower (twins, dec.); m. Michael Joseph O'Shea, Dec. 29, 1980. BA in History magna cum laude, Emory U., 1966. Mktg. staff mem. Time Inc., N.Y.C., 1966-69; mktg. adminstr. Collier-Macmillan Internat., N.Y.C., 1970-71; circulation mgr. Coll. Entrance Exam. Bd., N.Y.C., 1971-73; spl. asst. to pres. Wayne Dressel Assocs. Exec. Search, N.Y.C., 1973-75; freelance writer, editor, pub. rels. Princeton, N.J., 1975-78; dir. constituency rels. Emory U., Atlanta, 1978-80; devel. assoc. U. Del., Newark, 1981-83; asst. to pres. Elizabethtown (Pa.) Coll., 1983-85; assoc. v.p. Beaver Coll., Glenside, Pa., 1985; cons. mktg. and pub. rels. Phila., S.C., 1985—. Co-author: 50 Secrets of Highly Successful Cats, 1994; editor Elizabethtown mag., 1983-85; contbr. articles to nat. mags. and profl. jours. Founder Helping Hands Internat.; Trustee Large Found., Newberry Opera House Found; Phi Mu Found. Mem. Pub. Rels. Soc. Am. (accredited), Mortar Bd., Phi Beta Kappa, Phi Mu.

O'SHEA, JOHN P., insurance executive; b. Poughkeepsie, N.Y., May 1, 1930; s. John P. and Mildred A. (Galbraith) O'S.; m. Nancy Ann Shaw; m. Michael, Patricia, Stephen, Sandra. BS, Fordham U., 1951. Various positions Marshall & Sterling Inc., Poughkeepsie, 1955-70, v.p., 1970-80, pres., 1980—; bd. dirs. Crabapple Ins. Co., vice chmn., 1992—, Bermuda, Riverside Bank, Poughkeepsie, 1987—, chmn. of bd., 1993—; chmn. bd. VBH Ins. Co., Barbados. Trustee ARea Fund Dutchess County, Poughkeepsie, 1983-89, Marist Coll., 1994—, Mid-Hudson Med. Ctr., 1991—, Bardavon Opera House, 1990-94; chmn. bd. dirs. Vassar Bros. Hosp. and VBH Corp., Poughkeepsie, 1986-88; bd. dirs. Poughkeepsie Partnership, 1993—. Lt. USNR, 1952-55, Korea; comdr., 1955-76. Mem. Poughkeepsie Area C. of C. (chmn. 1982-83), Dutchess Golf and Country Club, Rotary (pres. Poughkeepsie 1968-69). Avocation: golf. Office: 110 Main St Poughkeepsie NY 12601-3083

O'SHEA, LYNNE EDEEN, advertising executive, educator; b. Chgo., Oct. 18, 1945; d. Edward Fisk and Mildred (Lessner) O'S. B.A., B.J. in Polit. Sci. and Advt, U. Mo., 1968, M.A. in Communications and Mktg. Research, 1971; PhD in Consumer Cultures, Northwestern U., 1977; postgrad., Sch. Mgmt. and Strategic Studies, U. Calif., 1988. Pres. O'Shea Advt. Agy., Dallas, 1968-69; congl. asst. Washington, 1969-70; brand mgr. Procter & Gamble Co., Cin., 1971-73; v.p. Foote, Cone & Belding, Inc., Chgo., 1973-79; v.p. corp. communications Internat. Harvester Co., Chgo., 1979-82; dir. communications Arthur Andersen & Co., Chgo., 1983-86; v.p. strategic planning Campbell-Ewald, Detroit and Los Angeles, 1986; v.p. bus. devel. Gannett Co., Inc., Chgo., 1987-94; group strategic planning dir. DDB Needham Worldwide, Inc., Chgo., 1995-96; exec. v.p. Mus. Broadcast Comm., Chgo., 1996—; prof. mktg. U. Chgo. Grad. Sch. Bus., 1979-80, Kellogg Grad. Sch. Mgmt., 1983-94; disting. vis. prof. Syracuse U., 1992—. Bd. dirs. Off-the-Street Club, Chgo., 1977-86; mem. adv. bd. U. Ill. Coll. Commerce, 1980—, Ctr. for Mature Industries, 1982—, Girl Scouts Am., 1985—, Chgo. Crime Commn., 1987—, Stephenson Rsch. Ctr., 1987—, DePaul U., 1989—, Roosevelt U., 1994—. Recipient numerous Eagle Fin. Advt. awards, Silver medalist Am. Advt. Fedn., 1989; named Advt. Woman of Yr. Chgo. Advt. Club, 1989; named Glass Ceiling Commn., 1991-95, Com. 21st Century, 1992—. Mem. Internat. Women's Forum (v.p. devel., v.p. communications, exec. com., bd. dir.), Chgo. Network, Women's Forum Chgo., Women's Forum Mich., Tarrytown Group, Social Venture Network, Execs. Club Chgo., Mid-Am. Club (bd. govs. 1990—). Office: Mus Broadcast Comm Chgo Cultural Ctr Michigan Ave at Washington St Chicago IL 60602-4801

O'SHEA, PATRICIA A., physician, educator; b. Syracuse, N.Y., June 14, 1944; d. John Daniel and Mildred (Olbeter) Allen; m. John S. O'Shea, July 5, 1969. BS summa cum laude, Le Moyne Coll., 1966; MD, Johns Hopkins U., 1970. Diplomate Am. Bd. Pathology, Am. Bd. Anatomic, Clin. and Pediat. Pathology. From intern to resident Duke U. Med. Ctr., Durham, N.C., 1970-74; from asst. to assoc. prof. pathology Brown U., Providence, 1974-90; assoc. prof. pathology Emory U., Atlanta, 1990—; mem. faculty Armed Forces Inst., Washington, 1989; short-course faculty U.S. and Can. Acad. Pathology, Augusta, Ga., 1992—. Contbr. articles to profl. jours. Fellow Am. Acad. Pediats., Coll. Am. Pathologists; m. Soc. Pediat. Pathology (mem. coun.). Avocations: tennis, opera, baseball, travel. Office: Egleston Children's Hosp Emory U 1405 Clifton Rd NE Atlanta GA 30322-1060

OSHEROFF, DOUGLAS DEAN, physicist, researcher; b. Aberdeen, Wash., Aug. 1, 1945; s. William and Bessie Anne (Ondov) O.; m. Phyllis S.K. Liu, Aug. 14, 1970. B.S. in Physics, Calif. Inst. Tech., 1967; M.S., Cornell U., 1969, Ph.D. in Physics, 1973. Mem. tech. staff Bell Labs., Murray Hill, N.Y., 1972-82, head solid state and low temperature physics research dept., 1982-87; prof. Stanford (Calif.) U., 1987—, J.G. Jackson and C.J. Wood prof. physics, 1992—; chair physics, 1993-96. Researcher on properties of matter near absolute zero of temperature; co-discoverer of superfluidity in liquid 3He, 1971, nuclear antiferromagnetic resonance in solid 3He, 1980. Co-recipient Simon Meml. prize Brit. Inst. Physics, 1976, Oliver E. Buckley Solid State Physics prize, 1981; John D. and Catherine T. MacArthur prize fellow, 1981. Fellow Am. Phys. Soc., Am. Acad. Arts and Scis., Nat. Acad. Scis. Office: Stanford U Dept Physics Stanford CA 94305-4060

O'SHIELDS, RICHARD LEE, retired natural gas company executive; b. Ozark, Ark., Aug. 12, 1926; s. Fay and Anna (Johnson) O'S.; m. Shirley Isabelle Washington, Nov. 8, 1947; children: Sharon Isabelle O'Shields Boles, Carolyn Jean, Richard Lee Jr. B.S. in Mech. Engring, U. Okla., 1949; M.S. in Petroleum Engring, La. State U., 1951. Registered profl. engr., Kans., Tex. Instr. petroleum engring. La. State U., 1949-51; prodn. engr. Pure Oil Co., 1951-53; sales engr., chief engr., v.p. Salt Water Control, Inc., Ft. Worth, 1953-59; cons. engr. Ralph H. Cummins Co., Ft. Worth, 1959-60; with Anadarko Prodn. Co. and parent co. Panhandle Eastern Pipe Line Co., 1960-88; pres. Anadarko Prodn. Co., 1966-68; exec. v.p. Panhandle Eastern Pipe Line Co., 1968-70, pres., chief exec. officer, 1970-79, chmn., chief exec. officer, 1979-83, chmn., 1983-88, also bd. dirs., 1969-93; pres., CEO Trunkline Gas Co., 1970-79, chmn., CEO, 1979-83, chmn., 1983-88; bd. dirs. Daniel Industries, chmn., Petrolite Corp. With USAAF, 1945. Mem. Am. Petroleum Inst., Soc. Petroleum Engrs., Ind. Natural Gas Assn. Am., Gas Research Inst., Ind. Petroleum Assn. Am., So. Gas Assn., Tau Beta Pi. Republican. Methodist. Lodge: Masons. Home: 3130 Camels Ridge Ln Colorado Springs CO 80904-1032

O'SHONEY, GLENN, church administrator. Exec. dir. Mission Svcs. of Luth. Ch. Mo. Synod Internat. Ctr., St. Louis. Office: Luth Ch Mo Synod Inter Ctr 1333 S Kirkwood Rd Saint Louis MO 63122-7295

OSIAS, RICHARD ALLEN, international financier, investor, real estate investment executive, corporate investor; b. N.Y.C., Nov. 13, 1938; s. Harry L. and Leah (Schenk) O.; m. Judy Delaine Bradford, Oct. 26, 1984; children: Kimberly, Alexandra Elizabeth. Grad., Columbia U., 1963; postgrad., David Lipscomb U., 1988—. Founder, chmn., CEO Osias Enterprises, Inc., numerous locations, 1953—; mem. bus. cabinet David Lipscomb U.; bd. dirs. Am. 21. Prin. works include city devel., residential and apt. units, founder City North Lauderdale, Fla., co-founder City of Lauderhill, Fla., complete residential housing communities, shopping centers, country clubs, golf courses, hotel chains, comprehensive housing communities; contributed Greystone Raquet and Tennis Club to Nolensville, Tenn.; owner, operator Coolsprings Exec. Plz., landmark office bldg., Internat. Common Market Shopping Complex and other office bldgs., shopping ctrs. in mid-southern region; co-author: South Florida Uniform Building Code. Mem. North Lauderdale City Coun., 1967—, mayor, 1968, pollice and fire commr., 1967—; mem. Gold Cir., Atlanta Ballet; benefactor Atlanta Symphony Soc.; founder Boys Clubs Broward County, Tower coun. Pine Crest Prep. Sch., Ft. Lauderdale; mem. condr.'s cir. Nashville Symphony; mem. bd. advisors Williamson-Davidson County chpt. MADD, 1990; mem. univ. bus. adv. cabinet David Lipscomb U., Nashville, 1988—; bd. dirs. Rape, Nashville chpt. Cystic Fibrosis, Citizens Against Sexual Exploitation, N.Y.C., Queens County Assn. for Prevention Cruelty to Children, 1973—, Easter Seal Soc. Tenn.; bd. dirs. Tenn. Children's Home, mem. adv. coun., 1973; hon. police commr., N.Y.C.; mem. Children's Abuse and Sexual Exploitation; mem. Ft. Lauderdale Better Bus. Bur., N.Y.C. Better Bus. Bur., Nashville Better Bus. Bur. Recipient Best Am. House award Am. Home mag., 1962, Westinghouse award, 1968, Cert. of Merit for outstanding achievement and contbn. to City of Atlanta by Mayor Andrew Young, 1982; named Builder of Yr., Sunshine State Info. Bur., Fla. and Sunshine State Sr. Citizen, Fla., 1967-70, Builder of Month, Builder/Arch. Mag., 1992; profiles on nat. and internat. media, including CBS TV and Fuji Network. Mem. Ft. Lauderdale BBB, N.Y. BBB, Nashville BBB, Offshore Power Boat Racing Assn., Fraternal Order Police Assn. (pres.), U.S. C. of C., Fla. C. of C., Margate C. of C., Ft. Lauderdale C. of C., Smithsonian Instn., Soc. Founders U. Miami, Tower Coun., Columns Soc., Pinecrest Prep. Sch. (founder), Nat. Assn. Home Builders, Bankers Club (Miami, Fla.), Bankers Top of First Club, Quarter Deck Club (Galveston, Tex.), Boca Raton (Fla.) Yacht and Country Club, Maunalua Bay Club (Honolulu), Tryall Golf and Country Club (Jamaica), Top of the Home Club, Svc. Plus Club (France), Ensworth Red Gables Soc., Cannes Island Yacht Club, Canary Islands Yacht Club, Venitian Bay Yacht Club, The Club Pelican Bay, Collier's Reserve Country Club (Naples, Fla.). Home: Club Le Ciel #1401 3991 Gulf Shore Blvd N Naples FL 33940 also: The Hillsborough 505 Almonte Ct Nashville TN 37215

OSIMITZ, DENNIS VICTOR, lawyer; b. Racine, Wis., May 28, 1951; s. Victor and Julianna (Wiernasz) O.; m. Mary Carol Rindt, June 5, 1976; children: Jeffrey Allen, Kevin James. BA, U. Wis., 1973, JD, 1976. Bar: Wis. 1976, Ill. 1976. U.S. Dist. Ct. (no. dist.) Ill. 1976. Assoc. Sidley & Austin, Chgo., 1976-83, ptnr., 1983—. Mem. ABA, Ill. Bar Assn., Chgo. Bar Assn., Union League Club, Chgo. Club. Roman Catholic. *

OSIPOW, SAMUEL HERMAN, psychology educator; b. Allentown, Pa., Apr. 18, 1934; s. Louis Morris and Tillie (Wolfe) O.; m. Sondra Beverly Feinstein, Aug. 26, 1956; children: Randall A., Jay I., Reva S., David S. B.A., Lafayette Coll., Easton, Pa., 1954; M.A., Columbia U., 1955; Ph.D., Syracuse U., 1959. Lectr. U. Wis., Madison, 1961; psychologist, asst. prof. Pa. State U., 1961-67; mem. faculty Ohio State U., Columbus, 1967—; prof. psychology Ohio State U., 1969—, chmn. dept., 1973-86; vis. prof. Tel-Aviv U., 1972, U. Md., 1980-81; vis. research assoc. Harvard U., 1965; cons. to govt. Author: Strategies in Counseling for Behavior Change, 1970, Theories of Career Development, 1983, 4th edit. 1995, Handbook of Vocational Psychology, 2 vols., 1983, 2d edit. 1995, A Survey of Counseling Methods, 1984; editor: Jour. Vocat. Behavior, 1970-75, Jour. Counseling Psychology, 1975-81, Applied and Preventative Psychology, 1993—. Served to 1st lt. U.S. Army, 1959-61. Mem. APA (bd. dirs. 1985-88), Nat. Register Health Svc. Providers in Psychology (bd. dirs. 1982-89, chmn. 1986-89). Home: 330 Eastmoor Blvd Columbus OH 43209-2022 Office: Ohio State U Psychology Dept Columbus OH 43210

OSIYOYE, ADEKUNLE, obstetrician/gynecologist, educator; b. Lagos, Nigeria, Jan. 5, 1951; came to U.S., 1972; s. Alfred and Grace (Apena) Oshiyoye; m. Toyin Osinowo Oshiyoye, Dec. 28, 1991; children: Adekunle Jr., Adedayo Justice. Student, Howard U., 1972-73; BS, U. State of N.Y., 1974; postgrad., Columbia U., 1974-78; MD, Am. U., Montserrat, West Indies, 1979. Intern South Chgo. Community Hosp., 1980-81; intern dept. obstetrics-gynecology Cook County Hosp., Chgo., 1981-82, resident physician, 1982-84, chief resident physician dept. obstetrics-gynecology, 1984-85; assoc. prof. dept. obstetrics-gynecology Chgo. Osteo. Coll. Medicine, 1986—; health physician, cons. physician City of Chgo. Dept. Health, 1989—; attending physician St. Bernard Hosp., Chgo., 1985—, Hyde Park Hosp., Chgo., 1986—, Mercy Hosp., Chgo., 1987—, Roseland Hosp., Chgo., 1985—, Columbus Hosp., Chgo., 1985—, Jackson Park Hosp., Chgo., 1985—; coord. emergency rm. Cook County Hosp., 1983-85. Med. editor African Connections, 1990—; med. columnist Newsbreed Mag., 1990—; founding mem. Ob-Gyn Video Jour. Am. Organizer Harold Washington Coalition, Chgo., 1983-87; operation mem. Operation P.U.S.H., Chgo., 1987—; active Chgo. Urban League, 1989—, Cook County Dem. Party, 1988—; mem. Mayor's Commn. on Human Rels., Chgo., 1990—, State of Ill. Inaugural Com., 1991. Shell scholar, 1965-69; recipient Fed. Govt. scholarship award, 1972, Howard Univ. scholarship award, 1973, Fed. Govt. Nigeria grad. med. scholarship award, 1975-79, Cerebral Palsy rsch. award, 1977, Ob-gyn. Video Jour. award, 1989, Role Model award Chgo. Police Dept., 1991, 92, Chgo. Bd. Edn., 1991, Chgo. 100 Black Men, 1991, Gov.'s Recognition award, 1992; named one of Best Dressed Men in Chgo., Chgo. Defender, 1990, 91. Fellow Am. Coll. Internat. Physicians, Am. Coll. Obstetricians & Gynecologists; mem. AMA (physician recognition award 1986), Am. Coll. Glegal Medicine (edn. com.), Am. Soc. Law Medicine, Am. Pub. Heart Assn., Nat. Med. Assn., Ill. Med. Soc., Chgo. Med. Assn., Chgo. Gynecol. Soc., Cook County Physician Assn., Nigerian Am. Forum (chmn. health com., chmn. election com.), Cook County Hosp. Surg. Alumni Assn., Howard U. Alumni Assn. (regent, chmn. scholarship com. Chgo. chpt.), Eureka Lodge (investigating com.), Masons, Shriners, Order of Eastern Star, Alpha Phi Alpha (life mem., mem. Labor Day com., dir. ednl. programs Xi Lambda chpt. 1990—, co-chmn. courtesy Black & Gold com. 1989, 90, Recognition award 1991), Pan Hellenic Action Coun. (chmn. pub. rels. com.), Ill. Maternal and Child Health Coalition, Beta Kappa Chi. Apostolic. Avocations: ping pong, fishing, golf, basketball, swimming. Home: PO Box 15187 Lansing MI 48901-5187 Office: Dept Health 37 W 47th St Chicago IL 60609-4657

OSKAM, GERARD LAMBERT, lawyer; b. East Orange, N.J., June 11, 1956; m. Denise L. Green; children: Monique, Michael, Johnny. AA, Orange Coast Coll., 1985; BS in Fin., U. So. Calif., 1987, AB in Philosophy, 1987; JD, Harvard U., 1990. Bar: Calif. 1990, Nev. 1993, U.S. Dist. Ct. Nev. Atty. Sheppard Mullin Richter and Hampton, Newport Beach, Calif., 1990-91, Stradling Yocca Carlson and Rauth, Newport Beach, 1991-93, McDonald Carano Wilson McCune Bergin Frankovich and Hicks, Reno, 1993—. Office: McDonald Carano et al 241 Ridge St Fl 4 Reno NV 89501-2028

OSLER, DOROTHY K., state legislator; b. Dayton, Ohio, Aug. 19, 1923; d. Carl M. and Pearl A. (Tobias) Karstaedt; BS cum laude in Bus. Adminstrn., Miami U., Oxford, Ohio, 1945; m. David K. Osler, Oct. 26, 1946; children: Scott C., David D. Mem. Conn. Ho. of Reps., 1973-92. Mem. Greenwich (Conn.) Rep. Town Meeting, 1968—, Eastern Greenwich Women's Rep. Club, 1970—; sec. Conn. Student Loan Found., 1973-83, v.p., 1983-84; mem. Spl. Edn. Cost Commn., 1976-77, Sch. Fin. Adv. Panel, 1977-78, Edn. Equity Study Com., 1980-81, Commn. on Goals for U. Conn. Health Ctr., 1975-76; bd. dirs. ARC, 1975. Mem. Nat. Order Women Legislators (sec. 1987-89), Conn. Order of Women Legislators (sec. 1983-84, pres. 1985-86), LWV (pres. Greenwich chpt. 1965-67, sec. Conn. chpt. 1967-72), AAUW (dir. 1971-73), Mortar Board, Phi Beta Kappa, Alpha Omicron Pi. Republican. Christian Scientist. Bi-weekly columnist local newspaper, 1973-83.

OSLER, GORDON PETER, retired utility company executive; b. Winnipeg, Man., Can., June 19, 1922; s. Hugh Farquarson and Kathleen (Harty) O.; m. Nancy A. Riley, Aug. 20, 1948; children: Sanford L., Susan Osler Matthews, Gillian Osler Fortier. Student, Queen's U., Kingston, Ont., Can., 1940-41. Pres. Osler, Hammond & Nanton Ltd., Winnipeg, 1952-64, UNAS Investments Ltd., Toronto, Ont., Can., 1964-72; chmn. Slater Steel Industries, Hamilton, Ont., Can., 1972-86, N.Am. Life Assurance Co., Toronto, 1986-95; chmn. TransCan. Pipelines, Toronto, 1983-89, ret., 1993; bd. dirs. Co-Steel Inc., Toronto. Lt. Can. Army, 1942-45, ETO. Mem. Toronto Club, York Club (Toronto), Everglades Club (Palm Beach, Fla.). Avocation: golf. Home: 17 Lamport Ave, Toronto, ON Canada M4W 1S7 Office: TransCan Pipelines, 55 Yonge St 8th Flr, Toronto, ON Canada M5E 1J4

OSLER, HOWARD LLOYD, controller; b. Camden, N.J., Nov. 24, 1927; s. Howard B. and Miriam (Locke) O.; m. Barbara C. Skufca, 1987; children by previous marriage: Carol, Peter, Andrew, Bruce. B.A., Antioch Coll., 1951. CPA, D.C. Pub. acct. Peat, Marwick Mitchell & Co., Boston, 1949-55; staff asst. to corp. contr. Gillette Co., Boston, 1957-59; gen. mgr. Panamanian subs. Gillette Co., 1959-61; asst. to pres. Gillette Co. Argentine subs., 1961-63; asst. to corp. contr. Gillette Co., Boston, 1963-65; contr. mil. Far East div. Gillette Co., 1965-67; contr. U.S. div. Foxboro Co., Mass., 1967-68; corp. contr. Foxboro Co., 1968-87, sec., clk., 1976-86, v.p., contr., 1981-87, ret., 1987. Trustee Gilman Cemeteries, 1988—, Trust Funds, 1990-91, 94—; commr. Gilmanton Corner Precinct, 1989—; mem. Gilmanton Budget Com., 1990—, Sch. Bldg. Com., 1988, 90, Zoning Bd. Adjustment, 1990-91; mem. Gilmanton Bd. Selectmen, 1991-94. Home: PO Box 413 Gilmanton NH 03237-0413

OSLIN, K. T. (KAY TOINETTE OSLIN), country singer; b. Crossett, Ark.. Student, Lon Morris Jr. Coll. Sang in folk trio; professional singing debut at Purple Onion, 1962; mem. road co. Hello, Dolly, also N.Y.C.; mem. cast Promise, Promises, revival West Side Story; songwriter; songs include Do Ya?, Round the Clock Lovin, Where Is A Woman To Go, Come Next Monday, Younger Men, others; albums: 80's Ladies (Grammy 1987, Country-Best Vocal Perfomance, Female), Hold Me (Grammy 1988, Country-Best Song, Country-Best Vocal Performance, Female), This Woman, 1988, Love in a Small Town, 1990, Songs From An Aging Sex Bomb: K.T. Oslin's Greatest Hits, 1993, New Way Home, 1993. Recipient Top Female Vocalist award Acad. Country Music, 1988. Office: Moress Nanas Shea c/o Stan Moress 1209 16th Ave S Nashville TN 37212-2901

OSMAN, EDITH GABRIELLA, lawyer; b. N.Y.C., Mar. 18, 1949; d. Arthur Abraham and Judith (Goldman) Udem; children: Jacqueline, Daniel. BA in Spanish, SUNY, Stony Brook, 1970; JD cum laude, U. Miami, 1983. Bar: Fla. 1983, U.S. Dist. Ct. (so. dist.) Fla. 1984, U.S. Dist. Ct. (mid. dist.) Fla. 1988, U.S. Ct. Appeals (11th cir.) 1985, U.S. Supreme Ct. 1987, U.S. Ct. Mil. Appeals 1990. Assoc. Kimbrell & Hamann, P.A., Miami, 1984-90, Dunn & Lodish, P.A., Miami, 1990-93; pvt. practice in law Miami, 1993—; spkr. in field. Mem. adv. com. for Implementation of the Victor Posner Judgement to Aid the Homeless, 1986-89; spkr. small firm and solo practitioner Town Hall Meetings, 1993; spkr. Bridge the Gap Seminar, Comml. Litigation, 1994. Mem. ABA (product liability com., corp. counsel com.), Fla. Bar Assn. (budget com. 1989-92, voluntary bar liaison com. 1989-90, spl. com. on formation of All-Bar Conf. 1988-89, chmn. mid-yr. conv. 1989, mem. long range planning com. 1988-90, bd. govs. 1991—, spl. commn. on delivery of legal svcs. to the indigent 1990-92, chair program evaluation com. bd. govs., 96—, mem. exec. com. 1992-93, 96—, rules and bylaws com. 1993-94, disciplinary rev. com. 1994—, investment com. 1994—, vice chair rules com. 1994—, Outstanding Past Voluntary Bar Pres. award 1996), Dade County Bar Assn. (fed. ct. rules com. 1985-86, chmn. program com. 1988-89, 90-91, exec. com. 1987-88, bus. law cert. com. 1995-96, practice law mgmt. com. 1995-96), Fla. Assn. Bar Assn. Pres. (bd. dirs. 1988-89, treas. 1989-90, v.p. 1990-91, pres. 1991-92), Fla. Assn. Women Lawyers (bd. dirs. 1985-86, v.p. Dade County chpt. 1986-87, pres. 1987-88, pres.-elect Fla. chpt. 1988-89, pres. 1989-90), Nat. Coun. Women's Bar Assn. (dir. nat. conf. 1990-91), Dade County Trial Lawyers Assn. Office: Edith G Osman PA Internat Place 100 SE 2nd St Ste 3920 Miami FL 33131-2148

OSMAN, MARY ELLA WILLIAMS, journal editor; b. Honea Path, S.C.; d. Humphrey Bates and Jennie Louise (Williams) Williams; student Coll. William and Mary, Ga. State Coll. for Women; A.B., Presbyn. Coll., 1939; B.S. in L.S., U. N.C., 1944; m. John Osman, Oct. 22, 1936. Asst. libr. Presbyn. Coll., Clinton, S.C., 1936-38, Union Theol. Sem., Richmond, Va., 1938-44; sr. cataloger, asst. libr. Rhodes Coll., Memphis, 1944-52; asst. test cities project Ford Found. Fund for Adult Edn., N.Y.C., 1952-57, assoc. dir. office of info., 1957-61, exec. asst. to pres., sec. to bd. dirs., 1960-61; asst. libr. AIA, Washington, 1962-68, asst. editor AIA Jour., 1969-72, assoc. editor, 1972-77, sr. editor, 1978-87. Mem. AIA (hon.), Chi Delta Phi, Kappa Delta. Presbyn. Contbr. to various mags. Home: 3600 Chateau Dr Apt 244 Columbia SC 29204-3971

OSMAN, STEPHEN EUGENE, historic site administrator; b. Berkeley, Calif., Aug. 8, 1949; s. Eugene Lee and June Elizabeth (Claus) O.; m. Wendy Kay Holmberg, June 21, 1975; children: Rachel Ann, Austin Thomas, Laurel Suzanne. BA in History and Edn. cum laude, St. Olaf Coll., 1971. Program mgr. Historic Ft. Snelling, St. Paul, 1971-85, dir., 1985—; program mgr. Legis. Commn. on Minn. Resources, 1985; mem. Coun. on Am.'s Mil. Past, Midwest Open Air Mus. Coord. Coun.; lectr. in field. Author: The Soldiers Handbook, 1825, 1972; contbr. articles to profl. jours. Fellow Co. Mil. Historians; mem. Assn. Living History Farms and Agrl. Mus., Living History Soc. Minn. Republican. Lutheran. Avocations: 19th Century military uniforms and equipment, historic crafts. Office: Minn Hist Soc Ft Snelling History Ctr Saint Paul MN 55111

OSMER, PATRICK STEWART, astronomer, educator; b. Jamestown, N.Y., Dec. 17, 1943; s. William Proudfit Jr. and Jane Briggs (Stewart) O.; m. Anita Amanda Bauza, Jan. 5, 1973; children—Katherine, Charlotte. B.S., Case Inst. Tech., 1965; Ph.D., Calif. Inst. Tech., 1970. Rsch. assoc. Cerro Tololo Inter-Am. Obs., La Serena, Chile, 1969-70, asst. astronomer, 1970-73, assoc. astronomer, 1973-76, astronomer, 1977-85, dir., 1981-85; astronomer Kitt Peak Nat. Obs., 1986-93; dep. dir. Nat. Optical Astronomy Obs., 1988-93; scientist 8-M telescope project Nat. Optical Astronomy Observatories, 1988-92, interim gemini project scientist, 1991-92; prof., chmn. astronomy dept. Ohio State U., 1993—. Contbr. articles to profl. jours. Chmn. telescope allocation com. Hubble Space Telescope, 1991. Fellow Woodrow Wilson Found., 1965, NSF, 1965-67. Mem. Am. Astron. Soc. (councillor 1985-88), Internat. Astron. Union, Astron. Soc. of Pacific, Tau Beta Pi. Avocations: running; tennis. Office: Ohio State U Dept Astronomy 174 W 18th Ave Columbus OH 43210-1106

OSMER-MCQUADE, MARGARET, business executive, broadcast journalist; b. N.Y.C.; d. Herbert Bernard and Margaret Normann (Brunjes) O.; m. Lawrence Carroll McQuade, Mar. 15, 1980; 1 son, Andrew. B.A., Cornell U., 1960. Assoc. producer UN Bur., CBS News, N.Y.C., 1962-69; producer 60 Minutes, N.Y.C., 1969-72; reporter, producer Bill Moyer's Jour., Pub. Broadcasting Service, N.Y.C., 1972-73, Reasoner Report, ABC News, N.Y.C., 1973-75; corr., anchor person Good Morning Am., ABC Morning News, Washington, 1975-77; corr. ABC TV News, Washington, 1977-79; v.p., dir. programs Council on Fgn. Relations, 1979-93; pres., CEO Qualitas Internat., N.Y.C., 1994—; dir. Dime Savs. Bank, 1980—; cons. pub. broadcasting; mem. program com. Ditchley Found. Producer, reporter: TV news shows Come Fly A Kite (Nat. Press Photographer's award 1974), Kissinger, 1970, No Tears for Rachel, 1972, Calder: Master of Mobiles, 1975; moderator, producer World in Focus, publ. TV series for Coun. Fgn. Relations/ Sta. WNYC, PBS, Worldnet, 1988-93. Mem. U.S. delegation World Conf. on Cambodian Refugees, Geneva, 1980; mem. Def. Adv. Com. on Women in the Service, 1978-82; trustee Cornell U.; mem. bd. overseers Cornell U. Med. Coll., pres.'s coun. Cornell Women; mem. program com. The Ritchley Found., 1994—, task force N.Y. Sch. Vols., 1994—; vol. Nat. Svc. Learning, 1994—. Recipient Peabody award Staff of 60 Minutes, 1970. Mem. NATAS, Coun. Fgn. Relations, program comm. The Mitching Found., Task Force N.Y. Sch. Vol., Nat. Press Club, Mid. Atlantic Club., vol. Nat. Svc. Learning. Club: Cosmopolitan, Century. *

OSMOND, DENNIS GORDON, medical educator, researcher; b. N.Y.C., Jan. 31, 1930; s. Ernest Gordon and Marjorie Bertha (Milton) O.; m. Anne Welsh, July 30, 1955; children: Roger Gordon, Martin Henry, David Richard. B.Sc. with first class honors, U. Bristol, Eng., 1951, M.B., Ch.B., 1954, D.Sc., 1975. House surgeon Royal Gwent Hosp., Newport, Eng., 1954-55; house physician Bristol Royal Infirmary, 1955; demonstrator, lectr. anatomy U. Bristol, 1957-60, 61-64; instr. anatomy U. Wash., Seattle, 1960-61; assoc. prof. anatomy McGill U., Montreal, Que., Can., 1965-67; prof. McGill U., 1967-74, Robert Reford prof. anatomy, 1974—, chmn. dept. anatomy and cell biology, 1985-95; vis. scientist Walter and Eliza Hall Inst. Med. Research, Melbourne, Australia, 1972-73; hon. sr. research fellow U. Birmingham, Eng., 1979; vis. scientist Basel Inst. Immunology, Switzerland, 1980. Contbr. numerous articles to profl. jours. Served with Royal Army Med. Corps, 1955-57. Fellow Royal Soc. Can.; mem. Am. Assn. Anatomists, Can. Assn. Anatomists, Anat. Soc. Gt. Britain and Ireland, Am., Can. assns. for immunology, Am. Assn. Immunology, Internat. Soc. for Exptl. Hematology. Home: 116 rue de Touraine, St Lambert, PQ Canada J4S 1H4 Office: Dept Anatomy McGill Univ, 3640 University St, Montreal, PQ Canada H3A 2B2

OSNES, LARRY G., academic administrator; b. Scottsbluff, Nebr., Oct. 30, 1941; s. Earl E. and Rose (DeRock) O.; m. Susan C.; 1 child, Justin. BA in History, Anderson Coll., 1963; MA in History, Wayne State Coll., 1965; PhD in History, U. Cin., 1970. Asst. prof. history and govt. U. Cin., 1967-69; dir. Am. studies Anderson (Ind.) Coll., 1970-75, chmn. dept. history, 1975-76, dean acadmeic devel., 1975-78, asst. corp. sec., dean academic devel. and pub. affairs, 1978-83; pres. Minn. Pvt. Coll. Coun., St. Paul, 1983-88, Hamline U., St. Paul, 1988—. Mem. Assoc. Colls. Twin Cities (chmn. 1988-90), Mpls. Club, St. Paul Athletic Club. Office: Hamline Univ 1536 Hewitt Ave Saint Paul MN 55104-1205

OSNES, PAMELA GRACE, special education educator; b. Burke, S.D., Sept. 10, 1955; d. John Ruben and Dortha Grace (Wilson) O.; children: Jocelyn Fern, Logan John. BS in Spl. Edn., U. S.D., 1977, BS in Elem. Edn., 1977; MA in Clin. Psychology, W.Va. U., 1981. Spl. edn. tchr. Sioux Falls (S.D.) Sch. Dist., 1977-79; instr. psychology dept. W.Va. U., Morgantown, 1982-85; dir. Carousel Preschool Program, Morgantown, 1982-85; assoc. prof. U. South Fla., Tampa, 1986-93. Mem. Assn. for Behavior Analysis, Coun. for Exceptional Children (div. early childhood, div. rsch., tchr. edn. div.), Coun. Adminstrs. Spl. Edn., Coun. for Children with Behavior Disorders.

OSNOS, DAVID MARVIN, lawyer; b. Detroit, Jan. 10, 1932; s. Max and Florence (Pollock) O.; m. Glenna DeWitt, Aug. 10, 1956; children: Matthew, Alison. A.B. summa cum laude, Harvard U., 1953, J.D. cum laude, 1956. Bar: D.C. 1956. Assoc. Arent, Fox, Kintner, Plotkin & Kahn, Washington, 1956-61, ptnr., 1962—, chmn. exec. com., 1978—; bd. dirs. EastGroup Properties, Jackson, Miss., VSE Corp., Alexandria, Va., Washington Real Estate Investment Trust, Kensington, Md., Washington Bullets Basketball Club, Landover, Md., Washington Capitals Hockey Club, Landover. Trustee Mt. St. Mary's Coll., Emmitsburg, Md., 1981-90; bd. dirs. Greater Washington Jewish Community Found., Rockville, Md., Jewish Community Ctr. Greater Washington, 1964-75. Avocations: tennis, music, enology. Office: Arent Fox Kintner 1050 Connecticut Ave NW Washington DC 20036-5339

OSNOS, GILBERT CHARLES, management consultant; b. Detroit, Nov. 23, 1929; s. Herman Sol and Helen (Yudkoff) O.; m. Margaret N. Paysner, Aug. 18, 1957; children: Steven, Elisabeth. BA, U. Mich., 1951; MBA, Harvard U., 1953. Dept. mgr. Sams, Inc., Detroit, 1956-57, asst. buyer, 1957-58, dir. store ops., 1958, buyer, 1958-59, mdse. buyer, 1959-62; buyer Topps Divsn. Interstate Dept. Stores, N.Y.C., 1962-65; mdse. mgr. Arlans Dept. Stores, N.Y.C., 1965-68; pres. Nazareth Mills divsn. Kayser Roth, N.Y.C., 1968-73, Rosenau Bros., Phila., 1973-75, Warnaco Men's Sportswear, 1975-78; with Grisanti and Galef, 1979-81, ptnr., 1981—; pres. Grisanti, Galef & Osnos, N.Y.C., 1983—; chmn. Osnos & Co., Inc., 1986—; bd. dirs. Mrs. Field's, Turnaround Mgmt. Assn., chmn., 1990-91; bd. dirs. Furrs Bishop. Lt. j.g. USNR, 1953-56. Mem. Am. Apparel Assn. (consumer affairs com.), Am. Bankruptcy Inst., Bus. Execs. for Nat. Security, Harvard Club, Holloween Yacht Club. Avocations: sailing, opera, classical music, photography, reading. Office: Osnos & Company Inc 230 Park Ave Ste C-301 New York NY 10169-0005

OSNOS, PETER LIONEL WINSTON, publishing executive; b. Bombay, India, Oct. 13, 1943; s. Joseph Lionel and Marta (Bychowski) O.; m. Susan R. Sherer, Aug. 18, 1973; children: Katherine Mason, Evan L.R. BA, Brandeis U., Waltham, Mass., 1964; MS in Journalism with honors, Columbia U., 1965. Editorial asst. I.F. Stone's Weekly, Washington, 1964-65; corr., editor The Washington Post, 1966-84; v.p. assoc. pub. Random House Trade Books and pub. Times Books, Random House, Inc., N.Y.C., 1984—. Contbr. articles to profl. publs. Bd. dirs. Human Rights Watch; vice chmn. Free Expression Project. Fellow NEH, 1973-74. Mem. Assn. Am. Pubs. (vice chmn. gen. pub. divsn.), Coun. on Fgn. Rels., Century Club. Office: Random House 201 E 50th St New York NY 10022-7703

OSOWIEC, DARLENE ANN, clinical psychologist, educator, consultant; b. Chgo., Feb. 16, 1951; d. Stephen Raymond and Estelle Marie Osowiec; m. Barry A. Leska. BS, Loyola U., Chgo., 1973; MA with honors, Roosevelt U., 1980; postgrad. in psychology, Saybrook Inst., San Francisco, 1985-88; PhD in Clin. Psychology, Calif. Inst. Integral Studies, 1992. Lic. clin. psychologist, Mo., Ill. Mental health therapist Ridgeway Hosp., Chgo., 1978; mem. faculty psychology dept. Coll. Lake County, Grayslake, Ill., 1981; counselor, supr. MA-level interns, chmn. pub. rels. com. Integral Counseling Ctr., San Francisco, 1983-84; clin. psychology intern Chgo.-Read Mental Health Ctr. Ill. Dept. Mental Health, 1985-86; mem. faculty dept. psychology Moraine Valley C.C., Palos Hills, Ill., 1988-89; lectr. psychology Daley Coll., Chgo., 1988-90; cons. Gordon & Assocs., Oak Lawn, Ill., 1989—; adolescent, child and family therapist Orland Twp. Youth Svcs., Orland Park, Ill., 1993; psychology fellow Sch. Medicine, St. Louis U., 1994-95; clin. psychologist in pvt. practice Chgo., 1996—. Ill. State scholar, 1969-73; Calif. Inst. Integral Studies scholar, 1983. Mem. APA, Am. Psychol. Soc., Am. Women in Psychology, Am. Statis. Assn., Ill. Psychol. Assn., Calif. Psychol. Assn., Mo. Psychol. Assn., Gerontol. Soc. Am., Am. Soc. Clin. Hypnosis, Internat. Platform Assn., Chgo. Coun. Hypnosis, NOW (chair legal advocate corps, Chgo. 1974-76), Registrant, Nat. Health svs. providers in Psychology. Avocations: playing piano, gardening, reading, backpacking, writing. Home: 6608 S Whipple St Chicago IL 60629-2916

OSRIN, RAYMOND HAROLD, retired political cartoonist; b. Bklyn., Oct. 5, 1928; s. Elkan and Amelia (Boll) O.; divorced 1978; children: Caren, Glenn Elliot; m. Stephanie Hearshen, Aug. 23, 1981; stepchildren: Calanit, Orli. Student, Art Students League, 1945-47. Free-lance cartoonist, comic book illustrator, comic strip ghost artist and TV animator, W.R. Smith Inc., Pitts., 1957-58, staff artist, Pitts. Press, 1958-63, Cleve. Plain Dealer, 1963-66, polit. cartoonist, 1966-93. Vol. New Internat. Mus. of Cartooning, Boca Raton. Recipient Freedom award, 1966, 67, Nat. Headliners award, 1970, 3d pl. award Internat. Salon de Cartoon, Montreal, Que., Can., 1975, award for excellence in journalism Press Club Cleve., 1978, 82, Disting. Service award Sigma Delta Chi, 1983. Excellence in Journalism 1st pl. award Cleve. Press Club, 1991; inducted into Cleve. Press Club Hall of Fame, 1986.

OSSERMAN, ROBERT, mathematician, educator; b. N.Y.C., Dec. 19, 1926; s. Herman Aaron and Charlotte (Adler) O.; m. Maria Anderson, June 15, 1952; 1 son, Paul; m. Janet Adelman, July 21, 1976; children—Brian, Stephen. B.A., NYU, 1946; postgrad., U. Zurich, U. Paris; M.A., Harvard U., 1948, Ph.D., 1955. Tchg. fellow Harvard U., 1949-52, vis. lectr., rsch. assoc., 1961-62; instr. U. Colo., 1952-53; mem. faculty Stanford U., 1955-94, prof. emeritus, 1994—, prof. math., 1966—, chmn. dept. math., 1973-79, Mellon Prof. Interdisciplinary Studies, 1987-90; dep. dir. Math. Scis. Rsch. Inst., Berkeley, Calif., 1990-95, dir. spl. projects, 1995—; mem. NYU Inst. Math. Scis., 1957-58, Math. Scis. Rsch. Inst., Berkeley., 1983-84, head math. br. Office Naval Rsch., 1960-61; researcher and author publs. on differential geometry, complex variables, differential equations, especially minimal surfaces, Laplace operator, isoperimetric inequalities, ergodic theory. Author: Two-Dimensional Calculus, 1968, A Survey of Minimal Surfaces, 1969, 2d edit., 1986, Poetry of the Universe, 1995. Fulbright lectr. U. Paris, 1965-66; Guggenheim fellow, 1976-77; vis. fellow U. Warwick, Imperial Coll., U. London. Fellow AAAS; mem. Am. Math. Soc., Math. Assn. Am. Office: Math Sci Rsch Inst 1000 Centennial Dr Berkeley CA 94720-5070

OSSIP-KLEIN, DEBORAH JANN, psychologist, educator; b. Miami Beach, Fla., June 2, 1955; d. Albert Edward and Kathrine (Freidkin) Ossip; m. Andrew Mark Ossip-Klein, Aug. 22, 1982; children: Jenna Eve, Alison Gwen. BA in Psychology and Sociology, U. Miami, Fla., 1975; MS in Clin. Psychology, U. Pitts., 1978, PhD in Clin. Psychology, 1981. Intern U. Miss. and Jackson VA Med. Ctr., 1980-81; asst. prof. psychology U. Rochester, N.Y., 1981-88, assoc. prof. psychology, 1988—; sr. scientist comty. and preventive medicine, 1994—; dir. smoking rsch. program U. Rochester, 1984—. Contbr. 25 articles to profl. jours., 5 chpts. to books. Research dir., co-founder Smoking Relapse-Prevention Hotline, 1981—; mem. smoking or health com. Am. Lung Assn., Rochester and Albany, N.Y., 1983-85; chmn. strategic planning com., Albany, 1984-85. Recipient Outstanding Performance award Dept. VA Med. Ctr., Canandaigua, N.Y., 1993; grantee Nat. Cancer Inst., 1984-91, Am. Cancer Soc., 1989-91, Nat. Inst. Aging, 1992-93, Dept. VA, 1993—. Mem. AAUP, APA, Soc. Behavioral Medicine. Jewish. Home: 12 San Rafael Dr Rochester NY 14618-3702 Office: U Rochester Sch Medicine Monroe Comty Hosp 435 E Henrietta Rd Rochester NY 14620-4658

OSSOFF, ROBERT HENRY, otolaryngological surgeon; b. Beverly, Mass., Mar. 25, 1947; s. Michael Max and Eve Joan (Kladky) O.; m. Lynn Spilman, 1984; 1 child, Leslin; 1 child by previous marriage, Jacob. BA, Bowdoin Coll., 1969; DMD, Tufts U., 1973, MD, 1975; MS in Otolaryngology, Northwestern U., 1981. Intern Northwestern Meml. Hosp., Chgo., 1975-76; resident in otolaryngology Northwestern Med. Sch., Chgo., 1976-80, NIH Rsch. fellow dept. otolaryngology, 1977-78, Am. Cancer Soc. clin. fellow, 1980-81, jr. faculty clin. fellow, 1981-84; pvt. practice medicine specializing in head and neck surgery, laryngology and care of the profl. voice, Chgo., 1975-86, Nashville, 1986—; chmn. dept. otolaryngology Vanderbilt U. Hosp., Nashville, 1986—, med. dir. Vanderbilt Voice Ctr., 1991—; mem. staff Children's Meml. Hosp., Chgo., 1980-81, Nashville VA Hosp., 1986—; chmn. div. otolaryngology Evanston (Ill.) Hosp., 1983-86; chief div. otolaryngology VA Lakeside Hosp., Chgo., 1982-86; mem. staff Northwestern Meml. Hosp., Chgo., 1981-86, Children's Meml. Hosp., Chgo., 1981-84; asst. prof. Northwestern U. Dental Sch., 1980-86, asst. prof. Northwestern U. Med. Sch., 1980-85, assoc. prof., 1985-86; Guy M. Maness prof., chmn. dept. otolaryngology Vanderbilt U. Sch. Medicine, 1986—; assoc. dir. Vanderbilt Free-Electron Laser Ctr. Med. and Materials Rsch., 1992—; assoc. vice-chancellor for health affairs and chief of staff, Vanderbilt U. Hosp., 1995—. Trustee Midwest Biolaser Inst., Chgo., 1981-86; bd. dirs. Laser Inst. Am., 1984-90, Am. Bd. Otolaryngology, 1995—. Recipient Lederer-Pierce award Chgo. Laryngol. and Otol. Soc., 1978. Fellow ACS, Am. Coll. Chest Physicians; mem. AMA, Am. Acad. Oral Medicine, Am. Acad. Oral Pathology, Am. Acad. Otolaryngology-Head and Neck Surgery (chmn. laser surgery com. 1983-89, chmn. self instl. package com. 1990—, Cert. of Honor 1984, bd. dirs. 1992-95), Am. Soc. Laser Medicine and Surgery (bd. dirs. 1985-88, pres.-elect 1988-89, pres. 1989-90, recipient William B. Mark award 1992), Soc. Head and Neck Surgeons, Am. Soc. Head and Neck Surgery (coun. 1991-94), Am. Broncho-esophagological Assn. (treas. 1980-84, pres.-elect 1994-95, pres. 1995—), Soc. Ear, Nose and Throat Advances in Children, The Triological Soc., Am. Laryngol. Assn., Cartesian Soc. Mem. editl. rev. bd. Otolaryngology-Head and Neck Surgery, 1988—; sr. editor Lasers in Surgery and Medicine, 1987-94, editor in chief-elect, 1994—, editor in chief 1995—; co-editor Complications in Head and Neck Surgery W.B. Saunders Co., 1993; mem. editl. bd. Jour. of Voice, 1987—, The Laryngoscope, 1988—, Operative Techniques in Otolaryngology-Head and Neck Surgery, 1989—, Jour. of Laser Applications, 1989—; contbr. chpts. to books, articles to profl. jours. Office: Vanderbilt U Med Ctr Dept Otolaryngology S-2100 Med Ctr N Nashville TN 37232-2559

OSTAR, ALLAN WILLIAM, academic administrator, higher education consultant; b. East Orange, N.J., Sept. 4, 1924; s. William and Rose (Mirmow) O.; m. Roberta Hutchison, Sept. 10, 1949; children: Karen, Rebecca, John. Cert. engring., U. Denver, 1943; B.A., Pa. State U., 1948; postgrad., U. Wis., 1949-55; LL.D., U. No. Colo., 1968, Eastern Ky. U., 1972, Whittier Coll., 1973; L.H.D., U. Maine, 1975; D.Letters, Central Mich. U., 1975; D.P.S., Bowling Green State U., 1975, R.I. Coll., 1983; D.Higher Edn., Morehead State U., 1977; L.H.D., Appalachian State U., 1977, No. Mich. U., 1978, Dickinson State Coll., N.D., 1979, Towson State U., 1980, Salem State Coll., 1980, Mont. Coll. Mineral Sci. and Tech., 1983, Ball State U., 1984; LL.D., U. Alaska, 1978, Ill. State U., 1983, Western Mich. U., 1984; D. Polit. Sci., Kyung Hee U., Korea, 1984; L.H.D., Fitchburg State Coll., 1986, Bridgwater State Coll., 1988, No. State Coll., 1988, Harris-Stowe State Coll., 1986; LLD, Edinboro U. Pa., 1987, Loch Haven U., Pa., 1989; LHD, No. Ariz. U., 1990, Shepherd (W.Va.) Coll., 1992, SUNY, 1993, Lincoln U., Mo., 1995. Dir. nat. pub. relations U.S. Nat. Student Assn., 1948-49; exec. asst. Commonwealth Fund, N.Y.C., 1952-53; asst. to dean extension div. U. Wis., 1949-52, dir. office communications services, 1954-58; dir. Joint Office Instnl. Research, Nat. Assn. State Univs. and Land Grant Colls., Washington, 1958-65; pres. Am. Assn. State Colls. and Univs., Washington, 1965-91; pres. emeritus Am. Assn. State Colls. and Univs., 1991—; sr. cons. Acad. Search Consultation Svc., 1991—; adj. prof. edn. Pa. State U., 1990—; mem. N.Y. Regents Commn. on Higher Edn.; bd. advisors Bowie State U., Pa. State U. Alumni Coun. Co-author: Colleges and Universities for Change, 1987; contbr. chpts. in books. Bd. visitors Air U. Mem. 42d (Rainbow) div. U.S. Army, 1943-46. Decorated 2 Bronze Stars; recipient Centennial award for disting. svcs. to edn. U. Akron, 1970, Fogelsanger award Shippensburg (Pa.) State Coll., 1974, World Peace Through Edn. medal Internat. Assn. U. Pres., 1975, Disting. Achievement award, U. So. Colo., 1979, Chancellor's award U. Wis., 1985, Chancellor's medal CUNY, 1986, Disting. Alumnus award Pa. State U., 1989, svc. award Coun. on Internat. Ednl. Exch., 1990, Chancellor's medal Internat. Svc. U. Ark., Little Rock, 1990, Disting. Pub. Svc. medal Dept. of Def., 1991; Alumni fellow Pa. State U., 1975. Unitarian-Universalist. Home: 5500 Friendship Blvd Chevy Chase MD 20815-7219 Office: Acad Search Cons Svc 1818 R St NW Washington DC 20009-1604

OSTASHEK, JOHN, government leader. Leader Govt. of Yukon Territory, Whitehorse, YT. Office: Office of Govt Leader, PO Box 2703, Whitehorse, YK Canada Y1A 2C6*

OSTBERG, HENRY DEAN, corporate executive; b. Bocholt, Germany, July 21, 1928; came to U.S., 1939, naturalized, 1945; s. Fred and Lotte (Hertz) O.; m. Sydelle Burns, Dec. 13, 1987; 1 child, Neal; stepchildren: Elysa Bari, Brent Adam, Ross Jay. LLB, N.Y. Law Sch., 1950; MBA, Ohio State U., 1953, PhD, 1957. Pres. H.D. Ostberg Assocs., N.Y.C., 1950—; chmn. bd. Admar Research Co., Inc., N.Y.C., 1960; dir. Self-Instructional Devel. Corp., Amherst Group, Porter Industries, Inc.; pres. Eastman Enterprises, Inc.; assoc. prof. mktg. NYU, 1954-63. Trustee Ostberg Found. Capt. USAF, 1950-53. Jewish. Contbr. articles to profl. jours. Home: 278 Fountain Rd Englewood NJ 07631-4403 Office: Admar Rsch Inc 225 Park Ave S New York NY 10003-1604

OSTBY, RONALD, dairy and food products company executive; b. 1937. BS, U. S.D., 1959. With Pillsbury Co., 1961-84, v.p. fin. planning; v.p., chief fin. officer AG Processing, 1984-86; group v.p., chief fin. officer Land O'Lakes, 1986—. Office: Land O'Lakes Inc 4001 Lexington Ave N Arden Hills MN 55126-2934

OSTEEN, CAROLYN MCCUE, lawyer; b. Spartanburg, S.C., June 3, 1943; d. Howard McDowell Jr. and Carolyn Hartwell (Moore) McCue; m. Robert Tilden Osteen, Dec. 21, 1963; children: Carolyn Willingham Moore, Sarah Lloyd. Student, Wellesley Coll., 1960-63; LLB, Duke U., 1966, LLM, 1970. Bar: N.C. 1966, Mass. 1971. Assoc. Robinson O. Everett, Durham, N.C., 1967-68, Cox, Smith, Smith, Hale & Guenther, San Antonio, 1969-70; assoc. Ropes & Gray, Boston, 1970-79, ptnr., 1979—; tchr. taxes Tex. Assn. Realtors, 1969-70. Co-author: Harvard Manual-Tax Aspects of Charitable Giving, 7 edits., 1980—; contbr. articles to legal publs. Bd. dirs., clk. Historic Boston, Inc., 1978—, Trustees of Reservations, Boston, 1982—. Mem. ABA, Boston Bar Assn. (vice-chmn. exempt orgns. com. 1987-92). Republican. Episcopalian. Office: Ropes & Gray 1 International Pl Boston MA 02110-2624

O'STEEN, SAM, film editor, director; b. Nov. 6, 1923. Asst. editor: (film) The Wrong Man, 1956; editor: (films) Youngblood Hawke, 1964, Kisses for My President, 1964, Robin and the Seven Hoods, 1964, Marriage on the Rocks, 1965, None But the Brave, 1965, Who's Afraid of Virginia Woolf?, 1966 (Academy award nomination best film editing 1966), Cool Hand Luke, 1967, The Graduate, 1967, Rosemary's Baby, 1968, The Sterile Cuckoo, 1969, Catch-22, 1970, Carnal Knowledge, 1971, Portnoy's Complaint, 1972, The Day of the Dolphin, 1973, Chinatown, 1974 (Academy award nomination best film editing 1974), (with Randy Roberts) Straight Time, 1978, Hurricane, 1979, Amityville II: The Possession, 1982, Silkwood, 1983 (Academy award nomination best film editing 1983), Heartburn, 1986, Nadine, 1987, Biloxi Blues, 1988, Frantic, 1988, Working Girl, 1988, (with Glenn Cunningham) A Dry White Season, 1989, Postcards from the Edge, 1990, Regarding Henry, 1991, Consenting Adults, 1992, Wolf, 1994; dir.: (films) Sparkle, 1976, (TV movies) A Brand New Life, 1973, I Love You, Goodbye, 1974, Queen of the Stardust Ballroom, 1975 (Emmy award nomination outstanding director of spl. program 1975), High Risk, 1976, Look What's Happened to Rosemary's Baby, 1976, The Best Little Girl in the World, 1981, Kids Don't Tell, 1985. Office: care Motion Picture Editors 7715 W Sunset Blvd Ste 220 Los Angeles CA 90046-3912

O'STEEN, WENDALL KEITH, neurobiology and anatomy educator; b. Meigs, Ga., July 3, 1928; s. Wellna Hubert and Lillian (Powell) O'S.; m. Sandra Lynn Kraeer, July 30, 1983; children: Lisa Diane, Kerry Keith, Buckley Powell. BA, Emory U., 1948, MS, 1950; PhD, Duke U., 1958. Asst. prof. Jr. Coll. Emory U., Valdosta, Ga., 1948-49; instr. Emory U., Atlanta, 1950-51, prof. Sch. Medicine, 1968-77; from asst. prof. to prof. med. br. U. Tex., 1958-67; asst. prof. Wofford Coll., Spartanburg, S.C., 1951-53; prof., chmn. dept. neurobiology and anatomy, Bowman Gray Sch. Med. Wake Forest U., Winston-Salem, N.C., 1977-93, prof. emeritus, 1993—; mem. anatomy com. Nat. Bd. Med. Examiners, Phila., 1982-87. Contbr. over 150 articles to books, nat. and internat. jours. Served to lt. col. USAR. Recipient Golden Apple teaching award Med. Br. U. Tex., Galveston, 1967, Outstanding Tchr. award Emory U., 1973, Williams Disting. Teaching award Emory U., 1974, award for teaching excellence Bowman Gray Sch. Medicine, Wake Forest U. Mem. Am. Assn. Anatomists (exec. com. 1980-84, v.p. 1990-92), Assn. Anatomy Chairmen (exec. com. 1982-84, pres. 1990-91), So. Soc. Anatomists (pres. 1975-76), Soc. for Neurosci., N.C. Soc. Neurosci. (pres. 1980-81), Western N.C. Soc. Neurosci. (pres. 1987-88), Assn. Rsch. in Vision and Ophthalmology, Alpha Omega Alpha. Republican. Methodist. Avocations: gardening, music. Office: Bowman Gray Sch of Medicine Wake Forest Univ Dept of Neurobiology & Anatomy Winston Salem NC 27157-1010

OSTEEN, WILLIAM L., SR., federal judge; b. 1931. BA, Guilford Coll., 1953; LLB, U. N.C., 1956. With Law Office of W.H. McElwee, Jr., North Wilkesboro, N.C., 1956-58; pvt. practice Greensboro, N.C., 1958-59; with Booth & Osteen, Greensboro, 1959-69; U.S. atty. U.S. Attys. Office, Greensboro, 1969-74; ptnr. Osteen, Adams & Osteen, Greensboro, 1974-91; fed. judge U.S. Dist. Ct. (mid. dist.) N.C., Greensboro, 1991—. With USAR, 1958-51. Fellow Am. Coll. Trial Lawyers; mem. ABA, N.C. State Bar, N.C. Bar Assn. (mem. and chair subcom. N.C. sentencing commn.), U. N.C. Law Alumni Assn. Office: US Dist Ct PO Box 3485 Greensboro NC 27402-3485*

OSTENDORF, LANCE STEPHEN, lawyer; b. New Orleans, Aug. 16, 1955. BBA summa cum laude, Loyola U., 1976, JD, 1980. Bar: La. 1980, U.S. Dist. Ct. (ea., we., mid. dists.) La.; U.S. Dist. Ct. La., U.S. Supreme Ct. Atty. McGlinchey Stafford Lang, New Orleans, 1980-92, Campbell McCranie, New Orleans, 1992—; atty. La. State U. Med. Found., New Orleans, 1992—. Home: 3445 N Causeway Blvd Metairie LA 70002

OSTENSO, NED ALLEN, oceanographer, government official; b. Fargo, N.D., June 22, 1930; s. Nels Andres and Estella (Temple) O.; m. Grace Elaine Laudon, June 29, 1963. BS, U. Wis., 1952, MS, 1953, PhD, 1962; postgrad., Johns Hopkins U., 1975. Scientist Arctic Inst. N.Am., Washington, 1956-66; asst. prof. geology and geophysics U. Wis., Madison, 1962-66; dir. marine geol. and geophys. programs Office Naval Rsch., Washington, 1966-69, sr. oceanographer, 1970-77; asst. Presdl. sci. advisor White House, Washington, 1969-70; dir. nat. sea grant coll. program NOAA, Washington, 1977-83, dir. Office Oceanic Rsch., 1983-89, chief scientist, 1989-90, asst. adminstr. for rsch., 1990-96, cons., 1996—; founder Joy/Mac Petroleum, Madison, 1959-65; fellow Fed. Execs. Inst., Charlottesville, Va., 1974, Am. Polit. Sci. Assn., Washington, 1975-76. Cotnbr. over 60 articles on polar regions, oceanography and geophysics to sci. jours., chpts. to books. 1st lt. Signal Corps, U.S. Army, 1953-56. Recipient Antarctic Svc. medal Dept. of Def., 1958, Meritorius Svc. citation NAS, 1959, Superior Accomplishment award USN, 1968; Mt. Ostenso named in his honor, 1963, Ostenso Seamount (Arctic Ocean) named in his honor, 1978. Fellow Geol. Soc. Am., Arctic Inst. N.Am., Marine Tech. Soc., Explorers Club; mem. Acad. Polit. Sci., Am. Geophys. Union, UN Assn. U.S.A., Cosmos Club. Home: 2871 Audubon Ter NW Washington DC 20008-2309

OSTER, JEFFREY WAYNE, marine corps officer; b. Milw., Nov. 11, 1941; s. Richard Alexander and Isabel Aagut (Jacobson) O.; m. Sherry Christine Holt, Feb. 1, 1969; children: Allison Brett, Jennifer Alexandria. BS in Geology, U. Wis., 1963, MBA, 1976; postgrad., Nat. War Coll., Washington, 1982-83. Commd. 2d lt. USMC, 1964, advanced through grades to major gen., 1992; various assignments USMC, U.S., Vietnam, Japan, 1964-81; exec. officer 4th marine rgt. 3d Marine Div., Okinawa, Japan, 1981-82; sec. gen. staff Hdqrs. USMC, Washington, 1983-86; ops. officer 1st Marine Div., Camp Pendleton, Calif., 1986-87, comdr. officer 7th marine rgt., 1987-89; comdg. gen. 9th Marine Expeditionary Brigade, Okinawa, 1989-90; comdr. Def. Electronics Supply Ctr., Dayton, Ohio, 1990-92; deputy chief of staff for Resources Hqrs. USMC, 1992—. Decorated Legion of Merit. Mem. Am. Def. Preparedness Assn. (bd. dirs. Tri-State chpt. 1990-92), Marine Corps Assn., Vietnam Vets. Am., U.S. Naval Inst., Dayton C. of C. (bd. dirs., vets. affairs com. 1990-92). Lutheran. Avocations: golf, running, computers. Home: 9367 Tartan View Dr Fairfax VA 22032-1209 Office: DCS For Programs & Resorces HQ MC Washington DC 20380-0001*

OSTER, LEWIS HENRY, manufacturing executive, engineering consultant; b. Mitchell, S.D., Jan. 18, 1923; s. Peter W. and Lucy (Goetsch) O.; m. Mary Mills, Aug. 17, 1948; children—David, Lewis, Nancy, Susan. B.S. in Engring., Iowa State U., 1948; M.B.A., Syracuse U., 1968. Registered profl. engr., Iowa. Mgr., Maytag Co., Newton, Iowa, 1953-59; sr. staff engr., mgr. Philco-Ford Corp., Phila., 1959-62; mgr. mech. and indsl. engring. Carrier Corp., Syracuse, N.Y., 1962-75; v.p. Superior Industries Internat., Van Nuys, Calif., 1981—; v.p., gen. mgr. Superior/Ideal, Inc., Oskaloosa, Iowa, 1975—; engring. cons., Louisville, 1951-53. Author: MTM Application Manual, 1957. Leader, Boy Scouts Am., Syracuse, 1965-73; fund chmn. United Fund, Syracuse, 1965-73. Served to lt. col. USAFR, 1942—; ETO. Mem. Am. Inst. Indsl. Engrs. (pres. 1951-53). Club: Oskaloosa Country. Lodge: Elks.

OSTER, MERRILL JAMES, entrepreneur, publisher, author, lecturer; b. Cedar Falls, Iowa, May 30, 1940; s. Harland James and Pearl Rosetta (Smith) O.; m. Carol Jane Dempster, June 1, 1962; children: David, Leah Jane. BS, Iowa State U., 1961; MS, U. Wis., 1962. Asst. radio-TV farm dir. Sta. WKOW, Madison, Wis., 1961-62; asst. editor Crops and Soils mag., Madison, 1962, Ford Farming and Ford Almanac mags., 1964-67; editor Top Farmer Intelligence, Woodstock, Ill., 1967-69; pres. Communication Cons., Cedar Falls, 1969—, Oster Farms and Pork Pro, Inc., Cedar Falls, 1971—; founder, pres. Profl. Farmers of Am., Inc., 1973—; pub. Futures Mag., Inc., 1975—; pres. Hometowner, Inc., 1976-84, Cedar Terrace Developers, Inc., 1977-91; Greenhill Estates, Inc., 1991—; pres. Oster Communications, Inc., 1981—, Greenhill Estates, Inc., 1991—; chmn. Future Source Inc., Lombard, Ill., 1981—; bd. dirs. Danish Mut. Ins. Co., Western

Home Inc.; instr. U. Wis. Grad. Sch. Banking, 1976-82, Land Buying Strategies Seminar, 1977-86; mem. Nat. Yr. of the Bible Com., 1983. Author: How Farmers Use Futures for Profit, 1978, Multiply Your Money Through Commodity Trading, 1979, Multiply Your Money Trading Soybeans, 1981, Farmland Buying Strategies, 1983, Becoming a Man of Honor, 1986, Becoming a Woman of Purpose, 1989, Vision-Driven Leadership, 1991; also booklets and articles on future of agr.; contbg. editor: AgriFinance, Banking mag., Successful Farming, Soybean Digest, 1969-75. Mem. Young Pres.'s Orgn., 1983-90, chmn. Iowa chpt., 1989. Named Outstanding Young Iowa State U. Alumnus, 1975, Iowa Entrepreneur of Yr. Inc. Mag., 1989, Cedar Falls Personality of Yr., 1991; recipient Blue Chip Enterprise Initiative award, 1992. Mem. Am. Assn. Agrl. Editors, Nat. Assn. Agrl. Marketers Assn., Mag. Pubs. Assn., Chief Execs. Orgn. World Pres. Orgn., Cedar Falls C. of C. (dir. 1975-76, v.p. 1989, pres. 1990-91), Athletic Congress of U.S., Beaver Hills Country Club, Alpha Zeta, Sigma Delta Chi. Republican. Home: RR 4 Cedar Falls IA 50613-9803 Office: 219 Parkade Cedar Falls IA 50613-2735

OSTER, ROSE MARIE GUNHILD, foreign language professional, educator; b. Stockholm, Feb. 26, 1934; came to U.S., 1958; d. Herbert Jonas and Emma Wilhelmina (Johnson) Hagetorn; m. Ludwig F. Oster, May 17, 1956; children: Ulrika, Mattias. Fil. mag., U. Stockholm, 1956; D. Phil., Kiel (Germany) U., 1958. Postdoctoral rsch. fellow linguistics Yale U., 1958-60, rsch. fellow Germanic langs., 1960-64, lectr. Swedish, 1964-66; mem. faculty U. Colo., Boulder, 1966-80; assoc. prof. Germanic langs. and lits. U. Colo., 1970-77, prof., 1977-80, chmn. dept., 1972-75; assoc. dean U. Colo. (Grad. Sch.), 1975-79, assoc. vice chancellor for grad. affairs, 1979-80; dean for grad. studies and research U. Md., College Park, 1980-83; prof. Germanic langs. and lits. U. Md., 1980—; mem. Fulbright Nat. Screening Com., Scandinavia, 1973, 83-87, chair, 1986-87; mem. selection com. Scandinavia Internat. Exch. of Scholars, 1982-86; cons. panelist Nat. Endowment for Humanities, 1975—, mem. bd. cons., 1980—; state coord. Am. Coun. on Edn., Colo., 1978-80, Md., 1981-83, dir. dept. leadership program, 1986-91; mem. exec. com. Assn. Grad. Schs., 1980-83; mem. dean's exec. com. African-Am. Inst., 1981-85; interim dir. Washington Sch. Psychiatry, 1994-95; cons. in field. Contbr. articles and revs. to profl. publs. Bd. dirs. Washington Sch. Psychiatry, Am.-Swedish Hist. Mus., Phila., Open Theatre, Washington. Carnegie fellow, 1974; grantee Swedish Govt., Am. Scandinavian Found.; grantee German Acad. Exchange Service. Mem. NOW, MLA (mem. Del. Assembly 1995—), AAUP, Soc. Advancement Scandinavian Studies (pres. 1979-80), Am. Scandinavian Assn. of Nat. Capital Area (pres. 1983-86), Am.-Scandinavian Found., Am. Assn. Higher Edn., Modern Lang. Assn. (mem. del. assembly). Home: 4977 Battery Ln Bethesda MD 20814-4931 Office: U Md Dept Germanic & Slavic College Park MD 20742

OSTERBERG, CHARLES LAMAR, marine radioecologist, oceanographer; b. Miami, Ariz., June 15, 1920; s. Arthur Edward and Grace Viola (Johnson) O.; m. Betty Peltier, Nov. 10, 1945; children: Cheryl Ann Osterberg Cheek, David Arthur, John Charles. BS, No. Ariz. U., 1948, MS, 1949; postgrad., Purdue U., 1958, U. Wash., 1960; PhD, Oreg. State U., 1962. Rsch. assoc. Lowell Obs., Flagstaff, Ariz., 1949-53; asst. scientist Atmospheric Rsch. Lab., No. Ariz. U., Flagstaff, 1953-56; tchr. high sch. Flagstaff, 1956-59; successively instr., asst. prof., assoc. prof., prof. oceanography Oreg. State U., 1962-67; asst. dir. vis. biomed. and environ. programs AEC, Washington, 1967-74; program mgr. environ. programs ERDA, Washington, 1974-76; dir. Internat. Lab. Marine Radioactivity, Mus. Océanographique, Monaco, 1976-79; marine scientist U.S. Dept. Energy, Washington, 1979-86, chmn. oceanography subcom., nuclear safety, Galileo and solar polar space project, ret., 1986; co-founder EnRad, Inc./Radon Testing and Engring., Inc., Gaithersburg, Md., 1986—; cons. Internat. Atomic Energy Agy., Vienna, Austria; participant NSF Acad. Yr. Inst., 1959-60. Contbr. numerous articles on radioecology to profl. jours. With AC, U.S. Army, 1940-45; PTO. Recipient Alumni Achievement award No. Ariz. U., 1983; USPHS fellow, 1962. Mem. Am. Soc. Limnology, Oceanography, Health Physics Soc., Am. Assn. Radon Scientists and Technologists (bd. dirs. 1988), Sigma Xi. Home: 14525 N Crown Point Dr Tucson AZ 85737-9322

OSTERBERG, JAMES NEWELL See POP, IGGY

OSTERBROCK, DONALD E(DWARD), astronomy educator; s. William Carl and Elsie (Wettlin) O.; m. Irene L. Hansen, Sept. 19, 1952; children: Carol Ann, William Carl, Laura Jane. PhB, U. Chgo., 1948, BS, 1948, SM, 1949, PhD, 1952; DSc (hon.), Ohio State U., 1986, U. Chgo., 1992. Postdoctoral fellow, mem. faculty Princeton, 1952-53; mem. faculty Calif. Inst. Tech., 1953-58; faculty U. Wis.-Madison, 1958-73, prof. astronomy, 1961-73, chmn. dept. astronomy, 1966-67, 69-72; prof. astronomy and astrophysics U. Calif., Santa Cruz, 1972-92, prof. emeritus, 1993—; dir. Lick Obs., 1972-81; mem. staff Mt. Wilson Obs., Palomar Obs., 1953-58; vis. prof. U. Chgo., 1963-64, Ohio State U., 1980, 86; Hill Family vis. prof. U. Minn., 1977-78. Author: Astrophysics of Gaseous Nebulae, 1974, James E. Keeler, Pioneer American Astrophysicist and the Early Development of American Astrophysics, 1984, (with John R. Gustafson and W.J. Shiloh Unruh) Eye on the Sky: Lick Observatory's First Century, 1988, Astrophysics of Gaseous Nebulae and Active Galactic Nuclei, 1989, Pauper and Prince: Ritchey, Hale, and Big American Telescopes, 1993; editor: (with C.R. O'Dell) Planetary Nebulae, 1968, (with Peter H. Raven) Origins and Extinctions, 1988, (with J.S. Miller) Active Galactic Nuclei, 1989; Stars and Galaxies: Citizens of the Universe, 1990; letters editor Astrophys. Jour., 1971-73. With USAAF, 1943-46. Recipient Profl. Achievement award U. Chgo. Alumni Assn., 1982, Antoinette de Vaucouleurs Meml. lecture and medal U. Tex., Austin, 1994; Guggenheim fellow Inst. Advanced Studies, Princeton, N.J., 1960-61, 82-83, Ambrose Monnell Found. fellow, 1989-90, NSF sr. postdoctoral rsch. fellow U. Coll., London, 1968-69. Mem. NAS (chmn. astronomy sect. 1971-74, sec. class math. and phys. sci. 1980-83, chmn. class math and phys. sci. 1983-85, councilor 1985-88), Am. Acad. Arts and Scis., Internat. Astron. Union (pres. commn. 34 1967-70), Royal Astron. Soc. (assoc.), Am. Astron. Soc. (councilor 1970-73, v.p. 1975-77, pres. 1988-90, vice chmn. hist. astronomy div. 1985-87, chmn. 1987-89, Henry Norris Russell lectr. 1991), Astron. Soc. Pacific (chmn. history com. 1982-86, Catherine Wolfe Bruce medal 1991, bd. dirs. 1992-95), Wis. Acad. Scis. Arts and Letters, Am. Philos. Soc. Congregationalist. Home: 120 Woodside Ave Santa Cruz CA 95060-3422

OSTERGARD, PAUL MICHAEL, bank executive; b. Akron, Ohio, Apr. 1, 1939; s. Paul and Janette Beryl (Laube) O.; m. Elizabeth K. McCombs, Jan. 1965 (div. Nov. 1971). A.B. magna cum laude, Case-Western Res. U., 1961; J.D., U. Mich., 1964; M.P.A., Harvard U., 1969; student, U. Madrid, Spain, 1959-60. Bar: Ohio 1964. Atty. U.S. Steel Corp., Pitts., 1967-69; gen. atty. TWA Inc., N.Y.C., 1969-71; v.p. adminstrn., sec., counsel Pa. Co. (now Penn Cen. Corp.), 1971-74, and subs. Buckeye Pipe Line Co., N.Y.C., 1972-74; pub. affairs exec. GE, Fairfield, Conn., 1974-84; pres. GE Found., Fairfield, Conn., 1984-90, Citicorp Found., N.Y.C., 1990—; bd. dirs. Citicorp Found. Mem. Nat. Hispanic Scholarship Bd., Am. Coun. on the Arts Bd., Inst. Ednl. Leadership Bd., Jr. Achievement of N.Y.; trustee U. Bridgeport, 1991; corp. adv. coun. ARC. Capt. USAF, 1965-68, Vietnam. Decorated Bronze Star, Legion of Merit (Vietnam); Univ. scholar, 1957-61; Littauer fellow, 1968-69. Mem. Ohio Bar Assn., Phi Beta Kappa, Omicron Delta Kappa. Episcopalian. Clubs: Harvard, Atrium (N.Y.C.). Home: Scout Hill Rd Mail Box 73A Mahopac NY 10541 Office: Citibank 850 3rd Ave Fl 13 New York NY 10022-6222

OSTERHAUS, WILLIAM ERIC, television executive; b. N.Y.C., July 31, 1935; s. Eric Hugo and Helen (McAuliff) O.; m. Nancy Jean Heinemann, June 19, 1960 (dec.); children: Eric Frank, Marc Andrew; m. Annemarie Clark, Dec. 28, 1985. Student, Fordham U., 1953-54, Harvard U. Bus. Sch., summer 1970. Staff producer news and spl. events dept. Sta. WNBC-AM-TV, N.Y.C., 1956-61; exec. producer Sta. KYW-TV, Cleve., 1961-64; exec. producer Sta. KPIX, San Francisco, 1964-67, gen. mgr., 1969-73; program mgr. Sta. KYW-TV, Phila., 1967-69; pres., gen. mgr. Sta. KQED Inc., San Francisco, 1973-78; pres. SiteLine Comms., Inc., San Francisco, 1979—; chmn. bd. VariCom Inc., San Francisco, 1982-86; chmn. TV adv. com. Calif. Pub. Broadcasting Commn., 1977-78; mem. joint com. on film and broadcasting Indo-U.S. Subcommn. on Edn. and Culture, 1975-85; chmn. TV com. San Rafael Redevel. Agy., Calif., 1977-78; mem. citizens adv. com. CATV, San Rafael, 1976-77, Dominican Coll., San Rafael, 1972-80. Bd. dirs., chmn. advocacy com. The Ctr. for the Arts, San Francisco, 1985—; bd. dirs. Studio for Tech. and the Arts, 1995—. 1st lt. U.S. Army, 1958-60. Recipient Peabody award and Hillman award for One Nation Indivisible documentary, 1968. Office: 1 Union St San Francisco CA 94111-1227

OSTERHELD, R(OBERT) KEITH, chemistry educator; b. Bklyn., Apr. 19, 1925; s. Albert Henry and Hilda Pearl (Heatlie) O.; m. Jean Drake Evans, June 28, 1952; children: Robert Keith, Albert Laighton, James Evans, Thomas Heatlie. BS in Chemistry, Poly. Inst. Bklyn., 1945; PhD in Inorganic Chemistry, U. Ill., 1950. Instr. Cornell U., Ithaca, N.Y., 1950-54; asst. prof. chemistry U. Mont., Missoula, 1954-58, assoc. prof., 1958-65, prof., 1965-90; prof. emeritus U. Mont., 1990—; chmn. dept. U. Mont., Missoula, 1973-90. Contbr. articles to profl. jours. Mem. Florence (Mont.) Sch. Bd., 1969-75, chmn., 1972-73, 74-75; bd. dirs. Mont. Sch. Bd. Assn., Helena, 1973-75; council mem. Florence-Carlton Community Ch., 1965-90, treas., 1965-90. Served to sgt. USAAF, 1945-47. Mem. Am. Chem. Soc., N.Am. Thermal Analysis Soc., Sigma Xi. Home: 524 Larry Creek Loop Florence MT 59833-6705 Office: U of Montana Dept Of Chemistry Missoula MT 59812

OSTERHOFF, JAMES MARVIN, retired telecommunications company executive; b. Lafayette, Ind., May 18, 1936; s. Abel Lyman and Mildred Paulene (Post) O.; m. Marilyn Ann Morrison, Aug. 24, 1958; children—Anne Michelle Bitsie, Amy Louise Olmsted, Susan Marie. B.S.M.E., Purdue U., 1958; M.B.A., Stanford U., 1963. Staff asst. FMC Corp., San Jose, Calif., 1963-64; with Ford Motor Co., Dearborn, Mich., 1964-84; v.p. fin. Ford Motor Credit Co., Dearborn, 1973-75; controller car ops. N. Am. Automotive Ops., Ford Motor Co., Dearborn, 1975-76; asst. controller N. Am. Automotive Ops., Ford Motor Co., 1976-79; controller tractor ops. Ford Motor Co., Troy, Mich., 1979-84; v.p. fin., CFO Digital Equipment Corp., Maynard, Mass., 1985-91; exec. v.p., CFO U.S.West Inc., Englewood, Colo., 1991-95; bd. dirs. GenCorp, Inc., FSA Holdings, Ltd., Pvt. Sector Coun.; mem. Conf. Bd. Fin. Coun. Served to lt. (j.g.) USN, 1958-61. Recipient Disting. Engring. Alumnus award Purdue U.; named Outstanding Mech. Engring. Alumnus, Purdue U. Mem. Fin. Execs. Inst. Office: US West Co 7800 E Orchard Rd Englewood CO 80111-2533

OSTERHOLM, J(OHN) ROGER, humanities educator; b. Worcester, Mass., Nov. 24, 1936; s. Walfred Anders and Ellen Olivia (Hendrickson) O.; m. Jo-Ann M. Doiron, Dec. 22, 1962 (div. 1981); children: Doreen, Jon R., Don J.; m. Diane Jane Ungerer, May 1, 1982. BA, Upsala Coll., 1959; MA, CCNY, 1966; PhD, U. Mass., 1978; postgrad., Tex. Tech U., 1961-62, Worcester (Mass.) State Coll., 1965-66, Clark U., 1972. Instr. Worcester Jr. Coll., 1962; supr. Aetna Life Ins. Co., N.Y.C., 1963-65; tchr. Wachusett Regional H.S., Holden, Mass., 1965-66; assoc. prof. Ctrl. N.E. Coll., Worcester, 1966-79, chmn. humanities, 1977-79; prof. Embry-Riddle Aero. U., Daytona Beach, Fla., 1979—; spkr. on aviation films and Bing Crosby. Author: Literary Career of Isaiah Thomas, 1978, Bing Crosby: A Bio-bibliography, 1994; editor: The Riddle Reader, 1988; co-author: MiG-15 to Freedom, 1996; contbr. articles to profl. jours. Dirs. Daytona Playhouse, Daytona Beach, 1980-83; lector Grace Luth. Ch., Ormond Beach, Fla., 1989—. With USAF, 1960-62. Recipient Best Supporting Actor award Daytona Playhouse, 1981. Mem. Popular Culture Assn., Air Force Assn., Soc. Collegiate Journalists, Internat. Crosby Circle. Republican. Avocations: acting, airplane models, computer simulations. Home: 303 Timberline Trl Ormond Beach FL 32174-8505 Office: Embry-Riddle Aero U Humanities Dept Daytona Beach FL 32114

OSTERHOUT, DAN RODERICK, insurance executive; b. Sharon, Pa., May 12, 1950; s. Donald Glenn and Phyllis Irene (Ellison) O.; m. D. Catherine Dear, July 26, 1970; children: Jason Ryan, Brandon Lee, Jordan Shane. BS in Fin., U. Balt., 1976; MBA, Loyola Coll., 1980. Various positions Alexander & Alexander, Balt., 1970-84; chief fin. officer Alexander & Alexander Europe, PLC., London, 1985-88; sr. v.p. Alexander & Alexander Svcs., Inc., N.Y.C., 1988—; pres., COO, Alexander & Alexander Inc., N.Y.C., 1993-94; chmn., CEO Alexander Underwriting Svcs., Inc., N.Y.C., 1994-95; pres., CEO Alexander Howden N.Am. Inc., N.Y.C., 1995; CEO Alexander Capital Markets, N.Y.C., 1996—. Office: Alexander Capital Markets 1185 6th Ave New York NY 10036

OSTERHOUT, SUYDAM, physician, educator; b. Bklyn., Nov. 25, 1925; s. Howard and Edna Cornell (Davison) O.; m. Shirley Elizabeth Kirkman, Sept. 17, 1960; children—Mark, Martin, Ann. B.A., Princeton, 1945; M.D. (Hanes fellow), Duke, 1949; Ph.D., Rockefeller U., 1959. Diplomate: Am. Bd. Internal Medicine. Intern pathology Cleve. City Hosp., 1950; intern internal medicine Mass. Meml. Hosp., Boston, 1950-51; resident Duke Hosp., 1953-56; faculty Duke Med. Sch., Durham, N.C., 1959—; now prof. medicine, prof. microbiology, asso. dean. Duke Med. Sch. Contbr. articles to profl. jours. Served with M.C. USAF, 1951-53. Recipient NIH Career Devel. award, 1960-65; Markle scholar in medicine, 1959-64. Fellow A.C.P.; mem. Am. Soc. Micro-Biology, Am. Fedn. Clin. Research, Sigma Xi, Alpha Omega Alpha. Home: 5133 N Willowhaven Dr Durham NC 27712-1956 Office: PO Box 3007 Durham NC 27715-3007

OSTERKAMP, DALENE MAY, psychology educator, artist; b. Davenport, Iowa, Dec. 1, 1932; d. James Hiram and Bernice Grace (La Grange) Simmons; m. Donald Edwin Osterkamp, Feb. 11, 1951 (dec. Sept. 1951). BA, San Jose State U., 1959, MA, 1962; PhD, Saybrook Inst., 1989. Lectr. San Jose (Calif.) State U., 1960-61, U. Santa Barbara (Calif.) Ext., 1970-76; prof. Bakersfield (Calif.) Coll., 1961-87, emeritus, 1987—; adj. faculty, counselor Calif. State U., Bakersfield, 1990—; gallery dir. Bakersfield Coll., 1964-72. Exhibited in group shows at Berkeley (Calif.) Art, Ctr., 1975, Libr. of Congress, 1961, Seattle Art Mus., 1962. Founder Kern Art Edn. Assn., Bakersfield, 1962, Bakersfield Printmakers, 1976. Staff sgt. USAF, 1952-55. Recipient 1st Ann. Svc. to Women award Am. Assn. Women in C.C., 1989. Mem. APA, Assn. for Women in Psychology, Assn. for Humanistic Psychology, Calif. Soc. Printmakers. Home: PO Box 387 Glennville CA 93226-0387 Office: Calif State Univ Stockdale Ave Bakersfield CA 93309

OSTERMAN, CONSTANTINE ELAINE, Canadian legislator; b. Acme, Alta., Can., June 23, 1936; m. Joe Osterman, Oct. 30, 1954; children: Theo, Kurt, Kim, Kelly, Joe Jr. MLA representing Three Hills constituency Alta. Legis. Assembly, 1979-92, party whip, mem. edn. caucus and agr. caucus coms., 1982-86, minister of consumer and corp. affairs, mem. social planning com. of cabinet, cabinet/caucus com. on legis. rev., agr. caucus com., 1986, minister of social svcs. and community health, 1986-89, minister career devel. and employment, chair econ. devel., 1989-92; retired Alta. Legis. Assembly, Three Hills, 1992; served select legis. com. to rev. surface rights issue, lead role in passing of Surface Rights Act, 1983. Active exec. bds. local ch., home and sch. assns., Carstairs, Alta., 1958—, surface rights area; commr., charter mem. Alta. Human Rights Commn., 1973-78; pres. Can. Assn. Statutory Human Rights Agys. Address: RR # 1, Carstairs, AB Canada

OSTERN, WILHELM CURT, retired holding company executive; b. Geisenheim am Rhein, Germany, Sept. 29, 1923; came to U.S., 1956, naturalized, 1970; s. Wilhelm A. and Margarete R. (Seul) O.; m. Beatrice Atkin, Jan. 3, 1992; children from previous marriage: Karen, Ellen, Wilhelm. Grad., Staatliches Realgymnasium, Geisenheim, 1941. With Bayer AG, and predecessor, 1941-88, officer and/or dir. subsidiaries and affiliates, 1956-89; vice chmn., chief fin. officer Mobay Corp., Pitts., 1974-86; vice chmn. Bayer USA, Inc., Pitts., 1986-88; bd. dirs. Schott Corp., Inc., Carl Zeiss, Inc., CDS Internat. Inc.; bd. dirs. World Trade Ctr., Pitts. With German Army, 1942-45. Hon. Consul Fed. Republic of Germany. Mem. Soc. Contemporary Crafts, Pitts. (bd. dirs.). Clubs: Brook (N.Y.C.); Duquesne (Pitts.). Home: Hartle Rd Sewickley PA 15143 Office: Bayer Corp 500 Grant St One Mellon Ctr Pittsburgh PA 15219-2502

OSTERTAG, ROBERT LOUIS, lawyer; b. N.Y.C., June 21, 1931; s. Frederick C. and Lillian (Bishop) O.; m. Ann Mary Flynn, Aug. 28, 1954; children—Thomas J., Daniel V., Debra A. B.A., Fordham U., 1953; LL.B., St. John's U., Bklyn., 1956; LL.M., Georgetown U., 1960. Bar: N.Y. 1957, U.S. Dist. Ct. (so. dist.) N.Y. 1969, U.S. Tax Ct. 1965, U.S. Ct. Mil. Appeals 1959, U.S. Supreme Ct. 1960. Atty. office chief counsel IRS, Washington, 1958-60; ptnr. Guernsey, Butts & Walsh, Poughkeepsie, N.Y., 1963-90, Guernsey, Butts, Ostertag & O'Leary, Poughkeepsie, N.Y., 1991-95, Ostertag & O'Leary, Poughkeepsie, 1995—; adj. prof. paralegal studies Marist Coll., Poughkeepsie, 1975-91; adj. prof. Fordham U. Sch. of Law, N.Y.C., 1993—; counsel Agr. Com., N.Y. State Assembly, 1967-68; mem. Gov.'s Jud. Screening Com., 1987-93; counsel to cons. and draftsman of proposed county charters and adminstrv. codes for Sullivan, Fulton, Orange and Onondaga Counties, N.Y., City of Poughkeepsie, N.Y.; mem. 9th Jud. Dist. Grievance Com., 1975-79, 9th Jud. Dist. Med. Malpractice Panel, 1975-91, mem. 9th Jud. Dist. Arbitration Panel, 1980—. Mem. adv. coun. Pace U. Sch. Law, 1975-84, paralegal adv. coun. Maris Coll., 1975—; bd. dirs. Com. for Modern Cts., 1975—; trustee Joseph F. Barnard Meml. Law Libr., Poughkeepsie, 1979—; mem. Dutchess County Charter Commn., N.Y., 1966-67, Dutchess County Bd. Health, 1964-70, pres., 1966-70; chmn. Dutchess County Charter Revision Task Force, 1979-88; dir. Hudson Valley Philharm. Soc., 1973-76; v.p., dir. High Tor Opera Co., 1967-70; dir. United Fund of Dutchess County, 1973-78, Dutchess County chpt. Am. Heart Assn., 1975-81, 84-89; trustee Sports Mus. Dutchess County, 1989-93, chmn., 1989-90; dir. Hudson Valley Stadium Corp., 1995—; dep. supr. Town of Poughkeepsie, 1976; dir. Standard Gage Co., 1972-88; dir. Hudson Valley Stadium Conf. Served to capt. JAGC, USAF, 1956-58. Recipient Recognition award Cen. Poughkeepsie Exch. Club, 1967, Marist Coll. Pres.'s award, 1991. Mem. Hudson Valley Estate Planning Council (pres. 1965-66, dir. 1969-74), ABA (chmn. conf. of state bar gen. practice leaders of gen. practice sect. 1980-87, mem. coun. 1982-86, chmn. by-laws com. 1988-89, chmn. litigation com. 1989-90, ho. of dels. 1985—, Gavel awards com. 1989—, standing com. on solo and small firm practitioners 1992-95), Am. Bar Found., N.Y. Bar Found., N.Y. State Bar Assn. (exec. com. 1983-85, 1986-93, ho. of dels. 1973-79, 80—, pres. 1991-92, chmn. unlawful practice of law com. 1977-81, chmn. com. on profl. econs. and efficiency rsch. 1982, chmn. sect. on gen. practice of law 1980-82, com. profl. ethics, 1986-90, chmn. long range planning com. 1992-95), Dutchess County Bar Assn. (sec. 1969-79, pres. 1984-85), Delta Theta Phi. Home: 5 Pat Dr Poughkeepsie NY 12603-5626 Office: 17 Collegeview Ave Poughkeepsie NY 12603

OSTFELD, ADRIAN MICHAEL, physician; b. St. Louis, Sept. 2, 1926; s. Simon and Margaret (Fisman) O.; m. Ruth Vogel, Dec. 31, 1950; children: Barbara Horowitz, Richard, Robin. Student, Washington U., St. Louis, 1943-44, 46-47, MD cum laude, 1951. Instr. Cornell U. Med. Coll., 1955-56; faculty U. Ill. Coll. Medicine Chgo., 1956-68, prof. preventive medicine, 1963-66, head dept., 1966-68; staff Research and Edn. Hosps., 1956-68; chmn. dept. epidemiology and pub. health Yale U., 1968-70, Anna Lauder prof. epidemiology and pub. health, 1970-94; prof. emeritus, 1994—; head div. chronic disease epidemiology Yale U., dir. med. student edn. Sch. Pub. Health, 1971-75; spl. cons. Surgeon Gen. USPHS, 1964—; chmn. ad hoc com. on life prolonging drugs NIH, 1973-76, mem. nat. adv. council on aging; cons. council on drugs AMA, 1964—; cons. human experimentation Nat. Inst. on Aging, 1977, cons., 1979, mem. overall program planning panel, 1981—; mem. Mayor's Com. on Elderly, New Haven, vice chmn., 1972, chmn., 1977-80; co-chmn. Nationwide Study Precursors of Stroke; dir. Conn. High Blood Pressure Program; cons. Am. Inst. Biol. Scis., Population Lab.; nat. cons. White House Conf. on Aging, 1981; mem. research rev. com. B Nat. Heart, Lung and Blood Inst., NIH, 1976—; mem. exec. com. Yale Center for Behavioral Medicine, 1977—; v.p. Conn. Heart Assn., 1978-80, pres., 1980-82; mem. nat. policy bd. on health and phys. fitness YMCA, 1979-81; chmn. Commrs. Council on Hypertension Conn.; mem. Interagy. Planning Group on Coronary Heart Disease Prevention, 1981; cons. Robert Wood Johnson Found., Commonwealth Found; mem. cardiac adv. com. N.Y. State Health Dept., 1989; mem. com. on drug use in the workplace NRC, 1991. Author: The Common Headache Syndromes, 1962, Epidemiology of Aging, 1975, Psychosocial Variables in Epidemiological Studies of Cardiovascular Disease, 1985, Established Populations for Epidemiologic Studies of Elderly, 1986, Stress, Crowding and Blood Pressure in Prisons, 1987; assoc. editor The Black American Elderly, 1989; editor Am. Jour. Epidemiology, 1979-91; mem. editorial bd. 5 med. jours.; also numerous articles. Mem. panel on nat. health care survey Nat. Rsch. Coun., 1989. Recipient Wisdom Soc. award, 1970; fellow Morse Coll., Yale U.; named one of Conn.'s most Disting. Citizens, Hartford Courant, 1985. Fellow Royal Soc. Health, Soc. Clin. Investigation, Royal Soc. Medicine; mem. NAS (com. on rsch. in the prevention of addiction 1989), Inst. Medicine (com. to evaluate artificial heart program Nat. Heart, Lung and Blood Inst., coord. health promotion and disease prevention for the second fifty 1990, com. on epidemiology and vets. studies 1991), Am. Epidemol. Soc., Am. Coll. Epidemiology, Am. Heart Assn. (fellow couns. on stroke and epidemiology, chmn. com. risk edn. in heart attack and stroke, Disting. Vol. award 1976, C-E. A. Winslow award 1976, Ivy award 1987), Am. Soc. for Pharmacology and Exptl. Therapeutics, Am. Coll. Preventive Medicine, Gerontol. Soc., Internat. Platform Assn., Am. Pub. Health Assn., Am. Coll. Preventive Medicine, Inst. of Medicine (program com.), Conn. Acad. Sci. and Engring., Am. Soc. Clin. Investigation, AAUP, Sigma Xi, Alpha Omega Alpha. Research on relevant social and psychol. factors in cardiovascular disease and high blood pressure, risk factors for stroke, health and social problems of aging. Home: 17 Marlborough Rd North Haven CT 06473-2928 Office: Yale Univ 60 College St New Haven CT 06510-3210

OSTFELD, ALEXANDER MARION, advertising agency executive; b. St. Louis, Feb. 13, 1932; s. Simon and Margaret (Fishmann) O.; B.S., Washington U., St. Louis, 1953; postgrad. St. Louis U., 1953-56. Mktg. mgr. lighting div. Emerson Electric Co., St. Louis, 1955-59; dir. research and media Frank Block Assos., St. Louis, 1959-61; research and media supr. Compton Advt., Chgo., 1961-65; media and mktg. supr. Leo Burnett Advt., Chgo., 1965-68; dir. mktg. and account planning, v.p. McCann-Erickson, Chgo., 1968-72, Kenyon & Eckhardt, Chgo., 1972; dir. Canadian and internat. ops. A. Eicoff & Co., Chgo.; owner Alex Ostfeld Co. Advt. and Mktg., Woodbridge, Conn. and Can. Cons. Am. Assn. Advt. Agys., Yale/New Haven Sci. Park. Mem. Am. Mktg. Assn. (sec. St. Louis 1956-57), Internat. Platform Assn., Broadcast Advt. Club, Am. Research Found. Clubs: Chgo. Exec., Woodbridge Hunt (Conn.). Home: 4 Ledge Rd Woodbridge CT 06525-1802 Office: 6 Ledge Rd Woodbridge CT 06525-1802

OSTFELD, LEONARD S., computer company executive; b. Passaic, N.J., Oct. 1, 1942; s. Edward and Anne (Grossman) O.; m. Barbara Molen, Aug. 22, 1965; children: Robert, Scott. BS in Acctg., NYU, 1964; MBA, Fairleigh Dickinson U., 1968. Sr. acct. Coopers & Lybrand, Newark, 1965-68, Ward Foods, N.Y.C., 1968-69; mgr. acctg. Reliance Group Inc., N.Y.C., 1969-78; v.p. acctg., treas. Ampal Am. Israel Corp., N.Y.C., 1978-81; v.p., controller CGA Computer Assocs., Holmdel, N.J., 1982-84; v.p., CFO, AGS Computers Inc., Mountainside, N.J., 1985-93; sr. v.p., CFO Princeton (N.J.) Fin. Sys., 1994-95; v.p., CFO Phoenix Info. Sys. Inc., St. Petersburg, Fla., 1995—. Mem. Am. Inst. CPAs, N.J. Soc. CPAs, Fin. Execs. Inst.

OSTHEIMER, GERARD WILLIAM, anesthesiology educator; b. Poughkeepsie, N.Y., Feb. 9, 1940; s. Gerard William and Margaret Amelia (Theil) O. BS, St. Francis Coll., Loretto, Pa., 1961; MD, U. Pa., 1965; MS (hon.), Harvard U., 1992. Diplomate Am. Bd. Anesthesiology. Rotating intern Misericordia Hosp., Phila., 1965-66; resident in anesthesiology Hosp. of U. Pa., Phila., 1966-68; instr. U. Pa., 1966-69; fellow in cardiovasc. anesthesiology Mayo Clinic, Rochester, Minn., 1968-69; rsch. fellow dept. anesthesia Mass. Gen. Hosp., Boston, 1969-70; rsch. fellow dept. anesthesia Harvard U. Med. Sch., Boston, 1969-70, instr., 1970, 72-76, asst. prof., 1976-83, assoc. prof., 1983-91, prof., 1991-95; anesthesiologist Brigham and Women's Hosp., Boston, 1972-95, dir. obstetric anesthesia, 1982-88, vice chmn. dept. anesthesia, 1988-91, 92-95; vis. prof. numerous univs., 1974-95, including U. Md., U. Wis., UCLA, 1990, U. Rochester, Columbia U., 1991, U. Ill., Chgo., 1992, 93, 94, Rush Med. Sch., Chgo., 1992, U. Cin., U. Conn., U. Colo., Denver, Med. Coll. Pa., Cornell U., 1993, Wake Forest U., Med. Coll. Wis., 1994; editl. reviewer Anesthesiology, Anesthesia and Analgesia, Ob-Gyn., Am. Jour. Ob-Gyn.; Astra Pharm. vis. prof., Australia and New Zealand, 1989; 1st Benjamin J. Covino lectr. Maimonides Med. Ctr., 1992, U. Mass. Sch. Medicine, 1992; Henry Ruth lectr. Hanhemann U., Phila., 1993; med. projects advisor Internat. Coun. on Edn., 1977-82; mem. ednl. materials project appraisal panel Assn. Am. Med. Colls., 1977-82; profl. cons. Internat. Childbirth Edn. Assn., 1980-82. Editor: Manual of Obstetric Anesthesia, 1984, 2d edit., 1992, (with S. Datta) Common Problems in Obstetric Anesthesia, 1987, (with Ferrante and Covino) Patient-Controlled Analgesia, 1989, Pain Relief and Anesthesia in Obstetrics, 1995; editor-in-chief Regional Anesthesia, 1990-95; mem. editl. bd. Jour. Cli. Anesthesia, 1988-95, Internat. Monitor, 1990-95, also others; contbr. numerous articles, revs. and abstracts to med. jours., chpts. to books. Maj. M.C., U.S. Army, 1970-72. Fellow Am. Coll. Anesthesiologists; mem. AMA, Am. Soc. Anesthesiologists, Internat. Anesthesia Rsch. Soc., Soc. for Obstetric Anesthesia and Perinatology (bd. dirs. 1973-81, pres. 1980-81), Mass. Soc. Anesthesiologists, New Eng. Soc. Anesthesiologists, Obstetric Anaesthetists Assn., Mass. Med. Soc. (com. on perinatal welfare 1977-95, com. on maternal welfare 1981-95), Norfolk Dist. Med. Soc., New Eng. Perinatal Soc., Assn. Univ. Anesthetists, World Fedn. Scocs. Anaesthesiologists (com. on obstetic anaesthesia and analgesia 1984-92), Am. Soc. Regional Anesthesia (bd. dirs. 1985-94, pres. 1991-92), European Soc. Regional Anesthesia, L.Am. Soc. Regional Anesthesia, Phi Rho Sigma. Avocations: fly fishing, weight training. *Died Oct. 1, 1995.*

OSTLER, SCOTT, newspaper sports columnist. Sports columnist San Francisco Chronicle. Office: San Francisco Chronicle 901 Mission St San Francisco CA 94103-2905

OSTLING, PAUL JAMES, lawyer; b. Jamaica, N.Y., Sept. 22, 1948; s. John Carl and Margaret Ruth (Reilly) O.; m. Jane B. Mahler, June 1, 1974 (div. 1980); m. Julie Eileen Boyum, Feb. 20, 1982 (div. 1988); m. Danita Kay Hoover, May 3, 1991. BS in Math. and Philosophy, Fordham U., 1969, JD, 1973. Bar: N.Y. 1974, U.S. Dist. Ct. (so. and ea. dists.) N.Y. 1974, U.S. Ct. Appeals (2d cir.) 1974, U.S. Ct. Appeals (4th, 5th, 9th, 10th, 11th cirs.) 1978. Assoc. Chadbourne Parke, N.Y.C., 1973-77; asst. gen. counsel Authur Young & Co., N.Y.C., 1977-79, assoc. gen. counsel, 1979-82, ptnr., assoc. gen. counsel, 1982, nat. dir. human resources, 1985-90; vice chmn. Ernst & Young, N.Y.C., 1990-94, assoc. gen. counsel, 1994—. Office: Ernst & Young 787 7th Ave New York NY 10019-6018

OSTLING, RICHARD NEIL, journalist, author, broadcaster; b. Endicott, N.Y., July 14, 1940; s. Acton Eric Sr. and Christine Cathryn (Cumins) O.; m. Joan Elaine Kerns, July 8, 1967; children: Margaret Anne, Elizabeth Anne. BA, U. Mich., 1962; MS in Journalism, Northwestern U., 1963; MA in Religion, George Washington U., 1970; LittD (hon.), Gordon (Mass.) Coll., 1989. Reporter, copyreader Morning News and Evening Jour., Wilmington, Del., 1963-64; asst. news editor Christianity Today mag., Washington, 1965-67, news editor, 1967-69; staff corr. Time mag., N.Y.C., 1969-74, religion writer, 1975-94, sr. corr., 1994—; broadcaster Report on Religion, CBS Radio Syndication, Washington, 1979—; religion corr. Newshour with Jim Lehrer formerly MacNeil/Lehrer Newshour, 1991—; adv. bd. Ctr. for Religion and the News Media, Northwestern U., 1994—. Author: Secrecy in the Church, 1974; co-author: Aborting America, 1979. Served with USNG, 1964-70. McCormick Found. fellow, 1962-63; recipient Supple, Templeton and Wilbur awards for religion writing. Mem. Religion Newswriters Assn. (pres. 1974-76), Phi Beta Kappa. Mem. Christian Reformed Ch. Home: 280 Hillcrest Rd Ridgewood NJ 07450-2400 Office: care Time Magazine 1271 Avenue Of The Americas New York NY 10020

OSTLUND, H. GOTE, atmospheric and marine scientist, educator; b. Stockholm, June 26, 1923; came to U.S., 1963; s. Sven and Ruth (Lundin) O.; m. Doris Beck, Sept. 30, 1950; children: Stellan, Goran. Fil Kand., U. Stockholm, 1949, Fil Lic., 1958; hon. doctorate, U. Gothenburg, 1984. Research asst. U. Stockholm, 1944-46; tchr. Technol. Night Coll., Stockholm, 1946-51; research asst. Royal Inst. Tech., Stockholm, 1947; asst. instr. Royal Inst. Tech., 1948-52; head of lab. Swedish Nitrogen Fertilizer Works, Ltd., 1952-54, Radioactive Dating Lab., Stockholm, 1954-63; asst. instr. Royal Inst. Tech., Stockholm, 1956-57; vis. research asso. prof. Inst. Marine Scis., U. Miami (Fla.), 1960-61, asso. prof. geochemistry, 1963-67, prof. marine and atmospheric chemistry Rosenstiel Sch. Marine and Atmospheric Sci., 1967—, chmn. div. chem. oceanography, 1970-72, coordinator Geochem. Oceans Sects., 1976-86, mem. exec. com. Geochem. Oceans Sects., 1973-86, coordinator Transient Tracers in Ocean, 1977-85. Assoc. editor: Revs. of Geophysics and Space Physics, 1974-76; mem. editorial bd.: Marine Chemistry, 1974-93; mem. adv. bd.: Tellus B; contbr. articles to profl. jours. Served in Royal Swedish Air Force, 1943-44, 46. Mem. Am. Geophys. Union, Am. Meteorol. Soc., AAAS, Swedish Chem. Soc., Swedish Geophys. Soc., Fla. Acad. Scis. Office: U Miami 4600 Rickenbacker Cswy Miami FL 33149-1031

OSTMAN, ELEANOR A., food writer; b. Hibbing, Minn., May 14, 1940; d. Ero Victor and Ellen Ina (Lapinoja) O.; m. Ronald Thomas Aune, June 20, 1965; 1 child, Aric Bruce. BA in Journalism, Macalester, 1962. Staff writer St. Paul Dispatch-Pioneer Press (now St. Paul Pioneer Press), 1962-65, home furnishings writer, 1965-70, food writer, 1967—. Chmn. residential crusade Am. Cancer Soc., St. Paul, 1985-86; chmn. St. Paul Jr. League 60th Anniversary, 1968. Recipient 6 Golden Carnation Nutrition writing awards Carnation Co., James Beard Journalism award, 1994, others. Mem. Assn. Food Journalists (founder, pres. 1976-78, Food Writing awards)), Internat. Food Media Conf. (bd. dirs. 1990—). Republican. Presbyterian. Avocations: travel, reading. Home: 853 Lincoln Ave Saint Paul MN 55105-3350 Office: St Paul Pioneer Press 345 Cedar St Saint Paul MN 55101-1014

OSTRAGER, BARRY ROBERT, lawyer; b. N.Y.C., July 14, 1947; m. Pamela Goodman, Apr. 8, 1972; children: Anne Elizabeth, Katie, Jane. BA, CCNY, 1968, MA, 1973; JD, NYU, 1972. Bar: N.Y. 1973. Sr. ptnr., trial lawyer Simpson Thacher & Bartlett, N.Y.C., 1973—. Co-author: Handbook on Insurance Coverage Disputes, 8th edit., 1995, Modern Reinsurance Law and Practice, 1996. Mem. Am. Law Inst., Assn. of Bar of City of N.Y. Office: Simpson Thacher & Bartlett 425 Lexington Ave New York NY 10017-3954

OSTRANDER, ROBERT EDWIN, retired United Nations interregional advisor, petroleum company executive; b. Pitts., June 30, 1931; s. Robert Jesse and Elizabeth Raymond (Comstock) O.; m. Margaret Valentina Servello, Dec. 21, 1958; children—Robert Glen, Roseanne. B.A., Cornell U., 1952. Cert. petroleum geologist; registered geol. scientist. Area reservoir engr. Mene Grande Oil Co., San Tome, Venezuela, 1956-61; dist. engr. Oasis Oil Co. of Libya, Tripoli, 1962-67; chief engr. Occidental Oil of Libya, Tripoli, 1967-71; div. head Iranian Oil Consortium, Ahwaz, Iran, 1972-75; mgr. ops. Ultramar Co. Ltd., Mt. Kisco, N.Y., 1975-81; v.p. engring. Weeks Petroleum Ltd., Westport, Conn., 1982-85; mng. dir. Reomag Inc., South Salem, N.Y., 1980—; cons. World Bank, Washington, 1981—; cons. UN Secretariat, 1994—; advisor to govts. of China, India, others in Asia, Africa, Middle East; guest lectr. Asian univs., internat. seminars. Contbr. articles to profl. jours. Sec. Rep. Com. Town of Lewisboro ; chair conservation advisory coun. Town of Lewisboro; sr. v.p., treas. Ostrander Family Assn.; Rep. Com. Westchester County; past dir. Oakridge Condominium Assn., Vista, N.Y. Served to 1st lt. U.S. Army, 1953-55. Mem. Am. Assn. Petroleum Geologists, Soc. Petroleum Engrs. Home: 159 Stonemeadow Ct South Salem NY 10590-2412

OSTRANDER, THOMAS WILLIAM, investment banker; b. Detroit, July 20, 1950; s. Roland J. and Sybil (Swartout) O.; m. Mary Ellen Gallagher, Mar. 17, 1979; children: John Charles, Elizabeth Ann, Brian Thomas. AB, U. Mich., 1972; MBA, Harvard U., 1976. CPA, Mich. Staff acct. Ernst & Whinney, Detroit, 1972-74, sr. acct., 1974; sr. acct. Ernst & Whinney, Cleve., 1975; assoc. Kidder, Peabody & Co., N.Y.C., 1976-78, asst. v.p., 1978-80, v.p., 1980-86, mng. dir., 1986-89; mng. dir. Salomon Bros., Inc., N.Y.C., 1989—; bd. dirs. Westmoreland Coal Co.; mem. adv. bd. Paton Sch. Accountancy U. Mich., 1984-87, mem. vis. com. Lit., Sci. and Arts Sch., 1988-90, 95—. Mem. AICPA, Met. Club, Harvard Club, Hasty Pudding Club, The Creek, Bond Club, Beaver Dam Winter Sports Club, Theta Delta Chi. Home: 60 E End Ave Apt 25B New York NY 10028-7906 Office: Salomon Bros Inc 7 World Trade Ctr New York NY 10048-1102

OSTRIKER, ALICIA SUSKIN, poet; b. N.Y.C., Nov. 11, 1937; d. David and Beatrice (Linnick) Suskin; m. Jeremiah P. Ostriker, 1958; children: Rebecca, Eve, Gabriel. BA, Brandeis U., 1959; MA, U. Wis., 1961, PhD, 1964. Asst. prof. Rutgers U., New Brunswick, N.J., 1965-68, assoc. prof., 1968-72, prof. English, 1972—. Author: Vision and Verse in William Blake, 1965, Songs, 1969, Once More Out of Darkness, and Other Poems, 1974, A Dream of Springtime, 1979, The Mother/Child Papers, 1980, A Woman Under the Surface: Poems and Prose Poems, 1982, Writing Like a Woman, 1983, The Imaginary Lover, 1986 (William Carlos Williams prize Poetry Soc. Am. 1986), Stealing the Language: The Emergence of Women's Poetry in America, 1986, Green Age, 1989, Feminist Revision and the Bible, 1993, The Nakedness of the Fathers: Biblical Vision and Revisions, 1994, The Crack in Everything, 1996; editor: William Blake: Complete Poems, 1977. Nat. Coun. on Humanities grantee, 1968; NEA fellow, 1976-77, N.J. Arts Coun. fellow, 1982, Guggenheim Found. fellow, 1984-85, faculty fellow Rutgers Ctr. for Hist. Analysis, 1995-96; recipient Strousse Poetry prize Prairie Schooner, 1986, Edward Stanley award Prairie Schooner, 1994, Anna David Rosenberg Poetry award, 1994. Office: Rutgers Univ Dept of English New Brunswick NJ 08903

OSTRIKER, JEREMIAH PAUL, astrophysicist, educator; b. N.Y.C., Apr. 13, 1937; s. Martin and Jeanne (Sumpf) O.; m. Alicia Suskin, Dec. 1, 1958; children—Rebecca, Eve, Gabriel. A.B., Harvard, 1959; Ph.D. (NSF fellow), U. Chgo., 1964; postgrad., U. Cambridge, Eng., 1964-65; hon. degree, U. Chgo., 1992. Rsch. assoc., lectr. astrophysics Princeton (N.J.) U., 1965-66, asst. prof., 1966-68, assoc. prof., 1968-71, prof., 1971—, chmn. dept. astronomy, dir. obs., 1979—, Charles A. Young prof. astronomy, 1982—, provost, 1995—. Author: Development of Large-Scale Structure in the Univers, 1991; mem. editl. bd., trustee Princeton U. Press; contbr. articles to profl. jours. Alfred P. Sloan Found. fellow, 1970-72. Fellow AAAS; mem. NAS (bd. govs. 1993—, counselor 1992—), Am. Astron. Soc. (councilor 1978-80, Warner prize 1972, Russel prize 1989), Internat. Astron. Union, Am. Philos. Soc., Am. Acad. Arts and Scis., Royal Astron. Soc. (assoc.). Home: 33 Philip Dr Princeton NJ 08540-5409 Office: Princeton Univ Office of the Provost 3 Nassau Hall Princeton NJ 08544

OSTROFF, ALLEN J., insurance company executive; b. Bklyn., Mar. 19, 1936; s. Irving and Sally (Cassoff) O.; m. Lenore, Oct. 29, 1967; children: Bruce, Gary, Stephen. BS, NYU, 1957. Ops. analyst N.Y. Hilton, 1964-66, corp. asst/ v.p., 1967-68, gen. mgr., 1972; mgr. Statler Hilton, N.Y.C., 1969-71; group v.p. Americana Hotel, N.Y.C., 1974-75; v.p. The Prudential, Newark, 1976-93, sr. v.p., 1993—; bd. dirs. Prime Hospitality Corp., Fairfield, N.J.; co-chair Am. Hotel Found., Inc., Washington; univ. lectr. in field. Mem. Cornell Soc. Hotelmen (chmn.), NYU Real Estate (chmn., inst. bd. exec. com.), Inst. Masters in Hospitality Program (chmn.), Am. Hotel and Motel Assn. Mgmt. (adv. com., co-chair Irefac, Washington). Avocations: teaching, boating. Office: The Prudential Realty Group 8 Campus Dr Parsippany NJ 07054-4493

OSTROFSKY, BENJAMIN, business and engineering management educator, industrial engineer; b. Phila., July 26, 1925; s. Eli and Edith (Segal) O.; m. Shirley Marcia Welcher, June 2, 1956; children: Keri Ellen Pearlson, Marc Howard. BSME, Drexel U., 1947; M in Engring., UCLA, 1962, PhD in Engring., 1968. Registered profl. engr., Tex., Calif. Lectr. Engring. Systems Design, UCLA, L.A., 1962-68; dir. ctr. mgmt. studies and analyses Coll. Bus. Adminstrn., Houston, 1970-72, prof. prodn. and logistics mgmt., 1969-73, chmn. dept., 1972-74; prof. indsl. engring. Cullen Coll. Engring., Houston, 1970—; prof. ops. mgmt. Coll. of Bus. Adminstrn., Houston, 1973—; lectr. Army Rsch. Inst. and various govt. and indsl. agys., also engring. industry, 1964-76; v.p. Tech. Soc. Logistics Engrs., 1974-76; nat. dir. Logistics Edn. Found., 1980—, acad. advisor, 1990—. Author: Design, Planning and Development Methodology, 1977; co-author: Manned Systems Design: Methods, Equipment and Applications, 1981. Program mgr. USAF Office of Sci. Rsch. project, 1977-86. Lt. U.S. Army, 1943-45, USAF, 1950-53. Fellow AAAS, Soc. Logistics Engrs. (cert. profl. logistician, chmn. nat. edn. com. 1972-74, sr. editor Annals 1986—, mng. editor 1986—, Armitage medal 1978, Eccles medal 1988, Founders medal 1993); mem. NSPE, Inst. Indsl. Engrs., Ops. Rsch. Soc. Am., Decision Scis. Inst., Am. Soc. for Engring. Edn., IEEE Engring. Mgmt. Soc., Blue Key, Sigma Xi, Tau Beta Pi, Phi Kappa Phi, Alpha Iota Delta, Alpha Pi Mu. Home: 14611 Carolcrest Dr Houston TX 77079-6405

OSTROM, DON, state legislator, political science educator; b. Chgo., Mar. 9, 1939; s. Irving and Margaret (Hedberg) O.; m. Florence Horan, Jan. 13, 1972; children: Erik, Rebecca, Katherine. BA, St. Olaf Coll., Northfield, Minn., 1960; MA, Washington U., 1970, PhD, 1972. Prof. polit. sci. Gustavus Adolphus Coll., St. Peter, Minn., 1972—; state rep. Minn. Ho. of Reps., St. Paul, 1988—. Democrat. Home: 405 N 4th St Saint Peter MN 56082-1921

OSTROM, JOHN H., vertebrate paleontologist, educator, museum curator; b. N.Y.C., Feb. 18, 1928; s. William C. and Norma (Beebe) O.; m. Nancy Grace Hartman, June 14, 1952; children: Karen Ann Ostrom, Alicia Jane Linstead. BS in Geology, Union Coll., Schenectady, 1951, DSc (hon.), 1991; PhD in Vertebrate Paleontology, Columbia U., 1960. Lectr. Bklyn. Coll., 1955-56; instr. Beloit (Wis.) Coll., 1956-58, asst. prof. geology, 1958-61; asst. prof. geology Yale U., 1961-66; assoc. prof., 1966-71, prof., 1971-93; asst. curator vertebrate paleontology Peabody Mus. Natural History, 1961-66, assoc. curator, 1966-71, curator, 1971-93; research asst. vertebrate paleontology Am. Mus. Natural History, N.Y.C., 1951-56; research assoc. Am. Mus. Natural History, 1965—. Author: The Strange World of Dinosaurs, 1964, (with John McIntosh) Marsh's Dinosaurs: The Collections from Como Bluff, 1966; editor: Bull. Soc. Vertebrate Paleontology, 1962-74, Am. Jour. Sci., 1970—, Bull. Peabody Mus., 1993; co-editor: Tectonics and Mountain Ranges, 1975, The Beginnings of Birds, 1985, Proterozoic Evolution and Environments, 1990; contbr. articles on new fossil vertebrates, particularly Mesozoic reptiles to profl. jours. Recipient Alexander von Humboldt U.S. Sr. Scientist award, 1976-77, F.V. Hayden medal, 1986; Guggenheim fellow, 1966-67, Am. Acad. Arts & Scis. fellow, 1994. Mem. AAAS, Soc. Vertebrate Paleontology (pres. 1969-70, Romer-Simpson medal 1994), Soc. Study Evolution, Soc. Systematic Zoology (coun. 1975-78, 83-85), Paleontol. Soc., Soc. Earth Sci. Editors, Sigma Xi (pres. Yale chpt. 1972-73). Home: 198 Towpath Ln Cheshire CT 06410-3314 Office: Yale U Dept Geology & Geophysics New Haven CT 06520

OSTROM, MEREDITH EGGERS, retired geologist; b. Rock Island, Ill., Nov. 16, 1930; s. Meredith Louis Hult and Alma (Eggers) O.; m. Ann Carolyn Postels, Aug. 1, 1953; children—Michael Eric, Craig Alan, Terry Scott. B.S., Augustana Coll., Rock Island, Ill., 1952; M.S., U. Ill., 1954, Ph.D., 1959. Geologist Ill. Geol. Survey, Urbana, 1955-59; geologist Wis. Geol. and Natural History Survey, Madison, 1959-62; asso. state geologist Wis. Geol. and Natural History Survey, 1962-72, state geologist, dir., 1972-90. Fellow Geol. Soc. Am.; mem. Am. Geol. Inst. (mem. governing bd. 1979-82), Am. Inst. Profl. Geologists (Pub. Svc. award 1991), Assn. Am. State Geologists (pres. 1982-83), Wis. Acad. Scis., Arts and Letters (pres. 1989), Masons. Unitarian. Home: 6802 Forest Glade Ct Middleton WI 53562-1711

OSTROM, PHILIP GARDNER, computer company executive; b. New Haven, Aug. 8, 1942; s. David McKellar and Barbara (Kingsbury) O.; m. Toni Hammons, Dec. 21, 1965; n. Nancy Jean Kahl, Apr. 2, 1983; children: Eric Craig, Paige Lynne. BS, U. Ariz., 1965; postgrad., U. Calif., 1992-94. Cert. sr. examiner quality control, Calif. Sales mgr. Procter & Gamble Co., Louisville, 1968-70, Dun & Bradstreet, L.A., 1970-71; internat. sales mgr. Memorex Corp., Santa Clara, Calif., 1971-82; dir. ops. Memtek Products, Campbell, Calif., 1982-86, Victor Techs., Scotts Valley, Calif., 1986-88; ops. mgr. Apple Computer, Cupertino, Calif., 1988-93; pres./CEO Ostrom & Assocs., San Jose, Calif., 1993—; ISO9000 lead assessor, 1992—. Spl. examiner CCQS, State of Calif., 1994—, presiding judge; examiner Malcolm Baldridge award, 1993—. Home: 1099 Maraschino Dr San Jose CA 95129-3317 Office: Ostrom & Assocs 1099 Maraschino Dr M/S07DGO San Jose CA 95129-3317

OSTROM, VINCENT A(LFRED), political science educator; b. Nooksack, Wash., Sept. 25, 1919; s. Alfred and Alma (Knudson) O.; m. Isabell Bender, May 20, 1942 (div. 1963); m. Elinor Awan, Nov. 23, 1963. BA in Polit. Sci., UCLA, 1942, MA in Polit. Sci., 1945, PhD in Polit. Sci., 1950. Tchr. Chaffey Union High Sch., Ontario, Calif., 1943-45; asst. prof. polit. sci. U. Wyo., Laramie, 1945-48; asst. prof. polit. sci. U. Oreg., Eugene, 1949-54, assoc. prof. polit. sci., 1954-58; assoc. prof. polit. sci. UCLA, 1958-64; prof. polit. sci. Ind. U., Bloomington, 1964-90, Arthur F. Bentley prof emeritus polit. sci., 1990—; Hooker disting. vis. scholar McMaster U., 1984-85; rsch. assoc. Bur. Mcpl. Rsch., 1950, Resources for Future, Inc., 1962-64; assoc. dir. Pacific NW Coop. Program in Ednl. Adminstrn., 1951-58; co-dir. Workshop in Polit. Theory and Policy Analysis, Ind. U., Bloomington, 1973—; cons. and lectr. in field. Author: Water and Politics, 1953, The Political Theory of a Compound Republic, 1971, 2d rev. edit., 1987, The Intellectual Crisis in American Public Administration, 1974, 2d edit., 1989, The Meaning of American Federalism, 1991; co-author: Understanding Urban Government, 1973, Local Government in the United States, 1988; author numerous monographs on polit. sci.; co-editor: Comparing Urban Service Delivery Systems, 1977, Guidance, Control and Evaluation in the Public Sector, 1986, Rethinking Institutional Analysis and Development, 1988, 2nd. edit. 1993; mem. bd. editors Publius, 1972—; mem. edit. bd. Constitutional Political Economy, 1989—; mem. founding bd. Committee on the Political Economy of the Good Society, 1990—; contbr. articles to profl. jours. Program coord. Wyo. Assessors' Sch., 1946-48, Budget Officer's Sch., 1947-48; exec. sec. Wyo. League of Municipalities, 1947-48; cons. Wyo. Legis. Interim Com., 1947-48, Nat. Resources, Alaska Constitutional Convention, 1955-56, Tenn. Water Policy Commn., 1956. Grantee and fellowships from numerous govt. and profl. agys. including Social Sci. Research Council, 1954-55, Ctr. Advanced Study in Behavioral Scis., 1955-56, Ctr. Interdisciplinary Rsch., 1981-82. Mem. Am. Polit. Sci. Assn. (special achievement award significant contbns. to study of federalism, 1991), Am. Econ. Assn., Am. Soc. Pub. Adminstrn., AAAS, Pub. Choice Soc., Internat. Polit. Sci. Assn. Home: 5883 E Lampkins Ridge Rd Bloomington IN 47401-9726 Office: Ind U Workshop in Polit Theory 513 N Park Ave Bloomington IN 47408-3829

OSTROSKI, GERALD B., utility company executive; b. Schofield, Wis., Jan. 18, 1941; s. Basil P. and Rose M. (Midlikowski) O.; m. Mary Ann Steif, June 6, 1964; children—Barbara, Michael, Gail, Scott. B.S.E.E., U. Wis., 1963. Registered profl. engr., Minn., N.D. Asst. planning engr. Minn. Power, Duluth, 1963-67, transmission planning engr., 1971-74, mgr. system planning, 1975-78, dir. info. and planning, 1978-82, v.p. info. and planning, 1982-88, v.p. info. and environ. svcs., 1988-90; pres. Synertec, 1990-95; pres. Synertec, 1995—; v.p. Minn. Power-Strategy & Growth, 1995—. Mem. IEEE, Duluth C. of C., Nat. Rifle Assn., Minn./Wis. Power Suppliers Group, Minn. High Technical Resources, Coun. Natural Resources Rsch. Inst. (adv. bd.), World Future Soc., Minn. C. of C. Roman Catholic. Club: Kitchi Gammi (Duluth). Lodge: Rotary. Office: Minnesota Power 30 W Superior St Duluth MN 55802-2030

OSTROSKI, RAYMOND B., lawyer; b. Wilkes-Barre, Pa., Nov. 24, 1954; s. Joseph Sr. and Lena (Lolli) O.; m. Pamela M. Mullay, Aug. 27, 1994; stepchildren: Charles R. Suppon, Lauren M. Suppon. Student, Pa. State U., Lehman, 1972-74; BA in Social Scis. summa cum laude, Wilkes Coll., 1976; JD, Temple U., 1983. Bar: U.S. Dist. Ct. (ea. dist.) Pa. 1983. Assoc. Hoegen & Marsh, Wilkes-Barre, Pa., 1983-85; assoc. counsel C-Tec Corp., Wilkes-Barre, 1985-88, corp. counsel, asst. corp. sec., 1988-91, v.p., gen. counsel, corp. sec., 1991-95, exec. v.p., gen. counsel, corp. sec., 1995—; bd. dirs. Mercom, Inc., Princeton, N.J., N.E. Netowrks Inc., White Plains, N.Y.; adj. prof. Pa. State U., Wilkes-Barre, Luzerne County C.C. Bd. dirs. Wilkes-Barre YMCA, 1993-94; bd. dirs., v.p. Make-A-Wish Found., Wilkes-Barre, 1990-94. Mem. ABA, Am. Soc. Corp. Secs., Am. Corp. Counsel Assn., Nat. Assn. Corp. Dirs., Pa. Bar Assn., Wilkes-Barre Law & Libr. Assn. Avocations: golf, basketball, softball, guitar. Home: 1667 Fairfield Rd Yardley PA 19067-3947 Office: C-Tec Corp 105 Carnegie Ctr Princeton NJ 08540-6215

OSTROW, JAY DONALD, gastroenterology educator, researcher; b. N.Y.C., Jan. 1, 1930; s. Herman and Anne Sylvia (Epstein) O.; m. Judith Fargo, Sept. 9, 1956; children: George Herman, Bruce Donald, Margaret Anne. B.S. in Chemistry, Yale U., 1950; M.D., Harvard U., 1954; M.Sc. in Biochemistry, Univ. Coll., London, 1970. Diplomate Am. Bd. Internal Medicine, Am. Bd. Gastroenterology. Intern Johns Hopkins Hosp., Balt., 1954-55; resident Peter Bent Brigham Hosp., Boston, 1957-58; NIH trainee in gastroenterology, 1958-59; NIH trainee in liver disease Thorndike Mem. Lab. Boston City Hosp., 1959-62; instr. in medicine Harvard U., Boston, 1959-62; asst. prof. medicine Case-Western Res. U., Cleve., 1962-70; assoc. prof. U. Pa., Phila., 1970-76, prof., 1977-78; Sprague prof. medicine Northwestern U., Chgo., 1978-89, prof. medicine, 1989-95, prof. emeritus, 1995—, chief gastroenterology sect., 1978-87; vis. prof. gastrointestinal and hepatology dept. Acad. Med. Ctr., U. Amsterdam, The Netherlands, 1995—; med. investigator VA Hosp., Phila., 1973-78, VA Med. Ctr. Lakeside, Chgo., 1990-95. Editor, contbg. author: Bile Pigments and Jaundice, 1986. Asst. scoutmaster Valley Forge council Boy Scouts Am., Merion, Pa., 1972-78; asst. scoutmaster Northeast Ill. council Boy Scouts Am., 1978-81; vestryman St. Matthew's Episcopal Ch., Evanston, Ill., 1979-82; treas. Classical Children's Chorale, Evanston, 1982. Served to lt. comdr. M.C. USN, 1955-57. Recipient Gastroenterology Rsch. award Beaumont Soc., El Paso, 1979, Sr. Disting. Scientist award Alexander von Humboldt Found., Germany, 1989-90; NIH fellow, 1958-62, grantee, 1962-92; VA grantee, 1970-95. Mem. Am. Assn. Study Liver Diseases (councillor 1983-85, v.p. 1985-86, pres. 1987), Am. Gastroent. Assn. (chmn. exhibit com. 1969-72, mem. undergrad. tchg. project 1972-88), Am. Soc. Clin. Investigation, Am. Physiol. Soc. (asst. editor 1979-84), Internat. Assn. Study Liver, Peripatetic Club. Office: U Amsterdam Acad Med Ctr, Meibergdreef 9 Rm C2-111, 1105 AZ Amsterdam The Netherlands

OSTROW, JOSEPH W., advertising executive; b. N.Y.C., Feb. 22, 1933; s. Meyer H. and Helen (Small) O.; m. Francine Lee Goldberg, Sept. 4, 1955; children: Elizabeth Sara, Peter Mathew, William Nathan. B.S. in Mktg., NYU, 1955. Researcher W.R. Simmons, N.Y.C., 1954-55; with Young & Rubicam, N.Y.C., 1955-87; sr. v.p., dir. communication planning Young & Rubicam, 1972-73, exec. v.p., dir., dir. communications services, 1973-87, mem. N.Y. exec. com., U.S.A. bd. dirs.; pres., chief operating officer worldwide Direct Mktg. Group of Cos., 1983-84; exec. v.p., dir. media worldwide Foote, Cone & Belding Co., N.Y.C., 1987-94; pres., CEO Cabletelevision Advt. Bur., N.Y.C., 1994—; lectr. in field; past chmn. Traffic Audit Bur.; dir. Audit Bur. Circulations; bd. dirs., past mem. exec. com. Advt. Info. Svcs., Advt. Rsch. Found. Mem. nat. coun. Boy Scouts Am. Mem. Media Dirs. Coun. (past pres.), Am. Assn. Advt. Agys. (past vice chmn. media policy com.), Internat. Radio and TV Found. (bd. dirs.), Advt. Coun. (bd. dirs.), John Reisenbach Found. (bd. dirs.). Office: Cable TV Advt Bur 757 3rd Ave New York NY 10017-2013 *It is important that one continue to set goals that seem unachievable and at the same time live by standards that remain consistently high. The maintenance of integrity and adherence to principles which support it, are especially critical when dealing with consumer commercial persuasion. Anything less would be detrimental to the proper pursuit of both personal and business achievements.*

OSTROW, RONA LYNN, librarian, educator; b. N.Y.C., Oct. 21, 1948; d. Morty and Jeane Goldberg; m. Steven A. Ostrow, June 25, 1972; 1 child, Ciné Justine. BA, CCNY, 1969; MS in LS, Columbia U., 1970; MA, Hunter Coll., 1975; postgrad., Rutgers U., 1990—. Cert. libr., N.Y. Br. adult and reference libr. N.Y. Pub. Libr., N.Y.C., 1970-73, rsch. libr., 1973-78; asst. libr. Fashion Inst. Tech., N.Y.C., 1978-80; assoc. dir. Grad. Bus. Resource Ctr., Baruch Coll., CUNY, 1980-90, assoc. prof., 1980-90; assoc. dean of librs. for pub. svcs. Adelphi U., Garden City, N.Y., 1990-94; chief libr. Marymount Manhattan Coll., N.Y.C., 1994—. Author: Dictionary of Retailing, 1984, Dictionary of Marketing, 1987; co-author: Cross Reference Index, 1989. Mem. ALA, AAUW, Libr. Info. and Tech. Assn., Assn. Coll. and Rsch. Librs. (chair N.Y.C. sect.). Office: Shanahan Libr Marymount Manhattan Coll 221 E 71st St New York NY 10021

OSTROW, STUART, theatrical producer, educator; b. N.Y.C.; m. Ann Elizabeth Gilbert; children: Julie Elizabeth, Katherine Ann, John Stuart. Cynthia Woods Mitchell chair, theatre prof. U. Houston; Pres. Stuart Ostrow Found., Inc., Musical Theatre Lab.; former mem. opera-musical theatre panel NEA; mem. bd. overseers com. to visit Loeb Drama Ctr., Harvard U. Producer: We Take the Town, 1961, The Apple Tree, 1966, 1776, 1969, Scratch, 1971, Pippin, 1972, The Moony Shapiro Songbook, 1981, American Passion, 1983, M. Butterly, 1988, La Bete, 1991, Face Value, 1993, Doll, 1995; producer, dir.: Here's Love, 1963, Swing, 1980; author, producer: Stages, 1978; assoc. dir.: Chicago, 1975. Served with USAF, 1952-55. Office: 5326 Mandell Houston TX 77005

OSTRUM, DEAN GARDNER, actor, writer, calligrapher; b. Russell, Kans., Jan. 2, 1922; s. Oscar and Helen Mae (Gross) O.; m. Sarepta Pierpont, Dec. 25, 1943 (div. Sept. 1980); children: Karna Hanna, John Pierpont, Daniel Gross, Peter Gardner. A.B. with honors in Polit. Sci, U. Kans., 1947; J.D., Yale U., 1950. Bar: Kans. 1950, Mo. 1954, Tex. 1955, Oreg. 1958, Wash. 1961, Ohio 1964, N.Y. 1975. Ptnr. Ostrum & Ostrum, Russell, 1950-54; asst. atty. gen. Kan., 1953-54; atty. Southwestern Bell Telephone Co., St. Louis, 1954-55; asst. gen. atty. Southwestern Bell

Telephone Co., Dallas, 1955-57; area. atty. Pacific Tel.&Tel. Co., Portland, Oreg., 1957-60; gen. atty. Pacific Tel.&Tel. Co., Seattle, 1960-61; v.p., gen. counsel Pacific N.W. Bell Telephone Co., Seattle, 1961-62, gen. comml. mgr., 1962-63; v.p., gen. counsel Ohio Bell Telephone Co., Cleve., 1963-74; v.p. regulatory matters Western Electric Co., Inc., N.Y.C., 1974-81; v.p., counsel AT&T Techs., Inc., 1981-85; dir. Nat. Corp. Theatre Fund, N.Y.C. Former trustee AT&T Found., Cleve. Playhouse, Cleve., Orch.; support care vol. St. Vincent's Hosp. Served with AUS, 1943-46, 50-52. Mem. AFTRA, SAG, Actors Equity Assn., Actor's Fund Am. (life mem.), Amateur Comedy Club N.Y.C., Phi Beta Kappa, Sigma Nu. Episcopalian (past vestryman). Home and Office: 45 Christopher St Ph A New York NY 10014-3533

OSTRY, BERNARD, broadcasting executive; b. Wadena, Sask., Can., June 10, 1927; s. Abraham and Tobie (Goldman) O.; m. Sylvia Knelman; children: Adam, Jonathan. B.A. with honors, U. Man., 1948; postgrad., U. London, 1948-52. Rsch. assoc. U. Birmingham, Eng., 1951-55; spl. asst. and advisor to leader of Indian del. to UN, 1951-52; David Davies fellow in internat. history U. London, London Sch. of Econs. and Polit. Sci., 1956-58; exec. sec.-treas. Commonwealth Inst. Social Rsch., 1959-61; moderator Nightline, CBC, 1960-63; sec.-treas. Social Sci. and Humanities Rsch. Couns. Can., 1961-63; supr. dept. pub. affairs radio and TV CBC, 1963-68; chief cons. to chmn. Can. Radio TV Commn., 1968-69; commr. Prime Min.'s Task Force on Govt. Info., 1968-70; asst. under-sec. of state Dept. of Sec. of State, Ottawa, Can., 1970-73; dep. min., sec.-gen. Nat. Mus. of Can., Ottawa, 1974-78; dep. min. of communications Govt. of Can., 1978-80; spl. adv. sec. state and min. of communications Paris, 1980-81; dep. min. of industry and tourism Govt. of Can., 1981-82, dep. min. of industry and trade, 1982-84; dep. min. of citizenship and culture Govt. of Can., Ont., 1984-85; chmn., chief exec. officer TVOnt., Toronto, 1985—; mem. adv. coun. Elgin and Winter Garden Project, 1988—; moderator, commentator CBC, radio and TV programs; mem. Can. Videotex Adv. Com. Author: Research in the Humanities and in the Social Sciences of Canada, 1962, The Cultural Connection, 1978; co-author: The Age of Mackenzie King: The Rise of the Leader, 1955, To Know and Be Known, 1969; also articles on Canadian social, labor, polit. and cultural history. Bd. govs. Heritage Can., 1975-80, Can. Conf. of Arts, 1977-82, 86—, U. Guelph, 1986—, Shaw Festival, 1986—; mem. adminstrv. coun. Internat. Fund for Promotion of Culture, UNESCO, Paris, 1975-80; mem. adv. com. on cultural policy Govt. of Can., 1979-80; hon. patron Wedge Entomol. Rsch. Found., McClellandville, S.C., 1975-80; bd. dirs. Festival of Festivals, 1982-84, Agy. for Instructional TV, 1985—, vice chmn., 1990; bd. dirs. Can. Native Arts Found., 1990—, Nat. Ballet Sch., 1990—; patron Bicentennial N.Am. Indian Art Exhibit; mem. nat. adv. coun. Can. Friends of Tel Aviv U., Inc.; mem. bd. advisors Festival Music of Can.; trustee Inst. for Jewish Learning, 1990—. Decorated officer Order of Can.; recipient Can. Film award for best documentary for The Style is Man Himself, 1968, numerous other awards for Twenty Million Questions. Mem. Canadian Hist. Assn. (life), Assn. Can. TV and Radio Artists (v.p. 1963), Can. Writer's Found., Assn. for Tele-Edn. in Can. (bd. dirs. 1985—), Internat. Inst. Communications (trustee 1979-85, founding mem. Can. chpt. 1980, chmn. of bd. nominating com. 1986-89), Can. Mediterranean Inst. (bd. dirs. 1986—), Children's Broadcast Inst. (bd. dirs. 1987—), Inst. Pub. Adminstrn. Can. Avocations: reading, travelling. Home: 44 Charles St W Apt 4111, Toronto, ON Canada M4Y 1R8 Office: TVOnt, PO Box 200 Stn Q, Toronto, ON Canada M4T 2T1

OSTRY, SYLVIA, academic administrator, economist; b. Winnipeg, Man., Can.; d. Morris J. and B. (Stoller) Knelman; m. Bernard Ostry; children: Adam, Jonathan. BA in Econs., McGill U., 1948, MA, 1950; PhD, Cambridge U. and McGill U., 1954; also 17 hon. degrees. Lectr., asst. prof. econs. McGill U.; research officer Inst. Stats., U. Oxford, Eng.; assoc. prof. U. Montreal, Can.; with dept. stats. Econ. Coun. Can., Ottawa, 1964-72, chmn., 1978-79; chief statistician Stats. Can., Ottawa, 1972-75; dep. minister consumer and corp. affairs Govt. Can., Ottawa, 1975-78, dep. minister internat. trade, coordinator internat. econ. relations, 1984-85, ambassador for multilateral trade negotiations, personal rep. of Prime Minister for Econ. Summit, 1985-88; chancellor U. Waterloo, 1991-97; head dept. econs. and stats. OECD, Paris, 1979-83; chmn. U. Toronto, Ont., Can., 1990—; lectr. Per Jacobssen Found., 1987; chmn. nat. coun. Can. Inst. Internat. Affairs, 1990-95; western co-chmn. Blue Ribbon Commn. for Hungary's Econ. Recovery, 1990-94; chmn. internat. adv. bd. Bank of Montreal; bd. dirs. Power Fin. Corp., mem. internat. adv. coun. UN U. World/World Inst. Devel. Econs. Rsch., Helsinki; expert advisor Commn. Transnat. Corps., UN; mem. internat. com. InterAm. Devel. Bank/Econ. Commn. L.A.-Caribbean Project; mem. acad. adv. bd. World Orgn. Rehab. through Tng., London. Author: Governments and Corporations in a Shrinking World: The Search for Stability, 1990, The Threat of Managed Trade to Transforming Economies; co-author: (with Richard Nelson) Technonationalism and Technoglobalism; Conflict and Cooperation, 1995; co-editor: Rethinking Federalism; Citizens, Markets and Governments in a Changing World, 1995; New Dimensions of Market Access, 1995, The Halifax G-7 Summit: Issues on the Table, 1995, Who's on First? The Post Coldwar Trading System, 1996; contbr. articles on empirical and policy-analytic subjects to more than 90 profl. publs. Decorated companion Order of Can.; recipient Outstanding Achievement award Govt. of Can., 1987, Hon. Assoc. award Conf. Bd. of Can., 1992; Disting. vis. fellow Volvo, 1989-90, U. Toronto fellow, 1989-90. Fellow Royal Soc. Can., Am. Statis. Assn.; mem. Am. Econ. Assn., Can. Econ. Assn., Royal Econ. Soc. (founding), Ctr. for European Policy Studies (internat. adv. coun.), Group of Thirty, Inst. for Internat. Econs. (adv. bd.). Avocations: films, theatre, contemporary reading. Office: U Toronto Ctr Int Studies, 170 Bloor St W 5th Fl, Toronto, ON Canada M5S 1T9

OSTWALD, MARTIN, classics educator emeritus; b. Dortmund, Germany, Jan. 15, 1922; came to U.S., 1946, naturalized, 1956; s. Max and Hedwig (Strauss) O.; m. Lore Ursula Weinberg, Dec. 27, 1948; children: Mark F., David H. B.A., U. Toronto, 1946; A.M., U. Chgo., 1948; Ph.D., Columbia U., 1952; Dr. (hon.), Fribourg (Switzerland) U., 1995. Instr. classics and humanities Wesleyan U., Middletown, Conn., 1950-51; from lectr. to asst. prof. Greek and Latin, Columbia U., 1951-58; mem. faculty Swarthmore Coll., 1958—, prof. classics, 1966-92; prof. classical studies U. Pa., 1968-92, prof. emeritus, 1992—; vis. assoc. prof. Princeton, spring 1964; vis. prof. U. Calif. at Berkeley, summer 1969, Tel-Aviv U., 1996; vis. fellow Balliol Coll., Oxford (Eng.) U., 1970-71, Wolfson Coll., Oxford, 1987, 91; dir. fellowships-in-residence in classics NEH, 1976-77, d'etudes, EHESS, Paris, 1991. Author: Autonomia, Its Genesis and Early History, 1982, From Popular Sovereignty to the Sovereignty of Law, 1987, Ananke in Thucydides, 1988, (with T.G. Rosenmeyer and J.W. Halporn) The Meters of Greek and Latin Poetry, 2d edit., 1980, Nomos and the Beginnings of the Athenian Democracy, 1969; translator with intro., notes and glossary Nicomachean Ethics (Aristotle), 1962; mem. editl. bd. Cambridge Ancient History, 1976-94; contbr. articles to profl. jours. Fulbright research fellow Greece, 1961-62; fellow Am. Council Learned Socs., 1965-66; fellow Nat. Endowment Humanities, 1970-71, 90-91; mem. Inst. for Advanced Study Princeton, 1974-75, 81-82, 90-91, Inst. Advanced Studies, Tel Aviv, 1994; Guggenheim fellow, 1977-78; Lang. fellow Swarthmore Coll., 1986-87. Fellow AAAS; mem. Am. Philos. Soc., Am. Philol. Assn. (pres. 1986-87), Classical Assn. Can., Soc. Promotion Hellenic Studies (hon.), Classical Assn. Atlantic States, Soc. Ancient Philosophy. Home: 408 Walnut Ln Swarthmore PA 19081-1137

O'SULLIVAN, BRENDAN PATRICK, lawyer; b. N.Y.C., May 26, 1930; s. Patrick Joseph and Rosaleen (McQuillan) O'S.; m. Maria Teresa Colonna, Sept. 8, 1957; children: Leslie, Laurie, James. Bar: N.Y. 1958, Fla. 1961, U.S. Dist. Ct. (so., mid. and no. dists.) Fla. 1961, U.S. Ct. Appeals (5th and 11th cirs.) 1961, U.S. Ct. Internat. Trade 1980, U.S. Supreme Ct. 1975. Staff atty. Maritime Adminstrn., Washington, 1958-60; assoc. Fowler, White, Gillen, Boggs, Villareal & Banker, P.A., Tampa, Fla., 1960-63, ptnr., 1963—. Coach, mgr. Tampa Bay Little League, Tampa, 1973-78. Lt. Comdr USNR-R, 1953-75. Mem. ABA, Fla. Bar Assn. (chmn. admiralty law com. 1979-80, admiralty and maritime law cert. com. 1995—), Hillsborough County Bar Assn., Maritime Law Assn. (sec. marine ins. com. 1988—, bd. dirs. 1993—), Fed. Bar Assn., Def. Rsch. Inst. (chmn. admiralty law com., 1988-91, editor newsletter, 1987—), Civil Trial Lawyers (bd. cert.), Nat. Bd. Trial Advocates, Tampa Bay Mariners Club (skipper 1979-80, speakers trophy, 1976), Gray-Gables-Bon Air Civic Club (pres. 1964-65), Southeastern Admiralty Law Inst. (bd. govs. 1974-77), University Club, Centre Club. Democrat. Roman Catholic. Avocations: tennis, swimming, jogging. Office: Fowler White Gillen Boggs Villareal & Banker PA 501 E Kennedy Blvd Tampa FL 33602-5200

O'SULLIVAN, CHRIS, collegiate hockey player; b. May 15, 1974; s. Joahn and Ann O'S. Wing Boston U. Hockey Team, 1992—; player U.S. Nat. Team at World Championships, 1995 (team finished sixth); leading scorer for USA Select Team at Tampera Cup in Finland; played on gold-medal winning Team South, 1994 Summer Sports Festival; played for U.S. Team at World Jr. Championships, Czechoslovakia, 1990-91, numerous others. Named Second Team All-Am., MVP of NCAA Tournament, NCAA All-Tournament Team, First Team All-New England Hockey East All-Star Team, MVP of Mariucci Classic, all 1994-95. Office: Boston Univ Sports Info Office 285 Babcock St Boston MA 02215

O'SULLIVAN, CHRISTINE, executive director social service agency; b. Washington, July 5, 1947; d. George Albert and Mary Ruth (Stalcup) Markward; m. Donald Phillip O'Sullivan, June 27, 1985; 1 child: Kimberly Molly. Sec. Gas Distributors Info. Svc., Washington, 1966-70; adminstr. asst. Nat. Airlines, Washington, 1970-71; office mgr. Tire Industry Safety Coun., Washington, 1971-75; pres. Type-Right Exec. Sec. Svc., Washington, Pitts., 1976-91; exec. dir. Eastside Cmty. Ministry, Zanesville, Ohio, 1991—; pres. FEMA Emer. Bd., Muskingum, Morgan and Perry Counties, Ohio, 1994-96; chair United Way Exec. Dirs. Coun., 1994-96; v.p. Muskingum County Hunger Network, Zanesville, 1993-95. Author: Write a Good Resume, 1976. V.p. Muskingum County Women's Rep. Club, 1994, sec., 1995; bd. dirs. Muskingum County Women's Coalition, 1994-96; pres. Downtown Clergy Assn., 1992-96, pres., 1995-96; mem. bd. human care ministry, Ohio Dist., Lutheran Ch., Mo. Synod; task force mem. Literacy Coun., 1993-96, Pro-Muskingum, 1995-96; bd. dirs. Families and Children First Coun., 1995-96; commr. Mo. Synod Luths. to Commn. on Religion in Appalachia; mem. steering com. Muskingum County Operation Feed, 1992-96. Recipient Excellence in Cmty. Svc. Muskingum Coun. DAR, 1994, Excellence in Cmty. Svc. award Aid Assn. Luths., 1993, Cert. of Achievement for Mil. Family Support, U.S. Army, 1991. Mem. Kiwanis, Richvale Grange. Avocations: creative writing, music. Home: 509 Van Horn Ave Zanesville OH 43701 Office: Eastside Cmty Ministry 40 N 6th St Zanesville OH 43701

O'SULLIVAN, EUGENE HENRY, retired advertising executive; b. Plainfield, N.J., June 8, 1942; s. Patrick J. and Helen (Callahan) O'S.; 1 child, Meredith. B.B.A., U. Notre Dame, 1964. Media buyer Foote Cone Belding, N.Y.C., 1967-68; account exec., mgmt. supr. Group Dtr, N.Y.C.; exec. v.p., dir. client svcs. Young & Rubicam, N.Y.C., 1968-84; sr. v.p., group dir. Ogilvy & Mather, N.Y.C., 1984-86, 87; exec. v.p. Hill, Holliday, Boston, 1986-87; exec. v.p., gen. mgr. McCann Erickson, N.Y.C., 1988-90; ret., 1990. Served to lt. (j.g.) USN, 1964-66. Mem. Lotos Club. Democrat. Home: 21 E 10th St New York NY 10003-5923

O'SULLIVAN, GERALD JOSEPH, association executive; b. Chgo., Dec. 9, 1941; s. Gerald Thomas and Norine Rita (Herbert) O'S.; m. Joan Griffin, June 14, 1992; children from previous marriage: Stacey Marie, Lauren Ann; 1 stepchild, Kelly. Student, Chgo. Tchrs. Coll., Roosevelt U.; MPA, Roosevelt U., 1974. Cert. tchr., Ill.; cert. law enforcement officer, Ill. Pub. health adminstr. Chgo. Dept. Health, 1968-76, dir. fiscal svcs., 1976-78, dir. mgmt. and ops., 1978-81, adminstrv. dir., 1981-83; dir. personnel Ill. Atty. Gen. Office, Chgo., 1983-86, dir. ops., 1986-91; dir. program devel. Genesis Schs., Inc., Chgo., 1991-93; sr. v.p. ops. World Trade Ctr. Chgo. Assn., 1993-94; sr. ops. mgr. Chgo. Mfg. Tech. Ctr., 1994-95; supt. Cook County Sheriff's Office Boot Camp, 1995—; community prof. Gov. State U., Chgo., 1986-88; prof. grad. program Roosevelt U., Chgo., 1974-81; cons E.W. Lynch Vocat. Sch., Chgo. Mem. steering com. Ill. Juvenile Justice Inst., 1992-93; bd. dirs. Apple Canyon Lake Property Owners' Assn., Apple River, Ill., 1988-90; mem. City of Chgo. Task Force Brownnfields Land Redevel., 1995. Staff sgt. U.S. Army, 1964-70. Mem. Soc. Human Resource Mgmt., Ill. Juvenile Justice Inst. (steering com. 1992-93), Chgo. Bar Assn. (justice for youth com. 1992-93), Ill. C. of C., Sierra Club, City of Chgo. Exec. Alumni (past v.p.), Thunderbird Internat. Sch. Mgmt. Alumni. Roman Catholic. Office: Cook County Sheriffs Office South Campus 3026 S California Ave Chicago IL 60608

O'SULLIVAN, JAMES MICHAEL, lawyer; b. Boston, Jan. 21, 1958; s. James M. and Edith I. (Fielding) O'S.; m. Mary Ann Hayes, Mar. 28, 1992; children: Mary Elizabeth, Sheila Joanne. BA, U. Mass.; JD, Northeastern U., Boston, 1983. Bar: Mass. 1983, U.S. Ct. Appeals (1st cir.) 1984, U.S. Dist. Ct. Mass. 1984, U.S. Supreme Ct. 1988. Mem. Thayer, Cannon & O'Sullivan, P.C., Quincy, Mass., 1986-90; prin. O'Sullivan & Gizzarelli, P.C., Norwell, Mass., 1990-92, O'Sullivan & Assocs., P.C., Norwell, 1992—; adj. instr. Ea. Nazerene Coll., Quincy, 1992—, New Eng. Banking Ins., Boston, 1989—; examiner Mass. Land Ct. Co-author: Bank Operations, 1990, 2d edit. 1994. Pres., bd. dirs. Cath. Alumni Sodality, Boston, 1984—, South Boston Cmty. Health Ctr., 1982—; mem. Vols. Lawyers Project. Mem. Mass. Bar Assn., Mass. Conveyancers Assn., KC. Democrat. Roman Catholic. Avocations: running, woodwork, reading. Office: O'Sullivan & Assocs PC 17 Accord Park Dr Norwell MA 02061

O'SULLIVAN, JOHN, editor; b. Liverpool, Eng., Apr. 25, 1942; s. Alfred and Margaret (Corner) O'S. B.A. (honors), London U., 1964. Jr. tutor Swinton (Eng.) Conservative Coll., 1965-67, sr. tutor, 1967-69; editor Swinton Jour., 1967-69; London corr. Irish Radio and TV, 1970-72; editorial writer, parliamentary sketchwriter London Daily Telegraph, 1972-79, asst. editor, polit. columnist, 1983-84; dir. studies Heritage Found., Washington, 1979-81; editor Policy Rev., Washington, 1979-83; columnist London Times, 1984-86, assoc. editor, 1986-87; editorial page editor N.Y. Post, 1984-86; spl. adv. Prime Min. Margaret Thatcher, London, 1987-88; editor Nat. Rev., N.Y.C., 1988—. Conservative candidate for Parliament, 1970; exec. adv. bd. Margaret Thatcher Found. Decorated comdr. Order British Empire, 1991; Harvard U. Inst. Politics fellow, 1983. Mem. Mont Pelerin Soc., Phil. Soc., Reform Club (London) Beefsteak Club (London). Avocations: theatre, films, reading, dining out. Office: Nat Review 150 E 35th St New York NY 10016-4178

O'SULLIVAN, JUDITH ROBERTA, government official, author; b. Pitts., Jan. 6, 1942; d. Robert Howard and Mary Olive (O'Donnell) Gallick; m. James Paul O'Sullivan, Feb. 1, 1964; children: Kathryn, James. BA, Carlow Coll., 1963; MA, U. Md., 1969, PhD, 1976; postgrad. in law, Georgetown U., 1992—. Editor Am. Film Inst., Washington, 1974-77; assoc. program coord. Smithsonian Resident Assocs., Washington, 1977-78; dir. instl. devel. Nat. Archives, Washington, 1978-79; exec. dir. Md. State Humanities Coun., Balt., 1979-81, 82-84, Ctr. for the Book, Libr. of Congress, Washington, 1981-82; dep. asst. dir. Nat. Mus. Am. Art, Washington, 1984-87, acting asst. dir., 1987-89; pres., CEO The Mus. at Stony Brook, N.Y., 1989-92; exec. dir. Nat. Assn. Women Judges, Washington, 1993; clk. Office Legal Adviser, U.S. Dept. State, Washington, 1994—; summer assoc. Piper & Marbury, Balt., 1995; chair Smithsonian Women's Coun., Washington, 1988-89; mem. editorial advisory bd. Am. Film Inst., 1979—. Author: The Art of the Comic Strip, 1971 (Gen. Excellence award Printing Industry Am.), Workers and Allies, 1975, (with Alan Fern) The Complete Prints of Leonard Baskin, 1984, The Great American Comic Strip, 1991; editor Am. Film Inst. Catalogue: Feature Films, 1961-70, 1974-77. Trustee Child Life Ctr., U. Md., College Pk., 1971-74; chair Smithsonian Women's Coun., 1988-89. Univ. fellow U. Md., 1967-70, Mus. fellow, 1970-71; Smithsonian fellow Nat. Collection Fine Arts, Washington, 1972-73. Mem. Assn. Assn. Art Mus. Dirs., Am. Assn. Mus., Mid-Atlantic Mus. Conf., AAUW. Avocations: mystery writing. Home: 17 F Ridge Rd Greenbelt MD 20770-1749 Office: Internat Claims and Investment Disputes US Dept State Office Legal Adviser Washington DC 20520

O'SULLIVAN, LYNDA TROUTMAN, lawyer; b. Oil City, Pa., Aug. 30, 1952; d. Perry John and Vivian Dorothy (Schreffler) Troutman; m. P. Kevin O'Sullivan, Dec. 15, 1979; children: John Perry, Michael Patrick. B.A., Am. U., 1974; J.D., Georgetown U., 1978, postgrad; Bar: D.C. 1978; assoc. firm Chapman, Duff & Paul, Washington, 1978-82, Gadsby & Hannah, Washington, 1983-85; ptnr. Perkins Coie, Washington, 1985-92, Fried, Frank, Harris, Shriver & Jacobson, Washington, 1993—; mem. adv. bd. Fed. Contracts Report; mem. faculty govt. contracts program George Washington U.; lectr. Contbr. articles to profl. jours. Mem. ABA (chair truth in negotiations com. 1991-94, vice chair 1985-93, coun. rep. 1993-95, acctg., cost and pricing com., coun. sect. pub. contract law 1993-95, chair membership com. 1994—, budget and fin. officer 1995—). Office: Fried Frank Harris Shriver and Jacobson 1001 Pennsylvania Ave NW Washington DC 20004-2505

O'SULLIVAN, MARK GILBERT, minister; b. Lawrence, Mass., Dec. 20, 1943; s. Martin William Sr. and Esther Christina (Lundquist) O'S.; m. Patricia Lynn Prahl, Feb. 8, 1970; children: Daniel, Michael, Erin. B in Ministry, Internat. Seminary, Plymouth, Fla., 1995. Cert. sr. law enforcement chaplain Internat. Conf. of Police Chaplains. Golf profl. Profl. Golfers Assn. Am., 1969-78; youth min. and pastor Kings Place Ministry, Auburn, Calif., 1979-85; police chaplain Greater Sacramento Law Enforcement Chaplaincy, 1986-87; sr. law enforcement chaplain Placer County Law Enforcement Chaplaincy, Newcastle, Calif., 1987-94, Law Enforcement Chaplaincy Sacramento, 1994—; bd. dirs. Internat. Conf. Police Chaplains, Livingston, Tex., 1987—; U.S. Olympic Security Team chaplain U.S. Olympic Com., Atlanta, 1996. Sgt. USAF, 1965-69. Mem. Calif. Assn. Hostage Negotiators (chaplain 1992—), Fed. Bur. Investigation (chaplain 1991—). Avocations: bass fishing, golfing. Office: Law Enforcement Chaplaincy 1023 H St Ste B Sacramento CA 95814

O'SULLIVAN, PAUL KEVIN, business executive, management and instructional systems consultant; b. Syracuse, N.Y., May 10, 1938; s. John Hugh and Helen Troy (Smith) O'S.; m. Lynda Troutman; children: Mary Kathleen and Karin Jennifer (twins), John Perry, Michael Patrick. A.B., Dartmouth Coll., 1960. Communications specialist Gen. Electric Co., Schenectady, N.Y., 1963-66; nat. inst. dir. Gen. Learning Corp., Washington, 1966-67; sr. con. ednl. systems. Aries Corp., McLean, Va., 1967-69; dir. profl. devel. Nat. Audio-Visual Assn., Fairfax, Va., 1969-74; exec. dir. Am. Soc. Tng. and Devel., Madison, Wis., 1974-80; sr. v.p. Sterling Inst., Washington, 1980-87, nat. account mgr. Orgnl. Dynamics, Inc., 1987-94; account exec. Zenger Miller, 1995-96, pres. The O'Sullivan Group, Inc., 1996—; staff dir. Nat. Audio-Visual Inst. for Effective Communications Ind. U., 1969-74; chief adminstr. Internat. Fedn. Tng. and Devel. Orgns., 1974-80; dir. Internat. Symposia for Tng. Communications in Switzerland, Australia and Middle East. Producer and dir. films and multi-media presentations; author communications and tng. courses, textbooks; contbr. articles to profl. jours. Served to lt. (j.g.), USNR, 1956-63. Recipient Honor medal for Literature Freedoms Found., 1963; Writers Gold Cup award Gen. Electric, 1966; Resolution for Outstanding Achievement Nat. Audio-Visual Assn., 1974, Pres.'s award for bus. achievement, 1989, 90, 91, 92, 93. Mem. Nat. Soc. for Performance and Instrn. (Presdl. citation 1977), Am. Soc. Assn. Execs. (Grand award for mgmt. achievement 1978), Am. Soc. Tng. and Devel. (hon. life).

O'SULLIVAN, THOMAS J., lawyer; b. New Haven, Apr. 7, 1940; s. Thomas J. and Marjorie (Hession) O'S.; m. Anita Brady, Aug. 10, 1968; children: Kathleen, Margaret, Mary Tess, Anne Elizabeth. BA in History, Yale U., 1961; LLB, Harvard U., 1966. Bar: Conn. 1966, U.S. Dist. Ct. Conn. 1967, N.Y. 1967, U.S. Dist. Ct. (so. and ea. dists.) N.Y. 1967, U.S. Ct. Appeals (2d cir.) 1971, U.S. Supreme Ct. 1971, U.S. Dist. Ct. (no. dist.) N.Y. 1976. Assoc. White & Case, N.Y.C., 1966-74, ptnr., 1974—. Served to 1st lt. U.S. Army, 1961-63. Mem. ABA, N.Y. State Bar Assn., Assn. of Bar of City of N.Y. Clubs: Milbrook (Greenwich, Conn.); Yale (N.Y.C.). Home: 56 Hillside Rd Greenwich CT 06830-4835 Office: White & Case 1155 Avenue Of The Americas New York NY 10036-2711

OSUMI, MASATO, utility company executive; b. Osaka, Japan, Aug. 20, 1942; s. Masahiro and Sachiko Osumi; m. Masako Nakajima, Apr. 21, 1968; children: Masanori, Koji, Yuko. BS, Yokohama Nat. U., 1966; MS, NYU, 1971; D in Engring., Kyoto U., 1978. Engr. Sanyo Elec. Co. Ltd., Hirakata, Osaka, 1966-71, chief researcher rsch. ctr., 1978-85, mgr., 1985-86, mgr. control systems rsch. ctr., 1987-89, div. mgr., 1989-92; gen. mgr. Sanyo Elec. Co. Ltd., 1992—; engr. Tokyo Sanyo Elec. Co. Ltd., Ohizumi-Cho, Gunma, Japan, 1971-73. Contbr. articles to profl. jours. Mem. Japanese Soc. Mech. Engrs. (bd. dirs. 1986-87), Japanese Soc. Precision Engrs, Heat Transfer Soc. of Japan. Avocation: golfing. Home: 3-10-8 Takiimotomachi, Moriguchi Osaka 570, Japan Office: Sanyo Elec Co Ltd 1-18-13, Hashiridani, Hirakata, Osaka 573, Japan

OSVER, ARTHUR, artist; b. Chgo., July 26, 1912; s. Harry and Yetta (Woodrow) O.; m. Ernestine Betsberg, Aug. 12, 1940. Student, Northwestern U., 1930-31, Art Inst. Chgo., 1931-36. Instr. art Washington U., St. Louis, 1960-83. Works exhbtd., Art Inst. Chgo., Pa. Acad. Art, Carnegie Inst., Whitney Mus., St. Louis Art Mus., Nelson Gallery, Atkins Mus., Corcoran Art Gallery, U. Ill. Ann., Mus. Modern Art, Met. Mus., others, works in permanent collections, Whitney Mus., Toledo Mus., Isaac Delgado Mus., Peabody Mus., Rio de Janeiro Mus.; artist in residence, U. Fla., 1954-55; trustee emeritus Am. Acad Rome, 1993, artist in residence, 1957-58, one man shows, Wilson Gallery, Chgo., 1940, Grand Central Moderns, N.Y.C., 1947, 49, 51, 56, U. Tenn., 1948, Syracuse U., 1949, Hamline U., 1950, U. Fla., 1951, 55, Fairweather-Hardin Gallery, Chgo., 1953, 55, 69, others. Recipient John Barton Paine medal Va. Mus., 1944, purchase prize U. Ill., 1949, Temple gold medal and purchase prize Pa. Acad., Prix de Rome, 1952, 53, J. Henry Schiedt prize Pa. Acad. Fine Arts, award Am. Acad. and Inst. Arts and Letters, 1991, Arts & Edn. Excellence in Painting award, Arts and Edn. Coun. Greater St. Louis, 1994; James Nelson Raymond traveling fellow, 1936-38; Guggenheim fellow, 1950-51; sabbatical leave grantee Nat. Endowment Arts. Mem. Audubon Artists, Artists Equity. Address: 465 Foote Ave Webster Groves MO 63119

OSWALD, EVA SUE ADEN, insurance executive; b. Ft. Dodge, Iowa, Feb. 2, 1949; d. Warren Dale Aden and Alice Rae (Gingerich) Aspeslet; m. Bruce Elliott Oswald, Nov. 27, 1976. BBS, U. Iowa, 1972. With Great Am. Ins. Co., 1975—; v.p. mktg. div. Great Am. Ins. Co., Orange, Calif., 1987, v.p. profit ctr., 1988-90; pres. Garden of Eva, Inc., 1990—; mem. Snelling-Selby Bus. Coun. Mem. Nat. Assn. Ins. Women, State Guarantee Fund (bd. dirs. 1986-87), Exec. Women St. Paul, Midway C. of C., White Bear Lake C. of C. Methodist. Office: 1585 Marshall Ave Saint Paul MN 55104-6222

OSWALD, GEORGE CHARLES, advertising executive, management and marketing consultant; b. Springfield, Ill.; s. William A. and Lucille (Harrison) O.; m. Wanda Lillian Hartmann, Sept. 6, 1938; children: William Allan, Suzanne Mae, George Charles, Nanette Marie. B.S., U. Ill., 1936. Copywriter J. Stirling Getchell, Inc., 1936-37; Washington corr. Popular Sci., Picture Mag., 1937-38; copywriter, account exec. William Esty Co., Inc., 1942-50; v.p., account supr. Cecil & Presbrey, Inc., 1950-52; v.p., dir. regional offices and internat. div. Kenyon & Eckhardt, 1952-61; exec. v.p., dir. Geyer, Morey, Ballard, Inc., N.Y.C., 1961-65; pres., chief exec. officer Geyer, Morey, Ballard, Inc., 1965-67; pres., chief exec. officer Geyer-Oswald, Inc., 1967-69, chmn. bd., chief exec. officer, 1969-70; vice chmn. bd. Lennen & Newell, Inc., 1970-72; chief exec. officer, dir. Bailey-Oswald, Inc., Dannemora, N.Y., 1972-75; dir., mgmt. assoc. Quadrant Mktg. Counselors, Ltd., N.Y.C., 1976-80; chmn. Mgmt. Assocs., N.Y.C., 1980—; bd. dirs. Farm Products Labs., Matrix, Inc., Satellite Beach, Fla., Realtime Assocs., Inc., Satellite Beach, Fla., Technocraft, Inc., McElhattan, Pa., Ameratec Corp.; pres., dir. Realmar, Inc.; dir. Piper Indsl. Complex, Inc. Mem. Am. Assn. Advt. Agys. (gov. Eastern region 1964-66, nat. gov. 1966-69), Nat. Outdoor Advt. Bur. (dir.), Am. Arbitration Assn., Delta Chi. Clubs: N.Y. Athletic, Adirondack League, Camp Fire Am., Winged Foot Golf (N.Y.C.). Home: 38 Edgewood Rd Scarsdale NY 10583-6421 also: Old Forge NY 13420

OSWALD, ROBERT BERNARD, science administrator, nuclear engineer; b. Detroit, May 25, 1932; s. Robert Bernard and Leona Virginia (LeFave) O.; m. Judith Ann Dick, Feb. 3, 1964; children: Robert Vernon, Susan Marie. BSME, U. Mich., 1957, BS in Math., 1957, MSME, 1958, PhD in Nuclear Engring., 1964. Rsch. physicist Harry Diamond Labs., U.S. Army, Washington, 1964-69, chief radiation, phys. br., 1970-72, chief rsch. lab., 1972-76; assoc. tech. dir. Harry Diamond Labs., U.S. Army, Adelphi, Md., 1976-79; asst. to dep. dir. sci. and tech. Def. Nuclear Agy., Alexandria, Va., 1979-81; tech. dir. Electronic R&D Command, U.S. Army, Adelphi, 1981-85; corp. v.p. Sci. Application Internat. Corp., McLean, Va., 1985-87; dir. R&D C.E. Washington, 1987—; exec. dir. strategic environ. R&D program, 1992-94; vis. prof. dept. nuclear engring. U. Mich., Ann Arbor, 1969-70. Contbr. articles to profl. jours. With USAF, 1950-53. Recipient Louis J. Hamilton award U. Mich., 1973, Disting. Exec. award Pres. of U.S., 1983,

Meritorious Exec. Pres. award, 1991; Boeing fellow, 1957-58, Atomic Energy Spl. fellow, 1961-63. Fellow IEEE; mem. Am. Phys. Soc., Soc. Mil. Engrs., Cath. Acad. Scis., Cosmos Club. Republican. Roman Catholic. Avocations: sailing, woodworking, gardening. Office: USA CE 20 Massachusetts Ave NW Washington DC 20314-0001

OSWALD, RUDOLPH A., economist; b. Milw., Aug. 4, 1932; s. Carl J. and Anne O.; m. Mary Louise Hurney. B.A., Holy Cross Coll., 1954; postgrad. (Fulbright scholar), U. Munich, W. Ger., 1954-55; M.S., U. Wis., Madison, 1958; Ph.D. in Econs, Georgetown U., 1965. Research and edn. dir. Internat. Assn. Fire Fighters, Washington, 1959-63; economist research dept. AFL-CIO, Washington, 1963-72; asst. dir. edn. dept. AFL-CIO, 1975-76, dir. research dept., 1976—; rsch. dir. Svc. Employees Internat. Union, Washington, 1972-75; adj. prof. econs. George Washington U.; mem. Fed. Employees Pay Coun., 1970-72, Sec. Navy's Adv. Bd. Edn. and Tng., 1975-78, Nat. Commn. Employment and Unemployment Stats., Fgn. Investment Adv. Com., 1978-83; mem. adv. coun. Indsl. Labor Rels. Sch., Cornell U., 1981-85, 95, 96, Sch. Bus. U. S.C. 1992-96; mem. Consumer Adv. Com. Securities and Exchange Com., 1994-96, Labor Rsch. Adv. Coun. to Bur. Labor Stats., mem. adv. com. on trade; mem adv. com. Ex-Im Bank, 1989-92. Bd. dirs. Nat. Industries for the Blind, 1965-71. Served with U.S. Army, 1956-57. Mem. Am. Econ. Assn., Am. Statis. Assn., Indsl. Rels. Rsch. Assn. (past pres.), Nat. Bur. Econ. Rsch. (dir.), Nat. Planning Assn. (dir.), Joint Coun. on Econ. Edn. (dir.). Home: 11804 Devilwood Dr Rockville MD 20854-3407 Office: AFL-CIO Dept Econ Rsch 815 16th St NW Ste 504 Washington DC 20006-4104

OSWALD, STANTON S., lawyer; b. Phila., Oct. 15, 1927; s. Sylvan J. and Myra (Steiger) O.; m. Bernice Boorstein, June 17, 1951; children: Jane Easley, Eve Robbins, David Oswald, Beth Oswald. BA, U. Pa., 1949; LLB magna cum laude, Harvard U., 1952. Bar: Pa., 1953. Law clk. to Judge William L. Hastie U.S. Ct. Appeals Third Circuit, Phila., 1952-53; assoc. Wolf, Block, Schorr & Solis-Cohen, Phila., 1953-63, ptnr., 1963-95, of counsel, 1995—. Trustee Jewish Fedn. Greater Phila.; trustee, hon. dir. Congregation Adath Jeshurun, Melrose Park; chmn. bd. dirs. Pa. affiliate Am. Diabetes Assn., past chmn. bd. dirs. Phila. chpt. With USAAF, 1946-47. Mem. ABA, Pa. Bar Assn., Phila. Bar Assn. Democrat. Jewish. Office: Wolf Block Schorr & Solis-Cohen 12th Fl Packard Bldg 15th and Chestnut St Philadelphia PA 19102-2625

OTA, TAKAO, American literature and studies educator; b. Minakuchi, Shiga, Japan, Mar. 25, 1942; s. Toshio and Chieko Ota; m. Reiko Arai, Feb. 26, 1946; children: Michiko, Takuo. BA in Math. and English, North Ctrl. Coll., Naperville, Ill., 1966; MA in Religion, Garrett-Evang. Theol. Sem., Evanston, Ill., 1975. Instr. English U. Hirosaki, Japan, 1975-78, assoc. prof., 1978-83; prof. ENglish Niijima Gakuen Women's Jr. Coll., Takasaki, Japan, 1983—, dean of acad. affairs, 1983-86, 93—. Chief editor: Marty, 1986, Printer's Measure, 1980, Crime in the Streets, 1993; editor periodicals Studies in Broadcasting Arts, Studies in Comparative Culture. Fulbright sr. rsch. fellow, 1981-82. Mem. United Ch. of Christ in Japan. Home: 3413-3 Saginomiya, Annaka 379-01, Japan Office: Niijima Gakuen Women's Jr Coll, 53 Showa-machi, Takasaki Japan

OTAYA, MICHIKO, nurse; b. Iwakuni-City, Japan, Mar. 14, 1949. AA, L.A. City Coll.; BSN, Calif. State U., L.A., 1974, BA in Japanese Lit., 1980. RN, Calif. Nurse trainee to charge nurse ICU L.A. County/U. So. Calif. Med. Ctr., 1975-79; pub. health nurse various clinics, L.A., 1979-87; clinic coord. L.A. County, Cen. Dist. Health Ctr., 1979-92; HIV/Tb rsch. nurse Los Angeles County/U. So. Calif. Med. Ctr., 1992—; speaker in field. Contbr. to The Japanese Jour. for the Pub. Health Nurse. Mem. Calif. Thoracic Soc., Am. Lung Assn. (edn. coms.), So. Calif. Pub. Health Assn., Temple City Toastmasters. Home: PO Box 1435 San Gabriel CA 91778

OTERO, JOAQUIN F., federal agency administrator; m. Carin Otero; 4 children. Trade unionist Transp. Comm. Internat. Union, 1957, internat. v.p., 1971-93; regional dir. L.Am. affairs Internat. Transport Workers' Fedn.; v.p. AFL-CIO, exec. coun.; dep. under sec. labor Bur. Internat. Labor Affairs U.S. Dept. Labor, Washington, 1993—; U.S. govt. rep. UN Internat. Labor Orgn., 1993—; mem. U.S. Bd. Fgn. Svc.; rep. of Sec. of Labor on Pres.'s Export Coun., various inter-agy. bds. Nat. pres. Labor Coun. for L.Am. Advancement; vice chmn. Nat. Dem. Party, 1989-93; mem. ITF World Exec. Bd. Recipient Hispanic Hero of the Yr. award U.S. Hispanic Leadership Conf., 1993. Office: US Dept Labor Internat Labor Affairs 200 Constitution Ave NW Washington DC 20210

OTERO-SMART, INGRID AMARILLYS, advertising executive; b. Santurce, P.R., Jan. 9, 1959; d. Angel Miguel and Carmen (Prann) Otero; m. Dean Edward Smart, May 4, 1991; 1 child, Jordan. BA in Communication, U. P.R., 1981. Traffic mgr. McCann-Erickson Corp., San Juan, P.R., 1981-82, media analyst, 1982, asst. account exec., 1982-83, account exec., 1983-84, sr. account exec., 1984-85, account dir., 1985-87; account supr. Mendoza-Dillon & Assocs., Newport Beach, Calif., 1987-89, sr. v.p. client svcs., 1989—. Mem. Youth Motivation Task Force, Santa Ana, Calif., 1989—; bd. dirs. Orange County Hispanic C. of C., Santa Ana, 1989-90, U.S. Hispanic Family of Yr.; mem. Santa Ana Project P.R.I.D.E., 1993. Avocations: reading, writing, antiques, music, theater. Office: Mendoza-Dillon & Assocs 4100 Newport Place Dr Ste 600 Newport Beach CA 92660-2451

OTEY, ORLANDO, music executive, educator, pianist, theorist; b. Mexico City, Mexico, Feb. 1, 1925; s. Ponciano O. and Dolores (Olin) O.; D. Mus., U. Mexico, 1945; student Curtis Inst. Music, Phila., 1945-48; also studied with Luis Moctezuma, Vladimir Sokoloff, Walter Gieseking, Manuel M. Ponce, Gian-Carlo Menotti; m. Diane E. McAnney, Feb. 22, 1974; 1 son, Nathaniel; children by previous marriage—Olivia, Alexander. Pianist appearing in Mexico, U.S., recitals and with orchs., 1929—; mem. faculty Nat. Sch. Music, U. Mex., 1941-45, Jenkintown Music Sch.; faculty Wilmington (Del.) Mus. Sch., 1965-70, exec. dir., 1966-70; musical dir. Brandywine Pops Orch., 1969-74, Jewish Community Ctr. Orch., 1974-78; dir. Otey Music Sch., 1970—. Gen. mgr. Am. Trade Export Corp., 1960-63; tech. translator export dept. S.S. White Co. (Pennwalt), 1957-60; one of 3 U.S. pianists at Chopin Centennial Festival, Warsaw, Poland, 1949; organist, choirmaster St. John's Episcopal Ch., Bala-Cynwyd, Pa., 1962-64, Christ Episcopal Ch., Media, Pa., 1965-67, Mt. Salem United Meth. Ch., Wilmington, Del., 1973-84. Composer: Mexican Fantasy, 1941, Etudes for Piano, 1941, Sonata Tenochtitlan, 1948, Arabesque, 1950, (songs) Sinfonia Breve, 1956, Suite for Strings, 1957, Tzintzuntzan for strings, 1958, Poetica for Soprano and orch., 1958; Poetica for solo trumpet and orch., 1970; Sonata Adelita, 1982. Program chmn. Tri-County Concerts Assn., Wayne Pa., 1955-57; v.p. Main Line Symphony Orch., 1956-58; mem. steering com. Cultural Center Commn. Wilmington. Bd. dirs. Del. Symphony Orch. Mem. Nat. Assn. Composers U.S.A. (pres. Phila. chpt. 1959-61), Nat. Edn. Assn. Jazz Educators, Am. Guild Organists, Am. String Tchrs. Assn. (life), Pan-Am. Assn., Curtis Inst. Music Alumni Assn. (life), Postal Commemorative Soc., Am. Symphony Orch. League, Phila. Art Alliance, Mus. Fund Soc. Phila., Nat. Music Tchrs. Assn. (Del. Music Tchr. of Yr. 1982), Phila. Music Tchrs. Assn., Del. Music Tchrs. Assn., Advancement Mus. Edn., Smithsonian Assocs., Nat. Hist. Soc. (charter), Del. Classical Guitar Soc., Wilmington Soc. Fine Arts, Del. Art Mus., Phila. Franklin Inst., Salem County (life), Valley Forge (life) hist. socs., Music Educators Nat. Conf., Internat. Platform Assn. Club: Rotary (pres. local club 1973). Author: Otey Music Teaching Method, 1973; discoverer formula of natural, exotic and non-septonic musical keys, 1978; rec. (albums) Sea of Galillee, Alacrán, 1992. Home and Office: 2391 Limestone Rd Wilmington DE 19808-4100

OTHERSEN, HENRY BIEMANN, JR., pediatric surgeon, physician, educator; b. Charleston, S.C., Aug. 26, 1930; s. Henry and Lydia Albertine (Smith) O.; m. Janelle Lester, Apr. 4, 1959; children: Megan, Mandy, Margaret, Henry Biemann III. B.S., Coll. Charleston, 1950; M.D., Med. Coll. S.C., 1953. Diplomate: Am. Bd. Surgery, Am. Bd. Thoracic Surgery, Am. Bd. Pediatric Surgery. Intern Phila. Gen. Hosp., 1953-54; postgrad. U. Pa., 1956-57; resident in gen. surgery Med. Coll. S.C., Charleston, 1957-62; resident in pediatric surgery Ohio State U. and Columbus Children's Hosp., 1962-64; research fellow Harvard U., Mass. Gen. Hosp., Boston, 1964-65; asst. prof. pediatric surgery Med. U. S.C., Charleston, 1965-68; assoc. prof. Med. U. S.C., 1968-72, prof., 1972—, chief pediatric surgery, 1972—; med. dir. Med. U. S.C. Hosp., 1981-85, Children's Hosp., 1985—. Editor The Pediatric Airway; mem. editorial bd. Jour. Pediatric Surgery, Jour. Parenteral and Enteral Nutrition; contbr. articles on pediatric oncology, esophageal, tracheal strictures to profl. jours. Bd. dirs., pres. S.C. div. Am. Cancer Soc., 1977-79. Served with USN, 1954-56, Korea. Fellow ACS, Am. Acad. Pediatrics; mem. Am. Pediatric Surg. Assn. (bd. govs. 1986-89, pres.-elect 1996), Brit. Assn. Pediatric Surgeons (overseas coun.), Am. Surg. Assn., So. Surg. Assn., Am. Trauma Soc., Charleston County Med. Soc. (pres. 1980), Alpha Omega Alpha (councilor 1978-94). Home: 171 Ashley Ave Charleston SC 29425-0001 Office: MUSC Children's Hosp 171 Ashley Ave Charleston SC 29425-0001 *A man ought to do what he thinks is right.*

OTHS, RICHARD PHILIP, health systems administrator, insurance executive; b. N.Y.C., July 3, 1935; s. Philip John and Florence Violet (Kraus) O.; m. Eleanor Fuerst, May 11, 1957; children—Philip, Lisa, Eleanor, Richard. BS in Pharmacy, Fordham U., 1956; MBA in Health Care Adminstrn., CUNY, 1976. Field sales rep. E.R. Squibb & Sons, N.Y.C., 1960-63; hosp. rep. E.R. Squibb & Sons, 1963-65; div. mgr. E.R. Squibb & Sons, Manhattan, 1965-68; adminstr. operating room Mt. Sinai Hosp., N.Y.C., 1968-69, dir. admitting, 1969-71, asst. dir. hosp., 1971-76; v.p., mgr. Bethesda Hosp. Oak, Cin., 1976-84; pres. Am. Health Capital HIBI Mgmt., Inc., N.Y.C., 1984-88; pres., CEO Morristown (N.J.) Meml. Hosp., 1988-96, Atlantic Health System, Florham Park, N.J., 1996—; Goldwater fellow in hosp. adminstr. Mt. Sinai Hosp., N.Y.C., 1973; cons. Physicians Protective Trust Fund-Fla. Served with USAF, 1957-60. Recipient award E.R. Squibb-AMA, 1964. Mem. APHA, ACHA, Am. Hosp. Assn. Republican. Roman Catholic. Home: 26 Glen Gary Dr Mendham NJ 07945-3030 Office: 325 Columbia Tpke Florham Park NJ

OTIS, ARTHUR BROOKS, physiologist, educator; b. Grafton, Maine, Sept. 11, 1913; s. Will Howe and Carrie (Brooks) O.; m. Eileen Macomber, Aug. 24, 1942; 1 son, Chandler Brooks. A.B., U. Maine, 1935; M.Ed., Springfield Coll., 1937; Sc.M., Brown U., 1939, Ph.D., 1941. Research assoc. cellular physiology State U. Iowa, 1941-42; instr. physiology U. Rochester Sch. Medicine, 1942-46, assoc. physiology, 1946-47, asst. prof. physiology, 1947-51; assoc. prof. physiology and surgery Johns Hopkins Sch. Medicine, 1952-56; prof. physiology U. Fla. Coll. Medicine, Gainesville, 1956-86; prof. emeritus U. Fla. Coll. Medicine, 1986—, head dept., 1956-80; civilian scientist OSRD, 1944; mem. physiology com. Nat. Bd. Med. Examiners, 1981-84. Author sci. papers; editor respiration sect.: Am. Jour. Physiology and Jour. Applied Physiology, 1962-64; editorial bd.: Respiration Physiology, 1970-81. Fulbright research scholar, 1950-51, 64-65. Mem. Am. Physiol. Soc., Soc. Gen. Physiologists, Phi Beta Kappa, Sigma Xi. Home: 2123 NW 4th Pl Gainesville FL 32603-1515 *I feel fortunate and grateful to have known so many fine people who, in one way or another, have given me so much help along the way.*

OTIS, GLENN KAY, retired army officer; b. Plattsburgh, N.Y., Mar. 15, 1929; s. Glenn Kirk and Violet Lucy (Hart) O.; m. Barbara Davies, June 6, 1953; children: Caren Otis, Nancee Otis Groh, Peter. BS, U.S. Mil. Acad., 1953; MS in Math., Rensselaer Poly. Inst., 1960; M in Mil. Sci., U.S. Army Command and Gen. Staff Coll., 1965. Commd. 2d lt. U.S. Army, 1953; gen.; dep. chief staff for ops. and plans Hdqrs. Dept. Army; comdg. gen. U.S. Army Tng. and Doctrine Command, Ft.Monroe, Va.; comdr. in chief U.S. Army Europe, Heidelberg, Federal Republic of Germany, 1983-88; ret. U.S. Army Europe, Heidelberg, 1988; exec. v.p. Coleman Rsch. Corp., 1989-95. Decorated D.S.C., Silver Star, Legion of Merit, Purple Heart. Roman Catholic. Home: 97 Normandy Ln Newport News VA 23606-1533

OTIS, JACK, social work educator; b. N.Y.C., Feb. 13, 1923; s. Abraham and Esther (Goldberg) O.; children: Elisabeth H., Erich R., Greta M., Marcus H., Alicia. A.B., Bklyn. Coll., 1946; M.S. in Social Work, U. Ill., 1948, M.Ed., 1955, Ph.D., 1957. Social worker Jewish Social Svc. Bur. Dade County, 1948-49; Psychiat. social worker Free Synagogue Social Service, N.Y. U., 1949-50; asso. prof. U. Ill., 1950-61; dep. dir. Office Juvenile Delinquency and Youth Devel., Dept. Health, Edn. and Welfare, 1961-65; dean Grad. Sch. Social Work U. Tex., 1965-77, prof. emeritus, 1993—; cons. to govt., 1961—; presenter Internat. Coun. on Social Welfare, Inter-Univ. Consortium for Internat. Social Devel., Internat. Assn. Schs. Social Work, 1994; mem. President's Com. Juvenile Delinquency and Youth Crime, 1961-65; spl. cons. for Am. social work edn. and rsch. European Ctr. for Social Welfare Tng. and Rsch., Vienna, Austria, 1976—. Author: (with George Barnett) Corporate Society and Education, 1961; contbr. article on child labor to Ency. Social Work, 1995. Bd. overseers Ctr. for Study Violence, Brandeis U., 1966-70. With AUS, 1943-46, PTO. Fulbright-Hays research fellow Austria, 1977-78. Mem. AAUP, Coun. on Social Work Edn. (commn. on accreditation), Philosophy of Edn. Soc., Nat. Assn. Social Workers, Am. Acad. Polit. and Social Sci., N.Y. Acad. Sci., Johannesburg Child Welfare Soc. (rsch. cons. South Africa chpt. 1990-91), Phi Kappa Phi (pres.). *The meaning of my life is whether I have added to the meaning of another's.*

OTIS, JAMES, JR., architect; b. Chgo., July 8, 1931; s. James and Edwina (Love) O.; m. Diane Cleveland, Apr. 9, 1955; children: James III, Julie C., David C. BArch cum laude, Princeton U., 1953; postgrad., U. Chgo., 1955-57. Registered architect, Ill., Ariz., Colo., Ind., Iowa, Wis. Designer Irvin A. Blietz Co., Wilmette, Ill., 1955-57; pres. Homefinders Constrn. Corp., Wilmette, 1957-59, O & F Constrn. Co., Northbrook, Ill., 1959-61; chmn. bd., chief exec. officer Otis Assocs., Inc., Northbrook, Ill., 1960-89; pres. Otis Co., 1981—; bd. dirs. Pioneer Bank, Chgo., So. Mineral Corp. Prin. works include GBC Corp. Hdqrs., Zurich Towers Office Complex, Schaumburg, Ill., AON Ins. Co. Corp. Hdqrs., Performing Arts Ctr., Northbrook, Ill., All State Regional Hdqrs., Skokie, Ill., Zurich Nat. Hdqrs.-Zurich Towers Schaumburg. Trustee Evanston (Ill.) Hosp., 1971-93, Better Govt. Assn., Chgo., Graham Found.; chmn. bd. trustees North Suburban YMCA, Northbrook, 1990—; governing mem. Shedd Aquarium; bd. govs. Chgo. Zool. Soc.; mem. adv. bd. Cook County Forest Preserve Dist.; mem. founder's coun. Field Mus., Chgo. Lt. USNR, 1953-55. Mem. AIA, Nat. Coun. Archtl. Registration Bds., Urban Land Inst., Northwestern U. Assocs., Chgo. Coun. Fgn. Rels. (assoc.), Internat. Wine and Food Soc., Princeton Club (pres. 1971-72), Econ. Club, Commonwealth Club, Chgo. Club, Comml. Club, Glen View Golf Club, Coleman Lake Club, Angler's Club. Republican. Episcopalian. Office: 310 Happ Rd Northfield IL 60093-3455

OTIS, JOHN JAMES, civil engineer; b. Syracuse, N.Y., Aug. 5, 1922; s. John Joseph and Anna (Dey) O.; m. Dorothy Fuller Otis, June 21, 1958; children: Mary Eileen Dawn, John Leon. B of Chem. Engring., Syracuse U., 1943, MBA, 1950, postgrad., 1951-55. Registered profl. engr., Ala., Tex.; cert. profl. for hazardous waste opns. and emergency response. Jr. process engr. GM, Syracuse, 1951-53, prodn. engr., 1954-58, process control engr., 1958-59, process engr., 1960-61; engr., writer GE, Syracuse, 1961-63; configuration control engr. GE, Phila., 1969; assoc. research engr. Boeing Co., Huntsville, Ala., 1963-65; assoc. Planning Rsch. Corp., Huntsville, 1965-67; prin. engr. Brown Engring. Co. subs. Teledyne Co., Huntsville, 1967-69; mech. designer Drever Co., Beth Ayres, Pa., 1970-71; civil engr. U.S. Army Corps Engrs., Mobile, Ala., 1971-74, Galveston, Tex., 1974—. Lector, lay minister Roman Cath. Ch. Served with USNR, 1944-50. Mem. Am. Inst. Indsl. Engrs. (past v.p. Syracuse and Huntsville chpts.), Tex. Soc. Profl. Engrs. (dir. Galveston County chpt. 1976-79, sec.-treas. 1979-80, v.p. 1980-81, pres. 1982-83), Am. Legion, Tau Beta Pi, Phi Kappa Tau, Alpha Chi Sigma, Chi Eta Sigma. Home: 2114 Yorktown Ct N League City TX 77573-5056 Office: US Army Corps Engrs Jadwin Bldg 2000 Fort Point Rd Galveston TX 77550-3038

OTIS, LEE LIBERMAN, lawyer, educator; b. N.Y.C., Aug. 19, 1956; d. James Benjamin and Deen (Freed) L.; m. William Graham Otis, Oct. 24, 1993. BA, Yale U., 1979; JD, U. Chgo., 1983. Bar: N.Y. 1985, D.C. 1994. Law clk. U.S. Ct. Appeals (D.C. cir.), Washington, 1983-84; spl. asst. to asst. atty. gen., civil div. U.S. Dept. Justice, Washington, 1984-86; dep. assoc. atty. gen. U.S. Dept. Justice, 1986, assoc. dep. atty. gen., 1986; law clk. to Justice Antonin Scalia U.S. Supreme Ct., Washington, 1986-87; asst. prof. law George Mason U., Arlington, Va., 1987-89; assoc. counsel to the Pres. Exec. Office of the Pres., Washington, 1989-92; assoc. Jones, Day, Reavis & Pogue, Washington, 1993-94; chief judiciary coun. U.S. Sen. Spence Abraham, 1995—; adj. prof. law Georgetown Law Sch., 1995, 96. Mem. Federalist Soc. for Law & Pub. Policy (founder, dir., nat. co-chmn.). Republican. Jewish. Avocations: sailing, computers.

O'TOOLE, ALLAN THOMAS, electric utility executive; b. Waterloo, Iowa, Dec. 22, 1925; s. Delmar C. and Elsie M. (Winkelman) O'T.; m. Barbara Joyce Boyd, Sept. 2, 1947; children: Kathy Lynn, Timothy Allan. BA, Westminster Coll., Fulton, Mo., 1948; postgrad., U. Mich., 1965. With Pub. Svc. Co. Okla., 1953-88, asst. treas., 1967-70, treas., 1970-73, v.p., contr., 1973-76, v.p. adminstrn., 1976-80, v.p. materiel and property mgmt., 1980-85, v.p. corp. svcs., 1985-88; ret., 1988. Bd. dirs., chmn. bd. Tulsa Area chpt. ARC, 1975—, regional chmn. midwestern ops. hdqrs., 1989-92; bd. dirs., pres. Tulsa Sr. Svcs., Inc., 1990—; with Okla. State Svc. Coun., 1995—. Lt. USNR, 1943-46, 51-53. Mem. Tulsa C. of C., Adminstrv. Mgmt. Soc. (bd. dirs., pres.), Westminster Coll. Alumni Assn. (pres., bd. trustees), K.C., Cedar Ridge Country Club, Kappa Alpha. Roman Catholic. Home: 8442 S Florence Ave Tulsa OK 74137-1435

O'TOOLE, DENNIS ALLEN, museum director; b. Scott AFB, Ill., Mar. 12, 1941; s. Roger Leslie and Emily May (Fisher) O'T.; m. Gertrude Lenore Probsting, July 10, 1965; children: Kara, Anne, Aaron. BA, Princeton U., 1963; MAT, Harvard U., 1965; PhD, Brown U., 1973; cert. exec. program, Dartmouth Coll., 1989. Tchr. Belmont (Mass.) H.S., 1965-67; curator of edn. Nat. Portrait Gallery, Washington, 1972-78; dir. group visits and ednl. programs Colonial Williamsburg (Va.), 1979; dep. dir. mus. ops. Colonial Williamsburg, Va., 1979-82, v.p. historic area programs and ops., 1982-88; v.p., chief edn. officer Colonial Williamsburg (Va.), 1988-92; exec. dir. Strawbery Banke, Inc., Portsmouth, N.H., 1992—; at-large coun. mem. Am. Assn. Mus., Washington, 1988-91; mem. coun. Am. Assn. State and Local History, Nashville, 1992—; mem. coun., exec. com. Inst. Early Am. History and Culture, Williamsburg, 1988-92. House minority clk. R.I. Ho. of Reps., Providence, 1968; bd. dirs. Friends of Williamsburg Regional Libr., 1990-92; mem. Portsmouth Advocates, 1993—. Mem. Rotary. Avocations: tennis, hiking, cross-country skiing, biking, reading. Office: Strawberry Bank Mus PO Box 300 Portsmouth NH 03802-0300

O'TOOLE, FRANCIS J., lawyer; b. Dublin, Ireland, Feb. 10, 1944; came to U.S., 1960; s. Francis Herbert and Josephine (McCarthy) O'T.; m. Carole Ann Leland, Apr. 11, 1977; children: Kathleen, Kirra. AB, Harvard U., 1967; JD, U. Maine, 1970. Bar: Maine 1970, U.S. Supreme Ct. 1977, U.S. Dist. Ct. D.C., U.S. Dist. Ct. (ea. dist.) Va., U.S. Ct. Appeals (1st, 2d, 4th, 5th, 7th, 8th, 9th and 10th cirs.). Assoc. Fried, Frank, Harris, Shriver & Jacobsen, Washington, 1971-78, ptnr., 1978-92; ptnr. Sidley & Austin, Washington, 1992—. Editor-in-chief U. Maine Law Rev., 1969-70; contbr. articles to profl. jours. Reginald Heber Smith fellow Calif. Indian Legal Services, 1970-71. Mem. ABA. Avocations: horse breeding and racing. Home: 7700 Burford Dr Mc Lean VA 22102-1716 Office: Sidley & Austin 1722 I St NW Washington DC 20006-3705

O'TOOLE, JAMES JOSEPH, business educator; b. San Francisco, Apr. 15, 1945; s. James Joseph and Irene (Nagy) O'T.; m. Marilyn Louise Burrill, June 17, 1967; children: Erin Kathleen, Kerry Louise. BA, U. So. Calif., L.A., 1966; DPhil, Oxford (Eng.) U., (Eng.), 1970. Corr. Time-Life News Service, L.A., 1967-68, Nairobi, Kenya, 1967-68; mgmt. cons. McKinsey & Co., San Francisco, 1969-70; coordinator field investigations Pres.'s Comm. on Campus Unrest, Washington, 1970; spl. asst. to sec. HEW, Washington, 1970-73; prof. mgmt. U. So. Calif.-Los Angeles, 1973-93, Univ. Assocs. Chair of Bus., 1982-93; chmn. sec.'s com. work in Am. HEW, Wshington, 1971-72; exec. dir. The Leadership Inst., 1990-93; v.p. Aspen Inst., 1994—; bd. dirs. Radica Games. Prin. author: Work in America, 1973, Energy and Social Change, 1976; author: Work, Learning and the American Future, 1977, Making America Work, 1982 (Phi Kappa Phi prize 1982), Vanguard Management, 1985, The Executive's Compass, 1993, Leading Change, 1995; bd. editors: Ency. Britannica, Chgo., 1981-87; editor: New Management, Los Angeles, 1983-89, The American Oxonian, 1996—. Mem. Project Paideia, Chgo., 1981-83. Rhodes scholar, 1966; recipient Mitchell prize Woodlands Conf., 1979. Mem. Phi Beta Kappa. Home: 19912 Pacific Coast Hwy Malibu CA 90265-5423 Office: The Aspen Inst 1000 N 3rd St Aspen CO 81611-1330

O'TOOLE, JOHN DUDLEY, retired utility executive, consultant; b. N.Y.C., Sept. 16, 1921; s. Lawrence Patrick and Mary Gertrude (Casey) O'T.; m. Constance Telfair, Jan. 17, 1952; children: John D. Jr., Paul L., Mary C., Michelle E. Hair, Jane C. Keating. M.E. with honors, Stevens Inst. Tech., 1949; postgrad., Poly. Inst. Bklyn., 1949-51. Registered profl. engr., Conn. Engr. Gibbs & Cox Inc., N.Y.C., 1949-54; engring. mgr. Union Carbide Nuclear Co., Paducah, Ky., 1954-55, Combustion Engring. Inc., Windsor, Conn., 1955-62, Westinghouse Electric Co., Pitts., 1962-66; engring. mgr., v.p. United Nuclear Corp. and Gulf United Nuclear Corp., Elmsford, N.Y., 1966-72; asst. to v.p., then v.p. Consol. Edison Co. of N.Y., N.Y.C., 1973-86; cons. Power Mgmt. Assocs., 1986—; nuclear div. com. Electric Power Research Inst., Palo Alto, Calif., 1980-86; vice chmn. Welding Research Council, N.Y.C., 1984-86; mem. vis. com. Lehigh U., Bethlehem, Pa., 1982-86. Contbr. tech. papers and articles to profl. jours. Mgmt. com. Nature Preserve, Nature Conservancy, Katonah, N.Y., 1970; nominating com. Katonah-Lewisboro Sch. Bd., 1970. Served with USN, 1943-46. N.Y. State War Service scholar N.Y. Dept. Edn., 1949. Home: 7 Thomas St Barrington RI 02806-4824

O'TOOLE, PETER, actor; b. County Galway, Ireland, Aug. 2, 1932; s. Patrick Joseph and Constance (Ferguson) O'T.; m. Sian Phillips, 1959 (div. 1979); children: Kate, Pat; m. Karen Brown, 1983 (div.); 1 child, Lorcan. Student, Royal Acad. Dramatic Arts. Actor Bristol Old Vic Co., 1955-58; London stage debut in Major Barbara, 1956; other stage appearances include Present Laughter, The Apple Cart, 1986, Pygmalion, 1987, Jeffrey Bervard is Unwell, 1989; films include Kidnapped, 1960, The Day They Robbed the Bank of England, 1960, Savage Innocents, 1961, Lawrence of Arabia, 1962, Becket, 1964, Lord Jim, 1965, What's New, Pussycat?, 1965, How to Steal a Million, 1966, The Bible... in the Beginning, 1966, The Night of the Generals, 1967, Great Catherine, 1968, The Lion in Winter, 1968, Goodbye Mr. Chips, 1969, Murphy's War, 1971, Under Milk Wood, 1971, Brotherly Love, The Ruling Class, 1972, Man of LaMancha, 1972, Rosebud, 1975, Man Friday, 1975, Foxtrot, 1976, Coup d'Etat, 1977, Zulu Dawn, 1978, Power Play, 1978, Caligula, 1979, Stuntman, 1980, The Antagonists, 1981, My Favorite Year, 1981, Supergirl, 1984, Creator, 1985, Club Paradise, 1985, The Last Emperor, 1987, High Spirits, 1988, On a Moonlit Night, 1989, Helena, Wings of Fame, The Pit and the Pendulum, King Ralph, 1991, Rebecca's Daughters, 1992, The Seventh Coin, 1993; appeared in: Rogue Male, BBC-TV, 1976, Strumpet City, RTE-TV, 1979; TV mini-series Masada, 1981, Svengali, 1982; TV film: Kim, 1983, The Dark Angel, BBC TV, 1988, Crossing to Freedom, 1990; autobiography Loitering with Intent, 1993. Decorated Comdr. des Arts et des Lettres, 1988. Office: William Morris Agy, 31-32 Soho Square, London W12 5DG, England*

O'TOOLE, ROBERT JOHN, II, telemarketing consultant; b. Binghamton, N.Y., Mar. 24, 1951; s. Robert John and Joan Ceclia (Martin) O'T.; m. Donna Sue Stevenson, Jan. 28, 1978 (div. 1984); children: Irene Grace, Erin Colleen, Robert John III; m. Karen Irene Cady, Dec. 21, 1994. Student, Corning (N.Y.) C.C., 1969-71, SUNY, Brockport, 1970-71; BA, Wake Forest U., 1973; MBA, Southwestern Coll., 1986. Asst. dir. devel. Duvall Home for Children, DeLand, Fla., 1978-81; gen. mgr. Royale Art Advt., Odessa, Tex., 1981-82; v.p. Barnes Assocs. Advt., Odessa, 1982-84, Tex. Assn. for Blind Athletes, Austin, 1985-86; sales mgr. Los Amables Pub., Albuquerque, 1987-88; dir. devel. Albuquerque (N.Mex.) Help for the Homeless, 1988-91; chmn., CEO Advantage Ventures, Inc. (formerly Advantage Mktg., Inc.), Albuquerque, 1991—; CEO LaCourt, Medina & Sterling, Albuquerque, 1993—; cons. Nat. Child Safety Coun., Austin, 1985, Assoc. Profl. Fire Fighters, Austin, 1985, Reynolds Aluminum, Austin, 1986, N.Mex. State Legis., 1990. Author: Telemarketing Tickets, 1988; founder, editor: (newspaper) Albuquerque Street News, 1990; publisher: (newspaper) The New Mexican, 1991; contbr. articles to jours. Founder Permian Basin Rehab. Ctr., Odessa, 1983, Albuquerque (N.Mex.) Help for the Homeless, Inc., 1988. Recipient Cert. of Merit, Small Bus. Adminstrn., Odessa, 1984. Mem. Direct Mktg. Assn., Amnesty Internat. Avocations: restoration of historic bldgs., archeo-geomantics, travel. Home: Historic Coke House 1023 2nd St SW Albuquerque NM 87102-4124 Office: Advantage Ventures Inc 201 Pacific Ave SW Albuquerque NM 87102-4176

O'TOOLE, ROBERT JOSEPH, manufacturing company executive; b. Chgo., Feb. 22, 1941; s. Francis John O'Toole; children: William, Patricia,

Timothy, Kathleen, John. BS in Acctg., Loyola U., Chgo., 1961. Fin. analyst A.O. Smith Corp., Milw., 1963-66, mgr. corp. fin. analysis and planning, 1966-68; contr. electric motor div. A.O. Smith Corp., Tipp City, Ohio, 1968-71; mng. dir. Bull Motors, Ipswich, Eng., 1971-74; gen. plant mgr. electric motor div. A.O. Smith Corp., Tipp City, 1974-79, v.p., gen. mgr., 1979-83; sr. v.p. A.O. Smith Corp., Milw., 1984-85, pres., chief oper. officer, 1986-89, pres., chief exec. officer, 1989—, also bd. dirs., now chmn. bd. dirs., 1992—; bd. dirs. 1st Wis. Nat. Bank, Milw.; mem. exec. com. TEC XIV, Milw., Mfrs. Alliance for Productivity and Innovation, Bus. Roundtable, Greater Milw. Com., Competitive Wis., Inc. Mem. Wis. Mgrs. and Commerce Assn. (exec. com.), Met. Milw. Assn. Commerce (bd. dirs.), Milw. Country Club, Univ. Club. Office: A O Smith Corp 1 Park Plz 11270 W Park Pl Milwaukee WI 53224-3623*

O'TOOLE, TARA J., federal official; d. Harold J. and Jeanne (Whalen) O'T. BA, Vassar Coll., 1974; MD, George Washington U., 1981; MPH, Johns Hopkins U., 1988. Diplomate Am. Bd. Internal Medicine, Am. Bd. Preventive/Occupational Medicine. Rsch. asst. Sloan-Kettering Cancer Inst., N.Y.C., 1974-77; resident in internal medicine Yale New Haven (Conn.) Hosp., 1981-84; physician Balt. Cmty. Health Ctrs., 1984-87; fellow in occupational medicine Johns Hopkins U., Balt., 1987-89; sr. analyst Office Tech. Assessment, Washington, 1989-93; asst. sec. energy for environ., safety and health Dept. Energy, Washington, 1993—. Democrat. Office: Dept of Energy Environ Safety & Health 1000 Independence Ave SW Washington DC 20585-0001*

O'TOOLE, TERRENCE J., lawyer; b. Mo., 1946. AB, St. Louis U., 1968; JD, U. Mo., 1972. Bar: Mo. 1973, U.S. Ct. Appeals (5th cir.) 1984, U.S. Ct. Appeals (3d cir.) 1988, U.S. Ct. Appeals (8th cir.) 1991. Asst. cir. atty. City St. Louis, 1973-76, 1st asst. cir. atty., 1977-78; ptnr. Bryan Cave, St. Louis. Mem. ABA. Office: Bryan Cave 211 N Broadway Saint Louis MO 63102-2733

OTOROWSKI, CHRISTOPHER LEE, lawyer; b. Teaneck, N.J., Nov. 20, 1953; s. Wladyslaw Jerzy and Betty Lee (Robbins) O.; m. Shawn Elizabeth McGovern, Aug. 4, 1978; children: Kirsten, Hilary. BSBA cum laude, U. Denver, 1974, MBA, 1977, JD, 1977. Bar: Wash. 1977, Colo. 1977, U.S. Dist Ct. (we. dist.) D.C. 1977, U.S. Dist. Ct. (we. dist.) Wash. 1978. Asst. atty. gen. Wash. State Atty. Gen., Spokane, 1978-79; atty. Bassett, Gemson & Morrison, Seattle, 1979-81; pvt. practice Seattle, 1981-88; atty. Sullivan, Golden & Otorowski, Seattle, 1988-91; pvt. practice Bainbridge Island, Wash., 1991—. Contbr. articles to profl. jours. Bd. dirs. Bainbridge Edn. Support Team, Bainbridge Island, 1991—. Mem. Fed. Bar Assn. We. Dist. Wash. (sec. 1979-82, trustee 1990-93), Wash. State Trial Lawyers Assn. (bd. govs. 1991-93), Assn. Trial Lawyers Am., Seattle Tennis Club, Seattle Yacht Club. Avocations: photography, sailing. Office: 298 Winslow Way W Bainbridge Island WA 98110

OTREMBA, BERNARD OTTO, marketing executive; b. Munich, Feb. 3, 1944; came to U.S., 1985; s. Louis E. and Burgl (Koppel) O.; m. Roswitha J. Pietrzyk, Dec. 27, 1984; children: Gabriele Yvonne, Sonya Charlotte. MBA in Econs., Munich Coll., 1970; PhD in Bus. Adminstrn., Pacific Western U., 1987. Pres. Import Export Ltd., Tehran, Iran, 1976-81; dir. bus. devel. Intergraph Europe, Inc., London and Amsterdam, The Netherlands, 1981-84; exec. v.p., gen. mgr. SSI Schaefer Systems Internat. Inc., Eatontown, N.J., 1985-88; pres. Gardner Internat. Ops. Ltd., Tampa, Fla., 1989-93; CEO, chmn. PFT Am. Inc., Phoenix, 1993—. Author: Industrial Psychology and Physiology in Contemporary Management, 1970, Can Computers Draw? CAD in Architecture, 1984, The Interdependence in the Economic Relations Between Industrial and Developing Countries, 1987. Mem. Rotary Internat., World Trade Ctr., German-Am. C. of C. Avocations: languages, traveling, boating. Home: 4218 W Charlotte Dr Glendale AZ 85310-3212

OTSTOTT, CHARLES PADDOCK, company executive, retired army officer; b. Ft. Worth, June 2, 1937; s. Daniel Dushane and Sarah May (Paddock) O.; m. Candice Lee Curley, Nov. 6, 1982; 1 child, Kelley Ann; 1 child from previous marriage, James Boyd. BS, U.S. Mil. Acad., West Point, N.Y., 1960; MS, Purdue U., 1967. Commd. 2d lt. U.S. Army, 1960, advanced through grades to lt. gen., 1990; bn. advisor Republic of Vietnam, 1964-65; co. cmdr., S-3, 2d bn. 502 Inf. (Airborne) 101st Airborne Div., 1967-68; comdr. 1st bn. 46 Inf., 1st Armored Div., Erlangen, Fed. Republic Germany, 1976-78; student Nat. War Coll., Ft. McNair, D.C., 1978-79; comdr. 2d brigade 9th High Tech. Light Div., Ft. Lewis, Wash., 1979-82; chief of staff 9th High Tech. Light Div., Ft. Lewis, 1982-83; exec. to SACEUR Supreme Hdqrs. Allied Powers Europe, Belgium, 1983-85; asst. div. comdr. 1st Armored Div., Bamberg, Fed. Republic Germany, 1985-86; comdg. gen. Combined Arms Combat Devel. Activity, Ft. Leavenworth, Kans., 1986-88, 25th Inf. Div. (Light), Schofield Barracks, Hawaii, 1988-90; dep. chmn. NATO Mil. Com., Brussels, 1990-92; ret., 1992, pvt. cons. strategic planning, 1992-94; with Innovative Logistics Techniques (Innolog, Inc.), 1994-96; v.p. advanced program devel. Bolt, Beranek, and Newman (BBN), 1996—; instr., then asst. prof. dept. physics U.S. Mil. Acad., West Point, 1968-71. Chmn. adv. com. Brussels Am. Sch., 1990-92. Decorated Def. D.S.M., Army D.S.M., Def. Superior Svc. medal, Silver Star, Legion of Merit. Avocations: handball, jogging, picture framing, woodworking.

OTT, CARL NEIL, environmental engineer; b. Alton, Ill., Nov. 6, 1948; s. Seldon Temple and Ruth Maxine (Eisenreich) Schumaker; m. Joan Hamilton Ott, Dec. 20, 1969; children: Amy Elizabeth, Nancy Rebecca. BS in Biol. Engring., Rose-Hulman Inst. Tech., Terre Haute, 1970. Sanitary engr. sanitary engr., Ind. State Bd. Health, Indpls., 1970-74; dir. Divsn. Pub. Water Supply Ind. State Bd. Health, Indpls., 1975-84; design engr. R.E. Curry & Assoc., Plainfield, Ind., 1984-85; dir. Engring. Howard Consultants, Pittsboro, Ind., 1985-86; pres. Phoenix Consulting, Pittsboro, Ind., 1986-90; v.p. Capitol Engring., Indpls., 1990—; bd. mem. Ind. Chpt. Am. Backflow Prevention Assn., Indpls., 1985-92; chmn. Short Sch. Com. Am. Water Works Assn., Indpls., 1976—. County surveyor Hendricks Co., Danville, Ind., 1991; mem. Rotary Internat. Brownsburg, Ind., 1987-93; pres. Jaycees N. Salem, Ind., 1976-77. Staff sgt. U.S. Army, 1970-76. Recipient Water Wheel award Am. Water Works Assn., Indpls., 1982, Bud Dale award Ind. Water Assn., Clarksville, 1987; named Honorary Life mem. Ind. Rural Water Assn., Nashville, Ind., 1984. Mem. NSPE, Am. Water Works Assn., Nat. Republican. Methodist. Avocations: nature activities, fossil hunting. Home: 7111 State Road 236 North Salem IN 46165-9565 Office: Capitol Engring Inc 9100 Keystone Xing 7th Fl Indianapolis IN 46240-4627

OTT, DAVID MICHAEL, engineering company executive; b. Glendale, Calif., Feb. 24, 1952; s. Frank Michael and Roberta (Michie) O.; m. Cynthia Dianne Bunce. BSEE, U. Calif., Berkeley, 1974. Electronic engr. Teknekron Inc., Berkeley, 1974-79; chief engr. TCI, Berkeley, 1979-83; div. mgr. Integrated Automation Inc., Alameda, Calif., 1983-87, Litton Indsl. Automation, Alameda, 1987-92; founder, chmn. Picture Elements Inc., Berkeley, 1992—. Inventor method for verifying denomination of currency, method for processing digited images, automatic document image revision. Mem. IEEE, AAAS, Assn. Computing Machinery, Union of Concerned Scientists. Office: Picture Elements Inc 777 Panoramic Way Berkeley CA 94704-2538

OTT, GEORGE WILLIAM, JR., management consulting executive; b. Chgo., May 5, 1932; s. George William and Isabelle (Salkeld) O.; m. Joan Virginia Vasseur; June 20, 1954; children: Lisa Joan, George William III, Robert Alexander. BSBA, U. So. Calif., L.A, 1954, MBA, 1960. CPA, Tex. Engr. adminstr. Douglas Aircraft, El Segundo, Calif., 1956-59; adminstrv. engr. Lear Corp., Santa Monica, Calif., 1959-61; co. adminstr. Plasmadyne Corp., Santa Ana, Calif., 1961-63; ptnr. Peat Marwick Mitchell & Co., L.A. and Houston, 1963-71; v.p. Korn/Ferry Internat., L.A., 1971-76; founder, pres., chief exec. officer Ott and Hansen, Inc., Pasadena, Calif., 1976—; bd. dirs. Virco Mfg. Co.; mem. adv. bd. Compensation Resource Group Inc., 1988—. Past pres., bd. dirs. Career Encores, 1989—; chmn., bd. dirs. Salvation Army, L.A. Metro, 1989—. Lt. (j.g.) USN, 1954-56. Mem. Nat. Assn. Corp. Dirs. (pres. So. Calif. chpt.), Calif. Exec. Recruiters Assn. (pres. 1992), Jonathan Club (L.A.), Rotary. Avocations: golf, model railroading. Office: Ott & Hansen 136 S Oak Knolls Ave Ste 300 Pasadena CA 91101-2624

OTT, GILBERT RUSSELL, JR., lawyer; b. Bklyn., Apr. 15, 1943; s. Gilbert Russell Sr. and Bettina Rose (Ferrel) O.; m. Lisa S. Weatherford, Apr. 12, 1986; children: Gilbert R. III, Laura Elisabeth. BA, Yale U., 1965; JD, Columbia U., 1969, MBA, 1969. Bar: N.Y. 1970. Assoc. Chadbourne, Parke, Whiteside & Wolff, N.Y.C., 1969-72, LeBoeuf, Lamb, Leiby & MacRae, N.Y.C., 1972-78; assoc. gen. counsel Kidder, Peabody & Co., Inc., N.Y.C., 1978—, asst. sec., 1978-91, asst. v.p., 1978-79, v.p., 1979-86, mng. dir., 1986-91, sr. v.p., sec., 1992—; v.p. Kidder, Peabody Group Inc., N.Y.C., 1989—; asst. sec., 1986—; bd. dirs. various subs. of Kidder, Peabody Group, Inc. Mem. Assn. of Bar of City of N.Y., Piping Rock Club, Univ. Club. Home: 260 Highwood Cir Oyster Bay NY 11771-3205 Office: Kidder Peabody & Co Inc 60 Broad St New York NY 10004

OTT, JAMES FORGAN, finance company executive; b. Chgo., Oct. 22, 1935; s. John Nash and Emily (Fentress) O.; m. Edna Cassinerio, July 8, 1961; children: Jeffery, Edna, Michael, Emily. A.B., Brown U., 1958; M.B.A., Northwestern U., 1961. C.P.A., Ill. Asso. investment banking White Weld & Co., Chgo., 1961-66; v.p. corp. fin. Eastman Dillion Union Securities & Co., Inc., Chgo., 1966-70; ptnr. Blunt Ellis & Simmons, Chgo., 1970-73; v.p. and treas., chief fin. officer The L.E. Myers Co., Chgo., 1973-83; sr. v.p., chief fin. officer Chgo. Title and Trust Co., 1983-86; v.p. fin., chief fin. officer, sec., treas. Middleby Corp., Chgo., 1987-93; sr. account mgr. Fin. Rels. Bd., Inc., Chgo., 1994. Mem. Ill. Soc. CPAs, Investment Analyst Soc. Chgo., Fin. Execs. Inst. Home: 25 Warrington Dr Lake Bluff IL 60044-1322

OTT, JOHN HARLOW, museum administrator; b. Ottawa, Ont., Can., Jan. 29, 1944; s. Thomas Gordon and Lois Elizabeth (Wright) O.; m. Lili Reineck, May 20, 1972; children—Jennie Elizabeth, Michael James Hutchins. B.A., Eastern Bapt. Coll., St. David's, Pa., 1966; M.A., SUNY-Oneonta, 1975; postgrad. Mus. Mgmt. Inst., U. Calif., Berkeley, 1987. Curator Hancock Shaker Village, Inc., Pittsfield, Mass., 1970-72, dir., 1972-83; exec. dir. Atlanta Hist. Soc., 1983-91, B&O R.R. Mus., Inc., Balt., 1991—; curator Ga. Hist. Soc., Savannah, 1983-87; mem. adv. bd. Concord (Mass.) Mus. Author: Hancock Shaker Village, 1976. Mem., chmn. arts com. Berkshire Hills Conf., Pittsfield, Mass., 1975-80; chmn. Pittsfield Civic Ctr. Commn., 1980-82; active Leadership Atlanta, 1984—; bd. dirs. Buckhead Bus. Assn., 1985-91, New Lebanon Shaker Heritage Found., N.Y.C., Hist. Ellicott City Restoration Found., 1992—; grad. 1993 Class of Leadership Balt.; mem. Mayor's Task Force on Greenways; mem. bd. dirs., exec. com. Balt. City C. of C., 1994—; mem. Mayor's Adv. Com. on Tourism, Entertainment and Culture, 1995; reviewer hist. and cultural mus. assistance program Md. Dept. Housing & Cmty. Devel., 1996. Decorated Bronze Star; named Mus. Profl. of Yr. in Ga., 1991. Mem. Am. Assn. Mus. (accrediting officer 1982—), Am. Assn. for State and Local History, Mid-Atlantic Mus. Assn., Ga. Soc. Assn. Execs., Nat. Hist. Communal Socs. Assn. (pres. 1983-84), Nat. Soc. Fund Raising Execs. (bd. dirs. Ga. chpt. 1985-91, bd. dirs. Md. chpt. 1993). Republican. Episcopalian. Office: B&O Railroad Mus 901 W Pratt St Baltimore MD 21223-2644

OTT, JURG, geneticist, educator; b. Schaffhausen, Switzerland, Apr. 11, 1939; came to U.S., 1970; s. Heinrich Paul and Anna Ida (Prag) O.; m. Susanne Rohr, 1968 (div. 1978); m. Salome Agathe Looser, Aug. 23, 1986. PhD, U. Zurich, Switzerland, 1968; MS, U. Wash., 1972. Asst. prof. U. Wash., Seattle, 1975-78; asst. dir. City Statistics Office, Zurich, 1979-85, dir., 1986; prof. Columbia U., N.Y.C., 1986—; research scientist N.Y. State Psychiat. Inst., 1986—. Author: Analysis of Human Genetic Linkage, 1991; (computer program) LIPED for Genetic Linkage, 1974; editor: Human Heredity, 1991—. NIMH grantee, 1989. Fellow Am. Psycho-Pathological Assn.; mem. Am. Soc. Human Genetics. Democrat. Avocation: piano. Office: Columbia U Box 58 722 W 168th St New York NY 10032-2603

OTT, KARL OTTO, nuclear engineering educator, consultant; b. Hanau, Germany, Dec. 24, 1925; came to U.S., 1967, naturalized, 1987; s. Johann Josef and Eva (Bergmann) O.; m. Gunhild G. Göring, Sept. 18, 1958 (div. 1986); children: Martina, Monika; m. Birgit Fehse, May 1, 1995. BS, J. W. von Goethe U., Frankfurt, Germany, 1948; MS, G. August U., Göttingen, Fed. Republic Germany, 1953, PhD, 1958. Physicist Nuclear Rsch. Ctr., Karlsruhe, Fed. Republic Germany, 1958-67, sect. head, 1962-67; prof. Sch. Nuclear Engring. Purdue U., West Lafayette, Ind., 1967—; cons. Argonne (Ill.) Nat. Lab., 1967—. Author: Nuclear Reactor Statics, 1983, 2nd edit., 1989, Nuclear Reactor Dynamics, 1985. Fellow Am. Nuclear Soc. Office: Sch Nuclear Engring Purdue U Lafayette IN 47907-1290

OTT, MICHAEL DUANE, lawyer; b. San Bernardino, Calif., June 9, 1948; s. Thomas Russell and Beverly Louise (Pentland) O.; m. Karen Hiroko Matsumoto, Dec. 23, 1967 (div. Jan. 1989); children: Jonathan Thomas, Steven Michael; m. Cynthia Lee Fontana, July 15, 1989. BA in History, U. Calif., San Diego, 1971; JD, U. Iowa, 1974. Bar: Calif., Oreg. Law clk. Hon. A. Andrew Hank, U.S. Dist. Ct., L.A., 1974-75; assoc. Mulvaney, Kahan, Dysart and Fraser, San Diego, 1975-77, 78-79; atty. Union Pacific R.R., Portland, Oreg., 1977; sr. dep. county counsel County of Lake, Lakeport, Calif., 1979-81, County of Fresno, Calif., 1981-83; county counsel County of Madera, Calif., 1983-88; ptnr. Borton, Petrini and Conron, Fresno, 1988—; new pos. Sandell, Olson & Ott; judge protem Madera County Superior Ct., 1986-88; jud. arbitration panel Fresno County, 1990—; paralegal adv. com. Fresno City Coll., 1992—. Editor Iowa Law Review, 1973-74; contbr. articles to profl. jours. Mem., vice chmn. Lake County Dem. Cen. Com., Lakeport, 1979-81; mem. Madera County Action Com., 1987-88. Mem. State Bar of Calif. (exec. com., Rep. sect. 1986-88), Fresno County Bar Bulletin (editorial bd. 1986-88), Madera County Bar Assn. (sec. 1986, treas. 1987), U. Calif. San Diego Alumni Assn. (bd. dirs. 1976-77, gen. counsel 1978-79). Avocations: tennis, golf. Office: Sandell Olson & Ott 2490 West Shaw Ave Ste 202 Fresno CA 93710*

OTT, WALTER RICHARD, academic administrator; b. Bklyn., Jan. 20, 1943; s. Harold Vincent and Mary Elizabeth (Butler) O; children: Regina Winter Burrell, Christina W., Walter R. Jr. BS in Ceramic Engring., Va. Poly. Inst. and State U., 1965; MS in Ceramic Engring., U. Ill., 1967; PhD in Ceramic Engring., Rutgers U., 1969. Registered profl. engr., Pa. Process engr. Corning Inc., Buckhannon, W.Va., 1965-66; staff research engr. Champion Spark Plug Co., Detroit, 1969-70; prof. engring. Rutgers U., New Brunswick, N.J., 1970-80; dean, assoc. provost N.Y. State Coll. Ceramics, Alfred, 1980-88; provost, chief acad. officer Alfred U., Alfred, 1988—; rsch. assoc. Atomic Energy Commn.-E.I. duPont de Nemours, Aiken, S.C., 1971; cons. Haight & Hofeldt Inc., Chgo., 1984-88, Pillsbury, Mpls., 1977-79, Ctr. for Profl. Advancement, New Brunswick, 1971-79, Hammond (Ind.) Lead Products, 1970-80; bd. dirs. Victor (N.Y.) Insulator Inc., UNIPEG, 1987-88; chmn. bd. dirs. Alfred Tech. Resources N.Y. Contbr. articles to profl. jours.; patentee in field. Recipient Ralph Teetor award Soc. Automotive Engrs., 1973, PACE award Nat. Inst. Ceramic Engrs., 1975, Ann. award Ceramic Assn. N.J., 1980; named to Greaves Walker Roll, Keramos, 1991. Fellow Am. Ceramic Soc. (trustee 1980-83, v.p. 1988-89); mem. Am. Soc. Engring. Educators, Ceramic Ednl. Coun. (pres. 1976-77), Ceramic Assn. N.Y. (treas. 1980-88, bd. dirs.), Ceramic Assn. N.J. (bd. dirs. 1974-80), Keramos (pres. 1982-84, Greaves-Walker Roll of Honor 1991), Tau Beta Pi. Avocations: tennis, reading. Home: 86 Maple Ave Wellsville NY 14895-1205 Office: Alfred U Provost Office Alfred NY 14802

OTT, WAYNE ROBERT, environmental engineer; b. San Mateo, Calif., Feb. 2, 1940; s. Florian Funstan and Evelyn Virginia (Smith) O.; m. Patricia Faustina Bertuzzi, June 28, 1967 (div. 1983). BA in Econs., Claremont McKenna Coll., 1962; BSEE, Stanford U., 1963, MS in Engring, 1965, MA in Comm., 1966, PhD in Environ. Engring., 1971. Commd. lt. USPHS, 1966, advanced to capt., 1986; chief lab. ops. br. U.S. EPA, Washington, 1971-73, sr. systems analyst, 1973-79, sr. rsch. engr., 1981-84, chief air toxics and radiation monitoring rsch. staff, 1984-90; vis. scientist dept. stats. Stanford (Calif.) U., 1979-81, 90—; vis. scholar Ctr. for Risk Analysis and dept. stats., civil engring., 1990-93; sr. environ. engr., EPA Atmospheric Rsch. and Exposure Assessment Lab, 1993-95; consulting prof. in civil engring. Stanford (Calif.) U., 1995—; dir. field studies Calif. Environ. Tobacco Smoke Study, 1993-95. Author: Environmental Indices: Theory and Practice, 1976, Environmental Statistics and Data Analysis, 1995; contbr. articles on indoor air pollution, total human exposure to chems., stochastic models of indoor exposure, motor vehicle exposures, personal monitoring instruments, and environ. tobacco smoke to profl. jours. Decorated Commendation medal USPHS, 1977; recipient Nat. Statistician award for outstanding contribution to environ. statistics EPA, 1995, Commendable Svc. Bronze medal for assessing human exposure from motor vehicle pollution, 1996. Mem. Internat. Soc. Exposure Analysis (v.p. 1989-90, Jerome J. Weselowski Internat. award for career achievement in exposure assessmemt 1995), Am. Statis. Assn., Am. Soc. for Quality Control, Air and Waste Mgmt. Assn., Internat. Soc. Indoor Air Quality and Climate, Phi Beta Kappa, Sigma Xi, Tau Beta Pi, Kappa Mu Epsilon. Democrat. Clubs: Theater, Jazz, Sierra. Avocations: hiking, photography, model trains, jazz recording. Developer nationally uniform air pollution index, first total human exposure activity pattern models. Home: 1008 Cardiff Ln Redwood City CA 94061-3678 Office: Stanford U Dept Stats Sequoia Hall Stanford CA 94305

OTT, WENDELL LORENZ, art museum director, artist; b. McCloud, Calif., Sept. 17, 1942; s. Wendell and Rose (Jacob) O. Student, San Francisco Art Inst., 1960-61, 62-63; B.A., Trinity U., San Antonio, 1968; M.F.A., U. Ariz., 1970; postgrad., Mus. Mgmt. Inst., U. Calif., 1984. Asst. dir. Roswell (N.Mex.) Mus. and Art Center, 1970-71, dir., 1971-86; dir. Tacoma (Wash.) Art Mus., 1986-92, Mus. of the Southwest, Tex., 1992-94, Tyler (Tex.) Mus. Art., 1995—; chmn. Roswell Humanities Series, 1972-73; instr. N.Mex. Mil. Inst., Roswell; mem. visual arts adv. com. Coll. of Santa Fe, 1985; grant reviewer Inst. Mus. Services, Washington, 1983. One man exhbns. include, Trinity U., 1967, 68, Men of Art Guild, San Antonio, 1967, 68, David Orr's Gallery, Roswell, 1976, G.W.V. Smith Art Mus., Springfield, Mass.; group exhbns. include Tex. Painting and Sculpture, Dallas Mus. Fine Arts, 1966, Witte Meml. Mus., San Antonio, 1967, 68, 1st ann. S.W. Arts Festival, Tucson, 1969, Graphics 69, Western N.Mex. U., 1969, 11th Ariz. ann. Phoenix Art Mus., 1969 (purchase awards), 9th ann., Security, Colo., 1969, 5th invitational Yuman Art Center, Yuma, Ariz., 1970, Juarez (Mexico) Mus. Art and History, 1973. Served with AUS, 1964-66. Mem. Am. Assn. Mus. (surveyor mus. assessment program 1984, pres. Washington arts consortium 1989—). Home: 5415 Old Bullard Rd # 108 Tyler TX 75703

OTTAWAY, JAMES HALLER, JR., newspaper publisher; b. Binghamton, N.Y., Mar. 24, 1938; s. James Haller and Ruth Blackburne (Hart) O.; m. Mary Warren Hyde, June 16, 1959; children—Alexandra, Christopher, Jay. Grad., Phillips Exeter Acad., 1955; B.A., Yale U., 1960; D.Journalism (hon.), Suffolk U., Boston, 1970; D.B.A. (hon.), Southeastern Mass. U., 1984. Reporter, mgmt. trainee New-Times, Danbury, Conn., 1960-62, Times Herald-Record, Middletown, N.Y., 1962-63; editor Pocono Record, Stroudsburg, Pa., 1963-65; publisher New Bedford (Mass.) Standard-Times, 1965-70; pres. Ottaway Newspapers, Inc., Campbell Hall, N.Y., 1970-85, chief exec. officer, 1976-88, chmn. bd., 1979—; v.p. Dow Jones & Co., 1980-86, sr. v.p., 1986—, also bd. dirs.; dir. Associated Press, 1982-91. Past. v.p. bd. trustees Phillips Exeter Acad.; trustee Am. Sch. Classical Studies at Athens, Storm King Art Ctr., Cornwall, N.Y., World Wildlife Fund USA, 1993—; chmn. World Press Freedom Com., 1996—; past pres., bd. dirs. Arden Hill Hosp. Found., Goshen, N.Y. Mem. Am. Newspaper Pubs. Assn., Am. Soc. Newspaper Editors. Episcopalian. Office: PO Box 401 Campbell Hall NY 10916-0401 also: Dow Jones & Co Inc 200 Liberty St New York NY 10281-1003

OTTAWAY, TERRI LOUISE, geologist, gemmologist; b. Toronto, Ont., Can., Nov. 17, 1957; d. Donald Gordon and Dorothy Kay (Parsons) O.; m. John Kenny, Nov. 26, 1983 (div.); m. Gary LaRose, Apr. 15, 1994. BSc with honors, U. Toronto, 1981, MSc, 1991. Mineral technician, gemmologist Royal Ont. Mus., Toronto, 1980—. Rsch. featured in cover story Nature, 1994. Fellow Can. Gemmological Assn., Gemmological Assn. Gt. Britain (diploma 1981); mem. Mineral. Soc. Am., Mineral. Assn. Can. Achievements include analysis of gases and solutions trapped inside Colombian crystal emeralds; development of a model which explains formation of emeralds in Colombian black shales. Avocations: herpetoculture, windsurfing. Office: Royal Ont Mus Dept Minerlgy, 100 Queens Park, Toronto, ON Canada M5S 2C6

OTTE, PAUL JOHN, academic administrator, consultant, trainer; b. Detroit, July 10, 1943; s. Melvin John Otte and Anne Marie (Meyers) Hirsch; children: Deanna, John. BS, Wayne State U., 1968, MBA, 1969; EdD, Western Mich. U., 1983. With Detroit Bank and Trust Co., 1965-68; teaching fellow Wayne State U., Detroit, 1968-69; auditor, mgr. Arthur Young & Co., Detroit, 1969-75; contr., dir. Macomb Community Coll., Warren, Mich., 1975-79, v.p. bus., 1979-86; pres. Franklin U., Columbus, Ohio, 1986—; owner, mgmt. trainer Otte and Assocs., Hilliard, Ohio, 1976—; prof. undergrad. and grad. programs Franklin U., Columbus, 1986—. Author various tng. manuals, 1982. Bd. dirs. Ohio Found. Ind. Colls., Mt. Carmel Coll. Nursing. Cpl. USMC, 1961-65. Teaching fellow Wayne State U., 1968-69. Mem. AICPA, Mich. Assn. CPAs (chmn. continuing profl. edn. com. 1980-82, leadership com. 1981-83), Nat. Assn. Coll. and Univ. Bus. Officers (acctg. prins. com. 1986), Assn. Ind. Colls. and Univs. Ohio (bd. dirs.), Mich. Community Colls. Bus. Officers Assn., Greater Detroit C. of C. (leadership award 1983), Columbus C. of C. (info. svc. com.). Roman Catholic. Avocations: travel, speaking engagements. Office: Franklin U 201 S Grant Ave Columbus OH 43215-5301

OTTE, RUTH L., cable television executive. V.p. mktg. MTV Networks Inc.; pres., COO Discovery Channel, 1986—. Office: Discovery Channel 7700 Wisconsin Ave Bethesda MD 20814-3578

OTTEN, ARTHUR EDWARD, JR., lawyer, corporate executive; b. Buffalo, Oct. 11, 1930; s. Arthur Edward Sr. and Margaret (Ambrusko) O.; m. Mary Therese Torri, Oct. 1, 1960; children: Margaret, Michael, Maureen Staley, Suzanne Hoodecheck, Jennifer. BA, Hamilton Coll., 1952; JD, Yale U., 1955. Bar: N.Y. 1955, Colo. 1959. Assoc. Hodges, Silverstein, Hodges & Harrington, Denver, 1959-64; ptnr. Hodges, Kerwin, Otten & Weeks (predecessor firms), Denver, 1964-73, Davis, Graham & Stubbs, Denver, 1973-86; pres., mem. Otten, Johnson, Robinson, Neff & Ragonetti, P.C., Denver, 1986—; rec. sec. Colo. Nat. Bankshares, Inc., Denver, 1983-93; gen. counsel Regis U., Denver, 1994—. Lt. USN, 1955-59. Mem. ABA, Colo. Bar Assn., Denver Bar Assn., Am. Arbitration Assn. (panel arbitrators, large complex case panel, mediator panel), Nat. Assn. Securities Dealers (bd. arbitrators), Law club, Univ. Club, Denver Mile High Rotary (pres. 1992-93), Phi Delta Phi. Republican. Roman Catholic. Avocations: hiking, biking, church activities. Home: 3774 S Niagara Way Denver CO 80237-1248 Office: Otten Johnson Robinson Neff & Ragonetti PC 1600 Colorado National Bldg Denver CO 80202-1056

OTTEN, JEFFREY, health facility administrator. CEO Brigham and Women's Hosp., Boston. Office: Brigham and Women's Hosp 75 Francis St Boston MA 02115-6195

OTTENBACHER, KENNETH JOHN, dean, educator; b. Missoula, Mont., Apr. 5, 1950; s. John and Florence (LaCasse) O.; m. Margaret E. Vaughn, May 7, 1975; children: Heather, Allison. BS, U. Mont., 1972, U. Ctrl. Ark., 1975; MS, U. Tenn., 1976; PhD, U. Mo., 1982. Registered occupational therapist. Prof. U. Wis., Madison, 1982-90; assoc. dean SUNY, Buffalo, 1990-95; vice dean U. Tex. Med. Br., Galveston, 1995—. Author: Evaluating Clinical Change, 1986; editor Occupational Therapy Jour. Rsch., 1987-91. Mem. Am. Acad. Sci., Am. Occupational Therapy Found. (charter), Acad. Rsch. (charter), Congress Rehab. Medicine. Home: 22 Quintana Dr Galveston TX 77554 Office: Salts Rm 4.202 301 University Blvd Galveston TX 77555-1028

OTTENBERG, JAMES SIMON, hospital executive; b. N.Y.C., Feb. 28, 1918; s. Irving Simon and Madeleine (Hirsh) O.; m. Margaret Anne Davies, May 10, 1941; children: Jeffrey, Betsy (Mrs. Michael Cherkasky), Jill (Mrs. Joshua Muscat). A.B., Swarthmore Coll., 1939; J.D., Harvard, 1942; M.Pub. Adminstrn., N.Y. U., 1963, postgrad., 1963-65. Bar: N.Y. bar 1945. Pvt. practice N.Y.C.; sec. to judge Gen. Sessions Ct., N.Y.C., 1955-58; exec. asst. commr. Marine and Aviation, N.Y.C., 1958-62; dep. commr. Mental Health Dept., N.Y.C., 1962-67; grant adminstr. Addiction Services Agy., N.Y.C., 1967-68; asst. dir. Child Study Assn. Am., N.Y.C., 1968-69, exec. dir., 1969-72; exec. dir. Edn. and Research Found. Better Bus. Bur. Met. N.Y., 1973-77; adminstr. Crotona Park Community Mental Health Center, N.Y.C., 1977-89; dir. med. adminstrn. Bronx-Lebanon Hosp., N.Y.C., 1989-92, adminstr. alcohol programs, 1992—; lectr. sch. continuing edn. NYU,

1969. Author: (with Rachele Thomas) You, Your Child and Drugs, 1971; annotated bibliography Political Reform, Machines and Big City Politics 1950-62, 1962. Active campaigns N.Y. Citizens for Stevenson, 1956, Kennedy and Johnson, 1960, Wagner, 1961, Robert F. Kennedy, 1964; Bd. dirs. Lenox Hill Neighborhood Assn., N.Y.C., 1954-66, Union Settlement, 1968-70. Served with USAAC, 1942-45. Recipient Lepesqueur award for highest scholarship Grad. Sch. Pub. Adminstrn., N.Y. U., 1963. Fellow Am. Pub. Health Assn. Home: 145 E 92nd St New York NY 10128-2431 Office: 321 E Tremont Ave Bronx NY 10457-5304

OTTENFELD, MARSHALL, marketing research company executive; b. Chgo., Jan. 15, 1937; s. Leo and Sadie (Patt) O.; B.A., U. Chgo., 1959; M.A., Roosevelt U., 1968; m. Gloria Jean Zilke, Dec. 28, 1960; children—David Joel, Jonathan Lawrence, Jennifer Lynn, Heather Anne. Study dir. Chgo. Tribune, 1962-64; project dir. Gardner Advt. Co., N.Y.C., 1964-65; research asso. Advt. Research Found., N.Y.C., 1965-66; research asso. pharm. products div. Abbott Labs., North Chicago, Ill., 1966-70; sr. v.p., dir. mktg. research D'Arcy-MacManus & Masius, Inc., Chgo., 1970-83; pres. Mid-Am. Research, Chgo., 1970—; pres., chief exec. officer Mid-Am. Research, Inc., 1983—; ptnr. Market Shares Corp., 1986—; lectr. mktg. Roosevelt U.; Assoc. editor Jour. Data Collection. Scout master Boy Scouts Am., Deerfield, Ill., 1980—. Served with AUS, 1961-62. Mem. Am. Mktg. Assn., Advt. Research Found., Research Practices Council, Qualitative Research Council, Am. Assn. Public Opinion Research, Midwest Assn. Public Opinion Research, Am. Assn. Advt. Agys., N.Y. Acad. Sci., Am. Acad. Polit. and Social Sci., Mktg. Research Assn., Zeta Beta Tau. Jewish. Club: Internat. Home: 1050 Summit Dr Deerfield IL 60015-1823 Office: Mid-America Rsch Inc 999 N Elmhurst Rd Mount Prospect IL 60056-1143

OTTENSMEYER, DAVID JOSEPH, neurosurgeon, health care executive; b. Nashville, Tenn., Jan. 29, 1930; s. Raymond Stanley and Glenda Jessie (Helpingstein) O.; m. Mary Jean Langley, June 30, 1954; children: Kathryn Joan, Martha Langley. BA, Wis. State U., Superior, 1951; MD, U. Wis., Madison, 1959; MS in Health Svcs. Adminstrn., Coll. St. Francis, 1985. Diplomate Am. Bd. Neurological Surgery. Intern then resident in gen. surgery Univ. Hosps., Madison, Wis., 1959-61; resident in neurol. surgery Univ. Hosps., 1962-65; staff neurosurgeon Marshfield Clinic, Wis., 1965-76; from instr. of neurol. surgery to clin. asst. prof. U. Wis. Med. Sch., Madison, 1964-77; CEO Lovelace Med. Ctr., Albuquerque, 1976-86, chmn., 1986-91; clin. prof. community medicine U. N.Mex., Albuquerque, 1977-79, clin. prof. neurol. surgery, 1979-92; exec. v.p., chief med. officer Equicor, 1986-90; v.p. Marshfield Clinic, 1970-71, pres., CEO, 1972-75; pres., CEO The Lovelace Insts., 1991-96; sr. v.p., chief med. officer Travelers Ins. Co., 1990-91; served on numerous adv. and com. posts. Contbr. articles to profl. jours. Col. USAR, 1960-90. Fellow ACS, Am. Coll. Physician Execs. (pres. 1985-86); mem. Am. Group Practice Assn. (pres. 1983-84), Am. Bd. Med. Mgmt. (bd. dirs. 1989-95, chmn. 1995). Republican. Episcopalian. Avocations: flying; golf; travel. Home: 2815 Ridgecrest Dr SE Albuquerque NM 87108-5132

OTTER, CLEMENT LEROY, lieutenant governor; b. Caldwell, Idaho, May 3, 1942; s. Joseph Bernard and Regina Mary (Buser) O.; m. Gay Corinne Simplot, Dec. 28, 1964; children: John Simplot, Carolyn Lee, Kimberly Dawn, Corinne Marie. BA in Polit. Sci., Coll. Idaho, 1967; PhD, Mindanao State U., 1980. Mgr. J.R. Simplot Co., Caldwell, Idaho, 1971-76, asst. to v.p. adminstrn., 1976-78, v.p. adminstrn., 1978-82, internat. pres., from 1982, now v.p.; lt. gov. State of Idaho, Boise, 1987—. Mem. Presdl. Task Force-AID, Washington, 1982-84; com. mem. invest tech. devel. State Adv. Council, Washington, 1983-84; mem. exec. council Bretton Woods Com., 1984—; mem. U.S. C. of C., Washington, 1983-84. Mem. Young Pres.' Orgn., Sales and Mktg. Execs., Idaho Assn. Commerce and Industry, Idaho Agrl. Leadership Council, Idaho Ctr. for Arts, Idaho Internat. Trade Council, Pacific N.W. Waterways Assn., N.W. Food Producers, Ducks Unltd. Republican. Roman Catholic. Clubs: Arid, Hillcrest Country. Lodge: Moose, Elks. Avocations: jogging, music, art collecting, horse training, fishing. Office: Office of the Lt Gov PO Box 83720 Boise ID 83720-0057*

OTTER, JOHN MARTIN, III, television advertising consultant, retired; b. Pottsville, Pa., Nov. 26, 1930; s. John Martin and Ruth A. (Knipe) O.; m. Susan Morgan Eaves, May 21, 1960; children—John Martin, IV, Robert Marshal. B.A., Cornell U., 1953. Comml. producer Arlene Frances Home Show, 1953-55; producer Dave Garroway Today Show, 1956-59; dir. spl. programs sales NBC-TV, 1959-61, v.p. nat. sales, 1962-64, v.p. charge sales, 1965-73; cons. sta. WNET-TV, Practising Law Inst., also Dragonwk Prodns., 1973-75; v.p., dir. network programming SSC&B Inc., 1975-78; sr. v.p., dir. network programming SSC&B Lintas Worldwide, N.Y.C., 1978-84; sr. v.p. dir. nat. broadcast McCann-Erickson U.S.A., N.Y.C., 1984-88; sr. v.p. spl. projects McCann-Erickson Worldwide, N.Y.C., 1988; pres. RETTO Internat. Inc., N.Y.C., 1989-94; retired, 1994. Mem. The Landings Club, The Landings Yacht Club. Republican. Episcopalian. Home: Four Seafarer's Cir Savannah GA 31411

OTTERBOURG, ROBERT KENNETH, public relations consultant, writer; b. N.Y.C., Jan. 26, 1930; s. Albert Marcus and Frances (Roset) O.; m. Susan Delman, Apr. 14, 1957; children—Laura Ann, Kenneth Douglas. BA, Colgate U., 1951; MS, Columbia U., 1954. Reporter, editor Fairchild Publs., N.Y.C., 1953-57; editor McGraw-Hill Pub. Co., 1957-59; v.p. pub. rels. Charles Mathieu & Co., 1959-61; pres. pub. rels. Otterbourg & Co., N.Y.C., 1962-69, 71—; sr. v.p. Daniel J. Edelman, 1970. Author: It's Never Too Late, 1993, Retire and Thrive, 1995; contbr. articles to profl. and consumer jours. Legis. asst. N.Y. State Senate, 1962-64; mem. exec. com. Columbia U. Sch. Journalism, N.Y.C., 1980-93, pres. exec. com., 1985-87; trustee Flat Rock Nature Ctr., pres., 1991-92; trustee Planned Parenthood Bergen County, 1985-88, v.p., 1986-88; trustee Urban League for Bergen County, 1988—; bd. dirs. Colgate U. Alumni Corp., 1969-93. 1st lt. USAF, 1951-53. Mem. Pub. Rels. Soc. Am., Columbia U. Grad. Sch. Journalism Alumni Assn. (pres. 1985-87). Democrat. Jewish. Home and Office: 68 Beverly Dr Durham NC 27707-2224

OTTERHOLT, BARRY L., technology management consultant; b. Richland, Wash., Aug. 15, 1953; s. Ernest D. and Jean T. Otterholt; m. Nancy L. Musgrave, Dec. 13, 1985; children: Casey J., Kris K., Cody M.E. BA in Computer Sci. Acctg., Western Wash. U., 1980; MBA in Bus. Administrn., Seattle Pacific U., 1982. Mgr. Robinson's, Wenatchee, Wash., 1971-75; purchasing agt. Sound Ctrs., Inc., Bellingham, Wash., 1975-79; chief oper. officer Speakerlab/Compulab, Seattle, 1979-82; mgmt. cons. Deloitte & Touche, Seattle, 1982-88; founder, prin. Solutions Consulting Group LLC, Bellevue, Wash., 1988—. Mem. Inst. Mgmt. Cons. (cert.). Office: Solutions Consulting Group 1400 112th Ave SE Bellevue WA 98004-6901

OTTERMAN, KENNETH JAMES, real estate investor, author, consultant; b. McKeesport, Pa., Jan. 21, 1949; s. Glenn Ewing Sr. and Beatrice May (Hill) O.; m. Deborah Jean Brown, Aug. 14, 1973; children: Kenneth J. Jr., Forrest G. BS in Bus., Pa. State U., 1973. exec. dir. Excel Telecomm. Prin., real estate investor Ken Otterman & Assocs., Reading, Pa., 1976; bd. advisors D.I.G., Phila., R.E.I.A., Reading; org. mem, investor Berks County Bank, Reading, 1987—; exec. dir. Excel Telecomms. Author: Real Estate Investing for Cash Flow, 1986, Home Ownership Bargains From Your Government, 1986, Rules of the Game, 1984, (course) Become a Real Estate Investor, 1984. Club: R.E.I.A. (Reading) (pres. 1982-85). Avocations: skiing, travel. Office: Four Homestead Rd Leesport PA 19533

OTTESON, SCHUYLER FRANKLIN, former university dean, educator; b. Mondovi, Wis., July 17, 1917; s. Hans and Elizabeth (Meyer) O.; m. Marie Lila Rothering, 1940; children: Judith Marie, Martha Jean, Karn Wilma, John Christian. Student, Eau Claire State Tchrs. Coll., 1935-37; Ph.B., U. Wis., 1939; M.B.A., Northwestern U., 1940; Ph.D., Ohio State U., 1948. Research asst. exec. com. Fair Store, Chgo., 1940-42; asst. buyer Montgomery Ward & Co., 1942-43; instr. econs. and bus. adminstrn. Ohio Wesleyan U., 1943-44, asst. prof., 1944-46; asst. prof. mktg. Ind. U., 1946-48, assoc. prof., 1948-52, prof., 1952—, assoc. dir. Bur. Bus. Research, 1947-49, dir. Bur. Bus. Research, 1954-60, chmn. of mktg. dept., 1960-65, chmn. Dr. Bus. Adminstrn. Program, 1965-71, acting dean Sch. Bus., 1971-72, dean, 1972-82, also dir. Internat. Bus. Research Inst.; bd. dirs. Circle Income Shares, Inc.; mem. ednl. adv. com. Chgo. Bd. Trade, 1952-55, chmn. com., 1954-55; bd. dirs. Am. Assembly Coll. Schs. of Bus., 1978-82, pres., 1981; chmn. Ctr. for Leadership Devel., 1976—. Author: (with T.N. Beckman) Cases in Credits and Collections, 1949, (with William G. Panschar and James M. Patterson) Marketing: The Firm's Viewpoint, 1964; Editor: Marketing—Current Problems and Theories, 1952, Business Horizons, 1957-66; Contbr. articles profl. publs. Recipient leather medal Sigma Delta Chi, 1960; named Sagamore of Wabash, gov. Ind., 1956. Mem. Am., Midwest econs. assns., Ind. Acad. Social Scis. (pres. 1969-70), Am. Marketing Assn. (pres. 1965-66), Alpha Delta Sigma, Beta Gamma Sigma (bd. govs.). Home: 512 S Jordan Ave Bloomington IN 47401-5120

OTTINO, JULIO MARIO, chemical engineering educator, scientist; b. La Plata, Buenos Aires, Argentina, May 22, 1951; came to U.S., 1976; naturalized, 1990; s. Julio Francisco and Nydia Judith (Zufriategui) O.; m. Alicia I. Löffler, Aug. 20, 1976; children: Jules Alessandro, Bertrand Julien. Diploma in Chem. Engring., U. La Plata, 1974; PhD in Chem. Engring., U. Minn., 1979; exec. program Kellogg Sch. Mgmt., Northwestern U., 1995. Instr. in chem. engring. U. Minn., Mpls., 1978-79; asst. prof. U. Mass., Amherst, 1979-83, adj. prof. polymer sci., 1979-91, assoc. prof. chem. engring., 1983-86, prof., 1986-91; Chevron vis. prof. chem. engring. Calif. Inst. Tech., Pasadena, 1985-86; sr. rsch. fellow Ctr. for Turbulence Rsch. Stanford (Calif.) U., 1989-90; Walter P.Murphy prof. chem. engring. Northwestern U., Evanston, Ill., 1991—, chmn. dept. chem. engring., 1992—; cons. in field; William N. Lacey lectureship Calif. Inst. Tech., 1994; Allan P. Colburn Meml. lectr. U. Del., 1987; Merck Sharp & Dohme lectr. U. P.R., 1989, Stanley Corrsin lectr. Johns Hopkins U., 1991; Centennial lectr. U. Md., 1994. Author: The Kinematics of Mixing: Stretching, Chaos and Transport, 1989; contbr. articles to profl. jours.; assoc. editor Physics Fluids A, 1991—; mem. editl. bd. Internat. Jour. Bifurc. Chaos, 1991—; cons. editor Am. Inst. Chem. Engring. Jour., 1991-95, assoc. editor., 1995—; one man art exhibit, La Plata, 1974. Recipient Presdl. Young Investigator award NSF, 1984; Univ. fellow U. Mass., 1988, Alpha Chi Sigma award AIChE, 1994. Fellow Am. Phys. Soc.; mem. AAAS, Soc. for Natural Philosophy (selection com. 1993—), Am. Chem. Soc., Am. Phys. Soc., Soc. Rheology, Am. Soc. Engring. Edn., Sigma Xi, Pau Beta Pi. Achievements include research in fluid dynamics, chaos, mixing and turbulence, granular flows, polymer processing. Home: 1182 Asbury Ave Winnetka IL 60093-1402 Office: Northwestern U Dept Chem Engring 2145 Sheridan Rd Evanston IL 60208-0834

OTTLEY, JEROLD DON, choral conductor, educator; b. Salt Lake City, Apr. 7, 1934; s. Sidney James and Alice (Warren) O.; m. JoAnn South, June 22, 1956; children: Brent Kay, Allison. B.A., Brigham Young U., Provo, Utah, 1961; M.Mus., U. Utah, 1967; Fulbright study grantee, Fed. Republic Germany, 1968-69; D.M.A. (grad. teaching fellow), U. Oreg., 1972. Tchr. public schs. Salt Lake City area, 1961-65; mem. faculty U. Utah, Salt Lake City, 1967—, asst. prof. music, 1971-78, adj. assoc. prof. music, 1978-81, adj. prof. music, 1981—; assoc. conductor Salt Lake Mormon Tabernacle Choir, 1974-75, conductor, 1975—; also guest conductor throughout U.S. Conducted Mormon Tabernacle Choir in 13 concert tours U.S., 25 fgn. countries, Utah Phila. and Milw. Orchestra in performance; rec. artist CBS Masterworks, London/Decca Records, Bonneville Records and Laserlight; prepared choirs for Eugene Ormandy, Maurice Avravanel, Stanislaw Skrowaczewski, Michael Tilson Thomas, Robert Shaw, Julius Rudel, Sir David Willcocks, Ling Tung. Past mem. gen. music coms. Mormon Ch., cultural arts com. Salt Lake City C. of C. (Honors in the Arts award), past bd. advs. Barlow Endowment Music Composition; v.p., past bd. dirs., com. chair Chorus Am. Served with U.S. Army, 1957-59. Faculty Study grantee U. Utah, 1971-72; recipient Brigham Young U. Alumni Achievement award, 1990. Mem. Am. Choral Dirs. Assn., Am. Choral Found., Master Tchr. Inst. Arts (past trustee), Great Music West Festival. Office: Mormon Tabernacle Choir 50 E North Temple Fl 20 Salt Lake City UT 84150-0002

OTTLEY, WILLIAM HENRY, professional association director, consultant; b. N.Y.C., Mar. 7, 1929; s. James Henry and Margaret (Deeble) O. BA, Yale U., 1950; spl. cert., Georgetown U., 1953; D of Aero. Sci. (hon.), Embry Riddle Aero. U., 1979. Dir. pub. rels. Thomas A. Edison Co., West Orange, N.J., 1953-56; exec. v.p. Career Publs., Inc., N.Y.C., 1956-60; dir. spl. exhibits N.Y. World's Fair, 1960-65; exec. dir. Nat. Pilots Assn., Washington, 1965-77, U.S. Parachute Assn., Washington, 1978-92, Nat. Aero. Assn., Washington, 1992-93; pres. Internat. Gen. Aviation Commn., Paris, 1994—; v.p. Fedn. Aero. Internat., Paris, 1994—. 1st lt. USAF, 1951-53. Recipient Skydiving Lifetime Achievement award, 1994. Mem. Am. Mus. Sport Parachuting (pres.), Met. Club Washington, Soc. of Cin. Republican. Episcopalian. Avocations: skydiving (world record holder 1982), flying (world record holder 1985), scuba diving, waterskiing, snow skiing. Home and Office: 2627 Woodley Pl NW Washington DC 20008-1525

OTTMANN, PETER, choreographer, ballet master; b. Renfrew, Ont., Can., Apr. 15, 1957; m. Karen Cameron. Grad., Nat. Ballet Sch., 1975; postgrad., Benesh Inst., London, 1993. Mem. Nat. Ballet of Can., Toronto, Ont., 1976—, 1st solosit, 1983-93, resident choreologist, ballet master, 1993-96, asst. to artistic dir., 1996—; mem. dancer exch. program Australian Ballet Co. Created roles of Reginald Hargreaves and Caterpillar in Glen Tetley's Alice, and for Café Dances, 1991; debuted as Lewis Carrol at Met. Opera House, N.Y.C., 1986; performed in The Nutcracker, Giseille, Romeo and Juliet, Don Quixote, The Miraculous Mandarin, La Ronde, 1987, Dream Dances, 1989, The Leaves Are Fading, 1990, the second detail, 1991, The Strangeness of a Kiss, 1991, Musings, 1991, The Taming of the Shrew, 1992, The Merry Widow, 1992, (in films) Alice, 1989, La Ronde, 1989, (TV prodn.) A Moving Picture; guest appearances at Spoleto Festival, Italy, Toronto Symphony Orch., 1986, Houston Ballet, 1993. Office: Nat Ballet Can, 157 King St E, Toronto, ON Canada M5C 1G9

OTTO, CHARLES EDWARD, health care administrator; b. Somerville, N.J., Nov. 12, 1946; s. Hans and Virginia (Hegeman) O.; m. Wendy Ann Halsey; June 26, 1971; children: Eric, C. Halsey, Robert. BA, Hobart Coll., Geneva, N.Y., 1968; MBA, U. Pa., 1973. Adminstrv. asst. Mass. Gen. Hosp., Boston, 1970-71; adminstrv. resident Hosp. of U. of Pa., Phila., 1973; adminstrv. asst. Norwalk (Conn.) Hosp., 1974-76; exec. dir. Waveny Care Ctr., New Canaan, Conn., 1977-93; adminstr. Avery Heights Retirement Village, Hartford, Conn., 1994—; bd. chmn. Conn. Assn. of Non-Profit Facilities for the Aged, Wallingford, 1984-86; chmn. regional adv. group Conn. Community Care, Inc., Norwalk, 1983-85. Bd. chmn. S.W. Fairfield Am. Cancer Soc., Norwalk, 1985-87. Served to lt. (j.g.) USNR, 1968-70. Mem. Wharton Healthcare Alumni Assn. (bd. dirs. 1993-94), Rocky Point Club. Episcopalian. Home: 12 Lake Dr S Riverside CT 06878-2016

OTTO, DONALD R., museum director; b. North Loup, Nebr., Oct. 7, 1943; s. Leonard R. and Lorraine E. (Lindsay) O.; B.A., Hastings (Nebr.) Coll., 1967; m. Sylvia D. Cook, Aug. 7, 1965; 1 dau., Allison Lindsay. With Kans.-Nebr. Natural Gas Co., Hastings, 1967-68; exhibits dir. Hastings Museum, 1968-72; asst. dir. Kans. State Hist. Soc., 1972-75; program dir. Ft. Worth Mus. Sci. and History, 1975-77, exec. dir., 1977—; pres. Kans. Mus. Assn., 1974, 75; officer Mountain Plains Mus. Conf., 1976-79, pres., 1977-78; spl. cons. mus. curriculum planning Coll. Liberal Studies, U. Okla., 1980. Mem. adminstrv. bd. 1st Meth. Ch., 1978-80, 81-83, 84-86; bd. dirs. Sci. Mus. Exhibit Collaborative, 1983—, Ft. Worth Conv. and Visitors Bur., 1986—, Internat. Space Theater Consortium, 1981—, pres. 1984-86, exec. com. 1991-92; mem. Ft. Worth Cultural Dist. Com., 1979—, Ft. Worth Air Power Coun., 1985—, Leadership Ft. Worth, 1988—, Forum Ft. Worth, 1989—; mem. grants com. Cultural Arts Coun. of Houston, 1988-89; mem. adv. coun. Ft. Worth Sr. Citizen Ctrs., 1986-88; trustee Big Bros.-Big Sisters, 1988-89; chmn. Ft. Worth Tourism Coun., 1983. Mem. Am. Assn. Mus. (accreditation on site com. 1974—), Mt. Plains Mus. Assoc. Bd., 1975-78, pres., 1977, Am. Assn. State and Local History, Am. Assn. Sci. and Tech. Ctrs. (bd. dirs. 1984-88), Assn. Sci. Mus. Dirs., Tex. Assn. Mus. (coun. 1980-82, v.p. 1983-84), Ft. Worth Aviation Heritage Soc. (bd. dirs. 1988—), Methodist. Clubs: Ridglea Country, Rotary (Ft. Worth). Office: Ft Worth Mus Sci & History 1501 Montgomery St Fort Worth TX 76107-3017

OTTO, FRED DOUGLAS, chemical engineering educator; b. Hardisty, Alta., Can., Jan. 12, 1935. BSc, U. Alta., 1957, MSc, 1959; BS in Chem. Engring., U. Mich., Ann Arbor, 1963. From asst. prof. to assoc. prof. U. Alta., Edmonton, 1962-70, chmn., 1975-84, prof. chem. engring., 19970—, dean engring., 1985-94; mem. governing coun. NRC, 1991-94. Fellow Can. Acad. Engring.; mem. AIChE, Can. Soc. Chem. Engrs. (pres. 1986-87), Am. Soc. Engring. Edn., Assn. Profl. Engrs., Geologists and Geophysicsts of Alta. (1st v.p. 1995-96, Centennial award 1993). Office: U Alta, 5-18 Chem-Mineral Engr Bldg, Edmonton, AB Canada T6G 2G6

OTTO, JEAN HAMMOND, journalist; b. Kenosha, Wis., Aug. 27, 1925; d. Laurence Cyril and Beatrice Jane (Slater) Hammond; m. John A. Otto, Aug. 22, 1946; children: Jane L. Rahman, Mary Ellen Takayama, Peter J. Otto; m. Lee W. Baker, Nov. 23, 1973. Student, Ripon Coll., 1944-46. Women's editor Appleton (Wis.) Post-Crescent, 1960-68; reporter Milw. Jour., 1968-72, editorial writer, 1972-77, editor Op Ed page, 1977-83; editorial page editor Rocky Mountain News, Denver, 1983-89, assoc. editor, 1989-92, reader rep., 1992—; Endowed chair U. Denver, 1992—. Founder, chmn. bd. trustees First Amendment Congress, 1979-85, chmn. exec. com., 1985-88, 89-91, pres. 1991—, mem. bd. trustees, 1979—; founding mem. Wis. Freedom of Info. Council. Recipient Headliner award Wis. Women in Communications, 1974; Outstanding Woman in Journalism award YWCA, Milw., 1977; Knight of Golden Quill Milw. Presss Club, 1979; spl. citation in Journalism Ball State U., 1980; James Madison award Nat. Broadcast Editorial Assn., 1981; spl. citation for contbn. to journalism Nat. Press Photographers Assn., 1981; Ralph D. Casey award, 1984; U. Colo. Regents award, 1985; John Peter Zenger award U. Ariz., 1988; Paul Miller Medallion award Okla. State U., 1990; Colo. SPJ Lowell Thomas award, 1990, Disting. Alumna award Ripon Coll., 1992, Hugh M. Hefner First Amendment Lifetime Achievement award Playboy Found., 1994. Mem. Colo. Press Assn. (chmn. freedom of info. com. 1983-89), Assn. Edn. in Journalism and Mass Communications (Disting. Svc. award 1984), Am. Soc. Newspaper Editors (bd. dirs. 1987-92), Soc. Profl. Journalists (nat. treas. 1975, nat. sec. 1977, pres.-elect 1978, pres. 1979-80, First Amendment award 1981, Wells Key 1984, pres. Sigma Delta Chi Found. 1989-92, chair Found. 1992-94), Milw. Press Club (mem. Hall of Fame 1993). Office: Rocky Mountain News 400 W Colfax Ave Denver CO 80204-2607

OTTO, KLAUS, physicist, physical chemist; b. Friedrichroda, Germany, Sept. 18, 1929; came to U.S., 1960, naturalized, 1967; s. Theodor M.W.A. and Gertrud (Gohla) O.; m. Christa Thomsen, Nov. 16, 1962; children: Ina N., Peter N. Vordiplom, U. Hamburg, Fed. Republic of Germany, 1954, Diplom, 1957, D of Natural Scis., 1960. Rsch. asst. U. Hamburg, 1959-60; postdoctoral fellow Argonne (Ill.) Nat. Lab., 1960-62; sr. rsch. scientist Ford Motor Co., Dearborn, Mich., 1962-73, prin. rsch. scientist assoc., 1973-81, staff scientist, 1981-95; ret., 1995; adj. prof. Mich. State U., 1986-95. Contbr. articles to profl. jours. Recipient Parravano award for excellence in catalysis rsch. and devel., 1986. Mem. AAAS, Am. Chem. Soc., German Bunsen Soc. of Electrochemistry, Mich. Catalysis Soc. (pres. 1980-81), N.Y. Acad. Scis., Sigma Xi (pres. Ford chpt. 1985-86). Home: 201 E Tonto Dr Sedona AZ 86351-7323

OTTO, MARGARET AMELIA, librarian; b. Boston, Oct. 22, 1937; d. Henry Earlen and Mary (McLennan) O.; children—Christopher, Peter. A.B., Boston U., 1960; M.S., Simmons Coll., 1963, M.A., 1970; M.A. (hon.), Dartmouth Coll., 1981. Asst. sci. librarian M.I.T., Cambridge, 1963; Lindgren librarian M.I.T., 1964-67, acting sci. librarian, 1967-69, asst. dir., 1969-75, asso. dir., 1976-79; librarian of coll. Dartmouth Coll., Hanover, N.H., 1979—; pres., chmn. bd. Universal Serials and Book Exch., Inc., 1980-81; bd. dirs. Rsch. Libr. Group; trustee Howe Libr., Hanover, 1988—, chmn., 1992—; mem. Brown Libr. Com., rsch. lbirs. adv. com. OCLC, 1991—, ARL; editl. com. Univ. Press New Eng., 1993—. Council on Library Resources fellow, 1974; elected to Collegium of Disting. Alumnus Boston U., 1980. Mem. ALA (task force on assn. membership issues 1993—, ad hoc working group on copyright issues), Assn. Rsch. Librs. (chair preservation com. 1983-85, bd. dirs. 1985-88, mem. stats. com., chair membership com. 1992—), Coun. on Libr. Resources (proposal rev. com. 1992—), Dartmouth Club (N.Y.C.), St. Botolph Club (Boston), Sloane Club (London). Home: 2 Berrill Farms Ln Hanover NH 03755-3205 Office: Dartmouth Coll 115 Baker Meml Libr Hanover NH 03755

OTTO, (BERTHA) MARIE, educational administrator, educational consulting company executive; b. Houston, July 11, 1930; d. Robert Lillard and Bertha Irene (Allen) Davis; m. Robert Lee Otto, Jan. 7, 1950; children: Lois Ann Otto Buschmann, Barbara Jeane Otto Hunt, Robert Lee Jr. Student, Tex. Christian U., 1947-49, Hardin-Simmons U., summers 1947, 49, 54; BA in Speech, Drama and Edn., Sul-Ross State U., 1954; postgrad., U. Wyo., 1961, U. Calif., Santa Barbara, 1962, Calif. State U., Northridge, 1964; MA, Calif. State U., Long Beach, 1969, postgrad., 1980-82. Lic. tchr., Tex., secondary tchr., Wyo., Calif.; lic. psychologist; lic. marriage and family counselor. Tchr. high schs., Tex., Wyo. and Calif., 1956-64; tchr., counselor Excelsior High Sch., Norwalk, Calif., 1964-66; counselor Neff High Sch., La Mirada, Calif., 1966-69; psychologist Huntington Beach (Calif.) Union High Sch. Dist., 1969-74, project mgr., dir. pupil pers., 1974-80, asst. supt., 1980-84, supt., 1984-88, supt. emeritus, 1988—; v.p. Poole-Young-Koehler Assocs., Inc., Long Beach, 1964-79; pvt. practice marriage and family counselor, Fountain Valley, Calif., 1970—; pres. Marie Otto Assocs., Fountain Valley, 1979—; supr. student tchrs. Chapman Univ. Orange, Calif., 1988—; sec.-treas., Ctr. for Teaching Thinking, Huntington Beach, 1991—. Mem. Fountain Valley Human Svcs. Com., Huntington Beach Human Resources Commn., state planning com. Girl Scouts U.S., Worland, Wyo., 1959-61; pres. Spl. Edn. Local Plan Orgn., 1983-84; bd. dirs. Humana Hosp. Huntington Beach, Golden West Coll. Found., Huntington Beach, Huntington Beach Community Clinic, Orange County chpt. ARC, Santa Ana, Calif. No on Drugs, 1988—; sec., treas. Ctr. for Teaching of Thinking, Huntington Beach, 1992—. Recipient numerous plaques, 1985—, including Fountain Valley Human Svcs. Com., 1979, City of Fountain Valley, 1975, 79, 88, City of Huntington Beach, 1988, Fountain Valley C. of C., 1988, City of Westminster, 1988, Orange Coast Coll., 1988, Golden West Coll., 1988, Ocean View Sch. Dist., 1988, Spl. Edn. Local Plan Orgn., 1984; named Woman of Yr., Soroptimist Club, Westminster, 1984, Disting. Alumnus, Grad. Sch. Edn. Calif. State U.-Long Beach, 1988. Home and Office: 16689 Mount Hoffman Cir Fountain Valley CA 92708

OTTOSON, HOWARD WARREN, agricultural economist, former university administrator; b. Detroit Lakes, Minn., Sept. 18, 1920; s. John Henry and Hilma Marie (Johnson) O.; m. Margaret Jane Featherstone, Oct. 22, 1944; children—Keith Richard, John Howard, David Thomas. B.S., U. Minn., 1942, M.S., 1950; Ph.D., Iowa State U., 1952. Chmn. dept. agrl. econs. U. Nebr., Lincoln, 1956-66, Bert Rodgers prof., 1965, dir., dean, 1966-79, asst. vice chancellor, 1979-81, vice chancellor, 1981-82, exec. v.p., provost, 1982-85, prof. agrl. econs. emeritus, 1985—; cons. USDA, Washington, 1961, 64, AID, Buenos Aires, Argentina, 1962, Colombian Inst. Agr., Bogota, 1970; mem. USDA Policy Adv. Com. on Feed Grains, Washington, 1966-68; chmn. Gt. Plains Agrl. Council, Lincoln, Nebr., 1971, 79; bd. dirs. Farm Found. Bd., Chgo., 1977-85. Sr. author: Land and People in the Northern Plains Tranition Area, 1966; sr. author Agrl. Land Tenure Research bull., 1962; editor: Land Use Problems and Policies in the U.S., 1963; co-editor: Transportation Problems and Policies in the Trans Missouri West, 1967. Pres. Lincoln Coun. Chs., Nebr., 1958-59, Nebr. divsn. UN Assn.-U.S.A., Lincoln, 1977-78; chmn. Mayor's Adv. Com. on Taxation, Lincoln, 1991; bd. dirs. LWV Nebr., 1993—. Served to lt. USNR, 1944-46, PTO. Mem. LWV (bd. dirs. Nebr. 1993—), Am. Agrl. Econs. Assn., Internat. Assn. Agrl. Economists (travel fellow 1958, 64), Open Forum (pres. 1991-92), Fifty-Fifty Club, Norden Club (pres. 1985-87), Farm House, Sigma Xi, Phi Kappa Phi, Gamma Sigma Delta, Phi Delta Kappa. Democrat. Presbyterian. Avocations: golf; skiing; woodwork; Civil War history; gardening. Home: 5811 Margo Dr Lincoln NE 68510-5029

OTWELL, RALPH MAURICE, retired newspaper editor; b. Hot Springs, Ark., June 17, 1926; s. Walter Clement and Pearl Oda (Tisdale) O.; m. Janet Barbara Smith, July 18, 1953; children—Brian Thornton, Douglas Keith, David Smith. Student, U. Ark., 1947-48; B.S., Northwestern U., 1951; postgrad. (Nieman fellow), Harvard, 1959-60. Reporter, telegraph editor So. Newspapers, Inc., Hot Springs, 1943-44, 47; asst. city editor Chgo. Sun-Times, 1953-59, news editor, 1959-63, asst. mng. editor, 1963-65, asst. to editor, 1965-68, mng. editor, 1968-76, editor, 1976-80, exec. v.p., editor, 1980-84; Mgmt. bd. newspaper div. Field Enterprises, Inc., 1967-84; lectr. Medill Sch. Journalism, Northwestern U., 1955—; charter mem. Nat. News Council, 1973-80. Trustee Garrett-Evang. Theol. Sem., 1965-79; Mem. nat. bd. Christian Social Concerns, United Meth. Ch., 1968-72; mem. bd. Community Renewal Soc., 1987-90, Chgo. Reporter, 1987-90, student publs. Northwestern U., 1968-72. Served to 1st lt. AUS, 1944-47, 51-53. Recipient

Page One award Chgo. Newspaper Guild, 1964; named Ill. Journalist of Year No. Ill. U., 1974. Mem. Am. Soc. Newspaper Editors (chmn. ethics com. 1976-77), AP Mng. Editors Assn., Soc. Profl. Journalists (dir. 1966-71, sec. 1971-72, v.p. 1972-73, pres. 1973-74), Northwestern U. Alumni Assn. (dir. 1965-68, 91-93, sec. 1993-94, Merit award 1969, Svc. award 1995), Sigma Delta Chi (pres. 1987-89), Kappa Tau Alpha, Econ. Club, Headline Club (pres. Chgo. chpt. 1965-66), Harvard Club Chgo., Chgo. Press Club (dir. 1968-77), Northwestern Club. Home: 2750 Hurd Ave Evanston IL 60201-1268

OUDENS, GERALD FRANCIS, architect, architectural firm executive; b. Manchester, N.H., May 18, 1934; s. John and Louise Esther (Wagner) O.; m. Monica Elizabeth Wohlfert, June 16, 1962; children: Elizabeth Marian, Matthew Thomas, Katherine Frances. BA in Architecture cum laude, Yale U., 1956, MArch, 1958. Registered arch., D.C., Va., Md., Pa., Ind., Nat. Coun. Archtl. Registration Bds. Intern architect Koehler & Isaak, Manchester, 1955-58; staff architect Office Surgeon Gen. USAF, Washington, 1958-61; assoc. Metcalf & Assocs., Washington, 1961-69; prin. Oudens & Knoop Architects, PC, Chevy Chase, Md., 1970—; vis. critic, thesis advisor dept. architecture Cath. U. Am., 1968-88; mem. adv. com. acad. med. ctr. study sch. architecture Rice U., 1975; mem. ambulatory care adv. panel U.S. VA, 1974-75; mem. adv. panel No. Ind. Health Systems Agy., 1977-81, AIA Rsch. Corp., 1978, Nat. Inst. Bldg. Scis., 1982-88; mem. design award juries Modern Healthcare Ann. Design Awards, 1992, Soc. for Critical Care Medicine/AACN/AIA ICU Design Awards, 1992-94, AIA Health Facilities Rev. Jury, 1995; presenter in field. Principal works include NIH Master Plan, Bethesda, Md., Sibley Meml. Hosp., Washington, D.C., Washington Adventist Hosp., Takoma Park, Md., Martha Jefferson Hosp., Charlottesville, Va., Marion (Ind.) Gen. Hosp., Humana Lucerne Hosp., Orlando, Fla., Hosp. de Pedregal, Mexico City, Fairfax Hosp., Falls Church, Va., Humana Audubon Hosp. and Heart Inst., Louisville, Ky., Humana Greensboro (N.C.) Hosp., Centre Universitaire des Sciences de la Sante, Yaounde, Cameroon, Washington Home and Hospice, Washington, D.C., Stoddard Bapt. Home, Washington, D.C., Cuttington U. Coll., Suakoko, Liberia, Escuela Agricola Panamericana, El Zamorano, FM, Honduras, others; contbr. articles to profl. jours. Recipient Nat. Capital Architecture award D.C. Coun. Engring. and Archtl. Socs./Washington Acad. Scis., 1961. Mem. AIA (acad. on architecture for health 1971—, past pres. and dir., nat. healthcare policy task force 1993—, mem. adv. com. Am. Collegiate Schs. Architecture coun. on archtl. rsch. 1994—, Henry Adams award 1958, Honor award Ky. chpt., 1980, Outstanding Leadership and Commitment to Healthcare Design award 1987, Merit award Washington Met. chpt. 1989, Citations for Design Excellence 1988, 1990, Am. Hosp. Assn. Grad. Fellowship Rev. Panel), Am. Hosp. Assn. (mem. faculty continuing edn. insts. 1972-76, adv. panel 1978), Internat. Hosp. Fedn., Forum for Health Care Planing. Office: Oudens & Knoop Architects PC 2 Wisconsin Cir Chevy Chase MD 20815-7003

OUELLET, ANDRÉ, former Canadian goverment official, corporate executive; b. St. Pascal, Quebec, Canada, Apr. 6, 1939; s. Albert and Rita (Turgeon) O.; m. Edith Carmichael, July 17, 1965; children: Sonia, Jean, Olga, Pierre. Postmaster gen. Canada, 1972; min. consumer and corp. affairs Canadian Parl., 1974, min. state urban affairs, 1974, min. public works, 1978, acting min. labor, 1978; min. consumer and corp. affairs, postmaster gen. Canada, 1980, min. resp. for Can. Post Corp., 1981, min. labor, 1983, min. resp. Crown Corps., 1984, min. foreign affairs, 1993-96; chmn. bd. Can. Post Corp., Ottawa, 1996—. Elected first mem. Parliament, 1967-93, Min. of the Crown. Office: Canada Post Corp, Ste N1250, 2701 Riverside Dr, Ottawa, ON Canada K1A 0B1

OUELLETTE, BERNARD CHARLES, pharmaceutical company executive; b. Windsor, Ont., Can., July 8, 1936; s. Edouard and Alice (Parent) O.; m. Mary Catherine Robert, Sept. 8, 1962; children: Timothy, Michelle, Maureen, Catherine, Suzanne. B.A., U. Windsor, 1964; M.B.A., Wayne State U., 1968; AMP, Harvard U., 1987. Pres. North York (Toronto) Cancer Soc., 1975-77; v.p. bus. devel. Connaught Biosciences Inc., 1975-78; exec. v.p. Winthrop Labs. Ltd., Toronto, Ont., Can., 1978-79; pres. Winthrop Labs. Ltd., 1979-80; exec. v.p. Winthrop Labs., N.Y.C., 1981-82, pres., 1982-83; pres. Pharm. Group Sterling Drug, Inc., N.Y.C., 1983-88, group v.p., 1984-88; pres., chief exec. officer Praxis Biologics Inc., Rochester, N.Y., 1988-89, also bd. dirs.; chief exec. officer Horus Therapeutics (formerly Biocare, Inc.), Rochester, 1989-90, chmn., pres., chief exec. officer, 1990—. Mem. Am. Mgmt. Assn. Roman Catholic. Home: 15 Merrycreek Crossing Pittsford NY 14534-1881

OUGHTON, JAMES HENRY, JR., corporate executive, farmer; b. Chgo., May 14, 1913; s. James H. and Barbara (Corbett) O.; student Dartmouth Coll., 1931-35; m. Jane Boyce, Jan. 23, 1940 (dec.); children: Diana (dec.), Carol Oughton Biondi, Pamela Oughton Armstrong, Deborah Oughton Callahan. Pres., dir. L.E. Keeley Co., Dwight, Ill., 1936—, Nev. Corp.; past adminstr. The Keeley Inst., Dwight, 1938-66; dir. 1st Nat. Bank of Dwight, Ill., 1939—, Ill. Valley Investment Co., 1945-89; farmer, farm mgr., livestock feeder, Ill.; sec., dir. Dwight Indsl. Assn., 1958-93; past mem. Ill. Ho. of Reps. Co-chmn. 1st Indsl. Conf. on Alcoholism, 1948; chmn. Midwest Seminar on Alcoholism for Pastors, 1957, 58, 59, 60; chmn. adv. bd. Ill. Dept. Corrections; chmn. Gov.'s Task Force on Mental Health Adminstrn., 1971-72; mem. adv. bd. Ill. Dept. Mental Health; dir., mem. exec. bd. W.D. Boyce council Boy Scouts Am.; del. 31st Internat. Congress on Alcoholism and Drug Dependence, Bangkok, 1975; mem. Internat. Council on Alcohol and Addictions, Lausanne, Switzerland, 1977; mem. Ill. Trade and Investment Mission to Japan and Korea, 1985; mem. adv. council Small Bus., Fed. Reserve Bank Chgo., 1985-86. Served as lt. (j.g.) USNR, 1944-46; PTO. Republican. Episcopalian. Clubs: Univ., Union League (Chgo.). Address: 103 W South St Dwight IL 60420-1329

OUREDNIK, PATRICIA ANN, accountant; b. Balt., Oct. 5, 1962; d. John Matthew and Patricia Ann (Ruzicka) O. BS in Acctg., U. Balt., 1984; MS in Mgmt. Info. Sys., Fla. Inst. Tech., 1991. CPA, Md. Acctg. clk. Cello Corp., Havre de Grace, Md., 1981-84; staff acct. KPMG Peat Marwick, Balt., 1984-85; audit supv. Coughlin & Mann, Chartered, Bel Air, Md., 1985-88, 89-92; CFO Kidde Sys., White Marsh, Md., 1988-89, FAMIC Corp., Columbia, Md., 1994—, Top Tools Automation Sys., Timonium, Md., 1992-93; contr. CRMA, Balt., 1995—. Cons. Shepherd's Clinic, Balt., 1992—. Mem. Md. Assn. CPAs, Assn. Retarded Citizens. Republican. Methodist. Home: 1618 Bramble Ct Bel Air MD 21015-1560 Office: CRMA 100 E Pratt St Baltimore MD 21202

OURIEFF, ARTHUR JACOB, psychiatrist; b. Boston, Jan. 20, 1924; s. James Leonard and Sigrid (Lewis) O.; m. Vernie Gusack, Aug. 17, 1947; children: Bruce, Martha, Sally. Student, Amherst Coll., 1941-43; MD, Harvard U., 1946. Intern Bellevue Hosp., N.Y.C., 1946-47; resident U. Ill., Chgo., 1947-51; psychoanalyst, psychiatrist L.A. Inst. Psychoanalysis with Adults and Children, 1953-59, pvt. practice, L.A., 1953—; asst. prof. psychiatry UCLA Med. Sch., L.A., 1970—. Lt (j.g.) USNR, 1949-51. Child Psychiatry fellow Inst. Juvenile Rsch., Chgo., 1951-53. Fellow Am. Psychoanalytic Assn.; mem. Am. Psychiat. Assn., So. Calif. Soc. Child Psychiatry. Democrat. Avocations: skiing, jogging, mountain climbing, Treking, travel. Home and Office: 320 N Cliffwood Ave Los Angeles CA 90049

OURSLER, FULTON, JR., editor-in-chief, writer; b. West Falmouth, Mass., June 27, 1932; s. Fulton and Grace (Perkins) O.; m. Anne Noel Nevill, Nov. 29, 1954; children: Theresa Noel, Fulton III, Mark Nevill, James Randall, Carroll Grace. B.A., Georgetown U., 1954. With Reader's Digest, Pleasantville, N.Y., 1956-87, book editor, 1968-70, sr. staff editor, 1970-72, asst. mng. editor, 1973, mng. editor, 1974-82, exec. editor, 1982-85, dep. editor-in-chief, 1986-87; editor-in-chief Guideposts mag., 1992—; editor-in-chief, founding editor Angels on Earth mag., 1995—. Established: Fulton Oursler Meml. Collection, Georgetown U. Library.; editor: (commentary) Behold This Dreamer, 1964. Bd. dirs. Georgetown U. Library Assocs. Served with U.S. Army, 1954-56. Mem. Friends of the Nyacks, Cath. Actors Guild, Univ. Club. Home: 2 Laveta Pl Nyack NY 10960-1604 Office: Reader's Digest Pleasantville NY 10570 *Man makes two journeys in life: one in matter, the other in spirit. The first journey is outward and manifest: it leads to family, society, and career. The second journey is inward and invisible: it leads to the kingdom of God. The first journey is limited by logic, flesh, and time. The second is infinite, and its pathway is paradox. Self-preservation is the strongest instinct on the first journey: freedom, maturity, self-knowledge, power, and abundance seem to be important goals. But on the second journey, one learns that to find our truest selves, we must lose the sense of self: that to grow we must become as a child: that freedom is won by surrender, that the one counts for more than the many, that the meek are powerful, and the poor are rich. On both journeys, to gain life one must lose it, and be reborn.*

OUSSANI, JAMES JOHN, stapling company executive; b. Bklyn., Jan. 3, 1920; s. John Thomas and Clara (Tager) O.; m. Lorraine G. Tutundgy, Apr. 25, 1954; children: James J., Gregory P., Rita C. B.M.E., Pratt Inst., 1938-42; J.D. (hon.), Coll. Boca Raton, Lynn U.; LLD. Dir. research, mfg. Supertronic Co., N.Y.C., 1943-46; sr. partner Perl-Oussani Machine Mfg. Co., N.Y.C., 1946-49; founder The Staplex Co., Bklyn., 1949, pres., 1949—; exec. dir. Lourdes Realty Corp.; dir. Junios Corp.; producer air sampling equipment for radioactive fallout AEC, 1951—. Mem. Bur. Research Air Pollution Control, Pres.'s Council on Youth Opportunity, Cardinal's Com. for Edn.; trustee Ch. of Virgin Mary; bd. dirs. St. Joan Arc Found., Boca Raton; founding mem. Lumen Christi-Palm Beach Diocese; founder, bd. dirs. Oussani Found.; founder James J. & Lorraine G. Oussani Scholarship Fund, Coll. Boca Raton; mem. cardinal's com. of laity, bishop's com. of laity; mem. Lumen Christi Found.; bd. overseers Lynn U., Boca Raton. Recipient Blue Ribbon Mining award, Sch. Mgmt. award, Aerospace Pride Achievement award; installed Knight of Jerusalem. Mem. Adminstrv. Mgmt. Soc., Office Adminstrn. Assn., Nat. Stationery and Office Equipment AssOffice Equipment Assn., Office Execs. Assn., Nat. Office Machine Mfg. Assn., Nat. Office Machine Dealers Assn., Nat. Office Products Assn., Bus. Equipment Mfrs. Assn., Our Lady Perpetual Help Holy Name Soc., Knights of Holy Sepulchre, Knights of St. Gregory, Knights of Malta, Rotary, Salaam Club, Mahopac Golf Club (Lake Mahopac, N.Y.), Internat. Club of Boca Raton, Boca Raton Hotel and Resort Club. Inventor automatic electric stapling machine. Patentee in field. Office: 777 5th Ave Brooklyn NY 11232-1626

OUTCALT, DAVID LEWIS, academic administrator, mathematician, educator; b. Los Angeles, Jan. 30, 1935; s. Earl Kinyon and Alberta Estes Ferguson O.; m. Marcia Lee Beach, July 1, 1956; children—Jeffrey David, Kevin Douglas, Gregory Mark, Eric Matthew. B.A. in Math., Pomona Coll., 1956; M.A. in Math., Claremont Grad. Sch., 1958; Ph.D. in Math., Ohio State U., 1963; D.Pub. Adminstrn. (hon.), Kyung Hee U., Korea, 1984. Asst. prof. math. Clarement McKenna Coll., 1962-64; asst. prof. to prof. math. U. Calif.-Santa Barbara, 1964-80, chmn. dept. math., 1969-72, dean instrnl. devel., 1977-80; vice chancellor acad. affairs U. Alaska, Anchorage, 1980-81, prof. math., 1980-86, chancellor, 1981-86; prof. natural and applied sci. U. Wis., Green Bay, 1986-93, chancellor, 1986-93, Hendrickson prof. econ. devel., 1994—; pres. Mid-Continent athletic conf., 1990-91. Author math. textbooks; contbr. articles on math. and higher edn. to profl. jours. Moderator bd. trustees Humana Hosp. Anchorage, 1982-83; mem. exec. bd. Western Alaska coun. Boy Scouts Am., 1982-86, Bay-Lakes coun., 1987—, v.p. exploring, 1988-92, v.p. ops., 1992-93, pres., 1993-94; mem. Anchorage Symphony bd., 1986, Green Bay Symphony Bd., 1988—, mem. Weidner Ctr. Presents Bd., 1994—. Grantee USAF Office Sci. Research, 1964-71, U. Calif., 1975-78, NSF, 1976-79. Mem. Math. Assn. Am., Internat. Assn. Univ. Pres.'s (exec. com. 1988—, vice chair N.Am. coun. 1988-94, newsletter editor 1994-95), Greater Green Bay C. of C. (advance bd. 1987—, bd. dirs. 1991-94, 95-96), Brown County Indsl. Devel. (pres. bd. dirs. 1994—), Rotary, Sigma Xi. Mem. Congregational Ch. Home: PO Box 89 Athelstane WI 54104-0089

OUTHWAITE, LUCILLE CONRAD, ballerina, educator; b. Peoria, Ill., Feb. 26, 1909; d. Frederick Albert and Della (Cornett) Conrad; m. Leonard Outhwaite, Mar. 1, 1936 (dec. 1978); children—Ann Outhwaite Maurer, Lynn Outhwaite Pulsifer. Student, U. Nebr., 1929-30, Mills Coll., 1931-32; student piano, Paris, 1933-35, Legat Sch., London, 1934, N.Y.C. Ballet, N.Y.C., 1936-41, Royal Ballet Sch., London, 1957-59. Tchr. ballet Perry Mansfield, Steamboat Springs, Colo., 1932, Cape Playhouse, Dennis, Mass., 1937-41, Jr. League, N.Y.C., 1937-41, King Coit Sch., N.Y.C., 1937-41; toured with Am. Ambassador Ballet, Europe and S. Am., 1933-35; owner, tchr. dance sch., Oyster Bay, N.Y., 1949-57. Producer, choreographer ballets Alice in Wonderland, 1951, Pied Piper of Hamlin, 1952. Author: Birds in Flight, 1992, Flowers in the Wind, 1994. Mem. English Speaking Union, Preservation Soc., Alliance Française, Delta Gamma. Republican. Methodist. Clubs: Mills Coll., Spouting Rock Beach, Clambake (Newport, R.I.). Office: Beachmound Bellevue Ave Newport RI 02840

OUTKA, GENE HAROLD, philosophy and Christian ethics educator; b. Sioux Falls, S.D., Feb. 24, 1937; s. Harold Irvin and Gertrude Anne (Elliott) O.; m. Carole Lee DeVore, June 26, 1960 (div. 1982); children: Paul Harold, Elizabeth Noelle; m. Susan Jane Owen, Dec. 29, 1984; 1 child, Jacqueline Elliott. B.A., U. Redlands, 1959; B.D., Yale U., 1962, M.A., 1964, Ph.D., 1967; L.H.D., U. Redlands, 1978. Instr. Princeton U., N.J., 1965-66, lectr., 1966-67, asst. prof., 1967-73, assoc. prof., 1973-75; assoc. prof. Yale U., New Haven, 1975-81, Dwight prof. philosophy and Christian ethics, 1981—; chair dept. religious studies, 1992-95; dir. resdl. seminar for coll. tchrs. NEH, New Haven, 1977-78; Mary Farnum Brown lectr. Haverford Coll., Pa., 1977; mem. faculty workshop on teaching of ethics Hastings Inst. of Soc., Ethics and Life Scis., Princeton, N.J., 1979; Merrick lectr. Ohio Wesleyan U., Delaware, Ohio, 1983; Williamson Meml. lectr. Meth. Theol. Sch. in Ohio, 1986. Author: Agape: An Ethical Analysis, 1972; co-editor, contbr.: Norm and Context In Christian Ethics, 1968, Religion and Morality, 1973, Prospects for a Common Morality, 1992; editorial bd. Jour. Religious Ethics. Service fellow office of spl. projects Health Services and Mental Health Adminstrn., HEW, Washington, 1972-73; mem. adv. com. social ethics Inst. Medicine Nat. Acad. Scis., 1975-77. Fellow Am. Council Learned Socs., 1968-69; fellow NEH, 1979-80, Woodrow Wilson Internat. Ctr. for Scholars, 1983; vis. scholar Kennedy Inst. of Ethics, Georgetown U., 1972-73. Mem. Am. Acad. Religion, Soc. Christian Ethics (bd. dirs.). ,Office: Yale U Dept Religious Studies 320 Temple St New Haven CT 06511-6601

OVENS, MARI CAMILLE, school system administrator, dietitian; b. Spokane, Wash., June 18, 1954; d. Harold Chester and May Eloise (Gundry) Chapman; m. Dana Preston Ovens, Dec. 18, 1985; children: Dylan Preston, Delaney Camille. BS in Dietetics, Ea. Wash. U., 1976; MS in Home Econs., Wash. State U., 1979. Registered dietitian, Wash. Dietary coord. City of Vancouver, Wash., 1978-83; clin. dietitian Eastmoreland Gen. Hosp., Portland, Oreg., 1983; supr. child nutrition Vancouver Sch. Dist. 37, 1983—; mem. culinary arts adv. bd. Clark Coll., Vancouver, 1983—; mem. task force Am. Heart Assns., Seattle, 1988—. Mem. Am. Sch. Food Svc. Assn., (registered dir., adminstr. III), Am. Dietetic Assn. (Recognized Young Dietitian of Yr. Wash. State 1983), Wash. Sch. Food Svc. Assn. (treas. 1989-91, trainer 1993—), Wash. State Dietetic Assn., Soroptimists (pres. Vancouver 1990-92). Office: Vancouver Sch Dist 37 PO Box 8937 Vancouver WA 98668-8937

OVERALL, JAMES CARNEY, JR., pediatrics laboratory medicine educator; b. Nashville, Sept. 27, 1937; s. James Carney and Evelyn Byrd (Duncan) O.; m. Marie Kathryn Pauli, Aug. 14, 1965; children: David, Paul. BS, Davidson Coll., 1959; MD, Vanderbilt U., 1963. Cert. pediatrics infectious diseases. Intern Vanderbilt U. Hosp., Nashville, 1963-64; resident Columbia Presbyn. Med. Ctr., N.Y.C., 1964-66; research assoc. Nat. Inst. Child Health, Bethesda, Md., 1966-68; instr. pediatrics Rochester, N.Y., 1968-70; asst. prof. pediatrics, microbiology U. Utah Sch. Med., Salt Lake City, 1970-74, assoc. prof. pediatrics, microbiology, 1974-79, prof. pediatrics, 1979—, prof. pathology, 1981—; chief pediatrics infectious diseases U. Utah Sch. Medicine, 1970-93, dir. virology course, 1980—, vice chmn. dept. pediatrics, 1982-92, med. dir. diagnostic virology lab., 1981—; bd. govs. Primary Children's Med. Ctr., Salt Lake City, 1976-78. Contbr. chpts. to textbooks, articles to profl. jours. vice moderator Holladay United Ch. Christ, Salt Lake City, 1982-85. Served to lt. comdr. USPHS, 1966-68. Recipient Investigator award Howard Hughes Med. Inst., 1974-80. Mem. Am. Pediatric Soc., Soc. Pediatric Rsch., Am. Soc. Virology, Infectious Diseases Soc. Am., Pan Am. Soc. for Clin. Virology (mem. coun.), Rapid Viral Diagnosis, Am. Bd. Pediatrics (sub-bd. for infectious diseases 1992-96), Am. Acad. Pediatrics (commn. on infectious diseases 1993—). United Ch. of Christ. Home: 896 18th Ave Salt Lake City UT 84103-3721 Office: Univ Utah Sch Med Dept Pediatrics Salt Lake City UT 84132

OVERBECK, GENE EDWARD, retired airline executive, lawyer; b. St. Louis, June 16, 1929; s. Harry C. and Edna (Kessler) O.; m. Patricia June Bay, Oct. 5, 1957; children: Richard, Thomas, Elizabeth, Katherine. B.A., U. Mich., 1951, J.D., 1953. Bar: Mich. 1953, Mo. 1954, N.Y. 1958, Tex. 1980. Asso. firm Sullivan & Cromwell, N.Y.C., 1957-59; gen. atty. Am. Airlines, 1959-67, v.p., gen. counsel, 1967-72, sr. v.p., 1972-90; dir. Stevens Internat., Inc. Served with AUS, 1954-57. Home: 4634 Charleston Terrace NW Washington DC 20007-1900

OVERBY, MONESSA MARY, clinical supervisor, counselor; b. Staples, Minn., Sept. 7, 1932; d. Joseph Melvin Overby and Marie Frances (Fellman) Vollstedt. BS, Coll. of St. Teresa, 1964; MS, Winona State U., 1978. Entered Franciscan Sisters, Roman Cath. Ch., 1953; nat. cert. counselor, Gestalt therapist, trainer. Elem. and jr. high tchr. Cath. Sch. System, Austin, Tracy, Lake City, Minn., 1955-67; sch. adminstr. McCahill Inst., Lake City, 1964-70; pastoral counselor and adult educator St. Edward's, Austin, Minn., 1970-76; adj. faculty and campus minister Winona (Minn.) State U., 1976-84; psychotherapist Family & Children's Ctr. and Human Devel. Assocs., La Crosse, Wis., 1978-84; family counselor Betty Ford Ctr., Rancho Mirage, Calif., 1987-89, clin. mgr. family and outpatient svcs., 1990—; workshop presenter in field. Mem. Am. Counseling Assn., Assn. for Specialists in Group Work, Minn. Assn. Specialists in Group Work (founding pres.). Democrat. Roman Catholic. Avocations: nursing home visitor, swimming, dog care, growing roses. Office: Betty Ford Ctr 39000 Bob Hope Dr Rancho Mirage CA 92270-3221

OVERBY, OSMUND RUDOLF, art historian, educator; b. Mpls., Nov. 8, 1931; s. Oscar Rudolph and Gertrude Christine (Boe) O.; m. Barbara Ruth Spande, Mar. 20, 1954; children: Paul, Katherine, Charlotte. B.A., St. Olaf Coll., 1953; B.Arch., U. Wash., 1958; M.A., Yale U., 1960, Ph.D., 1963. Asst. in instruction dept. of history of art Yale U., 1959-60, 61-62; architect Hist. Am. Bldgs. Survey, U.S. Nat. Park Service, 1960-61, summers 1959, 62, 63, 65, 68, 69, 70, 73, 85; lectr. dept. fine arts U. Toronto, Ont., Can., 1963-64; faculty dept. art history and archaeology U. Mo., Columbia, 1964—; dept. chmn. U. Mo., 1967-70, 75-77, prof. art history, 1979—, dir. Mus. of Art and Archaeology, 1977-83; vis. prof. dept. architecture U. Calif., Berkeley, 1980; Morgan prof. U. Louisville, 1989; bd. advisors Nat. Trust for Hist. Preservation, 1974-83; cons., panelist Nat. Endowment for Humanities, 1974—; bd. Mo. Mansion Preservation Commn., 1974-87; advisor Heritage/St. Louis Survey, 1974-76; counsellor to St. Louis Landmarks Assn., 1977—; chmn. Task Force on Hist. Preservation City of Columbia, 1977-78; cons. on hist. preservation; active Mo. Adv. Council on Hist. Preservation, 1967-82; lectr., exhibitor profl. confs. in field. Author: Historic American Buildings Survey, Rhode Island Catalog, 1972; co-author: Laclede's Landing, a History and Architectural Guide, 1977, The Saint Louis Old Post Office, A History and Architectural Guide to the Building and Its Neighborhood, 1979; co-author, editor: Illustrated Museum Handbook, A Guide to the Collections in the Museum of Art and Archaeology, University of Missouri-Columbia, 1982; editor in chief Buildings of the United States series; contbr. sects. to books, articles to profl. publs. in field. Served with U.S. Army, 1953-55. Recipient various fellowships and grants in field. Mem. Soc. Archtl. Historians (bd. dirs. 1968-73, 78-81, Jour. editor 1968-73, dir. Mo. Valley chpt., session chmn. ann. meeting 1976, v.p. 1982-86, pres. 1986-88, chmn. coms.), Mid-Continent Am. Studies Assn. (editorial bd. American Studies 1965-70), Midwest Art History Soc. (bd. 1975-78, gen. chmn. annual meeting 1977), Mid-Am. Coll. Art Assn. (session chmn. annual meeting 1975), Mo. Heritage Trust (pres. 1976-79, 81-83, bd. dirs. 1979—), Coll. Art Assn., Landmarks Assn. St. Louis, Soc. for Hist. Archaeology. Lutheran. Home: 1118 W Rollins Rd Columbia MO 65203-2221 Office: U Mo Dept Art History & Archaeology Columbia MO 65211

OVERFIELD, ROBERT EDWARD, physicist; b. Buffalo, Dec. 5, 1951; s. Russell Benton and Viola (Schavey) O.; m. Nancy Marie Dalesandro, Aug. 8, 1975; children: Brett Viola, Lindsay Grace, Anna Karina, Emily Patricia. BS in Physics, U. Rochester, 1974; PhD in Biophysics, U. Ill., 1979. Mech. engring. aide Xerox Corp., Webster, N.Y., 1974-75; grad. teaching and rsch. asst. U. Ill., Urbana, 1974-78, postdoctoral rsch. fellow, 1979-80; rsch. physicist Exxon Rsch. and Engring. Co., Linden, N.J., 1980-85; group leader hydrocarbon chemistry Exxon Rsch. and Engring. Co., Clinton, N.J., 1985-87; supr. analytical and materials Esso Resources Canada Ltd., Calgary, Alberta, 1987-91; mgr. oil sands R&D Imperial Oil Resources Ltd., Calgary, 1991-94; materials rsch. supr. Exxon Prodn. Rsch. Co., Houston, 1994—; chmn. organizing com. Canadian Oil Sands Network for R&D, Calgary, 1993-94. Contbr. articles to profl. jours. Eagle Scout Boy Scouts Am., Tonawanda, N.Y., 1966, asst. scoutmaster, 1970-74. Fellow NIH, 1975-78. Mem. Am. Chem. Soc. (divsn. petroleum chemistry). Achievements include several U.S. patents; development of innovation in molecular characterization used in heavy oil refining worldwide. Office: Exxon Prodn Rsch Co 3120 Buffalo Speedway Houston TX 77098-1806

OVERGAARD, MITCHELL JERSILD, lawyer; b. Chgo., Jan. 9, 1931; s. Kristen Mikkelsen and Rose Eunice (Jersild) O.; m. Joan Marquardt, Aug. 2, 1958; children: Wade, Kristin Bond, Neil. BA, U. Chgo., 1950, JD, 1953. Bar: Ill. 1957, U.S. Supreme Ct. 1975. Assoc. Dale, Haffner & Grow, Chgo., 1957-63; ptnr. Overgaard & Davis, Chgo., 1963—; Dir. Community Bank of Homewood-Flossmoor, Homewood, Ill., 1973-83. Trustee Village of Homewood, 1965-69, 85-95; commr. Homewood-Flossmoor Park Dist., 1969-77; past pres., bd. dirs. Family Svcs. and Mental Health Ctr. of South Cook County, Homewood Youth Coun.; bd. dirs. Ill. Philharm. Orch., 1992-95. With U.S. Army, 1953-56. Mem. Ill. Bar Assn., Chgo. Bar Assn. Mem. Reformed Ch. in America (elder). Home: 19137 Loomis Ave Homewood IL 60430-4431 Office: Overgaard & Davis 134 N La Salle St Chicago IL 60602-1086

OVERGAARD, ROBERT MILTON, religious organization administrator; b. Ashby, Minn., Nov. 6, 1929; s. Gust and Ella (Johnson) O.; m. Sally Lee Stephenson, Dec. 29, 1949; children: Catherine Jean Overgaard Thuleen, Robert Milton, Elizabeth Dianne Overgaard Almendinger, Barbara, Craig, David (dec.), Lori Overgaard Noack. Cert., Luth. Brethren Sem., 1954; BS, Mayville (N.D.) State U., 1959; MS, U. Oreg., 1970. Ordained to ministry Ch. Luth. Brethren Am., 1954. Pastor Elim Luth. Ch., Frontier, Sask., Can., 1954-57, Ebenezer Luth. Ch., Mayville, 1957-60, Immanuel Luth. Ch., Eugene, Oreg., 1960-63, 59th Street Luth. Ch., Bklyn., 1963-68, Immanuel Luth. Ch., Pasadena, Calif., 1969-73; exec. dir. world missions Ch. Luth. Brethren Am., Fergus Falls, Minn., 1973-86, pres., 1986—; Editor Faith and Fellowship, 1967-75. Home: 806 W Channing Ave Fergus Falls MN 56537-3221 Office: Ch Luth Brethren Am PO Box 655 Fergus Falls MN 56538-0655

OVERGAARD, WILLARD MICHELE, retired political scientist, jurisprudent; b. Montpelier, Idaho, Oct. 16, 1925; s. Elias Nielsen and Myrtle LaVerne (Humphrey) O.; m. Lucia Clare Cochrane, June 14, 1946; children: Eric Willard, Mark Fredrik, Alisa Claire. B.A., U. Oreg., 1949; Fulbright scholar, U. Oslo, 1949-50; M.A. (non-resident scholar 1954-55), U. Wis., Madison, 1955; Ph.D. in Polit. Sci. (adminstrv. fellow 1955-56, research fellow 1962-64), U. Minn., 1969. Instr., Soviet and internat. affairs Intelligence Sch., U.S. Army, Europe, 1956-62; dir. intelligence rsch. tng. program Intelligence Sch., U.S. Army, 1958-61; asst. prof. internat. affairs George Washington U., 1964-67; sr. staff polit. scientist Ops. Research Inst., U.S. Army Inst. Advanced Studies, Carlisle, Pa., 1967-70; assoc. prof. polit. sci., chmn. dept., dir. Internat. Studies Inst., Westminster Coll., New Wilmington, Pa., 1970-72; prof. polit. sci. and pub. law Boise (Idaho) State U., 1972-94, chmn. dept., 1972-87, acad. dir. M.P.A. degree program, personnel adminstr., mem. humanities council interdisciplinary studies in humanities, 1976-87, prof. of pub. law emeritus, 1994—, dir. Taft Inst. Seminars for Pub. Sch. Tchrs., 1985-87, coord. Legal Asst. Program, 1990-95; mem. comml. panel Am. Arbitration Assn., 1974—; mem. Consortium for Idaho's Future, 1974-75; adv. com. Idaho Statewide Tng. Program Local Govt. Ofcls., 1974-78; adv. group Gov. Idaho Task Force Local Govt., 1977; co-dir. Idaho State Exec. Inst., Office of Gov., 1979-83; grievance hearing officer City of Boise, 1981-85; arbitrator U.S. Postal Svc., 1988-90; cons. in field. Author: The Schematic System of Soviet Totalitarianism, 3 vols, 1961, Legal Norms and Normative Bases for the Progressive Development of International Law as Defined in Soviet Treaty Relations, 1945-64, 1969; co-author: The Communist Bloc in Europe, 1959; editor: Continuity and Change in International Politics, 1972; chief editor: Idaho Jour. Politics, 1974-76. Served with

USAAF, 1943-45; with AUS, 1951-54; ret. maj. USAR. Named Disting. Citizen of Idaho Idaho Statesman, 1979; named Outstanding Prof. of Sch. Social Scis. and Pub. Affairs, Boise State U., 1988. Mem. ABA (assoc.), Res. Officers Assn. (life). Home: 2023 S Five Mile Rd Boise ID 83709-2316

OVERHAUSER, ALBERT WARNER, physicist; b. San Diego, Aug. 17, 1925; s. Clarence Albert and Gertrude Irene (Pehrson) O.; m. Margaret Mary Casey, Aug. 25, 1951; children—Teresa, Catherine, Joan, Paul, John, David, Susan, Steven. A.B., U. Calif. at Berkeley, 1948, Ph.D., 1951; D.Sc. (hon.), U. Chgo., 1979. Research asso. U. Ill., 1951-53; asst. prof. physics Cornell U., 1953-56, asso. prof., 1956-58; supr. solid state physics Ford Motor Co., Dearborn, Mich., 1958-62; mgr. theoret. scis. Ford Motor Co., 1962-69, asst. dir. phys. scis., 1969-72, dir. phys. scis., 1972-73; prof. physics Purdue U., West Lafayette, Ind., 1973-74; Stuart disting. prof. physics Purdue U., 1974—. With USNR, 1944-46. Recipient Alexander von Humboldt sr. U.S. scientist award, 1979, Nat. Medal of Sci., Pres. of U.S., 1994. Fellow Am. Phys. Soc. (Oliver E. Buckley Solid State Physics prize 1975), Am. Acad. Arts and Scis.; mem. NAS. Home: 236 Pawnee Dr West Lafayette IN 47906-2115 Office: Purdue U Dept Of Physics West Lafayette IN 47907

OVERHOLT, HUGH ROBERT, lawyer, retired army officer; b. Beebe, Ark., Oct. 29, 1933; s. Harold R. and Cuma E. (Hall) O.; m. Laura Annell Arnold, May 5, 1961; children: Sharon, Scott. Student, Coll. of Ozarks, 1951-53; B.A., U. Ark., 1955, LL.B., 1957. Bar: Ark. 1957. Commd. 1st lt. U.S. Army, 1957, advanced through grades to maj. gen., 1981; chief Criminal Law Div., JAG Sch., Charlottesville, Va., 1971-73; chief personnel, plans and tng. Office of JAG, U.S. Army, Washington, 1973-75; staff judge adv. XVIII Airborne Corps, Ft. Bragg, N.C., 1976-78; spl. asst. for legal and selected policy matters Office of Dep. Asst., 1978-79; asst. judge adv. gen. for mil. law Office of JAG, Washington, 1979-81; asst. judge adv. gen. Office of JAG, 1981-85, judge adv. gen, 1985-89. Notes and comment editor Ark. Law Rev, 1956-57. Decorated Army Meritorious Service medal with oak leaf cluster, Army Commendation medal with 2 oak leaf clusters., Legion of Merit, Def. Meritorious Service medal, D.S.M. Mem. ABA, N.C. Bar Assn., Ark. Bar Assn., Assn. U.S. Army, Delta Theta Phi, Omicron Delta Kappa, Sigma Pi. Presbyterian. Office: Ward and Smith 1001 College Ct New Bern NC 28563

OVERHOLT, MILES HARVARD, III, management consultant, family therapist; b. L.A., July 7, 1948; s. Miles Harvard and Jessie Louise (Foster) O.; m. Deborah Jean Robinson, Nov. 22, 1970; 1 child, Rebecca Robinson. BA, Lafayette Coll., 1970; MSW, U. Pa., 1976, D in Social Work, 1979. Cert. social worker; lic. marriage and family therapist, N.J.; cert. mgmt. cons.; cert. clin. hypnotherapist. Youth dir. Camden County YMCA, Haddonfield, N.J., 1970-71; dir. multi-service ctr. Community YMCA, Red Bank, N.J., 1972-74; indsl. cons. NE Community Mental Health/Mental Retardation, Phila., 1977; therapist Marriage and Family Therapy Assns., Wilingboro, Marlton, N.J., 1976-82; mgmt. cons., owner Ambler and Overholt Cons., Inc., Cherry Hill, N.J., 1979-85; therapist, ptnr. Affiliated Counseling and Therapy Assocs., Moorestown, N.J., 1982—; owner, cons. Applied Orgnl. Devel., Inc., Palmyra, N.J., 1985-90; instr. Burlington County Coll., Willingboro, 1978-80; mem. co-adj. faculty Rutgers U., 1978-80; prin. Riverton Mgmt. Cons. Group (formerly Comm. Link Co.), 1990—. Author: Building Flexible Organizations: A People Centered Approach, 1996; contbr. articles to profl. jours. Mem. Phila. Human Resource Planning Group Bd., 1996—. Mott scholar YMCA, 1974-75. Mem. NASW, Inst. Mgmt. Cons. (bd. dirs. Phila. chpt. 1987, nat. bd. dirs. 1988-91), Assn. Mgmt. Cons. (bd. dirs. 1985—, nat. conf. chmn. 1985, regional v.p. 1986-88, pres. 1988-90), Am. Assn. Marriage and Family Therapy (editor N.J. newsletter 1989), Coun. Cons. Orgns. (bd. dirs. 1989-93, sec., officer 1991-93), APICS (mem. nat. planning com. 1996—). Avocations: running, model trains. Office: Riverton Mgmt Cons Group 303 E Broad St Palmyra NJ 08065-1607

OVERMAN, DEAN LEE, lawyer, investor, author; b. Cook County, Ill., Oct. 9, 1943; s. Harold Levon and Violet Elsa (True) O.; m. Linda Jane Olsen, Sept. 6, 1969; children: Elizabeth True, Chrstiana Hart. BA, Hope Coll., 1965; student, Princeton Sem. and U., 1965-66; JD, U. Calif., Berkeley, 1969; postgrad. in bus., U. Chgo., 1974, U. Calif. Bar: Ill. 1969, D.C. 1977. Assoc. to ptnr. D'Ancona, Pflaum et al., Chgo., 1970-75; White House fellow, asst. to v.p. Nelson Rockefeller, Washington, 1975-76; assoc. dir. Domestic Council The White House, Washington, 1976-77; sr. ptnr. Winston & Strawn, Washington, 1977—; cons. White House; spl. counsel to Gov. James Thompson, Springfield, Ill.; adj. faculty in secured financing U. Va. Law Sch., Charlottesville; vice chmn. J.F. Forstmann Co.; chmn. Holland nvestment Co.; adj. fellow Ctr. for Strategic and Internat. Studies, 1993-95; vis. scholar, officer Harvard U., 1994-95. Author: Toward a National Policy on State and Local Government Finance, 1976, Effective Writing Tecniques, 1980, (with others) Financing Equipment, 1973, Sales and Financing Under the Revised UCC, 1975; monthly newspaper column Chgo. Daily Law Bull.; contbr. articles to profl. jours. Commencement spkr. Hope Coll., Holland, Mich., 1978; bd. dirs. Internat. Bus. Inst., White House Fellows Assn., Cities for Schs., Inc.; adv. bd. The Beacon Group; former bd. dirs. U.S. Decathlon Assn. Reginald Heber Smith fellow U. Pa., 1969-70. Mem. Menta, Intertel, ALA, Ill. Bar Assn., D.C. Bar Assn., Chgo. Bar Assn., Met. Club (D.C.), Internat. Philos. Enquiry, Triple Nine Soc., Burning Tree Club (Bethesda, Md.), Country Club (Bethesda), Harvard Club of N.Y.C., Macatawa (Mich.) Bay Yacht Club. Office: Winston & Strawn 1400 L St NW Washington DC 20005-3509

OVERMAN, GLENN DELBERT, college dean emeritus; b. Camden, Ark., Apr. 23, 1916; s. George D. and Mattie D. (Scott) O.; m. Roberta Marie Thomas, May 20, 1939; children—Priscilla Ann, George Dan. B.S., Central State U., Edmond, Okla., 1937; M.S., Okla. State U., 1946; D.B.A., Ind. U., 1954. Cert. for labor arbitration Fed. Mediation and Conciliation Service, also Am. Arbitration Assn. Tchr. bus. high sch. Fairfax, Okla., 1937-39; Okla. rep. South-Western Publishing Co., 1939-42; dir. Sch. Intensive Bus. Tng., Okla. State U. Coll. Bus., 1946-50; dean Oklahoma City U. Sch. Bus., 1952-56; dean Ariz. State U. Coll. Bus. Adminstrn., 1956-85, dean emeritus, 1985—; hon. prof. Autonomous U. Guadalajara, Mex., 1990—; mem. Dept. Navy, Naval Audit Svc. U.S.A., 1972-75. Author: Economics Concepts Everyone Should Know, 1956. Mem. law adv. bd. S.W. Found. Med. Rsch. and Edn.; mem. U.S. Office Edn. Appeal Bd., 1985-88. Served to lt. (s.g.), Supply Corps USNR, 1942-46. Mem. Soc. Advancement Mgmt., Financial Execs. Inst., Systems and Procedures Assn. Am., Am. Marketing Assn., Newcomen Soc. Am., Red Red Rose, Am. Right of Way Assn., Beta Gamma Sigma, Delta Sigma Pi, Pi Sigma Epsilon, Lambda Chi Alpha, Phi Kappa Phi, Delta Pi Epsilon, Phi Delta Kappa, Alpha Phi Sigma, Kappa Delta Pi, Delta Nu Alpha. Methodist. Home: 512 E Fairmont Dr Tempe AZ 85282-3723

OVERMAN, LARRY EUGENE, chemistry educator; b. Chgo., Mar. 9, 1943; s. Lemoine Emerson and Dorothy Jane (Riggin) O.; m. Joanne Louise Dewey, June 5, 1966; children: Michael, Jackie. BA in Chemistry, Earlham Coll., 1965; PhD in Organic Chemistry, U. Wis., 1969. Asst. prof. chemistry U. Calif., Irvine, 1971-76, assoc. prof. chemistry, 1976-79, prof. chemistry, 1979—, chair dept. chemistry, 1990-93, disting. prof. chemistry, 1994—; bd. dirs. Organic Reactions, 1993—; mem. sci. adv. bd. Pharmacopeia, Inc., 1993—. Bd. editors Organic Reactions, 1984—, Organic Synthesis, 1986-94; mem. editl. adv. bd. Ann. Reports in Hetero Chem., 1989—, Synlett, 1989—, Jour. Am. Chem. Soc., 1996—, Chem. Revs., 1996—; mem. consulting editors Tetrahedron Publs., 1995—. NIH fellow, 1969-71, A.P. Sloan Found. fellow, 1975-77; Arthur C. Cope scholar, 1989; Guggenheim fellow, 1993-94; recipient Sr. Scientist award Alexander von Humboldt Found., 1985-87, Jacob Javits award Nat. Inst. Neurol. Sci., 1985-91, 92—. Fellow NAS, Am. Acad. Arts and Scis.; mem. Am. Chem. Soc. (exec. com. organic divsn., Creative Work in Synthetic Organic Chemistry award 1995), Japanese Chem. Soc., Swiss Chem. Soc., German Chem. Soc., Royal Soc. Chemistry. Achievements include research in new methods for organic synthesis, natural products synthesis, medicinal chemistry. Office: U Calif Irvine Dept Chemistry Irvine CA 92717-2025

OVERMYER, DANIEL LEE, Asian studies educator; b. Columbus, Ohio, Aug. 20, 1935; s. Elmer Earl and Bernice Alma (Hesselbart) O.; m. Estella Velazquez, June 19, 1965; children—Rebecca Lynn, Mark Edward. B.A., Westmar Coll., LeMars, Iowa, 1957; B.D., Evang. Theol. Sem., Naperville, Ill., 1960; M.A., U. Chgo., 1966, Ph.D., 1971. Pastor Evangel. United Brethren Ch., Chgo., 1960-64; asst. prof. dept. religion Oberlin Coll., Ohio, 1970-73; prof. Asian studies U. B.C., Vancouver, Can., 1973—, acting head religious studies, 1984-85, head Asian studies, 1986-91; vis. prof. U. Heidelberg, 1993; prof. Chinese U. Hong Kong, 1996—. Author: Folk Buddhist Religion, 1976; Religions of China, 1986; (with David Jordan) The Flying Phoenix, 1986. Contbr. articles to encys. and profl. jours. Chmn. Sch. Consultative Com., Vancouver, 1976-77; coord. Vancouver Boys Soccer League, 1979-81; adult edn. coord. United Ch. Can., Vancouver, 1981-84; co-chmn. Endowment Lands Regional Park Com., 1987-90; co-chair China and Inner Asia Coun., Assn. Asian Studies, 1992—. With USNR, 1953-61. Recipient Killam faculty rsch. prize U. B.C., 1986; NEH fellow, 1978, 79, China Rsch. fellow, 1981, sr. fellow coun. humanities Princeton U., 1983, Wang Inst. Grad. Studies fellow, 1985-86. Fellow Royal Soc. Can.; mem. Soc. Study Chinese Religions (pres. 1985-88), Assn. Asian Studies, Can. Asian Studies Assn. Democrat. Methodist. Avocations: photography, swimming, hiking, gardening. Home: 3393 W 26th Ave V, Vancouver, BC Canada V6S 1N4 Office: U BC, Dept Asian Studies, Vancouver, BC Canada V6T 1Z2

OVERSETH, OLIVER ENOCH, physicist, educator; b. N.Y.C., May 11, 1928; s. Oliver Enoch and Ione (Johnson) O.; m. Anneke deBruyn, Aug. 28, 1954 (divorced); children—Alison, Tenley. B.S., U. Chgo., 1953; Ph.D., Brown U., 1958. Instr. physics Princeton, 1957-60; mem. faculty U. Mich., Ann Arbor, 1961—; prof. physics U. Mich., 1968—; assoc. physicist Cern, Geneva, 1983—. Office: Cern PPE Div, CH-1211 Geneva Switzerland

OVERSTREET, JIM, public relations executive; b. Savannah, Ga., Dec. 11, 1947. Reporter Atlanta Constitution, 1967-69; asst. sports editor Marietta Daily Jour., 1969-73; mktg. dir. Lake Lanier Islands Resorts, 1973-77; gen. mgr. Harlequin Theatre, 1977-78; acct. exec. Cohn & Wolfe, 1978-80, acct. supr., 1980-83, dir. acct. svc., 1983-84, exec. v.p., gen. mgr., 1984-92, vice chmn., gen. mgr., 1993—. Office: Cohn & Wolfe 225 Peachtree St NE Atlanta GA 30303-1701

OVERTON, BENJAMIN FREDERICK, state supreme court justice; b. Green Bay, Wis., Dec. 15, 1926; s. Benjamin H. and Esther M. (Wiese) O.; m. Marilyn Louise Smith, June 9, 1951; children: William Hunter, Robert Murray, Catherine Louise. B.S. in Bus. Adminstrn., U. Fla., 1951, J.D., 1952; LL.D. (hon.), Stetson U., 1975, Nova U., 1977; LL.M., U. Va., 1984. Bar: Fla. 1952. With Office Fla. Atty. Gen., 1952; with firms in St. Petersburg, Fla., 1952-64; city atty. St. Petersburg Beach, Fla., 1954-57; circuit judge 6th Jud. Circuit Fla., 1964-74, chief judge, 1968-71; chmn. Fla. Conf. Circuit Judges, 1973; justice Supreme Ct. Fla., Tallahassee, 1974—; chief justice Supreme Ct. Fla., 1976-78; past adj. faculty Stetson U. Coll., Law and Fla. St. U. Coll. Law; bd. dirs. Nat. Jud. Coll., 1976-87; mem. Fla. Car Continuing Legal Edn. Com., 1963-74, chmn., 1971-74; 1st chmn. Fla. Inst. Judiciary, 1972; mem. exec. com. Appellate Judges Conf.; chmn. Appellate Structure Commn., 1978-79, Article Rev. Commn., 1983-84, Matrimonial Law Commn., 1982-85; chmn. Jud. Coun. Fla., 1985-89.; chmn. adv. com. for LLM program for appellate judges U. Va., 1985-94. Contbr. legal publs. Past reader, vestryman, sr. warden St. Albans Episcopal Ch., St. Petersburg; chmn. U.S. Constn. Bicentennial Commn. Fla. 1987-91; ch. Family Ct. Commn., 1990-91; ch. Death Case Postconviction Relief Proceeding 1990-91. Fellow Am. Bar Found.; mem. ABA (chmn. criminal justice task force to rev. trial and discovery standards 1991—), Fla. Bar Assn., Am. Judicature Soc. (dir., sec.). Democrat. Lodge: Rotary. Office: Fla Supreme Ct Supreme Ct Bldg Tallahassee FL 32399

OVERTON, BRUCE, personnel executive, consultant; b. Caldwell, N.J., June 27, 1941; s. E.F. and V.B. Overton; m. Charlene Gayle Overton; children: Julie, Diane, Sharon. BS, Widener U., 1963. Personnel mgr. Xerox Corp., Rochester, N.Y., 1965-71; prin. cons. Sibson and Co., Princeton, N.J., 1971-77; v.p. compensation RJR Nabisco, Inc., Atlanta, 1977-87, v.p. pers., 1987-89; ptnr. Ernst and Young, Atlanta, 1989-90; pres. Overton & Assocs., 1990-93; prnt. HR Mgmt. Inc., 1993—. Author articles on compensation and personnel mgmt., 1979—. Bd. dirs. Cobb County YMCA; bd. trustees Kennesaw Coll. Served to 1st lt. U.S. Army, 1963-65. Mem. Am. Compensation Assn. (chmn. bd. 1986-87). Republican. Presbyterian. Avocation: boating. Office: 3901 Roswell Rd Ste 330 Marietta GA 30062-6277

OVERTON, GEORGE WASHINGTON, lawyer; b. Hinsdale, Ill., Jan. 25, 1918; s. George Washington and Florence Mary (Darlington) O.; m. Jane Vincent Harper, Sept. 1, 1941; children—Samuel Harper, Peter Darlington, Ann Vincent. A.B., Harvard U., 1940; J.D., U. Chgo., 1946. Bar: Ill. 1947, U.S. Dist. Ct. (no. dist.) Ill. 1947, U.S. Supreme Ct. 1951. Assoc. Pope & Ballard, Chgo., 1946-48; ptnr. Overton & Babcock, Chgo., 1948-51, Taylor, Miller, Busch & Magner, Chgo., 1951-60; pvt. practice Chgo., 1960; sr. prin. Overton, Schwartz & Fritts and predecessor cos., Chgo., 1961-81; of counsel Wildman Harrold Allen & Dixon, Chgo., 1981—; bd. dirs. Ill. Inst. Continuing Legal Edn., 1974-81, chmn. 1980-81; mem. com. on profl. responsibility of Ill. Supreme Ct., 1986—, chmn., 1990-93. Contbr. articles to profl. jours. Bd. dirs. Open Lands Project, 1961—, pres., 1978-81; bd. dirs. Canal Corridor Assn., 1981—, chmn., 1981-84. 1st lt. U.S. Army, 1942-45. Mem. ABA (mem. com. on counsel responsibility 1985—, com. on nonprofit corps.), Ill. Bar Assn., Chgo. Bar Assn. (bd. mgrs. 1981-83), Assn. of Bar of City of N.Y., Am. Law Inst., Univ. Club. Office: Wildman Harrold Allen & Dixon 225 W Wacker Dr Chicago IL 60606-1224

OVERTON, JANE VINCENT HARPER, biology educator; b. Chgo., Jan. 17, 1919; d. Paul Vincent and Isabel (Vincent) Harper; m. George W. Overton, Jr., Sept. 1, 1941; children: Samuel, Peter, Ann. AB, Bryn Mawr Coll., 1941; PhD, U. Chgo., 1950. Rsch. asst. U. Chgo., 1950-52, mem. faculty, 1952-89, prof. biology, 1972-89; prof. emeritus, 1989. Author articles embryology, cell biology. NIH, NSF research grantee, 1965-87. Home: 1700 E 56th St Apt 2901 Chicago IL 60637-1935 Office: U Chgo 1103 E 57th St Chicago IL 60637-1503

OVERTON, JOHN BLAIR, lawyer; b. Newburgh, N.Y., Dec. 23, 1949; s. Jesse Woodhull and Joan (Blair) O. BA, Columbia U., 1972; JD, Golden Gate U., 1979. Bar: Calif. 1981, U.S. Dist. Co. (no. dist.) Calif. 1981, U.S. Dist. Ct. (ctrl. dist.) Calif. 1985, U.S. Ct. Appeals (9th cir.) 1986, U.S. Supreme Ct. 1990. Sole practice Sausalito, Calif., 1981—; bd. dirs. Ind. Feature Project of No. Calif. Author: Oregon Clean Water Handbook, 1975. Mem. ABA (chmn. subcom. 1985—), Phi Beta Kappa. Avocations: fly fishing, playing music. Office: 2401 Marinship Way Sausalito CA 94965-2854

OVERTON, JOSEPH ALLEN, JR., trade association administrator; b. Parkersburg, W.Va., Apr. 17, 1921; s. Joseph Allen and Edith (Wharton) O.; m. Bette Crosswhite, May 15, 1943; children: Joseph Allen III, Rebecca A., Mallory E. LL.B., Washington and Lee U., 1946, J.D., 1970. Bar: W.Va. 1947. Mem. firm Handlan, Overton & Earley, Parkersburg, 1947-54; spl. asst. to gen. counsel Dept. Commerce, 1955-56, spl. asst. to sec. commerce, 1955-59, dep. gen. counsel, 1956-59; mem. U.S. Tariff Commn., 1959-62, vice chmn., 1959-60; also prin. adviser on fgn. trade matters to U.S. del. to GATT meetings Japan and Europe; adminstrv. v.p. Am. Mining Congress, Washington, 1962; exec. v.p. Am. Mining Congress, 1963-72, pres., 1972-86, pub. Mining Congress Jour., 1963-82; pub. Am. Mining Congress Jour., 1983-86. Mem. W.Va. Legislature, 1948-50; bd. dirs. Eisenhower World Affairs Inst., 1985—. Served from pvt. to 1st lt. USAAF, 1941-46. Named Disting. fellow D.C. Nat. Def. U., 1985—. Mem. Am., W.Va., Fed. bar assns., Am. Legion, 40 and 8, Phi Kappa Psi. Episcopalian. Clubs: Elks, F Street, Internat. Army and Navy. Home: 140 Gloucester Rd Front Royal VA 22630-3706

OVERTON, MARCUS LEE, performing arts administrator, actor, writer; b. Calhoun, Ga., Aug. 13, 1943; s. Marcus Burl Jr. and Eva Mae (Greene) O. BS in Speech and Theatre, Northwestern U., 1965. Actor, tchr. Southeastern Shakespeare Festival, Atlanta, summer 1965; actor, company mgr. Eagles Mere Assocs. Repertory Co., Chgo., 1966; prodn. stage mgr. Lyric Opera of Chgo., 1966-72; mgr. Ravinia Festival, Highland Park, Ill., 1973-77; performing arts program mgr. Smithsonian Instn., Washington, 1983-92; exec. dir., prod. dir. Spoleto Festival U.S.A., Charleston, S.C., 1992-94; instr. in theatre and arts mgmt. Coll. Charleston, 1995—; narrator talking books Libr. Congress, Washington, 1982-83; adv. panelist Nat. Endowment for Arts, 1977-79, D.C. Commn. on Arts and Humanities, 1989, 90, 92; bd. dirs. Nat. Cultural Resources, 1989-90, Performing Arts Assistance Corp., 1992—; cons. in field. Producer Falstaff (L.A. Philharm.), 1981-82. Northwestern U. scholar, 1961-65. Avocations: travel, prehistoric cave art, motorcycle touring, linguistics, French culture. Office: 210 Little Oak Island Dr Folly Beach SC 29439-1486

OVERTON, ROSILYN GAY HOFFMAN, financial services executive; b. Corsicana, Tex., July 10, 1942; d. Billy Clarence and Ima Elise (Gay) Hoffman; m. Aaron Lewis Overton, Jr., July 2, 1960 (div. Mar. 1975); children: Aaron Lewis III, Adam Jerome; m. Mardiros Hatsakorzian, 1990. BS in Math., Wright State U., Dayton, Ohio, 1972, MS in Applied Econs. (fellow), 1973; postgrad. N.Y. U. Grad. Sch. Bus., 1974-76; Cert. Coll. Fin. Planning, 1987. CFP. Research analyst Nat. Security Agy., Dept. Def., 1962-67; bus. reporter Dayton Jour.-Herald, 1973-74; economist First Nat. City Bank, N.Y.C., 1974, A.T. & T. Co., 1974-75; broker Merrill Lynch, N.Y.C., 1975-80; asst. v.p. E.F. Hutton & Co., N.Y.C., 1980-84; v.p., nat. mktg. dir. investment products Manhattan Nat. Corp., 1984-86; pres. R.H. Overton Co., N.Y.C., 1986—; ptnr. Brown & Overton Fin. Svcs., 1987—. Named Businesswoman of Yr., N.Y.C., 1976. Mem. Inst. Cert. Planners, Internat. Assn. Fin. Planning (exec. v.p. N.Y. chpt.), Gotham Bus. and Profl. Womens Club, Rotary Internat., Wright State U. Alumni Assn., Mensa, Zonta. Methodist. Office: 142-05 Roosevelt Ave Ste 603 Flushing NY 11354-6007

OVERTON, SARITA ROSA, psychologist; b. South Haven, Mich., June 7, 1954; d. Samuel Edward and Rosa Jane (McGuire) O. BA in Psychology with honors, Mich. State U., 1976, MA in Rehab. Counseling, 1978, MA in Counseling Psychology, 1987, PhD in Counseling Psychology, 1988. Lic. psychologist, Mich. Dir. Job Club, Capital Area Community Svcs., Lansing, Mich., 1978-84; instr. rehab. counseling master's program Mich. State U., East Lansing, 1981-82, program teaching asst., 1985-87, coord. career assistance project, 1984, 84-85, clin. trainee Counseling Ctr., 1986, rsch. asst. disability mgmt. project, 1985-87; clin. trainee St. Lawrence Hosp., Lansing, 1986-87, psychologist Psychol. Svcs. and Addictions Clinic, 1987-91; psychologist Comprehensive Psychol. Svcs., P.C., East Lansing, 1990-95; pvt. practice psychologist Meridian Health and Wellness Ctr., East Lansing, 1995—; conf. and clin. presenter in field. Contbr. articles to profl. publs. Recipient Presdl. recognition award Mich. Rehab. Assn., 1986; grantee Nat. Inst. Handicapped Rsch., 1985; dissertation rsch. fellow Mich. State U., 1985. Mem. APA. Democrat. Avocations: reading, aquarist, yoga, meditation, imagery, Tai Chi Chuan. Office: Meridian Health and Wellness 139 Lake Lansing Rd Ste 200 East Lansing MI 48823

OVERTON, STANLEY DIXON, banking executive; b. Dickson, Tenn., May 2, 1928; s. Dallas Stanley and Ova (Dixon) O.; m. Carolyn Ruane, Feb. 14, 1976; children—Stanley D. Jr., James Stanton; 1 stepchild, Cecelia Halter. Student Fall's Bus. Coll., Nashville, 1948-49; Acctg. degree Internat. Accts. Soc., 1952; student Savs. & Loan Grad. Sch. Ind. U., 1961-63. With Fidelity Fed. Bank, FSB, Nashville, 1950-92, exec. v.p., 1963-67, pres., 1967-74, chmn., pres., 1974-84, chmn., chief exec. officer, 1984-92; chmn., chief exec. officer, Union Planters Bank of Middle Tenn., 1992-94, chmn., 1994—, also bd. dirs. Union Planters Corp.; past bd. dirs. Fed. Home Loan Bank Bd., Cin. United Way, Nashville; bd. dirs. YMCA, Nashville, Fellowship of Christian Athletes, Nashville. Served with USNR, 1946-48. Mem. C. of C. (past bd. govs.), Tenn. League Savs. Assns. (pres. 1969-70), U.S. League Savs. Assns., Am. Savs. and Loan Inst. (past pres.), Found. for Savs. Instns. (trustee). Clubs: Hillwood Country,Nashville City. Lodges: Masons, Shriners, Kiwanis. Home: 7 Warwick Ln Nashville TN 37205 Office: Union Planters Bank of Middle Tenn 401 Union St Nashville TN 37219

OVERTON-ADKINS, BETTY JEAN, foundation administrator; b. Jacksonville, Fla., Oct. 10, 1949; d. Henry and Miriam (Gordon) Crawford; children from previous marriage: Joseph Alonzo III, Jermaine Lamar; m. Eugene Adkins, Apr. 24, 1992. BA in English, Tenn. State U., 1970, MA in English, 1974; PhD in English, Vanderbilt U., 1980; student Inst. Ednl. Mgmt., Harvard U., 1990. Reporter Race Rels. Reporter Mag., Nashville, 1970-71; tchr. Met. Nashville Sch. System, 1971-72; instr., project dir. Tenn. State U., Nashville, 1972-76; asst. prof. Nashville State Tech. Inst., 1976-78, Fisk U., Nashville, 1978-83; assoc. dean. grad. sch. U. Ark., Little Rock, 1983-85, dean grad. sch., 1985-91; program dir. Kellogg Found., Battle Creek, Mich., 1991—; asst. dir. Kellogg Nat. Fellowship Program, Battle Creek, Mich., 1991-94; coord. higher edn. programs Kellogg Found., Battle Creek, 1994—; instr. U. Tenn., Nashville, 1976-82; dir. rsch. sponsored programs U. Ark., 1986-88; bd. dirs. Ark. Sci. and Info. Liaison Office, 1984-91. Bd. dirs. Ark. Sci. and Tech. Authority, Little Rock, 1989—, Women's Project, 1986—, Ark. Pub. Policy Panel, 1988-91, No. Bank Women's Adv. Bd., 1988-91, Nashville Panel, 1974-83, Ctrl. Ark. Libr. Sys., 1990-91, Ark. coun. NCCJ, 1990-92, Bread for World, 1990-95; mem. Commn. on Edn. Credits and Credentials, Am. Coun. on Edn., 1989-95; chmn. bi-racial adv. com. Little Rock Sch. Dist., 1987—. Fellow Am. Coun. Edn., 1981-82, W.K. Kellogg Found., 1988-93. Mem. Nat. Coun. Tchrs. of English, Coun. Grad. Schs., Coun. So. Grad. Schs., Women Color United Against Domestic Violence (pres.), An. Assn. High Edn., Rotary, Alpha Kappa Alpha. Democrat. Roman Catholic. Office: W K Kellogg Found One Michigan Ave E Battle Creek MI 49017

OVESON, W(ILFORD) VAL, state official, accountant; b. Provo, Utah, Feb. 11, 1952; s. Wilford W. and LaVon Oveson; m. Emilee Nebeker, Sept. 1, 1973; children: Polly, Libby, Peter, Benjamin. Student, U. Utah, 1973-74; BS in Acctg., Brigham Young U., 1976. CPA, Utah. Acct. Squire and Co., Orem, Utah, 1975-79; pvt. practice acctg. Squire and Co., Orem, 1979-80; state auditor State of Utah, Salt Lake City, 1981-84, lt. gov., 1985-93; sr. mgr. KPMG Peat Marwick, 1993; chmn. Utah Tax Commn., Salt Lake City, 1993—; mem. dist. export coun. U.S. Dept. Commerce, 1985—, mem. bd. examiners, State of Utah, 1981-84; chmn. State Records Com., 1981-84. Bd. dirs., unit campaign dir. United Way of Greater Salt Lake, 1985-86; trustee Travis Found., 1985-88; treas. Utah County Rep. Party; mem. State Platform Com., 1982, 84; mem. exec. com. Utah State Rep. Party, 1981—. Mem. AICPA (mem. governing coun. 1986), Utah Assn. CPAs (Pub. Svc. award 1984). Republican. Mem. LDS Ch. Avocations: skiing, personal finance, computers, house plants, fishing. Home: 2125 S 900 E Bountiful UT 84010-3105

OVITSKY, STEVEN ALAN, musician, symphony orchestra executive; b. Chgo., Oct. 12, 1947; s. Martin N. and Ruth (Katz) O.; m. Camille Levy; 1 child, David Isaac. MusB, U. Mich., 1968; MusM, No. Ill. U., 1975. Fine arts dir. Sta. WNIU-FM Pub. Radio, Dekalb, Ill., 1972-76; program mgr. Sta. WMHT-FM Pub. Radio, Schenectady, N.Y., 1976-79; gen. mgr., artistic dir. Grant Park Concerts, Chgo., 1979-90; v.p., gen. mgr. Minn. Orch., Mpls., 1990-95; exec. dir. Milw. Symphony Orch., 1995—; panelist Ill. Arts Coun., 1986, 87, 88, Chgo. Artists Abroad, 1987-91, Nat. Endowment for the Arts, 1987-89; bd. dirs. Ill. Arts Alliance, Chamber Music Chgo.; hon. dir. Chgo. Sinfonietta. With U.S. Army, 1968-71, Korea. Mem. NARAS, Am. Symphony Orch. League. Jewish. Avocations: audio, record collecting, softball. Office: Milw Symphony 330 E Kilbourn Ave Ste 900 Milwaukee WI 53202

OVITZ, MICHAEL S., communications executive; b. 1946; m. Judy Reich, 1969; 3 children. Grad., UCLA, 1968. With William Morris Agy., 1968-75; co-founder, chmn. Creative Artists Agy., L.A., 1975-95; pres. Walt Disney Co., Burbank, Calif., 1995—; mem. bd. advisors Med. Sch. UCLA, bd. dirs. Sch. Theatre, Film and TV. Trustee St. John's Hosp. and Health Ctr., Santa Monica, Calif., Mus. Modern Art, N.Y.C.; bd. govs. Cedars-Sinai Hosp., L.A.; mem. exec. adv. bd. Pediatric AIDS Found.; bd. dirs. Calif. Inst. Arts, Sundance Inst. Mem. Zeta Beta Tau. Avocations: contemporary art, African antiques, Chinese furniture. Office: Walt Disney Co 500 S Buena Vista St Burbank CA 91521*

OVSHINSKY, STANFORD ROBERT, physicist, inventor, energy and information company executive; b. Akron, Ohio, Nov. 24, 1922; s. Benjamin and Bertha T. (Munitz) O.; m. Iris L. Miroy, Nov. 24, 1959; children—Benjamin, Harvey, Dale, Robin Dibner, Steven Dibner. Student public schs., Akron; DSc (hon.), Lawrence Inst. Tech., 1980; DEng (hon.), Bowling Green State U., 1981; DSc (hon.), Jordan Coll., Cedar Springs, Mich., 1989. Pres. Stanford Roberts Mfg. Co., Akron, 1946-50; mgr. centre drive dept. New Britain Machine Co., Conn., 1950-52; dir. research Hupp Corp., Detroit, 1952-55; pres. Gen. Automation, Inc., Detroit, 1955-58, Ovitron Corp., Detroit, 1958-59; pres., chmn. bd. Energy Conversion Devices, Inc., Troy, Mich., 1960-78; pres., chief exec. officer, chief scientist Energy Conversion Devices, Inc., 1978—; adj. prof. engring. scis. Coll. Engring., Wayne State U.; hon. advisor for sci. and tech. Beijing (China) Inst. Aeronautics and Astronautics (name changed to Beijing U. Aeros. and Astronautics); chmn. Inst. for Amorphous Studies. Contbr. articles on physics of amorphous materials, neurophysiology and neuropsychiatry to profl. jours. Recipient Diesel Gold medal German Inventors Assn., 1968, Coors Am. Ingenuity award, 1988; named to Mich. Chem. Engring. Hall of Fame, 1983, Mich. Scientist of Yr., Impression 5 Sci. Mus., 1987. Fellow AAAS, Am. Phys. Soc.; mem. IEEE (sr.), Soc. Automotive Engrs., N.Y. Acad. Scis., Electrochem. Soc., Engring. Soc. Detroit, Cranbrook Inst. Sci. (bd. govs. 1981). Office: Energy Conversion Devices Inc 1675 W Maple Rd Troy MI 48084-7118

OWEISS, IBRAHIM MOHAMED, economist, educator; b. Egypt, Sept. 25, 1931; came to U.S., 1960; s. Mohamed Zaki and Warda (Zeiden) O.; m. Celine M. J. Lesuisse, July 19, 1975; children: Yasmeen, Kareem. B.Com., Alexandria U., Egypt, 1952; M.A., U. Minn., 1961, Ph.D., 1969. Tchr., 1953-55; econ. dir. indsl. projects Cairo, 1958-60; mem. faculty U. Minn., Mpls., 1961-67; mem. faculty Georgetown U., Washington, 1967—, prof. econs., 1973—; mem. faculty Johns Hopkins U., 1971-74; first undersec. state econ. affairs Govt. Egypt, Cairo, 1977; ambassador, 1977-79; chief Egyptian Econ. Mission to U.S., 1977-79; cons. econs., 1971—. Author: Pricing of Oil in World Trade, 1974, The Israeli Economy, 1974; editor: The Dynamics of U.S.-Arab Economic Relations, 1980, Economic Development of Egypt, 1982, Arab Civilization, Challenges and Responses, 1988, Political Economy of Contemporary Egypt, 1990. Pres. Assn. Egyptian-Am. Scholars, 1984-88; chmn. bd. dirs. Arab-Am. Bus. and Profl. Assn., Howard and Georgeanna Jones Inst. for Reproductive Medicine, 1984-90, Egyptian Am. Cultural Assn., 1975-77, Faith and Hope Project, 1975-77. Officer Egyptian Army, 1955-58. Decorated Egyptian Merit decoration 1st Order, Order of St. John; Ford Found. fellow, 1979-80. Mem. Am. Econ. Assn. Moslem. Club: University (N.Y.C.). Home: 4017 Glenridge St Kensington MD 20895-3708 Office: Georgetown University Dept Econs Washington DC 20057

OWEN, AMY, library director; b. Brigham City, Utah, June 26, 1944; d. John Wallace and Bertha (Jensen) O. BA, Brigham Young U., 1966, MLS, 1968. Systems libr. Utah State Libr., Salt Lake City, 1968-72, dir. reference svcs., 1972-74, dir. tech. svcs., 1974-81, dep. dir., 1981-87; dir., 1987—; serials com. chmn. Utah Coll. Libr. Coun., Salt Lake City, 1975-77, exec. sec., 1978-84, coun. mem. 1987—; mem. staff Gov.'s Utah Systems Planning Task Force, Salt Lake City, 1982; staff liaison Utah Gov.'s Conf. on Libr. and Info. Svcs., 1977-79, chair exec. planning com., 1990-91; mem. pres.'s adv. panel Baker & Taylor Co., Somerville, N.J., 1977-78; panelist U.S. Dept. Edn., 1992; mem. rsch. project adv. com. U. Wis. Sch. Libr. and Info., Madison, 1992-94; mem. adv. panel Nat. Commn. Libr. and Info. Svcs., 1985; Alumni Honor lectr. Coll. Humanities, Brigham Young U., 1990. Contbr. chpts. to books, also contbg. author various manuals; cons. and trainer in field. Coun. mem. Utah Endowment for Humanities, 1986-91, vice chmn., 1987-88, chair, 1988-90; trustee Bibliographic Ctr. for Rsch., 1987—, pers. com., 1988-89, chmn. pers. com., 1989-90, nominating com., 1984, v.p. bd. trustees, 1989-91, pres, 1991-93; active Chief Officers of State Libr. Agys., 1987—, stats. com., 1988-93, mem. network com., 1993—, state info. policy workshop com., 1988, bd. dirs., 1992—; mem. conf. program com. Fedn. of State Humanities Couns., 1988; mem. coop. pub. libr. data system task force Nat. Commn. on Libr. and Info. Svcs., 1988-90; grant rev. panelist NEH, 1988, 92, panel mem. reading and discussion groups, 1988; regional project mgmt. bd. mem. Intermountain Community Learning and Info. Ctr. Project, 1987-90; mem. midcontinental regional adv. com. Nat. Libr. Medicine 1991-94; mem. adv. com. Brigham Young U. Sch. Libr. and Info. Svcs. Named Libr. of Yr., Libr. Jour., 1990. Mem. Utah Libr. Assn. (pres. 1978-79, exec. bd. 1976-80, Spl. Svc. award 1989), Mountain Plains Libr. Assn. (rec. sec. 1979-80, fin. com. 1982-84, Disting. Svc. award 1989), ALA (bd. dirs. ASCLA divsn. 1984-86, 93—, pres. ASCLA divsn. 1994-95, fin. com. 1984-86, 89-92, 93—, planning, orgn. and bylaws com. 1981-85, SLAS program com. 1984-86, pres. program com. 1986, exec. bd. mem., 1988-90, 93-94; clene roundtable mem. com. 1984-86, nominations com. 1986-87, nat. adv. bd. office communications svcs., voices and visions project 1988-89; LITA div. Satellite Conf. Task Force mem. 1982; PLA div. editor column. 1987-89, PLA div. goals, guidelines and standards com. 1987-90, chair, 1990-91, PLA pub. libr. data svc. adv. com. 1988-91, PLA Kellogg Phase III EIC project adv. com. chair 1990-92, PLA strategic issues and directions com., 1991-92, PLA non MLS involvement com., 1990-91, ALA Office for Rsch. coop. pub. libr. data system adv. com. 1985-89), Dynix Snowbird Leadership Inst. (nat. adv. bd. 1990—), Phi Kappa Phi, Alpha Lambda Delta. Home: 7453 Lost Canyon Cir Salt Lake City UT 84121-4624 Office: Utah State Libr 2150 S 300 W Ste 16 Salt Lake City UT 84115-2536

OWEN, BERNICE DOYLE, nursing educator. BS, U. Iowa, 1963; MS in Pub. Health Nursing, U. Minn., 1964; PhD, U. Wis., 1982. Staff nurse VA Hosp., Madison, Wis., 1964-65; pub. health nurse Dane County Health Dept., Madison, 1965-66; instr. pub. health nursing U. Wis. Madison Sch. Nursing, 1966-69, asst. prof., head pub. health nursing, 1969-72, assoc. clin. prof. pub. health nursing, 1972-77, chairperson primary health care div., 1975-77, lectr., 1977-82, asst. prof., 1982-88, assoc. prof., 1988-91, prof., 1991—; part time asst. prof. U. Wis.-Milw., Sch. Nursing, 1984; mem. expert panel to develop clin. guidelines for low back disorders Agy. for Health Care Policy and Rsch., U.S. Dept. Health and Human Svcs., 1991-92; cons. and presenter in field. Ad hoc reviewer: Rsch. in Nursing and Health, 1987-88, 92; reviewer for manuscripts: Nat. Inst. for Occupational Safety and Health, 1985-91, Lippincott, Inc.; contbr. articles to profl. jours. Recipient scholarship Fireman's Fund Ins. Co., 1980-81, 1981-82, Schering award for occupational health nursing for WIs., 1990, Pres. Vol. Action award Point of Light Found., 1993; numerous rsch. and ednl. grants. Mem. ANA, APHA, Wis. Nurses' Assn., Madison Dist. Nurses Assn., Am. Assn. Occupational Health Nurses, Am. Assn. Occupational Health Nurses of South Cen. Wis. (treas. 1984-88, sec. 1994-96), Wis. State Assn. Occupational Health Nurses (bd. dirs. 1988-90), Wis. Pub. Health Assn. (legis. com. 1968-69, bd. dirs. 1973-75, aging com. 1974-75, injury prevention com. 1984—, co-chair membership com. 1991-93, v.p. 1994-96). Assn. Comty. Health Nursing Educators, Sigma Theta Tau (Beta Eta chpt. chair eligibility com. 1990-92, others). Avocations: photography, swimming, reading, fishing, gardening. Home: 1001 Pflaum Rd Madison WI 53716-2827 Office: U Wis Sch Nursing 600 Highland Ave # H6 242 Madison WI 53792-0001

OWEN, CHRISTINA L., lawyer; b. Oakland, Calif., Sept. 22, 1946. BS, U. Calif., Berkeley, 1968; JD, U. So. Calif., 1971. Bar: Calif. 1972. Ptnr. Baker & Hostetler, Long Beach, Calif. Mem. State Bar Calif., Maritime Law Assn. U.S. Office: Baker & Hostetler 300 Oceangate Ste 620 Long Beach CA 90802-6801

OWEN, CLAUDE BERNARD, JR., tobacco company executive; b. Danville, Va., June 12, 1945; s. Claude Bernard and Mildred Carter (Fulton) O.; m. Mary Lamar Lewis, Aug. 14, 1965; children: Christopher E., Jennifer L. BA in Econs., Davidson Coll., 1967; MBA in Fin., U. Md., 1969. Fin. analyst Dibrell Bros., Inc., Danville, 1971-73, asst. v.p., 1973-76, v.p., 1976-81, sr. v.p., 1981-84, exec. v.p., 1984-86, pres., 1986-89, chmn., CEO, 1990-95; chmn., CEO Dimon Inc., 1995—; bd. dirs. Am. Nat. Bankshares, Danville; chmn. bd. Richfood Holdings Inc., Richmond. Trustee Averett Coll., Danville, 1985, chmn. bd. trustees, 1991; pres. Danville-Pittsylvania County United Way, 1989. Served to 1st lt. U.S. Army, 1969-71. Mem. Va. C. of C. (bd. dirs. 1992—), Va. Mfg. Assn. (vice chmn. 1992, chmn. 1995—), Danville Golf Club (v.p. 1984-86), Commonwealth Club (Richmond), Country Club of Va. (Richmond), Rotary. Methodist. Avocations: golfing, raquetball, skiing. Office: Dibrell Bros Inc 512 Bridge St Danville VA 24541-1406*

OWEN, DUNCAN SHAW, JR., physician, medical educator; b. Fayetteville, N.C., Oct. 24, 1935; s. Duncan S. and Mary Gwyn (Hickerson) O.; m. Irene Lacy Rose, Oct. 22, 1966; children: Duncan Shaw III, Robert Burwell, Frances Gwyn. BS, U. N.C., 1957, MD, 1960. Diplomate Am. Bd. Internal Medicine (proctor 1977—). Intern Med. Coll. Va., Richmond, 1960-61; jr. asst. resident in medicine N.C. Meml. Hosp., Chapel Hill, 1961-62; asst. resident in medicine Med. Coll. Va., Richmond, 1964-65, fellow in rheumatic diseases, 1965-66; practice medicine specializing in internal medicine and rheumatology Richmond, Va., 1966—; instr. in medicine Med. Coll. Va., Richmond, 1966-67, asst. prof., 1967-71, assoc. prof., 1971-78, prof. dept. internal medicine, 1978—; Taliaferro/Scott Disting. prof. internal medicine Med. Coll. Va., Va. Commonwealth U., 1989—; dir. residency tng. Med. Coll. Va. Hosp.; dir. Rheumatology Clinics; mem. staff McGuire VA; dir. clin. tng. divsn. rheumatology, allergy, immunology, chmn. clin. activities comm., dept. internal mediine; chmn. med. adv. com. Richmond br. Arthritis Found., 1966-75, bd. dirs. 1966—, mem. nat. patient edn. com., 1979-80; med. advisor Social Security Adminstrn., HHS, 1967—; bd. dirs. Blue Shield Va., 1975-77, co-chmn. arthritis project Va. Regional Med. Program, 1975-76; bd. dirs. Univ. Internal Medicine Found., 1979—; prodr. Your Health TV series Va. Ednl. TV, 1978-79; prodr. Update in Medicine, Good Morning Virginia TV show, 1980; mem. various coms. in field. Contbr. numerous papers, chpts. in books, articles to profl. jours.; assoc. editor: Va. Med., 1978—; editorial reviewer Jour. AMA, 1979—, Arthritis Rheumatism, 1981—, Jour. Rheumatology, 1984—. Mem. usher's guild First Presbyn. Ch., Richmond, Va., 1966-70, deacon, 1974-77, chmn. of diaconate, 1976-77, elder, 1978—, chmn. witness com., 1978-80; co-chmn. physicians statewide capital funds campaign Va. Commn. U., 1986-87; bd. dirs. Mooreland Farms Assn., 1971-73, 77-81, Va. chpt. Arthitis Found., 1970-85; mem. Va. Mus., Richmond Symphony; bd. dirs. Richmond Area Health Care Coalition, 1980-84. Served to capt. MC, 1962-64. Recipient Army Commendation medal, 1964. Nat. Inst. Arthritis and Metabolic Diseases fellow, 1965-66; recipient Gerard B. Lambert award, 1974-75, Disting. Service award Arthritis Found., 1971. Fellow ACP, Am. Coll. Rheumatology; mem. AMA (expert on diagnostic and therapeutic tech. assessment program), Am. Rheumatism Assn. (exec. com. 1979-80), Richmond Acad. Medicine (pres. 1982, chmn. bd. 1983, parliamenarian 1988—), Med. Soc. Va. (com. on aging 1980-89, v.p. 1973, 75, del. 1972—, scholarship com. 1980-89), Richmond Soc. Internal Medicine (bd. dirs. 1971-73), Met. Richmond C. of C. (bd. dirs. 1981-94), Jr. Clin. Club (emeritus), Country Club Va., Custis Hunting and Fishing Club, Alpha Omega Alpha. Avocations: hunting, fishing, photography, amateur radio. Home: 8910 Brieryle Rd Richmond VA 23229-7704 Office: Med Coll Va Ambulatory Care Ctr PO Box 980647 Richmond VA 23298-0647

OWEN, H. MARTYN, lawyer; b. Decatur, Ill., Oct. 23, 1929; s. Honore Martyn and Virginia (Hunt) O.; m. Candace Catlin Benjamin, June 21, 1952; children—Leslie W., Peter H., Douglas P. A.B., Princeton U., 1951; LL.B., Harvard U., 1954. Bar: Conn. 1954. Assoc. Shipman & Goodwin, Hartford, Conn., 1958-61, ptnr., 1961-94, of counsel, 1995—. Mem. Simsbury (Conn.) Zoning Bd. Appeals, 1961-67, Simsbury Zoning Commn., 1967-79; sec. Capitol Region Planning Agy., 1965-66; bd. dirs. Symphony Soc. Greater Hartford, 1967-73; trustee Renbrook Sch., West Hartford, Conn., 1963-72, treas., 1964-68, pres., 1968-72, hon. life trustee, 1972—; trustee Simsbury Free Library, 1970-84; pres. Hartford Grammar Sch., 1987—, trustee; corporator Hartford Hosp. Lt. USNR, 1954-57. Mem. ABA, Conn. Bar Assn., Hartford County Bar Assn., Am. Law Inst. Republican. Episcopalian. Clubs: Princeton (N.Y.C.); Ivy (Princeton, N.J.); Dauntless (Essex, Conn.). Home: 44 Pinnacle Mountain Rd Simsbury CT 06070-1809 Office: One American Row Hartford CT 06103-2819

OWEN, HARRIES, editor; b. Garnant, Wales, U.K., Mar. 29, 1930; s. David and Maud (Jones) H.; m. Dorothy Richrds, Dec. 28, 1953; children: Jane Cathryn, Rowena. BA with honors, U. Wales, 1950; MA with honors, U.Oxford, Eng., 1952. Lectr./sr. lectr. U. Sydney, Australia, 1955-65; assoc. prof. U. N.S.W., Sydney, 1966-76; head policy planning Dept. Fgn. Affairs, Fed. Govt. Australia, Canberra, 1977-79, sr. advisor to prime minister, 1979-81; amb. to UNESCO Dept. Fgn. Affairs, Fed. Govt. Australia, Paris, 1982-83; Olin vis.fellow Heritage Found., Washington, 1983-84; editor-in-chief Nat. Interest, Washington, 1985—. Editor: America's Purpose, 1991; contbr. over 100 articles to periodicals, newspapers including Fgn. Affairs, Commentary, The New Republic, Harpers, Nat. Rev., N.Y. Times, Times (London), Wall St. Jour., Washington Post, others. Founding mem. Australia-Japan Found., Sydney, 1978-80. With RAF, 1953-54. Fellow Heritage Found. (adj.), Am. Enterprise Inst. (adj.); mem. Ctr. for Strategic and Internat. Studies (sr. assoc.). Avocations: reading, bridge, chess, golf. Home: 4101 Cathedral Ave NW Washington DC 20016 Office: The National Interest 1112 16th St NW Washington DC 20036

OWEN, HENRY, former ambassador, consultant; b. N.Y.C., Aug. 26, 1920. A.B., Harvard U., 1941. Economist Dept. State, Washington, 1946-55, mem. policy planning staff, 1955-62, dep. counselor, vice chmn. policy planning coun., 1962-66, chmn. coun., 1966-69; dir. fgn. policy studies Brookings Instn., 1969-77; personal rep. of Pres. U.S. with rank of ambassador to participate in preparations for summit meetings, 1977-81; cons. Salomon Bros., 1981—. Editor: Next Phase of U.S. Foreign Policy, 1971, (with Charles Schultze) Setting National Priorities, 1976. Served to lt. USN, 1942-46. Office: 1616 H St NW Washington DC 20006-4903

OWEN, HOWARD WAYNE, journalist, writer; b. Fayetteville, N.C., Mar. 1, 1949; s. E.F. and Roxie Geddie (Bulla) O.; m. Karen Lane Van Neste, Aug. 18, 1973. BA in Journalism, U. N.C., 1971; MA in English, Va. Commonwealth U., 1981. Sports writer Martinsville (Va.) Bulletin, 1971-73; sports editor Gastonia (N.C.) Gazette, 1973-74, Chapel Hill (N.C.) Newspaper, 1974-77; exec. sports editor Tallahassee Dem., 1977-78; asst. sports editor Richmond (Va.) Times-Dispatch, 1978-83, sports new editor, 1983-92, sports editor, 1992-95, dep. mng. editor, 1995—; founder Scholar/Athlete Awards, Richmond, 1986—. Author: Littlejohn, 1992, Fat Lightning, 1994, Answers to Lucky, 1996. Recipient Ark. Traveler award State of Ark., 1993. Mem. AP Sports Editors (regional chmn. 1986-87), Va. Writers Club, PEN Am. Ctr., 300 Club. Democrat. Avocations: travel, reading, cooking, sports, jogging. Home: 12836 Ashtree Rd Midlothian VA 23113-3095 Office: Richmond Newspapers Inc 333 E Grace St Richmond VA 23293-1000

OWEN, JACK WALDEN, retired hospital association administrator; b. Union City, Pa., Sept. 21, 1928; s. Wallace A. and Rosamond (Walden) O.; m. Charlotte Keller Owen, Sept. 14, 1957; children: Linda, Lisa, Jack II. BS, Western Mich. U., 1951, BA, 1953; MBA, U. Chgo., 1957. Chmn., CEO Princeton (N.J.) Ins. Co., 1975-83; pres. N.J. Hosp. Assn., Princeton, 1962-82; exec. v.p. Am. Hosp. Assn., Washington, 1982-89; pres. Am. Hosp. Assn., Chgo., 1991; pres. Am. Hosp. Assn. Svcs., Chgo., 1988-94, ret., 1994; bd. dirs. Robert W. Johnson Found., Princeton; chmn. Nat. Com. Prot. S.S., Washington, 1989—; assoc. trustee Suburban Hosp., Bethesda, Md., 1993—. Contbr. articles to profl. jours. Mem. Rocky Hill (N.J.) Sch. Bd., 1974-82. Cpl. U.S. Army, 1953-55. Recipient medal of honor U. Med. and Dentistry, Newark, 1980. Mem. City Tavern Club (Georgetown). Lutheran. Avocations: fishing, golf, woodworking. Home: 3249 Sandown Park Rd Keswick VA 22947

OWEN, JAMES CHURCHILL, JR., lawyer; b. Beverly, Mass., July 30, 1926; s. James Churchill and Alice Wright (Mann) O.; m. Garvene Hales, Feb. 3, 1950 (div. Feb. 1963); children: James Churchill III, Taylor Mann. Student, Yale U., 1944-47; BS, JD, U. Denver, 1956. Bar: Colo. 1957, U.S. Dist. Ct. Colo. 1957. Reporter Oklahoma City Times, 1947-50; writer Phila. Bull., 1951-54; assoc. Holme Roberts & Owen, Denver, 1957-60, ptnr., 1961—; mem. faculty Colo. Grad. Sch. Banking, Boulder, 1975-86; cmty. bd. dirs. Norwest Bank Colo., N.A. Mem. com. on acquistions Denver Pub. Libr. Friends Found., 1991—; trustee Denver Bot. Gardens, 1976-81, Denver Bot. Gardens Endowment, Inc., 1994—, Denver Zool. Found., 1992—; chmn. law alumni fund U. Denver Coll. Law, 1988-89, chmn. law alumni coun., 1989-91, mem. centennial planning com.; former mem. Colo. Gov.'s Coun. Advisors on Consumer Credit; bd. dirs. Rocky Mountain chpt. Juvenile Diabetes Found., 1993-96. Mem. ABA, Colo. Bar Assn. (past chmn. banking com. corp., banking and bus. law sect.), Denver Bar Assn., Colo. Bar Found., Econ. Club Colo. (co-founder, bd. dirs., sec.), Assn. Bank Holding Cos. (past chmn. lawyers' com.), Denver Country Club, Univ. Club, Law Club, Denver Club. Republican. Episcopalian. Avocation: classic cars. Office: Holme Roberts & Owen 1700 Lincoln St Ste 4100 Denver CO 80203-4541

OWEN, JOHN, retired newspaper editor; b. Helena, Mont., June 10, 1929; s. John Earl and Ella Jean (McMillian) O.; m. Alice Winnifred Kesler, June 9, 1951; children—David Scott, Kathy Lynn. B.A. in Journalism, U. Mont., 1951. Sports editor Bismarck (N.D.) Tribune, 1953-55; wire editor Yakima (Wash.) Herald, 1956; with Seattle Post-Intelligencer, 1956-94, sports editor, 1968-80, assoc. editor, 1980-94, columnist, 1968-94. Author: Intermediate Eater Cookbook, 1974, Gourmand Gutbusters Cookbook, 1980, Seattle Cookbook, 1983, Great Grub Hunt Cookbook, 1989, Press Pass, 1994; also short stories. Served with AUS, 1951-52. Named Top Sports Writer in Wash. Nat. Sportswriters Orgn., 1966, 68, 69, 71, 74, 85, 88. Home: 611 Bell St Apt 4 Edmonds WA 98020-3065

OWEN, JOHN ATKINSON, JR., physician, educator; b. South Boston, Va., Sept. 24, 1924; s. John Atkinson and Mary Helen (Carrington) O.; m. Wanda Earle Reamy, Nov. 29, 1952; children—John Atkinson III, Ryland R. BS., Hampden-Sydney Coll., 1944; M.D., U. Va., 1948. Intern Cin. Gen. Hosp., 1948-49; resident, fellow U. Va. Hosp., 1950-52; rsch. fellow Duke Med. Center, 1954-56; asst. prof. medicine Med. Coll. Ga., 1956-58, George Washington U. Med. Sch., 1958-60; mem. faculty U. Va. Sch. Medicine, 1960—, prof., 1970—, vice chmn. dept. internal medicine, 1972-74, James M. Moss prof. diabetes, sr. assoc. dean, 1995—; mem. Va. Vol. Formulary Bd.; Mem. exec. com. U.S. Pharmacopeia, 1970-75, pres., 1975-80, trustee, 1975-85. Mem. editorial bd.: Jour. Clin. Pharmacology, 1971-84; editor-in-chief: Hosp. Formulary, 1974-83. Served with USNR, 1942-45, 48-50, 52-53; capt. M.C. Res. Recipient Raven award U. Va., 1948; co-recipient Horsley Research prize, 1962. Mem. AMA, Am. Fedn. Clin. Rsch., So. Soc. Clin. Investigation, Med. Soc. Va. (pres. 1990-91), Am. Diabetes Assn., Endocrine Soc. Presbyterian. (elder 1965—). Home: 106 Tally Ho Dr Charlottesville VA 22901-2034 Office: U Va Sch Medicine PO Box 242 Charlottesville VA 22908-0242

OWEN, JOHN LAVERTY, human resources executive, consultant; b. Mayfield, Ky., July 28, 1923; s. John Clarence and Lydia (Laverty) O.; m. Marjory Clara Wallace, June 29, 1946; children: John Wallace, David William, Jeffrey Daniel. BA magna cum laude, Westminster (Mo.) Coll., 1944; postgrad., Purdue U., 1945; MS in Psychology, Pa. State U., 1951. Lic. psychologist, Pa. With Hamilton Watch Co., Lancaster, Pa., 1946-70, staff pers. svcs. dir., 1963-70; dir. corp. employee rels. HMW Industries, Inc., Lancaster, Pa., 1970-77; dir. human resources Hamilton Tech., Inc., Lancaster, Pa., 1977-80, v.p. human resources and public rels., 1980-84, sec., v.p. human resources and pub. rels., 1984-85; v.p. human resources Gen. Def. Corp., York, Pa., 1985-88; pres. Performance Systems Internat., 1984—, cons., 1984—; v.p., cons. Greenfield Assocs., Lancaster, 1988-91. Bd. dirs. Lancaster County United Way, 1972-78, 84-86, Lancaster chpt. Nat. Urban League, 1972-81, Assocs. in Downtown Lancaster, 1981-86, Lancaster YMCA, 1984-86, Lancaster Area Arts Coun., 1987-89; bd. dirs. Lancaster Guidance Clinic, 1959-63, pres., 1961-63. Mem. Am. Psychol. Assn., Pa. Psychol. Assn., Ea. Psychol. Assn., Am. Mgmt. Assn., Soc. Human Resource Mgmt. (cert. sr. profl. human resources), Am. Soc. Tng. and Devel., Lancaster Chamber Commerce and Industry, Omicron Delta Kappa, Psi Chi, Phi Kappa Phi, Delta Tau Delta. Republican. Presbyterian.

OWEN, MICHAEL, ballet dancer; b. Carlisle, Pa.. Studied with Marcia Weary; student, Pa. Ballet Sch., Sch. Am. Ballet, Am. Ballet Theatre Sch. Mem. Ballet Reportory Co.; with Am. Ballet Theatre, 1974—, soloist, 1977-87, prin. dancer, 1987—. Appeared in ballets including La Bayadere, Coppelia, Fall River Legend, Giselle, Jardin aux Lilas, The Leaves are Fading, Manon, Pillar of Fire, Romeo and Juliet, The Sleeping Beauty, Swan Lake, Undertow. Office: Am Ballet Theatre 890 Broadway New York NY 10003-1211

OWEN, MICHAEL LEE, lawyer; b. L.A., Aug. 17, 1942; s. Richard M. Owen and Betty Hamilton; m. Espy Bolivar. AB in Econ. with distinction, Stanford U., 1964; LLB, Harvard U., 1967. Bar: Calif., 1968, N.Y. 1968. Assoc. Reid & Priest, N.Y.C., 1967-69; mem. legal dept. Bank of Am. NT&SA, San Francisco, 1969-81; corp. sec. BRE Corp., San Francisco, 1970-75; v.p., assoc. gen. counsel Bank of Am. NT&SA, L.A., 1980-81; ptnr. & chair of Latin Amer. practice group Paul, Hastings, Janofsky & Walker, L.A., 1981—; mem. exec. com. Asia Pacific Dispute Resolution Ctr., NAFTA com. Am. Arbitration Assn.; mem. adv. bd. Southwestern Legal Found. Internat. and Comparative Law Ctr. Contbr. articles to profl. jours. regarding legal issues affecting financing and investment in Latin Amer. Office: Paul Hastings Janofsky & Walker 555 S Flower St Fl 24 Los Angeles CA 90071-2300

OWEN, NATHAN RICHARD, manufacturing company executive; b. Burnt Hills, N.Y., May 3, 1919; s. George H. and Mildred T. (Sharpley) O.; m. Janet M. Smith, Sept. 26, 1942; children: Patricia O. Smith, David G., Lorinda O. Clauson. B.S. in Mech. Engring, Mass. Inst. Tech., 1941, M.S., 1942; D.Sc., Clarkson Coll., 1979. With Chase Brass & Copper Co., 1946-47; with J.H. Whitney & Co., N.Y.C., 1947-62, ptnr., 1951-62; chmn. bd. Gen. Signal Corp., 1962-84, chmn. exec. com., 1980-95; chmn. emeritus, 1995—; bd. dirs. TechnoServe, Inc., Braille Internat., Inc., Enabling Techs., Inc. Served to lt. USN, 1942-46. Home: 1100 SW Shoreline Dr Palm City FL 34990 Office: PO Box 10351 Stamford CT 06904-2351

OWEN, RAY DAVID, biology educator; b. Genesee, Wis., Oct. 30, 1915; s. Dave and Ida (Hoeft) O.; m. June J. Weissenberg, June 24, 1939; 1 son, David G. BS, Carroll Coll., Wis., 1937, ScD, 1962; PhD, U. Wis., 1941, ScD, 1979; ScD, U. of Pacific, 1965. Asst. prof. genetics, zoology U. Wis., 1944-47; Gosney fellow Calif. Inst. Tech., Pasadena, 1946-47; assoc. prof. div. biology Calif. Inst. Tech., 1947-53, prof. biology, 1953-83, also chmn., v.p. for student affairs, dean of students, prof. emeritus, 1983—; research participant Oak Ridge Nat. Lab., 1957-58; Cons. Oak Ridge Inst. Nuclear Studies; mem. Pres.'s Cancer Panel. Author: (with A.M. Srb) General Genetics, 1952, 2d edit. (with A.M. Srb, R. Edgar), 1965; Contbr. articles to sci. jours. Recipient Gregor Mendel medal Czech Acad. Scis., 1965. Fellow AAAS; mem. Genetics Soc. Am. (pres., Thomas Hunt Morgan medal 1993), Am. Assn. Immunologists, Am. Soc. Human Genetics, Western Soc. Naturalists, Am. Soc. Zoologists, Am. Genetics Assn., Nat. Acad. Scis., Am. Acad. Arts and Scis., Am. Philos. Soc., Am. Acad. Allergy and Immunology (hon.), Internat. Soc. Animal Genetics (hon.), Sigma Xi. Home: 1583 Rose Villa St Pasadena CA 91106-3524 Office: Calif Inst Tech 156-29 Dean Students Office Pasadena CA 91125

OWEN, RAYMOND HAROLD, minister; b. Gleason, Tenn., Apr. 21, 1932; s. Charlie Emerson and Lula (Page) O.; m. Lavell Coburn, Oct. 4, 1952; children: Dana (dec.), Darryl R., Dyton L. BA in Religion, Oklahoma City U., 1964; ThM, So. Meth. U., 1967; MA in Evangelism, Scarritt Coll., Nashville, 1972; DD (hon.), Oklahoma City U., 1979. Ordained to ministry United Meth. Ch., 1967. Pastor 1st United Meth. Ch., Hugo, Okla.; dist. supt. Meth. Ch., Bartlesville Dist., Okla., 1977-82; sr. min. Epworth United Meth. Ch., Oklahoma City, 1971-73, New Haven United Meth. Ch., Tulsa, 1973-77, 1st United Meth. Ch., Bartlesville, Okla., 1982—; del. Jurisdictional Conf. S.W. United Meth. Ch., 1976, 80, 84, 88—, Gen. Conf., 1980, 84, 88, 90; mem. exec. com. World Meth. Coun. 1986—; bd. dirs. Green Co. Retirement Villa, Bartlesville. Author: Probingins in Prayer, 1975, Seedtime and Harvest, 1980, Questions That Shape Destiny, 1983, Listening To Life, 1987. 2d lt. U.S. Army, 1954-60. Mem. Rotary. Office: First United Meth Ch 500 S Johnstone Ave Bartlesville OK 74003-6621 *It is never very far from the mediocre to the exceptional; it is just more painful.*

OWEN, RICHARD, federal judge; b. N.Y.C., Dec. 11, 1922; s. Carl Maynard and Shirley (Barnes) O.; m. Lynn Rasmussen, June 6, 1960; children: Carl R., David R., Richard. AB, Dartmouth Coll., 1947; LLB, Harvard U., 1950; MusD (hon.), Manhattan Sch. Music, 1989. Bar: N.Y. 1950. Practiced in N.Y.C., 1950-74; assoc. Willkie Owen Farr Gallagher & Walton, 1950-53, Willkie Farr Gallagher Walton & Fitzgibbon, 1958-60; pvt. practice, 1960-65; ptnr. Owen & Aarons, 1965-66, Owen & Turchin, 1966-74; asst. U.S. atty. So. Dist. N.Y., 1953-55; trial atty. antitrust div. U.S. Dept. Justice, 1955-58; U.S. dist. judge So. Dist. N.Y., 1974—; asst. prof. N.Y. Law Sch., 1951-53; assoc. counsel N.Y. State Moreland Com. on Alcoholic Beverage Control Laws, 1963-64. Composer, librettist operas A Moment of War, 1958, A Fisherman Called Peter, 1965, Mary Dyer, 1976, The Death of the Virgin, 1980, Abigail Adams, 1987, Tom Sawyer, 1989. Trustee Manhattan Sch. Music, N.Y.C.; founder, bd. dirs. Maine Opera Assn., 1975-85; pres., bd. dirs. N.Y. Lyric Opera Co. 1st lt. USAAF, 1942-45. Decorated D.F.C. with oak leaf cluster, Air medal with 3 oak leaf clusters. Mem. ASCAP, Century Assn., Chelsea Yacht Club. Republican. Mem. Soc.

of Friends. Office: US Dist Ct US Courthouse Foley Sq New York NY 10007-1501

OWEN, ROBERT HUBERT, lawyer, real estate broker; b. Birmingham, Ala., Aug. 3, 1928; s. Robert Clay and Mattie Lou (Hubert) O.; m. Mary Dane Hicks, Mar. 14, 1954; children: Mary Kathryn, Robert Hubert. B.S., U. Ala., 1950; J.D., Birmingham Sch. Law, 1956. Bar: Ala. 1957, Ga. 1965. Methods and procedures analyst, supr. Ala. Power Co., Birmingham, 1952-58; assoc. Martin, Vogtle, Balch & Bingham, Birmingham, 1958-63; asst. sec. So. Services, Atlanta, 1963-69; sec. Southern Co., Atlanta, 1969-71; sec., asst. treas. Southern Co., 1971-77; exec. v.p., sec., gen. counsel, dir. Proverbs 31 Corp., Atlanta, 1978-81, 90—; broker Bob Owen Realty, Atlanta, 1990—; pvt. practice law Marietta, 1978-85; v.p., gen. counsel Hubert Properties, 1985-86. Atlanta area rep. Inst. Basic Youth Conflicts, 1970-80. Served to maj. USAF, 1951-52, 61-62. Mem. Jasons, Delta Chi, Omicron Delta Kappa, Beta Gamma Sigma, Delta Sigma Pi, Phi Eta Sigma. Baptist. Home and Office: 6590 Bridgewood Valley Rd NW Atlanta GA 30328-2906

OWEN, ROBERT RANDOLPH, accountant; b. Ardmore, Okla., June 24, 1939; s. Buford Randolph and Ruth Marie (Cleeton) O.; m. Patra Malinda Randolph, June 20, 1958; children: Stacy Malinda Owen Hodges, Mindy Carol Owen Long. BBA with high honors, So. Meth. U., 1961; postgrad., Harvard U., 1985. CPA, Tex. Various positions Alford, Meroney & Co., Dallas, 1961-80, mgr., 1967-69, ptnr., 1969-73, mng. ptnr. Dallas office, 1975-78, firm mng. ptnr., 1978-80; dep. regional mng. ptnr. S.W. region Arthur Young & Co., Dallas, 1980-83, ptnr., nat. dir. entrepreneurial svcs., 1983-86, ptnr., nat. dir. indsl. specialization, 1986-89; ptnr., nat. dir. industry svcs. Ernst & Young, 1990—. Author, editor: The Arthur Young Guide to Financing for Growth, 1986, The Ernst & Young Guide to Raising Capital, 1991. Capt. USAF, 1961-64. Mem. Tex. Soc. CPAs (pres. 1994-95, pres. Dallas chpt. 1988-89, bd. dirs. 1986—), AICPA. Baptist. Office: Ernst & Young LLP 2121 San Jacinto St Ste 500 Dallas TX 75201-6706

OWEN, ROBERT ROY, retired manufacturing company executive; b. Somerton, Ariz., Aug. 29, 1921; s. Wilbur Parker and Flossye Bell (White) O.; m. Barbara Dean Burton, Apr. 3, 1943; children—Melinne, Claudia, Christina, Rebecca, Jennifer. B.S., U. Calif. at Davis, 1942. Plantation engr. Del Monte, Hawaii, 1946-49; tech. rep. E.I. duPont de Nemours & Co., 1949-50; head engring. Pineapple Research Inst. of Hawaii, 1950-56; farm implement planning mgr., product planning and programming mgr., asst. chief engr., gen. mgr. equipment operations Tractor and Implement div. Ford Motor Co., Birmingham, Mich., 1956-68; pres. Gt. Western Sugar Co., Denver, 1968-71, Gt. Western Producers Coop., Englewood, Colo., 1971-76, Eversman Mfg. Co., Denver, 1976-95; dir. Ivancie Cellars, Inc.; Gen. chmn. Birmingham Arts Festival, 1960; pres. Evergreen Homes Assn., 1969-71; mem. U.S. Dept. Agr. Joint Council Food and Agrl. Scis., 1983-86. Contbr. articles to profl. jours. Served with AUS, 1942-46; brig. gen. Res. Recipient Centennial citation U. Calif., 1968, Distinguished Service award Colo. State U., 1971. Fellow Am. Soc. Agrl. Engrs.; mem. Newcomen Soc., Internat. Wine and Food Soc., Denver Club, Hiwan Country Club. Patentee in field. Office: Eversman Mfg Co 7475 W 5th Ave Ste 214 Lakewood CO 80226-1674

OWEN, ROBERT VAUGHAN, financial company executive; b. No. Adams, Mass., June 2, 1920; s. William and Lucy Anne (Morgan) O.; m. Jean Ann Gebauer, Dec. 6, 1946; children: Robert, Nancy, Bruce, Elizabeth. BA cum laude, Dartmouth Coll., 1946; MBA, Amos Tuck Sch., 1947. Fin. mgr. Gen. Electric Co., various locations, 1950-62; sr. budget dir. Citibank, N.Y.C., 1962-68, v.p., 1968-78, mng. dir., 1978-83; pres., chief exec. officer Bob Owen Assocs., Inc., Darien, Conn., 1984—. Contbr. articles to profl. jours. With USNR, 1943-45. Mem. N.Y. Fin. Execs. Inst. (pres. 1976). Republican. Roman Catholic. Office: Bob Owen Assocs Inc 10 Haskell Ln Darien CT 06820-3301

OWEN, ROBERTS BISHOP, lawyer; b. Boston, Feb. 11, 1926; s. Roberts Bishop and Monica Benedict (Burrell) O.; m. Kathleen Comstock von Schrader, Aug. 27, 1966; children—David Roberts, Lucy Leffingwell, William Atreus. Student, Dartmouth Coll., 1943-44; A.B. cum laude, Harvard U., 1948, LL.B. cum laude, 1951; Dip.C.L.S., Cambridge U., Eng., 1952. Bar: D.C. 1952, U.S. Ct. Appeals (D.C. cir.) 1953, U.S. Supreme Ct. 1958. Assoc. Covington & Burling, Washington, 1952-60; ptnr. Covington & Burling, 1960-79, 81—; the legal advisor U.S. Dept. State, Washington, 1979-81; sr. advisor Sec. of State former Yugoslavia, 1995; arbitrator Fedn. Bosnia and Herzegovina, 1995; mem. Permanent Ct. Arbitration, The Hague, The Netherlands, 1980-86, 93—; mem. arbitration panel Internat. Ctr. for Settlement of Investment Disputes, 1995—. Served to ensign USN, 1943-46. Fulbright scholar, 1951-52; recipient Disting Honor award Dept. of State, 1981, Sec. of State Disting. Svc. award, 1996, Sec. of Defense's medal for outstanding pub. svc., 1996. Fellow Am. Coll. Trial Lawyers; mem. ABA, Council Fgn. Relations, Am. Soc. Internat. Law (exec. council 1981-85). Clubs: Royal Ocean Racing (London); Metropolitan, City (Washington). Office: Covington & Burling Po Box 7566 1201 Pennsylvania Ave NW Washington DC 20044

OWEN, STEPHEN LEE, lawyer; b. Danville, Va., Mar. 25, 1952; s. L. Davis and Ann (Brodie) O.; m. Catherine Bryan Mabry; children: Hillary Brodie, Stephen Grayson. BA, Hampden-Sydney Coll., Va., 1974; JD, Coll. of William and Mary, Williamsburg, Va., 1977. Bar: Va. 1977, Md. 1977, U.S. Tax Ct. 1978, U.S. Dist. Ct. Md., D.C. 1990. Assoc. Venable, Baetjer & Howard, Balt., 1977-84, ptnr., 1985-93; ptnr. Piper & Marbury, Balt., 1993—. Co-author: Federal Taxation of Estates, Gifts & Trusts, 1988; co-author newsletter Real Estate Tax Ideas, 1985-; contbr. articles to profl. jours.; editorial bd. Jour. Partnership Taxation, 1984—, The Practical Tax Lawyer, 1985—. Bd. dirs. Balt. City Found., 1979-89. Mem. Am. Law Inst., Md. Bar Assn. (chmn. sect. of taxation 1989-90), Balt. Country Club, Caves Valley Golf Club. Avocation: golf. Office: Piper & Marbury 36 S Charles St Baltimore MD 21201-3020

OWEN, SUZANNE, retired savings and loan executive; b. Lincoln, Nebr., Oct. 6, 1926; d. Arthur C. and Hazel E. (Edwards) O. BSBA, U. Nebr., Lincoln, 1948. With G.F. Lessenhop & Sons, Inc., Lincoln, 1948-57; with First Fed. Lincoln, 1963-91; v.p., dir. personnel, 1975-81, 1st v.p., 1981-87, sr. v.p., 1987-91, ret., 1991; mem. pers. bd. City of Lincoln, 1989—. Mem. Lincoln Human Resources Mgmt. Assn., Lincoln Mgmt. Soc., Phi Chi Theta. Republican. Christian Scientist. Clubs: Wooden Spoon, Exec. Women's Breakfast Group, Community Women's. Lodges: Pi Beta Phi Alumnae, Order of Eastern Star (Lincoln).

OWEN, SYLVIA, interior design executive; d. Manfred and Maria Curry; grad. in Interior Design, U. Munich, 1963, N.Y. Sch. Interior Design, 1965; m. Christopher Owen, Oct. 9, 1965; 1 dau., Tjasa. With Internat. Knoll Planning Unit, N.Y.C., 1968-71; sr. interior designer, assoc. John Carl Warnecke and Assocs., N.Y.C., 1971-78; ptnr. Innerplan, N.Y.C., 1978-82; founder, operator Owen & Mandolfo, Inc., 1982—. Mem. Am. Soc. Interior Designers, AIA (assoc.). Projects include Chase Manhattan Bank, Chemical Bank, Republic Nat. Bank, AT&T Hdqrs., Bedminster, N.J., Sun Co. Hdqrs., Radnor, Pa., Globtik Tankers' exec. offices, N.Y.C. (first prize for corp. interiors Interior Design mag. 1976), Am. Hosp. in Paris expansion, CCNY, Commerzbank, N.Y.C., Restoration Villard Houses for Capital Cities Communications, Inc., N.Y.C., Beneficial Mgmt. Corp., Peapack, N.J., David Murdock Assocs., N.Y.C.; developing Gen. Telephone Electric hdqrs. bldg., Stamford, Conn., Dime Savings Banks, L.I., Christian Dior stores, N.Y.C. and Bal Harbour, Fla., tower stes. Waldorf Astoria Hotel, Trump Tower stores, numerous others; redesigning Neiman-Marcus store, San Francisco; developing new image Charles Jourdan stores, Davidoff of Geneva, L.A.; designing numerous pvt. residences. Works pub. in Archtl. Record, Interior Design, Interiors, N.Y. Mag., N.Y. Times, Archtl. Digest. Named one of 100 Best Interior Designers Worldwide, Archtl. Digest; recipient Outstanding Achievement award and 1st prize best of competition by Inst. Bus. Designers and Interior Design Mag., 1992, 1st prize for best design Am. Soc. Interior Designers, 1992; featured in Women of Design by Rizzoli. Office: Owen & Mandolfo Inc 192 Lexington Ave New York NY 10016-6823*

OWEN, THOMAS BARRON, retired naval officer, space company executive; b. Seattle, Mar. 19, 1920; s. Thomas Barron and Ruth (Deane) O.; m. Rosemary Stolz, Dec. 24, 1944; children—Catherine Adams, Thomas Barron, James Rowell, Nancy Deane. B.S. cum laude, U. Wash., 1940; postgrad., U.S. Naval Postgrad. Sch., 1946-47; Ph.D. in Chemistry, Cornell U., 1950; postgrad., U. Amsterdam, 1950-51, Indsl. Coll. Armed Forces, 1961-62, Harvard Grad. Sch. Bus. Adminstrn., 1964. Commd. ensign U.S. Navy, 1940, advanced through grades to rear adm., 1967, combat duty with Pacific Fleet, 1940-45; officer distbn. div. Bur. Naval Personnel, 1945-46; with armaments br. and mil. operations br. Office Naval Research, 1951-53; asst. repair supt. (hull) and prodn. analysis supt. Long Beach (Calif.) Naval Shipyard, 1953-57; dir. applied scis. div., dir. research and devel. planning div. Navy Bur. Ships, 1957-61; mil. asst. to dep. dir. def. research and engring. engring. and chemistry, 1962-63; assigned Office Asst. Sec. Navy Research and Devel., 1963; dir. support services Naval Research Lab., 1963-65, dir., 1965-67; chief naval research, 1967-70, ret., 1970; asst. dir. nat. and internat. programs NSF, 1970-74; assoc. dean grad. affairs and rsch. Am. U., Washington, 1974-76; asst. provost Am. U., 1976-79; asst. adminstr. NOAA, Dept. Commerce, Rockville, Md., 1979-81; mgr. program planning Fairchild Space & Electronics Co., Germantown, Md., 1981-83; sr. dir. systems effectiveness Fairchild Space Co., Germantown, 1983-84, v.p. procurement, 1984-86. Author profl. papers. Decorated D.S.M., Silver Star, Bronze Star. Fellow AAAS; mem. Am. Chem. Soc., U.S. Naval Inst., Philos. Soc. Washington, Sigma Xi, Phi Kappa Phi, Phi Lambda Upsilon, Tau Beta Pi, Chi Psi. Club: Cosmos (Washington). Home: 8409 Magruder Mill Ct Bethesda MD 20817-2746 *Demand high standards of excellence for self and others. Achieve respect of others through own performance. Be direct; avoid circumspection. Develop empathy; listen; consider feelings and rights of others. Maintain philosophy of "Onward and Upward!".*

OWEN, THOMAS LLEWELLYN, investment executive; b. Patchogue, N.Y., June 24, 1928; s. Griffith Robert and Jeanette Roberts (Hatfield) O.; A.B. in Econs., Coll. William and Mary, 1951; postgrad. Columbia U., 1952, N.Y. Inst. Fin., 1960-62; M.B.A., N.Y. U., 1966. Exec. trainee Shell Oil Co., N.Y.C. and Indpls., 1951-59, supr., 1958-59; petroleum and chem. investment analyst Paine, Webber, Jackson & Curtis, N.Y.C., 1959-62; sr. oil investment analyst DuPont Investment Interests, Wilmington, Del., N.Y.C., 1962-66, dir. research, 1964-66; v.p., sr. investment officer, mem. policy, investment coms. Nat. Securities and Research Corp., N.Y.C., 1966-75; sr. investment exec., v.p., portfolio mgr. F. Eberstadt & Co. and Eberstadt Asset Mgmt., Inc., N.Y.C., 1975-85, mem. policy com., 1979-85, also dir. portfolio rev. com.; sr. investment exec., portfolio mgr. Brown Brothers Harriman, N.Y.C., 1985-89; pres., CEO Owen Capital Mgmt., N.Y.C., 1989—. Mem. N.Y. Soc. Security Analysts, Assn. of Investment Mgmt. and Rsch., Oil Analysts Group N.Y., Am. Econ. Assn., Investment Assn. N.Y., Am. Petroleum Inst., Nat. Assn. Petroleum Investment Analysts, Internat. Assn. Energy Economists. Contbr. chpt. "Oil and Gas Industries" to Financial Analysts Handbook, 1975. Home and Office: 251 E 32nd St New York NY 10016-6304 *Perseverance and hard work are essential. But intense desire and strong convictions in conjunction with ethical principles are the ingredients of an outstanding leader. When your peers recognize your abilities and accomplishments, you have reached the pinnacle of success. It can be lonely at the top ..... but so gratifying and rewarding.*

OWEN, THOMAS WALKER, banker, broker; b. Everett, Wash., June 7, 1925; s. Thomas Walker and Frances (Yantis) O.; m. Barbara May Neils, Oct. 20, 1951; children: Thomas W., Gerhard, Caroline, Jeffrey; m. Ingrid Lundgren, June 7, 1975. B.A., U. Wash., 1949, MA in Finance, 1953; postgrad., Pacific Coast Banking Sch., 1956. Adminstrv. trainee Seattle Trust & Savs. Bank, 1949-54, asst. br. mgr., 1954-56, trust investment officer, 1956-57, mgr. investment dept., chmn. investment com., 1957-59; v.p., mgr. investment dept. Nat. Bank Wash., Tacoma, 1959-66, vice chmn., 1967-71; exec. v.p. bank adminstrn. Pacific Nat. Bank Wash., 1971-73; v.p. Reeder, Owen & Co., Inc., 1975-92; pres., chmn. Owen, Reeder, Inc., Merrill Lynch, 1991-92; bd. dirs. West One Bank Wash., Tacoma, 1981-93. Served with AUS, 1943-45. Decorated Bronze Star, Purple Heart. Mem. N.W. Forum, Wash. Athletic Club, Tacoma Club (past pres.), Tacoma Country and Golf Club, Phi Gamma Delta. Home: 10819 Evergreen Ter SW Tacoma WA 98498-6701

OWEN, WALTER SHEPHERD, materials science and engineering educator; b. Liverpool, Eng., Mar. 13, 1920; s. Walter L. and Dorothea (Lunt) O. B.Engring., U. Liverpool, 1940, M.Engring., 1942, Ph.D., 1950, D.Eng., 1972. Metallurgist English Electric Co., 1940-46; mem. research staff MIT, 1951-57; prof. metallurgy U. Liverpool, 1957-66; prof., dir. materials sci. and engring. Cornell U., 1966-70; dean Tech. Inst., 1970-71; v.p. sci. and research Northwestern U., Evanston, Ill., 1971-73; prof. and head materials sci. and engring. MIT, 1973-82, prof. phys. metallurgy, 1982-85, prof. emeritus, sr. lectr. materials sci. and engring., 1985—; Cons. to industry. Author research papers. Commonwealth Fund fellow, 1951. Fellow ASM; mem. NAE, AIME, Instn. Metallurgists, N.Y. Acad. Scis., Inst. Metals, Materials Rsch. Soc., Japan Inst. Metals (hon.). Office: MIT Rm 13-5114 Cambridge MA 02139

OWEN, WILLIAM HAROLD, JR., academic administrator; b. Stilwell, Okla., Aug. 2, 1933; s. William Harold Sr. and Nellie (Whiteside) O.; m. Mary Ann Fryar, Mar. 10, 1956; children: David G., John F. AA, Jr. Agrl. Coll., Beebe, Ark., 1953; BS, Ark. State Tchrs. Coll., 1957, MS in Edn., 1960. Tchr. Beebe Pub. Schs., 1957-59; asst. prof. social scis. Ark. State U., Beebe, 1959-69, dean students, registrar, 1969-81, chancellor, 1981—; bd. dirs. Beebe Indsl. Devel. Corp. Corp. sec. White County Meml. Hosp., Searcy, Ark., 1987—. With USAF, 1953-55. Mem. Ark. Assn. Two-Yr. Colls. (chmn. bd. dirs. 1989-90), Ark. Higher Edn. Coun., Beebe C. of C. (bd. dirs. 1985—), Beebe Kiwanis (past pres.). Presbyterian. Avocations: hunting, fishing, woodworking. Office: Ark State Univ PO Drawer H Beebe AR 72012

OWEN, WILLIAM MICHAEL, real estate developer; b. Houston, Sept. 27, 1950; s. W. Frank and Lois Marie (Nelson) O.; m. Debra Ann Phillips, Jan. 9, 1971 (div.); 1 child, Heather Ann; m. Pamela C. Birkhead, Feb. 18, 1983; 1 child, Sean Michael. BA in Econs., U. North Tex., 1992, MBA in Fin., 1994. Pres. Owen Resource & Devel., Inc., Denton, Tex., 1992—; pub., editor The Profit Connection Fin. Newsletter, 1994—; v.p. Ivey & Owen Investments, Inc., Las Vegas, 1992—; pres. Owen Fin. Group, Houston, 1978—. Office: Owen Resource & Develop Inc 309 Hollyhill Ln Denton TX 76205-7811

OWENDOFF, JAMES M., federal agency administrator; m. Marilyn Miller; children: Nate, John. BS in Mech. Engring, Va. Poly. Inst., 1968; MS in Mech. Engring., Cornell U.; graduate, U.S. Army War Coll. Asst. Office of Chief Air Force Environ. Restoration Divsn., Office of Dep. Under Sec. Defense Environ. Security; dep. asst. sec. environ. restoration U.S. Dept. Energy, Washington. Col. USAF. Office: Dept Energy Environ Restoration 1000 Independence Ave SW Washington DC 20505

OWENS, ALEXANDRA CANTOR, professional society administrator; b. N.Y.C., Nov. 22, 1961; d. Murray A. and Lois (Van Arsdel) C.; m. Michael R. Owens. BA, William Smith Coll., 1983. Exec. sec. Nissel & Nissel, CPAs, N.Y.C., 1983-85, Am. Soc. Journalists and Authors Charitable Trust, N.Y.C., 1986—; exec. dir. Am. Soc. Journalists and Authors, N.Y.C., 1985—. Contbg. author: Tools of the Writer's Trade, 1990; editor Sitzmark newsletter of High Life Ski Club, Rockaway, N.J., 1994—. Office: Am Soc of Journalists 1501 Broadway Ste 302 New York NY 10036-5501

OWENS, BUCK (ALVIS EDGAR, JR.), singer, musician, songwriter; b. Sherman, Tex., Aug. 12, 1929; s. Alvis Edgar and Maicie A.; m. Bonnie Owens, 1947 (div. 1955); children: Buddy, Mike; m. Phyllis Owens (div. 1972); 1 son, John; m. Jennifer, 1978. Attended pub. schs., Mesa, Ariz. Pres. Buck Owens Prodns.; owner stas. KUZZ-FM, KCWR-AM, Bakersfield, Calif., stas. KCWW-AM, KNIX-FM, Phoenix, sta. KUZZ-TV, Bakersfield, Owens Enterprises, Bakersfield, Home Preview and Camera Ads Publs. Rec. artist, Capitol Records, 1958-76, 88—, Warner Bros. Records 1976-80; star syndicated TV shows Buck Owens Ranch Show; leader, Buck Owens' Buckaroos Band, 1960—; star of TV show Hee Haw, 1969-86. Records include Under Your Spell Again, Above and Beyond, Excuse Me, I Think I've Got a Heartache, Fooling Around, Under the Influence of Love, My Heart Skips a Beat, Act Naturally, Waitin' in the Welfare Line, Sam's Place, How Long Will My Baby Be Gone, Tall Dark Stranger, Too Old to Cut the Mustard, Rollin' in My Sweet Baby's Arms, The Kansas City Song, We're Gonna Get Together, albums include All Time Greatest Hits Vol. 1, 1990, vol. 2, 1992, vol. 3, 1993, The Buck Owens Collection (1959-90), 92; others. Recipient Instrumental Group of Year award Country Music Assn., 1967-68; named Artist of Decade Capitol Records, Country Artist of Year for 5 consecutive years Billboard, Cash Box and Record World; awarded 28 consecutive No. 1 records. Office: Buck Owens Prodns 3223 N Sillect Ave Bakersfield CA 93308-6332

OWENS, CHARLES VINCENT, JR., diagnostic company executive and consultant; b. Kansas City, Mo., May 15, 1927; s. Charles Vincent and Helen (Barrett) O.; m. Cheryl Kreighbaum, Feb. 12, 1955; children: Melody, Kevin, Michael, John, Barbara. B.S., U. Notre Dame, 1948; M.S. (Univ. fellow), U. N.C., 1949. Public health educator Richmond County (N.C.) Health Dept., 1949-51; with Miles Labs., Inc., Elkhart, Ind., 1951-82; pres. Ames Co. div. Miles Labs., Inc., 1967-71, group v.p. profl. products group, 1971-77, exec. v.p. internat. ops., 1977-82; chmn., chief exec. officer Kyoto Diagnostics, Inc., 1983-85; bd. dirs. Genesis Labs., Inc., St. Jude Med. Inc., Chronimed Inc.; chief exec. officer Genesis Inc., 1985-88, chmn., 1988—. Bd. dirs. Elkhart YWCA, 1972-76; vice chmn. Elkhart County Bd. Health, 1973-77; chmn. Child Abuse Task Force, Elkhart County, Ind., 1977-78. Served with M.C., USAAF, 1945-47. Mem. Am. Public Health Assn., Health Industry Mfg. Assn. (dir.), Pharm. Mfrs. Assn., Nat. Pharm. Council (pres. 1970-71, dir. 1965-73), Am. Mgmt. Assn., Am. Diabetes Assn., Am. Assn. Diabetes Educators, Internat. Diabetes Fedn., Am. Soc. Med. Tech. Republican. Roman Catholic.

OWENS, CHARLES WESLEY, university executive; b. Billings, Okla., Oct. 27, 1935; s. Fred Charles and Mary Isabel (Metheney) O.; m. Barbara Jeanne Williams, Dec. 18, 1955; children: Charles E., Wesley A., Michael L., Janet K. BS, Colo. Coll., 1957; PhD, U. Kans., 1963. Chemist Phillips Chem. Co., Borger, Tex., 1957-58; from asst. prof. to assoc. prof. to prof. dept. chemistry U. N.H., 1963-89, chair dept. chemistry, 1979-82, assoc. v.p. for acad. affairs, 1983-87, interim v.p. for fin. and adminstrn., 1987-88, interim v.p. for acad. affairs, 1988-89; v.p. for acad. affairs, prof. chemistry Radford (Va.) U., 1989—, acting pres., 1994—; program chmn. New Eng. Assn. Chemistry Tchrs.; congl. sci. counselor to U.S. senators T. J. McIntyre and Gordon Humphrey; mem. NSF Rev. Panel for Coll. Tchr. Programs; NSF vis. scientist to NE h.s.'s; mem., chair vis. teams Commn. on Colls., SACS; mem. task force on dependent benefits Joint Ops. Com., New Eng. Land Grant Univs.; bd. trustees N.H. Higher Edn. Assistance Found.; faculty fellow in acad. affairs U. N.H.; summer rsch. participant Oak Ridge Nat. Lab.; guest assoc. chemist Brookhaven Nat. Lab.; vis. prof. chemistry U. San Marcos, Lima, Peru; rsch. assoc. U. Kans.; cons. Boston Felt Co., Rochester, N.H., Random House, Inc., McGraw-Hill Book Co. Contbr. articles to profl. jours. Bd. trustees Sci. Mus. Western Va.; mem. Radford City Commn. on Arts and Events, 1995. 2d lt. U.S. Army, 1957-58. Mem. Am. Assn. Higher Edn., Am. Chem. Soc. (membership com. N.E. sect., com. on profl. tng.), Rotary Internat., Soc. for Coll. and Univ. Planning, Phi Beta Kappa, Delta Epsilon, Phi Kappa Phi, Phi Lambda Upsilon, Sigma Xi. Avocations: flying, hiking, tennis, painting, video production. Office: Radford U Box 6890 Preston Hall Radford VA 24142

OWENS, DONALD D., church officer; m. Adeline Owens; children: Donna Bean, Debbi Bohi, Darlene Conyers. MA in Religion, Bethany Nazarene Coll.; MA and PhD in Cultural Anthropology, U. Okla. Established Ch. of the Nazarene, Korea, 1954-66; tchr. Nazarene Theol. Sem., Kansas City, Mo., 1975-81, Bethany (Okla.) Nazarene Coll., 1966-74; founding pres. Asia Pacific Nazarene Theol. Sem., Manila, 1981-84; regional dir. Asia Pacific World Mission Divsn., Manila, 1981-85; pres. MidAm. Nazarene Coll., Olathe, 1985—; mem. bd. gen. supts. Ch. of the Nazarene, Indpls., 1989—; founder Korea Nazarene Theol. Coll. Author: Challenge in Korea, Church Behind the Bamboo Curtain, Revival Fires in Korea, Sing Ye Islands. Office: Church of Nazarene 6401 Paseo Blvd Kansas City MO 64131-1213

OWENS, DORIS JERKINS, insurance underwriter; b. Range, Ala., June 16, 1940; d. Arthur Charles and Jennie (Lee) Jerkins; m. Gilbert Landers Owens, Jan. 29, 1959; 1 child, Alan Dale. Student Massey Draughon Bus. Coll., 1958-59, Auburn U., Montgomery, 1980, 81, 82. Cert. ins. counselor, profl. ins. woman. Exec. sec. Henry C. Barnet, Gen. Agt., Montgomery, Ala., 1959-66; sr. underwriter personal lines So. Guaranty Ins. Co., Montgomery, 1966—. Author: Bike Safety, 1976. Instr. Coop. State Dept. Defensive Driver Instr., 1975, 78; instr. ins. classes; v.p. Montgomery Citizens Fire Safety, 1981; panelist Gov.'s Safety Conf., Montgomery, 1975—; mem., panelist Women Annual Hwy. Safety Leaders, Montgomery, 1976, 78, 80; apptd. mem. Alliance Against Drugs, 1989. Recipient Able Toastmaster award Dist. 48 Toastmasters, 1979, Outstanding Lt. Gov. award, 1981, Outstanding Area Gov. award, 1980; named Ins. Woman of Year, 1979. Mem. Ins. Women Montgomery (pres. 1961, 85-86), Internat. Platform Assn., Blue-Gray Civitan Club. Office: So Guaranty Ins Co 2545 Taylor Rd Montgomery AL 36117-4706

OWENS, FLORA CONCEPCION, critical care nurse; b. Manila, Nov. 23, 1949; d. Felix and Marieta (Obsuna) Concepcion; m. George Owens, Feb. 13, 1976. Grad., San Juan de Dios Sch. Nursing, Pasay City, The Philippines, 1970; BSN, Concordia Coll., Manila, 1971. RN, Ill., Ark.; cert. in ACLS; CCRN. Staff nurse San Juan de Dios Hosp., 1970-71, Jefferson Meml. Hosp., Mt. Vernon, Ill., 1972, Russellville (Ark.) Nursing Home Ctr., 1973-76; staff nurse, relief supr. St. Mary's Regional Med. Ctr., Russellville, 1972-74, head nurse med. fl., 1975-76, insvc. coord. and unit mgr. med.-surg. ICU, 1976-90, staff nurse, charge nurse med.-surg. ICU, 1990—; instr. basic coronary care class, 1979-90, basic arrythmia class, 1979-91. Mem. AACCN, CCRN, Ark. Tech. Nurse Soc.

OWENS, GARY, broadcast personality, entrepreneur, author; b. Mitchell, S.D., May 10; s. Bernard and Vennetta O.; m. Arleta Lee Markell, June 26; children: Scott, Christopher. Student (speech and psychology scholar), Dakota Wesleyan U., Mitchell; student, Mpls. Art Inst. With Sta. KMPC, L.A., 1962-82; with Sta. KPRZ, L.A., 1982—, Sta KFI, L.A., 1986-90; pres. Foonman & Sons, Inc., 1987—; v.p., creative dir. GoldenWest Broadcasters, 1981-82; v.p., nat. creative dir. Gannett Broadcasting, 1984; TV performer, 1963—. writer Jay Ward Prodns., 1961-62; syndicated radio show The G.O. Spl. Report, from 1969; host: world-wide syndicated show Soundtrack of the 60's, 1981—, Biff Owens Sports Exclusive, 1981—; USA Today, Mut. Broadcasting System, 1982-83; radio host Gary Owens Music Weekend, Lorimar Telepictures, 1987—; performer, writer: world-wide syndicated show Sesame St, 1969—, Electric Co, 1969—, Dirkniblick (Mathnet) CTW, 1988; performer over 2500 animated cartoons including Dyno-Mutt, ABC-TV, 1975, Roger Ramjet, 1965, Space Ghost, 1968, Perils of Penelope Pitstop, 1970, Square One, 1987, Godzilla's Power Hour, 1979, Space Heroes, 1981, Mighty Orbots, 1984, World's Greatest Adventures, 1986, Garfield, Cops, Bobby's World, 1990, The 3 Musketeers, Return of Roger Ramjet, Alice in Wonderland, The Count of Monte Cristo, 20,000 Leagues Under the Sea, Godzilla, Mickey Mouse, Donald Duck, Goofy Chip N'Dale, Bill & Ted's Great Adventure, Tom & Jerry Jr., Eek the Cat, Swat Kats, Two Stupid Dogs, Ren & Stimpy, Bonkers, Dirk Niblick, numerous others, 1990; appeared: in films The Love Bug, 1968, Prisoner of Second Ave., 1975, Hysterical, 1982, Nat. Lampoon's European Vacation, 1985, I'm Gonna Get You Sucka, 1988, Kill Crazy, 1988, How I Got Into College, 1988, Say Bye Bye, 1989, Green Hornet, 1966 Regular on series; performer on camera more than 1000 nat. TV shows; performer: Rowan and Martin's Laugh-in, 1968-73; TV host: Gong Show, ABC-TV, 1976, Monty Pythons Flying Circus, 1975; regular performer: TV Games People Play, 1980-81, Breakaway, 1983; TV spls. include Bob Hope Spls., Like Hep, The Muppets Go Hollywood, Perry Como Visits Hollywood, The Gary Owens All-Nonsense News Network, Jonathan Winters & Friends, NBC's 50 Years, CBS's 50 Years, Battle of Beverly Hills, America's Choice. The American Comedy Awards, 1986—, Flip Wilson's Spls., Saturday Night at the Superbowl, Mickey Mouse's 50th Birthday; author: Elephants, Grapes and Pickles, 1963; 12 printings The Gary Owens What To Do While You're Holding the Phone Book, revised edit., 1973, A Gary Owens Chrestomathy, 1980; host Encore Pay TV, 1992; author: (screenplay) Three Caraway Seeds and an Agent's Heart, 1979; columnist: Radio and Records newspaper, 1978—, Hollywood Citizen-News, 1965-67, Hollywood mag., 1983—, The Daily News, 1981—; rec. artist MGM, ABC, Epic, Warner Bros., RCA, Reprise, Decca; TV announcer NBC, 1968-80, ABC, 1980—; host many top video's in U.S. including Dinosaurs, More Dinosaurs, Son of Dinosaurs, TV's Greatest Bits; host: How to Collect Comic Books, Aliens, Dragons, Monsters and Me, Gone Fishing, 1993, The Gary Owens All-Nonsense News Network. Chmn. Multiple Sclerosis dr. L.A., 1972; chmn., grand marshall So. Calif. Diabetes Dr., 1974—; mayor City of Encino, Calif., 1972-74; bd. govs. Grammy Awards, 1968—, Emmy Awards, 1972; mem. adv. bd. Pasadena (Calif.) City Coll., 1969—, Sugar Ray Robinson Youth Found., 1971—; mem. nat. miracle com. Juvenile Diabetes Found., 1981—, nat. com. for Carousel Ball Children's Diabetes Found. Denver; radio adv. bd. U. So. Calif., 1980—; hon. chmn. Goodwill Industries Sporting Goods Dr., 1986, chmn., 1986; active telethons Cerebral Palsy, 1980, DARE program, 1985—, S.A.N.E. program, 1985—, comic relief to help U.S. Homeless, 1986. Named outstanding radio personality in U.S., 1965-79, top Radio Personality in World, Internat. Radio Forum, Toronto, 1977, Man of Yr. All-Cities Employees Assn., City of Los Angeles, 1968, Top RadAssn. Broadcasters, 1986, Radio Man of Yr. Nat. Assn. Broadcasters, 1986; recipient Distinguished Service award Hollywood Jaycees, 1966, David award, 1978, Hollywood Hall of Fame award, 1980, Am. award Cypress Coll., 1981, Carbon Mike award Pacific Broadcasters, 1987, 5 Grammy nominations, Emmy award for More Dinosaurs, 1986; Star on Hollywood Walk of Fame, 1981; honored by U.S. Dept. Treasury, 1985, Am. Diabetes Assn., 1990, Variety Clubs Internat., 1990; inducted into Nat. Broadcasters Hall of Fame, 1994, Radio Hall of Fame, 1994, Nat. Assn. Broadcasters Hall of Fame, 1995. Mem. Nat. Cartoonists Soc., So. Calif. Cartoonists Assn., Cartoonists and Artists Profl. Soc. Office: 2444 Wilshire Blvd Ste 506 Santa Monica CA 90403-5813 *Without sounding like a coffee break Voltaire, the apothegm that "Everyman is his own Pygmalion" may be correct. I have tried to enrich my life by performing, reading, writing, creating, and helping others whenever possible. I try to stand up for what I believe, for it is better to give ulcers than to receive! Humor has helped protect me from the bruises of life, in addition to a daily supply of fantasy and illusion.*

OWENS, GREGORY RANDOLPH, physician, medical educator; b. Glendale, W. Va., Oct. 3, 1948; s. Elmer Herman and Anne Elizabeth (Kroggel) O.; m. Jane Marie Fleming, June 1, 1974; children: Gregory R. Jr., Allison Fleming. AB cum laude, Princeton U., 1970; MD, U. Pa., 1974. Diplomate Am. Bd. Internal Medicine, Am. Bd. Pulmonary Medicine, Am. Bd. Critical Care Medicine. Intern in internal medicine Hosp. U. Pa., Phila., 1974-75, residency in internal medicine, 1975-77, fellowship pulmonary disease, 1977-78, chief med. resident, 1978-79, fellowship pulmonary disease, 1979-80; asst. prof. medicine U. Pitts., 1980-86, assoc. prof. medicine, 1986-93, prof. medicine, 1993—, assoc. chief div. pulmonary medicine, 1984—; chief Montefiore U. Hosp., Pitts, 1991—; dir. Pulmonary Exercise Physiology Lab., Presbyn.-Univ. Hosp., Pitts., 1980-92, co-dir. Pulmonary Function Lab., 1980-92; co-dir. Occupl. Lung Clinic, Falk Clinic, Pitts., 1983-88. Contbr. articles to New Eng. Jour. Medicine, Am. Jour. Medicine, Jour. Lab. Clin. Medicine and others, presenter at profl. confs. Coach Oakmont (Pa.) Athletic Assn., 1988—, bd. dirs. Am. Lung Assn. Recipient Future Leaders Pulmonary Medicine award, Chgo., 1984, Preventive Pulmonary Acad. award NIH, 1988-93; grantee Health Rsch. and Svc. Found., 1980-85, NIH Lung Health Study, 1984-94, Lung Health Study II, 1994—. Mem. ACP, Am. Coll. Chest Physicians (Pa. gov. 1993—), Am. Thoracic Soc., Am. Fedn. for Clin. Rsch., Pa. Thoracic Soc. (pres. 1993-96). Avocations: golfing, gardening. Office: U Pitts Sch Medicine 440 Scaife Hall 3550 Terrace St Pittsburgh PA 15261

OWENS, HELEN DAWN, elementary school educator, reading consultant; b. Eastman, Ga., Oct. 9, 1949; d. Eli B. and Irene (Harrell) Branch; m. Bobby Lee Owens, Dec. 9, 1967; children: Leslie Owens-McDonald, Monica Dawn. AA, Miami (Fla.) Dade Jr. Coll., 1969; BS, Fla. Internat. U., 1978; MEd, Mercer U., 1986, EdS, 1991. Cert. presch.-12th grade, reading specialist, early childhood edn. specialist, Ga. Youth ctr. dir. Dept. Def., Clark AFB, Philippines, 1969-70; English lang. instr. Chinese Mil. Acad., Feng Shan, Taiwan, 1973-75; tchr., music instr. ABC Presch., Miami, 1976-78; kindergarten and music tchr. Berkshire Sch., Homestead, Fla., 1978-79; tchr., reading specialist Perdue Elem. Sch. Houston County Bd. Edn., Warner Robins, Ga., 1979—; mem. nominating com. mem. Ga. picture book of yr. U. Ga., Athens, 1990-91; reading cons. for schs., county edn. bds., regional reading ctrs., Ctrl. Ga., 1990—. Author: With Loving Hands and Tender Hearts, 1975. Exec. bd. dirs. Ladies Ministries, Ch. of God., Warner Robins, 1990-94; dir. Internat. City Girls' Club, Warner Robins, 1990-94. Recipient 25-Yr. Bible Tchr. Svc. award Internat. City Ch. of God., 1991; named Fla. State Family Tng. Dir. of Yr., Fla. Ch. of God, 1979, Ga. Girls' Club Coord. of the Year, 1995. Mem. Internat. Reading Assn. (mem. Ga. coun. 1979-96, dir. mem. devel. 1993-96, v.p. 1996-97, past pres. HOPE coun. 1990-92), Profl. Assn. Ga. Edn. Republican. Avocations: reading, sewing, touring foreign countries, swimming, storytelling. Home: 111 Crestwood Rd Warner Robins GA 31093-6803 Office: Perdue Elem Sch 856 Highway 96 Warner Robins GA 31088-2222

OWENS, HILDA FAYE, management/leadership development consultant, human resource trainer; b. Fountain, N.C., Mar. 23, 1939; d. Floyd Curtis and Essie Lee (Gay) O. BS in Edn. and Psychology, East Carolina U., 1961, MA in Edn., 1965; PhD in Higher Edn., Fla. State U., 1973; postgrad., Western Carolina U., 1962, U. Louisville, 1967, U. N.C., 1968. Tchr. New Bern (N.C.) City Schs., 1961-65; dir. counseling svcs., prof. Mt. Olive (N.C.) Coll., 1965-71, dean students, prof., 1973-77; coord. student affairs, rsch. assoc. bd. regents State Univ. System Fla., Tallahassee, 1971-73; assoc. prof. higher edn. U. S.C., Columbia, 1977-83; v.p. acad. affairs, prof. Spartanburg (S.C.) Meth. Coll., 1985-90; exec. asst. to pres. for planning and rsch., cons. Spartanburg (S.C.) Meth. Coll., 1990-91; pres. Excel Resource Assocs., Spartanburg, 1991—; mem. bd. dirs. The Haven; numerous presentations in field; speaker bus., ednl., civic and ch. meetings, confs. and workshops. Editor: Risk Management and the Student Affairs Professional, 1984, (with Witten and Bailey) College Student Personnel Administration: An Anthology, 1982; mem. editl. bd. Jour. Staff, Orgn. and Program Devel., Assn. Student Pers. Adminstrs. Jour., Nat. Assn. Student Pers. Adminstrs. Monograph Bd., Coll. Student Affairs Jour.; contbr. articles to profl. jours., over 40 chpts. to books. Grad. Leadership Spartanburg, 1987; adminstrv. bd. Bethel United Meth. Ch.; mem. exec. bd. Tuscarora coun. Boy Scouts Am. S.C. Coll. Pers. Assn. named Rsch. and Writing award in her honor, 1995; named One of 45 Outstanding S.C. Women, 1980, Disting. Grad. award Fla. State U., 1981, Outstanding Bus. and Profl. Woman of Yr. Spartanburg Bus. and Profl. Women, 1986, Capital Bus. and Profl. Women, 1982, Mt. Olive Bus. and Profl. Women, 1977; recipient Meritorious Svc. award S.C. Coll. Pers. Assn., 1990. Mem. NAFE, ASTD, Am. Mgmt. Assn., Nat. Assn. Student Pers. Adminstrs. (adv. bd. region III, Disting. Svc. award), Am. Assn. Higher Edn., Carolinas Soc. Tng. and Devel., Nat. Orgn. on Legal Problems in Edn., S.C. Pers. Assn. (pres., award named in honor 1994), Bus. and Profl. Women S.C. (pres., bd. dirs. Ednl. Found.), Internat. Platform Assn., Spartan West Rotary Club (bd. dirs.), Pi Delta Kappa (pres. U. S.C. chpt.). Democrat. Avocations: coin collecting, golf, movies, basketball, reading. Home: 230 Old Towne Rd Spartanburg SC 29301-3555 Office: Excel Resource Assocs PO Box 17248 Spartanburg SC 29301-0103

OWENS, JACK BYRON, lawyer; b. Orange, Calif., Oct. 14, 1944; s. Jack Byron and Lenna Mildred (Gobar) O.; children: John Byron, David Harold, James Paul, Alexandra Grace. A.B., Stanford U., 1966, J.D., 1969. Bar: Calif. 1970, D.C. 1970. Law clk. U.S. Ct. Appeals 9th Circuit, 1969-70; asso. firm Wilmer, Cutler & Pickering, Washington, 1970-71, 74-75; atty. adv. Dept. Air Force, 1971-73; law clk. U.S. Supreme Ct., 1973-74; prof. law Boalt Law Sch., U. Calif., Berkeley, 1975-79; partner firm Orrick, Herrington & Sutcliffe, San Francisco, 1978-81; exec. v.p., gen. counsel E & J Gallo Winery, 1981—; adj. prof. Georgetown U. Law Sch. Contbr. articles legal publns. Served with USAF, 1971-73. Mem. Am. Law Inst., Am. Bar Assn., Phi Beta Kappa, Order of Coif. Office: E & J Gallo Winery PO Box 1130 600 Yosemite Blvd Modesto CA 95353

OWENS, JANA JAE, entertainer; b. Great Falls, Mont., Aug. 30, 1943; d. Jacob G. Meyer and Bette P. (Sprague) Hopper; m. Sidney Greif (div.); children: Matthew N., Sydni C.; m. Buck Owens. Student, Interlochen Music Camp, 1959, Internat. String Congress, 1960, Vienna (Austria) Acad. Music, 1963-64; BA magna cum laude, Colo. Womens Coll., 1965, MusB magna cum laude, 1965. Tchr. music Ontario (Oreg.) Pub. Schs., 1965-67, Redding (Calif.) Pub. Schs., 1969-74; entertainer Buck Owens Enterprises, Bakersfield, Calif., 1974-78, Tulsa, 1979—; concertmistress Boise (Idaho) Philharm., 1965-67, Shasta Symphony, Redding, 1969-74. Rec. artist (violinist, vocalist) Lark Records, 1978—. Avocations: skiing, tennis, swimming. Office: Jana Jae Enterprises Lake Record Prodns Inc PO Box 35726 Tulsa OK 74153

OWENS, JOHN MURRY, dean; b. Livermore, Calif., Feb. 13, 1942; s. John Stephen and Hazel Mae (Murry) O.; m. Diane Davis, June 12, 1971; children: John, Jennifer, Mark. AA, Orange Coast Coll., 1961; BSEE, U. Calif., Berkeley, 1963; MSEE, Stanford U., 1964, PhD, 1968. Registered profl. engr., Tex. Prof. elec. engring. U. Tex., Arlington, 1979-87, dir. bur. engring., 1983-85, asst. dean rsch. coll. engring., 1983-85, dir. ctr. for advanced electron devices, 1984-87; prof., chmn. elec. engring. dept. Santa Clara (Calif.) U., 1987-89; program dir. NSF, Washington, 1989-91; prof., dir. engring. exptl. sta., assoc. dean for rsch. Auburn (Ala.) U., 1991—; cons. Microwave and Electronic Systems Ltd., Edinburgh, United Kingdom, Ivory and Sime Ltd., Edinburgh, Herbies Foods, Fort Worth, Tex. Instruments, Dallas, Rockwell Internat., Anaheim, Calif., Westinghouse Electric, Pitts., E.W. Communication Inc., Palo Alto, Calif., Telsar, Inc., Campbell, Calif., ITT Aerospace and Optical, Ft. Wayne, Ind., SMA, Inc., Florence, Italy, many others. Patentee in field. Bd. dirs. Arlington Swim Club; dist. chmn. boy Scouts Am., Auburn; bd. dirs. Arlington Gifted and Talented Assn.; pres. Masters of Upper Tex. Swimmers. Fellow IEEE; mem. Am. Soc. Engring. Edn., Kiwanis (bd. dirs. Arlington club), Tau Beta Pi, Eta Kappa Nu, Sigma Xi. Avocations: swimming, water skiing, camping, hiking, airplanes. Office: Auburn U 108 Ramsay Hall Auburn AL 36849

OWENS, JOSEPH, clergyman; b. Saint John, N.B., Can., Apr. 17, 1908; s. Louis Michael and Josephine (Quinn) O. Student, St. Mary's Coll., 1922-27, St. Anne's Coll., Montreal, Que. Can., 1928-30, St. Alphonsus Coll., Woodstock, Ont., Can., 1930-34; M.S.D., Pontifical Inst. Mediaeval Studies, Toronto, 1951. Ordained priest Roman Cath. Ch., 1933; parish asst. St. Joseph's Ch., Moose Jaw, Sask., Can., 1934-35, St. Patrick's Ch., Toronto, 1935-36, Maria-Hilf Ch., Tomslake, B.C., Can., 1940-44; instr. philosophy St. Alphonsus Sem., Woodstock, Ont., Can., 1936-40, 48-51, 53, Assumption U., Windsor, Ont., Can., 1954; with Pontifical Inst. of Mediaeval Studies, Toronto, 1954—; prof. Pontifical Inst. of Mediaeval Studies, 1960—; instr. mediaeval moral doctrine Accademia Alfonsiana, Rome, Italy, 1952-53; mem. faculty dept. philosophy Sch. Grad. Studies, U. Toronto. Mem. editorial bd.: The Monist, 1961—; Contbr. numerous articles to religious and profl. jours. Mem. Canadian Philos. Assn. (pres. 1981-82), Am. Catholic Philos. Assn. (pres. 1965-66), Metaphys. Soc. Am. (councillor 1965-67, pres. 1971-72), Soc. Ancient Greek Philosophy (pres. 1971-72), Catholic Commn. Intellectual and Cultural Affairs, Royal Soc. Can. Home: 141 McCaul St, Toronto, ON Canada M5T 1W3 Office: 59 Queen's Park Crescent, Toronto, ON Canada M5S 2C4

OWENS, LEWIS E., newspaper executive; b. Knoxville, Tenn., Mar. 11, 1934; m. Janetta Owens. B.S., Gainesville Coll. Retail advt. salesman Fort Worth Press, 1956-59; advt. dir. Gainesville Daily Register, 1959-62; asst. retail advt. mgr. Charlotte Observer and News, N.C., 1962-66; retail advt. mgr. Tallahassee Democrat, Fla., 1966-68, Charlotte Observer and News, 1968-75; advt. dir. Lexington Herald-Leader, Ky., 1975-78, v.p. sales and mktg., 1978-82, then v.p. and gen. mgr., now pres., pub. Sec. bd. dirs. Lexington Arts Council; v.p. Central Ky. Blood Ctr.; pres. United Way of the Bluegrass, 1978, 79, campaign chmn., 1977. Mem. Greater Lexington Area C. of C. (pres.-elect), Ky. Press Assn. (v.p.). Avocations: golf; racquetball; travel; sports. Office: Lexington Herald-Leader Co 100 Midland Ave Lexington KY 40508-1943

OWENS, MAJOR ROBERT ODELL, congressman; b. Memphis, June 28, 1936; m. Marie Cuprill; children: Christopher, Geoffrey, Millard, Carlos, Cecilia. Grad. with high honors, Morehouse Coll., 1956; M.S., Atlanta U., 1957. Mem. Internat. Commn. on Ways of Implementing Social Policy to Ensure Maximum Pub. Participation and Social Justice for Minorities, The Hague, Netherlands, 1972, 98th-104th Congresses from 12th (now 11th) N.Y. dist., 1983—; chmn. select edn. & civil rights subcom., edn. and labor com., 1987, ranking minority mem. econ. and ednl. opportunity subcom. on worker protections, mem. govt. reform and oversight com.; featured speaker White House Conf. on Librs., 1979. Pub. author and lectr. on library sci. Chmn. Bklyn. Congress Racial Equality; v.p. Met. Coun. on Housing, 1964; community coord. Bklyn. Pub. Library, 1964-66; exec. dir. Brownsville Community Coun., 1966-68; commr. N.Y.C. Community Devel. Agy., 1968-73; bd. dirs. community media program Columbia U., N.Y.C., 1973-75; mem. N.Y. State Senate, 1975-82, chmn. Dem. Ops. Com. Major R. Owens Day, named in his honor, City Bklyn., 1971. Office: US Ho of Reps 2305 Rayburn HOB Washington DC 20515-2311*

OWENS, MARVIN FRANKLIN, JR., oil company executive; b. Oklahoma City, Feb. 20, 1916; s. Marvin Franklin and Lewis (Coley) O.; m. Jessie Ruth Hay, June 15, 1941; children: Marvin Franklin III, William Earl, Jack Hay. B.S., U. Okla., 1937; postgrad., Stonier Grad. Sch. Banking Rutgers U., 1960-62. Petroleum engr. Brit. Am. Oil Producing Co., Oklahoma City, 1937-41; chief petroleum engr. Bay Petroleum Corp., Denver, 1946-54; sr. v.p. Cen. Bank of Denver, 1954-81. Elder Presbyn. Ch., Denver. With U.S. Army, 1941-46; col. Res. ret. Mem. Cherry Hills Country Club. Home: 3899 S Glencoe St Denver CO 80237-1024

OWENS, MARY JO, electronic guidance services company executive; b. Asheville, N.C., Nov. 26, 1936; d. William James and Mamie Laura (Simms) O.; children: Lolita Omaria, Ionita. BS, N.C. State U., 1963; MS in Edn., Iona Coll., 1973; DLitt, Knightsbridge U., Copenhagen, 1995; PhD (hon.), World Acad., Germany, England, 1995, Australian Inst. Coord. Rsch., 1995, London Inst. Applied Rsch., 1995. Prof. English N.C. State U., Greensboro, 1961-62, prof. French, 1962-63; instr. French Phillips Sr. High Sch., Battleboro, N.C., 1963-64, Farmville (N.C.) Sr. High Sch., 1964-65; instr. French, English Jordan Sellars Sr. High Sch., Burlington, N.C., 1965-66; program coord. Project Aware, Fed. Grant Program, Greensboro, 1966-67; instr. French, English Westchester County Schs., Mt. Vernon, N.Y., 1967-88; instr. Spanish evening sch. Bedford Park Acad., Bronx, N.Y., 1976-79; realty broker, owner M.J. Howell and Co. Inc., Stanfordville, N.Y., 1982—; founder, owner Electronic Guidance Svcs. Corp., Hunns Lake, N.Y., 1988—; dep. Internat. Parliament for Safety and Peace, Palermo, Italy. Author: An No Clouds Over My Sun, 1973 (Demale Writers award 1975), Native American Images and Resipes, 1991, Through the Glass, Clearly a Character Study of the "Half-Breed" in America, 1992. Founder Children of Profls. Orgn., Westchester County, N.Y., 1991—; pres. New Rochelle (N.Y.) Assn. Women Voters, 1981-89. Recipient Ludwig von Beethoven Medal of Honor, 1995, Albert Einstein Medal of Honor, 1995, Henri Dunant Medal of Honor, 1995; Am. Sch. Honors scholar, 1959; City of Mt. Vernon grantee, 1982-84. Mem. Internat. Culture Club (pres. 1982—), N.Y. Profl. Women (pres. 1990-92), N.Y. State Tchrs. Fedn., N.Y. State Retired Tchrs. Assn., Westchester County Minority Bus. Assn. (pres. 1982—), Westchester County Minority Real Estate Bd. (bd. dirs. 1982—), Cherokee Child Orgn. (chmn. 1988-92, Native Am. Visionary award 1992, Inner Man award 1991). Avocations: writing, drama, art, piano, voice. Home: PO Box 310 Stanfordville NY 12581-0310 Office: Electronic Guidance Svcs PO Box 27 Stanfordville NY 12581-0027

OWENS, MERLE WAYNE, executive search consultant; b. Barnsdall, Okla., Mar. 30, 1933; s. Jesse Raymond and Beulah Juanita (Thompson) O.; m. Nettie Natalie Norris, June 6, 1953; children: Jesse Wayne, Jennifer Lee. BBA, U. Okla., 1955. Sales engr. Nat. Supply Co., Tulsa, 1956-60; underwriter Allstate Ins., Dallas, 1960-63; regional mgr. Blue Cross Blue Shield, Dallas, 1963-78; sr. v.p. Paul R. Ray & Co., Ft. worth, 1978-93; owner Merle Owens & Assocs., Ft. worth, 1993—. 1st lt. U.S. Army, 1955-56. Republican. Baptist. Avocations: hunting, fishing, woodworking. Home: 420 Blue Jay Ct Bedford TX 76021-3201 Office: Merle W Owens & Assocs 201 Main St Ste 600 Fort Worth TX 76102-3110

OWENS, MICHAEL, camera graphics expert, executive. Student fil prodn., history, criticism. Freelance editor, prodn. mgr., asst. cameraman, gaffer, grip L.A. area, 1975-81; asst. cameraman, effects cameraman Indsl. Light & Magic, San Rafael, Calif., 1981—; freelance photography dir. 1981—. Asst. cameraman (films) ET: The Extraterrestrial, 1982, Star Trek II: The Wrath of Kahn, 1982; effects cameraman (films) Return of the Jedi, 1983, Indiana Jones and the Temple of Doom, 1984, Young Sherlock Holmes, 1985, Witches of Eastwick, 1987 (Brit. Acad. award); visual effects supr. The Burbs, 1989, Skin Deep, 1989, Switch, 1990, The Doors, 1990; dir. Robin Williams trailer for Mill Valley Film Festival. Office: Indsl Light & Magic PO Box 2459 San Rafael CA 94912-2459

OWENS, ROCHELLE, poet, playwright; b. Bklyn., Apr. 2, 1936; d. Max and Molly (Adler) Bass; m. George Economou, June 17, 1962. Fellow, Yale Sch. Drama, 1968. writer-in-residence, Brown U., 1989; tchr. U. Calif. 1982, U. Okla., 1985, 87, 88. Author: plays The String Game, 1965, Istanboul, 1965, Futz, 1967, Homo, 1966, Beclch, 1966, Futz and What Came After, 1968, He Wants Shih, 1969, Farmers Almanac, 1969, The Queen of Greece, 1969, Kontraption, 1970, The Karl Marx Play, 1971, O.K. Certaldo, 1975, Emma Instigated Me, 1976, The Widow and the Colonel, 1977, Mountain Rites, 1977, Who Do You Want, Peire Vidal, 1978, Chucky's Hunch, 1981, Who Do You Want, Peire Vidal, 1982; poetry Not be Essence That Cannot Be, 1961, Salt and Core, 1968, I am the Babe of Joseph Stalin's Daughter, Poems from Joe's Garage, The Joe 82 Creation Poems, The Karl Marx Play & Others, The Joe Chronicles, Part 2, Four Young Lady Poets, 1962, Shemuel, 1979, French Light, 1984, Constructs, 1985, Anthropologists at a Dinner Party, 1985, Who Do You Want Peire Vidal, 1986, W.C. Fields in French Light, 1986, How Much Paint Does the Painting Need, 1988, Selected Poems: 1961-1994, Black Chalk, 1992, Rubbed Stones: Poems from 1960-1992, 1994; (radio play) Sweet Potatoes, 1979 (Obie award 1982); (feature film) Futz, 1969; editor: (plays) Spontaneous Combustion; (Obie award 1967), Cimmarron Rev.; recs. include: From a Shaman's Notebook, 1968, The Karl Marx Play, 1974, Totally Corrupt, 1976, Black Box 17, 1979, (play) Three Front, 1990; (radio play) A Guerre Trois, 1991; reading performances at St. Mark's Poetry Project, Mus. Modern Art, Guggenheim, Whitney Mus., Oxford U., Am. Coll., Paris; host of The Writer's Mind; producer radio show, U. Okla.; (video) Oklahoma Too, 1987, How Much Paint Does The Painting Need, 1992; translator Festival Franco-Anglais, 1991, The Passersby, 1993; (video) Black Chalk, 1994. Founding mem. N.Y. Theatre Strategy, Women's Theatre Council. Ford Found. grantee, 1965, Creative Arts Pub. Svc. grantee, 1973, Nat. Endowment for Arts grantee, 1974, Rockfeller Found. grantee, 1974; Guggenheim fellow, 1971; honors N.Y. Drama Critics Cir.; Rockefeller Found. Bellagio resident, 1993; recipient Nomination in poetry Okla. Ctr. for the Book, 1995. Mem. Dramatists Guild, ASCAP. Included in anthologies. Address: 1401 Magnolia St Norman OK 73072-6827 *Creativity, idealism and mental concentration have enabled me to pursue the world of ideas, transforming itself always into art.*

OWENS, RODNEY JOE, lawyer; b. Dallas, Mar. 7, 1950; s. Hubert L. and Billie Jo (Foust) O.; m. Sherry Lyn Bailey, June 10, 1972; 1 child, Jonathan Rockwell. BBA, So. Meth. U., 1972, JD, 1975. Bar: Tex. 1975, U.S. Dist. Ct. (no. dist.) Tex. 1975, U.S. Tax Ct. 1975, U.S. Ct. Appeals (5th cir.) 1975. Assoc. Durant & Mankoff, Dallas, 1975-78, ptnr., 1978-83; ptnr. Meadows, Owens, Collier, Reed, Cousins & Blau, Dallas, 1983—. Contbr. articles to profl. jours. Baptist. Home: 6919 N Jan Mar Dr Dallas TX 75230-3111 Office: Meadows Owens Collier Reed 3700 Nations Bank Plz 901 Main St Dallas TX 75202-3714

OWENS, STEPHEN THOMAS, lawyer; b. San Jose, Calif., Aug. 2, 1948; s. Thomas Cunnane and Patricia Ann (Howie) O.; m. Joyce Ruckman, June 15, 1970 (div. Dec. 1972); 1 child, Eric Albert; m. Janet Lynn Gattuccio, Aug. 28, 1977; 1 child, Monica Lisa Cali. Diplôme des Etudes Franç, Université de Provence, Aix-en-Provence, France, 1973; BA, San Jose State U., 1974; JD, UCLA, 1978. Bar: Calif. 1978, U.S. Ct. Appeals (9th cir.) 1980, U.S. Dist. Ct. (no, cen., ea. & so. dists.) Calif., U.S. Dist. Ct. (ea. dist.) Ark. Assoc. Graham & James, L.A., 1978-84, ptnr., 1985—. Vol. atty. Pub. Counsel, L.A., 1990—, bd. dirs., 1992—. Recipient Pro Bono Svc. award State Bar of Calif., 1992, John Minor Wisdom Profl. and Pub. Svc. award ABA, 1993. Avocations: sailing, skiing, sea kayaking. Office: Graham & James 801 S Figueroa St Fl 14 Los Angeles CA 90017-2573*

OWENS, WILBUR DAWSON, JR., federal judge; b. Albany, Ga., Feb. 1, 1930; s. Wilbur Dawson and Estelle (McKenzie) O.; m. Mary Elizabeth Glenn, June 21, 1958; children: Lindsey, Wilbur Dawson III, Estelle, John. Student, Emory U., 1947-48; JD, U. Ga., 1952. Bar: Ga. 1952. Mem. firm Smith, Gardner & Owens, Albany, 1954-55; v.p., trust officer Bank of Albany, 1955-59; sec.-treas. Southeastern Mortgage Co., Albany, 1959-65; asst. U.S. atty. Middle Dist. Ga., Macon, 1962-65; assoc., then ptnr. Bloch, Hall, Hawkins & Owens, Macon, 1965-72; judge U.S. Dist. Ct. for Mid. Dist. Ga., Macon, 1972—, now sr. U.S. dist. judge. Served to 1st lt., JAG USAF, 1952-54. Mem. State Bar Ga., Macon Bar Assn., Am. Judicature Soc., Phi Delta Theta, Phi Delta Phi. Republican. Presbyterian. Clubs: Rotarian, Idle Hour Golf and Country. Office: US Dist Ct PO Box 65 Macon GA 31202-0065

OWENS, WILLIAM ARTHUR, military officer; b. Bismarck, N.D., May 8, 1940; s. Earl and Ruth (Arthur) O.; m. Monika Bastian, Sept. 30, 1967; 1 child, Todd. BS, U.S. Naval Acad., 1962; BA, MA, U. Oxford, Eng., 1974; MBA, George Washington U., 1976. Registered profl. engr.,. Commd. ensign USN, 1962, advanced through ranks to admiral, 1994, multiple assignments in nuclear submarines, 1962-77; comdg. officer USS Sam Houston (SSBN609), Honolulu, 1977-80, USS Corpus Christi (SSN705), New London, Conn., 1980-81, Submarine Squadron 4, Charleston, S.C., 1984-85, Submarine Group 6, Charleston, S.C., 1987-88; dir. USN Strategic Think Tank Washington, 1988, sr. mil. asst. to Sec. Def., 1988-90; comdr. 6th Fleet, Gaeta, Italy, 1990-92; dep. chief naval ops. Resources, Warfare Requirements & Assessments, Washington, 1992-94; vice-chmn. Joint Chiefs of Staff The Pentagon, Washington, 1994—. Author: Future of the Maritime Strategy, 1988, High Seas, 1994. Mem. Submarine League, U.S. Naval Acad. Alumni Assn., Oxford Soc., Coun. Fgn. Rels. Republican. Episcopalian. Avocations: golf, tennis.

OWENS, WILLIAM DON, anesthesiology educator; b. St. Louis, Dec. 12, 1939; s. Don and Caroline Wilhemena (Raaf) O.; m. Patricia Gail Brown, Dec. 12, 1964; children: Pamela, David, Susan. AB, Westminster Coll., 1961; MD, U. Mich., 1965. Diplomate Am. Bd. Anesthesiology. Resident and fellow Mass. Gen. Hosp. and Harvard Med. Sch., Boston, 1969-72; instr. Harvard Med. Sch., Boston, 1972-73; asst. prof. anesthesiology Washington U. Sch. Medicine, St. Louis, 1973-76, assoc. prof., 1976-82, prof., 1982—, chmn. dept., 1982-92; trustee Barnes Hosp., St. Louis, 1987-89; bd. dirs. Found. for Anesthesia Edn. and Rsch., 1990-95, Anesthesia Found.; bd. dirs. Am. Bd. Anesthesiology, 1984—, sec.-treas., 1991-94, pres., 1994—. Assoc. editor Survey of Anesthesiology, 1977-92; contbr. 50 articles to profl. jours., 7 chpts. to books. Served to lt. comdr. USN, 1966-69. Fellow Am. Coll. Anesthesiology; mem. Am. Soc. Anesthesiologists (bd. dirs. 1989-95, 1st v.p. 1995—), Internat. Anesthesia Rsch.Soc., Acad. Anesthesiology, Assn. Univ. Anesthesiologists. Office: Washington U Sch Med Dept Anesthesiology 660 S Euclid Ave Saint Louis MO 63110-1010 also: Am Bd Anesthesiology The Summit Ste 510 4101 Lake Boone Trail Raleigh NC 27607-7506

OWEN-TOWLE, CAROLYN SHEETS, clergywoman; b. Upland, Calif., July 27, 1935; d. Millard Owen and Mary (Baskerville) Sheets; m. Charles Russell Chapman, June 29, 1957 (div. 1973); children: Christopher Charles, Jennifer Anne, Russell Owen; m. Thomas Allan Owen-Towle, Nov. 16, 1973. BS in Art and Art History, Scripps Coll., 1957; postgrad. in religion, U. Iowa, 1977. Ordained to ministry Unitarian-Universalist Ch., 1978. Minister 1st Unitarian Universalist Ch., San Diego, 1978—; pres. Ministerial Sisterhood, Unitarian Universalist Ch., 1980-82; mem. Unitarian Universalist Svc. Com., 1979-85, pres., 1983-85. Bd. dirs. Planned Parenthood, San Diego, 1980-86; mem. clergy adv. com. to Hospice, San Diego, 1980-83; mem. U.S. Rep. Jim Bates Hunger Adv. Com., San Diego, 1983-87; chaplain Interfaith AIDS Task Force, San Diego, 1988—. Mem. Unitarian Universalist Ministers Assn. (exec. com. 1988, pres. 1989-91). Avocations: reading, walking, combating racism, promoting human rights, designing environments. Office: 1st Unitarian Universalist Ch 4190 Front St San Diego CA 92103-2030

OWERS, BRIAN CHARLES, retired holding company executive; b. London, 1934. Grad., U. of London, 1955. Sec. The Rank Orgn. Plc; sec., bd. dirs. Rank RX Holdings Ltd.; sec. A. Kershaw & Sons Plc; bd. dirs. Rank Holdings (UK) Ltd., Rank Overseas Holdings Ltd. Office: The Rank Organisation Plc, 6 Connaught Pl, London W2 2EZ, England

OWINGS, DONALD HENRY, psychology educator; b. Atlanta, Dec. 7, 1943; s. Markley James and Loyce Erin (White) O.; m. Sharon Elizabeth Calhoun, Jan. 29, 1966; children: Ragon Matthew, Anna Rebekah. BA in Psychology, U. Tex., 1965; PhD, U. Wash., 1972. Asst. prof. psychology U. Calif., Davis, 1971-78, assoc. prof., 1978-83, prof., 1983—, chair dept., 1989-93. Contbr. articles to profl. jours., book chpts. NSF rsch. grantee, 1978-80, 82-84. Fellow Animal Behavior Soc.; mem. Internat. Soc. for Ecol. Psychology, Internat. Soc. for Behavioral Ecology, Internat. Soc. for Comparative Psychology, Am. Psychol. Soc. Democrat. Avocations: hiking, music, bird watching, reading. Home: 815 Oeste Dr Davis CA 95616-1856 Office: U Calif Dept Psychology Davis CA 95616-8686

OWINGS, FRANCIS BARRE, surgeon; b. McColl, S.C., Mar. 9, 1941; s. Ralph Seer and Antoinette (Moore) O.; B.S., U. Miss., 1963, M.D., 1966; m. Judith Myers, Feb. 14, 1976; children—F. Patterson, Caroline C. Intern, San Francisco Gen. Hosp., 1966-67; resident in surgery U. Calif., San Francisco, 1969-74; surg. registrar Norfolk and Norwich Hosp., Norwich, Eng., 1971-72; practice medicine specializing in surgery, Atlanta, 1974—; mem. staff Crawford Long Hosp., pres. med. staff, 1981-82; mem. staff Piedmont Hosp.; clin. instr. surgery Emory U. Served to capt. USAF, 1967-69. Diplomate Am. Bd. Surgery. Fellow ACS, Southeastern Surg. Congress; mem. Med. Assn. Atlanta, Med. Assn. Ga., Naffziger Surg. Soc., Alpha Epsilon Delta, Sigma Chi, Phi Chi. Republican. Methodist. Home: 3400 Wood Valley Rd NW Atlanta GA 30327-1518 Office: 478 Peachtree NE Atlanta GA 30308

OWINGS, MALCOLM WILLIAM, retired management consultant; b. Cin., Feb. 5, 1925; s. William Malcolm and Margaret (Benvie) O.; m. Margie M. Gehiker, Sept. 4, 1948; children: Lynn A., Sandra S., Wendy K., Cheryl M. B.S. in Bus. Adminstrn., Miami U., Oxford, Ohio, 1950, LL.D., 1976; A.M.P., Harvard U., 1975. With Continental Can Co., 1950-83, corp. v.p., from 1971; v.p., gen. mgr. pub. affairs Continental Packaging Co (Continental Group, Inc.), 1982-83; owner, pres. Owings Assocs., Inc., Pinehurst, N.C., 1983-92; dir. First Bank, Pinehurst, N.C.; adviser to Am. del. Internat. Tin Council, 1978-82. Dean's assoc. exec. in residence Sch. Bus., Miami U., 1973, mem. alumni coun., 1958-65, mem. pres.'s devel. coun., 1965-69, meem. resource devel. bd., 1982; trustee Village of Thiensville, Wis., 1956-59; mem. N.C. Clean, 1985-94, chmn., 1986-93; bd. dirs. Barrington Area Devel. Coun., 1974-79, Sales Mgmt. Execs. Grad. Sch., Am. Soc. Environment, 1976, Keep Am. Beautiful, 1980-81, also chmn., 1990; chmn. Keep N.C. Beautiful Coun., Raleigh, 1988-92, Moore Meml. Hosp. Found., Pinehurse, N.C., 1986-89; mem. Moore Regional Hosp. Scroll Soc., 1991—, chmn., 1992-93; chmn. Moore County (N.C.) Rep. Party, 1986-88; co-founder Rep. Presdl. Task Force; mem. U.S. Senate Bus. Adv. Bd., 1981-91; commr. Moore County, 1988—, re-elected, 1992, Youth Svcs., 1993-95; apptd. to N.C. Watershed Protection Adv. Com. by N.C. Environ. Mgmt. Commn., 1990-92; bd. dirs. Pub. Edn. Found., 1994—, Ptnrs. for Children and Family, 1994—, Drug-Free Moore County Inc., 1995—, Dispute Settlement Ctr. of Moore County, 1995—; mem. Moore County Bd. of Health, 1994—. Recipient Cert. of Meritorious Svc. Miami U., 1967, Meritorious Svc. award Keep Moore County Beautiful, Inc., 1993-94; named Alumnus of Yr. Miami U., 1970; 1st Am. recipient Order of Apteryx Earth Awareness Found., 1971. Mem. Ill. C. of C. (bd. dirs. 1976-78), Miami U. Alumni Assn. (nat. pres. 1964-65), Omicron Delta Kappa, Sigma Chi, Delta Sigma Pi. Clubs: Pinehurst Country, Country of N.C. (Pinehurst). Home and Office: 805 Diamond Head Dr S Pinehurst NC 28374-9773 *The Golden Rule - "treating others as thyself" is not only a cornerstone for success, it is the foundation of personal happiness. However, it is well to remember that none of this is possible without political freedom and the contingent responsibilities that freedom requires.*

OWINGS, MARGARET WENTWORTH, conservationist, artist; b. Berkeley, Calif., Apr. 29, 1913; d. Frank W. and Jean (Pond) Wentworth; m. Malcolm Millard, 1937; 1 child, Wendy Millard Benjamin; m. Nathaniel Alexander Owings, Dec. 30, 1953. A.B., Mills Coll., 1934; postgrad., Radcliffe Coll., 1935; LHD (hon.), Mills Coll., 1993. One-woman shows include Santa Barbara (Calif.) Mus. Art, 1940, Stanford Art Gallery, 1951, stitchery exhbns. at M.H. De Young Mus., San Francisco, 1963, Internat. Folk Art Mus., Santa Fe, 1965. Commr. Calif. Parks, 1963-69, mem., Nat. Parks Found. Bd, 1968-69; bd. dirs. African Wildlife Leadership Found., 1968-80, Defenders of Wildlife, 1969-74; founder, pres. Friends of the Sea Otter, 1969-90; chair Calif. Mountain Lion Preservation Found., 1987; trustee Environmental Def. Fund, 1972-83; Regional trustee Mills Coll., 1962-68. Recipient Gold medal, Conservation Svc. award U.S. Dept. Interior, 1975, Converation award Calif. Acad. Scis., 1979, Am. Motors Conservation award, 1980, Joseph Wood Krutch medal Humane Soc. U.S., Nat. Audubon Soc. medal, 1983, A. Starker Leopole award Calif. Nature Conservancy, 1986, Gold medal UN Environment Program, 1988, Conservation award DAR, 1990, Disting. Svc. award Sierra Club, 1991. Home: Grimes Point Big Sur CA 93920

OWNBEY, PAMELA JEAN, civil engineer, environmental engineer; b. Eugene, Oreg., Sept. 5, 1953; d. Jelde Gene and Irene Neva (Beshears) Meyer; m. Anthony William Ownbey, May 2, 1972; children: Jill Suzanne, David Timothy. BS in Civil Engring. with high honors, Oregon State U., 1986, MS in Civil Engering., 1987. Registered profl. envirn. and civil engr., Oreg. Assoc. engr. Brown & Caldwell, Eugene, Oreg., 1987-89; civil engr. USDA-Willamette NF, Eugene, Oreg., 1989-95; environ. engr. Cascade Group, Eugene, Oreg., 1989—; civil engr. David Evans and Assocs., Bend, Oreg., 1995—. Guest speaker Childrens Miracle Network Telethon, Eugene, 1989; vol. Childrens Relief Nursery, Buena Vista Spanish Sch., Eugene, 1990-95; asst. coach Kidsports, Eugene, 1992-94. GPOP fellow EPA, 1986. Mem. ASCE, Am. Waterworks Assn., Water and Environ. Fedn., Internat. Conf. Bldg. Ofcls. Home: PO Box 10921 Eugene OR 97440-2921

OWNBY, CHARLOTTE LEDBETTER, anatomy educator; b. Amory, Miss., July 27, 1947; d. William Moss and Anna Faye (Long) Ledbetter; m. James Donald Ownby, Sept. 6, 1969; children: Holly Ruth, Mary Faye. BS in Zoology, U. Tenn., 1969, MS in Zoology, 1971; PhD in Anatomy, Colo. State U., 1975. Instr. Okla. State U., Stillwater, 1974-75, asst. prof., 1975-80, assoc. prof., 1980-84, prof., 1984—; dir. electron microscope lab. Okla. State U., Stillwater, 1977-87, head dept., 1990-95. Editor Proc. 9th World Congress Internat. Soc. Toxicology, 1989; editorial bd. Toxion, 1984—. Recipient SmithKline-Beecham award for rsch. excellence, 1992; NIH, USPHS grantee, 1979-92. Mem. Okla. Soc. Electron Microscopy (pres. 1977-78), Pan Am. Soc. Toxinology (pres. 1994—), Phi Beta Kappa, Sigma Xi, Phi Kappa Phi. Avocations: butterfly photography, bird watching, hiking, camping. Office: Okla State U Dept Physiol Scis 264 Vet Medicine Stillwater OK 74078

OWNBY, DENNIS RANDALL, pediatrician, allergist, educator, researcher; b. Athens, Ohio, July 14, 1948; s. Dillard Ralph and Miriam (Lee) O.; m. Helen Louise Engelbrecht, May 24, 1970; children: David Randall, Kathryn Louise. BS, Ohio U., 1969; MD, Med. Coll. Ohio, 1972. Diplomate Am. Bd. Allergy and Immunology, Am. Bd. Pediatrics, Nat. Bd. Med. Examiners. Intern and resident Duke U. Sch. Medicine, Durham, N.C., 1972-74, asst. prof., 1977-80; staff physician Henry Ford Hosp., Detroit, 1980—, dir. Allergy Rsch. Lab., 1986—; clin. asst. prof. pediat. U. Mich., Ann Arbor, 1980-86, clin. assoc. prof., 1986-95. Contbr. articles to med. jours., chpts. to books. Recipient Young Investigator award Nat. Inst. Allergy and Infectious Disease, 1978. Fellow Am. Acad. Pediatrics, Am. Acad. Allergy. Office: Henry Ford Hosp Dept Allergy & Clin Immunology 2799 W Grand Blvd Detroit MI 48202-2608

OWNBY, JERRY STEVE, landscape architect, educator; b. Shawnee, Okla., Jan. 25, 1939; s. Hugh H. and N. Lorraine (Hopkins) O.; children by previous marriage: Gregory Steve, Mitchell Hugh; m. Arnola Colson, Dec. 19, 1971; 1 child, Steven Cory. BS, Okla. State U., 1961; MS in Landscape Architecture, Kans. State U., 1964, M in Landscape Architecture, 1970. Coun. Landscape Archtl. Registration Bds. cert. and registered landscape architect, Ariz., Kans., Okla., Mo., Tex. Extension landscape architect Kans. State U., Manhattan, 1963-64, instr., 1969-70; landscape architect Beardsley & Talley, Seattle, 1964-65; extension specialist Okla. State U., Stillwater, 1965-69, from asst. prof. to prof. landscape architecture and coordinator landscape architecture, 1970-85; pvt. practice, 1985—; chmn. Okla. Landscape Architect Registration Bd., 1980-85; mem. 1985 Expert Panel for Uniform Nat. Exam., 1984-85; gov.'s appointee Mo. Coun. Landscape Architects, 1991—. Designs include Las Laderas residence, 1978 (Merit award 1981), Student Union courtyard Okla. State U., 1981 (Honor award 1983). Chmn. Oklahomans for Landscape Architecture, 1979-80; chmn., vice chmn. Stillwater Park and Recreation Adv. Bd., Okla., 1971-79. Recipient Outstanding Prof. award Okla. State U. chpt. Alpha Zeta, 1975, svc. award Stillwater City Commn., 1980, design awards Springfield Planning and Zoning Commn.., 1988, 89, 90, design award Springfield Environ. Adv. Bd., 1990, Gov.'s landscape design award for Andy Williams' Moon River Theatre, Branson, Mo., 1992, for Charley Pride Theater, Branson, 1995, design award Watershed Com., 1993; alumni fellow Kans. State U., 1995. Fellow Am. Soc. Landscape Architects (v.p. 1983-85, Okla. chpt. Svc. award 1980); mem. Nat. Coun. State Garden Clubs (accredited instr. 1964—), Nat. Coun. of Educators in Landscape Architecture, Mo. Assn. of Landscape Architects, Coun. Landscape Archtl. Registration Bds. (cert.), Phi Kappa Phi, Sigma Lambda Alpha. Republican. Baptist. Avocations: travel; photography; fishing. Home and Office: 1161 S Virginia Ave Springfield MO 65807-1727

OWSIA, NASRIN AKBARNIA, pediatrician; b. Babol, Iran, Dec. 5, 1940; came to U.S., 1968; d. Ahmad and Hoora O.; m. Behrooz A. Akbarnia, Mar. 19, 1968; children: Halleh, Ladan, Ramin. MD, Tehran (Iran) U., 1966. Intern in pediatrics Berkshire Med. Ctr. Hosp., Pittsfield, Mass., 1968-69; resident in pediatrics Albany (N.Y.) Med. Ctr. Hosp., 1969-72; pediatric gastroenterologist St. Christopher Hosp. for Children, Phila., 1972-73; asst. prof. Albany Med. Coll., 1973-76, Tehran U., 1976-80; asst. prof. St. Louis U. Med. Ctr., 1981-89, clin. assoc. prof., 1989-90; pvt. practice San Diego, 1990—. Bd. mem. Persian Cultural Ctr., San Diego, 1993—. Recipient award AMA. Fellow Am. Acad. Pediatrics; mem. Allergy and Asthma Found., Calif. Med. Soc., San Diego Med. Soc. Avocations: knitting, downhill skiing. Office: 8010 Frost St Ste 414 San Diego CA 92123-4284

OWSLEY, DAVID THOMAS, art consultant, appraiser, lecturer, author; b. Dallas, Aug. 20, 1929; s. Alvin Mansfield and Lucy (Ball) O. Grad., Phillips Andover Acad., 1947; A.B., Harvard, 1951; M.F.A., N.Y. U., 1964; fellow, Met. Mus. Am. Wing, 1964. Asst. curator dept. decorative arts and sculpture Boston Mus. Fine Arts, 1965-66; visitor Victoria and Albert Mus., London, Eng., 1966-68; curator antiquities, Oriental and decorative arts Mus. Art, Carnegie Inst., Pitts., 1968-78; mem. collections com. Dallas Mus. Art, 1994—. Served to 1st lt. USAF, 1952-54. Recipient Pres.' medal of Distinction Ball State U., 1989, Westmoreland Soc. Gold medal, 1991. Clubs: D.U. (Harvard Coll.); Leland Country (Mich.); Knickerbocker (N.Y.C.). Home: 116 E 68th St New York NY 10021-5956 *I have tried to pursue beautiful and significant works of art and to encourage others to share my love and respect for them.*

OWSLEY, TINA KATHLEEN, special education educator; b. Ponca City, Okla., Apr. 3, 1953; d. Lindsey C. Jr. and Nina Jane (Lotts) O. BA in Edn., Northeastern Okla. State U., 1975, MS in Edn., 1978; cert. in deaf edn., Tex. Woman's U., 1981; cert. in spl. edn. adminstrn., Gallaudet U., Washington, 1984. Cert. speech correction, learning disabilities, Mo., speech therapy, learning disabilites, deaf edn., Okla., speech pathology, learning disabilities, deaf edn., educable mentally handicapped, physically impaired, Kans. Tchr. learning disabilities, speech pathologist Perry County Schs., Perryville, Mo., 1975-77; tchr. learning disabilities Vinita (Okla.) Pub. Schs., 1977-78; cons. hearing impaired Sequoyah County Spl. Edn. Coop., Sallisaw, Okla., 1978-80; tchr. hearing impaired Ft. Gibson (Okla.) Pub. Schs., 1980-83; asst. to the v.p. Gallaudet U., 1983-84; coord., tchr. hearing impaired Shawnee County Spl. Edn. Coop., Topeka, 1984—; parent advisor Project ECHO, Okla. Dept. Edn., Oklahoma City, 1978-83; early interventionist Hearing Cons., Topeka, 1989—. Co-author: Curriculum Guide - Presch. Hearing Impaired Children, 1991. Bd. dirs. Florence Crittendon, 1995—. Mem. Nat. Assn. for Edn. of Young Children (Kans. chpt., pres. Topeka Assn. 1988-89), NEA (Kans. chpt., mem. Topeka spl. edn. com. 1991—, polit. action com. 1991—, bldg. rep. 1993-95), Coun. for Exceptional Children (pres. Chpt. 204 1989—, v.p. Kans. Fedn. 1991-92, pres.-elect Kans. Fedn. 1992-93, pres. 1993-94, immediate past pres. 1994-95, chmn. Spl. Edn. Day at the Legis. Kans. Coun. 1991, 95), Kans. Divsn. Early Childhood (pres. 1989-90, mem. chair 1993—), Kans. Educators of Hearing Impaired (pres. 1989-90), Kans. Commn. for Deaf and Hearing Impaired (chair Early Identification and Intervention Coun. 1990-95), Soroptimist Internat. Am. (corr. sec. local chpt. 1991-92, cmty. svc. chair 1991-95, del. 1992-94, bd. dirs. 1992-93, 95—, rec. sec. 1993-94, chair Youth Citizenship Award/Tng. Award Program 1995—, Soroptimist of the Yr. 1993), Sertoma Internat. (publicity chair 1992-94), Topeka Tots Team (sec. 1991—), Jr. Deaf Club (sponsor 1992—), Camp Fire Coun. (bd. dirs. 1993-96, chair program/membership 1993-96). Republican. Mem. Christian Ch. (Disciples of Christ). Avocations: counted cross-stitch, reading, gardening. Home: 4711 SE Girard St Topeka KS 66609-1838 Office: Shawnee County Spl Edn Coop 1725 SW Arnold Ave Topeka KS 66604-3306

OWSLEY, WILLIAM CLINTON, JR., radiologist; b. Austin, Tex., Oct. 6, 1923; s. William Clinton and Lois (Lamar) O.; B.A., U. Tex., 1944; M.D., U. Pa., 1946; m. Betty Pinckard, 1949; 2 children. Intern, Hermann Hosp., Houston, 1946-47; resident Hosp. of U. Pa., Phila., 1949-52; instr. radiology U. Pa., 1950-52; practice medicine specializing in radiology, Houston, 1952—; mem. staff Hermann Hosp., Twelve Oaks Hosp., Bellville Hosp., St. Elizabeth Hosp., Brazos Valley Hosp.; assoc. clin. prof. radiology U. Tex. Served with USNR, 1947-48. Diplomate Am. Bd. Radiology. Fellow Royal Soc. Medicine (U.K.), Am. Coll. Radiology; mem. Am. Roentgen Ray Soc., Radiol. Soc. N.Am., Interam. Coll. Radiology, AMA. Republican. Baptist. Office: 4710 Greeley St Ste 230 Houston TX 77006-6254

OWYANG, CHUNG, gastroenterologist, researcher; b. Chung King, China, Nov. 20, 1945; arrived in Can., 1965; s. Chi and Ching-Ying (Fung) O.; m. Jeannette Lim; children: Stephanie, Christopher. BS with honors, McGill U., Montreal, Can., 1968, MD, 1972. Diplomate Am. Bd. Internal Medicine, Gastroenterology; lic. Gen. Med. Coun., U.K., Que., Can., Min. Med. lic., Mich. med. lic. Intern in internal medicine Montreal Gen. Hosp./McGill U., 1972-73, resident in internal medicine, 1973-75; clin. teaching fellow in internal medicine McGill U., 1974-75; fellow in gastroenterology Mayo Clinic and Found., Rochester, Minn., 1975-78; instr. internal medicine Mayo Med. Sch., Rochester, 1977-78; asst. prof. U. Mich., 1978-84, assoc. prof., 1984-88, assoc. chief divsn. gastroenterology, 1984-90, prof., 1988—, chief divsn. gastroenterology, 1991—, dir. med. procedures unit, 1992—, dir. Digestive Health Inst., 1992—; assoc. dir. Gastrointestinal Peptide Rsch. Ctr., U. Mich., 1984-95, dir. 1996—; cons. Rsch. Coun. Janssen Pharmaceutica Inc., 1985—, Ann Arbor VA Med. Ctr., 1978—, NIH, Bethesda, Md., 1989-94, FDA, Bethesda, 1995—; H. Marvin Pollard chair in gastroenterology, U. Mich., 1996—; speaker, presenter in field. Co-author: Textbook of Gastroenterology, 1991, 2d edit. 1995, Atlas of Gastroenterology, 1992; mem. edit. bd. Pancreas, 1986—, Am. Jour. Physiology, 1988—, Regulatory Peptide Letter, 1988—, Gastroenterology, 1990—, guest editor, 1991—, Digestive Diseases, 1993—; contbr. numerous chpts. to books, articles to profl. jours., jours. refereed. Grantee in field. Fellow ACP; mem. Am. Assn. Physicians, Am. Soc. Clin. Investigation, Am. Gastroenterological Assn., Am. Pancreatic Assn., Am. Diabetes Assn., Am. Fedn. Clin. Rsch., Am. Motility Soc., Ctrl. Soc. Clin. Rsch., Internat. Assn. Pancreatology, Midwest Gut Club. Office: U Mich Med Ctr 3912 Taubman Ctr Ann Arbor MI 48109

OWYOUNG, STEVEN DAVID, curator; b. San Francisco, Jan. 14, 1947; s. Fay and Ethel (Woo) O.; m. Diana Lee Wong, Aug. 29, 1971; children: Christopher Mark, Todd Alexander. BA, U. Hawaii, 1973; MA, U. Mich., 1977, postgrad., 1978. Lectr., editor Nat. Palace Mus., Taipei, Taiwan, 1971-72; curatorial assoc. Fogg Art Mus., Harvard U., Cambridge, Mass., 1980-82, asst. curator, 1982-83; curator Asian arts St. Louis Art Mus., 1983—; sec. commn. bd. commrs. St. Louis Art Mus., 1991-93; vis. Washington U., St. Louis, 1990—; cons. Getty Art History Info. Program, 1993. Bd. dirs. World Affairs Coun. St. Louis, 1984-86, Nanjing-St. Louis Sister Cities, 1989-90; del. Chinese painting historians to People's Republic China, 1980. Charles L. Freer fellow Freer Gallery Art, 1976, 77, Horace H. Rackham predoctoral fellow, 1978, Louise W. Hackney fellow Am. Oriental Soc., 1978-79, Fulbright-Hays fellow, 1978-79, Social Sci. Rsch. Coun. and Am. Coun. Learned Socs. fellow, 1978-80; Samuel H. Kress Found. grantee, 1980, Horace H. Rackham grantee, 1980, Asian Cultural Coun. grantee, 1990. Mem. Asian Art Soc. Washington U. (bd. dirs. 1983—). Office: St Louis Art Mus Forest Pk Saint Louis MO 63110

OXELL, LOIE GWENDOLYN, fashion and beauty educator, consultant, columnist; b. Sioux City, Iowa, Nov. 17, 1917; d. Lyman Stanley and Loie Erma (Crill) Barton; m. Eugene Edwin Eschenbrenner, Aug. 8, 1936 (dec. 1954); children: Patricia Gene, Eugene Edward (dec. Feb. 1994); m. Henry J. Oxell, Nov. 3, 1956 (dec. July 1994). AS in Fashion Merchandising, Broward C.C., Davie, Fla., 1978. Fashion rep. Crestmoor Suit & Coat Co., St. Louis, 1951-56; with "To the Ladies" TV show KSD-TV, St. Louis, 1953-56; cons./instr. Miami-Herald Newspaper Glamor Clinic, Miami, Fla., 1957-71; pres./owner Loie's (Loy's) Inc., Miami, Fla., 1958-71; owner West Coast East Talent Agy.; pres./owner W. Coast E. Talent Agy.; instr./lectr. Charron-Williams Coll., Miami, 1973-77; instr. Fashion Inst. Ft. Lauderdale, Fla., 1977-86; pres./owner Image Power Unltd., Plantation, Fla., 1992—; lectr. in field; columnist Sr. Life News, Fla., Sr. Beacon, Tex., 1995—, Sr. Life and Boomer Times, Fla., 1995—, others. Author: I'd Like You to Meet My Wife, 1964; appeared on weekly TV show To the Ladies, 1950s, Del Russo Beauty Show, 1960s, Red Skelton TV show, also fashion commentary, TV commls. Vol. The Work Force, lectr., instr. The AARP Sr. Cmty. Svc. Employment Program (SCSEP), Ft. Lauderdale, Hollywood, Fla., 1987—, SCSEP Product Dirs., Charlestown, S.C., 1986; life mem. women's com. Miami Children's Hosp.; faculty advisor Nu Tau Sigma sorority Charron Williams Coll., 1973-77; pres. Venice of Am. chpt. Am. Bus. Women's Assn., 1975-76. Recipient Cert. of Appreciation Dade County Welfare Dept. Youth Hall, Miami, 1966, Community TV Found., Miami, 1966, 71, Woman of the Yr. award Am. Bus. Women's Assn. (Venice of Am. chpt.), 1976-77, Award for Svc. AARP Sr. Community Svc. Program, 1993. Mem. The Fashion Group Internat. (life, womens com. Miami Childrens Hosp.). Avocations: bridge, golf. Office: Image Power Unltd 1859 N Pine Island Rd # 339 Plantation FL 33322-5224

OXENBURY, HELEN, children's writer, illustrator; b. Suffolk, Eng., June 2, 1938; d. Thomas Bernard and Muriel (Taylor) O.; m. John Burningham, Aug. 15, 1965; children: Lucy, William Benedict. Stage designer Colchester, Eng., 1960, Tel-Aviv, 1961; TV designer London, 1963. Author, illustrator: Number of Things, 1967, ABC of Things, 1971, Pig Tale, 1973, The Queen and Rosie Randall, 1979, 729 Curious Creatures, 1980, 729 Merry Mix-ips, 1980, 729 Puzzle People, 1989, 729 Animal Allsorts, 1980, Crazy Creatures, 1980, Assorted Animals, 1980, Bill and Stanley, 1981, Bedtime, 1982, Monkey See, Monkey Do, 1982, Holidays, 1982, Helping, 1982, Mother's Helper, 1982, Animals, 1982, Bearch Day, 1982, Shopping Trip, 1982, Good Night, Good Morning, 1982, The Birthday Party, 1983, The Dancing Class, 1983, Eating Out, 1983, The Car Trip, 1983, The Drive, 1983, The Checkup, 1983, First Day of School, 1983, First Day at Playschool, 1983, Playschool, 1983, Grandma and Grandpa, 1984, Our Dog, 1984, The Important Visitor, 1984, Helen Oxenbury Nursery Story Book, 1985, Tom and Pippo Go Shopping, 1988, Tom and Pippo's Day, 1988, Tom and Pippo in the Garden, 1988, Tom and Pippo Go for a Walk, 1988, Tom and Pippo Make a Mess, 1988, Tom and Pippo Read a Story, 1988, Tom and Pippo See the Moon, 1988, Tom and Pippo and the Washing Machine, 1988, Pippo Gets Lost, 1989, Tom and Pippo and the Dog, 1989, Tom and Pippo in the Snow, 1989, Tom and Pippo Make a Friend, 1989, Tom and Pippo on the Beach, 1993, It's My Birthday, 1994, First Nursery Stories, 1994; (with Fay Maschler): A Child's Book of Manners: Verses, 1978; illustrator: The Great Big Enormous Turnip, 1968, The Quangle-Wangle's Hat, 1969, Letters of Thanks, 1969, The Dragon of an Ordinary Family, 1969, The Hunting of the Snark, 1970, Meal One, 1971, Cakes and Custard: Children's Rhymes, 1974, Balooky Klujypop, 1975, Animal House, 1976, Tiny Tim: Verses for Children, 1981, We're Going on a Bear Hunt, 1989, Farmer Duck, 1992, The Three Little Wolves and the Big Bad Pig, 1993, So Much, 1994. Office: care Greene and Heaton Ltd, 37 Goldhawk Rd, London W12 8QQ, England also: 5 E Heath Rd Hampstead, London NW3 1BN, England

OXENHANDLER, NEAL, language educator, writer; b. St. Louis, Feb. 3, 1926; s. Joseph and Billie (Lutsky) O.; m. Jean Romano (div. May 1976); children: Noelle, Daniel, Alicia; m. Judith I. Josel, Dec. 12, 1979. AB, U. Chgo., 1948; MA, Columbia U., 1951; PhD, Yale U., 1955; MA (hon.), Dartmouth Coll., 1973. Lectr. French St. Louis U., 1951-52; asst. instr. Yale U., New Haven, Conn., 1952-54, instr., 1954-57; asst. prof. UCLA, 1957-60, assoc. prof., 1960-65; assoc. prof. U. Calif., Santa Cruz, 1965-66, prof., 1966-69; prof. Dartmouth Coll., Hanover, N.H., 1969—, Edward Tuck prof., 1987—, chmn. dept. French and Italian, 1987-91; dir. NEH Summer Seminar in Comparative Lit., 1981. Author: Scandal and Parade: Theater of Jean Cocteau, 1957, Aspects of French Literature, 1961, French Literary Criticism: The Basis of Judgment, 1966, Max Jacob and Les Feux de Paris, 1964, (novel) A Change of Gods, 1962, Looking for Heroes in Post-War France, 1995; adv. editor Film Quar., Berkeley, 1958-91; mem. editl. com. U. Calif. Press, Berkeley, 1966-69; asst. editor French Rev., 1969-73; contbr. articles, revs., poetry and translations to profl. jours. With U.S. Army, 1941-43, ETO, PTO. Fulbright scholar, Italy, 1953; Cross-Disciplinary fellow Soc. for Values in Higher Edn., France, 1966; Guggenheim fellow, France, 1962, Inst. for Shipboard Edn., 1995. Mem. MLA (adv. editor proc. 1977-80), Internat. Assn. Philosophy and Lit., Internat. Comparative Lit. Assn. Democrat. Roman Catholic. Avocations: skiing, fly-fishing. Home: 468 Monroe Dr Sarasota FL 34236-1715 Office: Dartmouth Coll Dept French Hanover NH 03755

OXENKRUG, GREGORY FAYVA, psychopharmacologist; b. St. Petersburg, Russia, Oct. 25, 1941; arrived in U.S., 1980; s. Faiva Moshe and Rose Gregory (Sherman) O.; m. Rachel Maria Izrina, May 3, 1972 (div. Feb. 1993); children: Alexander, Daniel. MD, St. Petersburg Med. Sch., 1965; PhD, Bekhterev Psyco. Rsch. Inst., 1970; MA, Brown U., 1990. Asst. to assoc. prof. Bekhterev Phychoneurol. Rsch. Inst., St. Petersburg, 1970-79; clin. assoc. prof. dept. psychiatry Boston U., 1980-82; assoc. to prof. dept. pharmacology and psychiatry Wayne State U., Detroit, 1982-87; prof. dept. psychiatry Brown U., Providence, 1987-94, Tufts U., Boston, 1995—; chmn. dept. psychiatry St. Elizabeth's Med. Ctr., Boston, 1994—; chief psychiatry svc. VA Ctrs., Providence, 1988-94; chief inpatient psychiatry Lafayette Clinic, Detroit, 1982-88; dir. Pineal Rsch. Lab., 1984—. Contbr. over 100 articles to profl. jours. Recipient merit Review grant Dept. Vet. Affairs, 1990—. Fellow Am. Coll. Neuropsychopharmacology (ethics com.), Am. Soc. Biol. Psychiatry. Jewish. Avocations: English, history. Office: St Elizabeths Medical Ctr 736 Cambridge St QN-3P Boston MA 02135

OXER, JOHN PAUL DANIELL, civil engineer; b. Atlanta, Sept. 7, 1950; s. Robert B. Sr. and Leila Marie (Hammond) O.; m. Catherine Ann Stevens, Jan. 8, 1977. BCE, Ga. Inst. Tech., 1973; postgrad., U. Tex., Arlington, 1982-83. Lic. profl. engr. Ala., Ark., Ariz., Calif., Colo., Conn., Fla., Ga., Hawaii, Idaho, Ind., Iowa, Kans., Ky., La., Maine, Mich., Minn., Miss., Mo., Mont., Nebr., Nev., N.H., N.J., N.Mex., N.C., N.D., Okla., Oreg., S.C., S.D., Tenn., Tex., Utah, Vt., Va., Wash., W.Va., Wis., Wyo.; diplomate Am. Acad. Environ. Engrs. Project engr. J.S. Ross & Assocs. Inc., Smyrna, Ga., 1973-75, Welker & Assocs. Inc., Marietta, Ga., 1976-78; sr. project. engr. Claude Terry & Assocs., Inc., Atlanta, 1978-79; chief environ. engr. Bernard Johnson Inc. (SE), Atlanta, 1979-80; chief civil engr. region VI Ecology & Environ., Inc., Dallas, 1981-84; S.E. regional mgr. Ecology & Environ., Inc., Tallahassee, Fla., 1984-88; dir. program devel. Ecology & Environ., Inc., Dallas, 1988-91, exec. asst. to the pres., 1991-92; exec. asst. to the pres. Ecology & Environ., Inc., Houston, 1992—; guest lectr. U. Fla., Gainesville, U. Louisville, U. Houston, Fla. State U.; mem. Industry Functional Adv. Com. on Stds. for Trade Policy Matters, 1993—. Executive producer video documentary; writer, producer video documentary; co-author, dir. video prodn. Mem. indsl. bd. advisors Speed Sci. Sch. U. Louisville, 1991—. Named Young Engr. of Yr., Ga. Soc. Profl. Engrs., 1980. Mem. NSPE, ASCE, Am. Pub. Works Assn., Am. Soc. Landscape Archs., Am. Soc. Agrl. Engrs., Nat. Def. Exec. Res. (assigned to Fed. Emergency Mgmt. Agy.), Fla. Bar Assn. (assoc.), Masons. Republican. Avocations: piano, biathlon, photography, gardening. Office: Ecology & Environ Inc 4801 Woodway Dr # 280-w Houston TX 77056-1805 also: Ecology & Environ Inc 1999 Bryan St Ste 2000 Dallas TX 75201-6811

OXFORD, CHARLES WILLIAM, university dean, chemical engineer; b. Texarkana, Tex., Nov. 16, 1921; s. Charles Edward and Ellen (Alphin) O.; m. Mary Rae Mauzy, Dec. 24, 1946; children—Constance Susan, Catherine Ellen. BS, U. Ark., 1944, LLD (hon.), 1992; postgrad., U. Minn., 1946-48;

PhD, U. Okla., 1952; DSc (hon.), U. Ark., Little Rock. Asst. chemist Koppers Co., 1941; control chemist W.S. Dickey, 1942; asst. prof. chem. engring. U. Ark., 1948-50, asso. prof., 1952-57, prof., 1957—; asso. dean U. Ark. (Coll. Engring.), 1960—; asso. dir. U. Ark. (Engring. Expt. Sta.), 1964—, adminstrv. v.p. univ., 1968-73, exec. v.p., 1973-79, v.p. acad. affairs, 1979-88, v.p. emeritus, 1987—; exec. dir. U. Ark. Found., Inc., 1989-91; research participant Union Carbide Co., 1952; research engr. Boeing Airplane Co., 1955; cons. to industry. Exec. dir. U. Ark. Found., 1988-91. Served with USNR, 1944-46. Mem. Am. Inst. Chem. Engrs., Am. Soc. Engring. Edn., Am. Soc. Profl. Engrs., Sigma Xi, Tau Beta Pi, Alpha Chi Sigma, Omicron Delta Kappa. Club: Lion. Home: 110 Cyndee St Fayetteville AR 72703-3987

OXFORD, SHARON M., insurance company executive; b. Ekalaka, Mont., Aug. 30, 1939; d. Price S. and Myrtle I. (Wilkoski) Purdum; m. James L. Oxford Jr., Sept. 7, 1958 (div. May 1973); children: James L. III, Dana Renee, Monica Lynn Oxford Jones; m. Ronald Butts, Jan. 1, 1990. Degree in bus. adminstrn., Nat. Coll. Bus., Rapid City, S.D., 1958; student, Mesa (Ariz.) Community Coll., 1979-80. CPCU; cert. ins. counselor. Office mgr. Foster Fritchle Ins. Co., Colorado Springs, Colo., 1968-71, Mikes Ives Ins./Profl. Ins. Exchange, Colorado Springs, 1971-73; asst. to pres. Tolley-Weidman Ins. Co., Colorado Springs, 1973-76; rater Home Ins. Co., Phoenix, 1976-78; mgr. adminstrn. Fred S. James & Co. Ariz., Phoenix and Tempe, 1978-84; v.p. Sedgwick James, Tempe, 1984-85; sr. v.p. Fred S. James & Co. Ariz., Tempe, 1985—. Vol. MADD, store monitor Red Ribbon campaign; corr. sec. Young Reps., Colo. Springs, 1967; v.p. Colorado Springs chpt. Parents Without Ptnrs., 1975; team mem. Red Cross DAT, Mass Care Com. Mem. Am. Inst. for Property and Liability Underwriters, Soc. Cert. Ins. Counselors, Jaycee Wives (pres. Colorado Springs chpt. 1970), Assoc. of Automated Mgmt. Republican. Avocations: dancing, square dancing. Office: Sedgwick James 1414 W Broadway Rd Ste 200 Tempe AZ 85282-1122

OXLEY, DWIGHT K(AHALA), pathologist; b. Wichita, Kans., Dec. 2, 1936; s. Dwight K. Jr. and Ruth Erdene (Warner) O.; m. Patricia Warren, June 18, 1961; children: Alice DeBloois, Thomas Oxley. AB, Harvard U., 1958; MD, U. Kans., 1962. Diplomate Am. Bd. Pathology (trustee 1992—), Am. Bd. Nuclear Medicine. Pathologist Wesley Med. Ctr., Wichita, 1969-74, Eisenhower Med. Ctr., Rancho Mirage, Calif., 1974-78, St. Joseph Health Ctr., Kansas City, Mo., 1978-88; chmn. dept. pathology Wesley Med. Ctr., 1988—. Bd. editors Archives of Pathology and Lab. MEdicine, Chgo., 1984-95, Clinica Chimica Acta, Amsterdam, 1980-86, Am. Jour. Clin. Pathology, Chgo., 1974-80. Sr. warden St. Stephens Episcopal Ch., Wichita, 1994. Lt. commdr. USN, 1964-69. Fellow Am. Soc. Clin. Pathologists (various offices), Coll. Am. Pathologists (various offices); mem. Am. Pathology Found. (bd. dirs. 1979-89), Kans. Soc. Pathologists (pres. 1993—). Republican. Avocations: music, athletics. Office: Wesley Med Ctr 550 N Hillside St Wichita KS 67214-4910

OXLEY, JOHN THURMAN, ranching and investments executive, former petroleum company executive; b. Bromide, Okla., July 26, 1909; s. Moses E. and Sallie E. (Cochran) O.; m. Mary K. Yetter, Aug. 17, 1935; children: John C., Mary J., Thomas E. Student, East Central Coll., Okla., Tulsa Bus. Coll., Tulsa Law Sch., U. Tulsa. With Amerada Petroleum Corp., 1927-35; with Warren Petroleum Corp., 1935-48; sec. and mgr. gasoline div., pres., dir. Tex. Natural Gasoline Corp., Tulsa, 1948-60; exec. v.p., dir. Union Tex. Petroleum Corp., 1960-63; cons. Union Tex. Petroleum (merged with Allied Chem. Corp.), 1963; part owner Oxley Petroleum Co., 1963—; chmn., pres., chief exec. officer, dir. Arkansas Valley Industries, Inc., 1964-69; dir. Apco Oil Corp. Mem. So. Hills Country Club, Royal Palm Polo Sports Club, Boca Raton, Fla. Office: Williams Center Tower I Ste 1305 Tulsa OK 74103

OXLEY, MARY BOONE, early childhood education educator; b. Brownwood, Tex., June 18, 1928; d. Virgil Earl and Olive (Boone) Wheeler; m. William R. Oxley, June 8, 1950 (dec. Sept. 1987); children: Paul, Claire. BS, Tex. Women's U., 1949; MS, Tex. A&M U., 1967. Cert. tchr., Tex. Tchr. grade 2 El Paso (Tex.) Ind. Sch. Dist., 1949-50, Antioch (Calif.) Ind. Sch. Dist., 1950-52; tchr. grades 1-3 Richmond (Calif.) Ind. Sch. Dist., 1952-54; tchr. kindergarten St. Thomas Early Learning Ctr., College Station, Tex., 1967-85; lectr. early childhood edn. Tex. A&M U., College Station, 1985—; presenter workshops in field. Author: Illustrated Guide to Kindergarten Instruction, 1976; contbr. articles to profl. jours. Bd. dirs. Magination Station (children's theater), Bryan, Tex., 1990-94; cons. St. Thomas Early Learning Ctr., College Station, 1985-94. Mem. Nat. Assn. for Edn. Young Children (chmn. program 1976), Tex. Assn. for Edn. Young Children, Assn. Childhood Edn. Internat. (advisor 1990-94), Nat. Coun. Social Studies, Phi Delta Kappa. Democrat. Episcopalian. Avocations: bird watching, travel, youth camps. Home: 1005 Arboles Cir College Station TX 77840-4817 Office: Tex A&M Univ Edn Curriculum Instrn College Station TX 77843-4232

OXLEY, MICHAEL GARVER, congressman; b. Findlay, Ohio, Feb. 11, 1944; s. George Garver and Marilyn Maxine (Wolfe) O.; m. Patricia Ann Pluguez, Nov. 27, 1971; 1 child, Michael Chadd. BA, Miami U., Oxford, Ohio, 1966; JD, Ohio State U., 1969. Bar: Ohio 1969, U.S. Supreme Ct. 1985. Agt. FBI, 1969-71; mem. Ohio Ho. of Reps., 1973-81, 97th-103rd Congresses from 4th Ohio dist., Washington, D.C., 1981—; mem. commerce com., chmn. subcom. commerce, trade and hazardous materials, vice chmn. subcom. telecomm. and fin. Mem. ABA, Ohio Bar Assn., Findlay Bar Assn., Soc. Former Spl. Agts. FBI, Ohio Farm Bur., Sigma Chi. Lodges: Rotary, Elks. Office: US Ho Reps 2233 Rayburn House Bldg Washington DC 20515*

OXMAN, DAVID CRAIG, lawyer; b. Summit, N.J., Mar. 10, 1941; s. Jacob H. and Kathryn (Grear) O.; m. Phyllis Statter; children—Elena, Lee. A.B., Princeton U., 1962; LL.B., Yale U., 1969. Bar: N.Y. 1970, N.J. 1974, U.S. Dist. Ct. (so. and ea. dists.) N.Y. 1974, U.S. Ct. Appeals (2d cir.) 1974, U.S. Tax Ct. 1977, U.S. Supreme Ct. 1974. Assoc. Davis Polk & Wardwell, N.Y.C., 1970-76, ptnr., 1977-95, sr. counsel, 1995—. Served with USN, 1962-66. Fellow Am. Coll. Trust and Estate Counsel; mem. ABA, N.Y. State Bar Assn., Assn. of Bar of City of N.Y., N.J. Bar Assn., N.Y. County Lawyers Assn. Office: Davis Polk & Wardwell 450 Lexington Ave New York NY 10017-3911

OXNARD, CHARLES ERNEST, anatomist, anthropologist, human biologist, educator; b. Durham, Eng., Sept. 9, 1933; arrived in Australia, 1987; s. Charles and Frances Ann (Golightly) O.; m. Eleanor Mary Arthur, Feb. 2, 1959; children: Hugh Charles Neville, David Charles Guy. B.Sci. with 1st class honors, U. Birmingham, Eng., 1955, M.B., Ch.B. in Medicine, 1958, Ph.D., 1962, D.Sc., 1975. Med. intern Queen Elizabeth Hosp., Birmingham, 1958-59; rsch. fellow U. Birmingham, 1959-62, lectr., 1962-65, sr. lectr., 1965-66, court govs., 1958-66; assoc. prof. anatomy, anthropology and evolutionary biology U. Chgo., 1966-70, prof., 1970-78, gov. biology collegiate div., 1970-78, dean coll., 1973-77; dean grad. sch. U. So. Calif., Los Angeles, 1978-83; univ. rsch. prof. biology and anatomy U. So. Calif., 1978-83, univ. prof., prof. anatomy and cell biology, prof. biol. scis., 1983-87; prof. anatomy and human biology, head dept. of anatomy and human biology U. Western Australia, 1987-90, 93-95, dir. ctr. for human biology, 1989—, head div. agr. and sci., 1990-92; rsch. assoc. Field Mus. Natural History, Chgo., 1967; overseas assoc. U. Birmingham, 1968—; Lo Yuk Tong lectr. U. Hong Kong, 1973, 94, hon. prof., 1978, Chan Shu Tzu lectr., 1980, Octagon lectr. U. Western Australia, 1987, Latta lectr. U. Nebr., Omaha, 1987; Stanley Wilkinson orator, 1991, Lo Yuk Tong Found. lectr., U. Hong Kong, 1994; rsch. assoc. L.A. County Natural History Mus., 1984—, George C. Page Mus., L.A., 1986; vis. scholar U. Hong Kong, 1995, Shaw Coll. Chinese U. of Hong Kong, 1995, U. of Hong Kong, 1996; bd. dirs. U. Western Australia Press, 1993-95; adv. on human biology World Sci. Pub. Co., 1993—. Author: Form and Pattern in Human Evolution, 1973, Uniqueness and Diversity in Human Evolution, 1973, Human Fossils: The New Revolution, 1977, The Order of Man, 1983, Humans, Apes, and Chinese Fossils, 1985, Anatomies and Lifestyles, 1990; series editor Recent Advances in Human Biology Series World Sci. Pub., Vol. I, The Origin and Past of Modern Humans, 1995, Vol. 2, Bone Structure and Remodeling, 1995, Perspectives in Human Biology, Vol. 1 Genes, Ethnicity and Aging, 1995; mem. editl. bd. Annals of Human Biology; cons. editor: Am. Jour. Primatology, Jour. Human Biology, Jour. Human Evolution: Australia com. mem. Ency. Britannica, 1991—; bibliographic referee Britannica On-Line, 1994, 95; contbr articles to anat. and anthrop. jours. Mem. Pasteur Found., 1988; bd. dirs. West Australian Inst. for Child Health, 1991—; mem. electoral bd. Freemantle Hosp., 1991-94. Recipient Book award Hong Kong Coun., 1984, S.T. Chan Silver medal U. Hong Kong, 1980; grantee USPHS, 1960-71, NIH, 1974-87, NSF, 1971-87, Raine Found., 1988-91, Viertel Found., 1993-94, Australian Acad. Sci., 1995. Fellow N.Y. Acad. Sci., AAAS, So. Calif. Acad. Sci. (bd. dirs. 1985); mem. Chgo. Acad. Soc. (hon. life), Australasian Soc. for Human Biology (pres. 1987-90), Australia and New Zealand Anat. Soc. (pres. 1989-90), Anat. Soc. Gt. Britain and Ireland (councillor 1992-94), Nat. Health and Med. Rsch. Coun. (grantee 1988—), Australian Rsch. Coun. (grantee 1988—), Soc. for Study Human Biology (treas. 1962-66), Sigma Xi (pres., nat. lectr. 1990—), Phi Beta Kappa (pres. chpt.), Phi Kappa Phi (pres., Book award 1984). Office: U Western Australia, Ctr Human Biology, Nedlands WA 6009, Australia

OXTOBY, DAVID WILLIAM, chemistry educator; b. Bryn Mawr, Pa., Oct. 17, 1951; s. John Corning and Jean (Shaffer) O., m. Claire Bennett, Dec. 17, 1977; children: Mary-Christina, John, Laura. BA, Harvard, 1972; PhD, U. Calif., Berkeley, 1975. Asst. prof. U. Chgo., 1977-82, assoc. prof., 1982-86, prof., 1986—, Mellon prof., 1987-92, dir. James Franck Inst., 1992-95; dean physical scis. divsn. James Franck Inst., 1995—. Co-author: Principles of Modern Chemistry, 1986, Chemistry: Science of Change, 1990. Trustee Bryn Mawr Coll., 1989—; mem. bd. govs. Argonne Nat. Lab., 1996—. Recipient Quantrell award U. Chgo., 1986; Alfred P. Sloan Found. fellow, 1979, John Simon Guggenheim Found. fellow, 1987; Camille and Henry Dreyfus Found. tchr.-scholar, 1980. Fellow Am. Phys. Soc.; mem. Am. Chem. Soc., Royal Soc. Chemistry (Marlow medal 1983), Phi Beta Kappa. Office: James Franck Inst U Chgo 5640 S Ellis Ave Chicago IL 60637-1433

OXTOBY, ROBERT BOYNTON, lawyer; b. Huron, S.D., May 8, 1921; s. Frederic Breading and Frieda (Boynton) O.; m. Carolyn Bartholf; children: Michael, Thomas, Susan. Student, Ill. Coll.; B.A., Carleton Coll., 1943; J.D., Northwestern U., 1949. Bar: Ill. 1949. Mem. firm Van Meter, Oxtoby & Funk, 1949—; asst. U.S. atty., 1953-57, spl. asst. atty. gen., 1970—. Chmn. Ill Capital Devel. Bd., 1991-95; bd. dirs. Downtown Park, Inc., Springfield Bd. Edn. Served to 1st lt. USMCR, 1943-46, PTO. Home: 1933 Outer Park Dr Springfield IL 62704-3323 Office: First Am Ctr 1 Old Capitol Pla N Springfield IL 62701

OYE, KENNETH A., political scientist, educator; b. Phila., Oct. 20, 1949; s. George M. and Kazae Y. O.; Willa K. Michener; 1 child, Mari Katherine Michener Oye. BA in Polit. Sci. and Econs. with highest honors, Swarthmore Coll., 1971; PhD in Polit. Sci., Harvard U., 1983. Lectr. polit. sci. U. Calif., Davis, 1976-79; asst. prof. politics Princeton U., 1980-89, faculty assoc. ctr. internat. studies, 1982-89; assoc. prof. polit. sci. Swarthmore Coll., 1989-90; assoc. prof. polit. sci. MIT, Cambridge, 1990—, dir. ctr. internat. studies, 1992—; lectr. summer program quantitative methods Kennedy Sch. Harvard U., 1974, 75; guest scholar The Brookings Instn., 1979-80; co-dir. seminar XXI program MIT, 1993—, mem. coun. global environment, 1994—; presenter in field. Author: Economic Discrimination and Political Exchange: World Political Economy in the 1930s and 1980s, 1993; editor: Cooperation under Anarchy, 1986, (with Robert J. Lieber and Donald Rothchild) Eagle Entangled: U.S. Foreign Policy in a Complex World, 1979, Eagle Defiant: United States Foreign Policy in the 1980s, 1983, Eagle Resurgent? The Reagan Era in United States Foreign Policy, 1987, Eagle in a New World: American Grand Strategy in the Post Cold War Era, 1992; mem. editorial com. World Politics, 1982-89, mem. editorial bd., 1989—; contbr. chpts. to books and articles to profl. jours. Econs. and Security grantee Pew Charitable Trusts, 1986; Grad. fellow Woodrow Wilson Found., 1971, NSF, 1971-74, MacArthur Found., 1995, Japan Found., 1996. Mem. Am. Econs. Assn., Am. Polit. Sci. Assn., Phi Beta Kappa. Office: MIT Ctr Internat Studies 292 Main St # E38 648 Cambridge MA 02139

OYLER, GREGORY KENNETH, lawyer; b. Moses Lake, Wash., Sept. 16, 1953; s. Eugene Milton and Annetta Diane (Williams) O.; m. Evelyn Hartwell Wright, Oct. 18, 1986; 1 child, Elizabeth Atwood. AB, Princeton U., 1975; JD, Georgetown U., 1978; LLM, NYU, 1981. Bar: Pa. 1978, U.S. Tax Ct. 1978, U.S. Ct. Appeals (D.C. cir.) 1979, D.C. 1981, U.S. Supreme Ct. 1982, U.S. Ct. Claims 1983, U.S. Ct. Appeals (fed. cir.) 1987. Law clk. to judges U.S. Tax Ct., Washington, 1978-80; assoc. Hamel & Park, Washington, Washington, 1981-85; ptnr. Hopkins & Sutter, Washington, 1985-95, Scribner, Hall & Thompson, Washington, 1995—. Mem. adv. com. IRS Info. Reporting Program, 1993-94. Mem. ABA (tax sect., ins. and govt. submissions coms.), D.C. Bar Assn. (tax sect.), Fed. Bar Assn., Soc. Preservation Md. Antiquities (bd. dirs. 1991—). Office: Scribner, Hall & Thompson 1850 K St NW Ste 1100 Washington DC 20006-2201

OZ, FRANK (FRANK RICHARD OZNOWICZ), puppeteer, film director; b. Hereford, Eng., May 25, 1944; s. Isidore and Frances Oznowicz. Student, Oakland City Coll., 1962. Puppeteer with the Muppets, N.Y.C., 1963—; characters performed include The Mighty Favag (Saturday Night Live 1975-76), Miss Piggy, Fozzie Bear, Animal, Sam the Eagle; now v.p. Jim Henson Prodns., N.Y.C.; creative cons. feature film The Great Muppet Caper; appeared in films The Blues Brothers, 1980, Trading Places, 1983, Labyrinth, 1986; voice of Yoda in films The Empire Strikes Back, 1980, Return of the Jedi, 1983; dir. films The Dark Crystal (with Jim Henson), 1982, The Muppets Take Manhattan, 1984, Little Shop of Horrors, 1986, Dirty Rotten Scoundrels, 1988, What About Bob?, 1991, Housesitter, 1992, The Indian in the Cupboard, 1995. Recipient 4 Emmy awards for outstanding performance. Mem. AFTRA, Dirs. Guild Am., Writers Guild Am., Screen Actors Guild, Acad. TV Arts and Scis. Office: Jim Henson Prodns 117 E 69th St New York NY 10021-5004

OZAKI, YOSEHARU, English literature educator; b. Osaka-shi, Osaka-fu, Japan, May 24, 1932; s. Jintaro and Shizue (Okajima) O.; m. Kimiko Ozaki, May 27, 1962; children: Katsuyoshi, Megumi. BA, Kyoto U., Japan, 1955, MA, 1957. Lectr. Kyoto U., Japan, 1960-64, asst. prof. English, 1964-69; assoc. prof. English Nara Women's U., Nara, Japan, 1969-77, prof. English, 1977-96; prof. English Seiwa Coll., Nishinomiya-shi, Japan, 1996—. Author: Shakespeare by the Riverside, 1994; co-author: (with others) A Shakespeare Handbook, 1969, Shakespeare's Dramatic Climate, 1975, Love and Death-Whereabouts of Eros, 1987. Mem. English Lit. Soc. Japan (councillor 1990-92), Shakespeare Soc. Japan (standing com. 1983-89, com. mem. 1989-93), Dramatic Soc. Japan, Internat. Shakespeare Assn. Avocations: theatre, opera, ballet, concerts, movies. Home: 1-14 Sujaku 4-chome, Nara Nara-ken 631, Japan Office: Seiwa Coll, 7-54 Okadayama, Nishinomiya-shi Hyôgo 662, Japan

OZAWA, MARTHA NAOKO, social work educator; b. Ashikaga, Tochigi, Japan, Sept. 30, 1933; came to U.S., 1963; d. Tokuichi and Fumi (Kawashima) O.; m. May 1959 (div. May 1966). BA in Econs., Aoyama Gakuin U., 1956; MS in Social Work, U. Wis., 1966, PhD in Social Welfare, 1969. Asst. prof. social work Portland (Oreg.) State U., 1969-70, assoc. prof. social work, 1970-72; assoc. rsch. prof. social work NYU, 1972-75; assoc. prof. social work Portland State U., 1975-76; prof. social work Washington U., St. Louis, 1976-85, Bettie Bofinger Brown prof. social policy, 1985—. Author: Income Maintenance and Work Incentives, 1982; editor: Women's Life Cycle: Japan-U.S. Comparison in Income Maintenance, 1989, Women's Life Cycle and Economic Insecurity: Problems and Proposals, 1989; editl. bd. Social Work, Silver Spring, Md., 1972-75, 85-88, New Eng. Jour. Human Svcs., Boston, 1987—, Ency. of Social Work, Silver Spring, 1974-77, 91-95, Jour. Social Svc. Rsch., 1977—, Children and Youth Svcs. Rev., 1991—, Social Work Rsch., 1994—, Jour. Poverty. Grantee Adminstrn. on Aging, Washington, 1979, 84, NIMH, 1990-93, Assn. for Pub. Policy Analysis and Mgmt. Mem. Nat. Assn. Social Workers, Nat. Acad. Social Ins., Nat. Conf. on Social Welfare (bd. dirs. 1981-87), The Gerontol. Soc. Am., Coun. Social Work Edn., Washington U. Faculty Club (bd. dirs. 1986-91), Soc. for Social Work and Rsch. Avocations: photography, tennis, swimming, gardening. Home: 13018 Tiger Lily Ct Saint Louis MO 63146-4339 Office: Washington U Campus PO Box 1196 Saint Louis MO 63130-4899

OZAWA, SEIJI, conductor, music director; b. Shenyang, China, Sept. 1, 1935; s. Kaisaku and Sakura Ozawa; m. Vera Motoki-Ilyin; children: Seira, Yukiyoshi. Student, Toho Sch. Music, Tokyo, Japan, 1953-59; studies with, Hideo Saito, Eugene Bigot, Herbert Von Karajan, Leonard Bernstein; student at the invitation of Charles Munch, Tanglewood, 1959; DMus (hon.), U. Mass., New England Conserv. Music, Wheaton Coll. Music dir. Boston Symphony Orch., 1973—. One of three asst. condrs., N.Y. Philharm., 1961-62 season, music dir. Ravinia Festival, 1964-68, music dir. Toronto Symphony Orch., 1965-69, San Francisco Symphony Orch., 1970-76, appointed artistic advisor Tanglewood Festival, 1970, condr. Boston Symphony Orch. Evening at Symphony (Emmy award); music advisor Boston Symphony Orch., 1972-73, Saito Kinen Orch., Japan, 1992, internat. tour and Dvorak Gala, Prague, 1993; guest condr. major orchs. Recipient 1st prize Internat. Competition Orch. Condrs., 1959, Koussevitzky prize Tanglewood Music Ctr., 1960, Inouye award for Lifetime Achievement, 1994; conducting fellow Tanglewood Music Ctr., summer 1959; named Laureate Fondation du Japon, 1988; Seiji Ozawa Hall named for him Tanglewood Music Ctr., 1994. Office: Columbia Artists Mgmt Inc care Ronald A Wilford 165 W 57th St New York NY 10019-2201

OZAWA, TED, electronics executive; b. 1937. V.p. Maxell Corp. of Am., Fair lawn, N.J.; treas. Battery Engring., Inc., Boston. Office: Maxell Corp of Am 22-08 State Rt 208 Fair Lawn NJ 07410-2609 also: Battery Engring Inc 1636 Hyde Park Ave Boston MA 02136

OZBUN, JIM L., academic administrator. Dean agr. and home econs. Wash. State U., Pullman, until 1988; pres. N.D. State U., Fargo, 1988—. Office: ND State U Office of Pres PO Box 5167 Fargo ND 58105-5167

OZERNOY, LEONID MOISSEY, astrophysicist; b. Moscow, May 19, 1939; came to U.S., 1986, naturalized citizen; m. Marianne Rosen; 2 children. BS in Physics, Moscow State U., 1961, MS in Astronomy, 1963; PhD in Astrophysics, Shternberg Astron. Inst., Moscow, 1966; DSc in Astrophysics, Lebedev Phys. Inst., USSR Acad. Scis., Moscow, 1971. Rsch. scientist, dept. theoretical physics Lebedev Phys. Inst., 1966-71, sr. rsch. scientist, 1971-86; asst. then assoc. prof. Moscow Physics and Tech. Inst., 1968-79, fired after applying for emigration from USSR; prof. astrophysics, disting. vis. scientist Ctr. for Astrophysics, Harvard Coll. Obs. and Smithsonian Astrophys. Obs., Cambridge, Mass., 1986-89; prof. astrophysics, disting. vis. scholar Inst. Geophysics and Planetary Physics, Los Alamos (N.Mex.) Nat. Lab., 1989-91; sr. assoc. Nat. Rsch. Coun. NAS Goddard Space Flight Ctr., NASA, Greenbelt, Md., 1991-92, cons., 1993—; sr. rsch. scientist U. Space Rsch. Assn., Greenbelt, Md., 1993; prof. computational sci. and space sci. Inst. Computation Sci. and Informatics, George Mason U., Fairfax, Va., 1993—, prof. physics and astron. dept., 1994—; vis. prof. Boston U., 1986-87, Harvard U., 1987; mem. sci. coun. on plasma astrophysics, Presidium of USSR Acad. Scis., 1971-75. Co-editor: Astrophysics and Space Scis. mag., 1976-86; author several books; contbr. over 240 sci. papers in theoretical astrophysics and realted fields. Recipient Silver medal USSR Exhbn. of Achievements in Nat. Economy, 1988; NRC/NAS fellowship, 1991. Fellow Am. Phys. Soc. (com. on internat. freedom of scientists 1988-90); mem. AAAS, Royal Astron. Soc., Internat. Astron. Union, N.Y. Acad. Scis., Am. Astron. Soc. (exec. com. high energy astrophysics div. 1989-90), Astron. Soc. Pacific, COSPAR (Com. Space Rsch., Internat. Coun. Sci. Unions), The Planetary Soc., Internat. Platform Assn. Achievements include establishment of mass-radius and mass-angular momentum relationships for galaxies, of methods for measuring/constraining the black hole mass at the center of the galaxy; research on theory for evolution of cosmological turbulence; and on theory for structure and evolution of supermassive, rotating, magnetized bodies (magnetoids). Office: George Mason U Inst Computat Sci & Informatics Sci and Tech Bldg I Fairfax VA 22030-4444

OZERO, BRIAN JOHN, chemical engineer; b. Winnipeg, Manitoba, Can., Dec. 14, 1932; came to U.S., 1963; s. Daniel and Mary (Karpiuk) O.; m. Ila Atlas, Dec. 14, 1985. BS in Chem. Engring., Queens U., Kingston, Ontario, Can., 1954; MS in Chem. Engring., NYU, 1968. Technologist Shell Oil Co., Montreal, Quebec, Can., 1954-60; design engr. Chem. Constrn. Co., London, 1960-63; sr. process engr. Sci. Design Co., N.Y.C., 1963-65, process mgr., 1965-75; tech. dir. Halcon SD Group Inc., N.Y.C., 1976-85; sr. process mgr. Tech. Evaluation and Devel. Assocs., Hoboken, N.J., 1986; pres., prin. cons. Scientech Assocs. Inc., N.Y.C., 1986—. Recognized expert in ethylene oxide/ethylene glycol; contbr. articles and chpts. to tech. jours. and encyclopedias in field; patentee in field. Pres. Barrier Beach Preservation Assn., Westhampton, N.Y., 1985-88. Mem. Am. Inst. Chem. Engrs., Rotary. Republican. Roman Catholic. Avocations: reading, tennis, skiing. Home: PO Box 1524 Westhampton Beach NY 11978-7524 Office: Scientech Assocs Inc 225 E 36th St Apt 19A New York NY 10016-3628

OZI, ELIZABETH, private school administrator; b. São Paulo, Brazil, Aug. 5, 1959; d. Heni and Firmina O. BA in Psychology, U. Las Vegas, 1987; postgrad., NOVA U., Fla., 1989—; cert. of continuing profl. edn., U. Nev., 1988. Cert. tchr. Tchr. Clark County Sch. Dist., Las Vegas, Nev., 1990-94; owner, sch. dir. Parent's Choice, Las Vegas, Nev., 1993—; dir. Home Base Bus., Las Vegas, Nev., 1993—. Interviewer (Radio Show Series) Recognizing Signs to Prevent Suicide, 1990. Counselor Suicide Prevention, Nev., 1988-90. Recipient Cert. of Leadership award Nat. U., Las Vegas, 1990. Mem. Psi Chi. Avocation: writing. Home: 4646 Grasshopper Dr Las Vegas NV 89122

OZICK, CYNTHIA, author; b. N.Y.C., Apr. 17, 1928; d. William and Celia (Regelson) O.; m. Bernard Hallote, Sept. 7, 1952; 1 dau., Rachel Sarah. BA cum laude with honors in English, NYU, 1949; MA, Ohio State U., 1950; LHD (hon.), Yeshiva U., 1984, Hebrew Union Coll., 1984, Williams Coll., 1986, Hunter Coll., 1987, Jewish Theol. Sem. Am., 1988, Adelphi U., 1988, SUNY, 1989, Brandeis U., 1990, Bard Coll., 1991, Spertus Coll., 1991, Skidmore Coll., 1992. Author: Trust, 1966, The Pagan Rabbi and Other Stories, 1971, Bloodshed and Three Novellas, 1976, Levitation: Five Fictions, 1982, Art and Ardor: Essays, 1983, The Cannibal Galaxy, 1983, The Messiah of Stockholm, 1987, Metaphor and Memory: Essays, 1989, The Shawl, 1989, Epodes: First Poems, 1992, What Henry James Knew, and Other Essays on Writers, 1994, The Cynthia Ozick Reader, 1996, Fame and Folly, 1996; (plays) Blue Light, 1994, The Shawl, 1996; also poetry, criticism, revs., transls., essays and fictions in numerous periodicals and anthologies. Phi Beta Kappa orator, Harvard U., 1985. Recipient Mildred and Harold Strauss Living award Am. Acad. Arts and Letters, 1983, Rea award for short story, 1986; Lucy Martin Donnelly fellow, Bryn Mawr Coll., 1992, Guggenheim fellow, 1982. Mem. PEN, Authors League, Am. Acad. of Arts and Scis., Am. Acad. of Arts and Letters, Dramatists Guild, Académie Universelle des Cultures (Paris), Phi Beta Kappa. Office: care Alfred A Knopf Co 201 E 50th St New York NY 10022-7703

OZIER, IRVING, physicist, educator; b. Montreal, Que., Can., Sept. 7, 1938; s. Harry and Peppi (Schwartzwald) O.; m. Joyce Ruth Weinstein, July 4, 1963; children: Elizabeth, David, Douglas. B.A., U. Toronto, 1960; A.M., Harvard U., 1961, Ph.D., 1965. Research fellow Harvard U., Cambridge, Mass., 1965-67, MIT, Cambridge, Mass., 1966-67; mem. tech. staff Sci. Ctr. Rockwell Internat., Thousand Oaks, Calif., 1966-70; assoc. prof. physics U. B.C., Vancouver, B.C., Can., 1970-77, prof., 1977—; vis. rsch. fellow Katholieke Universiteit, Nijmegen, The Netherlands, 1976-77; vis. rsch. officer Nat. Rsch. Coun. Can., Ottawa, 1982-83; vis. prof. Eidgenossische Technische Hochschule, Zurich, Switzerland, 1988-89. Author research articles in molecular spectroscopy. Alfred P. Sloan research fellow, 1972-74; Izaak Walton Killiam Meml. Sr. fellow U. B.C., 1982-83. Mem. Am. Phys. Soc., Can. Assn. Physicists. Office: Dept Physics Univ BC, 6224 Agriculture Rd, Vancouver, BC Canada V6T 1Z1

OZIO, DAVID, professional bowler. Winner Firestone Tournament of Champions, 1991. Office: c/o Profl Bowlers Assn 1720 Merriman Rd Akron OH 44313-5252*

OZMENT, STEVEN, historian, educator; b. McComb, Miss., Feb. 21, 1939; s. Lowell V. and Shirley M. (Edgar) O.; m. Andrea Todd Foster, Apr. 30, 1977; children: Amanda, Emma; children by previous marriage: Joel, Matthew, Katherine. B.A., Hendrix Coll., 1960; B.D., Drew Theol. Sch., 1964; Ph.D., Harvard U., 1967; M.A. (hon.), Yale U., 1975. Asst. prof. Inst. Late Medieval and Reformation Studies, U. Tübingen, Fed. Republic Germany, 1966-68; asst. prof. history and religious studies Yale U., New Haven, 1968-72; assoc. prof. Yale U., 1972-75, prof., 1975-79; prof. history

Harvard U., 1979—, McLean prof. ancient and modern history, 1991—, assoc. dean undergrad. edn., 1984-87; Bonsall vis. prof. Stanford U., 1991. Author: Homo Spiritualis, 1969, The Reformation in Medieval Perspective, 1971, Mysticism and Dissent, 1973, The Reformation in the Cities, 1975, (with others) The Western Heritage, 1979, 5th edit., 1994, The Age of Reform, 1980 (winner Schaff prize, Am. Book Award nominee 1980), Reformation Europe: A Guide to Research, 1982, When Fathers Ruled: Family Life in Reformation Europe, 1983, (with others) The Heritage of World Civilizations, 1985, 4th edit., 1996, Magdalena and Balthasar: An Intimate Portrait of Life in 16th Century Europe, 1986, Three Behaim Boys: Growing Up in Early Modern Germany, 1990, Protestants: The Birth of a Revolution, 1992, The Bürgermeister's Daughter: Scandal in a 16th Century German Town, 1996; mem. editl. bd. Archive for Reformation History, 1976-93, Sixteenth Century Jour., 1976—, Jour. Am. Acad. Religion, 1972-77, Jour. Hist. Ideas, 1986—, Netherlands Archive for Church History, 1987—. Morse fellow, 1970-71, Guggenheim fellow, 1978, Cabot fellow, 1992. Mem. Am. Soc. Reformation Rsch. (dir. 1979-83). Home: 69 High Rd Newbury MA 01951-1725 Office: Harvard Univ Robinson Hall Cambridge MA 02138

OZMON, KENNETH LAWRENCE, university president, educator; b. Portsmouth, Va., Sept. 4, 1931; emigrated to Can.; s. Howard Augustine and Anna Josephine (Lynch) O.; m. Elizabeth Ann Morrison, July 6, 1968; children: Angela Francene, Kendi Elizabeth. BA in Philosophy and History magna cum laude, St. Bernard Coll., Ala., 1955; MA in Psychology, Cath. U., 1963; PhD in Psychology, U. Maine, 1968. Lic. psychologist, N.S. Instr. U. Maine, Orono, 1966-68; vis. lectr. St. Dunstan's U., P.E.I., Can., 1967; asst. prof. Calif. State U., Chico, 1968-69; chmn. dept. psychology U. P.E.I., Charlottetown, 1969-72, dean of arts, 1972-79; pres. St. Mary's U., Halifax, N.S., 1979—; chmn. Pres.' Council N.S. U., 1982-85; chmn. Met. Halifax U. Pres.' Com., 1982-84, 86-87, 92—; co-chmn. coordinating com. Nat. U. Week, 1983, 86-87. Contbr. numerous articles to psychol. jours. Bd. dirs. United Way Halifax-Dartmouth, 1980-82, Friends N.S. Mus. Industry Soc., 1993—; bd. dirs. Interuniv. Svcs., Inc., 1987-94, chmn., 1992-94; provincial bd. dirs. Can. Assn. Mentally Retarded, 1980-82; co-chmn. Found. for Irish and Can. Studies, 1993; mem. nat. coun. Can. Human Rights Found., 1976; mem. selection com. J.H. Moore Awards for Excellence, Toronto, 1983-92; hon. chmn. ann. campaign N.S. div. Can. Paraplegic Assn., 1985-86; mem. fundraising com. Phoenix House, 1986-88, Charitable Irish Soc. Halifax; chmn. Human Rights Commn., 1990; mem. adv. coun. Order of Can., 1991-95; area chair for N.S. Internat. Coun. Psychologists, 1992-93. Recipient Gov. Gen. of Can. award, 1993; named hon. prof. U. Internat. Bus. and Econs., Beijing, People's Republic of China; trustee scholar U. Maine, 1965-67; NDEA fellow, 1967-68. Mem. Assn. Atlantic Univs. (vice chmn. 1983-85, chmn. 1985-87), Assn. Commonwealth Univs (governing coun. 1988-91), Assn. Univs. and Colls. Can. (exec. coun. 1985-89, vice chmn. 1990-91, chmn., 1991-93, mem. audit com. 1991—, chmn. exec. com. 1991—, vice-chmn. nominating com. 1990-91), Can. Psychol. Assn. (Nat. Univ. Week coordinating com. 1983, co-chmn. 1986-87, audit com. 1985—, co-chmn. steering com. Halifax Met. Econ. Summit II 1994), Halifax Bd. Trade (internat. trade com. 1985-91, bd. dirs. 1989-91), Halifax Press Club, Halifax Club, Ashburn Golf Club, Saraguay Club. Roman Catholic. Avocations: fishing, golf, running. Home: 5895 Gorsebrook Ave, Halifax, NS Canada B3H 1G3 Office: St Mary's U, Pres Office, Halifax, NS Canada B3H 3C3

OZNOWICZ, FRANK RICHARD See OZ, FRANK

OZOLEK, JOHN ANTHONY, pediatrician, neonatologist; b. Dubois, Pa., Feb. 24, 1963; s. Anthony John and Ann Elaine (Castrilla) O.; m. Jamie Lynn McCombe, Oct. 29, 1994. BS in Biology, Case Western Res. U., 1985; MD, U. Pitts., 1989. Diplomate Am. Bd. Pediatrics. Intern in pediatrics Children's Hosp., Pitts., 1989-90, resident in pediatrics, 1990-92; fellow in neonatology Magee Women's Hosp., Pitts., 1992-95; physician rep. medication rev. com. neonatal ICU Magee Women's Hosp., Pitts., 1994—. Contbr. articles to profl. jours. Fellow Soc. Pediatric Rsch.; mem. AMA, Am. Acad. Pediatrics, Pa. med. Soc., Allegheny County Med. Soc. Roman Catholic. Avocations: bowling, poetry. Home: 9501 Point Aux Chenes Ocean Springs MS 39564 Office: Dept Pediatrics Divsn Neonatology Keesler Med Ctr Biloxi MS 39534

PAALZ, ANTHONY L., beverage company executive; b. Louisville, Apr. 18, 1924; s. Leon A. and Rose M. (Westendick) P.; m. Elaine Wolf, Feb. 11, 1956 (dec. Dec. 1981); children: Teresa Dawson, Eileen Baldwin, Anthony L. Jr.; m. Alison Kerr, May 3, 1986. BS, U. Ind., 1949. Chief acct. J.E. Seagram & Sons Inc., N.Y.C., 1959-69, asst. controller, 1969-72, dir. of taxes, 1972-84, v.p. taxes, 1984—. Served with USN, 1943-45, PTO. Decorated numerous battle stars. Mem. Tax Execs. Inst. Avocation: golf. Home: 29 Treeview Dr Melville NY 11747-2413 Office: Joseph E Seagram & Sons Inc 800 3rd Ave New York NY 10022-7604

PAANANEN, VICTOR NILES, English educator; b. Ashtabula, Ohio, Jan. 31, 1938; s. Niles Henry and Anni Margaret (Iloranta) P.; m. Donna Mae Jones, Aug. 15, 1964; children: Karl, Neil. AB magna cum laude, Harvard U., 1960; MA, U. Wis., 1964, PhD, 1967. Instr. English Wofford Coll., Spartanburg, S.C., 1962-63; asst. prof. Williams Coll., Williamstown, Mass., 1966-68; asst. prof. Mich. State U., East Lansing, 1968-73, assoc. prof., 1973-82, prof., 1982—, asst. dean Grad. Sch., 1977-82, chmn. dept. English, 1986-94; vis. prof. Roehampton Inst., London, 1982, 96, hon. fellow, 1992. Author: William Blake, 1982, 2d edit., 1996; contbr. articles to profl. and scholarly jours. Univ. fellow U. Wis., 1962, 63-64, Roehampton Inst. hon. fellow, London, 1992—; Harvard Nat. scholar, 1956-60. Mem. MLA, AAUP, Labor Party Advocates. Episcopalian. Home: 152 Orchard St East Lansing MI 48823-4536 Office: Mich State Univ Dept of English Morrill Hall East Lansing MI 48824-1036

PAAS, JOHN ROGER, German language educator; b. Chgo., Mar. 14, 1945; s. Walter V. and Doris (Marinoff) P.; m. Martha Clem White, Aug. 24, 1968; children: Emily, Anne. BA summa cum laude, Hamilton Coll., Clinton, N.Y., 1967; PhD, Bryn Mawr Coll., 1973. Part-time asst. prof. Bryn Mawr (Pa.) Coll., 1973-74; prof. German Carleton Coll., Northfield, Minn., 1974—, dept chair, 1985-88. Author: The German Political Broadsheet 1600-1700, 5 vols., 1985—, Effigies et Poesis: An Illustrated Catalogue of Printed Portraits with Laidatory Verses by German Baroque Poets, 2 vols., 1988; editor: Unbekannte Gedichte und Lieder des Sigmund von Birken, 1990, Hollsteon's German Engravings Etchings and Woodcuts, 1400-1700, vols. 38-41, 1994-95, Der Franken Rom: Nurnbergs Blutezeit in der zweiten Halfte des 17 Jhts., 1995, (with Wolfgang Harms, Michael Schilling and Andreas Wang) Illustrierte Flugblatter des Barock: Eine Auswahl, 1983; contbr. articles to profl. jours. Sgt. U.S. Army, 1969-71. Summer grantee German Acad. Exch. Svc., 1975, 78, 83, Andrew W. Mellon Found., 1976, Faculty Devel. grantee Bush Found., 1978, Carleton Coll., 1985, NEH grantee, 1990, 92-93; vis. fellow Beinecke Libr., Yale U., 1991, IREX fellow, 1978, Fulbright sr. rsch. fellow, 1988-89, 96—. Mem. MLA, Am. Assn. Tchrs. German, Soc. German Renaissance and Baroque Lit., Internationaler Arbeitskreis für Barockliteratur, Frühe Neuzeit Interdisziplinär. Home: 107 College St Northfield MN 55057-2222 Office: Carleton College 1 N College St Northfield MN 55057-4001

PAASWELL, ROBERT EMIL, civil engineer, educator; b. Red Wing, Minn., Jan. 15, 1937; s. George and Evelyn (Cohen) P.; m. Rosalind Snyder, May 31, 1958; children: Judith Marjorie, George Harold. B.A. (Ford Found. fellow), Columbia U., 1956, B.S., 1957, M.S., 1961; Ph.D., Rutgers U., 1965. Field engring. asst. Spencer White & Prentis, Washington, 1954-56; engr. Spencer White & Prentis, N.Y.C., 1957-59; rsch. scientist Davidson Lab., N.J., 1964; rsch. fellow Greater London Council, 1971-72; rsch. and teaching asst. Columbia U., 1959-62; asst. prof. civil engring. SUNY, Buffalo, 1964-68; chmn. bd. govs. Urban Studies Coll., 1973-76, assoc. prof., 1968-76, prof. civil engring., 1976-82; dir. Center for Transp. Studies and Research, 1979-82, chmn. dept. environ. design and planning, 1980-82; prof. transp. engring. U. Ill., Chgo., 1982-86, 89-90, dir. Urban Transp. Ctr., 1982-86; exec. dir. Chgo. Transit Authority, 1986-89; dir. transp. rsch. consortium, prof. civil engring. CCNY, 1990—, disting. prof., 1991—; faculty-on-leave Dept. Transp., 1976-77, cons., 1981—; v.p. Faculty Tech. Cons., Inc., Midwest Sys. Scis., Inc., 1982-86; dir. Urban Mass Transp. Adminstrn. Summer Faculty Workshop, 1980, 81; cons. transp. planning, energy and soil mechanics; spl. cons. to Congressman T. Tulski, 1973; vis. expert lectr. Jilin U. Tech., Changchun, Peoples Republic of China, 1985, hon. prof. transp., 1986—; bd. dirs. El'Escuto Archs. and Engrs., Chig, Hickling Co., Ottawa, Can., Transic Devel. Corp.; chmn. transp. steering adv. bd. Office of Tech. Assessment for Infrastructure and the Urban Core Project, 1994—; faculty Lincoln Inst. of Land Policy, 1994-95; vis. scholar Te. Aviv U., Israel, 1995—; arbitrator in productivity Met. Transp. Authority, N.Y.C., 1996—. Author: Problems of the Carless, 1977; editor: Site Traffic Impact Assessment, 1992; contbg. author: Decisions for the Great Lakes, 1982, World Book Encyclopedia, 1992, 93, 94, Transport and Urban Development, 1995; mem. bd. editors Jour. Environ. Systems, 1974—, Transp., 1978—, Jour. Urban Tech., 1992—; contbr. articles to profl. jours. Mem. Buffalo Environ. Mgmt. Commn., 1972-74; mem. Area Com. for Transit, Mayor's Energy Adv. Bd., 1974, Block Grant Rev. Com., City of Buffalo; chmn. com. on transp., mem. rev. adv. bd. Rsch. and Planning Coun. Western N.Y.; mem. transp. com. Chgo. 1992 Worlds Fair; mem. citizens' adv. bd. Chgo. Transit Authority, 1985—; mem. strategic planning com. Regional Transp. Authority, 1985; mem. steering com. Nat. Transit Coop. Rsch. Program, 1991—, Borough pres. (Manhattan) Trans. Adv. Bd., Bronx Ctr. Devel. Project; bd. dirs. Transit Devel. Corp., 1992—. Recipient Dept. Transp. award, 1977; SUNY faculty fellow, 1965-66. Fellow ASCE (past pres. Buffalo sect., chmn. steering com. 1992 specialty conf. traffic impact analysis); mem. AAAS, Transp. Rsch. Bd. (chmn. com. on transp. disadvantaged, mem. exec. com., peer rev. com. nat. transp. ctrs. 1988—), Inst. Transp. Engrs. (transit coun., exec. com., chmn. legis. policy com., rsch. com. surface transp. policy project 1995—), N.Y. Acad. Scis., Sigma Xi. Office: CCNY Inst Transp Systems Rm 220-Y 135th St and Convent Ave New York NY 10031

PABST, EDMUND G., retired insurance company executive, lawyer; b. Chgo., Apr. 22, 1916. Student, U. Calif-Berkeley; LL.D., B.S.L., Northwestern U., 1940. Bar: Ill., D.C. Mem. firm Leonard & Leonard, Chgo., 1940-41; atty. FTC, Washington, 1941-42; civilian lawyer U.S. Army, 1942-43; trial atty. OPA, Chgo., 1946-47; atty. Combined Ins. Co. Am., Chgo., 1947, v.p., asst. gen. counsel, 1954-59, sec., 1959-62, exec. v.p. adminstrn., 1962-76, W.Ger. Ops., 1976-78, v.p., gen. counsel, 1978-81, dir., 1952-83, mem. exec. com., 1958-76; officer, dir., mem. exec. com. Combined Am. Ins. Co., 1960-76; officer, dir.,mem. exec. com. Combined Ins. Co. Wis., 1953-76; officer, dir., mem. exec. com. Combined Life Ins. Co. N.Y., 1971-76; pres. Combined Opportunities, 1972-76. Bd. dirs. Uptown Chgo. Commn., pres., 1959-61; pres. S.E. Evanston Assn., 1968-70, 87-88; founding mem. Dewey Community Orgn., Evanston; mem. Evanston Zoning Bd. Appeals, 1969-76; mem. Evanston Zoning Amendment Com., 1980-88; bd. dirs. St. Francis Hosp., Evanston, 1980-89; trustee Mundelein Coll., 1971-88; me. Commonwealth Edison Task Force City of Evanston, 1988-93; chmn. Foster Reading Ctr., 1992—. Mem. ABA, Ill. Bar Assn., Chgo. Bar Assn. (civil rights com. 1959-70, chmn. 1966-67, ins. law com. 1947-60, chmn. 1951-52), Health Ins. Assn. Am. (sec. bd. dirs. 1969-73), U.S. C. of C. (internat. ins. adv. council 1978-81), ACLU (dir. Ill. div., treas. 1969-76). Home: 425 Grove St Apt 7C Evanston IL 60201-4632

PACALA, LEON, retired assocation executive; b. Indpls., May 3, 1926; s. John and Anna (Ferician) P.; m. Janet Lefforge, Dec. 28, 1947 (dec. July 1987); children: Mark, Stephen, James; m. Virginia Strasenburgh, Mar. 10, 1990. AB, Franklin (Ind.) Coll., 1949; BD, Colgate Rochester Div. Sch., 1952; PhD, Yale U., 1960; LLD (hon.), Nazareth Coll., 1980; LHD (hon.), Franklin Coll., 1987. Ordained to ministry Baptist Ch., 1952. Asst. prof. philosophy and religion DePauw U., 1956-61; participant study religion undergrad. coll. Lilly Found., 1957-59; assoc. prof. religion Bucknell U., 1961-68, prof., 1968-73, chmn. dept., 1961-64, dean, 1962-73; pres. Colgate Rochester (N.Y.) Div. Sch.; also Bexley Hall, Crozer Theol. Sem., 1973-80; exec. dir. Assn. Theol. Schs. in U.S. and Can., 1980-91; cons. acad. adminstrn. Beirut Coll. Women, 1972. Contbr. articles to profl. jours. Exec. com. Christian Faith in Higher Edn. Projects, 1965-68; trustee Franklin Coll., 1967-73; bd. dirs. Rohesters Jobs, Inc., 1973-80; trustee Rochester Area Colls., 1973-80; dir. Nat. Housing Ministries, Am. Bapt. Chs., 1976-80. With USAAF, 1944-45. Internat. Rotary scholar, Louvain U., Belgium, 1952-53. Mem. Am. Conf. Acad. Deans (exec. com., treas., chmn., presiding officer 1973-74), Am. Assn. Higher Edn., Assn. Am. Colls. (commn. religion higher edn.), Assn. Theol. Schs. (com. accreditation), World Conf. Assns. Theol. Instns. (v.p. 1988—), Am. Bapt. Assn. Sem. Adminstrs. (chmn 1975-80). Home: 3515 Elmwood Ave Rochester NY 14610-3464

PACE, CHARLES ROBERT, psychologist, educator; b. St. Paul, Sept. 7, 1912; s. Charles N. and Lenore (Lee) P.; m. Rosella Gaarder, Dec. 18, 1937; children: Rosalind, Jenifer. B.A., De Pauw U., 1933; M.A., U. Minn., 1935, Ph.D., 1937. Instr. in gen. coll. U. Minn., 1937-40; research asso. Am. Council Edn., 1941-42; research psychologist Bur. Naval Personnel, Navy Dept., 1943-47; mem. faculty Syracuse U., 1947-61, asso. dir., then dir. evaluation service center, 1947-52, asst. to chancellor, 1948-52, prof. psychology, chmn. dept., dir. psychol. research center, 1952-61; prof. higher edn. UCLA, 1961-82, prof. emeritus, 1982—; Mem. adv. coms. Am. Council Edn., Coll. Entrance Exam. Bd., Social Sci. Research Council. Author: They Went to College, 1941, (with M. E. Troyer) Evaluation in Teacher Education, 1944, (with F.H. Bowles and J.C. Stone) How to Get into College, 1968, College and University Environment Scales, 2d edit, 1969, Education and Evangelism, 1972, The Demise of Diversity?, 1974, Measuring Outcomes of College, 1979, Measuring the Quality of College Student Experiences, 1984, The Undergraduates, 1990. Post-doctoral fellow Rockefeller Found., 1940-41; fellow Center Advanced Study Behavioral Scis., 1959-60; recipient citation for meritorious civilian service Navy Dept., 1946, E.F. Lindquist award Am. Edn. Research Assn. and Am. Coll. Testing Program, 1984, Suslow award for outstanding svc. Assn. for Instl. Rsch., 1989. Mem. Am. Psychol. Assn., Am. Ednl. Research Assn., Assn. for Study Higher Edn. (Disting. Career award 1989), Am. Assn. Pub. Opinion Research.

PACE, ERIC DWIGHT, journalist; b. N.Y.C., Oct. 13, 1936; s. Eric and Eleanor Robertson (Jones) Paepcke; m. Suzanne Monique Wiedel, June 12, 1976 (div. Jan. 1987); children: Christine, Lydia. Grad., Phillips Exeter Acad., 1953; student, U. Heidelberg, Germany, 1955-56; B.A. magna cum laude, Yale, 1957; M.A., Johns Hopkins, 1959. Reporter San Angelo (Tex.) Standard Times and Evening Standard, 1957-58; mem. staff Life mag., N.Y.C., 1959-61; assigned to Life mag., Bonn, 1961, Paris, 1961-62; corr. Time mag., Bonn., 1962-63, Hong Kong, 1963-65; mem. staff New York Times, N.Y.C., 1965-66; assigned to New York Times, Saigon, 1966, Cairo, 1966-69, Paris, 1969-70, Beirut, 1970-71, N.Y.C., 1971-74, Teheran, 1974-77, N.Y.C., 1977—. Author: novels Saberlegs, 1970, Any War Will Do, 1973, Nightingale, 1979; contbr. articles to Fgn. Affairs, also others. Served with AUS, 1957. Recipient George Polk Meml. award Overseas Press Club, 1968, Page One award N.Y.C. Newspaper Guild, 1968. Mem. Mystery Writers Am., Authors Guild, Crime Writers Assn. (Gt. Britain), Am. P.E.N. Unitarian. Clubs: Century (N.Y.C.), Squadron A (N.Y.C.). Office: New York Times 229 W 43rd St New York NY 10036-3913

PACE, JOHN EDWARD, III, chemical engineer; b. Ridgeway, Va., Apr. 6, 1948; s. John Edward Jr. and Retta Jean Stanley Sheppard; m. Carolyn Ann Gray, Aug. 31, 1969; children: Brian Edward, Kimberly Carol. BSChemE, Va. Poly. Inst. and State U., 1971, MS in Chem. Engring., 1972. Registered profl. engr., W.Va. Summer engr. Exxon, Baytown, Tex., 1971; devel. engr. Dow Badische, Anderson, S.C., 1972-76; process devel. engr. Borg Warner, Parkersburg, W.Va., 1976-88, GE Plastics, Parkersburg, 1988—. Contbr. articles to profl. jours. Pres. Bethel Place Homeowners Assn., Washington, W.Va., 1984. Mem. AIChE, Elfuns. Republican. Baptist. Achievements include 3 patents on ABS processes; development of bulk SAN and bulk ABS processes. Home: 51 Bethel Pl Washington WV 26181 Office: General Electric Plastics PO Box 68 Washington WV 26181

PACE, KAREN YVONNE, mathematics and computer science educator; b. Jefferson City, Mo., Dec. 29, 1957; d. William John and Georgia (Loesch) Sippel; m. Charles Edward Pace, Dec. 27, 1982. EdB, Mo. State U., 1980; EdM, Drury U., 1985. Cert. secondary tchr. Tchr. Salem (Mo.) Sch. Dist., 1980—, Southwest Bapt. U., Boliver, Mo., 1985—; dist. chair Career Ladder Com., Salem, 1991-92; treas. Cmty. Tchrs. Orgn., Salem, 1992-93; assessment expert Salem Sch. Dist., 1993-94; sr. leader Mo. Assessment Project 2000, 1994. Pres. Community Cause Club, Salem, 1994. Mem. Salem Tchrs. Assn. (budget com. chair 1992-94). Democrat. Avocation: music. Home: PO Box 795 Salem MO 65560-0795 Office: Salem Sch Dist 1400 W 3rd St Salem MO 65560-2730

PACE, LEONARD, retired management consultant; b. Torrington, Conn., Oct. 24, 1924; s. Anthony and Maria G. P.; m. Maureen Therese Murphy, Sept. 15, 1956; children: Leonard Anthony, Susan Maria, Daniel Graham, Thomas William, Mary Macaire, Cathleen Anne. Student, Syracuse U., 1943; B.S.M.E., U. Conn., 1949; postgrad., N.Y. U., 1951-52, Wayne U., 1955. Cert. mgmt. cons. With GAF, 1949-57, asst. to div. controller, 1954-57; with Deloitte Haskins and Sells, N.Y.C., 1957—, head N.Y. mgmt. adv. services, 1965-67, head Eastern region, 1967-76, nat. dir. mgmt. adv. services, 1976-85, chmn. internat. mgmt. adv. svcs. com. Served as officer, pilot USAAF, 1943-45. Mem. Am. Mgmt. Assn., Inst. Mgmt. Cons. (dir., chmn. profl. standards com.). Clubs: Baltusrol Golf, Union League, Circumnavigators. Home: 35 Little Wolf Rd Summit NJ 07901-3112

PACE, STANLEY CARTER, retired aeronautical engineer; b. Waterview, Ky., Sept. 14, 1921; s. Stanley Dan and Pearl Eagle (Carter) P.; m. Elaine Marilyn Cutchall, Aug. 21, 1945; children: Stanley Dan, Lawrence Timothy, Richard Yost. Student. U. Ky., 1939-40; B.S., U.S. Mil. Acad., 1943; M.S. in Aero. Engring., Calif. Inst. Tech., 1949; LLD (hon.), Maryville Coll., 1987. Commd. 2d lt. USAAF, 1943, advanced through grades to col., 1953; pilot, flight leader B-24 Group, 15th Air Force, 1943-44; chief power plant br., procurement div. Hdqrs. Air Materiel Command Wright-Patterson AFB, Ohio, 1945-48; assignments, procurement div. Hdqrs. Air Materiel Command, 1949-53, dep. chief prodn. Hdqrs. Air Materiel Command, 1952-53, resigned, 1954; with TRW, Inc., Cleve., 1954-85, successively sales mgr., asst. mgr., mgr. West Coast plant; mgr. jet div. Tapco plant, Cleve.; asst. mgr. Tapco group, 1954-58, v.p., gen. mgr., 1958-65, exec. v.p. co., 1965-77, pres., 1977-85, vice chmn., 1985, dir., 1965-85; vice chmn., dir. Gen. Dynamics Corp., St. Louis, 1985, chmn., chief exec. officer, 1985-90, also bd. dirs. Head United Way drive, Cleve., 1984; former council commr., pres. Great Cleve. Council Boy Scouts Am.; former trustee Nat. Jr. Achievement, Denison U., Washington U., Judson Park; former chmn. Greater Cleve. Roundtable, Cleve. Found. Distbn. Com., Nat. Assn. Mfrs. Decorated Air medal with oak leaf clusters. Mem. AIAA, Aerospace Industries Assn. (chmn.), Soc. Automotive Engrs., Union Club, Country Club, Chagrin Valley Hunt Club, Pepper Pike Club, Eldorado Country Club, Rolling Rock Club, St. Louis Country Club, Delta Tau Delta. Home: 1709 Berkshire Rd Gates Mills OH 44040

PACE, STEPHEN SHELL, artist, educator; b. Charleston, Mo., Dec. 12, 1918; s. John C. and Ora K. (Reeves) P.; m. Palmina Natalini, Feb. 26, 1949. Student, Inst. Fine Arts, San Miguel, 1945-46, Art Students League, N.Y.C., 1948-49, Grande Chaumiere, Paris, 1950, Inst. D'Arte Statale, Florence, Italy, 1951, Hans Hofmann Sch., N.Y.C., 1951-52. Artist in residence Washington U., 1959; instr. painting Pratt Inst., N.Y.C., 1961-69; artist in residence Des Moines Art Ctr., 1970; vis. artist U. Calif., 1968; asso. prof. Bard Coll., 1969-71, Am. U., 1975-83. One-man show include Hendler Gallery, 1953, Artists Gallery, 1954, Poindexter Gallery, 1956, 57, Washington U., St. Louis, 1959, Holland-Goldowsky Gallery, Chgo., 1960, Howard Wise Gallery, Cleve., 1960, N.Y., 1960, 61, 63, 64, Dilexi Gallery, San Francisco, 1960, HCE Gallery, 1956-59, 61-63, 66, Dwan Gallery, Los Angeles, 1961, Hayden Gallery, Cambridge, Mass., 1961, Ridley Gallery, Evansville, Ind., 1966, U. Calif. at Berkeley, 1968, Graham Gallery, N.Y.C., 1969, Des Moines Art Center, 1970, U. Tex., Austin, 1970, Kansas City Art Inst., 1973, A.M. Sachs Gallery, N.Y.C., 1974, 76, 77, 78, 79, 81, 83, 85, Drew U., 1975, Bard Coll., 1975, Am. U., 1976, Roberto Polo Gallery, Washington, 1976, New Harmony (Ind.) Gallery, 1977, Farm Gallery, Far Hill, N.J., 1978, Barbara Fiedler Gallery, Washington, 1980, Chastenet Gallery, Washington, 1981, Katherina Rich Perlow Gallery, N.Y.C., 1987, 89, 91, 94, Vanderwoude-Tananbaum Gallery, N.Y.C., 1991, U. N.C., Greensboro, 1991, Evansville Mus., 1992, Maine Coast Artists, Rockport, 1994, Bates Coll. Mus., Lewiston, Maine, 1994; exhibited in group shows in U.S., Europe, Japan, Middle East, India, Burma, Australia, N.Z., Hawaii, Central and S.Am.; represented in permanent collections, Whitney Mus., Chrysler Mus., Norfolk, Va., Provincetown (Mass.) Mus., Evansville (Ind.) Mus., U. So. Ill., Carbondale, Michener Found., Walker Art Center, U. Calif., CIBA-Geigy Collection, Hallmark Collection, Bundy Art Gallery, U. N.C., Greensboro, Chase Manhattan Bank, Munson-Williams-Procter Inst., Utica, N.Y., Des Moines Art Center, Boston Mus. Fine Arts, Met. Mus., N.Y.C., Phillips Collection, Washington, Am. U., Washington, Corcoran Gallery, Washington, J. Patrick Lannan Mus., Venice, Calif., Curie Inst., Paris, Hirshhorn Mus., Washington, Bristol Myers Collection, Indpls. Mus., Portland (Maine) Mus., Bowdoin Coll. Mus., Brown U., Providence, Oberlin (Ohio) Coll. Mus, Farmsworth Art Mus., Rockland, Maine, Bates Coll. Mus., Lewiston, Maine. Served with AUS, 1941-45, ETO. Recipient Dolian Lorian award for promising Am. painters, 1954; Hallmark award, 1961; Guggenheim fellow, 1980; Creative Artists Pub. Service Program grantee, 1973. Mem. Nat. Acad. of Design (Benjamin Altman prize 1993). Office: 164 11th Ave New York NY 10011-1005

PACE, THOMAS M., lawyer; b. Mesa, Ariz., Feb. 5, 1952; s. Lemuel Max and Ann (Green) P.; m. Vi Garrett Pace, Jan. 24, 1981; children: Melanie, Brittany. BA, Stanford U., 1973; JD, U. Ariz., 1976. Bar: Ariz.; cert. real estate specialist. Assoc. Martin, Feldhacker & Friedl, Phoenix, 1976-77, Trew & Woodford, Phoenix, 1977-78; ptnr. Hecker, Phillips & Hooker, Tucson, 1978-88; sr. ptnr. O'Connor Cavanagh, Tucson, 1988-95. Mem. Mayor's Housing Task Force, Tucson, 1993; bd. dirs. Tucson Urban League, 1986—; chmn. So. Ariz. Homebuilders Polit. Action Com., 1995. Mem. So. Ariz. Homebuilders (tech. com), Stanford Club So. Ariz. Democrat. Office: 3443 N Campbell Ave Ste 145 Tucson AZ 85719-2379

PACH, PETER BARNARD, newspaper columnist and editor; b. Bklyn., Aug. 3, 1951; s. Stewart Warner and Constance (Barnard) P.; m. Kathleen Ann Megan, Sept. 7, 1985; children: Nell, Samuel. BA in English, Union Coll., 1973. Reporter Record Jour., Meriden, Conn., 1974-78, Wallingford bur. chief, 1978-83; Middletown bur. chief Hartford Courant, Conn., 1983-84, columnist, 1984-95; mem. editorial bd. Hartford (Conn.) Courant, 1992—; vis. instr. Wesleyan U., Middletown, Conn., 1985—. Recipient First Bus. and Econ. Reporting award New England Press Ass., 1977. Mem. Dedham County and Polo Club. Avocations: running, skiing, golf, gardening, reading. Home: PO Box 46 Middle Haddam CT 06456-0046 Office: Hartford Courant 285 Broad St Hartford CT 06115-2500

PACHECO, FELIPE RAMON, lawyer; b. Sagua la Grande, Las Villas, Cuba, Aug. 22, 1924; came to U.S., 1962; s. Felipe and Eugenia America (Rodriguez) P.; m. Maria Infiesta, Apr. 5, 1945; children: Carmen Pacheco Weber, Lilian C. Porter. D in philosophy and art, U. Havana, Cuba, 1947, D of laws, 1953; MS, Syracuse U., 1967; JD, U. Fla., 1975. Bar: Fla. 1975, U.S. Dist. Ct. (mid. dist.) Fla. 1976. Dir. librs. Ctrl. U. Las Villas, Santa Clara, Cuba, 1953-61; asst., assoc. catalog libr. Cornell U., Ithaca, N.Y., 1962-68, asst. law libr., 1969-70; law libr. Carlton, Fields, Tampa, Fla., 1971-75; pvt. practice Tampa, 1976—. Roman Catholic. Office: 4509 N Armenia Ave Tampa FL 33603-2703

PACHECO, MANUEL TRINIDAD, academic administrator; b. Rocky Ford, Colo., May 30, 1941; s. Manuel J. and Elizabeth (Lopez) P.; m. Karen M. King, Aug. 27, 1966; children: Daniel Mark, Andrew Charles, Sylvia Lois Elizabeth. BA, N.Mex. Highlands U., 1962; MA, Ohio State U., 1966, PhD, 1969. Prof. edn., univ. dean Tex. A&I U., Laredo, 1972-77, exec. dir. Bilingual Edn. Ctr., Kingsville, 1980-82; prof. multicultural edn., chmn. dept. San Diego State U., 1977-78; prof. Spanish and edn. Laredo State U., 1978-80, pres., 1984-88; assoc. dean Coll. Edn. U. Tex., El Paso, 1982-84, exec. dir. for planning, 1984; chief policy aide for edn. to gov. N.Mex., 1984; pres. U. Houston-Downtown, 1988-91, U. Ariz., Tucson, 1991—; cons. lang. div. Ency. Britannica, 1965-72; bd. dirs. Valley Nat. Bank Corp., Nat. Security Edn. Program.; mem. exec. com. Bus.-Higher Edn. Forum. Co-editor: Handbook for Planning and Managing Instruction in Basic Skills for Limited English Proficient Students, 1983; producer: (videotapes) Teacher Training, 1976. Treas. adv. com. U.S. Commn. on Civil Rights, L.A., 1987-91; trustee United Way of Houston, 1988-91; chmn. pub. rels. Buffalo Bayou Partnership, Houston, 1988-91; bd. dirs. Ctr. for Addiction and Substance Abuse, Greater Tucson Econ. Coun., Ariz. Econ. Coun., Ariz. Town Hall. Recipient Disting. Alumnus award Ohio State U., Columbus, 1984; named Most Prominent Am.-Hispancis Spanish Today mag., 1984, one of 100 Outstanding Hispanics Hispanic bus., 1988, Man of Yr. Hispanic Profl. Action Com., 1991; Fulbright fellow U. de Montepellier, France, 1962. Mem. Am. Assn. State Colls. and Univs., Nat. Acad. of Pub. Adminstrn., Hispanic Assn. Colls. and Univs., Tex. Assn. of Chicanos in Higher Edn., Rotary, Phi Delta Kappa. Office: U Ariz Office of Pres Tucson AZ 85721

PACHECO-RANSANZ, ARSENIO, Hispanic and Italian studies educator; b. Barcelona, Spain, Feb. 8, 1932; s. Arsenio Pacheco and Jacoba Ransanz-Alvarez; m. Mercedes Olivella-Sole, Sept. 1, 1956; children: Arsenio-Andrew, David-George. MA, U. Barcelona, 1954, PhD, 1958. Tutor Colegio Mayor Hispanoamericano Fray Junipero Serra, Barcelona, 1954-56; lectr. Hochschüle für Wirtschaft und Sozialwissenschaften, Nurnberg, 1956; asst. lectr. U. Glasgow, Scotland, 1957-59; lectr. U. St. Andrews, Scotland, 1960-70; vis. prof. U. Pitts., 1966; prof. Hispanic and Italian studies U. B.C., Vancouver, Can., 1970—. Editor: Historia de Xacob Xalabin, 1964, Testament de Bernat Serradell, 1971, Varia fortuna del soldado Pindaro, 1975; contbr. articles to profl. jours. Bd. dirs. Can. Fedn. Humanities, 1981-84. Fellow Royal Soc. Can.; mem. Can. Assn. Hispanists (pres. 1978-81), Asociacion Internacional de Hispanists, MLA, Assn. Hispanists Gt. Britain and Ireland, N.Am. Catalan Soc. (v.p. 1984-87, pres. 1987-90), Anglo Catalan Soc., Associacio Internacional de Llengua i Literaturea Catalana. Roman Catholic. Office: U BC, Hispanic and Italian Studies, Vancouver, BC Canada V6T 1Z1

PACHEPSKY, LUDMILA BAUDINOVNA, ecologist; b. Ukhta, Komi, Russia, Mar. 19, 1946; d. Baudin Nuraddin Islamov and Valentina Grigorievna (Tyrina) Islamova; m. Yakov Aronovich Pachepsky, June 8, 1978; children: Anna, Elizaveta. Diploma, Moscow State U., Russia, 1969, postgrad., 1969-72. Engr. Inst. Agrochemistry and Soil Sci. of Soviet Acad. Scis., Pushchino/Moscow, 1972-74, minor rsch. scientist, 1974-80, rsch. scientist, 1980-92; rsch. asst. U. Md., College Park, 1993-94; sr. rsch. scholar Duke U., Durham, N.C., 1994—; invited lectr. Moscow State U., 1990-91, U. Ekaterinburgh, Russia, 1990. Editor: Institute of Soil Science and Photosynthesis, 1983-86; author: Computer Modeling of Water and Salt Movement in Soils, 1973, Modeling of Soil Salinization and Alkalinization Processes, 1979, 86, Stable Characteristics and a Model of Ecosystems in Northern Prikaspy, 1982, Dynamic Model of the Tea Plantations Productivity, 1985, Photosynthetic Apparatus and Productivity of Triticale, 1991; contbr. articles to profl. jours. Recipient Spl. award for Efficient Sci. Govt. of Reg. of Georgia, USSR, 1985; rsch. grantee Terrestial Ecosystems Regional Rsch. and Analysis, USA, 1994, others. Mem. Am. Soc. Plant Physiologists, Am. Soc. for Gravitational and Space Biology, Am. Soc. Agronomy, Nat. Geographic Soc. Russian Orthodox. Home: 10403 Snowden Rd Laurel MD 20708 Office: USDA:ARS:Systems Rsch Lab Bldg 007 Rm 008 BARC-W 10300 Baltimore Ave Beltsville MD 20705

PACHMAN, DANIEL J., physician, educator; b. N.Y.C., Dec. 20, 1911; s. Louis and Ann (Kleinman) P.; m. Vivian Allison Futter, Nov. 8, 1935; children—Lauren Merle, Grace Allison. A.B., U. N.C., 1931; M.D., Duke U., 1934. Diplomate Nat. Bd. Med. Examiners, Am. Bd. Pediatrics. Intern pediatrics U. Chgo., 1934-35, instr. pediatrics, 1937-40; intern pediatrics N.Y. Hosp., 1935-36; resident pediatrics, attending pediatrician Duke Hosp., Durham, N.C., 1936-37; instr. Duke U., 1936-37, Northwestern U., 1940-42; practice medicine specializing in pediatrics Chgo., 1940-96; ret., 1996; clin. asst. prof. pediatrics U. Ill., 1950-59, clin. assoc. prof., 1960-67, clin. prof., 1967-81, emeritus prof., 1981—; attending pediatrician Ill. Research and Edn. Hosp., 1950-81; cons. Presbyn.-St. Luke's Hosp., Chgo., 1971-81, South Shore Hosp., 1955-60, Ill. Central Hosp., 1970-72, chmn. dept. pediatrics, 1962-70; attending pediatrician Trinity Hosp., 1971—; prof. pediatrics Rush Med. Coll., 1971-81, emeritus prof., 1981—; staff Children's Meml. Hosp.; courtesy staff Chgo. Lying-in Hosp; Med. cons. Bd. Edn., S. Shore High Sch., 1954-56; mem. advisory com. on sch. health Chgo. Bd. Health, 1962—, Chgo. Bd. Edn., 1962-66; pediatric cons. Ill. Council for Mentally Retarded Children, 1960-66; chmn. subcom. on sch. health Chgo. Med. Sch., 1961-67; chmn. Ill. Pediatric Coordinating Council, 1969-76. Contbr. numerous articles to profl. jours. Mem. com. on rights of minors Ill. Commn. on Children, 1975-77; mem. Mayor's Com. on Sch. Bd. Nominations, 1965-68; mem., co-chmn. Ill. Bd. for Opinions on Profl. Nursing, 1980—. Served to lt. col. M.C. U.S. Army, 1942-46. Recipient Archibald L. Hoyne award Chgo. Pediatric Soc., 1977. Fellow Am. Acad. Pediatrics (mem. exec. com. Ill. 1961-69, rep. to adv. council on child health Nat. Congress Parents and Tchrs., chmn. sci. exhibits com. 1964-72), Am. Cancer Soc. (pub. edn. com. 1967-69), Chgo. Inst. Medicine (mem.-at-large jt. com. on sch. services 1961-64), Chgo. Med. Soc. (past chmn. child health com.), Chgo. Pediatric Soc., AMA (med./edn. com. on sch. and coll. health), Phi Beta Kappa, Sigma Xi. Club: Quadrangle (bd. dirs. 1969-72), Carlton. Home: 1212 N Lake Shore Dr Chicago IL 60610-2371 Office: 2315 E 93rd St Chicago IL 60617-3948 *Knowledge, perception and an outlook of acceptance and encouragement make the life of a pediatrician an interesting and disciplined adventure.*

PACHOLSKI, RICHARD FRANCIS, retired securities company executive, financial advisor, consultant; b. Seattle, June 18, 1947; s. Theodore Francis and Nellie (Tarabochia) P.; m. Dorothy Irene Nelson, May 25, 1974; children: Nicolas, Tara. BA cum laude, U. Wash., 1969, MBA summa cum laude, 1970. CPA, Wash. Mgr. Arthur Andersen & Co., Seattle, 1970-76; v.p., contr. SNW Enterprises, Seattle, 1976-82; sr. v.p., treas., sec., dir. Seattle N.W. Securities, 1982-93; cons. Carl & Co., Portland, Oreg., 1984-88, Ellis & Carl Inc., Portland, 1979-83; pres. R. Pacholski, P.C., Redmond, Wash., 1979—; adj. prof. U. Wash., Seattle, 1976-80; bd. dirs. Seattle N.W. Securities. Mem. AICPA, Wash. Soc. CPAs, Nat. Assn. Securities Dealers (past bd. dirs. local dist.), Wash. Athletic Club, PacWest Club (Redmond, Wash.). Roman Catholic. Home and Office: 5060 164th Ct NE Redmond WA 98052-5294

PACHT, ERIC REED, pulmonary and critical care physician; b. Madison, Wis., Mar. 24, 1954; s. Asher Roger and Perle (Landau) P.; m. Karen Sue Dalpiaz, Aug. 7, 1982; children: Ben, Lora. BA summa cum laude, Lawrence U., 1976; MD cum laude, U. Wis., Madison, 1980. Diplomate Nat. Bd. Med. Examiners, Am. Bd. Internal Medicine. Intern, resident Ohio State U. Hosps., 1980-83, fellow in pulmonary and critical care medicine, 1983-86; asst. prof. Ohio State U., 1986-91, assoc. prof., 1991—; asst. dir. pulmonary and critical care Ohio State U., 1988—, dir. pulmonary and critical care fellowship tng. program, 1988—, med. sch. rep. to Am. Fedn. for Clin. Rsch., 1990-94, med. dir. lung transplantation program, 1992—, dir. clin. rsch., 1993—. Contbr. articles to profl. jours. Vol. Am. Lung Assn., Columbus, Ohio, Columbus Cancer Clinic. Recipient numerous rsch. awards. Fellow Am. Coll. Chest Physicians; mem. Am. Thoracic Soc., Ohio Thoracic Soc., Am. Fedn. Clin. Rsch., Phi Beta Kappa. Achievements include description of new form of respiratory failure and emphysema in patients with HIV. Home: 1224 Leicester Pl Columbus OH 43235-2181 Office: Ohio State U Divsn Pulmonary Medicine 1654 Upham Dr Columbus OH 43210-1250

PACHTER, IRWIN JACOB, pharmaceutical consultant; b. N.Y.C., July 15, 1925; s. Nathan and Ethel Lillian (Thomases) P.; m. Elaine Anna White, Aug. 23, 1953; children: Wendy, Jonathan. B.S., UCLA, 1947; M.S., U. N.Mex., 1949; Ph.D., U. So. Calif., 1951; postgrad., U. Ill., 1951-52, Harvard U., 1952-53. Research chemist Ethyl Corp., 1953-55; asso. research chemist Smith Kline & French, 1955-62, asst. sec. head, 1962; dir. medicinal chemistry Endo Labs., 1962-66; dir. research Endo div. du Pont Co., 1967-70; v.p. research and devel. Bristol Labs. div. Bristol-Myers Co., 1970-82; lectr. Adelphi U., 1963-69. Contbr. articles to profl. jours.; patentee in field. Trustee Gordon Research Conf., 1972-75; chmn. medicinal chemistry study group Walter Reed Inst. Research, 1975-77. Served with USN, 1944-46. Mem. Am. Chem. Soc. (chmn. div. medicinal chemistry 1974-76), Pharm. Mfrs. Assn. (chmn. research and devel. sect. 1975-76). Home: 101 Woodberry Ln Fayetteville NY 13066-1745

PACIFICO, ALBERT DOMINICK, cardiovascular surgeon; b. Bklyn., Sept. 24, 1940; s. Dominick Vincent and Amelia Catherine (Jannelli) P.; m. Vicki Lynne Overton, May 16, 1980; children: Albert D., Nicole M., Paul V. B.S., St. Johns U., 1960; M.D., N.J. Coll. Medicine, 1964. Diplomate Am. Bd. Surgery, Am. Bd. Thoracic Surgery. Med. intern Jersey City Med. Ctr., Seton Gall Coll. Medicine, 1964-65; asst. resident in surgery Mayo Clinic, Rochester, Minn., 1965-67; research fellow in surgery U. Ala., Birmingham, 1967-69, sr. resident, then chief resident surgery, resident in thoracic and cardiovascular surgery, 1968-72, mem. faculty dept. surgery, 1970—, prof. surgery, 1978-83, John W. Kirklin prof. cardiovascular surgery, 1983—, vice chmn. dept. surgery, 1990, dir. div. cardiothoracic surgery, 1984—, dir. Congenital Heart Disease Diagnosis and Treatment Ctr., 1985—; mem. staff gen., thoracic and cardiovascular surgery Univ. Hosp., Birmingham, 1972—, VA Hosp., Birmingham, 1972—; mem. staff Children's Hosp., Birmingham, 1971—, chief gen., thoracic and cardiovascular surgery, 1984—. Author: (with others) Pediatric Cardiac Surgery, 1985, Cardiology, 1985, Textbook of Surgery, 13th edit., 1986, The Treatment of Congenital Cardiac Anomalies, 1986, Perspectives in Pediatric Cardiology, 1988, Current Therapy in Cardiothoracic Surgery, 1989, Decision Making in Surgery of the Chest, 1989, Cardiac Surgery: Cyanotic Congential Heart Disease, 1989, Reoperation in Cardiac Surgery, 1989, others; mem. editorial bd. Am. Jour. Cardiology, 1983—, Heart and Vessel, 1985—, Jour. Cardiac Surgery, 1985—; cons. editorial referee Ala. Jour. Med. Scis., 1974-75; contbr. articles to med. jours. Fellow ACS, Am. Coll. Cardiology, Am. Surg. Assn.; mem. AMA, Ala. State Med. Soc., Jefferson County Med. Soc., Am. Heart Assn. (Paul Dudley White Internat. Svc. Citation 1977), Am. Assn. Thoracic Surgery, Soc. Thoracic Surgeons, Am. Surg. Soc., Internat. Coll. Pediatrics, John Kirklin Soc., Congentital Heart Surgeons Soc., Assn. Acad. Surgery, Ala. chpt. Mayo Clinic Alumni Assn., Panamanian Soc. Cardiology (hon.), Peruvian Soc. Thoracic and Cardiovascular Surgery (hon.), Soc. Nat. Inst. Cardiology Mex. (hon.), Cardiac Soc. Australia and New Zealand (corr.), Peruvian Soc. Cardiology (corr.), Alpha Omega Alpha. Republican. Roman Catholic. Office: Univ Ala UAB Station Dept Surgery Birmingham AL 35294

PACINO, AL (ALFREDO JAMES PACINO), actor; b. N.Y.C., Apr. 25, 1940; s. Salvatore and Rose P. Student, High Sch. of Performing Arts, N.Y.C., Actors Studio, from 1966. Formerly mail deliverer editorial offices Commentary Mag.; formerly messenger, movie theatre usher, bldg. supt.; co-artistic dir. The Actors Studio, Inc., N.Y.C., 1982-84. Served apprenticeship as actor, dir. and comedy writer in Off-Off Broadway theatres, Elaine Stewart's Cafe La Mama, Julian Beck & Judith Malina's Living Theatre; appeared in New Theatre Workshop prodn. of The Peace Creeps, Dec., 1966; joined Charles Playhouse, Boston, fall, 1967, and performed in New Theatre Workshop prodn. of America Hurrah and Awake and Sing; appeared in a one-act play Off Broadway The Indian Wants the Bronx, opened Astor Pl. Theater on Jan. 17, 1968 (Obie as best actor in Off-Broadway prodn. 1967-68); made Broadway debut in Does A Tiger Wear A Necktie?, 1969 (Tony award as best dramatic actor in a supporting role, named most promising new Broadway actor in a Variety poll of metropolitan drama critics); appeared in The Local Stigmatic at Actors Playhouse, N.Y.C., opening 1969; joined Repertory Theater of Lincoln Center, N.Y.C.; other plays include The Basic Training of Pavlo Hummel, Boston Repertory Theater, 1972, Camino Real, Richard III, 1973, 79, Jungle of Cities, 1979, The Connection, Hello Out There, Tiger at the Gates, American Buffalo, Julius Caesar, 1988, Salome, Chinese Coffee, Circle in the Square, 1992; (films) debut in Me, Natalie, 1969, Panic in Needle Park, 1971, The Godfather, 1972 (Best Actor award Nat. Soc. Film Critics, Acad. award nominee), Scarecrow, 1973, Serpico, 1973 (Acad. award nominee), The Godfather, Part II, 1974 (Acad. award nominee), Dog Day Afternoon (Acad. award nominee), 1975, Bobby Deerfield, 1977, And Justice for All, 1979 (Acad. Award nomination), Cruising, 1980, Author! Author!, 1982, Scarface, 1983, Revolution, 1985, Sea of Love, 1990, Dick Tracy, 1990 (Acad. award nominee), The Godfather Part III, 1990, Frankie and Johnny, 1991, Glengarry Glen Ross, 1992 (Acad. award nominee), Scent of a Woman, 1992 (Acad. award for Best Actor), Carlito's Way, 1993, Two Bits, 1994, Heat, 1995, City Hall, 1996, Donny Brasco, 1996; actor, prodr., dir., writer Looking for Richard, 1996. Recipient Am. Comedy award film Dick Tracy, 1991. Office: Chal Productions 301 W 57th St New York NY 10019-3101*

PACK, ALLEN S., retired coal company executive; b. Bramwell, W.Va., Dec. 11, 1930; s. Paul Meador and Mable Blanche (Hale) P.; m. Glenna Rae Christian, June 21, 1952; children: Allen Scott Jr., David Christian, Mark Frederick, Andrew Ray. BS., W.Va. U., 1952. Gen. mgr. Island Coal Co., Holden, W.Va., 1969-70, pres., 1970-73; v.p. adminstrn. Island Coal Co., Lexington, Ky., 1973-75; exec. v.p. Cannelton Holding Co., Charleston, W.Va., 1975-77, pres., chief ops. officer, 1977-80, pres., chief exec. officer, 1980-91; chmn., 1991-93, ret., 1993. Bd. dirs. Bucksin coun. Boy Scouts Am., Charleston, 1976—, pres., 1980, chmn., 1994, 95, 96; bd. dirs. W.Va. Univ. Found., Morgantown, 1978—; trustee Davis and Elkins Coll., 1981. Capt. USMC, 1952-54. Recipient Silver Beaver award Boy Scouts Am., 1981. Presbyterian.

PACK, EMILY LLOYD See LLOYD, EMILY

PACK, LEONARD BRECHER, lawyer; b. Seattle, Feb. 7, 1944; s. Howard David and Vivian (Brecher) P.; m. Barbara-Jane Lunin (div. Sept. 1978); children: Jesse, Justin; m. Adele Susan Weisman, Jan. 7, 1979; 1 child, Anna Rae. BA, Columbia U., 1966, JD, 1970, MIA, 1970. Bar: N.Y. 1971. Law clk. to judge U.S. Ct. Appeals D.C. Circuit, 1970-71; assoc. Fried, Frank, Harris, Shriver & Jacobson, N.Y.C., 1971-78; sec., assoc. gen. counsel Metromedia, Inc., Secaucus, N.J., 1979-86; sr. v.p., gen. counsel Orion Pictures Corp., N.Y.C., 1986-90; ptnr. Berger Steingut & Stern, N.Y.C., 1990-93; pvt. practice N.Y.C., 1993—. Bd. dirs., v.p. Dance Theatre Workshop. Mem. ABA. Democrat. Jewish. Avocation: music. Office: 1500 Broadway 21st Fl New York NY 10036

PACK, PHOEBE KATHERINE FINLEY, civic worker; b. Portland, Oreg., Feb. 2, 1907; d. William Lovell and Irene (Barnhart) Finley; student U. Calif., Berkeley, 1926-27; B.A., U. Oreg., 1930; m. Arthur Newton Pack, June 11, 1936; children: Charles Lathrop, Phoebe Irene. Layman referee Pima County Juvenile Ct., Tucson, 1958-71; mem. pres.'s council Menninger Found., Topeka; mem. Alcoholism Council So. Ariz., 1960—; bd. dirs. Kress Nursing Sch., Tucson, 1957-67, Pima County Assn. for Mental Health, 1958—, Ariz. Assn. for Mental Health, Phoenix, 1963—, U. Ariz. Found., Casa de los Niños Crisis Nursery; co-founder Ariz.-Sonora Desert Mus., Tucson, 1975—, Ghost Ranch Found., N.Mex.; bd. dirs. Tucson Urban League, Tucson YMCA Youth Found. Mem. Mt. Vernon Ladies Assn. Union (state vice regent, 1962-84),Mt. Vernon One Hundred (founder), Nature Conservancy (life), Alpha Phi. Home: Villa Compana 6653 E Carondelet Dr Apt 415 Tucson AZ 85710-2153

PACK, RICHARD MORRIS, broadcasting executive; b. N.Y.C., Nov. 22, 1915; s. Charles and Bertha (Gross) P.; m. Laura Lipkin, June 27, 1940; children: Robert N., Judith (dec.). A.B., NYU, 1938. Dir. publicity and continuity Sta. WNYC, N.Y.C., 1938-40; dir. publicity Sta. WOR, N.Y.C., 1942-47; dir. programming Sta. WNEW, N.Y.C., 1949-52; dir. programming and ops. Sta. WNBC and WNBT-TV, N.Y.C., 1952-54; v.p. programming Westinghouse Broadcasting Co., Inc., N.Y.C., 1955-65, sr. v.p. programming and prodn., 1965-72; pres. Group W Films, 1966-72; exec. adviser to chmn. Westinghouse Broadcasting Co., 1972-76; creative cons. Post-Newsweek Stas., Washington, 1972-76; disting. vis. lectr. telecommunications and film San Diego State U., 1988. Exec. producer film: One Day in the Life of Ivan Denisovich; author: (with Jo Ranson) Opportunities in Radio, 1948, Opportunities in Television, 1950; editor TV Quar., 1981—. Mem. pres.'s coun. social work edn. NYU, 1963-73. With USAAF, 1943-46.

PACK, RUSSELL T, theoretical chemist; b. Grace, Idaho, Nov. 20, 1937; s. John Terrell and Mardean (Izatt) P.; m. Marion Myrth Hassell, Aug. 21, 1962; children: John R., Nathan H., Allen H., Miriam, Elizabeth, Quinn R., Howard H. BS, Brigham Young U., 1962; PhD, U. Wis., 1967. Postdoctoral fellow U. Minn., Mpls., 1966-67; asst. prof. Brigham Young U., Provo, 1967-71; assoc. prof. Brigham Young U., 1971-75, adj. prof., 1975-88; staff scientist Los Alamos (N.Mex.) Nat. Lab., 1975-83, fellow, 1983—, assoc. grp. leader, 1979-81; vis. prof. Max Planck Institut, Gottingen, 1981; chmn. Gordon Rsch. Conf., 1982; lectr. in field. Contbr. articles to profl. jours. Named Sr. U.S. Scientist, Alexander Vol Humboldt Found., 1981. Fellow Am. Phys. Soc. (sec.-treas. div. Chem. Physics 1990-93); mem. Am. Chem. Soc., Sigma Xi. Mem. Ch. of Jesus Christ of Latter Day Saints. Home: 240 Kimberly Ln Los Alamos NM 87544-3526 Office: Los Alamos National Lab T-12 Ms # B268 Los Alamos NM 87545

PACKARD, BARBARA BAUGH, science institute administrator, physician, physiologist; b. Uniontown, Pa., Mar. 10, 1938; d. Walter Ray and Yolande (Ciarlo) Baugh; m. Lawrence Arthur Krames, Nov. 24, 1963 (div. 1971); m. John E. Packard III, July 14, 1979. B.S., Waynesburg Coll., 1960; M.S., W. Va. U., 1961, Ph.D., 1964; M.D., U. Ala.-Birmingham, 1974. Rsch. assoc. Boston U., 1966; instr. biology, rsch. assoc. in medicine U. Chgo., 1966-67; physiologist myocardial infarction br. Nat. Heart Inst., Bethesda, Md., 1967-71; rsch. assoc. U. Ala., Birmingham, 1971-74; Osler med. intern Johns Hopkins Hosp., Balt., 1974-75; sr. med. scientist adminstr. cardiac disease br. div. heart and vascular disease Nat. Heart, Lung, and Blood Inst., Bethesda, Md., 1975-79, assoc. dir. cardiology, 1979-82, dir. div. heart and vascular diseases, 1980-86, assoc. dir. for sci. program operation, 1986—. Trustee Waynesburg Coll., 1991—. Asst. surgeon gen. USPHS, 1975—. Recipient Commendation medal USPHS, 1978, Outstanding Svc. medal, 1987, Meritorious Svc. medal, 1988, Disting. Svc. medal, 1991; Disting. Pa. Coll. Alumni citation, 1991, Disting. Alumna of Yr. award Waynesburg Coll., 1996. Fellow Am. Coll. Cardiology (bd. govs. 1992-95); mem. Am. Physiol. Soc., Am. Heart Assn., Johns Hopkins Med. and Surg. Soc., Assn. Mil. Surgeons, Sigma Xi. Office: Nat Heart Lung & Blood Inst Bldg 31 Rm 5A03 9000 Rockville Pike Bethesda MD 20892-0001

PACKARD, BONNIE BENNETT, state legislator; b. Concord, N.H., Nov. 9, 1946; d. James Oliver and Caro Lucia (Arsenault) Bennett; m. David Bartlett Packard, Oct. 1, 1983. Mem. N.H. Ho. of Reps., Concord, 1981-82, 85—, vice chair ho. econ. devel. com., 1992, chair ho. commerce com., 1993—; v.p., treas. Dodd Ins. Agy., Contoocook, N.H., 1984-85; bd. dirs. Bus. Fin. Authority. State pres. N.H. Fedn. Rep. Women, 1982-83; chmn. Merrimack County (N.H.) Rep. Com., 1979-80; mem. Hillsborough County Rep. Com., 1995, chair Hillsborough County Del., 1995—; mem. Bd. Selectmen, New Ipswich, N.H., 1989-90; nat. del. trustee Nat. Kidney Found., 1990-91, 1st v.p. N.H. chpt., 1990-91. Mem. New Ipswich Hist. Soc., Greenville Women's Club. Episcopalian. Avocations: sketching, antiques, political campaigns. Home: 6 Joy Ln New Ipswich NH 03071-3610 Office: NH Ho of Reps Legis Office Building Rm 302 Concord NH 03301

PACKARD, ELEANOR GOULD See GOULD, ELEANOR LOIS

PACKARD, GEORGE RANDOLPH, journalist, educator; b. Phila., May 27, 1932; s. George Randolph and Anita Porter (Clothier) P.; m. Mary Biddle Lloyd, June 26, 1954 (div. Aug. 1978); children: Frank Randolph, Mary Wingate, William Clothier, Andrew Lloyd, Benjamin Wood, Alexander Barnes, Kent Elizabeth Davis-Packard; m. Lavinia Fletcher Plumley, July 1990. A.B., Princeton U., 1954; Ph.D., Fletcher Sch. Law and Diplomacy, 1963; research scholar, Tokyo U., 1961-62. Spl. asst. to U.S. ambassador to Japan, 1963-65; chief diplomatic corr. Newsweek mag., Washington, 1965-67; mng. editor Phila. Bull., 1969-73, exec. editor, 1973-75; dep. dir. Woodrow Wilson Internat. Center for Scholars, Smithsonian Instn., Washington, 1976-79; prof. Sch. Advanced Internat. Studies Johns Hopkins U., 1967-68, 94—, dean Sch. Advanced Internat. Studies, 1979-93; vis. pres. Internat. U. Japan, 1994—. Author: Protest in Tokyo: The Security Treaty Crisis of 1960, 1966, Japan, Korea and China, 1979, also articles. Candidate for U.S. Senate from Pa., 1975-76; bd. dirs. Asia Found., San Francisco, Atlantic Council U.S. Served to 1st lt. AUS, 1956. Ford fellow, 1960-62. Mem. Assn. Asian Studies, Japan Soc. N.Y., Council Fgn. Relations N.Y., Phi Beta Kappa. Club: Metropolitan (Washington). Home: 4425 Garfield St NW Washington DC 20007-1143 Office: Johns Hopkins U Sch Advanced Internat Study 1619 Massachusetts Ave NW 1740 Massachusetts Ave NW Washington DC 20036

PACKARD, JOHN MALLORY, physician; b. Saranac Lake, N.Y., Sept. 25, 1920; s. Edward Newman and Mary Bissell (Betts) P.; m. Ann Maurine Schoonover, June 15, 1944; children: Michael David, John Mallory, Ann Maurine, Mary Betts, Charles Edward, Kris Asvananda, Frank Schoonover, Charlotte Mellen. B.A., Yale U., 1942; M.D., Harvard U., 1945. Diplomate Am. Bd. Internal Medicine. Intern Presbyn. Hosp., N.Y.C., 1945-46; resident in internal medicine Peter Bent Brigham Hosp., Boston, 1948-49; practice medicine specializing in internal medicine and cardiology Pensacola, Fla., 1954-68; prof. medicine, asso. dean Med. Sch. U. Ala., Birmingham, 1968-76; exec. dir. Ala. Regional Med. Program, Birmingham, 1968-73; corp. v.p. med. edn. Bapt. Med. Centers, Birmingham, 1976-92; ret. Contbr. articles to med. jours. Served with USN, 1946-54. Fellow ACP, Am. Coll. Cardiology, Council Clin. Cardiology; mem. Jefferson County Med. Soc., Med. Assn. Ala., AMA, Am. Soc. Internal Medicine, Ala. Soc. Internal Medicine (pres. 1981-82), Alpha Omega Alpha. Republican. Episcopalian.

PACKARD, ROBERT CHARLES, lawyer; b. L.A., Sept. 21, 1919; s. Charles W. and Gertrude (Vern) P.; m. Nanette Taylor, Dec. 21, 1973 (dec.). B.S., U. So. Calif., 1941, J.D., 1947. Bar: Calif. 1948. Sr. ptnr. Kirtland & Packard, L.A., 1948-94, of counsel, 1994—. Fellow Am. Coll. Trial Lawyers; mem. ABA, L.A. Bar Assn. (substantive law com.), Intrenat. Bar Assn., Los Angeles County Bar Assn., Lawyer Pilots Bar Assn., Internat. Assn. Ins. Counsel (aviation com.), Am. Bd. Trial Advs., Am. Judicature Soc., Internat. Soc. Barristers, Calif. Club, Los Angeles Country Club, La Quinta Country Club, Phi Delta Phi. Home: 11445 Waterford St Los Angeles CA 90049-3438 Office: 1900 Avenue Of The Stars Los Angeles CA 90067-4301

PACKARD, ROCHELLE SYBIL, elementary school educator; b. June 25, 1951; d. Dave Wallace and Jeanette (Goddy) P. BA in Early Childhood Edn., Point Park Coll., 1973; MEd in Elem. Edn., U. Pitts., 1975. Instrnl. II permanent tchg. cert., Pa. Substitute tchr. Pitts. Pub. Bd. Edn., 1973-77, tchr. kindergarten, 1st grade, 2d grade, 1977—. Chair Israel Day Parade, Pitts., 1981; mem. Hadassah, Pitts., 1983—, Pioneer Women, Pitts., 1982—, ORT, Pitts., 1975—. Mem. Pitts. Fedn. Tchrs., Pitts. State Edn. Agy. Democrat. Jewish. Home: 4100 Lydia St Pittsburgh PA 15207

PACKARD, RONALD, congressman; b. Meridian, Idaho, Jan. 19, 1931; m. Jean Sorenson, 1952; children: Chris, Debbie, Jeff, Vicki, Scott, Lisa, Theresa. Student, Brigham Young U., 1948-50, Portland State U., 1952-53; D.M.D., U. Oreg., Portland, 1953-57. Gen. practice dentistry Carlsbad, Calif., 1959-82; mem. 98th-104th Congresses from 43rd (now 48th) Dist. Calif., 1983—; chmn. appropriations legis. subcom., former mem. pub. works and transp. com., sci., space, tech., also mem. appropriations fgn. ops. and transp. subcoms. Mem. Carlsbad Sch. Dist. Bd., 1962-74; bd. dirs. Carlsbad C. of C., 1972-76; mem. Carlsbad Planning Commn., 1974-76, Carlsbad City Coun., 1976-78; Carlsbad chmn. Boy Scouts Am., 1977-79; mayor City of Carlsbad, 1978-82; mem. North County Armed Svcs. YMCA, North County Transit Dist., San Diego Assn. Govts., Coastal Policy Com., Transp. Policy Com.; pres. San Diego div. Calif. League of Cities. Served with Dental Corps USN, 1957-59. Republican. Mem. Ch. LDS. Office: US Ho of Reps 2162 Rayburn HOB Washington DC 20515

PACKARD, SANDRA PODOLIN, education educator, consultant; b. Buffalo, Sept. 13, 1942; d. Mathew and Ethel (Zolte) P.; m. Martin Packard, Aug. 2, 1964; children: Dawn Esther, Shana Fanny. B.F.A., Syracuse U., 1964; M.S.Ed., Ind. U., 1966, Ed.D., 1973. Cert. tchr. art K-12, N.Y. Asst. prof. art SUNY-Buffalo, 1972-74; assoc. prof. art Miami U., Oxford, Ohio, 1974-81, spl. asst. to provost, 1979-80, assoc. provost, spl. programs, 1980-81; dean Coll. Edn. Bowling Green State U., Ohio, 1981-85; provost and vice chancellor for acad. affairs U. Tenn., Chattanooga, 1985-92; pres. Oakland U., Rochester, Mich., 1992-95; prof. edn., 1995—; sr. fellow, dir. tech. in edn. Am. Assn. State Colls. and Univs., 1995; prof. Oakland U., Rochester, Mich., 1995—; cons. Butler County Health Ctr., Hamilton, Ohio, 1976-78; vis. prof. art therapy Simmons Coll., 1979, Mary Mount Coll., Milw., 1981; bd. dirs. SE Ctr. for Arts in Edn., 1994—; mem. corp. adv. com. Corp. Detroit Mag., 1994-95. Sr. editor Studies in Art Edn. jour., 1979-81; editorial adv. bd. Jour. Aesthetic Edn., 1984-90; editor: The Leading Edge, 1986; contbr. articles to profl. jours., chpts. to conf. papers. Chmn. com. Commn. on Edn. Excellence, Ohio, 1982-83, Tenn. State Peformance Funding Task Force, 1988, Tenn. State Task Force on Minority Tchrs., 1988; reviewer art curriculum N.Y. Bd. Edn., 1985; mem. supt. search com. Chattanooga Pub. Schs., 1987-88; mem. Chattanooga Met. Coun., 1987-88, Chattanooga Ballet Bd., 1986-88, Fund for Excellence in Pub. Edn., 1986-90, Tenn. Aquarium Bd. Advisors, 1989-92, Team Evaluation Ctr. Bd., 1988-90; mem. Strategic Planning Action Team, Chattanooga City Schs., 1987-88, Siskin Hosp. Bd., 1989-92, Blue Ribbon Task Force Pontiac 2010: A New Reality, City of Pontiac Planning Divsn., 1992—; steering com., cultural action bd. Chattanooga, planning com United Way, 1987; Jewish Fedn. Bd.,

1986-91; mem. coun. for policy studies Art Edn. Adv. Bd., 1982-91; ex-officio mem. Meadow Brook Theatre Guild, 1992-95; bd. chair Meadow Brook Performing Arts Co., 1992-95; chair World Cup Soccer Edn. Com./Mich. Host Com. 1993-95; bd. dirs. Ptnrs. for Preferred Future, Rochester Cmty. Schs., 1992-95, Traffic Improvement Assn. Oakland County, 1992-95, Oakland County Bus. Roundtable, 1993-95; Rochester C. of C. host com. chair on edn. World Cup, 1992-95; bd. dirs. United Way Southeastern Mich.: active United Way Oakland County, Pontiac 2010: A New Reality, mayor's transition team city/sch. rels. task force: team evaluation leader Dept. of State Am. Univ. Bulgaria, 1995. Am. Coun. on Edn. and Mellon fellow Miami U., 1978-79; recipient Cracking the Glass Ceiling award Pontiac Area Urban League, 1992. Fellow Nat. Art Edn. Assn. (disting.); mem. Am. Assn. Colls. for Tchr. Edn. (com. chair 1982-85), Am. Art Therapy Assn. (registered), Nat. Art Edn. Assn. Women's Caucus (founder, pres. 1976-78, McFee award 1986), Am. Assn. State Colls. and Univs. (com. profl. devel. 1993-95, state rep. 1994-95), Econ. Club Detroit (bd. dirs. 1992-95), Rotary Club, Phi Delta Kappa (Leadership award 1985). Avocation: sailing. Home: 5192 Mirror Lake Ct West Bloomfield MI 48323 Office: Oakland U 503 O'Dowd Hall Rochester MI 48309

PACKARD, VANCE OAKLEY, writer; b. Granville Summit, Pa., May 22, 1914; s. Philip Joseph and Mabel (Case) P.; m. Mamie Virginia Mathews, Nov. 25, 1938; children: Vance Philip, Randall Mathews, Cynthia Ann. BA, Pa. State U., 1936; MS, Columbia U., 1937; LittD, Monmouth Coll., 1975. Reporter Centre Daily Times, State College, Pa., 1936; columnist Boston Record, 1937-38; writer, editor Asso. Press Feature Service, 1938-42; editor, staff writer Am. mag., 1942-56; staff writer Collier's mag., 1956; lectr. reporting, mag. writing Columbia, 1941-44, N.Y.U., 1945-57; guest lectr. several hundred colls. and univs., U.S. and 13 other countries. Author: Animal IQ, 1950, The Hidden Persuaders, 1957, The Status Seekers, 1959, The Waste Makers, 1960, The Pyramid Climbers, 1962, The Naked Society, 1964, The Sexual Wilderness, 1968, A Nation of Strangers, 1972, The People Shapers, 1977 (Notable Book of 1977, ALA), Our Endangered Children, 1983, The Ultra Rich, 1988;. Mem. planning commn., New Canaan, Conn., 1954-56; pres. Chappaquiddick Island Assn., 1977-78; mem. nat. bd. Nat. Book Com.; Trustee Silvermine Coll. Art. Recipient Distinguished Alumni award Pa. State U., 1961; Outstanding Alumni award Grad. Sch. Journalism, Columbia, 1963. Mem. Soc. Mag. Writers (pres. 1961); mem. Am. Sociol. Assn., Authors' Guild, Am. Acad. Polit. and Social Sci., Population Resource Ctr. (bd. dirs.), Ctr. for Study of Commercialism (bd. advisors). Home: Star Rt Chappaquiddick Edgartown MA 02539

PACKENHAM, RICHARD DANIEL, lawyer; b. Newton, Pa., June 23, 1953; s. John Richard and Mary Margaret (Maroney) P.; m. Susan Patricia Smillie, Aug. 20, 1983. BA, Harvard U., 1975; JD, Boston Coll., 1978; LLM in Taxation, Boston U., 1985. Bar: Mass. 1978, Conn. 1979, U.S. Dist. Ct. Mass. 1979, U.S. Dist. Ct. Conn. 1979, U.S. Ct. Appeals (1st cir.) 1981, U.S. Supreme Ct. 1985. Staff atty. Conn. Superior Ct., 1978-79; ptnr. McGrath & Kane, Boston, 1979-94, Packenham, Schmidt & Federico, Boston, 1994—. Mem. ABA, Mass. Bar Assn., Conn. Bar Assn., Boston Bar Assn., Mass CLE (faculty). Democrat. Roman Catholic. Club: Harvard (Boston). Home: 1062 North St Walpole MA 02081 Office: Packenham Schmidt & Federico 4 Longfellow Pl Boston MA 02114-2838

PACKER, BOYD K., church official. Mem. Quorum of the Twelve, Ch. of Jesus Christ of Latter-Day Saints. Office: LDS Church 50 E North Temple Salt Lake City UT 84150-0002

PACKER, DIANA, reference librarian; b. Cleve., Sept. 4; d. Herman and Sabina (Hochman) Reich; m. Herbert Packer, June 21, 1964 (dec.); children: Cynthia, Jeremy, Todd. BA, Case Western Res. U., 1951, MLS, 1952. Libr. Horizons Rsch. Inc., Cleve., 1952-64, Cleveland Heights (Ohio) University Heights Pub. Libr., 1969—. Officer Cleveland Heights PTA, 1971-84; bd. dirs. LWV, Cleveland Heights, 1974—; officer Spl. Librs. Assn., 1952-64. Mem. Ohio Libr. Assn. Avocations: travel, theater, art, music, reading. Home: 2201 Acacia Park Dr Apt 522 Lyndhurst OH 44124-3841

PACKER, KATHERINE HELEN, retired library educator; b. Toronto, Ont., Can., Mar. 20, 1918; d. Cleve Alexander and Rosa Ruel (Dibblee) Smith; m. William A. Packer, Sept. 27, 1941; 1 dau., Marianne Katherine. B.A., U. Toronto, 1941; A.M.L.S., U. Mich., 1953; Ph.D., U. Md., 1975. Cataloguer William L Clements Library, U. Mich., 1953-55, U. Man. (Can.) Library, Winnipeg, 1956-59; cataloguer U. Toronto Library, 1959-63; asst. prof. Faculty Library Sci., 1967-75, asso. prof., 1975-78, prof., dean, 1979-84, prof. emeritus, 1984—; head cataloguer York U. Library, Toronto, 1963-64; chief librarian Ont. Coll. Edn., Toronto, 1964-67. Author: Early American School Books, 1954. Mem. property tax working group Ont. Fair Tax Commn., 1991-92; mem. assessment reform working group City of Toronto, 1992—. Recipient Disting. Alumnus award U. Mich., 1981. Mem. Can. Library Assn. (Howard Phalin award 1972), Phi Kappa Phi. Home: 53 Gormley Ave, Toronto, ON Canada M4V 1Y9 Office: U Toronto, Faculty Info Studies, 140 Saint George St, Toronto, ON Canada M5S 1A1

PACKER, MARK BARRY, lawyer, financial consultant, foundation official; b. Phila., Sept. 18, 1944; s. Samuel and Eve (Devine) P.; m. Donna Elizabeth Ferguson (div. 1994); children: Daniel Joshua, Benjamin Dov, David Johannes; m. Helen Margaret (Jones) Klinedinst, July, 1995. AB magna cum laude, Harvard U., 1965, LLB, 1968. Bar: Wash. 1969, Mass. 1971. Assoc. Ziontz, Pirtle & Fulle, Seattle, 1968-70; pvt. practice, Bellingham, Wash., 1972—; bd. dirs., corp. sec. BMJ Holdings (formerly No. Sales Co., Inc.), 1977—; trustee No. Sales Profit Sharing Plan, 1977—; bd. dirs. Whatcom State Bank, 1995—. Mem. Bellingham Planning and Devel. Commn., 1975-84, chmn., 1977-81, mem. shoreline subcom., 1976-82; mem. Bellingham Mcpl. Arts Commn., 1986-91, landmark rev. bd., 1987-91; chmn. Bellingham campaign United Jewish Appeal, 1979-90; bd. dirs. Whatcom Community Coll. Found., 1989-92; trustee, chmn. program com. Bellingham Pub. Sch. Found., 1991—; Heavy Culture classic lit. group, 1991—, Jewish studies group, 1993—; trustee Kenneth L. Kellar Found., 1995—; mng. trustee Bernard M. & Audrey Jaffe Found; trustee, treas. Congregation Eytz Chaim, Bellingham, 1995—. Recipient Blood Donor award ARC, 1979, 8-Gallon Pin, 1988, Mayor's Arts award City of Bellingham, 1993. Mem. ABA (sec. real property probate and trust), Wash. State Bar Assn. (sec. environ. and land use law, sec. bus. law, sec. real property, probate and trust, com. law examiners 1992-94). Office: PO Box 1151 Bellingham WA 98227-1151

PACKER, ROGER JOSEPH, neurologist, neuro-oncologist; b. Chgo., May 14, 1951; s. Harry and Mania (Kelmanowski) P.; m. Bernice Ruth Cizek, Mar. 28, 1976; children: Michael Joseph, Zehava Sarah. MB, Northwestern U., 1973, MD, 1976. Resident pediatrics Cin. (Ohio) Childrens Hosp., 1976-78; fellow child neurology Children's Hosp. Phila., Pa., 1978-81; attending neurologist Children's Hosp. Phila., 1981-89; prof. neurology and pediatrics U. Pa., Phila., 1981-89; chmn. neurology Childrens Nat. Med. Ctr., Washington, 1989—; prof. neurology and pediatrics George Washington U., Washington, 1989—; clin. prof. neurology Georgetown U., Washington, 1992—; clin. prof. neurosurgery U. Va., Charlottesville, Va., 1993—; chmn. brain tumor strategy group Childrens Cancer Group, Arcadia, Calif., 1989—. Author: New Trends in Neuro-Oncology, 1991; contbr. chpts. to books and articles to profl. jours. Grantee NIH, Am. Cancer Inst., others. Fellow Am. Acad. Pediatrics, Am. Acad. Neurology (chair sci. selection 1992—, chair neuro-oncology 1981), Child Neurology Soc. (chief liaison health plan reform 1991—). Avocation: sports. Office: Childrens Nat Med Ctr 111 Michigan Ave NW Washington DC 20010-2970

PACKERT, GAYLA BETH, lawyer; b. Corpus Christi, Tex., Sept. 25, 1953; d. Gilbert Norris and Virginia Elizabeth (Pearce) P.; m. James Michael Hall, Jan. 1, 1974 (div. 1985); m. Richard Christopher Burke, July 18, 1987; children: Christopher Geoffrey Makepeace Burke Packert, Jeremy Eliot Marvell Packert Burke. BA, La. Tech. U., 1973; MA, U. Ark., 1976; post-grad., U. Ill., 1975-81, JD, 1985. Bar: Ill. 1985, U.S. Dist. Ct. (no. dist.) Ill. 1985, U.S. Ct. Appeals (7th cir.) 1987, Va. 1988, U.S. Dist. Ct. (we. dist.) Va. 1989. Assoc. Jenner & Block, Chgo., 1985-88; law clk. U.S. Dist. Ct. Va. (we. dist.), Danville, 1988-89; asst. commonwealth atty. Commonwealth of Va., Lynchburg, Va., 1989-95; pvt. practice Lynchburg, 1995—. Notes and comments editor U. Ill. Law Rev., 1984-85. Mem. ABA, Phi Beta Kappa. Home: 3900 Faculty Dr Lynchburg VA 24501-3110 Office: 725 Church St Ste 15B PO Box 529 Lynchburg VA 24505

PACKHAM, MARIAN AITCHISON, biochemistry educator; b. Toronto, Ont., Can., Dec. 13, 1927; d. James and Clara Louise (Campbell) A.; m. James Lennox Packham, June 25, 1949; children: Neil Lennox, Janet Melissa. BA, U. Toronto, 1949, PhD, 1954. Sr. fellow dept. biochemistry U. Toronto, 1954-58, lectr. dept. biochemistry, 1958-63, 66-67; rsch. assoc. dept. physiol. scis. Ont. Vet. Coll., U. Guelph, 1963-65; rsch. assoc. blood and cardiovascular disease rsch. unit U. Toronto, 1965-66; asst. prof. U. Toronto dept. biochemistry, 1967-72, assoc. prof., 1972-75, prof., 1975-89, acting chmn. dept. biochemistry, 1983, univ. prof., 1989—. Contbr. articles to profl. jours. Royal Soc. Can. fellow, 1991; recipient Lt. Govs. Silver medal Victoria Coll., 1949; co-recipient J. Allyn Taylor Internat. prize in Medicine, 1988. Mem. Can. Biochem. Soc., Am. Soc. Hematology, Can. Soc. Hematology, Can. Soc. Clin. Investigation, Am. Soc. Investigative Pathology, Am. Heart Assn. (coun. on thrombosis), Internat. Soc. Thrombosis and Haemostasis, Can. Atherosclerosis. Avocation: skiing. Office: U Toronto, Dept Biochemistry, Toronto, ON Canada M5S 1A8

PACKWOOD, BOB, senator; b. Portland, Oreg., Sept. 11, 1932; s. Frederick William and Gladys (Taft) P.; children: William Henderson, Shyla. BA, Willamette U., 1954; LLB, NYU, 1957; LLB (hon.), Yeshiva U., 1982, Gallaudet Coll., 1983. Bar: Oreg. Law clerk to Justice Harold J. Warner Oreg. Supreme Ct., 1957-58; pvt. atty., 1958-68; chmn. Multnomah County Rep. Cen. Com., 1960-62; mem. Oreg. Legislature, 1963-69; U.S. senator from Oreg., 1969-95, chmn. small bus. com., 1981-84, chmn. commerce com., 1981-85, chmn. fin. com., 1985-86, ranking min. mem. fin. com., 1987-94, chmn. fin. com., 1995, resigned, 1995. Mem. Internat. Working Group of Parliamentarians on Population and Devel., 1977; mem. Pres.'s Commn. on Population Growth and the Am. Future, 1972; chmn. Nat. Rep. Senatorial Com., 1977-78, 81-82; bd. dirs. NYU, 1970; bd. overseers Lewis and Clark Coll., Portland, 1966. Named One of Three Outstanding Young Men of Oreg., 1967; Portland's Jr. 1st Citizen, 1966; Oreg. Speaker of Yr., 1968; recipient Arthur T. Vanderbilt award NYU Sch. Law, 1970; Anti-Defamation League Brotherhood award, 1971; Torch of Liberty award B'nai B'rith, 1971; Richard L. Neuberger award Oreg. Environ. Coun., 1972; Conservation award Omaha Woodmen Life Ins. Soc., 1974; Monongahela Forestry Leadership award, 1976; Solar Man of Yr., Solar Energy Industries Assn., 1980; Guardian of Small Bus. award Nat. Fedn. Ind. Bus., 1980; Forester of Yr., Western Forest Industries Assn., 1980; Am. Israel Friendship award B'nai Zion, 1982; Grover C. Cobb award Nat. Assn. Broadcasters, 1982; Religious Freedom award, Religious Coalition for Abortion Rights, 1983; 22d Ann. Conv. award, Oreg. State Bldg. and Constrn. Trade Council, 1983; United Cerebral Palsy Humanitarian award, 1984; Am. Heart Assn. Pub. Affairs award, 1985; Margaret Sanger award Planned Parenthood Assn., 1985; Worth his Wheat in Gold award for leadership on tax reform Gen. Mills., 1986; Am. Assn. Homes for the Aging for Outstanding Svc. in cause of elderly, 1987; NARAL award for congrl. leadership, 1987; James Madison award Nat. Broadcast Editorial Assn., 1987; Pub. Excellence award First Ann. Jacob K. Javits, 1987; Golden Bulldog award Watchdogs of Treasury, Inc., 1988, 90; Sound Dollar award, 1989; Golden Eagle award Nurse Anesthetists, 1990; John F. Hogan Disting. Svc. award Radio-TV News Dirs. for def. of First Amendment, 1991; Nat. Conf. Soviet Jewry recognition, 1992, Space Shuttle Endeavor recognition, 1993, Spirit of Enterprise award U.S. C. of C., 1994, numerous others. Mem. Oreg. Bar Assn., D.C. Bar Assn., Beta Theta Pi. Office: 2201 Wisconsin Ave NW Ste 120 Washington DC 20007

PACTER, PAUL ALLAN, accounting standards researcher; b. N.Y.C., Jan. 26, 1943; s. Bernard David and Hilda Libby (Margolies) P. B.S., Syracuse U., 1964; Ph.D., Mich. State U., 1967. C.P.A., N.Y. Asst. prof. N.Y.U., 1967-69; rsch. mgr. Peat Marwick, N.Y.C., 1969-73; exec. dir. Fin. Acctg. Standards Bd., Stamford, Conn., 1973-84; commr. fin. City of Stamford, 1984-90; prof. acctg., MBA program U. Conn., Stamford, 1990-96, adj. prof., 1982-84; adj. prof. NYU, 1982-84; project cons. Fin. Acctg. Standards Bd., 1990-96, fellow Internat. Acctg. Standards Com., London, 1993—. Consulting editor The Jour. of Accountancy, 1968-73. Chmn. Stamford Commn. on Human Rights, 1977-84, Stamford Film Commn., 1984-90; mem. Charter Revision Commn., Stamford, 1979-80, Gov.'s Tourism Coun., Conn., 1984-90, acctg. adv. coun. U. Conn., 1984-90; pres. N. Stamford Dem. Club, 1983-84, treas., 1987-95; dir. Stamford Coliseum Authority, 1984-90; vice chmn. govtl. acctg. stds. adv. coun., 1984-91; treas. Conn. Tourism Assn., 1987-90, North Stamford Assn., 1993-94; bd. dirs. Stamford Ctr. for the Arts, United Way Stamford, Stamford Theatre Works, Stamford Cmty. Fund, Housing Devel. Fund of Fairfield County. Earhart Found. fellow Mich. State U., 1966-67; U.S. Office of Edn. grantee, 1967. Mem. AICPA, Am. Acctg. Assn. (coun.), N.Y. State Soc. CPA's, Beta Gamma Sigma, Beta Alpha Psi. Jewish. Office: Internat Acctg Standards Com, 167 Fleet St, EC4A 2ES London England

PACUN, NORMAN, lawyer; b. Bklyn., Mar. 1, 1932; s. Joseph J. and Tillie (Demburg) P.; m. Carol Yvonne Anderson, June 8, 1957; children: Catherine Elizabeth, David Edward. A.B. magna cum laude, U. So. Calif., 1953; LL.B., Harvard U., 1958. Bar: N.Y. 1959. With firm Kirlin, Campbell & Keating, N.Y.C., 1958-61; with Crane Co., 1961-76, sec., gen. counsel, 1964-68, v.p., sec., gen. counsel, 1968-76; v.p., gen. counsel Ingersoll-Rand Co., Woodcliff Lake, N.J., 1977-82, cons., 1982-83; cons. corporate devel. Crane Co., 1985-86; dir. Huttig Sash and Door Co., 1971-76, CF&I Steel Corp., 1974-76. Sec.-treas. Mid-Atlantic Legal Found., 1977-81, bd. dirs., 1980-85, treas., vice chmn., 1981-84; mem. com. Ctr. for Pub. Resources Legal Program, 1981-82; mem. Scarsdale Vol. Ambulance Corps, 1983-87, treas., 1985-87; emergency med. technician, N.Y., 1986-89; call firefichter and emergency med. technician Chatham Fire Rescue, 1989—; bd. dirs. Chatham Fire Assn., 1993—; mem., chmn. Chatham Hist. Commn., 1989—; mem. Chatham Long-Range Planning Commn., 1993-94. Served with AUS, 1953-55. Mem. ABA, Assn. Bar City N.Y., Am. Soc. Internat. Law, Harvard Club of Boston, Chatham Beach and Tennis Club (trustee 1994—), Chatham Platform Paddle Club (bd. govs. 1993—), Phi Beta Kappa. Home and Office: 14 Sunset Ln Chatham MA 02633-2461

PADBERG, DANIEL IVAN, agricultural economics educator, researcher; b. Summersville, Mo., Nov. 9, 1931; s. Christopher Edward and Ruth (Badgley) P.; m. Mildred Frances True, Aug. 5, 1956; children: Susan Elizabeth, Jean Ellen, Carol Natalie. B.S., U. Mo., 1953, M.S., 1955; Ph.D., U. Calif.-Berkeley, 1961. Asst. prof. Ohio State U., Columbus, 1961-65; project leader Nat. Commn. on Food Mktg., Washington, 1965-66; prof. Cornell U., Ithaca, N.Y., 1966-75; head dept. agrl. econs. U. Ill., Urbana, 1975-81; dean U. Mass., Amherst, 1981-83, prof. agrl. econs., 1983; cons. Farm Credit System, 1983-84; head dept. agrl. econs. Tex. A&M U., College Station, 1984-90, prof., 1990-95, ret., 1995; mem. White House Task Force on Farmer Bargaining, Washington, 1968; mem. food and nutrition bd. Nat. Acad. Sci., Washington, 1974-77; cons. Office Tech. Assessment, Washington, 1975-82; pres. Am. Agrl. Econs. Assn., 1987-88; exec. dir. Food and Agrl. Mktg. Consortium, 1993—; chmn. Nat. Adv. Com. on Concentration in Agrl., 1996. Author: Economics of Food Retailing, 1968, Todays Food Broker, 1971; editorial council: Am. Jour. Agrl. Econs., 1970-73, Jour. Consumer Affairs, 1974-76. Pres. council First Congregational Ch., Ithaca, 1971-72. Served to lt. (j.g.) USN, 1955-58, PTO. Consumer Research Inst. grantee, 1970; FDA grantee, 1971; USDA/NRI grantee, 1992; Simon research fellow U. Manchester, Eng., 1972-73. Mem. Am. Agrl. Econs. Assn. (Quality of Discovery award 1975, Quality of Communication in Research award 1977, chmn. awards 1979-80). Home: 90 Highland Ave # 216 Tarpon Springs FL 34689 *Not always right, but never in doubt.*

PADBERG, MANFRED WILHELM, mathematics educator, researcher; b. Bottrop, North-Rhine, Westphalia, Fed. Republic Germany, Oct. 10, 1941; came to U.S., 1968; s. Fritz Georg and Franziska (Grosse-Wilde) P.; m. Brigitte Anna Trager, July 7, 1967 (div. 1980); children:Britta, Marc Oliver. Diploma in mathematics Westfälische Wilhelms U., 1967; M.S. in Industrial Adminstrn., Carnegie-Mellon U., 1971, Ph.D., 1971. Scientific asst. Universitat, Mannheim, Fed. Republic Germany, 1967-68; rsch. fellow IIM, Berlin, 1971-74; assoc. prof. NYU, N.Y.C., 1974-78, prof. ops. rsch., 1978—, rsch. prof. ops. rsch., 1988—; vis. prof. Bonn (Fed. Republic Germany) U., 1974, IBM Rsch., Yorktown Heights, N.Y., 1975-76, Westfälische Wilhelms U., Münster, Fed. Republic Germany, 1978, Inst. Nat. de Recherche en Informatique et d'Automatique, Rocquencourt, France, 1980-81, Univ. Cath. de Louvain, Belgium, 1981-82, Centro Nat. di Riccerche Roma, 1982, U. Scientifique et Med. de Grenoble, France, 1984, SUNY, Stony Brook, 1987, Cen. Nat. de la Recherche Sci., Paris, 1988, others; vis. dir. rsch. Ecole Poly., Paris, 1989-90; vis. disting. rsch. prof. George Mason U., 1990-95; vis. prof. Augsburg U., Germany, 1990-91; cons. in field. Author: Linear Optimization and Extensions, 1995; co-author: Location, Scheduling Design and Integer Programming, 1996; editor: Combinatorial Optimization, 1980; co-editor: Polyhedra and Discrete Optimization, 1989, Algorithms and Discrete Optimization, 1989; contbr. numerous articles to profl. jours. Recipient Alexander-von-Humboldt Rsch. award, 1990-91. Mem. Ops. Research Soc. (Lanchester prize 1983), Math. Programming Soc. (G.B. Dantzig prize 1985). Avocation: traveling. Office: NYU Dept Math Washington Sq New York NY 10003

PADDOCK, ANTHONY CONAWAY, financial consultant; b. Paris, July 9, 1935; came to U.S., 1940; s. H. Watson and Mildred V. (Decker) P.; m. Wendy E. Brewer, Apr. 24, 1971. AB, Harvard U., 1957, JD, 1960; MBA, Columbia U., 1961. Bar: N.Y. 1961. Assoc. investment bank Merrill Lynch & Co., N.Y.C., 1961-69; v.p. Chase Manhattan Bank, N.Y.C., 1970-78, Standard Rsch. Cons., N.Y.C., 1978-84; mng. dir. Benchmark Valuation Cons., N.Y.C., 1978-84; prin. KPMG Peat Marwick, N.Y.C., 1984—; adj. prof. NYU, 1979-90. Mem. Assoc. for Corp. Growth, Inst. Mgmt. Cons. (cert.). Episcopalian. Home: 14 N Chatsworth Ave Larchmont NY 10538 Office: KPMG Peat Marwick 345 Park Ave New York NY 10154-0004

PADDOCK, AUSTIN JOSEPH, engineering executive; b. Washington Court House, Ohio, July 18, 1908; s. Leon A. and Nellie (Hare) P.; m. Janet Nevin, Aug. 3, 1934 (dec. Aug. 1964); children: Larry C. and Linda M. (twins), Jane M.; m. JoAnn Rourke, May 1966; 1 child, Jennifer Jo. BSCE, U. Mich., 1929. With Am. Bridge div. U.S. Steel Corp., 1929-61; from timekeeper constrn. dept., through ops. and sales to pres.; corp. adminstrv. v.p. fabrication and mfg. U.S. Steel Corp., 1961-69; chmn. bd., pres., chief exec. officer Blount, Inc., 1969-75; exec. v.p., chief oper. officer Pa. Engring. Corp., Pitts., 1975-78; vice chmn. bd., dir. Pa. Engring. Corp., 1978-87; dir., mem. exec. com. Pitts.-Des Moines Corp.; past dir. bldg. research adv. bd. Nat. Acad. Sci.; past dir. Am. Standards Inst., Steel Structures Paint Council; past dir. constrn. affairs com. U.S. C. of C.; past chmn. research tech. com. Am. Iron and Steel Inst. Past bd. dirs. Allegheny council Boy Scouts Am. Past dir. NAM. Clubs: Duquesne (Pitts.), Longue Vue Country (Pitts.); Montgomery Country, Men of Montgomery, Capital City. Home: 3875 Taylor Rd Montgomery AL 36116-6514

PADDOCK, JOHN, professional hockey team head coach; b. Oak River, Man., Can.; m. JIll Paddock; children: Jenny, Sally, Anna. Coach Maine Mariners, 1983-84, Hershey Bears, 1988-89; asst. gen. mgr. Phila. Flyers, 1989-90; coach Binghamton Rangers, 1990-91; head coach Winnipeg (Man.) Jets, 1991—, also gen. mgr. Twice named Am. League Coach of Yr.

PADDOCK, STUART R., JR., publishing executive. Bd. chmn. Daily Herald/Sunday Herald, Arlington Heights, Ill. Office: Daily Herald/Sunday Herald Paddock Publs PO Box 280 Arlington Heights IL 60006-0280*

PADEREWSKI, CLARENCE JOSEPH, architect; b. Cleve., July 23, 1908. BArch, U. Calif., 1932. Chief draftsman Sam W. Hamill, 1939-44; with Heitschmidt-Matcham-Blanchard-Gill & Hamill (architects), 1943; then practiced as C.J. Paderewski, 1944-48; pres. Paderewski, Dean & Asso., Inc. (and predecessor), San Diego, 1948-78; instr. adult edn. San Diego city schs., 1939-44, U. Calif. extension div., 1945, 56; Lectr. in field. Prin. works include Charactron Labs, Gen. Dynamics Corp., Convair, S.D., 1954, South Bay Elem. Schs., S.D., 1948-74; additions to El Cortez Hotel; including first passenger glass elevator in the world and New Travolator Motor Hotel, S.D., 1959, Palomar Coll., San Marcos, 1951-80, San Diego County U. Gen. Hosp., San Diego Internat. Airport Terminal Bldgs., Fallbrook Elem. Schs., 1948-74, Silver Strand Elem. Sch., Coronado, Tourmaline Terrace Apt. Bldg., San Diego Salvation Army Office Bldg. Mem. adv. bd. Bayside Social Service Center, 1953-75, San Diego Polonia Newspaper, 1994—; mem. San Diego Urban Design Com.; mem. adv. bd. Camp Oliver, 1963—, pres., 1975-76; bd. dirs. San Diego Symphony Orch. Assn., 1954-62, San Diego chpt. ARC, 1971-74; bd. dirs., chmn. coms., pres. San Diego Downtown Assn., 1963—; bd. dirs. Nat. Council Archtl. Registration Bds., 1958-66, bd. dirs. other offices, 1961-64, pres., 1965-66, chmn. internat. relations com., 1967-68, Salvation Army, vice chmn., 1989, life mem. adv. bd., 1993—, Copernicus Found., 1994—; mem. Calif. Bd. Archtl. Examiners, 1949-61, past pres., commr., 1961—; mem. Nat. Panel Arbitrators, 1953—, Nat. Council on Schoolhouse Constrn.; bd. dirs. Salvation Army, vice chmn., 1989, mem. coms., life mem. adv. bd., 1993—; hon. chmn. Ignacy Jan Paderewski Meml. Com., 1991. Decorated Knight Order Polonia Restituta, Polish govt. in exile, 1982; recipient Award of Merit for San Diego County Gen. Hosp., San Diego chpt., AIA, 1961, Honor award for San Diego Internat. Airport Terminal, Honor award Portland Cement Co., Golden Trowel award Plastering Inst., 1958-60, 4 awards Masonry Inst., 1961, award Prestressed Concrete Inst., 1976, Outstanding Community Leadership award San Diego Downtown Assn., 1963, 64, 65, 80. Fellow AIA (pres. San Diego chpt. 1948, 49, bd. dirs. 1947-53, chmn. several coms., spl. award 1977, Calif. Coun. Spl. award 1979, Calif. Coun. Disting. Svc. award 1982); mem. San Diego C. of C. (bd. dirs. 1959-62, 64-67), Am. Arbitration Assn. (San Diego adv. coun. 1969—), Sister City Soc. (bd. dirs.), Lions (past pres. Hillcrest Club, Lion of Yr. 1990, fellow internat. found. 1991), Father Serra Club (charter, past pres.), Outboard Boating Club San Diego, Chi Alpha Kappa, Delta Sigma Chi.*. Home: 2837 Kalmia Pl San Diego CA 92104-5418

PADGETT, NANCY WEEKS, law librarian, consultant, lawyer; b. Newberry, S.C., June 3, 1932; d. Price John and Caroline (Weeks) P.; m. David Lazar, Aug. 6, 1953 (div. Feb. 1994). BS, Northwestern U., 1953; MLS, U. Md., 1972; JD, Georgetown U., 1977. Bar: D.C. 1977. Asst. law libr. U.S. Ct. Appeals for D.C. Dist., Washington, 1972-74, supervisory law libr., 1974-84, circuit libr., 1984—. Mem. ALA, D.C. Bar Assn., Am. Assn. Law Librs. (profl. law libr. cert.). Home: 5301 Duvall Dr Bethesda MD 20816-1873 Office: US Ct Appeals for DC Cir Judges' Libr 3518 US Court House Washington DC 20002-5618

PADGETT, SHELTON EDWARD, lawyer; b. San Marcos, Tex., June 9, 1948; s. Sidney Curtis and Sybil (Dobie) P.; 1 child, Shelton Edward Jr. BS in Edn., S.W. Tex. U., 1970; JD, St. Mary's U., San Antonio, Tex., 1973. Bar: Tex. 1973. Briefing atty. Supreme Ct. Tex., Austin, 1973-74; assoc. Bracewell & Patterson, Houston, 1974-76; ptnr. Manitzas, Harris & Padgett, San Antonio, 1976-87, Kaufman, Becker, Clare & Padgett, San Antonio, 1987-89, Akin, Gump, Strauss, Hauer & Feld, San Antonio, 1989—. Bd. dirs. Bexar County Vol. Ctr., 1982-85, Beeville (Tex.) Meml. Hosp., 1982-85, Tex. Lyceum, Austin, 1984-86, Luth. Gen. Hosp., San Antonio, 1984-87; mem. labor law adv. com. to Tex. Bd. Legal Specialization, 1987—; mem. S.W. Tex. State U. Devel. Found., 1978—; mem. adv. commn. City of San Antonio Baseball Stadium, 1992—. Roman Catholic. Avocation: baseball. Office: Akin Gump Strauss Hauer & Feld 1500 Nationsbank Plz 300 Convent St San Antonio TX 78205-3701*

PADILLA, ELSA NORMA, special education educator, administrator; b. Guines, Havana, Cuba, Feb. 25, 1947; came to U.S., 1962; d. Regulo and Esther (Beato) Cuesta; m. Pedro Manuel Padilla, June 10, 1967; children: Jorge Alberto, Alejandro Manuel. BA, U. Ariz., 1970, MEd, 1972, cert. administration, 1982. Cert. elem. tchr. bilingual endorsement, spl. edn., adminstrn., Ariz. Spl. edn. tchr. Tucson Unified Sch. Dist., 1970, 1972-76, spl. edn. program specialist, 1976-78, spl. edn. tchr., 1978-81, bilingual diagnostician, 1981-84, asst dir. spl. edn., 1984-89; principal Ochoa Elem. Sch. Tucson Unified Sch. Dist., 1989-96, compliance monitor, 1996—; part time instr. Ariz. Dept. Edn., 1980-87, No. Ariz. U., 1983-89, U. Ariz., Tucson, 1983-88; mem. Bilingual Diagnostic Team, Tucson Sch. Dist., 1978, author Bilingual Spl. Edn. Program, 1980; prin. in restructuring of sch. project funded by Charles Stewart Mott Found.; cons. in field. Co-author: Courage to Change. Bd. dirs. TETRA Corp., Tucson, 1988-94, Vista Adv. Coun., Tucson, 1990-93; mem. City of South Tucson Econ. Devel. Adv. Bd. Grantee: U.S. Dept. Edn., Tucson, 1984; recipient NEA Excellence award, 1994. Mem. ASCD, Tucson Assn. for Bilingual Edn., Tucson Adminstrs. Inc., Nat. Assn. for Bilingual Edn., Assn. Cubana de Tucson. Democrat. Avocations: cooking, swimming. Office: Morrow Edn Ctr 1010 E 10th St Tucson AZ 85719

PADILLA, JAMES EARL, lawyer; b. Miami, Fla., Dec. 28, 1953; s. Earl George and Patricia (Bauer) P. BA, Northwestern U., 1975; JD, Duke U., 1978. Bar: Ill. 1978, U.S. Ct. Appeals (5th and 7th cir.) 1978, U.S. Supreme Ct. 1981, Colo. 1982, U.S. Ct. Appeals (10th cir.) 1982, D.C. 1985, N.Y. 1989. Assoc. Mayer, Brown & Platt, Chgo. and Denver, 1978-84; ptnr. Mayer, Brown & Platt, Denver, 1985-87, N.Y.C., 1988-96; private investor, 1996—. Contbg. author: Mineral Financing, 1982, Illinois Continuing Legal Education, 1993. Mem. ABA, Ill. Bar Assn., D.C. Bar Assn., Colo. Bar Assn., N.Y. State Bar Assn., Denver Bar Assn. Avocation: golf. Office: 1900 Summer St Unit 19 Stamford CT 01905-5024

PADOS, FRANK JOHN, JR., investment company executive; b. Easton, Pa., Feb. 9, 1944; s. Frank John and Mary Helen (Pokrifscak) P.; m. Barbara Janselwitz, July 6, 1968; children—Frank John (dec.), Kelly Ann, Kristin, Matthew John, Kaitlyn. B.A. cum laude in Econs, Boston Coll., 1966; M.B.A., U. Pa., 1968. Securities analyst Tchrs. Ins. and Annuity Assn., N.Y.C., 1971-74; investment officer Tchrs. Ins. and Annuity Assn., 1975-77, v.p., 1977-78, sr. v.p., mgr. securities div., 1978-83; mng. dir. Trust Co. of the West, 1983-95; exec. v.p. Desai Capital Mgmt., N.Y.C., 1995—; dir. Eyecare Ctrs. of Am. Served with U.S. Army, 1969-70. Decorated Bronze Star. Mem. Wharton Club, Sky Club. Roman Catholic. Home: 57 Thornley Dr Chatham NJ 07928-1360 Office: 540 Madison Ave New York NY 10022

PADOVA, JOHN R., federal judge; b. 1935. AB, Villanova U., 1956; JD, Temple U., 1959. With Marcu & Marcu, 1960; ptnr. Solo, Bergman & Trommer, 1962-65, Solo, Abrams, Bergman, Trommer & Padova, 1965-71, Solo, Bergman, Trommer, Padova & Albert, 1971-74, Solo, Bergman & Padova, 1974-75, Solo & Padova, 1975-77, 84-86, Solo, Padova & Lisi, 1977-84, Padova & Hinman, 1986-91, Padova & Lisi, 1991-92; fed. judge U.S. Dist. Ct. (ea. dist.) Pa., 1992—. With USNGR, 1959-64, USAR, 1964-68. Mem. ABA, Am. Trial Lawyers Assn., Phila. Bar Assn., Nat. Bd. Trial Advocacy, Pa. Trial Lawyers Assn., Phila. Trial Lawyers Assn. Office: US Dist Ct 601 Market St # 20316 Philadelphia PA 19106-1510*

PADOVANO, ANTHONY THOMAS, theologian, educator; b. Harrison, N.J., Sept. 18, 1934; s. Thomas Henry and Mary Rose (Cierzo) P.; m. Theresa Lackamp, 1974; children—Mark, Andrew, Paul, Rosemarie. B.A. magna cum laude, Seton Hall U., 1956; S.T.B. magna cum laude, Pontifical Gregorian U., Rome, Italy, 1958, S.T.L. magna cum laude, 1960, S.T.D. magna cum laude, 1962; Ph.L. magna cum laude, St. Thomas Pontifical Internat. U., Rome, 1962; M.A., NYU, 1971; Ph.D., Fordham U., 1980. Ordained priest Roman Cath. Ch., 1959. Asst. chaplain Med. Center, Jersey City, 1960; asst. St. Paul of the Cross Ch., Jersey City, 1962, St. Catharine Ch., Glen Rock, N.J., 1963; prof. systematic theology Darlington Sem., Mahwah, N.J., 1962-74; prof. Am. lit. Ramapo Coll., N.J., 1971—; founding faculty mem., adj. prof. theology/religious studies Fordham U., 1973-93; mem. Archdiocesan Commn. Ecumenical and Interreligious Affairs, 1965, Commn. Instrn. Clergy in Documents Vatican II, 1966; del. dialogue group Luth.-Roman Cath. Theol. Conversations, 1969; del.-at-large senate of priests Archdiocese of Newark; Danforth assoc., 1975—; Cath. pastor Inclusive Cmty. World Coun. Chs., 1986—; lectr. in field, also appearances on radio and TV; parish min. St. Margaret of Scotland, Morristown, N.J. Author: The Cross of Christ, the Measure of the World, 1962, The Estranged God, 1966, Who is Christ, 1967, Belief in Human Life, 1969, American Culture and the Quest for Christ, 1970, Dawn Without Darkness, 1971, Free to be Faithful, 1972, Eden and Easter, 1974, A Case for Worship, 1975, America: Its People, Its Promise, 1975, Presence and Structure, 1975, The Human Journey, 1982, Trilogy, 1982, Contemplation and Compassion, 1984, Winter Rain: A Play, 1985, His Name is John: A Play, 1986, Christmas to Calvary, 1987, Love and Destiny, 1987, Summer Lightening: A Play, 1988, Conscience and Conflict, 1989, Reform and Renewal, 1990, A Celebration of Life, 1990, The Church Today: Belonging and Believing, 1990, Scripture in the Streets, 1992, A Retreat with Thomas Merton, 1996; editor: Centenary Issue Roman Echoes, 1959; editl. bd. The Advocate, 1966-73; contbr. articles to mags., Padovano Collection, personal and profl. papers, Archives, U. Notre Dame. Active Diocese Paterson Ecumenical Commn.; founding pres. Justice and Peace Commn., Diocese of Paterson, active Resigned Priests Com. Mem. Cath. Theol. Soc. Am., Mariological Soc. Am., Nat. Fedn. Priests Councils (ofcl. rep. to Constl. Conv., Chgo. 1968), Corpus (pres.), Fedn. Christian Ministries, Internat. Fedn. of Married Cath. Priests (v.p. for N.Am.). Home: 9 Millstone Dr Morris Plains NJ 07950-1536 Office: Ramapo Coll New Jersey Mahwah NJ 07430 *People rather than ideas have been most formative in my life. More accurately, people, as they embodied certain ideals have proved most decisive. There is nothing more persuasive than an idea which becomes so vital that it transforms the person who proclaims it.*

PADULA, FRED DAVID, filmmaker; b. Santa Barbara, Calif., Oct. 25, 1937; s. Fred and Mary (Adams) P.; married; 1 child. B.A. in Music, San Francisco State U., M.A. in Art, 1965. Adj. faculty U. Calif., San Francisco Art Inst., San Francisco State U.; artist-in-residence U. Minn., Mpls. Filmmaker: Ephesus, 1965 (1st pl. award San Francisco Internat. Film Festival, awards N.Y. Film Festival, Chgo. Internat. Film Festival, others), The Artist Speaks, Two Photographers: Wynn Bullock and Imogen Cunningham, Little Jesus (Hippy Hill), Anthology of Boats, David and My Porch, Salmon River Run, El Capitan (awards: Grand Prize Festival Internat. de Film D'Aventure Uecue, La Plagne, France, Grand Prize Film Festival Internat. Montagna Esplorazione, Trento, Italy, Grand Prize Banff Festival of Mountain Films, Can., Grand Prize Mountain Film, Telluride, Colo., Gold medal Festival Internat. du Film Alpine, Les Diablerets, Switzerland; electronic music compositions include: Barking Dogs, Charnet Loops, others; one-man shows (photography) include aerial photographic survey of Mayan Indian Ruins, Yucatan, Mex., 1989, San Francisco Internat. Airport, San Francisco Mus. Modern Art, Kalamazoo Inst. Arts, DeYoung Mus., San Francisco, San Fernando Valley State Coll., Bekersfield Coll., Wash. State U., George Eastman House, represented in permanent collections, Kalamazoo Inst. Arts, State of Calif., George Eastman House, San Francisco Internat. Airport, Crocker Art Mus., Oakland Mus. Art, 1004 Gallery, Port Towsend, Wash., New Horizons Nat. Bank Hdqs., San Rafael, Calif. Address: 47 Shell Rd Mill Valley CA 94941-1551

PADULO, LOUIS, university administrator; b. Athens, Ala., Dec. 14, 1936; s. Louis and Helen (Yarbrough) P.; m. Katharine Seamans, Jan. 28, 1963; children: Robert, Joseph. BSEE, Fairleigh Dickinson U., 1959; MSEE, Stanford U., 1962; PhD, Ga. Inst. Tech., 1966. Engr. design and devel. Radio Corp. Am., 1959-60; asst. prof. elec. engring. San Jose State Coll., 1962-63; asst. prof. math. Ga. State U., 1966-67; assoc. prof. Columbia U., summer 1969, Harvard U., summer 1970; assoc. prof. Morehouse Coll., 1967-68, assoc. prof., chmn. dept. math., 1968-71; dir. exchange student program Stanford U., 1969-71, assoc. prof. elec. engring., 1971-75, assoc. prof. math., summers 1971-75, dir. MITE program, 1975; prof. elec. engring. and math., dean Coll. Engring. Boston U., 1975-88, assoc. v.p., 1986-87; pres. U. Ala., Huntsville, 1988-90; pres., chief exec. officer Univ. City Sci. Ctr., Phila., 1991—; vis. assoc. prof. Stanford U., 1969-71; vis. prof. U. Tokyo, 1986-88, MIT, 1987-88; program dir. Inst. on Computers, Logic and Automata Theory, NSF, 1969; founder, dir. dual degree program Atlanta U. Ctr. and Ga. Inst. Tech., 1968-70; numerical analyst Airesearch Corp., L.A., 1969; vis. scientist MIT, 1990-91; dir. Cmty of Sci., Inc., Nemawashi, Inc., Carver Fund. Author: System Theory, 1973, Minorities in Engineering, 1974; contbr. chpts. to books. Pres. Valley Found., Huntsville, Ala., 1988-89, Ala. Engring. Found., Huntsville, 1989; mem. task force Vision 2000, Huntsville, 1989; bd. dirs. North Ala. Intenat. Trade Assn., 1989, Ala. Supercomputer Network, 1989, Vision 2000, Am. Poetry ctr., 1992, Benjamin Franklin Tech. Ctr., 1991; pres. Higher Edn. Congress, 1992—; bd. dirs. U.S. Japan Soc., 1990—; adv. com. United Negro Coll. Fund; trustee Fairleigh Dickinson U., 1989—, Presbyn. Found. Phila., 1993—, Phila. Fund for Edn., 1995—, Internat. House; vis. com. sch. engring. Tuskegee U., Coll. Engring. Drexel U., 1993—; mem. Huntsville Army Cmty. Rels. Com.; bd. vis. Grad. Sch. Edn. U. Pa., 1996—, sch. bus. Temple U., 1993—. Recipient Excellence in Sci. and Engring. Edn. award Nat. Consortium for Black Profl. Devel., 1977, Reginald H. Jones Disting. Svc. award GE Found. and Nat. Action Coun. Minorities in Engring., 1983. Fellow IEEE, Am. Soc. Engring. Edn. (Western Electric Fund Excellence in Teaching award 1973, Vincent Bendix award 1984); mem. AAAS, ACM, Mass. Engrs. Coun., Math. Assn. Am., Union League of Phila., NAACP (life). Office: Univ City Sci Ctr 3624 Market St Philadelphia PA 19104-2614

PÁEZ, RAFAEL ROBERTO, holding company executive; b. Monterrey, Nuevo Leon, Mex., May 20, 1931; s. Rafael Páez Margain and Maria Garza Guerra; m. Maria Teresa Yrigoyen y Diaz González, May 14, 1955; children: Maria de Lourdes, Maria de los Angeles, Maria Teresa, Martha Cecilia, Maria Eugenia, Lucia, Maria del Carmen, Rafael Roberto. Degree in mech. and elec. engring., Inst. Tech. Estudios Superior, Monterrey, 1953, M Adminstrn., 1966. Mgr. finishing dept. Hojalata y Lamina, S.A., Monterrey, 1953-57, asst. supt., 1957-59, supt. gen., 1959-68; dir. ops. steel div. HYLSA, Monterrey, 1968-69, dir. gen. steel div., 1969-78; dir. gen. steel div. Alfa, Monterrey, 1978-81; pres., chief exec. officer Grupo Indsl. Alfa, S.A. de C.V., Monterrey, 1981-94; ret., 1994; cons. Vitro Envases, Monterrey, 1980—, Gas Indsl. de Monterrey, 1980, Grupo Financiero Serafin, 1986—, Conek, S.A. de Capital Veriable, Monterrey, 1989—, Bancomer S.A., Monterrey, 1992, Grupo Financiero GBM Atlántico, 1992, Korn/Ferry Internat., L.A., 1994. Roman Catholic. Avocations: tennis, swimming. Office: ALFA SA de CV, Av Gomez Morin 1111 Sur, 66254 Garza Garcia Nuevo Leon, Mexico

PAFFENBARGER, RALPH SEAL, JR., epidemiologist, educator; b. Columbus, Ohio, Oct. 21, 1922; s. Ralph Seal and Viola Elizabeth (Link) P.; m. Mary Dale Higdon, Sept. 19, 1943 (dec.); children—Ralph, James, Ann, Charles, John (dec.), Timothy; m. Jo Ann Schroeder, July 20, 1991. A.B., Ohio State U., 1944; M.B., Northwestern U., 1946, M.D., 1947; M.P.H., Johns Hopkins U., 1952, Dr.P.H., 1954. Intern Evanston (Ill.) Hosp., 1946-47; research asst. pediatrics La. State U. and Charity Hosp., New Orleans, 1949-50; practice medicine, specializing in geriatrics Framingham, Mass., 1960-68; clin. asst. prof. preventive medicine U. Cin., 1955-60; lectr. biostatistics Sch. Pub. Health, Harvard U., 1961-62, clin. assoc. preventive medicine Med. Sch., 1963-65, lectr. epidemiology Sch. Pub. Health, 1965-68, vis. lectr., 1968-83, vis. prof. epidemiology, 1983-85, vis. lectr., 1986-88, adj. prof. epidemiology, 1988—; prof. epidemiology in-residence U. Calif. Sch. Pub. Health, Berkeley, 1968-69, adj. prof., 1969-80; prof. epidemiology Stanford U., 1977-93, prof. emeritus, 1993—; rsch. epidemiologist U. Calif., Berkeley, 1993—; commd. officer USPHS, 1947, med. dir., Atlanta, Ga., 1947-53, Bethesda, Md., 1953-55, Cin., 1955-60, Framingham, 1960-68, ret., 1968; mem. epidemiology and disease control study sect. NIH, 1972-76. Assoc. editor: Am. Jour. Epidemiology, 1972-75, 80—, editor, 1975-79; contbr. articles to profl. publs. Served with AUS, 1943-47. Mem. AAAS, AMA, APHA, Am. Epidemiol. Soc., Am. Heart Assn., Internat. Epidemiol. Assn., Soc. Epidemiol. Rsch., Rsch. Soc. Am., Internat. Soc. Cardiology, Am. Assn. Suicidology, Marcé Soc., Am. Coll. Sports Medicine, Am. Acad. Sports Physicians, Nat. Fitness Leaders Assn., Royal Soc. Medicine, Phi Eta Sigma, Pi Kappa Epsilon, Delta Omega. Home: 892 Arlington Ave Berkeley CA 94707-1938 Office: Stanford U Sch Medicine Stanford CA 94305

PAGALA, MURALI KRISHNA, physiologist; b. Sri Kalahasti, Andhra, India, Oct. 2, 1942; came to U.S., 1970; s. Lakshmaiah and Radhamma (Bhimavaram) P.; m. Vijaya Bhimavaram, Dec. 12, 1969; children: Sobhan, Suresh. PhD in Zoology, S. V. Univ., Tirupati, A.P., India, 1969; MS in Computer Sci., Pratt Inst., N.Y., 1985. Postdoctoral fellow Inst. for Muscle Disease, N.Y.C., 1970-73, asst. mem., 1974; assoc. rsch. scientist NYU, N.Y.C., 1974-75; asst. to dir. Neuromus Disease Div. Maimonides Med. Ctr., Bklyn., 1975-89, dir. neuromuscular rsch., 1990—; vis. scientist II Physiol. Inst., U. Saarlandes, Hamburg, Germany, 1981, 82; sci. cons. UNDP/TOKTEN Program, Calcutta, India, 1990, NIGMS/FASEB MARC Program Grambling State U., La., 1992, 95; chair sci. confs., participated in Sci. Congress, Germany, 1990, Israel, 1992, Japan, 1994, 95. Reviewed and contbr. articles to profl. jours. Life mem. Telugu Assn. of North Am., 1989; sci. fair judge N.Y. Acad. Scis., N.Y.C., 1986—. Named Best speaker Zool. Soc. of S. V. Univ., 1964, Best Basic Rsch. paper Maimonides Med. Ctr., 1983, 88, 94; Fatigue Rsch. grantee Maimonides Rsch. Devel. Found., 1986—, Drug Rsch. grantee Maimonides Rsch. Devel. Found., 1989—, Aging Rsch. grantee Maimonides Rsch. Devel. Found., 1995—. Mem. N.Y. Acad. Scis., Am. Physiol. Soc., Assn. Scientists of Indian Origin in Am. (pres. 1993-94). Democrat. Hindu. Achievements include devel. in vitro electromyographic, electrocardiographic and multi-muscle chambers to evaluate the function of skeletal muscle, heart and smooth muscule preparations from experimental animals and human subjects; and development of consumer products. Home: 82 Pacific Ave Staten Island NY 10312-6212 Office: Maimonides Med Ctr 4802 10th Ave Brooklyn NY 11219-2916

PAGÁN, GILBERTO, JR., clinical psychologist; b. San Juan, P.R., Dec. 30, 1950; s. Gilberto Sr. and Juanita (Quiñones) P.; m. Grissele Camacho, Aug. 6, 1972; children: Mariel, Lauren. Exch. student, SUNY, Albany, 1969-70; BA in Psychology magna cum laude, U. P.R., 1972; MS in Devel. Psychology, Rutgers U., 1974, PhD in Clin. Psychology, 1984. Lic. psychologist, N.J.; cert. sch. psychology. Psychometrician Well Baby Clinic of New Brunswick, N.J., 1972-73; staff psychologist Community Orgn. for Mental Health and Retardation, Inc., Phila., 1976-77; intern in clin. psychology Multimodal Therapy Inst., Kingston, N.J., 1979-80; sch. psychologist New Brunswick Pub. Sch. System, 1980-83; mental health clinician Community Mental Health Ctr. U. Medicine and Dentistry N.J., Piscataway, 1983-93; sch. psychologist Perth Amboy Pub. Sch. Sys., 1993-95; pvt. practice clin. psychology Newark, 1988—; sch. psychologist Jersey City Pub. Sch. Sys., 1995—; assoc. in psychiatry Univ. of Medicine and Dentistry of N.J., Piscataway, 1988—; field supr. Rutgers U., New Brunswick, N.J., 1988—; cons. in field to clients including Bloomfield Pub. Sch. System, Div. of Youth and Family Svcs. of State of N.J., Project Head Start, Plainfield, N.J. Columnist San Juan Star, 1990-93, El Hispano, Phila., 1977-78; contbr. profl. publs.; presenter in field. Pres. N.J. chpt. Nat. Com. for Puerto Rican Statehood, 1990-95. NIMH fellow, 1978-79; predoctoral rsch. fellow Inst. for Rsch. in Human Devel., Divsn. Psychol. Studies of Ednl. Testing Svc., Princeton, N.J., 1974-75; recipient P.R. Psychol. Assn. award, 1972, Puerto Rican Action Bds. Parents Assn. award 1985; inducted into Nat. Honor Soc. in Psychology, 1973. Mem. APA, Am. Fedn. Tchrs., N.J. Psychol. Assn., Psi Chi. Democrat. Roman Catholic. Home: 422 Johnstone St Perth Amboy NJ 08861 Office: 467 Mount Prospect Ave Newark NJ 07104-2907

PAGAN, JOHN RUSTON, law educator; b. Little Rock, Aug. 4, 1951; s. John Frank and Betty (Hardin) P. BA, Coll. of William and Mary, 1973; MLitt, Oxford U., 1975; JD, Harvard U., 1978. Bar: Ark. 1979, Va. 1982, D.C. 1984, N.Y. 1996. From asst. to assoc. prof. Marshall-Whyte Sch. of Law Coll. of William and Mary, Williamsburg, Va., 1979-84; assoc. prof. Sch. of Law U. Ark., Little Rock, 1984-86, prof. Sch. of Law, 1986-95; prof. Sch. of Law NYU, 1996—. Contbr. articles to profl. jours. Ark. state senator, Little Rock, 1991-92; legislator Pulaski County Quorum Ct., Little Rock, 1987-90. Mem. Assn. of Marshall Scholars, Phi Beta Kappa. Democrat. Avocation: historical research. Home: 240 Mercer St Apt 1902 New York NY 10012 Office: NYU Sch Law 40 Washington Sq S New York NY 10012-1099

PAGANELLI, CHARLES VICTOR, physiologist; b. N.Y.C., Feb. 13, 1929; s. Charles Victor and Mary Barone (Spalla) P.; m. Barbara Harriet Slauson, Sept. 24, 1954; children: William, Kathryn, Peter, Robert, John. AB, Hamilton Coll., Clinton, N.Y., 1950; MA, Harvard U., 1953, PhD, 1957. Instr. physiology U. Buffalo, 1958-60, asst. prof., 1960-63; assoc. prof. SUNY, Buffalo, 1963-71, prof. physiology, 1971—. Editor: Physiological Function in Special Environments, 1990; contbr. articles to profl. jours. Recipient Elliott Coues award Am. Ornithologists Union, 1981. Mem. Sigma Xi, Phi Beta Kappa.

PAGANI, ALBERT LOUIS, aerospace system engineer; b. Jersey City, Feb. 19, 1936; s. Alexander C. and Anne (Salvati) P.; m. Beverly Cameron, Feb. 23, 1971; children: Penelope, Deborah, Michael. BSEE, U.S. Naval Acad., 1957; MBA, So. Ill. U., 1971. Commd. 2d lt. USAF, 1957, advanced through grades to col., 1978; navigator USAF, Lake Charles, La., 1957-63; pilot USAF, McGuire AFB, N.J., 1963-65; command pilot USAF, Anchorage, Alaska, 1965-68; mgr. airlift USAF, Saigon, Socialist Republic of Vietnam, 1968-69; chief spl. missions USAF, Scott AFB, Ill., 1969-74; commd. tactical airlift group USAF Europe, Mildenhall, Eng., 1974-76; dep. comdr. Rhein Main Air Base USAF Europe, Frankfurt, Fed. Republic Germany, 1976-78; chief airlift mgmt. USAF Military Airlift Command, Scott AFB, Ill., 1978-81, dir. tech. plans and concepts, 1981, dir. command and control, 1982-85; ret., 1985; program mgr. Lockheed Missile and Space Co., Sunnyvale, Calif., 1985-94; dir. data applications, dir. adv. programs PAR Govt. Systems Corp., New Hartford, NY, 1994—. V.p. Cath. Ch. Council, Mildenhall, 1974, pres., 1975. Decorated Legion of Merit, Bronze Star, Air medal, Vietnam Cross of Gallantry. Mem. Nat. Def. Transp. Assn., Soc. Logistics Engrs., Air Force Assn., Armed Forces Communication and Electronics Assn., Air Lift Assn., Daedalions, Mensa. Avocation: snow skiing. Home: 8592 Red Hill Rd Clinton NY 13323 Office: PAR Govt Systems New Hartford NY 13413

PAGAN MARTINEZ, JUAN, administrative corps officer; b. Cartagena, Murcia, Spain, Apr. 6, 1938; arrived in U.S., 1979; s. Juan and Rosa (Martinez) Pagan Lopez; m. Josefina Serrano Botella, Mar. 19, 1964; children: Rosa, Juan Carlos, Cristina. Degree, Escuela Pericial de Comercio, Cartagena, Spain, 1963. Warehouse, acctg. chief Almirante Bastarreche Profl. Sch., Cartagena, 1956-77; adminstrv. corps officer Spanish Navy, Cartagena, 1961-79, Embassy of Spain, Washington, 1979—. Contbr. articles to profl. jours. Centurion Franco's Youth Front, Cartagena, 1955; bandurria player Spanish Dance Soc., Washington, 1991—; sec. Sports and Phys. Edn. Coun., Cartagena, 1972-79. Recipient Golden Poet award World of Poetry, 1990, 91, Honorable mention, 1990, Blue Ribbon award So. Poetry Assn., 1990. Mem. Washington Spanish Club (sec. 1992-94, pres. 1994—). Avocations: poetry, music composer, bandurria, lute, guitar, sax player. Home: 1009 1st St Rockville MD 20850-1451

PAGANO, FILIPPO FRANK, financial broker, commercial loan consultant; b. East Paterson, N.J., Feb. 4, 1939; s. Frank and Katherine (Tavano) P.; m. Rose Ann Melisi, June 10, 1960 (div. Dec. 1972); children: Paul, Cynthia Pagano Grube, Stefanie; m. Darlene Ann Coryea, Mar. 1987. BS in Pharmacy, Rutgers U., 1960. Registered pharmacist, profl. ski instr.; lic. capt. master USCG. System analyst Parke-Davis & Co., Detroit, 1964-72; sr. mktg. analyst internat. Schering-Plough Pharm. Co., Kenilworth, N.J., 1972-73; v.p. Robert S. First, N.Y.C., 1973-74; pres. M-P Consultations Inc., N.Y.C., 1974-75; chief exec. officer Nordic Inn, Landgrove, Vt., 1975-83; sea capt. Bahamas, 1983-85; food and beverage dir. Meredith Guest House, Durham, 1985-86, gen. mgr., 1986-88; pres. Flagship Yachts, Durham, N.C., 1988—; gen. mgr. Inter-Global Capital, Raleigh, N.C., 1989—. Co-author: Nordic Inn Book of Soups, 1979; contbr. articles on skiing to newspapers and mags. Mem. Vt. Ski Touring Operators Assn. (pres. 1979-81), Beaufort Off-Shore Sailing Soc., Boss Club (Beaufort), Kappa Psi. Republican. Roman Catholic. Avocations: sailing, snow skiing, culinary interests. Home and Office: 405 Hardscrabble Dr Hillsborough NC 27278-9766

PAGANO, JON ALAIN, data processing consultant; b. Kankakee, Ill., Dec. 26, 1958; s. Antoine and Agnes P.; m. Linda S. Gound, Dec. 22, 1983. BA in Philosophy, U. Ill., 1979; BA in Computer Sci., North Cen. Coll., 1989. Computer ops. staff Roper Inc., Kankakee, 1979-81; programmer Harris Bankcorp, Chgo., 1981-84; cons. Circle Cons., Kankakee, 1984; sr. programmer/analyst First Nat. Bank, Chgo., 1984-86; programmer/analyst Internet Systems Corp., Chgo., 1986-87; sr. systems analyst, mgr. Concord Computing Corp., Elk Grove, Ill., 1987-89; pres. Circle Cons., Naperville, Ill., 1989—. Ednl. lobbying U. Ill., Urbana, 1986—, alumni networking North Cen. Coll., 1991—. Mem. ACM, IEEE, U. Ill. Alumni Assn. (Pres.'s Coun. 1988—, Bronze Circle 1988), Pres. Club North Ctrl. Coll. Avocations: running, camping, hiking, bouldering. Home: 344 Westbrook Cir Naperville IL 60565-3242 Office: Circle Cons 344 Westbrook Cir Naperville IL 60565-3242

PAGANO, JOSEPH STEPHEN, physician, researcher, educator; b. Rochester, N.Y., Dec. 29, 1931; s. Angelo Pagano and Marian (Vinci) Signorino; m. Anna Louise Reynolds, June 8, 1957; children: Stephen Reynolds, Christopher Joseph. A.B. with honors, U. Rochester, 1953; M.D., Yale U., 1957. Resident Peter Bent Brigham Hosp. Harvard U., Boston, 1960-61; fellow Karolinska Inst., Stockholm, 1961-62; mem. Wistar Inst., Phila., 1962-65; asst. prof., then assoc. prof. U. N.C., Chapel Hill, 1965-73, prof. medicine, 1974—, dir. div. infectious diseases, 1972-75; dir. U. N.C. Lineberger Comprehensive Cancer Ctr., Chapel Hill, 1974—; attending physician N.C. Meml. Hosp., Chapel Hill; vis. prof. Swiss Inst. Cancer Rsch., Lausanne, 1970-71, Lineberger prof. cancer rsch., 1986—; mem. virology study sect. NIH, Bethesda, Md., 1973-79; cons. Burroughs Wellcome Co., Research Triangle Park, N.C., 1978-95; mem. recombinant DNA adv. com. USPHS, 1986-90; mem. chancellor's adv. com. U. N.C., 1985-91, chair 1990-91; bd. dirs. Burroughs Wellcome Fund, 1993; mem. adv. com. N.C. Cancer Coord. and Control, 1993—; mem. N.C. planning commn. for N.C. Inst. Medicine to Organize research! America, 1993. Mem. editorial bd. Jour. Virology, 1974-90; bd. assoc. editors Cancer Rsch., 1976-80; assoc. editor Jour. Gen. Virology, 1979-84, Antimicrobial Agts. and Chemotherapy, 1984-93; contbr. numerous articles to profl. publs., chpts. to books. Bd. dirs. Am. Cancer Soc., N.C., 1980—; mem. Carolina Fedn. of Environtl. Programs, 1994-96. Recipient Sinsheimer award, 1966-68, USPHS Research Career award NIH, 1968-73; named Harry F. Dowling lecturer, 1991. Mem. AAAS (Newcomb Anderson prize selection com. 1984-88), Infectious Disease Soc. Am., Am. Soc. Microbiology, Am. Soc. Clin. Investigation, Am. Soc. Virology, Am. Assn. Physicians, Internat. Assn. for Rsch. in Epstein-Barr Virus and Assocs. Diseases (pres. 1991-94, 1st Gertrude and Werner Henle lectr. on viral oncology 1990), Chapel Hill Country Club, Chapel Hill Tennis Club (pres. 1980-82), Carolina Club, Baldhead Island Club. Episcopalian. Avocations: tennis, squash. Home: 114 Laurel Hill Rd Chapel Hill NC 27514-4323 Office: U NC Lineberger Comp Cancer Ctr Chapel Hill NC 27599-7295

PAGANUCCI, PAUL DONNELLY, banker, lawyer, former college official; b. Waterville, Maine, Apr. 18, 1931; s. Romeo J. and Martha (Donnelly) P.; m. Marilyn McLean, Sept. 10, 1966; children: Thomas Donnelly, Elizabeth Mary. A.B., Dartmouth Coll., 1953; M.B.A., Amos Tuck Sch. Bus. Adminstrn., 1954; J.D., Harvard U., 1957. Bar: N.Y. 1958, N.H. 1972. Staff asst. to pres. W.R. Grace & Co., N.Y.C., 1958-61, vice chmn., bd. dirs., 1986-89, chmn. exec. com., bd. dirs., 1989-91; pres., treas., bd. dirs. Lombard, Vitalis, Paganucci & Nelson, Inc., N.Y.C., 1961-72; prof. bus. adminstrn. Amos Tuck Sch. Dartmouth Coll., Hanover, N.H., 1972-77, assoc. dean, 1972-76, sr. investment officer, 1976-77, v.p., 1977-84, v.p. and treas., 1984-85; chmn. Ledyard Nat. Bank, Hanover, 1991—; bd. dirs. Grace Inst., N.Y.C., Filene's Basement, Inc., Allmerica Securities Trust, HRE Properties, Hypertherm, Inc.; allied mem. N.Y. Stock Exch., 1961-72. Chmn. bd. trustees Dartmouth Cath. Student Ctr., 1973-85, overseer, 1973—; trustee Colby Coll., 1975-85, 87—, Casque and Gauntlet; mem. Pres.'s Pvt. Sector Survey on Cost Control. Served with AUS, 1956-62. Mem. Inst. Chartered Fin. Analysts. Clubs: Dartmouth of N.Y. (dir., v.p., pres.); Union (Boston); Knights of Malta. Home: 33 Ropeferry Rd Hanover NH 03755-1404 Office: 38 S Main St Hanover NH 03755-2015

PAGE, ALAN CEDRIC, judge; b. Canton, Ohio, Aug. 7, 1945; s. Howard F. and Georgianna (Umbles) P.; m. Diane Sims, June 5, 1973; children: Nina, Georgianna, Justin, Khamsin. BA, U. Notre Dame, 1967; JD, U. Minn., 1978; LLD, U. Notre Dame, 1993; LLD (hon.), St. John's U., 1994, Westfield State Coll., 1994, Luther Coll., 1995. Bar: Minn. 1979, U.S. Dist. Ct. Minn. 1979, U.S. Supreme Ct. 1988. Profl. athlete Minn. Vikings, Mpls., 1967-78, Chgo. Bears, 1978-81; assoc. Lindquist & Vennum, Mpls., 1979-85; former atty. Minn. Atty. Gen.'s Office, Mpls., 1985-92; assoc. justice Minn. Supreme Ct., St. Paul, 1993—; cons. NFL Players Assn., Washington, 1979-84. Commentator Nat. Pub. Radio, 1982-83. Founder Page Edn. Found., 1988. Named NFL's Most Valuable Player, 1971, one of 10 Outstanding Young Men Am., U.S. Jaycees, 1981; named to NFL Hall of Fame, 1988, Coll. Football Hall of Fame, 1993. Mem. ABA, Minn. Bar Assn., Hennepin County Bar Assn., Minn. Minority Lawyers Assn. Avocations: running, biking. Office: 427 Minnesota Judicial Ctr 25 Constitution Ave Saint Paul MN 55155-1500

PAGE, ALBERT LEE, soil science educator, researcher; b. New Lenox, Ill., Mar. 19, 1927; s. Thomas E. and Hattie O. (Pease) Pugh; m. Shirley L. Jessmore, Sept. 14, 1952; children—Nancy, Thomas. BA in Chemistry, U. Calif.-Riverside, 1956; PhD in Soil Sci., U. Calif.-Davis, 1960. Prof. soil sci. U. Calif.-Riverside, 1960—; dir. Kearney Found., Univ. Calif.-Riverside, program of excellence in energy research. Editor: Methods of Soil Analysis, 1983, Utilization of Municipal Wastewater and Sludge on Land, 1983, Heavy Metals in the Environment, 1977. Served as QMQ1 USN, 1945-52. Recipient Environ. Quality Research award Am. Soc. Agronomy, 1984, Disting. Teaching award U. Calif., Riverside, 1976, Disting. Svc. award USDA, 1991; Fullbright scholar, 1966-67; Guggenheim Meml. Found. fellow, 1966-67. Fellow Am. Soc. Agronomy, Soil Sci. Soc. Am.; mem.

Internat. Soil Sci. Soc., Western Soil Sci. Soc., Soc. Environ. Geochemistry and Health, Sigma Xi. Lodge: Elks. Home: 5555 Canyon Crest Dr Apt 1F Riverside CA 92507-6443 Office: Univ of Calif Dept Soil & Environ Sci Riverside CA 92521

PAGE, AUSTIN P., construction technology and property development company executive; b. Sherbrooke, Que., Can., 1936. Grad., Sir George Williams U., 1966. Exec. v.p., CFO Tridel Enterprises Inc., Toronto; pres., CEO Aluma Systems Corp., Toronto; bd. dirs. Banca Commerciale Italiana of Can. Office: Tridel Enterprises Inc 4800 Dufferin St, Downsview, ON Canada M3H 5S9 also Office: Aluma Systems Corp. 4810 Dufferin St, Toronto, ON Canada M3H 5S8

PAGE, BENJAMIN INGRIM, political science educator, researcher; b. Los Angeles, Sept. 17, 1940; s. Benjamin Markham and Virginia Claire (Ingrim) P.; m. Mary Herbert Robertson, Dec. 30, 1964; children: Benjamin R., Alexandra C., Timothy M., Eleanor St. J. AB in History, Stanford U., 1961, PhD in Polit. Sci., 1973; LLB, Harvard U., 1965. Asst. prof. govt. Dartmouth Coll., 1971-73; asst. prof. polit. sci. U. Chgo., 1973-77, assoc. prof., 1978-82, prof., 1982-83; assoc. prof. U. Wis.-Madison, 1977-78; Frank C. Erwin Jr. Centennial chair in govt. U. Tex., Austin, 1983-88; Gordon Scott Fulcher prof. of decision making Northwestern U., 1988—; rsch. assoc. Nat. Opinion Rsch. Ctr., Chgo., 1978-82; bd. overseers Nat. Election Studies, Ann Arbor, Mich., 1975-81; cons. in field. Author: (with Sullivan, Pressman and Lyons) The Politics of Representation, 1974, Choices and Echoes in Presidential Elections, 1978, (with Petracca) The American Presidency, 1983, Who Gets What From Government, 1983, (with Shapiro) The Rational Public, 1992, (with Greenberg) The Struggle for Democracy, 1993, Who Deliberates?, 1996; contbr. articles to numerous jours. Recipient Law Week award Bur. of Nat. Affairs, 1965; fellow Social Sci. Research Council, 1972-73, Hoover Instn., 1981-82. Mem. AASS, Am. Polit. Sci. Assn. (governing coun. 1984-86), Midwest Polit. Sci. Assn. (v.p. 1991-93), Pub. Choice Soc., Am. Assn. Pub. Opinion Rsch., Am. Econs. Assn., Phi Beta Kappa. Democrat. Episcopalian. Home: 1633 Asbury Ave Evanston IL 60201-4101 Office: Northwestern U Polit Sci Dept Evanston IL 60208

PAGE, CLARENCE E., newspaper columnist; b. Dayton, Ohio, June 2, 1947; m. Lisa Johnson Cole, May 3, 1987. BS in Journalism, Ohio U., 1969. Reporter, asst. city editor Chgo. Tribune, 1969-80; dir. community affairs dept. Sta. WBBM-TV, 1980-82, reporter, planning editor, 1982-84; columnist, mem. editorial bd. Chgo. Tribune, 1984—. Frequent guest Sta. WTTW-TV, Chicago Tonight, Chicago in Review; contbr. articles to profl. jours. Participant 1972 Chgo. Tribune Task Force Series on Vote Fraud which won the Pulitzer Prize. Recipient Community Svc. award Ill. UPI, 1980, James P. McGuire award CLU, 1987, Pulitzer Prize for commentary, 1989. Office: Tribune Media Svcs 435 N Michigan Ave Ste 600 Chicago IL 60611-4001*

PAGE, CURTIS MATTHEWSON, minister; b. Columbus, Ohio, Oct. 24, 1946; s. Charles N. and Alice Matthewson P.; m. Martha Poitevin, Feb. 12, 1977; children: Allison, Charles, Abigail. BS, Ariz. State U., 1968; MDiv, San Francisco Theol. Sem., 1971, D Ministry, 1985. Ordained to ministry Presbyn. Ch., 1971. Pastor Ketchum (Idaho) Presbyn. Ch., 1972-80, Kirk O'The Valley Presbyn. Ch., Reseda, Calif., 1980-90; campaign dir. Kids 1st Edn. Reform Partnership, L.A., 1990-91; sr. pastor Orangewood Presbyn. Ch., Phoenix, 1991-93, First Meridian Heights Presbyn. Ch., Indpls., 1993—; mem. com. Ch. Devel., Ind., 1995—; bd. dirs. Express Pub., Ketchum. Bd. dirs. Mary Magdalene Home, Reseda; chmn. com. on preparation for the ministry, San Fernando, Calif., 1988-90; chmn. Ketchum City Zoning Commn., 1979-80; mem. Ketchum Master Planning Commn., 1974, L.A. Mayor's Citizen's Adv. Task Force on Ethics, 1990; co-chmn. Voice Cmty. Orgn. in San Fernando Valley, 1988-90; chair Family Cares, Indpls., 1995—. Avocations: amateur radio, tennis, snow skiing. Office: First Meridian Heights Pres 4701 Central Ave Indianapolis IN 46205-1828

PAGE, DAVID RANDALL, hospital administrator; b. Plainfield, N.J., Oct. 30, 1940; married;. BA, Davidson Coll., 1962; MA, Duke U., 1964. Administrv. resident Durham County Gen. Hosp., Durham, N.C., 1964; administrv. resident Duke U. Hosp., Durham, N.C., 1963-64, administrv. asst., 1964-65; asst. dir. Children's Mercy Hosp., Kansas City, 1968-69; asst. dir. Meml. Mission Hosp., Asheville, N.C., 1969-71, assoc. dir., 1971-81; exec. v.p., dir. Ochsner Fedn. Hosp., New Orleans, 1981-93; pres. Hermann Hosp., Houston, 1993—. Fellow ACHE; mem. AHA. Office: Hermann Hosp 6411 Fannin St Houston TX 77030-1501

PAGE, DOZZIE LYONS, vocational school educator; b. Tiptonville, Tenn., Apr. 13, 1921; d. Lessie LeRoy and Carrie (Oldham) Lyons; children: Rita, Gerald. BS in Edn., Chgo. Tchrs. Coll., 1968; MS in Psychology, Counseling and Guidance Chgo. State U., 1976; MA in Bus. Edn., Govs. State U., 1979. Cashier receptionist Unity Mut. Life Ins. Co., Chgo., 1939-47; sec. United Transport Service Employees Union, Chgo., 1947-51; sec. to dir. West Side YWCA, Chgo., 1951-53; sec., office mgr. Joint Council Dining Car Employees AFL CIO, Chgo., 1957-59; sr. stenographer Chgo. Police Dept., 1962-65; tchr. office practice Manpower Devel. Tng. Act, Chgo. Bd. Edn., 1965-67; tchr. office occupations Dunbar Vocat. High Sch., Chgo., 1968-71, tchr., coord. distributive edn., 1971-90; mem. NAACP, DuSable Mus. African-Am. History. Mem. Office Occupations Club, Distributive Edn. Assn., Assn. for Supervision and Curriculum Devel., Chgo. Urban League, Chgo. Bus. Edn. Assn. (exec. bd. 1983—, Enos Perry award 1987, pres. 1991-92), Ill. Pers. and Guidance Assn., Am. Pers. and Guidance Assn., Am. Vocat. Assn., Chgo. Urban League, Nat. Bus. Edn. Assn., Ill. Bus. Edn. Assn., Chgo. Bus. Edn. Assn., Chgo. State U. Alumni Assn., Governor's State U. Alumni Assn., Phi Delta Kappa. Home: 6127 S Justine St Chicago IL 60636-2327

PAGE, ELLIS BATTEN, behavioral scientist, educator, corporate officer; b. San Diego, Apr. 29, 1924; s. Frank Homer and Dorothy (Batten) P.; m. Elizabeth Latimer Thaxton, June 21, 1952; children: Ellis Batten (Tim), Elizabeth Page Sigman, Richard Leighton. A.B., Pomona Coll., 1947; M.A., San Diego State U., 1955; Ed.D., UCLA, 1958; postdoctoral (NSF fellow), U. Mich., 1959; postdoctoral (IBM fellow), MIT, 1966-67. Tchr. secondary schs. Calif., 1952-56; mem. psychology dept. San Diego City Coll., 1957-58; dir. guidance and testing Eastern Mich. U., 1958-60; dean Coll. Edn., prof. edn. and psychology Tex. Woman's U., 1960-62; dir. Bur. Ednl. Rsch. U. Conn., 1962-70, prof. ednl. psychology, 1962-79; prof. ednl. psychology and research Duke U., 1979—; vis. prof. U. Wis., 1960, 62, Harvard U., 1968-69, U. Javeriana, Bogotá, 1975; leader Ford Found. rsch. adv. team Venezuelan Ministry Edn., Caracas, 1969-70; vis. prof. Spanish Ministry Edn., 1972, 80, 82-85; rsch. cons. U.S. Office Edn., USN, Nat. Inst. Edn., Bur. Edn. Handicapped; chmn. nat. planning com. Nat. Ctr. Edn. Stats.; adviser Brazilian Ministry Edn., 1973, 80; chief Ministerial Commn. Edn., Bermuda, 1983-85; mem. Adv. Coun. for Edn. Stats., U.S. Dept. Edn., 1987-90; pres. TruJudge, Inc., 1993—. Author, editor in field. Capt. USMCR, 1943-46. Recipient Disting. Alumnus award San Diego State U., 1980. Fellow AAAS (life), APA (pres. ednl. psychology 1976-77), Am. Psychol. Soc., John Dewey Soc., Am. Assn. Applied and Preventive Psychology, Nat. Conf. Rsch. English, Philosophy Edn. Soc.; mem. Am. Coun. Assn., Am. Ednl. Rsch. Assn. (pres. 1979-80), Am. Statis. Assn. (officer N.C. chpt.), Assn. Computational Linguistics, Nat. Assn. Scholars, N.C. Assn. Rsch. Edn. (Disting. Rsch. award 1981, 91, pres. 1984-85), Rhetoric Soc. Am. (dir.), Psychometric Soc., Sociedad Espanola de Pedagogia (hon.), Sigma Xi, Phi Kappa Phi, Phi Gamma Delta, Psi Chi, Kappa Delta Pi, Phi Delta Kappa (life, svc. key). Anglican. Home: 110 Oakstone Dr Chapel Hill NC 27514-9585 Office: Duke U 213 W Duke Bldg Durham NC 27708

PAGE, ERNEST, medical educator; b. Cologne, Germany, May 30, 1927; came to U.S., 1936, naturalized, 1942; s. Max Ernest and Eleanor (Kohn) P.; m. Eva Veronica Gross, June 5, 1967; 1 son, Thomas J. A.B., Calif., Berkeley, 1949; M.D., Calif., San Francisco, 1952. Intern Peter Bent Brigham Hosp., Boston, 1952-53; resident Peter Bent Brigham Hosp., 1953-54, 57-58; research assoc. Harvard Med. Sch., 1957-65; assoc. prof. medicine and Physiology U. Chgo. Med. Sch., 1965-69, prof., 1969—. Editor: Am. Jour. Physiology: Heart and Circulatory Physiology, 1981-86. Served with AUS, 1945-46. Established investigator Am. Heart Assn., 1959-65. Mem. Am. Physiol. Soc., Biophys. Soc., Am. Soc. Cell Biology, Soc. Gen. Physiologists, Assn. Am. Physicians. Home: 5606 S Harper Ave Chicago IL 60637-1832 Office: U Chgo Med Sch 5841 S Maryland Ave Chicago IL 60637-1463

PAGE, FREDERICK WEST, business consultant; b. East Orange, N.J., Oct. 19, 1932; s. Frederick West and Dorothy (Donham) P.; m. Miriam Lowell Jones, Feb. 14, 1959; children: William, Janet, Thomas, James. A.B., Dartmouth Coll., 1954; postgrad., Wharton Grad. Sch. Bus., U. Pa., 1956-57; M.B.A., NYU, 1960. With Schering Corp. (now Schering-Plough), 1957-91, various mktg. positions, 1957-73, gen. mgr. animal health products, 1973-80, pres. U.S. Animal Health Products Div., 1980-83, v.p. pharm. ops., 1983-91; pres. Bus. Cons. Svcs., 1991—. Served with U.S. Army, 1954-56. Mem. Animal Health Inst. (exec. com. 1978-81, chmn. 1979-80). Republican. Club: Phi Kappa Psi. Home and Office: 22 Martin Rd West Caldwell NJ 07006

PAGE, GEORGE KEITH, banker; b. Rolling Prairie, Ind., July 7, 1917; s. Glenn Keith and Ruth (Mansfield) P.; m. Carmen Bailey; children: Kay, Susan, John Michael. Ed., U. Ala. Coll. Commerce and Bus. Adminstrn. Asst. cashier Baldwin County Bank, Bay Minette, Ala., 1938-43; pres., dir. Baldwin County Savs. & Loan Assn., Robertsdale and Fairhope, Ala., 1943-58; chmn. bd., chief exec. officer United First Fed. Savs. & Loan Assn. (merger Barnett Bank S.W. Fla.), Sarasota, Fla., 1958-86; sr. chmn. Barnett Bank S.W. Fla., 1986-89; also bd. dirs. Barnett Bank S.W. Fla., Sarasota, Fla.; ret., 1989; trustees Found. for Savs. Instns., 1984-86. Pres. Ala. Savs. and Loan League, 1956; past pres., gen. campaign chmn., bd. dirs., mem. adv. coun. Sarasota United Way; past chmn. Sarasota Housing Authority; past bd. dirs. Met. YMCA Sarasota-Manatee Counties; past bd. dirs., treas. Sarasota County Libr. Bldg. Fund; trustee Sarasota Meml. Hosp. Found., 1986-92, 93-94, chmn. endowment com., 1987-92; bd. dirs. Sarasota Opera Assn., Inc., 1992—; mem. adv. bd. Sunny Land coun. Boy Scouts Am.; past trustee Argus Found.; past bd. dirs. Indsl. Devel. Corp. Fla.; gen. chmn. capital campaign funds Sarasota YMCA, 1969. With USN, WWII. Recipient cert. of honor City Commn. and C. of C., Fairhope, 1958, Silver Beaver award Boy Scouts Am., Mobile, 1949, named Disting. Eagle Scout, 1982, Outstanding Citizen award Sarasota Jaycees, 1978, recipient Brotherhood award NCCJ, 1979. Mem. Fla. Savs. and Loan League (pres. 1970-71), Sarasota County C. of C. (past treas., bd. dirs.), Sarasota U. Club (past pres., bd. dirs.), Oaks Country Club, Field Club (bd. dirs. 1968-71), Masons (32d degree), Shriners. Avocation: golf. Office: 1800 2nd St Ste 808 Sarasota FL 34236-5904

PAGE, HARRY ROBERT, business administration educator; b. Milw., Mar. 22, 1915; s. Harry Allen and Lydia (Rosendahl) P.; m. Jeanne Tompkins, Apr. 1, 1945; children: Patricia Jeanne, Margaret Berenice. A.B., Mich. State U., 1941; postgrad., U.S. Army Command and Staff Coll., 1945-46, Indsl. Coll. Armed Forces, 1958-59; M.B.A., Harvard, 1950; Ph.D., Am. U., 1966. Served from 2d lt. to lt. col. U.S. Army, 1941-46; from lt. col. to col. USAF, 1947-61; exec. officer logistics directorate U.S. Joint Chiefs of Staff, Washington, 1959-61; asst. prof. bus. adminstrn. George Washington U., Washington, 1961-65; assoc. prof., chmn. dept. George Washington U., 1965-69, prof., chmn. dept. bus. adminstrn., 1970-74, assoc. dean, 1975-80, prof. emeritus, 1981—; cons. Advanced Study program Brookings Instn., Washington, 1966-70, Ednl. Svcs. Inst., U.S. Postal Svc., 1985-92. Author: Church Budget Development, 1964, An Analysis of the Defense Procurement Program Decision-Making Process, 1966, Public Purchasing and Materials Management, 1980, rev. edit., 1989; co-author: Federal Contributions to Management, 1972. Chmn. task force edn. and tng. Commn. Govt. Procurement, 1972-73; bd. dirs., treas. Coun. Chs., Greater Washington, 1963-68; bd. dirs. Hunter Assocs. Lab., Inc.; deacon Rock Spring Congregational Ch., 1994—. Decorated Air medal, Purple Heart, Legion of Merit. Fellow Nat. Contract Mgmt. Assn.; mem. Acad. mgmt., Nat. Assn. Purchasing Mgmt., Internat. Fedn. Purchasing and Materials Mgmt., Harvard Bus. Sch. Assn., Air Force Assn., Nat. Parks and Conservation Assn. (trustee), Air Force Sgts. Assn. (trustee, chmn. scholarship bd. 1971—), Harvard Bus. Club, Sch. of Wash. Club (dir., pres. 1980-81), Alpha Phi Omega, Lambda Chi Alpha Kappa Psi, Pi Sigma Alpha, Beta Gamma Sigma. Home: 3612 N Glebe Rd Arlington VA 22207-4317 Office: 710 21st St NE Washington DC 20002-4108

PAGE, J. BOYD, lawyer; b. Kingsport, Tenn., Sept. 27, 1948; s. James H. and Valda (Stone) P.; m. Patti Harmon, Oct. 10, 1987; 1 child, James Charles. BS in Commerce with distinction, U. Va., 1970, JD, 1973. Bar: Ga. 1973, U.S. Dist. Ct. (no., mid. and so. dists.) Ga. 1973. Assoc. Cofer, Beauchamp & Hawes, Atlanta, 1973-78, ptnr., 1978-84; sr. ptnr. Page & Logue, Atlanta, 1985-87, Page & Bacek, Atlanta, 1987—; adj. prof. law Emory U., Atlanta, 1980-83. Contbr. articles to profl. jours. Mem. ABA, ATLA, NASD (arbitration policy task force), AAA (securities adv. com.), State Bar Ga., Pub. Investors Arbitration Bar Assn. (dir., officer). Avocation: golf. Home: 190 Grogans Lndg Atlanta GA 30350-3113 Office: Page & Bacek 3490 Piedmont Rd NE Ste 900 Atlanta GA 30305-4809

PAGE, JOHN BOYD, physics educator; b. Columbus, Ohio, Sept. 4, 1938; s. John Boyd and Helen (Young) P.; m. Norma Kay Christensen, July 28, 1966; children: Rebecca, Elizabeth. BS, U. Utah, 1960, PhD, 1966. Rsch. assoc. Inst. for Theoretical Physics U. Frankfurt/Main, Fed. Republic of Germany, 1966-67; rsch. assoc. Cornell U., Ithaca, N.Y., 1968-69; asst. prof. physics Ariz. State U., 1969-75, assoc. prof., 1975-80, prof., 1980—; vis. prof. dept. physics Cornell U., 1989. Contbr. articles to profl. jours. Recipient Humboldt Rsch. award, 1991; NSF grantee, 1972-77, 77-80, 80-82, 82-86, 90-92, 91-94, 95—. Fellow Am. Phys. Soc.; mem. Am. Assn. Physics Tchrs., Phi Beta Kappa, Sigma Xi, Phi Kappa Phi, Phi Eta Sigma. Office: Ariz State U Physics Dept Tempe AZ 85287-1504

PAGE, JOHN HENRY, JR., artist, educator; b. Ann Arbor, Mich., Jan. 18, 1923; s. John Henry and Lucille (Bennett) P.; m. Mary Lou Franks, July 22, 1945; children: Jonathan, Marilyn, Jeremy. Student, Mpls. Sch. Art, 1940-42; B.Design, U. Mich., 1948; M.F.A., U. Iowa, 1950. Instr. Mankato (Minn.) State Coll., 1950-54; asst. prof. art U. No. Iowa, Cedar Falls, 1954-55; asst. prof. U. No. Iowa, 1955-59, assoc. prof., 1959-64, prof., 1964-87, acting head dept. art, 1984-85; head art dept. U. Omaha, 1959-60. One-man exhbns. include Luther Coll., Decorah, Iowa, 1981, Laura Musser Mus., Muscatine, Iowa, 1978, Coe Coll., Cedar Rapids, Iowa, 1975, Sheldon Gallery, Lincoln, Nebr., 1974, Creighton U., Omaha, 1969, Augustana Coll., Rock Island, Ill., 1964, Muskegon (Mich.) Mus. Art, 1983, retrospective (in three parts) Gallery of Art U. No. Iowa, Hearst Ctr. for the Arts, Cedar Falls, Iowa, Waterloo (Iowa) Mus. of Art, 1992; group exhbns. include 10th Nat. Print Show Bklyn. Mus., 1956, 9 Iowa Artists Gov. Exhbn., 1971-72, Walker Art Ctr., Mpls., 1973, Regional Invitational Exhbn., U. Omaha, 1978, Fragile Giants, Brunner Gallery, 1994-96; represented in permanent collections, Library of Congress, Walker Art Center, Des Moines Art Center, Joslyn Art Mus., Omaha, Carnegie Inst., Pitts. Served with U.S. Army, 1943-45. Nat. Endowment Arts grantee, 1975. Unitarian. Home: 114 E Los Arcos Green Valley AZ 85614-2429

PAGE, JONATHAN ROY, investment analyst; b. Harrisburg, Pa., Sept. 10, 1946; s. John and Ellen (Smith) P.; m. Patrice Marie Margerm, May 17, 1975; children: Elizabeth, Gregory, Richard, Brian. B.A., Dartmouth Coll., 1968; M.B.A., Tuck Sch. Dartmouth, 1969. Chartered fin. analyst. Investment officer Irving Trust Co., N.Y.C., 1970-75; sr. v.p., portfolio mgr. Dean Witter Intercapital Funds, N.Y.C., 1975—. Vestry person St. John's Ch., Ramsey, N.J., 1984-88. Mem. N.Y. Soc. Security Analysts, Fin. Analysts Fedn. Republican. Episcopalian. Avocations: tennis, golf, skiing, landscaping. Home: 36 Sturbridge Dr Saddle River NJ 07458-1742 Office: Dean Witter Intercapital Funds 2 World Trade Ctr Fl 72 New York NY 10048-0203

PAGE, JOSEPH ANTHONY, law educator; b. Boston, Apr. 13, 1934; s. Joseph E. and Eleanor M. (Santosuosso) P.; m. Martha Gil-Montero, May 18, 1984. AB, Harvard U., 1955, LLB, 1958, LLM, 1964. Asst. prof. coll. law U. Denver, 1964-67, assoc. prof., 1967-68; assoc. prof. law ctr. Georgetown U., 1968-73, prof., 1973—; bd. dirs. Pub. Citizen, Inc., Washington. Author: The Revolution That Never Was, 1972, The Law of Premises Liability, 1976, Peron: A Biography, 1984, The Brazilians, 1995; co-author: Bitter Wages, 1973. Lt. USCGR, 1959-67. Office: Georgetown U Law Ctr 600 New Jersey Ave NW Washington DC 20001-2075

PAGE, LARRY KEITH, neurosurgeon, educator; b. Rayville, La., July 7, 1933; s. Ardie Lee and Edris Estelle (Chaney) P.; m. Joan Marie Doherty, Aug. 27, 1960; children: Matthew, Elizabeth, Jennifer. BS, La. State U., 1955, MD, 1958. Diplomate: Am. Bd. Neurol. Surgery. Intern Grad. Hosp., U. Pa., Phila., 1958-59; resident Children's Hosp. and Peter Bent Brigham Hosp., Boston, 1962-66; assoc. neurosurgeon Children's Hosp., assoc. surgeon Peter Bent Brigham Hosp., 1966-71; cons. Beverly Hosp., Mass., Robert Breck Brigham Hosp., Boston, Pondville Hosp., Boston, West Roxbury VA Hosp., Boston VA Hosp.; clin. instr. neurosurgery Harvard U., Boston, 1966-71; prof., vice chmn. dept. neurosurgery U. Miami, Fla., 1971-95, prof. emeritus, 1995—, chief div. pediatric neurosurgery, 1971-95; neurosurgeon VA Hosp., Miami, 1971-88; neurosurgeon Jackson Meml. Hosp., Miami, 1971-95, dir. neurosurgery, 1994-95; chief neurosurgery Mt. Sinai Hosp., Miami, 1990-94; neurosurg. cons. FDA; neurosurg. cons. NASA. Mem. editorial bds., contbr. articles to profl. jours. Served to lt. USN, 1959-62. Mem. ACS, Am. Acad. Pediatrics, Am. Assn. Neurol. Surgeons, Internat. Soc. Pediatric Neurosurgery, Am. Soc. Pediatric Neurosurgery, Congress Neurol. Surgeons, Fellowship of Acad. Neurosurgeons, Internat. Neurosurg. Forum, Royal Soc. Medicine, Soc. for Rsch. in Hydrocephalus and Spina Bifida, New Eng. Neurosurg. Soc., Fla. Neurosurg. Soc. (pres. 1989-90), Mass. Med. Soc., Dade County Med. Assn., Internat. Palm Soc., Alpha Omega Alpha. Roman Catholic. Home and Office: 13845 SW 73rd Ct Miami FL 33158-1213

PAGE, LESLIE ANDREW, disinfectant manufacturing company executive; b. Mpls., June 5, 1924; s. Henry R. and Amelia Kathryn (Steinmetz) P.; m. DeEtte Abernethy Griswold, July 6, 1952 (div. Sept. 1975); children: Randolph, Michael, Kathryn, Caroline; m. Mary Ellen Decker, Nov. 26, 1976. BA, U. Minn., 1949; MA, U. Calif., Berkeley, 1953; PhD, U. Calif., 1956. Asst. microbiologist, lectr. U. Calif., Davis, 1956-61; cons. San Diego Zoological Soc. Zoo Hosp., 1957-60; microbiologist, research leader Nat. Animal Disease Ctr., USDA, Ames, Iowa, 1961-79; ret., 1979, specialist in Chlamydial nomenclature and disease; med. text cons. Bay St. Louis, Miss., 1979-85; founder, pres., chmn. bd. Steri-Derm Corp., Escondido, Calif., 1987—; cons. McCormick Distilling Co., Weston, Mo., 1994-95; specialist in chlamydial nomenclature and disease. Editor: Jour. Wildlife Diseases, 1965-68, Wildlife Diseases, 1976; contbr. chpts. to med. texts, over 70 articles to profl. jours.; patentee Liquid Antiseptic Composition. Pres. Garden Island Comty. Assn., Bay St. Louis, Miss., 1980-81; chief commr. East Hancock fire Protection Dist., Bay St. Louis, 1982-83; treas. Woodridge Escondido Property Owners Assn., 1986-88. Fellow Am. Acad. Microbiology (emeritus); mem. Wildlife Disease Assn. (pres. 1972-73, Disting. Svc. award 1980), Am. Soc. for Microbiology, Zool. Soc. San Diego, Sigma Xi, Phi Zeta (hon.). Home and Office: 1784 Deavers Dr San Marcos CA 92069

PAGE, LEWIS WENDELL, JR., lawyer; b. Scottsboro, Ala., Nov. 6, 1947; s. Lewis Wendell and Maymie Elizabeth (Parks) P.; m. Dollie Lucretia Roberts, Dec. 24, 1977; children—Margaret Amelia, Katherine Elizabeth. B.A., Auburn U., 1970; J.D., U. Ala., 1973; LL.M., George Washington U., 1975. Bar: Ala. 1973, U.S. Dist. Ct. (no. dist.) Ala. 1974, U.S. Ct. Appeals (5th cir.) 1973, U.S. Ct. Appeals (11th cir.) 1978, U.S. Supreme Ct. 1982. Assoc. firm Sadler, Sadler, Sullivan & Sharp, Birmingham, Ala., 1973-74; assoc. firm Lange, Simpson, Robinson & Somerville, Birmingham, 1975-80, ptnr. 1980-93, Page Law Firm, 1993—. Served to 2d lt. U.S. Army, 1973. Mem. Ala. State Bar Assn. (chmn. antitrust sect. 1983-84, co-chmn. permanent code commn. 1986-88), Birmingham Bar Assn. (panel chmn. grievance com. 1983-84, chmn. fee arbitration com. 1984-85), ABA (antitrust sect., litigation sect., patent, copyright and trademark sect.), Auburn U. Bar Assn. (pres. 1993-94), Tau Kappa Epsilon (sec.-treas. 1980-86). Office: Page Law Firm 1901 6th Ave N Ste 1540 Birmingham AL 35203-2618

PAGE, LINDA KAY, banking executive; b. Wadsworth, Ohio, Oct. 4, 1943; s. Frederick Meredith and Martha Irene (Vance) P. Student Sch. Banking, Ohio U., 1976-77; cert. Nat. Pers. Sch., U. Md.-Am. Bankers Assn., 1981; grad. banking program U. Wis., Madison, 1982-84; BA Capital U. Asst. v.p., gen. mgr. Bancohio Corp., Columbus, Ohio, 1975-78, v.p., dist. mgr., 1979-80, v.p., mgr. employee rels., 1980-81, v.p., divsn. mgr., 1982-83; commr. of banks State of Ohio, Columbus, 1983-87, dir. Commerce, 1988-90; pres., CEO Star Bank Cen. Ohio, Columbus, 1990-92; state dir. FMHA-USDA, 1993—. Bd. dirs. Clark County Mental Health Bd., Springfield, Ohio, 1982-83, Springfield Met. Housing, 1982-83; bd. advisers Orgn. Indsl. Standards, Springfield, 1982-83; trustee League Against Child Abuse, 1986-90; treas. Ohio Housing Fin. Agy., 1988-90; vice chair Fed. Reserve Bd.-Consumer Adv. Coun., 1989-91. Bd. dirs. Pvt. Industry Coun. Franklin County, 1990—, Ohio Higher Edn. Facilities Commn., 1990-93, Ohio Devel. Corp., 1995—; trustee, treas. Columbus State Community Coll. Found., 1990—; bd. dirs. Columbus Urban League, 1992—. Recipient Leadership Columbus award Sta. WTVN and Columbus Leadership Program, 1975, 82, Outstanding Svc. award Clark County Mental Health Bd., 1983. Mem. Nat. Assn. Bank Women (pres. 1980-81), Am. Bankers Assn. (pres. rels. coun. 1990-92), Women Execs. in State Govt., LWV (treas. edn. fund 1992—), Conf. State Bank Suprs. (bd. dirs., sec./treas. 1985-90), dist. chmn. 1984-85), Ohio Bankers Assn. (bd. dirs. 1982-83, 91-92), Internat. Womens Forum, Zonta. Democrat. Avocations: tennis, animal protection, reading, golf. Home: 641 Mirandy Pl Reynoldsburg OH 43068-1602 Office: 200 N High St Columbus OH 43215-2408

PAGE, LORNE ALBERT, physicist, educator; b. Buffalo, July 28, 1921; s. John Otway and Laura (Stewart) P.; m. Muriel Emily Jamieson, Sept. 7, 1946; children: J. Douglas, Kenneth L., James F., Donald S., David K. BSc, Queen's U., Can., 1944; PhD, Cornell U., 1950. Faculty U. Pitts., 1950—, prof. physics, 1958-86, prof. emeritus, 1987—. Contbr. articles to Phys. Rev., Rev. Modern Physics, Ann. Rev. Nuc. and Particle Sci. Served to lt. Royal Canadian Navy, 1944-45. Guggenheim fellow Upsala U., Sweden, 1957-58; Alfred P. Sloan research fellow, 1961-63. Fellow Am. Phys. Soc. Episcopalian. Achievements include measurement of the positron's mass, identification of positronium in condensed matter; development of method for analyzing circular polarization of high energy x-rays, first measurement of inherent polarization of positive beta particle. Home: 157 Lloyd Ave Pittsburgh PA 15218-1645

PAGE, LYMAN ALEXANDER, JR., physicist; b. San Francisco, Sept. 24, 1957; s. Lyman Alexander and Gillet (Thomas) P.; m. Elizabeth Olson, Feb. 12, 1990; children: William, James. BA with high honors, Bowdoin Coll., 1978; PhD, MIT, 1987. Rsch. technician Bartol Rsch. Found., Newark, Del., 1978-80; postdoctoral rsch. fellow MIT, 1989-90; instr. physics Princeton (N.J.) U., 1990-91, asst. prof. physics, 1991-95, assoc. prof., 1995—. Contbr. numerous sci. papers on cosmic microwave background Astrophys. Jour., 1979—. Surdna fellow Bowdoin Coll., 1978, NASA grad. student rschrs. program fellow MIT, 1987-89, David and Lucile Packard fellow Princeton U., 1994; Rsch. Corp. Cottrell scholar Princeton U., 1994. Mem. Am. Phys. Soc., Am. Astron. Soc. Achievements include measurement of tiny spatial variations in the temperature of the radiation thought to be the afterglow of the big-bang. Office: Princeton U Dept Physics Jadwin Hall Princeton NJ 08544-1019

PAGE, MARCUS WILLIAM, federal official; b. Washington, Sept. 20, 1937; s. Marcus William and Edna May (Horner) Pugh; m. Mary Jane Bitting, Dec. 10, 1989; 1 child from previous marriage, David Stephen. BA, Duke U., 1959; postgrad., George Washington U., 1961-65. Chief fin. svcs. FDA, Washington, 1965-68; chief fin. mgmt. br. Environ. Health Svc., Washington, 1968-70; chief acctg. ops. EPA, Washington, 1970-77, dir. fin. mgmt., 1977-81; dir. govt. acctg. systems Fin. Mgmt. Svc., Washington, 1981-83, dir. systems devel., 1983-84, dep. commr., 1984-87; dep. fiscal asst. sec. U.S. Treasury, Washington, 1987-95. Columnist Govt. Computer News, Washington, 1984-86; contbr. articles to various jours. Recipient Fin. Mgmt. Improvement award Joint Fin. Mgmt. Ipmrovement Program, Washington, 1980, Disting. Leadership award No. Va. Assn. Govt. Accts., 1986, Commrs. award Fin. Mgmt. Svc., 1987, Sec.'s Disting. Svc. award, 1995. Mem. Assn. Govt. Accts. (bd. dirs. 1981-85, pres. 1992-93), Planning Execs. Inst. (pres. 1973-74), Treasury Hist. Assn. (sec. 1990-92, chmn. bd. 1995—), Fed. Exec. Inst. Alumni Assn., C&O Canal Assn., Theta Chi. Avocations: hiking, science fiction, historic building restoration. Office: US Treasury 1500 Pennsylvania Ave Washington DC 20220-0001

PAGE, MICHEL, biochemist; b. Quebec, Que., Can., Feb. 18, 1940; s. Hector and Alma (Dussault) P.; m. Marthe Boudreau, Dec. 17, 1966; children: Brigitte, Marie, Charles, Madeleine. B.A., Laval U., 1960; B.Sc., Ottawa U., 1965, Ph.D., 1969. Nat. Cancer Inst. postdoctoral fellow U. Colo., Boulder, 1968-70; research fellow Mt. Sinai Sch. Medicine, N.Y.C., 1970-71; clin. biochemist Hotel Dieu Hosp., Quebec, 1971-81; research scholar Nat. Cancer Inst. Can., 1975-81; prof. biochemistry U. Laval, Quebec City, 1982—; pres., founder BCM Biotech, Inc., 1988, BCM Développement Inc., 1993; mem. grant panels Med. Rsch. Coun., Nat. Cancer Inst.; pres. BCH Biotech Inc., BCH Devel. Inc. Author: La cuisine sans cholesterol, 1975, Cancer, 1983, Cancérologie expérimentale, 1993; contbr. over 125 articles to sci. publls. Mem. Ordre des Chimistes du Que., AAAS, Canadian Biochem. Soc., Canadian Immunol. Soc., Am. Soc. Cell Biology., Am. Assn. Clin. Research. Roman Catholic. Home: 9175 Pl Lavalliere, 125 Rue Dalhousie Ste 218, Quebec City, PQ Canada G1K 4C5 Office: Faculty of Medicine, U Laval, Quebec, PQ Canada G1K 7P4

PAGE, OSCAR CLETICE, academic administrator; b. Bowling Green, Ky., Dec. 22, 1939; s. Elizabeth P.; m. Anna Laura Hood, June 12, 1965; children: Kristen, Matt. BA in Social Sci., Western Ky. U., 1962; MA in History, U. Ky., 1963, PhD in Early Modern European History, 1967. Instr. history Western Ky. U., Bowling Green, 1964; asst. prof., asst. chair history dept. U. Ga., Athens, 1967-71; dean Wesleyan Coll., Macon, Ga., 1971-78; v.p. acad. affairs Lander Coll., Greenwood, S.C., 1978-86, acting pres., 1985, provost, v.p. acad. affairs, 1986-88; pres. Austin Peay State U., Clarksville, Tenn., 1988-94, Austin Coll., Sherman, Tex., 1994—; mem. adv. com. Master of Mil. Art & Sci. Program, Leavenworth, Kans., 1994-96. Bd. dirs. United Way, Sherman, 1994—, Meml. Hosp., Clarksville, 1989-94, Nations Bank, Clarksville, 1988-94; mem. pres.'s commn. NCAA, 1990-94. Mem. Rotary, Sherman C. of C. Office: Austin Coll 900 N Grand Ave Sherman TX 75090-4440

PAGE, RICHARD LEIGHTON, cardiologist, medical educator, clinical researcher; b. San Diego, Mar. 8, 1958; s. Ellis Batten and Elizabeth Latimer (Thaxton) P.; m. Jean Reynolds, Oct. 12, 1985; children: Franklin Reynolds, Gillian Grace, Edward Batten. BS in Zoology magna cum laude, Duke U., 1980, MD, 1984. Diplomate Nat. Bd. Med. Examiners, Am. Bd. Internal Medicine, subspecialties cardiovascular disease and clin. cardiac electrophysiology; lic. physician, Tex. Rsch. fellow in pharmacology Columbia Presbyn. Med. Ctr., 1982-83; intern dept. medicine Mass. Gen. Hosp., Boston, 1984-85, resident, dept. medicine, 1985-87; cardiology fellow clin. electrophysiology Duke U. Med. Ctr., Durham, N.C., 1987-89, clin. cardiology fellow, 1989-90, lectr. medicine divsn. cardiology, 1989-90, assoc. in medicine, 1990, asst. prof. medicine, dir. clin. electrophysiology lab., 1990-92; asst. prof. medicine U. Tex. Southwestern Med. Ctr., Dallas, 1992-95, assoc. prof. medicine, 1995—, dir. sect. clin. cardiac electrophysiology, 1992—; dir. Stanley J. Sarnoff Endowment for Rsch. in Cardiovascular Sci., Inc., Bethesda, Md., 1990—, co-chmn., 1992; dir. sect. clin. electrophysiology U. Tex. Southwestern Med. Ctr., Dallas, 1992—; dir. clin. electrophysiology lab., arrhythmia and pacemaker service, Parkland Meml. Hosp., Dallas, 1992—. Editorial bd. Cardiac Chronicle, 1993, Author: Manual of Clinical problems in cardiology, 5th ed., 1995; contbr. articles to profl. jours., chpt. to book. Sarnoff Endowment fellow, 1982, Sarnoff scholar, 1987. Fellow Stanley J. Sarnoff Soc., Am. Heart Assn., Am. Coll. Cardiology; mem. North Am. Soc. Pacing and Electrophysiology, Tex. Med. Assn., Dallas County Med. Soc., North Tex. Electrophysiology Soc. (trustee), Sigma Xi, Alpha Omega Alpha. Episcopalian. Avocations: tennis, swimming. Home: 1500 Ramsgate Cir Plano TX 75093-5044 Office: U Tex Southwestern Med Ctr 5323 Harry Hines Blvd Dallas TX 75235-9047

PAGE, ROBERT HENRY, engineer, educator, researcher; b. Phila., Nov. 5, 1927; s. Ernest Fraser and Marguerite (MacFarl) P.; m. Lola Marie Griffin, Nov. 12, 1948; children: Lola Linda, Patricia Jean, William Ernest, Nancy Lee, Martin Fraser. BS in Mech. Engring, Ohio U., 1949; MS, U. Ill., 1951, PhD, 1955. Instr., research assoc. U. Ill., 1949-55; research engr. fluid dynamics Esso Research & Engring. Co., 1955-57; vis. lectr. Stevens Inst. Tech., 1956-57, dir. fluid dynamics lab., prof. mech. engring., 1957-61; prof. mech. engring., chmn. dept. mech., indsl. and aerospace engring. Rutgers-The State U., 1961-76, prof., research cons., 1976-79; dean engring. Tex. A&M U., 1979-83, Forsyth prof., 1983-93, prof. emeritus mech. engring., 1994—; spl. research base pressure and heat transfer, wake flow and flow separation. Author papers in field. Served with AUS, 1945-47, Pacific Theatre of Operations. Recipient Western Electric Fund award for excellence in engring. edn. Am. Soc. Engring Edn., 1968; Lindback Found. award for distinguished teaching, 1969; Disting. Alumnus award U. Ill., 1971; Disting. Service award, 1973; Life Quality Engring. award, 1974, James Harry Potter Gold medal, 1983, Ohio U. medal, 1983; named hon. prof. Ruhr U., Buchum, Fed. Republic Germany, 1984. Fellow AAAS, AIAA (assoc.), ABET, Am. Astron. Soc. (chmn. nat. space engring. com. 1969-70, 72-76), Am. Soc. Engring. Edn. (Centennial medal 1993); mem. ASME (hon. mem. award 1988), Am. Phys. Soc. Home: 1905 Comal Cir College Station TX 77840-4818

PAGE, ROBERT WESLEY, engineering and construction company executive, federal official; b. Dallas, Jan. 22, 1927; s. Arch Cleo and Zelma (Tyler) P.; m. Nancy Ann Eaton, Sept. 17, 1952; children: Robert W. Jr., David, Mark, Margaret. B.S. in Archtl. Engring., Tex. A&M U., 1950. Asst. prof. Am. Univ., Beirut, Lebanon, 1952-54; project mgr. Aramco, The Hague and Saudi Arabia, 1954-56; dir. constrn. and devel. Internat. Coll., Beirut, N.Y.C., 1956-58; internat. mgr. Bechtel Co., N.Y.C., 1958-64; v.p. Rockresorts Co., N.Y.C., 1964-71; pres., chief exec. officer George A. Fuller Co., N.Y.C., from 1971; corp. v.p. Northrop Corp., N.Y.C., from 1971; pres., chief exec. officer Rust Engring. Co., Birmingham, Ala., 1976-81; pres., chief exec. officer Kellogg Rust Inc., Houston, 1981-85, chmn., chief exec. officer, dir., 1985-86; pres., chief exec. officer PM Co., Houston, 1986; asst. sec. U.S. Dept. of Army, Washington, 1987-90; chmn. Panama Canal Commn., 1989-90; exec. v.p. McDermott Internat., Washington, 1990—; sr. lectr. MIT, 1993; chmn. Pegasus Cons., Inc.; adj. prof. Georgetown U.; bd. dirs. I.C.F./Kaiser Internat.; bd. dirs. Thormatrix, Inc., San Jose, Calif. Trustee Internat. Coll. Beirut; mem. Pres.'s Coun., U. Ala.; bd. dirs. Coll. Football Hall of Fame. With USNR, 1944-46, PTO. Trustee Am. U. in Cairo; trustee Wortham Theatre Ctr., Houston, Internat. Coll. Beirut; mem. Pres.'s Council, U. Ala.; mem. adv. bd. John E. Gray Inst., Lamar U.; bd. dirs. Coll. Football Hall of Fame. Served with USNR, 1944-46, PTO. Mem. ASME, ASCE, Rolling Rock Club (Ligoner, Pa.), Internat. Club (Washington), Army-Navy Club (Washington), Georgetown Club (Washington), Sakonnet Country Club (Little Compton, R.I.), Tau Beta Pi. Home: 3025 P St NW Washington DC 20007-3054 Office: 1850 K St NW Ste 950 Washington DC 20006-2213

PAGE, ROY CHRISTOPHER, periodontist, educator; b. Campobello, S.C., Feb. 7, 1932; s. Milton and Anny Mae (Eubanks) P. BA, Berea Coll., 1953; DDS, U. Md., 1957; PhD, U. Wash., 1967; ScD (hon.), Loyola U., Chgo., 1983. Cert. in periodontics. Pvt. practice periodontics Seattle, 1963—; asst. prof. U. Wash. Schs. Medicine and Dentistry, Seattle, 1967-70, prof., 1974—, dir. Ctr. Research in Oral Biology, 1976-96; dir. grad. edn. U. Wash. Sch. Dentistry, 1976-80; dir. rsch. U. Wash. Sch. Dentistry, Seattle, 1976-94, assoc. dean rsch., 1994—; vis. scientist MRC Labs., London, 1971-72; cons., lectr. in field. Author: Periodontal Disease, 1977, 2d edit., 1990, Periodontitis in Man and Other Animals, 1982. Recipient Gold Medal award U. Md., 1957; recipient Career Devel. award NIH, 1967-72. Fellow Internat. Coll. Dentists, Am. Coll. Dentists, Am. Acad. Periodontology (Gies award 1982, fellowship award 1989); mem. ADA, Am. Assn. Dental Rsch. (pres. 1982-83), Am. Soc. Exptl. Pathology, Internat. Assn. Dental Rsch. (pres. 1987, basic periodontal rsch. award 1977). Home: 8631 Inverness Dr NE Seattle WA 98115-3935

PAGE, TAMMY, education consultant; b. Bklyn., May 26, 1960; d. Jesse and Carolyn Page. AA, Manhattan C.C., 1980; BA, Hunter Coll., 1987; MA, Adelphi U., 1988. Cert. adminstr./supr. Adminstrv. asst. CUNY, N.Y.C., 1979-83; tchr. multi-cultural sch. N.Y.C. Bd. Edn., Bklyn., 1987-90, tchr. sch. for gifted, 1990-93; staff developer for curriculum and instrn., cons. N.Y.C. Bd. Edn., N.Y.C., 1993—; tchr. liaison with parents, N.Y. Bd. Edn., 1989-91, workshop coord., N.Y.C., 1990-91, 91-93; presenter in field. Recipient Pres.'s Excellence in Teaching award City U. Avocations: reading, poetry writing, gardening, chess. Office: Spl Educator Support Progrm United Fedn of Tchrs 260 Park Ave S New York NY 10010-7214

PAGE, THOMAS ALEXANDER, utility executive; b. Niagara Falls, N.Y., Mar. 24, 1933; m. Evelyn Rainnie, July 16, 1960; children: Christopher, Catherine. B.S. in Civil Engring, Purdue U., 1955, M.S. in Indsl. Adminstrn, 1963. Registered profl. engr., N.Y. C.P.A., Wis., Tex. Comptroller, treas. Wis. Power & Light Co., Madison, 1970-73; treas. Gulf States Utilities Co., Beaumont, Tex., 1973-75, sr. v.p. fin., 1975, exec. v.p., 1975-78, also bd. dirs.; exec. v.p., chief operating officer San Diego Gas & Electric Co., 1978-81, pres., chief exec. officer, 1981-92, chmn., 1983-92, chmn., chief exec. officer, 1992—, also pres., also bd. dirs. Mem. Dane County Bd. Suprs., Wis., 1968-72. Served to capt. USAF, 1955-57. Home: 1904 Hidden Crest Dr El Cajon CA 92019-3653 Office: San Diego Gas & Electric Co PO Box 1831 San Diego CA 92112

PAGE, WILLIAM MARION, lawyer; b. Columbus, Ga., July 31, 1917; s. Roger McKeene and Louise Olivia (Seals) P.; m. Lucy Quillian Page, Feb. 8, 1941 (dec. 1982); children: John Roger, Jane Quillian Page McCamy, William Franklin; m. Barbara Brown Waddell, May 10, 1985. LLB, U. Ga., 1939, JD. Bar: Ga. 1938, U.S. Supreme Ct. 1955. Ptnr. Page Scrantom Sprouse Tucker & Ford P.C., Columbus, Ga., 1939—. Bd. visitors U. Ga. Law Sch., 1969-74. With U.S. Army, 1941-46. Fellow Am. Coll. Trial Lawyers; mem. State Bar Ga. (bd. govs. 1964-71), ABA, Chattahoochee Circuit Bar Assn. (pres. 1948-49), Columbus Bar Assn. (pres. 1946-47), Am. Judicature Soc., Big Eddy Club, Kiwanis. Home: 916 Overlook Dr Columbus GA 31906-3029 Office: PO Box 1199 Columbus GA 31902-1199

PAGE, WILLIS, conductor; b. Rochester, N.Y., Sept. 18, 1918. Grad. with distinction, Eastman Sch. Music, Rochester., 1939. Mem. Rochester Philharm., 1937-40, Rochester Civic, 1939-40; prof. conducting Eastman Sch. Music, 1967-69; prof. conducting, dir. orchestral activities Drake U., Des Moines, 1969-71; guest condr. Sony concerts, Chiba, Japan, 1992. Mem. Boston Symphony Orch., 1940-55; prin. bass Boston Pops, 1947-55; condr. Cecilia Soc. Boston, 1952-54, New Orchestral Soc. Boston; assoc. condr. Buffalo Philharm., 1955-59; music dir./condr. Nashville Symphony Orch., 1959-67; music dir. Linwood Music Sch., 1955-59; 1st condr. Yomiuri Nippon Symphony, Tokyo, 1962-63; condr. Des Moines Symphony, 1969-71, Jacksonville (Fla.) Symphony Orch., 1971-83; founder, condr. St. John's River City Band, 1985-86; guest condr. Boston Pops, Toronto, Rochester Civic, Eastman-Rochester, Denver, Muncie, Jerusalem, St. Louis, Colorado Springs, Memphis, Hartford orchs., Yomiuri Nippon Symphony, 1988; founding condr., exec. dir. First Coast Pops Orch., 1989; condr. all-state orchs. of N.Y., Iowa, Ky., Tenn., Fla., also regional festivals; condr. 13 L.P. recordings including Symphony of the Air (Roger Williams soloist), Boston Festival Orch., Cook Labs., Nashville Symphony. Sgt. 95th inf. divsn. U.S. Army, 1943-45. Decorated Bronze Star; recipient Ford Found. European travel award, 1967.

PAGELS, JÜRGEN HEINRICH, balletmaster, dance educator, dancer, choreographer, author; b. Lübeck, Fed. Republic Germany, Apr. 16, 1925; came to U.S., 1955; s. Heinrich and Margret (Haas) P. Artists diploma, Hamburg (Fed. Republic Germany) State Exam Bd., 1947; advanced soloist exam. with honors, Assn. Russian Ballet, London, 1952, advanced tchrs. exam. with honors, 1961, sr. tchrs. exam. with honors, 1969; DFA, Pacific Western U., 1988. Ballet soloist Atlantic Theater, Lübeck, 1945-46, Stadt-Theater, Lübeck, 1946-47; prin. dancer Dortmund, Fed. Republic Germany, 1947-48, Operette and Stattl. Schauspielhaus Theater, Hamburg, 1949-50; ballet soloist Ballet Theater Co., Hamburg, 1950-51; prin. dancer Ballet Legat, London, 1951-52, Ballet Legat and Yugoslav Nat. Ballet, touring throughout Europe, 1952-53; guest ballet soloist Ballet Etoile, Paris Opera, Paris, 1954; dir., owner Pagels Legat Sch. Ballet, Dallas, 1955-62; guest tchr. ballet numerous dance acads. and ballet cos., worldwide, 1962-70; prof. dance Ind. Univ., Bloomington, 1970-90; prof. emeritus Ind. U., Bloomington, 1990—; guest tchr. ballet numerous orgns. including Vaganova Choreography Inst., Leningrad, USSR, Ballet do Rio de Janeiro, Egypt Nat. Ballet of Cairo, Ballet Intezet, Hungary, Nat. Ballet, Istanbul, Turkey, Royal Danish Ballet, Tex. Christian Univ., Ft. Worth, Nat. Ballet, Nicaragua; condr. master classes for Ballet Guatemala, Escuala Nacional de Danza, San Salvador, Academia de Danza Classica, Costa Rica, Nat. Ballet Venezuela, T.W. Univ., Nat. U. Costa Rica, Bellas Artes, Honduras, Ballet Nacional Nicaragua; co-founder, dir. Dallas Civic Ballet; art dir. Ballet Guatemala, 1978-79, Nat. Ballet Salvador, Ulm Theatre, Germany, Ballet Co., 1995, Artemis, Amsterdam, Holland; Internat. Ballet competition Managuq, Nicaraqua, 1995. Author of character dance books in English, German and Spanish, 1984, 85, and ballet dance books; collaborator and coach to Dame Margot Fonteyn. U.S. judge Internat. Ballet Competition, Trujillo, Peru, 1989, 90. Served as sgt. German Army, 1942-45. Research grantee Ind. Univ., 1977. Avocations: exhibited sculptor, tennis, deep-sea fishing. Home: 934 E Maxwell Ter Apt A Bloomington IN 47401-5278 Office: Ind U Sch Music Ballet Dept Bloomington IN 47405 also: Curtius Str 6, 23568 Lübeck Germany

PAGENKOPF, ANDREA LESUER, university official; b. Hamilton, Mont., July 28, 1942; d. Andrew and Martha Gail (Thompson) LeSuer; m. Gordon Kyle Pagenkopf, June 12, 1964 (dec. Feb. 1987); 1 child, Sarah Lynn. BA, U. Mont., 1964; PhD, Purdue U., 1968. Registered dietitian; lic. nutritionist. Asst. prof. Purdue U., West Lafayette, Ind., 1968, U. Ill., Champaign, 1968-69; asst. prof. Mont. State U., Bozeman, 1969-76, assoc. prof., 1976-86, prof. nutrition, 1986-91, dir. extension, 1991—, vice provost for outreach, 1993—. Author: (with others) Grow Healthy Kids, 1980. Worship commn. chair United Meth. Ch., Bozeman, 1989-90; cons. Gallatin Hospice, Bozeman, 1986-91. Recipient Excellence in Nutrition Edn. award Western Dairy Coun., 1987, Silver Buffalo award Mont. Extension, 1989, Mid-Career award Extension Hon., 1988; named Home Econs. Leader, Mont. Home Econs. Assn., 1990. Mem. Am. Dietetic Assn., Soc. Nutrition Edn. (interest group chair 1990-91), Am. Home Econs. Assn. Avocations: fly fishing, racquet ball, jogging. Office: Mont State U Extension 211 N Montana Hall Bozeman MT 59717

PAGET, JOHN ARTHUR, mechanical engineer; b. Ft. Frances, Ont., Can., Sept. 15, 1922; s. John and Ethel (Bishop) P.; B. in Applied Sci., Toronto, 1946; m. Vicenta Herrera Nunez, Dec. 16, 1963; children: Cynthia Ellen, Kevin Arthur, Keith William. Chief draftsman Gutta Percha & Rubber, Ltd., Toronto, Ont., 1946-49; chief draftsman Viceroy Mfg. Co., Toronto, 1949-52; supr., design engr. C.D. Howe Co. Ltd., Montreal, Que., Can., 1952-58, sr. design engr. Combustion Engring., Montreal, 1958-59; sr. staff engr. Gen. Atomic, Inc., La Jolla, 1959-81. Mem. ASME, Soc. for History Tech., Inst. Mech. Engrs., Brit. Nuclear Energy Soc. Patentee in field. Home: 3183 Magellan St San Diego CA 92154-1515

PAGILLO, CARL ROBERT, elementary school educator; b. Bklyn., Apr. 11, 1950; s. Nicholas and Rachel (Rhyne) P.; m. Joanne Ferro, Aug. 1, 1992. BA, Queens Coll., 1973, MS in Elem. Edn., 1975; advanced in edn. adminstrn., Bklyn. Coll., 1993. Tchr. grade 3, 5, and 6 Pub. Sch. 207 Queens, Howard Beach, N.Y., 1983-93; tchr. multimedia PS 20 YQ, Howard Beach, N.Y., 1983-93; tchr. lang. arts PS 56 Q, Richmond Hill, N.Y., 1993—. Pres., founder Catherine St. Block Assn., Lynbrook, 1987-91; baseball coach, mgr. Little League, Pony League and Baby Ruth League, Nassau County, 1974-92; capt. Lynbrook 4.0. tennis team, 1984-93. Recipient Ely Trachtenberg award United Fedn. of Tchrs., 1986. Mem. Phi Delta Kappa. Avocation: tennis. Home: 17 Catherine St Lynbrook NY 11563-1207

PAGLIA, CAMILLE, writer, humanities educator; b. Endicott, N.Y., 1947; d. Pasquale John and Lydia (Colapietro) P. BA in English summa cum laude with highest honors, SUNY, Binghamton, 1968; MPhil, Yale U., 1971, PhD in English, 1974. Mem. faculty Bennington (Vt.) Coll., 1972-80; vis. lectr. Wesleyan U., 1980, Yale U., New Haven, 1980-84; prof. humanities U. Arts, Phila., 1984—. Author: Sexual Personae: Art and Decadence from Nefertiti to Emily Dickinson, 1990, Sex, Art, and American Culture, 1992, Vamps and Tramps: New Essays, 1994. Office: Univ Arts 320 S Broad St Philadelphia PA 19102-4901

PAGLIARINI, JAMES, broadcast executive. AB, Princeton U., 1975; MEd, Temple U., 1976. Asst. to gen. mgr. Sta. KTEH-TV, San Jose, Calif., 1976-80; co-founder Sta. KNPB-TV, Reno, Nev., 1980—, sta. mgr., 1982-83, gen. mgr., CEO, 1983—; bd. dirs. Agy. Instrnl. T.V., Pub. Broadcasting, Western Indsl. Nev.; chmn. bd. govs. Pacific Mountain network, 1987—; mem. Cable Access Bd., Reno, PBS assessment policy com., 1988-89, funding task force, 1991, task force on nat. prodns., 1992-93, exec. com., 1995-96, program pricing policy task force, 1995-96; mem. TV policy task force Corp. for Pub. Broadcasting, 1995-96. Chmn. community adv. com. U. Nev. Sch. Engring., Reno; past bd. dirs. Planned Parenthood No. Nev., Boy Scouts Am., We. Nev. Clean Cities Com. Mem. Nev. Pub. Broadcasting Assn. (pres.), Small Sta. Assn. (pres. 1991-92). Office: Station KNPB 1670 N Virginia St Reno NV 89503

PAGLIARO, HAROLD EMIL, English language educator; b. N.Y.C., June 19, 1925; s. Harry E. and Linda (Ricci) P.; m. Judith Marie Egan, Sept. 16, 1966; children: Blake, Robert, Susanna, John. AB, Columbia U., 1947, MA, 1948, PhD, 1961. Instr. English, Columbia U., N.Y.C., 1956-60; asst. prof. Columbia U., 1961-63, faculty fellow, 1962, dir. honors sch. gen. studies, 1962-64; asst. prof. Swarthmore (Pa.) Coll., 1964-65, asso. prof., 1966-69, prof., 1970—, Alexander Griswold Cummins prof. English lit., 1982—, chmn. dept. English lit., 1970-74, 86-91, provost, 1974-79, Alexander Griswold Cummins prof. emeritus English, provost emeritus, 1992—; mem. sr. common room St. Edmund Hall, Oxford (Eng.) U., 1973-74, 79-80; assoc. Columbia U. Seminar 18th Century European Culture, 1982—. Author: Selfhood and Redemption in Blakes's "Songs", 1987, Naked Heart: A Soldier's Journey to the Front, 1996; editor: Fielding's Journal of a Voyage to Lisbon, 1963, Major English Writers of the Eighteenth Century, 1969, Studies in Eighteenth Century Culture, Vol. 2, 1972, Vol. 3, 1973, Vol. 4, 1974; contbr. articles to profl. jours. Mem. coll. evaluation bd. Middle States Assn., 1966—. Served with AUS, 1943-45. Decorated Purple Heart; NEH sr. fellow, 1983-84; George Becker fellow, 1988-89. Mem. MLA, Am. Soc. for Eighteenth-Century Studies (editor Proc. 1971-75), Am. Soc. Eighteenth-Century Studies (mem. publs. com. 1974-76). Home: 536 Ogden Ave Swarthmore PA 19081-1129

PAGLIARO, JAMES DOMENIC, lawyer; b. Phila., Aug. 18, 1951; s. Domenic A. and Nancy I. (D'Amore) P.; m. Susan B. Boag, Aug. 25, 1973; children: Jamie C., Justin A. BA cum laude, LaSalle U., 1973; JD, Dickinson Law Sch., 1976. Bar: Pa. 1976, U.S. Dist. Ct. (ea. dist.) Pa. 1977, U.S. Ct. Appeals (3d, 8th, 9th and 10th cirs.) 1989, U.S. Supreme Ct. 1989. Regional atty. Gov. of Pa., Phila., 1976-79; sr. trial atty. office regional solicitor U.S. Dept. Labor, Phila., 1979-85; assoc. Morgan, Lewis & Bockius, LLP, Phila., 1985-88; ptnr. litigation Morgan, Lewis & Bockius, Phila., 1988—. Chmn. Home & Sch. Bd. Norwood Acad., Chestnut Hill, Pa., 1983-87; vestry Hist. St. Paul's Ch., Elkins Park, Pa., 1993-94. Mem. ABA, Pa. Bar Assn. (speaker continuing legal edn. 1987—), Phila. Bar Assn., Woolsach Honors Soc., Pyramid Club. Avocations: history, swimming, numismatics. Home: 404 Westview Rd Elkins Park PA 19027-2428 Office: Morgan Lewis & Bockius LLP 2000 One Logan Sq Philadelphia PA 19103

PAGLIO, LYDIA ELIZABETH, editor; b. Providence; d. Victor and Lydia Anne (DiPrete) P. BA, NYU. Researcher Young Pres. Orgn., 1970-71; editorial asst. Sport mag., N.Y.C., 1971-72; assoc. editor True Experience, also True Love mags., N.Y.C., 1972-73; editor True Experience mag., 1973-81; assoc. editor Dell Pub., N.Y.C., 1983; editor Dell Pub., 1983-84, sr. editor, 1984-87, dir. Candlelight Ecstasy Romances, 1984-87; sr. editor Zebra Books, Pinnacle Books, 1987-89; pres., owner Sutton Press, Inc., N.Y.C., 1991—; pub. cons., N.Y.C., 1989—; dir. publicity Dancer's World, Springfield, Mass., 1978-80. Author articles. Pres., sec., mem. exec. com. West Side Community Recycling Corp., 1979-81; pres. 41 W 82 St. Tenants, 1989—. Mem. Editl. Free-lance Assn. (bd. dirs. 1984).

PAGNI, PATRICK JOHN, mechanical and fire safety engineering science educator ,; b. Chgo., Nov. 28, 1942; s. Frank and Helen Boyle Pagni; m. Carol DeSantis, Dec. 26, 1970; children: Christina Marie, Catherine Ann, Patrick John Jr. B in Aeronautical Engring. magna cum laude, U. Detroit, 1965; SM, MIT, 1967, ME, 1969, PhD, 1970. Registered profl. mechanical engr., Calif., fire protection engr., Calif. Research asst. MIT, Cambridge, 1965-70; asst. prof. Mech. Engring. Dept. U. Calif., Berkeley, 1970-76, assoc. prof., 1976-81, prof., 1981—, vice chmn. grad. study, 1986-89; acting assoc. dean Coll. Engring. U. Calif., 1990; assoc. faculty scientist Lawrence Berkeley Lab., 1976—; vis. scientist Factory Mut. Research Corp., Norwood, Mass., 1980; cons. on fire safety sci. various orgns., 1972—. Editor: Fire Science for Fire Safety, 1984, Fire Safety Science--Procs. of the First Internat. Symposium, 1986, Procs. of the Second Internat. Symposium, 1989; contbr. articles to profl. jours. Grantee NSF, NASA, Nat. Bur. Standards, Nat. Inst. Standards and Tech., 1971—; Applied Mechanics fellow Harvard U., 1974, 77; Pullman Found. scholar, 1960. Mem. ASME, Am. Phys. Soc., Combustion Inst., Soc. Fire Protection Engrs., Internat. Assn. Fire Safety Sci. (exec. com., chmn. awards com.), Ta u Beta Pi, Pi Tau Sigma, Alpha Sigma Nu. Democrat. Roman Catholic. Home: 1901 Ascot Dr Moraga CA 94556-1412 Office: Univ of Calif Coll of Engring Mech Engring Dept Berkeley CA 94720-1740

PAGNOZZI, AMY, columnist. Columnist The N.Y. Post, until 1993, The Daily News, N.Y.C., 1993—; also contbr. Mirabella, Elle, N.Y.C. Office: The Daily News 220 E 42nd St New York NY 10017-5806

PAGONIS, WILLIAM GUS, retired army general; b. Charleroi, Pa., Apr. 30, 1941; s. Constantinos V. and Jennie (Kontos) P.; m. Cheryl Elaine Miller, June 4, 1964; children: Gust, Robert. BS, Pa. State U., 1964, MBA in Bus. Logistics, 1970. Commd. 2d lt. U.S. Army, 1964, advanced through grades to lt. gen., 1991; comdr. 1097th Transp. Co., Vietnam, 1968; div. transp. officer, then exec. officer 2d bn., 501st inf., 101st Airborne Div., Vietnam, 1970-71; pers. staff officer U.S. Army Mil. Pers. Ctr., Alexandria, Va., 1973-75; staff officer Office Chief of Legis. Liaison, Washington, 1975-76; comdr. 10th transp. bn. 7th Transp. Group, Ft. Eustis, Va., 1977-78; dep. chief of staff, then ops. and rsch. systems analyst U.S. Army Transp. Sch. and Ctr., Ft. Eustis, 1978-79; dir. logistics, dir. indsl. ops., then chief of staff 193d Inf. Brigade, Panama, 1980-81, comdr. Logistics Support Command, 1981-82; comdr. Div. Support Command, 4th Inf. Div., Ft. Carson, Colo., 1982-85; spl. asst. to dep. comdg. gen. 21st Support Command, U.S. Army Europe, 1985-86, dep. comdg. gen., 1986-88; dir. plans and ops. Office Dep. Chief of Staff for Logistics, Washington, 1988-89, dir. transp., energy and troop support, 1989-90; comdg. gen. 22d Support Command, Dhahran, Saudi Arabia, 1990-91, U.S. Cen. Command/22d Support Command, Dhahran, 1991-92; comdr. 21st Theater Army Command, Germany, 1992-93; lt. gen., ret. U.S. Army, 1993; exec. v.p. logistics Sears & Roebuck Co., Hoffman Estates, Ill., 1993—. Author: Moving Mountains (Logistics Leadership and Management of the Gulf War), (one of top 30 best bus. books of 1992, top leadership book 1992 Soundview Exec. Book Summaries, 1992), 1992. Decorated D.S.M., Silver Star, Legion of Merit with oak leaf cluster, Bronze Star with 3 oak leaf clusters, Air medal with 2 oak leaf clusters, Meritorious Svc. medal with 4 oak leaf clusters, King Abdul Aziz 2d Class award Chief of Staff, Saudi Arabian Army, 1991, Kuwait Liberation medal Chief of Staff, Kuwait Army, 1992; recipient Merit and Honor award Govt. of Greece, 1991, Joseph C. Scheleen award Am. Soc. Transp. and Logistics, 1991, Man of Yr. award Modern Materials Handling, 1991, Grad. Man of Yr. award Alpha Chi Rho, 1991, AHEPA Man of Yr., 1992, Disting. Alumni award Pa. State U., 1994; named Hellenic Man of Yr., 1992; Pa. State U. fellow, 1992. Mem. Soc. Logistics Engrs. (hon.), Am. Legion, Am. Vets. Home: 25190 North Pawnee Rd Barrington IL 60010-1354 Office: Sears Roebuck & Co 3333 Beverly Rd Hoffman Estates IL 60179

PAGOTTO, LOUISE, English language educator; b. Montreal, June 22, 1950; came to U.S., 1980; d. Albert and Elena (Tibi) P. BA, Marianopolis Coll., Montreal, 1971; TESL Diploma, U. Papua New Guinea, 1975; MA, McGill U., 1980; PhD, U. Hawaii at Manoa, Honolulu, 1987. Tchr. Yarapos High Sch., Wewak, Papua New Guinea, 1971-73, Electricity Commn. Tng. Coll., Port Moresby, Papua New Guinea, 1975-76, Coll. of the Marshall Islands, Majuro, summers 1983-91, Leeward C.C., Pearl City, Hawaii, 1988-89, Kapiolani C.C., Honolulu, 1989—; presenter at confs. Contbr. articles to profl. jours. McConnell fellow McGill U., 1979, Can. Coun. fellow, 1980-83; recipient Excellence in Teaching award Bd. of Regents, 1993. Mem. AAUW, Linguistic Soc. Am., Nat. Coun. Tchrs. English, Hawaii Coun. Tchrs. English. Avocations: water sports (swimming, bodyboarding), walking. Office: Kapiolani CC 4303 Diamond Head Rd Honolulu HI 96816-4421

PAGTER, CARL RICHARD, lawyer; b. Balt., Feb. 13, 1934; s. Charles Ralph and Mina (Amelung) P.; m. Judith Elaine Cox, May 6, 1978; 1 child by previous marriage: Corbin Christopher. AA, Diablo Valley Coll., 1953; BA, San Jose State U., 1956; LLB, U. Calif., Berkeley, 1964. Bar:Calif. 1965, D.C. 1977, U.S. Supreme Ct. 1976. Law clk. Kaiser Industries Corp., Oakland, Calif., 1963-64, counsel, 1964-70; assoc. counsel Kaiser Industries Corp., Washington, 1970-73; counsel Kaiser Industries Corp., Oakland, Calif., 1973-75; dir. govt. affairs Kaiser Industries Corp., Washington, 1975-76; v.p., sec., gen. counsel Kaiser Cement Corp., Oakland, Calif., 1976-88; cons., gen. counsel Kaiser Cement Corp., San Ramon, 1988—. Author: (with A. Dundes) Urban Folklore from the Paperwork Empire, 1975, More Urban Folklore from the Paperwork Empire, 1987, Never Try to Teach a Pig to Sing, 1991, Sometimes the Dragon Wins, 1996. Served with USNR, 1957-61, to comdr., 1978. Mem. ABA, Contra Costa County Bar Assn., Am. Folklore Soc., Calif. Folklore Soc., Calif. Bluegrass Assn. (founder), Oakland Athletic Club, University Club. Republican. Home: 17 Julianne Ct Walnut Creek CA 94595-2610 Office: Kaiser Cement Corp Ste 225 2680 Bishop Dr San Ramon CA 94583-9999

PAHNICHAPUTT, MOMLUANG MOMRASAWONG ANANCHANOK, English and American literature educator; b. Bangkok, June 3, 1936; d. M.R. Boonarong Latavalya and Klia Amatyakul; m. Wanchai Pahnichaputt, Apr. 24, 1964; children: Anisa, Chayakorn. BA with honors, Chulalongkorn U., Bangkok, 1959, MA in English, 1961; MA in English, U. Denver, 1962, PhD in English, 1977. Prof. Faculty Arts Chulalongkorn U., Bangkok, 1986—, chair grad. com. for comprehensive examinations, 1977—, exec. com. mem. Grad. Sch., 1985-87, bd. mem. Grad. Sch., 1985-86; vis. fellow Amherst (Mass.) Coll., 1981-82, Yale U., New Haven, 1991, Harvard U., Cambridge, Mass., 1994. Author: American Literature: 1620-1858, 1982, Emily Dickinson's World, 1984, Imagery in Shakespeare's Tragedies, 1985, Modern American Novels, 1993, The Realm of Henry James, 1995. Fulbright grantee U.S. Govt., 1961-62; fellow Am. Coun. Learned Socs., 1981-82. Mem. MLA, Am. Studies Assn. in Thailand (charter mem. 1989—, bd. mem. 1989-92, founding editor Am. Studies jour. 1989), Am. Studies Assn., Mark Twain Circle. Avocations: oil painting, photography, music, reading. Office: Chulalongkorn Univ-English, Phyathai Rd, Bangkok 10330, Thailand

PAI, ANANTHA MANGALORE, electrical engineering educator, consultant; b. Mangalore, Karnataka, India, Oct. 5, 1931; came to U.S., 1979; s. Ramachandra M. and Janaki (Kamath) P.; m. Nandini Kamath, Nov. 25, 1956; children: Sunanda, Sujata, Shona, Gurudutt. BS, Madras U., India, 1953; MS, U. Calif., Berkeley, 1958, PhD, 1961. Elec. engr. Bombay Electric Supply Co., 1953-57; prof. Indian Inst. Tech., India, 1963-81, dean R&D, 1976-78; prof. U. Ill., Urbana, 1981—. Author: Computers in Power System, 1979, Power System Stability, 1981, Energy Functions, 1989. Recipient Bhatnagar award Govt. of India, 1974. Fellow IEEE, Indian Nat. Sci. Acad., NAE (India), Instn. Engrs. (India). Hindu. Office: U Ill Dept Elec Engring 1406 W Green St Urbana IL 61801-2918

PAI, SHIH I., Aeronautical engineer, educator; b. Tatung, Anhwei, China, Sept. 30, 1913; s. Hsi Chuan and Swe Lin (Cha) P.; BS in Elec. Engring., Nat. Central U. China, 1935; MS in Elec. Engring., MIT, 1938; PhD in Aeronautics and Math., Calif. Inst. Tech., 1940; D (hon.) Tech. U. Vienna, 1968; m. Alice Jen-Lan Wang, July 2, 1960; children: Stephen Ming Pai, Sue Pai Yang, Robert Yang Pai, Lou Lung Pai. Prof. aerodynamics Nat. Central U., China, 1940-47; vis. prof. Cornell U., 1947-49; rsch. prof. Inst. Phys. Sci. and Tech. (formerly, Inst. Fluid Dynamics and Applied Math.), U. Md., College Park, 1949-83, prof. emeritus, 1983-96; vis. prof. Tokyo U., 1966, Tech. U. Vienna, 1967, Tech. U. Denmark, 1974, U. Karlsruhe (Germany), 1980-81, U. Paris, 1981; hon. prof. Northwestern Poly. U., Peoples Republic China, 1980-96, Zhejiang U., Peoples Republic China, 1985-96; cons. Gen. Electric Co., N. Am. Aviation, Boeing Co., Martin Co. Served with Chinese Air Force, 1937-40. Guggenheim fellow, 1957-58, sr. scientist fellow NSF, 1966; recipient Alexander von Humboldt award, 1980, Centennial medal A. James Clark Sch. Engring. U. Md., 1994. Fellow Academia Sinica; mem. AIAA, Am. Phys. Soc., German Soc. Applied Math. and Mechanics, Internat. Acad. Astronautics (corr.). Author: 14 tech. books in fluid dynamics, latest being Two-Phase Flows, 1977; Modern Fluid Mechanics, 1981, (with Shijin Lu) The Theroetical and Computational Dynamics of a Compressible Flow, 1991; contbr. over 130 articles to profl. jours.; first to experimentally show the importance of coherent structure in turbulent flow, the authority of jet flow from low speed aerodynamics to hyperionic flow; contbr. modern fluid mechanics including magnetic fluid dynamics, radiation gas dynamics and two phase flows. Died May 23, 1996.

PAIDOUSSIS, MICHAEL PANDELI, mechanical engineering educator; b. Nicosia, Cyprus, Aug. 20, 1935; emigrated to Can., 1953, naturalized, 1976; s. Pandelis Aristeidis and Parthenope (Leptou) P. B in Engring., McGill U., 1958; PhD in Engring., U. Cambridge, 1963. Overseas fellow Gen. Electric Co., Erith, Kent, Eng., 1958-60; rsch. officer Atomic Energy of Can., Chalk River, Ont., 1963-67; with McGill U., Montreal, 1967—, prof., dept. mech. engring., 1976—, chmn., 1977-86, Thomas Workman prof., 1986—; cons. and rschr. in field. Editor Jour. Fluids and Structures; contbr. articles in field. Pres. Hellenic-Can. Solidarity Com. for Cyprus, 1974-80, Com. Pan-Can. de Solidarite pour Chypre, 1978-83; hon. consul gen. Republic of Cyprus, Montreal, 1983—. Recipient Brit. Assn. medal for high distinction in mech. engring., 1958, George Stephenson prize Inst. Mech. Engrs., 1976, commemorative medal for 125th ann. of Confederation of Can., 1993, medal Can. Congress Applied Mechs., 1995. Fellow Instn. of Mech. Engrs., ASME, Can. Soc. Mech. Engring., Royal Soc. Can., Am. Acad. Mechanics; mem. Internat. Assn. Hydraulic Rsch., Internat. Assn. Structural Mechanics in Reactor Tech., Order Engrs. Que. Home: 2930 Edouard Montpetit #PH2, Montreal, PQ Canada H3T 1J7 Office: 817 Ouest Rue Sherbrooke, Montreal, PQ Canada H3A 2K6

PAIER, ADOLF ARTHUR, computer software and services company executive; b. Branford, Conn., Oct. 27, 1938; s. Adolf Arthur and Margaret Mary (Almond) P.; m. Geraldine Shnakis, Sept. 17, 1966; children: Nathaniel Jason, Andrew Joseph, Alena Catherine. AA, Quinnipiac Coll., 1958; BS in Econs., U. Pa., 1960. Audit mgr. Touche Ross & Co., Phila., 1960-67; pres., dir. Safeguard Scientifics, Inc., Wayne, Pa., 1967-92; chmn., CEO, pres. Healthworks Alliance, Inc., Wayne, Pa., 1992—; pres., CEO Novus Corp., Radnor, Pa., 1992—; bd. dirs. Deltapaper, Croydon, Pa. Bd. dirs. Univ. of Arts, Phila., Lincoln Ctr. Family and Youth, Bridgeport, Pa.; mem. adv. bd. Sol C. Snider Entrepreneurial Ctr., Phila., Analytical Graphics, Inc., King of Prussia, Pa. Mem. AICPA, Chief Execs. Orgn., Phila. Pres. Orgn. Office: Novus Corp 259 Radnor Chester Rd Ste 145 Radnor PA 19087-5240

PAIGE, ANITA PARKER, retired English language educator; b. Valparaiso, Ind., Feb. 5, 1908; d. Eugene Mark and Grace Agnes (Noon) Parker; m. Robert Myron Paige, Aug. 12, 1933 (dec. 1965); children: Susan Marlowe Paige Morrison, Amy Woods Paige Dunker, Caroline Parker Paige McClennan. AB, Vassar Coll., 1929; MA, U. Chgo., 1930, postgrad., 1931-32. Instr. English Hillsdale (Mich.) Coll., 1930-31, asst. prof., 1931-33; bd. edn. Anglo-Am. Schs., Athens, Greece, 1948-51; tchr. secondary sch. Am. Sch., Teheran, Iran, 1957-58; instr. English Republic of China Mil. Cartographic Sec. group, Taipei, Taiwan, 1960-61; instr. dept. English Nat. Taiwan U., Taipei, 1961-62; intermittent lectr., 1988—; bd. dirs. Ginling Girls Mid. Sch., Taipei, 1960-62. Bd. dirs. (Presbyn.) Cmty. Ch., Teheran, 1957-58. Mem. LWV (chmn. Cook County, Ill. child welfare dept. 1933-36, mem. bd. Overseas Edn. Fund 1966-68), Diplomatic and Consular Officers Ret., Am. Women's Group of Paris, Assn., Am. Fgn. Svc. Women, Asian Am. Forum (founding mem.), Friends of Soochow U., Phi Beta Kappa. Democrat.

PAIGE, GLENN DURLAND, political scientist, educator; b. Brockton, Mass., June 28, 1929; s. Lester Norman and Rita Irene (Marshall) P.; m. Betty Gail Grenier, Jan. 2, 1949 (div.); children: Gail, Jan, Donn, Sean, Sharon, Van; m. Glenda Hatsuko Naito, Sept. 1, 1973. Grad., Phillips Exeter Acad., 1947; A.B., Princeton U., 1955; M.A., Harvard U., 1957; Ph. D., Northwestern U., 1959; PhD (hon.), Soka U., 1992. Asst. prof. pub. adminstrn. Seoul Nat. U., 1959-61; asst. to assoc. prof. politics Princeton U., 1961-67; prof. polit. sci. U. Hawaii, Honolulu, 1967-92, prof. emeritus, 1992—. Author: The Korean Decision, 1968, The Scientific Study of Political Leadership, 1977, To Nonviolent Political Science, 1993; editor: Political Leadership, 1972, (with George Chaplin) Hawaii 2000, 1973, (with Sarah Gilliatt) Nonviolence in Hawaii's Spiritual Traditions, 1991, Buddhism and Nonviolent Global Problem-Solving, 1991, (of Petra K. Kelly) Nonviolence Speaks to Power, 1993, (with Chaiwat Satha-Anand) Islam and Nonviolence, 1993; social sci. editor: Biography, 1977—. Program chmn. Hawaii Gov.'s Conf. on Yr. 2000, 1970; leader U.S. Group 103, Amnesty Internat., 1977-78; cons. UN Univ., 1980-86; coord. planning project Ctr. for Global Nonviolence, U. Hawaii Spark M. Matsunaga Inst. for Peace, 1988-95; pres. Ctr. for Global Nonviolence, 1994—; mem. nat. adv. group Martin Luther King Jr. Inst. for Nonviolence, State of N.Y., 1989-90., With U.S. Army, 1948-52. Decorated Commendation medal; recipient Seikyo Culture prize, 1982, Dr. G. Ramachandran award for internat. understanding, 1986, Anuvrat award for internat. peace, 1987, Jai Tulsi Anuvrat award, 1995; named Woodrow Wilson nat. fellow, 1955-56, Princeton U. Class of 1955 award, 1987, 3rd Gandhi Meml. lectr., New Delhi, 1990, Disting. life fellow Delhi Sch. Nonviolence, 1992. Mem. Internat. Peace Rsch. Assn. (co-convenor nonviolence study group 1989-91), Internat. Polit. Sci. Assn., World Future Studies Fedn., Phi Beta Kappa. Home: 3653 Tantalus Dr Honolulu HI 96822-5033 *Political science is a science that can liberate humankind from violence. To do so, it must first liberate itself. This will require five related transformations: normative, empirical, theoretical, institutional, and educational. The tasks of political scientists at the end of the 20th century are to begin these transformations. Twenty-first century successors must carry them forward, consolidate them, and extend their influence throughout global society.*

PAIGE, HILLIARD WEGNER, corporate director, consultant; b. Hartford, Conn., Oct. 2, 1919; s. Joseph Wegner and Ruth (Hill) P.; m. Dorothea Magner, Dec. 8, 1945; children—Elizabeth, Deborah, Hilliard, Jr. BSME, Worcester Poly. Inst., 1941, D Engring. (hon), 1971. Sr. v.p. Gen. Electric, N.Y.C., 1941-71; pres. Gen. Dynamics, St. Louis, 1971-73; chmn., chief exec. officer Satellite Bus. Systems, Inc., Washington, 1973-76; vice chmn. bd. Internat. Energy Assocs., Ltd., Washington, 1976-85; chmn. bd. H.A. Knott, Ltd., Silver Spring, Md., 1984-89; dir. The Atlantic Coun. of U.S., 1987—, Computer Data Systems, Inc., Videoconferencing Systems, Inc., Gen. Environ. & Energy, Inc., Gallager Marine Systems, Inc. Patentee in field; contbr. articles to profl. jours. Mem. Def. Sci. Bd. U.S. Dept. Def., Washington, 1973-78; trustee Worcester Poly. Inst., Mass., 1974—. Recipient Pub. Service award NASA, 1969, Order of Merit Italy, 1970, Engr. of Year award Greater Phila. Engring Council, 1960. Fellow AIAA; mem. Nat. Acad. Engring. Republican. Congregationalist. Clubs: Metropolitan, Chevy Chase (Washington); Conquistadores del Cielo. Avocations: skiing, tennis, scuba diving, golf. Home and Office: 5163 Filden St Washington DC 20016

PAIGE, JEFFERY MAYLAND, sociologist, educator; b. Providence, June 15, 1942; s. Charles Warren and Dorothy Frances (Rice) P.; m. Karen Ericksen, Apr. 30, 1966 (div. 1980). AB summa cum laude, Harvard U., 1964; PhD, U. Mich., 1968. Asst. prof. U. Calif., Berkeley, 1968-76; assoc. prof. U. Mich., Ann Arbor, 1976-82, prof., 1982—, dir. ctr. for rsch. on social orgn., 1992—; vis. lectr. U. Ctrl. Am., San Salvador, El Salvador, 1990, Fla. Internat. U., Miami, 1992; internat. observer Nicaraguan Nat. Adv. Commn. on Atlantic Coast, Managua, 1986. Author: Agrarian Revolution, 1975 (Sorokin award 1976); co-author: The Politics of Reproductive Ritual, 1981. Fulbright fellow, 1990, Kellog fellow, 1991; rsch. grantee NSF, 1990-92. Mem. Am. Sociol. Assn. (coun. chair polit. econ. of world sys. sect. 1987-89), Latin Am. Studies Assn., Sociol. Rsch. Assn. Democrat. Avocations: hiking, Nordic and alpine skiing, sailing. Office: U Mich Dept Sociology Ann Arbor MI 48109

PAIGE, NORMA, lawyer, corporate executive; b. Lomza, Poland, Oct. 11, 1922; came to U.S., 1927; d. Morris and Edith (Kachourek) Zelaso; children: Holly Paige Russek, Madelyn Paige Givant. BA, NYU, 1944, JD, 1946; postgrad. in bus. adminstrn., CCNY, 1953, NYU, 1969. Bar: N.Y. 1946, U.S. Supreme Ct. 1951. Ptnr. Paige and Paige, N.Y.C., 1948—; v.p., bd. dirs. Astronautics Corp. Am., Milw., 1959—, chmn. bd., 1984—; exec. v.p., bd. dirs. Kearfott Guidance & Navigation Corp., Wayne, N.J., 1988—; bd. dirs. Astronautics C.A., Ltd., Israel. Recipient Jabotinsky Centennial medal Prime Minister of Israel, 1980, Tribute to Women in Indsl. Industry Twin II award YWCA, 1981, NYU Sch. Law Outstanding Alumnus of Yr. award, 1991, Judge Edward Weinfeld award, 1996. Mem. N.Y. Women's Bar Assn. (pres. 1958-59). Office: Astronautics Corp Am 4115 N Teutonia Ave Milwaukee WI 53209-6731

PAIGE, RICHARD ALAN, nursing educator; b. Wichita, Sept. 27, 1935; s. Clarence Francis Paige and Marilyn Dezaree (Lagneou) Hust; m. Cindy M. McCormack, Oct. 5, 1991. AS in Nursing, SUNY, Albany, 1982; B of Health Care Mgmt., U. La Verne, 1987; postgrad., U. West L.A., 1991-92. RN Calif. Staff nurse Riverside Hosp., North Hollywood, Calif., 1978-80, Profl. Staffing, Northridge, Calif., 1980-82, Sherman Oaks (Calif.) Cmty. Hosp., 1982-83; paramedic, trauma coord. Mayo Newhall Meml. Hosp., Valencia, Calif., 1983-89; staff nurse Pacifica Hosp. of the Valley, Sun Valley, Calif., 1989-91; instr. ACLS Life Support Assocs., Acton, Calif., 1990-92; nusring supr. Westlake (Calif.) Hosp., 1992-93; staff nurse Granada Hills (Calif.) Hosp., 1992-93; clin. nurse educator Northridge Hosp., 1993—. Coauthor: Management of Gunshot Wounds, 1987. Mem. Emergency Nurses Assn. Republican. Avocation: computers. Office: Northridge Hosp 18300 Roscoe Blvd Northridge CA 91328

PAIGE, SANDRA KRISTINE, psychologist; b. Chgo., Dec. 3, 1961; d. Lesly Wade and Barbara Ann (Chambers) Johnson; m. Ray Anthony Paige, Nov. 9, 1991. BA in Psychology, U. Detroit, 1983, MA in Clin. Psychology, 1985, PhD in Clin. Psychology, 1988. Lic. clin. psychologist, Mich. Psychology trainee Mt. Carmel Mercy Hosp., Detroit, 1984-85; clin. intern Oakland County Ct., Pontiac, Mich., 1985-86, Harper-Grace Hosp., Detroit, 1986-87; sr. clin. psychologist State Jud. Counsel, Detroit, 1987—; assoc. psychologist Clark & Assocs., P.C., Southfield, Mich., 1988-94; cons. psychologist Children's Hosp., Detroit, 1988-89, Detroit Counseling Ctr., 1991—, Detroit Police Dept., 1993—; self-employed clin. supr., Detroit, 1993—. Guest commentator radio talk shows, 1991, 92. Mem. APA, Nat. Assn. Self Employed, Govt. Adminstr.'s Assn. (Appreciation award 1989, 91, 92), Zonta Internat., Alpha Kappa Alpha. Democrat. Avocations: writing, reading, physical fitness. Office: S K Paige PhD Psychol Svcs 3800 Woodward Ave Ste 518 Detroit MI 48201-2030

PAIGE, SUSANNE LYNN, financial consultant; b. Bklyn., Feb. 25, 1950; d. Abraham and Florence Roslyn (Rosenfeld) P.; divorced. BA cum laude, C.W. Post Coll., 1972, postgrad., 1975. Lic. mortgage broker, N.Y. Buyer B. Gertz and Sons, Inc., Jamaica, N.Y., 1973-76; nat. field sales mgr. LeVison Care Products, Inc., New City, N.Y., 1976-82, Am. Vitamin Products, Inc., Lakewood, N.J., 1984-85; prin. Paige & Assocs., Scarsdale, 1982-87; loan officer and fin. cons. Bayside Fed. Savs. and Loan, Jericho, N.Y., 1987-88; prin. Paige Capital Enterprises, Inc., Rye, N.Y., 1988—; mem. Comml. Investment Divsn./Westchester Bd. Realtors, White Plains, N.Y.; pub. spkr. and lectr. in field. Author: Closing the Deal in Today's Volatile Market, 1994; satarist/polit. cartoonist C.W. Post Coll. News and Editorial, Brookville, N.Y., 1968-72; contbr. articles to profl. jours. Recipient award for Best Original Essay, Newsday Harry F. Guggenheim award, Garden City, N.Y., 1967, Hon. Mention award C.W. Post Coll. Gallery, 1982, Hon. Mention (sculpture) Fresh Meadows (N.Y.) Merchant's Assn., 1971, meritorious notation Real Estate Weekly, 1991-93; selected as Comml. Deal-Maker of Yr., N.Y. Real Estate Jour., 1992, Real Estate Personality, 1993, Northeast Fin. Work-Out Specialist N.Y. and New Eng. Real Estate Jours., 1990-93, also meritorious notation, 1990-93. Mem. Alumni Assn. C.W. Post Coll., 60's East Realty Club, Westchester Bd. Realtors, White Plains, N.Y., Assn. Commercial Real Estate. Avocations: speaker for fin. seminars, writer, traveling. Office: Paige Capital Enterprises Inc PO Box 1234 Scarsdale NY 10583-9234

PAIGEN, KENNETH, geneticist, research director; b. N.Y.C., Nov. 14, 1927; s. Alexander and Ida (Kantor) P.; m. Beverly Vandermolen, June 14, 1970; children: Susan, Gina, Mark, David, Jennifer. A.B., Johns Hopkins U., Balt., 1946; Ph.D., Calif. Inst. Tech., Pasadena, 1950. Staff mem. Roswell Park Meml. Inst., Buffalo, 1955-72, dept. head, 1972-82; prof. dept. genetics U. Calif., Berkeley, 1982-89; dir., sr. staff scientist Jackson Lab., Bar Harbor, Maine, 1989—. Mem. AAAS, Am. Assn. for Cancer Rsch., Internat. Mammalian Genome Soc., Human Genome Orgn., Genetics Soc. Am., Am. Soc. for Biochemistry and Molecular Biology, Sigma Xi, Phi Beta Kappa. Democrat. Jewish. Avocation: sailing. Home: Old Farm Rd Bar Harbor ME 04609 Office: Jackson Lab 600 Main St Bar Harbor ME 04609-1523

PAIK, JOHN KEE, structural engineer; b. Seoul; came to U.S., 1955; s. Nam Suk and Kyong Ock (Yun) P.; m. Aine Fenoula Ievers, Feb. 20, 1970; 1 child, Brian Ievers Paik. BSCE, So. Meth. U., 1961; PhD, NYU, 1975. Lic. profl. engr. N.Y., N.J., Conn., Pa., Md., Mass., Vt., Ga., Fla. Chief engr. T.Y. Lin and Assocs., N.Y.C., 1960-67; chief structural engr. Soros Assocs., N.Y.C., 1967-68; sr. project engr. Stauffer Chem. Co., Dobbs Ferry, N.Y., 1975-77; prin., founder Paik and Assocs., Westchester County, N.Y., 1977—; chmn., founder The Future Home Tech. Inc., Port Jervis, N.Y., 1986—; chmn., pres. J.K.P. Constrn. Co. Inc., Mohegan Lake, N.Y., 1989—; adj. assoc. prof. Grad. Sch. Engring. Manhattan Coll., Bronx, 1985; lectr. Grad. Sch. Engring. Polytech. U., Bklyn., 1973-85, Cooper Union, N.Y.C., 1972. Mem. ASCE, Am. Inst. Steel Constrn., Prestressed Concrete Inst., N.Y Acad. Scis., Am. Concrete Inst., Post Tensioning Inst., Nat. Soc. Profl. Engrs., Constrn. Specifications Inst., Am. Arbitration Assn. (dispute arbitrator, constrn.), So. Meth. U. Alumni Club (pres. 1964), Chi Epsilon. Republican. Methodist. Achievements include the design of over 100 million sq. feet of comml., residential, indsl. and instnl. structures including several highrise bldgs. over 40 stories in N.Y.C. Home: Dyckman Dr Mohegan Lake NY 10547 Office: Paik and Assocs 100 Summit Lake Dr Valhalla NY 10595-1339

PAIKOWSKY, SANDRA ROSLYN, art historian; b. St. John, N.B., Can., Dec. 29, 1945; d. Morton Ernest and Bessie Frances (Rabkin) P.; m. John Richard Fox, Dec. 11, 1982. B.A., Sir. George Williams U., Montreal, Que., Can., 1967; M.A., U. Toronto, 1969. Curatorial asst. Royal Ont. Mus., Toronto, 1967-68; prof. art history Concordia U., Montreal, 1969—; curator Concordia Art Gallery, Montreal, 1981-93. Co-editor. Jour. Can. Art History, 1972-91, co-pub., 1981-91, editor, pub., 1991—; author exhbn. catalogues. Mem. Can. Mus. Assn., Univ. Art Assn. Can. Office: Concordia U Fine Arts BC 210-4, 1455 de Maisonneuve Blvd W, Montreal, PQ Canada H3G 1M8

PAIN, BETSY M., lawyer; b. Albertville, Ala., Aug. 29, 1950; d. Charles Riley and Jean Faye (Rains) Stone; m. William F. Pain, Nov. 18, 1977; children: Taylor Holland, Emily Anne Pain. AA, Northeastern Okla. A&M, Miami, Okla., 1970; BA, U. Okla., 1974, JD, 1976. Bar: Okla. 1977; U.S. Dist. Ct. (we. dist.) 1979. Staff atty. Okla. Dept. Corrections, Oklahoma City, 1978-79; gen. counsel Okla. Pardon and Parole Bd., Oklahoma City, 1979-84, exec. dir., 1984-88; corp. counsel Roberts, Schornick & Assocs., Inc., Norman, Okla., 1990—. Editor: (newsletter) RSA Environmental Report, 1991—. With extended family program Juvenile Svcs., Inc. Cleveland County, Okla., 1983-91. Mem. Okla. Bar Assn. (environ. law sect. 1977—), Am. Corp. Counsel Assn. Democrat. Methodist. Avocations: reading, needlework, church activities. Office: Roberts Schornick & Assoc Inc 3700 W Robinson St Ste 200 Norman OK 73072-3639

PAIN, CHARLES LESLIE, lawyer; b. Austin, Tex., Apr. 26, 1913; s. William Francis and Ruby (Gates) P.; m. Roberta Wilmoth, Mar. 27, 1942; children—Charles Laurence, William Francis, Glenn David. B.A., LL.B., U. Okla., 1935. Bar: Okla. 1935. Asst. atty. Southwestern Light & Power Co., 1935-40; practice in Anadarko, 1956—; partner Pain & Garland, 1956—; Exec. sec. to Congressman Toby Morris, 1951-53; Mem. Okla. Bd. Bar Examiners, 1969-78. Pres. Black Beaver council Boy Scouts Am., 1971-72; bd. dirs. Okla. Baptist Found., Inc., 1984-85, vice chmn., 1985-87. Served with AUS, 1940-46; col. Res. (Ret.). Recipient Silver Beaver award Boy Scouts Am. Mem. Am., Okla., Caddo County bar assns., Am. Legion, Res. Officers Assn., Order of Coif, Phi Beta Kappa, Phi Eta Sigma, Phi Alpha Delta, Sigma Chi. Democrat. Baptist. Club: Lion (past dist. gov.). Office: 111 SW 2nd St Anadarko OK 73005-3401

PAINE, ANDREW J., JR., banker; b. Chgo., Oct. 18, 1937; s. Andrew J. and Louise (Kelly) P.; m. Jane Medaris, June 25, 1960; children: Linda, Stephanie, Andrew. B.A., DePauw U., 1959; M.B.A., Ind. U., 1967; grad., Stonier Grad. Sch. Banking, 1969. Asst. cashier Ind. Nat. Bank, Indpls., 1964-66; asst. v.p. Ind. Nat. Bank, 1966-68, v.p., 1968-72, sr. v.p., 1972-76, exec. v.p. corp. devel., 1976-77, exec. v.p. corp. banking, 1977-79, pres., 1979—, chief oper. officer; also vice chmn. Ind. Nat. Corp. (now NBD Bank, N.A.); now pres., ceo; vice chmn. Ind. Nat. Corp., 1981—; dir. Indpls. Life Ins. Co., Hammond Co., Newport Beach, Calif. Mem. past pres.'s council Jr. Achievement Central Ind.; nat. bd. dirs. Jr. Achievement Inc.; trustee Children's Mus., DePauw U.; bd. dirs. Community Service Council Met. Indpls.; bd. govs. United Way, chmn. campaign, 1983. Recipient Key Man award Indpls. Jaycees, 1972; Alumni citation DePauw U., 1978. Mem. Am. Bankers Assn. (chmn. govt. relations council), Young Presidents Orgn., Ind. U. Sch. Bus. Alumni Assn. (past pres.). Methodist. Clubs: Columbia, Meridian Hills Country. Office: NBD Bank, N.A. 1 Indiana Sq # 501 Indianapolis IN 46266*

PAINE, JAMES CARRIGER, federal judge; b. Valdosta, Ga., May 20, 1924; s. Leon Alexander and Josie Carriger (Jones) P.; m. Ruth Ellen Bailey, Sept. 8, 1950; children: James Carriger, Jonathan Jones, JoEllen. B.S., Columbia U., 1947; LL.B., U. Va., 1950, J.D., 1970. Bar: Fla. 1950. Mem. firm Earnest, Lewis, Smith & Jones, West Palm Beach, Fla., 1950-54, Jones Adams Paine & Foster, 1954-60, Jones Paine & Foster, 1960-79; judge U.S. Dist. Ct. (so. dist.) Fla., West Palm Beach, 1979—. Bd. dirs., pres. Children's Home Soc. Fla., 1978-80; mem. bd. Episcopal Diocese S.E. Fla. Served to lt. USNR, 1943-47. Mem. Greater West Palm Beach C. of C. (pres. 1973-74), Palm Beach County Bar Assn. Democrat. Office: US Dist Ct 701 Clematis St West Palm Beach FL 33401-5101

PAINE, LOUIS BURR, JR., lawyer; b. Dallas, Dec. 22, 1932; s. Louis Burr and Winifred (Baker) P.; m. Lynne Murphy, July 23, 1960; children: Louis, Preston, Jeffrey. BA, U. Tex., 1954, LLB, 1956. Bar: Tex. 1956. Assoc. Butler & Binion, Houston, 1960-70, ptnr., 1970—, mng. ptnr., 1985-95. Lt. USN, 1956-60. Fellow Am. Bar Found., Am. Law Inst., Tex. Bar Found., Houston Bar Found., Houston Country Club. Presbyterian. Home: 107 Glynn Way Dr Houston TX 77056-1111 Office: Butler & Binion LLP 1600 1st Interstate Bank Plz Houston TX 77002

PAINTER, CARL ERIC, manufacturing company executive; b. Balt., Aug. 1, 1946; s. Walter Savery and Eleanor (Johnson) P.; m. Roxann Dawn Caprio. BSEE, Lehigh U., 1968; MBA, Harvard U., 1975. With Phelps Dodge Cable & Wire Co., Yonkers, N.Y., 1975-79; plant mgr. Phelps Dodge Cable & Wire Co., DuQuoin, Ill., 1979-83; dir. mktg. Phelps Dodge Cable & Wire Co., Greenwich, Conn., 1983-84; v.p. ops. & mktg. Cablec Corp., New City, N.Y., 1984-87; pres. Cablec Utility Cable Co. divsn. BICC Cables Corp., West Nyack, N.Y., 1987-93; exec. v.p. BICC Cables Corp., West Nyack, N.Y., 1990-92, pres., COO, 1992-93, pres., chmn., CEO, 1993—; bd. dirs. BICC plc, Phillips Cables. Lt. USN, 1968-72. Office: BICC Cables Corp 1 Crossfield Ave West Nyack NY 10994-2221

PAINTER, JACK TIMBERLAKE, civil engineer; b. Kincaid, W.Va., July 23, 1930; s. Troy Earl and Nannie Bell (Proffit) P. BSCE, W.Va. U., 1950, MSCE, 1955. Instr. civil engring. W.Va. U., 1950-51, 53-55; mem. faculty La. Tech U., Ruston, 1955—; prof. civil engring. La. Tech. U., 1962-92, prof. emeritus, 1992—; Alumni Found. prof. La. Tech U., 1977-78; vis. lectr. Manhattan Coll., Coll. Forestry, SUNY, Syracuse, Cornell U., U. Wis., summers 1954-60. Nat. pres. Circus Fans Assn. Am., 1967; lic. layreader Episcopal Ch. Served with USNR, 1951-52. Faculty fellow NSF, 1958-59; named Man of Year Omicron Delta Kappa, 1972. Fellow ASCE; mem. Am. Congress Surveying and Mapping, La. Engring. Soc. (Charles M. Kerr Pub. Rels. award 1990), Am. Soc. Engring. Edn., Tau Beta Pi (Outstanding Prof. award 1963, 68, 74, 78), Chi Epsilon (Excellent Teaching award 1985). Address: 1303 Hodges Ave Ruston LA 71270-5507

PAINTER, JOHN HOYT, electrical engineer; b. Winfield, Kans., Mar. 27, 1934; s. John Paul and Marjorie Marietta (Slack) P.; m. Joy Lou Vaughan, June 7, 1955; children—John Mark, Paul Burton, William Vaughan, Joy Lynn. B.S., U. Ill., Urbana, 1961; Gen. Electric Found. fellow, M.S., 1962;

Ph.D., So. Meth. U., 1972; postgrad., Coll. William and Mary, 1967-69. Communications engr. NASA Manned Spacecraft Center, Houston, 1962-65; sr. engr. Motorola Govt. Electronics div., Scottsdale, Ariz., 1965-67; research engr. NASA Langley Research Center, Hampton, Va., 1967-74; asso. prof., elec. engring. Tex. A&M U., College Station, 1974-79, prof., 1979—; pres. ALTAIR Corps. cons., College Station, 1980—; tchr. Christian seminars. Served with USAF, 1953-58. Recipient Recognition cert. NASA, 1975. Mem. IEEE (sr.). Patentee digital communications processing. Home: 1119 Merry Oaks Dr College Station TX 77840-2606 Office: Tex A&M U Dept Elec Engring College Station TX 77843 *No matter how big one's thinking, there is always a concept bigger. Realizing that God is the ultimate upper bound brings relief from mental striving.*

PAINTER, MARY E. (MARY PAINTER YARBROUGH), editor; b. Tulsa, July 15, 1920; d. Ernest Balf Parker and Maggie Mae (Renaud) P.; BA, Oklahoma City U., 1943; postgrad. Columbia U., 1944; m. Charles J. Yarbrough, Apr. 7, 1946; children: Kirby John, Kevin Lee. Editorial asst., feature writer Office War Info., 1943-46; feature writer, news editor Dept. State, 1946-53; with USIA, Washington, 1953-78, editor USIA World, 1967-78; with U.S. Internat. Communication Agy., 1978-80, editor USICA World, 1978-80; with Food Policy Center News/Views, Washington, 1981-84, mng. editor Food Policy Center News/Views, 1981-84; assoc. editor Food Monitor, 1981-83, editor, 1986-88; editor WHY Mag., 1989—. World Hunger Yr., N.Y.C., 1981—; editor USIAAA Newsletter, Washington, 1980-88, Reston (Va.) Interfaith Newsletter, 1982-90. Recipient Meritorious Service award USIA, 1964, Spl. Commendation, 1974; Dir.'s award for Outstanding Creativity, U.S. Internat. Communication Agy., 1980. Mem. NOW, Women's Action Orgn., Assn. Am. Fgn. Svc. Women, Am. Fgn. Svc. Assn. Democrat. Baptist. Home: 12132 Quorn Ln Reston VA 22091-2635 Office: World Hunger Yr 505 8th Ave Fl 21 New York NY 10018-6582

PAINTER, MICHAEL ROBERT, landscape architect, urban designer; b. L.A., Jan. 27, 1935; s. John Guy and Lillias (Armour) P.; m. Susan Margaret Collins, Jan. 3, 1959; children: Melissa Ann, Joshua Michael. BS, U. Calif., Berkeley, 1956; M Landscape Architecture in Urban Design, Harvard U., 1966. Registered landscape architect, Calif., N.Y., Nev., Pa., Tex. Jr. designer Lawrence Halprin & Assoc., San Francisco, 1956-58; ptnr. John Carl Warnecke & Assoc., San Francisco, 1958-69; pres. Michael Painter & Assoc., San Francisco, 1969-87, MPA Design, San Francisco, 1987—. Maj. archtl. works include Kennedy Gravesite, Arlington, Va., 1968 (honor award Am. Soc. Landscape Architects 1970), Lafayette Pk., Washington, 1970 (merit award Am. Soc. Landscape Architects 1972), corp. campus PacBell Adminstrn. Ctr., San Ramon, Calif., 1988 (merit award Am. Soc. Landscape Architects 1989), waterfront restoration Gt. Hwy./Ocean Beach, San Francisco, 1989 (honor award Am. Soc. Landscape Architects 1989), Doyle Drive Scenic Pkwy. Plan (merit award Am. Soc. Landscape Architects, Cmty. Svc. award San Francisco chpt. AIA, 1993). Past pres., bd. dirs. Friends of Recreation and Pks., San Francisco, 1969—; bd. dirs., advisor San Francisco Planning and Urban Rsch., 1972—; bd. dirs. Exploratorium, San Francisco, 1974—; coun. Grad. Sch. Design, Harvard U., 1983-86; chmn. Citizens Adv. Com., San Francisco. Fellow Am. Soc. Landscape Arch. (com. chair 1968-69, v.p. No. Calif. chpt. 1970-72, honor awards 1978, 82, merit awards 1981, 84); mem. Urban Land Inst. (assoc.), Calif. Coun. Landscape Arch. (design jury 1991), U. Calif. Coll. Environ. Design Alumni Assn. (bd. dirs. 1990-95), Mill Valley Tennis Club, Lambda Alpha. Avocations: gardening, hiking, swimming, historical research. Office: MPA Design 414 Mason St San Francisco CA 94102-1719

PAINTER, WILLIAM HALL, law educator; b. Pitts., May 2, 1927; s. John Littleton Dawson and Eleanor Cramer (Hall); m. Marion Symmes Homer, July 9, 1955; children: Richard William, Edward Homer. A.B., Princeton U., 1950; J.D., Harvard U., 1954. Bar: N.Y. 1955. Assoc. Debevoise, Plimpton & McLean, N.Y.C., 1954-58; teaching fellow Harvard U.Law Sch., Cambridge, Mass., 1958-59; prof. Villanova U. Law Sch., Phila., 1959-65; vis. prof. U. Mich. Law Sch., Ann Arbor, 1965; prof. U. Mo., Kansas City, 1965-71; spl. counsel, dir. study securities industry U.S. Ho. Reps., Washington, 1971-72; prof. U. Ill. Coll. Law, Champaign, 1972-81, Albert E. Jenner Jr. prof., 1981-87; Theodore Rinehart prof. law George Washington U., Washington, 1987—. Author: Federal Regulation of Insider Trading, 1968, Corporate and Tax Aspects of Closely Held Corporations, 1971, 2d edit., 1981, Problems and Materials in Business Planning, 1975, 3d edit., 1994, The Federal Securities Code and Corporate Disclosure, 1979, Painter on Close Corporations, 1991; contbr. articles to legal publs. Mem. Ill. Bus. Corp. Act Revision Com., 1981-83. Mem. ABA (fed. securities commn. sect. corp., banking and bus. law, chmn. subcom. on legis. 1974-81), Assn. Am. Law Schs. (chmn. sect. bus. assn. 1976), Am. Law Inst., Phi Beta Kappa. Home: 6652 32nd St NW Washington DC 20015-2310 Office: George Washington U Nat Law Ctr 720 20th St NW Washington DC 20052

PAINTON, IRA WAYNE, retired securities executive; b. Longdale, Okla., Nov. 3, 1917; s. Ira W. and Leatha (Ball) P.; m. Jane Tiffin, Apr. 9, 1941; children: Ann Painton Anderson, Scott W. A.B., Northwestern State U., Okla., 1940; postgrad., So. Meth. U., 1953. C.L.U. Mng. ptnr. Waynoka Motor Co., Okla., 1946-50; br. mgr. Am. Nat. Ins. Co., Omaha, 1953-57; dir. tng. Pacific Mut. Life Ins. Co., Los Angeles, 1957-61; dir. recruiting and tng. Fin. Programs, Inc., Denver, 1962-66; v.p. Securities Mgmt. & Research, Inc., Galveston, Tex., 1967; pres. Securities Mgmt. & Research, Inc., 1967-83; pres., dir. Am. Nat. Growth, Income and Bond Funds. Served to capt. Signal Corps, AUS, 1940-46, 50-52, Korea. Decorated Bronze Star. Mem. Am. Assn. CLUs, Northwestern Okla. State U. Alumni Assn. (Outstanding Bus./Profl. award 1992, chmn. foun. bd. 1993—). Home: 12004 Dahoon Dr Oklahoma City OK 73120-8131 *I believe real success, like beauty, is in the mind of the beholder. And as long as we persist in trying there can be no final failure, since success is usually a series of failures that turn out all right.*

PAINTON, RUSSELL ELLIOTT, lawyer, mechanical engineer; b. Port Arthur, Tex., Dec. 5, 1940; s. Clifford Elliott and Edith Virginia (McCutcheon) P.; m. Elizabeth Ann Mullins, July 2, 1965 (div. Dec. 1977); 1 child, Todd Elliott; m. Mary Lynn Weber, May 9, 1981. BS in Mech. Engring., U. Tex.-Austin, 1963, JD, 1972. Bar: Tex. 1972; registered profl. engr., Tex. Engr. Gulf States Utilities, Beaumont, Tex., 1963-66; engr. Tracor, Inc., Austin, Tex., 1966-70, corp. counsel, 1973-83, v.p., gen. counsel, 1983—, corp. sec., 1991—; atty. Brown, Maroney, Rose, Baker & Barber, Austin, 1972-73, Childs, Fortenbach, Beck & Guyton, Houston, 1973; corp. sec. Westmark Systems, Inc., Austin, 1990-91. Gen. counsel Paramount Theatre for Performing Arts, 1977-83, 2d vice chmn., 1978-80, 1st vice chmn., 1980-82, chmn. bd., 1982-84, retiring chmn., 1984-85; mem. Centex chpt. ARC; mem. adv. bd. Austin Sci. Acad., 1985-88, 93—; mem. adv. coun. Austin Transp., 1985-88; bd. dirs. Tex. Industries for the Blind and Handicapped, 1988-95, vice chmn., 1990-91. Named Boss of Yr. Austin Legal Secs. Assn., 1981. Mem. ABA, Tex. Bar Assn. (treas. corp. counsel sect. 1982-83), Travis County Bar Assn., Nat. Chamber Litigation Ctr., Better Bus. Bur. (arbitrator 1983—), Am. Electronics Assn. (chmn. Austin coun. 1985-86), Austin Yacht Club (race comdr. 1968-69, treas. 1970-71, sec. 1972, 75, vice commodore 1980, commodore 1981, fleet comdr. 1986), Order Blue Gavel, Houston Yacht Club, Delta Theta Phi. Republican. Episcopalian. Office: Tracor Inc 6500 Tracor Ln Austin TX 78725-2151

PAIROLERO, PETER CHARLES, surgeon; b. Bessemer, Mich., 1938. MD, U. Mich., 1963. Diplomate Am. Bd. Surgeons, Am. Bd. Thoracic Surgeons, Am. Bd. Gen. Vascular Surgeons. Intern St. Mary's Hosp., Duluth, Minn., 1963-64; resident gen. surgery Mayo Grad. Sch. Medicine, Rochester, Minn., 1966-71; fellow cerebral vascular resch. Mayo Grad. Sch. Medicine, Rochester, 1968-69, resident thoracic-cardio surgery, 1971-73. Mem. AMA. Office: 200 1st St SW Rochester MN 55905-0001*

PAIS, ABRAHAM, physicist, educator; b. Amsterdam, Holland, May 19, 1918; s. Jesaja and Kaatje (van Kleeff) P.; m. Lila Atwill, Dec. 15, 1956 (div. 1962); 1 child, Joshua; m. Agnes Ida Benedicte Nicolaisen, Mar. 15, 1990. B.Sc., U. Amsterdam, 1938; M.Sc., U. Utrecht, 1940, Ph.D., 1941. Research fellow Inst. Theoretical Physics, Copenhagen, Denmark, 1946; prof. Inst. Advanced Study, Princeton, N.J., 1950-63; prof. physics Rockefeller U., N.Y.C., 1963-81, Detlev Bronk prof., 1981—, prof. emeritus, 1988—; Balfour prof. Weizmann Inst., Israel, 1977. Author: Subtle is the Lord (Am. Book award 1983, Am. Inst. Physics award 1983), Inward Bound, 1986, Niels Bohr's Times, 1991, Einstein Lived Here, 1994. Decorated officer Order of Oranje Nassau (The Netherlands); recipient J.R. Oppenheimer Meml. prize, 1979, Physica prize The Netherlands, 1992, Gemant award Am. Inst. Physics, 1993, Lewis Thomas prize, 1995; Guggenheim fellow, 1960. Fellow Am. Phys. Soc.; mem. Royal Acad. Scis. Holland (corr., medal of sci. 1993), Royal Acad. Scis. and Letters, Denmark, Am. Acad. Arts and Scis., Am. Philos. Soc., Nat. Acad. Scis., Council on Fgn. Relations. Home: 1161 York Ave New York NY 10021-7940 Office: Rockefeller Univ Dept of Physics New York NY 10021

PAISLEY, KEITH WATKINS, state senator, small business owner; b. Mpls., Dec. 29, 1928; s. Manley G. and Maxine Alice (Watkins) P.; m. Jean Clare Robson, Sept. 23, 1950; children: Mark, Susan, Julie, Jeanne. BA, Hamline U., 1950. Rep. State of S.D., Pierre, 1981-84, senator, 1985—; owner Robson Hardware, Sioux Falls, S.D., 1972-93. Lutheran. Home: 2409 S Elmwood Ave Sioux Falls SD 57105-3315 Office: Robson Hardware 2322 W 12th St Sioux Falls SD 57104-3811

PAIVIO, ALLAN URHO, psychology educator; b. Thunder Bay, Ont., Can., Mar. 29, 1925; s. Aku and Ida Julia (Hanninen) P.; m. Kathleen Laura Blanche Austin, Jan. 9, 1946; children—Sandra, Anna Lee, Heather, Eric, Karina. B.Sc., McGill U., 1949, M.Sc., 1957, Ph.D., 1959. Lectr. Sir George Williams U., Montreal, 1957; research psychologist Cornell U., Ithaca, N.Y., 1958-59; asst. prof. psychology U. New Brunswick, Can., 1959-62; asst. prof. U. Western Ont., London, Can., 1962-63, assoc. prof., 1963-67, prof., 1967-92; prof. emeritus U. Western Ont., London, 1992—. Author: Imagery and Verbal Processes, 1971, Mental Representations: A Dual Coding Approach, 1986, Images in Mind: The Evolution of a Theory, 1991. Served with Royal Can. Navy, 1944-45. Recipient Queen's Silver Jubilee medal Can., 1977. Fellow Am. Psychol. Assn., Can. Psychol. Assn. (Disting. Contbns. to Psychology award 1982), Royal Soc. Can.; mem. Psychonomic Soc. Home: 919 Waterloo St, London, ON Canada N6A 3X2 Office: Univ of Western Ont, Dept Psychology, London, ON Canada

PAJOR, ROBERT E., paint and plastics company executive; b. 1936. BS, Roosevelt U., 1958; MBA, U. Calif., Berkeley, 1964. With The Richardson Co., Melrose Park, Ill., 1959, De Soto Chems., 1958-59; with Valspar Corp., Mpls., 1959-69, v.p., 1974-81, pres., COO, 1981-94, vice chmn., 1994—, also bd. dirs. With U.S. Army, 1959. Office: Valspar Corp 1101 S 3rd St Minneapolis MN 55415-1211*

PAK, HYUNG WOONG, foundation executive, educator; b. Ham-Hoong, Korea, Nov. 6, 1932; came to U.S., 1955, naturalized, 1968; s. Kyung-Koo and Myung-Sook (Lee) P.; m. Diana Lee Steen Woodruff, 1975; children: Jonathan Tong-Hee, Michelle Hyun-Mi Lee. AB, U. Chgo., 1958. Editor and publisher Chgo. Rev., 1958-63, cons., 1963-65; assoc. editor Ency. Britannica Press, Chgo., 1963-64; sr. editor social scis. and humanities Ency. Britannica Press, 1964-66; ednl. dir. Bantam Books, Inc., N.Y.C., 1966-69; gen. mgr. sch. dept. Appleton-Century-Crofts/New Century, N.Y.C., 1970-72; v.p., editorial dir. D. Van Nostrand Co., N.Y.C., 1972-74; pres. D. Van Nostrand Co., 1974-76, Chatham Sq. Press, N.Y.C., 1976-83; pub. Urizen Books, Inc., N.Y.C., 1978-81; exec. v.p. Bus. Software Mag., Palo Alto, Calif., 1983-84; pub., editor Asian High-Tech. Report, 1984-90; exec. dir. The Philip Jaisohn Meml. Found., Inc., Phila., 1990—; fellow Hoover Instn., Stanford, Calif., 1984-85. Author: The Pacific Rim, 1990; columnist The Phila. Bus. Rev., 1993—. Mem. Bd. Sch. Dist. Cheltenham Twp., Pa., 1987-94; mem. Asian task force Phila. Sch. Dist., 1988-95; co-chmn. bus. adv. com. Montgomery County, Pa., 1991-93; del. Citizens' Assembly for a Greater Phila., 1991-95; chmn. Pan Asian Assn. Greater Phila., 1992—, mem. bd. fellowship commn., 1992-95; bd. dirs. Brandywine Workshop, 1996—; trusee Abington Meml. Hosp. Found., 1996—. Served with Republic of Korea Army, 1950-54. Mem. ACLU (life), Phila. Mus. Art. Home: 1015 Sharpless Rd Philadelphia PA 19027-3040 also: Philip Jaisohn Meml Found 6705 Old York Rd Philadelphia PA 19126-2841

PAKE, GEORGE EDWARD, research executive, physicist; b. Jeffersonville, Ohio, Apr. 1, 1924; s. Edward Howe and Mary Mabel (Fry) P.; m. Marjorie Elizabeth Semon, May 31, 1947; children—Warren E., Catherine E., Stephen G., Bruce E. B.S., M.S., Carnegie Inst. Tech., 1945; Ph.D., Harvard U., 1948. Physicist Westinghouse Research Labs., 1945-46; mem. faculty Washington U., St. Louis, 1948-56, 62-70; prof. physics, provost Washington U., 1962-69, exec. vice chancellor, 1965-69, Edward Mallinckrodt prof. physics, 1969-70; v.p. Xerox Corp.; mgr. Xerox Palo Alto (Calif.) Research Center, 1970-78, v.p. corp. research, 1978-83, group v.p., 1983-86; dir. Inst. for Research on Learning, Palo Alto, Calif., 1987-91, dir. emeritus, 1991—; prof. physics Stanford U., 1956-62. Author: (with E. Feenberg) Quantum Theory of Angular Momentum, 1953, Paramagnetic Resonance, 1962, (with T. Estle) The Physical Principles of Electron Paramagnetic Resonance, 1973. Mem. gov. bd. Am. Inst. Physics, 1957-59; bd. dirs. St. Louis Research Council, 1964-70; mem. physics adv. panel NSF, 1958-60, 63- 66; chmn. physics survey com. Nat. Acad. Sci.-NRC, 1964-66; Mem. St. Louis County Bus. and Indl. Devel. Commn., 1963-66; chmn. bd. Regional Indsl. Devel. Corp., St. Louis, 1966-67, St. Louis Research Council, 1967-70; mem. President's Sci. Adv. Com., 1965-69; Bd. dirs. St. Louis Country Day Sch., 1964-70, Central Inst. for Deaf, 1965-70; trustee Washington U., 1970—, Danforth Found., 1971—, U. Rochester, 1982—; trustee Ctr. for Advanced Study in Behavioral Scis., Palo Alto, 1986-92, The Exploratorium, San Francisco, 1987—; bd. overseers Superconducting Super Collider, Univs. Rsch. Assn., 1984-89. Fellow Am. Phys. Soc. (pres. 1977); mem. Am. Assn. Physics Tchrs., AAUP, AAAS, Am. Acad. Arts and Scis., Nat. Acad. Sci., Sigma Xi, Tau Beta Pi. Home: 2 Yerba Buena Ave Los Altos CA 94022-2208 Office: Inst for Rsch on Learning 66 Willow Pl Menlo Park CA 94025

PAKISER, LOUIS CHARLES, JR., geophysicist; b. Denver, Feb. 8, 1919; s. Louis C. and Lila E. (Hanson) P.; m. Helen L. Meineke, Oct. 9, 1939. Geol. Engr., Colo. Sch. Mines, 1937-42; postgrad., U. Nancy, France, 1945, Stanford, U. Colo., 1958-60. Geophysicist Carter Oil Co., 1942-49; first nat. exec. dir. Am. Vets. Com., 1949-52; also mng. editor AVC Bull.; mem. nat. planning com.; geophysicist U.S. Geol. Survey, 1952-92; rep. geophysics br. U.S. Geol. Survey, Denver, 1958-60; chief maj. crustal studies U.S. Geol. Survey, 1960-61, chief br. crustal studies, 1961-65; acting chief Nat. Center Earthquake Research, 1965-67, chmn. exec. com. of center, 1967-68; chief Office Earthquake Research and Crustal Studies, 1967-70, research geophysicist, 1970-79, annuitant research geophysicist, 1979-92, chief br. seismicity and earth structure and nat. earthquake info. service, 1975-77; ad hoc panel on earthquake prediction OST, 1964-68; disting. lectr. Soc. Exploration Geophysicists, 1964; spl. lectr. U. New Orleans, 1982-83; chmn. interagy. staff group on minority participation in sci. and engring. U.S. Dept. Interior, 1972-74; adv. com. Am. Indian Ednl. Opportunity Program U. Colo., 1981-84; vis. com. geophysics dept. Colo. Sch. Mines, 1986-94. Chmn. land use adv. com. Douglas County, Colo., 1975-76, chmn. mineral extraction planning task force, 1989-90; mem. sci. stds. com. Douglas County Sch. Dist.; bd. dirs. Nat. Consortium for Black Profl. Devel., 1976-79; mem. adv. coun. Am. Vets. Com., 1960-61; mem. steering com. Nat. Civil Liberties Clearing House, 1950-52; mem. Amnesty Internat.; assoc. charter mem. U.S. Holocaust Meml. Mus. Recipient Distinguished Service award U.S. Dept. Interior, 1970. Mem. NAACP (exec. com. Tulsa br. 1949, co-chmn. membership com. 1949), AAAS, Anti-Defamation League, Am. Indian Sci. and Engring. Soc., Am. Geophys. Union, Soc. Advancement Chicanos and Native Ams. in Sci., Am. Geol. Inst. (chmn. adv. com. to minority participation program 1973-75), Geol. Soc. Am. (chmn. com. on minority participation in geol. scis. 1975-80). Unitarian Universalist. Home: 111 Emerson St Apt 1142 Denver CO 80218

PAKULA, ALAN J., producer, director; b. N.Y.C., Apr. 7, 1928; m. Hannah Cohn Boorstin, 1973. BA, Yale U., 1948. Producer's apprentice Metro Goldwyn-Mayer, Los Angeles, 1950; producer's asst. Paramount Pictures, Los Angeles, 1951; producer various studios, 1955—; founder, co-owner Pakula-Mulligan Prodns., Inc., Los Angeles; owner Pakula Prodns., Inc., N.Y.C. Producer: (play) There Must Be a Pony, (films) Fear Strikes Out, 1957, To Kill a Mockingbird, 1963, Love With the Proper Stranger, 1963, Baby, the Rain Must Fall, 1965, Inside Daisy Clover, 1965, Up the Down Staircase, 1967, The Stalking Moon, 1968; dir., producer: (films) The Sterile Cuckoo, 1969, Klute, 1971 (London Film Critics Best Dir. award), Love and Pain and the Whole Damned Thing, 1972, The Parallax View, 1974, (with James L. Brooks) Starting Over, 1979, (with Jon Boorstin) Dream Lover, 1986 (grand prize Avoriaz Film Festival), (with Susan Solt), Orphans, 1987; dir.: (films) All The President's Men, 1976 (Best Dir. award N.Y. Film Critics, Best Dir. award Nat. Bd. Rev.), Comes A Horseman, 1978, Rollover, 1981; dir., screenwriter, producer: (film) (with Keith Barish) Sophie's Choice, 1982, See You in the Morning, 1989, Presumed Innocent, 1990, The Pelican Brief, 1993. Office: Pakula Prodns Inc 330 W 58th St # 508 New York NY 10019-1827

PAL, PRABIR KUMAR, aluminium company executive; b. Chittagong, Bengal, India, Feb. 17, 1936; arrived in Can., 1969; s. Niranjan and Renuka (Mitter) P.; m. Nandinee Majumdar, Dec. 13, 1960; 1 child, Nobina. BA with honors in law, Cambridge U., 1958, MA, 1972; Diploma in Indsl. Mgmt., Geneva U., Geneva, 1964. Legal asst. Indian Aluminium Co. Ltd. (subs. Alcan), Calcutta, India, 1959-69, sec., 1972-76; fin. analyst Alcan Aluminium Ltd., Montreal, Que., Can., 1969-72, sr. legal and fin. officer, 1976-82, v.p., chief legal officer, 1987-88, v.p., chief legal officer, sec., 1988—; chief legal officer, treas. Alcan Europe, Geneva, 1982-84; chief legal and fin. officer Alcan Pacific, Vancouver, B.C., Can., 1984-86. Fellow Inst. Chartered Secs. and Adminstrs.; mem. Internat. Bar Assn., Univ. Club Montreal. Avocations: photography, rowing. Office: Alcan Aluminium Ltd, 1188 Sherbrooke St W, Montreal, PQ Canada H3A 3G2

PAL, PRATAPADITYA, museum curator; b. Bangladesh, Sept. 1, 1935; came to U.S., 1967; s. Gopesh Chandra and Bidyut Kana (Dam) P.; m. Chitralekha Bose, Apr. 20, 1968; children—Shalmali, Lopamudra. M.A., U. Calcutta, 1958, D.Phil., 1962; Ph.D. (U. K. Commonwealth Scholar), U. Cambridge, Eng., 1965. Research assoc. Am. Acad. of Benares, India, 1966-67; keeper Indian collections Mus. Fine Arts, Boston, 1967-69; sr. curator Indian and Southeast Asian art Los Angeles County Mus. Art, L.A., 1970-95, acting dir., 1979; vis. curator Indian and S.E. Asian art Art Inst. Chgo., 1995—; cons. curator Norton Simon Mus., Pasadena, Calif., 1995—; adj. prof. fine arts U. So. Calif., 1971-89; vis. prof. U. Calif., Santa Barbara, 1980, Irvine, 1994-95; William Cohn lectr. Oxford U., 1983; Catherine Mead meml. lectr. Pierpont Morgan Libr., N.Y.C., 1986; Ananda K. Coomaraswamy meml. lectr. Prince of Wales Mus., Bombay, 1987; D.J. Sibley prehistoric art lectr. U. Tex., Austin, 1989; Anthony Gardner meml. lectr. Victoria and Albert Mus., London, 1993, keynote spkr. 1st Internat. Conf. on Tibetan Art, 1994; mem. commr.'s art adv. panel IRS, Washington. Author: The Arts of Nepal, vol. 1, 1974, vol. 2, 1979, The Sensuous Immortals, 1977, The Ideal Image: Gupta Sculptures and its Influence, 1978, The Classical Tradition in Rajput Painting, 1978, Elephants and Ivories, 1981, A Buddhist Paradise: Murals of Alchi, 1982, Art of Tibet, 1983, Tibetan Painting, 1984, Art of Nepal, 1985, From Merchants to Emperors, 1986, Indian Sculpture, vol. 1, 1986, Icons of Piety, Images of Whimsey, 1987, Indian Sculpture, vol. 2, 1988, Buddhist Book Illuminations, 1988, Romance of the Taj Mahal, 1989, Art of the Himalayas, 1991, Pleasure Gardens of the Mind, 1993; Indian Painting, vol. 1, 1993, The Peaceful Liberators: Jain Art from India, 1994; gen. editor: Marg mag., 1993—. Bd. dirs. Music Circle, Pasadena, Calif. John D. Rockefeller III Fund fellow, 1964, 69, fellow NEA, 1974; Getty scholar, 1995-96. Fellow Asia Soc. (hon., Bombay); mem. Asiatic Soc. (Calcutta, B.C. Law gold medal 1993). *The guiding principles of my life have been hard work, total commitment to everything I do, whether work or play, fairness in all my dealings and treat everybody equally, whether a prince or a pauper.*

PALADE, GEORGE EMIL, biologist, educator; b. Jassy, Romania, Nov. 19, 1912; came to U.S., 1946, naturalized, 1952; s. Emil and Constanta (Cantemir) P.; m. Irina Malaxa, June 12, 1941 (dec. 1969); children—Georgia Teodora, Philip Theodore; m. Marilyn G. Farquhar, 1970. Bachelor, Hasdeu Lyceum, Buzau, Romania; M.D., U. Bucharest, Romania. Instr., asst. prof., then assoc. prof. anatomy Sch. Medicine, U. Bucharest, 1935-45; vis. investigator, asst. assoc., prof. cell biology Rockefeller U., 1946-73; prof. cell biology Yale U., New Haven, 1973-83; sr. research scientist Yale U., 1983-89; prof.-in-residence, dean sci. affairs Med. Sch., U. Calif., San Diego, 1990—. Author sci. papers. Recipient Albert Lasker Basic Research award, 1966, Gairdner Spl. award, 1967, Horwitz prize, 1970, Nobel prize in Physiology or Medicine, 1974, Nat. Medal Sci., 1986. Fellow Am. Acad. Arts and Scis.; mem. Nat. Acad. Sci., Pontifical Acad. Sci., Royal Soc. (London), Leopoldina Acad. (Halle), Romanian Acad., Royal Belgian Acad. Medicine. Research interests correlated biochem. and morphological analysis cell structures.

PALADINO, ALBERT EDWARD, venture capitalist; b. N.Y.C., Aug. 4, 1932; s. Albert E. and Jennie (Fiato) P.; m. Dorothy M. Hayes (div. June 1979); children: Thomas A., Robert E., Catherine J., Paul F.; m. Susan Flynn, June 11, 1983. BS in Ceramic Engring., Alfred U., 1954, MS in Ceramic Engring., 1956; ScD in Materials Sci., MIT, 1962. Registered profl. engr., Mass. Staff mem. Raytheon Co. Rsch. Div., Waltham, Mass., 1955-59; mgr. materials and crystal growth lab. Raytheon Co. Rsch. Div., Waltham, 1962-69; mgr. materials and techniques group Raytheon Co. Microwave & Power Tube Div., Waltham, 1969-72, mgr. electronics materials group, 1972-75; program mgr. materials Office of Tech. Assessment U.S. Congress, Washington, 1975-78; asst. dir. telephone ops. tech. ctr. GTE Labs., Waltham, 1978-79; dep. dir. Office Energy Programs U.S. Dept. Commerce, Nat. Inst. Standards and Tech., Washington, 1979-81; mng. ptnr. Advanced Tech. Ventures, Boston, 1981—; chmn. bd. dirs. Millitech Corp., South Deerfield, Mass., 1988—, Electro-Scan Corp., Billerica, Mass., 1990-95; bd. dirs. TranSwitch Corp., Shelton, Conn., 1988—, Microwave Networks, Houston, 1990-95, Micro Devices, Greensboro, N.C., 1992—, Thunderbird Techs., Morrisville, N.C., 1992—. Contbr. articles profl. jours.; patentee in field. Pres. West Needham (Mass.) Civic Assn., 1967-69; bd. trustees Alfred U., 1991—; mem. Needham Town Meeting, 1973-74, Rep. Nat. Com., 1988—. Recipient Disting. Svc. resolution Office of Tech. Assessment U.S. Congress, 1978. Fellow Am. Ceramic Soc. (chmn. basic sci. div. 1968-69, chmn. New Eng. sect. 1969-70, Disting. New Eng. Ceramic award), Nat. Venture Capital Assn. Avocations: painting, music, physical fitness, hiking, tennis, reading. Office: Advanced Tech Ventures 10 Post Office Sq Boston MA 02109-4603

PALADINO, JOSEPH ANTHONY, clinical pharmacist; b. Utica, N.Y., May 5, 1953; s. Paul Francis and Jacqueline Ann (Monaco) P.; m. Carol Ann Jenny, June 5, 1976; children: Nicholas Joseph, Matthew Jerome, Kathryn Elizabeth. BS in Biology, Siena Coll., Loudonville, N.Y., 1975; BS in Pharmacy, Mass. Coll. Pharmacy, 1977; D Pharmacy, Med. U. S.C., 1982. Acting dir. pharmacy Utica (N.Y.) Psychiat. Ctr., 1978-80; decentralized pharmacist Med. U. Hosp., Charleston, S.C., 1980-82; asst. dir. pharmacy Rochester (N.Y.) Gen. Hosp., 1982-87, adj. med. staff, 1986-87; clin. instr. pediatrics U. Rochester Sch. Medicine, 1985-87; clin. asst. prof. pharmacy SUNY, Buffalo, 1989-93, clin. assoc. prof., 1994—; dir. pharmacokinetics Millard Fillmore Suburban Hosp., Williamsville, N.Y., 1987—; dir. clin. outcomes and econs. rsch. Millard Fillmore Health System, Buffalo; editorial adv. bd. Jour. of Infectious Disease Pharmacotherapy, 1993—; mem. adv. bd. several major pharm. cos.; 1st vis. prof. pharmacy Tayside Health Bd., Dundee, Scotland, 1992. Big Bro., Big Bros. and Big Sisters, Albany, N.Y., 1972-80; bd. mem., den leader Cub Scouts, Clarence, N.Y., 1989-91; founding bd., coach Clarence Little League Football, 1992-94. Mem. Am. Coll. Clin. Pharmacy (founder, 1st chmn. Outcomes and Econs. Practice and Rsch. Network), Am. Soc. Microbiology, Soc. Infectious Diseases Pharmacists, N.Y. Acad. Scis. Achievements include pioneering a method of treating certain infectious diseases with an early switch from intravenous to oral antibiotics; co-development of a standardized format for dosing charts for critical intravenous medications; discovery of drug interaction between secobarbital and theophylline; integration of switch therapy with pharmacodynamics, outcomes therapy, and health care economics. Office: Millard Fillmore Suburban Hosp 1540 Maple Rd Williamsville NY 14221-3647 *Do not work at a job; it is far bettr to find a career and enjoy your work. Be persistent, take reasoned risks, and understand that what is obvious to you may not be apparent to others - what is easy for you may be arduous for others.*

PALAHNIUK, RICHARD JOHN, anesthesiology educator, researcher; b. Winnipeg, Man., Can., Dec. 5, 1944; s. George and Teenie (Lukinchuk) P.; m. Patricia June Smando, July 15, 1967; children: Christopher, Daniel, Andrew. BS in Medicine, U. Man., 1968, MD, 1968. Head obstetric anaesthesia Health Scis. Ctr., Winnipeg, 1973-79; prof. and chmn. of anaesthesia U. Man., Winnipeg, 1979-89; prof. anesthesiology, head dept. U. Minn., Mpls., 1989—. Contbr. papers and book chpts. to profl. publs.; mem.

editorial bd. Can. Jour. Anaesthesia, Toronto, 1985-89. Fellow Med. Rsch. Coun. Can., 1972, rsch. grantee, 1974-79. Fellow Royal Coll. Physicians of Can.; mem. Can. Anaesthetists' Soc., Am. Soc. Anesthesiology, Internat. Anesthesia Rsch. Soc. (editorial bd. Cleve. chpt. 1987—). Roman Catholic. Avocations: running, fishing, carpentry. Office: U Minn Med Sch 420 Delaware St SE Minneapolis MN 55455-0374

PALAIMA, THOMAS GERARD, classics educator, researcher; b. Cleve., Oct. 6, 1951; s. Michael Aloysius and Ann Dolores (Schulz) P. BA in Math. and Classics, Boston Coll., 1973; PhD in Classics, U. Wis., 1980; HHD (hon.), U. Uppsala, 1994. Asst. prof. Classics Fordham U., Bronx, N.Y., 1980-86; assoc. prof. U. Tex., Austin, 1986-91, Dickson Centennial prof. # 2, 1991—, chair dept., 1994—; dir. summer session Am. Sch. Classical Studies, Athens, 1984; dir. Aegean scripts and prehistory program U. Tex., Austin, 1986—; mem. mng. com. Am. Sch. Classical Studies, 1980—; mem. Mycenaean com. Austrian Acad. Scis., 1993—. Author: The Scribes of Pylos, 1988; editor: Pylos Comes Alive, 1984, Texts, Tablets and Scribes, 1988, Problems in Decipherment, 1989, Studia Mycenaea 1988, 1989, Aegean Seals, Sealings and Administration, 1990; book rev. editor Minos, 1989—. Fulbright fellow, Greece, 1979-80, Austria, 1992-93, Am. Coun. Learned Socs. fellow, 1983, MacArthur Found. fellow, 1985-90; NEH grantee, 1984, 89. Mem. Archaeol. Inst. Am., Am. Philolog. Assn. Democrat. Home: 505 E 40th Austin TX 78751-5103 Office: U Tex Dept Classics Wag 123 Austin TX 78712-1181

PALANCE, JACK, actor; b. Lattimer, Pa., Feb. 18; s. John and Anna (Gramiak) Palahnuik; m. Virginia Baker, Apr. 21, 1949 (div. 1969); children: Holly Kathleen, Brook Gabrielle, Cody John; m. Elaine Rochelle Rogers, May 6, 1987. Student, U. N.C., Stanford U. Appeared in stage plays The Big Two, 1947, Temporary Island, 1948, The Vigil, A Street Car Named Desire, 1948, The Silver Tassle, 1949, Darkness at Noon, 1950, Julius Caesar, The Tempest, 1955; motion pictures include Panic in the Streets, 1950, Halls of Montezuma, Sudden Fear (Acad. award nominee best supporting actor 1952), Shane (Acad. award nominee best supporting actor 1953), Arrowhead, Flight to Tangier, The Silver Chalice, Kiss of Fire, Attack!, Ten Seconds to Hell, The Big Knife, Man in the Attic, Warriors Five, Barabbas, I Died A 1000 Times, The Lonely Man, House of Numbers, Contempt, Torture Garden, Kill a Dragon, They Came to Rob Las Vegas, The Desperadoes, The Mercenary, Justine, Legion of the Damned, A Bullet for Rommel, The McMasters, The Professionals, Chato's Land, Companeros, Che, Oklahoma Crude, Craze, The Four Deuces, The Diamond, Hawk the Slayer, Gor, Bagdad Cafe, Young Guns, The Getaway, The Horsemen, The Shape of Things to Come, Hawk the Slayer, Without Warning, Tango & Cash, Batman 1989, Solar Crisis, 1990, City Slickers, 1991 (Acad. award for Best Supporting Actor 1991), Cops and Robbersons, 1994, City Slickers II: The Legend of Curley's Gold, 1994, Natural Born Killers, 1994, (voice) The Swan Princess, 1994, others; appeared on TV: Requiem for a Heavyweight (Sylvania award), Dr. Jekyll and Mr. Hyde, Dracula, (series) Bronk, 1975-76, (series host) Ripley's Believe It Or Not, (miniseries) Buffalo Girls, 1995. With AC, U.S. Army. Named Most Prominent Newcomer Theatre World, Best Screen Newcomer Look mag. Office: Martin Herwitz 427 N Canon Dr Ste 215 Beverly Hills CA 90210*

PALANS, LLOYD ALEX, lawyer; b. St. Louis, Aug. 6, 1946; s. Hyman Robert and Mae (Sherman) P.; m. Deborah Regn, Aug. 5, 1972; children: Emily Rebecca, Samantha Jane. BS, Tulane U., 1968; JD, U. Mo., 1972. Bar: Mo. 1972, U.S. Dist. Ct. (ea. and we. dists.) Mo. 1972, U.S. Ct. Appeals (8th cir.) 1972, U.S. Ct. Appeals (5th cir.) 1974, U.S. Supreme Ct. 1975, U.S. Ct. Appeals (9th cir.) 1992. Ptnr. Kramer, Chused, Kramer, Shostak & Kohn, St. Louis, 1972-77, Blumenfeld, Marx & Tureen, P.C., St. Louis, 1978-81, Gallop, Johnson & Neuman, St. Louis, 1981-90, Bryan Cave, St. Louis, 1990—; adj. prof. Washington U. Sch. Law, St. Louis, 1989—. Bd. dirs. St. Louis Chpt. ARC, 1987—, St. Louis Chpt. Leukemia Soc., 1988—, Combined Health Appeal Greater St. Louis, 1988—, Combined Health Appeal of Am., 1990. Mem. ABA, Mo. Bar, St. Louis Met. Bar Assn. Office: Bryan Cave 1 Metro Sq 211 N Broadway Saint Louis MO 63102-2733

PALAST, GERI D., federal agency administrator. BA in Polit. Sci., Stanford U., 1972; JD, NYU, 1976. Atty., legis. program analyst Am. Fedn. State County and Mcpl. Employees, Washington, 1976-77; legal counsel, field rep. Nat. Treasury Employers Union, Washington, 1977-79; dir., supervising atty. Nat. Employment Law Project, Washington, 1979-81; dir. politics and legislation Svc. Employees Internat. Union, AFL-CIO, Washington, 1981-93; asst. sec. congrl. and intergovtl. affairs Dept. Labor, Washington, 1993—. Office: Dept Labor Congl & Intergovtl Affairs 200 Constitution Ave NW Washington DC 20210-0001

PALAY, GILBERT, temporary help services company executive; b. 1927. BBA, U. Wis. CPA. Ptnr. Zetley and Palay, 1960-76; with Manpower Inc., 1976—, v.p., 1976-77, v.p. planning and devel., from 1977, since exec. v.p., now sr. exec. v.p.; now cons. Office: Manpower Inc Box 2053 5301 N Ironwood Ln Milwaukee WI 53217-4910*

PALAY, SANFORD LOUIS, retired scientist, educator; b. Cleve., Sept. 23, 1918; s. Harry and Lena (Sugarman) P.; m. Victoria Chan Curtis, 1970 (div. Nov. 1990); children: Victoria Li-Mei, Rebecca Li-Ming. A.B., Oberlin Coll., 1940; M.D. (Hoover prize scholar 1943), Western Res. U., 1943. Teaching fellow medicine, rsch. assoc. anatomy Western Res. U., Cleve., 1945-46; NRC fellow med. scis. Rockefeller Inst., 1948, vis. investigator, 1953; from instr. anatomy to assoc. prof. anatomy Yale U., 1949-56; chief sect. neurocytology, lab. neuroanatomical scis. Nat. Inst. Neurol. Diseases and Blindness, NIH, Washington, 1956-61; chief lab. neuroanatomical scis. Nat. Inst. Neurol. Diseases and Blindness, NIH, 1960-61; Bullard prof. neuroanatomy Harvard, Boston, 1961-89, prof. emeritus, 1989—; Linnean Soc. lectr., London, 1959; vis. investigator Middlesex Hosp. (Bland-Sutton Inst.), London, Eng., 1961; Phillips lectr. Haverford Coll., 1959; Ramsay Henderson Trust lectr. U. Edinburgh, Scotland, 1962; George H. Bishop lectr.. Washington U., St. Louis, 1990; Disting. Scientist lectr. Tulane U. Sch. Medicine, 1969, 75; vis. prof. U. Wash., 1969; Rogowski Meml. lectr. Yale, 1973; Disting. lectr. biol. structure U. Miami, 1974; Disting. Scientist lectr. U. Ark., 1977; Disting. scholar-in-residence dept. biology Boston Coll., Chestnut Hill, Mass., 1994—; other Disting. lectureships; vis. prof. U. Osaka, Japan, 1978, Nat. U. Singapore, 1983; spl. vis. prof. U. Osaka, 1988; chmn. study sect. on behavioral and neural scis. NIH, 1984-86; mem. fellowship bd. NIH, 1958-61, cell biology study sect., 1959-65, adv. com. high voltage electron microscope resources, 1973-80, mem. rev. com. behavioral and neurol. scis. fellowships, 1979-86; chmn. Gordon Research Conf. Cell Structure and Metabolism, 1960; assoc. Neurosci. Research Program, 1962-67, cons. assoc., 1975—; mem. anat. scis. tng. com. Nat. Inst. Gen. Med. Scis., 1968-72; mem. sci. adv. com. Oreg. Regional Primate Research Center, 1971-76. Author: The Fine Structure of the Nervous System, 1970, 3d edit., 1991, Cerebellar Cortex, Cytology and Organization, 1974; editor: Frontiers of Cytology, 1958, The Cerebellum, New Vistas, 1982; mem. sci. coun. Progress in Neuropharmacology and Jour. Neuropharmacology, 1961-66; mem. editorial bd. Exptl. Neurology, 1959-76, Jour. Cell Biology, 1962-67, Brain Research, 1965-71, Jour. Comparative Neurology, 1966—, Jour. Ultrastructure Research, 1966-86, Jour. of Neurocytology, 1972-87, Exptl. Brain Research, 1965-76, Neurosci, 1975-95, Anatomy and Embryology, 1968; co-mng. editor, 1978-88; editor in chief Jour. Comparative Neurology, 1981-93, editor emeritus, 1994—; mem. adv. bd. editors Jour. Neuropathology and Exptl. Neurology, 1963-82, Internat. Jour. Neurosci, 1969-74, Tissue and Cell, 1969-86; contbr. articles to profl. jours. Served to capt. M.C. AUS, 1946-47. Recipient 50 Best Books of 1974 award Internat. Book Fair, Frankfurt, Fed. Republic Germany, Best Book in Profl. Readership award Am. Med. Writers Assn., 1975, Biomed. Rsch. award Assn. Am. Med. Colls., 1989, Lashley award Am. Philos. Soc., 1991, Camillo Golgi award Fidia Rsch. Found., 1992; Guggenheim fellow, 1971-72; Fogarty scholar-in-residence NIH, Bethesda, 1980-81. Fellow Am. Acad. Arts and Scis.; mem. NAS, Am. Assn. Anatomists (chmn. nominating com. 1964, mem. exec. com. 1970-74, anat. nomenclature com. 1975-78, pres. 1980-81, Henry Gray award 1990), Histochem. Soc., Electron Microscope Soc. Am., AAAS, Am. Soc. Cell Biology (program com. 1975), Internat. Soc. Cell Biology, Soc. for Neurosci. (Gerard award 1990), Washington Soc. Electron Microscopy (organizing com., sec.-treas. 1956-58), Soc. Francaise de Microscopie Electronique (hon.), Royal Microscopical Soc. (hon.), Golgi Soc. (hon.), Anat. Soc. Gr. Britain and Ireland (hon.), Cajal Club (pres. 1973-74), Phi Beta Kappa, Sigma Xi, Alpha Omega Alpha. Home: 78 Temple Rd Concord MA 01742-1520

PALAZZI, JOSEPH L(AZARRO), manufacturing executive; b. New Haven, July 5, 1947; s. Joseph Anthony and Helen (Volosovich) P.; m. Lorna May Mickiewicz, May 27, 1978. BS, Quinnipiac Coll., 1969; MBA, U. New Haven, 1973. Mgr. budgets The Stanley Works, New Britian, Conn., 1972-76; mgr. planning Bangor Punta Corp., Greenwich, Conn., 1976-79; asst. corp. controller Pepperidge Farm, Norwalk, Conn., 1979-81, dir. fin. services, 1981-82, group controller, 1982-83; corp. controller Plessey, Inc., White Plains, N.Y., 1983-84, v.p. finance, 1984-86, chief fin. officer, 1986-89; v.p. fin., chief fin. officer BTR Inc., Stanford, Ct., 1990-92; pres. Fasco Industries Inc., Chesterfield, Mo., 1992—. Mem. Rep. Town Com., Newtown, Conn., 1981; bd. dirs. Danbury Hosp., 1987-92. Served with U.S. Army, 1969-76. Mem. AICPA, Nat. Assn. Accts., Sigma Six Flying Club. Episcopalian. Avocations: sailing, tennis, golf, flying. Home: 39 Villa Coublay Saint Louis MO 63131-2730 Office: Fasco Industries Inc 500 Chesterfield Ctr Ste 200 Chesterfield MO 63017-4823

PALDUS, JOSEF, mathematics educator; b. Bzi, Czechoslovakia, Nov. 25, 1935; emigrated to Can., 1968; s. Josef and Ludmila (Danicek) P.; m. Eva Zdena Bajer, Jan. 26, 1961; 1 dau., Barbara Alice. MSc, Charles U., Prague, 1958, DrSc, 1995; PhD, Czechoslovak Acad. Sci., Prague, 1961. Research scientist Czechoslovak Acad. Scis., Prague, 1961-62, 64-68; postdoctoral fellow NRC, Ottawa, Can., 1962-64; assoc. prof. applied math. U. Waterloo, Ont., Can., 1968-75, prof., 1975—; assoc. dir. Fields Inst., 1992-95; vis. prof. U. Rheims, 1973, U. Louis Pasteur, Strasbourg, France, 1975-76, 82-83, Cath. U., Nijmegen, Holland, 1981, Technion, Haifa, Israel, 1983; vis. scientist NRC, Ottawa, 1966-68, Free U. Berlin, 1981; adj. prof. chemistry U. Fla., Gainesville, 1984—; fellow Inst. for Advanced Study, Berlin, 1986-87. Mem. editl. bd. Comtex Sci., 1981-83, Advances in Quantum Chemistry, 1986, Jour. Chem. Physics, 1987-89, Can. Jour. Chemistry, 1994, Internat. Jour. Quantum Chemistry, 1996; mem. adv. editl. bd. Internat. Jour. Quantum Chemistry, 1977-88, Theoretica Chimica Acta, 1988-94, Jour. Math. Chemistry, Switzerland, 1989; contbr. numerous articles to profl. jours., chpts. to books. Killam Rsch. fellow, 1987-89; recipient prize Chemistry divsn. Czechoslovak Acad. Scis., 1962, 67, J. Heyrovsky Gold medal Czechoslovak Acad. Sci., 1992, Gold medal Faculty of Math and Physics, Comenius U., Slovakia, 1994, Alexander von Humboldt Sr. Scientist award, 1996. Fellow Royal Soc. Can.; mem. Internat. Acad. Quantum Molecular Sci., Internat. Soc. Theoretical Chem. Physics (bd. dirs.), European Acad. Scis., Czech Learned Soc. (hon. mem.), Arts and Letters (corr.), Am. Inst. Physics, N.Y. Acad. Scis., Applied Math. Soc. Can., Can. Soc. for Chemistry, Chem. Inst. Can. Roman Catholic. Office: U Waterloo Dept Applied Math, University Ave, Waterloo, ON Canada N2L 3G1

PALECEK, SANDRA MARIE, reading education specialist; b. Ashland, Wis., Oct. 31, 1940; d. Francis Joseph and Martha Evelyn (Verville) Bonneville; m. John Allan Palecek, Oct. 3, 1964; children: Stephanie Lynn, Michael John. BS in Elem. Edn., U. River Falls, 1971; MS in Reading, U. Superior, 1981. Tchr. grades 2 and 3 Spring Valley (Wis.) Sch., 1959-62; tchr. grade 2 Pleasant Hill Sch., Waukesha, Wis., 1962-64; tchr. grades 2 and 3 Glidden (Wis.) Sch., 1964-65; Chpt. I tchr. Butternut (Wis.) Sch., 1966-68; Chpt. I reading specialist Glidden Schs., 1968—; amb. of reading People to People to China, 1993. Pres. Chequmegon Reading Coun., Park Falls, Wis., 1981. Herb Kohl fellow, 1994; recipient Outstanding Svc. award Title I Program, Glidden, 1980, Significant Contbns. award Chpt. I Program, Madison, Wis., 1990; named Dist. Tchr. of Yr., Dept. Pub. Instrn., Madison, 1980, 94, Exemplary Remedial Reading award, 1989, 30 Yr. Svc. award Chpt. I, New Orleans, 1996. Mem. Internat. Reading Assn., Wis. State Reading Assn., Glidden Fedn. Tchrs. Union (v.p., then pres.). Avocations: reading, hiking, cross-country skiing, bowling. Home: N15517 Town Hall Rd Park Falls WI 54552-8069 Office: Glidden Sch Glidden WI 54527

PALERMO, ANTHONY ROBERT, lawyer; b. Rochester, N.Y., Sept. 30, 1929; s. Anthony C. and Mary (Palvino) P.; m. Mary Ann Coyne, Jan. 2, 1960; children: Mark Henry, Christopher Coyne, Peter Stuart, Elisabeth Megan McCarthy, Julie Coyne Lawther, Gregg Anthony. BA, U. Mich., 1951; JD, Georgetown U., 1956. Bar: D.C. 1956, N.Y. 1957, U.S. Supreme Ct. 1961. Trial atty. U.S. Dept. Justice, Washington, 1956-58; asst. atty. U.S. Dept. Justice, N.Y.C., 1958-60; asst. U.S. atty. in charge U.S. Dept. Justice, Rochester, N.Y., 1960-61; ptnr. Brennan, Centner, Palermo & Blauvelt, Rochester, 1962-81, Harter, Secrest & Emery, Rochester, 1981-94, Hodgson, Russ, Andrews, Woods & Goodyear, Rochester, 1994—. Note editor Georgetown Law Jour., 1956. Bd. dirs. McQuaid Jesuit H.S., Rochester, 1978-84, St. Ann's Home for Aged, Rochester, 1978-84, St. Ann's Home for Aged, Rochester, 1974—; bd. dirs., sec. St. Ann's Home Found., Rochester, 1989—; trustee, charter chmn. Clients' Security Fund N.Y., 1981-90; chmn. Govs. Jud. Screening Com. 4th Jud. Dept., mem. statewide com., 1987-89; chair magistrate selection com. U.S. Dist. Ct. (we. dist.) N.Y., 1995. Fellow Am. Bar Found., N.Y. State Bar Found. (bd. dirs. 1978-91), Am. Coll. Trial Lawyers; mem. ABA (ho. dels. 1980—, state del. 1982-85, bd. govs. 1985-88, 1989-93, sec. 1990-93), N.Y. State Bar Assn. (pres. 1979-80, ho. dels. 1973-75, 77—), Monroe County Bar Assn. (pres. 1973), Oak Hill Country Club. Roman Catholic. Avocation: golf. Home: 38 Huntington Meadow Rochester NY 14625

PALERMO, DAVID STUART, retired psychology educator and administrator. BS in Psychology and Edn., Lynchburg Coll., 1951; MS in Psychology, U. Mass., 1953; PhD, U. Iowa, 1955. Rsch. assoc. Iowa Child Welfare Rsch. Sta. U. Iowa, 1955; asst. prof. psychology So. Ill. U., Carbondale, 1955-58; asst. prof. Inst. Child Devel. U. Minn., Mpls., 1958-63; vis. prof. dept. psychology U. Edinburgh, Scotland, 1969-70; sr. Fulbright scholar dept. psychology U. Sydney, Australia, 1975; prof. Inst. Advanced Psychol. Studies Adelphi U., Garden City, L.I., N.Y., 1978-79; assoc. prof. Pa. State U., University Park, 1963-66, prof., 1966—, assoc. dir. Ctr. for the Study of Child, Adolescent Devel., 1984-88, assoc. dean for rsch. and grad. studies, Coll. Liberal Arts, 1988-92; prof. emeritus, 1992—; assoc. The Behavioral and Brain Scis., 1982—. Editor Child Development Abstracts and Bibliography, 1971-74; editor Jour. Exptl. Child Psychology, 1973-83, mem. editorial bd., 1966—; mem. editorial bd. Jour. Verbal Learning and Verbal Behavior, 1964-77, Metaphor and Symbolic Activity, 1983—, Cognitive Devel., 1990-93; contbr. numerous articles to profl. jours. Recipient Career Devel. award Nat. Inst. of Child Health and Human Devel. award, 1965-70. Fellow APA; mem. Soc. for Rsch. in Child Devel., Ea. Psychol. Assn., Jean Piaget Soc., Sigma Xi,.

PALERMO, GREGORY SEBASTIAN, architect; b. Westfield, N.Y., Oct. 28, 1946; s. Sebastian and Frances Joan (Ciminella) P.; divorced; children: Mark Sebastian, Christopher Anthony. BArch, Carnegie Mellon U., 1969; MArch in Urban Design, Wash. U., 1976. Registered architect, Mo., Calif., N.Y., Iowa. Architect PGAV Inc., St. Louis, 1976-79; sr. v.p. HOK, Inc., St. Louis, 1980-87; sr. assoc. Mackey Assocs., St. Louis, 1987-89; v.p., prin. Stone Marraccini Patterson, St. Louis, 1989-91; affiliate asst. prof. Washington U. Sch. Arch., 1984-90; vis. assoc. prof. Iowa State U. Dept. Arch., 1992-95, assoc. prof., 1995—; chair Des Moines Archtl. Adv. Com., 1996; mem. Des Moines Gateway Planning Com., 1996. Editorial bd. Iowa Architect mag., 1992—, assoc. ed., 1995—. Mem. Light Rail Transit Rev. Com., 1985, St. Louis Mayoral Task Force, 1986; exec/coun. Arts in Transit Com., St. Louis, 1987—; chmn. design rev. com.,St. Louis Metrolink Transit System, 1989-91; chair Nat. AIA Edn. Task Force, 1990; mem. Leadership St. Louis, 1990-91, Archtl. Adv. Commn. city of Des Moines, 1992—. Fellow AIA (bd. dirs., nat. v.p.); mem. Nat. Archtl. Accreditation Bd (pres. 1993-94). Office: Iowa State U Rm 156 Dept Architecture Ames IA 50011-3093

PALERMO, PETER M., JR., photography equipment company executive; b. Rochester, N.Y., Aug. 21, 1941; s. Peter M. and Adeline M. (Bruno) P.; m. Marcia G. Hendershott, Aug. 25, 1962; children: Peter M., Lisa M., Michelle A. B.A., Bowling Green U., 1963; M.B.A., U. Rochester, 1973. Mgr. mktg. Kodak Caribbean, Ltd., San Juan, P.R., 1976-79; gen. mgr. Kodak Philippines Ltd., Manila, 1979-81; gen. mgr. Mexican Ops. Eastman Kodak Co. Internat. Photo div., Mexico City, 1983-84; corp. v.p., gen. mgr. Eastman Kodak Co. Health Scis. div., Rochester, N.Y., 1984-86; corp. v.p., gen. mgr. consumer products div. Eastman Kodak Co., Rochester, 1986—, corp. v.p., gen. mgr. consumer imaging, 1991-93, v.p., dir. mktg., sr. v.p. imaging, 1993—; pres., CEO The Jason Found. for Edn., Pittsford, N.Y., 1993—; pres. Ultra Techs. div. Eastman Tech., Inc. (subs. Eastman Kodak Co.), 1989—; adj. faculty mem. Rochester Inst. of Tech., 1965-69. Contbr. articles to profl. jours. Bd. dirs. Spl. Olympics, 1990. Recipient Catholic Media award Pope John Paul II, Manila, 1981; named one of Outstanding Young Men of Am., 1973. Fellow Profl. Photog. Soc. of Philippines; mem. Health Industry Mfrs. Assn. (corp. mem., trustee 4-H com. 1990), Internat. Mgmt. Assn. (corp. mem.), Photo Mktg. Assn. Internat. (corp. mem.), Assn. Photog. Mfrs. Mex. Republican. Roman Catholic. Clubs: Manila Polo, Dorado Beach Country P.R. Lodge: Rotary (dir. Manila, 1979-81). Avocations: scuba diving; writing; photography; tennis. Office: Pres/CEO The Jason Fund for Edn 40A Grove St Pittsford NY 14534-1326

PALERMO, STEVE, sportscaster, color analyst, former umpire; b. Worcester, Mass., Oct. 9, 1949; m. Debbie, 1991. Attended, Norwich U., Worcester State Coll. Umpire N.Y. Penn League, 1972; umpire winter baseball P.R., Fla., and, Dominican Republic, 1972-74; umpire, single A baseball Carolina League, 1973; umpire, double A baseball Ea. League, 1973-74; umpire, triple A baseball Am. Assn., 1975-76; umpire Am. League Baseball, 1977-91; sports caster Seattle Mariners, 1992-94; sports caster MSG Network, 1994—, back-up color analyst, 1994—; sports analyst The Baseball Network, 1994—; umpire Am. League Championships, 1980, 82, 84, 89, World Series, 1983, Baseball All-Star Game, 1986; spl. asst. Major League Baseball Exec. Coun., 1994—. Co-founder Steve Palermo Found. for Spinal Cord Injuries, Overland Park, Kans. Recipient over 25 awards for courage and dedication, Arthur Ashe Courage award, 1994; named Sporting News # 1 Rated Am. League Umpire, 1991. Office: MSG Network 2 Penn Plz 14th fl New York NY 10121

PALESKY, CAROL EAST, tax accountant; b. Orange, N.J., May 13, 1940; d. Neil Norell and Marie R. Reiss; m. Jacob Palesky; children: Donna, Lewis. AB, Am. Inst., Pleasantville, N.J., 1973; postgrad., Am. Inst., Portland, Maine, 1980; student, Atlantic C.C., Mays Landing, N.J., 1971-73. With mgmt. First Nat. Bank of South Jersey (now First Fidelity), Pleasantville, N.J., 1967-74; loan officer Maine Savs. Bank, Portland, 1980-81; acct., owner East Assocs., Topsham, Maine, 1985—. Treas., bd. dirs. Congl. Term Limits Coalition, Topsham, 1993—; bd. dirs. Maine Citizens Rev. Bd., Portland, 1993—. Scholar Nat. Taxpayer Union, 1992, 94; recipient United to Serve Am. award, 1992. Mem. Nat. Assn. Small Business Owners, Maine Taxpayers Action Network (pres. 1990—), Topsham Taxpayer Assn. (pres. 1991—). Roman Catholic. Home and Office: 24 Sokokis Cir Topsham ME 04086-1615

PALEY, ALBERT RAYMOND, art educator, sculptor; b. Phila., Mar. 28, 1944; s. Albert Raymond and Dorothy (Appelgren) P.; B.F.A., Temple U., 1966, M.F.A., 1969; PhD (hon.), U. Rochester, 1989. Instr. art Tyler Sch. Art, Temple U., Phila., 1962-66; asst. prof. Sch. Am. Craftsmen, Rochester Inst. Tech., N.Y., 1969-72, prof. Coll. Fine and Applied Arts, 1984—; Morris Endowed Chair Coll. Fine and Applied Arts Sch. Am. Crafts, Rochester Inst. Tech., 1985-87; prof. art SUNY-Brockport, 1972-84; now Endowed artist in res. Paley Studio; cons. Rochester Inst. Tech., 1978, Haystack Sch. Crafts, Deer Isle, Maine, 1979, Pa. Ave. Devel. Corp., Washington, 1979, Margaret Woodbury Strong Mus., Rochester, N.Y., 1980. Prin. works include portal gates Renwick Gallery, Smithsonian Instn., Washington, sculpture court enclosure Hunter Mus. Art, Chattanooga, portal gates N.Y. State Senate, Albany, exterior sculpture Margaret Woodbury Strong Mus., Rochester, 800 tree grates & 30 benches, Pa. Ave. Devel. Corp., Washington, poster cases Port Authority of Allegheny County, Pitts., exterior sculpture Harro Theatre East, Rochester, N.Y., gates Va. Mus. Fine Arts, Richmond, sculpture The Willard, Washington, sculptures Wortham Theater Ctr., Houston, Milk Street Sta., Boston, Mus. of Fine Arts, Boston, Hartford, Conn. City Courthouse, Marco Philharmonic, Naples, Fla., Birmingham (Ala.) Mus. of Fine Art, Cornell U., Lasdon Biomed. Rsch. Ctr., N.Y.C., Washington Hebrew Congregation, Main Street Bridge Railings, Rochester; exterior sculpture Olympia at Promenade Two Bldg., The Landmarks Group, 1990, sculpture Aurora at Roanoke (Va.) Regional Airport, 1990, Ceremonial Gates at Ariz. State U., 1991; jewelry exhbn. at Renwick Gallery, Washington, Nat. Mus. Am. Art, 1992; exterior sculpture Criss Cross, Silver Spring, Md., 1992, interior sculpture screens for Fed. Courthouse, Camden, N.J., 1993. Nat. Endowment for Arts grantee, 1975, 76, 79, 84; recipient award of excellence Rochester chpt. AIAA, 1982; design in steel award Iron and Steel Inst., 1975, Artists fellow N.Y. Found. Arts, 1991; Lillian Fairchild award, U. Rochester, 1975; certificate of honor Tyler Sch. Art, Temple U., 1981. Mem. Artist and Blacksmith Assn. N.Am., Am. Craftsman Council. Office: Paley Studio Ltd 25 N Washington St Rochester NY 14614-1110*

PALEY, ALFRED IRVING, value engineering and consulting company executive, lecturer; b. Monticello, N.Y., Apr. 12, 1927; s. Max and Dora (Gutkin) P.; m. Sylvia Tiffel, June 26, 1949; children: Maureen, Howard, Doreen. BEE, Poly. Inst. Bklyn., 1949. Sr. engr. W.L. Maxson Corp., N.Y.C., 1950-58; chief engr. Acoustica Assocs., Mineola, N.Y., 1958-60; staff scientist in acoustics Am. Bosch Arma Corp., Garden City, N.Y., 1960-62; chief engr. in elec. acoustics Janus Products, Syosset, N.Y., 1962-63; mgr. Anti-Submarine Warfare systems Gyrodyne Co. of Am., St. James, N.Y., 1963-67; mgr. cost and value control Loral Electronic Systems, Yonkers, N.Y., 1967-80; v.p. program mgmt. FEL Corp., Farmingdale, N.J., 1980-84; pres. NRI Assocs., 1984—; value engrng. program mgr. CECOM, U.S. Army, Ft. Monmouth, N.J., 1985-95, ret. 1995; assoc. prof. Poly. Inst. Bklyn., 1955-65, Hofstra U., Hempstead, N.Y., 1974-79; lectr. Am. Mgmt. Assn., N.Y.C., 1973-80. Contbr. articles to profl. jours. Patentee in field. Bd. dirs. Suburban Temple, Wantagh, N.Y., 1964-80, Monmouth Reform Temple, Tinton Falls, N.J., 1983-91. Served with USN, 1945-46. Recipient Outstanding Achivement Through Value Engrng. award Dept. Def., 1995. Mem. Project Mgmt. Inst., Soc. Info. Display, (sec. 1978), Nat. Mgmt. Assn. (pres. chpt. 1975-76), Soc. Am. Value Engrs. (fellow, cert. tech. v.p. svcs. 1993—, pres. met. N.Y. chpt. 1986-91, Value Engr. of Yr. 1985-86, 88-89, Disting. Svc. award 1991). Democrat. Jewish. Home and Office: 5442 N Whitethorn Pl Tucson AZ 85704-2634

PALEY, GERALD LARRY, lawyer; b. Albany, N.Y., Sept. 11, 1939; s. Arthur and Mary (Peckner) P.; m. Joyce R., June 25, 1961 (div. June 1985); children: Jonathan, Eric, Suzanne; m. Sheryl Gae, Aug. 14, 1985. BA, Union Coll., 1961; JD with distinction, Cornell U., 1964. Bar: N.Y. 1964. Assoc. Nixon, Hargrave, Devans & Doyle, Rochester, N.Y., 1964-69; assoc. solicitor Dept. Labor, Washington, 1969-71; ptnr. Nixon, Hargrave, Devans & Doyle, Rochester, 1971-87, Phillips, Lytle, Hitchcock, Blaine & Huber, Rochester, 1987—. Author: Handbook of Federal Labor Relations Laws, 1981, Understand Employee Regulations, 1984. Mem. ABA. Republican. Jewish. Office: Phillips Lytle Hitchcock et al 1400 First Federal Pla Rochester NY 14614

PALEY, GRACE, author, educator; b. N.Y.C., Dec. 11, 1922; d. Isaac and Mary (Ridnyik) Goodside; m. Jess Paley, June 20, 1942; children: Nora, Dan.; m. Robert Nichols, 1972. Ed., Hunter Coll., NYU. Formerly tchr. Columbia, Syracuse U.; ret. mem. lit. faculty Sarah Lawrence Coll., Stanford, Johns Hopkins, Dartmouth. Author: The Little Disturbances of Man, 1959, Enormous Changes at the Last Minute, 1974, Leaning Forward, 1985, Later the Same Day, 1985, Long Walks and Intimate Talks, 1991, New and Collected Poems, 1992, The Collected Stories, 1994 (Nat. Book award nomination 1994); stories published in Atlantic, Esquire, Ikon, Genesis West, Accent, others. Sec. N.Y. Greenwich Village Peace Center. Recipient Literary award for short story writing Nat. Inst. Arts and Letters, 1970, Edith Wharton award N.Y. State, 1988, 89, Rea award for short story, 1993, Vt. Gov.'s award for Excellence in the Arts, 1993, award for contbn. to Jewish culture Nat. Found. Jewish Culture; Guggenheim fellow. Mem. Am. Acad. and Inst. Arts and Letters. Office: PO Box 620 Thetford VT 05074-0620

PALIA, ASPY PHIROZE, marketing educator, researcher, consultant; b. Bombay, Nov. 27, 1944; came to U.S., 1973; s. Phiroze E. and Homai P. (Irani) P. BE in Mech. Engring., U. Bangalore, 1966; MBA, U. Hawaii at Manoa, 1976; DBA, Kent State U., 1985. Sales engr. Larsen & Toubro Ltd., 1966-72, export sales engr., 1972-73; teaching fellow Coll. Bus. Adminstrn. Kent State U., 1977-80, instr. Coll. Bus. Adminstrn., 1982-84; asst. prof. Coll. Bus. Adminstrn. U. Hawaii, Manoa, 1984-89, assoc. prof., 1990—, pres. faculty coun., 1995-96; vis. prof. Coll. Mgmt. Nat. Sun Yat-sen U.,

Kaohsiung, Taiwan, 1992, Chulalongkorn U., Bangkok, Thailand, 1992, 93, U. Otago, New Zealand, 1995, Adminstrv. Staff Coll. India, Hyderabad, 1992; mem. U. Hawaii Manoa Ctr. for Teaching Excellence Faculty Adv. Group, 1991; mem. mktg. plan adv. com. U. Hawaii, Manoa, 1994, mem. honors and awards com., 1990-91, pres. faculty coun. 1995-96; vis. scholar faculty bus. adminstrn. Nat. U. Singapore, 1991, Mktg. Inst. Singapore Exec. Devel. Seminars, 1991, 94-95; affiliate faculty Japan Am. Inst. Mgmt. Sci., Honolulu, 1989—; vis. prof. Grad. Sch. Internat. Mgmt., Internat. U. Japan, Uhrasa, Yamato-machi, 1991, U. Internat. Bus. and Econs., Beijing, 1991, U. Kebangsaan Malaysia, Bangi-Selangor, Kuala Lumpur, Malaysia, 1991, 92; lectr., cons., presenter in field. Editor: (with Dennis A. Rondinelli) Project Planning and Implementation in Developing Countries, 1976; contbr. conf. procs. and articles to profl. jours. and books, including Indsl. Mktg. Mgmt., Internat. Bus. Jour., Asia-Pacific Jour. Mgmt., Internat. Mktg. Rev., Fgn. Trade Rev., Internat. Rev. Econs. & Bus., others; contbr. to numerous confs. and symposia in field; developer various mktg. decision support systems and decision-making tools for use in strategic market planning and in marketing simulations. Mem. various program rev. coms. Pacific and Asian Mgmt. Inst., Acad. Internat. Bus., Assn. Bus. Simulation and Exptl. Learning, others; bd. examiners Nat. U. Singapore Sch. Postgrad. Mgmt. Studies, 1991; mem. adv. bd. Soc. Coll. of Bus. Adminstrn. Alumni and Friends Exec. Com., 1991-93; adv. bd. Salvation Army Resdl. Treatment Facilities for Children and Youth Adv. Coun., 1989—, vice chair, 1987-89; treas., bd. dirs. Kings Gate Homeowners Assn., 1994—. Univ. fellow Kent State U., 1983; East-West Ctr. scholar East-West Ctr., 1973-75; Ednl. Improvement Fund grantee, 1989, Instrl. Travel and Devel. Fund grantee Office Faculty Devel. and Acad. Support, 1991, 95, joint rsch. grants U. Kebangsaan Malaysia, Nat. U. Singapore, U. So. Queensland, Australia, U. Otago, New Zealand; recipient Internat. Agreements Fund award Office Internat. Programs and Svcs., 1990-91, 91-92, ORA travel award U. Rsch. Coun., 1986, 88, 89, 91, 92, 94, 95. Mem. Am. Mktg. Assn. (academia editor Honolulu chpt. 1986-87), Acad. Internat. Bus. (chair Pacific Basin Region 1995, chair Pacific Basin chpt. 1996), Pacific Asian Consortium for Internat. Bus. Edn. and Rsch., Assn. for Bus. Simulation and Exptl. Learning, Pan-Pacific Bus. Assn. (charter), Mortar Bd. (Outstanding Educator award 1993, Mentor award 1995), East-West Ctr. Alumni Assn. U.S. (v.p. Hawaii chpt. 1987-89, ad campaign com. 1987-88), Beta Gamma Sigma (faculty advisor, sec.-treas. Alpha of Hawaii chpt. 1990—, Outstanding Svc. award 1992-93), Mu Kappa Tau, Pi Sigma Epsilon. Avocations: music, photography, swimming, reading, hiking. Home: 2724 Kahoaloha Ln Apt 1605 Honolulu HI 96826-3337 Office: U Hawaii Manoa Dept Mktg 2404 Maile Way Honolulu HI 96822-2223

PALIHNICH, NICHOLAS JOSEPH, JR., retail chain executive; b. Montclair, N.J., Nov. 9, 1939; s. Nicholas Joseph and Lucille (Pflugh) P.; m. Diane Lorraine Parise, Nov. 12, 1966; children: Nicholas, Kristin, Danielle. B.B.A., U. Notre Dame, 1961. Retail buyer R.H. Macy, N.Y.C., 1961-66, Korvettes, Inc., N.Y.C., 1966-69; retail v.p., gen. mdse. mgr. Mangurians Inc., Ft. Lauderdale, Fla., 1970-72; sr. v.p. retail mgmt. Korvettes Inc., N.Y.C., 1973-79; pres. Korvettes Inc., 1979-81; sr. v.p. retail mgmt. Lane Bryant, 1981-83; pres. retail mgmt. Dan Inc., 1984-86; exec. v.p. retail Bally U.S.A, 1987-93; dir. retail The Rockport Co., Marlborough, Mass., 1994—. Served with U.S. Army, 1962. Republican. Roman Catholic. Office: 220 Donald Lynch Blvd Marlborough MA 01752-4708

PALIN, MICHAEL EDWARD, actor, screenwriter, author; b. May 5, 1943; s. Edward and Mary P.; m. Helen M. Gibbons, 1966; 3 children. BA, U. Oxford, Eng., 1965. Writer, performer BBC Corp., 1965-69. Actor, writer: (TV shows) Monty Python's Flying Circus, 1969-74, Ripping Yarns, 1976-80; (films) And Now for Something Completely Different, 1970, Monty Python and the Holy Grail, 1974, Monty Python's Life of Brian, 1978, Time Bandits, 1980, Monty Python's The Meaning of Life, 1982, American Friends, 1991; TV presenter, writer Around the World in 80 Days, 1989, Pole to Pole, 1993, Palin's Column, 1994; actor: (TV shows) Three Men in a Boat, 1975, GBH, 1991; (films) Jabberwocky, 1976, A Private Function, 1984, Brazil, 1985, A Fish Called Wanda (Best Supporting Actor Brit. Acad. Film and TV Arts, 1989); actor, writer and co-producer: The Missionary, 1982; writer (stage play) The Weekend, 1994; author: Monty Python's Brand New Book, 1973, Dr. Fegg's Encyclopaedia of All World Knowledge, 1984, Limericks, 1985, Around the World in 80 Days, 1989, Pole to Pole, 1993, Pole to Pole: The Photographs, 1994, Hemingway's Chair 1995; (children's books) Small Harry and the Toothache Pills, 1981, The Mirrorstone, 1986, The Cyril Stories, 1986. Co-recipient (with Monty Python) Michael Balcon award for outstanding contribution to cinema British Academy of Film and TV Arts, 1987. Avocations: reading, running, railways. Office: 68 A Delancey St, London NW1 7RY, England

PALINSKY, CONSTANCE GENEVIEVE, hypnotherapist, educator; b. Flint, Mich., May 31, 1927; d. George and Genevieve Treasa (Pisarski) Ignace; m. Joseph Palinsky, July 3, 1947; children: Joseph II, Mark Robert. Art student, Flint Inst. Arts, Oriental Artists Sch., others; numerous hypnosis studies including, Ethical Tng. Hypnosis Ctr., N.J. and Fla., Mid-West Inst., Hypnodye Found, Ill. and Fla.; tng., Nat. Guild Hypnotherapists. Cert NLP practitioner, neuro linguistics programmer. Owner, operator Palinsky Gallery of Art and Antiques, Flint, 1970-80; art lectr. Genesee County Grade Sch. System Flint Inst. Arts, 1972-74; owner, hypnosis cons. Hypno-Tech. Ctr., Flint, 1975-80; asst. mgr. Wethered-Rice Fine Jewelry, Flint, 1982-83; hypnotherapist, sr. cons. Dailey Life Ctr., Flint, 1985-95; mem. Am. Bd. Hypnotherapy, Calif.; numerous radio and TV shows and guest appearances, Flint, 1957—, ABC Nat. Network, 1959, Flint Calbe TV, 1972, others. Author: Constructive Personality Development, 1987, Secrets Revealed for Hypnosys Scripting, 1989, Designing Hypnosis Scripts for Relief of Multiple Sclerosis, 1994, Substance Abuse Issues Revealed of Effective Hypnosis Interventions, 1994, Light Tough Therapy for Stress-Headache and Back Pain Relief--A Form of Hypno-Acupressure, 1995; one-woman show Dell's Aircraft Gallery, 1958; group shows at Flint Inst. Arts, U. Mich., Purdue U., Lafayette, Inc., Flint Artist Market, Saginaw, Detrout and Grand Rapids, Mich., Japan, others; contbr. articles to profl. jours.; author scripts and software in hypnosis field. Bd. dirs. The Chapel of The Angles Bldg. Fund for Lapeer County, 1974-75; pub. speaker various civic orgns. Named Oil Colorist of Yr. Profl. Photographers of Mich., 1959; recipient Pub. Svc. award Genesee County Sheriff's Dept., 1974. Mem. Internat. Soc. Profl. Hypnosis (regional v.p. 1977-79), Internat. Soc. Profl. Hypnotists and Counselors, Internat. Med. and Dental Hypnotherapist Assn., Nat. Guild Hypnotherapists, Nat. Guild Hypnotists (rsch. award for hypnosis for relief of multiple sclerosis 1991), Questers Antique Study Group (various offices including pres. 1972-90), Internat. Psychic Arts Rsch. (founder, pres. 1974-75), Flint Artist Market Group (program dir., treas.), Flint Soc. Arts and Crafts (v.p., pres. 1958-59), Quota Club, others. Republican. Roman Catholic. Avocations: writing, painting, sculpting, travel, water skiing. Home: 2362 Nolen Dr Flint MI 48504-5201

PALISCA, CLAUDE VICTOR, musicologist, educator; b. Rijeka, Croatia, Nov. 24, 1921; came to U.S., 1930; s. Matthew and Gisella (Fleischhacker) P.; m. Jane Agnes Pyne, June 12, 1960 (div. Feb. 1987); children: Carl Pyne, Madeline Grace; m. Elizabeth Ann Keitel, Apr. 4, 1987. B.A., Queens Coll., 1943; M.A., Harvard U., 1948, Ph.D., 1954; M.A. (hon.), Yale U., 1964. Instr., then asst. prof. music U. Ill. at Urbana, 1953-59; asso. prof. history music Yale U., New Haven, 1959—, prof., 1964-80, Henry L. and Lucy G. Moses prof. music, 1980-92, emeritus, 1992—, dir. grad. studies music, 1967-69, 87-92, chmn. music dept., 1969-75, chmn., dir. grad. studies in Renaissance studies, 1977-80; chmn. council on humanities Yale U., 1977-79, fellow Silliman Coll., 1963—; sr. fellow council humanities Princeton U., 1961; cons. U.S. Office Edn., 1963—, NEH, 1967—; dir. Nat. Seminar Music Edn., 1963. Author: Girolamo Mei: Letters on Ancient and Modern Music, 1960, 2d edit., 1977, (with others) Musicology, 1963, Baroque Music, 1968, 3d edit., 1991, (with Donald Grout) History of Western Music, 5th edit., 1996, Humanism in Italian Renaissance Musical Thought, 1985 (Internat. Musicol. Soc. award 1987), The Florentine Camerata, 1989, Studies in the History of Italian Music and Music Theory, 1994; translator: (with Guy Marco) Zarlino, The Art of Counterpoint, 1968; editor: Hucbald, Guido and John on Music: Three Medieval Treatises, 1978, Norton Anthology of Western Music, 1980, 3rd edit., 1996, (with D. Kern Holloman) Musicology in the 1980's, 1982, Zarlino, On the Modes, 1983, Yale Music Theory Translation Series, Boethius, Fundamentals of Music, 1989, The Theory of Music (Franchino Gaffurio) 1993; mem. editorial and adv. bds. Studies in Music (Western Australia); mem. exec. com.: New Grove Dictionary, Jour. History of Ideas, Jour. Music Theory; contbr. articles to publs. Bd. dirs., exec. com. Arts Council Greater New Haven, 1964-77, Neighborhood Music Sch., 1966-69; mem. exec. com. Ednl. Center for Arts, New Haven, 1973-83, chmn., 1979-80; bd. dirs., chmn. edn. com. New Haven Symphony Soc., 1966-72, v.p., 1968-72; mem. ednl. adv. bd. J.S. Guggenheim Meml. Found., 1983-92. Served with AUS, 1943-46. John Knowles Paine traveling fellow, 1949-50; Fulbright fellow, 1950-52; Guggenheim fellow, 1959-60, 81-82; Nat. Endowment for the Humanities sr. fellow, 1972-73; Misha Strassberg sr. fellow in creative arts U. Western Australia, summer, 1984. Fellow AAAS, Am. Coun. Arts in Edn. (pres. 1967-69); mem. Internat. Musicol. Soc. (dir., v.p. 1977-82), Am. Musicol. Soc. (hon., pres. 1970-72), Coll. Music Soc. (coun.), Renaissance Soc. (coun. 1973-74, exec. com. 1978-87), ACLS-Soviet Union of Composers Commn. on Music Composition and Musicology (co-chmn. 1986-90). Office: Yale Univ PO Box 208310 New Haven CT 06520-8310

PALISI, ANTHONY THOMAS, psychologist, educator; b. Rahway, N.J., Mar. 8, 1930; s. Anthony Francis and Marianne Catherine (Picone) P.; m. Dyane Cassidy, Apr. 19, 1954; children: Jane, Anthony Francis II, Phyllis, Damian-Marie. BS, Seton Hall U., 1951, MA, 1958; EdD, Temple U., 1973. Cert. secondary tchr., elem. prin., psychologist, rehab. counselor, N.J.; mem. Nat. Register Health Care Profls. in Psychology. Tchr., coach pub. schs. Rahway, 1953-60; sports editor Rahway News-Record, 1950-60; prin. elem. pub. sch. Franklin Twp., N.J., 1960-65; asst. prof. edn. Seton Hall U., 1965-73, assoc. prof., 1974-77, prof., 1977-82, acting grad. dean, 1976-77, dir., 1969-80, indsl. cons. group dynamics, 1967—. Contbr. articles and short stories to profl. jours. and popular periodicals. Mem. Rahway Bd. Edn. 1961-62; trustee Rahway Libr., 1961-68, pres. 1967-68. Recipient award N.J. Sportswriters' Assn., 1953. Mem. APA, ACA, Am. Mgmt. Assn. (co-author video tng. program), N.J. Psychol. Assn., Assn. for Specialists in Group Work (mem. rsch. com. 1980-82), N.Y. Acad. Scis., Nat. Acad. Counselors and Family Therapists (chmn., exec. dir. 1988-93), Nat. Register of Health Svc. Providers in Psychology. Roman Catholic.

PALITZ, BERNARD G., finance company executive; b. N.Y.C., Aug. 21, 1924; s. Clarence Y. and Ruth (Krummas) P.; m. Louise Beringer; children: Bernard G. Jr., Anne L. BS, MIT, 1947. Chmn. bd. Comml. Alliance Corp., N.Y.C., 1963-88, Credit Alliance Corp., N.Y.C., 1963-88, Leasing Svc. Corp., N.Y.C., 1963-88, Fin. Guaranty Ins. Co., Wilmington, Del., 1975—, Colonial Surety Co., Pitts., 1976—, Fin. Fed. Corp., 1989—; pres. Am. Credit Mgmt., Inc., N.Y.C. Trustee Coun. for Arts, MIT, 1979—, Haverford Coll., Pa., 1979-82, Rockefeller U. Coun.; incorporator Worcester (Mass.) Art Mus. Mem. Harmonie Club (N.Y.C.), Quaker Ridge Club (Scarsdale, N.Y.), Beach Point Club (Mamaroneck, N.Y.), Econ. Club of N.Y. Home: PO Box 287 221 E 70th St New York NY 10021-5203 Office: Am Credit Mgmt Inc 400 Park Ave New York NY 10022

PALITZ, CLARENCE YALE, JR., commercial finance executive; b. N.Y.C., Jan. 21, 1931; s. Clarence Yale and Ruth (Kromnes) P.; m. Muriel Dobson (div. Nov., 1988), children: Michael, Suzanne; m. Anka Kriser. B.A., Dartmouth Coll., 1952; M.B.A., NYU, 1953. With Bankers Trust Co., N.Y.C., 1952-53; v.p., dir. Credit Am. Corp., N.Y.C., 1956-58; asst. sec. James Talcott, Inc., N.Y.C., 1958-60; v.p., mng. dir. Shopper's Park-Westmount, Ltd., Edmonton, Alta., Can., 1958-74; pres., dir. 140 E 72d St. Corp., N.Y.C., 1962-65, Comml. Alliance Corp., N.Y.C., 1963-88, Credit Alliance Corp., N.Y.C., 1963-88, Leasing Service Corp., N.Y.C., 1963-88, Colonial Surety Co., Pitts., 1976—, Fin. Guaranty Ins. Co., Wilmington, Del., 1976—, Kidde Credit Corp., N.Y.C., 1976-80, First Interstate Comml. Alliance Corp., 1984-88, Fin. Fed. Corp., 1989—; pres., chmn. bd. dirs. First Land Devel. Inc., Allamuchy, N.J., 1987—; chmn. bd. Fin. Fed. Credit Inc., Houston; bd. dirs. City & Suburban Fin. Corp. Served to lt. (j.g.) USN, 1953-56. Office: Fin Fed Credit Inc 300 Frank W Burr Blvd Teaneck NJ 07666-6703

PALIZZI, ANTHONY N., lawyer, retail corporation executive; b. Wyandotte, Mich., Oct. 27, 1942; s. Vincenzo and Nunziata (Dagostini) P.; m. Bonnie Marie Kirkwood, Mar. 11, 1966; children—A. Michael, Nicholas A. PhB, Wayne State U., 1964, JD, 1966; LLM, Yale U., 1967. Bar: Mich. 1967. Prof. law Fla. State U., Tallahassee, 1967-69; prof. law Tex. Tech U., Lubbock, 1969-71; atty. Kmart Corp., Troy, Mich., 1971-74, asst. sec., 1974-77, asst. gen. counsel, 1977-85, v.p., assoc. gen. counsel, 1985-91, sr. v.p., gen. counsel, 1991-92, exec. v.p., gen. counsel, 1992—. Editor law rev. Wayne State U., 1964-66. Chmn. Brandon Police and Fire Bd., Mich., 1982-87. Mem. ABA, Am. Corp. Counsel Assn., Mich. State Bar Assn. Roman Catholic.

PALKO, MICHAEL JAMES, finance company executive; b. Passaic, N.J., Sept. 4, 1936; s. Michael and Josephine Marie (Jasper) P.; m. Alexandra S. Palko; children: Timothy, Christopher. Student, Upsala Coll., 1955; BSBA, U. Denver, 1963. CPA, Calif., Colo., Mich., N.J. Acct. Ernst & Young, Denver, 1963-66, Marquette, Mich., 1966-69, Trenton, N.J., 1969-72; v.p. First Interstate Bancorp., Los Angeles, 1972-74, H.F. Ahmanson & Co., Los Angeles, 1974-80; sr. v.p. Gt. Western Fin. Corp., Chatsworth, Calif., 1980—. Chmn. United Fund, Marquette, 1969; pres. Trenton, N.J. chpt. ARC, 1972; fin. chmn. Diocese of Marquette, Roman Cath. Ch., 1968-69. Served with USAF, 1955-59. Mem. AICPA, Calif. Soc. CPAs, Savs. and Cmty. Bankers of Am. (chair, tax com. 1993-94), Am. Fin. Svcs. Assn. (chair tax com. 1990-92), Western League of Savs. Instns. (former chair tax com.), Tax Execs. Inst., L.A. Taxpayers Assn. (bd. dirs. 1984-89), Kiwanis (past officer), Beta Gamma Sigma. Republican. Office: Gt Western Fin Corp 9200 Oakdale Ave N 11 21 Chatsworth CA 91311-6519

PALKOVITZ, HERBERT, lawyer; b. McKeesport, Pa., Dec. 1, 1942. BA, Washington & Jefferson Coll., 1964; JD, Cleve. U., 1968. Bar: Ohio 1969, U.S. Dist. Ct. (no. dist.) Ohio 1970, U.S. Supreme Ct. 1972, U.S. Ct. Appeals (6th cir.) 1982. Pvt. practice Cleve., 1969—; mem. alt. dispute com. Ohio Supreme Ct., Columbus. Chmn. mediation adv. bd. Jewish Family Svc. Assn., Cleve. Fellow Internat. Acad. Matrimonial Lawyers, Am. Acad. Matrimonial Lawyers (pres. Ohio chpt., bd. govs. 1990—); mem. ABA, Cleve. Bar Assn. (chair family law sect.), Cuyahoga County Bar Assn. (chair family law sect.). Office: 1600 Standard Bldg Cleveland OH 44113

PALLADINO, NUNZIO JOSEPH, retired nuclear engineer; b. Allentown, Pa., Nov. 10, 1916; s. Joseph and Angelina (Trentalange) P.; m. Virginia Marchetto, June 16, 1945; children: Linda Susan, Lisa Anne, Cynthia Madaline. B.S., Lehigh U., 1938, M.S., 1939, D.Eng. (hon.), 1964. Registered profl. engr., Pa. Engr. Westinghouse Electric Co., Phila., 1939-42; nuclear reactor designer Oak Ridge Nat. Lab., 1946-48; staff asst. to div. mgr. Argonne Nat. Lab., Lemont, Ill., 1948-50; mgr. PWR reactor design subdiv. Westinghouse Electric Corp., Pitts., 1950-59; head nuclear engring. dept. Pa. State U., University Park, 1959-66, dean Coll. Engring., 1966-81; chmn. Nuclear Regulatory Commn., Washington, 1981-86; past mem. Pa. Gov.'s Sci. Adv. Com., Gov.'s Energy Coun., Pa.'s Commn. To Investigate Three Mile Island; mem. Nat. Nuclear Accrediting Bd., 1989-92. Contbr. tech. articles to profl. jours. Served to capt. AUS, 1942-45. Recipient Order of Merit Westinghouse Electric Corp. Fellow ASME (Prime Movers award), Am. Nuclear Soc. (past pres., A.H. Compton award, W. Zinn award), Am. Soc. Engring. Edn.; mem. NAE, NSPE, Argonne Univs. Assn. (past interim pres., past bd. dirs.). Roman Catholic. Club: Rotary. *Do it right the first time.*

PALLADINO, VINCENT NEIL, lawyer; b. Phila., Dec. 5, 1950; s. Vincent Salvatore and Agnes (Ludwig) P.; m. Laurel Ruth Tanner, Apr. 15, 1984; children: Alissa Kathryn, Samantha Leigh. BA, Yale U., 1972; JD, Columbia U., 1975. Bar: N.Y. 1976. Atty. Nims, Howes, Collison & Isner, N.Y.C., 1975-77; atty. Fish & Neave, N.Y.C., 1977—, ptnr., 1987—. Editor-in-chief The Trademark Reporter, N.Y.C., 1986-88, mem. adv. bd., 1988—. Mem. ABA, Assn. Bar City of N.Y., N.Y. Intellectual Property Law Assn., Internat. Trademark Assn., Copyright Soc. U.S.A. Avocations: reading, running. Office: Fish & Neave 1251 6th Ave New York NY 10020-1104

PALLADINO-CRAIG, ALLYS, museum director; b. Pontiac, Mich., Mar. 23, 1947; d. Stephan Vincent and Mary (Anderson) Palladino; m. Malcolm Arnold Craig, Aug. 20, 1967; children—Ansel, Reed, Nicholas. BA in English, Fla. State U., 1967; grad., U. Toronto, Ont., Can., 1969; MFA, Fla. State U., 1978, ABD in Humanities, 1993. Editorial asst. project U. Va. Press, Charlottesville, 1970-76; instr. English Inst. Franco Americain, Rennes, France, 1974; adj. instr. Fla. State U., Tallahassee, 1978-79, dir. Four Arts Ctr., 1979-82, dir. U. Mus. of Fine Arts, 1982—. Curator, contbg. editor carious articles and exhbn. catalogues, 1982—, including Nocturnes and Nightmares, Monochrome/Polychrome and Choma; gen. editor Athanor I-XV, 1980—; represented in permanent collections Fla. Ho. of Reps., Barnett Bank, IBM. Individual artist fellow Fla. Arts Coun., 1979. Mem. Am. Assn. Mus., Fla. Art Mus. Dirs. Assn. (sec. 1989-91), Phi Beta Kappa. Democrat. Avocation: antique American fountain pen collecting. Home: 1410 Grape St Tallahassee FL 32303-5636 Office: Fla State U Mus of Fine Arts 250 Fine Arts Bldg Tallahassee FL 32306-2055

PALLAM, JOHN JAMES, lawyer; b. Cleve., May 19, 1940; s. James John and Coralia (Gatsos) P.; m. Evanthia Venizelos, Nov. 29, 1969; 1 child, Alethea. BA, Case Western Res. U., 1962; JD, Ohio State U., 1965. Bar: Ohio 1965, U.S. Ct. Claims 1969, U.S. Ct. Mil. Appeals 1969, U.S. Supreme Ct. 1970. Law clk. to presiding justice Cuyahoga County Ct., Cleve., 1965-66; assoc. Burke, Habor & Berick, Cleve., 1970-73; corp. atty. Midland Ross Corp., Cleve., 1973-80, corp. counsel, 1980-87; v.p., gen. counsel Brush Wellman Corp., Cleve., 1987—; guest lectr. Nat. Foundry Assn., Chgo., 1986—. Contbr. articles on labor and environ. matters to jours. Legal advisor Am. Hellenic and Prog. Assn., Cleve., 1966—. Served to capt. JAGC U.S. Army, 1966-70, Vietnam. Decorated Bronze Star with oak leaf cluster. Mem. Ohio Bar Assn. (committeeman 1984—), Cleve. Bar Assn. (merit svc. award 1972), Hellenic Bar Assn., Hellenic Univ. Club, Rowfant. Greek Orthodox. Avocations: history, antiques, golfing, rare books, railroading. Office: 17876 Saint Clair Ave Cleveland OH 44110-2602

PALLAS, CHRISTOPHER WILLIAM, cardiologist; b. Chattanooga, Mar. 27, 1956; s. William Charles and Katherine (Rigas) P. Student, Vanderbilt U., 1974-75; BA in Biology, U. Tenn., 1978; MD, Wake Forest U., 1982. Diplomate Am. Bd. Internal Medicine, Am. Bd. Cardiology. Intern Med. Coll. Ga., Augusta, 1982-83, resident, 1983-85, chief med. resident, 1985-86, clin. fellow cardiology, 1986-88, instr. in cardiology, 1988-89, attending physician, 1988—, asst. prof. cardiology, 1989—, researcher clin. and basic cardiology, 1989—; cons. cardiovascular diseases VA Med. Ctr., Dublin, Ga., 1988-89, dir. coronary care unit, Augusta, 1988—. Contbr. articles to profl. jours. Fellow Am. Coll. Chest Physicians, Am. Coll. Cardiology; mem. AMA, Med. Assn. Ga., Richmond County Med. Soc. Greek Orthodox. Avocations: golf, collecting antiques. Home: Ste 1601 # 1 Seventh St Augusta GA 30901 Office: Med Coll Ga Cardiology BA-A535 1120 15th St Augusta GA 30901-3157

PALLASCH, B. MICHAEL, lawyer; b. Chgo., Mar. 30, 1933; s. Bernhard Michael and Magdalena Helena (Fixari) P.; m. Josephine Catherine O'Leary, Aug. 15, 1981; children: Bernhard Michael III and Madeleine Josephine (twins). B.S.S., Georgetown U., 1954; J.D., Harvard U., 1957; postgrad., John Marshall Law Sch., 1974. Bar: Ill. 1957, U.S. Dist. Ct. (no. dist.) Ill. 1958, U.S. Tax Ct. 1961, U.S. Ct. Claims 1961, U.S. Ct. Appeals (7th cir.) 1962. Assoc. Winston & Strawn, Chgo., 1958-66; resident mgr. br. office Winston & Strawn, Paris, 1963-65; ptnr. Winston & Strawn, Chgo., 1966-70, sr. capital ptnr., 1971-91; sr. ptnr. B. Michael Pallasch & Assocs., 1991—; dir., corp. sec. Tanis, Inc., Calumet, Mich., 1972—, Greenbank Engring. Corp., Dover, Del., 1976-91, C.B.P. Engring. Corp., Chgo., 1976-91, Chgo. Cutting Svcs. Corp., 1977-88; corp. sec. Arthur Andersen Assocs., Inc., Chgo., 1976—, L'hotel de France of Ill., Inc., Chgo., 1980-85, Water & Effluent Screening Co., Chgo., 1988-91; dir. Bosch Devel. Co., Longview, Tex., 1977-87, Lor Inc., Houghton, Mich., 1977-87, Rana Inc., Madison, Wis., 1978-87, Woodlak Co., Houghton, 1977-87, Zipatone, Inc., Hillside, Ill., 1975-82, Keco Inc., Madison, 1977-81. Bd. dirs. Martin D'Arcy Mus. Medieval and Renaissance Art, Chgo., 1975—; bd. dirs. Katherine M. Bosch Found., 1978—; asst. sec. Hundred Club of Cook County, Chgo., 1966-73, bd. dirs., sec., 1974—. Served with USAFR, 1957-63. Knight of Merit Sacred Mil. Constantinian Order of St. George of Royal House of Bourbon of two Sicilies, knight Sovereign Mil. Order of temple of Jerusalem; named youth mayor City of chgo., 1950; recipient Outstanding Woodland Mgmt. Forestry award Monroe County (Wis.) Soil and Water Conservation Dist., 1975. Mem. Ill. Bar Assn. (tax lectr. 1961), Advs. Soc., Field Mus. Natural History (life), Max McGraw Wildlife Found., English Speaking Union. Roman Catholic. Clubs: Travellers (Paris); Saddle and Cycle (Chgo.). Home: 737 W Hutchinson St Chicago IL 60613-1519 Office: 35 W Wacker Dr Ste 4700 Chicago IL 60601-1614 *Personal philosophy: We define and measure success in various ways: achievement, position, wealth: and attribute it to the application of various attributes but is there any degree of success that we can achieve that is worthier than the knowledge that we have faithfully served those who depend upon and trust in us?.*

PALLIN, IRVING M., anesthesiologist; b. Boston, Feb. 11, 1910; s. Abraham and Lillian (Stoler) P.; m. Ann Gertrude Lear, 1940; children: Samuel Lear, Mary Jane, Carol Sue, Jonathan Jacob. B.S., Tufts U., 1932, M.D., 1937. Diplomate: Am. Bd. Anesthesiology. Intern W.W. Backus Hosp., 1937-39; resident anesthesiology N.Y. Postgrad. Med. Sch. and Hosp., 1939-41; practice medicine specializing in anesthesiology N.Y.C., 1941-70, Sun City, Ariz., 1970-80; attending anesthesiologist Jewish Hosp. Bklyn., 1942-54, sec. med. bd., 1951-70, pres. med. bd., 1962-63, dir. dept. anesthesiology, 1954-70; cons. anesthesiologist VA Hosp., Bklyn., 1950-65; dir. anesthesiology Cumberland Hosp., 1948-55; dir. dept. anesthesiology Queens Gen. Hosp., 1955-66; former prof. clin. anesthesiology SUNY Coll. Medicine, Bklyn.; chief anesthesia Boswell Meml. Hosp., Sun City, Ariz., 1970-77; dir. Asso. Hosp. Service (Blue Cross) Greater N.Y.; chmn. advisers of AMA to Am. Assn. Med. Assts., 1968-70. Contbr. articles to profl. publs. Co-chmn. Bklyn. physicians div. United Jewish Appeal, 1953-56; pres. Sun City unit Am. Cancer Soc., 1981-85, bd. dirs. Ariz. div., 1982—; pres. Beth Shalom Congregation of Sun City, 1976-78, Brotherhood, 1980, 81, pres. 1982-83; bd. dirs. Ariz. Endowment of Jewish Welfare, 1982-85. Recipient Heritage award State of Israel Bonds, 1983. Fellow Am. Coll. Anesthesiologists, N.Y. Acad. Medicine, N.Y. Acad. Scis.; mem. AMA (del. 1964—), Kings County Med. Soc. (pres. 1960-61, hon.), N.Y. Med. Soc. (ho. dels. 1952-54, sec. sect. anesthesiology 1952057), Acad. Medicine Bklyn. (pres. 1961), Am. Soc. Anesthesiologists (pres. 1957), N.Y. Soc. Anesthesiologists (pres. 1949-50, chmn. jud. com. 1951-56, hon.), Tam O'Shanter Golf Club (pres. 1960-63, Union Hills Country Club. Home: 10358 Highwood Ln Sun City AZ 85373

PALLIN, SAMUEL LEAR, ophthalmologist; b. N.Y., May 8, 1941; s. Irving and Gertrude (Lear) P. BA, Hofstra U., 1963; MD, SUNY, Bklyn., 1968. Diplomate Nat. Bd. Med. Examiners, Am. Bd. Ophthalmology. Intern L.I. Jewish Med. Ctr., 1968-69; resident Bklyn. Eye and Ear Hosp., 1972-75; prin. The Lear Eye Clinic, Ltd., Sun City, Ariz., 1975—; mem. staff Walter O. Boswell Meml. Hosp., Del E. Webb Meml. Hosp., Scottsdale Meml. Hosp., St. Luke's Med. Ctr., Thunderbird Samaritan Hosp.; presenter in field. Patentee in method of making self-sealing episcleral incision. Trustee Congr. Beth El Endowment Fund, 1987; mem. exec. bd. Ariz. chpt. Israel Bonds, 1988. With USAF, 1969-71. Mem. AMA, ACS, Am. Soc. Cataract and Refractive Surgery, Am. Acad. Ophthalmology, Ariz. Med. Assn., Ariz. Easter Seal Soc. (bd. dirs. 1989, life dir.), Maricopa County Med. Assn., Outpatient Ophthalmic Surgery Soc., Lions; hon. mem. Mex. Ophthalmology Soc. N.E., Mex. Intraocular Implant Soc., Ctrl. Mex. Ophthalmol. Soc. Office: The Lear Eye Clinic Ltd Bldg A-100 10615 W Thunderbird Blvd Sun City AZ 85351

PALLISER, CHARLES, writer, educator; b. Holyoke, Mass., Dec. 11, 1947. BA, Oxford U., 1970, BLitt, 1975. Lectr. Strathclyde U., Scotland, 1974-90. Author: The Quincunx, 1989, The Sensationist, 1991, Betrayals, 1995. Recipient Sue Kaufman 1st fiction prize Am. Acad. & Inst. Arts and Letters, N.Y.C., 1991.

PALLMEYER, REBECCA RUTH, federal judge; b. Tokyo, Sept. 13, 1954; came to U.S., 1957; d. Paul Henry and Ruth (Schrieber) P.; m. Dan P. McAdams, Aug. 20, 1977; children: Ruth, Amanda. BA, Valparaiso (Ind.) U., 1976; JD, U. Chgo., 1979. Bar: Ill. 1980, U.S. Ct. Appeals (7th cir.) 1980, U.S. Ct. Appeals 11th and 5th cirs.) 1982. Jud. clk. Minn. Supreme Ct., St. Paul, 1979-80; assoc. Hopkins & Sutter, Chgo., 1980-85; judge administrv. law Ill. Human Rights Commn., Chgo., 1985-91; magistrate judge U.S. Dist. Ct., Chgo., 1991—; mem. jud. resources com. Jud. Conf. of U.S., 1994—. Bd. govs. Augustana Ctr., 1990-91. Mem. Fed. Bar Assn. (bd. mgrs. Chgo. chpt. 1995-96), Womens Bar Assn. Ill. (bd. mgrs. 1996—), Nat.

Assn. Women Judges, Fed. Magistrate Judges Assn. (bd. dirs. 1994—), Chgo. Bar Assn. (chair devel. law com. 1992-93, David C. Hilliard award 1990-91), Valparaiso U. Alumni Assn. (bd. dirs. 1992-94). Lutheran. Avocations: choral music, sewing, running. Office: US Dist Ct Rm 2402 219 S Dearborn St Chicago IL 60604-1802

PALLONE, ADRIAN JOSEPH, research scientist; b. Lille, France, Apr. 8, 1928; came to US., 1946; s. Giovanni and Laurina (Caccia) P.; m. Teresa Maria Violino, June 12, 1954; children—John M., Anne Marie, Janet M., Joan L. B.S. in Aero. Engring., Poly Inst. Bklyn., 1952, M.S. in Aero. Engring., 1953, Ph.D. in Applied Mechanics, 1959; cert., Sloan Sch. Mgmt., MIT, 1984. Research assoc. Poly. Inst. Bklyn., 1955-59; mgr. Avco Systems Div., Wilmington, Mass., 1959-63; mem. faculty NYU, N.Y.C., 1963-67; dir. Avco Systems Div., Wilmington, 1967-78; chief scientist Avco Systems Div., 1978-87; aerospace cons. Textron Def. Systems, Wilmington, 1987-91; pres. Aerophysics Systems & Tech., Inc., Silver Lake, N.H., 1992—. Patentee in field. Contbr. articles to sci. jours. Fellow AIAA; mem. N.Y. Acad. Scis., Sigma Xi, Sigma Gamma Tau. Roman Catholic. Avocations: skiing; sailing; hiking. Office: Aerophysics Systems & Tech Inc PO Box 189 Silver Lake NH 03875-0189

PALLONE, FRANK, JR., congressman; b. Long Branch, N.J., Oct. 30, 1951. Grad. cum. laude, Middlebury Coll., 1973; MA, Tufts U., 1974; JD, Rutgers U., 1978. Councilman City of Long Branch, 1982-88; mem. N.J. Senate, 1984-88, 101st-104th Congresses from 3d (now 6th) N.J. dist., 1988—; ranking minority mem. commerce subcom. on energy and power. Democrat. Roman Catholic. Office: US Ho of Reps 420 Condon Ter SE Washington DC 20032-3710 Address: 540 Broadway Ste 118 Long Branch NJ 07740-5905*

PALLOT, JOSEPH WEDELES, lawyer; b. Coral Gables, Fla., Dec. 23, 1959; s. Richard Allen Pallot and Rosalind Brown (Wedeles) Spak; m. Linda Fried, Oct. 12, 1956; children: Richard Allen, Maxwell Ross. BS, Jacksonville U., 1981; JD cum laude, U. Miami, Coral Gables, Fla., 1986. Bar: Fla. 1986. Comml. lending officer S.E. Bank, N.A., Miami, 1981-83; ptnr. Steel Hector & Davis, Miami, 1986—. Bd. dirs. MOSAIC: Jewish Mus. of Fla., Miami Beach, 1993—; gov. Fla. Philharm. Orch., Coral Gables, 1994—. Mem. Miami City Club. Avocations: golf, tennis. Office: Steel Hector & Davis 200 S Biscayne Blvd Miami FL 33131

PALLOTTI, MARIANNE MARGUERITE, foundation administrator; b. Hartford, Conn., Apr. 23, 1937; d. Rocco D. and Marguerite (Long) P. BA, NYU, 1968, MA, 1972. Asst. to pres. Wilson, Haight & Welch, Hartford, 1964-65; exec. asst. Ford Found., N.Y.C., 1965-77; corp. sec. Hewlett Found., Menlo Park, Calif., 1977-84, v.p., 1985—; bd. dirs. Overseas Devel. Network. Bd. dirs. N.Y. Theatre Ballet, N.Y.C., 1986—, Consortium for Global Devel., 1992, Miramonte Mental Health Svcs., Palo Alto, Calif., 1989, Austin Montessori Sch., 1993. Mem. Women in Founds., No. Calif. Grantmakers, Peninsula Grantmakers. Avocations: running, skiing, hiking. Home: 532 Marine World Pky # 6203 Redwood Shores CA 94065 Office: William & Flora Hewlett Found 525 Middlefield Rd Ste 200 Menlo Park CA 94025-3447

PALM, CHARLES GILMAN, university official; b. Havre, Mont., Apr. 25, 1944; s. Victor F. and Laura (McKinnie) P.; m. Miriam Willits, Sept. 15, 1968. AB, Stanford U., 1966; MA, U. Wyo., 1967; MLS, U. Oreg., 1970. Asst. archivist Hoover Instn., Stanford (Calif.) U., 1971-74, dep. archivist, 1974-84, archivist, 1984-87, head libr., 1986-87, assoc. dir., 1987-90, dep. dir., 1990—. Co-author: Guide to Hoover Institution Archives, 1980, Herbert Hoover, Register of His Papers in the Hoover Institution Archives, 1983. Mem. Calif. Heritage Preservation Commn., Sacramento, 1988—, vice chmn., 1993—; mem. Nat. Hist. Records and Publs. Commn., Washington, 1990—. Fellow Soc. Am. Archivists; mem. Am. Hist. Assn., Soc. Calif. Archivists (pres. 1983-84). Republican. Office: Hoover Instn Stanford CA 94305

PALM, GARY HOWARD, lawyer, educator; b. Toledo, Sept. 2, 1942; s. Clarence William, Jr. and Emily Marie (Braunschweiger) P. AB, Wittenberg U., 1964; JD, U. Chgo., 1967. Bar: Ill. 1967, U.S. Dist. Ct. (no. dist.) Ill. 1967, U.S. Ct. Appeals (7th cir.) 1970, U.S. Supreme Ct. 1974. Assoc. Schiff Hardin & Waite, Chgo., 1967-70; dir. Edwin F. Mandel Legal Aid Clinic, Chgo., 1970-91, atty., 1991—; asst. prof. law U. Chgo., 1970-75, assoc. prof., 1975-83, prof., 1983-91, clin. prof., 1991—; peer rev. reader, clin. edn. grants U.S. Dept. Edn., Washington, 1980, 81, 83, 84, 86, 87, Legal Svcs. Corp., 1986-87; chairperson-elect, chairperson sect. clin. legal edn. Assn. Am. Law Schs., 1985, 86. Vol. ACLU, Chgo., 1968-75. Mem. ABA (clin. edn. com. 1974-80, membership com. 1984-85, skills tng. com. 1985-90, accreditation for Law Schs., 1987-94, mem. coun. sect. on legal edn. and admissions to the bar 1994—), Chgo. Bar Assn., Chgo. Council Lawyers, Ill. State Bar Assn. (legal edn., admission and competence com. 1985-91, 93—), Am. Trial Lawyers Assn., Assn. Am. Law Schs. (clin. teaching conferences 1985, 86, 87, 89, recipient Award for Outstanding Contbn. to Clin. Edn., sect on clin. legal edn., 1989, co-recipient of the award, 1994), Inter Univ. Consortium on Poverty Law, Ill. Task Force on Child Support. Democrat. Home: 2800 N Lake Shore Dr Apt 3706 Chicago IL 60657-6254 Office: Mandel Legal Aid Clinic 6020 S University Ave Chicago IL 60637-2704 *Notable cases include: Logan vs. Zimmerman Brush Co.; Buckhalter vs. Pepsi-Cola Gen. Bottlers, Inc.; Scott vs. Ill.; Slate vs. McFetridge.*

PALM, GERALD ALBERT, lawyer; b. Seattle, Nov. 4, 1942; s. Albert Nels and Gladys Elizabeth (Danberg) P.; m. Nancy Lee Himes, Dec. 6, 1969; children: Jason E., Kimberly A. BA, Dartmouth Coll., 1964; LLB, Harvard U., 1967. Bar: Wash. 1967, U.S. Dist. Ct. (we. dist.) Wash. 1967, U.S. Ct. Appeals (9th cir.) 1981, U.S. Dist. Ct. (ea. dist.) Wash. 1982. Assoc. Jones, Grey, Bayley, Kehoe, Hooper & Olsen, Seattle, 1967-68; assoc. Williams, Kastner and Gibbs, Seattle, 1968-74, ptnr., 1974-95; sole practitioner Seattle, 1995—. Youth basketball coach Jewish Community Ctr., Mercer Island, Wash., 1984-88; deacon, youth commn. Mercer Island Covenant Ch., 1988-95. Mem. FBA, Am. Bd. Trial Advocates (pres. Wash. chpt. 1989), Def. Rsch. Inst., Wash. Def. Trial Lawyers Assn. (trustee 1971), Wash. State Bar Assn., King County Bar Assn., Dartmouth Lawyers Assn., Mercer Island Country Club (trustee 1991-94, pres. 1993-94), Wash. Athletic Club, Mercer Island Kiwanis (pres. 1986-87). Republican. Mem. Covenant Ch. Avocations: tennis, water skiing, snow skiing, running, attending musicals and theatre. Home: 7400 E Mercer Way Mercer Island WA 98040-5819 Office: Law Office of Gerald A Palm Washington Mut Tower 1201 3d Ave Ste 2830 Seattle WA 98101

PALM, MARY EGDAHL, mycologist; b. Mpls., Jan. 27, 1954; d. Lauren and Mary E.; children: Natalie Elizabeth, Christopher Steven. BA in Biology, St. Olaf Coll., 1976; MSc in Plant Pathology (mycology), U. Minn., 1979, PhD in Plant Pathology (mycology), 1983. Lab. asst. St. Olaf Coll. Biology Dept., Northfield, Minn., 1974; tchg. asst. St. Olaf Coll. Biology Dept., Northfield, 1975-76; rsch. asst. U. Minn. plant pathology dept., Mpls., 1976-83, post doctoral rsch. assoc., 1983-84; mycologist (botanist GS12) USDA/APHIS biol. assessment and support staff, Beltsville, Md., 1984-91; mycologist (botanist GS13) biol. assessment and taxonomic support USDA/Animal and Plant Health Inspection Svc., Beltsville, 1991—; instr., coord. seminars and tng. sessions for USDA and ednl. sci. group, 1982—; adj. assoc. prof. plant pathology Pa. State U., State College, 1995. Co-author: (books) Deutermycetes and Selected Ascomycetes That Occur on or in Wood: An Indexed Bibliography, 1979, An Indexed Bibliography and Guide to Taxonomic Literature, 1988, A Literature Guide for the Identification of Plant Pathogenic Fungi, 1987, Mycology in Sustainable Development: Expanding Concepts, Vanishing Borders, 1996, Fungi on Rhodendron: A World Reference, 1996; contbr. articles to profl. jours. including Mycologia, Plant Disease, Can. Jour. Botany, Mycotaxon., Mycol. Rsch., others. Recipient St. Olaf Coll. Hon. Biology scholarship, 1976; grantee U. Minn. Computer Ctr. 1979, 80, 81, 82. Mem. Am. Phytopathol. Soc. (chairperson mycology com. 1988, 89, vice chairperson 1987, mem. 1985, 86, regulatory plant pathology com. 1993—, organizer, moderator colloquim on systematics of plant pathogenic fungi 1987), Mycol. Soc. Am. (sec. 1991-94, Am. Inst. Biol. Scis. rep. 1994—, v.p. 1995-96, pres.-elect 1996-97, pres. 1997-98, other coms.), L.Am. Mycol. Assn. (U.S. liaison), Internat. Assn. Plant Taxonomy (subcom. C of com. on fungi and lichens 1986, 87, 88). Office: USDA Rm 329 B-011A 10300 Baltimore Ave Beltsville MD 20705

PALMA, DOLORES PATRICIA, urban planner, consultant, lecturer, author; b. Bklyn.; d. Anthony Michael Resse and Eleanor Dorothea (Palma) Graffeo; m. Doyle G. Hyett, Apr. 12, 1986. BA, CUNY, Bklyn., 1972; M of Urban Planning, U. Mich., 1974. Student intern Mich. Mcpl. League, Ann Arbor, 1973-74; park planner Metro Bd. Parks and Recreation, Nashville, 1975; preservation planner Metro. Hist. Commn., Nashville, 1976; sr. community planner Metro Planning Commn., Nashville, 1977-79; exec. dir. Metro Hist. Zoning Commn., Nashville, 1980-82; asst. dir. Mid-Atlantic Regional Office, Nat. Trust for Hist. Preservation, Washington, 1983, dir. Office of Neighborhood Conservation, 1984, project dir. Urban Demonstration Program Nat. Main St. Ctr., 1985-87; pres. Hyett-Palma Inc. 1985—, Hyett-Palma Publs. 1988—; del. Nat. Assn. Neighborhoods Platform Conv., 1979. Founder Neighborhood Reinvestment Corp., Nashville, 1978; mayoral appointee Neighborhood Housing Services, Nashville, 1979-82; dir. Restore the U.S. Capitol Campaign, 1983. Author: Salaries, Wages and Fringe Benefits in Michigan Cities and Villages, 1973; Nashville: Conserving a Heritage, 1977; Neighborhood Commercial Buildings: A Survey and Analysis of Metropolitan Nashville, 1983; Business Enhancement Plan for Downtown Poughkeepsie, N.Y., 1987; Future Directions for Seward, Alaska, 1987; Action Agenda for Gay Street, Knoxville, 1987; Agenda for Economic Enhancement of Haymarket Lincoln, Nebraska, 1987; Management of Downtown Palmer, Alaska, 1988; Successful Business Recruitment Strategies in the U.S., 1988, Business Clustering: How to Leverage Sales, 1988, Business Plans for Business Districts, 1988, Office Tenant Recruitment for Pittsfield, Mass., 1989, Business Plan for the Heart of Corpus Christi, Tex., 1989, Retail Recruitment Strategies for Reading, Pa., 1989, Seward 2000: Comprehensive Plan, Seward, Alaska, 1989, Business Plan for Downtown Rocky Mount, N.C., 1990, Retail and Restaurant Audit for Rosslyn, Va., 1990, Market Analysis and Enhancement Strategies for Liberal, Kans., 1990, Market Analysis and Enhancement Strategies for Geneva, N.Y., 1990, Building the Vision: Washington Street Corridor, Falls Church, Va., 1990, The Magnetic Mile Vision, Glendale, Ariz., 1990, Downtown Hopkinsville (Ky.) Business Plan, 1990, Downtown Denton (Md.) Devel. Plan, 1991. East Downtown Dearborn (Mich.) Bus. Plan, 1991, Leavenworth/Lansing Market Analysis, 1991; (with Nat. League of Cities) City Commercial Centers Reborn: Building Commercial District Dynamism, 1990, Downtown Visions, 1992, Focus Groups for Downtown, 1992, Business Retention and Expansion, 1993, Winning Ways, 1993, Downtowns and Utilities, 1994, Downtown Safety: Addressing the Myths and the Realities, 1994, Downtown Parking Management, 1995, Downtown Public Space Maintenance, 1995, Accepting the Challenge: The Rebirth of America's Downtown, 1995; project dir.: A Market and Design Study for the Broadway National Register Historic District, 1982; author studies, pamphlet, articles; contbr. newsletters; editor Edgefield News, Nashville, 1979-80. Publicity dir. Hist. Edgefield, Inc., 1979; ptnr. Nat. League of Cities The Rebirth of Am's. Downtowns Pilot Program, 1993-94, Nat. League of Cities Am. Downtown: New Thinking New Life, 1995—; hon. mem. Tenn. State Legislature, 1980. Woodlawn scholar Nat. Trust for Hist. Preservation, 1976; named one of Outstanding Young Women of Am., 1985, award of excellence Va. Downtown Devel. Assn., 1990, Am. Planning Assn., 1991. Office: Hyett-Palma Inc 1600 Prince St Ste 110 Alexandria VA 22314-2836

PALMEIRO, RAFAEL CORRALES, professional baseball player; b. Havana, Cuba, Oct. 24, 1964. Degree in Comml. Art, Miss. State U. With Chgo. Cubs, 1986-88, Tex. Rangers, 1988-93; first baseman Balt. Orioles, 1994—. Named to Coll. All-Am. Team, 1985, to Nat. League All-Star Team, 1988, 95, to Am. League All-Star Team, 1991; named Eastern League Most Valuable Player, 1986. Office: Balt Orioles 333 W Camden St Baltimore MD 21201

PALMER, ALICE EUGENIA, retired physician, educator; b. Chgo., Sept. 17, 1910; d. Charles Grover and Eugenia Marie (Sundquist) P.; m. Lawrence A. Pratt, 1935; m. Clyde K. Bowles, 1973; children: Lawrene Alice Porter, Dorothy Jane Pratt (Mrs. John D. Shilling). BSc, U. Chgo., 1932, MS in Physiology, 1937; MD, Wayne State U., 1938. Diplomate Am. Bd. Dermatology (preceptor 1956—). Resident pathology Detroit Receiving Hosp., 1938, resident physician dermatology, 1939-42; practice medicine specializing in dermatology Detroit, 1942-61, 65-71, Sun City, Ariz., 1971-90; instr. pathology Sch. Medicine, Wayne State U., Detroit, 1938, assoc. clin. prof. medicine, 1946-61, 65-68, adj. clin. prof., 1968-71; chmn. dept. dermatology Grace Hosp., Detroit, 1956-61, 68-71; sr. cons. dermatology Jennings Hosp., Detroit, 1954-71; med. educator U.S. AID, 1961, chief med. edn. project, Vietnam, 1961-65, med. cons., Vietnam and East Asia, 1965-68; mem. 3-man team for Survey S.E. Asian Med. Rsch. Instns., 1966; vis. prof. dermatology faculty medicine U. Saigon, 1961, 62, 63, 64, 71-73; mem. Nat. Program Dermatology, 1969-75; served Clinica Adelante, Surprise, Ariz. Assoc. editor Detroit Med. News, 1959-60. Bd. dirs., exec. bd. YWCA, Detroit, 1965-70. Recipient Disting. Alumni award Wayne State U., 1987, Disting. Svc. award Sch. Medicine, Key to the City of Detroit, 1959, U.S. Civilia Svc. medal Vietnam; named one of 10 Top Women in Detroit, 1959; Julius Stieglitz fellow in chemistry U. Chgo., 1932. Mem. AMA, Ariz. Med. Soc., Mich. Med. Soc. (chmn. dermatology 1959), Pacific Dermatol. Soc., Detroit Dermatol. Soc. (pres. 1959), Phoenix Dermatol. Soc. (v.p. 1977), Am. Acad. Dermatology (mem. internat. com., mem. internat. task force 1971-75), Maricopa County Med. Soc., Internat. Soc. Tropical Dermatology, Am. Soc. Dermatologic Surgery, Am. Geriatric Soc., Am. Acad. Cosmetic Surgery, Am. Soc. Lipo-Suction Surgery, Am. Acad. Facial Plastic and Reconstructive Surgery, S.W. Derm. Soc. (sec.-treas. 1978—, pres. 1980-81), Women's Econ. Club Detroit (bd. dirs.), Pilot Club (pres.), Sigma Xi, Alpha Omega Alpha. Home and Office: 18170 N 91st Ave Apt 1155 Peoria AZ 85382-0868

PALMER, ANN THERESE DARIN, lawyer; b. Detroit, Apr. 25, 1951; d. Americo and Theresa (Del Favero) Darin; m. Robert Towne Palmer, Nov. 9, 1974; children: Justin Darin, Christian Darin. BA, U. Notre Dame, 1973, MBA, 1975; JD, Loyola U., Chgo., 1978. Bar: Ill. 1978, U.S. Supreme Ct. 1981. Reporter Wall Street Jour., Detroit, 1974; freelancer Time Inc. Fin. Publs., Chgo., 1975-77, extern, Midwest regional solicitor U.S. Dept. Labor, 1976-78; tax atty. Esmark Inc., 1978; counsel Chgo. United, 1978-81; ind. contractor Legal Tax Rsch., 1981-89; fin. and legal news contbr. The Chgo. Tribune, 1991—, Bus. Week Chgo. Bur., 1991—, Automotive News, 1993—, Crain's Chgo. Bus., 1994—. Mem. Saddle and Cycle Club of Chgo., Detroit Golf Club. Roman Catholic. Home: 873 Forest Hill Rd Lake Forest IL 60045-3905

PALMER, ARNOLD DANIEL, former professional golfer; b. Youngstown, Pa., Sept. 10, 1929; s. Milfred Jerome and Doris M. Palmer; m. Winnie Walzer, Dec. 20, 1954; children: Peggy Palmer Wears, Amy Palmer Saunders. Student, Wake Forest Coll., LLD, 1970. Profl. golfer, 1954-95, businessman, entrepreneur, 1960—; nat. spokesman Pennzoil Petroleum Products, Sears Can., Rolex, Lofts Seed, Cadillac Motor Car, GTE, Golf mag., Rayovac, Textron, 84 Lumber, Lexington Furniture, Office Depot; designer numerous golf courses. Author: Arnold Palmer's Golf Book, 1961, Portrait of a Professional Golfer, 1964, My Game and Yours, 1965, rev. edit., 1983, Situation Golf, 1970, Go for Broke, 1973, Arnold Palmer's Best 54 Holes of Golf, 1977, Arnold Palmer's Complete Book of Putting, 1986, Play Great Golf, 1987. With USCG, 1951-54. Winner over 90 major golf tournaments, 1955—, including Masters Championship, 1958, 60, 62, 94, U.S. Open, 1960, U.S. Amateur, 1954, Brit. Open, 1961, 62; recipient numerous golf awards including Bob Jones award U.S. Golf Assn., William D. Richardson award Golf Writers Assn. Am., Herb Graffis award Nat. Golf Found.; named Athlete of Decade PA, 1969, Sportsman of Yr. Sports Illustrated mag., 1960, Player of Yr. Profl. Golfers Assn., 1960, 62; Profl. Golfers Assn. Tour Money Leader, 1958, 60, 62, 63; elected to World Golf Hall of Fame, Profl. Golfers Assn. Hall of Fame. Mem. Latrobe (Pa.) Country Club, Laurel Valley Golf Club, Rolling Rock Club (Ligonier, Pa.), Bay Hill Club, Duquesne Club (Pitts.). Avocation: aviation. Home and Office: PO Box 52 Youngstown PA 15696-0052

PALMER, B.J., investment advisor; b. Sweetwater, Tex., July 2, 1934; s. Franklin and Hazel (Pugh) P.; m. Kay Monica McCosley, Feb. 15, 1964; children: Robert Fitzgerald, David Patrick. AS, Schreiner Mil. Inst., 1953; BA, U. Nebr., 1967; MS, U. George Washington, 1973. CFP. Commdr. 2nd lt. USMC, 1957, advanced through grades to col., 1979, ret., 1986; investment advisor Am. Express Fin. Advisors, Virginia Beach, VA., 1986—; tchr., mgr. Am. Express Fin. Advisors, Virginia Beach, 1991—; vol. tchr. fin. local H.S., Virginia Beach, 1992—. Sec. Ret. NATO Officers, Virginia Beach, 1989-91; fund raiser Rep. Party of Va., 1990—. Decorated two DFC, USMC, Vietnam, 1966, 69, Bronze star USMC, Vietnam, 1969. Mem. Internat. Assn. for Fin. Planners (pres. 1991-93), Inst. CFP (sec. 1993—), The Ret. Officers Assn. (v.p. 1993—). Republican. Avocations: pilot fixed wing A/C, pilot hang gliders, racquetball, tennis instructing. Office: Am Express Fin Advisors 1169 Selwood Dr Virginia Beach VA 23464-5810

PALMER, BRIAN EUGENE, lawyer; b. Mpls., May 16, 1948; s. Eugene Philip and Virginia Breeze (Rolfshus) P.; m. Julia Washburn Morrison, Dec. 29, 1972; 1 child, Julia Hunter. AB, Brown U., 1970; JD, William Mitchell Coll. of Law, 1974. Bar: Minn. 1974, U.S. Dist. Ct. Minn. 1975, U.S. Ct. Appeals (8th cir.) 1980, U.S. Ct. Fed. Claims 1984, U.S. Supreme Ct. 1980. Asst. pub. defender Hennepin County Pub. Defender, Mpls., 1974-78; assoc. Dorsey & Whitney, Mpls., 1978-82, ptnr., 1983—. Home: 1190 Lyman Ave Wayzata MN 55391-9671 Office: Dorsey & Whitney Pillsbury Ctr S 220 S 6th St Minneapolis MN 55402-1498

PALMER, CRUISE, newspaper editor; b. Kansas City, Kans., Apr. 9, 1917; s. Thomas Potter and Margaret Scroggs (McFadden) P.; m. Dorraine Humphreys, Sept. 7, 1946; children: Thomas Cruise, Martha D. Sprague. B.S. in Journalism, Kans. State U., 1938. With Kansas City (Mo.) Star, 1938—, news editor, 1963-64, mng. editor, 1965-66; exec. editor and bd. Star and Times, 1967-77, cons., 1978—; dir. Purtec Systems, Inc. Mem. bd. govs. Am. Royal Live Stock and Horse Show Assn., 1967-91; bd. dirs. ARC, 1978-91, Kansas City Mayor's Corps Progress, 1978-91; found. trustee Kans. State U.; trustee Kansas City Sister Cities Commn., 1978-91. Served to lt. (j.g.) USNR, 1943-46. Recipient Distinguished Service award Kans. State U., 1967; First Place award Pro-Am. Southgate Open Golf Tournament, 1973; Second Place award Pro-Am. Hawaiian Open, 1973, 85; Third Place, 1981; First Place award Jim Colbert Celebrity Tournament, 1981, First Place Team award Kansas City area Am. Cancer Soc. Golf Tournament, 1986. Mem. Am. Soc. Newspaper Editors, Mo.-Kans. A.P. Editors and Pubs., Soc. Profl. Journalists, Kansas City Sr. Golf Assn., Mo. Sr. Golf Assn., Kansas City Press Club (pres. 1953-54, 64-65, permanent trustee, pres. scholarship found. 1989), Kansas City Club, Chiefs Red Coat Club, Milburn Golf and Country Club, Beta Theta Pi (Greater Kansas City Beta of Yr. 1980). Episcopalian (former vestryman and lay reader). Home: 4900 W 64th Ter Shawnee Mission KS 66208-1340 Office: 1729 Grand Ave Kansas City MO 64108-1413

PALMER, CURTIS HOWARD, diversified company executive, lawyer; b. Oakland, Calif., 1908; s. Howard H. and Catherine May (Larkin) P.; m. Helen Hayes, Apr. 8, 1936. LL.B., U. Calif., 1932. Sole practice, 1932-35; tax counsel Calif. Bd. of Equalization, 1935-43; gen. counsel Alfred Hart, Los Angeles, 1943-60; exec. officer City Nat. Bank, Beverly Hills, Calif., 1960-75, chmn. bd., 1975; chmn. bd. Arden Group, Inc., Beverly Hills, 1976—; dir. Internat. Aluminum Corp.; chmn. bd. dirs. Arden Group Inc. Office: Arden Mayfair Inc 2020 S Central Ave Compton CA 90220-5302*

PALMER, DANIEL LEE, data communication manufacturing company executive; b. Norman, Okla., July 6, 1958; s. James Daniel and Margret (Kupka) P.; m. Kathleen Marie Connolly, Aug. 31, 1985; children: Jonathan Daniel, Elizabeth Marie, Robert Edward. BSEE, U. Colo., 1980; MSEE, U. Santa Clara, 1985. Engr. GTE Lenkurt, San Carlos, Calif., 1980-82; div. mgr. Granger Assocs., Santa Clara, Calif., 1982-84; v.p. DSC Comm., Santa Clara, 1984-89; v.p. engring., corp. officer Digital Link, Sunnyvale, Calif., 1989-95, pres., COO, 1995—. Contbr. articles to profl. jours. Mem. IEEE, Eta Kappa Nu. Avocations: piano, exercise, windsurfing, skiing, kids. Home: 36532 Montecito Dr Fremont CA 94536-2614 Office: Digital Link Corp 217 Humboldt Ct Sunnyvale CA 94089-1300

PALMER, DANNA SWAIN, special education educator; b. Greenville, N.C., Nov. 16, 1955; d. Thomas Ryan and Kristina (Massie) Swain; m. Charles Edward Palmer, July 26, 1980; children: Thad Edward, Kyle Thomas, Cory Leonard. BS in Music Edn., East Carolina U., 1978; M in Elem. Edn. with high honors, Wilmington Coll., 1993; spl. edn. cert., U. Del., 1994, Del. State U., 1994. Typing, swimming and music tchr. Norfolk (Va.) Acad., 1979-80; pvt. piano tchr. Seaford, Del., 1981-88; choral music tchr. Crusader Christian Acad., Salisbury, Md., 1989; 3d grade tchr., French tchr. Epworth Christian Sch., Laurel, Del., 1989-91; elem. tchr., asst. Woodbridge Schs., Greenwood, Del., 1992-93; spl. edn. tchr. Seaford (Del.) Sch. Dist., 1993—; mem., parent rep. Prin.'s Adv. Coun., Seaford, 1991-92, Supt.'s Adv. Coun., Seaford, 1993-94; mem., profl. rep. Supt.'s Profl. Adv. Coun., Seaford, 1994; del., spl. edn. rep. Project 21 Team Rsch., Dover, Del., 1994; swimming instr. ARC, Georgetown, Del., 1973-80, Seaford Jaycee Pool, 1974-94. Song leader, co-chair Pioneer Clubs, Seaford, 1986-91; choir dir. children's ministries St. John's United Meth. Ch., Seaford, 1980-85; V.p., sec. PTA of Seaford Mid. Sch., 1992-94, sec. 1992—; legislative liaison Seaford Mid. Sch., 1994—. Mem. Music Educator's Nat. Conf., Del. Music Educator's Assn., Music Tchr.'s Nat. Assn., Nat. Coun. for Tchrs. of Lang. Arts, Coun. for Exceptional Children, TESOL, Del. Limited English Proficiency Speakers. Republican. Avocations: music, biking, swimming, writing, sewing. Home: 531 N Phillips St Seaford DE 19973-2307 Office: Seaford Sch Dist 500 E Stein Hwy Seaford DE 19973-1528

PALMER, DAVE RICHARD, educator, military officer; b. Ada, Okla., May 31, 1934; s. David Furman and Lorena Marie (Clardy) P.; m. LuDelia Clemmer, Apr. 13, 1957; children: Allison, J. Kersten. BS, U.S. Military Acad., 1956; MA in History, Duke U., 1966; postgrad., Army War Coll., 1972-73; PhD (hon.), Duke U., 1990. Commd. U.S. Army, 1956, advanced through grades to lt. gen.; mem. faculty dept. history U.S. Mil. Acad., 1966-69; mem. staff (Pentagon), 1973-76, Joint Chiefs of Staff, 1979-81; comdr. Baumholder Mil. Community, W. Ger., 1981-83; dep. comdt. Command and Gen. Staff Coll., Ft. Leavenworth, Kans., 1983-85; comdg. gen. 1st Armored Div., W.Ger., 1985-86; supt. U.S. Mil. Acad., 1986-91, ret., 1991; pres. Walden U., 1995—. Author: The River and the Rock, 1969, The Way of the Fox, 1975, Summons of the Trumpet, 1978, 1794-America, Its Army, and The Birth of the Nation, 1994. Bd. dirs. Walden U., 1992-94. Decorated Legion of Merit (3); Bronze Star (2), D.S.M.(2). Mem. Assn. U.S. Army, Armor Assn., Mil. Conflict Inst., Coun. on America's Mil. Past, Soc. Mil. History, Soc. Cin.

PALMER, DAVID, dancer; b. Cairns, Australia. Attended, Saill Acad. of Dance, Sydney, Australia; studied with Janice Breen. Dancer Australian Ballet, Joffrey Ballet, Miami City Ballet, Royal Ballet of Flanders; prin. dancer San Francisco Ballet, 1994—; guest artist Sydney Dance Co., Ballet du Nord, France, Pact Ballet of South Africa, Queensland Ballet, Australian Ballet, Ballet Theatre of Miami. Dance performances include Prodigal Son, Apollo, Scotch Symphony, Rubies, Donizetti Variations, La Source, Bugaku, Diverimento No. 15, Tchaikovsky Pas de Deux, Minkus Pas de Trois, Sylvia Pas de Deux, Stars and Stripes, Diana and Acteon, Taming of the Shrew, Romeo & Juliet, Jeu Des Cartes, Lady and the Fool, La Fille mal gardée, Illuminations, Valentine, Jamboree, Kettantanz, Suite Saint-Säens, Trinity, Light Rain, Forgotten Land, Return to a Strange Land, Dream Dances, Arden Court, Aureole, Cloven Kingdom, Reus, Transtangos, Movillisimanoble, Caoticos, Contropical, Concerto for La Donna, The Moor's Pavane, Threshold, Rosalinda, La Bayadere, Nutcracker, Beyond Twelve, Surfacing, Aerial, The Huntchback of Notre Dame, Le Corsaire Pas de Deux, The Three Muscateers, Valses Poeticos, Maestrom, In the Night, The Concert, Company B, Rodeo, others; (film) To Dream of Roses, 1990; choreographer Aerial, Memories, Beauty and the Beast, Intimacy Pas de Deux, Collage. Office: San Francisco Ballet 455 Franklin St San Francisco CA 94102-4438

PALMER, DAVID GILBERT, lawyer; b. Lakewood, N.J., Jan. 10, 1945; s. Robert Dayton and Lois (Gilbert) P.; m. Susan Edmundson Walsh, Aug. 17, 1968; children: Jonathan, Megan. AB, Johns Hopkins U., 1967; JD, U. Colo., 1970. Bar: Colo. 1970, U.S. Dist. Ct. Colo. 1970, U.S. Ct. Appeals (9th and 10th cirs.) 1970, U.S. Supreme Ct. 1970. Ptnr., chmn. litigation dept. Holland & Hart, Denver, 1970-87, Gibson, Dunn & Crutcher, Denver, 1987—. Chmn. N.W. region Am. Heart Assn., Dallas, 1986—, bd. dirs., 1986—, sec., 1990—, chmn. elect, 1991-92, chmn., 1992-93; pres., bd. dirs. Colo. Heart Assn., Denver, 1974; bd. dirs. C. H. Kempe Nat. Ctr. for Prevention of Child Abuse, Denver, 1984-90, pres., 1989-90; bd. dirs. Goodwill Industries, Denver, 1981-84. Mem. ABA, Colo. Bar Assn., Denver Law Club. Clubs: University, Mile High (Denver). Home: 3120 Ramshorn

Dr Castle Rock CO 80104-9073 Office: Gibson Dunn & Crutcher 1801 California St Ste 4100 Denver CO 80202-2642

PALMER, DAVID SCOTT, political scientist, educator; b. Boston, July 16, 1937; s. Walter S. and Jean (Stuart) P.; m. Sarah Crawford, 1955 (dec. Nov. 1985); children: Walter Scott, Henry Crawford, Asa MacAdam. BA in Internat. Rels. cum laude, Dartmouth Coll., 1959; MA in Hispanic Am. Studies, Stanford U., 1962; PhD in Comparative Govt., Cornell U., 1973. Vol. leader Peace Corps, Peru, 1962-64; asst. dean freshmen, asst. to dir. admissions Dartmouth Coll., Hanover, N.H., 1964-68; from instr. to asst. prof. dept. govt. Bowdoin Coll., 1972-76; professorial lectr. Sch. Advanced Internat. Studies Johns Hopkins U., Washington, 1977-88; assoc. dean for programs Fgn. Svc. Inst., Dept. State, 1984-88, chair Latin Am. and Caribbean studies, 1976-88; prof. polit. sci. Boston U., 1988—, prof. internat. rels., 1990—, dir. Latin Am. studies, 1991-94; vis. lectr. Princeton U., 1978-79, Georgetown U., 1985. Author: Peru: The Authoritarian Tradition, 1980, (with Kevin Middlebrook) Military Government and Political Development: Lessons from Peru, 1975 (with Robert Wesson and others) The Latin American Military Institution, 1985; editor, contbr.: Shining Path of Peru, 1992, 2d edit., 1994; contbr. chpts. to books, articles and revs. to profl. jours. Recipient Meritorious Honor award U.S. Dept. of State, 1981; Daniel Webster nat. scholar, 1955-59; Edward John Noble Found. leadership grantee 1959-62. Mem. Latin Am. Studies Assn. (exec. com. 1983-86), New Eng. Coun. Latin Am. Studies (exec. com. 1989—, pres. 1993-94), Interam. Coun. of Washington (pres. 1978-79), Phi Beta Delta, Phi Kappa Phi, Sigma Delta Pi. Home: 69 Waverley St Belmont MA 02178-1958 Office: Boston U 152 Bay State Rd Boston MA 02215-1501

PALMER, DEBORAH JEAN, lawyer; b. Williston, N.D., Oct. 25, 1947; d. Everett Edwin and Doris Irene (Harberg) P.; m. Kenneth L. Rich, Mar. 29, 1980; children: Andrew, Stephanie. BA, Carleton Coll., 1969; JD cum laude, Northwestern U., 1973. Bar: Minn. 1973, U.S. Dist. Ct. Minn. 1973, U.S. Ct. Appeals (8th cir.) 1975, U.S. Supreme Ct. 1978. Econ. analyst Harris Trust & Savs. Bank, Chgo., 1969-70; assoc. Robins, Kaplan, Miller & Ciresi, Mpls., 1973-79, ptnr., 1979—. Trustee Carleton Coll., 1984-88; mem. bd. religious edn. Plymouth Congl. Ch., 1992-95. Mem. ABA, Minn. Bar Assn., Minn. Women Lawyers Assn. (sec. 1976-78), Hennepin County Bar Assn., Hennepin County Bar Found. (bd. dirs. 1978-81), Carleton Coll. Alumni Assn. (bd. dirs. 1978-82, sec. 1980-82), Women's Assn. of Minn. Orch. (bd. dirs. 1980-85, treas. 1981-83). Home: 1787 Colfax Ave S Minneapolis MN 55403-3008 Office: Robins Kaplan Miller & Ciresi 800 Lasalle Ave Minneapolis MN 55402-2006

PALMER, DENNIS DALE, lawyer; b. Alliance, Nebr., Apr. 30, 1945; s. Vernon D. Palmer and Marie E. (Nelson) Fellers; m. Rebecca Ann Turner, Mar. 23, 1979; children: Lisa Marie, Jonathan Paul. BA, U. Mo., 1967, JD, 1970. Bar: Mo. 1970, U.S. Dist. Ct. (we. dist.) Mo. 1970, U.S. Ct. Appeals (8th and 10th cirs.) 1973, U.S. Supreme Ct. 1980. Staff atty. Legal Aid Soc. Western Mo., Kansas City, 1970-73; assoc. Shughart, Thomson & Kilroy, P.C., Kansas City, 1973-76, ptnr., bd. dirs., 1976—. Contbr. articles on franchise and employment law to legal jours. Bd. dirs., chmn. legal assts. adv. bd. Avila Coll., Kansas City, 1984-87. 2d lt. U.S. Army, 1970. Mem. ABA (litigation com. 1980, forum com. on franchising 1987), Mo. Bar Assn. (antitrust com. 1975—, civil practice com. 1975—), Kansas City Bar Assn. (chmn. franchise law com. 1987—), Univ. Club. Avocations: jogging, golf, tennis, outdoor activities, reading. Home: 13100 Canterbury Leawood KS 66209-1003 Office: Shughart Thomson & Kilroy 12 Wyandotte Plz 120 W 12th St Fl 16 Kansas City MO 64105-1902

PALMER, DONALD CURTIS, interdenominational missionary society executive; b. Nelson, Minn., Oct. 8, 1934; s. Roy August Adn Cora (Bergner) P.; m. Dorothy Mae Nordquist, Mar. 16, 1962; children: Jean Marie, John Eric. Student, U. Minn., 1952-55; BS in Bible, Briercrest Bible Coll., Caronport, Can., 1958; MA in Missions, Trinity Divinity Sch., Deerfield, Ill., 1967; D in Ministry, Trinity Divinity Sch., 1989. Missionary Colombia GMU Internat., Kansas City, Mo., 1959-71; dir. evangelism GMU Internat., 1969-71, field sec. Latin Am., 1971-73, v.p. field ministries for Latin Am., 1973-85, v.p. research and strategy, 1985-92; gen. dir. Am. Missionary Fellowship, Villanova, Pa., 1992—; vis. prof. Grace Coll. of the Bible, Omaha, 1982-92; mem. Frontier People's Com., 1985-92, Evang. Missiological Soc., 1991—. Author: Explosion of People Evangelism, 1974; (with others) Dynamic Religious Movements, 1978, Managing Conflict Creatively, 1990. Republican. Baptist. Avocations: golf, tennis, hiking. Home: 200 Cohasset Ln West Chester PA 19380-6504 Office: Am Missionary Fellowship 672 Conestoga Rd Villanova PA 19085-1428 *The greatest inner quality that a person can possess is a thankful, grateful spirit.*

PALMER, DORA DEEN POPE, English and French language educator; b. Jackson, Miss., June 26, 1946; d. Melvin Sr. and Gladys (Wolfe) Pope; m. Carey Palmer Jr.; 1 child, Cawandra V. AA, Utica Jr. Coll., 1966; BS in Edn., Jackson State U., 1968, MA in Edn., 1976. Cert. English and French tchr. Tchr. English and French McCullough H. S., Monticello, Miss., 1968-69, Topeka-Tilton H.S., Monticello, 1969-70, Crystal Springs (Miss.) H.S., 1971-93; tchr. French Jackson (Miss.) Pub. Sch. Dist., 1993—; chair English Dept., Crystal Springs, 1983-93; lectr. Jackson State Upward Bound, Jackson, 1984-94; chair Crystal Springs H.S. steering and editing com. So. Assn. Colls. and Schs.; prodr., sponsor black history projects. Drama coach N.W. Mid. Sch., Jackson, 1993—; sponsor Beta Club, Crystal Springs, 1979; sec. Expo-Social & Civic Club, Jackson, 1988—; pianist Mount Wade Missionary Bapt. Ch., 1965-80, Terry Mission Missionary Bapt. Ch., 1979-87. Named Tchr. of Month, Tiger Pause newspaper, 1989, Star Tchr. Jackson State Upward Bound, 1992, Tchr. of Yr. Crystal Springs H.S., 1993; recipient Tchr. Appreciation award The Tiger ann., 1987, Outstanding Svc. award Terry Mission Bapt. Ch., 1983. Mem. Nat. Assn. Edn., Miss. Assn. Edn. Democrat. Avocations: playing piano, reading, cooking Southern dishes, sewing. Home: 316 S Denver St Jackson MS 39209-6303 Office: Jackson Pub Schs N W Jackson 7020 Hwy 49 N Jackson MS 39213

PALMER, EDWARD L., social psychology educator, television researcher, writer; b. Hagerstown, Md., Aug. 11, 1938; s. Ralph Leon and Eva Irene (Brandenburg) P.; children: Edward Lee, Jennifer Lynn. BA, Gettysburg Coll., 1960; BD, Luth. Theol. Sem., Gettysburg, 1964; MS, Ohio U., 1967, PhD, 1970. Asst. prof. Western Md. Coll., Westminster, 1968-70; asst. prof. Davidson Coll., N.C., 1970-77, assoc. prof., 1977-86, chair, 1985—, prof., 1986—, Watson prof., 1991—; guest rschr. Harvard U., Cambridge, Mass., 1977; vis. scholar UCLA, 1984; cons. Council on Children, Media, Merchandising, 1978-79, 1st Union Bank Corp., Charlotte, N.C., 1975-79; NSF proposal reviewer, 1978—. Editl. reviewer Jour. Broadcasting and Electronic Media, 1978—; editor: Children and the Faces of TV, 1980; author: (book) Children in the Cradle of TV, 1987; contbr. to Wiley Ency. of Psychology, 1984; author jour. articles. Sec. A. Mecklenburg Child Devel. Assn., Davidson and Cornelius, N.C., 1974-78; bd. mem. pub. radio sta. WDAV, 1970-90. Telecommunications task force Rutgers U., 1981. Recipient Thomas Jefferson Teaching award Robert Earl McConnell Found., 1993. Mem. APA, Soc. Rsch. in Child Devel., Am. Psychol. Soc., Assn. Heads Depts. Psychology (chair 1994-96), Southeastern Psychol. Assn., Southeastern Soc. Social Psychologists, So. Assn. Pub. Opinion Rsch., Phi Beta Kappa (pres. Davidson chpt. 1985-86). Avocations: sunrise and sunset walks, writing poetry, bird watching, music composition and performance. Office: Davidson Coll PO Box 1719 Davidson NC 28036-1719

PALMER, EDWARD LEWIS, banker; b. N.Y.C., Aug. 12, 1917; s. William and Cecelia (Tierney) P.; m. Margaret Preston, Jan. 5, 1940; children: Edward Preston, Jane Lewis. A.B., Brown U., 1938. With N.Y. Trust Co., 1941-59, v.p., 1952-59; with Citibank, N.A., N.Y.C., 1959-82; sr. v.p. Citibank, N.A., 1962-65, exec. v.p., 1965-70, dir., chmn. exec. com., 1970-82; pres. Mill Neck Group, Inc., 1982; bd. dirs. Devon Group, Inc., SunResorts Ltd., Holmes Protection Group Inc.; dir. emeritus Cornign Inc.; trustee emeritus Mut. N.Y. Trustee emeritus Met. Mus. Art, Brown U. Served to lt. comdr. USNR, 1942-46. Mem. Phi Gamma Delta. Home: Horseshoe Rd Mill Neck NY 11765 Office: 399 Park Ave New York NY 10022-4614

PALMER, FORREST CHARLES, librarian, educator; b. Burlington, Wis., Oct. 17, 1924; s. Forrest Blaire and Marie Florence (Rubach) P.; m. Lois Mae Davis, June 12, 1946; children: Forrest Charles, Beth Elaine, Janet Lorrayne. Student, U. Pitts., 1943-44; B.A., Valparaiso U., 1948; B.S. in L.S, George Peabody Coll., 1949, M.S. in L.S, 1953. Head catalog dept. Janesville (Wis.) Pub. Library, 1949-50; serials cataloger N.C. State U., Raleigh, 1950-51; head serials dept. N.C. State U., 1951-55; dir. libraries Miss. State U., State College, 1955-62; librarian, head dept. library sci. James Madison U., Harrisonburg, Va., 1962-70, head librarian, 1970-74, prof. library sci., documents librarian, 1973-89, ret., 1989, prof. emeritus, 1990—, mem. faculty senate, 1982-86, faculty marshall, 1983-85, treas. senate, 1985-86; mem. library com. Va. Higher Edn. Study Commn.; sec. joint law library com. Laird L. Conrad Meml. Library, Harrisonburg, 1974-89; adv. com. Va. Council Higher Edn.; Madison Coll. rep. Library Affairs Va. U. Center. Editor: Virginia Librarian, 1963-65. Contbr. articles and book revs. to profl. publs. Mem. edn. com. Starkville (Miss.) Youth Ctr., 1956; chmn. adv. bd. YMCA, State College, Miss., 1957-59; vice-chmn. Rep. city com., Harrisonburg, 1979-81; mem. land use adv. com. Ctrl. Shenandoah Planning Dist. Commn., 1979; mem. Bd. Zoning Appeals, Harrisonburg, 1981-91, vice chmn., 1983-85, chmn., 1985-91; ruling elder Presbyn. Ch. U.S., clk. of session, 1982-84; mem. task force on maintenance Synod of Mid-Atlantic, Presbyn. Ch., Massanetta Springs, 1991; mem. Ft. Delaware Soc., 1992, life mem., 1995—. With Signal Corps AUS, PTO, 1943-46. Recipient Golden Triangle award YMCA. Mem. ALA (liaison com. Library Instrn. Round Table 1978-80, com. on instrn. in use of libraries 1977-79, mem. Govt. Documents Round Table 1983-89), Southeastern Library Assn. (chmn. coll. sect. 1960-62, treas., mem. exec. bd. 1975-76, budget com. 1974-80, hdqrts. liason com., 1987-91), Miss. Library Assn. (chmn. standards and planning com. 1958-59, chmn. coll. sect. 1959-60), Va. Library Assn. (activities com. 1962-65, chmn. publs. com. 1963-65, 1st v.p. 1968, pres. 1969-70), Pi Gamma Mu, Alpha Beta Alpha (adviser 1962-70), Beta Phi Mu. Republican. Presbyterian. Home: 60 E Weaver Ave Harrisonburg VA 22801-3041 *Long-lasting and meaningful contributions to society are those made out of consideration for others, not those where another individual is harmed.*

PALMER, FRANK GARRATT, police executive; b. Wellington, Ont., Can., Mar. 24, 1939; m. Joyce Palmer, July 6, 1963; children: Jill, Brock. LLB, U. Manitoba, 1975; LLM, Dalhousie U., 1976. Joined Royal Can. Mounted Police, 1959-65; deputy chief Assiniboia Police Dept., Winnipeg, Man., Can., 1965-68; rejoined Royal Can. Mounted Police, 1968-1984; dir. econ. crime hdqs. Royal Can. Mounted Police, Ottawa, 1984-86; officer in charge criminal ops. Royal Can. Mounted Police, Toronto, 1986-87; officer in charge fed. policing Royal Can. Mounted Police, British Columbia, 1987-89; officer in charge criminal ops. Royal Can. Mounted Police, British Columbia, B.C., 1989-94; apptd. deputy commr. ops. Royal Can. Mounted Police, 1994-96; dep. commr. Northwestern region Royal Can. Mounted Police, Ottawa, 1996—. Mem. Can. Bar Assn., Internat. Soc. Reform or Criminal Law (dir.), B.C./Can. Criminal Justice Assn. (dir.). Office: Royal Canadian Mounted Police, 1200 Vanier Pkwy, Ottawa, ON Canada K1A 0R2

PALMER, GARY ANDREW, portfolio manager; b. Stamford, Conn., Dec. 30, 1953; s. Andrew and Edna Balz (Brogan) P.; m. Suzanne Branyon, Oct. 10, 1981; children: Gregory Allen, Kimberly Lynn. BS in Bus. Adminstrn., U. Vt., 1977; MBA, U. N.C., 1979. Sr. fin. analyst Carolina Power and Light Co., Raleigh, N.C., 1979-80; dir. fin. planning and analysis Fed. Home Loan Mortgage Corp., Washington, 1980-85; sr. v.p. capital markets Imperial Corp. of Am., San Diego, 1985-90; sr. v.p., treas. Pacific 1st Fin. Corp., Seattle, 1990-92, Gentral Capital Corp., Seattle, 1993-95; CFO So. Pacific Funding Corp., Lake Oswego, Ore., 1995—.

PALMER, GARY STEPHEN, health services administrator; b. Murphy, N.C., Jan. 19, 1949; s. Bruce and Mary Frances (Patterson) P.; m. Kathleen Hart Middleton, June 12, 1976; children: Eric S., Brian S. BS in Bus. Adminstrn., U. N.C., 1971; MHA, Baylor U., 1982. Commd. U.S. Army, 1972, advanced through grades to lt. col., 1990; dir. program budget Letterman Army Med. Ctr., San Francisco, 1979-80; adminstrv. resident Womack Community Hosp., Fayetteville, N.C., 1981-82, ambulatory healthcare adminstr., 1982-83, asst. adminstr. profl. svcs., 1983-85; ambulatory healthcare adminstr. USA Health Svcs., San Antonio, 1985-88; COO U.S. Army Den Rl Activity, Killeen, Tex., 1988-91; dir. managed care Tripler Army Med. Ctr., Honolulu, 1991-93; inspector gen. Womack Army Med. Ctr., Ft. Bragg, N.C., 1993-94; assoc. dir. exec. master's program Sch. Pub. Health U. N.C., Chapel Hill, 1994—. Fellow Am. Coll. Healthcare Execs. (army regent's adv. coun. 1988-92, Elua Alii chpt. Honolulu 1991-93); mem. Med. Group Mgmt. Assn. Home: 103 William White Ct Carrboro NC 27510-4120 Office: U NC Sch Pub Health CB 7400 Dept Health Policy/Adminstn Chapel Hill NC 27599-7400

PALMER, HANS CHRISTIAN, economics educator; b. N.Y.C., Sept. 21, 1933; s. Hans P. and Dagny E. (Stockel) P.; m. Beverly Wilson, June 28, 1963; children: Margaret D., David E. B.A., U. Calif.-Berkeley, 1954, M.A., 1955, Ph.D., 1965. Instr. econs. Pomona Coll., Claremont, Calif., 1962-65, asst. prof., 1965-70, assoc. prof., 1970-77, prof. econs., 1977—. Co-author: Financial Barrier to Higher Education in California, 1965; co-author, co-editor: Long-Term Care: Perspectives from Research and Demonstrations, 1983. Served to 1st lt. U.S. Army, 1955-57. Grantee NSF, 1975-76. Mem. Am. Econs. Assn., Assn. Health Services Research, Econ. History Assn., Econ. History Soc. (U.K.), History of Econs. Soc., Assn. Comparative Econ. Studies. Office: Dept Econs Pomona Coll Claremont CA 91711

PALMER, HARVEY JOHN, chemical engineering educator, consultant; b. N.Y.C., Apr. 3, 1946; s. Harvey Anthony and Pearl Edna (Weber) P.; m. Donna Mary Partigan, July 11, 1966; children—Harvey D., Angeline, Thomas. B.S.C.E., U. Rochester, 1967; Ph.D. in Chem. Engring., U. Wash., 1971. Lic. profl. engr., N.Y. Asst. prof. chem. engring. U. Rochester, N.Y., 1971-77, assoc. prof., 1977-84, prof., 1984—, assoc. dean for grad. studies, 1983-89, chair dept. chem. engring., 1990—; cons. Pfaudler Co., Rochester, 1978-79, Eastman Kodak Co., Rochester, 1982-92, Helios Corp., Mumford, N.Y., 1983-91, Boehringer Mannheim Corp., Indpls., 1993; bd. dirs. Transmation Inc., Rochester. Contbr. articles to profl. jours. Mem. sch. bd. Honeoye Falls-Lima Central Schs., N.Y., 1983-92, pres., 1988-90. Recipient Undergrad. Teaching award Coll. Engring., U. Rochester, 1979, 82. Mem. Am. Inst. Chem. Engrs. (sec. Rochester sect. 1976-77), Sigma Xi. Office: Univ Rochester Dept Chem Engring Rochester NY 14627

PALMER, IRENE SABELBERG, university dean and educator emeritus, nurse, researcher, historian; b. Franklin, N.J., May 28, 1923; d. John Joseph and May (Heiser) Sabelberg; 1 son, Andrew C. B.S., N.J. State Tchrs. Coll., 1945; diploma, Jersey City Med. Center Sch. Nursing, 1945; M.A., N.Y. U., 1951, Ph.D., 1963. Edn. dir. Diploma Schs. Nursing, N.J., Mass., 1948-52; ednl. dir. Glenn Dale (Md.) Hosp., D.C. Dept. Pub. Health, 1956, dir. nursing svc. and edn., 1956-61; assoc. clin. prof. nursing Georgetown U., 1960-61; USPHS trainee, 1961-62; assoc. chief nursing svc. for rsch. VA Hosp., San Francisco, 1963-64; rsch. nurse cons. HEW, USPHS, Div. Nursing, Nursing Rsch. Field Center, San Francisco, 1964-66; asst. dean, assoc. prof. nursing U. Colo. Sch. Nursing, Denver, 1966-68; dean, prof. nursing Boston U. Sch. Nursing, 1968-74; prof. Hahn Sch. Nursing, U. San Diego, 1974-91, prof. emeritus, 1991—, dean, 1974-87, dean emeritus, 1988—; lectr. Clasical Alliance of the western States, Uskudar, Turkey. Editor: Nursing Clinics of North America, 1970; Contbr. articles to profl. jours. Served to capt. Nurse Corps U.S. Army, 1953-56. Internat. Nightingale scholar; Nat. Health Svc. fellow; recipient Excellence in Nursing Scholarship award Orgn. Nurse Execs., 1993. Fellow Nat. League Nursing (bd. visitors 1977-87), Am Acad. Nursing; mem. ANA, Am. Assn. History Nursing, Am. Assn. Colls. Nursing (hon.), Boston U. Nursing Archives, German Rsch. Assn. (pres. 1995), Sigma Theta Tau (Leadership award Zeta Mu chpt. 1986, Excellence in Nursing award 1991).

PALMER, JAMES ALVIN, baseball commentator; b. N.Y.C., Oct. 15, 1945; children: Jamie, Kelly. Student, Ariz. State U., Towson (Md.) State Coll. Pitcher Balt. Orioles, 1966-84; commentator ABC Sports, 1984—; also appears in TV and print advertisements. Author: (with Jack Clary) Jim Palmer's Way to Fitness, 1985. Recipient Cy Young Meml. award Am. League, 1973, 75, 76; named Am. League Pitcher of Year The Sporting News, 1973, 75, 76; elected to Baseball Hall of Fame, 1990. Played All-Star Game, 1970, 71, 72, 77, 78.

PALMER, JAMES DANIEL, information technology educator; b. Washington, Mar. 8, 1930; s. Martin Lyle and Sarah Elizabeth (Hall) P.; m. Margret Kupka, June 21, 1952; children: Stephen Robert, Daniel Lee, John Keith. AA, Fullerton Jr. Coll., 1953; BS (Alumni scholar), U. Calif., Berkeley, 1955, MS, 1957; PhD, U. Okla., 1963; DPS (hon.), Regis Coll., Denver, 1977. Chief engr. Motor vehicle and Illumination Lab. U. Calif., Berkeley, 1955-57; assoc. prof. U. Okla., Norman, 1957-63; prof. U. Okla., 1963-66, asst. to dir. Rsch. Inst., 1960-63, cons. Rsch. Inst., 1966-69, dir. Sch. Elec. Engring., 1963-66, dir. Systems Rsch. Center, 1964-66; dean sci. and engring., prof. elec. engring. Union Coll., Schenectady, 1966-71; pres. Met. State Coll., Denver, 1971-78; rsch. and spl. programs adminstr. Dept. Transp., Washington, 1978-79; v.p., gen. mgr. rsch. and devel. div. Mech. Tech., Inc., Latham, N.Y., 1979-82; exec. v.p. J.J. Henry Co., Inc., Moorestown, N.J., 1982-85; BDM internat. prof. info. tech. George Mason U., Fairfax, Va., 1985—; bd. dirs. J.J. Henry Co., Inc.; cons. Sym Mgmt. Co., Boston, Higher Edn. Exec. Assocs., Denver, PERI, Princeton; adj. prof. U. Colo. Co-author: (with A.P. Sage) Software Systems Engineering, (with Aseltine, Beam and Sage) Introduction to Computer Systems, Analysis, Design and Application. Bd. dirs., exec. v.p. adv. com. U.S.A. Vols. for Internat. Tech. Assistance, 1967-83, exec. v.p., 1970-71, chmn. exec. com.; trustee, vice chmn. Nat. Commn. on Coop. Edn.; mem. exec. policy bd. Alaska Natural Gas Pipeline, 1978-79; trustee Auraria Higher Edn. Program, Denver; mem. Fulbright fellow Selection Com., Colo.; bd. mgrs., mem. exec. com. Hudson-Mohawk Assn. Colls. and Univs., trustee, chmn. bd., 1970-71; adv. com. USCG Acad., 1972-82, chmn. adv. com., 1979-82; mem. Colo. Gov.'s Sci. and Tech. Adv. Council; pres. Denver Cath. Community Services Bd.; mem. Archdiocesan Catholic Charities and Community Services; mem. bd. U. Okla. Rsch. Inst.; mem. adv. com. Mile-Hi Red Cross. With USMC, 1950-51. Case-Western Res. Centennial scholar, 1981; recipient U.S. Coast Guard award and medal for meritorious pub. service, 1983. Fellow IEEE (exec. and adminstrv. coms., v.p. long-range planning and finance, chmn. com. on large scale systems, Joseph E. Wahl Outstanding Career Achievement award 1993); mem. Systems, Man and Cybernetics Soc. (pres., Outstanding Contbns. award 1981), alumni assns. U. Calif. and U. Okla., Inst. Internat. Edn. (bd. dir. Rocky Mt. sect.), Soc. Naval Architects and Marine Engrs., Am. Soc. Engring. Edn., Am. Mil. Engrs., N.Y. Acad. Sci., Navy League, Sigma Xi, Eta Kappa Nu, Pi Mu Epsilon, Alpha Gamma Sigma. Home: 860 Cashew Way Fremont CA 94536 Office: George Mason U Sch of Info Tech & Engring Fairfax VA 22030

PALMER, JAMES EDWARD, public relations executive; b. Evansville, Ind., July 30, 1935; s. James Edward and Verble (Hearin) P. B.A. in English, N.Y.U., 1955. Reporter Evansville Courier, 1955-59; non-fiction editor Cosmopolitan mag., N.Y.C., 1959-61; exec. editor Cosmopolitan mag., 1961-65; editor Mag. Mgmt. Co., Inc., 1971-72; editor-in-chief Liberty mag., N.Y.C., 1972-73; dir. mag. and book dept. Carl Byoir & Assos., N.Y.C., 1973-76; corp. public relations dir. Macmillan, Inc., N.Y.C., 1977-80; pres. James Palmer Assos., N.Y.C., 1980-88, The Palmer Group, Houston, 1988—. Mem. Sigma Chi. Office: PO Box 90422 Houston TX 77290-0422

PALMER, JEFFRESS GARY, hematologist, educator; b. Bklyn., Oct. 7, 1921; s. William Ware and Margaret Lee (Boswell) P.; m. Jane Ann Cartwright, Feb. 2, 1951; children: Kristin Cartwright, Julie Mitchell. BS, Emory U., 1942, MD, 1944. Intern N.C. Bapt. Hosp., 1944-45; resident in medicine Emory U., Atlanta, 1947-49; fellow hematology U. Utah, Salt Lake City, 1949-52; from asst. prof. to prof. medicine U. N.C., Chapel Hill, 1952—. Capt. M.C. AUS, 1945-47. Mem. AAAS, AAUP, AMA, Am. Fedn. for Clin. Rsch., So. Soc. for Clin. Investigation, N.Y. Acad. Scis., Am. Soc. Hematology. Home: Morgan Creek Rd Chapel Hill NC 27514

PALMER, JOHN BERNARD, III, lawyer; b. Ft. Wayne, Ind., May 18, 1952; s. John Bernard and Dorothy Alma (Lauer) P. B.A., Mich. State U., 1974, J.D. U. Mich., 1977. Bar: Ill. 1977, U.S. Dist. Ct. (no. dist.) Ill. 1977, U.S. Tax Ct. 1979. Assoc. Mayer Brown & Platt, Chgo., 1977-80; assoc. Hopkins & Sutter, Chgo., 1980-83, ptnr., 1983—; adj. prof. Ill. Inst. Tech.-Kent Coll. of Law, Chgo., 1984—. Mem. ABA. Office: Hopkins & Sutter Three First Nat Plaza Chicago IL 60602

PALMER, JOHN L., social sciences researcher, educator; b. Upper Darby, Pa., Apr. 10, 1943; s. Richard Sidwell and Helen (Logan) P.; m. Nancy Hetenyi, June 29, 1968 (div. Dec. 1984); 1 child, Georgina; m. Stephanie Graham Gould, June 21, 1986; 1 child, Joanna. BA in Math., Williams Coll., 1965; PhD in Econs., Stanford U., 1970. Asst. prof. econs. Stanford U., Calif., 1969-71; dir. office income security policy HEW, Washington, 1971-75; asst. sec. HHS, Washington, 1979-81; sr. fellow The Brookings Instn., Washington, 1975-79, The Urban Inst., Washington, 1981-88; dean Maxwell Sch. Syracuse U., 1988—; adj. faculty Harvard U., Cambridge, Mass., 1982-84; cons. numerous govt. agys. and pvt. founds., 1975-79, 81—. Author, editor 12 books; contbr. numerous articles on econs., social and budgetary concerns and policies. Woodrow Wilson fellow, 1965, NDEA scholar, Stanford U. Fellow Nat. Acad. Pub. Adminstrn.; mem. Am. Econ. Assn., Assn. Pub. Policy Analysis and Mgmt., NAS (various coms.), Nat. Acad. Social Ins. Home: 6980 Woodchuck Hill Rd Fayetteville NY 13066-9760 Office: Syracuse U 200 Eggers Hall Syracuse NY 13244-1090

PALMER, JOHN M., medical administrator. AB, William Jewell Coll., 1967; MDiv, Gen. Sem. of Episcopal Ch., 1970. Ordained priest Episcopal Ch. Asst. to bishop Diocese of S.E. Fla., 1973-77; rector Ch. of the Transfiguration, 1977-79; dir. spl. parish ministries Trinity Ch., N.Y.C., 1979-86; exec. dir. Helen Keller Inst., N.Y.C., 1986—. Bd. dirs. Roosa Sch. Music, 1984-86, Village Nursing Home, 1984-86, Nat. Inst. Tng., 1982-86; chair Diocesan Com. on World Peace and Disarmament, 1983-86; chmn. bd. dis. Wyatt Cmty. Trust, 1977-79; mem. adv. com. WHO, 1986—; sec. Found. for Integrative Studies, 1990—; exec. com. World Blind Union, 1989—; exec. com. Interaction, 1986-91, Prvt. Agys. Collaborating Together, 1987-91; chmn. Partnership of Internat. Non-Govtl. Orgns. to Prevent Blindness, 1990—. Address: Helen Keller International 90 Washington St, 15th Fl New York NY 10006*

PALMER, LANGDON, banker; b. Montclair, N.J., Mar. 4, 1928; s. Lubin and Marjorie (Maxfield) P.; m. Millicent M. Lott, June 27, 1954; children—Jennifer Leigh, Langdon Jr., Christopher Lott. B. in Comml. Sci., Dartmouth Coll., 1951; M.B.A., NYU, 1959; postgrad. in advanced mgmt., Harvard Bus. Sch., 1968. Sr. v.p. Chase Manhattan Bank, N.Y.C., 1953-83; chmn., chief exec. officer Horizon Bank, Morristown, N.J., 1984-89; ret., 1989; bd. dirs. Chem. Bank N.J., N.A., 1989-92, now mem. adv. bd. Exec. v.p. Greater N.Y. coun. Boy Scouts Am., unitl 1983, Morris Sussex coun., 1984—; bd. dirs. N.J. Conservation Fund, Morris County Agrl. Devel. Bd., until 1993, Morris County Park Commn.; bd. dirs. Nature Conservancy, chmn. N.J. chpt.; trustee Morris County Parks and Conservation Found.; chmn. bd. Morris 2000, until 1994. Decorated Bronze Star; named Knight Great Commander of Liberian Humane Order of African Redemption, 1983; Ordre National Republic of Guinee, 1982; recipient Silver Beaver award Boy Scouts Am., 1977, Disting. Eagle award, 1989. Mem. Morris County C. of C. (bd. dirs. 1984—, vice chmn. 1987—, chmn. 1988). Republican. Episcopalian. Clubs: Morristown (N.J.); Anglers (N.Y.C.). Avocation: fly fishing.

PALMER, LARRY ISAAC, lawyer, educator; b. 1944. AB, Harvard U., 1966; LLB, Yale U., 1969. Bar: Calif. 1970. Asst. prof. Rutgers U., Camden, N.J., 1970-73, assoc. prof., 1973-75; assoc. prof. Cornell U., Ithaca, N.Y., 1975-79, prof. of law, 1979—, vice provost, 1979-84, v.p. acad. programs, 1987-91, v.p. acad. program and campus affairs, 1991-94; vis. fellow Cambridge U., 1984-85. Mem. Am. Law Inst. Office: Cornell U Law Sch 120 Myron Taylor Hall Ithaca NY 14853-4901

PALMER, LESTER DAVIS, minister; b. Augusta, Ga., Oct. 6, 1929; s. Lawton Evans and Gwendolyn (Ramsbotham) P.; m. Janelle Griffin, May 6, 1951; children: Gwen Palmer Chandler, Kathy Palmer Hagemier, Sandra Palmer Wood, Leslie. BA, Johnson Bible Coll., 1952; MDiv, Lexington Theol. Sem., 1958; postgrad., Boston U., 1961-63; DD, Bethany Coll., 1989, Christian Theol. Sem., 1995; DHL, Eureka Coll., 1996. Ordained to ministry Christian Ch. (Disciples of Christ), 1951; CLU, 1981, ChFC, 1984. Assoc. gen. min. Christian Ch. Ky., Lexington, 1957-61; assoc. prof. ch. adminstrn. Lexington Theol. Sem., 1963-66; v.p. Pension Fund of Christian Ch., Indpls., 1966-83, pres., 1984—. Editor Promotional and Interpretive Bull., 1984—; contbr. articles to profl. jours. Home: 5953 Manning Rd Indianapolis IN 46208-1082 Office: Pension Fund of Christian Ch 130 E Washington Indianapolis IN 46204-3645

PALMER, MADELYN STEWART SILVER, family practice physician; b. Denver, July 18, 1964; d. Barnard Stewart and Cherry (Bushman) Silver; m. James Michael Palmer, Sept. 26, 1992; children: Adoniram Jacob, Benjamin Kern. BA cum laude, Wellesley (Mass.) Coll., 1986; MD, U. Utah, 1990. Family practice resident Mercy Med. Ctr., Denver, 1990-93; physician South Fed. Family Practice, Denver, 1993-95, South West Family Pracice, Littleton, Colo., 1995—; staff St. Anthony Ctrl. Hosp., Denver, Porter Hosp., Denver, Swedish Hosp. Ward Young Women's pres. LDS Ch., Littleton, ward primary sec., Englewood. Mem. AMA, Am. Acad. Family Practice, Colo. Acad. Family Practice, Colo. Med. Soc. Achievements include research on physician practices and underimmunization of children. Home: 543 E Maplewood Dr Littleton CO 80121 Office: 6169 S Balsam Way Littleton CO 80123

PALMER, MARCIA STIBAL, food and wine retailer, interior designer, real estate investor; b. Berea, Ky., Mar. 31, 1948; d. Earl and Marie (Gabbard) Harrison; m. George E. Palmer; children: Anthony Craig, Everrett Todd, Melony Brook. Grad. high sch., Richmond, Ky., 1967. Prin. Hanna Hardware, Ft. Lauderdale, Fla., 1971-81, J-Mar-J-Design, Ft. Lauderdale and L.A., 1980—, Fernando's Internat. Market & Vintage Winery, Ft. Lauderdale, 1996—; pvt. practice real estate investing Ft. Lauderdale, 1971—. Mgr. campaign Rocky Rodriguez for City Commr., Ft. Lauderdale, 1987-88; del. Rep. State Conv., 1985—, Rep. Nat. Com., Washington, 1985—; active on Holy Cross Hosp. Aux., Ft. Lauderdale, 1984—. Mem. Nat. Safety Coun., Police Benevolent Assn., Hon. Order of Ky. Cols. (Frankfort), Ft. Lauderdale C. of C., Lauderdale-by-the-Sea. Baptist. Avocations: photography, sketching, art, antique collecting. Home and Office: 340 Sunset Dr Apt 1510 Fort Lauderdale FL 33301-2649

PALMER, MICHAEL ERIK, retail executive; b. Portsmouth, Va., Aug. 30, 1968; s. Curtis Ray and Elizabeth Ann (Crawford) P. AS, Ind. Vocat. Tech. Coll., Evansville, 1987; BS, U. So. Ind., Evansville, 1994. Comml. maintenanceman Betty's Laundry, Evansville, 1980-84, Wanda's Washerette, Evansville, 1985-87; indsl. maintenanceman Decora', Huntingburg, Ind., 1990; mgmt. exec. Budjet Video Warehouse, Huntingburg, 1986—; owner, pres. Spl. Details, Huntingburg, 1994—. Mem. Hutingburg Jaycees. Republican. Methodist. Avocations: Tae kwon do, power weight lifting, motorcyclist, welding. Home: RR 2 Box 395-a Dale IN 47523-9462 Office: 1103 N Main St Huntingburg IN 47542-1051

PALMER, PATRICK EDWARD, radio astronomer, educator; b. St. Johns, Mich., Dec. 6, 1940; s. Don Edward and Nina Louise (Kyes) P.; m. Joan Claire Merlin, June 9, 1963; children—Laura Katherine, Aidan Edward, David Elijah. S.B., U. Chgo., 1963; M.A., Harvard U., 1965, Ph.D., 1968. Radio astronomer Harvard U., Cambridge, Mass., 1968; asst. prof. astronomy and astrophysics U. Chgo., 1968-70, asso. prof., 1970-75, prof., 1975—; vis. assoc. prof. astronomy Calif. Inst. Tech., Pasadena, 1972; vis. radio astronomer Cambridge (Eng.) U., 1973; vis. rsch. astronomer U. Calif., Berkeley, 1977, 86; vis. scientist Nat. Radio Astronomer Obs., 1980-95. Contbr. articles on radio astron. investigations of comets and interstellar medium to tech. jours. Recipient Bart J. Bok prize for contbns. to galactic astronomy, 1969, Alfred P. Sloan Found. fellow, 1970-72, Helen B. Warner prize, 1975. Fellow AAAS (Chmn. sect. D astronomy 1984); mem. Am. Astron. Soc. (chmn. nominating com. 1981, publs. bd. 1985-86, Warner Prize selection com. 1977-78), Royal Astron. Soc., Internat. Astron. Union, AAUP. Club: U. Chgo. Track. Home: 5549 S Dorchester Ave Chicago IL 60637-1720 Office: Univ Chgo Astronomy & Astrophysics Ctr 5640 S Ellis Ave Chicago IL 60637-1433

PALMER, PHILIP EDWARD STEPHEN, radiologist; b. London, Apr. 26, 1921. Ed., Kelly Coll., Tavistock, Eng., 1938; M.B., B.S., U. London, 1944, D.M.R., 1946, D.M.R.T., 1947. Intern, then resident Westminster Hosp.; cons. radiologist West Cornwall (Eng.) Hosp. Group, 1947-54; sr. govt. radiologist Matabeleland, Rhodesia-Zimbabwe, 1954-64; prof. radiology U. Cape Town, South Africa, 1964-68; prof. U. Pa., 1968-70; prof. diagnostic radiology and vet. radiology U. Calif., Davis, 1970—; WHO cons. in field. Author: The Radiology of Tropical Diseases, 1980; contbr. articles to profl. pubs. Recipient German Röentgen award, 1993, 1st Béclère medal Internat. Soc. Radiology, 1996, 1st Antoine Béclère lectr. Internat. Soc. Radiology, 1996. Fellow Calif. Radiol. Assn., Royal Coll. Physicians (Edinburgh), Royal Coll. Radiologists (Eng.), Romanian Soc. Radiol. and Nuclear Med.; mem. Brit. Inst. Radiology, Brit. Med. Assn., Calif. Med. Assn., Internat. Skeletal Soc., Assn. Univ. Radiologists, Radiol. Soc. N. Am., Kenya Radiol. Soc., South African Coll. Medicine, Egyptian Soc. Radiology and Nuclear Medicine, Yugoslav Assn. for Ultrasound, West African Assn. Radiologists. Address: 821 Miller Dr Davis CA 95616-3622

PALMER, RAYMOND A., administrator, librarian; b. Louisville, May 8, 1939. BA in Biology, U. Louisville, 1961; MLS, U. Ky., 1966. Adminstrv. asst. Johns Hopkins Med. Libr., Balt., 1966-69; asst. librarian Harvard Med. Libr., Boston, 1969-74; health scis. librarian Wright State U., Dayton, Ohio, 1974-82, assoc. prof. library adminstrn., 1974-82; exec. dir. Med. Libr. Assn., Chgo., 1982-92, Am. Assn. Immunologists, Bethesda, Md., 1992-95; dir. edn. Nat. Ctr. Edn. in Maternal and Child Health, Arlington, Va., 1995—; cons. Acad. Mil. Med. Scis. Libr., Beijing, 1990, Alzheimer's Assn., Chgo., 1991. AUthor: Management of Library Associations; mng. editor: Jour. Immunology, 1992—; contbr. articles to profl. jours. Mem. ALA, Am. Soc. Assn. Execs., Greater Washington Soc. Assn. Execs., Spl. Librs. Assn., Biomed. Communication Network (chmn. 1980-82), Am. Mgmt. Assn. (strategic planning adv. coun. 1987-91), Coun. Biology Editors, Friends of Nat. Libr. Medicine (bd. dirs. 1989-92, 94—), Internat. Fedn. Libr. Assns. and Instns. (exec. com. Round Table for Mgmt. of Libr. Orgns. 1989-92), Med. Libr. Assn., Spl. Libr. Assn.

PALMER, RICHARD ALAN, chemistry educator; b. Austin, Tex., Nov. 13, 1935; s. Ernest Austin and Eugenia Rosalie (Robey) P.; m. Janice Leah Boyce, June 30, 1961; children: William D., Leah D., Sarah L., Benjamin C. BS, U. Tex., 1957; MS, U. Ill., 1962, PhD, 1965. Asst. prof. chemistry Duke U., 1966-71, assoc. prof., 1971-78, prof., 1978—, dir. grad. studies dept. chemistry, 1979-82, dir. Chemistry for Executives Program, 1992—. Author: Problems in Structural Inorganic Chemistry, 1971; mem. editorial bd. Applied Spectroscopy, 1990—. Served with USN, 1957-60. NIH fellow, 1965-66; NSF Internat. Study grantee, 1980-81. Mem. Am. Chem. Soc. (nat. coun. 1993—), Soc. Applied Spectroscopy, Coblentz Soc. (bd. mgrs. 1992—), Phi Beta Kappa, Sigma Xi, Phi Lambda Upsilon. Home: 126 Pinecrest Rd Durham NC 27705-5813 Office: Duke U Chemistry Dept Durham NC 27706

PALMER, RICHARD N., judge; b. Hartford, Conn., May 27, 1950. BA, Trinity Coll., 1972; JD with high honors, U. Conn., 1977. Bar: Conn. 1977, U.S. Dist. Ct. Conn. 1978, D.C. 1980, U.S. Ct. Appeals (2nd cir.) 1981. Law clk. to Hon. Jon O. Newman U.S. Ct. Appeals (2nd cir.), 1977-78; assoc. Shipman & Goodwin, 1978-80; asst. U.S. atty. Office U.S. Atty. Conn., 1980-83, 87-90, U.S. atty. dist. Conn., 1991, chief state's atty. Conn., 1991-93; ptnr. Chatigny and Palmer, 1984-86; assoc. justice Conn. Supreme Ct., Hartford, 1993—. Mem. Phi Beta Kappa. Office: 231 Capitol Ave Hartford CT 06106-1537

PALMER, RICHARD WARE, lawyer; b. Boston, Oct. 20, 1919; s. George Ware and Ruth French (Judkins) P.; m. Nancy Fernald Shaw, July 8, 1950; children: Richard Ware Jr., John Wentworth, Anne Fernald. AB, Harvard U., 1942, JD, 1948. Bar: N.Y. State 1950, Pa. 1959. Sec., dir. N.Am. Mfg. Co., Natick, Mass., 1946-48; assoc. Burlingham, Veeder, Clark & Hupper, Burlingham, Hupper & Kennedy, N.Y.C., 1949-57; ptnr. Rawle & Henderson, Phila., 1958-79, Palmer, Biezup & Henderson, Phila., 1979—; sec., bd. dirs. Underwater Technics, Inc., Camden, N.J., 1967-85; adv. on admiralty law to U.S. del. Inter-Govtl. Maritime Consultative Orgn., London, 1967; mem. U.S. Shipping Coordinating Com., Washington legal sub com., 1967—; U.S. del. 30th-34th internat. confs. Titular mem. Comité Maritime International; v.p., sec., bd. dirs. Phila. Belt Line R.R.; bd. dirs. Mather (Bermuda) Ltd. Editor: Maritime Law Reporter. Mem., permanent adv. bd. Tulane Admiralty Law Inst., Tulane U. Law Sch., New Orleans, 1975—; trustee Seamen's Ch. Inst., Phila., 1967—, pres., 1972-84; Harvard Law Sch. Assn., Phila., Pa. (exec. com. 1986—); bd. dirs. Havrford (Pa.) Civic Assn., 1972-85, pres., 1976-79; consul for Denmark in State of Pa., 1980-91. Lt. comdr. USNR, 1942-46. Fellow World Acad. Art and Sci. (treas. 1986—); mem. ABA (former chmn. stdg. com. on admiralty and maritime law 1978-79), N.Y.C. Bar Assn., Phila. Bar Assn., Am. Judicature Soc., Maritime Law Assn. (chmn. limitation liability com. 1977-83, 2d v.p. 1984-86, 1st v.p. 1986-88, pres. 1988-90, immediate past pres. 1990-92), Internat. Bar Assn., Internat. Assn. Def. Counsel, Assn. Average Adjusters USA and Bt. Britain, Port of Phila. Maritime Soc., Harvard Law Sch. Assn. of Phila. (exec. com. 1986—), Danish Order of Dannebrog, Phila. Club, Union League Club, Rittenhouse Club, India House, Harvard Club of N.Y.C. and Phila. (v.p., mem. exec. com. 1983-86, 94—). Republican. Episcopalian. Home: 318 Grays Ln Haverford PA 19041-1907 Office: Palmer Biezup & Henderson Pub Ledger Bldg 620 Chestnut St Philadelphia PA 19106-3409

PALMER, ROBERT B., computer company executive; b. 1940. BS, Tex. Tech U., MS. V.p. semiconductor ops. Digital Equipment Corp., v.p. mfg., pres., CEO, 1992—, now also chmn., 1995—. Office: Digital Equipment Corp 111 Powdermill Rd Maynard MA 01754-1499*

PALMER, ROBERT BAYLIS, librarian; b. Rockville Centre, N.Y., Apr. 5, 1938; s. John Frederick and Marion (Baylis) P.; divorced; 1 child, Michele Palmer Fracasso. A.B., Kenyon Coll., Gambier, Ohio, 1960; M.S. in L.S. Simmons Coll., Boston, 1965; M.A. in English, Middlebury (Vt.) Coll., 1965. Tchr. Brooks Sch., North Andover, Mass., 1960-65; librarian Brooks Sch., 1961-65; acting librarian Columbia Coll., 1965-66; asst. to dir. libraries Columbia U., 1965-67; dir. Barnard Coll. Library, 1967-81; Fulbright lectr. Tribhuvan U. Library, Kathmandu, Nepal, 1972-73, Kathmandu, 1980; vol. lectr. USIS, library cons., Asia, 1976; Fulbright lectr. Wuhan, Peoples Republic China, 1984-85; library cons., advisor, Peoples Republic China, 1986-87, Zanzibar, Tanzania, 1988; lectr., cons. Kenya, Ethiopia, Zimbabwe, 1988; English lang. escort officer U.S. Dept. State, 1989—. Mem. ALA. Address: 190 Riverside Dr New York NY 10024-1008 *Viewing one's country through the eyes of international guests, one can be both amazed and appalled by our human progress. Such experiences reconfirm the belief that there is much more to life than accumulating wealth.*

PALMER, ROBERT BLUNDEN, newspaper, printing executive; b. Port Huron, Mich., Nov. 25, 1917; s. Joseph Frank and Hazel Quinn (Blunden) P.; m. Mary Bellatti (dec.), Feb. 11, 1946; children: Robert L. Palmer, Frances Lobpries, Barbara Caldwell. Office mgr. Palmer Circulation Co., Midwest, 1933-41; reporter, bus. mgr. Titus County Tribune, Mt. Pleasant, Tex., 1941-42, editor, 1946-57; pub., editor Daily Tribune, Mt. Pleasant, Tex., 1957-88; pres. Palmer Media, Inc., Mt. Pleasant, Tex., 1972—, NorTex Press, Inc., Mt. Pleasant, Tex., 1973—, F.V.P. Network, Inc., Mt. Pleasant, Tex., 1989; owner Palmer Real Estate, 1968—. Capt. U.S. Army, 1942-46, ETO. Presbyterian. Avocations: reading, golf, travel, music. Office: Palmer Media Inc. 1705 Industrial Rd Mount Pleasant TX 75455-2235

PALMER, ROBERT JEFFREY, special education educator; b. Clarksburg, W.Va., June 25, 1961; s. Robert Edward and Katherine Elizabeth (Snopps) P. BS in Phys. Edn., W.Va. U., 1984, MA in Spl. Edn., 1994. Cert. tchr. phys. edn. 7-12, safety edn. 7-12, spl. edn. K-12. Tchr. Berkeley County Schs., Martinsburg, W.Va., 1988-89; tchr. spl. edn. Morgan County Schs., Berkeley Springs, W.Va., 1989—; mem. staff devel. coun. Morgan County Schs., 1994—. Mem. Coun. for Exceptional Children, W.Va. Edn. Assn., Moos, Lions. Democrat. Disciples of Christ. Avocations: motorcycles, music, reading, golf, baseball. Home: PO Box 455 435 Moser Ave Paw Paw WV 25434 Office: Paw Paw High Sch 422 Moser Ave Paw Paw WV 25434-9501

PALMER, ROBERT ROSWELL, historian, educator; b. Chgo., Jan. 11, 1909; s. Roswell Roy and Blanche (Steere) P.; m. Esther Howard, Dec. 19, 1942; children: Stanley, Richard, Emily. Ph.B., U. Chgo., 1931, LL.D., 1963; Ph.D., Cornell U., 1934; Litt.D., Washington U., St. Louis, 1962; L.H.D., Kenyon Coll., 1963, U. New Haven, 1980; Dr. honoris causa, U. Toulouse, France, 1965, U. Uppsala, Sweden, 1977. Mem. faculty Princeton U., 1936-63, 66-69, prof. history, 1946-63, Dodge prof. history, 1952-63; dean faculty arts and sci., prof. history Washington U., St. Louis, 1963-66; prof. history Yale U., 1969-77, emeritus, 1977; adj. prof. U. Mich., 1977-80; vis. prof. U. Chgo., summer 1947, U. Colo., summer 1951, U. Calif. at Berkeley, summer 1962, U. Mich., 1969, 75. Author: Catholics and Unbelievers in 18th Century France, 1939, Twelve Who Ruled, 1941, A History of the Modern World, 1950, (with Joel Colton) A History of the Modern World, 8th edit., 1994, also in Swedish, Italian, Finnish, Spanish and Chinese, The Age of the Democratic Revolution, 1959, vol. II, 1964, also German, Italian edits., World of the French Revolution, 1971, also in French, School of the French Revolution, 1975, The Improvement of Humanity: Education and the French Revolution, 1985, The Two Tocquevilles, Father and Son on the Coming of the French Revolution, 1987; co-author: Organization of Ground Combat Troops, 1947, Procurement and Training of Ground Combat Troops, 1948; editor: Rand McNally Atlas of World History, 1957. Served hist. div. U.S. Army, 1943-45. Recipient of ACLS Spl. prize, 1960, Bancroft prize, 1960, Antonio Feltrinelli Internat. prize, Rome, 1990. Mem. Am. Acad. Arts and Scis., Mass. Hist. Soc., Am. Philos. Soc., Am. Hist. Assn. (pres. 1970), Soc. French Hist. Studies (pres. 1961), Acad. Naz. dei Lincei. Home: Pennswood Village # K205 Newtown PA 18940-2401

PALMER, ROBERT TOWNE, lawyer; b. Chgo., May 25, 1947; s. Adrian Bernhardt and Gladys (Towne) P.; m. Ann Therese Darin, Nov. 9, 1974; children: Justin Darin, Christian Darin. BA, Colgate U., 1969; JD, U. Notre Dame, 1974. Bar: Ill. 1974, D.C. 1978, U.S. Supreme Ct. 1978. Law clk. Hon. Walter V. Schaefer, Ill. Supreme Ct., 1974-75; assoc. McDermott, Will & Emery, Chgo., 1975-81, ptnr., 1982-86; ptnr. Chadwell & Kayser, Ltd., 1987-88, Connelly, Mustes, Palmer & Schroeder, 1988-89; of counsel Garfield & Merel Ltd., 1990—; mem. adj. faculty Chgo. Kent Law Sch., 1975-77, Loyola U., 1976-78; mem. adv. com. Fed. Home Loan Mortgage Corp., 1988-89; bd. dir. Lincoln Legal Found., Cen. Fed. Savs. & Loan Assn. of Chgo.; mem. Chgo. Ctr. Adv. Bd. Voyageur Outward Bound Sch., 1988-91. Mem. ABA, Ill. State Bar Assn. (Lincoln award 1983), Chgo. Bar Assn., Internat. Assn. Def. Counsel, Chgo. Club, Dairymen's Country Club, Lambda Alpha. Contbr. articles to legal jours. and textbooks. Office: Garfield & Merel Ltd 211 W Wacker Dr Ste 1500 Chicago IL 60606-1217

PALMER, R(OBIE MARCUS HOOKER) MARK, banker; b. Ann Arbor, Mich., July 14, 1941; s. Robie Ellis and Katherine (Hooker) P.; m. Sushma Palmer. BA, Yale U., 1963. Copy asst. N.Y. Times, N.Y.C., 1963; asst. to producer WNDT-TV, N.Y.C., 1963-64; entered U.S. Fgn. Service, 1964; third sec. U.S. Embassy, New Delhi, India, 1964-66; internat. relations officer NATO affiars, Dept State, Washington, 1966-68; second sec. U.S. Embassy, Moscow, 1968-71; prin. speechwriter Sec. of State Rogers, Kissinger, Washington, 1971-75; counselor for polit. affairs U.S. Embassy, Belgrade, Yugoslavia, 1975-78; dir. office disarmament and control of arms Bur. of Polit.-Mil. Affairs Dept. State, Washington, 1978-81, dep. to undersec. for polit. affairs, 1981-82, dep. asst. sec. state for European affairs, 1982-86; amb. U.S. Embassy, Budapest, Hungary, 1986-90; pres., chief exec. officer Cen. European Devel. Corp., 1990—; chmn. bd. NOVA TV. Czech Republic Berlin-Brandenburg TV; Gen. Banking and Trust, Budapest. Author: speeches for five Secs. of State and three Presidents. Recipient Superior Honor award Dept. State, 1980, Presdl. Meritorious Service award, award, 1984. Mem. Council Fgn. Relations, Am. Fgn. Service Assn., Phi Beta Kappa. Episcopalian. Avocation: tennis. Home: Gelferstr 17A, D-14195 Berlin-Dahlem Germany Office: Mauerstrasse, 10117 Berlin 93, Germany

PALMER, ROGER CAIN, information scientist; b. Corning, N.Y., Oct. 14, 1943; s. Wilbur Clarence and Eleanor Louise (Cain) P. AA, Corning (N.Y.) C.C., 1964; BA, Hartwick Coll., 1966; MLS, SUNY, Albany, 1972; PhD, U. Mich., 1978. Tchr. Penn Yan (N.Y.) Acad., 1966-68, 70-71; dep. head, grad. libr. SUNY, Buffalo, 1972-75; asst. prof. UCLA, 1978-83; sr. tech. writer Quotron Sys., Culver City, 1984; sr. sys. analyst Getty Art History Info., Santa Monica, Calif., 1984-90, mgr. tech. devel., 1990-93; mgr. internal cons. group The J. Paul Getty Trust, Santa Monica, 1993—; gen. ptnr. Liu-Palmer, L.A., 1989—. Author: Online Reference and Information Retrieval, 1987, dBase II and dBase III: An Introduction, 1984, Introduction to Computer Programming, 1983. With U.S. Army, 1968-70. Mem. IEEE Computer Soc., ALA, Am. Soc. for Info. Scis., Spl. Librs. Assn., Art Librs. Soc. of N.Am., Assn. for Computing Machinery, Pi Delta Epsilon, Beta Phi Mu. Home: 1045 N Kings Rd Ste 310 West Hollywood CA 90069 Office: The J Paul Getty Trust 401 Wilshire Blvd Ste 1100 Santa Monica CA 90401-1430

PALMER, ROGER FARLEY, pharmacology educator; b. Albany, N.Y., Sept. 23, 1931; m. Nelida Santiago, Apr. 1994. B.S. in Chemistry, St. Louis U., 1953; postgrad., Fla. State U., 1955-56, Woods Hole Marine Biology Lab., 1956; M.D., U. Fla., 1960. Intern Johns Hopkins Hosp., 1960-61, resident in medicine, 1961-62; asst. dept. biochemistry U. Fla., Gainesville, 1957; asst. medicine Osler Med. Service, 1960-62; instr. pharmacology and therapeutics U. Fla., 1962, asst. prof. pharmacology, therapeutics and medicine, 1964-67, assoc. prof. pharmacology and medicine, 1967-69, prof. medicine, chief div. clin. pharmacology, 1969-70, 81-82; prof., chmn. dept. pharmacology, prof. medicine U. Miami, Fla., 1970-81; clin. prof. medicine U. Miami, 1982—; chmn. pharmacology sect. Nat. Bd. Med Examiners, 1977-81; cons. Nat. Acad. Scis.; chmn. pharmacology sect. Nat. Bd. Med. Examiners, 1977-81. Editorial bd. Pharmacol. Revs.; assoc. editor Advances in Molecular Pharmacology; ad hoc editor Am. Heart Jour.; editor Horizons in Clinical Pharmacology, 1976; author abstracts; contbr. articles to profl. jours. Served with USAR. Mosby scholar, 1957-60; Markle scholar in acad. medicine, 1965-70; recipient Basic Sci. Teaching award U. Miami, 1975-76; Meritorious Service medal Am. Heart Assn., 1972; citation for meritorious Service So. Region Am. Heart Assn., 1979; Visitante Distinguido award, Costa Rica, 1979; Outstanding Tchr. award U. Miami, 1982. Mem. Am. Coll. Clin. Pharmacology, Am. Fedn. Clin. Rsch., Am. Therapeutic Soc. (prize essay award 1970), Am. Soc. Pharmacology and Exptl. Therapeutics, N.Y. Acad. Sci., So. Soc. Clin. Investigation, U.S. Pharmacopeia Revision Com., Internat. Study Group Rsch. Cardiac Metabolism, Royal Soc. Health, Am. Soc. for Internal Medicine, Key Biscayne Yacht Club (bd. govs. 1994—), Sigma Xi. Office: 24 W Enid Dr Key Biscayne FL 33149-2009

PALMER, ROGER RAYMOND, accounting educator; b. N.Y.C., Dec. 31, 1926; s. Archibald and Sophie (Jarnow) P.; m. Martha West Hopkins, June 7, 1986; children by previous marriage: Kathryn Sue, Daniel Stephen, Susan Jo. B.S., U. Wis., 1949; M.B.A., Cornell U., 1951; student, NYU Grad. Sch. Bus. Adminstrn., 1951-54. Auditor, Ernst and Ernst (C.P.A.s), N.Y.C., 1953-54; auditor Gen. Dynamics Corp., 1956-60; mgr. corp. audits Tex. Instruments, 1960-64; auditor First National Bank, St. Paul, 1964-68; v.p. planning First National Bank, 1968-69, v.p., comptroller, 1969-75, sr. v.p., controller, 1975-82; asst. prof. fin. and acctg. Coll. St. Thomas, 1982—; dir. First Met. Travel, Inc.; guest lectr. U. Minn., 1966; conf. leader, speaker, 1959—. Contbr. articles to publs. Bd. dirs. Waterford (Conn.) Civic Assn., 1959-60, Friends of St. Paul Pub. Library, 1967, Mpls. Citizens League; chmn. bd. dirs. Film in the Cities, 1983-85; mem. acctg. adv. council U. Minn.; trustee Hazelton Found. Served with U.S. Maritime Service, 1945-47; with AUS, 1954-56. Mem. Inst. Internal Auditors (pres. So. New Eng chpt. 1957-60, edn. chmn. Dallas 1961, Twin City chpt. 1965-66), Nat. Assn. Accts. (dir. Norwich, Conn. chpt. 1958-60), Nat. Assn. Accountants (St. Paul chpt. 1967), Assn. Bank Audit, Control and Operation, Am. Inst. Banking, Fin. Execs. Inst., Planning Forum (pres. Twin Cities chpt. 1984-85), Univ. Club (St. Paul). Club: St. Paul Athletic. Home: 1411 Lincoln Ave Saint Paul MN 55105-2217 Office: U St Thomas Dept Fin & Acctg Saint Paul MN 55105

PALMER, RONALD DEWAYNE FAISAL, retired diplomat, educator, consultant; b. Uniontown, Pa., May 22, 1932; s. Wilbur Fortune and Ethel Danya (Roberts) P.; m. Tengku Intan Badariah Abubakar; children: Derek Ronald, Alyson Cecily, Natasha Elina, Nadiah Raha. BA, Howard U., 1954; MA in Internat. Studies, Johns Hopkins U., 1957. Assigned to U.S. Mil. Acad., Indonesia, Denmark, Malaysia, The Philippines, prior to 1976; amb. to Togo, 1976-78; dep. dir. gen. Fgn. Service State Dept., 1978-81; amb. to Malaysia Kuala Lumpur, 1981-83; sr. scholar, mem. adv. bd. Ctr. Strategic and Internat. Studies, Washington, 1983-86; amb. to Mauritius Port Louis, 1986-89; ret., 1989; prof., diplomatic con. internat. studies George Washington U., 1990—. Author: Building Cooperation - 20 Years of ASEAN, 1987. Decorated Order of Mono, Togo, Most Hon. Order of Johor Sultan of Johor Bahru, Malaysia; recipient Sr. Fgn. Svc. Performance award U.S. Dept. State, 1985. Mem. Am. Fgn. Svc. Assn., Coun. on Fgn. Rels., Inst. Strategic Studies, Assn. Black Am. Ambs. (pres.), Malaysia-Am. Soc., U.S. Indonesia Soc. (mem. adv. bd.), Royal Asia Soc., Wash. Inst. Fgn. Affairs, Asia Soc. Office: George Washington U Eliott Sch Internat Affairs 2013 G St NW # 4600 Washington DC 20052 also: care State Dept Fgn Svc Mailroom 2201 C St NW Washington DC 20520-0001

PALMER, RONALD LEIGH, lawyer; b. Blossburg, Pa., Feb. 22, 1939; s. Leigh Judson and Henrietta (Stevens) P.; m. Deanna Ruth Doss, Nov. 22, 1962; 1 child, Ashley Christine. BSME, U. Cin., 1962; LLB, So. Meth. U., 1966. Bar: Tex. 1966, U.S. Dist. Ct. (all dists.) Tex. 1968, U.S. Ct. Appeals (5th cir.) 1968. Law clk. to Judge Joe Ingraham, Houston, 1966-68; assoc. Baker & Botts, Houston, 1968-75, ptnr., 1975-85, sr. ptnr., 1985—; speaker numerous seminars, 1977—. Contbr. articles to profl. jours. Bd. councillors U. Dallas, 1990—; mem. exec. bd. So. Meth. U. Law Sch., 1992—. Republican. Presbyterian. Avocations: archeology, golf, computers. Home: 3301 Hanover Ave Dallas TX 75225-7642 Office: Baker & Botts LP 2001 Ross Ave Dallas TX 75201-2980*

PALMER, RUSSELL EUGENE, investment executive; b. Jackson, Mich., Aug. 13, 1934; s. Russell E. and Margarite M. (Briles) P.; m. Phyllis Anne Hartung, Sept. 8, 1956; children: Bradley Carl, Stephen Russell, Russell Eugene, III, Karen Jean. BA with honors, Mich. State U., 1956; D in Comml. Sci. (hon.), Drexel U., 1980; MA (hon.), U. Pa., 1984; PhD (hon.), Chulalongkorn U., 1988, Free U. of Brussels, 1989, York Coll., 1989. With Touche Ross & Co., N.Y.C., 1956-83, mng. ptnr., CEO, 1972-82, also bd. dirs., exec. coms.; mng. dir., CEO Touche Ross Internat., 1974-83; dean, Reliance prof. mgmt. and pvt. enterprise Wharton Sch. U. Pa., 1983-90, CEO; bd. dirs. GTE Corp., The May Dept. Stores Co., Bankers Trust Co., Allied-Signal, Inc., Imasco Ltd.; corp. bd. Safeguard Scientifics, Inc., Fed. Home Loan Mortgage Corp.; adv. bd. Cassidy & Assocs. Mem. pub. bds. Dirs. & Bds., Mergers & Aquisitions, Directory Corp. Affiliations, Directory Leading Pvt. Cos. Pres. Fin. Acctg. Found., 1979-82; trustee Acctg. Hall of Fame; bd. dirs. Joint Coun. Econ. Edn., 1978-83, United Fund Greater N.Y., 1980-83, UN Assn. U.S.A.; mem. Bus. Com. Arts, 1977-83; mem. Pres.'s Mgmt. Improvement Coun., 1979-80; mem. N.Y. adv. bd. Salvation Army, past mem. nat. adv. bd.; former mem. adv. coun. Sch. Internat. and Pub. Affairs Columbia U., Grad. Sch. Bus. Stanford U., Womens Way; mem. assocs. coun. Bus. Sch. Oxford U.; mem. adv. panel Comptr. Gen. U.S.; mem. U.S. Sec. Labor's Commn. on Workforce Quality and Labor Market Efficiency; pub. mem. Hudson Inst., mem. adv. bd. Radnor Venture Ptnrs.; bd. dirs. SEI Ctr. for Advanced Studies in Mgmt. Recipient Gavin Meml. award Beta Theta Pi, 1956, Disting. Community Svc. award Brandeis U., 1974, Outstanding Alumnus award Mich. State U., 1978, Humanitarian award Fedn. Jewish Philanthropies, 1979, Disting. Aux. Svc. award Salvation Army, 1979, LEAD Bus. award, 1984, Good Scout award Phila. coun. Boy Scouts Am., 1987. Mem. Cts. of Phila. Club, Merion Cricket Club, Merion Golf Club, Round Hill Club, Lost Tree Country Club, Conf. Bd. (bd. dirs.), Beta Gamma Sigma (mem. bd. govs.). Presbyterian. Office: The Palmer Group 3600 Market St Fl 530 Philadelphia PA 19104-2611

PALMER, SAMUEL COPELAND, III, lawyer; b. Phila., June 9, 1934; s. Samuel Copeland Jr. and Vivian Gertrude (Plumb) P.; divorced; children: Samuel C. IV, Sarah Anne, Bryan Douglas. Grad., Harvard Sch., Los Angeles, 1952; student, Yale U., 1953; A.B., Stanford U., 1955; JD, Loyola-Marymount U., Marymount, 1958. Bar: Calif. 1959, U.S. Dist. Ct. (cen., ea. and so. dists. Calif.) 1959, U.S. Ct. Appeals (9th cir.) 1970, U.S. Supreme Ct. 1971. Dep. city atty. Los Angeles, 1959-60; assoc. firm Pollock & Deutz, Los Angeles, 1960-63; ptnr. firm Pollock & Palmer, Los Angeles, 1963-70, Palmer & Bartenetti, Los Angeles, 1970-81, Samuel C. Palmer III, P.C., 1981-85; ptnr. Thomas, Snell, Jamison, Russell & Asperger, 1985—; adj. prof. Calif. State U., Fresno, 1993. Trustee Western Ctr. Law and Poverty; bd. dirs. Big Bros./Big Sisters, Fresno, Lively Arts Found., Nat. Sleep Found., Vols. in Parole; pres., bd. dirs. Poverello House; founder, pres. Fresno Crime Stoppers. Mem. ABA, State Bar Calif. (disciplinary subcom., bar examiners subcom.), Fresno County Bar Assn. (pres., bd. dirs. 1988-93), Pickwick Soc., Am. Bd. Trial Advocates, Chancery Club, Downtown Club, Calif. Club, Fig Garden Tennis Club, Rotary, Delta Upsilon, Phi Delta Phi. Home: 4607 N Wilson Ave Fresno CA 93704-3038 Office: 2445 Capitol St Fresno CA 93721-2224

PALMER, STACY ELLA, periodical editor; b. Middletown, Conn., Oct. 25, 1960; d. Marvin Jerome Palmer and Eileen Sondra (Cohen) Palmer Burke. B in Liberal Arts and Internat. Rels., Brown U., 1982. Asst. editor Chronicle of Higher Edn., Washington, 1982-86, sr. editor, 1986-88; news editor Chronicle of Philanthropy, Washington, 1988-93, mng. editor, 1993—. Bd. dirs. Brown Alumni Monthly, Providence, 1988-91, vice chmn., 1991-93. Mem. Comm. Network in Philanthropy, Investigative Reporters and Editors, Brown Club Washington (bd. dirs. 1993—, pres. 1994—). Avocations: swimming, bicycling, travel. Home: 1015 33rd St #806 Washington DC 20007 Office: Chronicle of Philanthropy 1255 23rd St NW Washington DC 20037-1125

PALMER, STEPHEN EUGENE, JR., government official; b. Superior, Wis., July 31, 1923; s. Stephen Eugene Sr. and Katharine (Greenslade) P.; m. Nancy Jane Swan, July 26, 1947 (div. 1986); children: Katharine Caldwell, Susan Greenslade, Stephen Eugene III; m. Patsy Elaine Simmons Lee, Sept. 7, 1989. A.B., Princeton U., 1944; postgrad., Columbia U., 1947-48, M.A., 1971; postgrad. Serbo-Croatian lang. and Balkan area, Ind. U., 1953-54; postgrad. in French Fgn. Service Inst., 1982-83. Tchr. Am. Community Sch., Tehran, Iran, 1946-47; with U.S. Govt., 1949-51; joined U.S. Fgn. Service, 1951; vice consul Nicosia, Cyprus, 1951-53; 3d sec., vice consul Belgrade, Yugoslavia, 1954; 2d sec., 1954-56, consul, 1956-57; consul, prin. officer Sarajevo, Yugoslavia, 1957-59; fgn. affairs officer Office UN Polit. Affairs, State Dept., 1959-63; 1st sec., chief polit. sect. Tel Aviv, Israel, 1963-66; 1st sec. polit. div. Middle Eastern and North African affairs Am. embassy, London, 1966-68; counselor for polit. affairs Am. embassy., Rawalpindi, Islamabad, Pakistan, 1968-71; consul gen. Madras, India, 1971-73; fellow Center for Internat. Affairs, Harvard, 1973-74; dir. Office Near Eastern and South Asian Regional Affairs, Dept. State, 1974-78; also staff dir. interdepartmental group for Near East and South Asia NSC, 1974-78; project dir. country reports on human rights and practices Dept. State, 1978; minister-counselor for refugee and humanitarian affairs U.S. Mission to Geneva, 1979, prin. dep. asst. sec. of state for human rights and humanitarian affairs, 1980-81, acting asst. sec., 1981; Dept. State mem. Congl. Commn. on Security and Cooperation in Europe, 1981-82; chmn. Fgn. Service Selection Bd., 1983, Project for Dissemination of the Laws of Armed Conflict, 1983-84; sr. advisor mgmt. systems and programs Dept. State, 1984-88, sr. cons., 1988-91, insp., 1991-93; cons. Booz, Allen & Hamilton, 1992—; mem. editorial team for country reports on human rights practices, 1993-94. Co-author: Yugoslav Communism and the Macedonian Question, 1971. Mem. Fairfax County Dem. Com. Served to 1st lt. USMCR, 1943-46. Recipient Superior Svc. awards U.S. Dept. of State, 1966, 82, Meritorious Honor award, 1971, John Jacobs Rogers award, 1988. Mem. Fgn. Svc. Res. Corps. Office: 2813 Bolling Rd Falls Church VA 22042-2012

PALMER, STEVEN MCGLONE, advertising agency executive; b. L.A., Aug. 28, 1965; s. Duane Burgess and Nancy (Magee) Pefley. BA in Sociology, U. Calif., Irvine, 1989. Media coord., then asst. media buyer Davis Ball & Colombatto Advt., L.A., 1990, asst. media planner, 1990-92, media planner, 1992-93, asst. account exec., 1993-94, account exec., 1994-95, sr. account exec., 1995—. Avocations: golf, playing guitar, skiing, tennis, soccer. Office: Davis Ball & Colombatto Advt 865 S Figueroa St Los Angeles CA 90017

PALMER, STEVEN O., federal official; b. Bowdle, S.D., Feb. 1, 1956; s. Richard James and Beverly Ann (Barlund) P.; m. Laurel Beach, July 17, 1982; children: Kristin Michelle, Lindsay Ann. BA in Polit. Sci., Kalamazoo Coll., 1978; MPA, U. Tex., Austin, 1980. Rschr. U. Tex., Austin, 1979-80; presdl. mgmt. intern Dept. Transp., 1980-82; mem. profl. staf com. budget U.S. Senate, Washington, 1982-83, sr. mem. staff subcom. on aviation, 1983-90, sr. mem. profl. staff subcom. sci., tech. and space, com. commerce , sci. and transp., 1990-93; asst. sec. govtl. affairs U.S. Dept. Transp., Washington, 1993—; team leader Clinton-Gore Presdl. Transition, 1992. Office: Dept Transp Govtl Affairs 400 7th St SW Rm 10408 Washington DC 20590-0001

PALMER, STUART HUNTER, sociology educator; b. N.Y.C., Apr. 29, 1924; s. Herman G. and Beatrice (Hunter) P.; m. Anne Barbara Scarborough, June 22, 1946; 1 dau., Catherine. B.A., Yale U., 1949, M.A., 1951, Ph.D., 1955. Asst. to dean Yale Coll., New Haven, 1949-51; instr. sociology New Haven Coll., 1949-51, 53-55; faculty U. N.H., Durham, 1955—; prof. U. N.H., 1964—, chmn. dept. sociology and anthropology, 1964-69, 79-82, dean Coll. Liberal Arts, 1982-95, dir. London program, 1995—; disting. vis. prof. SUNY, Albany, 1970-71; vis. behavioral scientist N.H. Div. Mental Health; vis. prof. U. Sussex, Eng., 1976, U. Ga., 1977; cons. U.S. Office Edn., USPHS, U.S. Office Delinquency and Youth Devel., Dept. Justice; mem. adv. com. for sociology Com. on Internat. Exchange of Persons; mem. exec. com. N.H. Gov.'s Commn. on Crime and Delinquency; co-chmn. Internat. Symposium on Univs. in Twenty-First Century; co-chmn. Internat. Confs. on Stress Rsch., Nat. Commn. Arts and Scis. Author: Understanding Other People, 1955, A Study of Murder, 1960, (with Brian R. Kay) The Challenge of Supervision, 1961, Deviance and Conformity, 1970, (with Arnold S. Linsky) Rebellion and Retreat, 1972, The Violent Society, 1972, The Prevention of Crime, 1973, (with John A. Humphrey) Deviant Behavior, 1980, Role Stress, 1981, Deviant Behavior: Patterns, Sources, and Controls, 1990; also articles. Chmn. bd. trustees Daniel Webster Coll., New Eng. Aero. Inst. Served to lt. AC AUS, 1942-45; Served to lt. AC USAF, 1951-53. Decorated Air medal with 3 oak leaf clusters; Henry Page fellow, 1953-55. Mem. Am. Sociol. Assn., Eastern Sociol. Soc., Internat. Sociol. Soc., Internat. Soc. Criminology, Internat. Soc. Forecasters, Am. Assn. Colls., Council for Liberal Learning, Am. Assn. Higher Edn., Council Colls. Arts and Scis., Nat. Assn. State Univs. and Land-Grant Colls., AAAS, Am. Acad. Polit. and Social Scis., N.Y. Acad. Scis., Am. Assn. Suicidology, Soc. Cross-Cultural Research, Am. Soc. Criminology, Assn. Gov. Bds. Univs. and Colls., Phi Beta Kappa (hon.), Sigma Xi, Alpha Kappa Delta. Home: Riverview Dr Durham NH 03824-3304 Office: U NH Coll Liberal Arts Murkland Hall Durham NH 03824 *Be honest with yourself.*

PALMER, STUART MICHAEL, microbiologist; b. Orange, N.J., Dec. 26, 1958; s. Victor Bernard and Adelaide Amy (Brothers) P.; m. Becky Elizabeth Buckley, Sept. 29, 1984; children: Jessica, Christopher, Kelly. BS in Microbiology and Biochemistry, Rutgers U., 1981, MS in Microbiology, 1984, PhD in Microbiology, 1986. Scientist in infectious diseases Abbott Diagnostics, Abbott Park, Ill., 1986-88, head sect. hepatitis tech. support, 1988-89, mgr. reagent process devel., 1989-90, mgr. TDxR tech. support, 1990-92; dir. therapeutic drug monitoring Roche Diagnostics, Somerville, N.J., 1992—; mem. tech. adv. bd. Abbott Diagnostics, 1991-92; del. rep. Nat. Com. on Clin. Lab. Stds., Somerville, 1994—; mem. Roche patent coord. com. Hoffmann-La Roche, Nutley, N.J., 1994—. Mem. United Way adv. bd. Roche Diagnostic Sys., Somerville, 1994; vol. Am. Heart Assn., Milburn, N.J., 1995; mem. Roche action com. Hoffmann-La Roche, 1994—. Charles and Joanna Busch Meml. Fund predoctoral fellow Rutgers U., 1985; recipient Student Presentation award Theobald Smith Soc. of Am. Soc. for Microbiology, New Brunswick, N.J., 1985. Fellow Assn. Clin. Scientists; mem. AAAS, Am. Assn. Clin. Chemistry, Am. Soc. Clin. Lab. Sci. Achievements include development of large-scale bioreactor processes for Rubella virsu and Toxoplasma gondii production; development of multiple fluorescence polarization assays for therapeutic drug monitoring tests on COBAS Integra chemistry system. Avocations: skiing, gardening. Office: Roche Diagnostics 1080 US Hwy 202 Somerville NJ 08876

PALMER, TEKLA FREDSALL, retired dietitian, consultant; b. Harwinton, Conn., Sept. 1, 1918; d. Frank Albert and Bertha Elena (Weingart) Fredsall; m. Charles Peter Palmer, Apr. 13, 1946; children: Peter F., Karen F. BS, Pratt Inst., 1945; MA, Columbia U., 1947; postgrad., NYU, 1964, Syracuse U., 1968, U. Rochester, 1976. Instr. nutrition Pratt Inst., Bklyn., 1945-48; cons. dietitian Grace Clinic, Bklyn., 1952-55; instr. Skidmore Coll. U. Hosp., N.Y.C., 1955-56; chief clin. dietitian Beth Israel Hosp., N.Y.C., 1966; lectr. Keuka (N.Y.) Coll., 1970-71, Rochester (N.Y.) Inst. Tech., 1975; lectr. nutrition Roberts Wesleyan Coll., Rochester, 1975-81; cons. Buffalo Regional Health Dept., 1967-75. Author: (lab. manual) Nutrition, Diet Therapy and Foods, 1954; com. chmn. The Long Island Diet Manual, 1st edit., 1966. Pratt Inst. scholar, Bklyn., 1943-44; Gen. Foods grantee, 1944-45. Mem. Am. Dietetic Assn. (registered), Va. Dietetic Assn., Richmond Dietetic Assn. (legis. chair 1989), Genesee Dietetic Assn. (pres. 1970-71), L.I. Dietetic Assn. (chair diet therapy 1965-66), Oxford Civic Assn., Nat. Parks and Conservation Assn. Methodist. Avocations: collecting antiques, visiting state and national parks and homes. Home: 8033 Ammonett Dr Richmond VA 23235-3201

PALMER, TIMOTHY JACKSON, bank executive; b. Albany, Ga., Dec. 22, 1946. BA in History, Ga. So. Coll., 1969, MBA in Fin., 1983. Loan officer First Nat. Bank, Vidalia, Ga., 1972-75; asst. registrar, data processing Ga. So. Coll., Statesboro, 1975-79; data processing/ops. officer Sea Island Bank, Statesboro, 1979-84; sr. v.p. Citizen's Bank, Gainesville, Ga., 1984-88; pres. Bank South, Douglas, Ga., 1988-90; pres., CEO FNC Bancorp, Inc., Douglas, 1990—, First Nat. Bank, Douglas, 1992—. With U.S. Army, 1969-72. Office: First National Bank PO Box 1699 Douglas GA 31534*

PALMER, WILLIAM JOSEPH, accountant; b. Lansing, Mich., Sept. 3, 1934; s. Joseph Flammin Lacchia and Henrietta (Yagerman) P.; m. Judith Pollock, Aug. 20, 1960 (div. Nov. 1980); children: William W., Kathryn E., Leslie A., Emily J.; m. Kathleen Francis Booth, June 30, 1990. BS, U. Calif., Berkeley, 1963; stepchildren: Blair T. Manwell, Lindsay A. Manwell. CPA. With Coopers and Lybrand, 1963-80, mng. ptnr., Sacramento, 1976-80; ptnr. Arthur Young & Co., San Francisco, 1980-89; ptnr. Ernst & Young, San Francisco, 1989-94; guest lectr. Stanford U. Engring. Sch., 1976; lectr. Golden Gate Coll., 1975; prof. U. Calif., Berkeley, 1994—. Author: (books) Businessman's Guide to Construction, 1981, Construction Management Book, 1984, Construction Accounting & Financial Management 5th Edition, 1994, Construction Litigation-Representing The Contractor, 1992, Construction Insurance, Bonding and Risk Management, 1996. Bd. dirs. Sacramento Met. YMCA, 1976-82, v.p., 1979-82; bd. dirs. Sacramento Symphony Found., 1977-80; asst. state fin. chmn. Calif. Reagan for Pres., 1980. Served to lt. USN, 1953-59. Mem. AICPA (vice chmn. com. constrn. industry, 1975-81), Nat. Assn. Accts. (pres. Oakland/East Bay chpt. 1972, Man of Yr. 1968), Calif. Soc. CPAs., Assn. Gen. Contractors Calif. (bd. dirs. 1971-74), World Trade Club, Commonwealth Club (San Francisco), Del Paso Country Club, Sutter Club, Comstock Club (Sacramento), Lambda Chi Alpha. Presbyterian. Avocations: antique boats, sailing, tennis, book collecting, pipe collecting. Home: 6 Heather Ln Orinda CA 94563-3508 Office: Ernst & Young 555 California St San Francisco CA 94104-1502

PALMER-CARFORA, LINDA LOUISE, special education educator; b. Derby, Conn., Mar. 6, 1950; d. Robert Roy and Ruth Mae (Borcherding) Palmer; m. John Michael Carfora, July 22, 1972; 1 child, Rachel Ellen. BS, So. Conn. State U., 1972; M of Edn. of the Deaf, Smith Coll., 1987. Learning disabilities tchr. Melissa Jones Sch., Guilford, Conn., 1972-76; tchr. Nat. Soc. for Autistic Children, London, 1977-79; clinician The Developmental Ctr., London, 1979-80; tchr. The Benhaven Sch., New Haven, Conn., 1982-84, Woodstock (Vt.) Developmental Ctr., 1984-86, Willie Ross Sch. for the Deaf, Longmeadow, Mass., 1988—; writer, edn. cons. Bloomington, Ind., 1994—; spl. edn. cons. Dalton (Mass.) Pub. Schs., 1990. Vol. clinician Elmira (N.Y.) Coll. Speech Clinic, 1968-69; vol. tutor New Haven Regional Ctr. for Mentally Retarded, 1969-70. Mem. Coun. for Exceptional Children, Smith Coll. Alumnae Assn. Congregationalist. Avocations: piano, poetry writing. Office: Willie Ross Sch Deaf 32 Norway St Longmeadow MA 01106

PALMER-HASS, LISA MICHELLE, state official; b. Nashville, Sept. 4, 1953; d. Raymond Alonzo Palmer and Anne Michelle (Jones) Davies; m. Joseph Monroe Hass, Jr. BSBA, Belmont Coll., 1975; AA in Interior Design, Internat. Fine Arts Coll., 1977; postgrad., Tenn. State U., 1991—. Interior designer Lisa Palmer Interior Designs, Nashville, 1977-84; sec. to pres. Hermitage Elect. Supply Corp., Nashville, 1981-83; sec. to dir. Tenn. Dept. Mental Health and Mental Retardation, Nashville, 1984-86; transp. planner Tenn. Dept. Transp., Nashville, 1986—. Mem. Nat. Arbor Day Found. Recipient cert. of appreciation Tenn. Dept. Mental Health and Mental Retardation, 1986; named Hon. Mem. Tenn. Ho. of Reps., 1990. Mem. NAFE, Nat. Wildlife Fedn., Profl. Secs. Internat. (cert.), Nashville Striders Club, The Music City Bop Club, Music City Bop Club Dance and Exhibn. Team, Mensa. Republican. Mem. Disciples of Christ Ch. Office: Tenn Dept Transp Environ Planning Office 505 Deaderick St Ste 900 Nashville TN 37243-0334

PALMESE, RICHARD DOMINICK, music company executive; b. Bklyn., Oct. 21, 1947; s. Dominick Arthur and Teresa Gertrude (Buonagura) P.; m. Lana Dee Beery, Oct. 20, 1951; children: Richard Andrew, Christina Marie. BA, St. Louis U., 1969. Disc jockey Sta. KSHE, St. Louis, 1966-70; sr. v.p. Arista Records, N.Y.C., 1975-83; exec. v.p., gen. mgr. MCA Records, L.A., 1983—, pres., 1990—. Named Promotion Exec. of Yr., Poe Pop Music Awards, 1979, 82, Exec. of Yr., 1983, 86, 90, Pres. of Yr., 1991. Democrat. Roman Catholic. Office: MCA Records Inc 70 Universal City Plz Universal City CA 91608

PALMETER, N. DAVID, lawyer; b. Elmira, N.Y., Jan. 29, 1938; s. Neal Henry and Elizabeth Jane (McHale) P.; m. Mary Lee Morken, 1964 (div. 1979); m. Mary Faith Tanney, Jan. 15, 1983; children: Stephen Michael, John David, Elizabeth Jane, James Martin. AB, Syracuse U., 1960; JD, U. Chgo., 1963. Bar: N.Y. 1963, D.C. 1969. Trial atty. U.S. Dept. Justice, Washington, 1966-68; assoc. Daniels & Houlihan, Washington, 1969-73, ptnr., 1973-75; ptnr. Daniels, Houlihan & Palmeter, Washington, 1975-84, Mudge, Rose, Guthrie, Alexander & Ferdon, Washington, 1984-95, Graham & James, Washington, 1995—. Contbr. articles to profl. publs. Mem. ABA, Internat. Bar Assn. (chmn. internat. trade and customs law com. 1989-93, liaison to World Trade Orgn. 1993—), Fed. Bar Assn., N.Y. State Bar Assn., D.C. Bar Assn., Washington Fgn. Law Soc. (pres. 1992-93), Am. Soc. Internat. Law, Can. Coun. on Internat. Law, Brit. Inst. Internat. and Comparative Law. Home: 2804 29th St NW Washington DC 20008-4112

PALMIERI, VICTOR HENRY, lawyer, business executive; b. Chgo., Feb. 16, 1930; s. Mario and Maria (Losacco) P.; children: Victor Henry, Matthew B., John W.; m. Cathryn Connors, July 6, 1990. AB in History, Stanford U., 1951, JD, 1954. Bar: Calif. 1954. Assoc. O'Melveny & Myers, L.A., 1955-59; exec. v.p. Janss Investment Corp., L.A., 1959-63, pres., 1963-68; chmn. Pa. Co. and its subs. Great S.W. Corp., 1969-77; chmn. bd. Palmieri Co., N.Y.C., 1969—; chmn. PHL Corp., Inc. (formerly Baldwin-United Inc.), Phila., 1983-87; trustee, CEO Colo.-Ute Electric Assn. Inc., 1990-92; spl. dep. rehabilitator Confedn. Life Ins. Co., 1994—; dep. rehabilitator, CEO Mut. Benefit Life Ins. Co., 1991-94; pres., CEO MBL Life Assurance Corp., 1994-95; dir. Ernest Home Ctr., Inc., 1992-95, William Carter Corp., 1992-95, William Carter Corp., 1992-95, Outlet Comms., Inc., 1993-95, Broadcasting Ptnrs. Inc., 1994-95, Mullin Cons. Inc., 1990—. Chmn. Am. Learning Corp., 1970-85; dep., exec. dir. Nat. Adv. Commn. on Civil Disorders, 1967-68; ambassador-at-large, U.S. coord. Refugee Affairs, Dept. State, 1979-81; trustee Rockefeller Found., 1979-89; pres., bd. dirs. Lincoln Ctr. Theater, 1985-89; chmn. Overseas Devel. Coun., 1985-91; mem. Coun. on Fgn. Rels.; bd. dirs. The Police Found., 1996—. Office: Palmieri Co 35th Fl 245 Park Ave Fl 35 New York NY 10167-0002

PALMINTERI, CHAZZ, actor; b. Bronx, N.Y., May 15, 1951. Actor: (theatre) The Guy in the Truck, 1982, Broadway, 1983, The King's Men, 22 Years, The Flatbush Faithful, 1985, (TV movies) Peter Gunn, 1990, (films) Oscar, 1991, Bullets Over Broadway, 1994 (Academy award nomination best supporting actor 1994), The Perez Family, 1994, The Usual Suspects, 1995, Jade, 1995, Faithful, 1996, Diabolique, 1996, Mulholland Falls, 1996; playwright, actor: (theatre) A Bronx Tale, 1989; screenwriter, actor: (film) A Bronx Tale, 1993. Office: William Morris Agency 151 El Camino Beverly Hills CA 90212*

PALMORE, JOHN STANLEY, JR., retired lawyer; b. Ancon, C.Z., Aug. 6, 1917; s. John Stanley and Antoinette Louise (Gonzalez) P.; m. Eleanor Anderson, July 31, 1938 (dec. 1980); 1 child, John Worsham (dec.). Student, Western Ky. State Coll., 1934-36; LL.B. cum laude, U. Louisville, 1939. Bar: Ky. 1938. Practice law Henderson, 1939-42, 47-59; judge Ct. Appeals Ky. (name changed to Supreme Ct. Ky. 1975), 1959-82, chief justice, 1966, 73, 77-82; practice law Frankfort, Ky., 1983-84; ptnr. Palmore & Sheffer, Henderson, 1984-86; sr. counsel Jackson & Kelly, Lexington, Ky., 1986-92; ret., 1992; city pros. atty., Henderson, 1949-53, city atty., 1953-55; commonwealth's atty. 5th Circuit Ct. Dist. Ky., 1955-59. Served to lt. USNR, 1942-46, 51-52. Mem. Ky. Bar Assn., Am. Legion, Ky. Hist. Soc., Frankfort Country Club, Lexington Club, Frankfort Rotary Club (pres. 1993-94), Masons, Shriners, Elks, Phi Alpha Delta. Episcopalian (past vestryman, sr. warden). Home: 2310 Peaks Mill Rd Frankfort KY 40601-9437

PALMORE, RODERICK ALAN, lawyer; b. Pitts., Feb. 14, 1952; s. Jefferson and Sophie (Spencer) Palmore; m. Lynne Avril Janifer, June 3, 1978; children: Jordan, Adam. BA, Yale U, 1974; JD, U. Chgo., 1977. Bar: Pa. 1977, Ill. 1982. Assoc. atty. Berkman Ruslander Pohl Lieber & Engel, Pitts., 1977-79; asst. U.S. atty. U.S. Atty's Office, Chgo., 1979-82; assoc. atty. Wildman Harrold Allen & Dixon, Chgo., Ill., 1982-86, ptnr., 1986-93; ptnr. Sonnenschein Nath & Rosenthal, Chgo., 1993—. Commr. Oak Park Plan Commn., 1988—, chair, 1994—; lectr. Youth Motivation Program Chgo. Coun. Commerce & Industry, 1989—; bd. govs. Am. Heart Assn. Met. Chgo., 1993-94; bd. dirs. Pub. Interest Law Initiative, Legal Assistance Found. Chgo. Named one of Outstanding African-Am. Businessmen, Dollars & Sense mag., Chgo., 1991. Mem. ABA (monirity ptnrs. conf. 1991—), Nat. Bar Assn., Cook County Bar Assn., Chgo. Bar Assn. (bd. dirs. 1992-94, co-chmn. minority clerkshop program 1991-92), Chgo. Com. on Minorities in Law Firms (bd. dirs. 1990-92), Chgo. Bar Found. (bd. dirs. 1993-94). Baptist. Avocations: running, biking, tennis, reading. Home: 507 N Euclid Ave Oak Park IL 60302-1617 Office: Sonnenschein Nath & Rosenthal 8000 Sears Tower Chicago IL 60606-6404

PALMREUTER, KENNETH RICHARD LOUIS, principal; b. Vassar, Mich., Feb. 8, 1939; s. Clarence L. and Louise M. (Koch) P.; m. Martha Marie Zoellick, June 16, 1962; children: Pauline, Karen, Joel. BS in Edn., Concordia Tchrs. Coll., 1962; MA in Elem. Sch. Adminstrn., U. Mich., 1967; postgrad., Wayne State U., 1976-78, U. Colo., 1988-89; LLD, Concordia Tchrs. Coll., Seward, Nebr., 1993. Tchr. Grace Luth. Sch., River Forest, Ill., 1960-61; tchr. Calvary Luth. Sch., Lincoln Park, Mich., 1962-63, prin., tchr. jr. high, 1963-76; asst. prin. Luth. High Sch. West, Detroit, 1976-78, prin., 1978-87; exec. dir., prin. Luth. High Sch., Denver, 1987—. Mem. Commn. on Theology and Ch. Rels., Luth. Ch.-Mo. Synod, 1995—, mem. planning coun. for mission and ministry, 1988-90; adv. team Luth. High Schs., 1984-88, 94—, Concordia Centennial adv. com., 1992; day sch. com. Rocky Mountain Dist., 1990-94, tchrs. conf. chmn., 1990-94, dist. conv. com., 1988, 91; nominations com. Mich. Dist., 1987, bd. social ministry, 1980-84, dist. conv. com., 1972, student aid com., 1974-78; conf. program com. Mich. Assn. Non-Pub. Schs., 1984-85; adv. coun. Wayne County Cmty. Coll., 1986-87. Named Outstanding Young Educator, Lincoln Park Jaycees, 1973; nominated Nat. Disting. Luth. Prin., 1992. Mem. NASSP, ASCD, Assn. Luth. Secondary Schs., Luth. Edn. Assn. Lutheran. Home: 2783 S Depew St Denver CO 80227-4106 Office: Lutheran High Sch 3201 W Arizona Ave Denver CO 80219-3941

PALMS, JOHN MICHAEL, academic administrator, physicist; b. Rijswijk, The Netherlands, June 6, 1935; naturalized, 1956; s. Peter Joannes and Mimi Adele (DeYong) P.; m. Norma Lee Cannon, June 2, 1958; children: John Michael, Daniele Maria, Lee Cannon. BS in Physics, The Citadel, 1958, DSc (hon.), 1980; MS in Physics, Emory U., 1959; PhD, U. N.Mex., 1966. Commd. 2d lt. USAF, 1958, retired capt. Res., 1970; lectr. physics dept. U. N.Mex., 1959-62; instr. physics dept. USAF Acad., 1961-62; staff mem. Western Electric Sandia Lab., 1961-62, U. Calif. Los Alamos Sci. Lab., 1962-66, Oak Ridge Nat. Lab., 1966; asst. prof. Emory U., Atlanta, 1966-69; assoc. prof. Emory U., 1969-73, chmn., assoc. prof. dept. physics, asso. prof. radiology dept. Med. Sch., 1973-74, prof., chmn. dept. physics, 1973-74, dean Coll. Arts. and Scis., 1974-80, acting chmn. dept. math. and computer sci., 1976-77, v.p. arts and scis., 1979-82, acting dean Emory Coll., 1979-80, acting dir. Emory U. Computing Ctr., 1980-82, v.p. acad. affairs, 1982-88, interim dean Grad. Sch., 1985-86, Charles Howard Candler prof. nuclear, radiation and environ. physics, 1988-90; pres., prof. physics Ga. State U., Atlanta, 1989-91, U. S.C., Columbia, 1991—; bd. dirs. Phila. Peco Energy Co., Fortis, Inc., N.Y.C., Carolina First, Greenville, S.C., Policy Mgmt. Sys. Corp., Columbia; adv. com. Oak Ridge Nat. Lab., 1984-89; mem. Nat. nuclear accredititng bd. Inst. Nuclear Power Ops., 1985-91, Inst., adv. coun., 1995; mem. panel for semiconductor detectors NAS/NRC, 1963-74; cons. Acad. Natural Scis., Phila., EG&G, INc., Santa Barbara, Calif., Tennelec, Inc., radiology dept. U. So. Calif. Med. Sch., Three Mile Island Environ. Study, Phila. Health Funds, ORTEC, Inc., Oak Ridge, Allied-Gulf Nuclear Svcs., Barnwell, S.C., TRW Space Sys. Divsn., L.A., AEC, Harshaw Chem. Co., Canberra Industries, dept. radiol. health Ga. Dept. Human Resources, Nat. Cancer Inst.; mem. high tech. task force Atlanta C. of C. Contbr. articles on nuclear, atomic, med. and environ. physics to profl. jours. Mem. adv. be. The Citadel, Oak Ridge Nat. Lab.; mem. exec. bd. Atlanta Area Coun. Boy Scouts of Am., 1989-90; mem. cmty. rels. bd. U.S. Penitentiary, Atlanta; trustee Inst. Def. Analysses, Wesleyan Coll., 1984-89, Pace Acad., 1984-89, St. Joseph's Hosp., Atlanta, 1987-89, Ga. Rsch. Alliance, 1988-89; mem. S.C. Univs. Rsch. and Ednl. Found. Bd., S.C. Rsch. Authority Bd.; bd. dirs. Civic-Atlanta Partnership Bus. and Edn., Inc., 1988-90, United Way. Mem. AAAS, Am. Phys. Soc., Am. Assn. Physics Tchrs., IEEE (Nuclear Sci. Group), Am. Nuclear Soc., Am. Coun. Edn., Coun. Provosts and Acad. V.P.s, Am. Conf. Acad. Deans, Soc. Nuclear Medicine, Health Physics Soc., Columbia C. of C. (bd. dirs.), Rotary, Phi Beta Kappa, Sigma Xi, Phi Kappa Phi, Omicron Delta Kappa, Sigma Pi Sigma. Home and Office: U SC House of the President Columbia SC 29208

PALMS, ROGER CURTIS, religious magazine editor, clergyman; b. Detroit, Sept. 13, 1936; s. Nelson Curtis and Winifred Jessie (Bennett) P.; m. Andrea Sisson, Aug. 22, 1959; children—Grant Curtis, Andrea Jane. B.A., Wayne State U., 1958; B.D., Eastern Baptist Sem., Phila, 1961, M.Div., 1971, D.D., 1977; M.A., Mich. State U., 1971. Ordained to ministry Am. Bapt. Chs., 1961. Pastor Ronceverte Bapt. Ch., W.Va., 1961-64; pastor 1st Bapt. Ch., Highland Park, N.J., 1964-67; chaplain Am. Bapt. Student Found., Mich. State U., East Lansing, 1967-73; assoc. editor Decision mag. Billy Graham Evang. Assn., Mpls., 1973-76, editor, 1976—; guest lectr. at schs of evangelism and writers' confs. Author over 13 books including Living on the Mountain, 1985, Enjoying the Closeness of God, 1989, Let God Help You Choose, 1989, Celebrate Life After 50, 1995; spkr. nationally syndicated radio program Something for You. Trustee No. Bapt. Theol. Sem., 1973—. Mem. Evang. Press Assn. (pres. 1991-93). Office: Decision Mag Billy Graham Evang Assn 1300 Harmon Pl Minneapolis MN 55403-1925 *Investing in people's spiritual lives, giving time and counsel, will bring multiplied results for generations. It is one of the most far-reaching ways I can put faith to work.*

PALO, NICHOLAS EDWIN, professional society administrator; b. Waukegan, Ill., Nov. 18, 1945; s. Edwin Arnold and Eevi Kustaava (Hukkala) P.; m. Lauren M. Reynolds, Aug. 18, 1990 (dec.). BA, U. Wis., Eau Claire, 1971; MS, U. Mo., 1975. Instr., coordinator U. Mo. Extension, Columbia, 1974-85; exec. officer Am. Bd. Profl. Psychology, Columbia, 1984—. Pres. Columbia Community Band, 1987; chmn. Arts Resources Coun., Columbia, 1988; adv. bd. Columbia Art League. Mem. Am. Soc. Assn. Execs., Psychology Execs. Roundtable, Mensa, Windjammers Unltd. Club, Am. Assn. Concert Bands Club, Internat. Trombone Assn., Phi Delta Kappa (hon.), Phi Mu Alpha (hon.). Democrat. Lutheran. Avocation: music. Home: 608 Spring Valley Rd Columbia MO 65203-2261 Office: Am Board of Profl Psychology 2100 E Broadway Ste 313 Columbia MO 65201-6082

PALOCHKO, ELEANOR LARIVERE, retired secondary education educator; b. Woonsocket, R.I., May 8, 1924; d. Albert E. and Rosella (Hernan) LaRivere; m. Raymond Francis Palochko, June 26, 1948; children: Ellen, David, Gary, Peggy. BS, U. Conn., 1945; postgrad., Columbia U., 1946, U. Conn., 1982, Cen. Conn. State U. Tchr. bus. Morgan High Sch., Clinton, Conn., 1945-46, Bassick High Sch., Bridgeport, Conn., 1947-49, Jonathan Law High Sch., Milford, Conn., 1961-92; ret., 1992. Former leader Girl Scouts U.S.A., Brownie Scouts; former treas., sec., v.p., pres. PTA, Milford; advisor Keyettes; vol. Milford Hosp. Aux., Bloodmobile drives ARC; sec. Friends of Counted Embroidery, Milford Sr. Ctr.; treas. Milford Hosp. Aux. Mem. NEA, AAUW (exec. bd., past v.p., sec., treas., Ednl. Found. gift in her name 1984-85), Conn. Edn. Assn., Milford Edn. Assn. (bldg rep.), New Eng. Bus. Educators Assn. (rep. profl. devel. com.), Conn. Bus. Educators Assn., Ret. Tchrs. of Bridgeport and New Haven, U. Conn. Alumni Assn., Ret. Profl. Women's Club, Conn. State Ret. Tchrs. Roman Catholic. Avocations: counted cross-stitch, reading, golf, Elderhostels travel. Home: 134 Corona Dr Milford CT 06460-3514

PALOMO, JUAN RAMÓN, columnist; b. Grafton, N.D., July 7, 1946; s. Domingo L. and Martina (López) P. AA, S.W. Tex. Jr. Coll., Uvalde, 1967; BS, S.W. Tex. State U., 1970; MA, Am. U., 1979. Cert. secondary tchr., Tex. Instr. art San Marcos (Tex.) High Sch., 1970-72; editor, pub. La Otra Voz, San Marcos, 1972; editor Hays County Citizen, San Marcos, 1972-76; gen. assignment/polit. reporter Houston Post, 1979-82; nat. reporter USA Today, Arlington, Va., 1982-83; Latin Am. and Caribbean corr. Houston Post, Barbados, 1984; Washington corr. Houston Post, 1985-90, columnist, editorial writer, 1990—; press asst. Carter-Mondale Tex. Hdqs., Austin, 1976; speech writer, press aide Warren Harding for State Treas., Austin, 1978. Mem. Tex. Dem. Exec. Com., Austin, 1976-78. Recipient 1st Pl. for Column Writing, Press Club Houston, 1989, 1st Pl. for Editorial Writing, Press Club Dallas, 1992, Tex. Associated Press Mng. Editors, 1992, Charles E. Green award Headliners Club Tex., 1992. Mem. Nat. Lesbian and Gay Journalists Assn. (bd. dirs. 1991-93, chair elections com. 1991), Nat. Assn. Hispanic Journalists, Nat. Conf. Editl. Writers, Houston Assn. Hispanic Media Profls., Parents, Family and Friends Lesbians and Gays. Avocations: painting, sketching. Home: 1636 Castle Ct Houston TX 77006-5708 Office: Houston Post PO Box 4747 Houston TX 77210-4747

PALOVICH, MARILYN LEE, elementary education educator; b. Trinidad, Colo., Apr. 24, 1943; d. Raymond Leon and Mary (Swigle) Swift; m. Joseph Lawrence Palovich, June 6, 1964; children: Milena Jo, Chad Michael. AA, Trinidad State Jr. Coll., 1963; BA, Adams State Coll., Alamosa, Colo., 1966. Cert. elem. edn. Tchr. grades 1-2-3-4 North Garcia Sch. Dist. No. 5, Trinidad, 1963-65; tchr. kindergarten Trinidad Sch. Dist. No. 1, 1965-68, tchrs. grades 3 and 5, 1970—; mem. adv. bd. Louden/Henritze Archaeology Mus., Trinidad, 1993—. Author: (poetry) Treasured Poems of America, 1994. Pres. Assn. Retarded Citizens, Trinidad, 1987-89; pres., v.p. So. Colo. Assn. to Aid the Handicapped, Trinidad, 1989—; mem. adv. bd., treas. So. Colo. Devel. Disability Svcs., Trinidad, 1987-89. Recipient Outstanding Elem. Tchr. award, 1974, 1st Pl. Nat. 5th Grade award Weekly Reader Editors, Middletown, 1994, Grand Prize Nat. 5th Grade award, 1995. Mem. NRA, Western Slavonic Assn., Colo. Fedn. Tchrs., Trinidad Fedn. Tchrs. Avocations: leather sewing and tooling, gun engraving, reading, writing poetry, handcrafts. Home: 733 Pine St Trinidad CO 81082-2314

PALOYAN, EDWARD, physician, educator, reseacher; b. Paris, Mar. 19, 1932; s. Michael and Renee (Palaian) P.; m. Geraldine Richveis, July 7, 1957; children—Vivian, Regina, Edmund, Grace. M.D., U. Chgo., 1956. Intern U. Chgo. hosps. and clinics, 1956-57; resident in surgery, 1957-58, 1960-65, asst. prof. surgery, 1965-68; asso. prof. surgery U. Chgo. Hosps. and Clinics, Pirtzker Sch. Medicine, 1968-73; prof. surgery Loyola U. Stritch Sch. Medicine, Maywood, Ill., 1973-94; chief endocrine surgery Loyola and Hines, Ill., 1980-94; assoc. chief of staff for rsch. VA Hosp., Hines, 1973-94; assoc. staff Hinsdale (Ill.) Hosp., 1991—. Author: (with A.M. Lawrence) Endocrine Surgery, 1976, (with A.M. Lawrence, F.H. Straus) Hyperparathyroidism, 1973. Served with USN, 1958-60. Recipient McClintock award U. Chgo. Med. Sch., 1971. Mem. Am. Surg. Assn., Soc. Univ. Surgeons, Endocrine Soc., Central Surg. Assn., Am. Assn. Endocrine Surgeons (pres. 1987). Home: 827 Taft Rd Hinsdale IL 60521-4836 also: 40 S Clay St Ste 217W Hinsdale IL 60521-3257

PALSER, BARBARA F., botany researcher, retired educator; b. Worcester, Mass., June 2, 1916; d. G. Norman and Cora A. (Munson) P. A.B., Mt. Holyoke Coll., 1938, A.M., 1940, D.Sc. (hon.), 1978; Ph.D., U. Chgo., 1942. From instr. to prof. botany U. Chgo., 1942-65; from assoc. prof. to prof. botany Rutgers U., New Brunswick, N.J., 1965-83, dir. grad. program in botany, 1973-80; adj. prof. botany U. Mass., Amherst, 1991—; Erskine fellow U. Canterbury, Christchurch, N.Z. 1969; vis. prof. Duke U., Durham, N.C., fall 1962; vis. research fellow U. Melbourne, Australia, fall 1984-85. Author lab. manual Principles of Botany, 1973, also numerous research papers in bot. jours.; bot. adviser Ency. Brit., Chgo., 1958-59; editor Bot. Gazette, Chgo., 1960-65. Named Outstanding Tchr., Rutgers Coll., 1977. Mem. Bot. Soc. Am. (sec. 1970-74, v.p. 1975, pres. 1976, Merit award 1985), Torrey Bot. Club (pres. 1968), Internat. Soc. Plant Morphologists, N.J. Acad. Scis. (pres. elect 1987-88, pres. 1988-89, Outstanding Svc. award 1985, 90), Am. Inst. Biol. Scis. Avocations: mountain hiking and climbing; stamp collecting; photography. Home: 330 Spencer Dr Amherst MA 01002-3367 Office: U Mass Dept Biology Morrill (South) PO Box 35810 Amherst MA 01003-5810

PALSHO, DOROTHEA COCCOLI, information services executive; b. Phila., June 9, 1947; d. John Charles and Dorothy Lucille (Decker) C.; m. Edward Robert Palsho; children: Christopher, Ryan, Erica (stepchild). BS, Villanova U., 1976; MBA, Temple U., 1977. V.p. info. svcs. Dow Jones & Co., Princeton, N.J., 1977—; now pres. bus. info. svcs. Named one of Class of Women Achievers YWCA Acad. of Women Achievers, 1985. Avocation: sports with the boys. Office: Dow Jones & Co Inc PO Box 300 Princeton NJ 08543-0300*

PALTER, ROBERT MONROE, philosophy and history educator; b. N.Y.C., June 19, 1924; s. Meyer and Mildred (Gilder) P.; m. Ruth Rappeport, July 15, 1945; 1 child, Alixe Daphne Cielo; m. Toni Ann Inmam, Apr. 5, 1955; children: Geoffrey Meyer, Jennifer Thorn, Nicholas Trask, Adam Finch; m. Annette B. Weiner, May 21, 1979 (div. 1982). AB, Columbia U., 1943; PhD, U. Chgo., 1952. From instr. to asso. prof. phys. scis. and philosophy U. Chgo., 1949-64; prof. philosophy and history U. Tex., Austin, 1964-82; Dana prof. history of sci. Trinity Coll., Hartford, Conn., 1983-91, prof. emeritus, 1991—. Author: Whitehead's Philosophy of Science, 1960; editor: Toward Modern Science, 1961, The Annus Mirabilis of Sir Isaac Newton, 1971. Served with AUS, 1944-46. Mem. Phi Beta Kappa.

PALTINEANU, IOAN CATON, agronomy engineer; b. Campina, Prahova, Romania, June 1, 1941; came to U.S., 1993; s. Caton and Ana (Gradin) P.; m. Rodica Stegaru Paltineanu, July 30, 1964 (dec. 1981); 1 child, Caton-Liviu; m. Nicoleta Popescu, Dec. 1, 1984; 1 child, Ioan. BS, Agronomic Inst., Bucharest, Romania, 1964, PhD, 1975. Engr. of agronomy Danube Embanked Island, Pietroiu Calarasi, Romania, 1964-67; rsch. leader Rsch. Inst. For Cereals and Indsl. Plants, Fundulea, Romania, 1967-78; FAO scholar agronomy dept. Colo. State U., Ft. Collins, Colo., 1970-71; dir. rsch. sta. for irrigated crops Valul lui Traian, Dobrogea, Romania, 1978-82; rsch. leader Rsch. Inst. for Pedology and Agrochemistry, Bucharest, 1982-83; dir. rsch. Inst. for Irrigation and Drainage, Baneasa Giurgiu, Romania, 1983-90; vis. scientist USDA-ARS Water Mgmt. Rsch. Lab., Fresno, Calif., 1993, USDA-ARS Natural Resources Inst., Environ. Chemistry Lab., Beltsville, Md., 1994—; expert prof. Quanta Engring Faculty of Atmospheric Scis., Tehran, 1977-78; state sec. land reclamation dept. Ministry of Agriculture, Bucharest, 1991-92. Contbr. articles to profl. jours. Mem. Am. Soc. of Agronomy and Soil Soc. of Am., U.S. Irrigation Assn. (tech.), Acad. of Agrl. and Forestry Scis., Romanian Soc. of Agronomy, Internat. Soil Sci. Soc. Achievements include research in soil physics, irrigation and nitrogen application efficiency for ground water pollution control using radioactive and nonradioactive methods; patentee in the field of concerning furrow, sprinkler and drip irrigation equipments, hydraulic lysimetry, laser detasseling of maize. Office: USDA-ARS-NRI Environ Chemistry Lab Bldg 007 10300 Baltimore Ave Rm 224 Beltsville MD 20705-2350

PALUMBO, BENJAMIN LEWIS, public affairs consulting company executive; b. Boston, Mar. 4, 1937; s. Guido Americo and Stella Marie (Lombardo) P.; m. Magdalene Julia Palinczar, Nov. 18, 1961; children: Matthew, Jason, Guy. BA, Rutgers U., 1959, MA, 1961. Adminstrv. asst. to Gov. Richard J. Hughes, N.J., 1963-65; dir. rsch. N.J. Dem. Com., Trenton, 1965-66; asst. to commr. N.J. Dept. Transp., Trenton, 1966-70; asst. dean Woodrow Wilsonn Sch., Princeton (N.J.) U., 1970-71; adminstrv. asst. to Senator Harrison Williams, U.S. Senate, Washington, 1971-73, staff dir. Dem. caucus, 1975-77, subcom. on govt. activities and transp., 1977-78; nat. campaign dir. Bentsen for Pres., Washington, 1973-75; dir. fed. govt. rels. Phillip Morris, Inc., Washington, 1978-83; pres. Palumbo & Cerrell, Inc., Washington, 1983—. Bd. dirs. Washington Performing Arts Soc., Arlington County Commn. on the Arts. Mem. Nat. Press Club, Rutgers Club Washington, Econ. Club Washington, Am. League Lobbyists, KC, Nat. Dem. Club. Democrat. Roman Catholic. Office: Palumbo & Cerrell Inc 1717 K St NW Ste 500 Washington DC 20006-1501

PALUMBO, DONALD R., metal products executive; b. 1936. Pres. Gold Coast Engring Inc., Chula Vista, Calif., 1980—. Office: Gold Coast Engring Inc PO Box 1109 Bonita CA 91908-1109*

PALUMBO, MATTHEW ALOYSIUS, marketing executive; b. Queens, N.Y., Sept. 17, 1961; s. John Christopher and Seiko (Murakami) P. BS, Cornell U., 1986; MBA in Mktg. Mgmt., St. John's U., 1990. Mortgage clk. Salomon Bros., Inc., N.Y.C., 1986; mut. fund adminstr. Bank of N.Y. Co., Inc., N.Y.C., 1986-88; copywriter Pierce Assocs., N.Y.C., 1988-90; dir. mktg. cons. Palumbo Assocs., S.I., 1989-90; adj. prof. St. John's U., S.I., 1990; mktg. dir., copy dir. Flaghouse Inc., Mt. Vernon, N.Y., 1990-93; spl. projects mgr., product mgr. Global Computer Supplies, Port Washington, N.Y., 1993—; guest lectr. Am. direct mktg. techniques Sheffield Halleron U. (Eng.), 1993; guest lectr. designed and acquired funding Cornell U., Ithaca, 1992—. N.Y. State Regents scholar, 1979, Annette Brodsky scholar, 1988. Mem. Am. Assn. MBA Execs., Hudson Valley Direct Mktg. Assn., Cornell Asian Alumni Assn. (v.p. alumni affairs 1993-95), Cornell ILR Alumni Assn., Direct Mktg. Club N.Y., Cornell Club N.Y., Cornell Club Fairfield County. Avocations: reading, sports, music. Home: 17 Willowbrook Ct Stamford CT 06902-6228

PALUMBO, RUTH ANN, state legislator; b. Lexington, Ky., July 7, 1949; d. James Keith and Dorothy Calvin (Carrier) Baker; m. John Anthony Palumbo II, June 29, 1974; children: John A. III (dec.), Joseph Edward, James Thomas, Stephen Baker. BA in Secondary Edn., U. Ky., 1972. Sales Chez Lissette Boutique, Leysin, Switzerland, 1966; sales, shoes Purcell's Dept. Store, Lexington, Ky., 1966-70; organist Ctrl. Bapt. Ch., Lexington, Ky., 1968; clk. Good Samaritan Hosp., Lexington, Ky., 1968-73; sec. Dr. Joseph Keith, Lexington, Ky., 1971-73; senate clk. aide Ky. Gen. Assembly, Frankfort, Ky., 1974; pub. rels. Palumbo Properties, Lexington, 1974-92; state rep. Ky. Gen. Assembly, 1991-92; mem. LWV, Lexington, 1990-92, Ky. Women's Polit. Caucus, Louisville, 1991-92, NAt. Order Women Legislators, Washington, 1992; sec. Ctrl. Ky. Caucus, Lexington, 1991-92. Mem. Greater Lexington Dem. Women, fin. v.p., 1982; mem. Nat. Order of Women Legislators, Washington, 1992; legis.liaison ACS Breast Cancer Detection Task Force, Ky., 1992; adv. coun. Bryan Sta. Youth Svcs. Ctr., Lexington, 1992; ball chmn. Lexington Philharmonic Women's Guild, 1990; govt. affairs Am. Symphony Orch. League Vol. Coun., Washington, 1992; bd. dirs. Philharmonic Women's Guild, pres., 1986-88; bd. dirs. Am. Cancer Soc., pres., 1988-89; bd. dirs. Lexington Phulharmonic Soc. Recipient Dorothy Moomaw Miles Svc. award Sayre Sch., 1986, Govs. Vol. Activist award Gov. Wallace G. Wilkinson, 1989, named Lexington's Outstanding Young Woman Bluegrass Jr. Woman's Club, 1982, Leadership Lexington, C. of C., 1988, Leadership Am. Found. for Women's Resources, Washington, 1989. Fellow U. Ky. Devel. Coun.; mem. Jr. League LExington (sec. 1989-90), Profl. Women's Forum, Gamma Phi Veta (pres. 1980-82). Baptist. Avocations: playing piano, singing, collecting stamps, music boxes, family. Home: 10 Deepwood Dr Lexington KY 40505-2106 Office: House of Reps State Capitol Anx Frankfort KY 40601

PALUSZEK, JOHN L., public relations firm executive; b. Bklyn., Nov. 3, 1933. BA in Mgmt., Manhattan Coll, 1955. Assoc. editor Petroleum Week, 1955-59; v.p., then sr. v.p., exec. v.p. Basford Pub. Rels., 1960-71; pres. Paluszek & Leslie Assocs., 1971-84; exec. v.p. Ketchum Pub. Rels., from 1984; now pres for pub. affairs Ketchum Pub. Rels., N.Y.C.; pres-elect Pub. Rels. Soc. Am., past pres. N.Y. chpt., past chmn., N.E. dist. Author articles in profl. jours. Office: Ketchum Pub Rels 220 East 42nd St New York NY 10017*

PALVINO, JACK ANTHONY, broadcasting executive; b. Rochester, N.Y., May 28, 1934; s. John Charles and Mary Aurelia P.; m. Joyce Ann Vilkaitis, Oct. 8, 1960; children: John Charles, Jill Marie, Jason Allen. B.S., St. John Fisher Coll., 1955. Broadcaster, program dir. Sta. WGVA, Geneva, N.Y., 1958-60; radio personality Sta. WBBF, Rochester, N.Y., 1958-78; pres. Sports and Spls. TV, 1970-73; co-owner, exec. v.p. Lincoln Group Ltd., 1978—; gen. mgr. Stas. WHAM, WVOR, WHTK, WPXY, Rochester, 1978—. Chmn. bd. trustees St. John Fisher Coll. Served with U.S. Army, 1957-58. Mem. St. John Fisher Alumni Assn., Nat. Assn. Broadcaster, Rochester Radio Broadcasters Assn. (pres. 1987—), N.Y. State Broadcasters Assn., Rochester C. of C. Roman Catholic. Clubs: University, Rochester Press Radio (pres. 1974), Rotary. Office: 207 Midtown Plz Rochester NY 14604-2016

PALVINO, NANCY MANGIN, librarian; b. Rochester, N.Y., Nov. 22, 1937; d. John Bernard and Miriam Lucille (Fox) Mangin; m. Lawrence Robert Palvino, July 2, 1960; children: Mark, Laurie, Lisa, Katharine, Thomas. BS, SUNY, Geneseo, 1959; MLS, U. Buffalo, 1993. Cert. libr., N.Y. Libr. Spencerport (N.Y.) Elem. Sch., 1959-60; tchr. East Greenbush (N.Y.) Elem. Sch., 1960-63; libr. # 41 Sch., Rochester, 1993—. Author: (bibliography) Autism, 1991. Fundraiser Rochester Philharm. Orgn., 1970; mem. women's bd. dirs. St. Mary's Hosp., Rochester, 1980—, giftshop chairperson, 1989-92, exec. coun., 1989-92, chmn. of ball, 1985, Imperial Ball Meml. Art Gallery, 1987, Holiday Open House, 1988; v.p. women's coun. Meml. Art Gallery, Rochester, 1989-91. Grantee DeWitt Wallace Reader's Digest Fund, 1994. Mem. N.Y. Libr. Assn. (scholarship 1992), Greater Rochester Areas Media Specialists (chmn. scholarship com. 1994-95, scholarship 1992). Avocations: golf, reading, walking, knitting. Home: 345 Kilbourn Rd Rochester NY 14618 Office: # 41 Sch 279 Ridge Rd W Rochester NY 14615-2927

PAMPLIN, ROBERT BOISSEAU, SR., textile manufacturing executive; b. Sutherland, Va., Nov. 25, 1911; s. John R. and Pauline (Beville) P.; m. Mary K. Reese, June 15, 1940; 1 child, Robert Boisseau Jr. BBA, Va. Poly. Inst. & State U., 1933; postgrad., Northwestern U., 1933-34; LLD (hon.), U. Portland (Oreg.), 1972; LHD (hon.), Warner Pacific Coll., 1976. With Ga.-Pacific Corp., Portland, 1934-76, sec., from 1936, adminstrv. v.p., 1952-55, exec. v.p., 1955-57, pres., 1957-67, chmn. bd., chief exec. officer, from 1967; ret., 1976; with R.B. Pamplin Corp., 1957—, chmn. bd., CEO, to 1996; chmn. bd., CEO Mt. Vernon Mills Inc. (subs. R.B. Pamplin Corp.), Greenville, S.C. Office: R B Pamplin Corp 900 SW 5th Ave Ste 1800 Portland OR 97204-1227

PAMPLIN, ROBERT BOISSEAU, JR., agricultural company executive, minister, writer; b. Augusta, Ga., Sept. 3, 1941; s. Robert Boisseau and Mary Katherine (Reese) P.; m. Marilyn Joan Hooper; children: Amy Louise, Anne Boisseau. Student Va. Poly. Inst., 1960-62; BSBA Lewis and Clark Coll., 1964, BS in Acctg., 1965, BS in Econs., 1966, LHD (hon.), 1995, DHL (hon.), 1995; MBA U. Portland, 1968, MEd, 1975, LLD (hon.), 1972, Western Bapt. Coll., 1989; MCL Western Conservative Bapt. Sem., 1978, DMin, 1982, PhD Calif. Coast U., DHL (hon.) Warner Pacific Coll., 1988, LLD (hon.) Western Bapt. Coll., 1989; cert. in wholesale mgmt. Ohio State U., 1970; cert. in labor mgmt. U. Portland, 1972; cert. in advanced mgmt. U. Hawaii, 1975; DD (hon.) Judson Bapt. Coll., 1984; DBA (hon.) Marquis Giuseppe Scicluna Internat. U. Found., 1986; LittD (hon.) Va. Tech. Inst. and State U., 1987, LHD (hon.); D of Sacred Letter (hon.) Western Conservation Bapt. Sem., 1991; DD Western Evang. Sem., 1994; LHD (hon.) Lewis and Clark Coll., 1995; DBA U. S.C., 1996. Pres., COO R.B. Pamplin Corp., Portland, Oreg., 1964—; chmn., CEO Columbia Empire Farms, Inc., Lake Oswego, Oreg., 1976—, United Tile Co., Pamplin Comms., Oreg. Wilbert Vault; chmn., CEO Mt. Vernon Mills Inc.; lectr. bus. adminstrn. Lewis and Clark Coll., 1968-69, trustee, 1989—; adj. asst. prof. bus. adminstrn., U. Portland, 1973-76; pastor Christ Cmty. Ch., Lake Oswego; lectr. in bus. adminstrn. and econs. U. Costa Rica, 1968, Va. Tech. Found., 1986; chmn. bd. dirs. United Tile Co., Christian Supply Ctrs., Inc. Author: Everything is Just Great, 1985, The Gift, 1986, Another Virginian: A Study of the Life and Beliefs of Robert Boisseau Pamplin, 1986, (with others): A Portrait of Colorado, 1976, Three in One, 1974, The Storybook Primer on Managing, 1974, One Who Believed, Vol. I, 1988, Vol. II, 1991, Climbing the Centuries, 1993, Heritage The Making of an American Family, 1994, American Heroes, 1995, Prelude to Surrender, 1995; editor Oreg. Mus. Sci. and Industry Press, 1973, trustee, 1971, 74—; editor Portrait of Oregon, 1973, (with others) Oregon Underfoot, 1975; hon. life pres. Western Conservative Bapt. Seminary; chmn. regents Western Sem., 1994. Mem. Nat. Adv. Coun. Vocat. Edn., 1975—; mem. Western Interstate Com. Higher Edn., 1981-84; co-chmn. Va. Tech. $50 million Campaign for Excellence, 1984-87, Va. Tech. Found., 1986—, Va.-Oreg. State Scholarship Commn., 1974—, chmn., 1976-78; mem. Portland dist. adv. coun. SBA, 1973-77; mem. rewards rev. com., City of Portland, 1973-78, chmn., 1973-78; bd. regents U. Portland, 1971-79, chmn. bd., 1975-79, regent emeritus, 1979—; trustee Oreg. Episc. Schs., 1979, Linfield Coll., U. Puget Sound, 1989—; chmn. bd. trustees Lewis and Clark Coll., 1991. Recipient Disting. Alumnus award Lewis and Clark Coll., 1974, ROTC Disting. Svc. award USAF, 1974, Albert Einstein Acad. Bronze medal, 1986, Disting. Leadership medal Freedoms Found., Disting. Bus. Alumnus award U. Portland, 1990, Nat. Caring award Caring Inst., 1991, Pride of Portland award Portland Lions Club, Hero Athlete award, 1994, Herman Lay Entrepreneurship award 1995; Va. Tech Coll. Bus. Adminstrn. renamed R.B. Pamplin Coll. Bus. Adminstrn. in his honor; Western Conservative Bapt. Sem. Lay Inst. for Leadership, Edn., Devel. and Rsch. named for R.B. Pamplin, Jr., 1988. Mem. Acad. Mgmt., Delta Epsilon Sigma, Beta Gamma Sigma, Sigma Phi Epsilon, Waverley Country Club, Arlington, Multnomah Athletic Club, Capitol Hill Club, Greenville Country Club, Poinsett Club, Eldorado Country Club, Thunderbird Country Club, Rotary. Republican. Episcopalian. Office: R B Pamplin Corp Inc 900 SW 5th Ave Portland OR 97204-1235

PAMPUSCH, ANITA MARIE, academic administrator; b. St. Paul, Aug. 28, 1938; d. Robert William and Lucille Elizabeth (Whaley) P. BA, Coll. of St. Catherine, St. Paul, 1962; MA, U. Notre Dame, 1970, PhD, 1972. Tchr. St. Joseph's Acad., St. Paul, 1962-66; instr. philosophy Coll. of St. Catherine, St. Paul, 1970-76, assoc. acad. dean, 1979, acad. dean, 1979-84, pres., 1984—; Am. Council Edn. fellow Goucher Coll., Balt., 1976-77; bd. dirs. St. Paul Cos.; head Women's Coll. Coalition, 1988-91. Author: (book rev.) Philological Quarterly, 1976; contbr. articles to profl. jours. Mem. adv. com. Instl. Leadership project, Columbia U., 1986—; dist. chmn. Rhodes Scholarship Selection com., Mo., Neb., Minn., Kans., N.D., S.D., 1987—; exec. com. Women's Coll. Coalition, Washington, 1985—. Mem. Coun. for Ind. Colls. (bd. dirs. 1987—, chair 1991—), Am. Philos. Assn., St. Paul C. of C. (bd. dirs. 1986—), St. Paul's Athletic Club, Mpls. Club, Phi Beta Kappa. Roman Catholic. Avocations: swimming, camping, reading, music. Office: Coll of St Catherine Office of the President 2004 Randolph Ave Saint Paul MN 55105-1789

PAN, CODA H. T., mechanical engineering educator, consultant, researcher; b. Shanghai, China, Feb. 10, 1929; came to U.S., 1948; s. Ming H. Pai and Chih S. Ling; m. Vivian Y.C. Chang, June 2, 1951; children—Lydia Codetta, Philip Daniel. Student, Tsing Hwa U., Beijing, China, 1946-48; B.S. in Mech. Engring., Ill. Inst. Tech., 1950; M.S. in Aero. Engring., Rensselaer Poly. Inst., 1958, Ph.D., 1961. Engr. Gen. Electric Co., Schenectady, 1950-61; dir. research Mech. Tech. Inc., Latham, N.Y., 1961-73; tech. dir. Shaker Research Corp., Ballston Lake, N.Y., 1973-81; prof. mech. engring. Columbia U., N.Y.C., 1981-87; sr. cons. engr. Digital Equipment Corp., Shrewsbury, Mass., 1987-92; adj. prof. Rensselaer Poly. Inst., 1961-81; vis. prof. Tech. U. Denmark, Copenhagen, 1971, U. Poitiers, France, 1987; mem. adv. panel rand Corp., 1974; engring. cons., 1992—, v.p. Indsl. Tribology Inst., Troy, N.Y., 1982—; co-prin. investigator Spacelab I, 1984. Contbg. author: Tribology, 1980, Structural Mechanical Software Series 3, 1980; contbr. articles to profl. jours.; patentee in field. Recipient IR-100 award, 1967; NIH fellow, 1972. Fellow ASME, Soc. Tribologists and Lubrication Engrs.; mem. AAAS, Am. Phys. Soc., Am. Acad. Mechanics. Home and Office: 6 Pinehurst Cir Millbury MA 01527-3361

PAN, LORETTA REN-QIU, retired educator; b. Changzhou, China, Oct. 1, 1917, came to U.S., 1951, naturalized, 1965; d. Ke-jun and Mei-ying (Xue) P.; B.A. in English Lit., Ginling Coll., 1940; cert. English Lit., Mt. Holyoke Coll., 1952. Instr. English, Nanking U., 1940-41; instr. English and Chinese, St. Mary's Girls Sch., Shanghai, 1941-44; instr. English, Ginling Coll., 1944-45; sr. translator info. dept. Brit. Embassy, Shanghai, 1945-48; Chinese editor U.S. Consulate Gen., Hong Kong, 1949-51; researcher, editorial asst. modern China project Columbia U., 1955-60, lectr. Chinese, 1960-67, sr. lectr., 1968-87. Methodist. Contbr. to various profl. publs. Home: 600 W 111th St New York NY 10025-1813

PANARESE, WILLIAM C., civil engineer; b. Framingham, Mass., Mar. 6, 1929; s. Angelo and Stephanie (De Profilo) P. B.S. in Civil Engring., Purdue U., 1952. Structural research engr. Assn. Am. Railroads, Chgo., 1952-55; with Portland Cement Assn., Chgo. and Skokie, Ill., 1957-76, 80-94; mgr. concrete tech. sect. Portland Cement Assn., 1973-76, assoc. mgr. bldg. constrn. sect., 1980-83, mgr. bldg. tech. dept., 1983-86, mgr. constrn. info. services dept., 1987-94. Author, editor Design and Control of Concrete Mixtures, Concrete Masonry handbook for Architects, Engineers, Builders, High Strength Concrete, Concrete Floors on Ground, Fiber Reinforced Concrete, Cement Mason's Guide, other bldg. guides and handbooks; editor: Concrete Constrn. mag., 1976-80, Concrete Technology Today newsletter, 1980-94. Served with C.E. U.S. Army, 1955-57. Fellow Am. Concrete Inst. (coms. 302 on constrn. of concrete floors, 332 on residential concrete work, chmn. 332 1984-88). Roman Catholic. Home: 942 Washington St Glenview IL 60025-4273

PANARETOS, JOHN, mathematics and statistics educator; b. Kythera, Lianianika, Greece, Feb. 23, 1948; s. Victor and Fotini (Kominu) P.; m. Evdokia Xekalaki; 1 child, Victor. First degree, U. Athens, 1972; MSc, U. Sheffield, Eng., 1974; PhD, U. Bradford, Eng., 1977. Lectr. U. Dublin, Ireland, 1979-80; asst. prof. U. Mo., Columbia, U.S, 1980-82; assoc. prof. U. Iowa, Iowa City, U.S., 1982-83, U. Crete, Iraklio, Greece, 1983-84; assoc. prof. div. applied math., Sch. Engring. U. Patras, Greece, 1984-87, prof., 1987-91, assoc. dean sch. engring., chmn. div. applied math., 1986-87, vice-rector, 1988-91; prof. Athens U. Econs., 1991—, chair dept. stats., 1993-96; pres. Nat. Coun. Edn. of Greece, 1996—; sec.-gen. Ministry Edn. and Religious Affairs, Greece, 1988-89, 95—. Contbr. articles to profl. jours. Mem. Sci. Coun. of Greek Parliament, 1987—; mem. ednl. com. OECD, 1994—; mem. governing bd. CERI of OECD, 1994—; chmn. rsch. com., pers. com. U. Patras, 1988-91. Mem. N.Y. Acad. Sci., Am. Statis. Assn., Inst. Math. Stats., Bernoulli Soc. for Probability and Math. Stats., Greek Math. Soc., Greek Statis. Inst., Internat. Statis. Inst. Office: Athens U Econs, PO Box 31466, 10035 Athens Greece

PANARO, VICTOR ANTHONY, radiologist; b. Buffalo, Aug. 7, 1928; s. Anthony and Teresa P.; m. Virginia Spann, Dec. 4, 1954; children: Denise, Lynn, Stephen. BA summa cum laude, U. Buffalo, 1948, MD, 1952. Diplomate Am. Bd. Radiology, Am. Bd. Nuclear Medicine, Am. Bd. Med. Examiners. Intern E. J. Meyer Meml. Hosp., Buffalo, 1952-53; resident E. J. Meyer Meml. Hosp., 1953-54, 56-58, Roswell Park Meml. Hosp. Cancer Inst., Buffalo, 1956-57; practice medicine specializing in radiology and nuclear medicine Buffalo, 1961—; mem. staff Erie County Med. Center, Buffalo, 1961—; assoc. dir. radiology dept. Erie County Med. Center, 1972—; mem. staff Westfield (N.Y.) Meml. Hosp., 1959-81, dir. radiology dept., 1959-81; mem. staff Buffalo Psychiat. Inst., 1974—, dir. radiology dept., 1974—; cons. nuclear medicine and radiology Brooks Meml. Hosp., 1970—; cons. VA Hosp., Buffalo; prof. radiology and nuclear medicine SUNY, Buffalo. Served as capt. M.C. U.S. Army, 1954-56. Fellow Am. Coll. Radiology; mem. AMA, N.Y. State Med. Soc., Erie County Med. Soc., Radiol. Soc. N.Am., Assn. Univ. Radiologists, Buffalo Radiol. Soc., Radiologists Bus. Mgrs. Assn., N.Y. State Radiol. Soc., Gibson Anatomical Soc., Gross Med. Soc., Cath. Physicians Guild Western N.Y., Phi Beta Kappa, Phi Chi. Republican. Roman Catholic. Clubs: Baccelli Med, Holy Name Soc, Romulus, Dante Allegiehri Soc. Home: 25 Elmhurst Rd Buffalo NY 14226-3539 Office: Erie County Med Center 462 Grider St Buffalo NY 14215-3075

PANATIER, M. J., gas industry executive. Sr. v.p., coo Phillips 66 Natural Gas Co. (now GPM Gas Corp.), Houston, 1986; now pres., ceo. Office: Phillips 66 Natural Gas Co 1300 Post Oak Blvd Houston TX 77056-3010*

PANAYIOTOU, GERGIOS KYRIAKOU See MICHAEL, GEORGE

PANCAKE, EDWINA HOWARD, science librarian; b. Butte, Mont., Nov. 10, 1942; d. Robert Evan and Edwina Howard (Handfield) P. Student, Miami U., 1960-63; BS in Biology, Baylor U., 1967; MLS, U. Tex., 1969. Sci. info. specialist U. Va., Charlottesville, 1969-73, acting dir. sci. and tech.

info. ctr., dir. sci. and engring libr., 1974-93, assoc. prof. emeritus, 1994—. NDEA fellow U. Tex., 1967-68. Fellow Spl. Libraries Assn. (bd. dirs. 1979-81, 83-84, 85-88, pres. 1994-95), Mensa. Episcopalian. Avocations: travel, theater, costuming, science fiction, editing newsletters.

PANCAKE, JOHN, newspaper editor. State news editor, environ. editor Miami Herald. Office: Miami Herald Pub Co One Herald Plz Miami FL 33132-1693

PANCHAL, JOAN, nursing educator; b. Pitts., Feb. 25, 1947; d. Edward and Gertrude (Kaminski) Dauginikas; m. Pravin D. Panchal, Aug. 20, 1970; children: Nita, Sheila, Lisa. A.D., Community Coll. Allegheny, Pitts., 1970; BSN, Pa. State U., 1981; MPH, U. Pitts., 1982, PhD, 1987. Surg. nurse South Side Hosp., Pitts., 1965-70; staff nurse-med. VA Hosp., Bronx, N.Y., 1970; head nurse Jewish Home and Hosp., Bronx, 1970-71; rehab. coord. Negley House, Pitts., 1978-81; instr. nursing Pa. State U., University Park, 1982-85, asst. prof., 1987—, grad. faculty, 1994—; cons., Pitts., 1978-88; with Pa. Dept. Health Nursing, Pub. Health Adminstrn., Pitts., 1982. Author book revs., course; author: (ednl. instrn.) Teaching the Cardiac Patient, 1991. Named for Edn. Excellence, Nightengale fo Pa., 1991. Mem. Pa. League for Nursing (pres. 1992-94, bd. dirs. 1989), NLN, ANA (item writer for cert. 1989), Pa. Nurses Assn. (provider unit 1990, bd. dirs. 1992—). Roman Catholic. Avocations: swimming, tennis. Office: Pa State U 201 Health And Human Dev E University Park PA 16802-6508

PANCOAST, EDWIN C., retired foreign service officer, writer, researcher; b. Stratford, N.J., Aug. 20, 1925; m. Eunice Billings, June 12, 1948; children: Laurence E., Karen L., Joanne L. B.A., Maryville Coll., 1949; M.S., George Washington U., 1971; grad., Nat. War Coll., Washington, 1971. Served U.S. Fgn. Svc., Dept. State, 1949-53, USIA, 1953-86; sr. policy officer USIA, Washington, 1984-86; chief of policy Voice of Am., 1975-79; U.S. consul, dir. Amerika Haus, Munich, 1979-84; ret., 1986; writer, researcher Chevy Chase, Md., 1986—. 1st lt. AUS, 1943-46, ETO. Address: 4813 Drummond Ave Chevy Chase MD 20815-5428

PANDE, KRISHNA PRASAD, electrical engineer, physicist; b. Basti, India, Jan. 3, 1946; came to U.S., 1977; s. Ram Milan and Sheetla Pandey; m. Malti Rani Shukla, June 6, 1973; children: Aru, Pari. PhD, Indian Inst. Tech., Madras, 1973. Scientist Nat. Phys. Lab., New Delhi, 1973-75; rsch. assoc. Rensselaer Poly. Inst., Troy, N.Y., 1977-79; asst. prof. Rutgers U., Piscataway, N.J., 1979-81; mgr. Bendix/Allied-Signal Corp., Columbia, Md., 1981-86; exec. v.p., gen. mgr. Microwave Signal, Inc., Clarksburg, Md., 1994-95; bd. dirs. Unisys, St. Paul, 1986-88; exec. dir. Comsat, Clarksburg, Md., 1988-93; pres. Synoptel, Inc. Mem. tech. adv. bd. NSF, Washington, 1985-92; mem. engring. bd. U. Cin., 1990-92; mem. math. rev. bd. Howard County, Md., 1985; mem. Comsat Quality Coun.; adv. bd. Hexawave Corp., Phoenix Microwave, Eagle Eye Tech., Princeton Electronic Sys., Crysind Electronics. Fellow IEEE (mem. admissions and adv. com. 1986-88); mem. AIAA (com. mem.), Am. Phys. Soc., N.Y. Acad. Scis., Electromagnetic Acad. Hindu. Achievements include research in InP transister technology and wireless communications. Home: 12200 Galesville Dr Gaithersburg MD 20878-2072

PANDEY, DHIRENDRA KUMAR, mechanical engineer,scientist; b. Jaunpur, India, July 1, 1951; came to U.S., 1978; s. Ram Raj and Ram Patti Pandey; m. Snehlata Pandey, Jan. 27, 1981; children: Nirnimesh, Nisheeth, Niket. BS, Banaras Hindu U., Varanasi, India, 1972, MS, 1974; PhD, U. Ill., Chgo., 1982. Asst. prof. H.B. Technol. Inst., Kanpur, India, 1976-78, Banaras Hindu U., 1975-76; teaching and rsch. asst. U. Ill., 1978-82; rsch. asst. prof. Old Dominion U., Norfolk, Va., 1982-85; rsch. scientist Info. & Control Systems, Hampton, Va., 1986-89; prin. scientist Hughes STX Corp., Hampton, Va., 1989-92; atmospheric scientist Sci. Applications Internat. Corp., Hampton, Va., 1992—. Contbr. articles to profl. jours.; patentee high temperature directional emissivity measurement system. Mem. Am. Meteorol. Soc., Am. Geophys. Union. Avocations: reading, writing. Home: 1 Carlisle Ct Hampton VA 23666-6024 Office: SAIC One Enterprise Pky Ste 250 Hampton VA 23666

PANDEY, RAMESH CHANDRA, chemist; b. Naugaon, India, Nov. 5, 1938; came to U.S., 1967; s. Gauri Dutt and Jivanti Pandey. B.Sc., U. Allahabad (India), 1958; M.Sc., U. Gorakhpur (India), 1960; Ph.D., U. Poona (India), 1965. Jr. research fellow C.S.I.R. Nat. Chem. Lab., Poona, India, 1960-64, research officer, 1965-67, scientist organic div., 1970-72; research assoc. dept. chemistry U. Ill., Urbana, 1967-70, vis. scientist, 1972-77; sr. scientist fermentation program Nat. Cancer Inst. Frederick (Md.) Cancer Research Facility, 1977-82, head chem. sect., 1982-83; sr. scientist Abbott Labs., North Chicago, Ill., 1983-84; pres. Xechem, Inc., Melrose Park, Ill., 1984-90, pres., chief exec. officer, dir. tech. devel., New Brunswick, N.J., 1990—; cons. Washington U. Sch. Medicine, St. Louis, 1976-85, LyphoMed, Inc., Melrose Park, 1984-85; vis. prof. Waksman Inst. Rutgers U., Piscataway, N.J., 1984-86. Mem. editorial bd. Internat. Jour. Antibiotics, 1986—; patentee graft thin layer chromatography. Fellow Am. Inst. Chemists; mem. Am. Chem. Soc., Am. Soc. Microbiology, Am. Soc. Mass Spectrometry, Am. Assn. Cancer Rsch., Am. Soc. Hosp. Pharmacists, Am. Soc. Pharmacognosy, Soc. Indsl. Microbiology, N.Y. Acad. Scis., Indian Sci. Congress Assn. Office: Xechem Inc Ste 310 100 Jersey Ave Bldg B New Brunswick NJ 08901-3200

PANDEYA, NIRMALENDU KUMAR, plastic surgeon, flight surgeon, military officer; b. Bihar, India, Feb. 9, 1940; came to U.S., 1958, naturalized, 1965; s. Balbhadra and Ramasawari (Tewari) P.; children: by previous wife Alok, Kiran; m. Haripriya Pradhan, June 15, 1988; 1 stepchild, Bibek. BSc, MS Coll., Bihar U.-Motihari, 1958; MS, U. Nebr., 1962; postgrad. U. Minn., 1959, Ft. Hays State Coll., 1961, D.O., Coll. Osteo. Medicine and Surgery, Des Moines, 1969, Hamilton Co. Pub. Hosp.; grad. Sch. Aerospace Medicine, U.S. Air Force, 1979. Diplomate Nat. Bd. Osteo. Med. Examiners. USPHS fellow dept. ob-gyn Coll. Medicine, U. Nebr., Omaha, 1963-65; intern Doctors Hosp., Columbus, Ohio, 1969-70; resident in gen. surgery Des Moines Gen. Hosp., 1970-72, Richmond Heights Gen. Hosp. (Ohio), 1972-73; fellow in plastic surgery Umea U. Hosp. (Sweden), 1973, Karolinska Hosp., Stockholm, 1974-75; mil. cons. in plastic surgery, USAF surgeon gen.; clin. prof. scis. Coll. Osteo. Medicine and Surgery, Des Moines, 1975-76, also adj. clin. prof. plastic and reconstructive surgery; chief flight surgeon Iowa Air Nat. Guard; practice in reconstructive and plastic surgery, Des Moines, 1975—; mem. staff Des Moines Gen. Hosp., Mercy Hosp. Med. Ctr., Charter Cmty. Hosp., Davenport Osteo. Hosp., Franklin Gen. Hosp., Ringgold County Hosp., Madison County Meml. Hosp., Winterset, Iowa, Mt. Ayr Surgery Ctr. of Des Moines, Hamilton County Hosp., Webster City Decatur County Hosp., Leon, Story County Hosp., Nev., Kirksville Osteopathic Med. Ctr., Grim Smith Hosp., Kirksville, St. Anthony's Hosp., Carroll, Iowa Meth. Hosp., Des Moines. Served to col. M.C., USAF; chief flight surgeon Iowa Air N.G. Regents fellow U. Nebr., Lincoln, 1961-62. Fellow Internat. Coll. Surgeons, Assn. Surgeons of India (life), Interam. Coll. Surgeons, Assn. Physicians India; mem. Assn. Plastic Surgeons of India (life), Assn. Mil. Surgeons of U.S. (life), Assn. Mil. Plastic Surgeons, AMA, Am. Osteo. Assn., Polk County Med. Soc., Iowa Soc. Osteo. Physicians and Surgeons, Polk County Soc. Osteo. Physicians and Surgeons (pres. 1978), Soc. U.S. Air Force Clin. Surgeons, Aerospace Med. Assn., Air N.G. Alliance of Flight Surgeons, AAUP, Am. Coll. Osteo. Surgeons, Am. Acad. Osteo. Surgeons (cert.), Soc. U.S. Air Force Flight surgeons. Hindu. Club: Army Navy. Contbr. numerous articles to profl. jours. Home: 4405 Mary Ann Cir West Des Moines IA 50265-5328 Office: Midwest Plas Surg Ctr 411 Laurel St Ste 1300 Des Moines IA 50314

PANDINA, ROBERT JOHN, neuropsychologist; b. Rochester, N.Y., July 19, 1945; s. Jack and Jane (Prezzevento) P.; 1 child, Gahan. BA in Psychology, Hartwick Coll., 1967; MA, U. Vt., 1969, PhD in Psychology, 1973. Prof. Ctr. of Alcohol Studies Rutgers U., Piscataway, 1976—, clin. psychology and neuroscis., 1976—, grad. faculty clin. psychology and neuroscis., 1976—, sci. dir. Ctr. Alcohol Studies, 1983—, prof. clin. psychology grad. sch. applied & profl. psych., 1990—, prof. psychology Ctr. Alcohol Studies, 1990—, dir. Ctr. Alcohol Studies, 1992—; lectr. Rutgers/Prodential Alcohol Edn. Workshops, Rutgers U., 1984—; cons. in field; mem. adv. bd. N.J. Collegiate Consortium for Health in Edn., 1991; mem. sci. adv. bd. Ctr. for Edn. and Drug Abuse Rsch., Western Psychiat. Inst. and Clinic, Pitts., 1991. Reviewer, mem. editorial bd. Am. Psychologist, Jour. Studies on Alcohol; reviewer Psychol. Bull., Jour. Abnormal Psychology; contbr. articles to profl. publs., chpts. to books. Trustee Alcohol Rsch. Documentation, Inc., Piscataway, 1982—, v.p., 1982-91, pres., 1991—. William James fellow; Nat. Inst. Drug Abuse grantee, 1982-83, 83-86, 86-88, 89-91, 91-94, Nat. Inst. Alcohol Abuse and Alcoholism grantee, 1983-86, 86-88, 88-91, Dept. Health, Human Svcs. Pub. Health Svc. grantee, 1978-81, Nat. Inst. Justice grantee, 1981-83. Mem. APA, Rsch. Soc. on Alcoholism, Soc. Psychologists in Addictive Behavior. Achievements include research on animal and human psychopharmacology, physiological and behavioral mechanisms in alsohol/drug related problems, experimental and clinical neuropsychology, neuropsychological models of mental disorders. Office: Rutgers U Ctr Alcohol Studies Busch Campus-Smithers Hall Piscataway NJ 08855-0969

PANEK, JAN, electrical power engineer, consultant; b. Benesov, Czechoslovakia, Aug. 10, 1930; came to U.S., 1971; s. Ludvik and Marie (Holzerova) P.; m. Eva Soukupova, Aug. 16, 1957; children: Hana, Paul. BSEE, Czech U. Engring., Prague, 1953, MSEE, 1956; PhD in Elec. Engring. Sci., Czechoslovak Acad. Scis., Prague. Rsch. engr. Rsch. Inst. Elec. Engring., Prague, 1953-65; elec. engring. expert UNESCO, Paris, 1965-71; chief tech. advisor UNESCO, Mexico City, 1969-71; cons. engr. GE, Phila., 1971-72, mgr. High Power Lab. switchgear div., 1972-74, cons. elec. power group tech. resources, 1975-78; mgr. transmission studies, elec. utility systems div. GE, Schenectady, 1978-85, mgr. transmission and distbn. studies system devel. engring. dept., 1985-87, sr. cons. dept. power systems engring., 1987-94; adj. prof. Rensselaer Poly. Inst., Troy, N.Y., 1994—; Pres. Electric Power Cons. Group, Inc., 1995—. Contbr. over 40 articles to profl. jours. Bd. dirs. Mental Health Orgn., Schenectady, 1985-92. Fellow Nat. Poly. Inst., Mexico City, 1971. Fellow IEEE (various offices 1971—, prize paper awards 1984, 85, 92), Conf. Internat. Grands Reseaux Electriques. Office: 711 Plank Rd Clifton Park NY 12065-2016

PANELLA, ELIZABETH M., secondary school principal. Prin. Fair Lawn (N.J.) High Sch. Recipient Blue Ribbon award U.S. Dept. Edn., 1990-91. Office: Fair Lawn High Sch Berdan Ave Fair Lawn NJ 07410

PANENKA, JAMES BRIAN JOSEPH, financial company executive; b. Milw., July 13, 1942; s. Alois J. and Jeanette (Buettner) P.; m. Kimberly A., Kerry A., Kristine A. BA, Marquette U., 1965. Sales rep. Pillsbury Corp., Milw., 1965-71; investment broker Marshall Co., Milw., 1971-72, E.F. Hutton, Milw., 1972-77; v.p. investments Dean Witter Inc., Milw., 1977-81; sr. v.p. investments Blunt Ellis & Loewi Inc./Kemper Securities, Inc./Everen Securities, Inc., Milw., 1981—; mem. Pres.'s Coun., Kemper Securities Group, Inc., 1981—. Bd. dirs. Mental Health Assn. of Wis., Milw., 1981-91, Sherri Steinhauer LPGA Mental Health Golf Tournament, Madison, Wis., 1991—; life mem. Marquette U. Pres.'s Coun., Milw., 1985—. Mem. Western Racquet Club (Elm Grove, Wis.), Geneva Nat. Golf Club (Lake Geneva, Wis.), Milw. Yacht Club. Roman Catholic. Avocations: tennis, golf, yachting. Office: Blunt Ellis & Loewi Kemper Securities Everen Securities 815 N Water St Milwaukee WI 53202-3526

PANES, JACK SAMUEL, publishing company executive; b. N.Y.C., Apr. 6, 1925; s. Max S. and Sophie (Levine) P.; m. Pearl Shaine, Dec. 25, 1949; children—Stephanie Jill, Michael Jonathan. B.A., Bklyn. Coll., 1947; M.S. in Journalism, Northwestern U., 1949. Editor, pub. The Howe Service, Inc., N.Y.C., 1949-54; founder, pub. Publs. for Industry, N.Y.C., 1955—, Panes Publs., Inc., N.Y.C., 1959—; owner Drug Products Display Service Advt. Co., N.Y.C., 1955—, Supplies for Industry Co., N.Y.C., 1956—; pres. Senap Devel. Corp., Great Neck, N.Y., 1972—. Pres. Russsell Woods Civic Assn., Great Neck. Served with inf. AUS, 1942-45, ETO. Decorated Silver Star medal, Bronze Star medal. Mem. Deadline Club, Sigma Delta Chi. Home: 21 Russell Woods Rd Great Neck NY 11021-4644 Office: Panes Publications Inc Great Neck NY 11021

PANETH, DONALD JOSEPH, editor, writer; b. N.Y.C., Feb. 28, 1927; s. Irving and Maud (Kramer) P.; m. Elma Olans, Apr. 10, 1949 (dec. 1987); children: Thea, Ira. BBA, CCNY, 1948; postgrad., Columbia U., 1949-50. Reporter N.Y. Times, 1947-49; free-lance journalist N.Y.C., 1950-56, 73-75, 77-83, 94—; rewriteman Daily Mirror, N.Y.C., 1956-63; copy editor The Morning Telegraph, N.Y.C., 1964-65; staff writer Med. Tribune, N.Y.C., 1966-72; copy editor L.I. Press, Queens, N.Y., 1975-77; editor-in-chief News Dictionary: People, Places and Events, 1977-80; editor, writer Yearbook of the UN, N.Y.C., 1986-93; documents editor UN Office Conf. Svcs., N.Y.C., 1993-94; adj. lectr. English York Coll., CUNY, 1983-86; cons. study of lit. of far right extremist groups in U.S. Anti-Defamation League, N.Y., 1995. Author: William Baziotes: A Literary Portrait, 1961, Current Affairs Atlas, 1979, The Ency. of American Journalism, 1983; contbr. articles to Commentary mag., The Nation, Village Voice, Peacework, WorldPaper, others; work included in anthologies Commentary on the American Scene, 1953, New York City Folklore, 1956. Mem. The Authors Guild, Willa Cather Pioneer Meml., Am.-Scandinavian Found. Democrat. Avocation: reading. Home and Office: 240 Cabrini Blvd Apt 1E New York NY 10033-1116

PANEYKO, STEPHEN HOBBS, banker; b. N.Y.C., June 30, 1942; s. Mirko and Leonore (Lane) P. Student, U. Pa., 1961-65. With Phila. Nat. Bank, 1965-66; v.p. Citibank, N.A., N.Y.C., 1970-82; exec. v.p. UJB Fin. Inc. (now Summit Bancorp.), Princeton, N.J., 1982-87; sr. exec. v.p. UJB Fin., Inc., Princeton, N.J., 1987—; chmn. bd. dirs. Gibraltar Corp., N.Y.C.; bd. dirs. UJB Mortgage Corp., Hackensack, N.J. Served to lt. USNR, 1966-70. Mem. Bankers Roundtable Assn. Republican. Congregationalist. Clubs: University (N.Y.C.); Baltusrol, Nassau, Bedens Brook. Home: 30 Duncan Ln Skillman NJ 08558-2313 Office: UJB Fin Corp 301 Carnegie Ctr Princeton NJ 08540-6227

PANG, FREDERICK F. Y., federal official; b. Honolulu, Nov. 16, 1936; s. Henry Kam and Constance Yu (Kyau) P.; m. Brenda W. I. Tom, Aug. 18, 1962; 2 children. BEd, U. Hawaii, 1959, MBA, 1972. Commd. 2d lt. USAF, 1959, advanced through grades to col., 1986, ret., 1986, adjudant 790th Aircraft Control and Warning Squadron, 1959-60; adjudant 1980th Aircraft Control and Warning Squadron USAF, Resolution Island, N.W.T., Can., 1960-61; dep. chief consolidated base pers. office USAF, 1961-62, dir. assignments hdqs. Pacific comm. area, 1963-65; dir. pers. 1964th Comm. Group USAF, Vietnam, 1965-68; dir. pers. plans hdqs. Pacific comm. area USAF, 1969-72, chief total officer force programs hdqs., 1972-77, asst. dir. office force structures, office asst. sec. def. manpower, res. affairs and logistics, 1977-80, dir.officer and enlisted pers. mgmt., 1980-84, dir. compensation, 1984-86, cons. office asst. sec. defense force mgmt. and pers., 1986-87; profl. mem. staff com. armed fordes U.S. Senate, Washington, 1987-93; asst. sec. Navy manpower and res. affairs The Pentagon, Washington, 1993-94, Asst. Sec. Def. (force mgmt. policy), 1994—. Decorated Bronze Star USAF. Mem. Alpha Phi Omega. Office: Asst Sec Defense Force Management Policy The Pentagon Rm 3E784 Washington DC 20301-4000

PANG, HERBERT GEORGE, ophthalmologist; b. Honolulu, Dec. 23, 1922; s. See Hung and Hong Jim (Chuu) P.; student St. Louis Coll., 1941; BS, Northwestern U., 1944, MD, 1947; m. Dorothea Lopez, Dec. 27, 1953. Intern Queen's Hosp., Honolulu, 1947-48; postgraduate course ophthalmology N.Y.U., Med. Sch., 1948-49; resident ophthalmology Jersey City Med. Ctr., 1949-50, Manhattan Eye, Ear, & Throat Hosp., N.Y.C., 1950-52; practice medicine specializing in ophthalmology, Honolulu, 1952-54, 56—; mem. staffs Kuakini Hosp., Children's Hosp., Castle Meml. Hosp., Queen's Hosp., St. Francis Hosp.; asst. clin. prof. ophthalmology U. Hawaii Sch. Medicine, 1966-73, now asso. clin. prof. Cons. Bur. Crippled Children, 1952-73, Kapiolani Maternity Hosp., 1952-73, Leahi Tb. Hosp., 1952-62. Capt. M.C., AUS, 1954-56, Diplomate Am. Bd. Ophthalmology. Mem. AMA, Am. Acad. Ophthalmology and Otolaryngology, Assn. for Rsch. Ophthalmology, ACS, Hawaii Med. Soc. (gov. med. practice com. 1958-62, chmn. med. speakers com. 1957-58), Hawaii Eye, Ear, Nose and Throat Soc. (pres. 1960), Pacific Coast Oto-Ophthalmological Soc., Pan Am. Assn. Ophthalmology, Mason, Shriner, Eye Study Club (pres. 1972—). Home: 346 Lewers St Honolulu HI 96815-2345

PANG, JOSHUA KEUN-UK, trade company executive; b. Chinnampo, Korea, Sept. 17, 1924; s. Ne-Too and Soon-Hei (Kim) P.; came to U.S., 1951, naturalized, 1968; m. He-Young Yoon, May 30, 1963; children: Ruth, Pauline, Grace. BS, Roosevelt U., 1959. Chemist, Realemon Co. Am., Chgo., 1957-61; chief-chemist chem. div. Bell & Gossett Co., Chgo., 1961-63, Fatty Acid Inc., div. Ziegler Chem. & Mineral Corp., Chgo., 1963-64; sr. chemist-supr. Gen. Mills Chems. Inc., Kankakee, Ill., 1964-70; pres., owner UJU Industries Inc., Broadview, Ill., 1971—, also dir. Bd. dirs. Dist. 92, Lindop Sch., Broadview, 1976-87; chmn. Proviso Area Sch. Bd. Assn., Proviso Twp., Cook County, Ill., 1976-77; bd. dirs. Korean Am. Community Svcs., Chgo., 1979-80; mem. governing bd. Proviso Area Exceptional Children, Spl. Edn. Joint Agreement, 1981-84, 85-87; alumni bd. govs. Roosevelt U., 1983-89; pres. Korean Am. Sr. Ctr., 1991-92; pres. Korean Am. Srs. Assn. Chicagoland, 1992—. Mem. Am. Chem. Soc., Am. Assn. Arts and Science, Am. Inst. Parliamentarians (region 2 treas. 1979-81, region 2 gov. 1981-82), Internat. Platform Assn., Ill. Sch. Bd. Assn., Nat. Assn. Sch. Bds., Chgo. Area Parliamentarians, Parliamentary Leaders in Action (pres. 1980-81), Nat. Speakers Assn. (dir. Ill. chpt. 1981-82, nat. parliamentarian 1982-84, 2d v.p. chpt. 1983-84), Toastmasters (dist. gov. 1969-1970), DADS Assn. U. Ill. (chmn. Cook County 1985—, bd. dirs. 1987-95, treas. 1990-91, v.p. 1991-92), Korean Am. Assn. of Chgo. (exec. dir. 1990), World Future Soc. (Chgo. area chpt. coord. 1988—, pres. Greater Chicagoland Futurists 1991-95), Chicagoland C. of C. (ednl., environ. and Pacific-Rim coms., internat. divsn.). Home: 2532 S 9th Ave Broadview IL 60153-4804 Office: UJU Industries Inc PO Box 6351 Broadview IL 60153-6351

PANG, MAYBELINE MIUSZE (CHAN), software and systems engineer, analyst; b. Shanghai, China, Sept. 9, 1945; came to U.S. from Hong Kong, 1964; d. Yee Sun and Margaret H. (Kong) Chan; m. Patrick Yewwah Pang, Aug. 4, 1968 (div. 1987); children: Elaine, Irene, George. BS in Physics/Math, Lincoln U., 1967; postgrad, U. Mo., 1967-68, U. Ariz., 1984-86. Application programmer Ariz. Health Sci. Ctr., Physiology Lab., Tucson, 1984-85; software engr. System and Software Engring. Dalmo Victor, Singer, Tucson, 1985-88, McDonnell Douglas Helicopter Co., Mesa, Ariz., 1988-90, Sperry Marine, Charlottesville, Va., 1990—; cons., worked with Air Force (F111 Weather Simulation), Army (Advanced Apache Helicopter), Navy (Seawolf weapons, ship control, CNO-Automatic Depth Finder) projects; comml. (Integrated Software Analysis Sys.; Sperry's docking sys.) projects; familiar with sys. analysis and design; software devel. and testing; algorithms, pulse processing, sys. engr. and analyst for Marine Sensors; active in new tech. group. Recipient Nat. Sci. Honor Soc. award, 1967, Teaching assistantship U. Mo., 1968. Avocations: Chinese healing and martial arts, spirit/mind/body medicine, religion, investments, reading and research. Home: 1517 Westfield Ct Charlottesville VA 22901-1602 Office: Sperry Marine Seminole Trail Charlottesville VA 22901

PANICH, DANUTA BEMBENISTA, lawyer; b. East Chicago, Ind., Apr. 9, 1954; d. Fred and Ann Stephanie (Grabowski) B.; m. Nikola Panich, July 30, 1977; children: Jennifer Anne, Michael Alexei. A.B., Ind. U., 1975, J.D., 1978. Bar: Ill. 1978, U.S. Dist. Ct. (no. dist.) Ill. 1978, U.S. Dist. Ct. (cen. dist.) Ill. 1987, U.S. Ct. Appeals, 1987. Assoc. Mayer Brown & Platt, Chgo., 1978-86, ptnr., 1986—. Mem. ABA, Ill. State Bar Assn. Republican. Roman Catholic. Office: Mayer Brown & Platt 190 S La Salle St Chicago IL 60603-3410

PANICHAS, GEORGE ANDREW, English language educator, critic, editor; b. Springfield, Mass., May 21, 1930; s. Andrew and Fotini (Dracouli) P. BA, Am. Internat. Coll., 1951, LittD (hon.), 1984; AM, Trinity Coll., Conn., 1952; PhD, Nottingham (Eng.) U., 1962. Instr., English and comparative lit. U. Md., College Park, 1962-63; asst. prof. U. Md., 1963-66, assoc. prof., 1966-68, prof., 1968-92; mem. Richard M. Weaver fellowship awards com., 1984-88, Ingersoll Prizes Jury Panel, 1986; co-chmn. Conf. on Irving Babbitt: Fifty Years Later, 1983. Author: Adventure in Consciousness: The Meaning of D.H. Lawrence's Religious Quest, 1964, Epicurus, 1967, The Reverent Discipline: Essays in Literary Criticism and Culture, 1974, The Burden of Vision: Dostoevsky's Spiritual Art, 1977, The Courage of Judgment: Essays in Criticism, Culture and Society, 1982, The Critic as Conservator: Essays in Literature, Society, and Culture, 1992; Editor: (with G.R. Hibbard and A. Rodway) Renaissance and Modern Essays: Presented to Vivian de Sola Pinto in Celebration of His Seventieth Birthday, 1966, Mansions of the Spirit: Essays in Literature and Religion, 1967, Promise of Greatness: The War of 1914-1918, 1968, The Politics of Twentieth-Century Novelists, 1971, The Simone Weil Reader, 1977, Irving Babbitt: Representative Writings, 1981, (with C. G. Ryn) Irving Babbitt in our Time, 1986; Modern Age: The First Twenty-Five Years, A Selection, 1988; editorial advisor Modern Age: A Quar. Rev., 1971-77; assoc. editor, 1978-83, editor, 1984—; adv. bd. Continuity: A Jour. of History, 1984-88, Humanitas, 1993—; contbr. articles and revs. to profl. jours. Mem. Acad. Bd. Nat. Humanities Inst., 1985—; trustee Found. for Faith in Search of Understanding, 1987. Grantee Earhart Found., 1982. Fellow Royal Soc. Arts (U.K.). Eastern Orthodox. Home and Office: PO Box Ab College Park MD 20741-3025 *In a profane age of unrest and breakdown, it is not enough for the critic to be purely and simply critical. He must work to conserve what is timeless, time-tested, time-honored. He must fight for causes he believes in, even if they appear to be lost causes. The critic's burden of responsibilty is also his vision of order.*

PANICO, ELAINE HARTMAN, nurse; b. Phila., July 13, 1924; d. Edward Earl and Eleanor Mayo (Adams) Hartman; children: Frederick, Robert, Eleanor, Lorne, Earl, John, William, Richard, Louise. BSN, State Coll. and Med. Ctr., 1946; BS in Edn., State Tchrs. Coll., 1946; postgrad., U. Pa., 1946-49. RN Summer Boys Camp, Winaukee, N.H., 1948; instr. Glassboro (N.J.) State Coll., 1948; coll. nurse, asst. Dean State Coll., Glassboro, 1946-48; asst. dir. nurses Osteo. Hosp., Phila., 1948-49, instr. pharm. math., 1948-49; eye surg. nurse Cornell-N.Y. Hosp., N.Y.C., 1949-50; surg. supr. Balt. City Hosps., 1950-52; nurse in charge Taj Mahal Med. Office, Atlantic City, N.J., 1990; surg. office nurse Ventnor, N.J., 1960—; pub. health spkr. elem. schs., Boston, 1950; RN internat. confs., Stony Brook, N.Y., 1980-85, A.C. Med. Ctr. Eye Clinic, Atlantic City, 1987-90; creator earliest postoperative surg. ICU, Balt. City Hosps., 1950-52. Cert. classic ballet, 1932-42. Bd. dirs. PTA, Ventnor, 1960-83, Atlantic Performing Arts Ctr., Atlantic City, 1970-90; mem. Holy Spirit Mothers Assn., Absecon, N.J., 1966-83; sponsor South Jersey Regional Theatre, Atlantic Community Concerts, Stockton Coll. Performing Arts; fin. sec. Atlantic City Med. Ctr. Aux., 1963; chmn. spl. projects Miss. Am. Pageant Scholarship Found., Very Important Hostess (V.I.H.), 1967—. Recipient Lifetime Recognition award Great Books Found., 1966-67, 15-yr. Gold award Miss Am. Pageant, 1982. Mem. AAUW, Atlantic County Med. Aux. (pres. 1984-90), U.S. Golf Assn., Internat. Platform Assn., RNs Cancer Heart Meml. Fund. (bd. dirs.), Hydrangea Club (chmn. 1964, Silver 15 Yr. award). Avocations: travel, oil painting, fishing, Chinese gourmet cooking, horseback riding, music. Home: 102 S Dudley Ave Ventnor City NJ 08406-2837 Office: 10 S Somerset Ave Ventnor City NJ 08406-2846

PANISH, MORTON B., physicial chemist, consultant; b. N.Y.C., Apr. 8, 1929; s. Isidore and Fanny (Glasser) P.; m. Evelyn Wally Chaim, Aug. 20, 1951; children: Steven, Paul, Deborah. Student, Bklyn. Coll., 1946-48; BS in Chemistry, Denver U., 1950; MS in Chemistry, Mich. State U., 1951, PhD in Phys. Chemistry, 1954. Chemist Oak Ridge (Tenn.) Nat. Lab., 1954-57; mem. tech. staff RAD div. AVCO Corp., Wilmington, Mass., 1957-61, sect. chief, 1961-64; mem. tech. staff Bell Telephone Labs. (now Bell Labs.), Murray Hill, N.J., 1964-69; dept. head Bell Telephone Labs. (now AT&T Bell Labs.), Murray Hill, N.J., 1969-86, disting. mem. tech. staff, 1986-92; cons., 1992—; mem. com. on microgravity rsch. NRC, 1991—, mem. com. on future of space sci. rsch. priorities, 1994-95; mem. com. on human rights NAS, 1996—. Co-author: Heterostructure Lasers, 1978, Gas Source Molecular Beam Epitaxy, 1993; contbr. numerous articles to profl. jours.; patentee in field. Mem. dean's adv. bd. Coll. Natural Sci., Mich. State U., 1990-95. Recipient Electrochem Soc. Electronics Divsn. award, 1972, Solid state medal, 1979, C&C Found. prize, Japan, 1986, Internat. Crystal Growth award Am. Assn. Crystal Growth, 1990, John Bardeen award The Minerals, Metals and Materials Soc., 1994. Fellow IEEE (Morris N. Liebmann Meml. award 1991), Am. Phys. Soc.; mem. Nat. Acad. Engring., Nat. Acad. Scis. Avocation: photography. Home and Office: 9 Persimmon Way Springfield NJ 07081-3605

PANITCH, MICHAEL B., brokerage house executive; b. 1939. Student, Mich. State U. With Sheason Lehman Hutton Inc., 1960-90, vice chmn.; with Smith Barney Harris Upham & Co., 1990-93, 94—, now vice chmn.

Office: Smith Barney Harris Upham & Co 388 Greenwich St New York NY 10013*

PANITZ, LAWRENCE HERBERT, lawyer; b. N.Y.C., Feb. 3, 1941; s. Abraham Alexander and Anita Rosyln (Zuckerberg) P.; m. Karin Blaschke, May 27, 1965. AB, Princeton U., 1962; JD, Columbia U., 1965. Bar: N.Y. 1965. Assoc., Wolf, Haldenstein, Adler, Freeman & Herz, N.Y.C., 1965-69; asst. chief fgn. counsel W.R. Grace & Co., N.Y.C., 1969-74; v.p., chief internat. counsel Revlon, Inc., N.Y.C., 1974-84; exec. v.p., chief adminstrv. officer ICN Pharms., Inc., Costa Mesa, Calif., 1985-87; ptnr. Myerson & Kuhn, N.Y.C., 1988-89, Frere Cholmeley, London, Brussels, Milan, Monte Carlo, Berlin, Paris, Rome, Barcelona, 1990-92; sr. v.p. corp. devel. Trefisco AG, Zürich, Switzerland, 1993; exec. v.p. corp. devel. Quantum Economic Devel., Ltd., Zürich, 1994—; arbitrator Am. Arbitration Assn., 1966—. Founder Park Ave. Malls Planting Project, 1984; patron Met. Opera, N.Y.C., 1987—. Princeton U. fellow, 1961. Mem. Assn. of Bar of City of N.Y., Presdl. Roundtable, Heritage Found. (assoc., inst. for econ. studies, adv. com.), Rep. Senatorial Inner Circle (U.S. senate bus. adv. bd.), Rep. Eagles, Knight of Malta, Order of St. John of Jerusalem. Republican. Home: Brandschenkestr 40, 8001 Zurich Switzerland Office: Quantum Economic Devel Ltd, Talstrasse 20, 8001 Zurich Switzerland

PANKEN, PETER MICHAEL, lawyer; b. N.Y.C., Dec. 30, 1936; s. Harold Ira and Sylvia Rita (Haimes) P.; m. Beverly Muriel Goldner, June 19, 1960; children: Aaron, Melinda. BA cum laude, Haverford Coll., 1957; LLB magna cum laude, Harvard U., 1962. Bar: N.Y. 1962, U.S. Dist. Ct. N.Y. 1962, U.S. Ct. Appeals (2d cir.) 1969, 3d cir. 1988, (10th cir.) 1989, U.S. Supreme Ct. 1989. Assoc. Paul Weiss Rifkind Wharton Garrison, N.Y.C., 1962-66, Poletti Freiden Prashker Feldman & Gartner, N.Y.C., 1966-67; assoc. Parker Chapin Flattau & Klimpl, N.Y.C., 1967-72, chair employment and labor law dept., 1986—. Editor: Harvard Law Rev., 1961-62; editor-in-chief: ALI-ABA Resource Materials on Labor and Employment Law (1st to 7th edits.), 1982—; contbr. articles on law and bus. to profl. jours. Pres., bd. dirs. Fedn. of Handicapped, N.Y.C., 1984-92; bd. dirs. Fedcap Rehab. Svcs., 1993—; pres. metro N.Y. chpt. Soc. for Human Resource Mgmt., 1990-92. Mem. ABA (labor and employment sect., com. on NLRB law), N.Y. State Bar Assn. (labor and employment law sect., continuing legal edn. com.), ABA-Am. Law Inst. (chmn. employment law programs), Am. Law Inst., SHRM (com. on employment practices). Office: Parker Chapin Flattau & Klimpl 1211 Avenue Of The Americas New York NY 10036-8701

PANKEY, EDGAR EDWARD, rancher; b. Irvine, Calif., May 22, 1916; s. John Henry and Emma (Bercaw) P.; m. Elizabeth Searles, Feb. 4, 1939; children—Victor Searles, James Henry, Peter Searles, Roberta Pankey Hurst. B.A., Pomona Coll., 1938. Owner Pankey Ranches, Inc., Tustin, Calif., 1949-64; owner Edgar E. Pankey Ranches, Tustin, 1945-80, Pankey Consolidated, Tustin, 1980—; grower agrl. crops, cattle in So. and Central Calif., Ariz., South Australia; owner, dir. Pankey-Blower Investment Corp., Riverside, Calif., 1963-74, Tustin East Corp., 1967-82; vice chmn. Bank of Irvine, 1973-77, chmn., 1977-83; vice chmn. Valley Irrigation Co., 1963-78; pres. Lake Woodmoor Assos., Colorado Springs, 1980-91, Sunwood, Carson City, 1992—; bd. dirs. Sunkist, Pyrotronics, Inc., Lilac; cons., fgn. agrl. visitors U.S. State Dept., 1961-75; mem. Fed. Orange Mktg. Com., 1968-74, Calif. Citrus Adv. Com., 1959-89; mem. study mission to European Common Market, 1963; v.p. Maricopa Mining Co., 1977-81. Mem. Tustin Sch. Bd., 1951-59, pres., 1957-59; pres. Orange County Sch. Bd. Assn., 1958-59, Calif. Lemon Men's Club, 1964-66; bd. dirs. Bowers Mus., NCCJ, Orange County Grand Jury Assn.; bd. dirs. Pioneer Coun., pres., 1990-93; pres. bd. dirs. Children's Hosp., Orange County; assoc. bd. dirs. Cmty. Hosp., Santa Ana; pres. World Affairs Coun., Orange, 1977-79, chmn., 1979-80; delegate Labor Policy, London, 1983, People to People Citriculture, China, 1986; bd. dirs. Chapman U., 1980-95, treas., 1987-95; fin. chmn. Children's Hosp., 1969-80, pres., 1981-82. Capt. USAAF, World War II. Mem. Asso. Farmers Orange County (pres. 1954), Calif. Farm Bur. (governing body 1957-58), Orange County Farm Bur. (pres. 1956-57), Orange County C. of C., Aircraft Owners and Pilots Assn., Naui Scuba. Presbyterian (trustee, pres. 1955-58). Lodge: Elks. Pioneered non-cultivation for citriculture; avocado variety expts. comml. users. Office: Pankey & Co 4800 Legray Rd Arvin CA 93203-9773

PANKEY, GEORGE ATKINSON, physician, educator; b. Shreveport, La., Aug. 11, 1933; s. George Edward and Annabel (Atkinson) P.; m. Patricia Ann Carreras, Sept. 22, 1972; children: Susan Margaret, Stephen Charles, Laura Atkinson, Edward Atkinson. Student, La. Poly. Inst., 1950-51; B.S., Tulane U., 1954, M.D., 1957; M.S., U. Minn., 1961. Diplomate Am. Bd. Internal Medicine, Am. Bd. Infectious Diseases. Intern U. Minn. Hosps., 1957-58, resident in internal medicine, 1958-60; resident in internal medicine Mpls. VA Hosp., Mpls. Gen. Hosp., 1960-61; practice medicine New Orleans, 1961—; partner Ochsner Clinic, New Orleans, 1968—; asst. vis. physician Charity Hosp. La., New Orleans, 1961-62; vis. physician Charity Hosp. La., 1962-75, sr. vis. physician, 1975-95; cons. infectious diseases Ochsner Clinic and Found. Hosp., 1963—, head sect. infectious diseases, 1972-94; instr. dept. medicine, div. infectious diseases Tulane U. Sch. Medicine, New Orleans, 1961-63; clin. instr. Tulane U. Sch. Medicine, 1963-65, clin. asst. prof. medicine, 1965-68, clin. asso. prof., 1968-73, clin. prof., 1973—; clin. prof. dept. medicine La. State U. Sch. Medicine, 1979—; clin. prof. oral diagnosis, medicine and radiology La. State U. Sch. Dentistry, 1983—; cons. World Health Info. Services Inc., 1974—; dir., founder Century Nat. Bank, New Orleans; mem. medicine test com. Nat. Bd. Med. Examiners, 1979-83; mem. infectious diseases adv. bd. Hoffman-LaRoche, 1982—. Author: A Manual of Antimicrobial Therapy, 1969; editor: (with Geoffrey A. Kalish) Outpatient Antimicrobial Therapy - Recent Advances, 1989, Infectious Diseases Digest, 1983-95, So. Med. Assn. Program for Infectious Diseases Dial-Access, 1983-92, Ochsner Clinic Reports on Serious Hosp. Infections, 1985—, Ochsner Clinic Reports on Geriatric Infectious Diseases, 1990-93, Ochsner Clinic Reports on the Management of Sepsis, 1991-93; bd. editors: Patient Care, 1969-75, Today in Medicine, 1990—; mem. editl. bd. Nat. Infectious Disease Info. Network, 1983—; mem. editl. adv. bd. Compendium Continuing Edn. in Dentistry, 1984-95, Quinolones Bull., 1985-93; contbr. numerous articles to profl. jours. Dir. Camp Fire Inc.; Pres. New Orleans Young Republican Club, 1969-71; adv. bd. Angie Nall Sch. Hosp., Beaumont, Tex.; trustee Nall Found. for Children, Beaumont. Recipient cert. merit Am. Acad. Gen. Practice, 1969, 70. Fellow ACP, Am. Coll. Preventive Medicine, Infectious Disease Soc. Am., Am. Coll. Chest Physicians, Royal Soc. Medicine; mem. Am. Assn. Contamination Control (chpt. pres. 1968-70), Am. Fedn. Clin. Research, So. Med. Assn. (certificate of award 1970), Am. Soc. Internal Medicine (del. ann. meeting 1971-72), Am. Soc. Microbiology, Am. Thoracic Soc., New Orleans Acad. Internal Medicine (pres. 1977-78), AMA, Aerospace Med. Assn., Am. Soc. Tropical Medicine and Hygiene, Am. Venereal Disease Assn., Am. Soc. Parasitologists, La. Soc. Internal Medicine (pres. 1972-73), La. Med. Soc., La. Thoracic Soc. (chmn. program com. 1968, governing council 1976-80), Surg. Infection Soc., Immunocompromised Host Soc., Musser Burch Soc., Orleans Parish Med. Soc., N.Y. Acad. Scis., Pan Am. Med. Assn. (diplomate mem. sect. internal medicine 1971, sect. pres. infectious diseases and virology 1978-85), SAR, Huguenot Soc. Founders Manakin in Colony of Va. Clubs: Masons (32 deg), Shriners. Home: 5910 Prytania St New Orleans LA 70115-4348 Office: Ochsner Clinic & Hosp 1514 Jefferson Hwy New Orleans LA 70121-2429

PANKO, JESSIE SYMINGTON, education educator; b. Jan. 19, 1935. Student, Hunter Coll., N.Y., 1959-62; BA, SUNY, 1969, MS, 1969; PhD, Syracuse U., 1974. Tchr. Anderson Elem. Sch., Mariana Islands, Guam, 1964-65; tchr. Herman Ave. Elem. Sch., Auburn, N.Y., 1969-71; asst. prof. edn. dept. SUNY, Cortland, N.Y., 1971-76, Utica, Rome, N.Y., 1974-76; asst. prof. applied scis. dept. Loop Coll., Chgo., 1976-77; assoc. prof. social scis. dept. Truman Coll., Chgo., 1977-81; dir. student teaching St. Xavier Coll., Chgo., 1976—, dir. undergrad. edn., 1977-79, dir. grad. edn., 1979-81, prof. edn. ctr., 1981-83, dir. grad. prog. in edn., 1983-86, dir. edn. ctr., 1986-89, dean sch. edn., 1989-92; bd. dirs. Queen of Peace, Acad. of Our Lady; mem. com. grad. programs St. Xavier Coll., 1986-89, tchr. edn. coun., 1976—, early childhood adv. bd., 1976-92. Moffett SUNY scholar, 1969. Mem. AAUP, ASCD, Am. Assn. Colls. of Tchr. Edn. (instnl. rep. 1987-92), Assn. Ind. Liberal Arts Colls. of Tchr. Edn. (instl. rep. 1986-92), Ill. Assn. of Tchr. Edn. in Pvt. Colls. (instnl. rep. 1985-96), Ill. Assn. Colls. Tchr. Edn. (coll. rep. 1981-96, sec. 1990-92), Assn. Tchr. Educators, Nat. Assn. Educatos Young Children, Ill. Dirs. Student Tchg., Chgo. Consortium Dirs. Student Tchg. (chairperson 1976—), Ill. Assn. Tchr. Educators, Pi Lambda Theta, Kappa Delta Pi. Office: St Xavier Coll 3700 W 103rd St Chicago IL 60655-3105

PANKOPF, ARTHUR, JR., lawyer; b. Malden, Mass., Feb. 1, 1931. BS in Marine Transp., Mass. Maritime Acad., 1951; BS in Fgn. Svc. and Internat. Transp., Georgetown U., 1957, JD, 1965. Bar: Md. 1965, D.C. 1966, U.S. Supreme Ct. 1977. Ea. area mgr. Trans Ocean Van Service of Consol. Freightway, 1958-61; with U.S. Maritime Adminstrn., 1961-65; assoc. firm Preston, Thorgrimson, Ellis & Holman, Washington, 1976-77; minority chief counsel Com. on Mcht. Marine & Fisheries U.S. Ho. of Reps., Washington, 1965-69; minority chief counsel, staff dir. Com. on Commerce, U.S. Senate, 1969-76; mng. dir. Fed. Maritime Commn., 1977-81; pvt. practice Washington, 1981-84; dir. legis. affairs Corp. Pub. Broadcasting, 1984-86, v.p., gen. counsel, sec., 1986-88; pvt. practice Washington, 1988-90, 96—; dir. fed. affairs Matson Navigation Co. Inc., Washington, 1190-95. Mem. Maritime Adminstrv. Bar Assn. (pres. 1995-96). Home: 7819 Hampden Ln Bethesda MD 20814-1108

PANKOVE, JACQUES ISAAC, physicist; b. Chernigov, Russia, Nov. 23, 1922; came to U.S., 1942, naturalized, 1944; s. Evsey Leib and Miriam (Simkine) Pantchechnikoff; m. Ethel Wasserman, Nov. 24, 1950; children: Martin, Simon. B.S.E.E., U. Calif., Berkeley, 1944, M.S.E.E., 1948; Ph.D. in Physics, U. Paris, 1960. Mem. tech. staff RCA Labs., Princeton, N.J., 1948-70; physicist, fellow RCA Labs., 1970-85; prof. U. Colo., Boulder, 1985-93, prof. emeritus, 1993—, Hudson Moore Jr. Univ. prof., 1989-93, program mgr. materials and devices Ctr. for Optoelectronic Computing Systems, 1986-89; Disting. Rsch. fellow Nat. Renewal Energy Lab. (formerly Solar Energy Rsch. Inst.), 1985-93; v.p. for rsch. and tech. Astralux, Inc., 1993—; vis. McKay lectr. U. Calif., Berkeley, 1968-69; vis. prof. U. Campinas, Brazil, 1975; Disting. vis. prof. U. Mo., Rolla, 1984; participant NAS sci. exch. program with Romania, 1970, Hungary, 1972, Yugoslavia, 1976. Mem. hon. editl. bd. Solid State Electronics, 1970-94, Solar Energy Materials, 1984—, Optoelectronics, 1986-95; regional editor Crystal Lattice Defects and Amorphous Materials, 1984-90; author: Optical Processes in Semiconductors, 1971, 75, (ednl. film) Energy Gap and Recombination Radiation, 1962; editor: Electroluminescence, 1977, Display Devices, 1980, Hydrogenated Amorphous Silicon, 1984; co-editor: Hydrogen in Semiconductors, 1991, Wide Bandgap Semiconductors, 1992; designer: laser sculpture, Bklyn. Mus., 1968; contbr. articles to profl. jours.; patentee in field. Trustee Princeton Art Assn., 1970-82; mem. Experiment-in-Arts-and-Tech., Berkeley, 1968-69. Served with U.S. Army, 1944-46. Recipient RCA achievement awards, 1952, 53, 63; David Sarnoff scholar, 1956. Fellow IEEE (J. J. Ebers award 1975, assoc. editor Jour. Quantum Electronics 1968-77, mem-at-large IEEE awards bd. 1992-95), Am. Phys. Soc.; mem. AAAS, NAE (hon.), Materials Rsch. Soc., Internat. Soc. for Optical Engring., Sigma Xi. Home: 2386 Vassar Dr Boulder CO 80303-5763 Office: U Colo Dept Elec Engring Boulder CO 80309-0425 also: Astralux Inc 2500 Central Ave Boulder CO 80301

PANKRATZ, HENRY J., management consultant; b. Brookdale, Man., Can., Feb. 19, 1939; s. John and Mary (Engbrecht) P.; m. Julia Marianna, May 30, 1981; children: Kathy, Karen, Lisa. Grad., Steinbach Collegiate, 1956; chartered acct., U. Man., 1962. Cert. FCA, FCMC. Mng. ptnr. Ernst & Young, Ottawa, Ont., Can., 1974-77; nat. dir., fin. planning and control Ernst & Young, Toronto, Ont., Can., 1977-84; mng. ptnr. Ernst & Young, Vancouver, B.C., Can., 1984-88, exec. ptnr., 1986—; chmn. Ernst & Young Cons., Toronto, 1988—; vice chmn. Ernst & Young. Former chmn. Comml. and Indsl. Devel. Commn. Ottawa-Carleton; former chmn. fin., chmn. long-range planning, mem. exec. com. Red Cross, Ont. Div. Fellow Inst. Chartered Accts. Ont., Inst. Cert. Mgmt. Cons. Can., (chmn. firm mem. com.). Office: Ernst & Young, PO Box 251 Toronto Dominion Ctr., Toronto, ON Canada M5K 1J7

PANLILIO, ADELISA LORNA, public health physician; b. Manila, Jan. 23, 1949; came to U.S., 1955; d. Filadelfo and Elsie Belle (Nessia) P. AB, Radcliffe Coll., 1969; MD, SUNY Downstate Med. Coll., Bklyn., 1973; MPH, Harvard Sch. Pub. Health, 1988. Intern in pediatrics Babies Hosp., Columbia-Presbyn., N.Y.C., 1973-74, resident in pediatrics, 1974-75; pediatric hematology fellow Downstate/Kings County Hosp. Med. Ctr., Bklyn., 1975-76; blood banking fellow Downstate/Kings Councty Hosp. Med. Ctr., Bklyn., 1976-77; asst. med. dir. ARC Blood Services, Nashville, 1977-80, med. dir., 1980-84, acting dir., 1984-85, med. dir., 1985-87; epidemic intelligence service officer Ctr. Disease Control, USPHS, Atlanta, 1988-90; med. epidemiologist Ctrs. for Disease Control and Prevention, Atlanta, 1988—; asst. clin. prof. pathology Vanderbilt U. Sch. Medicine, Nashville, 1977-87. Contbr. articles to med. jours. V.p., bd. dirs. Nashville CARES, 1986-87. Mem. Am. Assn. Blood Banks, Alpha Omega Alpha. Office: Ctr Disease Control 1600 Clifton Rd NE Atlanta GA 30329-4046

PANNEBAKER, JAMES BOYD, lawyer; b. Middletown, Pa., Mar. 9, 1936; s. Boyd Alton and Kathryn Kennedy (Brindle) P.; divorced; children: Jeffery B., Renee E. Pannebaker Bench, Traci Lee Pannebaker. BS, Elizabethtown Coll., 1958; JD, U. Mich., 1961. Bar: Pa. 1962, U.S. Dist. Ct. (mid. dist.) Pa., U.S. Ct. Appeals (3d cir.), U.S. Supreme Ct. 1969. Pvt. practice, Harrisburg, 1965-86; pres. Pannebaker & Jones, P.C., Middletown, 1986—; mem. regional adv. bd. Mellon Bank, Harrisburg, 1980—. Bd. dirs. Cmty. Gen. Osteo. Hosp., Harrisburg, 1970—; trustee Elizabethtown (Pa.) Coll., 1972-78; mem. adv. bd. Villa Teresa Nursing Home, Harrisburg, 1985—; vice chmn. Middletown chpt. ARC. Capt. U.S. Army, 1962-65. Mem. Am. Legion, Masons, Shriners, Elks. Republican. Methodist. Avocations: skiing, sailing, horseback riding, outdoor activities. Office: Pannebaker & Jones PC 4000 Vine St Middletown PA 17057

PANNER, BERNARD J., pathologist, educator; b. Youngstown, Ohio, Oct. 9, 1928; s. Morris W. and Matilda (Giber) P.; m. Molly R. Seidenberg, Feb. 11, 1962; children—Morris J., Aaron M., Daniel Z. A.B., Western Res. U., 1949, M.D., 1953. Diplomate Am. Bd. Pathology. Intern in internal medicine Kings County Hosp., Bklyn., 1953-54; resident in pathology Boston City Hosp., 1954-55, Strong Meml. Hosp., Rochester, N.Y., 1958-60; asst. prof. pathology Sch. Medicine, U. Rochester, 1960-67, assoc. prof., 1967-72, prof., 1972—; pathologist Strong Meml. Hosp., Rochester, 1972—; cons. Genesee Hosp., Rochester, 1974—. Contbr. articles to profl. jours. Served with USNR, 1955-57. Recipient Mapstone Teaching prize Sch. Medicine, U. Rochester, 1981. Mem. Internat. Acad. Pathology, Am. Assn. Pathologists, Internat. Soc. Nephrology, Am. Soc. Nephrology, Sigma Xi. Democrat. Jewish. Home: 330 Wilmot Rd Rochester NY 14618-2947 Office: U Rochester Sch Medicine Dept Pathology 601 Elmwood Ave Rochester NY 14642-0001

PANNER, JEANNIE HARRIGAN, electrical engineer; b. Malone, N.Y., Jan. 4, 1948; d. Martin Thomas and Marjorie (Boyea) Harrigan; m. John Charles Panner, Aug. 17, 1974. BS summa cum laude, SUNY, Plattsburgh, 1970; MA in Math., U. Vt., 1974, MSEE, 1993. Programmer Microelectronics Divsn. IBM, Burlington, Vt., 1970-71, assoc. programmer, 1971-74, sr. assoc. programmer, 1974-79, staff engr., 1979-85, adv. engr., 1985-90, sr. engr., 1990—. Contbr. articles to engring. jours.; patentee in field. Mem. IEEE, ACM. Avocations: golf, travel, gardening. Home: RR 1 Box 1310 Underhill VT 05489-9405 Office: IBM Microelectronics Divsn 1000 River St G07/863H Essex Junction VT 05452-4201

PANNER, OWEN M., federal judge; b. 1924. Student, U. Okla., 1941-43, LL.B., 1949. Atty. Panner, Johnson, Marceau, Karnopp, Kennedy & Nash, 1950-80; judge, now sr. judge U.S. Dist. Ct. Oreg., Portland, 1980—. Office: US Dist Ct 335 US Courthouse 620 SW Main St Portland OR 97205-3037

PANNETON, JACQUES, librarian; b. Trois-Rivières, Que., Can., May 7, 1943; s. Marcel and Bernadette (Page) P.; married; children—Anne-Marie, Luce. B.L.S., U. Montréal, 1964. Catalogueur Bibliothèque de Trois-Rivières, 1964-65; dep. librarian, then head librarian Bibliothèque Centrale de Pret de la Mauricie, Trois-Rivières, 1965-74; head librarian Bibliothèque de la Ville de Montréal, 1974—; prof. pub. libraries U. Montréal Library Sch., 1974-75; mem. Com. Cons. du Livre, Govt. Que., 1976; mem. adv. bd. Nat. Library Can., 1978—; mem. com. d'étude sur bibliothèques publiques Govt. Qué., 1987; invited guest German libraries, German Fed. Republic, summer 1976, Brit. libraries, spring 1978. Contbr. articles to profl. jours. Mem. Canadian, Am., Que. library assns., Corp. Profl. Librarians Que. (past pres.), Assn. pour l'avancement des sci. et des techniques de la documentation, Council Adminstrs. Large Urban Pub. Libraries, Internat. Fedn. Library Assns., Internat. Assn. Met. City Libraries. Office: Bibliothèque de Montreal, 5650 d'Iberville St Ste 400, Montreal, PQ Canada H2G 3E4

PANNKE, PEGGY M., insurance agency executive; b. Chgo., Oct. 26; d. Victor E. and Leona (O'Leary) Stich; children: Thomas Scott, David Suvanne, Heidi Mireille, Peter Helmut. Office mgr. DeHaan & Richter P.C., Chgo. and Des Plaines, Ill., 1983-86; v.p. long term care ins. Sales & Seminars, Des Plaines, 1986-90; pres., founder. Nat. Consumer Oriented Agy., Des Plaines, 1990—; cons. on long-term care ins. The Travelers, Tchrs. Ins. & Annuity Assocs., and numerous other ins. cos., N.Y.C., Hartford, Conn. and throughout U.S.; speaker Exec. Enterprises, N.Y.C., 1988-93. Contbr. articles on long-term care ins. to profl. jours.; columnist Senior News. Sponsor Ill. Alliance for Aging, Chgo., 1990—, Ill. Assn. Homes for Aging, 1990-91; bd. govs. St. Matthew Luth. Home, Park Ridge, Ill., 1993-95. Recipient Speakers awards Health Ins. Assn. Am., Washington, 1990, Retired Officers Assn., Glenview, Ill., 1991, 93, Nat. Assn. Sr. Living Industries, Denver, 1992, Exec. Enterprises, N.Y.C., 1993. Mem. Nat. Assn. Sr. Living Industries, Nat. Assn. Long Term Care Profls. (charter), Ctr. for Applied Gerontology, Nat. Coun. on Aging, Mature Ams. (ad hoc com.), Am. Mensa of Ill. (program dir. 1983-85), Kiwanis (bd. dirs. Park Ridge 1992—, pres. 1996—), Am. Soc. on Aging, Internat. Soc. for Retirement Planning. Avocations: songwriting, travel, sketching wildflowers, reading. Office: Nat Consumer Oriented Agy 2200 E Devon Ste 356 Des Plaines IL 60018-4503

PANOFSKY, WOLFGANG KURT HERMANN, physicist, educator; b. Berlin, Germany, Apr. 24, 1919; came to U.S., 1934, naturalized, 1942; s. Erwin and Dorothea (Mosse) P.; m. Adele Du Mond, July 21, 1942; children: Richard, Margaret, Edward, Carol, Steven. A.B., Princeton U., 1938, DSc (hon.), 1983; Ph.D., Calif. Inst. Tech., 1942; D.Sc. (hon.), Case Inst. Tech., 1963, U. Sask., 1964, Columbia U., 1977, U. Hamburg, Fed. Republic Germany, 1984, Yale U., 1985; hon. degree, U. Beijing, Peoples Republic China, 1987; DSc (hon.), U. Rome, 1988; hon. degree, Uppsala U., Sweden, 1991. Mem. staff mem. radiation lab. U. Calif., 1945-51, asst. prof., 1946-48, asso. prof., 1948-51; prof. physics Stanford U., 1951-62, prof. Stanford Linear Accelerator Ctr., 1962-89, prof. emeritus, 1989—; dir. Stanford (High Energy Physics Lab., Stanford Linear Accelerator Center), 1962-84, dir. emeritus, 1984—; Am. del. Conf. Cessation Nuclear Tests, Geneva, 1959; mem. President's Sci. Adv. Com., 1960-65; cons. Office Sci. and Tech., Exec. Office Pres., 1965-73, U.S. ACDA, 1968-81; mem. gen. adv. com. to White House, 1977-81; mem. panel Office of Sci. and Tech. Policy, 1977; with nat. def. rsch. Calif. Inst. Tech. and Los Alamos, 1942-45; chmn. bd. overseers Superconducting Supercollider Univs. Rsch. Assn., 1984-93; mem. com. to provide interim oversight DOE nuc. weapons complex NAS, 1988-89, mem. DOE panel on nuc. warhead dismantlement and spl. nuc. materials control, 1991-92; active Commn. Particles and Field of Internat. Union of Pure and Applied Physics, 1985-93. Decorated officer Legion of Honor; recipient Lawrence prize AEC, 1961; Nat. Medal Sci., 1969; Franklin medal, 1970; Ann. Pub. Service award Fedn. Am. Scientists, 1973; Enrico Fermi award Dept. Energy, 1979; Shoong Found. award for sci., 1983, Hilliard Roderick prize Sci. AAAS, 1991; named Calif. Scientist Yr., 1966. Mem. NAS (chmn. com. on internat. security and arms control 1985-93, mem. scis. com. on scholarly comm. with People's Republic of China 1987-92), AAAS, Am. Phys. Soc. (v.p., pres. 1974), Phi Beta Kappa, Sigma Xi. Home: 25671 Chapin Rd Los Altos CA 94022-3413 Office: Stanford Linear Accelerator Ctr PO Box 4349 Palo Alto CA 94309-4349

PANSINI, MICHAEL SAMUEL, energy company executive, consultant; b. Molfetta, Italy, July 12, 1928; came to U.S., 1935; s. Ralph and Isabel (Cirilli) P.; m. Anna D'Angelo, June 5, 1949 (div. 1970); children: Elizabeth, Valerie, Michael; m. Elizabeth Bischoff, Oct. 3, 1970 (div. Feb. 1992); 1 child, Elissa Michelle. B.S., NYU, 1950, M.B.A., 1952, LL.M., 1960; LL.D., Fordham U., 1956. Bar: N.Y. 1956, U.S. Tax Ct. Tax mgr. Pfizer Corp., N.Y.C., 1951-64; asst. treas. Hooker Chem. Corp., N.Y.C., 1964-69; treas., dir. United Indsl. Corp., N.Y.C., 1969-72; sr. v.p., gen. counsel Beker Industries Corp., Greenwich, Conn., 1972-87; pres., dir. Panmer, Inc., 1987—; tax, fin. cons., 1988—; v.p., corp. counsel Champion Energy Corp. and affiliates, 1991-93, Champion Holdings Co. and affiliates, 1993-96; v.p., chmn. various coms. Tax Exec. Inst., N.Y.C., 1963-72; pres., dir. Fed. Tax Forum, Inc., N.Y.C., 1961-72; dir. Intelligent Bus. Communications Corp. Mem. Rep. Town Com. 19th Dist., Stamford, Conn., 1993—; commr. Econ. Devel. Commn., Stamford, 1994—. Republican. Home and Office: 76 Lawrence Hill Rd Stamford CT 06903-2120

PANSKY, EMIL JOHN, entrepreneur; b. Manhattan, N.Y., June 1, 1921; s. Stanislaus and Anna (Jankovic) P.; m. Billie B. Byrne, May 27, 1955; 1 adopted child, Jimmy. BME, Cooper Union Coll., 1941; MBA, Harvard U., 1949; MADE, NYU, 1950. Registered profl. engr., Mich. Chief insp. flight line Republic Aviation, Farmingdale, L.I., 1941-45, salvage engr., 1946-47; product control supr. to product control mgr. Ford Motor, Detroit, 1949-51; asst. plant mgr. Anderson Brass, Birmingham, Ala., 1951-53; asst. v.p. to v.p. mfg. Cummins Engine, Columbus, Ind., 1953-54; pvt. practice Emil J. Pansky Assoc., San Leandro, Calif., 1954—; pres. Calif. Mfrs. Tech. Assn., San Francisco, 1978-80; cons. in field. Patentee die cast auto wheels, 1965. Pres. Menlo Circus Club, Menlo Park, Calif., 1974-81, Home Owners Assn., Kanuela, Hawaii, 1989-95; bd. dirs. No. Calif. Tennis Assn., San Francisco, 1984-87. Mem. ASME (life), Harvard Club San Francisco (bd. dirs. 1986-92), Harvard Bus. Sch. Club San Francisco (bd. dirs. 1970-73, cons. 1994-95). Democrat. Avocations: tennis, chess. Home: 901 Jackling Dr Hillsborough CA 94010-6127 Office: Emil J Pansky Assoc 1666 Timothy Dr San Leandro CA 94577-2312

PANTAGES, LOUIS JAMES, lawyer; b. Plainfield, N.J., Apr. 29, 1916; s. Dimitrios Louis and Bessie (Massas) P.; m. Dorothea Carol Adams, Dec. 16, 1950; children: James, Peter, Elaine Marie. A.B., Rutgers U., 1938, LL.B., 1940. Bar: N.J. 1941, U.S. Dist. Ct. N.J. 1941, U.S. Dist. Ct. (so. dist.) N.Y. 1955, U.S. Supreme Ct. 1960, U.S. Ct. Appeals (3d cir.) 1967. Since practiced in Newark; with firm Cox & Walburg, 1938-54; partner Mead, Gleeson, Hansen & Pantages, 1954-68, Gleeson, Hansen & Pantages, 1968-72, Hansen, Pantages, Sellar & Zavesky, 1972-77, Pantages Sellar Richardson & Stuart, 1977-82, Stein, Bliablias, McGuire, Pantages & Gigl, 1982—; trial lawyer in cts. of N.J., U.S. Dist. cts. of N.J., U.S. Dist. Ct., So. Dist. N.Y., U.S. Supreme Ct., others. Capt. M.I., AUS, 1942-46; Capt. M.I., U.S. Army, 1950-52. Fellow Am. Coll. Trial Lawyers, Internat. Acad. Law and Sci.; mem. ABA, N.J. Bar Assn., Essex County Bar Assn., Am. Judicature Soc., Trial Attys. N.J., N.J. Def. Assn., Internat. Assn. Def. Counsel, Fedn. Ins. and Corp. Counsel, Def. Rsch. Inst., Am. Arbitration Assn., Arbitration Forums, Inc., Rutgers Law Sch. Alumni Assn., Essex Fells Country Club, Hellenic Univ. Club N.Y. Republican. Greek Orthodox. Avocations: art, antiques, music. Home: 36 Windemere Rd Upper Montclair NJ 07043-2544 Office: 354 Eisenhower Pky Livingston NJ 07039-1023

PANTALEO, THEODORE THOMAS, III, medical care development officer. BS, Regis Coll., 1979; M Healthcare Adminstrn., Golden Gate U., 1987. Commd. 2d lt. USAF, 1980, advanced through grades to maj.; dir. respiratory svcs. USAF Hosp., Grand Forks AFB, N.D., 1980-81; chief med. recruiting 3550th USAF Recruiting Squadron, Indpls., 1980-83; dir. pers. svcs. USAF Hosp., Mather AFB, Calif., 1986, dir. pat. svcs., 1986-89; pres. Pantaleo Cons., Enid, Okla., 1989; adminstr. USAF Clinic Vance, Vance AFB, Okla., 1989-92; managed care devel. officer HQ USAF/SGHA, Bolling AFB, D.C., 92—. Contbr. articles to profl. jours. Active various cmty. orgns. Fellow Am. Coll. Health Care Execs. Home: HQ USAF/SGHA 400 Luke Ave Washington DC 20332 Office: HQ USAF/SGHA Bolling AFB 170 Luke Ave Ste 400 Washington DC 20332-5113*

PANTAZELOS, PETER GEORGE, financial executive; b. Cambridge, Mass., Dec. 8, 1930; s. George P. and Marion (Nichols) P.; m. Hytho Haseotes, May 26, 1963; children—George, Marion. BSEE, Northeastern U., 1953; MSEE, MIT, 1955; Acctg. Cert., Bentley Corp., Waltham, Mass., 1975. Mem. engring. dept. Thermo Electron Engring. Corp., Waltham, Mass., 1960-68; v.p. corp. planning Thermo Electron Corp., Waltham, Mass., 1968-72, v.p. ops. fin., 1972-80, exec. v.p., 1980—. Mem. IEEE, Am. Mgmt. Assn., Fin. Execs. Inst., Eta Kappa Nu, Tau Beta Pi, Sigma Xi. Mem. Greek Orthodox Ch. Club: Brae Burn (Newton, Mass.). Avocations:

golfing; gardening. Office: Thermo Electron Corp 81 Wyman St Waltham MA 02254

PANTEL, GLENN STEVEN, lawyer; b. Plainfield, N.J., Sept. 25, 1953; s. Donald and Sarah Libby (Pearlman) P.; m. Lisa Pamela Krop, June 28, 1981; 1 child, Adam Scott. AB, Johns Hopkins U., 1975; JD, U. Pa., 1978. Bar: N.J. 1978, U.S. Dist. Ct. N.J. 1978, Pa. 1978, Fla. 1980, U.S. Ct. Appeals (3d cir.) 1982. Law clk. to presiding judge U.S. Dist. Ct. (so. dist.), Miami, Fla., 1978-79; from assoc. to ptnr. Shanley & Fisher P.C., Morristown, N.J., 1979—, also bd. dirs. Trustee Friday Evening Club Cultural Presenters, Morristown, 1984—, Integrity, Inc., Drug and Alcohol Abuse Program, Newark; trustee, mem. scholarship com. 200 Club of Somerset County. Mem. ABA, Fla. Bar Assn., N.J. Bar Assn., Morris County Bar Assn., Phi Beta Kappa. Avocations: skiing, sailing. Home: 3 Cross Way Mendham NJ 07945-3120 Office: Shanley & Fisher PC 131 Madison Ave Morristown NJ 07960-6086

PANTEL, STAN ROY, newspaper publishing executive; b. Victoria, Tex., 1950. Degree, U. Tex. V.p. ops. Atlanta Jour.-Constitution. Office: Atlanta Journal-Constitution 72 Marietta St NW Atlanta GA 30303-2804

PANTENBURG, MICHEL, hospital administrator, health educator, holistic health coordinator; b. Denver, Oct. 6, 1926; d. Arthur Robert and Alice (McKenna) P. Diploma, Providence Nursing Sch., Kansas City, Kans., 1951; B.S. in Nursing Edn., St. Mary Coll., Leavenworth, Kans., 1958; M. in Nursing, Cath. U. Am., 1960. Joined Sisters of Charity, Roman Catholic Ch., 1945; lic. amateur radio operator. Dir. nursing Providence Hosp., Kansas City, Kans., 1958-62; nursing coordinator Sisters of Charity, Leavenworth, 1962-67; hosp. adminstr. St. Mary Hosp., Grand Junction, Colo., 1967-73, St. Vincent Hosp., Billings, Mont., 1973-84; dir. focus on leadership program Gonzaga U., Spokane, Wash., 1985-92; chaplain pastoral care dept. St. Marys Hosp. and Med. Ctr., Grand Junction, Colo., 1994—; dir. Norwest Bank, Billings. Co-author, editor: Management of Nursing (CHA award 1969), 1967. Bd. dirs. De Paul Hosp., Cheyenne, Wyo., 1980-96, Ronald McDonald House, Billings, 1982-85, St. Joseph Hosp., Denver. Named Woman of Yr., Bus. and Profl. Women, Billings, 1979. Mem. Cath. Hosp. Assn. (bd. dirs., sec.), Am. Hosp. Assn. (regional del. 1975-80), Am. Coll. Hosp. Adminstrn., Mont. Hosp. Assn. (pres.), Billings C. of C. (v.p. 1977-78). Avocations: hiking; skiing. Office: Pastoral Care Dept St Marys Hosp & Med Ctr Grand Junction CO 81501

PANTOLIANO, JOE, actor; b. Hoboken, N.J., Sept. 12, 1951. Actor: (stage prodns.) Brothers, 1982, Orphans, 1983, One Flew Over the Cuckoo's Nest, Italian American Reconciliation, The Death Star, Visions of Kerouac, (feature films) The Godfather Part II, 1974, The Idol Maker, 1980, Monsignor, 1982, Risky Business, 1983, Eddie and the Cruisers, 1983, The Mean Season, 1985, Goonies, 1985, Running Scared, 1986, The In Crowd, 1987, The Squeeze, 1987, Scenes from the Goldmine, 1987, Amazon Women on the Moon, 1987, La Bamba, 1987, Empire of the Sun, 1987, Midnight Run, 1988, Downtown, 1990, The Last of the Finest, 1990, Short Time, 1990, Zandalee, 1991, Used People, 1992, Three of Hearts, 1993, The Fugitive, 1993, Baby's Day Out, 1994, Calendar Girl, 1994, Steal Big, Steal Little, 1995, Bad Boys, 1995; (TV movies) More Than Friends, 1978, Alcatraz: The Whole Shocking Story, 1980, Destination: America, 1987, El Diablo, 1990, One Special Victory, 1991, Through the Eyes of a Killer, 1992, (TV mini-series) From Here to Eternity, 1979, Robert Kennedy and His Times, 1985, (TV spl.) Mr. Roberts, 1984 (TV Series) Free Country, 1978, The Fanelli Boys, 1990-91, (guest) Tales From the Crypt, Amazing Stories, L.A. Law, The Hitchhiker. Office: UTA 9560 Wilshire Blvd Fl 5 Beverly Hills CA 90212-2401*

PANTUSO, VINCENT JOSEPH, food service consultant; b. Charleston, W.Va., Aug. 13, 1940; s. Fortunato F. Pantuso and Josephine Malcom (Ginestra) Pantuso Messer; m. Carol Barber, Dec. 10, 1964 (div. 1976); children: Lisa, Barbara, Tina; m. Nancy Josephine Chellman, Sept. 30, 1978 (div. 1995). Student, Drexel U.; BSBA, St. Joseph's U., 1968; postgrad., Rollins Coll., 1984-85. Asst. mgr. Marriott Hotels, Inc., Bethesda, Md., 1962-64; v.p. sales mktg. ARA Services, Inc., Phila., 1964-72; sr. v.p. Interstate United Corp., Chgo., 1972-84; pres. V.J. Pantuso Services, Inc., Orlando, Fla., 1984—, New Vista Services, Inc., 1988—. Mem. Nat. Assn. Concessionaires (bd. dirs. 1982—, pres. 1989-91, chmn. 1991-94, Master Concessionaire, Chgo. 1985), Nat. Assn. Food Equipment Mfrs. (doctorate 1989). Republican. Episcopalian. Club: Citrus (Orlando). Avocation: fishing. Home: 9325 Bay Vista Estate Blvd Orlando FL 32836-6304

PANUSKA, JOSEPH ALLAN, academic administrator; b. Balt., July 3, 1927; s. Joseph William and Barbara Agnes (Preller) P. BS, Loyola Coll., Balt., 1948; PhD, St. Louis U., 1958; STL, Woodstock Coll., 1961; LLD (hon.), U. Scranton, 1974. Joined S.J., 1948; ordained priest Roman Cath. Ch., 1960. Instr. dept. physiology Emory U. Sch. Medicine, 1962-63; asst. prof. biology Georgetown U., 1963-66, assoc. prof., 1966-72, prof., 1973; provincial, bd. dirs. Jesuit Conf. Md. Province (S.J.), 1973-79; acad. v.p., dean faculties, prof. biology Boston Coll., 1979-82; pres. U. Scranton, Pa., 1982—; mem. Pa. Commn. Ind. Colls. and Univs., 1982—, mem. exec. com., treas., 1987-91, vice chmn., 1988-89, chmn., 1990-91; mem. President's Commn., NCAA, 1989-90. Mem. editl. bd. Cryobiology, 1968-88, editor-in-chief, 1971-74; contbr. chpts. to books, articles to sci. rsch. jours. Mem. corp. Am. Found. Biol. Rsch., 1967-85, pres. bd. dirs., 1974-79, v.p., 1979-83; trustee Loyola Coll., 1979-85, St. Joseph's U., 1979-84, U. Scranton, 1970-73, St. Peter's Coll., 1971-72, Woodstock Coll., 1973-76, Fordham U., 1982-88, Cambridge Ctr. for Social Studies, 1973-79 (pres. 1973-79), Corp. Roman Cath. Clergymen, 1973-79 (pres. 1973-79); rector Jesuit Community at Georgetown U., 1970-73; bd. dirs. United Way Pa., 1985-87, Scranton Preparatory Sch., 1984-90; chmn. Pa. Commn. for Ind. Colls. and Univs., 1990-91; bd. dirs. John Carroll U., 1992—, Nat. Inst. Environ. Renewal, 1992—. NIH postdoctoral trainee, 1962-63; Danforth Found. Harbison prize for disting. teaching, 1969; vis. fellow St. Edmunds Coll., Cambridge U., 1969. Mem. Am. Physiol. Soc., Soc. for Cryobiology, Soc. Exptl. Biology and Medicine, Assn. Jesuit Colls. and Univs. (bd. dirs. 1982—, treas. 1993—), Pa. Assn. Colls. and Univs. (exec. com., adv. com. to State Bd. Edn. 1990-91), Scranton C. of C. Home and Office: U Scranton Office of Pres Scranton PA 18510 *In order to be happy in a leadership role and to succeed in it, I have to possess a sense of coherence with my life values. I also need to recognize that my own activity makes a real difference in the empowerment of others so that there is a multiplier effect which extends me beyond my own person and activity.*

PANY, KURT JOSEPH, accounting educator, consultant; b. St. Louis, Mar. 31, 1946; s. Joseph Francis and Ruth Elizabeth (Westerman) P.; m. Darlene Dee Zabish, June 3, 1971; children: Jeffrey, Michael. BSBA, U. Ariz., 1968; MBA in Mgmt., U. Minn., 1971; PhD in Accountancy, U. Ill., 1977. CPA, Ariz., cert. fraud examiner. Staff auditor Arthur Andersen & Co., Mpls., 1968-69, Touche Ross & Co., Phoenix, 1971-73; teaching asst. U. Minn., Mpls., 1969-71; teaching asst. auditing and acctg. U. Ill., Urbana, 1972-76; asst. prof. acctg. Ariz. State U., Tempe, 1977-81, assoc. prof., 1981-85, Arthur Andersen/Don Dupont prof. acctg., 1985-91; mem. acctg. and auditing standards com. State of Ariz., Phoenix, 1989—; reviewer Jour. Acctg. and Pub. Policy, 1983—. Contbg. author: CPA Exam. Rev., 1983—; co-author: Principles of Auditing, 1988—, Auditing, 1993—; co-editor Auditing: A Jour. Practice and Theory, 1984-88; mem. editl. bd. Advances in Acctg., 1982—, Jour. Acctg. Edn., 1983—; reviewer Acctg. Rev., 1984—, ad hoc editor, 1989—; contbr. numerous articles to profl. jours. Active various child-related orgns. Peat, Marwick, Mitchell & Co. Found. grantee, 1985. Fellow AICPA (auditing stds. divsn. 1989-90, acctg. lit. selection com. 1989-90, acctg. lit. awards com. 1979-83, mem. auditing stds. bd. 1995—); mem. Am. Acctg. Assn. (tech. program com. 1980-81, chairperson Western region auditing sect. 1981-83, acctg. lit. nominating com. 1982-84, 88-89, acctg. lit. selection com. 1989-90, dir. auditing stds., chmn. auditing stds. com. 1989-90), Ariz. Soc. CPA's (auditing stds. com. 1978-81, ethics com. 1981-84). Avocation: baseball. Office: Ariz State U Sch of Accountancy Tempe AZ 85287

PANZER, MARY CAROLINE, museum curator; b. Flint, Mich., May 29, 1955; d. Milton and Caroline Alice (Weis) P. BA, Yale U.; MA, Columbia U., 1980; PhD, Boston U., 1990. Asst. prof. U. Kans., Lawrence, 1989-91; curator photographs Spencer Mus. Art, Lawrence, 1989-91; asst. dir. SMART Mus. Art, Chgo., 1991; curator photographs Nat. Portrait Gallery Smithsonian Instn., Washington, 1992—. Mem. Am. Studies Assn., Coll. Art Assn., Oracle, Mid-Atlantic Radical Historians Orgn., Orgn. Am. Historians. Office: Nat Portrait Gallery Smithsonian Instn Mrc # 213 Washington DC 20560

PANZER, MARY E., state legislator; b. Waupun, Wis., Sept. 19, 1951; d. Frank E. and Verna L. P.; 1 adopted child, Melissa. BA, U. Wis., 1974; mem., Wis. State Ho. Reps. from 53rd dist. Rep. State of Wis., Madison, 1980-93, senator, 1993—. Home: 635 W Tamarack Dr West Bend WI 53095-3653 Office: Wis State Senate State Capital Madison WI 53702

PANZER, MITCHELL EMANUEL, lawyer; b. Phila., Aug. 2, 1917; s. Max and Cecelia P.; m. Edith Budin, Apr. 13, 1943; children: Marcy C., Leslie S. Katz. AB with distinction and 1st honors, Temple U., 1937; JD magna cum laude, U. Pa., 1940; LLD honoris causa, Gratz Coll., 1972. Bar: Pa. 1942, U.S. Dist. Ct. (ea. dist.) Pa. 1948, U.S. Ct. Appeals (3d cir.) 1949, U.S. Supreme Ct. 1961. Gowen Meml. fellow U. Pa. Law Sch., 1940-41; law clk. Phila. Ct. Common Pleas, No. 7, 1941-42; assoc. Wolf, Block, Schorr and Solis-Cohen, Phila., 1946-54, ptnr., 1954-88, of counsel, 1988—; spl. adv. counsel Fed. Home Loan Mortgage Corp., Fed. Nat. Mortgage Assn., 1972-82; dir. emeritus, former counsel St. Edmond's Savs. and Loan Assn.; former dir. State Chartered Group, Pa. Bldg. and Loan Assn. Treas., Jewish Fedn. Greater Phila., 1981-82, v.p., 1982-86, trustee, 1963—, mem. exec. com., 1981-86, hon. life trustee, 1992—; trustee emeritus Pa. Land Title Inst., 1992—; bd. overseers Gratz Coll., 1958—, pres., 1962-68. Served to capt. USAF, 1942-46. Decorated Bronze Star medal; recipient Man of Year award Gratz Coll. Alumni Assn., 1964. Mem. Am. Coll. Real Estate Lawyers, ABA (chmn. spl. com. on residential real estate transactions 1972-73), Pa. Bar Assn. (mem. spl. com. on land titles), Phila. Bar Assn. (chmn. com. censors 1966, chmn. bd. govs. 1971, parliamentarian 1965-67, 71, chmn. charter and by-laws com. 1972), Jewish Publ. Soc. (trustee 1966-81, 85-88, v.p. 1972-75, sec. 1975-78), Order of Coif (pres. 1961-63, exec. com.). Jewish. Clubs: 21 Jewel Square (Phila.); Masons. Patentee in field. Home: 505 Oak Ter Merion Station PA 19066-1340 Office: Wolf Block Schorr & Solis-Cohen 12th Fl Packard Bldg 15th And Chestnut St Philadelphia PA 19102-2625

PAO, YIH-HSING, engineer, educator; b. Nanking, China, Jan. 19, 1930; s. Te-Cheng and Tsin-Han (Hsiao) P.; m. Amelia K.T. Shih, Sept. 7, 1957; children: Winston, May, Sophia. B.Eng., Nat. Taiwan U., Taiwan, Republic of China, 1952; M.S. in Mechanics, Rensselaer Polytech. Inst., N.Y., 1955; Ph.D. in Applied Mechanics, Columbia U., N.Y.C., 1959. Asst. prof. Cornell U., Ithaca, N.Y., 1958-62, assoc. prof., 1962-68, prof., 1968-84; chmn. dept. theoretical and applied mechanics Cornell U., Ithaca, 1974-80; Joseph C. Ford prof. Cornell U., Ithaca, N.Y., 1984—; dir. Inst. Applied Mechanics, Nat. Taiwan U., 1984-86, 89-94, prof., 1984—. Co-author: Diffraction of Elastic Waves and Dynamic Stress Concentration, 1972; contbr. chpts. to books, articles to profl. jours.; editor in field. Fellow ASME, Am. Acad. Mechanics; mem. U.S. NAE, Academia Sinica, ROC. Office: Inst Applied Mechs, Nat Taiwan U, Taipei 107, Taiwan

PAOLINI, GILBERT, literature and science educator; b. L'Aquila, Italy; naturalized citizen, 1954; s. John and Assunta A. (Turavani) P.; m. Claire Jacqueline Landro; children: Angela Janet, John Frank. B.A., U. Buffalo, 1957, M.A., 1959; postgrad., Middlebury Coll., summer 1960, 61; Ph.D., U. Minn., 1965. Lectr. Spanish Rosary Hill Coll., Buffalo, 1957-58; instr. Italian and Latin lit. U. Mass., Amherst, 1958-60; instr. Spanish and Italian Syracuse U., 1962-65, asst. prof., 1965-67; assoc. prof. Spanish lit. Tulane U., New Orleans, 1967-76, prof., 1976—; dir. Tulane scholars and honors program Tulane U., 1981-83, chmn. colloquia dept., 1981-83; originator Spanish Culture Week, New Orleans, 1977, 79; chmn. adv. com. Jambalaya program Nat. Endowment Humanities, New Orleans, 1975-80; Spanish essay reader Ednl. Testing Svc., Princeton, 1979-85; co-founder, gen. chmn. La. Conf. on Hispanic Langs. and Lits., 1981, 83, 85, 87, 89, 93, 95. Author: Bartolome Soler: novelista: Procedimientos estilísticos, 1963; An Aspect of Spiritualistic Naturalism in the Novel of B.P. Galdos: Charity, 1969; mem. editorial bd.: Forum Italicum, 1967-71, Critica Hispanica, 1979—, Discurso Literario, 1985—, Letras Peninsulares, 1987—; assoc. editor: South Central MLA Bull, 1978-80; editor: La Chispa'81: Selected Procs., 1981, Papers on Romance Literary Relations, 1983, La Chispa '83: Selected Procs., 1983, La Chispa '85: Selected Procs., 1985, La Chispa '87: Selected Procs. 1987, La Chispa '89: Selected Prods., 1989, La Chispa '93: Selected Procs. 1993; cons. editor South Central Rec., 1988-92; contbr. articles to profl. jours. With AUS, 1952-54, USAFRES, 1954-57. Recipient Disting. Service award Sociedad Espanola, 1979, Knight Cross of Order of Isabel the Catholic, 1984. Mem. MLA, AAUP, Am. Assn. Tchrs. Spanish and Portuguese (chmn. pub. rels. com. 1981-86, pres. La. chpt. 1979-81, 88-89), Am. Assn. Tchrs. Italian, Am. Assn. Advancement Humanities, Soc. for Lit. and Sci., Asociacion Internacional de Hispanistas, Southeastern Am. Soc. 18th Century Studies (exec. v.p.), Asociacion Internacional de Galdosistas, Phi Sigma Iota, Sigma Delta Pi (v.p. for S.W. 1989-92). Office: Tulane Univ 304 Newcomb Hall New Orleans LA 70118

PAOLINO, RICHARD FRANCIS, manufacturing company executive; b. Fall River, Mass., Feb. 16, 1945; s. Emelio and Sylvia (Fasciani) P.; m. Elizabeth Jane Maloney, Sept. 9, 1973; children: Christopher Matthew, Kathryn Elizabeth. AB in Engring. Sci., Dartmouth Coll., 1967; MBA in Mktg. and Fin., U. Chgo., 1973. Plant engr. Polaroid Corp., Cambridge, Mass., 1967; from salesman to asst. br. mgr., Fed. Products Corp., Chgo., 1967-74; area mgr., nat. accounts mgr., Husky Injection Molding Systems, Chgo. and Toronto, Can., 1974-76; v.p. mktg. Quality Measurement Systems Inc., Penfield, N.Y., 1976-78; dir. mktg. Automation and Measurement div. Bendix Corp., Dayton, Ohio, 1978-82; gen. mgr. Boice div. MTI, Latham, N.Y., 1982-85; v.p., gen. mgr. coordinate Measuring Sys. Divsn., Brown & Sharpe Mfg. Co., North Kingstown, R.I., 1985-94; v.p., gen. mgr. comml. ops. Measuring Sys. Group Worldwide, 1995—; pres., CEO DEA SpA, Turin, Italy; pres., mng. dir. DEA Iberica, Barcelona, Spain, DEA France, Villebon Sur Yvette, France, Brown and Sharpe Cos.; condr. seminars, lectr. in field. Bd. dirs. Automation Software, Inc., Providence, R.I., Leitz Messtechnik GmbH, Wetzlar, Germany, Brown & Sharpe-Precizika, Vilnius, Lithuania. 1st lt. USMCR, 1967-69. Mem. Soc. Mfg. Engrs. (past chmn. quality assurance tech. coun.), Am. Soc. Quality Control, Machinery and Allied Products Mktg. Coun., Mfr.'s Alliance for Productivity and Innovation (gen. mgrs. coun.), Assn. Mfg. Tech. Address: 16 Quincy Adams Rd Barrington RI 02806-5024 Office: Brown & Sharpe Mfg Co 200 Frenchtown Rd North Kingstown RI 02852-1711

PAOLINO, RONALD MARIO, clinical psychologist, consultant, psychopharmacologist, pharmacist; b. Providence, Mar. 15, 1938; s. Lawrence and Mary Corinne (Guglielmi) P.; m. Eileen Frances Quimby, June 18, 1960; children: Lisa Katherine, David Lawrence. Student, Providence Coll., 1955-56; BS in Pharmacy, U. R.I., 1959; MS in Pharmacology, Purdue U., 1961, PhD in Pharmacology/Toxicology, 1963, postdoctoral studies in clin. psychology, 1972-74; postdoctoral studies in existential analytic psychotherapy, Okla. Inst. Existential Analysis and Psychotherapy, 1974-75; Hostage Negotiation, FBI, 1991, Advanced Hostage Negotiation, 1995; Crisis Negotaition, FBI Acad., 1994; MA (hon.), Brown U., 1977. Lic. psychologist, R.I., pharmacist R.I.; nat. registered health svc. provider in psychology; cert. arbitrator; cert. nat. registered group psycho-therapists; cert. edn. provider N.Y. Intern dept. psychiatry and behavioral scis. U. Okla. Health Scis. Ctr., 1974-75; David Ross predoctoral fellow dept. pharmacology/toxicology Purdue U., 1961-63; NIMH postdoctoral fellow in psychology dept. psychology Yale U., 1963-65; asst. prof. pharmacology U. Conn. Sch. Pharmacy, 1965-67; assoc. prof. psychopharmacology Purdue U., 1967-74; NIMH fellow in clin. psychology U. Okla. Health Scis. Ctr., 1974-75; coord. group psychotherapy tng. program Brown U. Program in Medicine, 1983-85, assoc. prof. psychiatry and human behavior, 1976-90; pvt. practice; chief drug dependency treatment program VA Med. Ctr., Providence, 1975-87, dir. biofeedback clinic, 1977-87; chief, crisis mgmt. program, primary hostage negotiator; mem. Pharmacology and Therapeutic Agts. Com., 1979-87, VA Med. Ctr., coord. VA Contracted Half-Way Project for Substance Dependent Vets., 1981-85, chmn. Pain Mgmt. Task Force, 1984-85, mem. Supervisory Level Pharmacy Profl. Standards Bd., 1990—, mem. Mgmt. Suicidal and Violent Patient Task Force, 1990-91, chmn. Com. Prevention & Mgmt. of Disturbed Behaviors, 1991—, chief crisis mgmt. program, 1993—, advisor FBI Hostage Negotiations, 1991—, chmn. Outpatient Psychiatry Svcs. Reorganization Task Force, 1991, mem. VA-Dept. Def. Desert Storm Emergency Plan Com., 1991; advisor OSHA Dept. Labor for Violence in the Work Place, 1994—; mem. E. Prov. Clergy & MH Prov., 1995—; mem. substance abuse and prevention grant application rev. com. R.I. Adv. Coun. on Substance Abuse, 1982—, prevention, edn. and tng. com. on substance abuse, 1981—, chmn. 1981-82; adj. assoc. prof. psychology, U. R.I., 1982—; mem. planning com. State Conf. on Substance Abuse in the Hispanic Community, 1986; mem. alcohol awareness commn. Episc. Diocese of R.I., 1983-85; gubernatorial appointee Gov.'s Permanent Coun. on Drug Abuse Control, 1978-82; mem. rev. com. for funding of state drug abuse programs R.I. Single State Agy. on Drug Abuse, R.I. Dept. Mental Health Retardation and Hosps., 1978-82; cons. Nurses Renewal Com., 1980-81, substance abuse prevention edn. for elem. sch. children R.I. chpt. ARC, 1977, mem. suicide prevention steering com., 1977; mem.Interagy. Drug Abuse Steering Com., Lafayette, Ind. 1969-72; bd. dirs. Providence VA Med. Ctr. Credit Union; mem. bd. cert. for alcoholism counselors R.I. Assn. Alcohol Counselors, 1979-81; mem. Gov.'s Task Force on Substance Abuse at Adult Correctional Instn., 1977-78, Gov.'s Task Force on Mental Health Svcs. at Adult Correctional Instn., 1977-78, chmn. reclassification of inmates com., 1977-78; chmn. com. on edn. and cert. biofeedback practioners Conn. Biofeedback Soc., 1977-78; summer faculty fellow U. Conn., 1967; vis. scientist lectr. Assn. Am. Colls. Pharmacy, 1972-73; cons. to bus., unions, law enforcement; instr. R.I. State Police Acad., 1994, drug recognition experts recertification program R.I. Dept. Health, 1995; mem. faculty Law Enforcement Mgmt./Command Sch. U. R.I., 1991—. Author: (2 chpts.) Drug Testing: Issues and Options, 1991; contbr. 37 articles to profl. jours. Bd. dirs. R.I. chpt. Samaritans Internat. Suicide Prevention Orgn. v.p. Experience Jesus Inc.; mem. cmty adv. bd. Cpina Bifida Assn. R.I., 1980-83; mem. R.I. East Bay Clergy and Mental Health Profls. Coun.; congressman appointee (Patrick J. Kennedy); mem. veterans adv. commn., 1995—. Recipient Citation award for svc. and contbns. to formulation of state policy for treatment and prevention of drug abuse Gov. R.I., 1983, Letter of Commendation, Gov.'s R.I. Adv. Coun. on Substance Abuse, 1986, vc. Recognition award DAV, 1990, Spl. Contbn. award Providence VA Med Ctr., 1990. Mem. APA, Am. Coll. Forensic Examiners, Am. Psychotherapy Assn., Am. Soc. Pharmacology Exptl. Therapeutics, Internat. Brain Rsch. Orgn., Internat. Narcotic Enforcement Officers Assn., R.I. Group Psychotherapy Soc. (pres. 1991-93, continuing edn. dir. psychologists 1990—, exec. bd. 1986—, tng. faculty 1985—, co-dir. tng. 1986-87, tng. adv. bd. 1985-86), R.I. Psychol. Assn. (chmn. substance abuse ins. subcom. 1986-87, rep. Gov.'s Coun. on Mental Health State Plan Com. 1982-84), Hostage Negotiators of Am., R.I. East Bay Clergy and Mental Health Profls. Office: PO Box 159 Barrington RI 02806-0159

PAOLUCCI, ANNE ATTURA, playwright, poet, English and comparative literature educator; b. Rome; d. Joseph and Lucy (Guidoni) Attura; m. Henry Paolucci. BA, Barnard Coll; MA, Columbia U., PhD, 1963; hon. degree, Lehman Coll., CUNY, 1995. Mem. faculty English dept. Brearley Sch., N.Y.C., 1957-59; asst. prof. English and comparative lit. CCNY, 1959-69; univ. research prof. St. John's U., Jamaica, N.Y., 1969—; prof. English St. John's U., 1975—, acting head dept. English, 1973-74, chmn. dept. English, 1982-91, dir. doctor of arts degree program in English, 1982—; Fulbright lectr. in Am. drama U. Naples, Italy, 1965-67; spl. lectr. U. Urbino, summers 1966-67, U. Bari, 1967, univs. Bologna, Catania, Messina, Palermo, Milan, Pisa, 1965-67; disting. adj. vis. prof. Queens Coll., CUNY; bd. dirs. World Centre for Shakespeare Studies, 1972—; spl. guest Yugoslavia Ministry of Culture, 1972; rep. U.S. at Internat. Poetry Festival, Yugoslavia, 1981; founder, exec. dir. Council on Nat. Lits., 1974—; mem. exec. com. Conf. Editors Learned Jours.-MLA, 1975—; del. to Fgn. Lang. Jours., 1977—; mem. adv. bd. Commn. on Tech. and Cultural Transformation, UNESCO, 1978—; vis. fellow Humanities Research Centre, Australian Nat. U., 1979; rep. U.S. woman playwright Inter-Am. Women Writers Congress, Ottawa, Ont., Can., 1978; organizer, chmn. profl. symposia, meetings; TV appearances; hostess Mags. in Focus, Channel 31, N.Y.C., 1971-72; mem. N.Am. Adv. Council Shakespeare Globe Theatre Center, 1981—; mem. Nat. Grad. Fellows Program Fellowship Bd., 1985—; mem. Nat. Garibaldi Centennial Com., 1981; mem. Nat. Grad. Fellows Program, 1985—; trustee Edn. Scholarship, Grants Com. of NIAF, 1990—; guest speaker with E. Albee Ohio No. State U., 1990. Author (with H. Paolucci) books, including: Hegel On Tragedy, 1962, From Tension to Tonic: The Plays of Edward Albee, 1972, Pirandello's Theater: The Recovery of the Modern Stage for Dramatic Art, 1974, Poems Written for Sbek's Mummies, Marie Menken, and Other Important Persons, Places, and Things, 1977, Eight Short Stories, 1977, Sepia Prints, 1985, 2nd edit., 1986; plays include: Minions of the Race (Medieval and Renaissance Conf. of Western Mich. U. Drama award 1972), Cipango!, 1985, pub. as book, 1985, 86, videotape excerpts, 1986, 92; performed N.Y.C. and Washington, 1987-88, Winterthur Mus., U. Del., 1990; The Actor in Search of His Mask, 1987, Italian translation and prodn., Genoa, 1987, The Short Season, Naples, 1967, Cubiculo, N.Y., 1973, German translation, Vienna, 1996; poems Riding the Mast Where It Swings, 1980, Gorbachev in Concert, 1991, Queensboro Bridge (and other Poems), 1995 (Pulitzer prize nominee 1995-96); contbr. numerous articles, rev. to profl. jours.; editor, author introduction to: Dante's Influence on American Writers, 1977; gen. editor tape-cassette series China, 1977, 78; founder Coun. on Nat. Lit.; gen. editor series Rev. Nat. Lits., 1970—, CNL/Quar. World Report, 1974-76, semi-ann., 1977-84, ann., 1985—; full-length TV tape of play Cipango! for pub. TV and ednl. TV with original music by Henry Paolucci, 1990. Bd. dirs. Italian Heritage and Culture City-wide com., 1986—; Pres. Reagan appointee Nat. Grad. Fellows Program Fellowship Bd., 1985-86, Nat. Coun. Humanities, 1986—, Ann. award, FIERI, 1990; pres. Columbus: Countdown, 1992 Fedn.; mem. Gov. Cuomo's Heritage Legacy Project for Schs., 1989—; bd. dirs. Am. Soc. Italian Legions of Merit (chmn. cultural com. 1990—). Named one of 10 Outstanding Italian Ams. in Washington, awarded medal by Amb. Rinaldo Petrignani, 1986; named Cavaliere Italian Republic, 1986, "Commendatore" of the Italian Republic Order of Merit, 1992; recipient Notable Rating for Mags. in Focus series N.Y. Times, 1972, Woman of Yr. award Dr. Herman Henry Scholarship Found., 1973, Amita award, 1970, award Women's Press Club N.Y., 1974, Order Merit, Italian Republic, 1986, Gold medal for Quincentenary Can. trustee NIIAF, 1990, ann. awards Consortium of Italian-Am. Assns., 1991, Am.-Italian Hist. Assn., 1991, 1st Columbus award Cath. Charities, 1991, Leone di San Marco award Italian Heritage Coun. of Bronx and Westchester Counties, 1992, Children of Columbus award Order of Sons of Italy in Am., 1993, 1st Nat. Elena Cornaro award Order of Sons of Italy, 1993; Columbia U. Woodbridge hon. fellow, 1961-62; Am. Council Learned Socs. grantee Internat. Pirandello Congress, Agrigento, Italy, 1978. Mem. Internat. Shakespeare Assn., Shakespeare Assn. Am., Renaissance Soc. Am., Renaissance Inst. Japan, Internat. Comparative Lit. Assn., Am. Comparative Lit. Assn., MLA, Am. PEN, Hegel Soc. Am., Dante Soc. Am. (v.p. 1976-77), Am. Found. Italian Arts and Letters (founder, pres.), Pirandello Soc. (pres. 1978—), Nat. Soc. Lit. and Arts, Nat. Book Critics Circle, Am. Soc. Italian Legions of Merit (bd. dirs. 1990—). Office: St John's U Dept English Jamaica NY 11439 *My own first practical premise has been to organize every task (even routine chores) so that there is always time and energy for whatever important projects come up. There is enough room in the day for doing a number of things—and for creating "space" every so often to do one's own special work (writing fiction or poetry or plays, in my case). Organization is all-important; but perhaps the basic premise in intellectual things is organic growth, letting "in" those things that are meaningful because they already suggest an intrinsic pattern. In my case, I discovered long after the projects and books themselves had taken shape and had been published, that I had been tending for a number of years more and more exclusively toward drama and dramatic criticism and theory. Well, that, obviously, was my own potential "law" organizing from within my various interests. One must continue to allow for new interests to revitalize those already familiar.*

PAONE, PETER, artist; b. Phila., Oct. 2, 1936; s. George and Angelina (Vitrella) P.; m. Alma Alabilikian, 1976. B.A., Phila. Mus. Coll. Art, 1958. Instr. Phila. Mus. Coll. Art, Pratt Inst., others; head graphics dept. Fleisher Art Meml., 1959-62; tchr. Pa. Acad. Fine Arts, 1978—, also chmn. graphics dept.; instr. Positano Art Sch., Italy, 1961. One man shows include Ft. Worth Mus., 1963, Grippi Gallery, 1959, 60, 61, Phila. Print Club, 1961-64, 83, Robinson Gallery, Houston, 1978-79, Pa. Acad. Fine Arts, 1983, Ryder Coll., Pa., 1991, Merlin Verlag, Hamburg, Germany, 1996; exhibited in group shows at Phila. Mus. Art, 1960, 61, 63, Contemporary Am., 1961, Lehigh (Pa.) U., Bklyn. Mus., 1962, Paris Biennial, 1963, Dallas Mus., Otis Art Inst., L.A., Syracuse U., 1964, La Escuela Nacional, Mexico City,

Vanderbilt U., N.Y. World's Fair, Exhbn. Pakistan, 1967, Clydie Jessop Gallery, London, 1968, David Gallery, Houston, Kennedy Gallery, N.Y.C., 1970-72, Hooks-Epstein Gallery, 1978, 80, 81, 82, 83, 85, 87, 88, 90, Rider Coll. N.J., 1991, Merlin Verlag, 1996, Dresden, Germany, 1996; represented in permanent collections of Libr. of Congress, Phila. Mus. Art, Sumner Found., N.Y. Mus. Modern Art, Princeton Libr., Phila. Libr., Gen. Mills, Phila. Print Club, Rosenwald Collection, Carl Sandburg Meml. Libr., Syracuse U., Ft. Worth Mus., Victoria and Albert Mus., Brit. Mus., Art Inst. Chgo., Yale U. Recipient award of merit Phila. Print Club, 1983; Tiffany Found. grantee, 1962, 64; John Simon Guggenheim fellow, 1965-66; grantee Penn Council for the Arts, 1985. Mem. NAD (assoc.). Home: 1027 W Westview St Philadelphia PA 19119-3718 *Somewhere between the world of realism and surrealism, there is a world that deals with the reality of relationships, favoring the substance of the imagination rather than the substance of everyday vision. Objects that seemingly have no real relationship to each other in their existence are juxtaposed in the life of the artist. They have touched each other and have become part of the vision, and in turn have become his iconography. There is no urgency in this vision. The private reality has always been there and always will be. The viewer is allowed to question his knowledge of it, and in doing so, he often is uneasy and bewildered before the assemblage. This, at first, implies fantasy; this is not true. Instead, this is a reconstruction of reality, not an escape from it.*

PAPA, MARK G., oil and gas industry executive; b. Monroeville, Pa., Sept. 16, 1946; s. Mark W. Papa and Jean Feiler; m. Susan Berryman, Dec. 21, 1970; 1 child, Christine. BS in Petroleum Engring., U. Pitts., 1968; MBA in Econs./Fin., U. Houston, 1980. Registered profl. engr., Tex. Various petroleum engring., supervisory & engring. positions Conoco, Inc., various locations, 1968-81; divsn. prodn. coord. Belco Petroleum, Houston, 1981-82, mgr. ops., 1982-83; v.p. drilling and prodn. Belnorth, Houston, 1983-84, sr. v.p. drilling and prodn., 1984-85; sr. v.p. ops. Enron Oil & Gas, Houston, 1986-87, 1987-94, pres. N.Am. ops., 1994—. Mem. Soc. Petroleum Engrs., Am. Assn. Petroleum Geologists, Natural Gas Supply Assn., Tex. Ind. Prodrs. Royalty Orgn. Avocation: tennis. Office: Enron Oil & Gas Co 1400 Smith Houston TX 77002

PAPA, VINCENT T., financial insurance company executive; b. Bklyn., Dec. 11, 1946; s. Frank R. and Carmela (Farruggia) P.; m. Karen Ann Conroy, July 4, 1969; children: Kimberly, Jennifer, Kristen. BBA, Hofstra U., 1969; AAS, Nassau Community Coll., 1967; CPA, N.Y. Staff acct. Arthur Andersen & Co., N.Y.C., 1969-72; comptroller Finserv Corp., N.Y.C., 1972-80; v.p. and treas. Orion Capital Corp., N.Y.C., 1980—; chmn. bd. dirs. William H. McGee & Co., Inc., N.Y.C. Mem. AICPA, Nat. Assn. Corp. Treas., Am. Mgmt. Assn. (mem. ins. and risk mgmt. coun.), N.Y. State Soc. CPAs, Ins. Soc. N.Y. Office: Orion Capital Corp 600 5th Ave New York NY 10020-2302

PAPADAKIS, CONSTANTINE N., university executive; b. Athens, Greece, Feb. 2, 1946; came to U.S., 1969; s. Nicholas and Rita (Masciotti) P.; m. Eliana Apostolides, Aug. 28, 1971; 1 child, Maria. Diploma in Civil Engring., Nat. Tech. U. Athens, 1969; MS in Civil Engring., U. Cin., 1970; PhD in Civil Engring., U. Mich., 1973. Registered profl. engr., Ohio, Greece. Engring. specialist, geotechnical group Bechtel, Inc., Gaithersburg, Md., 1974-76; supr. and asst. chief engr. geotechnical group Bechtel, Inc., Ann Arbor, Mich., 1976-81; v.p., bd. dirs. water resources div. STS Cons. Ltd., Ann Arbor, 1981-84; v.p. water and environ. resources dept. Tetra Tech-Honeywell, Pasadena, Calif., 1984; head dept. civil engring. Colo. State U., Ft. Collins, 1984-86; dean Coll. Engring. U. Cin., 1986-95, dir. Groundwater Rsch. Ctr., 1986-95; dir. Ctr. Hill Solid and Hazardous Waste Rsch. Ctr. EPA, Cin., 1986-93; pres. Drexel U., Phila., 1995—; adj. prof. civil engring. U. Mich., 1976-83; cons. Gaines & Stern Co., Cleve., 1983-84, Honeywell Europe, Maintal, Fed. Republic of Germany, 1984-85, Arthur D. Little, Boston, 1984-85, Camargo Assocs., Ltd., Cin., 1986, King Fahd U. Rsch. Inst., Dhahran, Saudi Arabia, 1987, King Abdulaziz City for Sci. and Tech., Riyadh, Saudi Arabia, 1991, Henderson & Bodwell Cons. Engrs. Inc., 1991, Cin. Met. Sewer Dist., 1992, Ohio River Valley Water Sanitation Commn., 1994; acting pres. Ohio Aerospace Inst., 1988-90; interim pres. Inst. Advanced Mfg. Scis. Ohio Edison Tech. Ctr., 1989-90; bd. govs. Edison Materials Tech. Ctr., 1988-95; Incubator, 1988-95; bd. dirs. Fidelity Fed. Bank. Author: Problems on Strength of Materials, 1968, Sewer Systems Design, 1969; editor: Fluid Transients and Acoustics, 1978, Pump-Turbine Schemes, 1979, Small Hydro Power Fluid Machinery, 1982; Megatrends in Hydraulics, 1987; contbr. more than 65 articles to profl. jours. Mem. Greater Cin. C. of C. Blue Chip Campaign for Econ. Devel. Task Force, 1988-93, bd. dirs. Bus. Assistance Ctr., 1989-95; mem. Ohio Coun. on Rsch. and Econ. Devel., 1988, Ohio Sci. and Tech. Commn. Adv. Group, 1989-90, 92-95; coun. mem. St. Nicholas Ch. Parish, Ann Arbor, 1981-84; mem. City of Ft. Collins Drainage Bd., 1984-86; bd. dirs. Dan Beard coun. Boy Scouts Am., 1995, Intelligent Vehicle Hwy. Soc. Ohio, 1994-95. Recipient Horace W. King scholarship civil engring. dept. U. Mich., 1971-73, 6 Bechtel Merit awards, 1974-79, Young Engr. of Yr. award Mich. Soc. Profl. Engrs., Ann Arbor, Mich., 1982, Disting. Engr. award Engrs. and Scientists Cin. Tech. Socs. Coun., 1989, Acad. of Achievement in Edn. award Am. Hellenic Ednl. Progressive Assn., 1995, Hellenic Univ. Club of Phila. Achievement award, 1996, Krikos Disting. Hellene Leader award, 1996. Fellow ASCE (pres. Ann Arbor br. 1980-81, pres.-elect Mich. sect. 1983-84, hydraulics divsn. publ. com. 1980-83), ASME (chmn. fluid transients com. 1978-80, mem. fluids engring. divsn. awards com. 1981-84), Am. Soc. Engring. Edn.; mem. NSPE (legis. and govt. affairs com. 1994-95, chair profl. engrs. in edn. divsn. 1995), Order of the Engr., Internat. Assn. for Hydraulic Rsch., Ohio Engring. Dean's Coun. (chmn.-elect 1989-91), Rotary, Sigma Xi, Chi Epsilon, Tau Beta Pi. Greek Orthodox. Avocations: photography, classical music, travel, swimming, racquetball. Office: Drexel Univ 3161 Chestnut St Philadelphia PA 19106

PAPADAKIS, EMMANUEL PHILIPPOS, physicist, consultant; b. N.Y.C., Dec. 25, 1934; s. Philippos E. and Helen (Eastman) P.; m. Stella Christopher, Sept. 4, 1960; children: Susan H., Philip E., Christopher E., Nicholas E. S.B. in Physics, M.I.T., 1956, Ph.D. in Physics, 1962; M.M. in Mgmt, U. Mich., 1979. Mem. tech. staff Bell Telephone Labs., Allentown, Pa., 1962-69; dept. head Panametrics, Inc., Waltham, Mass., 1969-73; prin. staff engr. Ford Motor Co., Detroit, 1973-75, supr., 1975-87; ptnr. E&S Antiques, Ames, Iowa, 1978—, pres. Quality Systems Concepts Inc., 1991—; assoc. dir. Ctr. for Nondestructive Evaluation, Iowa State U., Ames, 1988-95; adj. prof. Northeastern U. ext., Waltham, 1970-73, elec. engring. and computer engring. Iowa State U., 1988-95; cons. quality, TQM, ISO-9000, acoustics and ultrasonic testing sys., 1969-73, 88—. Contbr. numerous articles on electronics, ultrasonics, acoustics, nondestructive testing, crystallography and quality to profl. jours.; assoc. editor IEEE Transactions on Ultras, Ferroelectrics and Frequency Control, 1972-92; assoc. tech. editor Materials Evaluation, 1975-87, rsch. coord., 1980-86, quality concepts coord., 1986-88, tech. editor, 1988—; reviewer various jours. in physics, testing materials and sci. instrumentation; reviewer proposals to various govtl. agencies. Fellow IEEE, Acoustical Soc. Am. (Biennial award 1968), Am. Soc. for Nondestructive Testing (Mehl honor lectr. 1979, tutorial award 1993); mem. ASTM, Am. Phys. Soc., Soc. Mfg. Engrs., Am. Soc. Quality Control, Soc. Automotive Engrs., Soc. Engring. Mechanics, Sigma Xi. Patentee in field; developer method and instrument for measuring ultrasonic velocity, method for bonding thin slabs to substrates, instrument for sheet metal texture determination, method using DSSS in ultrasonic flaw detection. Office: QSC Inc PO Box 1229 1205 Ridgewood Ave Ames IA 50010-5207

PAPADAKIS, MYRON PHILIP, lawyer, educator, pilot; b. N.Y.C., Dec. 11, 1940; s. Philip E. and Helen (Eastman) P.; m. Ann Hall, Sept. 1968; children: Wade, Nicholas. BS in Mech. Engring., U. Nebr., 1963; JD, South Tex. Coll. Law, 1974. Bar: Tex. 1975. Pilot, capt. Delta Airlines, Houston, 1970—; pvt. practice Papadakis et al, Houston, 1975-90; of counsel Slack & Davis, Austin, Tex., 1994—; adj. prof. South Tex. Coll. Law, Houston, 1980—. Co-author: Best of Trial-Products Liability, 1991, Aviation Accident Reconstruction and Litigation, 1995; contbr. articles to profl. jours. Lt. USN, 1963-69. Fellow Internat. Soc. Air Safety Investigators (chmn. ethics com. 1986-92). Avocations: flying, test flying, photography, fishing. Home: 5214 Buckman Mtn Austin TX 78746 Office: Slack and Davis Ste 2110 8911 N Capital of Tex Hwy Austin TX 78759-7247

PAPADAKIS, PANAGIOTIS AGAMEMNON, banker, international business executive; b. Athens, Greece, Mar. 29, 1935; s. Agamemnon Ioannou and Anna Karyatis (Kyriakopoulou) P.; m. Alexandra Argyropoulou, July 12, 1959. Student, U. Athens, 1953-57. Registered rep., Del., Athens, Greece, Zurich, Switzerland, Washington, 50 other countries. Pub., owner newspaper Peristeri, Athens, 1953-64; owner, gen. dir. printing house, advt. office, ins. agy., Athens, 1953-64; leader Nat. Radical Party Youth, Athens, 1958-59; founder, gen. dir. Servis Advt., Athens, 1963-78, Book-Servis, Athens, 1974-78; pres. Investments Promotions and Assocs. of Chgo., Athens, 1979-85; chmn. Internat. Investments World Co. Inc., Athens and Zurich, 1985—, Internat. Bus. Co. Inc., Internat. Comml. Co. Inc., Athens and Zurich, 1985—, Papadakis Internat. Fin. Co. Inc., Guarantor Co. Inc., Athens and Zurich, 1992—, Internat. Banker Fin. Co. Inc., Athens and Zurich, 1992—; chmn. Internat. Pap Financing and Investment Group, Vaduz Liechtenstein, Konekt Financing Investment Group AG, Griscaviation AG, Graubunden, Switzerland. Author, editor: Historical Biography of President Karamanlis, 1974-77; author: Why the Revolution of 21 April 1967 Happened, 1968; author numerous articles in Recently Humanity '93, Human Rights. Mem. Internat. C. of C., Internat. Soc. Financiers, World Trade Ctr. of Basel, Acad. Scis. Zurich (hon.), Assn. de Soutier A L'Universite De Dalout (hon.). Mem. New Democracy Party. Christian Orthodox. Home and Office: Usteristrasse 23, 8001 Zurich Switzerland Home: Karlihof 11, Malans Graubunden Switzerland also: Char Trikoupi 113, Kifissia Athens Greece Office: Internat Investment World Group Cos, Bahnhofstrasse 52, 8001 Zurich Switzerland also: Pontou 24, Ilissia Athens Greece also: 1329 Connecticut Ave Washington DC 20036

PAPADEMETRIOU, GEORGE CONSTANTINE, priest, director, educator; b. Thasos, Greece, Apr. 11, 1932; came to U.S., 1947; s. Constantine G. and Ourania C. (Katsifas) P.; m. Athanasia Antoniou, June 26, 1960; children: Dean, Jane, Tom. BTh, Holy Cross Orthodox Sem., 1959; MTh, Tex. Christian U., 1966; PhD, Temple U., 1977; MLS, Simmons Coll., 1983. Pastor Greek Orthodox Archdiocese, 1960—; libr. dir. Hellenic Coll., 1981—; assoc. prof. theology and philosophy Holy Cross Orthodox Sem., Brookline, Mass., 1978—. Author: Introduction to Saint Gregory Palamas, 1973, Essays on Orthodox Christian-Jewish Relations, 1990, Maimonides and Palamas on God, 1994. Mem. AHEPA, Mass. Commn. on Christian Unity, Orthodox Theol. Soc. Am., Am. Acad. Religion, Am. Theol. Libr. Assn. Office: Hellenic Coll 50 Goddard Ave Brookline MA 02146-7415

PAPADIMITRIOU, DIMITRI BASIL, economist, college administrator; b. Salonica, Greece, June 9, 1946; came to U.S., 1965, naturalized, 1974; s. Basil John and Ellen (Tacas) P.; m. Viki Fokas, Aug. 26, 1967; children: Jennifer E., Elizabeth R. BA, Columbia U., 1970; PhD, New Sch. Social Rsch., 1986. V.p., asst. sec. ITT Life Ins. Co. N.Y., N.Y.C., 1970-73; exec. v.p., sec., treas. William Penn Life Ins. Co. N.Y., N.Y.C., 1973-78, also dir.; exec. v.p., provost Bard Coll., 1978—, Jerome Levy Inst. prof. econs., 1978—, exec. dir. Bard Ctr., 1980—, Jerome Levy Econs. Inst., 1988—; adj. lectr. econs. New Sch. Social Rsch., 1975-76; fellow Ctr. for Advanced Econ. Studies, 1983; bd. dirs. William Penn Life Ins. Co. N.Y.; mem. adv. com. Hudsonia, Inc.; bd. govs. Jerome Levy Econs. Inst., 1986—; mem. subcoun. capital allocation Competitiveness Policy Coun.; mem. adv. com. Women's World Banking; radio econs. commentator Sta. WAMC, Monitor Radio, NPR, Money Radio. Bd. editors Ea. Econ. Jour.; book reviewer Econ. Jour. Bd. dirs. Catskill Ballet Theatre; trustee ACHAEA Found., Am. Symphony Orch. Mem. Am. Econ. Assn., Am.-Hellenic Banker Assn., Royal Econ. Soc., Am. Fin. Assn., European Econ. Assn., Eastern Economic Assn., Econ. Sci. Chamber of Greece. Home and Office: Bard Coll Annandale On Hudson NY 12504

PAPAGEORGE, TOD, photographer, educator; b. Portsmouth, N.H., Aug. 1, 1940; s. Theodore and Eileen Elizabeth (Flanigan) P.; m. Pauline Whitcomb, Feb. 3, 1962 (div. 1970); m. Deborah Flomenhaft, June 21, 1987; 1 child, Theo. BA in English Lit., U. N.H., 1962; MA, Yale U., 1979. Lectr. in photography MIT, Cambridge, Mass., 1974-75; lectr. in visual studies Harvard U., Cambridge, 1975-76; Walker Evans prof. of photography Yale U., New Haven, 1978—; vis. instr. in photography The Parsons Sch. Design, N.Y.C., 1969-72, The Pratt Inst. of Art, N.Y.C., 1971-74, The Cooper Union Sch. Art, N.Y.C., 1971-74; adj. lectr. in photography Queens Coll., N.Y.C., 1972-74. Guest dir. exhbn., Mus. Modern Art, N.Y.C., 1977, Yale Art Gallery, 1981; one-man shows include Light Gallery, N.Y.C., 1973, 79, Cronin Gallery, Houston, 1977, Art Inst. Chgo., 1978, Galerie Zabriskie, Paris, 1979, Stills Photography Group, Edinburgh, Scotland, 1980, Daniel Wolf Gallery, N.Y.C., 1981, 85, Akron (Ohio) Art Mus., 1981, Sheldon Meml. Art Gallery, Lincoln, Nebr., 1981, Franklin Parrasch Gallery, N.Y.C., 1991; group shows include Mus. Modern Art, N.Y.C., 1971, 73, 74, 76, 77, 78, 79, 91, Lowe Art Mus., Coral Gables, Fla., 1974, Balt. Mus. Art, 1975, Mus. Fine Arts, Boston, 1976, 91, Thomas Gibson Gallery, London, 1976, Galerie Zabriskie, Paris, 1977, 87, U. Colo., 1977, Houston Mus. Fine Arts, 1977, Art Inst. Chgo., 1979, Corcoran Gallery Art, Washington, 1980, Fraenkel Gallery, San Francisco, 1981, Daniel Wolf Gallery, N.Y.C., 1982, 83, 86, Albright-Knox Mus., Buffalo, 1983, The Whitney Mus. Art, N.Y.C., 1983, The Photographer's Gallery, London, 1983, Nat. Mus. Am. Art, Washington, 1984, The Dog Mus., N.Y.C., 1984, The Barbican Nat. Gallery, London, 1985, Light Gallery, N.Y.C., 1985, Centro Reina Sophia, Madrid, Spain, 1987, N.Y. State Mus., Albany, 1987, Worcester (Mass.) Art Mus., 1990, 94, Jewish Mus. Art, Wellesley, Mass., 1990, Musee De La Photographie, Mont-Sur-Marchienne, Belgium, 1991, Franklin Parrasch Gallery, N.Y.C., 1992, others; represented in permanent collections Mus. Modern Art, Art Inst. Chgo., Boston Mus. Fine Arts, Yale U. Art Gallery, Bibliothéque Nationale, Paris, Mus. Fine Arts, Houston, Dallas Mus. Fine Arts, Nat. Mus. Am. Art, Washington, J.B. Speed Mus., Louisville, Seattle Art Mus., Kunsthaus, Zurich, Switzerland, others; commd. by Aperture, Inc., 1975, Balt. Mus. Art, 1975, Seagrams Corp., 1975, Mus. Modern Art, N.Y., 1977, AT&T, 1978, Yale U. Art Gallery, 1981, Warner Comm., 1983; author: Walker Evans and Robert Frank: An Essay on Influence, 1981; editor: Public Relations: The Photographs of Garry Winogrand, 1977. Guggenheim fellow, 1970, 77; Nat. Endowment Arts fellow, 1973, 76. Subject of numerous articles and publs. Home: 122 Cottage St New Haven CT 06511-2406 Office: Yale U Sch Art PO Box 208270 New Haven CT 06520-8270

PAPAGEORGIOU, JOHN CONSTANTINE, management science educator; b. Kallithea, Greece, Nov. 22, 1935; came to U.S., 1969, naturalized, 1975; m. Thalia Christidou, 1969; children: Constantine, Elena, Demetrios, Antigone. B.Sc., Athens (Greece) Sch. Econs. and Bus. Scis., 1957; diploma tech. sci., U. Manchester, Eng., 1963, Ph.D. in Mgmt. Scis, 1965. Lectr. Athens Sch. Econs. and Bus. Scis.; also postgrad. Inst. Bus. Adminstrn., Athens, 1966-68; asst. prof. Faculty Adminstrv. Studies, York U., Toronto, Ont., Can., 1968-69; asst. prof. mgmt. Wayne State U., 1969-71; assoc. prof. mgmt. scis. St. Louis U., 1971-72; vis. prof. ops. rsch. Athens Sch. Econs. and Bus. Scis., 1972-73; assoc. prof. ops. analysis U. Toledo, 1974-76; assoc. prof. mgmt. sci. and coord. Coll. Profl. Studies, U. Mass., Boston, 1976-78; prof., coord. Coll. Profl. Studies, U. Mass., 1978-80; prof. mgmt. scis. dept. Coll. Mgmt. U. Mass., 1980—, chmn. mgmt. scis. dept., 1980-85; assoc. dean Coll. Mgmt. U. Mass., 1995; head dept. econ. research Agrl. Bank Greece, 1966-67; ops. analyst Esso-Pappas Indsl. Co., Greece, 1967-68; spl. adv. Center Planning and Econ. Research, Greece, 1972-73; cons. in field; condr. seminars. Author: Introduction to Operations Research (in Greek), 1973, Fundamentals of Operations Research, 1973, Management Science and Environmental Problems, 1980; co-author: Data on the Greek Economy, 1966; assoc. editor technos: Ops. Mgmt. Newsletter; spl. issues editor: Interfaces; guest editor: Internat. Jour. Tech. Mgmt.; mem. editorial bd. Jour. Managerial Issues, Southwestern Bus. Rev.; editor: TIMS COLIME Newsletter; contbr. articles to profl. jours. Served to 2d lt. Greek Army, 1958-60. Greek Govt. scholar, 1962-65; NATO postdoctoral fellow, 1965; Air Force Office Sci. Research fellow, summer 1980. Fellow AAAS; mem. Ops. Rsch. Soc. Am. (1985 nat. meeting program com., 1994 jo8int nat. meeting program chmn.), Inst. Mgmt. Scis. (chmn. nat. meeting com. 1985, faculty-in-residence com., coll. officer, chpt. officer, activities com.), Am. Inst. Decision Scis. (nat. innovative edn. com. 1981, programs and meetings com. 1983), Sigma Xi. Address: 14 Putney Rd Wellesley MA 02181-5315 *Our achievements are a function of our goals. I usually set ambitious but achievable goals and I try to achieve them through hard work, persistence, and belief in God's help. I believe that there is always room for improvement in the status-quo and that a continuous search for improvements is the major factor for continuous progress.*

PAPAGEORGIOU, PANAGIOTIS, medical educator; b. Thessaloniki, Greece, Dec. 23, 1959. MD, Aristotelian U., Thessaloniki, 1984; PhD in Physiology, Harvard U., 1990. Cert. Ednl. Com. for Fgn. Med. Grads., FLEX; diplomate Am. Bd. Internal Medicine, subspecialty in cardiovasc. disease; lic. physician, Mass. Rsch. fellow Am. Heart Assn., Mass. affiliate, 1989-90; intern in medicine Beth Israel Hosp., Harvard Med. Sch., Boston, 1990-91, jr. asst. resident internal medicine, 1991-92, clin. cardiology fellow cardiovascular divsn., 1992-94, clin. electrophysiology fellow cardiovascular divsn., 1994-96, staff electrophysiologist, 1996—; tchg. fellow dept. cellular and molecular physiology Harvard U., 1985-90, clin. fellow medicine, 1990-95, instr., 1995—. Contbr. articles to profl. jours., chpts. to books. Greek Nat. scholar, 1977-84, Albert J. Ryan scholar Harvard Med. Sch., 1987-90; recipient clinician-investigator devel. award NIH, 1995, Clinician Scientist awrd AHA, Nat. Ctr., 1995. Mem. ACP, AMA, Tessaloniki Med. Soc., Am. Heart Assn., Mass. Med. Soc., Biophys. Soc., Am. Heart Assn. Basic Rsch. Coun., Am. Coll. Cardiology. Office: Beth Israel Hosp 330 Brookline Ave Boston MA 02215

PAPAI, BEVERLY DAFFERN, library director; b. Amarillo, Tex., Aug. 31, 1949; d. Clarence Wilbur and Dora Mae (Henderson) Daffern; m. Joseph Andrew Papai, Apr. 3, 1976. BS in Polit. Sci., West Tex. State U., Canyon, 1972; MSLS, Wayne State U., 1973. Head extension dept. and Oakland County Subregional Libr. The Farmington Cmty. Libr., Farmington Hills, Mich., 1973-79, coord. adult svcs., br. head, 1980-83, asst. dir., 1983-85, dir., 1985—; cons. U.S. Office of Edn., 1978, Battelle Meml. Inst., Columbis, Ohio, 1980; presenter in field. Contbr. articles to profl. jours. Bd. dirs. Mich. Consortium, 1987-91; trustee Libr. of Mich., 1989-92, vice chair, 1991, chair, 1992; del. White House Conf. on Librs. and Info. Svcs., 1991; founder, treas., fiscal agt. METRO NET Libr. Consortium, 1993—. Recipient Athena award Farmington/Farmington Hills C. of C. and Gen. Motors, 1994; Amarillo Pub. Libr. Friends Group fellow, 1972, Wayne State U. Inst. of Gerontology fellow, 1972. Mem. ALA (officer), Mich. Libr. Assn. (chair specialized libr. svcs. roundtable 1975, chair conf. program 1982, chair pub. policy com. 1988-89, chair devel. com. 1994-95, chair ann. conf. and program coms. 1995-96, pres. 1996—, Loleta D. Fyan award 1975), LWV of Mich., Farmington Exch. Club, Coun. on Resource Devel. Democrat. Roman Catholic. Home: 6805 Wing Lake Rd Bloomfield Hills MI 48301 Office: The Farmington Cmty Libr 32737 W Twelve Mile Rd Farmington Hills MI 48334

PAPALEO, ANTHONY See FRANCIOSA, ANTHONY

PAPALIA, DIANE ELLEN, human development educator; b. Englewood, N.J., Apr. 26, 1947; d. Edward Peter and Madeline (Borrin) P.; m. Jonathan Finlay, June 19, 1976; 1 child, Anna Victoria Finlay. A.B., Vassar Coll., 1968; M.S., W.Va. U., 1970, Ph.D. (NSF fellow), 1971. Asst. prof. child and family studies U. Wis., Madison, 1971-75; assoc. prof. U. Wis., 1975-78, prof., 1978-87, coordinator child and family studies, 1977-79; adj. prof. psychology in pediatrics U. Pa. Sch. Medicine, 1987-89. Co-author: (with Sally W. Olds) A Child's World: Infancy Through Adolescence, 1975, 7th edit., 1996, Human Development, 1978, 6th edit., 1995, Psychology, 1985, 2d edit., 1988, (with Cameron J. Camp and Ruth Duskin Feldman) Adult Development and Aging, 1996; contbr. articles to profl. jours. Am. Council on Edn. fellow, 1979-80; U. Wis. grantee. Fellow Gerontol. Soc.; mem. Am. Psychol. Assn., Soc. Research in Child Devel., Nat. Council Family Relations, Psi Chi. Home: 316 E 18th St New York NY 10003

PAPALIOLIOS, COSTAS DEMETRIOS, physics educator; b. Brooklyn, N.Y., May 15, 1931; s. Demetrios K. and Helen (Georgiou) P.; m. Alice Wochele, Sept. 7, 1963; children—Andreas, Dimitri. B.S., Rensselaer Poly. Inst., 1953; A.M., Harvard, 1960, Ph.D., 1965. Mem. tech. staff Bell Telephone Labs., 1953-55; prof. physics Harvard, 1966—; physicist Smithsonian Astrophys. Obs., 1965. Served with AUS, 1955-57. Home: 40 Long Ridge Rd Carlisle MA 01741-1837 Office: Harvard U Dept. Physics Cambridge MA 02138

PAPANEK, GUSTAV FRITZ, economist, educator; b. Vienna, Austria, July 12, 1926; s. Ernst and Helene P.; m. Hanna Kaiser, June 13, 1947; children: Thomas H., Joanne R. Papanek Orlando. BA in Agrl. Econs, Cornell U., 1947; MA in Econs, Harvard U., 1949, PhD, 1951. Economist, dep. dir. program planning for Asia, tech. coop. adminstrn. Dept. State, 1951-53; econ. adv., then dir. adv. group to planning commn. Harvard U., Pakistan, 1954-58; dep. dir., then dir. Devel. Adv. Svc. Harvard U., 1958-70; dir. adv. group to planning commn. Harvard U., Indonesia, 1971-73; prof. econs. Boston U., 1974-92, prof. emeritus, 1992—, chmn. dept., 1974-83, interim dir., 1977-80, dir. Ctr. for Asian Devel. Studies, 1983-90, dir. Asian program, 1991-92; dir., cons. team devel. studies to planning commn. Govt. of Indonesia, 1987-89; pres. Boston Inst. for Developing Econs., Ltd. (BIDE), 1987—; dir. policy adv. team to Federated States of Micronesia, 1995—; cons. in field. Author: Pakistan's Development: Social Goals and Private Incentives, 1967, The Indonesian Economy, 1980, Development Strategy, Growth Equity and the Political process in Southern Asia, 1986; co-author: Decision Making for Economic Development, 1971, The Indian Economy, 1988; several other books; contbr. articles to profls. jours. With AUS, 1944-46. Grantee Ford Found., AID, World Bank, UN Devel. Program, UN Univ., HEW, Asian Devel. Bank. Mem. Am. Econs. Assn., Am. Agrl. Econs. Assn., Soc. Internat. Devel. (past mem. exec. com.), Assn. Comparative Econ. Studies (pres. 1982), Assn. Asian Studies (pres. New Eng. conf. 1975-77), Pakistan Econ. Assn. Home and Office: 2 Mason St Lexington MA 02173-6315

PAPANEK, VICTOR, designer, educator, writer; b. Vienna, Austria, Nov. 22, 1926; came to U.S., 1939; s. Richard Franz Josef and Helene (Von Spitz) P.; m. Winifred Nelson, 1951 (div. 1957); 1 child, Nicolette; m. Harlanne Herdman, July 29, 1966 (div. 1989); 1 child, Jennifer Satu. BArch, BFA in Design, Cooper Union, 1950; student with, Frank Lloyd Wright, 1949; cert., Inst. Gen. Semantics, Chgo., 1956; M.S., MIT, 1955; D.H.L. (hon.), Marycrest Coll., 1983; Ph.D. (hon.), U. Victoria, 1984, U. Zagreb, Yugoslavia, 1986. Head Ind. Design and Product Devel. Office, 1964—; instr. Ont. Coll. Art U. Toronto, 1954-59; vis. guest prof. creative engring. R.I. Sch. Design, Providence, 1959; assoc. prof. art and design SUNY-Buffalo, 1959-62; head dept. product design and assoc. prof. design N.C. State Coll., 1962-64; vis. guest critic Penland Sch. Crafts, N.C., summers 1963-67; assoc. prof. art and design Purdue U., Lafayette, Ind., 1964-68, prof., 1968-70, chmn. environ. and indsl. design dept., 1968-70; prof. Calif. Inst. Arts, Valencia, Calif., 1970-71, dean, 1971-72; vis. guest prof. Kunstakademiets Arkitekskole, Copenhagen, Denmark, 1972-73; vis. prin. lectr. Faculty of Art and Design Manchester Poly. Inst., 1973-75; vis. guest prof. architecture and indsl. design Carleton U., Ottawa, Ont., Can., 1975-76; prof., chmn. dept. design Kansas City Art Inst., 1976-81; J.L. Constant Disting. prof. design U. Kans., Lawrence, 1981—; scholar in residence Schumacher Coll., Dartington, Eng., 1991-93; design cons. WHO, Geneva, 1969—, Planet Products Pty. Australia, 1979—, Dartington Industries, South Devon, Eng., 1980-83, Croatia Products, Zagreb, Yugoslavia, 1984—. Author: Creative Engineering: Students Workbook, 1961, Creative Engineering: Instructor's Handbook, 1961, Miljon Och Miljonerna: Design Som Tjanst Eller Fortjanst, 1970, Design for the Real World: Human Ecology and Social Change, 1971, Big Character Poster No. 1: Work Chart for Designers, 1973, (with Jim Hennessey) Nomadic Furniture: Where to Buy and How to Build Furniture that Folds, Stacks, Inflates, Is Light-Weight for Moving, or Can Be Thrown Away and Recycled, 1973, Nomadic Furniture 2: More About Where to Buy and How to Build Furniture that Folds, Stacks, Inflates, Is Light-Weight for Moving, or Can Be Thrown Away and Be Recycled, 1974, (with Jim Hennessey) How Things Don't Work, 1977, Viewing the World Whole, 1983, Design for Human Scale, 1984, Design for the Real World, revised edit., 1985, The Green Imperative: Ecology and Ethics in Design and Architecture, 1995; contbr. chpts. to books, articles to profl. jours.; exhibitions: Mus. of Modern Art, N.Y.C., 1962, Internat. Design Ctr., West Berlin, 1973, Gallery Grada Zagreb, 1974. Recipient Design award UNESCO, 1963, Gold medal Art Dirs. Club Am., 1968, Honours award Internat. Coun. Socs. Indsl. Design, 1981, Augustus St. Gaudens medal Cooper Union, 1987, IKEA Internat. award Sweden and Holland, 1989, Lewis Mumford award for environment Architects, Designers & Planners for Social Responsibility, 1995. Fellow Chartered Soc. Designers, Am. Scandinavian Found. (hon.), Design Student Coun. New Zealand, Soc. Designers in Ireland, Design Soc. Mex. (diplomat), Creative Edn. Found.; mem. Internat. Congress Socs. of Indsl.

Design, Developing Countries Design Info. Group (co-founder), Industrielle Designere Danmark, Indsl. Design Inst. Australia, Indsl. Designers Soc. Am., Soc. Designers Ireland (hon. life), Croatian Designers Soc., Gliding Assn. Australia, Am. Soaring Soc., Grafik Design Austria. Anglican. Avocations: flying gliders and soaring planes; cookery; writing science fiction. Office: U Kans Sch Architecture Marvin Hall 417 Lawrence KS 66045

PAPARELLA, MICHAEL M., otolaryngologist; b. Detroit, Feb. 13, 1933; s. Vincent Paparella and Angela Creat; m. Treva Buzard, Oct. 2, 1992; children: Mark, Steven, Lisa. BS, U. Mich., 1953, MD, 1957. Diplomate Am. Bd. Otolaryngology (guest examiner 1967-75, bd. dirs. 1976, mem. standards and residencies com. 1976, fgn. med. grads. com. 1978, credentials com. 1984-85, examiner 1976—); lic. physician, Mich., Mass., Ohio, Minn. Rotating intern Emanuel Hosp., Portland, Oreg., 1957-58; resident in otolaryngology Henry Ford Hosp., Detroit, 1958-61, jr. mem. staff, 1960-61; mem. geographic staff, asst. Mass. Eye and Ear Infirmary, Boston, 1963-64; instr. Harvard U. Med. Sch., Boston, 1963-64; asst. prof. otolaryngology, dir. otological research lab. Ohio State U., Columbus, 1964-67; mem. staff dept. otolaryngology Ohio State U. Hosps., 1964-67; prof., chmn. dept. otolaryngology U. Minn., Mpls., 1967-84, dir. otopathology lab., 1967—, clin. prof., 1984—; mem. staff U. Minn. Hosps., 1967-84; pres. Minn. Ear, Head and Neck Clinic, Mpls., 1984—; dir. Nat. Temporal Bone Bank Program Midwestern Ctr., Mpls., 1979—; cons. VA Hosp., Dayton, Ohio, 1964-67. Mem. editl. bd. Minn. Med. Assn. Medicine, The Laryngoscope, Modern Medicine, Am. Jour. Clin. Rsch, Am. Jour. Otolaryngology, Annals Otology, Rhinology & Larynology, Acta Oto-Laryngologica; editor: (films) Surgical Techniques and Auditory Rsch., Surgical Treatment for Intractable External Otitis, Tympanoplasty, parts 1 and 2, Endolymphatic Sac, Canalplasty; (books) Atlas of Ear Surgery, 1968, 2d ed., 1971, 3d ed., 1980, Biochemical Mechanisms in Hearing and Deafness, 1970, Clinical Otology: An International Symposium, 1971, Year Book of the Ear, Nose and Throat, 1972-75, Otolarynology: Basic Sciences and Related Disciplines, 1973, 2d ed. vol I, 1980, Otolarynology: Ear, vol. II, 1973, 2d ed., 1980, Otolayrnology: Head and Neck, vol. III, 1973, 2d ed., 1980, Year Book of Otolarynology, 1976—, Boies's Fundamentals of Otolarynology: A Textbook of Ear, Nose and Throat Diseases, 5th ed., 1978, Ear Clinics International, vols. I-III. 1982, Medicassette Otolarynolgy, 1986; also contbr. numerous article to profl. pubs. Founder, sec., bd. dirs. Internat. Hearing Found., 1984—; mem. Presch. Med. Survey Vision and Hearing. Grantee NIH, Am. Otological Soc., Deafness Research Found., Hartford Found., Guggenheim Found., Bodman Found.; recipient Kobrak Research award, 1960, Amicitiae Sacrum honor Collegium Oto-Rhino-Laryngologicum, 1976; named Brinkman lectr. U. Nijmegen, Holland, 1986, Guest of Honor 5th Asia-Oceanic Meeting, Korea, 1983. Fellow ACS, Am. Acad. Ophthalmology and Otolaryngology (assoc. sec. continuing edn., assoc. sec., chmn. undergrad. edn. subcom., chmn. otorhinolaryngology self-improvement com., chmn. subcom. on evaluation new info. and edn. of hearing and equilibrium com., head and neck surgery equilibrium subcom. 1984-86, Merit award 1975); mem. Acad. Medicine Columbus County, Acad. Medicine Franklin County, Am. Assn. for Lab. Animal Scis., AMA, Am. Neurotology Soc. (audiology study com. 1976), Am. Otological Soc. (trustee research fund, pres.), Assn. Acad. Depts. Otolaryngology (pres. pro tem, organizer 1971-72, sec.-treas. 1972-74, pres. elect 1974-76, pres. 1976-78), Barany Soc., Better Hearing Inst. (adv. bd.), Deafness Research Found. (trustee, Centurion Club), Collegium Oto-Rhino-Laryngologicum Amicitiae Sacrum, Columbus Ophthalmology and Otolaryngological Soc., Hennepin County Med. Soc., Mpls. Hearing Soc. (bd. dirs.), Minn. Acad. Medicine, Minn. Acad. Ophthalmology and Otolaryngology (council), Minn. Coll. Surgeons, New England Otolaryngological Soc., Ohio State Med. Soc., Pan Am. Med. Assn., Soc. Univ. Otolaryngologists (exec. council 1969-71), Triological Soc. (v.p. middle sect. 1976, council mem. 1976, asst. editor), Alpha Kappa Kappa, Sigma Xi. Lodge: Lions (dir. hearing ctr., adv. council hearing ctr.). Office: 701 25th Ave S # 200 Minneapolis MN 55454-1443

PAPARELLI, ANGELO A., lawyer; b. Mich., 1949. BA, U. Mich., 1971; JD, Wayne State U., 1976. Bar: Mich. 1976, U.S. Supreme Ct. 1980, U.S. Ct. Appeals (6th cir.) 1980, Calif. 1981, U.S. Ct. Appeals (9th cir.) 1982. Law clk. to Hon. Dorothy C. Riley Mich. Ct. Appeals, 1976-78; ptnr. Bryan Cave, LLP, L.A. and Irvine, Calif. Mem. ABA (mem. immigration coordinating com. 1989-92, chmn. immigration nationality com., sect. internat. law and practice 1991—), Am. Immigration Lawyers Assn. (bd. govs. 1988-94, chair com. office mgmt. and budget/paperwork reduction act 1991-93, co-chair visa practice com. 1989-90, chair treaty investors and traders com. 1988-89, 90-91, 93-94, vice chair Dept. State visa office liaison com. 1987-88, chair task force on consular rev. and representation 1985, treas. 1985-86, vice chair 1986-87, chair 1987-88, So. Calif. chpt.), L.A. County Bar Assn. (mem. immigration sect. exec. bd. dirs. 1985—), State Bar Calif. (mem. standing com. profl. responsibility and conduct 1986-87). Office: Bryan Cave LLP Ste 1500 18881 Von Karman Blvd Irvine CA 92715-1500

PAPAS, IRENE KALANDROS, English language educator, writer, poet; b. Balt., Mar. 16, 1931; d. Louis and Kounia (Stamatakis) Kalandros; m. Steve S. Papas, Sept. 10, 1952; children: Fotene Stephenie Tina, Barbara Counia. AA with highest honors, Balt. C.C.; BA magna cum laude, Goucher Coll., 1968; MA in English Lang. and Lit., U. Md., 1974, postgrad., 1980—; postgrad., U. West Fla., 1990. Lic. theology profl.; cert. ESL tchr./tutor; cert. TV prodr. Tchr./tutor various schs., Balt., 1965—; tchr. theology U. Md. Free Univ., College Park, 1979—; author/pub. Ledger Publs., Silver Spring, Md., 1982—; TV producer Arts and Humanities Prodns., Silver Spring, 1991—; lectr. in English, philosophy, Montgomery Coll., Goucher Coll.; instr. English Composition, World Literature, U. Md., College Park, 1968—; adj. faculty various colls.; active White House Dept. Correspondence for Pres., 1993-94. Author: Irene's Ledger Songs of Deliverance, 1982, Irene's Ledger Song at Sabbatyon, 1986, Hawthorne's Ethan Brand: A Survey of Criticism and Comment, 1993, series Down to the Sea in Small Ships, 1991—, Small Meditations, Leaves for Healing, 1994; prodr./dir. tv. progs. Vol. prog. coord. Storyhour, All Saints Sch. Libr., Balt., 1960s, broadcasting/radio reading for the blind, Washington Ear, Silver Spring, 1970s; tutorial literary; election judge, Montgomery County (Md.) Suprs. Bd. of Elections, 1980's, 90's; mem. Byzantine Ch. Choir. Recipient First Prize Arts and Culture Category Smithsonian Inst., 1991; honored 6th Annual Awards Ceremony Montgomery Community T.V., Montgomery Coll. Performing Arts Ctr., 1991, 7th Ann. Awards Ceremony, 1992; also various grants. Mem. AAUP, Internat. Platform Assn., Nat. Poetry Assn., Phi Beta Kappa. Democrat. Greek Orthodox. Avocations: art/iconography, calligraphy, music, needlepoint. Office: PO Box 10303 Silver Spring MD 20914-0303

PAPAZIAN, DENNIS RICHARD, history educator, political commentator; b. Augusta, Ga., Dec. 15, 1931; s. Nahabed Charles and Armanouhe Marie (Pehlevanian) P.; m. Mary Arshagouni. BA, Wayne State U., 1954; MA, U. Mich., 1958; NDG, Moscow State U., 1962; PhD, U. Mich., 1966. Head dept. social and behavioral scis. U. Mich., Dearborn, 1966-69, head div. lit., sci. and the arts, 1969-73, assoc. dean acad. affairs, 1973-74; dir. Armenian Assembly Am., Washington, 1975-79; dir. grad. studies U. Mich., Dearborn, 1979-85, prof. history, dir. Armenian Rsch. Ctr., 1985—; fellow Ctr. for Russian and East-European Studies, U. Mich., Ann Arbor, 1982-92; chmn. bd. dirs. Mich. Ethnic Heritage Studies Ctr., U. Mich., 1987-92. Author: St. John's Armenian Church, 1974; editor: The Armenian Church, 1983, Out of Turkey, 1994; editor Jour. of Soc. Armenian Studies, 1995—. Bd. dirs. Armenian Apostolic Soc., Southfield, Mich., 1968-78; chmn. bd. dirs. Alex Manoogian Found., Taylor, Mich., 1969-77; mem. evaluation team Ind. Schs. Assn. Ctrl. States, Chgo., 1985; polit. commentator WXYZ-TV, ABC, Detroit, Southfield, 1984—, WWJ-Radio, Detroit, 1984—; bd. dirs. Southeastern Mich. chpt. ARC, 1988—, chmn. internat. svcs. com., 1988—, disaster and mil. family svcs. com., 1988—. Scholar/diplomat U.S. Dept. State, Washington, 1976; grantee NEH, Washington, 1977, AID, Washington, 1978, Knights of Vartan, 1984; recipient Dadian Armenian Heritage award, 1993. Mem. AAUP (chpt. pres. 1962-65), Nat. Assn. Armenian Studies and Rsch. (bd. dirs. 1961-91), Nat. Ethnic Studies Assn. (bd. dirs. 1976-85), Am. Hist. Assn., Soc. Armenian Studies (pres. exec. com. 1988-91, sec./treas. exec. com. 1991-95), Am. Assn. Advancement of Slavic Studies, Am. Acad. Polit. Sci., Armenian Students Assn. (Arthur S. Dadian Armenian Heritage award 1993), Knights of Vartan. Armenian Orthodox. Avocations: reading; travel. Home: 1935 Bluff Ct Troy MI 48098-6616 Office: U Mich 4901 Evergreen Rd Southfield MI 48075

PAPE, ARTHUR EDWARD, lawyer; b. Hartford, Conn., Oct. 30, 1939; s. Edward N. and Janet Pape; m. Barbara Nichols, Dec. 1962; children: Ann, Amy Pape Bloomberg. BA in English cum laude, U. Pitts., 1963; JD, Harvard U., 1965. Bar: Ohio 1965, Ill. 1976. Atty. Thompson, Hine & Flory, Cleve., 1965-73; ptnr. real estate devel. co. Bossel, Pape & Assoc., Cleve., 1973-75; sr. atty. 1st Nat. Bank Chgo., 1975-78, counsel, 1978-81; ptnr. Greenberger and Kaufmann, Chgo., 1981-86, Katten, Muchin & Zavis, Chgo., 1986—. Mem. ABA, Am. Coll. Real Estate Lawyers, Ill. Bar Assn. Chgo. Bar Assn., Lambda Alpha Internat. Home: 1002 S Wheaton Ave Wheaton IL 60187-6470 Office: Katten Muchin & Zavis 525 W Monroe St Ste 1600 Chicago IL 60661-3629

PAPE, PATRICIA ANN, social worker, consultant; b. Aurora, Ill., Aug. 2, 1940; d. Robert Frank and Helen Louise (Hanks) Grover; children: Scott Allen, Debra Lynn. BA in Sociology, Northwestern U., 1962; MSW, George Williams Coll., 1979. Cert. addictions counselor, Ill.; lic. clin. social worker, sch. social worker, Ill. Pvt. practice family counseling, 1979—; coord. community resources DuPage Probation Dept., Wheaton, Ill., 1977-80; dir. The Abbey Alcoholism Treatment Ctr., Winfield, Ill., 1980-81; prin. Pape & Assocs., Wheaton, 1982—; dir. alcoholism counselor tng. program Coll. of DuPage, Glen Ellyn, Ill., 1982-87; Chgo. affiliate Employee Assistance Program, 1982—; cons. Luth. Soc. Services Ill., 1979-82. Contbr. articles to profl. jours. Mem. alcohol drug task force Ill. Synod Luth. Ch. Am., Chgo., 1985—. Named Woman of Yr., Entrepreneur Women in Mgmt., Oak Brook, Ill, 1986. Mem. Assn. Labor-Mgmt. Adminstrs. Cons. Alcoholism (women's issues com. 1984—), Acad. Cert. Social Workers, Am. Assn. Marriage Family Therapists, Nat. Assn. Soc. Workers, Women in Mgmt. Home: 26w360 Churchill Rd Winfield IL 60190-2104 Office: Pape & Assocs 618 S West St Wheaton IL 60187-5038

PAPE, WILLIAM JAMES, II, newspaper publisher; b. Waterbury, Conn., Aug. 14, 1931; s. William B. and Helen (Cronan) P.; m. Patricia Moran, Oct. 15, 1959; children: William B. II, Andrew J. BS, U.S. Naval Acad., 1953; MBA, Harvard U., 1959; LHD (hon.), Teikyo Post U., 1991. Commd. ensign USN, 1953, advanced through grades to lt., 1955, resigned, 1957; asst. treas. Ea. Color Printing Co., Waterbury, 1959-63; pres., treas. Ea. Color Printing Co., Avon, Conn., 1977-87; v.p., asst. treas. Am.-Republican Inc., Waterbury, 1963-64, asst. publisher, comptroller, v.p., treas., 1964-72, pres., treas., 1972-88; pub. Waterbury Republican-Am., 1972—, editor, 1988—; also bd. dirs.; v.p., asst. treas. & dir. Paper Delivery, Inc., 1972-88; bd. dirs. Platt Bros., Waterbury. Bd. dirs. Conn. Coun. Freedom of Info., 1968-88, Conn. Bus. and Industry Assn., 1980-83, Naugatuck Valley Devel. Corp., Regional Action Coun., Waterbury, 1991; bd. dirs. Conn. Citizens for Jud. Modernization, pres., 1973-75; bd. dirs. Waterbury YMCA, 1970-78, trustee, 1972—, chmn. trustees, 1976-85; trustee Northeast Utilities, 1974—, Greater Waterbury Health Network Inc., 1993-95; mem. Conn. Pub. Expenditure Coun. Inc., 1974-77, dir. Conn. policy and econ. coun., 1994—; mem. Teikyo Post U., 1976—; grants com. Waterbury Found., 1980-87; pub. affairs com. Waterbury Hosp., 1984-90, past trustee; incorporator Conn. Found. for Open Govt. Inc.; active Conn. Legislature Commn. to Study Modernization and Unification of Cts., 1973-75, Citizens for Better Govt. Through Reorganization, 1977. Mem. Am. Judicature Soc. (assoc. dir. 1975-76), New England Newspaper Assn. (Conn. bd. govs. 1983-87), Conn. Bar Assn. (task force conflict of interest 1979—), Conn. Daily Newspaper Assn. (pres. 1970, exec. com. 1971-91), Waterbury C. of C. (exec. com., v.p. 1975, chmn. 1977-79, dir. 1980-83, vice-chmn. transp. 1981—), Navy League U.S. (communications bd. 1982), Waterbury Club, Madison Beach Club, Highfield. Republican. Roman Catholic. Avocations: sailing, firearms, walking, carpentry. Home: Old Sherman Hill Rd Woodbury CT 06798 Office: Waterbury Rep-Am PO Box 2090 389 Meadow St Waterbury CT 06722-2090

PAPENFUSE, EDWARD CARL, JR., archivist, state official; b. Toledo, Oct. 15, 1943; m. Sallie Fisher; children: Eric, David. BA in Polit. Sci., Am. U., 1965; MA in History, U. Colo., 1967; PhD, Johns Hopkins U., 1973. Assoc. editor Am. Hist. Rev., Washington, 1970-73; asst. archivist Md. Hall of Records, Annapolis, 1973-75, archivist, 1975—, commr. land patents, 1975—. Author: In Pursuit of Profit: The Annapolis Merchants in the Era of the American Revolution, 1975, (with others) Directory of Maryland Legislators, 1635-1789, 1974, (with others) Maryland: A New Guide to the Old Line State, 1976, The Hammond-Harwood House Atlas of Historical Maps of Maryland, 1608-1908, 1982, Doing Good to Posterity, 1995; also articles and revs. Mem. Johns Hopkins U. Med. Archives. NEH grantee; recipient Disting. Svc. award to State Govt. Nat. Gov.'s Assn., 1985, Marylander of Yr. award Md. Colonial Soc., 1985. Fellow Soc. Am. Archivists, Md. Hist. Soc., Am. Antiquarian Soc. Home: 206 Oakdale Rd Baltimore MD 21210-2520 Office: Md State Archives 350 Rowe Blvd Annapolis MD 21401-1685

PAPER, LEWIS J., lawyer, educator; b. Newark, Oct. 13, 1946; s. Sidney and Dorothy (Neiman) P.; m. Jan Clachko, Sept. 4, 1972; children—Lindsay, Brett. B.A., U. Mich., 1968; J.D., Harvard U., 1971; LL.M., Georgetown U., 1972. Bar: D.C. 1971, N.J. 1975, Md. 1984. Fellow, Inst. Pub. Interest Representation, Georgetown U. Law Sch., Washington, 1971-72; staff atty. Citizens Communications Ctr., Washington, 1972-73; legis. counsel to Sen. Gaylord Nelson, U.S. Senate, 1973-75; assoc. atty. Lowenstein, Sandler, Brochin, Kohl & Fisher, Newark, 1975-78; asst. gen. counsel Fed. Communications Commn., Washington, 1978-79, assoc. gen. counsel, 1979-81; ptnr. Grove, Engelberg & Gross, Washington, 1981-86, Keck, Mahin & Cate, 1986-95, Dickstein, Shapiro & Morin, LLP, Washington, 1995—; adj. prof. law Georgetown U. Law Sch., Washington, 1983-86. Author: John F. Kennedy: The Promise and the Performance, 1975, 79, Brandeis: An Intimate Biography, 1983, Empire: William S. Paley and the Making of CBS, 1987. Contbr. articles to newspapers, mags., and profl. jours. Office: Dickstein Shapiro & Morin LLP 2101 L St NW Washington DC 20037

PAPERNIK, JOEL IRA, lawyer; b. N.Y.C., May 4, 1944; s. Herman and Ida (Titefsky) P.; m. Barbara Ann Barker, July 28, 1972; children: Deborah, Ilana. BA, Yale U., 1965; JD cum laude, Columbia U., 1968. Bar: N.Y. 1969. Assoc. Shea & Gould, N.Y.C., 1968-76, ptnr., 1976-91; sr. ptnr., chmn. corp. and securities dept., mem. exec. com. Squadron, Ellenoff, Plesent & Sheinfeld, N.Y.C., 1991—; lectr. various panels. Author: Risks of Private Foreign Investments in the U.S. Served with USAR, 1967-73. Mem. ABA (sect. on corp. law, mem. forum on sports and entertainment law), N.Y. Sate Bar Assn. (lectr. various panels, mem. securities law com.), Assn. of Bar of City of N.Y. (chmn., lectr., mem. corp. law com., mem. securities regulation com. 1992-95(, N.Y. Tri-Bar Opinion Com., Yale Club. Office: Squadron Ellenoff Plesent & Sheinfeld 551 5th Ave New York NY 10176

PAPIANO, NEIL LEO, lawyer; b. Salt Lake City, Nov. 25, 1933; s. Leo and Ruth Ida (Cotten) P. B.A., Stanford, 1956, M.A. in Polit. Sci, 1957; J.D., Vanderbilt U., 1961. Bar: Calif. bar 1961. Partner Iverson, Yoakum, Papiano & Hatch (and predecessor firm), Los Angeles, 1961—; bd. dirs. Nederlander Orgn. and related cos., SCOA Industries, Inc., Ocean Tech., Inc., King Nutronics, Inc. V.p. Los Angeles County Welfare Planning Coun., 1966-71; chmn. L.A. Forward, 1970-71; vice chmn. Cal. Com. for Welfare Reform, 1972; mem. Calif. Jud. Selection Com., 1972-74; co-finance chmn. Rep. State Central Com., 1975; treas. L.A. Opera Co., 1964, bd. dirs., 1965; treas. So. Calif. Choral Music Assn., 1964, bd. dirs., 1964-73; bd. dirs. Citizens Adv. Coun. on Pub. Transp., Orthopedic Hosp., Stanford U. Athletic Bd., Nat. Athletic Health Inst., L.A. Music Ctr. Operating Co., L.A. Light Opera; bd. govs. USO, 1967-71, Performing Arts Coun. L.A. Music Ctr., 1981-87, Greater L.A. Homeless Partnership, 1985—, L.A. Olympic Com., 1986-88; bd. trustees The Am. U., 1980—. Mem. Am., Calif. bar assns., Los Angeles Area C. of C. (pres. 1966, dir. 1964-67, 72-75), California Club, Los Angeles Country Club, Rotary, Phi Delta Theta. Office: Iverson Yoakum Papiano & Hatch One Wilshire Bldg 27th Floor 624 S Grand Ave Ste 2700 Los Angeles CA 90017-3328

PAPINEAU-COUTURE, JEAN, composer, educator; b. Montreal, Que., Can., Nov. 12, 1916; s. Armand and Marie-Anne (Dostaler) P.-C.; m. Isabelle Baudouin, June 15, 1944 (dec. Oct. 1987); children—Nadia, Ghilaine, François. Doctorat honorifique, U. Sask., 1967. Prof. Conservatoire de Que., 1946-64; mem. faculté de musique U. Montreal, 1951-85; sec. faculté U. Montréal, 1953-67, vice-doyen, 1968, doyen, 1968-73. Composer several commd. works for, CBC also Zagreb Bienale, 1969—. Pres. Centre de Musique Canadienne, 1973-74, Société de musique contemporaine du Québec, 1966-73, Canadian Music Council, 1968-69; mem. Conseil canadien de Recherches pour les Scis. humaines, 1973-79; bd. dirs. Ency. Canadian Music. Recipient Prix Calixa Lavallée, 1962, Ordre du Can., 1968, Companion of Order of Can. 1994, médaille Centre Canadien de la musique, 1973, Prix Denise Pelletier, 1981, Diplôme D'Honneur of Can. Conf. of Arts, 1986, Gov. Gens. Performing Arts award, 1994; decorated grand officer de l'Ordre du Quebec, 1989. Mem. SOCAN. Home: 4694 Lacombe, Montreal, PQ Canada H3W 1R3

PAPKIN, ROBERT DAVID, lawyer; b. New Bedford, Mass., Feb. 26, 1933; s. Barney and Rose (Shuster) P.; m. Rachel Friedberg, Aug. 29, 1965; children: Steven C., Daniel M. AB, Harvard U., 1954, LLB, 1957. Bar: Mass. 1957, D.C. 1964. Legal asst. NRLB, Washington, 1958-61; assoc. Cox, Langford & Brown, Washington, 1963-66, ptnr., 1966-73; ptnr. Squire, Sanders & Dempsey, Washington, 1973—. Trustee Art Svcs. Internat., 1990—, Am. Friends of the Venezuelan Indians, 1991—. Served with U.S. Army, 1957-58, 61-62. Mem. ABA, D.C. Bar Assn., Fed. Bar Assn., Internat. Bar Assn., Met. Club Washington D.C., Cosmos Club. Democrat. Jewish. Home: 9702 Leeds Landing Cir Easton MD 21601 Office: Squire Sanders & Dempsey PO Box 407 1201 Pennsylvania Ave NW Washington DC 20004-2401

PAPP, LASZLO GEORGE, architect; b. Debrecen, Hungary, Apr. 28, 1929; came to U.S., 1956; m. Judith Liptak, Apr. 12, 1952; children: Andrea, Laszlo-Mark (dec. 1978). Archtl. Engr., Poly. U. Budapest, 1955; MArch, Pratt Inst., 1960. Designer Harrison & Abramovitz, Architects, N.Y.C., 1958-63; ptnr. Whiteside & Papp, Architects, White Plains, N.Y., 1963-67; pres. Papp Architects, P.C., White Plains, N.Y., 1967-96, chmn. Mem. Pres.'s Adv. Com. on Pvt. Sector Initiatives; mem. adv. com. Westchester C.C., 1971-75, Iona Coll., New Rochelle, N.Y., 1982-87, Norwalk State Tech. Coll., 1983—; v.p. Clearview Sch., 1985-89, pres., 1990-91; mem. Town Coun. New Canaan, Conn., 1993—. Fellow AIA (reg. dir. 1983-85); mem. Internat. Union Architects (rep. habitat com. 1986-90), N.Y. State Assn. Architects (v.p. 1977-80, pres. 1981), Am.-Hungarian Engrs. Assn. (bd. dirs. 1978-90), Am. Coun. World Fedn. Hungarians (pres. 1993—), Hungarian Univ. Assn. (pres. 1958-60), Westchester County C. of C. (bd. dirs. 1968-71, vice chmn. bd. for area devel. 1983-89, chmn. bd. dirs. 1989-90), Am.-Hungarian C. of C. (charter 1989—). Home: 1197 Valley Rd New Canaan CT 06840-2428 Office: Papp Architects PC 7-11 S Broadway White Plains NY 10601-3531

PAPP, LEANN ILSE KLINE, respiratory therapy educator; b. Niles, Ohio, June 18, 1944; d. Lee Andrew and Mildred Alice (Vaughan) Kline; m. Roger John Papp, July 11, 1964; 1 child, Lisa Marie. Student, John Carroll U., 1962-63; AAS in Respiratory Therapy, Sinclair C.C., Dayton, Ohio, 1975; ADN, Manatee Jr. Coll., Bradenton, Fla., 1983; B in Allied Health Edn., Ottawa U. of Kansas City, Overland Park, Kans., 1988; MS in Health and Wellness, Calif. Coll. Health Scis., 1995. RN, Fla., Ark.; cert. respiratory therapy technologist, registered respiratory therapist, BCLS instr., Am. Heart Assn., cert. hypnotherapist. Staff therapist Childrens' Med. Ctr., Dayton, 1975-79; staff therapist L.W. Blake Hosp., Bradenton, Fla., 1979; chief therapist The Breath Ctr., Sarasota, Fla., 1979-83; mem. clin. faculty Sarasota Meml. Hosp., 1983-84; spl. procedures therapist, mem. clin. faculty North Little Rock (Ark.) Meml. Hosp., 1984-85; clin. edn. coord. St. Vincent Infirmary, Little Rock, 1985-86; dir. clin. edn. for respiratory therapy tech. Pulaski Vo-Tech, North Little Rock, 1986-88; staff therapist Cobb Gen. Hosp., Austell, Ga., 1988-89; program dir. respiratory therapy tech. Coosa Valley Tech. Inst., Rome, Ga., 1989—; cons. Applied Measurement Profls., Lenexa, Kans, 1991-92, 93-94; faculty Am. Heart Assn., Marietta, Ga., 1989—; advisor Ga. Coun. on Vocat. Edn., Atlanta, 1991-94; mem. ednl. commn. Author: Nosocomial Infection and Control, 1993; co-author: Georgia State Standards-Respiratory Therapy Technology, 1989-90, 93-94. Co-chairperson Cystic Fibrosis Found., Atlanta, 1990; mem. Am. Lung Assn., 1995, bd. dirs., 1995. Recipient Commr.'s award of Excellence Ga. Dept. Tech. and Adult Edn., 1994. Mem. Am. Assn. Respiratory Care, Ga. Soc. Respiratory Care (mem. edn. com. 1993—, mem. health care reform com. 1995), Ga. Vocat. Assn., Health Occupations Educators (Outstanding New Tchr. award 1992), Lambda Beta Soc. Office: Coosa Valley Tech Inst 785 Cedar Ave Rome GA 30161

PAPPAGIANIS, DEMOSTHENES, microbiology educator, physician; b. San Diego, Mar. 31, 1928; s. George John and Mary (Terzakis) P.; m. Alice Ertel, Jan. 28, 1956; children: Michele, Marika. A.B., U. Calif.-Berkeley, 1949, M.A., 1951, Ph.D., 1956; M.D., Stanford U., 1962. Diplomate Am. Bd. Microbiology. Rotating intern Walter Reed Gen. Hosp., Washington, 1962-63; asso. prof. Sch. Public Health, U. Calif., Berkeley, 1963-67; prof. med. microbiology Sch. Medicine, U. Calif., Davis, 1967—; chmn. dept. med. microbiology Sch. Medicine, U. Calif., 1968-85; asso. mem. Armed Forces Epidemiol. Bd. Contbr. to profl. jours. and books. Served from 1st lt. to capt. M.C. U.S. Army, 1962-63. Recipient Meridian award Med. Mycol. Soc. Ams., 1986, Calif. medal Am. Lung Assn. Calif., 1988, Rhoda Benham award Med. Mycol. Soc. Am., 1992, Charles E. Smith Meml. award Coccidioidomycosis Study Group, 1994. Fellow Infectious Disease Soc. Am.; mem. Am. Soc. Microbiology, Am. Thoracic Soc., Calif. Thoracic Soc., Internat. Soc. Human and Animal Mycology, Sigma Xi, Alpha Omega Alpha. Home: 1523 Orange Ln Davis CA 95616-0912 Office: U Calif Sch Medicine Dept Med Microbiology Davis CA 95616

PAPPANO, ROBERT DANIEL, financial company executive; b. Chgo., Apr. 8, 1942; s. John Robert and Lucille Carmelita (Metallo) P.; m. Karen Marie Muellner, July 2, 1966; children: John, Kimberly, Robert, William. BS in Commerce, DePaul U., Chgo., 1964; MBA, Roosevelt U., Chgo., 1982. CPA, Ill. Audit supr. Alexander Grant & Co., Chgo., 1964-73; with W.W. Grainger, Inc., Skokie, Ill., 1973—, asst. to contr., 1973-75, contr., corp. acct., 1975-78, contr., asst. treas., 1978-84, v.p., contr., asst. treas., 1984-85, v.p., treas., asst sec., 1985-95; v.p. financial reporting and investor rels., 1995—. 1st lt. U.S. Army, 1965-67, Vietnam. Mem. AICPA, Ill. CPA Soc., Fin. Execs. Inst. Roman Catholic. Office: W W Grainger Inc 5500 Howard St Skokie IL 60077-2620

PAPPAS, ALCESTE THETIS, consulting company executive, educator; b. Dix Hills, N.Y., May 5, 1945; d. Costas Ernest and Thetis (Hero) P.; m. Sylvan V. Endich, Sept. 13, 1987. AB, U. Calif.-Berkeley, 1967, PhD, 1978; EdM, Harvard U., 1969. Cert. guidance counselor, Mass., secondary sch. tchr., Mass. Dir. student-young alumni affairs Calif. Alumni Assn., Berkeley, 1969-71; dir. residential programs U. Calif., Berkeley, 1971-73, dir. housing and childcare, 1973-79; sr. cons., mgr. Peat, Marwick, Mitchell & Co., N.Y.C., 1979-80, 80-82, sr. mgr., 1982-84; ptnr. in charge edn., other instns. Peat, Marwick, Main & Co., N.Y.C., 1984-93; pres. Pappas Cons. Group, Inc., Greenwich, Conn., 1993—; spkr. in field. Author: Reengineering Your Non-Profit Organization: A Guide to Strategic Transformation, 1996; contbr. articles to profl. jours., author monographs. Mem. Merola Opera Bd., San Francisco, 1978-80, Calif. Alumni Council, 1976-79; bd. overseers Regents Coll., 1986-89; bd. dirs., mem. fin. com. Hellenic Coll. and Holy Cross Sch. Theology, Brookline, Mass., 1983-87, Seabury Western Theol. Sem., Evanston, Ill., 1983-89; bd. dirs. N.Y. Chiropractic Coll., 1986-88, Com. on Econ. Devel., 1986-88, Greek Orthodox Archdiocese Council, N.Y.C., 1985-89; bd. dirs., vice chmn. St. Basil Acad., 1983-87; bd. dirs., mem. exec. com. YWCA, N.Y.C., 1985-90, Catalyst, 1988-90; chairperson capital campaign com. U. Calif., Berkeley, exec. v.p. exec. coun. Coll. Letters and Sci.; trustee Clark U., U. Calif. Found., 1993; bd. dirs. Empire Coll., 1983-87. Named mem. Acad. Women Achievers, YWCA, N.Y.C., 1984. Mem. Mid. States Assn. Schs. and Colls. (bd. dirs., fin. com. 1984-89, planning com. 1988-89), Mortar Bd., Pi Lambda, Lambda Theat, Prytanean. Avocations: opera; gourmet cooking; travel. Office: Pappas Cons Group Inc 2 Greenwich Plz Ste 100 Greenwich CT 06830-3000

PAPPAS, CHARLES ENGELOS, plastic surgeon; b. Phila., May 20, 1946; s.Engelos George and Angelina (Biniaris) P.; m. Marilyn Ann Pappas; children: Evan, Angela, Chrysten. BA, BS, U. Pa., 1968; MD, Temple U., 1972. Intern, then resident in gen. surgery Johns Hopkins Hosp., Balt., 1972-75; resident in gen. surgery Temple U. Hosp., Phila., 1975-76, resident in plastic surgery, 1976-78, chmn. dept. plastic surgery, 1978-81, clin. assoc. prof. surgery, 1981—; chief dept. plastic surgery Meml. Hosp., Phila., 1986—; clin. assoc. plastic surgery Chestnut Hill Hosp., Phila., 1979—, chief/dir. dept. plastic surgery, 1994—; dir. Inst. for Aesthetic Plastic Surgery, Ft.

Washington, Pa., 1985—; chmn. bd. Am. Gaming Industries, 1984—; dir., ptnr. Tristate Quicklube Co., 1982-91, Medars; pres., dir. two carwash cos., Phila., 1989—. Contbr. articles to profl. jours. Trustee Germantown Acad., Ft. Washington, 1986—, Commonwealth Nat. Country Club, Horsham, 1988—, Patrons' Charity Found. Fellow ACS, Royal Coll. Surgeons; mem. Am. Soc. Plastic Reconstructive Surgeons (diplomate), Am. Soc. Aesthetic Plastic Surgeons (diplomate), Phila. Soc. Plastic Surgeons (pres. 1990-92). Greek Orthodox. Avocations: golf, tennis, investing, skiing. Office: Inst Aesthetic Plastic Surgery 467 Pennsylvania Ave Ste 202 Fort Washington PA 19034-3420

PAPPAS, EDWARD HARVEY, lawyer; b. Midland, Mich., Nov. 24, 1947; s. Charles and Sydell (Sheinberg) P.; m. Laurie Weston, Aug. 6, 1972; children: Gregory Alan, Steven Michael. BBA, U. Mich., 1969, JD, 1973. Bar: Mich. 1973, U.S. Dist. Ct. (ea. dist.) Mich. 1973, U.S. Dist. Ct. (we. dist.) Mich. 1980, U.S. Ct. Appeals (6th cir.) 1983, U.S. Supreme Ct. 1983. Ptnr. firm Dickinson, Wright, Moon, Van Dusen & Freeman, Detroit and Bloomfield Hills, Mich., 1973—; mediator Oakland County Cir. Ct., Pontiac, Mich., 1983—; hearing panelist Mich. Atty. Discipline Bd., Detroit, 1983—, chmn., 1987—; mem. bus. tort subcom. Mich. Supreme Ct. Com. Standard Jury Instructions, 1992-94. Trustee Oakland Community Coll., Mich., 1982-90, Oakland-Livingston Legal Aid, 1982-90, v.p., 1982-85, pres., 1985-87; trustee, adv. bd. Mich. Regional Anti-Defamation League of B'nai B'rith, Detroit, 1983-90; mem. nat. and community rels. agy. div. Jewish Welfare Fedn.; planning commr. Village of Franklin, Mich., 1987-91, chmn. 1989-91, councilman, 1991-92, chmn. charter com., 1993-94; bd. dirs. Franklin Found., 1989-92; trustee The Settlement Ctr., 1992—. Fellow Mich. State Bar Found., Oakland Bar-Adams Pratt Found., ABA Found.; mem. ABA, Fed. Bar Assn., State Bar Mich. (co-chmn. nat. moot ct. competition com. 1974, 76, com. on legal aid, chmn. standing com. on atty. grievances 1989-92, comml. litigation com., civil procedure com. 1992-94), Oakland County Bar Assn. (vice-chmn. continuing legal edn. com., chmn. continuing legal edn. com. 1985-86, mediation com. 1989-90, chmn. mediation com. 1990-91, bd. dirs. 1990—, chmn. select com. Oakland County cir. ct. settlement week 1991, chmn. strategic planning com. 1992-93, editor Laches monthly mag. 1986-88, co-chair task force to improve justice systems in Oakland County 1993—), Am. Judicature Soc., Mich. Def. Trial Lawyers, Def. Rsch. and Trial Lawyers Assn., (com. practice and procedure), B'nai B'rith Barristers. Home: 32223 Scenic Ln Franklin MI 48025-1702 Office: Dickinson Wright Moon Van Dusen & Freeman 525 N Woodward Ave Bloomfield Hills MI 48304-2971

PAPPAS, EFFIE VAMIS, English and business educator, writer; b. Cleve., Dec. 26, 1924; d. James Jacob and Helen Joy (Nicholson) Vamis; m. Leonard G. Pappas, Nov. 3, 1945; children: Karen Pappas Morabito, Leonard J., Ellen Pappas Daniels, David James. BBA, Western Res. U., 1948; MA in Edn., Case Western Res. U., 1964; MA in English Lit., Cleve. State U., 1986; postgrad., Indiana U. Pa., 1979-80, 81-86. Cert. elem. and secondary tchr., Ohio. Tchr. elem. schs., Ohio, 1963-70; office mgr. Cleve. State U., 1970-72, adminstr. pub. relations, 1972-73; med. adminstr. Brecksville (Ohio) VA Hosp., 1974-78; lectr. English, bus. mgmt., math., comm., composition Cuyahoga C.C., Cleve., 1978-92; tchg. asst. Case Western Reserve U., 1979-80; lectr. bus. comms. Cleve. State U., 1980; participant in Sci. and Cultural Exch. dels. Am. Inst. Chemists, to Peoples Republic of China, 1984 and to Soviet Union, 1989. Feature writer The Voice, 1970-78; editor, writer Cleve. State U. newsletter and mag., 1970-73. Cub scout den mother Boy Scouts Am., Brecksville, 1960; mem. local coun. PTA, 1965-70; sec. St. Paul's Coun., 1990-91; Sunday Sch. tchr., mem. choir Brecksville United Ch. of Christ, 1975-76, mem. bd. missions, 1966-67, membership com. 1993, St. Paul Ladies Philoptohos, 1990-96; mem. Women's Econ. Action League. Recipient Editor's Choice award for outstanding achievement in poetry, Nat. Libr. of Poetry, 1995; grantee Cuyahoga C.C., 1982; named to Nat. Women's Hall of Fame. Mem. NEA, NAFE, AAUW (legis. chair, del. Ohio meetings 1993, 94, del. Ohio Coalition for Change, 1993, 94, mem. Ohio and Cleve. br. del. Gt. Lakes regional meeting 1994, internat. co-chair Cleve. br. 1994, del. to Internat. Fedn. Univ. Women triennial meeting Stanford U. 1992), AARP, Ohio Edn. Assn. (rep. assembly Columbus 1994), Nat. Mus. Women in Arts (hon. roll mem.), Nat. Trust for Hist. Preservation, Case Western Res. U. Planning Com. for Edn. Forum, Greater Cleve. Learning Project, Nature Conservancy, Smithsonian Instn., Internat. Soc. Poets. Avocations: entertaining, travel, reading, theater, correspondence with nat., internat. friends. Home: 8681 Brecksville Rd Cleveland OH 44141-1912

PAPPAS, GEORGE DEMETRIOS, anatomy and cell biology educator, scientist; b. Portland, Maine, Nov. 26, 1926; James and Anna (Dracopoulos) Pappatheodoros; m. Bernice Levine, Jan. 14, 1952; children: Zoe Alexandra, Clio Nicollette. BA, Bowdoin Coll., 1947; MS, Ohio State U., 1948, PhD, 1952; DSc (hon.), U. Athens, Greece, 1988. Vis. investigator Rockefeller Inst., N.Y.C., 1952-54; assoc. in anatomy Coll. Physicians and Surgeons, Columbia U., N.Y.C., 1956-57, asst. prof. anatomy, 1957-63, assoc. prof., 1963-66; prof. anatomy Albert Einstein Coll. Medicine, Yeshiva U., N.Y.C., 1967-77, prof. neurosci., 1974-77, vis. prof. neurosci., 1977—; prof., head dept. anatomy and cell biology U. Ill. Coll. Medicine, Chgo., 1977—; trustee Marine Biol. Lab., Woods Hole, Mass., 1975-81. Author: (with others) The Structure of the Eye, 1961, Growth and Maturation of the Brain, vol. IV, 1964, Nerve as a Tissue, 1966, The Thalmus, 1966, Pathology of the Nervous System, vol. 1, 1968, Structure and Function of Synapses, 1972, Methodological Approaches to the Study of Brain Maturation and Its Abnormalities, 1974, Advances in Neurology, vol.12, 1975, The Nervous System, vol. 1 The Basic Neurosciences, 1975, Cellular and Molecular Basis of Synaptic Transmission, 1988, also author many conf. procs.; contbr. over 200 articles to profl. jours.; former mem. editorial bd. Anatomical Record, Biol. Bull., Brain Rsch., Jour. Neurocytology, Microstructure; patentee method inducing analgesia by implantation of cells releasing neuroactive substances. Arthritis and Rheumatism Found. fellow, 1954-56; recipient career devel. award Columbia U., 1964-66; rsch. grantee NIH. Fellow AAAS, N.Y. Acad. Scis., Inst. Medicine Chgo.; mem. Am. Soc. Cell Biology (pres. 1974-75), Am. Assn. Anatomists (chmn. pub. policy com. 1981-82), Assn. Anatomy Chmn. (exec. com. 1978-80, pres. 1981-82), Electron Microscopy Soc. Am. (program chmn. 1984-85), N.Y. Soc. Electron Microscopy (pres. 1967-68), Soc. for Neurosci. (pres. Chgo. chpt. 1985-86), Harvey Soc., Internat. Brain Rsch. Orgn., Cajal Club, Sigma Xi. Home: 506 W Roscoe St Chicago IL 60657-3535 Office: U Ill Coll Medicine Dept Anatomy & Cell Biology 808 S Wood St Chicago IL 60612-7300

PAPPAS, GEORGE FRANK, lawyer; b. Washington, Oct. 5, 1950; s. Frank George and Lora Marie (Stauber) P.; m. Susan Elizabeth Bradshaw, Apr. 25, 1980; children: Christine Bradshaw, Alexandra Stauber. BA, U. Md., 1972, JD, 1975. Bar: Md. 1976, D.C. 1991, U.S. Dist. Ct. Md. 1976, U.S. Dist. Ct. (D.C. cir.) 1986, U.S. Dist. Ct. (we. dist.) Tex. 1993, U.S. Ct. Appeals (4th cir.) 1976, U.S. Ct. Appeals (D.C. cir.) 1984, U.S. Ct. Appeals (fed. cir.) 1991, U.S. Ct. Appeals (2d cir.) 1993, U.S. Ct. Appeals (6th and 7th cirs.) 1994, U.S. Supreme Ct. 1984, U.S. Ct. of Fed. Claims, 1995. Assoc. H. Russell Smouse, Balt., 1976-81; assoc. Melnicove, Kaufman, Wiener & Smouse, Balt., 1981-83, prin., 1983-88; ptnr. Venable, Baetjer and Howard, Balt., 1988—; lectr. Wash. Coll. Law, Am. U., Washington, 1980-84; mem. moot ct. bd., 1974-75; Master of the Bench , Inn XIII, Am. Inns of Ct., 1989. Founding editor-in-chief Internat. Trade Law Jour., 1974-75. 1st lt. USAF, 1972-76. Mem. ABA, Nat. Assn. R.R. Trial Counsel, Internat. Assn. Def. Counsel, Md. Bar Assn. (chmn. internat. coml. law sect., 1980-81), Am. Intellectual Property Law Assn., U.S. Trademark Assn., Omicron Delta Kappa, Phi Kappa Phi, Phi Beta Kappa. Republican. Greek Orthodox. Club: L'Hirondelle. Home: 9 Roland Ct Baltimore MD 21204-3550 Office: Venable Baetjer & Howard 2 Hopkins Plaza Baltimore MD 21201 also: 1201 New York Ave NW Ste 1000 Washington DC 20005-3917

PAPPAS, JOHN GEORGE, secondary school educator; b. Munich, Germany, May 8, 1962; parents U.S. citizens; s. Michael Thomas and Sophie Athens (Stambolis) P. BS in Bus. Adminstrn. and Mgmt., La Roche Coll., 1985; math./secondary education cert., California U. Pa., 1993. Acct., bookkeeper South Hills Anesthesia Assocs., Pitts., 1986-87; personal fitness instr. and sales profl. Prince's Gym, Canonsburg, Pa., 1988-92; math. tchr. Baldwin-Whitehall Sch. Dist., Pitts., 1993—; sponsor Freshmen Class, Pitts., 1993—. Asst. coord. Spl. Olympics, Baldwin H.S., 1994. Mem. Nat. Coun. Tchrs. Math., Baldwin Transition Team. Home: 2009 Clearfork Rd Bridgeville PA 15017-1605

PAPPAS, MARIA ELENI, nurse; b. Encino, Calif., Oct. 1, 1960; d. Nicholas Constantine and Helen Cleo (Tannors) P. BSN, U. San Francisco, 1985; M in Nursing, UCLA, 1991. Cert. critical care nurse, pub. health nurse. Staff med./surg. nurse VA Med. Ctr., West L.A., 1985-87; staff nurse ICU VA Med. Ctr., San Francisco, 1987-88; staff nurse SICU St. Mary's Hosp., San Francisco, 1988-89; staff nurse ICU St. Joseph's Hosp., Burbank, Calif., 1989-91; clin. nurse specialist Northridge (Calif.) Hosp. Med. Ctr., 1991-95; asst. clin. prof. Sch. Nursing, UCLA, 1993—. Co-author: (manual) Brain Death Policy Manual, 1993. VA scholar U. San Francisco, 1984, Reynolds Estate scholar UCLA, 1991. Mem. Sigma Theta Tau (Outstanding Contbn. award 1989). Greek Orthodox. Avocations: tennis, cross-stitch, swimming, pistol range, skiing. Home: 8012 Comanche Ave Winnetka CA 91306-1832 Office: GHCH/UCLA Heart Ctr 10445 Balboa Blvd Granada Hills CA 91394-9400

PAPPAS, PHILIP JAMES, real estate company executive; b. Chgo., Sept. 29, 1954; s. Nicholas James and Ann (Nicholson) P.; m. Ana Lucia Sant'Anna; children: Tiago, Marcelo, Amanda. BA, Shimer Coll., 1975. Mgr. Cook County Hosp., Chgo., 1975-77, purchasing agt., 1977-81; pres. L.G. Properties, Chgo., 1980—, Tiamar Real Estate, 1990—; docent Chgo. Archictecture Found., 1976-78. Life mem. OSA Boy Scouts Am.; v.p. Lincoln Park Builders Assn., Lake View Developers, pres., 1988-89. Recipient 1st pl. award for best interior restoration Nat. Hist. Trust for Preservation, 1991, Good Neighbor award for exceptional property restoration Northwide Real Estate Bd. Chgo. and Nat. Assn. Realtors, 1992, 95. Mem. Oxford Union Soc. (life), Chgo. Assn. Realtors. Greek Orthodox. Office: L G Properties 3654 N Lincoln Chicago IL 60613

PAPPE, STUART H., film editor. Editor: (films) The Killers, 1964, The Loved One, 1965, The President's Analyst, 1967, Bob & Carol & Ted & Alice, 1969, Alex in Wonderland, 1970, (with Gordon Scott and Maury Winetrobe) The Gumball Rally, 1976, An Unmarried Woman, 1978, Oliver's Story, 1978, (with Ronald Roose) The Wanderers, 1979, Carny, 1980, Class, 1983, Songwriter, 1984, (with Robert Lawrence) 8 Million Ways to Die, 1986, The Big Town, 1987, Moon Over Parador, 1988, Enemies, A Love Story, 1989, Scenes from a Mall, 1991, What's Love Got to Do with It?, 1993, (with John Carter and Pembroke Herring) Sister Act 2: Back in the Habit, 1993. Office: care Motion Picture Editors 7715 W Sunset Blvd Ste 220 Los Angeles CA 90046-3912

PAPPENFUS, MABEL LOUISE, retired educator; b. Porter, Minn., Sept. 21, 1926; d. Clarence Nels and Sadie Elizabeth (Gillespie) Rasmussen; m. Ben Pappenfus, June 13, 1957 (dec. Sept. 1989); 1 child, Bettyann. BS, St. Cloud (Minn.) State U., 1956. Elem. tchr. pub. schs., Aurora, Minn., 19544-56, Hutchinson, Minn., 1956-57; elem. tchr. Benton County Rurala Schs., Foley, Minn., 1957-62, Sch. Dist. 742, St. Cloud, 1968-85; supt. schs. Benton County, 1962-68; dir. Sch. Bd. Dist. 51, Foley, 1985-93; ret., 1993. Mem. coun. Gethsemane Luth. Ch., Oak Park, Minn., 1975—, also treas. Ch. Women and other offices; dir. Benton County Dem.-Farmer-Labor Party, 1983-94. Recipient Friend of Edn. award Ea. Minn. Uniserv, 1992, Dem.-Farmer Labor award for dedicated svc., 1995. Mem. NEA (life), Minn. Edn. Assn. (life), Future Farmers Am. (hon. mem. Foley chpt.), Benton County 4-H Leaders Assn. (Pioneer award 1989), Kiwanis. Avocations: reading, sewing, football, Scrabble, baking. Home: 1128 Laurel Ave Saint Paul MN 55104-6921

PAPPER, EMANUEL MARTIN, anesthesiologist; b. N.Y.C., July 12, 1915; s. Max and Lillian (Weitzner) P.; m. Patricia Meyer, Nov. 30, 1975; children: Richard Nelson Papper, Patrick Goldstein, Amy Goldstein. AB, Columbia U., 1935; MD, NYU, 1938; MD (hon.), Univ. Uppsala, Sweden, 1964, U. Turin, Italy, 1969, U. Vienna, Austria, 1977; DSc (hon.), Columbia U., 1988; PhD, U. Miami, 1990. Diplomate Am. Bd. Anesthesiology (dir. 1956-65, pres. 1964-65). Fellow medicine NYU, 1938-39, fellow physiology, 1940, asst. prof., 1946-49, assoc. prof., 1949; intern Bellevue Hosp., 1939-40, resident in anesthesiology, 1940-42; prof. anesthesiology, chmn. dept. Columbia U.; also dir. anesthesiology service Presbyn. Hosp., 1949- 69; dir. anesthesiology, vis. anesthesiologist Francis Delafield Hosp., 1951-69; v.p. med affairs, dean, prof. anesthesiology U. Miami, 1969-81, prof. pharmacology, 1972-81; dir. Abbott Labs., No. Trust Bank of Fla., Miami; cons. div. med. scis. NRC, 1954-69, Huntington (N.Y.) Hosp., 1949-69; nat. cons. surgeon gen. USAF, 1963-70; mem. surgery study sect. NIH, 1958-62; civilian cons. First Army, USN; prin. cons. Nat. Inst. Gen. Med. Scis., 1965-66, chmn. project com. gen. med. research program, 1966-70; mem. nat. heart council NIH, 1962-66; hon. cons. Royal Prince Alfred Hosp., Sydney, Australia. Author 250 sci. papers pub. in various med. jours., 3 textbooks. Bd. dirs. PBS-Channel 2, Miami, 1984—. Served from 1st lt. to maj. M.C. U.S. Army, 1942-46; chief anesthesiology sect. Torney, Dibble and Walter Reed hosps. Recipient Silver medal City of Paris, 1972; established E.M. Papper chair in anesthesiology Columbia U. Coll. Physicians and Surgeons, 1984, E.M. Papper lectures in anesthesiology Columbia U. and UCLA, 1978. Hon. fellow Royal Coll. Anaesthetists (England), Royal Coll. Surgeons (Ireland, faculty anaesthetists), Royal Soc. Medicine (England); mem. N.Y. Acad. Medicine (1st pres. sect. anesthesiology), Am. Surg. Assn., Am. Soc. Anesthesiologists (pres. 1967-68), N.Y. State Soc. Anesthesiologists (past pres.), NRC (chmn. com. anesthesia 1962-67), Am. Coll. Anesthesiologists, World Fedn. Soc. Anesthesiologists (v.p.), Am. Soc. Pharmacology and Exptl. Therapeutics, AMA, N.Y. Acad. Scis., N.Y. Co. Med. Soc., Am., N.Y. socs. anesthesiologists, AAAS, Am. Assn. Thoracic Surgery, Harvey Soc, Am. Soc. Clin. Investigation, Am. Thoracic Soc., Assn. Univ. Anesthetists (co-founder, 1st pres.), Pan Am. Med. Assn., Assn. Anaesthetists Gt. Britain and Ireland (hon.), Swedish Soc. Anesthesiologists (hon. mem.), Finnish Soc. Anesthesiologists (hon. mem.), Israeli Soc. Anesthesiologists (hon. mem.), Australian Soc. Anaesthesiologists (hon. mem.), N.Y. State Soc. Anesthesiologists (hon. mem.), D.C. Soc. Anesthesiologists (hon. mem.), Calif. Soc. Anesthesiologists (hon. mem.), German Soc. Anesthesiologists (hon. mem.), Halsted Soc., Japan Soc. Anesthesiologists (hon.), Am. Soc. Anesthesiologists (pres. 1969), European Acad. Anesthesiology (hon., Gold medal), Phi Beta Kappa, Sigma Xi, Alpha Omega Alpha. Clubs: Cosmos (Washington); Century Assn. (N.Y.C.). Home: 1 Grove Isle Dr Miami FL 33133 Office: PO Box 016370 Miami FL 33101-6370

PAPSIDERO, JOSEPH ANTHONY, social scientist, educator; b. Niagara Falls, N.Y., Nov. 7, 1929; s. Vincent and Mary Angela (Gallo) P.; m. Wilma Alice Toye, Aug. 26, 1950; children: Michael J., John A., Mary J., Mark V. EdB, U. Buffalo, 1953, EdM, 1956; MPH, U. N.C., 1961; EdD, Case Western Res. U., 1970. Health educator North Tonawanda (N.Y.) Dept. Pub. Health, 1953-56; health educator, asst. exec. dir. Tb and Heart Assn. of Montgomery County, Md., 1956-61; USPHS trainee, 1960-61; program dir. Tb and Respiratory Disease Assn. of Cleve., 1961-67; planning assoc. Health Planning and Devel. Commn., Health and Welfare Fedn. of Cleve., 1967-69; planning cons. Met. Health Planning Corp., Cleve., 1969-71; sr. instr. dept. cmty. health Sch. Medicine, Case Western Res. U., Cleve., 1969-71; asst. prof. human medicine Mich. State U., East Lansing, 1971-73, assoc. prof., 1973-77, prof., 1977-78, prof. community health scis. Coll. Human Medicine and Coll. Osteo. Medicine, 1978-85, assoc. dir. Office Health Services, Edn. and Research, Coll. Human Medicine, 1973-78, chmn. dept. cmty. health sci., 1983-93, dir. divsn. geriatrics and long term care dept. physical medicine and rehab., 1993—, dir. cmty. integrated med. programs and studies Coll. Osteo. Medicine, 1993—, co-dir. Ctr. for Aging Studies, Geriat. Edn. Ctr., 1988-90, dir. Ctr. for Policy Analysis in Aging and Long-Term Care, 1987—; dir. Geriat. Edn. Ctr. Mich.; cons. to pub. and pvt. orgns. and agys.; pres. Active Life Sys. Inc.; vis. prof. U. Rome, 1992—. Editor, contbg. author: (with others) Chance for Change: Implications of the Chronic Disease Module Study, 1979; mem. editorial bd. Aging: Clin. and Exptl. Rsch.; contbr. articles to profl. jours. Mem. APA, APHA, Assn. Tchrs. of Preventive Medicine, Am. Coll. Epidemiology, Gerontol. Soc. Am., Am. Geriat. Soc. Roman Catholic. Research gerontology/geriatrics, long-term care, epidemiology, health services and policy. Office: Mich State U B215 W Fee Hall East Lansing MI 48824

PAQUETTE, DEAN RICHARD, retired computer company executive, consultant; b. Detroit, July 15, 1930; s. William Roy and Neta Norine (Hadder) P.; B.A., U. Md., 1970; M.S., George Washington U., 1971; grad. Nat. War Coll.; m. Emma Shirley Jones, July 2, 1952; children—Neta E., Diane R., Kingsley W. Joined U.S. Army, 1946, Commd. 2d lt. U.S. Army, 1952, advanced through grades to col., 1972; mil. advisor to Indonesian Army, Djakarta, 1963-64; action officer army aviation directorate, The Pentagon, 1965-68, dep. dir. facilities engring. Chief of Engrs., 1975-76; div. chief, support requirements, 1973-75, divsn. chief, dep. chief ops. hdqs., 1973-75; sr. Army rep. in Australia, 1971-73; sr. Army liasion Internat. Civil Aviation Orgn., FAA, 1965-68; chief, research and devel. facilities constrn., 1969-71; chief of ops., mem. faculty Army Engr. Sch., 1958-61; ret., 1976; mgr. def. and space planning Control Data Corp., Alexandria, Va., 1977—. Vice pres. Waynewood (Va.) PTA, 1967. Decorated D.F.C., Purple Heart, Legion of Merit with 2 oak leaf clusters, Air medal with 8 oak leaf clusters. Mem. Army Engr. Assn. Corps of Engrs. (disting., Hall of Fame), Order of Purple Heart, Daedalions, Order of Carabao, Assn. U.S. Army, Army Aviation Assn. Club: Pinewild Country Club. Home: 23 Lasswade Dr Pinehurst NC 28374-6703

PAQUETTE, ELISE GOOSSEN, rehabilitation nurse; b. Mt. Kisco, N.Y., Nov. 20, 1956; d. Frederick Lawrence and Angela Rita (Menichelli) Goossen; m. J. Steven Paquette, Aug. 20, 1977; children: Justin, Gregory, Courtney. Diploma in Nursing, Albany Med. Ctr. Sch. Nursing, N.Y., 1977. CRRN. Staff nurse orthopedics Hahnemann Hosp., Phila., 1977-78; staff nurse rehab. Thomas Jefferson U. Hosp., Phila., 1978-79; staff nurse orthopedics, day charge arthritis unit Presbyn. U. Hosp., Pitts., 1979-82; orthopedic nurse to pvt. phys. practice Oakland Orthopedic Assocs., Pitts., 1982-84; sr. rehab. staff nurse George Washington U. Hosp., Washington, 1984-89, asst. head nurse, 1989-90; cons. Comprehensive Rehab. Assocs., Vienna, Va.; unit coord. (head nurse) New Medico Head Injury, Lynn, Mass., 1991; dir. orthopedic rehab. program Reconditioning Program Northeast Rehab. Hosp., Salem, N.H., 1992-94, cons. to clin. programs, 1994—, facilitator cmty. amputee support group, 1992; mem. arthritis subcom. Presbyn. U. Hosp., Pitts., 1987. Mem. com. Boy Scouts Am., Boxford, Mass., 1990-94; bd. dirs. Topsfield/Boxford Newcomers Club, 1991-92. Mem. Assn. Rehab. Nurses, Inst. Children's Lit. Avocations: drama, reading, gardening, writing children's literature. Office: Northeast Rehab Hosp 70 Butler St Salem NH 03079-3925

PAQUETTE, JACK KENNETH, management consultant, antiques dealer; b. Toledo, Ohio, Aug. 14, 1925; s. Hector J. and Nellie (McCormick) P.; m. Jane Russell, Sept. 13, 1947; children: Jan Eriksen, Mark Russell, Mary Beth, John Eric. Student, Baldwin-Wallace Coll., 1943-44, Marquette U., 1944; B.A., Ohio State U., 1949, M.A., 1951; postgrad., Wayne State U., 1966. Editor monthly pub. Bur. Motor Vehicles, State of Ohio, 1947-49; asst. city editor, copy editor Ohio State Jour., 1949-51; copywriter Owens-Ill., Inc., Toledo, 1951-53; copy chief mktg. dept. Owens-Ill., Inc., 1953-55, asst. advt. mgr. mktg. dept., 1955-59; advt. mgr. Owens-Ill., Inc. (Libbey div.), 1959-61; mgr. advt. and sales promotion Owens-Ill., Inc. (Libbey products), 1961-64, mgr. customer mktg. services glass container div., 1964-67, dir. corporate orgn. planning, 1967-69, v.p. adminstrv. div., dir. corp. relations, 1969-70, corporate v.p., dir. corp. relations, 1970-80, corp. v.p., asst. to chmn. bd., 1980-84, cons., 1984-86; pres. Paquette Enterprises, 1984—; owner The Trumpeting Angel, antiques, 1985—; mem. adv. bd. Cresset Chem. Co., 1987—. Author: A History of Owens-Illinois Inc., (1818-1984), 1985, The Glassmakers, 1994. Bd. dirs. Toledo YMCA, 1970-74, Vis. Nurse Svc., 1970-73, Children's Services Bd., 1973-80, Toledo council Boy Scouts Am., trustee, v.p. fin., 1978-84; trustee Owens Tech. Coll. Fund, 1978-81; mem. Advt. Club Toledo, 1951-75, trustee, 1960-62; hon. bd. dirs. Greater Toledo area chpt. ARC, 1970—; mem. adv. bd. Mercy Hosp., Toledo, 1981-84, Mary's Adult Day Care Ctr., 1989-93, St. Anthony's Children's Ctr., 1993; mem. pub. rels. com. Catholic U. Am., 1979-82; chmn. U.S. Savs. Bonds, Lucas County, 1977-79; trustee Bowling Green State U. Found., 1976-83, pres., 1980-82; mem. Nat. Commn. on a Free and Responsible Press, 1980-83; v.p. trustee Toledo Repertoire Theatre, 1984-88; trustee Crosby Gardens, 1983-89, chmn. 1987-88; trustee Toledo Botanical Gardens, 1989-90, chmn. emeritus and hon. lifetime trustee, 1990—; mem. pres.'s council Toledo Mus. Art, Bowling Green State U.; trustee Riverside Hosp. Found., 1984-94, chmn. 1986-89; mem. Juvenile Justice Adv. Bd., 1986-87; advisor R.B. Hayes Presdl. Ctr., 1990-92. With USNR, 1943-46, PTO. Recipient Gold Key award Pub. Rel. News, 1970, Silver Anvil award Pub. Rel. Soc., 1971, 72; named to Toledo Clean Hall of Fame, 1983. Mem. Ohio Mfrs. Assn. (v.p., trustee 1969-84), Keep Am. Beautiful, Inc. (nat. chmn., exec. com., 1978-84, chmn. emeritus, mem. nat. adv. coun. 1984—), Bus. Com. for the Arts (corp. liason 1980-84), Pub. Affairs Council, Glass Packaging Inst. (chmn. com. govtl. relations 1973-80), NAM, U.S. C. of C., Toledo C. of C. (cons. affairs com.), Martin County (Fla.) Hist. Soc., Western Great Lakes Hist. Soc., Toy Soldier Collectors of Am. Soc., Glass Collectors Club Toledo, USN Armed Guard Assn., Sampson WWII Navy Vets. Assn., OSU Alumni Assn. (life), Am. Legion (Toledo post), Pi Sigma Alpha. Clubs: Toledo Press (founding trustee), Toledo, Torch, Rotary. Home and Office: 2355 Parliament Sq Toledo OH 43617-1256

PAQUETTE, JOSEPH F., JR., utility company executive; b. Norwood, Miss., Aug. 24, 1934; married. BS in Civil Engring., Yale U., 1956. Pres. CMS Energy Corp., until 1988; chmn., pres., chief exec. officer Phila. Electric Co., 1956-86, 88-90; chmn., ceo, dir. Phila. Electric Co. (PECO Energy), 1990—; cfo, exec. v.p. Consumer Power Co., 1986-87, vice chmn., cfo, since 1987; also chmn. Susquehanna Electric Co. Office: PECO Energy 2301 Market St Philadelphia PA 19101*

PAQUETTE, RICHARD, airport executive. V.p. airport devel. Calgary Airport, AB, Can. Mem. Calgary Conv. and Visitors Bureau, Alta. Aviation Coun. Mem. Am. Assn. Airport Execs., Calgary C. of C., Calgary Rotary Club. Avocations: golf, skiing, bike riding, photography, hockey. Office: Calgary International Airport, 2000 Airport Rd NE, Calgary, AB Canada T2E 6W5

PAQUIN, ANNA, actress; b. New Zealand, 1983; d. Mary P. Appeared in (film) The Piano, 1993 (Academy Award best supporting actress 1993, Golden Globe nomination best supporting actress 1993), Jane Eyre, 1995. Office: William Morris Agency 151 S El Camino Dr Beverly Hills CA 90212-2704*

PAQUIN, THOMAS CHRISTOPHER, lawyer; b. Quincy, Mass., Feb. 12, 1947; s. Henry Frederick and Rita Marie (St. Louis) P.; m. Jean Jacqueline O'Neill, Aug. 5, 1972; children: Martha, Edward. BS in Acctg., Bentley Coll., 1969; JD, U. Notre Dame, 1974. Bar: Mass. 1974, U.S. Dist. Ct. Mass. 1976. Tax atty. Coopers and Lybrand, Boston, 1974-76; assoc. Cargill, Masterman & Cahill, Boston, 1976, Wilson, Curran & Malkasian, Wellesley, Mass., 1976-77; ptnr. Bianchi and Paquin, Hyannis, Mass., 1977—; bd. dirs., chmn. nominating com. Elder svcs. Cape Cod and Islands, Inc., Dennis, Mass., 1986-91; bd. dirs., corporator Vis. Nurse Assn. Cape Cod Found., Inc., Dennis, 1988—; pres. Life Svcs. Inc., 1991-95. Mem. Bass River Golf Commn., Yarmouth, Mass., 1980-83, chmn., 1982-83; chmn. Yarmouth Golf Course Bldg. Com., 1985-89; mem. hearing com. bd. Bar Overseers of the Supreme Jud. Ct., 1989-95; bd. dirs. Project Coach, Inc., 1990—; conciliator Barnstable Superior Ct., 1992—. Fellow Mass. Bar Found.; mem. ABA, Mass. Bar Assn. (del. 1986-87, mem. com. on bicentennial U.S. Constn. 1986-88, fee arbitration bd. 1985-86, chmn. speakers and writers subcom. 1986-88), Barnstable County Bar Assn. (chmn. seminar com. 1979-83, mem. exec. com. 1981-84, v.p. 1984-86, pres. 1986-87), Estate Planning Coun. Cape Cod (exec. com. 1985—, sec. 1991-93, pres.-elect 1993-95, pres. 1995—), Mass. Conveyancers Assn., Mid-Cape Men's Club (v.p. 1992—, pres. 1993). Office: Bianchi and Paquin 55 Sea Street Ext Hyannis MA 02601-5109

PARADIS, ANDRE, librarian; b. Quebec City, Que., Can., June 26, 1938; s. Theodule and Marcelle (Letarte) P.; m. Helene Legare, July 1, 1968. B.A., Seminaire de Quebec, 1960; diplome bibliotheconomie, U. Laval, 1963; baccalaureat en bibliotheconomie, U. Montreal, 1966. With Bibliotheque Municipale de Quebec, Quebec City, 1962-76; head br. office Bibliotheque Municipale de Quebec, 1963-65, chief librarian, 1966-75, chief tech. services, 1975-76; with Que. Pub. Libraries Service, 1976—. Mem. Corporation des Bibliothecaires Professionnels du Quebec. Home: 8580 De Marseille St, Charlesbourg, PQ Canada G1G 3S6 Office: 225 Grande-Allee Est, Bloc B 3d Floor, Quebec, PQ Canada

PARADIS, JAMES GARDINER, historian; b. Walker, Minn., Oct. 3, 1942; s. Louis Adelard and Rosalie Jane (Gardiner) P.; m. Judith Ellen Schmuckler, July 3, 1970; children: Emily, Rosalind. BS in Natural Sci., St.

John's U., 1964; AM in English, NYU, 1971; PhD in English, U. Wash., 1976. Chemistry instr. Harar Tchr. Tng. Inst., Harar, Ethiopia, 1964-66; sci. tchr. Pub. Sch. 143, N.Y.C., 1966-71; English instr. Univ. Wash., Seattle, 1974-76; asst. prof. sci. and tech. communication MIT, Cambridge, Mass., 1977-79, assoc. prof., 1980-89, chmn. writing prog., 1982-85, prof., 1990—; communications cons. Exxon Chemicals Corp., Baton Rouge, La., 1982-83, U.S. Dept. of Interior, Anchorage, Alaska, 1983, Brookhaven Nat. Lab., L.I., N.Y., 1978-90. Author: Thomas Henry Huxley, 1978; co-editor: Victorian Science and Values, 1981, Evolution and Ethics, 1989, Textual Dynamics of the Professions, 1991; editorial cons. MIT Press/Harvard U., 1980-89. Adv. com. Driscoll Elem. Sch., Brookline, Mass., 1990-91. Recipient devel. grant Internat. Bus. Machines, 1986-87, rsch. grant NEH, 1979-80, Am. Philos. Soc., 1976-77. Mem. Modern Lang. Assn., History of Sci. Soc., Soc. for Tech. Communications, British Soc. for History of Sci. Avocations: rock and ice climbing, cycling, winter mountaineering. Home: 26 Salisbury Rd Brookline MA 02146-2105 Office: MIT 77 Massachusetts Ave Cambridge MA 02139-4301

PARADISE, LOUIS VINCENT, educational psychology educator, university official; b. Scranton, Pa., Apr. 19, 1946; s. Louis Benjamin and Lucille (Bochicchio) P.; children: Christopher, Gabrielle,Victoria. BS, Pa. State U., 1968; MS, Bucknell U., 1974; PhD, U. Va., 1976. Lic. psychologist, profl. counselor; cert. sch. psychologist. Assoc. prof. Cath. U. Am., Washington, 1976-83; prof. edn., chmn. edn. leadership U. New Orleans, 1983-90, dean Coll. Edn., 1990-92, univ. exec. vice chancellor and provost, 1992-94, exec. vice chancellor for acad. affairs, 1994—. Author: Ethics in Counseling and Psychotherapy, 1979, Questioning: Skills for the Helping Process, 1979, Counseling in Community College, 1982. 1st lt. U.S. Army, 1968-72. Du-Pont scholar U. Va., 1974. Mem. APA, ACA (ethics com. 1986-89), Am. Edn. Rsch. Assn., So. Assn. Counselor Edn. (chmn. ethics com. 1988-89), Chi Sigma Iota (founding chpt. pres. 1985-87). Roman Catholic. Avocations: running, cycling. Office: U New Orleans Office Acad Affairs New Orleans LA 70148

PARADISE, PHIL(IP HERSCHEL), artist; b. Ontario, Oreg., Aug. 26, 1905; s. Joseph Richard and Bessie Ana (Green) P.; m. Virginia Dare McCormick, Oct. 21, 1934 (dec. 1953); children: Virginia Gail, Philip Lee; m. Alice Hancock Johns, Nov. 5, 1959. Grad., Chouinard Art Inst., Los Angeles, 1927. tchr. Chouinard Art Inst., 1932-40, dir. fine arts dept., 1936-40; summer guest instr. U. Calif. at Santa Barbara, Calif. Arts and Crafts, Oakland, Tex. Western Coll.; lectr. Scripps Coll. Exhibited all prin. invitational and competitive exhbns. in U.S., including, Pa. Acad. Fine Arts, Whitney Mus. Am. Art, Met. Mus. Art, Los Angeles County, Denver, San Diego mus., Nat. Gallery Art, Art. Inst. Chgo.; represented in permanent collections, Library of Congress Print Collection, Pa. Acad. Fine Arts, Cornell U., Spokane Art Assn., Los Angeles County Fair Assns., others; editorial illustrations in True; motion picture prodn. design and art dir. major studios. Recipient award Oakland Ann. Watercolor Exhbn., 1938, award Los Angeles County Fair Assn., 1938, Dana medal Pa. Acad. Fine Arts, 1939, 2d pl. oil Calif. State Fair Assn., 1949, Smithsonian Archives Am. Art award, 1990, Life Time Achievements award Laguna Beach Mus., 1991, others. Mem. Calif. Watercolor Soc. (pres. 1939), Am. Watercolor Soc. (life), NAD, Soc. Motion Picture Art Dirs. Address: 31 W Carrillo St Santa Barbara CA 93101-3212

PARADISE, ROBERT RICHARD, publishing executive; b. Bklyn., Nov. 29, 1934; s. Vincent James and Marie (Sangermano) P.; m. Camille Teresa Cosenza, July 11, 1964; children: Christine, Caren M., Robert V., Steven C. BA, St. Bonaventure U., 1956; MBA, NYU, 1972. Advt. sales rep. The Wall Street Jour., N.Y.C., 1961-63, retail advt. sales mgr., 1963-66, fin. advt. sales mgr., 1966-70, assoc. advt. sales mgr., 1970-74, ea. advt. sales mgr., 1974-80, nat. dir. advt. svc., 1980-85; v.p. adminstrn., mag. & internat. group Dow Jones & Co., Inc., N.Y.C., 1985—; bd. dirs. Am. Demographics, Ithaca, N.Y., 1986, Dow Jones So. Holding Co., Inc., 1988; assoc. pub. Barron's Nat. Bus. and Fin. Weekly, V.P. mag. group , 1988, pub., 1989—. Mem. bd. edn. Scarsdale (N.Y.) Schs., 1986-92. Served to lt. USNR, 1956-61. Mem. Advt. Club of N.Y., Fin. Com. Soc., Nat. Investors Rels. Inst. Roman Catholic. Club: Coveleigh (Rye, N.Y.) (bd. govs. 1987). Avocations: tennis, boating. Home: 8 Woods Ln Scarsdale NY 10583-6408 Office: Dow Jones & Co Inc Barron's Nat Bus 200 Liberty St New York NY 10281-1003*

PARADY, JOHN EDWARD, information systems executive, consultant; b. Inglewood, Calif., Sept. 26, 1939; s. Raymond Oliver and Ella Louise (Timm) P.; m. Barbara Lyn Pettit, Aug. 13, 1966; children: John, Renee, Stacy. BS, Calif. State U., Los Angeles, 1966; MS, U. So. Calif., 1968. Cert. data processing. Dir. info. systems Weyerhauser Co., Tacoma, Wash., 1975-82; exec. dir. McKenna, Conner & Cuneo, Los Angeles, 1982-83; sr. v.p. Bank of Am., San Francisco, 1983-85; pvt. practice cons. L.A., 1986-88; exec. v.p. Pacific Stock Exchange, Los Angeles, 1988-93; chief info. officer Coldwell Banker Corp., Mission Viejo, 1994—; mem. The Rsch. Bd., N.Y.C., 1983-86; bd. dirs. The Ctr. for Info. Systems Rsch., Cambridge, Mass., 1977-85; bd. dirs. The Molding Corp., Am., Cal-Air, Inc. Served to 2d lt., U.S. Army, 1959-64. Served to 2d lt., U.S. Army, 1959-64. Republican. Mormon. Avocations: fishing, camping, woodworking. Home: 1004 Vista Del Valley Rd La Canada Flintridge CA 91011-1805 Office: 27211 Las Ramblas Mission Viejo CA 92691

PARAISO, JOHNNA KAYE, elementary education educator; b. Wyandotte, Mich., Nov. 17, 1961; d. John Calvin and Ruth (Hughes) Underwood; m. Normandy Paraiso, Oct. 6, 1984; children: Sophia Elisabeth, Abigail Mahalia, Genevieve Christine. BS, Bob Jones U., 1983. Cert. ACSI, educator K-8 (all subjects). Tchr. fifth grade Temple Christian Sch., Redford, Mich., 1983-86; music tchr. Fairlane Christian Sch., Dearborn Heights, Mich., 1986-90; tchr. 2d grade Internat. Christian Sch., San Francisco, 1992-93, dept. head primary childhood edn., 1992-93; freelance musician children's concerts; leader Curriculum Selection Com.; initiator Elem. Music Program; dir. several dramatic prodns.; tchr. piano, guitar. Children's minister 1st Bapt. Ch., San Francisco, 1991-94. Mem. Pi Lambda Theta. Home: 2024 Stonebrook Rd Murfreesboro TN 37129

PARALEZ, LINDA LEE, technology management consultant; b. Raton, N.Mex., Oct. 29, 1955. AS, Amarillo Coll., 1975; student West Tex. State U., 1975-77, BBA, Century U., Beverly Hills, Calif., 1984, MBA, 1987, PhD in Bus. Mgmt. and Econ. Century U. Teaching asst. Amarillo (Tex.) Coll., 1974-75; drafter natural gas div. Pioneer Corp., Amarillo, 1975-76, sr. drafter exploration div. Amarillo Oil Co. 1976-77; drafting supr., engring. svcs. supr., dir. speakers' bur. Thunder Basin Coal Co., Atlantic Richfield Co., Wright, Wyo., 1977-86; ptnr., tech. and adminstrv. cons. Rose Enterprises, 1986—; prof. U. Phoenix, Utah; adj. prof. Weber State U., Ogden, Utah; tech. writer Eaton Corp., Riverton, Wyo., 1986-88; cons. State Wyo. Office on Family Violence and Sexual Assault, Cheyenne, 1986-89; Diamond L Industries, Inc., Gillette, Wyo., 1986-88; tech. writer, pubs. cons. Thiokol Corp., Brigham City, Utah, 1987-89, design specialist space ops., 1989-90, mgr. total quality mgmt. ctr. space ops., 1990—, cons. organizational effectiveness and quality mgmt. principles; cons. incident investigation team NASA Solid Rocket Booster Program, Huntsville, Ala.; cons. process improvement Puget Power, Seattle, Wash., Pub. Svc. Co. of Colo., W.R. White Co.; cons. process design Microsoft Corp., Seattle. Author: (poetry) God was Here, But He Left Early, 1976, Gift of Wings, 1980, 89; columnist Wytech Digest; contbr. numerous articles to profl. jours. Vol. NASA Young Astronauts Program Adv. Com., 1991—; bd. dirs. Campbell County Drafting Adv. Coun., 1984-85; sec. bd. dir. exec. com. Am. Inst. Design and Drafting, 1984-85, tech. publ. chairperson, 1984-85; vol. educator, data specialist child abuse prevention coun. Ogden. Named Most Outstanding Woman, Beta Sigma Phi, 1980, 81; recipient Woman in the Industry recognition Internat. Reprographics Assn., 1980; grand prize winner Wyo. Art Show with painting titled Energy, 1976. Mem. AAUW, NAFE, NOW, Am. Soc. Quality Control, Am. Productivity and Quality Coun., Am. Legion Aux., Ocean Rsch. Edn. Soc., Gloucester, Mass. (grant proposal writer, 1984), Soc. Tech. Communications, 4-H Club. Home: 2888 N 1300 E Ogden UT 84414-2607

PARAN, MARK LLOYD, lawyer; b. Cleve., Feb. 1, 1953; s. Edward Walter and Margaret Gertrude (Ebert) P. AB cum laude in Sociology, Harvard U., 1977, JD, 1980. Bar: Ill. 1980, Mass. 1986, Tex. 1993. Assoc. Wilson & McIlvaine, Chgo., 1980-83, Lurie Sklar & Simon, Ltd., Chgo., 1983-85, Sullivan & Worcester, Boston, 1985-92; pvt. practice, Boston, 1992; pvt. practice, Euless, Tex., 1992—. Mem. ABA, State Bar Tex. Avocations: tornado hunting, observation of severe thunderstorms, photography. Home and Office: 1050 W Ash Ln Apt 1015 Euless TX 76039-2161

PARASCOS, EDWARD THEMISTOCLES, utilities executive; b. N.Y.C., Oct. 20, 1931; s. Christos and Nina (Demitrovich) P.; BSME, CCNY, 1956, MSME, 1958; postgrad. ops. rsch. N.Y.U., 1964; m. Jenny Morris, July 14, 1978; children: Jennifer Melissa, Edward Themistocles. Design engr. Ford Instrument, 1957-61; reliability engring. supr. Kearfott div. Gen. Precision Inc., 1961-63; staff cons. Am. Power Jet, 1963-64; reliability mgr. Perkin Elmer Corp., 1964-66; dir. system effectiveness CBS Labs., Stamford, Conn., 1966-72; pres. Dipar Cons. Svcs. Ltd., East Elmhurst, N.Y., Lapa Trading Corp.; gen. mgr., prin. reliability engr. engring. Consol. Edison Co., N.Y.C., 1972—; pres., chmn. bd. RAM Cons. Assocs.; pres. , 1978-80; chmn. 1st Reliability Engring. Conf. Electric Power Industry, 1974, also 4th and 18th confs.; chmn. bd. Inter-Ram Q Conf. for electric power industry; gen. chmn. 18th Inter-Ramq Conf. for electric power industry; lectr. in field. Registered profl. engr., Calif. Fellow Am. Soc. Quality Control (vice chmn. Reliability div. 1968-70, sr. mem.); mem. ASME, Soc. Reliabilty Engrs., Edison Engring. Soc. Home: 30-02 83rd St Flushing NY 11370-1919 Office: 31-01 20th Ave Astoria NY 11105-2014

PARASKEVOPOULOS, GEORGE, aerospace engineer; b. Patras, Greece, Dec. 2, 1951; came to U.S., 1978; s. Chris and Anastasia (Rhodes) P.; m. Linda Anne Mohr, July 11, 1986; children: Chris, Anastasia. BS in Aeronautics with honors, U. London (Eng.), 1978; MS in Aeronautics, Iowa State U., Ames, 1980. Registered profl. engr., Greece. Aero. engr. Nat. Hellenic Corp., Athens, 1980-82; instr. Embry-Riddle Aero. U., Fla., 1982-84, U. Md., University College, 1984-86; sr. elec. engr. V.S.E., Alexandria, Va., 1987-90; head reliability dept. T.A.M.S.CO, Beltsville, Md., 1990—; cons. USCG, Washington, 1990—. Author: History of Wing Aircraft Design, 1978, Solutions to Air Influx at Main Entrance of University of Iowa Hospital, 1979. Engring. Rsch. Inst. grantee Iowa State U., 1978. Sr. mem. AIAA; assoc. mem. Royal Aero. Soc. Greek Orthodox. Avocations: sailing, tennis. Home: 239 N Cameron Ct Sterling VA 20164

PARCELLS, BILL (DUANE CHARLES PARCELLS), professional football coach; b. Englewood, N.J., Aug. 22, 1941; m. Judith Parcells; children: Suzy, Jill, Dallas. B.A., Wichita State U., 1964. Asst. coach Hastings Coll. (Nebr.), 1964, Wichita State U. (Kans.), 1969, U.S. Mil. Acad., 1966-69, Fla. State U., Tallahassee, 1970-72, Vanderbilt U., Nashville, 1973-74, Tex. Tech U., Lubbock, 1975-77; head coach U.S. Air Force Acad., Colorado Springs, Colo., 1978; asst. coach New Eng. Patriots, NFL, 1980; asst. coach N.Y. Giants, NFL, 1981-82, head coach, 1983-91; NFL studio analyst NBC Sports, 1991-92; head coach New England Patriots, NFL, 1993—. Coach NFL championship team N.Y. Giants, 1986. Address: New England Patriots RR 1 Foxboro MA 02035*

PARCH, GRACE DOLORES, librarian; b. Cleve., May ; d. Joseph Charles and Josephine Dorothy (Kumel) P. B.A., Case Western Res. U., 1946, postgrad., 1947-50; B.L.S., McGill U., 1951; M.L.S., Kent State U., 1983; postgrad., Newspaper Library Workshop, Kent State U., 1970, Cooper Sch. Art, 1971-72, API Newspaper Library Seminar, Columbia U., 1971, Coll. Librarianship, U. Wales, 1984, 85. Cert. literacy instr., Ohio. Publicity librarian Spl. Services U.S. Army, Germany, 1951; post librarian Spl. Services U.S. Army, Italy, 1952; USAF base librarian, 1953-54; br. librarian Cleveland Heights (Ohio) Pub. Library, 1954-63; asst. head reference div. Va. State Library, Richmond, 1964; dir. Twinsburg (Ohio) Pub. Library, 1965-70; dir. newspaper library Cleve. Plain Dealer, 1970-83; county librarian N.C., 1987-92; cons. Cath. Library Assn., 1961-64; mem. home econs. adv. com., Summit County, 1969, books/job com., 1968; mem. adv. com. Guide to Ohio Newspapers, 1793-1973, 1971-74; appointed to del. spl. librs. for People-to-People Program in Russia, 1995. Contbr. articles to Plain Dealer, N. Summit Times, Twinsburg Bull., Sun Press; author: Where In the World But in the Plain Dealer Library, 1971; Editor: Directory of Newspaper Libraries in the U.S. and Canada, 1976. Recipient MacArthur Found. award, 1988, Libr. of Am. award, 1988. Mem. McGill U. Alumnae Assn. (sec. 1973), Kent State U. Alumni Assn., ALA (rep. on joint com. with Cath. Library Assn. 1967-70), John Cotton Dana award 1967, Library Pub. Rels. Coun. award 1972), Cath. Library Assn. (co-chmn. 1960-63), Spl. Libraries Assn. (chmn. newspaper library directory com. 1974-76, chmn. pub. relations Cleve. chpt. 1973, chmn. edn. com. newspaper div. 1982-83, mem. edn. com. nominating com. 1984), Ohio Library Assn., Western Res. Hist. Soc., Am. Soc. Indexers, Cleve. Mus. Art Assn., Coll. and Research Librarians, Nat. Micrographic Assn., Women Space, Women's Nat. Book Com., Nat. Trust Hist. Preservation. Roman Catholic. Clubs: Cleve. Athletic, Cleve. Women's City. Home: 688 Jefferson St Bedford OH 44146-3711 *Greatness results in adapting aspects or ideas in other disciplines to one's own simplicity.*

PARCHER, JAMES VERNON, civil engineering educator, consultant; b. Drumright, Okla., July 21, 1920; s. James Augustus and Pearl (Sharp) P.; m. Martha Hoff Ruckman, Aug. 7, 1943; children: Carol Susan Parcher McLeod, James Robert, David Loris, Dee Ellen Parcher Casey, Kay Elaine Parcher Heiserman. BS, Okla. State U., 1941, MS, 1948; MA, Harvard U., 1967; PhD, U. Ark., 1968. Maintenance engr. Remington Arms Co., Kings Mills, Ohio, 1941-42; instr. Okla. State U., Stillwater, 1947-48; asst. prof. Okla. State U., 1948-54, asso. prof., 1954-67, prof., 1967-85, prof. emeritus, 1985—, head dept. civil engring., 1969-83. Author: A History of the Oklahoma State University College of Engineering, Architecture and Technology, 1988, (with R.E. Means) Physical Properties of Soils, 1962, Soil Mechanics and Foundations, 1968. Served with C.E. AUS, 1942-46, 50-52. Mem. ASCE, NSPE, Okla. Soc. Profl. Engrs., Res. Officers Assn., Am. Assn. Retired People, Phi Kappa Phi, Sigma Tau, Chi Epsilon. Home: 1024 W Knapp Ave Stillwater OK 74075-2709

PARDEE, ARTHUR BECK, biochemist, educator; b. Chgo., July 13, 1921; s. Charles A. and Elizabeth B. (Beck) P.; m. Ruth Sager; children by previous marriage: Michael, Richard, Thomas. B.S., U. Calif. at Berkeley, 1942; M.S., Calif. Inst. Tech., 1943, Ph.D., 1947; D (hon.), U. Paris, 1993. Merck postdoctoral fellow U. Wis., 1947-49; mem. faculty U. Calif. at Berkeley, 1949-61, assoc. prof., 1957-61; NSF fellow Pasteur Inst., 1957-58; prof. biology, chmn. dept. biochem. scis. Princeton, 1961-67; prof. biochemistry Princeton U., 1961-75; Donner prof. sci. Princeton, 1966; prof. Dana Farber Cancer Inst. and biochem. pharmacology dept. Harvard Med. Sch., Boston, 1975—; Mem. research adv. council Am. Cancer Soc., 1967-71. Co-author: Experiments in Biochemical Research Techniques, 1957; editor: Biochemica et Biophysica Acta, 1962-68. Trustee Cold Spring Harbor Lab. Quantitative Biology, 1963-69. Recipient Young Biochemists travel award NSF, 1952, Krebs Medal Fedn. European Biochem. Socs., 1973, Rosenstiel award Brandeis U., 1975, 3M award Fedn. Am. Socs., Exptl. Biology, 1980, CIIT Prize, 1993; Princess Takamatu lectr., 1990. Fellow AAAS; mem. NAS (editl. bd. proc. 1971-73, com. on scis. and pub. policy 1973-76), Am. Chem. Soc. (Paul Lewis award 1960), Am. Soc. Biol. Chemists (treas. 1964-70, pres. 1980-81), Am. Assn. Cancer Rsch. (pres. 1985-86), Am. Soc. Microbiologists, Japanese Biochem. Soc., Ludwig Inst. Cancer Rsch. (sci. com. 1988—), Chem. Industry Inst. Toxicology (Founders award), D. Home: 30 Codman Rd Brookline MA 02146-7555 Office: Dana-Farber Cancer Inst 375 Longwood Ave Boston MA 02215-5328

PARDEE, MARGARET ROSS, violinist, violist, educator; b. Valdosta, Ga., May 10, 1920; d. William Augustus and Frances Ross (Burton) P.; diploma Inst. Mus. Art, Juilliard Sch. Music, 1940, grad. diploma, 1942, diploma Juilliard Grad. Sch., 1945; m. Daniel Rogers Butterly, July 5, 1944. Instr. violin and viola Manhattanville Coll. Sacred Heart, N.Y.C., 1942-54, Juilliard Sch., N.Y.C., 1942—, Meadowmount Sch. Music, Westport, N.Y., 1956-84, 88-92, Bowdoin Coll. Music Festival and Sch., Maine, summer 1987; faculty Estherwood Sch. and Summer Festival, 1984-86, Killington (Vt.) Music Festival, 1993—; concert master Great Neck (L.I.) Symphony, 1954-85; adj. assoc. prof. music Queens Coll., Flushing, N.Y., 1978—; adj. assoc. prof. Adelphi U., Garden City, N.Y., 1979-83; adj. prof. SUNY, Purchase, 1980-93; vis. prof. Simon Bolivar Youth Orch. and Conservatory, Caracas and Barquisimeto, Venezuela, 1988, 89, Conservatoria de la Orch. Nat. Juvenil, Caracas, Venezuela, 1988, 89; debut N.Y. Town Hall, 1952; toured U.S. as soloist and in chamber music groups; soloed with symphony orchs. in Miss., N.J., D.C. and N.Y.; mem. jury for internat. competitions; guest artist prof. 1st Internat. Festival for Young Violinists, Caracas, 1988, guest vis. prof. Orch. Filarmónica Nacional & Municipal Sinfonica de Caracas, Venezuela, 1991—. Recipient Merit award and citation for exceptional leadership Am. String Tchrs. Assn, 1990, Andres Bello award Minister Edn. of Venezuela, 1993. Bd. dirs. Meadowmount Sch. Music. Mem. Soc. for Strings (dir. 1965-92), Associated Music Tchrs. League N.Y. (cert.), N.Y. State Music Tchrs. Assn. (cert., citation 1989), Music Tchrs. Nat. Assn., Am. String Tchrs. Assn. (Citation award 1990), Am. Fedn. Musicians, Viola Rsch. Soc. Office: care Juilliard Sch Lincoln Ctr Plz New York NY 10023

PARDEE, OTWAY O'MEARA, computer science educator; b. Seattle, June 26, 1920; s. Otway and Mary Gertrude (O'Meara) P.; m. Marilynn Lowrie, Aug. 9, 1946; children—Irene, Loraine, Suzanne. B.S. in Elec. Engring., U. Wash., 1941; Ph.D. in Elec. Engring., Stanford U., 1948. Instr. math. Syracuse U., N.Y., 1948-52, asst. to assoc. prof., 1952-69, dir. Computing Ctr., 1962-69, prof. computer sci., 1969-86; prof. emeritus Syracuse U., 1986—. Served with U.S. Navy (USNR) 1944-46. Mem. AAUP (pres. Syracuse U. chpt. 1960), Assn. Computing Machinery (chmn. Syracuse chpt. 1963), Am. Math. Soc., Math. Assn. Am., Am. Phys. Soc., IEEE, Sigma XI, Tau Beta Pi. Avocations: camping; photography. Home: 843 Maryland Ave Syracuse NY 13210-2502 Office: Syracuse U Ctr for Sci and Tech Ste 2-120 Syracuse NY 13244-4100

PARDEE, SCOTT EDWARD, securities dealer; b. New Haven, Oct. 11, 1936; s. William Durley and Catherine (Eames) P.; m. Aida Milagros Fuentes Tavarez, Jan. 29, 1966; 1 child, Alan Alexander. B.A., Dartmouth Coll., 1958; Ph.D., MIT, 1962. Research asst. Fed. Res. Bank, Boston, 1959-62; teaching asst. in econs. MIT, Cambridge, Mass., 1961-62; research economist Fed. Res. Bank N.Y., N.Y.C., 1962-66, mgr. fgn. dept., 1967-70, asst. v.p. fgn. dept., 1970-74, v.p. fgn. dept., 1974-79; tchr. banking and fin. NYU, 1965-67, Am. Inst. Banking, 1969-72; adj. prof. Grad. Sch. Bus. Columbia U., N.Y.C., 1972-75; dep. mgr. fgn. ops. Fed. Res. System Open Market Account, 1975-79, mgr. fgn. ops., 1979-81; exec. v.p., dir. Discount Corp. N.Y., N.Y.C., 1981-86; dir. Am. Internat. Group, 1982-86; vice chmn. Yamaichi Internat. Am. Inc., N.Y.C., 1986-88, chmn., 1988-95, sr. advisor, 1995—. Author: A Study of Inter-City Wage Differentials, 1962. Trustee Geonomics Inst., 1994—, Woodrow Wilson Fellowship Found., 1994—; mem. coun. Rockefeller U., 1994—; mem. Coun. on Fgn. Rels., 1995—. Woodrow Wilson fellow MIT, 1958-59; recipient Dr. Louis M. Spadaro award Fordham U., 1980. Mem. Coun. on Fgn. Rels., Phi Beta Kappa. Home: 250 South End Ave New York NY 10280-1074 Office: Yamaichi Internat Am Inc 2 World Trade Ctr Ste 9650 New York NY 10048-0203

PARDEN, ROBERT JAMES, engineering educator, management consultant; b. Mason City, Iowa, Apr. 17, 1922; s. James Ambrose and Mary Ellen (Fahey) P.; m. Elizabeth Jane Taylor, June 15, 1955; children—Patricia Gale, James A., John R., Nancy Ann. B.S. in Mech. Engring, State U. Iowa, 1947, M.S., 1951, Ph.D., 1953. Reg. profl. engr. Iowa, Calif.; lic. gen. contractor Calif. Indsl. engr. LaCrosse Rubber Mills, 1947-50; asso. dir. Iowa Mgmt. Course, 1951-53; asso. prof. indsl. engring. Ill. Inst. Tech., 1953-54; prof. engring. mgmt. Santa Clara U., 1955—, dean Sch. Engring., 1955-82; prin. Saratoga Cons. Group (Calif.), 1982—; Mem. Sec. Navy's Survey Bd. Grad. Edn., 1964. Mem. Saratoga Planning Commn., 1959-61. Served to 1st lt., Q.M.C. AUS, 1943-46. Named to Silicon Valley Engring. Hall of Fame Silicon Valley Engring. Coun., 1993. Mem. ASME (chmn. Santa Clara Valley sect. 1958), Am. Soc. Engring. Edn. (chmn. Pacific N.W. sect. 1960), Am. Inst. Indsl. Engrs. (edn. chmn. 1958-63, dir. ASEE-ECPD affairs 1963-68), Nat. Soc. Profl. Engrs., Engrs. Council Profl. Devel. (dir. 1964-65, 66-69), Soc. Advancement Mgmt., ASEM, Sigma Xi, Tau Beta Pi. Roman Catholic. Home: 19832 Bonnie Ridge Way Saratoga CA 95070-5010 Office: Santa Clara U Sch Engring Santa Clara CA 95053

PARDES, HERBERT, psychiatrist, educator; b. Bronx, N.Y., July 7, 1934; s. Louis and Frances (Bergman) P.; m. Judith Ellen Silber, June 9, 1957; children: Stephen, Lawrence, James. BS, Rutgers U., 1956, MD, SUNY, Bklyn., 1960; DSc (hon.) SUNY, 1990. Straight med. intern Kings County Hosp., 1960-61, resident in psychiatry, 1961-62, 64-66; asst. prof. psychiatry Downstate Med. Ctr., Bklyn., 1968-72, prof., chmn. dept., 1972-75; dir. psychiat. services Kings County Hosp., Bklyn., 1972-75; prof., chmn. dept. psychiatry U. Colo. Med. Sch., 1975-78; dir. psychiat. services Colo. Psychiat. Hosp., Denver, 1975-78; dir. NIMH, Rockville, Md., 1978-84; asst. surgeon gen. USPHS, 1978-84; prof. psychiatry Columbia U., N.Y.C., 1984—, chmn. dept., 1984—, dir. Psychiat. Inst., 1984-89, v.p. for health scis. and dean faculty of medicine, 1989—. Committeeman, Kings County Dem. Com., 1972-75; pres. sci. bd. Nat. Alliance for Research on Schizophrenia and Depression. Capt. M.C., AUS, 1962-64. Decorated Army Commendation medal; ann. hon. lectr. Downstate Med. Ctr. Alumni Assn., 1972, recipient Alumni Achievement medal, 1980, William Menninger award ACP, 1992, Dorothy Dix award Mental Illness Fedn., 1992, Vester Mark award, 1993. Mem. Assn. Am. Med. Colls. (chair-elect 1994-95, chair 1995-96), Am. Psychiat. Assn. (v.p. 1986-88, pres. 1989-90, Disting. Svc. award 1993), Inst. Medicine, Am. Psychoanalytic Assn., Coun. of Deans (adminstrv. bd., chair-elect 1993-94, chair 1994-95), Phi Beta Kappa, Alpha Omega Alpha. Contbr. articles to med. jours. Home: 15 Claremont Ave Apt 93 New York NY 10027-6814 Office: Columbia U Coll Phys & Surgeons Dept Psychiatry 630 W 168th St New York NY 10032-3702 also: NY State Psychiat Inst 722 W 168th St New York NY 10032-2603

PARDINI, SHARON KAY BROWN, architectural and interior designer; b. Grand Junction, Iowa, Apr. 15, 1938; d. Loyal Melvin Blanshan and Frances Mildred (Brown) Manen; m. Frederick Brown, Oct. 19, 1957 (div. Apr. 1963); 1 child Randal Alan; m. Joseph Leslie Pardini, Nov. 11, 1975; 1 child, Tiana Margaret. BA in Cosmetology, Lee Ann Acad., 1957; AA, U. Calif., Berkeley, 1966; BBA, U. Calif. Owner Sharon's Hair Fashions Salons, Oakland, Calif., 1958-80; v.p., sec., treas. Western Container Transp. Inc., 1978-87; pres. Par-West Inc. Design Firm, 1983—; mem. adv. bd. Bd. Cosmetology, Oakland, 1965-69; owner The Collection Designer Gallery, Lafayette, Calif., 1987-93. Mem. Republican Task Force, Washington, 1981-89; mem. svc. league Santa Catalina Sch., Monterey, Calif., 1986. Mem. Calif. Cosmetologist Assn. (v.p. 1973-75, bd. dirs. 1970-77), Mission Hills Country Club. Avocations; studying architecture and designing, horticulture, writing, furniture designing.

PARDO, DOMINICK GEORGE (DON PARDO), broadcasting announcer; b. Westfield, Mass., Feb. 22, 1918; s. Dominik J. and Waleria (Romaniak) P.; m. Catherine A. Lyons, Aug. 22, 1939; children: Paula Kay, Dona Marie, Michael D., David J., Katherine A. Student, Emerson Coll., 1942. Announcer Sta. WJAR, 1942-44. Actor, 20th Century Players, Sta. WJAR, Providence, 1938-40; announcer radio and TV, NBC, N.Y.C., 1944—; announcer for radio shows Pepper Young's Family, The Doctors; announcer TV shows Ford 50th Anniversary Show, 1953 (Sylvania TV award), Fred Allen's Judge for Yourself, Martha Raye Shows, 1953-58, Arthur Murray Party, Four Star Revue, Colgate Comedy Hour, Kate Smith Hour, Show of Shows, Caesar's Hour, Jonathan Winters Show; TV game shows Winner Take All, 1950, Price is Right (original), 1956-83, Jeopardy, 1964-75, Saturday Night Live, 1975-81, 83—; numerous other shows, including, Bill Stern's Sports, Magnificent Montague; others; newscaster, 1944-54.

PARDUE, DWIGHT EDWARD, venture capitalist; b. North Wilkesboro, N.C., Aug. 3, 1928; s. Gilbert F. and Nina (Glass) P.; m. Annie Eller, Mar. 24, 1951; children: Richard S., Dwight E. Cert., Clevenger Bus. Coll., 1956. Dir. warehousing Lowe's Co., Inc., North Wilkesboro, 1956-57; store mgr. Lowe's Co., Inc., Sparta, N.C., 1957-59, Richmond, Va., 1959-70; regional v.p. Lowe's Co., Inc., North Wilkesboro, 1970-75, sr. v.p. store ops., 1975-78, exec. v.p. sales and store ops., 1978-86, sr. exec. v.p., 1986-90; pres., investor D. Pardue & Assocs., Wilkesboro, N.C., 1990—; mem. steering com. Home Ctr. Leadership Coun., Nat. Home Ctr. Home Improvement Congress and Exposition, 1983-86; bd. dirs. Wilkes Nat. Bank, North Wilkesboro, N.C.; chmn. bd. Community Bancshares, Inc., Wilkesboro, 1992—. Served with U.S. Army, 1950-52. Mem. Oakwoods Country Club, Jefferson Landing Golf Club, Masons. Office: D Pardue & Assocs PO Box 791 North Wilkesboro NC 28659-0791

PARDUE, HARRY L., chemist, educator; b. Big Creek, W.Va., May 3, 1934; m. Mary Schultz; 1 child, Jonathan. BS, Marshall U., 1956, MS, 1957; PhD in Chemistry, U. Ill., 1961. From asst. to assoc. prof. Purdue U., West Lafayette, Ind., 1961-70, prof. chemistry, 1970—, head dept. chemistry, 1983-87. Recipient Am. Chem Soc. award in Analytical Chemistry, 1995. Mem. Am. Chem. Soc. (Chem. Instrumentation award Analytical Chem. divsn. 1982, Analytical Chemistry award 1995), Am. Assn. Clin. Chemists (award 1979, Samuel Natelson award 1982, Anachem award 1990). Achievements include research in instrumentation for chemical research, chemical kinetics. Office: Purdue U Dept Chem 1393 Brown Bldg W West Lafayette IN 47907-1393

PARDUE, KAREN REIKO, elementary education educator; b. Honolulu, June 13, 1947; d. Rex Shinzen and Ruth Fujiko (Arakawa) Ishiara; m. Jerry Thomas Pardue, Oct. 21, 1978 (dec. Sept. 1994); 1 child, Holly. BS, Western Ill. U., 1969; MA, U. No. Colo., 1971, 72. Tchr. home econs. Galesburg (Ill.) High Sch., 1969-70; tchr. spl. edn. Jefferson County Pub. Schs., Golden, Colo., 1973-85, 87-94; tchr. 3d & 3d grades Englewood (Colo.) Christian Sch., 1985-86; tchr. 2d grade Jefferson County Pub. Schs., 1994—; adj. instr. Colo. Christian U., Lakewood, 1989—; mem. recommended basic list com. Jefferson County Pub. Schs., 1993-95. Colo. Dept. Edn. Mini grantee, 1976, Jefferson Found. Venture grantee, 1988. Mem. ASCD, Colo. Coun. LEarning Disabilities, Jefferson County Ednl. Assn., Jefferson County Internat. Reading Assn., Delta Kappa Gamma (rec. sec. 1988-89, pres. 1990-92, treas. 1994—). Avocations: reading, sewing.

PARDUE, LARRY G., botanical garden administrator, educator; b. Glasgow, Ky., Dec. 6, 1944; s. Samuel Robert and Etta Belle (Napier) P.; children: James, Robert, Mathew. BA, U. South Fla., 1967, MA, 1970. Plant info. officer N.Y. Botanical Garden, N.Y.C., 1969-75; v.p. Wild Flower Preservation Soc., N.Y.C., 1970-73; exec. dir. Hort. Soc. N.Y., N.Y.C., 1975-88, Marie Selby Botanical Garden, Sarasota, Fla., 1988-93, Crosby Arboretum, Picayune, Miss., 1994—. Office: Crosby Arboretum PO Box 190 370 Ridge Rd Picayune MS 39466

PARDUE, MARY LOU, biology educator; b. Lexington, Ky., Sept. 15, 1933; d. Louis Arthur and Mary Allie (Marshall) P. B.S., William and Mary Coll., 1955; M.S., U. Tenn., 1959; Ph.D., Yale U., 1970; D.Sc. (hon.), Bard Coll., 1985. Postdoctoral fellow Inst. Animal Genetics, Edinburgh, Scotland, 1970-72; assoc. prof. biology MIT, Cambridge, 1972-80; prof. MIT, 1980—, Boris Magasanik prof. biology, 1995—; summer course organizer Cold Spring Harbor Lab., N.Y., 1971-80; mem. rev. com. NIH, 1974-78, 80-84, nat. adv. gen. med. scis. coun., 1984-86, sci. adv. com. Wistar Inst., Phila, 1976—; mem. health and environ. rsch. adv. com. U.S. Dept. Energy, 1987-94; bd. trustees Associated Universities, Inc., 1995—. Mem. editorial bd. Chromsoma, Molecular and Cellular Biology, Biochemistry; contbr. articles to profl. jours. Mem. rev. com. Am. Cancer Soc., 1990-93, Howard Hughes Med. Inst. Adv. Bd., 1993—. Recipient Esther Langer award Langer Cancer Rsch. Found., 1977, Lucius Wilbur Cross medal Yale Grad. Sch., 1989; grantee NIH, NSF, Am. Cancer Soc. Fellow AAAS, NAS (chmn. genetics sect. 1991-94, coun. 1995—), Am. Acad. Arts and Sci. (coun. mem. 1992-96); mem. NRC (bd. on biology 1989-95), Genetics Soc. Am. (pres. 1982-83), Am. Soc. Cell Biology (coun. 1977-80, pres. 1985-86), Assoc. Univ., Inc. (bd. trustees 1995—), Phi Beta Kappa, Phi Kappa Phi. Office: MIT Dept Biology 68-670 77 Massachusetts Ave Cambridge MA 02139-4301

PARDUS, DONALD GENE, utility executive; b. Stafford Springs, Conn., Aug. 1, 1940; s. William L. and Marion (Wondrasck) P.; m. Marilyn L. Riquier, June 10, 1961; children: David J., Susan L., Linda M. BS in Bus. Adminstrn, U. Hartford, Conn., 1966; grad., Harvard U., 1977. Internal auditor Conn. Light and Power Co., Berlin, 1958-67; fin. asst., then asst. treas. N.E. Utilities Svc. Co., Berlin, 1967-79; v.p., CFO, treas. Eastern Utilities, Boston, 1979-85, pres., CFO, 1985-87, pres., COO, trustee, 1987-89, pres., CEO, trustee, 1989-90, chmn., CEO, trustee, 1990—; chmn., dir. Blackstone Valley Electric Co., Newport Electric Corp., Eastern Edison Co., Montaup Electric Co., EUA Svc. Corp., EUA Investment Corp., EUA Ocean State Corp., EUA Cogenex Corp.; bd. dirs. Yankee Atomic Elec. Co., Conn., Maine and Vt. Office: Eastern Utilities Assocs PO Box 2333 1 Liberty Sq Boston MA 02107

PARÉ, JEAN-JACQUES, civil engineer, geotechnical and dam safety consultant; b. Quebec City, Que., Can., Mar. 14, 1929; s. Charles-Auguste and Anna (Delorme) P.; m. Germaine Everell, Sept. 7, 1955; children: Pierre, Marc, Louis, Francois. BA, Coll. St. Jean-Eudes, Quebec City, 1950; BSCE, Laval U., Quebec City, 1955; diploma in concrete, Imperial Coll., London, 1956, diploma in soil mechanics, 1957. Registered profl. engr., Que. Soil engr. Que. Hwy. Dept., Quebec City, 1957-60; lectr. soil mechanics U. Sherbrooke, Que., 1960-65; head soil mechanics TECSULT, Montreal, Que., 1965-72; head geotechnique dept. James Bay Energy Corp., Montreal, 1973-87; geotech. advisor Shawinigan-Lavalin, Montreal, 1988-91, SNC-Shawinigan, Montreal, 1991-93; pvt. practice cons. Verdun, 1994—. Contbr. over 50 articles on dam engring. to profl. jours. Pres. Monseigneur Codère Found., Montreal, 1979-82. Recipient best paper medal Civil Engring. Inst. Can., 1987; Athlone fellow, London, 1955-57. Fellow Engring. Inst. Can.; mem. Can. Geotech. Soc., Internat. Congress Large Dams, Profl. Engrs. Que. Avocations: tennis, skiing. Home and Office: 100 Berlioz Apt 1707, Verdun, PQ Canada H3E 1N4

PAREDES, AMERICO, English language educator; b. Brownsville, Tex., Sept. 3, 1915; s. Justo and Clotilde (Manzano-Vidal) Paredes-Cisneros; m. Amelia Sidzu Nagamine, May 28, 1948; children: Julia, Americo, Alan, Vicente. B.A., U. Tex., Austin, 1951, M.A., 1953, Ph.D., 1956. Journalist, 1936-50; mem. faculty U. Tex., Austin, 1951—; Ashbel Smith prof. English and anthropology U. Tex., 1981-83, Dickson, Allen and Anderson Centennial prof., 1983—, Dickson, Allen and Anderson Centennial prof. emeritus, 1985—. Author: With His Pistol in His Hand, 1958, Folktales of Mexico, 1970, A Texas-Mexican Cancionero, 1976, George Washington Gomez, 1990, Between Two Worlds, 1991, Uncle Remus Con Chile, 1993, Folklore and Culture on the Tex.-Mex. Border, 1993, The Hammon and the Beans and Other Stories, 1994; editor: Jour. Am. Folklore, 1968-1973. With AUS, 1944-46. Decorated Order of Aztec Eagle (Mex.), 1990, Order of José de Escandón (Mex.), 1991; recipient Charles Frankel prize NEH, 1989, award for lifetime achievement Tex. Inst. Letters, 1995; Guggenheim fellow, 1962. Mem. Am. Folklore Soc. (award 1990), Acad. Norteamericana de la Lengua Espanola, Mex. Acad. History. Office: Univ Tex Dept English Austin TX 78712

PAREDES, JAMES ANTHONY, anthropologist, educator; b. N.Y.C., Sept. 29, 1939; s. Antonio and Mildred Olene (Brown) P.; m. Anna Hamilton, Nov. 25, 1959 (div. 1984); children: J. Anthony Jr., Anna Teresa P. Lesinski, Sara Caroline P. Campbell; m. Elizabeth Dixon Purdum, Aug. 10, 1985 (div. 1994): 1 stepchild, David Joseph Plante. BA, Oglethorpe U., 1961; MA, U. N.Mex., 1964, PhD, 1969. Rsch. coord. Upper Miss. Mental Health Ctr., Bemidji, Minn., 1964-67; asst. prof., acting dir. Am. Ind. Studies Bemidji State Coll., 1967-68; community devel. specialist U. Minn. Agrl. Extension Svc., Bemidji, 1967-68; asst. prof. dept. anthropology Fla. State U., Tallahassee, 1969-74, assoc. prof., 1974-78, prof., 1979—, chmn. dept., 1974-77, 84-90; adj. prof. dept. anthropology U. Fla., Gainesville, 1979—; cons. Nat. Marine Fisheries Svc., Galveston, Tex., 1987-88, Bur. Indian Affairs, Washington, 1985, 92, Fed. Recognition Panel, Assn. on Am. Indian Affairs, N.Y.C., 1987-88. Author: Indios de los Estados Unidos Anglosajones, 1992; editor: Anishinabe: Six Studies of Modern Chippewa, 1980, Indians of the Southeastern United States in the Late 20th Century, 1992; author or co-author numerous articles, chpts. in books, revs. Mem. Sci. and Statis. Com., Gulf of Mex. Fishery Mgmt. Coun., Tampa, Fla., 1978-88. Recipient svc. award Poarch Creek Indians, 1990, Woodrow Wilson Found. fellow U. N.Mex., 1961-62; Nat. Inst. Mental Health predoctoral fellow U. N.Mex., 1968-69; Rockefeller Ctr. for Study of So. Culture and Religion fellow, Fla. State U., 1978. Fellow Am. Anthrop. Assn., Soc. for Applied Anthropology (assoc. editor 1983-88, pres. 1993-95); mem. So. Anthrop. Soc. (pres. 1988-89), Fla. Acad. Scis. (sect. chair 1984-85), Sigma Xi (Fla. State U. chpt. pres. 1977-78). Democrat. Avocation: walking. Office: Fla State U Dept Anthropology Tallahassee FL 32306

PARELL, MARY LITTLE, federal judge, former banking commissioner; b. Fond du Lac, Wis., Aug. 13, 1946; d. Ashley Jewell and Gertrude (McCoy) Little; m. John Francis Parell, May 28, 1972 (div. 1990); children: Christie, Morgan, Shawn, John Brady. AB in Polit. Sci. cum laude, Bryn Mawr Coll., 1968; JD, Villanova U., 1972; LLD (hon.), Georgian Ct. Coll., 1987. Bar. N.J. 1972. Assoc. McCarter & English, Newark, 1972-80, ptnr., 1980-84; commr. N.J. Dept. Banking, Trenton, 1984-90; assoc. gen. counsel Prudential Property & Casualty Ins. Co., Holmdel, N.J., 1991-92; judge U.S. Dist. Ct. N.J., 1992—; chmn. bd. Pinelands Devel. Credt Bank. Bd. trustees Exec. Commn. Ethical Standards, Trenton, 1984-90, Corp. Bus. Assistance, Trenton, 1984-91, N.J. Housing & Mortgage Fin. Agy., Trenton, 1984-90, N.J. Cemetery Bd. Assn., 1984-90, N.J. Hist. Soc., 1976-79, YMCA of Greater Newark, 1973-76, Diocesan Investment; mem. Supreme Ct. N.J. Civil Practice Com., 1982-84, Supreme Ct. N.J. Dist. Ethics Com., 1982-84; lay assesor Ecclesiastical Ct. Episc. Diocese Newark, 1980-84. Fellow Am. Bar Found.; mem. ABA, N.J. Bar Assn., Princeton Bar Assn. Office: US Courthouse 402 E State St Trenton NJ 08608-1507*

PARENT, ANDRÉ, neurobiology educator, researcher; b. Montreal, Que., Can., Oct. 3, 1944; s. Lucien and Yvette (Gagné) P.; m. Doris Côté, July 8, 1970; children: Geneviève, Philippe, Martin. BSc, U. Montreal, 1967; PhD in Neurobiology, U. Laval, Quebec City, Que., 1970; postgrad., Max-Planck Inst., Frankfurt, Germany, 1971. Asst. prof. anatomy Laval U. Med. Sch., 1971-76, assoc. prof., 1976-81, prof., 1981—, sci. dir. Neurobiology Rsch. Ctr., 1985-92. Author: Comparative Neurobiology of the Basal Ganglia, 1986, Human Neuroanatomy, 9th edit., 1996. Studentship Med. Rsch. Coun. Can., 1967-70, fellow, Frankfurt, 1970-71, scholar, 1973-78. Mem. Royal Soc. Can., Internat. Brain Rsch. Orgn. Avocations: music, reading. Office: Enfant Jesus Hosp Neurobiology Ctr, 1401 18th St, Quebec, PQ Canada G1J 1Z4

PARENT, GILBERT, member Canadian House of Commons; b. Mattawa, Ont., Can., July 25, 1935; m. Joan Davis, Aug. 23, 1958; children: Michèle Hundertmark, Monique Finley, madeleine Thomas, Thérèse. BSc, St. Joseph's Coll.; MA, Niagara U.; MEdn, U. N.Y. M.P. Ho. of Commons, Ottawa, Ont., Can., 1974; re-elected, 1979, 88; Parliamentary Sec.to Min. Veterans Affairs Ottawa, Ont., Can., 1977-79, Parliamentary Sec. to Min. of Labour, 1979-81, Parliamentary Sec. to Min. Fitness and Amateur Sports, 1981-83; Speaker of the House Ho. of Commons, Ottawa, Ont., Can., 1994; appted. Critic for Youth, 1989, Labour, 1992; assoc. critic CIDA, 1989, Industry, 1992. Mem. Can.-U.S. Parliamentary Assn. (vice-chair). Office: House of Commons, Rm 328-N Centre Block, Ottawa, ON Canada K1A 0A6

PARENT, LOUISE MARIE, lawyer; b. San Francisco, Aug. 28, 1950; d. Jules D. and Mary Louise (Bartholomew) P.; m. John P. Casaly, Jan. 5, 1980. AB, Smith Coll., 1972; JD, Georgetown U., 1975. Bar: N.Y. 1976, U.S. Dist. Ct. (so. dist.) N.Y. 1976. Assoc. Donovan Leisure, N.Y.C., 1975-77; various positions, then gen. counsel Am. Express Info. Svcs. Corp., N.Y.C., 1977-92; dep. gen. counsel Am. Express Co., N.Y.C., 1992-93, exec. v.p., gen. counsel, 1993—; mem. legal adv. com. N.Y. Stock Exch. Bd. dirs. A Better Chance Inc., Cooke Found. Spl. Edn. Mem. ABA (com. depts. corp. law). Home: 1170 5th Ave New York NY 10029-6527 Office: Am Express Co Am Express Tower World Fin Ctr New York NY 10285

PARENT, RODOLPHE JEAN, Canadian air force official, pilot; b. Thurso, Que., Can., June 16, 1937; s. Eugène Jean and Eliane Marie (Raby) P.; m. Michelle Marie Masse, Aug. 10, 1963; children—Stéphane, Nathalie, Cynthia. Student, Coll. Militaire Royal de St-Jean, 1958-61; B.Sc., Royal Mil. Coll. Can., Kingston, Ont., 1963. Commd. Royal Can. Air Force, 1958; advanced through grades to brig.-gen., 1984; joined 425 Squadron for ops. on CF-101 aircraft Bagotville, Que., 1964-69; worked for Directorate of Recruiting and Selection at Nat. Def. Hdqrs., Ottawa, Ont., Can., 1969-71; chief of ops. 433 Tactical Fighter Squadron, Bagotville, 1972-75, Can. Forces Base Bagotville, 1975-76; comdg. officer 433 Tactical Fighter Squadron, 1976-80; asst. dir. personnel careers Nat. Def. Hdqrs., Ottawa, 1980-81; base comdr. Can. Forces Base Lahr, Federal Republic Germany, 1981-83; commandant Coll. Militaire Royal de Saint-Jean, Que., 1983-86; dir. gen. personnel careers other ranks Nat. Def. Hdqrs., Ottawa, 1986-89; def. attaché Paris, 1989-92; ret., 1992. Decorated Order of Mil. Merit, Order of St. John of Jerusalem. Roman Catholic. Avocations: hockey; tennis; windsurfing.

PARENTE, WILLIAM JOSEPH, political science educator; b. Chgo., July 7, 1937; s. Salvatore S. and Genevieve (Rooney) P.; m. Diane Alpern, Nov. 30, 1963; children: Elizabeth, Margaret, William Joseph, Caroline, Rebecca, Catherine, Abigail, Christopher, Natalya. A.B. cum laude, Xavier U., Ohio, 1961; Ph.D. (Woodrow Wilson fellow, Woodrow Wilson dissertation fellow), Georgetown U., 1970. Woodrow Wilson intern Wilberforce (Ohio) U., 1965-66; asst. prof., chmn. polit. sci. dept. Antioch Coll., 1966-69, assoc. dean faculty, 1969-70; dean Coll. Arts and Scis., U. Scranton, Pa., 1970-85; assoc. prof. polit. sci. Coll. Arts and Scis., U. Scranton, 1970-73, prof., 1973—; Fulbright scholar Chulalongkorn U., Bangkok, Thailand, 1985-86, Inst. for Policy Studies, Washington, 1986-87; mem. nat. Fulbright screening com. for East Asia, Southeast Asia; mem. adv. com. Inst. Internat. Edn.; cons. on world affairs to Peace Corps. Author articles in field. Fellow Inst. Acad. Deans, 1971, Inst. Ednl. Mgmt., Harvard Bus. Sch., 1972, Fulbright fellow, Korea, 1974, Indonesia, 1978, Germany, 1980, Thailand, 1985-86, fellow NEH Seminar, U. Va., 1976, Harvard U., 1985, Columbia U., 1988, George Mason U., Va., 1990, UCLA, 1991, U. Mich., 1992, William and Mary, 1993, U. Iowa, 1994; scholar-diplomat program State Dept., 1970, 73; vis. scholar in humanities NYU, 1989. Fellow Union Experimenting Colls. and Univs., Inst. for Policy Studies, Soc. for Religion in Higher Edn.; mem. Am. Polit. Sci. Assn., Assn. Jesuit Colls. and Univs. (chmn. conf. on internat. edn. 1981-85), Alpha Sigma Nu (nat. sec.-treas. 1979-82, nat. pres. 1983-85), Pi Sigma Alpha, Eta Sigma Phi, Alpha Sigma Lambda, Tau Kappa Alpha, Phi Alpha Theta. Roman Catholic. Office: U Scranton Coll Arts & Sciences Scranton PA 18510

PARESKY, DAVID S., travel company executive; b. Boston, Sept. 27, 1938; s. Paul and Ada (Rudnick) P.; m. Linda Kotzen, Aug. 18, 1963; children: Pamela, Laura, Mark. BA, Williams Coll., 1960; JD, Harvard U., 1963, MBA, 1965. Bar: Mass. Pres., chmn. bd. Crimson Travel Service, Inc., Cambridge, Mass., 1965-89; pres., CEO Thomas Cook Travel, Cambridge, 1989-94, also chmn. bd. dirs. Dir., Gov.'s Mgmt. Task Force, Boston, 1979-83, Mass. Port Authority, Boston, 1980-83; mem. Bd. Higher Edn., Boston, 1980; trustee New Eng. Med. Ctr., 1982-83; mem. Bd. Regents of Higher Edn., Boston, 1980-86. Mem. Mass. Bar Assn., Am. Soc. Travel Agts., Travel Trust Internat., Greater Boston C. of C., Young Pres. Orgn. (chmn. New Eng. chpt. 1985), Phi Beta Kappa. Home: 231 Winter St Weston MA 02193-1034

PARET, PETER, historian; b. Berlin, Apr. 13, 1924; s. Hans and Suzanne Aimée (Cassirer) P.; m. Isabel Harris, Sept. 23, 1961; children: Suzanne Aimée, Paul Louis Michel. BA, U. Calif., Berkeley, 1949; Ph.D., U. London, 1960, DLitt, 1992; LittD, U. S.C., 1995; DHL, Coll. of Wooster, 1996. Resident tutor, delegacy of extramural studies Oxford U., 1959-60; research assoc. Center of Internat. Studies, Princeton U., 1960-62, 63; vis. asst. prof. U. Calif., Davis, 1962-63; assoc. prof. U. Calif., 1963-66, prof., 1966-69; prof. history Stanford U., 1969-77, Raymond A. Spruance prof. internat. history, 1977-86; Andrew W. Mellon Prof. in humanities Inst. Advanced Study, Princeton, N.J., 1986—; mem. Inst. for Advanced Study, Princeton, 1966-67; fellow Ctr. for Advanced Study in Behavioral Scis., Stanford, Calif., 1968-69; vis. fellow London Sch. Econs., 1972-73; NEH fellow, 1979-80; sr. fellow Hoover Instn., Stanford U., 1988-93. Author: (with John Shy) Guerrillas in the 1960's, 1962, French Revolutionary Warfare from Indochina to Algeria, 1964, Yorck and the Era of Prussian Reform, 1966, Clausewitz and the State, 1976, rev. edit., 1985; The Berlin Secession, 1980, Art as History, 1988, (with Beth Irwin Lewis and Paul Paret) Persuasive Images, 1992, Understanding War, 1992; editor, translator: (with Michael Howard) On War (C. v. Clausewitz), 1976, (with Daniel Moran) Historical and Political Writings (C. v. Clausewitz), 1992; editor: Frederick the Great, 1968, Frederick the Great—A Historical Profile, 1972, Sisyphus or the Limits of Education, 1973, The Age of German Liberation, 1977, Berliner Secession, 1981, Makers of Modern Strategy, 1986, (with Ekkehard Mai) Sammler, Stifter & Museen, 1993. Served with inf. U.S. Army, 1943-46. Fellow AAAS, Royal Hist. Soc., Hist. Kom zu Berlin, Leo Baeck Inst., London Sch. Econs. (hon.); mem. Am. Philos. Soc. (Jefferson medal), Soc. for Mil. History (Samuel Eliot Morison medal). Office: Sch Hist Studies Inst Advanced Study Princeton NJ 08540

PARETSKY, SARA N., writer; b. Ames, Iowa, June 8, 1947; d. David Paretsky and Mary E. Edwards; m. S. Courtenay Wright, June 19, 1976; children: Kimball Courtenay, Timothy Charles, Philip William. BA, U. Kans., 1967; MBA, PhD, U. Chgo., 1977. Mgr. Urban Rsch Ctr., Chgo., 1971-74, CNA Ins. Co., Chgo., 1977-85; writer, 1985—. Author: (novels) Indemnity Only, 1982, Deadlock, 1984 (Friends of Am. Writers award 1985), Killing Orders, 1985, Bitter Medicine, 1987, Blood Shot, 1988 (Silver Dagger award Crime Writers Assn., 1988), Burn Marks, 1990, Guardian Angel, 1992, Tunnel Vision, 1994, also numerous articles and short stories. Pres. Sisters in Crime, Chgo., 1986-88; dir. Nat. Abortion Rights Action League Ill., 1987—. Named Woman of Yr. Ms mag., N.Y.C., 1987. Mem. Crime Writers Assn. (Silver Dagger award 1988), Mystery Writers Am. (v.p. 1989), Authors Guild, Chgo. Network. Avocations: baseball, opera. *

PARFIT, GAVIN J., international management executive; b. Durban, South Africa, Oct. 15, 1947; m. Isabel Barzun; children: Elizabeth, Emily. ACIS, U. Natal, South Africa, 1970; MBA, Cranfield Inst. Tech., U.K., 1974. CEO Henry Vale & Co., South Africa, 1966-72; pres., CEO Golodetz Corp., N.Y.C., 1987—; dir. Chem. Bank Internat., Ltd., N.Y.C., London, 1983-87; v.p. Chemical Bank, N.Y., London, 1975-83; now ceo Delta Commodities Inc., N.Y. Trustee Turtle Bay Music Sch., N.Y.C., 1993. With South African Air Force, 1965. Home: 150 E 77th St Apt 5A New York NY 10021-1927 Office: Delta Commodities Inc 142 W 57th St 8th fl New York NY 10019-3300*

PARHAM, CAROL S., school system administrator; b. Balt.; m. William N. Parham, Jr.; children: William N. III, Julie T. BA in Social Studies Edn., U. Md.; M in Edn. Guidance and Counseling, Johns Hopkins U., postgrad. studies. Social studies tchr. Balt. City Schs., personnel specialist, acting staff specialist, personnel assoc.; supr. office personnel Howard County Pub. Schs., 1985-89; dir. personnel Anne Arundel County Pub. Schs., 1989—. Bd. dirs. Anne Arundel Trade Coun., United Way Ctrl. Md.; mem. task force Md. State Dept. Edn.; mem. edn. adv. com. JOhns Hopkins U. Sch. Continuing Studies; mem. adv. bd. Leadership Anne Arundel. Recipient Outstanding Achievement in Leadership award Md. State Tchrs. Assn., Outstanding Leadership in Edn. award St. John United Meth. Women; Good Scout award Baltimore Area Coun. Boy Scouts Am.; named Woman of Yr., Glen Burnie Chpt. Nat. Fedn. Bus. Profl. Women, Md. Supt. of Yr., 1995. Mem. Pub. Sch. Supts. Assn. Md., Assn. Sch. Bus. Officials Md. and DC (past pres.), Md. Personnel Assn. (past pres.), Coalition 100 Black Women, Rotary, Delta Sigma Theta. Office: Office of Supt 2644 Riva Rd Annapolis MD 21401

PARHAM, ELLEN SPEIDEN, nutrition educator; b. Mitchells, Va., July 15, 1938; d. Marion Coote and Rebecca Virginia (McNiel) Speiden; m. Arthur Robert Parham, Jr., Dec. 16, 1961; children: Katharine Alma, Cordelia Alyx. BS in Nutrition, Va. Poly. Inst., 1960; PhD in Nutrition, U. Tenn., 1967, MSEd in Counseling, 1994. Registered dietitian. Asst. prof. to prof. No. Ill. U., DeKalb, Ill., 1966—; coord. programs in dietetics No. Ill. U., DeKalb, 1981-86, 90—, coord. grad. faculty in Human and Family Resources, 1985-87; cons. on nutrition various hosps., clins. and bus., Ill., 1980—; founder, dir. Horizons Weight Control Program, DeKalb, 1983-91; founder, leader "Escaping the Tyranny of the Scale" Group, 1994—; co-chair Nutrition Coalition for Ill., 1989-90; pres., mgr. Design on Fabric, 1986—. Bd. editors Jour. Nutrition Edn., 1985-90, Jour. Am. Dietetic Assn., 1991—; contbr. articles to profl. jours. Mem. Am. Inst. Nutrition, Soc. Nutrition Edn., Am. Dietetic Assn., Am. Home Econs. Assn., Soc. Nutrition Edn. (treas. 1991-94, chair divsn. nutrition and weight realities 1995-96), N.Am. Assn. Study Obesity. Avocations: painting in watercolor, gardening, reading.

PARHAM, JAMES ROBERT, lawyer; b. East St. Louis, Ill., June 3, 1921; s. James Elbert and Edith Virginia (May) P.; m. Caroline Short, Nov. 4, 1950 (dec.); m. Elizabeth Joan Rinck, June 29, 1957; children: James R., Jr., Joseph R., J. Randolph. A.B., Princeton U., 1943; J.D. with honors, U. Ill., 1948. Bar: Ill. 1948, U.S. Dist. Ct. (so. dist.) Ill. 1948, U.S. Supreme Ct. 1968. Assoc., Pope & Driemeyer, East St. Louis, 1948-59, ptnr., Belleville, Ill., 1960-84, Thompson & Mitchell, 1985—; mem. adv. council Ill. Inst. for Continuing Legal Edn., Springfield, Ill., 1965-74. Contbr. articles to profl. jours. Sec., YMCA of S.W. Ill., Belleville, 1979-84. Served with U.S. Air Corps, 1943, 45, USAFR, 1950-53. Recipient Man of Yr. award Bicounty YMCA, Belleville, 1973; Disting. Service award Ill. Inst. Continuing Edn., 1974. Fellow Am. Bar Found., Ill. State Bar Found.; mem. Ill. State Bar Assn. (chmn. state tax sect. 1974), ABA, Met. St. Louis Bar Assn., Res. Officers Assn., Order of Coif. Republican. Methodist. Clubs: St. Clair Country (Belleville, v.p. 1955-56); Grey Oaks Country Club (Naples, Fla.). Lodge: Rotary (pres. East St. Louis club 1976-77). Home: 7535 Claymont Ct # 3 Belleville IL 62223-2218 Office: Thompson & Mitchell 525 W Main St PO Box 750 Belleville IL 62222

PARIKH, INDU, biomedical scientist, pharmaceutical executive; b. Bhavnagar, India; came to U.S., 1968; m. Emma Mosimann-Parikh; 1 child, Rayan. PhD, U. Zurich, Switzerland, 1965. Postdoctoral fellow Weizmann Inst., Rehovot, Israel, 1967-68; vis. scientist NIH, Bethesda, Md., 1968-70; asst. prof. pharmacology and medicine Sch. Medicine Johns Hopkins U., Balt., 1970-75; group leader dept. molecular biology Burroughs Wellcome Co., Research Triangle Park, N.C., 1975-77, asst. dept. head, 1977-82, dept. head, 1982-86; dir. biochemistry divsn. Glaxo, Inc., Research Triangle Park, 1986-90; v.p. R & D Research Triangle Pharms., Ltd., Durham, N.C., 1990—; mem. sci. adv. bds. 3 biotech. cos., 1990—. Co-editor: Affinity Chromatography and Biological Recognition, 1983; mem. editl. bd. 3 sci. jours.; contbr. over 70 articles to sci. publs. Exec. v.p., bd. dirs. Alopecia Areata Rsch. Found., 1983-90. Rsch. grantee NIH, U.S. Army Med. Command, 1970-75, Small Bus. Innovation Rsch., 1992-94. Mem. Am. Soc. Pharmacology and Exptl. Therapeutics, Am. Soc. Biochemistry and Molecular Biology, Am. Assn. Pharm. Scientists, Assn. for Rsch. in Vision and Ophthalmology, Control Release Soc., Internat. Soc. for Bioreecognition Tech. (mem. governing coun. 1984-90), NAS (hon., India), Soc. Biol. Chemistry India (hon. life). Achievements include 6 patents in field. Office: Research Triangle Pharm Ltd 4364 S Alston Ave Ste 200 Durham NC 27713

PARINS, ROBERT JAMES, professional football team executive, judge; b. Green Bay, Wis., Aug. 23, 1918; s. Frank and Nettie (Denissen) P.; m. Elizabeth L. Carroll, Feb. 8, 1941; children: Claire, Andrée, Richard, Teresa, Lu Ann. B.A., U. Wis., 1940, LL.B., 1942. Bar: Wis. Supreme Ct. 1942. Pvt. practice Green Bay, Wis., 1942-68; dist. atty. Brown County, Wis., 1949-50, cir. judge, 1968-82, res. judge, 1982—; pres. Green Bay Packers, Inc., 1982-90, chmn. bd., 1990-92; hon. chmn. bd., 1992-94. Mem. Wis. State Bar Assn. Roman Catholic. Office: Green Bay Packers PO Box 10628 Green Bay WI 54307-0628

PARIS, DEMETRIUS THEODORE, electrical engineering educator; b. Stavroupolis, Thrace, Greece, Sept. 27, 1928; came to U.S., 1947, naturalized, 1954; s. Theodore P. and Aspasia (Yannakis) Paraskevopoulos; m. Elsie Edwards, Jan. 5, 1952. B.S., Miss. State U., 1951; M.S., Ga. Inst. Tech., 1958, Ph.D., 1962. With Westinghouse Electric Corp., 1952-58, Lockheed-Ga. Co., 1958-59; asst. prof. elec. engring. Ga. Inst. Tech., 1959-63, assoc. prof., 1963-66, prof., 1966—, asst. dir. elec. engring., 1966-69, dir., 1969-89, v.p for rsch. and grad. programs, 1989-95; cons.Sci.-Atlanta, Inc., Lockheed-Ga. Co., U.S. Army Ltd. War Lab., Aberdeen, Md.; chair internat. activities com. Accreditation Bd. for Engring. and Tech., 1991—. Author: Basic Electromagnetic Theory, 1969. Recipient Sigma Xi award for best research paper by a mem. Ga. Inst. Tech. faculty, 1965. Fellow Accreditation Bd. for Engring. and Tech., IEEE (editor trans. on edn. 1976-79, Centennial medal 1984, ednl. activities bd. meritorious svc. citation 1989, IEEE rep. to Accreditation Bd. for Engring. and Tech. bd. dirs. 1990-95); mem. IEEE Edn. Soc. (Achievement award 1980, pres. 1986), Am. Soc. Engring. Edn., Sigma Xi, Kappa Mu Epsilon, Tau Beta Pi, Eta Kappa Nu, Phi Kappa Phi. Home: 2797 Alpine Rd NE Atlanta GA 30305-3401

PARÍS, KEVIN, English educator; b. N.Y.C., Oct. 14, 1953; s. Ferdinand and Minerva (Alicea) P.; m. Miriam Celeste Pérez, Dec. 20, 1975; children:

Kevin, Miriam. BA in English and Secondary Edn., U. P.R., 1977, MEd in English and Secondary Edn., 1979. Cert. tchr., P.R., Tex. Instr., tchr. trainer Cath. U. P.R., Ponce, 1980-82, asst. prof., tchr. trainer, 1983-85; tchg. asst. East Tex. State U., Commerce, 1982-83; secondary tchr., tchr. trainer Dallas Ind. Sch. Dist., 1985-91; prof. ESL and English Brookhaven Coll., Farmers Branch, Tex., 1991—; writing cons. region 10 Edn. Svc. Ctr., Richardson, Tex., 1986; mem. adv. bd. Tex. Higher Edn. Coordinating Bd., Austin, 1994—; writer curricula in field. Founding pres. Mesquite (Tex.) H.S. Band Parent Orgn., 1993-94. Mem. Tex. TESOL, TESOL, Nat. Inst. for Staff and Orgnl. Devel. Home: 410 Barton Dr Mesquite TX 75149-5984 Office: Brookhaven Coll 3939 Valley View Ln Farmers Branch TX 75244-4997

PARIS, PAUL CROCE, mechanics educator, engineering consultant, researcher; b. Buffalo, Aug. 7, 1930; s. Russell Horace and Martha Elizabeth (Robertson) P.; m. Elizabeth Alderman, Jan. 13, 1963 (div. 1974); children: Gail Elizabeth, Anthony James; m. Christine Ellen Anders, Jan. 10, 1980. BS in Engring. Mechanics, U. Mich., 1953; MS in Applied Mechanics, Lehigh U., 1955, PhD in Applied Mechanics, 1962. Instr. mechanics Lehigh U., Bethlehem, Pa., 1955-57, asst. prof., 1962-63, assoc. prof., 1963-65, prof., 1965-72, asst. dir. Inst. Rsch., 1962-64; asst. prof. civil engring. U. Wash., Seattle, 1957-62; pres., chief exec. officer Del. Rsch. Corp., Hellertown, Pa., 1968—; prof. mechanics Washington U., St. Louis, 1976—; program dir. NSF, Washington, 1964-65; vis. prof. Brown U., Providence, 1974-76; cons. Westinghouse, U.S. Steel, Boeing Co., Lawrence Radiation Lab., Rand Corp., NRC, NASA, others. Co-author: The Stress Analysis of Cracks Handbook, 1973, 2d edit., 1985; contbr. numerous articles to profl. jours. Fellow ASTM (award of merit 1972, Fracture Mechanics medal 1987), Internat. Congress on Fracture (hon.), Internat. Fatigue Series (hon. life); mem. Commanderie de Bordeaux (comdr. 1980—), Commanderie de Laupiac, Sigma Xi. Avocations: piloting, wildlife conservation. Home: PO Box 13 Cherryville MO 65446-0013 Office: Washington U Dept Mech Engring Saint Louis MO 63130

PARIS, PETER JUNIOR, religion educator, minister; b. New Glasgow, N.S., Can., May 30, 1933; s. Freeman Archibald and Violet Agatha (Jewell) P.; m. Shirley Ann McMillen, May 13, 1961; children: Valerie Lynn ToKunbo, Peter Brett. BA, Acadia U., Wolfville, N.S., 1956, BD, 1958; MA, U. Chgo., 1969, PhD, 1975; DD (hon.), McGill U., 1989, Acadia U., 1990. Ordained minister African United Bapt. Assn. N.S. Gen. sec. U. Alta. chpt. Student Christian Movement Can., Edmonton, 1958-61, spl. travelling sec., Toronto, 1964-65; nat. travelling sec. Student Christian Movement Nigeria, Ibadan, 1961-64; instr. urban studies Associated Coll. of Mid-West, Chgo., 1969-70; instr. ethics and soc. Howard U. Div. Sch., Washington, 1970-72; asst. prof. ethics and soc. Vanderbilt U. Div. Sch., Nashville, 1972-77, assoc. prof., 1977-83, prof., 1983-85; Elmer G. Homrighausen prof. Christian social ethics Princeton (N.J.) Theol. Seminary, 1985—; sr. fellow Mathey Coll., Princeton U., 1988—; cons. Assn. Theol. Schs., Indpls., 1986—, W.E.B. DuBois Inst., Harvard U., 1988—; lectr. U. S.Africa, Pretoria, Aug., 1988; fellow W.E.B. DuBois Inst., Harvard U., 1990. Author: Black Leaders in Conflict, 1978 (excerpts in Congl. Record May 1981), rev. as Black Religious Leaders: Conflict in Unity, 1991, The Social Teaching of the Black Churches, 1985; co-editor: Justice and the Holy, 1989; mem. editorial bd. Soundings: An Interdisciplinary Jour., Jour. Religion, Jour. Religious Ethics; author essays and chpts. in books. Ford Found. fellow Ctr. Urban Studies, U. Chgo., 1968-70, Woodrow Wilson fellow, 1990; rsch. grantee Lilly Endowment, Vanderbilt U., NRC, Princeton Theol. Seminary. Fellow Soc. for Values in Higher Edn.; mem. Am. Acad. Religion (assoc. dir. 1983-85, v.p. 1993, pres.-elect 1994, pres. 1995), Soc. Christian Ethics (bd. dirs. 1977-82, v.p. 1990, pres. 1991), Soc. for Study Black Religion (founding), Am. Theol. Soc. Democrat. Office: Princeton Theol Sem Dept of Theology CN 821 Princeton NJ 08542*

PARIS, ZACHARY T., lawyer; b. Cleve., Aug. 30, 1948. BA, Yale U., 1970, JD, 1973. Bar: Ohio 1973. Law clk. U.S. Dist. Ct. (no. dist.) Ohio; ptnr. Jones, Day, Reavis & Pogue, Cleve. Mem. Phi Beta Kappa. Office: Jones Day Reavis & Pogue North Point 901 Lakeside Ave E Cleveland OH 44114-1116

PARISER, RUDOLPH, chemicals company executive, consultant; b. Harbin, China, Dec. 8, 1923; came to U.S., 1941, naturalized, 1944; s. Ludwig Jacob and Lia (Rubinstein) P.; m. Margaret Louise Marsh, July 31, 1972. BS in Chemistry, U. Calif., Berkeley, 1944; PhD in Phys. Chemistry, U. Minn., 1950. With E.I. du Pont de Nemours & Co., Wilmington, Del., 1950-89, with elastomer chems. dept., 1967-79, dir. pioneering rsch., 1974-79, rsch. dir. polymer products dept., 1980-81, dir. polymer sci. cen. R & D dept., 1981-86, dir. advanced materials sci. cen. R & D dept., 1986-89; cons., pres. R. Pariser & Co., Inc., Hockessin, Del., 1989—; mem. materials rsch. adv. com. Nat. Sci. Found., 1986-89. Assoc. editor Jour. Chem. Physics, 1966-69, Chem. Physics Letters, 1967-70, Du Pont Innnovation, 1969-75; mem. adv. bd. Jour. Polymer Sci., 1980-89; mem. editorial bd. New Polymeric Materials, 1985-92; patentee in field; contbr. articles to profl. jours. With U.S. Army, 1944-46. Mem. AAAS, Am. Chem. Soc., Am. Phys. Soc., Internat. Union Pure and Applied Chemistry, Phila. Interlocuters (pres. 1972-76), Sigma Xi, Phi Lambda Upsilon, Du Pont Country Club, Rodney Sq. Club, Univ. and Whist Club Wilmington. Avocations: skiing, tennis, golf, sailing, gardening.

PARISH, J. MICHAEL, lawyer, writer; b. Decatur, Ill., Nov. 9, 1943; s. John Mitchell and Gladys Margaret (Daulton) P.; m. Susan Lee Sgarlat, July 24, 1976 (div.); m. Ellen R. Harnett, Dec. 3, 1991; children: Margaret Ruth, William Walter. AB cum laude, Princeton U., 1965; LLB, Yale U., 1968. Assoc. LeBoeuf Lamb et al, N.Y.C., 1968-73, ptnr., 1974-89; ptnr. Winthrop Stimson Putnam & Roberts, N.Y.C., 1989-95, Reid & Priest, N.Y.C., N.Y.C., 1995—; bd. dirs. Forum Funds, Portland, Maine, Core Trust. Contbr. poetry to mags. Dir. PBS Am. Poetry Project, 1985-90; coord. Yale Law Sch. Clinton Election com.. Univ. scholar Princeton U., 1965. Mem. Princeton Club N.Y. Avocations: soccer referee, coach Little League, poetry, fiction, nonfiction. Home: 100 Riverside Dr New York NY 10024-4822 Office: Reid & Priest 40 W 57th St New York NY 10019-4001

PARISH, JAMES ROBERT, author, cinema historian; b. Cambridge, Mass., Apr. 21, 1944; s. Fred Arthur and Ann Lois (Magilevy) P. BA, U. Pa., 1964, LLB, 1967. Pres. Entertainment Copyright Rsch.Co. Inc., N.Y.C., 1967-68; film reporter, reviewer, interviewer Variety, Motion Picture Daily, 1968-69; entertainment publicist Harold Rand & Co., 1969-70; freelance writer, publicist, film book cons., film reviewer, novelist, 1970—. Author: (with P. Michael) The Emmy Awards: A Pictorial History, 1970, The Fox Girls, 1971, The Great Movie Series, 1971 (with A.H. Marill) The Cinema of Edward G. Robinson, 1972, The Slapstick Queens, 1972, The Paramount Pretties, 1972, (with R. Bowers) The MGM Stock Company, 1973, Actors TV Credits, 1950-72, 73, Good Dames, 1973, (with M.R. Pitts) The Great Spy Pictures, 1973, The RKO Gals, 1973, (with S. Whitney), The George Raft File, 1973, (with M.R. Pitts) Film Directors: A Guide to Their American Pictures, 1974, Hollywood's Great Love Teams, 1974, (with S. Whitney) Vincent Price Unmasked, 1974, The Great Movie Heroes, 1975, (with D. Stanke), The Glamour Girls, 1975, The Debonairs, 1975, (with L. DeCarl) Hollywood Players: The Forties, 1975, (with J. Ano) Liza! (The Liza Minnelli Story), 1975, (with M.R. Pitts) The Great Gangster Pictures, 1975, The Elvis Presley Scrapbook, 1975, (with W. Leonard) Hollywood Players: The Thirties, 1976, (with D. Stanke) The All Americans, 1976, Film Directors: A Guide for Western Europe, 1976, Great Child Stars, 1976, The Jeanette McDonald Story, 1976, (with D. Stanke) The Leading Ladies, 1977, (with M.R. Pitts) The Great Science Fiction Pictures, 1977, Film Actors Guide: Western Europe, 1977, The Elvis Presley Scrapbook (update), 1977, (with M. Trost) Actors TV Credits: Supplement One, 1977, (with M.R. Pitts) Hollywood on Hollywood, 1978, (with R. Braff et al) Hollywood Character Actors, 1978, (with G. Mank and D. Stanke) The Hollywood Beauties, 1978, (with W. Leonard) The Funsters, 1979, (with D. Stanke) The Forties Gals, 1980, (with G. Mank) The Hollywood Reliables, 1980, The Great American Movies Book, 1980, (with G. Mank) The Best of MGM, 1981, (with M.R. Pitts) The Great Spy Pictures II, 1986, (with M.R. Pitts) The Great Gangster Pictures II, 1987, (with M.R. Pitts) The Great Western Pictures II, 1988, Black Action Pictures from Hollywood, 1989, (with M.R. Pitts) The Great Science Fiction Pictures II, 1990, (with V. Terrace) Complete Actors TV Credits, 1990, (with M.R. Pitts) Hollywood Songsters, 1990, The Great Cop Pictures, 1990, Prison Pictures from Hollywood, 1991, (with M.R. Pitts) Hollywood's Great Musicals, 1992, (with D. Stanke) Hollywood Baby Boomers, 1992, Prostitution in Hollywood Film, 1992, The Hollywood Death Book, 1992; Let's Talk: America's Favorite Talk Show Hosts, 1993, Gays and Lesbians in Mainstream Hollywood, 1993, Hollywood's Celebrity Death Book, updated and expanded, 1994, Ghosts and Angels on the Hollywood Screen, 1995, Today's Black Hollywood, 1995, Pirates and Seafaring Swashbucklers, 1995; assoc. editor: The American Movies Reference Book, 1969, TV Movies, 1969, The Great American Movie Book, 1980. Mem. Phi Beta Kappa. Avocations: docent, reading, writing. Address: 4338 Gentry Ave Apt 1 Studio City CA 91604-1764 *To succeed in one's ambitions requires an unyielding avoidance of other people's skepticisms.*

PARISH, JOHN COOK, insurance executive; b. Montezuma, Iowa, Mar. 26, 1910; s. Ariel Robert and Mary Ora (Cook) P.; m. Elizabeth Myers, Sept. 2, 1936; children: John C., Michael Myers, Judith, Robert S. Student, UCLA; B.A., Dartmouth Coll., 1936. Officer Dollar S.S. Lines, Seattle, 1930-31; with Ginn & Co. (pubs.), Manila, 1933-34; sec. to U.S. rep. Warsaw, Poland, 1934; with St. Paul Fire & Marine Ins. Co., 1936—, exec. spl. agt., 1943-44, asst. mgr. Pacific dept., 1947-48, asst. sec., 1948-50, sec., 1950-68, v.p., 1968—; also dir.; sec. St. Paul Mercury Ins. Co., 1950-68, v.p., 1968—; also dir.; v.p. St. Paul Ins. Co., 1968—. Mem. Bishop's council Minn. Episcopal Diocese; past pres., treas. Summit Sch. for Girls, St. Paul; past pres. Indianhead council Boy Scouts Am., past regional chmn. and mem. nat. exec. bd., internat. commr., v.p., 1972-78; hon. v.p. U.S. Found. for Internat. Scouting; chmn. St. Paul United Fund, 1963, pres., 1966; trustee Endowment Fund, Seabury Western Theol. Sem., Am. Humanics Found.; v.p. U.S. Found. Internat. Scouting, Salem Found.; bd. dirs. Inst. Ecumenical and Cultural Research, St. John's Coll.; mem. World Scout Com.; bd. trustees Naples (Fla.) Community Hosp.; sr. warden Trinity By the Cove Episcopal Ch., Naples, 1981-82. Decorated Cross of St. George Colombia; recipient Silver Tamaraw award Philippine Islands, Inter-Am. award Svc. to Youth, Silver Beaver, Silver Antelope, Silver Buffalo and Disting. Eagle award Boy Scouts Am., Bronze Wolf award for svc. to youth of world, Emerald Flower award Republic of China; Baden Powell fellow World Scout Found., 1982. Mem. St. Paul C. of C. (dir. 1973—), Beta Theta Pi. Clubs: Somerset Country (St. Paul), Minn. (St. Paul) (dir. 1968); Royal Poinciana (Naples, Fla.) (past pres. and dir.). Home: 122 Moorings Park Dr Apt G607 Naples FL 33942-2116

PARISH, LAWRENCE CHARLES, physician, editor; b. Cambridge, Mass., Oct. 12, 1938; s. Fred A. and Ann Lois (Magilavy) P.; m. Sheila Gail Rovner, July 31, 1966; children: Daniel Howard, Jennifer Leigh. Student, U. Mich., 1955-56; AB, U. Pa., 1959; MD, Tufts U., 1963. Diplomate Am. Bd. Dermatology, 1969. Asst. prof. dermatology U. Pa., Phila., 1969-73, clin. assoc. prof., 1973-80, adj. assoc. prof. comparative dermatology Sch. Vet. Medicine, 1973-87, prof. comparative dermatology, 1987—; clin. assoc. prof. Jefferson Med. Coll., Phila., 1980-84, clin. prof., 1984—; dir. Jefferson Ctr. for Internat. Dermatology, 1987—; vis. prof. Yonsei U., Seoul, Korea, 1983—, Zagazig U., Egypt, 1990—. Author: Louis A. Duhring, Pathfinder for Dermatology, 1967, (with John Crissey) The Dermatology and Syphilology of the 19th Century, 1981, (with others) Cutaneous Infestations of Man and Animal, 1983, Practical Management of the Dermatologic Patient, 1986, (with John Pettit) Manual of Tropical Dermatology, 1984, (with F.G. Gschnait) Manual of Sexually Transmitted Diseases, 1989, (with others) Pediatric Dermatology, 1989, (with Gary P. Lask) Aesthetic Dermatology, 1991, (with others) Color Atlas of Sexually Transmitted Diseases, 1991, Color Atlas of Difficult Diagnoses in Dermatology, 1994, Global Dermatology, 1994, Manual of Medical Mycology, 1995, Color Atlas of Cutaneous Infections, 1995, The Decubitus Ulcer in Clinical Practice, 1996; editor-in-chief Internat. Jour. Dermatology, 1981, Clinics in Dermatology, 1983—; editl. bd. Cutis, P&T, Clin. Therapeutics Chronical Dermatologica, Annali Italiani di Dermatologia, Jour. European Acad. Dermatology and Venereology, Drug Therapy, Medicina Cutanea Ibero-Latino-Am., Advances in Therapeutics, Gulf Jour. Dermatology; assoc. editor Concepts, 1994. Served to maj. U.S. Army, 1967-69; Korea. Recipient Andreus Bello award First Order of Venezuela. Fellow ACP, Coll. Physicians Phila. (chair sect. med. history 1975-78, founding chair sect. dermatology 1982-85); hon. mem. Polish Acad. Dermatology, British Assn. Dermatologists, Am. Acad. Vet. Dermatology, Venezuela Soc. Dermatology, Bulgarian Soc. Dermatology; corr. mem. French Soc. Dermatology and Venereology, Italian Soc. Dermatology and Venereology, Israeli Soc. Dermatology, Istanbul Dermatol. Soc.; mem. Am. Dermatol. Assn., Can. Dermatology Assn., Internat. Soc. Dermatology, History of Dermatology Soc. (founding pres. 1972—), Masons, B'nai Brith. Jewish. Avocations: gardening, travel, history of medicine, genealogy, collecting majollica and bargeware. Home: 941 Bryn Mawr Ave Penn Valley PA 19072-1524 Office: 1819 John F Kennedy Blvd Philadelphia PA 19103-1733

PARISH, RICHARD LEE, engineer, consultant; b. Kansas City, Mo., May 31, 1945; s. Charles Lee and Ruth (Duncan) P.; m. Patricia Ann Erickson, June 2, 1968; children: Christie Lynn White, Kerry Anne Parish-Philp. BS in Agrl. Engring., U. Mo., 1967, MS in Agrl. Engring., 1968, PhD, 1970. Registered profl. engr., Ohio. Asst., then assoc. prof. engring. Univ. Ark., Fayetteville, 1969-74; mgr. mech. research and devel. O.M. Scott & Sons Co., Marysville, Ohio, 1974-83; assoc. prof., then prof. La. State U., Baton Rouge, 1983—; pvt. practice engring. cons. Baton Rouge and Hammond, La., 1984—; prof. Hammond Rsch. Sta., 1995—; cons. in equipment design and evaluation, expert witness testimony in agrl. and hort. equipment, 1984—. Contbr. over 100 articles to profl. jours. and trade pubs.; patentee in field (3). Bd. dirs. Agrl. Missions Found. Recipient Quality award ITT, 1979, Rsch. Dirs. award O.M. Scott Co., 1978; NSF fellow, 1967-69; rsch. grantee Cotton Inc., Raleigh, N.C., 1970-74, 91-93, 95, La. Dept. Natural Resources, 1985-87, Italian Trade Commn., 1988-90. Mem. Am. Soc. Agrl. Engrs. (chmn. agrl. chem. application com. 1982-83, power and machinery div. program com. 1986-87), La. Vegetable Growers Assn., Am. Soc. Hort. Sci. Republican. Baptist. Avocations: gardening, woodwork, bicycling. Home: 21135 Hwy 16 Amite LA 70422 Office: Hammond Rsch Sta 21549 Old Covington Hwy Hammond LA 70403

PARISH, ROBERT LEE (CHIEF PARISH), professional basketball player; b. Shreveport, La., Aug. 30, 1953; m. Nancy Parish; 1 child, Justin. Student, Centenary Coll., 1972-76. Center Golden State Warriors, San Francisco, 1976-80, Boston Celtics, 1980-94; with Charlotte Hornets, 1994—; player NBA Championship Teams, 1981, 84. Named to Sporting News All-Am. First Team, 1976, NBA All-Star Team, 1981-87, 90-91. Office: Charlotte Hornets One Hive Dr Charlotte NC 28217*

PARISH, THOMAS SCANLAN, human development educator; b. Oak Park, Ill., Jan. 24, 1944; s. Robert S. and Florence Catherine (Fleming) P.; m. Joycelyn Pingel, Oct. 2, 1964; children: Robert V., Kimberly E., David G., Thomas P., Kathryn E. BA, No. Ill. U., 1968; MA, Ill. State U., 1969; PhD, U. Ill., 1972. Instr. psychology Parkland Coll., Champaign, Ill., 1971-72; asst. prof. Okla. State U., Stillwater, 1972-76; assoc. prof. Kans. State U., Manhattan, 1976-80, prof., 1980—, asst. to dean of edn., 1992—; assoc. dir. ARIOS-Kan., 1994—; rsch. coord. for Midwest Desegration Asst. Ct., 1994—. Assoc. editor: Jour. of Social Studies Rsch., 1994—; cons. editor Jour. Genetic Psychology, 1984—, Jour. Reality Therapy, 1992—, The Genetic, Social and General Psychology Monographs, 1984—; contbr. articles to profl. jours. Bd. dirs. Friendship Tutoring Program, Manhattan, 1982-91, Stillwater Awareness Coun., 1973-74; co-founder, bd. dirs. Youth Alternatives, Inc., Champaign, 1971-72. Fellow Am. Psychol. Soc.; mem. Am. Ednl. Rsch. Assn., APA, Assn. Reality Therapists, Soc. for Rsch. in Child Devel., Phi Delta Kappa, Phi Kappa Phi. Home: 3313 Germann Dr Manhattan KS 66503-8446 Office: Kans State U Coll of Edn Bluemont Hall Manhattan KS 66506

PARISI, CHERYL LYNN, elementary school educator; b. Hackensack, N.J., Aug. 26, 1955; d. Elza A. and Constance Leah (Sculley) Sockey; m. Albert J. Parisi, Apr. 18, 1981; 1 child, Christopher Thomas. BA, Fairleigh Dickinson U., 1977. Cert. tchr., N.J. Piano instr. Bergen County, N.J., 1972-79; art tchr. Meml. Sch., South Hackensack, N.J., 1979-80, Hackensack Mid. Sch., 1980-84, Nellie K. Parker Sch., Hackensack, 1984—. Exhibited in group shows at The Jacob Javits Conv. Ctr., N.Y.C., 1990, The Designer Craftsmen's Gallery, New Brunswick, N.J., 1993, Gloucester County Coll., Sewell, N.J., 1993, Johnson and Johnson Corp., Titusville, N.J., 1993, Arts Coun. Princeton, N.J., 1993, Montclair State U., Upper Montclair, N.J., 1992, 94. Recipient Art Educator Achievement award Fantasy Fund Inc. at the Cathedral of St. John the Divine, N.Y.C., 1992; grantee Hackensack Edn. Found., 1991; NEH fellow Princeton U., 1991. Mem. Art Educators N.J. (chairperson 1993 Yr. of the Am. Craft 1991-93, publicity 50th anniversary conf. 1990; pres. Bergen County chpt. 1984-86, Achievement award 1989), Nat. Art Edn. Assn. Avocations: playing the piano, reading. Home: 167 Godwin Ave Wyckoff NJ 07481-2004 Office: Nellie K Parker Sch 261 Maple Hill Dr Hackensack NJ 07601-1401

PARISI, JOSEPH (ANTHONY), magazine editor, writer-consultant, educator; b. Duluth, Minn., Nov. 18, 1944; s. Joseph Carl Parisi and Phyllis Susan (Quaranta) Schlecht. B.A. with honors, Coll. St. Thomas, 1966; M.A., U. Chgo., 1967, Ph.D. with honors, 1973. Asst. prof. Roosevelt U., Chgo., 1969-78; assoc. editor POETRY Mag., Chgo., 1976-83; acting editor POETRY Mag., 1983-85, editor, 1985—; vis. prof. U. Ill., Chgo., 1978-87; cons., writer ALA, Chgo., 1980—; cons. NEH, 1983—. Author: The Poetry Anthology, 1912-1977, 1978, Voices and Visions Reader's Guide, 1987, Marianne Moore: The Art of a Modernist, 1990, (listener's guide) Poets in Person, 1992; contbr. articles and reviews to profl. jours.; producer, dir. (audio series on NPR) Poets in Person, 1991. Recipient Alvin Bentley award Duns Scotus Coll., 1963; fellow U. Chgo., 1966-69. Mem. Delta Epsilon Sigma. Club: Cliff Dwellers. Avocations: piano, photography, book and record collecting. Office: Poetry Mag 60 W Walton St Chicago IL 60610-3305

PARIZA, MICHAEL WILLARD, research institute executive, microbiology and toxicology educator; b. Waukesha, Wis., Mar. 10, 1943; married; 3 children. BSc in Bacteriology, U. Wis., 1967; MSc in Microbiology, Kans. State U., 1969, PhD in Microbiology, 1973. Postdoctoral trainee McArdle Lab. for Cancer Rsch. U. Wis., Madison, 1973-76, asst. prof. Food Rsch. Inst. dept. Food Microbiology and Toxicology, 1976-81, assoc. prof., 1981-84, prof., 1984—, assoc. dept. chmn., 1981-82, dept. chmn. food microbiology and toxicology, 1982—, dir. Food Rsch. Inst., 1986—, disting. prof., 1993—; with Wis. Clin. Cancer Ctr., Environ. Toxicology Ctr., Dept. Nutritional Scis., Dept. Food Sci.; mem. Inst. Medicine's Food Forum; mem. com. on comparative toxicity naturally occurring carcinogens NAS; trustee Internat. Life Scis. Inst.-N.Am., 1986—. With U.S. Army, 1969-71. Office: U Wis Food Rsch Inst 1925 Willow Dr Madison WI 53706-1103

PARIZEAU, JACQUES, former Canadian government official; b. Montréal, Aug. 9, 1930; s. Gérard and Germaine (Biron) P.; m. Alicja Poznanska, Apr. 12, 1956 (dec. 1990); children: Bernard, Isabelle; m. Lisette LaPointe, Dec. 12, 1992. Degree, Inst. d'études politiques, Paris, 1952; PhD in Econs., London Sch. Econs., 1955. Prof. École des Hautes Études commerciales, Montréal, 1955-65, 67-70, 85-89; chmn. Inst. Applied Econs., Montréal, 1970-73; mem. Can. Nat. Assembly, Que., 1976-84, 89—; pres. Parti Québécois Can. Nat. Assembly, 1988—; min. fin. Québec Govt., 1976-84, min. revenue, 1976-84, pres. treasury bd., 1976-81, min. fin. instns., 1981-82, chmn. ministerial econ. devel. com., 1981-82, prime min., 1994-95; econ. and fin. adviser Premiers of Québec: Lesage, Johnson, Bertrand, Que., 1961-69; pres. Que. Fin. Instns. Task Force, 1970-73; chmn. Comm. of Enquiry on Future of Municipalities, Que., 1985. Editor L'Actualité économique, Montréal, 1955-61; chmn. bd. dirs. Daily Le Jour, Montréal, 1974-75; bd. dirs. Daily Le Devoir, Montréal, 1985-87. Bd. dirs. U. Montréal, 1969-74; bd. dirs., bd. govs. Théâtre du Nouveau-Monde, Montréal, 1988-92; pres. No com. Referendum on Charlottetown Accord, Que., 1992. Mem. Club de la Garnison (Que.), Knowlton Golf and Country Club (Lac Brome). Roman Catholic. Avocations: reading, music, gardening. Office: Parti Québécois, 7370 St-Hubert, Montreal, PQ Canada H2R 2N3

PARIZEK, ELDON JOSEPH, geologist, college dean; b. Iowa City, Apr. 30, 1920; s. William Joseph and Libbie S. P.; m. Mildred Marie Burger, Aug. 9, 1944; children—Richard, Marianne, Elizabeth, Amy. B.S., U. Iowa, 1942, M.S., 1946, Ph.D., 1949. Instr. U. Iowa, 1947-49; asst. prof. geology U. Ga., 1949-54, assoc. prof., 1954-56; asso. prof. U. Kansas City, 1956-63; prof. U. Mo., Kansas City, 1963—; chmn. dept. geoscis. U. Mo., 1968-78; dean U. Mo. (Coll. Arts and Scis.), 1979-86. Served with USN, 1942-45. Fellow Geol. Soc. Am.; mem. AAUP, Assn. Mo. Geologists, AAAS, Sigma Xi. Roman Catholic. Research, numerous publs. on mass wasting, slope failure, underground space, geology of West Mo. Home: 6913 W 100th Shawnee Mission KS 66212 Office: 5100 Rockhill Rd Kansas City MO 64110-2446

PARK, ALICE MARY CRANDALL, genealogist; b. Loda, Ill., Oct. 4, 1901; d. Frederick Adam and Sarah Elizabeth (Clemens) Crandall; m. Lee I. Park, Aug. 29, 1925 (dec. Aug. 24, 1978); children: Lee Crandall, Nancy Park Kern. BS, U. Chgo., 1924. Tchr. U. Chgo. Lab. Sch., 1924-25; genealogy rschr. Washington, 1925—. Author: Park/e/s and Bunch on the Trail West, 1974, rev. edit., 1982, Schenck and Related Families in New Netherlands, 1992, One Crandall Family 1651-1995, 1996. Pres. Falls Church (Va.) PTA, 1941-42, LWV, Fairfax County, Va., 1947-48. Mem. Chevy Chase Club, Met. Club Washington. Avocations: gardening, travel, cooking, music. Home: 4200 Cathedral Ave NW Washington DC 20016-4931

PARK, BEVERLY GOODMAN, public relations professional; b. Boston, Nov. 10, 1937; d. Morris and Mary (Keller) Goodman; divorced; children: Glynis Forcht, Seth, Elyse. BS, Simmons Coll., 1959; MS, Ea. Conn. State U., 1968; postgrad., Western N.E. Coll. Law, 1994—. Asst. dir. comty. svc. Hartford (Conn.) Courant, 1976-79; mayor Borough of Colchester, Conn., 1979-83; lifestyle editor Chronicle, Willimantic, Conn., 1980-82, suburban editor, 1982-84; officer mktg. & comm. U. Conn. Health Ctr., Farmington, 1984—; selected team mem. radiation exposure info. study Belorussia, 1993; mem. adv. bd. Hosp. News; mem. women's affairs com. U. Conn. Health Ctr. Women's Networking Task Force; mem. Univ. Adminstrv. Staff Coun.; mem. minority awards com. U. Conn. Health Ctr., mem. John N. Dempsey hosp. disaster plan com. Designer: (libr. studies curriculum) Classroom Instruction on the Use of Books and Libraries, 1972; pub.: (ednl. booklets) Have You Made Plans for the Future?, 1977-78; editor of edn. holiday and bridal supplements The Chronicle, 1980-84; editor: U. Conn. Health Ctr. Anniversary Mag., 1986, U. Conn. Health Ctr. Med. Catalog, 1986—, (ann. pub.) Salute, 1988—, U. Conn. Health Ctr. 30th Anniversary Supplement, 1991. Bd. dirs. Ea. Conn. Found. for Pub. Giving, Norwich, 1990—; women's club officer Dem. Town Com., Colchester, Conn., 1963-90; active Hadassah, Northampton/Amherst, 1996—, Women's League for Conservative Judaism. Recipient Lifestyle Page award New Eng. Press Assn., 1980, Media Excellence in Covering Human Svcs. award Conn. chpt. NASW, 1982, Ragan Report Arnold's Admirables award for excellence in graphics and typography, 1985, Gold award Healthcare Mktg. Report, 1987, award for video ACS, 1990. Mem. NOW (membership com. Southeastern chpt., mem. legis. task force, Meritorious Svc. award Southeastern Conn. chpt. 1985), Am. Soc. for Hosp. Mktg. and Pub. Rels., Am. Mktg. Assn., Assn. Am. Med. Colls. (group on pub. affairs), Conn. Hosp. Assn. (hosp. pub. rels. conf.), State of Conn. Pub. Info. Coun. (steering com.), New Eng. Hosp. Pub. Rels. and Mktg. Assn. (bd. dirs. 1987, 88). Avocations: swimming, hiking, spending time with grandchildren. Home: 111 Rick Dr Florence MA 01060

PARK, CHARLES DONALD, SR., financial executive; b. N.Y.C., Aug. 1, 1945; s. Charles and Madeline (Springer) P.; m. Pauline De Meo; children: Paula, Madeline. BA, Pace U., 1968, MBA, 1970. Coord. fin. reports Gen. Telephone & Electronics, N.Y.C., 1968-70; mgr. fin. analysis Mobil Corp., N.Y.C., 1970-73; mgr. corp. bus. planning and analysis Gen. Instrument, N.Y.C., 1973-74; controller Microelectronics Group Gen. Instrument, Hicksville, N.Y., 1974-77, chief fin. officer, 1977-81; corp. dir., fin. analysis Bendix, Southfield, Mich., 1981-82; v.p. fin. and adminstrn. MCI Internat., Inc., Rye Brook, N.Y., 1982-86; sr. v.p. fin. Sprague Techs., Inc., Stamford, Conn., 1987-89; exec. v.p., CFO Briggs Industries, Tampa, Fla., 1989—.

PARK, CHUNG IL, librarian; b. Chang-won, Korea, Aug. 25, 1938; s. Zung S. and Bong-y (Choo) P.; m. Jung Yoo, Aug. 30, 1969; children: Charlotte, Sue, Andrew. BA, Yonsei U., 1961; MLS, U. So. Calif., L.A., 1971; postgrad., U. Ill., 1975. Libr., mem. faculty Malcolm X Coll., Chgo., 1972—. Compiler, editor: (books) Best Sellers and Best Choices 1980-83, Best Books by Consensus 1984-88, Advertisement Digest: Library and Information Services, 1979; editor COINT, 1980-88; contbr. articles to profl. jours. Mem.

ALA, Am. Fedn. Tchrs. Avocation: automobile travel. Home: 9302 Parkside Ave Morton Grove IL 60053-1570 Office: Malcolm X Coll 1900 W Van Buren Chicago IL 60612

PARK, DAVID ALLEN, physicist, educator; b. N.Y.C., Oct. 13, 1919; s. Edwin Avery and Frances (Paine) P.; m. Clara Justine Claiborne, Aug. 18, 1945; children: Katharine, Rachel, Paul, Jessica. A.B., Harvard, 1941; Ph.D., U. Mich., 1950. Instr. Williams Coll., 1941-44; ops. research on radar countermeasures Harvard U. and Eng., 1944-45; instr. U. Mich., 1950; mem. Inst. Advanced Study, Princeton, 1950-51; mem. faculty Williams Coll., 1952-88, prof. physics, 1960-88, emeritus, 1988—; sr. vis. Cambridge (Eng.) U., 1962-63; vis. lectr. U. Ceylon, 1955-56, 72, Mass. Inst. Tech., 1966; vis. prof. U. N.C., 1964. Author: Quantum Theory, 1964, 3d edit., 1991, Contemporary Physics, 1964, Strong Interactions, 1966, Classical Dynamics and Its Quantum Analogues, 1979, 2d edit., 1990, The Image of Eternity, 1980, (with P.J. Davis) No Way, 1987, The How and the Why, 1988. Fellow Am. Phys. Soc.; mem. Internat. Soc. for Study Time (pres. 1973-76). Office: Williams Coll Dept Physics Williamstown MA 01267

PARK, ESTHER, retired association executive; b. Democratic People's Republic of Korea, Oct. 18, 1902; came to U.S., 1904; d. Chong Soo and Kyung Kun (Kim) P. BA, U. Hawaii, 1926; postgrad., UCLA, 1936; ACSW cert., Western Res. U., 1941; PhD (hon.), Ewha Womans U., Seoul, Korea, 1964. Tchr. pub. jr. high sch. Hilo, Hawaii, 1926-28; teenage sec. Honolulu YWCA, 1928-40, bus. and profl. women sec., 1940-47; Am. adv. sec. to Korea YWCA internat. divsn. YWCA U.S.A., N.Y.C., 1947-80; internat. vol. Nat. YWCA Korea, 1970-80; ret., 1980. Contbr. weekly articles to The Times, 1964-68. Mem. Korea Child Welfare Com., 1952-62, USO Coun., 1956—; v.p., treas. Korea com. World Univ. Svc., 1955; active Fulbright Commn., 1955-69; mem. adv. com. Korea Ch. World Svc., 1963-70; com. mem. social welfare bur. KNCC, 1964. Recipient citation Nat. Reconstruction Movement Korea and Ewha Womans U., 1962, Pub. Welfare medal Pres. of Republic of Korea, 1966, Seongru medal, 1972, Moran medal, 1980, Korean Coun. Women award, 1968, Mother of Yr. award Saessak Children's Assn., 1971, Nat. YWCA award, 1972, Plaque of Appreciation, U.S. Govt., AID, 1980; named Hon. Citizen, City of Seoul, 1969. Mem. NASW (cert.), BPW, Korea Assn. Vol. Agys. (adviser 1955-80), Royal Asiatic Soc., Am. Women's Club. Republican. Congregationalist. Avocations: music, reading, arts. Home: 1434 Punahou St Apt 732 Honolulu HI 96822-4729

PARK, HYE-SOOK, physicist, consultant; b. Cheon-Ju, Korea, Jan. 3, 1959; d. Jong-Yeol Park and Jong-Nim Kim; m. Richard Marshall Bionta, Sept. 27, 1985; 1 child, Mina Renee Bionta. BS, Pfeiffer Coll., 1980; MS, U. Mich., 1983, PhD, 1985. Rsch. asst. U. Mich., Ann Arbor, 1980-85; postdoctoral scholar U. Calif., Berkeley, 1985-87; postdoctoral scholar Lawrence Livermore Nat. Lab., Livermore, Calif., 1987-90, physicist, 1990—. Contbr. articles to profl. jours. Recipient Bruno Rossi prize Am. Astron. Soc., 1989. Mem. Internat. Soc. Optical Engring., Am. Phys. Soc. Avocations: bicycling, skiing, reading. Office: Lawrence Livermore Nat Lab PO Box 808 L-274 Livermore CA 94550

PARK, JAMES THEODORE, microbiologist, educator; b. Palo Alto, Calif., Aug. 3, 1922; s. Charles V. and Frances (Odenheimer) P.; m. Helen Sternberg, Dec. 13, 1952; children: Jane Frances, David Franklin, Elizabeth Ann. A.B., Central Mich. U., 1943, D.Sc., 1963; M.S., U. Wis., 1944, Ph.D., 1949. Biochemist Ft. Detrick, Md., 1949-53; germ-free animal research unit Walter Reed Army Med. Center, 1953-57; asso. prof., then prof. microbiology Vanderbilt U. Sch. Medicine, 1958-62; chmn. dept. Tufts U. Sch. Medicine, 1962-70, prof., 1962-93, prof. emeritus microbiology, 1993—; mem. study sect. biochem. microbiology Nat. Inst. Allergy and Infectious Diseases, 1964-68; microbiology tng. com. Nat. Inst. Gen. Med. Scis., 1971-73; chmn. microbial physiology and genetics study sect. NIH, 1985-88; vis. scientist Karolinska Inst. Stockholm, 1995. Editorial bd.: Jour. Bacteriology, 1964-69, Antimicrobial Agts. and Chemotherapy, 1983-86. NSF sr. postdoctoral research fellow Cambridge (Eng.) U., 1957-58; NIH spl. fellow U. Umea, Sweden, 1969-70. Mem. Am. Acad. Arts and Scis., Am. Soc. Biol. Chemists, Am. Soc. Microbiology, Soc. Gen. Microbiology. Home: 11 Bradford Rd Weston MA 02193-2104 Office: 136 Harrison Ave Boston MA 02111-1800

PARK, JOHN THORNTON, academic administrator; b. Phillipsburg, N.J., Jan. 3, 1935; s. Dawson J. and Margaret M. (Thornton) P.; m. Dorcas M Marshall; June 1, 1956; children: Janet Ernst, Karen Daily. BA in Physics with distinction, Nebr. Wesleyan U., 1956; PhD, U. Nebr., 1963. NSF postdoctoral fellow Univ. Coll., London, 1963-64; asst. prof. physics U. Mo., Rolla, 1964-68, assoc. prof. physics, 1968-71, prof., 1971—, chmn. dept. physics, 1977-83, vice chancellor acad. affairs, 1983-85, 86-91, interim chancellor, 1985-86, 91-92, chancellor, 1992—; vis. assoc. prof. NYU, 1970-71; pres. Talema Electronics, Inc., St. James, Mo., 1983—; prin. investigator NSF Rsch. Grants, 1966—; bd. dirs. Mo. Tech. Corp., Jefferson City, Mo., 1994—. Contbr. articles to profl. jours. Recipient Most Disting. Scientist award Mo. Acad. Sci., 1994. Fellow Am. Phys. Soc. (mem. divsn. elec. and atomic physics); mem. Am. Assn. Physics Tchrs., Rotary. Methodist.

PARK, LEE CRANDALL, psychiatrist; b. Washington, July 15, 1926; s. Lee I. and Alice (Crandall) P.; m. Barbara Anne Merrick, July 1, 1953; children: Thomas Joseph, Jeffrey Rawson; m. Mary Woodfill Banerjee, Apr. 27, 1985; stepchildren: Stephen Kumar, Scott Kumar. Grad., Putney Prep. Sch., Vt.; B.S. in Zoology, Yale, 1948; M.D., Johns Hopkins, 1952. Diplomate Nat. Bd. Med. Examiners, Am. Bd. Psychiatry and Neurology. Intern medicine Johns Hopkins Hosp., Osler Clinic, Balt., 1952-53; resident psychiatry USN Hosp., Oakland, Calif., 1954; resident psychiatry Henry Phipps Psychiat. Clinic Johns Hopkins Hosp., Balt., 1955-59; asst. psychiatrist Henry Phipps Psychiat. Clinic, 1955-59, staff psychiatrist, 1959—, staff dept. medicine, 1970—, dir. psychiat. outpatient svcs. and community psychiatry program, 1972-74, asst. dir. clin. svcs. dept. psychiatry, 1973-74, mem. departmental coun., 1974-76; fellow psychiatry Johns Hopkins U., 1955-59, faculty in psychiatry, 1959—, assoc. prof., 1971—, physician charge psychiat. svcs. student health svc., 1961-73; vis. psychiatrist Balt. City Hosp., 1960-61; co-prin., prin. investigator NIMH Psychopharmacology Rsch. Br. Outpatient Study of Drug-Set Interaction, 1960-68, co-dir. (with Eugene Meyer) Time-Limited Psychotherapy Rsch. Grant, 1969-73; pvt. practice psychiatry, 1964—; cons. Met. Balt. Assn. Mental Health, 1961-63, Bur. Disability Ins., Social Security Adminstrn., 1964-81; attending staff Seton Psychiat. Inst., 1966-73, exec. bd., 1970-73; staff Sheppard and Enoch Pratt Hosp., 1974—; rsch. includes borderline and narcissistic conditions, long-term effects of childhood emotional abuse, interrelationships of psychotherapy and pharmacotherapy, time ltd. psychotherapy, ethical considerations in clin. rsch. Contbr. articles and chpts. to profl. jours. and books. Served to lt. M.C., USNR, 1953-55, div. psychiatrist 1st Marine Div., Korea, staff psychiatrist USN Hosp., Camp Pendelton, Calif., 1954-55. Fellow Am. Psychiat. Assn. (life mem. assembly 1983-93), AAAS; mem. AMA, AAUP, Am. Psychosomatic Soc., Internat. Soc. Study of Personality Disorders, Am. Soc. Adolescent Psychiatry, Am. Coll. Neuropsychopharmacology, Am. Assn. Pvt. Practicing Psychiatrists, Md. Psychiat. Soc. (pres. 1978-79), Soc. Psychotherapy Rsch., N.Y. Acad. Scis., Group Therapy Network, Md. Interdisciplinary Coun. Children and Adolescents (treas. 1980-87), Med. and Chirug. Faculty Md., Balt. City, Balt. County Med. Socs., Johns Hopkins Med. and Surg. Assn., Md. Assn. Pvt. Practicing Psychiatrists, SAR, Crandall, Parke, Van Kouwenhoven-Conover and Vag Voorhees Socs., Nat. Soc. of the Sons and Daus. of the Pilgrims, Johns Hopkins Club (Balt.), Met. Club (Washington), Farmington Country Club (Charlottesville, Va.), Chevy Chase (Md.) Country Club, Phi Beta Pi. Home: 308 Tunbridge Rd Baltimore MD 21212-3803 Office: 1205 York Rd Ste 35 Lutherville Timonium MD 21093-6268

PARK, LELAND MADISON, librarian; b. Alexandria, La., Oct. 21, 1941; s. Arthur Harris and Jane Rebecca (Leland) P. Student, McCallie Sch., 1957-59; A.B., Davidson Coll., 1963; M.L.S., Emory U., 1964; postgrad., Simmons Coll., 1968; Adv.M. in L.S., Fla. State U., 1973, Ph.D., 1974. Reference librarian Pub. Library of Charlotte and Mecklenburg County, N.C., 1964-65; head reference and student personnel Davidson (N.C.) Coll. Library, 1967-70, asst. dir., 1970-75, dir., 1975—; cons. coll. cons. network So. Assn. Colls and Schs.; vis. lectr. Emory U., summer 1972; temporary instr. Fla. State U., 1973; libr. cons.; conf. spkr.; chmn. state adv. com. Libr. Svcs. and Constrn. Act, 1975-79; mem. N.C. State Libr. Commn., 1983-85, 87-92, chmn., 1989-92; mem. Dividson (N.C.) Town Appearance Commn., 1986-93, Hist. Preservation Commn., 1994-96. Editor Southeastern Librarian, 1976-78; acad. sect. editor N.C. Libraries, 1972-77; contbr. articles to profl. jours. Mem. Wake County Citizens for Better Librs., N.C., 1965-67; sec. com. libr. affairs Piedmont U. Ctr., 1969-70, chmn., 1970-72; mem. nat. bd. cons. NEH, 1976—; clk. mission com. St. Alban's Episcopal Mission, Davidson, N.C., 1969-72, layreader, 1970-75, treas., 1975-86. Recipient H.W. Wilson library periodical award, 1979, Alumni Achievement award The McCallie Sch., 1989, Order of Long Leaf Pine presented by N.C. Gov. James G. Martin, 1993. Mem. ALA, Southeastern Libr. Assn. (chmn. coll. and univ. sect. 1976-78, exec. bd. 1976-78), N.C. Libr. Assn. (2d v.p. 1975-77, 1st v.p. 1981-83, pres. 1983-85), Metrolina Libr. Assn. (pres. 1969-71), Mecklenburg County Libr. Assn. (treas. 1969-70), Soc. of Cin. (2d v.p. Ga. Soc. 1982-83), SAR, Mil. Order World Wars, Raleigh Jaycees (chmn. libr. com. 1965-67), Res. Officer Assn., SCV, Soc. Colonial Wars, S.C. Huguenot Soc., Beta Phi Mu, Sigma Nu, Omicron Delta Kappa. Democrat. Lodge: Rotary. Home: PO Box 777 235 Ney Circle Davidson NC 28036 Office: Davidson Coll E H Little Libr PO Box 1837 Davidson NC 28036-1837

PARK, MARY WOODFILL, information consultant; b. Nevada, Mo., Nov. 20, 1944; d. John Prossor and Elizabeth (Devine) Woodfill; m. Salil Kumar Banerjee, Dec. 29, 1967 (div. 1983); children: Stephen Kumar, Scott Kumar; m. Lee Crandall Park, Apr. 27, 1985; stepchildren: Thomas Joseph, Jeffrey Rawson. BA, Marywood Coll., 1966; postgrad., Johns Hopkins U., 1983, Goucher Coll., 1986. Asst. to dir. U. Pa. Librs., Phila., 1968-69; investment libr. Del. Funds, Phila., 1969-71; investment officer Investment Counselors Md., Balt., 1980-84, 1st Nat. Bank Md., Balt., 1984-85; founder Info. Consultancy, Balt., 1985—; lectr. Villa Julie Coll., Balt., 1989, Loyola Coll., Balt., 1991-92, Cath. U., 1993. Editor, contbr. to profl. publs. Vol. Internat. Visitors' Ctr., Balt., 1979-80, 91; del. White House Conf. on Librs.; v.p. bd. dirs. Friends of Goucher Libr., 1988-90; mem. industry applications com. Info. Tech. Bd., State of Md., 1993—; mem. info. tech. com. of the Tech. Coun., Greater Balt. Com., 1993—. Named One of Md.'s Top 100 Women, Warfield's Bus. Publn., 1996. Mem. Spl. Librs. Assn. (pres. Balt. chpt. 1991-92, mem. network coord. coun. Sailor project 1993-95), Am. Soc. Info. Sci., Assn. Ind. Info. Profls., Md. Libr. Assn., Info. Futures Inst., Hamilton St. Club (bd. dirs. 1989-92), Soc. Competetive Intelligence Profls. Office: The Info Consultancy 308 Tunbridge Rd Baltimore MD 21212-3803

PARK, ROBERT MCILWRAITH, science and engineering educator; b. Glasgow, Scotland, July 28, 1957; came to U.S., 1988; s. Robert McIlwraith and Elsie (Black) P.; m. Katherine Jean Angers, Dec. 21, 1985. BSc with honors, U. Glasgow, 1978, PhD, 1982. Sr. rsch. scientist 3M Can., Inc., Toronto, 1982-86, rsch. specialist, 1986-88; assoc. prof. dept. materials sci. and engring. U. Fla., Gainesville, 1988-93, prof., 1993—. Contbr. chpts. to books, over 60 articles to profl. jours. Recipient 3M Circle of Tech. Excellence award 1986, Rsch. Initiation awrd NSF, 1989, Rank prize for Optoelectronics, 1993. Achievements include patent for invention of a P-type doping process for the semiconductor zinc selenide. Office: U Fla Dept Materials Sci and Engring Gainesville FL 32611

PARK, RODERIC BRUCE, academic administrator; b. Cannes, France, Jan. 7, 1932; came to U.S., 1932; s. Malcolm Sewell and Dorothea (Turner) P.; m. Marijke DeJong, Aug. 29, 1953; children: Barbara, Marina, Malcolm. AB, Harvard U., 1953; PhD, Calif. Inst. Tech., 1958. Postdoctoral fellow Calif. Inst. Tech., 1958, Lawrence Radiation Lab., Berkeley, Calif., 1958-60; prof. botany U. Calif., Berkeley, 1960-89, prof. plant biology, 1989-93, prof. emeritus, 1993—; chmn. dept. instrn. in biology U. Calif., 1965-68; provost, dean U. Calif. (Coll. Letters and Sci.), 1972-80, vice chancellor 1980-90; chancellor U. Colo., Boulder, 1994—; pres. Brickyard Cove Harbors, Inc., 1975-77; dir. William Kaufmann, Inc., 1976-86; mem. corp. Woods Hole Oceanographic Instn., 1974-80; mem. Harvard Vis. Com. on Biochemistry and Molecular Biology, 1990-93. Co-author: Cell Ultrastructure, 51967, Papers on Biological Membrane Structure, 1968; Biology editor, W.H. Freeman & Co., 1966-74; Contbr. articles to profl. jours. Trustee Athenian Sch., 1980—, U. Calif.-Berkeley Found., 1986-90; pres. Jepson Endowment, 1992—, pres., 1994—; bd. dirs. Assoc. Harvard Alumni, 1976-79; bd. overseers Harvard U., 1981-87; mem. exec. com. Coun. Acad. Affairs, 1986-90, chmn., 1988-89; mem. exec. com. Nat. Assn. State Univs. and Land Grant Colls., 1988-90; mem. vis. com. Arnold Arboretum, 1981-88, chmn., 1986-88; acting dir. Univ. and Jepson Herbaria, 1991-93. Recipient New York Bot. Gardens award, 1962. Fellow AAAS; mem. Am. Soc. Plant Physiologists, Am. Bot. Soc., Am. Soc. Photobiology, Danforth Assn. (pres. San Francisco chpt. 1972), Richmond Yacht Club (commodore 1972, dir. found. 1992—), Transpacific Yacht Club, Explorers Club. Home: Office 301 256 Cactus Ct Boulder CO 80304-1001 Office: U Colo Office of the Chancellor Boulder CO 80309-0017

PARK, ROGER COOK, law educator; b. Atlanta, Jan. 4, 1942; s. Hugh and Alice (Cook) P.; m. Rosemarie J. Lilliker, June 14, 1967 (div. 1979); 1 child, Matthew; m. Suzanne Nicole Howard, Feb. 18, 1984; stepchildren: Sophie Currier, Nicholas Currier. BA cum laude, Harvard U., 1964, JD magna cum laude, 1969. Bar: Mass. 1969, Minn. 1973. Law clk. to Hon. Bailey Aldrich U.S. Ct. Appeals (1st Cir.), Boston, 1969-70; with Zalkind & Silverglate, Boston, 1970-73; prof. Law Sch. U. Minn., Mpls., 1973-95, Fredrikson and Byron prof. Law Sch., 1990-95; Disting. prof. law U. Calif./Hastings Coll. Law, San Francisco, 1995—; vis. prof. Law Sch. Stanford U., Palo Alto, Calif., summer 1977, Sch. Law Boston U., 1981-82, Law Sch. U. Mich., Ann Arbor, fall 1984; bd. dirs. Ctr. for Computer-Aided Legal Instrn., 1982—; reporter adv. group Civil Justice Reform Act, Dist. of Minn.; mem. evidence adv. com. Minn. Supreme Ct., 1988-95. Author: Computer Aided Exercises in Civil Procedure, 1979, 4th edit., 1995, (with McFarland) Trial Objections Handbook, 1991, Waltz and Park Casebook on Evidence, 8th edit., 1994; contbr. articles to profl. jours. Lt. U.S. Army, 1964-66, Vietnam. Mem. ABA (mem. subcom. on fed. rules of evidence, mem. rules of criminal procedure adn evidence com. criminal justice sect. 1988—), Am. Law Inst., Am. Assn. Law Schs. (chairperson evidence sect. 1994). Office: Hastings Coll of Law 200 McAllister St San Francisco CA 94102

PARK, ROY HAMPTON, JR., advertising executive; b. Raleigh N.C., July 23, 1938; s. Roy Hampton and Dorothy Goodwin (Dent) P.; m. Elizabeth Tetlow Parham, July 29, 1961; children: Elizabeth P. Fowler, Roy H., III. BA in Journalism, U. N.C., 1961; MBA, Cornell U., 1963. Sr. account exec., rev. bd. exec., advt. planning dir., awards chmn., pers. group head J. Walter Thompson Co., N.Y.C., and Miami, Fla., 1963-70; v.p. mktg. and account mgmt. Kincaid Advt. Agy., div. First Union Nat. BanCorp, Inc., Charlotte, N.C., 1970-71; v.p. Park Outdoor Advt., Ithaca, N.Y., 1971-75; v.p. advt. and promotion Park Broadcasting, Inc., Ithaca, 1976-81; mng. editor Park Communications Newsletter, 1976-81; mng. dir. Ag Rsch. Advt. Agy., Ithaca, 1976-84; v.p. and gen. mgr. Park Outdoor Advt., 1981-84; pres., chief exec. officer, dir. Park Outdoor Advt. of N.Y., Inc., 1984—; pres. Outdoor Advt. Coun. N.Y., Inc., 1986-91, chmn., dir., 1992-95; dir. Park Comm., Inc., 1993-95; dir., sr. v.p. RHP, Inc., 1994—, RHP Properties, Inc., 1994—; dir. Boyce Thompson Inst. for Plant Rsch., Inc., 1995—; trustee Park Found., Inc., 1995—. Mem. region I plans bd. Inst. Outdoor Advt., 1984-86; founding mem. alumni exec. coun. Cornell U. Johnson Grad. Sch. Mgmt., 1984-88; bd. vis. U. N.C. Sch. Journalism & Mass. Comm., 1994—; mem. N.C. Soc. of N.Y., 1994—; chmn. Ithaca Assembly Cotillion, 1979-81; dir. pub. rels. Tompkins County Conf. and Tourist Coun., 1976; exec. com. Tompkins County Rep. Fin. Com. 1983-84; chmn. Fin. Com. MacNeil for Assembly, 1984-86, co-chmn., 1978-82; bd. dirs. Tompkins County Coun. Arts, 1976; chmn. pub. relations com. United Way Tompkins County, 1973-74, loaned publicity exec. 1977; bd. chmn., publicity dir. Junior Olympics 1973-74; dir. pub. rels. United Fund Raleigh, N.C., 1971; fin. com. Special Children's Ctr., 1979. Recipient Project of Yr. award, 1974. Mem. Tompkins County C. of C. (chmn. legis. action com. 1976, acting chmn. nominating com. 1976, chmn. sign ordinance com. 1975-76, pub. rels. coun. 1976, chmn. sign ordinance com. recognition award 1975), Charlotte (N.C.) C. of C. (pub. rels. com. 1970-71), adv. Beach Preservation Assn. Pine Knoll Shores, N.C., Ithaca Yacht Club, Ithaca Country Club. Republican. Presbyterian. Office: Park Outdoor Advt PO Box 6477 Ithaca NY 14851-6477

PARK, SAM-KOO, transportation executive. BA in Econs., Yonsei U., 1967. Exec. dir. internat. trading Samyang Tire Indsl. Co., 1967-68; mng. dir. Korea Synthetic Rubber Indusl. Co., 1968-73; mng. dir. Kumho & Co., 1973-74, pres. L.A. br., 1974-79, v.p., 1979-80, pres., 1980-91; pres., CEO Asiana Airlines, Inc., 1991—. Office: Asiana Airlines Inc 3530 Wilshire Blvd Ste 1450 Los Angeles CA 90010

PARK, SOONG-KOOK, internist, researcher; b. Pyung-Yang, Korea, Aug. 9, 1938; s. Tae-Soo and Wha-Sil (Lee) P.; m. Sine-Ja, Oct. 9, 1965; children: Han-Kil, See-Nae, Han-Sol. BA, MD, Kyung-Pook Nat. U., Taegu, Korea, 1963. Med. diplomate. Surgeon gen. Republic of Korea, 1963-67; hosp. intern Bklyn. Jewish Hosp., 1968-69; resident in internal medicine Grassland Hosp., Valhalla, N.Y., 1969-72; fellow in gastroenterology Lahey Clinic, Boston, 1972-74; chief internal medicine Dongsan Presbyn. Hosp., Taegu, Korea, 1974-76; cons. in internal medicine, chief staff Mariana Med. Ctr., Guam, 1977-78; chief internal medicine Bak Hosp., Seoul, Korea, 1978, Dongsan Presbyn. Hosp., Taegu, 1978-90; prof. Keimyung U. Med. Sch., Taegu, 1980—; supt. Dongsan Med. Ctr., Taegu, 1990-94, Kyungju Dongsan Hosp., Kyungju, Korea, 1994-96; v.p. for med. affairs Keimyung U., 1996—; dir. Dongsan Med. Ctr., 1996—. Elder Sungji Presbyn. Ch., Taegu, 1976—; bd. dirs. YMCA, Taegu, 1980—; dist. gov. Y's Men's Internat., Taegu, 1987-88; comdt. Med. Drs. Soccer Team, Taegu, 1990-94, 96—. Recipient Elmar Crown, Y's Men's Club Internat., 1988. Mem. Korean Assn. Internal Medicine (councilor 1980), Korean Assn. Gastroenterology (councilor 1980—), Korean Soc. Gastrointestinal Endoscopy (coun. 1988—, pres. 1996), Korean Soc. Gastrointestinal Motility Study (pres. 1993), Am. Coll. Gastroenterology (internat.) N.Y. Acad. Scis. Presbyterian. Avocations: tennis, soccer, choir. Home: 424 Dongsan-Dong, Taegu 700-310, Republic of Korea Office: Dongsan Med Ctr, 194 Dongsan-Dong, Taegu 700-310, Republic of Korea

PARK, SUEGIE JA, clinical pharmacist; b. Seoul, Korea, May 3, 1942; came to U.S., 1975; d. Ung s. and Jung K. (Lee) Chun; m. Nobok Park, Oct. 3, 1967; children: Sung H., Eun H. BS in Pharmacy, Duck Sung Womens Coll., Seoul, 1969, U. Colo., 1983; MTh, So. Calif. Theol. Sem., 1993; postgrad., Idaho State U., 1994—. Registered pharmacist; cert. pastoral counseling; cert. coronary pulmonary resuscitation; cert. acute coronary life support. Pharmacist self drug store, Seoul, 1969-75; pharmacy intern St. Luke's Hosp., Denver, 1980-81, Fitzsimons Army Med. Ctr., Aurora, Colo., 1980-83, VA Hosp., Denver, 1982, Presbyn. Denver Hosp., 1982-84; clin. pharmacist The Children's Hosp., Denver, 1987-90, Presbyn./St. Luke's Med. Ctr., Denver, 1984—; mem. Asian Edn. Adv. Coun. in Denver Pub. Sch., 1988—; mem. HIV/AIDS Resources and Planning Coun., Denver Mayor's Office, 1993—. Author: (brochure) Education and Prevention of HIV/AIDS, 1992. With U.S. Army, 1976-79. Recipient Svc. award Asian Edn. Adv. Coun., Denver Pub. Sch., 1992, Disting. Svc. award Korean Assn. Colo., 1995. Mem. ACA, Korean Scientists and Engrs. Am., Colo. Soc. Hosp. Pharmacists, Rocky Mountain Korea Lions Club (chmn. scholarship com., appreciation and recognition award 1993). Avocations: reading, listening to classical music, travel, sports. Home: 2920 E Colorado Ave Denver CO 80210-3525 Office: Presbyn/St Luke's Med Ctr Pharmacy Dept 1719 E 19th Ave Denver CO 80218

PARK, THOMAS JOSEPH, biology researcher, educator; b. Balt., June 8, 1958; s. Lee Crandall and Barbara Ann (Merrick) P.; m. Stephanie Suzanne Reynolds, June 22, 1985; 1 child, Nicholas Timothy. BA, Johns Hopkins U., 1982; PhD, U. Md., 1988. Vis. scientist Coll. of France, Paris, 1988-89; rsch. fellow U. Tex., Austin, 1989-94; Alexander von Humboldt rsch. fellow U. Munich, 1994-95; with U. Ill. dept biol scis., Chgo., 1995—. Contbr. chpt. to book, articles to Jour. Neurosci., Jour. Comparative Psychology, Hearing Rsch., Jour. Neurophysiol. Grantee NIMH, 1986, Nat. Ctr. Sci. Rsch., Paris, 1988, NIH. Mem. AAAS, Soc. for Neurosci., Assn. for Rsch. in Otolaryngology. Office: U Ill at Chgo Dept Biol Scis Chicago IL 60607

PARK, U. YOUNG, nuclear engineer; b. Seoul, Republic of Korea, Oct. 12, 1940; came to U.S., 1968; s. Myung W. and Duk-Jo (Chang) P.; children: Tara Lynne, Thomas Robert, Kyung Gi. BS, Seoul Nat. U., 1963; MS, U. Cin., 1970. Registered profl. engr., Ohio, Calif. Nuclear engr. State of Ohio, Columbus, 1975-78, Batelle Columbus (Ohio) Labs., 1978-81, Bechtel, San Francisco, 1981-88; program mgr. Savannah River Site U.S. Dept. Energy, Aiken, S.C., 1988-95; Bechtel nuclear project advisor Korea Electric Power Corp, Seoul, 1993—. Mem. Am. Nuclear Soc. Address: Bechtel Korea Project 50 Beale St San Francisco CA 94105-1813

PARK, WILLIAM H(ERRON), financial executive; b. Monongahela, Pa. Sept. 19, 1947; s. William M. and Marjorie (Herron) P.; m. Mary Cornell, June 25, 1977; children: William H., Douglas C. BS in Indsl. Engring. with distinction Cornell U., 1969, MBA, 1970. Engr. True Temper Corp., Geneva, Ohio, 1970-72; with Price Waterhouse & Co., Boston, 1972-82; exec. v.p., CFO United Asset Mgmt. Corp., Boston, 1982—; v.p. The UAM Funds, 1992—; pres. No. Light Asset Mgmt., 1992—; bd. dirs. The Chautauqua Found., Inc., 1992—. Treas., trustee Tower Sch. in Marblehead, 1982-92. Mem. AICPAs, Mass. Soc. CPAs, Pleon Yacht Club (dir. and treas. 1987-92). Home: 3 Ft Sewall Ter Marblehead MA 01945-3505 Office: United Asset Mgmt Corp One Internat Pl Boston MA 02110

PARK, WILLIAM WYNNEWOOD, law educator; b. Philadelphia, Pa., July 2, 1947; s. Oliver William and Christine (Lindes) P. BA, Yale U., 1969; JD, Columbia U., 1972; MA, Cambridge U., 1975. Bar: Mass. 1972, D.C. 1980. Assoc. Coudert Frères, Paris, 1972-75; fellow Selwyn Coll., U. Cambridge, Eng., 1975-77; assoc. Hughes, Hubbard & Reed, Paris, 1977-79; prof. law Boston U., 1979—; counsel Ropes & Gray, Boston; v.p. London Ct. Internat. Arbitration; dir. Boston U. Ctr. Banking Law Studies, 1990-93; adj. prof. Fletcher Sch. Tufts U., Medford, Mass., 1980-86; vis. prof. U. Dijon, France, 1983-84, Inst. Univ. de Hautes Etudes Internat., Geneva, 1983. Author: International Chamber of Commerce Arbitration, 1984, 2nd edit., 1990, International Forum Selection, 1995; contbr. articles and book revs. to profl. jours. Trustee Mass. Bible Soc. Fellow Chartered Inst. Arbitrators; mem. Am. Soc. Internat. Law, Union Internat. Advocats, Soc. of Cin. Republican. Unitarian. Home: 36 King St Cohasset MA 02025-1304 Office: Boston U Law Sch 765 Commonwealth Ave Boston MA 02215-1401 also: Ropes and Gray 1 International Pl Boston MA 02110-2600

PARKANY, JOHN, business educator, international financial consultant; b. Budapest, Hungary, Jan. 28, 1921; came to U.S., 1947; s. Sandor and Renee (Linksz) P.; m. Betty Ruth Baird, Oct. 30, 1954; children: John Stephen, Ann Emily, Nancy. J.D., U. Budapest (Hungary), 1945; M.A., Georgetown U., 1949; Ph.D., Columbia U., 1955. Mktg. research mgr. Formica Corp., Cin., 1956-61; assoc. prof. Xavier U., Cin., 1961-62; mgr. econ. research Weyerhaeuser Co., Tacoma, Wash., 1962-73; v.p., sr. internat. economist Wells Fargo Bank N.A., San Francisco, 1973-80; Richard S. Reynolds Jr. prof. bus. adminstrn. Coll. of William and Mary, Williamsburg, Va., 1980-91; prof. emeritus Coll. of William and Mary, Williamsburg, 1991—. Mem. council econ. advisors Gov. Wash. State, Olympia, 1967-73; pres. Council Fgn. Affairs, Tacoma, Wash., 1968-69. Mem. Nat. Assn. Bus. Economists (v.p. San Francisco chpt. 1973-74), Am. Econ. Assn. Home: 151 Ridings Cv Williamsburg VA 23185-3903

PARKAS, IVA RICHEY, educator, historian, curator, paralegal; b. Comanche County, Tex., June 28, 1907; d. Andrew J. Richey and Pearl Lucretia (Kennedy) Richey; grad. Wayland Coll., 1927; B.A., Tex. Tech. U., 1935; M.Litt., U. Pitts., 1950; postgrad. UCLA, 1960, Pa. State U., 1961, U. Calif., Berkeley, 1962, Duquesne U., 1963, Carnegie-Mellon U., 1968; m. George Eduardo Parkas, May 5, 1945. Curator, historian Fort Pitt Blockhouse, Pitts., 1946-52, asst. curator-historian, 1964-84; tchr. U.S. history Pitts. sr. high schs., 1953-72; paralegal Allegheny County (Pa.) Law Dept., 1977-82. Del., White House Conf. on Children and Youth, Washington, 1960, 70; World Food Conf., Rome, 1974; U.S. Congl. Sr. Citizens intern, Washington, 1984. Named Disting. Alumnae, U. Pitts., 1978; recipient Classroom Tchr.'s medal Freedoms Found. Valley Forge, 1960; Henry Clay Frick Ednl. fellow; NDEA grantee; Greater Pitts. Air Force Squadron scholar, Pitts. Press scholar, 1960. Mem. NEA (life), AAUW (pres. Pitts. br. 1974-76), Hist. Soc. Western Pa., Western Pa. Council Social Studies (pres. 1969-71), DAR (regent Pitts. chpt. 1986-89), U. Pitts. Alumnae Assn. (bd. dirs. 1978—, v.p. 1984), Pa. Retired Pub. Sch. Employees Assn. (chairperson Am. revolution bicentennial 1974-76), Western Pa. Hist. Soc., Allegheny County Bicentennial Commn., Greater Pitts. Commn. for Women, Delta Kappa Gamma, Phi Alpha Theta. Commonwealth editor: So Your Children Can Tell Their Children, 1976; contbr. articles on hist. subjects to newspapers, mags. Home: 5520 5th Ave Apt C5 Pittsburgh PA 15232-2342

PARKE, ROBERT LEON, communications executive; b. Jersey City, Aug. 28, 1940; s. Edwin Gager and Alice Elizabeth (Servis) P.; m. Geraldine R. Pavlick, Sept. 2, 1967; children: Cheryl Lynn, Tracy Ann, David Scott. Grad. high sch., Jersey City. Asst. bookkeeper Snow-Kist Frozen Foods, Jersey City, 1964-67; supr. accounts receivable Swift Line Transfer Co., Inc., North Bergen, N.J., 1967-69; contr. Imperial Cartage Co., Inc., Jersey City, 1969-79; supr. inventory mgmt. Vista United Telecommunications, Lake Buena Vista, Fla., 1980—; corp. sec. Imperial Warehouse Co., Inc., Jersey City, 1968-79, Arbe Transfer Co. Inc., 1968-79; v.p. Cole Foods, Inc., Jersey City, 1968-79;. Spl. min. of the eucharist Diocese Orlando, Fla., 1992; vol. Gave Kids The World, Kissimmee, Fla.; mem. Pemberton Twp. Zoning Bd., Browns Mills, N.J., 1977-79; trustee, bd. dirs. Browns Mills Improvement Assn., 1974-79; trustee Rebecca Worf Meml. Fund Browns Mills, N.J., Parke Soc., S.E. Milw. Recipient Cert. Appreciation Am. Indian Relief Coun., 1996; Bob Parke day proclaimed by Twp. of Pemberton, 1979; named scholar NAPM Ctrl. Fla., Inc. Mem. Nat. Notary Assn., Fla. Notary Assn., Am. Soc. Notaries, Purchasing Mgmt. Assn. Ctrl. Fla., Nat. Assn. Purchasing Mgmt. (scholarship for continued edn., Ctrl. Fla. Most Suportive Mem. 1994). Office: Vista United Telecommunications 3100 Bonnet Creek Rd Lake Buena Vista FL 32830 *Everyone can have a dream, but only those that care and show perseverance will achieve success.*

PARKER, ALAN JOHN, veterinary neurologist, educator, researcher; b. Portsmouth, Eng., Oct. 28, 1944; came to U.S., 1969; s. William Barton and Emily (Begley) P.; m. Heather Margaret Nicholson, Oct. 30, 1971; children: Alyxander John, Robert William. B.Sc. with honors, Bristol U., 1966, B.V.Sc. with honors, 1968; M.S., U. Ill., 1973, Ph.D., 1976. Diplomate Am. Coll. Vet. Internal Medicine-Neurology, European Coll. Vet. Neurology. Intern Vet. Coll., U. Calif.-Davis, 1969-70; instr. vet. clin. medicine U. Ill., Urbana, 1970-71, 72-76, asst. prof., 1976-77, assoc. prof., 1977-82, prof., 1982—; cons. pharm. cos., seminar presenter; cons. in neurology Berwyn Vet. Hosp., Chgo., 1973—, Lake Shore Animal Hosp., Chgo., 1978—. Contbr. numerous articles to sci. jours., chpts. to books. Active Boy Scouts Am., Champaign, Ill., 1982—; active Presbyn. Ch., Monticello, Ill., 1979—. Recipient Vigil Honor and Founder's award Order of the Arrow, Boy Scouts Am.; sci. grantee various orgns., 1972—. Mem. AVMA, Am. Animal Hosp. Assn., Brit. Vet. Assn., Ill. State Vet. Assn. Republican. Office: U Ill Coll Vet Medicine 1008 W Hazelwood Dr Urbana IL 61801-4714

PARKER, ALAN WILLIAM, film director, writer; b. London, Feb. 14, 1944; s. William Leslie and Elsie Ellen P.; m. Annie Inglis, July 30, 1966; children: Lucy Kate, Alexander James, Jake William, Nathan Charles. Student Brit. schs. Advt. copywriter, 1966-69, dir. TV commls. Author: screenplay Melody, 1968; novel Bugsy Malone, 1975, Puddles in the Lane, 1977; author, dir.: No Hard Feelings, 1972, Our Cissy, 1973, Footsteps, 1973, Bugsy Malone, 1975 (5 Brit. Acad. awards) Come See the Paradise, 1990; dir.: The Evacuees (Brit. Acad. award, Internat. Emmy award, Press Guild U.K. award), Midnight Express (6 Golden Globe awards, 3 Brit. Acad. awards, 2 Oscar awards), Fame, 1980 (Brit. Acad. award, Golden Globe award, 2 Oscar awards), Shoot the Moon, 1982, Pink Floyd-The Wall, 1982, Birdy, 1984 (Grand Prix Spl. du Jury, Cannes Film Festival), A Turnip Head's Guide to the British Cinema, 1986, Angel Heart, 1987, Mississippi Burning, 1988 (Oscar award), The Commitments, 1991, The Road to Wellville, 1994, Evita, 1996. Recipient 4 Brit. Acad. awards. Mem. Brit. Acad. Film and TV Arts, Dirs. Guild Am., Writers Guild G.B., Writers Guild Am., Dirs. Guild G.B. Office: care Michael Wimer Creative Artists Agy 9830 Wilshire Blvd Beverly Hills CA 90212-1804

PARKER, ANGELO PAN, lawyer; b. Detroit, Feb. 10, 1945; s. Pan A. and Clementine (Kaplanis) P.; m. Dena Apostle, Mar. 9, 1975; children: Denise, Alyssa. BBA, St. Mary's U., San Antonio, Tex., 1967, JD, 1970. Bar: Tex. 1970, Nebr. 1973. Ptnr. Kutak Rock, Omaha, 1973-80, McCall, Parkhurst & Horton, Dallas, 1980-85, Strasburger & Price, L.L.P., Dallas, 1986—. 1st lt. U.S. Army, 1970-73. Office: Strasburger & Price LLP 4200 Nations Bank Plz 901 Main St Dallas TX 75202-3714

PARKER, ANN (ANN PARKER NEAL), photographer, graphic artist; b. London, Mar. 6, 1934; d. Russell Johnston and Mildred Grace (Best) P.; m. Avon Neal, Oct. 31, 1964. Student, R.I. Sch. Design, 1952-54; B.F.A., Yale U., 1956. V.p. Thistle Hill Press, North Brookfield, Mass., 1979—; artist-in-residence Altos de Chavon, Dominican Republic, 1983, 84; panel mem. Fulbright Hays Com. for Photography, Film and Video, 1983, 85, 86. Freelance photographer and graphic artist, 1956—; exhbns. include Santa Fe Ctr. Photography, 1982, Focus Gallery, San Francisco, 1983, Altos de Chavon, Dominican Republic, 1984, 86, 87, Nat. Mus. Art, La Paz, Bolivia, 1985, Princeton U. Libr., 1986, Instituto Dominicano de Cultura Hispanica, Santa Domingo, Dominican Republic, 1987, Gallery of Graphic Arts, N.Y.C., 1987, Maxwell Mus. Anthropology, U. N.Mex., Albuquerque, 1988, Gallery Twerenbold, Luzern, Switzerland, 1991, San Antonio Mus. Assns., 1992, Worcester (Mass.) Art Mus., 1993, Gallery of Graphic Arts, N.Y.C., 1994, Lumina Gallery, Taos, N.Mex., 1995, Gallery of Graphic Arts, N.Y.C., 1995, U. Conn., 1996, U. Mass. Med. Ctr., 1996, Ute Stebich Gallery, Lenox (Mass.), 1996; work pub. in Smithsonian mag., Am. Heritage Life, Americana, Aperture, Natural History, others; works in permanent collections N.Y. Pub. Libr., George Eastman House, Rochester, N.Y., Met. Mus. Art, N.Y.C., Mus. Modern Art, N.Y.C., Mus. Fine Arts, Boston, Ctr. Creative Photography, Tucson, MIT, Libr. of Congress, Smithsonian Instn., Rosenwald Collection, Mellon Collection, Whitney Mus., others; art books Ephemeral Folk Figures, 1969, Molas, 1977, Scarecrows, 1978, Early American Stone Sculpture, 1982, Los Ambulantes, 1982, Hajj Paintings, 1995, Folk Art of the Great Pilgrimage, 1995. Recipient 1st pl. award Mass. Open Photography, 1978, Am. Inst. Graphic Design awards, 1956, 77, 79, Mass. Arts Coun. award, 1988, 96; Ford Found. grantee, 1962-63m 63-64. Address: Thistle Hill North Brookfield MA 01535

PARKER, BARBARA Z., bank executive. Trust and investment mgr. Midlantic Corp., Edison, N.J.; now exec. v.p. Midlantic Bank NA. Office: Midlantic Bank NA 499 Thornall St Edison NJ 08837-2235*

PARKER, BARRINGTON D., JR., lawyer; b. Aug. 21, 1944. BA, Yale U., 1965, JD, 1969. Bar: N.Y. 1971. Law clk. to Hon. Aubret E. Robinson U.S. Dist. Ct. (D.C.), 1969-70; mem. Morrison & Foerster, N.Y.C.; bd. dirs., v.p. NAACP Legal Def. and Educational Fund, Inc., 1980—; com. on grievances, com. on civil discovery U.S. Dist. Ct. (so. dist.) N.Y., 1983—; com. on pre-trial phase civil cases U.S. Ct. Appeals (2nd cir.) 1983—. Mem. ABA, Assn. of Bar of City of N.Y. (com. on the judiciary 1978-82, exec. com. 1982-86, nominating com. 1987). Office: US Dist Ct 101 E Post Rd White Plains NY 10601

PARKER, BARRY JAMES CHARLES, retail executive; b. St. Louis, Sept. 9, 1947; s. James M.C. and Ruth E. (Cummings) P.; m. Donna Nardin, June 19, 1970; children: Thomas J.J., Michael B.B. BA, Washington U., St. Louis, 1969; MBA, U. Pa., 1971. Buyer, dist. merchandise mgr. F & R Lazarus & Co., Columbus, Ohio, 1971-75; v.p. and gen. merchandise mgr., sr. v.p. The Children's Place, Pinebrook, N.J., 1975-85; pres. County Seat Stores Inc., Dallas, 1985—, chmn. bd., pres., chief exec. officer, 1989—. Mem. Internat. Coun. Shopping Ctrs., Nat. Retail Fedn., Young Pres.'s Orgn. Roman Catholic. Avocations: tennis, skiing, golf. Office: County Seat Stores Inc 17950 Preston Rd Ste 1000 Dallas TX 75252-5638

PARKER, BOBBY EUGENE, SR., college president; b. Wortham, Tex., May 28, 1925; s. Thomas W. and Stacy (Beasley) P.; m. Marietta Vickrey, Sept. 1, 1946; children: Bobby Eugene Jr., Mark. AA, Westminster Jr. Coll., 1948; BS, Sam Houston State Coll., 1951; MS, Baylor U., 1954, EdD, 1964; LLD (hon.), Houston Bapt. U., 1990. Prin., counselor pub. schs. Richland and Mexia, Tex., 1948-57; dean students Howard Payne Coll., Brownwood, Tex., 1957-59; mem. faculty Baylor U., Waco, Tex., 1960-69; v.p. Mary Hardin-Baylor Coll., Belton, Tex., 1969-71; pres. U. Mary Hardin-Baylro, 1971-91, chancellor, 1991—; hon. chancellor Ebino (Japan) Kohgen Internat. Coll., 1994; hon. pres. Allen Jr. Coll., Kuji Iwate Japan, 1992. Mem. King's Daus. Hosp. Assn., Heart O' Tex. coun. nat. Boy Scouts Am., pres. 1995; trustee Bell County Mus. History and Art; bd. dirs. Greater Waco Safety Coun., 1963-67, Waco Girl's Club, 1967-69, Tex. Safety Assn., 1963; pres. coun. Heart of Tex. Athletic Conf. With USNR, 1943-46. Recipient Spl. Safety award Tex. Safety Assn., 1965, Exemplary medal San Marcos Bapt. Acad., 1991; named Man of Yr. Belton Area C. of C., 1978, Outstanding Christian Educator Mexican Bapt. Conv.; fellow Paul Harris. Mem. Internat. Platform Assn., Tex. Baptist Sch. Adminstrs. Assn., Tex. Found. Vol. Supported Colls. and Univs. (former chmn. bd.), Assn. Am. Colls., Am. Council Edn., Ind. Colls. and Univs. of Tex. (former mem. exec. bd.), Nat. Assn. Intercollegiate Athletics (former pres. adv. com.), Belton C. of C. (past bd. dirs.), East Tex. C. of C., Killeen C. of C., Temple C. of C., Friends of Scott and White. Lodge: Rotary Internat. (Gov. 1984, Dist. Gov.'s Role of Fame; Gov. Dist. 587. 1986-87). Home: 2506 River Oaks Dr Belton TX 76513-1654 Office: U Mary Hardin Baylor PO Box 8440 Belton TX 76513-0999

PARKER, BRENT MERSHON, retired medical educator, internist, cardiologist; b. St. Louis, July 3, 1927; s. William Bahlmann and Florence (Mershon) P.; m. Martha Shelton, Aug. 1, 1953; children: Martha Parker Burgess, Elizabeth, Margaret. MD cum laude, Wash. U., St. Louis, 1952. Diplomate Am. Bd. Internal Medicine. Intern and asst. resident N.Y. Hosp.-Cornell, N.Y.C., 1952-54; asst. resident, fellow Barnes Hosp., Wash. U., St. Louis, 1954-57; cardiology sect. chief VA Hosp., U. Oreg., Portland, 1957-59; asst. prof. to assoc. prof., co-dir. cardiovascular div., chief adult cardiac catherization Wash. U. Sch. Medicine, St. Louis, 1959-73; prof. medicine U. Mo., Columbia, 1973-89, prof. emeritus, 1989-94, chief of staff, assoc. dean, 1976-82, chief of cardiology, 1983-89; mem. colloquium faculty Merck, Sharp and Dohme, West Point, Pa., 1980-86. Author or co-author 58 papers in referred jours., 6 book chpts., teaching papers, others. Bd. dirs. St. Louis Heart Assn., 1962-73, v.p. 1972-73; bd. dirs. Mo. Heart Assn., 1965-75, pres. 1970-71. Served with USN, 1945-46. Recipient Arthur Strauss award St. Louis Heart Assn., 1973, 3 teaching awards U. Mo. Sch. Medicine, 1974, 75, 86, Preventive Cardiology Acad. award, Nat. Heart Lung and Blood Inst., 1982-87, Alumni Achievement award Washington Univ. Sch. Medicine, 1992; Brent Mershon Parker professorship estab. in honor U. Mo., 1989. Fellow ACP, Am. Coll. Cardiology (Mo., Kans. council rep. 1973-77), Clin. Cardiology Soc. Am. Heart Assn.; mem. Am. Fedn. Clin. Research, Cen. Soc. for Clin. Research, Alpha Omega Alpha, Sigma Xi. Episcopalian. Avocations: choral singing, jogging, camping, back packing.

PARKER, BRIAN PRESCOTT, forensic scientist; b. Norfolk, Va., Aug. 31, 1929; s. Milton Ellsworth and Louise Randall (Smith) P.; BS in Quantitative Biology, M.I.T., 1953; JD, Northwestern U., 1957; M.Criminology, U. Calif., Berkeley, 1961, D.Criminology, 1967; m. Sonia Garcia Rosario, Dec. 23, 1960; children: Robin Marie, Augustin Keith. Research asst. U. P.R. Med. Sch., 1961; cons. P.R. Justice Dept., 1961-63; spl. asst. FDA, Washington, 1964; lectr., then asst. prof. criminology U. Calif., Berkeley, 1964-70; sr. criminalist, then sr. forensic scientist Stanford Research Inst., Menlo Park, Calif., 1971-73; prof. forensic sci. and criminal justice Calif. State U., Sacramento, 1973-92; prof. emeritus, 1988—; project dir. phys. evidence Dept. Justice, 1969-70; vis. fellow Nat. Police Research Unit, Australia, 1985; vis. prof. Elton Mayo Sch. Mgmt., South Australia Inst. Tech., 1985. Mem. Am. Chem. Soc. Co-author: Physical Evidence in the Administration of Criminal Justice, 1970, The Role of Criminalistics in the World of the Future, 1972; asso. editor Law, Medicine, Science—and Justice, 1964; contbr. to Ency. Crime and Justice, 1983. Home: 5117 Ridgegate Way Fair Oaks CA 95628-3603

PARKER, CAMILLE KILLIAN, physician, surgeon; b. Columbus, Ohio, June 28, 1918; d. John Vincent and Myrtle (Kagy) Hill; m. E.W. Killian, Apr. 25, 1943 (dec.); children—Paul Wesley, Clyde Bernard; m. Francis W. Parker, Dec. 7, 1958. Student, U. Chgo., 1942-43; B.S., U. Ill., 1945; M.D., 1946; postgrad. in ophthalmology, Northwestern U., 1947-48. Diplomate Am. Bd. Ophthalmology. Intern Wesley Meml. Hosp., Chgo., 1946-47; resident in ophthalmology Ill. Eye and Ear Infirmary, Chgo., 1949-51; practice medicine specializing in med. and surg. ophthalmology Logansport, Ind., 1951—; sec. staff Meml. Hosp., Logansport, 1959; pres. med. staff St. Joseph Hosp., Logansport, 1965. Pres., Logansport Council for Pub. Schs., 1961,62; mem. Lake Maxinkuckee Mgmt. Com., Culver, Ind., 1981—; chmn. social concern Meth. Ch., 1963-65, ofcl. bd., 1961-65. Recipient Service award Culver Mil. Acad., 1969. Fellow Am. Acad. Ophthalmology and Otolaryngology; mem. AMA (physicians recognition award 1971, 75, 79, 82, 85, 88, 93, 94), Soc. Eye Surgeons (charter), Logansport C. of C., Cass County Med. Soc. (pres. 1971), Ind. State Med. Assn., Ind. Acad. Ophthalmology and Otolaryngology (pres. 1979-80). Republican. Clubs: Altrusa (v.p. 1967-69), Culver Mothers (pres. 1968-69). Home and Office: 2500 E Broadway Logansport IN 46947-2002

PARKER, CAROL JEAN, psychotherapist, consultant; b. Plant City, Fla., Sept. 4, 1946; d. Fennimore Blaine and Verna Melissa (Robinson) Bowman; m. Charles Bridges, June 1, 1968 (div. 1979); children: James, Nova. AA, Hillsborough C.C., Tampa, Fla., 1979; BA, Internat. Coll., L.A., 1981, MA, 1983. Asst. Dr. Clarke Weeks, Plant City, 1964-65; med. transcriber Tampa Gen. Hosp., 1965-71, St. Joseph's Hosp., Tampa, 1976-80; psychotherapist Discovery Inst., Tampa, 1980-85; owner, dir. Ananda Counseling Ctr., Tampa, 1985—; clinician Human Devel. Ctr., New Port Richey, Fla., 1979-81; exec. dir. women's program, The Manors Hosp., Tarpon Springs, Fla., 1992—. Participant Task Force on Prostitution and Female Offender Diversion Program, Tampa, 1988. Mem. ACA, Am. Assn. on Mental Health, Am. Assn. Clin. Hypnotists, Internat. Soc. for Study Multiple Personality Disorders and Disassociation, Tampa Bay Assn. Women Therapists (bd. dirs.), Tampa Bay Study Group on Multiple Personality Disorders and Dissociation (chmn. bd. 1990—, Outstanding Mem. award 1991). Office: Ananda Counseling Ctr 420 W Platt St Tampa FL 33606-2244

PARKER, CHARLES WALTER, JR., consultant, retired equipment company executive; b. nr. Ahoskie, N.C., Nov. 22, 1922; s. Charles Walter and Minnie Louise (Williamson) P.; m. Sophie Nash Riddick, Nov. 26, 1949; children: Mary Parker Hutto, Caroline Parker Robertson, Charles Walter III, Thomas Williamson. B.S. in Elec. Engring. Va. Mil. Inst., 1947; Dr. Engring. (hon.), Milw. Sch. Engring., 1980. With Allis-Chalmers Corp., 1947-87; dist. mgr. Allis-Chalmers Corp., Richmond, Va., 1955-57, Phila., 1957-58; dir. sales promotion industries group Allis-Chalmers Corp., Milw., 1958-61; gen. mktg. mgr. new products Allis-Chalmers Corp., 1961-62, mgr. mktg. services, 1962-66, v.p. mktg. and public relations services, 1966-70, v.p., dep. group exec., 1970-72, staff group exec. communications and public affairs, 1972-87, ret., 1987; prin. Charles Parker & Assocs., Ltd., Milw., 1987—; retired chmn. bd. dirs. Associated Dental Svc. Inc., Milw., 1989-93; founding mem. World Mktg. Contact Group, London; bd. dirs. Internat. Gen. Ins. Corp., Dinermite Corp. Gen. chmn. United Fund Greater Milw. Area, 1975; trustee Boy Scouts Am. Trust Fund, Milw.; bd. dirs. Jr. Achievement; pres. bd. trustees Univ. Sch. Milw., 1978-80; trustee Carroll Coll., Waukesha, Wis.; bd. dirs. Milw. Children's Hosp.; bd. regents Milw. Sch. Engring.; mem. Greater Milw. Com.; chmn. bd. dirs. Milw. Found., 1987-89. Served to capt. AUS, 1943-46, ETO. Decorated Bronze Star. Mem. NAM (dir.), IEEE (assoc.), Wis. C. of C. (pres. 1974-76), Sales and Mktg. Execs. Internat. (pres., CEO 1974, 75, Eduardo Rihan Internat. Mktg. Exec. of Yr. award 1979), Wis. Mfrs. and Commerce Assn. (exec. com.), Pi Sigma Epsilon (pres. 1976-77, trustee and chmn. nat. edn. found. 1979-86), Kappa Alpha. Home: 4973 N Newhall St Milwaukee WI 53217-6049 Office: PO Box 92398 828 N Broadway Milwaukee WI 53202-3611

PARKER, CHRISTOPHER WILLIAM, lawyer; b. Evanston, Ill., Oct. 26, 1947; s. Robert H. and Dorothy Boynton P.; m. Mary Ann P., Dec. 28, 1984. BA, Tufts U., 1969; JD, Northeastern U., 1976. Bar: Mass. 1977, U.S. Dist. Ct. Mass. 1977, U.S. Dist. Ct. (we. dist.) Tex. 1986, U.S. Ct. Appeals (1st cir.) 1988, U.S. Supreme Ct. 1988. Law clk. to judge U.S. Bankruptcy Ct. Mass. dist., Boston, 1976-77; assoc. Fletcher, Tilton & Whipple, Worcester, Mass., 1977-79; counsel U.S. Trustee, Boston, 1979-81; assoc. Craig and Macauley P.C., Boston, 1982-84, ptnr., 1984-87; counsel Hinckley, Allen, Snyder & Comen, Boston, 1987-88, ptnr., 1989-91; ptnr. McDermott, Will & Emery, Boston, 1991—. Mem. ABA, Mass. Bar Assn., Am. Bankruptcy Inst. Boston Bar Assn., Comml. Law League. Club: Union Boat (Boston). Home: 45 Walnut St Lynnfield MA 01940-2009 Office: McDermott Will & Emery 75 State St Boston MA 02109-1807

PARKER, CLEA EDWARD, retired university president; b. Talisheek, La., Apr. 2, 1927; s. William A. and Lutritia (Davis) P.; m. Peggy Ann Faciane, June 21, 1953; children—Brian, Stephen, Karen, Robin. B.A., Southeastern La. U., 1948; M.Ed., La. State U., 1952, Ed.D., 1965. Coach, tchr. Rugby Acad., New Orleans, 1948-50; tchr., prin., supr. instr., dir. curriculum and instrn. St. Tammany Parish Sch. Bd., 1950-67; prof. edn., head dept. student teaching Nicholls State Coll., Thibodaux, La., 1967-68; acting pres. Southeastern La. U., Hammond, 1968; pres. Southeastern La. U., 1968-80, pres. emeritus, 1980—; liaison La. State Dept. Edn., Higher Edn. and Bds. for Edn. in La., 1986; vis. lectr. La. State U., 1965-69; Past pres. St. Tammany Parish Tchrs. Assn., La. Assn. Supervision and Curriculum Devel.; past pres. elementary dept. La. Tchrs. Assn.; chmn. Pres.'s Council La. Bd. Edn., 1972-73; v.p. Conf. La. Colls. and Univs., 1973-74, pres., 1974-75; pres. elect Gulf South Conf., 1974-75, pres., 1975-76; mem. Steering Com. on Curriculum Devel. and Revision for Career Edn. for State La., 1973; mem. adv. council for State Plan for Career Edn., 1973. Mem. planning com. Gov.'s Conf. on Aging, 1976; v.p. chpt. 15 La. Good Samaritans, 1987-88; bd. dirs. Assn. for Retarded Citizens, pres.-elect, 1981; mem. Zemurray Park Recreation Commn., Hammond, 1992-95; chmn. bd. dirs. Lallie Kemp Meml. Hosp., 1993-94; bd. dirs. Lallie Kemp Med. Ctr., 1994—, chmn., 1994-95. With USCGR, 1945, 93-94. Named Hon. State Farmer La., 1970; Distinguished Alumnus of Yr. Southeastern La. U. Alumni Assn., 1977, 91, 92. Mem. Am. Assn. State Colls. and Univs. (com. on nat. svc. 1972-73, task force on aging 1975-76, 78-79, nominating com. 1977—, state Rep. for La. 1979—, com. agr. renewable resources and rural devel. 1979-80, Svc. to Edn. award 1980), Hammond C. of C., La. Assn. for Sch. Execs., Ozone Ramblers Camping Club (pres. 1988), KC (lectr. 1982, 85, 90-91, chancellor 1983-84, 87—, dep. grand knight 1995-96), Rotary (bd. dirs. Hammond, internat. svc. dir. 1972), Phi Delta Kappa, Kappa Delta Pi. Home: 10 Golden Dr Hammond LA 70401-1010

PARKER, DAVID FORSTER, real estate development consultant; b. Sarnia, Ont., Can., July 4, 1934; s. George William and Bessie Havergal (Forster) P.; m. Marilynn Catherine McFadden, Oct. 15, 1960; children: John Christopher, Stephen, David, Daniel. Student, U. Toronto, Ont., Can., 1954-57; BS, Mich. State U., 1964, M in Urban Planning, 1965; D in Pub. Adminstrn., SUNY, Albany, 1980. Prin. Tricon Ltd. Builders, Sarnia, Ont., 1957-62; urban planner N.Y. State Dept. Transp., Albany, 1965-66; asst. to dir. N.Y. State Budget, Albany, 1967-69; pres. Audubon Devel. Corp., Buffalo, 1969-76; dep. dir. Sadat City, Cairo, Egypt, 1976-79; cons. Milton Keynes (Eng.), 1979-80; v.p. Bos Corp., Jacksonville, Fla., 1980-82; prin. Clark Parker Assocs., Jacksonville, 1982-90, Parker Assocs., Jacksonville, 1990—, Clark Parker Realty, Jacksonville, 1982-92; pres. Fla. Real Estate Clinic, Inc., 1991-94; real estate broker, 1992—; pres. PFE, Inc., 1994—. Author: Marketing New Homes, 1990 (recognition 1990), Selling New Homes, 1990 (recognition 1990); contbr. articles to profl. jours. Chmn. Albany Citizens Against Poverty, 1966-67, Ctrl. Jacksonville Residential Task Force, 1986-88, Mayor's Housing Com., Jacksonville, 1990—. Mem. Inst. Residential Mktg., Nat. Assn. Home Builders, C. of C., S.E. Resort Real Estate Coun., Urban Land Inst., Comty. Devel. Coun., Am. Inst. Cert. Planners, SPEBSQSA (greater Jacksonville chpt. pres. 1990-92, sunshine dist. dir. 1993—, v.p. 1995-96), Selva Marina Country Club, Phi Kappa Phi, Beta Alpha Sigma, Phi Sigma Alpha. Home: 1739 Live Oak Ln Jacksonville FL 32233-5605 Office: Parker Assocs 14500 Beach Blvd Jacksonville FL 32250-9999

PARKER, DONALD FRED, college dean, human resources management educator; b. Oilton, Okla., Nov. 7, 1934; s. Robert Fred Parker and Georgia Marie (Culley) Meek; m. Jo Ellen Dunfee, Apr. 6, 1963; children: Margaret Elizabeth, Emily Lyle. BA in Sociology, U. Okla., 1957; MS in Personnel Adminstrn., George Washington U., 1966; PhD in Human Resource Mgmt., Cornell U., 1975. Commd. ensign USN, 1957, advanced through grades to capt., 1977; staff officer with chief naval ops. USN, Washington, 1969-71; comdg. officer, exec. officer, Patrol Squadron Ten USN, Brunswick, Maine, 1974-76; prof. Naval War Coll. USN, Newport, R.I., 1976-78; comdg. officer Navy Personnel Research & Devel. Ctr. USN, San Diego, 1978-80; ret. USN, 1980; asst. prof. Grad. Sch. Bus., U. Mich., Ann Arbor, 1980-84; prof. human resources mgmt., dean Coll. Commerce and Industry U. Wyo., Laramie, 1984-91; Sara Hart Kimball dean bus., prof. human resources mgmt. Oreg. State U., Corvallis, 1991—; advisor U.S. West Wyo. State Bd. Advisors, Cheyenne, 1986-91; bd. dirs. Unicover Corp., Rocky Mountain FSB; ex-officio dir. Wyo. Indsl. Devel. Corp., Casper, 1987; vis. prof. Acad. Internat. Econ. Affairs, Hsinchu, Taiwan, 1986-91. Author numerous articles, book chpts., case studies. Mem. Acad. of Mgmt. (human resource mgmt. divsn. dir. 1983-85), Midwest Assn. Deans and Dept. Chairs in Bus. (pres.), Western Assn. Collegiate Schs. Bus. (bd. dirs., sec./treas. elect 1996), Phi Kappa Phi. Avocations: jogging, skiing, hiking. Home: 4400 NW Honeysuckle Dr Corvallis OR 97330-3355 Office: Oreg State U Coll Bus Bexell Hall # 200 Corvallis OR 97331-2603

PARKER, DONALD HENRY, psychologist, author; b. Syracuse, N.Y., Apr. 18, 1912; s. Henry Melvin and Ethel (Madden) P.; m. Fritzi Taylor; 1 child, Dona Jean (Mrs. Roger Sell). B.A. cum laude, U. Fla., 1950, M.A. in Psychology, 1952; Ed.D. in Guidance, Columbia U., 1957. With Sears, Roebuck & Co., 1930-43; propr. Personnel Research Counselors (psychol. testing and guidance), Jacksonville, Fla., 1946-50; psychologist Childrens Home Soc. Fla., 1948-50; psychologist, reading cons. Bradford County schs., Fla., 1950-51; lectr., dir. Reading Lab., U. N.C., 1951-53; dir. Reading Center, Charlotte pub. schs., also Charlotte Coll., N.C., 1954-55; reading cons. Westchester County pub. schs., N.Y.; also instr. reading Columbia U., 1955-57; prof. edn., dir. Reading Lab., U. Bridgeport, Conn., 1957-58; multilevel cons. Sci. Research Assos., Chgo., 1957-64; dir. Inst. for Multilevel Learning Internat., 1964—, Biofeedback Counseling Center, Monterey, Calif., 1976-79; lectr. on multilevel philosophy (application of psychology of individual differences, devel. psychology and psychology of learning to theory that schooling consists of tng. and edn.), 1950—; cons. U.S. AID, Venezuela, 1965-67; participant, lectr. photopsychography, body-mind harmony and health 1st World Congress Parapsychology and Psychotronics, Prague, Czechoslovakia, 1973, 2d world congress, Monte Carlo, 1975; lectr. in Europe, 1960, 63, 71, 78, S.E. Asia, Australia, N.Z., 1969, Africa, India, Thailand, Hong Kong, Philippines, 1971; ednl. cons. to China, 1980, U.S.S.R., 1985. Author: SRA Reading Labs., 1957— (used by over 61,000, 000 students in 62 countries), Schooling for Individual Excellence, 1961, Schooling for What?, 1970, Photopsychography: New Image of Man, 1974, SRA Reading Power for Home Schooling, 1991; founder (with Sean Shanahan, Patricia Larkin), Gateway Literacy Project, 1992, Failing Schools! Why?, 1993; contbr. articles to profl. jours. Served with USN, 1943-46. Mem. Am. Psychol. Assn., Internat Reading Assn., Assn. Supervision and Curriculum Devel., Internat. Assn. Psychotronics Research, Am. Personnel and Guidance Assn., Phi Delta Kappa. Address: Heartsong House 148 San Remo Rd Carmel CA 93923-9763 *Increasingly, during the last few years of my eighty-two on Planet Earth, I have been influenced by the ancient Oriental philosophy of Yin-Yang, the dynamism and, yes, the continuum of possibility between good-bad, black-white, day-night, man-woman, and so on. While we may decry the one and cherish the other, we cannot have the one without the other. Still further, the truth usually lies somewhere along a line between the two. When I discover that truth, I act upon it to the best of my ability.*

PARKER, DONALD HOWARD, landscape architect; b. Boston, July 27, 1922; s. Glennes Arthur Sheldon and Vida Mary (Kendrew) P.; m. Ella Mae Stinson, Sept. 8, 1945 (dec. 1983); children—Randall Tebow, Sheldon Kendrew, Susan Bowen, Elizabeth Stinson; m. Helen Jackson Anthony, June 19, 1987; 1 stepchild, Scott Douglas Paul. B.S., U. Mass., Amherst, 1946, B. in Landscape Architecture, 1947. Registered landscape architect Va., N.C., N.Y., Mass. Landscape draftsman L.E. Moore, C.E., Boston, 1947-48, Leo A. Novick, L.A., N.Y.C., 1948-49; asst. landscape architect Colonial Williamsburg (Va.) Found., 1949-60, chief landscape architect, 1960-85; pvt. practice landscape architecture Williamsburg, 1949—; adv. com. Hist. Am. Bldg. Survey, 1969-71, Smithsonian Instn., 1977-80. Contbr. chpts. to books, articles to profl. jours. Active, Boy Scouts Am., 1958-84. Served to 2d lt. U.S. Army, 1942-45. Recipient Dist. Grad. award Dept. Land Architecture, U. Mass., 1984; Paul Harris fellow Rotary Found., 1981. Fellow Am. Soc. Landscape Architects (trustee Potomac chpt. 1977, Va. chpt. 1978-83, treas. Va. chpt. 1984-86, Disting. Svc. award Va. chpt. 1994); mem. Assn. Preservation Va. Antiquities (bd. dirs. 1995—), 20th Century Art Gallery (bd. dirs. 1980-84, treas. 1992-96), Williamsburg Inn Lawn

Bowling Club (pres. 1985-90, sec.-treas. 1991-93, treas. 1994—, tournament dir. 1985-94), Rotary (pres. Williamsburg club 1979-80). Avocations: sports, gardening, canoeing, traveling, lawn bowling. Home and Office: 108 Archers Hope Rd Williamsburg VA 23185-4406

PARKER, DONALD LESTER, technology company executive; b. Mobile, Ala., Dec. 19, 1944; s. Orin Harvey and Lois B. (Burdette) P.; m. Linda Jean Busby, Dec. 18, 1970; children: Amanda Leigh, Allison Ann. BS, Spring Hill Coll., 1966; PhD, Mich. State U., 1971. Research asst. Mich. State U., 1968-71; asst. prof. Iowa State U., Ames, 1975-79, assoc. prof., 1980; v.p. research & devel. QMS, Inc., Mobile, Ala., 1981-82; sr. v.p. QMS, Inc., Mobile, 1983-84, sr. v.p. corp. technology, 1985-86, sr. v.p. mktg. and technology, 1987, exec. v.p. products and technology, 1987—; adj. prof. computer & info. scis., U. So. Ala., 1986—. Contbr. articles to profl. jours. Mem. AAUP, Assn. Computing Machinery, IEEE, Am. Assn. for Artificial Intelligence, Ala. Acad. Sci., Am. Electronics Assn., Am. Mgmt. Assn., Am. Phys. Soc., AAAS, Fedn. Am. Scientists, Tech. Assn. Graphic Arts, Ala. State Research Resource Adv. Com., Nat. Computer Graphics Assn., World Future Soc. Home: 6420 Tokeneak Trl Mobile AL 36695-2940 Office: QMS Inc 1 Magnum Pass Mobile AL 36689*

PARKER, DOUGLAS MARTIN, lawyer; b. Chgo., Mar. 6, 1935; s. Lewis Wallace and Elaine (Schulz) P.; m. Angela Macintosh, June 5, 1965; children: Heather Louise, Melissa Meredith. A.B., Cornell U., 1956, LL.B., 1958. Bar: N.Y. 1959, U.S. Supreme Ct. 1966, D.C. 1969. Assoc. Mudge Rose Guthrie Alexander & Ferdon, N.Y.C., 1958-59, 62-69, ptnr., 1977-94, of counsel, 1995; ptnr, Lankler & Parker, Washington, 1969-73; with Office of Counsel to Pres., 1973; dep. gen. counsel HUD, 1974-77. Served to capt. U.S. Army, 1959-62. Mem. Am. Arbitration Assn. (mem. regional panel of neutrals, CPR Inst. for Dispute Resolution). Republican. Congregationalist. Home: 7 Highwood Rd South Orleans MA 02662

PARKER, EDNA G., federal judge; b. Johnston County, N.C., 1930; 1 child, Douglas Benjamin. Student, N.J. Coll. for Women (now Douglass Coll.); B.A. with honors, U. Ariz., 1953; postgrad., U. Ariz. Law Sch.; LL.B., George Washington U., 1957. Bar: D.C. Law clk. U.S. Ct. Claims, 1957-59; atty.-advisor Office of Gen. Counsel, Dept. Navy, 1959-60; trial atty. civil and tax div. Dept. Justice, 1960-69; adminstrv. judge Contract Appeals Bd., Dept. Transp., 1969-77; spl. trial judge U.S. Tax Ct., 1977-80, judge, 1980—. Mem. ABA, Fed. Bar Assn., D.C. Bar, D.C. Bar Assn., Women's Bar Assn. of D.C., Nat. Assn. Women Lawyers, Nat. Assn. Women Judges. Office: US Tax Ct 400 2nd St NW Washington DC 20217-0001*

PARKER, ELLIS D., retired career officer, electronics executive; b. Adams, Tenn., Nov. 1, 1932; s. Ellis A. and Lorene (Qualls) P.; m. Judy C. Matthews, Dec. 24, 1952; children: Donald S., Phillip R., David B. BS in Psychology, U. Nebr., 1972; MPA, Shippensburg U., 1979; LLD, Miles U., 1989. Rated aviator FAA. Commd. 2d lt. U.S. Army, Korea, 1957; advanced through ranks to lt. gen. U.S. Army, 1992; aviation officer, comdr. 17th aviation brigade U.S. Army, Korea, 1978-80; asst. divsn. commdr. 101st airborne divsn. U.S. Army, Fort Campbell, Ky., 1983-84; cmmdg. gen. Army Aviation County Sch. U.S. Army, Fort Rucker, Ala., 1984-89; dir. requirements army staff Pentagon, Washington, 1980-83, dir. army staff, 1989-92; dir. Cobro Corp., Saint Louis, 1993—; bd. dirs. Canadian Electronics, Toronto and Binghamton, N.Y., 1993—; v.p. aviation Lear Siegler, Oklahoma City, 1992-94. Contbr. articles to profl. jours. Chmn. Fort Rucker Mus. Found., 1995—; mem. presdl. search com. Enterprise (Ala.0 Jr. Coll.; adv. bd. Troy State U., Dotham, 1992—; chair retiree coun. for chief of staff U.S. Army. Decorated Disting. Flying Cross, 1969, Legion of Merit, 1991, Bronze Star, 1970, 71, 79, Disting. Svc. medals, Air medals, Army Commendation medals; named to Hall of Honor Gov. Ala., 1993—. Mem. Army Aviation Assn. Am. (Order of St. Michel, Gold 1992), Assn. U.S. Army (mem. exec. com. Fort Rucker chpt. 1994), Enterprise (Ala.) C. of C. (dir. 1995—), Enterprise Rotary Club (chmn. allocations com. 1993—). Republican. Avocations: flying, hunting, fishing, volunteering in community. Home and Office: 128 Deer Run Strut Enterprise AL 36330

PARKER, EUGENE NEWMAN, retired physicist, educator; b. Houghton, Mich., June 10, 1927; s. Glenn H. and Helen (MacNair) P.; m. Niesje Meuter, 1954; children—Joyce, Eric. BS, Mich. State U., 1948; PhD, Calif. Inst. Tech., 1951; DSc, Mich. State U., 1975; Doctor Honoris Causa in Physics and Math., Univ. Utrecht, The Netherlands, 1986; Doctor of Philosophy Honoris Causa in Theoretical Physics, U. Oslo, 1991. Instr. math. and astronomy U. Utah, 1951-53, asst. prof. physics, 1953-55; mem. faculty physics U. Chgo., 1955-95, prof. dept. physics, 1962-95, prof. dept. astronomy and astrophysics, 1967-95, prof. emeritus, 1995—. Author: Interplanetary Dynamical Processes, 1963, Cosmical Magnetic Fields, 1979, Spontaneous Current Sheets in Magnetic Fields, 1994. Recipient Space Sci. award AIAA, 1964, Chapman medal Royal Astron. Soc., 1979, Gold medal, 1992, Disting. Alumni award Calif. Inst. Tech., 1980, Karl Schwarzschild award Astronomische Gesselschaft, 1990; named James Arthur Prize Lectr. Harvard-Smithsonian Ctr. Astrophysics, 1986. Mem. NAS (H. K. Arctowski award 1969, U.S. Nat. Medal of Sci. award 1989), Am. Astron. Soc. (Henry Norris Russell lectr. 1969, George Ellery Hale award 1978), Am. Geophys. Union (John Adam Fleming award 1968, William Bowie medal 1990), Am. Acad. Arts and Scis., Norwegian Acad. Sci. and Letters. Achievements include development of theory of the origin of the dipole magnetic field of Earth; of prediction and theory of the solar wind and heliosphere; of theoretical basis for the X-ray emission from the Sun and stars. Home: 1323 Evergreen Rd Homewood IL 60430-3410

PARKER, EVERETT CARLTON, clergyman; b. Chgo., Jan. 17, 1913; s. Harry Everett and Lillian (Stern) P.; m. Geneva M. Jones, May 5, 1939; children: Ruth A. (Mrs. Peter Weiss), Eunice L. (Mrs. George Kolczun, Jr.), Truman E. AB, U. Chgo., 1935; BD magna cum laude, Chgo. Theol. Sem., 1943, Blatchford fellow, 1944-45, DD, 1964; DD, Catawba Coll., Salisbury, N.C., 1958; L.H.D., Fordham U., 1978, Tougaloo Coll., 1987. Pastor Waveland Ave. Congl. Christian Ch., 1943; asst. pub. service and war program mgr. NBC, 1943-45; founder-dir. Protestant Radio Commn., 1945-50; lectr. communication Yale Div. Sch., 1946-58, dir. communications research project, 1950-54; dir. Office Communication United Ch. Christ, 1954-83; sr. research assoc., adj. prof. Fordham U., 1983—; founder citizen movement to protect minority rights in media, 1963—; chmn. broadcasting and film commn. Nat. Coun. Chs., 1969-72, mem. gen. bd., 1966-72; chair Study Commn. on Theology, Edn. and Electronic Media, 1985-87; founder Found. for Minority Interests in Media, 1985—, treas., 1985—, Hispanic Telecommunications Network, 1986—; mem. adv. com. on advanced TV svcs., Consumer Adv. Group FCC, 1988-92. Producer-dir.: nat. TV programs including series Off to Adventure, 1956, Tangled World, 1965; originator: series Six American Families, PBS-TV, 1977; Author: Religious Radio, 1948, Film Use in the Church, 1953, The Television-Radio Audience and Religion, 1955, Religious Television, 1961, (with others) Television, Radio, Film for Churchmen, 1969, Fiber Optics to the Home: The Changing Future of Cable, TV and The Telephone, 1989, Social Responsibility of Television in the United States, 1994. Recipient Human Relations award Am. Jewish Com., 1966, Faith and Freedom award Religious Heritage Found., 1966, 77, Alfred I. DuPont-Columbia U. award pub. service in broadcasting, 1969; Roman Cath. Broadcasters Gabriel award pub. service, 1970; Lincoln U. award significant contbn. human relations, 1971; Racial Justice award Com. for Racial Justice, United Ch. Christ, 1973; Ch. Leadership award Council for Christian Social Action, 1973; Public Service award Black Citizens for a Fair Media, 1979, Pioneer award World Assn. for Christian Communication, 1988; Congl. citation, 1993. Club: Yale (N.Y.C.). Home: 11 Midland Ave White Plains NY 10606-2828 Office: Fordham University Dept Communications Bronx NY 10458

PARKER, FRANK LEON, environmental engineering educator, consultant; b. Somerville, Mass., Mar. 23, 1926; s. Benjamin James and Bertha (Cohen) P.; m. Elaine Marilyn Goldman, Aug. 22, 1954; children: Nina Madeline, Aaron Bennet, Stephan Alexander, David Seth. BS, MIT, 1948; MS, Harvard U., 1950, PhD, 1955. Registered profl. engr., N.Y. Engr. U.S. Bur. Reclamation, Riverton, Wyo., 1948; field engr. Rockland Light & Power Co., Nyack, N.Y., 1949-50; cons. Howard M. Turner, Boston, 1955; sect. chief IAEA, Vienna, Austria, 1960-61; chief radioactive waste disposal research sect. Oak Ridge Nat. Lab., 1956-66; prof. environ. engring. Vanderbilt U., Nashville, 1967-89, Disting. prof. environ. and water resources engring., 1989—, Alexander Heard Disting. prof., 1988; Westinghouse Savannah River Disting. Sci. prof. Clemson (S.C.) U., 1991—, Harvie Branscomb Disting. prof., 1994-95; cons. Adv. Com. on Reactor Safeguards, 1970-90, sci. adv. bd. Panel EPA, 1982-83, U.S. Dept. Energy, Hanford, Wash., 1970-93, Office Nuclear Waste Isolation, Battelle, 1975-87, chmn. bd. radioactive waste mgmt. NAS, 1985-91; commr. Monitored Retrievable Storage Rev. Commn., 1988-89. Mem. Port Authority Nashville, 1979-90; mem. Nashville Appeals Bd., 1979-88; mem. Jewish Community Rels. Coun., Nashville, 1981-87. With U.S. Army, 1943-46. Mem. NAE, Soc. Risk Analysis, AAAS, Am. Nuclear Soc., Am. Geophys. Union, Health Physics Soc., Nat. Coun. Radiation Protection and Measurements (consociate). Co-author: Physical and Engineering Aspects of Thermal Pollution, 1970; Engineering Aspects of Thermal Pollution, 1969; Biological Aspects of Thermal Pollution, 1969. Home: 4400 Iroquois Ave Nashville TN 37205-3832 Office: PO Box 1596 Nashville TN 37202-1596

PARKER, FRANKLIN, writer, educator; b. N.Y.C., June 2, 1921; m. Betty June Parker, June 12, 1950. BA, Berea Coll., 1949; MS, U. Ill., 1950; EdD, Peabody Coll. of Vanderbilt U., 1956. Librarian, speech tchr. Ferrum (Va.) Coll., 1950-52; librarian Belmont Coll., Nashville, 1952-54; circulation librarian George Peabody Coll. Tchrs. Vanderbilt U., Nashville, 1955-56; assoc. prof. edn. SUNY; New Paltz, 1956-57, U. Tex., Austin, 1957-64; prof. edn. U. Okla., Norman, 1964-68; Benedum prof. edn. emeritus W. Va. U., Morgantown, 1968-86; prof. emeritus, 1986; disting. vis. prof. Ctr. for Excellence in Edn. No. Ariz. U., 1986-89; disting. vis. prof. Coll. Edn. and Psychology Western Carolina U., 1989-94; research fellow U. Coll. Rhodesia, Africa, 1957-58, Rhodes-Livingstone Inst. Social Research, Africa, 1961-62; vis. prof. edn. U. Calgary, Alta., Can., summer 1969, U. Alta., Edmonton, summer 1970, No. Ariz. U., Flagstaff, summer 1971, U. Lethbridge, Can., (summers) 1971-73, Meml. U., Nfld., summer 1974; mem. Internat. Conf. African Adminstrn., Cambridge, (Eng.) U., 1957, European Bur. Adult Edn., Finland and Fed. Republic of Germany, 1966, nat. conf. White House Conf. on Edn., 1965, Nat. Fgn. Policy Conf. of Educators Dept. State, 1966; cons. Office Edn. HEW, 1970-75, NSF, 1980-86; cons. pubs. Macmillan, Merrill, Tchrs. Coll. Press, Wm. C. Brown, 1988—. Author: African Development and Education in Southern Rhodesia, 1960, 74, Africa South of the Sahara, 1966, George Peabody, A Biography, 1971, rev. edit., 1995, The Battle of the Books: Kanawha Country, 1975, What Can We Learn from the Schools of China?, 1977, British Schools and Ours, 1979; co-author: John Dewey: Master Educator, 2d rev. edit., 1961, Government Policy and International Education, 1965, Church and State in Education, 1966, Strategies for Curriculum Change: Cases from 13 Nations, 1968, Dimensions of Physical Education, 1969, International Education: Understandings and Misunderstandings, 1969, Understanding the American Public High School, 1969, Education in Southern Africa, 1970, Curriculum for Man in an International World, 1971, Administrative Dimensions of Health and Physical Education Programs, Including Athletics, 1971, Education and the Many Faces of the Disadvantaged, 1972, The Saber-Tooth Curriculum, meml. edit., 1972, Accelerated Development in Southern Africa, 1974, Myth and Reality: A Reader in Education, 1975, Six Questions: Controversy and Conflict in Education, 1975, Crucial Issues in Education, 6th rev. edit., 1977, Censorship and Education, 1981, Academic Profiles in Higher Education, 1993; series compiler and editor American Dissertations on Foreign Education, A Bibliography with Abstracts, vol. I Can., 1971, vol. II India, 1972, vol III Japan, 1972, vol. IV Africa, 1973, vol. V Scandinavia, 1974, vol. VI China, 1975, vol. VII Korea, 1976, vol. VIII Mex., 1976, vol. IX South Am., 1977, vol. X Cen. Am., 1978, vol. XI Pakistan, Bangladesh, 1979, Vol. XII Iran and Iraq, 1980, vol. XIII Israel, 1980, vol. XIV Middle East, 1981, vol. XV Thailand, 1983, vol. XVI Asia, 1985, vol. XVII Pacific, 1986, vol. XVIII Philippines, 1986, vol. XIX Australia and New Zealand, 1988, vol. XX Great Britain, 1990; (with Betty June Parker) Education in Puerto Rico and of Puerto Ricans in the U.S.A., vol. I, 1978, vol. II, 1984; Women's Education--A World View: Annotated Bibliography of Doctoral Dissertations vol. I, 1979; U.S. Higher Education: A Guide to Information Sources, 1980; Women's Education--A World View: Annotated Bibliography of Books and Reports, vol. II, 1981, Education in the People's Republic of China, Past and Present: Annotated Bibliography, 1986, Education in England and Wales: An Annotated Bibliography, 1991; spl. cons. U.S. and internat. edn. terms The Random House Dictionary of the English Language, 2d edit., 1987; mem. editorial bd. Jour. of Thought, 1965-80, Western Carolina U. Jour. Edn., 1969-76, W. Va. U. Mag., 1969-78, Ednl. Studies, 1975-77, Rev. Edn., 1977-86, Cor (Collected Original Resources in Edn.), 1977—, Internat. Jour African Hist. Studies, 1977-86 Edn. Digest, 1976-80, U.S.A. Today, 1981—, Collier's Yearbook, 1965-72, Compton's Yearbook, 1965-66, Dictionary of Am. Biography, supplement 5, 1951-55, 77, Dictionary of Scientific Biography, vol. 8, 1973, vol. 10, 1974, vol. 14, 1976, McGraw-Hill Ency. of World Biography, 1973, Acad. Am. Ency., 1979, Reader's Digest Almanac and Yearbook, 1968-73, others; mem. editorial bd., regular contbr. Americana Ann., 1961-89. Served with USAAF, 1942-46. Sr. Fulbright research scholar, 1961-62. Mem. African Studies Assn., S.W. Philosophy Edn. Soc. (pres. 1960), Am. Acad. Polit. and Social Sci., Am. Ednl. Research Assn., US Comparative and Internat. Edn. Soc. (feature writer 1963-68, v.p. 1963-64, internat. sec. 1965-68), Can. Comparative and Internat. Edn. Soc., Comparative Edn. Soc. Europe, History Edn. Soc. (pres. 1963-64), Appalachian Writers Assn., Kappa Delta Pi (life mem., Harold R.W. Benjamin fellow internat. edn. 1957-58, sec. com. on internat. edn. 1968-70), Phi Delta Kappa (life, research award chmn. commn. on internat. relations in edn. 1963-67), Phi Gamma Mu, Phi Kappa Phi (life).

PARKER, FRED I., federal judge; b. 1938. BA, U. Mass., 1962; LLB, Georgetown U., 1965. With Lyne, Woodworth & Everts, Boston, 1965-66, Office Atty. Gen., Montpelier, Vt., 1969-72, Langrock and Sperry, Middlebury, Vt., 1972-75; ptnr. Langrock, Sperry, Parker & Stahl, Middlebury, 1975-82, Langrock, Sperry, Parker & Wool, Middlebury, 1982-90; fed. judge U.S. Dist. Ct. (Vt. dist.), 1990-91, chief judge, 1991-94; fed. judge U.S. Ct. Appeals (2d cir.), 1994—; mem. conduct bd. Vt. Supreme Ct., 1975-79, jud. conduct bd., 1982-88. Active Vt. Lawyers Project. Mem. Vt. Bar Assn. (chair spl. com. reform of judiciary 1988-89), Chittenden County Bar Assn. Office: US Dist Ct 11 Elmwood Ave Fl 5 Burlington VT 05401-4366*

PARKER, GARRY OTIS, mission executive, missiologist; b. Ft. Smith, Ark., Sept. 13, 1942; s. Garry Cecil and Louise Elizabeth (Boring) P.; m. Sarah Merrick Whittum, June 10, 1967; children: Elizabeth Louise Parker-Sloat, Rebekah Lynne. AB, Taylor U., 1964; MDiv, Asbury Theol. Sem., 1968; postgrad., Cornell U., 1972, Princeton Theol. Sem., 1982-85, Johns Hopkins U., 1984. Ordained clergy United Meth. Ch., 1967. Missionary supr. OMS Internat., Malang, Indonesia, 1972-78; missionary, pastor The Union Ch., San Salvador, El Salvador, 1979-81; pastor Cmty. United Meth. Ch., Royal Oak, Md., 1981-84, Wesley United Meth., Elkton, Md., 1984-87; exec. cons. Gen. Bd. Global Ministry/United Meth. Ch., N.Y.C., 1987-89; pastor Tilghman (Md.) United Meth. Ch., 1989-91; pres., CEO The Mustard Seed, Pasadena, Calif., 1991—; corp. pres. The Mustard Seed, Pasadena, 1993—; Am. sch. bd. mem. Am. Sch. in El Salvador, San Salvador, 1980-81; global min. Peninsula Conf. Bd. United Meth. Ch., Dover, Del., 1982-88; bd. mem. Mission Compassion, San Francisco, 1995. Contbr. chpt. to book and articles to profl. jours. Chaplain Vol. Fire Dept., Tilghman, 1988-91. John Wesley fellow A Fund for Theol. Edn., Lexington, 1982. Mem. Christian Mgmt. Assn. Office: The Mustard Seed 1539 E Howard St Pasadena CA 91104

PARKER, GEORGE, retired pen manufacturing company executive; b. Janesville, Wis., Nov. 9, 1929; s. Russell C. and Eleanor (Jackson) P.; m. Nancy E. Bauhan, Aug. 11, 1951; children: George Safford III, Elizabeth, Martha, Patricia. B.A., Brown U., 1951, LL.D. (hon.), 1986; M.A., U. Mich., 1952; LL.D. (hon.), Milton Coll., 1974. With Parker Pen Co., Janesville, 1952-86; beginning as asst. to gen. mgr. Gilman Engring. Co. subs. Parker Pen Co., successively asst. domestic advt. mgr., fgn. advt. mgr., dir. fgn. sales, dir. domestic sales, v.p., gen. mgr., 1958-60, exec. v.p., 1960-66, pres., 1966-77, 81-82, chief exec. officer, 1966-80, 81-82, chmn. bd., 1976-86; chmn. bd. Manpower Inc., 1976-86; pres., chmn. Caxambas Assocs. of Fla., Inc., 1986—; chmn. bd. BANCWIS Corp., 1971-84, dir. emeritus, chmn. bd. 1971-84; bd. dirs. Bank of Wis.; chmn. bd. Moebius Printing Co., Milw., 1992-93. Chmn. Wis. Rep. Fin. Com., 1971-73, state chmn., 1974-76; mem. Nat. Rep. Fin. Com., 1971-73; mem. Rep. Nat. Com., 1974-76; chmn. bd. dirs., chief exec. officer Janesville Found.; bd. dirs., pres. Marco Island Taxpayers Assn., 1993-94; fellow Lake Forest Acad.; trustee emeritus Brown U., Beloit Coll.; chmn. emeritus bd. fellows Beloit Coll.; dir. Wis. Acad. Found., 1994—.

PARKER, GEORGE EDWARD, III, lawyer; b. Detroit, Sept. 26, 1934; s. George Edward and Lucia Helen (Muir) P.; m. Margaret G. Koehler; children—George, David, Benjamin. AB, Princeton U., 1956; JD, U. Mich., 1959. Bar: Mich. 1959, D.C. 1981, Fla. 1982. Assoc. Miller, Canfield, Paddock & Stone, Detroit, 1959-68; ptnr. Miller, Canfield, Paddock & Stone, 1968—. Bd. dirs. Detroit Econ. Growth Corp.; ctrl. allocations com. United Way; trustee David Whitney Fund, Grayling Fund. Republican. Office: Miller Canfield Paddock et al 150 W Jefferson Ave Ste 2500 Detroit MI 48226-4415

PARKER, GERALD WILLIAM, physician, medical center administrator, retired air force officer; b. Susquehanna, Pa., Oct. 22, 1929; m. Susan Emerson, May 4, 1985. BS, Union Coll., Schenectady, 1951; MD, N.Y. Med. Coll., 1955. Diplomate Nat. Bd. Med. Examiners, Am. Bd. Internal Medicine; lic. physician, N.Y., Tex., D.C. Intern Ellis Hosp., Schenectady, 1955-56; resident internal medicine Wilford Hall, USAF Med. Ctr., San Antonio, 1958-61; resident in gastroenterology Water Reed Army Med. Ctr., Washington, 1965-66; commd. capt. U.S. Air Force, 1956, advanced through grades to brig. gen., 1980, retired, 1986; chair dept. medicine USAF Hosp., Clark AFB, Philippines, 1967-69; chief internal medicine Malcolm Grow USAF Med. Ctr., Andrews AFB, Washington, 1969-70; chair dept. medicine Malcolm Grow USAF Med. Ctr., 1970-72, Wilford Hall USAF Med. Ctr., Lackland AFB, Tex., 1972-75; dir. hosp. services Wilford Hall USAF Med. Ctr., 1975-77; comdr USAF Hosp., Torrejon Air Base, Spain, 1977-78; dep. dir. med. plans and resources Office of Surgeon Gen. USAF, Washington, 1978-80; dir. med. plans and resources Office of Surgeon Gen. USAF, 1980-81; dir. med. inspection AF Inspection and Safety Ctr., Norton AFB, Calif., 1981-83; dep. surgeon gen. for ops. AF Med. Service Ctr., Brooks AFB, Tex., 1983-85; dir. profl. affairs and quality assurance Office of Surg. Gen., USAF, Washington, 1985-86; dep. dir., chief profl. services King Health Ctr., U.S. Soldiers and Airmens Home, Washington, 1986—; adj. prof. Health Care Scis., George Washington Univ., 1987—; clinical prof. medicine Uniformed Svcs. Univ. of Health Scis., 1988—. Decorated Air Force D.S.M. with oak leaf cluster, Legion of Merit with oak leaf cluster, Bronze Star, Air Medal with oak leaf cluster, ACP Laureate award, 1996. Fellow ACP; mem. AMA, Soc. AF Physicians, D.C. Med. Soc., Am. Geriatric Soc., ACP Execs., Alpha Omega Alpha. Office: King Health Ctr USSAH 3700 N Capitol St NW Washington DC 20317-0001

PARKER, H. LAWRENCE, rancher, investor, retired investment banker; b. Portchester, N.Y., June 16, 1926; s. Raeburn H. and Alice (Lawrence) P.; m. Eleanor Sage, Mar. 3, 1951 (div. 1967); children: Katherine, Richard, Michael, Douglas (dec.); m. Regine Hawes, Nov. 15, 1994. B.A., Yale U., 1949. With Morgan Stanley & Co., N.Y.C., 1950—; ptnr. Morgan Stanley & Co., 1959-75, mng. dir., 1975-83, adv. dir., 1984—; pres. Morgan Stanley Can. Ltd., 1976-79, chmn., 1979-84; mem. adv. bd. on edn. and tng. Sec. Navy, 1985-87. Trustee Green Mountain Valley Sch., Waitsfield, Vt., 1981-91. Served with USMCR, 1944-46. Mem. Investment Bankers Assn. Am. (bd. govs. 1966-70, pres. 1969), Nat. Assn. Securities Dealers (gov. 1981-84), Sublette County Hist. Soc. (trustee 1987-91). Clubs: Nat. Golf Links Am., Links (N.Y.C.), Blind Brook, Augusta Nat. Golf (Ga.), Bedford Golf and Tennis, Jupiter Island, Seminole Golf. Home: One Angas Trail Hobe Sound FL 33455

PARKER, HAROLD TALBOT, history educator; b. Cin., Dec. 26, 1907; s. Samuel Chester and Lucile (Jones) P.; m. Louise Salley, July 9, 1980. PhB, U. Chgo., 1928, PhD, 1934; postgrad., Cornell U., 1929-30. Mem. faculty Duke U., Durham, N.C., 1939—, assoc. prof., 1950-57, prof. history, 1957-77, emeritus, 1977—; adj. prof. U. Ala., Huntsville, 1978-81; faculty U. N.C., Chapel Hill, 1984. Author: The Cult of Antiquity and the French Revolutionaries, 1937, Three Napoleonic Battles, 1944, 83, (with Marvin Brown) Major Themes in Modern European History, 3 vols., 1974, Bureau of Commerce in 1781, 1979, An Administrative Bureau During the Old Regime, 1993; editor: (with Richard Herr) Ideas in History, 1965, Problems in European History, 1979, (with Georg Iggers) International Handbook of Historical Studies, 1979, Theory and Social History, 1980, (with L.S. Parker) Proc. Consortium of Revolutionary Europe, 1981, 84, 85, 86; assoc. editor Historical Dictionary of Napoleonic France, 1985; regional editor, contbg. author: Great Historians of the Modern Age, 1991; contbr. articles to profl. jours. With USAAF, 1942-45. Recipient Disting. Svc. award Consortium on Revolutionary Europe, 1993, Disting Svc. award So. Hist. Assn. European History Sect., 1993. Mem. Soc. for French Hist. Studies (pres. 1957, Disting. Svc. award 1989), AAUP (pres. Duke U. chpt. 1960), Phi Beta Kappa (pres. Duke chpt. 1961). Episcopalian. Home: 5-A Exum Dr West Columbia SC 29169

PARKER, HARRY JOHN, retired psychologist, educator; b. Sioux City, Iowa, Jan. 18, 1923. A.B., Elmhurst Coll., 1947; M.A., Northwestern U., 1953, Ph.D., 1956, postgrad., 1958; postgrad., Roosevelt U., 1957-58; LittD, Elmhurst Coll., 1990. Lic. psychologist, Okla. Tex. Counselor Northwestern U. Counseling Ctr., Chgo., 1952-56; counseling psychologist Northwestern U. Counseling Ctr., 1956-59, asst. dir., 1957-58, dir., 1958-59; pvt. practice counseling psychologist Chgo., 1956-59, Okla., 1959-69, Tex., 1969—; prof. edn. U. Okla., 1959-69; dir. manpower planning, regional med. program and Sch. Health Related Professions U. Okla. Med. Ctr., Oklahoma City, 1967-69; prof. preventive medicine and pub. health U. Okla. Med. Ctr., 1966-69, prof. human ecology, 1969; assoc. dean Sch. Allied Health Scis. U. Tex. Southwestern Med. Ctr., Dallas, 1969-74; prof. phys. medicine and rehab. U. Tex. Southwestern Med. Ctr., 1969-90; prof. psychiatry U. Tex. Southwestern Med. Ctr., 1969-90, prof. rehab. sci., 1970-90; adj. prof. rehab. U. N. Tex., 1990; adj. prof. psychology Ill. Inst. Tech., 1990—, Tex. Woman's U., 1991—; adj. prof. allied health edn. U. Tex. Southwestern Med. Ctr., Dallas, 1990—. Contbr. articles to profl. jours. Served with U.S. Army, 1943-46. Fellow Am. Psychol. Assn.; mem. Southwestern Psychol. Assn., Dallas Psychol. Assn., Tex. Psychol. Assn., Sigma Xi, Phi Delta Phi, Alpha Eta.

PARKER, HARRY LAMBERT, university rowing coach; b. Fitchburg, Mass., Oct. 28, 1935; s. Lambert Achilles and Ruth Margaret (Burnham) P.; m. Kathryn E. Keeler, Aug. 10, 1985; children: George Franklin, David Lambert, Abigail Keeler. A.B., U. Pa., 1957. Rowing coach Harvard U., 1960—; coach U.S. Olympic team, 1964, 68, 72, 80, 84; mem. U.S. Olympic Rowing com., 1964-68, 72-84; head coach U.S. Women's Olympic rowing team, 1976. Mem. town meeting, Winchester (Mass.), 1971-73. Served with USNR, 1957-60. Mem. Rowing Hall of Fame., U.S. Rowing Assn. (dir. 1966-85). Coach U.S. eight-oared crew, silver medalist 1972 Olympics, nat. intercollegiate championship crews Harvard U., 1983, 85, 87, 88, 89, 92; coach Harvard U. crew winners Grand Challenge Cup, Henley Royal Regatta, 1985, Ladies Challenge Plate, 1973, 90, Brittania Challenge Cup, 1993. Home: 26 Hancock St Winchester MA 01890-2002 Office: Harvard Univ 60 John Fitzgerald Kennedy St. Cambridge MA 02138-4933

PARKER, HARRY LEE, retired military officer, counselor; b. Birmingham, Ala., Feb. 20, 1944; s. Guy Milburn and Grace (Lee) P.; m. Sheri Lynn Pogue (div. Oct. 1973); children: John Lee, Suzanne Grace, Stephen Scott; m. Melanie Louise Cox, Apr. 20, 1979; 1 child, Christopher Robert. BA, Miss. State U., 1966; MS, Johns Hopkins U., 1980; postgrad., U.S. Army Command & Staff Coll, 1982. Commd. 2d lt. U.S. Army, 1966, advanced through grades to lt. col.; maintenance officer 85th Maintenance Bn., Hanau, Fed. Republic of Germany, 1967-69; commanding officer 143d Engr. Co. and A Co. 34th Engr. Bn., Long Binh, Vietnam, 1969-70; chief plans and ops. div. Dir. of Logistics, Ft. Rucker, Ala., 1971-73; supply and maintenance officer 97th Signal Bn. NATO, Mannehim, Fed. Republic of Germany, 1973-76; asst. materiel officer 8th Maintenance Battalion, Grossalheim, Fed. Republic Germany, 1977; tng. evaluator HQ 1st US Army, Ft. Meade, Md., 1978-81; logistics coord. Cuban Task Force, Ft. Indiantown Gap, Pa., 1980; project officer Dept. Def., Project Office, Mobile Electric Power, Washington, 1982-85; chief of maintenance U.S. Army South, Ft. Clayton, Panama, 1985-88; prof. mil. Sci. Army ROTC, Miss. State U., Starkville, Miss., 1988-90; ops. officer 101st area support group, Guardian City, Saudia Arabia, logistics officer, 1st Corps Support Command, XVIII Airborne Corps., Damman, Saudi Arabia (Desert Shield and Desert Storm), 1990-91; career/coop. edn. counselor Cen. Fla. C.C., Ocala, Fla., 1992-95.

Presbyn. elder. Decorated 2 Bronze Stars, 3 Meritorious Svc. medals, 5 Army Commendation medals. Mem. Ret. Officers Asn., Am. Legion, Miss. State U. Alumni Assn., Sigma Chi (life). Avocations: woodworking, pilot, scuba diving, boating, computers. Home: 7514 NW 42nd Ave Gainesville FL 32606

PARKER, HERBERT GERALD, state official; b. Fayetteville, Ark., May 13, 1929; s. Otis James and Anna Berthina (Fisher) P.; m. Florida Lucylle Fisher, June 27, 1959; 1 child, Christie Lynne. BS, U. Nebr., Omaha, 1962; MS, N.C. A&T State U., Greensboro, 1970; PhD, Fla. State U., Tallahassee, 1982. Commd. 2d. lt. U.S. Army, 1947, advanced through grades to col., 1969; served advisor mil. assistance advisory group Republic of China, Taiwan, 1962-65; prof. mil. sci. N.C. A&T State U., Greensboro, 1965-68; comdr. all U.S. Spl. Forces units the Delta, S. Vietnam, 1968-69; dir. non-resident instrn. U.S. Army Civil Affairs Sch., Ft. Gordon, Ga., 1969-71, commandant and dir., Ft. Bragg, N.C., 1971-73; prof. mil. sci., dept. head Fla. A&M U., Tallahassee, 1973-77; ret., 1977; chief Crimes Compensation Bur., State of Fla., 1979-87, chief internal auditor Fla. Dept. Edn., 1988-91, dir. of adminstrn. Fla. dept. edn., 1991-94. Bd. dirs. Opportunities Industrialization Centers, Leon County United Way, 1977-81, Fla. Victim/Witness Network, 1985-87; bd. dirs. Nat. Assn. Crime Victims Compensation Bds., 1981-87 (pres. 1984-86); mem. Nat. Urban League; pres. Fla. A&M U Boosters Club, 1983-85; bd. dirs. Tallahassee Urban League, 1982—, pres., 1985-87; bd. dirs. Tallahassee Cmty. Rels., 1993—, Tallahasse Sr. Citizens Found., 1994—, Tallahassee Sr. Citizens Adv. Bd., 1994—, pres., 1996—, adv. bd. Tallahassee Cmty. Justice Ctr., 1995—. Decorated Silver Star, Legion of Merit (2), Bronze Star (3), Purple Heart, Air Medal (3); recipient disting. service award Boy Scouts Am., 1969, James A. Fogarty award Fla. Victim/Witness Network, 1990. Mem. Nat. Assn. Social Scientists, U.S. Army Civil Affairs Assn. (Disting. Service award, 1973), Assn. Parents and Teachers, Tallahassee C. of C., Fla. State U. Coll. Edn. Alumni Assn. (sec. 1991-93), Mil. Order of the World Wars, 555th Parachute Infantry Assn., Inc., Capital Chordsmen (treas. 1991-94, 96—), Capital Rotary Club (Paul Harris fellow), Sigma Pi Phi (Sire Archon/pres. 1992-94), Kappa Alpha Psi, Phi Kappa Phi. Democrat. Methodist. Clubs: Jack and Jill of Am., Am. Bowling Congress, Univ. Men's League (pres.), Fla. A&M Credit Union Bowling League (pres.), Champion Chevrolet Men's Classic Bowling League, Hilaman Park Men's Golf Assn., Bass Anglers Sportsman Soc., Winewood Men's Golf Assn. (v.p.), Toastmasters Internat. (assn. v.p., pres. Ft. Bragg chpt. 1971-73), Nat. Geog. Soc. Home: 3510 Tullamore Ln Tallahassee FL 32308-3127 Office: Dir of Adminstrn Fla Dept Edn The Capitol Tallahassee FL 32399

PARKER, ISRAEL FRANK, national association consultant; b. Sylvania, Ga., Oct. 29, 1917; s. Cornelius Dean and Mary Eunice (Lewis) P.; m. Mary Alice, Dec. 26, 1938; 1 dau., Rebecca Gaye. Student, Ga. So. U., 1935-36, U. Ala., Birmingham, 1942-43, 49-50. Bus. mgr. United Bakery Workers Local 441, Birmingham, 1941-42; internat. rep. Retail, Wholesale and Dept. Store Union, AFL-CIO, Birmingham, 1942-52, asst. regional dir. So. area, 1957-60; regional dir. So. area Retail, Wholesale and Dept. Store Union, AFL-CIO, 1970-76; internat. sec.-treas. Retail, Wholesale and Dept. Store Union, AFL-CIO, N.Y.C., 1976-80; bd. govs. Nat. Assn. of Unemployment Ins. Appellate Bds., 1989-90; mem. bd. appeals Ala. Unemployment Compensation; trustee Retail, Wholesale and Dept. Store Internat. Union and Industry Health and Benefit Fund and Pension Fund; past chmn. Internat. Found. Employee Benefit Plans; chmn. Ala. Trade Union Coun. for Histadrut, 1970; bd. dirs. Found. for Internat. Meetings. Treas. Canterbury Meth. Men., 1993. Served with USN, 1944-46. Named Man of Yr. Birmingham Frat. Order Police, 1972. Mem. Altadena Valley Golf and Country Club. Home: 745 Bentley Dr Birmingham AL 35213-2543

PARKER, JACK, collegiate athletic coach; b. Somerville, Mass., Mar. 11, 1945; m. Jacqueline Gibson; children: Allison, Jacqueline. Head hockey coach Boston U., 1973—. Winner two NCAA titles, four consecutive Eastern crowns, others; recipient Spencer Penrose Meml. trophy as NCAA Coach of Yr., 1975, 1978; named New Eng. Coach of Yr., 1978, 84, 86, Hockey East Coach of Yr., 1986, 92, Gridiron Club Co-Coach of Yr., 1992; inducted into B.U. Athletic Hall of Fame, 1994; recipient Disting. Alum award Boston U., 1992. Mem. Am. Hockey Coaches Assn. (past pres.). Achievements include being the Terrier's all-time winningest coach with a 493-241-37 record, coaching the team to 13 NCAA Tournament appearances. Office: Boston Univ Sports Info 285 Babcock St Boston MA 02215

PARKER, JACK ROYAL, engineering executive; b. N.Y.C., Apr. 25, 1919; s. Harry and Clara (Saxe) P.; m. Selma Blossom, Dec. 8, 1946 (dec. Dec. 1991); children: Leslie Janet, Andrew Charles. Student, Bklyn. Poly. Inst., 1943; D.Sc. (hon.), Pacific Internat. U., 1956. Instr. Indsl. Tng. Inst., 1938-39; engr. Brewster Aero Corp., 1939-40; pres. Am. Drafting Co., 1940; design engr., plan div. Navy Dept., 1941-44; also supr. instr. N.Y. Drafting Inst.; instr. Gasoline Handling Sch., also Inert Gas Sch., U.S.N.T.S., Newport, R.I., 1944-46; cons. Todd Shipyards Corp., 1947-54; tech. adviser to pres. Rollins Coll., 1949-50; v.p. Wattpar Corp., 1947-54; pres. Parco Co. Can. Ltd., 1951-55; pres., dir., chief project mgr. Royalpar Industries, Inc., N.Y.C., 1947-75; chmn. Med. Engrs. Ltd., Nassau, Bahamas, 1957-60; pres. Parco Chem. Systems, Inc., 1965-69; pres., dir. Parco Internat., Inc., 1965-69; pres. Guyana Oil Refining Ltd., S.A., 1966-69, Refineria Peruana del Sur S.A., 1965-68; v.p., dir., founder Refinadora Costarricense de Petreoleo, S.A., 1963-73; pres. Oleoducto Trans Costa Rica, 1970-73, Trans Costa Rica Pipeline Operating Co., 1970-73, Due Diligence, Inc., 1985—; gen. mgr. Kellex power services Pullman Kellogg Co., 1975-77; past pres., sec., dir. Vernitron Corp., Amsterdam Fund, European securities Pub. Co.; Cons., Dominican Republic, 1964, Republic Costa Rica, 1964-65; Cons. Malta Indsl. Devel. Study Co. Ltd., 1965-67, Hambros Bank Ltd., London, 1967-68, Stone & Webster Engring. Corp., Boston, 1957-75, Hambro Am. Bank & Trust Co., N.Y.C., 1968-70; pres. J. Royal Parker Assos., Inc., 1975—, pres. Due Diligence, Inc., 1985—; Internat. Mfg. Centers, Inc., 1977-81, Delaware Valley Fgn. Trade Zone, Inc., 1977-80, Brown & Root (Delaware Valley) Inc., 1980-84; chmn. Summa Engring. Ltd., 1985-86; lectr. One World Club, Cornell U., 1963; chmn. project fin. panel Global Energy Forum '84; chmn., chief exec. officer Export Refinery Western Hemisphere Ltd., Castries, St. Lucia, W.I., 1991., 1991—; chmn., CEO Euro-Siberia Export Refining Corp., Siberia, Russia, 1992, chmn. Russian Trading Corp., Wilmington, Del., 1993—; rep. U.S. Merchant Marine Acad., Kings Point, N.Y., 1993—. Author: Gasoline Systems, 1945; also articles; developer Due Diligence process for project fin. analysis; patentee in field. Mem. adv. bd. Drafting Ednl. Adv. Commn. N.Y.C. Bd. Edn., 1968; founder museum U.S. Mcht. Marine Acad., 1977 (Disting. Service award 1987); pres. Am. Mcht. Marine Mus. Found., U.S. Mcht. Marine Acad., Kings Point, N.Y., 1981-87, pres. emeritus 1987—; Trustee Coll. Adv. Sci., Canaan, N.H. Decorated knight Order St. John of Jersusalem.; recipient Humanitarian award Fairleigh Dickinson U., 1974, Disting. Service award U.S. Merchant Marine Acad. Alumni Found., 1987. Fellow A.A.A.S.; mem. Inst. Engring. Designers (London), Am. Petroleum Inst., Soc. Am. Mil. Engrs., Presidents Assn., Am. Mgmt. Assn., Am. Inst. Chem. Engrs., Am. Inst. Dsgn. and Drafting. Republican. Clubs: Masons; Marco Polo (N.Y.C.); Royal Automobile (London). Achievements include invention of Lazy Golfer; development of Operation Centraport (Limon Costa Rica Internat. Freezone Trade). Home: 1117 Society Hill Blvd Cherry Hill NJ 08003-2421 Office: Woodcrest Sta PO Box 945 Cherry Hill NJ 08003-0945 *I do not consider myself successful as measured by most yardsticks. Success will be mine when I can create a meaningful life for people in so-called underdeveloped countries. Only then can life be rewarding and satisfying.*

PARKER, JACK STEELE, retired manufacturing company executive; b. Palo Alto, Calif., July 6, 1918; s. William Leonard and Mary Isabel (Steele) P.; m. Elaine Elizabeth Simons; 1 child, Kaaren Parker Gray. BSME, Stanford U., 1939; DBA (hon.), Southeastern Mass. U., 1970; LLD (hon.), Clark U., 1972, Renssalaer Poly. Inst., 1986. Engr. Western Pipe & Steel Co., San Francisco, 1939-40; marine surveyor Am. Bur. Shipping, Seattle, 1940-42; supt. steel constrn. Todd Shipyards, Houston, 1942-44; supt. outfitting Todd Shipyards, L.A., 1944-46; asst. chief engr. Am. Potash & Chem., Trona, Calif., 1946-50; mgr. separations div. GE, Hanford Works, Wash., 1950-52; div. mgr., v.p. aircraft gas turbines GE, Cin., 1952-57; v.p. corp. rels. GE, N.Y.C., 1957-61, v.p., group exec. aerospace and electronics, 1961-68, vice chmn., exec. officer, dir., 1968-80, dir. emeritus, 1980—; bd. dirs. L.A. Whitehall Corp. Overseer Hoover Instn., Stanford U., chmn. 1974-76; trustee Monterey Bay Aquarium Found., Heard Mus., Phoenix, Ariz.; hon. trustee Renssalaer Poly. Inst., Troy, N.Y.; bd. dirs. Smithsonian Instn., 1985-91; mem. bd. advisors Stanford Rsch. Inst. Fellow AIAA, ASME; mem. NAE, NAS (Pres.'s Circle), The Conf. Bd. (councilor for life, chmn. 1971-73), Aerospace Industries Assn. (chmn. 1966-68, hon. dir.), Sky Club, Augusta (Ga.) Nat. Golf Club, Desert Forest Golf Club, Desert Mountain Club, Bohemian Club, Boone & Crocket Club, Conquistadores del Cielo, Forest Highlands Club. Avocations: fishing, shooting, golf. Home: 6972 Stage Coach Pass Carefree AZ 85377 Office: GE 260 Long Ridge Rd Stamford CT 06927-1600

PARKER, JAMES, retired curator; b. Boston, Jan. 22, 1924; s. Cortlandt and Elizabeth (Gray) P. A.B., Harvard U., 1946. Fellow in European decorative arts, 16th-19th centuries Met. Mus. Art, N.Y.C., 1951; asst. Met. Mus. Art, 1952-54, asst. curator, 1954-62, assoc. curator, 1962-68, curator, 1968-93; adj. prof. Inst. Fine Arts, NYU, 1968-69, 71-72, 80. Author: (with others) Decorative Art from the Samuel H. Kress Collection at the Metropolitan Museum of Art, 1964; Contbr. articles to museum bulls. Trustee French Inst.-Alliance Francaise, N.Y.C. Served with F.A. AUS, 1944-45, PTO. Club: Union (N.Y.C.). Home: 17 E 89th St New York NY 10128-0615 Office: Met Mus Art Fifth Ave # 82nd St New York NY 10028

PARKER, JAMES AUBREY, federal judge; b. Houston, Jan. 8, 1937; s. Lewis Almeron and Emily Helen (Stuessy) P.; m. Florence Fisher, Aug. 26, 1960; children: Roger Alan, Pamela Elizabeth. BA, Rice U., 1959; LLB, U. Tex., 1962. Bar: Tex. 1962, N.Mex. 1963. With Modrall, Sperling, Roehl, Harris & Sisk, Albuquerque, 1962-87; judge U.S. Dist. Ct. N.Mex., Albuquerque, 1987—; mem. Standing Commn. on Rules of Practice and Procedures of U.S. Cts., N.Mex. Commn. on Professionalism, 1986—. Articles editor Tex. Law Rev., 1961-62. Mem. ABA, Fed. Judges Assn., Am. Judicature Soc., Am. Bd. Trial Advocates, Tex. Bar Assn., N.Mex. Bar Assn., Albuquerque Bar Assn., Order of Coif, Chancellors, Phi Delta Phi. Avocations: ranching, fly fishing, running, skiing. Office: US Dist Ct PO Box 566 Albuquerque NM 87103-0566

PARKER, JAMES FRANCIS, lawyer, airline executive; b. San Antonio, Jan. 1, 1947; s. Raymond Francis and Libbie Olivia (Dusek) P.; m. Patricia Elaine Lorang, May 15, 1971; children: James, Jennifer. BA with hons., U. Tex., 1969, JD with hons., 1971. Bar: Tex., U.S. Dist. Ct. (ea., we., so. no. dists.) Tex., U.S. Ct. Appeals (5th and 11th cirs.), U.S. Supreme Ct. Law clk. to presiding judge U.S. Dist. Ct., Austin, Tex., 1972-76; asst. atty. gen. State of Tex., Austin, 1976-79; atty. Oppenheimer, Rosenberg, Kelleher & Wheatley, San Antonio, 1979-86; v.p., gen. counsel SW Airlines Co., Dallas, 1986—. Mem. ABA, Tex. Bar Assn. Democrat. Lutheran. Office: SW Airlines Co 2702 Love Field Dr Dallas TX 75235-1908

PARKER, JAMES ROGER, chemist; b. L.A., July 19, 1936. BS, Pomona Coll., 1958; PhD, Iowa State U., 1964. Lab. asst. Ames (Iowa) Lab Atomic Energy Commn., 1958-64; analytical supr. PPG Industries, Natrium, W.Va., 1964-73, Corpus Christi, Tex., 1973-82; agrl. chemist PPG Industries, Barberton, Ohio, 1982-89; infrared spectroscopist PPG Industries, Monroeville, Pa., 1989-96, scientist, 1996—. Contbr. articles to profl. jours. Mem. Am. Chem. Soc., Soc. for Applied Spectroscopy, Spectroscopy Soc. Pitts., Soc. for Analytical Chemists Pitts., Phi Lambda Upsilon. Achievements include research in analytical chemistry of metal halides, iodine compounds, alkali metal oxides, coordination chemistry of phosphine oxides, qualitative identifications with proton magnetic resonance spectroscopy and polymer analyses with photoacoustic infrared spectroscopy. Office: PPG Industries 440 College Park Dr Monroeville PA 15146-1536

PARKER, JEFFREY ALAN, metal manufacturing company executive; b. Flint, Mich., Feb. 14, 1955; s. Wesley Francis and Rita Agnes (Fallon) P.; m. Darlien Cindy Thornton, Apr. 16, 1977; 1 child, Yvonne-Marie. Grad. high sch. Quality mgr. Amplaco Plastic, Rochester, N.Y., 1981-89; quality assurance mgr. Innex Industries, Rochester, 1989-90; lead inspector Acro Industries, Rochester, 1990-91, quality engr., 1991-94, dir. quality assurance, 1994—. Mem. Greater Rochester Quality Coun., 1994—; pres. Charlotte Cmty. Assn., Rochester, 1991, exec. bd., 1988-93; civilian vol. coord. Rochester Police Dept., 1993—. Recipient various vol. honors and awards City of Rochester, Rochester Police Dept., various cmty. assns. Mem. Am. Soc. Quality Control (sr. mem., exec. com. 1994—, editor Rochester sect. 1993—). Republican. Roman Catholic. Avocations: neighborhood crime prevention, gardening, roller coasters. Office: Acro Industries Inc 554 Colfax St Rochester NY 14606-3112

PARKER, JEFFREY SCOTT, law educator, university official; b. Alexandria, Va., Sept. 6, 1952; s. Clarence Franklin and Mary Florence (Partlow) P. B in Indsl. Engring., Ga. Inst. Tech., 1975; JD, U. Va., 1978. Bar: N.Y. 1979, U.S. Dist. Ct. (ea. and so. dists.) N.Y. 1979, U.S. Ct. Appeals (3d cir.) 1981, U.S. Ct. Appeals (2d cir.) 1984, U.S. Supreme Ct. 1984, U.S. Ct. Appeals (fed. cir.) 1985, U.S. Ct. Appeals (4th cir.) 1992. Assoc. Sullivan & Cromwell, N.Y.C., 1978-86, Sacks Montgomery, N.Y.C., 1986-87; dep. chief counsel U.S. Sentencing Commn., Washington, 1987-88; of counsel Sacks Montgomery, N.Y.C., 1988-90; assoc. prof. of law George Mason U., Arlington, Va., 1990-94; prof. law, assoc. dean acad. affairs George Mason U. Sch. Law, 1994—; cons. counsel U.S. Sentencing Commn., Washington, 1988-89. Contbr. articles to law revs.; mem. editorial bd. Va. Law Rev., 1976-78. Mem. ABA, Assn. of Bar of City of N.Y., N.Y. State Bar Assn., Am. Law and Econs. Assn., Am. Econs. Assn. Office: George Mason U Sch of Law 3401 N Fairfax Dr Arlington VA 22201-4411

PARKER, JENNIFER WARE, chemical engineer, researcher; b. Berkeley, Calif., Apr. 18, 1959; d. Raymond Paul and Maureen Christina (Trehearne) Ware; m. Henrik Davidson Parker, July 30, 1983; children: Katherine Joyce, Nathaniel Henrikson. BSChemE, Princeton U., 1980; MSChemE, UCLA, 1983, PhDCHemE, 1986. Devel. engr. Am. Pharmaseal, Glendale, Calif., 1980-81; rsch. engr. Crump Inst. Med. Engring, UCLA, 1986-87; sr. engr. The BOC Group, Murray Hill, N.J., 1987-90, lead engr., 1990-92; sr. rsch. engr. CFM Techs., Inc., West Chester, Pa., 1993—. Contbr. articles to profl. jours. Mem. Am. Inst. Chem. Engrs., N.Y. Acad. Scis. Avocations: sports, music, gardening. Home: 201 W Country Club Ln Wallingford PA 19086-6507

PARKER, JOHN GARRETT, lawyer; b. Roanoke Rapids, N.C., Mar. 6, 1947; s. Ben Thatch and Sarah Louise (Lessiter) P.; m. Helen Shell Nethercutt, Aug. 23, 1969; 1 child, Sarah Helen. BA in Econs., U. N.C., 1969, JD, 1976. Bar: Ga. 1976, U.S. Dist. Ct. (no. dist.) Ga. 1977, U.S. Ct. Appeals (5th and 11th cirs.) 1981, U.S. Ct. Appeals (9th cir.) 1986, U.S. Dist. Ct. (mid. dist.) Ga. 1989, U.S. Ct. Appeals (8th cir.) 1993. Assoc. atty. Hensell, Post, Brandon & Dorsey, Atlanta, 1976-83; ptnr. Hansell & Post, Atlanta, 1983-87, Paul, Hastings, Janofsky & Walker, Atlanta, 1987—. Co-chair Clark for Cong. com., Cobb County, Ga., 1992. Lt. U.S. Army, 1970-73. Mem. ABA, Atlanta Bar Assn., State Bar of Ga., Order of Coif. Republican. Episcopal. Avocations: hunting, golf. Home: 650 Mt Paran Rd Atlanta GA 30327 Office; Paul Hastings Janofsky & Walker 600 Peachtree St Ste 2400 Atlanta GA 30308

PARKER, JOHN MALCOLM, management and financial consultant; b. Halifax, N.S., Can., June 13, 1920; s. Charles Fisher and Mabel (Hennigar) P.; came to U.S., 1936, naturalized, 1942; m. Irene Wilson Davis, Oct. 11, 1942 (dec. Nov. 1987); 1 child, Elane Parker Jones; m. Kathryn Harvey Smithey, Apr. 22, 1989. Cert. internal auditor. With Standard Oil Co. N.J., Charlotte, N.C., 1941, Duke Power Co., Charlotte, 1941-42, So. Bell Tel. & Tel. Co., Charlotte, 1946-50, Atlanta, 1950-68, with South Central Bell Telephone Co., Birmingham, Ala., 1968-83, asst. v.p., gen. internal auditor; pres. Omega Assocs., Inc., 1983—; commr. gen. assembly Presbyn. Ch. of U.S., 1968, 81. Served with AUS, 1942-46. Mem. Inst. Mgmt. Accts. (pres. local chpt. 1972-73, nat. dir.), Am. Mgmt. Assn., Inst. Internal Auditors (pres. chpt. 1978-79, dist. dir. 1979-81, regional dir. 1981-83, internat. vice chmn. 1983-84, internat. bd. dirs. 1979-87, v.p. found. 1984-85). Internat. Platform Assn. Republican. Home: 4509 Clairmont Ave S Birmingham AL 35222-4438 Office: Omega Assocs Inc PO Box 530452 Birmingham AL 35253-0452

PARKER, JOHN MARCHBANK, consulting geologist; b. Manhattan, Kans., Sept. 13, 1920; s. John Huntington and Marjorie Elizabeth (Marchbank) P.; m. Agnes Elizabeth Potts, Mar. 17, 1978; m. Jan Goble, July 18, 1941 (div. 1968); children—Susan Kelly, Elizabeth Douglass, Deirdre Parker, John Eric; m. Nancy Booth, Jan. 24, 1970 (div. 1974). Student U. Minn., 1937, U. Wyo., 1938; B.S., Kans. State U., 1941. Cert. petroleum geologist Am. Inst. Profl. Geologists. Geologist, U.S. Pub. Roads Adminstrn., Alaska Hwy., Can., 1942-43; Field geologist Imperial Oil Ltd., Northwest Ter., Can., 1943-44; dist. geologist Stanolind Oil & Gas Co., Casper, Wyo., 1944-52; v.p. exploration Kirby Petroleum Co., Houston, 1952-74; v.p. exploration Northwest Exploration Co., Denver, 1974-75; cons. geologist Denver, 1975—. Contbr. articles to profl. jours. Recipient Disting. Service in Geology award Kans. State U., 1983. Fellow AAAS, Geol. Soc. Am.; mem. Am. Assn. Petroleum Geologists (pres. 1982-83, adv. council Tulsa 1983-84, Hon. Mem. award), Rocky Mountain Assn. Geologists (explorer of yr. 1979; pres. 1980-81). Home: 2615 Oak Dr No 32 Lakewood CO 80215 Office: PO Box 150187 Lakewood CO 80215-0187

PARKER, JOHN VICTOR, federal judge; b. Baton Rouge, La., Oct. 14, 1928; s. Fred Charles and LaVerne (Sessions) P.; m. Mary Elizabeth Fridge, Sept. 3, 1949; children: John Michael, Robert Fridge, Linda Anne. B.A., La. State U., 1949, J.D., 1952. Bar: La. 1952. Atty. Parker & Parker, Baton Rouge, 1954-66; asst. parish atty. City of Baton Rouge, Parish of East Baton Rouge, 1956-66; atty. Sanders, Downing, Kean & Cazedessus, Baton Rouge, 1966-79; chief judge U.S. Dist. Ct., Middle Dist. La., Baton Rouge, 1979—; vis. lectr. law La. State U. Law Sch. Served with Judge Adv. Gen.'s Corps U.S. Army, 1952-54. Mem. ABA, Am. Judicature Soc., Am. Arbitration Assn., La. State Bar Assn. (past mem. bd. govs.), Baton Rouge Bar Assn. (past pres.), Order of Coif, Phi Delta Phi. Democrat. Club: Baton Rouge Country. Lodges: Masons (32 deg.); Kiwanis (past pres.). Office: Russell B Long Fed Bldg & Courthouse 777 Florida St Ste 355 Baton Rouge LA 70801-1712

PARKER, JOHN WILLIAM, pathology educator, investigator; b. Clifton, Ariz., Jan. 5, 1931; s. Vilas William and Helen E. Parker; m. Barbara A. Atkinson, June 8, 1957; children: Ann Elizabeth, Joy Noelle, John David, Heidi Susan. BS, U. Ariz., 1953; MD, Harvard U., 1957. Diplomate Am. Bd. Pathology. Clin. instr. pathology U. Calif. Sch. Medicine, San Francisco, 1962-64; asst. prof. U. So. Calif. Sch. Medicine, L.A., 1964-68, assoc. prof., 1968-75, prof., 1975—, dir. clin. labs., 1974-94, vice chmn. dept. pathology, 1985—, dir. pathology reference labs., 1991-94; assoc. dean sci. affairs U. So. Calif., 1987-89; co-chmn. 15th Internat. Leucocyte Culture Conf., Asilomar, Calif., 1982; chmn. 2d Internat. Lymphoma Conf., Athens, Greece, 1981; v.p. faculty senate U. So. Calif., 1991-92; bd. dirs. ann. meeting Clin. Applications of Cytometry, Charleston, S.C., 1988—. Founding editor (jour.) Hematological Oncology, 1982-93; assoc. editor Jour. Clin. Lab. Analysis, 1985—; co-editor: Intercellular Communication in Leucocyte Function, 1983; founding co-editor (jour.) Communications in Clin. Cytometry, 1994—; contbr. over 150 articles to profl. jours., chpts. to books. Named sr. oncology fellow Am. Cancer Soc., U. So. Calif. Sch. Medicine, 1964-69, Nat. Cancer Inst. vis. fellow Walter and Eliza Hall Inst. for Med. Research, Melbourne, Australia, 1972-73. Fellow Coll. Am. Pathologists, Am. Soc. Clin. Pathologists; mem. Am. Assn. Pathologists, Am. Soc. Hematology, Internat. Acad. Pathology, Clin. Cytometry Soc. (v.p. 1993, pres.-elect 1994-95, pres. 1995—), Phi Beta Kappa, Phi Kappa Phi. Avocations: gardening, reading, hiking. Office: U So Calif Sch Medicine CSC 108 2250 Alcazar St Los Angeles CA 90033-4523

PARKER, JOSEPH B., JR., psychiatrist, educator; b. Knox County, Tenn., July 8, 1916; s. Joseph B. and Sue (York) P.; m. Phyllis Maxine Foster, May 25, 1946; children: Suzanna Margaret, Joseph B. III. B.S., U. Tenn., 1939, M.D., 1941. Diplomate: Am. Bd. Psychiatry and Neurology. Intern Knoxville Gen. Hosp., 1941-42; resident Duke U. Hosp., Durham, N.C., 1946-48; resident in psychiatry St. Elizabeth Hosp., Washington, 1944-45; practice medicine specializing in psychiatry Durham, 1948-49, 53-59, Memphis, 1949-53, Lexington, Ky., 1959-70; instr. psychiatry Duke U., 1948-49, assoc. prof., 1953-59; assoc. prof. psychiatry, dir. Child Guidance Clinic U. Tenn. Coll. Medicine, 1949-53; chief psychiatry VA Hosp., Durham, 1953-59; prof., chmn. dept. psychiatry U. Ky. Med. Ctr., 1959-69; prof. psychiatry Duke Med. Ctr., 1970-83, prof. emeritus, 1983—; vis. faculty U. Pitts., 1967, Harvard, 1968-69; cons. USPHS Hosp., VA Hosp., Lexington. Editor: Psychotherapeutics, 1979. Mem. prof. adv. com. Cerebral Palsy; mem. prof. adv. com. Jr. League Opportunity Workshop; mem. Gov. Ky. Adv. Council Mental Health, 1962—, Gov. Ky. Manpower Commn., 1963—; exec. com., trustee Central Ky. Mental Health Bd. Served to lt. comdr., M.C. USNR, 1942-46. Fellow Am. Psychiat. Assn. (cons. continuing edn. project 1971—), Am. Coll. Psychiatrists, So. Psychiat. Assn. (regent, pres. 1972), Ky. Psychiat. Assn. (past pres.); mem. Am. Psychopath. Assn., Soc. Biol. Psychiatry, Delta Tau Delta, Phi Chi, Delta Phi Alpha, Alpha Omega Alpha. Address: 24 Stoneridge Cir Durham NC 27705-5510

PARKER, JOSEPH CORBIN, JR., pathologist; b. Richmond, Va., Aug. 1, 1937; s. Joseph Corbin and Alice Cabell (Horsley) P.; m. Patricia Singleton, June 24, 1961; children: John Randolph, Nancy Jordan. BA, Va. Mil. Inst., 1958; MD, Med. Coll. Va., 1962; MS in Pathology, U. Minn., 1968. Fellow Mayo Clinic, Rochester, Minn., 1963-68; asst. prof. Duke U., Durham, N.C., 1969-70, Harvard U., Boston, 1970-71; assoc. prof. U. Ky., Lexington, 1971-75; prof. U. Miami, Fla., 1975-81; assoc. dean, prof. U. Tenn., Knoxville, 1981-86; prof. pathology, chmn. U. Mo., Kansas City, 1986-92; prof., chair dept. pathology U. Louisville Sch. Medicine, 1992—; bd. dirs. Truman Med. Ctr., Kansas City, Mo., Hosp. Hill Health Svc., Kansas City. Author 4 chpts. in books; contbr. 100 articles to profl. jours. Bd. dirs. Multiple Sclerosis Soc., Knoxville, Tenn., 1985, Alzheimers Assn., Kansas City, 1988-91, U. Louisville Med. Sch. Fund. 1st lt. USAR, 1958-67. Recipient 1st Jackson -Hope medal Va. Mil. Inst., 1958; Caldwell award Alzheimers Assn., 1986. Fellow Am. Asns. Neuropathology, Am. Soc. Clin. Pathology, Coll. Am. Pathology, Assn. Clin. Scientists; mem. So. Med. Assn., Am. Soc. Neurol. Surgeons. Democrat. Unitarian. Achievements include discovery of autosomal recessive neonatal adrenal leuko-distrophy. Home: 4606 Wolf Creek Pky Louisville KY 40241-5502 Office: U Louisville Sch Medicine Dept Pathology Louisville KY 40292

PARKER, JOSEPH MAYON, printing and publishing executive; b. Washington, N.C., Oct. 11, 1931; s. James Mayon and Mildred (Poe) P.; m. Lauretta Owen Dyer, Mar, 23, 1957; children: Katherine Suzanne, Joseph Wilbur. Student, Davidson Coll., 1949-51; BA, U. N.C., 1953, MPA, 1992; postgrad., Carnegie Inst. Tech., 1955-56. Mgr. print div. Parker Bros., Inc., Ahoskie, N.C., 1956-71, chief editorialist, 1961-77, gen. mgr., 1971-77, pres., chief exec. officer, 1977—; dir. Governor's Hwy. Safety Program, 1993—; treas. Chowan Graphic Arts Found., Murfreesboro, N.C., 1971-90, pres. 1990-92. Editor, columnist five community newspapers, N.C.; panelist: (TV talk show) North Carolina This Week, 1986-89. Mem. Ind. Devel. Commn., 1974-86; vice chmn. N.C. Goals and Policy Bd., Raleigh, 1977-84; trustee Pitt County Meml. Hosp., 1980-88; pres. Com. of 100, Winton, N.C., 1984-87; chmn. Northeastern N.C. Tomorrow, Elizabeth City, 1981-84, sec., 1984-90; del. Dem. Nat. Conv., N.Y.C., 1980, platform com., 1988; dist. chmn. N.C. Dem. Ctrl. Com., 1980-82. With U.S. Army, 1953-54, col. USAR, 1954-88. Mem. Soc. Profl. Journalists, East N.C. Press Assn. (past pres.), N.C. Press Assn., Nat. Newspaper Assn. (state chmn. 1976-83), Roanoke Island Hist. Assn. (vice-chmn. 1987-89), Ea. C. of C. (past chmn.), Rotary, Raleigh Exec. Club. Democrat. Methodist. Avocations: golf, reading. Home: 4500 Connell Dr Raleigh NC 27612-5600 Office: 215 E Lane St Raleigh NC 27601-1035

PARKER, JOSEPHUS DERWARD, lumber company executive; b. Elm City, N.C., Nov. 16, 1906; s. Josephus and Elizabeth (Edwards) P.; m. Mary Wright, Jan. 15, 1934 (dec. Dec. 1937); children: Mary Wright (Mrs. Henry Avon Perry), Josephus Derward; m. Helen Hodges Hackney, Jan. 24, 1940; children: Thomas Hackney, Alton Person, Derward Hodges, Sarah Helen (Mrs. Robert Seavey). AB, U. of the South, 1928; postgrad., Tulane U., 1928-29, U. N.C., 1929-30, Wake Forest Med. Coll., 1930-31. Founder, chmn. bd. J.D. Parker & Sons, Inc., Elm City, 1955—, Parker Tree Farms, Inc., 1956—; founder, pres. Invader, Inc., 1961-63; pres. dir. Brady Lumber Co., Inc., 1957-62; v.p., dir. Atlantic Limestone, Inc., Elm City, 1970—; owner, operator Parker Airport, Eagle Springs, N.C., 1940-62; founder, pres. Parkhurst Plantation, Inc., Elm City; pres. Toisnot Farms Inc., Elm City. Author: The Parker Family, 1987, The Red Wedding Gown, 1992. Served to capt. USAF, 1944-47. Mem. Moose, Lions, Wilson (N.C.) Country Club. Episcopalian. Home: PO Box 905 Elm City NC 27822-0905

PARKER, KELLIS E., SR., legal educator, lawyer, musician; b. 1942. J.D., Howard U., 1968. Bar: Colo. 1970. Law clk to presiding judge U.S. Ct. Appeals, 1968-69; acting prof. U. Calif., Davis, 1969-72; assoc. prof. Columbia U., N.Y.C., 1972-75, prof., 1975—; prof. law Seville and Isidor Sulzbacher, Columbia U. Law Sch., 1994—. Mem. bd. dirs. City Club (N.Y.C.); cons. Legal Def. and Edn. Funds, Inc., NAACP, 1972—; mem. exec. com. Nat. Com. Against Discrimination in Housing, 1974—. Author: Modern Judicial Remedies, 1975. Office: Columbia U Sch Law 435 W 116th St New York NY 10027-7201

PARKER, KEVIN JAMES, electrical engineer educator. BS in Engring. Sci. summa cum laude, SUNY, Buffalo, 1976; MSEE, MIT, 1978, PhD, 1981. Rsch. assoc. lab. for med. ultrasound MIT, Cambridge, 1977-81; asst. prof. dept. electrical engring. U. Rochester, N.Y., 1981-85, assoc. prof., 1985-91, prof., chair, 1992—, assoc. prof. dept. radiology, 1989-91, prof., 1992—; dir. Rochester Ctr. Biomedical Ultrasound, 1990—; com. mem. Internat. Symposium on Ultrasound Imaging, 1989—. Editorial bd. Ultras. Med. Biology, 1989—; contbr. numerous articles to profl. jours., chpts. to books. Fellow NIH, 1979, Lilly Teaching fellow, 1982; named IBM Supercomputing Contest Finalist, 1989; recipient Ultrasound in Medicine and Biology prize World Fed., 1991, Outstanding Innovation award Eastman Kodak Co., 1991. Mem. IEEE (sr. mem., Ultrasound Symposium Tech. Com. 1985—), Acoustical Soc. Am., Am. Inst. Ultrasound in Medicine (ethics com. 1987—, standards com. 1990—). Achievements include three patents in field. Office: Univ of Rochester Ctr for Biomedical Ultrasound 309 Hopeman Engineering Bldg Rochester NY 14627

PARKER, LEONARD S., architect, educator; b. Warsaw, Poland, Jan. 16, 1923; came to U.S. 1923; s. Rueben and Sarah (Kollica) Popuch; m. Betty Mae Buegen, Sept. 1, 1948 (dec. 1983); children—Bruce Aaron, Jonathan Arthur, Nancy Anne, Andrew David. BArch., U. Minn., 1948; MArch., MIT, 1950. Sr. designer Eero Saarinen Assocs., Bloomfield Hills, Mich., 1950-56; CEO, chmn. bd., pres., dir. design The Leonard Parker Assocs., Mpls., 1957—; pres., dir. design The Alliance Southwest, Phoenix, 1981-91; prof. grad. program Sch. Architecture, U. Minn., Mpls., 1959—; pres. Minn. Archtl. Found., 1991. Author: Abandoning the Catalogs, 1979, Rivers of Modernism, 1986, Collaboration-Same Bed, Different Dream?. Panel mem. Mpls. City Hall Restoration Com., Am. Arbitration Assn., USAF bd. visitors (chmn.). Served with U.S. Army, 1943-46; ETO. Firm has received 84 nat. and regional awards for design excellence. Fellow AIA; mem. Minn. Soc. Architects (pres. 1981, Gold medal 1986, pres. Mpls. chpt. 1979), Tau Sigma Delta. Home: 3936 Willmatt Hl Hopkins MN 55305-5142 Office: The Leonard Parker Assocs 430 Oak Grove St Minneapolis MN 55403-3253

PARKER, LYNDA MICHELE, psychiatrist; b. Phila., Sept. 28, 1947; d. Albert Francis and Dorothy Thomasinia (Herriott) P.; B.A., C. W. Post Coll., 1968; M.A. (Martin Luther King Jr. scholar 1968-70), N.Y.U., 1970; M.D., Cornell U., 1974; postgrad. N.Y. Psychoanalytic Inst., 1977-82. Intern, N.Y. Hosp., N.Y.C., 1975; resident in psychiatry Payne Whitney Clinic, N.Y.C., 1975-78; psychiatrist in charge day program Cabrini Med. Center, N.Y.C., 1978-79, attending psychiatrist, 1978—; admitting psychiatrist inpatient psychiat. treatment Payne Whitney Clinic, N.Y.C., 1978—, supr. psychiatry residents, 1978—, supr. long-term psychotherapy, 1980-82; attending psychiatrist N.Y. Hosp., Cornell Med. Center, 1979—; practice medicine specializing in psychiatry, N.Y.C., 1979—; instr. psychiatry Cornell U. Med. Coll., 1979-86, asst. prof., 1986—; instr. psychiatry, N.Y. Med. Coll., 1978—; psychiat. cons. Bldg. Service 32BJ Health Fund, 1983-89, Inwood House, N.Y.C., 1983-86, Time-Life Inc., 1986—, Ind. Med. Examiners, 1986—, Epilepsy Inst., 1986-87, asst. med. dir., 1987-88, med. dir., 1988; ind. med. examiner Rep. Health Care Rev. Sys. Mem. adv. bd. St. Bartholomew Community Presch., N.Y.C., 1990—. Mem. Am. Psychiat. Assn., Am. Womens Med. Assn. Episcopalian. Office: 219 E 69th St Apt 1J New York NY 10021-5453

PARKER, MACEO, jazz musician, alto saxophone; b. Kinston, N.C.. Student, Agrl. and Tech. Coll. N.C. (now N.C. Agrl. and Tech. U.). Musician James Brown, 1964-84, Own Group, 1984—. Albums include: Roots Revisited, 1990, Mo' Roots, 1991, 92, Live on Planet Groove, 1992, Southern Exposure, 1994. Office: Verve Digital Records 825 8th Ave New York NY 10019-7416

PARKER, MARY ALTHEA, painter, art educator; b. Oxford, N.C., Nov. 20, 1906; d. Richard Joseph and Lottie Lee (Barnes) P. BA, Rhodes Coll., 1928; MA, Case Western Res. U., 1944; postgrad., Cleve. Sch. Art, 1942-44, Hans Hofmann Sch. Art, 1950, 54. RN, 1931. Psychiat. and occupational therapy nurse Highland Hosp., Asheville, N.C., 1931-42; prof. art history Colby-Sawyer Coll., New London, N.H., 1944-72; tchr. art Kingswood-Cranbrook Summer Inst., Bloomfield Hills, Mich., summers 1948-49, Brevard (N.C.) Music Ctr., summers 1951-55; prof. art, art history Claflin Coll., Orangeburg, S.C., 1973-77; prof. sr. grad. faculty workshop Western Carolina U., Cullowhee, N.C., summer 1991, prof. sr. grad. faculty in painting, 1991-93; ret., 1993; represented by Art Gallery Ltd., New Bern, N.C.; bd. dirs. Black Mountain (N.C.) Coll. Mus. Arts Ctr. One-woman retrospective show at World Gallery, Asheville, N.C., 1990; exhibited in group shows at Art Gallery Ltd., Zone One Contemporary, Asheville. Mem. Sister City Pairing Project-Russia, Black Mountain, 1989—. Fellow Va. Ctr. for Creative Arts, The McDowell Colony; mem. LWV, Women's Internat. League for Peace and Freedom. Democrat. Mem. Religious Soc. of Friends. Avocations: music, reading. Home: 21 Wagon Trl Black Mountain NC 28711-2557

PARKER, MARY EVELYN, former state treasurer; b. Fullerton, La., Nov. 8, 1920; d. Racia E. and Addie (Graham) Dickerson; m. W. Bryant Parker, Oct. 31, 1954; children: Mary Bryant, Ann Graham. BA, Northwestern State U., La., 1941, hon. doctorate, 1987; diploma in social welfare, La. State U., 1943. Social worker Allen Parish, La., 1941-42; personnel adminstr. War Dept., Camp Claiborne, La., 1943-47; editor Oakdale, La., 1947-48; exec. dir. La. Dept. Commerce and Industry, Baton Rouge, 1948-52; with Mut. of N.Y., Baton Rouge, 1952-56; chmn. La. Bd. Pub. Welfare, Baton Rouge, 1950-51; commr. La. Dept. Pub. Welfare, Baton Rouge, 1956-63, La. Div. Adminstrn., 1964-67; treas. State of La., 1968-87. Chmn. White House Conf. on Children and Youth, 1960; pres. La. Conf. on Social Welfare, 1959-61; mem. Democratic Nat. Com., 1948-52; bd. dirs. Woman's Hosp., Baton Rouge; trustee Episcopal High Sch., Baton Rouge Gen. Hosp. Found.; mem. adv. council Coll. Bus., Tulane U., New Orleans. Named Baton Rouge Woman of Yr., 1976. Baptist. Home: 141 Duster Dr Natchez MS 39120-5263

PARKER, MARY-LOUISE, actress; b. Ft. Jackson, S.C., Aug. 2, 1964. Attended, Bard Coll. Actress: (theatre) Hay Fever, 1987, The Miser, 1988, The Art of Success, 1989, The Importance of Being Earnest, 1989, Prelude to a Kiss, Broadway, 1990-91 (Theatre World award 1990), Babylon Gardens, 1991, (films) Signs of Life, 1989, Longtime Companion, 1990, Grand Canyon, 1991, Fried Green Tomatoes, 1991, Mr. Wonderful, 1993, Naked in New York, 1994, The Client, 1994, Bullets Over Broadway, 1994, Boys on the Side, 1995, (TV movies) Too Young the Hero, 1988, A Place for Annie, 1994. Office: William Morris Agency 151 El Camino Beverly Hills CA 90212*

PARKER, MAYNARD MICHAEL, journalist, magazine executive; b. L.A., July 28, 1940; s. Clarence Newton and Virginia Esther (Boyce) P.; m. Judith Karen Seaborg, Dec. 11, 1965 (div.); 1 child, Francesca Lynn; m. Susan Fraker, Sept. 15, 1985; children: Nicholas Maynard, Hugh Fraker. B.A., Stanford U., 1962; M.A., Columbia U., 1963. Reporter Life mag., 1963-64, corr. Hong Kong Bur., 1966-67; corr. Hong Kong Bur. Newsweek, 1967-69; Saigon bur. chief Newsweek, Vietnam, 1969-70; chief Hong Kong Bur. Newsweek, 1969-73, sr. nat. affairs editor, 1975-77, asst. mng. editor, 1977-80, exec. editor, 1980-82, editor, 1982—; mng. editor Newsweek Internat. Newsweek, N.Y.C., 1973-75. Contbr. articles to Fgn. Affairs, Fgn. Policy, Reporter, Atlantic. Chmn. Stanford Alumni Bd. 1st lt. inf. U.S. Army, 1964-66. Mem. Am. soc. Mag. Editors (bd. dirs.), Coun. on Fgn. Rels., Stanford U. Alumni Bd. (chmn. emeritus), Overseas Press Club. Episcopalian. Avocations: reading, skiing, tennis, fly-fishing. Office: Newsweek Mag 251 W 57th St New York NY 10019

PARKER, MEL, editor; b. N.Y.C., Feb. 11, 1949; s. David Parker and Mollie (Kantorowicz) Lederman; m. Diane Nancy Goldberg, June 27, 1971; children: Emily, David. AB, Rutgers U., 1971; AM in English, N.Y.U., 1973. Editorial researcher Esquire Mag., N.Y.C., 1973; grad. asst. NYU, 1974-77; adj. lectr. CUNY, 1977-78; editor Leisure Books, N.Y.C., 1978-81; sr. editor Playboy Paperbacks, N.Y.C., 1981-82; sr. editor Berkley Pub. Group, N.Y.C., 1982-85, exec. editor, 1985-86, editor-in-chief, 1986-87; v.p., editor in chief Warner Paperbacks, N.Y.C., 1987-90, pub., 1990—. Office: Warner Books Inc Time-Life 1271 Avenue Of The Americas New York NY 10020

PARKER, MICHAEL (MIKE PARKER), congressman; b. Laurel, Miss., Oct. 31, 1949; m. Rosemary Prather; children: Adrian, Marisa, Thomas. BA, William Carey Coll., 1970. Operator various businesses; mem. vet. affairs com., textile caucus, sunbelt caucus, arts caucus 101st-104th Congresses from 4th Miss. dist., 1989—, mem. pub. works and transp. com., economic devel. subcom., water resources subcom., aviation subcom., 1989—. Presbyterian. Office: US Ho of Reps 2445 Rayburn Bldg Washington DC 20515-0004*

PARKER, NANCY WINSLOW, artist, writer; b. Maplewood, N.J., Oct. 18, 1930; d. Winslow Aurelius and Beatrice (Gaunt) P. B.A., Mills Coll., 1952; student, Sch. Visual Art, N.Y.C., Art Students League. Pub. relations exec. N.Y. Soccer Club, N.Y.C., 1961-63; with RCA, N.Y.C., 1964-67; art dir. Appleton-Century-Crofts, N.Y.C., 1968-70; staff designer Holt Reinhart & Winston, N.Y.C., 1970-73; free lance writer, illustrator, 1974—. Author, illustrator: The Man with The Take-Apart Head, 1974, The Party at the Old Farm, 1975, Mrs. Wilson Wanders Off, 1976, Love from Uncle Clyde, 1977, The Crocodile Under Louis Finneberg's Bed, 1978, The President's Cabinet, 1978, rev. edit., 1991, The Ordeal of Byron B. Blackbear, 1979, Puddums, The Cathcarts' Orange Cat, 1980, Poofy Loves Company, 1980 (ALA Notable Book 1980), The Spotted Dog, 1980, The President's Car, 1981, Cooper, The McNallys' Big Black Dog, 1981, Love from Aunt Betty, 1983, The Christmas Camel, 1983, The United Nations from A to Z, 1985; co-author: Bugs, 1987, Frogs, Toads, Lizards and Salamanders, 1990, Working Frog, 1992, Money, Money, Money, 1995, Locks, Crocs and Skeeters, The Story of the Panama Canal, 1996; illustrator: Oh, A Hunting We Will Go!, 1974, Warm as Wool, Cool as Cotton, The Story of Natural Fibers, 1975, The Goat in the Rug, 1976, Willy Bear, 1976 (Christopher award 1976), Sweetly Sings the Donkey, 1976, The Substitute, 1977, Hot Cross Buns and Other Old Street Cries, 1978, No Bath Tonight, 1978, My Mom Travels a Lot, 1981 (Christopher 1981), Paul Revere's Ride, 1985, General Store, 1988, Aren't You Coming Too?, 1988, Peter's Pockets, 1988, the Jacket I Wear in the Snow, 1989, At Grammy's House, 1990, Black Crow, Black Crow, 1991, When The Rooster Crowed, 1991, Barbara Frietchie, 1992, The Dress I'll Wear to the Party, 1992, Sheridan's Ride, 1993, Here Comes Henny, 1994, The Bag I'm Taking to Grandma's, 1995, We're Making Breakfast for Mother, 1996. Sec. East 74th St. Block Assn., 1974-83. Recipient various awards, 1974—; Jane Tinkham Broughton fellow, 1975. Mem. Author's Guild, Mills Coll. Club of N.Y., Mantoloking Yacht Club. Home: 51 E 74th St New York NY 10021-2716

PARKER, OLIVIA, photographer; b. Boston, June 10, 1941; d. Harvey Perley and Barbara Ellen (Churchill) Hood; m. John Otis Parker, Apr. 4, 1964; children: John Otis, Helen Elizabeth. B.A., Wellesley Coll., 1963. Tchr. photog. workshops, 1975—; trustee Friends of Photography, 1981-92, 95—, v.p., 1985-89. Photographer, 1969—; Author: (monographs) Signs of Life, 1978, Under the Looking Glass, 1983, Weighing the Planets, 1987; portfolios of black and white photographs Ephemera, 1977, Lost Objects, 1980; one-woman shows include, Vision Gallery, Boston, 1976, 77, 79, 82, 83, 86, 87, Friends of Photography, Carmel, Calif., 1979, 81, Marcuse Pfeifer, N.Y.C., 1980, 83, George Eastman House, Rochester, N.Y., 1981, Art Inst. Chgo., 1982, Photo Gallery Internat., Tokyo, 1983, 84, 87, Fotografie Forum Gallery, Frankfurt, Germany, 1985, Lieberman and Saul, N.Y.C., 1988, Mus. Photographic Arts, San Diego, 1988, Photographers' Gallery, London, 1990, Brent Sikkema, N.Y.C., 1990, 91, Parco, Tokyo, 1991, ICAC/Weston, Tokyo, 1992, Vision, San Francisco, 1993, Robert Klein, Boston, 1993, 96; group shows include, Mus. Fine Arts, Boston, 1978, 92, 93, 96. Chgo. Art Inst., 1978, Internat. Ctr. Photography, N.Y.C., 1985, 87, Fogg Art Mus. Harvard U., 1989; represented in permanent collections, Mus. Modern Art, N.Y.C., Art Inst. Chgo., Boston Mus. Fine Arts, Victoria and Albert Mus., London. Bd. dirs. MacDowell Colony, 1988—; trustee Art Inst. Boston, 1992—. Artists Found. fellow, 1978; recipient Wellesley College Alumnae Achievement award, 1996. Mem. Soc. for Photog. Edn. Club: Chilton. Office: Robert Klein 4th Fl 38 Newbury St Boston MA 02116-9999 *I am interested in the way people think about the unknown. New idea form, the old are shattered, and sometimes old ideas pop up among the new life graffiti on a wall.All is uncertainty and change, but optimists and bingo players are on the look out for moments of perfect knowledge and perfect cards.*

PARKER, OMAR SIGMUND, JR., lawyer; b. Jacksonville, Fla., Apr. 10, 1945; s. Omar Sigmund and Dorothea (Heath) P.; children: Omar Sigmund, Christopher Michael, Julie Anne, Melissa Suzanne, Amy Kathleen. BA, U. Wash., 1968; JD, U. Oreg., 1971. Bar: Wash. 1971, U.S. Dist. Ct. (we. dist.) Wash. 1971, U.S. Ct. Appeals, 1972. Ptnr. Perkins Coie, Seattle, 1971—. Contbr. articles to profl. jours. Bd. dirs. YMCA Youth and Govt. Program, Seattle, 1973-75. Mem. ABA, Wash. State Bar Assn., King County Bar Assn., Am. Coll. Real Estate Lawyers, Am. Coll. Mortgage Attys., Overlake Golf and Country Club, Order of Coif. Avocations: golf, youth coaching. Office: Perkins Coie 1201 3d Ave 40th Fl Seattle WA 98101-3099

PARKER, PATRICK STREETER, manufacturing executive; b. Cleve., 1929. BA, Williams Coll., 1951; MBA, Harvard U., 1953. With Parker-Hannifin Corp. and predecessor, Cleve., 1953—, sales mgr. fittings div., 1957-63, mgr. aerospace products div., 1963-65, pres. Parker Seal Co. div., 1965-67, corp. v.p., 1967-69, pres., 1969-71, pres. and chief exec. officer, 1971-77, chmn. bd. and chief exec. officer, 1977-84, chmn. bd., 1984—, pres., 1982-84, also bd. dirs., 1982—. Bd. trustees Case Western Res. U.; With USN, 1954-57. Mem. Union Club, Country Club, Pepper Pike Club. Office: Parker Hannifin Corp 17325 Euclid Ave Cleveland OH 44112-1209

PARKER, PAULETTE ANN, academic administrator; b. Detroit, Sept. 17, 1951; d. Charles Louis and Vera Ernestine (Dobiyash) Payor; m. James Hodges Parker Jr.; children: J. Daniel, Rebekah, Joshua. Student, U. Mich., 1969-71; BA in Govt. cum laude, Coll. William and Mary, 1992, MA in Govt., 1995. Intern U.S. Congress Ho. of Reps., Washington, summer 1971; adminstr. fgn. lang. houses Coll. of William and Mary, Williamsburg, Va., 1988-90, sec. dept. econs., 1990-93. Vol. Am. Cancer Soc., Am. Lung Assn., Am. Heart Assn., Va. Arthritis Found.; tchr. Williamsburg Comty. Ctr. Sunday Sch., 1988-91; vol. Am. Cancer Soc., Newport News chpt., 1990-91, PTA Breton H.S., 1990-91; active Union of Couns. for Soviet Jews, Washington, 1983-91. Mem. AAUW, Internat. Studies Assn. (presenter papers),, So. Polit. Sci. Assn. (presenter papers), Women in Internat. Security (presenter papers), Women's Caucus for Polit. Sci., Am. Polit. Sci. Assn., Pi Sigma Alpha. Avocations: reading, tennis, water sports, gardening, traveling.

PARKER, PETER D.M., physicist, educator, researcher; b. N.Y.C., Dec. 14, 1936; s. Allan Ellwood and Alice Francis (Heywood) P.; m. Judith Maxfield CUrren, Dec. 27, 1958; children: Stephanie, Gregory, Gretchen. BA, Amherst Coll., 1958; PhD, Calif. Tech., 1963. Physicist Brookhaven Nat. Labs., Upton, N.Y., 1963-66; prof. Yale U., New Haven, Conn., 1966—. Office: Yale U Physics Dept Wright Nuclear Structure 272 Whitney Ave New Haven CT 06520-8124

PARKER, PIERSON, minister, religion educator; b. Shanghai, China, May 27, 1905; s. Alvin Pierson and Susie Estelle (Williams) P.; m. Mildred Ruth Sorg, June 12, 1933; 1 son, Peter Pierson. A.B., U. Calif., 1927; student, So. Meth. U., 1928-29; M.A., Pacific Sch. Religion, 1933, Th.D. magna cum laude, 1934; S.T.D., Ch. Div. Sch. of Pacific, 1964. Ordained to ministry Congregational Ch., 1936, Episcopal Ch., 1944; instr. Bibl. lang. and lit. Pacific Sch. Religion, 1934-36; pastor North Congl. Ch., Berkeley, Calif., 1936-44; St. Andrew's Episc. Ch., Oakland, Calif., 1944-47; pres. No. Calif. Congl. Conf., 1938-39; lectr. Bibl. lit. Ch. Div. Sch. Pacific, 1940-43, instr., 1943-44, asst. prof., 1944-47, assoc. prof., 1947-49; Glorvina Rossell Hoffman prof. N.T. lit. and interpretation Gen. Theol. Sem., N.Y.C., 1949-74; sub-dean Gen. Theol. Sem., 1972-74; chaplain to seminarians Diocese of Los Angeles, 1974-83; disting. prof.-in-residence Cathedral of St. John the Divine, N.Y.C., 1975; prof. N.T. Grad. Sch. Theology, U. of South, 1951-52, 54-55, 56-57, 58-60, 67-69, 71-74; priest-in-charge Trinity Cathedral, Newark, 1953-54; research scholar Oxford U., 1957; lectr. N.T., St. Augustine's Coll., Canterbury, Eng., 1955; seminar asso. Columbia U.; vis. prof. Pacific Sch. of Religion, Ch. Div. Sch. Pacific, 1965, 1966, Seminario del Caribe, 1970, NT Maryknoll Sem., Ossining, N.Y. 1971-73, U. of South, 1975, Bloy Episc. Sch. Theology, 1978-79; priest-in-charge Ch. of Holy Spirit, Nice, France, 1962, St. Helena's Ch., Istanbul, Turkey, 1969; canon Cathedral Ch. of St. Paul, Los Angeles, 1977-81, Diocese of Los Angeles, 1981—; assoc. rector St. Ambrose Ch., Claremont, Calif., 1990—. Author: Interpreters' Bible (vol. on Deuteronomy), 1951, (with H.H. Shires, G.E. WRight) The Gospel Before Mark, 1953, Inherit the Promise, 1957, Christ Our Hope, 1958, Meditations on the Life of Christ, 1959, Good News in Matthew, 1976, A China Childhood, 1993; co-author: New Synoptic Studies, 1983; mem. editorial bd. Anglican Theol. Rev., 1949, Jour. Bibl. Lit., 1960-74; contbr. religious publs., Ency. Am. Mem. Studiorum Novi Testamenti Societas, Soc. Bibl. Lit. (pres. Pacific Coast sect. 1946-48, mem. council 1944, v.p. Middle Atlantic sect. 1959-60, pres. 1960-61, archivist 1976-83, nat. hon. pres. 1978), Pacific Theol. Group, Inst. Antiquity and Christianity, Pacific Sch. Religion Alumni Assn. (pres. 1943-46), Alpha Sigma Phi. Home: 650 W Harrison Ave Claremont CA 91711-4595

PARKER, R. JOSEPH, lawyer; b. St. Louis, June 29, 1944; s. George Joseph and Ann Rosalie (VanVactor) P.; m. Theresa Gaynor, Aug. 26, 1967; children: Christa Michele, Kevin Blake. AB, Georgetown U., 1966; JD, Boston Coll., 1969. Bar: Ohio 1969. Law clk. to judge U.S. Ct. Appeals (6th Cir.), Akron, Ohio, 1969-70; assoc. Taft, Stettinius & Hollister, Cin., 1970-78; ptnr. Taft, Stettinius & Hollister, Cin., 1978—; arbitrator Am. Arbitration Assn., Cin., 1980—; faculty Nat. Inst. for Trial Advocacy, 1990—; faculty advanced trial advocacy program IRS, 1993. Editor Law Rev. Ann. Survey Mass. Law, 1967-69. Bd. dirs. West End Health Ctr., Inc., Cin., 1972-76, Legal Aid Soc. Cin., 1982-85; chmn. bd. dirs. Vol. Lawyers for Poor Found., Cin., 1986-88; master Am. Inn of Court, 1984—. Fellow Am. Coll. Trial Lawyers; mem. Ohio State Bar Assn., Cin. Bar Assn., Cin. Country Club, Order of Coif. Democrat. Roman Catholic. Avocations: golf, squash. Office: 1800 Star Bank Bldg 425 Walnut St Cincinnati OH 45202-3904

PARKER, RICHARD E., building products manufacturing company executive. Formerly v.p., now exec. v.p. Morgan Products Ltd. (now ABTco), Oshkosh, Wis.; exec. v.p. hardboard /plastics div. Troy, Wis., 1992. Office: Abtco Inc 3250 W. Big Beaver Rd Ste 200 Troy WI 48084*

PARKER, ROBERT ALLAN RIDLEY, transportation execuive, astronaut; b. N.Y.C., Dec. 14, 1936; s. Allan Elwood and Alice (Heywood) P.; m. Joan Audrey Capers, June 14, 1958 (div. 1980); children: Kimberly Ellen, Brian David Capers; m. Judith S. Woodruff, Apr. 2, 1981. A.B., Amherst Coll., 1958; Ph.D., Calif. Inst. Tech., 1962. NSF postdoctoral fellow U. Wis., 1962-63, asst. prof., then assoc. prof. astronomy, 1963-74; astronaut NASA, Johnson Space Ctr., 1967-91; dir. policy plan Office Space Flight, NASA Hdqs., Washington, 1991, dir. space ops. utilization program, 1992—; mem. support crew Apollo XV and XVII, mission scientist Apollo XVII, program scientist Skylab program, mission specialist for Spacelab 1, 1983, ASTRO-1, 1990. Mem. Am. Astron. Soc., Phi Beta Kappa. Office: Code MO NASA-HQ Washington DC 20546

PARKER, ROBERT BROWN, novelist; b. Springfield, Mass., Sept. 17, 1932; s. Carroll Snow and Mary Pauline (Murphy) P.; m. Joan Hall, Aug. 26, 1956; children: David, Daniel. BA, Colby Coll., 1954; MA, Boston U., 1957, PhD, 1971; LittD (hon.), Northeastern U., 1987. Various bus. and advt. positions N.Y.C. and Boston, 1956-62; lectr. Boston U., 1962-64; mem. faculty Lowell (Mass.) State Coll., 1964-66, Bridgewater State Coll., 1966-68; asst. prof. English Northeastern U., Boston, 1968-73, assoc. prof., 1973-76, prof., 1976-79; lectr. Suffolk U., 1965-66; co-chmn. Parker-Farman Co., 1960-62. Author: (with others) The Personal Response to Literature, 1970, (with Peter L. Sandberg) Order and Diversity: The Craft of Prose, 1973, Godwulf Manuscript, 1974, God Save the Child, 1974, (with John R. Marsh) Sports Illustrated Weight Training, 1974, Mortal Stakes, 1975, Promised Land, 1976 (Edgar Allan Poe award for best novel Mystery Writers Am. 1976), The Judas Goat, 1978, (with Joan Parker) Three Weeks in Spring, 1978, Wilderness, 1979, Looking for Rachel Wallace, 1980, Early Autumn, 1981, A Savage Place, 1981, Surrogate: A Spenser Short Story, 1982, Ceremony, 1982, The Widening Gyre, 1983, Love and Glory, 1983, Valediction, 1984, The Private Eye in Hammett and Chandler, 1984, A Catskill Eagle, 1985, Parker on Writing, 1985, Taming a Seahorse, 1986, Pale Kings and Princes, 1987, Crimson Joy, 1988, Playmates, 1989, (with Raymond Chandler) Poodle Springs, 1989, Stardust, 1990, Perchance to Dream, 1990, A Year at the Races, 1990, Pastime, 1991, Double Deuce, 1992, Paper Doll, 1993, Walking Shadow, 1994, All Our Yesterdays, 1994, Spenser's Boston, 1994; screenwriter with Joan Parker: (TV movies) Spenser: Ceremony, 1993, Spenser: Pale Kings and Princes, 1993; contbr., cons.: (TV series) Spenser: For Hire, 1985-88, A Man Called Hawk, 1989-90. Served with U.S. Army, 1954-56. Mem. Writers Guild Am. Avocations: jogging, weightlifting.

PARKER, ROBERT DALE, civil engineer; b. Watertown, N.Y., July 21, 1951; s. Edson Adelbert Parker and Marjorie Lois (Goheen) Parker-Clark; m. Daphne Quinta, Aug. 25, 1978; children: April Beth, Amy Lynn. AAS, Canton Agrl. & Tech. Inst., 1972; B Tech., Rochester Inst. Tech., 1975. Registered profl. engr., Mich., N.Y. Process operator Monroe County Pure Waters, Rochester, N.Y., 1975-77; process ops. engr. Consoer, Townsend & Assocs., Chgo., 1978-79; engr. Rist Frost Assocs., Watertown and Glens Falls, N.Y., 1980-81; project rep. Stearns & Wheler Engrs., Cazenovia, N.Y., 1979, 82, 83; design engr. Bernier Carr & Assocs., P.C., Watertown, 1983-90, sr. design engr., 1990-92, assoc. engr., 1992—. Author wastewater treatment facilities operation and maintenance manuals. Mem. bd. edn. Faith Fellowship Christian Sch., Watertown, 1987-94; elder River of Life Fellowship Ch., Copenhagen, N.Y., 1994—. Recipient cert. Nat. Coun. Examiners for Engring. and Surveying, 1991. Mem. NSPE, ASCE, Water Environ. Fedn., N.Y. State Soc. Profl. Engrs. Republican. Achievements include design of innovative alternative technology wastewater collection and treatment facilities. Home: 13825 County Rte 156 Watertown NY 13601

PARKER, ROBERT FREDERIC, university dean emeritus; b. St. Louis, Oct. 29, 1907; s. Charles T. and Lydia (Gronemeyer) P.; m. Mary L. Warner, June 20, 1934; children: David Frederic, Jane Eleanor (Mrs. Howard H. Hush, Jr.). B.S., Washington U., St. Louis, 1925, M.D., 1929. Diplomate: Am. Bd. Microbiology. Asst. radiology Washington U. Med. Sch., 1929-30, instr. medicine, 1932-33; asst. Rockefeller Inst., 1933-36; mem. faculty Case Western Res. U., 1936—, prof. microbiology, 1954-77, prof. emeritus, 1977—, assoc. dean, 1965-73, dean, 1973-76, dean emeritus, 1976—. Mem. Cleve. Acad. Medicine (past bd. dirs.), Am. Soc. Clin. Investigation, Central Soc. Clin. Research, Am. Acad. Microbiology, Sigma Xi, Alpha Omega Alpha. Spl. research virus immunology, quantitative aspects virus infection, tissue culture, action of antibiotics. Home: 1890 E 107th St Apt 436 Cleveland OH 44106-2243 Office: 2085 Adelbert Rd Cleveland OH 44106-2622

PARKER, ROBERT GEORGE, radiation oncology educator, academic administrator; b. Detroit, Mich., Jan. 29, 1925; s. Clifford Robert and Velma (Ashman) P.; m. Diana Davis, June 30, 1977; children by previous marriage: Thomas Clifford, James Richardson. BS, U. Wis., 1946, MD., 1948. Diplomate Am. Bd. Radiology (trustee 1978—, pres. 1988-90). Intern U. Nebr. Hosp., Omaha, 1948-49; resident in pathology Western Res. U., Cleve., 1949-50; resident in radiology U. Mich., Ann Arbor, 1950, 52-54, instr. in radiology, 1954-55; staff radiotherapist Swedish Hosp. Tumor Inst., Seattle, 1955-58; prof. radiology U. Wash., Seattle, 1958-77; prof. radiation oncology UCLA, 1977—. Lt. USN, 1950-52. Fellow Am. Coll. Radiology; mem. AMA (radiology residence rev. com.), Am. Soc. Therapeutic Radiologists (pres. 1975-76), Radiol. Soc. N.Am. (bd. dirs. 1984-90, pres. 1991-92), Am. Radium Soc. (bd. dirs. 1988-92, pres. 1992). Office: UCLA Ste B265 200 UCLA Medicine Plz Los Angeles CA 90095-6951

PARKER, ROBERT LEE, SR., petroleum engineer, drilling company executive; b. Tulsa, July 16, 1923; s. Gifford Clevel and Gladys Carolyn (Baker) P.; m. Catherine Mae McDaniel, Dec. 16, 1944; children: Robert Lee, Carolyn Louise, Debra Ann. B.S., U. Tex., 1944; LL.D. (hon.), John Brown U., 1967, Oral Roberts U., 1977. With Parker Drilling Co., 1947—, owner, mgr., 1953—, pres., 1954-92, chmn. bd., 1967—; bd. dirs. CWI, Inc.; dir. Bank Okla., Enterra Corp., Mapco Inc.; chmn. Nat. Energy Task Force, 1981-82. Chmn. St. Francis Hosp., Tulsa, U. Tex. Engring. Found.; trustee U. Tulsa, 1st Methodist Ch., Tulsa; bd. dirs. Tulsa YMCA, Jr. Achievement, So. Meth. U.; active Boy Scouts Am. Served with U.S. Army, 1945-47. Named Distinguished Engring. Grad. U. Tex., 1969. Mem. Am. Petroleum Inst., Internat. Assn. Drilling Contractors, Okla. Ind. Petroleum Assn., Soc. Profl. Engrs. Republican. Clubs: So. Hills Country, Tulsa, Houston, Odessa Country. Office: Parker Drilling Co 8 E 3rd St Tulsa OK 74103-3616 *A discipline of character and work, an enthusiasm for life and an awareness of God's constant help have all had positive impacts on my life.*

PARKER, ROBERT LEE, JR., drilling company executive; b. Midland, Tex., Nov. 9, 1948; s. Robert Lee and Catherine Mae (McDaniel) P.; m. Carolyn Diane Daniel, June 1971 (div. 1974); 1 dau., Christy Diane; m. 2d, Patricia Ann Dollarhite, Oct. 21, 1977 (div. 1984); children—Robert Lee III, Austin Leeann; m. Risa Elaine Blackman, Nov. 24, 1986. Student Okla. State U., 1967-68; M.B.A., U. Tex., 1972. Contract rep. Parker Drilling Co., Tulsa, 1972-73, mgr. U.S. ops., 1973-74, v.p., 1974-76, exec. v.p., 1976-77, pres., chief operating officer, 1977-91, pres., chief exec. officer, 1991—, also dir.; bd. dirs. Alaska Air Group Inc. Bd. dirs. United Way, Tulsa, 1983-88, ARC, Tulsa chpt., 1985—. Recipient 3d place award Tex. Trophy Hunters Assn., 1983. Republican. Methodist. Office: Parker Drilling Co 8 E 3rd St Tulsa OK 74103-3616

PARKER, ROBERT M., federal judge; b. 1937. BBA, U. Tex., 1961, JD, 1964. Bar: Tex. 1964. Ptnr. Parish & Parker, Gilmer, Tex., 1964-65, Kenley & Boyland, Longview, Tex., 1965, Roberts, Smith & Parker, Longview, 1966-71, Rutledge & Parker, Ft. Worth, 1971-72, Nichols & Parker, Longview, 1972-79; judge U.S. Dist. Ct. (ea. dist.) Tex., 1979-94, chief judge, 1991-94; judge U.S. Ct. Appeals (5th Cir.), Tyler, Tex. Mem. Tex. Bar Assn. Office: 221 W Ferguson St Ste 400 Tyler TX 75702-7200

PARKER, SAM, financial executive; b. N.Y.C., June 30, 1935; s. John and Ida; B.B.A. in Public Acctg., Baruch Coll., City U. N.Y., 1962; m. Mary Rengifo, Oct. 5, 1970. Auditor, Eisner and Lubin, C.P.A.s, N.Y.C., 1962-65; mng. partner Parker and Mulligan, C.P.A.s, N.Y.C., 1965-67; asst. controller Korvettes Stores, N.Y.C., 1967-70; auditor Peat Marwick Main & Co., C.P.A.s, N.Y.C., 1970-74; dir. fin. and adminstrn. Nat. Bur. Econ. Research, Inc., Cambridge, Mass., 1974—; cons. in field. Served with AUS, 1958. C.P.A., N.Y., Mass. Mem. Am. Inst. C.P.A.s, Greater Boston C. of C. (Exec. Club), Pan Am. Soc. New Eng. (treas. 1981-82). Author articles in field. Office: Nat Bur of Econ Rsch 1050 Massachusetts Ave Cambridge MA 02138-5317*

PARKER, SARA ANN, librarian; b. Cassville, Mo., Feb. 19, 1939; d. Howard Franklin and Vera Irene (Thomas) P. B.A., Okla. State U., 1961; M.L.S., Emporia State U., Kans., 1968. Adult svcs. librarian Springfield Pub. Libr., Mo., 1972-75, bookmobile dir., 1975-76; coord. S.W. Mo. Libr. Network, Springfield, 1976-78; libr. developer Colo. State Libr., Denver, 1978-82; state librarian Mont. State Libr., Helena, 1982-88, State Libr. Pa., Harrisburg, 1988-90; Pa. commr. librs., dep. sec. edn. State of Pa., Harrisburg, 1990-95; state libr. State of Mo., Jefferson City, 1995—; cons. and lectr. in field. Author, editor, compiler in field; contbr. articles to profl. jours. Sec., Western Coun. State Librs., Reno, 1984-88, mem. Mont. State Data Adv. Coun., 1983-88, Mont. Telecommunications Coun., 1985-88, WLN Network Coun., 1984-87, Kellogg ICLIS Project Mgmt. Bd., 1986-88. Recipient President's award Nature Conservancy, 1989, Friends award Pa. Assn. Ednl. Communications and Techs., 1989; fellow Inst. Ednl. Leadership, 1982. Mem. ALA, Chief Officers State Libr. Agys. (chair N.E. 1991-92, v.p., pres. elect 1994—), Mont. Libr. Assn. (bd. dirs. 1982-88), Mountain Plains Libr. Assn. (sec. chmn. 1980, pres. 1987-88). Home: PO Box 554 Jefferson City MO 65102 Office: Mo State Libr PO Box 387 600 W Main St Jefferson City MO 65102

PARKER, SARAH JESSICA, actress; b. Nelsonville, Ohio, Mar. 25, 1965. Actress: (theatre) The Innocents, 1976, The Sound of Music, 1977, Annie, 1978, The War Brides, 1981, The Death of a Miner, 1982, To Gillian on Her 37th Birthday, 1983, 84, Terry Neal's Future, 1986, The Heidi Chronicles, 1989, (films) Rich Kids, 1979, Somewhere Tomorrow, 1983, Firstborn, 1984, Footloose, 1984, Girls Just Want to Have Fun, 1985, Flight of the Navigator, 1986, L.A. Story, 1991, Honeymoon in Vegas, 1992, Hocus Pocus, 1993, Striking Distance, 1993, Ed Wood, 1994, Miami Rhapsody, 1995, (TV movies) My Body, My Child, 1982, Going for the Gold: The Bill Johnson Story, 1985, A Year in the Life, 1986, The Room Upstairs, 1987, Dadah Is Death, 1988, The Ryan White Story, 1989, Twist of Fate, 1989, In the Best Interest of the Children, 1992, (TV series) Square Pegs, 1982-83, A Year in the Life, 1987-88, Equal Justice, 1990-91, (TV pilots) The Alan King Show, 1986. Office: CAA 9830 Wilshire Blvd Beverly Hills CA 90212*

PARKER, SCOTT JACKSON, theatre manager; b. Ft. Bragg, N.C., July 28, 1945; s. John William and Darice Lee (Jackson) P. MA, U. N.C., 1971; MFA, U. Va., 1978. Mng. dir. Duke U. Theatre, Durham, N.C., 1970-76; gen. mgr. East Carolina U. Theatre, Greenville, 1980-85; producer The Lost Colony Outdoor Drama, Manteo, N.C., 1986-89; dir. Inst. of Outdoor Drama U. N.C., Chapel Hill, N.C., 1990—; v.p. Paul Green Found., nationwide, 1989—. Producer, mgr., dir., scene designer. With U.S. Army, 1969-70. Mem. Nat. Theatre Conf. (sec. 1994—), Assn. for Theatre in Higher Edn. (founding mem. 1987), Southeastern Theatre Conf. (pres. 1982), Arts Advs. of N.C. (pres. 1993-94), The Players Club N.Y.C. Democrat. Baptist. Avocations: white water Kayaking, camping, hiking. Office: U NC Inst Outdoor Drama Cb # 3240 Chapel Hill NC 27599

PARKER, SCOTT LANE, management consultant; b. Phila., Feb. 23, 1946; s. Waldo G. and Nettie M. (Fulton) P.; m. Irene H. Lewis (div. Sept. 1969); m. Claudia E. Nebel, June 14, 1948; children: Adam Michael, Jay Maxwell, Zachary Scott. BA in Econs., U. Va., 1969, MBA, 1971. Mgmt. cons. The MAC Group, 1971-88, co-mng. dir., 1988-90; sr. v.p. operational support Gemini Consulting, 1991-92; sr. v.p. global strategic initiatives Gemini Consulting, Morristown, N.J., 1993-94; adj. prof. strategic mgmt. U. Md., College Park, 1994—; pres. Parker & Co., McLean, Va., 1995—. William Michael Shermet scholar U. Va., 1970; U.S. Steel fellow, U. Va., 1970.

PARKER, SCOTT SMITH, hospital administrator; b. Salt Lake City, Mar. 3, 1935; married. BA, U. Utah, 1960; MA, U. Minn., 1962. Adminstrv. resident Northwestern Hosp., Mpls., 1961-62, asst. adminstr., 1962-67; adminstr. Southside Hosp., Mesa, Ariz., 1967-71; v.p. Good Samaritan Med. Ctr., Phoenix, 1971-73; adminstr. Hoag Meml. Hosp. Presbyn., Newport Beach, Calif., 1973-75; pres. Intermountain Health Care, Salt Lake City, 1975—. Mem. Am. Hosp. Assn. (bd. dirs. 1980-83, chmn. elect, 1985-86, chair 1986-87, past chmn. 1987), Internat. Hosp. Fed. (exec. com. 1991—, pres. elect 1993), Ariz. Hosp. Assn. (pres. 1972). Home: 1014 Woodmoor Dr Bountiful UT 84010-1952 Office: Intermountain Health Care Inc 36 S State St Fl 22 Salt Lake City UT 84111*

PARKER, SUSAN BROOKS, healthcare executive; b. Newport, N.H., Nov. 7, 1945; d. Ronald Elliott and Elizabeth Louise (Wiggins) P.; married; children: Jeffrey Roberts Avery, Mark Brooks Avery. BS in English and French, U. Vt., 1968; MSW in Social Planning, Boston Coll., 1978. Activities dir. Avery Vt. Inns, Fairlee, 1968-71, retail buyer, 1969-75, mgr., 1972-74; aftercare worker Orange County Mental Health, Bradford, Vt., 1974-76; adminstrn. asst. Mass. Assn. for Mental Health, Boston, 1976-77; mental health planner Tri-City Area Office, Malden, Mass., 1977-78; exec. dir. Grafton County Human Services Commn., Lebanon, N.H., 1978-80, N.H. Developmental Disabilities Council, Concord, N.H., 1980-87; commr. Dept. of Mental Health, Augusta, Maine, 1987-89; assoc. commr. U.S. Social Security Adminstrn., Balt., 1989-93; sec. gen. Rehab. Internat., N.Y.C., 1994—; cons. Nat. Gov.'s Assn., Washington, 1985-86, Office of Health and Developmental Services, Washington, 1987; directorship Nat. Assn. of Devel. Disabilities, Washington, 1983-87, Cen. N.H. Mental Health Ctr., Concord, 1985-87; cons. in field. Author: poetry collection Scheme, 1965; contbr. articles to newspapers and profl. jours. Pres. PTO, Fairlee, Vt., 1972-73; dir. Ford Sayre Ski Program, Fairlee, 1972-76, United Way, Concord, 1983-86; bd. dirs. PTO Rundlett Jr. H.S., Concord, 1982-85; pres. U.S. Coun. for Internat. Rehab., 1993. Recipient Assn. Retarded Citizens Children's Disability Pub. Policy award, 1992, Kathryn C. Arneson award People to People, 1992, Commr.'s citation for outstanding efforts in developing policy Social Security Adminstrn., 1992, Dep. Commn.'s citation for outstanding exec. leadership, 1993; named Outstanding Alumnus Boston Coll., 1991, Adminstrn. Devel. Disabilities prin. investigator grantee, 1986. Mem. Am. Assn. Mental Retardation, Nat. Assn. State Mental Health Program Dirs., Nat. Assn. Retarded Citizens, Concord Luncheon Club. Avocations: skiing, canoeing, mountain climbing, reading, travel. Office: Rehab Internat 25 E 21st St New York NY 10010-6207

PARKER, THOMAS LEE, business executive; b. Ft. Worth, Aug. 23, 1921; s. J.T. Parker and Frances Gertrude (Rogers) Heer; m. Frances N. Newlon, Dec. 14, 1943 (dec. 1981); children: Richard T. (dec.), Pamela Parker Gartin. BSBA, Ohio State U., 1943. Sales rep. Frozen Drumstick Sales Co., Columbus, Ohio, 1946-47; sec.-treas., gen. mgr. Cream Cone Machine Co., Columbus, 1948-57; pres. Drumstick Inc., Columbus, 1958-62; pres. Big Drum, Inc., Columbus, 1962-83, chmn. bd., 1983-86; dir. Ohio Semitronics. Mem. nat. adv. coun. Boy Scouts Am., Dallas. Maj. U.S. Army, 1943-46, ETO. Decorated Bronze Star; recipient Service to Mankind Columbus Sertoma Club, 1975, Silver Beaver Boy Scouts Am., 1975, Silver Antelope Boy Scouts Am., 1977, Silver Buffalo Boy Scouts Am., 1986; Baden Powell fellow World Scouts, Geneva, 1982. Mem. Scioto Country Club (pres. 1977), Athletic Club (pres. 1971), Masons, Delta Tau Delta. Republican.

PARKER, WILLIAM ELBRIDGE, consulting civil engineer; b. Seattle, Mar. 18, 1913; s. Charles Elbridge and Florence E. (Plumb) P.; m. Dorris Laurie Freeman, June 15, 1935; children—Dorris Laurie, Jane Elizabeth. B.S., U.S. Naval Acad., 1935. Party chief King County Engrs., 1935-39; exec. sec., cons. engr. State Wash., 1946-49; city engr., chmn. Bd. Pub. Works, City of Seattle, 1953-57; cons. City of San Diego, 1957; ptnr. Parker-Fisher & Assocs., 1958-66; cons. engr. Minish & Webb Engrs., Seattle, 1966-70; city engr. City of Bremerton (Wash.), 1970-76; owner Parker & Assocs., Seattle, 1976—. Served to capt. C.E.C., USNR, 1939-45, 51-53. Named to Broadway Hall of Fame. Registered profl. engr., Wash. Mem. Am. Pub. Works Assn., U.S. Naval Inst., Pioneers of State Wash. (pres.), U.S. Naval Acad. Alumni Assn. (chpt. pres.), College Club (Seattle). Lodges: Masons, Shriners.

PARKER, WILLIAM H., III, federal official; b. Westbrook, Maine, May 4, 1937; s. William H. II and Anne Marney (Delaney) P.; m. Joan Moody Currier, June 17, 1959; children: Laurie Jean, Michael Currier, Suzan Elizabeth, Julie Ann. BS, U. Maine, 1960; MS, Northeastern U., 1966; MEM, U. Detroit, 1981, MBA, 1982; postgrad., Nova U. Diplomate Am. Acad. Environ. Engrs. Project engr. Camp Dresser & McKee, Boston, 1962-72, v.p., 1972-75; v.p. E.C. Jordan, Portland, Maine, 1975-77; sr. v.p., reg. mgr. Camp Dresser & McKee, Detroit, 1977-87, bd. dirs., 1982-87; sr. v.p. CDM Fed. Programs Corp., Washington, 1987-88, bd. dirs., 1987-88; dep. asst. sec. Dept. of Def., Washington, 1988-90; dir. environ. programs EG&G Inc., Wellesley, Mass., 1990—; bd. dirs. Parker Currier Inc., Brunswick, Maine; fin. cons. VMI, treas., pres., 1993—, White River Junction, Vt., 1987-90; presenter Congl. test, 1988-90; keynote speaker tech. and profl. socs., 1988—. Contbr. articles to profl. jours. Mem., chmn. planning bd. Town of Reading, Maine, 1968-73; mem. Town Meeting, Reading, 1969-75, Mcpl. Light Bd., Reading, 1974-75. 1st lt. U.S. Army, 1960-62. Recipient Outstanding Pub. Svc. medal Sec. of Def., 1989. Mem. ASCE, NSPE, Mass. Soc. Profl. Engrs (Young Engr. of Yr. award 1971), Am. Def. Preparedness Assoc., Engring. Socs. New Eng. (New Eng. award 1990), Soc. Am. Mil. Engrs., Nat. Security Industries Assn. (hon.), Water Pollution Control Fedn., Am. Water Works Assn., Mass. Jaycees (Reading) (local pres., state v.p. 1970-72, Econ. Club Detroit, Detroit Club, Sigma Xi, Tau Beta Pi, Alpha Kappa Psi, Beta Gamma Sigma, Phi Kappa Phi, Chi Epsilon. Republican. Roman Catholic. Avocations: reading, writing, traveling. Home: 15 Montclair Rd West Newbury MA 01985-2216 Office: EG&G Inc 45 William St Wellesley MA 02181-4004

PARKER, WILLIAM NELSON, economics educator; b. Columbus, Ohio, June 14, 1919; s. Murray Nelson and Evalyn Mae (Gares) P.; m. Josephine Yvonne Forbus, Sept. 20, 1948; children: Yvonne Victoria, Jarrett Nelson. A.B. magna cum laude, Harvard, 1939, M.A., 1941, Ph.D., 1951; M.A., Yale, 1962. Economist atomic energy com. U.S. Senate, 1946, Dept. State, 1947-48; cons. President's Materials Policy Commn., 1951; asst. prof. econs. Williams Coll., 1951-56; assoc. prof., then prof. econs. U. N.C. at Chapel Hill, 1956-62; prof. econs. Yale, 1962-89, emeritus, 1989—, dir. grad. studies in econs., 1968-72, 74-78; Del. to Am. Coun. Learned Socs., 1975-78; chmn. Coun. on West European Studies, 1985-89; dir. Mellon West European Project, 1987-92. Co-author: Coal and Steel in Western Europe, 1957; Editor, contbr.: Trends in the American Economy in the Nineteenth Century, 1958, The Structure of the Cotton Economy of the Antebellum South, 1970, American Economic Growth, 1972, European Peasants and Their Markets, 1976; Economic History and the Modern Economist, 1986; co-editor: Jour. Econ. History, 1960-66; author: Europe, America, and the Wider World, Vol. I, 1984, Vol. II, 1990. Served to maj. AUS, 1941-45. Nat. fellow Harvard U., 1935-41, Social Sci. Rsch. Coun. fellow, 1948-51, 62-63, Ford Faculty fellow, 1958-59, Resources for Future rsch. fellow, 1955-57, Guggenheim fellow, 1966-67, St. Anthony's Coll. fellow, 1972-73, Australian Nat. U. vis. fellow, 1983, 89. Mem. Am. Philos. Soc., Econ. History Assn. (pres. 1969-70, Hughes prize for excellence in tchg. 1995), Agrl. History Assn. (pres. 1979-80), Am. Econ. Assn. (rep. adv. com. U.S. Archives 1978-81), Am. Acad. Arts and Scis. Contbr. 1st Internat. Conf. Econ. History, Stockholm, Sweden, 1960, 3d conf., Munich, Germany, 1965, 7th conf., Edinburgh, 1978; U.S./USSR Historians Conf., Moscow, 1978, Tallinn, 1987; Sapporo Am. Studies Conf., Japan, 1981; French-Am. Fedn. prof. Ecole Des Hautes Etudes, Paris, 1984-85. Home: 144 Edgehill Rd Hamden CT 06517-4011

PARKERSON, HARDY MARTELL, lawyer; b. Longview, Tex., Aug. 22, 1942; s. Winifred Lenore (Robertson) P.; m. Janice Carol Johnson, Aug. 3, 1968; children: James Blaine Parkerson, Stanley Andrew Parkerson, Paul Hardy Parkerson. BA, McNeese State U., Lake Charles, La.; JD, Tulane U., 1966. Bar: La. 1966, U.S. Supreme Ct. 1971. Assoc. Rogers, McHale & St. Romain, Lake Charles, 1967-69; pvt. practice Lake Charles, 1969—; chmn. 7th Congl. Dist. Crime and Justice Task Force, La. Priorities for the Future, 1980; asst. prof. criminal justice La. State U., 1986. Bd. dirs. 1st Assembly of God Ch., Lake Charles, 1980—; bd. regents So. Christian U., Lake Charles, 1993—; mem. La. Dem. State Ctrl. Com., 1992—, Calcasieu Parish Dem. Com., 1988— (sec.-treas., exec. com., 1988—); former mem. Gulf Assistance Program, Lake Charles; 7th Congl. Dist. La. mem. Imports and Exports Trust Authority, Baton Rouge, 1984-88. Mem. Pi Kappa Housing Corp. of Lake Charles (bd. dirs., sec.-treas. 1985—), Optimists, Pi Kappa Phi (Beta Mu chpt.). Democrat. Mem. Assembly of God Ch. Avocations: political activist, television talk show host. Home: 127 Greenway St Lake Charles LA 70605-6821 Office: The Parkerson Law Firm 807 Alamo St Lake Charles LA 70601-8665

PARKES, KENNETH CARROLL, ornithologist; b. Hackensack, N.J., Aug. 8, 1922; s. Walter Carroll and Lillian Carolyn (Capelle) P.; m. Ellen Pierce Stone, Sept. 6, 1953. B.S., Cornell U., 1943, M.S., 1948, Ph.D., 1952. Curator birds Cornell U., 1947-52; mem. staff Carnegie Mus. of Natural History, Pitts., 1953—; curator birds Carnegie Mus., 1962-86, chief curator life scis., 1975-85, sr. curator birds, 1986—; research fellow epidemiology and microbiology U. Pitts., 1956, vis. lectr. Pymatuning Field Lab., 1957, adj. mem. grad. faculty, 1963—; mem. adminstrv. bd. Lab. Ornithology, Cornell U., 1962-68, 70-75; bd. trustees Del. Mus. Natural History, 1976-90. Taxonomic editor: Avian Biology, 1971-75; co-editor, 1977-93; cons. on bird art to artists, pubs.; contbr. articles to profl. jours., encys. Served with AUS, 1943-46. Fellow Am. Ornithologists Union (2d v.p. 1975-76); mem. Audubon Soc. Western Pa. (trustee 1982-91), Wilson Ornithol. Soc. (pres. 1973-75), numerous other profl. socs. Democrat. Unitarian. Office: Carnegie Museum Natural History 4400 Forbes Ave Pittsburgh PA 15213-4007

PARKEY, ROBERT WAYNE, radiology and nuclear medicine educator, research radiologist; b. Dallas, July 17, 1938; s. Jack and Gloria Alfreda (Perry) P.; m. Nancy June Knox, Aug. 9, 1958; children: Wendell Wade, Robert Todd, Amy Elizabeth. BS in Physics, U. Tex., 1960; MD, S.W. Med. Sch., U. Tex., Dallas, 1965. Diplomate Am. Bd. Radiology, Am. Bd. Nuclear Medicine. Intern St. Paul Hosp., Dallas, 1965-66; resident in radiology U. Tex. Health Sci. Ctr., Dallas, 1966-69, asst. prof. radiology, 1970-74, assoc. prof., 1974-77, prof., chmn. dept. radiology, 1977—, Effie and Wofford Cain Disting. chair in diagnostic imaging, 1994—; chief nuc. medicine Parkland Meml. Hosp., Dallas, 1974-79, chief dept. radiology, 1977—. Contbr. numerous chpts., articles and abstracts to profl. publs. Served as capt. M.C., Army N.G., 1965-72. NIH fellow Nat. Inst. Gen. Med. Sci., U. Mo., Columbia, 1969-70; Nat. Acad. Scis.-NRC scholar in radiol. research James Picker Found., 1971-74. Fellow Am. Coll. Cardiology, Am. Coll. Radiology; mem. Am. Coll. Nuclear Physicians (charter, ho. of dels. 1974—), Council on Cardiovascular Radiology of Am. Heart Assn., AMA, Assn. Univ. Radiologists, Dallas County Med. Assn., Dallas Ft. Worth Radiol. Soc., Radiol. Soc. N.Am., Soc. Chairmen of Acad. Radiology Depts., Soc. Nuclear Medicine (acad. council), Tex. Med. Assn., Tex. Radiol. Soc., Sigma Xi, Alpha Omega Alpha. Avocations: gardening, golf, tennis. Academic research interests: nuclear cardiology, development of new imaging technologies, medical education. Office: U Tex Southwestern Med Ctr Dallas Dept Radiology 5323 Harry Hines Blvd Dallas TX 75235-8896

PARKHILL, HAROLD LOYAL, artist; b. Fresno, Ohio, Feb. 16, 1928; s. Jesse Blair and Ella (Buser) P.; m. Rosalee Lavonne Croup, Aug. 5, 1950 (div. Nov. 1969); children: Lorie Cathrine, Scott Thomas, Cynthia Anne, Carrie Sue. Grad. high sch., Keene, Ohio. Farmer Fresno, 1947-52, 1964-80; bus driver Western Greyhound Lines, Calif., Ariz., N.Mex. and Tex., 1952-61; dispatcher Ea. Greyhound Lines, Cin., 1963; artist Coshocton, Ohio, 1980—. Represented in permanent collections Zanesville Art Ctr., Pomerene Fine Art Ctr.; represented in various corp. collections; works included in Modern Maturity's Seasoned Eye 3 Show, 1990-91; works shown in 4th, 5th, 6th and 8th edits. of Ency. of Living Artists; represented in group show at Kennedy Ctr., 1991. Past trustee Coshocton Pomerene Fine Art Ctr. With USNR, 1945-46, PTO. Recipient numerous best of show awards in oil and watercolor art, incl. award, 25th anniversary art show Internat. Platform Assn., Washington, 1989, 1st Pl. Painting, Internat. Platform Assn. 26th ann. art show, 1990. Mem. VFW, Internat. Platform Assn., Am. Legion, Ohio Realist Group, Am. Artists Profl. League, Elks. Republican. Methodist. Avocations: travel, gun collecting. Home: PO Box 85 Coshocton OH 43812-0085

PARKHURST, CHARLES, retired museum director, art historian; b. Columbus, Ohio, Jan. 23, 1913; s. Charles Percy and Isabella (Woodbridge) P.; m. Elizabeth Huntington Rusling, June 15, 1938 (div. 1962); children: Andrew, Christopher, Bruce; m. Rima Zevin Julyan, Sept. 1, 1962 (div. 1972); 1 child, Brooke; stepchildren: Candace, David, Mark; m. Carol Canda Clark, July 18, 1986. BA, Williams Coll., 1935; AM, Oberlin Coll., 1938; MFA, Princeton U., 1941. Rd. and bridge constrn. worker Danali Park Alaska Rd. Commn.; tchr. music, coach basketball Wasilla, Alaska, 1935-37; asst. curator (registrar) Nat. Gallery of Art, Washington, 1942-43; dep. chief, monuments, fine arts and archives sect. Allied Mil. Govt. in both U.S. Zones, Germany, 1945-46; asst. curator Albright Art Gallery, Buffalo, 1946-47; asst. prof. art and archaeology Princeton (N.J.) U.; asst. dir. Princeton (N.J.) Art Mus., 1947-49; head dept. fine arts, dir. Art Mus., prof. history and appreciation of art Oberlin (Ohio) Coll., 1949-62; dir. Balt. Mus. Art, 1962-70; asst. dir., chief curator Nat. Gallery Art, Washington, 1971-83, ret., 1983; co-dir. Mus. Art Williams Coll., 1983-84, mem. vis. faculty, 1980, Clark vis. prof., 1985-86, acting dir. grad. program in art history, 1986-87, dir. M.B. Prendergrast Systematic Catalogue project, 1983-87; interim dir. Smith Coll. Mus. Art, 1991-92, emeritus dir., 1992; faculty fellow Fund for Advancement Edn., 1952-53; Fulbright rsch. scholar U. Utrecht, Netherlands, 1956-57; vis. faculty U. Minn., 1953, UCLA, 1964, Johns Hopkins U., 1971, U. Wis., 1979, Williams Coll., 1980-92; lectr. on art, color theory and museology; chmn. Md. Arts Coun., 1967-68; chmn. Md. Revolutionary War Bicentennial Commn., 1968-70, Gov.'s Coun. on Arts in Md., 1966-68; trustee, officer Williamstown Regional Art Conservation Lab., 1983-90; ind. cons. Asian Art Mus., 1993-94. Contbr. articles to profl. jours. Commr. Nat. Mus. Am. Art, 1983-93; overseer Case Western Res. U., Cleve., 1982-86; trustee Amon Carter Mus., 1977-85, Hill-Stead Mus., Farmington, Conn., 1994—. With USNR, 1943-62. Decorated chevalier Legion d'Honneur de la République Française, 1947; recipient research grants Am. Council Learned Socs. and Am. Philos. Soc., 1961. Mem. Coll. Art Assn. (pres. 1958-60, bd. dirs.), Intermus. Conservation Assn. (co-founder), Assn. Art Mus. Dirs., Am. Assn. Mus. (pres. 1966-68, founder, mem. mus. accreditation com. 1970-76). Office: 33 Dana Pl Amherst MA 01002-2212

PARKIN, GERARD FRANCIS RALPH, chemistry educator, researcher; b. Middlesbrough, Cleveland, Eng., Feb. 15, 1959; s. Ralph and Clementine (Gill) P.; m. Rita K. Upmacis. BA with honors, Oxford (Eng.) U., 1981, MA, 1984, PhD, 1985. NATO/SERC (U.K.) postdoctoral rsch. fellow Calif. Inst. Tech., 1985-88; asst. prof. Columbia U., N.Y.C., 1988-91, assoc. prof., 1991-94; prof., 1994—. Contbr. more than 90 articles to profl. jours. Recipient Camille and Henry Dreyfus Tchr.-Scholar award, 1991, award in pure chemistry Am. Chem. Soc., 1994, Corday Morgan medal Royal Soc. Chemistry, 1995; A.P. Sloan rsch. fellow; NSF Presdl. faculty fellow, 1992—. Roman Catholic. Achievements include discovery that bond stretch isomerism in an artifact. Office: Columbia U 116th St And Broadway New York NY 10027

PARKIN, STUART S. P., materials scientist. Rsch. staff mem. IBM Almaden Rsch. Ctr., San Jose, Calif. Recipient Internat. prize for new materials Am. Phys. Soc., 1994, C.V. Boys prize Inst. Physics, London, 1991, Inaugural Outstanding Young Investigator award Materials Rsch. Soc., 1991. Office: IBM Almaden Rsch Ctr K11/D2 650 Harry Rd San Jose CA 95120-6099

PARKINS, FREDERICK MILTON, dental educator, university dean; b. Princeton, N.J., Sept. 8, 1935; s. William Milton and Phyllis Virginia (Plyler) P.; m. Carolyn V. Rude; children: Bradford, Christopher, Eric. Student, Carleton Coll., 1953-56; D.D.S., U. Pa., 1960; M.S.D. in Pedodontics, U. N.C., Chapel Hill, 1965; Ph.D. in Physiology, 1969. Instr. pedodontics U. N.C., 1965-67; asst. prof. pedodontics U. Pa., 1967-68, dir. Dental Aux. Utilization program, chmn. pedodontics, 1968-69; assoc. prof., head pedodontics U. Iowa, Iowa City, 1969-72; prof., head pedodontics U. Iowa, 1972-75; asst. dean acad. affairs U. Iowa (Coll. Dentistry), 1974-75, asso. dean acad. affairs, 1975-79, dir. continuing edn., 1975-77; prof. pedodontics, dean Sch. Dentistry, U. Louisville, 1979-85, prof. pediatric dentistry, 1985—; mem. Hillenbrand Fellowship adv. com. Am. Fund Dental Health, 1980-85; cons. Div. Dental Health USPHS, 1969-72; dental cons., med. staff Children's Hosp. Phila., 1968-71; med. staff Kosair Children's Hosp. Louisville, 1983—; cons., mem. pedodontic adv. com. Council Dental Edn., 1974-80, chmn. pedodontic adv. com., 1978-80, cons. council on legislation, 1978-79; dental cons. Aux. Utilization VA, 1968-69; cons. Bur. Health Resources Devel., 1974-76, Dept. Army, 1980—, numerous others. Assoc. editor: Jour. Preventive Dentistry, 1973-79; editorial bd., 1980-83; editorial reviewer: Jour. Pediatrics, 1969—, Jour. Dental Edn, 1978—, Jour. AMA, 1979—; asso. editor: Jour. Clin. Preventive Dentistry, 1979-84; Contbr. chpts. to textbooks, articles to profl. publs. Bd. govs. Youth Performing Arts Coun., Louisville-Jefferson County Sch. Dist., 1980-89, pres., 1986-88; bd. govs. Regional Cancer Ctr., U. Louisville, 1979-84, Univ. Hosp., 1979-84; mem. human studies com. U. Louisville, 1988-90. Robert Wood Johnson Congl. fellow Inst. of Medicine, 1977-78; USPHS postdoctoral fellow, 1963-67; NIH grantee, 1971-75; Recipient Earle Banks Hoyt Teaching award, 1969. Fellow AAAS, Am. Acad. Pediat. Dentistry (chmn. rsch. com. 1972-73, Ann. Rsch. award 1968, chmn. advanced edn. com. 1974-75, chmn. dental care programs com. 1978-80); mem. ADA, Am. Coll. Dentistry, Am. Soc. Dentistry for Children (exec. bd. Iowa unit 1969-75, award com. 1973-76, edn. com. 1974-77, chmn. rsch. adv. com. 1973-76), Biophys. Soc., Internat. Assn. Dental Rsch., N.Y. Acad. Dentistry, Key Dental Assn. (exec. bd. 1979-84), Am. Assn. Dental Schs. (coun. deans 1979-85, chmn. pedodontics sect. 1976, chmn. continuing edn. sect. 1979, legis. com. 1978-83), Louisville Dental Alumni Assn. (bd. govs. 1979-84), Am. Assn. Dental Rsch. (nat. affairs com. 1978-85), Acad. Laser Dentistry (vice-chmn. rsch. and edn. 1996, cert. com.), Southeastern Soc. Pediat. Dentistry, U.S. Power Squadron (bd. govs. 1987-93, sec. 1989, adminstrv. officer 1990, exec. officer 1991, comdr. 1992), Omicron Kappa Upsilon (pres. Wa. chpt. 1991-92), Louisville Boat Club, Rotary. Unitarian. Home: 6424 Marina Dr Prospect KY 40059-8846 Office:

U Louisville Sch Dentistry Dept Orthodontic Pediatric & Geriatric Denistry Rm 306 Louisville KY 40292

PARKINSON, ANDREW, communications executive; b. L.I., 1958. BA in Econs., Wesleyan U., 1980. Asst. brand mgr. Citrus Hill orange juice Procter & Gamble Co.'s, 1980-83; brand mgr., mgr. strategy and acquisitions, cheese divsn. Kraft Singles, 1983-87; mem. U.S. Board Sailing Team, 1987-89; pres. Peapod, Evanston, Ill., 1989—. Office: Peapod 1840 Oak Ave Evanston IL 60201*

PARKINSON, BRADFORD WELLS, aeronautical engineer, educator; b. Madison, Wis., Feb. 16, 1935; s. Herbert and Metta Tisdale (Smith) P.; m. Virginia Pinkham Wier, Nov. 26, 1977; children: Leslie, Bradford II, Eric, Ian, Bruce, Jared Bradford. BS, U.S. Naval Acad., 1957; MS, MIT, 1961; PhD, Stanford U., 1966. Commd. 2d lt. USAF, 1957, advanced through grades to col., 1972, ret., 1978; prof. mech. engring. Colo. State U., Ft. Collins, 1978-79; v.p. advanced engring. Rockwell Internat., Downey, Calif., 1979-80; gen. mgr., v.p. Intermetrics, Inc., Cambridge, Mass., 1980-84; prof., dir. gravity probe-B Stanford (Calif.) U., 1984—; chair adv. coun. NASA; dir. Trimble Navigation Ltd., Sunnyvale, Calif., Draper Lab., Cambridge. Decorated Bronze Star, Legion of Merit, Air medal with oak leaf cluster; recipient Thurlow award Inst. Navigation, 1986, Kepler award, 1991, von Karman Lectureship Am. Inst. of Aeronautics and Astronautics, 1996. Fellow AIAA, Royal Inst. Navigation (Gold medal 1983); mem. IEEE (Pioneer award 1994), AAS, NAE, Sigma Xi, Tau Beta Pi. Avocations: hiking, skiing, running. Home: 817 Santa Rita Rd Los Altos CA 94022-1131 Office: HEPL Stanford U Stanford CA 94305

PARKINSON, ETHELYN MINERVA, author; b. nr. Oconto, Wis., Sept. 13, 1906; d. James Nelson and Ethel Mabelle (Bigelow) P. Teaching certificate, County Normal Sch., Oconto Falls, Wis., 1923; R.N., Bellin Meml. Sch. Nursing, 1928. Author: Double Trouble for Rupert, 1958, Triple Trouble for Rupert, 1960, Good Old Archibald, 1960, The Merry Mad Bachelors, 1961, The Terrible Troubles of Rupert Piper, 1963, The Operation that Happened to Rupert Piper, 1966, Today I Am a Ham, 1968, Higgins of the Railroad Museum, 1970, Elf King Joe, 1970, Never Go Anywhere with Digby, 1971, Rupert Piper and Megan, the Valuable Girl, 1972, Rupert Piper and the Dear, Dear Birds, 1976 (Jr. Lit. Guild selection), Rupert Piper and the Boy Who Could Knit, 1979. Recipient Wis. Dramatic Soc. 1st place for playwriting, 1933; 1st place children's fiction Scholastic Book Services, 1957; Abingdon award, 1970; award of merit Wis. Hist. Soc., 1971. Republican. Presbyn. Address: 1031 Anderson Dr Green Bay WI 54304-5000 *I look at any success I may have had most humbly and most thankfully. I'm humble because I have a feeling that I haven't done things, but rather that things have happened to me. Perhaps that's because people have inspired and so helped me, all the way, children especially. I'm dedicated to giving as much happiness as I can to children, through my writing, and other ways. Childhood seems shorter now than ever, and when one of my stories makes children happy, makes them laugh, I am happy, too, and grateful.*

PARKINSON, GEORGINA, ballet mistress; b. Brighton, Eng., Aug. 20, 1938. Studied with Royal Ballet Sch. Mem. Royal Ballet, London, from 1955, soloist, from 1959, then prin.; ballet mistress Am. Ballet Theatre, N.Y.C., 1978—. Created roles in: La Belle Dame Sans Merci (Andree Howard), The Invitation (Kenneth MacMillan), Romeo and Juliet (Kenneth MacMillan), Mayerling (Kenneth MacMillan), The Concert (Jerome Robbins), Enigma Variations (Sir Frederick Ashton), Daphnis and Chloe (John Cranko), Everlast (Twyla Tharp). Office: care Am Ballet Theatre 890 Broadway New York NY 10003-1211

PARKINSON, JAMES THOMAS, III, investment consultant; b. Richmond, Va., July 10, 1940; s. James Thomas and Elizabeth (Hopkins) P.; m. Molly O Owens, June 16, 1962; children: James Thomas, Glenn Walser. BA, U. Va., 1962; MBA, U. Pa., 1964. Trainee Chem. Bank, N.Y.C., 1964-66; assoc., corp. fin. dept. Blyth & Co., Inc., N.Y.C., 1968-69; v.p., corp. fin. dept. Clark Dodge & Co., Inc., N.Y.C., 1969-74; pvt. practice investment mgmt., N.Y.C., 1974-85, 87—; v.p. Pleasantville Advisors, Inc., N.Y.C., 1986-87; instr. corp. fin. Ind. U., 1966-68. Sr. warden Ch. of Holy Trinity, N.Y.C., 1978-79; trustee Am. Bible Soc.; vestry Saint Thomas Ch., N.Y.C. With AUS, 1966-68. Republican. Episcopalian. Clubs: Univ., (N.Y.C.); Va. Country (Richmond). Office: 575 Madison Ave Ste 1006 New York NY 10022-2511

PARKINSON, JOSEPH L., electronics company executive, lawyer; b. San Antonio, Aug. 6, 1945; s. Douglas R. and Jane E. (Peck) P.; child by previous marriage, Jay Curtis. BA, Columbia Coll., 1967; JD, Tulane U., 1971; LLM in Taxation, NYU, 1972. Bar: La. 1971, Idaho 1975. Law clk. to judge U.S. Ct. Appeals (5th cir.), New Orleans, 1972-73; asst. prof. law Tulane U., New Orleans, 1973-74; cons. Baker & McKenzie, N.Y.C., 1974-75; asst. prof. law NYU, 1974-75; assoc. Moffatt, Thomas, Barrett & Blanton, Boise, Idaho, 1975-77; ptnr. Lloyd & Parkinson, Boise, 1978-80, Parkinson, Lojek & Penland, Boise, 1980-84; pres. Micron Tech., Inc., Boise, 1980-85, chmn., chief exec. officer, 1985—; now chmn., ceo 8x8, Santa Clara, CA; bd. dirs. Sematech, Austin, Tex., Standard Microsystems, Long Island, N.Y. Trustee Boise State U. Found., 1985—; bd. dirs. Idaho Health Facilities Authority, Boise, 1986—. Mem. Semiconductor Industry Assn. (bd. dirs. 1988—), Arid Club, Crane Creek Country Club. Avocations: hunting, fishing, skiing, ranching. Office: 8X8 2445 Mission College Blvd Santa Clara CA 95054*

PARKINSON, MARK VINCENT, state legislator, lawyer; b. Wichita, Kans., June 24, 1957; s. Henry Filson and Barbara Ann (Gilbert) Horton; m. Stacy Abbott, Mar. 7, 1983; children: Alex Atticus, Sam Filson, Kit Harlan. BA in Edn., Wichita State U., 1980; JD, Kans. U., 1984. Assoc. Payne and Jones Law Firm, Olathe, Kans., 1984-86; ptnr. Parkinson, Foth & Reynolds, Lenexa, Kans., 1986—; mem. Kans. Ho. Reps., 1990-92, Kans. Senate, 1993—. Mem. ABA, Johnson County Bar Found. (pres. 1993—), Kans. Bar Assn. Republican. Avocations: travel, running, movies. Office: Parkinson Foth & Reynolds 13628 W 95th St Lenexa KS 66215-3304

PARKINSON, RICHARD A., consumer products company executive. With First Security Bank, 1973-81, Rick Warner Ford, 1981-84; exec. v. pres., assistant gen. manager Assoc. Food Store Inc., Salt Lake City, 1984—; now pres., ceo. Office: Assoc Food Stores Inc 1850 W 2100 South Salt Lake City UT 84119-1304*

PARKINSON, THOMAS IGNATIUS, JR., lawyer; b. N.Y.C., Jan. 27, 1914; s. Thomas I. and Georgia (Weed) P.; AB, Harvard U., 1934; LLB, U. Pa., 1937; m. Geralda E. Moore, Sept. 23, 1937; children: Thomas Ignatius III, Geoffrey Moore, Cynthia Moore. Admitted to N.Y. bar, 1938, since practiced in N.Y.C.; assoc. Milbank, Tweed, Hope & Hadley, 1937-47, partner, 1947-56; pres. Mar Ltd., 1951—; pres. Breecom Corp., 1972-80, chmn. bd., 1980—; dir., exec. com. Pine St. Fund, Inc., N.Y.C., 1949-83, Trustee State Communities Aid Assn., 1949-83; dir. Fgn. Policy Assn., 1949-53; bd. dirs., exec. com. Milbank Meml. Fund, 1948-84. Mem. Am. Bar Assn., Assn. Bar City N.Y., Pilgrims U.S.A., Brit. War Relief Soc. (officer), Met. Unit Found., Phi Beta Kappa. Clubs: Down Town Assn., Knickerbocker, Union. Office: Windrove Svc Corp 780 3rd Ave Fl 25 New York NY 10017-2078

PARKINSON, WILLIAM CHARLES, physicist, educator; b. Jarvis, Ont., Can., Feb. 11, 1918; came to U.S., 1925, naturalized, 1941; s. Charles Franklin and Euphemia Alice (Johnston) P.; m. Martha Bennett Capron, Aug. 2, 1944; children: Martha Reed, William Reid. B.S.E., U. Mich., Ann Arbor, 1940, M.S., 1941, Ph.D., 1948. Physicist Applied Physics Lab., Johns Hopkins U., 1942-46, OSRD, 1943-44; mem. faculty U. Mich., 1947—, prof. physics, 1958-88, prof. emeritus physics, 1988—, dir. cyclotron lab., 1962-77; mem. subcom. nuclear structure NRC, 1959-68; mem. nuclear physics sub panel mgmt. and costs nuclear program, 1969-70; adv. panel physics NSF, 1966-69; cons. grad. sci. facilities, 1968, chmn. postdoctoral fellowship evaluation panel, 1969, cons. to govt. and industry, 1955—. Quondam mem. Trinity Coll., Cambridge, Eng. Recipient Ordnance Devel. award Navy Dept., 1946; Fulbright research scholar Cavendish Lab., Cambridge U., 1952-53. Fellow Am. Phys. Soc.; mem. N.Y. Acad. Scis., Biophys. Soc., Grad. "M" Club (awarded hon. "M" 1991), Sigma Xi, Phi Kappa Phi, Kappa Kappa Psi. Patentee in field. Home: 1600 Sheridan Dr Ann Arbor MI 48104-4052 Office: Univ Mich Dept Physics Ann Arbor MI 48109

PARKS, BEATRICE GRIFFIN, elementary school educator; b. Columbus, Miss., Jan. 3; d. James D. and Jimmie (McCottrell) Griffin; m. Orbia Ray Parks, Aug. 12, 1956 (div. May 1987); children: Donna Raye, Monica Lynn, David Griffin. BS in Edn., Lincoln U., Jefferson City, Mo., 1954. Elem. tchr. Cape Girardeau (Mo.) Pub. Schs., 1954-55, East St. Louis (Ill.) Bd. Edn., 1955-56; tchr. U.S. Army, Germany, 1956-57; elem. tchr. St. Louis Bd. Edn., 1960—, art specialist, 1980-94; floral designer Silk Expressions by Bea, St. Louis, 1991—; interior decorator Trans Designs, St. Louis, 1987-89. Arts chairperson Visual/Performing Arts Ctr., St. Louis, 1985-90; mem. Phyllis Wheatley YWCA. Recipient Svc. award Visual and Performing Arts Ctr., St. Louis, 1983-84, Art Excellence award, 1985-86. Mem. Nat. Art Edn. Assn., Mo. Art Edn. Assn., St. Louis Tchrs. Assn., Nat. Lincoln U. Alumni Assn., Greater St. Louis Lincoln U. Alumni Assn., Alpha Kappa Alpha (Founders award 1985, Arts and Heritage award 1988-89, Soror of Yr. 1992). United Ch. of Christ. Avocations: music, theater, writing. Home: 7192 White Oak Ln Saint Louis MO 63130-1816 Office: Silk Expressions by Bea PO Box 3087 Saint Louis MO 63130-0487

PARKS, DONALD LEE, mechanical engineer, human factors engineer; b. Delphos, Kans., Feb. 23, 1931; s. George Delbert and Erma Josephine (Boucek) P.; student Kans. Wesleyan U., 1948-50; BSME, Kans. State U., 1957, BS in Bus. Adminstrn., 1957, MS in Psychology, 1959; cert. profl. Ergonomist; m. Bessie Lou Schur, Dec. 24, 1952; children: Elizabeth Parks Anderson, Patricia Parks-Holbrook, Donna, Charles, Sandra. Elem. tchr., 1950-51; with Kans. State U. Placement Svc., 1957-59; human factors engr., systems engr. Boeing Co., Seattle, 1959-90, sr. specialist engr., 1972-74, sr. engring. supr., 1974-90; pres. D-Square Assocs. Engring. Cons., 1990—; adj. lectr. UCLA Engring. Extension, 1989—; cons., lectr. in field; participant workshops on guidelines in profl. areas, NATO, NSF, Nat. Acad. Sci., NRC. Mem. Derby (Kans.) Planning Commn., 1961-62, chmn., 1962; del. King County (Wash.) Republican Conv., 1972. With AUS, 1952-54. Mem. Human Factors Soc. (Puget Sound Pres.'s award 1969), Assn. Aviation Psychologists, ASME, Am. Psychol. Assn., Midwestern Psychol. Assn., Elks. Presbyterian. Contbr. over 80 articles to publs., chpts. to 8 books. Home: 6232 127th Ave SE Bellevue WA 98006-3943

PARKS, FREDRICK SCOTT, systems engineer; b. Phoenix, Ariz., Jan. 7, 1961; s. David Walker and Carrie Ellen (Abbott) P.; m. Kimberly Louise Kubeja, May 8, 1993. BS, Rensselaer Poly. Inst., 1982, MS, 1984. Rsch. material physicist DSM, Geleen, The Netherlands, 1982; sr. engr. analyst Anser Inc., Arlington, Va., 1983-93; sr. systems engr. Lockheed Missiles and Space Co., Inc., Sunnyvale, Calif., 1993-96; assoc. systems engr. Steven Myers & Assocs, Newport Beach, Calif., 1996—. Contbr. articles to profl. jours. Emergency Planning Coun. ARC, Arlington, 1985-92; EMT, 1990-91. Mem. AIAA, INCOSE, Am. Def. Preparedness Assn. Achievements include development of first detailed system architecture to enable multi-shot theater missile defense doctrine, development of Integrated Theater High Altitude Area Defense system architecture. Home: 663 S Bernardo Ave Ste M Sunnyvale CA 94087 Office: Steven Myers & Assocs 1301 Dove St Fl 7 Newport Beach CA 92660

PARKS, GEORGE RICHARD, librarian; b. Boston, Apr. 11, 1935; m. Carol A. Richmond; children: Elizabeth, Jennifer, Geoffrey. A.B. summa cum laude, U. N.H., 1959; M.A.L.S., U. Mich., 1962; postgrad., Johns Hopkins, 1959-65; EFM cert. Sch. Theology, U. of the South, 1985. Preprofl. young adult librarian Enoch Pratt Free Library, Balt., 1960-61; ctrl., br. librarian Enoch Pratt Free Library, 1962-65, asst. to asst. dir., 1965-66; asst. dir. for adminstrn., libraries U. Rochester, 1966-68, chief adminstrv. officer, 1968-69; dean of libraries U. R.I., 1969-80; univ. librarian Colgate U., 1980-85, U. So. Maine, Portland, 1985—; lectr. in field, cons. libr. bldg.; cons. antique map collection; mem. exec. bd. Greater Portland Theol. Libr., 1986-88, Maine Community Cultural Alliance, 1992—; mem. exec. bd. So. Maine Libr. Dist., 1990—, chmn., 1993. Apptd. Maine State Libr. Commn., 1994—. Recipient Margaret Mann award U. Mich., 1962; Phillips Exeter Acad. scholar, 1952-54; U. N.H. scholar, 1955-59; Johns Hopkins U. scholar, 1959-60; Enoch Pratt Free Library scholar, 1961-62. Mem. ALA, Assn. Coll. Rsch. Librs. (pres. New Eng. chpt. 1975, chmn. nat. conf. 1978, coll. librs. sect. planning com. 1994—), Consortium R.I. Acad. Rsch. Librs. (chmn. 1972-73), Maine Libr. Assn., New Eng. Libr. Assn. (conf. planning com. 1992—, v.p./pres. elect 1995—), Libr. Adminstrn. and Mgmt. Assn. (exec. bd. bldgs. and equipment sect., libr. bldg. awards com. 1983-85), Phi Beta Kappa, Phi Kappa Phi, Beta Phi Mu. Home: 4 Pierce St Westbrook ME 04092-2331 Office: U So Maine Libr PO Box 9301 314 Forest Ave Portland ME 04104-9301

PARKS, GORDON ROGER ALEXANDER BUCHANAN, film director, author, photographer, composer; b. Ft. Scott, Kans., Nov. 30, 1912; s. Jackson and Sarah (Ross) P.; m. Sally Alvis, 1933 (div. 1961); m. Elizabeth Campbell, 1962 (div. 1973); m. Genevieve Young, Aug. 26, 1973 (div. 1979); children by previous marriage: Gordon (dec.), Toni Parks Parsons, David, Leslie. Student pub. schs., Fort Scott, St. Paul; DFA (hon.), Md. Inst., 1968, Fairfield U., 1969; D (hon.), Boston U., 1969; LittD (hon.), Kans. State U., 1970; LHD (hon.), St. Olaf Coll., 1973; DFA (hon.), Colby Coll., 1974; DLit (hon.), MacAlester Coll., 1974; D (hon.), Lincoln U., 1975; HHD (hon.), Thiel Coll., 1976; DA (hon.), Columbia Coll., 1977; DFA (hon.), Rutgers U., 1980, Pratt Inst., 1981; LHD (hon.), Suffolk U., 1982; DFA (hon.), Kansas City Art Inst., 1984; LHD (hon.), Art Ctr. Coll. Design, 1986; DA (hon.), Hamline U., 1987; DFA (hon.), Am. Internat. Coll., 1988; HHD (hon.), Savannah Coll. Art and Design, 1988; D (hon.), U. Bradford, Eng., 1989; DFA (hon.), Rochester Inst. Tech., 1989, SUNY, 1990, R.I. Coll., 1990, Parsons Sch. Design, 1991, Manhattanville Coll., 1992, Coll. New Rochelle, 1992, Skidmore Coll., 1993; LittD (hon.), Montclair State U., 1994. Freelance fashion photographer Mpls., 1937-42; photographer Farm Security Adminstrn., 1942-43, OWI, 1944, Standard Oil Co., N.J., 1945-48, Life mag., 1948-68; ind. photographer, film maker, 1954—; color and black and white cons. various motion picture prodns., U.S. and Europe, 1954—. Writer, producer, dir.: The Learning Tree, 1969; dir.: (films) Shaft, 1972, Shaft's Big Score, 1972, The Super Cops, 1974, Leadbelly, 1976, Odyssey of Solomon Northup, 1984, Moments Without Proper Names, 1986 (Silver medal Internat. Film Festival 1989); creator, composer, dir. Martin, 1990; TV documentary: Diary of a Harlem Family, 1968 (Emmy award); author: Flash Photography, 1947, Camera Portraits: The Techniques and Principals of Documentary Portraiture, 1948, The Learning Tree, 1963, A Choice of Weapons, 1966 (Notable Book award ALA 1966), A Poet and His Camera, 1968, Whispers of Intimate Things, 1971, Born Black, 1971, In Love, 1971, (poetry) Moments Without Proper Names, 1975, Flavio, 1977 (Christopher award 1978), To Smile in Autumn, 1979, (novel) Shannon, 1981, Voices in the Mirror, 1990, (photography, paint and poetry) Arias in Silence, 1994; founder, editorial dir. Essence mag., 1970-73; composer Piano Concerto, 1953, Tree Symphony, 1967, 3 piano sonatas, 1956, 58, 60, modern works for piano and wind instruments, (film scores) The Learning Tree (Libr. Congress Nat. Film Registry Classics film honor, 1989), Shaft's Big Score, The Odyssey of Solomon Northup, Moments Without Proper Names; dir., composer (film) Ballet for Martin Luther King, 1991; poetry: Gordon Parks: A Poet and His Camera, Gordon Parks: Whispers of Intimate Things, In Love, Moments Without Proper Names; traveling exhibits in U.S. and abroad, 1990. Bd. dirs. Schomburg Ctr. for Research in Black Culture, Am. Arts. Alliance, W. Eugene Smith Meml. Fund, Black Tennis and Sports Found., Rondo Ave. Inc., St. Paul; Harlem Symphony Orch., N.Y.C.; mem. adv. com. Kans. Ctr. for the Book; bd. advocates Planned Parenthood Fedn. Am. Inc.; patron N.Y. City Housing Authority Symphony; supporter Apple Corps Theatre, N.Y.C., Quindaro Project, Kans., numerous other civic activities. Decorated Comdr. de l'Ordre des Arts et des Lettres (Republique Francaise); recipient Julius Rosenwald award for photography, 1942, award NCCJ, 1964, awards Syracuse U. Sch. Journalism, 1961, Newhouse citation Syracuse U., 1963, awards Phila. Mus. Art, 1964, awards N.Y. Art Dirs. Club, 1964, 68, Frederic W. Brehm award, 1962, Carr Van Anda Journalism award Ohio U., 1970, Carr Van Anda Journalism award U. Miami, 1964, Pres.'s fellow award R.I. Sch. Design, 1984, Am. Soc. Mag. Photographers award, 1985, Nat. Medal Arts award Commonwealth Mass. Communications, 1988, Kans. Gov.'s medal, 1986, Nat. medal of Arts, 1988, World Press Photo awa, 1988, N.Y.C. Mayor's award, 1989, Artist of Merit Josef Sudek medal, 1989, award Internat. Ctr. Photography, 1990; named Kansan of Yr. Sons and Daus. Kans., 1985. Mem. Urban League N.Y., ASCAP, Writers Guild, NAACP (Spingarn award 1972, Hall of Fame 1984), Acad. Motion Pictures Arts and Scis., AFTRA, Am. Inst. Pub. Service, Nat. Urban League Guild, Internat. Mark Twain Soc. (hon.), Newspaper Guild, Assn. Composers and Dirs., Dirs. Guild (nat. dir.), Dirs. Guild N.Y., Am. Soc. Mag. Photographers (Photographer of Yr. award 1960, 85), Nat. Assn. for Am. Coposers and Condrs., Stylus Soc. (hon.), U.S. Tennis Assn. Inc., Am. film Inst.Kappa Alpha Mu. Clubs: Pen; Black Tennis and Sports Found. (bd. dirs.). Home: 860 United Nations Plz New York NY 10017-1810

PARKS, HAROLD FRANCIS, anatomist, educator; b. Anna, Ill., Sept. 28, 1920; s. Guy Clay and Margaret (McCumiskey) P.; m. Margaret Bryner, Sept. 11, 1948; children—Edwin Thomas, Margaret Caroline. B.Ed., So. Ill. U., 1942; Ph.D., Cornell U., 1950. Tchr. music Martinsville (Ill.) High Sch., 1942; asst. band dir. Cornell U., 1942-43, dir. bands, 1943-46, teaching asst. comparative anatomy and histology and embryology, 1945-50, prof. zoology, 1961-64; instr., then asst. prof. anatomy U. N.C. Med. Sch., 1950-54; asst. prof., then assoc. prof. anatomy U. Rochester Sch. Medicine and Dentistry, 1954-61; prof. anatomy U. Ky. Med. Center, 1964-91, chmn. dept., 1964-79; vis. scientist Karolinska Inst., 1956; Exec. com. Ky.-Mich.-Ohio Regional Med. Library Program. Mem. AAAS, Am. Inst. Biol. Scis., Am. Assn. Anatomists (com. on status of women in anatomy 1978-80), Am. Soc. Cell Biology, Electron Microscopy Soc. Am., Am. Soc. Zoologists, So. Soc. Anatomists (council 1968-69), Assn. Anatomy Chmn. (council 1971-72), Sigma Xi, Omicron Kappa Upsilon (hon.), Phi Kappa Phi. Home: 837 Cahaba Rd Lexington KY 40502-3318

PARKS, HAROLD RAYMOND, mathematician, educator; b. Wilmington, Del., May 22, 1949; s. Lytle Raymond Jr. and Marjorie Ruth (Chambers) P.; m. Paula Sue Beaulieu, Aug. 21, 1971 (div. 1984); children: Paul Raymond, David Austin; m. Susan Irene Taylor, June 6, 1985; 1 stepchild, Kathryn McLaughlin. AB, Dartmouth Coll., 1971; PhD, Princeton U., 1974. Tamarkin instr. Brown U., Providence, 1974-77; asst. prof. Oreg. State U., Corvallis, 1977-82, assoc. prof., 1982-89, prof. math., 1989—; vis. assoc. prof. Ind. U., Bloomington, 1982-83. Author: Explicit Determination of Area Minimizing Hypersurfaces, vol. II, 1986, (with Steven G. Krantz) A Primer of Real Analytic Functions, 1992; contbr. articles to profl. publs. Cubmaster Oregon Trail Coun. Boy Scouts Am., 1990-92. NSF fellow, 1971-74. Mem. Am. Math. Soc., Math. Assn. Am., Soc. Indsl. and Applied Math., Phi Beta Kappa. Republican. Mem. Soc. of Friends. Home: 33194 Dorset Ln Philomath OR 97370-9555 Office: Oreg State U Dept Math Corvallis OR 97331-4605

PARKS, JAMES WILLIAM, II, public facilities executive, lawyer; b. Wabash, Ind., July 30, 1956; s. James William and Joyce Arlene (Lillibridge) P.; m. Neil Ann Armstrong, Aug. 21, 1982; children: Elizabeth Joyce, Helen Frances, James William III. BS, Ball State U., 1978; JD, U. Miami, 1981. Bar: La. 1981, Fla. 1982, U.S. Dist. Ct. (ea. dist.) La. 1981, U.S. Dist. Ct. (mid. dist.) La. 1982, U.S. Ct. Appeals (5th cir. and 11th cir.) 1981. Atty. Jones, Walker, Waechter, Poitevent, Carrere et al., New Orleans, 1981-83, Foley & Judell, New Orleans, 1983-88, McCollister & McCleary, pc, Baton Rouge, 1988-96; exec. dir. La. Pub. Facilities Authority, Baton Rouge, 1996—; adv. bd. Progressive Healthcare Providers, Inc., Atlanta, 1994—. Mem. AICPA, Nat. Assn. Bond Lawyers, La. State Bar Assn., Fla. Bar Assn., Assn. for Gifted and Talented Students, Baton Rouge (treas. 1994-96), Soc. La. CPA (govt. acctg. and auditing com. 1994-95). Avocations: travel, computers. Home: 5966 Tennyson Dr Baton Rouge LA 70817-2933 Office: La Pub Facilities Authority Ste 650 2237 S Acadian Thruway Baton Rouge LA 70808

PARKS, JESSICA L., federal agency administrator; b. Chattanooga, Feb. 4, 1953; d. Jesse C., Jr. and Mary Louise (Fox) P.; m. Edgar M. Swindell, Jan. 12, 1980; children: Allison Parks, Catherine Parks. Student, U. Ga., 1970-72; BA cum laude, Tulane U., 1974; JD, U. Tenn., 1980. Bar: N.C. 1980, U.S. Dist. Ct. (ea. dist.) N.C., U.S. Ct. Appeals (6th cir.). Law clk. to chief counsel George C. Marshall Space Flight Ctr., NASA, Huntsville, Ala.; pvt. practice, 1980-81; assoc. Bowers & Sledge, New Bern, N.C.; agy. counsel Craven County N.C. Dept. Social Svcs., 1981-82; adminstrv. judge U.S. Merit Systems Protection Bd., Washington, 1982-85, bd. mem., 1990-93, vice chmn., 1993—; assoc. regional counsel Office of Gen. Counsel, Dept. Housing and Urban Devel., 1985-90. Office: Kator Scott & Heller Ste 950 1275 K St NW Washington DC 20005

PARKS, JOE BENJAMIN, state legislator; b. McAlester, Okla., Dec. 17, 1915; s. James Allen and Mary Florence (Youngblood) P.; m. Florence M. Evans, Oct. 25, 1941; children: Anne, Kathryn. BS in Pub. Adminstrn., Okla. State U., 1939. Div. dir. U.S. VA, Washington, 1946-56; spl. asst., cons. U.S. GSA, Washington, 1957-58; mgr. dist. EDP div. RCA Corp., Washington, 1959-65; mgr. Ea. region Dashew Bus. Machines, Arlington, Va., 1966-68; assoc. adminstr. social and rehab. svc. U.S. Dept. Health, Edn. & Welfare, Washington, 1969-73; dir. mktg. govt. systems div. Booz, Allen & Hamilton, Washington, 1974-75; ptnr. Forbes & Parks, Dover, N.H., 1976—; mem. N.H. State Legislature, Concord, 1985-92, chmn. joint com. on elderly affairs, 1987-92; mem. com. on health, human svcs. and elderly N.H. State Legislature, 1987-90; chmn. subcom. mileage and electronic roll call, 1989-90, vice chmn. legis. adminstrn. com., 1990-91, mem. appropriations com., 1991-92; proprietor Portsmouth (N.H.) Athenaeum, 1992—; corporator Wentworth Douglas Hosp., Dover, 1980-89; pres. Berr Par, Inc., 1994—. Columnist Nat. Antiques Rev., 1975-77, Boston Globe N.H. Weekly 1987-88, Foster's Daily Democrat (Dover, N.H.), 1988-90; freelance writer, 1990—. Vice chmn. N.H. State Rep. Com., 1987-88; chmn. Strafford County Reps., 1988. Decorated Bronze Star. Congregationalist. Avocation: rhododendron hybridizing. Home and Office: 195 Long Hill Rd Dover NH 03820-6108

PARKS, JOHN MORRIS, metallurgist; b. Lafayette, Ind., July 16, 1917; s. Morris Randlette and Ruby Mildred (Beeker) P.; m. Martha Mac Elhose, June 8, 1944 (dec. Mar. 1978); children: Lorinda Ruth Parks Wiggins, Sarah Ann, Victoria Parks Nice, Daniel Sandford. B Chem. Engring. with distinction, Purdue U., 1939; M. Metall. Engring., Rensselaer Poly. Inst., 1941, PhD, 1942. Registered profl. engr., Ohio. Instr. metallurgy Rensselaer Poly. Inst., Troy, N.Y., 1939-45; editor Am. Soc. Metals, Cleve., 1945-46; supr. welding rsch. Armour Rsch. Found., Chgo., 1946-53; mgr. materials rsch. Air Reduction Co., Murray Hill, N.J., 1953-56; head sci. dept. Lincoln Electric Co., Euclid, Ohio, 1956—. Achievements include 99.98% ductile rod for making welding electrode, innershield welding electrode; computer programs for solidification temperatures of cast and weld metal; thermodynamic calculations (precision to 7 significant figures); metallographic and impact properties of weld metal and its relationship to solidification structure of steel; surface tension transfer welder. Home: 5151 Som Center Rd Solon OH 44139-1455 Office: Lincoln Electric Co 22801 Saint Clair Ave Euclid OH 44117-2524

PARKS, JULIA ETTA, retired education educator; b. Kansas City, Kans., Apr. 5, 1923; d. Hays and Idella Long; BEd, Washburn U., 1959, MEd, 1965; EdD, U. Kans., 1980; m. James A. Parks, Aug. 10, 1941; 1 child, James Hays. Tchr., concert vocalist, tchr. Lowman Hill Elem. Sch., 1959-64; faculty Washburn U., Topeka, Kans., 1964-93, prof. edn. 1981-92, mem. pres.'s adv. council, 1981-84, chair edn., phys. edn., health and recreation div., multicultural com., dept. edn., 1986-92; insvc. lectr. reading instrns. Kans. Pub. Schs., 1960-93; lectr. Topeka Pub. Schs. Mem. acad. sabbatical com., Washburn U., 1987-90, vis. teams Nat. Council for Accreditation of Tchr. Edn., 1974-86, prof. emeritus, 1993. Bd. dirs. Children's Hour, 1981-84, Mulvane Art Ctr., 1974-78; judge, All Kans. Spelling Bees, 1982-86; sec. Brown Decision Sculpture Com., 1974-85; oral record account of experiences as a miniority student in integrated Topeka High Sch., 1984. Mem. multicultural non-sexist com. Topeka Pub. Sch., 1967—; apptd. to Kans. Equal Edn. Opportunities Adv. Com., 1988; marshall Washburn U. Commencements, 1980-92; mem. State of Kans. Task Force in Edn., 1991-92; presenter in field. Designer stained glass windows for Ikenoue Christ Ch., Tokyo, 1995. Recipient Educator's award Living the Dream com., Local award for Excellence and Equity in Edn., The Brown Found.; named to Topeka High Sch. Hall of Fame, 1991; The Julia Etta Parks Honor Award created in her honor, Edn. Dept. Washburn Univ. Mem. Kans. Intergenerational Network, Washburn U. Alumni Assn. (contbr. alumni mag. 1989, recipient Teaching

Excellence award 1983), Internat. Reading Assn., Kans. Inst. Higher Edn. (mem. pres. adv. council, 1981-83), Kans. Reading Assn., Kans. Reading Profls. Higher Edn., Topeka High Sch. Hist. Soc., Links Club (pres. 1982-84, chairperson scholarship com. 1984-93, Topeka Back Home Reunion Club (historian, v.p. 1991—), Delta Kappa Gamma, Phi Delta Kappa, NONOSO Women's Hon. Sorority. Methodist. Office: Washburn U Dept Edn 1700 SW College Ave Topeka KS 66621-0001

PARKS, LLOYD LEE, oil company executive; b. Kiefer, Okla., Dec. 9, 1929; s. Homer Harrison and Avis Pearl (Motes) P.; m. Mary Ellen Scott, Aug. 20, 1948; children: Connie Jo, Karyn Ann, Rebecca Lee. Student, Okla. State U., 1948-50, Tulsa U., 1950-51, Harvard U. Bus. Sch., 1965. Acct. Deep Rock Oil Corp., 1951-54; chief acct. Blackwell Oil & Gas Co., Tulsa, 1954-60; sec. treas. Blackwell Oil & Gas Co., 1960-62; v.p., controller Amax Oil & Gas Inc., Houston, 1962-67, pres., CEO, 1968—92; v.p. Amax, Inc., 1975-92; pvt. practice oil and gas and real estate imvestment Salado, Tex., 1992—. Served with AUS, 1946-48, 50-51. Mem. Ind. Petroleum Assn. Am. (dir.), Mill Creek Country Club, Wildflower Country Club (Temple, Tex.), Lions Club. Republican. Office: PO Box 1021 Salado TX 76571-1021 *Work hard, work smart and believe in yourself. You can and will be successful; if you want to be.*

PARKS, MADELYN N., nurse, retired army officer, university official; b. Jordan, Okla., Diploma, Corpus Christi (Tex.) Sch. Nursing, 1943; B.S.N., Incarnate Word Coll., San Antonio, 1961; M.H.A. in Health Care Adminstrn, Baylor U., 1965. Commd. 2d lt. Army Nurse Corps, 1943, advanced through grades to brig. gen., 1975; basic tng. Fort Meade, Md., 1944; staff nurse eye ward Valley Forge (Pa.) Gen. Hosp., 1944; served in India, Iran, Italy, 1944-45; gen. duty staff nurse Fort Polk, La., 1951; nurse eye clinic Tripler Army Med. Center, Hawaii, 1951-54; staff nurse eye, ear, nose and throat ward Brooke Army Med. Center, San Antonio, 1954-57; edn!. coordinator Fort Dix, N.J., 1957-58; instr., supr. enlisted med. tng. U.S. Army Med. Tng. Center, Fort Sam Houston, Tex., 1959-61; chief nurse surg. field hosp. 62d Med. Group, Germany, 1961-62, sr. nurse coordinator, 1962-63; adminstrn. resident Letterman Gen. Hosp., San Francisco, 1964-65; dir. clin. specialist course Letterman Gen. Hosp., 1965-67; chief nurse 85th Evacuation Hosp., Qui Nhon, Vietnam, 1967-68; asst. chief nursing sci. div., asst. prof. Med. Field Service Sch., U.S. Army-Baylor U. Program in Health Care Adminstrn., 1968-72; chief nurse surgeons office Hdqrs. Continental Army Command, Fort Monroe, Va., 1972-73; chief dept. nursing Walter Reed Army Med. Center, Washington, 1973-75; chief Army Nurse Corps, Office of Surgeon Gen., Dept. Army, Washington, 1975-79; ret. Army Nurse Corps, Office of Surgeon Gen., Dept. Army, 1979; faculty assoc. adminstr. U. Md., 1974-78. Decorated D.S.M., Army Commendation medal with 2 oak leaf clusters, Legion of Merit, Meritorious Service medal; recipient Alumna of Distinction award Incarnate Word Coll., 1981. Mem. Ret. Officers Assn., AMEDD Mus. Found. Address: 5211 Metcalf San Antonio TX 78239-1933

PARKS, MICHAEL CHRISTOPHER, journalist; b. Detroit, Nov. 17, 1943; s. Robert James and Rosalind (Smith) P.; m. Linda Katherine Durocher, Dec. 26, 1964; children: Danielle Anne, Christopher, Matthew. AB, U. Windsor, Ont., Can., 1965. Reporter Detroit News, 1962-65; corr. Time-Life News Service, N.Y.C., 1965-66; asst. city editor Suffolk Sun, Long Island, N.Y., 1966-68; polit. reporter, foreign corr. The Balt. Sun, Saigon, Singapore, Moscow, Cairo, Hong Kong, Peking, 1968-80; fgn. corr. L.A. Times, L.A., Peking, Johannesburg, Moscow, Jerusalem, 1980-95, dpty. fgn. editor, 1995-96; mng. editor, 1996—. Recipient Pulitzer Prize, 1987. Mem. Royal Commonwealth Soc. London, Soc. Profl. Journalists, Fgn. Corr. Club (Hong Kong). Office: L A Times Times Mirror Sq Los Angeles CA 90012

PARKS, PATRICIA JEAN, lawyer; b. Portland, Oreg., Apr. 2, 1945; d. Robert and Marion (Crosby) P.; m. David F. Jurca, Oct. 17, 1971 (div. 1976). BA in History, Stanford U., 1963-67; JD, U. Penn., Phila., 1967-70. Bar: N.Y. 1971, Wash. 1974. Assoc. Milbank, Tweed, Hadley & McCoy, N.Y.C., 1970-73; assoc. Shidler, McBroom, Gates & Lucas, Seattle, 1974-81, ptnr., 1981-90; ptnr. Preston, Thorgrimson, Shidler, Gates & Ellis, Seattle, 1990-93; pvt. practice Seattle, 1993—. Active Vashon Allied Arts, Mountaineers, N.W. Women's Law Ctr., Wash. State Women's Polit. Caucus. Mem. NOW, ABA, Wash. State Bar Assn. (past pres. tax sect., past chair gift and estate tax com.), Washington Women in Tax, Washington Women Lawyers, Seattle-King County Bar Assn., Employee Stock Ownership Plan Assn., Western Pension Conf., Pension Roundtable, Wash. Athletic Club. Avocations: kayaking, hiking, Contra dancing, bird watching. Office: 1301 5th Ave Ste 3800 Seattle WA 98101-2603

PARKS, PAUL, corporate executive; b. Indpls., May 7, 1923; s. Cleab Jiles and Hazel (Crenshaw) P.; m. Virginia Loftman, Sept. 18, 1971; children: Paul, Pamela, Stacey. BS in Civil Engring., Purdue U., 1949; postgrad., MIT, 1958, U. Mass.; DEng, Northeastern U., 1994. Registered profl. engr., Mass. With Ind. State Hwy. Commn., Indpls., 1949-51; designer Stone & Webster Engring., Boston, 1951, Fay, Spofford & Thorndike, Boston, 1951-52; missile designer Chance Vought Aircraft, Boston, 1952-53; nuclear engr. Pratt & Whitney Aircraft, Boston, 1953-57; pntr. architecture and engring. firm, Boston, 1957-67; adminstr. Boston Model City Adminstrn., 1968-76; sec. ednl. affairs Commonwealth of Mass., Boston, 1976—; pres. Paul Parks and Assocs. Inc., Boston, 1979—; lectr. Tufts U. Sch. Civil Engring., 1968—; mem. northeastern regional bd. Fannie Mae, 1994—; corp. mem. Ptnrs. Healthcare Coop. Cons. gen. acctg. office Mayor's Com. Adminstrn. Justice; mem. Atty. Gen.'s Adv. Com. Civil Rights, 1969-71; mem. health task force Boston Fed. Exec. Bd.; adviser Boston Mothers for Adequate Welfare, 1966-68; speech therapist Vets. Lang. Clinic, Mass. Gen. Hosp., 1964-66; mem. Mass. Adv. Coun. on Edn., 1968-71, Mass. Com. Children and Youth, 1962-67; chmn. Mass. adv. com. to U.S. Civil Rights Commn., 1961-73; chmn. urban affairs com. Mass. Fedn. Fair Housing and Equal Rights, 1961-67; mem. Community Ednl. Coun., 1961-73; pres. Com. for Community Ednl. Devel. Inc., 1968-74; presdl. adv. commn. Nat. Coun. Ednl. Programs for Women, 1976-81; pres. Boston Pub. Libr.; mem. zoning bd. appeals City of Boston; adult leader youth programs Roxbury YMCA, 1951-58; trustee Brigham Hosp., Women's Hosp.; bd. dirs. Mass. Planned Parenthood Assn., Mass. Mental Health Assn., Mass. Soc. Prevention Blindness, Boston Coll. Upward Bound Program; chmn. sch. com. City of Boston, 1992—; mem. regional adv. coun. Fannie Mae. Served with AUS, 1943-46, ETO, PTO. Mem. ASCE, NSPE, NAACP (co-chmn. edn. com. 1960-68, v.p. Boston br. 1965-70), Nat. Acad. Pub. Adminstrn., Ams. Dem. Action (nat. bd. 1971-74, state bd. 1970-74), Greater Boston C. of C. (edn. com.). Mem. United Ch. of Christ (mem. nat. social action bd. 1963-68). Home: 78 Woodhaven St Mattapan MA 02126-1730 Office: 100 Boylston St Ste 815 Boston MA 02116-4610

PARKS, ROBERT EMMETT, JR., medical science educator; b. Glendale, N.Y., July 29, 1921; s. Robert Emmett and Carolyn M. (Heinemann) P.; m. Margaret Ellen Ward, June 15, 1945; children: Robert Emmett III, Walter Ward, Christopher Carr. AB, Brown U., 1944; MD, Harvard U., 1945; PhD, U. Wis., 1954. Intern Boston's Children's Hosp., 1945-46; rsch. assoc. Amherst (Mass.) Coll., 1948-51; postdoctoral fellow Enzyme Inst., Madison, Wis., 1951-54; mem. faculty U. Wis. Med. Sch., 1954-63, prof. pharmacology, 1961-63; prof. med. sci. Brown U., Providence, 1963-91, prof. emeritus, 1991—, dir. grad. program in pharmacology and exptl. pathology, 1978-81, chmn. sect. biochem. pharmacology, 1963-78, 83-91; cons. in field. Contbr. articles to profl. jours. With AUS, 1943-45, 46-48. Acad. medicine scholar John and Mary Markle Found., 1956-61. Mem. Am. Soc. Pharmacology and Exptl. Therapeutics, Am. Soc. Biol. Chemists, Am. Assn. Cancer Rsch. (bd. dirs. 1982-86), Sigma Xi. Home: 62 Alumni Ave Providence RI 02906-2310 Office: Brown U 429 Biomed Ctr Providence RI 02912

PARKS, ROBERT HENRY, consulting economist, educator; b. New Orleans, Sept. 20, 1924; s. Charles Samuel and Amelia (England) P.; m. Inta Kondrats, Sept. 20, 1958; children: Karen E., Robert R., Alison J.; m. Annette Fiechter, Dec. 10, 1982 (div.). A.B. in Econs., Swarthmore Coll., 1949; M.A., Ph.D. in Econs., U. Pa., 1958. Economist Econ. Forecasting div. Gen. Electric Co., 1958-61; dir. econ. research Life Ins. Assn. Am., 1961-68; chief economist Maj. Wall St. Investment Firms, 1968-80; pres. Robert H. Parks & Assocs., Inc., N.Y.C., 1980—; cons. to instnl. investment officers; prof. fin., dir. Inst. Internat. Fin. Pace U., Wharton Sch. (U. Pa.), Baruch (CUNY); prof. fin. Lehigh U. Author: The Witch Doctor of Wall Street, 1996; contbr. articles to profl. jours. Democrat. Home and Office: 31 Sherwood Rd Short Hills NJ 07078-2038

PARKS, R(OBERT) KEITH, missionary, religious organization administrator; b. Memphis, Tex., Oct. 23, 1927; s. Robert Crews and Allie Myrtle (Cowger) P.; m. Helen Jean Bond, May 24, 1952; children: Randall, Kent, Eloise, Stanley. BA, U. North Tex., 1948; BD, Southwestern Bapt. Theol. Sem., 1951, ThD, 1955; LittD (hon.), Hardin-Simmons U., 1976; D Missions (hon.), Calif. Bapt. Coll., 1980; STD (hon.), S.W. Bapt. Coll., Bolivar, Mo., 1981; DD (hon.), U. Richmond, 1987; HHD (hon.), Mercer U., 1992. Ordained to ministry So. Bapt. Conv., 1950. Pastor Red Springs (Tex.) Bapt. Ch., 1950-54; instr. Bible Hardin-Simmons U., Abilene, Tex., 1953-54; missionary Fgn. Mission Bd., So. Bapt. Conv., Indonesia, 1954-68; area dir. S.E. Asia Fgn. Mission Bd., So. Bapt. Conv., Richmond, Va., 1968-75, dir. div. mission support, 1975-79, pres., 1980-92; global missions coord. Coop. Bapt. Fellowship, Atlanta, 1993—; mem., past chmn. Inter-Agy. Coun., So. Bapt. Conv., 1980-92; trustee Bapt. Joint Com. on Pub. Affairs, Washington, 1980-91. Author: Crosscurrents, 1966, World in View, 1987; also numerous articles. Recipient Disting. Alumnus award Southwestern Bapt. Theol. Sem., 1980, U. North Tex., 1991, E.Y. Mullins Denominational Svc. award So. Bapt. Theol. Sem., 1989. Office: Coop Bapt Fellowship PO Box 450329 Atlanta GA 31145-0329

PARKS, ROBERT MYERS, appliance manufacturing company executive; b. Nevada, Mo., July 18, 1927; s. Cecil R. and Marcella (Myers) P.; m. Audrey Lenora Jones, June 18, 1955; children—John Robert, Janet M. Parks Huston. B.S., U. Mo., 1949; M.B.A., Harvard, 1952. Asst. dept. mgr. Jewett & Sherman Co., Kansas City, Mo., 1949-50; staff cons. Harbridge House, Inc., Boston, 1952; v.p. Electronic Splty. Co., Inc., Los Angeles, 1952-57; pres. Parks Products, Inc., Hollywood, Calif., 1957—, Generalist Industries, Inc., Hollywood, 1960-73; chmn. bd. Shaver Corp. Am., Los Angeles, 1965—; lectr. mktg. UCLA Extension div., 1960-61. Contbr. articles on mktg. and bus. mgmt. to profl. publs.; patentee in field. Active YMCA; bd. dirs. Hollywood Presbyn. Med. Center Found.; mem. dean's adv. council U. Mo. Bus. Sch., mayor's task force on L.A. River Cahuenga Pass Coalition. Served with USNR, 1944-45. Mem. Sales and Marketing Execs. Assn., C. of C., Navy League, World Affairs Council, Calif. Caballeros, Rangers, Vaqueros del Desierto, Los Caballeros, Rancheros Visitadores, E Clampus Vitus, Delta Sigma Pi, Sigma Chi. Presbyn. Clubs: Mason (Shriner), Los Angeles Breakfast, Braemar Country, Saddle and Sirloin. Home: 7421 Woodrow Wilson Dr Los Angeles CA 90046-1322 Office: 3611 Cahuenga Blvd Hollywood CA 90068-1205

PARKS, SALLIE ANN, county official, public relations executive, marketing professional; b. Detroit, Sept. 5, 1936; d. Bert A. Rennie and Edna V. (Lampman) Moran; m. Donald K. Parks, Aug. 22, 1959 (div. 1983); children: Sheri Lynn, Steven Rennie; m. Alden Matthews, Apr. 4, 1996. BA, Cen. Mich. U., 1959; postgrad., Mich. State U., 1962. Cert. accredited pub. relations profl. Editor Pinellas Classroom Tchrs. Assn., Clearwater, Fla., 1967-73; sub. tchr. Pinellas County Schs., Fla., 1972-74; real estate mgmt. Clearwater, 1971-74, bus. mgr., 1974-76; exec. dir. Pinellas County Arts Coun., Clearwater, 1976-81; dir. community relations Mease Health Care, Dunedin, Fla., 1981-86; pub. relations cons., tchr. Tokyo, Japan, 1986-87; dir. pub. rels. and mktg. Mease Health Care, Dunedin, 1987-92; county commr. Pinellas County, Clearwater, Fla., 1992-96, chairwoman, 1996; chair long term care subcom. Nat. Assn. Counties; bd dirs. Fla. Assn. Counties; chair Dist. V Juvenile Justice Bd.; mem. Met. Planning Orgn. Pinellas County, Pinellas County Arts Coun., Juvenile Welfare Bd. Pinellas County, Cmty. Health Purchasing Alliance Dist. V, Tampa Bay Regional Planning Coun. Area Agy. on Aging and Long Term Care subcom., Pinellas County Juvenile Boot Camp Task Force, Success by Six Task Force. Pres. Am. Heart Assn., Suncoast chpt., Clearwater, 1990-92; vice chairperson Clearwater Pub. Libr. Found., 1989; pres. LWV, Clearwater, 1972, PEO Sisterhood, Clearwater, 1975; trustee Pinellas Marine Inst. Recipient Athena award, Women in Communications, 1983, Leadership in the Arts award, Soroptimist Internat., 1980. Mem. Nat. Press Women, Fla. Pub. Rels. Assn. (past pres.). Republican. Presbyterian. Avocations: travel, theatre, music. Office: Office Bd Commrs 315 Court St Clearwater FL 34616-5165

PARKS, STEPHEN ROBERT, curator; b. Columbus, Ohio, July 18, 1940. BA, Yale U., 1961; PhD, Cambridge U., U.K., 1964. Assoc. curator James Marshall and Marie-Louise Osborn Collection, 1967—. Author: Sale Catalogues of Libraries of Eminent Persons, 1972, John Dunton and the English Book Trade: A Study of his Career with a Checklist of his Publications, 1975, The Elizabethan Club of Yale University and its Library, 1986, (with P.J. Croft) English Literary Autographs, 1984; editor Yale U.L. Gazette, 1980—; contbr. articles to profl. jours. Postdoctoral fellow U. Edinburgh, 1964-67. Home: 248 Bradley St New Haven CT 06510 Office: Beinecke Libr Yale U PO Box 208240 New Haven CT 06520

PARKS, THOMAS W., electrical engineering educator, consultant; b. Buffalo, Mar. 16, 1939; s. William K. and Mildred (Walzer) P.; m. Martha B., May 4, 1963; children: Alice J., Thomas M., Susan E. B.E.E., Cornell U., 1961, M.S., 1964, Ph.D., 1967. Co-op. engr. Cornell Aero Lab., Buffalo, 1958-61; elec. engr. Gen. Electric Advanced Electronics Center, Ithaca, N.Y., 1961-63; asst. prof. elec. engring. dept. Rice U., Houston, 1967-72, assoc. prof., 1972-77, prof. elec. engring., 1977-86; prof. elec. engring. Cornell U., Ithaca, N.Y., 1986—. Editor: IEEE Acoustics Speech and Signal Processing Soc., 1979-80. Recipient sr. scientist award A.V. Humboldt Found., Bonn, West Germany, 1972, Sr. Fulbright fellow Fulbright Found., 1973. Fellow IEEE (mem. com. 1978-80, tech. achievement award 1981); mem. IEEE Acoustics Speech and Signal Soc. (award 1988, Spira award for excellence in teaching 1992). Office: Sch of Elec Engring Cornell U Ithaca NY 14853

PARKYN, JOHN WILLIAM, editor, writer; b. London, Dec. 7, 1931; came to U.S., 1967; citizen, 1973; s. James R. and Eva M. (Dix) P.; m. Sybil (Judy) Hetherington; 1 child, Elaine. Student, Dulwich Coll., 1943-48. Staff writer Bus. Mag., London, 1954-56, Amalgamated Press, London, 1956-58; features editor Woman's Illustrated mag., London, 1958-60; staff writer Internat. Pub. Corp., London, 1960-61; editor Westward mag. Daily News Ltd., London, 1961-64; assoc. editor Daily Telegraph mag., London, 1964-66; features editor King mag. Europress, Ltd., London, 1966-67; assoc. editor Tropic mag. Miami (Fla.) Herald, 1967-69; editor Tropic mag., 1969-77; editor Calif. Today mag. San Jose (Calif.) Mercury News, 1977-83; editor Sunshine: The Mag. of South Fla. Sun-Sentinel Co. (subs. Tribune Co.), Ft. Lauderdale, Fla., 1983-96; cons. Het Parool newspaper, Amsterdam, 1965. Contbr. numerous articles to Am. and European mags. Chmn. Sunday Mag. Editors Conf., Louisville, 1973. With RAF, 1950-52. Recipient Outstanding Use of Editl. Color award Editor & Pub. mag., 1974, 75, 77, Nat. Headliner award, 1976, 79; named Editor Best Weekly Mag. in State Fla. Press Club, 1985-93, 95. Mem. Sunday Mag. Editors Assn. Office: 505 Beachland Blvd Ste 1-275 Vero Beach FL 32963

PARLIN, CHARLES C., JR., retired lawyer; b. Trenton, Feb. 12, 1928; s. Charles C. and Miriam (Boyd) P.; m. Joan Bona, June 28, 1948; children: C. Christopher, Robert B., Timothy B. B.A., U. Chgo., 1946; LL.B., U. Pa., 1949. Bar: N.Y. 1951. Assoc. firm. Shearman & Sterling, N.Y.C., 1950-59, ptnr., 1959-90, of counsel, 1990-92, ret., 1992. Home: Pudding Ln Silver Bay NY 12874

PARMELEE, ARTHUR HAWLEY, JR., pediatric medical educator; b. Chgo., Oct. 29, 1917; s. Arthur Hawley and Ruth Frances (Brown) P.; m. Jean Kern Rheinfrank, Nov. 11, 1939; children: Arthur Hawley III, Ann (Mrs. John C. Minahan Jr.), Timothy, Ruth Ellen. BS, U. Chgo., 1940, MD, 1943. Diplomate Am. Bd. Pediatrics (examiner 1966—). Intern U.S. Naval Hosp., Bethesda, Md., 1943-44; extern Yale Inst. Child Devel., 1947, New Haven Hosp., 1947-48, L.A. Children's Hosp., 1948-49; mem. faculty UCLA Med. Sch., 1951—, prof. pediat., 1967-88, prof. emeritus, 1988, dir. divsn. child devel., 1964-88; mem. Brain Rsch. Inst., 1966-88, Mental Retardation Rsch. Ctr., 1970-88; rsch. prof. pediat. U. Göttingen, Germany, 1967-68; mem. com. child devel. rsch. and pub. policy NRC, 1977-81; cons. Nat. Inst. Child Health and Human Devel., 1963-70, Holy Family Adoption Svc., 1949-80. Author articles, chpts. in books. Trustee Los Angeles Children's Mus., 1979. Served with USN, 1943-47. Recipient C. Anderson Aldrich award in child devel., 1975; Commonwealth fellow Centre de Recherches Biologiques Neonatales, Clinique Obstetricale Baudelocque, Paris, 1959-60; fellow Ctr. Advanced Study in Behavioral Scis., Stanford U., 1984-85; hon. lectr. Soc. for Developmental and Behavioral Pediat., 1996. Mem. AMA, Am. Pediat. Soc., Soc. Pediat. Rsch., Western Soc. Pediat. Rsch., Am. Acad. Pediat. (chmn. com. sect. child devel. 1966), Assn. Ambulatory Pediat. (mem. coun. 1966-69), Soc. Rsch. in Child Devel. (pres. 1983-85, Disting. Sci. Contbns. to Child Devel. award 1993), Assn. Psychophysiol. Study of Sleep, Los Angeles County Med. Soc., Phi Beta Kappa. Home: 764 Iliff St Pacific Palisades CA 90272-3927 Office: Univ Calif Dept Pediatrics Los Angeles CA 90024

PARMELEE, DAVID FREELAND, biologist, educator; b. Oshkosh, Wis., June 20, 1924; s. Gale Freeland and Helen Dale (MacNaughton) P.; m. Jean Marie Peterson, Dec. 4, 1943; 1 dau., Helen Gale. BA, Lawrence U., Appleton, Wis., 1950; MS, U. Mich., 1952; PhD, U. Okla., 1957. Grad. asst., then instr. U. Okla., 1952-58; from asst. prof. to prof. biology Kans. State U., Emporia, 1958-70; prof. ecology and behavioral biology U. Minn., Mpls., 1970-92, chmn. field biology program, 1970-84; curator birds Bell Mus. U. Minn., 1985-92; rsch. curator ornithology U. Nev., Las Vegas, 1992—; dir. field ops. bird virus and parasite rsch. studies U. Okla. Med. Ctr., 1963-65; program dir. U. Minn. Forestry and Biol. Sta., Lake Itasca, 1970-86, Cedar Creek Natrual History Area, 1970-84; lectr. on cruise vessels to Arctic and Antarctic for Travel Dynamics, N.Y.C., 1988—, Space Expedition, Inc., Seattle, 1993—, Cheesemans' Ecology Safaris, 1994—. Served with USMCR, 1943-46. Recipient Native Son award Rotary Internat., 1982; grantee NSF-U.S. Antarctic Research Program, 1972-90, Canadian Arctic Research Programs-NSF-Arctic Inst. N.Am.-Nat. Museum Can., 1953-71; recipient Conservation Edn. award Kans. Wildlife Fedn., Conservation Edn. award Sears-Roebuck Found., 1965; Antarctic site named Parmelee Massif in his honor. Fellow Explorers Club: mem. Orgn. Biol. Field Stas. (pres. 1984-85), Brit. Ornithol. Union, Cooper Ornithol. Soc., Wilson Ornithol. Soc., Nature Conservancy, Brit. Ornithologists' Club.

PARMENTER, CHARLES STEDMAN, chemistry educator; b. Phila., Oct. 12, 1933; s. Charles Leroy and Hazeltene Lois (Stedman) P.; m. Patricia Jean Patton, Mar. 31, 1956; children: Tighe Stedman, Kyle Kirkland, Leigh Patton. BA, U. Pa., 1955; PhD in Phys. Chemistry, U. Rochester, 1963. Tech. rep. photo products E.I. du Pont de Nemours & Co., 1958; NSF fellow chemistry Harvard U., Boston, 1962-63, NIH rsch. fellow, 1963-64, from asst. prof. to prof., 1964-88; Disting. prof. chemistry Ind. U., Bloomington, 1988—; Simon H. Guggenheim fellow U. Cambridge, 1971-72; vis. fellow Joint Inst. Lab. Astrophysics, Nat. Bur. Standards and U. Colo., 1977-78, 92. Lt. USAF, 1956-58. Recipient Humboldt Sr. Scientist award Tech. U. Munchen, 1986; Fulbright Sr. Scholar Griffith U., Australia, 1980. Earle K. Plyler Prize, Am. Physical Soc., 1996. Fellow AAAS, Am. Phys. Soc. (Ealre K. Plyler prize 1996); mem. NAS, Am. Acad. Arts and Scis., Am. Chem. Soc. (chmn. div. phys. chemistry 1986-87). Research in photochemistry, laser spectroscopy, energy transfer. Office: Ind U Dept of Chemistry Bloomington IN 47405

PARMENTER, ROBERT HALEY, physics educator; b. Portland, Maine, Sept. 19, 1925; s. LeClare Fall and Esther (Haley) P.; m. Elizabeth Kinnecom, Oct. 27, 1951; children: David Alan, Douglas Ian. B.S., U. Maine, 1947; Ph.D., Mass. Inst. Tech., 1952. Mem. staff solid state and molecular theory group Mass. Inst. Tech., 1951-54; guest scientist Brookhaven Nat. Lab., 1951-52; mem. staff Lincoln Lab., 1952-54, RCA Labs., 1954-66; vis. scientists RCA Labs., Zurich, Switzerland, 1958; acting head solid state research group RCA Labs., 1962-65; prof. physics U. Ariz., 1966—, chmn. dept., 1977-83; mem. NASA rsch. adv. com. electrophysics, 1964-68, chmn., 1966-68, mem. rsch. and tech. adv. com. basic rsch., 1966-68; vis. lectr. Princeton (N.J.) U., 1960-61. Served with USNR, 1944-46. Fellow AAAS, Am. Phys. Soc. (chmn. div. condensed matter physics 1967-68); mem. Sigma Xi, Tau Beta Pi. Achievements include predicting the existence of the acoustoelectric effect, the enhancement of the transition temperature of a superconductor by means of tunneling extraction; demonstration of the conditions under which deterministic chaos occurs in quantum mechanical systems. Home: 1440 E Ina Rd Tucson AZ 85718-1175 Office: U Ariz Physics Dept Tucson AZ 85721

PARMENTIER, EDGAR MARC, geology educator; b. Waynesburg, Pa., Oct. 29, 1945. BS, W.Va. U., 1968; M in Engring., Cornell U., 1969, PhD, 1975. Rsch. scientist/engr. AVCO-Everett Rsch. Lab., 1969-72; rsch. fellow geol. scis. Oxford U., 1975-77; from asst. prof. to assoc. prof. geol. scis. Brown U., Providence, R.I., 1977—. Mem. Am. Geophys. Union, Sigma Xi. Office: Brown U Dept Geological Sciences Providence RI 02912-9100*

PARMER, DAN GERALD, veterinarian; b. Wetumpka, Ala., July 3, 1926; s. James Lonnie and Virginia Gertrude (Guy) P.; 1 child by previous marriage, Linda Leigh; m. Donna Louise Kesler, June 7, 1980; 1 child, Dan Gerald. Student L.A. City Coll., 1945-46; DVM, Auburn U., 1950. Gen. practice vet. medicine, Galveston, Tex., 1950-54, Chgo., 1959-83; vet. in charge Chgo. Commn. Animal Care and Control, 1974-88; med. dir. food protection divsn. Chgo. Dept. Health, 1988-93; ret. 1993; chmn. Ill. Impaired Vets. Com.; tchr. Highlands U., 1959; humane officer Elmore County, 1994—; dir. sales for south, southeast and lower midwest Am. Vet. Identification Devices, Norco, Calif., 1993—. Pres. Elmore County Humane Soc. Served with USNR, 1943-45, PTO; served as staff vet. and 2d and 5th Air Force vet. chief USAF, 1954-59. Decorated 9 Battle Stars; recipient Vet. Appreciation award U. Ill., 1971, Commendation, Chgo. Commn. Animal Care and Control, 1987. Mem. VFW, AVMA (nat. com. for impaired vets., coun. pub. health and regulatory medicine 1990—), Ill. Vet. Medicine Assn. (chmn. civil def. and package disaster hosps. 1968-71, Pres.' award 1986), Chgo. Vet. Medicine Assn. (bd. govs. 1969-72, 74-81, pres. 1982), South Chgo. Vet. Medicine Assn. (pres. 1965-66), Am. Animal Hosp. Assn. (dir.), Ill. Acad. Vet. Practice (pres. 1993), Nat. Assn. of Professions, Am. Assn. Zoo Vets., Am. Assn. Zool. Parks and Aquariums, Elmore County Humane Soc. (pres. 1994-95), Midlothian Country Club, Valley Internat. Country Club, Masons, Shriners, Kiwanis. Democrat. Discoverer Bartonellosis in cattle in N.Am. and Western Hemisphere, 1951; co-developer bite-size high altitude in-flight feeding program USAF, 1954-56. Address: 6720 Post Oak Ln Montgomery AL 36117-2424 Office: Am Vet Identification Devices 3179 Hamner Ave Norco CA 91760

PARMER, JESS NORMAN, university official, educator; b. Elkhart, Ind., Nov. 23, 1925; s. Jess Noah and Zayda Irene (Tressler) P.; m. Bessie Norma Peterson, September 12, 1948; children: Thomas Norman, Sarah Irene. B.A., Ind. U., 1949; M.A., U. Conn., 1951; Ph.D., Cornell U., 1957. Resident in Malaya, Southeast Asia program, Cornell U., 1952-55; instr., then asst. prof. history U. Md., 1956-59; mem. faculty No. Ill. U., 1959-67, prof. history, 1960-67, chmn. dept., 1959-63; assoc. dean Coll. Arts and Scis. Ohio U., also dir. Center Internat. Studies, 1967-69, asst. dean faculties for internat. studies, 1969-75; v.p. acad. affairs Trinity U., San Antonio, 1975-82, prof. history, 1975-92; scholar in residence and dir. of special projects Ohio U., Athens, 1993—; cons. business, govt., edn.; Peace Corps rep. in Malaya, 1961-63, Tanzania, summer 1965, Malawi, summer, 1966, Korea, 1967; lectr. Fgn. Service Inst., 1958, 61, 65; vis. prof. history Nat. U. Malaysia, 1984; cons. social scis. com. Ill. Curriculum Program, 1961; cons. various corps.; vis. fellow Cornell U., 1987-88, vis. prof. 1989; luce scholar in res. Ohio U., 1990-91. Author: Governments and Politics of Southeast Asia, 2d edit., 1964, Colonial Labor Policy and Administration, 1960, Southeast Asia: Documents of Political Development and Change, 1974, People and Progress: A Global History, 1977; contbr. chpts. The World of Asia, 1995. Served with inf. AUS, 1944-46, ETO. Mem. AAUP, ACLU, Assn. Asian Studies (chmn. S.E. Asia regional coun. 1968-72, dir. 1969-72), Midwest Conf. Asian Affairs (chmn. library com. 1960-61), Southwest Conf. Asian Studies (pres. 1982-83), Am. Hist. Assn., Sons of the Am. Revolution, Torch Internat., Soc. of Ind. Pioneers, Tex. Soc. War of 1812. Office: Ohio U Ctr Internat Studies 56 East Union St Athens OH 45701-2987 *I find my life full of opportunity, excitement and satisfaction. Satisfaction comes from seeing ideas find institutional or behavioral expression and influencing people in positive ways. Self-fulfillment, hard work, respect for others, and honesty have been guiding principles and I have found them compatible and rewarding.*

PARMET, HERBERT SAMUEL, historian, educator; b. N.Y.C., Sept. 28, 1929; s. Isaac and Fanny (Scharf) P.; m. Joan Kronish, Sept. 12, 1948; 1 child, Wendy. BS, SUNY, Oswego, 1951; MA, Queens Coll., 1957; postgrad., Columbia U., 1958-62. Prof. history Grad. Sch. CUNY, 1968-95, disting. prof. history, 1983-95, prof. emeritus, 1995—; cons. ABC-TV, N.Y.C., 1983, KERA-TV, Dallas, 1986-91, WGBH-TV, Boston, 1988-91. Author: Aaron Burr: Portrait of an Ambitious Man, 1967, Never Again: President Runs for a Third Term, 1968, Eisenhower and the American Crusades, 1972, The Democrats, 1976, Jack: The Struggles of John F. Kennedy, 1980, JFK: The Presidency of John F. Kennedy, 1983, Richard Nixon and His America, 1990; editorial bd. Presdl. Studies Quar. Cpl. U.S. Army, 1952-54. Grantee, NEH, 1987. Fellow Soc. Am. Historians; mem. Am. Hist. Assn., Orgn. Am. Historians, Authors Guild. Avocation: photography. Home: 36 Marsten Ln Hillsdale NY 12529-5816

PARMITER, JAMES DARLIN, safety engineer; b. McKeesport, Pa., Apr. 5, 1934; s. James Harry and Ruth Adeline (Ulm) P.; student Pa. State U., 1952-56; m. Nancy Jane Light, Aug. 24, 1954; children: James Victor, David Baird. With Gen. Motors Co., Wilmington, Del., 1962-65; with Boeing Helicopter Co., Ridley Park, Pa., 1965-84, mgr. safety and indsl. hygiene, 1967-84; occupational safety and health mgr. Phila. Naval Shipyard, 1984-94, dir. occupational safety, health, and environ., 1994—; mem. faculty Pa. State U., Cheyney State Coll., West Chester U., Del. County Community Coll.; also cons. Mem. Gov.'s Adv. Com. on Occupational Safety and Health for Pa., 1967-84, Adv. Com. on Occupational Safety and Health Pa. State U., 1967-83; mem. Springfild Sch. Bd., 1969-75, Delaware County Sch. Bd., 1969-75. With USN, 1953-63, comdr. res. (ret.). Recipient Ben Franklin award Greater Phila. Safety Coun., 1981; Phila. Vision award Phila. Optometric Soc., 1972. Mem. Nat. Safety Coun. (aerospace sect. gen. chmn. 1974-76), Am. Soc. Safety Engrs. (pres. Phila. 1980-82, Safety Profl. of Yr. for region XII, 1982), Phila. Safety Coun. (chmn. bd. 1974-75), Am. Helicopter Soc., Am. Indsl. Hygiene Assn., Assn. Fed. Safety and Health Profls., Nat. Assn. Supts. Shore Establishments, Fed. Mgrs. Assn., Am. Philatelic Assn., Pa. State U. Alumni Assn., Masons., Shriners. Republican. Methodist. Home: 242 Brock Rd Springfield PA 19064-3116 also: 5525 Bay Ave Ocean City NJ 08226-1241 Office: Phila Naval Shipyard Code 106 Philadelphia PA 19112-5087

PARMLEY, LOREN FRANCIS, JR., medical educator; b. El Paso, Tex., Sept. 19, 1921; s. Loren Francis and Hope (Bartholomew) P.; m. Dorothy Louise Turner, Apr. 4, 1942; children—Richard Turner, Robert James, Kathryn Louise. B.A., U. Va., 1941, M.D., 1943. Diplomate Am. Bd. Internal Medicine, Am. Bd. Internal Medicine-Cardiovascular Disease. Commd. 1st lt. U.S. Army, 1944; advanced through grades to col., 1968; intern Med. Coll. Va., 1944; resident in internal medicine Brooke Gen. Hosp., San Antonio, 1948-49, U. Wis. Gen. Hosp., Madison, 1949-51; asst. prof. mil. med. sci. Med. Coll. U. Wis., Madison, 1949-51; asst. attache (med.) U.S. Embassy, New Delhi, 1953-55; fellow in cardiovascular disease Walter Reed Gen. Hosp., Washington, 1956-57; chief medicine and cardiology Letterman Gen. Hosp., San Francisco, 1958-63; med. and cardiology cons. U.S. Army Europe, Heidelberg, Germany, 1963-64; chief medicine Walter Reed Gen. Hosp., Washington, 1965-68; prof. medicine, asst. dean Med. U. S.C., Spartanburg, 1968-75; dir. med. edn. Spartanburg Gen. Hosp., Spartanburg, 1968-75; prof. medicine U. South Ala., Mobile, 1975-87, chief div. cardiology, 1980-87, prof. emeritus medicine, 1988—; lectr. medicine U. Calif.-San Francisco, 1959-63; clin. assoc. prof. medicine Georgetown U., Washington, 1967-68; clin. prof. medicine Med. Coll. Ga., Augusta, 1969-75; cons. internal medicine Surgeon Gen. U.S. Army, Washington, 1966-68. Contbg. author: The Heart, 1966, 70, 74, 78 Cardiac Diagnosis and Treatment, 1976, 80, The Heart in Industry, 1960, 70. Recipient Gold award sci. exhibit Am. Soc. Clin. Pathologists and Coll. Am. Pathologists, 1959; Certificate of Achievement in cardio-vascular disease Surgeon Gen. U.S.A., Washington, 1962; Bronze Medallion Meritorious Service, Am. Heart Assn., S.C., Columbia, 1969, 73; decorated Legion of Merit. Fellow ACP, Am. Coll. Cardiology (bd. govs. U.S Army 1967, S.C. 1969-73), Am. Coll. Chest Physicians; mem. Am. Heart Assn. (fellow coun. on clin. cardiology), Soc. Med. Cons. to Armed Forces, Kiwanis. Republican. Episcopalian. Avocations: golf, swimming. Home: 549 Fairway Dr Kerrville TX 78028-6440 also: 5862 Falls Church Rd E Mobile AL 36608-2961 Office: U South Ala Coll Medicine Dept Medicine Mastin Bldg 2451 Fillingim St Rm 414 Mobile AL 36617-2238

PARNAS, DAVID LORGE, computer scientist, engineer, educator; b. Plattsburgh, N.Y., Feb. 10, 1941; s. Jacob M. and Hildegarde Marienne (Lorge) P.; m. Lillian Lai Ngan Chik, Nov. 7, 1979; children: Jacob McNeil, Henrietta Heng Li. BS, Carnegie Inst. Tech., 1961, MS, 1964, PhD, 1965; Dr. honoris causa, Eidgenössische Technische Hochshule, Zürich, Switzerland, 1986. Mem. faculty Carnegie Mellon U., 1965-73, U. Md., 1965; vis. advisor Philips-Electrologica, Apeldoorn, Netherlands, 1969-70; prof. Technische Hochschule Darmstadt, W. Ger., 1973-76; prof. computer sci. U. N.C., Chapel Hill, 1976-82; vis. scientist IBM, Bethesda, Md., 1980-82; computer scientist Naval Rsch. Lab., Washington, 1972-86; prof. computer sci. U. Victoria, B.C., Can., 1982-86; mem. faculty McMaster U., Hamilton, Ont., Can., 1991—; cons. Bell Labs., TRW, Inc., DEC, BNR. Recipient Norbert Wiener award, 1987. Fellow Royal Soc. Can., Assn. Computing Machinery; mem. IEEE (sr.), Gesellschaft fur Informatik. Home: 551 Old Dundas Rd, Ancaster, ON Canada L9G 3J3 Office: McMaster U Comm Rsch Lab, Dept Elec/Computer Enging, 1280 Main St W, Hamilton, ON Canada L85 4K1 *Only the truth allows us to be free. Science is a search for the truth.*

PARNELL, CHARLES L., speechwriter; b. Myrtis, La., Feb. 13, 1938; s. Forrest L. and Dorothy D. (Jones) P. BA, Rice U., 1960; M Bus. and Pub. Adminstrn., Southeastern U., 1977. Commd. ens. USN, 1960, advanced through grades to comdr., 1975, ret., 1987; speechwriter Mead Data Cen., Dayton, Ohio, 1987-89, Nationwide Ins. Co., Columbus, Ohio, 1989-90; exec. speechwriter Miller Brewing Co., Milw., 1990—. Contbr. articles to profl. publs. Mem. U.S. Naval Inst., Ret. Officers Assn., World Future Soc. Avocations: reading, writing, travel. Office: Miller Brewing Co 3939 W Highland Blvd Milwaukee WI 53208-2816

PARNELL, FRANCIS WILLIAM, JR., physician; b. Woonsocket, R.I., May 22, 1940; s. Francis W. and Dorothy V. (Lalor) P.; m. Diana DeAngelis, Feb. 27, 1965; children: Cheryl Lynn, John Francis, Kathleen Diana, Alison Anne, Thomas William. Student, Coll. Holy Cross, 1957-58; AB, Clark U., 1961; MD, Georgetown U., 1965. Diplomate: Nat. Bd. Med. Examiners, Am. Bd. Otolaryngology. Intern Univ. Hosps., Madison, Wis., 1965-66; resident in gen. surgery Univ. Hosps., Madison, 1966-67, otolaryngology, 1967-70; pvt. practice medicine specializing in otolaryngology San Rafael, Calif., 1972-75, Greenbrae, Calif., 1972-75, 78—; chmn., pres., CEO Parnell Pharms., Larkspur, Calif., 1982—; cons. corp. med. affairs, 1978-82; corp. med. dir. Becton, Dickinson & Co., Rutherford, N.J., 1976-78; clin. instr. U. Calif. at San Francisco, 1972-75, asst. clin. prof., 1975-76; Alt. del., U.S. Del. 27th World Health Assembly WHO, Geneva, 1974. Contbr. articles to profl. jours. Candidate Calif. State Assembly, 1988; bd. dirs. Marin Coalition, 1980—, chmn., 1986-87; trustee Ross (Calif.) Sch. Dist., 1981-89; mem. governing bd. Marin Cmty. Coll. Dist., 1995—. Maj. M.C. AUS, 1970-72, lt. col. M.C., USAR, 1985-94. Fellow ACS (gov. 1988-94), Am. Acad. Otolaryngology. Home: PO Box 998 Ross CA 94957-0998 Office: 1100 S Eliseo Dr Greenbrae CA 94904-2004

PARNELL, THOMAS ALFRED, physicist; b. Lumberton, N.C., Nov. 24, 1931; s. Johnathan Alfred and Lula Beale (Lashley) P.; m. Elizabeth G. Brite, June 4, 1955; children: Marc Thomas, Gina Ann. B.S. in Physics, U. N.C., 1954, M.S. in Physics, 1962, Ph.D. in Physics, 1965. Rsch. adj., dept. physics U. N.C., Chapel Hill, 1962-65; ops. analyst U.S. Air Force Europe, Wiesbaden, W. Ger., 1965-66; asst. prof. physics Marshall U., Huntington, W.Va., 1966-67; physicist NASA-Marshall Space Flight Center, Huntsville, Ala., 1967—; chief astrophysics br. NASA-Marshall Space Flight Center, 1969—; mem. grad. faculty U. Ala., Huntsville. Mem. editorial bd. Nuclear Measurements; contbr. articles to profl. jours. Served to capt. USNR, 1975-91. Recipient Exceptional Sci. Achievement medal, Outstanding Leadership medal NASA, U.S. Antartica Svc. medal. Mem. Am. Phys. Soc., Sigma Xi. Club: Monte Sano (Huntsville). Home: 907 Corinth Cir SE Huntsville AL 35801-2064 Office: Marshall Space Flight Ctr ES 84 Huntsville AL 35812

PARODE, ANN, banker, lawyer; b. L.A., Mar. 3, 1947; d. Lowell Carr and Sabine (Phelps) P. BA, Pomona Coll., 1968; JD, UCLA, 1971. Bar: Calif. 1972, U.S. Dist. Ct. (so. dist.) Calif. 1972, U.S. Ct. Appeals (9th cir.) 1975. Assoc. Luce, Forward et al, San Diego, 1971-75; gen. counsel, exec. v.p., sec. San Diego Trust & Savings, 1975-94; judge pro tem San Diego Mcpl. Ct., 1978-84. Bd. dirs. San Diego Cmty. Found., 1989—, chmn., 1994-96; bd. dirs. The Burnham Inst., 1995—. Mem. Calif. Bar Assn. (corp. law com. 1980-83, client trust fund commn. 1986-90, chmn. 1989-90), San Diego County Bar Found. (founder, bd. dirs., pres. 1980-83), San Diego Bar Asns. (bd. dirs. 1977-81, v.p. 1977-78, 80-81, treas. 1979-80), Law Libr. Justice Found. (pres. 1994).

PARR, CAROLYN MILLER, federal court judge; b. Palatka, Fla., Apr. 17, 1937; d. Arthur Charles and Audrey Ellen (Dunklin) Miller; m. Jerry Studstill Parr, Oct. 12, 1959; children: Kimberly Parr Trapasso, Jennifer Parr Turek, Patricia Audrey. BA, Stetson U., 1959; MA, Vanderbilt U., 1960; JD, Georgetown U., 1977; LLD (hon.), Stetson U., 1986. Bar: Md. 1977, U.S. Tax Ct. 1977, D.C. 1979, U.S. Supreme Ct. 1983. Gen. trial atty. IRS, Washington, 1977-81, sr. trial atty. office of chief counsel, 1982; spl. counsel to asst. atty. gen. tax divsn. U.S. Dept. Justice, Washington, 1982-85; judge U.S. Tax Ct., Washington, 1985—. Nat. Def. fellow Vanderbilt U., 1959-60; fellow Georgetown U., 1975-76; recipient Spl. Achievement award U.S. Treasury, 1979. Mem. ABA, Md. Bar Assn., Nat. Assn. Women Judges, D.C. Bar Assn., Am. Judges Assn. Office: US Tax Ct 400 2nd St NW Washington DC 20217-0001

PARR, GRANT VAN SICLEN, surgeon; b. N.Y.C., Dec. 30, 1942; s. Ferdinand Van Siclen and Helene H. P.; m. Helen Mushat Frye, July 1, 1967; children: Kathleen Gage, Helen Johnston. A.B. with honors, Wesleyan U., 1965; M.D., Cornell U., 1969. Diplomate: Am. Bd. Thoracic Surgery, Am. Bd. Surgery. Intern, resident U. Hosps. of Cleve., 1969-71; resident in surgery U. Ala. Hosps., Birmingham, 1971-74; chief resident in surgery U. Ala. Hosps., 1974-75, resident in cardiovascular and thoracic surgery, 1975-77; practice medicine specializing in thoracic surgery Hershey, Pa., 1978-82; mem. staff Presbyn.-U. Pa. Med. Ctr., Phila., 1982-88, chief div. Thoracic surgery, 1984-88, acting chmn. Dept. Surgery, 1988; chief cardiovascular surgery Presbyn.-U. Pa. Med. Ctr., 1984-88; asst. prof. cardiothoracic surgery M.S. Hershey Med. Center, Hershey, Pa., 1987-88; chief cardiovascular surgery Morristown (N.J.) Meml. Hosp., 1988—; asst. prof. Pa. State U., 1978-82; clin. assoc. prof. surgery U. Pa., 1982-89; assoc. prof. clin. surgery Columbia U., 1992—; chief cardiovascular surgery Overlook Hosp., 1988—, Atlantic Health Systems, 1988—. Contbr. articles on thoracic surgery to med. jours. Fellow Am. Coll. Cardiology, ACS, Am. Coll. Chest Physicians, Phila. Coll. Physicians; mem. Internat. Cardiovascular Soc., Assn. of Acad. Surgeons, Am. Assn. Thoracic Surgery, Phila. County Med. Soc., Soc. Thoracic Surgeons, Soc. Critical Care Medicine, Pa., Thoracic Surg. Soc., John W. Kirklin Soc., AMA, Pa. Med. Assn., Morris County Golf Club, NYU Club, Beacon Hill Club. Office: Morristown Meml Hosp 100 Madison Ave Morristown NJ 07960-6013

PARR, HARRY EDWARD, JR., financial executive; b. Dayton, Ohio, Sept. 2, 1928; s. Harry Edward and Naomi Theresa (Oesbeck) P.; m. Suzanne Johnson, Oct. 3, 1953; children: Constance, Cynthia, Claudia, Brian, Patrick. BSBA, U. Dayton, 1951. With Chrysler Corp., Detroit, 1953-66; v.p., controller Diebold, Inc., Canton, Ohio, 1966-78, v.p., treas., 1978-82, sr. v.p. fin., treas., 1982-91, also bd. dirs., ret., 1991. Bd. dirs. Jr. Achievement Stark County, Canton United Way; trustee Walsh Coll., Canton, Canton Cultural Ctr. for Arts; trustee, mem. devel. bd. Stark County; bd. dirs. Aultman Hosp. Served to 1st lt. U.S. Army, 1951-53. Mem. Fin. Execs. Inst., Nat. Assn. Accts., Planning Execs. Inst., Canton C. of C. (former trustee). Club: Brookside Country (Canton).

PARR, JAMES GORDON, writer; b. Peterborough, Eng., May 26, 1927; went to Can., 1953; s. Reuben Scotney and Edith Grace (Rollings) P.; children: Mark Anthony, Katharine Elizabeth, Daniel John; m. Carole Elizabeth Vaughan, Dec. 1975. BSc, U. Leeds, Eng., 1947; PhD, U. Liverpool, Eng., 1953; LLD (hon.), U. Windsor, 1984. Registered profl. engr., Ont. Lectr. U. Liverpool, 1948-53; research assoc., lectr. U. B.C., Vancouver, 1953-55; assoc. prof., then prof. U. Alta., Edmonton, 1955-64; dean applied sci. U. Windsor, Ont., Can., 1964-72; chmn. com. univ. affairs Govt. Ont., Toronto, 1972; dep. minister Ministry Colls. and Univs., Govt. Ont., 1973-79; chmn., chief exec. officer TVOnt., Toronto, 1979-85; dir. gen. Ont. Sci. Ctr., Don Mills, 1985-88; founding pres. Indsl. Research Inst., U. Windsor, 1967-72. Author: Man, Metals and Modern Magic, 1958, (with A. Hanson) An Introduction to Stainless Steel, 1965, (with A. Hanson) The Engineer's Guide to Steel, 1965, Any Other Business, 1977, Is There Anybody There? Collected Verse, 1979, Megafart, a novel, 1990, Essays, 1992. Recipient Centennial medal Can., 1967, Jubilee medal, 1977. Fellow Royal Soc. Can., Am. Soc. Materials Internat., Ryerson Polytech. Inst., Ont. Inst. for Studies in Edn., Arts and Letters Club (Toronto) (pres. 1982-84). Home: 10 Governor's Rd, Toronto, ON Canada M4W 2G1

PARR, LLOYD BYRON, state official; b. Arvada, Colo., Oct. 27, 1931; s. Earle Ruly and Leva Corinne (Livengood) P.; m. Fransess Clyde Durham, Dec. 30, 1951; children: Russell Owen, Christopher Lee, Ryan Whitney. Diploma, Compton (Calif.) Jr. Coll., 1950; student, No. Mont. State U., 1964-65, U. Ark., Little Rock, 1969-70. Lic. civil engring. technician. Enlisted USN, 1950, aviation machinist mate, 1950-54; surveyor Denver Water Bd., 1955-56; enlisted USAF, 1957, advanced through grades to master sgt., 1971; site developer USAF, Korea, Okinawa, Turkey, Vietnam, 1957-73; ret. USAF, 1973; airport engr. State of Mo., Jefferson City, 1974-80, adminstr. aviation, 1981—. Sunday sch. tchr. Ch. of Christ, Eldon, Mo., 1973—. Decorated Bronze Star. Mem. Nat. Assn. State Aviation Ofcls. (bd. dirs. 1991-92, fin. com. 1988-93, treas. 1993-94, 2d v.p. 1994-95, 1st v.p. 1995-96, pres. 1996-97), Am. Assn. State Hwy. and Transp. Ofcls. (aviation com. 1986-95). Office: Mo Hwy & Transp Dept Capital and Jefferson Sts PO Box 270 Jefferson City MO 65102-0270 *Few of we mortals have the opportunity to contribute something truly unique to our world. Most of us can either add a few bricks to the wall of life or, if we choose to, we can tear down what others have built. I can only hope that the few bricks I add during my life will lend strength and color to the wall.*

PARR, RICK VINCENT, professional relations manager; b. Dyersburg, Tenn., Oct. 26, 1950; s. Dallas A. and Eloise (Carson) P.; m. Queen Ester Moore-Parr, Sept. 27, 1984; 1 child, Rickey Vincent Jr. BA, U. S.C., 1988. Cert. addictions counselor, 1988, mediator, 1994. Mgr. Greer, Parr & Parr, Inc., employment agy., Memphis, 1974-78; substance abuse counselor USMC, Parris Island, S.C., 1978-89, Charter Hosp., Savannah, Ga., 1989-91; profl. rels. mgr. Poplar Springs Hosp., Petersburg, Va., 1991—, customer svc. cons., 1994—; mem. substance abuse adv. bd. Savannah State Coll., 1989-91, Va. State U., Petersburg, 1992-95. Author: How to Thrive, Not Just Survive, 1995; writer, dir. docudrama Family in Crisis: The Intervention, 1993; author essays. Mem. Chesterfield County Youth Svcs. Bd., Chesterfield, Va., 1993-95; bd. dirs. Richmond (Va.) Urban League, 1994—; bd. dirs. Va. Assn. Alcohol and Drug Abuse Counselors, 1995—. Recipient gov.'s award for substance abuse edn. Commonwealth of Va., 1993. Mem. Nat. Assn. Alcohol and Drug Abuse Counselors, Va. Alliance for Mentally Ill (membership com. 1993—). Avocations: substance abuse education, public speaking, chess, basketball. Home: 144 Crater Woods Ct Petersburg VA 23805 Office: Columbia/HCA Poplar Springs Hosp 350 Poplar Dr Petersburg VA 23805-9367

PARR, ROBERT GHORMLEY, chemistry educator; b. Chgo., Sept. 22, 1921; s. Leland Wilbur and Grace (Ghormley) P.; m. Jane Bolstad, May 28, 1944; children: Steven Robert, Jeanne Karen, Carol Jane. AB magna cum laude with high honors in Chemistry, Brown U., 1942; PhD in Phys. Chemistry, U. Minn., 1947; D (hon.), U. Leuven, 1986. Asst. prof. chemistry U. Minn., 1947-48; mem. faculty Carnegie Inst. Tech., 1948-62, prof. chemistry, 1957-62; prof. chemistry Johns Hopkins U., 1962-74, chmn. dept., 1969-72; William R. Kenan, Jr. prof. theoretical chemistry U. N.C., Chapel Hill, 1974-90, Wassily Hoeffding prof. chem. physics, 1990—; vis. prof. chemistry, mem. Center Advanced Study U. Ill., 1962; distinguished vis. prof. State U. N.Y. at Buffalo, also Pa. State U., 1967; vis. prof. Japan Soc. Promotion Sci., 1968, 79, U. Haifa, 1977, Free U. Berlin, 1977; Firth prof. U. Sheffield, 1976; Coochbehar prof. Indian Assn. Cultivation of Sci., 1990; Sandoval Vallarta prof. UAM-Iztapalapa, 1992; chmn. com. postdoctoral fellowships in chemistry Nat. Acad. Sci.-NRC, 1961-63; chmn. panel theoretical chemistry Westheimer com. survey chemistry Nat. Acad. Sci., 1964; mem. coun. Gordon Rsch. Conf., 1974-76; mem. Commn. on Human Resources, NRC, 1979-82; mem. coun. Inst. for Molecular Sci., Okazaki, Japan, 1986-88; bd. trustees Inst. for Fundamental Chemistry, Kyoto, Japan, 1988—. Author: Quantum Theory of Molecular Electronic Structure, 1963, Density-Functional Theory of Atoms and Molecules, 1989, also numerous articles.; Asso. editor: Jour. Chem. Physics, 1956-58, Chem. Revs, 1961-63, Jour. Phys. Chemistry, 1963-67, 77-79, Am. Chem. Soc. Monographs, 1966-71, Theoretica Chimica Acta, 1966-69, 92—; bd. editors: Jour. Am. Chem. Soc, 1969-77; adv. editorial bd.: Internat. Jour. Quantum Chemistry, 1967—, Chem. Physics Letters, 1967-79. Recipient Outstanding Achievement award U. Minn., 1968, N.C. Disting. Chemist award, 1982; fellow U. Chgo., 1949; research asso., 1957; Fulbright scholar U. Cambridge, Eng., 1953-54; Guggenheim fellow, 1953-54; NSF sr. postdoctoral fellow U. Oxford (Eng.) and Commonwealth Sci. and Indsl. Research Orgn., Melbourne, Australia, 1967-68; Sloan fellow, 1956-60. Fellow AAAS, Am. Phys. Soc. (chmn. divsn. chem. physics 1963-64); mem. NAS, AAUP, Am. Chem. Soc. (chmn. divsn. phys. chemistry 1978, Irving Langmuir award in chem. physics 1994), Am. Acad. Arts and Sci., Indian Nat. Sci. Acad., Internat. Acad. Quantum Molecular Sci. (pres. 1991—), Phi Beta Kappa, Sigma Xi, Phi Lambda Upsilon, Pi Mu Epsilon. Home: 701 Kenmore Rd Chapel Hill NC 27514-2019 Office: U NC Dept Chemistry Chapel Hill NC 27599-3290

PARR, SANDRA HARDY, government affairs administrator; b. Atlanta, Dec. 30, 1952; d. Raymond William Hardy and Ruth (Berry) Yancey; m. James Parr Jr., Apr. 14, 1978; 1 child, James Andrew Parr III. Student, Lurleen B. Wallace Jr. Coll., 1972. Sales adminstr. Etec Corp., Hayward, Calif., 1976-77; adminstrv. sec. Cities Svc. Co., Atlanta, 1977-82; sales and planning coord. Intermodal Transp. Co., Norcross, Ga., 1982-83; freelance temp. sec. Atlanta met. area, 1983-86; freelance word processor, cons. Amoco Container Co., Norcross, 1986-88; psychiat. rev. asst. Am. Psychiat. Assn., Atlanta, 1988-89; support svcs. mgr. Parkside Health Mgmt. Corp., Atlanta, 1989-90; med. staff coord. C.P.C. Parkwood Hosp., Atlanta, 1991—; health svcs. asst. Ciba Vision Corp., 1991-93. Del. internat. nursing conf., citizen amb. program to People's Republic China, Seattle Washington People to People, Beijing, 1989; part-time exercise instr. Mem. NAFE. Avocations: creative writing, reading, exercising, calenetics instructing, ceramics. Home: 1301 Eugenia Ter Lawrenceville GA 30245-7437 Office: CPC Parkwood Hosp 1999 Cliff Valley Way NE Atlanta GA 30329-2420 Address: Philip Morris Mgmt Corp Govt Affairs 3 Ravinia Dr Ste 1560 Atlanta GA 30346-2118

PARRAMORE, BARBARA MITCHELL, education educator; b. Guilford County, N.C., Aug. 29, 1932; d. Samuel Spencer and Nellie Gray (Glosson) Mitchell; m. Lyman Griffis Worthington, Dec. 23, 1956 (div. 1961); m. Thomas Custis Parramore, Jan. 22, 1966; children: Lisa Gray, Lynn Stuart. AB, U. N.C., Greensboro, 1954; MEd, N.C. State U., 1959; EdD, Duke U., 1968. Counselor, thcr. Raleigh City Schs., 1954-59, sch. prin., 1959-65; prof. dept. of curriculum and instrn. N.C. State U., 19770-96, prof. emeritus, 1996—; acad. specialist Office Internat. Edn., U.S. Info. Svcs., sec. sch. initative program, The Philippines, 1987. Author: The People of North Carolina, 1972, 3rd edit. 1983. Japan Inst. Social and Econ. Affairs fellow, 1980; N.C. AAUW award for juvenile lit., 1973, Holladay medal for excellence N.C. State U., 1994. Mem. ASCD, N.C. ASCD (pres. 1994-96), N.C. Coun. for Social Studies (pres. 1985-87), Assn. Tchr. Educators, Delta Kappa Gamma, Kappa Delta Pi. Home: 5012 Tanglewood Dr Raleigh NC 27612-3135

PARRETT, SHERMAN O., lawyer; b. Cin., Jan. 8, 1943; s. Earl and Ruby (Angel) P.; m. Rosalind K. Brooks, Sept. 21, 1985; children: Laura, Samantha. BSEE, U. Cin., 1965; JD with honors, George Washington U., 1969. Bar: Calif. 1970, D.C. 1975, Ariz. 1992. Assoc. Flehr, Hohbach et al., San Francisco, 1970-73; ptnr. Cushman, Darby & Cushman, Washington, 1973-86, Irell & Manella, L.A., 1986-91, Streich Lang, Phoenix, 1991-94, Snell & Wilmer, Phoenix, 1994—. Office: Snell & Wilmer One Arizonia Ctr Phoenix AZ 85004-0001

PARRIGIN, ELIZABETH ELLINGTON, lawyer; b. Colon, Panama, May 23, 1932; d. Jesse Cox and Elizabeth (Roark) Ellington; m. Perry G. Parrigin, Oct. 8, 1975. BA, Agnes Scott Coll., 1954; JD, U. Va., 1959. Bar: Tex. 1959, Mo. 1980. Atty. San Antonio, 1960-69; law libr. U. Mo., Columbia, 1969-77, rsch. assoc., 1977-82; atty. pvt. practice, Columbia, 1982—. Elder, clk. of session First Presbyn. Ch., Columbia; mem. permanent jud. commn. Presbyn. Ch. U.S., 1977-83, mem. advisory com. on constitution, 1983-90. Mem. ABA, Mo. Bar Assn. (chmn. sub-com. revision of Mo. trsut law 1988-92). Democrat. Presbyterian. Avocations: music, gardening, reading. Home: 400 Conley Ave Columbia MO 65201-4219 Office: 224 N 8th St Columbia MO 65201-4844

PARRIOTT, JAMES DEFORIS, retired oil company executive, consultant; b. Moundsville, W. Va., Aug. 21, 1923; s. James D. and Bessie (Sadler) P.; m. Marynette Sonneland, Aug. 3, 1946; children—James Deforis III, Sara Graham. Student, Ohio Wesleyan U., 1941-43; LL.B., U. Colo., 1949. Bar: Colo. bar 1949, practice in Denver 1949-53. Asst. city atty. Denver, 1950-51; asst. atty. gen. Colo., 1952-53; chief counsel Bur. Land Mgmt., Dept. Interior, 1953, assoc. solicitor lands and minerals, 1954-56; atty. Ohio Oil Co., Washington, 1956-60, Findlay, Ohio, 1960-62; mgr. employee relations Marathon Oil Co., 1962-69, dir. pub. affairs, 1969-74, dir. pub. and govt. affairs, 1974-85; sr. cons. Hill and Knowton, Inc., Los Angeles. Pilot, USAAF, 1943-46. Mem. ABA, Fed. Bar Assn., Pacific Corinthian Yacht Club, Phi Alpha Delta, Phi Gamma Delta. Episcopalian. Home: 2825 Harbor Blvd Oxnard CA 93035-3952

PARRIS, FLORENCE MAE, elementary education educator; b. Waynesboro, Ga., Dec. 7, 1959; d. John Sr. and Ina Mae (Bowles) Rogers; m. David Anderson Parris, May 12, 1984; children: David II, India. BS in Early Childhood Edn., Paine Coll., 1983; MEd in Adminstrn. and Supervision, Trevecca Nazarene Coll., 1992. Film processor Colorcraft-Augusta (Ga.) Divsn.; switchboard operator Meharry-Hubbard Hosp., Nashville; vol. tchr. Meharry Day Care, Nashville; kindergarten tchr. Cousins Elem., Sardis, Ga.; first grade tchr. Mary Ann Garber Elem., Chattanooga; office mgr. Your Family Dentist, Chattanooga; kindergarten tchr. Lakeside Elem., Chattanooga; non-graded sch. tchr. Piney Woods Elem., Chattanooga; elem. tchr. Waynesboro (Ga.) Elem.; vol. tchr. Reading Summer Program, Nevis, West Indies, 1994. Named Educator of Month, Tchr. Retirement Assn., Waynesboro, 1990, Tchr. of Yr. Cousins Elem. Sch., 1989-90, 90-91. Mem. Tenn. Assn. Educators, Chattanooga Edn. Assn., Zeta Phi Beta Sorority Inc., Ea. Stars. Avocations: drawing, reading, aerobics. Home: 234 Anderson Rd Waynesboro GA 30830

PARRIS, MARK, federal agency official; b. Mpls.; m. Joan Elizabeth Gardner; 2 children. BS magna cum laude, Georgetown U., 1974. With Fgn. Svc., 1972-77; polit. counselor Fgn. Svc., Moscow, 1982-85, dir. Office Soviet Union Affairs, 1985-88; dep. chief mission U.S. Embassy, Tel Aviv, 1989-92; spl. asst. pres., sr. dir. Nat. Security Coun., Washington, 1995—. Mem. policy bd. Una Chapman Cox Found., U.S.-Israel Edn. Found. Phi Beta Kappa. Office: Nat Security Council Near East & S Asian Affairs 1600 Pennsylvania Ave NW Washington DC 20500

PARRIS, NINA GUMPERT, curator, writer, researcher, photographer; b. Berlin, Ger., Sept. 11, 1927; came to U.S., 1937, naturalized, 1944; d. Martin and Charlotte (Blaschko) Gumpert; m. Arthur Parris, Feb. 13, 1949 (div. 1974); children: Carl Joseph, Thomas Martin. BA, Bryn Mawr Coll., 1968; MA, U. Pa., 1969, PhD, 1979. Teaching fellow U. Mich., Ann Arbor, 1969-70; lectr. Phila. Coll. Art, 1970-71; research asst. Phila. Mus. Art, 1970-71; curator, lectr. U. Vt. Robert Hall Fleming Mus., Burlington, 1971-79; chief curator Columbia Mus., S.C., 1979-89; resident faculty visual arts Vt. Coll. Norwich Univ., 1991—. Author: Prints, Paintings and Drawings in Collection of Robert Hall Fleming Mus., 1979, (exhibition catalogue) Through a Master Printer, 1985, The South Carolina Collection of the Columbia Museum, 1987; columnist State newspaper, Columbia, 1984-88; exhibited in one person show at Living Learning Ctr., U. Vt., 1994, Meteor Gallery, Columbia, S.C., 1994, St. Michael's Coll. McArthur Arts Ctr., Colburn Gallery, U. Vt. Bd. dirs. Photography Cooperative, Montpelier, Vt., 1977-

79, Chittenden Arts Coun., Burlington, Vt., 1976-78. Woodrow Wilson fellow, 1968, Univ. fellow Ford Found., 1968-72; grantee NEA, NEH, S.C. Com. Humanities, Vt. Coun. Arts. Mem. Am. Assn. Museums (pres. curator's com. 1985-87, v.p. 1983-85).

PARRIS, ROBERT, composer; b. Phila., May 21, 1924; s. Louis and Rae (Oettinger) P. B.S. in Music Edn, U. Pa., 1945, M.S., 1946; B.S., Juilliard Sch. Music, 1948; student, Ecole Normale de Musique, Paris, Frnace, 1952-53. Mem. faculty Wash. State Coll., 1948-49, Juilliard Summer Sch., 1948; pvt. tchr., 1949-63; prof. music George Washington U., 1963—; mem. Broadcast Music, Inc. Composer: Concerto for Five Kettledrums and Orchestra, 1955, Fantasy and Fugue for Solo Cello; Lamentations and Praises, 1966, Sonata for Solo Violin, 1964, The Messengers for Orchestra, 1974; rec. artist: (albums) Concerto for Trombone and Orchestral Book of Imaginary Beings; Symphonic variations commd. by Nat. Endowment for Arts, Rostropovich and Nat. Symphony Orch., 1987, Parabolae Salomonis, 1995; solo recitals on harpsichord and piano, also in chamber music. Home: 3307 Cummings Ln Bethesda MD 20815-3239 Office: George Washington U Acad Ctr 21st And I St NW Washington DC 20052

PARRIS, THOMAS GODFREY, JR., medical facility administrator; b. Phila., Jan. 30, 1937; married. BS, Pa. State U., 1958; M Health Care Adminstrn., U. Pitts., 1965. Adminstrv. resident Homestead (Pa.) Hosp., 1964-65; exec. assoc. to v.p. Assocs. Hosp. Svcs. of N.Y., N.Y.C., 1965-67; asst. adminstr. Hackensack (N.J.) Med. Ctr., 1967-68; assoc. exec. dir. Met. Hosp. Ctr., N.Y.C., 1968-73; adminstr., CEO Women and Infants Hosp. of R.I., Providence, 1973-76, exec. v.p., CEO, 1976-79, pres., CEO, 1979—. Contbr. articles to profl. publs. Active various cmty. orgns. Fellow Am. Coll. Health Care Execs. (regent R.II. 1984-90); mem. Am. Hosp. Assn. (mem. com., del., trustee 1985-88), R.I. Hosp. Assn. (bd. dirs. 1973—, exec. com. 1974-79, chair 1978-79, del. 1979-80). Office: Women & Infants Hosp RI 101 Dudley St Providence RI 02905*

PARRISH, ALVIN EDWARD, former university dean, medical educator; b. Washington, Sept. 6, 1922; s. John Edward and Thyrza Carrie (Morse) P.; m. Mary Wharton Votaw, June 2, 1945; children—Karen Marie, Anne Elizabeth. M.D., George Washington U., 1945. Intern D.C. Gen. Hosp., Washington, 1945-46; instr. physiology George Washington U., 1947-48; resident medicine Gallinger Municipal Hosp. and VA Hosp., Washington, 1948-50; chief resident medicine Gallinger Municipal Hosp., 1950-51; asst. chief med. service VA Hosp., Washington, 1951-57; chief metabolic lab. VA Hosp., 1955-57; assoc. dean Sch. Medicine, George Washington U., 1957-66, prof. medicine, 1964-91, prof. medicine emeritus, 1991—; chief renal lab. George Washington div. D.C. Gen. Hosp., 1957-66, clin. coordinator, 1960-66; dir. div. renal diseases George Washington Univ. Medical Center, 1967-79; dir. office of human rsch. George Washington U. Hosp., 1979-89. Author books, articles. Served to capt., M.C. AUS, 1946-47; lt. col. Res. Mem. A.C.P., AMA, Am. Diabetes Assn., N.Y. Acad. Sci., AAAS, So. Soc. Clin. Investigation, Am. Soc. Nephrology, Am. Fedn. Clin. Research, Flying Physicians Assn., Pi Kappa Alpha. Home: 5908 Calla Dr Mc Lean VA 22101-3307 Office: George Washington Univ Hosp Sch Medicine Washington DC 20037

PARRISH, BARRY JAY, marketing executive; b. Chgo., Sept. 3, 1946; s. Hy J. and Shirley F. (Fimoff) Perelgut; 1 child, Jeffrey Scott. BA, Columbia Coll., 1968; MBA, U. Chgo., 1971. Asst. advt. mgr. Libby McNeill & Libby, Chgo., 1965-67; advt. and promotion mgr. McGraw-Hill Publs. Co., Chgo., 1967-69; creative dir., account exec. Holt Communication div. Bozell & Jacobs, Chgo., 1969-72; account supr. Linder Advt. div. Dailey & Assocs., San Francisco, 1972-75; v.p., account supr. internat. Arthur E. Wilk Advt., Chgo., 1975-76; exec. v.p. Shaffer/MacGill & Assocs., Chgo., 1976-81; v.p., dir. Grey II, Grey Advt., Chgo., 1981-88; exec. v.p. Gardner, Stein & Frank, Inc., Chgo., 1988-89; v.p. mktg. Reno-Sparks Conv. and Visitors Authority, 1989-90; sr. v.p. sales and mktg. N.W. Lodging, Inc., Seattle, 1991; v.p. sales & mktg. Howard Johnson/Hospitality Franchise Systems, Inc., Parsippany, N.J., 1991—. Contbr. articles to profl. jours., newspapers, mags. TV commls. judge CLIO awards, 1978, 79, U.S. Film Festival, 1980-81, 84; chmn. Reno/Tahoe Rsch. Coun., Reno/Tahoe Tourism Task Force. Served with USMC, to 1972. Recipient awards Houston Internat. Film Festival, Nat. Employment Assn., Coun. Sales Promotion Agys., Internat. Specialty Advt. Assn., others. Home: 16 Fells Manor Rd Caldwell NJ 07006-6126 Office: Howard Johnson Franchise Systems 339 Jefferson Rd Parsippany NJ 07054-3707

PARRISH, CARMELITA, secondary school educator; b. Varina, N.C., Mar. 19, 1934; d. James Robert and Nita Mae (Webb) Beal; m. John J. Parrish, July 24, 1953 (dec.); children: Deborah Joy Parrish White, Toni Lynne Parrish Altenburg. AA, Mid. Ga. Coll., 1979; BS in Edn., Ga. So. U., 1981; MEd, Valdosta State U., 1988, U. Ga., 1993. Secondary tchr. English, graphic arts, Spanish Ware County Bd. Edn., Waycross, Ga., 1981-91; tchr. Spanish, English Telfair County Bd. Edn., McRae, Ga., 1991-92, Pickens County H.S., Jasper, Ga., 1992—; co-advisor Spanish Club; advisor yearbook; tchr. Spanish, journalism. Former leader Girl Scouts U.S., Spain; tchr. area Sunday sch.; band chaperone tour leader student travel in Europe, 1985—. Recipient Star Tchr. award, 1987. Mem. ASCD, NEA, Nat. Coun. Tchrs. of English, Ga. Assn. Educators (local assoc. pres., legislator contact team), So. Assn. Colls. and Schs. (mem. evaluation com.), Phi Kappa Phi. Home: 119 Navaho Trl Jasper GA 30143-1207 Office: 670 W Church St Jasper GA 30143-1410

PARRISH, DAVID WALKER, JR., legal publishing company executive; b. Bristol, Tenn., Feb. 8, 1923. BA, Emory & Henry Coll., 1948, LLD, 1978; BS, U.S. Merchant Marine Acad., 1950; LLB, U. Va., 1951. Pres. The Michie Co., Charlottesville, Va., 1969-89, vice chmn., 1989-96; pub. cons., 1996—. Home: 114 Falcon Dr Charlottesville VA 22901-2013 Office: 300 Preston Ave Ste 103 Charlottesville VA 22902

PARRISH, EDGAR LEE, financial services executive; b. Washington, Apr. 11, 1948; s. Frank Jennings Parrish and Lorene (Lomax) Parrish.; m. Katherine Ellen MacLachlan, Sept. 12, 1987; children: Robert Alexander Wilson, Stephen Edgar MacLachlan. BS in Commerce, U. Va., 1970. Sr. v.p. Wheat, First Securities, Inc., Washington, 1971-79; v.p. Merrill Lynch, Pierce, Fenner & Smith, Inc., Washington, 1979-82, Phila., 1982-85; sr. v.p., fin. cons. Shearson Lehman Bros., Inc., Phila., 1985-87; sr. v.p., fin. cons., mem. chmn.'s coun. Shearson Lehman Bros., Inc., Washington, 1987-93, mem. dirs. coun., 1986; sr. v.p. investments PaineWebber, Inc., Washington, 1993—; pres. HESCO Corp., Manassas, Va., 1989—, also bd. dirs. Capt. USAFR, 1970-76. Mem. U. Va. Club (Washington), U. Va. Alumni Assn., Investment Mgmt. Conss. Assn. Democrat. Episcopalian. Home: 4502 Wetherill Rd Bethesda MD 20816-1813 Office: PaineWebber Inc Franklin Sq 1300 I St NW Washington DC 20005-3314

PARRISH, FRANK JENNINGS, food company executive; b. Manassas, Va., Dec. 29, 1923; s. Edgar Goodloe and Alverda (Jennings) P.; m. Lorene Lomax, Feb. 11, 1944 (div. Apr. 1984); children: Edgar Lee, Julia Lorene; m. Mary Jane Biser, Aug. 25, 1984. Student, Va. Poly. Inst., 1942-43; grad., Indsl. Coll. Armed Forces, 1972. Pres. Manassas Frozen Foods, Inc., 1946—; pres., mgr. Certified Food Buyers Service, Inc., 1953—; pres. First Nat. Acceptance Co., 1966—; v.p. Manassas Ice & Fuel Co. Mem. bus. adminstrn. adv. com. No. Va. Community Coll.; chmn. bd. North Va. coun. Am. Heart Assn., 1987-88; mem. inaugural com., 1961, vice-chmn. inaugural parade com. Maj. USAAF, 1943-46, CBI; ret. brig. gen. comdr. 909th TAC Airlift Group 1969-73, USAF; moblzn. asst. DCS plans and ops. Hdqrs., 1973-79. Decorated Legion of Merit, Air medal. Mem. Nat. Inst. Locker and Freezer Provisioners Am. (past pres., Industry Leadership award 1968), Va. Frozen Foods Assn. (past pres., dir.), Hump Pilots Assn., Va. Assn. Meat Processors (pres. 1986-90), Kiwanis. Methodist (chmn. bd. trustees 1958-66). Home: 9107 Park Ave Manassas VA 22110-4350 Office: 9414 Main St Manassas VA 22110-5424 *Do unto others as you would have them do unto you.*

PARRISH, JAY See PIFER, ALAN

PARRISH, JEANNE ELAINE, mayor, city councilwoman, former health services administrator, nurse; b. Great Falls, Mont., Sept. 7, 1921; d. Robert Edwin and Golda Mae (Jones) Cunningham; m. Charles Edward Parrish, Nov. 9, 1940; children: Charles Edwin, Carol Jean Parrish Wixted. BA, Calif. State Coll., San Diego, 1957, MA, 1959; MPH, U. Calif., Berkeley, 1962. RN, Calif. Staff nurse Rsch. Hosp., Kansas City, Mo., 1945, VNA, 1946; office nurse Rsch. Hosp., San Diego, 1947-50, pub. health nurse, 1950-52; supr. pediatrics San Diego County Hosp., 1952-54, clin. instr. pediatrics, 1955-58; dir. vocat. nurse program Grossmont, Calif., 1958-59; adminstrv. resident Cedars Sinai Hosp., L.A., 1962; exec. asst. nursing L.A. County Hosp., 1962-65; sr. asst. adminstr. Hollywood Presbyn. Hosp., L.A., 1965-75; med./legal analyst Farmers Ins., L.A., 1975-77; mental health cons. Calif. State Dept. of Mental Health, L.A., 1977-78, pub. health cons., 1978-84, med. area mgr., 1984-87; ret., 1987; elected city councilwoman City of Rancho Mirage, Calif., 1992-93, mayor, 1993—. Mem. Womens Club of Rancho Mirage, 1992; mem. Rep. Womens Fedn., Rancho Mirage, 1991; bd. dirs., past pres. Desert Coun. for Aging, Riverside, 1990; bd. dirs., sec. Retired Sr. Vol. Program, Palm Desert, 1992; bd. dirs. Coachella Valley ARC, 1990. Republican. Avocations: volunteering, consulting, teaching. Home: 3 Vista Loma Rancho Mirage CA 92270 Office: City Hall of Ranco Mirage 69825 Highway 11 Rancho Mirage CA 92270

PARRISH, JOHN ALBERT, dermatologist, research administrator; b. Louisville, Ky., Oct. 19, 1939; Children: Lynn, Susan, Mark. BA, Duke U., 1961; MD, Yale U., 1965. Diplomate Am. Bd. Dermatology. Medicine intern U. Mich., Ann Arbor, 1965-67; dermatology resident Harvard Med. Sch., Boston, 1969-72; dermatologist Mass. Gen. Hosp., Boston, 1972-87, dir. Wellman labs., 1975—, dir. cutaneous biology rsch. lab. Harvard, 1987—; chief dermatology Harvard Med. Sch., Boston, 1987—; dermatology cons. Beth Israel Hosp., Boston, 1973—. Author: A Doctor's Year in Vietnam, 1972, Dermatology and Skin Care, 1975, Effects of Ultraviolet Radiation on the Immune System, 1983; co-author: Science of Photomedicine, 1982, Photoimmunology, 1983. Lt. Commdr. USN, 1968-89. Decorated Vietnamese Cross Gallantry with gold; recipient Outstanding Gen. Med. Officer award USN, 1969; Dohi lectr. Japanese Soc. Dermatology, 1990. Mem. Am. Soc. Dermatology (photobiology task force 1972—, Marion B. Sulzberger award 1988), Am. Soc. Lasers in Surgery and Medicine (pres. 1987-88), Am. Soc. Photobiology (coun. 1978-82), Soc. Investigative Dermatology (Wm. Montagna award 1982). Achievements include developing novel and safe effective treatment of psoriasis. Office: Mass Gen Hosp Derm Wel 2 32 Fruit St Boston MA 02114-2620

PARRISH, JOHN BRETT, manufacturing executive; b. Clinton, Ill., Sept. 9, 1934; s. John Craig and Mary Lucille (Brett) P.; m. Lori Ann Burge, Mar. 15, 1990; children from previous marriage: Michael, Douglas, Lynn, Scott. AB in Econs., U. Ill., 1960. With GE Co., 1960-81; vice pres. fin. GE do Brazil S.A., Sao Paulo, 1976-79, v.p. and gen. mgr. consumer products, 1979-81; v.p. fin. services Burlington No. Inc., Seattle, 1981-82, v.p. and treas., 1982, sr. v.p. and chief fin. officer, 1982-83; chmn. and chief exec. officer Glacier Park Co. affiliate Burlington No., Inc., Seattle, 1983-85; exec. v.p. CEM Assocs., Inc., Bellevue, Wash., 1985-86; pres. Parrish, Inc., Seattle, 1986—. Woodrow Wilson fellow, 1960. Mem. Phi Beta Kappa. Home: 16742 45th Ave NE Seattle WA 98155-5616

PARRISH, OVERTON BURGIN, JR., pharmaceutical corporation executive; b. Cin., May 26, 1933; s. Overton Burgin and Geneva Opal (Shinn) P. B.S., Lawrence U., 1955; M.B.A., U. Chgo., 1959. With Pfizer Inc., 1959-74; salesman Pfizer Labs., Chgo., 1959-62; asst. mktg. product mgr. Pfizer Labs., N.Y.C., 1962-63; product mgr. Pfizer Labs., 1964-66; group product mgr. Pfizer Inc., 1966-67, mktg. mgr., 1967-68, v.p. mktg., 1969-70; v.p., dir. ops. Pfizer Labs., 1970-71; exec. v.p. domestic pharm. div. Prizer Labs., 1971-72; exec. v.p., dir. Pfizer Internat. Divsn., 1972-74; pres., chief operating officer G.D. Searle Internat., Skokie, Ill., 1974-75, pres., chief exec. officer, 1975-77; pres. Worldwide Pharm./Consumer Products Group, 1977-86; pres., chief exec. officer Phoenix Health Care, Chgo., 1987—; chmn., CEO, bd. dirs. Wis. Pharmiacal Co., Inc., 1990-96; co-chmn. Inhalon Pharms., 1991-95, also bd. dirs.; chmn. ViatiCare Ltd., 1993—, also bd. dirs.; chmn., CEO, bd. dirs. The Female Health Co., 1996—. Author: The Future Pharmaceutical Marketing; International Drug Pricing, 1971. Trustee Mktg. Sci. Inst.; trustee Food and Drug Law Inst., 1979—, Lawrence U., 1983—. Served to 1st lt. USAF, 1955-57. Mem. Am. Mktg. Assn., Am. Mgmt. Assn., Beta Gamma Sigma, Phi Kappa Tau. Home: 505 N Lake Shore Dr Chicago IL 60611-3427 Office: Phoenix Health Care 919 N Michigan Ave Chicago IL 60611-1601

PARRISH, ROBERT ALTON, retired pediatric surgeon, educator; b. Augusta, Ga., Sept. 10, 1930; s. Robert Alton and Thelma Elizabeth (Roney) P.; children: Joyce Ann, Cynthia Ann. A.B., Mercer U., 1951; M.S., U. Ga., 1953; M.D., Med. Coll. Ga., 1956. Diplomate: Am. Bd. Surgery. Intern Bapt. Meml. Hosp., Memphis, 1956-57; resident in surgery U. Tenn., Memphis, 1957-62; gen. surgeon Med. Coll. Ga., Aususta, 1962-64; asst. prof. surgery Med. Coll. Ga., Augusta, 1964-67, assoc. prof., 1967-70, prof. pediatric surgery, chief pediatric surgery, 1970-93, prof. emeritus pediatric surgery, 1993—; cons. to hosps. Named Outstanding Tchr. of Yr. Med. Found. Ga., Med. Coll. Ga., 1966. Fellow ACS; mem. Am. Assn. Surgery of Trauma, So. Surg. Assn., Am. Acad. Pediatrics, Alpha Omega Alpha, Phi Sigma, Alpha Epsilon Delta. Methodist. Home: 433 Scott Way Augusta GA 30909-9591

PARRISH, SHERRY DYE, elementary school educator; b. Birmingham, Ala., Oct. 18, 1957; d. Charles Max and Peggy Gail (Doss) Dye; m. James Wiley Parrish, June 13, 1987; 1 child, Taylor Austin Shaw. BS in Elem. Edn., Samford U., 1979; MS in Elem. Edn., U. Ala., 1995. Cert. tchr. Rank I, Class A., Ala. Tchr. Franklin Acad., Birmingham, Ala., 1979-83, Shades Cahaba Elem. Sch., Homewood, Ala., 1986-94, Trace Crossings Sch., Hoover, Ala., 1994-95, South Shades Crest Sch., Hoover, Ala., 1995—; chairperson sci. fair Shades Cahaba Elem. Sch., Homewood, 1990-94; mem. accreditation team, Warrior (Ala.) Sch., 1990; presenter Homewood City Schs., 1988, Constructivist Conf., Birmingham, 1994, 95, co-presenter NCTM regional conf., 1995, presenter Mid-South Whole Lang. Conf., Birmingham, 1995. Rsch. participant (book) Theme Immersion: Inquiry Based Curriculum in Elementary and Middle Schools, 1994. Founder, tchr. Women in Transition, Shades Mt. Baptist Ch., Birmingham, 1993—; presenter Festival of Marriage, Ridgecrest N.C, 1994, Dayspring Women's Conf., Birmingham, 1994. Mem. Nat. Coun. Teachers of Math., Am. Edn. Rsch. Assn., Educator's Forum. Avocations: reading, tennis, travel. Office: South Shades Crest Elem 3770 South Shades Crest Rd Hoover AL 35244

PARRISH, THOMAS KIRKPATRICK, III, marketing consultant; b. Richmond, Va., May 18, 1930; s. Thomas Kirkpatrick and Sally Cary (Friend) P.; divorced; children: Linn Cary, Wayne Elizabeth, Susan Scott, Thomas Kirkpatrick IV. A.B., Princeton U., 1952. Product mgr. Vick Chem. Co., N.Y.C., 1955-58; v.p. Benton & Bowles Advt. Agy., N.Y.C., 1958-65; pres. Am. Chicle Co. div. Warner-Lambert Co., Morris Plains, N.J., 1965-70, Life Savers Inc. div. Squibb Corp., N.Y.C., 1970-73, Lanvin-Charles of Ritz Inc. subs. Squibb Corp., N.Y.C., 1974-76; dir. parent co. Squibb Corp., 1974-77; group dir. new bus. devel. Gillette Co., Boston, 1977-78; exec. v.p. SSC & B, Inc., N.Y.C., 1978-81; sr. assoc. Am. Cons. Corp., 1982-86; prin. The Parrish Co., N.Y.C., 1986—. Mem. N.Y. State Republican Com., 1962-63; bd. dirs. YMCA Ctr. for Internat. Mgmt. Studies, N.Y.C., 1970-85. Served to lt., jr. grade USN, 1952-55. Home: 215 E 73rd St New York NY 10021-3653

PARRISH, WILLIAM EARL, history educator; b. Garden City, Kans., Apr. 7, 1931; s. Earl Milton and Anna Maye (Stoker) P.; m. Ellen Kaye Vickers, June 14, 1959 (div. 1971); m. Helen Sue Lewis Stoppel, June 2, 1972; children: Elizabeth Ann, William Lewis. BS with honors, Kans. State U., 1952; MA, U. Mo., 1953, PhD, 1955. Asst. prof. to Harry S. Truman prof. in Am. history Westminster Coll., Fulton, Mo., 1955-78, dean of coll., 1973-75; prof. history Miss. State U., Mississippi State, 1978—, head dept. history, 1978-85. Author: David Rice Atchison of Missouri, 1961, Turbulent Partnership, Missouri and the Union, 1963, Missouri Under Radical Rule, 1865-1870, 1965, A History of Missouri, Vol. III, 1860-1875, 1973, (with Charles T. Jones, Jr. and Lawrence Christensen) Missouri: The Heart of the Nation, 1992; gen. editor Sesquicentennial History of Missouri, 5 vols., 1971—. Mem. Mo. Adv. Coun. on Hist. Preservation, 1967-78; chmn. Mo. Am. Revolution Bicentennial Com., 1974-77; nat. adv. bd. Soc. of Civil War Historians, 1986—; mem. State Hist. Records Adv. Bd., 1980—. Recipient proclamation for quarter century of svc. Gov. of Mo., 1978, award of merit Am. Assn. State and Local History, 1974. Mem. Orgn. Am. Historians, Western History Assn., So. Hist. Assn., Nat. Trust Hist. Preservation, Miss. Hist. Soc. (pres. 1995-96), State Hist. Soc. Mo. (life), Rotary, Phi Alpha Theta (internat. pres. 1985-87), Phi Gamma Delta (historian 1989—). Presbyterian. Avocation: deltiology. Office: Miss State U Dept History Drawer H Mississippi State MS 39762 Home: 703 Bonnie Rd Starkville MS 39759-2104

PARR-JOHNSTON, ELIZABETH, academic administrator; b. N.Y.C., Aug. 15, 1939; d. Ferdinand Van Siclen and Helene Elizabeth (Ham) Parr; m. David E. Bond, Dec. 28, 1962 (div. July 1975); children: Peter, Kristina Aline; m. Archibald F. Johnston, Mar. 6, 1982; children: James, Heather, Alexandra, Margaret. BA, Wellesley Coll., 1961; MA, Yale U., 1962, PhD, 1973; postgrad., Harvard U., 1986. Various positions Govt. of Can., Ottawa, Ont., 1973-76, INCO Ltd., Toronto, 1976-79; chief of staff, sr. policy advisor Minstry of Employment and Immigration, Govt. of Can., 1979-80; various positions Shell Can. Ltd., Calgary, Alta., 1980-90; pres. Parr-Johnston & Assocs., Calgary, 1990-91; pres., vice chancellor Mt. St. Vincent U., Halifax, Nova Scotia, N.S., 1991-96; pres., vice-chancellor The U. N.B., Fredericton, Can., 1996—; instr. U. Western Ont., London, Ont., 1964-67, U. B.C., Vancouver, 1967-71; vis. scholar Wesleyan U., Middletown, Conn., 1971-72; acad. rsch. assoc. Carleton U., Ottawa, 1972-73; bd. dirs. Nova Scotia Power, Bank of Nova Scotia, Fishery Products Internat., The Empire Co.; spkr. and presenter in field. Mem. editorial bd. Can. Econ. Jour., 1980-83; contbr. articles to profl. jours. Bd. dirs. Dellcrest Home, 1980-84, Calgary S.W. Fed. Riding Assn., 1985-91, The Learning Ctr., Calgary, 1989-91, Halifax United Way, 1991-92, North/South Inst., 1992—, Vol. Planning N.S., 1992-93; planning chmn. John Howard Soc., 1980-84; mem. policy adv. com. C.D. Howe, 1980-85; mem. Ont. Econ. Coun., 1981-84. Woodrow Wilson fellow, 1962. Mem. Assn. Atlantic Univs. (chair 1994—), Assn. Univs. and Colls. in Can. (bd. dirs., mem. exec. com. 1994—), Coun. for Can. Unity (bd. dirs.), Women in Acad. Adminstrn. (adv. bd. 1991—), Calgary Coun. Advanced Tech. (exec. 1990-91), Can. Econs. Assn., Inst. Pub. Adminstrn. Can., Sr. Women Acad. Adminstrs. Can., Phi Beta Kappa. Anglican. Avocations: skiing, golf, sailing. Office: The Univ N B Office of the Pres PO Box 4400 Fredcericton NB

PARROTT, CHARLES NORMAN, bank executive; b. West Chester, Pa., June 5, 1947; s. Charles Orrin and Dorothy Emma (Rissel) P.; m. Karol Ellen Gress, Sept. 6, 1986. BS in Psychology, U. Cin., 1972, BS in Econs., 1975; postgrad., Stonier Grad. Sch. Banking, Rutgers, N.J., 1982. Cert: CLU, CFP, ChFC, CMFC, cert. trust and fin. adv. Asst. br. mgr. Cen. Trust Co., Cin., 1967-76; trust officer Bank of Pa., Reading, 1976-83; v.p. Lebanon Valley Nat. Bank, Lebanon, Pa., 1983—. Past pres. Sertoma, Lebanon, 1987; chmn. Mid Atlantic Air Mus., 1994; pres. The Salvation Army, Lebanon, 1994; vice chmn. The Am. Red Cross, 1994. Recipient Presdl. citation Am. Banking Assn., 1984; scholar Rotary Found., 1980. Mem. Lebanon Valley Sertoma Club, Annville Rotary Club. Avocations: photography, tennis, rail fan. Home: 1650 Robin Rd Lebanon PA 17042-6433 Office: Lebanon Valley Nat Bank 555 Willow St Lebanon PA 17046-4869

PARROTT, ROBERT HAROLD, pediatrician, educator; b. Jackson Heights, N.Y., Dec. 29, 1923; s. Harold Leslie and Ruth Mabel (Hargrove) P.; m. Paula McDonough, June 2, 1951; children: Timothy, Maureen, Daniel, Theresa, Christopher, Edward. Student, Fordham U.; M.D., Georgetown U., 1949. Intern Hosp. of St. Raphael, New Haven, Conn., 1949-50; resident Children's Hosp. of D.C., 1950-52; staff pediatrician, chief Pediatric Unit, Lab. of Clin. Investigation, Nat. Inst. Allergy and Infectious Diseases, NIH, Bethesda, Md., 1952-56; physician-in-chief, dir. Research Found., Children's Hosp. of D.C., Washington, 1956-62, dir., 1962-85, dir. emeritus, 1985—; prof. pediatrics George Washington U., Washington. Mem. AMA, Am. Acad. Pediatrics, Am. Pediatric Soc., Am. Acad. Med. Dirs., Am. Coll. Physician Execs., D.C. Med. Soc., Infectious Diseases Soc. Club: Cosmos (Washington). Home: 13064 Deanmar Dr Highland MD 20777-9519 Office: Children's Nat Med Ctr 111 Michigan Ave NW Washington DC 20010-2970

PARROTT, SHARON LEE, elementary educator; b. Ostrander, Ohio, Oct. 15, 1949; d. Fay Llewellyn and Thelma Irene (Reed) P. BS in Elem. Edn., Ind. Wesleyan U., 1975. From kindergarten assoc. tchr. to asst. tchr. Columbus (Ohio) Children's Coll., 1975; 1st grade tchr. Kayenta (Ariz.) Unified Sch. Dist. 27, 1975-84, presch. tchr., 1986-95; substitute tchr. Delaware and Union County Schs., Ohio, 1984-86. Tchr. Kayenta Bible Ch., 1981—, recorder, 1991-93. Mem. ASCD, Internat. Reading Assn., Nat. Coun. Tchrs. English, Assn. for Childhood Edn. Internat. Avocations: cooking, reading, outdoor activities. Home: PO Box 2172 Kayenta AZ 86033-2172 Office: Kayenta Unified Sch Dist 27 PO Box 337 Kayenta AZ 86033-0337

PARROTT-FONSECA, JOAN, federal agency administrator. BA in History, Howard U.; MA in Human Resource Mgmt., Georgetown U., JD. Acting dir., dep. dir. D.C.'s Dept. Consumer and Regulatory Affairs; former assoc. adminstr. Office of Enterprise Devel./U.S. Gen. Svcs. Adminstrn.; dir. Minority Bus. Devel. Agy./U.S. Dept. Commerce, 1995—. Office: US Dept of Commerce Minority Bus Devel Agy 14th & Constitution Ave NW Washington DC 20230

PARRY, ATWELL J., JR., state senator, retailer; b. Ogden, Utah, June 14, 1925; s. John Atwell and Nina Virginia (McEntire) P.; m. Elaine Hughes, Feb. 6, 1946; children—Bonnie, Michael, Jay, Donald, David, Delbert, Kent. Student pub. schs., Nampa, Idaho. Salesman, King's Packing Co., Nampa, 1947-54, credit mgr., 1954-55; plant mgr. Stone Poultry Co., Nampa, 1955-56; salesman Nestle Chocolate Co., 1956-64; owner, mgr. Melba Foods, Idaho, 1964-82; mem. Idaho Senate, 1981—; bd. dirs. Western Idaho Tng. Ctr., 1987-90; chmn. Senate Finance Com. and co-chmn. Joint Fin. and Appropriations Com., 1987—; chmn. Idaho State Bd. for Nat. Ctr. for Constl. Studies, 1988-90. Bd dirs. Alcohol Treatment Ctr., Nampa, 1978-82; mem. adv. bd. Mercy Med. Ctr., Nampa, 1976-81; mem. Melba City Council, 1971-74. Recipient Silver Beaver award Boy Scouts Am., 1959, Service award Mercy Med. Ctr., Outstanding Rep. Legislator in Idaho State award, 1993. Republican. Mormon.

PARRY, BARBARA DREPPERD, educational administrator; b. Coral Gables, Fla., Sept. 6, 1935; d. Clarence Hartsel and Mildred (Orme) Drepperd; m. William J. Parry, Nov. 3, 1978; children: William H. Glassford, Robert K. Glassford. BEd, U. Miami, 1957; MS in Ednl. Leadership, Nova U., 1993. Cert POP observer, Fla. Tchr. Dade County Pub. Schs., Miami, Fla., Montpelier (Vt.) Pub. Schs.; tkchr. Longmeadow (Mass.) Pub. Schs.; prin. Lower Sch. Gulliver Acad., Coral Gables. Mem. ASCD, NAESP, Nat. Coun. Tchrs. Math., AAUW, Delta Kappa Gamma. Office: Gulliver Acad 12595 Red Rd Miami FL 33156-6397

PARRY, DALE D., newspaper editor. BS in Journalism cum laude, Ball State U., Muncie, Ind., 1981. Feature writer, editor and columnist Richmond (Ind.) Palladium-Item, 1981-84; feature writer Cin. Enquirer, 1984-86, asst. editor Today sect., 1986-87; editor Today section The Dallas Morning News, 1987-90; assignment editor The Way We Live sect. Detroit Free Press, 1990-92, dep. features editor, 1992-94, features editor, 1993—. Mem. Am. Assn. Sun. and Feature Editors. Office: Detroit Free Press 321 W Lafayette Blvd Detroit MI 48226-2705

PARRY, HUGH JONES (JAMES CROSS), social scientist, educator, author; b. London, Mar. 10, 1916; came to U.S., 1919, naturalized, 1924; s. John and Jane Myfanwy (Jones) P.; m. Helen Mason Weston, May 30, 1941 (div. 1960); 1 son, John; m. Betty Brawer, Mar. 10, 1961; 1 son, Brian. A.B., Yale, 1937, postgrad., 1938; M.S., Columbia, 1939; Ph.D., U. So. Calif., 1949. Asso. dir. Opinion Research Center, U. Denver, 1947-49; also prof. sociology; asst. dir. Troop Attitude Research br., U.S. Forces in Europe, 1950-52; project dir. evaluation staff U.S. High Commn. for Germany, 1952-53; research officer Am. embassy, Paris, 1956-58; chief Western European br., survey research div. USIA, 1958-61; survey dir. Office Research and Analysis, 1961-62, chief of survey research and analysis, 1961-62, chief of survey research div., 1962-63; dir. research Office Research and Analysis, Western Europe, 1963-66; asso. dir. Social Research Group; prof. sociology George Washington U., Washington, 1966-82; research cons., editor, writer, 1983—. Author: (with Leo P. Crespi) Public Opinion in Western Europe, 1953, Root of Evil, 1957, The Dark Road, 1959, The Grave of Heroes, 1961, To Hell for Half a Crown, 1967. Served to lt. USNR, 1942-46. Winner PEN short story contest, 1987; Creative Writing fellow Nat. Endowment for Lit., 1975; Va. Ctr. for the Creative Arts felow, 1990, 92, 93, 95. Mem. Am. Assn. Pub. Opinion Rsch., Am. Hist. Assn., Am. Sociol. Soc., Cosmos Club (Washington), Phi Beta Kappa, Phi Delta Theta. Home: 4814 Falstone Ave Bethesda MD 20815-5542

PARRY, JAMES, insurance executive. Chmn. bd. Sedgwick of N.Y., Inc. Office: 1290 6th Ave Lobby 6 New York NY 10104

PARRY, LANCE AARON, newspaper executive; b. Allentown, Pa., Sept. 4, 1947; s. Harwood Clayton Bachman and Iola Mary (Johnson) P.; m. Virginia Eleanor Ford, Apr. 24, 1971; children: Halloran Lee, Christine Ford. BS in Edn., Kutztown U., 1969; postgrad., W.Va. U., 1970. With Call-Chronicle Newspapers, Allentown, 1970-81, mng. editor, 1979-81; asst. news editor The Phila. Inquirer, 1981-82, systems editor, 1982-84, night news editor, 1984-86, news editor daily edit., 1986-87, news editor Sunday edit., 1987-89, sr. editor/systems and tech., 1989-93, page design dir., 1993-94, features news editor, 1994—; news editor Sunday edit. Recipient 1st Place award for front page design Pa. Newspaper Pubs. Assn./Pa. Soc. Newspaper Editors, 1985, 87, 88, Disting. Alumnus award Kutztown U., 1992; Sigma Delta Chi scholar, 1969. Mem. Soc. Profl. Journalists, Pen and Pencil Club. Democrat. Presbyterian. Home: 16 Salisbury Ln Malvern PA 19355-2836 Office: The Phila Inquirer 400 N Broad St Philadelphia PA 19130-4015

PARRY, ROBERT TROUTT, bank executive, economist; b. Harrisburg, Pa., May 16, 1939; s. Anthony C. and Margaret R. (Troutt) P.; m. Brenda Louise Grumbine, Dec. 27, 1956; children: Robert Richard, Lisa Louise. BA magna cum laude, Gettysburg (Pa.) Coll., 1960; MA in Econs., U. Pa., 1961, PhD, 1967. Asst. prof. econs. Phila. Coll. Textiles and Sci., 1963-65; economist Fed. Res. Bd., Washington, 1965-70; v.p., chief economist Security Pacific Nat. Bank, Los Angeles, 1970-76, sr. v.p., chief economist, 1976-81, exec. v.p., chief economist, 1981-86; pres., chief exec. officer Fed. Res. Bank San Francisco, 1986—; bd. dirs. Nat. Bur. Econ. Rsch.; mem. adv. bd. Pacific Rim Bankers Program; mem. policy adv. bd. Ctr. for Real Estate and Urban Econs., U. Calif., Berkeley, mem. exec. com. Inst. Bus. and Econs. Rsch.; bd. dirs. San Francisco Bay Area Coun.; mem. Bay Area Econ. Forum; lectr. Pacific Coast Banking Sch., 1976-78; mem. adv. coun. SRI Internat. Mem. econ. vis. com. U. Pa.; mem. exec. bd. Boy Scouts Am., 1993—; bd. dirs. United Way, 1995. NDEA fellow, 1960-63. Mem. Nat. Assn. Bus. Economists (pres. 1979-80), Am. Econ. Assn. Home: 90 Overhill Rd Orinda CA 94563-3131 Office: Fed Res Bank San Francisco PO Box 7702 San Francisco CA 94120-7702

PARRY, ROBERT WALTER, chemistry educator; b. Ogden, Utah, Oct. 1, 1917; s. Walter and Jeanette (Petterson) P.; m. Marjorie J. Nelson, July 6, 1945; children: Robert Bryce, Mark Nelson. BS, Utah State Agr. Coll., 1940; MS, Cornell U., 1942; PhD, U. Ill., 1946; DSc (hon.), Utah State U., 1985. Research asst. NDRC Munitions Devel. Lab., U. Ill. at Urbana, 1943-45, teaching fellow 1945-46; mem. faculty U. Mich., 1946-69, prof. chemistry, 1958-69; Distinguished prof. chemistry U. Utah, 1969—; indsl. cons., 1952—; chmn. bd. trustees Gordon Rsch. Conf., 1967-68. Chmn. com. teaching chemistry Internat. Union Pure and Applied Chemistry 1968-74. Recipient Mfg. Chemists award for coll. teaching, 1972, Sr. U.S. Scientist award Alexander Von Humboldt-Stiftung (W. Ger.), 1980, First Govs. medal of Sci. State Utah, 1987. Mem. Am. Chem. Soc. (Utah award Utah Sect. 1978, past chmn. inorganic div. and div. chem. edn., award for distinguished service to inorganic chemistry 1965, for chem. edn., 1977, dir. 1973-83, bd. editors jour. 1969-80, pres.-elect 1981-82, pres. 1982-83, Priestly medal 1993), Internat. Union Pure and Applied Chemistry (chmn. U.S. nat. com.), AAAS, Sigma Xi. Founding editor Inorganic Chemistry, 1960-63. Research, publs. on some structural problems of inorganic chemistry, and incorporation results into theoretical models; chemistry of phosphorus, boron and fluorine. Home: 5002 Fairbrook Ln Salt Lake City UT 84117-6205 Office: U Utah Dept Chemistry Henry Eyring Bldg Salt Lake City UT 84112-1194

PARRY, WILLIAM DEWITT, lawyer; b. Hartford, Conn., June 4, 1941; s. William Brown and Mary Elizabeth (Caton) p.; m. Andrea Hannah Lewis, June 30, 1973; children: Sara, Jessica. BA, U. Mass., 1963; JD, U. Pa., 1966. Bar: N.J. 1987, Pa. 1967, U.S. Dist. Ct. (ea. dist.) Pa. 1974, U.S. Ct. Appeals (3d cir.) 1980, U.S. Supreme Ct. 1980. Assoc. Shapiro, Cook & Bressler, Phila., 1966-67; asst. dir. ABA joint com on continuing egal edn. Am. Law Inst., Phila., 1967-73; assoc. Lowenschuss Assocs., Phila., 1973-85; of counsel Weiss, Golden & Pierson, Phila., 1985-88; pvt. practice Phila., 1988—; ptnr. Rubin, Quinn, Moss & Patterson, Phila., 1989-93; pvt. practice Phila., 1993—. Author: Understanding and Controlling Stuttering: A Comprehensive New Approach Based on the Valsalva Hypothesis, 1994; editor U. Pa. Law Rev., 1964-66, The Practical Lawyer, 1967-73. Founder Phila. area chpt. Nat. Stuttering Project, 1985—, dir. Nat. Stuttering Project, 1996—; trustee Unitarian Soc. Germantown, Phila., 1983-86. Mem. ABA, Assn. Trial Lawyers Am., Phila. Bar Assn., Pa. Trial Lawyers Assn. Democrat. Avocations: writing, lecturing. Home: 520 Baird Rd Merion Station PA 19066-1302 Office: 1608 Walnut St Ste 900 Philadelphia PA 19103-5443

PARSEGIAN, V(OZKEN) ADRIAN, biophysicist; b. Boston, May 28, 1939; s. Voscan Lawrence and Varsenig (Boyajian) P.; m. Valerie Phillips, Mar. 2, 1963; children: Andrew, Homer, Aram. AB in Physics magna cum laude, Dartmouth Coll., Hanover, N.H., 1960; ed., Weizmann Inst., Rehovoth, Israel, 1962-64; PhD in Biophysics, Harvard U., 1965. With comm. biophysics lab. MIT, Cambridge, 1961-62;, 1967-95; chief lab. structural biology Divsn. Computer Rsch. & Tech., NIH, Bethesda, Md., 1995—; with Hansen Biophys. Lab. Stanford (Calif.) U., summer 1965; rsch. physicist phys. scis. lab. divsn. computer rsch./tech. NIH, Bethesda, Md., 1967-93, chief lab. structural biology divsn. computer rsch./tech., 1993—; head unit on molecular forces, lab. biochemistry and metabolism, NIDDK, NIH, 1984—; vis. prof. dept. physics Princeton (N.J.) U., 1990-91; mem. biophysics panel NSF, 1987-91, mem. materials synthesis and processing program panel, 1992; mem. coun. Gordon Rsch. Confs., 1988-91, mem. site and scheduling com., 1988-92, chmn. conf. on transport in bilayers and biol. membranes, 1985, chmn. conf. on chemistry at interfaces, 1986, chmn. conf. on water and aqueous solutions, 1994. Editor Biophys. Jour., 1977-80, Biophys. Discussions, 1978-92; contbr. over 100 articles to profl. jours.; editl. bd. 10 jours. Mem. Biophys. Soc. (pres. 1983-84, mem. coun. 1974-80, mem. exec. com. 1974-75, program chmn. ann. meeting 1981, mem. publ. com. 1980-83, chmn. publ. com. 1981-83, founding editor Biophys. Discussions, 1978-92, editor Biophys. Jour. 1977-80, Disting. Svc. award 1994), Sigma Xi, Phi Beta Kappa. Achievements include research in cell membranes, lipid bilayers and non-lamellar phases nucleic acids, particularly DNA, poolysaccarides, and proteins, particularly ionic channels, allosteric systems; in molecular assembly, protein conformation and function, ion transport, and membrane fusion; in hydration, hydrophobic solvation forces, van der Waals interactions, electrostatic forces, and mechanical forces of membrane or molecular fluctuation; in colloid and interface science, liquid-crystals, macromolecules, and surface physics; research to develop a relevant physics of forces and energies organizing biological macromolecules with direct measurement, theoretical analysis, and practical formulation for computation; use of computers in scientific publication and communication.

PARSELL, DAVID BEATTY, modern language educator; b. Charleston, S.C., Dec. 4, 1941; s. Sidney Irving and Jean Wesley (Beatty) P.; m. Sharon Youngblood, Apr. 7, 1967; children: Margaret Lindsey, John Benjamin. AB with honors, Hamilton Coll., 1963; MA, Vanderbilt U., 1968, PhD, 1970. Instr. French Grinnell (Iowa) Coll., 1967-69; from instr. to prof. modern languages Furman U., Greenville, S.C., 1969—. Author: Louis Auchincloss, 1988, Michel de Ghelderode, 1993; contbr. articles to books and profl. jours. Fulbright Travel grantee, 1965-66. Mem. Southern Comparative Literature Assn. (adv. bd. 1976-79, editorial bd. 1977—, editor newsletter 1988-92). Democrat. Episcopalian. Avocations: writing, photography, travel. Home: 8 Oakleaf Rd # 12 Greenville SC 29609-6652 Office: Furman U Box 30972 Greenville SC 29613

PARSHALL, GEORGE WILLIAM, research chemist; b. Hackensack, Minn., Sept. 19, 1929; s. George Clarence and Frances (Virnig) P.; m. Naomi B. Simpson, Oct. 9, 1954; children: William, Jonathan, David. B.S., U. Minn., 1951; Ph.D., U. Ill., 1954. Research chemist E.I. duPont de Nemours & Co., Wilmington, Del., 1954-65, research supr., 1965-79, dir. chem. sci., 1979-92, cons., 1992—, mem. com. on environ. mgmt. techs., 1994—; mem. chem. stockpile disposal com. NRC, Washington, 1992—; bd. chem. sci. NRC, Washington, 1983-86; Reilly lectr. Notre Dame U., 1980; Ipatieff lectr. Northwestern U., 1994. Author: Homogeneous Catalysis, 1980, 2d rev. edit. 1992; editor: Inorganic Syntheses, 1974, Jour. Molecular Catalysis, 1977-80. Recipient Ballar Inorganic Chemistry medal U. Ill., 1976. Mem. NAS, Inst. Chemists (Chem. Pioneer award 1992, Gold medal award 1995), Am. Chem. Soc. (award in inorganic chemistry 1983, award for leadership in chem. rsch. mgmt. 1989), Am. Acad. Arts Scis., Guild Episcopal Scholars (treas. 1994—). Episcopalian. Home: 2504 Delaware Ave Wilmington DE 19806-1220

PARSHALL, GERALD, journalist; b. St. Paul, Apr. 24, 1941; s. William Elmer and Evelyn (Steckling) P.; m. Sandra Grant, Dec. 20, 1970. B.A., U. Minn., 1963; M.A., U. Mich., 1964; grad. fellow, U. Chgo., 1966-67. Reporter York (Pa.) Gazette and Daily, 1968, Balt. Evening Sun, 1968-71; Capitol Hill staff U.S. News & World Report, Washington, 1971-77; sr. editor U.S. News & World Report, 1977-79, asst. mng. editor, 1979-90, sr. writer, 1990—; mem. Exec. Com. of Periodical Corrs., U.S. Congress, 1974-80, chmn., 1979-80. Served to 1st lt. U.S. Army, 1964-66. Recipient Front Page award Washington-Balt. Newspaper Guild, 1971, Silver Gavel award ABA, 1983. Home: 1004 Congress Ln McLean VA 22101-2116 Office: 2400 N St NW Washington DC 20037-1153

PARSKY, GERALD LAWRENCE, lawyer; b. West Hartford, Conn., Oct. 18, 1942; s. Isadore and Nettie (Sanders) P.; m. Susan Haas, June 26, 1966; children: Laura, David; m. Robin Cleary, Jan. 27, 1980. A.B., Princeton U., 1964; J.D., U. Va., 1968. Bar: N.Y. 1969, D.C. 1974, Calif. 1983. Assoc. Mudge Rose Guthrie & Alexander, N.Y.C., 1968-71; spl. asst. to under sec. U.S. Treasury Dept., Washington, 1971-73; exec. asst. to dep. sec. Fed. Energy Office U.S. Treasury Dept., 1973-74, asst. sec. internat. affairs, 1974-77; sr. ptnr. Gibson, Dunn & Crutcher, Los Angeles, 1977-90; of counsel Gibson, Dunn & Cruther, L.A., 1990-92; chmn. Aurora Capital Ptnrs., L.A., 1990—. Bd. govs. Performing Arts Council, Los Angeles Music Ctr. Recipient Alexander Hamilton award U.S. Treasury, 1976. Mem. ABA, Coun. Fgn. Rels., N.Y. Princeton Club, Calif. Club, Racquet Club, Anandale Club, Beach Club. Office: Aurora Capital Ptnrs 1800 Century Park E Los Angeles CA 90067-1501

PARSLEY, ROBERT HORACE, lawyer; b. Erwin, Tenn., Apr. 9, 1923; s. Millard Fillmore and Daisy Laurel (Garland) P.; m. Georganna Alice Strake, Apr. 11, 1952; children—Robert, Sharon, Brian, Sandra, Sally, David, John, Daniel, Jana. J.D.S., U. Va., 1949. Assoc. Baker & Botts, Houston, 1949-53; assoc. Butler & Binion, Houston, 1953-55, ptnr., 1955-94, of counsel, 1994—; bd. dirs. Stewart and Stevenson Svcs. Inc., Houston; trustee Southwestern Legal Found., Dallas, 1980, Southwestern Law Enforcement Inst., Dallas, 1980. Mem. Tex. State Commn. for Mental Health and Mental Retardation, Austin, 1972-78; vice chmn. Tex. State Commn. on Jud. Conduct, Austin, 1983-89; pres. bd. trustees St. Elizabeth Hosp. Found., Houston, 1984-90; bd. dirs. Strake Jesuit Coll. Prep., Houston, 1973—, San Jose Clinic, 1990—, South Tex. Sch. Law, 1994—; pres. St. Joseph's Hosp. Found., 1993-95, trustee, 1988—. Served to lt. USAAF, 1942-46, Panama. Recipient Order of Benemerenti (Vatican). Fellow Tex. Bar Found.; mem. ABA, Tex. Bar Assn., Houston Bar Assn. Republican. Presbyterian. Clubs: Houston, Houston Country. Home: 12 E Broad Oaks Dr Houston TX 77056-1202 Office: Butler & Binion 1600 1st Interstate Bank Plz Houston TX 77002

PARSON, BEVERLY A., foundation administrator; b. Saint Louis, Nov. 10, 1952; d. William Porter and Lovie (Woods) West; m. Edward Kenneth Parson, Mar. 25, 1972; 1 child, Leslie Nicole. B Liberal Studies, St. Louis U., 1983. Cons. dental practice mgmt. Dental Directions Svcs., St. Louis, 1983-87; dir. program and svcs. ea. Mo. chpt. Arthritis Found., St. Louis, 1987—; cons. dental practice mgmt. multi specialty groups, Mo., Ill., 1983-87; developer-medically underserved ednl. programming, St. Louis, 1989-93; cons. Guide to Working with Medically Underserved Populations, Atlanta, 1990-93; creator First Com. for Medically Underserved Population, St. Louis, 1990-93; bd. mem. Mo. State Task Force Arthritis in the Working Years, 1990-93; mem. patient svcs. subcom. Nat. Arthritis Found., 1992-93; mem. adv. bd. Mo. Boothill Edn. Program, 1993. Advocate, speaker St. Louis U.-Geriatric Summer Inst., St. Louis, 1992, United Way, St. Louis, 1990-93, Gov.'s Conf. on Aging, St. Louis, 1993; bd. dirs. Grace Hill Wellness Initiative, 1991-93. Recipient award of excellence Nat. Arthritis Found., Atlanta, 1992, Profl. Achievement award, 1993, Yes I Can award Sentinel Newspaper, St. Louis, 1993. Mem. Arthritis Found. Staff Assn. (grants and recognition com. 1991-93, profl. achievement award 1993). Democrat. Avocations: access to care for medically underserved, motivational speaking, reading. Home: 810 Leonard Dr Saint Louis MO 63119-1330 Office: Arthritis Found Ea Mo 8390 Delmar Blvd Saint Louis MO 63124-2107

PARSON, SARAH JANE, retired insurance executive; b. Phila., Nov. 11, 1931; d. Harry and Dorothy (Beatty) P. Grad. high sch., Phila., 1949. Typist, clk. Hartford Steam Boiler I & I Co., Phila., 1949-69, underwriter, 1969-86, sr. mktg. exec., 1986-93; acct. exec. Murray Ins. Agy., Scranton, Pa., 1994-95; ret., 1995. Contbr. articles to profl. jours. Recipient Ins. Women of Yr. award Greater Scranton Ins. Women, 1991, Rep. award Ins. Systems Unltd., 1991. Mem. Nat. Assn. Ins. Women, Northeastern Pa. Inst. Assn. (past pres. 1991-92), The Scranton Club, Order Eastern Star (worthy matron 1966-67, 81-82, 90-91). Democrat. Baptist. Avocations: golf, gardening, music, cameras, old movies. Home: 6817 Guyer Ave Philadelphia PA 19142-2518

PARSONS, ANDREW JOHN, management consultant; b. Kingston, Surrey, Eng., July 22, 1943; came to U.S., 1968; s. S. John and Hylda P. (Wili) P.; m. Carol Ann Iannucci, June 6, 1970; children: Alexandra, Katherine. BA, MA, Oxford U., 1965; MBA, Harvard U., 1970. Account exec. Leo Burnett, London, 1965-68; from strategic planning dir. to v.p. mktg. Prestige Group Ltd. div. Am. Home Products, N.Y.C. and London, 1970-76; v.p. mktg. Kurzweil Computer Products div. Xerox Corp., Cambridge, Mass., 1979-80; assoc. McKinsey & Co., Inc., N.Y.C., 1976-82, prin., 1982-88, dir. consumer industries sector, mktg. ctr., sr. ptnr., 1988—; underwriting mem. Lloyds of London, 1986—. Contbr. articles to profl. jours. Chmn. adv. bd. Salvation Army, Greater N.Y., 1983—; bd. dirs. United Way, N.Y.C., 1988—; trustee Sarah Lawrence Coll., Bronxville, N.Y., 1993—. Baker scholar Harvard Bus. Sch., 1970. Mem. Siwanoy Country Club, Watch Hill Yacht Club. Home: 56 Hereford Rd Bronxville NY 10708-5408 Office: McKinsey & Co Inc 55 E 52nd St New York NY 10055-0002

PARSONS, DANIEL LANKESTER, pharmaceutics educator; b. Biscoe, N.C., Sept. 10, 1953; s. Solomon Lankester and Doris Eva (Bost) P. BS in Pharmacy, U. Ga., 1975, PhD, 1979. Asst. prof. pharmaceutics U. Ariz., Tucson, 1979-82; asst. prof. Auburn (Ala.) U., 1982-86, assoc. prof., 1986-91, prof., 1991—, chmn. divsn., 1990—; cons. Wyeth-Ayerst, Phila., 1989-93, Technomics, Ardsley, N.Y., 1990-93; presenter in field. Author: (with G.V. Betageri and S.A. Jenkins) Liposome Drug Delivery Systems, 1993. Named Disting. Alumni Sandhills Coll., 1990, Tchr. of Yr., Pharmacy Student Coun., 1987, Grad. Faculty Mem. of Yr., Grad. Student Orgn., 1994. Mem. Am. Pharm. Assn., Am. Assn. Pharm. Scientists, Am. Coll. Clin. Pharmacology (mem. coun. 1990-93), Phi Kappa Phi, Kappa Psi (advisor 1990-95, Svc. award 1990, 95, Advisor award 1992, nat. scholarship com. 1995). Achievements include research on plasma protein binding of drugs and effects of perfluorochemical blood substitutes on such binding. Office: Auburn U Sch Pharmacy Auburn AL 36849

PARSONS, DAVID, artistic director, choreographer. Dancer Paul Taylor Dance Co., 1978-87; founder, artistic dir. Parsons Dance Co., 1987—. Choreographer The Envelope, 1984, Sleep Study, 1987, Caught, 1987, Elysian Fields, 1988, Reflections of Four, 1991, A Hairy Night on Bald Mountain, 1991, Bachiana, 1993, Destines, 1993, Ring Around the Rosie, 1993; performed with N.Y.C. Ballet, Berlin Opera, White Oak Dance Project. Choreography fellow Nat. Endowment for the Arts, 1988-89, 95. Office: Parsons Dance Co c/o Sheldon Soffer Mgt Inc 130 W 56th St New York NY 10019-3818

PARSONS, DONALD D., bishop. Bishop of Alaska Evang. Luth. Ch. in Am., Anchorage. Office: Synod of Alaska 1847 W Northern Lights Blvd # 2 Anchorage AK 99517-3343

PARSONS, DONALD JAMES, retired bishop; b. Phila., Mar. 28, 1922; s. Earl and Helen (Drabble) P.; m. Mary Russell, Sept. 17, 1955; children—Mary, Rebecca, Bradford. B.A., Temple U., 1943; M.Div., Phila. Div. Sch., 1946, Th.D., 1951, D.D. (hon.), 1964; postgrad., U. Nottingham, Eng., 1968; D.C.L., Nashotah (Wis.) House, 1973. Ordained priest Episcopal Ch., 1946, consecrated bishop, 1973; curate Immanual Ch., Wilmington, Del., 1946-49; rector St. Peter's Ch., Smyrna, Del., 1949-50; prof. N.T., Nashotah House, 1950-73, pres., dean, 1963-73; bishop Diocese of Quincy, Ill., 1973-88. Author: A Life-time Road to God, 1966, In Time with Jesus, 1973, Holy Eucharist: Rite Two, 1976. Home: 308 W Edgevale Pl Peoria IL 61604-1607

PARSONS, EDMUND MORRIS, investment company executive; b. Houston, Oct. 19, 1936; s. Alfred Morris and Virgina (Hanna) P. AB Harvard U., 1958; MBA, U. Pa., 1961; MS, MIT, 1970. Pres. Fredonia Enterprises, Inc., Houston, Tex., 1990—; fgn. service officer U.S. Dept. State, Washington, 1965-90; 1st sec. Am. Embassy, Mexico City, 1973-76; economist Fed. Res. Bank N.Y., N.Y.C., 1976-77; chief food aid div. U.S. Dept. State, Washington, 1977-80, dir. office devel., 1981-82, dir. office econ. policy, 1983-84; dep. chief mission U.S. Mission to FAO, Rome, 1985-86; dir. Office Ecology and Natural Resources U.S. Dept. State, Washington, 1986-88; dir. Office of Internat. Narcotics Control Programs, 1988-89; min.-counselor for econ. affairs Am. Embassy, Mexico City, 1989-90; pres. Fredonia Enterprises, Inc., Houston, 1990—; co-chmn. Tropical Forest Task Force, Washington, 1986-88; dep. U.S. rep. UN FAO, Rome, 1985-86; alt. U.S. rep. to environ. program U.S. Del. Nairobi, Kenya, 1987. Capt. USAF, 1962-72. Mem. Am. Fgn. Svc. Assn., Houston Restaurant Assn. (bd. dirs. 1992—), Houston World Affairs Coun. (bd. dirs. 1995—), Consular Corps of Houston (hon.), Houston Hispanic C. of C., Coun. Fgn. Rels. (Houston com.), Univ. Club (Houston). Republican. Methodist. Avocation: geneology. Office: 2727 Fondren Rd Ste 2A Houston TX 77063

PARSONS, EDWIN SPENCER, clergyman, educator; b. Brockton, Mass., Feb. 16, 1919; s. Edwin Webber and Ethel Faunce (Marsh) P.; m. Eleanor Millard, Nov. 3, 1944; children: William Spencer, Ellen, James Millard, Bradford Delano. A.B., Denison U., 1941, D.D., 1967; B.D., Andover Newton Theol. Sch., 1945; D.D., Kalamazoo Coll., 1966; L.H.D., Chgo. Coll. Osteo. Medicine, 1978. Ordained to ministry Am. Baptist Ch., 1944; asst. minister First Bapt. Ch., Newton Centre, Mass., 1945-47; exec. dir. Bapt. Student Found., Inc., Cambridge, Mass., 1947-59; pastor Hyde Park Union Ch., Chgo., 1959-65; assoc. prof. ethics U. Chgo. Div. Sch., 1965-78, prof., 1978-81; dir. ministerial field edn., 1977-79, asst. to dean, 1981-88; dean Rockefeller Meml. Chapel, 1965-79; v.p., dir. New Eng. office Health Resources Ltd., Kansas City, Mo., 1979-89; cons. dept. ch. and soc. Am. Bapt. Chs. of Mass., 1979-86, also editor Mass. Bapt. News, 1983-85; chmn. strategy and action com., bd. dirs. Mass. Council Chs., 1983-85; adj. prof. Andover Newton Theol. Sch., 1981-85. Author: The Christian Yes or No, 1964; contbr.: Belief and Ethics, 1978. Pres. Council Hyde Park-Kenwood Chs. and Synagogues, 1963; chmn. Abortion Rights Assn. Ill., 1974-79; founder, chmn. Ill. Religious Coalition for Abortion Rights, 1975, Ill. Clergy Consultation Services on Problem Pregnancies, 1971-79; bd. dirs., chmn. clergy adv. com. Planned Parenthood Assn., Chgo., 1977-79; bd. dirs. Hyde Park YMCA, Facing History and Ourselves Nat. Found., 1983-87; bd. govs. Internat. House, Chgo., 1969-79; trustee Packard Manse (Mass.), Bapt. Theol. Union, 1960-70, 81—; pres., bd. mgrs. Ministers and Missionaries Benefit Bd., 1975-81; mem. policy council Religious Coalition for Abortion Rights of Mass., 1980-86; sec., treas. Bolton Inst. for Sustainable Future, 1983-87; mem. gen. bd., mem. exec. com., mem. commn. on Christian unity Am. Bapt. Chs., 1963-72, 74-81; bd. dirs. Planned Parenthood League of Mass., 1984-92; interim assoc. dir. Mass Coun. Chs., 1988-89. Democrat. Home: 69 Fort Point Rd Weymouth MA 02191-2146

PARSONS, ELMER EARL, retired clergyman; b. Cloverland, Wash., Oct. 4, 1919; s. Claud Solomon and Bessie Lillian (Campbell) P.; m. Marjorie Emma Carlson, Aug. 29, 1942; children—Karl Elmer, James Myron, Helen Joy, Ann Elizabeth, Lois Marie, Louise Melba. B.A., Seattle Pacific U., 1942; S.T.B., N.Y. Theol. Sem., 1945; S.T.M., Asbury Theol. Sem., Wilmore, Ky., 1955; D.D. (hon.), Greenville (Ill.) Coll., 1958. Ordained to ministry Free Methodist Ch., 1944; acad. dean Wessington Springs (S.D.) Coll., 1945-47; missionary to China, 1947-49, missionary to Japan, 1949-54; supt. Japan Free Meth. Mission, 1950-54; pres. Central Coll., McPherson, Kans., 1955-64, Osaka (Japan) Christian Coll., 1964-74; Asia area sec., Free Meth. Ch., 1964-74; bishop Free Meth. Ch. N.Am., 1974-85. Author: Witness to the Resurrection, 1967. Chmn. Free Meth. Study Commn. on Doctrine, 1990-95. Named Alumnus of Year Seattle Pacific U., 1976. Mem. Wesleyan Theol. Soc.

PARSONS, ESTELLE, actress; b. Lynn, Mass., Nov. 20, 1927; d. Eben and Elinor (Mattson) P.; m. Richard Gehman, Dec. 19, 1953 (div. Aug. 1958); children: Martha and Abbie (twins); m. Peter L. Zimroth, Jan. 2, 1983; 1 child, Abraham. B.A. in Polit. Sci., Conn. Coll. Women, 1949; student, Boston U. Law Sch., 1949-50. Stage appearances include: Happy Hunting, 1957, Whoop Up, 1958, Beg, Borrow or Steal, 1960, Threepenny Opera, 1960, Mrs. Dally Has a Lover, 1962, Ready When You Are C.B, 1964, Malcolm, 1965, Seven Descents of Myrtle, 1968, And Miss Reardon Drinks a Little, 1971, Mert and Phil, 1974, The Norman Conquests, 1975-76, Ladies of the Alamo, 1977, Miss Margarida's Way, 1977-78, The Pirates of Penzance, 1981, The Shadow Box, 1994; adapted, dir., performer Orgasmo Adulto Escapes from the Zoo, 1983, The Unguided Missile, Baba Goya, 1989, Shimada, 1992; film appearances include: Bonnie and Clyde, 1966; Rachel, Rachel, 1967, I Never Sang for My Father, 1969, Dick Tracy, 1990, Boys On The Side, 1995; TV appearances include: Roseanne, 1990—; artistic dir. N.Y. Shakespeare Festival Players, 1986. Recipient Theatre World award, 1962-63, Obie award, 1964; recipient award Motion Picture Acad. Arts and Scis., 1967; Recipient Medal of Honor, Conn. Coll., 1969. Home: 505 W End Ave New York NY 10024-4305 *It's in attempting all, that one succeeds.*

PARSONS, FREDERICK AMBROSE, retired educator; b. Mpls. Feb. 21, 1916; s. Olof and Volborg (Anderson) P.; B.E., St. Cloud State Coll., 1939; postgrad. Colo. U., 1941; M.A., U. Minn., 1947, Ed.S., 1970; m. Margaret C. Anderson, June 20, 1943; children: Gretchen, Mark, Christine. Tchr., Delano (Minn.) H.S., 1940-43, prin., 1943-47; supt. schs. Delano, 1947-82. Mem. Am., Minn., Assns. Sch. Adminstrs., Met. Supts. Assn., U. Minn. Alumni Assn., Tau Kappa Alpha, Kappa Delta Pi, Phi Delta Kappa. Mason. Address: 428 St Peter Ave Delano MN 55328

PARSONS, GEORGE RAYMOND, JR., lawyer; b. N.Y.C., May 5, 1938; s. George Raymond and Gertrude (Blackburn) P.; m. Katharine P. Sook, Oct. 16, 1982; children: Timothy, Geoffrey, Amy, Julia, Elizabeth. BA with distinction, Wesleyan U., 1959; LLB with honors, Cornell U., 1962. Bar: N.Y. 1962, U.S. Dist. Ct. (we. and no. dists.) N.Y. 1962, Fla. 1974. Assoc. Nixon, Hargrave, Davans & Doyle LLP, Rochester, N.Y., 1962-69, ptnr., 1970—; lectr. continuing legal edn. programs. Editor-in-chief, contbr. articles to Cornell Law Rev., 1961-62, New Republic; contbr. John Updike Newsletter. Officer, bd. dirs. Rochester Philharm. Orch., 1976-83; pres. Friends of Rochester Pub. Libr., 1972-75; trustee Monroe County Libr. Sys., 1986-87, 94—, Reynolds Libr., 1987—, Rochester Regional Libr. Coun., 1988—, pres. 1994—; bd. dirs. Rundel Libr. Found., Inc., 1989—; pres. Friends of U. Rochester Librs., 1989-91; trustee Rochester Pub. Libr., 1978-81, 83—, pres. 1986-87, 94-96; bd. dirs. Writers and Books, 1991—; del. N.Y. State Gov.'s Conf. on Librs. and Info. Svcs., 1990; mem. trustee's vis. com. on librs. U. Rochester, 1991-95; trustee Halycon Hill Found., 1992—. Mem. ABA, N.Y. Bar Assn., Monroe County Bar Assn., Am. Coll. of Trust and Estate Counsel, Estate Planning Council Rochester. Democrat. Office: Nixon Hargrave et al Clinton Sq PO Box 1051 Rochester NY 14603-1051

PARSONS, GEORGE WILLIAM, city planner, educator; b. West Monroe, La., Aug. 1, 1930; s. Henry Vardaman and Virgie Mae (Hosch) P.; m. Beth

Nale, Aug. 2, 1991; children: Lauren, Layne, Lonn. BS, La. Tech. U.; MS, La. State U. Planning engr. USAF, Riverside, Calif., 1955-58; dir. Monroe-Ouachita Regional Planning Commn., Monroe, La., 1958-72; exec. dir. Shreveport (La.) Met. Planning Commn., 1972-76, City Planning & Devel. Programs, Monroe, 1976-79; dir. Dept. Planning & Policy Gov.'s Office State of Miss., Jackson, 1980-83; coord. Miss. Main Street program Small Town Ctr. Miss. State U., Mississippi State, 1983-86, assoc. prof., 1983—, dir. Ctr. for Small Town rsch. and design, 1986—, dir. Commn., Econ. Devel. Ctr., 1989—; interim exec. dir. Oktibbeha County Exec. Devel., Starkville, Miss., 1989-90. Pres. Riverside Swim & Tennis Club, 1975; bd. dirs. Chauvin Racquet Club, Monroe, 1978-79; disting. pres. Monroe Optimist Club. Recipient Disting. Svc. award Jaycees, Monroe, named Outstanding Man of the Yr., 1963. Mem. Am. Inst. Cert. Planners, Am. Soc. Landscape Architects, Am. Mgmt. Assn., Coun. State Planning Agys. (bd. dirs. 1981-83), Coun. State Community Action Agys. (exec. com. 1982-83), Miss. Gov.'s Policy Coun. Home: 227 Hiwassee Dr Starkville MS 39759-2117 Office: Community/Econ Devel Ctr Ctr for Small Town Rsch & Design 240 Giles Barr Ave Mississippi State MS 39762

PARSONS, GEORGE WILLIAMS, retired medical center administrator, cattle rancher; b. Natural Bridge, Va., Jan. 21, 1918; s. George Washington and Mary Elizabeth (Williams) P.; m. Miriam Rebecca Boyer, May 2, 1942; children: Mary Locke Parsons Black, Anne Boyer Parsons Talkington, George Russell. Student, Washington and Lee U., 1935-37; B.S. in Edn., U. Va., 1941; grad., USNR Tng. Sch., 1942, USNR Officer Candidate Sch., 1944, USNR Command Sch., 1944, Ind. Coll. Armed Forces, 1963, Fed. Health Care Inst., 1966. Tchr. Winchester, Va., 1941-42; asst. phys. dir. VA Hosp., Roanoke, Va., 1946-47; asst. chief spl. services VA Hosp., 1947-51; chief spl. services VA Hosp., Lyons, N.J., 1951-58; spl. asst. to hosp. mgr. VA Hosp., Pitts., 1958-62; asst. dir. VA Hosp., Clarksburg, W.Va., 1962-67, Erie, Pa., 1967-69, Marion, Ind., 1969-72, Bklyn., 1972-75; dir. VA Outpatient Clinic, Lubbock, Tex., 1975-76; dir. VA Med. Center, Bklyn., 1976-82, Alexandria, La., 1982-86; faculty, preceptor M.P.H./M.B.A. Program in Health Adminstrn., Columbia U.; faculty NYU; mem. dean's com. Tulane U. Sch. Medicine, New Orleans, 1982-86; chmn. Fed. Exec. Bd., N.Y.C., 1982; cluster leader Presdl. Mgmt. Intern Program, Nat. Inst. Public Affairs, 1980-82; mem. dist. bd. Health Systems Agy., Bklyn.; chmn. Combined Fed. Campaign for all VA Med. Facilities in N.Y.C., all fed. agys. in Rapides Parish (La.), 1984; mem. Rockbridge County (Va.) Farm Bur., Natural Bridge Ruritan Club; aide de camp Gov. David Treen, State of La., 1982, Gov. Edwin Edwards, State of La., 1985. Lt. comdr. USNR, 1942-46; PTO. Decorated 11 decorations and awards including two Presdl. Unit Commendations; recipient Outstanding Achievement award Am. Legion, 1975, Disting. Svc. award, 1975, Recognition award, 1978, Recognition award VFW, 1975, 83, United Vets. Assn. award Queens, N.Y., 1979; 9 citations and awards, 1980; 7 awards and citations, 1982; Outstanding Career award VA, 1986; also numerous other awards and commendations from VA, vets., civic orgns., 1946-86. Fellow Am. Coll. Healthcare Execs. (oral examiner), Royal Soc. Health; mem. Assn. Mil. Surgeons U.S. (pres. N.Y. chpt. 1979-80), Am. Hosp. Assn., La. Hosp. Assn. (pres. Central Dist. 1983-84), Sr. Exec. Service U.S. Govt., Fed. Hosp. Inst. Alumni Assn., N.Y. Acad. Scis., Res. Officers Assn. U.S.A. (pres. W.Va. chpt. 1967), Greater Alexandria/Pineville C. of C. (mil. affairs com. 1982-86), VFW (comdr Post 484 1949-50). Club: Rotary (pres. 1958, 71). Home: 1905 Canterbury Ln Apt 20 Sun City Center FL 33573-5641

PARSONS, HARRY GLENWOOD, retired surgeon; b. San Bernardino, Calif., Mar. 5, 1919; s. Harry Glenwood and Evelen May (Peris) P.; m. Rubyann Kattenhorn, Sept. 28, 1986. AB, Stanford (Calif.) U., 1942, MD, 1946. Diplomate Am. Bd. Surgery, Am. Bd. Thoracic Cardio-Vascular Surgery. Intern Stanford Hosp., San Francisco, 1941-42, Rockor fellow in surg. rsch., 1944-45, asst. resident in surgery, 1945-52, chief resident in surgery, 1952-53, Boyd fellow in thoracic cardiovasc. surgery, 1953-54; asst. clin. prof. surgery Stanford Med. Sch., 1955-65; med. dir., faculty head Weimar (Calif.) Med. Ctr., 1955-72; ret. Capt. M.C. U.S. Army, 1940-44. Fellow ACS; mem. AMA, Western Thoracic Surg. Soc., Placer Nevada County Med. Assn. (pres. 1979), Calif. Med. Assn. (del.), Alpha Omega Alpha. Avocation: flying.

PARSONS, HELGA LUND, writer; b. Seattle, Sept. 5, 1906; d. Gunnar and Marie Pauline (Vognild) Lund; m. Durwin David Algyer, June 6, 1937 (dec. 1971); children: Deanne Algyer Mathisen, Marilyn A. McIntosh; m. James Stewart Parsons, Sept. 30, 1972 (dec. 1988). Grad., Columbia Coll. Expression, Chgo., 1926. Lead actress Repertory Playhouse, Seattle, 1929-34; assoc. prof. drama U. Wash., 1931-32; dir. apprentice group Repertory Playhouse, Seattle 1932-34; writer, anchor radio programs Bon Marche Dept. Store, Seattle 1933-35; v.p. creative dir. Norwegian Am. Mus., Decorah, Iowa 1960-66. Author: Norway Travel Newspaper Series, Seattle, 1930, Concert Touring, Monodramas, 1936, (novelized version) Blondie and Dagwood King Features, 1946; script writer serials for WOR, CBS, NBC, N.Y.C.; appeared in Solid Gold Cadillac, I Remember Mama; editor Surfsedge Newsletter. Activities chmn. Glenview, Naples. Mem. Norwegian Am. Mus. (life), MIT (hon.). Republican. Avocations: family, fitness, interior decorating.

PARSONS, HENRY MCILVAINE, psychologist; b. Lenox, Mass., Aug. 31, 1911; s. Herbert and Elsie Worthington (Clews) P.; m. Renee Oakman, 1938 (div. 1945); 1 son, Robert; m. Marina Svetlova, 1949 (div. 1957); m. Marjorie Thorson, 1957. BA, Yale U., 1933; MA, Columbia U., 1947; PhD, U. Calif., Los Angeles, 1963. Reporter N.Y. Herald Tribune, 1935-42; organizer N.Y. Newspaper Guild, 1942; asst., then lectr. psychology Columbia U., 1947-52; research asso. N.Y. U., 1951-52; supr. Electronics Research Labs., Columbia U., 1952-58; mem. human factors staff Douglas Aircraft Co., Long Beach and Santa Monica, Calif., 1956-58; sr. human factors scientist, br. head System Devel. Corp., Santa Monica and Falls Church, Va., 1958-68; self-employed cons., 1968-69; 70-73; v.p. research Riverside Research Inst., N.Y.C., 1969-70; exec. dir. Inst. Behavioral Research Inc., Silver Spring, Md., 1974-79; pres. Exptl. Coll. of Inst. Behavioral Research, Silver Spring, 1974-80; mgr. human factors projects Human Resources Research Orgn., Alexandria, Va., 1980-83; sr. staff scientist Essex Corp., Alexandria, Va., 1983-90; mgr. Ctr. for Human Factors Human Resources Rsch. Orgn., Alexandria, 1990—; adj. prof. Lehigh U., 1983-84. Author: Man-Machine System Experiments, 1972; also chpts. in books, articles in jours. Served with USNR, 1942-45. Fellow AAAS, APA (pres. divsn. 21 1975-76, Franklin V. Taylor award 1992), Human Factors Soc. (pres. 1968-69, Pres.'s Disting. Svc. award 1993), Washington Acad. Scis., Am. Psychol. Soc.; mem. N.Y. Acad. Scis., Ergonomics Soc., Sigma Xi. Clubs: Century (N.Y.C.); Cosmos (Washington). Home: 1600 S Eads St Apt 1223 N Arlington VA 22202-2924 Office: Human Resources Rsch Orgn 66 Canal Center Plz Alexandria VA 22314-1591

PARSONS, IRENE, management consultant; b. North Wilkesboro, N.C.; d. Everett T. and Martha (Minton) P. B.S. in Bus. Edn. and Adminstrn, U. N.C., 1941, LL.D. (hon.), 1967; M.S. in Pub. Adminstrn, George Washington U., 1965. Tchr. Roanoake Rapids (N.C.) High Sch., 1941-42; rep. U.S. Civil Service Commn., 1942-43; with VA, 1946-74, asst. adminstr. vets. affairs, dir. personnel, dir. equal employment opportunity, 1965-74; mgmt. cons., 1974—; Exec. com. Pres.'s Study Group Careers for Women. Served to lt. USCGR, 1943-46. Recipient Fed. Woman's Outstanding Achievement award, 1966, Silver Helmet award Amvets, 1971, Career Svc. award Nat. Civil Svc. League, 1972, Disting. Alumni Achievement award George Washington U., 1973; named to Brevard Coll. Hall of Fame, 1984. Mem. Assn. Fed. Woman's Award Recipients (chmn. 1972-76). Address: PO Box 2046 North Wilkesboro NC 28659

PARSONS, JAMES JEROME, geographer, educator; b. Cortland, N.Y., Nov. 15, 1915; s. James Jerome and Edith (Gere) P.; m. Betty Rupp, Oct. 30, 1942; children—David, John, Sally. A.B., U. Calif. at Berkeley, 1937, M.A., 1939, Ph.D., 1948. Mem. faculty U. Calif. at Berkeley, 1946—, prof. geography, 1959—, chmn. dept. geography, 1960-66, 75-80. Author: Antioqueño Colonization in Western Colombia, 1949, San Andrés and Providencia, 1955, The Green Turtle and Man, 1962, Antioquia's Corridor to the Sea, 1967, Hispanic Lands and Peoples: Selected Writings of James J. Parsons, 1988, Las Regiones Tropicales Americanas: Vision Geografica, 1992. Served to maj. USAAF, 1941-45. Recipient Pedro Justo Berrio medal Dept. Antioquia, Colombia, 1987; Guggenheim fellow in Spain, 1959-60. Mem. AAAS, Assn. Am. Geographers (pres. 1974-75), Am. Geog. Soc. (David Livingstone medal 1985), Assn. Pacific Coast Geographers (pres. 1952), Acad. Colombiana de Historia (hon.). Home: 670 Woodmont Ave Berkeley CA 94708-1234

PARSONS, JEFFREY ROBINSON, anthropologist, educator; b. Washington, Oct. 9, 1939; s. Merton Stanley and Elisabeth (Oldenburg) P.; m. Mary Thomson Hrones, Apr. 27, 1968; 1 child, Apphia Hrones. B.S., Pa. State U., 1961; Ph.D., U. Mich., 1966. Asst. prof. anthropology U. Mich., Ann Arbor, 1966-71; assoc. prof. U. Mich., 1971-76, prof., 1976—, dir. mus. anthropology, 1983-86; vis. prof. Universidad Nacional Autonoma de Mexico, 1987; vis. prof. Universidad Buenos Aires, 1994. Author: Prehistoric Settlement Patterns in the Texcoco Region, Mexico, 1971; (with William T. Sanders and Robert Stanley) The Basin of Mexico: The Cultural Ecology of a Civilization, 1979, (with E. Brumfield) Prehispanic Settlement Patterns in the Southern Valley of Mexico, 1982, (with M. Parsons) Chinampa Agriculture and Aztec Urbanization in the Valley of Mexico, 1985, (with Mary H. Parsons) Maguey Utilization in Highland Central Mexico, 1990, The Production of Consumption of Salt During Postclassic Times in the Valley of Mexico, 1994. Research grantee NSF, 1967, 70, 72-73, 75-76, 81, Nat. Geog. Soc., 1984, 86, 88. Mem. Am. Anthrop. Assn., Soc. Am. Archaeology, AAAS, Inst. Andean Rsch., Inst. Andean Studies, Sociedad Mexicana de Antropologia, Sociedad Argentina de Antropologia. Office: Museum of Anthropology U Mich Ann Arbor MI 48109

PARSONS, JOHN R., actuary; b. Worcester, Mass., Apr. 12, 1931; s. Arthur Carleton and Miriam (Lyon) P.; m. Mona Jean Violette, Dec. 31, 1953 (dec. Aug. 1994); m. Joyce Piper, July 16, 1995; children: Richard, Jennifer, Thomas, Susan, Steven. BA, Wesleyan U., 1953. Cert. Mem. Am. Acad. of Actuaries, Enrolled Actuary DOI/IRS, Fellow Conf. of Actuaries, Mem. Soc. of Pension Actuaries. Pres. Parsons McKee Sommers, Inc., Westlake, Ohio, 1976-93, chmn., 1993—. Pfc. U.S. Army, 1953-55. Office: Parsons McKee Sommers & Co 2001 Crocker Rd Ste 300 Westlake OH 44145-1954

PARSONS, JUDSON ASPINWALL, JR., lawyer; b. Rochester, N.Y., Dec. 15, 1929; s. Judson A. and Frances (Holsopple) P.; m. Chesley Kahmann, Aug. 8, 1959; children: Ames, Brockett. BA, Amherst Coll., 1951; LLB, Harvard U., 1954. Bar: N.Y. 1954, N.J. 1973. Asst. U.S. atty. So. Dist. N.Y., N.Y.C., 1954-55; assoc. Dewey, Ballantine, Bushby, Palmer & Wood, N.Y.C., 1958-65, ptnr., 1966-82; pres. Orbiting Clef Prodns., Inc., Summit, N.J., 1982-86; spl. counsel Laughlin, Markensohn, Lagani & Pegg, P.C., Morristown, N.J., 1986-90, Parsons & Pegg, Morristown, 1990-91; sole practice, 1991—. Served to 1st lt. U.S. Army, 1955-58. Office: 108 Woodland Ave Summit NJ 07901-2003

PARSONS, KEITH I., lawyer; b. Davenport, Iowa, Apr. 28, 1912; s. Alfred and Cora Pearl (McDowell) P.; m. Lorraine Watson, June 28, 1939; children: Robert, Susan, James. Ph.B., U. Chgo., 1933, J.D., 1937. Bar: Ill. 1938. Asst. to sec. U. Chgo., 1934-37; since practiced in Chgo.; asst. chief, later chief legal div. Chgo. Ordnance Dist., 1942-46; ptnr. firm Milliken, Vollers & Parsons, 1946-64, Ross, Hardies, O'Keefe, Babcock & Parsons, 1965-83; of counsel firm Ross & Hardies, 1983—. Mem. Hinsdale (Ill.) Bd. Edn., 1957-63, pres., 1959-63; mem. bd. govs. Ill. State Colls. and Univs., 1970-73. Served to lt. col. AUS, 1942-46. Mem. ABA, Ill. Bar Assn., Chgo. Bar Assn. (past chmn. corp. law com., mem. bd. mgrs. 1967-69), Chgo. Law Club, Legal Club (past pres.), Phi Beta Kappa, Psi Upsilon, Hinsdale Golf Club, Chikaming Country Club. Home: 315 N La Grange Rd La Grange IL 60525-5600 Office: 150 N Michigan Ave Ste 2500 Chicago IL 60601-7525

PARSONS, LEONARD JON, marketing educator, consultant; b. Pitts., Sept. 1, 1942; s. Leonard J. and Marion Jane (Williams) P.; m. Julia Grieve, Jan. 23, 1965; children: Lorelei, Leonard Jon Jr. BSChemE, MIT, 1964; MS in Indsl. Adminstrn., Purdue U., 1965, PhD in Indsl. Adminstrn., 1968. Asst. prof. Ind. U., Bloomington, 1968-70; assoc. prof. Claremont (Calif.) Grad. Sch., 1970-77; prof. marketing Ga. Inst. Tech., 1977—; vis. scholar MIT, Cambridge, fall 1973; Fulbright-Hays sr. scholar Cath. U. Leuven, Belgium, spring 1977; vis. prof. INSEAD, France, fall 1984, Norwegian Sch. Mktg., Oslo, fall 1989, UCLA, spring 1990, Advt. Edn. Found., Anheuser Busch, St. Louis, summer 1993, CREER/FUCAM, Belgium, Fall 1995; mem. rsch. and test devel. com. Grad. Mgmt. Admissions Coun., 1988-90. Author: Using Microcomputers in Marketing, 1986; co-author: Market Response Models, 1990, Marketing Management, 1995, others; edtl. bd. Jour. Mktg. Rsch., 1970-80, 83-85, Jour. Bus. Rsch., 1973-79, Jour. Mktg., 1978-80; assoc. editor: Decision Scis., 1976-79; mktg. dept. editor: Mgmt. Sci., 1980-82; contbr. numerous chpts. to books, articles to profl. jours. Recipient first prize rsch. design contest Am. Mktg. Assn., 1971-72. Mem. Am. Statis. Assn. (chmn. stats. in mktg. sect. 1995), European Mktg. Acad. (mem. exec. com. 1981-84), Theta Delta Chi, Beta Gamma Sigma, Phi Kappa Phi. Office: Ga Inst Tech Dupree Sch Mgmt Atlanta GA 30332-0520

PARSONS, MERRIBELL MADDUX, museum administrator; b. San Antonio. BFA, Newcomb Coll., 1964; MA, M.Phil., Inst. Fine Arts, NYU, 1968. Curator of sculpture and decorative arts Mpls. Inst. Arts, 1969-74, chief curator, 1974-79; vice-dir. for edn. Met. Mus. Art, N.Y.C., 1979-87; dir. Columbus Mus. Art, Ohio, 1987-95; exec. dir. Julian Wood Glass Jr. Mus. Inc., Winchester, Va., 1995—. Author: Sculpture: David Daniels Collection; editor, author exhbn. catalogues and articles. Mem. pub. art com. Greater Columbus Arts Coun., 1989, Downtown Planning Group, Columbus, 1989. Clawson Mills fellow Met. Mus. Art, 1967; NEA professional grantee, Washington, 1972. Mem. Assn. Art Mus. Dirs., Am. Assn. Mus., Columbus C. of C. (bd. dirs. 1990-92). Office: 486 E Olmos Dr San Antonio TX 78212

PARSONS, RICHARD DEAN, banker, lawyer; b. N.Y.C., Apr. 4, 1948; s. Lorenzo Locklair and Isabelle (Judd) P.; m. Laura Ann Bush, Aug. 30, 1968; children: Gregory, Leslie, Rebecca. Student, U. Hawaii, 1968; JD, Union U., Albany, N.Y., 1971; LLD (hon.), Adelphi U., 1990, Medgar Evers Coll., N.Y.C., 1991. Bar: N.Y. 1972. Asst. counsel to gov. State of N.Y., Albany, 1971-73, 1st asst. counsel to gov., 1973-74; dep. counsel to v.p. Office of V.P., Washington, 1975; gen. counsel, assoc. dir. domestic coun. White House, Washington, 1975-77; ptnr. Patterson Belknap Webb & Tyler, N.Y.C., 1977-88; pres., chief oper. officer Dime Savs. Bank N.Y., N.Y.C., 1988-90, chmn., chief exec. officer, 1990-95; pres. Time Warner, N.Y.C., 1995—; bd. dirs. Fed. Nat. Mortgage Assn., Washington, 1989—, Philip Morris Cos., N.Y.C., Time Warner Inc., N.Y.C. Trustee Rockefeller Bros. Fund, N.Y.C., 1989—, Howard U., Washington, 1989—, Met. Mus. Art, N.Y.C., 1990—. Office: Time Warner 75 Rockerfeller Plaza New York NY 10019*

PARSONS, ROBERT EUGENE, transportation consultant; b. Cin., Apr. 19, 1931; s. Charles Eugene and Samantha Ellen (Snider) P.; m. Beverly Greenhalgh, Dec. 30, 1949; children: Brian Scott, Barry Lawrence, Robert Stephen, Kimberly Ann. ME, U. Cinn., 1954; MSME, Drexel Inst. Tech., 1959. Registered profl. engr., Calif., Nev., Md., Ohio. Asst. project engr. The Martin Co., Balt., 1956-62, sect. mgr., 1962-64; dep. dir. Supersonic Transp. Office FAA, Washington, 1964-71; dir. rsch. and devel. plans U.S. Dept. Transp., Washington, 1971; assoc. adminstr. Fed. RR Adminstrn., Washington, 1975-80; dir. ctr. field methods Nat. Bur. Standards, Gaithersburg, Md., 1980-81; dir. RR rsch. and devel. program U. Calif., Berkeley, 1981-84; cons. Walnut Creek, Calif., 1986-90; dir. program on advanced technology for hwy. U. Calif. Berkeley, 1984—; prin. Parsons Transp. Assocs., Midlothian, Va.; ons. Assn. Am. R.R.s, Washington, U. Calif., Calif. Dept. Transp., U.S. Dept. T ransp., Radar Control Sys., Rand, Sys. Control Tech., Intelligent Vehicle Hwy. Soc. Techs., Inc., Lawrence Livermore Nat. Lab., French Inst. Transp. Safety, Intelligent Vehicle Hwy. Soc. Am., chmn. sys. arch. com.; cons. IMRA Am., Inc. JKH & Assocs., Sci. Atlanta, Va. Tech., Va. Dept. Transp.; active transp. rsch. bd. groups. Contbr. articles to profl. jours. Mem. SAE, Intelligent Transp. Soc. Am. (chair system arch. com), Intelligent Transp. Sys. of Va. (bd. mem., chmn. strategic planning com.), ITS World (editorial bd.). Methodist. Avocations: computer work, woodworking. Home: 3106 Cove Ridge Rd Midlothian VA 23112-4354

PARSONS, SCOTTIE, artist; b. Watonga, Okla., Nov. 6, 1925; d. Robert Lee and Flora Elizabeth (Tuel) Hatcher; m. Frank Duane Stewart, Dec. 22, 1948 (dec.); children: Mark Duane, Mary Jan Stewart McDonald; m. Clyde Wallace Parsons Jr., Nov. 6, 1971. BS in Art Edn., Midwestern State U., 1968, student, 1968, 69, 84; student, So. Meth. U., Dallas, 1982-83. Tchr. art Wichita Falls (Tex.) Pub. Schs., 1969-70; owner Fine Arts Gallery, Wichita Falls, 1971; tchr. in field; studio artist, Wichita Falls, 1978—. One-person shows include LewAllen Gallery, 1991, William Campbell Contemporary Gallery, 1992, 94; exhibited in group shows at Invitational Fund Raiser Exhbn., 1988-94, LewAllen Gallery, Santa Fe, 1988—, William Campbell Contemporary Gallery, Ft. Worth, 1989—, Horwitch LewAllen Gallery, 1994, 95, Arlington (Tex.) Mus. Fine Art, 1993. Named to Women's Hall of Fame, North Tex. Com., 1988. Mem. Tex. Fine Arts Assn. (bd. dirs. 1988-94, Citation winner 1978, 80, 83, 84, 85, Juror's Choice award, 1983), Wichita Falls Art Assn. (pres. 1987-89, 91-93), Alum Santa Fe Inst. Fine Arts Alumni Assn. Republican. Presbyterian. Avocations: studying humanities, traveling, art, writing, photography. Home: 2614 Amherst Dr Wichita Falls TX 76308-5324 Office: Studio Artist Atelier 2629 Plaza Pky Wichita Falls TX 76308-3874

PARSONS, VINSON ADAIR, retired computer software company executive; b. Frankfort, Ky., Oct. 22, 1932; s. Richard Adair and Nina (Mefford) P.; m. Elizabeth Ann Peltier, June 2, 1956. A.S., Mitchell Coll., 1959; B.S., U. Conn., 1960; AMP, Harvard U., 1985. Auditor, Price Waterhouse & Co. (C.P.A.s), Hartford, Conn., 1960-65; controller Pervel Industries Inc., Plainfield, Conn., 1965-70; v.p., controller Akzo Am. Inc., Asheville, N.C., 1970-71, 73-83, v.p., chief fin. officer, 1983-86; v.p., chief fin. officer System Software Assocs. Inc., Chgo., 1986-89, also bd. dirs.; ret., 1990; dir. Am. Tape Co., BRIntec Co., Control Tech. Corp. Elected commr. Town of Weaverville Bd. Commrs., 1994—. With USN, 1953-57. Mem. Am. Mgmt. Assn., Fin. Execs. Inst., Inst. Mgmt. Accts. (pres. local chpt. 1969-70). Clubs: Asheville Country; University (N.Y.C.); Reems Creek Golf. Home and Office: 15 Preston Ct Weaverville NC 28787-8907

PARTAIN, CLARENCE LEON, radiologist, nuclear medicine physician, educator, administrator; b. Memphis, July 12, 1940; s. Archie Leon and Vergie (Young) P.; m. Judith Stafford, Jan., 1964; children: David Blane, Teri Ellyn, Amy Leigh. B.S.N.E., U. Tenn., 1963; M.S.N.E., Purdue U., 1965, Ph.D. in Nuclear Engring., 1967; M.D., Washington U., St. Louis, 1975. Diplomate: Am. Bd. Nuclear Medicine, Am. Bd. Radiology; registered profl. engr., Mo. Asst. prof. nuclear engring. U. Mo.-Columbia, 1968-71, assoc. prof., 1971-75; resident N.C. Meml. Hosp., Chapel Hill, 1975-79; assoc. prof. radiology U. N.C.-Chapel Hill, 1978-79; assoc. prof. Vanderbilt U., Nashville, 1980-85; prof. radiology and biomed. engring. Vanderbilt U., 1985—, vice chmn. radiology, 1989-92, dir. nuclear medicine, 1981-85, dir. magnetic resonance imaging, 1983-92, chmn. radiology, radiologist in chief, 1992—; cons. NIH, Bethesda, Md., 1980—. Author: Nuclear Magnetic Resonance (NMR) Imaging, 1983, NMR Imaging: Clinical Utility and Correlation, 1984, Thyroid and Parathyroid Imaging, 1986, Magnetic Resonance Imaging, 2d edit., 1988, Correlative Image: Nuclear Medicine, Magnetic Resonance, Computer Tomography, Ultrasound, 1988; editl. bd. Acad. Radiology, Magnetic Resonance Imaging, Jour. Magnetic Resonance Imaging, Jour. Nuclear Medicine. AEC Spl. fellow, 1964-66; grantee Nat. Inst. Neurosci., Communicative Diseases and Stroke, 1977-78. Fellow Am. Coll. Nuclear Physicians, Am. Coll. Radiology, Soc. Magnetic Resonance Imaging (bd. dirs.); mem. AMA, IEEE, Radiol. Soc. N.Am., Assn. Univ. Radiologists (exec. com.), Soc. Nuclear Medicine (trustee, Benedict Casson lectr. 1981), Am. Roentgen Ray Soc. (exec. coun.), Soc. Magnetic Resonance in Medicine (trustee), Sigma Phi Epsilon. Baptist. Home: 211 High Lea Rd Brentwood TN 37027-4944 Office: Vanderbilt U Med Ctr 1611 21st Ave S Nashville TN 37212-3103

PARTAIN, EUGENE GARTLY, lawyer; b. Memphis, Oct. 4, 1930; s. Eugene Gardner and Zoe (Allen) P.; m. Ute Agnes Reinsch, July 8, 1952; children—Gia Michele, Matthew Reinsch. B.A., Duke U., 1952, LL.B., 1958; M.A., Northwestern U., 1959. Bar: Ga. 1961, U.S. Supreme Ct. 1980. Sr. ptnr. King & Spalding, Atlanta. Served to capt. USAF, 1952-54. Fellow Am. Coll. Trial Lawyers, Internat. Acad. Trial Lawyers, Internat. Soc. Barristers, Am. Bd. Trial Advocates; mem. ABA, Atlanta Bar Assn. (exec. com.), Ga. Def. Lawyers Assn. (pres. 1982-83), Best Lawyers in Am., Old War Horse Lawyers Club, Lawyers Club of Atlanta. Presbyterian. Office: King & Spalding 191 Peachtree St NE Ste 4900 Atlanta GA 30303-1763

PARTAIN, LARRY DEAN, solar research engineer; b. McKinney, Tex., Apr. 27, 1942; s. Archie Leon and Vergie Ann (Young) P.; m. Deborah Patton, July 1986; children: Lauren Elizabeth, Catherine Ann. BSEE, U. Tenn., 1965; PhD, Johns Hopkins U., 1971. Assoc. prof. elec. engring. U. Del., Newark, 1971-78; engr. Engring. Research div. Lawrence Livermore Nat. Lab., Calif., 1978-80; sr. research engr. Chevron Research Co., Richmond, Calif., 1980-87; sr. scientist, mktg. mgr. Varian Ginzton Research Ctr., Palo Alto, Calif., 1987—. Co-author/editor: Solar Cells and Their Applications, 1995; contbr. articles to tech. jours.; patentee microwave sensor, solar cells, solar arrays, optical switch. Solar Energy Rsch. Inst. grantee, 1978-79, 84-86; duPont rsch. grantee, 1974-75; grantee USAF Wright Aero. Lab., 1984-85, 88-90, 91-93, Sandia Nat. Labs., 1985-86, Naval Surface Warfare Ctr., 1994, 95. Mem. IEEE. Office: Varian Rsch Ctr 3075 Hansen Way Palo Alto CA 94304-1025 *Technical advances are keyed to the pragmatic scientists' search for simple, accurate, and predictive physical models. This contrasts with the search for truth—a seductive and distracting abstraction better left to philosophers and theologians.*

PARTAN, DANIEL GORDON, lawyer, educator; b. Gardner, Mass., Aug. 2, 1933; s. Toivo Antero and Lempi Sivia (Adamson) P.; m. Doris Liepmann, June 8, 1957; children: Andrew Stewart, Matthew Alexander, Sarah Ruth, Iliana Maria, Juan Carlos. AB, Cornell U., 1955; LLB, Harvard U., 1958, LLM, 1961. Bar: Mass. 1959. Rsch. assoc. Harvard Law Sch., 1961, Rule of Law Ctr., Duke U. Law Sch., 1962-65; assoc. prof. U. N.D., 1964-65; assoc. prof. law Boston U., 1965-68, prof., 1968—; mem. NAFTA dispute settlement roster and binat. dispute panel U.S.-Can. Free Trade Agreement; cons. Dept. State, UN Devel. Program, Am. Acad. Arts and Sci.; pres., chmn. bd. dirs. UN Assn. Greater Boston, 1969-71, 76-77; chmn. Brookline Selectmen's Com. on Harvard Energy Plant, 1976—; vis. scholar Harvard Law Sch., 1977-78; vis. fellow Cambridge (Eng.) U., 1972. Author: Population in the United Nations System, 1973, Documentary Study of the Politicization of UNESCO, 2 vols., 1975, The International Law Process, 1992; co-author: Legal Problems of International Administration, 1968, The United States and the International Labor Organization, 1980; co-editor: Corporate Disclosure of Environmental Risks: U.S. and European Law, 1990; contbr. articles to books and jours. Mem. ABA, Boston Bar Assn., Bretton Woods Com., Commn. to Study the ORgn. Peace, Am. Law Inst., Acad. Coun. UN System, Am. Soc. Internat. Law, Internat. Law Assn., European Communities Studies Assn., UN Assn. Office: 765 Commonwealth Ave Boston MA 02215-1401

PARTANEN, CARL RICHARD, biology educator; b. Portland, Oreg., Nov. 23, 1921; s. Emil and Ellen (Engstrom) P.; m. Jane Nelson, June 24, 1961; children: Karen, Kirsten, Richard (dec.). Student, Multnomah Jr. Coll., 1946-48; B.A., Lewis and Clark Coll., 1950; M.A., Harvard, 1951, Ph.D., 1954. Am. Cancer Soc. postdoctoral research fellow Columbia, 1954-55, Harvard, 1955-57; research asso. Childrens Cancer Research Found., Boston, 1957-61; asso. prof. biology U. Pitts., 1961-64, prof. biology, 1964-86, chmn. biology, 1964-70, prof. emeritus, 1987—; Research fellow U. Edinburgh, Scotland, 1971-72, U. Nottingham, Eng., 1978-79. Contbr. articles to profl. jours. Served with AUS, 1942-45, ETO. Recipient Distinguished Achievement award Lewis and Clark Coll., 1968. Mem. Am. Genetic Assn., Bot. Soc. Am., Soc. for Devel. Biology, Soc. for In Vitro Biology, Am. Inst. Biol. Sci. Home: 1112 Farragut St Pittsburgh PA 15206-1746 Office: U Pitts Dept Biol Scis Pittsburgh PA 15260

PARTCH, KENNETH PAUL, editor, consultant; b. Mt. Vernon, N.Y., June 22, 1925; s. Edward Augustus and Grace Jane (Crabb) P.; m. Dorothy Sophia Iversen, July 16, 1953; children—Marjorie, Stephen, Jessica. A.B., Bklyn. Coll., 1949. Mng. editor Moore Publishing Co., 1955, Chain Store Age mag., 1955-59, Sales Mgmt. mag., 1961; editor Food Topics mag., 1961-68; dir. mktg. Grocery Mfrs. Am., 1969-70; editor Chain Store Age-Supermarket Group, N.Y.C., 1970-77; cons. to supermarket industry, 1977-80; editor-in-chief Supermarket Bus. mag., 1980—. Contbr. to Wharton Mag. Served with USAAF, 1943-46. Decorated Air medal; recipient Jesse Neal award Assoc. Bus. Press, 1968, Grand award ABP Points of Light

Award, 1991. Mem. Sigma Delta Chi. Home: 20 Devils Gardens Rd Norwalk CT 06854-3315

PARTEE, BARBARA HALL, linguist, educator; b. Englewood, N.J., June 23, 1940; d. David B. and Helen M. Hall; m. Morriss Henry Partee, 1966 (div. 1971); children: Morriss M., David M., Joel T.; m. Emmon Werner Bach, 1973 (div. 1996). BA with high honors in Math., Swarthmore Coll., 1961; PhD in Linguistics, MIT, 1965; DSc (hon.), Swarthmore Coll., 1989, Charles U., Prague, Czechoslovakia, 1992. Asst. prof. UCLA, 1965-69, assoc. prof., 1969-73; assoc. prof. linguistics and philosophy U. Mass., Amherst, 1972-73, prof., 1973-90, Disting. Univ. prof., 1990—, head dept. linguistics, 1987-93; fellow Ctr. for Advanced Study in Behavior Scis., 1976-77; mem. bd. mgrs. Swarthmore Coll., 1990—. Author: (with Stockwell and Schachter) The Major Syntactic Structures of English, 1972, Fundamentals of Mathematics for Linguists, 1979, (with ter Meulen and Wall) Mathematical Methods in Linguistics, 1990; editor: Montague Grammar, 1976; co-editor: (with Chierchia and Turner) Properties, Types and Meaning, Vol. I: Foundational Issues, Vol. II: Semantic Issues, 1989, (with Bach, Jelinek and Kratzer) Quantification in Natural Languages, 1995; mem. editoral bd: Language, 1967-73, Linguistic Inquiry, 1972-79, Theoretical Linguistics, 1974—, Linguistics and Philosophy, 1977—. Recipient Chancellor's medal U. Mass., 1977; NEH fellow, 1982-83; Internat. Rsch. and Exchanges Bd. fellow, 1989-90, 95. Mem. NAS (chair anthropology sect. 1993-96), Linguistic Soc. Am. (pres. 1986), Am. Philos. Assn., Assn. Computational Linguistics, Am. Acad. Arts and Scis., Sigma Xi. Home: 50 Hobart Ln Amherst MA 01002-1321 Office: U Mass Dept Linguistics Amherst MA 01003 *I had the good fortune to have loving and encouraging parents and stimulating teachers, to find a field of inquiry which I love and can contribute to, and to have the constant inspiration of wonderful collegues, wonderful students and wonderful family.*

PARTHASARATHY, RAJAGOPAL, writer, literature educator; b. Tirupparaitturai, India, Aug. 20, 1934; came to U.S., 1982; s. Krishnaswamy and Ambujam Rajagopal; m. Shobhan Koppikar, Oct. 26, 1969; children: Gautam, Arjun. BA, Bombay U., 1957, MA, 1959; Diploma in English Studies, Leeds (Eng.) U., 1964; PhD, U. Tex., 1987. Lectr. in English Ismail Yusuf Coll., Bombay, 1959-62, Mithibai Coll., Bombay, 1962-63, 64-65; lectr. in English lang. teaching Brit. Coun., Bombay, 1965-66; asst. prof. English Presidency Coll., Madras, 1966-67; lectr. in English South Indian Edn. Soc. Coll., Bombay, 1967-71; regional editor Oxford U. Press, Madras, 1971-78; editor Oxford U. Press, Delhi, 1978-82; asst. prof. English Skidmore Coll., Saratoga Springs, N.Y., 1986-92, assoc. prof., 1992—, dir. program in Asian studies, 1994—; dir. poetry workshop Stella Maris Coll., Madras, 1972-75; part-time lectr. in book pub. Coll. Vocat. Guidance, Delhi U., New Delhi, 1979-81. Author: (verse) Rough Passage, 1977; editor (verse) Ten Twentieth-Century Indian Poets, 1976, (with J.J. Healy) Poetry from Leeds, 1968; translator: (verse and prose) The Tale of an Anklet: An Epic of South India (The Cilappatikaram of Ilanko Atikal), 1993. Brit. Coun. scholar, 1963; recipient Ulka Poetry prize Poetry India, 1966, PEN/Book-of-the-Month Club Translation citation, 1994, Translation prize Sahitya Akademi (Nat. Acad. Letters India), 1995; U.S. Dept. State exch. visitor, 1978. Mem. MLA, Am. Lit. Translators Assn., Assn. for Asian Studies, Phi Kappa Phi. Avocations: travel, classical music, gardening. Home: 8 Salem Dr Saratoga Springs NY 12866-3726 Office: Skidmore Coll Dept English 815 N Broadway Saratoga Springs NY 12866-1632

PARTHUM, CHARLES ALBERT, civil engineer; b. Lawrence, Mass., Sept. 26, 1929; s. Albert and Elsie Ida (Eichner) P.; m. Mary Catherine Wiggin, Oct. 20, 1956; children: Stephen Charles, Julie Elizabeth. BSCE, Northeastern U., 1951. With Camp Dresser & McKee, Inc., Boston, 1951—; ptnr. Camp Dresser & McKee, Inc., 1967—, sr. v.p., dir., 1971-92; cons., 1992—; cons. EPA, 1980. Treas., deacon, moderator, clk. Tabernacle Ch., Salem, Mass.; chmn. Engr.-Joint Contacts Documents Com., 1980. With USN, 1952-55. Recipient Outstanding Civil Engring. Alumnus award Northeastern U., 1989. Mem. NSPE, ASCE (bd. dirs. 1987-90, pres. 1995-96, William H. Wisely Am. Civil Engr. award 1993), Am. Acad. Environ. Engrs. (diplomate), Boston Soc. Civil Engrs. (hon., pres. 1975-76), Water Pollution Control Fedn. (chmn. constrn. and bylaws com. 1972-77), Am. Water Resources Assn., Mass. Soc. Profl. Engrs., Am. Water Works Assn., New England Water Works Assn., New England Water Pollution Control Assn., Chi Epsilon (hon.). Office: One Cambridge Ctr Cambridge MA 02142

PARTIDA, GILBERT A., chamber of commerce executive; b. Nogales, Ariz., July 27, 1962; s. Enrique Gilberto and Mary Lou (Flores) P.; m. Soncee Ray Brown, July 30, 1992. BA with distinction, U. Ariz., 1984; JD cum laude, Pepperdine U., 1987; LLD (hon.), Calif. Western Sch Law, San Diego, 1993. V.p., bd. mem. Partida Brokerage, Inc., Nogales, 1983-91; law clk. Office of Ariz. Atty. Gen., Tucson, 1985; assoc. Gray, Cary, Ames & Frye, San Diego, 1986-89, sr. assoc., 1990-92; chmn. Mex. Practice Group Gray, Cary, Ames & Frye, 1992; pres. Greater San Diego C. of C., 1993—; corp. counsel San Diego Incubator Corp., 1990—. Contbr. articles to profl. jours. Mem. United Way Latino Future Scan Com., 1990; mentor Puente, 1991; leadership tng. mentor Chicano Fedn., 1992; dinner com. Young at Art, 1991; mem. Children's Initiative, 1993, Superbowl Task Force, 1993, San Diego Dialogue, 1993; hon. mem. Sister City, 1993, LEAD, 1993; hon. chair Easter Seals Telethon, 1994; vice chmn. Border Trade Alliance, 1989-91; mem. nat. gala com. HDI Ednl. Svcs., 1990; Calif. state del. U.S.-Mexico Border Govs.' Conf., 1990, 92; exec. com. San Diego Conv. and Visitors Bur. Mem. San Diego County Hispanic C. of C. (chmn. 1991, pres. 1990-91, v.p. 1989-90, internat. com. chair 1989-90, sec. 1989, founding bd. mem. 1988), Consejo Nacional de Maquiladoras, Calif. Hispanic C. of C. (state conv. joint venture com. 1991, spl. projects chair 1991), San Diego/Tijuana Sister Cities Soc. (adv. coun. 1993—), San Diego County Bar Assn. (U.S./Mexico liaison com.), ABA (U.S./Mexico bar liaison com.), Hispanic Alliance for Free Trade, Rotary Club San Diego. Avocations: tennis, running, creative writing. Office: Greater San Diego C of C 402 W Broadway Ste 1000 San Diego CA 92101-8507

PARTINGTON, JAMES WOOD, naval officer; b. Omaha, Jan. 16, 1939; s. Lee Edward and Carol Virginia (Wood) P.; m. Barbara Jean Arline, July 15, 1961; children: Jennifer, Kathleen, Mary Elizabeth. BA, U. R.I., 1970; grad., Naval War Coll., 1971. Commd. ensign USN, 1961, advanced through grades to rear adm., 1989; ops. officer Attack Squadron 122, Lemoore, Calif., 1974-77; comdg. officer Attack Squadron 27, Lemoore, 1977-80, Strike Fighter Squadron 125, Lemoore, 1980-82; coord. F/A 18 program Chief Naval Ops., Washington, 1982-84; comdg. officer Naval Air Sta., Lemoore, 1984-86; chief of staff Cruiser Destroyer Group 5, San Diego, 1986-87; dir. Naval Aviation Officer Assignments, Washington, 1987-88; comdr. Strike Fighter Wings Atlantic, Jacksonville, Fla., 1988-90, Naval Tng. Ctr., Great Lakes, Ill., 1990-92; v.p., dir. corp. planning Sr. Technologies Inc., 1992-94; pres. Partington and Associates, Lincoln, 1994—. Decorated Legion of Merit (5), DFC, Air medal (28), Meritorious Svc. medal. Mem. U.S. Naval Inst., Assn. Naval Aviation, Naval Order of U.S. Roman Catholic. Avocations: sailing, tennis, scuba diving.

PARTNOY, RONALD ALLEN, lawyer; b. Norwalk, Conn., Dec. 23, 1933; s. Maurice and Ethel Marguerite (Roselle) P.; m. Diane Catherine Keenan, Sept. 18, 1965. B.A., Yale U., 1956; LL.B., Harvard U., 1961; LL.M., Boston U., 1965. Bar: Mass. 1962, Conn. 1966. Atty. Liberty Mut. Ins. Co., Boston, 1961-65; assoc. counsel Remington Arms Co., Bridgeport, Conn., 1965-70; gen. counsel Remington Arms Co., 1970-88, sec., 1983-93; sr. counsel E.I. du Pont de Nemours & Co., Wilmington, Del., 1985—. Served with USN, 1956-58; to capt. USNR (ret.). Mem. ABA, Sporting Arms and Ammunition Mfrs. Inst. (chmn. legis. and legal affairs com. 1971-86), Am. Judicature Soc., U.S. Navy League (pres. Bridgeport coun. 1975-77, nat. dir., Conn. pres. 1977-80, v.p. Empire region 1980-85), Naval Res. Assn. (3d dist. pres., nat. exec. com. 1981-85), Chancery Club, Harvard Club of Boston, Harvard Club of Phila., Yale Club of N.Y.C. Home: 616 Bayard Rd Kennett Square PA 19348-2504 Office: 1007 Market St Wilmington DE 19898

PARTON, DOLLY REBECCA, singer, composer, actress; b. Sevier County, Tenn., Jan. 19, 1946; d. Robert Lee and Avie Lee (Owens) P.; m. Carl Dean, May 30, 1966. Country music singer, rec. artist, composer, actress, radio and TV personality; entrepreneur, owner entertainment park Dollywood, established 1985. Radio appearances include Grand Ole Opry, WSM Radio, Nashville, Cass Walker program, Knoxville; TV appearances include Porter Wagoner Show, from 1967, Cass Walker program, Bill Anderson Show, Wilburn Bros. Show, Barbara Mandrell Show; rec. artist, Mercury, Monument, RCA , CBS record cos.; star movie Nine to Five, 1980, The Best Little Whorehouse in Texas, 1982, Rhinestone, 1984, Steel Magnolias, 1989, Straight Talk, 1991; albums include Here You Come Again (Grammy award 1978), Real Love, 1985, Just the Way I Am, 1986, Portrait, 1986, Think About Love, 1986, Trio (with Emmylou Harris, Linda Ronstadt) (Grammy award 1988), 1987, Heartbreaker, Great Balls of Fire, Rainbow, 1988, White Limozeen, 1989, Home for Christmas, 1990, Eagle When She Flies, 1991, Slow Dancing with the Moon, 1993 (Grammy nomination, Best Country Vocal Collaboration for Romeo (with Tanya Tucker, Billy Ray Cyrus, Kathy Mattea, Pam Tillis, & Mary-Chapin Carpenter), (with Tammy Wynette and Loretta Lynn) Honky Tonk Angels, 1994; composer numerous songs including Nine to Five (Grammy award 1981, Acad. award nominee and Golden Globe award nominee 1981); author: Dolly, 1994. Recipient (with Porter Wagoner) Vocal Group of Yr. award, 1968; Vocal Duo of Yr. award All Country Music Assn., 1970, 71; Nashville Metronome award, 1979; Am. Music award for best duo performance (with Kenny Rogers), 1984; named Female Vocalist of Yr., 1975, 76; Country Star of Yr., Sullivan Prodns., 1977; Entertainer of Yr., Country Music Assn., 1978; People's Choice award, 1980, 88; Female Vocalist of Yr., Acad. Country Music, 1980; Dolly Parton Day proclaimed, Sevier County, Tenn., designated Oct. 7, 1967, Los Angeles, Sept. 20, 1979; recipient Grammy awards for best female country vocalist, 1978, 81, for best country song, 1981, for best country vocal performance with group, 1987; co-recipient (with Emmylou Harris and Linda Ronstadt) Acad. Country Music award for album of the yr., 1987; named to Small Town of Am. Hall of Fame, 1988, East Tenn. Hall of Fame, 1988.

PARTON, JAMES, historian; b. Newburyport, Mass., Dec. 10, 1912; s. Hugo and Agnes (Leach) P.; m. Jane Audra Bourne, Dec. 9, 1950 (dec. 1962); children: James III, Dana (dec.), Sara. A.B., Harvard U., 1934. Asst. E.L. Bernays, N.Y.C., 1934-35; aviation editor Time Mag., 1935-36, bus. and financial editor, 1937-39, asst. gen. mgr., 1940, bus. mgr. air express edit., 1941; promotion mgr. Time-Life Internat., 1945; editorial dir. Pacific Coast news burs. Time, Inc., 1947; editor and pub. Los Angeles Ind., 1948-49; cons. U.S. Dept. State, 1949; promotion dir. N.Y. Herald Tribune, 1950; asst. to pres., chmn. Herald Tribune Forum and dir. N.Y. Herald Tribune, Inc., 1951-53; v.p., treas. Thorndike, Jensen & Parton, Inc., 1953-57; founder, pres. Am. Heritage Pub. Co., Inc., 1954-70; pres. Ency. Brit. Ednl. Corp., Chgo., 1970-72; chmn. exec. com. Ency. Brit. Ednl. Corp., 1973; pres. James Parton & Co., N.Y.C., 1973-81, Parton Enterprises, Inc., 1981-84; dir. planning study Custom House Inst., N.Y.C., 1973; chmn. Nat. Advt. Rev. Bd., 1974-76; asst. librarian for pub. edn. Library of Congress, 1976-77; chmn. exec. com. Hist. Times, Inc., 1979-81; chmn. U.S. Army com. which produced ofcl. Eighth Air Force book Target-Germany, 1943. Author: "Air Force Spoken Here", General Ira Eaker and the Command of the Air, 1986. Editor, pub. Impact, The Army Air Forces Confidential Picture History of World War II, 8 vols, 1980. Trustee Loomis Inst., 1952—, pres., 1964-66, chmn., 1967-70; trustee USAF Hist. Found., 1955—; bd. visitors Air U., 1988-91. Commd. 2d lt. in USAAF, 1942; advanced through grades to lt. col. 1944. Decorated Legion of Merit, Bronze Star, European Theater ribbon with 4 battle stars. Mem. Harvard Club (N.Y.C.), Army and Navy Club (Washington). Home: PO Box 796 Hanover NH 03755-0796

PARTRIDGE, BRUCE JAMES, lawyer, educator; b. June 4, 1926, Syracuse, N.Y.; came to Can., 1969; s. Bert James and Lida Marion (Rice) P.; m. Mary Janice Smith, June 13, 1948 (dec. 1986); children: Heather Leigh, Eric James, Brian Lloyd, Bonnie Joyce; m. May S. Archer, May 28, 1988; stepchildren: Sheila Archer, Laurel Archer. AB cum laude, Oberlin Coll., Ohio, 1946; LLB, Blackstone Coll., Chgo., 1950, JD, 1952; LLB, U. B.C., 1974. Bar: B.C. 1976, N.W.T. 1980. Rsch. physicist Am. Gas Assn., Cleve., 1946-48; bus. adminstr. Rochester Inst. Tech., N.Y., 1953-58, Baldwin-Wallace Coll., Berea, Ohio, 1951-53, Cazenovia (N.Y.) Coll., 1948-51; v.p. bus. and mgmt., U. Del., Newark, Del., 1958-63; v.p. adminstrn. Johns Hopkins U., Balt., 1963-69; pres. U. Victoria, B.C., Can., 1969-72; assoc. Clark, Wilson & Co., Vancouver, B.C., 1975-78; successively solicitor, mng. solicitor, gen. solicitor, v.p. law and gen. counsel, sec. Cominco Ltd., Vancouver, 1978-88; exec. dir. Baker & McKenzie, Hong Kong, 1988-90; v.p. Pacific Creations Inc., 1990-92; faculty Camosun Coll., 1992—. Co-author: College and University Business Administration, 1968. Chmn. editorial com. Purchasing for Higher Education, 1962. Contbr. numerous articles to profl. jours. Chmn. commn. on adminstrv. affairs Am. Council on Edn., Washington, 1966-69; mem. Pres.'s Com. on Employment of Handicapped, Washington, 1967-69; mem. adv. council Ctr. for Resource Studies, Queen's U.; bd. dirs. L'Arche in the Americas; mem. adv. council Westwater Research Centre, U. B.C. Mem. Law Soc. B.C., Law Soc. of N.W. Ters., Assn. Can. Gen. Counsel, Fedn. Ins. and Corp. Counsel, Def. Research Inst. (product liability com.), Am. Corp. Counsel Assn., Vancouver Club, Aberdeen Marine Club, Hong Kong Football Club. Unitarian. Office: Camosun Coll, 4461 Interurban Rd, Victoria, BC Canada V8X 3X1

PARTRIDGE, MARK VAN BUREN, lawyer; b. Rochester, Minn., Oct. 16, 1954; s. John V.B. and Constance (Brainerd) P.; m. Mary Roberta Moffitt, Apr. 30, 1983; children: Caitlin, Lindsay, Christopher. BA, U. Nebr., 1978; JD, Harvard U., 1981. Bar: Ill. 1981, U.S. Dist. Ct. (no. dist.) Ill. 1981, U.S. Dist. Ct. (ea. dist.) Mich. 1983, U.S. Ct. Appeals (fed. cir.) 1983, U.S. Ct. Appeals (4th cir.) 1986, U.S. Ct. Appeals (5th cir.) 1993. Assoc. Pattishall, McAuliffe, Newbury, Hilliard & Geraldson, Chgo., 1981-88, ptnr., 1988—; adj. prof. John Marshall Law Sch., Chgo., 1990—; arbitrator Cook County Mandatory Arbitration Program, 1989—; v.p. Harvard Legal Aid Bur., 1980-81. Author: (with others) Winning With Computers, 1993; co-author: (article) Developments in Trademark and Unfair Competition Law, 1990; mem. editl. bd. The Trademark Reporter, 1994—; adv. bd. IP Litigator, 1995—. Vol. Chgo. Vol. Legal Svcs., 1983—. Mem. ABA (com. chmn. 1989—), Am. Intellectual Property Law Assn. (com. chmn. 1989-91), Intellectual Property Law Assn. Chgo. (com. chmn. 1993—, Brand Names Ednl. Found., moot ct. regional chmn. 1994—), Legal Club, Executives' Club, Union League Club. Avocations: genealogy, travel, computers. Office: Pattishall McAuliffe Newbury Hilliard & Geraldson 311 S Wacker Dr Chicago IL 60606-6618

PARTRIDGE, ROBERT BRUCE, astronomy educator; b. Honolulu, May 16, 1940; s. Robert B. and Laura Lea (Johnson) P.; m. Jane C. Widseth, Aug. 28, 1976; children: John D. W., Carl E. W. AB, Princeton U., 1962; PhD, U. Oxford, Eng., 1965. From instr. to asst. prof. Princeton (N.J.) U., 1965-70; assoc. prof. Haverford (Pa.) Coll., 1970-76, dean, 1982-85, prof., 1976—, Bettye and Howard Marshall prof. of natural scis., 1981—, provost, 1990-95; cons. NASA, NSF, 1988—. Contbr. numerous articles to profl. jours. Rhodes scholar, U. Oxford, 1962-65; Alfred Sloan fellow, 1971-76, Fulbright fellow, Norway, 1979-80, Guggenheim fellow, 1988-89. Home: 628 Overhill Rd Ardmore PA 19003-1007 Office: Haverford Coll Astronomy Dept Haverford PA 19041

PARTRIDGE, WILLIAM SCHAUBEL, retired physicist, research company executive; b. Ranchester, Wyo., Jan. 20, 1922; s. William Clayton and Elsie (Schaubel) P.; m. Jeannette Noble, Mar. 21, 1942; children—Nancy, Dianne, William Noble, Carol, Murray Noble (dec.). B.A., U. Wyo., 1946, M.A., 1948; Ph.D., U. Utah, 1951. Staff scientist U. Calif., Los Alamos, 1951-52; asst. dir. explosives research group U. Utah, Salt Lake City, 1952-55; assoc. research prof., dir. high velocity research lab. U. Utah, 1955-58, v.p. for research, 1966-79; pres. U. Utah Rsch. Inst., 1972-83, Utah Bioresearch, 1983-89, ret.; chmn. bd. Tech. Rsch. Assocs., Inc., 1983-89; pres., gen. mgr. Utah R & D Co., Salt Lake City, 1958-64; staff scientist Jet Propulsion Lab., Pasadena, Calif., 1964-66; mem. exec. com. Nat. Coun. Univ. Rsch. Adminstrs., 1969-71; pres., gen. mgr. U. Utah Rsch. Inst., 1972-83; mem. nat. adv. com. on planning and instl. affairs NSF, 1971-73; nat. adv. rsch. resources coun. NIH, 1974-78, mem. adv. com. to dir. NIH, 1981-84. Contbr. articles to profl. jours. Served to capt. USAAF, World War II. Patentee in field. Home: 11843 S Pond Ridge Dr Draper UT 84020

PARVER, JANE W., lawyer. AB summa cum laude, Tufts U.; MA, Fletcher Sch. Law and Diplomacy; JD, Columbia U., 1972. Bar: N.Y. 1973. Law clerk so. dist. N.Y. U.S. Dist. Ct., 1972-73; asst U.S. atty. so. dist. N.Y. criminal divsn. U.S. Atty's. Office, 1976-81; chief Major Crimes Unit, 1981-84; exec. asst. U.S. Atty., chief Pub. Corruption Unit, 1984-85; ptnr. Kaye, Scholer, Fierman, Hays & Handler, N.Y.C. Office: Kaye Scholer Fierman Hayes & Handler 425 Park Ave New York NY 10022-3506*

PARVIN, PHILIP E., retired agricultural researcher and educator; b. Manatee, Fla., July 3, 1927; s. Clinton Fisk and Beatrice (Ward) P. MS, Miss. State U., Starkeville, 1950; PhD, Mich. State U., 1965. Asst. prof. U. Fla., Gainesville, 1952-55; extension specialist U. Calif., Davis, 1963-66; gen. mgr. Rod McLellan Co., San Francisco, 1966-68; horticulturist Maui Agrl. Rsch. Ctr. U. Hawaii, Kula, 1968-93. Contbr. over 100 articles to profl. jours. With U.S. Army, 1945-46. Fellow Am. Soc. for Hort. Sci.; mem. Am. Acad. Floriculture (hon.), South African Protea Prodrs. and Exporters (hon. life), Internat. Protea Assn. (hon. life, chmn. rsch. com. 1983-89), Protea Growers Assn. Hawaii (hon. life), Rotary (pres. Maui chpt. 1981-82). Republican. Methodist. Achievements include development of Hawaii protea industry. Home: 2395 Nuremberg Blvd Punta Gorda FL 33983-2626

PARZEN, EMANUEL, statistical scientist; b. N.Y.C., Apr. 21, 1929; s. Samuel and Sarah (Getzel) P.; m. Carol Tenowitz, July 12, 1959; children: Sara Leah, Michael Isaac. AB in Math., Harvard U., 1949; MA, U. Calif., Berkeley, 1951, PhD, 1953. Research scientist Columbia, 1953-56, asst. prof. math. statistics, 1955-56; faculty Stanford, 1956-70, asso. prof. statistics, 1959-64, prof., 1964-70; prof. statistics State U. N.Y. at Buffalo, 1970-73, prof. stats. sci., 1973-78; distinguished prof. statistics Tex. A and M U., College Station, 1978—; guest prof. IMperial Coll., London, 1961-62; vis. prof. MIT, 1964-65, Harvard U., 1976, 88, Ctr. for Advanced Study in Behavioral Scis., 1983-84. Author: Stochastic Processes, 1962, Modern Probability Theory and its Applications, 1960, Time Series Analysis Papers, 1967, also articles. Fellow AAAS, Internat. Statis. Inst., Am. Statis. Assn., Royal Statis. Soc., Inst. Math. Statistics; mem. Am. Math. Soc., Soc. Indsl. and Applied Math., Bernoulli Soc., N.Y. Acad. Scis., Phi Beta Kappa, Sigma Xi. Research in time series analysis, non-parametric statistical data modeling, change analysis. Office: Tex A&M U Dept Stats College Station TX 77843-3143

PARZEN, STANLEY JULIUS, lawyer; b. N.Y.C., Feb. 6, 1952. BA, Earlham Coll., 1973; LLB cum laude, Harvard U., 1976. Bar: Ill. 1978, U.S. Dist. Ct. (no. dist.) Ill. 1978, U.S. Dist. Ct. (no. dist.) Calif. 1989, U.s. Dist. Ct. (we. dist.) Mich. 1995, U.S. Ct. Appeals (7th cir.) 1981, U.S. Ct. Appeals (8th cir.) 1983, U.S. Ct. Appeals (5th cir.) 1992, U.S. Ct. appeals (D.C. cir.) 1992, U.S. Ct. Appeals (2d cir.) 1990, U.S. Ct. Appeals (9th cir.) 1996. Law clk. to judge U.S. Ct. Appeals 4th cir., 1976-77; ptnr. Mayer, Brown & Platt, Chgo. Mem. Phi Beta Kappa. Office: Mayer Brown & Platt 190 S La Salle St Chicago IL 60603-3410

PASACHOFF, JAY MYRON, astronomer, educator; b. N.Y.C., July 1, 1943; s. Samuel S. and Anne (Traub) P.; m. Naomi Schwartz, Mar. 31, 1974; children: Eloise Hilary, Deborah Donna. A.B., Harvard U., 1963, A.M. (NSF fellow), 1965, Ph.D. (NSF fellow, N.Y. State Regents fellow for advanced grad. study), 1969. Research physicist Air Force Cambridge Research Labs., Bedford, Mass., 1968-69; Menzel research fellow Harvard Coll. Obs., Cambridge, Mass., 1969-70; research fellow Hale Obs., Carnegie Instn., Washington, and Calif. Inst. Tech., Pasadena, 1970-72; dir. Hopkins Obs. Williams Coll., Williamstown, Mass., 1972—; chmn. astronomy dept. Williams Coll., 1972-77, 91-92, asst. prof. astronomy, 1972-77, assoc. prof., 1977-84, prof., 1984, Field Meml. prof. of astronomy, 1984—; adj. asst. prof. astronomy U. Mass., Amherst, 1975-77, adj. assoc. prof., 1977-83, adj. prof., 1986—; vis. colleague and vis. assoc. prof. astronomy Inst. for Astronomy, U. Hawaii, 1980-81; vis. scientist Inst. d'Astrophysique, Paris, 1988; mem. Inst. Advanced Study, Princeton, 1989-90, Harvard-Smithsonian Ctr. for Astrophysics, 1993-94; total and other solar eclipse expdns., Mass., 1959, Que., Can., 1963, Mex., 1970, asst. dir. Harvard-Smithsonian-Nat. Geog. Expdn., P.E.I., Can., 1972, NSF expdn., Harvard-Smithsonian-Williams Expdn., Kenya, 1973; NSF expdn., Colombia, 1973 (annular eclipse), Australia, 1974, Pacific Ocean, 1977, Man., Can., 1979, NSF expdn., India, 1980, Pacific Ocean, 1981, Java, Indonesia, 1983, Miss., 1984 (annular eclipse), Papua, New Guinea, 1984, Sumatra, Indonesia, 1988, Hawaii 1989 (partial), Finland, 1990, Hawaii, 1991, Calif., 1992 (annular eclipse), Pacific near Africa, 1992, N.H., 1994 (annular eclipse), Chile, 1994, India, 1995; rsch. fellow Owens Valley Radio Obs., 1974; guest investigator NASA Orbiting Solar Obs.-8, 1975-79. Author: Contemporary Astronomy, 1977, 4th edit., 1989, Astronomy Now, 1978, Astronomy: From Earth to the Universe, 1979, 4th edit. 1991, subsequent versions 1993, 95; A Brief View of Astronomy, 1986, First Guide to Astronomy, 1988, First Guide to the Solar System, 1990, Journey Through the Universe, 1992; co-author: (with Marc L. Kutner, Naomi Pasachoff) Student Study Guide to Contemporary Astronomy, 1977, (with Kutner, Pasachoff and N.P. Kutner) Student Study Guide to Astronomy Now, 1978; (with M.L. Kutner) University Astronomy, 1978, Invitation to Physics, 1981; (with N. Pasachoff, T. Cooney) Physical Science, 1983, 2d edit., 1990, Earth Science, 1983, 2d edit., 1990; (with D.H. Menzel) A Field Guide to the Stars and Planets, 2d edit., 1983, 3d edit., 1992; (with R. Wolfson) Physics, 1987, 2nd edit., 1995, (Extended with Modern Physics, 1989, 2nd edit. 1995), (with N. Pasachoff, R.W. Clark, M.H. Westermann) Physical Science Today, 1987; (with N. Pasachoff and others) Discover Science, 7 vols., 1989; (with Michael Covington) Cambridge Eclipse Photography Guide, 1993; (with Len Holder and James DeFranza) Calculus, 1994, Single Variable Calculus, 1994, Multivariable Calculus, 1995; (with Edward Cheng, Patrick Osmer and Hyron Spinrad) The Farthest Things in the Universe, 1994; editor (with J. Percy) The Teaching of Astronomy, 1990; assoc. editor: Jour. Irreproducible Results, 1972-94, Annals of Improbable Rsch., 1994—; abstractor from Am. jours. for Solar Physics, 1968-78; cons. editor McGraw-Hill Ency. Sci. and Tech., 1983—; co-editor-in-chief (with S.P. Parker), McGraw-Hill Ency. of Astronomy, 1993; cons. Random House Dictionary, 1983-86, Nat. Geographic Atlas, 5th edit., 1981, 6th edit., 1990; phys. sci. com. World Book Encyclopedia, 1989-95, cons., 1996—; contbr. articles to profl. jours. and encys., articles and photographs to non-tech. publs. Recipient Bronze medal Nikon Photo Contest Internat., 1971, photograph aboard NASA Voyagers, 1977, Dudley award Dudley Obs., 1985; grantee: NSF, 1973-75, 79-83, 88-96, Nat. Geog. Soc., 1973-86, 91-95, Rsch. Corp., 1973-74, 75-78, 82-88, Getty Found., 1994-95. Fellow AAAS (chair sec D 1987-88), Royal Astron. Soc., Am. Phys. Soc. (mem.-at-large Am. Phys. Soc./Am. Assn. Physics Tchrs. Forum on Edn. 1995—), N.Y. Acad. Sci., Internat. Planetarium Soc.; mem. AAUP (chpt. pres. 1977-80), Internat. Astron. Union (U.S. nat. rep. Commn. on Tchg. Astronomy 1976—, chair Eclipse Working Group 1991—, rep. to Com. on Tchg. Sci. of Internat. Coun. Sci. Unions 1991-93), Am. Astron. Soc. (astronomy edn. adv. bd. 1990—, astronomy news com. 1991—), Astron. Soc. Pacific, Union Radio Sci., Am. Assn. Physics Tchrs. (astronomy com. 1983-87), Sigma Xi (chpt. pres. 1973-74, 95—, nat. lectr. 1993—). Home: 1305 Main St Williamstown MA 01267-2630 Office: Hopkins Obs Williams Coll Williamstown MA 01267-2565

PASAHOW, LYNN H(AROLD), lawyer; b. Ft. Eutiss, Va., Mar. 13, 1947; s. Samuel and Cecelia (Newman) P.; m. Leslie Aileen Cobb, June 11, 1969; 1 child, Michael Alexander. AB, Stanford U., 1969; JD, U. Calif., Berkeley, 1972. Bar: Calif. 1972, U.S. Ct. Appeals (9th cir.) 1972, U.S. Dist. Ct. (no. dist.) Calif. 1973, U.S. Dist. Ct. (cen. dist.) Calif. 1974, U.S. Supreme Ct. 1976, U.S. Dist. Ct. (ea. dist.) Calif. 1977, U.S. Ct. Appeals (fed. cir.) 1990. Law clk. judge U.S. Dist. Ct. (no. dist.) Calif., San Francisco, 1972-73; assoc. McCutchen, Doyle, Brown & Enersen, San Francisco, 1973-79, ptnr., 1979—; dir. Copyright Soc. No. Calif., San Francisco; mem. lawyer's com. Bay Area Biosci. Ctr., 1993—, attys. adv. panel, 1993—; moderator Lexis Counsel Connect Nat. Patent Forum, 1996—. Author: Pretrial and Settlement Conferences in Federal Court, 1983; co-author: Civil Discovery and Mandatory Disclosure: A Guide to Effective Practice, 1994; contbr. articles to profl. jours. Mem. ABA, Calif. Bar Assn., Am. Intellectual Property Law Assn. Democrat. Office: McCutchen Doyle Brown & Enersen 3 Embarcadero Ctr 28th Fl San Francisco CA 94111 *Notable cases include: duPont vs. Cetus, PCR patent litigation, nicotine patch patent litigation.*

PASANELLA, GIOVANNI, architect, architectural educator; b. N.Y.C., Jan. 13, 1931; children: Marco, Nicolas. Student, Cooper Union, 1949-53, Yale U., 1953-58. Registered architect, N.Y. Designer Edward L. Barnes, N.Y.C., 1959-64; prin. Giovanni Pasanella, N.Y.C., 1964-76; co-owner Pasanella & Klein, N.Y.C., 1976—; critic architecture U. Ky., Lexington, 1963, Yale U., New Haven, 1964; adj. prof. architecture Columbia U., N.Y.C., 1965-87; vis. fellow urban studies Inst. of Architecture, 1975.

Project dir. Inst. of Urban Environ. Columbia U., N.Y.C., 1965-68; cons. architecture to chmn. N.Y.C. Planning Commn., 1967; cons. urban design City of Lucca, Italy, 1985; bd. trustees Il Piccolo Teatro dell' Opera, Bklyn., 1986. Yale U. traveling fellow, 1958-59; Architecture award Archtl. Record, 1974, 75. Fellow AIA (Residential award N.Y. Soc. 1971); mem. Soc. of Archtl. Historians, Mcpl. Arts Soc. Office: Pasanella & Klein Architects 330 W 42nd St New York NY 10036-6902 Home: Cannizzaro, Via Fondi CAmaiore, Lucca Italy

PASANELLA, MARCO, furniture designer; s. Giovanni and Ann P. BA cum laude, Yale U., 1984. Pres., creative dir. The Pasanella Co., Inc., N.Y.C., 1986—; instr. Parsons Sch. of Design, 1993—; freelance writer, photographer for Elle, Casa Vogue, others, 1987—; co-founder Nat. Initiative for Courtesy & Etiquette, 1991-92. Contbg. editor Taxi Mag., 1987-90; rocking chair acquired by Cooper-Hewitt Mus., Smithsonian Inst. Nat. Mus. Design for permanent collection, 1991, etiquette placemat and napkin prodn. series, 1993, rocking chair acquired by Pres. Bill Clinton for pvt. quarters of White House; contbr. numerous articles to newspapers and profl. jours. Vol. project coord. Bailey House; organized renovation AIDS hospice lounge, 1987-88; mem. renewable energy com. Creative Coalition of Arts, 1990-91; mem. exec. com. Contemporary Arts Coun. of Mus. Modern Art, 1987-89. Named to Internat. Design 40: A Guide to Am.'s Leading Design Innovators, 1993, to Met. Home's Design 100: The Best Am. Has to Offer, 1994; recipient spl. recognition for excellence in design Internat. Contemporary Furniture Fair, N.Y.C., 1992; winner nat. design competition 2001: How Will We Live? Sony Corp., Metropolis Mag., Parsons Sch. Design, 1991. Mem. Furniture N.Y. (charter 1991—). Address: 420 Riverside Dr New York NY 10025

PASCAL, C(ECIL) BENNETT, classics educator; b. Chgo., May 4, 1926; s. Jack and Goldie (Zeff) P.; m. Ilene Joy Shulman, Feb. 1, 1959; 1 child, Keith Irwin. BA, UCLA, 1949, MA, 1950; MA, Harvard U., 1953, PhD, 1956. Instr. U. Ill., Champaign, 1955-56, Cornell U., Ithaca, N.Y., 1957-60; asst. prof. U. Oreg., Eugene, 1960-75, prof. classics, 1975-96, prof. emeritus, 1996—, head dept., various years - 1965-85. Author: Cults of Cisalpine Gaul, 1964; contbr. articles to profl. jours. Mem. Eugene Bicycle Com., 1971-83. Served with USN, 1944-46. Traveling fellow, Italy, Harvard U., 1956-57, Fulbright-Hays fellow, Rome, 1967-68. Mem. Am. Philol. Assn., Classical Assn. Pacific N.W. (pres. 1965-66), AAUP, Archeol. Inst. of Am. (past pres., sec. Eugene Soc.). Democrat. Jewish. Avocations: skiing, fishing, novel writing. Home: 330 Fulvue Dr Eugene OR 97405-2788 Office: U of Oreg Dept Classics Eugene OR 97403

PASCAL, DAVID, artist; b. N.Y.C., Aug. 16, 1918; s. Boucour and Carolina (Finor) P.; m. Theresa Auerbach, Aug. 24, 1962; 1 child, Jeffrey B. Student, Am. Artists Sch., 1936-38; M Practioner, N.Y. Tng. Inst. Neuro-Linguistic Programming, 1992. Instr. Sch. Visual Arts, N.Y.C., 1955-58; lectr. mus., schs., congresses N.Y., Paris, Italy, Sao Paulo, Buenos Aires, Argentina; organizer 1st Am. Internat. Congress Comics, N.Y.C., 1972; artistic counselor to bd. dirs. Lucca Internat. Comics Congresses, 1976—; participant overseas tours for Def. Dept., 1957, 58, 61; Auditor Coll. de Pataphysique, Paris. One-man show Librairie Le Kiosque, Paris, 1965, Museu de Arte, Sao Paulo, Brazil, Graham Gallery, N.Y.C., 1973, Museude Arte Moderna Rio de Janeiro, Brazil, 1973, Man and His World, Montreal, 1974, 75, World Gallery, N.Y.C., 1977, Musee d'Angouleme, France, 1983, 1st Cartoon Biennale Invitational, Davos, Switzerland, 1986, group show, Musee des Arts Decoratifs, 1967, Pinocchio/Graphis Invitational Exhbn., Venice, 1987, École Nat. Supérieure des Beaux-Arts, Paris, 1989 ; drawings appeared in Paris-Match; others; 73 1971); author, illustrator: The Art of Inferior Decorating, 1963, 15 Fables of Krylov, 1965 (in permanent exhibit at Congl. Library), The Silly Knight, 1967, Perspectives, 1985; also publ.: comics An American Expressionism (in archives Mus. of Art, Sao Paulo); editor "An American in Paris" issue Pilote Mag., Paris, 1988; co-editor spl. internat. comics issues Graphis mag, Zurich, Switzerland, Goofus, Paris, 1975; regular contbr. to The New Yorker. Served with U.S. Mcht. Marine, 1940-45. Recipient Dattero d'Oro Salone Intdelle Umorismo, Italy 1963, Illustrator's award Nat. Cartoonists Soc. 1969, 77, Phenix award, Paris 1971. Mem. Nat. Cartoonists Soc. (fgn. affairs sec. 1963—), Internat. Comics Orgn. (Am. rep. 1970—), Association des Auteurs de Comics et de Cartoons (Am. rep.). Home and Studio: 133 Wooster St New York NY 10012-3176 *Work is adult play. Knowing what you really want to do and finding the best ways to do it are the keys to joy of life.*

PASCAL, FRANCINE, writer; b. N.Y.C., May 13, 1937; d. William and Kate (Dunitz) Rubin; m. Jerome Offenberg, Sept. 9, 1958; children: Jamie, Laurie, Susan; m. John Robert Pascal, Aug. 18, 1964 (dec. 1981). BS, NYU, 1958. Author: Hanging Out With Cici, 1977, My First Love and Other Disasters, 1979, Hand Me Down, Kid, 1980 (Dorothy Canfield Fisher award, 1982, Meml. Childrens Book award, Bernard Versele award, Brussels), Save Johanna!, 1981, Love and Betrayal, 1985, Hold the Mayo, 1985, If Wishes Were Horses, 1994; collaborator on book of musical George M!, 1968; creator young adult book series Sweet Valley High, 1983, Sweet Valley Twins, 1986, Sweet Valley Kids, 1989, Sweet Valley University, 1993. Mem. PEN, NOW, Dramatist's Guild, Writer's League, Screen Writer's Guild.

PASCAL, ROGER, lawyer; b. Chgo., Mar. 16, 1941; s. Samuel A. and Harriet E. (Hartman) P.; m. Martha Hecht, June 16, 1963; children: Deborah, Diane, David. AB with distinction, U. Mich, 1962; JD cum laude, Harvard U., 1965. Bar: Ill. 1965, U.S. Dist. Ct. (no. dist.) Ill. 1965, U.S. Ct. Appeals (7th cir.) 1969, U.S. Supreme Ct. 1976, Wis. 1985, U.S. Ct. Appeals (2d and 9th cirs.) 1986. Assoc. Schiff Hardin & Waite, Chgo., 1965-71, ptnr., 1972—; adj. prof. law Northwestern U. Law Sch., 1994—. Bd. dirs., mem. exec. com. Chgo. Law Enforcement Study Group, 1975-80, pres., 1978-80; pres. Harvard Law Soc. Ill., 1976-78; bd. dirs. ACLU of Ill., 1984—, gen. counsel, 1986—. Mem. ABA (antitrust and litigation sects.), Pub. Interest Law Initiative (bd. dirs. 1989—), Fund for Justice (v.p., bd. dirs. 1986—), Chgo. Coun. Lawyers (bd. dirs. 1970-74, 80-84), Chgo. Legal Assistance Found. (bd. dirs. 1985-88), Phi Beta Kappa, Univ. Club, Met. Club. Office: Schiff Hardin & Waite 7200 Sears Tower Chicago IL 60606

PASCALE, DANIEL RICHARD, courts administrator; b. Racine, Wis., Mar. 22, 1940; s. Domenic and Fannie Colette (Julian) P.; m. Mary Sara McDonald, June 28, 1986; 1 child, Alexander. AB cum laude, Harvard U., 1962; JD, U. Chgo., 1965. Bar: Ill. 1966, U.S. Ct. Appeals (7th cir.) 1967, U.S. Dist. Ct. (no. dist.) Ill. 1969, U.S. Supreme Ct. 1972. Asst. corp. counsel City of Chgo., 1966-72, chief appellate atty., 1972-79, 1st dep. corp. counsel, 1979-84; assoc. Rudnick & Wolfe, Chgo., 1984-87, ptnr., 1987-90; judge Circuit Ct. of Cook County, Ill., 1990-94; adminstrv. dir. Adminstrv. Office of Ill. Cts., Chgo., 1995—. Bd. dirs. DeKoven Found., Racine, 1986—; adv. bd. Art Resources in Teaching, Chgo., 1987-94; v.p. Episcopal Homes Mgmt., Inc., Milw., 1988—. Mem. ABA, Ill. Bar Assn., Chgo. Bar Assn., Chgo. Coun. Lawyers, Woman's Bar Assn., Justinian Soc., Union League Club Chgo. Democrat. Episcopalian. Office: 160 N La Salle St Chicago IL 60601-3103

PASCARELLA, PERRY JAMES, author, editor, speaker; b. Bradford, Pa., Apr. 11, 1934; s. James and Lucille Margaret (Monti) P.; m. Carol Ruth Taylor, May 4, 1957; children: Cynthia, Elizabeth. AB, Kenyon Coll., 1956; Coll. William and Mary, William and Mary Coll., 1957; postgrad., George Washington U., 1958. Credit reporter Dun & Bradstreet, Cleve., 1956, 60; asst. editor Steel mag., Cleve., 1961-63, assoc. editor, 1963-67, bus. editor, 1968-69, mng. editor, 1969; mng. editor Industry Week mag., Cleve., 1970-71, exec. editor, 1971-86, editor-in-chief, 1986-89; v.p. editorial Penton Pub. Inc., 1989-96; lectr. in field. Author: Technology-Fire in a Dark World, 1979, Humanagement in the Future Corporation, 1981, The New Achievers, 1984, The Purpose-Driven Organization, 1989, The Ten Commandments of the Workplace, 1996; contbg. author: Optimistic Outlooks, 1982, Creating a Global Agenda, 1984, Leadership in a New Era, 1994, The New Bottom Line, 1996. Lt. comdr. USNR, 1957-60. Recipient Disting. Service award Kenyon Coll., 1975, 81, Am. Bus. Press Crain award, 1992; Carnegie scholar, 1952-56. Mem. World Future Soc., U. Akron Inst. for Future Studies (bd. advisors). Presbyterian (elder). Home: 30413 Winsor Dr Cleveland OH 44140-1143

PASCH, ALAN, philosopher, educator; b. Cleve., Dec. 1, 1925; s. P. Jerome and Esther (Broverman) P.; m. Eleanor Kudlich Berna, Dec. 27, 1950; 1 child, Rachel. B.A., U. Mich., 1949; M.A., New Sch. Social Research, 1952; Ph.D., Princeton U., 1955; Bamford fellow, 1955-56. Instr. philosophy Ohio State U., 1956-59, asst. prof., 1959-60; assoc. prof. philosophy U. Md., College Park, 1960-67, prof., 1967—. Author: Experience and the Analytic, 1958; also articles, revs. Active ACLU. Served with AUS, 1944-46, PTO. Mem. AAUP, Am. Philos. Assn. (exec. dir. 1969-72, sec.-treas. Eastern div. 1965-68), Metaphys. Soc. Am., Washington Philosophy Club (pres. 1978-79), Washington Rare Book Group. Office: U Md Dept Philosophy College Park MD 20742

PASCHAL, JAMES ALPHONSO, counselor, educator secondary school; b. Americus, Ga., Aug. 11, 1931; s. Bouie L. and Mary L. (Jackson) P.; widower Mar. 24, 1988; 1 child, Maret E. BA, Xavier U., New Orleans, 1957; MS, Ft. Valley State Coll., 1963; EdD, U. S.C., 1977. Cert. adminstr., tchr. counselor, social worker, S.C. Tchr. grade 5 East View Elem. Sch., Americus, Ga., 1957-59; libr., counselor Staley Jr. H.S., Americus, 1959-65; sch. social worker Americus City System, 1965-67; coord. student svcs. Augusta (Ga.) Tech., 1967-78; dir. student affairs Benedict Coll., Columbia, S.C., 1978-82; coord. facilities S.C. Commn. on Higher Edn., Columbia, 1982-89; counselor Swainsboro (Ga.) H.S., 1990-91, Monroe H.S., Albany, Ga., 1991—; vol. Caritas, New Orleans, 1953-57, Friendship House, New Orleans, 1955-56. With U.S. Army, 1951-53, Korea. Recipient scholarship Ft. Valley (Ga.) State Coll., 1948, grad. assistantship, Ft. Valley State Coll., 1962-63. Mem. NEA, ACA. Ga. Counseling Assn., Alpha Phi Alpha (v.p. 1972-74). Republican. Roman Catholic. Avocations: reading, walking, helping others. Home: PO Box 5523 Albany GA 31706-5523

PASCHALL, LEE MCQUERTER, retired communications consultant; b. Sterling, Colo., Jan. 21, 1922; s. Lee McQuerter and Agnes (Woldridge) P.; m. Bonnie Jean Edwards, Oct. 24, 1942; children: Patricia Ann Grillos, Stephen Lee, David Edward. B.A., U. Ala., 1957; M.A., George Washington U., 1964. Served with U.S. Army, 1940-46; communications engr. Colo. Air N.G., Denver, 1946-51; commd. maj. U.S. Air Force, 1951, advanced through grades to lt. gen., 1974, ret., 1978; ind. cons. Springfield, Va., 1978-81; pres., chief exec. officer Am. Satellite Co., Rockville, Md., 1981-84, chmn., 1984-85; dir. Gen. Data Comm. Industries. Contbr. numerous articles to profl. publs. Mem. com. rev. nat. communications system initiatives NRC, 1982-88. Decorated Legion of Merit with oak leaf cluster; decorated disting. service medals; recipient Eascon IEEE, 1979. Mem. Armed Forces Comms.-Electronics Assn. (chpt. pres., nat. bd. dirs. Disting. Svc.), Air Force Assn., Phi Beta Kappa. Mem. Disciples of Christ. Home and Office: 1513 Hampton Hills Cir Mc Lean VA 22101-6018

PASCHALL, ROD, writer; b. San Antonio, Sept. 1, 1935; s. Samuel and Helen (Roddy) P.; m. Patricia Diane Greenwalt, May 17, 1969; children: Christen, Karen Elizabeth. BA, U.S. Mil. Acad., 1959; MS, George Washington U., 1970; MA, Duke U., 1971. Asst. prof. U.S. Mil. Acad., West Point, N.Y., 1971-74; officer U.S. Embassy, Cambodia, 1974; comdr. 3rd Battalion 5th Spl. Force, Ft. Bragg, N.C., 1975-80; plans officer Office Joint Chiefs of Staff, Washington, 1979-80; comdr. Delta Force, Ft. Bragg, 1980-82; dir. Spl. Warfare Devels., Ft. Bragg, 1983-84, Mil. History Inst., Carlisle Barracks, Pa., 1984-89; cons. Office of Internat. Criminal Justice, Chgo., 1989—; book author, cons. Carlisle, 1989—. Author: Defeat of Imperial Germany, 1989, Low Intensity Conflict, 2010, 1990, Critical Incident Management, 1992, Witness To War: Korea, 1995. Decorated with Silver Star, 1967, Purple Heart, 1966.

PASCHANG, JOHN LINUS, retired bishop; b. Hemingford, Nebr., Oct. 5, 1895; s. Casper Paschang and Gertrude Fischer. D of Canon Law, Cath. U. Am., Washington, 1925, MA, 1926, PhD, 1927; JD (hon.), Creighton U., 1960. Pastor St. Rose Ch., Hooper, Nebr., 1921-23, Holy Cross Ch., Omaha, 1927-51; bishop Grand Island, Nebr., 1951-72; ret., 1972. Author: The Sacramentals, 1925, The Popes and Revival of Learning, 1927. Mem. KC (state chaplain 1938-42). Republican. Roman Catholic. Avocation: missionary work. Home: St Josephs Home 320 E Decatur St West Point NE 68788

PASCHKE, DONALD VERNON, music educator; b. Menominee, Mich., Oct. 22, 1929; s. Leo Carl Ferdinand and Augusta O. (Fritz) P.; m. Helen Inez Burton, Feb. 17, 1951; children: David Vernon, Celeste Eileen. MusB, BS in Choral Music Edn., U. Ill., 1957, MusM in Voice, 1958; D Mus. Arts, U. Colo., 1972. Instr. music Berea (Ky.) Coll., 1958-62; asst. prof. music Eastern N.Mex. U., Portales, 1962-71, assoc. prof., 1971-76, prof., 1976-94; prof. emeritus, 1994. Translator, editor: A Complete Treatise on the Art of Singing, Part Two (Manuel Garcia II), 1975; Part One, 1984. Songleader Portales Men's Breakfast, 1976—, pres., 1975-76, 90-91, v.p. 1974-75, 89-90; chancel choir dir. 1st Presbyn. Ch., Clovis, N.Mex., 1976-95. With U.S. Army, 1951-53. Mem. Nat. Edn. Assn., Nat. Assn. Tchrs. Singing (lt. gov. N.Mex. 1968-72, v.p. Gt. Plains chpt. 1972-74, chpt. pres. 1974-78), Pi Kappa Lambda, Phi Kappa Phi. Republican. Presbyterian. Avocations: photography, do-it-yourself projects. Home: 228 Kansas Dr Portales NM 88130-7121

PASCO, HANSELL MERRILL, retired lawyer; b. Thomasville, Ga., Oct. 7, 1915; s. John and Katherine (Merrill) P.; m. Williamine Carrington Lancaster, June 28, 1941; children: Hansell Merrill, Dabney, Robert, Elizabeth, Carrington. B.A., Va. Mil. Inst., 1937; LL.B., U. Va., 1940. Bar: Va. bar 1939. Ptnr. Hunton & Williams, Richmond, Va., 1948-81, sr. counsel, 1981—; mng. partner Hunton & Williams, 1968-76. Chmn. State Counsel Higher Edn. for Va., 1978-80; trustee Protestant Episcopal Sem., Alexandria, Va., 1980-85. Served with U.S. Army, 1940-45. Office: Hunton & Williams Riverfront Plz E Tower 951 E Byrd St Richmond VA 23219-4040

PASEWARK, WILLIAM ROBERT, author, management consultant; b. Mt. Vernon, N.Y., Sept. 9, 1924; s. William and Barbara (Hermann) P.; m. Jean McHarg, Mar. 17, 1956; children: William Robert, Lisabeth Jean, Jan Alison, Carolyn Ann, Scott Graham, Susan Gayle. B.S., NYU, 1949, M.A., 1950, Ph.D., 1956. Instr. NYU, 1949-51; assoc. prof. Meredith Coll., Raleigh, N.C., 1951-52; asst. prof. Mich. State U., 1952-56; prof. Tex. Tech. U., Lubbock, 1956-82; author, owner Office Mgmt. Cons., 1982—; cons. bus. and ednl. agys., lectr. in field, 1955—; field reader rsch. div. U.S. Office Edn., 1966—; mem. commn. to revise curricula Tex. Edn. Agy., 1974—; mem. adv. com. Lubbock Vocat. Office Edn.; mem. regional bd. examiners Am. Assn. Bus. Colls.; vis. prof. Calif. State U., Fresno, 1959, No. Ariz. State U., 1969, Ctrl. Conn. State Coll., 1974. Author: Individualized Instruction in Business and Office Education, 1973, Electronic and Mechanical Printing Calculator Course, 1974, Electronic Display Calculator Course, 1975, 2d edit., 1984, Clerical Office Procedures, 6th edit., 1978, Rotary Calculator Course, 1962, Ten-Key Listing Machine, 5th edit., 1981, Key-Driven Calculator Course, 1962, Full-Keyboard Adding Listing Machine Course, 3d edit., 1963, Secretarial Office Procedures, 10th edit., 1982, Duplicating Machine Processes, 1971, 2d edit., 1975, Office Machines Course, 1971, 5th edit., 1979, Curso de Máquinas de Oficina, 1977, Técnicas Secretariales y Procedimientos de Oficina, 1978, Machine Transcription Word Processing, 1979, 2d edit., 1987, Electronic Printing Calculator Course, Canadian edit., 1980, Electronic Printing Calculator, 3d edit., 1990, Electronic Calculating Machines Simulation, 4th edit., 1991, Procedures for the Modern Office, 7th edit., 1983, Electronic Display-Printing Calculator, 1983, Reprographics, 1983, Super Calc 3 Learning, Using, and Mastering, 1986, Electronic Office Machines, 6th edit., 1987, The Office: Procedures and Technology, 1987, 2nd edit., 1993 (Textbook Excellence award in bus. Text and Acad. Authors Assn. 1994, William Holmes McGuffy award for textbook excellence and longevity Text and Acad. Authors Assn. 1994), Working With SuperCalc 4, 1987 (Danish transl. 1987), Machine Transcription, Dictation, and Proofreading: An Introduction, 1987, Danish Translation of Supercalc 4, 1987, Microsoft Works: Tutorial and Applications IBM Version, 1991, Calculating Machines Simulation, A Short Course, 1991, Electronic Calculators: Display, Print, Display-Print, 2d edit., 1992, Microsoft Works: Tutorial and Applications Macintosh Version, 1992, Calculator Math for Job and Personal Use, 1992, Ten-Key Skill Builder, 1992, PFS: First Publisher: Tutorial and Applications, IBM 3.0, 4.0, 1993, Publish It!: Tutorial and Applications, IBM version 2.0, 1993, Publish It! Apple version, 1993, Microsoft Works for Windows, 1994, Microsoft Works 3.0 Macintosh, 1994 (Textbook Excellence award in computer text Text & Acad. Authors Assn. 1994), Microsoft Works for Windows 3.0 Tutorial and Applications, Express Publisher Tutorial and Applications, 1994, Microsoft Works DOS 3.0 Quick Course, 1994, Microsoft Works for Windows 3.0 Quick Course, 1995, Microsoft Works Macintosh 4.0 Quick Course, 1995, Microsoft Works 2.0/3.0 DOS: Applications for Reinforcement, 1995, Microsoft Works 2.0/3/0 for Windows: Applications for Reinforcement, 1995, Microsoft Works 4.0 for Macintosh: Tutorial and Applications, 1995, Microsoft Works 4.0 for Windows 95: Tutorial and Applications, 1996, Microsoft Office for Windows 95: Tutorial and Applications, 1996, ClarisWorks 4.0 for Macintosh: Tutorial and Applications, 1996, Pagemaker 5.0 for Windows and Macintosh: QuickTorial, 1996, Microsoft Works 95: QuickTorial, 1996, Microsoft Office 4.3 for Windows: Tutorial and Applications, 1996, and numerous others; assoc. editor: Am. Bus. Edn. Yearbook, 1953; contbr. articles to profl. jours. Adviser Lubbock Opportunities Industrialization Center; mem. Tex. Bus. Tchr. Edn. Council; v.p. Lubbock Econ. Council, 1983, pres., 1984; pres. Lubbock Area Presbyn. Council, 1969; chmn. Lubbock City-County Child Welfare Bd., 1973-74; active local Boy Scouts Am., United Fund. Served with USMCR, 1943-46. Recipient Founders Day award N.Y.U., 1956; Outstanding Educator of Am. award, 1970; citation Tex. Ho. of Reps., 1973; Tex. Bus. Tchr. of Year award, 1973. Mem. Nat. Bus. Edn. Assn., Nat. Assn. Bus. Tchr. Edn., Mountain-Plains Bus. Edn. Assn., Tex. Bus. Edn. Assn. (chmn. legislative com. 1973-80), Nat. Assn. Tchr. Edn. for Bus. and Office Edn., Edn. for Bus. Coordinating Council, Bus. Edn. State Suprs. and Tchr. Educators (nat. planning com.), W. Tex. Bus. Edn. Assn. (pres. 1958), Better Bus. Bur. (edn. com.), Am. Vocat. Assn. (pres. bus. and office div. 1976-77, dir. 1976-77, nat. adv. council 1976-84, award of merit 1978), Office Systems Research Assn., Text and Acad. Authors Assn., Authors Guild, Internat. Platform Assn., Lubbock Execs. Assn. (bd. dirs.), Lubbock C. of C., PTA (local pres. 1972), Delta Pi Epsilon, Phi Delta Kappa, Kappa Phi Kappa, Pi Omega Pi, Alpha Kappa Psi, Kappa Delta Pi. Clubs: Lion (past dir.), Lubbock Country. Research in office adminstrn. and ednl. systems. Home: 4403 11th St Lubbock TX 79416-4814 Office: 1901 University Ave Ste 504A Lubbock TX 79410-1556

PASHAYEV, HAFIZ MIR JALAL, diplomat, physics educator; b. Baku, Azerbaijan, May 2, 1941; s. Mirjalal Ali and Pusta (Kazymova) P.; m. Rena Musa Aliyeva, Apr. 8, 1967; children: Mirjamal, Jamila. M Physics, Baku (Azerbaijan) State U., 1963; PhD in Physics, Inst. Atomic Energy, Moscow, 1971; DSc, Acad. Scis., Baku, 1984. Researcher Inst. Physics, Baku, 1963-75; PhD fellow Inst. Atomic Energy, Moscow, 1967-71; postdoctoral fellow U. Calif., Irvine, 1975-76; head metall. physics lab. Acad. Scis., Baku, 1976-92; amb. to U.S.A. from Azerbaijan Washington, 1993—. Author 3 books in physics; co-author 2 dictionaries, 1991-92; contrb. articles to phys. jours. and mass media. Avocations: drawing, sports. Office: Embassy of Azerbaijan 927 15th St NW Ste 700 Washington DC 20005-2304

PASHEK, ROBERT DONALD, economics educator emeritus; b. The Dalles, Oreg., Feb. 27, 1921; s. Gregory and Mary M. (Bonomi) P.; children: William J., Nicole M. A.B., Central Wash. Coll., 1949; M.A., State U. Iowa, 1950; Ph.D., U. Ill., 1955; postgrad., Columbia U., 1947, Inst. Minerva, Zurich, 1947-48. Asst. prof. U. Wichita, 1953-55; asst. prof. Pa. State U., 1956-58, prof., 1960—, head dept. bus. logistics, 1964-73; assoc. dean Pa. State U. (Coll. Bus. Adminstrn.), 1973-87, dir. internat. programs, 1987-89, prof. emeritus, 1989; vis. prof. San Francisco State U., 1963-64; cons. Commonwealth of Pa., U.S. AID, U.S. Dept. Commerce. Served with AUS, 1944-46. Named Transp. Man of Year Delta Nu Alpha, 1964. Mem. Coun. Transp. Rsch. Ctrs. (pres. 1981-82), Am. Soc. Transp. and Logistics (past pres., dir. Joseph C. Scholeen award for excellence 1985), Am. Econ. Assn. (Disting. Mem. award Pub. Utilities Group 1985), Transp. Rsch. Forum, Beta Gamma Sigma, Alpha Kappa Psi. Research on econ. and social impact hwys., transport systems planning, logistic systems design and planning. Home: 5102 Wallingford Ave N Seattle WA 98103-6143 Office: Bus Adminstrn Bldg Pa State Univ University Park PA 16802

PASHGIAN, MARGARET HELEN, artist; b. Pasadena, Calif., Nov. 7, 1934; d. Aram John and Margaret (Howell) P. BA, Pomona Coll., 1956; MA in Fine Arts, Boston Univ., 1958; student, Columbia U., 1957. Art instr. Harvard-Newton Program Occidental Coll., Newton, Mass., 1959-62, instr. art, 1977-78; artist in residence Calif. Inst. Tech., 1970-71; grants panelist Calif. Arts Coun., Sacramento, 1993. Artist: solo shows include Rex Evans Gallery, L.A., 1965, 67, Occidental Coll., 1967, Kornblee Gallery, N.Y.C., 1969-72, U. Calif., Irvine, 1975, U. Calif. Santa Barbara, 1976, Stella Polaries Gallery, L.A., 1981, 82, Kaufman Galleries, Houston, 1982, Modernism Gallery, San Francisco, 1983, Works Gallery, Long Beach, Costa Mesa, Calif., 1986, 87, 88, 89, 90, 91, 92; group exhibitions include Pasadena Art Mus., 1965, Carson Pirie Scott, Chgo., 1965, Calif. Palace of Legion of Honor, San Francisco, 1967, Esther Bear Gallery, Santa Barbara, 1967, 69, Lytton Ctr. of the Visual Arts, L.A., 1968, Salt Lake Art Inst., Salt Lake City, 1968, Mus. Contemporary Crafts, Internat. Plastics Exhibition, 1969, Second Flint (Mich.) Invitational, 1969, Milw. Art Ctr., 1969, U.S.I.S. Mus., N.Y.C., Mus. Contemporary Art, Chgo., 1970, Studio Merconi, Milan, 1970, Calif. Inst. Tech., Baxter Art Galley, 1971, 1980, Calif. Innovations, Palm Springs Dessert Mus., 1981, Calif. Internat. Arts Found. Mus. of Modern Art, Paris, 1982, L.A. Artists in Seoul, Donsangbang Gallery, 1982, An Artistic Conversation, 1931-82, Poland, USA, Ulster Mus., Belfast, Ireland, 1983, Madison (Wis.) Art Ctr., 1994, Calif. State U., Fullerton, 1995, Oakland (Calif.) Mus., 1995; represented in pub. collections at River Forest (Ill.) State Bank, Atlantic Richfield Co., Dallas, Frederic Weisman Collection, L.A., Security Pacific Bank, L.A., Singapore, Andrew Dickson White Mus. of Art, Cornell U., Ithaca, N.Y., L.A. County Mus. of Art, Santa Barbara Art Mus., Laguna Beach Mus. of Art. Trustee, Pomona Coll, Claremont, Calif., 1987—; parade judge Tournament of RosesCentennial Parade, Pasadena, 1987; bd. dirs. L.A. Master Chorale, 1992—.

PASHLEY, MARY MARTHA, corporate finance educator; b. Oak Ridge, Tenn., May 12, 1956; d. John Hamilton and Wilogene (Queener) P. BA, Vanderbilt U., 1976; MS, U. Tenn., 1978, MBA, 1985, PhD, 1986. Teaching asst. U. Tenn., Knoxville, 1978-82, rsch. asst., 1982-83, lectr., 1983-85; asst. prof. fin. Tenn. Tech. U., Cookeville, 1986-93, assoc. prof., 1993—, assoc. dir. honors program; textbook reviewer Scott, Foresman & Co., 1988; ad hoc referee Fin. Mgmt., 1988, Applied Fin. Econs., 1991—, Fin. Rev., 1988—. Treas Mastersingers Community Chorus, 1988-89. Walter Melville Bonham Meml. scholar U. Tenn., 1982-93. Mem. Am. Bus. Women's Assn. (charter v.p. Chilhowee Bandstand chpt. 1984), Fin. Mgmt. Assn. (faculty liaison 1986—, presenter 1980, 82, 87, 94), Nat. Collegiate Hons. Coun., Mensa proctor 1990-94, registrar 1992, 94, Mid Tenn.), Beta Gamma Sigma, (chpt. sec.-treas. 1987-88, pres. 1988-89), Phi Kappa Phi, Omicron Delta Kappa. Avocations: music, travelling, psychology, art, dance. Office: Tenn Tech U Dept Econs & Fin Cookeville TN 38505

PASINETTI, PIER MARIA, author; b. Venice, Italy, June 24, 1913; came to U.S., 1946, naturalized, 1952; s. Carlo and Maria (Ciardi) P. Dottore in Lettere, U. Padua, Italy, 1935; Ph.D. in Comparative Lit., Yale U., 1949. Fellow La. State U., 1935-36, U. Calif. at Berkeley, 1936-37; lectr. U. Stockholm, 1942-46; prof. Italian and comparative lit. UCLA, 1949—. Author: L'ira di Dio, 1942, Venetian Red, 1960, The Smile on the Face of the Lion, 1965, From the Academy Bridge, 1970, Suddenly Tomorrow, 1971, Dall' Estrema America, 1975, Il Centro, 1979, Dorsoduro, 1983, Life for Art's Sake: Studies in the Literary Myth of the Romantic Artist, 1985, Melodramma, 1993, Piccole Veneziane Complicate, 1996; also articles, revs., film scripts. Recipient Fiction award Nat. Inst. Arts and Letters, 1965. Mem. Authors Guild. Club: Elizabethan Yale. Office: 1259 Dorsoduro, Venice Italy 30123

PASK, JOSEPH ADAM, ceramic engineering educator; b. Chgo., Feb. 14, 1913; s. Adam Poskoczem and Catherine (Ramanauskas) P.; m. Margaret J. Gault, June 11, 1938; children: Thomas Joseph, Kathryn Edyth. B.S., U. Ill., 1934, Ph.D., 1941; M.S., U. Wash., 1935. Ceramic engr. Willamina Clay Products Co., Oreg., 1935-36; teaching asst. ceramic engring. U. Ill., 1938, instr., 1938-41; asst. ceramic engr. electrotech. lab. U.S. Bur. Mines, 1941; assoc. ceramic engr. N.W. Exptl. Sta., 1942-43; asst. prof. ceramic engring., head dept. Coll. of Mines, U. Wash., Seattle, 1941-43; research ceramist, lamp div. Westinghouse Electric Corp., N.J., 1943-46; research engr. ceramic sect. Westinghouse Electric Corp., 1946-48; assoc. prof. ceramic engring., head ceramic group div. materials sci. and engring. U. Calif. at Berkeley, 1948-53, founder program ceramic engring. and sci., 1948, prof., 1953-80, prof. emeritus, 1980—, vice chmn. div., 1956-57, chmn. dept., 1957-61; asso. dean grad. student affairs U. Calif. at Berkeley (Coll. Engring.), 1969-80; sr.

faculty scientist Lawrence Berkeley Lab.; John Dorn Meml. lectr. Northwestern U., 1977; Mem. clay mineral com. NRC; mem. materials adv. bd., chmn. ad hoc com. ceramic processing, adv. commn. metallurgy div. U.S. Bur. Standards; chmn. NSF study objective criteria in ceramic engring. edn., U.S.-China Seminar on Basic Sci. of Ceramics, Shanghai, 1983. Recipient John F. Bergeron Meml. Svc. award Ceramic Engring. div. U. Wash., Seattle, 1969, gold medal for research and devel. French Soc. for Research and Devel., 1979, Berkeley citation U. Calif., 1980, Alumni honor award for disting. service in engring. U. Ill. Coll. Engring., 1982, Outstanding Achievement in Edn. award Com. of Confucius, 1982, Internat. Prize Japan Fine Ceramics Assn., 1988, Engring. Alumni Achievement award U. Wash. Coll. Engring., 1991. Fellow AAAS, Am. Ceramic Soc. (disting. life mem., v.p. 1953-54, pres. ednl. coun. 1954-55, trustee 1959-62, chmn. electronics div. 1959-60, John Jeppson award 1967, Ross Coffin Purdy award 1979), Mineral Soc., Acad. Dental Materials; mem. NAE, Nat. Inst. Ceramics Engrs., N.Y. Acad. Scis., Am. Soc. Matls, Brit. Ceramic Soc., Internat. Acad. Ceramics,, Am. Soc. Engring. Edn. (chmn. materials com. 1961-63, Centennial Cert. 1993), Clay Minerals Soc., Ceramics Soc. Japan (hon., Centennial medal 1991), Materials Rsch. Soc. Japan (hon.), Keramos, Sigma XI, Tau Bet Pi, Alpha Sigma Mu. Home: 994 Euclid Ave Berkeley CA 94708-1437 Office: U Calif Dept Material Sci & Mineral Eng Berkeley CA 94720 *Whatever success I have had can be attributed to hard work generated by a desire for success and recognition by my peers. This attitude was generated by my mother who came to this country, a land of opportunities, as an immigrant from Lithuania at the age of 16 without any knowledge of English. There was no question in her mind—and consequently mine—that I would get an education and be successful.*

PASKAWICZ, JEANNE FRANCES, pain practitioner; b. Phila., Mar. 3, 1954; d. Alex and Lillian (Pyluck) P. BSc, Phila. Coll. Pharmacy; MA, Villanova U., 1973; postgrad., St. Joseph U., 1979; PhD, Kensington U., 1984. Mem. anesthesiology staff Einstein Med. Ctr., Phila., 1990-94, Temple U. Hosp., 1994—; mem. detox./rehab. staff Presbyn. Med. Ctr., Phila., 1984—; house officer MCD-Elkins Park (Pa.) Campus, 1990—; mem. psychiatry staff Hahnemann U. Hosp., Phila., 1984-90; hostage negotiator Office of Mental Health, Phila., 1984-90; mem. surgery/anesthesiology staff Mt. Sinai Hosp., Phila., 1989-91. Bd. dirs. Phila. Coll. Pharmacy, St. Joseph U. Mem. NAFE, Am. Pain Soc., Nat. Parks Conservation Assn., North Shore Animal League, Amvets, DAV Comdrs. Club, Lambda Kappa Sigma.

PASMANICK, KENNETH, bassoonist; b. Rochester, N.Y., Aug. 23, 1924; s. Philip and Rose (Levitt) P.; m. Frances Virginia Cohen, Dec. 22, 1946; children: Philip, Anne. Student, Eastman Sch. Music, 1942-43, Juilliard Sch. Music, 1946-47; BA, Am. U., 1962. Am. specialist abroad for Dept. State, El Salvador and Costa Rica, 1966-67; instr. bassoon Am. U., Washington; prof. U. Md. Performed with Martha Graham Ballet tour and at Ziegfield Theater, 1946; prin. bassoonist Nat. Symphony Orch., 1947—, Washington Opera Soc.; performed (world premiere) Serenata for Bassoon and Chamber Orch. (Gian Francesca Malipiero), 1962, The Windhover (Robert Evett); performed (world premiere) Bassoon Concerto (David Amram), 1972, (N.Y. premiere), 1993; performed Concerto for Bassoon and Orch., 1971; performed (U.S. premiere) Concerto for Bassoon and Orch. (Gunther Schuller), 1985; performed (European premiere) Radio Orch. of Saarbrücken, Germany, 1992; rec. with Newport Classics Recs., Saarbrücken Radio Orch. for GM Recs., 1992; rec. (CD) Air for Bassoon and Strings (Alec Wilder) with Manhattan Chamber Orch., 1994. Served in USAAF, 1943-46. Recipient Gold medal for cultural contbn. in Costa Rica. Mem. Nat. Symphony Wind Soloists (founder). Home: 5227 Chevy Chase Pky NW Washington DC 20015-1747 *Irrational culturally induced ideas aside, I see no limits on the creative capacities of humans to forge a just and rational world for all its inhabitants.*

PASNICK, RAYMOND WALLACE, labor union official, editor; b. New Kensington, Pa., Apr. 29, 1916; s. Stanley and Mary Ann (Grzewienska) P.; m. Margaret Solberg, Mar. 3, 1937; children: Victor Keith, Raymond Gene. Ed. pub. schs. Editor Aluminum Workers Jour., New Kensington, 1936-37; publicity dir. Aluminum Workers Am., Pitts., 1937-44; asst. editor Steel Labor, Pitts., 1944-46; editor Steel Labor, 1962-78; Midwest editor, also Midwest dir. edn. United Steelworkers Am., Chgo., 1946-62; nat. editor, dir. comm. United Steelworkers Am., 1962-65; dir. pub. rels. United Steelworker Am., Pitts., 1965-78; editor OLDTIMER quar., 1978-86; vol. editor Steelworker Oldtimer, 1986—. Pub. mem. Chgo. Bd. Edn., 1955-66. Recipient of Civil Rights award Jewish Labor Com. Chgo., 1962, Man of Year award Chgo. unit Nat. Frontiersmen, 1963. Mem. Internat. Labor Press Assn. (pres. 1972-74), Am. Fedn. Tchrs., Chgo. Newspaper Guild (treas. 1948-56, v.p. 1957). Democrat. Roman Catholic. Home and Office: 2248 Country Club Dr Pittsburgh PA 15241-2335 *Living for one's self alone can be self-defeating. I have learned that the right way to live is to find others with common goals and work together with them. This is the most effective way to confront mutual challenges and make genuine social and economic progress.*

PASQUA, THOMAS MARIO, JR., journalism educator; b. L.A., Aug. 13, 1938; s. Thomas Mario and Ann Ione (Anderson) P.; m. Sandra Mae Liddell; children: Bruce Burks, Julie Burks, Geoffrey, Alexis. BA, Whittier (Calif.) Coll., 1960; MA, UCLA, 1961; PhD, U. Tex., 1973. Cert. secondary tchr. Reporter, photographer Whittier Daily News, 1954-65; tchr. LaSerna High Sch., Whittier, 1961-63, 64-65; lectr. Calif. State U., Fullerton, 1973-75, Mesa Coll., San Diego, 1978-83, U. San Diego, 1979-80, San Diego State U., 1985; prof. Southwestern Coll., Chula Vista, Calif., 1965—. Co-author: Excellence in College Journalism, 1983, Mass Media in the Information Age, 1990, Historical Perspectives in Popular Music, 1993; editor C.C. Journalist, 1983—; bibliographer Journalism Quar., 1974-92; contbr. articles to profl. jours. Mem. ch. coun. St. Andrew Luth. Ch., Whittier, 1965; mem. Chula Vista Bd. of Ethics, 1978-86; mem. Chula Vista Charter Rev. Com., 1969; mem. adv. bd. Bay Gen. Hosp., Chula Vista, 1985-87; mem. ch. coun. Victory Luth. Ch., Chula Vista, 1989-90; adv. com. Otay Valley Regional Park, 1990—. Wall St. Jour. Newspaper Fund fellow U. Wash., 1962; recipient Nat. Teaching award Poynter Inst. Media Studies, 1987. Mem. C.C. Journalism Assn. (archivist 1989—, charter inductee Hall of Fame, 1994), Journalism Assn. C.C.'s (exec. sec. 1975-81), Assn. for Edn. in Journalism and Mass Comm. (Markham prize 1974), Internat. Comm. Assn., Coll. Media Advisers, Am. Fedn. Tchrs. (pres. Southwestern Coll. 1977-78, 81-87), Phi Kappa Phi, Kappa Tau Alpha, Pi Sigma Alpha. Democrat. Avocations: gardening, cats, reading mysteries. Home: 760 Monterey Ave Chula Vista CA 91910-6318 Office: Southwestern Coll 900 Otay Lakes Rd Chula Vista CA 91910-7223

PASQUARELLI, JOSEPH J., real estate development, engineering and construction executive; b. N.Y.C., Mar. 5, 1927; s. Joseph and Helen (Casabona) P.; B.C.E. cum laude, Manhattan Coll., 1949; m. JoAnne Brienza, June 20, 1964; children: Ronald, Richard, June, Joy. Engr., Madigan-Hyland, N.Y.C. and Burns & Roe Inc., N.Y.C., 1949-56; sr. engr., asst. to exec. dir. Office of Sch. Bldgs., N.Y.C. Bd. Edn., 1956-67; dir. design and constrn. mgmt. City U. N.Y., 1967-72; dir. constrn. mgmt. Morse/Diesel Inc., N.Y.C., 1972-76; dir. projects and proposals Burns & Roe Indsl. Svcs. Corp., Oradell, N.J., 1976-80, dir. facilities and infrastructure, 1980-86; dir. design engring., constrn., devel. mgmt. Xerox Realty Corp., Stamford, Ct., 1986-89; exec. v.p. The Galvin Group N.Y.C., 1989-90; assoc. prin. Pei/Galvin Holdings, Ltd., N.Y.C., 1990-93; sr. v.p. Pei Group Holdings, Ltd., N.Y.C., 1993—. Served with U.S. Army, 1944-46. Licensed profl. engr., N.Y., N.J. Fellow ASCE; mem. N.Y. Bldg. Congress (past gov., chmn. legis. com.), NSPE, Mcpl. Engrs., Am. Arbitration Assn., Chi Epsilon. Club: Essex Fells Country. Contbr. articles to profl. jours. Home: 38 Oak Pl N Caldwell NJ 07006-4554 Office: Pei Group Holdings Ltd 10 Rockefeller Plz New York NY 10020-1903

PASQUERILLA, FRANK JAMES, real estate developer and manager; b. Johnstown, Pa., Sept. 4, 1926; s. Harry and Sabina (D'Alfonso) P.; m. Sylvia Theresa Guarino, Jan. 12, 1957; children—Mark E., Leah M. Student, Internat. Corr. Schs., 1944-50; LLD (hon.), U. Notre Dame, 1982; HHD (hon.), St. Francis Coll., Loretto, Pa., 1969, Mt. St. Mary's Coll., Emmitsburg, Md., 1990. With Phila. Q.M. Depot, 1944-46; hwy. insp. Pa. Dept. Hwys., Hollidaysburg, 1946-50; with Crown Am. Realty Trust (formerly Crown Constrn. Co.), Johnstown, Pa., 1951—, pres., 1956—, also chmn. bd., 1988—; bd. dirs. Johnstown Area Regional Industries, 1974—; dir., mem. exec. com. U.S. Nat. Bank, Johnstown. Pres. Johnstown Jaycees, 1950-51, Pa. Jaycees, 1953-54; nat. v.p. U.S. Jaycees, 1954-55; del. Pa. Constl. Conv., 1967; trustee U. Notre Dame, 1984—. Decorated knight comdr. Order St. Gregory the Gt. (Vatican); Solidarity Order (Italy); Prime Minister's Silver Anniversary medal (Israel); recipient Assisi award St. Francis Coll., Loretto, Pa., 1980, Humanitarian award Nat. Italian Am. Found., 1990; named Man of Yr. Order Sons of Italy in Am., 1990. Mem. Internat. Council Shopping Ctrs. (trustee 1983), Italian Sons and Daus. Am., Sunnehanna Club, Travelers Club, Elks. Republican. Roman Catholic. Avocations: opera, travel, football. Home: 945 Menoher Blvd Johnstown PA 15905-2566 Office: Crown Am Pasquerilla Plz Johnstown PA 15907*

PASQUIER, JOËL, music educator; b. Montmorency, France, Sept. 25, 1943; arrived in Can., 1967; s. Jean and Raymonde (Gourdin) P.; m. Anne Vachon, Nov. 28, 1970; 1 child, Ariane. Grad. in piano and chamber music, Conservatoire Nat. Superieur de Musique, Paris, 1962. Prof. Conservatoire de Musique de St. Germain-en-Laye, France, 1964-65; grad. asst. Sch. Music, Ind. U., Bloomington, 1965-67; tchr. piano Ecole de Musique, U. Laval, Quebec, Can., 1967—; dir. Ecole de Musique, U. Laval, Quebec, 1988-91. Appeared as solo pianist concert halls, radio, TV, with chamber and symphony orchs. in France, U.S., Can., The Netherlands. Fulbright scholar Ind. U., 1965. Mem. Que. Yacht Club. Office: U Laval Sch Music, Pavillon Casault, Sainte Foy, PQ Canada G1K 7P4

PASS, BOBBY CLIFTON, entomology educator; b. Cleveland, Ala., Nov. 4, 1931; s. Rufus Clifton and Alma Antoinette (Payne) P.; m. Annie Ruth Rutherford, Aug. 17, 1955; 1 child, Kevin Clifton. Student, Snead Jr. Coll., 1949-50; BS in Agr. Edn., Auburn U., 1952, MS in Entomology, 1960; PhD in Entomology, Clemson U., 1962. Rsch. asst. Auburn (Ala.) U., 1958-60, Clemson (S.C.) U., 1960-62; asst. prof. U. Ky., Lexington, 1962-67, assoc. prof., 1967-68, assoc. prof., chair, 1968, prof., chmn., 1969—; cons. USAID/Indonesia, 1985—, UK/Shandong Agr. U., People's Republic China, 1986—. Contbr. articles on insect mgmt. to profl. jours. Mem. Entomological Soc. Am. (pres. 1986-87, governing bd. 1983-88), Am. Registry Profl. Entomologists (cert., pres. 1979-80), Can. Entomological Soc., Internat. Orgn. for Biol. Control, S.C. Entomological Soc., Kans. Entomological Soc., Ky. Acad. Sci., Soc. Sigma Xi, Gamma Sigma Delta, Phi Kappa Phi. Democrat. Methodist. Home: 3234 Pepperhill Rd Lexington KY 40502-3545 Office: U Ky Dept Entomology Lexington KY 40546-0091

PASSAGE, DAVID, diplomat; b. Charlotte, N.C., June 16, 1942; s. John T. and Virginia (Beam) P. BA, U. Denver, 1964; MS, Georgetown U., 1966. With U.S. State Dept., 1966—; various positions U.S. State Dept., London, Australia, Ecuador, Vietnam, El Salvador, Botswana; dep. spokesman U.S. State Dept., Washington, spl. asst. to Sec. of State Henry Kissinger; dir. for Africa Nat. Security Coun. Staff, The White House, Washington; U.S. amb. to Botswana; polit. adviser to U.S. Spl. Opers. Command MacDill AFB, Fla.; dir. Andean affairs Dept. State, Washington, 1996—. Avocations: environment and conservation. Home: 2416 Chain Bridge Rd NW Washington DC 20016

PASSAGE, STEPHEN SCOTT, energy company executive; b. Miami, Oct. 10, 1946; s. John Thompson and Virginia Frances (Beam) P.; m. Ellen Shapiro, Aug. 21, 1988. BS in Civil Engring., Pol. Sci., MIT, 1969; MA in Pol. Sci., New Sch. Soc. Rsch., 1972, MA in Econs., 1975. Cer. Profl. Engr. Mem. engring. dept. Port Authority N.Y. and N.J., 1969-86; pres. Montenay Power Corp., N.Y., 1986—; chmn. IWSA. Contbr. articles to profl. jours. Chmn. 607 West End Ave Corp., 1991—. Mem. ASME, NSPE. Avocations: chess, hiking, tennis, canoeing, reading. Office: Montenay Power Corp 800 3rd Ave New York NY 10022-7604

PASSAGLIA, CANDACE V., special education educator; b. Woodstock, Ill., Nov. 17, 1951; d. Vaughn D. and Phyllis (Higgins) Heidenreich; m. Roger Michael Passaglia, Dec. 29, 1973; children: Ryan James, Shannon Marie. BS in Edn./Spl. Edn., No. Ill. U., 1973, MS in Spl. Edn. Adminstrn., 1995; learning disabilities/physically handicapped cert., U. Calif., Irvine, 1986. Cert. elem. edn., Ill., Calif.; cert. spl. edn. K-12. Tchr. grade 4 Woodstock (Ill.) Cmty. Sch. Dist. 200, 1973; exec. sec. various cos., 1974-83; instrnl. aide, substitute tchr. various sch. dists., Calif., 1984-87; resource specialist Irvine Unified Sch. Dist., 1987-89; learning disabilities tchr. Cary (Ill.) Elem. Sch. Dist. # 26, 1989-95; learning disabilities specialist Wilmette (Ill.) Sch. Dist. 39, 1995-96; tchr. grade 5 Cary Elem. Sch. Dist. 26, 1996—; instr. No. Ill. U. Grad. Sch., 1996—; tech. com., sys. operator computer network, mem. sch. improvement com. Cary (Ill.) Sch. Dist. # 26, 1990—; lectr. No. Ill. U., DeKalb, 1993, 94; keynote spkr. Kans. State U., Manhattan, 1994, 95. Author, editor: (nat. newsletter) Co-Teaching Network News, 1992—. Bd. dirs. Mission Viejo (Calif.) Little League Assn., 1985-87; mem. Cary (Ill.)-Grove H.S. Baseball Parent's Assn., 1990-94; oboist Crystal Lake Cmty. Band, 1989-91; 1st soprano The New Oratorio Singers, 1991-92; mem. Cary Cmty. Theatre, 1995—. Mem. ASCD, United Learning Disabilities Assn. Avocations: computers, writing, gardening, family time, reading. Office: Three Oaks Sch Cary Elem Sch Dist 26 15 S 2nd St Cary IL 60013

PASSANO, E. MAGRUDER, JR., publishing executive; b. Balt., Oct. 2, 1942; s. Edward M. and Mildred P. (Nelson) P.; m. Helen C. Marikle, Sept. 4, 1971; children: Catherine, Tammy, Sarah. BS, Johns Hopkins U., 1967, MLA, 1969. With Waverly, Inc., Balt., 1965—, salesman, 1970-73, v.p., 1973-75, v.p. adminstrn., sec., 1975-90. vice chmn., sec., 1990—. Pres., Passano Found., Balt., 1982—, Am. Lung Assn. Md., 1982-84; mem. exec. com. Vol. Coun. Equal Opportunity, Balt., 1978—, chmn., 1995—; bd. dirs. Combined Health Appeal Am.; pres. (CHA) Combined Health Agys., Md., 1985-87, chmn. exec. com., 1987-95; pres. 12:30 Club Balt., 1981-83; mem. exec. com. Balt. City Life Museums, 1982-93, v.p. 1987-93, trustee emeritus, 1993—; mem. adv. coun. Johns Hopkins U. Sch. Continuing Studies, 1984—, exec. chair alumni chpt., 1986-89, chair edn. cmty. devel. iniative, 1995—; mem. Md. Gov.'s Commn. on High Blood Pressure and Related Cardiovascular Risk Factors, 1986—; bd. govs. Md. New Directions, Inc., 1987-94; bd. dirs., mem. exec. com. YMCA Ctrl. Md., 1988-96; bd. dirs., chair edn. com. Pride of Balt., 1990—; bd. dirs. Independent Coll. Fund Md., 1994—; bd. vis. Towson State U., 1994—, Sch. Medicine U. Md., 1995—; mem. planning com. Md. Bus. Responsive Govt., 1994—. Served with USN, 1963-65. Recipient Prince Hall Bicentennial award Masons, 1975; citations Mayor of Balt., 1976, City of Balt., 1977, Vol. of Yr. award for outstanding svc. to CICHA, 1984-85, Presdl. award for outstanding svc. to Am. Lung Assn. Md., 1985, Outstanding Vol., 1988, Disting. Svc. award Soc. Profl. Journalists, 1987, Outstanding Svc. award Am. Heart Assn., 1988, Outstanding Vol. Svc. award Balt. Assn. Retarded Citizens, 1990, Vol. of Yr./Outstanding Leadership and Dedication award Combined Health Agys., 1991-92. Mem. Purchasing Mgmt. Assn. Md. (chmn. com. 1968-70), Balt. Jaycees (v.p. 1974-76, internat. senator 1975), Greater Balt. Minority Purchasing Coun. (Service award 1978), Soc. Colonial Wars (chpt. gov., 1989-91), Johns Hopkins U. Alumni Assn. (pres. Balt. 1984-86, Univ. Heritage award 1987). Democrat. Episcopalian. Home: 3925 Linkwood Rd Baltimore MD 21210-3001 Office: Waverly Inc 351 W Camden St Baltimore MD 21201-2436

PASSANO, EDWARD MAGRUDER, printing company executive; b. Towson, Md., Dec. 22, 1904; s. Edward Boetler and Eleanor (Isaac) P.; m. Mary Troy Fleming, Apr. 2, 1982; 1 son, Edward Magruder. B.S. in Econs., Johns Hopkins U., 1927. With Waverly Press, Inc. (name changed to Waverly Inc. 1988), Balt., 1927-82, treas., 1946-68, pres., 1963-71, chmn. exec. com., 1971-75, also bd. dirs., ret., 1982. Bd. dirs., treas. Passano Found., Inc., 1970—. Mem. Soc. Colonial Wars (life, gen. coun.). Republican. Episcopalian. Home: 6873 Travelers Rest Pt Easton MD 21601-7631 Office: Waverly Inc 351 W Camden St Baltimore MD 21201-2436

PASSANTINO, RICHARD J., architect; b. N.Y.C., Apr. 4, 1934; s. Charles V. and Ruth M. (Defina) P.; m. Erika F. Dethlefs, Sept. 1, 1962; children: Stefan C., Fiona R. BS in Architecture, U. Cin., 1957. Registered arch., D.C., Md., Va., Ga., Fla., Ky., Mo., N.J., S.C.; cert. Nat. Coun. Archtl. Registration Bds. Rsch. assoc. McLeod, Ferrara, Ensign, Washington, 1960-70; founding prin. Richard J. Passantino, AIA Architects, Bethesda, Md., 1970-80; pres. SAIC Architects, McLean, Va., 1980-90, LEA/Passantino & Bavier, Arlington, Va., 1990-94, Passantino & Bavier subs. Facility Group Smyrna, Ga., Bethesda, Md., 1994—; spkr. to various ednl. instn. in U.S., AIA rep. Union Internat. Archs., 1985-88; mem. nat. archtl. juries throughout U.S., 1975—. Co-author: Urban Schools in Europe, 1963; contbr. numerous articles to profl. jours.; designer 7 earthquake resistant schs. in So. Italy, 1985-88, Early Childhood Ctr., Buffalo, 1995, psychiat. hosp., Leesburg, Va., 1979, Haile Selassie U., Addis Ababa, Ethiopia; designer modifications Am. Consulate Gen., Ecuador, Am. embassies, Papua-New Guinea, The Philippines, Liberia, Ghana, others. Bd. dirs. Nat. Child Rsch. Ctr., Washington, 1969-74. 1st lt. USAF, 1958-60; capt. USAFR, 1960-62. Recipient award for sch. architecture exhbn. Am. Assn. Sch. Bd. Adminstrs., 1984. Mem. AIA (corp., steering com. architecture for edn. 19794), Coun. for Ednl. Facilities Planners (co-recipient Projects of Distinction award 1993), Assn. for Childhood Edn. Internat., Assn. Sch. Bus. Ofcls. Internat. (award of excellence 1986), Nat. Hist. Trust, Soc. Am. Mil. Engrs. Avocations: tennis, photography, travel. Office: Passantino & Bavier Archs Ste 250 2401 Lake Park Dr Smyrna GA 30080

PASSEY, GEORGE EDWARD, psychology educator; b. Stratford, Conn., Sept. 28, 1920; s. Henry Richard and Elizabeth (Angus) P.; m. Algie Aldridge Ashe, Nov. 18, 1950; children—Richard Ashe, Elizabeth Aldridge, Mary Louise. B.S., Springfield Coll., 1942; M.A., Clark U., 1947; Ph.D., Tulane U., 1950. Asst. prof. U. Ala., Tuscaloosa, 1952-55; assoc. prof. U. Ala., 1955-56, 57-59, prof., 1959-63; prof. psychology, chmn. div. social and behavioral scis. U. Ala., Birmingham, 1967-73; prof. engring. U. Ala., 1969-84, Disting. Service prof. psychology, 1984-85, Disting Service prof. emeritus, 1985—; dean U. Ala. (Sch. Social and Behavioral Scis.), 1973-84; research scientist Lockheed Ga. Co., Marietta, Ga., 1956-57, 63-65, cons., 1965-67; prof. Ga. Inst. Tech., 1965-67. Served with USNR, 1942-46, PTO; with USAF, 1951-52. Fellow Am. Psychol. Assn.; mem. So. Soc. for Philosophy and Psychology, Southeastern Psychol. Assn., Ala. Psychol. Assn., Pine Harbor Golf and Racquet Club, Coosa Pines Golf Club, Sigma Xi. Home: 7141 Skyline Dr Pell City AL 35125-9304 *Whatever success I have enjoyed ought to be attributed to the attempt I have made to carry out the admonitions of my parents to make choices only after having appraised the alternatives in terms of their consequences, to weigh ethical considerations above all others, never to demand of others what one is unwilling to give of himself, and to work untiringly for those causes to which one is committed.*

PASSI, BETH, school administrator. Dir. Blake Lower Sch., Hopkins, Minn., 1982—. Recipient elem. sch. recognition award U.S. Dept. Edn., 1989-90, 93-94, Bush prin. leadership fellow, 1993-94. Office: Blake Lower Sch 110 Blake Rd Hopkins MN 55343

PASSMORE, HOWARD CLINTON, JR., geneticist, biological sciences educator; b. Drexel Hill, Pa., Sept. 12, 1942; s. Howard Clinton and Thelma (Walter) P.; m. Irene Grace Wrigley, Aug. 22, 1964; children: Lisa, Heather. AB, Franklin and Marshall Coll., 1964; PhD, U. Mich., 1970. Asst. prof. genetics Rutgers U., New Brunswick, N.J., 1971-77, assoc. prof., 1977-88, prof., 1988—, dir. grad. program in microbiology and molecular genetics, 1995—; assoc. dir. Bur. Biol. Rsch., 1982-85; mem. mammalian genetics study sect. NIH, 1988-92. Rsch. grantee NIH, 1978—. Mem. Am. Assn. Immunologists, Genetics Soc. Am., Am. Soc. Human Genetics. Home: 21 W Mill Rd Long Valley NJ 07853-3435 Office: Rutgers U Bur of Biol Rsch PO Box 1059 Piscataway NJ 08855-1059

PASSMORE, JAN WILLIAM, private investor; b. Winchester, Ind., Nov. 5, 1940; s. Gale Orth and Helen Louise (Hoskinson) P.; m. Pamela Boa, Feb. 14, 1964. Student Nebr. State U., 1959-61; BS, Ball State U., 1963. With Aetna Life & Casualty, 1964-75, Western region dir., San Jose, Calif., 1972-75; broker, Sanders & Sullivan, San Jose, 1975-78, partner, 1978-80, pres., 1979-81; pres., CEO Corcoran & Black, San Jose, 1981-88, chmn. 1988-90; pres. First Richmond Corp., First Richmond Realtors, 1991-93; v.p. Prestwick, Inc. 1991-93; pres. Industries, Inc., 1990-96; chmn. nat. adv. council INA Marketdyne, 1980-82; chmn. bd. Econ. Devel. Corp. Wayne County, Ind., 1993; chmn. Nat. Adv. Coun. Cigna Corp., 1983-86; chmn. Aetna Life & Casualty Regional Adv. Council, 1982-84, 87-89. Chmn. bd. Goodwill Industries, 1978-80, 86-89; pres. Boy Scouts Am., 1981-83; bd. dirs. Music and Arts Found., 1980-85, Alexian Bros. Hosp. Found., 1978-85, Small Bus. Devel. Ctr. Region # 9, 1993-95, chmn., 1994; chmn. bd. Hope Rehab., 1985-87; chmn. bd. dirs. Santa Clara County United Way; mem. San Jose Trolley Commn.; past pres. bd. trustees Alum Rock United Meth. Ch.; past pres. bd. trustees 1st Meth. Ch. San Jose; nat. council rep. Boy Scouts Am., 1985-90; chmn. bd. Mayor's Blue Ribbon Commn. Fin. City of Richmond, Ind., 1993.; chmn. fin. 1st Meth. Ch., Richmond. Recipient Silver Beaver award, Benefactors award Boy Scouts Am., Mayoral Proclamation City of San Jose, Suprs. Proclamation County of Santa Clara, Proclamation from Calif. State Assembly; named Citizen of Yr., Aetna Life & Casualty Co., 1975, Disting. Citizen of Yr. Santa Clara County, 1985; INA-Marketdyne Golden Circle, 1977-82, 87; named hon. Ky. Col. Mem. Western Assn. Ins. Brokers (trustee 1987-90), Nat. Assn. Ind. Ins. Agts., Richmond-Wayne County C. of C. (chmn. 1993, bd. dirs. 1990-95, disting. svc. award 1996). Republican. Clubs: San Jose Country Club (treas., bd. dirs.), Scotts Boys Club (pres. 1994-96, trustee 1992—), Sainte Claire, Spartan Found., Pres.'s Council San Jose State U., Aetna Life and Casualty Gt. Performers, Forest Hills Country Club, Columbia Club, Masons, Shriners, Kiwanis (pres. Mechanicsburg, Pa. chpt. 1969, lt. gov. Pa. 1970-72, pres. San Jose chpt. 1986, mem. Richmond club 1990—, bd. dirs. 1991-93, Hero award 1995, MVP award 1991-95), Kiwanis Internat. (legion of honor 30 years). Home: 729 Toddsbury Ln Richmond IN 47374-5752 Office: PO Box 1441 Richmond IN 47375-1441 *A lot of people have provided opportunities for me - I have tried to recognize them as a trust and give each a 100% effort.*

PASSMORE, MICHAEL FORREST, environmental administrator; b. Oroville, Calif., July 9, 1947; s. Audley Forrest and Betty Beryle (Elkin) P.; m. Laura Ann Travis, Sept. 7, 1968 (div. 1985); children: Travis Forrest, Robert Bryan; m. Elise Jean Bechtold, Nov. 9, 1985; 1 child, Heather Elise. BS, Oreg. State U., 1974, MS, 1977; PhD, Tex. A&M U., 1981. Research asst. Oreg. State U., Corvallis, 1974-77, research assoc., 1977; grad. fellow Rob and Bessie Welder Wildlife Found., Sinton, Tex., 1977-80; wildlife biologist Environ. Resources Br. U.S. Army Corps Engrs., Walla Walla, Wash., 1980-87; asst. chief Environ. Rsch. Br. U.S. Army Corps Engrs., Walla Walla, 1986-87, chief, 1987-96; chief stewardship br. waterways experiment sta. Vicksburg, Miss., 1996—; master bird bander Fish and Wildlife Svc., 1981-90; citizen ambassador, wildlife biology del. People-to-People Internat., China, 1987; cert. wildlife biologist, 1987—. Co-author: Raptors on COE Lands, 1986, Ecology of Band-tailed Pigeons in Oregon, 1992; contbr. articles to profl. publs. Coach youth sports, 1984-92; vol. Boy Scouts Am., Walla Walla, 1986-95. Mem. The Wildlife Soc. (mem. spl. award com. 1987-88, Wilson Ornithol. Soc., Western Bird Banding Assn., Nat. Mil. Fish and Wildlife Assn. Methodist. Avocations: hunting, wildlife photography, camping, softball.

PASSON, RICHARD HENRY, academic administrator; b. Hazleton, Pa., Aug. 18, 1939; s. Henry Richard and Grace Miriam (Bernstein) P.; m. Margaret Rose Ferdinand, Aug. 14, 1965; children—Michael, Rebecca, Christopher. B.A. (Bishop Hafey scholar), King's Coll., Pa., 1961; M.A., U. Notre Dame, 1963, Ph.D. (NDEA fellow), 1965. From instr. to prof. English U. Scranton, 1964-73, chmn. English dept., 1970-73, fgn. student adviser, 1965-67; dean Coll. Arts and Scis., Creighton U., Omaha, 1973-77; acad. v.p. St. Joseph's U., Phila., 1977-84; provost U. Scranton, Pa., 1984—. Contbr. articles profl. jours. Recipient grant Nat. Assn. Fgn. Students, 1966. Mem. Modern Lang. Assn., Am. Assn. Higher Edn., Am. Assn. Acad. Deans. Democrat. Roman Catholic. Office: U Scranton Office of Provost Scranton PA 18510

PASSWATER, BARBARA GAYHART, real estate broker; b. Phila., July 10, 1945; d. Clarence Leonard and Margaret Jamison; m. Richard Albert Passwater, June 2, 1964; children: Richard Alan, Michael Eric. AA, Goldey-Beacom Coll., 1963; BA, Salisbury State U., 1981. Notary pub., Md. Sec. DuPont, Wilmington, Del., 1963-65, Nuclear-Chgo., Silver Spring, Md., 1965-67; office mgr. Montgomery County Sch. System, Wheaton, Md., 1977-79; adminstrv. asst. Solgar Nutritional Rsch. Ctr., Berlin, Md., 1979-94, asst. to dir. rsch., 1995—; assoc. broker Prudential-Groff Realty, Berlin, Md., 1983-87, ReMax, Inc., Berlin, Md., 1987-88; broker, mgr., developers rep. River Run Sales Ctr., Berlin, Md., 1988-96; pvt. practice Berlin, Berlin, 1996—. Treas. Ocean Pines (Md.) Vol. Fire Dept. Aux., 1981-84; emergency med. tech. Ocean Pines (Md.) Vol. Fire Dept., 1983-95; sec. Ocean Pines (Md.) Fire Dept., 1990-95; mem. Foster Care Review Bd., Snow Hill, Md., 1984—; life mem. Ocean Pines Vol. Fire Dept., 1996—. Mem. Beta Sigma Phi, Phi Kappa Phi. Avocations: photography, nature studies. Office: Solgar Nutritional Rsch Ctr 11017 Manklin Meadows Ln Berlin MD 21811

PASSWATER, RICHARD ALBERT, biochemist, author; b. Wilmington, Del., Oct. 13, 1937; s. Stanley Leroy and Mabel Rosetta (King) P. BS, U. Del., 1959; PhD, Bernadean U., 1976. Cert. firefighter; m. Barbara Sarah Gayhart, June 2, 1964; children: Richard Alan, Michael Eric. Supr. instrumental analysis lab. Allied Chem. Corp., Marcus Hook, Pa., 1959-64; tech. svcs. rep. F&M Sci. Corp., Avondale, Pa., 1965; dir. applications lab. Am. Instrument Co., Silver Spring, Md., 1965-77; dir. Am. Gen. Enterprises, Minn.; former daily broadcaster Sta. WMCA, N.Y.C., 1980-88; former daily broadcaster Sta. WRNG, Atlanta, 1982-85; rsch. dir. Solgar Nutritional Rsch. Ctr., 1978—, corp. v.p. Solgar Co., Inc.; chmn. Worcester County Emergency Planning Com.; bd. dirs. Worcester Meml. Hosp., Atlantic Gen. Hosp., River Run Assn; pres. 1989-92, Subaqueous Exploration and Archeology Ltd. Author: Guide to Fluorescence Literature, vol. 1, 1967, vol. 2 1970, vol. 3, 1974, Supernutrition, 1975, Supernutrition For Healthy Hearts, 1977, Super Calorie, Carbohydrate Counter, 1978, Cancer and Its Nutritional Therapies, 1978, 83, 93, The Easy No-Flab Diet, 1979, Selenium As Food and Medicine, 1980, The Slendernow Diet, 1982, (with Dr. E. Cranton) Trace Elements, Hair Analysis and Nutrition, 1983, The New Supernutrition, 1991, The Longevity Factor, 1993, Cancer Prevention and Nutritional Therapy, 1993, (with Ben Friedrich and Hans Kugler) Heart Health, 1994, Pycnogenol: The Super Protector Nutrient, 1994, Lipoic Acid: The Metabolic Antioxidant, 1995; contbg. author: Fire Protection Guide to Hazardous Materials, 1991; editor Fluorescence News, 1966-77, Jour. Applied Health Scis., 1982-83; mem. editorial bd. Nutritional Perspectives, 1978-96, The Body Forum, 1979-80, Jour. Holistic Medicine, 1981-88, VIM Newsletter, 1979—; contbg. editor Firehouse Mag., 1988-94, Jour Applied Nutrition; contbr. over 400 health articles to mags.; co-editor booklet series Your Good Health; sci. adv. and columnist Whole Foods mag.; patentee in field. bd. dirs. Sci. Documentation Ctr., Dunfermline, Eng.; Am. Found. Firefighter Health and Safety; chief Ocean Pines Vol. Fire Dept., 1984-93; active Emergency Med. Tech.; adviser Nat. Inst. Nutrition Edn.; past adv. bd. Stephen Decatur High Sch., Worcester County Dept. Edn. Cubmaster, 1975-79. Named Citizen of Yr. Ocean Pines, Md., 1987, 5th Ann. Achievement award, 1989, VFW Cert. of Commendation, 1988, Industry award Nat. Inst. Nutritional Edn., 1991; inducted into Delmarva Fireman's Hall of Fame, 1993. Fellow Internat. Acad. Preventive Medicine, Am. Inst. Chemists; mem. ASTM, AAAS, Am. Chem. Soc., Gerontology Soc., Am. Geriatric Soc., Am. Aging Assn., Soc. Applied Spectroscopy, Internat. Found. Preventive Medicine (v.p.), Internat. Union Pure and Applied Chemistry, Royal Soc. Chemistry (London), Internat. Acad. Holistic Health and Medicine, Capital Chem. Soc., Nutrition Today Soc., Am. Acad. Applied Health Scis. (pres., bd. dir.), Internat. Found. Preventive Medicine (v.p., dir.), Inst. Nutritional Rsch., Internat. Platform Assn., N.Y. Acad. Scis., Nat. Fire Protection Assn. (cert. firefighter level III, com. on properties of hazardous chemicals), Pi Kappa Alpha. Office: 11017 Manklin Meadows Ln Berlin MD 21811-9340

PASSY, CHARLES, arts critic; b. N.Y., Jan. 9, 1964; s. Victor and Beverly (Green) P.; m. Leslie M. Olsen, Dec. 15, 1989; 1 child, Jacob E. BA, Columbia U., 1985. Assoc. Jay K. Hoffman and Assocs., N.Y., 1983-87; sr. editor, mng. editor Ovation Mag., N.Y., 1988-89; editor Classical Mag., N.Y., 1989-91; editor-in-chief Musical Am. Pub., N.Y., 1991-92; staff writer The Palm Beach Post, West Palm Beach, 1992—; announcer, prodr. WNYC FM, N.Y., 1984-85; entertainment stringer N.Y. Newsday, 1987-92. Author: (with others) New Voices: Selected University and College Prize Winning Poems, 1989, The New Grove Dictionary of Jazz, The New Grove Dictionary of Music and Musicians in the United States, 1989; editor: (with others) The Letters of Virgil Thomson, 1988; contbr. numerous articles to jours. in field. Recipient Poetry award Acad. Am. Poets Columbia U., 1985, Criticism awards Soc. Profl. Journalists, 1995, Fla. Press Club, 1993, Fla. Soc. Newspaper Editors, 1993; fellow Knight Ctr. for Specialized Journalism, 1993. Mem. Music Critics Assn., Louis August Jonas Found. Avocations: poetry, baseball, theater, collecting sports memorabilia, reading. Home: 5481 Eagle Lake Dr Palm Bch Gdns FL 33418-1546 Office: Palm Beach Newspapers Inc 2751 S Dixie Hwy West Palm Beach FL 33405-1233

PASTAN, IRA HARRY, biomedical science researcher; b. Winthrop, Mass., June 1, 1931; s. Jacob and Miriam (Ceder) P.; m. Linda Olenik, June 14, 1953; children—Stephen, Peter, Rachel. B.S., Tufts U., 1953, M.D., 1957. Med. house officer Yale U. New Haven Hosp., 1957-59; clin. assoc. Nat. Inst. Arthritis and Metabolic Disease, NIH, Bethesda, Md., 1959-61, sr. investigator sect. on endocrine biochemistry, clin. endocrinology br., 1963-69; postdoctoral fellow Lab. of Cellular Physiology Nat Heart and Lung Inst. NIH, Bethesda, Md., 1961-62; head molecular biology sect. endocrinology br. Nat. Cancer Inst., NIH, Bethesda, Md., 1969-70, chief lab. molecular biology, 1970—. Author: An Atlas of Immunofluorescence, 1985; author, editor: Endocytosis, 1985; contbr. articles to profl. jours. Recipient Van Meter prize Am. Thyroid Assn., 1971, Superior Service award Dept. HEW and NIH, 1973, Meritorious Service medal USPHS, NIH, Nat. Cancer Inst., 1983, Disting. Service medal, 1985. Mem. AAAS, Am. Soc. Clin. Investigation, Am. Soc. Biol. Chemists, Am. Soc. for Microbiology, Am. Soc. for Cell Biology, Peripatetic Club, Nat. Acad. Scis., Clin. Immunology Soc., Am. Assn. Physicians, Am. Acad. Arts and Scis., Molecular Medicine Soc., Alpha Omega Alpha. Office: Lab Molecular Biology NCI/NIH Bldg 37 Rm 4E16 Convent Dr MSC 4255 Bethesda MD 20892-4255

PASTAN, LINDA OLENIK, poet; b. N.Y.C., May 27, 1932; d. Jacob L. and Bess (Schwartz) Olenik; m. Ira Pastan, 1953; children: Stephen, Peter, Rachel. BA, Radcliffe Coll., 1954; MLS, Simmons Coll., 1955; MA, Brandeis U., 1957. Author: (poetry) A Perfect Circle of Sun, 1971, On the Way to the Zoo, 1975, Aspects of Eve, 1975, The Five Stages of Grief, 1978 (Alice Fay di Castagnola award Poetry Soc. Am. 1978), Setting the Table, 1980, Waiting for My Life, 1981, PM/AM: New and Selected Poems, 1983 (Am. Book award nomination 1983), A Fraction of Darkness: Poems, 1985, The Imperfect Paradise, 1988, Heroes in Disguise, 1991, An Early Afterlife, 1995. Recipient Dylan Thomas Poetry award Mademoiselle, 1958, Virginia Faulkner award Prarie Schooner, 1992, Charity Randall citation Internat. Poetry Forum, 1996; NEA fellow; grantee Md. Arts Coun. Jewish. Office: 11710 Beall Mountain Rd Potomac MD 20854-1105

PASTER, HOWARD G., public relations, public affairs company executive; b. N.Y.C., Dec. 23, 1944. BA with honors, Alfred U., 1966; MS in Journalism, Columbia U., 1967. Legis. dir. UAW, 1977-80; exec. v.p. Timmons & Co., 1980-92; asst. to pres. and dir. Office Legis. Affairs White House, Washington, 1993; chmn., CEO Hill and Knowlton, Inc., N.Y.C., 1994—; bd. dirs. Ctr. Nat. Policy. Bd. dirs. Christmas-in-April. Office: Hill and Knowlton Inc 466 Lexington Ave New York NY 10017-3140

PASTERNACK, ROBERT FRANCIS, chemistry educator; b. N.Y.C., Sept. 20, 1936; 2 children. B.A., Cornell U., 1957, Ph.D. in Chemistry, 1962. Research assoc. in chemistry U. Ill., Champaign, 1962-63; from asst. to prof. chemistry Ithaca Coll., N.Y., 1963-66, Charles A. Dana Endowed prof. chemistry, 1976-82; Edmund Allen prof. chemistry Swarthmore Coll., Pa., 1984—; invited speaker seminars, colls., univs., nat., internat. meetings, confs. including Bioinorganic Chem., Italy, Portugal, Gordon Rsch. Confs., Spanish Royal Soc. Chem., many others; lectr. series Nankai U., China, U. Messina, Italy; mem. adv. com. Rsch. Corp.; mem. sci. & art com. Franklin Inst.; co-organizer, chmn. workshop on rsch. at undergrad. instn. NSF, mem. undergrad. curriculm chem.; vis. prof., vis. rschr. U Messina, U. Paris, Nakai, Rome, King's Coll., London, Fritz Haber Inst., Berlin; co-developer A Unified Lab. Program; initiator, chmn. C.P. Snow Lectr. Series. Author, co-author more than 100 sci. publs. Mem. com. on sci. and the arts Franklin Inst., 1992—. Grantee NSF, 1965-66, 69-72, 77-78, 83-84, 86-94, 95—, Petroleum Rsch. Fund, 1967-74, 86-88, NIH, 1971-89, Monsanto Corp., 1986-92, Rsch. Corp., 1974-75, 78-79, 84-85, Danforth Assocs., 1978-84, Camille and Henry Dreyfus Found., 1981, 95, NATO, 1979, 88-89, 95-96; recipient Camille and Henry Dreyfus Tchg./Scholar award, 1987-89, NSF Manpower Improvement award, King's Coll., U. London, 1977-78; NSF sci. faculty fellow U. Rome, 1968-70. Mem. AAAS. Am. Chem. Soc., N.Y. Acad. Sci., Sigma Xi. Office: Swarthmore Coll Dept Chemistry Swarthmore PA 19081

PASTERNACKI, LINDA LEA, critical care nurse; b. Green Bay, Wis., May 26, 1947; d. Paul John and Marion M. (Zagzebski) P.; (div.); children: Sam, Dan, Rachel Marie. Nursing diploma, St. Francis Sch. Nursing, Wichita, Kans., 1968; BS, Coll. St. Francis, Joliet, Ill., 1981, MS in Health Adminstrn., 1986. RN med.-surg., geriatrics, psychiatry St. Francis Hosp., Wichita, 1968-70; RN ICU-critical care unit Sunrise Hosp., Las Vegas, Nev., 1970-72; RN critical care unit Presbyn. Hosp., Albuquerque, 1972-75; RN med. ICU, surg. ICU VA Hosp., Albuquerque, 1976-81; RN emergency rm. Univ. Heights Hosp., Albuquerque, 1981-82; RN ICU, critical care unit Lovelace Med. Ctr., Albuquerque, 1982-86; RN ICU, emergency rm., surg. cornary care, intensive recovery room Presbyn. Hosp., Albuquerque, 1986-94; RN emergency rm., ICU, critical care unit St. Joseph Med. Ctr., Albuquerque, 1992-94; RN ICU, med.-surg. unit Transitional Hosp. Corp., Albuquerque, 1994—, admissions coord., 1995; hyperbaric therapy instr. Presbyn. Hosp., Albuquerque, 1975; clin. instr. U. N.Mex. EMT Sch., Albuquerque, 1980. Mem. AACN. Home: 10605 Central Park Dr NE Albuquerque NM 87123-4844 Office: Transitional Hosp Corp 700 High NE Albuquerque NM 87102

PASTERNAK, JOANNA MURRAY, special education and gifted and talented educator; b. Houston, Feb. 9, 1953; d. Lee Roy and Evelyn Mary (Kirmss) Murray; children: Sheila Ann Tanner, Lawrence Ross Tanner IV; m. Allen Pasternak, Jan. 9, 1993. BA in Liberal Arts with honors, Our Lady of the Lake, San Antonio, 1990. Acctg. clk. Houston Post, 1981-85; owner, art cons. Tanner Fine Art, Houston, 1985-92; spl. edn. tchr. Houston Ind. Sch. Dist., 1991-94, dept. chmn., 1994—; art cons. Plz. Gallery, Houston, 1985; mem. benefits com. Houston Ind. Sch. Dist., 1992—; presenter Am. Fedn. Tchrs. Nat. Edn. Conf., 1994. Contbr. articles to profl. jours. Vol. Nat. Health Care Campaign, legis. com. AFL-CIO; bd. dirs. PTA, SDMC; mem., pres. Westlawn Terr. Civic Club; Dem. campaign worker, 1993—; mem. precinct, state del. Dem. Senate, 1994; sec. Dist. 13 Dem. Conv., 1996. Mem. Tex. Fedn. Tchrs. (bd. dirs. quality ednl. stds. in tchg. 1993), Houston Fedn. Tchrs. (chairperson legis. liaison com. 1993, v.p. 1992—, chairperson legis. com. 1995-96), Delta Mu Delta. Democrat. Avocations: civic and political activities. Home: 2141 Colquitt St Houston TX 77098-3310 Office: Houston Fedn Tchrs 3202 Weslayan St Ste 102 Houston TX 77027-5748

PASTIN, MARK JOSEPH, association executive, consultant, educator; b. Ellwood City, Pa., July 6, 1949; s. Joseph and Patricia Jean (Camenite) P.; m. Joanne Marie Reagle, May 30, 1970 (div. Mar. 1982); m. Carrie Patricia Class, Dec. 22, 1984 (div. June 1990); m. Christina M. Brecto, June 15, 1991. BA summa cum laude, U. Pitts., 1970; MA, Harvard U., 1972, PhD, 1973. Asst. prof. Ind. U., Bloomington, 1973-78, assoc. prof., 1978-80; founder, bd. CTG, Inc., 1983—; chmn., CEO, pres. Coun. Ethical Orgns., Alexandria, Va., 1986—; prof. mgmt., dir. Ariz. State U., Tempe, 1988-92, prof. emeritus, 1996—; prof. emeritus, 1996—; chair Health Ethics Trust, 1995—; adv. bd. Aberdeen Holdings, San Diego, 1988-90; dir. Sandpiper Group, Inc., N.Y.C., 1987—, S.W. Projects, Inc., San Diego, 1988-90, Learned Nicholson, Ltd., 1990-91; bd. Japan Am. Soc. Phoenix, Found. for Ethical Orgns.; cons. GTE, Southwestern Bell, 1987-89, Tex. Instruments, MicroAge Computers, Med-Tronic, Blood Sys., Inc., Opus Corp., GTE, NyNex, Am. Express Bank, Kaiko Bussan Co., Japan, Arex Co., Japan, Century Audit Co., Japan, Scottsdale Meml. Hosp., Consanti Found., Lincoln Electric Co., Tenet Healthcare Corp.; vis. faculty Harvard U., 1980; invited presenter Australian Inst. Mgmt., Nippon Tel. & Tel., Hong Kong Commn. Against Corruption, 1984, Young Pres.'s Orgn. Internat. U., 1990, Nat. Assn. Indsl. & Office Parks, 1990, ABA, 1991, Govt. of Brazil, 1991, Tzuzuki Edn. Sys., 1995. Author: Hard Problems of Management, 1986 (Book of Yr. award Armed Forces Mil. Comtrs. 1986, Japanese edit. 1994), Power by Association, 1991, The State of Ethics in Arizona, 1991, Planning Forum, 1992; editor: Public-Private Sector Ethics, 1979; columnist Bus. Jour. Founding bd. mem. Tempe Leadership, 1985-89; bd. mem. Ctr. for Behavioral Health, Phoenix, 1986-89, Tempe YMCA, 1986—, Valley Leadership Alumni Assn., 1989—; mem. Clean Air Com., Phoenix, 1987-90. Nat. Sci. Found. fellow, Cambridge, Mass., 1971-73; Nat. Endowment for the Humanities fellow, 1975; Exxon Edn. Found. grant, 1982-83. Mem. Strategic Mgmt. Soc. (invited presenter 1985), Am. Soc. Assn. Execs. (invited presenter 1987-95), Bus. Ethics Soc. (founding bd. dirs. 1983), Found. Ethical Orgns. (chmn. 1988, pres.), Pres.'s Assn., Am. Mgmt. Assn., Golden Key, Harvard Club, Ariz. Club, Phi Beta Kappa. Avocations: golf, racquetball, running. Home: 7206 Park Terrace Dr Alexandria VA 22307-2035 Office: 1216 King St Ste 300 Alexandria VA 22314-2825

PASTINE, MAUREEN DIANE, university librarian; b. Hays, Kans., Nov. 21, 1944; d. Gerhard Walter and Ada Marie (Hillman) Hillman; m. Jerry Joel Pastine, Feb. 5, 1966. AB, in English, Ft. Hays State U., 1967; MLS, Emporia State U., 1970. Reference librarian U. Nebr.-Omaha, 1971-77; undergrad. libr. U. Ill., Urbana, 1977-79; reference librarian, 1979-80; univ. libr. San Jose State U.-Calif., 1980-85; dir. librs. Wash. State U., Pullman, 1985-89; ctrl. univ. libr. So. Meth. U., 1989—; mem. adv. bd. Foothill Coll. Libr. 1983-85; leader ednl. del. librs. to People's Republic of China, 1985, Australia/New Zealand, 1986, Soviet Union, 1988, East & West Germany, Czechoslovakia, Hungary, Austria, 1991, Rio de Janeiro, 1993. Co-author: Library and Library Related Publications: A Directory of Publishing Opportunities, 1973; asst. compiler: Women's Work and Women's Studies, 1973-74, 1975; compiler procs. Teaching Bibliographic Instruction in Graduate Schools of Library Science, 1981; editor: Integrating Library Use Skills into the General Education Curriculum, 1989; co-editor: In the Spirit of 1991: Access to Western European Libraries and Literature, 1992; contbr. articles to profl. pubs. Recipient Disting. Alumni Grad. award Emporia State U., 1986, Dudley Bibliog. Instruction Libr. of Yr. award, 1989. Mem. ALA (chmn. World Book-ALA Goal awards jury 1984-85), Assn. Coll. and Rsch. Librs. (editorial adv. bd. BIS Think Tank 1982-85, chmn. bibliographic instrn. sect. 1983-84, editorial bd. Choice 1983-85, chmn. Miriam Dudley Bibliographic Instrn. Libr. of Yr. award com. 1984-85, mem. task force on librarians as instrs. 1986—, chair task force internat. rels. 1987-89, BIS Libr. of Yr. 1989, rep. to AAAS/CAIP, 1989—, chair internat. rels. com. 1990-94, rsch. libr. of yr. award's com. 1994—, ALA pay equity com. 1994—), Libr. Adminstrn. and Mgmt. Assn. (chmn. stats. sect. com. on devel., orgn., planning and programming 1982-83, sec. stats. sect. exec. com. 1982-83, mem. at large 1986—), ALA Library Instrn. Round Table (long range planning com. 1986-94), ALA Libr. Rsch. Round Table, Wash. Libr. Assn., Assn. Libr. Collections & Tech. Svcs. Divsn., Libr. and Info. Tech. Assn., Assn. Specialized and Coop. Libr. Agencies (chair multi-lincs internat. networking discussion group 1990-92), Libr. Rsch. Roundtable, Women's Studies Sect., Eng. and Am. Lit. Studies Discussion Group, Tex. Libr. Assn., Pacific N.W. Libr. Assn., Phi Kappa Phi, Beta Phi Mu. Home: 8720 Hanford Dr Dallas TX 75243-6416 Office: So Meth U Cen Univ Librs Fondren Libr Dallas TX 75275-0135

PASTOR, ED, congressman; b. June 28, 1943. Mem. Maricopa County Bd. Suprs., Phoenix, Ariz., 1976-91; mem. 102nd-104th Congresses from Ariz. 2nd dist., 1991—. Office: House of Representatives Washington DC 20515

PASTORE, THOMAS MICHAEL, telecommunications sales executive; b. Bronx, N.Y., Jan. 25, 1959; s. Philip J. and Olga E. (DeGenito) P.; m. Kimberly A. Coppersmith, Dec. 13, 1986; children: Gabriela Maria, Thomas John. BA in Bus., Western State Coll., 1981. Sales rep. Victor Technologies Inc., Denver, 1981-84; account mgr. No. Telecom Inc., Denver, 1984-87, v.p. sales coun., 1985—, sales engr., 1987-92, dist. sales mgr., 1992—. Mem. Better Air Campaign, 1990—; sec. Warren Sq. Homeowners Assn., Denver, 1987-92; player, contbr. Dale Tooley Tennis Tournament, 1991-92; fundraiser Am. Cancer Soc., Denver, 1991—; mem. Denver Art Mus., 1991-92. Republican. Roman Catholic. Avocations: skiing, tennis, biking. Home and Office: No Telecom Inc 16095 Quarry Hill Dr Parker CO 80134-9553

PASTORELLE, PETER JOHN, film company executive, radiological services and waste management company executive; b. White Plains, N.Y., Jan. 23, 1933; s. Dominic John and Marguerite Delphine (Xavier) P.; m. Maria Rita Delcampo, Oct. 10, 1970; children: Betchie, Jomar. B.S., Fordham U., 1955; M.A., NYU, 1961; B.D., SUNY-Maryknoll, 1963. Radio news writer Western Conn. Broadcasting, Stamford, 1964-65; producer, dir. United Nations TV, N.Y.C., 1965-70; pres. The NDL Orgn., Inc., Peekskill, N.Y., 1965—, now chief exec. officer; pres. Peter Pastorelle Prodns., Mount Kisco, N.Y., 1970—, NDL Transport, Inc., 1984—, NDL Radon Services, Inc., 1988—; lectr. Am. Inst. Plant Engrs., Phila., 1981, Am. Chem. Soc., Phila., 1981, Low Level Radioactive Waste Mgmt. Decision Makers Forum, Fla., 1993; Blue Ribbon panelist NATAS, N.Y.C., 1980—; mem. Maxey Flats Steering Com.; mem. exec. com. N.Y. State Low Level Waste Group. Producer, writer films; Face of Hunger, 1976 (Dept. Commerce award), Samoa: Culture in Crisis, 1982 (Gold award), Water, 1978 (Silver award), composer film scores for UN including Faces of My Brother, Face of Hunger, Messengers of Peace; contbg. writer Radwaste Mag., 1994—. Mem. del. Citizen Amb. Program Nuclear Fuels Mgmt., Russia, Ukraine; mem. chmn.'s adv. bd. Rep. Nat. Com., 1994—; mem. Eisenhower Commn., 1995—. Served with U.S. Army, 1956-58. Mem. Health Physics Soc., Am. Nuclear Soc., Radiation Research Soc., N.Y. Acad. Sci., Pres.'s Club Fordham U. Republican. Roman Catholic. Home: PO Box 318 Mount Kisco NY 10549-0318 Office: The NDL Orgn Inc PO Box 791 Mount Kisco NY 10549-0791

PASTRANA, RONALD RAY, Christian ministry counselor, theology and biblical studies educator, former school system administrator; b. N.Y.C., Sept. 5, 1939; s. Anthony and Mildred Pastrana; m. Josephine Pastrana; children: Christine, Therese. BA in History/Sci. Edn., Queens Coll., 1963; advanced sci. cert., Pace U., 1964-68; MS in Counseling Edn., St. John's U., 1967; diploma, U.S. Acad. of Health Sci., 1975, U.S. Army Command and Gen. Staff Coll., 1979; D Ministry, Sch. Bible Theology Sem., 1996. Tchr. sci. Marie Curie Jr. High Sch., Bayside, N.Y., 1963-68; guidance counselor Half Hollow Hills High Sch., Dix Hills, N.Y., 1969-71; guidance counselor Walt Whitman High Sch., Huntington Station, N.Y., 1968-69, coord. occupational svcs., 1971-74; guidance coord. Dutchess County Bd. Coop. Ednl. Svcs. Tech. Edn. Ctr., Poughkeepsie, N.Y., 1974-86; coord. guidance and related acads. Dutchess County BOCES Tech. Edn. Ctr., Poughkeepsie, N.Y., 1986-96; asst. dir. Reach Out Sch. of Ministry, Hyde Park, N.Y., 1996—; ednl. cons. N.Y. State Edn. Dept., Albany, 1975-83, Armed Forces Vocat. Testing Group, Dept. of Def., Washington, 1975-77; cert. educator Lunar Edn. Project NASA, 1986-87. Author: Career Guidance in the Classroom, 1974, A Curriculum Guide to the Study of the Seven Dispensations and Eight Covenants, 1996. NSF sci. study grantee, 1964-68; recipient: Dutchess County Counselor of the Year award, 1995. Mem. Am. Counselors Assn., Am. Mental Health Counselors Assn., Nat. Career Devel. Assn., Am. Assn. Christian Counselors, N.Y. Acad. Scis., N.Y. State Assn. for Counseling and Devel., Sch. Adminstrs. Assn. N.Y. State, Dutchess County Counseling Assn. (exec. bd. 1989-96), Phi Delta Kappa. Avocations: rock and mineral collecting, fitness activities, canoeing, hiking. Home: 26 Greentree Dr S Hyde Park NY 12538-2132 Office: Reach Out Sch of Ministry PO Box 2035 251 Crum Elbow Rd Hyde Park NY 12538

PASTREICH, PETER, orchestra executive director; b. Bklyn., Sept. 13, 1938; s. Ben and Hortense (Davis) P.; m. Jamie Garrard Whittington; children by previous marriages: Anna, Milena, Emanuel, Michael. A.B. magna cum laude, Yale Coll., 1959; postgrad., N.Y. U. Sch. Medicine, 1959-60; studied trumpet, with Robert Nagle at Yale U., with Raymond Sabarich, Paris. Asst. mgr. Denver Symphony, Balt. Symphony; mgr. Greenwich Village Symphony, N.Y.C., 1960-63; gen. mgr. Nashville Symphony, 1963-65, Kansas City Philharmonic, 1965-66; asst. mgr., mgr. St. Louis Symphony, 1966-78, exec. dir., 1966-78; exec. dir. San Francisco Symphony, 1978—; instr. orch. mgmt. Am. Symphony Orch. League; bd. dirs. Nat. Com. for Symphony Orch. Support; founder San Francisco Youth Orch.; rep. planning and constrn. Davies Symphony Hall, San Francisco Symphony, 1980. Author: TV comml., 1969 (CLIO award); contbr. articles to various newspapers. Mem. recommendation bd. of the Avery Fisher Artist Program, Yale U. Council com. on music; past mem. adv. panel Nat. Endowment for the Arts, co-chmn. music panel, 1985; founding mem. bd. dirs. St. Louis Conservatory, mem. policy com. Maj. Orch. Mgrs. Conf., chmn., 1980; bd. dirs. Laumeier Sculpture Park, St. Louis, Stern Grove Festival, San Francisco Conv. and Visitors Bur.; chmn. fund campaign French-Am. Internat. Sch., San Francisco. Served with U.S. Army, 1960. Recipient First Disting. Alumnus award Yale U. Band, 1977, cert. Merit Yale Sch. Music, 1984. Mem. Am. Symphony Orch. League (dir., chmn., former chmn. task force on mgmt. tng.; mem. exec. and long-range planning com., chmn. standing com. on adminstrv. policy), Assn. Calif. Symphony Orchs. (dir.), Bankers Club of San Francisco. Club: Yale (N.Y.C.). Office: San Francisco Symphony Davies Symphony Hall San Francisco CA 94102

PASTRICK, HAROLD LEE, aeronautical engineer; b. Ambridge, Pa., June 28, 1936; s. Samuel and Mary (Makara) P.; m. Vivienne Lee Nusser Heinricher, June 3, 1961; children: Tracy Lee, Gregory Harold, Michael Joseph Samuel. BSEE, Carnegie-Mellon U., 1958; postgrad., Rutgers U., 1959-61, CCNY, 1961-63, U. Ala. Huntsville, 1964-66, 68-73; student, MIT, summers 1961-63; MS in Aeronautics & Astronautics, Stanford U., 1967, engr. in Aeronautics & Astronautics, 1972; PhD in Engring., Calif. Western U., 1977. Registered prof. engr., Ala. Metallurgical engring. aide Jones & Laughlin Steel Corp., Aliquippa, Pa., 1955-56; asst. engr., designer Am. Bridge Divsn., U.S. Steel Corp., Ambridge, 1957; electronics engr. Avionics Divsn., U.S. Army Signal R&D Labs., Ft. Monmouth, N.J., 1958-63; aerospace engr., Inertial Systems Team Missile R&D Labs., Redstone Arsenal, Ala., 1963-64; tech. dir. Army Inertial Guidance & Tech. Ctr., Redstone Arsenal, 1964-66; project engr. Inertial Guidance Br., Redstone Arsenal, 1967-71; rsch. aerospace engr. Guidance & Control Br., Redstone Arsenal, 1971-73; group leader Terminal Homing Missile Analysis, Redstone Arsenal, 1973-79; staff specialist, asst. to dir., land warfare Office of Under Sec. Def., Rsch. and Engring., Washington, 1979-80; chief, guidance and control analysis U.S. Army Missile Command, Redstone Arsenal, Ala., 1980-81; v.p. engring. Control Dynamics Co., Huntsville, 1981-83; asst. v.p., engring. analysis divsn. Sci. Applications Internat. Corp., Huntsville, 1983-86; v.p. theater missile def. and system analysis operation, 1986-91; corp. v.p., gen. mgr. SRS Technologies, Huntsville, 1991—; lectr. Sch. of Sci. and Engring., U. Ala., Huntsville, 1967-83; lectr. dept. continuing edn. George Washington U., 1985-87; engring. seminar dir. Applied Tech. Inst., Frankfurt, Germany, 1984, Singapore, 1986; tech. tng. dir. Tech. Tng. Corp., Tel Aviv, 1988; lectr. Advanced Tech. Internat., Ltd., London, 1985; guidance and control cons. various labs Dept. of Def., Washington, 1971-93; lectr., rsch. advisor Southeastern Inst. Tech., Huntsville, 1978-84; lectr., seminar leader Guidance and Control Technologies, U.S., Europe, Asia, Mex., 1980-94. Contbr. over 120 articles to profl. jours. Chmn. combined fed. campaign ARDEC, United Way, Redstone Arsenal, 1976; mem. Huntsville Econ. Devel. Coun., 1994; chmn. indsl. contbns. C. of C., Armed Forces Week, Huntsville-Madison County, 1993, 94, vice chmn. mil. affairs com., 1994-95, chmn., 1996; program chmn. tech. and bus. exhbn. and symposium, Huntsville, 1994-95, gen. chmn., 1995-96; pres. Greek Orthodox Ch., 1967, 73. Capt. U.S. Army, 1958-64. Fellow AIAA (assoc. missile tech. com. 1989-91, guest editor Jour. Guidance and Control 1981, vice-chmn. Huntsville chpt. 1979); mem. IEEE (sr., chpt. program chmn. 1972-73), Am. Def. Preparedness Assn. (vice-chmn. Huntsville chpt. 1974-75), Soc. for Computer Simulation, Assn. of U.S. Army, Inst. of Navigation, Ala. Acad. Sci. (vice chmn. 1978-79, engring. chmn. 1979-81), Rotary (dir. internat. svc. Greater Huntsville Club 1992-93, sec. 1994-95, pres.-elect 1995-96, pres. 1996—), Heritage Club (Huntsville), Greenwhyche Club (v.p. 1979), Redstone Golf Club. Achievements include pioneering hardware in the loop simulations for testing laser semi-active guided missiles. Avocations: golf, weight tng., choral music, reading, running. Home: 2624 Trailway Rd SE Huntsville AL 35801-1474 Office: SRS Technologies 500 Discovery Dr NW Huntsville AL 35806-2810

PASVOLSKY, RICHARD LLOYD, parks, recreation, and environment educator; b. Englewood, N.J., Feb. 16, 1924; s. Valentine and Ellen Isabel (Stoughton) P.; m. Jo Anne Evans, June 16, 1968. BEd, Panzer Coll., 1950; MA in Edn., NYU, 1955; D in Recreation, Ind. U., 1973. Asst. supt. recreation City of Rutland, Vt., 1951-53; supt. recreation City of Montpelier, Vt., 1953-55; dir. parks and recreation Twp. of Parsippany-Troy Hills, N.J., 1955-62; asst. prof. outdoor and environ. edn. N.J. State Sch. Conservation, Branchville, 1962-71; assoc. prof. edn. Ramapo Coll. N.J., Mahwah, 1972-84, coach archery, 1973-84; adj. prof. Kean Coll. N.J., Union, 1985—; instr. archery, dir. dance and recreation World Archery Ctr., Pomfret, Conn., 1964-92; dir. N.J. State Coll. divsn. Nat. Archery Asns., 1978-84. Advisor to choreographer, cons. prodn. office closing ceremonies Statue of Liberty Centennial Celebration, 1986; rec. artist: Square Dances, 1961, 91, mag. articles, 1954-66; columnist Lines About Squares, 1983—. Instr. dance camp staff Lloyd Shaw Found., 1981—, bd. dirs., 1982-88; bd. trustees Sussex County Sr. Legal Resources Ctr., 1992-94. With U.S. Army, 1943-46, ETO. Recipient Alumni award Panzer Coll. N.J., 1979, Spl. Alumni award, 1987; named to Ramapo Coll. Athletic Hall of Fame, 1993. Mem. AAHPERD (Recreator of Yr. Ea. Dist. 1977), N.J. Alliance Health, Phys. Edn., Recreation and Dance, Callers Coun. N.J., Callerlab, Phi Delta Kappa. Avocations: calling square dances, ballroom dancing, skiing, golf, tennis. Home: 31 Newton Ave Branchville NJ 07826-4203 Office: Kean Coll NJ Phys Edn Dept Union NJ 07083

PATAI, RAPHAEL, former anthropology educator; b. Budapest, Hungary, Nov. 22, 1910; s. Joseph and Edith (Ehrenfeld) P.; children: Jennifer Patai Schneider, Daphne. Ph.D., U. Budapest, 1933, Hebrew U. Jerusalem, 1936. Mem. faculty Hebrew U., 1937-47; dir., founder Palestine Inst. Folklore and Ethnology, 1944-48; prof. anthropology Dropsie Coll., Phila., 1948-57; vis. lectr. Columbia U., 1948, 54-56, 60-61, New Sch. Social Research, 1948; vis. prof. U. Pa., 1948-49, Ohio State U., 1956; lectr. N.Y. U., 1951-53; vis. lectr. Princeton U., 1952-54; dir. research Theodor Herzl Inst., N.Y.C.; editor Herzl Press, 1956-71; prof. anthropology Fairleigh Dickinson U., 1966-76; vis. prof. Judaic studies Bklyn. Coll., 1971-72. Adv. editor Judaism: Ency. Americana, 1959—; author: numerous books, including The Hebrew Goddess, 1967, 2d edit., 1978, 3rd edit., 1990, The Arab Mind, 1973, 83, (with Jennifer Patai) The Myth of the Jewish Race, 1975, 2d. edit., 89, The Jewish Mind, 1977, rev. edit., 1996, The Messiah Texts, 1979, Gates to the Old City, 1980, 81, The Vanished Worlds of Jewry, 1980, On Jewish Folklore, 1983, The Seed of Abraham: Jews and Arabs in Contact and Conflict, 1986, Nahum Goldmann: His Missions to the Gentiles, 1987, Ignaz Goldziher and His Oriental Diary, 1987, Apprentice in Budapest: Memories of a World That Is No More, 1988, Robert Graves and the Hebrew Myths, 1992, Between Budapest and Jerusalem, 1992, Journeyman in Jerusalem, 1992 , The Jewish Alchemists: A History and Source Book, 1994, The Jews of Hungary: History, Culture, Psychology, 1996, Jadid al-Islam: The Jews of Meshhed, 1996; editor: Herzl Yr. Book, 1958-71, Ency. of Zionism and Israel, 1971, Erich Brauer's The Jews of Kurdistan, 1993, (with Emanuel S. Goldsmith) Thinkers and Teachers of Modern Judaism, 1994, (with Goldsmith) Events and Movements in Modern Judaism, 1995; gen. editor Jewish Folklore and Anthropology Series, 1980—. Pres. Am. Friends of Tel Aviv U., 1956-68; dir. Syria-Lebanon-Jordan research project Human Relations Area Files, Inc., New Haven, 1955-56. Home: 39 Bow St Forest Hills NY 11375-5262

PATAKI, ANDREW, bishop; b. Palmerton, Pa., Aug. 30, 1927. Student, St. Vincent Coll., St. Procopious Coll., Lisle, Ill., Sts. Cyril and Methodius, Byzantine Cath. Sem., Grigorian U., Rome. Ordained priest Roman Cath. Ch., 1952. App. aux. bishop of Passaic, N.J. Byzantine Cath. diocese, 1983; bishop of Parma Ohio, 1984—. Home: 8924 Stover Ln Cleveland OH 44141-2033 Office: 1900 Carlton Rd Cleveland OH 44134-3129*

PATAKI, GEORGE E., governor; b. Peekskill, N.Y., June 24, 1945; m. Elizabeth (Libby) Rowland; children: Emily, Teddy, Allison, George Owen. BA, Yale U., 1967; JD, Columbia U. Sch. Law, 1970. Mayor City of Peekskill, Westchester, N.Y., 1982-84; elected mem. State Assembly, N.Y., 1985-92, State Senate, N.Y., 1993—; assoc. Law Firm of Dewey, Ballantine, Bushby, Palmer & Wood, 1970-74; ptnr. Law Firm Plunckett & Jaffe, P.C., N.Y.C., White Plains,, Albany and Peekskill, 1974-89; co-proprietor Pataki Farm, Peekskill, N.Y.; governor State of New York, 1996—. Advanceman Friends of Rockefeller Team, 1970; upstate campaign coord. Com. to Elect Gov. Wilson, 1974; mem. Peekskill Rep. City Com., 1974—, chmn. 1977-83; mem. N.Y. State Rep. Com., 1980-85. Address: Office of the Gov State Capitol Albany NY 12224*

PATAKI-SCHWEIZER, KERRY JOSEF, behavioral scientist, medical anthropologist; b. Peekskill, N.Y., Nov. 1, 1935; s. John Josef and Helen Ida (Schweizer) Pataki; S.B., U. Chgo., 1960; M.A., U. Wash., Seattle, 1965, Ph.D., 1968; m. Lalitha Shirin Harben, Nov. 16, 1973; children: Nicholas Josef, Kiran Sarah, Christopher Halim. Asst. prof. anthropology and humanities Reed Coll., Portland, Oreg., 1967-69; research asso. Inst. Behavioral Sci., vis. lectr. U. Colo., 1970; asst. research anthropologist U. Calif., San Francisco, 1971-73, research asso. dept. epidemiology and internat. health, 1979—; sr. lectr. community medicine U. Papua New Guinea, 1974-82, assoc. prof. behavioral sci. and med. anthropology, 1983—; guest prof. Max-Planck-Institut, Fed. Republic of Germany, 1987-88; cons. WHO, World Bank, USAID, Papua New Guinea Dept. Health. Served with AUS, 1955-56. Woodrow Wilson fellow, 1961; NIMH fellow, 1965-66; recipient French Govt. award for translation, 1960. Fellow Am. Anthrop. Assn., Internat. Coll. Psychosomatic Medicine, Royal Anthrop. Soc., Soc. Applied Athropology, World Assn. Social Psychiatry; mem. Am. Assn. Acad. Psychiatry. Malaysian Soc. Parasitology and Tropical Medicine, Papua New Guinea Med. Soc., Soc. Med. Anthropology, Soc. Psychol. Anthropology. Clubs: S. Pacific Aero, Royal Port Moresby Yacht, PNG Petroleum Club, Aviat Club, Returned Servicemen's League. Author: A New Guinea Landscape: Community, Space and Time of the Eastern Highlands, 1980, The Ethics of Development, 1987; also articles. Home: Box 5623, Boroko Papua New Guinea Office: U Calif Dept Of Epidemiology San Francisco CA 94143

PATARCA, ROBERTO, immunologist, molecular biologist, physician; b. Caracas, Venezuela, Feb. 12, 1958; came to U.S., 1981; s. Umberto Jose and Ivonne Noemi (Montero) P. MS, Ctrl. U. Venezuela, Caracas, 1981; PhD, Harvard U., 1987; MD, U. Miami, 1994. Computer programmer, systems analyst Centro Medico Docente La Trinidad, Caracas, 1978-81; rsch. fellow Mt. Sinai Sch. Medicine and Columbia U., N.Y.C., 1981-82, MIT-NASA Program, Boston, 1982; from rsch. fellow to asst. prof. pathology Harvard Med. Sch., Boston, 1982-90; asst. prof. medicine/immunology/microbiology U. Miami, Fla., Fla., 1994—; sci. dir. E.M. Papper lab. clin. immunology U. Miami, Fla., 1994—; high complexity clin. lab. dir. Am. Bd. Bioanalysts; teaching asst. Ctr. and Met. U., Caracas, 1977-80; lectr. and presenter in field. Co-editor jour. Chronic Fatigue Syndrome and Critical Review in Oncogenesis/Clinical Management of Chronic Fatigue Syndrome, 1994—; contbr. articles to profl. jours. Sub-guide Boy Scouts Am., Caracas, 1971-73; stake missionary Ch. of Jesus Christ of Latter Day Sts., Boston, 1985. Decorated Order of Merit (Venezuela); recipient Licha Lopez award Harvard Med. Sch., 1984, Richard A. Smith Rsch. award Dana-Farber Cancer Inst., 1989, Rsch. Distinction in Immunology U. Miami, 1994; Conicit and Gran Mariscal de Ayacucho Found. scholar, 1976-87, Am. Found. AIDS Rsch. scholar, 1990-93. Mem. AAAS, AMA, Fla. and Dade County Med. Assn., Clin. Immunology Soc., N.Y. Acad. Scis., Peruvian Soc. Immunology and Allergy, Alpha Omega Alpha. Avocations: classical guitar, tap dancing, swimming. Home: 16445 Collins Ave Apt 328 Miami FL 33160-4562 Office: U Miami Sch Medicine PO Box 016960 Miami FL 33138

PATCH, LAUREN NELSON, insurance company, chief executive officer; b. Lexington, Ky., Apr. 14, 1951; s. Nathaniel M. and Gertrude (Lasseter) P.; m. Helen Sloneker, June 30, 1973; children: Henry L., John Stewart. BS, U. Ky., 1973; attended exec. program, U. Mich., 1990. With Ohio Casualty Ins. Co., Hamilton, 1973—, pres., 1991, also bd. dirs., 1987—; pres., CEO Ohio Casualty Corp.; bd. dirs. Ins. Svcs. Office; dir. First Fin. Bancorp. Bd. dirs. Hamilton-Fairfield Arts Coun., 1990—, Dan Beard Coun. Boy Scouts. Mem. Young Pres. Assn. (Cin. chpt.), Wyoming Golf Club (bd. dirs. 1989—). Republican. Episcopalian. Avocations: golf, reading. Office: Ohio Casualty Ins Co 136 N 3rd St Hamilton OH 45025-0002*

PATCHAN, JOSEPH, lawyer; b. Bklyn., June 29, 1922; m. Nancy Joy Letaw, Jan. 7, 1952; children: Reed, Judith, David. B.S., Miami U., Oxford, Ohio, 1943; J.D., Cleve. State U., 1952. Bar: Ohio 1952, D.C. 1977. Pvt. practice law, 1955-69; judge U.S. Bankruptcy Ct., No. Dist. Ohio, 1969-75; ptnr. Baker & Hostetler, Cleve., 1975-91; dep. gen. counsel Resolution Trust Corp., Washington, 1991-94; dir. exec. Office for U.S. Trustees, U.S. Dept. Justice, Washington, 1994—; mem. adj. faculty Cleve. State U. Law Sch., 1959-74; mem. faculty Nat. Bankruptcy Seminar, Fed. Jud. Ctr., Washington, 1971-77; mem. adv. com. bankruptcy rules U.S. Jud. Conf., 1978-91; lectr. bankruptcy law seminars. Author: Practice Comments to Rules of Bankruptcy Procedure, 1973-91; contbr. articles on bankruptcy law to profl. publs. Served with USN, 1943-46. Fellow Am. Coll. Bankruptcy; mem. ABA (rep. nat. conf. lawyers and collection agys., chmn. 1985-88), Ohio Bar Assn., Cleve. Bar Assn. (chmn. bankruptcy and comml. law sect. 1984-86), D.C. Bar Assn., Nat. Conf. Bankruptcy Judges (assoc.), Am. Judicature Soc., Am. Bankruptcy Inst., Army and Navy Club (Washington). Jewish. Office: 901 E St NW # 700 Washington DC 20004-2037

PATE, JACQUELINE HAIL, retired data processing company manager; b. Amarillo, Tex., Apr. 7, 1930; d. Ewen and Virginia Smith (Crosland) Hail; student Southwestern U., Georgetown, Tex., 1947-48; children: Charles (dec.), John Durst, Virginia Pate Edgecomb, Christopher. Exec. sec. Western Gear Corp., Houston, 1974-76; adminstr., treas., dir. Aberrant Behavior Ctr., Personality Profiles, Inc., Corp. Procedures, Inc., Dallas, 1976-79; mgr. regional site svcs programs Digital Equipment Corp., Dallas, 1979-92, ret. 1992; realtor Keller Williams Realty, Austin, Tex., 1996—; mem. Austin Bd. Realtors. Active PTA, Dallas, 1958-73. Mem. Daus. Republic Tex. (treas. French legation state com. 1996). Methodist. Home: 5505-B Buffalo Pass Austin TX 78745

PATE, JAMES LEONARD, oil company executive; b. Mt. Sterling, Ill., Sept. 6, 1935; s. Virgil Leonard and Mammie Elizabeth (Taylor) P.; m. Donna Charlene Pate, Oct. 23, 1955; children: David Charles, Gary Leonard, Jennifer Elizabeth. Prof. econs. Monmouth (Ill.) Coll., 1965-68; sr. economist Fed. Res. Bank Cleve., 1968-72; chief economist B.F. Goodrich Co., Akron, Ohio, 1972-74; asst. sec. Dept. Commerce, Washington, Ohio, 1974-76, spl. adviser to White House, 1976, sr. v.p. fin., 1976; v.p. fin. Pennzoil Co., Houston, Ohio, 1976-89, exec. v.p., 1989, exec. v.p., chief oper. officer, 1990, pres., chief exec. officer, 1990—, also chmn. bd., 1994—. Contbr. articles to profl. jours. and text books. Bd. govs. Rice U.; mem. Senate Monmouth Coll.; bd. dirs. Am. Petroleum Inst., Nat. Petroleum Coun. Fellow Royal Econ. Soc.; mem. Pi Gamma Mu. Republican. Office: Pennzoil Co PO Box 2967 Houston TX 77252-2967*

PATE, JOHN GILLIS, JR., financial consultant, accounting educator; b. Chattanooga, Jan. 27, 1928; s. John Gillis Pate and Iona Estelle (Bowman) Pate Ketchman; m. Daphne Mae Davis, Feb. 8, 1946; children: John Gillis III, Daphne Iona, Donna Gay. Student U. Tampa, 1947-48; AA with highest honors, U. Fla., 1950; BS cum laude, Fla. State U., 1953, MS, 1958; PhD, Columbia U., 1968. Cert. Cost Analyst, cert. Office Automation Profl. Mgr. Grocery Concession, Albany, Ga., 1944-45, Variety Store, Panama City, Fla., 1946-47; asst. to CPA Standard Brands, Inc., Birmingham, Ala., 1951-53, acctg. supervisory trainee, Birmingham, Ala., 1953-54; grad. asst. Fla. State U., Tallahassee, 1957-58; asst. to CPA, Pensacola, Fla., 1956-58; pub. acct., Pensacola, 1958; asst. prof. U. Ga., Athens, 1958-60; lectr. Columbia U., N.Y.C., 1961-64; asst. prof. Bernard M. Baruch Coll. of CUNY, 1963-69; prof. acctg. U. Tex.-El Paso, 1969-85, U. S.C., Spartanburg, 1988-93; cons., resource person Personnel Dept. City of El Paso, 1981-88; cons. resource person finance and human resources Charles Lea Ctr., Spartanburg, 1988—, dir. Internal Audit, 1994—. Co-author: Accounting Trends and Techniques, 1967-88; Author: Index C.P.A. Exams and Unofficial Answers, 1974-81, Index to Accounting and Auditing Services, 1971; contbr. articles to ann. profl. publs. Tither, Coronado Bapt. Ch., El Paso, 1969-86, Buck Creek Bapt. Ch., Spartanburg, 1987—; cons. Alderman of El Paso, 1982, County Councilman of Spartanburg, 1991—. Served as lt. j.g. USN, 1955-56. Columbia U. fellow, 1960; Earhart Found. fellow, 1960; Am. Acctg. Assn. fellow, 1960; recipient Haskins and Sells award, 1960; Ford Found. fellow, 1961-62. Mem. AICPAs (cons.), Am. Acctg. Assn., Inst. Cost Analysis, Office Automation Soc. Internat., Beta Alpha Psi, Beta Alpha Chi. Republican. Club: Sertoma. Lodges: Moose, Masons, Shriners. Home and Office: 106 Lori Cir Spartanburg SC 29303-5527

PATE, MICHAEL LYNN, lawyer; b. Ft. Worth, Tex., July 9, 1951; s. J.B. and Mary Anna (Hable) P.; m. Barbara Ann Linch, May 28, 1977. AA, Schreiner Coll., 1971; BS, Tex. Wesleyan Coll., 1973; JD, U. Tex., 1975. Bar: Tex. 1976, D.C. 1983, U.S. Tax Ct. 1986, U.S. Supreme Ct. 1987. Adminstrv. asst. to Senator Sherman, counsel natural resources com. Tex. Senate, 1976-77; adminstrv. asst. to Lt. Gov. Bill Hobby, Austin, Tex., 1977-79; legis. asst. Senator Bentsen, Washington, 1979-81, legis. dir., 1981-86; ptnr. Bracewell & Patterson, Washington, 1986—. Mem. ABA, Tex. Bar Assn., D.C. Bar Assn. Democrat. Methodist. Avocations: basketball, tennis, golf. Office: Bracewell & Patterson 2000 K St NW Ste 500 Washington DC 20006-1809

PATE, PAUL DANNY, state senator, business executive, entrepreneur; b. Ottumwa, Iowa, May 1, 1958; s. Paul Devern and Velma Marie (McConnell) P.; m. Jane Ann Wacker, July 15, 1978; children: Jennifer Ann, Paul Daniel III, Amber Lynn. AA in Bus., Kirkwood Coll., 1978; grad. in fin. mgmt., U. Pa., 1990. Exec. dir. Jr. Achievement, Cedar Rapids, Iowa, 1978-82; pres. PM Systems Corp., Cedar Rapids, 1982—; pres., pub. DAVCO Inc., Cedar Rapids, 1985—; senator Iowa State Senate, Des Moines, 1989—; Sec. of State State of Iowa. Chmn. Iowa Young Reps., Des Moines, 1989—, Rep. Senate Campaign Com., 1990; co-chmn. Young Rep. Nat. Platform Com., Miami, Fla., 1991; bd. dirs. Iowa Right to Work Com., Linn County Hist. Soc. Recipient Guardian Small Bus. award Nat. Fedn. Independent Bus., 1990; named Young Entrepreneur of Yr. U.S. Small Bus. Adminstrn., Iowa, 1988, Alumnus of Yr. Kirkwood Coll., Cedar Rapids, 1990. Methodist. Avocations: private pilot, water skiing. Home: 2670 27th Ave Marion IA 52302-1240 Office: Off of State Senate Capitol Bldg Des Moines IA 50319*

PATE, ROBERT HEWITT, JR., counselor educator; b. Abingdon, Va., Apr. 5, 1938; s. Robert Hewitt and Esther Frances (Kirk) P.; m. Ellen O'Neal Pope, Dec. 11, 1960; children: Robert Hewitt III, Mary Ellen Pate Barton. AB, Davidson Coll., 1960; MEd, U. Va., 1965; PhD, U. N.C., 1968. Lic. prof. counselor, Va. Marketer Sinclair Refining Co., Abingdon, Va., 1960-61, 63-64; counselor St. Andrews Presbyn. Coll., Laurinburg, N.C., 1965-66; prof. counselor edn. U. Va., Charlottesville, 1968—, interim dean, 1994-95, sr. assoc. dean, 1995—; mem. adj. faculty Fed. Exec. Inst., Charlottesville, 1978—. Author: Being A Counselor, 1983. Elder local Presbyn. ch. 1st lt. U.S. Army 1961-63. Mem. Am. Counseling Assn., Va. Counselors Assn. (pres. 1983-84), Nat. Bd. Cert. Counselors (chair-elect, chair 1996-97). Avocation: reading. Home: 836 Flordon Dr Charlottesville VA 22901-7810 Office: U Va Ruffner Hall 405 Emmet St S Charlottesville VA 22903-2424

PATÉ-CORNELL, MARIE-ELISABETH LUCIENNE, industrial engineering educator; b. Dakar, Sènègal, Aug. 17, 1948; came to U.S., 1971; d. Edouard Pierre Lucien and Madeleine (Tournissa) Paté; m. C. Allin Cornell, Jan. 3, 1981; children: Phillip, Ariane. Eng. Degree, Inst. Polytechnique de Grenoble (France), 1971; MS in Ops. Rsch., Stanford U., 1972, PhD in Engring.-Econ. Systems, 1978. Asst. prof. in civil engring. MIT, 1978-81; asst. prof. indsl. engring. Stanford (Calif.) U., 1981-84, assoc. prof. indsl. engring., 1984-91, prof. indsl. engring., 1991—; cons. U.S. Water Resource Coun., 1979, EPA, 1980, Electric Power Rsch. Inst., 1985, WHO, 1988, Shell Oil, 1990, Texaco, 1991. Contbr. numerous articles to profl. jours. Numerous rsch. grants. Mem. Soc. for Risk Analysis (councilor 1985-86, pres. 1995), Ops. Rsch. Soc. Am., Inst. for Mgmt. Scis., Nat. Acad. Engring. Avocations: tennis, swimming, chess, music. Home: 110 Coquito Way Menlo Park CA 94028-7404 Office: Stanford U Dept Indsl Engring Stanford CA 94305

PATEL, CHANDRA KUMAR NARANBHAI, communications company executive, educator, researcher; b. Baramati, India, July 2, 1938; came to U.S., 1958, naturalized, 1970; s. Naranbhai Chaturbhai and Maniben P.; m. Shela Dixit, Aug. 20, 1961; children: Neela, Meena. B.Engring., Poona U., 1958; M.S., Stanford U., 1959, Ph.D., 1961. Mem. tech. staff Bell Telephone Labs., Murray Hill, N.J., 1961-93, head infrared physics and electronics rsch. dept., 1967-70, dir. electronics rsch. dept., 1970-76, dir. phys. rsch. lab., 1976-81, exec. dir. rsch. physics and acad. affairs div., 1981-87, exec. dir. rsch., materials sci., engring. and acad. affairs div., 1987-93; trustee Aerospace Corp., L.A., 1979-88; vice chancellor rsch. UCLA, 1993—; mem. governing bd. NRC, 1990-91; bd. dirs. Newport Corp., Fountain Valley, Calif., Cal Micro Devices Corp., Milpitas, Calif., Accuware Corp., Santa Monica, Calif., chmn. bd. Contbr. articles to tech. jours. Chmn. Calif. Biomed. Found., 1994—; mem. exec. bd. Calif. Healthcare Inst., 1995—. Recipient Gallantine medal Franklin Inst., 1968, Coblentz award Am. Chem. Soc., 1974, Honor award Assn. Indians in Am., 1975, Founders prize Tex. Instruments Found., 1978, award N.Y. sect. Soc. Applied Spectroscopy, 1982, Schawlow medal Laser Inst. Am., 1984, Thomas Alva Edison Sci. award N.J. Gov., 1987, William T. Ennor Mfg. Tech. award ASME, 1995; William T. Ennor Manufacturing Technology awd Am. Soc. of Mechanical Engineers, 1995. Fellow AAAS, IEEE (Lamme medal 1976, medal of honor 1989), Am. Acad. Arts and Scis., Am. Phys. Soc. (coun. 1987-91, exec. com. 1987-90, George E. Pake prize 1988, pres. 1995—), Optical Soc. Am. (Adolph Lomb medal 1966, Townes medal 1982, Ives medal 1989), Indian Nat. Sci. Acad. (fng.); mem. NAS (coun. 1988-91, exec. com. 1989-91), NAE (Zworykin award 1976), Gynecol. Laser Surgery Soc. (hon.), Am. Soc. for Laser Medicine and Surgery (hon.), Third World Acad. Scis. (assoc.), Calif. Biomed. Found. (pres. 1994—), Calif. Healthcare Inst. (exec. com. 1995—), Sigma Xi (pres. 1994—). Home: 1171 Roberto Ln Los Angeles CA 90077-2302 Office: UCLA Vice Chancellor Rsch PO Box 951405 Los Angeles CA 90095-1415

PATEL, HOMI BURJOR, apparel company executive; b. Bombay, June 28, 1949; s. Burjor Ratan and Roshen Burjor (Marfatia) P.; married; children: Neville H., Cyrus H., Natasha E. BS in Stats., U. Bombay, 1973; MBA in Fin. and Mktg., Columbia U., 1975. Exec. asst. to pres. Corbin Ltd., N.Y.C., 1976, dir. mktg., 1978; with subs. Hartmarx Corp., Chgo., 1979—; v.p., gen. mgr. Fashionaire Apparel Inc., Chgo., 1979-81; exec. v.p. Austin Reed of Regent St., Chgo., 1981-82, M. Wile and Co., Buffalo, 1982-84; pres., chief exec. officer M. Wile & Co., Johnny Carson Apparel, Intercontinental Apparel, Buffalo, 1984—; group exec. v.p. Hartmarx Mens Apparel Group Corp., Buffalo, 1987-91; chmn., ceo Hartmarx Mens Apparel Group Corp., Chgo., 1991-92; pres., COO Hartmarx Corp., Chgo., 1992—; bd. dirs., 1994—. Mem. Clothing Mfrs. Assn. Am. (bd. dirs. 1984—, chmn. mills rels. com. 1986—, exec. v.p. 1989—, pres. 1991, chief labor negotiator for U.S. tailored clothing industry), Univ. Club N.Y., Chgo. Club. Office: Hartmarx Corp 101 N Wacker Dr Fl 23 Chicago IL 60606-1718

PATEL, JASMIN RAMBHAI, medicinal chemist, consultant, researcher; b. Nadiad, India, Apr. 25, 1964; came to U.S., 1984; s. Rambhai G. and Smruti R. Patel; m. Rena Patel, Nov. 10, 1988. B in Pharm. with hons., Bombay U., India, 1984; PhD, Duquesne U., 1991. PPG post doctoral fellow The Scripps Rsch. Inst., La Jolla, Calif., 1990-92; rsch. scientist Gen-Probe, Inc., San Diego, 1992-95; sr. rsch. scientist Chugai Biopharmaceuticals, Inc., San Diego, 1995—; pres. Soc. of Fellows Scripps Rsch. Inst., La Jolla, Calif., 1991-92; cons. Am. Inst. Biol. Scis., Washington, 1994—. Author: (book chpt.) Chemistry and Biology of Pteridines, 1990; contbr. articles to profl. jours. including Internat. Jour. Cancer, Anticancer Rsch., Cancer Jour., Jour. Medicinal Chemistry. Recipient Bombay U. Gold medal, 1984, G.P. Nair award Indian Drug Mfrs. Assn., 1984, J.N. Tata scholarship J.N. Tata Endowment; Nat. Merit scholar Indian Ministry Edn. and Culture. Mem. Am. Chem. Soc. (chair publicity com. We. region 1995), Am. Assn. Pharm. Scientists, Am. Assn. Cancer Rsch., Rho Chi. Achievements include 4 filed U.S. Patent Applications; first synthesis of 5, 10-methylene-tetrahydro-5-deaza folate. Home: 10030 Scripps Vista Way San Diego CA 92131 Office: Chugai Biopharmaceuticals 6275 Nancy Ridge Dr San Diego CA 92121

PATEL, MARILYN HALL, federal judge; b. Amsterdam, N.Y., Sept. 2, 1938; d. Lloyd Manning and Nina J. (Thorpe) Hall; m. Magan C. Patel, Sept. 2, 1966; children: Brian, Gian. B.A., Wheaton Coll., 1959; J.D., Fordham U., 1963. Bar: N.Y. 1963, Calif. 1970. Mng. atty. Benson & Morris, Esq., N.Y.C., 1962-64; sole practice N.Y.C., 1964-67; atty. U.S. Immigration and Naturalization Svc., San Francisco, 1967-71; sole practive San Francisco, 1971-76; judge Alameda County Mcpl. Ct., Oakland, Calif., 1976-80, U.S. Dist. Ct. (no. dist.) Calif., San Francisco, 1980—; adj. prof. law Hastings Coll. of Law, San Francisco, 1974-76. Author: Immigration and Nationality Law, 1974; also numerous articles. Mem. bd. visitors Fordham U. Sch. Law. Mem. ABA (litigation sect., jud. adminstrn. sect.), ACLU (former bd. dirs.), NOW (former bd. dirs.), Am. law Inst., Am. Judicature Soc. (bd. dirs.), Calif Conf. Judges, Nat. Assn. Women Judges (founding mem.), Internat. Inst. (bd. dirs.), Advs. for Women (co-founder), Assn. Bus. Trial Lawyers (bd. dirs.). Democrat. Avocations: piano playing; travel. Office: US Dist Ct PO Box 36060 450 Golden Gate Ave San Francisco CA 94102

PATEL, MUKUND RANCHHODLAL, electrical engineer, researcher; b. Bavla, India, Apr. 21, 1942; came to U.S., 1966; s. Ranchhodlal N. and Shakariben M. Patel; m. Sarla Shantilal, Nov. 4, 1967; children: Ketan, Bina, Vijal. BEng, Sardar U., Vidyanagar, India; MEng with honors, Gujarat U., Ahmedabad, India; PhD in Engring., Rensselaer Poly. Inst., 1972. Registered profl. engr., Pa.; chartered mech. engr., U.K. Lectr. elec. engring. Sardar U., Vidyanagar, India, 1965-66; sr. devel. engr. GE, Pittsfield, Mass., 1967-76; mgr. R & D, Bharat Bijlee (Siemens) Ltd., Bombay, 1976-80; fellow engr. Westinghouse R & D Ctr., Churchill, Pa., 1980-84, mem. senate, 1982-84; pres. Induction Gen., Inc., Pitts., 1984-86; prin. engr. rsch. and devel. Space Divsn. GE, Princeton, Pa., 1986—; cons. Nat. Productivity Coun., New Delhi, 1976-80. Assoc. editor IEEE Insulation Mag.; contbr. articles to nat. and internat. profl. jours. Fellow Instn. Mech. Engrs.; mem. IEEE (sr.), Am. Soc. Sci. Rsch. (hon., nat. com. on electric power engring. edn.), Elfun Soc. Vols., Tau Beta Pi, Eta Kappa Nu, Omega Rho. Achievements include patents and invention awards on electromechanical design of superconducting generators; NASA award for research on space power systems; international authority in the area of electromechanical design of large power transformers. Home: 1199 Cobblestone Ct Yardley PA 19067-4751 Office: GE Astro Space PO Box 800 Princeton NJ 08543-0800

PATEL, MULCHAND SHAMBHUBHAI, biochemist, researcher; b. Sipor, India, Sept. 9, 1939; came to U.S., 1965; s. Shambhubhai J. and Puriben (Patel) P.; m. Kankuben M. Patel; children: Sumitra, Yashomati, Mayank. BS, Gujarat U., 1961; MS, U. Baroda, 1964; PhD, U. Ill., 1968. Asst. prof. pediatric rsch. Sch. Medicine Temple U., Phila., 1970-72, rsch. asst. prof. medicine, 1972-75, rsch. asst. prof. biochemistry, 1970-75, rsch. assoc. prof. biochem. medicine, 1975-78; assoc. prof. biochemistry Case Western Res. U. Sch. Medicine, Cleve., 1978-86, prof., 1986-93; prof., chmn. biochemistry SUNY, Buffalo, 1993—; mem. NIH biochem. study sect. 2, 1984-88; mem. editl. bd. Jour. Biol. Chem., 1991—. Author, co-author research articles. Recipient Gold Medal in Biochemistry, U. Baroda, 1973, Fulbright Research Scholar award to India, 1987; prin. investigator, research grantee NIH. Mem. Am. Soc. for Biochemistry and Molecular Biology, Am. Inst. Nutrition, Biochem. Soc. London, Am. Soc. Neurochemists, Internat. Soc. Neurochemistry. Office: SUNY-Dept Biochemistry Sch Medicine 140 Farber Hall 3435 Main St Buffalo NY 14214

PATEL, RAMANLAL L., engineering executive; b. Gujarat, India, Nov. 12, 1945; came to U.S., 1966; s. L.V. and J.L. Patel; m. Manju Patel; children: Prakash, Amit. BS, Gujarat U., 1966; BSME, U. Toledo, 1969, MBA, 1976. With Bendix Corp., 1969-81; exec. v.p. ops. Bendix-Toledo Stamping (Allied-Signal Corp.), Toledo, 1982-85; pres. Andrews Corp. (The Henley Group), Spartanburg, S.C., 1985-88, Johnson Filtration Sys. Inc. divsn. Wheelabrator, St. Paul, 1988-91; group pres. Wheelabrator Clean Water Group, 1990-91; pres., CEO Wheelabrator Engineered Sys. Inc., St. Paul, 1991—. Author: Automation, 1982; patentee for intake-exhaust rocker arm design-function, others. Mem. steering com. Soc. Automotive Engrs., 1976-78. Office: Wheelabrator Water Tech Inc 3003 Butterfield Rd Oak Brook IL 60521

PATEL, RONALD ANTHONY, newspaper editor; b. Detroit, Oct. 7, 1947; s. Chhotalal Ukabhai and Joan (Kaczynski) P.; m. Jane Elizabeth Douglas-Willan, Sept. 5, 1974; 1 child, Wendy Elizabeth; m. Susan Florence Winters, Nov. 16, 1982. Student, Wayne State U., 1965-69. Asst. city editor Royal Oak (Mich.) Daily Tribune, 1967-69; rewriteman, copyeditor Detroit News, 1969-70; asst. news editor Newsday, Garden City, N.Y., 1970-73; news editor Phila. Inquirer, 1973-80, asst. mng. editor, 1980-86, assoc. mng. editor for features, 1986-95, Sunday editor, 1995—. Contbr. to Elements of Newspaper Design (Steven Ames), 1989, Your Career in the Comics (Andrews and McNeal), 1995. Mem. Am. Assn. Sunday and Feature Editors (sec. 1979, pres. 1982), Newspaper Features Coun. (bd. dirs. 1990, meeting chmn. 1991, sec.-treas. 1992, pres. 1993-95), Pen and Pencil Club (pres. 1990—), Sigma Delta Chi. Office: Phila Inquirer 400 N Broad St Philadelphia PA 19130-4015

PATEL, VIRENDRA CHATURBHAI, mechanical engineering educator; b. Mombasa, Kenya, Nov. 9, 1938; came to U.S., 1969, naturalized, 1975; s. Chaturbhai S. and Kantaben N. (Rai) P.; m. Manjula Patel, May 29, 1966; children: Sanjay, Bindiya. BSc with honors, Imperial Coll., London, 1962; PhD, Cambridge (Eng.) U., 1965; Doctor honoris causa, Tech. U. Civil

Engring., Bucharest, Romania, 1994. Sr. asst. in research Cambridge U., 1965-69; vis. prof. Indian Inst. Tech., Kharagpur, 1966; cons. Lockheed Ga. Co., Marietta, 1969-70; mem. faculty U. Iowa, Iowa City, 1971—; prof. mech. engring. U. Iowa, 1975—, chmn. div., 1976-82, chmn. mech. engring., 1978-82, U. Iowa Found. Disting. prof., 1990—; research engr. Iowa Inst. Hydraulic Research, 1971—, dir., 1994—; mem. Iowa Gov. Sci. Advisory Council, 1977-83; mem. resistance com. Internat. Towing Tank Conf., 1978-87; vis. prof. U. Karlsruhe, W. Ger., 1980-81, Ecole Nationale Superieure de Mechanique, Nantes, France, 1984; jubilee prof. Chalmers Inst. Tech., Goteborg, Sweden, 1988; cons. in field. Author: Three Dimensional Turbulent Boundary Layers, 1972, also articles; assoc. editor AIAA Jour., 1987-90. Recipient Sr. Scientist award Alexander von Humboldt Found., 1980, 93. Fellow ASME, AIAA (assoc.); mem. Am. Soc. Engring. Edn., Soc. Naval Archtl. Marine Engrs., Sigma Xi., Pi Tau Sigma. Home: 1212 Teg Dr Iowa City IA 52246-4622 Office: Inst Hydraulic Research U Iowa 404 Hydraulics Lab Iowa City IA 52242-1585

PATELL, MAHESH, pharmacist, researcher; b. Ahmedabad, Gujarat, India, June 14, 1937; came to U.S., 1962.; s. Kantilal K. and Maniben K. Patell; m. Rajeshvari S. Amin, Sept. 6, 1967; children: Milan, Rupel. BS in Pharmacy, L.M. Coll. of Pharmacy, Ahmedabad, 1960; MS in Pharmacy, St Louis Coll., 1964. Rsch. pharmacist Rexall Drug Co., St. Louis, 1968-74; mgr. tech. info. svcs. Cord Labs., Bloomfield, Colo., 1974-77; rsch. investigator K.V. Pharms., St. Louis, 1977-79; section head-health care product devel. Bristol Myers-Squibb, Hillside, N.J., 1979—. Mem. Am. Assn. Pharmaceutical Scientists, Controlled Release Soc., Pa. Mfg. Confectioners Assn. Hindu. Achievements include patents for enteric coated tablet and process of making, uniquely designed capsule shaped tablets, taste masking pharmaceutical agents. Home: 4 Farrington St Edison NJ 08820-1921 Office: Bristol Myers Squibb 1350 Liberty Ave Hillside NJ 07205-1805

PATENT, DOROTHY HINSHAW, author, photographer; b. Rochester, Minn., Apr. 30, 1940; d. Horton Corwin and Dorothy Kate (Youmans) Hinshaw; m. Gregory Joseph Patent, Mar. 21, 1964; children: David Gregory, Jason Daniel. BS, Stanford U., 1962; MA, U. Calif., Berkeley, 1965, PhD, 1968; postgrad., U. Wash., 1965-67. Postdoctoral fellow Sinai Hosp., Detroit, 1968-69, Stazione Zoologica, Naples, Italy, 1969-70; acting asst. prof. U. Mont., Missoula, 1977. Author: Buffalo: The American Bison Today, 1986, The Way of the Grizzly, 1987, Christmas Trees, 1987 (Jr. Lit. Guild selection 1987), Wheat, The Golden Harvest, 1987, The Whooping Crane: A Comeback Story, 1988, Babies!, 1988, A Horse of a Different Color, 1988, Looking at Dolphins and Porpoises, 1989, Where the Wild Horses Roam, 1989, How Smart Are Animals?, Places of Refuge, 1992, Feathers, 1992, Nutrition: What's in the Food We Eat?, 1992, Dogs: The Wolf Within, 1993, Horses: Understanding Animal Behavior, 1994, What Good is a Tail?, 1994, Deer and Elk, 1994, Alligators, 1994, The Vanishing Feast, 1994, Return of the Wolf, 1995, West by Covered Wagon, 1995, Biodiversity, 1996, Children Save the Rain Forest, 1996, Prairies, 1996, Quetzel: Sacred Bird of the Cloud Forest, 1996, others. Recipient Eva L. Gordon award Am. Nature Study Soc., 1986. Mem. Am. Inst. Biol. Scis., Soc. Children's Book Writers and Illustrators, Authors Guild. Avocations: gardening, racquetball, travel.

PATERNO, JOSEPH VINCENT, college football coach; b. Bklyn., Dec. 21, 1926; s. Angelo Lafayette and Florence (de LaSalle) P.; m. Suzanne Pohland, May 12, 1962; children: Diana Lynne, Mary Kathryn, David, Joseph Vincent, George Scott. B.A., Brown U., 1950, LL.D., 1975. Asst. football coach Pa. State U., 1950-66, head football coach, 1966—. Author (with Bernard Asbell): The Paterno Principle, 1989; Paterno: By the Book, 1989. Served with AUS, 1945-46. Named Coach of Yr. Walter Camp Football Found., 1972, Coach of Yr. Washington Touchdown Club, 1973, 86, Coach of Yr. Football Writers Assn. Am., 1978, 82, 86; coached Nat. Collegiate Champions, 1982, 86, Named Sports Illustrated's 1986 Sportsman of the Yr. Mem. Am. Football Coaches Assn. (dir., Coach of Yr. awards 1968, 78, 82, 86). Ranked 4th in All-Time Divsn. IA Coaching Victories, 1st among active coaches. Office: Pa State U Dept Athletics University Park PA 16802*

PATERSON, BASIL ALEXANDER, lawyer; b. N.Y.C., Apr. 27, 1926; s. Leonard J. and Evangeline (Rondon) P.; m. Portia Hairston, 1953; children: Daniel, David. BS, St. John's Coll., 1948; JD, St. John's U., 1951. Bar: N.Y. 1952. Ptnr. Paterson, Michael, Jones and Cherot, N.Y.C., 1956-77, Meyer, Suozzi, English & Klein, P.C., Mineola, N.Y., 1983—; mem. N.Y. State Senate, 1965-70; dep. mayor for labor rels. City of N.Y., 1978; sec. of state State of N.Y., 1979-82; pres. Inst. Mediation and Conflict Resolution, 1971-77; chmn. 2d Jud. Screening Com., 1985-95; assoc. chmn. N.Y. State Sentencing Guidelines Com.; commr. Port Authority N.Y. and N.J., 1989-95. vice chmn. Dem. Nat. Com., 1972-78, mem., 1972-78. Recipient Eagleton Inst. Politics award, Disting. Svc. award Guardians Assn. N.Y. Police Dept., City Club N.Y. award, Black Expo award, Excellence medal St. John's U., Kibbe award CUNY. Roman Catholic. Office: Meyer Suozzi English & Klein PC 1505 Kellum Pl Mineola NY 11501-4811

PATERSON, KATHERINE WOMELDORF, writer; b. Qing Jiang, China, Oct. 31, 1932; came to U.S., 1940; d. George Raymond and Mary Elizabeth (Goetchius) Womeldorf; m. John Barstow Paterson, July 14, 1962; children: Elizabeth Polin, John Barstow, David Lord, Mary Katherine Nah-he-sah-pe-che-a. A.B., King Coll., Bristol, Tenn., 1954, Litt.D. (hon.), 1978; M.A., Presbyn. Sch. Christian Edn., 1957; postgrad., Kobe Sch. of Japanese Lang., 1957-60, Union Theol. Sem., 1961-62; M.R.E., Union Theol. Sem., 1962; hon. degree, Otterbein Coll., U. Md., St. Mary's of the Woods, Shenandoah Coll., Washington and Lee U., Norwich U., Mount St. Vincent U., Halifax, N.S., Can. Tchr. Lovettsville (Va.) Elementary Sch., 1954-55; missionary Presbyn. Ch., Japan, 1957-61; master sacred studies and English Pennington (N.J.) Sch. for Boys, 1963-65. Author: The Sign of the Chrysanthemum, 1973, Of Nightingales That Weep, 1974, The Master Puppeteer, 1976, Bridge to Terabithia, 1977, The Great Gilly Hopkins, 1978, Angels and Other Strangers, 1979, Jacob Have I Loved, 1980, Rebels of the Heavenly Kingdom, 1983, Come Sing, Jimmy Jo, 1985, (with John Paterson) Consider the Lilies, 1986, Park's Quest, 1988, The Tale of the Mandarin Ducks, 1990, The Smallest Cow in the World, 1991, Lyddie, 1991, The King's Equal, 1992, Who Am I?, 1992, Flip-Flop Girl, 1994, A Midnight Clear: Stories for the Christmas Season, 1995, A Sense of Wonder, 1995, The Angel and the Donkey, 1996, Jip: His Story, 1996; translator: The Crane Wife, 1981, The Tongue-Cut Sparrow, 1987. U.S. nominee for Hans Christian Andersen award, 1979, 89; recipient Nat. Book award, 1977, 79, Newbery medal, 1978, 91, Newbery honor, 1979, New Eng. Book award New Eng. Booksellers Assn., 1982, Union medal Union Theol. Sem., 1992. Mem. Authors Guild, PEN, Children's Book Guild Washington. Democrat. Office: Lodestar/Dutton 375 Hudson St New York NY 10014-3658

PATERSON, RICHARD DENIS, financial executive; b. Ottawa, Ont., Can., Oct. 13, 1942; m. Antoinette Paterson; children: Christopher, Russell, Kathlyn, Victoria, Connor. B in Commerce, Concordia U., Montreal, Que., Can., 1964. Auditor Coopers & Lybrand, Montreal, 1964-67; acct. Genstar Corp., Montreal, 1967-69; dir. fin. and adminstrn. Indussa Corp. (subs. Genstar Corp.), N.Y.C., 1969-73; v.p., comptroller Genstar Corp., Montreal and San Francisco, 1973-83; sr. v.p., CFO Genstar Corp., San Francisco, 1983-87; exec. v.p. Genstar Investment Corp., San Francisco, 1987-95; mng. dir. Genstar Capital LLC, Foster City, 1996—; bd. dirs. Gentek Bldg. Products, Inc.; chmn. bd. dirs. Prestolite Electric Inc., Andros Inc.; chmn., bd. dirs. Seaspan Internat. Ltd. Mem. Order Chartered Accts. Que. Office: Genstar Investment Corp Metro Tower Ste 1170 950 Tower Ln Foster City CA 94404-2121

PATERSON, ROBERT E., trading stamp company executive; b. Kearny, N.J., Nov. 30, 1926; s. Robert McKinley and Ethel (Brookes) P.; m. Eileen Josephine Connolly; children: Carol, Joan, Robert, Richard, Donald, Jeffrey. MBA, Columbia U., 1971. Cert. fin. planner. Sr. v.p. fin., treas. The Sperry & Hutchinson Co., Inc., N.Y.C., 1952-87, also bd. dirs.; mem. Nat. Assn. Accts., 1954-89, nat. treas., 1985-88; bd. dirs. Govt. Obligations Fund, 1986-87. Elected mem. Borough Coun., 1991—, coun. pres., 1995-96. Served with U.S. Army, 1944-45, PTO.

PATHAK, SUNIT RAWLY, business owner, consultant, journalist; b. Calcutta, India, Feb. 14, 1953; came to U.S., 1973.; s. Santosh K. and Bira (Laharry) P.; m. Koruna Dutt; 1 child, Adrit. BA, Calcutta U., 1972; BBA, U. Ga., 1975; MBA, U. Ark., 1978. Sr. analyst Norton-Christensen, Oklahoma City, 1981-84; bus. cons. Cactus Feeders, Inc., Dumas, Tex., 1984-85; analyst, controller Grindwell-Norton, Calcutta, 1985-87; prin. Tech. Venture Cons., Inc., Amarillo, Tex., 1985-93, Venture Mktg. Cons., Inc., Santa Barbara, Calif., 1985—; journalist Morris Communications, Amarillo, 1987-92; ptnr. Internat. Mktg. Inc./Venture Mktg. Cons., Inc., Amarillo, 1989-93; assoc. N.W. Environ. Tng. Inst., Amarillo, 1992-93; mng. editor Claude (Tex.) News, 1992-93; adj. faculty econs. Allan Hancock Coll., Santa Maria, Calif.; assoc. Dameron Petroleum, Midland, Tex., Cease Fire, Inc., Southfield, Mich., Tech. Spray, Amarillo, Tex., Eco-Adventures, USA, Santa Maria, Willcorp Industries, Oxnard, Calif. Fundraiser United Way, Oklahoma City, 1983; patron Nitish Laharry Children's Libr., Calcutta, 1984—. Recipient English Lit. prize Brit. Coun., 1969; Rotary Dist. 690 scholar, 1973. Mem. Inst. Mgmt. Accts. (v.p. membership Amarillo chpt. 1989-90), Meeting Planners Internat., Tex. Press Assn., Santa Barbara C. of C., Petroleum Club (Bakersfield, Calif.), Calcutta Cricket Club, Indian Polo Assn., Dalhart Country Club, Calcutta Club, Santa Barbara Polo & Racquet Club. Hindu. Avocations: polo, tennis, international air travel. Office: Tech Venture Cons Inc PO Box 744 Port Hueneme CA 93044-0744

PATILLO, SYLVIA JANE, human resources executive, educator; b. Kansas City, Mo., Nov. 15, 1946; d. John W. and Lola Mae (Williams) Jamierson; divorced; children: Rochelle D. Brown, Jason L. Patillo. AA, Penn. Valley Community Coll., Kansas City, 1981; BS, Park Coll., 1988; MA, Ottawa U., 1992. Computer operator Interstate Brands Corp., Kansas City, 1976-85, sec., 1986-88, personnel asst., 1988-89; employment specialist Gov. Employees Hosp. Assn., Independence, Mo., 1989—. Recording sec. Nat. Black MBA Assn., Kansas City, 1993—; vol. Urban League of Kansas City, 1986—; bd. dirs. Rose Brooks Ctr. Shelter for Women, Kansas City, 1987-90. Recipient scholarship Am. Bus. Womens Assn., 1987, 88. Mem. Soc. Human Resource Mgrs. Office: Van Kampen Am Capital 7501 NW Tiffany Springs Pky Kansas City MO 64153-1386

PATINKIN, MANDY, actor; b. Chgo., Nov. 30, 1952; s. Lester and Doris (Sinton) P.; m. Kathryn Grody, June 15, 1980. Student, U. Kans., 1970-72, Juilliard Sch. Drama, 1972-74. Actor N.Y. Shakespeare Festival, 1975-81; plays include Hotspur in Henry IV, Part 1, Hudson Guild, N.Y.C., Rebel Women, Hamlet, Leave it to Beaver is Dead, Savages; (Broadway) Evita (Tony award 1980), Shadow Box, Sunday in the Park with George, 1984, The Knife, 1987, The Winter's Tale, 1989, Mandy Patinkin in Concert: Dress Casual, 1989, The Secret Garden, 1991; films include The Big Fix, 1979, Ragtime, 1981, Yentl, 1983, Daniel, 1983, French Postcards, 1979, The Last Embrace, 1979, Night of the Juggler, Maxie, 1985, The Princess Bride, 1987, The House on Carroll Street, 1988, Alien Nation, 1988, Dick Tracy, 1990, The Doctor, 1991, True Colors, 1991, The Music of Chance, 1993, Life with Mikey, 1993, Indian Warrior, 1994; TV appearances include That Thing on ABC, That Second Thing on ABC, Taxi, Midnight Special, (series) Chicago Hope, 1994-95 (Emmy award, 1995); albums: Mandy Patinkin, 1989, Mr. Arthur's Place, Experiment, 1994. Recipient Music Achievement award Drama League, 1989. Mem. AFTRA, Screen Actors Guild, Actors Equity Assn.

PATINO, DOUGLAS XAVIER, foundation and university administrator; b. Calexico, Calif., Apr. 11, 1939; s. Jose Luis and Maria Teresa (Seymour) P.; m. Barbel Wilma Hoyer, Aug. 13, 1970; 1 child, Viktor Xavier. AA, Imperial Valley Coll., 1960; BA, Calif. State U., San Diego, 1962, MA, 1966; PhD, U.S. Internat. U., 1972. Deputy dir. Sacramento (Calif.) Concilio, Inc., 1968-69; v.p. student affairs U. So. Colo., Pueblo, 1973-75; dep. dir. for planning and rev. svc. br. to dir. Calif. Employment Devel. Dept., dir.; sec. Calif. Health & Welfare Agy., 1975-83; dir. Ariz. Dept. of Econ. Security, Phoenix, 1983-87; pres., chief exec. officer Marin Community Found., Larkspur, Calif., 1987-91; pres. New Partnership Found. and Patino Group, San Rafael, Calif., 1991-93; vice chancellor Calif. State U., Long Beach, 1993—; commr. Wm. T. Grand Found., 1986-88, Enterprize for the Ams., Washington, 1994—; trustee C.S. Mott Found., Flint, Mich., 1995—. Mem. Sec. of U.S. Dept. of Labor Task Force, Ariz., 1985-86, Staff Adv. Com. of the Human Resource Com., Nat. Gov. Assn., Washington, 1983-86; bd. dirs. Calif. Leadershp, Santa Cruz, Calif., 1985-95, No. Calif. Grantmakers, 1990-91, Ariz. Assn. Bus., 1984; chair U.S. Savs. Bond Dr. for State of Calif., 1982; trustee Nat. Hispanic U., Oakland, Calif., 1987-90, Hispanic Community Fund, San Francisco, 1989-95, C.S. Mott Found., 1995—; bd. dirs. Calif. Sch. Profl. Psychology, 1989-94, Coun. on Found., Washington, 1990—, Found. Ctr., N.Y., 1993. Recipient Azteca award Human Devel. Corp., 1991, Leadership award Nat. Concilors of Am. and United Way of Bay Area, 1990, Disting. Performance award, Nat. Alliance of Bus., Washington, 1985, Superior Svc. Mgmt. award, Am. Soc. Pub. Adminstrn., 1985, Humanitarian award, Los Padrinos, Inc., 1981, Small and Minority Bus. award for the State of Calif. 1982, Disting. Alumni award, Calif. Jr. Community Coll. Assn., Sacramento, 1982, Silver Spur award, Nat. Fedn. of Charros in Guadalajaro, Jalisco, Mex., 1974, Calif. Community Svc. award, Former Gov. Ronald Reagan, Sacramento, 1973. Mem. chair, Hispanics in Philanthropy, Am. Pub. Welfare Assn. (bd. dirs., Leadership award 1987), Rotary, 1987-93. Office: Calif State U 400 Golden Shore St # 116 Long Beach CA 90802-4209 Office: Calif State U 400 Golden Shore #116 Long Beach CA 90802-4275

PATINO, ISIDRO FRANK, law enforcement educator; b. San Antonio, Mar. 10, 1943; s. Isidro F. and Maria (Narro) P.; children: Michael, Rebecca, Karleen. BS, Calif. State U., L.A., 1973; MBA, U. Redlands, 1995. Records comdr. Placentia (Calif.) Police Dept., 1980-85; asst. dean Criminal Justice Tng. Ctr. Golden West Coll., Huntington Beach, Calif., 1986-89, assoc. dean instrn., 1989-92; divsn. dean dept. pub. svc. Rio Hondo Coll., Whittier, Calif., 1992—; pres., mem. State Chancellors Adv. Com. Pub. Safety Edn., 1991—; chmn. So. Calif. Pub. Safety Tng. Consortium, 1994—, active, 1993—; bd. suprs. L.A. County Spl. Task Force on Pub. Safety Tng., 1995—. Mem. Calif. Law Enforcement Assn. Records Suprs. (pres. so. chpt. 1985-87, state pres. 1986-87), Calif. Acad. Dirs. Assn. (chmn. 1988-89), Am. Soc. Criminologists, Acad. Criminal Justice Scis., Western and Pacific Assn. Criminal Justice Educators, Calif. Assn. Adminstrn. of Justice Educators (v.p. 1996-97), Calif. Peace Officers Stds. and Tng. Basic Course Consortium (chmn. instrn. com. 1987-88)m World Future Soc. (pres. Orange County-Long Beach chpt. 1988-92), Nat. Assn. Field Tng. Officers (nat. pres. 1992-93), Nat. Assn. Chiefs of Police, Am. Soc. Law Enforcement Trainers. Roman Catholic.

PATKAU, JOHN, architect; b. Winnipeg, Man., Can., Aug. 18, 1947; s. Abe John and Bertha (Klassen) P.; m. Patricia Frances Gargett, Aug. 10, 1974. BA, U. Manitoba, 1969, BA in Environ. Studies, 1969, MArch, 1972. Registered architect, B.C., Ont. Prin. John Patkau Architect Ltd., Edmonton, Can., 1977-83; ptnr. Patkau Archs. Inc., Vancouver, B.C., Can., 1984—; chmn. edn. com. Alta. Assn. Architects, 1981; vis. critic U. Calgary, 1981, 92, U. Waterloo, 1987, 89, U. Pa., 1987, Tech. U. N.S., 1987, U. B.C., 1988, 89, UCLA, 1989; design critic U. B.C., 1985-86; urban design panel Vancouver, 1990-92; vis. prof. William Lyon Somerville Lectureship U. Calgary, 1994; Eliot Noyes vis. design critic Harvard U., 1995. Recipient Progressive Architecture citation, 1981, Progressive Architecture award, 1993, 95, Can. Architects award, 1983, 86, 87, 89, 90, 92, 94, Wood Coun. First award, 1984, Gov. Gen. medal, 1986, 90, 92, 94, Gov. Gen. award, 1990, Lt. Gov. Archtl. medal, 1992, Honor award, 1992. Fellow Royal Archtl. Inst. Can. (chmn. design com. 1987); mem. Archtl. Inst. B.C., Royal Can. Coll. Art, Ont. Assn. Architects. Office: Patkau Archs, 560 Beatty St Ste L110, Vancouver, BC Canada V6B 2L3

PATKAU, PATRICIA, architect, architecture educator; b. Winnipeg, Manitoba, Can., Feb. 25, 1950; d. John Frederick and Aileen Constance (Emmett) Gargett; m. John Robert Patkau, Aug. 10, 1974. BA in Interior Design, U. Manitoba, 1973; MA in Architecture, Yale, New Haven, Conn., 1978. Ptnr. Patkau Archs., Vancouver, B.C., Can., 1983—; asst. prof. Sch. Architecture UCLA, U.S.A., 1988-90; assoc. prof. Sch. Architecture U. B.C., Can., 1992—; vis. critic U. Calgary, 1981, 87, U. Waterloo, 1987, U. Pa., U.S.A., 1987, U. Toronto, 1988, Southern Calif. Inst. Architecture, U.S.A., 1990, UCLA, 1991, U. Oreg., U.S.A., 1992, MIT, U.S.A., 1993, Yale U., 1993; design critic U. B.C., 1984-87; vis. prof. Harvard U., U.S.A., 1993, U. Calgary, 1994. Ctrl. Mortgage and Housing fellow, 1977, 78; recipient Manitoba Gold medal, 1973, Progressive Architecture citation, 1981, 93, Can. Architect Excellence award, 1983, 86, 87, 89, 90, 92, 94, Can. Wood Coun. First award, 1984, Honor award, 1992, Gov. Gen. Architecture medal, 1986, 90, 92, 94, Gov. Gen. Architecture award, 1990, Lt. Gov. Architecture medal, 1992, Can. Wood Coun. award, 1991. Fellow Royal Archtl. Inst. Can.; mem. Archtl. Inst. B.C. (Honor award 1988). Office: Patkau Archs, 560 Beatty St Ste L110, Vancouver, BC Canada V6B 2L3

PATMOS, ADRIAN EDWARD, university dean emeritus; b. Paterson, N.J., June 29, 1914; s. Adrian and Myra (Van Splinter) P.; m. Pearl Van Den Heuvel, Apr. 25, 1942; children: Adrian Edward III, Bruce Douglas. A.B. magna cum laude, N.Y.U., 1935, A.M., 1936; LLD, Wittenburg U., 1996; Penfield scholar, 1937-38; grad. study, Am. U., 1936-37. Asst. prof. econs. Wittenberg U., 1938-47, assoc. prof., head dept., 1947-50, prof. econs., 1950—, head dept., 1950-64, dir. mgmt. devel. program, 1952-79, eve. sessions, 1952-78; dean Wittenberg U. (Sch. Community Edn.), 1955-79, dean emeritus, 1979—; jr. accountant Def. Plant Corp., Curtiss-Wright Corp., summer 1943; vis. instr. Ohio Wesleyan U., summer 1944; spl. field rep. NLRB, 1946; vis. lectr. econs. N.Y.U., 1946-47, summer 1948; vis. prof. econs. USAF Inst. Tech., 1949, 50; cons. Clark C.C., 1982-84, Urbana U., 1983-94. Chmn. Clark County Health Facilities Planning Com., 1965-66, City commr., Springfield, Ohio, 1958-62, mayor, 1960-62; Trustee United Way, Springfield and Clark County, 1960-74; trustee Clark Tech. Coll., 1965-78, chmn., 1969-71; trustee Springfield Community Hosp., 1975-84, Elderly United, 1979-92. Recipient Wittenberg award for meritorious svc. to univ., 1964, Silver Knight award Nat. Mgmt. Assn., Sta. WIZE award for outstanding cmty. svc., Cmty. Svc. award C. of C., 1979, award of distinction Bd. of Realtors, Outstanding Svc. in Cmty. Labor-Mgmt. Relationships award Fed. Mediation Svc., citation as one of Ohio's foremost educators Ohio Senate, Medal of Honor for leadership in liberal arts edn., 1987; named Jr. Achievement Hall of Fame laureate, 1996. Mem. Ohio Coll. Assn. (pres. adult edn. sect. 1959-60), Am. Econs. Assn., Kiwanis (Disting. Svc. to Cmty. award), Phi Beta Kappa, Phi Gamma Delta, Blude Key. Baptist.

PATNAUDE, WILLIAM E., architect; b. Sanger, Calif., Sept. 24, 1937; s. Eugene Joseph Patnaude and Vera Mae (Giles) Patnaude Fagan; m. Mary Esther Simerly, Aug. 22, 1971 (div. 1987); children—Nathaniel, Matthew. B.Arch., U. Calif., Berkeley, 1961; postgrad., Calif. State U.-Fresno, 1968-72. Registered architect, Calif., Oreg., Wash., Idaho, Nev., N.Mex., Colo., Utah, Ariz., Mont., Ind., Iowa, Nebr., Ohio. Draftsman, architect Robert Stevens Assoc., Santa Cruz, Calif., 1963-66; architect Llewelyn Davies, Weeks & Ptnrs., London, 1966; architect Allen Y. Lew, Fresno, Calif., 1967-69, assoc., 1969-74; v.p., architect Lew & Patnaude, Inc., Fresno, Calif., 1978-84; pres. Lew & Patnaude, Inc., 1985—; instr. Calif. State U., Fresno, 1968-81. Constn. arbitrator Am. Arbitration Assn., 1976—; chair ctrl. area plan citizen's adv. com. City of Fresno, 1991-93, chair gen. plan update com., 1994-96; bd. dirs. Fresno Arts Ctr., 1971-74, Fresno County Alliance for the Arts, 1986-88, 91-94. With USNR, 1961-63. Recipient Award of Merit, Calif. Hist. Preservation Conf., Orange County, 1983; Award of Excellence Woodwork Inst. Calif., 1982. Fellow AIA (nat. dir. 1983-85, pres. Calif. coun. 1982, San Joaquin chpt. 1978, Awards of Excellence, 1972-95; mem. Constrn. Specifications Inst. (pres. Fresno chpt. 1977). Democrat. Avocations: photography; fine wines. Home: 4190 N Van Ness Blvd Fresno CA 93704-4213 Office: Lew & Patnaude Inc 1050 S St Fresno CA 93721-1407

PATON, LELAND B., investment banker; b. Worcester, Mass., Nov. 30, 1943; s. Andrew John and Anne Louise (Kehoe) P.; m. Nancy Carlon Nation, May 13, 1978;children: Scott Bartlett, Mark Grosvenor, Elisabeth Anne. Asst. sec. New England Mcht. Nat. Bank, Boston, 1965-69; with Prudential Bache Securities Inc. Prudential Securities Inc., 1969—; mgr. N.Y. instl. sales, N.Y.C., 1976-77; dir.mktg., from 1977, sr. v.p., from 1977, also dir., mem. exec. com.; mem. operating com. Prudential Securities Inc.; exchange ofcl. Am. Stock Exchange; bd. dirs. Chgo. Bd. of Options Exchange. Mem. N.Y. Stock Exchange, Securities Industry Assn. (chmn. mktg. com. 1981, bd. dirs.), Securities Ind. Inst. (bd. dirs.), Am.Mktg. Assn., Bond Club, N.Y., Apawamis Club, Harvard Club, Mid-Ocean Club, Long Cove Club. Office: Prudential Securities Inc One New York Plz New York NY 10292-2015

PATON WALSH, JILL, author; b. London, England, Apr. 29, 1937; d. John Llewelyn and Patricia (Dubern) Buss; m. Antony Edmund Paton Walsh, Aug. 5, 1961; Children: Edmund, Margaret, Clare. Author: Hengest's Tale, 1966, The Dolphin Crossing, 1967, Fireweed, 1969, (with Kevin Crossley-Holland, World Book Festival award 1970), Wordhoard, 1969, Goldengrove 1972, Farewell Great King, 1972, Toolmaker, 1973, The Dawnstone, 1973, The Emporer's Winding Sheet, 1974 (Whitbread prize 1974), The Huffler, 1975, The Island Sunrise: Preshistoric Culture in the British Isles, 1975, Unleaving, 1976 (Boston Globe, Horn Book award 1976), Children of the Fox: Crossing to Salamis, 1977, The Walls of Athens, 1978, Persian Gold, 1978, A Chance Child, 1978, The Green Book, 1981, Babylon, 1982, Parcell of Patterns, 1983 (Universe prize 1984), Lost and Found, 1984, Gaffer Samson's Luck, 1984 (Smarties Grand prix 1984), Lapsing, 1985, A School for Lovers, 1989, Birdy and the Ghosties, 1990, "Grace", 1991, Matthew and the Sea Singers, 1992, When Grandma Came, 1992, The Wydham Case, 1993, Knowledge of Angels, 1994, A Piece of Justice, 1995, Connie Came to Play, 1995, Thomas and the Tinners, 1995. Fellow Royal Soc. of Lit. (CBE award 1996). Addres: care David Higham Assocs, 5-8 Lower John St, Golden Sq London W1R 3PE, England

PATRICELLI, ROBERT E., health care company executive; b. Hartford, Conn., Dec. 9, 1939; s. Leonard J. and Lydia E. Patricelli; m. Margaret Patricelli; children—Thomas, Alison. A.B. with high honors, Wesleyan U., Middletown, Conn., 1961; LL.B. cum laude, Harvard U., 1965. Bar: N.Y. 1967. White House fellow U.S. Dept. State, Washington, 1965-66; minority counsel U.S. Senate Subcom. Employment, Manpower and Poverty, Washington, 1966-69; dep. asst. sec., dep. undersec. HEW, Washington, 1969-71; v.p. Greater Hartford Process, Devco, Conn., 1971-75; adminstr. Urban Mass Transp. Adminstrn., U.S. Dept. Transp., Washington, 1975-77; v.p. govt. relations CIGNA Corp., Hartford, Conn., 1977-79, v.p., sr. v.p., exec. v.p. corp. services, 1979-83, pres. affiliated bus. group, 1983-86; chmn., chief exec. officer Value Health Inc., Avon, Conn., 1987—. Bd. dirs. Hartford Hosp., 1994—, Health Spring, Inc., 1994-95; bd. dirs. U.S. C. of C., 1990—, chmn. health and employee benefits com., 1990-94; trustee N.E. Utilities Corp., 1993—, Wesleyan U., 1993—. Recipient Disting. Alumnus award Wesleyan U., 1986; Fulbright scholar U. Paris, 1962. Mem. Inst. of Medicine. Office: Value Health Inc 22 Waterville Rd Avon CT 06001-2066

PATRICK, CARL LLOYD, theatre executive; b. Honaker, Va., Dec. 6, 1918; s. Deward and Virginia Mae (McGraw) P.; m. Frances Estelle Wynn, Feb. 14, 1943; children: Carl Lloyd Jr., Michael Wynn. Ed. high sch., Dublin, Md. Gen. mgr. Martin Theatres, Columbus, Ga., 1945-69, pres., 1969-70; pres. Fuqua Industries, Inc., Atlanta, 1970-78, vice chmn., 1978-82; chmn. Carmike Cinemas, Inc., Columbus, 1982—; bd. dirs. Columbus Bank & Trust Co. Trustee Columbus Mus., 1983—, Ga. Southwestern Coll., Americus, 1984—, Columbus Coll., 1985—; bd. dirs. Columbus Tech. Inst., 1988—. Maj. U.S. Army, 1941-45. Mem. Nat. Assn. Theatre Owners (Sherrill Corwin award 1984, Hassanein Humanitarian award 1986, Exhibitor of the Decade award 1990). Methodist. Avocation: golf. Home: 2701 Lynda Ln Columbus GA 31906-1248 Office: Carmike Cinemas 1301 1st Ave Columbus GA 31901-2109

PATRICK, CHARLES WILLIAM, JR., lawyer; b. Monroe, N.C., Oct. 9, 1954; s. Charles William and Louise (Nisbet) P.; m. Celeste Hunt, June 5, 1976; children: Laura Elizabeth, Charles William III. BA magna cum laude, Furman U., 1976; JD, U. S.C., 1979. Bar: S.C. 1979, U.S. Dist. Ct. S.C. 1981, U.S. Ct. Appeals (11th cir.) 1981, U.S. Ct. Appeals (10th cir.) 1983, U.S. Ct. Appeals (4th cir.) 1986. Law clk. to presiding judge 9th Cir. Ct. State of S.C., Charleston, 1979-80; assoc. Ness, Motley, Loadholt, Richardson and Poole and predecessor firm Blatt and Fales, Charleston, 1980—; assoc. Motley, Loadholt, Richardson and Poole and predecessor firm Blatt and Fales, Charleston, 1980-84, ptnr., 1984—. Exec. editor S.C. Law Review, 1978; contbr. articles to profl. jours. Mem. ABA, Assn. Trial Lawyers Am., S.C. Assn. Trial Lawyers, Trial Lawyers for Pub. Justice, Phi Beta Kappa. Democrat. Presbyterian. Avocations: boating, skiing, fishing. Home: 38 Church St Charleston SC 29401-2742 Office: Ness Motley

Loadholt Richardson & Poole 151 Meeting St Box 1137 Charleston SC 29402

PATRICK, CRAIG, professional hockey team executive; b. Detroit, May 20, 1946; s. Lynn P.; m. Sue Patrick; children—Erin, Cory, Ryan. M.B.A., U. Denver. Hockey player Calif. Golden Seals, 1971-74; hockey player St. Louis Blues, 1974-75, Kansas City, 1975-76, World Hockey Assn., Minn., 1976-77, Washington Capitals, 1977-79; v.p., gen. mgr. N.Y. Rangers, N.Y.C., 1981-86; dir. athletics and recreation Univ. Denver, 1987-89; gen. mgr., exec. v.p. Pitts. Penguins, 1989—. Capt., U.S. Nat. Team, World Championships, Moscow, 1979; asst. mgr. and asst. coach U.S. Olympic Hockey Team, 1980. Office: Pitts Penguins Civic Arena Gate # 9 Pittsburgh PA 15219*

PATRICK, DAN, sportscaster; b. May 15, 1957; married; 2 children. BA in Broadcasting, U. Dayton, 1979. Morning sports and news reporter WTUE-Radio, Dayton, Ohio, 1979-81; weekend sports anchor, reporter WDTN-TV, Dayton, Ohio, 1981-83, CNN, 1983-89; sports dir. WKLS-AM, Atlanta, 1987-91; reporter weekday sports Laser 103, Milw., WLVQ-AM, Columbus, 1989-91; anchor, reporter SportsCenter ESPN, Bristol, Conn., 1989—; reporter weekday sports KSEG-AM, Sacramento, 1991. Office: ESPN Inc Comms Dept ESPN Plz Bristol CT 06010*

PATRICK, DEVAL LAURDINE, lawyer; b. Chgo., July 31, 1956; s. Laurdine Kenneth and Emily Mae (Wintersmith) P.; m. Diane Louise Bemus, May 5, 1984; children: Sarah Baker, Katherine Wintersmith. AB cum laude, Harvard Coll., 1978, JD, 1982; JD (hon.), Dist. Columbia Law Sch., 1994. Bar: Calif. 1983, D.C. 1985, Mass. 1987, U.S. Dist. Ct. Mass. 1987, U.S. Dist. Ct. (cen. dist.) Calif. 1983, U.S. Ct. Appeals (1st and 5th cirs.) 1984, U.S. Ct. Appeals (9th and 11th cirs.) 1984, U.S. Supreme Ct. 1988. Law clk. to Hon. Stephen Reinhardt U.S. Ct. Appeals (9th cir.), L.A., 1982-83; asst. counsel NAACP Legal Def. Fund, N.Y.C., 1983-86; ptnr. Hill & Barlow, Boston, 1986-94; asst. atty. gen. civil rights divsn. U.S. Dept. Justice, Washington, 1994—. Dir., mem. exec. com., chmn. New Eng. steering com. NAACP Legal Def. and Edn. Fund., Inc., 1991-94, vice chmn. Mass. Jud. Nominating Coun., 1991-93; trustee, mem. exec. com. Milton Acad., 1985—; overseer WGBH, 1993-94; corporator Milton Hosp., 1991-94. Recipient George Leisure award Harvard Law Sch., 1981; Rockefeller Traveling fellow, 1978. Mem. ABA (numerous bds. and coms.), Mass. Bar Assn., Mass. Black Lawyers Assn., Boston Bar Assn. (coun. mem. 1993), Harvard Club of Boston, Harvard Alumni Assn. (dir. 1993—). Avocations: squash, cooking, gardening.

PATRICK, H. HUNTER, lawyer, judge; b. Gasville, Ark., Aug. 19, 1939; s. H. Hunter Sr. and Nelle Frances (Robinson) P.; m. Charlotte Anne Wilson, July 9, 1966; children: Michael Hunter, Colleen Annette. BA, U. Wyo., 1961, JD, 1966. Bar: Wyo. 1966, U.S. Dist. Ct. Wyo. 1966, Colo. 1967, U.S. Supreme Ct. 1975. Mcpl. judge City of Powell (Wyo.), 1967-68; sole practice law Powell, 1966-88; atty. City of Powell, 1969-88; justice of the peace County of Park, Wyo., 1971-88; bus. law instr. Northwest Community Coll., Powell, 1968—; dist. judge State of Wyo. 5th Jud. Dist., 1988—; mem. Wyo. Dist. Judges Conf., sec.-treas., 1993-94, vice chair, 1994-95, chair, 1995-96. Editor: Bench Book for Judges of Courts of Limited Jurisdiction in the State of Wyoming, 1980-90. Dir. cts. Wyo. Girls State, Powell, 1982-85, 89-96. Recipient Wyo. Crime Victims Compensation Commn. Judicial award, 1995. Mem. ABA (Wyo. state del. to ho. of dels. 1994—, Wyo. del. judicial adminstrn. divsn., Pub. Svc. award for ct.-sponsored Law Day programs 1990, 92), Wyo. Bar Assn., Colo. Bar Assn., Park County Bar Assn. (sec. 1969-70, pres. 1970-71), Wyo. Assn. Cts. Ltd. Jurisdiction (pres. 1973-80), Am. Judicature Soc. Presbyterian (elder, deacon). Avocations: photography, travel, fishing, camping, bicycling. Home: PO Box 941 Powell WY 82435-0941 Office: PO Box 1868 Cody WY 82414-1868

PATRICK, HUGH TALBOT, economist, educator; b. Goldsboro, N.C., Feb. 22, 1930; s. Talbot and Paula (Miller) P.; B.A., Yale U., 1951; M.A. in Far Eastern Studies, U. Mich., 1955, M.A. in Econs., 1957; Ph.D. in Econs., 1960; M.A. (hon.), Yale U., 1968; children—Stephen, Matthew, Catherine. Econ. analyst U.S. Govt., 1951-52; lectr. econs. U. Mich., 1958-60; asst. prof. econs. Yale U., New Haven, 1960-64, assoc. prof., 1964-68, prof. Far Eastern econs., 1968-84, dir. Yale Econ. Growth Center 1976-79, 80-83; R.D. Calkins prof. internat. bus. Columbia U., 1984—; vis. prof. U. Bombay, 1961-62; mem. Japan-U.S. Econ. Relations Group, 1978-81, Nat. Com. for Pacific Econ. Coop.; dir. Ctr. on Japanese Econ. and Bus., Columbia U., 1986—. Ford Found. fellow, 1957-58; Am. Council Learned Socs. grantee, 1962; Guggenheim fellow, 1964-65; Fulbright research prof., 1964-65; Fulbright-Hays NDEA fellow, 1968-69; Assn. Asian Studies Disting. lectr., 1977. Mem. Japan Soc. (dir. 1973-79, 81—), Social Sci. Research Council (dir., chmn. 1985-88), Pacific Basin Inst., Pacific Trade and Devel. Confs. (chmn.). Democrat. Editor: Japanese Industrialization and Its Social Consequences, 1976, Japanese High Technology Industries-Lessons and Limitations of Industrial Policy, 1986; co-author, co-editor: Asia's New Giant-How the Japanese Economy Works, 1976; chapter author: (co-editor with Masahiko Aoki) The Japanese Finance Main Bank System: Its Relevance for Developing and Transforming Economies, 1994, (co-editor with Larry Meissner) Pacific Basin Industries in Distress: Structural Adjustment and Trade Policy in Nine Industrialized Economies, 1991 (Masayoshi Ohira Meml. prize, 1992); co-editor: (with Yung Chul Park) The Financial Development of Japan, Korea, and Taiwan: Growth, Repression and Liberalization, 1994. Office: Columbia U 522 Uris Hall 3022 Broadway New York NY 10027-7004

PATRICK, JANE AUSTIN, association executive; b. Memphis, May 27, 1930; d. Wilfred Jack and Evelyn Eudora (Branch) Austin; m. William Thomas Spencer, Sept. 11, 1952 (dec Apr. 1970); children: Duke Anthony-Spencer Austin, ToniLee Candice Spencer Hughes; m. George Milton Patrick, Oct. 1, 1971. Student Memphis State U., 1946-47; BSBA, Ohio State U., 1979. Svc. rep. So. Bell Tel. and Tel., Memphis, 1947-52; placement dir. Mgmt. Pers., Memphis, 1965-66; pers. asst. to exec. v.p. E & E Ins. Co., Columbus, Ohio, 1966-69; Ohio exec. dir. Nat. Soc. for Prevention of Blindness, Columbus, 1969-73; regional dir. Ohio and Ky. CARE and MEDICO, Columbus, 1979-87; v.p. Career Execs. of Columbus, 1987-91; v.p., owner, pres. Patrick Distribution, 1987—; lectr., cons. in field. Mem. choir 1st Cmty. Ch., Columbus, Ohio State Univ. Svc. Bd.; bd. dirs. Columbus Coun. on World Affairs, 1980-92, sec., 1983-91, chmn. devel. com.; chmn. pers. com. Ohio Hunger Task Force, 1989-90. Recipient commendations Nat. Soc. Prevention Blindness and Ctrl. Ohio Lions Eye Bank, 1973. Plaques for Svc. award Upper Arlington Pub. Schs., 1986. Mem. Non-Profit Orgn. Mgmt. Inst. (pres.), Nat. Soc. Fund-Raising Execs. (cert., nat. dir.), Pub. Rels. Soc. Am. (cert., membership com. chairperson), Ins. Inst. Am. (cert.), Mensa Internat., Columbus Dental Soc. Aux. (historian and publicity chair), Alpha Gamma Delta, Epsilon Sigma Alpha (pres.). Home: 2620 Love Dr Columbus OH 43221-2645

PATRICK, JANET CLINE, personnel company executive; b. San Francisco, June 30, 1934; d. John Wesley and Edith Bertha (Corde) Cline; m. Robert John Patrick Jr., June 13, 1959 (div. 1988); children: John McKinnon, Stewart McLellan, William Robert. BA with distinction, Stanford U., 1955; postgrad. U. Calif.-Berkeley, 1957, George Washington U., 1978-82. English tchr. George Washington H.S., San Francisco, 1957, K.D. Burke Sch., San Francisco, 1957-59, Berkeley Inst., Bklyn., 1959-63; placement counselor Washington Sch. Secs., Washington, 1976-78, asst. dir. placement, 1978-81; mgr. med. personnel service Med. Soc. D.C., 1981-89, pres. Med. Pers. Svcs. Inc., 1989— . Chmn. area 2 planning com. Montgomery County Pub. Schs. (Md.), 1974-75; mem. vestry, corr. sec., Christ Ch., Kensington, Md., 1982-84, vestry, sr. warden, 1984-85, vestry, chmn. ann. giving com., 1986-89; chmn. long-range planning com., 1989-92, sec., 1992-93, jr. warden, 1994, co-chair capital campaign, 1996; fin. com. Montgomery County Pvt. Industry Coun., 1994. Mem. Met. D.C. Med. Group Mgmt. Assn., Phi Beta Kappa. Republican. Episcopalian. Club: Jr. League (Washington). Home: 5206 Carlton St Bethesda MD 20816-2306 Office: Med Personnel Svcs Inc 1707 L St NW Ste 250 Washington DC 20036-4201

PATRICK, JOHN JOSEPH, social sciences educator; b. East Chicago, Ind., Apr. 14, 1935; s. John W. and Elizabeth (Lazar) P.; m. Patricia Grant, Aug. 17, 1963; children—Rebecca, Barbara. A.B., Dartmouth Coll., 1957; Ed.D., Ind. U., 1969. Social studies tchr. Roosevelt High Sch., East Chicago, 1957-62; social studies tchr. Lab. High Sch., U. Chgo., 1962-65; research assoc. Sch. Edn., Ind. U., Bloomington, 1965-69, asst. prof., 1969-74, assoc. prof., 1974-77, prof. edn., 1977—, dir. social studies devel. ctr., 1986—, dir. ERIC clearinghouse for social studies, social sci. edn., 1986—; bd. dirs. Biol. Scis. Curriculum Study, 1980-83; ednl. cons. Author: Progress of the Afro-American, 1968, The Young Voter, 1974; (with L. Ehman, Howard Mehlinger) Toward Effective Instruction in Secondary Social Studies, 1974, Lessons on the Northwest Ordinance, 1987; (with R. Remy) Civics for Americans, 1980, rev. edit. 1986; (with Mehlinger) American Political Behavior, 1972, rev. edit. 1980, (with C. Keller) Lessons on the Federalist Papers, 1987; America Past and Present, 1983; (with Carol Berkin) History of the American Nation, 1984, rev. edit., 1987; Lessons on the Constitution, 1985, James Madison and the Federalist Papers, 1990, How to Teach the Bill of Rights, 1991, Ideas of the Founders on Constitutional Government: Resources for Teachers of History and Government, 1991, Young Oxford Companion to the Supreme Court of the United States, 1994, Founding the Republic: A Documentary History, 1995. Bd. dirs. Law in Am. Soc. Found., 1984-88, Social Sci. Edn. consortium, 1984—; mem. Gov.'s Task Force on Citizenship Edn., Ind., 1982-87; active Ind. Commn. on Bicentennial of U.S. Constn., 1986-92; bd. dirs. Coun. for the Advancement of Citizenship, Nat. History Edn. Network, 1994—; mem. Natr. Coun. for History Standards, 1991-94. Mem. ASCD, Nat. Coun. Social Studies, Social Sci. Edn. Consortium (v.p. 1985-87), Coun. for Basic Edn., Am. Polit. Sci. Assn., Am. Hist. Assn., Orgn. Am. Historians, Phi Delta Kappa. Home: 1209 E University St Bloomington IN 47401-5045 Office: Ind U 2805 E 10th St Bloomington IN 47408-2601

PATRICK, LYNN ALLEN, lawyer, construction and land development company executive; b. Stettler, Alta., Can., Dec. 7, 1935; s. Allen Russell and Florence Lorene (Lynn) P.; m. Roberta Colleen Hughes, May 9, 1959; children: Diane Elizabeth, Ross Gordon. B.Sc., U. Alta., Edmonton, Can., 1957, LL.B., 1960. Bar: Alta. 1961. Ptnr. Cormie Kennedy, Edmonton, Alta., 1961-83; sr. v.p., gen. counsel Mutual Fund Group, Edmonton, 1983-88; pres. Stuart Olson Constrn., Inc., Edmonton, 1989-92; v.p., corp. counsel, sec. The Churchill Corp., 1992—. Past pres., trustee Minerva Found., Edmonton; adv. council mem. Minster of Edn., Alta.; gov. Banff Ctr. Mem. Can. Bar Assn., Edmonton Bar Assn., Law Soc. Alta., Royal Glenora Club (Edmonton). Progessive. Home: 64 Quesnell Rd, Edmonton, AB Canada T5R 5N2 Office: The Churchill Corp, 10180 101st St Ste 2280, Edmonton, AB Canada T5J 3S4

PATRICK, MARTY, lawyer; b. N.Y.C., May 10, 1949; s. Harry and Evelyn (Beroza) P.; m. Madelaine Joyce Benjamin, Dec. 2, 1984; 1 child, Jason; BS, L.I. U., 1971; Cert. Inst. for Leadership Devel., Jerusalem, 1974; JD, Nova Southeastern U., 1981. Exec. dir. Zionist Orgn. Am., Miami Beach, Fla., 1975-78; pres. Enigma Enterprises, Inc., Miami, Fla., 1978-82; ptnr. firm Martin Howard Patrick, P.A. Miami Beach, 1982—; pres. Patrick Law Ctr., Miami Beach, 1983-89; pres. First Fla. Title & Abstract Co., Miami, 1983—; chief exec. officer Atlantic Coast Title Co., 1989—; CEO Laughing in the Dark Prodns., 1994—. Horovitz scholar, 1980. Mem. ABA, Ga. Bar Assn., Fla. Bar Assn. Lodges: Mensa. Contbr. articles to profl. jours. Home: 12910 Oleander Rd Keystone Point FL 33181-2356 Office: 1141 Kane Concourse Bay Harbor Islands FL 33154-2012

PATRICK, RICHARD M., professional hockey team executive; b. Victoria, B.C., Can., Oct. 20, 1946; married; 3 children. Ed., Dartmouth Coll., Am. U. Washington. Exec. v.p. Washington Capitals Hockey Team, Landover, Md.; now pres, gov. Washington Capitals, 1992—. Office: Washington Capitals Usair Arena Landover MD 20785

PATRICK, RUTH (MRS. RUTH HODGE VAN DUSEN), limnologist, diatom taxonomist, educator; b. Topeka, Kans.; d. Frank and Myrtle (Jetmore) P.; m. Charles Hodge, IV, July 10, 1931; 1 son, Charles, V. BS, Coker Coll., 1929, LLD, 1971; MA, U. Va., 1931, PhD, 1934; DSc, Beaver Coll., 1970, PMC Colls., 1971, Phila. Coll. Pharmacy and Sci., 1973, Wilkes Coll., 1974, Cedar Crest Coll., 1974, U. New Haven, 1975, Hood Coll., 1975, Med. Coll. Pa., 1975, Drexel U., 1975, Swarthmore Coll., 1975, Bucknell U., 1976, Rensselaer Poly. Inst., 1976, St. Lawrence U., 1978; LHD, Chestnut Hill Coll, 1974; DSc, U. Mass., 1980, Princeton U., 1980, Lehigh U., 1983, U. Pa., 1984, Temple U., 1985, Emory U., 1986, Wake Forest U., 1986, U. S.C., 1989, Clemson, 1989, Glassboro State Coll., 1992. Asso. curator microscopy dept. Acad. Natural Scis., Phila., 1939-47; curator Leidy Micros. Soc., 1937-47, curator limnology dept., 1947—, chmn. limnology dept., 1947-73; occupant Francis Boyer Research Chair, 1973—, chmn. bd. trustees, 1973-76, hon. chmn. bd. trustees, 1976—; lectr. U. Pa., 1950-70, adj. prof., 1970—; guest Fellow of Saybrook Yale, 1975; participant Am. Philos. Soc. limnology expdn. to, Mexico, 1947; leader Catherwood Found. expdn. to, Peru and Brazil, 1955; del. Gen. Assembly, Internat. Union Biol. Scis., Bergen, Norway, 1973; Dir. E.I. duPont, Pa. Power and Light Co.; Chmn. algae com. Smithsonian Oceanographic Sorting Center, 1963-68; mem. panel on water blooms Pres.'s Sci. Adv. Com., 1966; mem. panel on water resources and water pollution Gov.'s Sci. Adv. Com., 1966; mem. nat. tech. adv. com. on water quality requirements for fish and other aquatic life and wildlife Dept. Interior, 1967-68; mem. citizen's adv. council Pa. Dept. Environ. Resources, 1971-73; mem. hazardous materials adv. com. EPA, 1971-74, exec. adv. com., 1974-79, chmn. com.'s panel on ecology, 1974-76; mem. Pa. Gov.'s Sci. Adv. Coun., 1972-78; mem. exec. adv. com. nat. power survey FPC., 1972-75; mem. coun. Smithsonian Instn., 1973—; mem. Phila. Adv. Council, 1973-76; mem. energy R & D adv. coun. Pres.'s, Energy Policy Office, 1973-74; mem. adv. coun. Renewable Natural Resources Found., 1973-76, Electric Power Rsch. Found., 1973-77; mem. adv. com. for rsrch. NSF., 1973-74; mem. gen. adv. com. ERDA, 1975-77; adv. bd. sec. energy, 1975-89; mem. com. on human resources NRC, 1975-76; mem. adv. council dept. biology Princeton, 1975-80; mem. com. on sci. and arts Franklin Inst., 1978—; mem. univ. council com. Yale Sch. Forestry and Environ. Studies, 1978-80; mem. sci. adv. council World Wildlife Fund-U.S., 1978-80; trustee Aquarium Soc. Phila., 1951-58, Henry Found.; bd. dirs. Wissahickon Valley Watershed Assn.; bd. govs. Nature Conservancy; bd. mgrs. Wistar Inst. Anatomy and Biology. Author: Rivers of the United States, Vol. 1, 1994, Rivers of the United States, Vol. 2—Chemical and Physical Characteristics, 1995, (with C.W. Reimer) Diatoms of the United States, Vol. 1, 1966, Vol. II, Part 1, 1975; author: (with others) Ground Water Contamination in the United States, 1983, 2d edit., 1987, Surface Water Quality: Have the Laws Been Successful?, 1992; mem. editorial bd. (with C.W. Reimer) Science, 1974-76, American Naturalist; trustee Biological Abstracts, 1974-76; contbr. over 150 articles to profl. jours. Recipient Disting. Dau. of Pa. award, 1952, Richard Hopper Day Meml. medal Acad. Natural Scis., 1969, Gimbel Phila. award, 1969; Gold medal YWCA, 1970, Lewis L. Dollinger Pure Environment award Franklin Inst., 1970, Pa. award for excellence in sci. and tech., 1970, Eminent Ecologist award Ecol. Soc. Am., 1972, Phila. award, 1973, Gold medal Pa. State Fish and Game Protective Assn., 1974, Internat. John and Alice Tyler Ecology award, 1975, Gold medal Phila. Soc. for Promoting Agr., 1975, Pub. Service award Dept. Interior, 1975, Iben award Am. Water Resources Assn., 1976, Outstanding Alumni award Coker Coll., 1977, Francis K. Hutchinson medal Garden Club of Am., 1977, Golden medal Royal Zool. Soc. Antwerp, 1978, Green World award N.Y. Bot. Garden, 1979, Hugo Black award U. Ala., 1979, Sci. award Gov. Pa., 1988, Founders award Soc. Environ. Toxicology and Chemistry, 1982, Environ. Regeneration award Rene Du Bois Ctr., 1985, Disting. Citizen award Pa., 1989, Excellence award N.Am. Benthological Soc., 1993; Sci. Edn. Ctr. named in her honor U. S.C., 1989; recipient Benjamin Franklin medal Am. Philosophical Society, 1993. Fellow AAAS (com. environ. alternatives 1973-74); mem. Nat. Acad. Scis. (chmn. panel com. on pollution 1966, mem. com. sci. and pub. policy 1973-77, mem. environ. measurements panel of com. on remote sensing programs for earth resource surveys 1973-74, mem. nominating com. 1973-75), Nat. Acad. Engring. (com. environ. engring.'s ad hoc study on explicit criteria for decisions in power plant siting 1973), Am. Philos. Soc. (Benjamin Franklin Outstanding Sci. Achievement award 1993), Assn. Metro. Sewage Agys. (Environ. award 1995), Am. Acad. Arts and Scis., Bot. Soc. Am. (mem. Darbarker prize com. 1956, Merit award 1971), Phycol. Soc. Am. (pres. 1954), Internat. Limnological Soc., Internat. Soc. Plant Taxonomists, Am. Soc. Plant Taxonomy, Am. Soc. Limnology and Oceanography, Water Pollution Control Fedn. (hon.), Soc. Study Evolution, Am. Soc. Naturalists (pres. 1975-76), Ecol. Soc. Am., Am. Inst. Biol. Scis., Internat. Phycol. Soc., Sigma Xi. Presbyterian. Office: Acad Natural Scis 19th at Benjamin Franklin Pkwy Philadelphia PA 19103

PATRICK, SUE FORD, diplomat; b. Union Springs, Ala., Nov. 9, 1946; d. Oscar Ford and Mildred (Hunter) Ford Carter; m. Henderson M. Patrick, Dec. 24, 1973; 1 child, Lauren. BA, Coll. Notre Dame of Md., 1967; postgrad., U. Va., 1967-69, 70-72; MA, Boston U., 1982; postgrad., Nat. War Coll., Washington, 1991-92. Joined Fgn. Svc., Dept. State, 1972; vice-consul Am. Consulate, Udorn, Thailand, 1973-74; desk officer Dept. State, Washington, 1976-78, 2d sec., 1982-84, spl. asst. refugee programs, 1984-85; 2d sec. U.S. Embassy, Nairobi, Kenya, 1978-81; 1st sec. polit. affairs U.S. Embassy, Abidjan, Ivory Coast, 1985-88; dep. chief of mission U.S. Embassy, Kigali, Rwanda, 1988-91, Nat. War Coll., Washington, 1991-92; adv. on NATO policy Office of Sec. of Def., The Pentagon, Washington, 1992-93, dir. office of fgn. civil. mil. affairs, 1993-94; congl. affairs advisor Office Regional Policy Bur. East Asian Pacific Affairs, Dept. State, Washington, 1994—. Mem. Am. Fgn. Svc. Assn. Roman Catholic. Avocations: jogging, climbing. Home: 2715 Colt Run Rd Oakton VA 22124-1101 Office: Regional Security Policy EAP/RSP Rm 4312 Dept State Washington DC 20520

PATRICK, THOMAS H., brokerage house executive; b. 1944. BA, Rutgers U., 1965; MBA, U. Pitts., 1966. Equity rsch. analyst Mellon Nat. Bank, 1966-68; prin. Sears, Chgo., 1970-72; with White Weld & Co., 1972-79; chief fin. officer, exec. v.p. Life Investors Inc., Cedar Rapids, Iowa, 1979-81; mng. dir. Merrill Lynch Capital Mkts., 1982-89; formerly chief fin. officer, exec. v.p. Merrill Lynch & Co. Inc., now exec. v.p. equity mkts. group. Office: Merrill Lynch & Co Inc World Financial Ctr 250 Vesey St New York NY 10281-1012*

PATRICK, WENDY LYNN, lawyer; b. Orange, Calif., Oct. 19, 1968; d. Robert Michael and Elizabeth (Alducka) P. BA, UCLA, 1990; JD, Calif. Western Sch. of Law, 1994. Bar: Calif. 1994, U.S. Dist. Ct. (so. dist.) Calif. 1994, U.S. Ct. Appeals (9th cir.) 1995. Media, pub. rels. dir. Curtiss Advt., Orange, Calif., 1985-91; lawyer San Diego Pub. Defenders Office, 1994—. Mem. Law Review Calif. Western Law Sch. Mem. Young Reps., Orange, 1990-92. Recipient First Place Gafford Mock Trial Competition, Calif. Western Sch. of Law, 1993, Five Am. Jurisprudence awards, 1991-94, First Pl. award San Diego Def. Lawyers Assn., 1992-93, Regional champion award ATLA, 1994, Nat. Competition award, 1994. Mem. San Diego County Bar Assn., San Diego Criminal Defense Bar Assn. Roman Catholic. Avocations: skiing, concert violinist, travel, karate. Office: San Diego Pub Defenders 233 A St Ste 900 San Diego CA 92101

PATRICK, WILLIAM BRADSHAW, lawyer; b. Indpls., Nov. 29, 1923; s. Fae William and Mary (Bradshaw) P.; m. Ursula Lantzsch, Dec. 28, 1956; children: William Bradshaw, Ursula, Nancy. AB, The Principia, 1947; LLB, Harvard U., 1950. Bar: Ind. Supreme ct. 1950, U.S. Dist. Ct. (so. dist.) Ind. 1950, U.S. Ct. Apls. (7th cir.) 1961. Ptnr., Patrick & Patrick, Indpls., 1950-53; sole practice, Indpls., 1953—; gen. counsel Met. Planning Commn. Marion County and Indpls., 1955-66; dep. prosecutor Marion County, Ind., 1960-62; past pres., dir. The Cemetery Co., operating Meml. Park Cemetery, Indpls.; sec., dir. Rogers Typesetting Co., Indpls., 1966-85. Pres. Indpls. Legal Aid Soc., 1963. Served to lt. (j.g.) USNR, 1942-46. Recipient DeMolay Legion of Honor. Mem. ABA, Ind. Bar Assn., Indpls. Bar Assn., Lawyers Assn. Indpls., Indpls. Estate Planning Coun., Am. Legion, SAR (sec. Ind. Soc. 1953-59), Svc. Club Indpls., U.S. Navy League, Mil. Order Loyal Legion, Mason (33 deg.), Shriner. Address: 7 N Meridian St Indianapolis IN 46204

PATRICK, WILLIAM HARDY, JR., wetland biogeochemist, educator, laboratory director; b. Johns, Miss., Nov. 9, 1925; s. William Hardy and Alma (Webb) P.; m. Ruth Martin, Dec. 21, 1951; children: Terry Lynn, William Hardy, Carol Ann, Henry Carr. B.S., La. State U., 1950, M.S., 1951; Ph.D., La State U., 1954; D.Honoris Causa, U. Ghent (Belgium), 1979. Asst. prof. agronomy dept. La. State U., Baton Rouge, 1953-56, assoc. prof., 1956-61, prof., 1961-76, prof. marine scis., 1977-78, Boyd prof. marine scis., 1978—; dir. Wetland Biogeochemistry Inst., Baton Rouge; Moore lectr. in ecology U. Va., 1985, York lectr. U. Fla., 1989; cons. numerous govt., indsl. orgns. Contbr. articles to sci. jours. Organizer, dir. La. Methodist World Hunger Scholarship Program, Baton Rouge, 1979—. Served with AUS, 1944-46. grantee numerous research orgns., 1963—. Fellow AAAS, Am. Soc. Agronomy, Soil Sci. Soc. Am. (Internat. award 1992, Rsch. award 1993); mem. Sigma Xi, Phi Kappa Phi. Republican. Methodist. Home: 888 Dubois Dr Baton Rouge LA 70808-5008 Office: Louisiana St Univ Wetland Biogeochemistry Baton Rouge LA 70803

PATRICKS, EDWARD J, elementary education educator; b. Chgo., Jan. 19, 1958; s. John Anthony and Marion Nora (Kinnavy) P. Ed, Ill. Benedictine, Lisle, Ill., 1981. Cert. tchr., Ill. Sci. tchr. St. Pius X, Stickney, Ill., 1981-84; dept. chair, sci. tchr. St. Giles Junior High, Oak Park, Ill., 1984—. Commr. City of Berwyn, 1991—, North Berwyn Pk. Dist., 1995—; past commr. St. Mary of Celle Little League; sponsor Berwyn Playground and Recreation Commn., Berwyn Blazers Taveling Soccer; bd. dirs. Dem. Orgn. Berwyn, St. Mary of Celle, St. Vincent De Paul Conf. Mem. ASCD, NSTA, Nat. Cath. Educators Assn., Ill. Assn. Pk. Dists., Ill. Sheriffs Assn., Suburban Pks. and Recreation Divsn., Nat. Recreation and Pk. Assn., Berwyn Devel. Corp., KC (4 degree). Home: 1809 Euclid Ave Berwyn IL 60402-1845 Office: Saint Giles 1030 Linden Ave Oak Park IL 60302-1351

PATRIKIS, ERNEST T., lawyer, banker; b. Lynn, Mass., Dec. 1, 1943; s. Theodore A. and Ethel (Stasinopolous) P.; m. Emily Herrick Trueblood, Mar. 18, 1972. BA, U. Mass., 1965; JD, Cornell U., 1968. Bar: N.Y. 1969. Exec. v.p., gen. counsel Fed. Res. Bank N.Y., 1968-95 1st v.p., 1995—; dep. gen. counsel Fed. Open Market Com., 1988-95. Contbr. articles to legal jours. Fellow Fgn. Policy Assn.; mem. Assn. of Bar of City of N.Y. (banking law com. 1982-84, 90—, futures regulation com. 1986-89); N.Y. State Bar Assn. (chmn. com. internat. banking, securities and fin. transaction 1987-91, banking law com. 1986—, vice chmn. internat. practice sect. 1991—), ABA (subcom. on gen. banking matters 1986), Coun. on Fgn. Rels. Home: 20 E 9th St New York NY 10003-5944 Office: Fed Reserve Bank NY 33 Liberty St New York NY 10045-0001

PATRON, JUNE EILEEN, former government official; b. N.Y.C., May 15; d. Irving B. and Mollie Patron; B.A. in Govt. with honors, Clark U., Worcester, Mass., 1965; M.A., Am. U., 1967. With U.S. Dept. of Labor, 1966-95, dir. Black Lung benefits program, 1976-79, asst. adminstr. pension and welfare benefit programs, 1979-84, assoc. dir. pension and welfare benefit programs, 1984-88, dir. program svcs., 1988-95, ret., 1995; mem. Sr. Exec. Svc. Recipient various awards Dept. Labor. Home: 3001 Veazey Ter NW Washington DC 20008-5454

PATRON, NICHOLAS VICTOR, special education educator; b. Canton, Ohio, Mar. 26, 1951; s. Nicholas Victor and Mary Josephine (Ottavio) P. BA, Walsh U., Canton, Ohio, 1973. Elem. tchr. Diocese of Youngstown Schs., Canton, 1973-87; spl. edn. tchr. Plain Local Schs., Canton, 1987—; bus. dir. Head of the Class, Canton, 1992—. Libr. substitute Stark County Libr., Canton, 1990—. Named Canton's Best Tchr., City of Canton, 1983; recipient Nat. Honor Soc. award Glen Oak H.S., 1994. Fellow NEA, Ohio Tchr.'s Retirement Assn. Avocations: art, reading, crafts, gardening, walking.

PATRON, SUSAN HALL, librarian, writer; b. San Gabriel, Calif., Mar. 18, 1948; d. George Thomas and Rubye Denver (Brewer) H.; m. René Albert Patron, July 27, 1969. BA, Pitzer Coll., 1969; MLS, Immaculate Heart Coll., 1972. Children's libr. LA Pub. Libr., 1972-79, sr. children's libr., 1980—; reviewer Sch. Libr. Jour., 1980—, Pubs. Weekly, 1986-91, The Five Owls, 1987—; mem. award com. Friends of Children and Lit. Award, 1984. Author: Burgoo Stew, 1991, Five Bad Boys, Billy Que, and the Dustdobbin, 1992, Maybe Yes, Maybe No, Maybe Maybe, 1993 (ALA Notable Book 1994), Bobbin Dustdobbin, 1993, Dark Cloud Strong Breeze, 1994, (with Christopher Weiman) Marbled Papers, 1979. Mem. ALA (Caldecott award com. 1988), PEN, Calif. Libr. Assn. (Patricia Beatty award com. 1987-89, 91-92), Internat. Bd. on Books for Young Children, Soc. Children's Book Writers and Illustrators, So. Calif. Coun. on Lit. for Children and Young People (awards com. 1985), Authors Guild. Office: LA Pub Libr Childrens Svcs 630 W 5th St Los Angeles CA 90071-2002

PATRONELLI, RAYMOND, church administrator. Asst. gen. overseer Christian Ch. of N. Am. Office: Christian Church of North Am 6203 Kelly Rd Plant City FL 33565-3567

PATTEN, BEBE HARRISON, minister, chancellor; b. Waverly, Tenn., Sept. 3, 1913; d. Newton Felix and Mattie Priscilla (Whitson) Harrison; m. Carl Thomas Patten, Oct. 23, 1935; children: Priscilla Carla and Bebe Rebecca (twins), Carl Thomas. D.D., McKinley-Roosevelt Coll., 1941; D.Litt., Temple Hall Coll. and Sem., 1943. Ordained to ministry Ministerial Assn. of Evangelism, 1935; evangelist in various cities of U.S., 1933-50; founder, pres. Christian Evang. Chs. Am., Inc., Oakland, Calif., 1944—, Patten Acad. Christian Edn., Oakland, 1944—, Patten Bible Coll., Oakland, 1944-83; chancellor Patten Coll., Oakland, 1983—; founder, pastor Christian Cathedral of Oakland, 1950—; held pvt. interviews with David Ben-Gurion, 1972, Menachim Begin, 1977, Yitzhak Shamir, 1991; condr. Sta. KUSW world-wide radio ministry, 70 countries around the world, 1989-90, Stas. WHRI and WWCR world coverage short wave, 1990—. Founder, condr.: radio program The Shepherd Hour, 1934—; daily TV, 1976—, nationwide telecast, 1979—; Author: Give Me Back My Soul, 1973; Editor: Trumpet Call, 1953—; composer 20 gospel and religious songs, 1945—. Mem. exec. bd. Bar-Ilan U. Assn., Israel, 1983; mem. global bd. trustees Bar-Ilan U., 1991. Recipient numerous awards including medallion Ministry of Religious Affairs, Israel, 1969; medal Govt. Press Office, Jerusalem, 1971; Christian honoree of yr. Jewish Nat. Fund of No. Calif., 1975; Hidden Heroine award San Francisco Bay coun. Girl Scouts U.S.A., 1976, Golden State award Who's Who Hist. Soc., 1988; Ben-Gurion medallion Ben-Gurion Rsch. Inst., 1977; Resolutions of Commendation, Calif. Senate Rules Com., 1978, 94; hon. fellow Bar-Ilan U., Israel, 1981; Dr. Bebe Patten Social Action chair established Bar-Ilan U., 1982. Mem. Am. Assn. for Higher Edn., Religious Edn. Assn., Am. Acad. Religion and Soc. Bibl. Lit., Zionist Orgn. Am., Am. Assn. Pres. of Ind. Colls. and Univs., Am. Jewish Hist. Soc., Am.-Isreal Pub. Affairs Com. Address: 2433 Coolidge Ave Oakland CA 94601-2630 *He that labors in any great or laudable undertaking has his fatigues first supported by hope, and afterwards rewarded by joy. To strive with difficulties, and to conquer them, is the highest human felicity. I am not afraid of tomorrow for I have seen yesterday and I love today.*

PATTEN, BERNARD MICHAEL, neurologist, writer, educator; b. N.Y.C., Mar. 23, 1941; s. Bernard M. and Olga (Vaccaro) P.; m. Ethel Doudine, June 18, 1964; children: Allegra, Craig. AB summa cum laude, Columbia Coll., 1962; MD, Columbia U., 1966. Med. intern N.Y. Hosp. Cornell Med. Ctr., N.Y.C., 1966-67; resident neurologist Columbia Presbyn. Med. Ctr., N.Y.C., 1967-69, chief resident neurologist, 1969-70; assoc. prof. neurology Baylor Coll. Medicine, Houston, 1973-95; asst. chief med. neurology NIH, Bethesda, Md., 1970-73; mem. med. bd. Nat. Myasthenia Gravis Found., 1973—, Nat. AmyoTrophic Lateral Sclerosis Found., 1982—, Nat. Myositis Assn., 1995—. Contbr. over 22 articles to profl. jours. With USPHS, 1970-73. Rsch. grantee NIH, pvt. founds., nat. health orgns. Fellow ACP, Royal Coll. Physicians. Roman Catholic. Achievements include discoverer (with others) L-Dopa for Parkinson's disease; pioneered use of immune suppression for myasthenia gravis, diagnosis and treatment of medical and neurologcal complications of breast implants. Home: 1019 Baronridge Dr Seabrook TX 77586-4001 Office: Baylor Coll Medicine 1 Baylor Plz Houston TX 77030-3411

PATTEN, CHARLES ANTHONY, management consultant, retired manufacturing company executive, author; b. Allentown, Pa., May 12, 1920; s. Charles Henerie and Mae (Doyle) P.; m. Kathleen Marie Breene, Jan. 6, 1951; children: Charles Anthony Jr., Amy Elizabeth Goddard, Nancy Kathleen Hansen. B.S.M.E., Lehigh U., 1942. With Joy Mfg. Co., 1947-63, works mgr., 1956-63; v.p. mfg. White Motor Corp., 1963-68, Colt Industries, 1968-69; With Dravo Corp., Pitts., 1942-47, 69-85; gen. mgr. engring. works div. Dravo Corp., 1970-71, corp. v.p., gen. mgr. engring. works div., 1971-75, corp. group v.p., chief exec. officer Dravo Mfg. Group, 1975-81, corp. sr. v.p., mem. corp. policy com., chief exec. officer Dravo Mfg. Group, 1981-83, corp. sr. v.p., asst. to pres. and chief exec. officer, mem. exec. com., 1984-85; pres. C.A. Patten Enterprises, 1985—; bd. dirs., v.p. Dravo (Can.) Ltd., 1975-85; dir., pres. Dravo-Okura Co. Ltd., 1974-79; dir. Dravo Mfg. (Can.) Ltd., 1975-83, Tru Weld Grating Inc., 1983-85; v.p. Dravo Internat., Inc., 1974-85. Trustee Ohio Valley Gen. Hosp., McKees Rocks, Pa., 1975-82, Marietta (Ohio) Coll., 1979-89, emeritus trustee, 1989—; bd. dirs. Vocat. Rehab. Center of Allegheny County, 1972-79, Jr. Achievement of S.W. Pa., 1975-80. Mem. ASME, Neville Island Mfrs. Assn. (pres. 1975-85), Am. Arbitration Assn. (panel of arbitrators, 1989-95), Duquesne Club. Republican. Roman Catholic. Home and Office: 2304 Clearvue Rd Pittsburgh PA 15237-1632 *The successful manager is a time-oriented goal setter. Without waiting for others to ask him, he envisions things that should happen and thinks through possible paths to reach the goals. When the goals are reached, he is quick to laud and praise his people for their accomplishment.*

PATTEN, DUNCAN THEUNISSEN, ecologist educator; b. Detroit, Oct. 13, 1934; s. Marc T. and Doris (Miller) P.; m. Eva Chittenden, July 27, 1957; children: Michael, Marc, Robin, Scott. BA, Amherst Coll., 1956; MS, U. Mass., Amherst, 1959; PhD, Duke U., 1962. Asst. prof. ecology Va. Poly. Inst., Blacksburg, 1962-65; asst. prof. ecology Ariz. State U., Tempe, 1965-67, assoc. prof., 1967-73, prof., 1973-95, prof. emeritus, 1995—, dir. ctr. environ. studies, 1980-95. Contbr. articles to profl. jours. Fellow AAAS, Ariz.-Nev. Acad. Sci.; mem. Ecol. Soc. Am. (bus. mgr. 1979-95), Brit. Ecol. Soc., Soc. Range Mgmt., Am. Inst. Biol. Scis., Soc. Wetland Scientists, Am. Water Resource Assn., Am. Geophys. Union, Soc. Conservation Biology, Sigma Xi. Office: Arizona State Univ Ctr for Environ Studies Box 873211 Tempe AZ 85287-3211

PATTEN, GERLAND PAUL, lawyer; b. Lewisville, Ark., Jan. 5, 1907; s. George Washington and Cleopatra (Sims) P.; m. Ira E. Barrett, June 10, 1927; children—Gerald William, Yvonne Claire. LL.B., Ark. Law Sch., 1938, J.D., 1980. Bar: Ark. 1933. Telegraph operator C., R.I.&P. Ry., 1923-31; since practiced in Little Rock; instr. Ark. Law Sch., 1935-44, prof., 1944-67, asst. dean, 1949-67; asst. U.S. atty. Little Rock, 1948-54; v.p., gen. counsel Nat. Investors Security Co., 1957-67; sec., treas., dir. Jess Odom Enterprises, Inc., Little Rock, Marifran Investments, Inc., Little Rock, Maryco Investments, Inc., Little Rock, State Investment Corp., Little Rock, Perryco Investments, Inc., Oklahoma City, Investors Equity Corp., Oklahoma City, Royal Investments Okla., Inc., Oklahoma City, to 1967; pres. Gerland P. Patten & Co., Little Rock, 1960—. Chmn. budget com. of Greater Little Rock Community Chest and Council, 1938; chmn. Pulaski County Welfare Bd., 1940-46; pres. Council Social Agys., Little Rock, 1943-44. Served as 2d lt. U.S. Army, 1944 46. Mem. Ark. Bar Assn. (sec. 1947-50), Pulaski County Bar Assn., Ark. Trial Lawyers (pres. 1973). Methodist. Home: 8 Sunset Cir Little Rock AR 72207-1718 Office: 1095 Union Nat Bank Bldg Little Rock AR 72201

PATTEN, JOHN W., magazine publisher; b. Summit, N.J., 1930. Grad., Dartmouth Coll., 1953. Pres. Bus. Week mag. Office: Bus Week 40th Fl 1221 Ave Of The Americas New York NY 10020-1001*

PATTEN, LANNY RAY, industrial gas industry executive; b. St. Joseph, Mo., July 31, 1934; s. E.L. and Sarah Catherine (Langner) P.; m. Ann Rogers Hall, Oct. 26, 1957; children: David, John, Jeffrey, Mark. BS in Engring., Iowa State U., 1956; AMP, Harvard U., 1976. Field engr. Carrier Corp., Kansas City, Mo., 1957; sales engr. Air Products and Chems., Inc., Allentown, Pitts., Chgo., 1960-63; dist. mgr. Air Products and Chems., Inc., Cleve., 1964-66; region mgr. Air Products and Chems., Inc., Pitts., 1966-68; div. gen. sales mgr. Air Products and Chems., Inc., Allentown, Pa., 1969-75; v.p., div. gen. mgr. Air Products and Chems., Inc., Allentown, 1975-88, sr. v.p., gases and equipment, 1988-90; pres., COO Airgas Inc., Radnor, Pa., 1990-91; pres., chief exec. officer CylServ, Inc., West Choshohocken, Pa., 1992—. Chmn. Lehigh U. Parents Assn., Bethlehem, Pa., 1977-90; campaign com. chmn. Good Shepherd Home, Allentown, 1989-90; mem. Boy Scouts Am., Allentown, 1978-90; pres., coach Youth Baseball Assn., Allentown, 1970-83. USAF Officer, 1957-60. Recipient PACE award for Engring. Achievement Iowa State U., 1990, Friend of Lehigh award, 1991. Mem. Compressed Gas Assn. (exec. bd. dirs. 1977-91), Internat. Oxygen Mfg. Assn. Allentown C. of C. (exec. bd. dirs. 1978-82), Kappa Sigma. Republican. Episcopalian. Avocations: baseball, golf, reading. Home: 1306 Club House Rd Gladwyne PA 19035-1006

PATTEN, ROBERT LOWRY, English language educator; b. Oklahoma City, Apr. 26, 1939; s. Charles H. and Helen (Lowry) P.; m. Faith L. Harris, June 12, 1960 (div. 1974); children: Jocelyn S., Christina S. BA, Swarthmore Coll., 1960; MA, Princeton U., 1963, PhD, 1965. Lectr. Bryn Mawr (Pa.) Coll., 1964-66, asst. prof. English, 1966-69; asst. prof. Rice U., Houston, 1969-71, assoc. prof., 1971-76, prof. English, 1976—, chair, dept. of English, 1991-92, master Grad. House, 1992-95; pres. PEN S.W., Houston, 1989-92. Author: Charles Dickens and His Publishers, 1978, George Cruikshank's Life, Times and Art, vol. 1, 1992, vol. 2, 1996; editor: (book by Charles Dickens) Pickwick Papers, 1972, George Cruikshank: A Revaluation, 1974, 2d edit., 1992, (with John O. Jordan) Literature in the Marketplace, 1995; editor SEL: Studies in English Lit., 1978-84, 90—. Bd. dirs. Cultural Arts Coun., Houston, 1979-80, Tex.Com. for the Humanities, 1979-80; pres., bd. dirs. Houston Ctr. for the Humanities, 1976-84. NEH fellow, 1968-69, 77-78, 87-88; Guggenheim fellow, 1980-81; Nat. Humanities Ctr. fellow, 1987-88; Nat. Gallery of Art Assoc., 1988-89. Mem. AAUP, MLA, PEN Am. Ctr., Dickens Fellowship, Dickens Soc., Grolier Club, Phi Beta Kappa (pres. Beta chpt. Tex. 1991-94). Episcopalian. Avocations: travel, opera. Office: Rice U Dept English MS 30 6100 Main St Houston TX 77005-1827

PATTEN, RONALD JAMES, university dean; b. Iron Mountain, Mich., July 17, 1935; s. Rudolph Joseph and Cecelia (Fuse) Pataconi; m. Shirley Ann Bierman, Sept. 5, 1959; children: Christine Marie, Cheryl Ann, Charlene Denise. BA, Mich. State U., 1957, MA, 1959; PhD, U. Ala., 1963. Acct. Price Waterhouse & Co., Detroit, 1958; instr. No. Ill. U., 1959-60; asst. prof. U. Colo., 1963-65; assoc. prof. Va. Poly. Inst. and State U., 1965-67, prof., 1967-73, head dept. accounting, 1966-73; dir. research Financial Accounting Standards Bd., Conn., 1973-74; dean Sch. Bus. Adminstrn., U. Conn., Storrs, 1974-88; chief of party-Eastern Caribbean Arthur D. Little Internat., 1988-89; dean Coll. Commerce and Kellstadt Grad. Sch. Bus. De Paul U., Chgo., 1989—; cons. to industry; bd. dirs. Transco Inc.; mem. individual investors adv. com. N.Y. Stock Exch., 1993—. Contbr. articles to profl. jours., chpts. to books. Bd. dirs. U.S. com. UNICEF, Chgo. 2d lt. F.A. AUS, 1958. Recipient Nat. Quartermaster award Nat. Quartermaster, Assn., 1956. Mem. AICPA, Am. Acctg. Assn., Inst. Mgmt. Accts., Acad. Internat. Bus. (Dean of Yr. award 1987), Internat. Assn. for Acctg. Edn. and Rsch., Chgo. Coun. Fgn. Rels., Ill. Coun. Econ. Edn. (Chgo., trustee 1989—), Execs. Club Chgo., Econ. Club Chgo., Pacioli Soc., Scabbard and Blade, Golden Key, Beta Gamma Sigma (mem. bd. govs. 1975-90, nat. sec.-treas. 1980-82, nat. v.p. 1982-84, nat. pres. 1984-86), Beta Alpha Psi (bd. dirs. 1992-94), Delta Sigma Pi, Phi Kappa Phi, Delta Mu Delta. Avocations: hiking, skiing, walking, golf, travel. Home: 334 N Montclair Ave Glen Ellyn IL 60137-5253

PATTEN, THOMAS HENRY, JR., management, human resources educator; b. Cambridge, Mass., Mar. 24, 1929; s. Thomas Henry and Lydia Mildred (Lindgren) P.; m. Jule Ann Miller, Aug. 27, 1972; children—Laurie Kathryn, Rhonda Josephine, Jenny Lydia. A.B., Brown U., 1953; M.S., Cornell U., 1955, Ph.D., 1959. Dir. program planning Ford Motor Co., Dearborn, Mich., 1957-65; prof. mgmt. and sociology U. Detroit, 1965-67; prof. orgnl. behavior and personnel mgmt. Sch. Labor and Indsl. Relations, Mich. State U., E. Lansing, 1967-84; prof. mgmt. and human resources Calif. State Poly. U., Pomona, 1984—; cons. in field. Author: The Foreman: The Forgotten Man of Management, 1968, Manpower Planning and the Development of Human Resources, 1971, OD-Emerging Dimensions and Concepts, 1973, A Bibliography of Compensation Planning and Administration, 1960-1974, 2d rev. edit., 1981, 3d rev. edit., 1987, Pay: Employee Compensation and Incentive Plans, 1977, Classics of Personnel Management, 1979, Organizational Development Through Teambuilding, 1981, A Manager's Guide to Performance Appraisal, 1982, Fair Pay: The Managerial Challenge of Comparable Job Worth and Job Evaluation, 1988. Served with USMC, 1946-51. Mem. ASTD (chmn. orgn. devel. div. 1972), Indsl. Rels. Rsch. Assn. (chpt. pres. 1970-71), Am. Sociol. Assn., Internat. Pers. Mgmt. Assn., Internat. Indsl. Rels. Assn., Orgnl. Behavior Teaching Soc., Inst. Applied Behavioral Sci., Acad. Mgmt., Am. Compensation Assn. Home: 353 Independence Dr Claremont CA 91711-1954 Office: Calif State Poly U Dept Mgmt & Human Resources 3801 W Temple Ave Pomona CA 91768-2557 *Human values come first.*

PATTEN, THOMAS LOUIS, lawyer; b. Mo., Oct. 3, 1945; m. Sherry V. Patten; children: Elizabeth, Caroline, Brooke. BS, U. Mo., 1967, JD, 1969. Bar: Mo. 1969, D.C. 1972, U.S. Dist. Ct. D.C. 1972, U.S. Claims Ct. 1972, U.S. Ct. Appeals (fed. cir.) 1972, U.S. Supreme Ct. 1972, U.S. Ct. Appeals (9th cir.) 1974, U.S. Ct. Appeals (4th cir.) 1981, Va. 1983, U.S. Dist. Ct. (ea. and we. dists.) Va. 1983. Ptnr Latham & Watkins, Washington. Fellow Am. Coll. Trial Lawyers. Office: Latham & Watkins Ste 1300 1001 Pennsylvania Ave NW Washington DC 20004-2505

PATTEN-VAN SERTIMA, JACQUELINE L., academic program director, photographer; b. N.Y.C., Jan. 6, 1948; d. Bernard Philip and Sarah Elizabeth (Gay) P.; children: LaCheun LaVette, LaSarah Renata; m. Ivan Van Sertima; stepchildren: Michael E. and Lawrence J. Van Sertima. BS in Psychology and Sociology, Hunter Coll., 1980, MS in Edn., 1982. Asst. theatre and dance photographer for Max Waldman, N.Y.C., 1978-80; free lance photographer and cons., N.Y.C., 1976—; art dir., cover designer Jour. African Civilizations, New Brunswick, N.J., also established audio div., Legacies, Inc., producer companion audio cassettes to vols., 1981—; dir. job location and devel. L.I. U., Bklyn., 1983-85, dir career svcs. 1985-87. Photog. exhbns. include Mus. City N.Y., 1976, Columbia U., 1979, Lincoln Ctr., 1980, Black Artists in Am., 1980, Nat. Urban League, 1980, NYU, 1981, Hunter Coll., 1981. Recipient Lincoln Ctr. photography award Womanart Galleries, 1980; 1st prize award Mademoiselle's 14th Ann. Photography Competition, 1980; internationally known for hand-painted photography and its significant contbn. to social awareness. Mem. Collective Black Photographers, Photog. Soc. Am., Am. Soc. Media Photographers. Home and Office: 347 Felton Ave Highland Park NJ 08904-2217

PATTERSON, ALAN BRUCE, obstetrician, gynecologist; b. Indpls., Apr. 23, 1953; s. Samuel S. and Eunice Selma (Brenner) P. BS, Tulane U., 1975; MD, Ind. U., Indpls., 1979. Diplomate Am. Bd. Ob-Gyn. Resident in ob-gyn St. Vincent Hosp., Indpls., 1979-83; mem. staff Metro Health., Indpls., 1983-91; pvt. practice Pompano Beach, Boca Raton, Fla., 1991—; mem. staff, cons., instr. Meth. Hosp., Indpls, 1983-91; instr. Nurse Pitocin Cert. Course, 1985; cons. Indpls. Planned Parenthood, 1982-83, United Parcel Service, Indpls., 1982-83. Recipient Outstanding Citizens award DAR, 1971. Fellow Am. Coll. Ob-Gyn; mem. Palm Beach County Med. Soc., Fla. Med. Assn., Am. Cancer Soc., Boca Raton C. of C., Phi Beta Kappa, Phi Eta Sigma, Beta Beta Beta. Jewish. Avocations: jogging, swimming, wine collecting, photography, racing. Home: 19090 Fox Landing Dr Boca Raton FL 33434-5154 Office: MDPA 550 SW 3rd St Ste 105 Pompano Beach FL 33060-6944 also: 1000 NW 9th Ct Ste 103 Boca Raton FL 33486-2268 also: 1500 University Dr #106 Coral Springs FL 33071

PATTERSON, ANITA MATTIE, union administrator; b. Birmingham, Ala., Feb. 19, 1940; d. John Evans Patterson and Flora Ella (Paul) Patterson/Mitchell; m. LeRoy Harold Walden, Mar. 19, 1958 (dec. Apr. 1966); children: Christopher Ann, DeRoy, Chanita. Student, Wayne State U., 1968-72, 72-78, Wayne State U., 1976-79. Sr. counselor City of Detroit, 1965-79; area dir. AFSCME, Washington, 1979—; exec. bd. Coalition Labor Union Women, Washington, exec. dir., 1975-77; chair nat. women's com. Coalition Black Trade Unionists, Washington, 1985—; tchg. fellow AFL-CIO Organizing Inst., Washington, 1992—; ofcl. election observer South Africa Election, 1994. Active So. Regional Coun., Atlanta, 1992—; mem. social svcs. com. Salem Bapt. Ch., Atlanta, 1990—. Recipient Cmty. Svcs. award A. Philip Randolph Inst., 1990, Cmty. Svcs. award So. Christian Leadership Coun., 1991, Leadership award Ga. State Legislature Black Caucus, 1992, Disting. Recognition award City of Detroit, 1989, Sojourner Truth award Coalition of Black Trade Unionists, 1994, Labor award Operation PUSH, 1994; named Addie L. Wyatt Women of Yr., Coalition of Black Trade Unionists, 1990, Ga. Labor Hall of Fame, 1996. Mem. Nat. Coun. Negro Women (ad hoc labor com. 1986—, Recognition award 1989, Svc. award 1988), Marracci Ct. # 32. Democrat. Avocations: reading, crossword puzzles, word games, golf, traveling. Office: AFSCME Internat Area Office 1720 Peachtree St NW Ste 150B Atlanta GA 30309-2439

PATTERSON, AUBREY BURNS, JR., banker; b. Grenada, Miss., Sept. 25, 1942; s. Aubrey Burns and Elizabeth (Staten) P.; m. Ruby Kathryn Clegg, Dec. 12, 1964; children: Aubrey B. III, Clayton H., Jennifer L. BBA, U. Miss., 1964; MBA, Mich. State U., 1969; student, Grad. Sch. Banking, U. Wis. With Bank of Miss., Tupelo, 1972—, pres., 1983—, chmn., chief exec. officer, 1990—; chmn., CEO BancorpSouth, Inc.; bd. dirs. Vol. Bank, Jackson, Tenn. Former chmn. bd. dirs. Salvation Army, Tupelo, 1978—; bd. dirs. Cmty. Devel. Found., chmn. bd., 1994-95; bd. dirs. Columbia Theol. Sem., Decatur, Ga., U. Miss. Found., Miss. Univ. for Women Found., Presbyn. Ch. U.S.A. Found., Miss. Econ. Coun., Jackson, 1986—, chmn., 1994; bd. dirs. North Miss. Health Svcs. Inc., 1987—, also exec. com.; moderator St. Andrews Presbytery Presbyn. Ch. USA. Capt. USAF, 1965-72. Decorated Air Force Commendation medal. Mem. Am. Bankers Assn., Miss. Bankers Assn. (pres. 1995—), Robert Morris Assocs., Soc. Internat. Bus. Fellows, Tupelo Country Club, Univ. Club, Kiwanis (pres. Tupelo 1987), Beta Gamma Sigma, Beta Alpha Psi. Presbyterian. Home: 1 Overdale Dr Tupelo MS 38801 Office: Bancorp Miss PO Box 789 Tupelo MS 38802

PATTERSON, BEVERLY ANN GROSS, fund raising consultant, social services administrator, poet; b. Pauls Valley, Okla., Aug. 5, 1938; d. Wilburn G. Jack and Mildred E. (Steward) Gross; m. Kenneth Dean Patterson, June 18, 1960 (div. 1976); children: Tracy Dean, Nancy Ann Patterson-McArthur, Beverly Jeanne Patterson-Wertman. AA, Modesto (Calif.) Jr. Coll., 1958; BA in Social Sci., Fresno (Calif.) State U., 1960; M in Community Counseling, Coll. Idaho; postgrad., Stanislaus State Coll., Turlock, Calif., U. Idaho, Boise (Idaho) State U. Cert. secondary tchr., Calif., Idaho, lic. real estate agt., Idaho. Secondary tchr. Ceres and Modesto Calif., Payette and Weiser Idaho, Ontario Oreg., 1960-67; dir. vol. svcs. mental retardation and child devel. State of Idaho, 1967-70, cons. dir. vol. svcs. health and welfare, 1970-72; dir. Ret. Sr. Vol. Program, Boise, 1972-74; exec. dir. Idaho Nurses Assn., Boise, 1974-76; community svcs. adminstr. City of Davis, Calif., 1976-78; devel. dir. and fundraising Mercy Med. Ctr., Nampa, Idaho, 1978-85; exec. dir. St. Alphonsus Med. Ctr. Found., Boise, 1985-87; dir. devel. and gift planning Idaho Youth Ranch, Boise, 1989-94; fund devel. cons. Mercy Housing, Nampa, Idaho, 1994-96, Pratt Ranch Boys Home, Emmett, Idaho, 1994-96, Northwest Childrens Home, Lewiston, Idaho, 1994-96, Idaho Spl. Olympics, Boise, 1994-95, Port of Hope Inc., Boise, 1994-95, Idaho Found. for Parks and Lands, Boise, 1994-95, St. Vincent de Paul, Inc., Boise, 1995—, Nampa Shelter Found., Inc., 1994-95, Turning Point Inc., Nampa, 1994-95, Port of Hope Treatment Ctr. Inc., Boise, 1995-96, Idaho Theater for Youth, Inc., Boise, 1995-96, Boise Tennis Coalition, Inc., 1995—, El Ada Cmty. Action Ctr., Boise, 1995; with Hemophilia Found. Idaho, 1995-96; incorporator, pres. Boise YWCA, 1996—, Melba (Idaho) Sch. Dist., 1996—; and many more; founder Fellowship Christian Adult Singles, Boise, 1974; cons., exec. dir. Boise Hotline, 1988-90; cons., fundraiser Cmty, Resources and Devel., 1980; co-dir. ACOA workshop leader Child Within Concepts, Inc., Boise, 1987—; cons. coord. Rural Hosp. Edn. Consortium, 1988; cons. hosp. fund devel. and cmty. resources Gritman Meml. Hosp., Moscow, Idaho, 1987-88; cons., conf. coord. State of Idaho, 1987-88; counsel Adult Children of Alcoholics, 1991; incorporator, pres. Nonprofit Solutions, Inc., Boise, 1995—; co-dir., incorporator Concepts, Inc., Meridian, 1996—; pres. Q&A Distbg. and Cons., Meridian, Idaho, 1994-95. Contbr. articles to profl. jours. Coord. Idaho Golf Angels Open Pro-Am Tournament, Boise, 1989-91; founding exec. v.p. Coll. Fund for Students Surviving Cancer, 1993—; bd. dirs. Arthritis Found., Idaho, 1984-86, Idaho Mental Health Assn., 1985-87, charitable fund raising coord., 1978—; founder Ctrl. Vol. Bur., Boise, 1971; mem. Idaho Devel. Network, 1990—. Named Idaho Statesman Disting. Citizen, 1985. Mem. Nat. Assn. for Hosp. Devel. (accredited, treas. 1980, accreditation chmn. 1984-86, conf. chmn. 1982, 85), Assn. Hosps. in Philanthropy (accredited), Nat. Soc. Fund Raising Execs. Mem. Community Christian Ch. Avocations: golf, family activities. Home and Office: 315 W Maple Ave Meridian ID 83642-2268 also: Child Within Concepts 2920 Raindrop Dr Boise ID 83706-4840

PATTERSON, CHARLES DAROLD, librarian, educator; b. Wahpeton, N.D., Aug. 8, 1928; s. Charles Irwin and Inez Fern (Slagg) P. B.Sc., Bemidji State U., 1950; M.A., U. Minn., 1956; M.Music, W.Va. U., 1964; advanced cert., U. Pitts., 1968, Ph.D., 1971. Tchr. music Fargo (N.D.) public schs., 1950; jr. reference librarian U. Minn. Libraries, 1954-55; head librarian Bemidji (Minn.) State U., 1955-58; dir. libraries, asst. prof. Glenville (W.Va.) State Coll., 1958-62; asst. prof. W.Va. U., 1962-66; instr. Grad. Sch. Library and Info. Scis. U. Pitts., 1966-71, asst. prof., 1971-72; assoc. prof. Sch. Library and Info. Sci. La. State U., Baton Rouge, 1972-78; prof. Sch. Library and Info. Sci. La. State U., 1978-93; prof. emeritus, 1993; Del. La. Gov.'s Conf. on Library and Info. Services, 1978. Author: Analysis of Library of Congress Music Subject Headings, 1971, JEL Cumulative Index, 1979, supplement, 1982, (with D.G. Davis) ARBA Guide to Library Science Literature, 1987; editor: W.Va. Libraries, 1963-66; mem. editorial bd.; Jour. of Edn. for Librarianship, 1975-79, editor, 1980-84; editor: Jour. Edn. for Library and Info. Sci., 1984-88; asst. editor Reference Services Review, 1986-93; contbr. articles to profl. jours. Served with U.S. Army, 1950-52. Recipient La. State U. Faculty Excellence award, 1984, ALA/Beta Phi Mu award, 1989. Mem. ALA (chmn. scholarship jury 1972-73), W.Va. Library Assn. (chmn. coll. and univ. library sect. 1960-61, exec. bd. 1960-61, 64-66), Assn. Coll. and Research Libraries (pres. Tri-state chpt. 1972), Assn. Am. Library Schs. (exec. bd. 1980-88), La. Library Assn., Southeastern Library Assn., AAUP (pres. chpt. 1985-86), Am. Guild Organists (dean chpt. 1985-86), Pitts. Bibliophiles, Univ. Chamber Music Soc. (pres., dir. 1979-80), Beta Phi Mu. (dir.-at-large 1982-85). Methodist. Home: 1480 Kenmore Ave Baton Rouge LA 70808-1130 also: Birchmont Beach Bemidji MN 56601 Office: La State U Sch Libr and Info Sci Baton Rouge LA 70803 *When one is confident in his own mind that he has, with given abilities, done his very best, then perhaps he has paid for his niche in eternity.*

PATTERSON, CHARLES ERNEST, lawyer; b. Rockford, Ill., Jan. 4, 1941; s. Alvin Maurice and Helen Mae (Mitchell) P. A.B. cum laude, U. Kans., 1963; J.D. with distinction U. Mich., 1966. Bar: Mo. 1966, U.S. Dist. Ct. (we. dist.) Mo. 1966, U.S. Ct. Mil. Appeals 1968, U.S. Supreme Ct. 1969, U.S. Ct. Appeals (8th cir.) 1971, Calif. 1985, U.S. Dist. Ct. (cen., no. dists.) Calif. 1985. Assoc. Watson, Ess, Marshall & Enggas, Kansas City, Mo., 1966-74, ptnr., 1974-85; ptnr. Lillick, McHose & Charles, Los Angeles; chmn. exec. com. 1987—; now ptnr. Pillsbury Madison & Sutro, L.A.; chmn. various coms. Def. Research Inst., 1978—; bd. govs. Legal Aid of Western Mo., 1978-80; mem. bench/bar com. Western div. Mo. Ct. Appeals, 1983—, 16th Jud. Cir. Ct. Mo., 1983—; mem. fed. practice com. U.S. Dist. Ct. (we. dist.) Mo. 1983— . Contbr. articles to profl. jours. Bd. dirs. Boys Clubs Greater Kansas City, Inc., 1974-78, Dismas House Kansas City, 1978-84, Mo. Assn. for Ex-Offenders, 1976-79, YMCA, 1976-79; v.p. Heart of Am. Rugby Football Union, Kansas City, 1976-78; pres. Pre Trial Diversion Services, Inc., Kansas City, 1976-78, Kansas City Vietnam Vets. Meml. Fund, 1984—; mem. bd. Kansas City Arts Council, 1984, Mo. Boys Town, Kansas City, 1983-84. Served to capt. USMC, 1966-69; Vietnam. Decorated Bronze Star medal with Combat V, Vietnamese Cross of Gallantry with Palm, Vietnamese Medal of Honor. Mem. ABA (ho. of dels. 1984—), Mo. Bar (bd. govs. 1978-84, pres. 1983-84, Award of Merit 1984, Jud. Conf. award 1984), Kansas City Bar Assn., Lawyers Assn. Kansas City, Western Mo. Def. Lawyers Assn. (pres. 1981-82), Mo. Orgn. Def. Lawyers (bd. dirs. 1984-85), Internat. Assn. Ins. Counsel. Clubs: Kansas City, Carriage (Kansas City, Mo.). Office: Pillsbury Madison & Sutro 725 S Figueroa St Ste 1200 Los Angeles CA 90017-5443*

PATTERSON, CHRISTOPHER NIDA, lawyer; b. Washington Courthouse, Ohio, Apr. 17, 1960; s. Donis Dean and JoAnne (Nida) O.; children: Travis, Kirsten. BA, Clemson U., 1982; JD, Nova U., 1985. Bar: Fla. 1985, U.S. Dist. Ct. (mid. dist.) Fla. 1985, U.S. Ct. Mil. Rev. 1986, U.S. Ct. Mil. Appeals 1987, U.S. Dist. Ct. (ea. dist.) Va. 1987, U.S. Supreme Ct. 1990, U.S. Ct. Appeals (11th cir.) 1992, U.S. Dist. Ct. (no. dist.) Fla. 1992, U.S. Dist. Ct. (so. dist.) Tex. 1995; cert. criminal trial lawyer Fla. Bar. and Nat. Bd. Trial Advocacy. Prosecutor Fla. State Attys. Office, Orlando, Fla., 1985; spl. asst. U.S. Atty. U.S. Dist. Ct. (ea. dist.) Va., 1987-90; ptnr. Patterson, Hauversburk and Cassidy, Panama City, Fla., 1992—; adj. prof. law Gulf Coast Coll. Author: Queen's Pawn, 1996. Capt. U.S. Army, 1986-92, Desert Storm. Mem. Nat. Assn. Criminal Def. Lawyers, Fla. Assn. Criminal Def. Lawyers, Acad. Fla. Trial Lawyers, Fla. Bar (criminal law sect., mil. law standing com., Pro Bono Svc. award), Bay County Bar Assn.

Episcopalian. Avocations: athletics, triathlons. Office: PO Box 1368 303 Magnolia Ave Panama City FL 32401-3124

PATTERSON, DAWN MARIE, dean, consultant, writer; b. Gloversville, N.Y., July 30; d. Robert Morris and Dora Margaret (Perham) P.; m. Robert Henry Hollenbeck, Aug. 3, 1958 (div. 1976); children: Adrienne Lyn, Nathaniel Conrad. BS in Edn., SUNY, Geneseo, 1962; MA, Mich. State U., 1973, PhD, 1977; postgrad., U. So. Calif. and Inst. Ednl. Leadership. Librarian Brighton (N.Y.) Cen. Schs., 1962-67; asst. to regional dir. Mich. State U. Ctr., Bloomfield Hills, 1973-74; grad. asst. Mich. State U., East Lansing, 1975-77; cons. Mich. Efficiency Task Force, 1977; asst. dean Coll. Continuing Edn., U. So. Calif., Los Angeles, 1978-84; dean, assoc. prof. continuing edn. Calif. State U., Los Angeles, 1985—; CEO Acclaims Enterprises Internat.; pres. Co-Pro Assocs. Mem. Air Univ. Bd. Visitors, 1986-90, Commn. on Extended Edn. Calif. State U. Calif., 1988-91; Hist. Soc., Los Angeles Town Hall, Los Angeles World Affairs Council. Dora Louden scholar, 1958-61; Langworthy fellow, 1961-62; Edn. Professions Devel. fellow, 1974-75; Ednl. Leadership Policy fellow, 1982-83; Leadership Calif., 1992, Leadership Am., 1994. Mem. AAUW (pres. Pasadena br. 1985-86), Am. Assn. Adult and Continuing Edn. (charter), Nat. Univ. Continuing Edn. Assn., Internat. Assn. Continuing Edn. and Tng. (bd. dirs. 1990—), Calif. Coll. and Mil. Educators Assn. (pres.), Los Angeles Airport Area Edn. Industry Assn. (pres. 1984), Rotary Club of Alhambra (bd. dirs.), Fine Arts (Pasadena), Zonta (pres. 1994—), Kappa Delta Pi, Phi Delta Kappa, Phi Beta Delta, Phi Kappa Phi. Republican. Unitarian. Office: 5151 State University Dr Los Angeles CA 90032-4221

PATTERSON, DENNIS GLEN, Canadian government official, lawyer; b. Vancouver, B.C., Can., Dec. 30, 1948; common law wife: Marie Uviluq; children: Bruce, George, Jessica, Alexander. BA with distinction, U. Alta., Edmonton, 1969; LLB, Dalhousie U., Halifax, N.S., 1972. Bar: N.S., 1972, B.C., 1974. Exec. dir. Maliiganik Tukisinniavik, Iqaluit, N.W.T., Can., 1975-81; mem. legis. assembly, Iqaluit Govt. of N.W.T., Yellowknife, 1979-93, minister edn., 1981-88, minister aboriginal rights and constl. devel., 1981-87, minister responsible for women, 1985-96; pvt. prctice, 1996—; govt. leader, 1987-91, mem. cabinet, 1991-92, now mem. legis. assembly. Avocations: seal hunting, piano. *

PATTERSON, DENNIS JOSEPH, management consultant; b. Honolulu, Apr. 13, 1948; s. Joseph John and Dorothy Elizabeth (Snajkowski) P.; m. Susan Tyra Pedlow, Dec. 31, 1981; children: Valerie Jean, Christina Elizabeth. BA, Elmhurst (Ill.) Coll., 1970; MA, George Washington U., 1973. Asst. dir. Vancouver (B.C.) Gen. Hosp., 1973-76, dir., 1975-76; v.p. Shaughnessy Hosp., Vancouver, 1976-79; pres. Westcare, Vancouver, 1979-84; mgr. Ernst & Whinney, Chgo., 1984-86, sr. mgr., 1986-88, ptnr., 1988-93; pres. FHP Internat. Cons. Group, Inc., Fountain Valley, Calif., 1993—. Contbr. articles to profl. jours. fin. mgr. Electoral Action Movement, Vancouver, 1978; trustee George Washington U., Calif. Sch. Profl. Psychology. Fellow Am. Coll. Healthcare Execs.; mem. Royal Vancouver Yacht Club, Va. Country Club, Manhattan Beach C.C., Phi Gamma Mu. Republican. Anglican. Avocation: sailboat racing, golf.

PATTERSON, DONALD FLOYD, human, medical and veterinary genetics educator; b. Maracaibo, Venezuela, Feb. 2, 1931; came to U.S., 1932; s. Carl Earl and Dayne (Murphy) P.; children: Russell H., Wade D. DVM, Okla. State U., 1954; DSc, U. Pa., 1967. Diplomate Am. Coll. Vet. Internal Medicine, Am. Bd. Vet. Internal Medicine, Am. Bd. Vet. Cariology. Intern Angell Meml. Hosp., Boston, 1954-56; instr. Okla. State U., Stillwater, 1956; instr., asst. prof. Vet. Sch. U. Pa., Phila., 1958-64, from assoc. prof. to prof. Vet. Sch., 1966-73, chief sect. med. genetics, 1966-95, Sheppard prof. med. genetics Vet. Sch., 1973—, prof. human genetics Med. Sch., 1974—; NIH spl. fellow divsn. med. genetics Johns Hopkins U., Balt., 1964-66; dir. Ctr. for Comparative Med. Genetics U. Pa., Phila., 1995—. Author computer program for canine genetic diseases; contbr. over 300 papers to sci. and med. jours. Capt. USAF, 1956-58. Recipient Merit award Am. Animal Hosp. Assn., 1982, NIH Merit award, 1989, 91, Med. Rsch. award World Congress Vet. Medicine, 1992. Fellow Am. Coll. Cardiology, Phila. Coll. Physicians; mem. AVMA (Gaines Rsch. award 1972, Career Rsch. Achievement award 1995), Am. Soc. Human Genetics. Democrat. Avocations: canoeing, poetry, literature. Office: U Pa Sch Vet Medicine 3900 Delancey St Philadelphia PA 19104-6010

PATTERSON, DONIS DEAN, bishop; b. Holmesville, Ohio, Apr. 27, 1930; s. Raymond J. and Louella Faye (Glasgo) P.; m. JoAnne Nida, Dec. 22, 1951; children: Christoper Nida, Andrew Joseph. BS, Ohio State U., 1952; STB, Episcopal Theol. Sch., 1957; M Div, Episcopal Divinity Sch., 1972; DD (hon.), Nashotah House Sem., 1984, U. of South, 1986. Rector St. Andrews Ch., Washington Court House, Ohio, 1957-63, St. Marks Ch., Venice, Fla., 1963-70, All Sts. Ch., Winter Park, Fla., 1970-83; bishop Episcopal Diocese Dallas, 1983-92; assisting bishop Episcopal Diocese of Ctrl. Gulf Coast, 1992-96;, 1996—; trustee Seabury Western Theol. Sem., Evanston, Ill., 1981-82, U. of South, 1983-92, Episcopal Theol. Sem. S.W., 1983-92. Chmn. Episcopal Ch. House of Bishops Armed Forces Com., 1989-93. Col., chaplain U.S. Army, 1952-54, Korea.

PATTERSON, EDWARD, investment banker; b. N.Y.C., Oct. 16, 1920; s. Arthur C. and Evelyn (Crimmins) P.; m. Joan Metzger, Jan. 10, 1947 (div. 1972); children: Patricia Kean, Lucinda, Elizabeth, Christina P. Fay. B.A., Yale U., 1943. Mem. N.Y. Stock Exch., N.Y.C., 1950-56; exec. v.p. Allen & Co., N.Y.C., 1956—, also bd. dirs.; dir. Teleprompter, 1980-82. Guest writer News Leader, Richmond, W.Va.; contbr. articles to N.Y. Times. Trustee Citizens Budget Commn., N.Y.C., 1957-80; trustee Garvan Collection, Yale U., 1968; mem. Fordham U. Council, N.Y.C., 1975; mem. Cardinal's Com. of the Laity. Lt. USNR, 1942-46, ETO. Roman Catholic. Clubs: Deepdale (Manhasset, N.Y.) (pres. 1970-75); Piping Rock (Locust Valley, N.Y.); Friendly Sons of St. Patrick. Office: Allen & Co 711 5th Ave New York NY 10022-3109

PATTERSON, ELIZABETH JOHNSTON, former congresswoman; b. Columbia, SC, Nov. 18, 1939; d. Olin DeWitt and Gladys (Atkinson) Johnston; m. Dwight Fleming Patterson, Jr., Apr. 15, 1967; children: Dwight Fleming, Olin DeWitt, Catherine Leigh. BA, Columbia Coll., 1961; postgrad. in polit. sci., U. S.C., 1961, 62, 64; LLD (hon.), Columbia Coll., 1987; D Pub. Svc. (hon.), Converse Coll., 1989. Pub. affairs officer Peace Corps, Washington, 1962-64; postgrad. VISTA, OEO, Washington, 1965-66; D Pub. Svc. Head Start and VISTA, OEO, Columbia, 1966-67; tri-county dir. Head Start, Piedmont Community Actions, Spartanburg, S.C., 1967-68; mem. Spartanburg County Coun., 1975-76, S.C. State Senate, 1979-86, 100th-102nd Congresses from 4th S.C. dist., 1987-93. Trustee Wofford Coll., 1975-81; bd. dirs. Charles Lea Ctr., 1978-90, Spartanburg Coun. on Aging; pres. Spartanburg Dem. Women, 1968; v.p. Spartanburg County Dem. party, 1968-70, sec., 1970-75; trustee Columbia Coll., 1991—. Mem. Bus. and Profl. Women's Club, Alpha Kappa Gamma. Methodist. Office: PO Box 5564 Spartanburg SC 29304-5564

PATTERSON, ELLMORE CLARK, banker; b. Western Springs, Ill., Nov. 29, 1913; s. Ellmore Clark and Harriet Emma (Wales) P.; m. Anne Hyde Choate, Sept. 28, 1940; children: Michael Ellmore, Arthur Choate, Robert Ellmore, David Choate, Thomas Hyde Choate. Grad., Lake Forest Acad., 1931; B.S., U. Chgo., 1935. With J. P. Morgan & Co., Inc., N.Y.C., 1935-39, 39-41, 46-59; v.p. J. P. Morgan & Co., Inc., 1951-59; exec. v.p. Morgan Guaranty Trust Co. N.Y. (merger J.P. Morgan and Guaranty Trust Co.), 1959-65, dir., chmn. exec. com., 1967-68, pres., 1969-71, chmn., 1971-77, chmn. exec. com., 1978; with Morgan Stanley & Co., 1939; dir. comml. Union Corp., Engelhard Hanovia, Inc.; chmn. dirs. adv. coun. Morgan Guaranty Trust Co.; mem. Presdl. Com. on Fin. Structure and Regulation, 1970-72. Bd. mgrs. Meml. Hosp. Cancer and Allied Diseases, N.Y.C.; Sloan-Kettering Inst. Cancer Center, N.Y.C., U. Chgo., Mass. Inst. Tech. Served from ensign to lt. comdr. USNR, 1941-46. Mem. Psi Upsilon. Episcopalian. Clubs: Links (N.Y.C.); Bedford (N.Y.); Golf and Tennis; Jupiter Island (Hobe Sound, Fla.); Fishers Island Country; Seminole Golf (Palm Beach, Pla.). Office: 23 Wall St New York NY 10260-1000

PATTERSON, EUGENE CORBETT, retired editor, publisher; b. Valdosta, Ga., Oct. 15, 1923; s. William C. and Annabel (Corbett) P.; m. Mary Sue Carter, Aug. 19, 1950; 1 child, Mary Patterson Fausch. Student, North Ga. Coll., Dahlonega, 1940-42; AB in Journalism, U. Ga., 1943; LL.D., Tusculum Coll., 1965, Harvard U., 1969, Duke U., 1978, Stetson U., 1984, Ind. U., 1990; Litt.D., Emory U., 1966, Oglethorpe Coll., 1966, Tuskegee U., 1966, Roanoke Coll., 1968, Mercer U., 1968, Eckerd Coll., 1977, U. South Fla., 1986, Dillard U., 1992; Colby Coll., 1994. Reporter Temple (Tex.) Daily Telegram and Macon (Ga.) Telegraph, 1947-48; mgr. for S.C. United Press, 1948-49; night bur. mgr. United Press, N.Y.C., 1949-53; mgr. London bur. United Press, also chief corr. U.K., 1953-56; v.p., exec. editor Atlanta Journal-Constitution, 1956-60; editor Atlanta Constitution, 1960-68; mng. editor Washington Post, 1968-71; prof. polit. sci. Duke U., 1971-72; editor, pres. St. Petersburg (Fla.) Times, 1972-84, chmn., chief exec. officer, 1978-88, editor emeritus, 1988—; editor, pres. Congl. Quar., Washington, 1972-86; chmn., chief exec. officer Congl. Quar., 1978-88; chmn. bd., chief exec. officer Fla. Trend mag., 1980-88, Ga. Trend mag., 1984-88, Ariz. Trend mag., 1986-88, Governing mag., 1987-88, Modern Graphic Arts, Inc., 1978-88, Poynter Inst. Media Studies, 1978-88, Poynter Fund, 1978-88. Vice chmn. U.S. Civil Rights Commn., 1964-68; mem. Pulitzer Prize Bd., 1973-84; trustee ASNE Found., 1981-84, U. Ga. Found., 1982-88, North Ga. Coll. Found., 1991-93, Am. Press Inst., Reston, Va., 1983-88, Duke U., 1988-94, Fla. Bar Found., 1992-93, LeRoy Collins Ctr. for Pub. Policy, 1990-93. Decorated Silver Star, Bronze Star with oak leaf cluster in 10th Armored Divsn., Gen. Patton's 3rd Army; recipient Pulitzer prize for editl. writing Columbia U., 1966, William Allen White Nat. Citation award U. Kans., 1980, Elijah Parish Lovejoy award Colby Coll., 1994. Fellow Soc. Profl. Journalists; mem. Am. Soc. Newspaper Editors (pres. 1977-78), St. Petersburg Yacht Club, Vinoy Club. Home: Snell Isle 1967 Brightwaters Blvd NE Saint Petersburg FL 33704-3007 Office: 535 Central Ave Saint Petersburg FL 33701-3703

PATTERSON, FLORENCE GHORAM, real estate broker; b. Savannah, Ga., Mar. 20, 1936; d. Ernest and Ida (Robinson) Ghoram; m. Carl Patterson (div. 1986); children: Chrysetta Patricia, Carl Jr. Student, CCNY. Lic. real estate broker, N.Y. Mgr. Am. Express Credit Card, N.Y.C., 1958-59; asst. v.p. Citicorp, N.Y.C., 1967-84; exec. dir., founder Pamoja Internat. Cultural Exch., Inc., Helena, N.Y., 1982—, editor Internat. Cookbook, 1992—; v.p. Parent Tchr. Support Group, Ft. Covington, N.Y., 1989-91, pres., 1991—; layout & design tech. PICEI Connected Publs., 1992—. Committeewoman Dem. Ctrl. Com., Suffolk County, N.Y., 1984; founder Deer Park (N.Y.) NAACP, 1968; v.p. United Civic Assn. Deer Park, 1982, pres., 1983-84; pres. PTA/PTSA Salmon River Ctrl. Sch., 1992-93, 95-96, v.p., 1994, rep. bldg. level team, 1994-95; facilitator secondary bldg. level team Compact for LEarning, 1994—; organizer Festival of Drums Multicultural Celebration. Recipient Cert. of Merit Universal Sons and Daus. of Ethopia, Inc., 1985, County Legis., Babylon, N.Y., 1985, Proclamation County Exec., Suffolk County, 1985, Town of Islip, N.Y., 1986, Personalities of Am. Cultural award, 1992, Vol. award Riverview N.Y. State Correctionsl Facility, 1995. Mem. NAFE, AMA, Nat. Trust for Hist. Presertion, Am. Mus. Natural History (hon. advisor), Nat. Arbor Day Found. Mem. Spiritual Ch. Avocations: ice skating, reading, dancing. Home and Office: 600 Smith Rd Brasher Falls NY 13613 also: Rt 37 Chatenuga St Fort Covington NY 12937

PATTERSON, GLENN WAYNE, botany educator; b. China Grove, N.C., Mar. 9, 1938; s. Simpson Wayne and Alice (Fisher) P.; m. Nancy Ann deLesdernier, Sept. 2, 1961; children: Steven, Eric, Alan. B.S., N.C. State U., 1960; M.S., U. Md., 1963, Ph.D., 1964. Asst. prof. dept. botany U. Md., College Park, 1964-69, assoc. prof., 1969-73, prof. botany, 1973—, chmn. dept., 1977-87, acting assoc. dean Colls. Agriculture and Life Scis., 1986-89. Recipient Biol. Scis. award Washington Acad. Scis., 1971. Mem. Am. Soc. Plant Physiologists, Am. Oil Chemists Soc. Office: Dept Botany Univ Md College Park MD 20742

PATTERSON, GRACE LIMERICK, library director; b. N.Y.C., Nov. 21, 1938; d. Robert and Frieda (Zeiontz) Limerick; m. Joseph Nathaniel Patterson (dec.); children: Lorrayne Carole, Joseph Nathaniel Jr. BA in Sociology, Edn., CUNY, 1971; MLS, Columbia U., 1975; MS in Comm., Coll. New Rochelle, 1989. Cert. libr. N.J. Exec. dir. Manhattanville Community Outreach, N.Y.C., 1971-74; br. and outreach svcs. Paterson (N.J.) Pub. Libr., 1975-79; media specialist II Passaic County C.C., Paterson, 1979-81; coord. outreach svcs. Irvington (N.J.) Pub. Libr., 1981-84; assoc. prof. libr. Rockland C.C., Suffern, N.Y., 1984-89; libr. dir. Hudson County C.C., Jersey City, 1989—. Editor jours. in field. Exec. bd. dirs. Essex-Hudson Region II, Orange, N.J., 1991; vol. Ridgewood (N.J.) Schs., 1981-83; Ridgewood Centennial Com. First Night, 1993. U.S. Dept. Edn. fellow, 1974-75. Mem. ALA (com., chairperson Black Caucus pub. rels. 1990-92), N.J. Libr. Assn. Avocations: photography, oral history, travel, geneology, public speaking. Office: Hudson County CC 25 Journal Square Jersey City NJ 07306-4300

PATTERSON, GRADY LESLIE, JR., financial advisor; b. Abbeville, S.C., Jan. 13, 1924; s. Grady Leslie and Claudia (McClain) P.; m. Marjorie Harrison Faucett, Dec. 22, 1951; children—Grady Leslie III, Steven G., M. Lynne, Laura A., Amy S., M. Beth. LLB, U. S.C., 1950, BS, 1975, LLD (hon.), 1980; LLD (hon.), The Citadel, 1985; HHD (hon.), Lander Coll., 1990; LLD (hon.), U. Charleston, S.C., 1992, Clemson U., 1992. Bar: S.C. 1950. County service officer Abbeville County, S.C., 1950; ops. officer S.C. Air N.G., Columbia, 1952-59; asst. atty. gen. State of S.C., Columbia, 1959-66, treas., 1967-94; fin. advisor, 1994—. Served with USAAF, 1943-46; maj. USAF, 1950-52, 61-61, ret. Maj. Gen. Decorated D.S.M. USAF. Mem. S.C. Bar Assn. Democrat. Presbyterian. Avocations: golf; jogging. Home: 3016 Petigru St Columbia SC 29204-3618

PATTERSON, HARLAN RAY, finance educator; b. Camden, Ohio, June 27, 1931; s. Ernest Newton and Beulah Irene (Hedrick) P.; children by previous marriage: Kristan Lee, Elizabeth Jane, Nolan Gene. BS cum laude, Miami U., Oxford, Ohio, 1953, MBA, 1959; PhD, Mich. State U., 1963. Asst. prof. fin. U. Ill., Champaign-Urbana, 1962-66; mem. faculty Ohio U., Athens, 1966—; prof. fin. Ohio U., 1977-94, prof. emeritus fin., 1994—; vis. prof., fellow Chgo. Merc. Exc., 1971; fin. cons., researcher projects for industry. Contbr. articles to acad. and profl. jours. Chmn. City of Athens Rainbow Adv. Bd., 1972-77; state chmn. scholarship com. for Ohio Rainbow Girls, 1975-87. Commd. officer USN, 1953-56. Recipient Fred Astaire Bronze I Achievement level; named Congressional Alternate to West Point, 1949; won competitive appointment U.S. Naval Acad., 1950; NROTC scholar, 1950; Stonier fellow, 1961, Mortgage Banking fellow, 1974, Found. Econ. Edn. fellow, 1965, 67, 69, 71. Mem. Internat. Platform Assn., Rotary Internat., Masons, Shriners, Order Eastern Star (worthy patron 1989, 92), Phi Beta Kappa (pres. faculty chpt. 1975), Beta Gamma Sigma (faculty adviser), Phi Eta Sigma, Alpha Kappa Psi, Delta Sigma Pi, Sigma Tau Alpha (adviser), Omicron Delta Epsilon, Pi Kappa Alpha. Republican. Avocation: dance classes. Home: 9B Station St Athens OH 45701-2758

PATTERSON, HELEN CROSBY, clinical psychologist; b. Jackson, Miss., Nov. 12, 1947; d. Thomas Atkinson and Helen Elizabeth (Crosby) Patterson; m. Fred C. Craig, July 7, 1967 (div. July 1970); 1 child, Erin Crosby. BA in Psychology, Millsaps Coll., 1972; MS in Clin. Psychology, U. Wyo., 1976, PhD in Clin. Psychology, 1978. Lic. clin. psychologist, Miss., N.Mex., Del. Coord., supervision and internships Antioch N.E. Grad. Sch., Keene, N.H., 1979-80; sr. clinician Jackson (Miss.) Mental Health Ctr., 1980-82; pvt. practice in Miss. and N.Mex., 1981—; clin. dir. Pain Mgmt. Ctr. St. Vincent Hosp., Santa Fe, N.Mex., 1990-91; psychol. cons. Disability Determination Svcs., Jackson, 1983—, Albuquerque, 1988-90, 91-93, Wilmington, Del., 1993-95; EAP cons., So. Beverage Co., Jackson, 1986-91, St. Vincent Hosp., Santa Fe, 1990-91. Mem. Hinds County Assn. for Children with Learning Disabilities, Jackson, 1985-88, Hinds County Mental Health Assn., Jackson, 1980-83. Mem. APA. Avocations: wholistic health studies, jyotish astrology, horses, ice skating, skiing. Office: 11 Northtown Dr Ste 205 Jackson MS 39211 also: 3817 Don Juan Ct NW Albuquerque NM 87107-2812

PATTERSON, JAMES, mayor; b. San Mateo, Calif., Feb. 18, 1948; m. Sharon LeTourneau, 1968; children: B.J., Jason, Lindsay. BA in Polit. Sci. summa cum laude, Calif. State U., Fresno, 1992. Radio broadcasting exec. Sta. KIRV-AM, Fresno, Calif., 1968—; mayor City of Fresno, 1993—. Chair San Joaquin River Conservancy; vice chair Fresno County Transp. Authority; bd. mem. Fresno City-County Consortium Agy.; chmn. NO on Measure H Com., 1989, Criminal Justice and Law Enforcement Commn., 1990-91; vice chmn. YES on Measure E Com., 1988; mem. Human Rels. Commn., City of Fresno, 1987-91; bd. dirs. Leadership Fresno Alumni Assn., 1989-91, Fresno County YFC/Campus Life, 1984-88. Mem. Fresno City and County C. of C. (chmn. local govt. affairs com. 1990-91, bd. dirs. FRESPAC 1990-91, city budget rev. com. 1989-91, privatization task force 1988-89, charter sect. 809 rev. task force 1987-88). Office: Office of the Mayor/City Coun City Hall 2600 Fresno St Fresno CA 93721-3620

PATTERSON, JAMES MILTON, marketing specialist, educator; b. DeQueen, Ark., Oct. 15, 1927; s. Charles Edward and Phoebe Allene (Steel) P.; m. Della Jeanne Hays, July 3, 1964; children—J. Marshall, Julia M.; children by previous marriage—Robert T., Donald A. B.S., U.S. Mcht. Marine Acad., 1948; M.B.A. (Teagle Found. fellow), Cornell U., 1954, Ph.D. (Ford Found. dissertation fellow), 1961. Third mate Esso Shipping Co., 1948-52; instr. in bus. adminstrn. Northwestern U., 1957-60; lectr. Center for Programs in Govt. Adminstrn., U. Chgo., 1959; asst. prof. mktg. Ind. U., 1960-63, asso. prof., 1963-69, prof., 1969—, chmn. dept. mktg., 1972-78, asso. dir. Poynter Ctr., 1980, acting dir., 1981, co-sec. U. Faculty Coun., pres. Bloomington Faculty Coun.; dir. Ind. U. Inst. for Advanced Study, 1994—; bd. dirs. Inst. Advanced Study; cons. petroleum mktg.; expert witness on antitrust and mktg. Author: Marketing: The Firm's Viewpoint, 1964, Highway Robbery: An Analysis of the Gasoline Crisis, 1974, Competition Ltd.: The Marketing of Gasoline, 1972. Served with USNR, 1945-48. Mem. Assn. for Practical & Profl. Ethics. Democrat. Home: 2431 N Dunn St Bloomington IN 47408-1117 Office: Ind U Inst Advanced Study Bloomington IN 47405

PATTERSON, JAMES RANDOLPH, physician; b. Lancaster, Pa., Jan. 30, 1942; m. Linda Lewis Patterson, Nov. 22, 1969. AB, U. Pa., 1964; MD, Columbia U., 1968. Diplomate Nat. Bd. Med. Examiners, Am. Bd. Internal Medicine, Subspecialty of Pulmonary Disease. Pulmonary and critical care specialist The Oregon Clinic, Portland, 1975—; clin. prof. medicine Oreg. health Scis. U., Portland, 1978—; mem. Am. Bd. Internal Medicine, Phila., 1995—; trustee Collins Med. Trust, Portland, Oreg., 1992—. Contbr. numerous articles to profl. jours. Recipient Class of 1964 award U. Pa., Van Loan award Am. Lung Assn. Oreg., 1990, Meritorious Achievement award Oreg. Health Scis. U., 1991; named Class Pres. Coll. Physicians and Surgeons of Columbia U., 1968, Tchr. of Yr. Providence Med. Ctr., Portland, Oreg., 1976, Internist of Yr., 1983, Best Doctors in Am., 1992-95. Mem. AMA, Am. Thoracic Soc., Am. Coll. Chest Physicians, Oreg. Lung Assn., North Pacific Soc. of Internal Medicine, Pacific Interurban Clin. Club, Multnomah County Med. Soc., Oreg. Med. Assn., Oreg. Soc. Ctirical Care Medicine. Office: The Oregon Clinic 507 NE 47th Ave Portland OR 97213

PATTERSON, JAMES WILLIS, pathology and dermatology educator; b. Takoma Park, Md., Dec. 29, 1946; s. James Clark and Helen (Hendricks) P.; m. Julie Wyatt, Dec. 30, 1989; 1 child, James Wyatt. BA, Johns Hopkins U., 1968; MD, Med. Coll. Va., 1972. Diplomate Am. Bd. Dermatology, Am. Bd. Dermatopathology, Nat. Bd. Med. Examiners. Fellow dermatopathology Armed Forces Inst. Pathology, Washington, 1979-80; rotating intern in medicine Med. Coll. Va., Richmond, 1972-73, resident in dermatology, 1973-76, assoc. prof. pathology and dermatology, 1982-89, prof., 1989-92, dir. dermatopathology, 1982-92; clin. prof. dermatology and pathology Med. Coll. of Va., 1992-96; with Dermatology Assocs. of Va., 1992-96, Va. Dermatopathology Svcs., Richmond, 1992-96; prof. pathology and dermatology U. Va., 1996—; clin. instr. dermatology U. Colo. Med. Ctr., Denver, 1980-82; cons. in pathology McGuire VA Hosp., Richmond, 1982-92; cons. in pathology and dermatology Kenner Army Hosp., Ft. Lee, Va., 1982-95. Author: Dermatology: A Concise Textbook, 1987; contbr. over 100 articles on dermatology and pathology to med. jours.; asst. editor Jour. Cutaneous Pathology, 1989-94. Mem. nat. alumni schs. com. Johns Hopkins U., 1986—. With M.C., U.S. Army, 1976-82, col. Res. Recipient Stuart McEwen award Assn. Mil. Dermatologists, 1980, 82. Fellow ACP, Am. Acad. Dermatology, Am. Soc. Dermatopathology; mem. Va. Dermatol. Soc. (sec.-treas. 1984-88, v.p. 1988-89, pres. 1989-90), Johns Hopkins U. Alumni Assn. (pres. cen. Va. chpt. 1989), Tau Epsilon Phi (life). Republican. Presbyterian. Avocations: American history, baseball, golf.

PATTERSON, JERRY EUGENE, author; b. Fort Worth, May 2, 1931; s. Charles Edward and Lois (Pruitt) P. B.A., U. Tex., 1952, M.A., 1955; postgrad., Yale U., 1955-57, Columbia U., 1958-60. Asst. editor Hispanic Am. Hist. Rev., 1954; manuscript. div. librarian Yale U. Library, 1955-57; cataloguer Edward Eberstadt & Sons, N.Y.C., 1958-61; with Parke-Bernet Galleries, N.Y.C., 1962-68; asst. v.p. Parke-Bernet Galleries, 1964-65, v.p., 1965-68; U.S. rep. Christie, Manson & Woods, N.Y.C., 1968-71; sr. v.p. Sotheby Parke Bernet Inc., 1980-83; Cons. Library of Congress, 1964-67. Author: Autographs, a Collectors Guide, 1973, A Collector's Guide to Relics and Memorabilia, 1974, Antiques of Sport, 1975, The City of New York, 1978, Porcelain, 1979, Living It Up: A Guide to the Named Apartment Houses of New York, 1984, The Vanderbilts, 1989; mng. editor: Artnewsletter, 1975-78; Contbr. to: Auction Antiques Ann, 1971, also articles on rare books, manuscripts and art market to Am. and fgn. periodicals. Republican. Episcopalian. Home: 176 E 77th St New York NY 10021-1909

PATTERSON, JOHN C., clinical psychology researcher; b. Asheville, N.C.. BS in Psychology, Stephen F. Austin State U., MS in Psychology; PhD in Psychology, Tex. A&M U., 1981. Resident in psychology Wiilford Hall USAF Med. Ctr., San Antonio, 1981; staff psychologist, maximum security unit Rusk State Psychiatric Hosp., Tex.; unit dir. USAF Sch. Aerospace Medicine; chief, aerospace clin. psychology function USAF Aeromed. Consultation Svc., 1985—; faculty mem. USAF Sch. Aerospace Medicine and U. Tex. Health Sci. Ctr., San Antonio (Psychiatry); internat. vis. lectr. in aeromed. neuropsychiatry; cons. in aerospace clin. psychology and neuropsychology evaluation; mem. NASA In-House Working Group on Astronaut Selection; cons. NASA. Contbr. over 30 articles to profl. jours.; rschr. in psychological factors associated with heart disease, aircrew and astronaut selection, spatial disorientation, aviator cognitive funcitoning, and airsickness; presenter in field. Mem. APA, Aerospace Med. Assn. (Raymond F. Longacre award 1995), Am. Soc. Clin. Hypnosis, Internat. Neuropsychology Soc., AF Soc. for Clin. Psychologists, Bexar County Psychol. Assn. Office: USAF Aeromed Consultation Armstrong Lab Brooks AFB TX 78235

PATTERSON, JOHN DE LA ROCHE, JR., lawyer; b. Schenectady, N.Y., July 8, 1941; s. John de la Roche Sr. and Jane C. (Clay) P.; m. Michele F. Demarest, Nov. 28, 1987; children: Daniel C., Sara R., Amy C. BA, Johns Hopkins U., 1963; LLB, Harvard U., 1966. Bar: Mass. 1968. Vol. Peace Corps, Chad, 1966-67; assoc. Foley, Hoag & Eliot, Boston, 1967-73, ptnr., 1974—, exec. com., 1989—. Chmn. Kodaly Ctr. Am. Inc., Newton, Mass., 1977-87. Mem. ABA, Boston Bar Assn. Democrat. Avocations: sailing, tennis, travel, reading. Office: Foley Hoag & Eliot 1 Post Office Sq Boston MA 02109-2103

PATTERSON, JOHN MALCOLM, judge; b. Goldville, Ala., Sept. 27, 1921; s. Albert Love and Agnes Louise (Benson) P.; m. Florentine M. Sawyers, Oct. 17, 1975; children—Albert L., Barbara Louise. J.D., U. Ala., 1949. Bar: Ala. bar 1949. Practiced in Phenix City, 1949-51, 53-55; atty. gen., securities commr. State of Ala., 1955-59; gov. of Ala., 1959-63; practice law Montgomery, Ala., 1963-84; judge Ala. Ct. Criminal Appeals, 1984—; chief judge Ct. of the Judiciary; cattle farmer. Bd. editors: Ala. Law Review, 1948-49. Chmn. bd. Lyman WArd Mil. Acad. Served to maj., F.A. AUS, 1940-45; maj. 1951-53. Nominated one of 10 outstanding young men of U.S., 1956, one of four outstanding young men of Ala. Jr. C. of C. Mem. ABA, Ala. Bar Assn., VFW, Am. Legion. Farrar Order of Jurisprudence, Ala. Acad. Honor, Alpha Tau Omega, Phi Alpha Delta, Sigma Delta Kappa, Phi Eta Sigma, Omicron Delta Kappa. Office: PO Box 301555 Montgomery AL 36130-1555

PATTERSON, JOSEPH REDWINE, lawyer; b. Corsicana, Tex., Apr. 16, 1927; s. Joseph Isham and Caroline Anderson (White) P.; m. Ann Louise Cumber, Mar. 9, 1956; children—Joseph Redwine, Amy Cumber. B.A. in Philosophy, So. Methodist U., 1948, M.A. in Govt, 1951, J.D., 1954. Bar: Tex. 1954. Asst. dist. atty. Dallas County, 1955-56; assoc. gen. counsel Traders and Gen. Ins. Co., Dallas, 1957; ptnr. firm Patterson, Lamberty, Stanford & Walls, Dallas, 1957—; ptnr. PLS Properties (real estate), Dallas, 1971—. Contbr. legal jours. Founding dir. Dallas chpt. Action on Smoking and Health; mem. chancel choir University Park United Meth. Ch., Dallas. Served with USN, 1945-46. Fellow Tex. Bar Found., Dallas Bar Found.;

mem. ABA, Tex. Bar Assn., Dallas Bar Assn., Cross Country Club Dallas. Democrat. Home: 6131 Meadow Rd Dallas TX 75230-5058 Office: 2011 Cedar Springs Rd Dallas TX 75201-1808

PATTERSON, KENT E., environmental services consultant, hydrogeologist; b. 1947. BS in Civil Engring., MS in Bio-Environ. Engring., Okla. State U., 1968. With Corps of Engrs., Tulsa, 1968-70, Roy F. Weston Inc., Richmond, Va., 1970-77; with Environ Resource Mgmt., 1977—, now pres., CEO. Office: Environ Resources Mgmt 855 Springdale Dr Exton PA 19341-2843*

PATTERSON, LLOYD CLIFFORD, psychiatrist; b. Toronto, Ont., Can., Jan. 16, 1917; came to U.S., 1942; s. William Henry and Florence May (Sonley) P.; m. Gloria May Patterson, Nov. 12, 1943; children: Diane Meisenheimer, Pamela DeBarr. MD, U. Western Ont., London, 1942. Diplomate Am. Bd. Psychiatry; cert. Am. Psychoanalytic Assn. Intern Hollywood Presybn. Hosp., L.A., 1942-43; fellow in intern medicine U. Calif. Hosp., San Francisco, 1943-44; resident in psychiatry Langley Porter Neuropsychiat. Inst., San Francisco, 1944-48; cons. psychiatrist student health U. Calif., Berkeley, 1960-70; assoc. clin. prof. U. Calif. Med. Sch., San Francisco, 1972—; dir. med. edn. Alta Bates Med. Ctr., Berkeley, 1988—; program chair Western Divisional Psychoanalytic meetings, San Francisco, 1966. Mem. East Bay Psychiat. Assn. (pres. 1962), No. Calif. Psychiat. Assn. (pres. 1968-69), San Francisco Psychoanalytic Soc. (pres. 1972-73), Am. Psychiat. Soc., Am. Psychoanalytic Soc., Calif. Med. Assn. (hosp. surveyor, mem. continuing med. edn. com. 1985-91, cons. CME com. 1992), Alameda Contra Costa Med. Assn. Avocations: tennis, golf. Home: 409 Cola Ballena Alameda CA 94501-3608 Office: 3021 Telegraph Ave Berkeley CA 94705-2013

PATTERSON, LYDIA ROSS, industrial relations specialist, consulting company executive; b. Carrabelle, Fla., Sept. 3, 1936; d. Richard D. Ross and Johnnie Mae (Thomas) Kelley; m. Edgar A. Corley, Aug. 1, 1964 (div.); 1 child, Derek Kelley; m. Berman W. Patterson, Dec. 18, 1981. BA, Hunter Coll., 1958. Indsl. rels. specialist U.S. Dept. Energy, N.Y.C., 1966-68; regional dir./mgr. Div. Human Rights State of N.Y., N.Y.C., 1962-66, 68-76; v.p. Bankers Trust Co., N.Y.C., 1976-87; pres., CEO Lydia Patterson Comm., N.Y.C., 1985-95; CEO Lydia Patterson Comms., 1996—; v.p., mgr. Merrill Lynch and Co. Inc., N.Y.C., 1987-90; seminar speaker Columbia U., Wharton Sch. Bus., Harvard U., Duke U., Cornell U., 1976-85; mem. conf. bd. Cornell U., Bus. Policy Rev. Coun., Exec. Leadership Coun. Bd. dirs. Project Discovery Columbia U., 1988, CUNY, Vocat. Edn. Adv. Coun., 1990. Mem. Nat. Urban League, Employment Mgrs. Assn., Fin. Women's Assn. (govt. and cmty. affairs com. 1986-87), Women's Forum, Employment Dissemination of Info., Wellington Cmty. Edn. Found. (bd. dirs. 1992—). Office: 12689 Coral Breeze Dr Wellington FL 33414-8070

PATTERSON, MADGE LENORE, elementary education educator; b. Vandergrift, Pa., Nov. 9, 1925; d. Paul Warren and Lucy Mae (Lemmon) Schaeffer; m. Stanley Clair Patterson, June 19, 1948 (dec.); 1 child, Stanley Kent. BS in Edn., Indiana State Tchrs. Coll., Pa., 1946, MEd, 1971. Elem. tchr. New Kensington (Pa.) Pub. Schs., 1946-49; elem. tchr. Armstrong Sch. Dist. Schs., Ford City, Pa., 1951-52, kindergarten tchr., 1967-93; kindergarten tchr. Rural Valley (Pa.) Presbyn. Ch., 1957-67; vol. tutor Adult Lit., Kittanning, Pa., 1993—; co-owner dairy farm. Sunday sch. tchr., choir mem., 1949—; sec. Rural Valley Presbyn. Ch. Women's Assn., 1988-92. Mem. NEA, Pa. Assn. Sch. Retirees, Clara Cockerille Reading Coun. (treas. 1994-96), Pa. State Edn. Assn., Internat. Reading Assn., Keystone Reading Assn., Assn. Early Childhood Edn., Rural Valley Bus. and Profl. Club, Women's Civic Club (Woman of Yr. 1994), Am. Assn. Ret. Persons, Rural Valley Grange (former lectr.). Democrat. Avocations: dancing (line, square, ballroom), reading, camping, music, travel. Home: RR 2 Box 182 Dayton PA 16222-8813

PATTERSON, MARION LOUISE, photographer, educator; b. San Francisco, Apr. 24, 1933; d. Morrie Leslie and Esther Elizabeth (Parker) P. BA, Stanford U., 1955; MA, Calif. State U., San Francisco, 1970. Clk. Best's Studio (Ansel Adams Gallery), Yosemite, Calif., 1958-61; asst. to photography editor Sunset Mag., Menlo Park, Calif., 1961-64; freelance photographer Oaxaca, Mex., 1964-66; communications cons. Projects to Advance Creative in Edn., San Mateo, Calif., 1966-68; instr. in photography, chair photography dept. Foothill Coll., Los Altos Hills, Calif., 1968—; instr. U. Calif., Santa Cruz, 1984—. One woman shows include West German Embassy in the Hague, Bayreuth, Republic of Germany, Kasteel Hoensbrueck, Netherlands, Daxaca, Mex., San Francisco Mus. of Modern Art, Focus Gallery, San Francisco, Oakland Mus., Monterey County Mus., Stanford U., Ansel Adams Gallery, Yosemite, and others; exhibited in group shows MIT, George Eastman House, Polaroid Corp., Art in the Embassies, Ind. U., U. of Ala., Critics Choice Traveling Exhibit, New Light, New Directions, Reclaiming Paradise, and others; contbr. photographs and articles in books and magazines. Mem. Am. Soc. Mag. Photographers, Soc. for Photographic Edn. Office: Foothill Coll 12345 El Monte Ave Los Altos CA 94022-4504

PATTERSON, MARTHA ELLEN, artist, art educator; b. Anderson, Ind., Mar. 12, 1914; d. Clarence and Corrine Ringwald; m. John Downey, Nov. 27, 1935 (div. 1946); 1 child, Linda Carol; m. Raymond George Patterson, May 6, 1947. Student, Dayton (Ohio) Art Inst., Bendell Art Sch., Bradenton, Fla. Beauty operator WRENS, Springfield, Ohio, 1932-40; co-owner Park Ave. Gallery, Dayton; window decorator, art tchr.; tchr. art; judge art shows. One-woman shows include N.C.R. Country Club, Bill Turner Interiors, U. Dayton, High Street Gallery, Trails End Club, The Designerie, Riverbend Park, Statesman Club, State Fidelity Bank, Wygerson's Garden Ctr., Pebble Springs, Backstreet, First City Fed. Bank, Bradenton, Fla., Alley Gallery, Merrill-Lynch, Miami U., Gem City Bank, Dayton, Ohio, Winters Bank, Dayton, Sherwin-Williams, Howard Johnsons, Dayton Woman's Club, Bergamo, Dayton Meml. Hall, Bob and Arts, Del Park Med. Soc., The Dayton Country Club, Christ Methodist Ch., Unitarian Ch., The Metropolitan, Rikes, Dr. Pavey's, Dr. Chaney's, Dayton Convention Ctr., The Yum Yum, Jan Strunk Interiors, Park Avenue Gallery; artist: (water colors, oils, acrylics, inks and pastels) exhibitions include: Dayton Art Inst., Meml. Hall of Dayton, Dayton Country Club, Bergamo, Womens Club of Dayton, Am. Watercolor Soc., Riverbend Park, First City Fed., NCR Country Club, Springfield (Ohio) Mus., Longboat Key Art Ctr., others; in private collections of Mr. and Mrs. Richard Nixon, Virginia Graham, Les Brown, Paul Lynde, Air Force Mus. at Wright Patterson, Mr. and Mrs. Charles Lange of NCR, U. Dayton-Ohio, Stephen House, Doug Yeager, and others. Vol. Christian Woman's Soc. of Am., Twig Children's Hosp., Dayton, The Utopians; mem. Tri Art Dayton, Long Boat Key Art Ctr., Fla. Recipient first prize Dayton Soc. Painters and Sculptors Show Rikes, First Prize, 1976, 77, First Prize, Best in Show, 1978, Beavercreek Art Assn. First Place, Best in Show, Artist and Sculpture Yearly Show, 1966, 68 2d place, Dayton Art Inst. 2d prize, Tri County Hon. Mention, Walker Motor Sales 2d place, Bendell Art Gallery 2d and 3d, Montgomery County Fair Best in Show. Mem. Art League of Manatee County (Fla.), Nat. Mus. Women in Art, Am. Watercolor Soc., Springfield Mus. Art, Dayton Soc. Painters, N.Y. Watercolor Soc., Long Boat Key Art League, Tri Art. Republican. Methodist. Avocations: art mus., books, music, travel, gourmet cooking. Home: 3853 Lawrenceville Dr Springfield OH 45504-4459 Winter Address: 5920 7th Ave W Bradenton FL 34209-3519

PATTERSON, MARY-MARGARET SHARP, writer, editor, media strategist; b. Fairmont, W.Va., July 12, 1944; d. H. Sutton Sharp and Columbia Strock; m. David Sands, June 15, 1968; 1 child, Scott Sutton. BA cum laude, Ohio State U., 1966, MA, 1967. Media coordinator Am. Hosp. Assn., Chgo., 1969; feature and mag. writer Chgo. Today newspaper, 1969-70; reporter Houston Chronicle, 1971-73; instr. journalism U. Houston, 1974-76; asst. prof. Utica (N.Y.) Coll. U. Syracuse, 1976-78; dir. undergrad. studies coll. journalism U. Md., College Park, 1978-82, editor, 1982; dir. information and devel. Audubon Naturalist Soc. Cen. Atlantic States, Inc., Chevy Chase, Md., 1982-89; dir. media rels. Defenders of Wildlife, Washington, 1989-90; resident Johns Hopkins-Nanjing U. Ctr. for Chinese and Am. Studies, Nanjing, China, 1990-91; writer, editor Am. Assn. Retired Persons, Washington, 1993-95; prin. Mary Margaret Patterson Writer, Editor, Media Cons., 1996—; cons. project Africa Carnegie Mellon U. Pitts., 1969; newspaper div. head summer journalism inst. Trinity U., San Antonio, 1979-81; columnist San Antonio Mag., 1976-79; cons. Callahan & Assoc., Washington, 1992—. Editor: Credit Unions On-Line, 1996—; contbr. numerous articles and book revs. to newspapers and mags. Mem. Chevy Chase Presbyn. Ch. Choir, Washington, 1980—, ruling elder, 1993-96. Recipient Reporting Excellence award The Newspaper Fund, Cleve., 1966; Univ. Grad. fellow Ohio State U., 1966, Nat. Grad. fellow Women in Communications, 1967. Mem. Soc. Profl. Journalists, Mortar Bd., Washington Ind. Writers, Inc., Nat.Press CLub Libr., Kappa Tau Alpha. Democrat. Avocations: music, swimming, walking, French, Chinese.

PATTERSON, MILDRED LUCAS, teaching specialist; b. Winston-Salem, N.C., Jan. 24, 1937; d. James Arthur and Lula Mae (Smith) Lucas; m. James Harrison Patterson Jr., Mar. 31, 1961; children: James Harrison III, Roger Lindsay. BA, Talladega Coll., 1958; MEd, St. Louis U., 1969; postgrad., Webster U., 1970. Classroom tchr. St. Louis Bd. Edn., 1961-72, reading specialist, 1972-88, co-host radio reading show, 1988-91; tchr. specialist Reading to Achieve Motivational Program, St. Louis, 1991—; bd. dirs. Supt.'s Adv. Com., University City, Mo., 1994—; presenter Chpt. I Regional Conf. Bd. dirs. Gateway Homes, St. Louis, 1989-93; mem. com. University City Sch. Bond Issue, 1994. Recipient Letter of Commendation, Chpt. I. Regional Conf., 1991, Founders' award Gamma Omega chpt. Alpha Kappa Alpha, 1985. Mem. Internat. Reading Assn. (Broadcast Media award for radio 1990, Bldg. Rep. award St. Louis chpt. 1990), St. Louis Alliance of Black Educators. Avocations: reading, arts and crafts, storytelling, motivational speaking.

PATTERSON, NONA SPARKS, small business owner; b. Tipton Hill, N.C., Sept. 9, 1935; d. Fred and Mary Jane (Byrd) Sparks; m. J. M. Patterson, Apr. 24, 1960; children: James Stacy, Jonathan Sparks. BS in Elem. Edn. and History, Berry Coll., 1958; postgrad., U. Ga. Tchr. Floyd County Sch. Sys., Ga., 1959-60; H.S. English tchr. Gwinnett County Sch. Sys., Ga., 1960-67; v.p. Furniture Village, Lawrenceville, Ga., 1967—. Past pres. Lawrenceville (Ga.) Elem. Sch., 1976-78, Lawrenceville Mid. Sch., 1978-80, Ctrl. High Sch., 1980-89; Sunday sch. tchr. United Meth. Ch., Lawrenceville, 1980—; bd. dirs. Swinnett Fine Arts Ctr., Duluth, Ga., 1984—; vol. Olympic Com.; del. Dem. Conv., Atlanta, 1984; mem. exec. bd. Swinnett (Ga.) Dem. Com., 1988—; active Jr. Svc. League, Atlanta, 1978—, Atlanta Children's Theatre, 1978-89, Atlanta Symphony Assn., 1989—. Mem. Ga. Home Furnishing Assn. (bd. dirs.). Avocations: snow skiiing, tennis, hiking, mountain climbing, basketball. Home: 1946 New Hope Rd Lawrenceville GA 30245-6565 Office: Furniture Village 194 Gwinnett Dr Lawrenceville GA 30245-5626

PATTERSON, ORLANDO, sociologist; b. Jamaica, June 5, 1940; came to U.S., 1970.; s. Charles A. Patterson and Almina Morris; m. Nerys Wyn Thomas, Sept. 5, 1965 (div. 1994); children: Rhiannon, Barbara; m. Anita Haya Goldman, Aug. 12, 1995. BS, U. of the West Indies, 1962; PhD, London Sch. of Econs., 1965; MA, Harvard U., Harvard, 1971; LHD (hon.), Trinity Coll., Conn., 1992. Asst. lectr. U. of London, London Sch. Econs. and Polit. Sci., 1965-67; lectr. U. of West Indies, 1967-70; vis. lectr. Harvard U., Cambridge, Mass., 1970-71, Allston Burr sr. tutor, 1971-73, prof. sociology, 1971-93, John Cowles prof. sociology, 1993—; vis. mem. Inst. Advanced Study, Princeton, N.J., 1975-76; vis. fellow, Wolfson Coll., Cambridge U., 1978-79; Phi Beta Kappa vis. scholar, 1988-89; mem. tech. advisory com. to prime min. and govt. of Jamaica, 1972-74, sp. advisor to prime min. of Jamaica, 1973-80. Author: (novels) The Children of Sisyphus, 1964 (1st prize Dakar Festival Negro Arts 1966), An Absence of Ruins, 1967, Die the Long Day, 1972, (nonfiction) The Sociology of Slavery, 1967, Ethnic Chauvinism, 1977, Slavery and Social Death, 1982 (co-winner Ralph Bunche award Am. Polit. Sci. Assn. 1983), Freedom; vol. 1, Freedom in the Making of Western Cluture, 1991 (Nat. Book award Nat Book Found. 1991); contbr. Stories from the Caribbean, 1965. Recipient UCLA medal, 1992; Guggenheim fellow, 1978-79. Mem. Am. Acad. Arts and Scis., Am. Sociol. Assn. (citation for disting. contbn. to scholarship 1983). Office: Harvard Univ Dept of Sociology William James 520 Cambridge MA 02138

PATTERSON, PAUL M., school administrator; b. Aberdeen, S.D., Sept. 29, 1946; s. Robert M. and Esther M. (Wellman) P.; m. Karen M. Brenner, June 1, 1974; 1 child, Jennifer K. BS, No. State U., 1964; MS, U. Ill., 1976, EdD, 1994. Tchr. Rapid City (S.D.) Pub. Schs., 1968-75, Rock Island (Ill.) Pub. Schs., 1975-76; tchr. Sch. Dist. U-46, Elgin, Ill., 1976-85, coord. fine arts, 1985-92, dir. instructional programs, 1992—; cons. Chgo. Pub. Schs., 1990, North Palos Dist. 117, North Palos Hills, Ill., 1993. Contbr. articles to profl. jours. Adv. bd. Ill. Arts Coun., Chgo., 1994—, Ill. Alliance for Arts Edn., Chgo., 1987—, Ill. State Bd. Edn. Fine Arts Com., Springfield, 1986-94; mem. Heritage Commn., Elgin, 1985-88. Ill. Adminstr. scholar Ill. Bd. Edn. and Nat. Gallery of Art, Washington, 1991. Mem. ASCD, Ill. ASCD, Am. Assn. Sch. Adminstr., Phi Delta Kappa, Kappa Delta Pi. Home: 931 Glenhome Ln Elgin IL 60123-2302 Office: School District 46 355 E Chicago St Elgin IL 60120-6543

PATTERSON, PERRY WILLIAM, economist, publishing company executive; b. Lancaster, Pa., Nov. 18, 1949; s. William and Helen (Bergmark) P.; m. A. Kimball Harrill, Mar. 3, 1984; children: Reed W., Amy M. BS in Econs., U. Hartford, 1972; MA, U. Mass., 1974; MBA, Rutgers U., 1983. From econ. analyst to dir. econs. Cahners Pub. Co., 1974-81; economist, asst. dir. Ctr. Internat. Bus. Cycle Rsch., Rutgers U., 1981-83; dir. corp. rsch. and devel. Gordon Publs., Inc., 1984-88; dir. prod. dev. Faulkner & Gray, 1988-89; group pub. Inst. Mgmt. and Adminstrn., N.Y.C., 1989—; founder, pres. IBC, 1988—. Designer aerospace products mag., 1986—, newsletters; contbg. editor: Bus. Mktg., 1982-91; contbr. articles to profl. jours. Mem. Am. Econ. Assn., Nat. Assn. Bus. Economists, Bus. Profl. Advt. Assn., Am. Bus. Press (rsch. com.). Home: 259 Forest Ave Glen Ridge NJ 07028-1728 Office: Inst Mgmt and Adminstrn 29 W 35th St New York NY 10001-2299

PATTERSON, POLLY REILLY (MRS. W. RAY PATTERSON), civic worker, retired communications company executive; b. Wilkinsburg, Pa., 1906; d. Thomas L. and Margaret (Coughey) Reilly; m. W. Ray Patterson, Sept. 2, 1943. Student, U. Pitts. With Bell Telephone Co. of Pa., Pitts., 1925-71, clk., mgmt. positions, 1935-64, assoc. pub. rels. staff, 1965-71. Asst. treas. Allegheny County (Pa.) Soc. for Crippled Children, 1962-66, v.p., 1966-70; bd. dirs. Jr. Achievement, Inc., SW Pa., 1950-71, Pa. Soc. Crippled Children and Adults, 1960-68, Pitts. YWCA, 1964-72, Chatham Village Homes, Inc., 1973-76; mem. Allegheny County United Way, 1972—, nat. ho. of dels. Nat. Soc. for Crippled Children and Adults, 1965-67. Named Pitts. Advt. Woman of Yr., 1958, one of Pitts.'s Ten Outstanding Women, Pitts. Sun Telegraph, 1959; recipient Crystal Prism award Am. Advt. Fedn., 1972, 75. Mem. Assn. Pitts. Clubs (bd. dirs. 1946-81, pres. 1952-53), Altrusa Internat. (pres. Pitts. Club 1950-51), Pitts. Advt. Club (v.p., sec. 1929-69), Pitts. Bus. and Profl. Women's Club, Telephone Pioneers Am.

PATTERSON, RICHARD NORTH, writer, lawyer; b. Berkeley, Calif., Feb. 22, 1947; s. Richard Wallace and Marjorie Frances (North) P.; m. Laurie Anderson, Apr. 13, 1993; children: Shannon Heath, Brooke North, Adam Chandler, Chase Kenyon, Katherine Jeanne Blunt, Stephen Thomas Blunt. BA History, Ohio Wesleyan U., 1968; JD, Case Western Reserve, 1971. Bar: Ohio, 1971, D.C., 1973, Ala., 1975, Calif., 1984. Asst. atty. gen. State of Ohio, 1971-73; with divsn. enforcement SEC, Washington, 1973-75, San Francisco, Calif., 1878-81; assoc. atty. Berkowitz, Lefkovits & Patrick, Birmingham, Ala., 1975-77, ptnr., 1978; assoc. McCutchen, Doyle, Brown & Enerson, San Francisco, Calif., 1985-87, ptnr., 1987-93, of counsel, 1993-94. Author: The Lasko Tangent, 1979, The Outside Man, 1981, Escape the Night, 1983, Private Screening, 1985, Degree of Guilt, 1993, Eyes of a Child, 1995, The Final Judgement, 1995. Mem. bd. trustees Ohio Wesleyan U. Recipient Edgar Allen Poe award for best 1st novel Mystery Writers Am., 1979, Grand Prix de Literateur Policiere, 1995. Home: 2609 Fillmore St San Francisco CA 94115-1235

PATTERSON, ROBERT ARTHUR, physician, health care consultant, retired health care company executive, retired air force officer; b. Palestine, Ill., Sept. 3, 1915; s. Robert Bruce and Nera (McColpin) P.; m. Judith Scheirer, May 15, 1961; children: Mary Kay, Elaine Alice Mills, Robert Arthur II, Victoria Patterson Goodrum. Student, U. Ill., 1933-35; M.D., U. Louisville, 1939. Diplomate: aerospace medicine Am. Bd. Preventive Medicine. Intern Detroit Receiving Hosp., 1939-40; joined Mich. N.G., 1940; commd. USAAF, 1946; advanced through grades to lt. gen. USAF, 1972; rated chief flight surgeon and command pilot; assigned U.S. and ETO, 1940-45; assigned U.S., Spain, Japan, Philippines, 1945-63; dep. dir. plans and hospitalization Office Surgeon Gen., USAF, Washington, 1963-65; dir. plans and hospitalization Office Surgeon Gen., USAF, 1965-68; surgeon Hdqrs. USAFE, Lindsey Air Sta., Germany, 1968-71, Hdqrs. SAC, Offutt AFB, 1971-72; surgeon gen. USAF, 1972-75, ret., 1975; health care cons. Arlington, Va., 1975; sr. v.p. sci. affairs Baxter Travenol Labs., Inc., Deerfield, Ill., 1976-86, health care cons., 1987—; Active Martin Meml. Community Coun., Stuart, Fla. Decorated D.S.M. with oak leaf cluster, Legion of Merit with oak leaf cluster, Air Force Commendation medal; recipient citation of honor Air Force Assn., citation of distinction Fed. Hosp. Execs., citation of distinction Am. Hosp. Assn. Fellow Am. Coll. Preventive Medicine, Aerospace Medicine Assn., Am. Coll. Physician Execs. (founder); mem. Assn. Mil. Surgeons (pres. 1972), AMA, Am. Acad. Med. Dirs., Air Force Assn., Ret. Officers Assn., Soc. Mil. Cons. to Armed Forces, Soc. Armed Forces Med. Labs. Scis., NIH Alumni, U. Ill. Alumni Assn., Aircraft Owners and Pilots Assn., Order Daedalians, Assn. for Advancement of Med. Instrumentation, Exptl. Aircraft Assn., Deutsch Kurzhaar Verband, N.A. Versatile Hunting Dog Assn., Uniformed Services U. Health Scis. Alumni Assn., Air Safety Found. Clubs: Mid-America (Chgo.), Exmoor Country (Highland Park, Ill.), Cen. Fla. Conservation and Hunt (Lake Wales, Fla.), Yacht and Country (bd. govs., Stuart, Fla.), Sunshine Gun, Yacht (Stuart, Fla.), Willoughby Golf Club (Stuart, Fla.). Home: Yacht & Coutry Club 3474 SE Fairway East Stuart FL 34997 Office: Baxter Healthcare Corp One Baxter Pkwy Deerfield IL 60015

PATTERSON, ROBERT EDWARD, lawyer; b. Los Angeles, Sept. 14, 1942; s. Ellis Elwood and Helen (Hjelte) P.; m. Christina Balboni, Oct. 2, 1971; 1 child, Victor Ellis. BA, UCLA, 1964; JD, Stanford U., 1972, grad. bus. exec. program, 1986. Bar: Calif. 1972. Ptnr. Graham & James, Palo Alto, Calif., 1972—; bd. dirs. Procyte Corp. Served to lt. comdr. USN, 1964-69. Mem. Rotary, Palo Alto Club, Menlo Circus Club, Bohemian Club. Democrat. Office: Graham & James LLP 600 Hansen Way Palo Alto CA 94304-1043

PATTERSON, ROBERT HUDSON, library director; b. Alexandria, La., Dec. 11, 1936; s. Hubert Hudson and Beth (Jones) P.; 1 child, Jennifer Bookhart. B.A., Millsaps Coll., Jackson, Miss., 1958; M.A., Tulane U., 1963; M.L.S., U. Calif., Berkeley, 1965. Mem. profl. staff Tulane U. Libr., New Orleans, 1965-69, 73-76, asst. dir. collection devel., 1973-76; head spl. collections cataloging U. Tex., Austin, 1970-73; dir. librs. U. Wyo., Laramie, 1976-81, U. Tulsa, 1981—; chmn. exec. bd. Wyo. State Libr. Adv. Com., 1976-81; mem. bd. Okla. State Libr. Adv. Com., 1981-84; mem. adv. coun. Bibliog. Ctr. for Rsch., Denver, 1978-81; past mem. exec. bd. S.E. La. Libr. Network; bd. dirs. Amigos Bibliog. Coun., 1983-86; cons. NEH, Harry Ransom Humanities Rsch. Ctr., U. Tex., Austin. Editor Conservation Adminstrn. News, 1979-93; contbr. articles to profl. jours. Pres. Western Conservation Congress, 1981-82. Sr. fellow CLR/UCLA, 1989. Fellow Internat. Boswell Inst.; mem ALA (various offices), Okla. Libr. Assn. (various offices).

PATTERSON, ROBERT LOGAN, librarian, country and western dance promoter; b. Pitts., Mar. 12, 1940; s. Walter Glenn and June (Logan) P. BA, U. Vt., 1962; MA, San Jose State Coll., 1965; MEd, Boston State Coll., 1979; cert. advanced grad. study Northeastern U., 1982; PhD, Saybrook Inst., 1983. With IBM, London, 1966-68, Info. Dynamics Corp., 1968-70; systems libr. Boston Theol. Inst., 1971-73, Dr. Solomon Carter Fuller Mental Health Clinic, Boston, 1978-79, Boston Evening Med. Ctr. Mental Health Clinic, 1979-81, Mystic Valley Mental Health Center, Arlington, Mass., 1981-82, Cambridgeport Problem Ctr., Cambridge, Mass., 1982-84, U. Mass., Boston, 1973—; owner Tex. Dance Workshops, Houston; psychology extern Boston Inst. Psychotherapies, 1981-82, Cambridge Hosp. Psychotherapy Center, 1982-84; prin. psychologist Mass. State Svc. Mem. SAR, Mass. Tchrs. Assn., Strictly Country Dancers, Tex. Country Western Dance Assn., New Eng. Country Two Steppers Club, Psi Chi, Kappa Delta Pi. Home: 8 Winthrop Ave Bedford MA 01730-2223 Office: U Mass Harbor Campus Boston MA 02125

PATTERSON, ROBERT PORTER, JR., federal judge; b. N.Y.C., July 11, 1923; s. Robert Porter and Margaret (Winchester) P.; m. Bevin C. Daly, Sept. 15, 1956; children: Anne, Robert, Margaret, Paul, Katherine. AB, Harvard U., 1947; LLB, Columbia U., 1950. Bar: N.Y. 1951, D.C. 1966. Law clk. Donovan, Leisure, Newton & Lumbard, N.Y.C., 1950-51; asst. counsel N.Y. State Crime Commn. Waterfront Investigation, 1952-53; asst. U.S. atty. Chief of Narcotics Prosecutions and Investigations, 1953-56; asst. counsel Senate Banking and Currency Com., 1954; assoc. Patterson, Belknap, Webb & Tyler, N.Y.C., 1956-60, ptnr., 1960-88; judge U.S. Dist. Ct. (so. dist.) N.Y., 1988—; counsel to minority select com. pursuant to house resolution no. 1, Washington, 1967; mem. Senator's Jud. Screening Panel, 1974-88, Gov.'s Jud. Screening Panel, 1975-82, Gov.'s Sentencing Com., 1978-79. Contbr. articles to profl. jours. Chmn. Wm. T. Grant Found., 1974-94, Prisoners' Legal Services N.Y., 1976-88; dir. Legal Aid Soc., 1961-88, pres., 1967-71; chmn. Nat. Citizens for Eisenhower, 1959-60, Scranton for Pres., N.Y. State, 1964; bd. mgrs. Havens Relief Fun Soc., 1994—, Millbrook Sch., 1966-78, Vera Inst. Justice, 1981—, New Sch. for Social Rsch., 1986-94, George C. Marshall Found., 1987-93; mem. exec. com. Lawyers Com. for Civil Rights Under Law, 1968-88; mem. Goldman Panel for Attica Disturbance, 1972, Temporary Commn. on State Ct. System, 1971-73, Rockefeller U. Council, 1986-88, exec. com. N.Y. Vietnam Vets. Meml. Commn., 1982-85, Mayor's Police Adv. Com., 1985-87. Served to capt. USAAF, 1942-46. Decorated D.F.C. with cluster, Air medal with clusters. Mem. ABA (ho. of dels. 1976-80), N.Y. State Bar Assn. (pres. 1978-79), Assn. Bar City N.Y. (v.p. 1974-75), N.Y. County Lawyers Assn., Am. Law Inst., Am. Judicature Soc. (bd. dirs. 1979). Republican. Episcopalian. Home: Fair Oaks Farm Cold Spring NY 10516 Office: US Court House 500 Pearl St New York NY 10007

PATTERSON, RONALD PAUL, publishing company executive, clergyman; b. Ashland, Ohio, Dec. 4, 1941; s. Donald Edward and Mildred (Niswender) P.; m. Marlene Pfahler, Sept. 1, 1962; children: Paul Edward, Mark Loren. BA, Malone Coll., 1963; MDiv, United Theol. Sem., Dayton, Ohio, 1967; MA, Syracuse U., 1970; DD, Cen. Meth. Coll., 1988. Ordained to ministry United Methodist Ch., 1967. Editor youth publs. Otterbein Press, Dayton, 1964-68; assoc. editor The Upper Room, Nashville, 1970-74; editor Word Books, Waco, Tex., 1974-77; editorial dir. Abingdon Press, Nashville, 1977-88; book editor United Meth. Ch. Pub. House, 1977-88, v.p., 1984-88, sr. editor Ch. Resources, 1988-92; pub., CEO United Meth. Reporter, Dallas, 1992—; v.p. Religious Pub. Rels. Coun. Nashville, 1970-74; jr. coll. instr. creative writing, Waco; leader writers' workshops. Author: (with others) The Kyle Rote Story, 1975; editor: Come On, Let's Pray, 1972; compiler: The Coming of Easter, 1973; founding editor Alive Now! devotional publ.; editorial dir. Quar. Rev., 1980-87; contbr. articles to mags. Tchr. Tenn. State Prison, Nashville, 1984-88; vice chmn. pastor-parish com., Hermitage, Tenn., 1984-86. Recipient George Washington Honor medal Nat. Freedom Found., Valley Forge, Pa., 1960, Paul M. Hinkhouse award Religious Pub. Relations Council, N.Y.C., 1973; named one of Outstanding Young Men Am., 1972. Mem. Am. Acad. Religion, Religion Pub. Group, Christian Publs. Assn., Southeastern Pubs. Assn. (exec. com. 1985-88), Pubs. Assn. of South (treas.), Evang. Christian Pubs. Assn. (bd. dirs. 1987-88), Protestant Ch.-owned Pubs. Assn. (bd. dirs.), Internat. Pubs. Assn. World Meth. Coun., Downtown Rotary Club (Dallas). Democrat. United Methodist. Avocations: boating, refinishing furniture, golf. Home: 1563 Waterside Ct Dallas TX 75218-4488 Office: 2520 W Commerce St Dallas TX 75212-4909

PATTERSON, RONALD R(OY), health care systems executive; b. Baton Rouge, Mar. 4, 1942. BS, U. Houston, 1965; MS, Trinity U., San Antonio, 1973. Asst. adminstr. Med. Br. Tex. U., Galveston, 1972-75; asst. v.p. Hosp. Affiliates Internat., Nashville, 1975-81; chief oper. officer Affiliated Hosp. Systems, Houston, 1981-82; sr. v.p. Republic Health Corp., Dallas, 1982-88; pres. Miller Patterson Inc., Plano, Tex., 1988-89; ind. healthcare mgmt. cons. Plano, 1989-90; sr. v.p. Harris Meth. Health System, Ft. Worth, Tex., 1990-91; exec. v.p., COO Champion Healthcare Corp., Houston, Tex., 1991—; bd. govs. Fedn. Am. Health Systems, 1996—. Fellow Am. Coll. Healthcare

Execs.: mem. Tex. Hosp. Assn. (vice chmn. multi-hosp. constituency 1987), Fedn. Am. Health Sys. (bd. govs. 1996—). Avocation: photography. Office: Champion Healthcare Corp 515 W Greens Rd Ste 800 Houston TX 77067

PATTERSON, ROY, physician, educator; b. Ironwood, Mich., Apr. 26, 1926; s. Donald I. and Helmi (Lantta) P. M.D., U. Mich., 1953. Diplomate: Am. Bd. Internal Medicine, Am. Bd. Allergy and Immunology. Intern U. Mich. Hosp., Ann Arbor, 1953-54; med. asst. research U. Mich. Hosp., 1954-55, med. resident, 1955-57, instr. dept. medicine, 1957-59; attending physician VA Research Hosp., Chgo., Northwestern Meml. Hosp.; mem. faculty Northwestern U. Med. Sch., Chgo., 1959—; prof. medicine Northwestern U. Med. Sch., 1964—, Ernest S. Bazley prof. medicine, chief sect. allergy-immunology dept. medicine. Editor: Jour. Allergy and Clin. Immunology, 1973-78. Served with USNR, 1944-46. Fellow Am. Acad. Allergy (pres. 1976), A.C.P.; mem. Central Soc. for Clin. Research (pres. 1978-79). Office: Northwestern U Med Sch Dept Medicine 303 E Chicago Ave Chicago IL 60611-3008

PATTERSON, RUSSELL, conductor, opera executive; b. Greenville, Miss., Aug. 31, 1930; s. Dudley Russell and Elizabeth (Taylor) P.; m. Teresa Gutierrez de Celis, Aug. 28, 1979; children: Richard Russell, Christopher Leonard. B.A., B.Mus., S.E. La. U., 1950; M.Mus., Kansas City Conservatory of Music, 1952; D.M.A., U. Mo. at Kansas City. Prof. music Kansas City Conservatory of Music, 1960-68; mem. profl. com. Met. Opera, 1962—; condr. Kansas City Symphony, 1982-83, artistic dir., 1982-86, condr. emeritus, 1986—; cons. Ford Found. Musician with Baton Rouge Symphony, 1948-50, Brevard Music Festival, 1947-49, Kansas City Philharmonic Orch., 1951-59, Bayrische Staatsoper, Munich, Germany, 1952-53; condr. Kansas City Philharmonic Orch., 1965-66, Point Lookout (Mo.) Festival, 1967—, Kansas City Ballet, 1965-66, Am. Ballet Co., European tour, 1958; gen. dir., Lyric Opera of Kansas City, 1958—, artistic dir., Missouri River Festival, 1976—; dir. Sunflower Music Festival, 1978—. Mem. opera com. Mo. Council Arts, 1965-69; mem. music panel Nat. Endowment Arts, 1970-72; mem. Univ. Assocs. U. Mo. at Kansas City, 1970—. Recipient Alice M. Ditson condrs. award Columbia U., 1982, W.F. Yates medalion William Jewell Coll.; named Disting. Alumni Southeast La. U. Mem. Friends of Art, Opera America (v.p. 1971-73), Phi Mu Alpha Sinfonia, Pi Kappa Lambda, Mensa. Home: 4618 Warwick Blvd Apt 1A Kansas City MO 64112-1751 Office: Lyric Opera Lyric Theater 1029 Central St Kansas City MO 64105-1619

PATTERSON, SAMUEL CHARLES, political science educator; b. Omaha, Nov. 29, 1931; s. Robert Foster and Garnet Marie (Jorgensen) P.; m. Suzanne Louise Dean, June 21, 1956; children—Polly Ann, Dean Foster, Grier Edmund. B.A., U. S.D., 1953; M.S., U. Wis., 1956, Ph.D., 1959. Asst. prof. polit. sci. Okla. State U., Stillwater, 1959-61; asst. prof. U. Iowa, Iowa City, 1961-64, assoc. prof., 1964-67, prof., 1967-85, Roy J. Carver prof., 1985-86; prof. Ohio State U., Columbus, 1986—; vis. prof. U. Wis., 1962, U. Okla., 1968-78, U. Essex, Colchester, Eng., 1969-70. Author: (with others) Representatives and Represented, 1975, A More Perfect Union, 4th edit., 1989; co-author: The Legislative Process in the United States, 4th edit., 1986, Comparing Legislatures, 1979; editor: American Legislative Behavior, 1968; co-editor: Comparative Legislative Behavior: Frontiers of Research, 1972, Parliaments in the Modern World, 1994, Handbook of Legislative Research, 1985, Political Leadership in Democratic Societies, 1991; editor Am. Jour. Polit. Sci., 1970-73; co-editor Legis Studies Quar., 1981-85; mng. editor am. Polit. Sci. rev., 1985-91. Served with U.S. Army, 1953-55. Recipient Disting. Scholar award Ohio State U., 1990; fellow social Sci. Rsch. Coun., 1961, 67, Guggenheim, 1984-85; vis. fellow Brookings Instn., 1984-85, Ctr. Advanced Study in Behavioral Scis., 1993-94; Fulbright Bologna chair, 1995. Mem. Internat. Polit. Sci. Assn., So. Polit. Sci. Assn., Can. Polit. Sci. Assn., Am. Polit. Sci. Assn., Midwest Polit. Sci. Assn. (pres. 1980-81), Phi Beta Kappa, Phi Kappa Phi, Pi Sigma Alpha. Office: Ohio State U Dept Polit Sci 2140 Derby Hall 154 N Oval Mall Columbus OH 43210-1373

PATTERSON, STEVE, professional hockey team executive; b. Beaver Dam, Wis., Sept. 21, 1957. BBA with honors, U. Tex., 1980, JD, 1984. Bar: Tex. 1984. Gen. mgr., profl. basketball team counsel Houston Rockets, 1984-89, profl. basketball mktg. exec. group ticket sales, mgr., bus. ops. exec., gen. mgr., 1989-94; pres. profl. hockey team Houston Aeros, 1994—; pres. Arena Oper. Co., Houston, 1995—. Office: Houston Aeros 24 E Greenway Plz Ste 800 Houston TX 77046-2409

PATTERSON, VEDA MALIA, equal opportunity specialist; b. Greensboro, N.C., Nov. 9, 1954; d. Walter and Dorothy Martelle (Dusenbury) P. BA, Howard U., 1976; MS, Am. U., 1987. Claims svc. rep. State Farm Ins. Co., Alexandria, Va., 1978-83; substitute tchr. Fairfax County, Arlington County and Alexandria City Schs., 1983-88; cons. pub. rels. United Black Fund, Washington, 1985-87; equal opportunity specialist U.S. Dept. Agriculture, Washington, 1988—; participant U.S. Dept. Agriculture Mgmt. Devel. Program, Washington, 1993-94; cons. in field. Co-founder No. Va. chpt. Nat. Polit. Congress of Black Women. Mem. Continental Socs., Inc. (No. Va. chpt. v.p. 1993—), Jr. League No. Va., Howard U. Alumni Assn. (No. Va. chpt. charter mem., past sec.), Alpha Kappa Alpha. Democrat. Presbyterian. Avocations: photography, travel, cultural activities, political trivia, writing. Home: 2000 Huntington Ave Apt 501 Alexandria VA 22303-1732

PATTERSON, VIRGINIA GOODWIN, social worker; b. Nashville, Feb. 21, 1917; d. Marsh and Lena Grace (Givens) Goodwin; BS, Peabody Coll., 1968; MSW, U. Tenn., 1970; lic. pvt. social work practitioner; lic. social worker; m. Fletcher Woodall Patterson, June 17, 1940; 1 child, Judith Ellen Patterson Murphy. Various secretarial positions, 1934-43; dir. day camp Cumberland Valley Girl Scout council, Nashville, summers 1953-62; sec. Centenary Methodist Community Center, Nashville, 1961-64; dir. resident camp Sycamore Hills, Ashland City, Tenn., summers 1963-65; case worker United Methodist Community Center, 1970-71; social case worker, dir. day care for elderly Sr. Citizens, Inc., Nashville, 1971-88; ret., 1988; v.p. Cumberland Valley Girl Scout council, 1963-64; youth tchr., counselor Dalewood Meth. Ch., 1950—, pres. Women's Soc. Christian Service. Pres. Isaac Litton High Sch. PTA, Nashville, 1959-61; dir. Ind. Svcs. Sr. Citizens, 1985; pres. United Meth. Women, 1990, 94; mem. choir Dale United Meth., 1990—; mem. adminstrv. bd. Coun. on Ministries. Recipient Thanks badge Girl Scouts, 1961. Mem. Nat. Assn. Social Workers (past chpt. registrar, corr. sec.), Tenn. Fedn. Aging (pres. 1982-84, sec. 1984-86, 91, bd. dirs. 1992-94), Nat. Council Aging, Pi Gamma Mu (past chpt. sec.). Republican. Lodges: Soroptimists of Nashville (pres. 1986), Civitan (pres. 1990-91, bd. dirs. 1992-94). Contbr. articles to profl. jours. Home: 1709 Sherwood Ln Nashville TN 37216-4023 Office: 1801 Broadway Nashville TN 37203

PATTERSON, W. MORGAN, college president; b. New Orleans, Oct. 1, 1925; s. E. Palmer and Jess Margaret (Wood) P.; m. Ernestine North, June 10, 1948; children—W. Morgan, II, Jay North. B.A., Stetson U., 1950, D.D. (hon.), 1979; M.Div., New Orleans Bapt. Theol. Sem., 1953, Th.D., 1956; postdoctoral, Oxford U., 1965-66, 72-73. Prof. ch. history New Orleans Bapt. Theol. Sem., 1956-59; prof. ch. history, David T. Porter prof. ch. history, dir. grad. studies So. Baptist Theol. Sem., Louisville, Ky., 1959-76; dean acad. affairs Golden Gate Bapt. Theol. Sem., Mill Valley, Calif., 1976-84; pres. Georgetown Coll., Ky., 1984-91; vis. prof. Midwestern Bapt. Theol. Sem., Kansas City, Mo., La. Coll., Pineville, 1991-92, Golden Gate Bapt. Theol. Sem., Mill Valley, Calif., 1992-94, New Orleans Bapt. Theol. Sem., 1995, 96; chmn. hist. commn. So. Bapt. Conv., Nashville, 1969-72; honored guest 2d Vatican Coun., Rome, 1965. Author: Baptist Successionism: A Critical View, 1969; co-editor: Professor in the Pulpit, 1963; contbr., editor: Ency. Southern Baptists; book rev. editor Review and Expositor, 1965-70. Served as flight officer USAAF, 1943-46. Recipient Disting. Alumnus award Stetson U., 1992, Disting. Svc. award for outstanding contbn. to Bapt. history Hist. Commn., So. Bapt. Conv., 1993; Am. Assn. Theol. Schs. fellow, 1965-66. Mem. Am. Soc. Ch. History, So. Bapt. Hist. Soc. (pres. 1979-80), William H. Whitsitt Bapt. Heritage Soc., Conf. on Faith and History, Commn. on Bapt. Heritage of Bapt. World Alliance. Avocations: travel; philately; collecting books. Home: 7 Pierce Dr Novato CA 94947-4450

PATTERSON, WILLIAM BRADFORD, surgical oncologist; b. New Rochelle, N.Y., June 25, 1921; s. Arthur Henry and Gertrude Claire (Hough) P.; m. Helen Russell Ross, May 17, 1943; children: William Bradford, Rebecca H. Bruns, Linda Stevens, Stuart Ross. A.B., Harvard U., 1943, M.D., 1950. Diplomate: Am. Bd. Surgery. Chemist E.I. DuPont Co., 1942-44; intern Peter Bent Brigham Hosp., Boston, 1950-51; resident in surgery, 1951-56; surgeon Boston City Hosp., 1956-59; practice medicine specializing in surgery Boston, 1963-70; chief Pondville Hosp., 1959-63; prof. surgery U. Rochester, N.Y., 1970-78; assoc. dir. for cancer control Dana Farber Cancer Inst., Boston, 1978-91; vis. prof. surgery Harvard Med. Sch., 1978-89; cons. Nat. Cancer Inst. Contbr. chpts. to books, articles to med. jours. Served with USNR, 1944-46. Fellow ACS; mem. Mass. Med. Soc., Boston Surg. Soc., New Eng. Surg. Soc., New Eng. Cancer Soc. Democrat. Congregationalist. Home: RR 1 Box 59 Middlebury VT 05753-9505

PATTERSON, WILLIAM BROWN, university dean, history educator; b. Charlotte, N.C., Apr. 8, 1930; s. William Brown and Eleanor Selden (Miller) P.; m. Evelyn Byrd Hawkins, Nov. 27, 1959; children: William Brown, Evelyn Byrd, Lucy Miller, Emily Norvell. BA, U. South, 1952; MA, Harvard U., 1954, PhD, 1966, cert. ednl. mgmt., 1982; BA, Oxford (Eng.) U., 1955, MA, 1959; MDiv, Episc. Div. Sch., Cambridge, Mass., 1958. Ordained to ministry Episcopal Ch. as deacon, 1958, as priest, 1959. Asst. prof. history Davidson (N.C.) Coll., 1963-66, assoc. prof., 1966-76, prof. history, 1976-80; dean Coll. Arts and Scis. U. South, Sewanee, Tenn., 1980-91, prof. of history, 1980—. Author: (with others) Discord, Dialogue, and Concord, 1977; mem. bd. editors St. Luke's Jour. Theology, Sewanee, 1982-90; contbr. numerous articles to profl. jours. Trustee U. South, 1968-71; mem. internat. adv. com. U. Buckingham, Eng., 1977—; pres. So. Coll. and Univ. Union; organizer Associated Colls. of South, 1988-89. Danforth Found. grad. fellow, 1952, Mellon Appalachian fellow U. Va., 1992-93, rsch. fellow NEH, 1967, Folger Shakespeare Libr., Washington, 1975, Inst. for Rsch. in Humanities, U. Wis., Madison, 1976, Newberry Libr., Chgo., 1979; Rhodes scholar, 1953. Mem. Am. Hist. Assn., Am. Soc. Ch. History, N.Am. Conf. on Brit. Studies, Eccles. History Soc. Eng., Renaissance Soc. Am., So. Hist. Assn., Soc. for Values in Higher Edn., Episcopal Div. Sch. Alumni/ae Assn. (mem. exec. com. 1984-87), Phi Beta Kappa, Beta Theta Pi. Avocations: gardening, tennis. Home: 195 North Carolina Ave Sewanee TN 37375 Office: U of the South Dept History Sewanee TN 37383-1000

PATTERSON, WILLIAM ROBERT, lawyer; b. Wathena, Kans., Feb. 25, 1924; s. George Richard and Jessie (Broadbent) P.; m. Lee Rhyne, Aug. 16, 1947; children: Martha, Robert, Elizabeth. Student, U. Rochester, 1943-44; A.B., Lenoir-Rhyne Coll., 1947; LL.B. with distinction, Duke U., 1950. Bar: Ga. 1951, D.C. 1962. Asso. firm Sutherland, Asbill & Brennan, Atlanta, 1950-58; partner Sutherland, Asbill & Brennan, 1958—; trustee Ga. Tax Conf., 1980-83, pres., 1980-82; lectr. in field. Mem. bd. visitors Duke U. Law Sch., 1973-87, chmn., 1977-87, life mem., 1987—; trustee Pace Acad., Atlanta, 1958-89, trustee emeritus, 1989—; mem. devel. bd. Lenoir-Rhyne Coll., 1976-79, trustee, 1980-89; elder Trinity Presbyterian Ch., Atlanta. With USN, 1942-46. Fellow Am. Coll. Mortgage Attys. (bd. regents 1993—); mem. ABA, Ga. State Bar, Atlanta Bar Assn., D.C. Bar Assn., Am. Coll. Real Estate Lawyers (bd. govs. 1987-90), Am. Law Inst., So. Fed. Tax Inst. (trustee 1957-90, adv. trustee 1990—, pres. 1974-75, chmn. 1975-76), Atlanta Tax Forum (trustee 1977-83, pres. 1981-82), Order of Coif, Cherokee Town and Country Club, Commerce Club, Peachtree Club. Home: 2939 Rivermeade Dr NW Atlanta GA 30327-2039 Office: Sutherland Asbill & Brennan First Union Pla 23d Fl 999 Peachtree St NE Atlanta GA 30309-3964

PATTERSON, WILLIAM S., lawyer; b. Kings Mountain, N.C., July 16, 1947. BA, Wake Forest U., 1969; JD with honors, U. N.C., 1973. Bar: N.C. 1973. Staff atty. interpretive divsn. Office Chief Counsel U.S. Dept. Treasury, 1973-75, staff atty. tax ct. litigation divsn., 1975-77; ptnr. Hunton & Williams, Raleigh, N.C. Office: Hunton & Williams PO Box 109 1 Hanover Sq 14th Fl Raleigh NC 27602*

PATTERSON, WILLIAM WAYNE, business executive; b. Overton, Tex., Mar. 23, 1943; s. Samuel Ashley and Marguerite (Robinson) P.; B.B.A., U. Tex., 1965, LL.B., 1967; postgrad. cert. comparative law Universidad Nacional de Mexico, 1967; m. Janie Chiles, Dec. 27, 1969; children: Perrin Ashli, Shawn Adair, Andrew Clay. Acct., Peat, Marwick, Mitchell & Co., Houston, 1968-74; controller Keystone Internat., Inc., Houston, 1974-76, sec.-treas., 1976-78, v.p. fin., 1978-86, exec. v.p., 1986-89, group pres. systems and controls group, 1985-86, also bd. dirs., 1978—; chmn., CEO Tex. Microsystems Inc., Houston, 1989—, Briskheat Corp., 1989—. Trustee Shriners Hosp. Crippled Children; mem. adv .bd. Child Abuse Prevention Council; bd. dirs. Ronald McDonald House. C.P.A., Tex. Mem. Am. Inst. C.P.A.s, ABA. Episcopalian. Clubs: Houstonian, Masons, Houston Country Club. Office: Tex Microsystems Inc PO Box 42963 Houston TX 77242-2963

PATTESON, ROY KINNEER, JR., clergyman, administrator; b. Richmond, Va., Oct. 27, 1928; s. Roy Kinneer and Mary (Anderson) P.; m. Edna Pauline Cox, Apr. 15, 1950; children: Stephen, David. B.A., U. Richmond, 1957; B.D., Union Theol. Sem., 1961; Th.M., Duke U., 1964, Ph.D., 1967. Ordained to ministry Presbyterian Ch. in U.S.A., 1961. Fellow Duke U. Inst. Medieval and Renaissance Studies, 1968; pres. So. Sem. Jr. Coll., 1970-72; v.p. Mary Baldwin Coll., 1972-77; pres. King Coll., Bristol, Tenn., 1977-79; asst. to pres. Va. Wesleyan Coll., 1979-81, v.p., 1981-85; v.p. Westminster-Canterbury of Hampton Rds., Inc., Virginia Beach, Va., 1985-88; asst. sec. bd. trustees Westminster-Canterbury of Hampton Rds., Inc., 1986-88; dir. Norfolk (Va.) Sr. Ctr., 1987-88; cons. Marts & Lundy Inc., Rockbridge Baths, Va., 1988-92; trustee, treas. Beverley St. Studio Sch., Staunton, Va., 1996—; pastor Pittsboro and Mt. Vernon Springs Presbyn. chs., Pittsboro, N.C., 1962-65; mem. mission council and chmn. budget com. Shenandoah Presbytery, 1973-77; chmn. com. on higher edn. Norfolk Presbytery, 1980-82; mem. community adv. bd. Madison Coll., 1975-77; bd. dirs. Tenn. Ind. Coll. Fund; v.p. Mid-Appalachian Coll. Council, 1978-79. Vice pres. Rockbridge Hist. Soc., Lexington, Va., 1970-77; chmn. edn. com. Staunton-Augusta C. of C. Served with U.S. Army, 1948-49; with U.S. N.G., 1949-52. Recipient Grad. Scholar award Duke U., 1966. Office: 342 Bellevue Ln Rockbridge Baths VA 24473

PATTI, ANDREW S., consumer products company executive; b. 1940. With Standard Brands, 1961-63, 65-67; pres. Armour Handcrafts Inc., Phoenix, 1982-86; now pres., chief exec. officer Armour Internat. Corp., Phoenix; with Dial Corp., Phoenix, 1986—, now pres., chief oper. officer. With U.S. Army, 1963-65. Office: Dial Corp Consumer Products Group 1850 N Central Ave Phoenix AZ 85077-0001*

PATTI, SISTER JOSEPHINE MARIE, health science facility administrator; b. Buffalo, July 5, 1934; d. Joseph John and Caroline Mary (Mayer) P. BS, D'Youville Coll., Buffalo, 1964; MHA, Xavier U., Cin., 1974. Joined Grey Nuns of Sacred Heart, Roman Cath. Ch., 1954. Med. technologist Griffin Meml. Hosp., Kodiak, Alaska, 1964-70; asst. supr., sr. med. tech. A.B. Hepburn Hosp., Ogdensburg, NY, 1970-72; adminstrv. res. St. Joseph's Infirmary, Atlanta, 1973-74; adminstr. Kodiak (Alaska) Island Hosp., 1974-78; adminstrv. asst. St. Joseph's Hosp. Inc., Atlanta, 1978-79; asst. adminstr. St. Joseph's Hosp., 1979-80; dir., misson effective St. Joseph's Hosp., Atlanta, 1986-88, asst. v.p., 1988-90, v.p. misc. effect, 1990-95; adminstr. Motherhouse, Grey Nuns of the Sacred Heart, Yardley, Pa., 1980-85; dir. St. Joseph's Mercy Care Corp., Atlanta, 1988-95; v.p. Mission St. Joseph Healthcare, NAshua, N.H., 1995—; chairperson bd. dirs. Atlanta Cmty. Health Program for the Homeless, 1988-91; vice chairperson bd. dirs. Mercy Mobile Health Program, 1991-94; dir. South Ctrl. Health Planning and Devel., Inc., Anchorage, 1976-77. Adv. bd. Lifelink Ga., 1988-91; mem. instnl. rev. bd. AIDS Rsch. Consortium, Atlanta, 1988-95; dir. North Atlanta Sr. Svcs., 1988-93; bd. dirs. Mercy Sr. Care, 1991-95, sec., 1991-93; mem. Hispanic Svcs. Adv. Bd., 1991-94; bd. dirs. Cath. Social Svcs., Inc., 1992-95. Fellow Am. Coll. Health Care Execs. Office: St Joseph Healthcare 172 Kinsley St PO Box 2013 Nashua NH 03061-2013

PATTILLO, MANNING MASON, JR., academic administrator; b. Charlottesville, Va., Oct. 11, 1919; s. Manning Mason and Margaret (Camblos) P.; m. Martha A. Crawford, June 8, 1946; children: Manning Mason III, Martha Crawford, John Landrum. Student, Johns Hopkins U., 1937-38; BA with highest honors, U. of South, 1941, DCL, 1993; student, U. Calif. at Berkeley, 1941-42; AM, U. Chgo., 1947, PhD, 1949; LLD, LeMoyne Coll., 1967, St. John's U., 1968, Oglethorpe U., 1994; LHD, U. Detroit, 1968, Coll. New Rochelle, 1967, Park Coll., 1973; LittD, St. Norbert Coll., 1967. From instr. to assoc. prof. higher edn. U. Chgo., 1949-56; assoc. dir. Lilly Endowment, Inc., Indpls., 1956-60; exec. dir. for edn. Lilly Endowment, Inc., 1961-62; dir. Danforth commn. on ch. colls. and univs., 1962-66; assoc. dir. The Danforth Found., 1964-66, v.p., 1966-67; pres. The Found. Center, N.Y.C., 1967-71; adj. prof. N.Y. U., 1968-71; dir. spl. projects U. Rochester, 1972-75; pres. Oglethorpe U., Atlanta, 1975-88, chancellor, 1988—; cons. in field; tech. asst., then assoc. sec. commn. on colls. and units North Cen. Assn. Colls. and Secondary Schs., 1948-56; cons. USAF Acad., 1952, Phillips Exeter Acad., 1974; chmn. IBM Incentive awards com., 1970-75; adv. com. Brookings Instn., 1970-71; vis. prof. Inst. Higher Edn., U. Ga., 1988—; bd. dirs. Fidelity Nat. Bank. Author: (with D.M. Mackenzie) Church Sponsored Higher Education in the United States, 1966, (with D.M. Mackenzie) Eight Hundred Colleges Face the Future, 1965, Private Higher Education in the United States, 1990, The Episcopal Church: Diagnosis and Reform, 1989; contbr. articles to profl. jours. Mem. pres.'s adv. coun. Wellesley Coll., 1969-72; trustee Seabury Press, Japan Internat. Christian U., 1970-72, Le Moyne Coll., 1970-83, Sacred Heart U., 1968-75, U. of South, 1984-88, St. Martin's Episc. Sch.; bd. dirs., chmn. Atlanta Coll. Art, 1984—, Howard Sch.; trustee Greater Rochester Community Found., 1973-75, pres., 1975; trustee, chmn. Nat. Coun. on Philanthropy, 1968-80; trustee, chmn. bd. trustees Park Coll., 1967-74; provost St. Mary's Coll. of Md., 1975; bd. visitors Kanuga Confs., Inc.; pres., life trustee Ga. Found. for Ind. Colls., 1977-79; chmn. Univ. Center in Ga., 1978-79; pres. Assn. Pvt. Colls. and Univs. of Ga., 1980-81; trustee, chmn. Ga. Spl. Olympics; trustee, mem. exec. com. Nat. Assn. Ind. Colls. and Univs., Ind. Coll. Funds of Am., 1982-86; co-dir. Coll. Cons. Network, So. Assn. Colls. and Schs., 1988—; mem. De Kalb County Community Relations Commn.; chmn. De Kalb Community Coun. on the Aging; mem. commn. on colls. and steering com. on revision accrediting procedures So. Assn. Colls. and Schs.; vice-chmn bd. dirs. Woodruff Arts Ctr.; mem. adv. coun. ARC. With AUS, 1942-46. Mem. Nat. Assn. Scholars, Assn. for Higher Edn., Nat. Assn. Ind. Schs. (bd. dirs.), Guild of Scholars, English Speaking Union (dir., pres. br., nat. bd. dirs.), Country Day Sch. Headmasters Assn. U.S. (hon.), Atlanta Hist. Soc., Dekalb C. of C. (dir., chmn.), Phi Beta Kappa, Omicron Delta Kappa, Kappa Sigma. Episcopalian (vestryman, sr. warden, mem. cathedral chpt., diocesan council, standing com.). Clubs: Century (N.Y.C.); Commerce, Capital City. Lodge: Rotary. Office: Office of Chancellor Oglethorpe Univ 4484 Peachtree Rd NE Atlanta GA 30319-2737

PATTIS, S. WILLIAM, publisher; b. Chgo., July 3, 1925; s. William Robert and Rose (Quint) P.; m. Bette Z. Levin, July 16, 1950; children: Mark Robert, Robin Quint Himovitz. BS, U. Ill., 1949; postgrad., Northwestern U., 1949-50. Exec. v.p., pub. United Bus. Publs., 1949-59; chmn., CEO 3M/Pattis, 1959-88; pres. NTC Pub. Group, Lincolnwood, Ill., 1961-96; dir. P-B Comm., Winnetka, Ill., 1978—; bd. dirs. 1st Colonial/Highwood; mem. book and libr. com. USIA, Washington, 1986-89, chmn., 1989-93; mem. exec. com. Pub. Hall of Fame, 1987—; chmn. U.S.-USSR Bilateral Info. Talks, Moscow, 1990. Mem. Pres.'s Coun. Youth Opportunity, 1968-70; bd. dirs. Photography Youth Found., 1970-73, Expt. in Internat. Living, 1970, Inst. Human Creativity, 1983—, Annenberg Ctr. for Health Scis., 1991—; trustee Eisenhower Med. Ctr., Rancho Mirage, Calif., 1989—; trustee Am. Coun. Tchrs. Russian, 1992—; bd. dirs. Nat. Security Edn. Act, Washington, 1993-94; lord of manor, Kirkbride, Eng., 1989—. Recipient Human Rels. award Am. Jewish Com., 1971, Paul Simon award Cen. States Conf. on Tchg. Fgn. Langs., 1992. Mem. Standard Club (Chgo.), Northmoor Country Club (Highland Park, Ill.), Tamarisk Country Club (Rancho Mirage). Home: 195 Elder Ln Highland Park IL 60035-5368 Office: NTC Pub Group 4255 W Touhy Ave Lincolnwood IL 60646

PATTISHALL, BEVERLY WYCKLIFFE, lawyer; b. Atlanta, May 23, 1916; s. Leon Jackson and Margaret Simkins (Woodfin) P.; children by previous marriage: Margaret Ann Arthur, Leslie Hansen, Beverly Wyckliffe, Paige Terhune Pattishall Watt, Woodfin Underwood; m. Dorothy Daniels Mashek, June 24, 1977; 1 stepchild, Lyssa Mashek Piette. BS, Northwestern U., 1938; JD, U. Va., 1941. Bar: Ill. 1941, D.C. 1971. Pvt. practice law Chgo., 1946—; ptnr. Pattishall, McAuliffe, Newbury, Hilliard & Geraldson and predecessor firms, Chgo.; dir. Juvenile Protective Assn. Chgo., 1946-79, pres., 1961-63, hon. dir., 1979—; dir. Vol. Interagy. Assn., 1975-78, sec., 1977-78; U.S. del. Diplomatic Confs. on Internat. Trademark Registration Treaty, Geneva, Vienna, 1970-73, Diplomatic Conf. on Revision of Paris Conv., Nairobi, 1981; mem. U.S. del. Geneva Conf. on Indsl. Property and Consumer Protection, 1978; adj. prof. trademark, trade identity and unfair trade practices law Northwestern U. Sch. Law, Chgo. Author: (with David C. Hilliard) Trademarks, Trade Identity and Unfair Trade Practices, 1974, Unfair Competition and Unfair Trade Practices, 1985, Trademarks, 1987, Trademarks and Unfair Competition, 1994, 2d edit., 1996; contbr. articles to profl. jours. Lt. comdr. USNR, WWII, ETO, PTO, ATO, ret. comdr. Fellow Am. Coll. Trial Lawyers (bd. regents 1979-83); mem. ABA (chmn. sect. patent, trademark copyright law 1963-64), Internat. Patent and Trademark Assn. (pres. 1955-57, exec. com. 1955—), Assn. Internat. Pour La Protection Propriete Indsl. (mem. of honor), Ill. Bar Assn., Chgo. Bar Assn., D.C. Bar Assn., Chgo. Bar Found. (dir. 1977-83), U.S. Trademark Assn. (dir. 1963-65), Legal Club, Law Club (pres. 1982-83), Econ. Club, Chikaming Country Club, Univ. Club, Mid-Am. Club, U. Va. Lile Law Soc. (sr. counselor), Selden Soc. (London, Ill. rep.). Office: Pattishall McAuliffe Newbury Hilliard & Geraldson 311 S Wacker Dr Ste 5000 Chicago IL 60606-6618

PATTISON, ABBOTT LAWRENCE, sculptor; b. Chgo., May 15, 1916; s. William L. and Bonnie (Abbott) P.; m. Mary Grant, June 2, 1945; children: William G., Grant A., Harry, Jean. BA, Yale, 1937, BFA, 1939. Tchr. Chgo. Art Inst., 1946-51; instr. Skowhegan Art Sch., 1955-56. Sculptor in residence U. Ga., 1953-54; affiliated Feingarten Gallery, Los Angeles, Fairweather Hardin Gallery, Chgo., Alwin Gallery, London; major commns. include Mayo Clinic, Rochester, Minn., Cen. Nat. Bank, Cleve., U. Chgo., Chgo. State U., Ill. Capitol Bldg., Lincoln Library, Springfield, Ill., Northbrook (Ill.) Library, New Trier West High Sch., Northfield Ill., Culligan Internat. & Commerce Plaza, Oak Brook, Ill.; 1st Logan prize and purchase Art Inst. Chgo. 1942, Eisendrath prize 1946, 1st Pauline Palmer prize for sculpture 1950, prize 1953, 3d prize contemporary sculpture show Met. Mus. Art 1951, 1st prize Chgo. Sculptor Show, Art Cen. 1955, 1st prize McCormick Pl. Art Show 1962, prize Bundy Mus., Waitsfield, Vt. 1963; work in China and Japan, 1940, Europe, 1950-51, 55-56, 58, 60-61, Italy, 1955-56, 58, 60-61; represented in collections Art Inst. Chgo., Corcoran Gallery, Washington, Phoenix Museum, Calif. Palace Legion of Honor, others; represented permanent collections at Whitney Mus., N.Y.C., Israel State Mus. Jerusalem, San Francisco Mus., Buckingham Palace, London, Eng., Yorkshire (England) Sculpture Park, U.S. State Dept., St. Louis Mus., Palm Springs Desert Mus., Portland (Maine) Mus., Addison Gallery Am. Art., Davenport Mus., Evansville Mus. Capt. USN, 1942-45. Recipient of Yale U.'s 1st traveling fellowship, 1939, 1st Logan prize Art Inst. Chgo., 1942. also: Caldbeck Gallery 12 Elm St Rockland ME 04841-2811

PATTISON, DELORIS JEAN, counselor, university official; b. Logansport, Ind., Oct. 3, 1931; d. John R. and Grace I. Gallagher (Yocum) Taylor; m. John A. Pattison, July 3, 1952; children: Traci (dec.), John A. II, Scott, Becky. BS in Secondary Edn., Goshen Coll., 1973; MA in Edn., Ball State U., 1977. Life cert. vocat. edn. tchr., Ind. Tchr. home econs. Marion (Ind.) H.S., 1973-78; dir. youth employment Logansport Cmty. Schs., 1979-83; substitute tchr. Ft. Wayne (Ind.) Cmty. Schs., 1983-87; employment counselor Ind. Dept. Employment, Marion, 1987-90; counselor, coord. adminstrv. career svcs. Ind. Wesleyan U., Marion, 1990—. Editor: A Teen Trace, 1971; also articles. Bd. dirs. Ind. Christian Coll. Consortium, 1990—. Named Outstanding Employee, Ind. Dept. Employment and Tng., 1989. Mem. Nat. Assn. Colls. and Employers, Midwest Coll. Placement Assn., Great Lake Assn. for Sch., Coll. and Univ. Staffing, Dist. Min. Spouse Assn. (sec. 1987-89), Am. Legion Aux. Methodist. Avocations: reading, walking, writing, travel. Home: 801 N Huntington #47 Hippensteel Dr Marion IN 46792 Office: Ind Wesleyan U 4201 S Washington St Marion IN 46953-4974

PATTISON, ROBERT MAYNICKE, architect; b. Colonia, N.J., Feb. 22, 1923; s. Maynicke Munn Pattison and Lillian Cornelia (Garretson) Pattison Fox; divorced; children: Jeannine (Mrs. D. Harper), Darrel Keith, Michael Shaun. Lic. architect, Ohio. Project coord. Walker & Weeks, Cleve., 1948-

60; project architect Shaefer, Flynn & Williams, Cleve., 1960-62; v.p. Williams-Pattison Assoc., Inc., Cleve., 1962-74; prin. Robert M. Pattison, Architect, Berea, Ohio, 1974-85, 90—; architect, plan examiner City of Cleve. Bldg Dept., 1985-90; project architect Dalton-Dalton-Newport A/E, Shaker Heights, Ohio, 1977-78; asst. supr. Turner Constrn., Inc., Cleve., 1980; architect Lawson Co., Cuyahoga Falls, Ohio, 1980-81. Co-author: IEEE White Book, 1979. With USN, 1943-45. Mem. Kiwanis (pres. Middleburg Heights club 1991-92). Republican. Home and Office: 444 Woodlawn Cir Berea OH 44017-1231

PATTON, ALTON DEWITT, electrical engineering educator, consultant, research administrator; b. Corpus Christi, Tex., Feb. 1, 1935; s. Alton G. and Civilia Louise (Taylor) P.; m. Nancy Jo Elder, Mar. 1, 1959; children: Elizabeth, Carolyn. BEE, U. Tex., Austin, 1957; MEE, U. Pitts., 1961; PhD in Elec. Engring., Tex. A&M U., 1972. Registered profl. engr., Tex. Engr. Westinghouse Electric Corp., Pitts., 1957-65; prof. elec. engring. dept. Tex. A&M U., College Station, 1965-79, 82—, head elec. engring. dept., 1992—, Brockett prof., 1986, Dresser prof., 1987, dir. Electric Power Inst., 1976-79, 85-92; rsch. fellow Tex. Engring. Expt. Sta., College Station, 1985; dir. Ctr. for Space Power Tex. Engring. Expt. Sta., 1987-92; pres. Associated Power Analysts Inc., College Station, Tex., 1973—. Contbr. articles to elec. engring. jours., 1960—. Fellow IEEE (prize paper award 1975, 94); mem. NSPE, Internat. Conf. on Large High Voltage Electric Systems, Internat. Astonautical Fedn. Republican. Presbyterian. Avocations: fishing, hunting, photography, stamp and coin collecting. Home: 1217 Merry Oaks Dr College Station TX 77840-2608 Office: Tex A&M U Elec Engring Dept College Station TX 77843

PATTON, BOB J., oil industry executive; b. Whitt, Tex., Nov. 5, 1925; s. John Elmer and Dora Althia (Davis) P.; m. Glenda Nell Colbert, May 30, 1950; children: Eva Diane, Elaine Gay, John Carl. BS in Physics, U. North Tex., 1949, MS in Physics, 1950. Instr. U. North Tex., Denton, 1950-51; rschr. Gulf R & D, Pitts., 1951-53; rsch. assoc. Mobil R & D, Dallas, 1953-80; mwd mgr. Gearhart Industries, Ft. Worth, 1980-82; pres. Patton Cons., Inc., Dallas, 1982—. Patentee in field. With USN, 1945-46. Mem. Soc. Petroleum Engrs., Aircraft Owners & Pilots Assn., Sigma Pi Sigma. Republican. Avocations: inventing, woodworking, flying. Home and Office: 2436 Monaco Ln Dallas TX 75233-2826

PATTON, CARL ELLIOTT, physics educator; b. San Antonio, Sept. 14, 1941; s. Carl Elliott and Geraldine Barnett (Perry) P. BS, MIT, 1963; MS, Calif. Inst. Tech., 1964, PhD, 1967. Sr. scientist Raytheon Co., Waltham, Mass., 1967-71; assoc. prof. physics Colo. State U., Ft. Collins, 1971-75, prof., 1975—; IEEE Magnetics Soc. Disting. lectr., 1993. editor-in-chief IEEE Transactions on Magnetics, 1987-91. Fellow IEEE, Am. Phys. Soc. Office: Colo State Univ Dept Physics Fort Collins CO 80523

PATTON, CARL VERNON, academic administrator, educator; b. Coral Gables, Fla., Oct. 22, 1944; s. Carl V. and Helen Eleanor (Benkert) P.; m. Gretchen West, July 29, 1967. BS in Community Planning, U. Cin., 1967; MS in Urban Planning U. Ill.-Urbana, 1969, MS in Pub. Adminstrn., 1970; MS in Pub. Policy, U. Calif.-Berkeley, 1975, PhD in Pub. Policy, 1976. Instr. to prof. U. Ill., 1968-83, dir. Bureau of Urban and Regional Planning Rsch., 1977-79, prof., chmn. dept., 1979-83; prof., dean Sch. Architecture and Urban Planning, U. Wis., Milw., 1983-89; v.p. acad. affairs, prof. polit. sci., geography and urban planning U. Toledo, 1989-92; pres. Ga. State U., Atlanta, 1992—. Author: Academia in Transition, 1979; (with others) The Metropolitan Midwest, 1985; (with David Sawicki) Basic Methods of Policy Analysis and Planning, 1986, rev. 2d edit., 1993; (with Kathleen Reed) Guide to Graduate Education in Urban and Regional Planning, 1986, 88; editor: Spontaneous Shelter: International Perspectives and Prospects, 1988, (with G. William Page) Quick Answers to Quantitative Problems: A Pocket Primer, 1991; assoc. editor Jour. of Planning Edn. and Rsch., 1983-87, mem. editl. bd., 1987-89; mem. editl. bd. Habitat International, 1993—, Atlanta International Magazine, 1993—; contbr. articles to profl. jours. Chmn. Community Devel. Commn., Urbana, 1978-82; mem. Civic Design Ctr., Milw., 1983-87; mem. City of Milw. Art Commn., 1988-89, ToledoVision, 1989-92, Toledo Art Ctr. Bd., 1989-92, City of Toledo Bd. Cmty. Rels., 1990-92; bd. dirs. Atlanta YMCA, The Downtown Atlanta Partnership, Ctrl. Atlanta Progress, Ga. Rsch. Alliance, Ctrl. Atlanta Hospitality Childcare, Inc., Atlanta Convention and Vis. Bur., Atlanta United Way, Woodruff Art Ctr., Fox Theatre; mem. exec. com. The Fairlie-Poplar Task Force, The Univ. Ctr. in Ga.; mem. Ga. Coun. on Econ. Edn., Atlanta Neighborhood Devel. Ptnrship. Fellow NIMH, 1973-75, U. Ill. Center for Advanced Studies, 1973-74. Mem. Am. Planning Assn., Am. Inst. Cert. Planners, Assn. Collegiate Schs of Planning (v.p. 1985-87, pres. 1989-91), Atlanta C. of C. Avocations: racquetball, jogging, photography, travel. Home: 3807 Tuxedo Rd NW Atlanta GA 30305-1042 Office: Ga State U Office of Pres University Plz Atlanta GA 30303-3083

PATTON, DAVID WAYNE, health care executive; b. Utica, N.Y., June 15, 1942; s. Dale Willard and Eleanor (Miller) P.; BS, Ariz. State U., 1964; MHA, U. Minn., 1966; MA, Claremont U., 1989, MBA, 1991; m. Barbara Jean; children: Jodi Lynn, Steven Wayne. Asst. adminstr. Maricopa County Gen. Hosp., Phoenix, 1969-71; adminstr. Holy Rosary Hosp., Miles City, Mont., 1971-74; exec. dir. St. Luke's Hosp., Aberdeen, S.D., 1974-79; pres., CEO Parkview Episcopal Med. Ctr., Pueblo, Colo., 1979-84; founder Leadership Pueblo, 1982; pres. Community Health Corp. and Riverside (Calif.) Community Hosp., 1984-92; pres. DevelopMed Inc., Fullerton, Calif., 1993-95; adminstr., chief exec. officer Kona Cmty. Hosp., Kealakekua, Hawaii, 1995—; Bd. dirs. San Louis Valley Health Maintenance Orgn., 1982-84, World Pres. Orgn., Riverside C. of C., 1986-91, pres. 1988-89; campaign chmn. United Way of the Inland Valleys, 1989-90; founder, chmn. Leadership Riverside, 1987-89. Served to capt. USAF, 1966-69. Fellow Am. Coll. Healthcare Execs. (regent 1976-79). Republican. Home: 78-7259 Puuloa Rd Kailua Kona HI 96740-9715

PATTON, DIANA LEE WILKOC, artist; b. New Rochelle, N.Y., June 28, 1940; d. August E. and Meta Diane (Neuburg) Wilkoc; m. Gardner C. Patton, Aug. 10, 1963; children: Michael, Talryn, Shawn. AB cum laude Brown U., 1962; postgrad. Pan-Am. Art Inst., 1962-63. Svc. mgr. Lord and Taylor, N.Y.C., 1962-63; tchr. adult edn., Mountain Lakes, N.J., 1972-74, Somerville, N.J., 1978-82, Bound Brook Adult Sch., 1982—; artist in watercolors, pen and ink, acrylics, jewelry created; one-woman and group shows N.E. U.S., Perth, Australia, 1977, spl. bicentennial exhibit, Trenton, 1976, Rutgers U., 1980, Brookdale Coll., 1982, Camden County Coll., 1986, Morris County Coll., 1988, Bergen Mus. Arts and Scis., 1987, 88, 90, 91, North Gallery, Far Hills, 1982, 86, Clarence Dillon Gallery, 1989, 91, Princeton Med. Ctr. 1993, 94, 96; work represented pvt. and public collections in U.S., Australia, N.Z., Germany, Luxembourg, Japan, Eng.; designer ofcl. poster N.J. Festival of Ballooning, 1990, Arc Challenge Races, 1993, 94; instr. in field; developer art appreciation courses for children and adults; toymaker, 1973-76. Winner bronze medal in watercolor Nat. Mystic (Conn.) Outdoor Art Festival, 1977; Mayor's Purchase prize Franklin Twp., 1976; Tri-State Watercolor award Somerset County Coll., 1978; Best in Show Raritan Valley Art Assn., 1978, 94; award Garden State Watercolor Soc., 1979, 1984, 95; 1st and 2d and Best in Show awards Somerset and Westfield Art Assns. shows; 1st place for profl. watercolor Plainfield Tri-State Arts Festival, 1983, 85, 87, N.E. Art Festival Caldwell Coll., 1990, 95; Tewksbury award, 1990; 2d place in watercolor Internat. Miniature Art Show, Washington, 1983; best in show and Grumbacher award Caldwell State show, 1984; 1st place Carrier Clinic Tri-State 1984; Grumbacher Bronze award, 1984, Grumbacher Silver award, 1985, 88, 94, Watercolor award Artists League Cen. N.J. show Cornelious Lowe Mus., 1986, Winsor-Newton award Am. Artists Proleague, 1987, Robert Simmons award, 1989, Basking Ridge Environmental Ctr. award, 1994; Best in Show N.J. State Juried, Piscataway, 1988; 2d place N.J. Miniature Art Soc., 1989; 1st pro Raritan Valley, 1992, 93, 1st mixed media B.R. Environ. Ctr., 1994; artist-in-residence grant Middlesex Librs., 1983-92, watercolor demonstrator, 1983—; TV appearances, State of the Arts-N.J., 1986, Midday (spl. art shows), 1986, TKR, 1995. Elisha Benjamin scholar Brown U., 1960. Mem. Garden State Watercolor Soc., Miniature Art Socs., Fla., Washington, AAUW (life, various offices 1963-73), art assns. Raritan Valley (pres. 1980-82), Somerset, Westfield, North Haven (Maine), Essex Watercolor Club, Am. Artists Profl. League. Presbyterian. Clubs: Hanover Squares (co-pres. 1972-73), Morris County Folk Dancers (co-pres. 1963). Home and Studio: 497 Stony Brook Dr Bridgewater NJ 08807-1945 *Be your own unique self (especially helpful in the arts!). Strive to be better, and measure up to your best standards, not others! But also be kind to yourself (and others), and fully enjoy exploring who you are and what you can do.*

PATTON, GEORGE SMITH, military officer; b. Boston, Dec. 24, 1923; s. George Smith, Jr. and Beatrice Banning (Ayer) P.; m. Joanne Holbrook, June 14, 1952; children: Margaret, George, Robert, Helen, Benjamin. BS, U.S. Mil. Acad., 1946; MPS, George Washington U., 1965. Commd. 2d lt. U.S. Army, 1946, advanced through grades to maj. gen., 1973; parachutist Germany, 1947-51; assigned Armor Br., 1949; instr. tank offense sect. Armored Sch. Fort Knox, Ky., 1952-53; comdr. Co. A, 140th Tank Bn. Korea, 1953, exec. officer I, Corps Reconnaissance Bn., 1953-54; co. tactical officer dept. tactics U.S. Mil. Acad., 1954-56; officer exec. dept. U.S. Naval Acad., 1956-57; assigned Command and Gen. Staff Coll., Fort Leavenworth, Kans., 1957-58; a.d.c. comdg. gen. 7th Army and comdr. in chief U.S. Army, Europe, 1958-60; exec. officer 1st squadron 11th Armored Cav. Regt. Straubing, Germany, 1960-61; assigned Armed Forces Staff Coll. Norfolk, Va., 1961-62; assigned U.S. Army War Coll. Carlisle Barracks, Pa., 1964-65; spl. forces ops. officer Mil. Assistance Command Vietnam, 1962-63; comdr. 2/81 Armor, 1st Armored Div. Fort Hood, Tex., 1963-64; chief Mainland S.E. Asia br. Far East-Pacific div. Office Dep. Chief Staff for Mil. Ops., Dept. Army, 1965-67; chief force devel. div. U.S. Army, Vietnam, 1967-68; comdg. officer 11th Armored Cav. Regt. Vietnam, 1968-69; assigned U.S. Army Primary Helicopter Ctr., Ft. Wolters, Tex., 1969-70, Ft. Rucker, Ala., 1969-70; asst. div. comdr. for support 4th Armored div. Hdqrs. U.S. Army, Europe, 1970-71; comdt. U.S. Army Armor Sch. Fort Knox, 1971-73; dir. security assistance Hdqrs. U.S. European Command, 1973-74, comdr. Army Readiness Region, 1974-75; comdr. 2d Armored Div. Fort Hood, 1975-77; dep. comdg. gen. U.S. VII Corps, 1977-79; dir. readiness Hdqrs. Dept. Army Materiel Devel. and Readiness Command Alexandria, Va., 1979-80; ret., 1980; instr. history U. Md., 1960-61. Mem. West Point Fund, Alexandria, Va.; trustee Essex Agrl. and Tech. Inst., Hathorne, Mass. Decorated D.S.C. with oak leaf cluster, Silver Star with oak leaf cluster, Legion of Merit with two oak leaf clusters, D.F.C., Bronze Star with oak leaf cluster, Purple Heart; Cross of Gallantry with gold, silver and bronze stars Vietnam; Army Forces Honor medal 1st class. Mem. Assn. U.S. Army, Armor Assn., Blackhorse Assn., Ducks Unltd., N.E. Farm Bur., Legion of Valor, Am. Legion. Home: 650 Asbury St South Hamilton MA 01982-1321

PATTON, JAMES LEELAND, JR., lawyer; b. Wilmington, Del., Sept. 28, 1956; s. James L. Patton and Eleanor Phillips Crawford Brown; m. Kathleen Long Patton, May 29, 1981; children: Kathryn Stuart, Diana Lantz. BA in Philosophy, Davidson (N.C.) Coll., 1979; JD, Dickinson Sch. Law, Carlisle, Pa., 1983. Bar: Del. 1983, U.S. Dist. Ct. Del. 1983, U.S. Ct. Appeals (3rd cir.) 1988, U.S. Supreme Ct. 1991. Ptnr., chair Bankruptcy Dept. Young Conaway Stargatt & Taylor, Wilmington, 1983—; trustee Pvt. Panel Bankruptcy Trustees, 1985-88. Contbr. (ref. ency.): Fletcher Corporate Bankruptcy, Reorganization and Dissolution, 1992. Mem. ABA, Del. State Bar Assn. (bankruptcy law subcom. chmn. 1986—). Avocation: photography, sailing. Office: Young Conaway et al PO Box 391 11th & Market Wilmington DE 19899

PATTON, JAMES RICHARD, JR., lawyer; b. Durham, N.C., Oct. 27, 1928; s. James Ralph and Bertha (Moye) P.; m. Mary Margot Maughan, Dec. 29, 1950; children: James Macon, Lindsay Fairfield. AB cum laude, U. N.C., 1948; postgrad., Yale U., 1948; JD, Harvard U., 1951. Bar: D.C. bar 1951, U.S. Supreme Ct. 1963. Attache of Embassy; spl. asst. to Am. ambassador to, Indochina, 1952-54; with Office Nat. Estimates, Washington, 1954-55; atty. Covington & Burling, Washington, 1956-61; founding ptnr., chmn. exec. com. Patton Boggs, LLP, Washington, 1962—; Lectr. internat. law Cornell Law Sch., 1963-64, U.S. Army Command and Gen. Staff Coll., 1967-68; Mem. Nat. Security Forum, U.S. Air War Coll., 1965, Nat. Strategy Seminar, U.S. Army War Coll., 1967-70, Global Strategy Discussions, U.S. Naval War Coll., 1968, Def. Orientation Conf., 1972; mem. Com. of 100 on Fed. City, Washington; mem. adv. council on nat. security and internat. affairs Nat. Republican Com., 1977-81; bd. dirs. Madeira Sch., Greenway, Va., 1975-81, Lawyers Com. for Civil Rights Under Law, Washington, Legal Aid Soc. Washington; mem. Industry Policy Adv. Com. for Trade Policy Matters, 1984-87; councillor of Atlantic Council of U.S., 1987-90; mem. visiting com. Ackland Art Mus. U. N.C., 1987—, Nat. Coun. Anderson Ranch Arts Ctr., 1987—. Adv. coun. mem. Johns Hopkins U. Sch. Advanced Internat. Studies, 1989-92; nat. bd. dirs. Aspen Mus., 1987-90; nat. coun. mem. Whitney Mus., 1992—; bd. dirs., exec. com. Nat. Mus. Natural History, Smithsonian, 1992—; trustee Aspen Music Assocs., 1993—. Mem. ABA (past com. chmn.), Inter-Am. Bar Assn. (past del.), Internat. Law Assn. (past com. chmn.), Am. Soc. Internat. Law (treas., exec. coun.), Washington Inst. Fgn. Affairs, Nat. Gallery (collectors com. 1988-91), Gerrard Soc., Met. Club (Washington), Phi Beta Kappa, Alpha Epsilon Delta.

PATTON, JOANNA, advertising agency owner; b. Quincy, Ill., Dec. 20, 1946; d. John H. and Jane Vandike P. Student Stetson U., 1964-66, Fla. State U., 1966-67. Para legal, Miami, Fla., 1968-74; exec. asst. Louis Nizer, Atty., N.Y.C., 1974-77; adminstrv. asst. to pres. Cosmair, N.Y.C., 1977-78, mgr. pub. rels., 1978, dir. pub. rels., 1978-79, mktg. dir., 1980-81; owner Joanna Patton Advt., N.Y.C., 1982-83; ptnr. Levinger & Patton, N.Y.C., 1983-86, Lotas Minard Patton McIver, Inc., 1986—. Hon. co-chair Cannes Advt. Film Festival Gala. Mem. Fashion Group, Advt. Women N.Y. Office: Lotas Minard Patton McIver 152 W 57th St New York NY 10019-3310

PATTON, JOSEPH DONALD, JR., management consultant; b. Washington, Pa., Jan. 4, 1938; s. Joseph Donald and Priscilla Ann (Johnson) P.; BS in Phys. Scis. and Math. Edn., Pa. State U., 1959; MBA in Mktg., U. Rochester (N.Y.), 1970; m. Susan Oertel, June 3, 1967; children: Jennifer Ann, Joseph Donald, III. Tchr., Aschaffenburg (W.Ger.) Am. Sch., 1963-64; with Xerox Corp., Rochester, 1964-75, mgr. field engring., 1973-75; pres. Patton Cons., Inc., Rochester, 1975-93, Hilton Head, S.C., 1993—; mem. adj. faculty Rochester Inst. Tech., SUNY, Geneseo. Served as capt. U.S. Army, 1959-63. Registered profl. quality engr., Calif.; cert. profl. logistician; cert. quality engr., cert. reliability engr.; cert. service exec. Fellow Am. Soc. Quality Control (reliability and maintainability tech. award 1982), Soc. Logistics Engrs. (Sole Armitage medal 1980, 82); sr. mem. Instrument Soc. Am.; mem. Assn. Field Service Mgrs. (publs. award 1981), Nat. Assn. Service Mgrs. (life cert. svc. exec.), Am. Prodn. and Inventory Control Soc. Republican. Presbyterian. Author 7 texts in field; contbr. over 100 articles to profl. jours. Office: Patton Consultants Inc 4 Covington Pl Hilton Head Island SC 29928-7665

PATTON, NANCY MATTHEWS, elementary education educator; b. Pitts., Apr. 7, 1942; d. Thomas Joseph and Sara Theresa (Jocunskas) Matthews; m. Jack E. Patton, July 20, 1974; children: Susan, Steven. BS in Ed., Ind. U. of Pa., 1963; grad. student, U. Pitts. 4th grade tchr. Elroy Sch., Pitts., 1980-91; 6th grade tchr. Brentwood Middle Sch., Pitts., 1991—; sponsor Brentwood Middle Sch. newspaper; coach Brentwood Varsity Cheerleaders, 1981-93. Councilperson Brentwood Borough Coun., 1988—, v.p., 1994—; sec. Brentwood Dem. Com., 1989-95; bd. trustees Brentwood Libr. Bd., 1988—; mem. Brentwood Econ. Devel. Corp., 1995—. Mem. NEA, Nat. Sci. Tchrs. Assn., Pa. State Edn. Assn., Brentwood Century Club. Democrat. Roman Catholic. Avocations: reading, community service. Home: 105 Hillson Ave Pittsburgh PA 15227-2941

PATTON, NORMAN S., church administrator. Pres. Ch. of God Fgn. Missionary Bd., Anderson, Ind. Office: Ch of God PO Box 2498 Anderson IN 46018-2498

PATTON, PAUL E., governor; b. Fallsburg, KY. Grad. in mech. engring., U. Ky., 1959. With coal bus., until 1979, dep. sec. transp.; judge-exec. Pike County, 1981; lt. gov., sec. econ. devel., pres. senate State of KY, Frankfort, KY, 1991—; governor State of Kentucky, 1995—; served on Ky. Crime Commn., Ky. Tourism Commn., Task Force for Workplace Literacy; former mem. Prichard Com. for Acad. Excellence. Mem. bd. overseers Bellarmine Coll., bd. trustees Pikeville Coll.; chmn. Ky. Dems., 1981-83; del. Dem. Nat. Conv.; served numerous terms Pike County Dem. Exec. Com. Office: Office the Governor The Capitol 700 Capitol Ave Frankfort KY 40601*

PATTON, RICHARD WESTON, mortgage company executive; b. Evanston, Ill., Sept. 26, 1931; s. Robert Ferry and Sue Buckley P.; m. Linda A. Kruse, Feb. 2, 1971; 1 child, Robert Weston. B.A., Amherst Coll., 1954. Sales engr. Thermo Fax Sales Corp., Chgo., 1958-60; account exec. Nat. Mortgage Investors, Inc., Chgo., 1960-61; sales mgr. Nat. Mortgage Investors, Inc., Pasadena, Calif., 1962-66; asst. v.p. Nat. Mortgage Investors, Inc., 1966-67, v.p., 1967-69, exec. v.p., 1969-73, pres., chief exec. officer, dir., 1973-84, vice-chmn. bd., 1984-90; pres. Richard W. Patton Enterprises, Pasadena, 1990—; pres., chmn. exec. com., dir. Ocean Park Restaurant Corp., Santa Monica, Calif., 1977-88; dir. Cenfed Bank, Cenfed Corp. Bd. dirs. Pasadena Boys' Club, 1963-66, Opera Assocs., 1984-90; mem. steering com. Amherst Coll. Capital Fund Drive, 1963-66. With USMCR, 1955-58. Mem. Amherst Coll. Alumni Assn. (bd. dirs. 1963—, pres. 1977-79, 86-89), Overland Club (sec., bd. dirs.), Kroenstadt Ski Club (past pres.). Office: Rich W Patton Enterprises 3644 San Pasqual St Pasadena CA 91107-5419

PATTON, ROBERT FREDERICK, lawyer, banker; b. New Castle, Pa., Dec. 9, 1927; s. Wylie E. and Lena Francis (Gardner) P.; m. Virginia Lee Reehl, Aug. 15, 1952; children: Thomas E., Barbara L., Susan G., Laura L. A.B., Westminster Coll., New Wilmington, Pa., 1950; J.D., Harvard U., 1953. Bar: Pa. 1954. Assoc. Buchanan, Ingersoll, Rodewald, Kyle & Buerger, Pitts., 1953-60, ptnr., 1960-83; chmn. Union Nat. Corp., 1983-89; vice chmn. Integra Fin. Corp., Pitts., 1989, now bd. dirs.; chmn. Bank Cons. Assocs., Pitts., 1990—; bd. dirs. Armstrong World Industries, Inc.; adj. prof. U. Pitts. Law Sch., 1978. Trustee Westminster Coll., 1976-91, sec., 1978-93, chmn., 1988-91; vice moderator Pitts. Presbytery, 1987; chmn. Allegheny County Mental Health/Mental Retardation Bd., 1977-80; trustee Montefiore Hosp., 1985-90, Jewish Healthcare Found., 1990-94. Mem. Am. Law Inst., Am. Bar Found., Allegheny Bar Assn., Duquesne Club, Chartiers Country Club, Nauset Beach Club. Republican. Home: 293 Dixon Ave Pittsburgh PA 15216-1207 Office: Bank Cons Assocs 5800 Usx Tower Pittsburgh PA 15219

PATTON, SHARLENE DARLAGE, nurse; b. Seymour, Ind., July 20, 1933; d. Alfred J. and Viora E. (Elkins) Darlage; children: Raye Ellen, Scott, Susan, Martha, Lisa, Elise. RN, Sch. Nursing Michael Reese Hosp., 1953; BA, Gov.'s State U., 1985. Head nurse Drug Abuse Program, Chgo.; nurse Tinley Park (Ill.) Mental Hosp. Mem. ANA. Address: 593 8th St Chicago Heights IL 60411-1926

PATTON, STEPHEN RAY, lawyer; b. Crawfordsville, Ind., Aug. 29, 1953; s. Don C. and Marlene (Miller) P.; m. Linda L. Wilson, Sept. 3, 1977; children: Andrew Caleb, Sean Patrick. BA, Ind. U., 1975; JD magna cum laude, Georgetown U., 1978. Bar: Ill. 1978, U.S. Dist. Ct. (no. dist.) Ill. 1978. Assoc. Kirkland & Ellis, Chgo., 1978-84, ptnr., 1984—; chmn. Lakeview Clinic, Chgo. Vol. Legal Svcs. Fund. Mem. ABA (litigation sect.). Office: Kirkland & Ellis Amoco Bldg 200 E Randolph St Chicago IL 60601-6436

PATTON, STUART, biochemist, educator; b. Ebenezer, N.Y., Nov. 2, 1920; s. George and Ina (Neher) P.; m. Colleen Cecelia Lavelle, May 17, 1945; children—John, Richard, Gail, Thomas, Mary Catherine, Patricia, Joseph. B.S., Pa. State U., 1943; M.S., Ohio State U., 1947, Ph.D., 1948. Chemist Borden Co., 1943-44; research fellow Ohio State U., Columbus, 1946-48; mem. faculty Pa. State U., University Park, 1949-80, prof., 1959-80; Evan Pugh rsch. prof. agr. Pa. State U., 1966-80; adj. prof. neurosci. Sch. Medicine U. Calif., San Diego, 1981—; vis. scientist Scripps Instn. Oceanography; cons. in field, 1950—. Author: (with Robert Jenness) Principles of Dairy Chemistry, 1959, (with Robert G. Jensen) Biomedical Aspects of Lactation, 1975. Served to lt. (j.g.) USNR, 1944-46. Recipient Borden award chemistry milk Am. Chem. Soc., 1957, Agrl. and Food Chemistry award, 1975; Alexander von Humboldt sr. scientist award, 1981. Mem. Am. Chem. Soc., Am. Dairy Assn., Am. Soc. Biochemistry and Molecular Biology, Am. Soc. Cell Biology. Home: 6208 Avenida Cresta La Jolla CA 92037-6510 Office: U Calif San Diego Ctr Molecular Genetics 0634-J La Jolla CA 92093

PATTON, SUSAN OERTEL, clinical social worker, educator; b. Syracuse, N.Y., May 18, 1946; d. Robert William and Jane (VanWormer) Oertel; m. Joseph D. Patton, Jr., June 3, 1967; children: Jennifer, Joseph D. III. BA, SUNY, Geneseo, 1984; MSW, SUNY, Buffalo, 1987. Cert. social worker, N.Y.; lic. ind. social worker, S.C.; cert. employee assistance profl.; qualified clin. social worker; bd. cert. fellow in managed mental health care; diplomate in clin. social work. Counselor Profl. Counseling Svc., Gowanda, N.Y., 1987-88, Mental Health Mgmt., Rochester, N.Y., 1988-93; counselor The Health Assn., Rochester, 1988-89, sr. counselor, 1989-90, asst. dir. mktg. and tng., 1990-92; pvt. practice Rochester, 1988-93; employee assistance program dir. Recovery Ctr. EAP, Hilton Head, S.C., 1993-95; pres., dir. Employee Assistance Program, Inc., Hilton Head Island, S.C., 1995—; instr. Medaille Coll., Buffalo, 1990-93. Co-author: Treating Perpetrators of Sexual Abuse, 1990. Mem. NASW, Acad. Cert. Social Workers, Am. Bd. Cert. Managed Care Providers, S.C. Counselors Assn., Employee Assistance Profls. Assn. Office: Employee Assistance Program Carolina Bldg Ste 110 10 Office Park Rd Hilton Head Island SC 29928-7541

PATTON, TAMARA J., foreign language educator; b. Balt., Dec. 6, 1957; d. Martin Hobert Patton and Dixie J. Sult. BA in French, U. N.C., Greensboro, 1980, MA in French, 1987; PhD student, U. N.C., Chapel Hill, 1991—; cert. in Egyptian hieroglyphs, Arabic Lang. Inst., Cairo, 1991. Grad. French instr. U. N.C., Greensboro, 1981-84; mgr. Magic Travel, Greensboro, N.C., 1986-87; French tchr. South Florence (S.C.) High Sch., 1987; French, Persian, Arabic and ESL instr. High Point (N.C.) U., 1988—; French instr. U. N.C., Chapel Hill, 1993-94; Spanish instr. Guilford Tech. C.C., 1995; mem. Spanish study group U. N.C., summer 1995, moderator Ann. French Lit. Symposium, 1994; presenter, lectr. in field; resided with Berber tribe in Morocco, summer 1994. Illustrator, artist textbooks and portraits; fgn. corr. (Moroccan newspaper) La Tribune of Fez, 1994—; translator of articles. Officer Greensboro (N.C.) Com. for Relocation of Refugees, 1990; bd. dirs. UNA of USA, Winston-Salem, N.C., 1993—; active Greensboro Jaycees, 1991-92, Prince of Peace Luth. Ch., Greensboro, 1990-92; organizer comty. watch program Sedge Lake Garden, Kernersville, N.C., 1995—. French Embassy scholar, 1992. Mem. MLA, Fgn. Lang. Assn. N.C., UN Assn. Am. (bd. dirs. 1993—), Univ. Women Am., Archael. Inst. Am., Piedmont Indep. Coll. Assn., Pi Delta Phi (pres. 1982-83, hon.). Avocations: Egyptology, fgn. langs., rsch. in ancient documents, tennis. Avocations: Egyptology, foreign languages, painting, literary criticism, research in ancient documents. Home: 5045 Toucan Ln Kernersville NC 27284-7865 Office: High Point U Dept Fgn Langs Montlieu Ave Univ Sta High Point NC 27262

PATTON, THOMAS EARL, lawyer; b. Nov. 25, 1940; s. Thomas E. and Alice F. (Rodarmel) P.; m. Patricia Mann, Aug. 12, 1965 (dec.); m. Barbara Wood, Sept. 21, 1974; 1 child, David Earl. A.B., Cath. U. Am., 1962, J.D. summa cum laude, 1965. Bar: N.Y. 1966, D.C. 1966, Va. 1982. Assoc. Sullivan & Cromwell, N.Y.C., 1965-69; mem. Williams Connolly & Califano, Washington, 1970-75; asst. gen. counsel U.S. Dept. Energy, Washington, 1977-78; ptnr. Schnader, Harrison, Segal & Lewis, Washington, 1979-94; disting. lectr. Cath. U. Am., 1970-90, 95—, bd. regents; nat. arbitrator Am. Arbitration Assn.; bd. dirs. Elcotel, Inc., Info. Exch., Inc. Author: Securities Litigation, 1989, Federal Procedure Casebook, 1990; contbr. articles to profl. jours.; editor in chief Cath. U. Am. Law Rev. Mem. Washington World Affairs Coun., 1980—. Mem. ABA, D.C. Bar (founder and chair litigation sect.), Cosmos Club, Internat. Club (Washington). Roman Catholic. Office: Tighe Patton Tabackman & Babbin 1750 Pennsylvania Ave NW Washington DC 20006

PATTON, THOMAS F., academic administrator, pharmaceutical chemist; b. McKeesport, Pa., Aug. 14, 1948; s. Floyd E. and Alberta I. (Trager) P.; m. Denise Pretzer, Mar. 1, 1986; 1 child, William Patrick. BS, U. Wis., 1971, MS, 1973, PhD, 1975. Prof. U. Kansas, Lawrence, 1975-86, assoc. vice chancellor, 1981-85; assoc. dir. The Upjohn Co., Kalamazoo, Mich., 1986-88; v.p. ops. Oread Labs., Lawrence, Kans., 1988-89; sr. dir. pharm. R&D Merck, Rahway, N.J., 1990-93; v.p. pharm. R&D Dupont-Merck, Wilmington, Del., 1993-94; pres. St. Louis Coll. Pharm., 1994—. Fellow AAAS Acd. Pharm. Scis., Am. Assn. Pharm. Scis., Sigma Xi, Rho Chi.

Office: St Louis Coll Pharmacy 4588 Parkview Pl Saint Louis MO 63110-1029

PATTON, THOMAS JAMES, sales and marketing executive; b. Cleve., Nov. 2, 1948; s. Michael Anthony and Delores (Bammerlin) P.; m. Thomasina Bernadette Cavallaro, Aug. 9, 1969; children: Thomasina, Thera V. A in Transp., Cleve. State U., 1971, BA in Mktg., 1973; BA, SUNY, Empire State, 1994. CLU; ChFC. Ins. salesman Manulife, Cleve., 1972-75, Mass. Mut., Cleve., 1976-80, Patton Ins. Assn., Inc., Avon Lake, Ohio, 1976—; ins. cons. Diversified Benefit Plans, Inc., Avon Lake, 1978-93, dir. sales and mktg., 1993—; pres. commerce Benefits Group, Inc. and Ins. Mktg. Group, Inc., 1995; prin. Cmty. Health Ptnrs., Ltd., Ill., 1994; pres. Commerce Benefits Group, Inc.; cons. Regional Sch. Consortium, Lorain County, Ohio, 1986—, County of Lorain, 1984—, City of Lorain, 1986—, County of Lorain, 1984—, City of Lorain, 1985—; prin. Comty. Health Ptnrs. Ltd.; bd. Italian Cultural Found. Pres. Lake Erie Rate Coun., Cleve., 1970-71; mem. Lorain County Dem. Ctrl. Com., Avon Lake, Ohio, 1986—; mem. com. Cleve. Leukemia Soc., 1985; bd. dirs. Villa Serena Sr. Housing, St. Francis Soc., Italian Cultural Found. Mem. Nat. Assn. Life Underwriters, Profl. Ins. Agts. Assn., Cert. Profl. Ins. Agts. Soc., Soc. Benefit Plan Adminstrn., Lorain County Life Underwriters, Irish Heritage, Order Italian Sons and Daus., Profl. Assn. Dive Instrs./Nat. Assn. Underwater Instrs. (SCUBA diving instr.). Roman Catholic. Avocations: fishing, skin and scuba diving, soccer, photography. Office: Diversified Benefit Plan Inc PO Box 900 Elyria OH 44036-0900

PATTON, WENDELL MELTON, JR., retired management educator, consulting psychologist, college president; b. Spartanburg, S.C., July 10, 1922; s. Wendell Melton and Emily Jane (Harris) P.; m. Martha Jane Matthews, July 5, 1944; children: Wendell III, Leland, Melissa, Brooks B. Student, Wofford Coll.; B.S., U. Ga., 1946, M.S., 1948; Ph.D., Purdue U., 1950; grad., Advanced Mgmt. Course, Colgate U.; LL.D., Wake Forest U., 1961. Lic. psychologist, N.C., Ga. Asst. registrar U. Ga., 1946-48, asst. prof., 1946-48; prof. edn. and psychology Lander Coll., 1948, treas., dept. head, 1948-52; sr. asso. Bruce Payne & Assos., Inc., mgmt. cons., 1952-55; v.p. pres. and asst. gen. mgr. Shuford Mills, Inc., Hickory, N.C., 1955-59; pres. High Point U., N.C., 1959-81; prof. mgmt. U. S.C., Conway, Coastal Carolina Coll., 1982-87; past dir. Furniture Library, N.C. Assn. Ind. Colls. and Univs., Piedmont U. Ctr., Guilford Tech. Coll., Wachovia Bank and Trust, Jefferson Pilot Mutual Funds. Contbr. articles to trade and profl. publs. Served as capt. Air Transport Command AUS, 1942-45. Mem. Am. Mgmt. Assn., Am. Psychol. Assn., SAR, Sigma Xi, Phi Kappa Phi, Delta Kappa Pi, Psi Chi. Methodist. Club: Rotarian. Home: 414 E Covenant Towers 5001 Little River Rd Myrtle Beach SC 29577-2478

PATTULLO, ANDREW, former foundation executive; b. Omaha, Feb. 12, 1917; s. Andrew and Dorothy Anna (Askwith) P.; m. Jean Harriet Fralick, May 1, 1941; children: Andrew, Douglas Ernest. B.S. in Bus. Adminstrn, U. Nebr., 1941, D.Sc. (hon.), 1979; M.B.A. in Hosp. Adminstrn, U. Chgo., 1943; D.Adm. (hon.), Can. Sch. Mgmt., 1981; D.Sc. (hon.), U. Alta., 1982, Georgetown U., 1983. Fellow W.K. Kellogg Found., Battle Creek, Mich., 1943-44; assoc. dir. div. hosps. W.K. Kellogg Found., 1944-51, dir. div. hosps., 1951-67, program dir., 1967-71, v.p. programs, 1971-75, v.p., 1975-78, sr. v.p., 1978-82; ret., 1982; trustee W.K. Kellogg Found., 1972-82; nonresident lectr. U. Mich. Sch. Public Health, 1960-88; mem. Fed. Hosp. Council, 1965-73; mem. Nat. Adv. Com. on Nursing Home Adminstrn., 1968-69; mem. com. on health careers Nat. Health Council, 1964-70; cons. USPHS, 1962-64, Bur. Health Services Research, Dept. HEW, 1968-78; mem. vis. com. for sponsored research M.I.T., 1976-79; mem. nat. adv. council Health Services Research Center, U. Mo.-Columbia, 1977-82; mem. adv. council Mich. Health Facilities, 1965-72, Mich. Mental Health Facilities (Gov.'s Action Com. on Health Care), 1963-66; chmn. community betterment award com. (Mich. Welfare League), 1962, 63; mem. (Mich. Adv. Hosp. Council), 1960-72, (Gov.'s Commn. on Govtl. Relations), 1954-56, (Adv. Commn. Prepaid Hosp. and Med. Care), 1962; hon. prof. Cayetana Hereida U. (Lima), Peru, 1982, U. Sao Paulo Sch. Pub. Health (Brazil), 1982. Mem. editorial bd.: Inquiry, 1980-81. Pres. Battle Creek Area United Fund, 1963, chmn. fund drive, 1960; pres. Battle Creek YMCA, 1959-60, Nottawa Trails council Boy Scouts Am., 1957-60; Trustee Calhoun County chpt. ARC, 1962-65; bd. dirs. Great Lakes Health and Edn. Found., 1973-74; bd. dirs. Calhoun County unit Am. Cancer Soc., 1976-78, chmn. com. on founds. Mich. div., 1978-79; trustee Mich. Health Council, 1951-74, pres., 1967; mem. Calhoun County Bd. Social Services, 1982-90; trustee Southwestern Mich. Rehab. Hosp., 1982—, First Congl. Ch., Battle Creek, 1982-89. Recipient Distinguished Service award U. Chgo. Hosp. Adminstrn. Alumni Assn., 1955; Tri-State Hosp. Assembly award, 1963; award of merit Am. Assn. Hosp. Planning, 1966; award for advancement edn. in hosp. adminstrn. Assn. U. Programs in Hosp. Adminstrn., 1968; Key award for meritorious service Mich. Hosp. Assn., 1970; Trustees award Am. Hosp. Assn., 1972; Disting. Service award Mich. Health Council, 1973; Disting. Achievement award Ohio State U. Hosp. Adminstrn. Alumni, 1982; George Findlay Stephens award Can. Hosp. Assn., 1982; named to Mich. Health Hall of Fame, 1978; Disting. Service award Hosp. Mgmt. Systems Soc. of Am. Hosp. Assn., 1974; Silver Beaver award Boy Scouts Am. Fellow Am. Pub. Health Assn., Am. Coll. Hosp. Adminstrs. (hon.); mem. Am. Hosp. Assn. (adv. coun. hosp. rsch. and ednl. trust 1960-67, mem. coun. rsch. and edn. 1959-62, life mem., chmn. adv. com. Ctr. for History of Hosps. and Healthcare Admnistrns., 1985—), Mich. Hosp. Assn. (trustee 1949-55, pres. 1954-55, life mem.), Internat. Hosp. Fedn., Mich. Pub. Health Assn., Can. Coll. Health Service Execs. (hon.), Latin Am. Hosp. Fedn. (hon.), Duke U. Hosp. Adminstrn. Alumni Assn. (hon.), Sao Paulo Hosp. Assn. (hon.). Home: 162 Feld Ave Battle Creek MI 49017-1312

PATTY, ANNA CHRISTINE, middle school educator; b. Atlanta, Aug. 25, 1937; d. Henry Richard and Gertrude (Smith) Johnson; children: Robert E., C. Wayne Jr., Christine E. BS in Math., U. Ga., 1959; MA in Edn., Va. Poly. Inst. and State U., 1991. Cert. tchr., Va. Mgr. Steak and Ale Restaurants, Inc., Dallas, 1982-84; bus. mgr. Nova Plaza Corp., Charlotte, N.C., 1984-86; asst. mgr. WoodLo, Inc., Charlotte, 1986-87; food activity mgr. Army and Air Force Exch. Svc., Schweinfurt, Fed. Republic Germany, 1987-89; substitute tchr. Montgomery County Schs., Christiansburg, Va., 1989-91; rsch. asst. Va. Poly. Inst. and State U., Blacksburg, 1990-91; math. and sci. middle sch. tchr. Hampton (Va.) City Schs., 1991—; mem. NSTA/APST Summer Inst., U.Md., 1992, NSTA Summer Inst., Sci. and Tech., SUNY, Stoney Brook, N.Y., 1995; EXCEL coach Christopher Newport U., 1993-95. With Operation Path Finders, Sandy Hook, N.J., 1994. Mem. NEA, Va. Educators Assn., Nat. Sci. Tchrs. Assn. (summer inst. participant 1992), Va. Middle Sch. Assn., Va. Sci. Tchrs., Nat. Coun. Tchrs. Math. Republican. Unitarian. Avocations: hiking, camping, herbs, wine tasting, cooking. Home: 811 Player Ln Newport News VA 23602

PATTY, CLAIBOURNE WATKINS, JR., lawyer; b. Cleve., Feb. 19, 1934; s. Claibourne Watkins and Eleanor (Todd) P.; m. Barbara Benton, May 4, 1968; children—Claibourne Watkins III, William Jordan. B.A., U. of South, 1955; J.D., U. Ark., 1961. Bar: Ark. 1961. Law clk. U.S. dist. judge, Ft. Smith, 1961-63; pvt. practice Little Rock, 1963-68; asst. ins. commr. State of Ark., 1968-69; trust officer Union Nat. Bank of Little Rock, 1969-77; asst. dean U. Ark. Sch. Law, Little Rock; also exec. dir. Ark. Inst. for Continuing Legal Edn., 1977-86; law clk. 2d Div. Chancery Ct., Pulaski County, 1986-89; of counsel Gruber Law Firm, Little Rock, 1989—; lectr. law Ark. Sch. Law, 1965; bd. dirs., chmn. Pulaski County Legal Aid Bur., 1966-69. Bd. dirs., pres. Family Svc. Agy. of Ctrl. Ark., 1976-81, 86-93; bd. dirs., pres. Good Shepherd Ecumenical Retirement Ctr., 1975—; mem. Ark. adv. com. U.S. Commn. on Civil Rights, 1985-89. With AUS, 1955-57. Mem. Beta Theta Pi, Phi Alpha Delta. Office: Gruber Law Firm 315 N Broadway St North Little Rock AR 72114-5379

PATTY, R. BRUCE, architect; b. Kansas City, Mo., Jan. 25, 1935; s. Charles Everett and Sarah Louise (Pendleton) P.; m. Donna Jean Watts, June 1, 1958; children—Kristen, Jennifer, Scott. B.S. in Architecture, U. Kans., 1958. Cert. Nat. Council Archtl. Registration Bds. V.p. Kivett & Myers (architects), Kansas City, Mo., 1959-70; prin. Patty Berkebile Nelson Immenschuh Architects Inc., Kansas City, Mo., 1970-90; pres. Patty/Archer/Architects/Engrs., Kansas City, 1991-94; v.p. mktg., dir. arch. design Burns & McDonnell, Kansas City, MO, 1994—; Mem. chancellors assos. U. Kans., 1980—; bd. dirs. Downtown, Inc., 1972—, v.p., 1978-79, U. Kans. Alumni Assn., 1990—. Prin. works include Kansas City Internat. Airport, 1968 (Design award Kans. chpt. AIA 1974), Truman Office Bldg, Jefferson City, Mo., 1975 (Design award State of Mo. 1976), Kansas City Police Sta, 1976 (Design award Central States AIA 1980). Recipient Disting. Alumni award U. Kans., 1983. Fellow AIA (pres. Kansas City chpt. 1974, nat. dir. 1980-82, nat. v.p. 1983, nat. pres. 1985), Royal Archtl. Inst. Can. (hon.); mem. Greater Kansas City C. of C. (bd. dirs.), Fedn. Collegicos Architects, Mex. (hon.), University Club (bd. dirs., pres. 1990), Indian Hills Country Club (bd. dirs.), Rotary (bd. dirs.). Presbyterian. Home: 3840 W 56th St Shawnee Mission KS 66205-2784 Office: Burns and McDonnell PO Box 419173 Kansas City MO 64141-6173

PATY, DONALD WINSTON, neurologist; b. Peking, China, Sept. 25, 1936; s. Robert Morris and Katherine (Behenna) P.; m. Jo Anne Haymore, Dec. 28, 1958; children: Morris Britten, Beverly Behenna, Breay Winston, Donald Blake. B.A., Emory U., 1958, M.D., 1962. Intern Duke U., 1962-63; resident in medicine and neurology Emory U., 1965-70; fellow in immunology MRC Demyelinating Diseases Unit, U. Newcastle-upon-Tyne, Eng., 1970-72; asst. prof., then prof. neurology U. Western Ont. (Can.) Med. Sch., 1972-80; prof. neurology, head div. U. B.C. Med. Sch., Vancouver, 1980—; sec.-gen. XV World Congress of Neurology, Vancouver, B.C., 1993; advisor London (Ont.) chpt. Multiple Sclerosis Soc. Can., 1972-80; sec. exec. com., med. adv. bd. Internat. Fedn. Multiple Sclerosis Socs. Author articles in field.; Mem. editorial bds. profl. jours. Bd. dirs. London Symphony, 1978-80; chmn. grants rev. com. Multiple Sclerosis Soc. of Can.; mem. exec. com. med. adv. bd., chmn. med. mgmt. com. Internat. Fed. Multiple Sclerosis Soc. With USPHS, 1963-65. Fellow Can. Life Ins. Assn., 1972-77; grantee Multiple Sclerosis Soc. Can.; grantee Med. Rsch. Coun. Can.; recipient John Dystel Rsch. award Multiple Sclerosis Soc./Am. Acad. Neurology, 1995, Sir Richard Cave award Multiple Sclerosis Soc. Gt. Britain and No. Ireland, 1995, Charcot award Internat. Fedn. of Multiple Sclerosis Socs., 1995. Fellow ACP, Royal Coll. Physicians and Surgeons Can. (chmn. com. in neurology 1982-86), Am. Acad. Neurology; mem. Can. Neurol. Soc. (pres. 1989-90), Am. Neurol. Assn., Brit. Assn. Neurologists (hon.), World Fedn. Neurology (chmn. multiple sclerosis rsch. group), Alpha Omega Alpha. Unitarian. Home: 3657 W 24th Ave, Vancouver, BC Canada V6S 1L7

PATZ, ARNALL, physician; b. Elberton, Ga., June 14, 1920; s. Samuel and Sarah (Berman) P.; m. Ellen B. Levy, Mar. 12, 1950; children: William, Susan, David, Jonathan. BS, Emory U., 1942, MD, 1945. Pvt. practice ophthalmology Balt., 1951-70; faculty ophthalmology Johns Hopkins Sch. Medicine, 1955—, prof., 1973—; William Holland Wilmer prof., chmn. dept. ophthalmology, dir. Wilmer Ophthal. Inst., 1979-89; mem. Nat. Diabetes Adv. Bd., 1977-80. First recipient Edward Lorenzo Holmes award Inst. Medicine Chgo., 1954, Helen Keller Prize for Vision Rsch. Helen Keller Rsch. Found., 1994; Sight-Saving award D.C. Soc. Prevention Blindness, 1954; E. Mead Johnson award Am. Acad. Pediatrics, 1956; Albert Lasker award Am. Pub. Health Assn., 1956; 1st Seeing Eye Research Prof. Ophthalmology award, 1970; Derrick Vail medal Ill. Soc. Prevention of Blindness, 1981; Jules Stein award for Disting. Ophthalmic Achievement Research to Prevent Blindness, 1981; David Rumbough Sci. award Juvenile Diabetes Found. Internat., 1983; 1st Issac C. Michaelson award Israel Acad. Scis. and Humanities, 1986; 1st Paul Henkind lectureship The Macula Soc., 1989. Mem. AMA (Billings silver medal 1973), Am. Acad. Ophthalmology (honor award 1973, sr. honor award 1981, pres.-elect 1986, pres. 1987), Assn. for Rsch. in Vision and Ophthalmology (Friedenwald Meml. award 1980, Weisenfeld award 1993), Nat. Soc. Prevention of Blindness (v.p. 1981—, 1st Disting. Scientist award), Am. Ophthal. Soc. (Howe medal 1991), Balt. City Med. Soc., Md. Soc. Prevention Blindness (past pres.), Pan-Am. Assn. Ophthalmology, Md. Soc. Eye Physicians and Surgeons. Home: 2A Slade Ave Baltimore MD 21208-5214 Office: Johns Hopkins Med Insts 600 N Wolfe St Baltimore MD 21205-2110

PATZ, EDWARD FRANK, lawyer; b. Balt., Aug. 25, 1932; s. Maurice A. and Violet (Furman) P.; m. Betty Seldner Levi, Nov. 18, 1956; children—Evelyn Anne, Edward Frank, Thomas L. B.S., U. Md., 1954, LL.B., 1959. Bar: Md. 1959. Partner firm Weinberg and Green and predecessor firms, Balt., 1959—. Bd. dirs. Jewish Family and Children's Service, 1965-71; mem. regional bd. dirs. NCCJ. Mem. ABA, Md. Bar Assn., Balt. Bar Assn., Comml. Law League Am., Am. Bankruptcy Inst., Ctr. Club, Suburban of Balt. Country Club (bd. govs., pres.), Caves Valley Golf Club, Hammock Dunes Club. Home: 15 Evan Way Baltimore MD 21208-1700 Office: Weinberg & Green 100 S Charles St Baltimore MD 21201-2725

PAUGH, THOMAS FRANCIS, magazine editor, writer, photographer; b. Newark, Mar. 15, 1929; s. George Ruel and Gladys (Organ) P.; m. Martha Anne Freeze, Apr. 10, 1954; children: Jennifer Paugh Kopp, Lawrence David (dec.). B.A., Colgate U., 1952. Photographer, reporter Ridgewood News, N.J., 1954-55; reporter Bergen Record, Hackensack, N.J., 1955-56; assoc. editor Sports Afield, N.Y.C., 1957-62, managing editor, 1962-67; field editor Sports Afield, Miami, Fla., 1967-76; regional editor Outdoor Life, Miami, 1977-78; editor-in-chief Sports Afield, N.Y.C., 1978-94, editor emeritus, 1994—. Columnist, Sports Afield, 1967-76, editor, The Sports Afield Treasury of Fly Fishing, 1989; contbr. articles to profl. jours. Served to 1st lt., USAF, 1952-54. Recipient Nat. Mag. award, 1987, 92. Mem. Outdoor Writers of Am. Avocations: fishing, hunting, photography, painting. Office: Sports Afield 250 W 55th St New York NY 10019-5201

PAUL, ANDREW MITCHELL, venture capitalist; b. N.Y.C., Feb. 10, 1956; s. John William and Bobba Lorraine (Ice) P.; m. Margaret Rae Batchelor, Sept. 19, 1987. BA, Cornell U., 1978; MBA, Harvard U., 1983. Mktg. rep. IBM Corp., N.Y.C., 1978-81; assoc. Hambrecht & Quist Venture Capital Co., San Francisco, 1983-84; gen. ptnr. Welsh, Carson, Anderson & Stowe, N.Y.C., 1984—; bd. dirs. Quorum Health Group, Nashville, Lincare Inc., St. Petersburg, Fla., nat. Surgery Ctrs., Inc., Chgo., Medcath, Inc., Charlotte, N.C., Am. Oncology Inc., EmCare Holdings Inc., Housecall Inc. Mem. Info. Industry Assn. (chmn. new bus. com. 1987—), Nat. Venture Capital Assn., N.Y. Venture Capital Assn., Bronxville Field Club, Siwanoy Country Club, Hudson Nat. Golf Club. Avocations: tennis, golf, skiing, biking, traveling. Home: 283 Pondfield Rd Bronxville NY 10708-4936 Office: Welsh Carson Anderson & Stowe One World Fin Ctr Ste 3601 New York NY 10281

PAUL, ARA GARO, university dean; b. New Castle, Pa., Mar. 1, 1929; s. John Hagop and Mary (Injejikian) P.; m. Shirley Elaine Waterman, Dec. 21, 1962; children: John Bartlett, Richard Goyan. B.S. in Pharmacy, Idaho State U., 1950; M.S., U. Conn., 1953, Ph.D. in Pharmacognosy, 1956. Cons. plant physiology Argonne (Ill.) Nat. Lab., 1955; asst. prof. pharmacognosy Butler U., Indpls., 1956-57; mem. faculty U. Mich., Ann Arbor, 1957—; prof. pharmacognosy U. Mich., 1969—; dean U. Mich. (Coll. Pharmacy), 1975-95; dean emeritus, prof. pharmacognosy; vis. prof. microbiology Tokyo U., 1965-66; mem. vis. chemistry faculty U. Calif., Berkeley, 1972-73; del. U.S. Pharmacopeial Conv., 1980, 90. Contbr. articles to profl. jours. Recipient Outstanding Tchr. award Coll. Pharmacy, U. Mich., 1969, Outstanding Alumnus award Idaho State U., 1976, Profl. Achievement award Coll. Pharmacy, Idaho State U., 1990; G. Pfeiffer Meml. fellow Am. Found. Pharm. Edn., 1965-66, Disting. Svc. Profile award Am. Found Pharm. Edn., 1992; fellow Eli Lily Found., 1951-53, Am. Found. Pharm. Edn., 1954-56, NIH, 1972-73. Fellow AAAS; mem. Am. Pharm. Assn., Mich. Pharm. Assn., Am. Soc. Pharmacognosy, Acad. Pharm. Scis., Am. Assn. Colls. Pharmacy, Washtenaw County Pharm. Soc., Am. Soc. Hosp. Pharmacists, Am. Assn. Pharm. Scientists, Phi Lambda Upsilon, Sigma Xi, Phi Delta Chi, Phi Sigma Kappa, Rho Chi. Home: 1415 Brooklyn Ave Ann Arbor MI 48104-4496 Office: U Mich Coll Pharmacy Ann Arbor MI 48109-1065

PAUL, ARTHUR, artist, graphic designer, illustrator, art and design consultant; b. Chgo., Jan. 18, 1925; s. William and Becky (Goldenberg) P.; m. Beatrice Miller, Dec. 24, 1949 (div. 1973); children: William Warren, Fredric; m. Suzanne Seed, Mar. 8, 1975; 1 dau., Nina. Student, Inst. Design, 1947-51. Vice-pres., art dir. HMH Pub. Co., Playboy, Chgo., 1962-82; also sr. art dir., corp. art dir. Playboy mag.; pres. Art Paul Design; freelance artist Chgo., 1984—; lectr. in field. Free lance illustrator, designer, 1951-53; designer 1st issue: Playboy mag, 1953, Playboy Rabbit symbol, 1953; exhibited in one man shows at, Etc. Gallery, 1949, 500D Gallery, 1965, U. Ill., 1965; organizer, exhibitor: travelling exhbn. Beyond Illustration-The Art of Playboy; museums, Europe, Asia, U.S., 1971-73, Can., 1976-77; author: Vision-Art Paul, 1983, Art of Playboy, 1986; designer PBS-TV title for humorous feature film presentations on American Playhouse; prodn. design cons. (PBS-TV movie) Who Am I This Time?. Trustee Chgo. Mus. Contemporary Art, 1970-86; apptd. trustee by Gov. of Ill. to Ill. Summer Sch. of Arts, 1987—. Served with USAAF, 1943-46. Recipient numerous art awards, 1951 including Polycube award Art Dirs. Club Phila., 1975, Art Direction Mag. award, 1975, Gold medal for Chgo. Film Festival poster Art Dirs. Club N.Y., 1980, Top Midwest Mktg. award Playboy TV Subscription Ad, 1979, 82, Gold medal for exhbn. Beyond Illustration City of Milan, 1971, Profl. Achievement award IIT Inst. Design Alumni Assn., 1983; Art Inst. scholar, 1943; named to Art Dirs. Hall of Fame, 1986. Mem. 27 Designers Chgo. (hon.), Alliance Graphique Internationale. Home: 175 E Delaware Pl Chicago IL 60611-1756 *Design is more than a sense of order for me. It is beauty and common sense. To draw, to paint and to look at art is in the fabric of my life. I enjoy working with ideas and seeing them develop into a reality, after which I am fortunate enough to learn whether they have performed as intended.*

PAUL, BENJAMIN DAVID, anthropologist, educator; b. N.Y.C., Jan. 25, 1911; s. Phillip and Esther (Kranz) P.; m. Lois Fleischman, Jan. 4, 1936; children: Robert Allen, Janice Carol. Student, U. Wis., 1928-29; AB, U. Chgo., 1938, PhD in Anthropology, 1942. Lectr., rsch. dir. Yale U., 1942-44; community orgn. expert Inter-Am. Ednl. Found., 1946; from lectr. to assoc. prof. anthropology Harvard U., 1946-62, dir. social sci. program Sch. Pub. Health, 1951-62; prof. anthropology Stanford (Calif.) U., 1963—, chmn. dept., 1967-71, dir. program in medicine and behavioral sci., 1963-70; cons. NIH, 1957—. Editor: Health, Culture and Community: Case Studies of Public Reactions to Health Programs, 1955, Changing Marriage Patterns in a Highland Guatemalan Community, 1963, The Maya Midwife as Sacred Professional, 1975, Mayan Migrants in Guatemala City, 1981, The Operation of a Death Squad in San Pedro la Laguna, 1988. 2d lt. AUS, 1944-46. Travelling fellow Social Sci. Rsch. Coun., 1940-41, Ctr. Advanced Study Behavioral Scis. fellow, 1962-63. Mem. Am. Anthropol. Assn. (Disting. Svc. award 1994), Phi Beta Kappa, Sigma Xi. Ethnographic field rsch. in Guatemala, 1941, 62, 64-65, 68-69, 73-79, 83-95. Home: 622 Salvatierra St Palo Alto CA 94305-8538 Office: Stanford U Dept Anthropology Stanford CA 94305

PAUL, CARL FREDERICK, lawyer, former judge; b. N.Y.C., June 10, 1910; s. Carl Frederick and Kate (Wagner) P.; m. Lilian Iris O'Neill, Apr. 18, 1953; children: Julie S., Carl F., Cynthia Marie, Celeste Wagner, Paul (dec. June 1982). AB magna cum laude, U. Rochester, 1932; LLB, Harvard U., 1935. Bar: N.Y. 1935, D.C. 1949, U.S. Supreme Ct. 1941. Assoc. Nixon, Hargrave, Devans & Doyle, Rochester, N.Y., 1935-41, 46-48; atty. Office Gen. Counsel HEW, Washington, 1958-59; commd. officer USN, 1941, advanced through grades to capt., ret., 1958; chief trial counsel NASA, Washington, 1959-74, judge Bd. Contract Appeals, 1974-79; assoc. Burch & Bennett, P.C., Washington, 1979—. Mem. ABA, Fed. Bar Assn. (pres. D.C. chpt., plaque 1995, 96), Inter-Am. Bar Assn., D.C. Bar Assn., Monroe County (N.Y.) Bar Assn., Washington Fgn. Law Soc. (pres.), Phi Beta Kappa, Theta Delta Chi. Clubs: Univ. (Rochester, N.Y.); Nat. Aviation (Washington). Home: 5702 Warwick Pl Chevy Chase MD 20815-5502

PAUL, CAROL ANN, academic administrator, biology educator; b. Brockton, Mass., Dec. 17, 1936; d. Joseph W. and Mary M. (DeMeulenaer) Bjork; m. Robert D. Paul, Dec. 21, 1957; children: Christine, Dana, Stephanie, Robert. BS, U. Mass., 1958; MAT, R.I. Coll., 1968, Brown U., 1970; EdD, Boston U., 1978. Tchr. biology Attleboro (Mass.) High Sch., 1965-68; asst. dean., mem. faculty biology North Shore Community Coll., Beverly, Mass., 1969-78; master planner N.J. Dept. for Higher Edn., Trenton, 1978-80; assoc. v.p. Fairleigh Dickinson U., Rutherford, N.J., 1980-86; v.p. acad. affairs Suffolk Community Coll., Selden, N.Y., 1986-94, assoc. prof. biology, 1994—; faculty devel. cons. various colls., 1979—, title III evaluator, 1985—. Author: (lab. manual and workbook) Minicourses and Labs for Biological Science, 1972 (rev. edit., 1975); (with others) Strategies and Attitudes, 1986; book reviewer, 1973-77. V.p. League of Women Voters, Beverly, 1970-74, Cranford, N.J., 1982-83; alumni rep. Brown U., Cranford, 1972—. Commonwealth Mass. scholar, 1958; recipient Acad. Yr. award NSF, 1968-69, Proclamation for Leadership award Suffolk County Exec., 1989. Mem. AAHE, AAWCC, Profls. and Orgn. Developers (planning com. 1977-79, nat. exec. bd. 1979-80), Nat. Coun. for Staff, Phi Theta Kappa, Pi Lambda Theta. Roman Catholic. Avocations: swimming, knitting. 5169243010: 75 Fairview Cir Middle Island NY 11953-2340 Office: Suffolk Community Coll 533 College Rd Selden NY 11784-2851

PAUL, CHARLES S., motion picture and television company executive; b. 1949. BA, Stanford U., 1971; JD, U. Santa Clara, 1975. Law clk. U.S. Supreme Ct., 1975-76; with Cooley Castro Huddleson & Tatum, 1976-79; with Atari Inc., 1979-85, sr. v.p., gen. counsel, pres. coin-operated games div., 1983-85; with MCA, Inc., Universal City, Calif., 1985—, v.p., pres. MCA Enterprises div., 1986-89, exec. v.p., 1989, also bd. dirs. Office: MCA 100 Universal City Plz Universal City CA 91608

PAUL, COURTLAND PRICE, landscape architect, planner; b. Pasadena, Calif., Mar. 11, 1927; s. Charles Price and Ethyle Louisa (Stanyer) P.; m. Kathryn Nadine Knauss, July 5, 1947; children: Pamela Kathryn, Courtland Scott, Kimberly Carol, Robyn Annette, Sanford Elliott. AA, John Muir Coll., 1948; student, Calif. Poly. U., 1948-49. Lic. landscape architect Ariz., Nebr., Nev., Calif. Founder, sr. prin., landscape architect Peridian Group, P.C., Pasadena, 1951—; apptd. Calif. State Bd. Landscape Architects, 1960, 1964, pres., 1964; lectr. Calif. Poly. U., Pomona, Tex. A&M U., UCLA, Orange Coast Coll. Bd. dirs. Landscape Architecture Found., 1981-85 (pres. 1983). Served with USN, 1944-46. Recipient Achievement award Calif. Landscape Contractors Assn., 1963, citation award Pasadena Beautiful Found., 1969, Landscape Architecture award of merit Calif. Garden Clubs, 1970, commendation resolution Calif. State Senate Rules Com.,1 986, Profl. of Yr. Life Mem. award, 1986, 1st outstanding svc. to industry and environ. award Long Beach/O.C., Meridian award Landscape Contractors Assn., Max Tipton Meml. award, 1993; named Man of Yr. Landscape and Irrigation mag., 1987. Fellow Am. Soc. Landscape Archs. (at-large coun. fellows); mem. Calif. Coun. Landscape Archs. (pres. 1958, Outstanding Svc. citation 1984). Office and Home: 27605 Avenida Larga San Juan Capistrano CA 92675-9999 *People!! A career must be based on people - family, friends, friends of friends, friends of your clientele. They have shaped and made my career!! Always be there for them! Be on time, produce more than is expected and always, ALWAYS be fair!!!.*

PAUL, DOUGLAS ALLAN, insurance executive; b. Chgo., Feb. 9, 1949; s. Eugene Frank and Flo Sinclair (Broomhead) P.; m. Pamela DeGroot, Oct. 20, 1984. BS, Rensselaer Polytechnic Inst., Troy, N.Y., 1971; MBA, U. Pa., 1976. Asst. dir. admissions and alumni affairs Rensselaer Polytechnic Inst., 1971-74; sr. mgr. McKinsey and Co. Inc., N.Y.C., 1977-82; v.p. strategic planning Am. Internat. Group, N.Y.C., 1983—; chmn. bd. dirs. AIG Designs Holdings, Inc.; bd. dirs. Fischbach Corp. Mem. Wall St. Planning Group (exec. dir. 1984—). Home: 284 W 11th St New York NY 10014-2413 Office: Am Internat Group Inc 70 Pine St New York NY 10270-0002

PAUL, ELDOR ALVIN, agriculture, ecology educator; b. Lamont, Alta., Can., Nov. 23, 1931; s. Reinhold and Ida (Mohr) P.; m. Phyllis Ellen Furhop, Aug. 3, 1955; children: Lynette, Linda. BSc, U. Alta., 1954, MSc, 1956; PhD, U. Minn., 1958. Asst. prof. U. Saskatchewan, Saskatoon, Can., 1959-64, assoc. prof., 1964-70, prof., 1970-80; mem. faculty, chmn. dept. plant and soil biology U. Calif., Berkeley, 1980-85; mem. faculty, chairperson dept. of crop and soil sciences Mich. State U., East Lansing, 1985-94; prof. crop and soil sci., 1994—; vis. prof. U. Ga., Athens, 1972-73, USDA, Ft. Collins, 1992-93. Author: Soil Microbiology and Biochemistry, 1988 editor: Soil Biochemistry, vols. 3-5, 1973-81, Isotopic Techniques in Plant Soil and Aquatic Biology, 1991-94; contbr. over 200 articles on microbial ecology and soil microbiology to sci. publs. Fellow AAAS, Soil Sci. Soc. Am., Can. Soc. Soil Sci., Am. Soc. Agronomy (Soil Sci. Rsch. award 1995); mem. Internat. Soc. Soil Sci. Soil Biology (chmn. 1978-82), Am. Soc. Microbiology, Am. Ecol. Soc. Home: 4232 Sugar Maple Ln Okemos MI 48864-3225 Office: Mich State U Dept Crop & Soil Scis East Lansing MI 48824

PAUL, ELIAS, food company consultant; b. Michigan City, Ind., Nov. 16, 1919; s. Phillip P. and Esther (Kranz) P.; m. Gloria Payne, Aug. 24, 1942;

children—Nancy E., Janet L. B.S., U. Ill., 1947. Exec., div. mgr. Swift & Co., Chgo., 1947-64; exec. operating com. Hygrade Food Products, Detroit, 1965; v.p., gen. mgr. meat div. Cudahy Co., Phoenix, 1966; pres. Cudahy Co., 1966-71; also chief exec. officer, dir.; chmn. bd. Am. Salt Co., Kansas City, Mo., 1966-71, Milk Specialties Co., Dundee, Ill.; ret. pres., chief exec. officer, dir. John Morrell & Co., Chgo.; chmn. bd. Golden Sun Feed Co., John Morrell & Co. Ltd.; dir. United Brands, Foster Grant, Baskin Robbins; cons. United Brands, Boston.; Vice chmn., dir. Am. Meat Inst., ret. Mem. Ariz. Retirement System Bd.; chmn. Investment Adv. Council. Served to maj. Chem. Corps, AUS, 1941-46. Mem. Chgo. Bd. Trade, Chgo. Merc. Exchange, Internat. Monetary Market, Phoenix Country Club, Forest Highlands Country Club, Gamma Sigma Delta, Phi Kappa Phi. Home: 140 E San Miguel Ave Phoenix AZ 85012-1339

PAUL, EVE W., lawyer; b. N.Y.C., June 16, 1930; d. Leo I. and Tamara (Sogolow) Weinschenker; m. Robert D. Paul, Apr. 9, 1952; children: Jeremy Ralph, Sarah Elizabeth. BA, Cornell U., 1950; JD, Columbia U., 1952. Bar: N.Y. 1952, Conn. 1960, U.S. Ct. Appeals (2nd cir.) 1975, U.S. Supreme Ct. 1977. Assoc. Botein, Hays, Sklar & Herzberg, N.Y.C., 1952-54; pvt. practice Stamford, Conn., 1960-70; staff atty. Legal Aid Soc., N.Y.C., 1970-71; assoc. Greenbaum, Wolff & Ernst, N.Y.C., 1972-78; v.p. legal affairs Planned Parenthood Fedn. Am., N.Y.C., 1979—, v.p., gen. counsel, 1991—. Contbr. articles to legal and health publs. Trustee Cornell U., Ithaca, N.Y., 1979-84; mem. Stamford Planning Bd., Conn., 1967-70; bd. mem. Stamford League Women Voters, 1960-62. Harlan Fiske Stone scholar Columbia Law Sch., 1952. Mem. ABA, Conn. Bar Assn., Assn. of Bar of City of N.Y., Stamford/Norwalk Regional Bar Assn., U.S. Trademark Assn. (chairperson dictionary listings com. 1988-90), Phi Beta Kappa, Phi Kappa Phi. Office: Planned Parenthood Fedn 810 7th Ave New York NY 10019-5818 *The ability to plan the number and timing of my children has made it possible for me to enjoy career, marriage and family.*

PAUL, FRANK, retired consulting company executive; b. Germany, Apr. 13, 1924; came to U.S., 1947, naturalized, 1953; s. Georg and Hedwig (Muenz) P.; m. Trudy Maier, Apr. 9, 1947; 1 son, Robert. B.B.A. summa cum laude, Baruch Coll., CCNY, 1960. Acctg. supr. S. Augstein Co., College Point, N.Y.C., 1953-58; controller Werner Mgmt. Cons., N.Y.C., 1958-61; v.p. fin. adminstrn. Werner Mgmt. Cons., 1961-67; exec. v.p. Werner Assocs., N.Y.C., 1968-84; also dir.; pres. ORU Group Inc., N.Y.C., 1973-84; bd. dirs. Treasurer Reliance Cons. Group Inc; cons., 1983-84.

PAUL, FRANK WATERS, mechanical engineer, educator, consultant; b. Jersey Shore, Pa., Aug. 28, 1938. BSME, Pa. State U., 1960, MSME, 1964; PhD in Mechanical Engring., Lehigh U., 1968. Registered profl. control engr., Calif. Control engr. Hamilton Standard div. United Techs. Corp., 1961-64; instr. mechanical engring. Lehigh U., Bethlehem, Pa., 1964-68; asst. prof. mechanical engring. Carnegie-Mellon U., Pitts., 1968-73, assoc. prof., 1973-77; assoc. prof. Clemson (S.C.) U., 1977-79, prof., 1979-83, McQueen Quattlebaum prof., 1983—; cons. numerous cos. including Westinghouse Electric, 1969, 82-83, Alcoa Rsch. Labs., 1976-80, State of N.J., Dept. Higher Edn., 1986, Dunlop Sports, Inc., 1988, BPM Tech.; hon. prof. engring. Hull U. Eng., 1990-93; Dora Jones vis. prof. of electronic engring., 1993; dir. Ctr. for Advanced Mfg., 1982; lectr. to colls. and univs., U.S. and abroad. Author: (book, with others) Progress in Heat and Mass Transfer, Vol. 6, 1972, Metals: Processing and Fabrication, Encyclopedia of Materials Science and Engineering, 1986; contbr. articles to IEEE Control Systems mag., Jour. of Engring. for Industry (ASME), Jour. of Dynamic Systems Measurement and Control (ASME), and other scholarly publs. Sabbatical United Techs. Rsch. Ctr., 1985-86, Hull U., 1993. Mem. ASME (participant and paper reviewer Dynamic Systems and Control divsn. 1968—, chmn. panel on robotics 1985-87), Am. Soc. Engring. Educators, Soc. Mech. Engrs. (charter mem. Robotics Internat.), Pi Tau Sigma, Tau Beta Pi, Sigma Tau, Sigma Xi. Achievements include patents related to manufacturing automation. Office: Clemson U Fluor Daniel Bldg Rm 100 Clemson SC 29634-0921

PAUL, GABRIEL (GABE PAUL), former professional baseball club executive; b. Rochester, N.Y., Jan. 4, 1910; s. Morris and Celia (Snyder) P.; m. Mary Frances Copps, Apr. 17, 1939; children: Gabriel, Warren, Michael, Jennie Lou, Henry. Ed. pub. schs., Rochester. Reporter Rochester Democrat and Chronicle, 1926-28; publicity mgr., ticket mgr. Rochester Baseball Club, 1928-34, traveling sec., dir., 1934-36; publicity dir. Cin. Reds Baseball Club, 1937, traveling sec., 1938-50, asst. to pres., 1948-49, v.p., 1949-60, gen. mgr., 1951-60, v.p., 1949-60; v.p., gen. mgr. Houston Astros Baseball Club, 1960-61; gen. mgr. Cleve. Indians Baseball Club, 1961-63, pres., treas., 1963-72, pres., 1978-84; pres. N.Y. Yankees, 1973-77, ret., 1984. Dir. or trustee various charitable instns. Served with inf. AUS, 1943-45. Named Major League Exec. of Yr. Sporting News, 1956, 74, Sports Exec. of Yr. Gen. Sports Time, 1956, Exec. of Yr., Braves 400 Club, 1974, Baseball Exec. Yr., Milw. Baseball Writers, 1976, Major League Exec. of Yr. UPI, 1976; recipient J. Lewis Comiskey Meml. award Chgo. chpt. Baseball Writers Assn. Am., 1961, Judge Emil Fuchs Meml. award Boston chpt., 1967, Bill Slocum award N.Y. chpt., 1975, Sports Torch of Learning award, 1976; named to Ohio Baseball Hall of Fame, 1980. Clubs: Palma Ceia Country (Tampa, Fla.), Centre Club (Tampa).

PAUL, GORDON LEE, behavioral scientist, psychologist; b. Marshalltown, Iowa, Sept. 2, 1935; s. Leon Dale and Ione Hickman (Perry) P.; m. Joan Marie Wyatt, Dec. 24, 1954; children: Dennis Leon, Dana Lee, Joni Lynn. Student, Marshalltown Community Coll., 1953-54, San Diego City Coll., 1955-57; B.A., U. Iowa, 1960; M.A., U. Ill., 1962, Ph.D., 1964. Social sci. analyst VA Hosp., Danville, Ill., 1962; counseling psychologist U. Ill., Urbana, 1963; clin. psychologist VA Hosp., Palo Alto, Calif., 1964-65; pvt. practice clin. psychology, 1964-65; asst. prof. psychology U. Ill., Champaign-Urbana, 1965-67; assoc. prof. U. Ill., 1967-70, prof., 1970-80; Cullen disting. prof. psychology U. Houston, 1980—; pvt. practice psychology Champaign, 1965-80, Houston, 1980—; psychotherapy rsch. cons., Palo Alto, 1964-65; cons. Ill. Dept. Mental Health, 1965-73, 78-82, NIMH, 1968-78; adviser Ont. (Can.) Mental Health Found., 1968-69, NSF, 1968-69, Can. Coun., 1969-75, VA, 1972, 80—, APA, 1970—, UCLA/VA Med. Ctr./Camarillo Schizophrenia Rsch. Ctr., 1978-93, Alliance for Mentally Ill, 1980—. Author: Insight vs. Desensitization in Psychotherapy, An Experiment in Anxiety Reduction, 1966, Anxiety and Clinical Problems, 1973, Psychosocial Treatment of Chronic Mental Patients, 1977, Assessment in Residential Treatment Settings, Part 1, 1986, Observational Assessment Instrumentation for Service and Research, Part 2, 1987, Part 3, 1988; mem. editl. bd. Behavior Therapy, 1969-75, Behavior Therapy and Exptl. Psychiatry, 1969—, Schizophrenia Bull., 1971—, Jour. Abnormal Psychology, 1972-76, Jour. Residential Treatment, 1983—, Jour. Psychopathology and Behavioral Assessment, 1985—; cons. editor Jour. Applied Behavior Analysis, 1966-77, 81—, Psychol. Bull., 1967—, Jour. Abnormal Psychology, 1970-72, 76—, Psychosomatic Medicine, 1971-77, Psychophysiology, 1972—, Archives Gen. Psychiatry, 1973-74, Behavior Therapy, 1976-87, Profl. Psychologist, 1977-87, Hosp. Community Psychiatry, 1980-94, Biobehavioral Revs., 1980-84, Jour. Cmty. Psychology, 1983, Am. Psychologist, 1983—, Brit. Jour. Clin. Psychology, 1985-87, Nervous and Mental Disease, 1992, Current Directions in Psychol. Sci., 1992—; contbr. articles to profl. jours. Served with USN, 1954-58. Recipient Creative Talent award Am. Inst. Rsch., 1964, Teaching award U. Ill., 1968, 75; rsch. award Mental Health Assn., 1985; listed among 353 best mental health experts in nation Good Housekeeping, 1994; NIMH fellow, 1963-64. Fellow Am. Psychol. Assn. (corr. com. 1965-70, pres. sect. III div. 12 1972-73, exec. com. div. 12 1974-77, Disting. Scientist award sect. III, div. 12 1977), Am. Psychol. Soc., Assn. Clin. Psychosocial Rsch., Am. Assn. Applied and Preventive Psychology; mem. Midwestern Psychol. Assn., Tex. Psychol. Assn., Houston Psychol. Assn., Assn. for Advancement Psychology, Phi Beta Kappa, Chi Gamma Iota. Subject of NIMH sci. report monograph, 1981: Treating and Assessing the Chronically Mentally Ill: The Pioneering Research of Gordon L. Paul. Home: 6239 S Braeswood Blvd Houston TX 77096-3715 Office: Psychology Dept U Houston Houston TX 77004

PAUL, GORDON WILBUR, marketing educator; b. Muskegon, Mich., Aug. 12, 1933; s. Wilbur M. and Ruth Hansen P.; m. Gloria W (Borns), Apr. 29, 1961; children: Christopher G., Bradley A. BS, Tulsa U., 1955; MBA, U. Tex., 1962; PhD, Mich. State U., 1966. Material controller Brunswick Corp., Muskegon, Mich., 1959-61; assoc. prof. La. State U., Baton Rouge, 1965-69; prof., chmn. U. Mass., Amherst, 1969-77; prof. U. Cen. Fla., Orlando, 1977—; lectr. in field; Fulbright lectr., Portugal, 1985, 90, Athens, Greece, 1974. Author: (with others): Consumer Behavior: An Integrated Approach, 1975, Marketing Management, 1994, Marketing Management Strategy and Programs, 1994. Served to capt. USAF, 1955-58. Mem. Am. Mktg. Assn., Am. Inst. Decision Scis., Sales and Mktg. Execs., So. Mktg. Assn. (v.p. 1987). Methodist. Avocation: boating.

PAUL, HERBERT MORTON, lawyer, accountant, taxation educator; b. N.Y.C.; s. Julius and Gussie Paul; m. Judith Paul; children: Leslie Beth, Andrea Lynn. BBA, Baruch Coll.; MBA, NYU, LLM; JD, Harvard U. Ptnr. Touche Ross & Co., N.Y.C.; assoc. dir.-tax Touche Ross & Co., dir. fin counseling; mng. ptnr. Herbert Paul, P.C., N.Y.C., 1983—; prof. taxation, trustee NYU. Author: Ordinary and Necessary Expenses; editor: Taxation of Banks; adv. tax editor The Practical Accountant; mem. adv. bd. Financial and Estate Planning, Tax Shelter Insider, Financial Planning Strategist, Tax Shelter Litigation Report; bd. dirs. Partnership Strategist, The Business Strategist; cons. Professional Practice Management Mag.; mem. panel The Hot Line; advisor The Partnership Letter, The Wealth Formula; cons. The Insider's Report for Physicians; mem. tax bd. Business Profit Digest; cons. editor physician's Tax Advisor; bd. fin. cons. Tax Strategies for Physicians; tax and bus. advisor Prentice Hall; contbg. editor. Jour. of Accountancy. Trustee NYU, mem. bd. overseers Grad. Sch. Bus.; mem. com. on trusts and estates Rockefeller U.; trustee Alvin Ailey Am. Dance Theatre, Associated Y's of N.Y.; chair NYU Alumni Assn., bd. dirs.; co-chmn. accts. divsn. Fedn. Philanthropies. Mem. Inst. Fed. Taxation (adv. com. chmn.), Internat. Inst. on Tax and Bus. Planning (adv. bd.), Assn. of Bar of City of N.Y., NYU Tax Soc. (pres.), Bur. Nat. Affairs-Tax Mgmt. (adv. com. on exec. compensation), Am. Inst. CPAs (com. on corp. taxation), Tax Study Group, ABA (tax sect.), N.Y. County Lawyers Assn., N.Y. State Soc. CPAs Dir. (chmn. tax div. com. on fed. taxation, gen. tax com., furtherance com., com. on relations with IRS, bd. dirs.), Nat. Assn. Accts., Assn. of Bar of City of N.Y., Accts. Club of Am., Pension Club, Nat. Assn. Estate Planners (bd. dirs.), N.Y. Estate Planning Coun. (bd. dirs.), N.Y. C. of C. (tax com.), Grad. Sch. Bus. of NYU Alumni Assn. (pres.), Pres. Council (NYU), NYU Alumni Assn. (chair). Clubs: Wall St., City Athletic (N.Y.C.), Inwood Country.

PAUL, HERMAN LOUIS, JR., valve manufacturing company executive; b. N.Y.C., Dec. 30, 1912; s. Herman Louis and Louise Emilie (Markert) P.; student Duke, 1931-32, Lehigh U., 1932-33; m. Janath Powers (dec. Jan. 1996); children—Robert E., Charles Thomas, Herman Louis III. Power plant engr. Paul's Machine Shop, N.Y.C., 1935-43; pres., chief engr. Paul's Machine Shop, N.Y.C., 1943-48; v.p., chief engr. Paul Valve Corp., East Orange, N.J., 1948-54; pres., chief engr. P-K Industries, Inc., North Arlington, N.J., 1954-59; v.p., dir. research Gen. Kinetics, Englewood, N.J., 1959-62; engring. cons., N.Y.C., 1962-65; v.p., dir. Hydromatics, Inc., Bloomfield, N.J., 1965-67; with P.J. Hydraulics, Inc., Myerstown, Pa., 1967—, pres., chief engr., 1968-80, dir. and stockholder, 1980-81; pres. Flomega Industries, Inc., Cornwall, Pa., 1982—; cons. to Metal Industries Devel. Center, Taiwan, 1979; engring. cons. valves and complimentary equipment, 1980—; valve cons. Continental Disc Corp., Kansas City, Mo., 1980—. Vice chmn. Nat. UN Day Com., 1977, 78, 79, 80. Mem. ASME, Instrument Soc. Am., Am. Soc. Naval Engrs., Internat. Platform Assn., The Navy League, The Naval Inst. Club: Heidelberg Country (Bernville, Pa.), Quentin (Pa.) Riding. Patentee in field. Home: RD 5 370 Dogwood Ln Lebanon PA 17042

PAUL, JAMES CAVERLY NEWLIN, law educator, former university dean; b. Chestnut Hill, Pa., Apr. 30, 1926; s. William Allen Butler and Adelaide Sims (Newlin) P.; m. Margaret Morris Clausen, June 25, 1948; children: Nicholas Newlin, Martha Morris, Adelaide Sims. B.A., Princeton U., 1948; J.D., U. Pa., 1951. Bar: Pa. bar 1952. Legal sec. to Chief Justice U.S., 1951-53; asst. prof. U. N.C., 1953-55; asst. dir. Inst. Govt., U. N.C., 1953-55; prof. law, dir. Inst. Legal Research, U. Pa., 1955-63; prof. law, dean and founder of faculty of law Haile Selassie U., Ethiopia, 1963-67; v.p. acad. affairs Haile Selassie U., 1967-69; exec. v.p. Ednl. and World Affairs, N.Y.C., 1969-70; dean Sch. Law, Rutgers U., Newark, 1970-74, prof. law, 1970—, Newhouse scholar in law, 1984—, William J. Brennan prof., 1988—; exec. sec., trustee Internat. Ctr. for Law in Devel., N.Y.C., 1974—; founding mem., sec.-treas. Internat. Third World Legal Studies Assn., N.Y.C., 1980—; adj. prof. Columbia U., 1973—; cons. Constl. Commn. of Transitional Govt. of Ethiopia, 1992-93. Author: Rift in the Democracy, 1951, (with others) Federal Censorship, 1961, Ethiopian Constitutional Development, 1969, Lawyers in the Third World, 1981, The International Context of Rural Poverty in the Third World, 1986. Candidate for U.S. Congress from 9th Dist. Pa., 1958; del. Dem. Nat. Conv., 1960. Served with USNR, 1943-46, PTO. Recipient spl. medal for distinguished service to univ. edn. in Ethiopia, 1969. Mem. Am., N.J., Pa. bar assns., Internat. Third World Legal Studies Assn. (sec.-treas. 1980—), Order of Coif. Club: Princeton (N.Y.C.). Home: 1352 Chancellor Pl Trappe MD 21673 Office: 15 Washington St Newark NJ 07102-3105 *My life in law and teaching about law gives satisfaction because it enables me to direct my energies towards thinking about social justice, individual dignity, and the possibilities of attaining more of the conditions enabling these ideals. But that satisfaction is tempered by constant realization of my own frailities and the failure everywhere of people, particularly those most fortunately endowed, to be guided by principled thinking.*

PAUL, JAMES WILLIAM, lawyer; b. Davenport, Iowa, May 3, 1945; s. Walter Henry and Margaret Helene (Hillers) P.; m. Sandra Kay Schmid, June 15, 1968; children: James William, Joseph Hillers. BA, Valparaiso U., 1967; JD, U. Chgo., 1970. Bar: N.Y. 1971, U.S. Ct. Appeals (2d cir.) 1971, U.S. Dist. Ct. (so. and ea. dists.) N.Y. 1972, U.S. Supreme Ct. 1977, U.S. Ct. Appeals (6th cir.) 1981, Ind. 1982, U.S. Dist. Ct. (no. dist.) Ind. 1982, U.S. Claims Ct. 1989, U.S. Dist. Ct. (ea. dist.) Mich. 1989, U.S. Ct. Appeals (fed. cir.) 1991. Assoc. Rogers & Wells, N.Y.C., 1970-78, ptnr., 1978—; dir., officer Musica Sacra, Inc., 1972-81. Bd. dirs. Turtle Bay Music Sch., Am. Lutheran Publicity Bur. Recipient Disting. Alumnus award Valparaiso U., 1994. Mem. ABA (antitrust sect. ins. com.), Assn. Bar City N.Y. (civil ct. com.), Fed. Bar Council (young lawyers com.). Democrat. Clubs: Yale (N.Y.C.), Sky (N.Y.C.); Quaker Hill Country (Pauling, N.Y.). Home: 500 E 85th St Apt 12H New York NY 10028-7406 also: 5 Curtis Dr Sherman CT 06784-1220 Office: Rogers & Wells 200 Park Ave Ste 5200 New York NY 10166-0005

PAUL, JOHN JOSEPH, bishop; b. La Crosse, Wis., Aug. 17, 1918; s. Roland Philip and Louise (Gilles) P. B.A., Loras Coll., Dubuque, Iowa, 1939; S.T.B., St. Mary's Sem., Balt., 1943; M.Ed., Marquette U., 1956. Ordained priest Roman Catholic Ch., 1943; prin. Regis High Sch., Eau Claire, Wis., 1948-55; rector Holy Cross Sem., La Crosse, 1955-66, St. Joseph's Cathedral, La Crosse, 1966-77; aux. bishop Diocese of La Crosse, 1977-83, bishop, 1983—. Office: PO Box 4004 La Crosse WI 54602-4004

PAUL, JOSEPH B., customer service administrator, desktop publisher; b. Bklyn., Jan. 21, 1961; s. Samuel and Ruth (Bassin) P.; m. Rose Jacklyn Futterman, Apr. 1, 1984. BS in Computer Sci., CUNY, S.I., 1983; MBA, Nova U., 1988. Computer programmer Office of Mgmt. and Budget, N.Y.C., 1981-83; programmer, analyst Harris Corp., Melbourne, Fla., 1983-84; sr. analyst AT&T, Maitland, Fla., 1984-85; project leader Fla. Power and Light, Miami, 1985-90; project mgr. S.E. Toyota Distbr., Deerfield Beach, Fla., 1990-93; dir. customer svcs. Data Net Corp., Miramar, Fla., 1993-95; v.p. PC support Citizens Fed. Bank, Ft. Lauderdale, Fla., 1995—; pres. S.E. Area Focus Users Group, Miami, 1986-89, Co-Log Users Group, Miramar, 1993-94. Mem. agy. rels. sub-com. United Way South Fla., Miami, 1988-90; pres. Archtl. Control Com., Sunrise, Fla., 1991-93. Mem. Am. Mgmt. Assn., Am. Mktg. Assn., Toastmasters, Tau Alpha Pi (pres. 1982-83). Republican. Jewish. Avocations: photography, woodworking, dog breeding, computers. Home: 13120 NW 11th Dr Sunrise FL 33323-2951 Office: Citizens Fed Bank 1100 W McNab Rd Fort Lauderdale FL 33309

PAUL, JUSTUS FREDRICK, historian, educator; b. Boonville, Mo., May 27, 1938; s. Firdel W. and Emma L. (Frankenfeld) P.; m. Barbara Jane Dotts, Sept. 10, 1960; children: Justus, Rebecca, Ellen. A.B., Doane Coll., Crete, Nebr., 1959; M.A., U. Wis., 1960; Ph.D., U. Nebr., 1966. Tchr. Wausau High Sch., Wis., 1960-62; instr. history U. Nebr., 1963-66; mem. faculty U. Wis., Stevens Point, 1966—; prof. history U. Wis., 1973—, chmn. dept., 1969-86, chmn. faculty senate, 1977-79, 83-85, dean Coll. Letters and Scis., 1986—. Author: Senator Hugh Butler and Nebraska Republicanism, 1976, The World is Ours: The History of the University of Wisconsin-Stevens Point, 1894-1994, 1994; editor: Selected Writings of Rhys W. Hays, 1977; co-editor: The Badger State: A Documentary History of Wisconsin, 1979; contbr. articles to profl. jours. Chmn. Portage County (Wis.) Bd. Adjustment, 1976-90; moderator 1st Congl. United Ch. of Christ, 1988-90; bd. dirs. Monteverdi Master Chorale, 1988-90, sec., 1988-89, pres., 1989-90, bd. govs., 1994—; bd. dirs. United Ch. Family Svcs., 1992—, sec., 1994, treas., 1995-96. Grantee State of Wis., 1974-80, Am. Assn. State and Local History, 1968-69; recipient Paul Kerenbrock Humanitarian award Doane Coll., 1996, Rothman award for local history, 1996. Mem. Am. Hist. Assn., Orgn. Am. Historians, Hist. Soc. Wis., Nebr. Hist. Soc. Mem. United Ch. Christ. Home: 2001 Country Club Dr Stevens Point WI 54481-7009 Office: Coll Letters and Scis U Wis 130 CCC Stevens Point WI 54481

PAUL, LEE GILMOUR, lawyer; b. Denver, July 27, 1907; s. Russell Barnett and Mary Ellen (Gilmour) P.; m. Gordon Dodge Leupp, Apr. 14, 1934; children: Jenifer Paul Bode, Mary Paul Collins, Deborah Paul Clemo. A.B., Bowdoin Coll., 1929, LL.D. (hon.), 1978; LL.B., Harvard, 1932. Bar: Calif. bar 1933. Pvt. practice Los Angeles, 1934-42; industry mem. Shipbldg. Commn., NWLB, 1942-46; partner Paul, Hastings, Janofsky & Walker, Los Angeles, 1946-80, of counsel, 1980—. Pres., Pasadena (Calif.) Child Guidance Clinic, 1964-65; Pres. Los Angeles Boys Club, 1973-80, Los Angeles Boys Club Found., 1980—; chmn. Pasadena Council Alcoholism, 1966-68; trustee Boys and Girls Aid Soc. Los Angeles County, 1968-72; bd. dirs. Pasadena's Charity Bank; trustee Pasadena Pub. Libr.; chmn. Criminal Justice Legal Found., 1989; trustee Pasadena Humane Soc. Mem. Am., Los Angeles County bar assns., Sigma Nu. Clubs: California (Los Angeles); Valley Hunt (Pasadena). Home: 230 S Arroyo Blvd Pasadena CA 91105-1507 also: 517 Emerald Bay Laguna Beach CA 92651 Office: Paul Hastings Janofsky & Walker 555 S Flower St Los Angeles CA 90071-2300 Address: 695 Town Center Dr Costa Mesa CA 92626-1924

PAUL, LES, entertainer, inventor; b. Waukesha, Wis., June 9, 1915; s. George and Evelyn (Stutz) Polfuss; m. Mary Ford (dec. 1977); children: Lester, Gene, Colleen, Robert, Mary. Student pub. schs., Waukesha. Appeared on numerous radio programs throughout Midwest, in 1920's and 1930's; formed Les Paul Trio, 1936-37, and appeared with Fred Waring, N.Y.C.; appeared on first television broadcast with an orch. from NBC, N.Y.C., 1939; mus. dir., WJJD and WIND, Chgo., 1941; appeared with Mary Ford on own television show, Mahwah, N.J., 1953-57; host: Edison 100th Anniversary of invention of phonograph at Edison Home, West Orange, N.J., 1977; numerous TV, club appearances, especially Fat Tuesday's, N.Y.C.; recs. include: Lover and Brazil, 1948, Nola, 1949, Goofus, 1950, Tennessee Waltz, 1950, Little Rock Getaway, 1950, Mockin' Bird Hill, 1951, Just One More Chance, 1951, Walkin' and Whistlin' Blues, 1951, How High The Moon, 1951 (Hall of Fame award 1979), Smoke Rings, 1952, The World's Waiting For The Sunrise, 1952, Tiger Rag, 1953, Meet Mr. Callaghan, 1953, Jazz Me Blues, 1952, Vaya Con Dios, 1954, Chester and Lester, 1976 (Grammy award), Guitar Monsters, 1977 (Grammy nominee), The Legend and the Legacy, 1991, The Best of the Capitol Masters with Mary Ford, 1992, The Guitar Artistry of Les Paul, Greatest Hits!, 1994. Served with Armed Forces Radio Service, World War II. Les Paul and Mary Ford named to Grammy Hall of Fame, 1977; Grammy Achievement award for contbns. to rec., musical instruments industry; named to Rock 'N' Roll Hall of Fame, 1988; named to Wis. Performing Artists Hall of Fame, 1990. Mem. AFTRA, ASCAP, SAG, Audio Engring. Soc., Am. Fedn. Musicians. Pioneer multi-track tape recorder; inventor 1st 8-track tape recorder; inventor sound-on-sound recording; creator Les Paul electric solid body guitars; consultant, Gibson Guitar Corp., Nashville. *To be successful requires hard work, determination, a positive attitude, believing in one's self, a God given talent and luck.**

PAUL, LINDA BAUM, geriatrics nurse, toy business owner; b. Syracuse, N.Y., Aug. 18, 1946; d. LeRoy Stanley and Evelyn Lucille (Miller) Baum; m. James Frederick Paul, Mar. 2, 1974; children: Patricia Ann, Sharon Joy, Sarah Leigh. LPN, Ctrl. Tech. Adult LPN Program, Syracuse, 1970; postgrad. in RN, Human Svc., Onondaga C.C., 1990-92, postgrad. in MSW/Counseling, 1996—. LPN, charge nurse Maple Lawn Nursing Home, Manlius, N.Y., 1970-73; nurse, foster parent, personal care provider Ofc. Mental Retardation & Devel. Disabilities/Sequin Cmty., Syracuse, 1974-87; LPN, charge nurse Cmty. Gen. Hosp., Syracuse, 1989-96; owner Wood-You Crafts, Manlius, 1987-92. Election insp. Dem. Com. Bd. Elections, Dewitt/Fayetteville, N.Y., 1986-87; mem. Jamesville-DeWitt PTG, 1974—; mem. ch. missions and ourtreach Manlius Meth. Ch., 1995—, choir dir., 1993; choir dir. Bridgeport Meth. Ch., 1974-76; soloist Syracuse Chorale; mem. ENABLE/United Cerebbral Palsy Ctr. Avocations: singing, piano, bowling. Home: 219 Hobson Ave Fayetteville NY 13066-1616

PAUL, M(ALCOLM) LEE, psychology educator; b. Shreveport, La., July 13, 1951; s. Francis Malcolm and Ava Aileen (Boyles) P.; m. Stephanie Maxfield, July 23, 1994; 1 child, Ryan Lee; 1 stepchild, Blake Wayne. BS, Abilene Christian U., 1974, MS, 1977; EdD, Nova Southeastern U., 1986. Lic. profl. counselor, Tex. Entertainer Six Flags Over Tex., Arlington, 1965-78; dir. univ. svcs. and rsch. Abilene Christian U., Dallas, 1977-82; v.p. for psychol. svcs. Security Rsch. Cons., Dallas, 1980-82; prof. of psychology Amber U., Garland, Tex., 1980—; assoc. prof. psychology Southwestern Christian Coll., Terrell, Tex., 1991—; pvt. practice psychotherapy, Dallas, 1982—; mem. ethics com. Baylor Hosp., Garland. Co-author: The Parable of Man, 1980. Named one of Outstanding Young Men of Am., 1979. Mem. APA, ACA. Mem. Ch. of Christ. Avocations: scuba diving, hunting, music. Office: Dr M Lee Paul 9535 Forest Ln Ste 200 Dallas TX 75243-5959

PAUL, MARTIN AMBROSE, physical chemist; b. N.Y.C., June 29, 1910; s. Martin and Rosena (Sing) P.; m. Genevieve Wells, June 28, 1935; children: Harriet (Mrs. J. Henry Jonquiere), Dorothy (Mrs. Duvall A. Jones). B.A., CCNY, 1930; M.A., Columbia U., 1931, Ph.D., 1936. Instr. CCNY, 1930-42; research supr. Explosives Research Lab., NDRC, Bruceton, Pa., 1942-45; asst. prof. chemistry Triple Cities Coll., Syracuse U., 1946-48, asso. prof., 1948-50; prof. chemistry Harpur Coll., State U. N.Y. at Binghamton, 1950-65, chmn. dept., 1950-60; exec. sec. div. chemistry and chem. tech. Nat. Acad. Scis.-NRC, Washington, 1965-74; cons., 1974—; Vis. prof. Cornell U., several summers, U. Calif. at Los Angeles, 1957-58, Columbia, 1960-61; Exec. sec. XXIII Internat. Congress Pure and Applied Chemistry, 1971, sec. commn. on symbols, terminology and units, 1967-71, chmn., 1971-73, sec. com. on nomenclature and symbols, 1975-79. Author: Principles of Chemical Thermodynamics, 1951, Physical Chemistry, 1962, (with King, Farinholt) General Chemistry, 1967; also articles. Recipient Naval Ordnance Devel. award, 1946; John Simon Guggenheim fellow, 1957. Fellow A.A.A.S. (v.p., chmn. chemistry sect. 1972); Benjamin Franklin fellow Royal Soc. Arts; mem. Am. Chem. Soc., AAUP, Phi Beta Kappa, Sigma Xi, Phi Lambda Upsilon. Club: Cosmos (Washington). Research on measurement of acidity in highly acid media, nature of indicators, catalysis by acids, thermodynamic properties of solutions, sci. policy. Home: 1772 Horatio Ave Merrick NY 11566-2949

PAUL, MAURICE M., federal judge; b. 1932. BSBA, U. Fla., 1954, LLB, 1960. Bar: Fla. 1960. Assoc. Sanders, McEwan, Mims & MacDonald, Orlando, Fla., 1960-64; ptnr. Akerman, Senterfitt, Eidson, Mesmer & Robinson, Orlando, 1965-66, Pitts, Eubanks, Ross & Paul, Orlando, 1968-69; judge U.S. Cir. Ct. (9th cir.) Fla., 1973-82; judge, now chief judge U.S. Dist. Ct. (no. dist.) Fla., 1982—. Office: US Dist Ct 110 E Park Ave Tallahassee FL 32301-7750*

PAUL, NORMAN LEO, psychiatrist, educator; b. Buffalo, N.Y., July 5, 1926; s. Samuel Joseph and Tannie (Goncharsky) P.; m. Betty Ann Byfield, June 6, 1951 (dec. May 1994); children: Marilyn, David Alexander. MD, U. Buffalo, 1948. Fellow pharmacology Coll. Medicine, U. Cin., Ohio, 1949-50; resident psychiatry Mass. Mental Health Ctr., Boston, 1952-55; fellow child psychiatry James Jackson Putnam Children's Ctr., Boston, 1957-58, 59, Mass. Gen. Hosp., Boston, 1958-59; chief psychiatrist Day Hosp. Mass. Mental Health Ctr., Boston, 1960-64; dir. conjoint family therapy Boston (Mass.) State Hosp., 1964-65, cons. in family psychiatry, 1965-70; assoc. clin. prof. dept. neurology Boston (Mass.) U. Sch. Medicine, 1977—; cons. Mental Health Ctr., Alaska Native Hosp., Anchorage, 1967, 68; cons. in family psychiatry Boston (Mass.) VA Hosp., 1967-71, Mass. Soc. for the Prevention of Cruelty to Children, Boston, 1993—; lectr. in psychiatry Harvard Med. Sch., Boston, 1976—; faculty assoc. Mgmt. Analysis Corp., Cambridge, Mass., 1979-82. Family therapist: (tv documentary) PBS-Trouble in the Family, 1965 (George Foster Peabody award 1965); co-author A Marital Puzzle, 1977, 86, German edit., 1987, French edit., 1995. Sponsor Mass. Orgn. to Repeal Abortion Laws, Boston, 1965-70; chair Audio Unit of Child Devel. and Mass Media, White House Conf. on Children and Youth, Washington, 1970; bd. trustees Cambridge (Mass.) Coll., 1977-89. Capt. USAF, 1950-52. Recipient Edward A. Strecker, M.D. award for young psychiatrist of yr., 1966, Cert. of Merit, Mass. Coun. on Family Life, Boston, 1967, Cert. of Commendation, Mass. Assn. for Mental Health, Boston, 1967, Disting. Achievement award Soc. for Family Therapy and Rsch., Boston, 1973. Fellow Royal Soc. Medicine, Am. Psychiat. Assn. (life); mem. Am. Assn. Marriage and Family Therapy (bd. dirs. 1983-86), Am. Family Therapy Assn. (v.p. 1982-83, Disting. Contbn. award 1984), Assn. for Rsch. in Nervous and Mental Disorders, Group for the Advancement Psychiatry (chair com. on the family 1982-84). Avocations: study of codes, travelling. Office: 394 Lowell St Ste 6 Lexington MA 02173-2575

PAUL, OGLESBY, physician; b. Villanova, Pa., May 3, 1916; s. Oglesby and Laura Little (Wilson) P.; m. Marguerite Black, May 29, 1943 (dec. Sept. 1979); children: Marguerite, Rodman; m. Jean Lithgow, Jan. 17, 1981. A.B. cum laude, Harvard U., 1938, M.D. cum laude, 1942. Diplomate: in cardiovascular disease Am. Bd. Internal Medicine. Intern. Mass. Gen. Hosp., Boston, 1942-43; asst. medicine Harvard Med. Sch., 1946-49; clin. asso. prof. medicine U. Ill., 1952-62, clin. prof. medicine, 1962; asst. attending physician Presbyn.-St. Luke's Hosp., 1951-54, asso. attending physician, 1954-59, attending physician, 1959-62; chief div. medicine Passavant Meml. Hosp., Chgo., 1963-72; prof. medicine Northwestern U., 1963-77; med. dir. Univ. Med. Assos., 1973-75, v.p. health scis., 1973-75; prof. medicine Harvard U. Sch. Medicine, Boston, 1977-82, prof. medicine emeritus, 1982—; dir. admissions Harvard U. Sch. Medicine, 1977-82; sr. physician Brigham and Women's Hosp., Boston, 1977-82, sr. physician emeritus, 1982—; cons. U.S. Naval Hosp., Great Lakes, Ill., 1959-74; Mem. joint U.S.-U.K. Com. for Study Coronary and Pulmonary Disease, 1959—. Chmn. gov.'s adv. com. Ill. Regional Med. Program on Heart Disease, Cancer and Stroke, 1967-70; dirs. Internat. Soc. Cardiology Found. Served from lt. (j.g.) to lt. M.C. USNR, 1943-46. Fellow ACP, Am. Coll. Cardiology, Royal Soc. Medicine (Eng.); mem. Assn. U. Cardiologists, Am. Heart Assn. (pres. 1960-61), Chgo. Heart Assn. (pres. 1966-67), Am. Epidemiol. Soc., Am. Clin. and Climatol. Assn. Home: 10 Longwood Dr # 322 Westwood MA 02090 Office: Harvard U Med Sch Countway Libr 10 Shattuck St Boston MA 02115-6011

PAUL, RICHARD WRIGHT, lawyer; b. Washington, May 23, 1953; s. Robert Henry Jr. and Betty (Carey) P.; m. Paula Ann Coolsaet, July 25, 1981; children: Richard Haven, Timothy Carey, Brian Davis. AB magna cum laude, Dartmouth Coll., 1975; JD, Boston Coll., 1978. Bar: Mich. 1978, U.S. Dist. Ct. (ea. dist.) Mich. 1978, U.S. Ct. Appeals (6th cir.) 1982, U.S. Supreme Ct. 1989, U.S. Dist. Ct. (we. dist.) Mich. 1991. Assoc. Dickinson, Wright, Moon, Van Dusen & Freeman, Detroit, 1978-85, ptnr., 1985—; mediator Wayne County Cir. Ct. Mem. ABA, Def. Rsch. Inst., Detroit Bar Assn., Mich. Def. Trial Counsel, Dartmouth Lawyers Assn., Oakland County Bar Assn., Assn. Def. Trial Counsel, Alumni Coun. Dartmouth Coll., Dartmouth Detroit Club (pres. 1980—). Avocations: tennis, cycling. Office: Dickinson Wright Moon Van Dusen and Freeman 525 N Woodward Ave Ste 2000 Bloomfield Hills MI 48304

PAUL, ROBERT ARTHUR, steel company executive; b. N.Y.C., Oct. 28, 1937; s. Isadore and Ruth (Goldstein) P.; m. Donna Rae Berkman, July 29, 1962; children: Laurence Edward, Stephen Eric, Karen Rachel. AB, Cornell U., 1959; JD, Harvard U., 1962, MBA, 1964. With Ampco-Pitts. Corp. (formerly Screw & Bolt Corp. Am.), 1964—, v.p., 1969-71, treas., 1973-79, exec. v.p., 1972-79, pres., COO, 1979-94, pres., CEO, 1994—, dir., 1969—; exec. v.p., bd. dirs. Louis Berkman Co.; bd. dirs. Nat. City Corp., Ribozyme Pharms., Inc.; gen. ptnr. Romar Trading Co.; instr. Grad. Sch. Indsl. Adminstrn. Carnegie Mellon U., 1966-69; trustee Cornell U. Trustee H.L. and Louis Berkman Found., Presbyn. Univ. Hosp.; trustee, pres. Fair Oaks Found.; vice chmn. Jewish Healthcare Found. Pitts. Mem. ABA, Mass. Bar Assn., Harvard Club (N.Y.), Concordia Club, Pitts. Athletic Club, Duquesne Club. Republican. Jewish. Office: Ampco-Pitts Corp 600 Grant St Pittsburgh PA 15219-2702

PAUL, ROBERT CAREY, lawyer; b. Washington, May 7, 1950; s. Robert Henry and Betty Jane (Carey) P. AB, Dartmouth Coll., 1972; JD, Georgetown U., 1978. Assoc. Milbank Tweed Hadley and McCloy, N.Y.C., 1978-85; ptnr. Dechert Price and Rhoads, N.Y.C., 1986-89, Kelley, Drye & Warren, Brussels, 1989-93; counsel Rockefeller & Co., Inc., N.Y.C., 1995—. Home: 310 E 46th St #9B New York NY 10017 Office: Rockefeller & Co Inc 30 Rockefeller Plz New York NY 10112

PAUL, ROBERT DAVID, management consultant; b. N.Y.C., Nov. 1, 1928; s. Joseph Wolf and Freda (Sturm) P.; m. Eve Weinschenker, Apr. 9, 1952; children: Jeremy Ralph, Sarah Elizabeth. BS in Engring., U. Mich., 1950. Administrv. asst. Martin E. Segal Co., N.Y.C., 1950; naval architect Gibbs & Cox, N.Y.C., 1951; with The Segal Co., N.Y.C., 1953—, pres., 1967-76, vice chmn., 1977-91, chmn., 1991-94; dir., cons. Segal Co., N.Y.C., 1994—; trustee Employee Benefit Rsch. Inst., Washington, 1978-94, chair fellow com., 1994; bd. dirs. Wiss, Janney, Elstner Assocs., Northbrook, Ill., Empire Blue Cross Blue Shield. Contbr. articles to profl. jours. Cpl. U.S. Army, 1951-53. Mem. Soc. Human Resources Mgmt., Am. Compensation Assn., Am. Benefits Conf., Internat. Found. Employee Benefit Plans (past chmn. corp. com.), Univ. Club. Avocations: naval and mil. history, jazz piano. Office: The Segal Co 1 Park Ave New York NY 10016-5802

PAUL, ROBERT GREGORY, electronic company executive; b. Rockford, Ill., Mar. 5, 1942; s. George A. and Leona (Mueller) P.; m. Margaret Kennedy, June 22, 1984; children: Katherine, Robert, Andrew. B.S.M.E., U. Wis., 1964; M.B.A., Stanford U., 1966. Asst. treas. The Allen Group Inc., Melville, N.Y., 1971-73, treas., 1973-74, v.p.-treas., 1974-76; v.p. fin. Antenna Specialists Co., Cleve., 1976-77, v.p. ops., 1977-78, pres., 1978—. Home: 1965 Mornington Ln Apt 14 Cleveland OH 44106-2871 Other: Allen Group Inc 25101 Chagrin Blvd # 350 Beachwood OH 44122-5619

PAUL, ROLAND ARTHUR, lawyer; b. Memphis, Jan. 19, 1937; s. Rol and Hattye (Mincer) P.; m. Barbara Schlesinger, June 10, 1962; children: Deborah Lynn, Arthur Eliot. B.A. summa cum laude, Yale U., 1958; LL.B. magna cum laude, Harvard U., 1961. Bar: N.Y. 1962, Mich. 1978, Conn. 1989. Law clk. to judge U.S. Ct. Appeals, 1961-62; fgn. affairs officer, spl. asst. to gen. counsel Dept. Def., 1962-64; assoc. firm Cravath, Swaine & Moore, N.Y.C., 1964-69; counsel fgn. relations subcom. security commitments U.S. Senate, 1969-71; assoc. firm Simpson Thacher Bartlett, N.Y.C., 1971-73; v.p., gen. counsel Howmet Corp., Greenwich, Conn., 1976—; v.p., gen. counsel, dir. Pechiney Corp., Greenwich, Conn., 1984-95. Author: American Military Commitments Abroad. Mem. Council Fgn. Relations, Am. Bar Assn., Mich. Bar Assn. Home: 8 Ellery Ln Westport CT 06880-5202 Office: Pechiney Corp 475 Steamboat Rd Greenwich CT 06830-7144

PAUL, RONALD NEALE, management consultant; b. Chgo., July 22, 1934; s. David Edward and Frances (Kusel) P.; m. Nona Maria Moore, Dec. 27, 1964 (div. Oct. 1981); children: Lisa, Karen, Brenda; m. Georgeann Elizabeth Lapkoff, Apr. 10, 1982. BS in Indsl. Engring., Northwestern U., 1957, MBA, 1958. Asst. to pres. Victor Comptometer Co., Chgo., 1958-64; cons. Corplan, Chgo., 1964-66; pres. Technomic Inc., Chgo., 1966—; mng. ptnr. L/P Ptnrs., Chgo., 1978—; bd. dirs. Summit Restaurants, Salt Lake City. Co-author: The 101 Best Performing Companies in America, 1986, Winning the Chain Restaurant Game, 1994. Mem. Am. Mktg. Assn., Am. Mgmt. Assn., Planners Forum, Pres.'s Assn., Product Devel. Mgmt. Assn., Beta Gamma Sigma. Avocations: reading, racquetball. Office: Technomic Inc 300 S Riverside Plz Ste 1940 Chicago IL 60606-6613

PAUL, RONALD STANLEY, research institute executive; b. Olympia, Wash., Jan. 19, 1923; s. Adolph and Olga (Klapstein) P.; m. Margery Jean Pengra, June 5, 1944; children: Kathleen Paul Crosby, Robert S., James N. Student, Linfield Coll., 1940-41, Reed Coll., 1943-44, Harvard U., 1945; BS, U. Oreg., 1947, MS, 1949, PhD, 1951. Physicist, research mgr. Gen. Electric Co., Richland, Wash., 1951-64; asso. dir. Battelle N.W. Labs., Richland, 1965-68; dir. Battelle N.W. Labs., 1971-72, Battelle Seattle Research Ctr., 1969-70; v.p. ops. Battelle Meml. Inst., Columbus, Ohio, 1973-76, sr. v.p., 1976-78, exec. v.p., 1978-81, pres., 1981-87, chief exec. officer, 1984-87, assoc. trustee, 1986-92; lectr. modern physics Ctr. for Grad. Studies, Richland, 1951-62; IAEA cons. to Japan, 1962; bd. dirs. LifeSpan Biosciences, Inc., bd. chmn. MicroPlanet, Ltd. Contbr. articles to profl. jours. Trustee Linfield Coll., 1970-73, Denison U., 1982-88, Oreg. Mus. Sci. and Industry, 1971-72, Columbus Ctr. Sci. and Industry, 1973-87, Columbus Cancer Clinic, 1974-87, Columbus Children's Hosp. Research Found., 1975-87, Franklin U., 1987; trustee Pacific Sci. Ctr., 1969-74, Found. assoc., 1989—; v.p. exec. bd. Cen. Ohio council Boy Scouts Am., 1976-87; mem. exec. bd. of fellows Seattle-Pacific Coll., 1970-73; bd. overseers Acad. for Contemporary Problems, 1971-75; mem. nat. adv. bd. Am. U., 1982-86, Ohio State U. Found., 1985-87; bd. dirs. Edward Lowe Found., 1985—. Served with USAAF, 1943-46. Recipient Silver Beaver award Boy Scouts Am., 1986. Mem. Am. Phys. Soc., Am. Nuclear Soc., Sigma Xi, Sigma Pi Sigma, Pi Mu Epsilon. Republican. Presbyterian. Home: 7706 173rd St SW Edmonds WA 98026-5018

PAUL, STEPHEN HOWARD, lawyer; b. Indpls., June 28, 1947; s. Alfred and Sophia (Nahmias) P.; m. Deborah Lynn Dorman, Jan. 22, 1969; children: Gabriel, Jonathan. AB, Ind. U., 1969, JD, 1972. Bar: Ind. 1972, U.S. Dist. Ct. (so. dist.) Ind. 1972. Assoc. Baker & Daniels, Indpls., 1972-78, ptnr., 1979—. Editor in chief Ind. U. Law Jour., 1971. Pres. Belle Meade Neighborhood Assn., Indpls., 1974-78; v.p., counsel Brentwood Neighborhood Assn., Carmel, Ind., 1985-88, pres., 1988-91. Mem. ABA (state and local tax com. 1985—, sports and entertainment law com.), Am. Property Tax Counsel (founding mem.), Ind. State Bar Assn., Order of Coif. Republican. Jewish. Office: Baker & Daniels 300 N Meridian St Indianapolis IN 46204-1755

PAUL, THOMAS A., book publisher. Pres. Gale Rsch. Co., Detroit, Mich., 1987-90; pres., CEO Internat. Thomson Pub., Stamford, Conn., 1990—. Office: Internat Thomson Pub 1 Station Pl Stamford CT 06902-6800

PAUL, THOMAS FRANK, lawyer; b. Aberdeen, Wash., Sept. 23, 1925; s. Thomas and Loretta (Ounstead) P.; m. Dolores Marion Zaugg, Apr. 1, 1950; chilren: Pamela, Peggy, Thomas Frank. BS in Psychology, Wash. State U., 1951; JD, U. Wash., 1957. Bar: Wash. 1958, U.S. Dist. Ct. (no. and so. dists.) Wash. 1958, U.S. Ct. Appeals (9th cir.) 1958, U.S. Supreme Ct. 1970. Ptnr., shareholder, dir. LeGros, Buchanan & Paul, Seattle, 1958—; lectr. on admiralty and maritime law. Mem. ABA (chmn. com. on admiralty and maritime litigation 1982-86), Wash. State Bar Assn., Maritime Law Assn. U.S.A. (com. on nav. and C.G. matters 1981-82, com. on U.S. Mcht. Marine program 1981-82, com. on practice and procedure 1982-86, com. on limitation of liability 1982-86, com. on maritime legislation 1982—), Asia Pacific Lawyers Assn., Rainier Club, Columbia Tower Club. Republican. Home: 1323 Willard Ave W Seattle WA 98119-3460 Office: LeGros Buchanan & Paul 701 5th Ave Seattle WA 98104-7016

PAUL, WILLIAM, physicist, educator; b. Deskford, Scotland, Mar. 31, 1926; came to U.S., 1952; s. William and Jean (Watson) P.; m. Barbara Anderson Forbes, Mar. 28, 1952; children—David, Fiona. M.A., Aberdeen U., Scotland, 1946; Ph.D., Aberdeen U., 1951; A.M. (hon.), Harvard U., 1960; D Honoris Causa, Paris, 1994. Asst. lectr., then lectr. Aberdeen U., 1946-52; mem. faculty Harvard U., 1953—, Gordon McKay prof. applied physics, 1963-91, Mallinckrodt prof. applied physics, 1991—, prof. physics, 1980—; professeur associé U. Paris, 1966-67; cons. solid state physics, 1954—; Ripon prof., Calcutta, 1984. Author: Handbook on Semiconductors: Band Theory and Transport Properties, 1982; co-editor: Solids Under Pressure, 1963, Amorphous and Liquid Semiconductors, 1980. Carnegie fellow, 1952-53; Guggenheim fellow, 1959-60; Humboldt awardee, 1990; fellow Clare Hall Cambridge U., 1974-75. Fellow Am. Phys. Soc., Brit. Inst. Physics, N.Y. Acad. Scis., Royal Soc. Edinburgh; mem. AAAS, Sigma Xi. Home: 2 Eustis St Lexington MA 02173-5612 Office: Harvard U Pierce Hall Cambridge MA 02138

PAUL, WILLIAM DEWITT, JR., artist, educator, photographer, museum director; b. Wadley, Ga., Sept. 26, 1934; s. William DeWitt and Sonoma Elizabeth (Tinley) P.; m. Dorothy Hefling, Sept. 2, 1962; children: Sarah Elizabeth, Barbara Susan, Dorothy Ann. Student, Emory U., summer 1952, U. Rome, summer 1953, Ga. State Coll. Bus. Adminstrn., Atlanta, 1953—, summer 1956; B.F.A., Atlanta Art Inst., 1955; A.B., U. Ga., 1958, M.F.A., 1959. Instr. art and art history Park Coll., Parkville, Mo., 1960-61; dir. exhbns., instr. art history Kansas City (Mo.) Art Inst., 1959-64, curator study collections, asst. prof. art, 1964-65; coordinator basic courses dept. art, asst. prof. art U. Ga., Athens, 1965-67; curator Ga. Mus. Art, asso. prof. art, 1967-69, dir., asso. prof., 1969-80; chmn. visual arts rev. panel Ga. Council for Arts and Humanities, 1976-77; v.p. Arts Festival Atlanta, 1982, 84, 85, trustee, 1982-93; guest artist Arts Festival Atlanta, 1987; mem. parents council Randolph-Macon Woman's Coll., Lynchburg, Va., 1986-87. Exhibited in one man shows at Ga. Mus. Art, 1959, Atlanta Art Assn., 1959, Unitarian Gallery, Kansas City, 1960, Palmer Gallery, Kansas City, 1965, Heath Gallery, Atlanta, 1976, Hunter Mus. Art, Chattanooga, 1976, Forum Gallery, N.Y.C., 1977, Madison (Ga.) Morgan Cultural Ctr., 1980, Columbus (Ga.) Mus. Arts and Scis., 1980, Macon (Ga.) Mus. Arts and Sci., 1980, Banks Haley Gallery, Albany, Ga., 1980, Augusta Richmond County (Ga.) Mus., 1980, Heath Gallery 1982, Moon Gallery, Berry Coll., Rome, Ga., 1983, Bathhouse Gallery, Atlanta, 1987, MIA Gallery, Seattle, 1988, Valencia C.C., Orlando, Fla., 1991, Gasperi Gallery, New Orleans, 1993, Contemporary Arts Ctr., New Orleans, 1994; numerous site-specific installations, 1986-87; exhibited group shows, New Arts Gallery, Atlanta, 1961, Kansas City Art Inst., 1960-64, Park Coll., 1960, Mulvane Art Ctr., Topeka, 1965, Palazzo Venezia, Rome, 1984, Elaine Benson Gallery, Bridgehampton, L.I., N.Y., 1986, Dulin Gallery Art, Knoxville, Tenn., 1986, 1987 Atlanta Biennale, Nexus Contemporary Art Ctr., Atlanta, Valencia C.C., Orlando, 1988, Greg Kucera Gallery, Atlanta, 1992, King Plow Arts Ctr., Atlanta, 1994, Leslie-Lohman Found., N.Y.C., 1995, others; represented in permanent collections Gen. Mills Inc., Mpls., Hallmark Cards, Kansas City, Little Rock Arts Ctr., Ga. Mus. Art, U. Ga. Ford Found. faculty enrichment grantee, 1978; recipient numerous awards for paintings. Mem. Am. Fedn. Arts (trustee 1969-81), Coll. Art Assn., Am. Assn. Museums (council 1981), Lovis Corinth Meml. Found., Ga. Alliance Arts Edn. (dir. 1975-77), Phi Kappa Phi. Home: 150 Bar H Ct Athens GA 30605-4702

PAUL, WILLIAM ERWIN, immunologist, researcher; b. Bklyn., June 12, 1936; s. Jack and Sylvia (Gleicher) P.; m. Marilyn Heller, Dec. 25, 1958; children: Jonathan M., Matthew E. A.B. summa cum laude, Bklyn. Coll., 1956; M.D. cum laude, SUNY-Downstate Med. Ctr., 1960, DSc (hon.), 1991. Intern, asst. resident Mass. Meml. Hosp., Boston, 1960-62; clin. assoc. Nat. Cancer Inst. NIH, Bethesda, Md., 1962-64; postdoctoral fellow, instr. NYU Sch. Medicine, N.Y.C., 1964-68; sr. investigator Lab. Immunology Nat. Inst. Allergy and Infectious Diseases, NIH, Bethesda, Md., 1968-70, chief Lab. Immunology, 1970—; dir. Office of AIDS Rsch. NIH, Bethesda, Md., assoc. dir. AIDS rsch., 1994—; mem. bd. sci. advisors Jane Coffin Childs Meml. Fund for Med. Research, 1982-90; G. Burroughs Mider lectr. NIH, 1982; mem. sci. rev. bd. Howard Hughes Med. Inst., 1979-85, 87-91, mem. med. adv. bd., 1992-96; mem. bd. sci. cons. Meml. Sloan-Kettering Cancer Ctr., N.Y.C., 1984-92; chmn. adv. com. Harold C. Simmons Arthritis Rsch. Ctr., 1984-90; bd. dirs. Fed. Am. Soc. Experimental Biology, 1985-88; mem. bd. basic biology Nat. Res. Council, 1986-89; mem. select com. Alfred P. Sloan Jr. Prize, Gen. Motors Cancer Res. Fedn., 1986-87; sci. adv. coun. Cancer Rsch. Inst., 1985-94; mem. com. to visit div. med. sci., bd. overseers Harvard Coll., 1987-93; Carl Moore lectr. Sch. Medicine, Washington U., St. Louis, 1986; mem. adv. com. Pew Scholars Program in Biomed. Scis., 1988-91; Richard Gershon lectr. Yale U. Sch. Medicine, 1986; Nelson Med. lectr., U. Calif., Davis, 1988; Disting. Alumnus lectr., Univ. Hosp., Boston, 1989; Anderson med. lectr. U. Va., 1990, La Jolla sci. lectr., 1991, Wellcome vis. prof. Wayne State U., 1991, mem. Adv. Com. dept. of Molecular Bio., Princeton U, 1993-94, annual lectr., Dutch Soc. for Immunology, 1992, Yamamura Meml. lectr. Osaka U., 1992, Kunkel lectr., Johns Hopkins U Sch. of Medicine, 1993; Welcome vis. prof. SUNY Stony Brook, 1993; Benacerraf lectr. Harvard Med. Sch., 1993; Sulkin lectr. U. Tex. Southwestern Med. Ctr., 1995. Editor: Fundamental Immunology, 1984, 3d edit., 1993, Ann. Rev. Immunology, Vols. 1-14, 1983—; adv. editor Jour. Exptl. Medicine, 1974—; assoc. editor Cell, 1985—; transmitting editor Internat. Immunology, 1989—; corr. editor Procs. Royal Soc. Series B, 1989-93; mem. editl. bd. Molecular Biology of Cell, 1990-92; contbg. editor Procs. NAS U.S.A., 1992-94; contbr. numerous articles to sci. jours. Served with USPHS, 1962-64, 75—. Recipient Founders' prize Tex. Instruments Found., 1979, Alumni medal SUNY Downstate Med. Ctr., 1981, Disting. Svc. medal USPHS, 1985, 3M Life Scis. award, 1988, Tovi Comet-Wallerstein prize CAIR Inst., Bar-Ilan U., 1992, 6th ann. award for excellence in immunologic rsch. Duke U., 1993, Alunni honors Bklyn. Coll., 1994. Fellow Am. Acad. Arts and Scis.; mem. NAS, Inst. Medicine NAS, Am. Soc. Clin. Investigation (pres. 1980-81), Am. Assn. Immunologists (pres. 1986-87), Assn. Am. Physicians, Scandinavian Soc. Immunology (hon.). Office: NIH Bldg 31 Rm 4C02 31 Center Dr MSC 2340 Bethesda MD 20892-2340

PAUL, WILLIAM F., manufacturing company executive. Previously pres., chief exec. officer Sikorsky Aircraft, Stratford, Conn.; now sr. v.p. defense and space systems United Techs. Corp., Hartford, Conn.; exec. v.p., chmn. intl. ops. United Techs Corp., Washington. Office: United Techs Co 1401 I St NW Ste 600 Washington DC 20005*

PAUL, WILLIAM GEORGE, lawyer; b. Pauls Valley, Okla., Nov. 25, 1930; s. Homer and Helen (Lafferty) P.; m. Barbara Elaine Brite, Sept. 27, 1963; children—George Lynn, Alison Elise, Laura Elaine, William Stephen. B.A., U. Okla., 1952, LL.B., 1956. Bar: Okla. bar 1956. Pvt. practice law Norman, 1956; ptnr. Oklahoma City, 1957-84, Crowe & Dunlevy, 1962-84, 96—; sr. v.p., gen. counsel Phillips Petroleum Co., Bartlesville, Okla., 1984-95; ptnr. Crowe & Dunlevy, Oklahoma City, 1996—; assoc. prof. law Oklahoma City U., 1964-68; adv. bd. Martindale Hubbell, 1990—. Author: (with Earl Sneed) Vernon's Oklahoma Practice, 1965. Bd. dirs. Nat. Ctr. for State Cts., 1993—, Am. Bar Endowment, 1986—. 1st lt. USMCR, 1952-54. Named Outstanding Young Man Oklahoma City, 1965, Outstanding Young Oklahoman, 1966. Fellow Am. Bar Found. (chmn. 1991), Am. Coll. Trial Lawyers; mem. ABA (bd. govs. 1995—), Okla. Bar Assn. (pres. 1976), Oklahoma County Bar Assn. (past pres.), Nat. Conf. Bar Pres. (pres. 1986), U. Okla. Alumni Assn. (pres. 1973), Order of Coif, Phi Beta Kappa, Phi Delta Phi, Delta Sigma Rho. Democrat. Presbyterian. Home: 13017 Burnt Oak Rd Oklahoma City OK 73120-8919 Office: Crowe & Dunlevy 1800 Mid-Am Tower 20 N Broadway Oklahoma City OK 73102-8273

PAUL, WILLIAM MCCANN, lawyer; b. Cambridge, Mass., Feb. 9, 1951; s. Kenneth William and Mary Jean (Lamson) P.; m. Janet Anne Forest, Feb. 25, 1984; children: Emily L'Engle, Andrew Angwin, Elizabeth Seton. Student, U. Freiburg, Fed. Republic of Germany, 1971-72; BA, Johns Hopkins U., 1973; JD, U. Mich., 1977. Bar: D.C. 1978, U.S. Dist. Ct. D.C. 1978, U.S. Ct. Claims 1984, U.S. Ct. Appeals (4th cir.) 1980, U.S. Ct. Appeals (fed. cir.) 1983, U.S. Tax Ct. 1990. Law clk. to judge U.S. Ct. Appeals (5th cir.), Austin, Tex., 1977-78; assoc. Covington & Burling, Washington, 1978-87, ptnr., 1987-88, 89—; dep. tax legis. counsel U.S. Treasury Dept., 1988-89. Mem. ABA, D.C. Bar Assn., Am. coll. Tax Counsel, Order of Coif. Presbyterian. Home: 5604 Chevy Chase Pky NW Washington DC 20015-2520 Office: Covington & Burling PO Box 7566 1201 Pennsylvania Ave NW Washington DC 20004-2401

PAULAUSKAS, EDMUND WALTER, real estate broker; b. Lowell, Mass., Nov. 16, 1937; s. Vladas and Barbara (Antonavicius) P.; m. Joyce Wagenhauser, Feb. 5, 1977. BS in Bus., Boston U., 1959; M Div., Oblate Coll. of SW, 1976; PhD in Psychology, Sussex U., Brighton, Eng., 1979. Lic. real estate broker, lic. mortgage broker, Fla.; ordained priest Roman Cath. Ch., 1970. Priest Diocese of Beaumont, Tex., 1970-77; psychotherapist Houston Dept. Pub. Health, 1979-84; pres., broker Vets. Realty, Ft. Lauderdale, Fla., 1984—. Producer TV program Catholic Church Today, 1975. Mem. Ft. Lauderdale Bd. Realtors. Home: 4250 Galt Ocean Dr Unit 1N Fort Lauderdale FL 33308

PAULEY, JANE, television journalist; b. Indpls., Oct. 31, 1950; m. Garry Trudeau; 3 children. BA in Polit. Sci, Ind. U., 1971; D. Journalism (hon.), DePauw U., 1978. Reporter Sta. WISH-TV, Indpls., 1972-75; co-anchor WMAQ-TV News, Chgo., 1975-76, The Today Show, NBC, N.Y.C., 1976-90; corr. NBC News, N.Y.C., 1976—; prin. writer, reporter NBC Nightly News, 1980-82, substitute anchor, 1990—; co-anchor Early Today, NBC, 1982-83; prin. corr. Real Life With Jane Pauley, NBC, 1990; co-anchor Dateline NBC, 1992—. Office: NBC News 30 Rockefeller Plz New York NY 10112

PAULEY, ROBERT REINHOLD, broadcasting executive, financial executive; b. New Canaan, Conn., Oct. 17, 1923; s. Edward Matthew and Grace Amanda (Smith) P.; m. Barbara Anne Cotton, June 22, 1946; children: Lucinda Teed, Nicholas Andrew, Robert Reinhold Jr., John Adams. Student, Harvard U., 1946, MBA, 1951; DSc (hon.), Curry Coll., 1966. With radio sta. WOR, 1951-52, NBC, 1953-56, CBS, 1956-57; account exec. ABC, 1957-59, sales mgr., 1959-60, v.p. in charge, 1960-61, pres., 1961-67; pres. Mutual Broadcasting System, N.Y.C., 1967-69; v.p. corp. fin. E.F. Hutton & Co., Inc., 1971-81; founder, chmn. TV News Inc., N.Y.C.; founder Nat. Black Network, N.Y.C.; founder, pres. Cablenet Internat. Corp. and Cablenet News, N.Y.C.; disting. lectr. U. S.C., Spartanburg. Trustee Curry Coll.; bd. dirs. Found. to Improve TV. Mem. Radio-TV Execs. Soc., SAR, St. Nicholas Soc. Clubs: Harvard (Boston, N.Y.C.), Myopia Hunt, Tryon Hounds. Home: PO Box 217 Landrum SC 29356-0217

PAULEY, STANLEY FRANK, manufacturing company executive; b. Winnipeg, Man., Can., Sept. 19, 1927; came to U.S., 1954, naturalized, 1961; s. Daniel and Anna (Tache) P.; m. Dorothy Ann Ruppel, Aug. 21, 1949; children: Katharine Ann, Lorna Jane. B.E.E., U. Man., 1949. With Canadian Industries Ltd., Kingston, Ont., 1949-53; sr. engring. asst. Canadian Industries Ltd., 1952-53; controls designer Standard Machine and Tool Co. Ltd., Windsor, Ont., 1953-54; prodn. supt. E.R. Carpenter Co., Richmond, Va., 1954-57, pres., 1957-83, chmn., CEO, 1983-94; chmn., CEO, Carpenter Co. (formerly E.R. Carpenter Co.), Richmond, 1994—, also bd. dirs.; bd. dirs. Carpenter Co. of Can., Carpenter de Mexico, Carpenter Plc., Carpenter S.a., Am. Filtrona Corp., Carpenter Gmbh, Mentor Portfolio Fund. Trustee U. richmond, Hampden-Sydney Coll., Va. Mus. Found., Va. Mus. Fine Arts, Va. Higher Edn. Tuition Trust Fund. Mem. Commonwealth Club, Forum Club, Country Club of Va. Republican. Presbyterian. Home: 314 St Davids Ln Richmond VA 23221-3708 Office: Carpenter Co 5016 Monument Ave Richmond VA 23230-3620

PAULIKAS, GEORGE ALGIS, physicist; b. Pagegiai, Lithuania, May 14, 1936; came to U.S., 1949, naturalized, 1955; s. George and Olga (Pacas) P.; m. Joan Marie Gross, Sept. 7, 1957; 1 child, Nancy Marie. B.S. in Engring. Physics, U. Ill., Chgo. and Urbana, 1957, M.S. (univ. fellow 1957-58), 1958; Ph.D. in Physics (NSF fellow 1958-61), U. Calif., Berkeley, 1961. With Aerospace Corp., El Segundo, Calif., 1961—, head space particles and fields dept., 1968, dir. space scis. lab., 1968-81, v.p. labs., 1981-85, group v.p. devel., 1985-89, group v.p. programs, 1989-94, exec. v.p., 1992—; mem. various ad hoc coms. NAS, 1970, 73, 79, 80, ann., 1984-87, 91-92, mem. com. solar and space physics, 1977-80; mem. adv. coun. geophysics U. Calif., 1973-75, exec. com. space scis. lab., Berkeley, 1978-81; mem. sci. adv. bd. USAF, 1975-82, 91-95; cons. Lawrence Berkeley Lab., 1961-66, Office Space Scis., NASA, 1975-82, Los Alamos phys. divsn. adv. com., 1983-96, Naval Rsch. Adv. Com., 1984-86, Naval Studies Bd., 1989-95; mem. def. space tech. com. NRC, 1987-92. Author papers in field; asso. editor: Jour. Geophys. Research, 1972-75. Trustee Calif. Mus. of Sci. and Industry, 1994—. Recipient Aerospace Corp. Trustees Disting. Achievement award, 1980; Meritorious Civilian Svc. award USAF, 1982, 95, U. Ill. Alumni Disting. Engring. award, 1992. Fellow AIAA (chmn. tech. com. space sci. and astronomy 1976-77), Am. Phys. Soc.; mem. Am. Geophys. Union, Sigma Xi. Home: 1537 Addison Rd Pls Vrds Est CA 90274-1808 Office: Aerospace Corporation 2350 E El Segundo Blvd El Segundo CA 90245-4609

PAULIN, AMY RUTH, civic activist, consultant; b. Bklyn., Nov. 29, 1955; d. Ben and Alice Lois (Roth) P.; m. Ira Schuman, May 25, 1980; children: Beth, Sarah, Joseph. BA, SUNY, Albany, 1977, MA, 1978, postgrad., 1979—. Instr. SUNY, Albany, 1978, Queens (N.Y.) House of Detention,

1979; fundraiser United Jewish Appeal Fedn., N.Y.C., 1979-83; dir. devel. Altro Health & Rehab., Bronx, N.Y., 1983-86; fundraising cons. N.Y.C., 1986-88; pres. LWV, Scarsdale, N.Y., 1990-92, Westchester, N.Y., 1992-95; trustee Scarsdale (N.Y.) Village, 1995—; bd. dirs. Westco Prodns. Mem. adv. coun. Family Ct.; chair county budget chair Westchester Womens Agenda; mem. adv. com. Fund for Women & Girls; bd. dirs. Mid. Sch. PTA, Westchester Coalition for Legal Abortion, Scarsdale Open Soc. Assn., 1992-95, United Jewish Appeal Fedn. Scarsdale Women's Campaign; v.p. Westchester Children's Assn.; troop leader Girl Scouts U.S.; mem. Town Club Edn. Com., 1983-89; mem. Scarsdale Bowl com., 1992—, chair, 1994-95; mem. Scarsdale Japanese Festival, 1992-93; mem. Westchester Women's Equality Day, 1987-92; mem. nominating com. Heathcote Neighborhood Assn., 1991-92; bd. dirs. Westchester Cmty. Found., 1994-95; mem. Scarsdale Village Youth Bd., 1992-95; mem. legislators task force on women and youth at risk Westchester County Bd., 1984—; mem. Updating Voting Equipment Com., 1994, chair, 1994-95; chair Cmtys. Tobacco Free Westchester; co-chair Parent Tchr. Coun. Sch. Budget Study, 1991-94; future planning chair Kids Base Bd., 1992-95; chair parking and traffic subcom. Village Downtown Devel. Com., 1994-95; mem. Westchester Commn. Campaign Fin. Reform, Westchester Commn. Child Abuse. Mem. LWV (bd. dirs. women and children's issues Westchester chpt., dir. devel. N.Y. state), N.Y. State Pub. Health Assn. (bd. dirs. Lower Hudson Valley chpt.). Avocations: swimming, dancing. Home: 12 Burgess Rd Scarsdale NY 10583-4410

PAULIN, HENRY SYLVESTER, antiques dealer, emeritus educator; b. Cleve., Nov. 8, 1927; s. Sylvester and Mary (Zimmerman) P.; m. Florence Caroline Schwegman, Aug. 30, 1952. B.S. in Edn, Kent (Ohio) State U., 1955; M.A., Ohio State U., 1958, Ph.D., 1964. Tchr. indsl. arts Brimfield Jr.-Sr. High Sch., Kent, 1954-55, Zanesville (Ohio) High Sch., 1955-57; instr. ceramics Art Inst., Zanesville, 1956-57; asst. prof., then asso. prof. indsl. arts State U. Coll., Oswego, N.Y., 1956-63; instr. Ohio State U., 1961-63; assoc. prof., coordinator Indsl. Arts Div., Kent State U., 1963-67; prof. and chmn. dept. design and industry San Francisco State U., 1967-80, prof. emeritus, 1980—; propr. Paulin Place (Fine Antiques and Paintings), Oxford, Ohio, 1980—; vis. prof. No. Ill. U., summer 1965. Served with AUS, 1946-48. Mem. Calif. Tchrs. Assn., Oxford C. of C., Oxford Retail Mchts. Assn., Epsilon Pi Tau, Phi Delta Kappa. Home: 6294 Fairfield Rd Oxford OH 45056-1555

PAULIN, SVEN JOSEF KARL, radiologist, educator; b. Oct. 18, 1926. Miriam H. Stoneman prof. radiology emeritus Harvard U., Cambridge, Mass.; with dept. radiology Beth Israel Hosp., Boston. Mem. Radiol. Soc. N.Am. Home: 260 Charles River St Needham MA 02192

PAULING, LINUS CARL, JR., health science administrator. Pres., chmn. Linus Pauling Inst. of Sci. and Medicine, Palo Alto, Calif. Recipient. Office: Linus Pauling Inst of Sci & Med 440 Page Mill Rd Palo Alto CA 94306

PAULL, LAWRENCE G., production designer; b. Chgo., Apr. 13, 1946; s. Albert and Sally (Miller) P.; m. Marcy Bolotin, Oct. 23, 1983; 1 child, Michael. BA, Univ. of Ariz., 1968. Prodn. designer: (films) Little Fauss and Big Halsey, 1970, Chandler, 1971, The Hired Hand, 1971, A Tattered Web, 1971, Star Spangled Girl, 1971, They Only Kill Their Masters, 1972, Murder Once Removed, 1972, She Waits, 1972, Second Chance, 1972, Heat of Anger, 1972, The Naked Ape, 1973, The Last American Hero, 1973, The Nickel Ride, 1974, Terror on the Fortieth Floor, 1974, The Stranger Who Looks Like Me, 1974, W. W. and the Dixie Dance Kings, 1975, The Bingo Long Traveling All-Stars and Motor Kings, 1976, Sherlock Holmes in New York, 1976, Which Way Is Up?, 1977, Tail Gunner Joe, 1977, The Storyteller, 1977, A Circle of Children, 1977, Blue Collar, 1978, FM, 1978, Friendly Fire, 1979, How to Beat the High Cost of Living, 1980, In God We Trust, 1980, Doctor Detroit, 1982, Rehearsal for Murder, 1982, Blade Runner, 1982 (Academy award nomination best art direction 1982, British Academy award best art direction 1983), (with Augustin Huarte) Romancing the Stone, 1984, American Flyers, 1985, (with Todd Hallowell) Back to the Future, 1985, (with Bill Elliot) Cross My Heart, 1987, Project X, 1987, License to Drive, 1988, Cocoon: The Return, 1988, Harlem Nights, 1989, (with Geoff Hubbard) The Last of the Finest, 1990, (with Hubbard) Predator 2, 1990, City Slickers, 1991, Unlawful Entry, 1992, Memoirs of an Invisible Man, 1992, Born Yesterday, 1993, (with Richard Hudolin) Another Stakeout, 1993, The Naked Gun 33 1/3: The Final Insult, 1994. Office: care Craig Jacobsen Hansen Jacobson & Teller 450 N Roxbury Dr 8th Fl Beverly Hills CA 90210

PAULL, RICHARD ALLEN, geologist, educator; b. Madison, Wis., May 20, 1930; s. Ethra Harold and Martha (Schaller) P.; m. Rachel Kay Krebs, Mar. 6, 1954; children: Kay Marie, Lynn Ellen, Judith Anne. B.S., U. Wis., 1952, M.S., 1953, Ph.D., 1957. Party chief Pan Am. Petroleum Co., 1955-57; research group leader Jersey Prodn. Research Co., 1957-62; mem. faculty U. Wis.-Milw., 1962—, chmn. dept. geol. scis., 1962-66, prof., 1966—; cons. in field, 1966—. Author books, papers in field. Served with USAF, 1953-55. Hon. curator Milw. Museum; recipient Amoco Distinguished Teaching award, 1975. Fellow Geol. Soc. Am. (chmn. ann. meeting 1970, tech. program com. 1970, 77, membership com. 1977-80, chmn. 1980); mem. AAAS, Am. Assn. Petroleum Geologists (chmn. sci. fair award com. 1980, membership com. 1981-87, vis. petroleum geologists com. 1982-87, pub. affairs com. 1982-85), Soc. Econ. Paleontologists and Mineralogists, Nat. Assn. Geology Tchrs. (v.p. 1976-77, pres. 1977-78), Am. Geol. Inst. (governing bd. 1977-79, sec. and exec. com. 1986-88), Nature Conservancy, Sigma Xi. Home: 722 E Carlisle Ave Milwaukee WI 53217-4834 Office: U Wis Dept Geoscis Milwaukee WI 53201

PAULLING, JOHN RANDOLPH, JR., naval architecture educator, consultant; b. Doniphan, Mo., Jan. 8, 1930; s. John Randolph and Ruth Elizabeth (Braschler) P.; m. Charlotte Lansing Peabody, Dec. 19, 1952; children: John Randolph III, Ruth Frances, Thomas Dudley. BS, MIT, 1952, MS, 1953, Naval Architect profl. degree, 1954; DEngring., U. Calif., Berkeley, 1958. From instr. to prof. U. Calif., Berkeley, 1954-91, prof. emeritus, 1991—; rsch. engr. Det Norske Veritas, Oslo, 1962-63; vis. prof. U. N.S.W., Sydney, Australia, 1975, U. Tokyo, 1979; vis. rsch. engr. Nat. Maritime Inst., London, 1980; mem. adv. com. USCG, 1988—. Contbr. articles to profl. jours. Named Eminent Ocean Engr. Japan Soc. for Promotion of Sci., 1979. Fellow Soc. Naval Architects and Marine Engrs. (v.p. 1985-88, David Taylor medal 1985), Royal Instn. Naval Architects; mem. NAE, Japan Soc. Naval Architects, Richmond Yacht Club. Avocations: sailing, woodworking. Office: U Calif Dept Naval Architecture PO Box 1064 Geyserville CA 95441

PAULSEN, DIANA, religious organization administrator. Exec. dir. Refomed Church in Am., N.Y.C. Office: Reformed Church in Am 475 Riverside Dr Rm 1811 New York NY 10027

PAULSEN, FRANK ROBERT, college dean emeritus; b. Logan, Utah, July 5, 1922; s. Frank and Ella (Ownby) P.; m. Marye Lucile Harris, July 31, 1942; 1 son, Robert Keith; m. Lydia Ransier Lowry, Nov. 1, 1969. B.S., Utah State U., 1947; M.S., U. Utah, 1948, Ed.D., 1956; Kellogg Found. postdoctoral fellow, U. Oreg., 1958; Carnegie Found. postdoctoral fellow, U. Mich., 1959-60. High sch. prin. Mt. Emmons, Utah, 1948-51; supt. schs. Cokeville, Wyo., 1951-55; from asst. prof. to assoc. prof. edn. U. Utah, 1955-61; prof. edn., dean Sch. Edn. U. Conn., 1961-64; dean Coll. Edn. U. Ariz., Tucson, 1964-84, dean emeritus, prof. emeritus higher edn., 1984—; scholar-in-residence Fed. Exec. Inst., Charlottesville, Va., 1970; Disting. prof. edn. U. Bridgeport, summer 1972; dir. Am. Jour. Nursing Pub. Co., N.Y.C., Am. Capital Growth Fund, Am. Series Portfolio Stock Co., Houston, Am. Gen. Equity Fund, Am. Capital Bond Fund, Am. Capital Convertible Securities Fund, Am. Capital Exchange Fund, Am. Series Portfolio Co., Am. Capital Income Trust; exec. com. New Eng. Council Advancement Sch. Adminstrn., 1962-64; trustee Common Sense Trust Co., Houston. Author: The Administration of Public Education in Utah, 1958, Contemporary Issues in American Education, 1966, American Education: Challenges and Images, 1967, Changing Dimensions in International Education, 1968, Higher Education: Dimensions and Directions, 1969, also numerous articles. Trustee Joint Council Econ. Edn., 1962-70; v.p., dir. Southwestern Coop. Ednl. Lab., 1965-67; bd. dirs. Nat. League for Nursing, 1967-69, mem. com. on perspectives, 1966-72; dir., chmn. exec. com. ERIC Clearinghouse on Tchr. Edn., 1968-70; bd. dirs. Tucson Mental Health Center, 1968-70. Served with AUS, 1942-46, PTO. Mem. Aerospace Med. Assn., NEA, Assn. Higher Edn., Am. Assn. Sch. Adminstrs., Am. Acad. Polit. and Social Sci., John Dewey Soc., Utah Acad. Letters, Arts and Scis., Ariz. Acad., Am. Assn. Colls. Tchrs. Edn. (Conn. liaison officer 1962-64, mem. studies com. 1962-68, dir.), Ariz. Assn. Colls. Tchr. Edn. (pres. 1972-80), AAAS, Am. Ednl. Research Assn., Kappa Delta Pi, Pi Sigma Alpha, Pi Gamma Mu., Phi Delta Kappa. Lodge: Rotary.

PAULSEN, JOANNA, publishing executive. Pres., sales manager Amereon House, Mattituck, N.Y. Office: Amereon House PO Box 1200 Mattituck NY 11952-0921

PAULSEN, SERENUS GLEN, architect, educator; b. Spooner, Wis., July 27, 1917; s. Serenus Justin and Edna Anne (Dalton) P.; m. Virginia C. Habel, Jan. 26, 1944; children: Thomas J., Nancy Lee (Mrs. John Marshall). Student, U. Ill., 1938-42; B.Arch. cum laude, U. Pa., 1947; Diploma in Architecture and City Planning, Royal Acad. Art, Stockholm, 1948. With Carroll, Grisdale & Van Alan (Architects), Phila., 1946-47, Eero Saarinen & Assos., Bloomfield Hills, Mich., 1949-51, 53-57; chief designer Reisner & Urbahn (Architects), N.Y.C., 1951-52; archtl. coordinator Knoll Assos., N.Y.C., 1952-53; prin. Glen Paulsen Assos., Birmingham, Mich., 1958-69; prin., v.p. Tarapata-MacMahon-Paulsen Assos., Inc. (Architects), Bloomfield Hills, 1969-77; pres. Cranbrook Acad. Art, head dept. architecture, 1966-70; prof., chmn. Masters Program in Architecture U. Mich., 1976-78, Emil Lorch prof. architecture, 1982-85, prof. emeritus, 1985—; Mem. Nat. Com. on Urban Planning and Design, 1971-72; archtl. commn. U. Wash., Seattle, 1968-76. (Recipient 3d prize Bi-Nat. Competition for Design Rainbow Center Plaza, Niagara Falls, N.Y. 1972). Gov. emeritus Cranbrook Acad. Art. Served with C.E. USAAF, 1942-46. Fellow AIA (honor awards Detroit chpt. for Shapero Hall of Pharmacy 1965, Our Shepherd Lutheran Ch. 1966, Ford Life Sci. Bldg. 1967, Birney Elementary Sch., Detroit 1971, Fed. Bldg., Ann Arbor, Mich. 1978, gold medal for 1980 Detroit chpt.); mem. Mich. Soc. Architects, (Robert F. Hastings award 1985). Home: 3 Southwick Ct Ann Arbor MI 48105-1409 Office: U Mich Coll Architecture and Urban Planning Ann Arbor MI 48109

PAULSON, BELDEN HENRY, political scientist; b. Oak Park, Ill., June 29, 1927; s. Henry Thomas and Evelina (Belden) P.; m. Louise D. Hill, Jan. 9, 1954; children: Eric, Steven. AB, Oberlin (Ohio) Coll., 1950; MA, U. Chgo., 1955, PhD, 1962. With Italian service mission Naples, 1950-53; organizer Homeless European Land Program, Sardinia, 1957-59; with UN High Commn. Refugees, Rome, 1960-61; mem. faculty U. Wis., Milw., also; U. Wis. extension, 1962—, prof. polit. sci., 1969—; chmn. Center Urban Community Devel., 1967-90; co-founder High Wind Assn. for Modeling an Alternative Cmty., 1980; co-founder, pres. Plymouth Inst. for Sustainable Devel., 1992—; hon. rsch. prof. Internat. Tech. and Economy Inst, Inst. for Sci. of Scis., Shanghai, China, 1990—. Author: The Searchers, 1966; also articles. Served with USNR, 1945-46. Findhorn Found. fellow; grantee Social Sci. Rsch. Coun., 1967-68. Mem. Am. Polit. Sci. Assn., World Future Soc., Internat. Ctr. Integrative Studies, Soc. Sustainable Futures. Home: W7122 County Rd U Plymouth WI 53073-4538 Office: U Wis Dept Urban Community Devel 161 W Wisconsin Ave 6th Fl Milwaukee WI 53203-1404

PAULSON, BERNARD ARTHUR, oil company executive, consultant; b. Lakeview, Mich., July 12, 1928; s. Arthur Bernard and Genevieve Talbard (Bushley) P.; m. Joan Lee Curtiss, Dec. 4, 1954; children: James, Joseph (dec.), Ann, Thomas (dec.), Bernadette, Patricia, Steven. B.S. in Chem. Engring., Mich. State U.-East Lansing, 1949. Registered profl. engr., Tex. Process engr. Mid-West Refineries Inc., Alma, Mich., 1949-57; plant mgr. Kerr-McGee Corp., Cleve. and Wynnewood, Okla., 1957-66; v.p. Coastal States Petrochemical, Corpus Christi, Tex., 1966-71, Koch Industries Inc., St. Paul and Wichita, 1974-88; cons. Koch Industries Inc., Corpus Christi, Tex., 1988-94; pres. Koch Refining Co., Wichita, 1981-88; chmn. bd. dirs. The Automation Group Inc.; bd. dirs. Hitox Corp. Am., Indtech Inc. Chmn., pres. Cleve. Area Hosp. Corp., 1962; dir. Ada Wilson Hosp. Found.; pres. Corpus Christ Bd. Trade. 1st lt. USAF, 1955-57. Recipient Claud R. Erickson Disting. Alumnus award Mich. State U., 1994. Mem. AIChE (fuels and petrochem. award 1989), Nat. Petroleum Refiners Assn., Refining Am. Petroleum Inst., Wichita Area C. of C. (bd. dirs.), Bd. Trade, North Shore Country Club, Corpus Christi Town Club (bd. dirs.), Elks. Home and Office: 5310 Greenbriar Dr Corpus Christi TX 78413-2827

PAULSON, DAVID L., newspaper publishing executive. Treas. Los Angeles Times. Office: Los Angeles Times Times Mirror Sq Los Angeles CA 90053

PAULSON, DONALD ROBERT, chemistry educator; b. Oak Park, Ill., Sept. 6, 1943; s. Robert Smith and Florence Teresa (Beese) P.; m. Elizabeth Anne Goodwin, Aug. 20, 1966; children: Matthew, Andrew. BA, Monmouth Coll., 1965; PhD, Ind. U., 1968. Asst. prof. chemistry Calif. State U., Los Angeles, 1970-74, assoc. prof., 1974-78, prof., 1979—, chmn. dept., 1982-90; vis. prof. U. B.C., Vancouver, Can., 1977-78, U. Sussex, Brighton, Eng., 1984-85. Author: Alicyclic Chemistry, 1976; contbr. articles to profl. jours. Named Outstanding Prof., Calif. State U., Los Angeles, 1978. Mem. Am. Chem. Soc., Chem. Soc. (London), InterAm. Photochem. Soc., Nat. Assn. Sci. Tchrs., Sigma Xi. Democrat. Episcopalian. Avocations: photography, hiking, soccer. Home: 1627 Laurel St South Pasadena CA 91030-4710 Office: Calif State U Dept Chemistry 5151 State University Dr Los Angeles CA 90032-4221

PAULSON, GLENN, environmental scientist; b. Sycamore, Ill., Sept. 14, 1941; s. Orville Madison and Clarice Hope (Lewis) P.; m. Linda Joyce Cooper, May 17, 1985. BA with honors, Northwestern U., 1963; PhD, Rockefeller U., 1971; ScD (hon.), L.I. U., 1972. Dir. sci. for citizen program New Sch. for Social Rsch., N.Y.C., 1967-69; exec. dir. Scientists' Com. for Pub. Info., N.Y.C., 1971-72; staff scientist, adminstr. sci. support prog. Natural Resources Def. Coun., N.Y.C., 1971-74; asst. commr. N.J. Dept. Environ. Protection, Trenton, 1974-79; v.p. Nat. Audubon Soc., N.Y.C., 1979-82, sr. v.p., 1982-84; v.p. Clean Sites, Inc., Alexandria, Va., 1984-88; dir. Ctr. for Hazardous Waste Mgmt. Ill. Inst. Tech., Chgo., 1988-90, rsch. prof. dept. environ. engring., 1988-95; pres. Paulson and Cooper, Inc., 1992—; chmn. environ. mgmt. adv. bd. Dept. Energy, 1992-94. Editor, author: Environment, USA, 1974; contbr. articles to profl. jours. Bd. dirs. Citizens for Clean Air, N.Y.C., 1965-74, Rene Dubos Ctr., N.Y.C., 1981-90. NSF grantee, 1976, A.W. Mellon Found. grantee, 1979-84, Coalition on Superfund grantee, 1988-89; Rockefeller Univ. fellow, 1963-71. Fellow AAAS, Am. Inst. Chemists; mem. Am. Chem. Soc., Soc. for Environ. Toxicology and Chemistry, Coun. for Advancement Sci. Writing (bd. dirs. 1968-95), Soc. Risk Assessment, Sec. Energy Adv. Bd. (charter mem. 1990-93). Avocation: outdoor activities. Office: Paulson and Cooper Inc PO Box 1541 Jackson Hole WY 83001

PAULSON, JAMES MARVIN, engineering educator; b. Wausau, Wis., Jan. 1, 1923; s. Gustav Victor and Susanna (Dracy) P.; m. Marjorie Beulah Burton, May 11, 1946; children—Vicki Rae, Michael James. B.S. in Civil Engring, The Citadel, 1947; M.S. in Civil Engring, Ill. Inst. Tech., 1949; Ph.D., U. Mich., 1958. Registered profl. engr., Mich. Draftsman Wausau Iron Works, 1946; engr. Charles Whitney Cons. Engr., Milw., 1948-49; faculty Wayne State U., Detroit, 1949—, prof., 1961-85, chmn. dept. civil engring., 1967-72, assoc. dean Coll. Engring., 1973-83, prof. emeritus, 1985—; v.p. Civil Engrs., Inc., 1954—; cons. in field. Served with AUS, 1943; Served with USMCR, 1943-46. Mem. ASCE (life), Mich. Soc. Profl. Engrs. (life), Am. Soc. for Engring. Edn., Sigma Xi, Tau Beta Pi, Chi Epsilon. Presbyterian. Home: PO Box 23 Greenbush MI 48738-0023

PAULSON, JOHN DORAN, newspaper editor, retired; b. Grand Forks, N.D., Oct. 1, 1915; s. Holger D. and Irene E. (Finkle) P.; m. Zoe Y. Bean Hensley, July 6, 1946 (dec. Aug. 1993); children: James L., Michael D., Christine R., David E., Patrick R. Student, U.N.D., 1932-34; B.S., U. Minn., 1936. Copy editor Mpls. Star, 1936; reporter The Forum, Fargo, N.D.-Moorhead, Minn., 1937-39; polit. writer The Forum, 1939-51, mng. editor, 1951-56, editor, 1957-80; v.p. Dakota Photographics Inc., Fargo, 1963-93. Del. N.D. Constl. Conv., 1971-72. Served with AUS, 1942-46. Mem. Am. Soc. Newspaper Editors. Home: 1362 2nd St N Fargo ND 58102-2725

PAULSON, KENNETH ALAN, executive newspaper editor; b. Chgo., Dec. 3, 1953; s. Knut Norman and Helen Elizabeth (Beardsley) P.; m. Peggy Jean Foot, June 12, 1976; children: Carrie Ann, David. BA in Journalism, U. Mo., Columbia, 1975; JD, U. Ill., Champaign, 1978. Bar: Ill., 1978, Fla. 1979. Exec. editor, v.p. news Gannett Suburban Newspapers, White Plains, N.Y.; 2d v.p. N.Y. Associated Press Bd., N.Y.C., 1995-96. Co-author: (book) Truly One Nation, 1988, Profiles of Power, 1988.

PAULSON, PAUL JOSEPH, advertising executive; b. White Plains, N.Y., Sept. 25, 1932; s. Paul and Ann (Loughlin) P.; m. Kathryn P. Keeler, June 30, 1962; children: Thomas, Mark, Kathryn, John, Clifford. BSBA, Ohio State U., 1954; MBA, U. Pa., 1959. With Compton Advt. Inc., N.Y.C., 1959-78; mgmt. supr. Compton Advt. Inc., 1965-78, sr. v.p., 1968-78, also dir.; pres., dir. Doyle Dane Bernbach Inc., N.Y.C., 1978-83; pres., chief exec. officer Isidore & Paulson, Inc., N.Y.C., 1983-93; chmn., pres., CEO Paulson & Co. Mktg. Svcs., Greenwich, 1993—; mem. Ohio State U. Alumni Adv. Coun., 1982—; pres. coun. mem. Ohio State U., 1993—. Author: Fundamentals of Consumer Goods Marketing, 1966. Chmn. Christmas for Underprivileged Children, N.Y.C., 1963—. Served to lt. (j.g.) USNR, 1955-58, MTO, ETO. Mem. Wharton Grad. Bus. Sch. Alumni Assn. (pres. N.Y.C. club 1963-65, dir. 1972—), Ohio State U. Alumni Assn., Wharton Grad. Bus. Sch. Roman Catholic. Clubs: N.Y. (dir.), Milbrook, Sigma Chi. Home: 45 W Brother Dr Greenwich CT 06830-6726

PAULSON, PETER JOHN, librarian, publishing company executive; b. N.Y.C., Jan. 30, 1928; s. Peter John and Lillian Agnes Elaine (Neuman) P.; m. Josephine C. Bowen, Dec. 5, 1953; children: David, Debora. B.Social Scis. cum laude, CCNY, 1949; M.A. in History, Columbia, 1950; M.A. in L.S, SUNY, Albany, 1955. Library asst. N.Y. State Library, Albany, 1952-55; head, gift and exchange sect. N.Y. State Library, 1955-65, head catalog sect., 1965-66, prin. librarian tech. services, 1966-71, dir., 1972-85; exec. dir. OCLC Forest Press, 1985—; adj. asst. prof. library sci. State U. N.Y. at Albany, 1960-71; Adv. com. Ohio Coll. Library Center, 1970-71; adv. council to pub. printer depository libraries, 1972-77, chmn., 1975-77; com. fed. depository library service N.Y. State, 1960-70, chairperson, 1960-70; bd. dirs. Capital Dist. Libr. Coun., Nat. Info. Standards Orgn., N.E. Document Conservation Ctr. Mem. ALA (chmn. com. on legislation 1980-82, pres. state library agy. sect. 1982-83), N.Y. Library Assn. (pres. 1975), Hudson-Mohawk Library Assn. (v.p. 1964), SUNY-OCLC Network (governing bd. 1980-82), Phi Beta Kappa. Home: 24 Tillinghast Ave Albany NY 12204-2312 Office: OCLC Forest Press 85 Watervliet Ave Albany NY 12206-2023

PAULSON, RONALD HOWARD, English and humanities educator; b. Bottineau, N.D., May 27, 1930; s. Howard Clarence and Ethel (Tvete) P.; m. Barbara Lee Appleton, May 25, 1957 (div. 1982); children: Andrew Meredith, Melissa Katherine. BA, Yale U., 1952, PhD, 1958. Instr. U. Ill., 1958-59, from asst. to assoc. prof., 1959-63; prof. English Rice U., Houston, 1963-67; prof. English Johns Hopkins U., Balt., 1967-75, chmn. dept., 1968-75, Andrew W. Mellon prof. humanities, 1973-75, Mayer prof. humanities, 1984—, chmn. dept., 1985-91; prof. English Yale U., New Haven, Conn., 1975-84, Thomas E. Donnelly prof., 1980-84, Ward Phillips lectr., 1978, Alexander lectr., 1979, Brown and Haley lectr., 1979, Hodges lectr., 1980. Author: Theme and Structure in Swift's Tale of a Tub, 1960, Fielding, 1962, Hogarth's Graphic Works, 1965, rev. edits., 1970, 89, Fictions of Satire, 1967, Satire and the Novel, 1967, (with Thomas F. Lockwood) Fielding: The Critical Heritage, 1969, Satire: Modern Essays in Criticism, 1971, Hogarth: His Life, Art and Times, 1971, Rowlandson: A New Interpretation, 1972, Emblem and Expression: Meaning in Eighteenth Century English Art, 1975, The Art of Hogarth, 1975, Popular and Polite Art in the Age of Hogarth and Fielding, 1979, Literary Landscape: Turner and Constable, 1982, Book and Painting: Shakespeare, Milton and the Bible, 1983, Representations of Revolution, 1983, Breaking and Remaking, 1989, Figure and Abstraction in Contemporary Painting, 1990, Hogarth Vol. 2: High Art and Low, Hogarth Vol. 3: Art and Politics, 1993, The Beautiful, Novel, and Strange: Aesthetics and Heterodoxy, 1996; also numerous essays. 1st lt. AUS, 1952-54. Sterling fellow 1957-85, Guggenheim fellow 1965-66, 1986-87, NEH fellow 1977-78. Fellow Am. Acad. Arts and Scis.; mem. Am. Soc. for 18th Century Studies (pres. 1986-87). Home: 2722 St Paul St Baltimore MD 21218-4332 Office: Johns Hopkins U Dept English Baltimore MD 21218

PAULSON, STANLEY FAY, edcuational association administrator; b. Atwater, Minn., Mar. 5, 1920; s. Adolph and Ida May (Fay) P.; m. Margaret Nan Appelquist, Sept. 8, 1944; children—Richard Stanley, Lynn Edith. B.A. in Philosophy, U. Minn., 1942, M.A., 1949, Ph.D., 1952; B.D., Bethel Theol. Sem., 1944. Instr. U. Minn., 1948-53; research asso. studies in lang. and behavior Bur. Naval Research, 1952-53; overseas instr. U. Md. Program in Germany and Eng., 1953-54; asst. prof. U. Minn., 1954-56; mem. faculty San Francisco State U., 1956-66, prof. speech, chmn. dept., 1959-62, v.p. acad. affairs, 1963-65, acting pres., 1965-66; prof., chmn. dept. speech Pa. State U., 1966-69, dean Coll. Liberal Arts, 1969-84; bd. dirs. Assn. Am. Colls., 1978-85, chmn. bd., 1983-84, v.p., 1985-87; presdl. search cons. Assn. Governing Bd. Univs. and Colls., Washington, 1987-88; sr. cons. Acad. Cons. Service, Washington, 1988—. Author: (with Bystrom, Ramsland) Communicating Through Speech, 1951; also articles. Served to lt. (j.g.) USNR, 1945-46. Fulbright lectr. Kanazawa (Japan) U., 1962-63. Mem. Speech Communication Assn. (vice chmn. group methods sect. 1961-62), Western Speech Assn. (counselor pub. address 1961—), AAUP, Internat. Communication Assn., Council Colls. Arts and Scis. (dir. 1971-75, v.p. 1972, pres. 1973). Home: 5500 Friendship Blvd Apt 2403N Bethesda MD 20815-7218 Office: Acad Search Consultation Svc 1818 R St NW Washington DC 20009-1604

PAULSON, WILLIAM LEE, state justice; b. Valley City, N.D., Sept. 3, 1913; s. Alfred Parker and Inga Gertina (Wold) P.; m. Jane E. Graves, Sept. 8, 1938; children: John T., Mary (Mrs. Mikal Simonson). B.A., Valley City State Tchrs. Coll., 1935; J.D., U. N.D., 1937. Bar: N.D. 1937. Practiced in Valley City, 1937-66; state's atty. Barnes County, 1941-50, 59-66; assoc. justice N.D. Supreme Ct., 1967-83, surrogate judge, 1983—; Pres. N.D. States Attys. Assn., 1964; dir. for N.D. Nat. Dist. Attys. Assn., 1963-65. Pres. Valley City Jaycees, 1943; dist. v.p. U.S. Jaycees, 1945-46; bd. dirs. Valley City C. of C., 1960-61; judge Am. Legion Oratorical Contest, 1970-72; mem. nat. awards jury Freedoms Found. at Valley Forge, 1969-71, 77; chancellor Episcopal Ch. N.D., from 1965; Mem. alumni adv. bd. U. N.D., from 1971. Mem. Am. Bar Assn., State Bar N.D., U. N.D. Alumni Assn. (pres. Valley City Area 1963-65, Sioux award 1973). Clubs: Elk, K.P, Eagle, Mason (Shriner). Home: 1009 E Highland Acres Rd Bismarck ND 58501-2417 Office: Box 444 Valley City ND 58072

PAULSTON, CHRISTINA BRATT, linguistics educator; b. Stockholm, Sweden, Dec. 30, 1932; came to U.S., 1951; d. Lennart and Elsa (Facht) Bratt; m. Rolland G. Paulston, July 26, 1963; children: Christopher-Rolland, Ian Rollandsson. B.A., Carleton Coll., 1953; M.A. in English and Comparative Lit., U. Minn., 1955; Ed.D., Columbia U., 1966. Cert. tchr., Minn. Tchr. Clara City and Pine Island High Schs., Minn., 1955-60, Am. Sch. of Tangier, Morocco, 1960-62, Katrineholm Allmanna Laroverk, Katrineholm, Sweden, 1962-63, East Asian Library, Columbia U., N.Y.C., 1963-64; asst. instr. Tchrs. Coll., Columbia U., 1964-66; instr. U. Punjab, Chandigarh, India, summer 1966, Pontificia Universidad Catolica Del Peru, Lima, 1966-67; cons. Instituto Linguistico de Verano, Lima, 1967-68; asst. prof. linguistics U. Pitts., 1969-75, prof., 1975—, asst. dir. English Lang. Inst., 1969-70, dir. English Lang. Inst., 1970—, acting dir. Lang. Acquistion Inst., fall 1971, acting chmn. dept. gen. linguistics, 1974-75, chmn., 1975-89. Author numerous books and articles on linguistics. Recipient research award Am. Ednl. Research Assn., 1980; Fulbright-Hays grantee, Uruguay, 1985. Mem. Assn. Tchrs. of English to Speakers of Other Langs. (2d v.p., conv., chmn. 1972, exec. com. 1972-75, rsch. com. 1973-75, 78-80, chmn. 1973-75, 1st v.p. 1975, pres. 1976), Linguistics Soc. Am. (com. linguistics and pub. interest 1973-77), Internat. Assn. of Tchrs. of English as a Fgn. Lang., Am. Council on Teaching of Fgn. Langs., MLA (exec. com. lang. and soc. 1975-76), Ctr. Applied Linguistics (trustee 1976-81, exec. com. 1980, publs. com. 1981, research com. 1981), Eastern Competitive Trailriding Assn. Democrat. Episcopalian. Office: U Pitts Linguistics Pittsburgh PA 15260

PAULUS, ELEANOR BOCK, professional speaker, author, consultant; b. N.Y.C., Mar. 12, 1933; d. Charles William Bock and Borghild (Nelson) Garrick; m. Chester William Paulus Jr., Sept. 6, 1952; children: Chester W.

III, Karl Derrick, Diane Paulus Henricks. Student, Smith Coll., 1952-53. Owner, founder Khan-Du Chinese Shar-Pei, Somerset, N.J., 1980—; dir. Pet Net, Santa Fe, N.Mex., 1992—; co-owner, CFO, exec. prod. Am. Dream TV Prodns.and Capitol Idea/Multi Media Prodns., Washington, 1995—; lectr., cons. on Chinese Shar-Pei and canine health, 1980—; internat. con., lectr. on pet care and health. Author: Health Care Handbook for Cats, Dogs and Birds, The Proper Care of Chinese Shar-Pei; contbr. articles to mags. and jours., chpts. to books. Dir. bd. trustees Rutgers Prep. Sch., Somerset, 1970-76, v.p. bd. trustees, 1976-81, pres. PTA, 1966-76; chmn. Raritan River Festival, New Brunswick, N.J., 1980-91. Named Woman of Yr., City of New Brunswick, 1982. Mem. Dog Writers Am. Assn., Dog Fanciers N.Y.C., Bonzai Clubs Internat., Koi Club N.Y., Raritan Valley Country Club, Chinese Shar-Pei Club of Am. (v.p. 1982-86, bd. dirs. east sect. 1980-82, Humanitarian award 1986). Avocations: travel, dog related activities, gardening, photography, geneaology, bonzai, koi. Home: 321 Skillmans Ln Somerset NJ 08873-5325 Office: E B Paulus 20 Sutton Pl S # 5A New York NY 10022-4165

PAULUS, JOHN DAVID, economist; b. Petoskey, Mich., July 26, 1943; s. George Emil and Daisy Helen (Hulbert) P.; m. Carol Ann Jones, Sept. 1, 1962; children—Susan, John, Andrew, Sharon. A.B., U. Mich.-Dearborn, 1965; Ph.D., U. Chgo., 1972. Programmer analyst Ford Motor Co., Dearborn, Mich., 1965-67; systems analyst Gen. Electric Co., Detroit, 1967-68; sr. economist Fed. Res. Bd., Washington, 1972-78; sr. v.p. Fed. Res. Bank Mpls., 1978-79; v.p. Goldman Sachs and Co., N.Y.C., 1979-82; mng. dir., chief economist Morgan Stanley and Co., N.Y.C., 1982—. Contbr. numerous articles to profl. jours., newspapers and mags. Mem. Am. Econ. Assn., Nat. Assn. Bus. Economists. Office: Morgan Stanley and Co 1251 Ave Of The Americas New York NY 10020-1104

PAULUS, NORMA JEAN PETERSEN, lawyer, state school system administrator; b. Belgrade, Nebr., Mar. 13, 1933; d. Paul Emil and Ella Marie (Hellbusch) Petersen; LL.B., Willamette Law Sch., 1962; LL.D., Linfield Coll., 1985; m. William G. Paulus, Aug. 16, 1958; children: Elizabeth, William Frederick. Sec. to Harney County Dist. Atty., 1950-53; legal sec., Salem, Oreg., 1953-55; sec. to chief justice Oreg. Supreme Ct., 1955-61; admitted to Oreg. bar, 1962; of counsel Paulus and Callaghan, Salem, mem. Oreg. Ho. of Reps., 1971-77; sec. state State of Oreg., Salem, 1977-85; of counsel firm Paulus, Rhoten & Lien, 1985-86; supt. pub. instrn. State of Oreg., 1990—; Oreg. exec. bd. US West, 1985—; adj. prof. Willamette U. Grad. Sch, 1985; mem. N.W. Power Planning Com., 1986-89. Fellow Eagleton Inst. Politics, 1971; mem. Pacific NW Power Planning Council, 1987-89; adv. com. Defense Adv. Com. for Women in the Service, 1986, Nat. Trust for Hist. Preservation, 1988—; trustee Willamette U., 1978—; bd. dirs. Benedictine Found. of Oreg., 1980—, Oreg. Grade. Instn. Sci. and Tech., 1985—, Mid Willamette Valley council Camp Fire Girls, 1985-87; overseer Whitman Coll., 1985—; bd. cons. Goodwill Industries of Oreg.; mem. Salem Human Relations Commn., 1967-70, Marion-Polk Boundary Commn., 1970-71; mem. Presdl. Commn. to Monitor Philippines Election, 1986. Recipient Distinguished Service award City of Salem, 1971; Path Breaker award Oreg. Women's Polit. Caucus, 1976; named One of 10 Women of Future, Ladies Home Jour., 1979. Woman of Yr., Oreg. Inst Managerial and Profl. Women, 1982, Oreg. Women Lawyers, 1982, Woman Who Made a Difference award Nat. Women's Forum, 1985. Mem. Oreg. State Bar, Nat. Order Women Legislators, Women Execs. in State Govt., Women's Polit. Caucus Bus. and Profl. Women's Club (Golden Torch award 1971), Zonta Internat., Delta Kappa Gamma.*

PAULUS, STEPHEN HARRISON, composer; b. Summit, N.J., Aug. 24, 1949; s. Harrison Child and Patricia Jean (Clark) P.; m. Patricia Ann, July 18, 1975; children: Gregory Stephen, Andrew Christopher. Student, Macalester Coll., 1967-69; B.A., U. Minn., 1969-71, M.A., 1972-74, Ph.D., 1974-78. Co-founder, fundraiser Minn. Composers Forum, St. Paul, 1973-84; Exxon/Rockefeller composer in residence Minn. Orch., Mpls., 1983-87; composer in residence Santa Fe Chamber Music Festival, summer 1986; Regent's lectr. U. Calif., Santa Barbara, Nov. 1986; composer in residence Atlanta Symphony Orch., 1988-92, Dale Warland Singers, 1991-92; composer in residence Aspen Festival, summer, 1992. Performances with Tanglewood Festival, 1980, Edinburgh Festival, 1983, Aldeburgh Festival, 1985; composer (orchestral works) Sinfonietta, Concertante, Ordway Overture, Concerto for Orchestra, Seven Short Pieces for Orchestra, Translucent Landscapes, Spectra, Reflections: Four Movements on a Theme of Wallace Stevens, Divertimento for Harp and Chamber Orchestra, Trumpet Concerto, Suite from Harmoonia, Suite from The Postman Always Rings Twice, Ground Breaker--An Overture for Constrn. Instruments and Orch., Symphony in Three Movements, Street Music, Manhattan Sinfonietta, Violin Concerto, Symphony for Strings, Concerto for Violin, Cello & Orch., Organ Concerto, Violin Concerto No. 2, (recordings) Violin Concerto, Concertante and Symphony for Strings, Songs: Bittersuite, All My Pretty Ones, Artsongs, (for orch.) Violin Concerto (Kennedy Ctr. Friedheim award for 3d pl. Am. Works for Orch., 1988), Symphony for Strings, Street Music, Echoes Between the Silent Peaks, (operas) The Woodlanders, The Postman Always Rings Twice, The Woman At Otowi Crossing, The Village Singer, Harmoonia, The Woman at Otowi Crossing; (for chorus and orch.), So Hallow'd Is the Time, (5 carols for chorus and strings) Christmas Tidings, Letters for the Times, North Shore, Canticles: Songs and Rituals for the Easter and the May, Voices, (chamber work) Seven for the Flowers Near the River, Seven Miniatures, Fantasy in Three Parts, Quartessence, others, also numerous works for chamber groups including Partita for Violin and Piano, Music for Contrasts (string Quartet), String Quartet No.2, Quartessence, (for soprano voice, piano, percussion and string quartet) Letters From Colette, American Vignettes (for cello and piano); (for solo voice) All My Pretty Ones, Artsongs, Mad Book, Shadow Book: Michael Morley's Songs, Elizabethan Songs, Bittersuite for baritone and piano, (solo voice/bass-baritone and vn, vc. pf.) The Long Shadow of Lincoln; (for solo instruments) Two Moments for Guitar, (piano) Translucent Landscapes; (for chorus) Madrigali di Michelangelo, Four Preludes on Playthings of The Wind, Peace, Personals, Marginalia, Echoes Between the Silent Peaks, Jesu Carols, Meditations of Li Po, Love's Philosophy, Three Songs for Mixed Chorus, The Earth Sines, The Elixir, (narrative and chamber orch.) Voices from the Gallery, (chamber) Music of the Night (for violin, voice and percussion), (choral) Visions from Hildegard, Part I (for flute, oboe, timpany, percussion, organ and chorus), Part Two (for brass quintet, percussion and chorus), (for narrator and chamber orch.) Voices from the Gallery, (vocal) Songs of Love and Longing, (chamber/instrumental) Air on Seurat, (chorus) Three Songs for Mixed Chorus, Christ Our Passover, (piano) Preludes, (organ duet) The Triumph of the Saint, (chorus and chamber ensemble) Whitman's Dream. Recipient Outstanding Achievement award U. Minn., 1991, Disting. Alumni award, 1991, Lancaster Symphony Orch. Composer's award, 1994; Guggenheim fellow, 1982-83, NEA fellow, 1978; NEA Consortium grantee, 1987. Mem. ASCAP (bd. dirs. 1990), Am. Music Ctr., Minn. Composers Forum (v.p. 1984-87, bd. dirs.). Avocations: tennis, reading. Home and Office: 1719 Summit Ave Saint Paul MN 55105-1833

PAULY, BRUCE HENRY, engineering consultant; b. Washington, Nov. 11, 1920; s. Elmer George and Charlotte May (Weck) P.; m. Dorothy Buhrman Rollins, June 20, 1945; 1 child, Margaret MacKenzie Pauly Price. B.S. in Mech. Engring., Va. Poly. Inst., 1941; M.S. in Engring. Adminstrn., Case Inst. Tech., 1965. Registered profl. engr., Pa. lic. pvt. pilot. Sect. mgr. Aviation Gas Turbine div., Westinghouse Electric Corp., Lester, Pa., 1945-52; sales mgr. aircraft (Pesco) Borg-Warner Corp., Bedford, Ohio, 1952-55; v.p. research and engring. Weatherhead Co., Cleve., 1955-69; v.p. engring. Eaton Corp., Cleve., 1969-82; co-owner, dir. Crystaloid Electronics Co., Hudson, Ohio, 1983-85; mem. vis. com. Fenn Coll. Engring., Cleve. State U., 1973-85; mem. engring. adv. com. Cuyahoga Community Coll., Cleve., 1979—; exec. com. Coll. Engring. Va. Poly Inst. and State U., Blacksburg, 1980—; mem. com. Transp. Research Bd. NRC, Washington, 1982-84. Patentee turbojet control, hydraulic pump, gas regulator, hose crimper. Mem. task force Pres.' Pvt. Sector Survey, Washington, 1982; mem. Cleve. Sr. Council, 1983—. Served to lt. col. USAAF, 1941-45, ETO; USAF Ret. Res., 1986—. Decorated Legion of Merit; decorated Bronze Star, Croix de Guerre (France). Mem. AIAA (co-chmn. nat. aerospace propulsion conf. Cleve 1982), Soc. Automotive Engrs. (chmn. motor vehicle council 1981-82), Nat. Conf. on Fluid Power (gen. chmn. 1977), Cleve. Engring. Soc. (bd. govs. 1979-81), Chagrin Valley C. of C., Mil. Order World Wars (comdr. Cleve. 1984-85), Res. Officers Assn., Cheshire Cheese Club (Cleve), Pi Tau Sigma, Pi Delta Epsilon. Republican. Episcopalian. Home: 143 Kenton Rd Chagrin Falls OH 44022-2503

PAULY, DANIEL MARC, fisheries educator; b. Paris, May 2, 1946; s. Louis and Renee (Clément) P.; m. Sandra W. Wade, Dec. 8, 1978; children: Ilya, Angela. Diploma, U. Kiel, Germany, 1974, D Natural Scis., 1979, Habilitaton, 1985. Postdoctoral fellow Internat. Ctr. for Living Aguatic Resources Mgmt., Manila, 1979-80, scientist, 1980-86, dir. resources assessment of mgmt., 1986-93, dir. life sci. div., 1994, prin. sci. adviser, 1994—; prof. Fisheries Ctr., U. B.C., Vancouver, Can., 1994—; cons. FAO, various countries, 1980-89, World Bank, Washington, 1989. Author: (essays) On the Sex of Fish and the Gender of Scientists, 1994; contbr. over 300 articles and reports on tropical fisheries and related areas to sci. jours. Avocations: writing, scuba diving. Office: U BC, Fisheries Ctr, Vancouver, BC Canada

PAULY, JOHN EDWARD, anatomist; b. Elgin, Ill., Sept. 17, 1927; s. Edward John and Gladys (Myhre) P.; m. Margaret Mary Oberle, Sept. 3, 1949; children: Stephen John, Susan Elizabeth, Kathleen Ann, Mark Edward. B.S., Northwestern U., 1950; M.S., Loyola U., Chgo., 1952, Ph.D., 1955. Grad. asst. gross anatomy Stritch Sch. Medicine, Loyola U., Chgo., 1953-54; rsch. asst. anatomy Chgo. Med. Sch., 1952-54, research instr., 1954-55, instr. in gross anatomy, 1955-57, assoc. in gross anatomy, 1957-59, asst. prof. anatomy, 1959-63, asst. to pres., 1960-62; asso. prof. anatomy Tulane U. Sch. Medicine, 1963-67; prof., head dept. anatomy U. Ark. for Med. Scis., Little Rock, 1967-83; prof., head dept. physiology and biophysics U. Ark. for Med. Scis., 1978-80, vice chancellor for acad. affairs and sponsored rsch., 1983-92, assoc. dean Grad. Sch., 1983-92, prof. anatomy, 1992-95, prof. emeritus, 1995—; tech. adviser Ency. Brit. Films, 1956; mem. safety and occupational health study sect. Nat. Inst. Occupational Safety and Health, Ctr. for Disease Control, 1975-79; vis. prof. faculty medicine Kuwait U., 1993, 94. Author: (with Hans Elias) Human Microanatomy, 1960, 3d edit. 1966, (with Elias and E. Robert Burns) Histology and Human Microanatomy, 1978; editor: (with Lawrence E. Scheving and Franz Halberg) Chronobiology, 1974, (with Heinz von Mayersbach and Lawrence E. Scheving) Biological Rhythms in Structure and Function, 1981, The American Association of Anatomists, 1888-1987. Essays on the History of Anatomy in America and a Report on the Membership-Past and Present, 1987, (with Lawrence E. Scheving) Advances in Chronobiology, 1987, (with Dora K. Hayes and Russel J. Reiter) Chronobiology: Its Role in Clinical Medicine, General Biology and Agriculture, 1990; editor Am. Jour. Anatomy, 1980-92; co-mng. editor Advances in Anatomy, Embryology and Cell Biology, 1980—; mem. adv. editorial bd. Internat. Jour. Chronobiology, 1973-83; contbr. articles to profl. jours. Served with USNR, 1945-47. Recipient merit certificates AMA, 1953, 59; Bronze award Ill. Med. Soc., 1959; Lederle Med. Faculty award, 1966. Fellow AAAS; mem. Am. Assn. Anatomists (sec.-treas. 1972-80, pres. 1982-83, Centennial award 1987, Henry Gray award 1995), So. Soc. Anatomists (pres. 1971-72), Assn. Anatomy Chmn. (sec.-treas. 1969-71), Am. Physiol. Soc., Internat. Soc. Chronobiology, Pan-Am. Assn. Anatomy, Internat. Soc. Electrophysiol. Kinesiology, Internat. Soc. Steriology, Consejo Nacional de Profesores de Ciencias Morfologicas (hon.), Sigma Xi, Sigma Alpha Epsilon. Roman Catholic.

PAUMGARTEN, NICHOLAS BIDDLE, investment banker; b. Phila., Apr. 30, 1945; s. Harald Paumgarten and Elise Biddle (Robinson) Tyson; m. Carol Marshall, June 24, 1966; children—Nicholas Biddle, Alexander. B.A., U. Pa., 1967; M.B.A., Columbia U., 1971. Mng. dir. 1st Boston Corp., N.Y.C., 1971—. Office: First Boston Corp Park Ave Pla 55 E 52nd St New York NY 10055-0002*

PAUP, BRYCE ERIC, professional football player; b. Scranton, Iowa, Feb. 29, 1968. Degree in Bus., U. No. Iowa. With Green Bay Packers, 1990-94; linebacker Buffalo Bills, 1995—. Selected to Pro Bowl, 1994-95. Office: Buffalo Bills 1 Bills Dr Orchard Park NY 14127

PAUSA, CLEMENTS EDWARD, electronics company executive; b. South Gate, Calif., Oct. 18, 1930; s. Oscar Clements and Kathleen Patricia (O'Toole) P.; m. Janice Mary Hanson, Jan. 22, 1955; children: Geoffrey Clements, Ronald Edward. Student, UCLA, 1948-50; BS, U. Calif., Berkeley, 1953, MS, 1954, cert. in bus., 1960. Product mgr. Fairchild Semiconductor Corp., 1959-62, mgr. plant, 1962-64; gen. mgr. Fairchild Hong Kong Ltd., 1964-67, dir. plant group, 1967-68; dir. internat. mfg. Nat. Semiconductor Corp., Santa Clara, Calif., 1968-70, gen. mgr. Far East ops., 1970-73, v.p. internat. mfg., 1973-86, corp. v.p. internat. mfg., 1986-90, corp. v.p. internat. mfg. emeritus, 1991—; dir. Coopers & Librand Cons.; bd. dirs. 8 subs. cos., 2 J.V. cos. Mem. internat. adv. bd. U. Santa Clara, 1984—. Served to capt. USNR, 1952-81. Mem. Naval Res. Assn., Res. Officer's Assn., Calif. Alumni Assn., Delta Chi Alumni Assn. (v.p., pres. 1978-86). Republican. Roman Catholic. Office: Coopers & Lybrand 10 Almaden Blvd San Jose CA 95113-2226

PAUSTIAN, BONITA JOYCE, school health administrator; b. Duluth, Minn., Apr. 17, 1935; d. Theodore Herald Oliver and Olga Magdalene (Bongey) Oliver-Spaulding; m. E. Earl Paustian, June 30 1956; children: Caprice, Lori, Leisa, Jodi, Jena. Diploma, Mercy Hosp. Sch. Nursing, 1956; BS, Colombia Pacific U., 1985. RN, Mich., Ind.; cert. Nat. Bd. for Cert. Sch. Nurses. Staff nurse Mercy Hosp., Benton Harbor, Mich., 1956-60; charge nurse rehab. unit Berrien Gen. Hosp., Berrien Center, Mich., 1960-61; charge nurse newborn nursery Meml. Hosp., St. Joseph, Mich., 1965-70; sch. nurse Berrien Springs Pub. Schs., 1970-88; in-svc. dir. Medco, South Bend, Ind., 1989; ins. examination nurse Exam Mgmt. Svcs., Kalamazoo, Mich., 1989—; health educator, 1989; supr. sch. health Buchanan (Mich.) Cmty. Schs., 1990—; lectr., presenter various programs in field; nurse cons., Mich., 1992—; OSHA/MIOSHA trainer, Mich., 1992—; pres. Sch. Nurse Consulting Svcs. Author: School Nurse Brochures, 1994; prodr., photographer slide show The Michigan School Nurse, 1988. Mem. choir Berrien Center Bible Ch., 1985—. Recipient Golden Nugget award Mich. Coun. for Exceptional Children, 1994, cert. of appreciation Optimist Club, Berrien County Day Program for Hearing Impaired Children, Ottawa Elem. Sch., Moccasin Elem. Sch. cert. of honor Am. Heart Assn.; named Mich. Sch. Nurse of Yr., 1987, One of Top 10 Nurses in Mich., Wayne State U. and Met. Woman's Mag., 1994. Mem. Mich. Assn. Sch. Nurses (pub. rels. chair 1993—, exec. bd., Pres. award 1993, Sch. Nurse of Yr. 1987), Nat. Assn. Sch. Nurses (exec. dir., state bd. dirs. 1994—, cert. recognition, 1995). Avocations: travel, reading, cross-stitch, freelance writing, vocal music. Home: 5703 Windy Acres Ln Berrien Springs MI 49103 Office: Buchanan Cmty Schs 401 W Chicago St Buchanan MI 49107-1044

PAVA, ESTHER SHUB, artist, educator; b. Hartford, Conn., June 29, 1921; d. Jacob H. and Rose (Rietkop) Shub; m. Jacob Pava, June 16, 1946; children: David Lauren, Jonathan Michael, Daniel Seth, Nathaniel Alexander. BFA, R.I. Sch. of Design, 1944; MA, San Francisco State U., 1971. Artist New Eng. Roto Engraving Co., Holyoke, Mass., 1944-46, Wyckoff Advt. Agy., San Francisco, 1947-48; tchr. San Francisco Unified Sch. Dist., 1963-66, Laguna Salada Sch. Dist., Pacifica, Calif., 1966-83; artist, educator Belmont, Calif., 1983—. Recipient numerous awards for artwork. Mem. Burlingame Art Soc. (pres. 1983-84), Thirty and One Artists (pres. 1992-93), Peninsula Art Assn., Soc. Western Artists (signature mem., exhibited in many juried shows), Belmont Art Assn., others. Avocations: world travel, book discussion groups, sketching. Home: 2318 Hastings Dr Belmont CA 94002-3318

PAVALON, EUGENE IRVING, lawyer; b. Chgo., Jan. 5, 1933; m. Lois M. Frenzel, Jan. 15, 1961; children: Betsy, Bruce, Lynn. BSL, Northwestern U., 1954, JD, 1956. Bar: Ill. 1956. Sr. ptnr. Pavalon & Gifford, Chgo., 1970—; mem. com. on discovery rules Ill. Supreme Ct., 1981—; lectr., mem. faculty various law schs.; bd. dirs. ATLA Mut. Ins. Co. Former mem. state bd. dirs. Ind. Voters Ill; bd. overseers Inst. Civil Justice, Rand Corp., 1993—; mem. vis. com. Northwestern U. Law Sch., 1990-96. Capt., USAF, 1956-59. Fellow Am. Coll. Trial Lawyers, Internat. Soc. Barristers, Internat. Acad. Trial Lawyers, Roscoe Pound Found. (life fellow, pres. 1988-90); mem. ABA, Chgo. Bar Assn. (bd. mgrs. 1978-79), Ill. Bar Assn., Ill. Trial Lawyers Assn. (pres. 1980-81), Trial Lawyers for Pub. Justice (founding mem., v.p. 1991-92, pres.-elect 1992-93, pres. 1993-94), Assn. Trial Lawyers Am. (parlimentarian 1983-84, sec. 1984-85, v.p. 1985-86, pres. elect 1986-87, pres. 1987-88), Am. Bd. of Profl. Liability Attys. (diplomate), Chgo. Athletic Assn., Standard Club. Author: Human Rights and Health Care Law, 1980, Your Medical Rights, 1990; contbr. articles to profl. jours., chpts. in books. Home: 1540 N Lake Shore Dr Chicago IL 60610-1623 Office: Pavalon & Gifford 2 N La Salle St Chicago IL 60602-3702

PAVÃO, LEONEL MAIA (LEE PAVÃO), advertising executive; b. Fall River, Mass., Jan. 30, 1934; s. Leonel M. and Maria (Raposo) P.; m. Joan Frances Hersey, Oct. 4, 1957; children: Mark, Christopher, Leah, Sarah. BS in Advt. Design, U Mass., Dartmouth, 1956. Art dir. to creative dir. J. Walter Thompson, N.Y., Holland, Miami, Spain, 1956-70; ptnr. Powers & Pavão, N.Y.C., 1970-73; v.p., nat. creative dir. JWT Brazil, 1974-76; mng. dir. J. Walter Thompson, Lima, Peru, 1976-80; pres., chief exec. officer J. Walter Thompson, São Paulo, Brazil, 1980-88; dir. J. Walter Thompson, worldwide, 1982-88; pres. Latin Am. region J. Walter Thompson, 1985-88; pres. Lee M. Pavão, Chapel Hill, N.C., 1988—. Designer U.S. stamp design Nat. Grange, 1967. Chair Chapel Hill Parks and Recreation Commn., 1990-93, chair, 1991-93; mem. exec. bd. Friends of Sr. Ctr., Chapel Hill, 1991-93; chair Space Location and Design Requirements Commn., 1991-96; vice chair exec. bd. The Childhood Trust serving dept. psychiatry U. N.C., Chapel Hill, 1990-93, chair, 1993-95, chair long range planning com., 1991-92; mem. Commodores Club, permanent sec., JWT archives endowment Duke U., 1989—; mem. Task Force on Aging, Orange County, 1990-91, Chapel Hill Town Coun., 1993—; bd. dirs. Chapel Hill/Orange County Visitors Bur., 1993, vice chair, 1994, chair, 1996; mem. Chapel Hill Mus. Study Com., 1994; bd. dirs. Ronald McDonald House, Chapel Hill, 1996—. With U.S. Army, 1957-59. Named Personality of Yr., Rio de Janeiro Stock Exch. Mag., 1983, Bursinessman of Yr., São Paulo Chamber, 1984; recipient Tendecia award Bloch Editors, Rio de Janeiro, 1984, Advt. Man of Yr. columnist's award Brazil, 1986, Outstanding Achievement in Bus. award McGraw Hill and Madia Assocs., 1987. Mem. Am. Chamber São Paulo, Am. Chamber Lima Peru (dir. 1977-79, distinction award 1979), Carolina Club, U.N.C., Chapel Hill, N.Y. Athletic Club (N.Y.C.), N.Y. Athletic Quarter Century Club, Lima Golf Club, San Francisco Golf Club São Paulo. Avocations: golf; photography; antique and classic car collecting. Office: 1507 E Franklin St Ste 35 Chapel Hill NC 27514-2887

PAVAROTTI, LUCIANO, lyric tenor; b. Modena, Italy, Oct. 12, 1935; s. Fernando and Adele (Venturi) P.; m. Adua Veroni, Sept. 30, 1961; children—Lorenza, Cristina, Giuliana. Diploma magistrale, Istituto Magistrale Carlo Sigonio, 1955; studies with, Arrigo Pola, Ettore Campogalliani. Formerly tchr. elem. schs.; salesman ins. Debut as Rodolfo in La Bohème, Reggio Emilia, Italy, 1961; roles include Edgardo in debut Lucia di Lammermoor, Amsterdam, 1963, the Duke in debut Rigoletto,Carpi, 1961, Rodolfo in La Bohème, Covent Garden, 1963, Tonio in debut The Daughter of the Regiment, Covent Garden, 1966, appeared in Lucia di Lammermoor, Australia, 1965, Am. debut, Miami, Fla., 1965; numerous European performances including Italy, Vienna Staatsoper, Paris; performed with San Francisco Opera, 1967, debut, Met. Opera, N.Y.C., 1968; appeared in The Daughter of the Regiment, Met. Opera, 1971, Elisir d'Amore, Met. Opera, 1973, La Bohème, Chgo. Opera, 1973, La Favorita, San Francisco Opera, 1973, Il Trovatore, San Francisco Opera, 1975, Bellini I Puritani, Met. Opera, 1976, Ponchielli La Gioconda, San Francisco Opera, 1979, Aida, San Francisco Opera, 1981, Mozart, Idomeneo, Met. Opera, 1982, Verdi, Ernani, Met. Opera, 1983, Tosca, Met. Opera, 1995; numerous internat. performances including La Scala, Milan, Hamburg, Teatro Colon, Buenos Aires, Australian Opera, Sydney; concert series of Am. and internat. cities, including Carnegie Hall, 1973, Buenos Aires, Moscow, Beijing, Hong Kong, Tokyo, including arena concerts, Madison Square Garden, 1984, and major cities in America, Europe, South America; appeared in film Yes, Giorgio, 1983; established Opera Co. of Philadelphia/Luciano Pavarotti Vocal Competition, 1980; rec. artist on Winner Concorso Internationale, Reggio Emilia, 1961, Amore, 1992, Pavorotti and Friends, 1993, Ti Amo-Puccini's Greatest Love Songs, 1993, Pavarotti and Friends 2, 1995; appeared in PBS TV spl. (with Placido Domingo & Jose Carreras) The Three Tenors, 1994. Named Artist of Yr. Gramophone, 1992; recipient Grammy award, 1981, 1988. Office: care Herbert Breslin 119 W 57th St New York NY 10019-2303*

PAVEN, NATHAN SAMUEL, lawyer; b. Malden, Mass., Aug. 17, 1925; s. Morris and Leah Paven; m. Ruth Marshall, June 22, 1952; children: Nathalie, Melissa Paven-Paquette, Andrew. AB, Harvard Coll., 1948, LLB, 1951. Bar: Mass. 1951, U.S. Dist. Ct. Mass. 1954, U.S. Ct. Appeals (1st cir.) 1958. Atty., advisor Office of Price Stabilization, Washington, 1951-53; assoc. Schlesinger & Manuelian, Boston, 1953-55; ptnr. Mason & Paven, Boston, 1955-71, Flamm, Paven & Feinberg, Boston, 1971-83, Paven & Norton, Braintree, Mass., 1983—; asst. atty. gen. Mass. Office of Atty. Gen., Boston, 1958-60, spl. asst. atty. gen., 1960-64. Mem. Mass. Consumer Coun., 1963-67. With U.S. Army, 1943-45, ETO. Democrat. Office: Paven & Norton 10 Forbes Rd Braintree MA 02184-2605

PAVILANIS, VYTAUTAS, microbiology educator, physician; b. Kaunas, Lithuania, June 7, 1920; s. Kazys and Antonina (Eimontas) P.; m. Irene Stencelis, Mar. 8, 1947; children: Alain, Christine Gaputis, Marina Pavilanis Branigan, Ingrid. MD, U. Kaunas, 1942; diploma in microbiology, Institut Pasteur, Paris, 1947, diploma in serology and hematology, 1948; hon. doctorate, U. Que., 1988, 89. Asst. prof. pathology U. Kaunas, 1942-44; resident physician Siegburg, Germany, 1944-45; asst. Institut Pasteur, Paris, 1945-48; asst. prof. U. Montreal, Can., 1948; head virus dept. Institut Armand-Frappier, Ville de Laval, Que., Can., 1948-75; sci. dir. Institut Armand-Frappier, 1970-75, research coordinator, 1975-78, dir. quality control, 1976-79, asst. dir. teaching and research, 1978-82; assoc. prof. U. Montreal, 1956-85, prof. emeritus, 1985—; prof. U. Que., 1974-85, prof. emeritus, 1985—; cons. in field. Contbr. articles to profl. jours. Recipient Queen's Jubilee medal Can., 1977, Prix d'excellence Province of Que., 1993. Fellow Royal Soc. Can., Royal Coll. Physicians (Can.); mem. Can. Soc. Microbiology (2d v.p. 1966, award 1984), Can. Public Health Assn. (chmn. lab. sect. 1969), Virology Club Montreal (pres. 1969), Coll. Physicians and Surgeons P.Q., Can. Med. Assn., Can. Assn. Med. Microbiologists, Soc. Microbiology P.Q., N.Y. Acad. Sci. Home: 4742 The Boulevard, Westmount, PQ Canada H3Y 1V3 Office: PO Box 100, Laval, PQ Canada H7N 4Z3

PAVIN, COREY, professional golfer. mem. Ryder Cup Team, 1993. PGA Tour top U.S. golfer, leading money winner, 1991, 6th on PGA Tour 1992; Tour Wins include: Honda Classic, 1992, L.A. Open, 1994, Nissan Open, 1995, U.S. Open, 1995. Address: care PGA Tour 112 Tpc Blvd Ponte Vedra Beach FL 32082-3046*

PAVLIK, JAMES WILLIAM, chemistry educator; b. Chgo., Sept. 22, 1937; s. Victor William and Rose (Jaros) P.; m. children—Claire, David, Anne. A.B., Carthage Coll., 1959; M.S., Va. Poly. Inst. and State U., 1961; Ph.D., George Washington U., 1970. Asst. prof. chemistry Haile Sellasie I U., Addis Ababa, Ethiopia, 1967-69; research scientist George Washington U., Washington, 1969-70; from asst. prof. to assoc. prof. chemistry U. Wis., River Falls, 1970-74; prof. chemistry Worcester Poly. Inst., Mass., 1974—; cons. in field. Contbr. articles to profl. jours. Recipient Award for Outstanding Teaching, Worcester Poly. Inst., 1981. Mem. Am. Chem. Soc., Inter-Am. Photochem. Soc., Sigma Xi. Home: 11 Sawyer Rd Northborough MA 01532-1353 Office: Dept Chemistry Worcester Poly Inst Institute Rd Worcester MA 01609-2706

PAVLIK, NANCY, convention services executive; b. Hamtramck, Mich., July 18, 1935; d. Frank and Helen (Vorobojoff) Phillips; m. G. Edward Pavlik, June 30, 1956; children: Kathleen, Christine, Laureen, Michael, Bonnie Jean. Student, U. Ariz., 1956-80. Exec. sec. Mich. Bell, Detroit, 1951-56, RCA, Camden, N.J., 1956-58; owner, pres. Southwest Events Etc., Scottsdale, Ariz., 1969—. Chmn. hospitality industry com. Scottsdale City Coun., 1989—; bd. dirs. Scottsdale Curatorial Bd., 1987-89. Mem. Soc. Incentive Travel Execs., Meeting Planners Internat., Am. Soc. Assn. Execs., Indian Arts and Crafts Assn., Scottsdale C. of C. (bd. dirs., tourism steering com. 1984-88), Contemporary Watercolorists Club. Democrat. Roman Catholic. Avocations: watercoloring, Indian arts, crafts. Home: 15417 Richwood Fountain Hills AZ 85268 Office: SW Events Etc 8233 E Paseo Del Norte A-600 Scottsdale AZ 85258

PAVLIK, WILLIAM BRUCE, psychologist, educator; b. Cleve., Feb. 29, 1932; s. William Frank and Mary (Maco) P.; m. Mary Katherine Findley, May 22, 1979; children by previous marriage: William James, Heather Ann,

Russell Matthew, James Clark; 1 child, Amelia Katherine. B.S., Western Res. U., 1953; M.A., Ohio State U., 1955, Ph.D., 1956. Asst. prof. psychology Western Mich. U., 1956-60; asst. prof., then asso. prof. Rutgers U., 1960-68; prof. psychology Va. Poly. Inst. and State U., 1968-77, chmn. dept., 1968-72; prof. psychology U. Ga., Athens, 1977-94; ret., head dept., 1977-84. Author articles in field. Mem. Eastern Psychol. Assn., Southeastern Psychol. Assn. (pres. 1985-86), Psychonomic Soc. Home: 555 Forest Rd Athens GA 30605-3823

PAVONY, WILLIAM H., retail executive; b. Bklyn., Mar. 1, 1940; s. Harry and Mollie (Leibell) P.; m. Geraldine Rice, June 10, 1961; 1 child, Sheryl. BBA cum laude, Hofstra U., 1960. CPA, N.Y., Tex. Mgr. Arthur Andersen & Co. Inc., N.Y.C., 1960-73; group sr. v.p. Purolator Svcs. Inc., New Hyde Park, N.Y., 1973-75; v.p., contr. Purolator Inc., Piscataway, N.J., 1975-78; sr. v.p. Zale Corp., Dallas, 1978-85; sr. v.p. fin., chief fin. officer Alexander's Inc., N.Y.C., 1985-88, exec. v.p., chief fin officer, 1988-89; exec. v.p. adminstrn. The Kobacker Co., Columbus, Ohio, 1989-93; also bd. dirs.; exec. v.p. Arthur Rutenberg Homes, Clearwater, Fla., 1993-94; CFO Color Tile, Inc., Ft. Worth, 1994—. Treas., bd. dirs. Tex. Vis. Nurses Assn., Dallas, 1984-85. Mem AICPA, Fin. Execs. Inst. (past bd. dirs. North Tex. chpt., sec. Columbus chpts.), N.Y. Soc. CPAs, Inst. Mgmt. Accts. Home: 7308 Monticello Pky Colleyville TX 76034-6856*

PAVSEK, DANIEL ALLAN, banker, educator; b. Cleve., Jan. 18, 1945; s. Daniel L. and Helen A. (Femec) P.; m. M. Ellen Canfield, Apr. 11, 1980 and July 26, 1985 (div. Sept. 1981 and Aug. 1989). A.B., Maryknoll Coll., Glen Ellyn, Ill., 1966; M.A., Maryknoll Sch. Theology, Ossining, N.Y., 1971, Cleve. State U., 1972; Ph.D., Case Western Res. U., 1981. Pres. Council Richmond Heights, Ohio, 1972-75; lectr. econs. Cleve. State U., 1972-75; asst. prof. Baldwin-Wallace Coll., Berea, Ohio, 1975-81; v.p., economist Ameritrust Co., Cleve., 1981-91; dean, prof. econs. Harry F. Byrd Jr. Sch. Bus. Shenandoah U., Winchester, Va., 1992—; adj. prof. bus. adminstrn. Baldwin-Wallace Coll., Berea, Ohio, 1981-91. Mem. Am. Econ. Assn., Nat. Tax Assn., Pub. Choice Soc., Nat. Assn. Bus. Econs. Democrat. Home: 231 Woodberry Ln Apt 119 Winchester VA 22601-3592

PAWELEC, WILLIAM JOHN, retired electronics company executive; b. Hammond, Ind., Feb. 15, 1917; s. John and Julia (Durnas) P.; BS in Acctg., Ind. U., 1939; m. Alice E. Brown, May 30, 1941 (dec. Dec. 1970); children: William John, Betty Jane Pawelec Conover; m. 2d, June A. Shepard, Nov. 27, 1976 (div. June 1980). Statistician, Ind. State Bd. Accounts, 1939-41; with RCA, 1941—, mgr. acctg. and budgets internat. div., 1957-61, controller internat. div., 1961-68, corp. mgr. internat. fin. ops. and controls, 1968-75, mgr. corp. acctg., 1975-77, dir. internat. acctg., 1977-81, ret., 1981; controller RCA Internat., Ltd., Electron Ins. Co., 1977, RCA Credit Corp., 1979; ret., 1981. Active Westfield United Fund, 1967—. Mem. Nat. Assn. Accts. (past nat. v.p.), Watchung Power Squadron, N.J. State C. of C., Commerce and Industry Assn. N.Y., Stuart Cameron McLeod Soc., Ind. U. Alumni Assn. (pres. N.J. chpt.), Beta Gamma Sigma, Sigma Epsilon Theta, Echo Lake Country Club. Home: 86 New England Ave Summit NJ 07901

PAWLEY, RAY LYNN, zoological park herpetology curator; b. Midland, Mich., Nov. 7, 1935; s. Lynn Richard and Alice Marie (Skelton) P.; m. Ethel Marie Condon, Feb. 19, 1955 (div. 1974); children: Ray Allyn, Shanna Sue, Cynthia Ann, Dawn Marie, Brandon Earl, Dareen Joy. Student in zoo adminstrn., Mich. State U., 1954-57. Asst. curator/lectr. Black Hills Reptile Gardens, Rapid City, S.D., summers 1952-53; owner, adminstr. Reptile Exhibit, St. Ignace, Mich., 1957-59; animal coord. Marlin Perkin's Wild Kingdom (Don Meier Prodns.), Chgo., 1961-62; zoologist Lincoln Park Zool. Gardens, Chgo., 1961-64; curator Brookfield (Ill.) Zoo, 1964—; assoc. dept. zoology Field Mus. Natural History, Chgo.; internat. zoo and conservation cons., Russia, Latvia, Mex., Kenya, China, Ecuador, Czechoslovakia; past instr. herpetology Field Mus., Coll. of DuPage, Triton Coll.; info. resource for fed. and state wildlife agys.; lectr., cons. in field. Contbr. oer 50 articles to profl. jours. and popular mags.; co-creator money bench Chgo. Children's Mus. Immediate past v.p. Ill. Endangered Species Protection Bd., Springfield; liaison Endangered Species Tech. Adv. Com., Springfield. Mem. Am. Zoo Assn. (3d Outstanding Svc. awards), Internat. Herpetological Alliance (officer), Chgo. Acad. Scis. (life), Chgo. Herpetological Soc. (life, cons.), Mensa. Avocations: hiking, archaeology, art, mechanics, paleontology. Home: PO Box 218 Hinsdale IL 60522-0218 Office: Chicago Zool Park Brookfield IL 60513

PAWLICZKO, GEORGE IHOR, academic administrator; b. Rochester, N.Y., Oct. 26, 1950; s. Roman and Irene Olha (Zubryckyj) P.; m. Ann Maria Lencyk, June 10, 1978. BA, St. John Fisher Coll., 1972; MA, Fordham U., 1974, MBA, 1986, PhD, 1989. Admissions counselor Fordham U., Bronx, N.Y., 1977-78; asst. dean Grad. Sch. of Bus. Fordham U., N.Y.C., 1978-81; asst. to pres., dir. mgmt. info. systems Marymount Coll., Tarrytown, N.Y., 1981-82; exec. dir. N.Y. Inst. Credit, N.Y.C., 1982-94, Am. Inst. Banking of Greater N.Y., N.Y.C., 1994—. Trustee St. Andrew's Ch., Hamptonburgh, N.Y., 1986—. Mem. Shevchenko Scientific Soc., Beta Gamma Sigma, Phi Alpha Theta. Office: Am Inst Banking of Greater NY 80 Maiden Ln New York NY 10038-4811

PAWLOSKI, SCOTT JACOB, civil engineer; b. Farmington, Mich., Aug. 6, 1966; s. Alger John and Sharon Ruth (Schumacher) P.; 1 child, Alicia Rene. BSCE cum laude, Mich. Tech. U., 1988. Registered profl. engr., Mich. Asst. engr. Alcona County Rd. Commn., Lincoln, Mich., 1986-87, Sanilac County Rd. Commn., Sandusky, Mich., 1989-93; staff engr. R.S. Scott Assocs., Inc., Alpena, Mich., 1993-94, project mgr., 1994—; county hwy. engr. Montmorency County Rd. Commn., Atlanta, Mich., 1994—. Judge awards presentation Jr. Achievement N.E. Mich., Alpena, 1995. Mem. NSPE, Mich. Soc. Profl. Engrs., Chi Epsilon. Home: 4649 Bean Creek Rd Lachine MI 49753 Office: R S Scott Assocs Inc 405 River St Alpena MI 49707

PAWLSON, LEONARD GREGORY, physician; b. Victoria, Tex., 1943. MD, U. Pitts., 1969; MPH, U. Wash., 1976. Diplomate Am. Bd. Internal Medicine. Intern, affiliate hosps. Stanford U., 1969-70, resident in medicine, 1970-71; fellow in endocrinology U. Wash., 1973-75, Robert Wood Johnson clin. scholar, 1975-76; asst. prof. medicine and health care scis. George Washington U., Washington, 1976-80, assoc. prof. med. and health care scis., 1980-85, prof. health care scis., medicine, and health svcs. mgmt. and policy, 1985—, assoc. chmn. dept. health care scis., 1978-90, Mudoch head prof. preventive medicine, 1995—, acting chmn., 1987-90, chmn., 1990—; attending physician George Washington Hosp., 1976—. Robert Wood Johnson health policy fellow, 1986-87; bd. dirs. Bon Secours Hosp. System, 1993—, U.S. Soliders and Airmans Home, 1992—. Robert Wood Johnson health policy fellow, 1986-87. Mem. ACP, Am. Geriatrics Soc. (past pres. and chmn. bd., editor law and pub. policy sect. Jour. Am. Geriatrics Soc.); mem. Soc. Gen. Internal Medicine (past bd. dirs.), Assn. Tchrs. Preventive Medicine (chair pub. policy com.). Office: George Washington U Med Ctr Dept Health Care Scis 2150 Pennsylvania Ave NW Washington DC 20037-2396

PAWSON, ANTHONY J., molecular biologist. Sr. scientist Samuel Lunenfeld Rsch. Inst., Toronto, Ont., Can. Recipient Internat. award Gairdner Found., 1994. Fellow Royal Soc. London, Royal Soc. Can. Office: Samuel Lunenfeld Rsch Inst, 600 University Ave, Toronto, ON Canada M5G 1X5

PAWULA, KENNETH JOHN, artist, educator; b. Chgo., Feb. 4, 1935; s. John and Clara (Brzezinski) P.; student Northwestern U., 1956, Art Inst. Chgo., 1956; B.F.A., U. Ill., 1959; M.A. in Painting, U. Calif., Berkeley, 1962. Graphic designer Motorola, Inc., Chgo., 1959-60; grad. asst. printmaking U. Calif., Berkeley, 1961-62, asso. in art, 1962-63; archaeol. delineator for Islamic excavation Am. Research Center, Egypt, 1964-65; instr. Sch. of Art, U. Wash., Seattle, 1965-67, asst. prof., 1967-73, asso. prof., 1974—; participant artist-in-residence program of Ecole Superieure Des Beaux-Arts D'Athenes at Rhodos Art Center, Greece, 1978; cons. to Wydawnictwo Interpress, Warsaw, Poland, 1978; mem. art jury ann. painting, drawing and sculpture show Art Mus. of Greater Victoria, Can., 1971, Unitarian Art Gallery, Seattle, 1968, Cellar Gallery, Kirkland, Wash., 1968, Lakewood Artist's Outdoor Exhibit, Tacoma, Wash., 1968; participant Painting Symposium, Janow Podlaski, Poland, 1977. One-man shows of paintings include: Univ. Unitarian Fine Arts Gallery, Seattle, 1970, Polly Friedlander Gallery, Seattle, 1970, Lynn Kottler Galleries, N.Y.C., 1971, U. Minn. Art Gallery, Mpls., 1971, Art Mus. of Greater Victoria, Can., 1972, Second Story Gallery, Seattle, 1972, Yuuhigaoka Gallery Osaka, Japan, Universidade Federal Fluminense Niteroi, Rio de Janiero, Brazil, 1990, Pyramid Gallery, N.Y.C., 1991; group shows include: Worth Ryder Gallery, U. Calif., Berkeley, 1962, Seattle Art Mus., 1964, 70, 65, 66, Frye Art Mus., Seattle, 1966, San Francisco Art Ins., 1966, Henry Gallery, U. Wash., Seattle, 1966, 67, 70, State Capitol Mus., Olympia, Wash., 1967, Attica Gallery, Seattle, 1967, 69, Sec. of State's Office, Olympia, 1968, Eastern Mich. U., Ypsilanti, 1968, Rogue Gallery, Medford, Oreg., 1968, Marylhurst Coll., Oreg., 1968, Spokane Art Mus., 1968, Cheney Cowles Mus., Spokane, 1969, Jade Gallery, Richland, Wash., 1969, Alaska U., 1970, Polly Friedlander Gallery, Mpls., 1971, Anchorage Art Mus., 1972, U. Nev. Art Gallery, 1972, Juneau (Alaska) Art Mus., 1972, Springfield (Mo.) Art Mus., 1973, U. N.D., Grand Forks, 1974, Washington and Jefferson Coll., Washington, Pa., 1975, MacMurray Coll., Jacksonville, Ill., 1976, Gallery of Fine Arts, Eastern Mont. Coll., 1976, Inst. of Culture, Janow Podlaski, Poland, 1977, Seattle Arts Commn., 1978, Polish Cultural Center, Buffalo, 1979, Cabo Frio Internat. Print Biennial, Brazil, 1983, Sunderland (Eng.) Poly. U. Faculty Exchange Exhbn., 1984, Internat Art Biennial Mus. Hosio Capranica-Viterbo, Italy, 1985; represented in permanent collections: San Francisco Art Mus., Seattle Art Mus., Henry Gallery, U. Wash., Seattle, Highline Coll., Midway, Wash., Marylhurst Coll., Art Mus., Janow Podlaski, Poland, Tacoma Nat. Bank, Fine Arts Gallery of San Diego. Mem. Coll. Art Assn., AAUP. Home: 2242 NE 177th St Seattle WA 98155-5241 Office: U Wash Coll Arts & Scis Sch Art Dm # 10 Seattle WA 98195

PAXON, L. WILLIAM, congressman; b. Buffalo, Apr. 29, 1954; s. Leon W. and Mary P. (Sellers) P. BA, Canisius Coll., 1977. Mem. Erie County Legis., N.Y., 1978-82, N.Y. State Assembly, 1983-89, 101st-104th Congresses from 31st (now 27th) N.Y. dist., 1989—; chair Nat. Rep. Congrl. Com.; mem. com. on commerce. Mem. Buffalo C. of C., Lions. Roman Catholic. Youngest mem. in history of Erie County Legislature. Office: US Ho of Reps 2436 Rayburn HOB Washington DC 20515-3227 also: 5500 Main St Williamsville NY 14221-6737*

PAXSON, LOWELL WHITE, television station executive; b. Rochester, N.Y., Apr. 17, 1935; s. Donald Earl and Maybelle L. (White) P.; m. Jean Louise Blauvelt, May 2, 1961 (div. Apr. 1977); children: Todd L., Devon W., Julie; m. Barbara Ann Chapman, Nov. 19, 1977 (div. Nov. 1988); children: Thomas, Jennifer; m. Marla J. Bright, Jan. 6, 1990; 1 child, Nicole. BA, Syracuse U., 1956. Pres., owner Sta. WACK-AM, Newark, N.Y., 1957-61, Sta. WKSN-AM/FM, Jamestown, N.Y., 1961-68, Sta. WNYP-TV, Jamestown, 1966-68, Sta. WTBY-AM, Waterbury, Conn., 1968-70, Sta. WYND-AM, Sarasota, Fla., 1968-74, Sta. WAVS-AM, Ft. Lauderdale, Fla., 1973-77, Sta. WWQT-AM, Clearwater, Fla., 1977-83, Sta. WHBS-FM, Holiday, Fla., 1977-83; pres. Full Circle Mktg., Fla., 1968-77; founder, pres emeritus Home Shopping Network, St. Petersburg, Fla., 1982-91; founder, pres. Paxson Broadcasting, St. Petersburg and Clearwater, 1991—; owner WHPT-FM/WHNX-AM, St. Petersburg, 1991—, WWNX-AM/FM, Orlando, WROO-FM, Jacksonville, Fla., WTZA-FM, Miami, Fla., WLVE-FM, Miami; operator WMGF-FM, Orlando, WVRI-FM, Orlando, WAIA-FM, Jacksonville, WZNZ-AM, Jacksonville, WNZS-AM, Jacksonville. Trustee Milligan Coll., Tenn., 1987—; bd. dirs. Broadcap, Washington, 1986—; mem. Coun. of 100 of Pinellas County, St. Petersburg, 1985—; chmn. City of Sarasota Planning and Zoning Commn., 1970-74. Capt. U.S. Army, 1956-57. Mem. Nat. Assn. Broadcasters, Nat. Cable TV Assn., Direct Mktg. Assn. Am., Roebling Soc. Republican. Avocations: yachting, deep sea fishing. Home: 700 Spottis Woode Ln Clearwater FL 34616-5266 Office: Paxson Broadcasting 18401 Us Highway 19 N Clearwater FL 34624-1739 also: Sta WMGF-FM 2500 Maitland Center Pky Maitland FL 32751-7224

PAXSON, RICHARD, newspaper editor. Editor Va. news desk, Va. weeklies The Washington Post. Office: The Washington Post 1150 15th St NW Washington DC 20071-0001

PAXTON, ALICE ADAMS, artist, architect and interior designer; b. Hagerstown, Md., May 19, 1914; d. William Albert and Josephine (Adams) Rosenberger; m. James Love Paxton Jr., June 26, 1942 (div.); 1 child, William Allen III (dec.). Student, Peabody Inst. Music, Balt., 1937-38; grad., Parson's Sch. Design, N.Y., 1940; studies with J. Laurie Wallace, 1944-46; studies with Augustus Dunbier, 1947-48, Sylvia Curtis, 1949, Milton Wolsky, 1950, Frank Sapousek, 1951. Freelance work archtl. renderings and interior design, N.Y., 1937-40; interior designer, designer spl. furnishings, muralist Orchard and Wilhelm, Omaha, 1940-42; tchr. art classes Alice Paxton Studio, Omaha, 1957-64; tchr. mech. drawing, archtl. rendering and mech. perspective Parson's Sch. Design, N.Y., 1937-40. Designer (interior) Chapel Boys' Town, Nebr., 1942; one-woman show of archtl. renderings Washington County Mus. Fine Arts, Hagerstown, 1944; exhibited group shows at Joslyn Mus., Omaha, 1943-44 (1st place), Ann. Exhbn. Cumberland Valley Artists, Hagerstown, 1945; represented in permanent collections at No. Natural Gas Co. Bldg., Omaha, Swanson Found., Omaha; also pvt. collections; vol. designer, decorator: recreation room Omaha Blood Bank, ARC, 1943, recreation room Creighton U., 1943, lounge psychiat. ward Lincoln (Nebr.) Army Hosp., 1944; planner, color coordinator Children's Hosp., Omaha, 1947, painted murals, 1948, decorated dental room, 1950; designed Candy Stripers' uniforms; painted and decorated straw elephant bag presented to Mrs. Richard Nixon, 1960; contbr. articles and photographs to Popular Home mag., 1958. Co-chair camp and hosp. coms. ARC, 1943-45, mem. county com. to select and send gifts to servicemen, 1943-46; mem. Ak-Sar-Ben Ball Com., Omaha, 1946-48, Nat. Mus. Women in the Arts, The Md. Hist. Soc.; judge select Easter Seal design, Joslyn Mus., 1946; mem. council Girl Scouts U.S., Omaha, 1943-47; spl. drs. chmn. Jr. League, Omaha, 1947-48, chair Jr. League Red Cross fund dr., 1947-48; bd. dirs., vol. worker Creche, Omaha, 1954-56; mem. Omaha Jr. League; chmn. Jr. League Community Chest Fund Dr., 1948-50; co-chair Infantile Paralysis Appeal, 1944; numerous vol. profl. activities for civic orgns., hosps., clubs, chs., community playhouse, and for establishing wildlife sanctuary. Recipient three teaching scholarships Parson's Sch. Design, 1937-40, presdl. citation ARC activities, 1946, 1st prize Ann. Midwest Show Joslyn Mus., 1943. Mem. Associated Artists Omaha (charter), Internat. Platform Assn., U.S. Hist. Soc., Nat. Mus. Women in Arts (charter), Md. Hist. Soc., Fountain Head Country Club. Republican. Episcopalian. Home: 19614 Meadowbrook Rd Hagerstown MD 21742-2519

PAXTON, BILL, actor, writer, director; b. Ft. Worth, May 17, 1955; s. John Lane and Mary Lou (Gray) P; m. Louise Newbury. Student, NYU; studies with Stella Adler, Vincent Chase. Actor: (feature films) Mortuary, 1981, Stripes, 1981, The Lords of Discipline, 1982, Streets of Fire, 1983, Impulse, 1983, Weird Science, 1984, Terminator, 1984, Commando, 1985, Aliens, 1985 (Saturn award Acad. of Sci. Fiction, Fantasy, and Horror Films 1986), Near Dark, 1986, Pass the Ammo, 1987, Next of Kin, 1989, The Last of the Finest, 1990, Navy Seals, 1990, Predator 2, 1990, One False Move, 1992, Hurricane, 1992, The Vagrant, 1992, Indian Summer, 1993, Boxing Helena, 1993, Tombstone, 1993, True Lies, 1994, Frank and Jesse, 1994, Apollo 13, 1995, Twister, 1995, Evening Star, 1996, The Last Supper, 1996, Traveler, 1996 (also prodr.), (TV movies) Deadly Lessons, 1983, The Atlanta Child Murders, 1985, An Early Frost, 1985, (TV mini-series) Fresno, 1986, (TV series) The Hitch-Hiker, 1986; dir. (theatrical short) Fish Heads, 1982 (Spl. Award Melbourne Film Festival 1982); prodr., co-author (theatrical short) Scoop, 1983. Mem. Screen Actors Guild. Address: Banner Entertainment Ste 301 9201 Wilshire Blvd Beverly Hills CA 90210

PAXTON, J. WILLENE, retired university counseling director; b. Birmingham, Ala., Oct. 30, 1930; d. Will and Elizabeth (Davis) P. AB, Birmingham So. Coll., 1950; MA, Mich. State U., 1951; EdD, Ind. U., 1971. Nat. cert. counselor, lic. profl. counselor, Tenn. Dormitory dir. Tex. Tech U., Lubbock, 1951-53; counselor Mich. State U., East Lansing, summer 1951, 52; dir. univ. ctr. and housing SUNY, Fredonia, 1953-56, assoc. dean of students, 1956-57; asst. dean of women U. N.Mex., Albuquerque, 1957-63; dean of women East Tenn. State U., Johnson City, 1963-68, 70-78, dir. counseling ctr., 1978-92; ret., 1992. Sec. adminstrv. bd. Meth. Ch., 1983-86, vice chmn., 1993, chmn., 1994—, chmn. social concerns com., 1991-93, program chmn. Good Timers fellowship, 1994-95, pres. Sunday Sch. class, 1994, chmn. fin. campaign, 1995, chair promotion and publicity, bldg. com., 1996—; tng. dir. Contact Teleministries, Inc., 1983-87, chmn., 1988, 95, vice chmn., 1993-95; bd. dirs. Asbury Cts., 1990—, chmn. policy com., 1994-96. Mem. APA, AAUW (br. pres.), Am. Counseling Assn., Tenn. Psychol. Assn., Assn. Univ. and Coll. Counseling Ctr. Dirs. (conv. planning com. 1991), Am. Coll. Pers. Assn. (media bd., newsletter editor), Nat. Assn. Women Deans, Adminstrs. and Counselors, Tenn. Assn. Women Deans and Counselors (state pres., v.p., program chmn.), East Tenn. Edn. Assn. (chmn. guidance divsn.), East Tenn. State U. Retirees Assn. (bd. dirs. 1994-95, program com., pres.-elect 1996), Gen. Federated Woman's Club (pres. 1980-81, 88-89, 95-96, 2d v.p. 1991-95), Univ. Women's Club (v.p. 1993-94, pres. 1994, 95), Delta Kappa Gamma (chpt. pres. 1974-76, state rec. sec. 1977-79, v.p. 1979-81, chmn. nominating com. 1981-83, chmn. leadership devel. com. 1983-85, internat. rsch. com. 1982-84, chmn. self-study com. 1985-87, com. to study exec. sec. 1987-89, state pres. 1989-91, parliamentarian 1991-93, internat. constn. com. 1992-94, awards com. 1993-95, chmn. internat. conv. meal functions com. 1994, state pers. com. 1995—, state achievement award 1987). Home: 1203 Lester Harris Rd Johnson City TN 37601-3335

PAXTON, LISA ANN, speech language pathologist; b. Laramie, Wyo., Feb. 29, 1968; d. LeRoy Dean and La Donna Mae (Roblyer) Smith; m. Camron Lee Paxton, Aug. 12, 1989; 1 child, Cy Hunter. BGS, Fort Hays State U., 1991, MS, 1992. Lic. speech lang. pathologist, Kans. Speech lang. pathologist N.W. Kans. Ednl. Svc. Ctr., Oakley, 1991-92, Unified Sch. Dist. # 352, Goodland, Kans., 1992—. Mem. Am. Speech Lang. Hearing Assn., Kans. Speech Lang. Hearing Assn. Home: 912 E 4th St Goodland KS 67735-2100

PAXTON, ROBERT OWEN, historian, educator; b. Lexington, Va., June 15, 1932; s. Matthew W. and Nell B. (Owen) P.; m. Sarah Plimpton, Dec. 9, 1983. B.A., Washington and Lee U., 1954, LittD (hon.), 1974; B.A., Oxford (Eng.) U., 1956, M.A., 1961; Ph.D., Harvard U., 1963; DHL (hon.), SUNY, Stony Brook, 1994; DL (hon.), U. Caen, France, 1994. Instr. history U. Calif., Berkeley, 1961-63, asst. prof., 1963-67; asso. prof. SUNY, Stony Brook, 1967-69; prof. history Columbia U., 1969—, chmn. dept., 1980-82, dir. Inst. on West Europe, 1991-95. Author: Parades and Politics at Vichy, 1966, Vichy France: Old Guard and New Order, 1940-44, 1972, Europe in the Twentieth Century, 1975, 2d edit., 1985; co-author: Vichy France and the Jews, 1981; co-editor: De Gaulle and the U.S., 1995. Served with USNR, 1956-58. Decorated chevalier Ordre National des Arts et des Lettres (France), officer Ordre National du Mérite (France); Rhodes scholar, 1954-56; Am. Coun. Learned Socs. fellow, 1974-75; Rockefeller Found. fellow, 1978-79; German Marshall Fund fellow, 1986. Fellow Am. Acad. Arts and Letters; mem. Am. Hist. Assn., Soc. d'histoire moderne, Linnaean Soc. N.Y. (pres. 1978-80). Home: 460 Riverside Dr Apt 72 New York NY 10027-6820 Office: Columbia U Dept History New York NY 10027

PAXTON, RONALD BRENT, aerospace engineer; b. Salt Lake City, Feb. 7, 1947; s. Baker James and Vauna Mae (Leany) P.; m. Lynda Mihlberger, Mar. 19, 1974 (div. Jan. 1990); children: Adam, Tami, Jason, Brett, Amy; m. Karen Rae Richardson Rousselle, Nov. 19, 1993. BS in Mech. Engring., U. Utah, 1976. Lic. profl. engr., bldg. insulation contractor, Utah. Insulation specialist Baker Insulation, Salt Lake City, 1965-69, 71-75, Suprior Insulation Co., Salt Lake City, 1975-76; supr. Propellant and Adhesive Structures Thiokol Corp. Space Divsn., Brigham City, Utah, 1986; with Thiokol Corp., 1976; sr. scientist Grain Structures Thiokol Corp., Utah Tactical Divsn., Brigham City, Utah, 1987-92; grain structural analyst Thiokol Corp. Sci. and Engring., Brigham City, Utah, 1992—. Contbr. propellant grain design and structural analysis of high performance solid rocket motors, publs. in field. Missionary to Navajo Indians, LDS Ch., 1969-71; explorer scout advisor Boy Scouts Am., Brigham City, Utah, 1979-83; FAA lic. pilot, search and rescue pilot for CAP (USAF aux.), Brigham City, Utah, 1985—. Recipient Franklin award Thiokol Corp., 1984, Trailblazer award USN, 1984. Mem. NSPE, Aircraft Owners and Pilots Assn., Exptl. Aircraft Assn., Utah Pilots Assn., NRA, Am. Mensa. Republican. Mem. LDS Ch. Avocations: flying, model building, shooting. Home: 2585 S Tess Pl Perry UT 84302-4142 Office: Thiokol Corp Brigham City UT 84302

PAXTON, TOM, songwriter, entertainer, author; b. Chgo., Oct. 31, 1937; s. George Burton and Esther Hildegard (Peterson) P.; m. Margaret Ann Cummings, Aug. 5, 1963; children: Jennifer Ann, Katherine Claire. BFA, U. Okla., 1959. Rec. artist with Elektra, Flying Fish, Hogeye, Reprise, Vanguard, Mountain Railroad, Pax Records, 1962—; owner Pax Records. Folk artist, U.S., Can., Gt. Brit., Scandanavia, France, Germany, Australia, N.Z., 1960—; albums include Ramblin' Boy, 1964, Ain't That News, 1965, Outward Bound, 1966, Morning Again, 1968, The Things I Notice Now, 1969, Number 6, 1970, The Compleat Tom Paxton, 1971, How Come the Sun, 1971, Peace Will Come, 1972, New Songs for Old Friends, 1973, Something in My Life, 1975, New Songs from the Briar Patch, 1977, Heroes, 1978, Up and Up, 1980, The Paxton Report, 1980, One Million Lawyers...and Other Disasters, 1986, The Marvelous Toy and Other Gallimaufry, 1987, Even a Gray Day, And Loving You, 1987, Politics, 1989, The Authentic Guitar of Tom Paxton, 1989, It Ain't Easy, 1991; author: (children's books) Jennifer's Rabbit, 1988, Belling The Cat, 1990, Englebert the Elephant, 1990, Aesop's Fables Retold in Verse, 1988, Androcles and The Lion, 1991. Bd. dirs. Kerrville Polk Festival, 1990. Mem. ASCAP, AFTRA, Am. Fedn. Musicians, Screen Actors Guild, World Folk Music Assn. (hon. chmn. bd.). Office: Pax Records 19 Railroad Ave East Hampton NY 11937-2471

PAYCHECK, JOHNNY, country western musician; b. Greenfield, Ohio, May 31, 1941. Played with Faron Young, George Jones, Ray Price; songs include A-11, 1965, Heartbreak Tennessee, 1966, The Lovin' Machine, 1966, Apartment No. 9, Touch My Heart, She's All I Got, Someone to Give My Love to, 1972, Love is a Good Thing, 1972, Something About You I Love, 1973, Mr. Lovemaker, 1973, Song and Dance Man, 1973, Slide Off Your Satin Sheets, 1974, I'm the Only Hell Mama Ever Raised, 1974, Take This Job and Shove It, 1974, Maybellene, 1978, You Can Have Her, 1979, You Better Move On, 1980, I Can't Hold Myself in Line, 1981, I Never Got Over You, 1983; albums include Double Trouble (with George Jones), Greatest Hits, Take This Job and Shove It, Armed and Crazy, Everybody's Got a Family, Back On The Job, Mr. Lovemaker.

PAYN, CLYDE FRANCIS, technology company executive, consultant; b. Auckland, New Zealand, Jan. 17, 1952; came to U.S., 1973; s. Phillip Francis and Ngaire Eunice P.; m. Betsy Ann Dannels, June 17, 1978; children: Tamara, Brittany, Erik. Cert., Auckland Inst. Tech., 1971; MBA, Vanderbilt U., 1980. Tech. mgr. Carborundum (N.Z.) Ltd., Auckland, 1968-73; mem. product application tech. staff Carborundum Co., Niagara Falls, N.Y., 1973-78; mgr. product mktg. Universal Abrasives, Phila., 1978-80; bus. mgr., catalyst advocate Johnson Matthey, Inc., Phila., 1980-84; pres. Catalyst Cons., Inc., Phila., 1984—; CEO Catalyst Group, Phila., 1988—. Pres. Hideaway Hill Civic Assn., Maple Glen, Pa., 1988, 89. Mem. AIChE, Am. Chem. Soc., Catalysis Soc., Comml. Devel. Assn., Chem. Mktg. Rsch. Assn., Polymer Mfg. Engrs. Assn. Achievements include development of new process technology, catalyst and product development for petroleum, petrochemical, chemical, polymer and environ. industries. Office: The Catalyst Group Inc PO Box 637 Spring House PA 19477-0637

PAYNE, ALMA JEANETTE, English educator and author; b. Highland Park, Ill., Oct. 28, 1918; d. Frederick Hutton and Ruth Ann (Colle) P. BA, Wooster (Ohio) Coll., 1940; MA, Case Western Res. U., 1941, PhD, 1956. Tchr. English, history, Latin Ohio Pub. Schs., Bucyrus and Canton, 1941-46; from instr. to prof. English and Am. studies Bowling Green (Ohio) State U., 1946-79, dir. Am. studies program, 1957-79, chmn. Am. culture PhD program, 1978-79, prof. emerita English, Am. studies, 1979—; adj. prof. Am. studies U. South Fla., 1982—. Author: Critical Bibliography of Louisa May Alcott, 1980, Discovering the American Nations, 1981; contbr. articles to profl. jours.; editor Nat. Am. Studies Assn. Newsletter; contbr. articles to profl. jours. Nat. Coun. for Innovation in Edn. grantee, Norway, U.S. Embassy and Norwegian Dept. Ch. and State, 1978-79. Mem. AAUW (pres. 1982-84), Soc. Descendants of the Mayflower in Fla. (state treas. 1985), Nat. Am. Studies Assn. (v.p. 1977-79), Phi Beta Kappa, Phi Kappa Phi, Kappa Delta Pi, Alpha Lambda Delta, Zonta. Republican. Presbyterian. Avocations: travel, gardening, baseball, photography, reading. Home and Office: 11077 Orangewood Dr Bonita Springs FL 33923-5720

PAYNE, DONALD M., congressman; b. Newark, July 16, 1934. BA, Seton Hall U. Freeholder Essex County, 1973-78; ins. co. exec., prior to 1989, former v.p. computer forms mfr.; mem. Newark Mcpl. Coun., 1982-89, 101st-104th Congresses from 10th N.J. dist., 1989—; mem. econ. and ednl. opportunity com., mem. internat. rels. com. Chmn. World YMCA Refugee and Rehab. Com., 1973-81; pres YMCA's of USA. Democrat. Office: US Ho of Reps 2244 Rayburn HOB Washington DC 20515-3010 also: 970 Broad St Rm 1435-b Newark NJ 07102-2506*

PAYNE, DOUGLAS DEFREES, cardiothoracic surgeon, educator; b. Dayton, Ohio, Feb. 13, 1940; s. William Gebhart and Elizabeth (Defrees) P.; m. Geraldine Rupp, June 10, 1966. BA, Harvard U., 1962, MD, 1966. Diplomate Am. Bd. Surgery, Am. Bd. Thoracic Surgery. Cardiothoracic surgeon New England Med. Ctr., Boston, 1975—, vice chmn. dept. cardiothoracic surgery, 1985-93, acting chmn. dept. cardiothoracic surgery, 1993-94, chief Divsn. Cariothoracic Surgery, 1994—; assoc. prof. surgery Tufts U., Boston, 1982-90, prof. surgery, 1990—. Lt. col. U.S. Army, 1973-75, Korea. Fellow ACS; mem. Am. Heart Assn., Am. Coll. Chest Physicians. Soc. Thoracic Surgeons, Internat. Soc. for Heart Transplantation, Internat. Cardiovascular Soc. Office: New Eng Med Ctr 750 Washington St Boston MA 02111-1533

PAYNE, EDWARD CARLTON, archbishop; b. Hartford, Conn., Aug. 4, 1928; s. Robert Carlton and Margaret Ilon (Bodnar-Donovan) P. Lic.Th., Santa Maria del Gracia, 1947; Lic.Sac.Th., St. Francis Sem., 1966; B.S., Peoples U., 1973, M.Div., 1976, D.S.M., 1971, D.A.E.H., 1973; D.D., St. Ephrem's Inst., 1974. Ordained deacon, 1947, archdeacon, 1951, presbyter, 1953, priest, 1966, archpriest, 1967; rector's asst. Grace Episcopal Ch., Hartford, Conn., 1947-51; asst. chaplain St. Mary and All Saints Episcopal Ch., Higganum, Conn., 1947-50; chaplain's asst. St. Elizabeth's Episcopal Chapel, Hartford, Conn., 1947-55; dir., prior Order of the Cross, Hartford, Conn., 1951—; rector's asst. Ch. of the Good Shepherd, Hartford, 1951-55, St. James Episcopal Ch., Hartford, 1956-57; rector Holy Cross Old Roman Cath. Ch., Hartford, 1966—; canon Old Cath. Cathedral Ch. of Christ-on-the-Mount, Mariavite-Russian Orthodox Ch., Woodstock, N.Y., 1967-68; sr. pastor Old Roman Cath. Cathedral Ch. of the Holy Saviour, Niagra Falls, N.Y., 1971-81; dean of Conn.-R.I. Old Roman Cath. Ch., 1968-69, bishop of Conn.-R.I., 1969-72, archbishop of New Eng., 1972—, metropolitan, exarch of Ugro-Finnic Peoples,, 1975—; patriarch Old Roman Cath. Hungarian Orthodox Ch. Patriarchate of N. Am., 1975—, Slavonic World Patriarchate of Am. World Patriarchates, 1994—; pastor West Community Ch., East Granby, Conn., 1976—; pres. Council of Bishops, Am. World Patriarchates of Byelorussian-Ukrainian Orthodox Cath. Ch., 1975-78, 94—; staff mem. Open Hearth Mission, Hartford, 1985-91; Patriarchate Hungarian-Slovonic Orthodox, 1994; moderator United Cath. Conf., Boston, 1967-69; interim pastor Christ Cath. Ch. of the Transfiguration, Boston, 1970-72; instr. Independent Cath. Seminarium, 1970—; mem. Synod of No.Am. Old Roman Ch., 1966-85; mem. Commn. on Liturgy and Music, 1968-70; hon. chaplain N.S.K.K. Motorcycle Club, Hartford, Conn., 1974-75; interim organist Our Saviour's Polish Nat. Cath. Ch., Hartford, Conn., 1957, Warburton Community Congregational Ch. (United Ch. of Christ), Hartford, Conn., 1959-60, Hartford Elks Lodge, 1962-64, organist, 1964—; chaplain, organist, counselor Culbro Tobacco Co., Windsor and Simsbury, Conn., 1967, 77-78. Editor: The Silver Cross, 1951—, The Independent Catholic, 1970—, The Associated Traditionalist, 1974-75; Asst. editor: The Augustinian, 1966-70. Chmn. Hartford Area Peter A. Reilly Def. Com., 1974-76; chmn. Bradley J. Ankuda Def. Com., 1977-78. Recipient God and Country award First Hartford Council Area, 1949; recipient cert. of appreciation Quirk Middle Sch., Hartford, Conn., 1978; prelate Order of St. Nicholas, Kent, Eng., 1971; nominee Cmdr. Orthodox Order of St. Gregory the Illuminator, Holy Russian Orthodox Ch. in Exile. Mem. Traditionalist Clergy Assn. (sec. 1974-75), Red Men Club, Elks. Republican. Performer, instr., composer, arranger tenor banjo, mandolin, bugle, piano, organ, and carillon. Office: PO Box 290261 Wethersfield CT 06129-0261 *Be "Furchtlos und Treu" ("Fearless and Faithful"). Never consider yourself to be a failure or you'll be one. Keep on keeping on, no matter what the odds. Go onward and upward, using all stumbling blocks as stepping stones, even though you have to burn bridges so that you don't retreat. And, above all, offer many prayers of thanks to God every day, for that's what the Eucharist means: THANKSGIVING.*

PAYNE, ELIZABETH ANN THOMAS, food service business owner; b. South Pittsburgh, Tenn., Jan. 9, 1951; d. Horace Lee and Elizabeth Pearl (Short) Thomas; m. John Edward Payne, May 9, 1969; children: John Brenton, William Ethan, Amanda Ann. Pvt. student apprentice to chef, Lucerne Sch., Switzerland, 1981-82; cert. in basic mgmt. and supervison, Cooking and Hospitality Inst., Chgo., 1988; apprenticeship to Chrsistine Bryant, 1987-89. Cert. in health svcs.; cert. in mgmt. Marrriott Corp. Mgr. Cheese Keg, Bartlesville, Okla., 1981-83; catering bus. Stavanger, Norway, 1983-85; asst. chef, cons. Coffee and Tea Market, Valparaiso, Ind., 1987-89; catering mgr. Marriott at Samford U., Birmingham, Ala., 1990-92; asst.mgr. R & S Mgmt., Charlotte, N.C., 1993; owner The Art of Food, Birmingham, Ala., 1994—; owner, prop. food svc. delivery and catering bus., Chatom, Ala., 1994—. Photographer travel publ. Fund raiser Tchrs. Orgn., Stavanger, 1984. Republican. Mem. Ch. of Christ. Avocations: antiques, photography, gardening, herbal medicien, fishing. Home and Office: RR 1 Box 75 Bridgeport AL 35740-9729

PAYNE, EUGENE EDGAR, insurance company executive; b. San Antonio, Aug. 9, 1942; s. Eugene Edgar and Louise (Speer) P.; m. Karen S. James, June 10, 1978; children: Kelly Lynn, Katherine Louise, Mary Patricia, Kerry Erin, Kimberley Ann, Thomas Julius. B.S., Tex. A&M U., 1964, M.S., 1965; Ph.D. (research fellow 1968-70), U. Okla., 1970. Mgmt. cons. E.I. DuPont de Nemours Co., Del., 1965-68; dir. mgmt. info. systems, spl. cons. Electronic Data Systems Corp., Dallas, 1970-71; dir. planning and mgmt. systems U. Tex., Dallas, 1971-74; v.p. fin. and mgmt. S.W. Tex. State U., San Marcos, 1974-81; v.p. fin. and adminstrn. Tex. Tech U., 1981-88, Tex. Tech Health Ctr., Lubbock, 1981-88; treas. Tex. Tech U. Found., 1981-88; exec. v.p. Investors Life Ins. of N.Am., Austin, Tex., 1988—, Investors Life of Calif., 1988—, Standard Life Ins. of Miss., 1988—, InterContinental Life of N.J., 1988—; exec. v.p. Family Life Ins. Co., 1991—, Fin. Industries Corp., Austin, Tex., 1991—; cons. in field. Contbr. articles to profl. jours. Vestry, fin. com. St. Christopher's Episc. Ch., 1983-86; chmn. bd. trustees All Saints Episc. Sch., Lubbock, 1985-89, Episc. Sem. of Southwest, Austin, Tex., 1985-89. NDEA fellow, 1969. Mem. Am. Inst. Indsl. Engrs. (Sr.), Inst. Mgmt. Scis., Ops. Research Soc. Am., Assn. Computing Machinery, Assn. Instl. Research, Soc. Coll. and Univ. Planning, Nat. Assn. Coll. and Univ. Bus. Officers, Rotary. Home: 1300 Circle Ridge Dr West Lake Hls TX 78746-3402 Office: FIC Ins Group 701 Brazos St Ste 1400 Austin TX 78701-3232

PAYNE, FLORA FERN, retired social service administrator; b. Carrollton, Mo., Sept. 25, 1932; d. George Earnest and Bernadine Alice (Schaefer) Chrisman; m. H.D. Matticks, Oct. 20, 1950 (div. Oct. 1959); children: Dennis Don, Kathi D.; m. S.L. Freeman, Nov. 25, 1960 (div. Jan. 1973); 1 child, Gary Mark; m. Vernon Ray Payne, Mar. 18, 1988. Student, S.E. C.C., Burlington, Iowa, 1976-77; cert. stenographer, Corr. Sch., Chgo., 1960-61. Social svc. designee Mo. League Nursing, 1991. Sec. to v.p. Moore Co., Marceline, Mo., 1973-75; steno to trainmaster A.T. & S.F. Rlwy. Co., Fort Madison, Iowa, 1975-88; with social svc. Brookfield (Mo.) Nursing Ctr., 1990-95; candidate for Linn County Pub. Adminstr., 1996. Mem. NAFE, Mo. Orgn. Social Svcs. Republican. Avocations: writing poetry, dancing, interior decorating. Home: 205 W 6th St Bucklin MO 64631-9097

PAYNE, FRANCES ANNE, literature educator, researcher; b. Harrisonburg, Va., Aug. 28, 1932; d. Charles Franklin and Willie (Tarvin) P. B.A., Shorter Coll, 1953, B.Mus., 1953; M.A., Yale U., 1954, Ph.D., 1960. Instr. Conn. Coll., New London, 1955-56; instr. U. Buffalo, 1958-60, lectr., 1960, asst. prof., 1960-67; assoc. prof. SUNY, Buffalo, 1967-75; prof. English and medieval lit. SUNY, 1975—; adj. fellow St. Anne's Coll., Oxford, Eng., 1966-67, 68-69. Author: King Alfred and Boethius, 1968; Chaucer and Menippean Satire, 1981. Contbr. articles to scholarly publs. AAUW fellow, Oxford, 1966-67; Research Found. grantee SUNY Central, Oxford, 1967, 68, 71, 72; recipient Julian Park award SUNY-Buffalo, 1979. Mem. Medieval Acad. Am., Internat. Arthurian Soc., New Chaucer Soc., Internat. Soc. Anglo-Saxonists, Pi Kappa Lambda. Office: SUNY-Buffalo 306 Clemens Hall Buffalo NY 14260

PAYNE, FRED R(AY), aerospace engineering educator, researcher; b. Mayfield, Ky., Jan. 26, 1931; s. Joe L. and Bonnie (Vincent) P.; m. Marilyn Maassen, Oct. 12, 1957; children: John P., Kevin R., Joel F. BS in Physics, U. Ky., 1952; MS Aero. Engring., Pa. State U., State College, 1964, PhD, 1966. Registered profl. engr., Tex. Commd. 2d lt. USAF, 1952, advanced through grades to maj., 1966, resigned, 1966; prof. Pa. State U., State Coll., 1966-68; design specialist Gen. Dynamics, Ft. Worth, 1968-69; prof. U. Tex., Arlington, 1969—, aero. engring. grad. advisor, 1973-82, 92-96; bd. dirs. TRL-Aero. Engring., U. Tex., 1972—; organizer profl. confs. Editor Integral Methods in Sci. Engring., 1986-91; editor newsletter Ft. Worth Chess Club, 1973-78, Tex. Chess Assn., 1977-78; contbr. articles to profl. jours. Chess instr. Dan Danciger Community Ctr., Ft. Worth, 1973-77; youth dir. Ft. Worth Chess Club, 1973-78. Rsch. grantee USN, NSF, NASA, 1963-67, 75-91, Orgn. Rsch. Fund, 1975-89; faculty fellow NASA Ames Rsch. Ctr., 1988, 89. Mem. Am. Math. Soc., Am. Phys. Soc., Am. Acad. Mechanics, Soc. for Indsl. and Applied Math., Ky. Chess Club, Tex. Chess Club (pres. 1950-52, 73-75), Sigma Xi (pres. U. Tex.-Arlington chpt. 1990-92). Avocations: chess master (postal), classical music, gardening. Office: U Tex Aerospace Engring Arlington TX 76019

PAYNE, GERALD LEW, physics educator; b. Columbus, Ohio, Mar. 11, 1938; s. Harry Moses and Lucy Loretta (Frabott) P.; m. Candia Walker Draves, Dec. 31, 1963; children: Tracy, Lucy, Karen. BS in Engring., MS in Physics, Ohio State U., 1961; PhD in Physics, U. Calif., San Diego, 1967. Rsch. assoc. U. Md., College Park, 1967-69; asst. prof. physics U. Iowa, Iowa City, 1969-74, assoc. prof., 1974-80, prof., 1980—, chmn. dept. physics and astronomy, 1991—; cons. Los Alamos (N.Mex.) Nat. Lab., 1975—, Lockheed Rsch. Lab., Palo Alto, Calif., 1977-86. Contbr. over 100 articles to profl. jours. Lt. comdr. USN, 1961-64. Fellow NSF, 1965. Fellow Am. Phys. Soc.; mem. AAAS, AAUP, Am. Assn. Physics Tchrs. Democrat. Office: U Iowa 305 Van Dept Physics Iowa City IA 52242

PAYNE, GERALD OLIVER, elementary education educator; b. East St. Louis, Ill., July 17, 1930; s. Amos Oliver and Suzanne Louise (Goussery) P.; m. Nancy Louise Ecklund, Aug. 8, 1959; children: Paul Clifton, Christopher Amos, Scott Eric, Miriam Louise, Susan Jeannette. BA, Yale U., 1953; MusB, U. Dubuque, Iowa, 1957; PhD, U. Wis., 1969. Tchr. pub. schs. Aspen, Colo., 1959-61; tchr. pub. schs. Madison, 1961-65; coord. fgn. langs., 1964-69, asst. dir. curriculum, 1967-69; assoc. prof. edn. SUNY, Buffalo, 1969-71, prof. edn., 1971-86, chmn. dept. curriculum and supervision, 1975-78, coord. cert. advanced studies in adminstrn. and supervision, 1969-75, 78-86, assoc. chmn. dept. elem. edn. and reading, 1985-86; chmn. dept. edn. and psychology Warren Wilson Coll., N.C., 1986-90, chmn. div. social sci. and profl. studies, 1987-90; tchr. Hendersonville County Schs., Hendersonville, N.C., 1990—; Mem. working com. Fgn. Lang. Educators Wis., 1968-69; mem. North Central Evaluation Teams, 1967, 68, 69; cons. Ednl. Prof. Devel. Assistance project Lackawanna (N.Y.) Pub. Schs., 1969-74; coll. rep. Coll. Assn. for Devel. Ednl. Adminstrn., N.Y. State, 1969-84; cons. middle sch. Cheektowaga (N.Y.) Central Schs., 1974; cons. Orchard Park (N.Y.) Middle Sch., 1974-76, Alden (N.Y.) Middle Sch., 1975, Geneva (N.Y.) Middle Sch., 1979. Contbr. articles to profl. jours. Chmn. troop com. Greater Niagara Frontier coun. Boy Scouts Am., Lewiston, N.Y., 1974-76, scoutmaster, 1976-79; advisor Explorer Post, 1979-83, Order of Arrow, 1978-83; elder 1st Presbyn. Ch., Lewiston, 1978-83, 1st Presbyn. Ch., Hendersonville, N.C., 1991-94. Mem. NEA (life), Western N.Y. Yale Alumni Assn. (mem. schs. com. 1972-83, dir. 1977-83), Nat. Middle Sch. Assn., Assn. for Supervision and Curriculum Devel., Phi Delta Kappa (exec. com. 1978-81, sec. 1985-86, pres.-elect 1986). Republican. Lodge: Masons. Home: RR 4 Box 287 Hendersonvlle NC 28739-9442 Office: Hendersonville County Schs 414 4th Ave W Hendersonville NC 28739-4254

PAYNE, GLORIA MARQUETTE, business educator; b. Elkins, W.Va., Dec. 21, 1923; d. Anthony and Roselyn Marquette; m. Carl Wesley Payne, Mar. 6, 1950; 1 child, Mary Debra Payne Moore. BA, Davis and Elkins Coll., MHL (hon.); MA, W.Va. U.; PhD, U. Pitts., 1975; postgrad., NYU Fashion Inst. Tech. Cert. designed appearance cons. Sec. Equitable Ins. Co., Elkins, 1943-44; tchr., dept. head Spencer (W.Va.) High Sch., 1944-45; prof. bus. Davis & Elkins Coll., Elkins, 1945-93; image cons. Elkins, 1988-93, bus. cons., 1970-93; mgr. Elkins Wallpaper Shop, 1945-65; owner Merle Norman Cosmetic Studio, Elkins, 1950-56; dir. tchr. workshops W.Va. U., Marshall U., State Dept. Edn., Charleston, W.Va., summers; dir. machine shorthand workshops for tchrs. throughout the U.S.; dir. designer appearance World Modeling Assn., N.Y.C., 1989—; instr. modeling Davis & Elkins Coll., 1980-93. Author: A Methods Class is Interesting and Challenging, 1970, The Oak or the Pumpkin; mem. editl. bd. Nat. Assn. of Business Teachers Edn. Pub., 1993, 94; contbr. articles to profl. jours. Chair Bi-Centennial, City of Elkins; dir. Elkins Fair, City of Elkins; pres. St. Brendans Parish; judge Mountain State Forest Festival Parades, 1988-94; rep. Region I at Dallas Nat. Conv., 1994 (one of five nat. finalists); div. chair bus., econs., and tourism. Recipient Outstanding Prof. award Sears-Roebuck Co., Lois Latham award for Excelence in Teaching, Community Svc. award Elkins C. of C., 1992, award for Outstanding Educator W.Va. Vocat. Assn., 1994, Region I award for Outstanding Vocational Educator; 1st recipient James S. McDonnell Found. Fully Endowed Acad. Chair in Bus. and Econs.; named Educator of Yr., W.Va. Women's Club, Outstanding Educator AAUW. Mem. Am. Bus. Writers Assn., W.Va. Edn. Assn. (past pres., Outstanding Prof., Outstanding Svc. award, Outstanding Bus. Educator award), Tri-State Bus. Edn. Assn. (historian, outstanding svc. award, Tchr.-Educator of the South award 1991), World Modeling Assn. (v.p. 1988-90, modeling award 1989), Designed Appearance U.S. (dir. 1990-95), W.Va. C. of C., The Fashion Club (advisor), Beta Sigma Phi (advisor), Beta Alpha Beta (advisor), Pi Beta Phi, Phi Beta Lambda (advisor). Democrat. Roman Catholic. Avocations: flower arranging, modeling. Home: 301 Davis St Elkins WV 26241-4030 Office: Davis & Elkins Coll 100 Sycamore St Elkins WV 26241-3996

PAYNE, HARRY CHARLES, historian, educator; b. Worcester, Mass., Mar. 25, 1947. BA, Yale U., 1969, MA, 1969; PhD, 1973; MPhil, Yale U., 1970; hon. degree, Hamilton Coll., 1988, Colgate U., 1989, Williams Coll., 1993, Amherst Coll., 1994. Mem. faculty Colgate U., Hamilton, N.Y., 1973-85, prof. history, 1982-85; provost, acting pres. Haverford (Pa.) Coll., 1985-88; pres. Hamilton Coll., Clinton, N.Y., 1988-93, Williams Coll., Williamstown, Mass., 1994—. Contbr. numerous articles and revs. to scholarly publs. Bd. dirs. Clark Art Inst., Williamstown Theatre Festival, Barnard Coll., Nat. Assn. Ind. Colls. and Univs., Mass. Mus. Contemporary Art. Overseas fellow Churchill Coll., Cambridge U., Eng., 1977. Mem. Am. Soc. 18th-Century Studies (Article prize 1977, pres. 1984-85). Office: Williams Coll Office of Pres Williamstown MA 01267

PAYNE, HARRY MORSE, JR., architect; b. Norwood, Mass., Nov. 3, 1922; s. Harry Morse and Edna May (Beardsley) P.; m. Helen Marion Beasley, Aug. 29, 1946; children: Harry Morse, Thomas Beasley, Amelia Morse. Student, Boston Archtl. Center, 1946-49, MIT, 1949-50. Draftsman William G. Upham, Norwood, 1946-47; designer William Riseman Assos., Boston, 1947-49, Harry J. Korslund, Norwood, 1949-51, William Hoskins Brown, Boston, 1951-52; designer, prin. dir. The Architects Collaborative, Cambridge, Mass., 1952-86; pres. The Architects Collaborative, 1975-77, emeritus, 1986—; emeritus Boston Archtl. Center, 1963-65, 71-73; asst. prof. Harvard U. Grad. Sch. Design, 1954-63. Prin. works include U.S. Embassy, Athens, Greece, U. Baghdad, Iraq, Temple Israel, Boston, Quincy Sch., Boston; author: The Survey System of the Old Colony, 1985, Name Change--Paine to Payne, 1992, Cape Code Land Strategy, 1994. Served with USN, 1943-46. Fellow AIA; mem. Boston Soc. Architects, Mass. State Assn. Architects, New Eng. Hist. and Geneal. Soc., The Colonial Soc. Mass., Mass. Soc. Genealogists (pres. 1986-88), Lincoln Hist. Soc. (pres. 1990-92). Home: 245 Aspen Cir Lincoln MA 01773-4922

PAYNE, HOWARD JAMES, insurance company executive; b. Des Moines, Iowa, Oct. 22, 1940; s. James W. and Wilma F. (Kever) P.; m. Mary J. Kellam, June 8, 1963; children: Scott D., Steven M. MBA, U. Iowa, 1986. CPCU; assoc. in underwriting, assoc. in mgmt. Underwiter Allied Ins. Co., Des Moines, 1963-70; br. underwriting mgr. Allied Ins. Co., Phoenix, 1973-75; asst. br. mgr. Allied Ins. Co., Santa Rosa, Calif., 1975-77; casualty underwriting mgr. Am. States Ins. Co., Indpls., 1970-73; asst. v.p. underwriting Lumberman's Mut. Ins. Co., Mansfield, Ohio, 1977-80; asst. v.p., underwriting mgr. Hastings (Mich.) Mutual Ins. Co., 1980-82; v.p. underwriting John Deere Ins. Co., Moline, Ill., 1982-86, v.p., regional mgr., 1986-90; v.p. credit ins. mgr. John Deere Ins. Co, Des Moines, 1990-93; v.p., spl. program mgr. John Deere Transp., Brookfield, Wis., 1993—; ins. instr. Am. States Ins. Co., Indpls., 1971-73, CPCU chpt., Phoenix, 1973-75; ins. instr. and adviser C.C. Mansfield, Ohio, 1978-80; pres. Am. States Credit Union, Indpls., 1973. Mem. CPCU Soc., West Des Moines C. of C. Republican. Avocations: tennis, physical fitness, reading. Home: 1641A S Coachlight Dr New Berlin WI 53151 Office: John Deere Transp 350 N Sunny Slope Rd Brookfield WI 53005-4846

PAYNE, JAMES RICHARD, environmental chemist; b. Anaheim, Calif., Sept. 3, 1947; s. Theodore L. and Laura P. (Schutz) P.; m. Marinee J. Pavlovich, June 29, 1968; children: Clayton Bennett, Taylor Sierra. BA with honors, Calif. State U., Fullerton, 1969; PhD, U. Wis., 1974. Chemist in engring. coll. unit N.Am. Rockwell Corp., Downey, Calif., 1968-69; tchg. asst., rsch. asst., and NIH predoctoral fellow U. Wis., Madison, 1969-74; postdoctoral scholar Woods Hole (Mass.) Oceanographic Inst., 1974-75; asst. rsch. chemist U. Calif. Bodega Marine Lab., Bodega Bay, 1975-78; sr. chemist, asst. v.p. Sci. Applications Internat. Corp., La Jolla, Calif., 1978-91; sr. v.p., dir. rsch. SOUND Environ. Svcs., Inc., Carlsbad, Calif., 1991—; also bd. dirs. SOUND Environ. Svcs., Inc., Carlsbad; mem. exec. sci. and tech. coun. Sci. Applications Internat. Corp., La Jolla, 1985-91; mem. NAS/NRC Marine Bd.: Com. on Effectiveness of Oil Spill Dispersants, Washington, 1985-88; ind. oil spill cons., Encinitas, Calif., 1991—. Co-author: Fate and Weathering of Petroleum Spills in the Marine Environment: A Literature Review and Synopsis, 1980, Petroleum Spills in the Marine Environment: The Chemistry and Formation of Water-in-Oil Emulsions and Tar Balls, 1985, Oil Spill Dispersants: Mechanisms of Action and Laboratory Tests, 1993. Achievements include participant in two NAS/NRC studies and coms. on oil pollution in the marine environment and the use of oil spill dispersants; research on oil weathering, oil/ice interactions, remediation of hazardous waste sites. Home: 1651 Linda Sue Ln Encinitas CA 92024-2427 Office: Sound Environ Svcs Inc 2236 Rutherford Rd Ste 103 Carlsbad CA 92008-8836

PAYNE, JOHN ROSS, rare books and archives appraisal consulting company executive, library science educator; b. Clarksville, Tex., Dec. 4, 1941. BA, Tex. Christian U., 1963; MLS, North Tex. State U., 1967. Successively acting dir., asst. to dir., assoc. libr. for acquisitions, assoc. libr. for ops., rsch. assoc. Harry Ransom Humanities Rsch. Ctr. U. Tex., Austin, 1969-85, prof. Grad. Sch. Libr. and Info. Sci., 1988-89, 91—, prof. grad. course in rare books and lit. manuscripts, 1989—; dir. Payne Assocs., 1978—. Author: A Bibliography of W. H. Hudson, 1977, Modern British Fiction: An Exhibit, 1972; co-author: (with Elizabeth Johnson) Katherine Mansfield: An Exhibit, 1973, (with Adrian Goldstone) A Bibliographical Catalogue of John Steinbeck, 1975; contbr. articles to profl. jours. Lilly fellow Ind. U., 1967-68. Mem. ALA, Am. Soc. Appraisers (state dep. dir.), Appraisers Assn. Am., Soc. Am. Archivists (hon., speaker at Atlanta meeting 1988), Manuscripts Soc., Tex. Libr. Assn., Tex. State Hist. Assn., Book Club of Tex., Grolier Club, Book Collectors of L.A. Home: 2309 Camino Alto Austin TX 78746-2404

PAYNE, JOYCE TAYLOR GILLENWATER, art specialist, art museum consultant, educator; b. Charleston, W.Va., Oct. 4, 1932; d. Clyde Matthew and Bessie Francis (Summers) Taylor; m. Jack W. Gillenwater, Aug. 26, 1950 (div. Mar. 1980); children: Jack William Gillenwater Jr., Brenda Joyce Gillenwater, Kevin David Gillenwater, Todd Gregory Gillenwater; m. Roy B. Payne Jr., Mar. 19, 1982. BS cum laude, W.Va. State Coll., Institute, 1969; MA in Art Edn., W.Va. U., 1976, psotgrad., 1976-89. Tchr. art Herbert Hoover H.S., Elkview, W.Va., 1970-71, Andrew Jackson Jr. H.S., Cross Lanes, W.Va., 1971-90; art specialist Cabell County Bd. Edn., Huntington, W.Va., 1990-94; instr. art edn. Shawnee State U., Portsmouth, Ohio, 1994—; mem. adv. bd. W.V.a Bd. Edn., Charleston, 1986-87, Kanawha County Bd. Edn., Charleston, 1986. Artist, working in painting, sculpture, pottery, fiber works. Mem. NEA (rep.), W.Va. Edn. Assn., W.Va. Art Edn. Assn., Kanawha County Tchrs. Assn., Kanawha County Art Edn. Assn., Cabell County Tchrs. Assn., Nat. Art Edn. Assn. Avocations: scuba diving, art works, reading, travel. Home: 283 Oakwood Ave Portsmouth OH 45663-8908

PAYNE, KENNETH EUGENE, lawyer; b. Kansas City, Kans., Jan. 12, 1936; s. Felton T. and Irene Elizabeth (Snyder) P.; m. Deidre Lee Hood, Aug. 11, 1957; children: Steven Scott, Kendra Ann. BS, U. Kans., 1959; JD, Am. U., 1965. Bar: Mo. 1965, D.C. 1967. Assoc., Irons, Birch, Swindler & McKie, Washington, 1966-69, Irons, Stockman, Sears & Santorelli, 1969-71; asst. gen. counsel U.S. Dept. Commerce, Washington, 1971-73; ptnr. Finnegan, Henderson, Farabow, Garrett & Dunner, Washington, 1973—; del. Inter-Am. Commn. on Sci. and Tech. Transfer, U.S. Dept. State; cons. UN Indsl. Devel. Orgn.; lectr. Practicing Law Inst., Licensing Law and Bus. Inst. Capt. U.S. Army, 1960-68. Mem. Licensing Execs. Soc. Internat. (treas. 1986-87, pres.-elect 1988, pres. 1989), Licensing Execs. Soc. U.S. and Can. (pres.-elect 1982-83, pres. 1983-84), ABA, Am. Patent Law Assn., Assn. Trial Lawyers Am. Republican. Methodist. Contbr. articles to profl. jours. Home: 4415 33rd St N Arlington VA 22207-4465 Office: Finnegan Henderson Farabow et al 1300 I St NW Ste 700 Washington DC 20005-3314

PAYNE, LADELL, college president; b. Birmingham, Ala., Dec. 6, 1933; s. Clyde Ladell and Martha Gerusia (McBrayer) P.; m. Mary Jean Taylor, Aug. 23, 1954; children: Lisa, Jennifer. BA with honors, Samford U., 1955; MA in English, La. State U., 1956; PhD in English, Stanford U., 1966; LttD, Samford U., 1996. From instr. to prof. English, chmn. dept. lit. and presdl. asst. Claremont McKenna Coll., Calif., 1960-79; pres. Randolph-Macon Coll., Ashland, Va., 1979—; Fulbright lectr. U. Vienna, Austria, 1971-72; nat. cons. Ctr. for Study So. Culture, U. Miss., Oxford, 1980—; adminstrv. assoc. Am. Coun. on Edn., Washington, 1979, mem. nat. panel, commn. on women in higher edn., 1981—; founding mem. pres.'s commn. Nat. Collegiate Athletic Assn., 1984—. Author: Thomas Wolfe, 1969, Black Novelists and the Southern Literary Tradition, 1981; contbr. articles on William Faulkner, Robert Penn Warren, Thomas Wolfe, and Ellen Glasgow to profl. jours. Mem. Va. bd. dirs. NCCJ, 1980-92, chmn. Va. region, Richmond, 1982-85; trustee, mem. exec. com. The Collegiate Schs., Richmond, 1986-89. NEH fellow, 1973. Mem. Nat. Assn. Ind. Colls. and Univs. (bd. dirs. 1990-93), Coun. on Postsecondary Accreditation (bd. dirs. 1991-93), Phi Kappa Phi. Methodist. Avocation: classical music. Office: Randolph-Macon Coll Office of the President Ashland VA 23005

PAYNE, LAWRENCE EDWARD, mathematics educator; b. Enfield, Ill., Oct. 2, 1923; s. Robert Ulysses and Harriet (Lasher) P.; m. Ruth Marian Winterstein, Dec. 27, 1948; children: Steven L., John E., Marcia G., Christopher J., Michele T. Student, Miami U., Oxford, Ohio, 1943-44; B.S. in Mech. Engring, Iowa State U., 1946, M.S. in Applied Math, 1948, Ph.D., 1950; DSc (hon.), Nat. U. Ireland, 1990. Jr. engr. Linde Air Products, North Tonawanda, N.Y., 1946-47; asst. prof. math. U. Ariz., 1950-51; research assoc. U. Md., 1951-52, asst. prof., 1952-55, asso. prof., 1955-60, prof., 1960-65; prof. Cornell U., Ithaca, N.Y., 1965-94; prof. emeritus Cornell U., Ithaca, N.y., 1994—; dir. Center for Applied Math. Cornell U., 1967-71, 76-77, 80-81; Lectr. in field; cons. Nat. Bur. Standards, 1958-65. Mem. editorial bd. Jour. of Elasticity, Applicable Analysis, Math. Methods in the Applied Sciences, Stability and Applied Analysis of Continuous Media; contbr. articles to profl. jours. Served with USNR, 1943-46. Recipient Sci. Achievement Math. award Washington Acad. Scis., 1962, Citation of Merit Iowa State U., 1992; NSF sr. postdoctoral fellow, 1958-59. Mem. Am. Math. Soc. (Steele prize in math. 1972), Soc. Indsl. Applied Math., Am. Acad. Mechanics, Soc. Engring. Sci., Soc. Natural Philosophy, Internat. Soc. for the Interaction Mechanics and Math., Royal Soc. of Edinburgh (elected hon. mem. 1991), Sigma Xi. Office: Cornell U Dept Math Ithaca NY 14853

PAYNE, LESLIE, newspaper editor, columnist, journalist, author; b. Tuscaloosa, Ala., July 12, 1941; m. Violet S. Cameron; children—Tamara Olympia, Jamal Kenyatta, Haile K. B.A., U. Conn., 1964. Reporter Newsday, L.I., N.Y., 1969-73, copy editor, mng. editor, 1973, minority affairs specialist, 1974-77, nat. corr., 1977-81, syndicated columnist, 1980—, nat. editor, 1981-85, asst. mng. editor, 1985—; judge Pulitzer Prize Selection Com., 1983, 84, Emmy Blue-Ribbon Panel, Acad. TV Arts and Scis., 1981, 83. Author: Life and Death of the Symbionese Liberation Army, 1976; co-author: Heroin Trail, 1974. Served to capt. U.S. Army, 1963-69. Decorated Bronze Star; recipient Pulitzer prize, 1974, Tobenkin award Columbia U., 1978, World Hunger Media award UN, 1983, Unity award Lincoln U., Journalism prize Howard U., AP and UPI awards (commentary), 1984, numerous other awards. Mem. Nat. Assn. Black Journalists (pres. 1981-83), Com. to Protect Journalists, Internat. Press Inst. Avocations: painting; softball; mountain climbing. Office: Newsday Inc 235 Pinelawn Rd Melville NY 11747-4226

PAYNE, LEWIS FRANKLIN, JR. (L.F. PAYNE), congressman; b. Amherst, Va., July 9, 1945; m. Susan King; children: Graham, Hunter, Sara, Anna. BA, Va. Mil. Inst., 1967; MBA, U. Va. Mem. 100th-104th Congresses from 5th Va. dist., Washington, 1988—. Democrat. Presbyterian. Office: US Ho of Reps 2412 Rayburn Washington DC 20515

PAYNE, MARY ALICE MCGILL, mental health quality consultant; b. Centreville, Miss., Jan. 2, 1936; d. Robert Malcolm and Alice (Brannon) McGill; m. Donald Ray Payne, Aug. 8, 1958; children: Patricia Alice, Margaret Jean, Donald Paul. Diploma, So. Bapt. Hosp. Sch. Nursing, New Orleans, 1958; BSN, Northwestern State U., 1962, postgrad. Psychiat. nursing instr. McNeese U., Lake Charles, La., 1964-67; drug rsch. nurse dept. psychiatry Med. Sch., Tulane U., New Orleans, 1969-79; psychiat. nurse East La. State Hosp., Jackson, 1959-80; acting CEO Feliciana Forensic Facility, Jackson, 1989, quality assurance dir., 1984-91. Mem. ANA, NAFE, Am. Psychiat. Nurses Assn., Am. Coll. Healthcare Execs. (assoc.), La. State Nurses Assn., Nat. Assn. Healthcare Quality, La. Assn. Healthcare Quality, Bapt. Nursing Fellowship, Feliciana Dist. Nurses Assn., Am. Soc. Quality Control, Nat. League for Nursing. Home: PO Box 144 3226 E College St Jackson LA 70748-0144

PAYNE, MARY LIBBY, judge; b. Gulfport, Miss., Mar. 27, 1932; d. Reece O. and Emily Augusta (Cook) Bickerstaff; m. Bobby R. Payne; children: Reece Allen, Glenn Russell. Student, Miss. Univ. Women, 1950-52; BA in Polit. Sci. with distinction, U. Miss., 1954, LLB, 1955. Bar: Miss. 1955. Ptnr. Bickerstaff & Bickerstaff, Gulfport, 1955-56; sec. Guaranty Title Co., Jackson, Miss., 1957; assoc. Henley, Jones, & Henley, Jackson, Miss., 1958-61; freelance rschr. Pearl, Miss., 1961-63; solo practitioner Brandon, Miss., 1963-68; exec. dir. Miss. Judiciary Commn., Jackson, 1968-70; chief drafting & rsch. Miss. Ho. Reps., Jackson, 1970-72; asst. atty. gen. State Atty. Gen. Office, Jackson, 1972-75; founding dean, assoc. prof. Sch. Law Miss. Coll., Jackson, 1975-78, prof., 1978-94; judge Miss. Ct. Appeals, Jackson, 1995—; adv. bd. Sarah Ison Ctr. Women Studies U. Miss., 1988-95; bd. disting. alumnae Miss. U. Women, 1988-95. Contbr. articles to profl. jours. Founder, bd. dirs. Christian Conciliation Svc., Jackson, 1983-93; counsel Christian Action Com. Rankin Bapt. Assn., Pearl, 1968-92. Recipient Book of Golden Deeds award Pearl Exch. Club, 1989, Excellence medallion Miss. U. Women, 1990; named Woman of Yr. Miss. Assn. Women Higher Edn., 1989. Fellow Am. Bar Found.; mem. Christian Legal Soc. (nat. bd. dirs., regional membership coord.). Baptist. Avocations: public speaking, travel, needlepoint, sewing, reading. Office: Ct Appeals PO Box 22847 Jackson MS 39225

PAYNE, MAXWELL CARR, JR., retired psychology educator; b. Nashville, Feb. 9, 1927; s. Carr and Mary Evans (Tarpley) P.; m. Juanita Campbell, Oct. 17, 1958; children: Maxwell Carr III, Elizabeth Campbell, Mary Allison. AB, Vanderbilt U., 1949; AM, Princeton U., 1950, PhD, 1951. Rsch. assoc. U. Ill., Urbana, 1951-54; asst. prof. psychology Ga. Inst. Tech., Atlanta, 1954-60, assoc. prof., 1961-65, prof., 1965-90, ret., 1991; cons. Lockheed-Ga. Co., Marietta, 1963; testing dir. Aircrew Ctr., Am. Insts. Rsch., Atlanta, 1960-75; faculty Atlanta Sch. Art, 1970; mem. Ga. State Bd. Examiners of Psychologists, 1970-74. Contbr. articles to profl. jours. Sunday Sch. tchr. Northside United Meth. Ch., Atlanta, 1989—. With USNR, 1944-46. Recipient Disting. Tchr. award Ga. Inst. Tech., 1970. Fellow AAAS; mem. Am. Psychol. Assn., Ga. Psychol. Assn. (Cert. of Merit), Southeastern Psychol. Assn., So. Soc. Philosophy and Psychology (treas. 1971-74, pres. 1985-86), Ga. Inst. Tech. Faculty Club (pres. 1970), Phi Beta Kappa, Sigma Xi, Phi Kappa Phi, Omicron Delta Kappa, Beta Theta Pi. Avocation: gardening. Home: 3035 Farmington Dr NW Atlanta GA 30339-4704

PAYNE, MICHAEL DAVID, English language educator; b. Dallas, Jan. 17, 1941; s. Fred G. Payne and Jocie Marie (Kirkham) Lundberg; children: Jeffrey, Jennifer, Albert, Edward. Student, U. Calif.-Berkeley, 1958-59, 61; B.A., So. Oreg. Coll., 1962; Ph.D., U. Oreg., 1969. Tchr. English, Medford (Oreg.) Sr. High Sch., 1962-63; instr. English, U. Oreg., Eugene, 1963-69; asst. prof. to prof. English, Bucknell U., Lewisburg, Pa., 1969—, chmn. dept. history, 1980-82, chmn. dept. English, 1982-88, 92-94, Presdl. prof., 1982-86, John P. Crozer prof. English lit., 1986—; dir. Bucknell Univ. Press, 1972-76; assoc. editor Bucknell Rev., 1970-85, editor, 1985-88. Author: Irony in Shakespeare's Roman Plays, 1974, Reading Theory, 1993; editor: Contemporary Essays on Style, 1969, Shakespeare: Contemporary Critical Approaches, 1979, Text, Interpretation, Theory, 1985, Perspective, 1986, Criticism, History and Intertextuality, 1987, The Senses of Stanley Cavell, 1988, Blackwell Dictionary of Cultural and Critical Theory, 1996; gen. editor Bucknell Lectures in Lit. Theory, 1990-95. Recipient Lindback award for disting. teaching, 1976, Disting. Svc. award CEA, 1988, Profl. Achievement award, 1993; Folger Shakespeare Libr. fellow, 1973, NEH fellow, 1974, Bucknell Alumni fellow, 1978-79. Mem. Johnson Soc. London, Inst. for Romance Studies (U. London), MLA, Coll. English Assn., Phi Beta Kappa (hon.). Home: 1704 Jefferson Ave Lewisburg PA 17837-1632

PAYNE, MICHAEL LEE, association management executive; b. Monroe, N.C., Aug. 6, 1948; s. Robert H. and Martha (Brooks) P. BA in History, U. S.C., 1970, BA in Journalism, 1971; BA in Polit. Sci., 1972. Program dir. Coastal Plains Reg. Commn., Washington, 1972-75; dir. fed. rels. Office Coastal Zone Mgmt. NOAA, Washington, 1975-80; investment specialist Econ. Dirs. Adminstrn. U.S. Dept. Commerce, Washington, 1980-82; dep. to asst. sec. for congl. affairs Office of Sec. U.S. Dept. Commerce, Washington, 1982-84; v.p. Smith-Bucklin Assocs., Washington, 1984—, sr. v.p.; bd. dirs. Smith-Bucklin Assoc.; presenter to hospitality industry. Author: Complete Guide to Non-Profit Management, 1993; contbr. numerous articles to profl. publs. Mem. Am. Soc. Assn. Execs., Profl. Convention Mgrs. Assn., Meeting Profls. Internat. Avocations: travel, tennis, fishing, handball, biking. Office: Smith-Bucklin Assoc 1200 19th St Washington DC 20036

PAYNE, NANCY SLOAN, visual arts educator; b. Johnstown, Pa., Aug. 5, 1937; d. Arthur J. and Esther Jenkins (Ashcom) Sloan; m. Randolph Allen Payne, Nov. 19, 1970; 1 child, Anna Sloan. BS in Art Edn., Pa. State U., 1959; MFA in Sculpture, George Washington U., 1981. Visual arts tchr. Alexandria (Va.) Schs., 1960-61; art tchr. sch. program Corcoran Gallery of Art, Washington, 1962; visual arts tchr. Montgomery County Schs., Rockville, Md., 1965-67; instr. No. Va. C.C., Alexandria, 1971-73, Mt. Vernon Coll., Washington, 1971-73; visual arts tchr. Arlington (Va.) County Schs., 1967-79; edn. coord. The Textile Mus., Washington, 1982-87; mid. sch. visual arts tchr., K-12 dept. chair St. Stephen's and St. Agnes Sch., Alexandria, 1988—; co-founder Fiber Art Study Group, Washington, 1988—; co-owner Art Gallery, Chincoteague Island, Va., 1989—. Exhibited in group shows at Craftsmen's Biennial Va. Commonwealth U. (Excellence in Textiles award), 1973, Va. Craftsmen Biennial The Va. Mus., 1980, Creative Crafts Coun. 15th Biennial, 1982, Alexandria's Sculpture Festival, 1983, 84, 13 Fiber Artists Exhbn. Foundry Gallery, Washington, 1985. Founding mem. Alexandria Soc. for Preservation Black Heritage, Alexandria, 1982—. Mem. Nat. Art Edn. Assn. Democrat. Avocations: growing flowers, collecting hub caps, McDonald toys, and polit./campaign items. Home: 600 Johnston Pl Alexandria VA 22301-2512 Office: St Stephen's & St Agnes Schs 4401 W Braddock Rd Alexandria VA 22304

PAYNE, PAUL D., finance company executive. Exec. v.p., coo Mercedes-Benz Credit Corp., Norwalk, Conn. Office: Mercedes-Benz Credit Corp 201 Merritt 7 # 7 700 Norwalk CT 06851-1056*

PAYNE, PAULA MARIE, minister; b. Waukegan, Ill., Jan. 13, 1952; d. Percy Howard and Annie Maude (Canady) P. BA, U. Ill., 1976; MA, U. San Francisco, 1986; MDiv, Wesley Theol. Sem., 1991, student, 1995—. Ordained to ministry United Meth. Ch., 1990. Chaplain for minority affairs Am. U., Washington, 1988-89; chaplain, intern NIH, Bethesda, Md., 1989-90; pastor Asbury United Meth. Ch., Charles Town, W.Va., 1990—; supt. ch. sch. United Meth. Ch., Oxon Hill, Md., 1989-90; mem. AIDS task force Wesley Theol. Sem., Washington, 1988-89; mem. retreat. com. Balt. Conf., 1990—; chair scholarship com. Asbury United Meth. Ch., 1990—. Bd. dirs. AIDS Task Force Jefferson County, Charles Town, 1991—, Community Ministries, Charles Town, 1991—. Tech sgt. USAF, 1984-88; chaplain Army N.G., Md. Recipient Cert. of Recognition, Ill. Ho. of Reps., 1988, 20th Century award of Achievement Internat. Biog. Ctr., Cambridge, Eng., 1993, 1st Five Hundred, Cambridge, 1994, Citizen's citation, City of Balt., 1994, others; Ethnic Minority scholar United Meth. Ch., 1988-89, Brandenburg scholar, 1988-89, Tadlock scholar, 1989-90, Calvary Fellow scholar Calvary United Meth. ch., 1989-90. Mem. U. Ill. Alumni Assn. (bd. dirs. 1987-88), Alpha Kappa Alpha (pres. local chpt. 1974-76, v.p. 1973). Democrat. Home: 8005 Richard Dr Forestville MD 20747 *What good is excellence in scholarship, if one cannot lead souls to Christ.*

PAYNE, ROBERT E., federal judge; b. 1941. BA in Polit. Sci., Washington and Lee U., 1963; LLB magna cum laude, Washington & Lee U., 1967. Assoc., ptnr. McGuire, Woods, Battle & Boothe, Richmond, Va., 1971-92; fed. judge U.S. Dist. Ct. (ea. dist.) Va., 1992—. Notes editor Wash. & Lee U. Law Rev. Capt. U.S. Army, 1967-71. Mem. ABA, Va. Bar Assn., Va. State Bar Assn., Va. Assn. Def. Attys. (chmn. comml. litigation sect. 1989-91), Richmond Bar Assn., Order of Coif. Episcopalian. Office: Lewis F Powell Jr US Courthouse 1000 E Main St Ste 334 Richmond VA 23219

PAYNE, ROBERT WALTER, psychologist, educator; b. Calgary, Alta., Can., Nov. 5, 1925; s. Reginald William and Nora (Cowdery) P.; m. Helen June Mayer, Dec. 1948 (div. 1972); children: Raymond William, Barbara Joan, Margaret June; m. Josephine Mary Riley Adams, Mar. 1977 (div. 1982); children: George Reginald Alexander, Robin Charles; m. Jean Isobel Dawson, Aug., 1983. B.A., U. Alta., 1949; Ph.D., U. London, Eng., 1954. Lectr. psychology Inst. Psychiatry U. London, 1952-59; prof. psychology Queens U., Kingston, Ont., 1959-65; prof. psychology, chmn. dept. behavioral sci. Temple U. Med. Sch., Phila., 1965-73; prof. dept. psychiatry Temple U. Med. Sch., 1973-78; med. research scientist III Eastern Pa. Psychiat. Inst., Phila., 1965-78; prof. psychology U. Victoria, B.C., Can., 1978-91, prof. emeritus, 1991—, dean Faculty Human and Social Devel., 1978-83. Contbr. articles to profl. jours. Recipient Stratton Research award, 1964. Fellow Am. Psychol. Assn., Brit. Psychol. Soc., Canadian Psychol. Assn., Am. Psychopath. Assn. Home: 2513 Sinclair Rd, Victoria, BC Canada V8N 1B5

PAYNE, ROGER LEE, geographer; b. Winston-Salem, N.C., Oct. 26, 1946; s. Irvin Lee and Gladys Odel (Binkley) P.; m. Sara Lucinda Parker, Aug. 16, 1970 (div. Feb. 1992); 1 child, Jennifer Nicole; m. Anne F. Remen, June 11, 1995. BA, East Carolina U., 1969, MA, 1972. Geographer, chief geog. names U.S. Geol. Survey, Reston, Va., 1974—; instr. geography and history Pan Am. Inst./U.S. Geog. Survey, 1989—; exec. sec. U.S. Bd. Names, U.S. Geol. Survey, Washington, 1990—; part-time instr. East Caroline U., Greenville, N.C., 1979-81, George Washington U., Washington, 1977—, George Mason U., Fairfax, Va., 1979-83, Benjamin Franklin U., Washington, 1985-87; del. UN, N.Y.C., 1987—, instr., 1995—; mem. scientist exch. Geol. Survey, Beijing, 1989; instr. Nat. Black Colls., Howard U., 1985. Author: Urban Development in South Africa, 1972, Place Names of Outer Banks, 1985, Manuals on Auto Names, 1987, 89; coord., editor: (book series) National Gazetter U.S., 1982—; contbr. articles, revs. to profl. jours. Chmn. E. Carolina Blood Dr., Greenville, 1969. Lt. USAF, 1970-72. Recipient Guy Buzzard award Gamma Theta Upsilon, 1970; Superior Svc. award Geol. Survey, 1988. Fellow Explorers Club; mem. Assn. Am. Geographers (various coms. 1969—, pres. mid-Atlantic divsn. 1981-82, treas., sec.), Am. Name Soc. (pres. 1989), Am. Nat. Std. Inst. (rep. 1986), Cosmos Club. Avocations: hiking, volleyball. Home: 47762 Hammerstone Way Sterling VA 20165-4769 Office: US Geol Survey 523 National Ctr 12201 Sunrise Valley Dr Reston VA 22091-3401

PAYNE, ROGER S., conservation organization executive; b. N.Y.C., Jan. 29, 1935; m. Katy Boynton, 1960 (div. 1985); chilren: John, Holly, Laura Sam; m. Lisa Harrow. AB in Aminal Behavior, Harvard U., 1957; PhD, Cornell U. Rsch. zoologist Inst. for Rsch. in Animal Behavior N.Y. Zool. Inst., N.Y.C., 1968-71; asst. prof. biology Rockefeller U., N.Y.C., 1968-71; founder, pres. Whale Conservation Inst., Lincoln, Mass., 1971—. Author: Among Whales, 1995; host (TV documentary) In the Company of Whales, 1992 (series) Ocean Planet, 1994-95. Co-recipient Albert Schweitzer medal Animal Welfare Inst., 1980; recipient Joseph Wood Krutch medal Humane Soc. U.S., 1989, Lyndhurst prize Lyndhurst Found., 1994; genius grantee John D. and Catherine T. MacArthur Found., 1984. *

PAYNE, ROY STEVEN, judge; b. New Orleans, Aug. 30, 1952; s. Fred J. and Dorothy Julia (Peck) P.; m. Laureen Fuller, Sept. 8, 1973; children: Julie Elizabeth, Kelly Kathryn, Alex Steven, Michael Lawrence. BA with distinction, U. Va., 1974; JD, La. State U., 1977; LLM, Harvard U., 1980. Bar: La. 1977, U.S. Dist. Ct. (we. dist.) La. 1980, U.S. Ct. Appeals (5th cir.) 1980, U.S. Supreme Ct. 1983. Law clk. to judge U.S. Dist. Ct., Shreveport, La., 1977-79; assoc. Blanchard, Walker, O'Quin & Roberts, Shreveport, 1980-83, ptnr., 1984-87; U.S. Magistrate judge, We. Dist. La., Shreveport, 1987—; instr. New Eng. Sch. Law, Boston, 1979-80. Contbr. articles to profl. jours. Chmn. Northwest La. Legal Svcs. Assn., Shreveport, 1984-85. Mem. 5th Cir. Bar Assn., 5th Cir. Jud. Coun. (magistrate judges com. 1992—), La. State Bar Assn. (editorial bd. Forum jour., 1983-87, legal aid com.), Fed. Magistrate Judges Assn., Shreveport Bar Assn., La. Assn. Def. Counsel (bd. dirs. 1987), Harry V. Booth Am. Inn of Ct. (pres. elect 1994-95, pres. 1996—), Order of Coif, Rotary, Phi Kappa Phi, Phi Delta Phi. Methodist. Home: 12494 Harts Island Rd Shreveport LA 71115-8505 Office: US Courthouse 300 Fannin St Ste 4300 Shreveport LA 71101-3121

PAYNE, R.W., JR., lawyer; b. Norfolk, Va., Mar. 16, 1936; s. Roland William and Margaret (Sawyer) P.; m. Gail Willingham, Sept. 16, 1961; children: Darrell, Preston, Darby, Clinton. BA in English, U. N.C., 1958, LLB, 1961; LLB, Stetson U., 1962. Bar: Fla. 1963, U.S. Dist. Ct. (so. dist.) 1964, U.S. Ct. Appeals (11th cir.) 1965, U.S. Supreme Ct. 1970. Assoc. Roney & Beach, St. Petersburg, Fla., 1963-64, Nichols, Giather, Beckham, Miami, Fla., 1964-67; ptnr. Spence, Payne, Masington, Miami, 1967-95, Payne, Leeds, Colby & Robinson, P.A., Miami, 1995—; presenter numerous profl. convs. and seminars. Contbr. articles to legal jours., legal edn. books. Mem. Ottawa Roughriders, Can. Football League, fall 1958; capt. football team U. N.C., 1957, bd. dirs., v.p. alumni bd., 1984-92, bd. dirs. ednl. found., 1988-92; bd. dirs. Chem. Dependency Tng. Inst.; past pres. Coral Gables (Fla.) Sr. H.S. Athletic Boosters Club; past bd. dirs. Coral Gables War Meml. Youth Ctr., 1st United Meth. Ch. Coral Gables; past mem. gov.'s coun. on phys. fitness and sports, Fla.; past assoc. mem. Jr. Orange Bowl Com. With USMC, 1959. Fellow Am. Coll. Trial Lawyers, Internat. Acad. Trial Lawyers; mem. ABA, Fla. Bar Assn., Acad. Fla. Trial Lawyers (past mem. bd. govs.), Dade County Bar Assn. (past bd. dirs.), Dade County Trial Lawyers Assn. (founder, past pres.), Bankers Club, Miami Club, Univ. Club, Coral Reef Yacht Club, Order of Golden Fleece, Order of Old Well, Sigma Chi, Phi Delta Phi. Avocations: boating, golf, diving. Office: Payne Leeds Colby Robinson Ste 300 2950 SW 27th Ave Miami FL 33133

PAYNE, SIDNEY STEWART, archbishop; b. Fogo, Nfld., Can., June 6, 1932; m. Selma Carlson, 1962; children: Carla Ann, Christopher Stewart, Robert Clement, Angela Marie Louise. BA, Meml. U., St. John's, Nfld., 1958; lic. of theology, Queen's Coll., St. John's, 1958; BDiv, Gen. Synod, 1968; DDiv (hon.), King's Coll., Halifax, N.S., Can., 1981. Ordained priest Anglican Ch., 1958, bishop, 1978, archbishop, 1990. Deacon Mission of Happy Valley, Goose Bay, Labrador, Nfld., Can., 1957-65; rector Parish of Bay Roberts, Nfld., Can., 1965-70, Parish of St. Anthony, Nfld., 1970-76, 1976-78; bishop Diocese of Western Nfld., 1978-90, archbishop of Western Nfld. and Met. Eccles. Province of Can., 1990—; pres. Diocesan Synod, chmn. exec. com., mem. ex-officio diocesan coms.; pres. Provincial Synod, Provincial Coun.; chair Provincial House of Bishops; mem. long range planning com., ministry com., mem. nat. exec. coun. Partners in World Mission, Stewardship and Fin. Devel. Com.; mem. Anglican/Roman Cath. Bishops' Dialogue, Can.; active Provincial and Nat. House of Bishops. Mem. Internat. Grenfell Assn. (past bd. dirs.). Avocations: reading, walking, gardening, cross-country skiing. Home: 13 Cobb Ln, Corner Brook, NF Canada A2H Office: Anglican Diocesan Ctr, 25 Main St, Corner Brook, NF Canada A2H 1C2

PAYNE, THOMAS CHARLES, architect; b. Chatham, Ont., Dec. 9, 1949; s. Lloyd George and Dorothy Elizabeth (Webster) P.; m. Irma Osadsa, Sept. 21, 1974; children: Natalia Sophia, Nicholas Alexander. AB, Princeton U., 1971; attended, Ecole des Beaux Arts, 1971-72; MArch, Yale Sch. Architecture, 1974. With Barton Myers Assocs., 1979-87; ptnr. Kuwabara Payne McKenna Blumberg Architects, 1987—; adj. asst. prof. arch. U. Toronto, 1986-89; guest critic Toronto, Harvard, Waterloo. Recent project include Art Gallery Ont. Stage III, Woodsworth Coll. U. of Toronto, Trinity Coll., Master Plan, Stratford Festival, Improvements, Stauffer Libr., Queen's U., The Fields Inst. U. Toronto, Nat. Ballet Ctr., Toronto Goodman Theatre, Chgo. Recipient Gov. Gen.'s award for Arch. Royal Arch. Inst. of Can., 1992; fellow Woodsworth Coll. U. Toronto, Toronto Arts award. Mem. Am. Inst. Architecture, Royal Archtl. Inst. Can., Ont. Archtl. Assn. Home: 200 Glen Rd, Toronto, ON Canada M4W 2X1 Office: Kuwabara Payne McKenna Blumberg Architects, 322 King St W 3rd Fl, Toronto, ON Canada M5V 1J2

PAYNE, THOMAS L., university official; b. Bakersfield, Calif., Oct. 17, 1941; s. Harry LeRoy and Opal Irene (Ansel) P.; m. S. Alice Lewis, Feb. 1, 1963; children: Jacob, Joanna. AA in Liberal Arts, Bakersfield (Calif.) Jr. Coll., 1962; BA in Zoology, U. Calif., Riverside, 1965, MS in Entomology, 1967, PhD in Entomology, 1969. Asst. prof. entomology and forest sci. Tex. A&M U., College Station, 1969-73, assoc. prof., 1973-78, prof., 1978-87, rsch. coord. USDA so. pine beetle program, 1974-78; prof. entomology, head dept. Va. Poly. and State U., Blacksburg, 1987-92; dir. Ohio Agrl. R & D Ctr., assoc. dean for rsch. Ohio State U. Coll. Agr., Wooster, 1993—; sec. protection sect. Nat. Planning Conf. for Rsch. in Forestry and assoc. Rangelands, 1977; bd. dirs. Urban Pest Control Rsch. Ctr. Endowment Fund, 1988—; dean's rep., ex officio mem. Va. Pesticide Control Bd., 1989—; vis. prof. Forest Zoology Inst., U. Freiburg, Germany, 1978. Editor: (with Birch and Kennedy) Mechanisms in Insect Olfaction, 1986; mem. editorial bd. Jour. Ga. Entomol. Soc., 1979-83; co-editor Jour. Insect Behavior, 1987—; contbr. chpts. to books. Pres., co-founder Brazos County Firefighters Assn., 1979-81; v.p., co-founder Precinct 2 Vol. Fire Dept., 1979-80, pres., 1982-86; author grant to build Edge Tex. Sr. Citizens Ctr., 1979; mem. Friends of Blacksburg Master Chorale. Recipient numerous awards, 1976—, including cert. of appreciation for svc. as rsch. coord. expanded so. pine beetle rsch. USDA, 1976, 78, 80, rsch. award Tex. Forestry Assn., 1977, awards Am. Registry Profl. Entomologists, 1979, Alexander von Humboldt Stiftung sr. U.S. scientist award, 1982, Faculty Disting. Achievement award in rsch. Assn. Former Students Tex. A&M U., 1985, A.D. Hopkins award for outstanding rsch.-adminstrn. in forest entomology, 1991; Volkswagenwerk fellow U. Freiburg, 1978. Mem. AAAS, Entomol. Soc. Am. (CIBA-GEIGY agrl. recognition award 1982), Internat. Soc. Chem. Ecology, Internat. Chemoreception Workshop on Insects, Internat. Union Forest Rsch. Orgns., Nat. Corn Growers Assn., So. Forest Insect Work Conf., Va. Agribus. Coun., Va. Agrl. Chem. and Soil Fertility Assn., Va. Hort. Soc. (exec. coun. 1989), Va. Corn Growers Assn., Va. Soybean Assn., Va. Pest Control Assn, Western Forest Insect Work Conf., Coll. Agr. and Life Scis. Agr. Faculty Assn., Sigma Xi, Gamma Sigma Delta. Office: Ohio State U Ohio Agrl R & D Ctr 1680 Madison Ave Wooster OH 44691-4114

PAYNE, TIMOTHY E., management consultant; b. Valdosta, Ga., Oct. 12, 1948; s. Ernest Elbert and Lorraine (Tomlinson) P. BS, Valdosta State U., 1971. Profl. safety cert. Nat. Safety Coun.; cert. assoc. in risk mgmt. Ins. Inst. Am. Sr. cons. Kent Watkins & Assocs., Miami, Fla., 1975-80; mgmt. engrng. coord. U. Fla., Gainesville, 1980-86; adminstrv. sys. mgr. Amelia Island (Fla.) Co., 1986-89; CEO, pres. Payne & Assocs., Gainesville, Fla., 1989—; cons. Grace Com., Gainesville, 1991; teaching asst. La. State U., New Orleans, 1971. Author: Industrial Location Survey, 1971, (workbook) Bonus Calculation Procedures, 1977; contbr. articles to Indsl. Mgmt. Jour., Compete, Jour. Competitive Techs. Internat. Gov.'s intern State Ga., Atlanta, 1971. Mem. Am. Soc. Safety Engrs., Nat. Safety Mgmt. Soc. (state v.p. 1994). Avocations: golf, tennis.

PAYNE, TYSON ELLIOTT, JR., retired insurance executive; b. Dallas, May 25, 1927; s. Tyson Elliott and Winnie Claris (Denman) P.; m. Billie Jane Spears, Aug. 28, 1948; children: David Tyson, Sally Jane. B.J., U. Tex., 1949. CLU, ChFC. Sports editor Lufkin (Tex.) News, 1949-51, Tyler (Tex.) Courier Times, 1951-53; with Am. Nat. Ins. Co., Galveston, Tex., 1953-88; v.p. health ins. ops. Am. Nat. Ins. Co., St. Louis, 1965-1970; v.p. mktg. Am. Nat. Ins. Co., Galveston, 1970-86; pvt. practice ins. agt. Austin, Tex., 1987-88; exec. v. p., dir. Sch. of Ins. & Fin. Svcs. at U. Houston, 1988-92; ret., 1992. Elder Presbyn. Ch. With USNR, 1945-46. Home: 8110 Cardin Dr Austin TX 78759-8704

PAYNE, WILLIAM BRUCE, lawyer; b. Tulsa, Apr. 18, 1943; s. Marvin Ream and Audrey Arlene (Jones) P.; m. Suzanne Cooper, June 4, 1966; children: Allison, Stephanie. BS, U. Okla., 1965, JD, 1968. Bar: Minn. 1968, U.S. Dist. Ct. Minn. 1968, U.S. Ct. Appeals (8th cir.) 1968. Fin. ptnr. Dorsey & Whitney, Mpls., 1968—; sec., bd. dirs. Deltak Corp., Mpls. 1st lt. USAR, 1968-74. Mem. ABA, Minn. Bar Assn., Minikahda Club. Office: Dorsey & Whitney 220 S 6th St Minneapolis MN 55402-1498*

PAYNE, WILLIAM JACKSON, microbiologist, educator; b. Chattanooga, Aug. 30, 1925; s. Henry Frederick and Maude (Fonda) P.; m. Jane Lindsey Marshall, June 16, 1949; children: William Jackson, Marshall, Lindsey. BS, Coll. William and Mary, 1950, DSc (hon.), 1996; MS, U. Tenn., 1952, PhD, 1955. Instr. bacteriology U. Tenn., 1953-54; mem. faculty U. Ga., 1955-95, prof. microbiology, head dept., 1962-77, Alumni Found. Disting. prof., 1982-95, acting dean Franklin Coll. Arts and Scis., 1977-78, dean Franklin Coll. Arts and Scis., 1978-88; vis. professorial fellow U. Wales, Cardiff, 1975, hon. professorial fellow, 1977-87; cons. U. Ala., 1959, 68, 70, 85, Philip Morris Co., 1981, Iowa State U., 1988, Howard U., 1989, U. Ctrl. Fla., 1992, U. Tenn., 1994—, Auburn U., 1995; summer rsch. participant Oak Ridge Nat. Lab., 1960; chmn. Com. Nat. Registry Microbiologists, 1966-72; cons. U.S. EPA, 1971; mem. biol. oceanography panel NSF, 1976-77; mem. nitrogen-fixation panel CRGO U.S. dept. Agr., 1982; mem. vis. com. So. Assn. Colls., Miss. State U., 1983; vis. lectr. Ctr. for Environ. Biotech., Danish univs.-Copenhagen, Aarhus, Aalborg, 1989; co-chair 1st Gordon Rsch. Conf. on nitric oxide in biochemsitry and biology, 1995. Author: (with D.R. Brown) Microbiology: A Programmed Presentation, 1968, 2d edit., 1972, (transl. to Spanish, 1975), Denitrification, 1981, also articles; mem. editl. bd. Applied and Environ. Microbiology, 1974-79, Environ. Ethics, 1982-95, U. Ga. Press, 1975-78, 88-91. Trustee Athens Acad., 1967-72. Served with USNR, 1943-46. Recipient M.G. Michael award 1960, creative rsch. award U. Ga., 1982, Alumni Achievement award McCallie Sch., 1993. Fellow Am. Acad. Microbiology; mem. Am. Soc. Microbiology (pres. southeastern br. 1963, found. lectr. 1972-73, dir. found. 1973-76, chmn. found. com. 1977-82, com. undergrad. and grad. edn. 1974-77, steering com. undergrad. faculty-mentor enhancement program 1988-90, P.R. Edwards award southeastern br. 1972, R.G. Eagon award 1995), Ga. Acad. Sci., Athens City Club, Sigma Xi (pres. U. Ga. chpt. 1963, rsch. award U. Ga. chpt. 1973), Phi Kappa Phi (pres. U. Ga. chpt. 1983), Sigma Alpha Epsilon. Episcopalian. Home: 111 Alpine Way Athens GA 30606-4002

PAYNE, W(ILLIAM) SPENCER, retired surgeon; b. St. Louis, Mar. 22, 1926; s. Richard Johnson and Mary (Matthews) P.; m. Maureen J.S. Divertie, Oct. 3, 1959; children: Susan Mary, William Spencer, Sarah Elspeth. Student, DePauw U., Greencastle, Ind., 1944-45, Haverford (Pa.) Coll., 1945-46; MD, Washington U., St. Louis, 1950; MS, U. Minn., 1960. Intern, then resident in internal medicine St. Louis City Hosp., 1950-52, resident in gen. surgery, 1954-55; resident in gen. surgery, then resident in thoracic surgery Mayo Grad. Sch., Rochester, Minn., 1955-61; practice medicine specializing in surgery Rochester, 1962-90, ret., 1990; cons. thoracic and cardiovascular surgery Mayo Clinic and Mayo Found., 1962—; prof. surgery Mayo Med. Sch., 1974—, James C. Masson prof. surgery, 1982-87; head sect. gen. thoracic surgery Mayo Clinic, 1987-90; mem. staff Rochester Meth., St. Mary's, Rochester State hosps.; bd. dirs. Am. Bd. Thoracic Surgery, 1985-89. Author: The Esophagus, 1974, Manual of Upper Gastrointestinal Surgery, 1985; contbr. 274 articles to profl. jours.; mem. editl. bd. Annals of Thoracic Surgery, 1987-89. Lt. M.C., USNR, 1952-54, Korea. Recipient Howard K. Gray award Mayo Assn., 1959; named James C. Masson prof. Mayo Found. Mem. ACS, Am. Surg. Assn., Am. Assn. Thoracic Surgery, Soc. Thoracic Surgeons, Am. Coll. Chest Physicians, Central Surg. Assn., Minn. Surg. Soc., Internat. Assn. Study Lung Cancer, Mayo

Alumni Soc. Thoracic Surgery, Priestly Soc., Internat. Soc. Diseases of the Esophagus (hon.), Esophageal Surg. Club (hon.), Soc. of Thoracic and Cardiovascular Surgeons of Great Britain and Ireland (hon.), U. Club (Rochester), Madeline Island Yacht Club (LaPointe, Wis.). Presbyterian. Office: Mayo Clinics 200 1st St SW Rochester MN 55905-0001

PAYNTER, HARRY ALVIN, retired trade association executive; b. Miami, Ariz., July 22, 1923; s. Harry and Mabel Vera (Moore) P.; m. Betty Clarice Wilkins, Dec. 3, 1944; children: Harry Alvin, Steven Wilkins, Barbara Elizabeth, Susan Moore. B.S., Okla. State U., 1948; M.B.A., Harvard U., 1954; postgrad., Air Command and Staff Coll., 1957, Armed Forces Staff Coll., 1961, Nat. War Coll., 1969. Commd. 2d lt. AC U.S. Army, 1943; advanced through grades to col. USAF, 1968; service as flight comdr. 8th Air Force, World War II and Berlin airlift; asst. air attache (Am. embassy), Karachi, Pakistan, 1958-60; air attache (Am. embassy), Quito, Ecuador, 1965-67, Vietnam, 1969; prof. aerospace studies Dartmouth, 1967-68; ret., 1970; mng. dir. Gas Appliance Mfrs. Assn., Inc., N.Y.C., 1970-73; pres. Gas Appliance Mfrs. Assn., Inc., Arlington, Va., 1973-88. Decorated D.F.C., Air medal with 3 oak leaf clusters, Purple Heart, Joint Services Commendation medal with oak leaf cluster U.S.; Abdon Calderon Ecuador; recipient Am. Bankers award, 1947; named Ecuador Hon. Command Pilot. Mem. Can. Gas Assn. (life), Guild Ancient Supplers (hon.), Am. Soc. Gas Engrs. (hon.), Air Force Assn., Ret. Officers Assn., Am. Soc. Assn. Execs., Nat. Press Club. Phi Kappa Phi. Presbyterian. Home: 1416 N Inglewood St Arlington VA 22205-2735

PAYNTER, VESTA LUCAS, pharmacist; b. Aiken County, S.C., May 29, 1922; d. James Redmond and Annie Lurline (Stroman) Lucas; m. Maurice Alden Paynter, Dec. 23, 1945 (dec. 1971); children: Sharon Lucinda, Maurice A. Jr., Doyle Gregg. BS in Pharmacy, U. S.C., 1943. Lic. pharmacist. Owner, pharmacist Cayce Drug Store, S.C., 1944-52, Dutch Fork Drug Store, Columbia, S.C., 1955-60, The Drug Ctr., Cayce, 1963-81; pharmacist Lane-Rexall, Columbia, 1952-55; dist. pharmacist S.C. Dept. Health and Environ. Control, Columbia, 1983-90, ret., 1990. Named Preceptor of Yr., Syntex Co., student body U. S.C., 1981. Fellow, 5th Dist. Pharm. Assn., S.C. Pharm. Assn., S.C. Pub. Health Assn., Alpha Epsilon Delta; mem. China, India, Burma VA Assn. (assoc.), 14th Air Force Assn. (assoc.). Baptist. Lodges: Order of Eastern Star, Order of Amaranth, Sinclair Lodge, White Shrine of Jerusalem, Palmetto Shrine. Avocations: travel, tennis, golf, art. Home: 2351 Vine St Cayce SC 29033-3000

PAYSON, HENRY EDWARDS, forensic psychiatrist, educator; b. N.Y.C., May 12, 1925; s. Aurin Eliot and Lois Elizabeth (Chickering) P.; m. Barbara Louise Jarvis, Mar. 29, 1958; children: Ann Elizabeth, John Eliot, Sally Lynn, Susan Gail. B.S., Harvard Coll., 1948; M.D., Columbia U., 1952; M.S.L., Yale U. Law Sch., 1978; A.M. (hon.), Dartmouth Coll., 1981. Diplomate: Am. Bd. Med. Examiners, Am. Bd. Psychiatry and Neurology, Am. Bd. Forensic Psychiatry. Research fellow in medicine Columbia U. unit Goldwater Meml. Hosp., 1952-53; intern Osler Clinic, Johns Hopkins Hosp., 1953-54; resident in psychiatry Phipps Clinic, 1955-58; resident in internal medicine Duke U. Hosp., 1954-55; asst. prof. psychiatry and medicine Yale U. Sch. Medicine; also attending physician Yale-New Haven Med. Center, 1958-63; asst. prof. psychiatry Dartmouth Med. Sch., 1963-68, assoc. prof., 1968-78, prof., 1978-90, prof. emeritus, 1990—, chief forensic psychiatry, dept. psychiatry; attending psychiatrist Hitchcock Clinic, Dartmouth-Hitchcock Med. Center, 1972-90; chief in-patient service Dartmouth-Hitchcock Mental Health Center, 1969-71; cons. VA Hosp., White River Junction, Vt., 1972-91, N.H. Hosp., 1980-87, VA Hosp., Manchester, N.H., 1981-91, N.H. Prison, 1984-88, Cottage Hosp., Woodsville, N.H., 1990—; dir. Disturbed Offender Project of N.H., 1972-73. Contbr. articles to profl. publs. Mem. N.H. Guardian Adv. Council, 1979-83. Served with AUS, 1943-46. NIMH career tchr., 1961-63. Fellow Am. Psychiat. Assn. (life); mem. AAAS, Am. Acad. Psychiatry and Law, N.H. Psychiat. Soc. (pres. 1977-78). Office: The Aldrich House PO Box 845 Norwich VT 05055-0845

PAYSON, MARTIN DAVID, entertainment company executive, lawyer; b. N.Y.C., Jan. 4, 1936; s. Joseph J. and Stella (Riemer) P.; m. Doris Leah Greenberg; children: Michele, Leslie, Eric. A.B., Cornell U., 1957; LL.B. cum laude, NYU, 1961. Bar: N.Y. 1961. Assoc. Paul Weiss Rifkind Wharton & Garrison, N.Y.C., 1961-67; instr. Law Sch., U. Mich., Ann Arbor, 1963-64; ptnr. Polier Tulin & Payson, N.Y.C., 1967-70; gen. counsel Warner Communications, Inc., N.Y.C., 1970—; also dir. Warner Communications, Inc.; now vice chmn. Time Warner Inc., N.Y.C. Chmn. entertainment div. United Jewish Appeal-Fedn. Joint Campaign, N.Y.C., 1982-84; mem. pres.'s council Tulane U., New Orleans, 1984—; trustee Fedn. Jewish Philanthropies N.Y., N.Y.C., 1983—. Mem. ABA, Assn. Bar City N.Y. Democrat. *

PAYSON, MARTIN FRED, lawyer; b. Bklyn., Dec. 25, 1940; m. Rhoda Shapiro, Oct. 8, 1961; children: Jacqueline, Marla. BBA, CCNY, 1961; JD, Bklyn. Law Sch., 1966. Bar: N.Y. 1967, Pa. 1989, U.S. Ct. Appeals (1st cir.) 1971, U.S. Ct. Appeals (2d and 3d cirs.) 1968, U.S. Ct. Appeals (4th cir.) 1969, U.S. Supreme Ct. 1970. Gen. ptnr. Jackson, Lewis, Schnitzler & Krupman, White Plains, N.Y., 1967—; lectr. in field. Contbr. articles to various publs. With U.S. Army, 1961-62. Mem. N.Y. State Bar Assn. (labor and employee rels. sects.), Soc. for Human Resource Mgmt. Avocations: photography, cycling. Office: Jackson Lewis Schnitzler & Krupman One N Broadway White Plains NY 10601

PAYSON, RONALD SEARS, biology educator; b. Springfield, Mass., Oct. 17, 1938; s. Peter Martin and Beatrice Thelma (Sears) Farrell; m. Cynthia Myrtle Henderson Smith, July 17, 1965 (div. Jan. 1977); children: Melinda Martha Payson-English, Ronald Sears Payson Jr., Angelique Payson-Bernstein, Marcus A. AASN, U. of the State of N.Y.; BS, U. Mass., MAT in Biology/Ecology. R.N. Prof. biol. scis. Columbia-Greene C.C., 1970-94, prof. emeritus; cons. Spinrut Hill Assocs., Craryville, N.Y., 1994—; dir. Ctr. for Effective Teaching, coord. distance edn. Hudson Valley (N.Y.) C.C., 1995—. Sec. bd. dirs. N.E. Marine Environ. Inst.; bd. dirs. Hudson River Sloop Clearwater; treas. Vol. Fire Co. Home: RR 1 Box 242 West Coxsackie NY 12192

PAYTON, BENJAMIN FRANKLIN, college president; b. Orangeburg, S.C., Dec. 27, 1932; s. Leroy Ralph and Sarah (Mack) P.; m. Thelma Louise Plane, Nov. 28, 1959; children: Mark Steven, Deborah Elizabeth. BA, S.C. State Coll., 1955; BD (Danforth grad. fellow 1955-63), Harvard U., 1958; MA, Columbia U., 1960; PhD, Yale U., 1963; LLD (hon.), Eastern Mich. U., 1972; LHD (hon.), Benedict Coll., 1972; LittD (hon.), Morgan State U., 1974, U. Md., 1987; LLD, Morris Brown Coll., Lehigh U., 1990. Asst. prof. sociology of religion and social ethics Howard U., Washington; also dir. Howard U. (Community Rsch.-Svc. Project), 1963-65; exec. dir. dept. social justice and Commn. on Religion and Race Nat. Coun. Chs. of Christ in U.S.A., 1966-67; pres. Benedict Coll., Columbia, S.C., 1967-72; program officer higher edn. and rsch. Ford Found., 1972-81; pres. Tuskegee (Ala.) U., 1981—; mem. nat. rev. bd. (Ctr. for Cultural and Tech. Exch. between U.S. and Asia); mem. commn. on Pre-Coll. Edn. in Math., Sci. and Tech. NSF; ednl. advisor to V.P. George Bush during Seven-Nation Tour of Africa, 1982; team leader U.S. Presdl. Task Force on Agrl. and Econ. Devel. to Zaire; bd. dirs. AmSouth Bancorp., ITT Corp., Libr. Corp., Praxair, Inc., Sonat, Inc.; mem. vis. com. Dept. Humanities MIT, 1988-90; vis. com. bd. overseers Harvard U., 1989-95. Author: (with Dr. Seymour Melman) A Strategy for the Next Stage in Civil Rights: Metropolitan-Rural Development for Equal Opportunity, 1966. Mem. nat. commn. on higher edn. issues Am. Coun. Edn.; bd. dirs. Ala. Shakespeare Festival. Recipient Billings Prize, 1st Pl., Harvard U., 1957, Gold medal award Napoleon Hill Found., 1987, Benjamin E. Mays award, 1988, Centennial Alumnus award S.C. State Coll., 1988; named South Carolinian of Yr. by statewide TV-Radio, 1972. Mem. NAACP, Am. Soc. Scholars, Soc. for Religion, Higher Edn. (dir.), Assn. Governing Bds. (pres.'s adv. coun.), Phi Beta Kappa, Alpha Phi Alpha, Alpha Kappa Mu, Sigma Pi Phi. Home: Grey Columns 399 Montgomery Rd Tuskegee AL 36083 Office: Office of the Pres Tuskegee Univ Tuskegee AL 36088

PAYTON, GARY DWAYNE, professional basketball player; b. Oakland, Calif., July 23, 1968; m. Monique Payton; children: Raquel, Gary Dwayne. Grad., Oreg. State U., 1990. Drafted NBA, 1990; guard Seattle Supersonics, 1990—. Named mem. All-Am. First Team, The Sporting News, 1990, Pacific-10 Conf. Player of Yr., 1990, NBA All-Star, 1994, 95, NBA Player of the Week; named to NBA All-Def. 1st Team, 1994, 95. Office: Seattle Supersonics Ste 200 190 Queen Anne Ave N Seattle WA 98109-9711

PAYTON, JACQUELINE N., mathematics educator; b. Louisa, Va., Aug. 7, 1937; d. Floyd R. and Juanita B. (Johnson) Nelson; m. Richard W. Payton, June 24, 1961; children: Richard Jr., Glennis, Charles, Sheree. BS, Va. State U., 1958, MEd, 1971; EdD, U. Va., 1987. Instr. math. Lancaster (Va.) County Sch. Bd., 1958-69, Chesterfield (Va.) County Sch. Bd., 1971-72, 73-74; assoc. prof. math. Va. State U., Petersburg, 1974—; instr. math. U. Va., Charlottesville, 1985, 86; project dir. Upward Bound Math. and Sci. Ctr. Va. State U., Petersburg, 1991—. Mem. Nat. Coun. Tchrs. Math., Internat. Soc. Tech. in Edn., Va. Coun. Tchrs. Math., Ea. Ednl. Rsch. Assn., Phi Delta Kappa, Kappa Mu Epsilon. Office: Va State U 306 S Hunter Mcdaniel Petersburg VA 23803

PAYTON, THOMAS WILLIAM, corporate finance consultant executive; b. Toronto, Ont., Can., Sept. 7, 1946. With Can. Imperial Bank of Commerce, Toronto; dir. Bramalea Ltd., Toronto, 1981-82, v.p., 1982-88, sr. v.p., 1988-90, sr. v.p., treas., 1991-93; pres. DelLyn Advisors Inc., 1993—; dir. Cadillac Fairview, Inc., 1994-95. Office: DelLyn Advisors Inc, 8 King St E Ste 810, Toronto, ON Canada M5C 1B5

PAYTON, WALTER (SWEETNESS PAYTON), professional race car driver, former professional football player; b. Columbia, Miss., July 25, 1954; s. Peter Edward and Alyne Payton; m. Connie Payton; children: Jarrett, Brittney. BA in Communications, Jackson State U. Running back Chgo. Bears, 1975-88; played Pro Bowl, 1976-86; mem. NFL Championship team, 1985; professional race car driver, 1993—. Representative for Food for Thought Program, Bryan Foods, 1993—. Named NFC Player of Yr., The Sporting News, 1976-77, to NFC All-Star Team, 1976-78, NFC Player of Yr., UPI, 1977, NFL Most Valuable Player, Profl. Football Writers Am., 1978, played in nine Pro Bowls, inducted into Pro Football Hall of Fame, 1993; Black Athlete of the Year, Gordon's Gin, 1985. NFL all-time rushing leader. *

PAZ, OCTAVIO, poet, Mexican diplomat; b. Mex., Mar. 31, 1914; s. Octavio Paz and Josephina Lozano; m. Elena Garro, 1937 (div.); m. Marie José Tramini, 1964. Student, U. Mex.; D (hon.), New Sch. Social Rsch. Sec. Mex. Embassy, Paris, 1945; chargé d'affaires Mex. Embassy, Tokyo, 1951, secretariat external affairs, 1953-58; extraordinary and plenipotentiary minister Mex. Embassy, Paris, 1959-62; Mex. amb. to India, 1962-68; vis. prof. U. Tex., Austin, U. Pitts., 1968-70; Simón Bolívar prof. Latin Am. studies, 1970; fellow Churchill Coll., Cambridge U., 1970-71; Charles Eliot Norton prof. poetry Harvard U., 1971-72; Regent's fellow U. Calif., San Diego; now dir. Revista Vuelta, Mexico City; founder literary rev. Barandal, 1931; mem. editorial bd., columnist El Popular; co-founder Taller, 1938; co-founder, editor El Hijo Prodigo, 1943-46; editor Plural, 1971-75; founder, editor Vuelta, 1976—. Author: (poetry) Luna Silvestre, 1933, No pasarán!, 1936, Raíz del hombre, 1937, Bajo tu clara sombra y otros poemas sobre España, 1937, Entre la piedra y la flor, 1941, A la orilla del mundo y primer dia, 1942, Libertad bajo palabra, 1949, Aguila o sol?, 1951 (pub. as Eagle or Sun?, 1970), Semillas para un himno, 1954, Piedra de sol, 1957 (pub. as Sun Stone, 1963), La estación violenta, 1958, Agua y viento, 1959, Libertad bajo palabra: obra poética 1935-1958, 1960, Salamandra 1958-1961, 1962, Selected Poems, 1935-1957, 1963, Viento entero, 1965, Vrindaban, Madurai, 1965, Blanco, 1967, Disco visuales, 1968, Ladera este (1962-1968), 1969, La centana: poemas 1935-1968, 1969, Configurations, 1958-1969, 1971, Renga, 1971, Topoemas, 1971, Early Poems 1935-1955, 1973, Pasado en claro, 1975, Vuelta, 1976, A Draft of Shadows and Other Poems, 1979, Selected Poems, 1979, Airborn/Hijos del aire, 1981, Poemas 1935-1975, 1981, Poemas recientes, 1981, Instante y revelación, 1982, Selected Poems, 1984, Cuatro chopos/The Four Poplars, 1985, Arbol adentro, 1987 (pub. as A Tree Within, 1988), Nineteen Ways of Looking at Wang Wei, 1987, The Collected Poems of Octavio Paz 1957-1987, 1988, Lo mejor de Octavio Paz: el fuego de cada día; (prose) El laberinto de la soledad, 1950 (pub. as The Labyrinth of Solitude: Life and Thought in Mexico, 1961), Aguila o Sole, 1951, El arco y la lira: el poema, la revelación poética, poésia e historia, 1956 (pub. as The Bow and the Lyre: The Poem, the Poetic Revelation, Poetry and History, 1973), Las peras del olmo, 1957, Tamayo en la pintura mexicana, 1959, Cuadrivio, 1965, Los signos en rotación, 1965, Puertas al campo, 1966, Claude Lévi-Strauss; o, El nuevo festín de Esopo, 1967 (pub. as Claude Lévi-Strauss: An Introduction, 1970), Corriente alterna, 1967 (pub. as Alternating Current, 1973), Marcel Duchamp; o, El castillo de la pureza, 1968 (pub. as Marcel Duchamp; or, The Castle of Purity, 1970), México: la última década, 1969, Conjunciones y disyunciones, 1969 (pub. as Conjunctions and Disjunctions, 1974), Posdata, 1970 (Pub. as The Other Mexico: Critique of the Pyramid, 1972), Las cosas en su sitio: sobre la literatura española del siglo XX, 1971, Los signos en rotación y otros ensayos, 1971, Traducción: literatura y literalidad, 1971, Apariencia desnuda: la obra de Marcel Duchamp, 1973 (pub. as Marcel Duchamp: Appearance Stripped Bare, 1979), El signo y el garabato, 1973, Solo a dos voces, 1973, Teatro de signos/transparencias, 1974, Versiones y diversiones, 1974, Los hijos del limo: del romanticismo a la vanguardia, 1974 (pub. as Children of the Mire: Modern Poetry from Romanticism to the Avant-Garde, 1974), El mono gramético, 1974 (pub. as The Monkey Grammarian, 1981), La búsqueda del comienzo: escritos sobre el surrealismo, 1974, The Siren and the Seashells and Other Essays on Poets and Poetry, 1976, Xavier Villaurrutia en persona y en obra, 1978, El ogro filantrópico: historia y política 1971-1978, 1979, Rufino Tamayo: Myth and Magic, 1979, México en la obra de Octavio Paz, 1979, Rufino Tamayo, 1982, Sor Juana Inés de la Cruz, o, Las trampas de la fe, 1982 (pub. as Sor Juana, or, The Traps of Faith, 1988), Tiempo nublado, 1983 (pub. as One Earth, Four or Five Worlds: Reflections on Contemporary History, 1985), Sombras de obras: arte y literatura, 1983, Günter Gerzo, 1983, Hombres en su siglo y otros ensayos, 1984 (pub. as On Poets and Others, 1986), Pasión critica: conversaciones con Octavio Paz, 1985, Convergences: Essays on Art and Literature, 1987, Generaciones y semblanzas: escritores y letras de México, 1987, El pelegrino en su patria: historia y política de México, 1987, Los privilegios de la vista: arte de México, 1987, Primeras letras, 1931-1943, 1988, One World or the Other, 1989, Poesía, mito, revolución, 1989, La otra voz: poesía y fin de siglo, 1990 (pub. as The Other Voice, 1992), Essays on Mexican Art, 1993, My Life With the Wave, 1994, The Double Flame, 1995; adapter: (plays) La hija de Rappaccini, 1956; editor: Voces de España, 1938, Laurel: antología de la poésia moderna en lengua española, 1941, Anthologie de la poésie mexicaine, 1952, Anthología poética, 1956, Anthology of Mexican Poetry, 1958, Tamayo el la pintura mexicana, 1959, Magia de la risa, 1962, Antología by Fernando Pessoa, 1962, Cuatro poetas contemporáneos de Suecia: Martinson, Lundkvist, Ekelöf, y Lindegren, 1963, Poesía en movimiento: Mexico 1915-1966, 1966, Remedios varo, 1966, Antologia by Xavier Villaurrutia, 1980; translator: Sendas de Oku by Basho, 1957, Veinte poemas by William Carlos Williams, 1973, 15 poemas by Guillaume Appollinaire, 1979; writer (film) Yo, la Peor de Todas, 1990. Guggenheim fellow, U.S., 1944; recipient Grand Prix Internat. de Poesie (Belgium), 1963, Jerusalem prize, 1977, Critics prize (Spain), 1977, Nat. prize for letters (Mex.), 1977, Grand Golden Eagle Internat. Festival (Paris) 1979, Grand Aigle d'Or (Nice), 1979, Premio Ollin Yoliztli (Mex.), 1980, Miguel de Cervantes prize (Spain), 1982, Neustadt Internat. prize for literature, 1982, Wilhelm Heinse medal (Germany), 1984, Fedn. German Book Trade Peace prize, 1984, Gran Cruz de Alfonso X el Sabrio, 1986, T.S. Eliot award for creative writing Ingersoll Found., 1987, Alexis de Toqueville prize Inst. France, 1988, Nobel Prize in literature, 1990. Mem. AAAL (hon.). Office: Revista Vuelta Amigos del Arte AC, Avenida Contreras 516 Piso 3, 10200 Mexico City Mexico also: care Churchill Coll, Cambridge England

PAZANDAK, CAROL HENDRICKSON, liberal arts educator; b. Mpls.; d. Norman Everard and Ruth (Buckley) Hendrickson; m. Bruce B. Pazandak (dec. 1986); children: David, Bradford, Christopher, Eric, Paul, Ann; m. Joseph P. O'Shaughnessy, May 1991. PhD, U. Minn., 1970. Asst. dir. admissions U. Minn., Mpls., 1970-72, asst. dean liberal arts, 1972-79, asst. to pres., 1979-85, office of internat. edn., acting dir., 1985-87, asst. prof. to assoc. to prof. liberal arts, 1970-96, prof. emerita, 1996—; vis. prof. U. Iceland, Reykjavik, 1984, periods in 1983, 86, 87, 88, 89, 90-92, 93, 94, 96; vis. rsch. prof. U. Oulu, Finland, 1993; exec. sec. Minn.-Iceland Adv. Com., U. Minn., 1984—; cons. U. Iceland, 1983—; co-chair Reunion of Sisters-Minn. and Finland Confs., 1986—; sec. Icelandic Assn. of Minn., 1995—. Editor: Improving Undergraduate Education in Large Universities, 1989. Past pres. Minn. Mrs. Jaycees, Mpls. Mrs. Jaycees; formerly bd. govs. St. John's Preparatory Sch., Collegeville, Minn.; former bd. trustees Coll. of St. Teresa, Winona, Minn.. Recipient Partnership award for contbn. to advancing shared interests of Iceland and Am., 1994; named to Order of the Falcon, Govt. of Iceland, 1990, Coll. Liberal Arts Alumna Notable Achievement, 1995. Mem. Am. Psychol. Assn., Am. Coun. Edn. (former steering com. Nat. Identification Program for Women in Higher Edn. Adminstrn. 1983-86), Soc. Advancement of Scandinavian Studies. Home: 1361 Prior Ave S Saint Paul MN 55116-2656 Office: U Minn N 247 Elliott Hall 75 E River Rd Minneapolis MN 55455-0280

PAZIRANDEH, MAHMOOD, rheumatologist, consultant; b. Hamadan, Iran, Jan. 1, 1932; came to U.S., 1966; naturalized U.S. Citizen, 1977; s. Rahim and Zahra (Shoushtar) P.; m. Parvin Danesh, Apr. 19, 1961; children: Bruce, Justin, Navid. MD, U. Tehran, 1958; postgrad., Eng., 1959-64, Pitts. U., 1967-68. Diplomate Am. Bd. Internal Medicine and Rheumatology. Asst. prof. Tehran U., Iran, 1964-67; clin. assoc. Cleve. Clinic Found., 1969-70; clin. instr. Case Western Res. U., Cleve., 1970-72, sr. clin. instr., 1972-78, clin. asst. prof., 1979-93, clin. assoc. prof., 1993—; dir. med. edn. Lake Hosp., Cleve., 1984-96, pres. med. staff, 1990-93; mem. CME com. Case Western Res. U. Sch. Medicine, 1994-96; dir. med. edn. Euclid Hosp., Cleve., 1971-73, dir. quality assurance, 1989-93. Contbr. articles to profl. jours. Speaker pub. edn. radio, TV and seminars, Cleve., 1984—; chmn. pub. forums Arthritis Found., Cleve., 1985—, trustee, 1986-96, chmn. pub. edn. com., 1987—. Recipient recognition svc. award Arthritis Found., 1976, Robert Stecher Vol. award, 1988, Nat. Vols. Svc. citation, 1989; Eng. and Iranian Govt. scholar, 1959-63. Fellow ACP, Am. Coll. Rheumatology; mem. Am. Soc. Internal Medicine, Ohio State Med. Assn. (del. 1989-96), Lake County Med. Soc. (pres. 1988—), Cleve. Rheumatism Soc. (pres. 1974), N.Y. Acad. Scis. Republican. Avocations: arts, antiques. Home: 124 Pheasant Ln Hunting Valley OH 44022-4043 Office: Case Western Res U 36100 Euclid Ave Willoughby OH 44094-4456

PAZMIÑO, PATRICIO AUGUSTO, physician, scientist, consultant; b. Quito, Ecuador, Nov. 7, 1943; came to U.S., 1967; s. Manuel Eduardo and Angela Alicia (Narvaez) P.; m. Lydia Zulema Bohorquez, 1970; children: Patricio, Pablo, Carlos, Katherine. BS, Gonzaga U., 1968; PhD, U. Ill., 1971; D of Medicine & Surgery, Ctrl. U. Ecuador, 1974. Diplomate Am. Bd. Internal Medicine, Am. Bd. Nephrology. Asst. prof. pharmacology Ctrl. U. Sch. Medicine, Quito, Ecuador, 1971-74; staff nephrologist, internist Nat. Naval Med. Ctr., Bethesda, 1979-84; asst. prof. medicine Uniformed Svcs. U. Health Scis., Bethesda, Md., 1980-83; head nephrology divsn. Nat. Naval Med. Ctr., Bethesda, 1983-84; med. dir. El Paso (Tex.) Dialysis Ctr., 1986-89, Nephrology, Internal Medicine & Hypertension Ctr., El Paso, 1987—; asst. prof. medicine Tex. Tech. Sch. Medicine, El Paso, 1989—; med. dir. BMA Dialysis Ctr., El Paso, 1989-95; dir. Total Renal Care, 1995—; staff internist, nephrologist Columbia Med. Ctrs., Sierra Med. Ctr., Southwestern Gen. Hosp., R.E. Thomason Gen. Hosp., Rio Vista Rehab. Ctr., Providence Meml. Hosp., William Beaumont Army Med. Ctr. Author: Farmacologia Hormonal, 1974; contbr. articles to profl. jours. Served with USN, 1979-84. Fellow ACP, Interam. Coll. Physicians and Surgeons; mem. AMA, Nat. Kidney Found., Tex. Med. Assn., El Paso County Med. Assn., Am. Heart Assn. (pres. 1996-97, bd. dirs. El Paso divsn. 1994—), S.W. Renal Soc. (pres. 1991-92), S.W. Assn. Hispanic Am. Physicians (pres. 1993, Outstanding Pres. award 1993), Ecuadorean Acad. Medicine. Avocations: photography, scientific research, travel, chess, sports cars. Office: NIH Ctr 1701 N Mesa St Ste 101 El Paso TX 79902-3503

PAZO, ROSA MERCADO, home health agency administrator; b. Ponce, P.R., Jan. 3, 1941; d. Clemente Mercado-Gonzalez and Ana L. (Rivera) Mercado; m. Tomas Pazo, Dec. 19, 1964; children: Tomas J., Rosana, Gilberto Luis, Tomas A. Diploma, Jose N. Gandara Sch. Nursing, Ponce, 1961; BSN, Cath. U. P.R., Ponce, 1970; grad., Sch. Nurse-Midwifery, Rio Piedras, P.R., 1962. RN, La., Tex., P.R., Va.; cert. nurse-midwife. Prof. nursing U. P.R., Mayaguez, 1969-70; gen. supr. nursing St. Lukes Home Care Program, Ponce, 1970-80; labor and delivery/post partum nurse Ochsner Med. Instn., Jefferson, La., 1980; unit coord. med.-surg. St. Jude Med. Ctr., Kenner, La., 1983-85; surg. ICU nurse Arlington (Tex.) Meml. Hosp., 1985-86; surg. ICU nurse VA Med. Ctr., New Orleans, 1980-85, emergency rm. nurse, 1986-93; exec. nursing dir. Best Home & Health Care, New Orleans, 1991-93; adminstrv. DON, co-owner Internat. HealthCare Network, Metairie, La., 1993—; instr. Sch. of Nurse-Midwifery, Ponce, 1965-69; nurse midwife Mcpl. Hosp. V. Tricoche, Ponce, 1963-65; labor and delivery nurse Ponce Dist. Hosp., 1962-63. Mem. Nat. Gerontol. Nursing Assn., La. Assn. Home Care Programs, Civic Club Orgn., Nat. Assn. Hispanic Nurses, Magnolia Women Civic Club, Nat. Assn. Home Care, State Assn. Home Care. Roman Catholic. Avocations: reading mystery novels, volunteering. Office: Internat Health Care Netwk 4051 Veterans Memorial Blvd Metairie LA 70002-5539

PAZUR, JOHN HOWARD, biochemist, educator; b. Zubne, Czechoslovakia, Jan. 17, 1922; came to U.S., 1946, naturalized, 1961; s. John and Mary (Bonko) P.; m. Jean Josephine Glabais, Nov. 22, 1950; children—Robert Leslie, Barbara Jean, Beverly Ann, Carolyn Jo. B.S., U. Guelph, 1944; M.S., McGill U., 1946; Ph.D., Iowa State U., 1950. Instr. chemistry Iowa State U., 1950-51; asst. prof. biol. chemistry U. Ill., 1951-52; mem. faculty U. Nebr., 1952-66, prof. biochemistry, 1959-66, chmn. dept., 1960-66; prof. biochemistry Pa. State U., 1966—, chmn. dept., 1966-74. Mem. Am. Chem. Soc., Am. Soc. Biol. Chemists. Home: Unit 306 403 S Allen St State College PA 16801-5252 Office: Penn State U 108 Althouse Lab University Park PA 16802-4500

PEABODY, DEBBIE KAY, elementary school educator; b. Wooster, Ohio, Apr. 9, 1954; d. Walter L. and Carolyn E. (Lee) Mussatto; m. David Leslie Peabody, Jan. 6, 1973; children: Dawn Kathleen, Lesli Kay. BS in Elem. Edn., Southwestern Adventist Coll., Keene, Tex., 1986. Cert. tchr. K-8, Ariz. Head tchr. SDA Elem. Sch., Camp Verde, Ariz., 1986-89; tchr. 6th grade Roosevelt Sch. Dist., Phoenix, 1989-93, jr. high reading tchr., 1993-94, collaborative peer tchr., 1994—; dist. assessment plan co-chair Roosevelt Sch. Dist., 1993—; mem. Greater Phoenix Curriculum Coun. Dist. Assessment Plan Writing Team, 1994—; CHAMPS coord. Sunland Elem. Sch., Phoenix, 1991-94. Co-author: (activity book) Explosion of ASAP Activities, 1994. Recipient Edn. of Merit award Southwestern Union Coll., 1985, 86. Mem. ASCD, NEA, Ariz. Edn. Assn., Roosevelt Edn. Assn., Nat. Coun. Tchrs. Math. Avocations: quilting, embroidery, biking, hiking, canoeing. Office: Roosevelt School Dist 6000 S 7th St Phoenix AZ 85040-4209

PEABODY, WILLIAM TYLER, JR., retired paper manufacturing company executive; b. Melrose, Mass., Mar. 17, 1921; s. William Tyler and Dorothy (Atkinson) P.; m. Florence Marshall Peabody, July 27, 1946 (dec.); children: Carol Peabody Moomey, William Tyler III, Janet Peabody Barrow, Marshall R. A.B. cum laude, Harvard U., 1942, postgrad. Grad. Sch. Arts and Scis., 1946-47, LL.B., 1949. Bar: N.Y. 1950. Asso. firm Root, Ballantine, Harlan, Bushby & Palmer, N.Y.C., 1949-54; with law div. Scott Paper Co., Phila., 1954-62, 67-85; asst. to gen. mgr. Scott Paper Co., Everett, Wash., 1962-67; asst. sec. Scott Paper Co., 1965-71, corp. sec., 1971-83, asst. sec., 1983-84, ret. Pres. Knollwood Terrace Civic Assn., Carle Place, N.Y., 1952-53; pres. Carle Place Taxpayers Assn., 1953-54; bd. dirs. Nether Providence Cmty. Assocs., Inc., Wallingford, Pa., 1969-75, pres., 1969-70; bd. dirs. Ethel Mason Day Care Ctr., Wallingford, 1976-81, pres., 1979-80; vestryman St. Mary's Episc. Ch., Carle Place, N.Y., 1953-54; vestryman, jr. warden Trinity Episc. Ch., Everett, Wash., 1965-67; chmn. Rose Valley Folk, 1977-78; bd. dirs. Helen Kate Furness Free Libr., Wallingford, 1984-87, v.p., 1986-87; Chester-Wallingford chpt. ARC, 1991—, exec. com., 1992—, 1st vice chmn., 1994-95, chmn., 1995—; bd. dirs. Everett, Wash. Area C. of C., 1965-67; Snohomish County Family Counseling Svc., Everett, 1962-67, pres., 1965; pres. Wallingford, Pa. Swim Club, 1960-61. Lt. USNR, 1942-46. Mem. ABA, Am. Soc. Corp. Secs. (dir. 1977-81, pres. Middle Atlantic group 1976-77), Harvard Club (Phila., sch. com. 1959-62, 76-90). Home: 15 Rose Valley Rd Moylan PA 19063-4217

PEACE, BARBARA LOU JEAN, education educator; b. Valdosta, Ga., Jan. 11, 1939; d. Billington Philip and Hattie Lougene (Dollar) Peace. Student, Valdosta State Coll., 1956-58; BA in English, Tenn. Temple U., 1961; postgrad., Fla. State U., 1962-63; MS in Indsl. and Orgnl.

Psychology, Valdosta State U., 1994. Receptionist ITT, Thompson Industries, Valdosta, Ga., 1961; child welfare worker Lowndes County Welfare Dept., Valdosta, 1961-62; supr. child welfare divsn. Muscogee County Dept. Family & Children Services, Columbus, Ga., 1963-66; dir. social work Valdosta-Lowndes County Headstart Program, 1966-67; tchr. English & Remedial Reading Valdosta City Sch. System, 1966-73; tchr. advisor English & Psychology Valdosta Technical Inst., 1973—; chmn. dept. psychology Valdosta Tech. Inst., 1994—; chair South Ga. Consortium Psychology Tchrs., 1994-95; advisor Vocat. Indsl. Clubs Am., 1981-88, 90—, adv. coun., 1982-86, planning com. regional leadership conf., 1984, coord. state leadership contests, state advisor officer tng., presenter leadership confs., 1986; advisor Valdosta Tech. Inst. 1981-88, 90—, quality coun. mem. 1994, quality coun. team leader 1995-96, chair blood drive, 1994-95; past vica craft adv. bd. Valdosta H.S., Lowndes H.S. Sponsor ARC Blood Drive, Valdosta, 1984-88, Ga. Sheriffs' Boys' Ranch, Arts, Inc.; vol. Am. Heart Assn., Am. Lung Assn., 1994—; contbr. Am. Cancer Soc., United Way; active personnel, finance, nominating and kindergarten and kitchen coms. Azalea City Bapt. Ch., adult choir, dir. children's choir, tchr. Sunday Sch., nursery worker; bd. dirs., pianist, advisor/counsellor, tutor Valdosta Korean Bapt. Ch., 1985-92. Mem. Am. Vocational Assn., Ga. Vocational Assn., Vocat. Ga. Assn., Vocational Edn. Spl. Needs Personnel, Action Travelers (bd. dirs. 1970—), Adventuretour Exchange Club (sponsor 1981-85). Republican. Baptist. Avocations: traveling, music, stamp collecting, gourmet cooking. Office: Valdosta Tech Inst 4089 Val Tech Rd Valdosta GA 31602-9801

PEACE, H. W., II, oil company executive; b. Clinton, Okla., May 21, 1935; s. Herman Wilbern and Bernice (Mitchell) P.; m. Norma June Williams; children: Hugh William, Susannah Lee. BS in Geology, U. Okla., 1959, MS in Geology, 1964; postgrad., U. S.W. La., 1968. Jr. geologist Union Oil Co. Calif., Houston, 1964-65; area geologist Union Oil Co. Calif., Lafayette, La., 1965-70; geologist dist. exploration Union Oil Co. Calif., Oklahoma City, 1970-77; mgr. Rocky Mountain exploration Union Oil Co. Calif., Casper, Wyo., 1977-80; mgr. div. exploration Cotton Petroleum Corp., Tulsa, 1980-83; v.p. exploration Hadson Petroleum Corp., Oklahoma City, 1983-85, exec. v.p., chief operating officer, 1985-88, also bd. dirs.; exec. v.p., chief ops. officer Mosswood Oil and Gas Co., Oklahoma City, 1985-88; exec. v.p., chief ops. officer Anadarko Supply Co., Oklahoma City, 1986-88, also bd. dirs.; mng. ptnr. EXAD, Oklahoma City, 1988-91; pres., chief exec. officer, dir. Panhandle Royalty Co., Oklahoma City, 1991—. Dir. sch. geology adv. com. U. Okla., Norman, 1984—, vice chmn. 1988-89, chmn. 1989-90, exec. com. 1990—. Lt. USN 1959-63, capt. USNR, 1963-82, retired list 1995. Mem. Am. Assn. Petroleum Geology (rep. del. or alt. 1984—), Soc. Exploration Geophysicists, Soc. Econ. Paleontologists and Mineralogists, Petroleum Assn. Wyo. (v.p. 1979-80), Tulsa Geol. Soc., Oklahoma City Geol. Soc. (chmn. profl. affairs 1976-77), Naval Res. Assn., Cherokee Hills Homeowners Assn. (pres. 1971-73), Fieldstone Homeowners Assn. (pres. 1983), Navy League. Republican. Lodge: Civitan. Avocations: golf, swimming, hiking. Office: Panhandle Royalty Co 5400 N Grand Blvd Ste 210 Oklahoma City OK 73112-5654

PEACH, PEGGY, mental health therapist, chemical dependency counselor; b. Middletown, Ohio, Sept. 14, 1946; children: Christina, Scott. BS in Edn., Ohio U., 1971; MA, U. Cin., 1987; PhD, Union Inst., Cin., 1994—. Pers. mgr. Import Store, Lebanon, Ohio, 1971-75; trainer Ohio Dept. Transp., Lebanon, 1975-80; family therapist Greene Hall, Xenia, Ohio, 1987-88; counselor, clin. dir. County Drug and Alcohol, Lebanon, 1989-90; therapist Bergamo, Dayton, Ohio, 1992; crisis counselor Eastway, Dayton, 1991-92; therapist A.V.O.I.S.E., Cin., 1991-94, Dartmouth Hosp., Dayton, 1992-94; condr. workshops in field. Mem. Ctrl. Com., Rep. Party, Warren County, Ohio, 1988; den mother cub scouts Boy Scouts Am., 1981; vol. Children's Svcs., Lebanon, 1986, Women Helping Women, Cin., 1987. Mem. Am. Counselors Assn., Assn. for Religious and Value Issues in Counseling, Nat. Cert. Reciprocity Consortium Alcohol and Other Drug Abuse. Roman Catholic. Avocations: needlework, fishing, reading.

PEACHEY, LEE DEBORDE, biology educator; b. Rochester, N.Y., Apr. 14, 1932; s. Clarence Henry and Eunice (DeBorde) P.; m. Helen Pauline Fuchs, June 7, 1958; children: Michael Stephen, Sarah Elizabeth Keating, Anne Palmer Lorenz. BS, Lehigh U., 1953; postgrad., U. Rochester, 1953-56; Ph.D. (Leitz fellow), Rockefeller U., 1959; MA (hon.), U. Pa., 1971. Research asso. Rockefeller U., 1959-60; asst. prof. zoology Columbia U., 1960-63, asso. prof., 1963-65; asso. prof. biochemistry and biophysics U. Pa., Phila., 1965-70; prof. biology U. Pa., 1970—; adj. prof. molecular, cellular and developmental biology U. Colo., 1969-84; mem. molecular biology study sect. NIH, 1969-73; mem. Biomed. Rsch. Tech. Rev. Com., NIH, 1994—; mem. Mayor's Sci. and Tech. Adv. Coun., Phila., 1972—; chmn. Gordon Rsch. Conf. on Muscle, 1983. Editor: Third and Fourth Conferences on Cellular Dynamics, N.Y. Acad. Scis., 1967, First and Second Confs. on Cellular Dynamics, 1968, Am. Physiol. Soc. Handbook on Skeletal Muscle, 1983; mem. editorial bd. Tissue and Cell, 1969—, Jour. Cell Biology, 1970-73, Pitman Series in Cellular and Development Biology, 1977—, Microscopy Rsch. and Technique, 1982-93, Advances in Optical and Electron Microscopy, 1983—, Neuroimage, 1991—, Jour. Microscopy, 1992—, Bioimages, 1993—; contbr. articles to sci. jours. Trustee Keith R. Porter Endowment for Cell Biology, Narberth, Pa., 1981—. Guggenheim and Fulbright-Hays fellow, 1967-68, Overseas fellow Churchill Coll., Cambridge, Eng., 1967-68, Fogarty Sr. Internat. fellow, 1979-80, hon. rsch. fellow U. Coll., London, 1979-80; Royal Soc. (London) guest rsch. fellow, Cambridge, 1986; grantee NSF, 1960-72, NIH, 1973—, Muscular Dystrophy Assn. Am., Inc. 1973-91. Fellow AAAS; Mem. Electron Microscopy Soc. Am. (council 1975-78, pres. 1982), Am. Soc. Cell Biology (program chmn. 1965, council 1966-69), Biophys. Soc. (program chmn. 1976, council 1976-80, exec. com. 1976-82, pres. 1981-82), Internat. Union Pure and Applied Biophysics (council 1978-84, v.p. 1984-87, pres. 1987-90, chmn. commn. on cell and membrane biophysics 1981-84, hon. v.p. 1990-93), Physiol. Soc. (Eng.); mem. Internat. Soc. Stereology (internat. stereology software com. 1982—), Soc. Gen. Physiologists. Achievements include research in mechanisms of muscle cell contraction; development of methods in light and electron microscopy; development of computer graphic methods for three-dimensional image analysis and reconstruction. Home: 606 Old Gulph Rd Narberth PA 19072-1622 Office: U Pa Dept Biology Philadelphia PA 19104-6018

PEACOCK, A(LVIN) WARD, textile company executive; b. Durham, N.C., June 17, 1929; s. Erle Ewart and Vera Louise (Ward) P.; m. Barbara Sheppard White, July 2, 1955; children: Alvin Ward, Stephen White, Nancy Lay. B.S. in Commerce, U. N.C., 1950; M.B.A., Harvard U., 1952. Asst. to v.p. Erwin Mills, Inc., Durham, 1953-55, sec., 1957-62, sec.-treas., 1962-64; v.p. Dixie Yarns, Inc., Chattanooga, 1964-76, sr. v.p., 1976-81; sr. v.p. Springs Industries, Fort Mill, S.C., 1981-86; exec. v.p. Springs Industries, Fort Mill, 1986-92; bd. dirs. Palmetto Seed Capital Corp.; regional dir. First Wachovia Corp., Charlotte, N.C., 1988-92. Trustee Holston Conf. Colls., Tenn., 1968-79, Sci. Mus. Charlotte, 1990-94; bd. dirs. Chattanooga Meml. Hosp., 1979-81, Charlotte Symphony, 1990-94, Greater Carolinas chpt. ARC, 1988-94; dir. Allied Arts Fund, 1978-81, Metrolina Food Bank, 1994—; mem. Chattanooga Wastewater Regulation Bd., 1978-81. 1st lt. USAF, 1955-57. Mem. Tenn. Mfrs. Assn. (chmn. bd. dirs. 1980-81), Chattanooga Mfrs. Assn. (pres. 1968-69), Am. Textile Mfrs. Inst., Univ. Club, River Hills Club, Phi Beta Kappa, Alpha Kappa Psi, Sigma Nu. Republican. Methodist. Home: 22 Wood Hollow Rd River Hills SC 29710

PEACOCK, ERLE EWART, JR., surgeon, lawyer, educator; b. Durham, N.C., Sept. 10, 1926; s. Erle Ewart and Vera Louise (Ward) P.; m. Mary Louise Lowrey, Apr. 17, 1954; children: James Lowrey, Susan Louise, Virginia Gayle. Cert. in medicine, U. N.C., 1947, BS, 1990; MD, Harvard U., 1949; JD, U.N.C., 1993. Bar: N.C. 1993. Intern, asst. resident surgery Roosevelt Hosp., N.Y.C., 1949-51; from asst. resident gen. surgery U. N.C. Hosps., Chapel Hill, 1953-54, chief resident gen. surgery, 1954-55; resident in plastic surgery Barnes Hosp., St. Louis, 1955-56; mem. faculty dept. surgery U. N.C., Chapel Hill, 1956-69; prof. surgery, head div. plastic surgery U. N.C., 1965-69; prof., chmn. dept. surgery U. Ariz., Tucson, 1969-77; prof. surgery Tulane U., New Orleans, 1977-82; pvt. practice surgery Chapel Hill, N.C., 1982—; vis. prof. surgery U. Va., Charlottesville, 1988—; chief hand surgery Valley Forge Army Hosp., Phoenixville, Pa., 1951-53; pres. Am. Bd. Plastic Surgery, 1975. Author: Wound Repair, 1977, 3d edit., 1982; assoc. editor: Am. Jour. Surgery, 1967—, Surgery Yearbook, 1970-89, Plastic and Reconstructive Surgery, 1972-78; asst. editor: Jour. Surg. Rsch., 1970-76. With USN, 1945-46; capt. M.C., U.S. Army, 1951-53. Served with U.S. Navy, 1945-46; served to capt. M.C. U.S. Army, 1951-53. Recipient Yandell medal Louisville Surg. Soc., 1972, McGraw medal Detroit Surg. Soc., 1973, Disting. Svc. award U. N.C., 1979, Jacob Markowitz award Acad. Surg. Rsch., 1993, Lifetime Achievement award Wound Healing Soc., 1994. Mem. AAAS, ACS, ABA, Womack Sur. Soc. (pres. 1979-80), Soc. U. Surgeons (pres. 1965-68), Plastic Surgery Rsch. Coun. (pres. 1966), Am. Surg. Assn., Am. Bd. Plastic Surgery (pres. 1976), Am. Bd. Gen. Surgery, Am. Assn. Plastic Surgeons (Clinician of Yr. 1985), Am. Soc. Surgery Hand, Internat. Soc. Surgeons, So. Surg. Assn., Rotary, Alpha Omega Alpha. Republican. Methodist. Home: 645 Rock Creek Rd Chapel Hill NC 27514-6714 Office: Patterson Dilthey Clay & Bryson Attys at Law 4020 Westchase Blvd Ste 550 Raleigh NC 27607-3942

PEACOCK, GEORGE ROWATT, retired life insurance company executive; b. Lakeland, Fla., Aug. 27, 1923; s. Robert and Annie Keane (Rowatt) P.; m. Virginia Jenkins, June 7, 1952; 1 child, Robert George. B.A., U. Fla., 1948, postgrad., 1948-49; postgrad., U. N.C., 1949-50, 51, Ind. U., summers 1966, 67. With Equitable Life Assurance Soc. U.S., 1952-88; v.p., head real estate dept. Equitable Life Assurance Soc. U.S., N.Y.C., 1974-77; sr. v.p., head equities sector Equitable Life Assurance Soc. U.S., 1977-80, sr. v.p., head real estate sector, 1980-84; chmn., chief exec. Equitable Real Estate Investment Mgmt., Inc., 1984-88; pres., chief exec. officer Carluke Inc., 1988—; past pres. Planters Redevel. Corp., St. Louis, 1984-87; trustee Equitable Life Mortgage & Realty Investors, 1981-83; bd. dirs. E.Q.K. Realty Investors, Arbor Properties Trust (formerly E.Q.K. Green Acres); emeritus mem. adv. bd. govs. Wharton Real Estate Ctr., U. Pa., 1985—. Author papers in field. Trustee Urban Land Inst., 1982-88; bd. dirs. Urban Land Found., 1994—; bd. govs. Ctrl. Atlanta Progress, 1984-86. With USAAF, 1942-45, with USAF, 1950-51. Decorated Purple Heart. Mem. Am. Soc. Real Estate Counselors, Urban Land Inst., Brit. Am. Property Investment Council, Am. Inst. Real Estate Appraisers, Real Estate Bd. N.Y. (past gov.), Phi Beta Kappa, Phi Kappa Phi, Phi Gamma Delta. Democrat. Office: 3414 Peachtree Rd NE Atlanta GA 30326-1113

PEACOCK, HUGH ANTHONY, agricultural research director; b. Cairo, Ga., May 30, 1928; s. Leslie Hugh and Annie John (Aldredge) P.; m. Mary Helen Willis, Oct. 8, 1949; children: Ramon Anthony, Elizabeth Ann, Mary Evelyn. BS in Agronomy, U. Fla., 1952, MS in Agronomy, 1953; PhD, Iowa State U., 1956. Rsch. assoc. Iowa State U., Ames, 1955-56; asst. agronomist U. Fla., Leesburg, 1957-58; rsch. agronomist Ga. Exptl. Sta. USDA, Experiment, 1959-73; dir. Agrl. Rsch. & Edn. Ctr. U. Fla., Jay, 1973—. Contbr. articles to Agronomy Jour., Crop Sci., Plant Disease, Jour. Nematology. Director Hist. Soc. Santa Rosa County, Milton, Fla., 1979-80, Kiwanis Club of Milton, 1988-89, chmn. agrl. com., 1987-89. Cpl. U.S. ARmy, 1946-47, CBI. John D. Rockefeller Inst. scholar, 1953. Mem. Environ. Enhancement Assn. West Fla. (bd. dirs. Pensacola chpt. 1976-96), Am. Soc. Agronomy (assoc. editor 1980-83), Am. Genetic Assn., Crop Sci. Soc. Am. (assoc. editor 1976-80), Alpha Zeta, Phi Kappa Phi, Sigma Xi, Gamma Sigma Delta. Methodist. Achievements include research in number of genes controlling defoliation vs. non-defoliation in cotton; effect of heterosis and combining ability on yield of cotton, effect of nitrogen fertilization on yield; effect of skip-row culture on fiber characteristics of cotton; yield response of cotton to spacing, effect of seed source on seedling vigor, yield and lint of upland cotton; a cone-type planter for experimental plots; subsurface sweep for applying herbicides; yield responses of soybean cultivars to Meloidogyne incognita; cotton responses to nitrogen fertilization. Office: U Fla Agr Rsch Ctr RR 3 Box 575 Jay FL 32565-8926

PEACOCK, JAMES DANIEL, lawyer; b. Moorestown, N.J., Dec. 19, 1930; s. L. Lawrence and Esther H. Peacock; m. Joan Peacock, June 14, 1953; children: Elizabeth Levine, Martha McLaughlin, Margaret Mae Daly, Mary Anne Freidman. AB, Duke U., 1952; LLB, U. Md., 1957. Bar: M. 1957, U.S. Ct. Appeals (4th cir.) 1959, U.S. Dist. Ct. Md. 1957, U.S. Supreme Ct. 1976. Of counsel Semmes Bowen & Semmes, Balt., 1957—. Trustee Sheppard & Enoch Pratt Hosp., Towson, Md., 1964— (chair 1993—). Fellow Am. Coll. Trial Lawyers (state chair 1985-86, adj. state chair 1992-93), ABA, Md. State Bar Assn., Am. Bar Found., Md. Bar Found.; mem. Balt. City Bar Assn., Balt. County Bar Assn., Wednesday Law Club (pres. 1987-88). Home: 105 Bonnie Hill Rd Baltimore MD 21204-4209 Office: Semmes Bowen & Semmes 401 Washington Ave Baltimore MD 21204-4821

PEACOCK, JUDITH ANN See ERWIN, JUDITH ANN

PEACOCK, LAMAR BATTS, retired physician; b. Albany, Ga., Sept. 21, 1920; s. Herbert A. and Helen Marian (LeVan) P.; m. Jane Bonner, June 7, 1947; children: Helen Lee (Mrs. Richard Paul Wade), Linda Jane (Mrs. Mathew Gossage), Lamar Bonner. BA, Emory U., 1941; MD, Med. Coll. Ga., 1946. Diplomate: Am. Bd. Internal Medicine. Intern Univ. Hosp., Augusta, 1946-47; resident Univ. Hosp., 1947-48; fellow internal medicine U. Va. Hosp., Charlottesville, 1948-49; resident Univ. Hosp., Augusta, 1949-50; practice medicine specializing in internal medicine and allergy Atlanta, 1950-91; mem. staff St. Joseph's Infirmary, Crawford Long Hosp., Piedmont Hosp., Grady Meml. Hosp., Hughes Spalding Pavilion, Northside Hosp., West Paces Ferry Hosp., all Atlanta, Cobb Gen. Hosp., Austell, Ga., Douglasville (Ga.) Hosp.; instr. internal medicine Ga. Bapt. Hosp., Atlanta, 1950-58, chief medicine, 1958-72; mem. faculty Emory U. Sch. Medicine, Atlanta, 1950—, asst. clin. prof. medicine, 1962—; instr. internal medicine Sch. Dentistry, 1958—. Chief med. br., health services Atlanta Met. Area Civil Def., 1960-63; mem. Ga. Pub. Health Assn., 1967-69, Ga. Bd. Health, 1966-72, Ga. Vocational Rehab. Council, 1973—; Pres. trustees Med. Coll. Ga. Found., 1963. Fellow ACP, Am. Coll. Allergy and Immunology (nat. pres. 1972-73), Am. Acad. Allergy and Immunology; mem. AMA, Am. Heart Assn., Ga. Heart Assn., Am. Soc. Internal Medicine, Ga. Soc. Internal Medicine, 5th Dist. Med. Soc., Ga. Thoracic Soc., Med. Assn. Atlanta (prs. 1965), Med. Assn. Ga. (1st v.p. 1966-67), Southeastern Allergy Assn. (pres. 1963-64), So. Med. Assn., Cherokee Town and Country Club. Episcopalian. Home: 3120 Verdun Dr NW Atlanta GA 30305-1940

PEACOCK, LELON JAMES, psychologist, educator; b. Brevard, N.C., May 25, 1928; s. L.J. and Dorothy (Barrett) P.; m. Marian Davis, June 8, 1945; children: Lynn Barrett, Janice Davis, Timothy Lee. Student, Emory U., 1945-47; A.B., Berea Coll., 1950; M.S., U. Ky., 1952, Ph.D., 1956. Psychophysiologist U.S. Army Med. Research Lab., Ft. Knox, Ky., 1954-56; rsch. assoc., acting dir. Yerkes Labs. of Primate Biology, Inc., Orange Park, Fla., 1956-59; assoc. prof. psychology U. Ga., Athens, 1959-65; prof. U. Ga., 1966-90, prof. emeritus, 1990—. Author: (with R.V. Heckel) Textbook of General Psychology, 1966; Contbr. articles profl. jours. Recipient U. Ga. M.G. Michael Research award, 1964. Fellow AAAS; mem. APA, So. Soc. Philosophy and Psychology (pres. 1973-74), Soc. Neurosci., Sigma Xi, Phi Kappa Phi. Home: 145 Woodland Way Athens GA 30606-4349

PEACOCK, MARKHAM LOVICK, JR., English educator; b. Shaw, Miss., Sept. 19, 1903; s. Markham Lovick and Mary (Patton) P.; m. Dora Greenlaw, Dec. 29, 1928. Grad., Webb Sch., 1921; B.A., Washington and Lee U., 1924, M.A., 1926; Ph.D., Johns Hopkins, 1942. Mem. faculty Va. Polytech. Inst., 1926—, prof. English, 1945—, chmn. dept., 1960-66. Author: The Critical Opinions of William Wordsworth, 1949, also critical, ednl. and lit. articles. Mem. Am. Assn. U. Profs., Nat. Council of Tchrs. English, Modern Lang. Assn., Internat. Fedn. of Modern Langs. and Lits., Modern Humanities Research Assn., Acad. Polit. Sci., N.E.A., Guild of Scholars, Omicron Delta Kappa, Lambda Chi Alpha, Sigma Upsilon, Phi Kappa Phi, Gold Triangle. Episcopalian. Clubs: Shenandoah; Tudor and Stuart (Balt.), Johns Hopkins (Balt.); Princeton. Home: 801 Draper Rd SW Blacksburg VA 24060-5117

PEACOCK, MARY WILLA, magazine editor; b. Evanston, Ill., Oct. 23, 1942; d. William Gilbert and Mary Willa (Young) P. B.A., Vassar Coll., 1964. Assoc. lit. editor Harper's Bazaar mag., N.Y.C., 1964-69; staff editor Innovation mag., N.Y.C., 1969-70; editor in chief, co-founder, sec.-treas., pres. Rags mag., N.Y.C., San Francisco, 1970-71; co-founder, features editor Ms. mag., N.Y.C., 1971-77; pub., pres. Rags mag., N.Y.C., 1977-80; sr. editor Village Voice, N.Y.C., 1980-85, style editor, 1985-89; editor-in-chief Model mag., N.Y.C., 1989—, editorial cons., 1991—; fashion dir. Lear's Mag., N.Y.C., 1992-93; dep. editor In Style Mag., 1993-94, Mirabella mag., 1994-95; cons., 1995—.

PEACOCK, MOLLY, poet; b. Buffalo, June 30, 1947; d. Edward Frank and Pauline Ruth (Wright) P. BA magna cum laude, Harpur Coll., Binghamton, N.Y., 1969; MA with honors, Johns Hopkins U., 1977. Adminstr., lectr. in English, SUNY-Binghamton, 1970-76; lectr. Johns Hopkins U., Balt., 1977-78, Barnard Coll., 1989-93; instr. English, Friends Sem., N.Y.C., 1981-92; poet-in-residence Del. Arts Coun., Wilmington, 1978-81, Bucknell U., NYU, Sarah Lawrence Coll., U. Western Ontario, 1995—. Author: And Live Apart, 1980; Raw Heaven, 1984, Take Heart, 1989, Original Love, 1995; contbg. writer House and Garden mag., 1996 contbr. poems to The New Yorker, The New Republic, The Nation. Danforth Found. fellow, 1976; Yaddo fellow, 1980, 82, 89, Ingram Merrill Found., 1981, 86, New Va. Rev., 1983; grantee Creative Artists Pub. Svc. Program, 1977, N.Y. Found. for Arts, 1985, NEA, 1991; Lila Wallace/Woodrow Wilson fellow, 1994, 95. Mem. PEN, Poetry Soc. Am. (governing bd. 1988—, pres. emeritus). Home: 505 E 14th St Apt 3G New York NY 10009-2903 also: 229 Emery St E, London, ON Canada N6C 2E3

PEACOR, DONALD RALPH, geology educator, research mineralogist; b. Somerville, Mass., Feb. 15, 1937; married 1960; 3 children. BS, Tufts U., 1958; MS, MIT, 1960, PhD in Crystallography, 1962. Instr. to assoc. prof. geology U. Mich., Ann Arbor, 1962-71, prof., 1971—. Mem. Mineral Soc. Am., Am. Crystallographic Assn. Office: University of Michigan Dept of Geological Sciences Ann Arbor MI 48109-1063*

PEAGLER, OWEN F., college administrator; b. New Milford, Conn., Nov. 28, 1936; s. Robert James and Myrtle (Gary) P.; m. Joyce Hancock (div. 1983); children: Catherine, Robert; m. Teresa Boone, Mar. 20, 1985; 1 child, Kirin. BS, Western Conn. State U., 1956; MA, NYU, 1959, profl. diploma, 1964. Tchr. New Milford Pub. Schs., 1955-56; dir. guidance White Plains (N.Y.) Pub. Schs., 1957-69; dean sch. continuing edn. Pace U., N.Y.C., 1969-78, Ea. Conn. State U., Willimantic, 1978—; chmn. bd. WAVE, Inc., Washington, 1976—; cons., V.I., 1970-73. Sec. dept. community affairs State of Del., Wilmington, 1982-83; asst. to N.Y. Rep. State Chmn. N.Y. Rep. State Com., Albany, 1970-78; chmn. Pres'. Adv. Coun. on Edn. Disadvantaged Children, Washington, 1973-78. Named N.Y. State Young Man of Yr. N.Y. Jr. C. of C., 1964; recipient Outstanding Coll. Programs award Conn. Nat. Guard, 1988. Home: 57 Boughton Rd Old Lyme CT 06371-1321 Office: Ea Conn State U Office of Dean Cont Edn 83 Windham St Willimantic CT 06226-2211

PEAKE, FRANK, middle school educator; b. Elgin, S.C., Oct. 25, 1939; s. Barney and Elrie (Branham) P. AA, Anderson Coll., 1966; BS, U. S.C., 1968; MA in Teaching, The Citadel, 1976. Cert. tchr., S.C. Classroom tchr. Berkeley Jr. High, Moncks Corner, S.C., 1968-70; classroom tchr. Berkeley Middle Sch., Moncks Corner, 1970-85, 90-95, ret., 1995; classroom tchr. Macedonia Middle Sch., Moncks Corner, 1986-88, North Ctrl. High, Kershaw, S.C., 1988-89. With S.C. Air Nat. Guard, 1959-65. Mem. Nat. Coun. Tchrs. Math., Mensa. Republican. Baptist. Avocations: reading. Home: 195 Peake Rd Elgin SC 29045

PEALE, RUTH STAFFORD (MRS. NORMAN VINCENT PEALE), religious leader; b. Fonda, Iowa, Sept. 10, 1906; d. Frank Burton and Anna Loretta (Crosby) Stafford; m. Norman Vincent Peale, June 20, 1930; children: Margaret Ann (Mrs. Paul F. Everett), John Stafford, Elizabeth Ruth (Mrs. John M. Allen). AB, Syracuse U., 1928, LLD, 1953; LittD, Hope Coll., 1962; LHD (hon.), Milw. Sch. Engring., 1985, Judson Coll., 1988; LHD, Milw. Sch. Engring., 1985. Tchr. math. Cen. High Sch., Syracuse, N.Y., 1928-31; nat. pres. women's bd. domestic missions Ref. Ch. Am., 1936-46; sec. Protestant Film Commn., 1946-51; chmn. Am. Mother's Com., 1948-49; pres., editor-in-chief, gen. sec., CEO, chmn. bd. dirs. Peale Ctr. for Christian Living, 1940—; nat. pres. bd. domestic missions Ref. Ch. in Am., 1955-56; mem. bd. N. Am. Missions, 1963-69, pres., 1967-69; mem. gen. program council Ref. Ch. in Am., 1968—; mem. com. of 24 for merger Ref. Ch. in Am. and Presbyn. Ch. U.S., 1966-69; v.p. Protestant Council N.Y.C., 1964-66; hon. chancellor Webber Coll., 1972—; co-founder, pub. Guideposts, N.Y.C., 1945—, pres., 1985-92, chmn. bd., 1992—; pres. Fleming H. Revell, Tarrytown, N.Y., 1985-92; founder Ruth Stafford Peale Ctr., Syracuse, 1989—. Appeared on: nat. TV program What's Your Trouble, 1952-68; Author: I Married a Minister, 1942, The Adventure of Being a Wife, 1971, Secrets of Staying in Love, 1984; founder, pub. (with Dr. Peale) Guidepost mag., 1957—; co-subject with husband: film One Man's Way, 1963. Trustee Hope Coll., Holland, Mich., Champlain Coll., Burlington, Vt., Stratford Coll., Danville, Va., Lenox Sch., N.Y.C., Interchurch Center Syracuse U., 1955-61; bd. dirs. Cook Christian Tng. Sch., Lord's Day Alliance U.S.; mem. bd. and exec. com. N.Y. Theol. Sem., N.Y.C.; sponsor Spafford Children's Convalescent Hosp., 1966—; bd. govs. Help Line Telephone Center, 1970—, Norman Vincent Peale Telephone Center, 1977; mem. nat. women's bd. Northwood Inst., 1981. Named N.Y. State Mother of Yr., 1963, Disting. Woman of Yr., Nat. Art Assn., Religious Heritage Am. Ch. Woman of Yr., 1969; recipient Cum Laude award Syracuse U. Alumni Assn. N.Y., 1965, Honor Iowans award Buena Vista Coll., 1966, Am. Mother's com. award for religion, 1970, Disting. Svc. award Coun. Chs., N.Y.C., 1973, Disting. Citizen award Champlain Coll., 1976, Disting. Svc. to Cmty. and Nation award Gen. Fedn. Women's Clubs, 1977, Horatio Alger award, 1977, Religious Heritage award, 1979, joint medallion with husband Soc. for Family of Man, 1981, Soc. Family of Man award, 1981, Alderson-Broaddus award, 1982, Marriage Achievement award Bride's mag., 1984, Gold Angel award Religion in Media, 1987, Adela Rogers St. John Roundtable award, 1987, Disting. Achievement award Am. Aging, 1987, Paul Harris award N.Y. Rotary, 1989, Leader's award Arthritis Found. Dutchess County, 1992, Dave Thomas Well Done! award, 1994, Norman Vincent Peale award for positive thinking, 1994, Master of Influence award Nat. Speakers Assn., 1995. Mem. Insts. Religion and Health (bd. exec. com.), Am. Bible Soc. (trustee 1948-93, hon. trustee 1993—), United Bible Soc. (v.p.), Interch. Ctr. (bd. dirs. 1957-92, chmn. 1982-90), Nat. Coun. Chs. (v.p. 1952-54, gen. bd.; treas. gen. dept. Uniteed Ch. Women, vice chmn. broadcasting and film commn. 1951-55, program chmn. gen. assembly 1966), N.Y. Fedn. Women's Clubs (chmn. religion 1951-53, 57-58), Home Missions Coun. N.A. (nat. pres. 1942-44, nat. chmn. migrant com. 1948-51), Internat. Platform Orgn. (bd. govs. 1994—, Norman Vincent Peale award 1994), PEO, Alpha Phi (Frances W. Willard award 1976). Republican. Office: Peale Ctr Christian Living 66 E Main St Pawling NY 12564-1409

PEALE, STANTON JERROLD, physics educator; b. Indpls., Jan. 23, 1937; s. Robert Frederick and Edith May (Murphy) P.; m. Priscilla Laing Cobb; June 25, 1960; children: Robert Edwin, Douglas Andrew. BSE, Purdue U., 1959; MS in Engring. Physics, Cornell U., 1962, PhD in Engring. Physics, 1965. Research asst. Cornell U., Ithaca, N.Y., 1962-64, research assoc., 1964-65; asst. research geophysicist, asst. prof. astronomy UCLA, 1965-68; asst. prof. physics U. Calif., Santa Barbara, 1968-70, assoc. prof., 1970-76, prof., 1976-94, prof. emeritus, rsch. prof., 1994—; mem. com. lunar and planetary exploration NAS-NRC, Washington, 1980-84, lunar and planetary geosci. rev. panel, 1979-80, 86-89, 94—, Planetary Sys. Sci. Working Group, 1988-93, Lunar and Planetary Sci. Coun., 1984-87; lunar sci. adv. group NASA-JPL, Pasadena, Calif., 1970-72. Assoc. editor: Jour. Geophys. Research, 1987; contbr. articles to profl. jours. Recipient Exceptional Scientific Achievement medal NASA, 1980, James Craig Watson award Nat. Acad. Scis., 1982; vis. fellowships U. Colo., Boulder, 1972-73, 1979-80. Fellow AAAS (Newcomb Cleveland prize 1979), Am. Geophys. Union; mem. Am. Astron. Soc. (divsns. planet sci. and dynamic astronomy, Dirk Brouwer award 1992), Internat. Astron. Union. Avocation: gardening. Office: U Calif Santa Barbara Dept Physics Santa Barbara CA 93106

PEAPPLES, GEORGE ALAN, automotive executive; b. Benton Harbor, Mich., Nov. 6, 1940; s. Arthur L. and Kathleen C. (Peters) P.; m. Rebecca Dean Sowers, June 27, 1962; children: Lucia Christine, Sarah Bouton. BA in Econs., U. Mich., 1962, MBA in Fin., 1963. Fin. analyst Gen. Motors Corp., Detroit, 1964-68; dir. capital analysis and investment N.Y.C., 1968-73; asst. div. comptroller Delco Moraine div. Dayton, Ohio, 1973-75; asst. treas. bank relations Detroit, 1975-77, asst. comptroller, 1980-82; group dir. strategic bus. planning Chevrolet-Pontiac-Canada group Warren, Mich., 1984-86; v.p. Detroit, 1986—; v.p., fin. mgr. Gen. Motors of Can., Ltd., Oshawa, Ont., 1982-84, pres., gen. mgr., 1986-94; asst. sec. of Navy U.S. Dept. Def., 1977-80; v.p. industry-govt. rels. GM, Washington, 1994—, now v.p. corp. affairs; bd. dirs. Nat. Assn. Mfrs., Am. Coalition for Traffic Safety and Fed. City Coun.; mem. vis. com. U. Mich. Mem. Coalition for Vehicle

Choice. Recipient Disting. Pub. Svc. award Washington, 1980. Mem. Phi Kappa Phi. Office: GM Corp. 1660 L St NW Ste 401 Washington DC 20036-5603 also: GM Bldg 3044 W Grand Blvd Detroit MI 48202-3091*

PEARCE, COLMAN CORMAC, conductor, pianist, composer; b. Dublin, Leinster, Ireland, Sept. 22, 1938; came to U.S., 1987; s. Charles Edward and Elizabeth Mary (Byrne) P.; m. Eithne McGrath, Jan. 25, 1964 (div. 1991); 1 child, Deborah. BMus, Nat. U. Ireland, Dublin, 1960; studied with Franco Ferrara, 1965, pvt. pupil of Hans Swarowsky, 1969. From staff condr. to prin. condr. Radio TV Ireland (RTE), Dublin, 1965-83; prin. condr., music dir. Miss. Symphony Orch., Jackson, 1987—; dir. orch. studies, Royal Irish Acad. Music, Dublin, 1970-78; music examiner, Dept. Edn., Dublin, 1965-87; choral arranger, Castle Tours, Limerick, Ireland, 1974—. Avocations: art collecting, reading, theatre, travel. Home: 5045 Meadow Oaks Park Dr Jackson MS 39211-4816 Office: Miss Symphony Orch PO Box 2052 201 E Pascagoula St Jackson MS 39201-4114

PEARCE, DAVID HARRY, biomedical engineer; b. Newport News, Va., July 20, 1943. BSEE, Va. Poly. Tech. and State U., 1966; PhD, U. Va., 1972. Registered profl. engr., Miss. Asst. prof. dept. physiology U. Miss. Med. Sch., Jackson, Miss., 1972-74, E. Tenn. State U. Sch. Medicine, JohnsonCity, Tenn., 1974-75; biomed. engr. Miss. Meth. Rehab. Ctr., Jackson, Miss., 1975-82, dir. biomedical engring., 1987—; v.p. Bobby J. Hall & Assocs., McComb, Miss., 1982-87; grant adminstr. HUD Block Grant, Magnolia, Miss., 1985-87. Contbr. articles to profl. jours. Young Investigator Pulmonary award NIH, 1973. Mem. IEEE, Am. Soc. Hosp. Engrs., Assn. Advancement of Med. Instrumentation, Jackson Photo Soc. (pres. 1980), Miss. Writers Assn. (treas. 1992). Avocations: photography, woodworking, writing. Home: 230 Greenfield Pl Brandon MS 39042-9008 Address: PO Box 5336 Brandon MS 39047-5336 Office: Miss Meth Rehab Ctr 1350 E Woodrow Wilson Ave Jackson MS 39216-5112

PEARCE, DONALD JOSLIN, retired librarian; b. Southampton, Eng., May 31, 1924; came to U.S., 1949, naturalized, 1952; s. Alfred Ernest and Constance May (Jeffrey) P.; m. June Inez Bond, Dec. 7, 1946; children—Kristin, Kim. Student, Sch. Oriental and African Studies, U. London, 1942-43; A.B., George Washington U., 1953; M.S. in L.S, Cath. U. Am., 1954. Part-time library asst. U.S. Dept. Agr., 1949-54; student asst. George Washington U. Library, 1950-53; circulation librarian Denison U., 1954-56; staff Ohio State U. Library, 1956-59, asst. acquisition librarian, 1958-59; head librarian, asst. prof. U. N.D., 1959-69, chief bibliographer, 1969-73, asst. dir. libraries, 1973-75, asst. prof. Oriental philosophy, 1969-75; library dir., asst. prof. philosophy U. Minn., Duluth, 1975-88, ret., 1988; Chmn. staff orgn. round table Ohio Library Assn., 1958-59. Served with Brit. Army, 1943-47. Mem. ALA, N.D. Library Assn. (pres. 1965-67), Minn. Library Assn. (sec. 1978-80, v.p. 1985, pres. 1986), Assn. Coll. Reference Librarians, Mountain Plains Library Assn. (v.p. 1968-69), Buddhist Assn., Phi Beta Kappa, Beta Phi Mu. Home: 1804 Vermilion Rd Duluth MN 55803-2509

PEARCE, ELI M., chemistry educator, administrator; b. Bklyn., May 1, 1929; s. Samuel and Sarah (Reitzen) Perlmutter; m. Maxine I. Horowitz, Feb. 21, 1951 (div. 1978); children:Russell Gane, Debra Nore; m. Judith Handler, May 29, 1980. BS, Bklyn. Coll., 1949; MS, NYU, 1951; PhD, Poly. Inst. Bklyn, 1958. Research chemist NYU-Bellevue Med. Ctr., N.Y.C., 1949-53, DuPont, Wilmington, Del., 1958-62; sec. mgr. J.T. Baker, Phillipsburg, N.J., 1962-68; tech. supr. Allied Corp., Morristown, N.J., 1968-72, research cons., 1972-73; dir. Dreyfus Lab. Research Triangle Inst., Research Triangle Park, N.C., 1973-74; prof. polymer chemistry and chem. engring. Poly. Inst. N.Y., Bklyn., 1974—, dir. Polymer Research Inst., 1981—, Univ. prof., 1990—, head dept. chemistry, 1976-82, dean arts and scis., 1982-90; cons. AMP, Inc., Harrisburg, Pa., Arco, Newton Square, Pa., Colgate, Piscataway, N.J., Dupont, Richmond, Va., Texaco, Beacon, N.Y. Co-author: Laboratory Experiments in Polymer Synthesis and Characterization, 1982, High Performance Thermosets; editor: Macromolecular Synthesis, Vol. 1, 1982; co-editor: Fiber Chemistry, 1983, Contemporary Topics in Polymer Science, vol. 2, 1977, Flame Retardance of Polymeric Materials, vols. 1-3, Jour. Polymer Sci.; mem. editl. bd. Ency. Materials Sci., 1983; contbr. over 220 articles on polymers to profl. jours. Bd. dirs. Petroleum Research Fund, 1982-84; bd. dirs. Nat. Materials Adv. Bd., 1975-77. Served with U.S. Army, 1953-55. Recipient Edn. Service award Plastics Inst. Am., 1973; recipient Disting. Faculty citation Poly. Inst. N.Y., 1980, Paul J. Flory Polymer Edn. award, 1992, Kaufman Lectr. award Ramapo Coll., 1992, Gold Medal award N.Y. Inst. Chemists, 1992, Reed-Lignin Lectr. award U. Wis., 1987. Fellow AAAS, Am. Inst. Chemists, N.Am. Thermal Analysis Soc., N.Y. Acad. Scis. (chmn. polymer sect. 1972-73), Soc. Plastics Engrs. (Internat. Edn. award 1988); mem. Am. Chem. Soc. (councilor 1978—, chmn. polymer divsn. 1980, coun. policy com., chmn. com. sci.), Sigma Xi. Home: 2 Fifth Ave New York NY 10011 Office: Polytech U Polymer Rsch Inst 6 Metrotech Ctr Brooklyn NY 11201-2907

PEARCE, GEORGE HAMILTON, archbishop; b. Boston, Jan. 9, 1921; s. George Hamilton and Marie Louise (Duval) P. BA, Marist Coll. and Sem., Framingham, Mass., 1943. Tchr. Marist Coll. & Sem., Bedford, Mass., 1947-48, St. Mary's High Sch., Van Buren, Maine, 1948-49; missionary Roman Catholic Vicariate of Samoa, 1949-67, vicar apostolic of Samoa, 1956-66; bishop Diocese of Samoa, 1966-67; archbishop Archdiocese of Suva, Suva, Fiji, 1967-76; apostolic adminstr. Diocese of Agana, Guam, 1969; pres. Episcopal Conf. of the Pacific, 1969-71; staff mem. Bethany House of Intercession, Hastings-on-Hudson, N.Y., 1977-83; asst. to bishop Diocese of Providence, 1983—. Home: 30 Fenner St Providence RI 02903-3603

PEARCE, HARRY JONATHAN, lawyer; b. Bismarck, N.D., Aug. 20, 1942; s. William R. and Jean Katherine (Murray) P.; m. Katherine B. Bruk, June 19, 1967; children: Shannon Pearce Baker, Susan J., Harry M. BS, USAF Acad., Colorado Springs, Colo., 1964; JD, Northwestern U., 1967. Bar: N.D. 1967, Mich. 1986. Mcpl. judge City of Bismarck, 1970-76, U.S. magistrate, 1970-76, police commr., 1976-80; sr. ptnr. Pearce & Durick, Bismarck, 1970-85; assoc. gen. counsel GM, Detroit, 1985-87, v.p., gen. counsel, 1987-92, exec. v.p., gen. counsel, 1992-94, exec. v.p., 1994-95, vice chmn., 1996—; bd. dirs. GM Corp., Hughes Electronics Corp., Electron Data Sys. Corp., GM Acceptance Corp., Am. Automobile Mfrs. Assn., Marriott Internat. Inc., Econ. Strategy Inst., United Way for Southeastern Mich. Mem. vis. com. Sch. Law, Northwestern U.; mem. bd. visitors U.S. Air Force Acad.; chmn. Product Liability Adv. Coun. Found.; founding mem. minority counsel demonstration program Commn. on Opportunities for Minorities in the Profession, ABA. Capt. USAF, 1964-70. Hardy scholar Northwestern U., Chgo., 1964-67, recipient Alumni Merit award, 1991. Fellow Am. Coll. Trial Lawyers, Internat. Soc. Barristers; mem. Am. Law Inst. Avocations: amateur radio, woodworking, sailing. Office: GM Corp Mail Code 482-114-132 3044 W Grand Blvd Detroit MI 48202

PEARCE, HERBERT HENRY, real estate company executive. Student, New Haven Coll.; LLD (hon.), U. New Haven, 1980; LHD (hon.), Albertus Magnus Coll., 1988. Various mgmt. positions A.C. Gilbert Co., New Haven, Conn., 1935-57; chmn., CEO H. Pearce Real Estate Co., North Haven, Conn., 1958—. Hon. chmn. YMCA Fund Raising Project; mem. Yale New Haven Hosp. Devel. Com.; nominations com. U. New Haven; bd. dirs. Nation Conf. Christians and Jews; mem. adv. bd. South Ctrl. Jr. Achievement; chmn. United Way Loaned Exec. Com.; chmn. mktg. and rsch. Conn. Regional Econ. Devel. Coun.; advisor Eli Whitney Mus. on A.C. Gilbert Project. Recipient Cmty. Leadership award Greater New Haven C. of C., Greater New Haven Realtor of Yr. award, Outstanding Achievement award Nat. Jr. Achievement Orgn., Humanitarian award Hunger Relief and Devel., Inc., YMCA Cmty. Leadership award; inducted into Jr. Achievement Free Enterprise Hall of Fame. Fellow Berkeley Coll. (assoc.), Yale U. (assoc.); mem. Conn. Assn. Realtors (past pres.), Greater New Haven Bd. Realtors (past pres.), Quinnipiack Club, New Haven Country Club, Mory's Assn., Kiwanis. Office: H Pearce Real Estate Co 393 State St North Haven CT 06473

PEARCE, JOAN DELAP, research company executive; b. Oakland, Calif., June 13, 1930; d. Robert Jerome and Wilhelmina (Reaume) DeLap; m. Gerald Allan Pearce, June 18, 1953; 1 child, Scott Ford. Student, U. Oreg., 1948-55. Rsch. assoc. deForest Rsch., L.A., 1966-78, assoc. dir., 1978-92; dir. rsch. Walt Disney Prodns., Burbank, Calif., 1978; pres., bd. dirs. Joan Pearce Rsch. Assocs., 1992—; lighting dir. Wilcoxen Players, Beverly Hills, Calif., 1955-60, Theatre 40, L.A., 1960-66. Bd. advisors Living History Ctr., Marin County, Calif., 1982-89, bd. dirs., 1989—. Mem. Am. Film Inst. Democrat. Avocations: photography; travel; theater; swimming. Home: 2621 Rutherford Dr Los Angeles CA 90068-3042 Office: Joan Pearce Rsch Assocs 8111 Beverly Blvd Ste 308 Los Angeles CA 90048-4525

PEARCE, PAUL FRANCIS, retired aerospace electronics company executive; b. Boston, Sept. 17, 1928; s. George Hamilton and Marie Louise (Duval) P.; m. Gilda Troisi, Apr. 11, 1953; children: Janet, Theresa, Diane. BSEE (Edwards scholar), MIT, 1950; M.S., Mass. Inst. Tech., L.A., 1952; postgrad. (Hughes fellow), U. Calif., Los Angeles, 1957-58, U. So., Calif., 1958-59, Inst. Mgmt. Northwestern U., 1966. Project engr. Trans-Sonics, Inc., Burlington, Mass., 1952-55; sect. head application engring., strategic systems Hughes Aircraft Co., Culver City, Calif., 1955-59; with Lockheed Electronics Co., Plainfield, N.J., 1959-67; gen. mgr. div. mil. systems Lockheed Electronics Co., 1964-65, v.p., gen. mgr., 1965-67; v.p., div. mgr. Tele-Dynamics div. AMBAC Industries, Inc., Ft. Washington, Pa, 1967-74; group v.p. comml. and aerospace electronics group AMBAC Industries, Inc., Carle Place, N.Y., 1973-80; pres. James G. Biddle Co., Blue Bell, Pa., 1980-93, ret.; bd. dirs. AVO Internat. Ltd., 1987-91. Mem. Armed Forces Communications and Electronics Assn. (pres. 1969-71), Inst. Nav., Delaware Valley Mfrs. Assn. (sr. vice chmn. 1987-89, chmn. 1990-92—), Greater Phila. C. of C., Ft. Washington Indsl. Park Mgmt. Assn. (gov. 1973-74), Sigma Xi. Clubs: Mfrs'. Golf and Country (Oreland, Pa.) (handicap chmn. 1987-90), St. David's Golf Club (Wayne, Pa.).

PEARCE, RONALD, retired cosmetic company executive; b. Whitstable, County of Kent, Eng., Apr. 29, 1920; came to U.S., 1949; s. Fernley Charles and Medora Kate (Lissenden) P.; m. Olive Stacey, Apr. 4, 1942; children: David Fernley, Jane Ryding Robertson. Cambridge matriculation, Lindisfarne Coll., Ruabon, North Wales, U.K., 1937. Chief cashier Westminster Bank, Croydon, Eng., 1947-48; comml. officer Brit. Consulate, Dallas, 1949-52; v.p. World Gift Co., Dallas, 1953-63, Nelson Electronics, Dallas, 1963-68; stockbroker Walston & Co., Dallas, 1968-73; dir. purchasing Mary Kay Cosmetics, Inc., Dallas, 1973-85; pres. Global Water Techs., Inc., 1992-95, Alpha Aqua Tech., 1996—. Chmn. bd. Dallas Lighthouse for the Blind, 1987. Served to flight lt. RAF, 1940-46. Republican. Episcopalian. Home: 6918 Lloyd Valley Ln Dallas TX 75230-3129

PEARCE, WILLIAM JOSEPH, public broadcasting executive; b. Ponca City, Okla., Jan. 15, 1925; s. William Thomas and Mary Madeline (Fitzgerald) P.; m. Michaele Evelyn Mitchell, Aug. 1, 1958 (div. June 1962); m. Mary Simmen, June 6, 1964 (div. Mar. 31, 1982); children: Margaret Wickens, Daniel Ethan.; m. Noel Knille, Sept. 1, 1983 (div. Dec. 1988); children: Ryder Fitzgerald and Tyler Lightsinger (twins); stepchildren: Laura Rutherford Stone, Alexandra Garret Stone. B.A., U. Miami, 1950; postgrad., U. Conn., 1952-53; M.S., Syracuse U., 1959; grad. Advanced Mgmt. Program, Harvard U., 1976, Wharton Sch., U. Pa. Tchr. public schs. East Lyme, Conn., 1953-56; tchr. Dept. Air Force, Japan, 1956-58; exec. producer TV N.Y. State Edn. Dept., Albany, 1959-60; dir. radio-TV Brown U., 1960-65; cons. ETV, Rochester (N.Y.) City Sch. Dist., 1966-68; gen. mgr. Sta. WLIW-TV, Plainview, N.Y., 1968-69; pres., gen. mgr. Sta. WXXI-TV-AM-FM, Rochester, 1969—; bd. dirs. Native Am. Pub. Telecommunications, Rochester Philharm. Orch., N.Y. State Gov.'s TV-Film Adv. Bd., Am. Program Svc., Rochester Sch. Arts; chmn. N.Y. State Pub. Broadcasting Stas., Brookings Inst. Ctr. Advanced Study, Rochester. Mem. bd. mgmt. Rochester YMCA Camps; dir. Hunt Hollow Devel. Corp.; v.p. fin. Urbanarium, Rochester Devel. Cmty. With Signal Corps, USN, 1943-46, PTO. Recipient George Foster Peabody award, numerous other spl. radio and TV programming and prodn. awards for public affairs and performance programs, Civic medal for edn. City of Rochester. Mem. Nat. Assn. Pub. TV Stas., Nat. Pub. Radio, Nat. Assn. Broadcasters, N.Y. State Broadcasters Assn. (bd. dirs.), Rochester Radio Reading Svc., Eastern Ednl. TV Network, Rochester C. of C., VFW, Univ. Club of Rochester (bd. dirs.), Tennis Club of Rochester, Rotary. Roman Catholic. Office: 280 State St Rochester NY 14614-1033 *I never had an idea I didn't get from reading. There is nosubstitute.*

PEARCE, WILLIAM MARTIN, history educator; b. Plainview, Tex., Mar. 11, 1913; s. Will Martin and Annie Eugenia (Bates) P.; m. Frances Elizabeth Campbell, Sept. 6, 1939; children—William Martin III, Richard Campbell. A.A., Kemper Mil. Sch., 1932; A.B., So. Meth. U., 1935; M.A., Tex. Tech U., 1937; Ph.D., U. Tex., 1952; LL.D., Tex. Wesleyan Coll., 1978. Instr. history Tex. Tech Coll., 1938-42, 46-47, asst. prof. history, 1949-53, asso. prof. history, 1953-55, prof., head dept. history, 1955-60, v.p. coll., 1960-68; dir. Tex. Tech Coll. (Archeol. Field Sch.), Glorieta, N.Mex., 1948, Tex. Tech Coll. (Valley of Mexico), 1949; pres. Tex. Wesleyan Coll., 1968-78; ret., 1978. Author: The Matador Land and Cattle Company, 1964. Served as lt. AUS, 1942-45. Decorated Bronze Star, Purple Heart; recipient Distinguished Alumnus award Tex. Tech U., 1975. Mem. Panhandle-Plains Hist. Soc. (dir.), Phi Alpha Theta, Pi Kappa Alpha, Phi Kappa Phi. Methodist. Home: 101 N Troy Ave #D Lubbock TX 79416-3029

PEARL, GEORGE CLAYTON, architect; b. London, Tex., Nov. 4, 1923; s. George William and Virgie Adlaid (Ford) P. BArch, U. Tex., 1950; DFA (hon.), U. N.Mex., 1996. Dir. design Stevens, Mallory, Pearl & Campbell, Albuquerque, 1953-89, dir. emeritus, 1989—. One man shows include St. Johns Coll., Santa Fe, 1987. Chmn. Albuquerque Landmarkers and Urban Conservation Commn., 1980-85; bd. advisors Nat. Trust for Hist. Preservation, Washington, 1976-86; bd. dirs. N.Mex. Archtl. Found., Santa Fe, 1988—, Hispanic Cultural Found., Albuquerque, 1985-90; active Commn. for Preservation Hist. N.Mex. Chs.; mem. Capitol Arts Found., 1990—, Guadaupe Hist. Found., 1991—; pres. N.Mex. Archtl. Found., 1991—. Recipient Bunting award Albuquerque Conservation Assn., 1988, Life Achievement award Historic Preservation State N.M.. 1993, Lifetime Achievement award Design and Historic Preservation Albuquerque Community Found. Fellow AIA (Silver medal western mountain region 1987). Democrat. Roman Catholic. Home: 215 12th St NW Albuquerque NM 87102-1815

PEARL, JUDEA, computer scientist, educator; b. Tel-Aviv, Sept. 4, 1936; U.S. citizen; married; 3 children. BSc, Israel Inst. Tech., 1960; MSc, Newark Coll. Engring., 1961; PhD in Elec. Engring., Poly. Inst. Bklyn., 1965. Rsch. engr. Dental Sch., NYU, 1960-61; mem. tech. staff RCA Rsch. Labs., 1961-65; dir. advanced memory devices Electronic Memories, Inc., Calif., 1966-69; prof. engring. sys. and computer scis. UCLA, 1969—; instr. Newark Coll. Engring., 1961; cons. Rand Corp., 1972, Integrated Sci. Corp., 1975, Hughes Aircraft, 1989. Recipient Outstanding Achievement award RCA Labs., 1965. Fellow IEEE, Am. Assn. Artificial Intelligence; mem. Nat. Acad. Engring. Office: UCLA Dept Computer Sci 4731 Boelter Hall Los Angeles CA 90024*

PEARLMAN, DAVID SAMUEL, allergist; b. Syracuse, N.Y., Jan. 20, 1934; s. Benjamin Norman and Sylvia Rene (Karp) P.; m. Doris Ann Greenberg, Apr. 16, 1966; children—Michael, Melanie. Student, Cornell U., 1951-54; M.D., SUNY, Syracuse, 1958. Diplomate Am. Bd. Allergy and Immunology (dir. 1973-78). Intern, then asst. resident in pediatrics Univ. Hosps., Cleve., 1958-60; chief resident in pediatrics U. Colo. Med. Center, Denver, 1960-61; mem. faculty U. Colo. Med. Center, 1962—, clin. prof. pediatrics, 1978—, dir. pediatric allergy tng. program, 1964-66, co-dir., 1966-73; practice medicine specializing in allergy Denver, 1972—; assoc. Colo. Allergy and Asthma Clinic, 1972—; acting chief dept. pediatric allergy Nat. Jewish Hosp. and Rsch. Ctr., 1972-73, sr. staff physician pediatrics allergy, 1973-92; mem. allergy and infectious disease tng. grant com. NIH, 1970-72. Contbr. articles to med. jours. Served to maj. M.C. AUS, 1967-69. Fellow U. Colo. Med. Center, 1961-62; Fellow NIH, 1963-66, 69-72. Fellow Am. Acad. Pediatrics (chmn. sect. on allergy and Clin. Immunology, 1992-94), Am. Acad. Allergy (exec. com. 1978-81), Am. Coll. Allergists; mem. Soc. Pediatric Rsch., Western Soc. Pediatric Rsch., AAAS, Am. Soc. Cert. Allergists, Am. Thoracic Soc., Am. Coll. Chest Physicians, Rocky Mountain Pediatric Soc., Colo. Allergy Soc., Joint Council Allergy and Immunology (bd. dirs. 1985-92, pres. 1988-90), Colo. Med. Soc., Denver Med. Soc., Adams-Aurora County Med. Soc., Friends of Chamber Music (dir. 1965-81). Jewish. Address: 6029 E Prentice Pl Englewood CO 80111-1415

PEARLMAN, JERRY KENT, electronics company executive; b. Des Moines, Mar. 27, 1939; s. Leo R. Pearlman; married; children: Gregory, Neal. BA cum laude, Princeton U., 1960; M.B.A., Harvard U., 1962. With Ford Motor Co., 1962-70; v.p. fin. dir. Behring Corp., 1970-71; controller Zenith Electronics Corp., Glenview, Ill., 1971-74, v.p., 1972-74, v.p. fin., 1974-78, sr. v.p. fin., 1978-81, sr. v.p. fin., group exec., 1981-83, chief exec. officer, 1983-95, chmn., 1984-95, also dir.; bd. dirs. Stone Container Corp., Am. Nat. Bank, Current Assets LLC. Bd. dirs. Evanston (Ill.) Hosp., Ctrl. Asia-Am. Enterprise Fund, Northwestern U. Office: 21 Linden Ave Wilmette IL 60091

PEARLMAN, MITZI ANN, elementary education educator; b. Houston, July 21, 1951; d. Bernard Joseph and Annie Mae (Gollob) P. BA in Sociology, U. Colo., Boulder, 1975; MA in Elem. Edn., U. Colo., Denver, 1988. Cert. elem. tchr., Colo. Tchr. 2d grade Cherry Creek Schs., Englewood, Colo., 1987-88; tchr. 2d, 3rd grades Douglas County Schs., Castle Rock, Colo., 1988—. Vol. Denver Zoo. Recipient Douglas County NOVA awards for Creative Excellence in Teaching, 1988, 89, 90, 91, 92, Innovative Instrn. award Bus. Week mag., 1990, Douglas County Edn. Found. grants, 1993, Pub. Svc. Intergenerational grant, 1993, Classroom Connection Disseminator grants, 1992, 93, Classroom Connection Adaptor grants, 1992, 93, 94, 95, Douglas County mini grant, 1989; named Channel 7 Tchr. of the Week, 1993. Mem. ASCD, Internat. Reading Assn., Douglas County Reading Assn. (treas. 1992-94), Colo. Assn. Sci. Tchrs., Phi Delta Kappa. Avocations: reading, pets, relaxing. Office: Acres Green Elem Sch 13524 Acres Green Dr Littleton CO 80124-2701

PEARLMAN, RONALD ALAN, lawyer; b. Hamilton, Ohio, July 10, 1940. A.B. with honors, Northwestern U., 1962, J.D. cum laude, 1965; LL.M. in Taxation, Georgetown U., 1967. Bar: D.C. 1991, U.S. Tax Ct. 1969, U.S. Supreme Ct. 1968. Atty. office chief counsel IRS, Washington, 1965-69; assoc. Thompson & Mitchell, St. Louis, 1969-70, ptnr., 1970-83; dep. asst. sec. for tax policy Dept. Treasury, Washington, 1983-84, asst. sec. tax policy, 1984-85; ptnr. Bryan, Cave, McPheeters & McRoberts, St. Louis, 1986-88; chief of staff joint com. on taxation U.S. Congress, Washington, 1988-90; ptnr. Covington & Burling, Washington, 1991—; adj. prof. Sch. Law Wash. U., St. Louis, 1972-83; vis. instr. Sch. Law U. Va., Charlottesville, 1995—; mem. BNA Tax Mgmt. Adv. Bd., 1986-88, 93—; participant ednl. seminars. Mem. bd. editors Northwestern U. Law Rev.; contbr. articles to various publs. Fellow Am. Coll. Tax Counsel; mem. ABA (chair govt. rels. com., mem. coun., tax sect. 1986-88), Fed. Bar Assn. (tax sect.), Am. Law Inst. (tax adv. group, cons. pass-through entities project and tax integration project), N.Y. State Bar Assn. (mem.-at-large exec. com., tax sect. 1991-93), Mo. Bar (chmn. taxation com. 1976-78), Met. St. Louis Bar Assn. (taxation sect. 1969-83, chmn. sect. 1974-75, exec. com. 1974-75), D.C. Bar (tax sect.), Mid-Am. Tax Conf. (chmn. planning com. 1979), Order of Coif. Office: Covington & Burling PO Box 7566 1201 Pennsylvania Ave NW Washington DC 20044-2401

PEARLMAN, SAMUEL SEGEL, lawyer; b. Pitts., May 28, 1942; s. Merle Maurice and Bernice Florence (Segel) P.; m. Cathy Schwartz, Aug. 16, 1964; children: Linda P. Kraner, Caren E. AB, U. Pa., 1963, LLB magna cum laude, 1966. Bar: Pa. 1966, Ohio, 1967, U.S. Ct. Appeals (3d cir.) 1967. Law clk. U.S. Dist. Ct. (Ea. dist.) Pa., 1966-67; assoc. Burke, Haber & Berick, Cleve., 1967-72, prin., 1973-86, prin. Berick, Pearlman & Mills, 1986—; lectr. law Case Western Res. U. Sch. Law, 1978-82; mem. registration com. Ohio Div. Securities, 1979-89; adv. dir. Midland Title Security, Inc. Trustee Realty ReFund Trust (NYSE). Mem. ABA, Ohio State Bar Assn., Greater Cleve. Bar Assn. (chmn. securities law sect. 1985-86), Order of Coif. Republican. Jewish. Author: Cases, Forms and Materials for Modern Real Estate Transactions, 1978, 82. Office: 1111 Superior Ave 1350 Eaton Ctr Cleveland OH 44114

PEARLMAN, SETH LEONARD, civil engineer; b. Steubenville, Ohio, Aug. 6, 1956; s. Abraham and Rita Joy (Morov) P.; m. Pamela Diane Bretton, Mar. 29, 1987; children: Isaac Joseph, Julian Brett. BSCE, Carnegie Mellon U., 1978, MSCE, 1979. Registered profl. engr., Pa., Va. Sr. engr. GAI Cons., Pitts., 1979-82; v.p. mktg. Belot Concrete Industries, Tiltonsville, Ohio, 1982-86; chief design engr. Nicholson Constrn. Co., Bridgeville, Pa., 1986-93, regional mktg. mgr., 1993-95; dir. bus. devel. Nicholson Constrn. Co., Bridgeville, 1995—; speaker, lectr. in field. Author conf. publs. Fundraiser United Jewish Fedn., Pitts., 1988—; bd. dirs. Beth El Congregation of the South Hills, Pitts., 1991—. Mem. ASCE (mem. geotech. sect. com. Pitts. chpt. 1990—), Am. Concrete Inst. (mem. fiber reinforced concrete com. 1982—, co-chair state of art report, mem. concrete piling com. 1989—, bd. dirs. Pitts. chpt. 1984-87), ADSC Internat. Assn. Found. Drilling (earth retention com.), Nat. Soc. Profl. Engrs. (pres. Wheeling, W.Va. chpt. 1986). Democrat. Home: 266 Twin Hills Dr Pittsburgh PA 15216-1108 Office: Nicholson Constrn PO Box 98 Bridgeville PA 15017-0098

PEARLSTEIN, LEONARD, advertising agency executive. Pres., chief exec. officer Keye/Donna/Pearlstein, L.A., until 1991; pres., chief operating officer Lord, Dentsu & Ptnrs., N.Y.C., 1991—; pres. The Pearlstein Grp, Los Angeles. Office: The Pearlstein Group 1900 Ave of the Stars Ste 1900 Los Angeles CA 90067*

PEARLSTEIN, PHILIP, artist; b. Pitts., May 24, 1924; s. David and Libbie (Kalser) P.; m. Dorothy Cantor, Aug. 20, 1950; children: William, Julia, Ellen. BFA, Carnegie Inst. Tech., 1949; MA, NYU, 1955. Instr. Pratt Inst., 1959-63; vis. critic Yale U., 1962-63; from asst. prof. to prof. art dept. Bklyn. Coll., 1963-82, now Disting. prof. emeritus. Shows include Tanager Gallery, N.Y.C., 1955, 59, Peridot Gallery, N.Y.C., 1956, 57, 59, Allan Frumkin Gallery, N.Y.C., 1962, 63, 65, 67, 69, 72, 74, 76, 78, 80, 83, Frumkin Gallery, Chgo., 1960, 65, 69, 73, 75, 80, 81, Hirschl & Adler Mod., N.Y.C., 1985, 88, 91, 92, 93, Robert Miller Gallery, N.Y.C., 1995, Kansas City Art Inst., 1962, Ceeje Gallery, 1965, 66, Reed Coll., 1965, 79, Galerie Thelen, Cologne, Germany, 1972, Galleri Ostergren, Malmo, Sweden, 1972, Galerie Kornfeld, Zurich, Switzerland, 1972, Staatliche Museen-Kupferstichkabinett, Berlin, 1972, Kunstverein, Hamburg, Germany, 1972, Editions La Tortue, Paris, 1973, Donald Morris Gallery, Detroit, 1973, 76, 80, 94, Gimpel Fils Ltd., London, 1975, 79, Marianne Friedland Gallery, Toronto, Ont., Can., 1975, 81, Springfield (Mo.) Art Mus., 1978, 95, Harkus Krakow Gallery, Boston, 1978-79, Myers Fine Arts Gallery, SUNY, Plattsburg, 1979, Galerie Jöllenbach, Cologne, Germany, 1979, 89, Carnegie-Mellon U., Pitts., 1979, Assoc. Am. Artists, 1980, FIAC, Paris, 1980, Brooke Alexander Gallery, 1980, 81, Ringling Mus. Art, Sarasota, Fla., 1981, San Antonio Mus. Art, 1981, (Retrospective) Milw. Art Mus., The Bklyn. Mus., The Pa. Acad. Fine Arts, Phila., The Toledo Mus. Art, 1983-84, Carnegie Inst. Mus. Art, Pitts., 1982, Brody's Gallery, Washington, 1983, Images Gallery, Toledo, 1984, Hirschl and Adler Modern, N.Y.C., 1985, 88, 92, 93, Galerie Rudolph Zwirner, Cologne, Germany, 1989, 91, Compass Rose Gallery, Chgo, 1991, Printworks Gallery, Chgo., 1990, Condeso Lawler Gallery, N.Y.C., 1991, P.S. 1, N.Y., 1992, Butler Art Inst, Youngstown, Ohio, 1992, Tokashima Art Mus., Japan, 1992; group shows at Carnegie Internat., 1955, 64, 67, Whitney Mus. Am. Art, 1955, 56, 58, 62, 65, 67, 70, 72, 73, 74, 79, 91, U. Ill., 1965, 67, 68, Providence Art Club, 1965, U. Mich. Mus., 1965, Corcoran Gallery, 1967, Vassar Coll., 1968, Milw. Art, 1969, Pa. Acad. Fine Arts, 1971-72, Indpls. Mus. Art, 1972, Galerie Lowenadler, Stockholm, Sweden, 1973, Nat. Acad. Arts and Letters, N.Y.C., 1973 (award), Yale U., 1973, 74, Hofstra U., 1973, Helsinki (Finland) Mus. Art, 1974, Art Inst. Chgo., 1974, Cleve. Mus. Art, 1974, America 1976 Bicentennial Exhbn., U.S. Dept. Interior, 1976, Wildenstein Gallery, N.Y.C., 1976, many others, retrospective exhbns., Finch Coll., 1974, U. Tex., Austin, 1974, Cranbrook Acad. Art, Mich., 1974, Notre Dame U., 1975, Grand Rapids (Mich.) Art Mus., 1975, Kalamazoo Inst. Arts, Tampa Bay Art, 1975, Miami Art, 1975, Philbrook Art, 1980, Chryler Mus., 1980, Akron Art Mus., 1981, San Antonio Mus., 1981, Honolulu Acad. of Art, 1994; represented in permanent collections, Phila. Mus. Art, San Antonio Mus. Assn., Pa. State U., Whitney Mus., Mus. Modern Art, N.Y. U., Met. Mus. of Art, Bklyn Mus. Carnegie Mus., Syracuse U., James A. Michener Found., Hirshhorn Mus., Corcoran Gallery, Art Inst. Chgo., Milw. Art Ctr., Ludwig Collection, Aachen, Germany, Sydney and Frances Lewis Found., Richmond, Va., Bklyn. Mus., Cleve. Mus. Art, Milw. Mus., others. Fulbright fellow to Italy, 1958-59; Guggenheim fellow, 1971-72; Nat. Endowment for the Arts grantee, 1968, grantee Am. Acad. Arts and Letters, 1992; NAD assoc., 1983.

PEARLSTEIN, SEYMOUR, artist; b. Bklyn., Oct. 14, 1923; s. Morris Lazarus and Anna (Bassiur) P.; m. Toby Tessie Rubinstein, Mar. 21, 1943; children: Judith Helene, Lawrence Jonathan. Cert., Pratt Inst., Bklyn., 1950, Art Students League N.Y., 1954; student of Jack Potter. Owner, illustrator, designer Sy Pearlstein Advt. Art Studio, N.Y.C., 1946-71; artist-painter rep. by Far Gallery, N.Y.C., 1969-81; prof. N.Y.C. Tech. Coll., CUNY, Bklyn., 1971-94, prof. emeritus, 1994—, chmn. art and advt. design dept., 1985-88. One-man shows Silvermine Guild of Artists, New Canaan, Conn., 1973, Far Gallery, 1973, 75, 78, Klitgord Ctr., N.Y.C., C.C., 1974, De Mers Gallery, Hilton Head, S.C., 1975, Adelphi U., Garden City, N.Y., 1979, Grace Gallery, N.Y.C. Tech. Coll., 1992; group shows A.M. Sachs Gallery, N.Y.C., 1971, Springfield (Mo.) Art Mus., 1971, Am. Acad. Arts and Letters, N.Y.C., 1975, 76, 77, NAD, N.Y.C., 1986, 87, 89, 91, 92, Butler Inst. Art, Ohio, 1975, Ball State U., Queens Mus., N.Y.C., 1978, 81, Dept. State Art in Embassies Program, N.Y. Hist. Soc., 1981, Colo. Heritage Mus., Denver, 1981, 82, 86, Am. Watercolor Soc., N.Y.C., Ingber Gallery, N.Y.C., 1985, Audubon Artists, N.Y.C., 1990, 91, 92, Allied Artists Am., N.Y.C., 1990, 91, 95, Phila. Mus. Sales and Loan Gallery, Nat. Arts Club, N.Y.C., 1989, others; represented in permanent collections Mus. N.Mex., Santa Fe, Mint Mus. Art, Charlotte, N.C., NAD, N.Y.C., Fine Arts Gallery, San Diego, Adelphi U., Queens Mus., N.Y.C., Munson-Williams-Proctor Inst., Utica, N.Y., N.Y.C. Tech. Coll., Bklyn. Served with AUS, 1942-46. Recipient Gold medal Nat. Acad. Design, 1969, Hassam Fund Purchase award Am. Acad. Arts and Letters, 1969, 77, Gold medal of honor Nat. Arts Club, 1970, Ranger Fund Purchase award NAD, 1971, 82, Gold medal Soc. Illustrators, 1972, Nat. Inst.-Am. Acad. Arts and Letters grant, 1975. Mem. NAD (sec. coun.) 1980-84, W.H. Leavin prize 1985), Am. Watercolor Soc. (bd. dirs. 1979-80, Watercolor U.S.A. award 1971), Art Students League of N.Y. (life), Allied Artists Am. (bd. dirs. 1976-79, E. Lowe award 1969, gold medal 1980, George Tweed Meml. award 1989, 92), Audubon Artists (bd. dirs. 1986-89, 91-93, Grumbacher award 1971, Fabri medal 1980), Alliance Figurative Artists (c0chmn. 1976-77), Profl. Staff Congress. Home: 52 Dartmouth St Forest Hills NY 11375-5142 Office: NYC Tech Coll CUNY 300 Jay St Brooklyn NY 11201-2902

PEARLSTINE, NORMAN, editor; b. Phila., Oct. 4, 1942; s. Raymond and Gladys (Cohen) P.; m. Nancy Colbert Friday, 1988. A.B., Haverford Coll., 1964; LL.B., U. Pa., 1967. Staff reporter Wall Street Jour., Dallas, Detroit, L.A., 1968-73; Tokyo bur. chief Wall Street Jour., 1973-76; mng. editor Asian Wall Street Jour., Hong Kong, 1976-78; exec. editor Forbes Mag., Los Angeles, 1978-80; nat. news editor Wall Street Jour., N.Y.C., 1980-82; editor, pub. Wall Street Jour./Europe, Brussels, 1982-83; mng. editor, v.p. Wall Street Jour., N.Y.C., 1983-91, exec. editor, 1991-92; pres., chief exec. officer Friday Holdings, L.P., N.Y.C., 1993-94; editor-in-chief Time Warner, Inc., N.Y.C., 1994—; dir. Dolan Media. Pres. Atsuko Chiba Found.; bd. dirs. Am. Woman's Econ. Devel. Recipient Editor of Yr. award Nat. Press Found., 1989. Mem. ABA, D.C. Bar Assn. (trustee), N.Y. Hist. Soc. (former chmn.), Coun. Fgn. Rels. Office: Time Warner Inc 1271 Avenue Of The Americas New York NY 10020

PEARMAN, REGINALD JAMES, educational administrator; b. N.Y.C., May 23, 1923; s. William H. Astoria Arabell (Webb) P.; children: Jeanita, Lydia, Reginald. B.S., NYU, 1950; Ed.D., U. Mass., 1974. Cert. tchr., N.Y. Tchr., N.Y.C. Pub. Schs., 1951-55, supr., 1955-62; with Fgn. Service, State Dept., Caracas, Venezuela, 1962-65, Peace Corps, Washington, 1965-67, AID, Washington, 1967-69; dir. job devel. N.Y.C. Human Resources Adminstrn., 1969-71; ednl. program specialist U.S. Dept. Edn., Washington, 1971-74; mem. adv. com. women's equity U.S. Office of Edn., 1974, task force arts and humanities, 1975-76, task force edn. of gifted, 1976-77, basic edn., 1977, urban edn., 1978, pub. sch. adminstrn., 1979; mem. adv. bd. internship program Am. Pub. Transit Assn., 1977-79; mem. White House Initiative for Historically Black Colls. and Univs., 1982-83; tchr. Calif. State Coll.-Los Angeles, 1966, Cornell U./N.Y. State Sch. Labor and Indsl. Relations, 1968, 70, U. Md., College Park, 1974-76; with Md. Dept. Employment and Tng., Wheaton, 1985-86; counseling coord. Montgomery Coll., 1987—; mem. scholarship selection com. Creative Edn. Found., 1991-92; discussion leader Creative Problem Solving Inst., SUNY, Buffalo, 1991-92; grad. adviser U. Mass./D.C. Publ. Sch. project; also cons. Served with U.S. Army, 1944-47; PTO. Bd. dirs. D.C. Striders youth sports club, Inst. Scholar Athletes, 1992; mem. Pres.'s Coun. Youth Opportunity, 1968; mem. D.C. ofcls. com. Nat. Youth Games, 1983; ofcl. Potomac Valey Track and Field Assn.; mem. platform com. N.Y. State Liberal Ind. party, 1968. Mem. NCAA All Am. Track Team, 1949, U.S. Olympic Team, Helsinki, 1952. NCCJ fellow, 1953; U. Havana scholar, 1955; U. Pitts. fellow, 1967; named to NYU Hall of Fame, 1974, Pa. Relay Carnival Hall of Fame, 1994; recipient Disting. Alumni award, 1977, Brotherhood in Sports award B'nai B'rith, 1954. Mem. Nat. Alliance Black Sch. Educators (higher edn. commn.), Inst. Scholar Athletes (bd. dirs.), Phi Delta Kappa. Lutheran. Established 4 Am. records and 3 world records in running events in middle distances. Home: 9118 September Ln Silver Spring MD 20901-3705

PEARSALL, GEORGE WILBUR, materials scientist, mechanical engineer, educator, consultant; b. Brentwood, N.Y., July 13, 1933; s. Milo Dickerson and Margaret Elizabeth (White) P.; m. Patricia Louise Stevens, Oct. 11, 1962. B. Metall. Engring., Rensselaer Poly. Inst., 1955; Sc.D. (Am. Soc. Metals fellow), MIT, 1961. Registered profl. engr., N.C. Research engr. Dow Chem. Co., Midland, Mich., 1955-57; research asst. MIT, 1959-60, asst. prof. metallurgy, 1960-64; assoc. prof. mech. engring. Duke U., 1964-66, prof., 1966-81, prof. mech. engring. and materials sci., 1981—, prof. pub. policy studies, 1982—, acting dean Sch. Engring., 1969-71, dean, 1971-74, 82-83; trustee Triangle Univs. Ctr. for Advanced Studies, 1976-92, chmn. exec. com., 1983-88; dir. Duke-IBM Product Safety Inst., 1979-90. Author: (with W.G. Moffatt and J. Wulff) The Structure and Properties of Materials, 1964; edtl. bd. Jour. Products Liability, Proceedings of the IEEE; contbr. articles to profl. jours. Served with AUS, 1957. Mem. AAAS, ASME, ASTM, Soc. Risk Analysis, Am. Soc. Metals, Am. Soc. Plastics Engrs., Sigma Xi, Phi Lambda Upsilon, Tau Beta Pi, Pi Tau Sigma. Home: 2941 Welcome Dr Durham NC 27705-5555

PEARSALL, GREGORY HOWARD, naval officer; b. Riverhead, N.Y., Nov. 2, 1951; s. Smith Gregory and Betty Irene (Tuthill) P.; m. Barbara Jean Hesler, Nov. 28, 1980; children: Christopher, Andrew, Kevin. BS in Mgmt., U.S. Naval Acad., Annapolis, Md., 1974; MS in Bus., Naval Postgrad. Sch., Monterey, Calif., 1986; MA in Fgn. Affairs, Naval War Coll., Newport, R.I., 1994. Supply officer USS Hermitage, Virginia Beach, Va., 1978-80, Naval Ordnance Sta., Indian Head, Md., 1980-83; asst. supply officer USS Shenandoah, Norfolk, Va., 1983-85; ADP project officer, comptroller Navy Fleet Material Support Office, Mechanicsburg, Pa., 1987-90; comptroller U.S. Naval Acad., Annapolis, 1990-92; supply officer USS Sierra, Charleston, S.C., 1992-93; dir. fleet/indsl. support group Navy Ships Parts Control Ctr., Mechanicsburg, 1994-95; exec. officer Navy Fleet Material Support Office, Mechanicsburg, 1995—; dir. Charles County Econ. Devel. Commn., Waldorf, Md., 1980-83; mem. Capital Region Econ. Devel. Corp., Camp Hill, Pa., 1995—. Coach St. Andrews Little League, Charleston, 1993, King Phillip Little League, Bristol, R.I., 1994, Bristol Youth Soccer Assn., 1994, Hampden Youth Soccer Assn., Mechanicsburg, 1995. Recipient Meritorious Svc. medal Pres. of the U.S., 1983, 90, 92, 93, Hammer award Nat. Performance Review, 1995. Avocations: gardening/landscaping, woodworking, coin/card collecting, sports. Office: Navy Fleet Material Support Office 5450 Carlisle Pike Box 2010 Mechanicsburg PA 17055

PEARSE, WARREN HARLAND, association executive, obstetrician and gynecologist; b. Detroit, Sept. 28, 1927; s. Harry Albridge and Frances (Wressell) P.; m. Jacqueline Anne Langan, June 15, 1950; children: Kathryn, Susan, Laurie, Martha. B.S., Mich. State U., 1948; M.B., M.D., Northwestern U., 1950. Intern. Univ. Hosp., Ann Arbor, Mich., 1950-51; resident obstetrics and gynecology, 1951-53, 55-56; practice medicine specializing obstetrics and gynecology Detroit, 1956-58; mem. faculty U. Nebr. Med. Center Omaha, 1959-71, Found. prof., chmn. dept. obstetrics and gynecology, 1962-71; asst. dean U. Nebr. Med. Center Omaha (Med. Coll.), 1963-71, mem. residency rev. com. obstetrics and gynecology, 1968-71; dean Med. Coll. Va., Richmond, 1971-75; exec. dir. Am. Coll. Obstetrics and Gynecology, 1975-93; cons., 1993—; Chmn. research adv. group Maternal Child Health Service, Health Scis. Mental Health Adminstrn., HEW, 1967—; cons. family planning Office Econ. Opportunity, 1970—. Author: (with R.W. Stander) Obstetrics and Gynecology at the University of Michigan, 1969; Contbr. chpts., articles tech. lit. Served from 1st lt. to capt. AUS, 1953-55. Mem. Am. Coll. Obstetrics and Gynecology (dist. sec., treas. 1964-68, vice chmn. 1968-71), Am. Gynecology Soc., Soc. Gynecology Investigation, Assn. Profs. Gynecology and Obstetrics (sec., treas. 1969—), Alpha Omega Alpha. Home: 350 S River Landing Rd Edgewater MD 21037-1549 Office: American College of Obs & Gyns 409 12th St SW Washington DC 20024

PEARSON, ALBERT MARCHANT, food science and nutrition educator; b. Oakley, Utah, Sept. 3, 1916; s. Levi and Mary (Marchant) P.; m. Harriet Eilenberger, Nov. 16, 1946; children—Richard A., Carol Jane, Marian Beth, Donna Gay, David C. B.S., Utah State U., 1940; M.S., Iowa State U., 1941; Ph.D., Cornell U., 1949. Grad. asst. Iowa State U., 1940-41, Cornell U., 1946-49; asst. prof., then assoc. prof. U. Fla., 1949-54; mem. faculty Mich. State U., 1954-89, prof. food sci. and human nutrition, 1961-89; adj. prof. animal sci. Brigham Young U., 1989-90; courtesy prof. anima sci. Oreg. State U., 1991—. Served with USMCR, 1942-45, PTO. Mem. Am. Soc. Animal Sci. (sec.-treas. 1965-68, pres. 1969-70), Reciprocal Meat Conf. (chmn. 1956), Sigma Xi, Phi Kappa Phi. Spl. research body composition, muscle proteins, flavor components in meat. Home: 7765 Bates Rd S Salem OR 97306-9419 Office: Oreg State U Dept Animal Sci Corvallis OR 97331

PEARSON, BELINDA KEMP, economist, consultant; b. Kansas City, Mo., Apr. 14, 1931; d. William Ewing and Margaret Norton (Johnson) Kemp; m. Carl Erik Pearson, Sept. 15, 1953; children: Erik, Frederick, Margaret. BA, Wellesley Coll., 1952; MA, Tufts U., 1954, PhD, 1958. Rsch. asst. Harvard U., Cambridge, Mass., 1954-55; instr. econs. Suffolk U., Boston, 1956-59; lectr. econs., Wellesley Coll., Mass., 1964-65; econ. analyst, asst. econs. Seafirst Bank, Seattle, 1966-79, v.p., 1974-85; chief economist, 1979-85; dir. Lektor, Inc., Issaquah, Wash., 1984—, pres., 1987—; mem. Wash. Gov's. Coun. Econ. Advisors, Olympia, 1979—; dir. Pacific N.W. Regional Econ. Conf., 1979—, chair, Seattle Conf., 1987; mem. Western Blue Chip Econ. Forecast Panel, 1988—; mem. King County, Wash., Land Capacity Task Force, 1995-96; mem. bd. regents Wash. State U., Pullman, 1985-90, v.p., 1988-90, Regents Found. Investment Com. of Wash. State U., 1987-91; mem. Wash. State Libr. Commn., Olympia, 1976-84. Fulbright scholar London Sch. Econs., 1952-53. Mem. Am. Econ. Assn., Nat. Assn. Bus. Economists (chmn. arrangements 1982 ann. meeting), Seattle Economists Club (pres. 1973-74), Mcpl. League, City Club (Seattle) (chmn. reports com. 1986-88), pres. LWV, Lake Wash. East, 1993-95. Office: Lektor Inc 4227 Providence Point Dr SE Issaquah WA 98029

PEARSON, CHARLES THOMAS, JR., lawyer; b. Fayetteville, Ark., Oct. 14, 1929; s. Charles Thomas and Doris (Pinkerton) P.; m. Wyma Lee Hampton, Sept. 9, 1988; children: Linda Sue, John Paddock. B.S., U. Ark., 1953, J.D., 1954; postgrad., U.S. Naval Postgrad. Sch., 1959; A.M., Boston U., 1963. Bar: Ark. bar 1954. Practice in Fayetteville, 1963—; dir. officer N.W. Comms., Inc., Dixieland Devel., Inc., Jonlin Investments, Inc., World Wide Travel Svc., Inc., Okliania Farms, Inc., N.W. Arl. Land & Devel., Inc., Garden Plaza Inns, Inc. Word Data, Inc., M.P.C. Farms, Inc., Fayetteville Enterprises, Inc., NWA Devel.Co., Delta Comm., Inc.; past. dir., organizer N.W. Nat. Bank. Adviser Explorer Scouts, 1968—; past pres. Washington County Draft Bd.; past pres. bd. Salvation Army. Served to comdr. Judge Adv. Gen. Corps USNR, 1955-63. Mem. ABA, Ark. Bar Assn., Washington County Bar Assn., Judge Advs. Assn., N.W. Ark. Ret. Officers Assn. (past pres.), Methodist Men (past pres), U. Ark. Alumni Assn. (past dir.), Sigma Chi (past pres. N.W. Ark. alumni, past chmn. house corp.), Alpha Kappa Psi, Phi Eta Sigma, Delta Theta Phi. Republican. Methodist. Clubs: Mason (32 deg., K.T., Shriner), Moose, Elk, Lion, Metropolitan. Office: 36 E Center St Fayetteville AR 72701-5301

PEARSON, CLARENCE EDWARD, management consultant; b. Chgo., Apr. 22, 1925; s. Edward and Irene (Silander) P.; m. June Waldhe, Apr. 21, 1951 (dec. 1967); 1 child, Scott; m. Laurie Norris, Apr. 25, 1995. BS, No. Ill. U., 1950; MPH, U. N.C., 1952. Instr. Mt. Prospect (Ill.) Pub. Schs., 1950-51; dir. health edn. DuPage County Health Dept., Wheaton, Ill., 1952-55; chief health edn. St. Louis Health Dept., 1955-57; dir. health and hosps. Health and Welfare Council, St. Louis, 1957-61; dir. health and safety Met. Life Ins. Co., N.Y.C., 1961-87; prof. edn. Columbia Tchrs. Coll., 1975—; prof. pub. health U. N.C., 1987—; pres. Universal Health Concepts, N.Y.C., 1984-87; Coun. Internat. Health, Washington, 1981-84; bd. dirs. Health Info. Co., Nat. Coun. Internat. Health, Washington, 1981-84; chmn. Profl. Exam. Svc., N.Y.C., 1996—; v.p. Peter Drucker Found. for Nonprofit Mgmt., 1994—; adv. bd. C. Everett Koop Inst.; bd. overseers Dartmouth Med. Sch., 1992—. Co-author: Managing Health Promotion, 1982; contbr. chpts. to books in field. Co-chmn. Scandinavian-Ams. for Rockefeller presdl. campaign, N.Y., 1968. Served as staff sgt. U.S. Army, 1943-46. Recipient Disting. Career award Am. Pub. Health Assn., Washington, 1981, Gold Medal for Achievement, Columbia U., N.Y.C., 1984, Internat. Health award Asia Pacific Consortium, Honolulu, 1984, Porter Prize, Pitts. Health Ctr., 1986. Fellow Am. Pub. Health Assn. (governing council 1970-78), The Univ. Club (N.Y.C.). Home: 530 E 23rd St New York NY 10010-5022 Office: Peter Drucker Found for Nonprofit Mgmt 320 Park Ave 3rd Fl New York NY 10022-6839

PEARSON, DANIEL S., lawyer; b. N.Y.C., Oct. 9, 1930; children: Elizabeth Oster, William M., Charles M.; m. Fredricka G. Smith, June 19, 1982; 1 child, Deardre Smith. BA, Amherst Coll., 1952; JD, Yale U., 1958. Bar: Fla. 1959, U.S. Supreme Ct. 1967, N.Y. 1982, U.S. Ct. Appeals (1st, 5th, 9th and 11th, DC cirs.). Asst. U.S. atty., Miami, 1961-63, pvt. practice, 1963-67; ptnr. Pearson, Josefsberg & Tarre, P.A., Miami, 1967-80; judge Dist. Ct. Appeal (3rd dist.), Miami, 1980-89; ptnr. Holland & Knight, Miami, 1989—; adj. prof. U. Miami Sch. Law; lectr. Practicing Law Inst., Fla. Bar; mem. Am. Bd. Trial Advs. Served with USCG, 1951-54. Mem. ABA, Am. Law Inst., Am. Coll. Trial Lawyers, Am. Acad. Appellate Lawyers, Am. Bd. Trial Advocates, Order of Barristers, Dade County Bar Assn. Home: 7580 Erwin Rd Miami FL 33143-6273 Office: Holland & Knight 701 Brickell Ave Miami FL 33131-2822

PEARSON, DAVID PETRI, chemist; b. Portland, Oreg., Oct. 24, 1926; s. Brewer Petri and Laura Alvine (Johnson) P.; m. Patricia Margaret Cowan, June 4, 1949; children—Kathryn A., James P., Rebecca L., Kristine R., Judith G. B.A. in Chemistry, Reed Coll., 1949; M.S. in Phys. Chemistry, Oreg. State U., 1953; Ph.D. in Phys. Chemistry, U. So. Calif., 1960. Research chemist Phillips Petroleum Co. (AEC), Idaho Falls, Idaho, 1957-62, Bartlesville, Okla., 1962-69; lectr. in chemistry, Portland State U., 1969-71; asst. prof. chemistry So. Oreg. State Coll., Ashland, 1971-72; research assoc. Oreg. Grad. Ctr., Beaverton, 1972-74; sr. chemist Portland Gen. Electric Co., 1975-87; ret., 1987. Patentee in field. Served to cpl. USAAF, 1946-47. Mem. Am. Chem. Soc. (treas. Portland sect. 1979-82, chmn. 1983), Electrochem. Soc. Clubs: Am. Alpine, Idaho Alpine (sec. Idaho Falls 1961, pres. 1962). Republican. Presbyterian. Home: 6324 SW Radcliffe St Portland OR 97219-5749

PEARSON, DAVIS, architect; b. Bryn Mawr, Pa., June 10, 1925; s. Rodney S. and Bertha (Bott) P.; m. Priscilla Ball (dec. 1990); children: Davis Jr., Leslie B Jessell, Donald S.; m. Anne Grim, 1991. BArch, U. Pa., 1950. Registered arch., Pa., N.J., Del., Fla.; cert. Nat. Coun. Archtl. Registration Bd. Assoc. Mirick Pearson Batcheler, Phila., 1954-60, ptnr., 1960-93; cons. HLM Archs., Phila., 1995—; chmn. Lower Merion Planning Commn., 1986-89, active, 1970-92; bd. dirs. Devon Manor Corp., also sec., Main Line Health, Inc. Prin. works include The Episc. Acad., various bldgs., Medford Leas, Cathedral Village, Dunwoody Village, Devon Manor Retirement Communities, others. Bd. mgrs., treas. Saunders House; trustee The Chapin Home; life trustee The Episc. Acad., trustee emeritus, 1991; past pres. The Merion Civic Assn.; bd. dirs. Merion Cmty. Assn., pres., 1976-92, Cmty. Health Affiliates; active The Carpenters Co., Phila. Mem. AIA, Tau Sigma Delta. Office: HLM/MPB Archs 262 S 23rd St Philadelphia PA 19103-5530

PEARSON, DONALD EMANUAL, chemist, educator; b. Madison, Wis., June 21, 1914; s. Gustav E. and Clara (Bjelde) P.; m. Gwen Smiseth, June 5, 1950; children: Donald T., Jeanah C., Sam S. Grad., U. Wis., 1936, U. Ill., 1940. Chemist Pitts. Plate Glass Co., Milw., 1940-42; tech. aide OSRD, 1942-45; chemist MIT, 1945-46; faculty Vanderbilt U., Nashville, 1946-79; prof. chemistry Vanderbilt U., 1954-79, prof. emeritus, 1979—; pvt. practice as cons., chem. rschr. Nashville; cons. in chem. and environ. problems, arson cases; rsch. dir Reclamation Svcs., Madisonville, Ky.; mem. com. for Reorgn. of Tenn. Dept. Health.; NSF resident to Tenn. Toxics Program. Author: (with R.C. Elderfield) Phenazines, 1956, (with C.A. Buehler) Survey of Organic Syntheses, 1970, Vol. II, 1977; also numerous articles. Mem. Am. Chem. Soc. Discoverer new method of substitution in aromatic compounds, new rearrangement hydrazone; research on mechanisms of Beckmann rearrangement, reactions in polyphosphoric acid; structure of diuretic mercuhydrin; synthesis of barbiturates, anti-malarials, plant regulatory substances and spin labels.

PEARSON, DONNA SUTHERLAND, lumber company executive. CEO Sutherland Lumber, Kansas City, Mo. Office: Sutherland Lumber Co 4000 Main St Kansas City MO 64111

PEARSON, DOUGLAS N., battery manufacturing company executive. Formerly v.p. Monroe (Mich.) Auto Equipment Co.; now exec. v.p. Exide Corp., Reading, Pa. Office: Exide Corp PO Box 14205 Reading PA 19612-4205*

PEARSON, GERALD LEON, food company executive; b. Mpls., June 24, 1925; s. Perry and Lillian (Peterson) P.; m. Beverly Mary Schultz, Nov. 10, 1946; children: Steven, Perry, Liecia. Grad., Trimont (Minn.) High Sch., 1943. Treas. Trimont Packing Co., 1946-52; v.p. Spencer Foods, Iowa, 1952-68, pres., chief exec. officer, 1969-80, chmn. bd., chief exec. officer, 1972-80; chmn. Beef Specialists of Iowa Inc., 1983-94; bd. dirs. Graffaloy, Inc., El Cajon, Calif., dir. applied mem. tech., Minnetonka, Minn.; chmn., CEO World Champions of Golf Inc.; owner Brooks Golf Club, Okoboji, Iowa. Pres. Pearson Art Found.; bd. dirs. Bethany Coll., Lindsborg; commr. Nat. Mus. Am. Art-Smithsonian Instn., 1995; founder World Jazz Hall of Fame. With USN, 1943-46. Mem. Swedish Royal Roundtable, Swedish Council Am. (bd. dirs.). Home: 7224 E Stagecoach Pass Carefree AZ 85262-5003 Office: World Champions of Golf &D PO Box 195 Spencer IA 51301

PEARSON, GERALD P., hospital administrator; b. 1944. With St. Joseph Hospital, Elgin, Ill., 1963-83; exec. v.p. Franciscan Sisters Health Care Corp., Frankfort, Ill., 1983-89, pres., 1989—. Office: Franciscan Sisters Health Care Corp 9223 W St Francis Rd Frankfort IL 60423*

PEARSON, HENRY CHARLES, artist; b. Kinston, N.C., Oct. 8, 1914; s. A. Louis and Estelle P. BA, U. N.C., 1935; MFA, Yale U., 1938; postgrad., Art Students League, 1953-56. Stage scene designer, 1937-42; instr. art New Sch. Social Research, N.Y.C., 1965—, Pa. Acad. Fine Arts, Phila., 1973-88. Exhbns. include Workshop Gallery, N.Y.C., 1958, Stephen Radich Gallery, N.Y.C., 1960-70, The Responsive Eye, Mus. Modern Art, 1965, 29th Biennial Exhbn., Corcoran Gallery Art, Washington, 1965, Retrospective N.C. Mus. Art, Raleigh, N.C., 1968, Drawings USA, Minn. Mus. Art, St. Paul, 1971-73, Betty Parsons Gallery, N.Y.C., 1971-76, Art Students League Centennial, 1975, Truman Gallery, N.Y.C., 1976-79, Marilyn Pearl Gallery, N.Y.C., 1980—; retrospective Columbia (S.C.) Mus. Art, 1988, Henry Pearson and Friends Arts Ctr., Kinston, N.C., 1993, Seamus Heaney & Henry Pearson, Gordon College, Wenham, Ma., 1996; represented in permanent collections Mus. Modern Art, N.Y.C., Met. Mus. Art, N.Y.C., Whitney Mus. Am. Art, N.Y.C., Albright-Knox Gallery, Buffalo, N.C. Mus. Art, Raleigh; represented in commd. works include List Art Posters, 1965, N.Y. Film Festival poster, 1968; illustrator: Rime of the Ancient Mariner, 1964, Five Psalms, 1969, Seamus Heaney's Sweeney Praises the Trees, 1981, Seamus Heaney's Poems and a Memoir, 1982, Seamus Heaney's Three Short Poems, 1993-94. With AUS, 1942-48, USAF, 1948-53. Ford Found. fellow, 1964; Recipient gold medal for achievement in the fine arts N.C. Gov., 1970. Mem. Am. Abstract Artists, Century Assn. Studio: 58 W 58th St New York NY 10019-2502

PEARSON, HENRY CLYDE, judge; b. Ocoonita, Lee County, Va., Mar. 12, 1925; s. Henry James and Nancy Elizabeth (Seals) P.; m. Jean Calton, July 26, 1956; children—Elizabeth, Frances, Timothy Clyde. Student Union Coll., 1947-49; LL.B., U. Richmond, 1952. Bar: Va. 1952, U.S. Ct. Appeals (4th cir.) 1957, U.S. Supreme Ct. 1958. Sole practice, Jonesville, Va., 1952-56; asst. U.S. atty. Western Dist. Va., Roanoke, 1956-61; ptnr. Hopkins, Pearson & Engleby, Roanoke, 1961-70; judge U.S. Bankruptcy Ct. Western Dist. Va., Roanoke, 1970—; participant Va. Continuing Edn. Seminars; mem. adv. com. fed. rules bankruptcy procedure. Mem. Va. Ho. of Reps., 1954-56, Va. Senate, 1968-70; Republican nominee Gov. of Va., 1961. Served with USN, 1943-46; PTO. Mem. Va. State Bar, ABA, Va. Trial Lawyers Assn., Assn. Trial Lawyers Am., Am. Judicature Soc., Am. Judges Assn., Fed. Bar Assn., Delta Theta Phi, Tribune Jefferson Senate, Am. Legion, VFW. Methodist. Clubs: Masons, Shriners. Editorial bd. Am. Survey Bankruptcy Law, 1979. Office: US Courthouse PO Box 2389 Roanoke VA 24010-2389

PEARSON, JAMES BOYD, JR., electrical engineering educator; b. McGehee, Ark., June 3, 1930; s. James Boyd and Lydia Frances (Lacey) P.; m. Marian Scarborough, Feb. 16, 1957; children: Sarah, Jane, Carol, Catherine, Susan, Joanne. BSEE, U. Ark., 1958, MSEE, 1959; PhD, Purdue U., 1962. Asst. prof. electrical engring. Purdue U., Lafayette, Ind., 1962-65; assoc. prof. Rice U., Houston, 1965-70, prof., 1970-79, J.S. Abercrombie prof., 1979—. Served to capt. USAR, 1952-55. Fellow IEEE. Office: Rice Univ Dept Elec and Computer Enging Houston TX 77251

PEARSON, JOHN, mechanical engineer; b. Leyburn, Yorkshire, U.K., Apr. 24, 1923; came to U.S., 1930, naturalized, 1944; s. William and Nellie Pearson; m. Ruth Ann Billhardt, July 10, 1944 (wid. Nov. 1984); children: John, Armin, Roger; m. Sharoll L. Chisolm, Sept. 8, 1993. B.S.M.E., Northwestern U., 1949, M.S., 1951. Registered profl. engr., Calif. Rsch. engr. Naval Ordnance Test Sta., China Lake, Calif., 1951-55, head warhead rsch. br., 1955-58, head solid dynamics br., 1958-59, head detonation physics group, 1959-67; head detonation physics div. Naval Weapons Ctr., China Lake, Calif., 1967-83, sr. rsch. scientist, 1983—; cons., lectr. in field; founding mem. adv. bd. Ctr. for High Energy Forming, U. Denver; mem. bd. examiners Sambalpur U., India, 1982-83. Author: Explosive Working of Metals, 1963; Behavior of Metals Under Impulsive Loads, 1954; contbr. articles to profl. publs; patentee impulsive loading, explosives applications. Charter mem. Sr. Exec. Svc. U.S., 1979. With C.E., U.S. Army, 1943-46, ETO. Recipient L.T.E. Thompson medal, 1965, William B. McLean medal, 1979, Superior Civilian Svc. medal USN, 1984, Haskell G. Wilson award, 1985, cert. of recognition Sec. Navy, 1975, merit award Dept. Navy, 1979, cert. of commendation Sec. Navy, 1981, Career Svcs. award Sec. Navy, 1988, John A. Ulrich award Am. Def. Preparedness Assn., 1991; 1st disting. fellow award Naval Weapons Ctr., 1989. Fellow ASME; mem. Am. Soc. Metals, Am. Phys. Soc., AIME, Fed. Exec. League, Sigma Xi, Tau Beta Pi, Pi Tau Sigma, Triangle. Home and Office: PO Box 1390 858 N Primavera St Ridgecrest CA 93555-7907

PEARSON, JOHN DAVIS, naval officer; b. Pinetops, N.C., June 22, 1939; s. Hugh Oliver Sr. and Lillian Marie (Williams) P.; m. Georgeanne Spalding, Dec. 29, 1962; children: Brian Davis, Elizabeth Ann. BS in Naval Sci., U.S. Naval Acad., Annapolis, Md., 1961; MS in Underwater Acoustics, U.S. Naval Postgrad. Sch., Monterey, Calif., 1970. Commd. ensign USN, 1961, advanced through ranks to rear adm., 1989; engr. officer USS California, Norfolk, Va., 1971-76; exec. officer USS Richmond K. Turner, Norfolk, 1976-77; instr. Prospective Engr. Officer Course, Idaho Falls, Idaho, 1977-79; comdg. officer USS Thomas C. Hart, Norfolk, 1979-81, USS Truxtun, San Diego, 1981-84; officer in charge Sr. Officer Ship Material Readiness Course, Idaho Falls, 1984-86; div. dir. Office Chief of Naval Ops., Washington, 1987-89; dep. commdr. Joint Task Force Four, Key West, Fla., 1989-91; commdr. Mine Warfare Command, Corpus Christi, Tex., 1991—. Decorated Legion of Merit. Avocations: golf, fishing, skiing. *

PEARSON, JOHN EDWARD, lawyer; b. Jamaica, N.Y., Aug. 20, 1946; s. Stanley Charles and Rose Margaret (Manning) P.; m. Laura Marie Johannes, Dec. 28, 1968; children: Laura Rose, Jack. BA, Manhattan Coll., 1968; JD, St. John's U., 1972. Bar: N.Y. 1973, Fla. 1981, U.S. Dist. Ct. (so. dist.) N.Y. 1977, U.S. Dist. Ct. (so. dist.) Fla. 1982, U.S. Ct. Appeals (11th cir.) 1982, U.S. Ct. Appeals (5th cir.) 1982. Assoc. Sage, Gray, Todd & Sims, N.Y.C., 1972-78, ptnr., 1979; ptnr. Sage, Gray, Todd & Sims, Miami, Fla., 1980-87; ptnr. Hughes, Hubbard & Reed, Miami, 1987-91, 94—, N.Y.C., 1992-93. Author jour. article (Best Article award 1971). With USMCR,

1968-69. Mem. ABA, Fla. Bar Assn., N.Y. State Bar Assn., Assn. Bar City N.Y., Dade County Bar Assn., N.Y. County Lawyers Assn., Greater Miami C. of C. (trustee). Republican. Roman Catholic. Avocations: sailing, running. Home: 276 Sea View Dr Key Biscayne FL 33149-2504 Office: Hughes Hubbard & Reed Miami Ctr Ste 2500 201 S Biscayne Blvd Ste Miami FL 33131-4332

PEARSON, LARRY LESTER, journalism educator, internet presence provider; b. Sioux Falls, S.D., Sept. 27, 1942; s. Lester Loren and Lois Ursula (Cochran) P.; m. Alice Marie Simons, Sept. 15, 1979; children: Gregory Eric, Hillary Yvette, Andrew Todd. BA cum.laude, U. Minn., 1964, PhD, 1990; MA, U. Wis., 1969. Newsman UPI, Mpls., 1962-63; newsman Daily American, Rome, Italy, 1964-65; instr. Journalism Sch., U. Wis., 1965-67; with Mpls. Tribune, 1967-85, wire editor, 1970-72, news editor, 1972-82; news editor Mpls. Star & Tribune, 1982; asst. prof. U. Alaska, Anchorage, 1985-92, assoc. prof., 1992—, dir. Ctr. for Info. Tech., 1990-92; spl. cons. to Alaska Ho. Com. on Telecomm., 1985-90; proprieter Online Design, 1995—. Mem. Internat. Communication Assn., Am. Soc. Newspaper Design, Assn. Edn. in Journalism and Mass Communication. Lutheran. Home: 2410 E 16th Ave Anchorage AK 99508-2906 Office: U Alaska Anchorage AK 99508

PEARSON, LOUISE MARY, retired manufacturing company executive; b. Inverness, Scotland, Dec. 14, 1919 (parents Am. citizens); d. Louis Houston and Jessie M. (McKenzie) Lenox; grad. high sch.; m. Nels Kenneth Pearson, June 28, 1941; children: Lorine Pearson Walters, Karla. Dir. Wauconda Tool & Engring. Co., Inc., Algonquin, Ill., 1950-86; reporter Oak Leaflet, Crystal Lake, Ill., 1944-47, Sidelights, Wilmette, Ill., 1969-72, 79-82. Active Girl Scouts U.S.A., 1955-65. Recipient award for appreciation work with Girl Scouts U.S., 1965. Clubs: Antique Automobile of Am. (Hershey, Pa.), Vet. Motor Car (Boston), Classic Car of Am. (Madison, N.J.), Hoseless Carriage Club. Home: 125 Dole Ave Crystal Lake IL 60014-5837

PEARSON, MARGARET DONOVAN, former mayor; b. Nashville, Oct. 29, 1921; d. Timothy Graham and Nelle Ligon (Schmidt) Donovan; m. Jimmie Wilson Pearson, Aug. 2, 1946 (dec. Oct. 1978). BS, Vanderbilt U., 1944, MA, 1950; MS, U. Tenn., 1954. Cryptanalysist Army Signal Corps, Washington, 1944-45; phys. edn. tchr. Nashville Bd. Edn., 1945-46; tchr. English, phys. edn. White County Bd. Edn., Sparta, Tenn., 1946-57; spl. edn. supr. Tenn. Dept. Edn., Cookeville, 1957-65; staff devel. dir. Tenn. Dept. Edn., Nashville, 1965-84; 1st woman alderman City of Sparta, 1987-91, 1st woman mayor, 1991-95. Mem. Tenn. Gov.'s Com. Employment of Disabled, 1989—, U.S. Ret. Sr. Vol. Program, 1985—. Am. Speech, Lang. and Hearing Assn. fellow, 1971; Ky. Col.; Tenn. Col. Mem. Tenn. Mcpl. League (dist. dir. 1987-94, 1st woman elected as v.p.), Sparta C. of C., Rotary (1st woman elected pres.). Methodist. Avocations: reading, knitting, needlepoint. Home: PO Box 22 114 Highland Dr Sparta TN 38583-0022

PEARSON, MARGIT LINNEA, real estate company executive; b. Weymouth, Mass., Nov. 6, 1950; d. Eric Gustav and Evelyn (Forest) P. BA, Simmons Coll., 1972; MBA, Harvard U., 1975. Sr. mgr. McKinsey & Co., Inc., N.Y.C., 1975-83; pres. Berkey, Inc., Greenwich, Conn., 1987-89, APC Corp., Hawthorne, N.J., 1990-91; mng. dir. Renaissance, N.Y.C., 1992-93; pres. Sunset Point Devel., Charleston, S.C., 1987—. Bd. dirs. NORMAL, Ctr. for Contemporary Art, Desert Chorale, Santa Fe, 1994—. Avocations: art, skiing, travel. Home: 9 E 96th St New York NY 10128-0778 Office: 1590 Canyon Rd Santa Fe NM 87501-6136

PEARSON, NATHAN WILLIAMS, investment management executive; b. N.Y.C., Nov. 26, 1911; s. James A. and Elizabeth (Williams) P.; m. Kathleen P. McMurtry, Apr. 9, 1947; children: James S. (dec.), Nathan Williams. A.B., Dartmouth Coll., 1932; M.B.A., Harvard, 1934; LLD (hon.), Thiel Coll., 1972. With U.S. Steel Corp., 1939-42; mgr. research Matson Navigation Co., 1946-47; controller Carborundum Co., 1947-48; with T. Mellon and Sons, Pitts., 1948-70; v.p., gov. T. Mellon and Sons, 1957-70; chmn., chief exec. officer, chmn. emeritus Mellon Bank N.A. & Mellon Bank Corp., Pitts., 1987—; fin. exec. for Paul Mellon, 1948—. Chmn. Pitts. Theol. Sem., 1987. Served from lt. (j.g.) to comdr. USNR, 1942-46. Mem. Allegheny Country Club, Harvard-Yale Princeton Club, Duquesne Club, Laurel Valley Golf Club, Edgeworth Club, Rolling Rock Club (Ligonier, Pa.), Racquet and Tennis Club. Republican. Presbyterian. Home: 10 Woodland Rd Sewickley PA 15143-1123 Office: Mellon Bank Corp 525 William Penn Pl Pittsburgh PA 15219-1711

PEARSON, NATHAN WILLIAMS, broadcast executive; b. Sewickley, Pa., Aug. 1, 1951; s. Nathan Williams Sr. and Kathleen Patricia (McMurtry) P.; m. Jane Ruth Wallace, Oct. 12, 1985; children: Nathan McMurtry, Howe Quinn, Henry Wallace. BA and MA in Music, Conn. Wesleyan U., 1974; MBA, Columbia U., 1982. Pvt. practice cons. N.Y.C. and Washington, 1974-82; with McKinsey & Co., N.Y.C. and L.A., 1982-88; exec. v.p., chief fin. officer, mng. prin., sec., treas. Broadcasting Ptnrs., Inc., N.Y.C., 1988-95; chmn. Broadcasting Ptnrs., L.L.C., Rye, N.Y., 1995—; vice chmn. Icelandic Broadcasting Corp., Reykjavik. Author: "Goin' to Kansas City," 1987; producer LP records, TV and radio programs; contbr. articles to profl. jours. Sec., bd. dirs. CityLore, Inc., N.Y.C., 1986—; v.p. bd. dirs. Young Audiences, N.Y., 1987-95, pres., 1995—. Mem. Soc. for Ethnomusicology, Am. Folklore Soc., Wadawanuck Club, Nat. Assn. Broadcasting, Beta Gamma Sigma. Avocations: boardsailing, river running, hiking. Home: 3 Holly Ln Rye NY 10580-3953 Office: Broadcasting Ptnrs LLC 3 Holly Ln Rye NY 10580

PEARSON, NORMAN, urban and regional planner, administrator, academic and planning consultant, writer; b. Stanley, County Durham, Eng., Oct. 24, 1928; arrived in Can., 1954; s. Joseph and Mary (Pearson) P.; m. Gerda Maria Josefine Riedl, July 25, 1972. BA in Fine Arts with honors in Town and Country Planning, U. Durham (Eng.), 1951; PhD in Land Economy and Ecol. Planning, Internat. Inst. Advanced Studies, 1979; MBA, Pacific Western U., Colo., 1980, DBA, 1982; PhD In Mgmt., Calif. U. for Advanced Studies, 1986. Cons. Stanley Urban Dist. Coun., U.K., 1946-47; planning asst. Accrington Town Plan and Bedford County Planning Survey, U. Durham Planning Team, U.K., 1947-49, Allen and Mattocks, cons. planners and landscape designers, Newcastle upon Tyne, U.K., 1949-51; adminstrv. asst. Scottish Div., Nat. Coal Bd., Edinburgh, Scotland, 1951-52; planning asst. London County Coun., Westminster, U.K., 1953-54; planner Ctrl. Mortgage and Housing Corp., Ottawa, Ont., Can., 1954-55; planning analyst City of Toronto (Ont.) Planning Bd., 1955-56; dir. planning Hamilton Wentworth Planning Area Bd., Hamilton, Ont., 1956-59, Burlington (Ont.) and Suburban Area Planning Bd., Can., 1959-62; commr. planning City of Burlington, Ont., 1959-62; pres. Tanfield Enterprises Ltd., London, Ont., Can., 1962—, Norman Pearson & Assocs. Ltd., London, Ont., Can., 1962—, Internat. Planning Mgmt. Cons., London, Ont., Can., 1962—, Leahy, Pearson, Toll & Assocs. Ltd., London, Ont., Can., 1993-95; cons. in urban, rural and regional planning, 1962—; life mem. U.S. Com. for Monetary Research and Edn., 1976—; spl. lectr. in planning McMaster U., Hamilton, 1956-64, Waterloo (Ont.) Luth. U., 1961-63; asst. prof. geography and planning U. Waterloo (Ont.), 1963-67; assoc. prof. geography U. Guelph (Ont.), 1967-72, chmn., dir. Ctr. for Resource Devel.; prof. polit. sci. U. Western Ont., London, 1972-78; chmn. bd. dirs. Alma Coll., St. Thomas, Ont., 1990—; adj. prof. of ecological planning and land econs. Internat. Inst. for Advanced Studies, Clayton, Mo., 1980-89; core faculty Doctoral Program in Adminstrn/Mgmt. Walden U., Mpls., 1986—, chair adminstrn.-mgmt., 1989—; mem. acad. coun. Walden U., 1992—; mem. bd. regents Calif. U. for Advanced Studies, Petaluma, 1987-94; mem. Social Scis., Econ. and Legal Aspects Com. of Rsch. Adv. Bd. Internat. Joint Commn., 1972-76; cons. to City of Waterloo, 1973-76, Province of Ont., 1969-70; advisor to Georgian Bay Regional Devel. Coun., 1968-72; real estate appraiser, province of Ont., 1976—; pres., chmn. bd. govs. Pacific Western U., Canada, 1983-84. Author: Franchise & Partnership: A New Concept of Urban Development, 1995, Pipelines & Farming, 1995, Resources Development Policies in Canada, 1995, Planning for Eastern Georgian Bay, 1996; (with others) An Inventory of Joint Programmes and Agreements Affecting Canada's Renewable Resources, 1964, An Emerald Light, 1994, Light Beyond the Craft in Canada, 1994; editor, co-author: Regional and Resource Planning in Canda, 1963, rev. edit., 1970; editor (with others): The Pollution Reader, 1968; contbr. numerous articles on town planning to profl. jours., chpts. to books. Pres. Unitarian Ch. of Hamilton, 1960-61. With RAF, 1951-53, RAFVR, 1953-68. Decorated knight of grace Sovereign Order St. John of Jerusalem, 1979, knight Order St. Lazarus of Jerusalem, 1991, Internat. Order of Merit, 1991, Order Internat. Fellowship, 1995. Fellow Royal Town Planning Inst. (Bronze medal 1957), Royal Econ. Soc., Lambda Alpha Internat.; mem. Am. Inst. Planners, Can. Inst. Planners, Can. Polit. Sci. Assn., Internat. Soc. City and Regional Planners, Internat. Assn. Engrs. and Drs. Indsl. pplied Scis., Empire Club, Univ. Club (London), Baconian Club. Office: PO Box 5362, Station A, London, ON Canada N6A 4L6

PEARSON, OSCAR HARRIS, plant breeder, geneticist; b. Stratham, N.H., Jan. 17, 1902; s. Frank Harris and Grace Eunice (Gowen) P.; m. Helen Ruth Monosmith, Dec. 15, 1929; children: Robert, David, Ann, Charles, George, Sandra. BS, U. N.H., 1923, MS, 1925; PhD, U. Calif., Berkeley, 1928. Jr. olericulturist U. Calif., Davis, 1928-33; head seed R & D Ea. States Farmers Exch., West Springfield, Mass., 1934-59; dir. seed R & D Seed Rsch. Specialists, Hollister, Calif., 1959-63, Niagara Seed, San Juan Bautista, Calif., 1963-67; sr. rsch. assoc. plant breeding dept. Cornell U., Ithaca, N.Y., 1967-70; cons. Bud Senegal, Dakar, 1970-75. Contbr. articles to profl. jours. Fellow AAAS, Am. Soc. Hort. Sci. (Asgrow award 1969). Achievements include basic program of hybrid cabbage seed production; development of Pearson tomato cultivar, the Butter and Sugar high quality bicolor hybrid sweet corn, other cultivars; isolation of a "n" male sterile cabbage for use in hybrid seed production. Office: 62 Reise Ter Portsmouth RI 02871-2710

PEARSON, PATRICIA KELLEY, marketing representative; b. Carrollton, Ga., Jan. 21, 1953; d. Ben and Edith (Kelley) Rhudy; m. Ray S. Pearson, June 4, 1976; children: Chad, Jonathan, Kelly. BA in Journalism, Ga. State U., 1974; BSN, West Ga. Coll., 1990. RN Fla. Pub. rels. asst. Grady Meml. Hosp., Atlanta, 1974-77; editorial asst. Childers & Sullivan, Huntsville, Ala., 1977-78; sales rep. AAA Employment Agy., Huntsville, 1978-80; editor Wright Pub. Co., Atlanta, 1980-82; elect./electronic drafter PRC Cons., Atlanta, 1980-87; researcher Dept. Nursing at West Ga. Coll., Carrollton, 1989-90; med./surg. nurse Tanner Med. Ctr., Carrollton, Ga., 1989-90, Delray Community Hosp., Delray Beach, Fla., 1990-91; sales rep. Innovative Med. Svcs., 1991-94; with staff devel., employee rels. Beverly Oaks Rehab. and Nursing Ctr., 1994-95; sales rep. Olsten-Kimberly Quality Care Home Health Svcs., 1996—. Vol. Project Response. All-Am. scholar U.S. Achievement Acad., 1990, recipient Nat. Coll. Nursing award, 1989. Mem. NOW, Space Coast Bus. Writer's Guild, Omicron Delta Kappa. Democrat. Home: 111 Boca Ciega Rd Cocoa Beach FL 32931-2825

PEARSON, PAUL DAVID, lawyer, mediator; b. Boston, Jan. 22, 1940; s. Bernard J. and Ruth (Bayla) Horblit; m. Carol A. Munschauer; children—David Todd, Lisa Kari. AB, Bucknell U., 1961; LLB, U. Pa., 1964. Bar: Mass. 1966, N.Y. 1987. Staff atty., tech. assoc. lab. of community psychiatry, dept. psychiatry Harvard Med. Sch., Boston, 1966-68; assoc. Snyder Tepper & Berlin, Boston, 1968-71, ptnr., 1971-77; with Hill & Barlow, Boston, 1977-87, ptnr., chmn. family law dept.; with Hodgson, Russ, Andrews, Woods and Goodyear, Buffalo, 1987—, ptnr., chmn family law dept., lectr. Mass. Continuing Legal Edn., New Eng. Law Inst.; instr. law and mental health Boston Psychoanalytic Soc. and Inst., 1975-87; lectr. in field. Trustee, v.p., legal counsel Boston Ballet Soc.; trustee, chmn., legal counsel Wayland (Mass.) Townhouse; trustee Family Counseling Service (region West); mem., chmn., clk. Wayland Zoning Bd. Appeals; v.p., counsel, Arts Wayland Found., 1982-87; vis. fellow Woodrow Wilson Found., 1985-87, Mass. Gov.'s Spl. Commn. on Divorce, 1985-87; lectr. dept. psychiatry SUNY-Buffalo Med. Sch., 1989—; bd. dirs. Jewish Community Ctr. Greater Buffalo and Buffalo chpt., Am. Jewish Com., 1991—, pres., 1995—, Arts Coun. Buffalo and Erie County, 1992—. Served to capt. Mil. Police Corps, USAR. Fellow Am. Acad. Matrimonial Lawyers (pres., bd. mgrs. Mass.); mem. ABA (family law com.), Mass. Bar Assn. (chmn. family law sect.), Boston Bar Assn. (family law com., legis. chmn.), N.Y. Bar Assn. (family law com.), Erie County Bar Assn. (chmn. alternative dispute resolution com., family law com.). Contbr. articles to profl. jours. Home: 605 Lebrun Rd Buffalo NY 14226-4232 Office: Hodgson Russ Andrews Woods & Goodyear M & T Plz Ste 1800 Buffalo NY 14203

PEARSON, PAUL GUY, academic administrator emeritus; b. Lake Worth, Fla., Dec. 5, 1926; s. Eric Conrad and Dora Wilma (Capen) P.; m. Winifred Clowe, June 30, 1951; children: Thomas, Jean, Andrew. Student, Palm Beach Jr. Coll., 1946-47; B.S. with honors, U. Fla., 1949, M.S., 1951, Ph.D., 1954; Litt.D. (hon.), Rutgers U., 1982; LL.D. (hon.), Juniata Coll., 1983; commandeu de L'ordre de merite, Grand Duchy of Luxembourg, 1988. Asst. prof. U. Tulsa, 1954-55; asst. prof. Rutgers U., New Brunswick, N.J., 1955-60; assoc. prof. Rutgers U., 1960-64, prof., 1964-81, assoc. provost, 1972-77, exec. v.p., 1977-81, acting pres., 1978; pres., prof. Miami U., Oxford, Ohio, 1981-92; bd. dirs. Union Ctrl. Life Ins., Cin., S.W. Ohio Sr. Svcs., Cin., Nat. Conservancy, Ohio. Mem. U.S. Army Sci. Bd., 1984-86. Served with USNR, 1944-46. Fellow AAAS; mem. Am. Inst. Biol. Scis. (governing bd. 1968-79, v.p. 1977, pres. 1978), Rotary Internat. (Paul Harris fellow), Phi Beta Kappa (assoc.). Home: 5110 Bonham Rd Oxford OH 45056-3606

PEARSON, PAUL HAMMOND, physician; b. Bolenge, Belgian Congo; s. Ernest B. and Evelyn (Utter) P. B.S., Northwestern, 1944, B.Medicine, 1946, M.D., 1947; M.P.H., UCLA, 1963. Diplomate: Am. Bd. Pediatrics. Intern Los Angeles County Gen. Hosp., 1946-47; resident Cin. Children's Hosp., 1949-51; fellow convulsive disorders and electroencephalography Johns Hopkins Hosp., Balt., 1951-53; resident in child psychiatry U. B.C., Can., Vancouver, 1976-77; practice medicine specializing in pediatrics L.A., 1953-62; chief mental retardation br. USPHS div. chronic disease, 1963-65; asst. dir. mental retardation program Nat. Inst. Child Health and Human Devel., NIH, 1965-66; spl. asst. to surgeon gen. USPHS, 1966-67; C.L. Meyer prof. child health, prof. pub. health and preventive medicine, dir. Meyer Children's Rehab. Inst., 1967-81, McGaw prof. adolescent medicine, dir. adolescent medicine, 1982-89, prof. emeritus dept. pediatrics, 1989—; mem. grad. faculty U. Nebr. Coll. Medicine, Omaha, 1967—; med. dir. Univ. Hosp. Eating Disorder Program U. Nebr. Coll. Medicine, 1983-89, sr. cons. Univ. Hosp. Eating Disorder Program, 1989—; from instr. to asst. clin. prof. U. So. Calif. Med. Sch., 1953-62; from assoc. clin. prof. pediatrics to clin. prof. pediatrics Georgetown U. Sch. Medicine, Washington, 1963-67; Cons., mem. profl. services program com. United Cerebral Palsy Assn., 1969-72, mem. nat. awards com., 1971; Am. Acad. Pediatrics liaison rep. to Am. Acad. Orthopedic Surgery, 1969-73; apptd. to Nat. Adv. Council Services and Facilities for Developmentally Disabled Dept. Health. Edn. and Welfare, 1971-75; councilor Accreditation Council Facilities for Mentally Retarded, Joint Commn. on Accreditation Hosps., 1973-74; fellow adolescent medicine Boston Children's Hosp. Med. Center, 1981. Cons. editor: Am. Jour. Mental Deficiency, 1970-72; Contbr. articles to profl. jours. Mem. com. on accessible environments Nat. Acad. Scis., 1974-77. Served to capt. MC AUS, 1947-49. Mem. Am. Acad. Pediatrcs (com. on children with handicaps 1969-75, com. sect. on child devel. 1974—), Am. Assn. Mental Deficiency, Nat. Assn. for Retarded Children, Greater Omaha Assn. for Retarded Children (dir.), Am. Pub. Health Assn., Am. Acad. Cerebral Palsy and Developmental Medicine (exec. com. 1971-76, chmn. sci. program com. 1972-74, sec. 1974-77, mem. research and awards com. 1977-78, pres. 1981-82, bd. dirs. 1982-84), Assn. Univ.-Affiliated Facilities (exec. com. 1973—, v.p. 1974-75, pres. 1975-76, dir. 1971-78), Soc. Adolescent MedicineAlpha Omega Alpha. Home: 1123 N 122nd St Omaha NE 68154-1411 Office: U Nebr Med Ctr Dept Pediatrics Omaha NE 68198

PEARSON, PAUL HOLDING, insurance company executive; b. Worcester, Mass., Feb. 14, 1940; s. Malcolm D. and Myra L. (Holding) P.; m. Judith N. Howe, July 13, 1958 (div. June 1974); children: Scott D., Todd E.; m. Anne Beck, July 26, 1974. BA in Bus. and Econs., U. Maine, 1961. C.L.U., 1971. Jr. life underwriter State Mut. Am., Worcester, 1961-63, life underwriter, 1963-67, sr. life underwriter, 1967-69; dir. life underwriting Security Mut. Life Ins. Co., Binghamton, N.Y., 1969, 2d v.p. underwriting, 1970, v.p., 1971-75, sr. v.p. ins. services div., 1975-79, exec. v.p., 1979-81, pres., 1981—, chief exec. officer, 1987—; chmn. Security Mutual Life Ins. Co. of N.Y., Binghamton, 1996—; chmn., CEO, bd. dirs. SML Properties corp., Binghamton, Security Equity Life Ins. Co., Binghamton, 1987-93. Trustee, treas. Lourdes Meml. Hosp., Binghamton, 1978-92; mem. SUNY Found., Binghamton, 1982-89; trustee, chmn. fin. com. Elmira Coll., 1983-87; bd. dirs. Broome C.C. Found., 1982-91, pres. 1985-86; pres. New Industries for Broome, Binghamton, 1985-95, N.Y. State Bus. Devel. Coun., 1987—; bd. dirs. Valley Devel. Found., 1987-91, Bus. Coun. N.Y., 1988—, Am. Coun. Life Ins., 1990—. Mem. Assn. for Advanced Life Underwriting, Nat. Assn. Life Underwriters, Broome County C. of C. (bd. dirs. 1980-88, chmn. 1986), Binghamton C/C Live Wire Club. Office: Security Mut Life Ins Co NY Court House Sq PO Box 1625 Binghamton NY 13902-1625

PEARSON, PHILLIP THEODORE, veterinary clinical sciences and biomedical engineering educator; b. Ames, Iowa, Nov. 21, 1932; s. Theodore B. and Hazel C. (Christianson) P.; m. Mary Jane Barlow, Aug. 28, 1954; children: Jane Catherine, Bryan Theodore, Todd Wallace, Julie Ann. DVM, Iowa State U., 1956, PhD, 1962. Intern Angell Meml. Animal Hosp., Boston, 1956-57; instr. Coll. Vet. Medicine Iowa State U., 1957-59, asst. prof., 1959-63, assoc. prof., 1963-64, prof. vet. clin. scis. and biomed. engring., 1965-72, 89-96, dean, 1972-89; dir. Vet. Med. Rsch. Inst., 1972-89; prof. Sch. Vet. Medicine, U. Mo., 1964-65. Bd. dirs. Iowa Sate Meml. Union, 1970-84; v.p. Iowa State Meml. Union, 1975; chmn. coun. of deans Assn. Am. Vet. Medicine Colls., 1978-79. Recipient Riser award, 1956; distinguished Tchr. award Norden Labs., 1962; Gaines award Gen. Foods Corp., 1966; Outstanding Tchr. award Iowa State U., 1968; Faculty citation, 1974; named Iowa Vet. of the Yr., 1988. Mem. AVMA, Iowa Vet. Medicine Assn., Am. Animal Hosp. Assn., Am. Assn. Vet. Clinicians, Am. Coll. Vet. Surgeons (bd. regents 1972, pres. 1977), Nat. Acad. Practice, Kiwanis (bd. dirs., pres. Ames 1966—), Sigma Xi, Phi Kappa Phi, Phi Zeta, Alpha Zeta, Gamma Sigma Delta (Alumni award of merit 1991). Home: 1610 Maxwell Ave Ames IA 50010-5536

PEARSON, RALPH GOTTFRID, chemistry educator; b. Chgo., Jan. 12, 1919; s. Gottfrid and Kerstin (Larson) P.; m. Lenore Olivia Johnson, June 15, 1941 (dec. June 1982); children—John Ralph, Barry Lee, Christie Ann. B.S., Lewis Inst., 1940; Ph.D., Northwestern U., 1943. Faculty Northwestern U., 1946-76, prof. chemistry, 1957-76; prof. chemistry U. Calif., Santa Barbara, 1976-89, prof. emeritus, 1989—; Cons. to industry and govt., 1951—. Co-author 5 books. Served to 1st lt. USAAF, 1944-46. Recipient Chemical Pioneer award Am. Inst. Chemists, 1995; Guggenheim fellow, 1951. Mem. Am. Chem. Soc. (Midwest award 1966, Inorganic Chemistry award 1969), Nat. Acad. Sci., Phi Beta Kappa, Sigma Xi, Phi Lambda Upsilon (hon.). Lutheran. Achievements include being originator prin. of hard and soft acids and bases.

PEARSON, RICHARD JOSEPH, archaeologist, educator; b. Kitchener, Ont., Can., May 2, 1938; s. John Cecil and Henrietta Anne (Wallwin) P.; m. Kazue Miyazaki, Dec. 12, 1964; 1 child, Sarina Riye. B.A. in Anthropology with honours, U. Toronto, 1960; Ph.D., Yale U., 1966. Asst. prof., then assoc. prof. archaeology U. Hawaii, 1966-71; mem. faculty U. B.C., Vancouver, 1971—; now prof. archaeology U. B.C. Author: The Archaeology of the Ryukyu Islands, 1969, Higashi Ajia no Kodai Shakai to Kokogaku, 1984, Windows on the Japanese Past, Studies in Archaeology and Prehistory, 1986, Ancient Japan, 1992; contbr. articles to profl. jours. Guggenheim fellow. Mem. Am. Anthrop. Assn., Soc. Am. Archaeology, Indo-Pacific Prehistory Assn., Assn. Asian Studies. Office: Dept Anthropology/Sociology, U BC, Vancouver, BC Canada V6T 1Z1

PEARSON, ROBERT GREENLEES, writing services company executive; b. Kansas City, Mo., Feb. 19, 1917; s. Ridley Stillson and Agnes (Greenlees) P.; m. Laura Gray Betsy Dodge, Jan. 3, 1945; children—Bradbury, Wendy, Robert Ridley. A.B. with honors, U. Kans., 1938. Mgr. corporate public relations Shell Oil Co. (N.Y. Head Office), 1938-71; v.p. public relations Council Better Bus. Bur. (N.Y. Hdqrs.), 1971-73; writer public affairs dept. Mobil Oil Corp., N.Y.C., 1973-74; sr. advisor Alcoholics Anonymous World Services, Inc., N.Y.C., 1974-85; pres. Robert Pearson Assocs., Writing Svcs., Riverside, Conn., 1985—; Bd. dirs. Nat. Safety Council; pres. Fairfield County (Conn.) Council on Alcoholism, 1962. Author: Oil for Victory, 1946, The J.C. Nichols Chronicle, 1994; contbr. articles to profl. jours. Served to lt. comdr. USNR, 1941-45. Congregationalist. Clubs: Riverside (Conn.); Yacht, Dutch Treat. Home: 17 Jones Park Dr Riverside CT 06878-2205 Office: PO Box 671 Riverside CT 06878-0671

PEARSON, ROGER, organization executive; b. London, Aug. 21, 1927; s. Edwin and Beatrice May (Woodbine) P.; m. Marion Primrose Simms, June 3, 1959; children: Edwin, Sigrid, Emma, Rupert. BS with honors, U. London, 1951, MS, 1954, PhD, 1969. Chmn. Pakistan Tea Assn., 1964; mng. dir. Octavius Steel & Co. of Pakistan Ltd., Chittagong, East Pakistan, 1959-65; chmn. Plummer Bros., Ltd., Chittagong, East Pakistan, 1959-65, Chittagong Warehouses, Ltd., Chittagong, East Pakistan, 1960-65; chmn. dept. sociology and anthropology Queens Coll., Charlotte, N.C., 1970-71; chmn. dept. anthropology U. So. Miss., Hattiesburg, 1971-74; dean acad. affairs, dir. research Mont. Coll. Mineral Sci. Tech., Butte, 1974-75; exec. dir. Council for Econ. and Social Studies, Washington, 1975—. Author: Eastern Interlude, 1954, Introduction to Anthropology, 1978, Anthropological Glossary, 1985, Race, Intelligence and Bias in Academe, 1991, Shockley on Eugenics and Race, 1992, Heredity and Humanity, 1996; editor: Ecology and Evolution, 1982; editor, pub. Jour. Indo-European Studies, 1973—, Jour. Social Polit. and Econ. Studies, 1976—. Trustee, Benjamin Franklin U., Washington, 1984-87. Served to lt. Brit. Indian Army, 1945-48. Fellow Inst. Chartered Secs. Adminstrs. (London), Inst. Dirs. (London), Oriental Club, Reform Club (London), Army and Navy Club (Washington). Office: Coun Econ and Social Studies 1133 13th St NW Apt C-2 Washington DC 20005-4203

PEARSON, ROGER LEE, library director; b. Galesburg, Ill., Dec. 7, 1940; s. Clifford Emmanuel and Lillian Louise (Fisher) P. B.A., Knox Coll., 1963; M.A. in Sociology, U. Nebr.-Omaha, 1968; M.A. in Library Sci., Rosary Coll., 1974. Vol. U.S. Peace Corps, Brazil, 1964-66; extension service supr. Brown County Libr., Green Bay, Wis., 1974-75; system adminstr. Nicolet Libr. System, Green Bay, 1976-77; exec. dir. South Central Libr. System, Madison, Wis., 1977-81; dir. Corpus Christi Pub. Librs., Tex., 1981-84, Naperville (Ill.) Pub. Librs., 1984-95, Sonoma County Libr., Santa Rosa, Calif., 1995—; lectr. Grad. Sch. Libr. and Info. Sci., Rosary Coll., River Forest, Ill., 1991-95. Mem. ALA, Rotary. Avocations: walking, travel research, train travel, Brazilian and Mexican studies. Home: 5225 Old Redwood Hwy Apt 1 Santa Rosa CA 95403 Office: Sonoma County Libr 3d and E Sts Santa Rosa CA 95404

PEARSON, RONALD DALE, retail food stores corporation executive; b. Des Moines, 1940; married. B.S. in Bus. Adminstrn., Drake U., 1962. With Hy-Vee Food Stores, Inc. (name changed to Hy-Vee, Inc. in 1996), Chariton, Iowa, 1962—; pres. Hy-Vee, Inc., Chariton, Iowa, 1983—; chmn., pres., & CEO Hy-Vee, Inc., 1989—; dir. Beverage Mfrs., Inc., Civic Ctr. Cts., Inc. Office: Hy-Vee Inc 5820 Westown Pkwy West Des Moines IA 50266*

PEARSON, ROY MESSER, JR., clergyman; b. Somerville, Mass., Mar. 10, 1914; s. Roy Messer and Bessie M. (Ricker) P.; m. Ruth Simmons, July 12, 1936; children: Beverly, Bradford; m. Barbara K. Cerello, Sept. 1, 1990. AB magna cum laude, Harvard U., 1935; BD cum laude, Andover Newton Theol. Sch., 1938; DD, Amherst Coll., 1957, Brown U., 1971; LLD, Emerson Coll., 1966, Colby Coll., 1967; LHD, Norwich U., 1968; DSO, Curry Coll., 1969. Minister Southville (Mass.) Federated Ch., 1936-38; ordained to ministry Congl. Ch., 1938; minister First Congl. Ch. Swanzey, N.H., 1938-40, Amherst, Mass., 1940-47; minister Hancock Congl. Ch., Lexington, Mass., 1947-54; lectr. Andover Newton Theol. Sch., 1951-54, dean, 1954-65, pres., 1965-79, also trustee; pres. Andover Theol. Sem., 1954-65, Bartlett prof. sacred rhetoric, 1954-79 ; preacher Nat. Council Chs. in Brit. Isles, 1951; regular radio preacher Mass. Council Chs., 1952-57; preacher Internat. Congl. Council Brit. Isles, 1957; interim minister, Peterborough, Newport, New London, Hanover, Hopkinton, and Warner, N.H., 1979-87. Author: Here's Faith for You, 1953, This Do-And Live, 1954, The Hard Commands of Jesus, 1957, Seeking and Finding God, 1958, The Ministry of Preaching, 1959; Contbg. Author: (ed. G. Paul Butler) Best Sermons of 1955, 1955, Hear Our Prayer, 1961, The Preacher: His Purpose and Practice, 1963, The Believer's Unbelief, 1963, Best Sermons of 1964, 1964, Best Sermons of 1968, 1968, Prayers for All Occasions, 1990; also articles religious periodicals. Served as 1st lt. Chaplains Corps AUS, 1944. Recipient Churchman award for best sermon of the year, 1948; Am. Assn. Theol. Schs. fellow, 1960. Mem. Phi Beta Kappa. Club: University (Boston). Home: 31 Stony Brook Rd PO Box 870 New London NH 03257 *With the advance of my age and the growth of my faith I find myself a Christian* *agnostic. It is not that I believe less. Rather, that I believe more. God is too great for me to comprehend his immensities.*

PEARSON, SCOTT ROBERTS, economics educator; b. Madison, Wis., Mar. 13, 1938; s. Carlyle Roberts and Edith Hope (Smith) P.; m. Sandra Carol Anderson, Sept. 12, 1962; children—Sarah Roberts, Elizabeth Hovden. BS, U. Wis.-Madison, 1961; MA, Johns Hopkins U., 1965; PhD, Harvard U., 1969. Asst. prof. Stanford U., Calif., 1968-74, assoc. prof., 1974-80, assoc. dir. Food Research Inst., 1977-84, dir., 1992—, prof. food econs., 1980—. Cons. AID, World Bank, Washington, 1965—; staff economist Commn. Internat. Trade, Washington, 1970-71. Author: Petroleum and the Nigerian Economy, 1970; (with others) Commodity Exports and African Economic Development, 1974, (with others) Rice in West Africa, Policy and Economics, 1981, (with others) Food Policy Analysis, 1983, (with others) The Cassava Economy of Java, 1984, (with others) Portuguese Agriculture in Transition, 1987, (with Eric Monke) The Policy Analysis Matrix, 1989, (with others) Rice Policy in Indonesia, 1991, (with others) Structural Change and Small-Farm Agriculture in Northwest Portugal, 1993, (with others) Agricultural Policy in Kenya, 1995. Mem. Am. Agrl. Econs. Assn., Am. Econ. Assn. Home: 691 Mirada Ave Palo Alto CA 94305-8477 Office: Stanford U Food Rsch Institute Stanford CA 94305

PEARSON, THOMAS ARTHUR, epidemiologist, educator; b. Berlin, Wis., Oct. 21, 1950; married; 2 children. BA, Johns Hopkins U., 1973, MD, 1976, MPH, 1976, PhD in Epidemiology, 1983. Fellow cardiology Johns Hopkins Sch. Medicine, 1981-83, from asst. prof. to assoc. prof. medicine, epidemiology, 1983-88; prof. epidemiology Columbia U., 1988—, prof. meeidcine, 1995—; dir. Mary Imogene Bassett Rsch. Inst., 1988—; prof. medicine, Jane Forbes Clark chair in health rsch. Columbia U., N.Y.C., 1995—; chmn. monitoring bd. CARDIA project Nat. Heart, Lung and Blood Inst., 1987—; mem. rsch. com. Md. Heart Assn., 1986-88; chmn. data safety monitoring bd. HIT trial VA, 1994—; commr. Md. Coun. Phys. Fitness, 1985-88; mem. clin. applications and prevention commn. NIH, 1987-91, chmn., 1990-91. Mem. ACP, Am. Heart Assn. (nat. rsch. com. 1987-92, coun. epidemiology 1987—, vice chmn. 1994-95, chmn. 1996-98), Am. Fedn. Clin. Rsch., Am. Coll. Epidemiology, Am. Coll. Preventive Medicine, Am. Coll. Cardiology (prevention com.), Soc. Epidemiol. Rsch. (rsch. prize 1978). Achievements include research in the etiology and pathogenesis of atherosclerosis. Office: Mary Imogene Bassett Med Rsch Inst 1 Atwell Rd Cooperstown NY 13326-1301

PEARSON, WALTER DONALD, editor, columnist; b. Pittsfield, Mass., Feb. 5, 1916; s. Edgar C. and Edna (Scott) P.; divorced; children: Florence, Donald, Sharon; m. Elsa Swanson; 1 child, Richard. Student, Dartmouth Coll., 1941-43. Advt. salesman, 1935-41; securities broker Charles A. Day Co., Boston, 1947-55; founder, owner, mgr. First New Eng. Securities Co., Inc., Southbridge, Mass., 1955-71; now owner, editor Pearson Investment Letter, Dover, Fla.; fin. columnist World Intelligence Rev.; free-lance columnist various publications; fin. advisor, investment mgr. Author: Investing for the Millions, 1990. With inf. U.S. Army, 1943-45, ETO. Decorated Bronze star, Croix de Guerre (France), Combat Infantry badge. Home: 1628 White Arrow Dr Dover FL 33527-5741

PEARSON, WILLARD, former army officer; b. West Elizabeth, Pa., July 4, 1915; s. John Alfred and Mary Catherine (Mehrmann) P.; m. Reba E. Barton, Sept. 12, 1947; children: Richard Barton, Joan Louise, Patricia Jean. Student, Douglas Bus. Coll., 1933-35; M.S., Columbia U., 1953; postgrad., Army War Coll., 1956-57; postgrad. in mgmt., U. Pitts., 1962; M.A., George Washington U., 1963. Commd. 2d lt. U.S. Army Res., 1936; advanced through grades to lt. gen. U.S. Army, 1971; comdg. gen. 1st Brigade, 101st Airborne Div. Vietnam, 1966-67; J3, USMACV Saigon, 1967-68; dir. individual tng. ODCSPER, Hdqrs. Dept. Army Washington, 1968-69; comdg. gen. Ft. Lewis, Wash., 1969-71, V Corps U.S. Army Europe, 1971-73; supt. Valley Forge Mil. Acad. and Jr. Coll., Wayne, Pa., 1973-85. Mem. Franklin Inst., Phila. Orchestra Assn., Friends Independence Nat. Hist. Park; bd. advisors Vietnam Veterans Meml. Inst.; trustee Chapel of 4 Chaplains, exec. com., 1984-87; bd. dirs. Citizens Crime Commn. Phila. Decorated D.S.M. with 2 oak leaf clusters, Silver Star medal with two oak leaf clusters, Legion of Merit with two oak leaf clusters, Bronze Star medal with two oak leaf clusters, Combat Inf. badge with star, Air medal with six oak leaf clusters; Republic of Korea Presdl. Commendation; Mil. Order of Merit Korea; Vietnamese Order 4th and 5th Classes; Vietnamese Gallantry Cross with palm; Grand Cross Merit with star Fed. Repub. Germany; Pa. D.S.M. Mem. Accuracy in Media, Am. Legion, Am. Security Coun., Assn. U.S. Army, Coun. for Inter-Am. Security, Mil. Order World Wars, Nat. Assn. Uniformed Svcs., 101st Airborne Divsn. Assn., Olympia Assn., Navy League, VFW, Res. Officers Assn., Nat. Sojourners Inc., Beta Gamma Sigma. Presbyterian. Club: Penn. Lodge: Masons (33 degree), Shriners (knight comdr. ct. honor). Master parachutist. Address: 375 Red Coat Ln Wayne PA 19087-1338

PEARSON, WILLIAM ROWLAND, nuclear engineer; b. New Bedford, Mass., Sept. 30, 1923; s. Rowland and Nellie (Hilton) P.; BS, Northeastern U., 1953; postgrad. U. Ohio, 1960; m. Arlene Cole Loveys, June 14, 1953; children: Denise, Robert, Rowland, Nancy. Engr., Goodyear Atomic Corp., Portsmouth, Ohio, 1953-63, Cabot Titania Corp., Ashtabula, Ohio, 1963-64; supr. United Nuclear, Wood River, R.I., 1964-72; sr. engr. Nuclear Materials and Equipment Co., Apollo, Pa., 1972-74; engr. U.S. Nuclear Regulatory Commn., Rockville, Md., 1974-90, ret., 1990. Served with USNR, 1942-45. Decorated Air medal. Mem. AAAS, Am. Nuclear Soc., Am. Inst. Chem. Engrs. (chmn. 1966-67). Republican. Baptist. Clubs: Masons, Elks. Home: 60 Meeting Hill Rd Hillsboro NH 03244-4856

PEASBACK, DAVID R., recruiting company executive; 1 child, Jennifer. B.A., Colgate U., 1955; LL.B., U. Va., 1961. Mgmt. trainee Proctor & Gamble, N.Y.C., 1955-56; assoc. Covington & Burling, Washington, 1961-64; litigation counsel Litton Industries, Inc., Beverly Hills, Calif., 1965-67; v.p. Bangor Punta Ops., Greenwich, Conn., 1968-71; assoc. Heidrick and Struggles, N.Y.C., 1972-76, ptnr., 1976-88, pres., chief exec. officer, 1983-87; vice-chmn., chief exec. officer Canny, Bowen, Inc., N.Y.C., 1988—. Served as sgt. USMC, 1956-58. Office: Canny Bowen Inc 200 Park Ave 49th Fl New York NY 10166*

PEASE, CAROL HELENE, oceanographer; b. Bay City, Mich., Dec. 29, 1949; d. George Olson and Mernabelle Hattie (Laabs) P.; m. Alexander Jeffrey Chester, June 16, 1974 (div. May 1978); m. Bruce William Rummel, Oct. 28, 1989. Student, U. Mich., 1968-71; BS in Math., U. Miami, 1972; MS in Phys. Oceanography, U. Wash., 1975, MS in Meteorology, 1981; PhD in Meteorology, U. Wash., Seattle, 1993. Rsch. asst. Arctic ice dynamics joint expt. U. Wash., Seattle, 1972-75; oceanographer Pacific Marine Environ. Lab. Nat. Oceanic and Atmospheric Adminstrn., Seattle, 1975-78, sea ice project leader Pacific Marine Environ. Lab., 1978—; U.S. rep. Internat. Sea Ice Commn. for Internat. Assn. Physical Scis. of the Ocean, 1991—. Contbr. articles to profl. jours. Mem. Arboretum Found., Seattle, 1975—, Seattle Art Mus., 1978—, Nat. Women's Polit. Caucus, Seattle, 1984—; sustaining mem. Friends of KUOW, KCTS Found., Seattle, 1978—, 82—. Recipient performance awards NOAA, 1977, 82, 85, 87, 88, 90, Adminstr.'s award, 1988. Mem. AAAS, Assn. Women in Sci., Am. Geophys. Union (session chair interdisciplinary sea ice studies 1992), Am. Meteorol. Soc. (session chair symposium meterology and oceanography N.Am. high latitudes 1984, mem. standing com. on polar meteorology and oceanography 1985-90, chmn. 1987-89, session chair, co-convener conf. on polar meteorology and oceanography 1988, session chair conf. on polar meteorology and oceanography 1992), Corinthian yacht Club, Valkyrien (sec. 1978-81, 1992-93, pres. 1994), Daus. Norway. Avocations: racing keelboats, gardening, genealogy. Office: NOAA Pacific Marine Environ Lab 7600 Sand Point Way NE Seattle WA 98115-6349

PEASE, DAVID GORDON, artist, educator; b. Bloomington, Ill., June 2, 1932; s. Gordon A. and June (Stephens) P.; m. Julie Jensen, Mar. 29, 1956; children: Lisa Kay, Kerry Susan. B.S., U. Wis., 1954, M.S., 1955, M.F.A., 1958. Instr. art Mich. State U., 1958-60; mem. faculty Tyler Sch. Art, Temple U., Phila., 1960-83; prof. Tyler Sch. Art, Temple U., 1970-83, chmn. painting dept., 1968-77, dean, 1977-83; prof., dean Yale U. Sch. Art, New Haven, 1983—; vis. faculty mem. Yale U. Summer Sch. Music and Art, 1970-72. One-man shows include Baylor U., 1972, U. Wis., 1972, Pa. Acad. Fine Arts, 1977, Terry Dintenfass Inc., N.Y.C., 1969, 71, 76, Phila. Art Alliance, 1961, 70; group exhbns. include Carnegie Internat., Pitts., 1961, Corcoran Biennial, Washington, 1961, 63, Whitney Annual, N.Y.C., 1963; represented in permanent collections Whitney Mus. Am. Art, Phila. Mus. Art, Pa. Acad. Fine Arts, Des Moines Art Center, Pa. State U., U. Wis., Temple U., Hallmark Cards Inc., Columbia Pictures, others. Trustee Louis Comfort Tiffany Found., 1988—. With U.S. Army, 1955-57. Recipient William A. Clark award Corcoran Biennial, 1963, Lindbeck Found. Disting. Teaching award, 1968, Disting. Alumni award U. Wis., 1991; Guggenheim Found. fellow, 1965-66; Tiffany Found. grantee, 1975-76. Mem. Coll. Art Assn. Am., Nat. Assn. Schs. Art, Nat. Coun. Art Adminstrs. (bd. dirs. 1984-87), Alliance Ind. Colls. of Art (bd. dirs. 1988-91), Assn. Ind. Colls. Art and Design (trustee 1992-96). Home: 95 Thankful Stow Rd Guilford CT 06437-2529 Office: Yale U Sch Art 180 York St New Haven CT 06511-4804

PEASE, EDWARD ALLAN, lawyer, former state senator, university official; b. Terre Haute, Ind., May 22, 1951; s. Robert Richard and Joanna Rose (Pilant) P.; A.B. with distinction (Wendell Willkie scholar), Ind. U., Bloomington, 1973, J.D. cum laude, Indpls., 1977; postgrad. Memphis State U., 1975-76, Ind. State U., 1978-85. Gen. law clk. appellate and contracts div. Office Ind. Atty. Gen., Indpls., 1974-75; nat. dir. alumni affairs Pi Kappa Alpha Frat., Memphis, 1975-76; admitted to Ind. bar, 1977; partner firm Thomas, Thomas & Pease, Brazil, Ind., 1977-84; of counsel firm Thomas & Thomas, Brazil, 1984—; v.p. Ind. State U., 1993; mem. Ind. Senate, 1980-92, chmn. Judiciary Com.; chmn. Ind. Commn. Trial Cts., 1987-89; mem. adv. bd. 1st Bank & Trust Co. Clay County; mem. exec. bd. Wabash Valley council Boy Scouts Am., 1972—, exec. bd. east cen. region, 1986-88, v.p., 1977-84, pres., 1984-88, mem. nat. Order of Arrow com., 1984—, nat. vice chmn., 1990-93, nat. chmn., 1993—. Recipient Silver Beaver award Boy Scouts Am., 1975, Silver Antelope, 1992, Disting. Eagle Scout award, 1995. Mem. Ind. Bar Assn., Phi Beta Kappa, Pi Kappa Alpha (nat. pres. 1988-90). Republican. Club: Columbia (Indpls.). Office: Ind State U 340 Gillum Hall ISU Terre Haute IN 47809

PEASE, ROGER FABIAN WEDGWOOD, electrical engineering educator; b. Cambridge, Eng., Oct. 24, 1936; came to U.S., 1964; s. Michael Stewart and Helen Bowen (Wedgwood) P.; m. Caroline Ann Bowring, Sept. 17, 1960; children: Emma Ruth, Joseph Henry Bowring, James Edward. BA, Cambridge U., Eng., 1960, MA, 1964, PhD, 1964. Rsch. fellow Trinity Coll., Cambridge, 1963-64; asst. prof. U. Calif., Berkeley, 1964-67; mem. tech. staff AT&T Bell Labs., Murray Hill, N.J., 1967-78; prof. elec. engring. Stanford (Calif.) U., 1978—; cons. IBM, San Jose, Calif., 1964-67, Xerox Corp., Palo Alto, Calif., 1978-84, Perkin Elmer Co., Hayward, Calif., 1979-90, Lawrence Livermore (Calif.) Labs., 1984-92, Affymax Rsch. Inst., 1989-93, Affymetrix, 1993—; mem. tech. adv. bd. Ultratech. Stepper, 1993—. Contbr. over 100 articles to profl. jours. Patentee (8) in field. Scoutmaster Boy Scouts Am., Holmdel, N.J., 1977-78. Pilot officer RAF, 1955-57. Fellow IEEE (Rappaport award 1982), San Jose Sailing Club. Avocations: sailboat racing, windsurfing. Home: 838 Esplanada Way Stanford CA 94305-1015 Office: Stanford U Dept Elec Engring Stanford CA 94305

PEASE-PRETTY ON TOP, JANINE B., community college administrator; b. Nespelem, Wash., Sept. 17, 1949; d. Benjamin and Margery Louise (Jordan) Pease; m. Sam Vernon Windy Boy, July 30, 1975 (div. Jan. 1983); children: Rosella L. Windy Boy, Sam Vernon Windy Boy; m. John Joseph Pretty On Top, Sept. 15, 1991. BA in Sociology, Anthropology, Ctrl. Wash. U., 1970; MEd, Mont. State U., 1987, EdD, 1994; HHD (hon.), Hood Coll., 1990; LLD (hon.), Gonzaga U., 1991; EdD (hon.), Whitman Coll., 1993. Dep. dir. Wash. State Youth Commn., Olympia, 1971; tutor student svcs. Big Bend C.C., Moses Lake, Wash., 1971-72, upward bound dir., 1972-75; women's counselor Navajo C.C., Many Farms, Ariz., 1972; dir. adult & continuing edn. Crow Ctrl. Edn. Commn., Crow Agy., Mont., 1975-79; ednl. cons. Box Elder, Mont., 1979-81; dir. Indian career svc. Ea. Mont. Coll., Billings, 1981-82; pres. Little Big Horn Coll., Crow Agency, 1982—; exec. com. Am. Indian Higher Ednl. Consortium, Washington, 1983—; bd. dirs. Am. Indian Coll. Fund, N.Y.C., 1988—; sec. Indian Nations at Risk U.S. Dept. Edn., Washington, 1990-91, collaborator task force, 1990-91; 2d vice chmn. Nat. Adv. Coun. Indian Edn., Washington, 1994—. Chmn. Bighorn County Dem. Ctrl. Com., Hardin, Mont., 1983-88; mem. coun. First Crow Indian Bapt. Ch., 1989—. MacArthur fellow John D. & Catharine MacArthur Found., 1994. Mem. Nat. Indian Edn. Assn. (Indian educator of yr. 1990), Crow Tribe Nighthawk Dance Soc. Office: Little Big Horn Coll PO Box 370 Crow Agency MT 59022

PEASLEE, JAMES M., lawyer; b. Scranton, Pa., Sept. 1, 1952; s. Robert Victor and Jean (Mark) P. BA, Yale U., 1973, MA, 1973; JD, Harvard U., 1976; LLM in Taxation, NYU, 1979. Bar: N.Y. 1977. Assoc. Cleary, Gottlieb, Steen & Hamilton, N.Y.C., 1976-84, ptnr., 1984—. Office: Cleary Gottlieb Steen & Hamilton 1 Liberty Plz New York NY 10006-1404

PEASLEE, MARGARET MAE HERMANEK, zoology educator; b. Chgo., June 15, 1935; d. Emil Frank and Magdalena Bessie (Cechota) Hermanek; m. David Raymond Peaslee, Dec. 6, 1957; 1 dau., Martha Magdelena Peaslee-Levine. A.A., Palm Beach Jr. Coll., 1956; B.S., Fla. So. Coll., 1959; med. technologist, Northwestern U., 1958, M.S., 1964, Ph.D., 1966. Med. technologist Passavant Hosp., Chgo., 1958-59; med. technologist St. James Hosp., Chicago Heights, Ill., 1960-63; asst. prof. biology Fla. So. Coll., Lakeland, 1966-68, U. S.D., Vermillion, 1968-71; assoc. prof. U. S.D., 1971-76, prof., 1976, acad. opportunity liaison, 1974-76; prof., head dept. zoology La. Tech. U., Ruston, 1976-90, assoc. dean, dir. grad. studies and rsch., prof. biol. scis. Coll. Life Scis., 1990-93; v.p. for acad. affairs U. Pitts. at Titusville, Pa., 1993—. Contbr. articles to profl. jours. Fellow AAAS; mem. AAUP, Am. Inst. Biol. Scis., Am. Soc. Zoologists, S.D. Acad. Sci. (sec.-treas. 1972-76), N.Y. Acad. Scis., Pa. Acad. Sci., La. Acad. Sci. (sec. 1979-81, pres. 1983), Sigma Xi, Phi Theta Kappa, Phi Rho Pi, Phi Sigma, Alpha Epsilon Delta. Office: U Pitts Office of Acad Affairs Titusville PA 16354-0287

PEAT, RANDALL DEAN, defense analysis company executive, retired air force officer; b. Chicago, July 6, 1935; s. Thomas R. and Lulu M. (Ray) P.; m. Joyce Enid Hunter, Sept. 15, 1956; children—Brian James, Sondra Lee Peat Gadell. B.S. in Journalism, Medill Sch. Journalism Northwestern U., Evanston, Ill., 1956, M.S. in Journalism Mgmt., 1957. Commd. officer U.S. Air Force, 1957, advanced through ranks to maj. gen.; pilot, instr. Strategic Air Command, Westover AFB and Clinton-Sherman, Okla., 1958-66; asst. air attache Am. Embassy, Djakarta, Indonesia, 1967; pilot Pacific Command Airborne Command Post, Hickam AFB, Hawaii, 1968-70; staff officer 7th Air Force, Saigon, Vietnam, 1971, Hdqrs. U.S. Air Force, Pentagon, D.C., 1972-75, SHAPE, Belgium, 1976-79, Hdqrs. U.S. Air Force, Pentagon, D.C., 1980-81; dep. dir. plans Office Joint Chief of Staff, Pentagon, D.C., 1982-84; asst. chief of staff ops. Supreme Hdqrs. Allied Powers Europe, Belgium, 1984-87; chief of staff Strategic Air Command, Offutt AFB, Nebr., 1987-89; v.p. R&D Assocs., Europe, 1989—. Decorated Air medal, Bronze Star, Meritorious Service medal, Def. Superior Service medal, Def. Disting. Service medal; Republic of Vietnam Cross of Gallantry with Palm, Republic of Vietnam Campaign medal. Mem. Daedalians (vice flight capt. 1976), Air Force Assn., Pi Alpha Mu. Avocations: cooking; hiking; painting; British mystery writers. Home: Rue des Allies 43, B-7870 Lens Belgium also: LOGICON RDA 6053 W Century Blvd Los Angeles CA 90045-5323

PEATTIE, LISA REDFIELD, urban anthropology educator; b. Chgo., Mar. 1, 1924; d. Robert and Margaret (Park) Redfield; m. Roderick Peattie, June 26, 1943 (dec. 1962); children: Christopher, Seth, Miranda, Julia; m. William A. Doebele, 1973 (div.). M.A., U. Chgo., 1950, Ph.D., 1968. Faculty mem. dept. urban studies MIT, Cambridge, 1965—, prof. urban anthropology, 1968-85; now prof. emeritus, sr. lectr. MIT; cons. World Bank, 1975, 76, 81, UN, 1980. Author: The View from the Barrio, 1968, Thinking About Development, 1982, (with W. Ronco) Making Work, 1983, (with Martin Rein) Women's Claims, 1983, Planning: Rethinking Ciudad Guayana, 1987. Recipient Paul Davidoff award Am. Soc. Collegiate Schs. of Planning, 1989. Mem. Am. Anthrop. Assn., Soc. Applied Anthropology. Office: Dept Urban Studies MIT Cambridge MA 02139

PEAVEY, HARTLEY DAVIS, electronics company executive; b. Meridian, Miss., Dec. 30, 1941; s. Joseph B. and Sarah (Davis) P.; m. Melia McRae, Nov. 18, 1977; children: Joseph Thomas, Marcus Clinton. BS, Miss. State U., 1965. Founder, owner, pres. Peavey Electronics, Miss., 1965—, Corby, Eng., 1986—; mem. industry sector adv. com. on consumer goods for trade policy matters Commerce Dept., Washington, 1987—; mem. adv. bd. Musicfest U.S.A.; industry spokesman music and audio field, mktg. and internat. trade. matters. Mem. Lauderdale County Econ. Devel. Authority, 1984-90; mem. adv. bd. Meridian Mcpl. Airport, 1986-90; mem., corp. sponsor Miss. World's Fair Council, 1984. Served with Miss. NG, 1965-71. Recipient Pres.'s "E" award for exports U.S. Commerce Dept., 1978, Indsl. Glove award Gov. of Miss., 1980, Nat. Heritage award Queen City Sertoma Club, 1982, Presdl. "E Star" award for excellence in exporting, 1985, Miss. Export Excellence award 1983, 86; honored as one of 84 most notable people in State of Miss., Miss. Mag., 1983; named Patron of Excellence Miss. State U., 1982, Mississippian of Yr. Miss. Broadcasting Assn., 1984, Man of Yr. Meridian Star, 1984, Outstanding Alumnus of Yr. Miss. Assn. Vocat. Educators, 1985, Capts. of Industry tribute State of Miss. Jackson Bus. Jour., 1988; Ann. Hartley Peavey Day named in his honor, Apr. 20, 1982, Meridian; inducted Rock Walk of Fame, Hollywood, Calif., 1990, Jr. Achievement Miss. Bus. Hall of Fame, 1990; Hartley Peavey Entrepreneurial award established in hisname bus. com. Meridian/Lauderdale C. of C., 1989, Hartley D. Peavey Auditorium named in his honor Ross Collin's Vocat. Sch., 1989. Mem. Nat. Assn. Musical Mchts. (bar code com. 1989, inducted Hall of Fame 1988), Nat. Assn. Mfrs. (state dir. 1989-90), Meridian Mfrs. Assn., Am. Music Conf. (bd. dirs. 1986-87), Audio Engring. Soc., Creative Audio & Music Electronics Orgn. (bd. dirs.), Nat. Assn. Young Music Merchants (hon.), City of Morton C. of C., City of Decatur C. of C., Meridian C. of C. Office: Peavey Electronics Co PO Box 2898 711 A St Meridian MS 39301-5422*

PEAVLER, NANCY JEAN, editor; b. Kansas City, Mo., Dec. 19, 1951; d. Elmer Alfred and Ruth Lenoris (Peterson) Zimmerli; m. Craig Eugene Peavler, Dec. 6, 1975; 1 child, Matthew Dean. Assoc., Kansas City (Kans.) Community Coll., 1976; BS in Human Resources Mgmt., Friends U., Wichita, Kans., 1995. Staff writer The Kansas City Kansan, 1972-73; assoc. editor Capper's Stauffer Communications, Topeka, 1976-87, editor, 1987—. Precinct com.-woman Shawnee County Rep. Party, Topeka, 1985-87. Mem. Women in Communications, Soc. Profl. Journalists. United Methodist. Office: Capper's 1503 SW 42nd St Topeka KS 66609-1214

PEAVY, HOMER LOUIS, JR., real estate executive, accountant; b. Okmulgee, Okla., Sept. 4, 1924; s. Homer Louis and Hattie Lee (Walker) P.; children: Homer Martin, Daryl Mark. Student Kent State U., 1944-49; grad. Hammel-Actual Coll., 1962. Sales supr. Kirby Sales, Akron, Ohio, 1948-49; sales mgr. Williams-Kirby Co., Detroit, 1949-50; area distributor Peavy-Kirby Co., Phila., 1953-54; salesman James L. Peavy Realty Co., Akron, 1954-65; owner Homer Louis Peavy, Jr., Real Estate Broker, Akron, 1965—; pvt. practice acctg., Akron, 1962—; fin. aid officer Buckeye Coll., Akron, 1982. Author: Watt Watts, 1969; poet: Magic of the Muse, 1978, P.S. I Love You, 1982; contbr. poetry to Am. Poetry Anthology, 1983, New Worlds Unlimited, 1984, Treasures of the Precious Moments, 1985, Our World's Most Cherished Poems, 1985; songs: Sh...Sh, Sheree, Sheree, 1976, In Akron O, 1979; teleplay: Revenge, 1980. Bd. dirs. Internat. Elvis Gold Soc., 1978—; charter mem. Statue of Liberty-Ellis Island Found., 1984, Nat. Mus. of Women in Arts, 1986, Nat. Mus. Am. Indian, U.S. Holocaust Meml. Mus.; mem. Nat. Trust for Hist. Preservation, Ohio Hist. Soc., Preservation/N.C., Japanese Am. Nat. Mus.; charter mem. USS Constn., Libr. Congress Nat. Assocs. Mus. Recipient Am. Film Inst. Cert. Recognition, 1982, Award of Merit cert. World of Poetry 10th ann. contest, 1985, Golden Poet award World of Poetry, 1985, 87, 88, 89. Mem. NAACP (mem.-at-large), Ohioana Library Assn., Internat. Black Writers Conf., Acad. Am. Poets, Poetry Soc. Am., Smithsonian Nat. Assocs., Manuscript Club Akron, Internat. Platform Assn., Ohio Theatre Alliance, Kent State U. Alumni Assn. Democrat. Home and Office: 1160 Cadillac Blvd Akron OH 44320-2858

PEAZY, ROBERT A., lawyer; b. Apr. 7, 1938. BA, U. Colo., 1961; JD, U. Tex., 1966. Bar: D.C. 1967, U.S. Supreme Ct. 1971, U.S. Claims Ct. 1988. Ptnr. Morgan, Lewis & Bockius, Washington. Mem. European Maritime Law Orgn. (dir. 1991—). Office: Morgan Lewis & Bockius 1800 M St NW Washington DC 20036-5802*

PECANO, DONALD CARL, truck, trailer and railcar manufacturing executive; b. Los Angeles, Dec. 2, 1948; s. Domenick Lawrence and Carlotta Noble (Martello) P.; m. Sandra Ann Tuminello, Apr. 26, 1969; children: Julie Ann, Melissa Ann, Donald Carl. B.S. in Acctg, Pa. State U., 1970; M.B.A. in Mktg, Youngstown State U., 1981; postgrad., Case Western Res. U., 1995. C.P.A., Pa. Contr. Atlas Guard Service subs. SERVISCO, East Orange, N.J., 1974-76; asst. to pres. SERVISCO, Hillside, N.J., 1976-77; v.p. fin. Columbus Svcs., Inc. subs. SERVISCO, New Castle, Pa., 1977-82; dir. fin. East Mfg. Corp. and subs. cos., 1982-88, v.p. fin. and adminstrn., 1988—, also mem. exec. com.; v.p. fin. Intermodal Techs. Inc., 1991—; v.p. East Railcar Corporation, 1993—; Weatherhead profl. fellow Case Western Res. U., 1995. Weatherhead profl. fellow Soc. Case Western Res. U., 1995. Republican. Roman Catholic. Office: 1871 State Route 44 Randolph OH 44265 *Placing the best interests of the company ahead of your own is ultimately in your own best interest.*

PECCARELLI, ANTHONY MARANDO, prosecutor; b. Newark, Apr. 12, 1928; s. Adolph and Mary (Marano) P.; m. Mary Dearborn Hutchison, Dec. 23, 1953; children: Andrew Louis, David Anthony, Laura Elizabeth. BS, Beloit Coll., 1953; JD, John Marshall Law Sch., 1959; M in Jud. Studies, U. Nev., 1990. Bar: Ill. 1961, U.S. Dist. Ct. (no. dist.) Ill., U.S. Supreme Ct. Supr. real estate and claims Gulf Oil Corp., Chgo., 1956-61; asst. state's atty. DuPage County, Wheaton, Ill., 1961-65; first asst. state's atty. DuPage County State's Atty., Wheaton, Ill., 1965-69; mem.-del. Ill. Constnl. Conv., Springfield, 1969-70; exec. dir. Ill. State's Atty. Assn., Elgin, 1970-71; ptnr. Barclay, Damisch & Sinson, Chgo., 1971-79; assoc. cir. judge 18th Jud. Cir. Ct., Wheaton, 1979-82; cir. judge, 1982-93; chief judge 18th Jud. Cir. Ct., Wheaton, 1989-93; presiding judge domestic rels. divsn., 1982-83, presiding judge law divsn., 1987-89; chief judge 18th Judicial Cir., 1989-93; justice 2nd dist. Ill. Appellate Ct., Wheaton, 1993-94; state's atty. DuPage County, Wheaton, Ill., 1995-96; chair Ill. Jud. Conf. Ill. Supreme Ct., Springfield, 1987-89. Contbr. articles to profl. jours. Bd. dirs., treas. DuPage Coun. for Child Devel.; bd. dirs. Ctrl. DuPage Pastoral Counseling Ctr.; chair Wheaton Com. for Jud. Reform, 1962; trustee Midwestern U., 1993—. Cpl. USMC, 1946-48. Mem. DuPage County Bar Assn. (pres. 1972-73), DuPage County Legal Assistance Fedn. (pres. 1973-74), DuPage County Lawyer Referral Svc. (pres. 1972),. Congregationalist.

PECHILIS, WILLIAM JOHN, lawyer; b. Brockton, Mass., May 13, 1924; s. John and Kaleroe (Karmeris) P.; m. Kay Dillon, June 7, 1958; children: Julie W., Karen P., John D. BA, Harvard U., 1946, LLB, 1951. Bar: Mass. 1951. Law clk. to assoc. justice Supreme Judicial Ct., Boston, 1951-52; assoc. Goodwin, Procter and Hoar, Boston, 1952-61, ptnr., 1961-94, of counsel, 1995—. Trustee Concord (Mass.) Acad., 1978-80, Wang Inst. Grad. Studies, Tyngsboro, Mass., 1979-87, Wang Ctr. for Performing Arts, 1983—, Anatolia Coll., Boston, 1984-91; mem. fin. com. Weston, Mass., 1972-74. With USNR, 1943-46, PTO. Fellow Am. Coll. Trust and Estate Counsel; mem. ABA, Mass. Bar Assn., Boston Bar Assn., Harvard Club, Weston Golf Club, Woods Hole Golf Club, Phi Beta Kappa. Avocation: golf. Home: 101 Ash St Weston MA 02193-1940 Office: Goodwin Procter and Hoar Exchange Pl Boston MA 02109-2808

PECHUKAS, PHILIP, chemistry educator; b. Akron, Ohio, Oct. 30, 1942; s. Alphonse and Evelyn (Grebenak) P.; children: Rolf Birkhoff, Maria Berenson, Sarah Landau, Fiona Veronese, Amy Hayes. BS, Yale U., 1963; PhD, U. Chgo., 1966. Asst. prof. chemistry Columbia U., N.Y.C., 1967-72, assoc. prof., 1972-78, prof., 1978—, chmn. dept. chemistry, 1984-87. Contbr. articles to profl. jours. Fellow Nat. Bur. Standards, 1966-67, Alfred P. Sloan Found., 1970-74, J.S. Guggenheim Found., 1975, Haverford Coll., 1985. Fellow Am. Phys. Soc.; mem. Am. Chem. Soc. (chmn. theoretical chemistry subdivision 1985-86), Humboldt Sen. Scientist, 1993-94. Office: Columbia U Dept Chemistry 116th St and Broadway New York NY 10027

PECK, ABRAHAM, editor, writer, educator, magazine consultant; b. N.Y.C., Jan. 18, 1945; s. Jacob and Lottie (Bell) Peckolick; m. Suzanne Wexler, Mar. 19, 1977; children: Douglas Benjamin, Robert Wexler. B.A., N.Y. U., 1965; postgrad., CUNY, 1965-67. Engaged in community organizing and tutoring, 1962-64; with N.Y.C. Welfare Dept., 1965-67; free-lance writer, 1967—; writer, organizer Chgo. Action Youth Internat. Party, 1968; editor Chgo. Seed, 1968-70; treas. Seed Pub., Inc., 1968-70; mem. coordinating com. Underground Press Syndicate, 1969; assoc. editor Rolling Stone mag., San Francisco, 1975, contbg. editor, 1976-96; cons. various mags., 1984—; ednl. cons. Asian Sources Media Group, Hong Kong, Manila, 1989—; feature writer Chgo. Daily News, 1977-78; with features dept. Chgo. Sun-Times, 1978-81; from asst. prof. to assoc. prof. Medill Sch. Journalism, Northwestern U., 1981-92, prof., 1992—, dir. M.S.J. mag. pub. program, 1982—, chmn. mag. program, 1988—, mem. sch. ops. com., 1990—, dir. Nat. Arts Journalism Program, 1993—; critic at large Sta. WBBM, 1979-82; editor, co-founder Sidetracks, alt. newspaper supplement, Chgo. Daily News, 1977-78; mem. exec. com. Assn. for Edn. in Journalism and Mass Communication, mag. divsn., 1987-89, 92—, pres., 1994-95; mem. adv. bd. Academe mag., Am. Assn. Univ. Profs., 1990—, Heartland Jour., 1990—, Technos, 1992—. Editor: Dancing Madness, 1976; author: Uncovering the Sixties: The Life and Times of the Underground Press, 1985, 91; cons. editor, contbr.: The Sixties, 1977; contbr.: The Eighties: A Look Back, 1979, Voices From the Underground, 1993. Served with AUS, 1967. Office: Northwestern U Medill Sch Journalism 1845 Sheridan Rd Evanston IL 60201-5004

PECK, ABRAHAM JOSEPH, historian; b. Landsberg, Fed. Republic of Germany, May 4, 1946; came to U.S., 1949; s. Shalom W. and Anna (Koltun) P.; m. Jean Marcus, June 21, 1969; children: Abby, Joel. BA, Am. U., 1968, MA, 1970; PhD, U. East Anglia, Eng., 1977; postgrad., U. Hamburg, Fed. Republic Germany, 1973-74. Adminstrv. dir. Am. Jewish Archives, Cin., 1976—; lectr. in Judaic studies U. Cin., 1980—; mem. internat. adv. bd. Internat. Ctr. for Holocaust Studies, 1986—; mem. adv. bd. Nat. Cath. Inst. for Holocaust Studies, 1988—; founding mem. Greater Cin. Interfaith Holocaust Found., 1986—. Author: Radicals and Reactionaries, 1978; editor Jews and Christians After the Holocaust, 1982; co-editor Am. Rabbinate: A Century of Continuity and Change 1883-1983, 1985, Studies in the American Jewish Experience II, 1984, Queen City Refuge: An Oral History of Cincinnati's Jewish Refugees from Nazism, 1989, Sephardim in the Americas: Studies in Culture and History, 1993; editor: The German-Jewish Legacy in America: From Bildung to the Bill of Rights, 1989, Selected Documents of World Jewish Congress, 1936-50, 2 vols., 1991; contbr. articles to profl. jours. Spl. advisor U.S. Holocaust Meml. Coun., Washington, 1982-86; bd. dirs. Am. Jewish Com., Cin., 1978-84, Anti-Defamation League of Ohio, Ind. and Ken., Columbus, 1982-86, Jewish Community Rels. Coun., Cin., 1980-86; mem. Am. Hist. Found., Orgn. Am. Historians. Fullbright Found. fellow, 1973-74; Ohio Program in the Humanities grantee, 1980, 83, 85. Mem. Assn. Jewish Studies, Soc. Scholarly Pub., Soc. Am. Archivists, Internat. P.E.N. Centre of German-Speaking Writers Abroad. Avocations: travel, raising dogs. Office: Am Jewish Archives 3101 Clifton Ave Cincinnati OH 45220-2404

PECK, ARTHUR JOHN, JR., diversified manufacturing executive, lawyer; b. Trenton, N.J., Mar. 2, 1940; s. Arthur John and Mary Ellen (Kelly) P.; m. Susan Williams Lodge, July 18, 1970; children: David A., Margaret E. BA in Hist., Yale U., 1962; LLB, Washington & Lee U., 1968. Admissions officer Lawrenceville Sch., N.J., 1962-65; atty. Shearman & Sterling, N.Y.C., 1968-72; asst., assoc. counsel Corning (N.Y.), Inc., 1972-81, asst. sec., 1981-88, sec., 1988—; sec. Teddington Co., Ltd., 1989—, Corning Inc. Found. 1981—, Corning Europe, Inc., 1989—, Corning Inc., 1988—; Corning Internat. Corp., 1991—; dir., sec. Corning Inc. Fgn. Sales Corp., 1992—; Watkins Glen Internat., Inc., 1983—; Corning Classic Charities, Inc., 1978—; asst. sec. Corning Enterprises, Inc., 1974—; Corning Mus. Glass, 1981—; Market St. Restoration Corp., 1974—; trustee, sec. The Rockwell Mus., 1983—; dir. Wisland, S.A., 1989—. Office: Corning Inc Riverfront Plaza Corning NY 14831

PECK, AUSTIN H., JR., lawyer; b. Pomona, Calif., Dec. 25, 1913; s. Austin H. and Helen (Templeton) P.; m. Jean Albertson, Nov. 9, 1939; children: Julie, Francesca, Lisa. A.B. with distinction, Stanford, 1935, J.D., 1938. Bar: Calif. 1938. Since practiced in Los Angeles; mem. firm Latham & Watkins, 1946-76, of counsel, 1976-92. Mem. nat. coun. House Ear Inst.; trustee Cancer Found. Santa Barbara, Calif. Mem. Am., Calif., Los Angeles bar assns., Zeta Psi, Phi Delta Phi. Clubs: California (L.A.), L.A. Country, Birnam Wood (Montecito, Calif.), Valley (Montecito), Cypress Point. Home: 770 San Ysidro Ln Santa Barbara CA 93108-1323 Office: 633 W 5th St Los Angeles CA 90071-2005

PECK, BERNARD SIDNEY, lawyer; b. Bridgeport, Conn., July 26, 1915; s. James and Sadie P.; m. Marjorie Eloise Dean, Apr. 10, 1943; children: Daniel Dean, Constance Lynn. B.A., Yale U., 1936, LL.B., 1939. Bar: Conn. 1939, Fla. 1979, N.Y. 1982. Pvt. practice Bridgeport, 1939-84; ptnr. Goldstein and Peck, 1946-84; judge Mcpl. Ct., Westport, Conn., 1951-55; ptnr. Peck & Peck, Naples, Fla., 1983-87, Porter, Wright, Morris & Arthur, Naples, 1987-90, Peck, Peck & Volpe, Naples, 1990-92, Peck, Volpe & Sullivan, Naples, 1992-94; Peck & Skrivan, Naples, 1994—. Moderator town meeting, Westport, 1950-51; mem. Westport Republican Town Com., 1951-79; pres. Westport YMCA, 1957, trustee, 1964-84; pres. endowment bd. YMCA Naples, 1987-88. Capt. AUS, 1942-46. Fellow Am. Coll. Trial Lawyers, Internat. Acad. Trial Lawyers; mem. ABA, Collier County Bar Assn., Phi Beta Kappa. Clubs: Linville (N.C.) Ridge Country; Royal Poinciana Golf (dir. 1983-90, pres. 1987-89), Yale (trustee 1985—) (Naples, Fla.). Home: 4951 Gulf Shore Blvd N Apt 202 Naples FL 33940-2685 Office: Peck & Skrivan 5801 Pelican Bay Blvd Ste 103 Naples FL 33963-2709 also: 21 Crest Trl Linville Ridge NC

PECK, CHARLES EDWARD, retired construction and mortgage executive; b. Newark, Dec. 1, 1925; s. Hubert Raymond and Helen (White) P.; m. Delphine Murphy, Oct. 15, 1949; children: Margaret Peck Iovino, Charles Edward, Katherine Peck Koustmer, Perry Anne Peck Flanagan. Grad., Phillips Acad., 1943; student, MIT, 1944; BS, U. Pa., 1949; PhD in Pub. Svc. (hon.), Univ. Coll., 1995. With Owens-Corning Fiberglas Corp., various locations, 1949-61; sales mgr. home bldg. products Owens-Corning Fiberglas Corp., Toledo, 1961-66; v.p. home bldg. products mktg. div. Owens-Corning Fiberglas Corp., 1966-68, v.p. constrn. group, 1968-75, v.p. bldg. materials group, 1976-78, exec. v.p., 1978-81, bd. dir.; co-chmn. The Ryland Group, Columbia, Md., 1981-82; chmn., chief exec. officer The Ryland Group, Columbia, 1982-90; dir. The Delaware Group of Funds, 1991—; sec. Enterprise Homes, Inc., 1992—; mem. statutory vis. com. U.S. Nat. Bur. Standards, 1972-77; mem. adv. com. Fed. Nat. Mortgage Assn., 1977-78, 85-86; mem. vis. com. MIT-Harvard Joint Ctr. for Urban Studies; chmn. Prodrs. Adv. Forum, 1977-81. Mem. vis. com. Harvard U. Grad. Sch. Design, 1981-86; chmn. Howard County United Way Campaign, Md., 1987, chmn. cmty. partnerships, 1991-94; bd. dirs. Nat. Inst. for Urban Wildlife, 1986-90, United Way Ctrl. Md., 1987-91, Howard County Gen. Hosp., 1988-94, Columbia Festival, Inc., 1988-91, NAHB Rsch. Found., 1989-92, Alliance to End Childhood Lead Poisoning, 1990-93; mem. adv. bd. U. Md. Engring. Sch., 1990—; mem. adv. bd. Continuing Edn. Johns Hopkins U., 1988-91; mem. policy adv. bd. Harvard Joint Ctr. Housing Studies, 1984-94; chmn. chancellor's adv. coun. U. Md. Sys., 1988—; chmn. Univ. Md. Found., 1990-94, bd. dirs., 1990—; exec. fellow Kennedy Sch., Harvard U., 1990-92; chmn. Affordable Housing Initiative, Columbia, Md., 1990-92; bd. overseers U. Md., College Park, 1994—; bd. visitors Sch. Law U. Md., Balt., 1996—; mem. Victory '94 com. Md. State Rep. party, chmn. election inquiry funding com., 1994-95; chmn. Children of Separation and Divorce Ctr., 1995—. 2d lt. USAAF, 1944-46. Mem. U.S. C. of C. (bd. dirs. 1975-81), Ohio C. of C. (bd. dirs. 1975-81), Depression and Related Affective Disorders Assn. (pres. 1986-89, bd. dirs. 1986—, pres. 1993-94, chmn. Children of Separation and Divorce), Rotary, Talbot Country Club, City Club, Ctr. Club, Caves Valley Golf Club, Phi Gamma Delta. Home: 7649 Woodstream Way Laurel MD 20723-1163 Office: PO Box 1108 Columbia MD 21044-0108

PECK, CLAUDIA JONES, associate dean; b. Ponca City, Okla., Feb. 1, 1943; d. Claude W. and Josephine Jones; children: Jody Athene, Cameron Guthrie. BS, U. Okla., 1972; MS, U. Mo., 1976; PhD, Iowa State U., 1981. Instr. econs. Iowa State U., Ames, 1980-81; asst. prof. consumer studies Okla. State U., Stillwater, 1981-85, assoc. prof., 1985-88, prof., 1988-89; assoc. dean for rsch. and grad. studies U. Ky., Lexington, 1989—, faculty assoc. Sanders-Brown Ctr. on Aging, 1991. Contbr. articles to profl. jours. Recipient Lela O'Toole Rsch. award Okla. Home Econs. Assn., 1988, Merrick Found. Teaching. award Okla. State U., 1987. Mem. Am. Assn. Family and Consumer Scientists (v.p. 1990-92), Am. Coun. on Consumer Interests (pres. 1994-95, Applied Rsch. award 1985), Missouri Valley Econ. Assn. (v.p. 1994-96), Sigma Xi (pres. 1993-94). Office: U Ky 102 Erikson Hall 0050 Lexington KY 40506-0050

PECK, DALLAS LYNN, retired geologist; b. Cheney, Wash., Mar. 28, 1929; s. Lynn Averill and Mary Hazel (Carlyle) P.; m. Tevis Sue Lewis, Mar. 28, 1951 (dec.); children: Ann, Stephen, Gerritt; m. Carmella M. Peck, Apr. 29, 1995. B.S., Calif. Inst. Tech., 1951, M.S., 1953; Ph.D., Harvard U., 1960. With U.S. Geol. Survey, 1954-95; asst. chief geologist, office of geochemistry and geophysics U.S. Geol. Survey, Washington, 1967-72, geologist, geologic div., 1972-77, chief geologist, 1977-81, dir., 1981-93, geologist, 1993-95, emeritus scientist, 1995—; mem. Lunar Sample Rev. Bd., 1970-71; chmn. earth scis. adv. com. NSF, 1970-72; vis. com. dept. geol. scis. Harvard U., 1972-78; mem. Earthscis. Adv. Bd., Stanford U., 1982-93; chmn. com. earth scis. Fed. Coord. Coun. Sci., Enring. and Tech., 1987-92; mem. sci., tech. com. UN Decade for Nat. Disaster Reduction, 1992-94. Recipient Meritorious Svc. award Dept. Interior, 1971, Disting. Svc. award, 1979; Presdl. Meritorious Exec. award, 1980, Disting. Alumni award Calif. Inst. Tech., 1985, Ian Campbell medal Am. Geol. Inst., 1994. Fellow AAAS (pres. sect. E. 1996—), Geol. Soc. Am., Am. Geophys. Union (pres. sect. volcanology, geochemistry and petrology 1976-78). Home: 2524 Heathcliff Ln Reston VA 22091-4225

PECK, DANIEL FARNUM, chemical company executive; b. Port Jervis, N.Y., Aug. 6, 1927; s. John Flint and Frances Ann (Farnum) P.; m. Ardyce Chase Hoover, July 14, 1951 (dec. July 1979); children: Cheryl H. Gerber, Daniel Farnum Jr., Laurie A. Peck Perry; m. Barbara Ann Gunning Gillinder, Sept. 5, 1980. BSChemE, Clarkson U., 1950. Field engr. Rsch. Corp., Bound Brook, N.J., 1950-51; process devel. engring. supr. Nat. Starch and Chem. Corp., Plainfield, N.J., 1951-55, prodn. dept. head, 1955-60; div. supr. Nat. Starch and Chem. Corp., Indpls., 1960-67; plant and mfg. mgr. Nat. Starch and Chem. Corp., Meredosia, Ill., 1967-72, dir. mfg., 1972-76, div. v.p., 1976-80, corp. v.p., 1980-84, group v.p., 1984-89, ret., 1989; also bd. dirs. Nat. Starch and Chem. Corp., Bridgewater, N.J. Mem. Envelope Mfrs. Assn., Soc. Chem. Industry, Adhesive Mfrs. Assn., Adhesive Sealant Coun. (pres. edn. found., bd. dirs.). Avocations: boating, golf, bridge, hunting, fishing.

PECK, DAVID BLACKMAN, electrical engineer; b. Whitewater, Wis.; s. Clarence Neil and Jean Briese (Blackman) P. BSEE, San Diego State U., 1976. Engring. specialist Litton Systems, Woodland Hills, Calif., 1977-89; engr., proprietor Cockpit Devices, Edgerton, Wis., 1989—. Mem. NSPE, IEEE. Avocations: private pilot, jazz trumpeter. Home: 913 Bliven Rd Edgerton WI 53534-9543 Office: Cockpit Devices Edgerton WI 53534

PECK, DEANA S., lawyer; b. Wichita, Kans., Nov. 6, 1947; d. Richard Rector Williams and Elva Alene (Davis) Williams; m. Frederick Page Peck, June 16, 1967 (div. Nov. 1981); 1 child, Paige. BA, Wichita State U., 1970; JD, U. Kans., 1975. Bar: Ariz. 1975, U.S. Dist. Ct. Ariz. 1975, U.S. Ct. Appeals (9th cir.) 1981, U.S. Ct. Appeals (10th cir.) 1990, U.S. Ct. Appeals (fed. cir.) 1991. Assoc. Streich Lang, Phoenix, 1975-80, ptnr., 1980—; vis. lectr. U. Kans. Sch. of Law, Lawrence, 1985. Mem. Phoenix Arts Commn. Mem. ABA, State Bar Ariz., Maricopa County Bar Assn., Kans. U. Law Soc. (bd. govs. 1980-82). Office: Renaissance One 2 N Central Ave Phoenix AZ 85004-2322

PECK, DIANNE KAWECKI, architect; b. Jersey City, June 13, 1945; d. Thaddeus Walter and Harriet Ann (Zlotkowski) Kawecki; m. Gerald Paul Peck, Sept. 1, 1968; children: Samantha Gillian, Alexis Hilary. BArch, Carnegie-Mellon U., 1968. Architect, P.O.D. R & D , 1968, Kohler-Daniels & Assos., Vienna, Va., 1969-71, Beery-Rio & Assocs., Annandale, Va., 1971-73; ptnr. Peck & Peck Architects, Occoquan, Va., 1973-74, Peck, Peck & Williams, Occoquan, 1974-81; corp. officer Peck Peck & Assoc., Inc., Woodbridge, Va., 1981—; CEO, interior design group Peck Peck & Assoc., 1988—. Work pub. in Am. Architecture, 1985. Vice pres. Vocat. Edn. Found., 1976; chairwoman architects and engrs. United Way; mem. Health Systems Agy. of No. Va., commendations, 1977; mem. Washington Profl. Women's Coop.; chairwoman Indsl. Devel. Authority of Prince William, 1976, vice chair, 1977, mem., 1975-79; mem. archtl. rev. bd. Prince William County, 1996—; developer research project Architecture for Adolescents, 1987-88; mem. inaugural class Leadership Am., 1988, Leadership Greater Washington; mem. D.C. Coun. Metrication, 1992—, D.C. Hist. Preservation League, Rep. Nat. Com.; mem. Prince William County Archtl. Review Bd., 1996—. Recipient commendation Prince William Bd. Suprs., 1976, State of Art award for Contel Hdqrs. design, 1985, Best Middle Sch. award Coun. of Ednl. Facilities Planners Internat., 1989, Creativity award Masonry Inst. Md., 1990, First award, 1990, Detailing award, 1990, Govt. Workplace award for renovations of Dept. of Labor Bldg., 1990, Creative Use of Materials award Inst. of Bus. Designers, 1991, 1st award Brick Inst. Md., 1993, award Brick Inst. Va., 1994, Bull Elephant award Prince William County Young Reps., 1995; named Best Instl. Project Nat. Comml. Builders Coun.; subject of PBS spl.: A Success in Howard Co. Mem. Soc. Am. Mil. Engrs., Prince William C. of C. (bd. dir.). Roman Catholic. Club: Soroptimist. Research on inner-city rehab., adolescents and the ednl. environ. Office: 2050 Old Bridge Rd Woodbridge VA 22192-2447

PECK, DONALD VINCENT, musician; b. Yakima, Wash., Jan. 26, 1930; s. Clarence Leon and Bertha A. (Compin) P. Diploma in Music, Curtis Inst. Music, 1951; student, Seattle U., 1948-49. With Seattle Symphony Orch., 1947-49, Nat. Symphony Orch., Washington, 1951-52; prin. flutist Kansas City Philharmonic Orch., 1955-57, Chgo. Symphony Orch., 1957—; instr. flute and woodwind ensemble DePaul U., Chgo.; guest soloist with various orchs. Served with USMCR, 1952-55. Office: care Chgo Symphony Orch 220 S Michigan Ave Chicago IL 60604-2508 also: Parsons Artists Mgmt PO Box 160 Highland Park IL 60035-0160

PECK, EDWARD LIONEL, retired foreign service officer, corporate executive; b. Los Angeles, Mar. 6, 1929; s. Alexander George and Rae (Lee) P.; m. Heather Dianne Hicks-Beach, Jan. 20, 1957 (div. July 1971); m. Ann Day Slevin, May 5, 1974; children—Heather Anne, Brian Michael, Thomas William, Julia Katherine. B.S., UCLA, 1956; M.B.A., George Washington U., 1973. Joined Fgn. Service Dept. State, Washington, 1957, intelligence specialist, 1968-71, spl. asst., 1971-74; econ. counselor U.S. Embassy, Cairo, 1974-77; chief of mission U.S. Interests Sect., Baghdad, Iraq, 1977-80; dir. Office of Egyptian affairs Washington, 1980-82; ambassador U.S. Embassy, Nouakchott, Mauritania, 1983-85; dep. dir. Vice Pres.' Task Force on Combatting Terrorism, 1985-86; dir. Office of Career Transition, 1986-88; ret., 1989; pres. Fgn. Svcs. Internat., 1989—; exec. sec. Am. Acad. Diplomacy, 1989-92; trainer, lectr., cons. on fgn. affairs, internat. bus., 1990—; dir. polit. tradecraft program Nat. Fgn. Affairs Tng. Ctr., Arlington, Va., 1991—; sr. assoc. Global Bus. Access Ltd., Washington, 1991—; Woodrow Wilson vis. fellow, 1993—. Served to capt. U.S. Army, 1946-49, 50-52. Recipient Meritorious Honor award Dept. State, 1967, 73, 77, 79, Superior Honor award Dept. State, 1974, 88, Wilbur J. Carr award, 1989; Rivkin award Am. Fgn. Svc. Assn., 1973. Home and Office: 106 Grafton St Bethesda MD 20815-3426

PECK, EDWIN RUSSELL, real estate management executive; b. Akron, Ohio, Aug. 19, 1931; s. Roy Zola and Mary Susan (Snyder) P.; m. Lou Ellen Smith, Oct. 28, 1949; children—Edwin Russell, Lori Rae. B.S. in Gen. Bus., San Diego State U., 1957. Mortgage trainee South Pacific Corp., San Diego, 1957-58; asst. sec., loan officer Southland Savs., Lamesa, Calif., 1958-60; supr. Phoenix Mut. Life Ins. Co., Hartford, Conn., 1960-63; v.p. comml. loan T.J. Bettes Co., Houston, 1963-68; sr. v.p. comml. loan Am. Mortgage Co., Houston, 1968-72; sr. v.p. real estate S.C.I., Houston, 1972-87, cons., 1987—. Served with USN, 1949-52; Japan/Korea. Republican. Presbyterian. Home: 11738 Oak Valley Dr Houston TX 77065-2937 Office: Service Corp Internat 1929 Allen Pky Houston TX 77019-2507

PECK, ELDRED GREGORY, actor; b. La Jolla, Calif., Apr. 5, 1916; m. Greta Rice, 1942 (div. 1949); m. Veronique Passani; 5 children. Ed., U. Calif., Neighborhood Playhouse Sch. Dramatics. Mem. Nat. Council on Arts, 1965—. Actor: (plays) including Sons and Soldiers, (films) including: Keys of the Kingdom, 1945, Valley of Decision, 1945, Spellbound, 1945, The Yearling, 1946, Duel in the Sun, 1947, The Macomber Affair, 1947, Gentlemen's Agreement, 1947, The Paradine Case, Yellow Sky, The Great Sinner, 1948, Twelve O'Clock High, 1949, The Gunfighter, 1950, Captain Horatio Hornblower, 1951, Only the Valiant, 1951, David and Bathsheba, 1951, Snows of Kilamanjaro, 1952, Roman Holiday, 1953, Night People, Man With a Million, Purple Plains, Moby Dick, 1954, Man in the Grey Flannel Suit, 1956, The Designing Woman, 1956, The Bravados, 1958, Pork Chop Hill, 1959, Beloved Infidel, 1959, On The Beach, 1959, Guns of Navarone, 1961, To Kill a Mockingbird (Acad. award as best actor 1962), Cape Fear, 1962, How the West Was Won, 1963, Captain Newman, M.D, 1963, Behold a Pale Horse, 1964, Mirage, 1965, Arabesque, 1966, Mackenna's Gold, 1967, The Chairman, 1968, The Stalking Moon, 1968, Marooned, 1969, I Walk the Line, 1970, Shootout, 1971, Billy Two-Hats, 1972, Amazing Grace and Chuck, 1987, Old Gringo, 1989, Cape Fear, 1991, Other People's Money, 1991; co-producer, star: (films) The Big Country, 1958; producer, star: (films) The Omen, 1976, MacArthur, 1977, The Boys from Brazil, 1978, The Sea Wolves, 1981, The Scarlet and Black, 1983, (TV miniseries) The Blue and the Gray, 1982, The Portrait, 1993, Sinatra: 80 Years My Way, 1995; voice: (TV miniseries) Baseball, 1994; rec.: (audio cassette) The New Testament, 1985-86. Nat. chmn. Am. Cancer Soc., 1966; founder, prodr. La Jolla Playhouse, 1947-52. Recipient Presdl. Medal of Freedom, Jean Hersholt Humanitarian award, 1968, Life Achievement award Am. Film Inst., 1989, Career award Cannes Film Festival, 1989, Kennedy Ctr. Honors, 1991, Lifetime Achievements award Lincoln Ctr., N.Y.C., 1992, Legion d'Honneur, France, 1993. Mem. Acad. Motion Picture Arts and Scis. (gov.; pres. 1967-70), Am. Film Inst. (founding chmn. bd. trustees 1967-69). *

PECK, ELLIE ENRIQUEZ, retired state administrator; b. Sacramento, Oct. 21, 1934; d. Rafael Enriquez and Eloisa Garcia Rivera; m. Raymond Charles Peck, Sept. 5, 1957; children: Reginaldo, Enrico, Francisca Guerrero, Teresa, Linda, Margaret, Raymond Charles, Christina. Student polit. sci. Sacramento State U., 1974. Tng. services coord. Calif. Div. Hwys., Sacramento, 1963-67; tech. and mgmt. cons., Sacramento, 1968-78; expert examiner Calif. Pers. Bd., 1976-78; tng. cons. Calif. Pers. Devel. Ctr., Sacramento, 1978; spl. cons. Calif. Commn. on Fair Employment and Housing, 1978; cmty. svcs. rep. U.S. Bur. of Census, No. Calif. counties, 1978-80; spl. cons. Calif. Dept. Consumer Affairs, Sacramento, 1980-83, project dir. Golden State Sr. Discount Program, 1980-83; dir. spl. programs for Calif. Lt. Gov., 1983-90, ret., 1990; pvt. cons., 1990—; cons., project dir. nat. sr. health issues summit Congress Calif. Srs. Edn. and Rsch. Fund, 1995; project dir. various post-White House Conf. on Aging seminars and roundtables, 1995—; coord. Calif. Sr. LEgis., 1995—; project dir. SSI/QMB Outreach Project, 1993-94. Author Calif. Dept. Consumer Affairs publ., 1981, U.S. Office Consumer Edn. publ., 1982. Bd. dirs Sacramento/Sierra Am. Diabetes Assn., 1989-90. Author: Diabetes and Ethnic Minorities: A Community at Risk. Trustee, Stanford Settlement, Inc., Sacramento, 1975-79; bd. dirs. Sacramento Emergency Housing Ctr., 1974-77, Sacramento Cmty. Svcs. Planning Coun., 1987-90, Calif. Advs. for Nursing Home Reform, 1990—, Calif. Human Devel. Corp., 1995—; campaign workshop dir. Chicano/Latino Youth Leadership Conf., 1982-95; v.p. Comision Femenil Nacional, Inc., 1987-90; del. Dem. Nat. Conv., 1976; mem. exec. bd. Calif. Dem. Cen. Com., 1977-89; chairperson ethnic minority task force Am. Diabetes Assn., 1988-90; steering com. Calif. Self-Esteem Minority Task Force, 1990-93; del. White House Conf. Aging, 1995. Recipient numerous awards including Outstanding Cmty. Svc. award Comuicaciones Unidos de Norte Atzlan, 1975, 77, Outstanding Svc. award, Chicano/Hispanic Dem. Caucus, 1979, Vol. Svc. award Calif. Human Devel. Corp., 1981, Dem. of Yr. award Sacramento County Dem. Com., 1987, Outstanding Advocate award Calif. Sr. Legis., 1988, 89, Calif. Assn. of Homes for Aging, Advocacy award, 1989, Resolution of Advocacy award, League Latin-Ams. Citizens, 1989, Meritorious Svc. to Hispanic Cmty. award Comite Patriotico, 1989, Meritorious Svc. Resolution award Lt. Gov. of Calif., 1989, Cert. Recognition award Sacramento County Human Rights Commn., 1991, Tish Sommers award Older Women's League/Joint Resolution Calif. Legislature, 1993, Latino Eagle award in govt. Tomas Lopez Meml. Found., 1994. Mem. Hispanic C. of C., Older Women's League, CongressCalif. Srs., Sacramento Gray Panthers, Latino Dem. Club Sacramento County (v.p. 1982-83). Home and Office: 2667 Coleman Way Sacramento CA 95818-4459

PECK, ERNEST JAMES, JR., academic administrator; b. Port Arthur, Tex., July 26, 1941; s. Ernest James and Karlton Maudean (Luttrell) P.; children from previous marriage: David Karl, John Walter; m. Frances R. Taylor; 1 stepchild, Michael R. Taylor. BA in Biology with honors, Rice U., 1963, PhD in Biochemistry, 1966. Rsch. assoc. Purdue U., West Lafayette, Ind., 1966-68, asst. prof., 1968-73; asst. prof. Baylor Coll. Medicine, Houston, 1973-74, assoc. prof., 1974-80, prof., 1980-82; prof., chmn. biochemistry Sch. Med. Sci., U. Ark., Little Rock, 1982-89; dean sci. and math. U. Nev., Las Vegas, 1989-95; vice chancellor acad. affairs U. Nebr., Omaha, 1995—; adj. prof. U. Ark., Pine Bluff, 1986-88; program dir. NSF, Washington, 1988-89; mem. edit. bd. Jour. Neurosci. Rsch., N.Y.C., 1982-92. Co-author: Female Sex Steroids, 1979, Brain Peptides, 1979. Recipient Rsch. Career award NIH, Nat. Inst. of Child Health and Human Devel., 1975-80; NIH fellow, 1964-66. Fellow AAAS; mem. Am. Chem. Soc., Am. Soc. Biochemistry and Molecular Biology, Am. Soc. Neurochemistry, Endocrine Soc., Sigma Xi. Avocations: fishing, hunting. Office: U Nebr-Omaha Vice Chancellor Acad Affair 60th and Dodge Sts Omaha NE 68182-0001

PECK, FRED NEIL, economist, educator; b. Bklyn., Oct. 17, 1945; s. Abraham Lincoln and Beatrice (Pikholtz) P.; m. Jean Claire Ginsberg, Aug. 14, 1971; children: Ron Evan, Jordan Shefer, Ethan David. BA, SUNY, Binghamton, 1966; MA, SUNY, Albany, 1969; PhM, NYU, 1984; PhD, Pacific Western U., 1984; MS in Edn., Coll. New Rochelle, 1993. Lectr. SUNY, Albany, 1969-70; research asst. N.Y. State Legislature, Albany, 1970; sales and research staff Pan Am. Trade Devel. Corp., N.Y.C., 1971; v.p., economist The First Boston Corp., N.Y.C., 1971-88; mng. dir. Sharpe's Capital Mkt. Assocs. Inc., N.Y.C., 1988-89; pres., chief economist Hillcrest Econs. Group, N.Y.C., 1989-93; dir. edn. The Ednl. Advantage, Inc., New City, N.Y., 1990-95; adj. prof. Hofstra U., Hempstead, N.Y., 1975; lectr. NYU, 1982; mem. faculty New Sch. for Social Rsch., N.Y.C., 1974-94; coord. computer aided instrn. N.Y.C. Bd. of Edn., 1990—. Author, editor: (biennial publ.) Handbook of Securities of U.S. Government, 1972-86. Mem. ASCD, Am. Econ. Assn., Ea. Econ. Assn., Econometric Soc., Nat. Assn. Bus. Economists, Am. Statis. Assn., Doctorate Assn. of N.Y. Educators, Beta Gamma Sigma (hon. soc.), Phi Delta Kappa. Democrat. Jewish. Lodges: Knights Pythias, Knights Khorassan. Office: PS 169 at JHS 60 420 E 12th St New York NY 10009 *March in one place long enough and eventually you will wind up leading the parade of progress...No one grows old. When you tire of learning, of experiencing new things your are old.*

PECK, GARNET EDWARD, pharmacist, educator; b. Windsor, Ont., Can., Feb. 4, 1930; s. William Crozier and Dorothy (Marentette) P.; m. Mary Ellen Hoffman, Aug. 24, 1957; children: Monique Elizabeth, Denise Anne, Philip Warren, John Edward. B.S. in Pharmacy with Distinction, Ohio No. U., 1957; M.S. in Indsl. Pharmacy, Purdue U., 1959, Ph.D., 1962. Sr. scientist Mead Johnson Research Center, 1962-65, group leader, 1965-67; assoc. prof. indsl. and phys. pharmacy Purdue U., West Lafayette, 1967-73; prof. Purdue U., 1973—, dir. indsl. pharmacy lab., 1975—, assoc. dept. head, 1989—; cons. in field. Contbr. articles to profl. jours. Mem. West Lafayette Mayor's Advisory Com. on Community Devel., 1973—; mem. West Lafayette Citizen's Safety Com., 1974-81; mem. West Lafayette Park Bd., 1981—, pres., 1983—. Served with U.S. Army, 1951-53. Recipient Lederle Faculty award Purdue U., 1976. Fellow AAAS, Am. Inst. Chem., Am. Assn. Pharmaceutical Scientists; mem. Am. Chem. Soc., Acad. of Rsch. and Sci. (Sidney Riegelman award 1994), Am. Assn. Colls. of Pharmacy, N.Y. Acad. Scis., KC. Roman Catholic. Office: Purdue U Sch Pharmacy & Pharm Scis Dept Industrial & Physical Pharm West Lafayette IN 47907

PECK, GARY LAWRENCE, dermatologist, researcher; b. Detroit, Oct. 15, 1938; s. Marvin Max Peck and Renee Louise (Lerman) Peck Dopulos; m. Harriet Lee Ceasar, June 19, 1960; children: Julie Marsha, Tobi Elizabeth, Rachel Catherine. MD, U. Mich., 1962. Diplomate Am. Bd. Dermatology. Intern St. Luke's Hosp., San Francisco, 1962-63; resident in dermatology U. Chgo. Hosps. and Clinics, 1963-66; sr. investigator dermatology br. Nat. Cancer Inst., NIH, Bethesda, Md., 1969-90; prof. dept. dermatology U. Md. Sch. Medicine, Balt., 1991-93; lectr. Am. Acad. Dermatology, 1977-87, U.

Md., and numerous others; cons. in field. Author chpts. in books; patentee in field for rsch. on vitamin A derivative as acne treatment; contbr. over 60 articles to profl. jours. Capt. USAF, 1966-68, med. dir. USPHS, 1976-90. Recipient fellowship USPHS, 1965-66, 68-69. Mem. Am. Acad. Dermatology, Soc. Investigative Dermatology, Washington, D.C. Dermatol. Soc., French Soc. Dermatology (foreign corr.). Avocations: international folk dancing, photography, travel. Office: Washington Cancer Inst Washington Hosp Ctr 110 Irving St NW Washington DC 20010-2931

PECK, HARRY, public relations executive. Exec. v.p. Charles Ryan Assoc. Inc. Office: Charles Ryan Assocs Inc PO Box 2464 1012 Kanawha Blvd E Charleston WV 25239*

PECK, JOAN KAY, systems engineer; b. Cedar Rapids, Iowa, Sept. 22, 1959; d. Leonard Allen and Mildred Jane (Keller) P. BS in Indsl. Engring., Iowa State U., 1983; MS in Space Tech., Fla. Inst. Tech., 1986. Student intern Rockwell-Collins, Cedar Rapids, 1979; coop. student Amana (Iowa) Refrigeration, 1981; sr. engr. Harris Govt. Aerospace Systems, Palm Bay, Fla., 1983-88; sr. systems engr. McDonnell Douglas Space Systems Co., Kennedy Space Ctr., Fla., 1988-94; clergy intern River City Met. Cmty. Ch., Sacramento, 1993—. V.p. programming Inst. Indsl. Engrs., Ames, 1982-83; victim advocate Sexual Assault Victims Svcs., Fla. State Attys. Office, Brevard County, 1991-92. Recipient Outstanding Achievement award NASA, 1991.

PECK, MARYLY VANLEER, college president, chemical engineer; b. Washington, June 29, 1930; d. Blake Ragsdale and Ella Lillian (Wall) VanLeer; m. Jordan B. Peck, Jr., June 15, 1951; children: Jordan B. III, Blake VanLeer, James Tarleton VanLeer, Virginia Ellaine.; m. 2d, Walter G. Ebert, Sept. 3, 1983 (dec. June 1990); m. 3d Edwin L. Carey, Apr. 13, 1991. Student, Ga. Inst. Tech., 1948, 55-58, Duke U., 1947-48; B.Ch.E., Vanderbilt U., 1951; M.S.E., U. Fla., 1955, Ph.D., 1963. Chem. engr. Naval Research Lab., Washington, 1951-52; chem. engr. Med. Field Research Lab., Camp LeJeune, N.C., 1952; asso. research and instr. U. Fla., Gainesville, 1953-55; chem. engr., research asso. Ga. Tech. Expt. Sta., Atlanta, 1956-58; lectr. Ga. State Coll., Atlanta, 1957-58; lectr. math. East Carolina Extension, Camp Lejeune, 1959; sr. research engr. Rocketdyne div. N.Am. Aviation Co., 1961-63; self-employed as lectr., 1963; assoc. prof. Campbell Coll., Buie's Creek, N.C., 1963-66; prof. Campbell Coll., 1966; acad. dir. St. John's Episcopal Sch., Upper Tumon, Guam, 1966-68; chmn., prof. phys. scis. U. Guam, Agana, 1968-73; dean Coll. Bus. and Applied Tech. U. Guam, 1973-74, dean Community Career Coll., 1974-77; pres. Cochise Coll., Douglas, Ariz., 1977-78; systems planning analyst Urban Pathfinders, Inc., Balt., 1978-79; dean undergrad. studies U. Md. Univ. Coll., College Park, 1979-82; pres. Polk Community Coll., Winter Haven, Fla., 1982—. Founder, pres. Guam Acad. Found., 1972-77; bd. dirs. Cochise Coll. Found., 1977-78; charter bd. dirs. Turnaround Inc., 1987-91, chmn. 1990—; bd. dirs. United Way Cen. Fla., 1986—, bd. dirs. All Saints Acad., 1994—, vice chmn., 1992, chair-elect, 1993, chmn. 1994; founding mem. Prince George's Ednl. TV Cable Coalition; mem. Prince George's Cable TV Ednl. Adv. Group, 1980-82, Polk County Coun. Econ. Edn., 1982; sec. Polk Community Coll. Found., 1982—; mem. Polk County Coordinating Coun. Vocat. Edn., 1982-91, PRIDE Adv. Coun.; vice chmn. Fla. Job Tng. Coordinating Coun., 1983-87, Fla. Edn. Fund Bd., 1988-93. Named Disting. Alumnus U. Fla., 1992, Woman of Distinction Girls Scouts U.S.A., 1994; fellow NSF, 1961-63; recipient She Knows Where She's Going award Girls Inc. of Winter Haven, 1995. Fellow Soc. Women Engrs. (nat. v.p. 1962-63); mem. AAUW, Am. Inst. Chem. Engrs., Am. Chem. Soc., NSPE, Am. Assn. for Higher Edn., Am. Assn. Community and Jr. Colls., Am. Assn. Univ. Adminstrs., Rotary, Sigma Xi, Tau Beta Pi, Chi Omicron Gamma, Phi Kappa Phi, Delta Kappa Gamma. Episcopalian. Home: 1290 Howard Ter NW Winter Haven FL 33881-3158 Office: Polk Community Coll 999 Avenue H NE Winter Haven FL 33881-4299

PECK, MERTON JOSEPH, economist, educator; b. Cleve., Dec. 17, 1925; s. Kenneth Richard and Charlotte (Hart) P.; m. Mary McClure Bosworth, June 13, 1949; children—Richard, Katherine, Sarah, David. AB, Oberlin Coll., 1949; AM, Harvard U., 1951, PhD, 1954; AM (hon.), Yale U., 1963. Teaching fellow, instr. econs. Harvard U., Boston, 1951-55, asst., then assoc. prof. bus. adminstrn., 1956-61; asst. prof. econs. U. Mich., Ann Arbor, 1955-56; dir. systems analysis Office Sec. Def., Washington, 1961-63; prof. econs. Yale U., New Haven, Conn., 1963—; chmn. dept. Yale U., New Haven, 1967-74, 77-84, acting dean sch. of orgn. and mgmt., 1987-88; Mem. Council Econ. Advisers, Exec. Office of Pres., 1968-69; cons. in field, 1954—. Author: (with others) The Economics of Competition in the Transportation Industries, 1959, Competition in the Aluminum Industry, 1945-58, 1961, (with F. Scherer) The Weapons Aquisition Process, An Economic Analysis, 1962, (with others) Technological Change, Economic Growth and Public Policy, 1967, Federal Regulation of Television, 1973; editor The World Aluminum Industry in a Changing Energy Era, 1988; co-editor: What Is To Be Done? Proposals for the Soviet Transition to the Market, 1991, Competitiveness ?, The Impact of Public Policy, 1992; contbr. (with others) articles to profl. jours. With AUS, 1944-46. Mem. Am. Econ. Assn., Am. Assn. U. Profs., Lawn Club, Yale Club. Home: 27 Temple Ct New Haven CT 06511-6820

PECK, RALPH BRAZELTON, civil engineering educator, consultant; b. Winnipeg, Man., Can., June 23, 1912; (parents Am. citizens); s. Orwin K. and Ethel Indie (Huyck) P.; m. Marjorie Elizabeth Truby, June 14, 1937; children: Nancy Jeanne Peck Young, James Leroy. D in Civil Engring., Rensselaer Poly. Inst., 1937; postgrad., Harvard U., 1938; D Eng. (hon.), Rensselaer Poly. Inst., 1974; DSc (hon)., Laval U., 1987. Registered profl. engr., structural engr., Ill.; civil engr., Calif. Structural detailer Am. Bridge Co., Ambridge, Pa., 1937; asst. subway engr. City of Chgo., 1939-43; chief engr. testing Holabird & Root, Scioto Ordnance Plant, Marion, Ohio, 1943; research asst. prof. soil mechanics U. Ill., Champaign-Urbana, 1943-48, research prof. found. engring., 1948-57, prof. found. engring., 1957-74, prof. emeritus, 1974—; cons. founds., tunnels, earth dams, landslides, throughout U.S. and various fgn. countries, 1943—. Author: (with K. Terzaghi and G. Mesri) Soil Mechanics in Engineering Practice, 1948, 3d edit., 1996, (with T.H. Thornburn and W.E. Hanson) Foundation Engineering, 1953, 2d edit., 1973, Judgment in Geotechnical Engineering: The Professional Legacy of Ralph B. Peck, 1984; author more than 300 tech. papers. Recipient Disting. Civilian Svc. award Dept. of Army, 1973, Moles Non-mem. award, 1973, Nat. Medal Sci. Pres. Gerald Ford, 1974, Golden Beaver award. 1983, Disting. Svc. award Deep Founds Inst., 1984, award of merit Am. Cons. Engrs. Coun., 1988. Fellow Geol. Soc. Am.; mem. NAE, ASCE (hon.; nat. dir. 1962-65; Norman medal 1944, Wellington prize 1965, Terzaghi award 1969, Washington award 1976, Pres.'s award 1986, John Fritz medal 1987, Rickey medal 1988), Am. Acad. Arts and Scis., Internat. Soc. Soil Mechanics and Found. Engring. (pres. 1969-73), Southeast Asian, Japanese, Mexican Socs. Soil Mechanics (hon.), NSPE (award 1972), Sigma Xi, Chi Epsilon, Tau Beta Pi, Phi Kappa Phi. Home: 1101 Warm Sands Dr SE Albuquerque NM 87123-4328

PECK, RICHARD EARL, academic administrator, playwright, novelist; b. Milw., Aug. 3, 1936; s. Earl Mason and Mary Amanda (Fry) P.; m. Donna Joy Krippner, Aug. 13, 1960; children: Mason, Laura. AB magna cum laude, Carroll Coll., Waukesha, Wis., 1961; MS, U. Wis., 1962, PhD, 1964. Asst. prof. U. Va., Charlottesville, 1964-67; assoc. dean, prof. Temple U., Phila., 1967-84; dean arts and scis. U. Ala., 1984-88; provost, v.p. academic affairs Ariz. State U., Tempe, 1988-89, interim pres., 1989-90; pres. U. N.Mex., Albuquerque, 1990—. Editor: Poems/Nathaniel Hawthorne, 1967, Poems/Floyd Stovall, 1967; author: (books) Final Solution, 1973 (nominated for John W. Campbell award as Best Sci. Fiction Novel of 1973 by Sci. Fiction Rsch. Assn.), Something for Joey, 1978, Passing Through, 1982, (plays) Sarah Bernhardt and the Bank, 1972, Don't Trip over the Money Pail, 1976, The Cubs Are in fourth Place and Fading, 1977, Phonecall, 1978, Bathnight, 1978, Prodigal Father, 1978, Lovers, Wives and Tennis Players, 1979, Curtains, 1980, A Party for Wally Pruett, 1982, Allergy Tests, 1982, Your Place or Mine, 1987, (films) Starting over Again, 1982, What Tangled Webs, 1974, Tutte le Strade Portanno a Roma, 1974, Il Diritto, 1974; contr. numerous scholarly articles to lit. jours., book revs., travel articles and humor columns to newspapers and mags., papers to univ. orgns. and writers' confs. Bd. dirs. East Valley Partnership (Econ. Devel. Orgn.), Sci. and Tech., Samaritan Health Svcs.; gubernatorial appointee, bd. dirs. Ala. Humanities Found.; mem. Nat. Found. for Post-Secondary Edn.; bd. dirs. Phila. Alliance for Teaching Humanities in the Schs., Dela. Valley Faculty Exch.; adv. bd. Ea. Pa. Theater Coun.; chmn. Temple U. Bicentennial Festival of Am. Arts, 1976; mem. Univ. Negotiating Team in re: Temple-AAUP faculty contract. Capt. USMC, 1954-59. Recipient Whitman Pub. scholarship, 1959-63, Woodrow Wilson fellowship, 1961-62, Knapp Found. fellowship, 1962-63, C. Brooks Fry award Theater Americana, Altadena, Calif., 1979. Mem. MLA, Northeast MLA. Conf. Univs. and Colls. Arts, Letters and Scis., Coun. Colls. Arts and Scis., Nat. Assn. State Univs. and Land-Grant Colls. Home: 1901 Roma Ave NE Albuquerque NM 87106-3824 Office: U NMex Office of Pres Albuquerque NM 87131

PECK, RICHARD HYDE, hospital administrator; b. Ft. McClelland, Ala., Aug. 30, 1941; s. Robert H. and Elizabeth M. P.; m. Barbara Mansfield, Dec. 27, 1964; children—Catherine, Nancy, Joanne. A.B. in Econs, U. N.C., 1963; M.S. in Health Adminstrn, Duke U., 1966. Adminstrv. asst. U. Hosps., Cleve., 1966-67, asst. adminstr., 1967-69; asst. dir. Duke U. Hosp., 1969-71, asso. dir., 1971-73, adminstrv. dir., 1973-81; asso. prof. health adminstrn. program Duke U.; chief exec. officer Eliza Coffee Meml. Hosp., Florence, Ala., 1981—; bd. dirs. Ala. Blue Cross and Blue Shield, 1986—; mem. med. ctr. adv. council U. Ala., Birmingham, 1983—. Campaign dir., pres.-elect The Shoals United Way, 1986. Mem. Am. Coll. Hosp. Adminstrs, Am. Hosp. Assn., Ala. Hosp. Assn. (bd. dirs. Trust 1983), Florence area C. of C. (bd. dirs.). Democrat. Presbyterian. Office: Pub Hosp Bd 205 S Marengo St Florence AL 35630-6033

PECK, RICHARD WAYNE, novelist; b. Decatur, Ill., Apr. 5, 1934; s. Wayne Morris and Virginia (Gray) P. Student, Exeter (Eng.) U., 1954-55; B.A., DePauw U., 1956; M.A., So. Ill. U., 1959. Mem. faculty Sch. Edn., Hunter Coll., 1965-71; lectr. in field; adj. prof. libr. sci. La. State U., 1996—. Author: books for adolescents, including Are You in the House Alone?, 1977 (Edgar Allen Poe award 1977), Father Figure, 1978, Secrets of the Shopping Mall, 1979; (poetry anthology) Sounds and Silences, 1970; (novels for adults) New York Time; Contbr. articles on architecture and local history to N.Y. Times. Asst. dir. Council Basic Edn., Washington, 1969-70. Served with U.S. Army, 1956-58. English-Speaking Union fellow Jesus Coll., Oxford (Eng.) U., 1973; winner Nat. Prize for Young People's Lit. ALA, 1990. Mem. Authors Guild, Authors League, Delta Chi. Republican. Methodist. Home: 155 E 72nd St New York NY 10021-4371

PECK, ROBERT A., newspaper publisher; b. Riverton, Wyo., Oct. 7, 1924; s. LeRoy E. and Elvira Eugenia (Sostrom) P.; m. Cordelia S. Peck, Oct. 5, 1949; children: Christopher, George, Steven. BA, U. Wyo., 1949. Pub. The Riverton Ranger, 1949—; mem. Wyoming State Senate, 1991—. Pres. Central Wyo. Coll. Bd., Riverton, 1966-81; sec. CWC Found., Riverton, 1968—. Staff sgt. U.S. Army, 1943-45, ETO. Mem. Soc. Profl. Journalists, Masons, Phi Beta Kappa. Republican. United Methodist. Office: The Riverton Ranger 421 E Main PO Box 993 Riverton WY 82501-0993

PECK, ROBERT DAVID, educational foundation administrator; b. Devil's Lake, N.D., June 1, 1929; s. Lester David and Bernice Marie (Peterson) P.; m. Lylia June Smith, Sept. 6, 1953; children: David Allan, Kathleen Marie. BA, Whitworth Coll., 1951; MDiv, Berkeley (Calif.) Bapt. Div. Sch., 1958; ThD, Pacific Sch. Religion, 1964; postgrad., U. Calif., Berkeley, 1959-60, 62-63, Wadham Coll., Oxford U., Eng., 1963. Music tchr. pub. schs. Bridgeport, Wash., 1954-55; prof., registrar Linfield Coll., McMinnville, Oreg., 1963-69; asst. dir. Ednl. Coordinating Coun., Salem, Oreg., 1969-75; assoc. prof. Pacific Luth. U., Tacoma, 1976-79, U. Puget Sound, Tacoma, 1977; v.p. John Minter Assocs., Boulder, Colo., 1979-81, Coun. Ind. Colls., Washington, 1981-84; adminstrv. v.p. Alaska Pacific U., Anchorage, 1984-88; pres. Phillips U., Enid, Okla., 1988-94, chancellor, 1994-95; chmn. The Pres. Found. for Support of Higher Edn., Washington, 1995—; pres. Phillips U. Ednl. Enterprises Inc., 1994-95; cons. Higher Edn. Exec. Assocs., Denver, 1984—; owner Tyee Marina, Tacoma, 1975-77; yacht broker Seattle, 1977-79. Author: Future Focusing: An Alternative to Strategic Planning, 1983, also articles. Dem. county chmn., McMinnville, 1968, Dem. candidate for state Ho. of Reps., McMinnville, 1969; pres. McMinnville Kiwanis, 1965-69. Cpl. Signal Corps, U.S. Army, 1952-54. Carnegie Corp. grantee, 1982, 84. Mem. Okla. Ind. Coll. Assn. (sec. 1989—). Mem. Christian Ch. Avocation: sailing, sculpting. Office: Pres Found for Support Higher Edn Western Office PO Box 529 Phoenix AZ 85001-0529

PECK, ROBERT MCCRACKEN, naturalist, science historian, writer; b. Phila., Dec. 15, 1952; s. Frederick William Gunster and Matilda (McCracken) P. BA in Art History, Princeton U., 1974; MA, U. Del., 1976. Dir. Pocono Lake (Pa.) Preserve Nature Ctr., 1971, 72; asst. to dir. Natural History Mus. Acad. Natural Scis., Phila., 1976-77; tech. dir. Bartram Heritage Study U.S. Dept. Interior and Bartram Trail Conf., Atlanta and Montgomery, Ala., 1977-78; spl. asst. to pres. Acad. Natural Scis., Phila., 1977-82, acting v.p. Nat. History Mus., 1982-83, fellow, 1983—; cons. BBC, Eng., 1987-92; bd. dirs. Phila. Conservationists, Natural Lands Trust, Phila., Libr. Co. of Phila., Phila. City Inst.; mng. editor Frontiers, 1979-82; lectr. in field. Author: A Celebration of Birds: The Life and Art of Louis Agassiz Fuertes, 1982, Headhunters and Hummingbirds: An Expedition Into Ecuador, 1987, Wild Birds of America: The Art of Basil Ede, 1991, Land of the Eagle: A Natural History of North America, 1991, German edit., 1992; author: (with others) William Bartram's Travels, 1980, John Cassin's Illustrations of the Birds of California, Texas, Oregon, British and Russian America, 1991; author: (foward) The Birds of America by John James Audubon, 1985; editor: Bartram Heritage Report, 1978; author (with others), editor: Philadelphia Wildfowl Exposition Catalog, 1979; contbr. chpts. to books, articles to mags. and newspapers including The New York Times. Trustee Chestnut Hill Acad., Phila.; bd. dirs. RARE Ctr. Tropical Bird Conservation, Mus. Coun. of Phila. Recipient Richard Hopper Day Meml. award Acad. Natural Scis. of Phila., 1991; Eleanor Garvey fellow in printing and graphic arts Houghton Libr., Harvard U., 1995. Fellow Royal Geographic Soc., Explorers Club (various coms. 1983—, Explorers award 1988); mem. Soc. History of Natural History, Sigma Xi. Achievements include discovery of a new species of frog, Eleutherodactylus pecki; rsch. on orthoptera indigenous to the Caribbean, status of invasive African Desert Locust in the West Indies, the Orinoco River and its tributaries, botanical, entomological, ichthyological, herpetological and malacological specimens for the Smithsonian Instn. and the Acad. of Natural Scis.; participation in expeditions which discovered several new species of fish in Guyana Shield, Venezuela, discovered several new species of amphibians and insects as well as two new races of birds in Ecuador, investigated the ecological, economic and political impact of instream-flow legislation on the Yellowstone River Basin, current projects include biological and cultural research in Mongolia. Office: Academy of Natural Sciences 1900 Benjamin Franklin Pky Philadelphia PA 19103-1101

PECK, ROBERT STEPHEN, lawyer, educator; b. Bklyn., Dec. 11, 1953; s. Irwin and Edith Rose (Welt) P.; m. Terre Garcia; 1 child, Zachary Madison. BA in Polit. Sci., George Washington U., 1975; JD, Cleve.-Marshall Law Sch., 1978; postgrad., NYU, 1978; LLM, Yale U., 1990. Bar: N.Y. 1979, U.S. Dist. Ct. (so. and ea. dists.) N.Y. 1979, D.C. 1989. Congl. aide U.S. Ho. of Reps., Washington, 1972-74; div. dir. Automated Correspondence, Washington, 1974-75; law clk. to presiding justice Cleve. Mcpl. Ct., 1976; editor Matthew Bender & Co., N.Y.C., 1977-78; legal dir. Pub. Edn. Assn., N.Y.C., 1978-82; staff dir. ABA, Chgo., 1982-87, Washington, 1987-89; jud. fellow U.S. Supreme Ct., 1990-91; legis. counsel ACLU, 1991-95; adj. prof. American U., Washington, 1991—; dir. legal affairs Assn. Trial Lawyers Am., 1995—; legal advisor Freedom to Read Found., Chgo., 1986—, exec. com. bd. trustees, 1987-90, 95—, pres., 1988-90, v.p., trustee, 1993—; bd. dirs. Nat. Constl. Ctr., 1990-93; lectr. on constl. law, legal ethics. Author: We the People, 1987, The Bill of Rights and the Politics of Interpretation, 1991; co-author: Speaking and Writing Truth, 1985; editor: Understanding the Law, 1983, Blessings of Liberty, 1986, To Govern A Changing Society, 1990; contbr. numerous articles on constl. law to law revs. Mem. N.Y. State Edn. Adv. Bd., Albany, N.Y., 1979-81; bd. dirs. Nat. Com. on Pub. Edn. and Religious Liberty, 1995—, Ams. for Religious Liberty, 1995—. NEH grantee 1983, 85. Mem. ABA (chmn. pub. election law com. 1983-85, 87-90). Democrat. Jewish. Avocations: tennis, music, travel. Office: Assn Trial Lawyers Am 1050 31st St NW Washington DC 20007

PECK, THOMAS, newspaper publishing executive. BS in Acctg., U. Conn.; MS Wharton Sch. Bus., U. Pa. CPA. Audit mgr. and computer audit specialist Ernst & Young, 1969-75; v.p. fin. and adminstrn. Orba Corp., 1975-83; controller and chief acctg. officer Esprit Systems, 1983-85; v.p. PRD Property Devel., 1985-89; asst. v.p. Mac Andrews & Forbes, 1989-90; CFO Daily News, L.P., 1990—. Office: NY Daily News Office of the CFO 450 W 33d St 3d Flr New York NY 10001

PECK, WILLIAM ARNO, physician, educator; b. New Britain, Conn., Sept. 28, 1933; s. Bernard Carl and Molla (Nair) P.; m. Patricia Hearn, July 10, 1982; children by previous marriage: Catherine, Edward Pershall, David Nathaniel; stepchildren: Andrea, Elizabeth, Katherine. A.B., Harvard U., 1955; M.D., U. Rochester, N.Y., 1960. Intern, then resident in internal medicine Barnes Hosp., St. Louis, 1960-62; fellow in metabolism Washington U. Sch. Medicine, St. Louis, 1963; mem. faculty U. Rochester Med. Sch., 1965-76, prof. medicine and biochemistry, 1973-76, head div. endocrinology and metabolism, 1969-76; John E. and Adaline Simon prof. medicine, co-chmn. dept. medicine Washington U. Sch. Medicine, St. Louis, 1976-89; physician in chief Jewish Hosp., St. Louis, 1976-89; prof. medicine and exec. vice chancellor med. affairs, dean sch. medicine, pres. univ. med. ctr. Washington U., St. Louis, 1989—; chmn. endocrinology and metabolism adv. com. FDA, 1976-78; chmn. gen. medicine study sect. NIH, 1979-81; chmn. Gordon Conf. Chemistry, PHysiology and Structure of Bones and Teeth, 1977; chmn. Consensus Devel. Conf. on Osteoporosis, NIH, 1984; co-chmn. Workshop on Future Directions in Osteoporosis, 1987; chmn. Spl. Topic Conf. on Osteoporosis, U.S. FDA, 1987; dir. Angelica Corp., Boatman's Trust Co., Allied Healthcare Products, Hologic, Reinsurance Group of Am. Editor Bone and Mineral Rsch. Anns., 1982-88; mem. editorial adv. bd. Osteoporosis Internat., other jours.; contbr. to med. jours. Pres. Nat. Osteoporosis Found., 1985-90. Served as med. officer USPHS, 1963-65. Recipient Mosby Book award Alpha Omega Alpha, 1960, Doran J. Stephens award U. Rochester Sch. Medicine, 1960, Lederle Med. Faculty award, 1967, NIH Career Program award, 1970-75, Commr.'s Spl. citation FDA, 1988, Humanitarian award Arthritis Found. Ea. Mo., 1995. Fellow ACP, AAAS; mem. Am. Assn. Clin. Endocrinologists, Am. Geriatric Soc., Am. Soc. for Biochemistry and Molecular Biology, Am. Soc. Clin. Investigation, Am. Fedn. Clin. Rsch., Am. Diabetes Assn., Internat. Bone and Mineral Soc. (pres. 1983-84), Assn. Am. Physicians, Endocrine Soc., Orthopedic Rsch. Soc., Nat. Inst. Arthritis, Musculoskeletal and Skin Diseases (adv. coun. 1986-89), Assn. Am. Med. Colls. (adminstrv. bd. Coun. of Deans 1993—, group on bus. affairs rsch. task force), Sigma Xi, Alpha Omega Alpha (bd. dirs. 1992-95). Home: 2 Apple Tree Ln Saint Louis MO 63124-1601 Office: Washington U Sch Medicine 600 S Euclid Ave Saint Louis MO 63110-1093

PECK, WILLIAM HENRY, museum curator, art historian, archaeologist, author, lecturer; b. Savannah, Ga., Oct. 2, 1932; s. William Henry Peck and Mildred (Bass) Peck Tuten; m. Ann Amelia Keller, Feb. 2, 1957 (dec. 1965); children: Alice Ann, Sarah Louise; m. Elsie Holmes, July 8, 1967; 1 child, William Henry IV. Student Ohio State U., 1950-53; BFA, Wayne State U., 1960, MA, 1961. Jr. curator Detroit Inst. Arts, 1960-62, asst. curator, 1962-64, assoc. curator, 1964-68, curator ancient art, 1968—, acting chief curator, 1984-88, sr. curator, 1988—; lectr. art history Cranbrook Acad. Art, Bloomfield Hills, Mich., 1963-65; vis. lectr. U. Mich., Ann Arbor, 1970; adj. prof. art history Wayne State U., Detroit, 1966—; excavations in Egypt, Mendes, 1964-66, Precinct of Mut, Karnak, 1978—; mem. Oriental Inst.-U. Chgo. Author: Drawings from Ancient Egypt, 1978, The Detroit Institute of Arts: A Brief History, 1991; co-author: Ancient Egypt: Discovering its Splendors, 1978; Mummies, Diseases and Ancient Cultures, 1980; also articles. With U.S. Army, 1953-55. Ford Motor Co. travel grantee, 1962; Am. Research Ctr. Egypt fellow, 1971; Smithsonian Instn. travel grantee, 1975; recipient Award in the Arts Wayne State U., 1985. Mem. Archaeol. Inst. Am., Am. Research Ctr. Egypt, Internat. Assn. Egyptologists, Soc. Study Egyptian Antiquities, Am. Assn. Mus. Democrat. Episcopalian. Avocations: origami, performance of early music, collecting T.E. Lawrence material. Office: Inst Arts 5200 Woodward Ave Detroit MI 48202-4008

PECKER, DAVID J., magazine publishing company executive, financial executive; b. N.Y.C., Sept. 24, 1951; m. Karen Balan, Oct. 31, 1987. BBA, Pace U., postgrad. CPA, N.Y. Sr. auditor Price Waterhouse & Co.; mgr. fin. reporting Diamandis Communications, Inc., N.Y.C., 1979; dir. fin. reporting Diamandis Communications, Inc., dir. acctg., asst. contr., 1983; COO, CFO, exec. v.p. pub. Hachette Mags., Inc., N.Y.C., 1990-91, pres., COO, 1991-92, pres., CEO, COO, 1992—; mem. Fashion Group's Internat. Adv. Bd., The N.Y. City Partnership Com.; mem. bd. dirs. The Madison Square Boys & Girls Club, Friends Indeed. Bd. dirs. Pace U., N.Y.C., Drug Enforcement Agents Found., 1995—. Mem. Am. Mgmt. Assn., Mag. Pubs. Am. (exec. com.). Office: Hachette Mags Inc 1633 Broadway New York NY 10019-6708

PECKHAM, BARRY, newspaper publishing executive. V.p. circulation The Dallas Morning News, Tex. Office: The Dallas Morning News Communication Ctr Young & Houston Sts Dallas TX 75202

PECKHAM, DONALD EUGENE, retired utilities company executive; b. Willis, Kans., Nov. 28, 1922; s. Rolland Claude and Winona Maude (Lewis) P.; m. Evelynn Darlene Dodson, Dec. 20, 1949 (dec.). B.A. cum laude in Acctg, Eastern N.Mex. U., 1953; M.B.A., U. Ariz., 1954. Acct. Ill. Power Co., Decatur, Ill., 1954-57; with Public Service Co. of N.Mex., Albuquerque, from 1957, sec., 1968-70; sec., asst. treas. Public Service Co. of N.Mex., 1970-74, sec., treas., 1974-79, sec., asst. treas., from 1979; sec. Paragon Resources, Inc., 1972-75, sec., asst. treas., from 1975; sec. Sunbelt Mining Co., Inc., 1980-81, sec., asst. treas., from 1981; sec. Meadows Resources, Inc., from 1981; now ret. Served with USMC, 1943-46. Republican. Lodge: Elks.

PECKHAM, JOHN MUNROE, III, investment executive, author, lecturer; b. Abington, Mass., July 25, 1933; s. John Munroe and Mildred (Davis) P.; m. Ann M. Peckham; children: Lisa, Holly, John M. IV. AB, Tufts U., 1955; postgrad., Columbia U., 1955-56. Pres. Peckham Boston Adv. Co., 1964—; pres., chmn. Boston Hall Corp., Boston, 1987—; pres. Boston Hall Pub. Co., 1988—. Founder Realtors Concerned for Realtors, Chgo., 1986—; mem. bd. advisors Kids Stop, Boston, 1988-89; bd. dirs. Am. Fedn. for Children and Youth, L.A., 1988-89. Lt. comdr. USN, 1956-62. Mem. Nat. Assn. Realtors (v.p.), Realtors Nat. Mktg. Inst. (v.p. 1988), Internat. Fedn. Realtors, Inst. Real Estate Mgmt., Ten Club (pres. Boston chpt. 1974-79), Friends of Bill W. Republican. Baptist. Avocations: bicycling, swimming, cribbage, speaking, reading. Office: Peckham Boston Advisory Co. 4 Longfellow Pl Apt 2003 Boston MA 02114-2817

PECKOL, JAMES KENNETH, consulting engineer; b. Cleve., Oct. 24, 1944; s. William John and Elinor Elizabeth (Bustard) P.; children: Erin, Robyn. BS Engring., Case Inst. Tech., 1966; MSEE, U. Wash., 1975, PhDEE, 1985. Cons. GE, Raytheon, Ling Temco Vought, RCA, Boeing Co., 1966-72; sr. staff engr. indsl. products bus. unit John Fluke Mfg. Co., Seattle, 1972-83, sr. staff engr. automated systems bus. unit, 1983-86, sr. staff engr. MR&D Bus. unit, 1986-93; founder Oxford Cons., Edmonds, Wash., 1987—; affiliate asst. prof. dept. elec. engring. U. Wash., Seattle, 1984-87, 95—; sr. lectr., assoc. prof. dept. elec. engring. U. Aberdeen, Scotland, 1987; lectr. dept. computer sci. Seattle U., 1989; lectr. dept. math. and sci. Shoreline C.C., Seattle, 1989—; lectr. dept. computer sci. Edmonds (Wash.) C.C., 1992—; assoc. prof. dept. engring./computer sci. U. Nantes, France, 1993; mem. computer sci. and elec. engring. curriculum adv. bd. Wash. State U., 1990—; lectr. various confs. and univs. Contbr. articles to profl. jours.; patentee in field. Mem. IEEE, Am. Assn. Artificial Intelligence, Assn. Computing Machinery, Tau Beta Pi. Home and Office: Oxford Cons Ltd 859 14th St SW Edmonds WA 98020-6611

PECKOLICK, ALAN, graphic designer; b. N.Y.C., Oct. 3, 1940; s. Charles and Belle (Binenbaum) P.; m. Jessica Margot Weber, June 3, 1984. AAS, Pratt Inst., Bklyn., 1968. Art dir. McCann-Erickson, 1964-68; graphic designer Herb Lubalin, 1968-72; v.p., creative dir. Lubalin, Smith, Carnase, Inc., N.Y.C., 1972-74, LCS & P Design Group, Inc., N.Y.C., 1974-76; pres. Lubalin Peckolick Assoc., N.Y.C., 1976-81, Pushpin, Lubalin, Peckolick, N.Y.C., 1981-86, Peckolick and Ptnrs., N.Y.C., 1986-89; design dir. Addison Design Cons., N.Y.C., 1989-91; chmn. Peckolick Inc., N.Y.C., 1991—; bd. advisors Designworld mag., Victoria, Australia, 1983—, Herb Lubalin Study

Ctr., N.Y.C.; lectr. Pratt Inst., Parsons Sch. Design, Sch. Visual Arts, also various orgns. Co-author, designer: Herb Lubalin Graphic Designer, 1986; exhibited at Sony Gallery, Tokyo, 1989. Bd. dirs. Glaucoma Found., 1993, Whale Conservation Inst., 1994. Recipient awards AIGA, Art Directors Club awards. Mem. N.Y. Art Dirs. Club (6 gold medals, over 50 awards), N.Y. Type Dirs. Club (bd. dirs.), Alliance Graphique Internationale, Art Dirs.Club Bergen (Norway) (hon.). Avocations: automobile racing, sculpting, collecting art and prints, cooking, travel. Home: 30 E 10th St New York NY 10003-6202 Office: Peckolick Inc 30 East 21st St New York NY 10010

PECORA, ROBERT, chemistry educator; b. Bklyn., Aug. 6, 1938; s. Alfonso Edward and Helen (Buscavage) P. A.B., Columbia U., 1959, A.M., 1960, Ph.D., 1962. Asst. prof. chemistry Stanford U., 1964-71, assoc. prof., 1971-78, prof., 1978—; chmn. chemistry, 1992—; vis. prof. U. Manchester, (Eng.), 1970-71, U. Nice, (France), 1978; cons. chemistry to maj. corps. Co-author: Dynamic Light Scattering, 1976; contbr. articles to profl. jours. Recipient Sr. Scientist award Alexander von Humboldt Found., 1985; NSF fellow, 1960-62, Am. Acad. Scis. postdoctoral fellow U. libre de Bruxelles, Belgium, 1963. Fellow AAAS, Am. Phys. Soc.; mem. Am. Chem. Soc. Home: 707 Continental Cir Mountain View CA 94040-3366 Office: Stanford U Dept Chemistry Stanford CA 94305

PECSOK, ROBERT LOUIS, chemist, educator; b. Cleve., Dec. 18, 1918; s. Michael C. and Katherine (Richter) P.; m. Mary Bodell, Oct. 12, 1940; children: Helen Pecsok Wong, Katherine, Jean Pecsok Nagle, Michael, Ruth Pecsok Hughes, Alice Pecsok Tominaga, Sara Pecsok Lima. S.B. summa cum laude, Harvard, 1940, Ph.D., 1948. Prodn. foreman Procter & Gamble Co., Balt., 1940-43; instr. chemistry Harvard, 1948; asst. prof. chemistry U. Calif. at Los Angeles, 1948-55, asso. prof., 1955-61, prof., 1961-71, vice chmn. dept., 1965-70; prof., chmn. dept. U. Hawaii, Honolulu, 1971-80; dean natural scis. U. Hawaii, 1981-89; sci. adviser FDA, 1966-69. Author: Principles and Practice of Gas Chromatography, 1959, Analytical Methods of Organic and Biochemistry, 1966, Modern Methods of Chemical Analysis, 1968, 2d edit., 1976, Modern Chemical Technology, 1970, rev. edit. 1989, Physicochemical Applications of Gas Chromatography, 1978. Served as lt. USNR, 1943-46. Recipient Tolman medal, 1971; Guggenheim fellow, 1956-57; Petroleum Research Fund Internat. fellow, 1963-64. Mem. Am. Chem. Soc., Am. Inst. Chemists, Phi Beta Kappa, Alpha Chi Sigma, Phi Lambda Upsilon. Home: 13855 Riverhead Ct San Diego CA 92129-3222

PEDDICORD, KENNETH LEE, academic administrator; b. Ottawa, Ill., Apr. 5, 1943; s. Kenneth Charles and Elizabeth May (Hughes) P.; m. Patricia Ann Cullen, Aug. 2, 1969; children: Joseph, Clare. BSME, U. Notre Dame, 1965; MSNE, U. Ill., 1967, PhD, 1972. Registered profl. engr., Tex. Rsch. nuclear engr. Swiss Fed. Inst. for Reactor Rsch., Würenlingen, Switzerland, 1972-75; asst. prof. nuclear engring. Oreg. State U., Eugene, 1975-79, assoc. prof. nuclear engring., 1979-82; prof. nuclear engring. Tex. A&M U., College Station, 1983—, head dept. nuclear engring., 1985-88, asst. dir. rsch. Tex. Engring. Experiment Sta., 1988-91, dir. Tex. Experiment Sta., 1991-93, assoc. dean coll. engring., 1990-91, interim dean coll. engring., 1991-93, interim dep. chancellor engring., 1993-94, assoc. vice chancellor for strategic programs, 1994—; vis. scientist Joint Rsch. Centre-Ispra Establishment, EURATOM, Ispra, Italy, 1981-82; cons. EG&G Idaho, Inc., Idaho Falls, Idaho, 1979, Portland (Oreg.) Gen. Electric Co., 1980, Battelle Human Affairs Rsch. Ctr., Bellevue, Va., 1984, Los Alamos (N.Mex.) Nat. Lab., 1984-89, Pa. Power & Light, Allentown, Pa., 1986, Argonne Nat. Lab., Idaho Falls, 1989, Univs. Space Rsch. Assn., Houston, 1989—, Ark. Dept. Higher Edn., Little Rock, 1990; speaker in field; mem. Nat. Rsch. Coun. Com. on Advanced Space Based High Power Techs., 1987-88, NASA OAET Aerospace Rsch. and Tech. subcom., 1987—, SP-100 Materials Sci. Rev. Com., DARPA/NASA/DOE, 1984-86, Nuclear Engring. Edn. for Disadvantaged, 1978—, sec., 1978-80, vice chair, 1985-88, chair, 1988-91; John and Muriel Landis Scholarship Com., 1979—, chair, 1985—; mem. adv. bd. for nuclear sci. and engring., 1984-86; mem. tech. program com. Internat. Conf. on Reliable Fuels for Liquid Metal Reactors, 1985-86; mem. Tex. Transp. Inst. Rsch. Coun., 1987—, Tex. A&M Rsch. Found. Users' Coun., 1989—. Contbr. articles to profl. jours. Recipient Best Paper award AIAA 9th Ann. Tech. Symposium Johnson Space Ctr., 1984. Mem. ASME, NSPE, Am. Nuclear Soc. (cert. governance 1983, 84, 85, Materials Sci. and Tech. Divsn. Chmn's. award 1989, mem. materials sci. and tech. divsn. exec. com. 1983-86, sec.-treas. 1985-86, vice-chmn./chair-elect 1986-87, chair 1987-88, bd. dirs. 1988-91, mem. edn. divsn. exec. com. 1979-82, sec.-treas. 1982-83, vice-chmn./chair-elect 1983-84, chair 1984-85, mem. student activities com. 1976—, chair 1978-81, Oreg. sect. Edn. com. 1976, 79, 80, Oreg. sect. bd. dirs. 1977), Am. Soc. Engring. Edn., Tex. Soc. Profl. Engrs., Univ. Space Rsch. Assn. (mem. sci. coun. engring.), Pi Tau Sigma, Alpha Nu Sigma. Office: Office of Chancellor John B Connally Bldg 301 Tarrow St Fl 7 College Station TX 77840-1801

PEDDICORD, ROLAND DALE, lawyer; b. Van Meter, Iowa, Mar. 29, 1936; s. Clifford Elwood and Juanitas Irene (Brittain) P.; m. Teri Linn O'Dell; children: Erin Sue, Robert Sean. BSBA with honors, Drake U., 1961, JD with honors, 1962. Bar: Iowa 1962; cert. civil trial specialist Nat. Bd. Trial Advs. Asst. atty. gen. State of Iowa, 1962-63; assoc. Steward, Crouch & Hopkins, Des Moines, 1962-65; ptnr. Peddicord, Wharton, Thune & Spencer, Des Moines, 1968—; lectr. in law Drake U., 1962-68; lectr. law Coll. Osteo. Medicine, Des Moines, 1965-72. Editor and chief Drake Law Rev., 1961-62. Past mem. nat. bd. dirs., nat. coun. YMCA of U.S.A., past vice chmn. nat. bd.; bd. dirs., past chmn. Greater Des Moines YMCA, 1968-89. With USMC, 1954-57. Mem. ABA, ATLA, Iowa Bar Assn., Polk County Bar Assn., Iowa Trial Lawyers Assn., Iowa Acad. Trial Lawyers, Am. Bd. Trial Advs. (pres. Iowa chpt., cert. civil trial specialist). Republican. Methodist. Office: 405 6th Ave Ste 700 Des Moines IA 50309-2412 Office: Peddicord Wharton Thune Spencer PO Box 9130 Des Moines IA 50306-9130

PEDEN, KATHERINE GRAHAM, industrial consultant; b. Hopkinsville, Ky., Jan. 2, 1926; d. William E. and Mary (Gorin) P. Student pub. schs. Vice pres. radio sta. WHOP-CBS, Hopkinsville, 1944-68; owner sta. WNVL, Nicholsville, Ky., 1961-71; commr. commerce Ky., 1963-67; mem. Gov. Ky. Cabinet, Frankfort, 1963-67; pres., cons. Katherine G. Peden & Assos. Inc., Louisville; indsl. and community developers Katherine G. Peden & Assos. Inc.; bd. dirs. Westvaco Corp.; mem. adv. bd. Norfolk So. Corp. Chmn. Louisville and Jefferson County Riverport Authority, 1975-80; civilian aide to Sec. of Army, 1978-82; mem. com. Pres.'s Commn. on Status of Women, 1961-62; mem. Pres.'s Commn. on Civil Disorders, 1967; pres. Ky. Derby Festival, 1979-80; Dem. nominee U.S. Senate, 1968; mem. adv. coun. U. Ky. Coll. Bus.; trustee Spalding U., 1980-86. Named Woman of Year Hopkinsville, 1952. Mem. Fedn. Bus., Profl. Women's Clubs (pres. state 1955-56, 1st nat. v.p. 1960-61, nat. pres. 1961-62). Mem. Christian Ch. (deaconess 1956-59, 60-63). Home: 3818 Washington Sq Louisville KY 40207 Office: PO Box 6268 Louisville KY 40206-0268

PEDERSEN, DARLENE DELCOURT, health science publishing consultant; b. Westbrook, Maine; 1 child, Jorgen David. BSN, U. Conn., 1967; postgrad., U. British Columbia, 1974-75; MSN, U. Pa., 1996. RN, Pa. Various nursing positions, psychiat.-comty health, 1967-79; assoc. editor JB Lippincott Co., Phila., 1979-84; acquisition editor WB Saunders Co., Phila., 1984-88, v.p., editor in chief, 1988-91, sr. v.p., editorial dir. books divsn., liaison to London office, 1991-95, cons., domestic and internat., 1995—. Author: (with others) Canadian Nurse, 1976; contbr. Basic Nursing Skills, 1977; oil painter. Mem. ANA, Am. Psychiat. Nurses Assn., Am. Med. Pubs. Assn., Assn. Am. Pubs., Internat. Soc. Psychiat. Consultation Liaison Nurses, Forum Exec. Women, The Manuscript Soc., Assn. Profl. Comm. Cons., Internat. Platform Assn., Soc. for Ednl. Rsch. in Psychiat. Mental Health Nursing. Avocations: autograph and art collection, travel, francophile, French music, reading. Office: Ste 200 516 Gordon Ave Penn Valley PA 19072

PEDERSEN, KAREN SUE, electrical engineer; b. Indianola, Iowa, Apr. 27, 1942; d. Donald Cecil and Dorothy Darlene (Frazier) Kading; m. Wendell Dean Pedersen, May 6, 1961; children: Debra Ann Pedersen Schwickerath, Michael Dean. AA, Grand View Coll., Des Moines, 1975; BSEE, Iowa State U., 1977; MBA, Bentley Coll., Waltham, Mass., 1988. Registered profl. engr., Mass. Engr. Iowa Power & Light Co., Des Moines, 1978-80, rate engr., 1980-84; sr. rsch. engr. Boston Edison Co., Boston, 1984-87, sr. engr., 1987-94, prin. rsch. analyst, 1994—. Ops. chmn. Old South Ch., Boston, 1989—. Mem. IEEE (chmn. Iowa ctrl. chpt. 1983-84), NSPE, Mass. Soc. Profl. Engrs. (pres. 1992-93, vice chair northeast region 1995—), Eta Kappa Nu. Republican. Congregationalist. Office: Boston Edison Co 800 Boylston P283A 800 Boylston P1706 Boston MA 02199

PEDERSEN, KEN, recording industry executive. CFO Virgin Records Am. Inc., Beverly Hills, Calif. Office: Virgin Records Am Inc 338 N Foothill Rd Beverly Hills CA 90210-3608*

PEDERSEN, KNUD GEORGE, economics educator, university president; b. Three Creeks, Alta., Can., June 13, 1931; s. Hjalmar Neilsen and Anna Marie (Jensen) P.; m. Joan Elaine Vanderwarker, Aug. 15, 1953 (dec. 1988); children: Greg, Lisa; m. Penny Ann Jones, Dec. 31, 1988. Diploma in Edn., Provincial Normal U., 1952; BA, U. B.C., 1959; MA, U. Wash., 1964; PhD, U. Chgo., 1969; LLD (hon.), McMaster U., 1996. Asst. prof. econs. of edn. U. Toronto; asst. prin. econs. of edn., assoc. dir. U. Chgo., 1970-72; dean, assoc. prof., then prof. U. Victoria, B.C., 1972-75; acad. v.p., prof. U. Victoria, 1975-79; pres., prof. Simon Fraser U., Vancouver, B.C., 1979-83, U. B.C., Vancouver, 1983-85; pres., vice-chancellor U. Western Ont., London, Can., 1985-94, prof. econs. of edn., 1985-96; interim pres. U. No. B.C., 1995; pres. Royal Roads U., 1995-96; bd. dirs. Assn. Univs. and Colls., Can., 1979-84, chmn., 1989-91; bd. dirs. Vancouver Bd. Trade, 1983-85; pres. Can. Club Vancouver, 1983-84; mem. coun. trustees Inst. for Rsch. on Pub. Policy, Ottawa, Ont., Can., 1983-89; chmn. Coun. Ont. Univs., 1989-91. Author: The Itinerant Schoolmaster, 1972; contbr. chpts. to books. Decorated officer Order of Can., Order of Ont.; recipient 125th Anniversary of Confedn. of Can. medal; fellow Ford Found., 1965-68, Can. Coll. Tchrs., 1977, Royal Soc. for Encouragement of Arts, 1984; also 11 major scholarships. Mem. Semiahmoo Golf and Country Club. Avocations: golf, fishing.

PEDERSEN, NORMAN A., lawyer; b. Modesto, Calif., Dec. 29, 1946; s. Melvin R. and Hilda R. (Akenhead) P. BA, U. Calif., Berkeley, 1970, MA, 1972; JD, UCLA, 1975. Bar: Calif., D.C. Trial atty. Fed. Power Commn., Washington, 1975-77; asst. to commr. Fed. Regulatory Commn., Washington, 1977-79; ptnr. Kadison, Pfaelzer, Woodard, Quinn & Rossi, Washington, 1979-87, Graham & James, Washington, 1987-88, Jones, Day, Reavis & Pogue, Washington, 1988—. Home: 5063 Loughboro Rd NW Washington DC 20016-2615 Office: Jones Day Reavis & Pogue 1450 G St NW Ste 700 Washington DC 20005-2001*

PEDERSEN, PAUL BODHOLDT, psychologist, educator; b. Ringsted, Iowa, May 19, 1936. BA in History and Philosophy, U. Minn., 1958, MA in Am. Studies, 1959; ThM, Luth. Sch. Theology, Chgo., 1962; MA in Ednl. Psychology, U. Minn., 1966; PhD in Asian Studies, Claremont (Calif.) Grad. Sch., 1968. Asst. prof. dept. psychoednl. studies, psychologist U. Minn., Mpls., 1971-75; sr. fellow Culture Learning Inst. East-West Ctr., Honolulu, 1975-76, sr. fellow coord., 1975-76; assoc. prof. dept. psychoednl. studies, psychologist U. Minn., 1975-79, higher edn. coord., 1976-77; sr. fellow Culture Learning Inst. East-West Ctr., 1979-81; prof., chmn. dept. counselor edn. Syracuse (N.Y.) U., 1982-90, prof. edn. dept. counseling and human svcs., 1989—, adj. prof. dept. internat. rels., 1993—; vis. lectr. Nommensen U., Medan, Sumatra, Indonesi, 1962-65, U. Malaya, 1969-71; vis. prof. dept. psychology U. Hawaii, 1978-81; spkr. in field. Author numerous books, chpts. to books, articles to profl. jours.; mem. editl. bd. Am. Jour. Multicultural Counseling and Devel.; editl. advisor Jour. Profl. Psychology, Jour. Simulation and Games, Internat. Jour. Intercultural Rels. Mem. APA, Am. Assn. Counseling and Devel. Internat. (mem. rels. com., editl. bd. Jour. Counseling and Devel., editor Internationally Speaking newsletter, mentor media com.), Internat. Assn. for Cros Cultural Psychology, Internat. Coun. Psychologists, Soc. Intercultural Tng. and Rsch. (exec. com. mem., program chairperson 1977, chairperson Pacific Com. 1977, pres. 1978-80, editl. bd. Jour. Intercultural Rels.). Office: Dept Human Studies U Ala 157 Education Bldg Birmingham AL 35294

PEDERSEN, PAUL RICHARD, composer, educator; b. Camrose, Alta., Can., Aug. 28, 1935; s. Richard and Anna (Rasmussen) P.; m. Jean Frances Stollery, Aug. 6, 1956; children: Rebecca, David (dec.), Katherine, Andrew. B.A., U. Sask., 1957; Mus.M., U. Toronto, 1961, Ph.D., 1970. Music dir. Camrose Lutheran Coll., 1962-64; prof. McGill U., Montreal, Que., 1966-90, chmn. dept. theory, 1970-74, dir. Electronic Music Studio, 1971-74, assoc. dean faculty of music, 1974-76, dean faculty of music, 1976-86, dir. McGill records, 1976-90; dean Faculty Music, U. Toronto, Ont., Can., 1990-95. Contbr. articles to music jours.; Composer: chamber music Woodwind Trio No. 1, 1956, Woodwind Trio No. 2, 1957, Chorale Prelude No. 2, 1958, Lament, 1958, Ricercare, 1958, Woodwind Quintet (commd. Saskatoon Summer Festival), 1959, Come Away, 1959, Fugue, 1959, Sonata for Violin and Piano (commd. Andrew Dawes), 1960, Serial Composition, 1965, An Old Song of the Sun and the Moon and the Fear of Loneliness, 1973, Wind Quintet No. 2, 1975; choral works Ecclesiastes XII, 1958, Psalm 117, 1959, All praise to Thee, 1960, Built on a Rock, 1961, Passion Oratorio, 1961, rev., 1990, God Himself is Present, 1961, O Darkest Woe, 1961, Psalm 134, 1961, On the Nativity of Christ, 1963; 12 Chorales, SAB Choir, 1974, chorale mass, SAB Choir, 1983, De Profundis Choir and Orch., 1987; electronic music The Lone Tree, 1964, Themes from the Old Testament, 1966, Fantasie, 1967, Origins, 1967, For Margaret, Motherhood and Mendellssohn, 1971; orchestral music Concerto for Orchestra, 1961, Lament, 1962. Recipient Can. Council awards, 1958, 59, 73; Queen Elizabeth II Ont. scholar, 1965; Province of Ont. grad. fellow, 1964-65. Mem. Candian League Composers. Home: 70 Indian Grove, Toronto, ON Canada M6R 2Y4 Office: U Toronto, Faculty Music, Toronto, ON Canada M5S 1A1

PEDERSEN, RICHARD FOOTE, diplomat and academic administrator; b. Miami, Ariz., Feb. 21, 1925; s. Ralph Martin and Gertrude May (Foote) P.; m. Nelda Newell Napier, May 9, 1953; children: Paige Elizabeth, Jonathan Foote, Kendra Gayle. BA summa cum laude, Coll. of Pacific, 1946; MA, Stanford U., 1947; PhD, Harvard U., 1950; LLD (hon.), George Williams Coll., 1964, U. of Pacific, 1966. Teaching fellow, tutor Harvard U., Cambridge, Mass., 1949-50; with UN econ. and social affairs Dept. State, Washington, 1950-53; adviser econs. and social affairs U.S. Mission to UN, N.Y.C., 1953-55, adviser polit. and security affairs, 1956-59, sr. advisor polit. and security affairs, 1959-64, minister, counselor, 1964-66, ambassador, sr. adviser to U.S. rep., 1966-67; ambassador, dep. U.S. rep. in UN security council UN, N.Y.C., 1967-69; counselor Dept. State, 1969-73; ambassador to Hungary, 1973-75; sr. v.p. internat. U.S. Trust Co., 1975-78; pres. Am. U., Cairo, 1978-90; dir. internat. programs Calif. Poly Pomona U., 1990-95; mem. adv. bd. Nat. Coun. U.S.-Arab Rels., 1985—; trustee Consortium for Internat. Devel., 1990-95. Mem. Nat. Coun. YMCAs, 1961-73; bd. dirs. Ctr. for Civic Edn., 1995—, Physicians for Peace, 1988-90; mem. Fulbright bd., Egypt, 1980-82, adv. bd. Fulbright Cultural Enrichment Program, So. Calif., 1991—. With AUS, 1943-45 ETO. Recipient Sumner Peace prize Harvard U., 1950, Outstanding Alumnus award U. Pacific, 1962; named to Order of Sacred Treasure, Gold and Silver Star, Govt. of Japan, 1987; named One of 10 Outstanding Young Men, U.S. Jr. C. of C., 1956; awarded Order of Scis. and Arts, first class Govt. of Egypt, 1990. Mem. Royal Inst. Internat. Affairs, Coun. Fgn. Rels., Am. Soc. Internat. Law, L.A. Coun. World Affairs, Am. Fgn. Svc. Assn., Middle East Inst., UN Assn. Am., Internat. Assn. Univ. Pres., Pacific Coun. Internat. Policy. Democrat. Congregationalist. Clubs: Harvard (N.Y.); Cosmos (Washington). Avocations: swimming, tennis, Egyptology, local history. Home: 2503 N Mountain Ave Claremont CA 91711-1545 also: 2503 N Mountain Ave Claremont CA 91711-1545

PEDERSEN, WESLEY NIELS, public relations and public affairs executive; b. South Sioux City, Nebr., July 10, 1922; s. Peder Westergaard and Marie Gertrude (Sorensen) P.; m. Angela Kathryn Vavra, Oct. 17, 1948; 1 son, Eric Wesley. Student, Tri-State Coll., Sioux City, Iowa, 1940-41; BA summa cum laude, Upper Iowa U.; postgrad., George Washington U., 1958-59. Editor, writer Sioux City Jour., 1941-50; corr. N.Y. Times, Life, Time, Fortune, 1948-50; editor Dept. State, 1950-53; fgn. svc. officer Dept. State, Hong Kong, 1960-63; fgn. affairs columnist, roving corr., counselor summit meetings and fgn. ministers confs. USIA, 1953-60, chief, worldwide spl. publs. and graphics programs, 1963-69; chief Office Spl. Projects, Washington, 1969-78, Office Spl. Projects, Internat. Communication Agy., 1978-79; v.p. Fraser Assocs., pub. rels., Washington, 1979-80; dir. communications and pub. rels. Pub. Affairs Coun., Washington, 1980—; lectr. creative communications Upper Iowa U., 1975; chmn., Europe, Ambassadorial Internat. Affairs Seminar, Fgn. Svc. Inst., 1975; lectr. internat. pub. rels. Pub. Rels. Inst., Am. U., 1976; lectr. bus. and mgmt. div. NYU, 1976, 77, 78; cons. pub. rels., editorial and design; del. founding sessions 1st Amendment Congress, Phila. and Williamsburg, Va., 1980, exec. com., 1980. Columnist Pub. Rels. Jour., 1980-85; author: Legacy of a President, 1964, American Heroes of Asian Wars, 1969; co-author: Effective Government Public Affairs, 1981; editor: Escape At Midnight and Other Stories (Pearl S. Buck), 1962, Exodus From China (Harry Redl), 1962, Macao, 1962, China's Men of Letters (K.E. Priestley), 1963, Children of China (Pearl S. Buck and Margaret Wylie), 1963, Destination the Moon (William Howard), 1964, Man on the Moon, 1964, Bounty From the Land, 1965, The Americans and the Arts (Howard Taubman), 1969, The Dance in America (Agnes de Mille), 1969, Getting the Most From Grassroots Public Affairs Programs, 1980, Computer Applications in Public Affairs, 1984, Cost-Effective Management for Today's Public Affairs, 1984, Making Community Relations Pay Off: Tools and Strategies, 1988, Winning at the Grassroots: How to Succeed in the Legislative Arena by Mobilizing Employees and Other Allies, 1989, Leveraging State Government Relations, 1990, Managing the Business-Employee PAC, 1992, Adding Value to the Public Affairs Function, 1994, Pub. Affairs Rev. mag., 1980-86, Impact newsletter on nat. and internat. pub. affairs, 1980—; contbr. to the Commissar, 1972, Informing the People: A Public Affairs Handbook, 1981, The Practice of Public Relations, 1984; mem. editl. bd. Pub. Rels. Quar., 1975—, Fgn. Svc. Jour.,1 975-81; mem. adv. bd. Pub. Rels. News, 1991—; contbr. articles to profl. jours. Founding chmn. bd. dirs. Nat. Inst. for Govt. Pub. Info. Rsch., Am. U., 1977-80. Served with USAAF, 1943-46. Recipient 2 awards A.P. Mng. Editors Assn., Iowa, 1949, Meritorious Svc. award USIA, 1963, Presdl. commendation, 1964, 1st prizes Fed. Editors Assn., 1970, 74-75, 1st prizes Soc. Tech. Comm., 1974, 75-76, Gold award Internat. Newsletter Conf., 1982, Silver award, 1985, Eddi award for design excellence Editor's Workshop, 1983, Gold Circle award for outstanding comm. Am. Soc. Assn. Execs., 1988-89, Editors' Forum award, 1988-90, 94, 95, Assn. Trends award, 1989-96, Grand prize Nat. Ann. Report Conf., 1989, Comm. Concepts awards, 1989-96, Grand prize, 1992, MerComm awards, 1990-96, Nat. Media Conf. award, 1989, 90, Internat. Acad. Comm. Arts and Scis. award, 1994, 96, Grand prize, 1995; named Most Outstanding Info. Officer in Exec. Br. Govt. Info. Orgn., 1975, Ky. Col. and Adm. Nebr. Navy, 1984. Mem. Am. Fgn. Svc. Assn., Internat. Assn. Bus. Communicators (Communicator of Yr. Washington chpt. 1978, various awards 1973, 76-78, 84, 90, 94, 95), Nat. Assn. Govt. Communicators (pres. 1978-79, Communicator of Yr. 1977, Disting. Svc. award 1978), Pub. Rels. Soc. Am. (mem. Counselor's Acad. 1980—, chmn. 1st Amendment task force 1980-81, co-recipient Thotrd 1980, 81, 94, recipient 1995), Fgn. Svc. Club, Nat. Press Club, Overseas Press Club. Episcopalian. Home: 5214 Sangamore Rd Bethesda MD 20816-2322 Office: Pub Affairs Coun 1019 19th St NW Ste 200 Washington DC 20036-5105 *Keenness of mind and an abundance of luck, it is said, are the key ingredients of personal success. The truth be told, however, I've performed only one act of brilliance in my lifetime: the selection of my parents. But I've had an enormous amount of good fortune, a fact manifestly clear to anyone who has ever met my wife and son. They, thank goodness, chose me.*

PEDERSEN, WILLIAM FRANCIS, JR., lawyer; b. N.Y.C., Apr. 4, 1943; s. William F. and Priscilla S. (Auchincloss) P.; m. Ellen L. Frost, Feb. 2, 1974; children: Mark Francis, Claire Ellen. BA, Harvard U., 1965, LLB, 1968. Bar: Mass. 1969, D.C. 1978. Assoc. Ropes & Gray, Boston, 1969-72; staff atty. EPA, Washington, 1972-75; dep. gen. counsel, then assoc. gen. counsel EPA, 1976-85; staff counsel Senate Com. on Govt. Ops., Washington, 1975-76; lectr. Harvard Law Sch., 1985-86; of counsel Perkins Coie, Washington, 1987—, ptnr., 1989-94; ptnr. Shaw, Pittman, Potts & Trowbridge, Washington, 1994—. Contbr. articles to profl. jours. Mem. ABA (standing com. on environ. law 1987-89). Democrat. Episcopalian. Office: Shaw Pittman Potts & Trowbridge 2300 N St NW Washington DC 20037-1122

PEDERSON, CARRIE ANN, systems engineer, product trainer; b. Port Townsend, Wash., Dec. 12, 1957; d. Joe Dell and Shirley Ann (Harris) Wall; m. Joseph Allen Bauer, May 5, 1979 (div. 1986); m. Roald Leif Pederson, May 23, 1987. AS in Computer Programming, So. Ohio Coll., 1981; cert. in data processing, Live Oaks Joint Vocat. Sch., Milford, Ohio, 1976; BBA in Info. Systems, Dallas Bapt. U., 1993. Programmer Procter & Gamble Co., Cin., 1976-87; systems analyst AMP Inc., Harrisburg, Pa., 1987-89; computer sys. cons. James Rich Computing, Corsicana, Tex., 1989-91; programmer/analyst Guardian Industries, Corsicana, 1991-93; project mgr. Intrix Systems Group, Sacramento, 1993-94; sys. engr., product trainer Objective Sys. Integrators, Folsom, Calif., 1994—; prof. Navarro Coll., Corsicana, 1989-93. Vol. Updowntowners, Cin., 1986-87; sponsor Ind. Order Odd Fellows Children's Home, Corsicana, 1989-90. Mem. Newcomers Club (corr. sec. 1990). Republican. Mem. Christian Ch. Avocation: community activities. Home: 110 Kershaw Ct Folsom CA 95630-8611

PEDERSON, CON, animator. Grad., UCLA. Former writer, animator Walt Disney; animator Graphic Films Corp.; co-founder Abel & Assocs.; sr. animator MetroLight Studios, L.A., 1987—; animator for Redstone rocket project, also Explorer Satellite program. Spl. effects supr., animated models designer (film) 2001: A Space Odyssey. Office: MetroLight Studios 5724 W 3rd St Ste 400 Los Angeles CA 90036-3078*

PEDERSON, GORDON ROY, state legislator, retired military officer; b. Gayville, S.D, Aug. 8, 1927; s. Roy E. and Gladys F. (Masker) P.; m. Betty L. Ballard, Mar. 8, 1955; children: James D., Carol A. Pederson Niemann, Nancy G. Pederson Holub, Gary W. Student, Yankton Coll., 1948-50, Fla. State U., 1963; advanced course, Infantry Sch., 1958-59. Drafted U.S. Army, 1945-47, commd. 2d lt., 1952, advanced through grades to lt. col., 1967, served Korean War, 1950-54; served CONUS World War II, platoon leader 17th infantry regiment, 7th infantry divsn. U.S. Army, Korea, 1953-54; rifle co. commdr. 10th mountain divsn. U.S. Army, Germany, 1955-58; instr., dir. instrn. U.S. Army Jungle Warfare Tng. Ctr. U.S. Army, Ft. Sherman, Canal Zone, 1961-63, comdr. post, 1963-64; 1st bri., 1st infantry divsn. U.S. Army, Vietnam, 1965-66; dir. tng. hdqs. U.S. Army, Ft. Leonard Wood, 1966-68; advisor Ministry of Nat. Def., Rep. China on Taiwan, Rep. China on Taiwan, 1969-70; retired U.S. Army, 1970; rep. S.D. Ho. Reps., Pierre, 1977—; operator Dairy Queen, Wall, S.D., 1990-95; chmn. transp. com. S.D. Ho. Reps., 1979-93. Del. S.D. Rep. Conv., 1974-78, 80, 82, 84, 86, 88, 90, 92, Rep. Conv. S.D., 1994, Nat. Rep. Conv., 1976, 80, 84, 88, 92; bd. dirs. Legis. Rsch. Coun., 1988, 90, 92. Decorated Bronze Star, Medal of Merit, U.S. Presdl. Unit Citation, Rep. Korea Presdl. Unit Citation, Rep. Vietnam Presdl. Unit Citation, Combat Infantry Badge with Star, Legion of Merit, Air Medal with 2 Oak Leaf Clusters, Army Accomodation medal with 2 oak leaf clusters, Cross of Gallantry with Palm, Republic Vietnam. Mem. VFW, DAV, Am. Legion, Retired Officers Assn., Wall C. of C., Internat. Lions Club. Lutheran. Home: PO Box 312 116 W 7th St Wall SD 57790 Office: SD Ho of Reps State Capitol Bldg Pierre SD 57501

PEDERSON, RENA, newspaper editor. Editorial page editor Dallas Morning News. Office: The Dallas Morning News 508 Young St Dallas TX 75202-4808

PEDERSON, TONY WELDON, newspaper editor; b. Waco, Tex., Oct. 27, 1950; s. Lloyd Moody and Ida Frances (Walker) P.; m. Julianne Kennedy, Mar. 21, 1974. B.A., Baylor U., 1973; M.A., Ohio State U., 1976. Sports writer Waco (Tex.) Tribune, Tex., 1970-73; sports writer Houston Chronicle, 1974-75, copy editor, 1976-80, sports editor, 1980-83, mng. editor, 1983—; adj. faculty U. Houston, 1977-79. Mem. Houston Com. Fgn. Rels. Mem. Nat. AP Mng. Editors Assn., Tex. AP Mng. Editors Assn. Methodist. Avocations: golf, reading. Office: Houston Chronicle Pub Co 801 Texas St Houston TX 77002-2906

PEDERSON, WILLIAM DAVID, political scientist, educator; b. Eugene, Oreg., Mar. 17, 1946; s. Jon Moritz and Rose Marie (Ryan) P. BS in Polit. Sci., U. Oreg., 1967, MA in Polit. Sci., 1972, PhD in Polit. Sci., 1979. Teaching asst. polit. sci. dept. U. Oreg., Eugene, 1975-77; instr. govt. dept. Lamar U., Beaumont, Tex., 1977-79; asst. prof. polit. sci. dept. Westminster Coll., Fulton, Mo., 1979-80; asst. prof., head polit. sci. and pre-law Yankton Coll. U. S.D., 1980-81; prof. polit. sci. dept. La. State U., Shreveport,

1981—; program analyst NIH, Bethesda, Md., summer 1973; assoc. prof. jr. state program Am. U., Washington, summer 1984; rsch. assoc. Russian and East European Ctr. U. Ill., Urbana, summers 1982-96; founding dir. Washington semester La. State U., Shreveport, 1982-91, 96—, Presdl. Conf. Series, 1992—, Am. Studies program, 1982—; editorial staff writer The Times, Shreveport, 1990. Author: The Rating Game in American Politics, 1987; editor: The Barberian Presidency, 1989; Congressional-Presidential Relations: Governmental Gridlock, 1991; co-editor: Grassroots Constitutionalism, 1988; Morality and Conviction in American Politics, 1990, Great Justices of the U.S. Supreme Court: Ratings and Case Studies, 1993, 2d edit., 1994, Lincoln and Leadership: A Model for a Summer Teachers Institute, 1993; Abraham Lincoln: Sources and Style of Leadership, 1994, Abraham Lincoln: Contemporary, 1995, 2d printing, 96; guest editor Quarterly Jour. Ideology, 1994; contbr. articles to profl. jours.; founder La. Lincolnator, 1994. Mem. Mayor's Comm. on the Bicentennial U.S. Constn., 1987; active Barnwell Ctr., Shreveport, 1984, Am. Rose Soc., Shreveport, 1982. Served with U.S. Army, 1968-70. Recipient Tng. award NIH 1973, Outstanding Prof. award Westminster Coll. 1980, La. State U., 1984, Cultural Olympiad award, 1995, Page Shreveport rose Shreveport Times Jour., 1995; grantee La. State U., 1982, La. Endowment for Humanities, 1987, 93, 95; fellow NEH, 1981-85. Fellow Am. Polit. Sci. Assn., Am. Judicature Soc.; mem. Abraham Lincoln Assn. (mem. bd. dirs. 1994, dir. conf. in the south, 1992, dir. 1st summer Inst. on Abraham Lincoln, 1993, grantee 1992, 93, Achievement award 1994), Ctr. Study Presidency, Internat. Soc. Polit. Psychology, Am. Studies Assn, Internat. Lincoln Assn. (bd. dirs. 1994—, pres. 1990-93). Office: La State U Dept Polit Sci One University Pl Shreveport LA 71115-2301

PEDESKY, GERALDINE GOLICK, design project professional; b. Hayward, Calif., Oct. 27, 1935; d. Charles Anthony and Dolores Irene (Lemon) Golick; m. Charles Francis Pedesky, Nov. 10, 1960. BA, San Jose State Coll., 1957. Flight attendant Trans Continental Airlines, Burbank, Calif., 1958-62; office mgr. The Hertz Corp., L.A., 1964-77; v.p. adminstr. Vitousek Real Estate Sch., Honolulu, 1977-94; project mgr. Philpotts & Assoc., Honolulu, 1994—; mem. sec. Hawaii Assn. Real Estate Schs., Honolulu, 1977-93. Trustee Bernice Pauahi Bishop Mus., Honolulu, 1988-94, mem. exec. com., 1994; mem. Bishop Mus. Assn., Honolulu, 1983-87 (past pres.), Bishop Mus. Svc. League, Honolulu, 1977-83 (pres. 1982); bd. dirs. Outrigger Duke Kahanamoku Found., Honollulu, 1986-94 (pres.1989). Mem. Outrigger Canoe Club (bd. dirs., sec.-treas., v.p. ops.), Honolulu Acad. Arts, Contemporary Mus. Art, Nature Conservancy, Bishop Mus. Assn. Avocations: outrigger canoe paddling (state champion, 1980, 83, 85-91, 93), hiking, runnning. Office: Philpotts & Assocs 925 Bethel St #200 Honolulu HI 96813

PEDICINI, LOUIS JAMES, manufacturing company executive; b. Detroit, June 29, 1926; s. Louis I. and Myra Ann (Bergan) P.; m. Ellen Sylvia Mulden, June 5, 1948; 1 child, Eric Louis. B.S.E.E., Wayne U., 1955. Dept. head Gen. Motors Corp., 1948-58; exec. v.p. Lester B. Knight & Assos., Inc., Chgo., 1959-76; exec. v.p. ops. Pullman Trailmobile, Chgo., 1976-81; mng. dir. Ingersoll Engrs. Inc., Rockford, Ill., 1981-82; pres. George Fischer Foundry Systems Inc., Holly, Mich., 1982-93; also bd. dirs.; chmn. George Fischer Corp., Bloomingdale, Ill., 1994—. Served with U.S. Army, 1944-46. Fellow Inst. Brit. Foundrymen; mem. Am. Foundrymen's Soc. (past bd. dirs., William H. McFadden gold medal 1994), Skokie Country Club, Plaza Club. Republican. Office: 230 Covington Dr Bloomingdale IL 60108-3106

PEDINI, KENNETH, radiologist; b. Hartford, Conn., Mar. 19, 1940; s. Daniel Victor and Elizabeth Catherine Pedini; m. Egle Damijonaitis; children: David D., Julian A. AB in Philosophy, Trinity Coll., 1962; MD, Boston U., 1966. Diplomate Nat. Bd. Med. Examiners, Am. Bd. Radiology. Resident radiology Boston City Hosp., 1967-70, chief resident radiology, 1969-70, jr. staff radiologist, 1970-71; jr. staff radiologist U. Hosp., Boston, 1970-71; ptnr. Shawsheen Radiology, Andover, Mass., 1971—; sr. radiologist Lawrence (Mass.) Gen. Hosp., 1971-75, dir. radiology, 1976-87; sr. radiologist Melrose (Mass.)-Wakefield Hosp., 1971-93, chief radiologist, 1993—; pres. L & M Radiology Inc, Andover, Mass., 1994—; bd. trustees Lawrence Gen. Hosp., 1984-89; pres. L&M Radiology Inc., Andover, Mass., 1994—. Trustee Lawrence Gen. Hosp. Health Enterprises, Inc., 1990-93; mem. fin. com. Lawrence Gen. Hosp., 1986—; co-founder Andover Sch. of Montessori, 1975—; mem. alumni adv. com. Trinity Coll., 1995. Fellow Am. Coll. Radiology (councilor 1979-81); mem. Mass. Radiol. Soc. (pres. 1985-86, pres.-elect 1984-85, v.p. 1983-84, exec. com. 1977-87), Mass. Med. Soc., Stonehorse Yatch Club.

PEDLEY, JOHN GRIFFITHS, archaeologist, educator; b. Burnley, Eng., July 19, 1931; came to U.S., 1959; s. George and Anne (Whitaker) P.; m. Mary Grace Sponberg, Aug. 30, 1969. BA, Cambridge (Eng.) U., 1953, MA, 1959; postgrad. (Norton fellow), Am. Sch. Classical Studies, Athens, Greece, 1963-64; PhD, Harvard U., 1965. Loeb research fellow in classical archaeology Harvard U., 1969-70; asst. prof. classical archaeology and Greek U. Mich., Ann Arbor, 1965-68; assoc. prof. U. Mich., 1968-74, acting chmn. dept. classical studies, 1971-72, 75-76; dir. Kelsey Mus. Archaeology, 1973-86, prof., 1974—; guest scholar J. Paul Getty Mus., vis. scholar UCLA, 1989; resident in archaeology Am. Acad. in Rome, 1990; mem. staff excavations, Sardis, Turkey, 1962-64, Pylos, Greece, 1964, co-dir. excavations, Apollonia, Libya, 1966-68; field dir. Corpus Ancient Mosaics, Tunisia, Thysdrus, 1972-73; co-prin. investigator excavations, Carthage, N.Africa, 1975-79, dir. excavations, Paestum, Italy, 1982-85. Author: Sardis in the Age of Croesus, 1968, Ancient Literary Sources on Sardis, 1972, Greek Sculpture of the Archaic Period: The Island Workshops, 1976, Paestum: Greeks and Romans in Southern Italy, 1990, Greek Art and Archaeology, 1992, The Sanctuary of Santa Venera at Paestum, Vol. 1, 1993; editor: New Light on Ancient Carthage, 1980; co-editor: Studies Presented to GMA Hanfmann, 1971. Am. Coun. Learned Socs. fellow, 1972-73; grantee Am. Philol. Soc., 1979, Nat. Endowment Arts Mus., 1974, 77, 79, 80, NEH, 1967, 75, 77, 83, 84; NEH fellow, 1986. Home: 1233 Baldwin Ave Ann Arbor MI 48104-3623 Office: Kelsey Mus U Mich Ann Arbor MI 48109

PEDOE, DANIEL, mathematician, writer, artist; b. London, Eng., Oct. 29, 1910; came to U.S., 1962, naturalized, 1972; B.Sc., U. London, 1930; B.A., Magdalene Coll., Cambridge, Eng., 1933, Ph.D., 1937; postgrad., Princeton U., 1935-36. Instr. Southampton U., Birmingham U., Eng., 1936-47; Leverhulme rsch. fellow Cambridge (Eng.) U., 1947-48; reader U. London, 1948-52; prof. U. Khartoum, 1952-59, U. Singapore, 1959-62, Purdue U., 1962-64; prof. math. U. Minn., Mpls., 1964-81. Author: Circles, 1957, Gentle Art of Mathematics, 1958, Projective Geometry, 1963, A Course in Geometry, 1970, Geometry and the Liberal Arts, 1976; co-author: Methods of Algebraic Geometry, 3 vols., 1947-53, Japanese Temple Geometry Problems, 1990. Recipient Lester R. Ford award for expository writing Math. Assn. Am., 1968. Mem. Am. Math. Assn. Home: 704 14th Ave SE Minneapolis MN 55414-1595

PEDONE, JOSEPH LAWRENCE, advertising executive; b. Teaneck, N.J., Dec. 13, 1947; s. Richard and Frances (Maenza) P.; m. Nancy Ann Tolve, June 19, 1982; children: Jill Marie, Leigh Ann. AA, Rockland Community Coll., 1968; BSBA, Youngstown State U., 1970. Asst. prodn. mgr. Pace Advt., N.Y.C., 1972-77; prodn. mgr. Doubleday Advt., N.Y.C., 1977-78, Smith Greenland, N.Y.C., 1978-79; assoc. promotion dir. Edwin Bird Wilson, N.Y.C., 1979-80; print/traffic dir. Bozell & Jacobs, Union, N.J., 1980-81; print, art svcs. dir. Saatchi & Saatchi Advt. Inc., N.Y.C., 1981—. Contbr. articles to profl. jours. Recipient Good Scout award Greater N.Y. Coun. Boy Scouts Am., 1988, Fellowship award N.Y. Club Printing House Craftsmen, 1989, Luminaire award Women in Prodn., 1991, Electronic Integration Pioneer award Lasers in Graphics Conf., 1992; inducted Pub. and Prodn. Exec.'s Hall of Fame, 1992. Mem. Am. Assn. Advt. Agys. (chmn. 1990-93), Gravure Advt. Coun. (vice chmn. 1990—), Pub. and Prodn. Execs. (editorial advisor 1989—), Specification for WEB Offset Pubs. (bd. dirs. 1991—), NYU Bd. Graphic comms. Mgmt. and Tech. Ctr., Digital Distribution of Advtsg. for Pubs. Assn. (chmn.). Republican. Roman Catholic. Office: Saatchi & Saatchi Advt Inc 375 Hudson St New York NY 10014-3658

PEDRAZA, PEDRO, research director; b. N.Y.C., Sept. 30, 1946; s. Pedro Pedraza Algarin and Catherine (Martinez) Pedraza; m. Irza Ortiz, Sept. 3, 1964 (div. 1980); children: Pedro III, Andre; m. Enercida Guerrero, June 14, 1985; children: Lucas, Xiomara, Roxanne. BA, Occidental Coll., 1968; MS, Columbia U., 1973. Rsch. dir. Ctr. for Puerto Rican Studies CUNY, N.Y.C., 1973—, acting dir. Ctr. for Puerto Rican Studies, 1994. Bd. dirs. Educators for Social Responsibility, N.Y.C., 1990-94, Advs. for Children, N.Y.C., 1987-94, Youth Action Program, El Barrio Popular Edn. Program, P.R./Latino Edn. Roundtable. Home and Office: Hunter Coll Ctr Puerto Rican Studies 160 E 107th St # 1 New York NY 10029

PEDROTTI, LENO STEPHANO, physics educator; b. Zeigler, Ill., May 21, 1927; s. Celeste Louis and Dolores (Galeaz) P.; m. Wilma Jean Sullivan, June 23, 1951; children—Daro Stephano, Michael Louis, Sandra Maria, Laura Jean, Catherine Ann, Leno Matthew, Mary Ann, John Owen. B.S. in Edn, Ill. State U., 1949; M.S. in Physics, U. Ill., 1951; Ph.D., U. Cin., 1961. Teaching asst. U. Ill., Urbana, 1949-51; prof. physics, chmn. dept. Air Force Inst. Tech., Wright-Patterson AFB, Ohio, 1951-82, prof. emeritus, 1982—; cons., editor Ctr. Occupational Rsch. & Devel., Waco, Tex., 1975-82, sr. v.p., 1982—; presenter in field, 1982—; author, editor, lectr. laser and electro-optics Engring. Tech., Inc., Waco, 1978—; mem. indsl. adv. com. laser electro-optics program Cin. Tech. Coll., 1981-82; tech. cons. Univ. Eye Surgeons, Inc., Ohio State U., 1979-82; mem. exec. com. joint svcs. optical program Optical Scis. Ctr., U. Ariz., 1975-82. Author: Principles of Technology, 1986, Introduction to Optics, 1987, rev. edit., 1993, Applied Mathematics, 1988; contbg. author: Technical Prep Associate Degree: A Win/Win Experience, 1991, The Science Technology, Society Movement, 1993; contbr. articles to profl. jours. Faculty fellow NSF, 1959. Mem. Am. Nuclear Soc., Am. Phys. Soc. (vice chmn. then chmn. So. Ohio sect. 1974-76), Laser Inst. Am. (bd. dirs 1974-84), Am. Assn. Physics Tchrs., Am. Soc. Engring. Edn., Optical Soc. Am., Am. Vocat. Assn. (Outstanding Mem. award 1988 vocat. instrnl. materials affiliate Ednl. Exhibitor Assn.-SHIP citation for outstanding commitment to vocat.-tech. edn. 1994), Nat. Coun. Tchrs. Math., Sigma Xi, Tau Beta Pi (Outstanding Tchr. award 1961, 62, 63, 68), Sigma Pi Sigma. Home: 11006 Trailwood Dr Waco TX 76712-3131 Office: Cord 601 Lake Air Dr Waco TX 76710-5841

PEEBLER, CHARLES DAVID, JR., advertising executive; b. Waterloo, June 8, 1936; s. Charles David and Mary E. (Barnett) P.; student Drake U., 1954-56; m. Susie Jacobs, June 5, 1958 (div. 1977); children: David Jacobs, Mark Walter; m. Tonita Worley, Nov. 12, 1979; 1 son, Todd Whitney. Asst. to exec. v.p. J.L. Brandeis & Sons, Omaha, 1956-58; with Bozell, Jacobs, Kenyon & Eckhardt (formerly Bozell & Jacobs), 1958—, v.p., mem. plans. bd. 1960-65, pres. mid-continent ops., Omaha, 1965-67, pres., CEO, 1967-86, CEO, 1986—. Hon. chmn. bd. dirs. Am. Craft Mus.; bd. dirs. Nat. Jr. Achievement of Am. Mem. Drake U., Southampton Hosp., Gtr. N.Y. Coun. Boy Scouts Am., Madison Square Boys and Girls Club, Nat. Ctr. Learning Disabilities, N.Y.C. Partnership; partnership corp. com. Central Park Conservancy; campaign steering com. Morehouse Sch. Medicine. Mem. Nat. Golf Links Am., CEO Orgn., Blind Brook Club (Purchase), Eldorado Country Club (Indian Wells), Old Baldy Club, Mill Reef Club, Meadow Club (Southampton). Home: 166 E 64th St New York NY 10021-7478 Office: Bozell, Jacobs, Kenyon& Eckhardt 40 W 23rd St New York NY 10010-5200*

PEEBLES, CARTER DAVID, lawyer; b. Chgo., July 9, 1934; s. Carter Davis and Vera Virginia (Howd) P.; m. Donna Ruth Hostetter, Aug. 3, 1957; children: John Carter, Mary Elizabeth, Sarah Anne. A.B., DePauw U., 1956; M.A., U. Stockholm, Sweden, 1955; J.D., U. Chgo., 1959. Bar: Ind. 1959, Ill. 1960. Ptnr. Peebles, Thompson, Rogers & Skekloff and predecessor firms, Ft. Wayne, Ind., 1976-91; pvt. practice law Ft. Wayne, 1991—; faculty labor relations Purdue U. Regional Campus; U.S. commr., 1961-71, U.S. magistrate, 1971-84. Author: (with others) Model Business Corporation Act, 3 vols, 1960, Indiana Bankruptcy Handbook, 2d edit, 1976, Business Practice Under the UCC, 1970, (with Daniel E. Johnson) Indiana Legal Business Forms, 2 vols, 1967, Forms and Comment, 2 vols, 1970, (with James A. Knauer) Indiana Collection Law, 1981, (with Jerald I. Ancel) Farm Foreclosure Prevention, 1983, (with Thomas L. Ryan) The Farmer in Financial Distress, 1985, (with David H. Kleiman) Farmers and Lenders - The Financial Dilemma, 1986, (with Daniel J. Skekoff) Basic Bankruptcy in Indiana, 1987, (with J.T. Massey) Farm Foreclosure Defense, 1990; contbr. articles to profl. jours. Bd. dirs. Antioch Found., Religious Instrn. Assn., Religious Heritage of Am. Mem. ABA, Ill., Ind., Allen County Bar Assns., Am. Bankruptcy Inst., Am. Agrl. Law Assn., Phi Delta Phi. Lodges: Masons, Shriners, Jesters. Home: 6737 Blue Mist Rd Fort Wayne IN 46819-1503 Office: 1325 Spy Run Ave Fort Wayne IN 46805-4027 *As a young man, I was passionate, and later compassionate. Now, cynicism has me. Men used to do business on a handshake; now, a lengthy contract seems made only to be broken. People seem to seek the unfair advantage, forgetting that the only "good deal" is the deal fair to both sides. Fortunately, most people don't want something for nothing, will recognize a moral obligation and, many times, possess deep moral courage. If there is revolution in this country, it will not be black against white or have against have-not, but care against care-not. It appears that compassion wins after all.*

PEEBLES, JAMES W., publishing executive. BTheology, Am. Baptist Theol. Seminary; BA Romance Langs., Music Edn., Tenn. State U., MA Romance Langs.; MA Linguistics, Bi-Cultural Studies, U. Maine; PhD, U. Madrid. Tchr. various pub., pvt. schs.; pres., founder Winston-Derek Pub. Group (Winston-Derek record co. subs. 1986), Nashville. Contbr. The Original African Heritage Study Bible, author over 750 books, papers in field. Office: Winston-Derek Publishing Co 1722 W End Ave Nashville TN 37203-2602

PEEBLES, PEYTON ZIMMERMAN, JR., electrical engineer, educator; b. Columbus, Ga., Sept. 10, 1934; s. Peyton Zimmerman Peebles Sr. and Maida Erlene (Denton) Dials; m. Barbara Ann Suydam, Sept. 6, 1969; children: Peyton Zimmerman III, Edward Arlen. BSEE, Evansville Coll., 1957; MSEE, Drexel Inst., 1963; PhD, U. Pa., 1967. Design engr. RCA, Moorestown, N.J., 1958-64, systems engr., 1966-69; prof. U. Tenn., Knoxville, 1969-75, 76-81; vis. prof. U. Hawaii, Honolulu, 1975-76; prof. U. Fla., Gainesville, 1981-84, 1990—, assoc. chmn., 1984-90; cons. in field. Author: Communication System Principles, 1976, Probability, Random Variables and Random Signal Principles, 1980, 3d edit., 1993, Digital Communication Systems, 1987; prin. author: Principles of Electrical Engineering, 1991; contbr. articles to profl. jours.; patentee in field. Capt. USAFR, 1957-61. David Sarnoff fellow, 1964-66. Fellow IEEE; mem. Sigma Xi, Eta Kappa Nu, Tau Beta Pi, Sigma Pi Sigma, Phi Beta Chi. Methodist. Avocations: fishing, painting, woodworking. Office: U Fla Elec Engring Dept Gainesville FL 32611

PEECHATKA, WALTER NORMAN, government official; b. East Stroudsburg, Pa., Sept. 3, 1939; s. Walter Clinton and Lillian Mae (Post) P.; m. Bonita Louise Umholtz, Apr. 20, 1968; children—Troy, Trent. B.S. in Forestry, Pa. State U., University Park, 1961. Asst. supt. coop. for mgmt. Dept. Forests and Waters, Harrisburg, Pa., 1967-69; program specialist State Soil and Water Conservation Commn., Harrisburg, 1969-71; dir. Bur. Soil and Water Conservation, Harrisburg, 1971-82; exec. vice. pres. Soil Conservation Soc. Am., Ankeny, Iowa, 1982-87; dir. Bur. Plant Industry Pa. Dept. Agr., Harrisburg, 1987-91, dep. sec. for regulatory programs, 1991-95, exec. dep. sec., 1995—. Served to capt. USAR, 1962-64. Recipient Pres.'s Citation, Soil Conservation Soc. Am., 1983, Disting. Svc. award Nat. Assn. Conservation Dists., 1986. Mem. Assn. Soil Conservation Adminstrv. Officers (pres. 1978), Pa. Forestry Assn. (pres. 1973-74). Lutheran. Office: Pa Dept Agr Exec Dep Sec Exec Office 2301 N Cameron St Harrisburg PA 17110-9408

PEEK, LINDA OLIVE, material specialist; b. East Orange, N.J., Jan. 25, 1949; d. Carl Henry Peek and Helen Florence (Dewar) Wutke; div. 1970; children: Michelle Ann Foust-Courtney, Robert Carlton Foust II-Higgins. Grad., Long Beach Evening High Sch., 1971. Lab receptionist Long Beach (Calif.) Meml. Hosp. Med. Ctr., 1969-71; office mgr. Dr. Francis A. Hurtubrise MD, Inc., Long Beach, 1971-72; lab. technician Long Beach Meml. Hosp. Med. Ctr., 1972-79, St. Mary's Hosp., Grand Junction, Colo., 1980-89; materiel specialist Antelope Valley Hosp., Lancaster, Calif., 1991—. Mem. "I Count" (lab. rep. 1992—), Employee's Assn. (mem.-at-large 1993-94, bd. Ernst Employee Scholarship Loan com. 1994—). Democrat. Avocations: walking, collecting coins, taping movies, scuba diving, motorcycling. Home: 44753 N 18th St W Lancaster CA 93534-2711 Office: Antelope Valley Hosp 1600 W Avenue J Lancaster CA 93534-2814

PEELE, ROGER, hospital administrator; b. Elizabeth City, N.C., Dec. 24, 1930; s. Joseph Emmett and Catherine (Groves) P.; m. Diana Egan, June 15, 1963 (dec.); children: Amy, Rodney, Holly; m. Gail Nelson Oct. 15, 1992. A.B., U. N.C., 1955; M.D., U. Tenn., 1960. Cert. adminstrv. psychiatry, 1970 cert. forensic psychiatry, 1982. Intern St. Elizabeths Hosp., Washington, 1960-61; resident in psychiatry St. Elizabeths Hosp., 1961-64, tng. officer, 1964-67, chief of service William A. White div., 1967-69; dir. Area D Community Mental Health Center, 1969-73, asst. supt., 1974-75, 77-79, acting supt., 1975-77, chmn. dept. psychiatry, 1979—; clin. instr. psychiatry George Washington U., 1965-67, asst. clin. prof., 1967-71, assoc. clin. prof., 1971-79, clin. prof., 1979—; asst. dir. NIMH, 1978-79; chief clin. officer D.C. Commn. on Mental Health, 1987-91. Contbr. articles on clin., forensic and adminstrv. issues in Am. psychiatry to profl. jours. Served with USAF, 1950-53. Superior Service award HEW, 1967. Fellow Am. Coll. Psychiatry, Am. Psychiat. Assn. (speaker 1986-87, Adminstr. of Yr. 1989); mem. AMA, D.C. Med. Soc., Am. Assn. Psychiat. Adminstrs. (past pres.), Group for Advancement Psychiatry, Med. Soc. St. Elizabeth's Hosp. (past pres.), Fed. Physicians Assn. (past pres.). Episcopalian. Home: 5302 41st St NW Washington DC 20015-1904 Office: PO Box 39249 Washington DC 20016 *A key to effective treatment is not to allow the seductiveness of logic to narrow one's observations.*

PEELER, BOB, lieutenant governor; b. Gaffney, S.C., 1952; s. Smith and Sally (Bratton) P.; m. Bett Carter; children: Caroline, Robert, Jr. V.p. Peeler's Milk; former chmn. Cherokee County Sch. Bd., S.C. State Bd. Edn.; now lt. gov. State of S.C.; founding mem. advancement bd. Coll. Commerce, Clemson U. Mem. S.C. Dairy Assn. (past pres.), Cherokee County C. of C. (past pres.), Sertoma Internat. (life), Rotary (Gaffney chpt.), Masons, York Rite. Republican. Methodist. Office: Office Lt Gov PO Box 142 Columbia SC 29202-0142

PEELER, SCOTT LOOMIS, JR., foreign language educator; b. Rome, Ga., Aug. 25, 1947; s. Scott Loomis Sr. and Emily Willis P. BA in Spanish and French, U. South Fla., 1969, MA in Spanish and Edn., 1974; EdD candidate, Ariz. State U., 1982-91. Cert. tchr., Fla. Tchr. Spanish Polk County Schs., Lakeland, Fla., 1969—; tchr. Brandon (Fla.) Adult and Community Sch., 1978-79, Hillborough C.C., Fla., 1986; grad. rsch. asst. Ctr. Indian Edn., Ariz. State U., Tmpe, 1983-84; bi-lingual census worker U.S. Dept. Census, Tampa, 1980; part-time tchr. tribal mgmt. program Scottsdale (Ariz.) C.C., 1988; lect. in field; part-time tour guide. Author: Historical Markers and Monuments in Tampa and Hillsborough County, Florida, 1994; contbr. articles to profl. jours. Donor Peeler Am. Indian Scholarship U. South Fla., 1986; active Ptnrs. of Ams., Sister Cities Internat., Tampa, 1972—, chair edn. com., bd. dirs., 1990—; mem. Tampa Hist. Soc., 1972—, bd. dirs., 1994, Mus. Cherokee Indian (life), Ybor City Mus. (charter); started ptnr. city relationship between Lakeland, Fla. and Valledupar, Cesar, Colombia, 1977; co-chair Ariz. Indian Edn./Native Am. Lang. Issues Conf., 1984; mem. pres.'s coun. U. South Fla.; mem. Sister Cities Com., Lakeland, Fla., del. on ofcl. visit to Japan, 1993; mem. Sons of Confederate Vets.; mem. minority task force Tampa Bay Area Blood Marrow Donor Program; vol. Tampa/Hillsborough County Conv. and Visitors Ctr. Recipient Teaching Incentive award Carnation Milk Corp., Phoenix, 1984, named one of Outstanding Young Men of Am., Montgomery, Ala., 1984; Am. Indian Leadership prog. grantee Ariz. State U., 1982-84; Newberry Library fellow Am. Indian Ctr. History, Chgo., 1981. Mem. Nat. Indian Edn. Assn. (Ariz. steering com. 1984), Huguenot Soc. S.C. (life), Fla. Geneal. Soc., U. South Fla. Alumni Assn., Christian Hope Indian Eskimo Fellowship, Cajun Connection, Alliance Francaise, L'Unione Italiana, Tampa Bay History Ctr. (charter), Ybor City Mus. (charter), Nat. Congress Am., Indians, Tampa Trolley Soc., Krewe of the Knights of Sant 'Yago, Tampa Bay Area Camellia Soc., Nat. Mus. Am. Indians (charter), Nat. Indian Adult Edn. Assn. (planned conf. in Tampa 1995), Sons of Confederate Vets. Home: 433 Summit Chase Dr Valrico FL 33594-3841 Office: George Jenkins High Sch 6000 Lakeland Highlands Rd Lakeland FL 33813-3877

PEELER, STUART THORNE, petroleum industry executive and independent oil operator; b. Los Angeles, Oct. 28, 1929; s. Joseph David and Elizabeth Fiske (Boggess) P.; m. Sylvia Frances Townley, Nov. 5, 1985. B.A., Stanford U., 1950, J.D., 1953. Bar: Calif. 1953. Ptnr. Musick, Peeler & Garrett, Los Angeles, 1958-73; with Santa Fe Internat. Corp., Orange, Calif., 1973-81; v.p., sec., assoc. gen. counsel Santa Fe Internat. Corp., 1973-74, sr. v.p., gen. counsel, dir., 1975-81; vice-chmn. bd., chmn. exec. com. Supron Energy Corp., 1978-82; chmn. bd., chief exec. officer Statex Petroleum, Inc., 1982-89; chmn., pres. and chief exec. officer Putumayo Prodn. Co., 1989—; bd. dirs. Cal Mat Co., Homestake Mining Co., Homestake Gold of Australia Ltd., Chieftain Internat. Inc. Trustee J. Paul Getty Trust; mem. U.S. Tuna Team, 1957-67, capt., 1966. Served with U.S. Army, 1953-55. Decorated Army Commendation medal. Mem. AIME, State Bar Calif., Am. Judicature Soc., Theta Chi, Phi Delta Phi, Tucson Country Club, Skyline Country Club. Republican. Congregationalist. Office: PO Box 35852 Tucson AZ 85740-5852

PEELMAN, JAMES MICHAEL, lawyer; b. Cleve., Feb. 7, 1958. AB, William and Mary, 1980; JD, U. Richmond, 1984. Bar: D.C., Va., Md. Ptnr. Mark & Peelman, Rockville, Md., 1994—. Mem. KC. Roman Catholic. Avocations: golf, woodworking, furniture fabrication. Office: Mark & Peelman 33 Wood Ln Rockville MD 20850-2228

PEEPLES, RUFUS RODERICK, JR. (RODDY PEEPLES), farm and ranch news radio broadcaster; b. Tehuacana, Tex., July 3, 1932; s. Rufus Roderick and Josephine (Gray) P.; m. Bettimae Scrivener, Aug. 8, 1953; children: James Roderick, Deidre Lynn. BA, Tex. A&M Coll., 1953. Farm dir. KADA Radio, Ada, Okla., 1953-56, KGNO Radio, Dodge City, Kans., 1956-59, KLIK Radio, Jefferson City, Mo., 1959; assoc. farm dir. KWFT Radio, Wichita Falls, Tex., 1959-64; farm and ranch dir. and owner Voice of S.W. Agt. Radio Network, San Angelo, Tex., 1964—; mem. adv. bd. Tex. Agrl. Lifetime Leadership Program, College Station, 1987—, West Tex. Boys Ranch, San Angelo, 1966—; mem. devel. coun. Tex. A&M U. Coll. Agr. and Life Scis., 1992—. Named Man of Yr. in Tex. Agr., Tex. Assn. County Agrl. Agts., 1984, Disting. Alumnus Coll. Agr. and Life Scis., Tex. A&M Univ., 1995; recipient Ann. Comms. award Tex. Profl. Agrl. Workers, 1982, Knapp-Porter award, Tex. Agrl. Extension Svc., 1995. Mem. Nat. Assn. Farm Broadcasters (pres. 1982, Farm Broadcaster of Yr. 1992), San Angelo C. of C. Republican. Methodist. Avocations: flying, music, photography.

PEEPLES, WILLIAM DEWEY, JR., mathematics educator; b. Bessemer, Ala., Apr. 19, 1928; s. William Dewey and Thelma Jeannette (Chastain) P.; m. Katie Ray Blackerby, Aug. 30, 1956; children: Mary Jeannette, William Dewey III, Gerald Lewis, Stephen Ray. B.S., Samford U., 1948; M.S., U. Wis., 1949; Ph.D., U. Ga., 1951. Rsch. mathematician Ballistics Rsch. Lab., Aberdeen, Md., summer 1951; mem. faculty Samford U., Birmingham, Ala., 1951-56, prof. math., 1959-95, head dept., 1967-95; mem. faculty Auburn U., 1956-59; ret., 1995; cons. Hayes Internat. Corp. Co-author: Modern Mathematics for Business Students, 1969, Finite Mathematics, 1974, Modern Mathematics with Applications to Business and the Social Sciences, 4th edit, 1986, Finite Mathematics with Applications to Business and the Social Sciences, 1981, 2d edit., 1987; Contbr. articles to profl. publs. Served to 1st lt. AUS, 1954-56. Mem. Am. Math. Soc., Math. Assn. Am., Nat. Council Tchrs. Math., Ala. Coll. Tchrs. Math. (pres. 1969), Sigma Xi, Pi Mu Epsilon, Phi Kappa Phi (pres. 1977), Lambda Chi Alpha. Baptist (deacon, chmn. 1986). Club: Mason (Shriner). Home: 419 Poinciana Dr Birmingham AL 35209-4129

PEER, GEORGE JOSEPH, metals company executive; b. St. Louis, Aug. 26, 1925; s. George J. and Melba (Rahning) P.; m. Mary Jane Hazlewood, Feb. 14, 1948; children—Linda, Gary, Steven, Scott. B.S., Purdue U., 1945, M.S., 1948; postgrad., Advanced Mgmt. Program, Harvard, 1967. Operating supr. Republic Steel Corp., Canton, Ohio, 1948-54; various sales positions to v.p. sales Basic, Inc., Chgo., Cleve., 1954-63; v.p. marketing Handy & Harman, N.Y.C., 1963-71; dir. Handy & Harman, 1971-75, group v.p. precious metals, 1972-75; chmn., pres., chief exec. officer Multi-Metal Wire Cloth, Inc., 1975-88; pres. Holyoke Wire Cloth Co., 1975-88, Multi-Wedge Corp., 1976-88, United-Holyoke Corp., 1980-86; pres., chief exec. officer

Liquid-Solids Separation Corp., 1988-93, dir., 1988—; bd. dirs. Lewis Corp.; chmn. Phillips Steel Fabricators, Inc., 1989-93. Chmn. bd. Lucas Milhaupt, Inc., Cudahy, Wis., 1967-75. Served with USNR, 1943-46, 51-53. Mem. Am. Mgmt. Assn., Nat. Indsl. Conf. Bd., Am. Inst. Mining and Metall. Engrs., Tau Beta Pi, Kappa Delta Rho. Republican. Conglist. Clubs: Landings Club (Savannah, Ga.), Cornell of N.Y. Home: 21-31 Croton Lake Rd Katonah NY 10536 Office: PO Box 9 Northvale NJ 07647-0009

PEER, LARRY HOWARD, literature educator; b. Ogden, Utah, Jan. 2, 1942; s. Howard Harvey and Edna Celina (Baron) P.; m. Janet Priday; 9 children. BA, Brigham Young U., 1963, MA, 1965; PhD, U. Md., 1969. From asst. to assoc. prof. U. Ga., Athens, 1968-75; assoc. prof. Brigham Young U., Provo, Utah, 1975-78, prof., 1978—; acting head dept. comparative lit. U. Ga., Athens, 1973-74, Brigham Young U., Provo, 1978-81; pres. Western Regional Honors Coun., 1978-79; exec. dir. Am. Conf. on Romanticism, 1992—. Author: Beyond Haworth, 1984, The Reasonable Romantic, 1986, The Romantic Manifesto, 1988. Mem. MLA, Am. Comparative Lit. Assn. (exec. officer 1988-94), Am. Soc. for Aesthetics, Rocky Mountain Soc. for Aesthetics (pres. 1986-87), Internat. Byron Soc., Internat. Brontë Soc. Mem. LDS Ch. Avocation: travel. Office: Brigham Young U Comparative Lit Dept Provo UT 84602

PEERCE, LARRY, film director; b. Bronx, N.Y.; s. Jan Peerce. Dir.: One Potato, Two Potato, 1964, The Incident, 1967, Goodbye Columbus, 1969, The Sporting Club, 1971, A Separate Peace, 1972, Ash Wednesday, 1973, The Other Side of the Mountain, 1975, Two Minute Warning, 1976, The Other Side of the Mountain-Part II, 1978, The Bell Jar, 1979, Why Would I Lie?, 1980, Love Child, 1982, Hard to Hold, 1984, Wired, 1989; TV films include A Stranger Who Looks Like Me, 1974, I Take These Men, 1983, Love Lives On, 1985, The Fifth Missile, 1986, Prison for Children, 1987, Elvis and Me, 1988, The Court-Martial of Jackie Robinson, 1990, Murder at the PTA Luncheon, 1990, A Woman Named Jackie, 1991, Child of Rage, 1992, Poisoned by Love: The Kern County Murders, 1993; miniseries include Queenie, 1987, The Neon Empire, 1989. Office: 12700 Ventura Blvd Studio City CA 91604-2469 also: 225 W 34th St Ste 1012 New York NY 10122-0049

PEERMAN, DEAN GORDON, magazine editor; b. Mattoon, Ill., Apr. 25, 1931; s. Staley Jacob and Irene (Monen) P. B.S. with highest distinction, Northwestern U., 1953; postgrad., Cornell U., 1953-54; B.D., Yale, 1959; D.D., Kalamazoo Coll., 1967. With Christian Century Found., 1959—; copy editor Christian Century mag., 1959-61, assoc. editor, 1961-64, mng. editor, 1964-81, exec. editor, 1981-85, sr. editor, 1985—. Author: (with M.E. Marty) Pen-ultimates, 1963, (with Marty, L.M. Delloff, J.M. Wall) A Century of The Century, 1987; editor: Frontline Theology, 1967; co-editor: (with Marty) New Theology 1-10, 1964-73, A Handbook of Christian Theologians, 1965, enlarged edit., 1984, (with Alan Geyer) Theological Crossings, 1971. Contbr.: Chile: Under Military Rule, 1974. Active Chgo. community theater groups. Recipient award for distinction in lay ministry within the church Yale Div. Sch., 1995. Mem. ACLU, Fellowship of Reconciliation, Amnesty Internat., Clergy and Laity Concerned, Phi Beta Kappa. Democrat. Baptist. Office: 407 S Dearborn St Chicago IL 60605-1111

PEERS, MICHAEL GEOFFREY, archbishop; b. Vancouver, B.C., Can., July 31, 1934; s. Geoffrey Hugh and Dorothy Enid (Mantle) P.; m. Dorothy Elizabeth Bradley, June 29, 1963; children: Valerie Anne Leslie, Richard Christopher Andre, Geoffrey Stephen Arthur. Zert.dolm., U. Heidelberg, Germany, 1955; BA, U. B.C., Vancouver, 1956; Licentiate in Theology, Trinity Coll., Toronto, Ont., 1959, DD (hon.), 1977; DD (hon.), St. John's Coll., Winnipeg, Man., 1981, Wycliffe Coll., Toronto, 1987, Kent U., Canterbury, Eng., 1988, Montreal Diocesan Coll., Que., Can., 1989, Coll. of Emmanuel and St. Chad, Sask., Can., 1990, Thorneloe U., 1991; DCL (hon.), Bishop's U., Lennoxville, Que., 1993. Ordained to ministry Anglican Ch. as deacon, 1959, as priest, 1960, consecrated bishop, 1977. Asst. curate St. Thomas Ch., Ottawa, 1959-61; chaplain U. Ottawa, 1961-66; rector St. Bede's Ch., Winnipeg, 1966-72, St. Martin's Ch., Winnipeg, 1972-74; dean of Qu'Appelle, Regina, Sask., 1974-77; bishop Qu'Appelle, 1977-82; archbishop Coll. of Emmanuel and St. Chad, 1982-86; instr. Ottawa Tchrs. Coll., 1962-66, St. Paul's High Sch., Winnipeg, 1967-69.

PEET, CHARLES D., JR., lawyer; b. N.Y.C., Sept. 3, 1935; s. Charles D. and Margaret Louise (Sherman) P.; children: Alisa, Amanda. B.A., Yale U., 1957; J.D., Harvard U., 1960. Bar: N.Y. 1962. Assoc. Milbank, Tweed, Hadley & McCloy, N.Y.C., 1960-68, ptnr., 1969—. Mem. ABA, N.Y. State Bar Assn., Assn. Bar N.Y.C., Internat. Bar Assn. Office: Milbank Tweed Hadley & McCloy 1 Chase Manhattan Plz New York NY 10005-1401

PEETE, CALVIN, professional golfer; b. Detroit, July 18, 1943; s. Dennis and Irenia (Bridgeford) P.; m. Christine Sears, Oct. 24, 1974; children: Charlotte, Calvin, Rickie, Dennis, Kalvanetta. Grad. in adult edn., Highland Park Sch., Detroit, 1982; cert. degree hon., Wayne State U., 1983. Profl. golfer Sawgrass, Fla., 1975-84; winner Greater Milw. Open, 1979, 82, Anheuser-Busch Classic, 1982, Atlanta Classic, 1983, Phoenix Open, 1985, Tournament Players Championship, 1985-86, U.S. F & G, 1986; exhibitionist Ptnrs. for Youth, Miami, Fla., 1982—, Desert Mahie Jr. Golf, Phoenix, 1983—, City of Atlanta Jr. Golf, 1983—, Calvin Peete-Augustus J. Calloway Golf Tournament, Detroit, 1983—; mem. U.S.A. Team vs. Japan, 1982-83, Ryder Cup Team, 1983, 85. Active supporter Sickle Cell Anemia Found., Palm Beach and Lee Counties (Fla.). Recipient Ben Hogan award, 1983, Good Guy award Gordin Gin, 1983, Jackie Robinson award for athletics Ebony Mag., 1983, Vardon trophy, 1984. Mem. Profl. Golfers Assn. Democrat. Baptist. Winner 12 PGA Tournaments, $2.3 million in prize money; led PGA tour in driving accuracy 10 consecutive years, 1981-90. Office: Calvin Peete Enterprises Inc 2050 Collier Ave Fort Myers FL 33901-8114*

PEETE, RUSSELL FITCH, JR., aircraft appraiser; b. Memphis, June 15, 1920; s. Russell Fitch and Louise Gift (Edmondson) P.; m. Esther Eletha Mosley, Feb. 7, 1942 (dec. Jan. 1987); children: Miriam, Russell III, William; m. Margery May George, Sept. 2, 1988. BS in Aerospace Engring., Miss. State U., 1942. Dredge hand U.S. Corp. Engrs., West Memphis, Ark., 1937; rodman U.S. Corp. Engrs., Mobile, Ala., 1939; rsch. engr. Chicago & Southern Airlines, Memphis, 1941-51; tech. sales rep. Lockheed Corp., Burbank, Calif., 1951-82; ops. analyst Flying Tiger Line, L.A., 1982; dir. sales engring. Cammacorp, El Segundo, Calif., 1982-85, Anacorp, Marina Del Rey, Calif., 1987-89; aviation cons. Avcons, Sedona, Ariz., 1985—; aircraft appraiser Nat. Aircraft Appraiser Assn., Tucson, 1993—; cons. Avcons, Camarillo, Calif., 1985-86. Sec. Conejo Y's Mens Clubs, Thousand Oaks, Calif., 1960-63. With U.S. Army, 1944-46. Mem. Soc. Automotive Engrs., Exptl. Aircraft Assn., Aircraft Owners and Pilots Assn., Confederate Air Force, Internat. Aerobatic Club, Nat. Aircraft Appraisers Assn. Republican. Lutheran. Avocations: flying, photography, golf, travel. Office: 63652 E Squash Blossom Ln Tucson AZ 85739-1263

PEETE, WILLIAM PETTWAY JONES, surgeon; b. Warrenton, N.C., Mar. 29, 1921; s. Charles Henry and Lucy Pettway (Jones) P.; m. Mary Frances Hart, Feb. 7, 1960; 1 child, Marianna Jones. AB, U. N.C., 1942; MD, Harvard U., 1947. Fellow in pathology Peter Bent Brigham Hosp., Boston, 1943-44; house officer Mass. Gen. Hosp., Boston, 1947-54; instr. Harvard U. Med. Sch., 1953-55; asst. to dean Duke U. Med. Sch., Durham, N.C., 1955-63; asst. prof., asso. prof. Duke U. Med. Sch., 1955-64, prof. surgery, 1964-92, prof. emeritus surgery, 1992—; bd. dirs. Nations Bank, Durham; cons. Physicians for Peace, Am. Family Life, Inc., Rsch. Triangle Park, Batelle Corp., Patient Problems. Moseley fellow, 1954-55. Mem. N.C., Surg. Assn., So. Surg. Assn., So. Surg. Club, Soc. for Surgery of Alimentary Tract.

PEGELS, C. CARL, management science and systems educator; b. Barendrecht, South Holland, Netherlands, Feb. 26, 1933; came to U.S., 1962, naturalized, 1968; s. Bertus and Adriana Maria (Denotter) P.; children—Janice Joy, Kevin Carl. BS in Mech. Engring., Detroit Inst. of Tech., 1961, MS, PhD; Mgmt., Purdue U., 1963, 66. Prodn. engr. Ford Motor, Windsor, Can., 1955-62; instr. Purdue U., W. Lafayette, Ind., 1962-66; prof. SUNY-Buffalo, 1966—; v.p. Ctr. for Mgmt. Systems, Buffalo, 1978-91. Author: Basic for Business, 1973, Health Care & Elderly, 1980, Japan vs The West, 1984, Q.C. in Health Care, 1985, Decision Support Systems for Production and Operations Management, 1986, Management and Industry in China, 1987, Strategic Management for Hospitals and Health Care Corporations, 1987, Health Care and the Older Citizen, 1988, Decision Support Systems for Management Science/Operations Research, 1989, Strategic Information Systems, 1993. Krannert fellow, 1966; Krannert scholar Purdue U., 1963. Mem. Ops. Research Soc. Am., Inst. Mgmt. Sci., Am. Inst. Decision Scis. Avocations: long distance runner. Home: 63 Ruskin Rd Buffalo NY 14226-4255 Office: SUNY at Buffalo Sch of Mgmt Buffalo NY 14260

PEGIS, ANTON GEORGE, English educator; b. Milw., Feb. 21, 1920; s. George Anton and Eugenia (Stathas) P.; m. Harriet Louise Stevens, June 1, 1949; children: Stefani Elizabeth, Penelope Eugenia. A.B., Western State Coll. Colo., 1949; M.A., Denver U., 1951, Ph.D., 1956. Jr. engr. N. Shore Gas Co., Waukegan, Ill., 1946-47; instr. Ft. Lewis Coll., 1952-53; process control technician Gates Rubber Co., Denver, 1953-54; prof. English Colo. Sch. Mines, Golden, 1954—; asst. to pres. Colo. Sch. Mines, 1964-68, v.p. for devel., 1968-73, v.p. for external affairs, 1973-74, prof. English, 1975-82, prof. emeritus, 1982—; cons. U.S. Bur. Mines, Office of Mineral Reports, Washington, Regional Tng. Center, Office of Personnel Mgmt., Denver, 1983, CSC, San Francisco, 1974-94. Author: Social Theory in the Novels of Ford Madox Ford, 1956, An Intensive Course in English for Foreign Engineering Students, 1957, Humanism and the Practical Order, 1964, Excellence and the Odyssean Philosophy, 1965, Platonism in the Renaissance Lyric, 1965, Education for Leadership, 1966, Totality in Engineering Education, 1968, Course Recommendations for the Resource Engineer, 1968, Encroachment of Competing Land Uses on Mineral Development, 1976. Chmn. United Way Fund; sec. Colo. Sch. Mines Found.; pres. Roland Valley Civic Assn., 1974-75. Served with AUS, 1940-46; maj. AUS, ret. Appointed hon. disting. sgt. 121st Field Arty. Regiment, 1988. Named Outstanding Prof., Tau Beta Pi, 1963, Hon. Colonel 115th Engring. Rgt., 1988; recipient Outstanding Prof. award Colo. Sch. Mines, 1976; Amoco Found. awards. Mem. Golden C. of C. (pres. 1968), Am. Soc. Engring. Edn. (chmn. Rocky Mountain sect.), Am. Alumni Council (chmn. dist. VII 1971-72), Modern Lang. Assn., Blue Key, Theta Chi, Alpha Psi Omega. Home: 415 Scenic Ct Golden CO 80401-2533

PEGRAM, JOHN BRAXTON, lawyer; b. Yeadon, Pa., June 29, 1938; s. William Bement and Marjorie (Rainey) P.; m. Patricia Jane Narbeth; Aug. 21, 1965; children: Catherine, Stephen. AB in Physics, Columbia U., 1960; LLB, NYU, 1965. Bar: N.Y. 1965, U.S. Dist. Ct. Del. 1994, U.S. Dist. Ct. (ea. anad so. dists.) N.Y. 1994, U.S. Supreme Ct. 1971. Engr. Fairchild Camera and Instrument Corp., Clifton, N.J., 1960-66; assoc. Hoxie Faithfull and Hapgood, N.Y.C., 1966-71; ptnr. Davis Hoxie Faithfull and Hapgood, N.Y.C., 1972-95; prin. Fish & Richardson P.C., 1995—; mem. intellectual property litig. adv. com. U.S. Dist. Ct. for the Dist. Del., 1994—; mem. neutral evaluation and mediation panels U.S. Dist. Ct. for the Eastern Dist. of N.Y., 1994—; mem. mediation panel U.S. Dist. Ct. for the So. Dist. N.Y., 1994—. Editor The Trademark Reporter jour., 1984-86, mem. editorial adv. bd., 1986—; contbr. articles to profl. jours. Fellow Am. Bar Found. (life); mem. IEEE, ABA (chmn. antitrust law sect. com. on patents, trademarks and know how 1986-89, mem. legal econs. sect., bus. law sect., chmn. intellectual property law divsn. IV 1995-96), Am. Phys. Soc. (life), Fed. Bar Coun., Fed. Cir. Bar Assn., N.Y. State Bar Assn., Assn. of Bar of City ofN.Y., Am. Intellectual Property Law Assn. (chmn. fed. practice and procedure com. 1974-76, chmn. unauthorized practice com. 1977-79, chmn. trade secrets com. 1992-94, mem. Japan practice com. 1992—, mem. editl. bd. Quar. Jour., 1994-95, chmn. fed. litig. com. 1995—), N.Y. Intellectual Property Law Assn. (sec. 1981-84, dir. 1984-86, pres. 1989-90), U .S. Bar/ Japan Patent Office Liaison Coun. (del. 1990—), Chartered Inst. Patent Agts. (fgn. mem.), Inst. Trade Mark Agts. (overseas mem.), Am. Judicature Soc., Internat. Intellectual Property Soc., Internat. Patent and Trademark Assn. (U.S. group AIPPI), Internat. Trademark Assn. (bd. dirs. 1985-87, fin. com. 1987-95). Office: Fish & Richardson PC 45 Rockefeller Plz New York NY 10111-0201

PEHL, GLEN EUGENE, risk and insurance consultant; b. Woodford, Wis., Aug. 10, 1932; s. Henry Earnest and Ella Viola Pehl; m. Mazie Lee McCrackin, July 9, 1960; children—Keith, Tracey. B.S. in Bus. Adminstrn., Ala. Poly. Inst., 1958. Indsl. account rep. Am. Mut. Liability Ins. Co., Charlotte, N.C., 1958-60, br. sales mgr., 1960-64, dist. sales mgr., 1964-66; chmn., pres., treas. Indsl. Ins. Mgmt. Corp. and Corp. Life Cons., Inc., Charlotte, 1966-91; vice chmn. McNeery Ins. Consulting Inc., Charlotte, 1991-92, pres., CEO, 1992—; dir. N.C. Self-Insurers Assn., 1976-80; lectr. Trustee Alexander Children's Home, Charlotte, 1982-87, dir., treas., 1992-95. Served with USAF, 1951-55. Decorated Nat. Def. medal. Mem. N.C. Citizens Assn. Republican. Presbyterian. Clubs: Charlotte City, Cedarwood Country. Lodge: Masons. Office: McNeery Ins Consulting Inc PO Box 220926 Charlotte NC 28222

PEHLKE, ROBERT DONALD, materials and metallurgical engineering educator; b. Ferndale, Mich., Feb. 11, 1933; s. Robert William and Florence Jenny (McLaren) P.; m. Julie Anne Kehoe, June 2, 1956; children: Robert Donald, Elizabeth Anne, David Richard. B.S. in Engring, U. Mich., 1955; S.M., Mass. Inst. Tech., 1958, Sc.D., 1960; postgrad., Tech. Inst., Aachen, Ger., 1956-57. Registered profl. engr., Mich. Mem. faculty U. Mich., 1960—, prof. materials sci. and engring., 1968—, chmn. dept., 1973-84; cons. to metall. industry; vis. prof. Tohoku U., Sendai, Japan, 1994. Author: Unit Processes of Extractive Metallurgy, 1973; Editor, contbr. numerous articles to profl. jours. Pres. Ann Arbor Amateur Hockey Assn., 1977-79. NSF fellow, 1955-56; Fulbright fellow, 1956-57. Fellow Am. Soc. Metals (mem. tech. divs. bd. 1982-84, sec. metals acad. com. 1977), Minerals, Metals and Materials Soc. of AIME (Gold Medal award extractive metallurgy div. 1976); mem. NSPE, Iron and Steel Soc. of AIME (Disting. life mem., chmn. process tech. div. 1976-77, dir. 1976-79, Howe meml. lectr. 1980), Germany, London, Japan Socs. Iron and Steel, Am. Foundrymen's Soc., Am. Soc. Engring. Edn., N.Y. Acad. Sci., Sigma Xi, Tau Beta Pi, Alpha Sigma Mu (pres. 1977-78). Home: 9 Regent Dr Ann Arbor MI 48104-1738 Office: U Mich Materials Sci & Engring Dow Bldg 2300 Hayward St Rm 2146B Ann Arbor MI 48109-2136

PEHRSON, GORDON OSCAR, JR., lawyer; b. San Antonio, Feb. 18, 1943; s. Gordon Oscar and Frances (Burns) P.; m. Janice Sue Hagedorn, May 17, 1969; children: Christopher Wells, Ashley Stewart; m. Sharon Ann McNellage, Jan. 1, 1983. AB, Coll. William and Mary, 1964; JD, U. Mich., 1967; postgrad., U. London, 1967-68. Bar: Ill. 1968, D.C. 1969, U.S. Ct. Claims 1968, U.S. Ct. Mil. Appeals 1968, U.S. Ct. Appeals (D.C. cir.) 1976, U.S. Supreme Ct. 1976, U.S. Ct. Appeals (3d and 5th cirs.) 1979, U.S. Ct. Appeals (Fed. cir.) 1982, U.S. Tax Ct. 1990. Assoc. Sutherland, Asbill & Brennan, Washington, 1970-75, ptnr., 1975—; adj. prof. law Georgetown U., Washington, 1977-81; bd. advisors The Ins. Tax Rev., 1986—. Contbr. articles on tax law to profl. jours.; editor The Ins. Tax Rev., 1986-94. Trustee U.S. Supreme Ct. Hist. Soc., 1993—, Food for All Seasons Found., 1992-94; bd. advisors Hartford Inst. Ins. Taxation, 1993—. Fellow in internat. law U. Mich., 1967. Mem. ABA (co-chair investment fin. and taxation, com. sect. torts, and ins. practice 1994-96, chair tax procedure com., sect. adminstrv. law and regulatory practice 1994—), Fed. Cir. Bar Assn. (chair tax appeals com. 1994-96), D.C. Bar Assn., Am. Law Inst. Econ. Club of Washington, Met. Club (Washington), Nat. Press Club (Washington), Order of Coif. Episcopalian. Home: 4517 Foxhall Cres NW Washington DC 20007-1056 Office: Sutherland Asbill & Brennan Ste 1000 1275 Pennsylvania Ave NW Washington DC 20004-2404

PEI, IEOH MING, architect; b. Canton, China, Apr. 26, 1917; came to U.S., 1935, naturalized, 1954; s. Tsu Yee Pei and Lien Kwun Chwong; m. Eileen Loo, June 20, 1942; children: T'ing Chung, Chien Chung, Li Chung, Liane. BArch, MIT, 1940; MArch, Harvard U., 1946; DFA (hon.), U. Pa., 1970, Rensselaer Poly. Inst., 1978, Carnegie Mellon U., 1980, U. Mass., 1980, Brown U., 1982, NYU, 1983, Dartmouth Coll., 1991, Northeastern U.; LLD, Chinese U., Hong Kong, 1970, Pace U.; LHD, Columbia U., 1980, U. Colo., 1982, U. Rochester, 1982, U. Hong Kong, 1990, Am. U., Paris, 1990. Practice architecture N.Y.C., 1939-42; asst. prof. Harvard Grad. Sch. Design, 1945-48; dir. archtl. div. Webb & Knapp, Inc., 1948-55; with Pei Cobb Freed & Partners (formerly I.M. Pei & Ptnrs., I.M. Pei & Assos.), N.Y.C., 1955—. Prin. projects include Mile High Ctr., Denver, Nat. Ctr. Atmospheric Rsch., Boulder, Colo., Dallas City Hall, John Fitzgerald Kennedy Libr., Boston, Can. Imperial Bank Commerce Complex, Toronto, Overseas Chinese Banking Corp. Ctr., Singapore, Dreyfus Chemistry Bldg. MIT, East-West Ctr. U. Hawaii, Honolulu, Mellon Art Ctr. and Choate Rosemary Hall Sci. Ctr., Wallingford, Conn., Univ. Plz. NYU, Johnson Mus. Art Cornell U., Ithaca, N.Y., Washington Sq. East, Phila, Everson Mus. Art, Syracuse, N.Y., Nat. Gallery Art, East Bldg., Washington, Wilmington Tower, Raffles City, Singapore, West Wing Mus. Fine Arts, Boston, expansion and modernization of Louvre Mus., Paris, Morton H. Meyerson Symphony Ctr., Dallas, MIT Arts and Media Ctr., Jacob K. Javits Conv. Ctr., N.Y.C., Fragrant Hill Hotel, Beijing, Tex. Commerce Tower, Houston, Bank of China, Hong Kong, Creative Artists Agy., Beverly Hills, Calif., Guggenheim Pavilion, Mount Sinai Med. Ctr., N.Y.C., Rock n' Roll Hall of Fame and Mus., Cleve., Mus. Modern Art, Athens, Greece, Miho Mus. of Art, Shiga, Japan, Bilbao (Spain) Estuary Project, Four Seasons Hotel, N.Y.C., others; planning projects include S.W. Washington Redevelopment Plan, Govt. Ctr. Redevelopment Plan, Boston, Oklahoma City Downtown Redevelopment Plan, Bedford Stuyvesant Super Block, Bklyn., master plan Columbia U. Mem. Nat. Def. Rsch. Com., Princeton, N.J., 1943-45, Nat. Coun. Humanities, 1966-70, Nat. Coun. on Arts, 1981-84. MIT traveling fellow, 1940, Wheelwright fellow Harvard, 1951; Thomas Jefferson Meml. medal for Architecture, 1976, gold medal for architecture Am. Acad. Arts and Letters, 1979, Nat. Arts Club Gold medal of honor, 1981, Mayor's award of Honor for Art and Culture, N.Y.C., 1981, La Grande Medaille D'or L'Académie d'Architecture, 1981, Pritzker Architecture prize, 1983, Medal of Liberty, 1986, Medal of French Legion of Honor, 1988, Nat. Medal of Art, 1988, Praemium Imperiale Japan Art Assn., 1989, UCLA Gold medal, 1990, Colbert Found. first award for Excellence, 1991, Excellence 2000 award, 1991, Freedom medal, 1993. Fellow AIA (Medal of Honor N.Y. chpt. 1963, Gold Medal 1979); hon. fellow ASID; mem. Nat. Inst. Arts and Letters (Arnold Brunner award 1961), Am. Acad. Arts and Scis., Am. Acad. and Inst. Arts and Letters (chancellor 1978-80), Royal Inst. Brit. Architects, NAD, Urban Design Council. Office: Pei Cobb Freed & Ptnrs 600 Madison Ave New York NY 10022-1615*

PEIFFER, RANDEL AARON, agricultural sciences educator, researcher; b. Ligonier, Pa., Aug. 4, 1944; s. Tony and Emma E. (Leighty) P. BS, Delaware Valley Coll., 1968; MS, Pa. State U., 1970, PhD, 1976. Rsch. asst. prof. Del. State U., Dover, 1986; asst. prof. Del. State Coll., Dover, 1986-93, assoc. prof., 1993—; vis. prof. Farmers Home Adminstrn. Advisor carpentry adv. com. Vocat. Tech. Sch., Kent County, Del., 1987—; mem. Del. Agr. Mus., Dover, 1986—; mem. tech. com. NE-SARE, 1994—. Recipient First Pl. Sci. Poster in Plant and Soil Sci., 9th Biennial Rsch. Symposium, Assn. Rsch. Dirs. 1890 Land-Grant Colls. and Univs., Atlanta, 1992—. Mem. Am. Soc. Agronomy, Crop Sci. Soc. Am., Fraternal Order Police, Silver Lake Fishing Club (editor newsletter Dover chpt. 1984—). Achievements include research inforage management and utilization, biological control of gypsy moth in urban forest and crop ecology. Office: Del State U Dept Agr Natural Resources Dover DE 19901

PEIMBERT, MANUEL, astronomer; b. Mexico City, June 9, 1941; s. Gonzalo Peimbert and Catalina Sierra; m. Silvia Torres, Aug. 25, 1962; children: Antonio, Mariana. BS, U. Nacional Autónoma de Mex., 1962; PhD in Astronomy, U. Calif., Berkeley, 1967. Postdoctoral fellow U. Calif., Berkeley, 1967-68; prof. astronomy U. Nacional Autónoma de Mex., Mexico City, 1968—. Author over 100 research articles, 1960—; editor Revista Mexicana de Fisica, 1981-85. Recipient Guillaume Budé medal Coll. de France, Paris, 1974, Nat. Prize of Scis. Govt. of Mex., 1981. Fellow Third World Acad. Scis.; mem. NAS (fgn. assoc.), Am. Astron. Soc. (councilor 1975-78), Internat. Astron. Union (v.p. 1982-88), Royal Astron. Soc. U.K. (fgn. assoc.), Acad. de la Investigacion Cientifica (Scis. prize 1971), Soc. Mexicana de Fisica. Office: Inst de Astronomia, APDO Postal 70-264, 04510 Mexico City Mexico

PEIPERL, ADAM, kinetic sculptor, photographer; b. Sosnowiec, Poland, June 4, 1935; came to U.S., 1953, naturalized, 1958; s. Jacob and Fanny (Alster) P.; m. Martha Rose Dorf, June 15, 1958; children: Maury, Laurence, Linda. Grad., Cours Complémentaire Général, Paris, 1952; B.S. in Chemistry, George Washington U., 1957; postgrad., Pa. State U., 1959. Cons. in Russian sci. lit. Libr. Congress, Washington, 1959-61, 66-67; chemist Nat. Bur. Standards, Washington, 1961-63; sci. translator Am. Inst. Physics, N.Y.C., 1973-94. One-man shows include Balt. Mus. Art, 1969, Pa. Acad. Fine Arts, 1969, Marlborough Gerson Gallery, N.Y.C., 1969, Smithsonian Mus. History and Tech., 1972, Electric Gallery, Toronto, Ont., Can., 1975, Phila. Art Alliance, 1978; group shows include Washington Gallery Modern Art, 1968, Corcoran Gallery Art, 1968, Kent State U., McKay Art Inst., San Antonio, 1969, NASA Manned Spacecraft, Houston, 1970-71, Nat. Mus. Am. Art, 1972-82, Meml. Art Gallery, U. Rochester, 1978, Foster Harmon Galleries Am. Art, Sarasota, Fla., 1982-83, Artworks Gallery, Santa Barbara, Calif., 1989; represented in permanent collections Pa. Acad. Fine Arts, Mus. Boymans-van Beuningen, Rotterdam, The Netherlands, John F. Kennedy Ctr. for Performing Arts, Hirshhorn Mus. and Sculpture Garden, Kreeger Mus.; made first kinetic polarized-light sculpture in water, 1968; designed polarized-light kaleidoscope interiors, 1989; kaleidoscope photographs pub. on book covers for Prentice-Hall, Inc., 1991, 92, Mayfield Pub. Co., 1992, 94, Modern Curriculum Press, 1993; poster for Elektra Entertainment, 1990 (reproduced in book 1995), art for Andersen Consulting brocure, 1995, Time-Life Book-of-the-Month, 1995; collaborated with choreographer Maida Rust Withers (multimedia dance theater work) Spirit Place * Spirit Planet * Tukuhnikivatz, 1996; photography represented by The Stock Market Photo Agy. Home: 1135 Loxford Ter Silver Spring MD 20901-1130

PEIPERT, JAMES RAYMOND, journalist; b. Alton, Ill., Nov. 15, 1942; s. Lawrence George and Virginia Pauline (Sieve) P.; m. Mary Ellen Finney, Aug. 1, 1970; children: Benjamin, Matthew, Thomas. BA, So. Ill. U., 1965. Reporter, editor AP, Chgo., 1965-68, N.Y.C., 1968-70; corr. AP, Moscow, 1970-74, London, 1974-80; news editor AP, Johannesburg, South Africa, 1980-81; East Africa bur. chief AP, Nairobi, Kenya, 1981-86; nat./fgn. editor Fort Worth Star-Telegram, 1986—. With U.S. Army, 1965-67. Roman Catholic. Avocations: bicycling, maintaining 1967 Mustang, reading. Office: Fort Worth Star Telegram PO Box 1870 Fort Worth TX 76101-1870

PEIRANO, LAWRENCE EDWARD, civil engineer; b. Stockton, Calif., May 13, 1929; s. Frank Lloyd and Esther Marie (Carigiet) P.; m. Mary Ellen Alabaster, July 26, 1952; children: Thomas Lawrence, Ellen Marie. BSCE, U. Calif., Berkeley, 1951, MSCE, 1952. Registered profl. engr., Calif., Nev.; diplomate Am. Acad. Environ. Engrs. Assoc. civil engr. Calif. Div. Water Resources, 1952-53; with Kennedy Engrs., Inc., San Francisco, 1955-94, project mgr., 1960-79, v.p., chief environ. engr., 1974-79; dir. ops. Kennedy/Jenks Engrs., Inc., San Francisco, 1979-86; sr. v.p., regional mgr. Kennedy/Jenks/Chilton, Inc., San Francisco, 1986-90; exec. v.p., chief tech. officer Kennedy/Jenks Cons., Inc. (formerly Kennedy Engrs., Inc.), San Francisco, 1990-94, also bd. dirs., chmn. bd., 1972-94; ret., 1994; spl. lectr. san. engring. U. Calif., Berkeley, 1976. Served in U.S. Army, 1953-55, Korea, Okinawa. James Monroe McDonald scholar, 1950-51. Fellow ASCE (life); mem. Water Environ. Fedn., U. Calif. Alumni Assn., U.S. Ski Assn., Sierra Club, Tau Beta Pi, Chi Epsilon. Republican. Roman Catholic. Home: 3435 Black Hawk Rd Lafayette CA 94549-2326 *Focus on serving clients and rewards will follow.*

PEIRCE, BROOKE, English language educator; b. Washington, Jan. 2, 1922; s. Charles Brooke, Jr. and Nancy Ley (Bass) P.; m. Carol Emily Marshall, July 12, 1952. B.A., U.Va., 1943; M.A., Harvard U., 1947, Ph.D., 1954. Teaching fellow Harvard U., 1948-51; instr. English U. Va., 1951-54; mem. faculty Goucher Coll., 1954-85, prof. English, 1966-85, prof. emeritus, 1985—, chmn. dept. English and dramatic arts, 1964-69, 72-75, chmn. faculty humanities, 1964-66, 72-73, 79; vis. prof. English, SUNY Coll.-Oswego, 1985-87; lectr. Villa Julie Coll., 1989—. Author: (with Carol Peirce) Introduction to English Literature, 2 vols., 1954. Treas. Edgar Allan Poe Soc., Balt., 1959-66, mem. bd., 1959—. Served with U.S. Army, 1943-45. Nat. Endowment for Humanities fellow, 1977-78; recipient Disting. Tchr. award, 1979. Mem. Modern Lang. Assn., Raven Soc. of U. Va., Classical Assn., Phi Beta Kappa. Democrat. Home: 705 Warren Rd Cockeysville Hunt Valley MD 21030-2824

PEIRCE, CAROL MARSHALL, English educator; b. Columbia, Mo., Feb. 1, 1922; d. Charles Hamilton and Helen Emily (Davault) Williams; m.

Brooke Peirce, July 12, 1952. AB, Fla. State U., 1942; MA, U. Va., 1943; PhD, Harvard U., 1951. Head English dept. Fairfax Hall, Waynesboro, Va., 1943-44; instr. English Cedar Crest Coll., Allentown, Pa., 1944-46, Harvard U., 1952-53; asst. dean instrn. Radcliffe Coll., Cambridge, 1950-53; head English extension home study U. Va., Charlottesville, 1953-54; asst. dir. admissions Goucher Coll., Towson, Md., 1956-62; prof. English and comm. design U. Balt., 1968—, chmn. dept., 1968-94, gen. edn. core coord., 1985-87, Disting. teaching prof. Coll. Liberal Arts, 1981-82, chmn. humanities div., 1972-79; gen. edn. dir., 1995—; chmn. bd. New Poets Series, 1975-85; vis. scholar Lucy Cavendish Coll., U. Cambridge, Eng., 1977-78; co-coord. On Miracle Ground: The Internat. Lawrence Durrell Conf., 1980, 82, 90; co-coord. conf. Evermore! Celebrating the 150th Anniversary of Edgar Allan Poe's "Raven," 1995. Author: (with Brooke Peirce) A Study of Literary Types and an Introduction to English Literature from Chaucer to the Eighteenth Century, 1954, A Study of Literary Types and an Introduction to English Literature from the Eighteenth Century to the Present, 1954; editor: (with Lawrence Markert) On Miracle Ground: Second Lawrence Durrell Conference Proceedings, 1984; guest editor: (with Ian S. MacNiven) Lawrence Durrell Issue, Parts I and II, Twentieth Century Literature, Fall, Winter, 1987; contbr. essays to: Poe and Our Times, 1986, Critical Essays on Lawrence Durrell, 1987, Into the Labyrinth: Essays on the Art of Lawrence Durrell, 1989, On Miracle Ground: Essays on the Fiction of Lawrence Durrell, 1990, Dictionary of Literary Biography Yearbook, 1990, St. James Reference Guide to English Literature, 1991, Poe's Pym: Critical Explorations, 1992, Selected Essays on the Humor of Lawrence Durrell, 1993, Lawrence Durrell: Comprehending The Whole, 1994; assoc editor: Deus Loci: The Lawrence Durrell Jour., 1990-92, co-editor, 1993—. McGregor fellow, DuPont fellow U. Va., 1943; Harvard tutor, Anne Radcliffe traveling fellow Harvard U., 1951. Mem. MLA, Edgar Allan Poe Soc. of Balt. (bd. dirs. 1973-89, pres. 1989—), Lawrence Durrell Soc. (nat. pres. 1980-82, internat. pres. 1994—), Md. Assn. Depts. English, Phi Beta Kappa, Chi Delta Phi, Phi Alpha theta, Phi Kappa Phi. Home: 705 Warren Rd Cockeysville Hunt Valley MD 21030-2824 Office: Univ Balt Dept Lang Lit and Comm Dsgn Baltimore MD 21201

PEIRCE, GEORGE LEIGHTON, airport administrator; b. Worcester, Mass., Mar. 9, 1933; s. George Leighton and Grace Hislop (McDougall) P.; m. Carolyn Janasy, Oct. 7, 1968; children: Jennifer Lindsey, Amanda Leighton. B.B.A., U. Mass., 1961. Supr. mgmt. engrng. services Port Authority of N.Y. and N.J., 1961-69; airport mgr. Stewart Airport, Newburgh, N.Y., 1970; asst. mgr. LaGuardia Airport, Flushing, N.Y., 1970-75; gen. mgr. LaGuardia Airport, 1975-94; bd. dirs. Lighthouse, Inc., N.Y.C., 1989-94, Americas' Sail, Huntington, N.Y. Mem. Queens adv. bd. Salvation Army, 1980-94; chmn. adv. bd. Queens Lighthouse for Blind, 1980-94; bd. dirs., treas., vice chmn. OPSAIL; bd. dirs. Couri Found. Ridgefield, Conn. With USAF, 1954-58, Mass. Air N.G., 1959-61. Recipient Outstanding Community Svc. award Greater N.Y. Coun. Boy Scouts Am., 1978, Outstanding Pub. Svc. award Dept. Transp., 1986, Meritorious Pub. Svc. award USCG, 1986, Pub. Svc. award N.Y. Urban League, 1991, Disting. Svc. award Port Authority N.Y., N.J., 1992, George W. Hixon fellow award Kiwanis Internat., 1996. Mem. Queens C. of C., Coll. Aeronautics, Acad. Aero. (adv. bd.), 1976-94, LaGuardia Kiwanis (bd. dirs., past pres.), North Beach Club (past pres., bd. dirs.). Home: 392 Brett Rd Fairfield CT 06430-1720

PEIRCE, JOHN WENTWORTH, architect; b. Boston, Feb. 9, 1912; s. Thomas W. and Gabrielle (Dexter) P.; m. Grace Minot, June 27, 1934; children—Thomas W., Lucy (Mrs. David Scanlon III), John W. A.B. cum laude, Harvard, 1933; postgrad. Archtl. Sch., 1933-35; M.Arch., MIT, 1947. Individual practice architecture Boston, 1938-42; assoc. Shepley, Bulfinch, Richardson & Abbott, Boston, 1948-60; ptnr. Peirce & Pierce, Boston, 1960-71, Peirce Pierce & Kramer, 1971-75; Mem. Mass. Bd. Registration for Architects, 1954-59, chmn., 1957; mem. Mass. Insp.-Gen. Council, 1981-85. Prin. archtl. works include Shields Warren Radiation Lab, N.E. Deaconess Hosp., Boston, Trinity Episcopal Ch, Topsfield, Mass., Loeb Marine Lab, Woods Hole, Mass., Art/Music Bldg., St. Mark's Sch., Southboro, Mass. Chmn. Topsfield Conservation Commn., 1965-71; commr. Ipswich River Watershed Dist., 1968—, chmn., 1976-80; bd. dirs. Ipswich River Watershed Assn., 1976-87; trustee Essex County Greenbelt Assn., 1961-71, pres., 1966-77, dir., 1977-80, hon. dir., 1980—; trustee Trustees Pub. Reservations, 1966-83; bd. dirs. Plymouth County Wildlands Trust, 1973-79, 81-84, 87-95, trustee, 1984-87. Served to lt. comdr. USNR, 1942-46. Recipient Ann. Conservation award Mass. Trustees of Reservations, 1975, Open Space award Mass. Conservation Council, 1977, Conservation award Ipswich River Watershed Assn., 1984, Conservation award New Eng. Wildflower Soc., 1988. Fellow AIA; mem. Mass. Assn. Architects (pres. 1968), Boston Soc. Architects (v.p. 1968, pres. 1969). Clubs: Bournes Cove Yacht (Wareham, Mass.) (commodore 1966-68); St. Botolph (Boston). Home and Office: Witch Hill 9 Garden St Topsfield MA 01983-2401

PEIRCE, NEAL R., journalist; b. Phila., Jan. 5, 1932; s. J. Trevor and Miriam deS. (Litchfield) P.; m. Barbara von dem Bach-Zelewski, Apr. 18, 1959; children: Celia, Andrea, Trevor. B.A., Princeton U., 1954; postgrad., Harvard U., 1957-58. Legis. asst. Office of U.S. Rep. Silvio Conte of Mass., 1959; polit. editor Congl. Quar., 1960-69; co-founder, contbg. editor Nat. Jour., Washington, 1969—; cons. and commentator elections CBS News, 1962, 67-76, NBC News, 1964-66; lectr. in field; syndicated newspaper columnist Washington Post Writers Group; dir. Peirce-Phelps, Inc., Phila.; mem. faculty Salzburg (Austria) Seminar, 1980, 84; first Weinberg prof. Princeton U.'s Woodrow Wilson Sch. Pub. and Internat. Affairs, 1992. Author: The People's President, 1968, 2d edit., 1981, The Megastates of America, 1972, The Pacific States of America, 1972, The Mountain States of America, 1972, The Great Plains States America, 1973, The Deep South States of America, 1974, The Border South States, 1975, The New England States, 1976, The Mid-Atlantic States of America, 1977, The Great Lakes States of America, 1980, The Book of America: Inside Fifty States Today, 1983, Citistates: How Urban America Can Prosper in A Competitive World, 1993, Breakthroughs: Recreating The American City, 1993; co-editor: Investing in America, 1982, Corrective Capitalism, 1987; editor spl. series Phoenix Republic and Gazette, 1987, Seattle Times, 1989, Balt. Sun, 1991, Owensboro Messenger-Inquirer, 1991, Dallas Morning News, 1991, St. Paul Pioneer-Press, 1991, Raleigh News & Observer, 1993, Spokane Spokesman-Rev., 1994, Phila. Inquirer, 1995, Charlotte Observer, 1995. Founder, chmn. S.W. Neighborhood Assembly and Cmty. Coun., Washington, 1963-65; mem. exec. com. Nat. Civic League, 1990-95; trustee German Marshall Fund of U.S., 1987—; adv. com. Trust for Pub. Land, 1984—, Nat. Acad. Pub. Adminstrn., 1992—, Alliance for Redesign of Govt., 1993—; bd. dirs. Inst. for Ednl. Leadership, 1987—; mem. Nat. Commn. State and Local Pub. Svc., 1991—. With CIC, AUS, 1954-57. Fellow Woodrow Wilson Internat. Center Scholars, 1971-74. Mem. Newfound Lake Regional Assn. (v.p. 1989-92), Phi Beta Kappa. Episcopalian. Club: Federal City (Washington). Home and Office: 610 G St SW Washington DC 20024-2440

PEIRSON, GEORGE EWELL, film producer, art director, educator; b. L.A., May 16, 1957; s. Malcolm Alan and Beth (Wanlass) P. BFA, Art Ctr. Coll. of Design, Pasadena, Calif., 1986. Photographer Griffith Park Observatory, L.A., 1981-84; owner, art dir. Peirson to Peirson Studio, West Hills, Calif., 1983—; instr. Art Workshops, L.A., 1988-89, Learning Tree U., Chatsworth, Calif., 1990-93. Art dir., films include Valentine's Day, 1986, Private Demons, 1986, The Courtyard, 1987, Hope of the Future, Escape from Lethargia, 1988, Time Scrambler, 1988, Star Quest, 1988, Star Runner, 1989, The World of Early Bird, 1989, Dominic's Castle, 1991, The Deadly Avenger, 1991, Hell Comes to Frogtown II, 1991, The Minister's Wife, 1991, Endangered, 1991, Hell Comes to Frogtown III, 1992, Eye of the Stranger, 1992, Showtime, 1992, Star Runners, 1992, Monty, 1992, Guyver, Dark Hero, 1993, Tiger Mask, The Star, 1994, Dragon Fury, 1994, Arizona Werewolf, 1994, Drifting School, 1994; prodr.: Jurassic Women, 1994, Wolves Carnival, 1995, King of Hearts, 1995, Rollergator, 1995, Lord Protector, 1996. Mem. Assn. for Astron. Arts (bd. mem., v.p. 1987-89), Costumers Guild West, Assn. of Sci. Fiction and Fantasy Artists. Republican. Avocations: computers, skiing, running, bicycling, scuba diving. Office: Peirson to Peirson Studio 23409 Gilmore St West Hills CA 91307-3314

PEISER, ROBERT ALAN, financial executive; b. N.Y.C., Apr. 17, 1948; s. Donald Edward and Natalie Audrey (Phillips) P.; m. Kathleen Lorraine Reilly, Jan. 11, 1970; children: Karyn, Brian, Craig, Scott. BA, U. Pa., 1969; MBA, Harvard U., 1972. Dir. corp. fin. TWA, N.Y.C., 1972-77, sr. v.p. fin., CFO, 1983-86, exec. v.p. fin , CFO, 1994—; treas. Hertz Corp., N.Y.C., 1977-80; staff v.p., treas. ops. RCA Corp., N.Y.C., 1980-81; v.p., treas., Trans World Corp., N.Y.C., 1982-83; sr. v.p., CFO ALC Comm. Corp., Birmingham, Mich., 1986-88; sr. v.p. fin., CFO Borman's Inc., Detroit, 1988-89; pres., CEO Orange-Co. Inc., Bartow, Fla., 1989-92; with Bahadur, Balen & Kazerski, Ltd., Southfield, Mich., 1992-94; bd. dirs. Phar-Mor, Inc., Youngstown, Ohio, 1995—. Trustee Mich. chpt. Leukemia Soc. Am. Mem. Fin. Execs. Inst., Birmingham Athletic Club, The Wyndgate Country Club. Home: 326 Lakewood Dr Bloomfield Hills MI 48304-3533 Office: TWA 1 City Ctr 515 N 6th St Fl 19 Saint Louis MO 63101-1842

PEISS, CLARENCE NORMAN, physiology educator, college dean; b. Ansonia, Conn., Jan. 3, 1922; s. Alexander and Rose P.; m. Evelyn Schwartz, July 17, 1949; children: Kathy Lee, Robert Laurence. A.B., Stanford U., 1946, A.M., 1948, Ph.D., 1949. Postdoctoral fellow Johns Hopkins U., 1949-50; sr. instr. St. Louis U. Sch. Medicine, 1950-52, asst. prof., 1952-54; mem. faculty Loyola U. of Chgo. Stritch Sch. Medicine, 1954—, prof. physiology, 1958-85, assoc. dean Grad. Sch., 1972-78, assoc. dean for acad. affairs, 1975-78; dean Loyola U. Chgo. Stritch Sch. Medicine, 1978-82, prof. and dean emeritus, 1985—; v.p. acad. affairs, dean Scholl Coll. Podiatric Medicine, Chgo., 1985-87; liaison scientist Office of Naval Research, London, 1965-66; mem. physiology study sect. NIH, 1966-70; cons. Nat. Heart Inst. Contbr. chpts. to books; articles to profl. jours. in field of tissue metabolsim, temperature regulation and central Nervous system control of cardiovascular and respiratory systems. Served with M.C. U.S. Army, 1943-46. Decorated Purple Heart, Bronze Star; Royall Victor scholar, 1939-43; Markle Scholar in Acad. Medicine, 1953-58. Mem. AAAS, Am. Physiol. Soc., AMA, Council Med. Deans.

PEIXOTO, JOSE ULYSSES, internist, researcher; b. Crato, Ceará, Brazil, Aug. 29, 1930; s. Adérito de Aquino Silva and Adelite Alencar Peixoto; m. Maria Isolda Teles Cartaxo, May 23, 1958; children: Jose Ulysses Peixoto Filho, Eunice Ulysséia Peixoto Maia, Jorge André Cartaxo Peixoto. 1st degree, State Coll. Goias, Brazil, 1942, postgrad., 1942-49; 2d degree, St. John Coll., Fortaleza, Brazil, 1949; postgrad., Fed. U., Recife, Brazil, 1955; Laurel, Cearense Med. Ctr., 1994. Med. resident St. Michael Hosp., Rio de Janeiro, 1956; intern St. Anthony Hosp., Iguatú, Ceará, 1957; founder Social Providence, Crato, Ceará, 1958-64; attendent St. Frances Hosp., Crato, 1958-69; founder St. Michael Hosp., Crato, 1967-93, pres., dir., 1983-93, internist, researcher, 1993—; founder Faculty of Law, Crato, 1977-78; lectr. faculty of medicine The Fed. U. of Ceará, 1976—. Recipient Good Svc. award Lyons Club, 1992. laurel Cearense Med. Ctr., 1994. Fellow Brazilian Med. Assn. (specialist); mem. AAAS, ACP, Brazilian Soc. Clin. Medicine (specialist), N.Y. Acad. Sci. Roman Catholic. Avocations: reading, walking in woods, cinema, farming.

PEKARSKY, MELVIN HIRSCH, artist; b. Chgo., Sept. 18, 1934; s. Abe and Inda (Levin) P. Student, Sch. of Art Inst., Chgo., 1951-52; B.A., Northwestern U., 1955, M.A., 1956. Faculty Northwestern U., 1955-56; faculty Kendall Coll., 1960-67, chmn. art dept., 1965-67; asst. dean Sch. Visual Arts, N.Y.C., 1967-68; assoc. dean Sch. Visual Arts, 1968-69; grad. faculty NYU, 1970-71; assoc. prof. art SUNY, Stony Brook, 1975-84, prof. art, 1984—; chmn. dept. SUNY, 1977-78, 84-89. One-man shows include Gimpel and Weitzenhoffer, N.Y.C., 1974, Lehigh U., 1975, Ball State U. Gallery, Muncie, Ind., 1975, G.W. Einstein Co., Inc., N.Y.C., 1975, 77, 78, 80, 81, 82, 84, 86, 88, 91, 95, Hull Gallery, Washington, 1978, Centro Colombo-Americano, Bogotá, Colombia, 1980, 112 Greene St. Gallery, N.Y.C., 1980, 82, Marianne Deson Gallery, Chgo., 1987, Butler Inst. Am. Art, Youngstown, Ohio, 1990, The Mus. at Stony Brook, 1993; group shows include Chgo. Art Inst., 1966, Whitney Mus., N.Y.C., 1971, Bklyn. Mus., 1974, Cleve. Mus., 1978, Cooper-Hewitt Mus., 1971, Mus. Modern Art Corp.,Lending and Adv. Svc. Exhbns., Kuznetsky-Most Galleries, Moscow, 1989, NAD, N.Y.C., 1990, public murals commns., Houston and Crosby Sts., N.Y.C., 1972, Lafayette and Bleecker Sts., N.Y.C., 1969; represented in permanent collections, Cleve. Mus., Fogg Mus. Art, Harvard U., Indpls. Mus., Westinghouse Corp., Corcoran Gallery Art, Yale U., Notre Dame U., AT&T, Chase Manhattan Bank, other pub. and corp. collections, also pvt. collections. Founding mem., v.p., bd. dirs. City Walls, 1969-71. Served with Combat Engrs. AUS, 1957-59. Recipient grants in public art through City Walls Kaplan Fund, 1969, City Walls Bernhard Found., 1971, City Walls N.Y. State Council on Arts, 1970, City Walls Nat. Endowment for the Arts, 1971. Mem. Coll. Art Assn. Am. Home: PO Box 1575 Stony Brook NY 11790-0875 Office: SUNY Art Dept Stony Brook NY 11794-5400

PEKER, ELYA ABEL, artist; b. Moscow, June 15, 1937; came to U.S. 1972; s. Aba Z. and Frieda I. (Warshavsky) P.; m. Katrina Friedman, May 19, 1977; 1 child, Benjamin E. Diploma of Artist for Theater Design, Art Inst., Moscow, 1956. Comml. artist N.Y.C., 1972-88. One-man shows include Nakhamkin Fine Art Gallery, N.Y.C., 1980-85; exhibited in group shows in Basel, Switzerland, Hong Kong, others; represented in permanent collections of Kennedy-Onassis family, Emil Wolf, Frank L'Angella, Campbell family, Benjamin family, others; contemporary flower and still-life poster series published 1991, reproductions published worldwide. Mem. Am. Biog. Inst. (dep. gov., order internat. ambs., Gold Record Achievement 1995, 20th Century Achievement award 1995, Internat. Cultural Diploma Honor 1996), Internat. Platform Assn., Licensing Industry Merchandiser's Assn. Address: 1673 E 16th St Ste 164 Brooklyn NY 11229-2901

PÉLADEAU, MARIUS BEAUDOIN, art consultant, retired museum director; b. Boston, Jan. 27, 1935; s. Marius and Lucienne (Beaudoin) P.; m. Mildred L. Cole, Feb. 26, 1972. B.A. cum laude, St. Michael's Coll., 1956; M.S., Boston U., 1957; M.A., Georgetown U., 1962. Assoc. editor Public Utilities Fortnightly, Washington, 1962-66; adminstrv. asst., press sec. to U.S. Congressman J. P. Vigorito, Washington, 1967-72; dir. Maine League Hist. Socs. and Mus.'s, Monmouth, 1972-76, William A. Farnsworth Library and Art Mus., Rockland, Maine, 1976-87; gen. mgr. The Theater at Monmouth, Maine, 1989; cons. in field, 1990—. Author: The Verse of Royall Tyler, 1968, The Prose of Royall Tyler, 1972, Chansonetta: The Life and Photographs of Chansonetta Stanely Emmons, 1858-1937, 1977. Trustee Jones Mus. Glass and Ceramics; guest curator L.C. Bates Mus., Hinckley, Maine. Fellow Co. Mil. Historians; mem. Vt. Hist. Soc. Democrat. Roman Catholic.

PELADEAU, PIERRE, publishing company executive; b. Montreal, Apr. 11, 1925; s. Henri and Elmire (Fortier) P.; m. Raymonde Chopin, May 26, 1954; children: Eric, Isabelle, Pierre-Karl, Anne-Marie; m. Line Parisien, May 24, 1979; children: Esther, Pierre Jr., Jean. L.Ph., U. Montreal, 1945, M.A., 1947; B.C.L., McGill U., Montreal, 1950; Dr honoris cause, U. Que., U. Sherbrooke. With Quebecor Inc.; pub., printing and forest products holding co. exec. Quebecor Inc., Montreal, 1965—; editor, pres., chief exec. officer Quebecor Inc., 1965—; bd. dirs. Donohue Inc., Sodarcan Inc. 1st chancelor Ste.-Anne U., Novia Scotia, 1988. Mem. Order of Can., Nat. Order Que. Club: Saint-Denis. Office: Quebecor inc, 612 Rue Saint-Jacques ouest, Montreal, PQ Canada H3C 4M8

PELAEZ, MARC Y.E., federal official, career naval officer; b. Hollywood, Fla., Apr. 1, 1946; s. Genaro Julio Jr. and Odette (Delorme) P.; m. Sheila Prom, June 8, 1968; children: Jeannine Lynn, John Marc. Grad., U.S. Naval Acad., 1968. Commd. ensign USN, 1968, advanced through grades to rear adm., 1993; various assignments USS Bolivar, 1969-72; assignment officer submarine/nuclear power divsn. Naval Mil. Pers. Command, 1972-75; engr. officer USS Tunny, 1976-79; exec. officer USS James Monroe, 1979-80; asst. rsch. and devel. submarines Naval Sea Systems Command, Washington, 1981-83; mgr. advanced submarine combat system Naval Sea Systems Command; comdr. USS Sunfish, 1984-88; program mgr. advanced submarine tech. program, exec. asst. to asst. sec. of Navy for rsch., devel. and acquisition Def. Advanced Rsch. Projects Agy.; chief naval rsch. Dept. of Navy, Arlington, Va. Decorated Def. Superior Svc. Medal, Legion of Merit with gold star. Avocation: sailing. Office: Chief Of Naval Research 800 N Quincy St Arlington VA 22203-1906

PELAEZ, ROLANDO FEDERICO, economics educator, consultant; b. Washington, May 5, 1940; s. Rolando Juan and Maria Gertrudis (Bringuier) P. BS, La. State U., 1962, MA, 1964; PhD in Econs., U. Houston, 1973; postgrad., Rice U., 1978-79. Teaching fellow U. Houston-Univ. Park, 1970-71, instr., 1971-73; asst. prof. N.Mex. State U., 1973-74, Southeastern La. U., 1976; asst. prof. U. Houston-Downtown, 1977-80, assoc. prof. fin. Coll. Bus., 1987—; assoc. prof. U. St. Thomas, 1980-87; expert witness forensic economist; vis. asst. prof. U. Houston-Univ. Park, 1974-75; spkr., presenter confs. in field. Contbr. articles to profl. jours. OAS doctoral fellow, 1970. Mem. Am. Econ. Assn., Am. Statis. Assn., So. Finance Assn., Southwestern Econ. Assn., Southwestern Finance Assn., Western Econ. Assn., Nat. Assn. Forensic Economists. Home: 8318 Daycoach Ln Houston TX 77064-8202

PELANDINI, THOMAS FRANCIS, marketing executive; b. Vallejo, Calif., Jan. 6, 1938; s. Francis Lee and Betty (Tucker) P.; m. Sandra Lee Holmes, Sept. 17, 1961; children: Jennifer Lynn, Beth Ann. BA in Comm., U. Wash., Seattle, 1961. Dir. div. public relations Pepsi-Cola Co., N.Y.C. and Chgo., 1966-68; account supr. Patton Agy., Phoenix, 1968-70; v.p. Hill & Knowlton, Inc. (public relations), Los Angeles, 1970-72; corp. dir. communications Avco Corp., Greenwich, Conn., 1972-75; v.p. public affairs Crocker Nat. Bank, San Francisco, 1975-82; sr. v.p. Hoefer-Amidei, Inc., San Francisco, 1982-83; exec. v.p. Manning, Selvage & Lee, Inc., San Jose, Calif., 1983-85; sr. v.p. corp. affairs Austec, Inc., San Jose, 1986-88; pres., chief operating officer Austec, Inc., San Jose, CA, 1988-90; v.p. corp. com. Businessland Inc., San Jose, Calif., 1990-92; v.p. worldwide sales and mktg. Sitka Corp., Alameda, Calif., 1992-93; pres. Channel Focus (Europe) Ltd., Reading, U.K., 1993—. Bd. dirs. Diablo Community Service Dist. 1st lt. USAF, 1962-65. Mem. Diablo Country Club. Home: Thimble Farm Diablo CA 94528

PELAVIN, MICHAEL ALLEN, lawyer; b. Flint, Mich., Sept. 5, 1936; s. B. Morris and Betty (Weiss) P.; m. Natalie Katz, June 18, 1960; children: Mark, Gordon. Student U. Mich., 1954-55, Wayne State U., 1955-57; JD, Detroit Coll. Law, 1960. Bar: Mich. 1960, U.S. Tax Ct. 1966, U.S. Ct. Appeals (6th cir.) 1969, N.Y. 1989. Assoc. Pelavin & Powers, P.C. (now Pelavin, Powers & Behm P.C.), Flint, Mich., 1960-63, ptnr., 1963-71, pres., 1980—; trustee Mut. of Am. Life Ins. Co., 1981—; chair Nat. Jewish Community Rels. Adv. Coun., 1986-89. Chmn. young leadership cabinet United Jewish Appeal, 1973; pres. Flint Jewish Fedn., 1974-77; chmn. Bishop Internat. Airport Authority, 1990—. Mem. ABA, N.Y. State Bar Assn., Assn. Trial Lawyers Am., Mich. Bar Assn. Democrat. Home: 6168 Sierra Pass Flint MI 48532-2134 Office: Pelavin & Powers PC 801 S Saginaw St Flint MI 48502-1511

PELAVIN, SOL HERBERT, research company executive; b. Detroit, Dec. 16, 1941; s. Norman J. and Alice A. (Levinson) P.; m. Diane Christine Blakemore, Aug. 14, 1966; children: Shayna Beth, Adam Blake. BA in Math., U. Chgo., 1965, MAT in Math., 1969; MS in Stats., Stanford U., 1974, PhD candidate in mathematical models of edn. research, 1975. Tchr. pub. schs., 1965-70. teaching rsch. asst. Stanford (Calif.) U., 1972-74; cons. Rand Corp., Santa Monica, Calif., 1975; policy analyst SRI Internat., Menlo Park, Calif., 1975-78; exec. officer NTS Research Corp., Durham, N.C., 1978-82; pres. Pelavin Assocs., Inc., Washington, 1982-94; exec. v.p., CFO Am. Inst. Rsch., 1994—; dir. Data Analysis and Tech. Support Ctr., Washington, 1989-93, Policy Analysis Support Ctr., Washington, 1993—; expert witness to U.S. Congress, 1977, 79, Cabinet briefing, 1983; cons. Frank, Bernstein, Conway and Goldman, Balt., 1980-81; dir. Ednl. Analysis Ctr., Washington, 1982-85. Author: (with others) Investigation of the Impact of the Emergency School Assistance Porgrams on Black, Male 10th Grade Student Achievement, 1975, (with P. Barker) A Study of the Generalizability of the Results of Standardized Achievement Tests, 1976, (with J.L. David) Research on the Effectiveness of Compensatory Education Programs: A Reanalysis of Data, 1977, (with others) Federal Expenditures for the Education of Children and Youth With Special Needs, 1981, (with D.C. Pelavin) An Evaluation of the Fund for the Improvement of Postsecondary Education, 1981, 83, (with others) Evaluation of the Commodity Supplemental Food Program, 1982, An Evaluation of the Bilingual Education Evaluation, Dissemination and Assessment Centers, 1984, A Study of a Year-Round School Program, 1978, An Evaluation of the Indian Education Act, Title IV, Part C, Education for Indian Adults, 1984, Teacher Preparation: A Review of State Certification Requirements, 1984, Analysis of the National Availability of Mathematics and Science Teachers, 1983, Minority Participation in Higher Education, 1988, Changing the Odds, 1990, others; contbr. articles to profl. jours. NSF fellow U. Chgo., 1968-69; Cuneo fellow Stanford U., 1973. Mem. AAAS, Am. Ednl. Research Assn., Am. Psychol. Assn. Democrat. Jewish. Office: American Inst Rsch 3333 K St NW Washington DC 20007

PELC, KAROL I., engineering management educator, researcher; b. Czestochowa, Poland, July 29, 1935; came to U.S., 1985; s. Stanislaw Pelc and Kamilla (Hecko) Pelc-Kosna; m. Ryszarda Lidia Ryglewicz, Sept. 24, 1959; 1 child, Dariusz. MScEE, Tech. U. Wroclaw, Poland, 1958, PhD in Econs., 1976; PhD in Electronics, U. Uppsala, Sweden, 1968. Electronic design engr. Rsch. Inst. Tech. U. Wroclaw, Poland, 1957-60; prodn. & engring. mgr. Energopomiar Co., Wroclaw, 1960-65; rsch. asst. dept. electronics U. Uppsala, 1961-62; assoc. dir. div. Inst. Electric Power Industry, Wroclaw, 1966-68; rsch. dir. Tech. U. Wroclaw, 1968-77; founder, dir. Forecasting Rsch. Ctr., Wroclaw, 1971-81; lectr., dir. Jelenia Gora Coll. br. Tech. U. Wroclaw, 1982-85; prof. Mich. Technol. U., Houghton, 1985—; vis. prof. Indian Inst. Tech., Bombay, 1981, Stevens Inst. Tech., Hoboken, N.J., 1993; vis. scholar Japan Ctr. for Mich. Univs., Hikone, 1992; mem. innovation task force Internat. Inst. for Applied Systems Analysis, Laxenburg, Austria, 1983-84; chmn. forecasting seminar Polish Acad. Scis., Warsaw, 1974-81; v.p. div. Soc. Mgmt. and Orgn., Wroclaw, 1979-80. Author: Planning of Research and Development, 1981; mem. editl. bd. Technol. Forecasting and Social Change, U.S. R&D Mgmt., Eng., Transformations, Poland; contbr. more than 80 articles to scholarly jours.; patentee in field. Mem. Internat. Assn. Mgmt. Tech., Internat. Assn. for Rsch. and Devel. Mgmt., Am. Soc. Engring. Mgmt., Engring. Mgmt. Soc. of IEEE, Acad. Mgmt. Roman Catholic. Avocations: classical music, tourism, cross-country skiing, bicycling. Office: Mich Technol Univ Sch Bus & Engring Adminstrn Houghton MI 49931

PELCZAR, MICHAEL JOSEPH, JR., microbiologist, educator; b. Balt., Jan. 28, 1916; s. Michael Joseph and Josephine (Polek) P.; m. Merna M. Foss, Aug. 28, 1941; children: Ann Foss, Patricia Mary, Michael Rafferty, Rita Margaret, Josephine Merna, Julia Foss. BS, U. Md., 1936, MS, 1938; PhD, U. Iowa, 1941; DSc (hon.), Utah State U., 1986. Diplomate: Am. Bd. Microbiology. Instr. bacteriology U. Iowa, 1940-41; asst. prof., assoc. prof. bacteriology U. Md., College Park, 1946-50; prof. microbiology U. Md., 1950-78; prof. emeritus, 1978—, v.p. grad. studies and research, 1966-78, v.p. emeritus, 1978—; pres. Council Grad. Schs. in U.S., Washington, 1978-84; pres. emeritus Council Grad. Schs. in U.S., 1984—; mem. microbiology adv. panel Office Naval Rsch., 1965-70; spl. cons. Random House Dictionary of English Lang., 1965; councilor Oak Ridge Assoc. Univs., Inc., 1959-66; also bd. dirs.; mem. So. Regional Edn. Bd., Coun. Grad. Edn. in Agrl. Scis., 1967; mem. departmental com. on biol. scis. U.S. Dept. Agr. Grad. Sch., 1967-76; chmn. Spl. Meeting on Neisseria WHO, Geneva, Switzerland, 1964, mem. expert adv. panel on bacterial diseases, 1967-77; mem. Gov.'s Sci. Adv. Bd., 1967—, chmn., 1967-72; mem. organizing com. for XVII Gen. Assembly NRC, div. biology and agr. Internat. Union Biol. Scis., 1968; chmn. bd. on human resource data and analysis Commn. on Human Resources, NRC, 1975-79; mem. exec. com. Coun. Grad. Schs., 1976-78; mem. Nat. Sea Grant Rev. Panel, 1979-89; mem. adv. com. Nat. Rsch. Coun., 1987—. Co-author: Microbiology, 5th edit, 1986, Elements of Microbiology, 1981, Microbiology: Concepts and Applications, 1993; editorial bd.: Jour. of Bacteriology, 1965-69; Contbr. sect. to: Ency. Brit, 1969, 94; articles to profl. jours. Ency. Ednl. Research. Recipient Nat. Sea Grant Assn. award, 1991, ASM Disting. Svc. award, 1995. Fellow AAUP (past br. pres.). Nat. Adminstrn. Acad. Univ. Rsch. (founding mem. 1985); mem. AAAS, Am. Acad. Microbiology, Am. Inst. Biol. Scis. (bd. govs., past vis. lectr.), Am. Soc. Microbiology (bd. govs., past com. chmn., councilor, br. pres., hon. mem. 1986—), Internat. Assn. Microbiology, Washington Acad. Scis., Nat. Assn. State Univs. and Land-Grant Colls. (chmn. coun. for rsch. policy and adminstrn., cons. higher edn. rsch. adminstrn.), Cosmos Club, Phi Beta Kappa (assoc. 1989), Sigma Xi (ann. award sci. achievement 1968), Phi Kappa Phi, Sigma Alpha Omicron. Research microbial physiology. Home: PO Box 133 300 Avalon Farm Ln Chester MD 21619

PELÉ (EDSON ARANTES DO NASCIMENTO), professional soccer player; b. Três Coracões, Minas Gerais, Brazil, Oct. 23, 1940; came to U.S., 1975; s. João Ramos do Nascimento and Celeste Arantes; m. Rosemeri Cholbi, Feb. 21, 1966 (div.); children: Kely Cristina, Edson, Jennifer; m. Assiria Lemos, April 30, 1994. Grad. in phys. edn., Santos U., 1972. Soccer player with Santos Football Club, Sao Paulo, 1956-74, N.Y. Cosmos,

N.Y.C., 1975-77; chmn. Pepsi Internat. Youth Soccer Program, 1972—; pres. Empresas Pelé, Santos; chmn. Pelé Soccer Camps, 1978—; dir. soccer clinics. Author: Eu Sou Pelé, 1962, Jogando com Pelé, 1974, My Life and the Beautiful Game, 1977, Pelé Soccer Training Program, 1982; appeared in: films Eu sou Pelé, 1964, A Marcha, 1973, Istoé Pelé, 1974, Pelé, The Master and His Method, 1973, Pelé's New World, 1975, Pelé, 1977, Os Trombadinhas, 1979, Victory, 1981, A Minor Miracle, 1983, Hot Shot, 1985; composer: numerous songs in Samba style including Saudacão Criança, 1969, Vexamão, 1970; soundtrack for film Pelé, 1977. Active Spl. Olympics, 1978—. Served with Brazilian Army, 1958. Recipient Internat. Peace award, 1978, WHO medal, 1989; named Athlete of Century, 1980. Player 4 World Cups, 1958, 62, 66, 70, won 3 times, Brazilian Nat. Team, 1957-71; scored 1, 282 goals (1,364 games) total; 1088 goals (1114 games) for Santos Football Club, 97 goals (111 games) for Brazilian Nat. Team, 65 goals (108 games) for Cosmos. Address: 75 Rockefeller Plz New York NY 10019-6908*

PELED, ABRAHAM, computer company executive; b. Suceava, Romania, Sept. 21, 1945; came to U.S., 1971; s. Leon and Laura (Pachter) B.; m. Judith Oberndorf, Aug. 22, 1967; 1 child, Daphna. BSEE, Technion U., Israel, 1967, MSEE, 1970; MAEE, Princeton U., 1973, PhDEE, 1974. Postdoctoral fellow IBM, Yorktown Heights, N.Y., 1974-76; mem. rsch. staff Haifa (Israel) Sci. Ctr. IBM, 1976-78; mgr. signal process T.J. Watson Rsch. Ctr. IBM, Yorktown Heights, 1978-80; function mgr. CS dept. San Jose (Calif.) Rsch. Lab. IBM, 1980-83; dir. tech. planning rsch. dir. IBM, Yorktown Heights, 1983-85, v.p. rsch. systems and software rsch. div., 1985-93; sr. v.p. bus. devel. Elron Electronic Industries, Haifa, Israel, 1993-95; CEO News Digital Syss., Ltd., London, 1995—. Author: Digital Signal Processing, 1976. Tech. officer Israeli Army Signal Corps, 1967-71. Fellow IEEE; mem. Univs. Space Rsch. Assn. (trustee 1987-92), Nat. Rsch. Coun. (elected mem. computer sci. and tech. bd. 1989-93).

PELHAM, FRAN O'BYRNE, writer, teacher; b. Phila., Oct. 16, 1939; d. Frederick Thomas and Frances Rebecca (Johns) O'Byrne; m. Donald Lacey Pelham, June 15, 1968; children: Mary Frances, Michael. BA, Holy Family Coll., 1967; M in English Edn., Trenton Coll., 1974; EdD, U. Pa., 1993. Cert. secondary tchr. Tchr. Sch. Dist. Bristol (Pa.) Twp., 1967-70; feature writer various publs., Phila. and others, 1980—; prof., dir. Writing Ctr. Holy Family Coll., Phila., 1982-89; asst. prof. lit. and writing LaSalle U., Phila., 1989—; dir. tech. communications Internat. Chem. Co., Phila., 1985-90; speaker, workshop leader various orgns. Author: Search for Atocha Treasure, 1989, Downtown America: Philadelphia, 1989; contbr. articles to mags. Participant Home and Sch. Assn., Jenkintown, Pa., 1983, Jenkintown Arts Festival, 1984, Campus Ministry Team Holy Family Coll., Phila., 1986-89, Alliance for a Living Ocean, 1991—, Phila. Children's Reading Roundtable, Authors Guild. Recipient Citation Mayor's Commn., 1988. Mem. Nat. Coun. Tchrs. Eng., Am. Conf. Irish Studies, Nat. League Am. Pen Women (br. pres. 1982-84), Phila. Writers' Conf. (bd. dirs. 1982-86), Pi Lambda Theta, Lambda Iota Tau, Phi Delta Kappa. Democrat. Roman Catholic. Avocations: scuba diving, tennis, boating, travel. Office: LaSalle U Olney Ave Philadelphia PA 19120

PELHAM, JUDITH, hospital administrator; b. Bristol, Conn., July 23, 1945; d. Marvin Curtis and Muriel (Chodos) P.; m. Jon N. Coffee, Dec. 30, 1992; children: Rachel, Molly, Edward. BA, Smith Coll., 1967; MPA, Harvard U., 1975. Various govt. postions, 1968-72; prin. analyst Urban Systems, Cambridge, Mass., 1972-73; dir. devel. and planning Roxbury Dental and Med. Group, Boston, 1975-76; asst. to dir. for gen. medicine and ambulatory care Peter B. Brigham Hosp., Boston, 1976-77, asst. dir. ambulatory care, 1977-79; asst. v.p. Brigham and Women's Hosp., Boston, 1980-81; dir. planning and mktg. Seton Med. Ctr., Austin, Tex., 1980-82, pres., 1982-92, chief exec. officer, 1987-92; pres., chief exec. officer Daughters of Charity Health Services, Austin, 1987-92; pres. Mercy Health Svcs., Farmington Hills, Mich., 1993—; cons. Robert W. Johnson Found., 1979-80; bd. dirs. Mercy Health Svcs., Healthcare Forum, Amgen, Mercy Health Found., Am. Healthcare Sys.; mem. mgmt. bd. Inst. for Diversity in Health Mgmt., 1994—. Author: Financial Management of Ambulatory Care, 1985; contbr. articles to profl. jours. Trustee A. Shivers Radiation Therapy Ctr., Austin, 1982-92, Marywood Maternity and Adoption Agy., 1982-86; bd. dirs. Quality of Life Found., Austin, 1985, Austin Rape Crisis Ctr., adv. bd., 1986-88; bd. dirs., trustee League House, 1982-93, Seton Fund, 1982-93, Greater Detroit Area Haelth Coun., 1994—; mem. Gov's Job Tng. Coordinating Council, 1983-85; adv. council U. Tex. Social Work Found., 1983-85; charter mem. Leadership Tex., Austin, 1983-93. Recipient Leadership award YWCA, Austin, 1986. Mem. Am. Coll. Healthcare Execs., Am. Hosp. Assn., Tex. Hosp. Assn. (mem. various coms. 1982-87), Austin Area Rsch. Orgn., Tex. Conf. Health Facilities (bd. dirs. 1985-89, pres. 1988), Cath. Health Assn. (bd. dirs. 1987-95, com. on govt. rels. 1984-91, sec., treas. 1982-95, chair fin. com. 1992-95). Office: Mercy Health Svcs 34605 W 12 Mile Rd Farmington Hills MI 48331

PELHAM, THOMAS GERALD, lawyer; b. Hartford, Ala., Nov. 23, 1943; s. Roy W. and Annie Louise (Blackburn) P.; m. Vivian Holden, Feb. 1, 1969; children: Christopher Holden, Evan Blackburn. BA, Fla. State U., 1965; MA, Duke U., 1967; JD, Fla. State U., 1971; LLM, Harvard U., 1977. Bar: Fla. 1971. Ptnr. Brown, Smith, Young & Pelham, Tallahassee, 1971-76; prof. law So. Meth. U., Dallas, 1977-80; ptnr. Carlton Fields Law Firm, Tallahassee, 1980-82, Akerman, Senterfitt & Edison, Tallahassee, 1982-84, Culpepper, Pelham, Turner & Mannheimer, Tallahassee, 1985-87; sec. Fla. Dept. Community Affairs, Tallahassee, 1987-91; ptnr. Holland & Knight, Tallahassee, 1991-93, Apgar & Pelham, Tallahassee, 1993—; adj. prof. law Fla. State U., Tallahassee, 1992—; chmn. bd. dirs. Legal Environ. Assistance Found., Tallahassee; mem. Gov.'s Environ. Land Mgmt. Study Com., Tallahassee, 1992. Author: State Land Use Planning and Regulation, 1979. Mem. Tallahassee-Leon County Planning Com., 1985-87, Capitol Ctr. Planning Commn., Tallahassee, 1982-85. Recipient Govtl. Conservationist of Yr. award Fla. Audubon Soc., 1990, Spl. Friend of Fla. award 1000 Friends of Fla., 1988, 90, Person of Yr. award Fla. Environ. Mag., 1990. Mem. ABA (state and local law sect.), Fla. Bar (chmn. environ. and lang use law sect. 1990-91), Am. Planning Assn. (Fla. chpt. v.p. chpt. affairs 1992-94, pres.-elect 1994—), Econ. Club Fla. Avocations: reading, travel, jazz, movies, jogging. Office: Apgar & Pelham 909 E Park Ave Tallahassee FL 32301-2646

PELIAS, NATALIE ANNE, employment consultant; b. New Orleans, Oct. 31, 1950; d. James Michael and Esther (Daley) Pelias; m. David Michael Herman, Dec. 11, 1991. Diploma, U. Grenoble, France, 1966; student, U. New Orleans, 1968-72. Adminstrv. asst. Prudential Bache, New Orleans, 1976-78; account exec. Acctg. Pers. Cons., New Orleans, 1978-80; ptnr. Glover-Pelias, New Orleans, 1980-82; pres. Pelias & Assocs., New Orleans/Louisville, 1982—; condr. workshops and seminars in field. Vol. WYES Pub. TV, New Orleans, 1976-78. Recipient Citizenship award DAR, 1964; named to Hon. Order of Ky. Cols., one of Outstanding Young Women of Am., 1984. Mem. Nat. Assn. Pers. Cons. (cert. CPC, life). Greek Orthodox. Avocations: literature, music, archaeology.

PELIKAN, JAROSLAV JAN, history educator; b. Akron, Ohio, Dec. 17, 1923; s. Jaroslav Jan and Anna (Buzek) P.; m. Sylvia Burica, June 9, 1946; children: Martin, Michael, Miriam. Grad. summa cum laude, Concordia Jr. Coll., Ft. Wayne, Ind., 1942; BD, Concordia Theol. Sem., St. Louis, 1946; PhD, U. Chgo., 1946; MA (hon.), Yale U., 1961; DD (hon.), Concordia Coll., Moorehead, Minn., 1960, Concordia Sem., 1967, Trinity Coll., Hartford, Conn., 1987, St. Vladimir's Orthodox Theol. Sem., 1988, Victoria U., Toronto, 1989, U. Aberdeen, Scotland, 1995; LittD (hon.), Wittenberg U., 1960, Wheeling Coll., 1966, Gettysburg Coll., 1967, Pacific Luth. U., 1967, Wabash Coll., 1988, Jewish Theol. Sem., 1991; HHD (hon.), Providence Coll., 1966, Moravian Coll., 1986, Jewish Theol. Sem., 1991; LLD (hon.), Keuka Coll., 1967, U. Notre Dame, 1979; LHD (hon.), Valparaiso U., 1966, Rockhurst Coll., 1967, Albertus Magnus Coll., 1973, Coe Coll., 1976, Cath. U. Am., 1977, St. Mary's Coll., 1978, St. Anselm Coll., 1983, U. Nebr.-Omaha, 1984, Tulane U., 1986, Assumption Coll., 1986, LaSalle U., 1987, Carthage Coll., 1991, U. Chgo., 1991, So. Meth. U., 1992, SUNY, Albany, 1993; ThD (hon.), U. Hamburg, 1971, St. Olaf Coll., 1972; STD, Dickinson Coll., 1986; DSc in Hist., Comenius U., Bratislava, 1992; ScD (hon.), Loyola U., Chgo., 1995. Faculty Valparaiso (Ind.) U., 1946-49, Concordia Sem., St. Louis, 1949-53, U. Chgo., 1953-62; Titus Street prof. eccles. history Yale U., 1962-72, Sterling prof. history, 1972—, William Clyde DeVane lectr., 1984-86, dir. div. humanities, 1974-75, chmn. Medieval studies, 1974-75, 78-80, dean Grad. Sch., 1973-78; Gray lectr. Duke U., 1960, Ingersoll lectr. Harvard U., 1963, Gauss lectr. Princeton U., 1980, Jefferson lectr. NEH, 1983, Richard lectr. U. Va., 1984, Rauschenbusch lectre. Colgate-Rochester Divinity Sch., 1984, Gilson lectr. U. Toronto, 1985, Hale lectr. Seabury-Western Sem., 1986, Mead-Swing lectr. Oberlin Coll., 1986, Gross lectr. Rutgers U., 1989; bd. dirs. Nat. Humanities Ctr., 1984-90, Univ. Support Svcs. Inc., 1992—; adv. bd. Ctr. Theol. Inquiry, 1984-90; mem. coun. The Smithsonian Instn., 1984-90; U.S. chmn. U.S. Czechoslovak Commn. on Humanities and Social Scis., 1987—. Author: From Luther to Kierkegaard, 1950, Fools for Christ, 1955, The Riddle of Roman Catholicism, 1959 (Abingdon award 1959), Luther the Expositor, 1959, The Shape of Death, 1961, The Light of the World, 1962, Obedient Rebels, 1964, The Finality of Jesus Christ in an Age of Universal History, 1965, The Christian Intellectual, 1966, Spirit Versus Structure, 1968, Development of Doctrine, 1969, Historical Theology, 1971, The Christian Tradition, 5 vols., 1971-89, Scholarship and Its Survival, 1983, The Vindication of Tradition, 1984, Jesus through the Centuries, 1985, The Mystery of Continuity, 1986, Bach Among the Theologians, 1986, The Excellent Empire, 1987, The Melody of Theology, 1988, Confessor Between East and West, 1990, Imago Dei, 1990, Eternal Feminines, 1990, The Idea of the University: A Reexamination, 1992, Christianity and Classical Culture, 1993, Faust the Theologian, 1995, The Reformation of the Bible/ The Bible of the Reformation, 1996, Mary through the Centuries, 1996, also introductions to works of others; editor, translator: Luther's Works, 22 vols., 1955-71, The Book of Concord, 1959; editor: Makers of Modern Theology, 5 vols., 1966-68, The Preaching of Chrysostom, 1967, Interpreters of Luther, 1968, Twentieth-Century Theology in the Making, 3 vols., 1969-70, The Preaching of Augustine, 1973, The World Treasury of Modern Religious Thought, 1991, Sacred Writings, 7 vols., 1992; mem. editorial bd. Collected Works of Erasmus, Classics of Western Spirituality, Evangelisches Kirchenlexikon, Emerson's Nature, 1986, The World Treasury of Modern Religious Thought, 1990; departmental editor Ency. Britannica, 1958-69; adminstrv. bd. Papers of Benjamin Franklin; chmn. publs. com. Yale Univ. Press, 1979-90, 92—, v.p. bd. govs., 1988—; contbr. to many sym, jours., encys. Pres. 4th Internat. Congress for Luther Research, 1971, New Eng. Congress on Grad. Edn., 1976-77. Recipient Abingdon award, 1959; Pax Christi award St. John's U., Collegeville, Minn., 1966, Colman J. Barry award, 1995; John Gilmary Shea prize Am. Cath. Hist. Assn., 1971, nat. award Slovak World Congress, 1973, religious book award Cath. Press Assn., 1974, Christian Unity award Atonement Friars, 1975, Bicentennial award Czechoslovak Soc. Arts and Scis., 1976, Wilbur Cross medal Yale U. Grad. Sch. Assn., 1979, Profl. Achievement award U. Chgo. Alumni Assn., 1980, Shaw medal Boston Coll., 1984, Comenius medal Moravian Coll., 1986, Alumnus of Yr. award U. Chgo. Div. Sch., 1986, Bicentennial medal Georgetown U., 1989, award for excellence Am. Acad. Religion 1989, Umanità award Newberry Libr., 1990; recipient Festschrift: Schools of Thought in the Christian Tradition, 1984; sr. fellow Carnegie Found. for Advancement Tchg., 1982-83. Fellow Medieval Acad. Am. (councillor, Haskins medal 1985); mem. Am. Hist. Assn., Am. Soc. Ch. History (pres. 1965), Internat. Congress Luther Rsch. (pres. 1971), Am. Acad. Arts and Scis. (v.p. 1976-94, pres. 1994), Am. Philos. Soc. (councillor 1984-87), Coun. Scholars of Libr. of Congress (founding chmn. 1980-83), Elizabethan Club, Mory's, Phi Beta Kappa (senator United chpts. 1985-90). Home: 156 Chestnut Ln Hamden CT 06518-1604 Office: Yale U Dept History 1504A Yale Sta New Haven CT 06520-7425

PELISEK, FRANK JOHN, lawyer; b. Wauwatosa, Wis., June 8, 1930; s. Frank Pelisek and Virginia Pancost; m. Jane Olga Bauman (div.), Susan M., David P.; m. Jill Ann Grootemaat, Apr. 4, 1975. BS in Econs., U. Wis., 1954, LLB, 1958; D in Comml. Sci. (hon.), U. Wis., Milw., 1990. Sr. ptnr. Michael, Best & Friedrich, Milw., 1958—. 1st lt. U.S. Army, 1954-56. Office: Michael Best & Friedrich 100 E Wisconsin Ave Milwaukee WI 53202-4107

PELL, ARTHUR ROBERT, human resources development consultant, author; b. N.Y.C., Jan. 22, 1920; s. Harry and Rae (Meyers) P.; m. Erica Frost, May 19, 1946; children—Douglas, Hilary. AB, NYU, 1939, MA, 1944; PhD, Calif. Coast U., 1977; profl. diploma, Cornell U., 1943. Personnel dir. Eagle-Electric Mfg. Co., Long Island City, N.Y., 1946-50, North Atlantic Constructors, N.Y.C., 1950-53; v.p. Harper Assos., Inc (personnel consultants), N.Y.C., 1953-75; cons. Human Resources Mgmt., 1975—; adj. asso. prof. mgmt. Sch. Continuing Edn., NYU, 1962-84; lectr. Baruch Sch. Bus. and Pub. Adminstrn. Coll. City N.Y., 1948-67; adj. asso. prof. mgmt. Coll. Bus. Adminstrn., St. John's U., 1971-76. Author: (with W.B. Patterson) Fire Officer's Guide to Leadership, rev. edit., 1963, Placing Salesmen, 1963, Placing Executives, 1964, Police Leadership, 1967, How to Get the Job You Want After 40, 1967, Recruiting and Selecting Personnel, 1969, (with M. Harper) Starting and Managing an Employment Agency, 1970, Recruiting, Training and Motivating Volunteer Workers, 1972, Be a Better Employment Interviewer, 1972, rev. edits., 1978, 86, 94, The College Graduate Guide to Job Finding, 1973, (with Wilma Rogalin) Women's Guide to Executive Positions, 1975, (with Albert Furbay) College Student's Guide to Career Planning, 1975, (with Dale Carnegie Assocs.) Managing Through People, 1975, rev. edits., 1978, 1987, Choosing a College Major: Business, 1978, Enrich Your Life: The Dale Carnegie Way, 1979, The Part Time Job Book, 1984, Making the Most of Medicare, 1987, rev. edit., 1990, (with George Sadek) Resumes for Engineers, 1982, Resumes for Computer Professionals, 1984, How to Sell Yourself on an Interview, 1982, The Job Finder's Kit, 1989, Getting the Most from Your People, 1990, Diagnosing Your Doctor, 1991, The Supervisor's Infobank, 1994; editorial cons. for revision Dale Carnegie's How to Win Friends and Influence People, 1981; author syndicated feature The Human Side; also articles. Served with AUS, 1942-46. Office: 111 Dietz St Hempstead NY 11550-7625

PELL, CLAIBORNE, senator; b. N.Y.C., Nov. 22, 1918; s. Herbert Claiborne and Matilda (Bigelow) P.; m. Nuala O'Donnell, Dec. 1944; children: Herbert Claiborne III, Christopher T. Hartford, Nuala Dallas Yates, Julia L.W. Student, St. George's Sch., Newport, R.I.; A.B. cum laude, Princeton U., 1940; A.M., Columbia U., 1946; 46 hon. degrees. Enlisted USCGR, 1941; served as seaman, ensign North Atlantic sea duty, Africa, Italy; hospitalized to U.S., 1944; instr. Navy Sch. Mil. Govt., Princeton, 1944-45; capt. USCGR; ret.; on loan to State Dept. at San Francisco Conf., 1945, State Dept., 1945-46, U.S. embassy, Czechoslovakia, 1946-47; established consulate gen. Bratislava, Czechoslovakia, 1947-48; vice consul Genoa, Italy, 1949; assigned State Dept., 1950-52; v.p., dir. Internat. Rescue Com.; senator from R.I., 1961-96; ranking minority mem. Fgn. Rels. Com., Labor and Human Resources Subcom. on Edn., Arts, and Humanities; mem. Rules and Adminstrn. Com., Joint Com. on Libr. and Congl. Intern Program, Senate Dem. Policy Com.; U.S. del. Internat. Maritime Consultative Orgn., London, 1959, 25th Gen. Assembly, 1970. Author: Megalopolis Unbound, 1966, (with Harold L. Goodwin) Challenge of the Seven Seas, 1966, Power and Policy, 1972. Hon. bd. dirs. World Affairs Council R.I.; trustee St. George's Sch.; trustee emeritus Brown U.; Cons. Democratic Nat. Com., 1953-60; exec. asst. to chmn. R.I. State Dem. Com., 1952-54; chmn. R.I. Dem. Fund drive, 1952, Dem. nat. registration, chmn., 1956, co-chmn., 1962; chief delegation tally clk. Dem. Nat. Conv., 1956, 60, 64, 68. Decorated knight Crown of Italy, Grand Cross Order of Merit Italy, Red Cross of Merit Portugal, Legion of Honor France, comdr. Order of Phoenix Greece, Grand Cross Order of Merit Liechtenstein, Grand Cross Order of Christ Portugal, Order of Henry the Navigator, Portugal, Grand Cross Order of N. Star Sweden, Grand Cross of Merit Knights of Malta, Grand Officer of Merit Luxembourg, Grand Comdr. Lebanon; recipient Caritas Elizabeth medal Cardinal Franz Koenig, Grand decoration of honor in silver with sash Austria, Gold medal of St. Barnabas (Cyprus), recipient Pres.'s Fellow award R.I. Sch. Design, medal Nat. Order of Cedar, Hugo Grotius Commemorative medal The Netherlands, recipient Harold W. McGraw, Jr. Prize in Education, McGraw-Hill, 1988. Mem. Soc. Cin. Episcopalian. Clubs: Hope (Providence); Knickerbocker (N.Y.C.), Racquet and Tennis (N.Y.C.), Brook (N.Y.C.); Metropolitan (Washington); Travellers (Paris); Reading Room (Newport); White's (London). Office: US Senate 335 Russell Senate Bldg Washington DC 20510 *I have a seven word definition of my job and of my life: "Translate ideas into events, and help people.".**

PELL, DANIEL MAX, lawyer; b. N.Y.C., July 19, 1949; s. Joseph C. and Hazel (Kowitz) P.; m. Joan Kohler, 1982 (dec. 1985); 1 child, Max Andrew. BA in Psychology, Lafayette Coll., 1971; JD, DePaul U., 1975. Bar: Pa., Md., Ill. U.S. Dist. Ct. (mid. and ea. dists.) Pa., U.S. Ct. Appeals (3d cir.), U.S. Supreme Ct. Pvt. practice, York, Pa.; bd. dirs., mem. exec. com. Ctrl. Pa. Legal Svcs., Lancaster, 1988-94; mem. fed. pub. defender's panel U.S. Dist. Ct. for Mid. Dist. Pa., 1985—; gen. counsel Wireless Telecom., Inc., York, 1994—. Active Internat. Campaign for Tibet, 1994-95. Mem. Pa. Bar Assn., York County Bar Assn. (pro bono rep. Chinese detainees of Golden Venture 1994—). Avocation: photography. Office: 309 E Market St York PA 17403

PELL, JONATHAN LAURENCE, artistic administrator; b. Memphis, Oct. 20, 1949; s. Burton Marshall and Eleanor (Leopold) P. BA, U. So. Calif., 1971. Interior designer Gene Morse Assocs., Wichita, Kans., 1971-77; mgr. Internat. Artists Mgmt., N.Y.C., 1977-79, Robert Lombardo Assocs., N.Y.C., 1979-80; TV producer Sta. WNET, N.Y.C., 1980-83; dir. artistic administration The Dallas Opera, 1984—; dir. publicity John Curry Skating Co., N.Y.C., 1983; prodr. Jerome Kern Centennary Gala Town Hall, N.Y.C., 1984; vocal competition judge Pavarotti Competition, Ctr. for Contemporary Opera, Marguerite McCammon Competition, San Antonio Opera Guild, Richard Tucker award, others; tchr. master classes for young singers Can. Opera Co., S.W. Chpt. NATS. Scenic and Costume designer for plays, musicals and ballets for various cos., 1970-76; host The Dallas Opera Radio Hour, WRR, 1994—. Mem. Richard Tucker award selection com. Mem. Opera Am. Office: Dallas Opera 3102 Oak Lawn Ave Ste 450 Dallas TX 75219-4259

PELL, WILBUR FRANK, JR., federal judge; b. Shelbyville, Ind., Dec. 6, 1915; s. Wilbur Frank and Nelle (Dickerson) P.; m. Mary Lane Chase, Sept. 14, 1940; children: Wilbur Frank III, Charles Chase. A.B., Ind. U., 1937, LL.D. (hon.), 1981; LL.B. cum laude, Harvard U., 1940; LL.D., Yonsei U., Seoul, Korea, 1972, John Marshall Sch. Law, 1973. Bar: Ind. 1940. Pvt. practice Shelbyville, 1940-42, 45-70; spl. agt. FBI, 1942-45; sr. ptnr. Pell & Good, 1949-56, Pell & Matchett, 1956-70; judge U.S. Ct. Appeals (7th cir.), 1970—, now sr. judge; mem. 3 judge spl. divsn. U.S. Ct. Appeals (D.C. cir.), appointing ind. counsel, 1987-92; dep. atty. gen., Ind., 1953-55; dir., chmn. Shelby Nat. Bank, 1947-70. Bd. dirs. Shelbyville Community Chest, 1947-49, Shelby County Fair Assn., 1951-53; dir. Shelby County Tb Assn., 1948-70, pres., 1965-66; dist. chmn. Boy Scouts Am., 1956-57; mem. pres.'s council Nat. Coll. Edn., 1972-87; dir. Westminster Found., Ind. U.; hon. dir. Korean Legal Center. Fellow Am. Coll. Probate Counsel, Am. Bar Found.; mem. ABA (judge Edward R. Finch Law Day USA Speech award 1973), Ind. Bar Assn. (pres. 1962-63, chmn. ho. of dels. 1968-69), Fed. Bar Assn., Ill. Bar Assn., Shelby County Bar Assn. (pres. 1957-58), 7th Fed. Cir. Bar Assn., Am. Judicature Soc., Am. Coun. Assn., Shelby County C. of C., Nat. Conf. Bar Pres.'s, Riley Meml. Assn., Ind. Soc. Chgo. (pres. 1978-79), Harvard Law Soc. Ill. (pres. 1980-81), Rotary (dist. gov. 1952-53, internat. dir 1959-61), Union League, Legal Club (pres. Chgo. 1976-77), Law Club (pres. Chgo. 1984-85), Kappa Sigma, Alpha Phi Omega, Theta Alpha Phi, Tau Kappa Alpha, Phi Alpha Delta (hon.). Republican. Presbyterian (elder, deacon). Office: US Ct Appeals 7th Cir 219 S Dearborn St Ste 2760 Chicago IL 60604-1803 *I have been fortunate - fortunate in having for 55 years a supportive, loving wife, for being selected for the President of the State Bar Association when the nominating committee was split between two others, for being selected as a Federal Judge although never in political office when one was expected to get the position.*

PELLA, MILTON ORVILLE, retired science educator; b. Wilmot, Wis., Feb. 13, 1914; s. Charles August and Ida Marie (Pagel) P.; m. Germaine Marie Reich, Dec. 9, 1944. B.E., Milw. State Tchrs. Coll., 1936; M.S., U. Wis., 1940, Ph.D., 1948. Tchr. sci. and math. Wyler Mil. Acad., 1937-38; tchr. elementary sch. Delavan Pub. Schs., 1938-39; tchr. sci. U. Wis. High Sch., 1939-42; prof. sci. edn. U. Wis., Madison, 1946-80, prof. emeritus, 1980—; With Fgn. Ednl. Service, Turkey, 1959, Iran, Turkey, Jordan, Syria, Lebanon, 1961, 62, Jordan, Lebanon, 1963, 64, 65, 66, 68, Costa Rica, 1967, Saudi Arabia, 1969, Nigeria, 1968, 69, Lebanon and Egypt, 1971-81. Author: Physical Science for Progress, 3d edit, 1970, Science Horizons—The Biological World, (with Branley and Urban), 1965-70. Served with AUS, 1942-46. Fellow A.A.A.S.; mem. Central Assn. Sci. and Math. (pres. 1955), Nat. Assn. for Research in Sci. Teaching (pres. 1966), Nat. Sci. Tchrs. Assn. (dir. 1950, 60). Club: Masons. Home: 5518 Varsity Hl Madison WI 53705-4652

PELLECCHIA, EVE WASSALL, management consultant; b. Columbus, Ohio, Dec. 7, 1956; d. Robert Byron Wassall and Constance Leona (Windey) Moult; m. Dennis John Pellecchia, Oct. 29, 1983; children: Kevin Patrick, Kara René. BS, Lebanon Valley Coll., 1978; MBA, Lehigh U., 1983. CFP. Ops. rsch. analyst Air Products & Chems., Inc., Trexlertown, Pa., 1978-83; ops. rsch. mng. analyst Air Products & Chems., Inc., Trexlertown, 1984-87, ops. rsch. mgr. gas. div., 1987-88; pvt. practice Wyomissing, Pa., 1990—. Mem. Reading Hosp. Aux., Wyomissing, 1987—; fundraiser Am. Heart Assn., 1991—. Avocations: skiing, tennis, photography, horseback riding. Home: 102 Robert Rd Wyomissing PA 19610-3116

PELLEGRENE, THOMAS JAMES, JR., editor, researcher; b. Wilmington, Del., Dec. 26, 1959; s. Thomas J. and MaryBelle (McGowan) P.; m. Pamela Heinecke, Apr. 5, 1986. BS in Journalism, Northwestern U., 1981, MS in Journalism, 1982. Staff writer Ft. Wayne (Ind.) Journal-Gazette, 1982-87, bus. editor, 1987-95, asst. metro editor, 1995—. Mem. Soc. Profl. Journalists. Office: Fort Wayne Journal-Gazette 600 W Main St Fort Wayne IN 46802-1408

PELLEGRIN, GILLES GEORGE, lawyer; b. Paris, Mar. 8, 1952; s. Jacques Robert Pellegrin and Nicole Deret; m. Litzie E. Gozlan, Dec. 22, 1981; children: Vanessa, Raphael. Cert., Inst. for Internat. and Fgn., Trade Law/Georgetown U., 1977; Dess de Droit des Rels. Comml. Indsl., U. Paris, 1977; M Comparative Jurisprudence, NYU, 1978. Assoc. Mudge, Rose, Guthrie & Alexander, N.Y.C., 1977, Debost, Borel, Carpentier & Falques, Paris, 1978; European counsel Tex. Instruments, Villeneuve-Louvet, France, 1980-84; legal advisor of the chmn. and CEO Honda France, Marne-La-Vallee, France, 1984-87; gen. counsel Sema Group, Montrouge, France/London, 1987-90; corp. gen. counsel Bull S.A., Paris, 1990—. Avocations: tennis, fencing, swimming, skiing, theater. Home: 170 Tremont Str Boston MA 02111 Office: Bull HN Info Systems Inc 300 Concord Rd Billerica MA 01821

PELLEGRINI, ANNA MARIA, soprano; b. Pretoro, Chieti, Italy, July 15, 1944; arrived in Can., 1959, naturalized, 1964; d. Vincenzo and Giuseppina (Pietrantonio) P.; m. Steven Murray Thomas, Aug. 13, 1974; 1 son, Vincent Thomas. Student, U. Toronto, Ont., Can., Faculty of Music, 1962-65. Tchr. voice Italian repertoire. Debut as Gilda in Rigoletto, Can. Opera Co., 1965; leading roles in: Cosi Fan Tutte, La Boheme, Turandot, I Pagliacci, Elektra; title roles in: Madama Butterfly, Manon Lescaut, Can. Broadcasting Corp. TV prodn. Madama Butterfly, 1977; appeared in maj. opera houses throughout the world. Recipient prize Met. Opera Nat. Auditions, 1966, Caravello d'Oro Ufficio Di Turismo, Genova, 1970, medallion honoring her and Puccini Sindico di Teatro Comunale di Treviso, 1974. Mem. Can. Actors Equity, Brit. Equity, Que. (Can.) Union des Artistes, Am. Guild Mus. Artists, Assn. Can. TV and Radio Artists. Office: Sardos Artist Mngmt Corp 180 W End Ave New York NY 10023-4902

PELLEGRINI, ROBERT J., psychology educator; b. Worcester, Mass., Oct. 21, 1941; s. Felix and Teresa (Di Muro) P.; 1 child, Robert Jerome. BA in Psychology, Clark U., 1963; MA in Psychology, U. Denver, 1966, PhD in Social Psychology, 1968. Prof. San Jose (Calif.) State U., 1967—; rsch. assoc. U. Calif., Santa Cruz, 1989-90; pres. Western Inst. for Human Devel., San Jose, 1985—. Author: Psychology for Correctional Education, Bringing Psychology to Life; contbr. articles to profl. jours. Recipient Warburton award for scholarly excellence, 1995, Disting. Tchr. of Yr. award Western Psychol. Assn., 1996. Mem. Phi Beta Kappa. Office: San Jose State U Dept Psychology San Jose CA 95192

PELLEGRINO, EDMUND DANIEL, physician, educator, former university president; b. Newark, June 22, 1920; s. Michael J. and Marie (Catone) P.; m. Clementine Coakley, Nov. 17, 1944; children: Thomas, Virginia, Michael, Andrea, Alice, Leah. BS, St. John's U., 1941, DSc (hon.), 1971; MD, NYU, 1944; 39 hon. degrees. Diplomate Am. Bd. Internal Medicine. Intern Bellevue Hosp., N.Y.C., 1944-45; asst. resident medicine Bellevue

Hosp., 1948-49; resident medicine Goldwater Meml. Hosp., N.Y.C., 1945-46; fellow medicine NYU, 1949-50; supervising Tb physician Homer Folks Hosp., Oneonta, N.Y., 1950-53; dir. internal medicine Hunterdon Med. Center, Flemington, N.J., 1953-59; med. dir. Hunterdon Med. Center, 1955-59; prof., chmn. dept. medicine U. Ky. Med. Center, 1959-66; prof. medicine SUNY, Stony Brook, 1966-72; v.p. for health scis., dir. Health Scis. Center SUNY, 1968-73, dean Sch. Medicine, 1968-72; v.p. health affairs U. Tenn. System; chancellor U. Tenn. Med. Units, Memphis, 1973-75; prof. med. Yale U., New Haven, 1975-78; pres. Yale-New Haven Med. Center, 1975-78, Cath. U. Am., Washington, 1978-82; prof. philosophy and biology Cath. U. Am., 1978-82; John Carroll prof. medicine and med. ethics Georgetown U., Washington, 1982—; dir. Kennedy Inst. Ethics, Washington, 1983-88; dir. Ctr. for Advanced Study Ethics Georgetown U., Washington, 1988-94, dir. Ctr. for Clin. Bioethics, 1991—, acting chief Divsn. Gen. Internal Medicine, 1993-94. Founding editor Jour. Medicine and Philosophy, 1983—. Served with USAAF, 1946-48. Master ACP; fellow N.Y. Acad. Medicine; mem. Inst. Medicine of NAS, AMA, Assn. Am. Physicians, Medieval Acad. Am., Metaphys. Soc. Am., N.Y. Acad. Sci., Am. Clin. and Climatol. Assn. Office: Georgetown U Ctr for Clin Bioethics Washington DC 20007

PELLEGRINO, JAMES WILLIAM, college dean, psychology educator; b. N.Y.C., Dec. 20, 1947; s. Vincent and Emily (Nicosia) P.; m. Barbara Jo Sposato, June 6, 1970 (div. 1975); 1 child, Christopher Michael; m. Susan Rosen Goldman, Dec. 23, 1978; children: Joshua Goldman, Seth Goldman. BS in Psychology, Colgate U., 1969; MS in Experimental, Quantitative Psychology, U. Colo., 1970, PhD in Experimental, Quantitative Psychology, 1973. Asst. prof. U. Pitts., 1973-78, assoc. prof., 1978-79; assoc. prof. U. Calif., Santa Barbara, 1979-83, prof., 1983-89; Frank Mayborn prof. Vanderbilt U., Nashville, Tenn., 1989—, dean Peabody Coll. Edn. and Human Devel., 1991—; co-dir. Learning Tech. Ctr. Vanderbilt U., 1989-91; proposal reviewer NSF, Can. Rsch. Coun., Australian Rsch. Coun.; presenter in field. Author: (with others) Cognitive Psychology and Instruction, 1978, Handbook of Semantic Word Norms, 1978, Memory Organization and Structure, 1979, Aptitude, Learning and Instruction: Cognitive Process Anayses, How Much and How Can Intelligence Be Increased, 1982, Advances in Instructional Psychology, vol. II, 1982, Handbook of Research Methods in Human Memory and Cognition, 1982, Advances in the Psychology of Human Intelligence, 1982, Individual Differences in Cognition, 1983, Human Abilities: An Information Processing Approach, 1984, Test Design: Developments in Psychology and Psychometrics, 1985, International Encyclopedia of Education, 1985, What is Intelligence?, 1986, Arthur Jensen: Consensus and Controversy, 1987, Intelligence and Cognition: Contemporary Frames of Reference, 1987, Metacognition, Motivation and Understanding, 1987, Test Validity, 1988, Learning and Individual Differences: Abilities, Motivation and Methodology, 1989, The Psychology of Learning and Motivation, 1989, The Proceedings of the 22nd Annual Hawaii International Conference on System Sciences, 1989, Vision and Action: The Control of Grasping, 1990, Learning Disabilities: Theoretical and Research Issues, 1990, Intelligence: Reconceptualization and Measurement, 1991, Philosophy of Science, Cognitive Psychology, and Educational Theory and Practice, 1992, New Approaches to Testing: Rethinking Aptitude, Achievement and Assessment, 1992, Cognitive Approaches to Automated Instruction, 1992; co-author: Human Intelligence: Perspectives and Prospects, 1985, Testing: Theoretical and Applied Perspectives, 1989, Instruction: Theoretical and Applied Perspectives, 1991; contbr. numerous articles to profl. jours. NIMH fellow; Colgate U. scholar, N.Y. State Regents scholar, Westchester County Golf Assn. Caddie scholar; recipient Austen Colgate award, Phil R. Miller award, Outstanding Young Men in Am. award. Mem. AAAS, Am. Ednl. Rsch. Assn. (various coms.), Midwestern Psychol. Assn., Rocky Mountain Psychol. Assn., N.Y. Acad. Sci., European Assn. Rsch. on Learning and Instrn., Cognitive Sci. Soc., Soc. Multivariate Experimental Psychology, Computers in Psychology, Soc. Mathematical Psychology, Soc. Rsch. and Child Devel., Psychonomic Soc., Sigma Xi, Phi Beta Kappa, Psi Chi. Avocations: sports, gardening, music. Home: 44 Park Crescent Cir Nashville TN 37215-6115 Office: Vanderbilt U Box 329 Peabody Coll Nashville TN 37203

PELLEGRINO, NANCY DAVIS, middle school educator; b. Newark, Feb. 10, 1944; d. William Francis and Doris (Williams) Davis; m. Donald Nicholas Spano (dec. May 1980); children: Donna, Donald; m. Anthony Joseph Pellegrino Jr., Mar. 17, 1984. BA in Sci., Rutgers U., 1965; MEd, Nat.-Louis U., 1994. Cert. tchr. biology, gen. sci. Biology tchr. Our Lady of Good Coun., Newark, N.J., 1964-67; 4th grade tchr. Most Holy Name of Jesus, Gulfport, Fla., 1974-80; tchr. dropout prevention Pinellas Park (Fla.) Mid. Sch., 1988-93, tchr. sci.-tech. edn. lab., 1993—; chmn. Sch. Adv. Coun., Pinellas Park, 1992-95, pro edn. facilitator, 1993-95; presenter Sci.-Tech. Conf., St. Petersburg, Fla., 1993, Edn. at Tech. Conv., Innisbrook, Fla., 1994; curriculum writer Fla. Dept. Edn., Tallahassee, 1994, PETC at U. South Fla., 1995, Improving Edn. in Orlando, 1995. SAPP Bookfair scholar Bookfair Assn., 1992. Mem. ASCD, Fla. Assn. Sch. Tchrs., Pinellas Assn. Sci. Tchrs. Avocations: model airplane building, computers. Office: Pinellas Park Mid Sch 6940 70th Ave Pinellas Park FL 34665-3907

PELLEGROM, DANIEL EARL, international health and development executive; b. Three Rivers, Mich., May 29, 1944; s. Francis Robert and Regina Elizabeth (Valentine) P.; m. Sally Margaret Stukenbroeker, Nov. 30, 1944; children: Daniel, Jr., Benjamin, Sara. BA, Western Mich. U., 1966; MDiv, Union Theol. Seminary, 1969. Ordained to ministry, Presbyn. Ch., 1970. Dir. coll. programs Planned Parenthood Fedn., N.Y.C., 1969-71; exec. dir. Memphis Planned Parenthood, 1971-75, Md. Planned Parenthood, Balt., 1975-85; pres. Pathfinder Internat., Watertown, Mass., 1985—; bd. dirs. Alan Guttmacher Inst., N.Y.C., Inter Action, Washington, 1988-92, Brush Found., Cleve., Advocates for Youth, Washington, treas., 1991—; bd. overseers Planned Parenthood League Mass., Cambridge. Mem. Gov.'s conf. on children and youth State of Md., Balt., 1978-80; assoc. sch. hygiene and pub. health Johns Hopkins U., Balt., 1984-85. Recipient Leadership award Greater Balt. Com., 1983-84; Pathfinder Internat. recipeint UN Population award, 1996. Mem. APHA. Democrat. Avocations: baseball, travel, hiking. Home: 48 Bound Brook Rd Newton MA 02161-2036 Office: Pathfinder Internat 9 Galen St Ste 217 Watertown MA 02172-4501

PELLERZI, LEO MAURICE, lawyer; b. Cumberland, Md., June 14, 1924; s. John and Ida Lezzer (Regis) P.; m. Betty Lou Mearkle, Jan. 17, 1946; children: Jon Lou, Cheryl M., John C., Michele S., Julie A., Laura M., Jeffrey C. LL.B., George Washington U., 1949, LL.M., 1950. Bar: D.C. bar 1949, also U.S. Supreme Ct 1949. Atty. ICC, 1949-51, ECA, 1951-52; atty. Subversive Activities Control Bd., 1952-56, asst. gen. counsel, 1956-59; adminstv. law judge ICC, 1959-65; gen. counsel U.S. Civil Svc. Commn., 1965-68; asst. atty. gen. for adminstrn. Dept. Justice, 1968-73; chmn. bd. Govt. Svcs., Inc., 1971-73; gen. counsel Am. Fedn. Govt. Employees, AFL-CIO, 1973-78; chmn. bd. Flag Filter Corp., 1978-85; pvt. practice law Washington, 1978-90. Gen. counsel Lafayette Fed. Credit Union, 1956-59; pres. Fed. Adminstrv. Law Judges Conf., 1963-65. Served with USAAF, 1943-45; lt. col. Res. Decorated Air medal with 4 oak leaf clusters.; recipient Commrs.'s award U.S. Civil Svc. Commn., 1968, Justice Tom C. Clark award Fed. Bar Assn., 1967. Mem. ABA, Fed. Bar Assn. (pres. D.C. chpt. 1962-63, chmn. com. gen. counsel 1966-67), George Washington U. Alumni Assn. Roman Catholic. Home: 106 Indian Spring Dr Silver Spring MD 20901-3017

PELLETIER, ARTHUR JOSEPH, state legislator, industrial arts and computer programming educator; b. Exeter, N.H., Dec. 13, 1946; s. Joseph Telesphor and Elsie Jane (Dillon) P.; m. Marsha Lynn Mingle, May 19, 1973; 1 child, John. Diploma N.H. Vocat. Tech. Inst., 1966; B.A., Kans. State U., 1970, M.S., 1972. Cert. in secondary edn., guidance. Asst. to dir. Kans. State U. Div. Continuing Edn., Manhattan, 1971-74; tchr. drafting Portsmouth High Sch., N.H., 1974-86; tchr. computer programming McIntosh Coll., Dover, N.H., 1982-84; assoc. prof. N.H. Vocat.-Tech. Coll., Stratham, N.H., 1986-87; kitchen designer Area Kitchen Ctr., Portsmouth, 1987; mem. N.H. Ho. Reps., 1993—; mem. legis. sci., tech. and energy com., 1993—; co-founder N.H. Coalition for Edn.; mem. bd. dirs. N.H. Citizen Action, 1991—; mem. Dover Ready to Learn Task Force, 1995—; mem. Dover Schs. Program Evaluation and Review Com.; mem. Partnership Healthier Cmty., 1995—, Ams. for Non-Smoker's Rights, 1996—; bd. advs. Hub Family Support Ctr., 1996—. Mem. World Future Soc., Seacoast I.B.M. Users Group, Friends of Dover Libr. Avocations: radio-controlled model aircraft; tennis; photography. Home: 94 Back River Rd Dover NH 03820-4411

PELLETIER, LOUIS CONRAD, surgeon, educator; b. Montreal, Que., Can., Mar. 15, 1940; s. Conrad L. and Lucienne (Rochette) P.; m. Louise Montpetit, June 26, 1965; children: Conrad R., Marie-Helene. BA, Brébeuf Coll., Montreal, 1959; MD, U. Montreal, 1964. Resident in cardiovascular and thoracic surgery U. Montreal, 1964-70, chmn. dept. surgery, 1986-94; rsch. asst. Mayo Clin. Found., Rochester, Minn., 1970-72; mem. dept. surgery Maisonneuve-Rosemont Hosp., Montreal, 1972-76, Sacré-Coeur Hosp., Montreal, 1972-80; mem. dept. surgery Montreal Heart Inst., 1979—, head dept. surgery, 1979-87. Contbr. articles to profl. jours. Mem. adminstrv. bd. College Stanislas, Montreal, 1979-86, Que. Heart Found., 1980-84, regional healthcare bd., 1991-92, Hotel-Dieu Hosp., 1993-95. Recipient Young Investigator's award Am. Coll. Cardiology, 1972; Med. Rsch. Coun. Can. scholar U. Montreal, 1973-78. Fellow Royal Coll. Physicians and Surgeons Can.; mem. ACS, Association des Medecins de Langue Francaise du Canada, Can. Med. Assn., Royal Coll. Can., Assn. Cardiovascular and Thoracic Surgery Que., Can. Cardiovascular Soc., Montreal Cardiac Soc., Clin. Rsch. Club Que., Soc. Thoracic Surgeons, Can. Assn. Clin. Surgeons, Sociedad de Cardiocirujanos, Coun. on Cardiovasular Surgery, Am. Heart Assn., Internat. Soc. for Heart Transplantation, Can. Soc. Cardiovascular and Thoracic Surgeons, Am. Assn. Thoracic Surgery, Am. Surgical Assn. Roman Catholic. Avocations: skiing, sailing. Office: Montreal Heart Inst, 5000 E Belanger, Montreal, PQ Canada H1T 1C8

PELLETIER, MARSHA LYNN, state legislator, secondary school educator; b. Mt. Pleasant, Mich., July 29, 1950; d. Eugene Russell and Mary Ellen (Edde) Mingle; m. Arthur Joseph Pelletier, May 19, 1973; 1 child, John Frederick. BS in Home Econs. and Edn., Kans. State U., 1971, MS in Edn. Guidance and Counseling, 1972. Lic. rela estate broker, N.H. Conf. coord., guidance counselor Kans. State U., Manhattan, 1971-73; tchr. home econs. Franklin (Mass.) H.S., 1974, Exeter (N.H.) H.S., 1974-75, Barrington (N.H.) Mid. Sch., 1975-81, Pentucket Regional Jr. H.S., West Newbury, Mass., 1981-82; realtor assoc. Century 21 Ocean and Norword Realty, Portsmouth, N.H., 1983-86; tchr. interior design, cons. U. N.H., Durham, 1986-87; tchr. home econs. Dover Jr. H.S., 1983—; rep. Dist. 12 Dover N.H. Ho. of Reps., Concord, 1992-94; ind. real estate broker Dover, 1986—. Bd. dirs. Dover Adult Learning Ctr., 1995—; mem. Health Task Force, Dover and Concord, 1993-94; mem. bd. trustees St. John's Meth. Ch., 1995—. Mem. NEA (local pres. negotiator, membership chair, leadership exec. com., rep. 1979—), Nat. Coalition for Consumer Edn., Alpha Delta Kappa. (v.p. historian altruistic chmn. 1984-89). Democrat. Avocations: gardening, aerobics, designing, sewing, cooking. Home: 94 Back River Rd Dover NH 03820-4411

PELLETIER, S. WILLIAM, chemistry educator; b. Kankakee, Ill., July 3, 1924; s. Anthony Amos and Estella Edith (Hays) P.; m. Leona Jane Bledsoe, June 18, 1949; children: William Timothy, Jonathan Daniel, Rebecca Jane, Lucy Ruth, David Mark, Sarah Lynn. B.S. with highest honors in Chem. Engring, U. Ill., 1947; Ph.D. in Organic Chemistry, Cornell U., 1950. Instr. chemistry U. Ill., 1950-51; mem. staff Rockefeller Inst., 1951-62, assoc. prof. organic chemistry, 1961-62; prof. chemistry, head dept. U. Ga., 1962-69, Alumni Found. disting. prof., 1969—, provost, 1969-76, Univ. prof., 1976—; dir. Inst. for Natural Products Research, 1976—; Gordon lectr., New Hampton, N.H., 1955, 59, 69; lectr. German Acad. Agrl. Scis., 1959; Am. Swiss Found. lectr., Zurich, Basel, Bern, Geneva, Switzerland, 1960; Commemorative dedication lectr. Shionogi Rsch. Lab., Osaka, Japan, 1961; Victor Coulter lectr. U. Miss., 1965; Nason-Piston lectr. Boston Pub. Libr., 1982; Plenary lectr. 32d Internat. Congress on Medicinal Plant Rsch., Antwerp, Belgium, 1984; lectr. for internat. symposia in Berlin, Melbourne, Hong Kong, Latvia, Prague, Stockholm, London, Riga, Latvia, Varna, Bulgaria, Istanbul, Turkey, also other lectures in Eng., Italy, India, Israel, Taiwan, Japan; mem. health medicinal chemistry study panel NIH, 1968-72. Author: Chemistry of the Alkaloids, 1970, Alkaloids: Chemical and Biological Perspectives, vols., 1-10, 1983-96, 7 monographs on Am. etcher John Taylor Arms, 1975-93, catalogue of etchings of Charles Meryon and Jean-Francois Millet, 1994, Adriaen van Ostade, Etchings of Peasant Life in Holland's Golden Age, 1994; editl. bd. Jour. Organic Chemistry, 1966-70, Heterocycles, 1979—, Jour. Natural Products, 1980—, Phytochem. Analysis, 1989—, Trends in Heterocycloc Chemistry, 1994—, Recent Rsch. Devel. in Heterocyclic Chemistry, 1994, also numerous articles. Pres. bd. Flushing Christian Day Sch., 1956-60; bd. advisers Ga. Mus. Art, 1968—; bd. dirs. Center for Research Libraries, Chgo., 1975-81. Served with USNR, 1944-46. Fellow AAAS, Royal Soc. Arts (London), Royal Soc. Chemistry (London); mem. Am. Chem. Soc. (chmn. N.E. Ga. sect. 1968, Charles Herty medal 1971, So. Chemists award 1972), Am. Soc. Pharmacognosy (Rsch. Achievement award 1991), Worldwide Discipleship Assn. (bd. dirs. 1980-88), Sigma Xi, Phi Eta Sigma, Tau Beta Pi, Sigma Tau. Presbyn. (elder). Spl. research structure and stereochemistry diterpenoid alkaloids, applications of carbon-13 nuclear magnetic resonance to structure determination, synthesis of terpenes, X-ray crystallographic structures of natural products. Office: U Ga Dept Chemistry Athens GA 30602-2556 *I have been working in the field of natural products for over forty years now. As we unravel the structures of complex natural products and illuminate their fascinating chemistry. I am impressed over and over with the marvelous design andhandiwork of the Creator. In a certain real sense, as I explore and discover new truth about the part of the universe in which I work, I believe that I am thinking God's thoughts after him.*

PELLETREAU, ROBERT HALSEY, diplomat; b. Patchogue, N.Y., July 9, 1935; s. Robert H. and Mary (Pigeon) P.; m. Pamela Day, Dec. 17, 1966; children: Katherine Day, Erica Pigeon, Elizabeth Anne. B.A., Yale U., 1957; LL.B., Harvard U., 1961. Bar: N.Y. 1961. Assoc. firm Chadbourne, Parke, Whiteside & Wolfe, N.Y.C., 1961-62; joined U.S. Fgn. Service, 1962; service in Morocco, Mauritania, Lebanon, Algeria, Jordan and Syria; ambassador to Bahrain, 1979-80, dep. asst. sec. def., 1980-81, 85-87, dep. asst. sec. state, 1983-85, ambassador to Tunisia, 1987-91, ambassador to Egypt, 1991-93; asst. sec. state U.S. Dept. State, Washington, 1994—. Served with USNR, 1957-58. Mem. Am. Fgn. Service Assn., Middle East Inst., Coun. Fgn. Rels. Office: US Dept State Rm 6242 (NEA) Washington DC 20520

PELLETT, HOWARD ARTHUR, tax investigator; b. Monterey Park, Calif., May 27, 1939; s. Howard Holland and Dorothy Lois (Judson) P.; m. Carol Lynn Underhill, Feb. 19, 1960; children: William, Michael, Stephen, Douglas, Matthew. AA, E. L.A. Coll., 1959; BS, L.A. State Coll., 1961. Agt. IRS, L.A., Bellingham, Wash., 1961-67, Anchorage, Juneau, Alaska, 1968-71; asst. dist. dir., group mgr. IRS, Anchorage, 1971-74; returns program mgr. IRS, Seattle, 1974-78; group mgr. IRS, Everett, Wash., 1978-80; agt. IRS, Seattle, 1980—. Sec.-treas. Friends of Skagit County, Mount Vernon, Wash., 1993—; pres. Guemes Island (Wash.) Property Owners Assn., 1991—. Mem. Beta Alpha Psi. Democrat. Avocations: public service, rational recovery group coordinator, gardening. Home: 421A Guemes Island Rd Anacortes WA 98221 Office: IRS 915 2nd Ave Ste 2290 Seattle WA 98174-1001

PELLEY, MARVIN HUGH, mining executive; b. St. Anthony, Nfld., Can., Nov. 24, 1947; s. Hugh Albert Pelley and Alma Josie (Harnett) Potter; m. Velma Delilah Gillard, Nov. 5, 1965; 1 child, Rhonda Mary-Jane. Diploma in engring., Meml. U. Nfld., St. John's, 1969, BSc, 1969; B in Engring. with distinction, Tech. U. N.S., Halifax, 1973. Registered profl. engr. Contract miner Whissel Mining Ltd., Nfld., 1969-71; planning engr. Kaiser, N.S., 1972; gen. foreman opers. Iron Ore Co. Can, Nfld., 1973-74, chief engr., 1975-78; exec. v.p./ptnr. Baumgartl & Assoc., Nfld., 1978-81; mgr. tech. svcs. Denison Mines Ltd. Quintette, B.C., 1981-86; v.p. engring./transp. Curragh Resources Inc., Y.T., 1986-87; exec. v.p. mining Curragh Resources Inc., Ont., 1987-91, pres. projects and coal, 1991-92, pres. corp. devel. and projects, 1992-93; pvt. cons., 1993-94; pres. Alagnak Enterprises, Inc., Mississauga, Ont., 1995—; presenter in field. Mem. Am. Inst. Mining Engring., Canadian Inst. Mining and Metallurgy, Assn. Profl. Engrs Nfld., Assn. Profl. Engrs. B.C., Assn. Profl. Engrs. Yukon, B.C. Mining Assn. (bd. dirs. 1989). Avocations: reading, outdoor activities, canoeing, fishing, golf. Office: 1527 Manorbrook Ct, Mississauga, ON Canada L5M 4A9

PELLEY, SHIRLEY NORENE, library director; b. Raymondville, Tex., Oct. 9, 1931; d. Llloyd Marshall and Lillian Norene (Southall) Ayres; m. May 14, 1954 (div.); children: Michael, Cynthia, Katheryne. BA in Music Edn., Bethany Nazarene Coll., 1954; MLS, U. Okla., 1966. Tchr. Hilldale Elem. Sch., Oklahoma City, 1954-56; music tchr. self-employed, Okla., Mo., 1956-64; circulation clk. Bethany (Okla.) Pub. Libr., 1964-65; libr. reference U. Okla. Libraries, Norman, 1966-83; dir. learning resource ctr. So. Nazarene U., Bethany, 1983—. Mem. ALA, Okla. Libr. Assn., Assn. Coll. and Rsch. Librs., Met. Librs. Network of Ctrl. Okla., Assn. Christian Librs. Republican. Nazarene. Avocations: reading, walking, travel. Office: So Nazarene U Learning Resource Ctr 4115 N College Ave Bethany OK 73008-2671

PELLI, CESAR, architect; b. Tucuman, Argentina, Oct. 12, 1926; came to U.S., 1952, naturalized, 1964; s. Victor V. and Teresa S. (Suppa) P.; m. Diana Balmori, Dec. 15, 1950; children: Denis G., Rafael A. BArch cum laude, U. Tucuman, 1949; MS in Architecture, U. Ill., 1954. Assoc. firm Eero Saarinen & Assocs. (Architects), 1954-64, Daniel, Mann, Johnson & Mendenhall, 1964-68, Gruen Assocs. Inc., L.A., 1968-77, Cesar Pelli & Assocs., New Haven, Conn., 1977—; dean Sch. Architecture, Yale U., New Haven, 1977-84. Works include Pacific Design Ctr. and Expansion, L.A. (Honor award So. Calif. chpt. AIA 1976, Design award from Progressive Architecture 1987), U.S. Embassy, Tokyo, Mus. Modern Art Expansion, N.Y.C., World Fin. Ctr. and Winter Garden, N.Y.C. (Bard award), Cleve. Clinic (Honor award AIA 1986), Herring Hall, Rice U., Houston (Honor award AIA 1986), Carnegie Hall Tower, N.Y.C. (Honor award AIA 1994, Design award AIA/Conn. 1991), Boyer Ctr. Molecular Medicine Yale U. (Design award AIA/Conn.), St. Luke's Med. Tower, Houston (Honor award Modern Healthcare/AIA 1991), NationsBank Corp. Ctr., Charlotte, NTT Corp. Hdqrs., Tokyo, New North Terminal, Washington Nat. Airport, Aronoff Ctr. for the Arts, Cin., Kuala Lumpur City Centre, Malaysia, Frances Lehman Loeb Art Ctr. Vassar Coll., Poughkeepsie, N..Y.; bd. govs. Perspecta mag.; editor Yale Seminars on Architecture, 1981, 82. Recipient Gold medal Am. Inst. of Architects, 1995. Fellow AIA (Firm award 1989, named to top ten list of living Am. archs. 1991, Gold medal 1995); mem. NAD (Arnold M. Brunner Meml. prize 1978), Am. Acad. Arts and Letters (academician), Internat. Acad. Architecture (academician). Office: Cesar Pelli & Assocs care Janet Kagan 1056 Chapel St New Haven CT 06510

PELLI, DENIS GUILLERMO, visual perception, psychology educator; b. Champaign, Ill., June 25, 1953; s. Cesar Pelli and Diana Balmori. BA in applied math. magna cum laude, Harvard U., 1975; PhD in physiology, Cambridge U., Eng., 1981. Rsch. fellow Psychology Dept. U. Minn., Mpls., 1979-81; prof. neurosci. Inst. Sensory Rsch. Syracuse (N.Y.) U., 1981-95; prof. psychology NYU, 1995—; dir., founder Computational Neurosci. Program Syracuse U. and SUNY Health Sci. Ctr., 1991-95; adj. prof. dept. psychology Syracuse U., 1991-95; rsch. prof. dept. ophthalmology, SUNY Syracuse Health Ctr., 1991—; freeman Worshipful Co. Spectacle Maker, Brit. Opticians Guild, 1979—; mem. Working Group on Visual Disability Com. on Vision NAS/NRC, Washington, 1993; co-chair low vision panel Nat. Adv. Eye Coun. Vision Rsch. Program Planning Com., 1989-90; mem. reviewers res. NIH, 1993—, visual scis. B study sect., 1989-93, external reviewer, 1989, ad hoc mem., 1986, 87, 88, visual scis. ad hoc study sect., 1986, low vision grants ad hoc study sect., 1985; site visit team mem. Nat. Inst. Aging, 1988; acad. rsch. enhancement awards ad hoc study sect., Nat. Eye Inst., 1985; reviewer NSF, Air Force Office Rsch., Tobacco-Related Disease Rsch. Program of U. Calif. Contbr. articles to profl. jours. Mem. AAAS, APA, Assn. Computing Machinery, Assn Edn. and Rehab. of Blind and Visually Handicapped, Assn. Rsch. Vision and Opthamology, Graphic Arts Tech. Found., IEEE Computer Soc., N.Y. Acad. Scis., Optical Soc. Am., Psychonomics, SIGGRAPH, Soc. Neurosci., Sigma Xi. Achievements include invention of ISR Video Attenuator, 1989, Letters-in-Noise chart, 1987, Pelli-Robson Contrast Sensitivity Chart, 1986, Blurscope and contrast reduction screen for control of resolution and contrast of vision of moving objects, 1986. Home: 110 Bleecker St Apt 15F New York NY 10012 Office: NYU Psychology Dept 6 Washington Pl New York NY 10003

PELLOW, DAVID MATTHEW, lawyer, law educator; b. Batavia, N.Y., Oct. 5, 1950; s. Louis Matthew and M. Beverly (Sizing) P.; m. Barbara Terry Walzer, Aug. 24, 1975; children—Matthew Aaron, Jonathan Adam. B.S. in Bus. Adminstrn., Boston Coll., 1972; J.D., U. Mich., 1975. Bar: N.Y. 1976, U.S. Dist. Ct. (no. dist.) N.Y. 1976, U.S. Ct. Appeals (3d cir.) 1980, U.S. Supreme Ct. 1981, U.S. Dist. Ct. (we. dist.) N.Y. 1985. Ptnr. Bond, Schoeneck & King, Syracuse, N.Y.; adj. asst. prof. labor law LeMoyne Coll., Syracuse, N.Y., 1981—; bd. dirs. Legal Services Central N.Y. Inc., Syracuse, 1978-81. Active N.Y. State Human Rights Arbitration Adv. Com., 1990—. Contbr. articles to profl. jours. Mem. ABA (labor and employment law sect.), N.Y. State Bar Assn., Indsl. Relations Research Assn. (v.p. central N.Y. chpt. 1981-82). Office: Bond Schoeneck & King 1 Lincoln Ctr Fl 18 Syracuse NY 13202-1324

PELOFSKY, JOEL, lawyer; b. Kansas City, Mo., June 23, 1937; s. Louis J. and Naomi (Hecht) P.; m. Brenda L. Greenblatt, June 19, 1960; children: Mark, Lisa, Carl. AB, Harvard U., 1959; LLB, 1962. Bar: Mo. 1962, U.S. Dist. Ct. (we. dist.) Mo. 1962, U.S. Ct. Appeals (8th cir.) 1968, U.S. Ct. Appeals (10th cir.) 1970. Law clk. to judge U.S. Dist. Ct. (we. dist.) Mo., 1962-63; mem. Miniace & Pelofsky, Kansas City, Mo., 1965-80; asst. pros. atty. Jackson County (Mo.), 1967-71; mem. Kans. City (Mo.) City Council, 1971-79; judge U.S. Bankruptcy Ct., Western Dist. Mo., Kansas City, 1980-85; ptnr. Shughart, Thomson & Kilroy P.C., Kansas City, 1986-95; apptd. U.S. trustee Ark., Mo., Nebr., 1995—; intermittent lectr. in law U. Mo.; mem. Region I, Law Enforcement Assistance Adminstrn. Bd. dirs. Greater Kansas City Mental Health Found.; mem. adv. bd. Urban League, Kansas City, Mo., chmn. human resource devel. com. Mo. Mcpl. League; bd. dirs., mem. exec. com. Truman Med. Ctr., Kansas City, Mo., pres. bd. 1988-90, chmn. bd., 1990-92; trustee Menorah Med. Ctr., Kansas City, Mo. Served to lt. U.S. Army, 1963-65. Mem. ABA, Mo. Bar, Kansas City Bar Assn., Comml. Law League. Office: US Trustee 818 Grand Ste 200 Kansas City MO 64105-1917

PELOQUIN, LOUIS OMER, lawyer; b. Tracy, Quebec, Can., June 15, 1957; came to U.S., 1986; s. Gilles and Andree (Gelinas) P.; m. Carole Plante, Aug. 21, 1987; children: Louis-Alexandre, Valerie. BBA, Laval U., Quebec City, Can., 1980; LLB, U. Montreal, Can., 1984; LLM, NYU, 1987. Bar: Que. 1985, N.Y. 1988. Assoc. Martineau Walker, Montreal, Que., Can., 1985-86, Paul, Weiss, Rifkind, Wharton & Garrison, N.Y.C., 1987-89, Shearman & Sterling, N.Y.C., 1989-91, McCarthy Tetrault, Montreal, 1991-93; v.p., gen. counsel, sec. Golden Star Resources Ltd., Denver, 1993—. Contbr. articles to profl. jours. Recipient Richard de Boo prize in Taxation, 1984. Mem. ABA, N.Y. Bar Assn., Quebec Bar Assn., Assn. Am. Corp. Counsel, Rocky Mountain Mineral Law Found. Avocations: golf, skiing, reading, painting. Home: 5300 E Nichols Dr Littleton CO 80122-3892 Office: Golden Star Resources Ltd 1700 Lincoln St # 1950 Denver CO 80203-4501

PELOSI, NANCY, congresswoman; b. Balt., Mar. 26, 1941; d. Thomas J. D'Alesandro Jr.; m. Paul Pelosi; children: Nancy Corinne, Christine, Jacqueline, Paul, Alexandra. Grad., Trinity Coll. Former chmn. Calif. State Dem. Com., 1981; committeewoman Dem. Nat. Com., 1976, 80, 84; fin. chmn. Dem. Senatorial Campaign Com., 1987; mem. 99th-102d Congresses from 5th Calif. dist., 1987-1992, 103rd Congress from 8th Calif. dist., 1993—; mem. appropriations com., subcoms. labor, HHD & edn., fgn. ops., D.C.; intelligence (select) com., standard official conduct com. Office: US House of Rep 2457 Rayburn Washington DC 20515-0508*

PELOSO, JOHN FRANCIS XAVIER, lawyer; b. N.Y., Oct. 7, 1934; s. Rocco C. and Victoria (Musco) P.; m. Elizabeth Byrne Peloso, Oct. 7, 1961; children: Alycia, John, Matthew. BA, Fordham U., 1956, LLB, 1960. Bar: N.Y. 1960, U.S. Dist. Ct. (so. dist.) N.Y. 1962, U.S. Ct. Appeals (2nd cir.) 1967, U.S. Supreme Ct. 1968. Law clk. to judge U.S. Dist. Ct. (so. dist.) N.Y., 1960-61; asst. to U.S. Atty. U.S. Atty.'s Office, N.Y., 1961-65; assoc. Carter Ledyard & Milburn, N.Y., 1965-70; chief trial counsel NYRO-SEC, N.Y., 1970-75; ptnr. Sage Gray Todd & Sims, N.Y., 1975-87, Morgan, Lewis & Bockius, N.Y., 1987—; speaker in field. Contbr. articles to profl. jours. Capt. inf. USAR, 1956-64. Mem. ABA (sect. corp., banking and bus. law, com. fed. regulation securities 1975—, com. bus. and corp. litigation, chair subcom. securities litigation 1993—, litigation co-chmn. com. securities 1983-87, com. on liaison with jud. 1987-88, coun. 1989-91, co-chmn. com. trial evidence 1994-95, co-chmn. task force on the ind. lawyer 1995—), Assn. of Bar of City of N.Y. (arbitration com. 1970-73, fed. legis. com. 1975-78, fed. cts. com. 1982-86), Nat. Assn. Securities Dealers (nat. panel arbitrators

1975—, nat. arbitration com. 1982-85). Office: Morgan Lewis & Bockius 101 Park Ave New York NY 10178

PELOTTE, DONALD EDMOND, bishop; b. Waterville, Maine, Apr. 13, 1945; s. Norris Albert and Margaret Yvonne (LaBrie) P. AA, Eymard Sem. and Jr. Coll., Hyde Park, N.Y., 1965; BA, John Carroll U., 1969; MA, Fordham U., 1971, PhD, 1975. Ordained priest Roman Cath. Ch., 1972. Provincial superior Blessed Sacrament, Cleve., from 1978; ordained coadjutor bishop Diocese of Gallup, N.Mex., 1986-90, bishop, 1990—; nat. bd. dirs. Maj. Superiors of Men, Silver Spring, Md., 1981-86, Tekakwitha Conf., Great Falls, Mont., 1981—. Author: John Courtney Murray: Theologian in Conflict, 1976. 1st native Am. bishop. Mem. Cath. Theol. Soc. Am., Am. Cath. Hist. Soc. *

PELSTER, WILLIAM C., lawyer; b. St. Louis, May 11, 1942; s. William R. and Marie C. (Graefe) P.; m. Terry C. Cuthbertson, Aug. 9, 1969. BA, Oberlin Coll., 1964; JD, U. Mich., 1967. Bar: Mo. 1967, N.Y. 1968, U.S. Dist. Ct. (so. dist.) N.Y. 1968, U.S. Ct. Appeals (2d cir.) 1968, U.S. Supreme Ct. 1972. Law clk. to presiding justice U.S. Ct. Appeals (2d cir.), N.Y.C., 1967-68; assoc. Donovan, Leisure, Newton & Irvine, N.Y.C., 1968-75; ptnr. Skadden, Arps, Slate, Meagher & Flom, N.Y.C., 1976—. Trustee Cancer Care Inc., N.Y.C., 1975—. Mem. ABA, Assn. of Bar of City of N.Y. Office: Skadden Arps Slate Meagher & Flom 919 3rd Ave New York NY 10022*

PELTASON, JACK WALTER, former university president, educator; b. St. Louis, Aug. 29, 1923; s. Walter B. and Emma (Hartman) P.; m. Suzanne Toll, Dec. 21,1946; children: Nancy Hartman, Timothy Walter H., Jill K. BA, U. Mo., 1943, MA, 1944, LLD (hon.), 1978; AM, Princeton U., 1946, PhD, 1947; LLD (hon.), U. Md., 1979, Ill. Coll., 1979, Gannon U., 1980, U. Maine, 1980, Union Coll., 1981, Moorehead (N.D.) State U., 1980; LHD (hon.), 1980, Ohio State U., 1980, Mont. Coll. Mineral Scis. and Tech., 1982, Buena Vista Coll., 1982, Assumption Coll., 1983, Chapman Coll., 1986, U. Ill., 1989. Asst. prof. Smith Coll., Mass., 1947-51; asst. prof. polit. sci. U. Ill., Urbana, 1951-52, assoc. prof., 1953-59, dean Coll. Liberal Arts and Scis., 1960-64, chancellor, 1967-77; vice chancellor acad. affairs U. Calif., Irvine, 1964-67, chancellor, 1984-92; pres. U. Calif. System, Oakland, 1992-95, Am. Coun. Edn., Washington, 1977-84; prof. emeritus dept. politics and soc. U. Calif., Irvine, 1995— ; Cons. Mass. Little Hoover Commn., 1950. Author: The Missouri Plan for the Selection of Judges, 1947, Federal Courts and the Political Process, 1957, Fifty-eight Lonely Men, 1961, Understanding the Constitution, 13th edit., 1994, orig. edition, 1949, (with James M. Burns) Government By the People, 16th edit., 1995, orig. edit., 1952; contbr. articles and revs. to profl. jours. Recipient James Madison medal Princeton U., 1982. Fellow Am. Acad. Arts and Scis.; mem. Am. Polit. Sci. Assn. (council 1952-54), Phi Beta Kappa, Phi Kappa Phi, Omicron Delta Kappa, Alpha Phi Omega, Beta Gamma Sigma. Home: 18 Whistler Ct Irvine CA 92715-4069 Office: U Calif Dept Politics and Society 18 Whistle Ct Irvine CA 92715-4069

PELTIER, EUGENE JOSEPH, civil engineer, former naval officer, business executive; b. Concordia, Kans., Mar. 28, 1910; s. Frederick and Emma Helen (Brasseau) P.; m. Lena Evelyn Gennette, June 28, 1932 (dec.); children: Marion Joyce, Eugene Joseph (dec.), Carole Josephine, Kenneth Noel, Judith Ann. B.S. in Civil Engring., Kans. State U., 1933, LL.D., 1961. Registered profl. engr., Mo., N.Y., Kans., Fla., Va., Calif. Commd. lt. (j.g.) U.S. Navy, 1936, advanced through grades to rear adm., 1957; asst. public works officer Great Lakes, Ill., 1940-42; sr. asst. supt. civil engr. Boston, 1942-44; officer in charge 137th Constrn. Bn. Okinawa, 1945, officer in charge 54th Constrn. Regt., 1945; officer various public works assignments Pensacola, Fla., 1945-46, Memphis, 1946-49, Jacksonville, Fla., 1949-51; dist. public works officer (14th Naval Dist.), 1951-53; asst. chief maintenance and materials Bur. Docks Washington, 1953-56; comdg. officer Pt. Hueneme, 1956-57; chief Bur. Yards and Docks, Navy Dept. Washington, 1957-62; chief of civil engrs., 1957-62, ret., 1962; instrumentman, resident engr. Kans. Hwy. Commn., Norton, Topeka, Chanute, 1934-40; v.p. Sverdrup & Parcel & Assocs., Inc., St. Louis, 1962-64; sr. v.p. Sverdrup & Parcel & Assos., Inc., 1964-66, exec. v.p., 1966-67, pres., dir., 1967-75, chief exec. officer, 1972-75, ptnr., 1966-75, cons., 1975-82; pres., dir. Sverdrup & Parcel & Assos., N.Y., Inc., 1967-75; dir. Sverdrup & Parcel Internat., Inc., 1967-75; v.p., dir. ARO, Inc., Tullahoma, Tenn., 1966-75; cons. EPA, 1976-80; dir. Merc. Trust Co., St. Louis, 1971-81. Mem. emeritus Civic Progress, Inc.; bd. dirs. YMCA, St. Louis, 1972-76. Decorated Legion of Merit; recipient citation Am. Inst. Steel Constrn., 1973. Mem. ASCE (hon.), Am. Public Works Assn. (1 of Top Ten Public Works Men of Year 1960), Soc. Mil. Engrs. (pres. 1960-61), Am. Concrete Inst., Am. Road and Transp. Builders Assn. (pres. 1972-73), Nat. Soc. Profl. Engrs., Mo. Soc. Profl. Engrs., Public Works Hist. Soc. (pres. 1977-78, trustee 1975-79), Nat. Acad. Engring., Cons. Engrs. Council (award of Merit 1962), Sigma Tau, Phi Kappa Phi. Clubs: Army-Navy Country (Washington); Old Warson Country (St. Louis).

PELTON, JAMES RODGER, librarian; b. St. Louis, Mar. 21, 1945; s. Norman C. and Leona V. (Schulte) P.; m. Sandra Lee Birdsell, Mar. 29, 1969; 2 daus., Joni Lee, Vicki Sue. B.A., U. Mo., 1967, M.L.S., 1969. Br. librarian Scenic Regional Library, Union, Mo., 1968-71; adminstr. Daniel Boone Regional Library - Columbia Center, Columbia, Mo., 1971-78; cons. La. State Library, Baton Rouge, 1978-80; dir. Shreve Meml. Library, Shreveport, La., 1980—. Mem. ALA, La. Library Assn. Home: 3201 Old Mooringsport Rd Shreveport LA 71107-3926 Office: 424 Texas St Shreveport LA 71101-3522

PELTON, JOHN STAFFORD, metal products executive; b. Windsor, Ont., Can., May 10, 1946; s. Stafford Baker and Gertrude Pelton; m. Ethelwyn Lillian Darlene Pelton, May 24, 1969; children: Sarah, Rebecca, Charles, Elizabeth. B in Comm., U. Toronto, Ont., 1969. Cert. acct., 1972. CFO Canavest House, Ltd., Toronto, 1973-74; CFO Fed. Industries Ltd., Winnipeg, Manitoba, Can., 1974-86, sr. v.p. corp. devel., 1986-87; sr. v.p., dir., head mergers and acquisitions Merrill Lynch Can. Inc., Toronto, 1987-88; pres., COO, dir. FT Capital Ltd. (formerly Fin. Trustco Capital Ltd.), Toronto, 1988-90, Morgan Fin. Corp., Toronto, 1988-91; pres., COO, mng. ptnr. Greystone Ptnrs. Inc., Toronto, 1989-91; pres., COO, dir. Fed. Industries Ltd., Winnipeg, 1991-92, pres., CEO, dir., 1992-95; chmn., CEO Fed. Industries Ltd. (renamed Russel Metals Inc. May, 1995), 1995—. Office: Russel Metals Inc, 210-1900 Minnesota Ct, Mississauga, ON Canada L5N 3C9

PELTON, RALPH A., insurance company executive; b. Milw., Jan. 26, 1932; s. Roman Henry and Anastasia Katherine (Kolasinski) Pelczynski; m. Barbara Ann Schoultz, May 11, 1957; children: Ann, Mark, David, Susan, Tim. BSBA in Fin., Marquette U., 1954. From trainee to v.p. Northwestern Mut. Life Ins. Co., Milw., 1956—. Pres. council Boy Scouts of Am., Milw., 1986-87. With U.S. Army, 1954-56. Roman Catholic. Office: Northwestern Mut Life Ins Co 720 E Wisconsin Ave Milwaukee WI 53202-4703*

PELTON, RUSSELL GILBERT, lawyer; b. Monticello, N.Y., July 23, 1914; s. William and May (Morgan) P.; m. Marion Gosart, Dec. 14, 1940; children: William, Marjorie, Marilyn Pelton Barringer. BS, Syracuse U., 1935; JD, George Washington U., 1944. Bar: D.C. 1944, N.Y. 1947, U.S. Supreme Ct. 1948, U.S. Dist. Ct. N.Y. 1947; U.S. Dist. Ct. (fed. dist.). Ptnr., Darby & Darby, N.Y.C., 1945-56; sr. v.p. N.Am. Philips Corp., N.Y.C., 1956-75; exec. v.p. U.S. Philips Corp., N.Y.C., 1968-75; of counsel Rogers, Hoge & Hills, N.Y.C., 1976-78; ptnr. Spellman, Joel & Pelton, White Plains, N.Y., 1979-81, Eslinger & Pelton, N.Y.C., 1983-85; officer, dir. Tech. Container Corp., N.Y.C., 1977—; former dir. Ferrocube Corp., Savgerties, N.Y., Polyseal Corp., N.Y.C.; lectr. Practising Law Inst., 1953-69; arbitrator, mediator Am. Arbitration Assn., 1985—. Vice-pres. Siwanoy council Boy Scouts Am., 1948-53; v.p. Rye Neck Bd. Edn., Mamaroneck, N.Y., 1952-62; mem. Zoning Bd. Appeals, 1966-70; town justice, 1970-85; trustee Syracuse U., 1967-73. Served with Signal Corps, U.S. Army, 1941-45. Mem. ABA, Am. Patent Law Assn. (past chmn. com. antitrust), N.Y. State Bar Assn. (ethics com., Iolta com.), N.Y. Patent Law Assn. (past bd. govs.), State Magistrates Assn., County Magistrates Assn. (treas., v.p., pres.), Westchester County Bar Assn. (dir., chmn. ethics com., ADR com.), Assn. Bar City N.Y. (patent com.), IEEE, Am. Radio Relay League, Aircraft Owners and Pilots Assn. Clubs: Wings, Cloud (N.Y.C.); Winged Foot Golf (Mamaroneck, N.Y.); Waccabuc Country (South Salem, N.Y.); Masons, Elks. Patentee in field. Home: 3 Oxford Rd Larchmont NY 10538-1428

PELTON, RUSSELL MEREDITH, JR., lawyer; b. Chgo., May 14, 1938; s. Russell Meredith and Mildred Helen (Baumrucker) P.; m. Patty Jane Rader, Aug. 12, 1961; children: James, Thomas, Michael, Margaret. BA, DePauw U., 1960; JD, U. Chgo., 1963. Bar: Ill. 1963, U.S. Supreme Ct. 1979. Assoc., Peterson, Ross, Schloerb & Seidel, Chgo., 1966-72, ptnr., 1972-90; ptnr. Oppenheimer, Wolff & Donnelly, 1990—, Chgo. mng. ptnr., 1992-95; co-founder, gen. counsel Chgo. Opportunities Industrialization Ctr., 1969-83; gen. counsel Delta Dental Plan Ill., 1979—; bd. dirs. First United Life Ins. Co., 1979-82. Pres. Wilmette Jaycees, 1970; chmn. Wilmette Sch. Bd. Caucus, 1970-71; Wilmette Dist. 39 Bd. Edn., 1972-80; gen. counsel Am. Assn. Neurol. Surgeons, 1981—; bd. dirs. Wilmette United Way, 1980-86, campaign chmn., 1983-85, pres., 1985-86; Wilmette Zoning Bd. Appeals, 1989—, chmn., 1990—. Served to capt. USAF, 1963-66. Mem. Chgo. Bar Assn., Ill. Bar Assn., ABA, Ill. Trial Lawyers Assn., Soc. Trial Lawyers. Office: Oppenheimer Wolff & Donnelly Two Prudential Plz 45th Fl 180 N Stetson Ave Chicago IL 60601-6710

PELTZ, ALAN HOWARD, manufacturing company executive; b. N.Y.C., July 16, 1944; s. Harry and Rachel (Hammer) P.; BBA in Acctg., CCNY, 1966; MBA in Fin., Pace U., 1971; grad. advanced mgmt. program, Harvard U., 1988; m. Frieda Wichter, Nov. 16, 1968; children: Jason, Elissa. Corp. auditor RCA, N.Y.C., 1966-69; sr. fin. analyst Celanese Chem. Co., N.Y.C., 1969-70; asst. treas. Baker Industries, Inc., Parsippany, N.J., 1970-74; v.p. fin., adminstrn., human resources, mgmt. info. systems Burndy Corp., Norwalk, Conn., 1974-93, v.p., CFO, 1993—; v.p. fin. Framatome Connectors Internat., Paris, 1993—; mem. faculty Fairfield (Conn.) U., 1979-80; mem. exec. adv. com. Western Conn. State Coll., 1979-80. Bd. dirs. Elderhouse, 1985, Friends of Norwalk Coll., 1986, Hallbrook Hosp. Served as sgt. USMC, 1967-68. Fellow Internat. House Columbia, 1965. Mem. Fin. Execs. Inst., Internat. Treasury Orgn., Norwalk C. of C. (bd. dirs. 1984—), Nat. Assn. Corp. Treas., Mfrs. Alliance Productivity and Innovation Inc. (fin. coun. II), Nat. Elec. Mfrs. Assn. (human resources). Republican. Jewish. Avocations: racquetball, skiing, tennis. Office: Burndy Corp Richards Ave Norwalk CT 06854-2318

PELTZ, ALICE JEAN, bacteriologist; b. Astoria, N.Y., Apr. 7, 1950; d. John Christopher and Alice Rose (Faltin) Rauth; m. Lowell J. Peltz, Oct. 12, 1974 (dec. Mar. 1987); adopted children: Laura Jean Scruggs, Randall Michael, James Julius. AAS in Biol. Tech., SUNY, Farmingdale, 1970; BA in Natural Sci., Adelphi U., 1989; MPA, L.I. U., 1992, cert. in gerontology, 1994. Lab. technician toxicology lab. drug abuse sect. Suffolk County Dept. Health Svcs., Hauppage, N.Y., 1973-81, bacteriologist pub. & environ. health lab. water bac. sect., 1981—; presenter confs. and workshops Adelphi U., Garden City, N.Y., 1992, 93, Hofstra U., Hempstead, N.Y., 1993, N.Y. Inst. Tech., Old Westbury, 1993, Suffolk Acad. Law, 1993, 94, Suffolk County C.C., Brentwood campus, 1994. Active Suffolk County Rep. Women, 1993, Huntington Breast Cancer Action Coalition, Family Svc. League Suffolk County, Inc.; intern Cath. Charities Meals on Wheels Program, 1994; mem. Nassau Assn. Continuing Cmty. Edn. Mem. NAFE, Am. Soc. for Pub. Adminstrn. (mem. environ. and natural resources sect.), Soc. Forensic Toxicologists, Inc., N.Y. State Pub. Health Assn., Suffolk County Assn. Mcpl. Employees (mem. polit. action com., sec.-treas., med. examiners' unit), Pi Alpha Alpha. Lutheran. Avocations: needlepoint, crafts. Home: 114A Wells Rd Northport NY 11768-3450 Office: Suffolk County Med Examiner Bldg 487 North Complex Smithtown NY 11787

PELTZER, DOUGLAS LEA, semiconductor device manufacturing company executive; b. Clinton, Ia., July 2, 1938; s. Albert and Mary Ardelle (Messer) P.; m. Nancy Jane Strickler, Dec. 22, 1959; children: Katharine, Eric, Kimberly. BA, Knox Coll., 1960; MS, N.Mex. State U., 1964; MBA, U. Phoenix, 1990. Rsch. engr. Gen. Electric Co., Advanced Computer Lab., Sunnyvale, Calif., 1964-67; large scale integrated circuit engr. Fairchild Camera & Instrument, Rsch. & Devel. Lab., Palo Alto, Calif., 1967-70, bipolar memory divsn., Mountain View, Calif., 1970-83, tech. dir., 1977-83; v.p. tech. ops. Trilogy Systems Corp., Cupertino, Calif., 1983-85; pres. Tactical Fabs, Inc., 1985-89; v.p. process devel. Chips and Techs. Inc., 1989-92; pres, CEO CAMLAN, Inc., San Jose, Calif., 1992-94; staff Chip Express, Santa Clara, Calif., 1994—; prin. Corp. Tech. Devel. Cons., Inc., 1994—. NSF fellow, 1962-63; recipient Sherman Fairchild award for tech. excellence, 1980, Semiconductor Equipment and Materials Inst. award, 1988; Inventor of Yr. award Peninsula Patent Law Assn., 1982. Mem. AAAS, IEEE, Sigma Pi Sigma. Inventor in field; patentee in field. Home: 10358 Bonny Dr Cupertino CA 95014-2908

PELTZIE, KENNETH GERALD, hospital administrator, educator; b. Kansas City, Nov. 17, 1933; s. Sam and Leah (Unell) P.; m. Suzan Francis Orringer, July 19, 1964; 1 child, Sharon Lynn. BA, Washington U., 1955; MS, Columbia U., 1958. Adminstrv. officer USAF Hosp., Dyess AFB, Tex., 1958-61; budget examiner Officer Mgmt. & Budget, 1961-66; assoc. adminstr. Sinai Hosp. Detroit, 1966-72; v.p. Chi Systems, Ann Arbor, Mich., 1972-80; sr. v.p. Robert Douglas Assocs., Houston, 1980-82; exec. v.p. Community Hosp. of Indpls., 1982-86; pres. Affiliated Hosps. Ind., Indpls., 1982-86; v.p. corp. strategy Bethesda Healthcare Corp., Boynton Beach, Fla., 1987—; adj. asst. prof. Fla. Atlantic U., Boca Raton, 1991—; mem. adv. bd. Stewart James Rsch. Ctr., Boca Raton, Fla., 1991—. Co-author: Continued Care & Cost Containment, 1974; contbr. articles to profl. jours. Mem. com. United Way of Palm Beach County, West Palm Beach, Fla., 1992-93; active Leadership Palm Beach. Fellow ACHE; mem. Am. Hosp. Assn., Internat. Hosp. Fedn., Soc. Healthcare Plannig & Mktg., Rotary Club Delray Beach. Office: Bethesda Meml Hosp 2815 S Seacrest Blvd Boynton Beach FL 33435-7934

PELTZMAN, SAM, economics educator; b. Bklyn., Jan. 24, 1940; s. Benjamin Raphael and Ceil (Heller) P.; m. Nancy Virginia Bradney, Sept. 7, 1952; children: Shira Malka, Talya Rose. BBA, CCNY, 1960; PhD, U. Chgo., 1965. Prof. econs. UCLA, 1964-73; sr. staff economist Council of Econ. Advisers, Washington, 1970-71; prof. econs. grad. sch. bus. U. Chgo., 1973-87, Sears, Roebuck prof., 1987—; dir. George J. Stigler Ctr. for Study The Economy and the State U. Chgo., U. Chgo., 1992—; vis. fellow Inst. for Advanced Study Hebrew U., Jerusalem, 1978. Co-author: Public Policy Toward Mergers, 1967; editor Jour. Law and Econs.; contbr. articles to profl. jours. Mem. Am. Econ. Assn., Mt. Pelerin Soc. Jewish. Office: U Chgo Grad Sch Bus 1101 E 58th St Chicago IL 60637-1511

PELUSO, DAVID ANTHONY, clinical pharmacist, consultant; b. Hartford, Conn., Dec. 21, 1957; s. Dominic Anthony and Mary (Carbone) P.; m. Annette Pope; 1 child, Anthony James. BS in Biology, BS in Pharmacy, U. Conn., 1981; advanced mgmt. tng. program, Jackson Meml. Med. Ctr., 1985; PharmD, Southeastern U. Health Scis., 1993. Lic. pharmacist Fla., S.C. Hosp. pharmacy technician U. Conn. Health Ctr., Farmington, Conn., 1979-81; ambulatory pharmacy technician Burgdorf Health Clinic, Hartford, 1980-81; clin. pharmacist I med. svcs. U. Miami/ Jackson Meml. Hosp., Miami, Fla., 1981-83, supr. pharmacy ops., 1983-89, clin. pharmacist med. svcs., 1989—, medication surveillance pharmacist, 1993-95; pharmacist Home Maintenance Solutions & Svcs., Ft. Lauderdale, Fla., 1993-95; adj. clin. instr. Nova S.E. U., 1995—; reviewer continuing edn. programs Power-Pak, 1995—. Mem. Am. Soc. Hosp. Pharmacists, Kappa Psi (pres. Nu chpt. 1980). Achievements include research in gastrointestinal disease, pharmacokinetics, asthma and colony stimulating factors.

PELZ, ROBERT LEON, lawyer; b. N.Y.C., Nov. 18, 1918; s. Leon S. and Fanny M. (Berk) P.; m. Mary Jane Gips, Feb. 11, 1949; children: Kathryn Louise, Robert Leon. AB, Columbia U., 1939, JD, 1942. Bar: N.Y. 1942. Since practiced in N.Y.C.; ptnr. Hess Segall Guterman Pelz Steiner & Barovick, 1953-86, Loeb and Loeb, N.Y.C., 1986—; chmn. bd. dirs. Commentary mag. Life trustee, former v.p. Fedn. Jewish Philanthropies; bd. dirs., chmn. legal com., former chmn. bd. dirs. Fedn. Jewish Philanthropies Svc. Corp.; past trustee Coll. Pharm. Scis. Columbia U.; former chmn. bd. trustees Am. Jewish Com. Capt. AUS, WWII. Office: Loeb and Loeb 345 Park Ave New York NY 10154-0004

PEMBERTON, BOBETTE MARIE (HARMAN), nursing administrator; b. San Mateo, Calif., Oct. 20, 1952; d. William Adolph and Agnes Marie (Costa) Harman; m. William Charles Pemberton (div. Sept. 1993). BSN, U. San Francisco, 1975, PHN. RN, Calif., Hawaii, Fla.; cert. pub. health nurse, flight nurse, OR nurse. Recreation supr. Burlingame (Calif.) Recreation Ctr., 1968-74; nursing asst. III Stanford U. Med. Ctr., Palo Alto, Calif., 1974-75, staff nurse, 1976-78; clin. edn. supr., mobile ops. supr. Irwin Meml. Blood Bank, San Francisco Med Soc., 1978-87; OR staff nurse U. Calif., Davis, 1987-88; asst. dir. blood svcs. ARC, Farmington, Conn., 1988-89; coord. blood bank St. Anthony's Med. Ctr., St. Petersburg, Fla., 1989-90; dir. donor svcs. Hunter Blood Ctr., Clearwater, Fla., 1990-93; dir. nursing svcs. Blood Bank of Hawaii, Honolulu, 1993—; chairperson nursing edn. com. Calif. Blood Bank System, No. Calif. region seminar Irwin Meml. Blood Bank; mem. sci. com. Blood Bank Nurses Calif., Calif. Blood Bank System; nursing rep. Local 535; lectr. in field. With USAFR, 1983—. Mem. NAFE, Am. Bus. Women's Assn. (rec. sec., chairperson spring conf. Burlingame charter chpt., del. Kansas City conv.), Am. Assn. Blood Banks, Calif. Blood Bank Soc. (nursing and donor svcs. com.), Air Force Assn., Air Force Res. Officers Assn. Republican. Roman Catholic. Avocations: swimming, country dancing, horseback riding, Civil War history. Home: 512 Marin Dr Burlingame CA 94010

PEMBERTON, DONALD T., church administrator. Dir. of pub. CH. of God. Office: Church of God PO Box 2430 Cleveland TN 37320

PEMBERTON, JOHN DE JARNETTE, JR., lawyer, educator; b. Rochester, Minn., Apr. 21, 1919; s. John de Jarnette and Anna Trego (Hogeland) P.; m. Frances E. Werner, July 23, 1973; children by previous marriage: Ann O., Sarah F., Caro G., Nancy S., James de Jarnette. B.A., Swarthmore (Pa.) Coll., 1940; LL.B., Harvard U., 1947. Bar: N.C. 1949, Minn. 1950, N.Y. 1969, Calif. 1976. Acting asst. prof., then assoc. prof Duke U. Law Sch., Durham, N.C., 1947-50; ptnr. Pemberton, Michaels, Bishop & Seeger, Rochester, 1950-62; nat. exec. dir. ACLU, 1962-70; prof. U. San Francisco Law Sch., 1973-86; dep. gen. counsel, then acting gen. counsel EEOC, 1971-73; regional atty. dist. office EEOC, San Francisco, 1986-94; adj. lectr. NYU Law Sch., 1968-70, U. San Francisco Law Sch., 1986—; mem. legal com. No. Calif. chpt. ACLU, 1973-86. Assoc. editor and/or editor sects. in law jours. Chmn. Olmsted County (Minn.) Republican Party, 1958-61; commnr. Minn. Fair Employment Practices Com., 1961-62; exec. com Leadership Conf. Civil Rights, 1967-68. Served with Am. Field Service, 1941-45. Mem. ABA, Calif. Bar Assn. Quaker. Home: 11739 Laurel Dell Ave Monte Rio CA 95462-9740

PEMBERTON, MELISSIE COLLINS, retired elementary education educator; b. Pembroke, Va., Dec. 25, 1907; d. Walter Wingo and Grace Moore (Musselman) Collins; m. Oakland Herbert Pemberton, May 17, 1930; children: Oakland Herbert Jr., Walter Scott, William Durwood. BA in Edn., George Washington U., 1962; MA equivalency, Md. Bd. Edn., 1968. Tchr. Giles County Bd. Edn., Newport, Va., 1925-30, D.C. Pub. Schs., Washington, 1945-47, Montgomery County Pub. Schs., Rockville, MD, 1955-59, 63-75; tchr. rep. Curriculum Materials Rev., Rockville, Md., 1967-68, Elem. Spl. Edn. Rev. and Evaluation Com. for Textbooks, Rockville, 1970; del. Montgomery Edn. Assn., Rockville, 1967. Leader Montgomery County Govt., Rockville, 1988, advisor, 1994-95; sponsor Rep. Nat. Com., Washington, 1988; radio operator U.S.A. FCC, Washington, 1942, mem. Vol. Svc. Motor Corps, Richmond, Va., 1942; sec. Bon Air Heights Civic Assn., 1994-95; sec. Ben Aid Heights Civic Assn., 1994—; adv. Montgomery County Govt., Rockville, Md., 1994—, Md. State Hwy. Adminstrn. Dept. Transp., 1994—. Named Civitan Internat. scholar, 1964. Mem. Bon Air Heights Civic Assn., Montgomery County Edn. Assn. (emeritus life mem. 1975), NEA, Md. State Tchrs. Assn., Pi Lamba Theta. Republican. Methodist. Avocations: stamp, coin and plate collecting, gardening, painting. Home: 6208 Macarthur Blvd Bethesda MD 20816-3212

PENA, DIANA C., mathematics educator; b. El Paso, Oct. 8, 1960; d. Rodolfo D. and Rosalie Pena. BSME, U. Tex., El Paso, 1986, MS in Mfg. Engring., 1994, MEd in Adminstrn., 1995. Cert. secondary math. tchr. Rschr. Honeywell Optoelectronics, Dallas, 1990-92; math. tchr. Ysleta Ind. Sch. Dist., El Paso, 1991-92, El Paso Ind. Sch. Dist., 1992—; supr. SEE Inst., El Paso, 1990-91; subsitute tchr. El Paso Ins. Sch. Dist., 1989-90; math. and computer sci. tchr. Crestline Sch., El Paso, 1989-91. Mem. St. Patrick's Ladies Altar Soc., El Paso, 1988—; funds solicitor Operation Noel, El Paso, 1991—. Mem. Kappa Delta Pi. Avocations: reading, tennis, badmitton, computers, jogging. Home: 1608 Winslow Rd El Paso TX 79915-1430

PEÑA, FEDERICO FABIAN, federal official; b. Laredo, Tex., Mar. 15, 1947; s. Gustavo J. and Lucille P.; m. Ellen Hart, May 1988. BA, U. Tex., Austin, 1969, JD, 1972. Bar: Colo. 1973. Ptnr. Pena & Pena, Denver, 1973-83; mayor City and County of Denver, 1983-91; pres. Peña Investment Advisors, Inc., Denver, 1991-93; sec. U.S. Dept. of Transp., Washington, 1993—; assoc. Harvard U. Ctr. for Law and Edn., Cambridge, Mass.; mem. Colo. Bd. Law Examiners. Mem. Colo. Ho. of Reps., 1979-83, Dem. leader, 1981. Named Outstanding House Dem. Legislator, Colo. Gen. Assembly, 1981. Roman Catholic. Home: 3517 Sterling Ave Alexandria VA 22304-1834 Office: Dept of Transportation Office Sec 400 7th St SW Washington DC 20590-0001*

PEÑA, HEATHER MARIA, internist; b. North Hampton, Mass., Sept. 30, 1955; d. Cesareo Dennis and Eloise Verna (Morrison) P.; m. Christopher Searl. BS summa cum laude, Tufts U., 1977; MD, Harvard U., 1981. Intern, resident in internal medicine UCLA Hosp. and Clinics, 1981-84; staff physician Santa Monica (Calif) Hosp., St. John's Hosp., 1992—, Oceanview Med. Group at Pritikin Long Ctr., Santa Monica, Calif., 1984—. Mem. Am. Heart Assn. Epidemiology Council. Mem. Am. Coll. Physicians (assoc.), Harvard Med. Hamilton-Hunt Soc., Phi Beta Kappa. Democrat.

PENA, MANUEL, JR., state senator; b. Cashion, Ariz., Nov. 17, 1924; s. Manuel and Elvira (Gomez) P.; student public schs.; m. Aurora Cruz, June 13, 1945; children: Yolanda, Mary, Henry, Steve, Patricia, Geraldine, Manuel III. Owner Pena Realty & Ins. Agy., Phoenix, 1951-90; ret.; pres. emeritus Pena Ins. Agy., 1990; pres. Penasco, Inc.; mem. Ariz. state adv. com. U.S. Commn. Civil Rights, 1974, Ariz. Ho. of Reps., Phoenix, 1967-72, Ariz. Senate, Phoenix, 1973—. Exec. sec. Ariz. Athletic Commn., 1964-66, 67-71; bd. dirs. Ariz. Consumers Coun., 1960—; commr. human rels. City of Phoenix, 1967-71. With U.S. Army, 1945-46. Mem. VFW, Am. Legion (comdr.). Democrat. Roman Catholic. Office: State Capitol Office of State Senate PO Box 6482 Phoenix AZ 85007

PENA, RAYMUNDO JOSEPH, bishop; b. Corpus Christi, Tex., Feb. 19, 1934; s. Cosme A. and Elisa (Ramon) P. D.D., Assumption Sem., San Antonio, 1957. Ordained priest Roman Catholic Ch., 1957; asst. pastor St. Peter's Ch., Laredo, Tex., 1957-60, St. Joseph's-Our Lady of Fatima, Alamo, Tex., 1960-63, Sacred Heart, Mathis, Tex., 1963-67, Christ the King and Our Lady of Pillar Parishes, Corpus Christi, 1967-69; pastor Our Lady of Guadalupe Parish, Corpus Christi, 1969-76; v.p. Corpus Christi Diocesan Senate of Priests, 1970-76; aux. bishop of San Antonio, 1976-80; bishop El Paso, 1980-95, Brownsville, Tex., 1995—; mem. secretariat to Prep. Synod of Bishops for Am. Mem. Nat. Conf. Cath. Bishops, U.S. Cath. Conf. (chmn. bishops' com. for hispanic affairs 1987-90, bishops' com. for ch. in L.Am. 1994—). Home: Rt 8 Box 629 7600 Old Military Rd Brownsville TX 78522 Office: PO Box 2279 Brownsville TX 78522-2279

PENALOZA, BETTY RAQUEL, international affairs consultant; b. Lima, Peru, Oct. 4, 1947; came to U.S., 1970; d. Hernan and America (Ortiz) P.; m. Ray D. Roy Sr., Mar. 23, 1974 (div. Feb. 1989). BBA, U. St. Thomas, 1992, postgrad., 1993-94. Adminstrv. asst. Petroperu, Lima, 1968-70; adminstrv. asst. Petroperu, Houston, 1970-74, buyer, 1974-88; petroleum attache Consulate of Peru, Houston, 1974-87; buyer Serpimpex, S.A., Houston, 1991-93; owner Am. Victoria Trading Co., Houston, 1994—. Vice-chair Loop Program, End Hunger Network, 1993; vol. Mayor's Office, NAFTA Liaison, 1993. Named First Woman Elected Sec. of the Consular Corps, Consular Corps Houston, 1987. Mem. Consular Corps (hon. life).

PENCE, IRA WILSON, JR., material handling research executive, engineer; b. Pontiac, Mich., June 18, 1939; s. Ira Wilson and Fern Elizabeth (Fraser) P.; m. JoAnna Springer, Sept. 5, 1959; children: Ira W. III, Teresa Ann, Deidre Lynn. BS, U. Mich., 1962, MSEE, 1964, PhD, 1970. Rsch. engr.

Willow Run Labs., Ypsilanti, Mich., 1960-67, Dow Lab., Ann Arbor, Mich., 1967-70, GE, Schenectady, N.Y., 1970-80; engring. mgr. GE, Charlottesville, Va., 1980-83; v.p. engring. Unimation, Inc., Danbury, Conn., 1983-87; dir. MHRC Ga. Inst. Tech., Atlanta, 1987-94; cons. Superior Motor, Hartford, 1987-89; bd. dirs. Wesley Foundation; adv. council Westinghouse, Pittsburgh, 1983-87. Editor: Progress in Material Handling and Logistics, 1988; Material Handling for 90's, 1990. Trustee United Meth. Ch., 1988—. Recipient New Product of Yr. award Innovation Today, 1985. Mem. IEEE (sr., sect. chmn. 1978), ASME (Materials Handling Engring. divsn. chair 1994). Republican. Methodist. Avocations: cabinet making, golf. Office: Ga Inst Tech 765 Forest Crossing Dr SW Atlanta GA 30331-7387

PENCE, MARTIN, federal judge; b. Sterling, Kans., Nov. 18, 1904; m. Eleanor Fisher, Apr. 12, 1975. Bar: Calif. 1928, Hawaii 1933. Practice law Hilo, Hawaii, 1936-45, 50-61; judge 3d Circuit Ct., Hawaii, 1945-50; chief judge U.S. Dist. Ct., Hawaii, 1961-74; sr. judge U.S. Dist. Ct., 1974—. Office: US Dist Ct 1036 Maunawili Loop Kailua HI 96734-4621*

PENCE, ROBERT DUDLEY, biomedical research administrator, hospital administrator; b. Hillsboro, Ohio, June 16, 1928; s. Glenn Roush and Mildred (Wright) P. BA cum laude, Miami U., Oxford, Ohio, 1950; postgrad., U. Montpellier, France, 1950-51. Mktg. rep. Tex. Petroleum Co., West Africa, 1956-58; mgr. lab. and office svcs. Sloan-Kettering Inst. for Cancer Rsch., N.Y.C., 1958-68; bus. mgr., cancer rsch. inst. New Eng. Deaconess Hosp., Boston, 1968-72, adminstr. Shields Warren Radiation Lab., 1970-78, asst. dir., 1972-86, adminstrv. dir., cancer rsch. inst., 1974-88, adminstrv. dir. Shields Warren Radiation Lab., 1978-88, dir. div. of rsch., 1986-88, cons., 1988—; field liaison fellow ACS, Chgo., 1981-88. Pres. Am. Cancer Soc., Brookline, Mass. Served to lt. (j.g.) USN, 1951-55. Fulbright scholar, Montpellier, 1950. Mem. Assn. Community Cancer Ctrs. (del.), Internat. Union Against Cancer (U.S. standing com.), Assn. Am. Cancer Insts., Soc. Rsch. Adminstrs. (charter), Nat. Coun. Univ. Rsch. Adminstrs., Nat. Tumor Registrars Assn. (advisor 1980—), Tumor Registrars Assn. New Eng. (bd. dirs. 1975—), Phi Beta Kappa. Home: 30 Driftwood Cir Norwood MA 02062-5505

PENCEK, CAROLYN CARLSON, treasurer; b. Appleton, Wis., June 13, 1946; d. Arthur Edward and Mary George (Notaras) Carlson; m. Richard David Pencek, July 10, 1971; children: Richard Carlson, Mallory Barbara Rowlinds. BA in Polit. Sci., Western Coll., 1968; Ma in Polit. Sci., Syracuse U., 1975; postgrad., Temple U., 1991—. Investment analysts asst. Bankers Trust Co., N.Y.C., 1969-71; substitute tchr. Lackawanna Trail Sch. Dist., Factoryville, Pa., 1971-81; instr. polit. sci. Keystone Coll., La Plume, Pa., 1972-73; USGS coding supr. Richard Walsh Assocs., Scranton, Pa., 1975-76; instr. polit. sci. Pa. State U., Dunmore, 1976-77; treas. Creative Planning Ltd., Dunmore, 1988—; bd. trustees Lourdesmont Sch., Clarks Summit, Pa., 1989—. Bd. dirs. Lackawanna County Child and Youth Svcs., Scranton, 1981—, pres., 1988-90; founding mem., sec. Leadership Lackawanna, 1982-84; bd. dirs. N.E. Pa. Regional Tissue and Transplant Bank, Scranton, 1984-88, Vol. Action Ctr., Scranton, 1986-91; founding mem. Women's Resource Ctr. Assn., Scranton, 1986—, pres., 1986-87; v.p. sch. improvement coun. Lackawanna Trail Sch. Dist., 1995-96. Named Vol. of Yr. nominee, Vol. Action Ctr., 1985; Temple U. fellow, Phila., 1991-92. Mem. AAUW (sec. 1973-75, state sel. com. 1979-81), Assn. Jr. Leagues Internat. (area II coun. mem. 1978-79), Jr. League Scranton (v.p. 1980, pres. 1981-83, Margaret L. Richards award 1984), Philharmonic League (v.p. 1976, pres. 1977). Episcopalian. Home: RR 2 Box 2489 Factoryville PA 18419-9649 Office: Creative Planning Ltd 1100 Dunham Dr Dunmore PA 18512-2653

PENDARVIS, DONNA KAYE, elementary secondary school educator, adminstrator; b. New Orleans, June 19, 1959; d. Ray Haddox and Nita Sims; 1 child, Krista. BS, U. So. Miss., 1979; MEd, William Carey Coll., 1982, EdS, 1984; MEd in Guidance and Counseling, Southeastern La. U., 1992. Cert. elem. tchr., Miss., La.; lic. profl. counselor. Tchr. Sumrall (Miss.) Elem. Sch., 1979-88; tchr. kindergarten Washington Parish Sch. Bd., Franklinton, La., 1988-89; elem. tchr. Columbia (Miss.) Acad., 1989-92; counselor and adminstr. St. Tammany Parish, Covington, La., 1992-94; counselor, adminstr. Varnado (La.) H.S., 1994—. Grantee Miss. Power Found. Mem. NEA, ASCD, Am. Assn. Math. Tchrs., Am. Fedn. Tchrs., Miss. Fedn. Tchrs., La. Edn. Assn., Lamar County Classroom Tchrs. Assn., Washington Parish Reading Assn., Miss. Pvt. Sch. Assn., La. Counselors Assn., La. Vocat. Assn., La. Adminstrn. Sch. Employees Assn., Chi Omega Iota. Home: PO Box 217 27195 Military Rd Varnado LA 70467-0217 Office: Varnado High School 25543 Washington St Angie LA 70426

PENDERECKI, KRZYSZTOF, composer, conductor; b. Debica, Poland, Nov. 23, 1933; s. Tadeusz and Zofia P.; m. Elzbieta Solecka; children: Lukasz, Dominique. Grad., State Acad. Music, Krakow, 1958; student, Arthur Malawski and Stanislaw Wiechowicz; Dr. honoris causa, U. Rochester, St. Olaf Coll., Northfield, Minn., Cath U., Leuven, Belgium, U. Bordeaux, France, Georgetown U., Belgrade U., Madrid U., Spain, Adam Mickiewicz U., Warsaw U., Poland, 1993, U. Catolica Argentina, Buenos Aires, 1994, Acad. Music, Cracow, 1994, Acad. Music, Warsaw, 1994, U. Glasgow, 1995. Prof. composition Krakow State Sch. Music, 1959-65, Folkwang Hochschule für Musik, Essen, Fed. Republic Germany, 1966-68; composer-in-residence Sch. Music, Yale U., alternate years; guest condr. London Symphony Orch., Polish Radio Orch., Berlin Philharm. Orch. Composer: Psalms of David for chorus and percussion, 1958, Emanations for 2 string orchs., 1959, Strophes for soprano, narrator and 10 instruments, 1959, Dimensions of time and silence, 1959-61, Anaklasis, 1959-60, Threnody for the Victims of Hiroshima, 1960, Psalmus for tape, 1961, Polymorphia, 1961; Fluorescences, 1961, Stabat Mater, 1962, Canon, 1962, Sonata for cello and orch., 1964, St. Luke Passion, 1965, De Natura Sonoris I, 1966, Dies Irae, 1967, Capriccio for violin and orch., 1967, Capriccio for cello Solo, 1968; opera The Devils of Loudun, 1968-69; Utrenja for double chorus, soloists and orch., 1969-71, Cosmogony, 1970, Utrenja II-Resurrection, 1971, Actions for jazz ensemble, 1971, Partita for harpsichord, 4 solo instruments and orch., 1971-72, Cello Concerto, 1967-72; for double chorus, soloists and orchestra Ecloga VIII for 6 male voices, 1972; Symphony 1, 1972-73, Canticum Canticorum Salomonis for 16 voices and chamber orch., 1970-73, Magnificat, 1973-74, When Jacob Awoke for orch., 1974, Violin Concerto, 1976-77, Paradise Lost (rappresentazione), 1976-78, (Christmas) Symphony No. 2, 1980, Te Deum, 1979-80, Lacrimosa, 1980, Agnus Dei for a cappella chorus, 1981, Cello Concerto No. 2, 1982, Requiem, 1983, Concerto per Viola, 1983, Polish Requiem, 1983-84, The Black Mask, 1986, Der Unterbrochene Gedanke, 1987, Adagio, 1989, Ubu Rex, 1991, Sinfonietta for orchestra, 1990-91, Symphony No. 5 for orchestra, 1991-92, Partita for orchestra, rev. edit., 1991, Flute concerto, 1992-93, Quartet for Clarinet and String Trio, 1993, Divertimento per Cello solo, 1994, Violin Concerto No. 2, 1992-95, Agnus Dei, 1995, Symphony No. 3, also other works; guest condr. NDR Symphony Orch., Hamburg, Federal Republic of Germany. Recipient 1st prize for Strophes Polish Composers Assn., 1959, UNESCO award, Fitelberg prize and Polish Ministry Culture award all for Threnody, 1960, Krakow composition prize for Canon, 1961, grand prize State N. Rhine-Westphalia for St. Luke Passion, 1966, Pax prize Poland, 1966, Jurzykowski prize Polish Inst. Arts and Scis., 1966, Sibelius award, 1967, Prix d'Italia, 1967-68, Polish 1st Class State award, 1968, Gottfried von Herder prize, 1977, prix Arthur Honegger, 1978, Sibelius prize Wihouri Found., 1983, Wolf Found. prize, 1987, 3 Grammy awards, Gamma prize Acad. Rec. Arts and Scis., 1988, Manuel de Falla Gold medal Accademia de Bellas Artes, Granada, 1989, Das Grosse Verdienstkreuz des Verdienstordens der Bundesrepublik Deutschland, 1990, 2 Grammy nominations, 1992, Grawermeyer Music award, 1992, Österreichische Ehrenzeichen für Wissenschaft und Kunst, 1994; grantee several founds., govts., insts. Mem. Royal Acad. Mus. London (hon.), Nat. Acad. of Santa Cecilia (Rome) (hon.), Royal Swedish Acad. Music, Acad. of Kuenste West Berlin (extraord. mem.), Nat. Acad. of Bellas Artes (Buenos Aires) (corr.), Internat. Acad. Philosophy and Art (Berne), Nat. Acad. Scis., Belles-lettres et Arts (Bordeaux), Acad. Scientiarium et Artium Europaea (Salzburg), L'Ordre de Saint Georges de Bourgogne (officer, Brussels). Creator original notational system allowing aleatory freedom for performer within sects. of precise duration. Home: ul Cisowa 22, 30229 Cracow Poland Office: ICM Artists Ltd 8942 Wilshire Blvd Beverly Hills CA 90211-1934 also: Panstwowa Wyzsza Szkola Muzyczna, ul Starowislna, 31-038 Cracow Poland

PENDERGAST, JOHN JOSEPH, III, lawyer; b. Lewiston, Maine, Jan. 29, 1936; s. John Joseph and Grace (McCarty) P.; m. Joan Shaw Cole, June 14, 1958; children: John Joseph IV, Timothy S., Terrence B., Mary R., Michael C., Joan M. B.A., Yale U., 1957, LL.B., 1960. Bar: R.I. 1961, U.S. dist. Ct. R.I. 1961, U.S. Ct. Appeals (1st cir.) 1963. Assoc. Hinckley, Allen, & Snyder, Providence, 1960-66, ptnr., chmn. labor dept., 1966—; instr. U. R.I., Kingston, 1984-88, adj. prof. Providence Coll., 1984-86. Author: (with others) The Developing Labor Law, 2d edit., 1983, Labor and Employment Arbitration, 1988, NLRA Law & Practice, 1992. Mem. Cath. Charities panel Diocese of Providence, 1976-94; bd. dirs. Smith Hill Center, Providence, 1978-93; v.p. Providence Boys Clubs, 1970-72, bd. dirs., 1990—. Mem. ABA (labor law sect.), The Best Lawyers in Am., Am. Coll. Hosp. Attys., Indsl. Rels. Rsch. Assn., Hosp. Assn. Labor Execs., R.I. Bar Assn., Sakonnet Yacht Club, University Club, Yale Club of R.I. (Providence). Avocations: antiques, fly fishing. Home: 21 Violet St Providence RI 02908-4825 Office: Hinckley Allen & Snyder 1500 Fleet Ctr Providence RI 02903

PENDERGAST, WILLIAM ROSS, lawyer; b. Kansas City, Mo., Oct. 1, 1931; s. Francis Gregory and Florence (Ross) P.; m. Dorothy Victoria Dusic, Aug. 5, 1961; children—William Ross, Patrick Fitzwilliam. B.S., Rockhurst Coll., 1952; J.D., U. Mo.-Columbia, 1957. Bar: Mo., D.C., U.S. Supreme Ct. Assoc. Meyer & Smith, Kansas City, Mo., 1957-61; trial atty. FDA, Washington, 1961-65; ptnr. McLean, Morton & Boustead, Washington, 1965-68, McMurray and Pendergast, Washington, 1968-79, 83, Arent, Fox, Kintner, Plotkin & Kahn, Washington, 1983—; chmn. ABA Food and Drug Com., Washington, 1970-79; dir. Nat. Source Vitamin E Assn., Washington, 1984—. Contbr. articles to profl. jours. Served with U.S. Army, 1950-52. Mem. ABA, Fed. Bar Assn. Democrat. Roman Catholic. Clubs: Metropolitan, Chevy Chase. Office: Arent Fox Kintner Plotkin & Kahn 1050 Connecticut Ave NW Washington DC 20036-5303

PENDERGHAST, THOMAS FREDERICK, business educator; b. Cin., Apr. 23, 1936; s. Elmer T. and Dolores C. (Huber) P.; BS, Marquette U., 1958; MBA, Calif. State U., Long Beach, 1967; D in Bus. Adminstrn. Nova U., 1987; m. Marjorie Craig, Aug. 12, 1983; children: Brian, Shawna, Steven, Dean, Maria. Sci. programmer Autonetics, Inc., Anaheim, Calif., 1960-64; bus. programmer Douglas Missile & Space Ctr., Huntington Beach, Calif., 1964-66; computer specialist N.Am. Rockwell Co., 1966-69; asst. prof. Calif. State U., Long Beach, 1969-72; prof. Sch. Bus. and Mgmt., Pepperdine U., Los Angeles, 1972—; spl. adviser Commn. on Engring. Edn., 1968; v.p. Visual Computing Co., 1969-71; founder, pres. Scoreboard Animation Systems, 1971-77; exec. v.p. Microfilm Identification Systems, 1977-79; pres. Data Processing Auditors, Inc., 1981—; data processing cons. designing computer system for fin. health and mfg. orgns., 1972—. Mem. Orange County Blue Ribbon Com. on Data Processing, 1973; mem. Orange County TEC Policy Bd., 1982-87; mgmt. and organization devel. cons. Assn. Psychological Type, 1993—. Served to lt. USNR, 1958-60. Cert. in data processing. Mem. Users of Automatic Info. Display Equipment (pres. 1966). Author: Entrepreneurial Simulation Program, 1988. Home: 17867 Bay St Fountain Valley CA 92708-4443

PENDERGRAFT, NORMAN ELVEIS, art history educator, art museum director; b. Durham, N.C., Mar. 4, 1934; s. Harvey W. and Essie (Wilson) P. AB, U. N.C., 1962, MA in Coll. Teaching, 1967; postgrad., Conservatory Music G. Rossini, Pesaro, Italy, 1963-65, Ohio U., 1969-71, U. Calif., Berkeley, 1979 (summer). Tchr. N.W. High Sch., Greensboro, N.C., 1961-62; tchr. English, The English Ctr., Ancona, Italy, 1964-65; prof. art dept. N.C. Ctrl. U., Durham, 1966—, dir. Art Mus., 1976—; guest curator Artistic Legacy: Collection of Art from CIAA Schs., Diggs Gallery at WSSU. Exhibit organizer, author catalog: Gullah Life Reflections: Painting by Jonathan Green, 1988, Where Myth Stirs: Paintings by Jim Moon, 1991, Joy of Living: Romance Bearden's Late Work, 1993, Charles Alston: New Negro Artist, 1994, Yohannes Gedamu: Painter, 1995. Bd. dirs. Stagville Hist. Preservation Soc., Durham County, 1989—; program chmn. Durham Hist. Preservation Soc., 1991-93. With USN, 1954-58. Recipient Friends of Arts award N.C. Art Edn. Assn., 1984, Profl. Svc. award N.C. Mus. Coun., 1995; selected to attend NEH Roman Painting 1480-1550: New Approaches seminar, Rome, 1992. Mem. AAUP, Am. Assn. Mus., Southeastern Mus. Conf., Coll. Art Assn., N.C. Mus. Coun. (past pres. art sect.). Democrat. Avocations: travel, walking. Home: 208 Watts St Durham NC 27701-2037 Office: NC Ctrl U NCCU Art Mus PO Box 19555 Durham NC 27707-0099

PENDERGRASS, HENRY PANCOAST, physician, radiology educator; b. Bryn Mawr, Pa., Jan. 29, 1925; s. Eugene Percival and Rebecca (Barker) P.; m. Carol Lowe Dodson, Aug. 27, 1960 (dec. Aug. 1993); children: Sharon (dec.), Lisa (dec.), Deborah, Margaret; m. Carol Minster Roberts, Oct. 2, 1994. Student, U.S. Naval Acad., 1944-46; A.B., Princeton U., 1948; M.D., U. Pa., 1952; M.P.H., Harvard U., 1969. Diplomate: Am. Bd. Radiology, Am. Bd. Nuclear Medicine. Intern Pa. Hosp., 1953-54; mem. staff and faculty U. Pa. Med. Sch. and Univ. Hosp., Phila., 1953-58, 60-61; clin. asst. in neuroradiology Inst. Neurology Queen Sq., London, 1959-60; mem. staff and faculty Harvard U. Med. Sch. and Mass. Gen. Hosp., Boston, 1958-59, 61-76; prof. radiology Vanderbilt U. Sch. Medicine, Nashville, 1976-95, prof. emeritus, 1995—, vice chmn., 1976-89. Mem. editorial bd. Am. Family Physician, 1980-94, Jour. Digital Imaging, 1987—; contbr. chpts. to books, articles to med. jours. Mem. cancer control rev. com. Nat. Cancer Inst., 1975-79; Bd. dirs. state and local div. Am. Cancer Soc., 1976-85; mem. Project Hope Med. Mission, Peru, 1962; trustee Harpeth Hall Sch., Nashville, 1983-88. With U.S. Army, USN, 1943-46. Am. Cancer Soc. grantee, 1956-57; Nat. Cancer Inst. grantee, 1957-58; Nat. Inst. Neurol. Disease and Blindness grantee, 1959-60; Nat. Inst. Gen. Med. Scis. grantee, 1968-69; Distinguished Service award Am. Medical Assn., 1994. Fellow Am. Coll. Radiology (life mem., benefactor, counselor, steering com. 1968-73, bd. chancellors 1977-81), AMA (mem. Ho. of Dels. 1986—, sect. coun. on radiology 1978—, sec. 1987—, sect. on med. schs. 1979—, Disting. Svc. Gold medal 1994, grad. med. edn. adv. com. 1994—), Coun. Med. Splty. Socs., Am. Roentgen Ray Soc., Brit. Inst. Radiology, Ea. Radiol. Soc. (pres., trustee 1968-72, sci. program chmn. 1964, 72, 79), Assn. Univ. Radiologists, Mass. Radiol. Soc. (v.p. 1967-68, 75-76), Mass. Med. Soc. (counselor 1968-76), Nashville Acad. Medicine (chmn. com. on ethics 1981-82, Nat. Bd. Med. Examiners 1995—), Radiol. Soc. N.Am. (bd. dirs. 1972-77, chmn. 1975-76, pres.-elect and pres. 1977-78, Gold medal 1984, trustee RSNA Rsch. and Edn. Fund 1984-90, fund sec.-treas 1988-90), Am. Soc. Emergency Radiology, Tenn. Med. Assn., Tenn. Radiol. Soc. (pres.-elect, then pres. 1985-86, exec. com. 1984-88), Mid. Tenn. Radiol. Soc. (pres. 1984-85, sec., treas. 1985-94), Soc. Thoracic Imaging, Soc. Magnetic Resonance in Medicine, Sigma Xi, Delta Psi. Clubs: Belle Meade Country, Merion golf, Merion Cricket, Amateur Ski (N.Y.), Cap and Gown (Princeton, N.J.). Office: Vanderbilt U Sch Medicine 1121 21st Ave S Nashville TN 37232-2675

PENDERGRASS, TEDDY (THEODORE D. PENDERGRASS), musician; b. Phila., Mar. 26, 1950; m. Karin Michelle Still, June 20, 1987; children: Tisha, Ladonna, Teddy. Student public schs. Drummer for various groups, 1966-69; Singer, lead singer Harold Melvin & Blue Notes, 1969-75; solo artist, 1975—; pres. Teddy Bear Enterprises, Phila. Squire, Memphis. albums include: Life Is a Song Worth Singing, 1978, Teddy, 1979, T.P., 1980, Live Coast to Coast, 1980, It's Time for Teddy, 1981, Teddy Pendergrass, 1982, This One's For You, 1982, Heaven Only Knows, 1983, Greatest Hits, 1984, Love Language, 1984, Workin' It Back, 1985, Joy, 1988, Truly Blessed, 1991, A Little More Magic, 1993. Recipient civic and pub. service awards., Image award NAACP, 1973, 80, Black Achievement award Ebony Mag., 1979, award outstanding mus. contbn. Afro-Am. Hist. Mus., 1983, award of merit City of Detroit, 12 gold and 7 platinum albums; recipity Keys to Cities, Lakeland (Fla.), Detroit, Savannah (Ga.), Memphis; named New Artist of 1977 for Top Pop Album Billboard Mag.

PENDERY, EDWARD STUART, deputy county judge; b. Dayton, Ky., June 1, 1931; s. Edward Stuart and Marguerite Garnet (Owens) P.; m. Nancy Jean Burck, Aug. 22, 1958; children: Michael Edward, Darren Frederick, Eric Christopher. Student, U.S. Tech. Sch., 1952. R.R. dep. chief clk. N.Y. Ctrl. R.R., Cin., 1950-51; R.R. comml. agt. C & WC Rlwy., Cin., 1955-58; salesman Pittsburg Paint & Glass, Cin., 1958-63; ops. mgr. Am. Laundry/Econo Sales, Cin., 1963-67; pvt. practice I.P.C.S. Pub., Ft. Thomas, Ky., 1967-68, 74-86; mag. sales and display ads staff Cin. (Ohio) Mag., 1969-74; dep. county judge Campbell County Ky., Newport, Ky., 1986—. Editor, originator: (tabloids) North Ky. Sports Scene, 1976—, Bellevue News, 1980—, Shopping Guides, 1980—. Chmn. site group North Ky. U., Highland Heights, 1968; chmn. study group Ft. Thomas (Ky.) Sch. Sys., 1970; dir. North Ky. U. Norse Club, Highland Heights, 1971-89, Famous Stars H.S. Program, Bellevue, Ky., 1978-94; mem. Bellevue Civic Assn., 1980—, North Ky. Adminstrs. Group, Newport, 1986-94, Libr. Site Com., Cold Spring, Ky., 1993-94, Nat. Alliance Bus., 1993. Staff sgt. USAF, 1951-55. Named Ky. Col., Ky. Gov., 1967; recipient Meritorious Svc. award Cub Scouts, 1968. Mem. Am. Assn. Ret. Persons, Elks, Am. Legion, North Ky. U. Norse Club. Democrat. Avocation: golf. Home: 38 Homestead Pl Fort Thomas KY 41075-1225

PENDLETON, BARBARA JEAN, retired banker; b. Independence, Mo., Aug. 14, 1924; d. Elmer Dean and Martha Lucille (Friess) P. Student, Cen. Mo. State Coll., 1942; D of Bus. Adminstrn. (hon.), Avila Coll., 1986. V.p. Grand Ave. Bank, Kansas City, Mo., 1962-76, exec. v.p., 1976-79; vice chmn. City Bank & Trust Co., Kansas City, 1979-82, chmn., 1982-83; exec. v.p. United Mo. Bank of Kansas City, 1983-93, United Mo. Bancshares, Inc., 1990-93; bd. dirs. Shepherd Ctrs. of Am., Inc., 1992—. Vice chmn., mem. Dept. Def. adv. com. Women in Svc., Washington, 1967-69; chmn. City of Kansas City Employee Retirement Fund, 1985—; mem. bd. dirs. YMCA USA, 1996—. Recipient Matrix award Press Women, 1963, Wohelo award Campfire, Inc., 1979. Mem. Fin. Women Internat. (nat. pres. 1972-73), Am. Humanics, Inc. (chmn. 1987-88). Club: Cen. Exchange (Kansas City) (pres. 1983-84).

PENDLETON, ELMER DEAN, JR., retired military officer, international consultant; b. Kansas City, Mo., June 26, 1927; s. Elmer Dean and Martha Lucille (Friess) P.; m. Anne Bittner, Sept. 10, 1971; children: V. Allison Connor, John K. Lange, Christian D. Pendleton. BS, U.S. Mil. Acad., West Point, 1951; MS, George Washington U., Washington, 1969. Commd. 2d lt. U.S. Army, 1951, advanced through grades to maj. gen., 1977, ret., 1986; platoon leader 11th airborne div., Fort Campbell, Ky., 1951-52; co. commdr. 7th infantry div., Korea, 1952-53, 82d airborne div., Fort Bragg, N.C., 1954-56; instr. Ranger Sch., Eglin AFB, Fla., 1957-58; aide to comdg. gen. Teheran, Iran, 1958; staff officer 3d inf. (Old Guard), Washington, 1958-59, Dept. of Army, Washington, 1960-63; bn. comdr. 24th inf. div., Berlin, Fed. Republic Germany, 1964-65; sector advisor Can Tho, Vietnam, 1965-66; bn. comdr. 1st inf. div., Vietnam, 1966-68; brigade comdr. 1st inf. div. and II field force, G-3, Vietnam, 1969-70; corps G-3 XVIII airborne corps, Fort Bragg, N.C., 1971-74; dep. chief of staff and chief of staff XVIII airborne corps, 1974-75; comdr. 1st corps Support Command, Fort Bragg, N.C., 1975-78, 19th Support Command, Taegu, Korea, 1978-80; logistics officer U.S. Readiness Command, MacDill AFB, Fla., 1980-81; ops. officer U.S. Readiness Command, 1981-82; chief Joint U.S. Mil. Mission for Aid to Turkey, Ankara, 1982-86; cons. Internat. Activities, Washington, 1986—. Decorated D.S.M., Def. D.S.M., Silver Star with 3 oak leaf clusters, Legion of Merit with 2 oak leaf clusters, D.F.C. with 2 oak leaf clusters, Bronze Star with 8 oak leaf clusters and V device, Combat Infantry Badge 2d award, 44 Air medals, Purple Heart, others. Mem. Am. Turkish Coun. (bd. dirs., chmn. def. and security affairs com.), ITEC, Inc. (pres.), Army-Navy Club (Washington). Home and Office: 3028 Knoll Dr Falls Church VA 22042-3111

PENDLETON, EUGENE BARBOUR, JR., business executive; b. nr. Louisa, Va., Apr. 2, 1913; s. Eugene Barbour and Virginia (Goodman) P.; m. Mildred McLean, June 18, 1938; children: Barbara Jane Pendleton Wootton, Sally Anne Pendleton Campbell, Nancy McLean Pendleton Wheeler, Susan Virginia Pendleton Hayden, Martha Christina Pendleton Perry. Student, Va. Mil. Inst., 1930-31, Hampden-Sydney Coll., 1931-34. Organizer, mgr. Gen. Ins. Agy., 1937-42; treas. Louisa County, Va., 1946-58; field rep. Va. Dept. Taxation, 1958-60; treas. State of Va., 1960-64; treas. So. States Coop., 1964-80, v.p. fin., 1977-78; v.p. fin. Truxmore Industries Inc., Richmond, Va., 1978-86, retired, 1986; mem. adv. bd. Jefferson Nat. Bank. Bd. dirs., past pres. Richmond Businessmen's Assn.; v.p., mem. exec. com. Atlantic Rural Expn.; past mem. exec. com. Richmond Home for Boys, Va. Edn. Fund; past bd. dirs. Richmond Symphony.; Mem. bd. suprs., Louisa County, 1937-42; mem. Ho. of Dels., Va. Gen. Assembly, 1966-70; Past pres. Va. Thanksgiving Festival. Served from ensign to lt. USNR, 1942-46, ETO. Mem. Va. Richmond chambers commerce, Bond Club Va., County and City Treas. Assn. Va. (past pres.), Nat. Assn. State Treas., Mil. Order World Wars (past comdr.), Navy League U.S. (pres.), 1st Families Va. (pres., coun.), Soc. of Va. (v.p.), Am. Legion, VFW (past comdr.), Downtown Club (Richmond, past pres.), commonwealth Club, Country Club of Va., Shriners, Masons, Willow Oakes Country Club (past pres.), Sigma Chi. Mem. Christian Ch. (past elder, chmn. bd.). Home: 8007 Dunsmore Rd Richmond VA 23229-7411

PENDLETON, GARY H(ERMAN), life insurance agent; b. Stuart, Va., Mar. 8, 1947; s. Herman P.; m. Laura Jeanes, Feb. 14, 1976; children: Blair J., Gray E. BS, SUNY, Albany. CLU, ChFC. Dir. intergovt. relations N.C. Dept. Transp., Raleigh, 1973-76; pres. Preferred Planning and Ins., Inc., Raleigh, 1976—; mem. N.C. State Banking Commn., 1985-89. Chmn., county commr. Wake County, N.C., 1992—; mem. N.C. Bd. C.C.'s, 1989-91, N.C. Econ. Devel. Bd., 1991-93. Presbyterian. Avocations: snow skiing, boating, fishing, hunting. Home: 2908 Lake Boone Pl Raleigh NC 27608-1151 Office: 2601 Oberlin Rd Ste 201 Raleigh NC 27608-1319

PENDLETON, MARY CATHERINE, foreign service officer; b. Louisville, Ky., June 15, 1940; d. Joseph S. and Katherine R. (Toebbe) P. BA, Spalding Coll., 1962; MA, Ind. U., 1969; cert., Nat. Def. U., 1990; D (hon.), U. N. Testemitanu, Moldova, 1994. Cert. secondary tchr., Ky. Tchr. Presentation Acad., Louisville, 1962-66; vol. Peace Corps, Tunis, Tunisia, 1966-68; employment counselor Ky. Dept. for Human Resources, Louisville, 1969-75; gen. svcs. Am. Embassy, Khartoum, Sudan, 1975-77; counsular officer Am. Embassy, Manila, Philippines, 1978-79; adminstrv. officer Am. Embassy, Bangui, Cen. African Republic, 1979-82, Lusaka, Zambia, 1982-84; post mgmt. officer Dept. of State Bur. European and Can. Affairs, Washington, 1984-87; adminstrv. counselor Am. Embassy, Bucharest, Romania, 1987-89; dir. adminstrv. tng. divsn. Fgn. Svc. Inst., Arlington, Va., 1990-92; ambassador Am. Embassy, Chisinau, Moldova, 1992-95; adminstrv. counselor Am. Embassy, Brussels, 1995—. Bd. dirs. Am. Sch. of Bucharest, 1987-89. Named to Honorable Order of Ky. Cols., 1988. Democrat. Roman Catholic. Avocations: family history research, outdoor activities. Home and Office: Emb USA, Blvd du Regent 27, B-1000 Brussels Belgium

PENDLETON, MOSES ROBERT ANDREW, dancer, choreographer; b. St. Johnsbury, Vt., Mar. 28, 1949; s. Nelson Augustus and Mary Elizabeth (Patchel) P. B.A., Dartmouth Coll., 1971. Co-founder, dir., choreographer, dancer Pilobolus Dance Theater, Washington, Conn., 1971—; founder, artistic dir. Momix Dance Theater, Washington, 1980—. Choreographer, dancer numerous works including Pilobolus, 1971, Anendrom, 1972, Walklyndon, 1972, Ocellus, 1972, Ciona, 1973, Monkshood's Farewell, 1974, Untitled, 1975, Eve of Samhain, 1977, Alraune, 1975, Lost in Fauna, 1976, Shizen, 1977, Bonsai, 1978, Day Two, 1981, Elva, 1987, Debut C, 1988, Accordion, 1989, Fantasy on a Variation on a Theme, 1989; choreographer Am. premiere of Jean Coeteau's Les Marie de la tour Eiffel, 1988; actor, dancer: (film) Pilobolus and Joan, 1974; choreographer: Erik Satie Festival, Paris Opera, 1978; co-choreographer: Molly's Not Dead, 1978; choreographer: (for Pilobolus Dance Theater) Day Two 1981, Stabat Mater, 1985, Carmina Burana Side II, 1985; Joffrey Ballet Relache, 1980, Closing Ceremonies 1980 Winter Olympics, Berlin Opera Tutuguri, 1981, Moses Pendleton Presents Moses Pendelton, 1982, Ballet de Nancy, France, Pulcinella, 1985, (for Momix Dance Theater) Kiss Off Spiderwoman, 1986, Spawning, 1986, Venus Envy, 1986, Medusa, 1986, Preface to Preview, 1986, excerpts from Gifts from the Sea, 1986, (opera for Spoleto Festival) Platee, 1987, Passion, 1991; tchr., artist-in-residence at univs. throughout U.S., 1977; tchr., condr. workshops. Recipient Edinborough Fringe Festival Scotman's award, 1973, Berlin Critic's prize, 1975; Nat. Endowment for Arts grantee, 1975-76; Guggenheim fellow in choreography, 1977. Democrat. Office: Momix PO Box 35 Washington Depot CT 06794-0035

PENDLETON, SUMNER ALDEN, financial consultant; b. Boston, May 2, 1918; s. Sumner Maynard and Ethel Parker (Phinney) P.; m. Nancy Curtiss Welles, June 8, 1941; children: Nancy Alden Pendleton Dyer, John Welles. SB cum laude, Harvard U., 1939, MBA, 1941. With Gen. Electric Co., 1945-50, Ford Motor Co., 1950-53; asst. to corp. contr. to contr. electronics div. Curtiss-Wright Corp., 1953-60; asst. contr. fin. analysis, audit and data processing methods ITT Corp., 1960-63; contr., asst. sec. Joy Mfg. Co., Pitts., 1963-67; v.p. fin. treas. Ryan Homes, Inc., Pitts., 1967-71, v.p. corp. devel., 1971-74; v.p., sec., treas. Ryan Homes Fin. Co., 1970-74; chmn., treas. Unidyne Corp., Pitts., also, 1975-80, Bergoo Coal Co., Pitts., 1975-78; assoc. exec. dir. budget and fin. United Presbyn. Ch. U.S.A., 1976-78; fin. cons., 1978-81; dir., v.p. fin., treas. Hytronics Corp., 1979-81; lic. sales assoc. VR Bus. Brokers, Clearwater, 1990-92, 95—; lic. sales assoc., bus. brokers Metro Bay Assocs., Clearwater, Fla., 1992-94; mgmt. fin. cons., 1974—; chmn., treas., bd. dirs. Consource Plastic Recycling Corp., Tampa, 1992—; mem. Svc. Corps Ret. Execs., 1981—, v.p., sec., treas. Pinellas chpt., 1983-85, pres., 1985-86, chmn., 1986-87. Gen. campaign chmn. Comty. Chest Ridgewood, Hohokus and Midland Park, N.J., 1959-60, pres., 1960-62; treas. Southminster Presbyn. Ch., Mt. Lebanon, Pa., 1966-76, trustee, 1965-68, elder, 1968-71, past deacon, head usher, Sunday sch. tchr. Lt. comdr. USNR, 1941-45, capt. USNR, ret. Decorated Silver Star; recipient Acctg. Profession Exec. of Yr. award Robert Morris Coll., 1973; Baker scholar Harvard Bus. Sch., 1941. Mem. Fin. Execs. Inst. (dir. Newark 1961-62), Nat. Assn. Accts. (Lybrand cert. 1955, pres. Paterson chpt. 1955-56, nat. dir. 1957-59, v.p. 1965-66, mem. exec. com. 1966-69), Stuart Cameron McLeod Soc. (pres. 1975-76), Harvard Bus. Sch. Assn. Pitts. (v.p. 1968-69, pres. 1969-70, chmn. bd. govs. 1970-71), Harvard Club of Fla. West Coast (v.p. 1982-84, pres. 1984-86, bd. dirs. 1986—), Harvard Bus. Sch. Club Fla. West Coast (bd. dirs. 1986—). Home: 2163 Waterside Dr Clearwater FL 34624-6658 Office: 4625 E Bay Dr Ste 305 Clearwater FL 34624-5747

PENDLETON, TERRY LEE, baseball player; b. L.A., July 16, 1960; m. Catherine Grindulo Marquey, Oct. 27, 1984. Student, Oxnard Coll., Calif., Fresno State U., Calif. Baseball player St. Louis Cardinals, 1982-90, Atlanta Braves, 1990—; with Fla. Marlins, 1994—. Winner Most Valuable Player award Baseball Writers' Assn. Am., 1991, Gold Glove award, 1987, 89, 92; mem Nat. League All-Star Team, 1992; Nat. League Batting Champion, 1991; named N.L. Comeback Player of the Yr. The Sporting News, 1991, Third Baseman on the Sporting News N.L. All-Star Team, 1991. Office: Fla Marlins 2269 NW 199th St Opa Locka FL 33056*

PENDLEY, WILLIAM TYLER, naval officer, international relations educator; b. Paris, Ky., June 21, 1936; s. Louis Tyler and Virginia Lorene (Poplin) P.; m. Anne Carrol Cooke, Dec. 13, 1958; children: Stephen Tyler, Robert Randolph, Lisa Carrol, Leslie Brooks. BS in Engring., U.S. Naval Acad., 1958; MA, Am. U., Washington, 1965. Commd. ens. USN, 1958, advanced through grades to rear adm., 1983; comdg. officer Patrol Squadron 45, Jacksonville, Fla., 1975-76; ops. officer Patrol Wing 11, U.S. Atlantic Fleet, Jacksonville, 1976-78, commdr., 1979-81; exec. sec. for joint chief of staff matters Chief Naval Ops., Washington, 1978-79, planner for joint chief of staff matters, 1981-82, dir. plans policy and strategy div., 1985-86; exec. asst. to comdr. in chief U.S. Pacific Fleet, Pearl Harbor, Hawaii, 1982-83; commdr. patrol wings U.S. Atlantic Fleet, Brunswick, Maine, 1983-85; commdr. Naval Forces Korea, Seoul, 1986-89; sr. mem. UN Mil. Armistice Commn., 1986-89; dir. strategic plans and policy USCINCPAC, Camp H. M. Smith, Hawaii, 1990-91; dep. asst. sec. def. for East Asia and Pacific affairs Dept. Defense, Washington, 1992-93; prof. internat. rels. Air War Coll., Maxwell AFB, Ala., 1993—; fellow Georgetown U. Leadership Seminar, Washington, 1985. Co-author: Nuclear Coexistence, 1994; contbr. articles to profl. jours. Decorated Def. D.S.M. with oak leaf cluster, Legion of Merit with 4 gold stars; named hon. Ky. Col., 1975; recipient Def. medal for disting. pub. svc., 1993. Mem. U.S. Naval Inst., Internat. Inst. Strategic Studies, Phi Kappa Phi, Pi Gamma Mu. Methodist. Avocations: flying, golf, tennis, skiing. Home: 6445 Eastwood Glen Dr Montgomery AL 36117-4713 Office: Air War Coll 325 Chennault Cir Maxwell AFB AL 36112-6427

PENFIELD, CAROLE H. (KATE PENFIELD), minister, church official. Grad., Andover Newton Theol. Sch. Co-pastor Ctrl. Bapt. Ch., Providence, 1st Bapt. Ch. Am., Providence; exec. dir. Ministers Coun. of ABC USA; mem. regional and nat. mins. coun. and senate Am. Bapt. Chs., v.p., 1994—; mem. state Senate ethics com. R.I. Legislature; pres. R.I. State Coun. Chs., 1987-89. Editor Ministry, Am. Bapt. Chs. Office: ABC in the USA PO Box 851 Valley Forge PA 19482-0851

PENFIELD, PAUL LIVINGSTONE, JR., electrical engineering educator; b. Detroit, May 28, 1933; s. Paul Livingstone and Charlotte Wentworth (Gilman) P.; m. Martha Elise Dieterle, Aug. 24, 1956 (dec. Apr. 1988); children: David Wesley, Patricia Jane, Michael Baldwin; m. Barbara Jean Buehrig Lory, July 22, 1989. BA, Amherst Coll., 1955; ScD, MIT, 1960. Asst. prof. elec. engring. MIT, Cambridge, 1960-64, assoc. prof., 1964-69, prof., 1969—, head dept. elec. engring. and computer sci., 1989—. Author: Frequency-Power Formulas, 1960, MARTHA User's Manual, 1971; co-author: Varactor Applications, 1962, Electrodynamics of Moving Media, 1967, Tellegen's Theorem and Electrical Networks, 1970. Sr. postdoctoral fellow NSF, 1966-67. Fellow IEEE (chmn. Boston sect. 1971-72, Darlington award 1983, Centennial medal 1984); mem. Nat. Acad. Engring., Am. Phys. Soc., Assn. for Computing Machinery, Audio Engring. Soc., Sigma Xi. Avocation: field identification of ferns and fern hybrids. Office: MIT Dept EECS Cambridge MA 02139

PENHUNE, JOHN PAUL, science company executive, electrical engineer; b. Flushing, N.Y., Feb. 13, 1936; s. Paul and Helene Marguerite (Beux) P.; m. Nancy Leigh Peabody, Sept. 6, 1958 (div. Apr. 1982); children: Virginia Burdet, James Peabody, Sarah Slipp; m. Marcellite Helen Porath, Feb. 15, 1986; 1 child, Marcellite Helen Broadhurst. BSEE, MIT, 1957, PhD in Elect. Engring., 1961; postgrad., U. Grenoble, France, 1959; postgrad. in bus., Harvard U., 1973. Asst. prof. elec. engring. MIT, Cambridge, 1962-64; mem. tech. staff Lincoln Lab MIT, Lexington, 1964-66; supr. radar group Bell Tel. Labs., Whippany, N.J., 1966-68; asst. dir. Advanced Ballistic Missile Def. Agy., Washington, 1968-69; pres. Concord Rsch. Corp., Burlington, Mass., 1969-73; ind. sci. cons. Carlisle, Mass., 1973-79; bd. dirs. Phys. Dynamics, Inc., La Jolla, Calif., 1979-81; sr. v.p. for rsch. Sci. Applications Internat. Corp., San Diego, 1981—; chmn. indsl. adv. bd. Inst. Biomed. Engring./U. Calif., San Diego, 1992—, CONNECT steering com., 1993—, adv. bd. dept. bioengring., 1995—; bd. visitors Coll. Engring./U. Calif., Davis, 1993—; human subjects com. Salk Inst., La Jolla, 1995—. Author: Case Studies in Electromagnetism, 1960; patentee in field. Bd. dirs. La Jolla (Calif.) Chamber Music Soc., 1985-87. 1st lt. U.S. Army, 1961-62. Recipient Meritorious Civilian Svc. award Dept. Army, 1968. Mem. N.Y. Acad. Scis., Cosmos Club (Washington), San Diego Yacht Club, Eta Kappa Nu, Tau Beta Pi, Sigma Xi, Phi Kappa Sigma. Avocations: boating, classical music. Home: 6730 Muirlands Dr La Jolla CA 92037-6315 Office: Sci Applications Internat Corp 1200 Prospect St Ste 400 La Jolla CA 92037

PENICK, GEORGE DIAL, JR., foundation executive; b. San Juan, P.R., Apr. 17, 1948; s. George Dial and Marguerite Murchison (Worth) P.; m. Carol Davis Bonham, Jan. 30, 1971; children: Holladay Bonham, Robert Anderson. BA, Davidson Coll., 1970; EdM, Harvard U., 1976, M in Pub. Adminstrn., 1977, EdD, 1982. Asst. to dir. Learning Inst. N.C., Durham, 1970-71; child devel. adminstr. N.C. Office for Children, Raleigh, 1973-75; sr. research asst. Harvard U.-MIT Joint Ctr. for Urban Studies, Cambridge, 1978-79; assoc. dir. Mary Reynolds Babcock Found., Winston-Salem, N.C., 1979-85; exec. dir. Jessie Ball duPont Fund, Jacksonville, Fla., 1986-90; pres. Found. for the MidSouth, Jackson, Miss., 1990—; bd. dirs. Miss. Chem. Corp.; bd. dirs. Nat. Charities Info. Bus., 1990—, chair, 1996—; bd. dirs. Nat. Cathedral Assn., 1993—, Coun. on Founds., 1994—; bd. dirs. Presiding Bishop's Fund for World Relief, 1994—; bd. dirs. Southeastern Coun. Founds., 1983-89. Mem. Leadership Jacksonville, 1987-88, Leadership La., 1994; bd. dirs. Practical and Cultural Edn. Ctr. for Girls, Jacksonville, 1987-90, pres., 1989-90; bd. dirs. Jacksonville Cmty. Coun., Inc., 1987-90, Greater Jackson Found., 1994—. 1st lt. U.S. Army, 1971-73. Democrat. Club: Harvard of N.Y.C. Avocations: jogging, stamp collecting, children. Home: 138 Highland Hills Ln Flora MS 39071-9536 Office: Found for the Mid South 308 E Pearl St 4th Fl Jackson MS 39201

PENICK, JOE EDWARD, petroleum consultant; b. Frederick, Okla., Nov. 8, 1920; s. Jesse Olin and Grace Ann (Lane) P.; m. Norma Gene Scott, Oct. 18, 1942; children: Joe Edward, David Scott. B.S., U. Okla., 1942; grad., Exec. Devel. Program, Cornell U., 1963. Research engr. Magnolia Petroleum Co., Dallas, 1942-46; with Mobil Oil Corp., 1942-85; refinery mgr. Mobil Oil Corp., Torrance, Calif., 1961-67; v.p. mfg. Mobil Oil Corp., N.Y.C., 1967-76; sr. v.p. for research and engring. Mobil Oil Corp., 1977-85; pres. Mobil Research and Devel. Corp., 1977-85. Mem. Dirs. Indsl. Rsch., Springdale Golf Club, Bedens Brook Club, Nassau Club. Patentee petroleum refining. Office: 181 Library Pl Princeton NJ 08540-3072

PENIKETT, ANTONY DAVID JOHN, Canadian government official; b. Nov. 14, 1945; s. Erik John Keith and Sarah Ann (Colwell) P.; m. Lula Mary Johns, 1974; children—John Tahmoh, Sarah Lahlil, Stephanie Yahsan. Exec. asst. to nat. leader New Dem. Party, Ottawa, Ont., Canada, 1975-76, nat. pres., 1981-85, fed. councillor, 1973—; leader New Dem. Party, Whitehorse, Y.T., Canada, 1980—; campaign mgr. New Dem. Party, N.W.T., Canada, 1972; city councillor City of Whitehorse, Y.T., Canada, 1977-79; elected mem. Yukon Legis. Assembly, 1978-95; opposition leader Yukon Legis. Assembly, Y.T., Canada, 1982-85, 92-95; elected govt. leader Yukon Terr. Yukon Legis. Assembly, 1985-92; sr. policy advisor, exec. coun. Govt. of Saskatchewan, 1995—. Author (film): The Mad Trapper, 1972; La Patrouille Perdue, 1974. Mem. Christian Socialist Ch. Office: Legislative Bldg Rm 37, Regina, SK Canada S4S 0B3

PENIN, LINDA MARGARET, elementary education educator; b. N.Y.C., May 18, 1946; d. Santos Rodriquez and Dorothea May (Fink) P. BA, Jersey City State Coll., 1969, MA, 1973. Cert. elem. tchr., reading tchr., reading specialist. Tchr. elem. Leonia (N.J.) Bd. Edn., 1969—. Recipient Gov.'s Tchr. Recognition award State of N.J., 1989. Mem. NEA, N.J. Edn. Assn., Bergen County Edn. Assn., Leonia Edn. Assn., Order of Ea. Star N.J. (officer). Republican. Methodist. Avocations: reading, bike riding, relaxing at beach. Home: 24 Kimble Ct Pompton Plains NJ 07444-1656 Office: Leonia Bd Edn 500 Broad Ave Leonia NJ 07605-1537

PENISTEN, GARY DEAN, entrepreneur; b. Lincoln, Nebr., May 14, 1931; s. Martin C. and Jayne (O'Dell) P.; m. Nancy Margaret Golding, June 3, 1951; children: Kris D., Janet L., Carol E., Noel M. B.S. in Bus. Adminstrn., U. Nebr., Omaha, 1953; LLD (hon.), Concordia Coll., 1993. With Gen. Electric Co., 1953-74; mgr. group fin. ops. power generation group Gen. Electric Co., N.Y.C., 1973-74; asst. sec. navy fin. mgmt., 1974-77; sr. v.p. fin., chief fin. officer, dir. Sterling Drug Inc., N.Y.C., 1977-89; sr. v.p. fin., health group Eastman Kodak Co., N.Y.C., 1989-90; bd. dirs. Foster Ptnrs. Inc., Food Ct. Entertainment Network Inc.; chmn. bd. dirs. Acme United Corp. Bd. dirs. Goodwill Industries Greater N.Y., Goodwill Industries Internat. Found., 1989—; nat. dir. Navy League of U.S.; mem. corp. adv. bd. Concordia Coll., Bronxville, N.Y., 1991—, U. Nebr. Coll. Bus., Omaha, 1990—. Recipient Disting. Public Service award Navy Dept., 1977; Alumni Achievement citation U. Nebr., Omaha, 1975. Mem. Fin. Execs. Inst., Rotary, Union League, Econs. Club (N.Y.C.), Siwanoy Country Club. Republican. Unitarian. Home and Office: 10 Fordal Rd Bronxville NY 10708-2416

PENKAVA, ROBERT RAY, radiologist, educator; b. Virginia, Nebr., Jan. 30, 1942; s. Joseph Evert and Velta Mae (Oviatt) P.; m. Kathy Bennett Secrest, Apr. 6, 1973; children: Ashley Secrest, J. Carson Bennett. AB BS, Peru State Coll., Nebr., 1963; MD, U. Nebr., Omaha, 1967. Intern Lincoln Gen. Hosp., Nebr., 1967-68; resident Menorah Med. Cen., Kansas City, 1968-71; chief resident Menorah Med. Ctr., Kansas City, 1970-71; adj. faculty U. Mo., Kansas City, 1970-71; staff radiologist Ireland Army Hosp., Ft. Knox, Ky., 1971-72, chief, dept. radiology & nuclear med., 1972-73; staff radiologist Deaconess Hosp., Evansville, Ind., 1973—, dir. dept. radiology, 1992—; mem. faculty U. So. Ind., Evansville, 1973—; assoc. faculty Ind. U. Coll. Med., Bloomington, 1973—; med. dir. Sch. Radiol. Tech. U. So. Ind., Evansville, 1978—; dep coroner Vanderburgh County, 1991—; chmn. So. Ind. Health Sys., 1980-83; pres. Vanderburgh County Med. Soc. Svc. Bur., 1979—; mem. roentgen soc. liaison com. Ind. Bd. Health, 1968. Author numerous articles on med. ultrasound, nuclear med., angiography, and computed tomography. Chmn. profl. div. United Way of So. Ind., 1983; bd. dirs. S.W. Ind. Pub. Broadcasting, 1978-84, S.W. Ind. PSRO, 1982; v.p. Mesker Zoo Found., bd. dirs., 1991—. Maj. U.S. Army, 1971-73. Named Sci. Tchr. of Year, Lewis & Clark Jr. High Sch., 1963. Mem. AMA, Evansville Med. Radiol. Assn. (treas. 1987—), Tri-State Radiology Assn. (pres.), Vanderburgh County Med. Soc. (pres.), Physicians Svc. Bur. (treas.), Magnetic Resonance Imaging, Inc. (treas.), Am. Coll. Radiology, Radiol. Soc. N.Am., Am. Roentgen Ray Soc., Am. Inst. Ultrasound in Medicine, Soc. Cardiovascular and Interventional Radiology. Avocations: golf, boating, flying. Office: 611 Harriet St Evansville IN 47710-1781

PENKOFF, DIANE WITMER, communication educator; b. Pasadena, Jan. 20, 1945; d. Stanley Lamar and Mary Evelyn Witmer; m. Robert D. Joyce (div. 1987); 1 child, David William Penkoff. AA, Golden West Coll., Huntington Beach, Calif., 1977; BS in BA, U. LaVerne (Calif.), 1980; MS in Sys. Mgmt., U. So. Calif., L.A., 1989; MA in Communication Arts, U. So. Calif., 1993, PhD in Orgnl. Comm., 1994. Dir. pub. rels. Weight Watchers, Santa Ana, Calif., 1980-84; dir. comm. March of Dimes, Costa Mesa, Calif., 1986-90; prin. Penkoff Comm. Resources, L.A., 1990-92; instr. Calif. State U., Fullerton, 1990-94; asst. lectr. comm. arts and scis. U. So. Calif., University Park, 1991-94; asst. prof. Purdue U., West Lafayette, Ind., 1994—. Editor, The Paper Weight, 1981-84. Chmn. award com. March of Dimes, Costa Mesa, nat. vol., 1980—, also chair speakers bur. Sagemore divsn., mem. exec. com. Mem. Pub. Rels. Soc. Am. (accredited mem.), U. So. Calif. Alumni Assn., Indpls. Symphony Chorus. Avocations: singing.

PENLAND, ARNOLD CLIFFORD, JR., college dean, educator; b. Asheville, N.C., Oct. 8, 1933; s. Arnold Clifford and Pearl (Bailey) P.; m. Jean Wall (div. 1967); 1 child, Marcia Jean; m. Joan Eudy; 1 child, Elizabeth Bailey. BS, Western Carolina U., 1956; MA, Vanderbilt U., 1959; MEd, Duke U., 1966; PhD, Fla. State U., 1983. Tchr. of music Reidsville (N.C.) Pub. Schs., 1956-60; supr. of music Raleigh (N.C.) Pub. Schs., 1960-67; supr. of music and rsch. Smoky Mt. Cultural Arts Devel. Assn., Sylva, N.C., 1967, 1968-69; state supr. of music State Dept. of Edn., Columbia, S.C., 1969-70; assoc. prof. of music U. of Fla., Gainesville, 1970-80, prof. of music, 1980—, assoc. dean and prof. Coll. of Fine Arts, 1981—; prog. dir. Raleigh Cultural Ctr., Inc., 1962-67; music dir. various ch. choirs, N.C. and Fla., 1956-80; ednl. cons. Nat. Grass Roots Opera, Co., Raleigh, 1962-67, bd. dirs. Fla. League of the Arts. Contbr. articles to profl. jours. Mem. Gainesville Cultural Commn., 1975-76, v.p. Alachua County Arts Coun., Inc., 1976-77; bd. dirs. Arts Coun. of Raleigh, Inc., 1963-65. Recipient Disting. Service Citation, Federated Music Clubs of N.C., 1966; grantee Office of Edn., 1967-69. Mem. Nat. Assn. Acad. Affairs Adminstrn. (pres. 1990-92, bd. dirs. 1992-96), Reg. Assn. Acad. Affairs Adminstrn. (pres. 1985-86), Music Educators Nat. Conf., Coll. Music Soc. (life), Lions (v.p. Raleigh chpt. 1963-66), Kiwanis (Kiwanian of Yr. 1989-90, bd. dirs. 1992-96), Order of Omega, Phi Delta Kappa (pres. North Ctrl. Fla. chpt. 1985-86), Sigma Phi Epsilon. Democrat. Presbyterian. Avocations: gardening, cooking. Office: U Fla Coll Fine Arts 115800 Gainesville FL 32611-5800 *In life one can do anything one chooses to do if one is genuinely committed.*

PENLAND, JOHN THOMAS, import and export and development companies executive; b. Guntersville, Ala., Mar. 31, 1930; s. James B. and Kathleen (Bolding) P.; m. Carolyn Joyce White, May 30, 1961; children—Jeffrey K., Mark A., Michael J. B.A., George Washington U., 1957. Vice pres., dir. Rouse, Brewer, Becker & Bryant, Inc., Washington, 1957-63; staff mem. SEC, Washington, 1963-67; pres., dir. INA Trading Corp., Phila., 1968-69; v.p. INA Security Corp., Phila., 1967-69; v.p. Shareholders Mgmt. Co., Los Angeles, 1969, sr. v.p., 1970, exec. v.p., 1970-73, pres., 1973-75, also bd. dirs.; v.p. Shareholders Capital Corp., L.A., 1972-73; v.p., dir. several mut. funds managed by Shareholders Mgmt. Co., 1970-75; pres., chmn., CEO, HMO Internat. and its subs., L.A., 1975; founder, pres., chmn. Pendlar Corp., Atlanta, 1977—; chmn., pres. Bella Vista Developers, Inc., Albuquerque, 1977—; chmn. CompuComp Corp., Atlanta, 1977-81; chmn., pres. Fran Stef Corp., N.Y.C., 1982-89; pres., chmn. Engineered Products Corp., Dandridge, Tenn., 1983-90; founder, chmn., CEO Am. Accessories Inc., Covington, Ga., 1983—; founder, pres., chmn. United Am. Products Corp., Dandridge, 1983-89; founder, chmn. Chamisa Properties, Inc., Albuquerque, 1988-94, Glorieux Ltd., Atlanta, 1988—, Ga. Ptnrs. Ltd., Covington, 1988-94; founder, chmn., dir. Premier Trading Internat., Inc., Atlanta, 1989—; founder, dir. Chamisa Enterprises, Inc., Covington, 1990—; founder, mng. ptnr. Ft. Hill Ptnrs., Knoxville, Tenn., 1990-93; chmn. Einson Freeman & Detroy Corp., Fair Lawn, N.J., 1978-83; founder, dir., pres. West Point Contract Packaging, Inc., Winston-Salem, N.C., 1991—; founder, mng. ptnr. Harbor View, Ltd., Fernandina Beach, Fla., 1992-94; founder, chmn. West Point Tech. Assembly, Inc., Winston-Salem, N.C., 1993—; dir., pres. BKP Industries, Inc., Monroe, Ga., 1995—. Served with AUS, 1948-55. Republican. Episcopalian. Home: PO Box 549 Social Circle GA 30279-0549 Office: 3261 Highway 278 NE Covington GA 30209-3103

PENLIDIS, ALEXANDER, chemical engineering educator; b. Kozani, Greece, Feb. 12, 1957; j. Diploma in engring., U. Thessaloniki, 1980; PhD in Chem. Engring., McMaster U., 1986. Rsch. assoc. Polymer Prodn. Techs., McMaster Inst., Can., 1985-86; from asst. prof. to assoc. prof. chem. engring. U. Waterloo, Ontario, Can., 1986-90; from assoc. prof. to prof., 1990-95; assoc. dir. Inst. Polymer Rsch. U. Waterloo, Ont., Can., 1990-95, dir., 1995—; cons. in field, 1985—. Founding co-editor Polymer Reaction Engring. Jour., 1990—. Mem. AIChE, Chem. Inst. Can., Am. Chem. Soc., Can. Soc. Chem. Engring. Office: Univ Waterloo Inst Polymer Rsch, Chem Engring Dept, Waterloo, ON Canada N2L 3G1

PENMAN, PAUL DUANE, nuclear power laboratory executive; b. Williston, N.D., Sept. 25, 1937; s. Robert Roy and Kathryn Erica (Hagstrom) P.; m. Cornelia Dennis, Jan. 9, 1960 (div. June 1986); children: Anne, Robert, Jill; m. Carrie B. Silverblatt, July 14, 1986. BS in Engring. Physics, U. Colo., 1959; MS in Physics, U. Louisville, 1965. Asst. prof. U. Louisville, 1962-65; engr. Bettis Atomic Power Lab., West Mifflin, Pa., 1965-71, mgr., 1971-77, in charge lab. ops., 1977-82, in charge nuclear core mfg., 1982-92; mgr. performance and quality Westinghouse Electro-Mech. Divsn., Cheswick, Pa., 1992-93, mgr. performance quality improvement, 1994—. Leader Boy Scouts Am., Pitts., 1977-80. Lt. USN, 1959-64. Mem. U.S. Naval Inst., Gyro Internat. (bd. dirs., pres. 1988-90), U. Colo. Alumni Assn. (pres. Pitts. 1971-8o). Republican. Home: 105 Urick Ct Monroeville PA 15146-4919 *Make all decisions on first principles - they will carry you through all storms.*

PENN, ARTHUR HILLER, film and theatre producer; b. Phila., Sept. 27, 1922; s. Harvy and Sonia (Greenberg) P.; m. Peggy Maurer, Jan. 27, 1955; children: Matthew, Molly. Student, Joshua Logan's Stage Co., Black Mountain Coll., Asheville, N.C., U. Perugia, Florence, Italy, Actors Studio, Los Angeles; studied with Michael Chekhov. Joined Army Theatre Co. during World War II; worked in TV, 1951-53; producer plays for Broadway theatre including The Miracle Worker (Tony award 1960), All The Way Home, Toys in the Attic, Two for the Seesaw, In the Council House, Wait Until Dark, Sly Fox, Monday After the Miracle; films include The Left-Handed Gun, 1957, The Miracle Worker, 1962, Mickey One, 1964, The Chase, 1965, Bonnie and Clyde, 1967, Alice's Restaurant, 1969, Little Big Man, 1971, Night Moves, 1975, The Missouri Breaks, 1976, Four Friends, 1981, Target, 1985, Dead of Winter, 1987; co-dir. film Visions of Eight, 1973; dir. theatre: Golden Boy, Hunting Cockroaches. Office: care Sam Cohn Internat Creative Mgmt 40 W 57th St New York NY 10019-4001 also: William Morris Agy 151 S El Camino Dr Beverly Hills CA 90212-2704

PENN, HUGH FRANKLIN, JR., psychology educator; b. Hartselle, Ala., Jan. 28, 1941; s. Hugh Franklin and Marynelle (Walter) P.; m. Susan Irwin Adams, June 5, 1976; children: Charles Bracken, Caryn Elizabeth. BS, Florence State Coll., 1964; MA, Florence State Univ., 1967; grad. ednl. specialist, U. Ala., 1972, PhD, 1982. Psychology tchr. Hartselle (Ala.) H.S., 1964-89, sch. counselor, 1989-91, spl. svcs. counselor, 1991—; psychology instr. Calhoun C.C., Decatur, Ala., 1970—; chmn. bd. North Ctrl. Ala. Mental Health Bd., 1984-87, bd. dirs.; pres. of advisors Ala. Assn. Student Couns., 1970; ea. states head advisor So. Assn. Student Couns., 1973-74; mem. adv. bd. Mental Health Assn. Morgan County, 1996—. Named Outstanding Young Educator of Ala., Ala. Jaycees, 1973. Mem. APA, ACA, Coun. for Exceptional Children, Learning Disabilities Assn., Am. Sch. Counselor Assn., Autism Soc. Am., Orton Dyslexia Soc., Hartselle C. of C. (Thomas Guyton Humanitarian award 1994). Methodist. Home: 412 Aquarius Dr SW Hartselle AL 35640-4000 Office: Hartselle City Schs 130 Petain St SW Hartselle AL 35640-3228

PENN, JOHN GARRETT, federal judge; b. Pittsfield, Mass., Mar. 19, 1932; s. John and Eugenie Gwendolyn (Heyliger) P.; m. Ann Elizabeth Rollison, May 7, 1966; cildren: John Garett II, Karen Renee, David Brandon. BA, U. Mass., 1954; LLB, Boston U., 1957; postgrad. pub. and internat. affairs, Princeton U., 1967-68. Bar: Mass 1957, D.C. 1970. Trial atty. Dept. Justice, Washington, 1961-65, atty. tax div., 1961-70; then reviewer, asst. chief gen. litigation sect., assoc. judge Superior Ct. of D.C., Washington, 1970-79; judge U.S. Dist. Ct. D.C., Washington, 1979-92, chief judge, 1992—. Ex-officio dir. day care program D.C. Dept. Recreation, 1978—. Served with JAGC U.S. Army, 1958-61. Nat. Inst. Pub. Affairs fellow, 1967. Mem. Nat. Bar Assn., Mass. Bar Assn., Washington Bar Assn., Bar Assn. D.C. (hon.), Am. Judicature Soc., Boston U. Law Sch. Alumni Assn. Episcopalian. Office: US Dist Ct DC US Courthouse 333 Constitution Ave NW Washington DC 20001

PENN, SEAN, actor; b. Burbank, Calif., Aug. 17, 1960; s. Leo and Eileen (Ryan) P.; m. Madonna Louise Ciccone, Aug. 16, 1985 (div.); 2 children: Dylan Frances, Hopper Jack. Appearences include (Broadway debut) Heartland, others include Slab Boys, Hurlyburly, 1988; (films) Taps, 1981, Fast Times at Ridgemont High, 1982, Bad Boys, 1983, Crackers, 1984, Racing with the Moon, 1984, The Falcon and the Snowman, 1985, At Close Range, 1986, Shanghai Surprise, 1986, Colors, 1988, Judgment in Berlin, 1988, Casualties of War, 1989, We're No Angels, 1989, State of Grace, 1990, Carlito's Way, 1993, Dead Man Walking, 1995 (Golden Globe award nominee for best actor 1995, Best Actor award Berlin Film Festival 1996, Acad. award nominee for best actor 1996); dir., writer: The Indian Runner, 1991, The Crossing Guard, 1995; (TV movie) The Killing of Randy Webster, 1981. Office: William Morris Agy 151 El Camino Beverly Hills CA 90211*

PENN, STANLEY WILLIAM, journalist; b. N.Y.C., Jan. 12, 1928; s. Murray and Lillian (Richman) P.; m. Esther Aronson, July 12, 1952; children—Michael, Laurel. Student, Bklyn. Coll., 1945-47; B. Journalism, U. Mo., 1949. With Wall St. Jour., 1952-90; investigative reporter N.Y. bur., 1957-90. (Co-recipient Pulitzer prize for nat. reporting 1967). Home: 380 Riverside Dr New York NY 10025-1858

PENNACCHIO, LINDA MARIE, secondary school educator; b. Boston, Oct. 8, 1947; d. Antonio and Florence (Delano) P. BA in Math., U. Mass., 1969; MEd in Guidance, Boston State Coll., 1974, cert. advanced study in adminstrn., 1976. Cert. math., guidance counselor, prin. Math. tchr. Abraham Lincoln Sch., Revere, Mass., 1969-91; computer tchr. grades K-8 Abraham Lincoln Sch., Revere, 1985-91; math. tchr. Beachmont Middle Sch., Revere, 1991—, equity coord., 1995; office asst. Mass. Gen. Hosp., Bunker Hill Health Ctr., Charlestown, Mass., 1982—; adviser Nat. Jr. Honor Soc., Revere, 1985-94; mem. math. Curriculum Revision Com., Revere, 1985-86, 94-95, Com. to Establish Gifted and Talented Program, Revere, 1988; participant U.S. Dept. Edn. Tech. Grant, Revere, 1989-92; mem. math. portfolio pilot study Commonwealth of Mass. Dept. Edn., 1992-95. Mem. ASCD, Nat. Coun. Tchrs. Math., Mass. Tchrs. Assn., Assn. Tchrs. Math. in Mass., Nat. Assn. Student Activity Advisers. Democrat. Roman Catholic. Office: Beachmont Sch 15 Everard Ave Revere MA 02151-5516

PENNANT-REA, RUPERT LASCELLES, banker, economist; b. Harare, Zimbabwe, Jan. 23, 1948; came to Britain, 1966; s. Peter Athelwold and Pauline Elizabeth (Creasy) Pennant-Rea; m. Louise Greer, Oct. 3, 1970 (div. 1976); m. Jane Trevelyan Hamilton, Aug. 18, 1979 (div. 1986); children: Emily Trevelyan, Rory Marcus; m. Helen Jay, June 24, 1986; 1 child, Edward Peter. B.A. with honors, Trinity Coll., Dublin, 1970; M.A., U. Manchester, 1972. Economist, Confedn. Irish Industry, Dublin, 1970-71, Gen. and Mcpl. Workers Union, Eng., 1972-73, Bank of Eng., 1973-77; journalist The Economist, London, 1977-93, editor, 1986-93; dep. gov. Bank of Eng., London, 1993-95; chmn. Caspian, London, 1995—. Author: Gold Foil, 1979; The Pocket Economist, 1983; The Economist Economics, 1986. Recipient Wincott prize for fin. journalism Wincott Found., London, 1984. Mem. Ch. of Eng. Clubs: Marylebone Cricket, Reform (London), Harare (Zimbabwe). Avocations: music; tennis. Office: Caspian, 199 Bishopsgate, London EC2, England

PENNARIO, LEONARD, concert pianist, composer; b. Buffalo, July 9, 1924; s. John D. and Mary (Chiarello) P. Student music, U. So. Calif., 1942; student piano with, Guy Maier, Isabelle Vengerova. Profl. debut Dallas Symphony, 1936; performed with Los Angeles Philharm., 1939, N.Y. Philharm. 1943; composer: Midnight on the Cliffs, (piano) Variations on the Kerry Dance, also piano concerto and other works for piano; soloist orchs. in Phila., Chgo., Boston, N.Y.C., Los Angeles, St. Louis, others; performed concerts in Eng., Italy, Fed. Republic of Germany, Holland, France, Scandinavian countries, Austria; toured in South Africa, 1959, Europe, 1960; featured pianist chamber music concerts with Heifetz & Piatigorsky; recorded albums for RCA, Angel, CBS Masterworks. Mem. Calif. Scholarship Fedn. Served with USAAF, World War II. Mem. Ephebian Soc., ASCAP. Roman Catholic.

PENNELL, WILLIAM BROOKE, lawyer; b. Mineral Ridge, Ohio, Oct. 28, 1935; s. George Albert and Katherine Nancy (McMeen) P. AB, Harvard U., 1957; LLB cum laude, U. Pa., 1961; m. Peggy Polsky, June 17, 1958; children: Katherine, Thomas Brooke. Bar: N.Y. 1963, U.S. Dist. Ct. (so. dist.) N.Y. 1964, U.S. Dist. Ct. (ea. dist.) N.Y. 1964, U.S. Ct. Appeals (2d cir.) 1966, U.S. Ct. Claims 1966, U.S. Tax Ct. 1967, U.S. Supreme Ct. 1967. Clk. U.S. Dist. Ct., (so. dist.) N.Y., N.Y.C., 1961-62; assoc. Shearman & Sterling, N.Y.C., 1962-71, ptnr., 1971-91. Recent case editor U. Pa. Law Rev., 1960-61. Bd. govs. Bklyn. Heights Assn., 1964-74, pres., 1969-71; chmn. bd. Willoughby House Settlement, 1972-95. Served with U.S. Army, 1957. Fellow Salzburg Seminar Am. Studies, 1965. Mem. Rembrandt Club. Office: PO Box 249 Canaan NY 12029

PENNEMAN, ROBERT ALLEN, retired chemist; b. Springfield, Ill., Feb. 5, 1919; s. Allen Frederick and Beryl (McNeeley) P.; m. Mary Ellen Emerick, July 25, 1942; children: Jacqueline, Cindy, Dean. A.B. summa cum laude, Millikin U., Decatur, Ill., 1941, Sc.D. (hon.), 1961; M.S., U. Ill., 1942, Ph.D. in Inorganic Chemistry, 1947. Chemist Ill. Hwy. Lab., Springfield, 1941; chemist metall. lab. U. Chgo., 1942-45; research assoc. Clinton Labs., Oak Ridge, 1945-46; chemist, staff mem., group and assoc. div. leader Los Alamos Nat. Lab., 1947-84, ret., 1984; adj. prof. U. N.Mex., 1950—; cons., lectr. in field. Editl. bd. Inorganic Cheistry, 1962-66 (founding mem.), Inorganic and Nuclear Chemistry Letters, 1968—; contbr. articles to profl. jours. Recipient Disting. Performance award Los Alamos Nat. Lab., 1981, award of excellence Los Alamos Nat. Lab., 1986, Seaborg award Actinide Separations Chemistry, 1995. Mem. Am. Chem. Soc. (chmn. N.Mex. chpt. 1956), Nat. Acad. Scis. (participant workshop 1983), Sigma Xi, Phi Kappa Phi, Alpha Chi Sigma. Home: 12201 LaVista Grande Dr Albuquerque NM 87111-6710 Office: Los Alamos Nat Lab PO Box 1663 Los Alamos NM 87545-0001

PENNER, HANS HENRY, historian; b. Sacramento, Jan. 29, 1934; s. Hans Henry and Frieda Marie (Haehnel) P.; m. Anna M. Tardiff, Sept. 27, 1958. D.B., U. Chgo., 1958, M.A., 1962, Ph.D., 1965. Instr. U. Vt., 1962-65; asst. prof. Dartmouth Coll., 1965-71, Preston Kelsey prof. religion, 1991—, dean faculty, 1980-85; Pres. Am. Acad. Religion New Eng., 1980-81. Author: Impasse and Resolution: A Critique of the Study of Religion, 1989; editl. bd. Am. Acad. Religion; contbr. articles to profl. jours. Danforth fellow, 1968-69; Dartmouth Faculty fellow, 1967; Fulbright research grantee, 1966; Am. Council Learned Socs. grantee, 1979. Mem. Assn. Asian Studie, Am. Soc. St. Religion, Internat. Assn. History of Religion. Home: PO Box 642 Hanover NH 03755-0642 Office: Dartmouth Coll 6306 Thornton Hanover NH 03755

PENNER, HARRY HAROLD HAMILTON, JR., pharmaceutical company executive, lawyer; b. Norfolk, Va., July 29, 1945; s. Harry H.H. and Leona F. (Vossler) P.; m. Irene Anne Uanino, June 22, 1968; children: Harry III, Emilie A., Stephanie M., Christopher D., Scott T., Rebecca S., Andrew E. BA, U. Va., 1967; JD, Fordham U., 1970; LLM in internat. law, NYU, 1975. Bar: N.Y. 1971. Assoc. Choate Regan Davis & Hollister, N.Y.C., 1971-75; counsel Pinkertons Inc., N.Y.C., 1975-78; atty. Boehringer Ingelheim Ltd., Ridgefield, Conn., 1978-81; v.p., gen. counsel Novo Labs. Inc., Wilton, Conn., 1981-85; exec. v.p., gen. counsel Novo Industri A/S, Bagsvaerd, Denmark, 1985-88; pres. Novo Nordisk of N.Am. Inc., N.Y.C., 1988-93; exec. v.p. Novo Nordisk A/S, Bagsvaerd, Denmark, 1985-93; pres., CEO, bd. dirs. Neurogen Corp., Branford, Conn., 1993—; bd. dirs. Anergen, Inc., Redwood City, Calif.; bd. dirs., exec. com. Conn. Tech. Coun.; profl. adv. bd. Conn. United for Rsch. Excellence. Republican. Roman Catholic. Office: Neurogen Corp 35 NE Industrial Rd Branford CT 06405-2844

PENNER, KEITH, Canadian government official; b. Sask., Can., May 1, 1933. BA, U. Alberta, Can., 1955; MEd, U. Ottawa, Can., 1971. Secondary sch. tchr. Dryden, Ont., Can., 1961-68; mem. parliament Cochrane-Superior, Ont., 1968-88; mem. Nat. Transp. Agy., Ottawa, Ont., 1988—; past parliamentary sec. to Min. of State for Sci. and Tech., past parliamentary sec. to Min. of Indian Affairs and No. Devel., past chmn. Standing Com. on Indian Affairs and No. Devel.; vis. fellow Sch. of Polit. Sci., Queen's U., 1987-88. Office: Nat Transp Agy, Ottawa, ON Canada K1A 0N9*

PENNER, STANFORD SOLOMON, engineering educator; b. Unna, Germany, July 5, 1921; came to U.S., 1936, naturalized, 1943; s. Heinrich and Regina (Saal) P.; m. Beverly Preston, Dec. 28, 1942; children: Merilynn Jean, Robert Clark. BS, Union Coll., 1942; MS, U. Wis., 1943, PhD, 1946; Dr. rer. nat. (hon.), Technische Hochschule Aachen, Germany, 1981. Research asso. Allegany Ballistics Lab., Cumberland, Md., 1944-45; research scientist Standard Oil Devel. Co., Esso Labs., Linden, N.J., 1946; sr. research engr. Jet Propulsion Lab., Pasadena, Calif., 1947-50; mem. faculty Calif. Inst. Tech., 1950-63, prof. div. engring., jet propulsion, 1957-63; dir. research engring. div. Inst. Def. Analyses, Washington, 1962-64; prof. engring. physics, chmn. dept. aerospace and mech. engring. U. Calif. at San Diego, 1964-68, vice chancellor for acad. affairs, 1968-69, dir. Inst. for Pure and Applied Phys. Scis., 1968-71, dir. Energy Ctr., 1973-91; bd. dirs. Ogden Corp., Optodyne Corp.; U.S. mem. adv. group aero. rsch. and devel. NATO, 1952-68, chmn. combustion and propulsion panel, 1958-60; mem. adv. com. engring. scis. USAF-Office Sci. Rsch., 1961-65; mem. subcom. on combustion NACA, 1954-58; mem. rsch. adv. com. on air-breathing engines NASA, 1962-64; mem. coms. on gas dynamics and edn. Internat. Acad. Astronautics, 1969-80; nat. lectr. Sigma Xi, 1977-79; chmn. fossil energy rsch. working group Dept. Energy, 1978-82, chmn. advanced fuel cell commercialization working group, 1993-95; chmn. assembly engring. NAE, 1978-82; chmn. NAS-NRC U.S. Nat. Com. IIASA, 1978-82; mem. commn. engring. tech. sys. NRC, 1982-84; spl. guest Internat. Coal Sci. Confs., 1983, 85, 87, 89, 91; mentor Def. Sci. Studies Group, 1985-93; chmn. studies mcpl. waste incineration NSF, 1988-89, Calif. Coun. Sci. Tech., 1992. Author: Chemical Reactions in Flow Systems, 1955, Chemistry Problems in Jet Propulsion, 1957, Quantitative Molecular Spectroscopy and Gas Emissivities, 1959, Chemical Rocket Propulsion and Combustion Research, 1962, Thermodynamics, 1968, Radiation and Reentry, 1968; sr. author: Energy, Vol. I (Demands, Resources, Impact, Technology and Policy), 1974, 81, Energy, Vol. II (Non-nuclear Energy Technologies), 1975, 77, 84, Energy, Vol. III (Nuclear Energy and Energy Policies), 1976; editor: Chemistry of Propellants, 1960, Advanced Propulsion Techniques, 1961, Detonations and Two-Phase Flow, 1962, Combustion and Propulsion, 1963, Advances in Tactical Rocket Propulsion, 1968, In Situ Shale Oil Recovery, 1975, New Sources of Oil and Gas, 1982, Coal Combustion and Applications, 1984, Advanced Fuel Cells, 1986, Coal Gasification: Direct Applications and Syntheses of Chemicals and Fuels, 1987, CO2 Emissions and Climate Change, 1991, Commercialization of Fuel Cells, 1995; assoc. editor Jour. Chem. Physics, 1953-56; editor Jour. Quantitative Spectroscopy and Radiative Transfer, 1960-92, Jour. Def. Rsch., 1963-67, Energy-The Internat. Jour., 1975—. Recipient spl. award People-to-People program, NATO, pub. svc. award U. Calif., San Diego, N. Manson medal Internat. Colloquia on Gasdynamics of Explosions and Reactive Systems, 1979, internat. Columbus award Internat. Inst. Comm., Genoa, Italy, 1981, disting. assoc. award U.S. Dept. Energy, 1990; Guggenheim fellow, 1971-72. Fellow Am. Phys. Soc., Optical Soc. Am., AAAS, N.Y. Acad. Scis., AIAA (dir. 1964-66, past chmn. com., G. Edward Pendray award 1975, Thermophysics award 1983, Energy Systems award 1983), Am. Acad. Arts and Scis.; mem. Nat. Acad. Engring., Internat. Acad. Astronautics, Am. Chem. Soc., Sigma Xi. Home: 5912 Avenida Chamnez La Jolla CA 92037-7402 Office: U Calif San Diego 9500 Gilman Dr La Jolla CA 92093-0411

PENNEY, ALPHONSUS LIGUORI, archbishop; b. St. John's, Nfld., Can., Sept. 17, 1924; s. Alphonsus Liguori and Catherine (Mullaly) P. L.Ph., U. Ottawa, 1945, L.Th., 1949; LL.D., Meml. U. Nfld., 1980. Ordained priest Roman Cath. Ch., 1949. Named vicar forane Roman Cath. Ch., 1960, vicar gen., 1971, prelate of honour, 1971, asst. priest, then parish priest, 1949-72; bishop Roman Cath. Ch., Grand Falls, Nfld., 1973-79; archbishop Roman Cath. Ch., St. John's, Nfld., 1979-91, archbishop emeritus, 1991—; chmn. Cath. Edn. Com., 1979-91. Served with RCAF, 1952-57. Address: Box 1029, Almonte, ON Canada K0A 1A0

PENNEY, CHARLES RAND, lawyer, civic worker; b. Buffalo, July 26, 1923; s. Charles Patterson and Gretchen (R) P. BA, Yale U., 1945; JD, U. Va., 1951; DFA (hon.), SUNY, 1995. Bar: Md. 1952, N.Y. 1958, U.S. Supreme Ct. 1958. Law sec. to U.S. Dist. Ct. Judge W.C. Coleman, Balt., 1951-52; dir. devel. office Children's Hosp., Buffalo, 1952-54; sales mgr. Amherst Mfg. Corp., Williamsville, N.Y., 1954-56, also; Delevan Electronics Corp., East Aurora, N.Y.; mem. firm Penney & Penney, Buffalo, 1958-61; pvt. practice, Niagara County, N.Y., 1961—. Numerous contemporary art collection exhbns. include Mus. Modern Art, N.Y.C., 1962, Whitney Mus. Am. Art, N.Y.C., 1963, 79, 80, Burchfield-Penney Art Ctr., 1973, 92-96, Meml. Art Gallery, Rochester, 1976, 78, 83, 88, U. Iowa, 1978, Columbus (Ohio) Gallery Fine Arts, 1979, Whitte Meml. Mus., San Antonio, 1979, U. N.C., 1979, Ga. Mus. Art, 1979, Hunter Mus. Art, Chattanoga, Tenn., 1980, Brooks Meml. Art Gallery, Memphis, 1980, Portland (Maine Mus. Art), 1980, Arts Ctr., South Bend, Ind., 1980, The Bowers Mus., Santa Ana, Calif., 1980, Beaumont (Tex.) Art Mus., 1981, 88, Meadows Mus. Art, Shreveport, La., 1981, 88, Cedar Rapids (Iowa) Mus. Art, 1983, Roland Gibson Art Gallery, Potsdam, N.Y., 1983, 84, Met. Mus. Art, 1984, San Jose Mus. Art, 1985, Tampa Mus., 1986, Boston Athenaeum, Mass., 1986, The New Britain (Conn.) Mus. Art, 1986, Currier Gallery Art, Manchester, N.H., 1987, Miss. Mus. Art, Jackson, 1987, others; selected works from art collections exhibited at Met. Mus. Art, N.Y. Hist. Soc., 1987, San Francisco Mus. Art, 1963, Walker Art Ctr., Mpls., 1963, Pa. Acad. Fine Arts, 1964, and 25 U.S. Embassies, 1965-72, U. Ariz., Tucson, 1965, 66, Albright-Knox Art Gallery, Buffalo, 1967, 87, Cleve. Mus., Art, 1972, Indpls. Mus. Art, 1973, Whitney Mus. Am. Art, N.Y., 1979, 80, Milw. Mus. Art, 1984, Wadsworth Atheneum, Hartford, 1986, Corcoran Gallery Art, Washington, 1987, U. Mich., 1993, Terra Mus. Am. Art, 1993. Bd. dirs. Buffalo State Coll. Found.; hon. life trustee Burchfield-Penney Art Ctr. 2d lt. U.S. Army, 1943-46. Recipient Pres.'s Disting. Svc. award Buffalo State Coll., 1991, Disting. Svc. to Culture award Coll. Arts and Scis., SUNY, Potsdam, 1983; named Disting. fellow Cultural Studies of the Burchfield-Penney Art Ctr., 1994. Fellow The Explorers Club: mem. AARP, Albright-Knox Art Gallery Buffalo (life), Buffalo Mus. Sci. (Life), Buffalo and Erie County Hist. Soc. (life), Niagara County Hist. Soc. (life), Old Ft. Niagara (life), Buffalo Soc. Artists (hon. trustee), Hist. Lockport (life), Landmark Soc. Western N.Y. (life), Nat. Trust Hist. Preservation, Am. Ceramic Cir., Hist. Lewiston (life), Friends of U. Rochester Librs. (life) Meml. Art Gallery U. Rochester (hon. bd. mgrs., hon. life), Winslow Homer Soc. of Dir.'s Cir., Smithsonian Instn., Rochester Hist. Soc. (life), Am. Hist. Print Collectors Soc. (bd. dirs.), Burchfield Homestead Soc. (hon. life), Archives Am. Art, Mark Twain Soc. (hon.), U. Rochester's Pres.'s Soc. (hon. life), U. Iowa's Pres.'s Club (hon. life), Va. Law Found., Nat. Geog. Soc. (life), Hist. Soc. of Tonawandas (life), Pres.'s Cir. Buffalo State Coll. (hon. life), Peanut Palls, Grolier Club, Pan Am. Expo Collectors Soc., Columbus (Ohio) Mus. of Art, Castellani Art Mus./Niagara U., Yale Club of N.Y.C., Chi Psi, Phi Alpha Delta. Clubs: Automobile (Lockport); Zwicker Aquatic, Niagara County Antiques (hon.); Rochester Art (hon. life). Office: 538 Bewley Building Lockport NY 14094-2934 *I have tried to strive for excellence in whatever I undertake, be it small or large. What success I may have achieved has required initiative, imagination, and dedication to the task at hand. Satisfaction comes from the hard work that leads to an objective. In all that I do I adhere to the Golden Rule and to fairness, honesty, and understanding in human relationships. I try to maintain a sense of humor at all times. And I enjoy living in a small community because it is from such areas that the strength of America comes.*

PENNEY, PEARCE JOHN, retired librarian; b. St. Anthony, Nfld., Can., Mar. 10, 1928; s. Edgar and Elsie Belle (Bussey) P.; m. Amy Parrill, Aug. 30, 1950; children—Wayne, David, Donald, Reneé. B.A., Mt. Allison U., 1957; M.Div., Pinehill Div. Sch., 1959; M.S. in Library Scis, Syracuse U., 1968. Tchr., 1946-50; ordained to ministry United Ch. of Can., 1959; pastor various chs., 1959-67; librarian, head of acquisitions Meml. U., St. John's, Nfld., 1968-71, U. Guelph, Ont., 1971-72; chief provincial librarian Nfld. Pub. Library Services, St. John's, 1972-93. Mem. Can. Libr. Assn., Atlantic Provinces Libr. Assn., Nfld. Libr. Assn. Home: 24 Parsons Rd, Saint John's, NF Canada A1A 2J1

PENNEY, SHERRY HOOD, university president, educator; b. Marlette, Mich., Sept. 4, 1937; d. Terrance and B. Jean (Stoutenburg) Hood; m. Carl Murray Penney, July 8, 1961 (div. 1978); children: Michael Murray, Jeffrey Hood; m. James Duane Livingston, Mar. 30, 1985. BA, Albion Coll., 1959, LLD (hon.), 1989; MA, U. Mich., 1961; PhD, SUNY, Albany, 1972. Vis. asst. prof. Union Coll., Schenectady, N.Y., 1972-73; assoc. higher edn. N.Y. State Edn. Dept., Albany, 1973-76; assoc. provost Yale U., New Haven, Conn., 1976-82; vice chancellor acad. programs, policy and planning SUNY System, Albany, 1982-88; acting pres. SUNY, Plattsburgh, 1986-87; chancellor U. Mass., Boston, 1988-95, pres., 1995—, chancellor, 1996—; chmn., bd. dirs. Nat. Higher Edn. Mgmt. Sys., Boulder, Colo., 1985-87; mem. commn. on higher edn. New Eng. Assn. Schs. and Colls., Boston, 1979-82, Mid. States Assn. Schs. and Colls., Phila., 1986-88; mem. commn. on women Am. Coun. Edn., Washington, 1979-81, commn. on govt. rels., 1990—; bd. dirs. Boston Edison Co., Am. Coun. on Edn., Carnegie Found. for Advancement of Teaching, 1994—, The Boston Pvt. Industry Coun., 1994—. Author: Patrician in Politics, 1974; editor: Women in Management in Higher Education, 1975; cons. editor Change mag. and Jour. Higher Edn. Mgmt.; contbr. articles to profl. jours. Mem. Internat. Trade Task Force, 1994—; mem. exec. com., Challenge to Leadership, 1988, chair, 1996; mem. Mid-Am. adv. bd. HERS, 1992—; trustee Berkeley Div. Sch., Yale U., 1978-82, John F. Kennedy Libr. Found.; bd. dirs. Albany Symphony Orch., 1982-88, U. Mass. Found., 1988—, Mcpl. Rsch. Bur., Boston, 1990—, New Eng. Coun., New Eng. Aquarium, Boston Plan for Excellence, Boston Pvt. Industry Coun., Greater Boston One to One Leadership Coun., Hers Mid Atlantic Adv. Bd., NASULGC Commn. Urban Affairs, The Ednl. Resource Inst., 1994, The Environ. Bus. Coun., 1991—; corp. mem. United Way, 1990—. Recipient Disting. Alumna award Albion Coll., 1978. Mem. Am. Coun. Edn. (bd. dirs.), Am. Assn. Higher Edn., Orgn. Am. Historians, Internat. Assn. Univ. Pres., Nat. Assn. State Univs. and Land Grant Colls., Greater Boston C. of C. (bd. dirs.), Yale Club (N.Y.C.) St. Botolph Club, Comml. Club (Boston). Unitarian. Office: U Mass Boston 100 Morrisey Blvd Boston MA 02125

PENNIMAN, CLARA, political scientist, educator; b. Steger, Ill., Apr. 5, 1914; d. Rae Ernest and Alethea (Bates) P. B.A., U. Wis., 1950, M.A., 1951; Ph.D., U. Minn., 1954. Legal sec., 1934-37; adminstrv. asst. Wis. Employment Service, 1937-47; mem. faculty U. Wis., 1953—, prof. polit. sci., 1961-84, prof. emeritus, 1984—, chmn. dept., 1963-66; dir. Center for Pub. Policy and Adminstrn., 1968-74, Oscar Rennebohm prof. pub. adminstrn., 1974-84; Asso. Brookings Instn., 1972-76; examiner-cons., mem. higher edn. commn. N. Central Assn. Colls.; vis. lectr. Johns Hopkins, summer 1958. Author: State Income Taxation, 1980; co-author: The Minnesota Department of Taxation, 1955, State Income Tax Administration, 1959, Government in the Fifty States, 1960; Contbr. to: Politics in the American States, 1965, 71, 76. Pres. League Women Voters, Madison, 1956-58; mem. Gov. Wis. Tax Impact Study Commn., 1959, Gov.'s Higher Edn. Merger Com., 1971-73; Mayor Madison Met. Com., 1957-58, Madison Redistricting Com., 1960-63; mem. adv. com. govts. div. Bur. Census, 1962-65, mem. state compensation study com., 1983. Recipient Outstanding Achievement award U. Minn., Disting. Service award U. Wis.-Madison. Mem. Am. Polit. Sci. Assn. (v.p. 1971-72, past mem. nat. coun.), Midwest Polit. Sci. Assn. (pres. 1965), ASPA, AAUP (pres. state conf. 1972-73), Nat. Assn. Schs. Pub. Adminstrn. (coun. 1973-75), Am. Acad. Pub. Adminstrn., Altrusa (pres. Madison chpt. 1968-69), Phi Beta Kappa, Phi Kappa Phi. Home: 6209 Mineral Pt Rd Apt 1402 Madison WI 53705-4558

PENNIMAN, NICHOLAS GRIFFITH, IV, newspaper publisher; b. Balt., Mar. 7, 1938; s. Nicholas Griffith Penniman III and Esther Cox Lony (Wight) Keeney; m. Linda Jane Simmons, Feb. 4, 1967; children: Rebecca Helmle, Nicholas G. V. AB, Princeton U., 1960. Asst. bus. mgr. Ill. State Jour. Register, Springfield, 1964-69, bus. mgr., 1969-75; asst. gen. mgr. St. Louis Post-Dispatch, 1975-84, gen. mgr., 1984-86, pub., 1986—. Chmn. Downtown St. Louis, Inc., 1988-90, Mo. Health and Ednl. Facilities Adminstrn., 1982-85, Ill. State Fair Bd., Springfield, 1973-75, St. Louis Sports Com., 1992-93; trustee St. Louis Country Day Sch., 1983-86; bd. dirs. St. Louis Arts and Edn. Coun., 1987—, St. Louis area Boy Scouts Am., 1987-96, Mercantile Libr., 1995—, Regional Commerce Assn., 1995—; v.p. Fair Found., Gateway Arch Park Extension; chmn. Forest Park Forever, 1991-93, Caring Found. for Children, 1988-91. With U.S. Army, 1962-67. Clubs: St. Louis Country, Noonday (pres. 1994). Avocation: tennis. Home: 7540 Maryland Ave Saint Louis MO 63105 Office: Pulitzer Pub Co 900 N Tucker Blvd Saint Louis MO 63101-1069

PENNIMAN, RICHARD WAYNE See LITTLE RICHARD

PENNIMAN, W. DAVID, information scientist, educator, consultant; b. St. Louis, Dec. 19, 1937; s. William Leon and Laura Mae (Van Winkle) P.; m. Charlotte Ann Meder, Mar. 17, 1973; children: Kara, Rachel, John; 1 child by previous marriage, Jessica. BS in ME, U. Ill., 1960, MS in Journalism, Communications, 1962; PhD in Communication Theory, Ohio State U., 1975. Registered profl. engr., Ohio. Assoc. dir. engring. publs. U. Ill. Coll. Engring., Urbana, 1965-66; research scientist info. systems Battelle Columbus Labs., Columbus, Ohio, 1966-69, assoc. mgr. info. systems, 1969-77; research scholar Internat. Inst. Applied Systems Analysis, Laxenburg, Austria, 1977; mgr. research Online Computer Library Ctr., Dublin, Ohio, 1978-79, dir. software devel., 1979-82, v.p. planning and research, 1982-84; dir. libraries and info. systems AT&T Bell Labs., Murray Hill, N.J., 1984-90, dir. info. svcs. group, 1990-91; pres. Coun. on Libr. Resources, Inc., Washington, 1991-95; dir. Ctr. for Info. Studies, 1995—; prof. sch. of Info. Scis. Univ. Tenn., 1995—; bd. dirs., chmn. Engring. Info. Inc., N.Y.C., 1983-91; governing com. Forest Press Inc., Albany, N.Y., 1985-88; adv. com. info. sci. Rutgers U., 1982-91. Author numerous book chpts. and articles in profl. jours. Advisor United Way, Columbus, 1981-83. Served with U.S. Army, 1963-65. Named Tech. Person of the Yr. Columbus Tech. Council, 1982, U.S. Del. to Internat. Inst. for Applied Systems Analysis, 1977. Fellow AAAS; mem. IEEE (sr.), ALA, Am. Soc. Info. Sci. (pres. 1988-89), Assn. for Computing Machinery. Avocations: antique automobiles, hiking. Home and Office: 114A Arcadian Ln Oak Ridge TN 37830 Office: U Tenn 804 Volunteer Blvd Knoxville TN 37996

PENNING, PATRICIA JEAN, elementary education educator; b. Springfield, Ill., Sept. 3, 1952; d. Howard Louis and Jean Lenore (Hartley) P. AA, Lincoln Land C.C., Springfield, 1972; BA, Millikin U., 1975. Cert. tchr. grades K-9. Receptionist Drs. Penning, Marty & Teich, Springfield, 1968-72; child care asst. La Petite Acad., Springfield, 1970-72; tchr. St. Agnes Sch., Springfield, 1975—; mail clk. St. John's Hosp., Springfield, 1977-88; mem. dir. instrnl. tv St. Agnes Sch., Springfield, 1981—, sec. primary level, 1993—, mem. reading com., 1994—, mem. social com., 1994—. Mem. St. Agnes Folk Choir, Springfield, 1976—; cantor, St. Agnes Ch., Springfield, 1976—. Recipient Outstanding Tchr. award Office Cath. Edn., Springfield, 1988, Golden Apple award Ch. 20 and Town and Country Bank, Springfield, 1993; named Apprentice Cathechist, Diocese of Springfield, Ill., 1992. Mem. Internat. Reading Assn., Nat. Coun. Math., Nat. Cath. Edn. Assn. (Grad. award 1991), Ill. State Assn. Curriculum and Devel. Roman Catholic. Avocations: reading, crafts, gardening, classical music. Home: 22 Westminster Rd Chatham IL 62629-1254 Office: St Agnes Sch 251 N Amos Ave Springfield IL 62702-4796

PENNINGER, FRIEDA ELAINE, retired English language educator; b. Marion, N.C., Apr. 11, 1927; d. Fred Hoyle and Lena Frances (Young) P. AB, U. N.C., Greensboro, 1948; MA, Duke U., 1950, PhD, 1961. Copywriter Sta. WSJS, Winston-Salem, N.C., 1948-49; asst. prof. English Flora Macdonald Coll., Red Springs, N.C., 1950-51; tchr. English Barnwell, S.C., 1951-52, Brunswick, Ga., 1952-53; instr. English U. Tenn., Knoxville, 1953-56; instr., asst. prof. Woman's Coll., U. N.C., Greensboro, 1956-58, 60-63; asst. prof., assoc. prof. U. Richmond (Va.), 1963-71; chair., dept. English Westhampton Coll., Richmond, 1971-78; prof. English U. Richmond, 1971-91, Bostwick prof. English, 1987-91; ret., 1991. Author: William Caxton, 1979, Chaucer's "Troilus and Criseyde" and "The Knight's Tale": Fictions Used, 1993, (novel) Look at Them, 1990; compiler, editor: English Drama to 1660, 1976; editor: Festschrift for Prof. Marguerite Roberts, 1976. Fellow Southeastern Inst. of Mediaeval and Renaissance Studies, 1965, 67, 69. Democrat. Presbyterian. Home: 2701 Camden Rd Greensboro NC 27403-1438

PENNINGTON, CATHERINE ANN, legal technology consultant; b. Washington, Jan. 4, 1950; d. William Carter and Marcia Moss (Lewis) Pennington; m. Zlatko Paunov, Mar. 6, 1996. BS, U. Md., 1975; MS, Am. U., 1977; MLS, Brigham Young U., 1980, JD, 1980. Bar: Tex. 1981. Acquisitions asst. Am. U., Washington, 1976-77; libr. asst. Brigham Young U., Provo, Utah, 1977-80; sr. reference libr. So. Meth. U., Dallas, 1980-81; law libr. Johnson & Swanson, Dallas, 1981-85; cons., sr. libr. N.Y. Pub. Libr., N.Y.C., 1985-86; assoc. law libr. St. John's U., Jamaica, N.Y., 1986-89, asst. prof. div. libr. and info. sci., 1987-89, adj. prof. law, 1988-89; dir. libr. svcs. Chadbourne & Parke, N.Y.C., 1989-94; prin. Pennington Consulting, 1994—. Author: Microcomputer Software Selection for Law Libraries, 1987-93, (with others) videotape Organizing a Small Law Firm Library, 1985, Planning the Small Law Office Library, 1994, Microsoft Word for Windows in One Hour for Lawyers, 1995. Dem. precinct chair Dallas County, Tex., 1983-85; sec. St. George Civic Assn., S.I., N.Y., 1988-90, v.p., 1990-92. Fellow Am. Bar Found., ABA (chair libr. com. 1987-90, chair rsch. skills 1990-92, law practice mgmt. sect. 1992, editor-in-chief network 2d 1992-94, coun. 1994—); mem. Am. Assn. Law Librs. (chair pvt. law libr. sect. 1985-86, Bender grantee 1981). Mormon. Avocations: quilting, swimming, skiing. Office: 17 Carroll Pl Staten Island NY 10301-1503

PENNINGTON, DONALD HARRIS, physician; b. Clarksville, Ark., Sept. 13, 1945; s. John Powers and Verna Olive (Harris) P.; m. Susan Myree Snyder, Aug. 27, 1966 (div. Aug. 1982); children: Thomas Walter, Aimee Myree, John Herrick. BA, U. of the Ozarks, 1968; MD, U. Ark., 1972; wine diploma, Calif. Dept. Agr., 1973. Intern St. Vincent Infirmary, Little Rock, 1973; physician, founding ptnr. Clarksville Med. Group, P.A., 1972-93; physician Mercy Med. Svcs., Inc., Ft. Smith, Ark., 1993—; cons. family planning svcs. Ark. State Bd. of Health, 1973-93. Founding mem., musician Ft. Douglas (Ark.) Backporch Bluegrass Symphony, 1976-91; acoustic double bassist River Valley Jazz Union, Russellville, Ark., 1991—. Bd. dirs. Johnson County Regional Hosp., Clarksville, 1973-82; asst. ch. organist 1st United Meth. Ch., Clarkville, 1968—, full time organist 1st Presbyn. Ch., 1994—; active ACLU, Planned Parenthood Fedn., The League to Make a Difference, Sierra Club Legal Defense Fund, The Nature Conservancy; mem. Nat. Trust for Hist. Preservation, 1982—. Mem. AMA, Assn. Am. Physicians for Human Rights, Nat. Trust for Historic Preservation, Ark. Med. Soc. (county del. 1972—), Ark. Acad. Family Practice, Sierra Club, Legal Def. Fund, Drug Policy Found., Am. Guild Organists. Democrat. Avocations: restoration of historic homes, antiques, family history, music, historical preservation. Home: 317 N Johnson St Clarksville AR 72830-2931 *I make as much music as I can; share joy with others, to a point; practice medicine as best as I know how, but remember there is a point where my responsibility ends. Keep breathing in and out - enjoy the happiness of the journey.*

PENNINGTON, JOHN WESLEY, III, lawyer, school system administrator; b. Peoria, Ill., Apr. 1, 1943; s. John W. Jr. and Clara Media (Hicks) P.; m. Marcia Gebhard, July 11, 1964; children: John W. IV, Joshua Wallace, Jennifer Kate. BSE with honors, U. South Fla., 1971; MS in Mgmt., Fla. Internat. U., 1974; JD, U. Miami, 1981. Bar: Fla. 1982; registered profl. engr., Fla., Md. Supr. construction Dade County Sch. Bd., Miami, Fla., 1972-79; dir. planning and constrn. U. Miami, 1979-81, M.R. Harrison Constrn. Co., Miami, 1981-85; v.p. ops., corp. counsel M.R. Harrison Constrn. Co., Miami, Fla., 1987-90; exec. v.p., corp. counsel Harvesters Group Inc., 1985-87; pres., CEO Am. Consolidated Group, Inc., Miami, 1987-90; asst. supt., staff atty. Dade County Sch. Bd., Miami, 1990—; vis. prof. Fla. Internat. U., Miami, 1978; mgmt. trustee Trowel Trades Union Funds, Miami, 1983-85; speaker in field. Editor (short stories) Clara Media Hicks Pennington, 1992; contbr. articles to profl. jours. V.p. Kendale Lakes (Fla.)

Condominium Assn., 1973-75; tchr. high sch. class Kendale United Meth. Ch., South Dade, Fla., 1988. Capt. USMC, 1961-68, Vietnam, ret. med. disability. Mem. Am. Inst. Indsl. Engrs. (sr.), Am. Arbitration Assn. (aribrator), Fla. Bar Assn., Dade County Bar Assn., Omicron Delta Kappa (pres. 1970-71), Pi Mu Epsilon, Phi Kappa Phi, Tau Beta Phi. Home: 8567 SW 137 Ave Miami FL 33183 Office: Office of Staff Atty Ste 428 1450 NE 2nd Ave Miami FL 33132

PENNINGTON, MARY ANNE, art museum director, museum management consultant, art educator; b. Franklin, Va., Apr. 12, 1943; d. James Clifton and Martha Julia (Futrell) P.; m. Walter Joseph Shackleford, Nov. 26, 1981. Student East Carolina U., 1962; BFA, Va. Commonwealth U., 1965, MFA, 1966; postgrad. Cameron U., 1970, East Carolina U., 1972, U. N.C., Chapel Hill, 1980. Instr. art Presbyn. Coll., Clinton, S.C., 1966-69; tchr. art in Pitt County, 1970-71, Greenville City (N.C.) Sch. Systems, 1971-73; instr. art Pitt Community Coll., 1972-73; coordinator visual arts and humanities program, Ludwigsberg, Fed. Republic Germany, 1974-76; vis. artist-in-residence Salt Pond Art Ctr., Blacksburg, Va., summer, 1978; asst. prof. art Pembroke State U., N.C., 1976-80; exec. dir. Greenville Mus. Art, 1980-87, The Lauren Rogers Mus. of Art, Laurel, Miss., 1987-93, Huntington (W.Va.) Mus. Art, 1994—; guest curator Slidell (La.) Arts Ctr., 1993, Artemis. Roanoke, Va., 1995; judge art competition, 1980—; speaker N.C. Dept. Corrections, 1980-87; guest lectr. art Converse Coll., Spartanburg, S.C., 1966, U. So. Miss., 1993; coord. cultural arts program Jones County Leadership Inst., 1989-90, participant, 1990-91, chair curriculum com., 1991-92, chair bd. dirs.; field reviewer Inst. Mus. Svcs., 1986-92; mem. project support grants panel Miss. Arts Commn., 1990-93; mem. Jones County Competitive Cmty. Program Team, chair edn. task force, 1991-92; adj. prof. visual art U. So. Miss. and Jones County Jr. Coll., 1993-94; mem. fed. art project rev. panel, 1994-96; co-chmn. Huntington 125th Anniversary Celebration, 1994-96. Author: Application of Industrial Sand Casting to Sculpture, 1966, Handbook to the Collection of the Lauren Rogers Mus. Art, 1989, Museum in The Schools Education Program, 1989, moderator Long Range Plan Panel, 1992, Ms. Conf. on the Arts; art columnist Laurel Leader Call, 1990-93, The Herald Dispatch, 1994—; also articles. Bd. dirs. Pitt-Greenville Arts Coun., InterMus. Lab. Consortium, 1996—, Our Jobs, Our Children, Our Future, Inc. 1994—; comm. com. Huntington C. of C., 1995—; program coordinator Pitt-Greenville Leadership Inst., 1982-87; bd. dirs., v.p. Parents As Resource Tchrs., 1990-91; advisory bd. chmn. Marshall Artists Series Edn. Com., 1994—; bd. dirs. Huntington Chamber Orch., 1994—. Recipient Vol. award N.C. Gov., 1981; 2 N.C. Arts Council scholarship awards, 1980, 87. Mem. Am. Assn. Mus. (accreditation surveyor 1990—, mus. assessment program surveyor 1990—), Southeastern Mus. Conf., Inc. (steering com. 1990-91), N.C. Mus. Council (bd. dirs. 1986-87), Miss. Mus. Assn. (bd. dirs. 1990-94, v.p. 1992-94), Miss. Inst. Arts and Letters (bd. govs. 1990-94, v.p. 1992-93, pres. 1993-94, chair Visual Arts Award, 1991, 92), Jones County C. of C. (adv. bd. dirs. 1990-93).

PENNINGTON, MERCEDES LARMOYEUX, medical, surgical nurse; b. Jacksonville, Fla., Feb. 26, 1921; d. Pierre Joseph Damian and Margaret Edwina (McMullen) Larmoyeux; m. Richard Charles Pennington, Sept. 30, 1942; children: Thomas, Donna, Douglas, John. AA, Fla. Jr. Coll., 1974, AS in Nursing, 1978. RN, Fla. Med. sec. to pathologist St. Vincent's Hosp., Jacksonville; staff nurse med.-surg. unit St. Luke's Hosp.-Mayo, Jacksonville. Home: 818 Leafy Ln Jacksonville FL 32216-2624

PENNINGTON, RICHARD MAIER, management consultant, retired insurance company executive, lawyer; b. Phila., Aug. 2, 1926; s. Richard and Mildred (Locke) P.; m. Apr. 20, 1963; children—Elizabeth Ann, Catherine Carter. BA, Haverford Coll., 1950; LL.B., Temple U., 1961. Bar: Pa. 1963. Claims work with INA, Phila., 1953-57, 1957-76, Asst. v.p., 1976-77; v.p. Atlantic Mut. Ins. Co., N.Y.C., 1977-78, sr. v.p., 1979-92; mem. exec. com. Ins. Com. for Arson Control, Chgo., 1982-91. Served with U.S. Army, 1945-46. Mem. ABA.

PENNINGTON, WILLIAM MARK, sportswriter; b. Hartford, Conn., Dec. 12, 1956; s. Albert William and Lillian Anne (Lewis) P.; m. Joyce Hand, July 14, 1990; children: Anne D'Amour, Elise Holly. BS, Boston U., 1978. Reporter The Bristol Press, Bristol, Conn., 1976-77, The Associated Press, Boston, 1977, The Providence Jour.-Bull., Providence, 1977-79, The Stamford Advocate, Stamford, Conn., 1979-84; reporter The Record, Hackensack, N.J., 1984-89, syndicated columnist, sr. writer, 1989—. Author: The Winning Spirit, 1991; contbg. author: (book) Best Sports Stories, 1983, 85, 87, 94. Recipient Best Story award Associated Press Sports Editors, 1985, 89, 91, 93, Best Columnist award, 1983, 89. Mem. Baseball Writers Assn. of Am., Boston U. Football Alumni Assn., New England Hist. Genealogical Soc. Roman Catholic. Office: The Record 150 River St Hackensack NJ 07601-7110

PENNISTEN, JOHN WILLIAM, computer scientist, linguist, actuary; b. Buffalo, Jan. 25, 1939; s. George William and Lucy Josephine (Gates) P. AB in Math. and Chemistry with honors, Hamilton Coll., 1960; postgrad., Harvard U., 1960-61, U.S. Army Lang. Sch., 1962-63; MS in Computer Sci. with honors, N.Y. Inst. Tech., 1987; cert. in taxation, NYU, 1982; cert. in profl. banking, Am. Inst. of Banking of Am. Bankers Assn., 1988.; cert. Asian Langs., NYU, 1992. Actuarial asst. New Eng. Mut. Life Ins. Co., Boston, 1965-66; asst. actuary Mass. Gen. Life Ins. Co., Boston, 1966-68; actuarial assoc. John Hancock Mut. Life Ins. Co., Boston, 1968-71; asst. actuary George B. Buck Cons. Actuaries, Inc., N.Y.C., 1971-75, Martin E. Segal Co., N.Y.C., 1975-80; actuary Laiken Siegel & Co., N.Y.C., 1980; cons. Bklyn., 1981—; timesharing and database analyst banklink corp. cash mgmt. div. Chem. Bank N.Y.C., 1983-85; programmer analyst Empire Blue Cross and Blue Shield, N.Y.C., 1986-88, Mt. Sinai Med. Ctr., N.Y.C., 1988-89, French Am. Banking Corp. (subs. Banque National de Paris), N.Y.C., 1989; sr. programmer analyst Dean Witter Reynolds, Inc., N.Y.C., 1989-92; computer specialist for software N.Y.C. Dept. Fin., 1992—; enrolled actuary U.S. Fed. Pension Legis. Bklyn., 1976—. Contbr. articles to profl. jours. With U.S. Army, 1961-64. Mem. AAAS, MLA, Soc. Actuaries (fellow), Practising Law Inst., Assn. Computing Machinery, IEEE Computer Soc., Am. Assn. Artificial Intelligence, Linguistic Soc. Am., Assn. Computational Linguistics, Am. Math. Soc., Math. Assn. Am., Nat. Model R.R. Assn. (life), Nat. Ry. Hist. Soc., Ry. and Locomotive Hist. Soc. (life), Bklyn. Heights Assn., Met. Opera Guild, Am. Friends of Covent Garden, Harvard Gra. Soc., Am. Legion, Phi Beta Kappa, others. Home: 135 Willow St Brooklyn NY 11201-2255

PENNOCK, DONALD WILLIAM, mechanical engineer; b. Ludlow, Ky., Aug. 8, 1915; s. Donald and Melvin (Evans) P.; B.S. in M.E., U. Ky., 1940, M.E., 1948; m. Vivian C. Kern, Aug. 11, 1951; 1 son, Douglas. Stationary engring., constrn. and maintenance Schenley Corp., 1935-39; mech. equipment design engr. mech. lab. U. of Ky., 1939; exptl. test engr. Wright Aero. Corp., Paterson, N.J., 1940, 1941, investigative and adv. engr. to personnel div., 1941-43; indsl. engr. Eastern Aircraft, div. Gen. Motors, Linden, N.J., 1943-45; factory engr. Carrier Corp., Syracuse, N.Y., 1945-58, sr. facilities engr., 1958-60, corporate material handling engr., 1960-63, mgr. facilities engring. dept., 1963-66, mgr. archtl. engring., 1966-68, mgr. facilities engring. dept., 1968-78. Staff, Indsl. Mgmt. Center, 1962, midwest work course U. Kan., 1959-67. Mem. munitions bd. SHIAC, 1950-52; trustee Primitive Hall Found., 1985—. Elected to Exec. and Profl. Hall of Fame, 1966. Registered profl. engr., Ky., N.J. Fellow Soc. Advancement Mgmt. (life mem., nat. v.p. material handling div. 1953-54); mem. ASME, NSPE, Am. Material Handling Soc. (dir. 1950-57, chmn. bd., pres. 1950-52), Am. Soc. Mil. Engrs., Am. Mgmt. Assn. (men. packaging council 1950-55, life mem. planning council), Nat. Material Handling Conf. (exec. com. 1951), Found. N.Am. Wild Sheep (life), Internat. Platform Assn., Tau Beta Pi. Protestant. Mng. editor Materials Handling Engring. (mag. sect.), 1949-50; mem. editorial adv. bd. Modern Materials Handling (mag.), 1949-52. Contbr. articles to tech. jours. Contbg., cons. editor Materials Handling Handbook, 1958. Home: 24 Pebble Hill Rd Syracuse NY 13214

PENNOYER, PAUL GEDDES, JR., lawyer; b. N.Y.C., Feb. 11, 1920; s. Paul G. and Frances (Morgan) P.; m. Cecily Henderson, Feb. 5, 1949; children—Jennifer, Deidre, Paul T., Sheldon K., William M. B.S., Harvard U., 1942, LL.B., 1948. Bar: N.Y. 1949, U.S. Dist. Ct. (so. and ea. dists.) N.Y. 1952, U.S. Supreme Ct. 1972, U.S. Ct. Appeals (2d cir.) 1964, U.S. Ct. Appeals (4th cir.) 1986, U.S. Ct. Appeals (11th cir.) 1987. Assoc. Bingham Englar Jones & Houston, N.Y.C., 1949-55, ptnr., 1955-63; ptnr. Chadbourne & Parke, N.Y.C., 1963-89; of counsel, 1989—. Vice pres., trustee Frick Collection, 1975—; trustee L.I. U., 1975-85. Served to lt. USN, 1942-45. Decorated Navy Cross, Air Medal (2). Mem. ABA, N.Y. State Bar Assn., Assn. Bar City N.Y., N.Y. Bar found., Am. Coll. Trial Lawyers, N.Y. Yacht Club. Republican. Episcopalian. Office: Chadbourne & Parke 30 Rockefeller Plz New York NY 10112

PENNOYER, ROBERT M., lawyer; b. N.Y.C., Apr. 9, 1925. B.A., Harvard U., 1946; LL.B., Columbia U., 1950. Bar: N.Y. 1951, U.S. Supreme Ct. 1971. Partner firm Patterson, Belknap, Webb & Tyler, N.Y.C., 1962—; asst. U.S. atty. criminal div. So. Dist., N.Y., 1953-55; asst. to gen. counsel Office of Sec. of Def., Dept. Def., Washington, 1955-57; spl. asst. to asst. sec. of def. for internat. security affairs Office of Sec. of Def., Dept. Def., 1957-58. Trustee Carnegie Instn., Washington, 1968-69, John Merck Fund, 1982—, Mrs. Giles Whiting Found., 1970—, Met. Mus. Art, 1966—, Pierpont Morgan Libr., 1969—, columbia U., 1982-88, Boyce Thompson Inst. for Plant Rsch., Cornell U., 1974—. Lt. (j.g.) USNR, 1944-46. Mem. ABA, N.Y. State Bar Assn., Assn. Bar City N.Y., Century Assn. Office: Patterson Belknap 1133 Avenue Of The Americas New York NY 10036-6710

PENNY, JOSEPHINE B., retired banker; b. N.Y.C., July 7, 1925; d. Charles and Delia (Fahey) Booy; student Columbia U., Am. Inst. Banking; grad. Sch. Bank Adminstrn. U. Wis., 1975; m. John T. Penny, July 15, 1950 (div.); children—John T., Charleen Penny DeMauro, Patricia Penny Paras. With Prentice-Hall, N.Y.C., 1942-43; with Trade Bank & Trust Co., 1943-52, 61-70; with Nat. Westminster Bank U.S.A., 1970-85, v.p., dep. auditor, 1978-85. Mem. Bank Adminstrn. Inst. (chpt. dir. 1983-85), Inst. Internal Auditing, Nat. Assn. Bank Women (chpt. chmn. 1980-81). Home: 221A Manchester Ln Jamesburg NJ 08831-1711

PENNY, LAURA JEAN, librarian; b. Union City, Tenn., June 25, 1956; d. Glen Jones and Harriet Smith (Gould) P. BS in Econs., Lambuth Coll., 1978; MLS, U. Ariz., 1980. Asst. libr. local history and genealogy Pikes Peak Libr. Dist., Colorado Springs, Colo., 1981-84; info. officer Inmos Corp., Colorado Springs, 1984-86; dir. libr. Colo. State Hosp., Pueblo, 1987—. Author: A Tempstuous Voyage, 1987, Abstracts of Strafford County, 1987, Abstracts of Washington County, 1988. Pres. El Paso County Dem. Women's Club, Colorado Springs, 1986-87; chmn. El Paso County Dem. Com., 1987—. Mem. Colo. Coun. Libr. Devel., Pikes Peak Geneal. Soc. (editor 1985-87). Methodist. Avocations: politics, genealogy, writing, skiing. Office: Colo State Hosp 1600 W 24th St Pueblo CO 81003-1411

PENNY, ROGER PRATT, management executive; b. Buffalo, July 13, 1936; s. George Albert and Louise (Mings) P.; m. Judith Stevens, Aug. 25, 1957; children: David, Sarah, Julia. BA in Adminstrv. Engring., Union Coll., 1958. Registered profl. engr., N.Y., Ind., Pa. From supt. to sr. mgr. Bethlehem Steel Corp., Lackawanna, N.Y., 1958-83; gen. mgr. Bethlehem Steel Corp., Burns Harbor, Ind., 1983-87; sr. v.p. Bethlehem (Pa.) Steel Corp., 1987-92, bd. dirs., bd. dirs., pres., chief oper. officer, 1992—. Mem. United Way, Buffalo, 1960-82; chmn. campaign United Way Porter County, Valparaiso, Ind., 1986; mem. Orchard Park Town Coun., 1970-82; mem. adv. bd. Purdue U., West Lafayette, Ind., 1985-86, Bus. Sch., Valparaiso U., 1986; bd. dirs. Minsi Trails coun. Boy Scouts Am., Lehigh Valley, Pa., 1988—, pres., 1996—; trustee St. Luke's Hosp. Mem. Am. Iron and Steel Inst., Assn. Iron and Steel Engrs., Valparaiso C. of C. (dir. 1985-86), Orchard Park C. of C., Buffalo C. of C., Sand Creek Club (pres. 1983-86), Buffalo Soccer Club (pres. 1960-75, sec.), Saucon Valley Country Club. Republican. Episcopalian. Office: Martin Tower 1170 8th Ave Bethlehem PA 18016-7600

PENROD, JAMES WILFORD, choreographer, dancer; b. Provo, Utah, July 22, 1934; s. Joseph Keller and Virginia Rose (Zobell) P. BA in English, U. So. Calif., 1964; MFA in Dance, U. Calif., Irvine, 1974; CMA, Inst. Movement Studies, 1990. Mem. faculty Am. Sch. Dance, Hollywood, Calif., 1958-68, U. So. Calif., Idyllwild, 1957-59; prof. dance U. Calif., Irvine, 1966—, chmn. dept., 1981-89, 91-94; co-artistic dir. Dancer's Dance Co., Los Angeles, 1968-69, Penrod Plastino Movement Theatre, Irvine, 1968-84, choreographer, 1958—. Profl. dancer on TV, in movies and on stage; choreographer original works.; Author: Movement for the Performing Artist, 1974; co-author: Dancer Prepares, 1970. Grantee U. Calif., 1967—. Mem. SAG, AFTRA, AGVA, Nat Dance Assn., Congress Rsch. in Dance (dir. 1983-85), Orange County Performing Arts Dance Alliance (bd. dirs. 1986-89), Dance Notation Bur. (adv. bd. dirs. 1988-90), Screen Extras Guild, Actors Equity, Am. Guild Mus. Artists. Home: 4645 Green Tree Ln Irvine CA 92715-2250

PENROD, KENNETH EARL, medical education consultant, retired; b. Blanchester, Ohio, Mar. 30, 1916; s. William F. and Josie Alma (Carman) P.; m. Virginia Hogue, June 29, 1942; children: Caroline (dec.), Bruce Hogue. B.S., Miami (Ohio) U., 1938; Ph.D., Iowa State Coll., 1942. Asst. prof. physiology Boston U. Sch. Medicine, 1946-50; asso. prof. physiology Duke U. Sch. Medicine, 1950-57, prof., 1957-59, asst. dean, 1952-59; founding v.p. for med. affairs, prof. physiology W.Va. U., 1959-65; provost for med. ctr., prof. physiology Ind. U., Indpls., 1965-69; vice chancellor for med. and health scis. State U. System Fla., Tallahassee, 1969-74; exec. dir. community hosp. grad. med. edn. program Fla. Bd. Regents, Tallahassee, 1974-85; retired, 1992; spl. cons. AID, Latin Am. Mem. editorial bd. Jour. Med. Edn, 1957-65; contbr. to sci. jours. in physiol. and health edn. Served from 2d lt. to capt. USAAF, 1942-46. Mem. Am. Physiol. Soc., Assn. for Acad. Health Centers (incorporator), Assn. Am. Med. Colls., AAAS, Rotary, Phi Beta Kappa, Sigma Xi, Phi Kappa Phi, Phi Kappa Tau, Alpha Omega Alpha. Presbyterian. Home: 913 Lasswade Dr Tallahassee FL 32312-2831

PENROSE, CHARLES, JR., professional society administrator; b. Phila., Oct. 9, 1921; s. Charles and Beatrice (d,Este) P.; m. Ann Lucille Cantwell, Apr. 17, 1943; children: James, Thomas, John. Grad., Episcopal Acad., Overbrook, Pa., 1940. Exec. sec. Newcomen Soc. N.Am. (N.A.), Phila., 1946-48; dist. sales mgr. Phila., for; Fitchburg Paper Co., Mass., 1948-50, 52-53; sales mgr. A.M. Collins Mfg. Co., Phila., 1953-54; v.p. sales A.M. Collins Mfg. Co., 1954-55; sales mgr. A.M. Collins div. Internat. Paper Co., N.Y.C., 1955; asst. to sales mgr. fine paper and bleached bd. div., 1956-57; sr. v.p., chief exec. officer Newcomen Soc. in N.Am., Downingtown, Pa., 1957-61; also dir. Newcomen Soc. in N.Am.; pres., CEO Newcomen Soc. U.S., 1961-87, chmn., 1987-89, chmn. emeritus, 1989—; sr. v.p. N. Am. Newcomen Soc., London, 1957-89, hon. v.p., 1989—; pres., CEO Newcomen publs. in N. Am., Inc., 1958-61, trustee, 1948-61; pres., dir. Rocaton, Inc., Darien, Conn., 1960-61. Author: They Live on a Rock in the Sea The Isles of Shoals in Colonial Days, 1957. Sec., asst. treas. Chester County Investment Fund Assn., Phila., 1959-64; v.p. Brit. Am. Ednl. Found., Inc., N.Y.C., 1968-70, pres., 1970-75, trustee, 1968-81; trustee The Stanley Mus., Kingfield, Maine, 1995—. Capt. USAAF, 1940-46, S.W. Pacific; capt. AUS, 1950-52, Germany. Mem. Most Venerable Order Hospice of St. John of Jerusalem (London). Mem. Newcomen Soc. U.S., Newcomen Soc. London, Royal Soc. Arts (Benjamin Franklin fellow 1980), Pilgrims of U.S., First Troop Phila. City Calvary (hon.), Nat. Inst. Social Scis., Soc. Am. Historians, Marine Hist. Assn., N.H. Hist. Soc., Mt. Washington Obs., Sandwich (N.H.) Hist. Soc. (trustee 1992-94, v.p. 1994—), Chi Psi Omicron. Republican. Episcopalian. Clubs: Tokeneke (Darien); Tamworth Outing (N.H.); Wonalancet Outdoors (N.H.). Home: Briar Farm North Sandwich NH 03259 Office: 412 Newcomen Rd Exton PA 19341-1934

PENSE, ALAN WIGGINS, metallurgical engineer, academic administrator; b. Sharon, Conn., Feb. 3, 1934; s. Arthur Wilton and May Beatrice (Wiggins) P.; m. Muriel Drews Taylor, June 28, 1958; children—Daniel Alan, Steven Taylor, Christine Muriel. B.Metall. Engring., Cornell U., 1957; M.S., Lehigh U., 1959, Ph.D., 1962. Research asst. Lehigh U., Bethlehem, Pa., 1957-59, instr., 1960-62, asst. prof., 1962-65, asso. prof., 1965-71, prof., 1971—, chmn. dept. metallurgy and materials engring., 1977-83, assoc. dean Coll. Engring. and Applied Scis., 1984-88, dean, 1988-90, v.p., provost, 1990—; assoc. dir. Ctr. Advanced Tech. for Large Structural Systems NSF, 1986-89; cons. adv. com. on reactor safeguards NRC, 1965-86. Author: (with R.M. Brick and R.B. Gordon) Structure and Properties of Engineering Materials, 4th edit, 1978; also articles. Recipient Robinson award Lehigh U., 1965, Stabler award, 1972; Danforth fellow, 1974-86. Fellow Am. Soc. Metals, Am. Welding Soc. (William Spraragan award 1963, Adams Membership award 1966, Jennings award 1970, Adams lectr. 1980, William Hobart medal 1982, Plummer lectr. 1995); mem. ASTM, Am. Soc. Engring. Edn. (Western Elec. award 1986), Internat. Inst. Welding, Nat. Acad. Engring. Republican. Evang. Congregationalist (pres. bd. trustees Evang. Sch. Theology). Home: 2227 West Blvd Bethlehem PA 18017-5025 Office: 27 Memorial Dr W Bethlehem PA 18015-3005 *Achievement of significant goals in our life must be balanced by the quality of that life itself, for what we are is as important as what we do.*

PENSKAR, MARK HOWARD, lawyer; b. Detroit, Mar. 4, 1953; s. Sol Leonard and Frances (Rosenthal) P.; m. Carol Ann Stewart, Aug. 7, 1977; children: David, Rebecca. BA, U. Mich., 1974, MPP, 1975, JD, 1977. Bar: Calif. 1977, U.S. Dist. Ct. (no. dist.) Calif. 1977, (ea. and cen. dists.) Calif. 1983, (so. dist.) 1988, U.S. Ct. Appeals (9th cir.) 1987, U.S. Tax Ct. 1993. Assoc. Pillsbury, Madison and Sutro, San Francisco, 1977-84, ptnr., 1985-96; sr. bus. litigation atty. Pacific Gas and Electric Co., San Francisco, 1996—; panelist Superior Court early settlement program, San Francisco. Mem. Com. for Sch. of Pub. Policy. Mem. ABA, San Francisco Bar Assn., Commonwealth Club, Phi Gamma Delta (past pres. Bay Area grad. chpt.), Phi Alpha Delta. Avocations: camping, golf, wine collecting. Home: 29 E Altarinda Dr Orinda CA 94563-2415 Office: Pacific Gas and Electric Co Law Dept B30A PO Box 7442 San Francisco CA 94120

PENSKE, ROGER S., manufacturing and transportation executive; b. 1937; married. Grad., Lehigh U., 1958. With Alcoa Aluminum, Pitts., 1958-63, George McKean Chevrolet, Phila., 1963-65; prin. Penske Corp., Red Bank, N.J., pres., chmn. bd.; chmn. bd. dirs., pres. Penske Transp. Inc., Detroit, Pa. Internat. Raceway, Nazareth, 1986—; CEO Detroit Diesel Corp., chmn. bd. dirs.; pres. Competition Tire West, inc., Brooklyn, Mich.; chmn. bd. dirs. Penske Truck Leasing Corp., Penske Speedway, Inc., Detroit, Penske Automotive Group, Detroit, Outer Drive Holidays, Inc., Detroit, D Longo, Inc., El Monte, Calif.; sec. Ilmore Engring., Inc., Redford, Mich. *

PENSON, EDWARD MARTIN, management consulting company executive; b. N.Y.C., Aug. 30, 1927; s. Michael and Cecile (Cohan) P.; m. Georgann Ellen McCune, June 25, 1975; children: Jeffery, Albert, Cynthia. B.A. cum laude, U. Fla., 1950, Ph.D., 1955; M.A., Ohio U., 1951. Prof. communication Ohio U., Athens, 1955-75, dean, 1965-68, v.p., 1969-75; pres., prof. Salem State Coll., Mass., 1975-78; prof., chancellor U. Wis.-Oshkosh, 1978-89, chancellor emeritus, 1989—; pres. Penson-Strawbridge, Inc., mgmt. cons., 1989—; cons. Royal McBee, Litton Industries, Ohio Credit Union, Battelle Meml. Inst., 1963-66, U. Nev., 1980-81, Paine Art Ctr., 1985, Acad. Ednl. Devel., King Fiesal U., 1986, OshKosh B'Gosh, Inc., 1987, Akron U., 1988, Baker Paper Co., 1990; bd. dirs. Valley Bank, Wis. Contbr. numerous articles to profl. jours., chpts. to books. Bd. dirs. Assn. Retarded Citizens, Salem, Mass., 1975-78; bd. dirs. Econ. Devel. Council, North Shore, Mass., 1976-78, Ohio student loan commr., Columbus, 1971-75. Mem. Communication Assn. Am., Internat. Communication Assn., Am. Assn. State Colls. and Univs., Nat. Assn. Student Personnel Adminstrs., Sigma Alpha Eta, Phi Kappa Phi, Alpha Lambda Delta, Psi Chi, Rotary (Salem, Mass. and Oshkosh, Wis.). Home and Office: 924 Summerbrooke Dr Tallahassee FL 32312

PENTKOWSKI, RAYMOND J., superintendent. Supt. Battenkill (Vt.) Valley Supervisory Union. Named state finalist Nat. Supt. of Yr. award, 1989. Office: East Arlington Rd Arlington VT 05250

PENTNEY, ROBERTA JEAN, neuroanatomist, educator; b. Van Nuys, Calif., Jan. 11, 1936; d. Bernard Andrew and Helen Amelia (Sahm) Pierson; m. William M. Pentney, July 5, 1975; 1 child, William Robert. BA, Coll. Notre Dame, Belmont, Calif., 1960; PhD, U. Notre Dame, 1965. Asst. then assoc. prof. Coll. Notre Dame, Belmont, 1965-71; spl. fellow Coll. Phys. Sci. and Surgery, Columbia U., N.Y.C., 1971-74; from asst. prof. to prof. Sch. Medicine and Biomed. Sci. SUNY, Buffalo, 1974—; interim chmn. dept. anat. cell biology Sch. Medicine and Biomed. Sci. SUNY, Buffalo, 1992—. Contbr. articles to profl. jours. Mem. Am. Assn. Anatomists, Soc. for Neuroscis., Rsch. Soc. on Alcohoism, Gerontol. Soc., Sigma Xi. Office: SUNY Dept Anatomy Cell Bio 317 Farber Hall Buffalo NY 14214

PENTZ, PAUL, hardware company executive; b. 1940. BS, Cornell U., 1969. With AmyNG, 1962-68, Gen. Foods Corp., 1962-69; v.p. Jewel Cos., 1969-78; group mdse. mgr. Servistar Corp., East Butler, Pa., 1978-79, v.p. mdse. advt., 1979-83, sr. v.p. advt. mdse., 1983-86, sr. v.p. mdse. advt. inventory control, 1986-93, CEO, 1993—. Office: Servistar 1 Servicestar Way East Butler PA 16029*

PENWELL, JONES CLARK, real estate appraiser, consultant; b. Crisp, Tex., Dec. 19, 1921; s. Clark Moses and Sarah Lucille (Jones) P.; BS, Colo. State U., 1949; m. A. Jerry Jones, July 1, 1967; children: Dale Maria, Alan Lee, John Steven, Laurel Anne, Tracy Lynn. Farm mgmt. supr. Farmers Home Adminstrn., Dept. Agr., 1949-58; rancher 1958-61; real estate appraiser/realty officer Dept. Interior, Tex., Calif., Ariz., Colo., Washington, 1961-78, chief appraiser Bur. Reclamation, Lakewood, Colo., 1978-80; ind. fee appraiser, cons., 1980-94; ret., 1995. Served with USN, 1940-46. Accredited rural appraiser; cert. review appraiser, gen. appraiser; recipient Outstanding Performance awards U.S. Bur. Reclamation, 1964, 75, 80. Mem. Am. Soc. Farm Mgns. and Rural Appraisers, Internat. Right-of-Way Assn., Nat. Assn. Rev. Appraisers (regional v.p. 1978-79), Jefferson County Bd. Realtors. Democrat. Presbyterian. Clubs: Elks, Rotary, Mt. Vernon Country. Author: Reviewing Condemnation Appraisal Reports, 1980; The Valuation of Easements, 1980. Home and office: 10100 W 21st Pl Lakewood CO 80215-1406 *Personal philosophy: Great personal satisfaction and benefit to society follows a person's development, constant improvement and marketing of talents in a line of work which is enjoyable and most comfortable for him to deliver.*

PENZ, ANTON JACOB, retired accounting educator; b. Cleve., Feb. 22, 1906; s. Stephen F. and Elizabeth (Prokosch) P.; (married); children—Alton Jeffry, David Alan. B.S. in Elec. Engring, Cleve. State U., 1933; M.A. in Edn, Western Res. U., 1936; M.B.A., Northwestern U., 1942; Ph.D., Ohio State U., 1947. Prof. Davis and Elkins Coll., 1937-40; lectr. Rensselaer Poly. Inst., 1944; asst. prof. La. State U., 1944-47; prof. accounting, head dept. U. Ala., 1947-71, prof. emeritus, 1971—; Distinguished vis. prof. U. Nev., Reno, spring 1972, U. Colo., Boulder, spring 1973, Va. Commonwealth U., Richmond, spring 1975, U. Md., College Park, spring 1979; cons., lectr. AID, Lima, Peru, 1965-66, Guyana, 1967. Author: Manual De Contabilidad Y Costos, 1966; Editor: Accounting Teachers Guide, 1953, Professional Developments: Accounting Teachers Guide, 1953, Accountancy, A Vocation and Profession, 1958, Guide to Accounting Instruction: Concepts and Practices, 1968, Introducing the Profession: A Guide to Accounting Instruction, 1968. Del. various congresses. Mem. Nat. Assn. Accountants (Lybrand award 1951), Fin. Execs. Inst., Am. Accounting Assn. (v.p. 1962-63), Beta Alpha Psi (pres. 1955-56, editor newsletter 1953-55). Home: Pine Valley # F-31 800 Rice Valley Rd N Tuscaloosa AL 35406-1671 Office: Box AC Tuscaloosa AL 35486

PENZER, MARK, lawyer, editor, corporate trainer, former publisher; b. Bklyn., Nov. 22, 1932; s. Ed and Fay (Weinberg) P.; m. Eileen Malen, Aug. 12, 1962; children: Matthew, Nicole; m. Nydia A. Rey, Nov. 25, 1984. B.B.A., CCNY; J.D., Fordham U. Bar: N.Y. 1968, D.C. 1973, Fla. 1982, U.S. Dist. Ct. (ea. dist.) N.Y. 1976, U.S. Dist. Ct. (so. dist.) Fla. 1991; cert. instr. DMA, 1986. Free-lance writer, 1950-83; editorial asst. Hearst mags., N.Y.C., 1955; asst. editor Hearst mags., 1956, assoc. editor, 1957-66; columnist N.Y. Jour.-Am., 1960-62; editor in chief Rudder mag., 1967-69, editorial dir., 1970-74; editor in chief True, 1970-73, editor at large, 1973-75; pub., editor in chief Jour. Energy Medicine, 1978-81; Medicare hearing officer Miami, Fla., 1981-82; pres. Success Internat., Inc., Coral Gables, Fla., 1984-85; adj. prof. bus. and tech. writing Fla. Internat. U., small bus. mgmt., U. Miami, 1986-89; pres. Heroica, Inc., Miami Lakes, Fla., 1989-90; pvt. practice Law Offices of Mark Penzer, Hialeah and Miami Lakes, Fla., 1991—; tchr. creative writing Dade County Off Campus Edn. Author: The Motorboatman's Bible, 1965, The Powerboatman's Bible, 1977; asst. editor: The Path of Least Resistance, 1989, Do It!, 1991. Served with AUS, 1953-55. Mem. Hialeah-Miami Lakes Bar Assn. (pres. 1990-92).

PENZIAS, ARNO ALLAN, astrophysicist, research scientist, information systems specialist; b. Munich, Germany, Apr. 26, 1933; came to U.S., 1940, naturalized, 1946; s. Karl and Justine (Eisenreich) P.; m. Anne Pearl Barras, Nov. 25, 1954; children: David Simon, Mindy Gail, Laurie Ruth. BS in Physics, CCNY, 1954; MA in Physics, Columbia U., 1958, PhD in Physics, 1962; Dr. honoris causa, Observatoire de Paris, 1976; ScD (hon.), Rutgers U., 1979, Wilkes Coll., 1979, CCNY, 1979, Yeshiva U., 1979, Bar Ilan U., 1983, Monmouth Coll., 1984, Technion-Israel Inst. Tech., 1986, U. Pitts., 1986, Ball State U., 1986, Kean Coll., 1986, U. Pa., 1992, Ohio State U., 1988, Iona Coll., 1988; Drew U., 1989; ScD (hon.), Lafayette Coll., 1990, Columbia U., 1990, George Washington U., 1992, Rensselaer Univ., 1992, U. Pa., 1992; Bloomfield Coll., 1994. Mem. tech. staff Bell Labs., Holmdel, N.J., 1961-72, head radiophysics rsch. dept., 1972-76; dir. radio research lab. Bell Labs., 1976-79, exec. dir. rsch., communications scis. div., 1979-81, v.p. rsch., 1981-95, v.p., chief scientist, 1995—; bd. dirs. A.D. Little, Duracell; adj. prof. earth and scis. SUNY, Stony Brook, 1974-84, Univ. Disting. lectr., 1990; lectr. dept. astrophys. scis. Princeton U., 1967-72, vis. prof., 1972-85; rsch. assoc. Harvard Coll. Obs., 1968-80; Edison lectr. U.S. Naval Rsch. Lab., 1979; Kompfner lectr. Stanford U., 1979; Gamow lectr. U. Colo., 1980; Jansky lectr. Nat. Radio Astronomy Obs., 1983; Michelson Meml. lectr., 1985; Grace Adams Tanner lectr., 1987; Klopsteg lectr. Northwestern U., 1987; grad. faculties alumni Columbia U., 1987-89; Regents' lectr. U. Calif., Berkeley, 1990; Lee Kuan Yew Disting. vis. nat. U. Singapore, 1991; mem. astronomy adv. panel NSF, 1978-79, mem. indsl. panel on sci. and tech., 1982—, disting. lectr., 1987, affiliate Max-Planck Inst. for Radioastronomie, 1978-85, chmn. Fachbeirat, 1981-83; rschr. in astrophysics, info. tech., its applications and impacts. Author: Ideas and Information Managing in a High-Tech World, 1989 (pub. in 10 langs.), Harmony-Business, Technology and Life After Paperwork, 1995; mem. editl. bd. Ann. Rev. Astronomy and Astrophysics, 1974-78; mem. editl. bd. AT&T Bell Labs. Tech. Jour., 1978-84, chmn., 1981-84; assoc. editor Astrophys. Jour., 1978-82; contbr. over 100 articles to tech. jours.; several patents in field. Trustee Trenton (N.J.) State Coll., 1977-79; mem. bd. overseers U. Pa. Sch. Engring. and Applied Sci., 1983-86; mem. vis. com. Calif. Inst. Tech., 1977-79; mem. Com. Concerned Scientists, 1975—, vice chmn., 1976—; mem. adv. bd. Union of Couns. for Soviet Jews, 1983—; bd. dirs. IMNET, 1986-91, Coun. on Competitiveness, 1989-92. With U.S. Army, 1954-56. Named to N.J Lit, Hall of Fame, 1991; recipient Herschel medal Royal Astron. Soc, 1977, Nobel prize in Physics, 1978, Townsend Harris medal CCNY, 1979, Newman award, 1983, Joseph Handleman prize in the scis., 1983, Grad. Faculties Alumni award Columbia U., 1984, Achievement in Science award Big Brothers Inc., N.Y.C., 1985, Priestly award Dickinson Coll., 1989, Pender award U. Pa., 1992. Mem. NAE, NAS (Henry Draper medal 1977), AAAS, IEEE (hon.), Am. Astron. Soc., Am. Phys. Soc. (Pake prize 1990), Internat. Astron. Union, World Acad. Arts and Sci.

PENZIEN, JOSEPH, structural engineering educator; b. Philip, S.D., Nov. 27, 1924; s. John Chris and Ella (Stebbins) P.; m. Jeanne Ellen Hunson, Apr. 29, 1950 (dec. 1985); children—Robert Joseph, Karen Estelle, Donna Marie, Charlene May; m. Mi-jung Park, June 16, 1988. Student, Coll. Idaho, 1942-43; B.S., U. Wash., 1945; Sc.D., Mass. Inst. Tech., 1950. Mem. staff Sandia Corp., 1950-51; sr. structures engr. Consol. Vultee Aircraft Corp., Fort Worth, 1951-53; asst. prof. U. Calif. at Berkeley, 1953-57, asso. prof., 1957-62, prof. structual engring., 1962-88, prof. emeritus, 1988—; dir. Earthquake Engring. Research Center, 1968-73, 77-80; cons. engring. firms; chief tech. adv. Internat. Inst. of Seismology and Earthquake Engring., Tokyo, Japan, 1964-65; chmn. bd. Ea. Internat. Engrs., Inc., 1980-90, Internat. Civil Engring. Cons., Inc., 1990—. NATO Sr. Sci. fellow., 1969. Fellow Am. Acad. Mechanics; hon. mem. ASCE (Walter Huber Research award, Alfred M. Freudenthal medal, Nathan M. Newmark medal), Earthquake Engring. Rsch. Inst. (hon., Hausner medal), IAEE (hon.); mem. Am. Concrete Inst., Structural Engrs. Assn. Calif., Seismol. Soc. Am., Nat. Acad. Engring. Home: 800 Solana Dr Lafayette CA 94549-5004 Office: Davis Hall Univ Calif Berkeley CA 94720

PEOPLES, DAVID WEBB, screenwriter; b. Middletown, CT; s. Joe Webb Peoples. B.A. English, UC Berkeley, 1962. Scripts include Blade Runner, 1982, Leviathan, 1989, Dead Fall, 1990, Unforgiven, 1992 (Academy award nomination best original screenplay 1992), Hero, 1992; dir., writer: The Blood of Heroes, 1990. Office: Shapiro/Lichtman Agy 8827 Beverly Blvd Los Angeles CA 90048-2405

PEOPLES, JOHN ARTHUR, JR., former university president, consultant; b. Starkville, Miss., Aug. 26, 1926; s. John Arthur and Maggie Rose (Peoples) P.; m. Mary E. Galloway, July 13, 1951; children: Kathleen, Mark Adam. B.S., Jackson State U., 1950; M.A., U. Chgo., 1951, Ph.D., 1961. Tchr. math. Froebel Sch., Gary, Ind., 1951-58; asst. prin. Lincoln Sch., Gary, 1958-62; prin. Banneker Sch., Gary, 1962-64; asst. to pres. Jackson (Miss.) State U., 1964-66, v.p., 1966-67, pres., 1967-84; Trustees disting. prof. Univs. Ctr. of Jackson, 1984-85; asst. to pres. SUNY, Binghamton, 1965-66; cons. in higher edn., 1985—; lectr. summers numerous univs. and colls. Contbr. articles to profl. jours. Active Boy Scouts Am.; bd. govs. So. Regional Edn. Bd.; bd. visitors Air U.; adv. com. U.S. Army Command and Gen. Staff Coll.; mem. Commn. Excellence Am. Assn. State Colls. and Univs.; bd. commrs. Jackson Airport Authority. Served with USMCR, 1944-47. Recipient Disting. Am. award Nat. Football Found., Presdl. citation, Lifetime Achievement award Nat. Black Coll. Alumni Found., 1993—; named to Southwestern Athletic Hall of Fame. Mem. Am. Council Edn. (chmn. dir. 1975), Am. Assn. Higher Edn. (dir. 1971-74), NEA, Miss. Tchrs. Assn., Jackson C. of C. (econ. council), Alpha Kappa Mu, Phi Kappa Phi, Phi Delta Kappa, Omega Psi Phi (Man of Year, Sigma Omega chpt. 1966), Sigma Pi Phi. Lodge: Masons (33 deg.).

PEOPLES, THOMAS EDWARD, publisher, executive, writer; b. Cleve., Oct. 26, 1915; s. Robert Stephen and Mary Frances (Box) P.; m. Helen Catherine Mullaney, Jan. 9, 1943; children—Michael Thomas, Mary Dennis, Thomas Edward, James Robert. Student, John Carroll U., 1933-37. Staff photographer Central Press Assn. div. Hearst Corp., 1938-41; staff photographer Internat. News Photos, Cleve., 1946, bur. mgr., 1947-52; picture editor Newspaper Enterprise Assn., Cleve., 1953-58; comics prodn. editor Newspaper Enterprise Assn., 1958-68, dir. comic art, 1968-76, v.p., 1972-76. Author: syndicated comic page Our Boarding House with Maj. Hoople, 1959-69, Major Hoople Football Forecast, 1959-91. Served to 1st lt. U.S. Army, 1941-46, PTO. Mem. Cleve. Newspaper and Newsreel Cameramens Assn. (pres. 1950-51), Newspaper Comics Council (exec. bd. 1968-76, promotion dir. 1972-73), Nat. Cartoonists Soc., Sigma Delta Chi. Democrat. Roman Catholic. Home: 1095 Circle Ter W # B Delray Beach FL 33445-2905 *Every day we should attempt to do some deed for the betterment of society and one's fellowmen. The performance of these deeds may or may not be anonymous but they must never be done with the aim of financial reward or personal or social gain. Our efforts to help our fellowmen may not be crowned with success every time, but it is in the trying we receive our reward.*

PEPE, FRANK A., cell and developmental biology educator; b. Schenectady, May 22, 1931; s. Rocco and Margherita (Ruggiero) P. B.S., Union Coll., 1953; Ph.D., Yale U., 1957. Instr. anatomy U. Pa., Phila., 1957-60, assoc. in anatomy, 1960-63, asst. prof., 1963-65, assoc. prof., 1965-70, prof., 1970-92, chmn. dept. anatomy, 1977-90, prof. cell. and devel. biology, 1992-96, emeritus prof., 1996—. Editor: Motility in Cell Function, 1979. Recipient Rsch. Career Devel. award USPHS, 1968-73, Raymond C. Truex Disting. Lecture award Hahneman U., 1988. Fellow AAAS; mem. Am. Assn. Anatomists, Am. Chem. Soc., Am. Inst. Biol. Scis., Am. Soc. Cell Biology, N.Y. Acad. Scis., Biophys. Soc., Microscopy Soc. Am., Sigma Xi. Home: 4614 Pine St Philadelphia PA 19143-1808 Office: U Pa Sch Medicine Philadelphia PA 19104-6508

PEPE, LOUIS ROBERT, lawyer; b. Derby, Conn., Mar. 7, 1943; s. Louis F. and Mildred R. (Vollaro) P.; m. Carole Anita Roman, June 8, 1969; children: Marissa Lee, Christopher Justin, Alexander Drew. B.Mgmt.Engring., Rensselaer Poly. Inst., 1964, M.S., 1967; J.D. with distinction, Cornell U., 1970. Bar: Conn. 1970, U.S. Dist. Ct. Conn. 1970, U.S. Ct. Appeals (2d cir.) 1971, U.S. Supreme Ct. 1975, U.S. Ct. Claims 1978. Assoc., Alcorn, Bakewell & Smith, Hartford, Conn., 1970-75, ptnr., 1975-82; sr. ptnr. Pepe & Hazard, Hartford, 1983—; dir. BayBank Conn., 1987-93; adj. assoc. prof. Hartford Grad. Ctr., 1972-87. Bd. dirs. No. Conn. chpt. Lukemia Soc. Am., Inc.; mem. New Hartford Planning and Zoning Commn., 1973-84, chmn., 1980-84; mem. New Hartford Inland Wetlands Commn., 1975-78, New Hartford Housing Authority, 1971-72. Served to 1st lt., U.S. Army, 1964-66. Decorated Army Commendation Medal; recipient Frazer prize and Robinson Moot Ct. award Cornell U., 1970. Fellow Am. Bar Found.; mem. ABA, Am. Coll. Trial Lawyers, Am. Bd. Trial Advs., Conn. Bar Assn. (chmn. constrn. law sect. 1989-92), Conn. Trial Lawyers Assn., Hartford County Bar Assn., Am. Legion, Phi Kappa Phi. Home: 3 Metacom Dr Simsbury CT 06070-1851 Office: Goodwin Sq Hartford CT 06103-4300

PEPE, MICHAEL, publishing executive; b. Chester, Pa., May 1, 1954; s. John F. and Adele (Davis) P.; m. Laurie Ann Huckins, June 12, 1976; children: Matthew Eliot, Gordon Michael. BA, U. Del., 1976; MBA, Harvard U., 1981. Area mgr. Surgicot, Inc., Hauppauge, N.Y., 1976-78, dir. mktg., 1978-79; assoc. Morgan Stanley & Co., N.Y.C., 1981-82; asst. brand mgr. Procter & Gamble, Cin., 1982-84; v.p. mktg. Patient Tech., Inc., Hauppauge, 1984, pres., chief operating officer, 1984-86; dir. strategic planning People mag. div. Time, Inc., N.Y.C., 1986-87, dir. prod., 1987—; Group Pub Fortune, N.Y.C. Walter C. Teagle fellow, Harvard U., 1979. Phi Beta Kappa. Club: Harvard. Avocations: fly fishing, running, cooking, wine. Office: Time Inc Time & Life Bldg Rockefeller Ctr New York NY 10020-1302*

PEPE, STEPHEN PHILLIP, lawyer; b. Paterson, N.J., Oct. 30, 1943; s. Vincent Attilio and Emma (Opletal) P.; m. Catherine B. Hagen, Dec. 8, 1990. BA, Montclair (N.J.) State Coll., 1965; JD, Duke U., 1968. Bar: Calif. 1969, J.S. Dist. Ct. (no., so., ea. and cen. dists.) Calif. 1975, U.S. Ct. Appeals (9th cir.) 1975, U.S. Sup. Ct. 1978. Assoc. O'Melveny & Myers, L.A., 1968-75, ptnr., 1976—, chmn. lab. and employment law dept., 1989-92. Co-author: Avoiding and Defending Wrongful Discharge Claims, 1987; co-editor: Guide to Acquiring and Managing a U.S. Business, 1992, Calif. Employment Law Letter, 1990—. Bd. visitors Duke Law Sch., 1992—; bd. trustees Montclair State Coll. Found., 1991; pres. Inst. Indsl. Rels. Assn. With USAR, 1969-75. Mem. Am. Hosp. Assn. (labor adv. com. 1975-90), Mchts. and Mfrs. Assn. (bd. dirs., chmn. legal com. 1989—), Calif. Club (chmn. employee rels. com., chmn. legal com. 1980—). Democrat. Roman Catholic. Club: Calif. (chmn. employee relations com., chmn. legal com. 1989—). Avocations: wine collecting, wine making, wine judging. Office: O'Melveny & Myers 610 Newport Center Dr Newport Beach CA 92660-6429*

PEPE, STEVEN DOUGLAS, U.S. magistrate judge; b. Indpls., Jan. 29, 1943; s. Wilfrid Julius and Roselda (Gehring) P. BA cum laude, U. Notre Dame, 1965; JD magna cum laude, U. Mich., 1968; postgrad., London Sch. Econs. and Polit. Sci., 1970-72; LLM, Harvard U., 1974. Bar: Ind. 1968, U.S. Dist. Ct. Ind. 1968, D.C. 1969, U.S. Dist. Ct. D.C. 1969, mass. 1973, Mich. 1974, U.S. Dist. Ct. (ea. dist.) Mich., 1983. Law clk. Hon. Harold Leventhal U.S. Cir. Ct. Appeals, Washington, 1968-69; staff atty. Neighborhood Legal Svcs. Program, 1969-70; cons. Office of Svcs. to Aging, Lansing, Mich., 1976-77, Administrn. Aging, Dept. Health and Human Svcs., 1976-78; U.S. magistrate judge Eastern Dist., Ann Arbor, Mich., 1983—; mem. Biregional Older Am. Advocacy Assistance Resource and Support Ctr., 1979-81; cons., bd. dirs. Ctr. Social Gerontology (1988-93); clin. prof. law, dir. Mich. Clin. Law Program, U. Mich. Law Sch., 1974-83; adj. prof. law Detroit Mercy Sch. Law, 1985; lectr. U. Mich. Law Sch., 1985-96. Editor Mich. Law Rev.; contbr. articles to profl. jours. Recipient Reginald Heber Smith Cmty. Lawyer fellowship, 1969-70; Mich.-Ford Internat. Studies fellow, 1970-72, Harvard Law Sch. Clin. Teaching fellow, 1972-73. Mem. ABA, State Bar Mich., State Bar Ind., D.C. Bar, Fed. Bar Assn., Washtenaw County Bar Assn., Am. Inn Court XI, U. Detroit Mercy, Pi Sigma Alpha, Order of Coif. Office: US District Court PO Box 7150 Ann Arbor MI 48107-7150

PEPER, CHRISTIAN BAIRD, lawyer; b. St. Louis, Dec. 5, 1910; s. Clarence F. and Christine (Baird) P.; m. Ethel C. Kingsland, June 5, 1935 (dec. Sept. 1995); children: Catherine K. Peper Larson, Anne Peper Sale, Christian B.; m. Barbara C. Pleiter, Jan. 25, 1996. AB cum laude, Harvard U., 1932; LLB, Washington U., 1935; LLM, Yale U., 1937. Bar: Mo. 1934. Since practiced in St. Louis; of counsel Peper, Martin, Jensen, Maichel & Hetlage.; lectr. various subjects Washington U. Law Sch., St. Louis, 1943-61; ptnr. A.G. Edwards & Sons, 1945-67; pres. St. Charles Gas Corp., 1953-72; bd. dirs. St. Louis Steel Casting Inc., Hydraulic Press Brick Co., El Dorado Paper Bag Mfg. Co., Inc. Editor: An Historian's Conscience: The Correspondence of Arnold J. Toynbee and Columba Cary-Elwes, 1986. Contbr. articles to profl. jours. Mem. vis. com. Harvard Div. Sch., 1964-70; counsel St. Louis Art Mus. Sterling fellow Yale U., 1937. Mem. ABA, Mo. Bar Assn., St. Louis Bar Assn., Noonday Club, Harvard Club, East India Club (London), Order of Coif, Phi Delta Phi. Roman Catholic. Home: 1454 Mason Rd Saint Louis MO 63131-1211 Office: 720 Olive St Saint Louis MO 63101-2338

PEPER, GEORGE FREDERICK, editor; b. Nyack, N.Y., Jan. 25, 1950; s. Gerhard Wilhelm and Doris Elene (Bargfrede) P.; m. Elizabeth Marshall White, May 20, 1978; children: Timothy William, Christopher Scott. BA in English and Comparative Lit., Princeton U., 1972; postgrad., Yale U., 1973. Assoc. editor Winchester Press, N.Y.C., 1973-75; communications dir. Met. Golf Assn., N.Y.C., 1976; assoc. editor, exec. editor Golf mag., N.Y.C., 1976-78; editor Golf mag., 1979-90; editor-in-chief Golf Mag., 1990—; editl. dir. Golf Mag. Properties, N.Y.C., 1992—, sr. v.p., editl. dir., 1994. Author: Scrambling Golf, 1977, Golf's Supershots, 1982, Masters Tournament anns., 1983—, The PGA Championship, 1916-84, 1985, Golf Courses of the PGA Tour, 1986, 94, Grand Slam Golf, 1991, Golfwatching: A Viewer's Guide to World Golf, 1995; (with Greg Norman) Shark Attack: Greg Norman's Guide to Aggressive Golf, 1988, Greg Norman's Instant Lessons, 1993; scriptwriter: Jack Nicklaus-The Year in Golf, 1994, Official U.S. Open Video, 1994, 95, Official PGA Championship Video, 1994, 95; editor: Golf in America: The First 100 Years, 1988, Shinnecock Hills Golf Club, 1891-91. Mem. Golf Writers Assn., Am. Met. Golf Writers Assn., Am. Soc. Mag. Editors, Sleepy Hollow Country Club (Scarborough, N.Y.), Loch Lomond Golf Club (Scotland), Royal and Ancient Golf Club of St Andrews (Scotland). Office: Golf Magazine 2 Park Ave New York NY 10016-5603

PEPIN, JOHN NELSON, materials research and design engineer; b. Lowell, Mass., June 5, 1946; s. Nelson Andre and Leanne Florine (Boucher) P. BS in Mech. Engring., Northeastern U., 1968; MS in Aerospace Engring., MIT, 1970. Aero. engr. Bradway STOL Amphibian Ltd., Raymond, Maine, 1979; staff engr. Fiber Materials, Inc., Biddeford, Maine, 1979-84; pres. Pepin Assocs., Inc., Greenville, Maine, 1984—; cons. Foster-Miller Engrs., Waltham, Mass., 1985—, Johnson & Johnson Orthopedic Divsn., Braintree, Mass., 1984-86, Allied Signal Aerospace, South Bend, Inc., 1985-93, B.F. Goodrich, Akron, Ohio and Marlboro, Mass., 1986-87. Patentee in field. Grantee, 1982-84, U.S. Dept. Transp. grantee, 1989—, U.S. Dept. of Energy grantee, 1990-93; grantee NIH, 1994—. Mem. Soc. for Advancement of Materials and Process Engring., Seaplane Pilots Assn., MIT Club of Maine (bd. dirs. Portland chpt. 1988). Roman Catholic. Achievements include reseach contributions in lightweight structures to contain turbine engine rotor failures, process to recycle plastics into automotive structures, and advanced bone replacement materials. Home: PO Box 143 Greenville ME 04441-0143

PÉPIN, MARCEL, broadcast executive; b. Ste-Cécile-de-Lévrard, Que., Can., 1941. BA, U. Ottawa, Can., 1961, Etudes supérieures en Lettres françaises, 1962-64; B in Pedagogy, U. Montreal, Can., 1962. Lectr. U. Ottawa, 1962-64; corr. Parliament Le Droit, Ottawa, 1964-68; gen. mgr. Conseil économique de l'Outaouais, 1968-69; asst. to mng. editor info. La presse, 1970-73, columnist labor sect., 1973-74; chief parliamentary bur. La presse, Ottawa, 1974-77; chief editor Le Soleil, Que., 1977-82; pres. Commn. d'accès à l'information, 1982-88; chief editor French Radio News CBC, 1988-90, gen. mgr. programs French Radio Info., 1990-91; v.p. French Radio SRC CBC, 1991—; pres. Communauté Radios Publiques Langue Française Radio France, 1993-95; former treas. Conseil de presse du Que.; former pres. Campagne Centraide 1994, Ministères et agences du govt. fed., Montreal et region met. Mem. conseil d'adm. Musée des religions de Nicolet. Recipient Prix Olivar-Asselin, 1982. Mem. La tribune des journalists (former bd. dirs.), Syndicat des journalistes de La Presse (former pres.), Fédn. professionnelle des journalistes du Que. (former v.p.). Office: PO Box 6000, 1400 René-Lévesque Blvd E, Montreal, PQ Canada H3C 3A8

PEPINE, CARL JOHN, physician, educator; b. Pitts., June 8, 1941; s. Charles John and Elizabeth (Hovan) P.; m. Lynn Divers, Aug. 3, 1963; children: Mary Lynn, Anne, Elizabeth. BS, U. Pitts., 1962; MD, N.J. Coll. Medicine, 1966. Intern Allegheny Gen. Hosp., U. Pitts., 1966-67; resident in internal medicine Jefferson Med. Coll. Hosp., Phila., 1967-68, naval med. ctr., 1968-69, fellow in physiology and cardiovascular disease, 1969-71; asst. prof. medicine Jefferson Med. Coll., Phila., 1971-74; asst. prof. medicine U. Fla., Gainesville, 1974-75, assoc. prof., 1975-79, prof., 1979—, co-dir. div. cardiovascular medicine, 1982—; dir. cardiology catheterization lab. Shands Hosp., U. Fla., Gainesville, 1974-86; chief cardiology VA Regional Med. Ctr., Gainesville, 1979-94. Mem. editl. bd. Revs. in Contemporary Pharmacotherapy, Aspirin Rsch. Update, Jour. Cardiovascular Mgmt., Am. Jour. Geriatric Cardiology, Cardiac Chronicle, Internat. Jour. Cardiology; editor in chief Jour. Myocardial Ischemia; contbr. articles to profl. jours.; developer catheters to measure blood flow and heart circulation. Served to comdr. USN, 1968-74. Recipient Faculty Rsch. prize in clin. sci., U. Fla., 1989-90, Pioneer Investigator award Internat. Soc. Holter Monitoring, 1990, Rsch. Achievement awards U. Fla., 1990-92, Paul Dudley White award Assn. Mil. Surgs., 1991; grantee Dept. of Def., 1971-74, VA, 1975-90, NHLBI, 1985—. Fellow Am. Coll. Cardiology (gov. for Fla. 1984-87, chmn. bd. govs. 1986-87, bd. trustees 1985-87, 90—, pres. Fla. chpt. 1986-87, chmn. ann. sci. sessions 1990), Am. Heart Assn. (coun. on clin. cardiology and on circulation, bronze award 1983), Am. Fedn. Clin. Rsch., Soc. Cardiac Angiography, Am. Soc. Clin. Investigation; mem. Assn. U. Cardiologists, Pi Kappa Alpha, Alpha Omega Alpha. Research on dynamics of coronary circulation, effects of coronary artery spasm and stenosis, silent myocardial ischemia, effects of lasers on blood vessels, calcium antagonists, ambulatory monitoring. Office: U Fla 1600 SW Archer Rd PO Box 100277 Gainesville FL 32610

PEPITONE, BYRON VINCENT, former government official; b. New Brunswick, N.J., June 9, 1918; s. Joseph James and Sarah Frances (Byron) P.; m. Marolynn Mary Mills, June 9, 1940; children: Byron II, James S. Student, U.S. Army Command and Gen. Staff Coll., 1944, Air. U. Air Command and Staff Coll., 1950, NATO Def. Coll., 1955. Commd. 2d lt. USAAF, 1942; advanced through grades to col. USAF, 1953; ret., 1970; dep. dir. SSS, Washington, 1970-72; acting dir. SSS, 1972-73, dir., 1973-77; ret., 1977. Decorated D.S.M., Legion of Merit with 2 oak leaf clusters, USAF Commendation medal, U.S. Army Commendation medal with oak leaf cluster; recipient Distinguished Service medal SSS, 1972. Mem. USAF Assn. Home: 2265 SW Creekside Dr Palm City FL 34990-2528

PEPLAU, HILDEGARD ELIZABETH, nursing educator; b. Reading, Pa., Sept. 1, 1909; d. Gustav and Ottylie (Elgert) P. Diploma, Pottstown Hosp. Sch. Nursing, 1931; BA, Bennington Coll., 1943; MA, Columbia U., 1947, EdD, 1953, DSc (hon.), 1983; cert., William Alanson White Inst., 1953; DSc (hon.), Alfred U., 1970, Duke U., 1974, Rutgers U., 1985, Ind. U., 1994, U. Ulster, No. Ireland, 1994; D of Nursing Sci. (hon.), Boston Coll., 1972; LHD (hon.), U. Indpls., 1987, Ohio State U., 1990. RN, N.J., Calif. Exec. officer Coll. Health Svc., Bennington (Vt.) Coll., 1938-43; dir. grad. program psychiatric nursing Tchrs. Coll., Columbia U., N.Y.C., 1948-53; exec. dir. ANA, Washington, 1969-70; dir. grad. program psychiatric nursing Rutgers U., New Brunswick, N.J., 1955-74, prof. emerita, 1974—. Author: Interpersonal Relations in Nursing, 1952; contbr. numerous articles to profl. publs. and jours., 1942—. 1st lt. Nurse Corps, U.S. Army, 1943-45. Mem. ANA, Am. Acad. Nursing (designated Living Legend 1994), Internat. Coun. Nurses (3d v.p. 1977-81, bd. dirs. 1973-77), Nat. League Nursing. Democrat. Lutheran. Home: 14024 Otsego St Sherman Oaks CA 91423-1225

PEPPAS, NIKOLAOS ATHANASSIOU, chemical engineering educator, consultant; b. Athens, Greece, Aug. 25, 1948; s. Athanassios Nikolaou Peppas and Alice Petrou Rousopoulou; m. Lisa Brannon, Aug. 10, 1988. Diploma in Engring., Nat. Tech. U., Athens, 1971; ScD, MIT, 1973. Rsch. assoc. MIT, Cambridge, Mass., 1975-76; asst. prof. chem. engring. Purdue U., West Lafayette, Ind., 1976-78, assoc. prof., 1978-81, prof., 1981—, Showalter Disting. prof., 1993—; vis. prof. U. Geneva, 1982-83, Calif. Inst. Tech., Pasadena, 1983, U. Paris, 1986, Hoshi U., Japan, 1994, Hebrew U., Jerusalem, 1994, U. Naples, 1995; adj. prof. U. Parma, Italy, 1987; cons. in field; mem. adv. bd. several cos. Author: Biomaterials, 1982, Hydrogels in Medicine and Pharmacy, 1987, One Hundred Years of Chemical Engineering, 1989, Pulsatile Drug Delivery, 1993, Biopolymers, 1993, Superabsorbent Polymers, 1994; contbr. articles and abstracts to jours. Active Indpls. Symphony Orch., Indpls. Mus. Arts, Holy Trinity Orthodox Ch. Indpls. Recipient APV Silver medal U. Parma. Fellow Am. Inst. Med. Biol. Engrs., Am. Assn. Pharm. Scientists, Soc. Biomaterials; mem. AIChE (chmn. materials divsn. 1988-90, dir. bioengring. divsn. 1994—, Materials Engring. Sci. award 1984, Bioengring. award 1994, Best Paper award 1994), Am. Chem. Soc., Am. Phys. Soc., N.Y. Acad. Sci., Controlled Release Soc. (pres. 1987-88, Founders award 1991), Soc. Biomaterials (Clemson award 1992), Am. Soc. Engring. Edn. (AT&T award 1982, Curtis McGraw award 1988, G. Westinghouse award 1992), Polymer Pioneer, numerous others. Avocations: linguistics, opera, rare maps, record collecting, wine collecting. Office: Purdue U Sch Chem Engring West Lafayette IN 47907

PEPPER, ALLAN MICHAEL, lawyer; b. Bklyn., July 5, 1943; s. Julius and Jeanette (Lasovsky) P.; m. Barbara Benjamin, Aug. 30, 1964; children—Leslie Anne, Joshua Benjamin, Adam Richard, Robert Benjamin. B.A. summa cum laude, Brandeis U., 1964; LL.B. magna cum laude, Harvard U., 1967. Bar: N.Y. 1968, U.S. Dist. Ct. (so. and ea. dists.) N.Y. 1968, U.S. Ct. Appeals (2d cir.) 1968, U.S. Supreme Ct. 1988. Law clk. U.S. Ct. Appeals for 2d Circuit, N.Y.C., 1967-68; assoc. Kaye, Scholer, Fierman, Hays & Handler, N.Y.C., 1968-74, ptnr., 1975—; lectr. in field. Mem. exec. com., assoc. nat. chmn. Brandeis U. Alumni Fund, 1979-82, nat. chmn., 1982-85, chmn. 25th Reunion gift com., 1989, devel. com., trustee, 1982-85, pres., councillor, 1980—; trustee Brandeis U., 1985-95, sec., 1992-93, budget and fin. com., 1988-95, chmn. com. strategic plan, 1990-91, acad. affairs com., 1985-92, student life and phys. facilities com., 1985-89, vice chmn. ad hoc by-laws com., 1988-89, long range planning com., 1989-91, chmn. audit com., 1991-95, exec. com., 1990-91; bd. dirs. Styles Brook Homeowners Assn., 1990—, exec. com., 1994—; nominating com. Edgemont Sch. Bd., 1992-93; trustee Edgemont Sch. Found., 1994—. Recipient Henry Jones-Golda Meier Bnai Brith Youth Services award, 1986, L.I. Press Valedictory medal, 1960; Felix Frankfurter scholar Harvard U. Law Sch., 1964-65; Louis D. Brandeis hon. scholar Brandeis U., 1964. Mem. ABA, Assn. of Bar of City of N.Y. (mem. law firm mgmt. com. 1987-91), N.Y. State Bar Assn. (comml. and fed. lit. sect., vice chmn. com. on discovery 1993—), Brandeis U. Alumni Assn. (exec. com. 1982-85, alumni giving strategic planning com., 1992, Alumni Svc. award 1988), Phi Beta Kappa (L.I. Alumni award 1960). Democrat. Jewish. Lodge: B'nai B'rith (pres. Henry Jones Lodge 1982-84, mem. Westchester-Putnam council 1982-85, bd. govs. dist. 1, 1985-86). Office: Kaye Scholer Fierman Hays & Handler 425 Park Ave New York NY 10022-3506

PEPPER, BEVERLY, artist, sculptor; b. Bklyn., Dec. 20, 1924; d. Irwin Edward and Beatrice Evadne (Horenstein) Stoll; m. Curtis G. Pepper, Oct. 11, 1949; children: Jorie Graham, John Randolph. Studied with, Fernand Leger, Andre L'Hote; student, Pratt Inst., 1939-41, D.F.A. (hon.), 1982; student, Art Students League, N.Y.C., 1944; D.F.A. (hon.), Md. Inst., 1983. Prof. meritus U. Perugia, Italy, 1987. One-woman shows include Marlborough Gallery, N.Y.C., 1969, Galerie Hella Nebelung, Dusseldorf, Ger., 1971, Piazza Margana, Rome, 1971, Parker St. Gallery, Boston, 1971, Qui Arte Contemporanea, Rome, 1972, Marlborough Galleria d'Arte, Rome, 1972, Tyler Sch. of Art, Temple U. Abroad, Rome, 1973, Hammarskjold Plaza Sculpture Garden, N.Y.C., 1975, Met. Mus. Art, Miami, Fla., 1976, San Francisco Mus. Art, 1976, 86, Seattle Mus. Art, 1977, Princeton U., 1978, Indpls. Mus. Art, 1978, Todi Piazza and Sala delle Pietra, 1979, Gimple-Hanover Gallery, Zurich, 1980, Ronald Greenberg Gallery, St. Louis, 1980, Davenport Art Gallery, 1981, Hansen Fuller Goldeen Gallery, San Francisco, 1981, Laumeier Internat. Sculpture Park, St. Louis, 1982 Galleria Il Ponte, Rome, 1982, John Berggrun Gallery, San Francisco, 1983, 1985, Adams-Middleton Gallery, Dallas, 1985, Andre Emmerich Gallery, N.Y.C., 1975, 77, 79, 80, 82, 84, 86, 87, 89, 90, 91, 93, Columbus (Ohio)

Mus. Art, 1986, Charles Cowles Gallery, N.Y.C., 1987, 90, 94, Albright-Knox Art Gallery 20 yr. traveling survey exhbn., 1986, Visual Arts Ctr. MIT, Cambridge, Mass., 1989, James Corcoran Gallery, Santa Monica, Calif., 1989, 90, Contemporary Sculpture Ctr., Tokyo, 1991, Met. Mus. Art, N.Y.C., 1991, Narni all Rocca, Narna, Italy, 1991; group shows include XXIII Biennale di Venezia, Venice, Italy, 1972, Mus. Phila. Civic Center, 1974, Finch Coll. Mus. Art, N.Y.C., 1974, Marlborough Gallery, N.Y.C., 1974, Janie C. Lee Gallery, Houston, 1975, New Orleans Mus. Art, 1976, Documenta 6, Kassel, Ger., 1977, Quadriennale di Roma, Rome, 1977, Seattle Mus., 1979, Bklyn. Mus. Art, 1986, 87, Bienale de Sculpture, Monte Carlo, 1991, Galleria Comunale d'Arte Moderna, Spoletto, Italy, 1992, Chelsea Harbour Sculpture '93, London, 1993, Queens Mus. Art, Corona Park, N.Y., 1994; represented in numerous permanent collections including Met. Mus. Art, N.Y.C., Fogg Mus., Cambridge, Mass., Albright-Knox Art Gallery, Buffalo, Jacksonville (Fla.) Mus. Modern Art, Galleria d'Arte Moderna, Florence, Italy, Walker Art Center, Mpls., Instituto Italiano di Cultura, Stockholm, Sweden, Power Inst. Fine Arts, Sydney, Australia, Galleria Civica d'Arte Moderna, Turin, Italy, Albertina Mus., Vienna, Hirshhorn Mus. and Sculpture Garden, Washington, Worcester (Mass.) Art Mus., Parkersburg (W.Va.) Art Mus., Smithsonian Inst., Washington, Dartmouth Coll., Hanover, N.H., Atlantic Richfield Co., L.A., Rutgers U., Wright, Runstad & Co., Seattle, Niagara Frontier Transp. Authority, Buffalo, Johns Hopkins Hosp., John Deere Foundry, East Moline, Ill.; commns. include Amphisculpture, AT&T, Bedminster, N.J., 1974-76, Dartmouth Coll., 1976-77, Sol i Onbra, 1986-91, City Barcelona, 1986—, Teatre Celle, Villa Celle, Postoia, Italy, 1989-91, Terana Altar II, Smithsonian Inst., Nat. Mus. Am. Art, Washington, 1990-91, Gotanno Community Park, Adachi-ku Machizukuri Corp., Neo-Hodos, Tokyo, 1992, Split Ritual, U.S. Nat. Arboretum, Washington, 1992, Palingenesis, Credit-Suisse, Zurich, 1992-94, The Garden at 26 Fed/ Plz., Gen. Svcs. Adminstrn., N.Y.C., 1992—, Jerusalem Ritual, Jerusalem Found., Israel, 1994. Recipient award Nat. Endowment of Arts, 1976, 79, award GSA, 1975, Honor award Nat. Women's Caucus for Art, 1994. Home: Torre Gentile di Todi (PG) Italy 06059 Office: Andre Emmerich Gallery 41 E 57th St New York NY 10022-1908

PEPPER, DAVID M., physicist, educator, author, inventor; b. L.A., Mar. 9, 1949; s. Harold and Edith (Kleinplatz) P.; m. Denise Danyelle Koster, Mar. 19, 1992. BS in Physics summa cum laude, UCLA, 1971; MS in Applied Physics, Calif. Inst. Tech., 1974, PhD in Applied Physics, 1980. Mem. tech. staff Hughes Rsch. Labs., Malibu, Calif., 1973-87, sr. staff physicist, 1987-91, head nonlinear and electro-optic devices sect., 1989-91, sr. scientist, 1991—; adj. prof. math. and physics Pepperdine U., Malibu, 1981—. co-author: Optical Phase Conjugation, 1983, Laser Handbook, Vol. 4, 1985, Optical Phase Conjugation, 1995, Spatial Light Modulator Technology, 1995, CRC Handbook of Laser Science and Technology, 1995; tech. referee profl. jours.; contbr. articles to tech. jours. including Sci. Am.; holder 15 patents. Mem. Sons and Daughters of 1939 Club, 2d Generation of Martyrs Meml., Mus. Holocaust. Recipient Rudolf Kingslake award Soc. Photo-Optical Instrumentation Engrs., 1982, Publ. of Yr. award Hughes Rsch. Lab., 1986; NSF trainee Calif. Inst. Tech., 1971; Howard Hughes fellow Hughes Aircraft Co., 1973-80. Fellow Optical Soc. Am; mem. AAAS, IEEE (guest editor, assoc. editor), SPIE (guest editor), N.Y. Acad. Scis., Am. Phys. Soc., Laser Inst. Am., Internat. Coun. Sci. Unions (com. on sci. and tech. in developing countries), Sigma Xi (v.p. 1986-87, chpt. pres. 1987-88, 90-91, 91-92), Sigma Pi Sigma. Jewish. Avocations: classical music, travel, sports, astronomy, nature. Office: Hughes Rsch Labs RL 65 RL 64 3011 Malibu Canyon Rd Malibu CA 90265-4737 *Personal philosophy: We all have a profound, meaningful purpose and mission in life—the challenge is to identify, appreciate, realize and embrace our dreams and goals.*

PEPPER, IAN L., environmental microbiologist, research scientist, educator; b. Tonypandy, Wales, U.K., Oct. 5, 1946. BSc in Chemistry, U. Birmingham, U.K., 1970; MS in Soil Biochemistry, Ohio State U., 1972, PhD in Soil Microbiology, 1975. Post-doctoral rsch. assoc. Wash. State U., 1975-76; asst. prof., asst. rsch. sci. dept. soils, water and engring. U. Ariz., 1971-81, assoc. prof., assoc. rsch. sci., 1971-88, prof., rsch. sci. dept. soil and water sci. and microbiology, 1988—, chair undergrad. program in environ. sci., 1993—. Contbr. articles to profl. jours. Recipient Ciba-Geigy award, 1983. Fellow Am. Acad. Microbiology, Am. Soc. Agronomy, Soil Sci. Soc. Am. Office: Univ of Arizona 429 Shantz Bldg Tucson AZ 85721

PEPPER, JEFFREY MACKENZIE, publishing executive; b. Dallas, June 11, 1957; s. Doris Jane (Mackenzie) P.; m. Martha Helen Stearns, July 27, 1985; children: Katherine McRaven, Anne Mackenzie. BA, Coll. Wooster, 1979. Sales rep. Acad. Press, N.Y.C., 1979-82; program editor Addison-Wesley Pub. Co., Reading, Mass., 1982-83, acquisitions editor, 1983-86; sr. editor Osborne McGraw-Hill, Berkeley, Calif., 1986-90, editor-in-chief, 1990-95; v.p., editl. dir. Acad. Press Profl., Chestnut Hill, Mass., 1995—. Contbr. articles to profl. jours. Avocations: storytelling, computers, gardening.

PEPPER, JOHN ENNIS, JR., consumer products company executive; b. Pottsville, Pa., Aug. 2, 1938; s. John Ennis Sr. and Irma Elizabeth (O'Connor) P.; m. Frances Graham Garber, Sept. 9, 1967; children: John, David, Douglas, Susan. BA, Yale U., 1960; PhD (hon.), Mt. St. Joseph Coll., St. Petersburg (Russia) U., Xavier U. From staff asst. to advt. mgr. Procter & Gamble Co., Cin., 1963-74, gen. mgr. Italian subs., 1974-77; v.p., gen. mgr. divsn. packaged soap and detergent Proctor & Gamble Co., Cin., 1977-80, group v.p. divsns. packaged soap and bar soap and household cleaning products, 1980-84, group v.p. European ops., 1981, exec. v.p., bd. dirs., 1984-86, pres. U.S. bus., 1986—, pres. internat. bus., 1990-95, chmn. bd., CEO, 1995—; bd. dirs. Xerox Corp., Motorola, Inc. Group chmn. Cin. United Appeal Campaign, 1980; trustee Xavier U., 1985-89, mem. exec. com., 1989; trustee Cin. Coun. World Affairs, Cin. Art Mus., Ctr. Strategic & Internat. Studies, Christ Ch. Endowment Fund, Yale Corp.; gen. chmn. United Way Campaign, 1994; co-chair Gov.'s Edn. Coun., State of Ohio; mem. adv. coun. Yale Sch. Mgmt.; mem. schs. com. Cin. Bus. Com.; co-chmn. Cin. Youth Collaborative; mem. Total Quality Leadership steering com. Served to lt. USN, 1960-63. Mem. Am. Soc. Corp. Execs., Grocery Mfrs. Am., Nat. Alliance Businessmen (chmn. communication com.), Soap and Detergent Assn. (bd. dirs.), The Bus. Coun., Bus. Roundtable, Yale Club, Queen City Club, Commonwealth Club, Comml. Club. Office: Procter & Gamble Co 1 Procter Gamble Plz Cincinnati OH 45202

PEPPER, JONATHAN L., newspaper columnist; b. Dearborn, Mich., Aug. 23, 1955; s. Joseph Daniel and Norma (McIntyre) P.; m. Diane Sharon Garelis, May 12, 1984; children: Jonathon Jay, Lauren Claire, Scott Joseph. BA, Mich. State U., 1977. Copywriter Detroit Free Press, 1977-84, reporter, 1984-87; nat. corr. Detroit News, 1987-91, bus. columnist, 1991—; host talk show Sta. WXYT, 1995—. Mem. Writers Guild Am. Office: The Detroit News 615 W Lafayette Blvd Detroit MI 48226-3124

PEPPER, NORMA JEAN, mental health nurse; b. Ellington, Iowa, Nov. 7, 1931; d. Victor F. and Grace Mae (Tate) Shadle; m. Bob Joseph Pepper, Dec. 28, 1956 (dec. Oct. 4, 1985); children: Joseph Victor, Barbara Jean, Susan Claire (dec.). Diploma in Nursing, Broadlawns Polk County Hosp., 1950-53; BSN, U. Iowa, 1953-55; MSN, U. Colo., 1955-60. Cert. mental health nurse. Head nurse Colo. Psychiatric Hosp., Denver, 1956; head nurse, Psychiatry Denver General Hosp., 1958-60; with Nurses Official Registry, Denver, 1960-73; staff nurse VA Med. Ctr., Denver, 1974-94; counselor VA Hosp. Employee Assistance Com., Denver, 1987-94. Mem. Colo. Nurses Assn. Home: 4836 W Tennessee Ave Denver CO 80219-3130

PEPPERDENE, MARGARET WILLIAMS, English educator; b. Vicksburg, Miss., Dec. 25, 1919; d. O.L. and Jane (Stocks) Williams. B.S., La. State U., 1941; M.A., Vanderbilt U., 1948, Ph.D., 1953. Div. Instr. English U. Oreg., 1946-47; teaching fellow Vanderbilt U., 1948-50; instr., then asst. prof. Miami U., Oxford, Ohio, 1952-56; mem. faculty Agnes Scott Coll., 1956—, prof. English, chmn. dept., 1967—. Author articles.; Editor: That Subtile Wreath: Lectures Presented at the Quartercentenary Celebratiom of the Birth of John Donne, 1973. Served to lt. USNR, 1943-46. Fulbright fellow, 1950-51; Ford Found. grad. fellow, 1951-52; AAUW fellow, 1954-55; research fellow Dublin Inst. Advanced Studies, 1954-55; Guggenheim fellow, 1956-57; recipient Gov.'s Award in Humanities, Ga., 1987. Home: 418 Glendale Ave Decatur GA 30030-1922

PEPPERS, JERRY P., lawyer; b. Cleve., Mar. 8, 1946; s. Jerry P. and Katherine M. Peppers; m. Sue E. Schafer, June 14, 1969; children: Amy E., Erica K., Christina A., Michele S. BBA, Ohio U., 1968; JD, Duke U., 1971. Bar: N.Y. 1972. Assoc. Winthrop, Stimson, Putnam & Roberts, N.Y.C., 1971-81, ptnr., 1982—; mgmt. com., 1995—; bd. dirs. Firth Rixson, Inc., Rochester, N.Y., Monroe Forgings, Inc., Rochester, Progenitor, Inc., Columbus, Ohio, Viking Metall. Corp., Reno; N. Am. pension oversight com. The Morgan Crucible Co., Windsor, U.K. Editor: (booklet) Outline of Mergers and Acquisitions in the United States, 14th edit., 1995. Trustee Ohio Univ. Found., Athens, 1991—, Fox Meadow Athletic Assn., Scarsdale, Scarsdale Youth Soccer Club, Inc., Scarsdale Maroon and White Club. Mem. ABA, Internat. Bar Assn., India House, Fox Meadow Tennis Club (Scarsdale, N.Y.). Avocation: coaching soccer (lic. FIFA). Office: Winthrop Stimson Putnam & Roberts 1 Battery Park Plz New York NY 10004-1405

PEPPET, RUSSELL FREDERICK, accountant; b. Chgo., Oct. 3, 1939; s. George Russell and Elizabeth (Foster) P.; m. Rosemary Meyer, June 18, 1960; children—Cynthia, Jeffrey, Scott. B.S. in Math, Mich. State U., 1960; M.B.A., Northwestern U., 1963. C.P.A., Ill., Minn. Cons. Peat, Marwick, Mitchell & Co., Chgo., 1961-68; head mgmt. cons. dept. Peat, Marwick, Mitchell & Co., Mpls., 1968-72; partner Peat, Marwick, Mitchell & Co., 1969-88; sr. cons. partner for Continental Europe, Paris, 1972-78, partner-in-charge mgmt. cons. dept., N.Y. office, 1978-81, vice chmn. mgmt. cons., 1981-86; mng. ptnr. San Jose Bus. Unit, 1986-88; v.p. internat. devel. Towers Perrin, N.Y.C., 1989-90; vice-chmn. Quirk Carson Peppet Inc., N.Y.C., 1990—; bd. dirs. AFS-USA, treas., 1991-92, chmn., 1992—. With U.S. Army, 1962-64. Mem. Am. Inst. C.P.A.'s. Club: Sky (N.Y.C.). Office: Quirk Carson Peppet Inc 99 Park Ave New York NY 10016

PEPPLER, DANIEL DARCY, advertising executive; b. Kitchener, Ont., Can., May 21, 1944; s. James Duffy and Grace Madeline (Pyne) P.; 1 child, Carolyn; m. Ann Beverly Govinda, Sept. 12, 1981; children: Michael, Kathryn. BSc in Advt. Design, Ariz. State U., 1969. Art dir. Ardiel Advt., Toronto, Ont., Can., 1969-72; writer, art dir. Baker Lovick Advt., Toronto, Ont., Can., 1972-74, Needham Harper & Steers, Toronto, Ont., Can., 1974-76; group creative dir. J. Walter Thompson, Toronto, Ont., Can., 1976-79; exec. v.p., dir. creative svcs. Needham Harper Worldwide, Toronto, Ont., Can., 1979-86; chmn., nat. creative dir. Schur Peppler, Toronto, Ont., Can., 1986-88; chmn., nat. creative dir. Doner Schur Peppler, Toronto, Ont., Can., 1988-91, CEO, nat. creative dir., 1991—. Mem. Foster Parent Plan of Can. Recipient 3d prize Am. Film Festival, 1978, Clio awards, 1989, Gold Mktg. award Honda Corp., 1990, Gold and Bronze Bessies, 1991. Roman Catholic. Avocation: tennis. Office: Doner Schur Peppler, 90 Eglinton Ave W 6th fl, Toronto, ON Canada M4R 2E4

PEPPLER, WILLIAM NORMAN, aviation association executive; b. Hanover, Ont., Can., June 29, 1925. Student public shcs., Hanover. Charter pilot Leavens Bros., Toronto, Ont., 1945-48; chief flying instr. Sky Harbour Air Service, Goderich, Ont., 1949-51; survey pilot Spartan Air Services, Ottawa, Ont., 1951-57; mgr. Can. Owners and Pilots Assn., Ottawa, 1957—; editor Can. Flight Mag., 1957—; Can. Gen. Aviation News, 1957—. Office: 77 Metcalfe, Ottawa, ON Canada K1P 5S4

PEPPLES, ERNEST, tobacco company executive; b. Louisville, Feb. 13, 1935; s. Ernest Clifton and Goldie Mae (Byington) P.; m. Martha Scott Norman; children: J. Craig, Eleanor Evans, Cindy. AB, Yale U., 1957; LLB, U. Va., 1963. Bar: Ky., 1963. Ptnr. Wyatt, Grafton & Sloss (name changed to Wyatt, Tarrant & Combs), Louisville, 1963-75; v.p., gen. counsel Brown & Williamson Tobacco Corp., Louisville, 1975-80, sr. v.p., 1980—, also bd. dirs.; chmn. bd. dirs. Tobacco Merchants Assn. U.S.A., Inc., Princeton, N.J.; bd. dirs. Tobacco Inst., Washington, Coun. for Tobacco Rsch., Inc., N.Y., Ky. Tobacco Rsch. Bd., Lexington. Pres. Louisville and Jefferson County Health and Welfare Council, 1972-73, Neighborhood Housing Services Inc., Louisville, 1986-87. Served to 1st lt. U.S. Army, 1957-60. Mem. ABA, Ky. Bar Assn., Tobacco Mchts. Assn. (bd. dirs. 1975—, chmn. 1990—). Democrat. Mem. Christian Ch. Clubs: Louisville Country, Pendennis, Tavern. Home: 2432 Ransdell Ave Louisville KY 40204-2113 Office: Brown & Williamson Tobacco Corp 1500 Brown & Williamson Tower Louisville KY 40202

PEPYNE, EDWARD WALTER, lawyer, former educator; b. Springfield, Mass., Dec. 27, 1925; s. Walter Henry and Frances A. (Carroll) P.; m. Carol Jean Dutcher, Aug. 2, 1958; children—Deborah, Edward, Jr., Susan, Byron, Shari, Randy, David, Allison, Jennifer. B.A., Am. Internat. Coll., 1948; M.S., U. Mass., 1951, Ed.D., 1968; postgrad., NYU, 1952-55; prof. diploma, U. Conn., 1964; J.D., Western New Eng. Coll., 1978. Bar: Mass. 1978, U.S. Supreme Ct. 1981. Prin., tchr. Gilbertville Grammar Sch., Hardwick, Mass., 1948-49; sch. counselor West Springfield High Sch., Mass., 1949-53; instr. NYU, 1953-54; supt. schs. New Shoreham, R.I., 1954-56; asst. prof. edn. Mich. State U., 1956-58; sch. psychologist, guidance dir. Pub. Sch. System, East Long, Mass., 1958-62; lectr. Westfield State Coll., 1961-65; dir. pupil services Chicopee Pub. Sch., 1965-68; assoc. prof. counselor edn. U. Hartford, West Hartford, Mass., 1968-71, prof., 1971-85, dir. Inst. Coll. Counselors Minority and Low Income Students, 1971-72, dir. Div. Human Services, 1972-77; cons. Aetna Life & Casualty Co., Hartford, 1962-75; hearing officer Conn. State Bd. Edn., 1980—; exec. dir. Sinapi Assocs., 1959-78; pvt. practice, Ashfield, Mass., 1978—. Co-author: Better Driving, 1958; assoc. editor: Highway Safety and Driver Education, 1954; chmn. editorial com.: Man and the Motor Car, 5th edit., 1954; contbr. numerous articles to profl. jours. Chief Welfare Svcs. Civil Def., Levittown, N.Y., 1953-54; chmn. Ashfield Planning Bd., Mass., 1979-83; moderator Town of Ashfield, 1980-81, town counsel, Charlemont, Mass., 1983-84; mem. jud. nominating coun. Western Regional Com., 1993—. Mem. ABA, APA, Mass. Bar Assn., Mass. Acad. Trial Attys., Am. Pers. and Guidance Assn., New Eng. Pers. and Guidance Assn. (bd. dirs.), New Eng. Ednl. Rsch. Orgn. (pres. 1971), Am. Assn. Sch. Adminstrs., Am. Ednl. Rsch. Assn., Mt. Tom Amateur Radio Assn., Franklin County Amateur Radio Club, Elks, Kiwanis (pres. 1988-89, lt. gov. div. 12, 1991-92), Masons (master 1994—), Shriners, Phi Delta Kappa. Home: PO Box 31 134 Ashfield Mountain Rd Ashfield MA 01330-9622 Office: PO Box 345 134 Ashfield Mountain Rd Ashfield MA 01330-9622

PERADOTTO, JOHN JOSEPH, classics educator, editor; b. Ottawa, Ill., May 11, 1933; s. John Joseph and Mary Louise (Giacometti) P.; m. Noreen Doran, Aug. 29, 1959 (div. 1982); m. Marlene Rosen, Aug. 29, 1992; children: Erin, Monica, Noreen, Nicole. B.A., St. Louis U., 1957, M.A., 1958; Ph.D., Northwestern U., 1963. Instr. classics and English Western Wash. U., Bellingham, 1960-61; instr. Georgetown U., 1961-63, asst. prof. classics, 1963-66; asst. prof. classics SUNY, Buffalo, 1966-69, asso. prof., 1969-73; prof., chmn. classics U. Tex., Austin, 1973-74; prof. classics SUNY-Buffalo, 1974—, Andrew V.V. Raymond prof. classics, 1984—, Disting. teaching prof., 1990—, chmn. dept., 1974-77, dean div. undergrad. edn., 1978-82; Martin lectr. Oberlin Coll., 1987; dir. summer seminar for coll. tchrs. NEH, 1976, for secondary sch. tchrs., 1984. Author: Classical Mythology: An Annotated Bibliographical Survey, 1973, Man in the Middle Voice: Name and Narration in the Odyssey, 1990; also articles and revs.; founding assoc. editor: Arethusa, editor-in-chief, 1974-95; mem. bd. editors SUNY Press, 1978-81; editor: SUNY Press Classical Series, 1981—, Classical Literature and Contemporary Literary Analysis, 1977, Women in the Ancient World, 1978, 83; co-editor: Population Policy in Plato and Aristotle, 1975, The New Archilochus, 1976, Augustan Poetry Books, 1980, Indo-European Roots of Classical Culture, 1980, Vergil: 2000 Years, 1981, Texts and Contexts: American Classical Studies in Honor of J.P. Vernant, 1982, Semiotics and Classical Studies, 1983, Audience-oriented Criticism and the Classics, 1986, Herodotus and the Invention of History, 1987, The Challenge of Black Athena, 1989, Pastoral Revisions, 1990, Reconsidering Ovid's Fasti, 1992, Bakhtin and Classical Studies, 1993, Rethinking the Classical Canon, 1994, Horace: 2000 Years, 1995, The New Simonides, 1996. Fellow Center for Hellenic Studies, 1972-73; Recipient Chancellor's award for teaching excellence State U. N.Y., 1975. Mem. Am. Philol. Assn. (dir. 1974-77, pres. 1990), Classical Assn. Atlantic States (exec. com. 1976-78). Office: Dept Classics State U NY Buffalo NY 14260

PERAHIA, MURRAY, pianist; b. N.Y.C., Apr. 19, 1947; m. Naomi Shohet, 1980; 2 children. MS, Mannes Coll. Music; student, Jeannette Haien, Artur Balsam, Mieczyslaw Horszowski. Appeared with Berlin Philharm., Chgo. Symphony Orch., English Chamber Orch., Boston Symphony Orch., N.Y. Philharm., Cleve. Orch., Los Angeles Philharm., Phila. Orch., others; performed with Budapest, Guarneri and Galimir string quartets; frequent performer, artistic dir.: Aldeburgh Festival, 1983-89; past participant: Marlboro Music Festival; recital tours in U.S., Can., Europe and Japan; recs. for SONY Classical; 1st Am. to record the Complete Mozart Concertos as condr. with English Chamber Orch., recorded complete Beethoven concertos with Haitink concertgebouw Orch. Recipient Kosciusko Chopin prize, 1965, Avery Fisher prize, 1975, numerous maj. rec. awards. Office: care Edna Landau IMG 22 E 71st St New York NY 10021-4911

PERCIASEPE, ROBERT, federal agency administratorr. BS in Environ. Scis., Cornell U.; MS in Planning, Syracuse U. Various positions county and regional planning agys. and SUNY; asst. dir. planning City of Balt.; asst. sec. for planning and capital programs Md. Dept. Environ., Annapolis, dep. sec., sec. of environ., 1991-93; asst. adminstr. for water EPA, Washington, 1993—; lectr. Johns Hopkins U., Morgan Stte U., U. Md.; former chmn. Md. Asbestos Oversight Com., Chesapeake Bay Agreement States' Nutrient Reduction Work Group; former vice chmn. Appalachian Low-Level Radioactive Waste Commn.; former 1st chmn. N.E. Ozone Transport Commn.; former mem. bd. dirs. Chesapeake Bay Trust; former mem. Md. Gov.'s Internat. Cabinet and Md. Gov.'s Commn. on Lead Paint Poisoning. Contbr. articles to profl. jours. Mem. profl. orgns. Avocations: biking, hiking, softball. Office: Water 401 M St SW Washington DC 20460*

PERCOCO, THELMA ANN, nurse, educator; b. Newton, Kans., Sept. 11, 1935; d. Menno J. and Lydia A. (Miller) Hirschler; m. Richard A. Percoco, June 5, 1960. Diploma in nursing, Bethel Deaconess Hosp., Newton, 1957; BS in Nursing, Fla. State U., 1960; MS in Nursing, Tex. Women's U., 1977. RN, Tex. Staff nurse, team leader VA Hosp., Albuquerque, 1957-58, 60; staff nurse State Tuberculosis Hosp., Tallahassee, 1960, West Haven (Conn.) VA Hosp., 1960, 61; staff nurse, team leader, than head nurse and surg. supr. Houston VA Hosp., 1961-79; instr. Lee Coll., Baytown, Tex., 1979—, Lead Inst., 1987-93; acting divsn. chair allied health Lee Coll., Baytown, Tex., 1993-94; com. mem. Am. Cancer Soc. Contbr. articles to various publs. Chair Pine Bluff Civic Assn., La Porte, Tex., 1984—. Named Tchr. of Yr., Lee Coll., 1987. Mem. ANA, Nat. League for Nursing, Tex. League for Nursing (pub. rels. com. 1990), Tex. Nurses Assn. (chair legis. com. 1987-91), Sigma Theta Tau (acting chair allied health divsn. 1992-93).d. Avocation: sailboat racing. Home: 1 Pine Bluff St La Porte TX 77571-6677 Office: Lee Coll 511 S Whiting St Baytown TX 77520-4703

PERCUS, JEROME KENNETH, physicist, educator; b. N.Y.C., June 21, 1926; s. Philip M. and Gertrude B. (Schweiger) P.; m. Ora Engelberg, May 20, 1965; children: Orin, Allon. B.S.E.E., Columbia U., 1947, M.A., 1948, Ph.D., 1954. Instr. elec. engring. Columbia U., N.Y.C., 1952-54; asst. prof. Stevens Inst. Tech., Hoboken, N.J., 1955-58; assoc. prof. NYU, N.Y.C., 1958-65; prof. physics NYU, 1965—; dir. Nat. Biomed. Research Found. Author: Many-Body Problem, 1963, Kinetic Theory and Statistical Mechanics, 1969, Combinatorial Methods, 1971, Combinatorial Methods in Developmental Biology, 1977, Mathematical Methods in Developmental Biology, 1978, Mathematical Methods in Enzymology, 1984, Lectures on the Mathematics of Immunology, 1986; editor: Pattern Recognition, Jour. Statis. Physics, Jour. Comp. Molecular Biology. With USN, 1944-46. Recipient Pregel Chemistry Physics award N.Y. Acad. Scis., 1975, Joel Henry Hildebrand award in the Theoretical and Exptl. Chemistry of Liquids, Am. Chem. Soc., 1993, Pattern Rec. Soc. award, 1992. Fellow AAAS, Am. Phys. Soc.; mem. Am. Math. Soc., Sigma Xi. Office: NYU 251 Mercer St New York NY 10012-1110

PERCY, LEE EDWARD, motion picture film editor; b. Kalamazoo, Feb. 10, 1953; s. Richard Noyes and Helen Louise (Sheffield) P. Student, Goodman Sch., Chgo., 1971, Juilliard Sch., 1972; AB, U. Calif., Santa Cruz, 1977. Radio news reporter McGovern Campaign, Chgo., 1972; cons. Kjos Pub. Co., Chgo., 1973-74; dir. VisArt, Ltd., San Francisco, 1977; ind. film editor L.A., 1978—. Editor: motion pictures: Re-Animator, 1984, Kiss of the Spiderwoman, 1985, Slam Dance, 1987, Checking Out, 1988, Blue Steel, 1989, Reversal of Fortune, 1990, Year of the Gun, 1991, Single White Female, 1992, Against the Wall, 1993 (Eddie award 1995, nominated for Cable ACE award), Corrina, Corrina, 1994, Kiss of Death, 1995, Before and After, 1995. Mem. Am. Cinema Editors, Editors Guild Hollywood, Motion Picture Editors N.Y.

PERCY, S. W., oil industry executive; b. 1946. BA in Mech. Engring, Rensselear Polytechnic Inst.; MBA, U. Mich.; JD, Cleve. State U. With Standard Oil Co., 1976—; exec. v.p. BP Am., Inc., BP Exploration & Oil Inc.; pres., CEO BP Oil Co. Divsn. Office: BP America Inc 200 Public Sq Cleveland OH 44114-2301

PERDIGAO, GEORGE MICHAEL, advertising executive; b. Sacramento, Jan. 23, 1965; s. George Vierra and Carolyn Sue (Creager) P. B in Journalism, U. So. Calif., 1987. Dir. advt. Mike Glickman Realty, Inc., Brentwood, Calif., 1987-90; sr. acct. exec. Bozell, Inc., West L.A., 1990-92; acct. supr. Dailey & Assocs., L.A., 1992—. Recipient Trojan 4th Estate award U. So. Calif., 1987. Home: 7320 Balboa Blvd # 123 Van Nuys CA 91406 Office: Dailey & Assocs 3055 Wilshire Blvd Los Angeles CA 90010-1108

PERDUE, BEVERLY MOORE, state legislator, geriatric consultant; b. Grundy, Va., Jan. 14, 1948; d. Alfred P. and Irene E. (Morefield) Moore; children: Garrett, Emmett. BA, U. Ky., 1969; MEd, U. Fla., 1974, PhD, 1976. Pvt. lectr., writer, cons., 1980-86; pres. The Perdue Co., New Bern, N.C., 1985—; rep. N.C. State Gen. Assembly, Raleigh, 1986-90; senator N.C. Gen. Assembly, Raleigh, 1990—; bd. dirs. Nations Bank, New Bern. Bd. dirs. N.C. United Way, Greensboro, 1990-92; exec. mem. N.C. Dem. Party, Raleigh, 1989—; mem. N.C. travel bd. Nat. Conf. State Legislators. Named Outstanding Legislator, N.C. Aging Network, 1989, 92, Toll fellow Nat. Conf. State Legislators, Lexington, Ky., 1992. Mem. Nat. Coun. on Aging, Bus. and Profl. Women, Rotary. Episcopalian. Home: 211 Wilson Point Rd New Bern NC 28562-7519 Office: Perdue & Co PO Box 991 507 Pollack St New Bern NC 28563 also: NC Senate Raleigh NC 27601

PERDUE, CHARLES L., JR., anthropology educator; b. Panthersville, Ga., Dec. 1, 1930; s. Charles L. Sr. and Eva Mae (Samples) P.; m. Nancy J. Martin; children: Martin Clay, Marc Charles, Kelly Scott, Kevin Barry (dec.). Student, North Ga. Coll., 1948-49, Santa Rosa (Calif.) Jr. Coll., 1953; AB in Geology, U. Calif., Berkeley, 1958, postgrad., 1958-59; MA in Folklore, U. Pa., 1968, PhD in Folklore, 1971. Engring. writer Convair Astronautics, Vandenberg AFB, Calif., 1959-60; geologist, mineral classification branch U.S. Geological Survey, Washington, 1960-67; asst. prof. English dept. U. Va., Charlottesville, 1971-72, asst. prof. English and sociology, anthropology depts., 1972-73, asst. prof. English and anthropology depts., 1973-76, assoc. prof., 1976-92, prof., 1992—; cons. in field. Author: Outwitting the Devil: Jack Tales from Wise County, Virginia, 1987, Pig's Foot Jelly and Persimmon Beer: Foodways from the Virginia Writers' Project, 1992, (with others) Weevils in the Wheat: Interviews with Virginia Ex-Slaves, 1976; contbr. articles to profl.jours. With US Army, 1951-54. Univ. Predoctoral fellow U. Pa., 1967-71; Wilson Gee Inst. Rsch. grant U. Va., 1974, 75; Rsch. grant NEH, 1980-81, 84; Sesquicentennial Assoc. award Ctr. for Advanced Studies U. Va. 1978-79, 87-88. Mem. Am. Folklore Soc. (exec. bd. 1980-83, book rev. editor jour. 1986-87), Mid. Atlantic Folklore Assn. (founding mem., bd. dirs.), Nat. Coun. for Traditional Arts (bd. dirs. 1971-87, pres. 1973-79), Va. Folklore Soc. (archivist/editor 1974-89, archivist 1990-94, archivist/pres. 1995—). Office: U Va Dept Anthropology Cabell Hall Charlottesville VA 22903

PERDUE, CHRISTINE H., lawyer; b. Huntington, W. Va., Mar. 18, 1949. BA, Oberlin Coll., 1971; JD, Duke U., 1974. Bar: Va. 1974, D.C. 1989. Ptnr. Hunton & Williams, Fairfax, Va.; adj. prof. U. Richmond, 1981-83. Mem. ABA, Va. Bar Assn. (chair labor law sect. 1992—), Fairfax Bar Assn., Phi Beta Kappa. Office: Hunton & Williams 3050 Chain Bridge Rd PO Box 1147 Fairfax VA 22030*

PERDUE, FRANKLIN P., poultry products company executive; m. Mitzi Henderson Ayala, July 1988. Chmn. exec. com. Perdue Farms Inc., Salisbury, Md., Perdue Inc. subs. Perdue Farms Inc., Salisbury; chrm., dir. Perdue Farms, Inc. Office: Perdue Farms Inc PO Box 1537 Salisbury MD 21802-1537*

PERDUE, JAMES, food products executive; b. 1949. BS, Wake Forest U., 1973; MA in Marine Biology, Southeastern Mass. U., 1976; PhD in Fisheries, U. Wash., 1983. With U. Md., Cambridge, 1976-78; chmn. bd. Perdue Transp., Inc., Salisbury, Md., 1983—, Perdue Farms Inc., 1983—. Office: Perdue Farms Inc Old Ocean City Rd Salisbury MD 21802*

PERDUE, JAMES EVERETT, university vice chancellor emeritus; b. Auburn, Nebr., June 24, 1916; s. James O. and Hazel D. Perdue; m. Raedeen Tibbetts, Apr. 9, 1939; children: Pamela Jane, Darcy Clare; m. 2d, June Harrison Ward, Aug. 14, 1988. Student, Nebr. Wesleyan U., 1933-34; A.B., Nebr. State Tchrs. Coll., 1937; A.M., No. Colo. State U., Greely, 1940; Ph.D., Stanford U., 1952; LL.D., U. Denver, 1965. Coach, tchr. social studies DeWitt High Sch., Nebr., 1937-38; head social sci. dept. Ft. Morgan High Sch., Colo., 1938-41; ednl. rep. Row, Peterson and Co., 1941-43; acting dean Coll. Arts and Scis., U. Denver, 1946-48, assoc. dean, 1948-51; univ. budget officer U. Denver, 1951-52, asst. to chancellor, 1952-53; prof. social sci., dean Coll. Arts and Scis., U. Denver, 1953-65; pres., prof. social sci. SUNY-Oswego, 1965-77; assoc. chancellor SUNY System, 1977-78, vice chancellor for acad. programs, policy and planning, 1978-81; acting v.p. acad. affairs SUNY-Oswego, 1981; founding dean Coll. Arts and Sci. Ark. State U., 1981-82; provost, chief operating officer U. Ark., 1983; cons. to colls. and univs., 1981—; cons. N.J. State System Higher Edn., 1988; interim v.p. Met. State Coll., Denver; trustee Oswego City Savs. Bank; dir. Oswego br. Marine Midland Trust Co. Author: (autobiography) The First 75 Years, 1991. Mem. adv. com. on higher edn. Legis. Council State of Colo.; mem. Colo. Mental Health Planning Com., Colo. Council on Instrn., Hosp. Rev. and Planning Council Central N.Y.; mem. Colo. Com. to Secure the Super Conducting Super Collider, 1988; bd. dirs. Acad. Collective Bargaining Service, 1973—, chmn., 1974—; chmn. Oswego County Heart Fund, 1973; vestry mem. St. Charles Episcopal Ch., 1988; bd. dirs. Heritage Found., 1990—; trustee Morgan C.C. Found., 1990-95, pres. 1992-95. Served as ops. and communications officer USNR, 1943-46. Recipient Disting. Ednl. Service award Peru State, 1966; Outstanding Male Educator award U. N.C., 1975; Meritorious Service award Am. Assn. State Colls. and Univs., 1972; Adminstrv. Leave award Danforth Found., 1972. Mem. Am. Conf. Acad. Deans (vice chmn. 1963-64, exec. bd. 1959-64, nat. chmn. 1965-66), Am. Assn. State Colls. and Univs. (dir. 1967-72, pres.-elect 1976), Ft. Morgan Country Club (trustee 1990-93), Phi Beta Kappa, Pi Gamma Mu, Phi Delta Kappa. Home: 504 E 6th Ave Fort Morgan CO 80701-3217

PERDUNN, RICHARD FRANCIS, management consultant; b. Trenton, N.J., Dec. 12, 1915; s. Francis R. and Edith (Nogle) P.; m. Eugenia E. Morel, June 7, 1941; 1 child, Justine Reneau; m. Doris D. Andrus, Jan. 30, 1993. B.S., Lehigh U., 1939; postgrad. student, U. Pitts., 1939-40, Johns Hopkins, 1941-42. With U.S. Steel Co., also Glenn L. Martin, 1939-43, supt. machine and assembly, 1941-43; partner Nelson & Perdunn (engrs. and cons., also); v.p. Penco Corp., 1947-49; with Merck & Co., 1949-54, mgr. adminstrn., 1951-54; with Stevenson, Jordan & Harrison (mgmt. engrs.), N.Y.C., 1954-68; exec. v.p. Stevenson, Jordan & Harrison (mgmt. engrs.), 1962-64, pres., 1964-68; pres., chief exec. officer Bachman-Jacks, Inc., Reading, Pa., 1968-71; sr. v.p. Golightly Internat., N.Y.C., 1971—; also dir. Golightly Internat.; chmn. Perdunn Assocs., Inc., 1979—, dir. West Point & Annapolis Text Book Pub. Co., 1948—, Indsl. Edn. Films Inc., 1966—, Eldun Corp., 1964—, Security Nat. Bank, Newark, 1964—, Surburban Life Ins. Co., 1966—, Mainstem Inc., 1965—, Greenhouse Decor Inc., 1961—, Neuwirth Mut. Fund Inc., 1975—; Lectr. on finance and mfg. in, U.S., Can., Eng., Sweden. Assoc. editor: Systems and Procedures Quar, 1948-51; Contbr. articles to profl. publs. Bd. dirs. Inst. Better Confs., Internat. Inst. Bus. Devel., Inst. Urban Affairs, People Care, Inc.; dir. finance Assn. Help for Retarded Children. Served with USAAF, 1942-47. Mem. N.Y.C. C. of C., Council Econ. Devel., Am. Mgmt. Assn., AIM (pres.'s council), Newcomen Soc. N.Am., Systems and Procedures Assn. Am., Soc. Advanced Mgmt. Address (winter): 99 Bird Song Way Apt D306 Hilton Head Island SC 29926-1373 also: 600 Square Brielle NJ 08730 Address (summer): 28 Bay Point Harbour Point Pleasant NJ 08742

PEREIRA, JULIO CESAR, middle school educator; b. Vila Nova Sintra, Cape Verde, Cape Verde, Oct. 12, 1937; came to U.S., 1983; s. Julio Feijoo Pereira and Beatriz Feijoo Pereira. Student, Mil. Sch., Coimbra, Portugal, 1958-61; MAEE, U. Lisbon, Portugal, 1976; cert. in teaching, Afonso Domingues, Lisbon, 1979, Ea. Nazarene Coll., Quincy, Mass., 1988. Registered profl. engr., Portugal. Vocat. sch. tchr. Portuguese Sch., Lisbon, 1969-83, dir. instrn., 1980-81; social studies tchr. Madison Park H.S., Boston, 1984-85; math. tchr. Dearborn Mid. Sch., Boston, 1985—. Inventor slide model for algebraic addition. Lt. Portuguese Army, 1961-65. Recipient Tchr. Appreciation award Algebra Project Boston, 1992, Multicultural Recognition award Mass. Dept. Edn., 1992, Ofcl. citation Mass. Senate, 1993, Presdl. award for Excellence in Math. Teaching, Pres. of U.S., 1994. Mem. Coun. Presdl. Awardees in Math. Avocations: reading, research, computer programming, gardening, travel. Home: 116 Park St Stoughton MA 02072-2925 Office: Dearborn Mid Sch 35 Greenville St Boston MA 02119-2315

PERELL, EDWARD ANDREW, lawyer; b. Stamford, Conn., Mar. 30, 1940; s. Sydney C. and Dorothy (Barger) P.; m. Nan Lifflander, Oct. 10, 1959; children: Stephanie Perell Krause, Timothy R. BA, Yale Coll., 1962, LLB, 1965. Bar: N.Y. 1966. Assoc. Debevoise & Plimpton, N.Y.C., 1965-72, ptnr., 1973-88, 93—; ptnr. Debevoise & Plimpton, N.Y.C. and London, 1989-93. Contbr. numerous articles on securities laws, mergers and acquisitions to profl. publs. Chmn. bd. dirs. Fedn. Protestant Welfare Agys., N.Y.C., 1983-87; pres., bd. dirs. Graham-Windham Family Svcs., N.Y.C., 1970-77. Mem. ABA, Assn. of Bar of City of N.Y., Internat. Bar Assn., Yale Clubs of N.Y. and London, Law Soc. of England and Wales. Home: Cricket Ln Dobbs Ferry NY 10522 also: 14 Sutton Pl S New York NY 10022-3071 Office: Debevoise & Plimpton 875 3rd Ave New York NY 10022-6225*

PERELLA, MARIE LOUISE, lawer; b. Akron, Ohio, Feb. 5, 1967; d. Manuel James and Jean Ann (Nalencz) P. BA in Spanish, John Carroll U., 1989; student, Univ. Ibero Americana, Mexico City, 1988; JD, Akron U., 1992. Bar: Ohio 1992, U.S. Dist. Ct. (no. dist.) Ohio 1993. Law clk. Akron Law Dept., 1990; legal intern Cuyahoga Falls (Ohio) Law Dept., 1990-92; law clk. Ticktin, Baron, Koepper & Co. LPA, Cleve., 1992, assoc. atty., 1992—. Guest spkr. Cleve. Legal Secs. Assn. meeting, 1995. Mem. ABA, ATLA, Ohio State Bar Assn., Cuyahoga County Bar Assn., Cleve. Bar Assn., Centro Cultural Hispano, Justinian Forum, Phi Alpha Delta (clk. intern/law sch./grant chpt. 1991-92), Sigma Delta Pi. Avocations: sports, travel, flute. Office: Ticktin Baron Koepper & Co LPA 1621 Euclid Ave 1700 Keith Bldg Cleveland OH 44115-2107

PERELLA, SUSANNE BRENNAN, librarian; b. Providence, Mar. 19, 1936; d. Laurence J. and Harriet E. (Delaplane) Brennan. B.A., U. Conn., 1960; M.L.S., U. Mich., 1967. Head M.B.A. Library, Univ. Conn., Hartford, 1964-66; asst. librarian Cornell Univ. Grad. Sch. Bus., Ithaca, N.Y., 1967-72; head reader's services FTC Library, Washington, 1972-79; library dir. FTC Library, 1979-92; libr. dir. Libr. and Info. Svcs. U.S. Treasury, Washington, 1992—. Mem. Law Librarians Soc., Spl. Libraries Assn., Am. Assn. Law Libraries, Fed. Library and Info. Ctr. Com. Office: US Dept Treasury Libr 1500 Pennsylvania Ave NW Washington DC 20005-1007

PERELLE, IRA B., psychologist; b. Mt. Vernon, N.Y., Sept. 16, 1925; s. Joseph Yale and Lillian (Schaffer) P.; student U. Tex.; grad. in elec. engring. R.C.A. Inst., 1951; student Iona Coll.; B.S., M.S., Ph.D., Fordham U.; m. Diane A. Granville, 1982; 1 child, Jessica Eve. Prodn. mgr. Arden Jewelry Case Co., 1946-49; became chief engr. Westlab Electronic Service Engrs., 1949; ptnr. Westlab, 1954; pres. Westlab, Inc., 1955-64, chmn. bd., 1956; pres. Westchester Research and Devel. Labs., 1953-65; exec. dir. Interlink, Ltd., 1966—; dir. Atlantic Research Inst., 1975—; cons. higher edn. divsn. U.S. Dept. of Edn., 1994—; cons. ednl. research Fordham U., Catholic U. of P.R., Bayamon (P.R.) Central U., World U., San Juan, P.R., John Jay Coll., N.Y.C., Rockland C.C., N.Y.; rsch. cons. So. Westchester County Bd. Coop. Ednl. Services; stats. cons. City of Mt. Vernon (N.Y.), Reader's Digest, Pleasantville, N.Y., GT&E Inc., CUNY; served as expert witness for N.Y. State Tax Ct.; assoc. Columbia U. Seminars; prof. dept. psychology NYU; prof. dept. bus. and econs., dept. psychology Mercy Coll., Dobbs Ferry, N.Y.; prof. Grad. Sch. Bus., L.I. U.; adj. prof. SUNY-Purchase, Fordham U., N.Y.C.; vis. prof. Fairleigh Dickenson U.; faculty adv. com. Mercer County Coll., 1969-73; conf. leader Nat. Conf. Ednl. Tech., 1971-73. Mem. staff Civil Def., 1954-74; bd. dirs. Mid-Hudson Inst., Dobbs Ferry, N.Y. Served as radio instr. USAAF, 1943-46. Mem. IEEE, AAAS, N.Y. Zool. Soc., Assn. Ednl. Communication and Tech., N.Y. State Ednl. Communication Assn., Audio Engring. Soc., Acoustical Soc. Am., Am. Inst. Physics, Am. Psychol. Assn., Am. Ednl. Rsch. Assn., Am. Statis. Assn., Animal Behavior Soc., Am. Genetic Soc., N.Y. Acad. Scis. Author: A Practical Guide to Educational Media for the Classroom Teacher, 1974; also articles; research on laterality for evolutionary biology. Discoverer Perelle Phenomenon, psychology-attention. Office: Mercy Coll Dobbs Ferry NY 10522

PERELMAN, LEON JOSEPH, paper manufacturing executive, university president; b. Phila., Aug. 28, 1911; s. Morris and Jennie (Davis) P.; m. Beverly Waxman, Jan. 27, 1945 (div. Apr. 1960); children: Cynthia, David. B.A., LaSalle Coll., 1933, LL.D., 1978; postgrad., U. Pa. Law Sch., 1933-35; L.H.D. (hon.), Dropsie U., 1976. Ptnr. Am. Paper Products Co. (later Am. Paper Products Inc.), Phila., 1935-42, pres., 1943—; pres. Am. Cone & Tube Co. Inc., Phila., 1953—, United Ammunition Container Inc., Phila., 1961—, Ajax Paper Tube Co., Phila., 1962—; vice chmn. bd. Belmont Industries, Phila., 1963—; pres. Dropsie U., Phila., 1978—. Author: Perelman Antique Toy Mus., 1972. Fin. chmn. Valley Forge council Boy Scouts Am., 1968; founder, bd. dirs. Perelman Antique Toy Mus., Phila., 1969; pres. West Park Hosp., 1975-78, 81—; trustee La Salle U., Balch Inst. Ethnic Studies. Served to 1st lt. USAAF, 1942-45. Recipient citation Jewish Theol. Sem., 1965; Beth Jacob award, 1966; award Pop Warner Little Scholars Inc., 1972; Cyrus Adler award Jewish Theol. Sem., 1976. Mem. AAUP, Jewish Publ. Soc. Am. (treas. 1983, v.p. 1991), Franklin Inst., Am. Assn. Mus. Republican. Jewish. Clubs: Union League (Phila.); Masons, Shriners. *One of the highlights of my life was the establishment of an antique toy museum to keep intact in a permanent place, in order to provide inspiration and pleasure for the general public and stimulate interest in old toys and to give students, antiquarians and collectors an opportunity for study and research in the history and development of one of the world's largest collections of children's toys during the past hundred years.*

PERELMAN, RONALD OWEN, diversified holding company executive; b. Greensboro, N.C., 1943; s. Raymond and Ruth (Caplan) P.; m. Claudia Cohen; 4 children. BA, U. Pa., 1964; MBA, Wharton Sch. Fin., 1966. With Belmont Industries Inc., 1966-78; chmn., chief exec. officer, dir. MacAndrews & Forbes Holdings Inc., Wilmington, Del., 1983—; chmn., chief exec. officer MacAndrews & Forbes Group Inc. (subs.), N.Y.C., 1978—; chmn., chief exec. officer, dir. Revlon Group Inc. (subs. MacAndrews & Forbes Group Inc.), N.Y.C., 1985—, Revlon Inc. (subs.), N.Y.C., 1985—; also chmn. Nat. Health Labs. Inc., La Jolla, Calif., 1985—, Andrews Group Inc., N.Y.C., 1985—. Jewish. Office: Revlon Group Inc 625 Madison Ave New York NY 10022 also: MacAndrews & Forbes Group Inc 38 E 63rd St New York NY 10021-8005*

PERENCHIO, ANDREW JERROLD, film and television executive; b. Fresno, Calif., Dec. 20, 1930; s. Andrew Joseph and Dorothea (Harvey) P.; m. Robin Green, July 16, 1954 (div.); children: Candace L., Catherine M., John Gardner; m. Jacquelyn Claire, Nov. 14, 1969. BS, UCLA, 1954. V.p. Music Corp. Am., 1958-62, Gen. Artists Corp., 1962-64; pres., owner theatrical agy. Chartwell Artists, Ltd., L.A., from 1964; chmn. bd. Tandem Prodns., Inc. and TAT Communications Co., L.A., 1973-83; pres., CEO Embassy Pictures, L.A., from 1983; now pres. Chartwell Partnerships Group, L.A. Promoter Muhammad Ali-Joe Frazier heavyweight fight, 1971, Bobby Riggs-Billie Jean King tennis match, 1973. Served to 1st lt. USAF, 1954-57. Clubs: Bel-Air Country (Los Angeles); Westchester (N.Y.) Country; Friars (N.Y.C.). Office: Chartwell Partnerships Group 1901 Avenue Of The Stars Los Angeles CA 90067-6008

PERERA, GEORGE A., physician; b. N.Y.C., Dec. 29, 1911; s. Lionello and Carolyn (Allen) P.; m. Anna Paxson Rhoads, Dec. 22, 1934; children: Marcia (Mrs. Nicholas B. Van Dyck), David Rhoads. A.B., Princeton U., 1933; M.D., Columbia U., 1937, Sc.D. in Medicine, 1942. Diplomate: Am. Bd. Internal Medicine (dir. 1957-64, vice chmn. 1963-64). Intern Presbyn. Hosp., N.Y.C., 1937-39; resident medicine Presbyn. Hosp., 1941-43; asst. resident Peter Bent Brigham Hosp., Boston, 1939-40; asst. physiology N.Y. U., 1940-41; mem. staff Presbyn. Hosp., 1943-71, attending physician, 1960-71; faculty Columbia U. Coll. Physicians and Surgeons, 1946-71, prof. medicine, 1958-71, asso. dean, 1962-70. Trustee Riverdale Country Sch., N.Y.C., 1949-80, pres., 1977-80; trustee Mary Imogene Bassett Hosp., Cooperstown, N.Y., 1961-80, Columbia U. Press, 1961-64, 66-69, Bridges of Understanding Found., 1973-77; trustee Concern for Dying, 1975-81, v.p., 1978-79, 80-81; alumni trustee Columbia U., 1974-80; mem. corp. Haverford Coll., 1979-87; bd. dirs. Kendal-Crosslands Comty., 1983-94. Fellow ACP, AAAS; mem. N.Y. Acad. Medicine (v.p. 1968-70, trustee 1973-78), Assn. Am. Physicians (emeritus), Alpha Omega Alpha. Home: 159 Kendal Dr Kennett Square PA 19348-2332

PERERA, LAWRENCE THACHER, lawyer; b. Boston, June 23, 1935; s. Guido R. and Faith (Phillips) P.; m. Elizabeth A. Wentworth, July 5, 1961; children: Alice V. Perera Lucey, Caroline F. Perera Barry, Lucy E., Lawrence Thacher. B.A., Harvard U., 1957, LL.B., 1961. Bar: Mass. 1961, U.S. Supreme Ct. 1973. Clk. Judge R. Ammi Cutter, Mass. Supreme Jud. Ct., Boston, 1961-62; assoc. firm Palmer & Dodge, Boston, 1962-69; ptnr. Palmer & Dodge, 1969-74; judge Middlesex County Probate Ct., East Cambridge, Mass., 1974-79; partner firm Hemenway & Barnes, Boston, 1979—; mem. faculty and nat. coun. Hon. Nat. Jud. Coll., Reno, prof./pres. Mass. Continuing Legal Edn., Inc., 1988-90. Chmn. Boston Fin. Commn., 1969-71; overseer Brigham & Women's Hosp., Boston, Boston Lyric Opera; chmn. bd. overseers Boston Opera Assn.; chmn. Back Bay Archtl. Commn., 1966-72; trustee emeritus Sta. WGBH Ednl. Found., Boston Athenaeum, Wang Ctr. Performing Arts. Fellow Am. Acad. Matrimonial Lawyers, Am. Coll. Trust and Estate Counsel; mem. ABA, Am. Bar Found., Am. Law Inst., Mass. Bar Assn., Mass. Bar Found., Boston Bar Assn.. Home: 18 Marlborough St Boston MA 02116-2101 Office: 60 State St Boston MA 02109-1803

PERES, JUDITH MAY, journalist; b. Chgo., June 30, 1946; d. Leonard H. and Eleanor (Seltzer) Zurakov; m. Michael Peres, June 27, 1972; children: Dana, Avital. BA, U. Ill., 1967. Acct. exec. Daniel J. Edelman Inc., Chgo., 1967-68; copy editor Jerusalem (Israel) Post, 1968-71, news editor, 1971-75, chief night editor, 1975-80, editor, style book, 1978-80; copy editor Chgo. Tribune, 1980-82, rewriter, 1982-84, assoc. fgn. editor, 1984-90, nat. editor, 1990-95, nat./fgn. editor, 1995—. Office: Chicago Tribune 435 N Michigan Ave Chicago IL 60611-4001

PERESS, MAURICE, symphony conductor, musicologist; b. N.Y.C., Mar. 18, 1930; s. Haskell Ben Ezra and Elka (Tygier) P. B.A., N.Y.U., 1951; postgrad., Mannes Coll. Music, NYU Grad. Sch. Musicology. Asst. condr. Mannes Coll. Music, 1957-60; music dir. NYU, 1958-61; asst. condr. New York Philharmonic, 1961-62; music dir. Corpus Christi (Tex.) Symphony, 1961-74, Austin Symphony, 1970-72, Kansas City Philharm., 1974-80; dir. Bur. Indian Affairs pilot project Communication through Music, 1968; faculty Queens Coll., 1969-70, 83—; mus. dir. world premiere Bernstein Mass, J.F. Kennedy Center, Washington, 1971. Pub.: musical adaptation and devel. Ellington Opera, Queenie Pie; orchestrations: Ellington, New World 'a Comin', Black Brown and Beige, Bernstein West Side Story Overture; reconstrn. Gershwin's "Strike Up the Band", 1929, Paul Whiteman's Historic Aeolian Hall concert of 1924 (recorded Musical Heritage Soc.), Duke Ellington's First Carnegie Hall concert, 1944; George Antheil's 1927 Carnegie Hall "Ballets Mécanique" concert (recorded Musical Heritage Soc.); James Reese Europes Clef Club concert, 1912, First "All Negro" concert composed and performed by African Ams. in Carnegie Hall; author: Some Music Lessons for American Indian Youngsters, 1968; contbr. articles profl. jours. Served with AUS, 1953-55. Named Millicent James fellow NYU, 1955; Mannes Coll. scholar, 1955-57. Mem. ASCAP, Conductor's Guild, The Friends of Earl Robinson (pres.), Dvorak Am. Soc. (bd. dirs.), Am. Soc. for Jewish Music (bd. dirs.). Jewish. Home: 310 W 72nd St New York NY 10023-2675

PERETTI, MARILYN GAY WOERNER, human services professional; b. Indpls., July 30, 1935; d. Philip E. and Harriet E. (Meyer) Woerner; children: Thomas A., Christopher P. BS, Purdue U., 1957; postgrad., Coll. DuPage, 1980—, U. Wis., 1981—. Nursery sch. lab. asst. Mary Baldwin Coll., Staunton, Va., 1957-58; tchr. 1st grade, nursery sch. No. Ill. area schs., 1958-61; asst. tchr. of blind Glenbard E. H.S., Lombard, Ill., 1978-80; adminstrv. asst. Elmhurst Coll., 1980-81; dir. vol. svcs. DuPage Convalescent Ctr., Wheaton, 1981-95; dir. cmty. outreach Sr. Home Sharing, Inc., Lombard, Ill., 1996—; developer new vol. pos. for vis. the non-verbal handicapped, 1994; prodr. 4 ednl. slide programs on devel. countries, 1988-91; initiator used book collection for library project U. Zululand, S. Africa, 1993-94. Editor, designer newsletter Our Developing World's Voices, 1994—. Bd. dirs. Lombard YMCA, 1977-83, pres., 1980; vol. Chgo. Uptown Ministry, 1979; participant fact finding trips El Salvador, 1988, Honduras, 1989, Nicaragua, 1989, Republic of South Africa, 1991; mem. Nature Artists Guild of Morton Arboretum; vol. PADS, 1994—. Mem. Nature Artists Guild of Morton Arboretum. Avocations: swimming, writing poetry, desktop publishing, Third World concerns, botanical watercolors. Office: Sr Home Sharing Inc 837 Westmore-Meyers Rd Lombard IL 60148

PEREY, RON, lawyer; b. Cleve., Feb. 2, 1943; s. John Perecinsky and Anne (Nagy) Disman; 1 child, Page Suzanne; m. Janice Ash, Aug. 19, 1995. BA in Polit. Sci., Miami U., Oxford, Ohio, 1965; JD cum laude, Ohio State U., 1968. Bar: Wash. 1968, U.S. Dist. Ct. (we. dist.) Wash. 1968, U.S. Ct. Appeals (9th cir.) 1973, U.S. Supreme Ct. 1985. Assoc. Reed McClure, Seattle, 1968-71, ptnr., 1971-82; ptnr. Perey & Smith, Seattle, 1982-86, Perey Langley, Seattle, 1986-92; owner Law Offices of Ron Perey, Seattle, 1992—; lectr. in field of personal injury and trial practice. Contbr. articles to profl jours. Roscoe Pound Found. fellow. Fellow Roscoe Pound Found.; mem. ATLA (state del. 1989-90), ABA (litigation sect.), King County Bar Assn. (chmn. med.-legal com. 1989-90), Wash. State Trial Lawyers Assn. (bd. govs. 1983-85, 89-91), Am. Bd. Trial Advs. (diplomate; nat. bd. rep. 1996—), Wash. State Bar Assn. (bd. govs. 1994—), Damage Attys. Round Table. Democrat. Avocations: travel, reading, weight lifting, tennis, hiking, jogging. Office: Market Place Tower 2025 1st Ave Ste 350 Seattle WA 98121-2100

PEREYRA-SUAREZ, CHARLES ALBERT, lawyer; b. Paysandu, Uruguay, Sept. 7, 1947; came to U.S., 1954, naturalized, 1962; s. Hector and Esther (Enriquez-Sarano) P.-S.; m. Susan H. Cross, Dec. 30, 1983. BA in History magna cum laude, Pacific Union Coll., 1970; postgrad., UCLA, 1970-71; JD, U. Calif., Berkeley, 1975. Bar: Calif. 1975, D.C. 1980. Staff atty. Western Ctr. Law and Poverty, Inc., Los Angeles, L.A., 1976; trial atty. civil rights div. U.S. Dept. Justice, Washington, 1976-79; asst. U.S. atty., criminal div. U.S. Dept. Justice, Los Angeles, L.A., 1979-82; sr. litigation assoc. Gibson, Dunn & Crutcher, Los Angeles, L.A., 1982-84; sole practice Los Angeles, L.A., 1984-86; ptnr. McKenna & Cuneo, Los Angeles, L.A., 1986-95, Davis Wright Tremaine, L.A., 1995—. Democrat. Avocations: tennis, jogging, travel.

PEREZ, ANDREW, III, architect; m. Cynthia A. Jonston; children: Andrew, Chrstina Alexia, David Alexander. Student, Georgetown U., 1958; BArch, U. Tex., 1961; postgrad., U. Calif., Berkeley, 1965-66. Registered architect, Tex., Calif.; cert. Nat. Coun. Archtl. Registration Bd. Founder, mng. ptnr. O'Neill & Perez, Architects, 1969-84, Andrew Perez Assocs., Architects, 1984—; dir., coord. architecture and interior design programs U. Tex., San Antonio, 1988—; prin.-in-charge master planning and urban design svcs. City of San Antonio, Pan Am. U., Ft. Hood, Tex., various Tex. communities; vis. lectr. Universidad Nacional Autonoma de Mex., Instituto Tecnologico de Nuevo Laredo y la Academia de Arquitectura, Tex. A&M u., U. Houston, 1987; vis. critic U. Tex., San Antonio, San Antonio Coll., Trinity U.; juror various archtl. design competitions. Prin. works include Bank of San Antonio, 1974 (Design Excellence award Bldg./Owners Mgmt. Assn., Pre-cast Concrete Inst. 1976), Gill Cos. Office Bldg., 1975 (Design Excellence award Bldg./Owners Mgmt. Assn. 1977), Mullins Ranch Ho., Muldoon, Tex., (Design Excellence award San Antonio chpt. AIA 1978, Honor award Tex. Soc. Architects 1979), Baird Residence, Marble Falls, Tex. (Honor award Tex. Soc. Architects 1978), Mexican Am. Unity Coun. Ctr., 1978 (Design Excellence award San Antonio chpt. AIA 1978, Adaptive Reuse award San Antonio Conservation Soc. 1979), Bandera br. Gill Savs. (Honor award Tex. Soc. Architects 1981, Design Excelllence award San Antonio chpt. AIA 1984), Victoria Cts. Phases I & II renovation, 1979-86 (Design Excellence award San Antonio chpt. AIA 1982), Child Care Ctr., Brooks AFB, Tex., 1981 (1st Honor award USAF Design Awards 1980, 1st Pl. Design award USAF Design Competition, 1980), St. Paul Sq. Block Improvements, 1982 (Honor award, Design Excellence award San Antonio chpt. AIA 1982), Diagnostic Unit Tex. Dept. Corrections, Huntsville, Tex., 1983, Straus Ranch Ho., Bexar County, Tex. (2 Design Excellence awards San Antonio chpt. AIA 1984, Honor award Tex. Soc. Architects 1984, one of 8 Outstanding Examples of Architecture in Tex. during Past 150 Yrs. Tex. Architect Mag. 1986), Logistical Systems Ops. Ctr., Kelly AFB, 1984, adminstrv. offices Alamo C.C. Dist., 1984, U.S. Border Patrol Sta., Eagle Pass, Tex., 1984 (Design Excellence award San Antonio chpt. AIA 1984), City Pub. Libr. & Lagoon/Pk. Devel., Farmers Branch, Tex., 1985 (Design Excellence, Honor award San Antonio chpt. AIA 1987), McAllister Ranch Ho., Magic Springs, Tex. (Design Excellence award San Antonio chpt. AIA 1985), U.S. Post Office, San Antonio, 1985, Consolidated Support Ctr., Brooks AFB, Tex., 1985, Univ. Ctr. U. Tex., San Antonio, 1986, Health & Phys. Edn. Facility Pan Am. U., 1986, Minten Residence, 1986 (Design Excellence award San Antonio chpt. AIA 1987), The Edn. Ctr., 1986 (John & Joyce Karr award Tex. Hist. Commn. 1987, Design Excellence award San Antonio chpt. AIA 1987), Manske Meml. Libr., Farmers Branch (1st Pl. Design award City of Farmers Branch Design Competition 1981, Design Excellence award San Antonio chpt. AIA 1987), County Line Rad Fire Sta., New Braunfels, Tex., 1987, Tex. Air N.G. Hdqs., 1990, Cahill Residence, San Antonio, 1991, Longoria Residence, Helotes, Tex., 1993-94, others. Pres. parents-tchrs. coun. St. Anthony Sch., 1979, founding treas., bd. dirs., 1985-88, mem. devel. com.; mem. parish bd. Our Lady Grace Ch., 1980-82; chmn. Mayor & City Coun.'s Hist. Sites and Structures Task Force, 1982-87, Task Force Redrafting San Antonio Hist. Preservation Ordinance, 1985-87, Master Plan Task Force for City of San Antonio, 1992, City of San Antonio Hist. Rev. Bd., 1991-92, City of San Antonio Hist. and Design Rev. Commn., 1992—; mem. Task Force Developing hist. Preservation Incentives Program, 1986; founder/v.p. San Antonio Hist. Found., 1988; bd. dirs. Stas. KSTX and KPAC, 1984—, San Antonio Mus. Assn., 1986—, chmn. facilities com., 1987—, sec. bd. dirs., 1991—. With USN, 1963-65, capt. Res. ellow AIA (past pres., v.p., sec. San Antonio chpt., mem. urban design com. 1984-86, mem. and past chmn. San Antonio chpt. found., co-chmn. graphic and publs. com. nat. conv. 1986); mem. Nat. Trust Hist. Preservation, Tex. Soc. Architects (bd. dirs. 1982-85), Urban Design Inst. Office: Andrew Perez Assocs Architects 3737 Broadway St Ste 300 San Antonio TX 78209-6547

PEREZ, BERTIN JOHN, investment banker; b. Havana, Cuba, Feb. 5, 1939; s. Bertin Porfirio and Otilia Maria (Padron) P.; m. Maria Luisa Miranda, Aug. 5, 1960; 1 child, Bertin Henry. Student, U. Havana, 1958; BBA in Acctg., U. Villanova, 1960; MBA, U. Miami, Fla., 1967. CPA, Fla. Auditor/analyst Hilton Hotels, N.Y.C., 1961-63; ptnr. Laventhol Howarth, Miami, 1964-68; treas. Caesar's World, Inc., 1969-72; v.p. fin., CFO Caesar's World, Inc., L.A., 1973-78, group v.p., 1979-82; cons. B.P. Assocs., L.A., 1983-87; mng. dir. Perlman Enterprises, Atlantic City, N.J., 1988-89; v.p., CFO Continental Health Affiliates, Englewood Cliffs, N.J., 1990-93; sr. v.p. Printon Kane Group, Short Hills, N.J., 1993-94; pres. Brtin J. Peres & Assocs., N.Y.C., 1994—; spkr.-lectr. Wash. State U., 1974-75. Mem. Republican Nat. Party, Washington, Nat. Geog. Soc., Washington, 1970-85, Nat. Rifle Assn., Washington. Mem. Financial Exec. Inst., Smithsonian Inst. Roman Catholic. Avocations: hunting, fishing, tennis. Home: 452 Piermont Rd Demarest NJ 07627-2421 Office: Bertin J Perez & Assocs Rm 316 1270 Avenue Of The Americas Fl 12 New York NY 10020-1702

PEREZ, CARLOS A., radiation oncologist, educator; b. Colombia, Nov. 10, 1934; came to U.S., 1960, naturalized, 1969; children: Carlos S., Bernardo, Edward P. B.S., U. de Antioquia, Medellin, 1952, M.D., 1960. Diplomate: Am. Bd. Radiology (trustee 1985—). Rotating intern Hosp. U. St. Vincente de Paul, Medellin and Caldas, 1958-59; resident Mallinckrodt Inst. Radiology, Washington U. Sch. Medicine, St. Louis, 1960-63; mem. faculty Mallinckrodt Inst. Radiology, Washington U. Sch. Medicine, 1964—, prof. radiology, 1972—, dir. radiation oncology ctr., 1976—; fellow radiotherapy M.D. Anderson Hosp. and Tumor Inst., U. Tex., Houston, 1963-64. Co-editor: Principles and Clinical Practice of radiation Oncology, Principles and Practice of Gynecologic Oncology; editl. bd. Internat. Jour. Radiation and Physics, 1975—, Cancer, 1993—; contbr. articles to med. jours. Fellow Am. Coll. Radiology; mem. AAAS, AMA, Internat. Assn. Study Lung Cancer, Am. Soc. Clin. Oncology, Am. Soc. Therapeutic Radiologists (pres. 1981-82, Gold medal 1992), Am. Radium Soc., Am. Assn. Cancer Rsch., Am. Assn. Cancer Edn., Radiol. Soc. N.Am., Brit. Inst. Radiology, Mo. Radiol. Soc., Mo. Acad. Sci., Mo. Med. Soc., St. Louis Med. Soc., Greater St. Louis Soc. Radiologists, Radiation Rsch. Soc. Home: 78 Lake Frst Saint Louis MO 63117-1359 Office: Washington U Radiation Oncology Ctr 4511 Forest Park Ave Saint Louis MO 63108-2138

PEREZ, CARLOS GROSS, professional baseball player; b. Nigua, Dominican Republic, Apr. 14, 1971. Pitcher Montreal Expos, 1995—. Selected to N.L. All-Star Team, 1995. Office: Montreal Expos, 4540 Pierre-de-Coubertin Av, Montreal, PQ Canada H1V 3N7*

PEREZ, GERARD VINCENT, art publishing company executive; b. LeMans, France, Oct. 5, 1946; came to U.S., 1971; s. Georges and Marie-Laurence (Anziani) P.; m. Nancy J. Rudin, Apr. 23, 1976; children: Samantha, Amanda. BA, B. Franklin Coll., Orleans, France, 1966; MBA, ESCAE Marseille, France, 1970; postgrad., Am. Grad. Sch. Internat. Mgmt., Glendale, Ariz., 1973. Owner, mgr. Mariettes Unltd., St. Tropez, France, 1967-69; sales engr. Paper Converting Machine Co., Inc., Green Bay, Wis., 1973-75; mgr. sales J.D. Marshall Internat., Skokie, Ill., 1975-77; pres. Fine Art Resources, Inc., Chgo., 1977-86, London Contemporary Art, Prospect Heights, Ill., 1986-91, Art Emotion Corp., Prospect Heights, 1991—. Served with French Armed Forces, 1970-71. Home: 1758 S Edgar St Palatine IL 60067-7435

PEREZ, JEAN-YVES, engineering company executive; b. 1945. Ingenieur Civil Engring., Ecole Centrale des Arts et Manufactures, Paris, 1967; MS, U. Ill., 1970. With Soletanche Enterprise, 1971-72; pres., CEO Woodward-Clyde Group, Inc., Denver, 1967-70, 73—. With French Air Force, 1970-71. Office: Woodward-Clyde Cons 4582 S Ulster St Ste 600 Denver CO 80237-2635

PEREZ, JOSEPHINE, psychiatrist, educator; b. Tijuana, Mex., Feb. 10, 1941; came to U.S., 1960, naturalized, 1968. BS in Biology, U. Santiago de Compostela, Spain, 1971; MD, 1975. Clerkships in internal medicine, gen. surgery, otorhinolaryngology, dermatology and venereology Gen. Hosp. of Galicia (Spain), 1972-75; resident in gen. psychiatry U. Miami (Fla.), Jackson Meml. Hosp. and VA Hosp., Miami, 1976-78; practice medicine specializing in psychiatry, marital and family therapy, individual psychotherapy, Miami, Fla., 1979—; nuclear medicine technician, EEG technician, supr. Electrographic Labs., Encino, Calif., 1963-71; emergency room physician Miami Dade Hosp., 1975; attending psychiatrist Jackson Meml. Hosp., 1979—, asst. dir. adolescent psychiat. unit, 1979-83; mem. clin. faculty U. Miami Sch. Medicine, 1979—, clin. instr. psychiatry, 1979—. Mem. AMA (Physicians' Recognition award 1980, 83, 86, 89), Am. Assn. for Marital and Family Therapy (cert. clin. mem., treas. 1982-84, pres.-elect 1985-87, pres. 1987-89), Am. Psychiat. Assn., Am. Med. Women's Assn., Assn. Women Psychiatrists, South Fla. Psychiat. Soc. Office: 420 S Dixie Hwy Ste 4A Coral Gables FL 33146

PEREZ, LOUIS MICHAEL, newspaper editor; b. Tampa, Fla., May 30, 1946; s. Louis H. and Mary Elizabeth (Mansell) P.; m. Betty Louise Yates, Mar. 22, 1969 (div. May 1980); 1 child, Christian Marcos; m. Donna Marie Pence, Oct. 8, 1982; children: Louis Michael Jr., Ty Pence, Shea Marie. Student, Loyola U., New Orleans, 1964-66; BS in Journalism, U. Fla., 1969. Reporter/corr. Tampa Tribune, Gainesville, Fla., 1966-69; asst. to dean Coll. Edn. U. Fla., Gainesville, 1969-70, adj. prof. Coll. Journalism, 1975-76; reporter Gainesville Sun, 1970-76, editorial writer, 1974-76; editorial page editor The Ledger, Lakeland, Fla., 1976-81, exec. editor, 1981—; vis. prof. Coll. Journalism U. Fla., 1982; judge journalism awards Scripps-Howard Found., 1988; juror Pultizer Prizes com., 1994, 95. Recipient Best Editorial award Fla. Bar Assn., 1977. Mem. Am. Soc. Newspaper Editors, Fla. Soc. Newspaper Editors (pres. 1981-82, bd. dirs. 1980-83, 88-90, 1st pl. Best Feature Article award 1972). Roman Catholic. Home: 5220 Waterwood Run Bartow FL 33830-9768 Office: The Ledger PO Box 408 Lakeland FL 33802-0408

PEREZ, MARY A(NGELICA), educational administrator; b. San Benito, Tex., Sept. 3; d. Refugio P. and Maria G. (Guerra) P. AA, Tex. Southmonost Coll., Brownsville, Tex., 1955; BS in Elem. Edn., Tex. A&I U. (now Tex. A&M U.), 1959. Cert. elem. tchr., Tex., Calif. Substitute tchr. Bassett Unified Sch. Dist., La Puente, Calif.; tchr. kindergarten West Covina (Calif.) Unified Sch. Dist., ret.; tchr. ESL Tulane U., New Orleans; tchr. bilingual kindergarten San Benito (Tex.) Consolidated Sch. Dist.; tchr. bilingual 4th grade Brownsville (Tex.) Consolidated Sch. Dist.; tchr., head coord. Headstart St. Benedict Ch., San Benito, Tex. Delta Kappa Gamma scholar, 1953; grantee NDEA, 1963, EEOC, 1969, U. Madrid, 1991. Mem. NEA, Nat. Assn. Bilingual Edn., Calif. Tchrs. Assn., Calif. Assn. Bilingual Educators, Tex. Tchrs. Assn. (pres. 1966), Catholic Tchrs. Guild (pres. Brownsville Diocese 1965), Hispanic Women's Coun.. Democrat. Roman Catholic. Avocation: making and selling crafts. Home: 1829 S Lark Ellen Ave West Covina CA 91792-1104

PEREZ, ROSIE, actress; b. Bklyn.; d. Ismael Serrano and Lydia Perez. dramatic appearances include: (T.V.) 21 Jump Street, WIOU, (film) Do the Right Thing, 1989, White Men Can't Jump, 1992, Night on Earth, 1992, Untamed Heart, 1993, Fearless, 1993 (Acad. award nom. Best Supporting Actress 1994), It Could Happen To You, 1994, Somebody to Love, 1995. Office: CAA 9830 Wilshire Blvd Beverly Hills CA 90212-1804*

PEREZ, VICTOR, medical technologist, laboratory director; b. Arecibo, P.R., Apr. 3, 1930; s. Perez Victor and Cintron Catalina; m. Iraida Quiñones, June 1, 1964; children: Victor Jaime, Victor Lucas, Victor Ramon, Maria Victoria. BS, CAAM, Mayaguez, P.R., 1952; grad. in Med. Tech., Sch. Medicine, San Juan, P.R., 1953. Cert. med. technologist. Med. technologist blood bank Sch. Medicine, San Juan, 1953-57, dir. exptl. surgery, 1957-71; lab. dir. Metro. Hosp. Clin. Lab., Rio Piedres, P.R., 1971—; pres. P.R. Bd. Med. Technologists, 1971-74, Coll. P.R. Med. Technologists, 1976-77, P.R. Bd. Examiners, mem., 1986—. Pres. Club Exchange-Cupey, Rio Piedres, 1960, Parent Tchr. Student Assn., San Jose Coll., Rio Piedres, 1972. Mem. Am. Soc. Med. Technicians, Coll. Med. Technologists (pres. 1976), Am. Assn. Med. Tech., N.Y. Acad. Scis., Am. Assn. Clin. Chemistry, P.R. Coll. Med. Technolgists, Nat. Cert. Agy., Omicron Sigma. Roman Catholic. Home: Sagrado Corazon Brigida # 1705 Rio Piedras San Juan PR 00926

PEREZ-CRUET, JORGE, psychiatrist, psychopharmacologist, psychophysiologist; b. Santurce, P.R., Oct. 15, 1931; s. Jose Maria Perez-Vicente and Emilia Cruet-Burgos; m. Anyes Heimendinger, Oct. 4, 1958; children: Antonio, Mick, Graciela, Isabelle. BS magna cum laude, U. P.R., 1953, MD, 1957; diploma psychiatry McGill U., Montreal, Que., Can., 1976. Diplomate Am. Bd. Psychiatry and Neurology, Nat. Bd. Med. Examiners, Am. Bd. Geriatric Psychiatry; lic. Can. Coun. Med. Examiners; cert. in quality assurance. Rotating intern Michael Reese Hosp., Chgo., 1957-58; fellow in psychiatry Johns Hopkins U. Med. Sch., 1958-60, instr., then asst. prof. psychiatry, 1962-73; lab. neurophysiologist and psychomatic lab. Walter Reed Army Inst. Rsch., Washington, 1960-62, cons., 1963-65; rsch. assoc. lab. chem. pharmacology NIH, Bethesda, Md., also rsch. assoc. adult psychiatry br. and lab. clin. sci. NIMH, Bethesda, 1969-73; psychiatry resident diploma course in psychiatry McGill U. Sch. Medicine, Montreal Gen. Hosp., 1973-76, Montreal Children's Hosp., 1975; prof. psychiatry U. Mo.-Mo. Inst. Psychiatry, St. Louis, 1976-78; chief psychiatry svc. San Juan (P.R.) VA Hosp., pharmacy and therapeutic com. 1978-92; also prof. psychiatry U. P.R. Med. Sch., 1978-92; prof. psychiatry U. Okla. Health Scis. Ctr., Okla. City VA Med. Ctr., 1992—; spl. adviser on mental health P.R. Senate, P.R. sec. health, 1989; spl. cons. NASA, 1965-69; cons. divsn. narcotic addiction and drug abuse NIDA, 1972-73. Capt. M.C., USAR, 1960-62; sr. surgeon USPHS, 1969-71, med. dir., 1971-73. Recipient Coronas award, 1957, Ruiz-Arnau award, 1957, Diaz-Garcia award, 1957, Geigy award, 1975, 76, AMA Recognition award, 1971, 76, 81, Horner's award, 1975, 76, Pavlovian award, 1978, Recognition cert. Senate of P.R., 1986, cert. of merit Gov. of P.R., 1986. Fellow Interam. Coll. Physicians and Surgeons, Royal Coll. Physicians and Surgeons Can. (sr., cert.); mem. Am. Psychiat. Assn., Am. Physiol. Soc., Pavlovian Soc., Am. Fedn. Clin. Rsch., Am. Assn. Geriatric Psychiatry, Am. Soc. Clin. Pharmacology and Therapeutics, Am. Soc. Pharmacology and Experimental Therapeutics, Soc. Neurosci., Nat. Assn. Healthcare Quality, Internat. Soc. Rsch. Aggression, Okla. Psychiat. Assn., Am. Soc. Clin. Psychopharmacology, Menninger Found., Okla. Assn. Health Care Quality. Roman Catholic. Home: 3304 Rosewood Ln Oklahoma City OK 73120-5604 Office: Oklahoma City VA Med Ctr 921 NE 13th St Oklahoma City OK 73104-5007

PEREZ-GIMENEZ, JUAN MANUEL, federal judge; b. San Juan, P.R., Mar. 28, 1941; s. Francisco and Elisa (Gimenez) P.; m. Carmen R. Ramirez, July 16, 1964; children: Carmen E., Juan C., Jorge E., Jose A., Magdalena. BBA, U. P.R., 1963, JD, 1968; MBA, George Washington U., 1965. Bar: P.R. 1968. Ptnr. Goldman, Antonetti & Davila, San Juan, 1968-71; asst. U.S. atty. San Juan, 1971-75, U.S. magistrate, 1975-79; judge U.S. Dist. Ct. P.R., San Juan, 1979—. Mem. ABA, Fed. Bar Assn., Colegio de Abogados. Roman Catholic. Office: US Courthouse CH-125 Fed Bldg 150 Carlos Chardon Ave San Juan PR 00918-1765*

PÉREZ-GONZALEZ, ESMERALDA, principal, educator; b. Alice, Tex., Sept. 7, 1963; d. Felipe Perez and Cora Cantu Perez Carrillo. BS, Corpus Christi State U., 1987, MS, 1993; AA, Del Mar Coll., 1987. Tchr. Holy Family Sch., Corpus Christi, Tex.; prin. Archbishop Oscar Romero Middle Sch., Corpus Christi, Tex. Title VII Bilingual Edn. Fellowship grantee, Gov. Fellowship award, 1994. Mem. Tex. Assn. Bilingual Edn., PTA, Nat. Cath. Edn. Assoc., Assoc. Supervision, Curriculum Devel., Nat. Assoc. Secondary Sch. Prin., Year Round Edn., Tex. Middle Sch. Assoc., Nat. Middle Sch. Assoc., Nat. Coun. of tchrs. of Math., tex. Coun. of Tchrs. of Math. Avocations: continuing education, walks on the beach, collecting sanddollars, family. Home: 7252 Mansions Dr Apt 3J Corpus Christi TX 78414-3713

PEREZ-MENDEZ, VICTOR, physics educator; b. Guatemala, Aug. 8, 1923; came to U.S., 1946; m. 1949; 2 children. MS, Hebrew U., Israel, 1947; PhD, Columbia U., 1951. Rsch. assoc. Columbia U., N.Y.C., 1951-53, staff physicist, 1953-61; sr. scientist Lawrence Berkeley Lab., U. Calif., Berkeley, 1960—; vis. lectr. Hebrew U., 1959—; prof. physics dept. radiology U. Calif., San Francisco, 1968—. Fellow IEEE, AAAS, Am. Phys. Soc., N.Y. Acad. Sci.; mem. Soc. Photo Instrumentation Engrs. Office: U Calif Lawrence Berkeley Lab Berkeley CA 94720

PÉREZ-RIVERA, FRANCISCO, writer; b. Vertientes, Cuba, Oct. 3, 1938; came to U.S., 1968, naturalized, 1974; s. Francisco Daniel Pérez and María Eloísa Rivera. BA, Camagüey Coll., Cuba, 1955; MA in Romance Langs., U. Munich, 1967. Newsman, script writer Bavarian Radio Svc., Munich, 1964-68; newsman Associated Press, N.Y.C., 1968-92, arts and entertainment editor, 1992—; dir. Spanish programs for lang. labs., 1987. Author: (poetry) Construcciones, 1979, (novel) Las sabanas y el tiempo, 1986, (short stories) Cuentos Cubanos, 1992; co-author: Introducción a la literatura española, 1982; short stories in the anthologies New Cuban Storytellers, 1961, Cuba: Nouvelles et contes d'aujourd'hui, 1985, Narrative and Liberty: Cuban Tales of the Dispersion, 1996. Grantee German Academic Exchange Svc., Munich, 1961-67; fellow Cintas Found., N.Y., 1980. Home: 212 E 77th St Apt 1G New York NY 10021-2111 Office: AP 50 Rockefeller Plz New York NY 10020-1605

PEREZ-SILVA, GLAISMA, special education teacher; b. Mayagüez, P.R., Oct. 19, 1957; d. Ismael Pérez and Gladys (Silva) Valentin; 1 child, Andrés Guillermo Figueroa. BA in Spl. Edn., Catholic U., Ponce, P.R., 1980; MS in Spl. Edn. summa cum laude, Interam. U., Rio Piedras, P.R., 1987. Spl. edn. tchr. Manuel G. Tavarez Sch., Ponce, P.R., 1980-81, Amalia Marin Sch., Rio Piedras, P.R., 1981-82, 83-87, Carmen Gomez Tejera Sch., Rio Piedras, 1982-83, Victor Pares Sch., Rio Piedras, 1987-88; bilingual spl. edn. tchr. R. J. Kinsella Cmty. Sch., Hartford, Conn., 1988—; spl. edn. monitor R. J. Kinsella Cmty. Sch., 1993-95, program coord. enrichment program, 1994-95, coord. cultural and artistic program, 1991—, mem. governance team, 1994—; spl. edn. tchr. Hartford Bd. Edn. Summer Cmp, 1989; site supr. Ctr. City Chs. Summer Camp, Hartford, 1992, 94; tchr. coord. The Village for Families and Children Summer Program, 1995; staff writer El Extra News, Hartford, 1992-95; Spanish music dir. WFCS-FM, New Britain, Conn., 1993—; spl. reporter WFCR-Tertulia, Amherst, Mass., 1994—; lectr. in field. Tchr. Spanish Noah Webster Enrichment Program, Hartford, 1991, bd. dirs. PTA, 1991-92; collaborator D.J. WRTC, Hartford, 1991-93, Guakia, Inc., Hartford, 1991-96, vis. artist, 1996—; bd. dirs. Kinsella's Union Sch. Com., Hartford, 1991-93, Padres Abriendo Puertas, 1994; mem. adv. bd. The Writers Voice, Fairfield, Conn., 1995; advisor Kinsella Sch. and Cmty. Partnership, 1992—; ednl. advisor cultural and cmty. issues Charter Oak Cultural Ctr., Hartford, 1993, bd. dirs., 1995; mem. steering com. P.R. Cultural Day Wadsworth Atheneum, Hartford, 1993-94, 94-96, co-chair, 1994-95, bd. electors, 1995; bd. dirs. Cimarrona: Centro de la Mujer Puertorriquena (Puerto Rican Woman Center), Hartford, 1995, pres., 1996—; advisory bd. mem. Centro de Reafirmaciñn Familiar, Hartford, 1996—. Mem. Hartford Fedn. Tchrs. Avocations: reading, drawing, crafts, music, poetry. Office: RJ Kinsella Community Sch 65 Van Block Ave Hartford CT 06106-2826

PEREZ-VALDES, YVONNE ANN, nurse, educator; b. Tampa, Fla., May 18, 1946; d. Raimundo Abal and Encarnita (Perez) P. ASN, St. Petersburg Jr. Coll., 1978. Cert. ob-gyn., pediatric ICU nurse, RN, Fla. Nurse St. Joseph Hosp., Tampa, Fla., 1966-71, cardiologist office nurse mgr., 1976-78; ICCU nurse U. Community Hosp., Tampa, Fla., 1979-80; emergency rm. charge nurse, ICCU asst. head nurse Centro Asturiano Hosp., Tampa, Fla., 1980-85; mem. faculty, head dept. nursing Tampa Coll., 1985-88; supr., dir. edn. Oakwood Nursing Home, Tampa, 1988-89; instr. health Hillsborough County Schs., Tampa, 1989-95; developer staff, mgr. risk, dir. edn. safety and pers. Meadowbrook Manor Tampa, 1994-95; faculty mem. Health Industry & Adv. Bd., Tampa, 1992-95; bilingual instr. for refugee asst. program Ideal Sch., Miami, Fla., 1980—; pvt. duty home health nurse, 1972-75; office nurse mgr. for cardiologist/internist, 1975-76. Author: Cry Out, I'm Listening. Mem.-at-large Nat. Rep. Com., Washington, 1991-92; mem. Presdl. Com., Washington, 1991-95, Senatorial Com., Washington, 1991-95. Name included Benefactor's Wall Am. Nursing Found. Bldg., Washington. Mem. ANA, ARC, Am. Cancer Assn., Am. Hispanic Nurses (chmn. 1992), Fla. Nurses Assn., Tampa Nurses Assn., St. Joseph's Hosp. Devel. Coun., Nat. Audubon Soc., Am. Diabetes Assn. Democrat. Roman Catholic. Avocations: photography, reading, boating, travel, writing. Office: Hillsborough County Schs Ctr for Tng 5410 N 20th St Tampa FL 33610-8213 also: Meadowbrook Manor Tampa 8720 Jackson Springs Rd Tampa FL 33615-3210

PERFIDO, RUTH S., lawyer; b. Pitts., Oct. 10, 1941. BA, Newcomb Coll., 1963; JD, U. Pitts., 1977. Bar: Pa. 1977. Ptnr. Reed Smith Shaw & McClay, Pitts. Office: Reed Smith Shaw & McClay Mellon Sq 435 6th Ave Pittsburgh PA 15219-1809*

PERHACH, JAMES LAWRENCE, pharmaceutical company executive; b. Pitts., Oct. 26, 1943; s. James Lawrence and Elizabeth Louise (Hoffman) P.; m. Judith Irene Selter, Apr. 15, 1967; children: Laura Anne, Amy Elizabeth. BS, U. Dayton, 1966; MS, U. Pitts., 1969, PhD, 1971. Sr. scientist dept. pharmacology Mead Johnson Rsch. Ctr., 1971-74, sr. investigator dept. biol. rsch., 1974-76, sr. rsch. assoc. dept. biol. rsch., 1976-77, sr. rsch. assoc. dept. pathology and toxicology, 1977-78, prin. rsch. assoc. dept. pathology and toxicology, 1978-80; dir. pharmacology Wallace Biol. Rsch., Wallace Labs. div. Carter-Wallace Inc., Cranbury, N.J., 1980, exec. dir. biol. rsch., 1980-84, assoc. dir. clin. rsch., 1984-85, dir. clin. investigation, 1985-87, v.p. clin. pharmacology and pharmacokinetics, 1987—; vis. asst. prof. dept. pharmacy practice and adminstrn. Coll. Pharmacy Rutgers U., 1993—; adj. prof. toxicology Phila. Coll. Pharmacy and Sci., 1981—; assoc. faculty Evansville Ctr. Med. Edn., Ind. U., 1973-80; lectr. grad. physiology U. Evansville, 1973-79; scientific adv. bd. Clin. Rsch. Ctr., U. Med. Dentistry, N.J., 1995— apptd. med. pharmacologist, 1993, sec., 1994, chmn., 1985-86; mem. drug utilization rev. coun. State of N.J., 1983—; mem. substance abuse com. Tri-State Area Health Planning Coun., Evansville, 1972-75; mem. addictions mem. edn. program Evansville Ctr. for Med. Edn., 1972-78. Fellow Am. Coll. Clin. Pharmacology; mem. AAAS, Am. Soc. Clin. Pharmacology and Therapeutics, Am. Soc. Pharmacology and Exptl. Therapeutics, Am. Coll. Toxicology, European Soc. Toxicology, Soc. Exptl. Biology and Medicine, Soc. Neurosci., N.Y. Acad. Sci., Physiol. Soc. Phila., Drug Info. Assn., Sigma Xi. Research in drug discovery, elucidation of mechanism of action and safety evaluation of new therapeutic agents. Home: 6 Highfield Ct Lawrenceville NJ 08648-1077 Office: Wallace LabsHalf Acre Rd PO Box 1001 301B College Rd E Princeton NJ 08512-6608

PERHACS, MARYLOUISE HELEN, musician, educator; b. Teaneck, N.J., June 15, 1944; d. John Andrew and Helen Audrey (Hosage) P.; m. Robert Theodore Sirinek, Jan. 27, 1968 (div. Jan. 1975). Student, Ithaca (N.Y.) Coll., 1962-64; BS, Juilliard Sch., 1967, MS, 1968; postgrad., Hunter Coll., 1976, St. Peter's Coll., Jersey City, N.J., 1977. Cert. music tchr., N.Y., N.J. Instr. Carnegie Hall, N.Y.C., 1966-69; program developer, coord., instr. urban edn. program Newburgh (N.Y.) Pub. Sch. System, 1968-69; adj. prof. dept. edn. St. Peter's Coll., Jersey City, 1976-92; tchr. brass instruments Indian Hills High Sch., Oakland, N.J., 1976; tchr. Jersey City Pub. Schs., 1976-77, N.Y.C. Pub. Sch., Bronx, 1980-84; pvt. tchr. Cliffside Park, N.J., 1976—; vocal music tchr. East Rutherford, N.J., 1990; tchr. music Bergen County Spl. Svcs. Sch. Dist., 1990-91; tchr. gen. music Little Ferry (N.J.) Pub. Schs., 1991-92; tchr. mid. sch. instrumental Paramus (N.J.) Pub. Schs., 1993-94; tchr. vocal music West New York (N.J.) Pub Schs., 1995—; Park Ridge N.J. High Sch. Summer Instrumental Music Pgm., 1995, and 1996, teacher, singer, trumpeter Norwegian Caribbean Lines, 1981-82, Jimmy Dorsey Band, Paris and London, 1974; music and edn. lecture cir., 1992—. Singer with Original PDQ Bach Okay Chorale, 1966, Live from Carnegie Hall Recordings, 1970, St. Louis Mcpl. Opera, 1970, Ed Sullivan Show, 1970; singer, dancer, actress (Broadway shows) Promises, Promises, 1969-71, Sugar, 1971-72, Lysistrata, 1972; trumpeter (Broadway shows) Jesus Christ Superstar, 1973, Debbie!, 1976, Sarava!, 1979, Fiddler on the Roof, Lincoln Ctr., 1981, Sophisticated Ladies, 1982; writer, host series on women in music Columbia Cable/United Artists, 1984; recordings: Carnegie Hall Live, Avery Fisher Hall, Lincoln Ctr. Cons. to cadette troop Girl Scouts U.S., Jersey City, 1967-68, Bergen County N.J. Coun., 1995—. Mem. NEA, AFTRA, Actors Equity Assn., Am. Fedn. Musicians (mem. theatre com. local 802 N.Y.C. 1972—, chmn. 1973), AFM Local N.J. 248, Music Educators Nat. Conf., N.J. Music Educators Assn., N.J. Sch. Music Assn., N.J. Edn. Assn., , Internat. Women's Brass Conf. (charter mem.), Internat. Trumpet Guild, Women of Accomplishment (charter mem. 1992), Mu Phi Epsilon. Democrat. Episcopalian. Avocations: cats, cake decorating, food sculpting, horticulture, sewing. Home and Office: 23 Crescent Ave Cliffside Park NJ 07010-3003

PERHAM, ROY GATES, III, industrial psychologist; b. Hackensack, N.J., Apr. 22, 1958; s. Roy Gates Jr. and Titania Joan (Robbitts) P. BA with honors, Bates Coll., 1980; MS, Stevens Inst. Tech., 1982, PhD, 1989. Intern Sen. Edmund S. Muskie, Washington, 1978; psychometrician Lab. Psychol. Studies Stevens Inst. Tech., Hoboken, N.J., 1981-83, instr., 1985, adj. asst. prof., 1990—; adj. asst. prof. Fairleigh Dickinson U., Rutherford, N.J., 1986; sr. assoc. AAI Orgnl. Performance Cons., Florham Park, N.J., 1990-94; assessment projects mgr. Tech. Employee Selection and Tng. Inc., Hasbrouck Heights, N.J., 1995—; WordStar coord. N.Y. Computer Soc., N.Y.C., 1985-88. Chmn. Juvenile Conf. Com., hasbrouck Heights and Wood-Ridge, N.J., 1985-95; mem. N.J. State Juvenile Delinquency Commn., Trenton, N.J., 1988-91; county exec.'s rep. Bergen County Youth Svcs. Commn., 1990—, chair, 1994-96; chair Bergen County Task Force on Youth Violence, 1993—; mem. adv. council to N.J. Juvenile Justice Commn., 1995—. Named Citizen of Yr., Lions Club of Hasbrouck Heights, N.J., 1988. Mem. APA, Am. Psychol. Soc., Met. N.Y. Assn. for Applied Psychology, Soc. for Indsl./Orgnl. Psychology, Inc., Phi Beta Kappa, Psi Chi. Home: 269 Raymond St Hasbrouck Heights NJ 07604-1723 Office: Technical Employee Selection & Tng Inc The Profl Bldg 248 Blvd Hasbrouck Heights NJ 07604

PERICH, TERRY MILLER, secondary school educator; b. Greensburg, Pa., Sept. 22, 1948; s. Miller and Eleanor Ann (Schmuck) P.; m. Kathleen Ann Ferrari, July 26, 1975. BA in Elem. Edn., Edinboro U., 1970; elem. cert., Pa. State U., 1973; Masters equivalency degree, U. Pitts., 1994; postgrad., Carlow Coll., 1994. Trained student assistance profl., Pa.; cert. tchr. elem. edn. Tchr. sci. and math. Penn Trafford Schs., Harrison City, Pa., 1970—; mentor, tchr. Tchr. Enhancement Inst. St. Vincent Coll., Latrobe, Pa.; selected tchr. Watershed Restoration St. Vincent Coll., Latrobe. County committeeman Dem. Party, Penn Twp., Pa., 1994—; lion tamer Bushy Run Lions Club, Claridge, Pa., 1993—, 3rd v.p., 1995, 2d v.p., 1996. Recipient Commendation, Pres.-elect Clinton, SAP award for working with students at risk St. Vincent Coll. Prevention Projects, 1991. Mem. NEA, ASCD, PACE, Nat. Sci. Tchrs. Assn., Pa. Tchrs. Edn. Assn., Pa. Sci. Tchrs. Assn., Westmoreland County Assn. Student Assistance Profls. (bd. dirs. 1992-94, mem. Westmoreland county student assistance team 1995-96), Penn Trafford Edn. Assn. (exec. bd. dirs. 1990-91). Roman Catholic. Avocations: travel, education. Home: 13 Rizzi Dr Irwin PA 15642-8902 Office: Penn Mid Sch PO Box 368 Watt Rd Claridge PA 15623

PERILLO, GIULIO, controller; b. Udine, Italy, May 16, 1946; came to U.S., 1947; m. Mary Kathleen Gore, June 29, 1968; children: Christopher, Tara. BA in Econs., Rutgers U., 1968; MBA in Mktg., Seton Hall U., 1977. Mgr. mfg. acctg. Ortho Pharm. Co., Sommerville, N.J., 1977-78, div. controller, 1978-80; group controller Ortho Pharm. Co., Raritan, N.J., 1980-83; v.p. fin., treas. Pitman-Moore, Inc., Washington Crossing, N.J., 1983-84; v.p. surg. products Rorer Group Inc., Ft. Washington, Pa., 1984-85, corp. controller, 1985-86, v.p., controller, 1986—. Served to 1st lt. U.S. Army, 1969-72. Home: 2085 Grantham Ave Berwyn PA 19312-2119 Office: Rhone Plenc Rrer Pharm 500 Arcola Rd Collegeville PA 19426-3930*

PERIN, DONALD WISE, JR., former association executive; b. Newton, Mass., Feb. 28, 1915; s. Donald Wise and Beatrice Franklin (Cobb) P.; m. Jean Newcomb Mulcahy, Dec. 5, 1942; children: William Kirk, Betsy Cobb, Donald Wise. Student, Norwich U., 1932-34; B.A., Columbia U., 1936. With Gt. Am. Indemnity Co., N.Y.C., 1936-50; asst. sec. Gt. Am. Indemnity Co., 1946-50; asst. sec.-treas. Nat. Assn. Ins. Agts., N.Y.C., 1950-54; v.p. Alexander & Co., Chgo., 1954-63, Great Am. Ins. Co., N.Y.C., 1964-69; dir. research Ind. Ins. Agts. of Am., N.Y.C., 1970-79; exec. v.p. Ind. Ins. Agts. of Am., 1979-81, exec. v.p. emeritus, 1981. Served with U.S. Army, 1940-46, PTO. Mem. Am. Soc. Assn. Execs., Soc. C.P.C.U.'s, Sigma Alpha Epsilon. Republican. Methodist. Home and Office: Monument Ave Bennington VT 05201

PERITORE, LAURA, law librarian; b. San Francisco, Nov. 28, 1945; d. Attilio and Anita (Firenzi) Marcenaro; children: Victor Anthony, Phillip Michael. BA, U. Calif., Santa Barbara, 1967, MA, 1970; MLS, U. Mo., 1974. Asst. libr. Mo. Hist. Soc., Columbia, 1971-74, 77-79; asst. libr. Hastings Law Libr., San Francisco, 1980-86, assoc. libr., 1986—; part-time tchr. legal rsch. City Coll., San Francisco, 1990-91. Author: Guide to California County Probate and Vital Records, 1994; contbr. articles and monographs to profl. jours. Mem. Am. Assn. Law Librs., No. Calif. Assn. Law Librs. (asst. editor newsletter 1984-86, workshop com. 1988, advt. editor 1990-91, sec. 1993-94, grantee 1984). Avocations: piano, yoga, cooking. Office: Hastings Law Libr 200 Mcallister St San Francisco CA 94102-4707

PERITZ, ABRAHAM DANIEL, business executive; b. Ellenville, N.Y., Aug. 12, 1940; s. Harry and Ida (Koblin) P.; m. Marleen Minkoff, Dec. 12, 1964; children—Alaine, Marc. B.A., Hartwick Coll., Oneonta, N.Y., 1962; postgrad., Baruch Coll., 1967. Asst. restaurant mgr. Concord Hotel, Kiamesha Lake, N.Y., 1962-64; with Ruder Finn, Inc., N.Y.C., 1965—, v.p., controller, 1972-75, chief fin. officer, 1976-82, treas., 1983—. Treas. Kingsley Sq. Townhouse Assn., Freehold, N.J., 1974-75. Served with USAR, 1964. Democrat. Jewish. Home: 127 Kingsley Way Freehold NJ 07728-1667 Office: Ruder Finn Inc 301 E 57th St New York NY 10022-2900

PERKIEL, MITCHEL H., lawyer; b. N.Y.C., Oct. 26, 1949; s. Frank and Ella Perkiel; m. Lois E. Perkiel, June 24, 1984; children: Joshua L., Alexa Kim, Griffin. BA, SUNY, Stony Brook, 1971; JD, New York Law Sch.,

1974. Bar: N.Y. 1975, U.S. Dist. Ct. (so. and ea. dists.) N.Y. 1975, U.S. Ct. Appeals (2d cir.) 1975, Conn. 1988. Law clk. to presiding justice N.Y. County Civil Ct., 1975; assoc. Levin & Weintraub & Crames, N.Y.C., 1975-80, ptnr., 1980-90; with Kaye, Scholer, Fierman, Hayes & Handler, N.Y.C. Notes and comments editor New York Law Rev., 1973-74. Served with USAR, 1969-73. Mem. ABA, Assn. of Bar of City of N.Y., Am. Bankruptcy Inst. Office: Kaye Scholer Fierman Hayes & Handler 425 Park Ave New York NY 10022-3506

PERKIN, GORDON WESLEY, international health agency executive; b. Toronto, Ont., Can., Apr. 25, 1935; came to U.S., 1962; s. Irvine Boyer and Jean (Laing) P.; m. Elizabeth Scott, Dec. 21, 1957; children: Scott, Stuart. MD, U. Toronto, 1959. Asst. dir. clin. research Ortho Research Found., Raritan, N.J., 1962-64; assoc. med. dir. Planned Parenthood Fedn. Am., N.Y.C., 1964-66; program advisor Ford Found., N.Y.C., 1966-67; regional program advisor Ford Found., Bangkok, 1967-69, Rio de Janeiro, 1973-76; program officer Ford Found., Mexico City, 1976-80; project specialist Ministry Fin. and Econ. Planning, Accra, Ghana, 1969-70; cons. World Health Orgn., Geneva, 1971-73; pres. Program for Appropriate Tech. in Health, Seattle, 1980—; affiliate prof. pub. health, U. Wash., Seattle. Contbr. numerous articles to profl. jours. Am. Pub. Health Assn. fellow, 1970. Mem. Planned Parenthood Fedn. Am. (bd. dirs. 1983-89), Planned Parenthood Seattle-King County (bd. dirs. 1982—, mem. exec. com. 1983-86), Nat. Coun. for Internat. Health (bd. govs. 1984-95), Nat. Acad. Scis. (com. mem. 1987-90), Alan Guttmacher Inst. (bd. dirs. 1985-90), Assn. Reproductive Health Profls., Alpha Omega Alpha. Office: PATH 4 Nickerson St Seattle WA 98109-1651

PERKIN, HAROLD JAMES, social historian, educator; b. Stoke-on-Trent, Eng., Nov. 11, 1926; s. Robert James and Hilda May (Dillon) P.; BA 1st class with distinction (major scholar coll., Bell exhibitioner univ.), Cambridge U., 1948, MA, 1952; m. Joan Griffiths, July 3, 1948; children: Deborah Jane, Julian Robert. Asst. lectr., then lectr. social history Manchester U., 1951-65; sr. lectr. Lancaster U., 1965-67, prof. social history, 1967-84, dir. centre social history, 1975-84; Andrew W. Mellon disting. prof. humanities Rice U., Houston, 1984; prof. history Northwestern U., Evanston, Ill., 1985—, prof. higher edn., 1987—; vis. fellow Princeton U., 1979-80; fellow Nat. Humanities Center, N.C., 1982-83. Served with RAF, 1948-50. Recipient Gold medal Nat. Inst. Ednl. Research, Tokyo, 1982. Fellow Royal Hist. Soc., 1969—, John Simon Guggenheim fellow, 1989-90; v.p. Social History Soc. U.K. (founding chmn. 1976), Econ. History Soc., Soc. Study Labour History, History of Edn. Soc., Assn. U. Tchrs. (pres. 1970-71). Author: The Origins of Modern English Society, 1780-1880, 1969; Key Profession: The History of the Association of University Teachers, 1969; New Universities in the U.K., 1969; The Age of the Railway, 1970; The Age of the Automobile, 1976; The Structured Crowd, 1980; Professionalism, Property and English Society since 1880, 1981; The Rise of Professional Society: England since 1880, 1989, Higher Education and English Society, Japanese translation, 1993, The Third Revolution: International Professional Elites in the Modern World, 1996. Home: 106 St Mary's Mansions, London W2 1SZ, England Office: Hist Dept Northwestern U 633 Clark St Evanston IL 60208-0001

PERKINS, BOB(BY) F(RANK), geologist, dean; b. Greenville, Tex., Dec. 9, 1929; s. William Frank and Vela Beatrice (Richey) P.; m. Patricia Katharine Woodhull, May 25, 1954; children: Katharine Harriet, Marianna Lea, Orrin Woodhull. B.S., So. Methodist U., 1949, M.S., 1950; Ph.D., U. Mich., 1956. Instr. geology and biology So. Meth. U., 1950-51, 53-56; asst. prof. geology U. Houston, 1956-57; rsch. paleontologist Shell Devel. Corp., Houston, 1957-66; prof. geology La. State U., Baton Rouge, 1966-75; chmn., dir. Sch. Geosci. La. State U., 1973-75; prof. geology, dean Grad. Sch. U. Tex., Arlington, 1975-95; also assoc. v.p. research Grad. Sch., U. Tex., Arlington, 1975-93; exec. dir. Gulf Coast sect. Soc. Econ. Paleontologists and Mineralogists Found., 1983—. Editor: 15 vol. series Geoscience and Man, 1970-75; contbr. articles to profl. jours. Fellow Geol. Soc. Am., AAAS, Tex. Acad. Sci.; mem. Paleontol. Soc., Am. Assn. Petroleum Geologists, Paleontol. Soc. Gt. Britain, Soc. Econ. Paleontologists and Mineralologists, Malacological Soc. London. Home: 165 Pinehurst Rd West Hartland CT 06091

PERKINS, BRADFORD, history educator; b. Rochester, N.Y., Mar. 6, 1925; s. Dexter and Wilma (Lord) P.; m. Nancy Nash Tucker, June 18, 1949 (dec.); children: Dexter III, Matthew Edward, Martha Nash. A.B., Harvard U., 1946, Ph.D., 1952. From instr. to asso. prof. history U. Calif. at, Los Angeles, 1952-62; prof. history U. Mich., 1962—, chmn. dept., 1971-72, 80-81; Commonwealth Fund lectr. Univ. Coll., London, Eng., 1964; vis. prof. history Brandeis U., 1970, Ecole des Hautes Etudes en Sciences Sociales, Paris, 1983; Albert Shaw lectr. Johns Hopkins U., 1979; mem. council Inst. Early Am. History and Culture, 1968-71; program dir. Nat. Endowment for Humanities Fellowships in Residence for Coll. Tchrs., 1974-75. Author: The First Rapprochement: England and the United States, 1795-1805, 1955, Youthful America, 1960, Prologue to War: England and the United States, 1805-1812, 1961, Causes of the War of 1812, 1962, Castlereagh and Adams: England and the United States, 1812- 1823, 1964, The Great Rapprochement: England and the United States, 1895-1914, 1968, The Creation of a Republican Empire, 1993. Served with AUS, 1943-45, ETO. Decorated Bronze Star.; Recipient Bancroft prize, 1965, Disting. Faculty award U. Mich., 1986; Warren fellow, 1969-70; Social Sci. Research Council faculty research fellow, 1957-60; Guggenheim fellow, 1962-63. Mem. Am. Hist. Assn., Soc. Am. Historians, Orgn. Am. Historians (coun. 1969-72), Soc. Historians Am. Fgn. Rels. (coun. 1967-72, pres. 1974, Graebner award 1992), Mass. Hist. Soc., Am. Antiquarian Soc. Home: 3401 Berry Rd Ypsilanti MI 48198-9423

PERKINS, CHARLES, III, newspaper editor; b. Brockton, Mass., July 25, 1952; s. Charles II and Barbara Perkins; m. Linda C. Burroughs, Jan. 4, 1985. BA, Dartmouth Coll., 1975. Editor Journal-Opinion, Bradford, Vt., 1977-78; reporter, editor The Union Leader and N.H. Sunday News, Manchester, N.H., 1978-81; Sunday editor N.H. Sunday News, Manchester, 1981-84; mng. editor The Union Leader and N.H. Sunday News, Manchester, 1984-92, exec. editor, 1992—. Office: PO Box 9555 Manchester NH 03108-9555

PERKINS, CHERYL GREEN, certified public accountant; b. Spokane, Wash., Dec. 16, 1945; d. Philip Benjamen and Vera Kay (Broyles) Green; m. T. Don Perkins, Sept. 27, 1976; 1 child, Alan Kent. BBA, Wash. State U., 1968; MBA, U. Oreg., 1969. CPA, Oreg. CPA KPMG Peat Marwick, San Francisco, Portland, Oreg., 1969-75; CPA, ptnr. Isler & Co., Portland, Oreg., 1976-81; CPA, shareholder Perkins Jeddeloh & Acheson, Portland, Oreg., 1981-86, Perkins & Co., P.C., Portland, Oreg., 1986—. Co-author: Real Estate Taxation, 1982. Community bd. mem. Meridian Park Hosp.; mem. deferred giving com. St. Vincent Hosp., Portland, 1987—; trustee Marylhurst (Oreg.) Coll., 1984-86. Named One of Best Tax Practioners in Oreg., Money Mag., 1987. Mem. AICPA, Oreg. Soc. CPAs (chmn. various coms. 1974—), Portland Tax Forum (bd. dirs. 1989—), Portland Estate Planning Coun. (bd. dirs. 1989-94), Multnomah Athletic Club. Republican. Office: Perkins & Co PC 1211 SW 5th Ste 1200 Portland OR 97204-3623

PERKINS, DAVID, English language educator; b. Philadelphia, Pa., Oct. 25, 1928; s. Dwight Goss and Esther M. (Williams) P. A.B., Harvard U., 1951, M.A., 1952, Ph.D., 1955. Mem. faculty Harvard U., 1957—, prof. English, 1964-94, chmn. dept. English, 1976-81, chmn. dept. lit., 1987-89, prof. emeritus, 1994—; vis. prof. Goettingen U., 1968-69. Author: The Quest for Permanence: the Symbolism of Wordsworth, Shelley and Keats, 1959, Wordsworth and the Poetry of Sincerity, 1964, English Romantic Writers, 1967, A History of Modern Poetry: From the 1890's to the High Modernist Mode, 1976, A History of Modern Poetry, Vol. 2, Modernism and After, 1987; (with W. Jackson Bate) British and American Poets: Chaucer to the Present, 1986, Is Literary History Possible, 1991; editor: The Teaching of Literature: What is Needed Now, 1988, Theoretical Issues in Literary History, 1991; mem. editorial adv. bd. Keats-Shelley Jour., 1962-89, The Wordsworth Circle. Served with AUS, 1955-57. Guggenheim fellow, 1962, 73; Fulbright fellow, 1968-69; Am. Council Learned Socs. fellow, 1977. Mem. Am. Acad. Arts and Scis., Cambridge Sci. Club. Home: 984 Memorial Dr # 304 Cambridge MA 02138-4701

PERKINS, DAVID LAYNE, SR., architect; b. Picayune, Miss., Mar. 3, 1925; s. Robert E. and Henrietta (Browne) P.; m. Edna Blanche Rice, Jan. 23, 1954; children—David Layne Jr., Richard Scott. B.Arch., Tulane U., 1954. Registered architect, La. Designer, draftsman Curtis & Davis Architects, New Orleans, 1948-53; designer M. Wayne Stoffle, Architect, New Orleans, 1954; asst. prof. of architecture U. Southwestern La., Lafayette, 1954-57, 86-87, 88; prin. David L. Perkins, Architect, Lafayette, 1955-75; pres., sr. ptnr. Perkins-Guidry-Young, Architects, Inc., Lafayette, 1975-88; pres., sr. ptnr., chmn. Perkins-Guidry-Beazley-Ostteen, Architects, Inc., Lafayette, 1985-90; pvt. practice cons. architect Lafayette, 1988—; bd. dirs. St. Joseph's Home; past pres., 1st v.p., treas., bd. dirs. Nat. Archtl. Accrediting Bd.; past dir. gulf states region AIA Nat Bd. Dirs.; past pres., v.p., bd. dirs. La. Architects Assn.; mem. dean's council Tulane U. Sch. Arch. Prin. works include office bldgs., Lafayette Pub. Library, neuropsychiat. clinic. Mem. adv. bd. Lafayette Cath. Service Ctr. Inc. Served to capt. USAF, 1943-45, 51-52. Fellow AIA (pres. So. La. chpt. 1963-64, honor award So. La. chpt. 1982, 83, 85, bd. dirs. 1975-78, award of excellence 1982); mem. La. Architects Assn. (honor award 1963, 64, 70, 74, 82, 83). Republican. Presbyterian. Avocation: boating, woodworking. Home: 503 Marjorie Blvd Lafayette LA 70503-3147 Office: PO Box 51762 Lafayette LA 70505-1762

PERKINS, DWIGHT HEALD, economics educator; b. Chgo., Oct. 20, 1934; s. Lawrence Bradford and Margery (Blair) P.; m. Julie Rate, June 15, 1957; children: Lucy Fitch, Dwight Edward, Caleb Blair. B.A., Cornell U., 1956; A.M., Harvard U., 1961, Ph.D., 1964. From instr. to assoc. prof. Harvard U., Cambridge, Mass., 1963-69, prof. econs., 1969-81, assoc. dir. East Asian Research Ctr., 1973-77, chmn. dept. econs., 1977-80, H.H. Burbank prof. polit. economy, 1981—; dir. Harvard Inst. Internat. Devel., Cambridge, 1980-95; dir. Nat. Com. on U.S.-China Rels., 1991—; trustee China Med. Bd., 1995—; cons. permanent subcom. on investigations U.S. Senate, 1974-80; H.M. Jackson vis. prof. Chinese studies U. Wash., 1985, Phi Beta Kappa lectr., 1992-93, Faculty Salzburg seminar, 1996; mem. Internat. Adv. Group to Prime Min. of Papua, New Guinea, 1991-92; cons. Korea Devel. Inst., 1972-80. Author: Agricultural Develoopment in China, 1368-1968, 1969, Market Control and Planning in Communist China, 1966, China: Asia's Next Economic Giant?, 1986, (with E.S. Mason and others) The Economic Modernization of Korea, 1980, (with S. Yusuf) Rural Development in China, 1984, (with M. Gillis and others) Economics of Development, 1983, 4th edit., 1996; editor: China's Modern Economy in Historical Perspective, 1975, (with M. Roemer) Reforming Economic Systems in Developing Countries, 1991. Mem. Vis. Com. Far Ea. Studies, U. Chgo., 1973-77; mem. bd. govs. East-West Ctr., Honolulu, 1979-82; co-moderator Aspen Inst. Seminar on Korea, Colo., 1980-83. Lt. (j.g.) USNR, 1956-58. Fgn. Area Tng. fellow Ford Found., N.Y., 1958-62; NSF Sci. Faculty fellow Tokyo, 1968-69. Mem. Assn. Asian Studies, Assn. Comparative Econ. Systems (past pres.), Am. Econ. Assn., Phi Beta Kappa. Home: 64 Pinehurst Rd Belmont MA 02178-1504 Office: Harvard Inst Internat Devel One Eliot St Cambridge MA 02138-5781

PERKINS, EDWARD J., diplomat; b. Sterlington, La., June 8, 1928; m. Lucy Liu; children: Katherine, Sarah. Student, U. Calif., Lewis and Clark Coll.; BA, U. Md., 1967; MPA, U. So. Calif., 1972, DPA, 1978; studied French, Fgn. Service Inst., 1983; LLD (hon.), U. Md., 1990, St. John's U., 1990, Lewis and Clark Coll., 1988; LHD (hon., Winston-Salem State U., 1990; LHD (hon.), Bowie State Coll., 1993; HHD (hon.), St. Augustine Coll., 1991, Beloit Coll., 1990, U. So. Calif., 1995. Chief of pers. Army and Air Force Exch. Svc., Taipei, Taiwan, 1958-62; dep. chief Army and Air Force Exch. Svc., Okinawa, Japan, 1962-64; chief pers. and adminstrn. Army and Air Force Exchange Service, Okinawa, Japan, 1964-66; asst. gen. svcs. officer Far East bur. AID, 1967-69, mgmt. analyst, 1969-70; asst. dir. for mgmt. U.S. Ops. Mission to Thailand, 1970-72; staff asst. Office of Dir. Gen. Fgn. Svc., 1972, personnel officer, 1972-74; adminstrv. officer Bur. Near Eastern and South Asian Affairs, 1974-75; mgmt. analysis officer Office Mgmt. Ops., Dept. State, 1975-78; counselor for polit. affairs Accra, Ghana, 1978-81; dep. chief of mission Monrovia, Liberia, 1981-83; dir. Office of West African Affairs, Bur. African Affairs, Dept. State, 1983-85; U.S. amb. to Liberia, 1985-86, U.S. amb. to South Africa, 1986-89; dir. gen., dir. pers. Fgn. Svc., Dept. of State, Washington, 1989-92; U.S. rep. to UN N.Y.C., 1992-93; U.S. amb. to Australia Canberra, 1993—. Contbr. articles to profl. publs. Bd. dirs. Lewis and Clark Coll., 1994—. Recipient Presdl. Meritorious Svc. award, 1987, Presdl. Disting. Svc. award, 1989, Meritorious Honor award AID, 1967, Disting. Alumni award U. So. Calif., 1991, Achievement award So. U., 1991, award for outstanding svc. as fgn. svc. officer Una Chapman Cox Found., 1989, Living Legend award The Links, Inc., 1989. Fellow Nat. Acad. Pub. Adminstrn.; mem. VFW, ASPA, Conf. Minority Pub. Adminstrs., Navy League, Sigma Pi Phi, Kappa Alpha Psi, Inc. (Laurel Wreath award 1993, C. Rodger Wilson Leadership Conf. award 1990, Disting. Svc. award 1989, Outstanding Achievement award for Fgn. Svc. 1986), Phi Kappa Phi. Office: Am Embassy Canberra Dept State Washington DC 20521-7800

PERKINS, ELIZABETH ANN, actress; b. Queens, N.Y.. Grad., Goodman Theatre, Chgo., 1981. Films include: About Last Night, 1986, From the Hip, 1987, Sweet Hearts Dance, 1988, Big, 1988, Love at Large, 1990, Enid is Sleeping, 1990, Avalon, 1990, He Said/She Said, 1991, The Doctor, 1991, Indian Summer, 1993, The Flintstones, 1994, Miracle on 34th Street, 1994, Moonlight and Valentino, 1995; TV film: For Their Own Good, 1993; theater: Brighton Beach Memoirs, 1984, Playwrights' Horizon, Ensemble Studio Theater, N.Y. Shakespeare Festival, Four Dogs and a Bone, 1995. Office: c/o Susan Culley & Assocs 150 S Rodeo Dr Ste 220 Beverly Hills CA 90212-1825

PERKINS, FRANK OVERTON, marine scientist, educator; b. Fork Union, Va., Feb. 14, 1938; s. Frank Otie and Mary Ella (Hughes) P.; m. Beverly Anne Weeks. BA, U. Va., 1960; MS, Fla. State U., Tallahassee, 1962, PhD, 1966. Marine scientist Va. Inst. Marine Sci., Coll. William and Mary, Gloucester Point, Va., 1966-69; sr. marine scientist Va. Inst. Marine Sci., Coll. William and Mary, Gloucester Point, 1969-77, asst. dir., 1977-81, dir., dean Sch. Marine Sci., 1981-91, prof. marine sci., 1991—. Baptist. Home: 101 Loblolly Ct Yorktown VA 23692-4252 Office: Va Inst of Marine Sci College of William and Mary Gloucester Point VA 23062

PERKINS, FREDERICK MYERS, retired oil company executive; b. Tallahassee, Fla., Oct. 7, 1928; s. Frederick Myers and Nancy Evelyn (Turner) P.; m. Rosemary Ross, Dec. 21, 1950; children: Lucille Lambert Reed, Nancy Evelyn Cavanagh, Matthew Myers. B.Ch.E., U. Fla., 1951, M.S., 1952. Prodn. research engr. Humble Oil & Refining Co., Houston, 1952-62, prodn. staff coordinator, 1963-65; reservoir engr. Humble Oil & Refining Co., New Orleans, 1965-66; prodn. mgr. Humble Oil & Refining Co., Corpus Chrisiti, Tex., 1966-70; petroleum economist Standard Oil Co. N.J., N.Y.C., 1962-63; dep. mng. dir. Esso Australia Ltd., Sydney, 1970-72; gen. mgr. natural gas Exxon Co. U.S.A., Houston, 1972-76, v.p. prodn., 1976-79, dep. mgr. producing Exxon Corp., 1979-80, v.p. gas, 1980-85, v.p. producing, 1985-86; pres. Exxon Prodn. Research Co., Houston, 1986-93; ret., 1993. Patentee in field. Served with U.S. Army, 1946-47, PTO. Mem. Soc. Petroleum Engrs., Galveston Country Club, Petroleum Club.

PERKINS, GEORGE HOLMES, architectural educator, architect; b. Cambridge, Mass., Oct. 10, 1904; s. George Howard and Josephine (Schock) P.; m. Georgia Hencken, June 3, 1933; children—Gray H., Jennifer H. Student, Phillips-Exeter Acad., 1920-22; A.B., Harvard U., 1926, M.Arch., 1929; LL.D., U. Pa., 1972. Instr. architecture U. Mich., 1929-30; instr. architecture Harvard, 1930-36, asst. prof., 1936-39, asso. prof., 1939-42, Norton prof. regional planning, chmn. dept., 1945-51; dean, chmn. dept. architecture Grad. Sch. Fine Arts, U. Pa., 1951-71, prof. architecture and urbanism, 1971—; practicing architect and city planner, 1933—; asst. regional rep., acting dir. urban devel. div. Nat. Housing Agy., 1942-45; cons. Brit. Ministry of Town and Country Planning, 1946, UN, 1946, 55-56; cons. to Govt. Turkey, 1958-60, Balt. Redevel. Authority, Cambridge Redevel. Authority, Worcester Redevel. Authority.; Mem. Cambridge Planning Bd., 1950-51; dir. Phila. Housing Assn., 1951-56, pres., 1953-56; dir. Citizens Council City Planning, 1951-54; chmn. Phila. Zoning Commn., 1955-58, Phila. City Planning Commn., 1958-68; dir. Phila. Port Corp., Old Phila. Devel. Corp., Phila. Indsl. Devel. Corp. Author: Comparative Outline of Architectural History, 1937; editor: Jour. Am. Inst. Planners, 1950-52; contbr. articles to profl. jours. Mem. Phila. Commn. Higher Edn.; Trustee Fairmount Park Art Assn., 1965—. Fellow A.I.A. (chancellor coll. fellows 1964-66); mem. Am. Inst. Planners, Am. Soc. Planning Ofcls., Nat. Assn. Housing Ofcls., World Soc. Ekistics; hon. corr. mem. Royal Inst. Architects Can. Clubs: The Country (Brookline); Franklin Inn (Phila.), Rittenhouse (Phila.), Philadelphia Cricket (Phila.), Art Alliance (Phila.); Century (N.Y.C.). Home: 82 Bethlehem Pike Philadelphia PA 19118-2821

PERKINS, GEORGE WILLIAM, II, financial services executive, film producer; b. Salem, Mass., Sept. 10, 1926; s. George William and Daisy A. (Chase) P.; m. Mildred Boyle, Oct. 6, 1951; children: George William III, Clifton Alfred Dow, Mark Paige. Student, Northeastern U., 1944-49; B.Sc., Curry Coll., 1952; postgrad., Eastern Sch. Photography, Boston U.; Cert., Coll. Financial Planning, Denver, 1974. Registered investment advisor. Travel lectr., color cinematographer, 1946—; in charge road testing Renault auto, Alcan Hwy., Alaska, 1949; pres. Neily Film Prodns., Inc., 1953-55; Eastern regional v.p. Western Res. Life Assurance Co., Ohio, 1973-75; pres., chmn. bd. Fin. Mktg. Systems, Inc., Nashua, N.H., 1976—; chmn. Holmes Travel Orgn., 1978—; chmn. bd., v.p. Fin. Cons. Group for Women, Inc., 1981—; registered prin. Fin. Cons., Stoneham, Mass., 1975-88, Linsco-Pvt. Ledger, Boston, 1988-96; div. mgr. Calif. Pacific Ins. Services Inc., 1977-80; pres. Fin. Benefits Planning Corp., 1983—; sr. v.p., treas. Penn Distbn. Co, Inc., 1983-87, Penn RE Life Ins. Co., 1984-88; v.p. Polymer Balloon Corp., 1984-88; dir., treas. Linsco Ins. Agy., Inc., 1987-96; registered prin. Linsco-Pvt. Ledger, 1988-96; sr. v.p. corp. rels. Capital Def. Corp., 1990—; dir. Fin. Cons. Mgmt. Corp., Sonolite Corp., Contrex Co., FBP, Inc., FMSINC, Capital Defence Corp., Security Trust Ins. Co.; speaker on sales and service motivation; assoc. prof. bus. adminstrn. Curry Coll., until 1963, also sr. mem. bd. trustees, mem. coll. corp., also chmn. reorgn., 1963; pvt. trustee and executor, 1972—. Narrator, film producer: Burton Holmes travelogues, 1950-70; appearances at Carnegie Hall, N.Y. Music Hall, Phila. Symphony Hall, Boston Nat. Geog. Soc., Washington, numerous other cities, U.S., Mexico and Can.; designer world's largest portable cinemascope motion picture screen; contbg. editor: monthly newsletter Fin. Strategies and Money Mgmt. for Women; contbr. articles on ins. and sales to various publ., documentary and world travel motion picture and video prodn. in 36 countries, also photographic and cinematographic publs. Served with USNR, World War II, PTO. Recipient Nat. Quality award Nat. Assn. Life Underwriters. Mem. Merrimack Valley Life Underwriters Assn. (v.p., dir. 1968-69), Boston Life Underwriters Assn., Advt. Club Greater Boston, Internat. Assn. Fin. Planners (charter pres. No. Mass. chpt.), Nat. Assn. Security Dealers (prin.), Northeastern U., Curry Coll. alumni assns., Mass. Brokers Assn., Inst. Cert. Fin. Planners, Ins. Conf. Planners Assn., Am. Soc. Assn. Execs., Masons, Rotary (charter pres. Chelmsford, Mass. 1967-68). Home: 278 Lowell St Lynnfield MA 01940-1115 Office: 33 Main St Nashua NH 03060-2776 *Life tends to be what you encourage it to be as you live it day by day.*

PERKINS, GLADYS PATRICIA, retired aerospace engineer; b. Crenshaw, Miss., Oct. 30, 1921; d. Douglas and Zula Francis (Crenshaw) Franklin; m. Benjamin Franklin Walker, Sept. 26, 1952 (dec.); m. William Silas Perkins, Sept. 16, 1956 (dec.). BS in Math., Le Moyne Coll., 1943; postgrad., U. Mich., 1949, U. Calif., L.A., 1955-62. Mathematician Nat. Adv. Com. for Aeronatics (now NASA), Hampton, Va., 1944-49, Nat. Bur. of Standards, L.A., 1950-53, Aberdeen Bombing Mission, L.A., 1953-55; assoc. engr. Lockheed Missiles Systems Div., Van Nuys, Calif., 1955-57; staff engr. Hughes Aircraft Co., El Segundo, Calif., 1957-80; engring. specialist Rockwell Internat., Downey, Calif., 1980-87, ret., 1987. Contbr. articles to profl. publs. Named Alumnus of Yr. Le Moyne-Owen Coll., 1952; recipient Nat. Assn. for Equal Opportunity in Higher Edn. award Le Moyne-Owen Coll. Mem. Soc. of Women Engrs., Assn. of Computing Machinery, Le Moyne-Owen Alumni Assn. (pres. 1984), U. Mich. Alumni Club, Alpha Kappa Alpha. Democrat. Congregationalist. Home: 4001 W 22nd Pl Los Angeles CA 90018-1029

PERKINS, HERBERT ASA, physician; b. Boston, Oct. 5, 1918; s. Louis and Anna (Robinson) P.; m. Frances Snyder, Sept. 2, 1942; children: Susan, Deborah, Dale, Karen, Erin. A.B. cum laude, Harvard U., 1940; M.D. summa cum laude, Tufts U., 1943. Intern Boston City Hosp., 1944, resident, 1947-48; practice medicine specializing in transfusion medicine, 1953—; clin. instr. Stanford Med. Sch., 1953-57, asst. clin. prof., 1957-58; hematologist Open Heart Surgery Team, Stanford Hosp., San Francisco, 1955-58, Jewish Hosp., St. Louis, 1958-59; dir. rsch. Irwin Meml. Blood Ctrs., San Francisco, 1959-78, med. and sci. dir., 1978-90, exec. dir., 1987-91, pres., 1991-93, sr. med. scientist, 1993—; asst. prof. medicine Washington U., St. Louis, 1958-59, U. Calif., San Francisco, 1959-66, assoc. prof., 1966-71, clin. prof., 1971—; v.p. Blood Rsch. & Devel. Found., 1995—. Co-editor: Hepatitis and Blood Transfusion, 1972; assoc. editor: Transfusion. Served to maj. M.C., U.S. Army, 1944-47. Mem. AAAS, Am. Assn. Blood Banks (chmn. sci. adv. com. 1972-73, chmn. standards com. 1968-71, chmn. com. on organ transplantation and tissue typing 1970-80, bd. dirs. 1982-86), Am. Soc. Hematology, Internat. Transfusion Soc., Transplantation Soc., Am. Fedn. Clin. Rsch., Am. Soc. Histocompatibility and Immunogenetics (pres. 1985-86), Nat. Marrow Donor Program (chair bd. dirs., chmn. com. on stds. 1987-94, chmn. fin. com. 1987-94). Home: 520 Berkeley Ave Menlo Park CA 94025-2323 Office: Irwin Meml Blood Ctrs 270 Masonic Ave San Francisco CA 94118-4417

PERKINS, HOMER GUY, manufacturing company executive; b. New Haven, Oct. 23, 1916; s. Frank W. and Emily (Oesting) P.; m. Dorothy C. Stock, Jan. 24, 1942; children: Maribeth Perkins Grant, Homer Guy Jr., Hazel Mary Perkins Adolphson, Dorothy Catherine, Caroline Ann, Faith Elizabeth Perkins Crotteau, Ruth Emily Perkins Sico. BA in Internat. Rels., Yale U., 1938; LLD (hon.), Westfield (Mass.) State Coll., 1977. With Stanhome, Inc. (formerly Stanley Home Products, Inc.), Westfield, 1939—, v.p., 1965-66, exec. v.p., 1966-70, pres., CEO, 1970-78, chmn., 1978-81, also bd. dirs. Treas. Stanley Park of Westfield, 1949—; pres. Citizens Scholarship Found., Easthampton, Mass., 1966-67, Easthampton Cmty. Chest, 1960-61; chmn. fin. com., bd. dirs. Western Mass. coun. Girl Scouts U.S., 1966-69; mem. devel. com. Clarke Sch. Deaf, Northampton, 1965-68; mem. fin. com. Town of Easthampton, 1962-70, chmn. fin. com., 1967-68; dir. Frank Stanley Beveridge Found., Westfield, 1956-95, pres., 1966-87; trustee Cooley Dickinson Hosp., Northampton, 1963-70, 84-92, chmn. bd. trustees, 1989-91; pres. bd. trustees Northampton Sch. for Girls, 1964-73; bd. dirs. Porter Phelps Huntington Found., Hadley, Mass., 1960-92, Guild of Holy Child, Westfield, 1969-76; mem. bd. overseers Williston Acad., Easthampton, 1961-64, Old Sturbridge (Mass.) Village, 1970-76; v.p. bd. trustees Williston-Northampton Sch., 1970-75, pres., 1975-78. With USAAF, 1942-46. Mem. Direct Selling Assn. (chmn. 1975, bd. dirs., mem. Hall of Fame), Paperweight Collectors Assn. (pres. 1991-95), Lions (past pres. Easthampton club). Home: 8 Carol Ave Easthampton MA 01027-1904

PERKINS, JACK EDWIN, lawyer; b. Portola, Calif., May 25, 1943; s. Charles James and Vira Almena (Wing) P.; m. Barbara Kay Nielson, Jan. 18, 1969; chidlren: Jill Christy, Kelli Anne. BA, San Jose State Coll., 1966; JD, Hastings Coll. Law, 1972. Bar: Calif. 1972, D.C. 1989. Asst. U.S. Atty., Dept. Justice, San Francisco, 1973-74; staff atty. Dept. Justice, Washington, 1972, 74-80, legis. counsel, 1980-86, dep. asst. atty. gen., 1986-90; chief adminstrv. hearing officer Exec. Office for Immigration Rev., Falls Church, Va., 1990—. Served to capt. USMC, 1966-69, Vietnam. Recipient John Marshall award Dept. Justice, 1986. Avocations: tennis, jogging, racquetball. Home: 3310 Fallen Tree Ct Alexandria VA 22310-2262 Office: Exec Office Immigration Rev 5107 Leesburg Pike Washington DC 20530-0864

PERKINS, JAMES FRANCIS, physicist; b. Hillsdale, Tenn., Jan. 3, 1924; s. Jim D. and Laura Pervis (Goad) P.; A.B., Vanderbilt U., 1948, M.A., 1949; Ph.D., 1953; m. Ida Virginia Phillips, Nov. 23, 1949; 1 son, James F. Sr. engr. Convair, Fort Worth, Tex., 1953-54; scientist Lockheed Aircraft, Marietta, Ga., 1954-61; physicist Army Missile Command Redstone Arsenal, Huntsville, Ala., 1961-77; cons. physicist, 1977—. Served with USAAF, 1943-46. AEC fellow, 1951-52. Mem. Am. Phys. Soc., Sigma Xi. Contbr. articles to profl. jours. Home and Office: 102 Mountain Wood Dr SE Huntsville AL 35801-1809

PERKINS, JAMES PATRICK, advertising executive; b. Chgo., Dec. 6, 1939; s. John Alfred and Mary Grace (Quinlan) P.; student U. Ill., 1959-60,

Western Ill. U., 1961; m. Sarah Reed Simkins, Sept. 13, 1975; children: Brian Patrick, Kevin Matthew, Quinn Cecile. Sales and mktg. exec. Glidden-Durkee, 1964-65; advt. mgr. Amvar Chem. Co., 1965-69; indsl. coatings rep. Benjamin Moore Co., 1969-71; account exec. JTC Advt., 1971-74; creative dir., pres. Laven, Fuller & Perkins Advt.-Mktg., Chgo., 1974—. Bd. dirs., mem. adv. bd. Booth Meml. Hosp., Salvation Army, Chgo., 1978-81. Sgt. U.S. Army, 1961-62. Mem. Chgo. Advt. Club, Orlando Ad Club, Employment Mgrs. Assn., Fla. Hosp. Adminstrs.,Barclay Club (Chgo.), Club Internat. (Chgo.), Submarine Club. Roman Catholic. Avocations: watercolor painting, railroading, reading, golf. Home: 1314 Scott Ave Winnetka IL 60093-1463 Office: 280 W Canton Ave Ste 104 Winter Park FL 32789-3146

PERKINS, JAMES WINSLOW, international business consultant, builder, contractor; b. Southington, Conn., Sept. 15, 1955; s. Robert Winslow and Florence Corinne (Angelone) P. Student, Tunxis Community Coll., Farmington, Conn., 1973-75. Owner Town & Country Club, Smithfield, R.I., 1975-80, Ad Mark of Mass, Inc., Ludlow, Mass., 1980-84, Car Stereo Distbrs., Inc., West Palm Beach, Fla., 1983-85, Internat. Imports, Lauderdale Lakes, Fla., 1985-88, Modern Sectional Homes, Inc., Southington, Conn., 1989-93. Mem. Nat. Assn. Realtors, Cen. Conn. Bd. Realtors, New Eng. Mfrd. Housing Assn., 100 Club of Conn. Republican. Avocations: sailing, water skiing. Home: 2587 Meriden-Wtby Rd Marion CT 06444 also: Modern Sectional Homes PO Box 153 Marion CT 06444-0153

PERKINS, JAMES WOOD, lawyer; b. New Bedford, Mass., Oct. 14, 1924; s. Ralph Chamberlain and Louise Bartlett (Allen) P.; m. Margaret Neale Heard, Feb. 3, 1951; children: Charles H., James A., George H. AB, Havard U., 1945, JD, 1948; ThM, Harvard Div. Sch., 1996. Bar: Mass. 1948, U.S. Dist. Ct. Mass. 1948. Engr. Sylvania Electric Products, Inc., Salem, Mass., 1944-45; assoc. Palmer & Dodge, Boston, 1948-54, ptnr., 1955-91, mng. ptnr., 1986-89, of counsel, 1992—. Mem. ABA (chmn. sect. local govt. law 1970-71, sect. del. 1974-78), Nat. Assn. Bond Lawyers (pres. 1985-86). Office: Palmer & Dodge 1 Beacon St Boston MA 02108-3106

PERKINS, JOHN ALLEN, lawyer; b. New Bedford, Mass., Sept. 13, 1919; s. Ralph Chamberlain and Louise Bartlett (Allen) P.; m. Lydia Bullard Cobb, Sept. 9, 1944; children: John A., Susan W., Robert C., William B. A.B., Harvard U., 1940, LL.B., 1943. Bar: Mass. Of counsel Palmer & Dodge, Boston; clk. Social Law Library, 1961-83; grad. researcher Univ. Coll., Oxford U., 1978; bd. dirs. Greater Boston Legal Services, Inc., 1972-91. Author: The Prudent Peace—Law as Foreign Policy, 1981; contbr. articles to profl. jours. Mem. Dedham (Mass.) Sch. Com., 1959-65, chmn., 1963-65, town counsel, Dedham, 1971-72. Mem. Am. Law Inst., Am. Coll. Trust and Estate Counsel, Mass. Bar Assn. (dir. 1973-75), Internat. Acad. Estate and Trust Law (exec. coun. 1990-94), Boston Bar Assn. (council 1972-75, v.p. 1981-82, pres. 1982-84). Home: 203 Highland St Dedham MA 02026-5835 Office: Palmer & Dodge 1 Beacon St Boston MA 02108-3106

PERKINS, LAWRENCE BRADFORD, JR., architect; b. Chgo., Jan. 13, 1943; s. Lawrence Bradford and Margery Isabella (Blair) P.; m. Phyllis Barbara Friedman, Sept. 11, 1966; children: Rachael Naomi, Judith Eve, Rebecca Abigail. BA, Cornell U., 1967; MBA, Stanford U., 1969; BArch, CCNY, 1976. Registered architect, N.Y., Ohio, Ill., Conn., Pa., Mass., Ill., N.J., Ga., Fla., Mo., Ariz., Tex. Pres. Perkins Eastman Archs., N.Y.C., 1983—, Omnidata Svcs., N.Y.C., 1971-73; mng. ptnr. Llewelyn-Davies Assocs., N.Y.C., 1973-77, Perkins & Will, N.Y.C., 1977-81; ptnr. Attia & Perkins, N.Y.C., 1981-83. Author chpts. to books; contbr. articles to profl. jours. Bd. dirs. Castle Gallery Coll. New Rochelle, N.Y., 1985—, Settlement Housing Fund, N.Y.C., 1991—, Helen Keller Internat., N.Y.C., 1993—, various other village bds. and coms. Fellow AIA (mem. various coms.), Am. Inst. Cert. Planners, Cornell U. Coun., Epsilon Assn. (pres. 1993—). Home: 4 Rectory Ln Scarsdale NY 10583-4314 Office: Perkins Eastman Archs 437 5th Ave New York NY 10016-2205

PERKINS, LEEMAN LLOYD, music educator, musicologist; b. Salina, Utah, Mar. 27, 1932; s. Milton Lloyd and Ida Margaret (Johnson) P.; m. Marianne Suzanne Contesse, Nov. 14, 1956; children: Eric Raymond, Bruce Philippe, Marc Christian (dec.), Patrick Thierry. BFA, U. Utah, 1954; PhD, Yale U., 1965. Instr. Boston U., 1964; instr. Yale U., 1964-67, asst. prof., 1967-71, dir. undergraduate studies in music history, 1969-70; assoc. prof. music history, coord. for musicology U. Tex., Austin, 1971-75, assoc. prof. music history, grad. adv. for musicology, 1976; prof. music Columbia U., N.Y.C., 1976—, chmn. dept music, 1985-90; instr. advanced seminar in Medieval History, Smith Coll., 1968; vis. assoc. prof. music Columbia U., 1975; vis. prof. Boston U., 1978; dir. NEH Summer Seminar, 1977. Editor: Johannes Lheritier Opera Omnia, 1969, (with Howard Garay) The Mellon Chansonnier, 1979; contbr. to profl. jours. Chmn. grad. musicology com., Columbia U., 1980-84. Sgt. U.S. Army, 1957-59. Recipient James Morris Whiton Fund award Yale U., 1965, The Otto Kinkeldey award Am. Musicological Soc., 1980; Trumbull Coll. fellow Yale U., 1966-71, Lewis-Farmington fellow Yale U., 1962-63, Morse fellow Yale U., 1967-68, Am. Coun. Learned Soc. fellow, 1973-74, NEH fellow, 1979, 1984-85, French Archival Scis. fellow Newberry Libr. Center for Renaissance Studies, 1991; Martha Baird Rockefeller grantee, 1963-64, Paul Mellon Found. grantee, 1972, Am. Coun. Learned Soc., 1972, 82, U. Tex. grantee, 1975,. Mem. Am. Musicological Soc. (chmn. program com. 1979, bd. dirs. 1980-81, adv. bd., 1985-86, chmn. ad hoc sub com., 1985-86, exec. com. delegate, 1989-92), Internat. Musicological Soc., The Renaissance Soc. of Am., Amici Thomae Mori, Phi Beta Kappa, Phi Kappa Phi. Mormon. Office: Columbia U Dept of Music Dodge Hall 703 New York NY 10027

PERKINS, LEIGH H., sporting goods company executive, conservationist. Chmn. The Orvis Co., Manchester, Vt.; fund raiser The Orvis-Perkins Found., The Perkins Charitable Found. Bd. govs. Wyo. chpt., bd. trustees The Nature Conservancy. Recipient Oak Leaf award The Nature Conservancy, 1995. Office: Orvis Co Inc US Route 7A Manchester VT 05254

PERKINS, LUCIAN, photographer. Grad., U. Texas. Intern The Washington Post, 1979, now staff photographer. Named Newspaper Photographer of Yr., Pictures of Yr. competition, 1993; recipient Pulitzer Prize for explanatory journalism, 1995, Photo of Yr. award World Press, 1996. Office: The Washington Post 1150 15th St NW Washington DC 20071-0001

PERKINS, MARVIN EARL, psychiatrist, educator; b. Moberly, Mo., June 1, 1920; s. Marvin Earl and Nannie Mae (Walden) P.; A.B., Albion Coll., 1942; M.D., Harvard U., 1946; M.P.H. (USPHS fellow), Johns Hopkins U., 1956; L.H.D., Albion Coll., 1968; grad. U.S. Army Command and Gen. Staff Coll., 1966, U.S. Army War Coll., 1972; m. Mary MacDonald, May 24, 1943 (div.); children: Keith, Sandra, Cynthia, Marvin, Mary, Irene; m. 2d, Sharon Johnstone, May 20, 1978; 1 dau., Sharon. Intern, Henry Ford Hosp., Detroit, 1946-47; post surgeon, hosp. comdg. officer Fort Eustis, Va., 1948; resident physician psychiatry Walter Reed Army Hosp., Washington, 1949-52; chief psychiatry br., psychiatry and neurology cons. div. Office U.S. Army Surgeon Gen., Washington, 1952-53, chief records rev. br., 1953-55; chief psychiat. svcs. div. D.C. Dept. Pub. Health, 1955-58, chief bur. mental health, 1959-60; lectr. Johns Hopkins U., Balt., 1960-65; adj. prof. Columbia U., 1961-67; prof. psychiatry Mt. Sinai Sch. Medicine of CUNY, 1967-72; clin. prof. psychiatry Coll. Physicians and Surgeons, Columbia U., 1972-77; prof. psychiatry N.Y. Coll. Medicine, 1977-78; prof. behavioral medicine and psychiatry U. Va. Sch. Medicine, 1978—; dir. N.Y.C. Community Mental Health Bd., 1960-68, commr. mental health svcs., 1961-68; dir. psychiatry Beth Israel Medical Center, N.Y.C., 1967-72, dir. Morris J. Bernstein Inst., 1968-72; dir. Community Mental Health Svcs. Westchester County, 1972-77; dir. psychiatry Westchester County Med. Center, 1977-78; med. dir. Mental Health Svcs. of Roanoke Valley, 1978-82; med. dir. Roanoke Valley Psychiat. Ctr., 1980-82, pres. med. staff, 1985-86; med. dir., pres. med. staff Catawba Hosp., 1988-91; psychiat., mental hygiene clinic VA Med. Ctr., Salem, Va., 1992-95; cons. psychiatrist Blue Ridge Cmty. Svcs., 1992—; med. dir. partial hospitalization program Alleghany Regional Hosp., Low Moor, Va., 1995—. With AUS, 1943-46; col. M.C. Res. ret. Diplomate in psychiatry Am. Bd. Psychiatry and Neurology; certified mental hosp. adminstr. Am. Psychiat. Assn. Fellow Am. Psychiat. Assn. (life), N.Y. Acad. Medicine (life); mem. AMA, Group Advancement Psychiatry, Roanoke Acad. Medicine, N.Y. Psychiat. Soc., Neuropsychiat. Soc. Va., Med. Soc. Va., State Hist. Soc. Mo. (life), Res. Officers Assn. (life) Mil. Order of World Wars (perpetual). Home: 3728 Forest Rd SW Roanoke VA 24015-4510 also: PO Box 20437 Roanoke VA 24018 Office: 1604 Boulevard Salem VA 24153 also: 865 Roanoke Rd Daleville VA 24083

PERKINS, MERLE LESTER, French language educator; b. West Lebanon, N.H., Apr. 16, 1919; s. Charles Elisha and Ethel (Armstrong) P.; m. Barbara Marion Cunningham, June 16, 1951; children: Elizabeth Cunningham, Janet Blair. AB, Dartmouth Coll., 1941; AM, Brown U., 1942, PhD in French, 1950. Instr. French Brown U., 1948-50, U. Chgo., 1950-53; mem. faculty U. Calif., Davis, 1953-67; prof. French U. Calif., 1963-67, chmn. dept. fgn. langs., 1962-65, chmn. dept. Italian and French, 1965-67; prof. French U. Wis., 1967—, chmn. grad. studies French, 1967-74, 77-89, Pickard Bascom prof. French, 1983—; dir. univs. Mich. and Wis. Year in France, Aix-en-Provence, 1976-77, chmn. admissions, 1979-89. Author: The Moral and Political Philosophy of the Abbé de Saint-Pierre, 1959, Voltaire's Concept of International Order, 1965, J.-J. Rousseau on History, Liberty, and National Survival, 1968, Jean-Jacques Rousseau on the Individual and Society, 1974, Diderot on the Time-Space Continuum, 1982, Montesquieu on National Power and International Rivalry, 1986, Six French Philosophes on International Rivalry and War, 1989, Marquis de Sade, His Ethics and Rhetoric: Suspense in Sade, 1989, Diderot: A Study Guide, 1990, Enlightenment Writers, Their Contributions to Two Revolutions, 1993, Ordeal of Arms, Air Combat, Europe and the Balkans, 1993, Recollections of Air Combat, World War II, 1996; also anthology, articles, reviews. Served with USAAF, 1942-45. Decorated Air medal with 3 oak leaf clusters.; Parker fellow Dartmouth Coll., 1941-42; Edwards fellow Brown U., 1948-49; Penrose Fund grantee Am. Philos. Soc., 1956-57, 72-73, 74-75; Fulbright research grantee France, 1960-61, 67-68. Mem. Am. Assn. Tchrs. French, Philol. Assn. Pacific Coast, Modern Lang. Assn. (grantee 1956-57), Internat. Assn. for 18th Century Studies, Modern Humanities Research Assn., Phi Beta Kappa. Episcopalian. Office: U Wis Dept French 1220 Linden Dr Madison WI 53706-1525

PERKINS, NINA ROSALIE, social worker; b. Huntington, W.Va., July 17, 1953; d. Lloyd William and Violet Macil (Elkins) Fowler; m. Homer Chester Bartoe, Jan. 30, 1972 (div. Dec. 1979); m. Gary Michael Lovejoy, Aug. 9, 1982 (div. Mar. 1989); m. Raymond Wesley Perkins, Apr. 14, 1989 (div. Nov. 1989); 1 child, Homer David. BSW, Marshall U., 1982; postgrad., W.Va. U., 1989-95. Lic. social worker, W.Va.; cert. personal care provider. Child care worker Charles W. Cammack Children's Ctr., Huntington, 1983-84; ins. underwriter Mut. of Omaha, Shreveport, La., 1984-86; banquet mgr. Ramada Inn, Shreveport, 1986-87; ctr. coord. Cabell County Community Svcs. Orgn., Inc., Huntington, 1987-90, case mgr. sr. svcs., 1990-92; minority AIDS program coord. W.Va. Dept. Health, Charleston, 1988-90, cons. instr., 1990-92; social worker Marshall U. Sch. Medicine, Frank E. Hanshaw Geriatric Ctr., Huntington, 1990—; owner, adminstr. Sr. Care Mgmt. Svcs., Huntington, W.Va., 1991-92; dir. social svcs. Wayne Continuous Care Ctr., 1992—; charter mem. Cabell County Com. for Drug Info., Huntington, 1990—; mem. Huntington Area AIDS Task Force, 1988—; social work cons. for Region 2, Area Agy. on Aging Adv. Com.; cons. and guest lectr., 1991-96; mem. ethics com. W.Va. Dept. HHS Office Social Svcs., 1995—; mem. partial hospitilization adv. com. Prestera Ctr. Mental Health. Mem. Dem. Women's Club, Cabell County. Recipient Cert. for Concerned Citizenship, State of W.Va., 1982. Mem. W.Va. Assn. Dirs. Sr. Programs, NAFE, Internat. Plaform Assn., Inst. Noetic Scis. Democrat. Baptist. Avocations: gardening, writing, swimming, reading. Office: Frank Hanshaw Geriatric Ctr 2900 1st Ave Huntington WV 25702-1271

PERKINS, RALPH LINWOOD, business executive, public health administration specialist; b. Orono, Maine, July 17, 1914; s. Ralph L. and Zilla (Sawyer) P.; m. Hilda Beatrice Morrison, Sept. 1, 1938; children: Sylvia Lucille Perkins Nespoli, Jacquelyn Sue Perkins Lowe-Vosburgh. BSME, U. Maine, 1935; MS in Hosp. Adminstrn., Columbia, 1950. With U.S. Engrs. Dept., Quoddy, Me., 1935-37, NYA in, Me., Ohio and W.Va., 1937-44; with USPHS, W.Va., Miss., La., D.C. and N.Y., 1944-48; asst. adminstrv. officer USPHS Hosp., S.I., 1949-50, adminstrv. officer, 1950-63; asso. dir. Hosp. U. Pa., 1963-64, exec. dir., 1964-74; sr. adviser Chi Systems, Inc., Ann Arbor, Mich., 1974-78; Lectr. Columbia Sch. Pub. Health and Adminstrv. Medicine, 1961-74. Past chmn. Delaware Valley Hosp. Council Forum.; Former bd. dirs. West Phila. Community Mental Health Consortium. Recipient Commendation Medal USPHS, 1963. Fellow Am. Coll. Health Care Execs. (life); mem. Am. Hosp. Assn. (life), Maine Hosp. Assn., Delaware Valley Hosp. Coun. (past dir., past pres. forum, sec.-treas.), Assn. Am. Med. Colls., Hosp. Assn. Pa. (past trustee), Commd. Officers Assn. USPHS (life). Methodist. Home and Office: 517 Fairfax Rd Drexel Hill PA 19026-1210

PERKINS, ROBERT LOUIS, physician, educator; b. Bradford, Pa., Feb. 20, 1931; s. Robert Marcell and Lola Ruth (Freeman) P.; m. Ruth Caloccia, Sept. 7, 1952 (dec. 1978); children: Cathy Lynn, Robert Louis; m. Penelope Joel Brodgen, Dec. 24, 1983. AB, W.Va. U., 1953, BS, 1954; MD, Johns Hopkins U., 1956; MS in Medicine, Ohio State U., 1962. Diplomate Am. Bd. Internal Medicine. Instr. medicine Ohio State U., Columbus, 1961-65, asst. prof., 1965-69, assoc. prof., 1969-73, prof. medicine, 1973—, prof. med. microbiology, 1974—, Pomerene prof., 1977-82, Saslaw prof., 1982-90, dir. infectious diseases div., 1971-87; dir. med. edn. Grant Med. Ctr., Columbus, 1990—. Contbr. chpts. to books, numerous articles to profl. jours. Served to capt. USAF, 1958-60. NIH fellow, 1960-62. Fellow ACP, Infectious Disease Soc. Am.; mem. Ctrl. Soc. for Clin. Rsch., Am. Fedn. Clin. Rsch. Republican. Methodist. Avocations: model aviation; golf. Home: 2285 Pinebrook Rd Columbus OH 43220-4327 Office: Grant Med Ctr Med Edn 111 S Grant Ave Columbus OH 43215-4701

PERKINS, ROGER ALLAN, lawyer; b. Port Chester, N.Y., Mar. 4, 1943; s. Francis Newton and Winifred Marcella (Smith) P.; m. Katherine Louise Howard, Nov. 10, 1984; children: Marshall, Morgan, Matthew, Justin, Ashley. BA, Pa. State U., 1965; postgrad., U. Ill., 1965-66; JD with honors, George Washington U., 1969. Bar: Md. 1969, Mass. 1975. Trial atty. Nationwide Ins. Co., Annapolis, Md., 1969-72; assoc. Arnold, Beauchemin & Huber, P.A., Balt., 1973; assoc., then ptnr. Goodman & Bloom, P.A., Annapolis, 1973-76; ptnr. Luff and Perkins, Annapolis, 1976-78; sole practice Anapolis, 1978—; temp. adminstrv. hearing officer Anne Arundel County, 1984—; asst. city atty., Annapolis, 1980-82; atty. Bd. Appeals of City of Annapolis, 1986—; mem. Appellate Jud. Nominating Commn., 1995—. Editl. adv. bd. Daily Record, 1996—. Mem. Gov.'s Task Force on Family Law, 1991-94; adv. coun. on family legal need of low income persons MLSC, 1991; coach youth sports. Fellow Am. Acad. Matrimonial Lawyers, Am. Bar Found., Md. Bar Found. (bd. dirs. 1992-95); mem. ABA (ho. dels. 1991-93, 94-96, standing com. on solo and small firm practitioners 1993—, chair 1996—), Md. State Bar Assn. (pres. 1992-93, treas. 1988-91, bd. govs. 1985-87, chair spl. com. on lawyer profl. responsibility 1994-95, family and juvenile law sect. coun. 1983-89, chair 1987-88), Anne Arundel County Bar Assn. (pres. 1984-85). Republican. Methodist. Home: 503 Bay Hills Dr Arnold MD 21012-2001 Office: The Courtyards 133 Defense Hwy Ste 202 Annapolis MD 21401-7015

PERKINS, ROSWELL BURCHARD, lawyer; b. Boston, May 21, 1926. A.B. cum laude, Harvard U., 1945, LL.B. cum laude, 1949, LLD (hon.), Bates Coll., 1988. Bar: Mass. 1949, N.Y. 1949. Assoc. Debevoise, Plimpton & McLean, N.Y.C., 1949-53; ptnr. Debevoise & Plimpton, and predecessor firms, N.Y.C., 1957—; asst. sec. U.S. Dept. Health, Edn. amd Welfare, 1954-56; counsel to Gov. Nelson A. Rockefeller, State of N.Y., 1959; asst. counsel spl. subcom. Senate Commerce Com. to investigate organized crime in interstate commerce, 1950; chmn. N.Y.C. Mayor's Task Force on Transp. Reorgn., 1966; mem. Pres.'s Adv. Panel on Personnel Interchange, 1968; chmn. adv. com. Medicare Adminstrn. Contracting Subcontracting HEW, 1973-74; dir. Fiduciary Trust Co. N.Y., 1963—; trustee Bowery Savs. Bank, 1975-82; mem. legal com. to bd. dirs. N.Y. Stock Exch., 1995—. Mem. N.Y. Lawyers Com. Civil Rights, 1970-73; mem. nat. exec. com., 1973—, co-chmn., 1973-75; mem. adv. coun. Woodrow Wilson Sch. Pub. and Internat. Affairs, Princeton U., 1967-69; bd. dirs. The Commonwealth Fund, 1974—; bd. dirs. Sch. Am. Ballet, 1974-85, chmn. bd., 1976-80; dir., sec. N.Y. Urban Coalition, 1967-74; trustee Pomfret Sch., 1961-76; The Brearley Sch., 1969-75; dir. Salzburg Seminar Am. Studies, 1970-80; mem. overseers vis. com. Kennedy Sch. Govt., Harvard U., 1971-77, Harvard and Radcliffe Colls., 1958-64, 1971-77. Recipient Spl. Merit Citation of Am. Judicature Soc., 1989, Harvard Law Sch. Assn. award, 1994. Mem. ABA (commn. on law and economy 1975-79; mem. house of dels. 1980-93), N.Y. State Bar Assn., Assn. Bar City of N.Y. (chmn. spl. com. on fed. conflict of interest laws 1958-60), Assn. Harvard Alumni (pres. 1970-71), Am. Law Inst. (mem. coun. 1969, pres. 1980-93, chmn. coun. 1993—), Am. Arbitration Assn. (bd. dirs. 1966-71). Author: The New Federal Conflict of Interest Law; editor Harvard Law Rev. Home: 1120 5th Ave New York NY 10128-0144 Office: Debevoise & Plimpton 875 3rd Ave New York NY 10022-6225

PERKINS, SAMUEL, lawyer; b. Boston, Dec. 16, 1948; s. Malcolm and Sheila D. (Redmond) P.; m. Nancy Joy Reed, June 21, 1975; children: Molly, Sara, Benjamin, Emily. AB cum laude, Harvard U., 1970; JD, Boston U., 1976. Bar: Vt. 1977, U.S. Dist. Ct. Vt. 1977, Mass. 1984, U.S. Dist. Ct. Mass. 1984, U.S. Ct. Appeals (1st cir.) 1992. Asst. atty. gen. Atty. Gen.'s Office, Montpelier, Vt., 1977-78; assoc. Welch & Graham, White River Junction, Vt., 1978-81; ptnr. Welch, Graham, Perkins & Manby, White River Junction, 1981-83; assoc. Morrison, Mahoney & Miller, Boston, 1983-87, ptnr., 1987-95; ptnr. Brody, Hardoon, Perkins & Kesten, Boston, 1995—. Mem. Mass. Bar Assn., Boston Bar Assn., Def. Rsch. Inst., Mass. Def. Lawyers Assn. Office: Brody Hardoon Perkins & Kesten 200 State St Mktplace Ctr Boston MA 02109

PERKINS, SUE DENE, journalism educator; b. Wichita Falls, Tex., Jan. 12, 1946; d. Darrye Clayton and Josephine Marie (Hall) P. BA, North Tex. State U., 1968; MA, Stephen F. Austin State U., 1980; postgrad., Angelo State U., 1979. Cert. tchr., Tex. Mag. editor Haire Pubs., N.Y.C., 1968-69; women's editor Arlington (Tex.) Daily News, 1970, police reporter editor, 1972; mag. editor Tex. Assn. Bus., Houston, 1972-74; editor in ho. pubs. P.R. Am. Assn. Respiratory Therapy, Dallas, 1974-76; asst. employee pub. rels. Gen. Telephone, San Angelo, 1976-79; dir. student pubs. Stephen F. Austin State U., Nacogdoches, Tex., 1980-83, founder Women in Comm. chpt., 1982; instr. journalism Tex. A&M Univ., College Station, 1983-84; owner photo supply Photo-Graphics Co., Lufkin, Tex., 1985-88; adv. student pubs. Diboll (Tex.) Ind. Sch. Dist., 1987—; computer cons. Deep East Tex. Coun. Govt., Lufkin, 1990, Region VII Edn. Svc. Ctr., Kilgore, Tex., 1994. Editor: (mags.) Handbags & Accessories, 1968-69, Tex. Industry, 1972-74, (newspaper) Arlington Daily News, 1970-72, (newsletter) Am. Assn. for Respiratory Therapy Bull., 1974-76. Pres. Wheeler Cemetery Assn., Corrigan, Tex., 1992, v.p., 1993; sec. Youth for Christ, Diboll, Tex., 1993-95. Named Outstanding Ex-Student Electra (Tex.) Alumni Assn., 1981-82. Mem. Journalism Educators Am., Tex. Journalism Edn. Assn., Tex. Classroom Tchrs.Assn., Order Ea. Star. Baptist. Avocations: outdoor photography, fishing. Home: RR 1 Box 106 Corrigan TX 75939-9739 Office: Diboll High Sch 1000 Harris St Diboll TX 75941-9762

PERKINS, THOMAS HAYES, III, furniture company executive; b. Brookhaven, Miss., Nov. 18, 1922; s. Thomas H. Jr. and Clara Louretta (Whittington) P. BS, La. State U. Owner T.H. Perkins Furniture, Inc. Chmn. Miss. Regional Housing Authority, McComb. With U.S. Army, 1943-44. Decorated Purple Heart, Bronze Star. Mem. Internat. Camellia Soc. (pres. 1988-94). Independent. Office: T H Perkins Furniture 520 Brookway Blvd Brookhaven MS 39601-0750

PERKINS, THOMAS JAMES, venture capital company executive; b. Oak Park, Ill., Jan. 7, 1932; s. Harry H. and Elizabeth P.; m. Gerd Thune-Ellefsen, Dec. 9, 1961; children: Tor Kristian, Elizabeth Siri. B.S.E.E., M.I.T., 1953; M.B.A., Harvard U., 1957. Gen. mgr. computer div. Hewlett Packard Co., Cupertino, Calif., 1965-70, dir. corp. devel., 1970-72; gen. partner Kleiner & Perkins, San Francisco, 1972-80; sr. ptnr. Kleiner Perkins Caufield & Byers, San Francisco, from 1980; chmn. bd. Tandem Computers, Inc., Cupertino, Calif.; chmn. bd. Tandem Computers, Genentech; dir. Spectra Physics., Corning Glass Works, Collagen Corp., LSI Logic Corp., Hybritech Inc., Econics Corp., Vitalink Communications Corp. Author: Classic Supercharged Sports Cars, 1984. Trustee San Francisco Ballet, 1980—. Mem. Nat. Venture Capital Assn. (chmn. 1981-82, pres. 1980-81). Clubs: N.Y. Yacht, Links, Am. Bugatti (pres. 1983—). Office: Tandem Computers Inc 10435 Tantau Ave Cupertino CA 95014-3548 also: Genentech Inc 460 Point San Bruno Blvd South San Francisco CA 94080-4918*

PERKINS, THOMAS KEEBLE, oil company researcher; b. Dallas, Jan. 31, 1932; s. James Thomas and Willie Fae (Keeble) P.; m. Anita Aliene Smith, July 20, 1963; children—Julia, Stephen. B.S., Tex. A&M U., 1952, M.S., 1953; Ph.D., U. Tex., 1957. Engr. Dow Chem. Co., Freeport, Tex., 1952; instr., asst. prof. U. Tex., Austin, 1955-57; from research engr. to disting. research adviser ARCO Exploration and Prodn. Tech., Plano, Tex., 1957-94, ret., 1994; trustee S.W. Rsch. Inst., San Antonio, 1994—, Dickinson Pl. Charitable Corp., Dallas, 1995—. Contbr. numerous articles to profl. jours.; patentee in field. Recipient Atlantic Richfield Tech. Achievement award, 1980, 90, 91. Mem. Soc. Petroleum Engrs. (C.K. Ferguson award com. 1973-75, Disting. lectr. 1977-78, Lester C. Uren award 1978, J. F. Carll award com. 1984-86, tech. editor jour. 1981-84, J.F. Carll award 1993), Nat. Acad. Engring. Republican. Methodist.

PERKINS, VAN L., university administrator, educator, conservationist; b. Standardville, Utah, May 22, 1930; s. Howard Edward and Maude (Larsen) P.; m. Colleen Campbell, Feb. 14, 1951 (div. Aug. 1984); children: Mark E., Cheryl, Scott C., Brett C., Regan; m. Katherine Marie Bennett, Jan. 17, 1986. BA, U. Utah, 1956; MA, Harvard U., 1958, PhD, 1966. Purchasing agt. Bechtel Corp., San Francisco, 1951-55; instr. to asst. prof. Brigham Young U., Provo, Utah, 1960-64; asst. prof. U. Calif., Riverside, 1964-68; assoc. prof. U. Calif., 1968-73, prof., 1973-91, prof. emeritus, 1991—; assoc. dean Grad. Sch. U. Calif., Riverside, 1971-73; vice chancellor U. Calif., Riverside, 1973-78, exec. vice chancellor, 1987-88; cons. in higher edn. mgmt., 1977—, mus. orgn. and mgmt., 1982. Author: Crisis in Agriculture, 1969; contbr. articles to profl. jours. Mgr. U.S. Senatorial and Ho. Reps. Campaigns, Dem., Utah and Calif., 1962, 64, 80; mem. adv. com. U.S. Commn. on Civil Rights, 1978-84; conservation chair Santa Fe group Sierra Club, 1992-94; polit. chair Rio Grande chpt. Sierra Club, 1993, 94, exec. com. chair, 1996—. With U.S. Army, 1950-52. Recipient George Emory Fellows prize U. Utah, 1956, Edwards Meml. prize Agrl. History Soc., 1965; Danforth fellow, 1956, co, 1962-64. Mem. ACLU, Sierra Club, Southern Utah Wilderness Alliance, Audubon Soc., Wilderness Soc., Phi Beta Kappa, Phi Kappa Phi. Democrat. Home: RR 19 Box 128H Santa Fe NM 87505-9286 Office: U Calif-Riverside 621 Old Santa Fe Trail Santa Fe NM 87501

PERKINS, WHITNEY TROW, political science educator emeritus; b. Boston, Feb. 28, 1921; s. Wesley Trow and Hazel Alice (Mason) P; m. Kathryn A. Sylvester, June 28, 1947; children—Rebecca, Mason, Wesley, Rachel. A.B., Tufts U., 1942; Ph.D., Fletcher Sch. Law and Diplomacy, 1948. Asst. prof. internat. relations U. Denver, 1948-53; from assoc. prof. to prof. polit. sci. Brown U., Providence, 1953-84; chmn. Internat. Relations Concentration, Brown U., 1955-84; cons. U.S.-P.R. Commn. on Status of Puerto Rico, 1965. Author: Denial of Empire: The United States and its Dependencies, 1962; Constraint of Empire: The United States and Caribbean Interventions, 1981. Served to capt. USAF, 1942-45, PTO. Recipient Fulbright Research award, 1951-52. Mem. Am. Polit. Sci. Assn., Internat. Studies Assn., Phi Beta Kappa. Democrat. Avocations: tennis; squash; hiking. Home: 11 Catalpa Rd Providence RI 02906-2614

PERKINS, WILLIAM CLINTON, company executive; b. Decatur, Ill., Mar. 7, 1920; s. Glen Rupert and Frances Lola (Clinton) P.; m. Eunice Cagle, Sept. 7, 1939 (div. 1954); stepchildren: William Rea Cagle, Howard Christy Cagle; 1 child, Clinton Colcord; m. Lillian Wuollet, Sept. 7, 1955 (div. 1965); m. Shirley Thomas, Oct. 24, 1969. BS Mil. Sci. and Meteorology, U. Md., 1954; MS in Bus. and Pub. Adminstrn., Sussex Coll., Eng., 1975. Commd. USAF, 1943-73, advanced through grades to col.; with Ship Systems div. Litton Ind., Culver City, Calif., 1973-75; dir. materiel Hughes Aircraft Co., Tehran, Iran, 1974-78; mgr. internat. s/c Northrop Corp., Dahran, Saudi Arabia, 1978-81; dir. materiel CRS, Riyadh, Saudi Arabia, 1981-83; head major subcontracts Lear Ziegler Corp., Santa Monica, Calif., 1984-88; pres., CEO Ice Village Ctrs., Inc., L.A., 1988—; bd. dirs. Ice Village Ctrs., Inc., L.A., Forefront Industries, Maywood, Calif. Bd. dirs. World Children's Transplant Fund, L.A., 1987-95; mem. Mayor's Space Adv. Com., L.A., 1970-74; mem. aerospace hist. com. Mus. Sci. and Industry, L.A., 1988—. Mem. AIAA (sec. chmn. 1970), Ret. Officers Assn.

(pres. 1992-95), Soc. for Non-destructive Testing (program chmn. 1973), Am. Soc. Quality Control, Am. Meterol. Soc., Sigma Alpha Epsilon (alumni chpt. pres. 1974-76). Avocations: golf, scuba diving, sailing, flying, gardening. Home: 8027 Hollywood Blvd Los Angeles CA 90046-2510

PERKINS, WILLIAM H., JR., finance company executive; b. Rushville, Ill., Aug. 4, 1921; s. William H. and Sarah Elizabeth (Logsdon) P.; m. Eileen Nelson, Jan. 14, 1949; 1 child, Gary Douglas. Ed., Ill. Coll. Pres. Howlett-Perkins Assos., Chgo.; mem. Ill. AEC, 1963-84, sec., 1970-84; mem. adv. bd. Nat. Armed Forces Mus., Smithsonian Instn., 1964-82. Sgt.-at-arms Democratic Nat. Conv., 1952, 56, del.-at-large, 1964, 68, 72; spl. asst. to chmn. Dem. Nat. Com., 1960; mem. Presdl. Inaugural Com., 1961, 65, 69, 73. Served with U.S. Army, 1944-46. Mem. Ill. Ins. Fedn. (pres. 1965-84), Ill. C. of C. (chmn. legis. com. 1971), Chgo. Assn. Commerce and Industry (legis. com., Raoul Wallenberg Humanitarian award 1993), Sangamo Club, Masons, Shriners. Methodist. Home: 52 N Cowley Rd Riverside IL 60546-2042 Office: 19 Riverside Rd Ste 6 Riverside IL 60546-2263

PERKINS, WILLIAM HUGHES, speech pathologist, educator; b. Kansas City, Mo., Feb. 21, 1923; s. William C. and Edna (Hughes) P.; m. Jill Thompson, June 16, 1952; children: Christopher, Scott, Alizon, Kyle. BS, Southwest Mo. State U., 1943; MA, U. Mo.-Columbia, 1949, PhD, 1952. Lic. speech pathologist, Calif. Asst. prof. communications arts and scis., dept. speech sci. and tech. U. So. Calif., L.A., 1952-56, assoc. prof., 1956-60, prof., 1960-88, dir. Stuttering Ctr., 1957-88, disting. prof. emeritus, 1988—; adv. editor Coll.-Hill Press, San Diego, 1980-87. Author: Speech Pathology, 1967, Human Perspectives in Speech and Language Disorders, 1977; editor Jour. Speech and Hearing Disorders, 1977-81, Current Therapy of Communications Disorders, 1983-84, Functional Anatomy of Speech, Language and Hearing, 1986; editor-in-chief Seminars in Speech and Language, 1983-90, Recent Advances in Communications Disorders, 1984, Stuttering Prevented: A Guide for Parens, 1991, Stuttering and Science, 1996. Served to lt. comdr. USN, 1943-46. Fellow Am. Speech and Hearing Assn. (Honors of Assn. award 1983). Home: 5425 Weatherford Dr Los Angeles CA 90008-1048

PERKINS SENN, KARON ELAINE, lawyer; b. Lexington, Ky., Nov. 9, 1959; d. John Robert and Sharon Lynn (Cook) Perkins; m. F. Anthony Senn. BA, Purdue U., 1980; cert. of proficiency, Pushkin Inst. Russian Lang., Moscow, 1980; JD, Ind. U., 1983. Bar: Ind. 1984, U.S. Dist. Ct. (so. dist.) Ind. 1984, U.S. Dist. Ct. (no. dist.) Ind. 1990. Internt. mktg. specialist Ind. Dept. Commerce, Indpls., 1980-81; law clk. Mendelson, Kennedy, Miller, Muller & Hall, Indpls., 1981-83; assoc. Jewell, Crump & Angermeier, Columbus, Ind., 1983-86; ptnr. Dalmbert, Marshall & Perkins, Columbus, 1986-92; pvt. practice Columbus, Ind., 1992—; asst. city atty. City of Columbus, 1985-95; town atty. Town of Hope (Ind.), 1987-89; course coord. law for non lawyers Ind. U.-Purdue U., Columbus, 1985-95; course coord. inst. law Sr. Citizen Crt., Columbus, 1990; author, speaker continuing legal edn. seminar, 1988, 89, 90, 91, 92, 94; bd. dirs., sec. Bartholomew Area Legal Aid, 1984-96. Mem. Leadership Bartholomew County, Columbus, 1986; bd. dirs. Salvation Army, Columbus, 1986-92, Columbus Dance Workshop; chmn. Bartholomew County Young Reps., 1986-88, 2d dist. Young Reps., 1987-91; treas. Columbus Task Force on Poor Relief, 1985-90. Recipient Outstanding Female Young Rep., Ind. Young Rep. Fedn., 1987, cert. of appreciation Ind. Tsk Force on Poor Relief, 1987; faculty alumni fellow Ind. U., 1983. Mem. ABA (del. young lawyers div. 1986-87), Ind. Bar Assn. (council, bd. dirs. young lawyers sect., sec.-treas., chair), Bartholomew Bar Assn. (sec., sec.-treas. 1984-90), Ind. Assn. Trial Lawyers, Columbus Jayshees (v.p. 1986, Outstanding New Mem. award 1985), Columbus Jaycees (bd. dirs. 1987), Zonta Club (purliamentarian Columbus 1986-88), Kiwanis. Baptist. Avocations: hiking, reading, sports. Home: 15830 E Lakeshore Dr N Ct Hope IN 47246 Office: 404 Washington St Ste 204 Columbus IN 47201-6758

PERKOFF, GERALD THOMAS, physician, educator; b. St. Louis, Sept. 22, 1926; s. Nat and Ann (Schwartz) P.; m. Marion Helen Maizner, June 7, 1947; children: David Alan, Judith Ilene, Susan Gail. M.D. cum laude, Washington U., 1948. Intern Salt Lake City Gen. Hosp., 1948-49, resident, 1950-52; from instr. to asso. prof. medicine U. Utah, 1954-63; chief med. service Salt Lake VA Hosp., 1961-63; asso. prof., then prof. medicine Washington U. Sch. Medicine, St. Louis, 1963-79; chief Med. Service, St. Louis City Hosp., 1963-68, prof. preventive medicine and pub. health, dir. div. health care research, 1968-79; Curators prof. and assoc. chmn. dept. family and community medicine and prof. medicine U. Mo., Columbia, 1979-91, Curators prof. emeritus, 1991—; co-dir. program health care and human values U. Mo., 1984-85; chmn. nat. adv. com. Robert Wood Johnson Clin. Scholars Program, 1989-96; dep. dir. Robert Wood Johnson Found. Generalist Physician Initiative, 1991—; career rsch. prof. neuromuscular diseases Nat. Found. Neuromuscular Diseases, 1961; founder, dir. Med. Care Group of Washington U., 1968-78. Contbr. articles profl jours. Served as jr. asst. surgeon USPHS, 1953-54. John and Mary R. Markle scholar med. sci., 1955-60; Henry J. Kaiser Sr. fellow Ctr. Advanced Studies in Behavioral Sci., Stanford, 1976-77, 85-86. Mem. Am. Soc. Clin. Investigation, Soc. Tchrs. Family Medicine, Assn. Am. Physicians, Inst. Medicine (Nat. Acad. Scis.). Home: 1300 Torrey Pines Dr Columbia MO 65203-4826 Office: U Mo Sch Medicine Dept Family & Community Medicine M228 Med Scis Columbia MO 65212

PERKOVIC, ROBERT BRANKO, international management consultant; b. Belgrade, Yugoslavia, Aug. 27, 1925; came to U.S., 1958, naturalized, 1961; s. Slavoljub and Ruza (Pantelic) P.; m. Jacquelyn Lee Lipscomb, Dec. 14, 1957; children: Bonnie Kathryn, Jennifer Lee. M.S. in Econs, U. Belgrade, 1954; B.F.T., Am. Grad. Sch. Internat. Mgmt., 1960; grad. Stanford exec. program, Stanford U., 1970. Auditor Gen. Foods Corp., White Plains, N.Y., 1960-62; controller Gen. Foods Corp., Mexico City, 1962-64; dir. planning Monsanto Co., Barcelona, Spain, 1964-67; dir. fin. Monsanto Co., Europe, Brussels, 1967-70; dir. fin. planning-internat. Monsanto Co., St. Louis, 1970-71; asst. treas. Monsanto Co., 1971-72, Brussels, 1972-74; corp. treas. Fiat-Allis Inc. & BV, Deerfield, Ill., 1974-78; v.p., treas. TRW Inc., Cleve., 1978-88; pres. RBP Internat. Cons., Cleve., 1988—; dir. U.S. Bus. Coun. for Southeastern Europe, Inc. Active Cleve. Commn. on Fgn. Relations. Inc. Served with Yugoslavian Army, 1944-47. Mem. Fin. Execs. Inst., Cleve. Treas. Club (bd. dirs., pres.), Mayfield Village (Ohio) Racquet Club. Office: RBP Internat Cons 26 Pepper Creek Dr Cleveland OH 44124-5248

PERKOWITZ, SIDNEY, physicist, educator, author; b. Bklyn., May 1, 1939; s. Morris and Sylvia (Gray) P.; m. Sandra Price; 1 child, Michael Abram. BS, N.Y. Poly., N.Y.C., 1960; MS, U. Pa., 1962, PhD, 1967. Rsch. physicist Gen. Telephone & Electronics Labs., Bayside, N.Y., 1966-69; asst. prof. physics Emory U., Atlanta, 1969-74, assoc. prof., 1974-79, prof., 1979-87, Charles Howard Candler prof., 1987—, chmn. dept., 1980-83; vis. prof. U. Calif.-Santa Barbara, 1983-84; cons. Santa Barbara Rsch. Ctr., 1983-87, Nat. Rsch. Coun. Can., Ottawa, 1988-91, NIST, Gaithersburg, Md., 1990-94; vis. scientist Southeastern Univs. Rsch. Assn., Washington, 1990-91; adj. prof. humanities Atlanta Coll. Arts, 1989—; mem. adv. panel Exptl. Gallery, Smithsonian Inst., Washington. Author: Optical Characterization of Semiconductors, 1993, Empire of Light, 1996; editor, contbr. numerous articles and essays to sci. publs. Grantee Sloan Found. Rsch. Corp., AEC, NIH, NSF, Office Naval Rsch., U.S. Dept. Energy, U.S. Dept. Def., TRW Corp., Korea Inst. Sci. and Tech., Lockheed Corp., Oak Ridge Nat. Lab. Mem. AAAS, Am. Phys. Soc., Soc. for Lit. and Sci. (v.p.), Phi Beta Kappa. Avocations: movies, crossword puzzles, music, hiking. Office: Emory U Rollins Rsch Ctr Physics Dept Atlanta GA 30322-2430

PERKOWSKI, JAN LOUIS, language and literature educator; b. Perth Amboy, N.J., Dec. 29, 1936; m. Liliana Asenova Daskalova, May 24, 1989. AB, Harvard U., 1959, AM, 1960, PhD, 1965. Asst. prof. U. Calif., Santa Barbara, 1964-65; assoc. prof. U. Tex., Austin, 1965-74; prof. U. Va., Charlottesville, 1974—. Author: A Kashubian Idiolect in U.S., 1969, Vampires, Dwarves & Witches Among the Ontario Kashubs, 1972, Vampires of the Slavs, 1976, Gusle & Ganga Among the Hercegovinians of Toronto, 1978, The Darkling-A Treatise on Slavic Vampirism, 1989; contbr. numerous articles to jours. Grantee, fellow Ford Found., Harvard U., Kościuszko Found., U. Tex., Am. Philos. Soc., Nat. Mus. Man, U. Va., NEH, Kennan Inst., numerous others. Mem. Am. Assn. for the Advancement of Slavic Studies, Am. Assn. Tchrs. of Slavic and East European Langs. Office: U Va Dept Slavic Langs & Lits 109 Cabell Hall Charlottesville VA 22903

PERKOWSKI, MAREK ANDRZEJ, electrical engineering educator; b. Warszawa, Poland, Oct. 6, 1946; came to U.S., 1981; s. Adam Perkowski and Hanna (Zielinska) Mystkowska; m. Ewa Kaja Wilkowska, Oct. 26, 1974; 1 child, Mateusz Jan. MS in Electronics with distinction, T.U. of Warsaw, 1970, PhD in Automatics with distinction, 1980. Sr. asst. Inst. of Automatics, T.U. of Warsaw, 1973-80, asst. prof., 1980-81; vis. asst. prof. Dept. Elec. Engring., U. Minn., Mpls., 1981-83; assoc. prof. Portland State U., 1983-94, prof., 1994—. Co-author: Theory of Automata, 3d edit., 1976, Problems in Theory of Logic Circuits, 4th edit., 1986, Theory of Logic Circuits-Selected Problems, 3d edit., 1984; contbr. 134 articles to profl. jours., 11 chpts. to books. Mem. Solidarity, Warsaw, 1980-81. Recipient Design Automation award SIGDA/ACM/DATC IEEE, 1986-91; Rsch. grantee NSF, 1991, 94, Commn. for Familites Roman Cath. Ch., Vatican, 1981, Air Force Ofice Sci. Rsch., 1995. Mem. IEEE (Computer Soc.), Polish Nat. Alliance, Assn. for Computing Machinery, Am. Soc. for Engring. Edn. Roman Catholic. Avocations: tourism, philosophy, woodcarving. Home: 15720 NW Perimeter Dr Beaverton OR 97006-5391 Office: Portland State U Dept Elec Engring PO Box 751 Portland OR 97207-0751

PERKOWSKI, PAUL JAMES, accountant; b. Glen Ridge, N.J., Feb. 19, 1956; s. Benjamin and Adele P.; m. Beth Vasselli, Sept. 17, 1978; children: Thomas, Katelyn. BS, Montclair State Coll., 1978. CPA. Auditor, sr. tax mgr. Ernst & Young, Hackensack, N.J.; ptnr. Perkowski & Assocs., CPAs, Spring Lake, N.J.; presenter in field. Mem. AICPA, Inst. Mgmt. Accts., N.J. Soc. CPAs, Internat. Assn. Fin. Planning (bd. dirs. 1988-94), Spring Lake C. of C. Roman Catholic. Office: Perkowski & Assocs CPAs 302 Washington Ave Spring Lake NJ 07762-1432

PERL, MARTIN LEWIS, physicist, educator; b. N.Y.C., June 24, 1927; children: Jed, Anne, Matthew, Joseph. B.Chem. Engring., Poly. Inst. Bklyn., 1948; Ph.D., Columbia U., 1955; ScD (hon.), U. Chgo., 1990. Chem. engr. Gen. Electric Co., 1948-50; asst. prof. physics U. Mich., 1955-58, asso. prof., 1958-63; prof. Stanford, 1963—. Author: High Energy Hadron Physics, 1975; contbr. articles on high energy physics and on relation of sci. to soc. to profl. jours. Served with U.S. Mcht. Marine, 1944-45; Served with AUS, 1945-46. Recipient Wolf prize in physics, 1982, Nobel Prize in Physics, 1995. Fellow Am. Phys. Soc.; mem. Nat. Acad. Scis., AAAS. Home: 3737 El Centro Ave Palo Alto CA 94306-2642 Office: Stanford U Stanford Linear Accelerator Ctr Stanford CA 94305

PERLBERG, JULES MARTIN, lawyer; b. Chgo., Jan. 28, 1931; s. Maurice and Louise Mae (Schonberger) P.; m. Dora Ann Morris, Dec. 22, 1968; children: Julia, Michael. BBA with high distinction, U. Mich., 1952, JD with high distinction, 1957. Bar: Ill. 1958, D.C. 1964; C.P.A., Ill. Acct. Arthur Andersen & Co., Chgo., 1954-55; faculty U. Mich. Law Sch., Ann Arbor, 1957-58; assoc. Sidley & Austin and predecessor firm, Chgo., 1958-65, ptnr., 1966—. Mem. Glencoe (Ill.) Bd. Edn., 1980-87, pres., 1985-86; bd. dirs. Juvenile Diabetes Found., Chgo., 1981—, v.p. 1983-85, treas., 1988-90; exec. bd. Am. Jewish Com., Chgo., 1978-88, v.p., 1981-83; trustee New Trier Twp. Schs., 1987-91, pres., 1989-91; class co-chairperson parents com. Duke U., 1992-94. 1st lt. U.S. Army, 1952-54. Recipient Gold medal Ill. Soc. C.P.A.s, 1955. Mem. ABA, Chgo. Bar Assn. Clubs: Legal, Law; Mid-Day (Chgo.); Standard. Home: 568 Westley Rd Glencoe IL 60022-1071 Office: Sidley & Austin 1 First Nat Plz Chicago IL 60603

PERLE, EUGENE GABRIEL, lawyer; b. N.Y.C., Dec. 21, 1922; s. Philip and Simme (Meschenberg) P.; m. Ellen Carlotta Kraus, Nov. 26, 1953 (dec. 1964); 1 child, Elizabeth Anne; m. Ruth Friedberg Lerner, May 23, 1972 (div. 1977); m. Patricia Fitzpatrick Sinnott, Jan. 24, 1981. BA, Queens Coll., 1943; JD, Yale U., 1949. Bar: N.Y. 1950. Assoc. Cravath, Swaine & Moore, N.Y.C., 1949-53; asst. counsel N.Y. State Moreland Commn. Investigation Harness Racing, N.Y.C., 1953-54; assoc. Gordon, Brady, Caffrey & Keller, N.Y.C., 1954-56; assoc. gen. atty. Time Inc., N.Y.C., 1956-66; pub. counsel Time Inc., 1966-73, v.p. law, 1973-80, corp. v.p. law, 1980-85; counsel Proskauer Rose Goetz & Mendelsohn, N.Y.C., 1985-92, Chapman & Fennell, 1992-94; mem. Ohlandt, Greeley, Ruggiero & Perle, Stamford, Conn., 1995—. Co-author: The Publishing Law Handbook, 1988-95; mem. editl. bd. Yale Law Jour., 1948-49; mem. adv. bd. Bur. Nat. Affairs Patent, Trademark and Copyright Jour., 1972-86; contbr. to Bull. Copyright Soc. U.S.A. Trustee Baron deHirsch Fund, 1959-87, hon. trustee, 1988—; commr. Nat. Commn. New Technol. Uses Copyrighted Works, 1975-78; bd. dirs. N.Y. Sch. for Circus Arts, Inc., 1979-87, Am. Arbitration Assn., 1979-84; justice of peace City of Norwalk, Conn., 1960-63. Lt. USNR, 1943-46. Mem. ABA (chmn. copyright divsn. 1970-71, 86-87, chmn. com. copyright and new tech. 1971-73, chmn. com. econs. profession 1976, coun. patent, trademark and copyright sect. 1979-83, governing bd. forum com. comms. law 1979-85, chmn. related fields and future devels. divsn. forum com. entertainment and sports industries 1979), Copyright Soc. U.S.A. (trustee 1962-64, 69-70, 71-74, pres. 1976-78, hon. trustee 1978—), U.S. Trademark Assn. (bd. dirs. 1969-72, 74-77, v.p. 1972-73), Assn. of Bar of City of N.Y., Sunningdale Country Club, Century Assn. Club, Adms. Cove Club. Democrat. Office: Ohlandt Greeley One Landmark Sq Stamford CT 06901

PERLE, GEORGE, composer; b. Bayonne, N.J., May 6, 1915; s. Joseph and Mary (Sanders) Perlman; m. Laura Slobe, 1940; m. Barbara Philips, Aug. 11, 1958 (dec.); children: Kathy, Annette; 1 stepchild, Max Massey; m. Shirley Gabis Rhoads, June 6, 1982; stepchildren: Paul Rhoads, Daisy Rhoads. MusB, DePaul U., 1938; MusM, Am. Conservatory of Music, 1942; Ph.D., NYU, 1956. Mem. faculty U. Louisville, 1949-57, U. Calif., 1957-61, Juilliard Sch. Music, 1963, Yale U., 1965-66, U. So. Calif., summer 1965, Tanglewood, summers 1967, 80, 87; from asst. prof. to assoc. prof. to prof. CUNY, 1961-85, prof. emeritus, 1985—; composer-in-residence San Francisco Symphony, 1989-91; vis. Birge-Cary prof. music SUNY, Buffalo, 1971-72; vis. prof. U. Pa., 1976, 80, Columbia U., 1979, 83; vis. Ernest Bloch prof. music U. Calif., Berkeley, 1989; vis. disting. prof. music NYU, N.Y.C., 1994. Author: Serial Composition and Atonality 1962, 6th edit., 1991, Twelve-Tone Tonality, 1977, 2d edit., 1996, The Operas of Alban Berg, vol. 1, 1980, vol. 2, 1985, The Listening Composer, 1990, The Right Notes, 1995, Style and Idea in the Lyric Suite of Alban Berg, 1995; contbr. articles in Am., fgn. mus. jours.; composer: Pantomime, Interlude and Fugue, 1937, Little Suite for Piano, 1939, Two Rilke Songs, 1941, Sonata for Solo Viola, 1942, Three Sonatas for Clarinet, 1943, Piano Piece, 1945, Hebrew Melodies for Cello, 1945, Lyric Piece for Cello and Piano, 1946, Six Preludes for Piano, 1946, Sonata for Solo Cello, 1947, Solemn Procession for Band, 1947, Sonata for Piano, 1950, Three Inventions for Piano, 1957, Quintet for Strings, 1958, Wind Quintet I, 1959, Sonata I for Solo Violin, 1959, Wind Quintet II, 1960, Fifth String Quartet, 1960-67, Three Movements for Orchestra, 1960, Monody I for flute, 1960, Music for The Birds of Aristophanes, 1961, Monody II for double bass 1962, Serenade I for Viola and Chamber Ensemble, 1962, Three Inventions for Bassoon, 1962, Sonata II for Solo Violin, 1963, Short Sonata for Piano, 1964, Solo Partita for Violin and Viola, 1965, Six Bagatelles for Orch., 1965, Concerto for Cello and Orch., 1966, Wind Quintet III, 1967, Serenade II for Chamber Ensemble, 1968, Toccata for Piano, 1969, Suite in C for Piano, 1970, Fantasy-Variations for Piano, 1971, Sonata Quasi una Fantasia for Clarinet and Piano, 1972, Seventh String Quartet, 1973, Songs of Praise and Lamentation for chorus and orch. 1974, Six Etudes for Piano, 1976, 13 Dickinson Songs, 1978, Concertino for Piano, Winds, and Timpani, 1979, A Short Symphony, 1980; Ballade for Piano, 1981, Sonata a quattro, 1982, Serenade III for Piano and Chamber Ensemble, 1983, Six New Etudes for Piano, 1984, Wind Quintet IV, 1984, Sonata for Cello and Piano, 1985, Sonatina for Piano, 1986, Sonata a cinque, 1986, Dance Fantasy for Orch., 1986, Lyric Intermezzo for chamber orch., 1987, Lyric Intermezzo for fifteen players, 1987, Lyric Intermezzo for piano, 1987, New Fanfares for brass ensemble, 1987, Sinfonietta, 1987, Windows of Order for string quartet, 1988, Sextet for winds and piano, 1988, Concerto for Piano and Orch., 1990, Sinfonietta II, 1990, Concerto No. 2 for Piano and Orch., 1992, Adagio for Orch., 1992, Transcendental Modulations (commd. for 150 anniversary N.Y. Philharmonic), 1993, Phantasyplay for Piano, 1994, Duos for French horn and string quartet, 1995, Six Celebratory Inventions, 1995. Served with AUS, 1943-46, ETO, PTO. Recipient Nat. Inst. Arts and Letters award, 1977, Pulitzer prize, 1986; Guggenheim fellow, 1966-67, 74-75, MacArthur fellow, 1986; grantee Am. Council Learned Socs., 1968-69, Nat. Endowment for the Arts, 1978-79, 85. Fellow Am. Acad. Arts and Scis.; mem. Am. Musicol. Soc., ASCAP (Deems Taylor award 1973, 78, 81), Am. Acad. Arts and Letters.

PERLE, RICHARD NORMAN, government official; b. N.Y.C., Sept. 16, 1941; s. Jack Harold and Martha Gloria (Needell) P.; m. Leslie Joan Barr, July 31, 1977; 1 child, Jonathan Barr. BA, U. So. Calif., 1964; postgrad. in econs., U. London, 1962-63; MA, Princeton U., 1967. Asst. sec. internat. security policy Dept. Def., Washington, 1981-87; prof. staff mem. subcom. nat. security Senate Com. on Govt. Ops., Washington, 1970-72; profl. staff mem. committee on armed services U.S. Senate, Washington, 1969-80; resident fellow Am. Enterprise Inst. for Pub. Policy Rsch., Washington, 1987—. Office: Am Enterprise Inst Pub Policy Rsch 1150 17th St NW Washington DC 20036-4603

PERLESS, ELLEN, advertising executive; b. N.Y.C., Sept. 9, 1941; d. Joseph B. and Bertha (Messinger) Kaplan; m. Robert L. Perless, July 2, 1965. Student, Smith Coll., 1958-59; BA, Bard Coll., 1962. Copywriter Doyle, Dane Bernbach, N.Y.C., 1964-70, Young & Rubicam, N.Y.C., 1970-74; creative supr. Young & Rubicam, 1974-76, v.p., creative supr., 1977, v.p., assoc. creative dir., 1978, sr. v.p., assoc. creative dir., 1979-84; v.p., assoc. creative dir. Leber Katz Ptnrs., 1984-85, sr. v.p., creative dir., 1986-87; sr. v.p., sr. creative dir. FCB/Leber Katz Ptnrs., N.Y.C., 1987-93, sr. v.p., group creative dir., 1994—. Recipient Clio awards, Andy awards, awards Art Dirs. Club N.Y., N.Y. Festivals, One Club. Home: 37 Langhorne Ln Greenwich CT 06831-2611 Office: FCB/Leber Katz Ptnrs 150 E 42 St New York NY 10017

PERLESS, ROBERT L., sculptor; b. N.Y.C., Apr. 23, 1938; s. Meyer and Ethel (Glassman) P.; m. Ellen R. Kaplan, July 2, 1965. Student, U. Miami, Fla., 1955-59. One-man exhbns. include Bodley Gallery, N.Y.C., 1968, 70, Galerie Simonne Stern, New Orleans, 1969, Bernard Danenberg Gallery, N.Y.C., 1970-72, Bonino Gallery, N.Y.C., 1976; group exhbns. include Bodley Gallery, 1970, Whitney Mus., 1970, Forum Gallery, N.Y.C., 1975, Bonino Gallery, 1975, Houston Gallery, 1976, Aldrich Mus., Ridgefield, Conn., 1978, Taft Mus., Cin., 1980, Aldrich Mus., 1987, 94, Stamford (Conn.) Mus., 1989, Bruce Mus., Greenwich, Conn., 1989, Andre Emmerich's Top Gallant Farm, 1991, 92, 93, 94, 95, 96; represented in permanent collections at Whitney Mus., Aldrich Mus., Chrysler Mus., Norfolk, Va., Everson Mus., Syracuse, N.Y., Okla. Art Ctr., Oklahoma City, Phoenix Art Mus., Stamford (Conn.) Mus. Address: 37 Langhorne Ln Greenwich CT 06831-2611

PERLIK, WILLIAM R., lawyer; b. Pitts., May 20, 1925; s. Charles A. and Teresa Anna (Kraft) P.; m. Annabel Virginia Shanklin, June 16, 1949; children—Ronald A., Lynn C. B.A., Oberlin Coll., 1948; J.D., Yale U., 1951. Bar: D.C. 1952, Va. 1955, U.S. Supreme Ct. 1974. Law clk. to judge U.S. Ct. Appeals, Washington, 1951-52; assoc., then ptnr. Cox Langford Stoddard & Cutler, Washington, 1952-62; ptnr., of counsel Wilmer Cutler & Pickering, Washington, 1962—; adj. prof. politics Oberlin Coll., Ohio, 1973—. Trustee, chmn., mem. exec. com. Oberlin Coll., 1980—; pres. Va. Sch. Bd. Assn., 1971-72; mem. and chmn. Fairfax County Sch. Bd., Va., 1964-72; pres. Fairfax County Fedn. Citizens Assns., 1958. Served with U.S. Army, 1943-46; ETO. Recipient Edn. award Fairfax Edn. Assn., 1960; Citizen of Yr. award Washington Evening Star, 1961. Mem. ABA. Avocations: music; hiking; gardening. Home: 1249 Daleview Dr Mc Lean VA 22102-1538 Office: Wilmer Cutler & Pickering 2445 M St NW Washington DC 20037-1435

PERLIN, ARTHUR SAUL, chemistry educator; b. Sydney, N.S., Can., July 7, 1923; s. Benjamin and Eva (Gaum) P.; m. Ruth Laurel Freedman, Nov. 18, 1950; children—Anna, Louise, Deborah, Myra, David. B.Sc., McGill U., Can., 1944, M.Sc., 1946, Ph.D., 1949. Research officer Nat. Research Council Can., Ottawa, Ont., Can., 1948-67; E.B. Eddy prof. chemistry McGill U., Montreal, Que., Can., 1967-91, prof. chemistry emeritus, 1991—; research scientist Pulp and Paper Research Inst. Can., Montreal, Que., 1967—. Contbr. articles to profl. jours., chpts. to books; patentee in field. Fellow Royal Soc. Can., Chem. Inst. Can.; mem. Am. Chem. Soc. (C.S. Hudson award 1979). Office: McGill U, Dept Chemistry, Montreal, PQ Canada H3C 3G1

PERLIN, SEYMOUR, psychiatrist, educator; b. Passaic, N.J., Sept. 27, 1925; s. Samuel and Fanny (Horowitz) P.; m. Ruth Joan Rudolph, Aug. 21, 1958; children: Jonathan Brian, Steven Michael, Jeremy Francis. Student, Johns Hopkins U., 1943-44; B.A. summa cum laude, Princeton U., 1946; M.D., Columbia U., 1950; grad., Washington Psychoanalytic Inst. Diplomate Am. Bd. Psychiatry and Neurology. Intern Univ. Hosp., Ann Arbor, Mich., 1951-52; resident N.Y. State Psychiat. Inst., 1950-51, 53-54, Manhattan State Hosp., 1952; practice medicine specializing in psychiatry and psychoanalysis Bethesda, Md., 1954-59, Stanford, Calif., 1959-60, N.Y.C., 1960-63, Balt., 1964-72, Bethesda, 1974—; chief div. psychiatry Montefiore Hosp., 1960-63; dir. clin. care and tng. Henry Phipps Psychiat. Clinic, Johns Hopkins Hosp., 1964-72; sr. research scholar Ctr. for Bioethics, Kennedy Inst., Georgetown U., Washington, 1974-78; clin. prof. psychiatry UCLA Sch. Medicine, 1973-74; clin. prof. psychiatry George Washington U. Sch. Medicine, 1974-76, prof., 1977—, also dir. residency tng., 1977-93; lectr. psychiatry Columbia U., 1963-64; assoc. prof. psychiatry Johns Hopkins Sch. Medicine, 1964-65, prof., 1966-72, dep. chmn. dept. psychiatry and behavioral scis., 1969-72; program dir. Fellowship Program in Suicidology, 1967-72; adv. council Univ. health services Princeton, 1970-82; vis. fellow Princeton U., 1973, Oxford U., 1974; Joseph P. Kennedy fellow medicine, law and ethics, 1974-75; chief sect. psychiatry Lab. Clin. Sci., NIMH, 1955-59, mem. clin. program-project com., 1967-70; fellow Ctr. Advanced Study in Behavioral Scis., 1959-60; chmn. mental health study sect. B, div. research grants NIH, 1964-66; cons. Community Mental Health Services, Md. Dept. Mental Hygiene, 1964-72; chmn. bd. dirs. Youth Suicide Nat. Ctr., 1985-87. Cons. editor: Jour. Suicide and Life Threatening Behavior, 1970-89; editorial bd.: Johns Hopkins Med. Jour, 1970-72; editor: Handbook for the Study of Suicide; co-editor: Ethical Issues in Death and Dying; contbr. numerous articles to med. jours. Served with USNR, 1944-46, with USPHS, 1954-58. Recipient Meirhoff award in pathology, 1950, Bicentennial Silver medal for achievement in psychiatry, 1967, both Coll. Phys. and Surg. Columbia. Fellow Am. Psychiat. Assn.; mem. Am. Coll. Psychiatry, Washington Psychoanalytic Soc., Med. Soc. D.C., Washington Psychiat. Soc., Am. Assn. Suicidology (pres. 1969-70, Dublin award 1978, ann. lectureship in suicidology in his name George Washington U. 1995). Home: 5125 Westbard Ave Bethesda MD 20816-1413 Office: Dept Psychiatry George Washington U Sch Medicine 2150 Pennsylvania Ave NW Washington DC 20037

PERLIS, DONALD M., artist; b. N.Y.C., July 29, 1941; s. Herman and Sylvia M. (Marks) P.; m. Theresa Brown, June 9, 1968. Student, Art Students League, 1961, Sch. Visual Arts, N.Y.C., 1965, Skowhegan Sch., 1965. One man show Sindin Gallery, N.Y.C., 1994, 95; exhibited paintings at Whitney Mus., N.Y.C., Graham Gallery, 1971, 75, Sindin Galleries, 1993, 95, Charas-Elbohio, 1993; documentary film on artist produced by Time Capsule Films, 1993; author monograph Allegories of Love, 1995. Mem. NAD. Home: 105 E 9th St New York NY 10003-5401

PERLIS, MICHAEL FREDRICK, lawyer; b. N.Y.C., June 3, 1947; s. Leo and Betty F. (Gantz) P.; children: Amy Hannah, David Matthew; m. Angela M. Rinaldi, Dec. 23, 1988. BS in Fgn. Svc., Georgetown U., 1968, JD, 1971. Bar: D.C. 1971, N.Y. 1993, U.S. Dist. Ct. D.C. 1971, U.S. Ct. Appeals 1971, D.C. Ct. Appeals 1971, Calif. 1980, U.S. Dist. Ct. (no. dist.) Calif. 1980, U.S. Dist. Ct. (cen. dist.) Calif. 1985, U.S. Ct. Appeals (9th cir.) 1980, U.S. Supreme Ct., 1980, N.Y. 1993. Law clerk D.C. Ct. Appeals, Washington, 1971-72; asst. corp. counsel D.C., Washington, 1972-74; counsel U.S. SEC, div. enforcement, Washington, 1974-75, br. chief, 1975-77, asst. dir., 1977-80; ptnr. Pettit & Martin, San Francisco, 1980-89, Stroock & Stroock & Lavan, L.A., 1989—; adj. prof. Cath. U. Am., 1979-80. Mem. ABA (co-chmn. subcom. securities and commodities litigation 1982-83), D.C. Bar Assn., Calif. State Bar Assn. Office: Stroock & Stroock & Lavan 2029 Century Park E Los Angeles CA 90067-2901

PERLIS, SHARON A., lawyer; b. New Orleans, Oct. 2, 1945; d. Rogers I. and Dorothy (Koehl) P. BA in French, Principia Coll., 1967; JD, Tulane U., 1970. Officer, dir. Perlis, Inc., New Orleans, 1973—; pres. SILREP

Internat. Co., Metairie, 1984-95; officer, dir. Internat. Adv. Svcs., Inc., New Orleans, 1985-89; prin. Perlis & Hogg, Metairie, 1985—; legal counsel La. Ins. Rating Commn., 1980-84; adminstrv. law judge State of La., 1980-84, mem. Econ. Devel. Adv. Coun., 1982-84; dir. The Chamber/New Orleans and The River Region, 1990-95, Bd. of Trade, 1990-96, exec. com. small bus. coun., 1987-89, chmn. small bus. coun., 1988, exec. com. East Jefferson coun., 1989—; dir. World Trade Co., 1985-96, vice-chmn. internat. bus. com.; dir. New Orleans br. Fed. Res. Bank of Atlanta, 1982-88, chmn., 1984, 86, 88; bd. of commr. Port of New Orleans, 1992-95, vice chmn., 1995, chmn., 1996. Mem. human rels commn. City of New Orleans, 1992-93; mem. exec. bd. La. Coun. Econ. Edn., 1986-89, Pvt. Enterprise Edn. Found., 1986-89; state del. White House Conf. on Small Bus., La. rep. internat. trade issues, 1986; dir. Metro YMCA, 1990-96; exec. com. agy. rels. United Way, 1987-90; mem. exec. com. Jr. Achievement Project Bus., 1987; vice chmn. La. Dist. Export Coun. Recipient Achiever's award Woman Bus. owners Assn., 1994, Jefferson Econ. Devel. Commn. award, 1994, Advocacy of Yr. award Small Bus. Adminstrn., 1988. Mem. Phi Alpha Eta. Avocations: reading, sailing, tennis. Office: Perlis & Hogg 3421 N Causeway Blvd Ste 404 Metairie LA 70002-3722

PERLMAN, BARRY STUART, electrical engineering executive, researcher; b. Bklyn., Dec. 5, 1939; s. Harold Wallace and Jane (Cohen) P.; m. Carolyn Amelia Francis; 1 child, David Matthew. BEE, CCNY, 1961; MSEE, Poly. Inst. N.Y., 1964, PhD in Electrophysics, 1973. Mem. tech. staff, comms. lab. RCA Corp., N.Y.C., 1961-68; mem. tech. staff RCA Labs., Princeton, N.J., 1968-81, mgr. microwave rsch. lab., 1981-86, head design automation rsch., 1986-88; chief microwave photonic devices br. Electronics and Power Source Directorate, Army Rsch. Lab., Ft. Monmouth, N.J., 1988-95; dir. electronics div. Phys. Scis. Directorate, Army Rsch. Lab., Ft. Monmouth, 1995—; pres., mem. bd. dirs. INTEREX, Los Altos, Calif., 1981-83; rep. adv. group on electron devices Group A, RF Components, Office of Under-sec. of Def.; mem. tech. adv. bd. U. R.I., Ctr. High Frequency Microelectronics, U. Mich.; mem. ind. adv. bd. Computer Applications to Electromagnetics Edn., NSF and U. Utah, 1990—, MIMICAD Ctr., U. Colo., 1989—; Ctr. prof. microwave/lightwave engring. Drexel U., Phila., 1992—. Editor: Advances in Microwaves, 1974; mem. editl. bd. Wiley Jour. MW.MMW CAD, 1992—; contbr. articles to profl. jours.; patentee in field. Bd. dirs. YMCA, Princeton, 1975-78; pres. Home Owners Assn., E. Windsor, N.J., 1976-78; instr. Am. Heart Assn., N.J., 1978-82; chief rescue squad, E. Windsor, 1978-82. Fellow IEEE (awards and advancement com. 1987—); mem. Microwave Theory and Tech. Soc. of IEEE (editl. bd., chmn. CAD com. MTT-1 1985-92, MTT adcom. 1990-94, others), Ultrasonics, Ferroelectrics and Frequency Control, Cirs. and Sys., Automated RF Techniques Group (treas. 1984-88, v.p. 1990-91). Avocations: scouting, woodworking, photography, camping, gardening, tennis. Office: Army Rsch Lab AMSRL-PS-E Fort Monmouth NJ 07703-5000

PERLMAN, BURTON, judge; b. New Haven, Dec. 17, 1924; s. Phillip and Minnie Perlman; m. Alice Weihl, May 20, 1956; children: Elizabeth, Sarah, Nancy, Daniel. B.E., Yale U., 1945, M.E., 1947; LL.B., U. Mich., 1952. Bar: Ohio, 1959, N.Y. 1953, Conn. 1952, U.S. Dist. Ct. (so. and ea. dists.) N.Y. 1954, U.S. Ct. Appeals (2d cir.) 1953, U.S. Ct. Appeals (6th cir.) 1959, U.S. Dist. Ct. (so. dist.) Ohio 1959. Assoc. Armand Lackenbach, N.Y.C., 1952-58; pvt. practice, Cin., 1958-61; assoc. Paxton and Seasongood, 1961-67; ptnr. Schmidt, Effton, Josselson and Weber, 1968-71; U.S. magistrate U.S. Dist. Ct. (so. dist.) Ohio, 1971-76; U.S. bankruptcy judge, 1976—; chief bankruptcy judge so. dist. Ohio, 1986-93; adj. prof. U. Cin. Law Sch., 1976—. Served with U.S. Army, 1944-46. Mem. ABA, Fed. Bar Assn., Am. Judicature Soc., Cin. Bar Assn. Office: US Bankruptcy Ct Atrium Two Ste 800 221 E 4th St Cincinnati OH 45202

PERLMAN, D(AVID), biochemist, educator; b. Madison, Wis., Feb. 6, 1920; s. Selig and Eva (Shaber) P.; m. Kató Lenárd, Aug. 18, 1968. B.A., U. Wis., 1941, M.S., 1943, Ph.D., 1945. Biochemist Hoffmann-LaRoche, Inc., 1945; microbiologist Merck & Co., 1945-47; biochemist Squibb Inst. for Med. Research, 1947-67; prof. Sch. Pharmacy, U. Wis., Madison, 1967—, dean, 1968-75; Chmn. 3d Internat. Congress Genetics of Indsl. Microorganisms, 1968-75, Kremers prof. pharm. biochemistry, 1979—; chmn. Conf. on Antimicrobial Agts. and Chemotherapy, 1966, 67, Gordon Research Conf. on Coenzymes and Metabolic Pathways, 1966. Editor: Advances Applied Microbiology, 1968—, Ann. Reports Fermentation Processes, 1977—; Contbr. articles to profl. jours. Guggenheim fellow, 1966. Fellow Am. Acad. Microbiology, N.Y. Acad. Scis., Acad. Pharm. Scis.; mem. Am. Chem. Soc. (Disting. Service award div. microbiol and biochem. tech. 1977, Marvin J. Johnson award (same div. 1978), Am. Soc. Microbiology (pres. found. 1974-75, Fisher Sci. Co. award 1979, Pasteur award Ill. sect. 1979), Am. Soc. Pharmacognosists, Tissue Culture Assn., Soc. for Gen. Microbiology, Am. Pharm. Assn., Am. Soc. Biol. Chemistry, Biochem. Soc., Soc. for Indsl. Microbiology (Charles Thom award 1979), Sigma Xi. Home: 1 Chippewa Ct Madison WI 53711-2803

PERLMAN, DAVID, science editor, journalist; b. Balt., Dec. 30, 1918; s. Jess and Sara P.; m. Anne Salz, Oct. 15, 1941; children: Katherine, Eric, Thomas. A.B., Columbia U., 1939, M.S., 1940. Reporter Bismarck (N.D.) Capital, 1940; reporter San Francisco Chronicle, 1940-41, reporter, sci. editor, 1952-77, city editor, 1977-79, assoc. editor, sci. editor, 1979—; reporter New York Herald Tribune, Paris, N.Y.C., 1945-49; European corr. Colliers mag. and New York Post, 1949-51; Regents prof. human biology U. Calif., San Francisco 1974; vis. lectr. China Assn. Sci. and Tech., Beijing, Chengdu and Shanghai, 1983; sci. writer-in-residence U. Wis., 1989. Contbr. articles to major mags. Founding dir. Squaw Valley (Calif.) Community of Writers; dir. Alan Guttmacher Inst., 1985—; trustee Scientists Inst. for Pub. Info., 1986-94. Served with inf. USAAF, 1941-45. Recipient Atomic Indls. Forum award, 1975, AAAS Sci. Writing award, 1976, Ralph Coates Roe medal ASME, 1978, Margaret Sanger Cmty. Svc. award, 1981, Fellows' medal Calif. Acad. Scis., 1984, Career Achievement award Soc. Profl. Journalists, 1989, Glenn T. Seaborg award Internat. Platform Assn., 1993; Poynter fellow Yale U., 1984, Carnegie Corp. fellow Stanford U., 1987. Fellow Calif. Acad. Scis.; mem. AAAS (adv. bd. Science-81-86 mag., com. Pub. Understanding of Sci. 1985-90), Coun. for Advancement Sci. Writing (pres. 1976-80), Nat. Assn. Sci. Writers (pres. 1970-71, Disting. Sci. Journalism award 1994), Astron. Soc. Pacific (dir. 1976-78), Sigma Xi. Office: Chronicle Pub Co 901 Mission St San Francisco CA 94103-2905

PERLMAN, GILBERT E., publishing executive; b. N.Y.C., Mar. 26, 1954; s. Michael G. and Annette (Posner) P.; m. Betsy R. Erlich, May 9, 1980; children: Michael, Alexandra. BS in Econs., U. Pa., 1976. Bus. mgr. Philo Records, North Ferrisburg, Vt., 1976-78; fin. analyst Ballantine Books, N.Y.C., 1978-80, bus. mgr., 1980-84, v.p. dir. bus. ops., 1984-88, sr. v.p. dir. bus. ops., 1988-93; exec. v.p. Ballantine Pub. Group, N.Y.C., 1994—. Office: Ballantine Pub Group 201 E 50th St New York NY 10022-7703

PERLMAN, ITZHAK, violinist; b. Tel Aviv, Aug. 31, 1945; s. Chaim and Shoshana P.; m. Toby Lynn Friedlander, 1967; 5 children. Student, Tel Aviv Acad. Music, Juilliard Sch., Meadowmount Sch. Music.; hon. degree in music, Tufts U., 1986. Appeared with N.Y. Philharm., Cleve. Orch., Phila. Orch., Nat. Symphony Orch., most orchs. in U.S., with Berlin Philharm., English Chamber Orch., London Symphony, London Philharm., Royal Philharm., BBC Orch., Vienna Philharm, Concertgebouw; participant numerous music festivals, including Ravinia Festival, Berkshire Music Festival, Aspen Music Festival, Israel Festival, Wolf Trap Summer Festival, recital tours, U.S., Can., S.Am., Europe, Israel, Australia, Far East; recorded for Angel, London, RCA Victor, DG, CBS records. Recipient Leventritt prize 1964; The Art of Perlman, (with Janet Goodman Guggenheim), Itzak Perlman's Greatest Hits (with Kathleen Battle) The Bach Album, (with Andre Previn) A Different Kind of Blues, (with Andre Previn) It's A Breeze, (with Pinchas Zucherman) Duets for Violins. Recipient Leventritt prize, 1964, Grammy awards, 1977, 78, 80-82, 87, Award - Medal of Liberty, 1986; hon. doctorates from Harvard U., Yale U, Brandeis U., Hebrew U.-Jerusalem. Address: EMI Classics/Angel Records care CEMA Distrs 21700 Oxnard St #700 Woodland Hills CA 91367

PERLMAN, LAWRENCE, business executive; b. St. Paul, Apr. 8, 1938; s. Irving and Ruth (Mirsky) P.; children: David, Sara. BA, Carleton Coll., 1960; JD, Harvard U., 1963. Bar: Minn. 1963. Law. clk. for fed. judge, 1963; assoc., ptnr. Fredrikson & Byron, Mpls., 1964-75; gen. counsel, exec. v.p. U.S. pacing ops. Medtronic, Inc., Mpls., 1975-78; sr. ptnr. Oppenheimer, Wolff & Donnelly, Mpls., 1978-80; sec., gen. counsel, v.p. corp. svcs. Control Data Corp., Mpls., 1980-82; pres. Comml. Credit Co., 1983-85, Imprimis Technology, 1985-88; pres., chief oper. officer Control Data Corp., Mpls., 1989; pres., chief exec. officer Control Data Corp. (now Ceridian Corp.), 1990-92; chmn., pres., CEO Ceridian Corp., Mpls., 1992—; bd. dirs. Ceridian Corp., Kmart Corp.,Inter-Regional Fin. Group, Inc., Seagate Tech., Inc., The Valspar Corp., Computer Network Tech.; mem. nat. adv. bd. Chem. Banking Corp. Chmn., bd. dirs. Walker Art Ctr.; regent Univ. of Minn., 1993-95. Mem. Bus. Roundtable (mem. policy com.). Office: Ceridian Corp 8100 34th Ave S Minneapolis MN 55425-1640

PERLMAN, MARK, economist, educator; b. Madison, Wis., Dec. 23, 1923; s. Selig and Eva (Shaber) P.; m. Naomi Gertrude Waxman, June 7, 1953; 1 child, Abigail Ruth Williams. B.A., M.A., U. Wis., 1947; Ph.D., Columbia, 1950. Asst. prof. U. Hawaii, 1951-52, Cornell U., 1952-55; asst. prof., then assoc. prof. Johns Hopkins U., 1955-63; prof. econs., history and pub. health U. Pitts., 1963-94, chmn. dept., 1965-70, univ. prof., 1969-94, prof. emeritus, 1994—; co-chmn. Internat. Econ. Assn. Conf. on Econs. of Health in Industrialized Nations, Tokyo, Japan, 1973, Conf. on Orgn. and Retrieval Econs. Data, Kiel, West Germany, 1975; vis. fellow Clare Hall U. Cambridge, 1977; ofcl. visitor faculty econs. and politics, U. Cambridge, 1976-77; co-chmn., co-editor Internat. Congress on Health Econs., Leyden, The Netherlands, 1980; mem. Princeton Inst. Adv. Study, 1981-82; adj. scholar Am. Enterprise Inst., 1981—; Österreichischer Länderbank Joseph Schumpeter prof. Technische Universität, Vienna, 1982; disting. vis. scholar Beijing Chinese Nat. Acad. Social Scis., 1983; Rockefeller Found. resident scholar Villa Serbelloni, Bellagio, Como, Italy, 1983; vis. prof. Inst. für Weltwirtschaft U. Kiel, 1987, U. Augsburg, 1992; mem. Internat. Com. for Documentation in the Social Scis., UNESCO, 1988—, exec. com. 1993—. Author: Judges in Industry: A Study of Labor Arbitration in Australia, 1954, Labor Union Theories in America, 1958, 2d edit., 1976, The Machinists: A New Study in American Trade Unionism, 1962, (with T.D. Baker) Health Manpower in a Developing Economy, 1967; editor: The Economics of Health and Medical Care, 1974, The Organization and Retrieval of Economic Knowledge, 1977, (with G.K. MacLeod) Health Care Capital: Competition and Control, 1978, (with K. Weiermair) Studies in Economic Rationality: X-Efficiency Examined and Extolled, 1990, (with A. Heertje) Evolving Technology and Market Structure: Studies in Schumpeterian Economics, 1990, (with N.H. Ornstein) Political Power and Social Change: The United States Faces a United Europe, 1991; (with C.E. Barfield) Capital Markets and Trade: The United States Faces a United Europe, 1991, Industry, Services, and Agriculture: The U.S. Faces a United Europe, 1991; Political Power and Social Change: The United States Faces a United Europe, 1991; (with F.M. Scherer), Entrepreneurship, Technological Innovation, and Economic Growth: Studies in Schumpeterian Economics, 1992, (with Yuichi Shionoya) Innovations in Technology Industries and Institutions, 1994; also articles, essays on health, population change, econ. devel., orgn. econ. knowledge and methodology, econ. productivity, history of econ. discipline; Festschrifts (Sir John Barry, Edgar M. Hoover), 1972; editor: series Cambridge Surveys of Contemporary Economics 1977-94, Cambridge Surveys of Economic Institutions and Policies, 1991—; cons. editor, later editorial cons. USIA publ., Portfolio on Internat. Econ. Perspectives, 1972-83; mng. co-editor Jour. Evolutionary Econs., 1989—; corr. Am. editor Revue d'Economie Politique, 1990—; series editor Great Economists of the World, 1990—. With U.S. Army, 1943-46. Social Sci. Research Council fellow, 1949-50; Ford Found. fellow, 1962-63; Fulbright lectr. Melbourne U., 1968. Mem. Am. Econ. Assn. (founding and mng. editor Jour. Econ. Lit. 1968-81), Royal Econ. Soc., Internat. Union Sci. Study Population, History Econs. Soc. (v.p. 1979-80, pres. elect 1983-84, pres. 1984-85), J.A. Schumpeter Intellectuale Geselleschaft (editor 1986—), Phi Beta Kappa. Jewish. Club: Athenaeum (London). Home: 5622 Bartlett St Pittsburgh PA 15217-1514

PERLMAN, MATTHEW SAUL, lawyer; b. Washington, Aug. 30, 1936; s. Jacob and Helen (Aronson) P.; m. Julia Gertrude Hawks, June 22, 1966; children—Penelope Leah, Deborah Jane, Sarah Louise, Jacob Henry. A.B., Brown U., 1957; LL.B., Harvard U., 1960. Bar: D.C. 1960, Md. 1960, U.S. Supreme Ct. 1965. Atty. Air Force Gen. Counsel's Office, Washington, 1960-65; mem. Armed Services Bd. of Contract Appeals, Washington, 1965-67; gen. counsel Pres.' Commn. on Postal Orgn., Washington, 1967; asst. gen. counsel Dept. Transp., Washington, 1967-69; ptnr. Arent, Fox, Kintner, Plotkin & Kahn, Washington, 1969—; mem. Pres. Reagan's Transition Team for GSA, Washington, 1980-81; mem. adv. bd. Fed. Contracts Report, Washington, 1969—; overseas corr. Internat. Constn. Law Rev., London, 1983—. Contbr. articles to profl. jours. Pres. Civic Assn. River Falls, Potomac, Md., 1975-77; mem. Montgomery County Md. Citizens Adv. Commn. for Rock Run AWT Plant, 1979-85. Served to capt. USAF, 1960-63. Mem. ABA (pub. contracts sect.), Fed. Bar Assn., Cosmos Club. Republican. Jewish. Home: 10517 Stable Ln Potomac MD 20854-3867 Office: Arent Fox Kintner Plotkin & Kahn 1050 Connecticut Ave NW Washington DC 20036-5303

PERLMAN, RHEA, actress; b. Bklyn., Mar. 31; m. Danny DeVito, Jan. 8, 1982; children: Lucy Chet, Gracie Far, Jake. Grad., Hunter Coll. Has appeared in numerous Broadway plays; founder Colonades Theatre Lab., N.Y.C.; various roles in TV movies include I Want to Keep My Baby!, 1976, Stalk the Wild Child, 1976 Intimate Strangers, 1977, Having Babies II, 1977, Mary Jane Harper Cried Last Night, 1977, Like Normal People, 1979, Drop Out Father, 1982, The Ratings Game (cable), 1984, Dangerous Affection, 1987, A Family Again, 1987, To Grandmothers House We Go, 1992, A Place To Be Loved, 1993; TV series include Taxi, Cheers, 1982-1993; motion pictures include Love Child, 1982, My Little Pony (voice only) 1986, Enid is Sleeping, 1990, Ted and Venus, 1991, Class Act, 1992, There Goes The Neighborhood, 1992, Canadian Bacon, 1995. Recipient Emmy award for Outstanding Supporting Actress in a Comedy Series, 1984, 85, 86, 89, Am. Comedy award for funniest supporting female-TV. Office: CAA 9830 Wilshire Blvd Beverly Hills CA 90212*

PERLMAN, RICHARD WILFRED, economist, educator; b. Mt. Vernon, N.Y., Dec. 15, 1923; s. Uriel and Annie (Feitelberg) P.; m. Irma Lowenthal, Sept. 18, 1949; children: Abel, David, Laura, Jennifer. AB, Cornell U., 1947; PhD, Columbia U., 1953. Asst. prof. econs. Adelphi U., Garden City, N.Y., 1953-57; assoc. prof. Adelphi U., 1957-64; prof. econs. U. Wis., Milw., 1964—, chmn. dept., 1965-68, 74-77; NRC prof. Brookings Instn., 1958-59; Fulbright lectr. Inst. Politecnico Nacional, Mexico City, 1964, Autonomous U. Madrid, 1972. Author: Economics of Education, 1973, Labor Theory, 1969, Economics of Poverty, 1976, (with others) An Anthology of Labor Economics, 1972, Economics of Unemployment, 1984, Issues in Labor Economics, 1989, Sex Discrimination in the Labor Market, 1994. Mem. President's Com. on EEO, 1963. Rsch. fellow U. Melbourne, Australia, 1985; hon. rsch. fellow U. Birmingham, 1990-93, sr. fellow, 1993-96; Fulbright rsch. scholar, Australia, 1987. Mem. Am. Econ. Assn., Indsl. Relations Research Assn., Phi Beta Kappa. Home: 3341 N Summit Ave Milwaukee WI 53211-2930

PERLMAN, WILLA M., publishing executive; b. Bklyn., Nov. 18, 1959; d. Amir Eytan Cohen, Mar. 24, 1991; 1 child, Jonathan. BA in Arts and Scis., Barnard Coll., 1981. Dir. children's books Harcourt Brace, San Diego, 1987-91; editorial dir. Willa Perlman book Harper Collins, N.Y.C., 1991-93; pres., pub. children's divsn. Simon & Schuster, N.Y.C., 1993—. Jewish. Office: Simon & Schuster 1230 6th Ave New York NY 10020

PERLMUTH, WILLIAM ALAN, lawyer; b. N.Y.C., Nov. 21, 1929; s. Charles and Roe (Schneider) P.; m. Loretta Kaufman, Mar. 14, 1951; children: Carolyn, Diane. AB, Wilkes Coll., 1951; LLB, Columbia U., 1953. Bar: N.Y. 1954. Assoc. Cravath, Swaine & Moore, N.Y.C., 1955-61; ptnr. Stroock & Stroock & Lavan, N.Y.C., 1962—; bd. dirs. Knogo North Am. Inc., Hauppauge, N.Y. Editor Columbia U. Law Rev., 1952-53. Trustee Aeroflex Found., N.Y.C., 1965—, City Ctr. 55th St. Theater Found., 1995—, Harkness Founds. for Dance, N.Y.C., 1976—, Wilkes U., Wilkes-Barre, Pa., 1980—, Weininger Found., 1985—, NYU Med. Ctr., 1995—; trustee Hosp. for Joint Diseases Orthopaedic Inst., N.Y.C., 1980—, chmn. bd. trustees, 1994—. Mem. N.Y. State Bar Assn., Assn. of Bar of City of N.Y., Harmonie Club. Jewish. Home: 880 Fifth Ave New York NY 10021-4951 Office: Stroock & Stroock & Lavan 7 Hanover Sq New York NY 10004-2616

PERLMUTTER, ALVIN HOWARD, television and film producer; b. Poughkeepsie, N.Y., Mar. 24, 1928; s. Fred and Jennie (Albert) P.; children: James F., Stephen H., Tom W. Student, Colgate U., 1945-47; B.A., Syracuse U., 1949. Dir. pub. affairs Sta. WNBC, also Sta. WNBC-TV, N.Y.C., 1957-59; program mgr. Sta. WNBC-TV, 1959-61; exec. producer Nat. Ednl. TV, 1961—; v.p. news documentaries NBC, from 1975; pres. Alvin H. Perlmutter Inc., N.Y.C.; instr. TV news and pub. affairs NYU, 1957, Fairleigh Dickinson U., 1962; cons. John and Mary Markle Found., Pub. Agenda Found.; chmn. Dore Schary Awards for film and TV, Anti-Defamation League. Producer: series Assignment America; Great American Machine, Consumer Reports Presents, Money Matters, Cover Story, Black Journal; various spl. programs including: Native Land, The Primal Mind, Adam Smith's Money World series, Family Computing series, Priceless Treasures of Dresden, The Perpetual People Puzzle; exec. producer: Report From Philadelphia, The Secret Government, The Power of Myth. Chair Dore Schary awards, Anti-Defamation League; bd. dirs. N.Y. Open Ctr. 1st lt. AUS, 1950-53. Recipient various citations and awards including 5 Emmy awards, Peabody award, Robert Kennedy award. Mem. Acad. TV Arts and Scis. (gov. N.Y. chpt., nat. trustee, chmn. awards com. 1968), Assn. Pub. TV Producers (chmn. 1969). Clubs: Overseas Press (N.Y.C.), University; Coffee House. Home: 27 W 86th St New York NY 10024-3615 Office: 45 W 45th St New York NY 10036-4602

PERLMUTTER, DAVID H., physician, educator; b. Bklyn., May 11, 1952; s. Herman Arthur and Ruth (Jacobs) P.; m. Barbara Ann Cohlan, Feb. 7, 1981; children: Andrew, Lisa. BA, U. Rochester, 1974; MD, St. Louis U., 1978. Intern then resident in pediatrics U. Pa. Sch. Medicine, Phila., 1978-81; fellow in pediatric gastroenterology Harvard U. Sch. Medicine, Boston, 1981-84, instr. pediatrics, 1983-85, asst. prof. pediatrics, 1985-86; asst. prof. pediatrics, cell biology Washington U. Sch. Medicine, St. Louis, 1986-89, assoc. prof. pediatrics, cell biology, 1989—. Editor: Pediatric Rsch., 1990—; editorial bd. Gastroenterology, 1990—; contbr. articles to profl. jours. Recipient Established Investigator award Am. Heart Assn., 1987, Rsch. Scholar award Am. Gastroent. Assn., 1985, RJR Nabisco Co., 1986. Mem. Soc. Pediatric Rsch. (coun. rep. 1990—), Am. Soc. Cell Biology, Am. Soc. Clin. Investigation. Home: 6344 Wydown Blvd Saint Louis MO 63105-2213 Office: Washington U Sch Medicine Dept Pediatrics 400 S Kingshighway Blvd Saint Louis MO 63110-1014

PERLMUTTER, DIANE F., communications executive; b. N.Y.C., Aug. 31, 1945; d. Bert H. and Frances (Smith) P. Student, NYU Grad. Sch. of Bus., 1969-70; AB in English, Miami U., Oxford, Ohio, 1967. Writer sales promotion Equitable Life Assurance, N.Y.C., 1967-68; adminstrv. asst. de Garmo, Inc., N.Y.C., 1968-69, asst. account exec., 1969-70, account exec., 1970-74, v.p., account supr., 1974-76; mgr. corp. advt. Avon Products, Inc., N.Y.C., 1976-79, dir. communications Latin Am., Spain, Can., 1979-80, dir. brochures, 1980-81, dir. category merchandising, 1981-82, group dir. motivational communications, 1982-83, group dir. sales promotion, 1983-84, v.p. sales promotion, 1984, v.p. internat. bus. devel., 1984-85, area v.p. Latin Am., 1985, v.p. advtg. and campaign mktg., 1985-87, v.p. U.S. operational planning, 1987; cons. N.Y.C., 1987-88; sr. v.p. Burson-Marsteller, N.Y.C., 1988-90, exec. v.p., mng. dir. consumer products, 1991-93, bd. dirs., 1992—, co-chief operating officer, 1993-94, chief operating officer, 1994—; chmn. mktg. practice/U.S., 1996—; chairperson ann. meeting Direct Selling Assn., Washington, 1982; v.p. Nat. Home Fashions League, N.Y.C., 1975-76; adj. instr. SUNY/Fashion Inst. Tech., 1992—; bd. dirs. Double L.P. Industries, Inc. Founding bd. mem. Am. Red Magen David for Israel, N.Y.C., 1970-75; mem. adv. coun. Miami Sch. Bus., 1986—, Miami Sch. Applied Scis., 1978-81. Mem. Pub. Rels. Soc. Am., Advt. Women of N.Y., Women in Communications, Miami U. Alumni Assn. (pres., chair 1986), Publicity Club N.Y. (bd. dirs. 1994—), Beta Gamma Sigma. Avocation: interior design. Office: Burson-Marsteller 230 Park Ave S New York NY 10003-1513

PERLMUTTER, DONNA, music and dance critic; b. Phila.; d. Myer and Bessie (Krasno) Stein; m. Jona Perlmutter, Mar. 21, 1964; children: Aaron, Matthew. BA, Pa. State U., 1958; MS, Yeshiva U., 1959. Music and dance critic L.A. Herald Examiner, 1975-84, L.A. Times, 1984-94, N.Y. Times Contbr., 1994—; dance critic Dance Mag., N.Y.C., 1980—; music critic Opera News, N.Y.C., 1981—, Ovation Mag., N.Y.C., 1983-89, N.Y. Mag., 1995—, L.A. Mag., 1996—, Daily News, L.A., 1996—; panelist, speaker various music and dance orgns. Author Shadowplay: The Life of Antony Tudor, 1991. Recipient Deems Taylor award for excellence in writing on music ASCAP, 1991. Mem. Music Critics Assn. Home: 10507 Le Conte Ave Los Angeles CA 90024-3305

PERLMUTTER, JACK, artist, lithographer; b. N.Y.C., Jan. 23, 1920; s. Morris and Rebecca (Schiffman) P.; m. Norma Mazo, Dec. 24, 1942; children: Judith Faye, Ellen. Staff Dickey Gallery, D.C. Tchrs. Coll., 1951-68, dir., 1962-68, prof. art; prof. art, chmn. printmaking dept. Corcoran Gallery Art, Washington, 1960-82; resident artist St. Olaf Coll., Minn., Gibbs Art Gallery, Charleston, S.C., Mus. Sch. Art, Greenville, S.C.; vis. prof. art U. Costa Rica, San Jose, 1983; Fulbright research prof. painting and printmaking Tokyo U. Arts, 1959-60; art cons. Pres.'s Com. to Hire Handicapped; now curator exhibits Cosmos Club, Washington. NASA artist for: 1st Saturn V moon rocket, Apollo 6, Apollo 16, Orbiter Columbia (space shuttle), Voyager II; contbg. editor: Art Voices South, 1979-80, Art Voices, 1980-82; numerous one-man shows, U.S. and Tokyo, including: Balt. Mus. Art, Brandeis U., Corcoran Gallery Art, Dintenfass Gallery, N.Y.C., Makler Gallery, Phila., Smithsonian Inst., Yoseido Gallery, Tokyo, C. Troup Gallery, Dallas, Nat. Acad. Scis., 1981, Arts Club Washington, 1981, Annapolis, Md., 1982, and gllleries in Amsterdam, Rotterdam, The Hague and Costa Rica; exhibited nat. shows, U.S., Switzerland, Yugoslavia, traveling exhibits, Europe, S.Am., Can.;permanent collections include Bklyn. Mus., Cin. Mus. Art, Carnegie Inst. Art, Corcoran Gallery Art, Library Congress, Met. Mus. Art, N.Y.C., Nat. Gallery Art, Washington, Phila. Mus. Art, Walker Gallery, Mpls., Nat. Mus. Modern Art, Tokyo, U.S. Embassies in Bucharest, Budapest, Bonn, Dublin, London, Prague, Tokyo, others. Recipient awards for paintings and prints from Balt. Mus. Art, Libr. Congress, Corcoran Gallery Art, Butler Inst. Arts, Smithsonian Inst., Soc. Am. Graphic Artists, First Internat. Exhbn. Fine Arts in Saigon, Mus. Fine Arts in Saigon, Mus. Fine Art, Boston, others. Fellow Internat. Inst. Arts and Letters; mem. Soc. Am. Graphic Artists. Club: Cosmos (Washington). Prints, drawings and biog. data in Art Archives Am. Studio: 2511 Cliffborne Pl NW Washington DC 20009-1511

PERLMUTTER, JEROME HERBERT, communications specialist; b. N.Y.C., Oct. 17, 1924; s. Morris and Rebecca (Shiffman) P.; m. Evelyn Lea Friedman, Sept. 19, 1948; children: Diane Muriel, Sandra Pauline, Bruce Steven. AB cum laude, George Washington U., 1949; MA, Am. U., 1957. Chief editor svc., prodn. editor NEA, Washington, 1949-50; editor in chief Jour. AAHPER, Washington, 1950-51; editor Rural Elec. News, REA, USDA, Washington, 1951-53; publ. writer Agrl. Rsch. Svc., 1953-56; chief, editor br. Office Info., 1956-60; sec. Outlook and Situation Bd., 1960-62; chief econ. reports Econ. Rsch. Svc., 1960-62; chief div. pub. and reprodn. svcs. U.S. Dept. State, Washington, 1962-79; pres. Perlmutter Assocs., 1979—; writing cons. CSC, 1956, World Bank, 1967—; communication cons. European Investment Bank, Can. Internat. Devel. Agy., Inter-Am. Devel. Bank, Internat. Monetary Fund; faculty agr. grad. sch. U. Md., also Fgn. Svc. Inst.; pub. cons. White House Conf. on Children and Youth, 1971. Author: A Practical Guide to Effective Writing, 1965; Contbr. articles profl. jours. Coord. fed. graphics Nat. Endowment for Arts, 1972-79, graphic designer, conv. of maj. polit. com., 1980. With USNR, 1943-46. Recipient award U.S. Jr. C. of C., 1963. Mem. Am. Assn. Agr. Coll. Editors, Assn. Editl. Bus. (bd. dirs.), Fed. Editors Assn., Am. Farm Econ. Assn., Soc. Tech. Comm. (bd. dirs.), Md. Literacy Coun., Soc. Profl. Journalists, Phi Beta Kappa, Phi Eta Sigma, Artus. Home: 15111 Glade Dr Silver Spring MD 20906

PERLMUTTER, LEONARD MICHAEL, concrete construction company executive; b. Denver, Oct. 16, 1925; s. Philip Permutter and Belle (Perlmutter); m. Alice Love Bristow, Nov. 17, 1951; children: Edwin George, Joseph Kent, Cassandra Love. B.A., U. Colo., 1948, postgrad., 1948-50. Ptnr. Perlmutter & Sons, Denver, 1947-58; v.p. Prestressed Concrete of Colo., Denver, 1952-60; pres. Stanley Structures, Inc., Denver, 1960-83; chmn. bd. Stanley Structures, Inc., 1983-87; dir. Colo. Nat. Bankshares, Inc.; adj. prof. Grad. Sch. Pub. Affairs U. Colo., Denver, 1987—; chief exec. officer Econ.

Devel. Gov.'s Office State of Colo., 1987-88; chmn. bd. Colo. Open Lands, 1989. Chmn. bd. U. Colo. Found., Boulder, 1979-81; dir. Santa Fe Opera Assn., N.Mex., 1976-85; v.p. Santa Fe Fedn., 1979-87; chmn. bd. Nat. Jewish Hops.-Nat. Asthma Ctr., Denver, 1983-86; pres. Denver Symphony Assn., 1983-84, chmn. bd., 1985; trustee Midwest Rsch. Inst., 1989—; pres. Nat. Jewish Ctr. for Immunology and Respiratory Medicine, 1991-93. Recipient Humanitarian Am. Jewish Com., 1981. Mem. Prestressed Concrete Inst. (pres. 1977, dir. 1973-74). Club: Rolling Hills Country (Golden) (pres. 1966-68). Home: 15125 Foothill Rd Golden CO 80401-2044 Office: LAP Inc 1515 Arapahoe St Denver CO 80202-2117

PERLMUTTER, LOUIS, investment banker, lawyer; b. Cambridge, Mass., Oct. 3, 1934; s. Kermit H. and Rachel (Ehrlich) P.; m. Barbara Patricia Sondik, Dec. 11, 1966; children: Kermit, Eric. B.A., Brandeis U., 1956; J.D., U. Mich., 1959; LHD (hon.), Brandeis U., 1995. Bar: Mass. 1959, N.Y. 1961. Law practice N.Y.C., 1960-65; asst. to pres. New Eng. Industries, N.Y.C., 1965-67; pres. Octagon Assocs., N.Y.C., 1967-75; sr. v.p. White Weld, N.Y.C., 1975-78; mgn. dir. Merrill Lynch, White, Weld, N.Y.C., 1978; mng. dir. Lazard Freres & Co. LLC, N.Y.C., 1978—. Contbr. articles to profl. and gen. interest publs. Chmn. bd. trustees Brandeis U., Waltham, Mass., 1988-95, Am. Jewish Congress, N.Y.C., 1988-94; chmn. exec. com., bd. govs. UN Assn. USA; mem. Coun. Fgn. Rels., Overseas Devel. Coun., Washington; mem. com. visitors U. Mich. Law Sch. Recipient Human Rels. award Am. Jewish Com., 1995. Mem. Econ. Club of N.Y. Home: 39 E 79th St New York NY 10021-0216 Office: Lazard Freres & Co LLC 30 Rockefeller Plz New York NY 10020-2001

PERLOE, SIDNEY IRWIN, psychologist, primatologist, educator; b. Bklyn., June 21, 1932; s. Herman and Helen (Cutler) P.; m. Judith Gregory, June 9, 1957 (dec. Feb. 1971); children: Deborah, Jonathan; m. Paulette Jellinek, May 20, 1977; children: Alexandra, Gabriel. AB, NYU, 1953; PhD, U. Mich., 1959. Asst. prof. Yale U., New Haven, Conn., 1958-61; asst. prof. Haverford (Pa.) Coll., 1961-64, assoc. prof., 1964-68, prof., 1968—. Contbr. articles to profl. jours. Mem. Am. Psychol. Soc., Am. Soc. Primatologists, Internat. Primatological Soc., Internat. Soc. Human Ethology. Office: Haverford Coll 370 Lancaster Ave Haverford PA 19041-1309

PERLOFF, JEAN MARCOSSON, lawyer; b. Lakewood, Ohio, June 25, 1942; d. John Solomon and Marcella Catherine (Borngen) Marcosson; m. Lawrence Storch, Sept. 8, 1991. BA magna cum laude, Lake Erie Coll., 1965; MA in Italian, UCLA, 1967; JD magna cum laude, Ventura Coll. Law, 1976. Bar: Calif. 1976, U.S. Dist. Ct. (cen. dist.) Calif. 1978. Assoc. in Italian U. Calif.-Santa Barbara, 1967-70; law clk., paralegal Ventura County Pub. Defender's Office, Ventura, Calif., 1975; sole practice, Ventura, 1976-79; coprin. Clabaugh & Perloff, A Profl. Corp., Ventura, 1979-82; sr. jud. atty. to presiding justice 6th div. 2d Dist. Ct. Appeals, L.A., 1982—; instr. Ventura Coll. Law, 1976-79. Pres., bd. dirs. Santa Barbara Zool. Gardens, 1987-88; bd. trustees Lake Erie Coll., 1993—. Named Woman of Yr., 18th Senatorial dist. and 35th Assembly dist. Calif. Legislature, 1992, Woman of Yr., Calif. Legislature, 1993; Mem. ABA, Calif. Bar Assn. (mem. appellate ct. com. 1993-95), Kappa Alpha Sigma. Democrat. Club: Fiesta City. Avocations: tennis, jogging, biking, reading, music. Home: 1384 Plaza Pacifica Santa Barbara CA 93108-2877 Office: 2d Dist Ct of Appeals Div 6 200 E Santa Clara Ventura CA 93001

PERLOFF, JOSEPH KAYLE, cardiologist; b. New Orleans, Dec. 21, 1924; s. Richard and Rose (Cohen) P.; m. Marjorie G. Mintz; children: Nancy L., Carey E. BA, Tulane U., 1945; pre-med. student, U. Chgo., 1946-47; MD, La. State U. at New Orleans, 1951; MA (hon.), U. Pa., 1973. Diplomate Am. Bd. Internal Medicine, Am. Bd. Cardiovascular Disease. Intern Mt. Sinai Hosp., N.Y.C., 1951-52, resident in pathology, 1952-53, resident in medicine, 1953-54; Fulbright fellow Inst. Cardiology, London, 1954-55; resident in medicine Georgetown U. Hosp., Washington, 1955-56, fellow in cardiology, 1956-57; clin. instr. medicine Georgetown U. Sch. Medicine, Washington, 1957-59, instr. medicine, 1959-61, asst. prof. medicine, 1961-66, assoc. prof., 1966-70, prof., 1970-72, dir. cardiac diagnostic lab., 1959-68, asst. dir. div. cardiology, 1968-72; prof. medicine and pediatrics U. Pa. Sch. Medicine, Phila., 1972-77, chief cardiovascular sect., 1972-77; prof. medicine and pediatrics UCLA Sch. Medicine, 1977—, Streisand/AMA chair in cardiology, 1983; cons. Nat. Heart, Blood and Lung Inst. Author: Physical Exam Heart and Circulation, 1990, Clinical Recognition of Congenital Heart Disease, 1987, The Cardiomyopathies, 1988, Congenital Heart Disease in Adults, 1991; co-author: Congenital Heart Disease After Surgery, 1983. Ensign USN, 1943-46, PTO. Recipient The Best of UCLA award Chancellor's Selection, 1987; Residency Career Devel. award NIH, 1959-69. Fellow ACP, Am. Coll. Cardiology; mem. Am. Fedn. Clin. Rsch., Assn. Univ. Cardiologists, Alpha Omega Alpha. Office: UCLA Sch Medicine Cardiology 47 123 Chs Los Angeles CA 90024

PERLOFF, MARJORIE GABRIELLE, English and comparative literature educator; b. Vienna, Austria, Sept. 28, 1931; d. Maximilian and Ilse (Schueller) Mintz; m. Joseph K. Perloff, July 31, 1953; children—Nancy Lynn, Carey Elizabeth. A.B., Barnard Coll., 1953; M.A., Cath. U., 1956, Ph.D., 1965. Asst. prof. English and comparative lit. Cath. U., Washington, 1966-68; asso. prof. Cath. U., 1969-71; asso. prof. U. Md., 1971-73, prof., 1973-76; Florence R. Scott prof. English U. So. Calif., Los Angeles, 1976—; prof. English and comparative lit. Stanford U., Calif., 1986—, Sadie Dernham prof. humanities, 1990—. Author: Rhyme and Meaning in the Poetry of Yeats, 1970, The Poetic Art of Robert Lowell, 1973, Frank O'Hara, Poet Among Painters, 1977, The Poetics of Indeterminacy: Rimbaud to Cage, 1981, The Dance of the Intellect: Studies in the Poetry of the Pound Tradition, 1985, The Futurist Moment: Avant-Garde, Avant-Guerre and the Language of Rupture, 1986, Poetic License: Essays in Modern and Postmodern Lyric, 1990, Radical Artifice: Writing Poetry in the Age of Media, 1991, Wittgenstein's Ladder: Poetic Language and the Strangeness of the Ordinary, 1996; editor: Postmodern Genres, 1990; co-editor: John Cage: Composed in America, 1994; contbg. editor: Columbia Literary History of the U.S., 1987; contbr. preface to Contemporary Poets, 1980, A John Cage Reader, 1983. Guggenheim fellow, 1981-82, NEA fellow, 1985; Phi Beta Kappa scholar, 1994-95. Mem. MLA (exec. coun. 1977-81, Am. lit. sect. 1993—), Comparative Lit. Assn. (pres. 1993-94), Lit. Studies Acad. Home: 1467 Amalfi Dr Pacific Palisades CA 90272-2752 Office: Stanford U Dept English Stanford CA 94305

PERLOFF, ROBERT, psychologist, educator; b. Phila., Feb. 3, 1921; s. Myer and Elizabeth (Sherman) P.; m. Evelyn Potechin, Sept. 22, 1946; children: Richard Mark, Linda Sue, Judith Kay. A.B., Temple U., 1949; M.A., Ohio State U., 1949, Ph.D., 1951; D.Sc. (hon.), Oreg. Grad. Sch. Profl. Psychology, 1984; D.Litt. (hon.), Calif. Sch. Profl. Psychology, 1985. Diplomate: Am. Bd. Profl. Psychology. Instr. edn. Antioch Coll., 1950-51; with personnel research br. Dept. Army, 1951-55, chief statis. research and cons. unit., 1953-55; dir. research and devel. Sci. Research Assos., Inc., Chgo., 1955-59; vis. lectr. Chgo. Tchrs. Coll., 1955-56; mem. faculty Purdue U., 1959-69, prof. psychology, 1964-69; field assessment officer univ. Peace Corps Chile III project, 1962; Disting. Svc. prof. bus. adminstrn. and psychology U. Pitts. Joseph M. Katz Grad. Sch. Bus., 1969-90, Disting. Svc. prof. emeritus, 1991—; dir. rsch. programs U. Pitts. Grad. Sch. Bus., 1969-77; dir. Consumer Panel, 1980-83; bd. dirs. Book Center.; cons. in field, 1959—; adv. com. assessment exptl. manpower R & D labs. Nat. Acad. Scis., 1972-74; mem. rsch. rev. com. NIMH, 1976-80, Stress and Families rsch. project, 1976-79. Contbr. articles to profl. jours.; editor Indsl. Psychologist, 1963-65, Evaluator Intervention: Pros and Cons; book rev. editor Personnel Psychology, 1952-55; co-editor: Values, Ethics and Standards Sourcebook, 1979, Improving Evaluations; bd. cons. editors Jour. Applied Psychology; bd. advs. Archives History Am. Psychology, Psychol. Svc. Pitts., Recorded Psychol. Jours.; guest editor Am. Psychologist, 1972, Edn. and Urban Soc., 1977, Profl. Psychology, 1977; adv. editor Contemporary Psychology, 1994—. Bd. dirs., v.p. Sr. Citizens Svc. Corp., Calif. Sch. Profl. Psychology, Greater Pitts. chpt. ACLU; chmn. Nat. adv. com. Inst. Govt. and Pub. Affairs, U. Ill., 1986-89. Decorated Bronze Star; Robert Perloff Grad. Rsch. Assistantship in Inst. Govt. and Pub. Affairs, U. Ill., named in his honor, 1990; Robert Perloff Career Achievement award Knowledge Utilization Soc., named in his honor, 1991. Fellow AAAS, APA (mem.-at-large exec. com. div. consumer psychology 1964-67, 70-71, pres. div. 1967-68, mem. coun. reps. 1965-68, 72-74, chmn. sci. affairs com., div. consumer psychology 1968-69, edn. and tng. bd. 1969-72, chmn. finance com., treas. 1975-84, dir. 1974-82, chmn. investment com. 1977-82, pres. 1985, mem. adv. bd., mem. bd. sci. affairs 1994—, mem task force intelligence and Intelligence Tests, author column Standard Deviations in jour.), Ea. Psychol. Assn. (pres. 1980-81, dir. 1977-80); mem. Am. Psychol. Soc., Internat. Assn. Applied Psychology, Pa. Psychol. Assn. (Disting. Svc. award 1985), Assn. for Consumer Rsch. (chmn. 1970-71), Am. Psychol. Found. (v.p. 1988-89, pres. 1990-92), Am. Evaluation Assn. (pres. 1977-78, trustee 1995—), Soc. Psychologists in Mgmt. (Disting. Contbn. to Psychology Mgmt. award 1989, pres. 1993-94), Knowledge Utilization Soc. (pres. 1993-95), Sigma Xi (pres. U. Pitts. chpt. 1989-91), Beta Gamma Sigma, Psi Chi. Home: 815 St James St Pittsburgh PA 15232-2112 *Experiment. Innovate responsibly. Take risks judiciously. Do not shrink from new ventures for fear of failure. No one is immune from adversity. The hallmark of a successful achieving person is his or her ability to snap back after misfortune, and to benefit from and not be immobilized by failure.*

PERLONGO, DANIEL JAMES, composer; b. Gaastra, Mich., Sept. 23, 1942; s. James and Camille (Fittante) P. Mus.B. in Composition, U. Mich., 1964, Mus.M., 1966; Corso di Perfezionamento, Accademia di S. Cecilia, Rome, 1968. Assoc. prof. music Indiana (Pa.) U., 1968—. Composer (for orchestra) Myriad, 1968, Ephemeron, 1972, Concertino, 1980, Lake Breezes, 1990, Concerto for Piano and Orchestra, 1992, Shortcut from Bratislava for Piano and Orch., 1994, (chamber orch.) Variations, 1973, Voyage, 1975, (chamber music) Improvision for Four, 1965, Improvisation 2, 1966, Eufonia, poetica e sonora, 1966, (string trio) Intervals, 1967, (ensemble pieces) Movement for 8 Players, 1967, Semblance for string quartet, 1969-70, String Quartet II, 1983, (percussion quartet) For Bichi, 1968, Movement in Brass, 1969, (various works) Process 7, 5, 3 for 6 in 12, for flute, oboe, clarinet, 3 percussions, 1969, Tre Tempi for flute, oboe, clarinet, violin, cello, 1971, Fragments for flute and cello, 1972, Structure, Semblance and Tune for tuba and percussion, 1973, (wind ensemble) Changes, 1970, (violin) Violin Solo, 1971, (double bass) Episodes, 1966, (for oboe, clarinet and bassoon) Ricercar, 1976, (solo piano) Piano Sonata, 1965, Suite for Piano, 1988, Serenade, 1977, First Set, 1990, (saxophone quartet) Aureole, 1978, (brass quintet) Summer Music, 1979, (solo bass clarinet) Soliloquy, 1980, (soprano voice and piano) Six Songs, 1980, (solo organ) Tapestry, 1981, (winds, percussion and piano) Montalvo Overture, 1984, (piano and woodwind quintet) A Day At Xochimilco, 1987, (trombone and organ) Novella, 1988, (mezzo soprano, violin, clarinet and piano) By Verse Distills, 1989, (wind ensemble) Preludes and Variations, 1991, (horn and harp) Arcadian Suite, 1993. Fulbright fellow Italy, 1966; Italian Govt. grantee, 1967; recipient Joseph Bearns prize Columbia U., 1966; Rome prize, 1971, 72; award Nat. Inst. Arts and Letters, 1975, Internat. Double Reed Soc. prize, 1979, New Music for Young Ensembles prize, 1979, Nebr. Sinfonia prize, 1981; Nat. Endowment Arts grantee, 1981, 95; Guggenheim fellow, 1982. Office: Indiana U of Pa Cogswell Hall Indiana PA 15701

PERLOV, DADIE, management consultant; b. N.Y.C., June 8, 1929; d. Aaron and Anna (Leight) Heitman; m. Norman B. Perlov, May 29, 1950; children—Nancy Perlov Rosenbach, Jane, Amy Perlov Schenkein. BA, NYU, 1950; postgrad., Adelphi U., 1963, Vanderbilt U., 1973. Cert. assn. exec., N.Y. Exec. dir. ops. Open City, N.Y.C., 1962-64; field svcs. dir. Nat. Coun. Jewish Women, N.Y.C., 1968-74; exec. dir. N.Y. Libr. Assn., N.Y.C., 1974-81, Nat. Coun. Jewish Women, N.Y.C., 1981-90; founder, prin. Consensus Mgmt. Group, N.Y.C. and Washington, 1989—; cons. HEW 1975-76; pres.-elect Internat. Coun. Libr. Assn. Execs., 1979-80; exec. mem. Conf. of Pres., 1981-90; strategic planner, lectr., merger facilitator, trainer in field. Contbr. articles to profl. jours. Dem. committeewoman, 1966; mem. N.Y. Zool. Soc., 1959—, adv. bd. Nat. Inst. Against Prejudice and Violence, 1985-89, profl. adv. com. for Hornstein program in Jewish communal svc. Brandeis U., 1986-90; bd. visitors Pratt Inst., Bklyn., 1980-84; bd. dirs. Pres. Coun. on Handicapped, 1981—; facilitator Nursing Summit, 1994. Recipient Recognition award N.Y. Libr. Assn., 1978, BUDDY award NOW Legal Def. and Edn. Found., 1989, cert. N.Y. State Legislature, 1978; named N.Y. State Exec. of Yr., 1980, One of Am.'s 100 Most Important Women, Ladies' Home Jour., 1988. Fellow Am. Soc. Assn. Execs. (cert. 1978, evaluator 1980-91, bd. dirs. 1987-90, bd. found. 1990-92, Excellence award 1983); mem. LWV (chpt. pres. 1960-62), N.Y. Soc. Assn. Execs, (pres. 1985, Outstanding Assn. Exec. 1989, Outstanding Svc. award 1991), Global Perspectives in Edn. (bd. dirs.), Nat. Orgn. Continuing Edn. (coun.), Audubon Soc., N.Y. Citizens Coun. on Librs. (bd. dirs. 1981-84), Am. Arbitration Assn. (mem. panel). Avocations: writing, mycology, history, music, art.

PERLOW, GILBERT J(EROME), physicist, editor; b. N.Y.C., Feb. 10, 1916; s. David and Esther (German) P.; m. Mina Rea Jones. AB, Cornell U., 1936, MA, 1937; PhD, U. Chgo., 1940. Instr. physics U. Minn., Mpls., 1940-41; physicist Naval Ordnance Lab., Washington, 1941-42, Naval Rsch. Lab., Washington, 1942-52; rsch. assoc. physics dept. U. Minn., Mpls., 1952-53; assoc. physicist Argonne (Ill.) Nat. Lab., 1953-57, sr. physicist, 1957—; editor Jour. Applied Physics Am. Inst. Physics/Argonne Nat. Lab., 1970-73, editor Applied Physics Letters, 1970-90, consulting editor Applied Physics Letters, 1990—; vis. assoc. prof. physics U. Wash., Seattle, 1957; vis. prof. German univs., Munich, Berlin; exch. physicist AERE Harwell, Berkshire, Eng., 1961. Contbr. over 70 articles to profl. jours., also chpts. to books; author numerous U.S. patents. Recipient Alexander von Humboldt award Alexander von Humboldt Found., Tech. U. Munich, 1972. Fellow Am. Phys. Soc.; mem. Chgo. Corinthian Yacht Club (life mem., commodore 1974). Avocations: sailing, woodworking, painting. Home: 4919 Northcott Ave Downers Grove IL 60515-3434 Office: Argonne Nat Lab Physics Divsn 9700 Cass Ave Argonne IL 60439-4803

PERLSTADT, SIDNEY MORRIS, lawyer; b. Warsaw, Poland, May 9, 1907; came to U.S. 1916, naturalized, 1920; s. Isaac H. and Sarah (Carmel) P.; m. Mildred Penn, Mar. 5, 1935 (dec.); children—Harry, Susan Perlstadt Serota; m. Bessie Lendrum, Jan. 25, 1961 (dec.). Ph.B., U. Chgo., 1928; J.D., DePaul U., 1942. C.P.A., Ill. Bar: Ill. 1943, U.S. Dist. Ct. (no. dist.) Ill. 1944, U.S. Tax Ct. 1944. Revenue agt. IRS, San Francisco and Chgo., 1935-43; ptnr. Sonnenschein, Nath & Rosenthal, Chgo., 1944—. Mem. Ill. Pub. Employees Pension Laws Commn., 1973-84; trustee Indsl. Areas Found. Mem. Chgo. Bar Assn., Ill. Bar Assn., ABA. Club: Cliff Dwellers (Chgo.). Home: 175 E Delaware Pl Chicago IL 60611-1750 Office: Sonnenschein Nath Rosenthal Suite 8000 233 S Wacker Dr Ste 8000 Chicago IL 60606-6404

PERLSTEIN, ABRAHAM PHILLIP, psychiatrist; b. N.Y.C., Apr. 15, 1926; s. Benjamin William and Pauline (Gittler) P.; m. Shirley Anne Rubenstein, July 10, 1949; children: Judith Paula, Susan Carol, Bernard William. BS, U. Oreg., 1949; MD, NYU, 1953. Diplomate Am. Bd. Psychiatry and Neurology. Cons. alcoholism dir. SUNY, Bklyn., 1958—, clin. asst. prof. psychiatry, 1957—; med. dir. Peninsula Counseling Ctr., Woodmere, N.Y., 1973-78, psychiat. cons. geriatrics, 1978-90; pvt. practice Elmont, N.Y., 1957-90; assoc. psychiat. dir. Frankling Gen. Hosp., Valley Stream, N.Y., 1980-82; attending psychiatrist Kings County Hosp. Ctr., Bklyn., 1957-90, SUNY, U. Hosp. Bklyn., 1963-90, Franklin Gen. Hosp., Valley Stream, 1969-90; adj. clin. asst. prof. psychiatry Cornell U. Med. Coll., N.Y.C., 1978-90; assoc. attending psychiatrist North Shore U. Hosp., Manhasset, N.Y., 1978-90. Sgt. U.S. Army, 1944-46. Fellow Am. Psychiat. Assn. (life). Avocations: music, art, sports. Office: Columbia River Mental Health Svcs PO Box 1337 1950 Ft Vancouver Way Ste A Vancouver WA 98666

PERLSTEIN, WILLIAM JAMES, lawyer; b. N.Y.C., Feb. 7, 1950; s. Justin Sol and Jane (Goldberg) P.; m. Teresa Catherine Lotito, Dec. 20, 1970; children—David, Jonathan. B.A. summa cum laude, Union Coll., 1971; student London Sch. Econs., 1969-70; J.D., Yale U., 1974. Bar: Conn. 1974, D.C. 1976, U.S. Dist. Ct. D.C. 1977, U.S. Ct. Appeals D.C. cir. 1978, U.S. Supreme Ct. 1993. Law clk. Judge Marvin Frankel, U.S. Dist. Ct., N.Y.C., 1974-75; assoc. Wilmer, Cutler & Pickering, Washington, 1975-82, ptnr., 1982—, mem. mgmt. com. 1995—. Mng. editor Yale Law Jour., 1973-74; contbg. author The Workout Game, 1987. Mem. ABA (bus. bankruptcy com. 1983—, vice-chmn. executory contracts subcom. of bus. bankruptcy com. 1988-90, bankruptcy cts. subcom. 1990—), Am. Bankruptcy Inst. (chmn. legis. com. 1986-89, bd. dirs. 1987-93), Am. Law Inst., Union Coll. Alumni Coun., Phi Beta Kappa. Jewish.

PERMAN, NORMAN WILFORD, graphic designer; b. Chgo., Feb. 17, 1928; s. Jacob and Ida (Ladenson) P.; m. Lorraine Shaffer, July 22, 1956; children: Jonathan Dean, Margot Bess. Student, Corcoran Sch. Art, Washington, 1946-47, Northwestern U., 1948-50; BFA, Art Inst. Chgo., 1951. Asst. to designer Everett McNear, Chgo., 1951-52; ind. graphic designer specializing booklets, annual reports, exhibits, packaging and books Chgo., 1953—; guest lectr. U. Ill., Chgo.; curator 75th Anniversary Exhbn. Arts Club of Chgo., 1992; lectr. in field; juror various nat. and regional exhbns. Designer: (records and ednl. materials) Invitations to Personal Reading, 165 vols., 1965, Sounds I Can Hear, Talkstarters, 1966, Health and Growth, 1970, Mathematics Around Us, 1974, Good for Life Exhibit, 1978, Invitation to Mathematics, 1984, Health for Life, 1986; editor: Form and Meaning, 1962; exhbns. include Art Inst. Chgo., 1954-62, 68, U. Ill., 1960, 62, 64, U. Wis., 1957, Am. Inst. Graphic Arts, 1958, 60-61, 63-64, 66, 68, 70, 72, 74, 76, 79-81, 83, State Dept. USSR, 1964, Art Dirs. Club, N.Y.C., 1961, 63, 65, 69, HUD Art in Architecture Exhibit, Smithsonian Instn., 1973, 50 Yrs. Graphic Design in Chgo. Exhibit, 1977; represented in numerous design jours., annuals and graphics books. With USN, 1946-48. Recipient award Art Dirs. Club, Chgo., 1960, 62, 65, 68, award Art Dirs. Club, N.Y.C., 1961-82, Gold medal Direct Mail Assn., 1961, 64. Fellow Am. Ctr. for Design (bd. dirs., chmn. Allerton Park Conf. 1962, nat. pres. 1965-66, exhibits 1952-89, award 1952-86); mem. Assn. Corp. Art Curators (v.p. 1982), Am. Inst. Graphic Arts (award 1960-85), 27 Chgo. Designers, Art Inst. Chgo. (chmn. alumni fund), Oriental Inst., Coun. Fgn. Rels., Arts Club of Chgo. (bd. dirs.). Democrat. Avocations: photography, mountain trekking, travel, music.

PERMUTT, SOLBERT, physiologist, physician; b. Birmingham, Ala., Mar. 6, 1925; s. Harry and Rachel (Damsky) P.; m. Loretta Paul, Jan. 17, 1952; children—Nina Rachel, Thomas Joshua, Lisa Ellen. M.D., U. So. Calif., 1949. Intern U. Chgo. Clinics, 1949-50, resident medicine, 1952, research assoc. dept. anatomy, 1950-52; resident medicine Montefiore Hosp., N.Y.C., 1954-56; fellow medicine and environmental medicine Johns Hopkins Med. Sch., 1956-58; chief div. cardiopulmonary physiology Nat. Jewish Hosp., Denver, 1958-61; asst. prof. physiology Sch. Medicine, U. Colo., 1960-61; mem. faculty Sch. Hygiene and Pub. Health, Johns Hopkins, 1961, prof. environ. health sci., 1965—; prof. medicine Johns Hopkins U. Sch. Med., 1972—, dir. respiratory div. dept. medicine, 1972-81, prof. anesthesiology, 1978—; head physiology div., environ. health sci. John Hopkins Sch. Hygiene and Pub. Health, 1976-79; dir. pulmonary div. Francis Scott Key Med. Ctr. (John Hopkins Med. Instn.), 1981-87, dir. pulmonary rsch., div. pulmonary medicine, 1986-87, dir. rsch. div. pulmonary and critical care medicine, 1988—; assoc. dir. Johns Hopkins Asthma and Allergy Ctr., 1990—; Cons. space sci. bd. Nat. Acad. Sci., 1966-67, mem. com. effects atmospheric contaminants human health, 1968-70; mem. project com. Heart and Lung Program, NIH, 1970-74; mem. sci. adv. council Children's Asthma Research Inst. and Hosp., Denver, 1973-75; mem. expert panel Nat. Inst. Allergy and Infectious Diseases, 1972-74; mem. nat. adv. com. for Cal. Primate Research Center, 1972-75; vice chmn. council on cardiopulmonary diseases Am. Heart Assn., 1974-75, chmn., 1976—, mem. research com., 1979-85; nat. adviser Aspen Lung Confs., 1974—; mem. pulmonary disease adv. com. HHS and NIH, 1979-83. Mem. editorial bd. publs. Am. Physiol. Soc. Circulation Research, 1965—, La Revue Française des Maladies Respiratories, 1975—; contbr. articles to profl. jours. Served with U.S. Army, 1943-46, 53-54. Recipient Gold medal Am. Coll. Chest Physicians, 1977, Louis and Artur Lucian award McGill U., 1980; fellow Nat. Found. Infantile Paralysis, 1956-58. Mem. Am. Lung Assn. (George Wills Comstock award 1988, Edward Livingston Trudeau medal 1992), Cardiovascular System Dynamics Soc., Am. Med. Assn. (reference panel for diagnostic and therapeutic tech. assessment-DATTA), Assn. Am. Physicians, Johns Hopkins Med. and Surg. Assn., Md. Soc. Med. Rsch., Am. Thoracic Soc., Am. Physiol. Soc., AAAS, Am. Heart Assn. (Citation for Disting. Svc. to Rsch. 1979-84, Disting. Achievement award Cardiopulmonary Coun. 1986). Home: 2303 Sulgrave Ave Baltimore MD 21209-4405

PERO, JOSEPH JOHN, retired insurance company executive; b. N.Y.C., Nov. 5, 1939; s. Joseph John and Grace Margaret (Picchione) P.; m. Margaret Ann Carey, July 11, 1964; children: Ann Marie, Christopher. B.S., Manhattan Coll., 1961; M.B.A., NYU, 1967. With GM, 1963-94; dir. profit and investment analysis Gen. Motors Corp., N.Y.C., 1973-76; asst. treas., sec. to exec. com. Gen. Motors Corp., Detroit, 1976-79, N.Y.C., 1980-81; exec. v.p.-fin. Motors Ins. Corp. (subs. Gen. Motors Corp.), Detroit, 1981-87, pres., 1987-94; ret., 1994. Bd. dirs. Inner City Bus. Improvement Forum, Detroit, 1978-79; trustee Mt. Elliot Cemetery Assn., 1978-79; bd. dirs., treas. Ryan Sr. Residences of Archdiocese of Detroit. With Army N.G., 1963-69. Mem. Nat. Assn. Ind. Insurers (bd. govs.), Forest Lake Country Club. Home: 4097 Waterwheel Ln Bloomfield Hills MI 48302-1871

PERONI, GERALDINE, film editor. Editor: (films) (with Francoise Coispeau) Vincent & Theo, 1990, The Player, 1992, Short Cuts, 1993.

PERONI, PETER A., II, psychologist, educator; b. Trenton, N.J., Nov. 14, 1942; s. Peter A. and Mary D. (DiLeo) P. BA, LaSalle U., 1964; MA, Trenton State Coll., 1967, MAT, 1969; EdD, Rutgers U., 1977. Cert. secondary sch. social studies, student pers. svcs.; lic. psychologist, Pa. Tchr. St. Anthony High Sch., Trenton, 1964-67, Lawrence Twp. (N.J.) Pub. Schs., 1967-68; counselor Bucks County C.C., Newtown, Pa., 1968-72, prof., 1972—; consulting psychologist N.J. Dept. Health, Trenton, 1977-84; dir. clin. svcs. New Horizon Treatment Svcs., Trenton, 1984-88. Author: The Burg: An Italian-American Community at Bay in Trenton, 1979; writer, coproducer (TV): The Burg: A State of Mind, 1980; author: Academic Success Through Self-Conditioning, 1982. N.J. Commn. for Humanities grantee, 1980. Avocation: motorcycle touring. Home: 52 Hollynoll Dr Trenton NJ 08619-2208

PEROT, H. ROSS, investments and real estate group executive, data processing services company executive; b. June 27, 1930; married; 4 children. Ed., U.S. Naval Acad. Data processing salesman IBM Corp., 1957-62; founder Electronic Data Systems Corp., Dallas, 1962-84, chmn., CEO, also dir., to 1986; now with The Perot Group, Dallas; chmn. Hillwood Devel. Corp., Dallas, 1984—; founder Perot Systems Corp., Washington, 1988—; independent cand. for Pres. of U.S., 1992. Author: Not For Sale at Any Price, 1993. Served with USN, 1953-57. Recipient Internat. Disting. Entrepreneur award, U. Man., 1988, The Winston Churchill award, 1986, The Raoul Wallenberg award, The Jefferson award, The patrick Henry award, The Nat. Bus. Hall of Fame award, The Sarnoff award, The Eisenhower award, The Smithsonian Computerworld award, The Horatio Alger award. Office: The Perot Group 12377 Merit Dr Ste 1700 Dallas TX 75251-2239*

PEROTTI, BEATRICE YEE-WA TAM, pharmacokineticist; b. Hong Kong, Nov. 16, 1964; came to U.S., 1984; d. Kin-Fan Tam and Kam-Sheung So; m. Ronald Anthony Perotti, Jan. 29, 1988. Internat. baccalaureate, Lester Pearson Coll. Pacific, Victoria, B.C., 1984; BA, Mills Coll., 1988; PhD, U. Calif., San Francisco, 1994. Rsch. scientist Pfizer Ctrl. Rsch., Groton, Conn., 1994—; guest lectr. U. Calif., San Francisco, 1993. Author: Burger's Medicinal Chemistry and Drug Discovery, 1995; producer, performer (soprano recital) 300 Years of Classical Songs, 1986, Love Songs From the East and West, 1987; contbr. articles to profl. jours. Tutor Upward Bound, Oakland, Calif., 1985-87; soloist Brookside Cmty. Ch., Oakland, 1988-94, youth counselor, charity coord., 1989-94; vol. Project Open Hands, Oakland, 1993-94. U. Calif. rsch. fellow, 1986, AFPE Assn. fellow, 1992-94; Sir. Jack Cater trust scholar Hong Kong Edn. Dept., 1982-84; recipient Hong Kong Mills Club scholarship, 1984-87, Hellman music award Mills Coll., 1986-87, Gordon Rsch. Conf. Student Travel award, 1993, Greater Victoria Music award Greater Victoria Music Festival Assn., 1993. Mem. AAAS, ISSX, Am. Assn. Pharm. Scientists (AAPS Travel award 1992). Avocations: B.S.A.C. class 3 diver, swimming, target shooting, in-line skating, golfing. Home: 268 Shore Rd Waterford CT 06385 Office: Pfizer Ctrl Rsch Eastern Point Rd Groton CT 06340

PERRAULT, GEORGES GABRIEL, chemical engineer; b. Vincennes, France, July 31, 1934; s. René and Georgette (Salin) P. Diploma in engring., Ecole Nat. Supérieure de Chimie de Strasbourg, France, 1958; D. U. Strasbourg, France, 1960, PhD, 1964. Rsch. scientist in phys. chemistry solids Nat. Ctr. for Scientific Rsch., Strasbourg, France, 1958-64; rsch. scientist electrochemistry Nat. Ctr. for Scientific Rsch., Meudon, France, 1964-67, Duke U., Durham, N.C., 1967-68, Meudon, 1968-88; rsch. scientist in biogeography and environment Nat. Ctr. for Sci. Rsch., Paris, 1988—. Editor: Nouvelle Revue Entomologie, 1984—; co-author: Encyclopedia of Electrochemistry Elements, 1978, Standard Potential of Aqueous Solutions, 1985, Biogeography of Carabidae of Mountains and Islands, 1991, Carabid Beetles: Ecology and Evolution, 1994; contbr. articles to profl. jours. Sgt. French Marines, 1961-63. Mem. N.Y. Acad. Scis., Electrochem. Soc. (treas. European sect. 1981-84, chmn. 1984—), French Soc. Chemistry (electrochem. group com. mem. 1991-92), N.Y. Entomological Soc., French Entomological Soc., Am. Entomological Soc., French Soc. Astronomy, Camping Club. Roman Catholic. Avocations: travel, photography.

PERREAULT, SISTER JEANNE, college president; b. Providence, Dec. 13, 1929; d. Alphonse and Malvina I. (Chevalier) P. BSEd, Cath. Tchrs. Coll., Providence, 1959; MS, Cath. U., Washington, 1968; EdD (hon.), Salve Regina U., 1990. Tchr. elem. sch. St. Ann Sch., West Warwick, R.I.; tchr. jr. high sch. St. John Jr. High Sch., West Warwick; tchr. high sch. Notre Dame High Sch., Berlin, N.H.; assoc. prof. Rivier Coll., Nashua, N.H., pres., 1980—; mem. Gov.'s Task Force for Edn. Mem. State of N.H. Post-Secondary Edn. Commn., Concord; bd. dirs. Ctr. for Econ. Devel. for Nashua Area, Bishop Guertin H.S., Nashua; commr. New Eng. Assn. Schs. & Colls.; provincial coun. Sisters of Presentation of Mary. Mem. AAUP, Am. Coun. Colls., Assn. Cath. Colls. and Univs., N.H. Coll. and Univ. Coun.

PERREAULT, WILLIAM DANIEL, JR., business administration educator; b. N.Y.C., Apr. 7, 1948; s. William Daniel Sr. and Barbara Louise (Peckham) P.; m. Pamela Pittard, May 27, 1972; children: Suzanne Elizabeth, William Daniel III. BS, U. N.C., 1970, PhD, 1973. Asst. prof. U. Ga., Athens, 1973-76; asst. prof. U. N.C., Chapel Hill, 1976-79, assoc. prof., 1979-81, prof., 1981-83, Hanes prof., 1983-88; vis. prof. Stanford (Calif.) U., 1986-87, assoc. dean, 1988-92. Kenan prof., 1988—. Co-author: The Marketing Game, 1994, Essentials Marketing, 1994, Basic Marketing, 1996; editor: Jour. Mktg. Rsch., 1982-85; contbr. articles to profl. jours. Chmn. adv. com. Bur. Census, Washington, 1982-86. Mem. Am. Mktg. Assn. (v.p. 1986, 95, bd. dirs. 1986-89, 949-95), Acad. Mktg. Sci. (Outstanding Edn. award 1995), Decision Scis. Inst. (coun. 1977), Assn. Dir. Consumer Rsch. Conf. (chmn. 1976—), Mktg. Sci. Inst. (trustee 1989-94), Phi Beta Kappa. Republican. Presbyterian. Office: U NC Cb 3490 Carroll Hall # 012A Chapel Hill NC 27599

PERRELLA, JAMES ELBERT, manufacturing company executive; b. Gloversville, N.Y., May 30, 1935; s. James E. and A. Irene (Ferguson) P.; m. Diane F. Campesi; 1 child, Joy. B.S.M.E., Purdue U., 1960, M.S.I.M., 1961. Gen. mgr. Centac div. Ingersoll-Rand Co., Mayfield, Ky., 1972-75; gen. mgr. Air Compressor Group Ingersoll-Rand Co., Woodcliff Lake, N.J., 1975-77, corp. v.p., pres. Air Compressor Group, 1977-82, exec. v.p., 1982-92, pres., 1992—, chmn., CEO, 1993—, also dir. Named Disting. Alumnus Sch. Mech. Engring., Purdue U., 1982; named Disting. Alumnus Krammert Mgmt. Sch., Purdue U., 1982. Office: Ingersoll-Rand Co 200 Chestnut Ridge Rd Woodcliff Lake NJ 07675*

PERRENOD, DOUGLAS ARTHUR, astronautical engineer; b. Weehawken, N.J., Sept. 13, 1947; s. George Edward and Eunice Lillian (Cohn) P. Student, Fla. Inst. Tech., 1968-72; B.A. in Interdisciplinary Sci. U. South Fla., 1973; postgrad. Calif. State U., 1982—; grad. engr. mgmt. cert. program Calif. Inst. Tech., 1987; bioenvironmental engr. USAF Sch. Aerospace Medicine, 1992. Cert. glider flight instr. FAA. Engr. trainee NASA Kennedy Space Ctr., Fla., 1969-73; quality control engr. Pelletech Corp., Fontana, Calif., 1976-77; electronics specialist Gen. Telephone Co., San Bernardino, Calif., 1977-79; aerospace and project engr. Rockwell Internat., Downey, Calif., 1979-85, Lockheed Corp., Ontario, Calif., 1986-87, Lockheed Engring. Mgmt. Svc. Co., 1987, Eagle Engring., 1988—, Eagle Tech. Svcs., 1989—; aviation cons., owner-founder Flight Unltd., Long Beach, Calif.; mission pilot, project engr. Flight Level 500 High Altitude Soaring Project. Vol. mem. Orange County Human Services Agy., 1981-86; active Big Bros. of Am., 1978. Lt. Col. USAFR, 1973—. Recipient Amelia Earhart award CAP, 1968, Manned Flight Awareness Apollo 11 medallion NASA, 1971, 1st Shuttle Flight award NASA, 1981, Aerospace Maintenance Officer of Yr. award USAFR, 1979; named to Engr. Honor Roll, Rockwell Internat., 1982, 83, 85. Mem. AIAA, Assn. Mil. Surgeons U.S., Res. Officers Assn., Officers Assn., Air Force Assn., Soc. Flight Test Engrs., Assoc. Glider Club of So. Calif., Long Beach Navy Aero. Club. Developed concept for, and co-authored unprecedented Inter-agency agreement between USAF and NASA for exchange of advanced environmental technology, 1994. Designer telescope mount for 1st astronomy obs. Fla. Inst. Tech., 1969. Home: 18511 Egret Bay Blvd Apt 612 Houston TX 77058-3275

PERRET, JOSEPH ALOYSIUS, banker, consultant; b. Phila., Feb. 26, 1929; s. Joseph Henry and Mary Rose (Martin) P.; m. Nancy S. Bott, June 24, 1950; children—Kathlyne, Robert, Susan, Michael. Student, U. Pa., 1953-57, Temple U., 1957-58, Stonier Grad. Sch. Banking, 1966. Head analyst Phila. Nat. Bank, 1953-57; spl. banking rep. Burroughs Corp., Phila., 1957-59; v.p. First Pa. Banking & Trust Co., Phila., 1959-66, Md. Nat. Bank, Balt., 1966-70; sr. v.p. Md. Nat. Bank, 1970-75, Comml. Credit Co., Balt., 1975-78, Sanwa Bank Calif., Los Angeles, 1978-91; cons., 1991—; chmn. bd. Star System, Inc., San Diego. Mem. Am. Bankers Assn., Data Processing Mgmt. Assn., Balt.-Washington Regional Clearing House (chmn. 1970), Calif. Bankers Cleanring House Assn. (chmn. 1990). Clubs: Country of Md; Merchants (Balt.); Friendly Hills Country (Whittier, Calif.). Home and Office: 3023 S Rio Claro Dr La Puente CA 91745-5954

PERRET, MAURICE EDMOND, geography educator; b. La Chaux-de-Fonds, Switzerland, May 19, 1911; s. Jules Henri and Henriette Marie (Leuba) P.; Gymnase La Chaux-de-Fonds, 1929; Bac. es Lettres, U. Zurich (Switzerland), 1930; Licence es Lettres, U. Neuchatel (Switzerland), 1940; M.A. (Internat. House fellow 1940-42), U. Calif. at Berkeley, 1942; Doctorat es Lettres, U. Lausanne (Switzerland), 1950. Tchr., Petropolis and Lycee Francais, Rio de Janeiro, Brazil, 1935-37; asst. consulate Switzerland, San Francisco, 1942-43; del. internat. com. Red Cross, Washington, 1943-45; del. Aid to Arab Refugees, Palestine, 1949-51; asst. Internat. Telecommunication Union, Geneva, Switzerland, 1951-52; librarian La Chaux-de-Fonds, Switzerland, 1953-54; asst. Oltremare, Rome, Italy, 1955-56; prof. Avenches, Switzerland, 1957-63; prof. geography, map librarian U. Wis., Stevens Point, 1963-81, prof. emeritus, 1981—. Curator Roman Mus., Avenches, Switzerland, 1960-63. Mem. city council Avenches, Switzerland, 1961-63. Served with Swiss Army, 1939-40. Initiator Hist. Mus. of Portage County Hist. Soc., Stevens Pt. Mem. Assn. Am. Geographers, Nat. Council Geog. Edn., Am. Geog. Soc., Wis. Acad. Scis., Arts and Letters, Société vaudoise de geographie (v.p. 1960-63), Fedn. Swiss Geog. Socs. (v.p. 1961-63). Club: Travelers Century. Editorial com. Atlas Switzerland, 1960-63. Pub.: Les Colonies Tessinoises en Californie, 1950, Portage County, Of Place and Time, 1992; contbr. articles to profl. jours. Office: U Wis Dept Geography Stevens Point WI 54481

PERRET, PETER JAMES, symphony conductor; b. Rochester, Minn., Mar. 25, 1941; s. George E. and Margaret (Minge) P.; m. Chao Mei-Wah, Mar. 23, 1966 (div. Apr. 1978); 1 child, Ondine; m. Debra Skeen, May 24, 1986; 1 child, Zachary. Student, Royal Conservatory, Brussels, 1964, Diplome Superieru, 1966. Chief producer Swiss Broadcasting Corp., Geneva, 1967-72; prin. condr. Capetown (Peoples Republic of Africa) Symphony, 1972-74; Exxon arts endowment condr. Buffalo Philharmonic, 1975-78; music dir. Winston-Salem (N.C.) Symphony, 1978—; vis. prof. U. Capetown, 1973-74; scholar-in-residence Canisius Coll., Buffalo, 1976, 77; prof. conducting N.C. Sch. of the Arts, Winston-Salem, 1980-88. Composer: (classical music) Symphonie Élégiaque, 1989; recordings on Koch Internat., Albany Records, Vienna Modern Masters. Avocations: cooking, tennis, sailing, mycology, reading. Home: 644 N Spring St Winston Salem NC 27101-1327 Office: Winston-Salem Symphony 610 Coliseum Dr Winston Salem NC 27106-5325

PERRETT, RHONDA ALLISON, elementary school educator; b. Miami Beach, Fla., Apr. 13, 1961; d. Carlton and Betty (Schachter) Fredericks; m. William Montague Perrett IV, Nov. 3, 1984. BS in Speech Comm., No. Mich. U., 1984; postgrad., Mt. St. Mary U., 1995. New patient educator Mountainview Med., West Nyack, N.Y., 1985-86; med. office mgr. Dr. Zack Zepher, New City, N.Y., 1986-87, Dr. H. K. Chaudhry, Montgomery, N.Y., 1989-92; spl. edn. para-profl. Valley Ctrl. Schs., Walden, N.Y., 1992—; media mail cons. Dr. Ronald Hoffman, N.Y.C., 1991—. Mem. Kappa Delta Pi, Delta Zeta. Republican. Jewish. Avocations: reading Russian literature, traveling, swimming, aerobics, dance. Home: 89 Bordens Rd Walden NY 12586-3226

PERRETTI, PETER NICHOLAS, JR., lawyer; b. Passaic, N.J., Oct. 4, 1931; s. Peter N. and Jessie (Ingram) P.; m. Ruth Mary Drechsler, Aug. 1, 1953; children: Peter N. III, Earl P., Ruth M. BA, Colgate U., 1953; JD, Cornell U., 1956. Bar: U.S. Supreme Ct., N.J., U.S. Ct. Appeals (3rd and 6th cirs.), U.S. Dist. Ct. N.J., U.S. Dist. Ct. (no. and ea. dists.) Ohio. Law sec. N.J. Superior Ct., Essex County, Newark, 1956-58; dep. atty. gen. Criminal Div., Exxex County, Newark, 1958-60; assoc. Riker, Danzig & Marsh, Newark, 1960-62; ptnr. Riker, Danzig, Scherer, Hyland & Perretti, Morristown, N.J., 1961-89, 90—; atty. gen. State of N.J., Trenton, 1989-90; bd. dirs. Jefferson Nat. Bank, Passaic, N.J. Trustee Middle Atlantic Assn. Colls. and Schs., Phila., Cornell Law Sch. Adv. Bd., Ithaca, N.Y., 1990—; bd. trustees Montclair (N.J.) Kimberley Acad.. Fellow Am. Bar Found., Am. Coll. Trial Lawyers; mem. ABA, Trial Attys. Assn. N.J. (hon.), N.J. State Bar Assn., Morris County Bar Assn., Fed. Bar Assn. of N.J., Am. Judicature Soc. Republican. Office: Riker Danzig Scherer Hyland & Perretti Hdqs Pla One Speedwell Ave Morristown NJ 07962-1981

PERRILL, FREDERICK EUGENE, information systems executive; b. Charlotte, N.C., Sept. 11, 1939; s. Frederick Eugene and Dorothy (Miller) P.; m. Kathryne Sims, June 1, 1963. BS in Engring., U.S. Naval Acad., 1962; MS in Bus., Naval Postgrad. Sch., 1969; postgrad., NAval War Coll., 1972-73. USCG Masters lic. Commd. ensign USN, 1962, advanced through grades to capt., 1982; supply officer USS Biddle DDG-5, 1962-63, USS Hermitage LSD-34, 1963-64; comptr. Amphibious Staff, 1964-68; dir. MIS systems, acctg., transp. Naval Supply Depot, Yokouka, Japan, 1969-72; project mgr. fin. systems design Asst. Sec. of Navy, 1973-76; dir. logistics USS Concord, 1976-78; project mgr. Fin. Systems, Washington, 1978-81; commanding officer Fin. and Acctg. Ctr., San Diego, 1981-83; dir. ops. Naval Supply Ctr., Oakland, 1984-85; asst. chief of staff MIS, COMMS. Naval Airforce Pacific, Coronado, Calif., 1985-86; ret. Naval Airforce Pacific, Coronado, 1986; sr. group mgr. Planning Rsch. Corp., San Diego, 1986-87; v.p. OPS/COO R.D. Ram Corp., San Diego, 1987-88; dir. Fourth Generation Tech., LaJolla, Calif., 1988-90; pres. Perrill Info. Systems, San Diego, 1990—; cons. Titan Corp. LaJolla, 1991—, Monger Industries, San Diego, 1988—, Delfin Corp., San Jose, 1990-91, Dobbs Ho., Memphis, 1986; farmer owner Pine Tree (property mgmt. co.), 1965—; owner, pres. Ancient Mariner Boat Svcs., 1990—. Contbr. articles to profl. jours. Asst. scout master Boy Scouts Am., Yokosuka, Japan, 1969-72; Protestant lay leader USS Concord AFS-5, Norfolk, Va., 1976-78. Mem. VFW, Naval Sailing Assn., Am. Legion, Humane Soc. of U.S., Disabled Am. Vets. Presbyterian. Avocations: sailing, skiing, camping. Home: 4785 Seda Dr San Diego CA 92124-2457

PERRILL, REBECCA LAURAN, elementary school educator; b. Columbus, Ohio, Mar. 20, 1954; d. Charles Howard and Helen Marie (Simons) P. BA in Elem. Edn., Ohio Wesleyan U., 1976; postgrad., Ohio State U., 1977-78, U. Dayton, Wright State U., Ashland U., Portland State U. Cert. elem. edn. tchr., Ohio. Tchr. 2nd and 4th grades Washington Court House (Ohio) City Schs., elem. tchr., grade 5. Mem. Kappa Delta Pi, Delta Kappa Gamma, Phi Delta Kappa. Home: 329 Gregg St Washington Court House OH 43160-1449

PERRIN, CHARLES R., light manufacturing executive; b. 1945. BA in History, Trinity Coll., 1967; MBA, Columbia U., 1969. With Gen. Foods Corp., 1969-73; various mgmt. positions with Chesebrough-Pond's, Inc., 1973-85; with Duracell Inc., Bethel, Conn., 1985—; v.p., pres. Duracell N.Am. Duracell Internat. Inc., 1988—, pres., COO internat. devel. markets, 1992—. Office: Duracell Internat Inc Berkshire Indsl Park Bethel CT 06801*

PERRIN, EDWARD BURTON, health services researcher, biostatistician, public health educator; b. Greensboro, Vt., Sept. 19, 1931; s. J. Newton and Dorothy E. (Willey) P.; m. Carol Anne Hendricks, Aug. 18, 1956; children: Jenifer, Scott. BA, Middlebury Coll., 1953; postgrad. (Fulbright scholar) in stats, Edinburgh (Scotland) U., 1953-54; MA in Math. Stats., Columbia U., 1956; PhD, Stanford U., 1960. Asst. prof. dept. biostats. U. Pitts., 1959-62; asst. prof. dept. preventive medicine U. Wash., Seattle, 1962-65; assoc. prof. U. Wash., 1965-69, prof., 1969-70, prof., chmn. dept. biostats., 1970-72, prof. dept. health svcs., adj. prof. dept. biostats., 1975—, chmn. dept., 1983-94; prof. (hon.) West China U. of Med. Scis., Szechwan, Peoples Republic of China, 1988—; overseas fellow Churchill Coll., Cambridge U., 1991-92; sr. scientist Seattle Vets. Affairs Med. Ctr., 1994—; clin. prof. dept. cmty. medicine and internat. health Sch. Medicine, Georgetown U., Washington, 1972-75; dep. dir. Nat. Ctr. for Health Stats., HEW, 1972-73, dir., 1973-75; rsch. scientist Health Care Study Ctr., Battelle Human Affairs Rsch. Ctrs., Seattle, 1975-76, dir., 1976-78; dir. Health and Population Study Ctr. Batelle Human Affairs Rsch. Ctrs., Seattle, 1978-83; sr. cons. biostats. Wash./Alaska regional med. programs, 1967-72; biometrician VA Co-op Study on Treatment of Esopageal Varices, 1961-73; mem. Epidemiology and Disease Control Study Sect., NIH, 1969-73; chmn. health svcs. rsch. study sect., HEW, 1976-79; chmn. health svcs. R&D field program rev. panel, VA, 1988-91; chmn. health svcs. info. steering com. State of Washington, 1993-94; mem. nat. adv. coun. Agy. for Health Care Policy and Rsch. Dept. Health and Human Svcs., U.S. Govt., 1994—; mem. com. on nat. stats. NRC, NAS, 1994—; chmn. scientific adv. com. Med. Outcomes Trust, 1994—. Contbr. articles on biostats., health services and population studies to profl. publs.; mem. editorial bd.: Jour. Family Practice, 1978-90, Public Health Nursing, 1992—. Mem. tech. bd. Milbank Meml. Fund, 1974-76. Recipient Outstanding Service citation HEW, 1975. Fellow AAAS, Am. Pub. Health Assn. (Spiegelman Health Stats. award 1970, program devel. bd. 1971, chmn. stats. sect. 1978-80, governing coun. 1983-85, stats. sect. recognition award 1989), Am. Statis. Assn. (mem. adv. com. to divsn. statis. policy 1975-77); mem. Assn. Health Svcs. Rsch. (pres. 1994-95), Inst. Medicine of Nat. Acad. Sci. (chmn. membership com. 1984-86, mem. bd. on health care svcs. 1987-96, forum health stats. 1994-95, chmn. com. on clin. evaluation 1990-93), Biometrics Soc. (pres. Western N.Am. Region 1971), Inst. Math. Stats., Internat. Epidemiologic Assn., Sigma Xi, Phi Beta Kappa. Home: 4900 NE 39th St Seattle WA 98105-5209 Office: U Wash Dept Health Svcs PO Box 357660 Seattle WA 98195-7660

PERRIN, GAIL, editor; b. Boston, Oct. 14, 1938; d. Hugh and Helen (Baxter) P. B.A., Wellesley Coll., 1960. Copy girl Washington Daily News, summers, 1954-57, reporter, 1958, 60-61, acting women's editor, food editor, 1961-62, rewrite reporter, 1963-65; reporter Honolulu Star Bull., 1959; women's editor Boston Globe, 1965-71, asst. met. editor, 1971-74, food editor, 1974-92; food cons., free-lance writer, 1992—. Mem. Assn. Food Journalists, Women's Culinary Guild.

PERRIN, KENNETH LYNN, university chancellor; b. L.A., July 29, 1937; s. Freeman Whitaker and Lois Eileen (Bowen) P.; m. Shirley Anne Cupp, Apr. 2, 1960; children: Steven, Lynne. BA, Occidental Coll., 1959; MA, Calif. State U., Long Beach, 1964; PhD, Stanford U., 1969. Lic. in speech pathology, Calif. Chmn. dept. communicative disorders U. Pacific, Stockton, Calif., 1969-77; dir. edn. and sci. programs Am. Speech-Lang.-Hearing Assn., Rockville, Md., 1977-80; dean Faculty Profl. Studies West Chester U., Pa., 1980-82; acting acad. v.p. West Chester U., 1982, pres., 1983-91; pres. Coun. on Postsecondary Edn., Washington, 1991-93; chancellor, system sr. v.p. U. Hawaii, Hilo and West Oahu, 1993—; cons. in field, 1969-76; pres. north region Calif. Speech Hearing Assn., 1975-76. Co-author: monograph Prevalence of Communicative Disorders, 1981; contbr. articles to profl. jours.; editor: Guide to Graduate Education Speech Pathology and Audiology, 1980. Chmn. Southeastern chpt. Greater Brandywine Br. ARC; trainee Vocat. Rehab. Adminstrn., 1965-69. Named Disting. Alumnus Sch. Humanities Calif. State U., Long Beach, 1988. Fellow Am. Speech-Lang.-Hearing Assn. (vice chmn. edn. tng. bd. 1975-77 cert. clin. competence in speech pathology); mem. West Chester C. of C. (pres. 1988). Home: 543 Kaanini St Hilo HI 96720 Office: 200 W Kawili St Hilo HI 96720-4075

PERRIN, MICHAEL WARREN, lawyer; b. Cameron, Tex., Nov. 10, 1946; s. Frank W. and Mary Ann (Green) P.; m. Melinda Elizabeth Hill, Aug. 9, 1969; children: Elizabeth, Carter, Hunter. BS, U. Tex., Austin, 1969, JD, 1971. Bar: Tex. 1972, U.S. Dist. Ct. (no., ea., we. and so. dists.) Tex., U.S. Ct. Appeals (5th and 11th cirs.), U.S. Supreme Ct. Assoc. Vinson & Elkins, Houston, 1972-73; assoc. Fisher, Roch & Gallagher, Houston, 1973-76; ptnr. Fisher, Gallagher, Perrin & Lewis, Houston, 1976-91; sole practice Houston, 1991—. Fellow Am. Coll. Trial Lawyers, Internat. Acad. Trial Lawyers, Internat. Soc. Barristers; mem. Am. Bd. Trial Advocates (assoc.), Houston Bar Assn., Houston Young Lawyers Assn. (sec. 1974-75), Tex. Young Lawyers Assn. (dir. 1976-78, chmn. bd. 1978-79), Houston Trial Lawyers Assn. (pres. 1987-88), Tex. Trial Lawyers Assn. (pres. 1989-90), Tex. Bar Found., Assn. Trial Lawyers Am. Democrat. Methodist. Office: 333 Clay Ste 4440 Three Allen Ctr Houston TX 77002

PERRIN, NANCY ANN, elementary music educator; b. Dayton, Ohio, June 13, 1948; d. Eugene Clark and Geneva Louise (Sease) Maupin; 1 child, Mike J. Brown; m. Keith A. Perrin, Dec. 5, 1987. BMusic, Ohio State U., 1970; MMusic in Edn., Wright State U., 1984, MEd, 1991. Cert. tchr., supr., elem. prin., h.s. prin., staff pers. adminstr., asst. supt., supr. instrnl. svcs., Ohio. Tchr. Tecumseh Local Schs., New Carlisle, Ohio, 1976—, head dept. music, 1989—; instr. Sinclair C.C., Dayton, Ohio, 1980—. Mem. ASCD, Am. Mathay Assn. (archivist 1986-91), Music Educators Nat. Conf., Ohio Assn. Elem. Sch. Adminstrs., Dayton Music Club. Avocations: playing keyboard and guitar, bicycling. Home: 270 Banbury Rd Centerville OH 45459-1706 Office: Tecumseh Local Bd Edn Park Layne Sch 9760 W National Rd New Carlisle OH 45344-9290

PERRIN, NOEL, environmental studies educator; b. N.Y.C., Sept. 18, 1927; s. Edwin Oscar and Blanche Browning (Chenery) P.; m. Nancy Hunnicutt, Nov. 26, 1960 (div. 1971); children: Elisabeth, Amy; m. 2d Annemarie Price, June 20, 1975 (div. 1980); m. Anne Spencer Lindbergh, Dec. 26, 1988 (dec. 1993). B.A., Williams Coll., 1949; M.A., Duke U., 1950; M.Litt., Cambridge U., 1958. Copy boy Daily News, N.Y.C., 1950-51; assoc. editor Med. Econs., Oradell, N.J., 1953-56; instr. U. N.C. Woman's Coll., Greensboro, 1956-59; from instr. to prof. English Dartmouth Coll., Hanover, N.H., 1959-90, prof. environ. studies, 1991—. Author: A Passport Secretly Green, 1961, Dr. Bowdler's Legacy, 1969, Giving Up the Gun, 1979, Second Person Rural, 1980, Third Person Rural, 1983, A Reader's Delight, 1988, A Noel Perrin Sampler, 1991, Last Person Rural, 1991, Solo: Life with an Electric Car, 1992; columnist, Washington Post Book World, 1980-86, 89-91. Served to 1st lt. arty. AUS, 1951-52. Decorated Bronze Star; Guggenheim Found. fellow, 1970, 85. Episcopalian. Home: RR 1 Box 8 Thetford Center VT 05075-9701 Office: Dartmouth College Environ Studies Program Hanover NH 03755

PERRIN, ROBERT, writer, consultant; b. Ann Arbor, Mich., Aug. 21, 1925; s. John Stephenson and Narcissa Elizabeth (Merkel) P.; m. Barbara J. Groom, June 25, 1949; children: Stephen, Jennifer Perrin Hummel. BS, U. Minn., 1945. Reporter United Press Assn., Detroit, 1948-49, Detroit Free Press, 1949-55; adminstrv. asst. U.S. Senate, Washington, 1955-66; asst. dir. U.S. Office Econ. Opportunity, Washington, 1966-68, dep. dir., 1968-70; v.p. Mich. State U., East Lansing, 1970-79; vice chancellor SUNY System, Albany, 1979-85; exec. v.p. Tchrs. Ins. and Annuity Assn.—Coll. Retirement Equities Fund, N.Y.C., 1987-92; cons. Dept. State, 1993-94. Contbr. articles to mags., newspapers. Mem. U.S.-Mex. Commn. on Border Devel., Washington, 1967-68. Lt. USNR, 1943-46, PTO. Fellow Reid Found., 1954.

PERRIN, SARAH ANN, lawyer; b. Neoga, Ill., Dec. 13, 1904; d. James Lee and Bertha Frances (Baker) Figenbaum; m. James Frank Perrin, Dec. 24, 1926. LLB, George Washington U., 1941, JD, 1964. Bar: D.C. 1942. Assoc. atty. Mabel Walker Willebrandt, law office, Washington, 1941-42; atty. various fed. housing agys., 1942-69, asst. gen. counsel FHA, Washington, 1959-60, asst. gen. counsel HUD, Washington, 1960-69; sec. Nat. Housing Conf., Washington, 1970-80; rsch. cons. housing and urban devel., Palmyra, Va., 1970-76; acting sec. Nat. Housing Rsch. Coun., Washington, 1973-80; bd. dirs. Nat. Housing Conf., 1972—. Mem. Rep. Presdl. Adv. Commn., 1991-92; trustee Found. for Coop. Housing, 1975-80; mem. Blue Ridge Presbytery Div. Mission, Presbyn. Ch., 1979-80, Friends of Fluvanna County Libr. Mem. ABA, Fed. Bar Assn., Women's Bar Assn. D.C. (pres. 1959-60), Nat. Assn. Women Lawyers, George Washington Law Assn., Charlottesville Area Women's Bar Assn., Fluvanna County Bar Assn., Fluvanna County Hist. Soc. (pres. 1973-75, exec. com. 1985-89), Order Eastern Star, Presbyn. Women (pres. Fork Union chpt. 1972-80, sec. 1980-94), Phi Alpha Delta (internat. pres. 1955-57, internat. adv. bd.). Home: Solitude Plantation Palmyra VA 22963

PERRINE, RICHARD LEROY, environmental engineering educator; b. Mountain View, Calif., May 15, 1924; s. George Alexander and Marie (Axelson) P.; m. Barbara Jean Gale, Apr. 12, 1945; children: Cynthia Gale, Jeffrey Richard. A.B., San Jose State Coll., 1949; M.S., Stanford U., 1950, Ph.D. in Chemistry, 1953. Cert. environ. profl., 1987. Research chemist Calif. Research Corp., La Habra, 1953-59; assoc. prof. UCLA, 1959-63, prof. engring. and applied sci., 1963-92, prof. emeritus, 1992—, chmn. environ. sci. and engring., 1971-82; prin. Aspen Environ. Group, 1990-93; v.p. Sage Resources, 1988-91; cons. environ. sci. and engring., energy resources, flow in porous media; mem. Los Angeles County Energy Commn., 1973-81; mem. adv. council South Coast Air Quality Mgmt. Dist., 1977-82; mem. air conservation com. Los Angeles County Lung Assn., 1970-84; mem. adv. com. energy div. Oak Ridge Nat. Lab., 1987-90; mem. policy bd. Inst. Environ. and Natural Resource Rsch. and Policy U. Wyo., 1994—. Editor in chief The Environ. Profl., 1985-90. Served with AUS, 1943-46. Recipient Outstanding Engr. Merit award in environ. engring. Inst. Advancement Engring., 1975; ACT-SO award in field of chemistry West Coast region NAACP, 1984. Mem. AAAS, Am. Chem. Soc., Soc. Petroleum Engrs., Am. Inst. Chem. Engrs., Can. Inst. Mining and Metallurgy, N.Am. Assn. Environ. Edn., Nat. Assn. Environ. Profls. (cert.), Air and Waste Mgmt. Assn., Assn. Environ. Engring. Profs., Sierra Club, Wilderness Soc., Audubon Soc., Sigma Xi, Tau Beta Pi, Phi Lambda Upsilon. Home: 22611 Kittridge St West Hills CA 91307-3609 Office: Univ Calif Engring Bldg I Rm 2066D Los Angeles CA 90024-1593

PERRINE, VALERIE, actress; b. Galveston, Tex., Sept. 3, 1943; d. Kenneth and Renee (McGinley) P. Student, U. Ariz., 1961. Screen debut Slaughterhouse Five, 1972; other films include The Last American Hero, 1973, Lenny, 1974 (Best actress award Cannes Film Festival, 1975, Best Supporting Actress, N.Y. Film Circle, 1975, Actress of Yr. award United Motion Pictures Assn., 1975, award most promising newcomer to leading film roles Brit. Acad., 1975), W.C. Fields and Me, 1976, Mr. Billion, 1977, Superman, 1978, The Electric Horseman, 1979, Magician of Lublin, 1979, Can't Stop the Music, 1980, Superman II, 1980, Agency, 1981, The Border, 1982, The Mask, 1985, Water, 1986, Maid to Order, 1987, Bright Angel, 1991, Boiling Point, 1994; TV movies include The Couple Takes A Wife, 1972, Steambath, 1972, Whenm the Girls Come Out To Play, 1974, Ziegfield 1978, Marian Rose White, 1982, Malibu, 1983, When Your Lover Leaves, 1983, Una Casa a Roma, 1987, Una Donna d'Affare, 1987, Sweet Bird of Youth, 1989, The Mountain of Diamonds, 1990; (TV series) Leo and Liz in Beverly Hills, 1986; (TV miniseries) The Secrets of Lake Success, 1993. Mem. SAG, AFTRA. Address: Borinstein Oreck & Bogart 8271 Melrose Ave Ste 110 Los Angeles CA 90046-6824*

PERRIS, TERRENCE GEORGE, lawyer; b. L.A., Oct. 18, 1947; s. Theodore John Grivas and Penny (Sfakianos) Perris. BA magna cum laude, U. Toledo, 1969; JD summa cum laude, U. Mich., 1972. Bar: Ohio 1972, U.S. Tax Ct. 1982, U.S. Ct. Claims 1983, U.S. Supreme Ct. 1983. Law clk. to judge U.S. Ct. Appeals (2d cir.), N.Y.C., 1972-73; law clk. to Justice Potter Stewart U.S. Supreme Ct., Washington, 1973-74; assoc. Squire, Sanders & Dempsey, Cleve., 1974-80, ptnr., 1980—; v.p., trustee SS&D Found., Cleve., 1984—; nat. coord. Taxation Practice Area, 1987—; chmn. Cleve. Tax Inst., 1993; vis. prof. law U. Mich., 1996; lectr. in field. Mem. vis. com. U. Mich. Law Sch., 1986—. Capt. U.S. Army, 1974. Mem. ABA, Ohio Bar Assn., Cleve. Bar Assn. (subchpt. C of internal revenue code task force), Supreme Ct. Hist. Soc., Tax Club Cleve., Order of Coif, Union Club of Cleve., U. Mich. Club of Cleve., The Club of Cleve., Pres.'s Club (Ann Arbor, Mich.), Phi Kappa Phi. Republican. Eastern Orthodox. Avocation: landscape gardening. Office: Squire Sanders & Dempsey 4900 Society Ctr 127 Public Sq Cleveland OH 44114-1216

PERRISH, ALBERT, steel company executive; b. Vancouver, B.C., Can., Nov. 18, 1914; came to U.S., 1920; s. Sam and Nettie (Prezant) P.; m. Leora Claire Quiat, Jan. 12, 1962 (dec. 1984); m. Helen Ann Frazin, June 11, 1985; children: Peggy, Kathleen. BSBA, UCLA, 1938. Commr. City of L.A. Harbor Dept., 1961-64, pres., 1964; exec. Ferro Union Inc., Torrance, Calif., 1964—; mem. adv. bd. U.S. Dept. Commerce, Washington, 1946-50, Small Bus. Adminstrn., Washington, 1955-56. Capt. USAAF, 1942-46. Recipient Star of Solidarity, Pres. of Italy, 1954, Order of Leopold, King of Belgium, 1962, Order of Merit, Govt. of France, 1962. Mem. Am. Inst. Internat. Steel (founder, pres. West Coast chpt. 1959—). Office: Ferro Union Inc 1000 W Francisco St Torrance CA 90502

PERRON, PIERRE O., science administrator; b. Louiseville, Que., Can., Aug. 19, 1939; m. Rachel DesRosiers. BA in Scis. with honors, Laval (Can.) U., 1959, BASc in Metall. Engring., 1963; PhD in Metallurgy, U. Strathclyde, Glasgow, Scotland, 1966. Rsch. officer Chalk River Nuclear Labs. Atomic Energy of Can. Ltd., 1966-68; mgr. radiation protection dept. Hydro Que., 1968-71; dir. material scis. Que. Indsl. Rsch. Ctr., 1971-75, dir. R&D, 1975-82; assoc. dep. minister Dept. Energy and Resources Govt. of Que., Quebec City, 1982-85, Dept. Energy, Mines and Resources Can., Ottawa, 1985-89; pres. Nat. Rsch. Coun. Can., Ottawa, Ont., 1989-94; ret., 1994.

PERRONE, NICHOLAS, mechanical engineer, business executive; b. Apr. 30, 1930. B. Aero. Engring., Poly. Inst. Bklyn., 1951, M.S., 1953, Ph.D., 1958. Research asst., then assoc. applied mechanics Bklyn. Poly. Inst., 1951-58; asst. prof., then assoc. prof. Pratt Inst., 1958-62; sr. scientist Structural Mechanics br. Office Naval Research, Washington, 1962-67; acting head dept. Structural Mechanics br. Office Naval Research, 1967-68, dir. program, 1968-69, 71-82; pres. CASA Gifts Inc., 1983-85; dep. to pres. Advanced Tech. and Research Inc., 1986-87; pres. Perrone Forensic Cons. Inc., 1987—; lectr. civil engring. Cath U. Am., 1962-64, adj. prof., 1965—; spl. research fellow NIH, Georgetown U., 1969-70; participant numerous workshops, confs., symposia; lectr. in field. Contbg. author: Biodynamics, 1980; editor or co-editor numerous monographs; editorial adv. bd.: Advances in Engring. Software, Computers and Structures, Engineering Fracture, Pressure Vessels and Piping; contbr. numerous articles to profl. jours. Fellow AAAS, ASME, Am. Acad. Mechanics; mem. ASCE, AIAA, N.Y. Acad. Sci., Am. Soc. Engring. Edn., Soc. Automotive Engrs., Soc. Mfg. Engrs. Address: 12207 Valerie Ln Laurel MD 20708-2837

PERROS, THEODORE PETER, chemist, educator; b. Cumberland, Md., Aug. 16, 1921; s. Peter G. and Christina (Sioris) P.; m. Electra Paula Zolotas, July 21, 1973 (div.). BS, George Washington U., 1946, MS, 1947, Ph.D., 1952; postgrad., Technische Hochschule, Munich, Germany. Analyst research div. U.S. Naval Ordnance Lab., 1943-46; faculty George Washington U., Washington, 1946—, prof. chemistry and forensic scis., 1960—, chmn. dept. forensic sci., 1971-73, chmn. dept. chemistry, 1980-88; v.p. Meridian-West Assos., 1978—; rsch. chemist Bur. Ordnance, 1949; rsch. dir. Air Force Office Sci. R&D, 1958-59; cons. U.S. Naval Ordnance Lab., 1953-56; fed. commr., chmn. bd. dirs. Interstate Commn. Potomac River Basin, 1980; sec. Ahepa Ednl. Found., 1969-78; mem. Chesapeake Bay Sci. and Tech. Adv. Com., 1993. Author: (with William F. Sager) Chemical Principles, 1961, (with C.R. Naeser, W. Harkness) Experiments in General Chemistry, 1961, College Chemistry, 1966; Contbr. (with C.R. Naeser, W. Harkness) articles to profl. jours. Pres. So. Intercollegiate Athletic Conf., 1968, Hellenic Rep. Club of Washington, 1968-70, D.C. Heritage Groups Coun., 1980; campaign chmn. Nat. Rep. Heritage Groups Coun., 1977-78, recipient Kurt Voldemars Meml. award for disting. svc., 1985; mem. D.C. Rep. State Com., 1980—; exec. com. Rep. Nat. Com., 1994-95; chmn. Nat. Rep. Heritage Groups Coun., 1994-95. Named Disting. Prof. in Edn. George Washington U., 1990, Award of Distinction, CHS Alumni Assn., 1992; NSF fellow, 1959; AEC grantee, 1951-53, Rsch. Corp. grantee, 1953-54. Fellow Am. Inst. Chemists, Am. Acad. Forensic Scis., Washington Acad. Scis.; mem. Am. Chem. Soc., Soc. Applied Spectroscopy, German Lang. Soc., Chem. Soc. London, Gesellschaft Deutscher Chemiker, Philos. Soc. Washington, Am. Hellenic Ednl. Progressive Assn. (pres. Inst. Arts and Scis., pres. Washington chpt. 1976-78, dist. gov. 1982-83, supreme gov. 1985-86, AHEPA Acad. Achievement award 1984), Sigma Xi, Omicron Delta Kappa, Alpha Chi Sigma (pres. 1964, bd. gov.'s 1986-88, Profl. Merit award 1985, Profl. Chemistry award 1985). Research on stabilities of inorganic coordination polymers, preparation and characterization fluorine containing compounds transition metals. Home: 5825 3rd Pl NW Washington DC 20011-2106

PERROT, PAUL NORMAN, museum director; b. Paris, France, July 28, 1926; came to U.S., 1946, naturalized, 1954; s. Paul and K. Norman (Derr) P.; m. Joanne Stovall, Oct. 23, 1954; children—Paul Latham, Chantal Marie Claire, Jeannine, Robert. Student, Ecole du Louvre, 1945-46, N.Y. U. Inst. Fine Arts, 1946-52. Asst. The Cloisters, Met. Mus. Art, 1948-52; asst. to dir. Corning (N.Y.) Mus. Glass, 1952-54, asst. dir. mus., 1954-60, dir., 1960-72; editor Jour. Glass Studies, 1959-72; asst. sec. for mus. programs Smithsonian Instn., Washington, 1972-84; dir. Va. Mus. Fine Arts, 1984-91; dir. Santa Barbara Mus. Art, 1991-94, mus. cons., 1995—; lectr. glass history, aesthetics, museology; past v.p. Internat. Coun. Mus. Found.; past pres. N.E. Conf. Mus.; past pres. Internat. Centre for Study of Preservation and Restoration of Cultural Property, Rome, mem. coun., 1974-88. Author: Three Great Centuries of Venetian Glass, 1958, also numerous articles on various hist. and archael. subjects. Former trustee Winterthur Mus.; former trustee, treas. Mus. Computer NEtwork; mem. Internat. Cons. Com. for the Preservation of Moenjodaro; chmn. adv. com. World Monuments Fund; mem. vis. com. Getty Conservation Inst. Mem. Am. Assn. Mus. (past v.p., coun. 1967-78), N.Y. State Assn. Mus. (past pres.), Internat. Assn. History Glass (past v.p.) Corning Friends of Library (past pres.), So. Tier Library System (past pres.). Home: 988 Blvd of the Arts #1010 Sarasota FL 34236-4836

PERROTTO, LARRY J., newspaper executive; married; 3 children. Degree, Edinboro U., 1959. Pres., CEO Am. Pub. Co.; mem. bd. dirs. Am. Pub. Co., West Frankfort, Ill., Argus Corp., Toronto, Ont., Barber Mine Timber Co., DuQuoin, Ill., Hollinger, Inc., Toronto, Shawnee Bancorp, Harrisburg, Ill., Western Dominion Investments, Vancouver, B.C. Recipient Disting. Alumni award U. Edinboro, 1991. Mem. Delta Sigma Chi. Home: 47 Frankfort Dr West Frankfort IL 62896 Office: President/CEO Chicago Sun Times 401 N Wabash Ave Chicago IL 60611

PERRUCCI, ROBERT, sociologist, educator; b. N.Y.C., Nov. 11, 1931; s. Dan and Inez (Mucci) P.; m. Carolyn Land Cummings, Aug. 4, 1965; children: Mark Robert, Celeste Ann, Christopher Robert, Alissa Cummings, Martin Cummings. B.S., SUNY, Cortland, 1958; M.S. (Social Sci. Research Council fellow), Purdue U., Ph.D., 1962. Asst. prof. sociology Purdue U., West Lafayette, Ind., 1962-65; asso. prof. Purdue U., 1965-67, prof., 1967—, head dept., 1978-87; vis. Simon prof. U. Manchester (Eng.), 1968-69; Bd. dirs. Ind. Center on Law and Poverty, 1973-76. Author: Sociology, 1983, Circle of Madness, 1974, Divided Loyalties, 1980, The Triple Revolution, 1971, Profession Without Community, 1968, The Engineers and the Social System, 1968, Mental Patients and Social Networks, 1982, Plant Closings: International Context and Local Consequences, 1988, Networks of Power, 1989, Japanese Auto Transplants in the Heartland: Corporatism and Community, 1994; editor: The American Sociologist, 1982—, Social Problems, 1993—; contbr. articles to profl. jours. Served with USMC, 1951-53. Recipient grants NSF, 1966-68, 76-78, grants NIMH, 1969-72. Mem. Am. Sociol. Assn., Soc. Study Social Problems (dir. 1980—), N. Central Sociol. Assn. (pres. 1973-74). Home: 305 Leslie Ave West Lafayette IN 47906-2411 Office: Dept Sociology Purdue U West Lafayette IN 47907

PERRY, A. MICHAEL, banker; b. Huntington, W.Va., May 31, 1936; s. Austin Lee and Virginia (Cole) P.; m. Henriella Mylar, 1958; children—Michele, Melanie, Audy. B.A., Marshall U., 1958; LL.B., W.Va. U., 1961. Ptnr. Huddleston, Bolen, Beatty, Porter, Copen, Huntington, 1961-81; chmn. bd., chief exec. officer 1st Huntington Nat. Bank, 1981-88, chmn. bd., 1981—; pres., chief exec. officer Key Bancshares W.Va., Inc., Huntington, 1983-85, Key Centurion Bancshares, Inc.,, 1985—. Trustee Alderson Broaddus Coll., 1984-89, Greater Ashland Found. Inc.; bd. dirs. Tri-State Cultural Devel. Plan; mem. adv. bd. Marshall Artists Series, Huntington, 1987-89; mem. bd. trustees U. W.Va. system, vice chairperson. Recipient Advocate of Yr. award SBA, 1985, Citizen of Yr. award Huntington newspaper, 1987. Mem. W.Va. Research League (bd. dirs., v.p.), W.Va. Bankers Assn. (bd. dirs., chmn. govt. and legis. com., chmn. interstate banking task force), W.Va. C. of C. (mem. exec. com., chmn.-elect 1989), Order of Coif, Omicron Delta Kappa. Baptist. Club: Rotary (past pres.). Avocations: farming, collecting farm and kitchen implements. Home: 3350 Harvey Rd Huntington WV 25704-9112 Office: Banc One Ctr Charleston WV 25301 also: PO Box 1113 Charleston WV 25324-1113*

PERRY, ANTHONY JOHN, retired hospital executive; b. Dighton, Mass., Oct. 19, 1919; s. Antone and Jessie P.; m. Harriet M. McGirr, Nov. 26, 1949; children: Joan Perry, Martha. B.S. in Edn, State Coll. Mass. at Bridgewater, 1942; MHA, Northwestern U., 1952. Flight supt. Trans World Airlines, Lisbon, Portugal, 1946-47; sta. mgr. Peruvian Internat. Airlines, N.Y.C., 1947-49; with adminstrn. Decatur and Macon County Hosp. (now Decatur Meml. Hosp.), Decatur, Ill., 1952-86, adminstr., 1961-69, exec. v.p., 1969-74, pres., CEO, 1974-86; ret., 1996; cons. in field, 1986—; bd. dirs. MMI Cos., 1985-95, chmn., 1985-94; pres. Mental Health Assn. Macon County, 1957; mem. Tech. Coun. Means and Methods of Financing Health Care for Ill. Bd. dirs. Macon County chpt. ARC, 1960-66, South Cen. Ill. Health Planning Council, 1969—, United Way Decatur and Macon County, 1960-66, Voluntary Hosps. Am., 1977-86; mem. adv. bd. Grad. Studies Ctr., Millikin U. Served with USAAF, 1942-46. Fellow Am. Coll. Hosp. Adminstrs.; mem. Am. Hosp. Assn. (trustee, mem. regional adv. bd., chmn. coun. on fin. 1975-79), Ill. Hosp. Assn. (pres. 1972, chmn. rate rev. steering com. 1979—), Decatur Country Club, La Quinta (Calif.) Resort Golf Club. Home: 421 Hackberry Dr Decatur IL 62521-5501 Office: Millikin Ct Suite 518 Decatur IL 62523

PERRY, BILL, photojournalist. Photo editor Gannett News Svc., Arlington, Va. Office: Gannett News Svc 100 Wilson Blvd 10th Fl Arlington VA 22229-0001*

PERRY, B(ILLY) DWIGHT, lawyer; b. Oklahoma City, Jan. 28, 1933; s. William C. and Julia Walton (Bray) P.; m. Shirley Andersen, June 16, 1959 (div. 1973); m. Suzanne Meyer , Sept. 15, 1973; children: Scott R., Ryan W., Samantha G., Devin D. BA, U. Okla., 1955; JD, Georgetown U., 1963. Bar: D.C. 1964, U.S. Supreme Ct. 1968. Law clk. to Judge E. Barrett Prettyman U.S. Ct. Appeals (D.C. cir.), 1963-64; assoc. McCarty & Wheatley, Washington, 1964-67; assoc., then ptnr. Dow, Lohnes & Albertson, Washington, 1967-91, mng. ptnr., 1991—. Lt. arty. U.S. Army, 1956-60. Mem. ABA, Fed. Communications Bar Assn., D.C. Bar Assn. (Young Lawyer of Yr. 1967-68), Washington Golf and Country Club. Episcopalian. Avocations: fishing, hunting, scuba diving. Office: Dow Lohnes & Albertson 1200 New Hampshire Ave Washington DC 20036-6802

PERRY, BLANCHE BELLE, physical therapist; b. New Bedford, Mass., Sept. 2, 1929; d. Joseph Rudolph and Beatrice (Faria) Andrews; BS, Ithaca (N.Y.) Coll., 1951; MA, Assumption Coll., Worcester, Mass., 1978; m. Louis Perry, Nov. 26, 1953; (dec. 1980); children: Marcia, Susan, Tracey, Evelyn. Office and hosp. phys. therapist, Mass. and N.Y., 1961-65; dir. rehab. svcs. St. Luke's Hosp., New Bedford, 1967-89; ret, 1989; profl. adv. com. Vis. Nurse Assn. Wareham, 1980; mem. faculty continuing edn. Newbury Coll., 1986; corporator New Bedford Five Cents Savs. Bank, Compass Bank for Savs. Chmn. Mattapoisett Sch. Com., 1970; vice chmn. Mass. Sch. Commn. Area IV, 1972-75; sec. Old Colony Regional Vocat. Sch. Com., 1973—; trustee Abner Pease Scholarship Found.; chmn. com. opportunity ctr. CARF, New Bedford, 1987; pres. St. Luke's Hosp. Retirees, 1996. Grantee Elks Nat. Found., 1965. Mem. Am. Phys. Therapy Assn., Nat. Rehab. Adminstrs. Assn., Delta Kappa Gamma. Republican. Club: Mattapoisett Women's (pres. 1996). Home: 41 Aucoot Rd Mattapoisett MA 02739-2401

PERRY, CATHERINE D., judge; b. 1952. BA, Univ. of Okla., 1977; JS, Wash. Univ. Sch. of Law, 1980. Sec., law clk. Gillespie, Perry & Gentry, Sentinel, Okla., 1970, 77-78; with Armstrong, Teasdale, Kramer & Vaughn, St. Louis, 1980-90; magistrate judge U.S. Dist. Ct. (Mo. ea. dist.), 8th circuit, St. Louis, 1990-94, district judge, 1994—. Mem. Fed. Magistrate Judges Assn., Nat. Assn. of Women Judges, Am. Bar Assn., Mo. Bar Assn., Bar Assn. of Metropolitan St. Louis, Women Lawyers Assn. of Greater St. Louis. Office: US Courthouse 1114 Market St Rm 840 Saint Louis MO 63101-2034*

PERRY, CHARLES OWEN, sculptor; b. Helena, Mont., Oct. 18, 1929; s. Owen Hindmarch and Margaret Carroll (Bache) P.; m. Sheila Alicia Henry, June 22, 1962; children—Paul, Carlo, Daniela, Patrick, Marco. Student, Columbia U., 1953; M.Arch., Yale U., 1958. Architect Skidmore Owings & Merrill, San Francisco, 1958-64, Prix de Rome Architecture, 1964-66; sculptor-in-residence Dartmouth Coll., 1973. One-man shows include Hansen Gallery, San Francisco, 1964, Waddell Gallery, N.Y.C., 1967, 70, Dartmouth Coll., 1973, Arts Club, Chgo., 1973; exhibited in group shows at Whitney Mus., 1964, 66, Spoleto Festival, 1967, Venice Biennale, 1970, Quadrienalle di Arte de Roma, 1977, Katonah Gallery, N.Y.; represented in permanent collections at Mus. Modern Art, N.Y.C., Art Inst. Chgo., San Francisco Mus. Art, U. Ind. Mus. Art, Dartmouth Coll., U. Mich., Nat. Air and Space Mus., IBM, Charlotte, N.C., Hyatt Regency, San Francisco, Fed. Res. Bank, Mpls., Barnett Plaza, Tampa, Lincoln Ctr., Dallas, Shell Oil Bldg., Melbourne, Australia, GE Hdqrs., Fairfield, Conn., Bushnell Park, Hartford, Conn., Crystal City, Arlington, Va.; patentee in furniture design field. Served with U.S. Army, 1951-53. Decorated Bronze star. Fellow Am. Acad. Rome, Nat. Acad. Design; mem. Sculptors Guild, Silvermine Guild, Century Assn. (N.Y.C.). Roman Catholic. Home: 20 Shorehaven Rd Norwalk CT 06855-2807 Studio: 3 Raymond St Norwalk CT 06854-3107

PERRY, DALE LYNN, chemist; b. Greenville, Tex., May 12, 1947; s. Francis Leon and Violet (Inabinette) P. BS, Midwestern U., 1969; MS, Lamar U., 1972; PhD, U. Houston, 1974. NSF fellow dept. chemistry Rice U., Houston, 1976-77; Miller Research fellow dept. chemistry U. Calif.-Berkeley, 1977-79; prin. investigator solid state chemistry and spectroscopy Lawrence Berkeley Lab. U. Calif., 1979—, sr. scientist, 1987—; lectr. Ana G. Mendez Ednl. Found., 1988. Author, editor: Instrumental Surface Analysis of Geologic Materials, 1990, Applications of Analytical Techniques to the Characterization of Materials, 1992, Applications of Synchrotron Radiation Techniques to Materials Science, 1993, Applications of Synchrotron Radiation Techniques to Materials Science II, 1995; contbr. articles to profl. jours. Recipient Sigma Xi Nat. Research award U. Houston, 1974. Fellow Royal Soc. Chemistry (London); mem. Am. Chem. Soc. (chmn. materials chemistry and engring. subdivsn., indsl. and engring. chemistry divsn., 1992-96), Soc. Applied Spectroscopy, Coblentz Soc., Materials Rsch. Soc. (corp. participation com. 1991—), Sigma Xi. Office: U Calif Lawrence Berkeley Lab Mail Stop 70A-1150 Berkeley CA 94720

PERRY, DAVID, priest. Ecumenical officer Nat. Episcopal Ch., N.Y.C. Office: Episcopal Ch Ctr 815 2nd Ave New York NY 10017-4503

PERRY, DONALD A., cable television consultant; b. Newport News, Va., July 18, 1938. With James Broadcasting, 1961; v.p., gen. mgr. Hampton Rds. Music Corp., Hampton Rds. Cablevision Corp., Danville Cablevision Corp., 1971-70; pres., treas. Donald A. Perry & Assocs., Inc., Gloucester, Va., 1970—; prin. Am. Cablevision Corp., 1970—; sec., treas. Communications East Corp.; sec., treas. 1st Commonwealth Communications, Inc., also chmn. bd. dirs.; pres., chief oper. officer 1st Commonwealth Cablevision, Ltd.; sec. Atlantic Metrovision Corp.; owner Gourmet Mkt., Ltd. With USCG, 1956-60. Recipient J.L. Johnson award, 1984; Paul Harris fellow. Mem. Nat. Cable TV Assn., Community Antenna TV Assn. (bd. dirs.), Va. Cable TV Assn. (past pres.), So. Cable TV Assn. (past officer, past dir.), Rotary (Newport News chpt., past pres.), Tower Club. Home: 201 Country Club Rd Newport News VA 23606-3705 Office: Donald A Perry & Assocs Inc PO Box 1275 Newport News VA 23601-0275 also: Summerville Plantation Gloucester VA 23061

PERRY, DONALD HOWARD, magazine publisher; b. N.Y.C., Feb. 13, 1927; s. Samuel Joseph and Rose (Felzen) P.; m. Florence Kjar, Apr. 17, 1966; 1 child, Lisa Robin; m. Marianne Savin, Feb. 8, 1987. Student, NYU, 1943-44. Ad mgr. shopping sect. Argosy Mag., N.Y.C., 1950; pub. rep. Many Mags., N.Y.C., 1951-60; editor, pub. Money Making Opportunities, Studio City, Calif., 1960—; instr. N.Y. State adult edn. program, 1958-59. Author: Insider's Mail Order, 1963. Ens. U.S. Maritime Svc., 1944-46. Mem. Braemar Country Club, Warner Ctr. Club. Office: Success Pub Internat 11071 Ventura Blvd Studio City CA 91604-3548

PERRY, DOUGLAS, opera singer. B.M., Wittenberg U.; M.A., Ball State U. Made debut as Don Basilio in Marriage of Figaro, with N.Y.C. Opera; appeared as King Kaspar in: Amahl and the Night Visitors; appeared as Timothy in: Help! Help! The Globolinks; appeared as Guillot in: Manon; Dancing Master and Brighella in: Ariadne auf Naxos; Met. Opera debut as scientist/first mate in: The Voyage (Philip Glass); European debut with Netherlands Opera as Mahatma Gandhi in Satyagraha (Philip Glass); appeared as analyst in A Quiet Place (Bernstein), La Scala and Vienna Stadtsoper; featured soloist on tours and recs. with Gregg Smith Singers and Camerata Singers; performed with Sante Fe Opera, also performed with Ft. Worth Opera, Chatauqua Opera, N.Y.C. Opera, Opera Co. of Boston, Houston Grand Opera, Balt. Opera., Miami Opera, Chgo. Lyric Opera, Seattle Opera, San Francisco Opera, Opera Co. Phila.; recs. include Satyagraha, Songs from Liquid Days, A Quiet Place, Mother of Us All. Address: 170 W End Ave New York NY 10023-5401 Office: Trawick Artists Mgmt Inc 1926 Broadway New York NY 10023-6915

PERRY, E. ELIZABETH, social worker, real estate manager; b. Balt., Oct. 2, 1954; d. James Glenn and Pearl Elizabeth (Christopher) P.; 1 child, Linden Andrew. AA, C.C. of Balt., 1973; B in Art, Psychology, Social Work, U. Md., Balt., 1975, MSW, 1978. Asst. grant coord. Md. Conf. Social Concern, Balt., 1975; dir. social svcs. West Balt. Cmty. Health Care Corp., 1978-80; tng. counselor NutriSystem Inc. of Md., Balt., 1983-86; counselor/psychotherapist Switlik Elem. Sch., Marathon, Fla., 1988-89; program dir. emergency shelter Children's Home Soc., Miami, 1990-91; health educator, spokesperson Rape Treatment Ctr., Miami, 1991-94; CEO, pres. bd. Child Assault Prevention Project, Miami, 1993—; self-employed in real estate rehab. and mgmt., 1980—; pub. spkr. on women's and children's issues/sexual assault issues, 1990—. Bd. dirs. Partnership Way, 1993-95, ACHIEVE, 1995—; pub. citizen Dem. Nat. Com. Mem. AAUW, NOW (bd. dirs. Dade County 1994-95), Nat. Abortion Rights Action League, Amnesty Internat., People for the Am. Way, Psi Chi, Phi Theta Kappa. Democrat. Avocations: hiking, skating, dogs, sewing, knitting. Home: 5161 Alton Rd Miami Beach FL 33140 Office: Child Assault Prev Project Omni Mall Ste 1195 1601 Biscayne Blvd Miami FL 33132

PERRY, EDNA BURRELL, retired elementary school principal; b. Washington, July 30, 1934; d. Harold Flowers and Annie Mae (Harrison) Burrell; m. Sidney Lee Perry, Jr., June 5, 1954; children: Angela, Andrea R. BME magna cum laude, Howard U., Washington, 1956; MA in Adminstrn./Supervision, Roosevelt U., Chgo., 1972. Cert. prin., nat. cert. counselor. Tchr. Healy Sch., Chgo., 1959-62; from asst. prin. to prin., counselor C.H. Wacker Sch., Chgo., 1962-94; ret.; team dir. Diamite Corp., Milpitas, Calif., 1986—. Vol. Am. Cancer Soc., Chgo., 1960-80; minister of music Ch. of the Good Shepherd, Chgo., 1959—, condr. choir, 1959—. Named Lay Person of the Yr., Ch. of Good Shepherd, 1980, Woman of the Yr., 1992, Music award, 1994. Mem. Nat. Assn. Negro Musicians, Nat. Pharm. Assn. Aux. (nat. pres. 1977-79, 90-93), Delta Sigma Theta. United Ch. of Christ. Avocations: nutritional counseling. Home: 9201 S Cregier Ave Chicago IL 60617-3602

PERRY, EDWIN CHARLES, lawyer; b. Lincoln, Nebr., Sept. 29, 1931; s. Arthur Edwin and Charlotte C. (Peterson) P.; m. Joan Mary Hanson, June 5, 1954; children: Mary Mills, Judy Phipps, James Perry, Greg Perry, Jack Perry, Pricilla Perry. BS, U. Nebr., 1953, JD, 1955. Bar: Nebr. 1955; U.S. Dist. Ct. Nebr., 1955; U.S. Ct. Appeals Nebr., 1968. Prin. Perry, Guthery, Haase & Gessford, P.C., Lincoln, 1957—. Chmn. Lincoln Lancaster County Planning Com., Madonna Rehab. Hosp. Fellow Am. Bar Found., Nebr. Bar Found.; mem. Nebr. State Bar Assn. (chair ho. dels. 1987-88, pres. 1991-92), Nebr. Coun. Sch. Attys. (pres. 1978-79), Lincoln Bar Assn. (pres. 1982-83). Republican. Roman Catholic. Office: Perry Guthery Haase & Gessford PC 1400 Firstier Brk Bldg Lincoln NE 68508

PERRY, ESTON LEE, real estate and equipment leasing company executive; b. Wartburg, Tenn., June 16, 1936; s. Eston Lee and Willimae (Heidle) P.; m. Alice Anne Schmidt, Oct. 21, 1961; children: Julie Anne, Jeffrey John, Jennifer Lee. B.S., Ind. State U., 1961. With Oakley Corp., 1961—, dir., 1965—, v.p., 1981-86, pres., 1986—; corp. officer Ind. State Bank, Terre Haute, 1975-80; pres. One Twenty Four Madison Corp., Terre Haute, 1979—, also bd. dirs., chmn. bd., 1981—. Bd. dirs. Aviation Commn., Terre Haute, pres., 1970; bd. dirs. Salvation Army, Terre Haute, 1975-91, mem. exec. adv. bd., 1979-87; bd. dirs. Vigo County Dept. Pub. Welfare, 1979-82, Jr. Achievement Wabash Valley, 1980-86; bd. dirs. United Way of Wabash Valley, 1984-89, chmn. fund campaign, 1984, bd. dirs. United Way of Ind., 1984-90, v.p., 1986, pres. 1988-89; trustee Oakley Found., 1970—; bd. dirs. Terre Haute Symphony Orch., 1984-87, Ind. State U. Found., 1988—, Goodwill Industries of Terre Haute, 1984—, Leadership Terre Haute, 1984-88, Cen. Eastside Assocs., 1984-88, pres., 1984-85; mem. exec. com. Ind. State U. Found., 1990-94; bd. dirs. City of Terre Haute Hulman Links Commn., pres., 1986-91; mem. President's Assocs., Ind. State U., adv. bd. Ctr. Econ. Devel., 1984—; bd. overseers Sheldon Swope Art Gallery of Terre Haute, 1984-87; nat. mem. Council on Founds.; mem. adv. com. comml. air service study Ind. Dept. Commerce; bd. assocs. Rose Hulman Inst. Tech., 1986—. Served with U.S. Army, 1955-57. Mem. Jaycees Terre Haute (v.p. 1967-69), C. of C. Terre Haute (bd. dirs. 1984-93, vice chmn. 1986-88, chmn. 1990), Wabash Valley Pilots Assn., Aircraft Owners and Pilots Assn., Air Safety Found., Aviation Trades Assn., Lambda Chi Alpha. Clubs: Country of Terre Haute (bd. dirs.), Aero of Terre Haute; Sycamore Varsity (Ind. State U.). Lodges: Lions (pres. Terre Haute 1983-84), Elks. Home: 25 Bogart Dr Terre Haute IN 47803-2401 Office: 8 S 16th St Terre Haute IN 47807-4102

PERRY, EVELYN REIS, communications company executive; b. N.Y.C., Mar. 9; d. Lou L. and Bertl (Wolf) Reis; m. Charles G. Perry III, Jan. 7, 1968; children: Charles G. IV, David Reis. BA, Univ. Wis., 1963; student Am. Acad. Dramatic Arts, 1958-59, Univ. N.Mex., 1963-64. Lic. real estate broker, N.C. Vol. ETV project Peace Corps, 1963-65; program officer-radio/tv Peace Corps, Washington, 1965-68; dir. Vols. in Svc. to Am. (VISTA), Raleigh, N.C., 1977-80; exec. dir. CETA Program for Displaced Homemakers, Raleigh, 1980-81; cons. exec. dir. to Recycle Raleigh for Food and Fuel, Theater in the Park, 1981-83, Artspace, Inc., Raleigh, 1983-84; pres., chief exec. officer Carolina Sound Communications, MUZAK, Charleston, S.C. and 12 counties in S.C., 1984—; pub. rels. account exec. various cos., Washington, Syracuse, N.Y., 1969-71; cons. pub. rels. and orgn. Olympic Organizing Com., Mexico City, 1968; cons. pub. rels., fundraising, arts mgmt. pub. speaking, Ill., Pa., N.C., 1971-77; organizational and pub. speaking cons. Perry & Assocs., Raleigh, 1980—. Mem. adv. bd. Gov.'s Office Citizen Affairs, Raleigh, 1981-85; mem. Involvement Coun. of Wake County, N.C., Raleigh, 1981-84; mem. Adv. Coun. to Vols. in Svc. to Am., Raleigh, 1980-84; mem. Pres.'s adv. bd. Peace Corps, Washington, 1980-82; v.p., bd. dirs. Voluntary Action Ctr., Raleigh, 1980-84, bd. dirs., Charleston, 1988-94; sec. bd. dirs. Temple Kahil Kadosh Beth Elohim, 1987-89, sec. fin., 1989-90, v.p. programming, 1990-93, v.p. adminstrn. 1993-95; bd. dirs. Chopstik Theater, Charleston, 1989-90; del., chmn. S.C. Delegation to White House Conf. Small Bus., 1995. Mem. N.C. Coun. of Women's Orgns. (pres., v.p. 1982-84), Charleston Hotel and Motel Assn., N.C. Assn. Vol. Adminstrs. (bd. dirs. 1980-84), S.C. Restaurant Assn., Nat. Assn. Women Bus. Owners, Internat. Planned Music Assn. (bd. dirs. 1986—, newsletter editor), NAFE, Nat. Fedn. Ind. Businesses (mem. adv. bd. 1987—, chmn. guardian adv. coun. 1994—), Internat. Platform Assn., Theaterworks (bd. dirs. 1994—), Charleston C. of C. Office: Carolina Sound Comm Inc 1941 Savage Rd Ste 200G Charleston SC 29407

PERRY, FLOYDE E., JR., bishop. Bishop of So. Ohio Ch. of God in Christ, Shaker Heights. Office: Ch of God in Christ PO Box 320 Memphis TN 38101-0320

PERRY, FRANK, motion picture executive, director, producer, writer; b. N.Y.C., 1930; m. Eleanor Perry (div. 1970); m. Barbara Goldsmith, 1976. Apprentice Westport (Conn.) Country Playhouse; theatre stage mgr., prodn. mgr., mng. dir.; dir.-observer Theatre Guild, 1955, also producer;

now pres., chief exec. officer Corsair Pictures; lectr. on film Harvard U., Yale U.; adj. prof. film studies NYU Grad. Film Sch.; adj. prof. film. Columbia U. Dir., producer: (films) David and Lisa, 1963, Ladybug, Ladybug, 1964, The Swimmer, 1968, Last Summer, 1969, Diary of a Mad Housewife, 1970, Doc, 1971, Play It as It Lays, 1972, Rancho Deluxe, 1975, Compromising Positions, 1985, Hello Again, 1986; dir.: (films) Man on a Swing, 1972, Mommie Dearest, 1981, Monsignor, 1983; producer film Miss Firecracker, 1989; producer/dir.: (TV spls.) The Capote Trilogy, including A Christmas Memory, starring Geraldine Page, ABC Premiere Episode TV series Skag, CBS drama Dummy, (screenplays) Mommie Dearest, A Shock to the System; dir. Broadway prodn. Ladies At The Alamo, 1978; dir. J.F.K.: A One-Man Show, 1983; co-author (with Truman Capote) Trilogy, An Experiment in Multimedia. Mem., bd. dirs. Lincoln Ctr. Theatre; trustee, mem. exec. com. Actors Studio, Guild Hall; founding chmn. Guild Hall Acad. Arts; v.p., sec. Goldsmith-Perry Philanthropies, Inc. With U.S. Army, 1952-54. Recipient 3 Peabody awards, and numerous internat. film and directorial awards. Mem. Acad. Motion Picture Arts and Scis.

PERRY, FREDERICK SAYWARD, JR., electronics company executive; b. Kittery Point, Maine, Aug. 14, 1940; s. Frederick Sayward Sr. and Rita Alice (Contant) P.; m. Judith Ann Golden, June 21, 1963 (div. 1973); 1 child, Elizabeth; m. Sarah Winthrop Smith, Aug. 26, 1979; children: Mariah, Justus. BA in Math., Harvard U., 1963. Applications engr. Block Engring. Inc., Cambridge, Mass., 1963-67, 69-71; sci. officer Arms Control and Disarmament Agy., Washington, 1967-69; sales mgr. Infrared Industries Inc., Waltham, Mass., 1971-75; mktg. rep. Honeywell Radiation Ctr., Lexington, Mass., 1975-77; pres. Boston Electronics Corp., Brookline, Mass., 1977—. Contbr. article to Laser Focus mag. Mem. Alexandria (Va.) Dem. Com., 1969-70, Brookline Town Meeting, 1988, mem. fin. com., 1993-95, conservation commr., 1995—; bd. dirs. Brookline Green Space Alliance, 1987—, v.p., 1995—. Mem. Optical Soc. Am., Laser Inst. Am., Internat. Soc. Optical Engring. Home: 32 Bowker St Brookline MA 02146-6955 Office: Boston Electronics Corp 72 Kent St Brookline MA 02146-7347

PERRY, GAYLORD JACKSON, former professional baseball player; b. Williamston, N.C., Sept. 15, 1938. Student, Campbell Coll. Began profl. career with St. Cloud team, No. League; pitcher San Francisco Giants, 1962-71, Cleve. Indians, 1972-75, Tex. Rangers, 1975-77, 80, San Diego Padres, 1978-79, N.Y. Yankees, 1980, Atlanta Braves, 1981, Seattle Mariners, 1982-83, Kansas City Royals, 1983. Co-author: Me and the Spitter: An Autobiographical Confession, 1974. Recipient Cy Young Mem. award Am. League, 1972, Cy Young award Nat. League, 1978; mem. Nat. League All-Star team, 1966, 70, 79, Am. League All-Star team, 1972, 74; inducted into Baseball Hall of Fame, Cooperstown, N.Y., 1991. Address: PO Box 1958 Kill Devil Hills NC 27948-1958

PERRY, GEORGE, neuroscience researcher; b. Lompoc, Calif., Apr. 12, 1953; s. George Richard and Mary Arlene (George) P.; m. Paloma Aguilar, May 21, 1983; children: Anne A., Elizabeth A. BA, U. Calif., Santa Barbara, 1974; PhD, U. Calif., Scripps Inst. of Oceanography, San Diego, 1979. Postdoctoral fellow Baylor Coll. Medicine, Houston, 1979-82; from asst. prof. to prof. pathology, neurosci. Case Western Res. U., Cleve., 1982—, chmn. med. sch. faculty coun., chmn. faculty senate, 1996—; chmn. study sect. NIH, Bethesda, Md., 1988-93. Editor: Alterations in the Neuronal Cytoskeleton in Alzheimer Disease, Clin. Neurosci.; assoc. editor Am. Jour. Pathology, 1994—; mem. 1992—; mem. editl. bd. Am. Jour. Pathology, 1992—, African Jour. Neuroscis., Alzheimer Assoc. Disorder, Alzehimer's Disease Review; contbr. papers to profl. publs. Fellow Muscular Dystrophy Assn., 1980; recipient Career Devel. award NIH, 1988; grantee NIH, 1988—. Mem. AAAS, Microcsopy Soc. N.E. Ohio (treas. 1986-88, trustee 1988-90, pres. 1990-91), Am. Soc. Cell Biology, Soc. Neurosci., Am. Assn. Investigative Pathologists, Am. Assn. Neuropathologists (awards com. 1992-96, coun. 1995—). Democrat. Roman Catholic. Home: 2500 Eaton Rd University Ht OH 44118-4339 Office: Case Western Res U 2085 Adelbert Rd Cleveland OH 44106-2622

PERRY, GEORGE LEWIS, research economist, consultant; b. N.Y.C., Jan. 23, 1934; s. Lewis G. and Helen L. (Couloumbis) P.; m. Jean Marion West, 1956; children: Elizabeth, Lewis G., George A.; m. 2d, Dina Needleman, 1987. BS, MIT, 1954, PhD, 1961. Editor Brookings Papers on Econ. Activity, 1970—; columnist L.A. Times, 1981-93; bd. dirs. State Farm Mut. Automobile Ins. Co., Bloomington, Ill., Dreyfus Mut. Funds, N.Y.C., Fed. Realty, Bethesda, Md.; co-dir. Brookings Panel Econ. Activity. Author: Unemployment, Money Wage Rates and Inflation, 1966; editor: Curing Chronic Inflation, 1978; contbr. articles to profl. jours. Mem. Am. Econs. Assn. Office: Brookings Instn 1775 Massachusetts Ave NW Washington DC 20036-2188

PERRY, GEORGE WILLIAMSON, lawyer; b. Cleve., Dec. 4, 1926; s. George William and Melda Patricia (Arther-Holt) P. B.A. in Econs., Yale U., 1949; J.D., U. Va., 1953. Bar: Ohio 1953, D.C. 1958, U.S. Supreme Ct. 1958, U.S. Ct. Appeals (D.C. cir.) 1959. Atty. U.S. Dept. Justice, Washington, 1954-56; assoc. Roberts and McInnis, Washington, 1957-59; atty. assoc. counsel Com. on Interstate Fgn. Commerce, U.S. Ho. of Reps., Washington, 1960-65; atty., advisor ICC, Washington, 1965-68; assoc. dir. devel. Yale U., New Haven, 1968-70; dir. tax research Pan Am. World Airways, N.Y.C., 1973-75; hearing officer Indsl. Commn. Ohio, Cleve., 1978-81; sole practice, Cleve., 1981—. Served with U.S. Army, 1945-46. Mem. Soc. of Cincinnati in State of Conn., Yale Alumni Assn. (Cleve.), Concord Coalition, Phi Delta Phi. Episcopalian.

PERRY, GEORGE WILSON, oil and gas company executive; b. Pampa, Tex., July 18, 1929; s. Frank M. and Ruth (Ingersoll) P.; m. Patricia Carberry Bowen; children: Sally, Jett Perry Pemrick, Susan Jeanne Perry Bynder, Virginia Anne Perry Haynie, Tobe Jackson Perry. BS in Petroleum Engring., U. Tulsa, 1952. Registered profl. engr., Tex. Engr. Stanolind Oil & Gas Co., Oklahoma City, 1952-53, Parker Drilling Co., Tulsa, 1953-54; drilling engr. Holm Drilling Co., Tulsa, 1954-55; drilling mgr. Mobil Oil, Victoria, Tex., Lake Charles, La., Paris, France, Anaco, Venezuela, N.Y.C., Tehran, Iran, Stavanger, Norway, New Orleans, La., 1955-79; exec. v.p. Loffland Bros. Co., Tulsa, 1979-89; pres., CEO Gas Well Properties, Inc., Dallas, 1989—; pres. George Perry Farms, Tunica, Miss., 1989—. Mem. Delta Tau Delta. Office: Gas Well Properties Inc PO Box 795302 5995 Summerside Dr Dallas TX 75379-5302

PERRY, HAROLD OTTO, dermatologist; b. Rochester, Minn., Nov. 18, 1921; s. Oliver and Hedwig Clara (Tornow) P.; m. Loraine Thelma Moehnke, Aug. 27, 1944; children—Preston, Oliver, Ann, John. AA, Rochester Jr. Coll., 1942; BS, U. Minn., 1944, MB, 1946, MD, 1947; MS, Mayo Grad. Sch. Medicine, 1953. Diplomate Am. Bd. Dermatology with spl. competence in dermatopathology (mem. bd. 1979-90, v.p. 1989, pres. 1990). Intern Naval Hosp., Oakland, Calif., 1946-47; resident in dermatology Mayo Grad. Sch. Medicine, 1949-52; practice medicine specializing in dermatology Rochester, 1953-86; mem. staff Mayo Clinic, 1953-86, mem. emeritus staff, 1987—; instr., asst. prof., assoc. prof. Mayo Med. Sch., 1953-86, prof., 1978-83, Robert H. Kieckhefer prof. dermatology, 1978-83, head dept. dermatology, 1975-83, emeritus prof. dermatology, 1987—; civilian cons. dermatology to surgeon gen. USAF, 1979—. Contbr. articles to med. jours. and, chpts. to books. With USNR, 1943-45, 46-49. Mem. AMA, Am. Acad. Dermatology (pres. 1981, Sulzberger internat. lectr. 1986), Am. Dermatol. Assn. (bd. dirs. 1985-89, pres. 1989-90), Noah Worcester Dermatol. Soc. (pres. 1969), Minn. Dermatol. Soc. (pres. 1967), Chgo. Dermatol. Soc., Internat. Soc. Tropical Dermatology, Minn. Med. Assn.; hon. mem. French Dermatol. Soc., Spanish Acad. Dermatology, Brazilian Dermatol. Soc., Ga. Dermatol. Soc., Iowa Dermatol. Soc., Korean Dermatol. Soc., Bolivar Soc. Dermatology, Jacksonville Dermatol. Soc., N.Am. Clin. Dermatol. Soc. Home: 3625 SW Bamber Valley Rd Rochester MN 55902 Office: Mayo Clinic Dermatology Dept Rochester MN 55905

PERRY, I. CHET, petroleum company executive; b. Phila., Jan. 18, 1943; s. Irving Chester Sr. and Erma Jackson (McNeil) P.; 1 child, London Schade. BA in Psychology, Bus., Lake Forest Coll., 1965. Lic. real estate broker, Ill. Sr. mgmt. trainee British Overseas Airways Corp., London, Eng., 1968-69; owner Itec Internat. Ltd., Barrington, Ill., 1970—; owner Itec Refining & Mktg. Co., Ltd., Barrington, 1970—, CEO, mng. dir., 1986—. Lt. U.S. Army, 1965-68, Vietnam. Decorated Bronze Star, Purple Heart. Mem. Am. Petroleum Inst., Barrington Bd. Realtors (bd. dirs. 1974-78) Forest Grove Club, Barrington Tennis Club. Republican. Quaker. Avocations: tennis, photography. Home: 444 W Russell St Barrington IL 60010-4123

PERRY, J. WARREN, health sciences educator, administrator; b. Richmond, Ind., Oct. 25, 1921; s. Charles Thomas and Zona M. (Ohler) P. BA, DePauw U., 1944; postgrad., Harvard U., 1948-49; MA, Northwestern U., 1952, PhD, 1955; DSc (hon.), D'Youville Coll., 1990. Instr. St. John's Mil. Acad., Delafield, Wis., 1944-47; counselor, asst. prof. psychology U. Ill.-Chgo., 1953-56; dir. prosthetic-orthotic edn., asst. prof. orthopaedic surgery Northwestern U. Med. Sch., 1957-61; lectr. psychology U. Chgo., 1957-61; asst. chief div. tng. Vocat. Rehab. Adminstrn., HEW, 1961-64, dep. asst. commr. research and tng., 1964-66; prof. health scis. adminstrn. SUNY-Buffalo, 1966-85, founding dean Sch. Health Related Professions, 1966-77, dean and prof. emeritus, 1985—; Mary E. Switzer Meml. lectr. Dallas, 1977, Lexington, 1991; mem. task force for Legislation for Allied Health Professions, 1966-67; com. edn. allied health professions and svcs., coun. med. edn. AMA, 1968-73; nat. adv. com. Am. Dietetic Assn., 1970-75, chmn., 1972-75; nat. rev. com., regional med. programs HEW, 1969-72; mem. Inst. Medicine, NAS, 1973—, steering com. on manppower policy for primary care, bd. health promotion and disease prevention, 1981-83, sr. advisor, com. to study the role allied health, com. to study med. manpower in VA, 1988-91; spl. med. adv. com. VA, 1974-77; task force on manpower for prevention Fogarty Internat. Inst., NIH, 1975-76; acad. planning com. Mass. Gen. Hosp. Founding editor: Jour. Allied Health, 1972-78, editor emeritus, 1985—; contbr. articles to profl. jours. Bd. dirs., dir. com. opera edn. Lyric Opera Guild, Chgo., 1957-61; chmn. acad. divsn. dr., coun. trustees Buffalo Philharm. Orch., 1987-93; bd. dirs. Goodwill Industries Buffalo, 1969-76; trustee Cmty. Music Sch. Buffalo, 1977-80; adv. bd., v.p. Sisters of Charity Hosp., Buffalo, 1969-87, pres., 1986-88; bd. visitors U. Pitts., 1977-80; coun. trustees D'Youville Coll., Buffalo, 1978-88, trustee emeritus, 1989-95; bd. dirs. Am. Lung Assn. Western N.Y., 1975-92, pres., 1983; bd. dirs. ARC, Buffalo, Artpark State Performing Arts Ctr., Lewiston, N.Y., 1986—; Am. Lung Assn. N.Y. State, 1981-85, exec. com., 1989-92; chmn. N.Y. State Coalition Smoking or Health, Albany, N.Y., 1987-91; trustee Theodore Roosevelt Inaugural Site Found., 1987, pres., 1991-94; bd. advisors Buffalo Coun. on World Affairs, 1987-88; trustee Buffalo Opera Co., 1989-94, chmn. opera adv. coun., 1995—. Recipient Sustained Superior Svc. award HEW, 1965, Disting. Svc. award Am. Orthotics-Prosthetics Assn., 1966, Buffalo Opera Co., 1995, Chancellors award for adminstrv. svc. SUNY, 1977, 1st Allied Health Leadership award, 1988, Disting. Author award Jour. Allied Health, 1978, Cert. of Merit, AMA, 1979, Pres. Cir. PIN, Buffalo State Coll., 1993, 50th Anniversary Alumni citation De Pauw U., 1994, Outstanding Svc. award Theodore Roosevelt Inaugural Site Found., 1994, Brotherhood/Sisterhood award in health NCCJ Western N.Y., 1995, Christmas Seal Hall of Fame award ALA N.Y. State, 1995, Disting. Citizenship award Mayor of Buffalo, 1995; named Outstanding Individual Philanthropist, Nat. Soc. Fundraising Execs. Western N.Y., 1992, Ky. Col., 1969, Nebr. admn., 1964; J. Warren Perry Disting. Author award named in his honor Jour. Allied Health, 1984—, J. Warren Perry Meml. lectr. named in his honor SUNY, 1990—, J. Warren Perry Outstanding Vol. Leadership award named in his honor Western N.Y. chpt. ALA, 1994—; Perry Scholarships presented in his honor U. Buffalo Found., 1991—. Fellow Assn. Schs. of Allied Health Professions (pres. 1969-70, cert. of merit 1977, Pres.'s award 1978, Honors of Society 1984); mem. APA, Am. Dietetics Assn. (hon.), Am. Personnel and Guidance Assn., Nat. Rehab. Assn., Phi Beta Kappa, Phi Delta Kappa (pres. 1955), Delta Tau Delta. Home: 83 Bryant St Buffalo NY 14209-1836

PERRY, JACQUELIN, orthopedic surgeon; b. Denver, May 31, 1918; d. John F. and Tirzah (Kuruptkat) P. B.E., U. Calif., Los Angeles, 1940; M.D., U. Calif., San Francisco, 1950. Intern Children's Hosp., San Francisco, 1950-57; resident in orthopedic surgery U. Calif., San Francisco, 1951-55; orthopedic surgeon Rancho Los Amigos Hosp., Downey, Calif., 1955—; chief pathokinesiology Rancho Los Amigos Med. Ctr., 1961—; chief stroke service Rancho Los Amigos Hosp., 1972-75; mem. faculty U. Calif. Med. Sch., San Francisco, 1966—; clin. prof. U. Calif. Med. Sch., 1973—; mem. faculty U. So. Calif. Med. Sch., 1969—, prof. orthopedic surgery, 1972—, dir. polio and gait clinic, 1972—; Disting. lectr. for hosp. for spl. surgery and Cornell U. Med. Coll., N.Y.C., 1977-78; Packard Meml. lectr. U. Colo. Med. Sch., 1970; Osgood lectr. Harvard Med. Sch., 1978; Summer lectr., Portland, 1977; Shands lectr.; cons. USAF; guest speaker sympsoia; cons. Biomechanics Lab. Centinela Hosp., 1979—. Served as phys. therapist U.S. Army, 1941-46. Recipient Disting. Svc. award Calif. Assn. Rehab. Facilities,1981, Pres.'s award, 1984, Milton Cohen award Nat. Assn. Rehab., 1993, Isabelle and Lenard Goldensen award for tech. United Cerebral Palsy Assn., 1981, Jow Dowling award, 1985, Profl. Achievement award UCLA, 1988, Armistad award Rancho Los Amigos Med. Ctr., Calif., 1990; named Woman of Yr. for Medicine in So. Calif., L.A. Times, 1959, Alumnus of Yr., U. Calif. Med. Sch., 1980, Physician of Yr. Calif. Employment Devel. Dept., 1994. Mem. AMA, Am. Acad. Orthop. Surgeons (Kappa Delta award for rsch. 1977), Am. Orthop. Assn. (Shands lectr. 1988), Western Orthop. Assn., Calif. Med. Soc., L.A. County Med. Soc., Am. Phys. Therapy Assn. (hon. Golden Pen award 1965), Am. Acad. Orthotists and Prosthetists (hon.), Scoliosis Rsch. Soc., LeRoy Abbott Soc., Am. Acad. Cerebral Palsy. Home: 12319 Brock Ave Downey CA 90242-3503 Office: Rancho Los Amigos Med Ctr 7601 Imperial Hwy Downey CA 90242-3456

PERRY, JAMES ALFRED, environmental scientist, consultant, educator, administrator; b. Dallas, Sept. 27, 1945. BA in Fisheries, Colo. State U., 1968; MA, Western State Coll., 1973; PhD, Idaho State U., 1981. Sr. water quality specialist Idaho Div. Environ., Pocatello, 1974-82; area mgr. Centrac Assocs., Salt Lake City, 1982; prof. forest water quality U. Minn., St. Paul, 1982—, dir. natural resources policy and mgmt., 1985—, dir. grad. studies in water resources, 1988-92; dep. dir. AID-funded Environ. Tng. Project for Ctrl. and Ea. Europe, 1992-96; spl. asst. to dean grad. sch. U. Minn., St. Paul, 1996—; vis. scholar Oxford U., Green College, Eng., 1990-91; internat. cons. in water quality. Charter mem. Leadership Devel. Acad., Lakewood, Minn., 1988. ACOP/ESCOP nat. leadership fellow, 1995—. Mem. Minn. Acad. Scis. (bd. dirs. 1987-90), Am. Water Resources Assn., Internat. Water Resources Assn., Internat. Soc. Theoretica and Applied Limnology, N.Am. Benthol Soc. (exec. bd. Albuquerque 190-91), Sigma Xi, Xi Sigma Pi, Gamma Sigma Delta. Office: U Minn Dept Forest Resource 115 Green Hall 1530 Cleveland Ave N Saint Paul MN 55108-1027

PERRY, JAMES FREDERIC, philosophy educator, author; b. Washington, Jan. 21, 1936; s. Albert Walter and Helene Anna Maria (Neumeyer) P.; m. Sandra Jean Huizing, Feb. 18, 1957 (div. May 1972); children: Sandra Elaine, James Frederic Jr., Bartholomew; m. Roberta Schofield, June 6, 1984. Student, Princeton U., 1953-56, Marietta (Ohio) Coll., 1958-60; BA with honors in Philosophy, Ind. U., 1962, PhD in Philosophy of Edn., 1972. NDEA fellow in philosophy U. N.C., 1962-65; instr. N.C. State U., Raleigh, 1965-66; Univ. fellow Ind. U., 1971; adj. lectr. Ind. U., Bloomington, 1972-75; prof. philosophy Hillsborough Community Coll., Tampa, Fla., 1975—. Author: Random, Routine, Reflective, 1989; contbr. articles to profl. jours. Precinct committeeman Dem. Party, Tampa, 1988—. Nat. Def. Edn. Act fellow U. N.C., 1962-65, Univ. fellow Ind. U., 1970-71. Mem. AAUP (pres. Fla. conf. 1986-89, chair com. "A" on acad. freedom 1989—), C.C. Humanities Assn. (so. divsn. exec. bd. 1981-89), Internat. Soc. Philos. Enquiry, Internat. Congress for Critical Thinking and Moral Critiques (founding mem. S.E. coun. 1991), Soc. for Values in Higher Edn., Princeton Alumni Assn. of Fla. Suncoast (sec. 1983-86, pres. 1986-95), Mensa, Authors Guild, Textbook and Acad. Authors Assn. Avocations: travel, foreign travel, genealogy, commercial piloting, flight instruction. Office: Hillsborough C C PO Box 10561 Tampa FL 33679-0561

PERRY, JAMES R., construction company executive; b. Mar. 23, 1936. BSCE, Case Inst. Tech., 1958; AMP, U. Hawaii, 1979; Cert., Japan-Am. Inst. Mgmt. Sci., 1983. With Great Lakes Dredge & Dock & Co., Ohio, 1958-67; various positions to exec. v.p. Hawaiian Dredging Constrn. Co., Honolulu, 1967-89; pres. Dillingham Constrn. Pacific Ltd., Honolulu, 1989-93; pres., COO Dillingham Constrn. Corp., Pleasanton, Calif., 1993—; pres., CEO Dillingham Constrn. Pacific, Ltd., 1990-93, Dillingham Constrn. Pacific Basin Ltd., 1990-93, Dillingham Constrn. Hong Kong Ltd., 1990-93, Hawaiian Dredging Constrn. Co., Honolulu, 1990-93; bd. dirs. Dillingham Constrn. Holdings, Inc. Past dir. Cement and Concrete Products Industry of Hawaii, Hawaii Humane Soc.; past pres. Kailua Youth Activities League; mem. Olomana Cmty. Assn.; constrn.mgr. Damien Meml. H.S.; chmn. trustees Hawaii Carpenters Mkt. Recovery Fund; mem. U. Hawaii Sch. of Arch. Fund; adv. com. for constrn. engring. and mgmt. specialization U. Hawaii Dept. Civil Engring. Mem. Hawaii Constrn. Industry Assn. (dir.), Am. Concrete Inst., Japan-Am. Inst. Mgmt. Sci., Constrn. Specification Inst., Hawaii C. of C., Gen. Contrs. Assn. (past pres., dir.), Gen. Contr.'s Labor Assn. (v.p.), The Beavers. Office: Dillingham Constrn Corp 5960 Inglewood Dr Pleasanton CA 94588-8535*

PERRY, JEAN LOUISE, dean; b. Richland, Wash., May 13, 1950; d. Russell S. and Sue W. Perry. BS, Miami U., Oxford, Ohio, 1972; MS, U. Ill., Urbana, 1973, PhD, 1976. Cons. ednl. placement office U. Ill., 1973-75; adminstrv. intern Coll. Applied Life Studies, 1975-76, asst. dean, 1976-77, assoc. dean, 1978-81, asst. prof. dept. phys. edn., 1976-81; assoc. prof. phys. edn. San Francisco State U., 1981-84, prof., 1984-90, chair, 1981-90; dean Coll. of Human and Community Scis. U. Nev., Reno, 1990—. Named to excellent tchr. list U. Ill., 1973-79. Mem. AAHPERD (fellow research consortium, pres. 1988-89), Am. Assn. Higher Edn., Am. Ednl. Research Assn., Nat. Assn. Phys. Edn. in Higher Edn., Nat. Assn. Girls and Women in Sports (guide coordinator, pres.), Delta Psi Kappa, Phi Delta Kappa. Home: 3713 Ranchview Ct Reno NV 89509-7437 Office: U Nev Coll Human and Cmty Scis/136 Reno NV 89557

PERRY, JEANNE ELYCE, principal; b. Ft. Collins, Colo., Jan. 23, 1953; d. Franklin Clyde and Ruth Caroline (Skoglund) Stewart; m. William Kay Perry, Dec. 28, 1974; children: Belinda Eve, Angela Marie. BA in Elem. Edn., Western State Coll., 1975; MA in Ednl. Leadership, U. No. Colo., 1992. Tchr. elem. sch. Soroco Sch. Dist., Oak Creek, Colo., 1977-86, L.A. Unified Sch. Dist., 1986-88; coord. elem. computer Weld RE-1 Sch. Dist., Gilcrest, Colo., 1988-93; prin. Delta (Colo.) Coun. Sch. Dist., 1993—. Leader Girl Scouts Am., Yampa, Colo., 1984-86, Platteville, Colo., 1988-89; precinct committeewoman Rep. Party, Platteville, 1991-93. Colo. Gov.'s grantee, 1990, 91. Mem. ASCD. Baptist. Avocations: hiking, skiing, gardening, crafts. Office: Cedaredge Mid Sch 360 N Grand Mesa Dr Cedaredge CO 81413-3321

PERRY, JOE, guitarist; b. Boston, Sept. 10, 1950. With Aerosmith, 1970-80, 84—, The Joe Perry Project, 1980-84. Albums: (with Aerosmith) Aerosmith, 1973, Get Your Wings, 1974, Toys in the Attic, 1975, Rocks, 1976, Pure Gold, 1976, Draw the Line, 1977, Live Bootleg, 1978, A Night in the Ruts, 1979, Greatest Hits, 1980, Rock in a Hard Place, 1982, Done with Mirrors, 1986, Classics Live, 1986, Permanent Vacation, 1987, Gems, 1989, Pump, 1989, Pandora's Box, 1991, Get a Grip, 1993, Big Ones, 1994, Box of Fire, 1994; (with Joe Perry Project) I've Got the Rock n' Rolls Again, Let the Music Do the Talking. Recipient (with Aerosmith) Grammy award Best Rock Group, 1994. Office: c/o Aerosmith Geffen/DGC Records 9130 W Sunset Blvd Los Angeles CA 90069-3110

PERRY, JOHN RICHARD, philosophy educator; b. Lincoln, Nebr., Jan. 16, 1943; s. Ralph Robert and Ann (Roscow) P.; m. Louise Elizabeth French, Mar. 31, 1962; children: James Merton, Sarah Louise, Joseph Glenn. BA, Doane Coll., Crete, Nebr., 1964; PhD, Cornell U., Ithaca, N.Y., 1968; DLitt (hon.), Doane Coll., 1982. Asst. prof. philosophy UCLA, 1968-72; vis. asst. prof. U. Mich., Ann Arbor, 1971-72; assoc. prof. UCLA, 1972-74, Stanford (Calif.) U., 1974-77; prof. Stanford U., 1977-85, Henry Waldgrave Stuart prof., 1985—, chmn. dept. philosophy, 1976-82, 90-91, dir. ctr. study lang. and info., 1985-86, 93—, resident fellow Soto House, 1985-91. Author: Dialogue on Identity and Immortality, 1978, (with Jon Barwise) Situations and Attitudes, 1983, The Problem of the Essential Indexical, 1993. Pres. Santa Monica Dem. Club, Calif., 1972-74. Woodrow Wilson fellow, 1964-65, Danforth fellow, 1964-68, Guggenheim fellow, 1975-76, NEH fellow, 1980-81. Mem. Am. Philos. Assn. (v.p. Pacific divsn. 1992-93, pres. 1993-94). Office: Stanford U Ctr Study Language & Information Stanford CA 94305

PERRY, JOHN WESLEY, SR., psychotherapist; b. Elleville, Ga., Mar. 30, 1934; s. West Charles and Mary (Willie) P.; m. Alma Perry, Dec 25, 1956; children: Sheranda Pearl, John Wesley Jr., Sheree Denise. AA, Edward Waters Coll., 1955; BS, Paul Quinn Coll., 1962; MEd, Prairie View U., 1967, 74; EdD, Calif. Coast U., 1989. Cert. clinical therapist, Tex., counselors tng., U. Ark., U.S. Dept. Labor; lic. profl. counselor Tex. State Bd. Profl. Counselors. Tchr. phys. edn., coach Bremond (Tex.) High Sch., 1962-65; counselor coord. Dept. of Labor, San Marcos, Tex., 1965-70; tchr. hist. Austin (Tex.) I.S.D., 1970-71, 71-72; sch. adminstr. Pearce Jr. High Sch., Austin, 1971-87; state parole officer Tex. State Parole Bd., Austin, 1987-88; psychotherapist child behavior Killeen, Tex., 1988—. Trustee bd. pro tempo A.M.E. Ch., Austin; active Boy Scouts, Austin. With U.S. Army, 1955-57. Recipient Stewart certificate Grant Chapel A.M.E. Ch., Austin, 1965, Bus. Mgr. award Nat. Alumni Paul Quinn Coll. Alumni, Waco, Tex., 1978, 79, v.p. award, 1980, Outstanding Civic award United Negro Coll. Fund, 1984; grantee Chapel A.M. E. Ch. Office: Dr J Wesley Perry Therapy Clinic 600 S Gray St Killeen TX 76541-7140

PERRY, KENNETH WALTER, integrated oil company executive; b. Shamrock, Tex., Feb. 24, 1932; s. Charles Bowman and Sunshine Virginia (Grady) P.; m. Mary Dean Sudderth, Aug. 28, 1953; children: Mary Martha Perry Mitchell, Kathryn Virginia. BSME, U. Okla., 1954. Sales engr. Mid-Continent Oil Well Supply Co., 1954-55; with Cosden Oil & Chem. Co., Big Spring, Tex., from 1957, jr. engr., 1957-59, project engr., 1959-60, chem. salesman, 1960-64, chem. products mgr., 1964-65, mktg. mgr., then v.p. mktg., 1965-69, v.p. chems., 1969-72, sr. v.p., 1972-76, pres., from 1976; group v.p. Am. Petrofina, Inc., Dallas, 1976-85, sr. v.p., 1985-86, pres., CEO, 1986-88, vice chmn., bd. dirs., 1989-92; CEO Nimir Petroleum Co. Ltd., Dallas, 1992—; chmn. bd. dirs. United Commerce Bank, Highland Village, Tex., 1989-92, CEO, 1990-91. Mem. bd. govs. Dallas Symphony Orch., 1987-93; bd. dirs. Dallas Coun. World Affairs, 1980; mem. engring. com. U. Okla. Aerospace, Nuclear, 1982; bd. dirs. Colo. Mcpl. Water Dist., 1972; bd. visitors Coll. Engring., U. Okla., 1990—. 1st lt. USASC, 1955-57. Mem. Am. Petroleum Inst. (bd. dirs. 1986-90), Nat. Petroleum Coun., Nat. Petroleum Refiners Assn. (chmn. petrochem. com. 1984-87), Ctr. Strategic and Internat. Studies, 25-Yr. Clubs, Petroleum Industry Club, Petrochem. Industry Club, Northwood Club, Dallas Petroleum Club. Office: Nimir Petroleum Co Ltd 5956 Sherry Ln Ste 801 Dallas TX 75225-8019*

PERRY, KENNETH WILBUR, accounting educator; b. Lawrenceburg, Ky., May 21, 1919; s. Ollie Townsend and Minnie (Monroe) P.; m. Shirley Jane Kimball, Sept. 5, 1942; 1 dau., Constance June (Mrs. Linden Warfel). B.S., Eastern Ky. U., 1942; M.S., Ohio U., 1949; Ph.D., U. Ill., 1953; LL.D., Eastern Ky. U., 1983. C.P.A., Ill. Instr. Berea Coll., 1949-50, U. Ky., summer 1950; teaching asst. U. Ill. at Champaign, 1950-53, asst. prof. accounting, 1953-55, asso. prof., 1955-58, prof., 1958—, Alexander Grant prof., 1975—; vis. prof. Northeastern U., summer 1966, Parsons Coll., 1966-67, Fla. A. and M. U., fall 1971; Carman G. Blough prof. U. Va., fall 1975; dir. Illini Pub. Co. Author: Accounting: An Introduction, 1971, Passing the C.P.A. Examination, 1964, (with N. Bedford and A. Wyatt) Advanced Accounting, 1960; contbg. author: Complete Guide to a Profitable Accounting Practice, 1965, C.P.A. Review Manual, 1971; Editor: The Ill. C.P.A, 1968-70; contbg. editor: Accountants' Cost Handbook, 1960. Served to maj. AUS, 1942-46; col. Res. ret. Named outstanding alumnus Eastern Ky. U., 1969. Mem. Am. Accounting Assn. (v.p. 1963, Outstanding Educator award 1974), Am. Inst. C.P.A.'s, Am. Statis. Assn., Nat. Assn. Accountants (dir. 1969-71), Ill. Soc. C.P.A.s (chair in accountancy), Beta Alpha Psi, Beta Gamma Sigma (Distinguished scholar 1977-78), Omicron Delta Kappa. Methodist. Home: 2314 Fields South Dr Champaign IL 61821-9302 Office: Commerce W U Ill Champaign IL 61820

PERRY, L. TOM, church official, merchant. Mem. Quorum of the Twelve, The Ch. of Jesus Christ of LDS, Salt Lake City; chmn. ZCMI, Salt Lake City. Office: LDS Ch 50 E North Temple Salt Lake City UT 84150-0002

PERRY, LAWRENCE STEVEN, lawyer; b. Chgo., Ill., Oct. 27, 1959; s. Bernard Norman and Shirley Ruth (Solomon) P.; m. Sheila, 1987 (div. 1989); m. Leslie Greenslet Perry, Apr. 21, 1991; 1 child, Graham Hayden Perry. BA in Biochemistry and Molecular Biology, Northwestern U., 1981; JD, IIT Chgo., 1984. Bar: Ill. 1984, U.S. Dist. Ct. (no. dist.) Ill. 1984, U.S. Ct.

Appeals (fed. cir.) 1985, U.S. Patent and Trademark Office 1985, N.Y. 1989, U.S. Dist. Ct. (so. dist.) N.Y. 1989. Legal intern McDermott, Will & Emery, Chgo., 1983-84; assoc. Laff, Whitesel, Conte & Saret, Chgo., 1984-85; assoc. Fitzpatrick, Cella, Harper & Scinto, N.Y.C., 1986-92, ptnr., 1992—; lectr. in field. Contbr. articles to profl. jours. Treas. Greenwich (Conn.) Dem. Town Com., chairperson fundraising, 1993-95, treas., 1994-95; chairperson fundraising Temple Israel, Westport, Conn., 1994-95. Mem. ABA (sect. on reeximination 1992—), AIPLA (com. biotechnology, interferences). Democrat. Jewish. Avocations: motorcycling, rock climbing. Office: Fitzpatrick Cella et al 277 Park Ave New York NY 10172

PERRY, LEE ROWAN, lawyer; b. Chgo., Sept. 23, 1933; s. Watson Bishop and Helen (Rowan) P.; m. Barbara Ashcraft Mitchell, July 2, 1955; children: Christopher, Constance, Geoffrey. B.A., U. Ariz., 1955, LL.B., 1961. Bar: Ariz. 1961. Since practiced in Phoenix; clk. Udall & Udall, Tucson, 1960-61; mem. firm Carson, Messinger, Elliott, Laughlin & Ragan, 1961—. Mem. law rev. staff, U. Ariz., 1959-61. Mem. bd. edn. Paradise Valley Elementary and High Sch. Dists., Phoenix, 1964-68, pres., 1968; treas. troop Boy Scouts Am., 1970-72; mem. Ariz. adv. bd. Girl Scouts U.S.A., 1972-74, mem. nominating bd., 1978-79; bd. dirs. Florence Crittenton Services Ariz., 1967-72, pres., 1970-72; bd. dirs. U. Ariz. Alumni, Phoenix, 1968-72, pres., 1969-70; bd. dirs. Family Service Phoenix, 1974-75; bd. dirs. Travelers Aid Assn. Am., 1985-89; bd. dirs. Vol. Bur. Maricopa County, 1975-81, 83-86, pres., 1984-85; bd. dirs. Ariz. div. Am. Cancer Soc., 1978-80, Florence Crittenton div. Child Welfare League Am., 1976-81; bd. dirs. Crisis Nursery for Prevention of Child Abuse, 1978-81, pres., 1978-80; Ariz. dir. Devereux Found., 1996—. Served to 1st lt. USAF, 1955-58. Mem. State Bar Ariz. (conv. chmn. 1972), Rotary (dir. 1971-77, 95-96, pres. 1975-76, West Leadership award 1989), Ariz. Club (bd. dirs. 1994—), Phoenix Country Club, Phi Delta Phi, Phi Delta Theta (pres. 1954). Republican. Episcopalian. Office: Carson Messinger Elliott Laughlin & Ragan Norwest Bank Tower PO Box 33907 Phoenix AZ 85067-3907

PERRY, LEWIS CURTIS, historian, educator; b. Somerville, Mass., Nov. 21, 1938; s. Albert Quillen and Irene (Lewis) P.; m. Ruth Opler, June 5, 1962 (div. 1970); 1 child, Curtis Allen; m. Elisabeth Israels, Nov. 26, 1970; children: Susanna Irene, David Mordecai. A.B., Oberlin Coll., 1960; M.S., Cornell U., Ithaca, N.Y., 1964; Ph.D., Cornell U., 1967. Asst. prof. history SUNY, Buffalo, 1966-72, assoc. prof., 1972-78; prof. Ind. U. Bloomington, 1978-84; Andrew Jackson prof. history Vanderbilt U., 1984—, dir. Am. Studies, 1992-95; Ampart lectr. U.S. Info. Service, India and Nepal, 1986, France, 1989; vis. prof. U. Leeds, 1988-89; vis. Raoul Wallenberg fellow Rutgers U., 1991-92. Author: Radical Abolitionism, 1973, reissue, 1995, Childhood, Marriage, and Reform, 1980, Intellectual Life in America, 1984, Boats Against the Current, 1993; co-author: Patterns of Anarchy, 1966, Antislavery Reconsidered, 1979; editor: Jour. Am. History, 1978-84, Twayne's American Thought and Culture Series, 1985—. Pres. Unitarian-Universalist Ch., Bloomington, 1983-84. N.Y. State Regents fellow, 1965-66, Am. Coun. Learned Socs. fellow, 1972-73, Nat. Humanities Inst. fellow, 1975-76, John Simon Guggenheim Found. fellow, 1991, NEH fellow, 1987-88. Mem. Orgn. Am. Historians (editor 1978-84, exec. bd. 1996-99), Am. Hist. Assn., Am. Studies Assn., Soc. Historians Early Am. Republic. Home: 1917 Capers Ave Nashville TN 37212 Office: Vanderbilt U PO Box 95B Nashville TN 37235-0095

PERRY, LOIS WANDA, safety consultant; b. Seattle, Dec. 29, 1937; d. William and Ethel Lenora (Benson) Abrahamson; m. S. Peter Perry, Jan. 12, 1991; stepchildren: Christopher, Tony. BA, Pacific Luth. U., 1962; postgrad., Gonzaga U., 1984. Cert. vocat. rehabilitaton counselor. Claims rep. Social Security Adminstrn., Calif. and Oreg., 1962-69; field rep. Oreg. Dept. of Labor and Industries, Salem, Oreg., 1969-72; safety cons. and trainer, regional safety coord. Wash. Dept. of Labor and Industries, Spokane, 1987—. Guardian Ad Litem Spokane County Juvenile Ct., 1989—. Mem. AAUW (membership v.p. Valley br. 1992-94, program v.p., co-chair 1994—, com. chair Downtown br. 1989-90, bd. dirs. 1989-90), ASTD (bd. dirs. Spokane-Inland N.W. chpt. 1992), Spokane Tng. Consortium. Democrat. Lutheran. Avocations: gardening, traveling, textile design. Home: 914 S Mckinzie Rd Liberty Lake WA 99019-9752 Office: Wash State Dept Labor & Industries 901 N Monroe St Ste 100 Spokane WA 99201-2148

PERRY, LOUIS BARNES, retired insurance company executive; b. Los Angeles, Mar. 4, 1918; s. Louis Henry and Julia (Stoddard) P.; m. Genevieve Patterson, Feb. 8, 1942; children: Robert Barnes, Barbara Ann, Donna Lou. B.A., UCLA, 1938, M.A., 1940, Ph.D., 1950; fellow in econs., Yale U., 1941; LL.D., Pacific U., 1964; L.H.D., Whitman Coll., 1967, Linfield Coll., 1981; D.C.S., Willamette U., 1977. Teaching asst. UCLA, 1940-41, research teaching asst., 1946-47; faculty Pomona Coll., 1947-59, asst. to pres., 1955-57, prof. econs., 1957-59; pres. Whitman Coll., Walla Walla, Wash., 1959-67; v.p., treas. Standard Ins. Co., Portland, Oreg., 1967-68; exec. v.p. Standard Ins. Co., 1968-71, pres., 1972-83, chmn., 1983-85, also bd. dirs.; investment counselor, broker Wagenseller & Durst, L.A., 1951-59; rsch. coord. So. Calif. Rsch. Coun., 1952-54; cons. Carnegie Survey Bus. Edn., 1957-58. Author: (with others) Our Needy Aged, 1954, A History of the Los Angeles Labor Movement, 1963; Contbr. (with others) articles to profl. jours. Mem. Oreg. Bd. Higher Edn., 1975-87, pres., 1975-80. Served to maj. AUS, World War II; lt. col. Res. Mem. Am. Coll. Life Underwriters (trustee 1972-81), Rotary, Phi Beta Kappa, Beta Gamma Sigma, Phi Delta Kappa, Pi Gamma Mu, Alpha Gamma Omega, Artus. Methodist. Home: 1585 Gray Lynn Dr Walla Walla WA 99362-9282 *In looking back over the years, an unspoken and oftentime subliminal guiding principle has been to reach beyond one's realistic grasp. This concept coupled with an interest in treating others as one would like to be treated has made it possible to react to new challenges. Successfully meeting the latter has provided a varied career in a number of different fields of activity.*

PERRY, LUKE (COY LUTHER PERRY, III), actor; b. Fredericktown, Ohio, Oct. 11, 1966; s. Coy Sr. and Ann Perry; m. Minnie Sharp, Nov. 18, 1993. Appeared in TV series Loving, 1987, Another World, 1989, Beverly Hills, 90210, 1990—, appeared in films Terminal Bliss, 1992, Buffy the Vampire Slayer, 1992, The Webbers, 1993, 8 Seconds, 1994. Office: Nigro Karlin & Segal 10100 Santa Monica Blvd Los Angeles CA 90067*

PERRY, MALCOLM BLYTHE, biologist; b. Birkenhead, Cheshire, Eng., Apr. 26, 1930; s. Cyril A. and Hilda (Blythe) P.; m. Eileen M. Perry, Aug. 10, 1956 (dec. 1981); children: Sara Jane, Judith Anne. B.Sc., U. Bristol, Eng., 1953; Ph.D., U. Bristol, 1956, D.Sc., 1969. Banting research fellow Queen's U., Kingston, Ont., Can., 1955; asst. prof. Queen's U., 1956-60, R.S. McLaughlin research prof., 1960-62; sr. research officer Nat. Research Council, Ottawa, Ont., 1962-81; prin. research officer Nat. Research Council, 1981—; scientist U. Cambridge, Eng., 1969, U. Paris, 1979; prof. U. Ottawa, 1982. Contbr. articles to profl. jours. Fellow Royal Soc. Can., Royal Inst. Chemistry; mem. Can. Soc. Microbiology (award 1991), Am. Soc. Microbiology. Home: 769 Hemlock Rd, Ottawa, ON Canada K1K 0K6 Office: NRC, 100 Sussex Dr, Ottawa, ON Canada K1A 0R6

PERRY, MALCOLM OLIVER, vascular surgeon; b. Allen, Tex., Sept. 3, 1929. BA, U. Tex., 1951; MD, U. Tex., Dallas, 1955. Diplomate Am. Bd. Surgery, Am. Bd. Gen. Vascular Surgery. Intern Letterman Army Hosp., San Francisco, 1955-56; resident in surgery Parkland Meml. Hosp., Dallas, 1958-62; fellow in vascular surgery U. Calif., San Francisco, 1962-63; asst. prof. surgery U. Tex., Dallas, 1962-67, assoc. prof. surgery, chief vascular surgery, 1967-71, prof. surgery, chief vascular surgery, 1971-74; prof. surgery U. Wash., Seattle, 1974-77; prof. surgery, chief vascular surgery Cornell U. Med. Coll., N.Y.C., 1978-87, Vanderbilt U. Sch. Medicine, Nashville, 1987-91; chief vascular surgery Tex. Tech U. Health Scis. Ctr., Lubbock, 1991-95. Capt. USAF, 1955-58; major Tex. Air N.G., 1960-66. Office: U Tex Dept Surgery Southwestern Med Sch 5323 Harry Hines Blvd Dallas TX 75235

PERRY, MARGARET, librarian, writer; b. Cin., Nov. 15, 1933; d. Rufus Patterson and Elizabeth Munford (Anthony) P. AB, Western Mich. U., 1954; Cert. d'etudes Francaises, U. Paris, 1956; MSLS, Cath. U. Am., 1959. Young adult and reference libr. N.Y. Pub. Libr., N.Y.C., 1954-55, 57-58; libr. U.S. Army, France and Germany, 1959-63, 64-67; chief circulation U.S. Mil. Libr., West Point, N.Y., 1967-70; head edn. libr. U. Rochester, N.Y., 1970-75, asst. prof., 1973-75, assoc. prof., 1975-82, asst. dir. librs. for reader svcs., 1975-82, acting dir. librs., 1976-77, 80; univ. libr. Valparaiso U., Ind., 1982-93; ret., 1993; mem. Task Force on Coop. Edn., Rochester, 1972; freelance writer Mich. Land Use Inst., 1995—. Author: A Bio-bibliography of Countee P. Cullen, 1903-1946, 1971, Silence to the Drums: A Survey of the Literature of the Harlem Renaissance, 1976, The Harlem Renaissance, 1982, The Short Fiction of Rudolph Fisher, 1987; also numerous short stories; contbr. articles to profl. jours. Bd. dirs. Urban League, 1978-80. Recipient 1st prize short story contest Armed Forces Writers League, 1966; 2d prize Frances Steloff Fiction prze, 1968, 1st prize short story Arts Alive, 1990, 2d prize short story Willow Rev., 1990; seminar scholar Schloss Leopoldskron, Salzburg, Austria, 1956, 3d prize short story West Shore C.C., Scottville, Mich., 1995. Mem. ALA, NOW. Democrat. Roman Catholic. Avocations: violin, collecting book marks, gardening, reading, travel. Home: 15050 Roaring Brook Rd Thompsonville MI 49683-9216

PERRY, MARILYN See PERRY-WIDNEY, MARILYN

PERRY, MARSHA GRATZ, legislator, professional skating coach; b. Niagara Falls, N.Y., Dec. 9, 1936; d. William Henry and Margarett Edna (Barr) Gratz; m. Robert X. Perry, Jr., Jan. 28, 1961; children: Robert, Margarett, David. Student, Elmira Coll., 1954-57; BILR, Cornell U., 1959. Coll. recruiter Inmont, N.Y.C., 1959-61; skating dir. City of Bowie (Md.), 1971-86; skating coach Benfield Pines Ice Rink, Millerville, Md., 1974—; mem. Md. Ho. of Dels.; mem. Md. Ho. of Dels.; summer hockey & skating coach Washington Capitals, Landover, Md., 1986—; co-dir. Prostart Hockey Programs; dir. U.S. Ice Forums. Dist. dir., v.p., planning zoning dir. Crofton (Md.) Civic Assn., 1974-86; pres. West County Fedn. Cmty. Assn.; mem. AACO Drug & Alcohol adv. coun.; bd. dirs. Am. Cancer Soc., Am. Heart Assn., Md. Hall Creative Arts. Named Citizen of Yr. Crofton Civic Assn., 1986. Mem. Women Legislators. Avocations: ice hockey, figure skating, sailing. Home: 1605 Edgerton Pl Crofton MD 21114-1504 Office: MD Ho of Dels State Capital Annapolis MD 21401

PERRY, MATTHEW, actor; b. Williamstown, Mass., Aug. 19. Actor Friends, 1994—. Appeared on TV series including Boys Will Be Boys, Sydney, Growing Pains; TV movies include Deadly Relations, Call Me Anna, Dance 'Til Dawn; films include A Night in the Life of Jimmy Reardon, 1988, She's Out of Control, 1989, Parrallel Lives, 1994. Office: William Morris Agy 151 El Camino Beverly Hills CA 90212*

PERRY, MATTHEW J., JR., federal judge; b. 1921. BS, S.C. State U., 1948, LLB, 1951. Bar: S.C. Atty. Spartanburg, S.C., 1951-61, Columbia, S.C., 1961-76; judge U.S. Ct. Mil. Appeals, Washington, 1976-79, U.S. Dist. Ct., Columbia, 1979—; instr. law U. S.C., 1973-75. Office: US Dist Ct 1845 Assembly St Columbia SC 29201-2431*

PERRY, MICHAEL CLINTON, physician, medical educator, academic administrator; b. Wyandotte, Mich., Jan. 27, 1945; s. Clarence Clinton and Hilda Grace (Wigginton) P.; m. Nancy Ann Kaluzny, June 22, 1968; children: Rebecca Carolyn, Katherine Grace. BA, Wayne State U., 1966, MD, 1970; MS in Medicine, U. Minn., 1975. Diplomate Am. Bd. Internal Medicine, Am. Bd. Hematology, Am. Bd. Oncology. Intern in internal medicine Mayo Grad. Sch. Medicine, Rochester, Minn., 1970-71, resident, 1971-72, fellow, 1972-75; instr. Mayo Med. Sch., Rochester, 1974-75; asst. prof. U. Mo., Columbia, 1975-80, assoc. prof., 1980-85, prof., 1985—, chmn. dept. medicine, 1983-91, sr. assoc. dean, 1991-94, Nellie A Smith chair oncology, dir. div. hematology/oncology, 1994—; prin. investigator Cancer and Leukemia Group B, Nat. Cancer Inst., Hanover, N.H., 1982—, exec. com., 1982-84, 1987-90. Author, co-author 30 book chpts.; editor: Toxicity of Chemotherapy, 1984, The Chemotherapy Source Book, 1992, 95, Comprehensive Textbook of Thoracic Oncology, 1995; contbr. articles to profl. jours. Recipient Faculty Alumni award U. Mo., Columbia, 1985, Disting. Alumnus award Wayne State U., 1995. Fellow ACP; mem. Am. Soc. Hematology, Am. Soc. Clin. Oncology, Cen. Soc. Clin. Research, Am. Soc. Internal Medicine (Young Internist of Yr. 1981), Sigma Xi, Alpha Omega Alpha. Home: 1112 Pheasant Run Columbia MO 65201-6254 Office: U Mo-Columbia 516 Ellis Fischel Cancer Ctr 115 Business Loop 70 W Columbia MO 65203-3244

PERRY, MICHAEL DEAN, professional football player; b. Aiken, S.C., Aug. 27, 1965. Student, Clemson. Defensive tackle Cleveland Browns, 1988-94, Denver Broncos, 1994—. Voted to Pro Bowl, 1989-91, 93; named defensive tackle The Sporting News All-Pro team, 1989-93. Office: Denver Broncos 13655 Broncos Pkwy Englewood CO 80112

PERRY, NELSON ALLEN, radiation physicist, radiological consultant; b. Louisville, Mar. 26, 1937; s. Leslie Irvin and Sue Helen (Harris) P.; m. Sarita Sue Cornn, Apr. 28, 1956; children: Melody S. Bruck, Kimberly D. Horne. AS, Campbellsville (Ky.) Coll., 1954; BS, U. Louisville, 1961; MS, U. Okla., 1966. Cert. hazard control mgr., hazart material mgt.; lic. med. physicist, Tex. Assoc. prof. Ind. Christian U., Indpls., 1974-76; asst. prof. Ind. U., Indpls., 1971-75; instr. Ind. Voc. Tech. Coll., Indpls., 1968-76; health physicist Michael Reese Hosp., Chgo., 1966-68; radiation safety officer St. Francis Hosp., Beech Grove, Ind., 1968-76, Ind. U., Indpls., 1971-75; radiation safety officer U. South Ala., Mobile, 1976—, assoc. prof., 1981—; radiol. cons., 1974—. Contbr. articles to profl. jours. Named Ky. Col., 1964; USPHS trainee, 1965-66. Mem. Am. Assn. Physicists in Medicine, Health Physics Soc. Republican. Baptist. Avocation: collecting miniatures. Office: U South Ala 257 CSAB Mobile AL 36688

PERRY, NORMAN ROBERT, priest, magazine editor; b. Cin., Dec. 17, 1929; s. Joseph Sylvester and May Ann (Hafertepe) P. B.A. cum laude, Duns Scotus Coll., 1954. Joined Franciscan Order, Roman Cath. Ch., 1950, ordained priest, 1958. Assoc. pastor St. Clement Ch., St. Bernard, Ohio, 1959-61, St. Therese Ch., Fort Wayne, Ind., 1961-62; tchr. Bishop Luers High Sch., Fort Wayne, 1961-62; preaching band Franciscan Friars, 1962-66; definitor St. John the Baptist Province, Cin., 1972-75; vicar provincial St. John the Baptist Province, 1975-81; editor St. Anthony Messenger, 1981—; visitator gen. Order of Friars Minor, Commissariat of the Holy Land, Washington, 1980, Acad. Am. Franciscan History, Washington, 1981; mem. office of due process Archdiocesan Adminstrv. Review Bd.; trustee Franciscan Terrace; pro-syndol judge Cin. Archdiocesan Tribunal. Author: Best of the Wiseman, 1981; assoc. editor St. Anthony Messenger, 1966-81. Recipient numerous awards for reporting, editorials, opinion and review writing. Home: St Francis Friary 1615 Vine St Cincinnati OH 45210-1200 Office: St Anthony Messenger 1615 Republic St Cincinnati OH 45210-1219

PERRY, PAUL ALVERSON, utility executive; b. Farwell, Mich., Apr. 19, 1929; s. LaVerne Seneca and Ruth Valeria (McNeal) P.; m. Mildred Mayhew Small, Apr. 13, 1957; children: Patricia Perry Larson, Ruth Perry Watkins, Robert Paul, Donna Jean. B.S.B.A., Central Mich. U., 1952. With Consumers Power Co., Jackson, Mich., 1954-84; asst. sec. Consumers Power Co., 1960-68, sec., 1968-84; sec., dir. Mich. Gas Storage Co., Jackson, 1969-84; dir. No. Mich. Exploration Co.; sec. Plateau Resources Ltd.; sec., dir. Mich. Utility Collection Service Co., Inc. Served with U.S. Army, 1952-54. Mem. Am. Soc. Corp. Secs. Home: 9110 42nd St Pinellas Park FL 34666-5606

PERRY, RALPH BARTON, III, lawyer; b. N.Y.C., Mar. 17, 1936; s. Ralph Barton and Harriet Armington (Seelye) P.; m. Mary Elizabeth Colburn, Sept. 2, 1961; children: Katherine Suzanne, Daniel Berenson. A.B., Harvard U., 1958; LL.B., Stanford U., 1963. Bar: Calif. 1964. Assoc. and mem. Keatinge & Sterling, Los Angeles, 1963-68; mem. firm Graven Perry Block Brody & Qualls, Los Angeles, 1968—. Bd. dirs. Planning and Conservation League, 1968—; v.p. Coalition for Clean Air, pres. 1972-80, 85-88. Served with U.S. Army, 1956-58. Mem. ABA (ho. of dels. 1975-95), State Bar Calif., L.S. County Bar Assn., Lawyers Club L.A. County (gov. 1968-82), Keep Tahoe Blue, Nat. Wildlife Fedn., Internat. Wildlife Fedn., Sierra Club. Club: Los Angeles Athletic. Home: 296 Redwood Dr Pasadena CA 91105-1339 Office: Graven Perry Block Brody & Qualls 523 W 6th St Ste 1130 Los Angeles CA 90014-1106

PERRY, RAYMOND CARVER, education educator; b. Anaheim, Calif., July 6, 1906; s. Arthur Raymond and Helen (Carver) P.; m. Evelyn Lucile Wright, July 7, 1940; children: Douglas Wright, David Wright. AB, Stanford U., 1926; MA, U. So. Calif., L.A., 1928, EdD, 1933. Cert. psychologist, Calif. Secondary tchr. Mexia (Tex.) Sch. Dist., 1926-27; elem. tchr. Artesia (Calif.) Sch. Dist., 1927-28; tchr. jr. high L.A. Sch. Dist., 1928-30, tchr. jr. coll., 1930-35; prof. and dean San Diego State Coll., 1935-40; divsn. chief Calif. Dept. Edn., Sacramento, 1940-45; prof. edn. U. So. Calif., L.A., 1940-72, prof. edn. emeritus, 1972—; curriculum cons., psychologist Fontana (Calif.) Sch. Dist., 1947-51; curriculum survey staff Melbo Assocs., L.A., 1948-71; curriculum cons. Sulphur Springs Sch. Dist., L.A. County, 1965-69. Author: Basic Mathematics for College Students, 1957, Group Factor Analysis of Adjustment Questionnaire, 1934, Cross My Heart, 1990; co-author: Review of Educational Research, 1965. Svc. group rep. City Coordination Coun., Long Beach, Calif., 1933-35. Lt. comdr. USNR, 1942-45. Mem. Nat. Coun. Tchrs. Math., Andrus Ctr. Assocs., U. So. Calif. Ret. Faculty, Phi Delta Kappa (San Diego chpt. pres. 1935-40). Republican. Presbyterian. Avocations: photography, travel.

PERRY, ROBERT, fine arts and performing arts educator; b. New Bedford, Mass., July 13, 1938; s. Antone and Mary (Sousa) P.; m. Elaine Delores Amaral, Sept. 5, 1959; children: LeslieAnn, Robert Jr., John Robert. B Music Edn. magna cum laude, U. Mass., Lowell, 1965; MusM, Boston U., 1972; EdD, U. Mass., Amherst, 1993. Cert. music tchr., supr., Mass. Jr. H.S. music tchr. Somerset (Mass.) Pub. Schs., 1965-66, supr. music grades K-8, 1966-69, supr. music grades K-12, 1969-94, coord. find and performing arts, 1994—; coord. music edn. U. Mass., Lowell, 1992-93; asst. student tchrs. Barrington (R.I.) Coll., 1973-77, Westfield (Mass.) State Coll., 1978-83; condr. marching band workshops Boston Conservatory, 1977-78; mem. focus com. Edn. Reform, Mass., 1993—; cons. in field, 1993—. Contbr. articles to profl. publs. Bd. dirs. Somerset Friends of Music, 1972—; pres. Somerset Arts Coun., 1980-82; founder Carl McDermott Scholarship, Somerset, 1987—; condr. R.I. All State Jr. H.S. Band, 1987, All Star Brasses, Zeiterion Theatre, New Bedford, Mass., 1994-95; organizer Somerset Friends of Music, Musictown Festivals, 1972; asst. mgr. Mass. All State Band, 1981, mgr., 1982; chair Mass. All State Concert, 1992; mem. Touch of Brass Quintet, 1980—. Mem. Mass. Music Educators Assn. (pres. elect 1993-95, pres. 1995—, Lowell Mason award 1992), Internat. Trumpet Guild, Somerset Adminstrs. Assn. (treas. 1982—), Educators Nat. Conf. Avocations: running, painting, aikido, reading, camping. Home: 51 Robin Ln Somerset MA 02726-3540 Office: Somerset Pub Schs 580 Whetstone Hill Rd Somerset MA 02726-3702

PERRY, ROBERT PALESE, molecular biologist, educator; b. Chgo., Jan. 10, 1931; s. Robert John and Gertrude Katherine (Hyman) Palese-Perry; m. Zoila Figueroa, Apr. 28, 1957; children—Rocco, Adele, Monique. B.S., Northwestern U., 1951; Ph.D., U. Chgo., 1956; Docteur Honoris Causa, U. Paris, 1983. Research assoc. Inst. for Cancer Research, Fox Chase Cancer Ctr., Phila., 1960-62, asst. mem., 1962-65, assoc. mem., 1965-69, sr. mem., 1969—; Stanley Reimann chair in rsch. Fox Chase Cancer Ctr., Phila., 1994—; assoc. dir. Inst. for Cancer Research, Fox Chase Cancer Ctr., 1971-74; prof. biophysics U. Pa., Phila., 1973—. Contbr. numerous research articles to profl. jours., 1957—. Guggenheim fellow, 1974; Nat. Acad. scholar USA/USSR Exch. Program, 1987. Mem. Nat. Acad. Scis. (com. on human rights 1979-86), Internat. Cell Rsch. Orgn. (pres. 1983-86), European Molecular Biology Organization. Home: 1808 Bustleton Pike Southampton PA 18966-4608 Office: Inst Cancer Research 7701 Burholme Ave Philadelphia PA 19111-2412

PERRY, RUTH EARLENE, physician; b. Phila., July 25, 1956; d. William Earl and Ruth Ann (Woodland) P.; m. Frederick Montgomery Walton, Sept. 20, 1986; children: Kendall Taylor, Courtney Eleanora. BA in Biology, Swarthmore Coll., 1978; MD, Temple U., 1982. Diplomate Am. Bd. Internal Medicine; diplomate Am. Bd. Emergency Medicine. Intern Med. Coll. Pa., 1982-83; resident in internal medicine Med. Coll. Pa., 1983-85; attending physician emergency rm. Albert Einstein Med. Ctr., Phila., 1985-92, dir. occupational health, 1991-92; med. dir. Bristol (Pa.) Site and Corp. Engring. Rohm & Haas Co., 1992—. Fellow Am. Bd. Emergency Medicine; mem. Am. Coll. Emergency Medicine, Am. Coll. Occupational Medicine, Pa. Med. Soc., Opera Guild. Avocations: gardening, playing flute and piano, art collecting, opera, ballet. Home: 702 Dominion Dr Moorestown NJ 08057-4404 Office: Rohm & Haas DVI Inc State Rd & Rte 413 Bristol PA 19007

PERRY, SARAH TERESA ANDERSON (TERI PERRY), nurse manager, critical care nurse; b. Flushing, N.Y., Jan. 14, 1957; d. John Thomas and Dorothy Reu (James) Anderson; m. Dennis Michael Perry Sr., Oct. 17, 1981; children: John Thomas, Clayton Foster. ADN, Augusta (Ga.) Coll. Sch. Nursing, 1979; BSN, Med. U. of S.C., 1985, MSN, 1987. Shift supr. ICU U. Hosp., Augusta, Ga.; staff nurse III Roper Hosp., Charleston, S.C.; nurse mgr. Med. U. of S.C. Med. Ctr., Charleston, mem. biomed. ethics com., 1988-94; nurse mgr. CCU Med. Coll. of Ga., Augusta, 1994—, Med. Coll. Ga., Augusta, 1995—; registry coord. Nat. Registry of Myocardial Infarction 2, 1994—. Mem. AACN (pres. Charleston chpt. 1989-90, officer CSRA chpt.), S.C. Nurses Assn., Sigma Theta Tau. Home: 4826 Rocky Shoals Cir Evans GA 30809

PERRY, SEYMOUR MONROE, physician; b. N.Y.C., May 26, 1921; s. Max and Manya (Rosenthal) P.; m. Judith Kaplan, Mar. 18, 1951; children: Grant Matthew, Anne Lisa, David Bennett. BA with honors, UCLA, 1943; MD with honors, U. So. Calif., 1947. Diplomate: Am. Bd. Internal Medicine. Intern L.A. County Hosp., 1946-48, resident, 1948-51, mem. staff outpatient dept., 1951; examining physician L.A. Pub. Schs., 1951-52; sr. asst. surgeon Phoenix Indian Gen. Hosp., USPHS, 1952; charge internal medicine USPHS Outpatient Clinic, Washington, 1952-54; fellow hematology UCLA, 1954-55, asst. rsch. physician atomic energy project, 1955-57; asst. prof. medicine, head Hematology Tng. Program, Med. Ctr., 1957-60; instr. medicine Coll. Med. Evangelists, 1951-57; attending specialist internal medicine Wadsworth VA Hosp., Los Angeles, 1958-61; sr. investigator, medicine br. Nat. Cancer Inst., 1961-65, chief medicine br., 1965-68, mem. clin. cancer tng. com., 1966-69, chief human tumor cell biology br., 1968-71, assoc. sci. director clin. trials, 1966-71, assoc. sci. dir. for program planning, div. cancer treatment, 1971-73, dep. dir., 1973-74, acting dir., 1974; spl. asst. to dir. NIH, 1974-78, assoc. dir., 1978-80, acting dep. asst. sec. health (tech.), 1978-79; acting dir. Nat. Ctr. Health Care Tech., OASH, 1978-80, dir., 1980-82; dep. dir. Inst. for Health Policy Analysis Georgetown U. Med. Ctr., Washington, 1983-89, prof. medicine, prof. community and family medicine, 1983-93; adj. prof., 1993—; interim chmn. dept. Georgetown U. Med. Ctr., Washington, 1989-90, chmn., 1990-93, dir. Inst. for Health Care Rsch. and Policy; sr. scholar Med. Tech. and Practice Patterns Inst., Washington, 1993—; dir. WHO Collaborating Ctr. on Health Tech., 1995—; mem. adv. com. on rsch. and on the therapy of cancer Am. Cancer Soc., 1966-70, adv. com. chemotherapy and hematology, 1975-77, chmn. epidemiology, diagnosis and therapy com., 1971, grantee, 1959-60; med. dir. USPHS, 1961-80; asst. surg. gen., 1980-82; mem. radiation com. NIH, 1963-70, co-chmn., 1971-73; pres. Nat. Blood Club, 1971; chmn. Interagy. Com. on New Therapies for Pain and Discomfort, 1978-80; mem. adv. panel on med. tech. and costs of medicare program Congress of U.S., 1982-84; chmn. criteria working group (bioseparation) NASA, 1984; cons. Nat. Ctr. Health Svcs. Rsch. and Health Care Tech., DHHS, 1985-90, Nat. Libr. of Medicine, 1985-89, Agy. for Health Care Policy and Rsch, DHHS, 1990—, Hosp. Assn. N.Y. State, 1990-91; mem. procedures rev. com. and profl. adv. panel Blue Cross/Blue Shield Nat. Capitol Area, 1987-93; advisor WHO Programme on Tech. Devel., Assessment and Transfer; mem. sci. com. Catalan office of Tech. Assessment, Barcelona, Spain, 1994—. Assoc. editor Internat. Jour. Tech. Assessment in Health Care, 1984—; mem. editl. bd. Jour. Health Care Tech., 1984-87, Health Tech.: Critical Issues for Decision Makers, 1987-90, Courts, Health and the Law, 1990-91. Bd. dirs. NIH Alumni Assn. Decorated comendador Order of Merit, Peru; comendador Orden Hipólito Unanue, Peru; Pub. Health Service commendation, 1967; Meritorious Service medal USPHS, 1980. Master ACP (adv. com. to gov. Md. on coll. affairs 1969-76, gov. for USPHS and HHS 1980-82, subcom. on clin. efficacy assessment 1982-85, chmn. health and pub. policy com. D.C. met. area 1987—, mem. gov.'s coun., D.C., 1992—); mem. APHA, Inst. Medicine of NAS (mem. evaluation panel coun. health care tech. 1987-90, com. on evaluation med. techs. in clin. use 1981-84, chmn. rev. com. on Inst. Medicine Report on Hip Fracture 1990, mem. rev. com. on renal disease 1990, rev. com. on artificial heart 1991), Patient Outcome Rsch. Team (chmn. adv. com. analysis of practice, hip fracture repair and hip replacement for osteoarthritis U. Md. 1990-94), Assn. Health Svcs. Rsch. (health svcs. rsch. adv. com. 1990-93), Assn. Acad. Health Ctrs., Internat. Soc. Tech. Assessment in Health Care (pres. 1985-87, bd. dirs. 1989-95), NIH Alumni Assn. (bd. dirs. 1993—), Cosmos Club.evements include elucidation of leukocyte physiology;

initiation of the consensus development process and the technology assessment forum method to resolve controversial issues in medical care. Office: Med Tech and Practice 2121 Wisconsin Ave NW Ste 220 Washington DC 20007-2258

PERRY, SUSAN MILLER, magazine editor. Editor-in-chief Longevity, N.Y.C., 1992—. Office: Gen Media Internat Inc 277 Park Ave 4th Fl New York NY 10172

PERRY, TIMOTHY A., criminal justice educator; b. San Diego, Apr. 11, 1939; s. Sidney Lilburn and May (Babler) P.; m. Sherry Grace Maxwell, Apr. 8, 1972. BA in Police Sci. and Adminstrn., Seattle U., 1976. Cert. coll. prof., vocat. instr., Wash. Police officer Seattle Police Dept., 1966-77, tng. officer, 1977-84, narcotics detective, 1985-90; chief of police Clyde Hill (Wash.) Police Dept., 1984-85; prof. criminal justice Shoreline C.C., Seattle, 1990—, dir. criminal justice edn., 1993—; appeared on nat. programs, include King TV, King Radio, Kiro TV, Kiro Radio, Komo TV; cons. with attys. in civil law suits involving police issues; v.p., author Palladium Publs., Seattle, 1984-92; expert witness, cons. in field, 1988—. Author: Basic Patrol Procedures, The Practical Mockscene Manual, The Art of Criminal Investigation. Mem. Wash. Assn. Police Trainers, Wash. State Law Enforcement Educators Assn., Pacific Assn. Law Enforcement Educators, Internat. Assn. Chiefs of Police. Office: Shoreline CC 16101 Greenwood Ave N Seattle WA 98133

PERRY, TROY D., clergyman, church administrator; divorced; 2 children. Student Midwest Bible Sch.; D in Ministry (hon.), Samaritan Coll., L.A.; D in Human Svcs., Sierra U., Santa Monica, Calif. Former pastor Ch. of God of Prophecy, Santa Ana, Calif.; founder, moderator Universal Fellowship Met. Community Chs., L.A.; rep. Met. Community Chs. and gay and lesbian rights movement numerous TV shows including 60 Minutes, Phil Donahue, The Mike Douglas Show. Author: The Lord is My Shepherd and Knows I'm Gay, Don't Be Afraid Anymore, 1991, (video) God, Gays & The Gospel: This is Our Story; contbg. editor Is Gay Good? Mem. Los Angeles County Commn. Human Rels. Recipient Humanitarian award ACLU Lesbian and Gay Rights chpt., 1978, Humanitarian award Gay Press Assn. Office: Universal Fellowship Met Comm Chs 5300 Santa Monica Blvd Ste 304 Los Angeles CA 90029-1131

PERRY, VINCENT ALOYSIUS, corporate executive; b. Weehawken, N.J.; s. Edwin Robert and Florence Loretta (Gutberlet) P.; m. Doris Lucille Wanckel, Dec. 3, 1944 (dec. July 1988); children: Cynthia Jeanne, Bradford Kimball. A.B., NYU, 1948, M.A., 1949. Asst. prof. fin. Lehigh U., Bethlehem, Pa., 1949-51; mgr. econs. and fin. analysis div. Gen. Foods Corp., White Plains, N.Y., 1951-59; v.p., treas. Universal Match Corp., St. Louis, 1959-61; asst. treas. Internat. Paper Co., N.Y.C., 1961-71; v.p., treas. Bangor Punta Corp., Greenwich, Conn., 1971-75; fin. v.p., treas. Ziff-Davis Pub. Co., N.Y.C., 1975-77; sr. v.p. fin. The Viguerie Co., Inc., Falls Church, Va., 1977-79. Treas. Workshop for Bus. Opportunities, N.Y.C., 1969-88. Served to capt. AUS, 1942-46, ETO. Mem. Lambda Chi Alpha. Home: 1301 Mill Hill Rd Southport CT 06490-1041

PERRY, WILLIAM JAMES, federal official, mathamatical scientist; b. Vandergrift, Pa., Oct. 11, 1927; s. Edward Martin and Mabelle Estelle (Dunlap) P.; m. Leonilla Mary Green, Dec. 29, 1947; children: David Carter, William Wick, Rebecca Lynn, Robin Lee, Mark Lloyd. B.S. in Math, Stanford U., 1949, M.S., 1950; Ph.D., Pa. State U., 1957. Instr. math. Pa. State U., 1951-54; sr. mathematician HRB-Singer Co., State College, Pa., 1952-54; dir. electronic def. labs. GTE Sylvania Co., Mountain View, Calif., 1954-64; pres. ESL, Inc., Sunnyvale, Calif., 1964-77; tech. cons. Dept. Def., Washington, 1967-77, under sec. def. for research and engring., 1977-81; mng. dir. Hambrecht & Quist (investment bankers), San Francisco, 1981-85; chmn. Tech. Strategies & Alliances, Menlo Park, Calif., 1985-93; prof., co-dir. Ctr. for Internat. Security and Arms Control Stanford U., 1989-93; apptd. Dep. Sec. Def. Pentagon, Washington, 1993-94, appt. Sec. Def., 1994—. Served with U.S. Army, 1946-47. Recipient Outstanding Civilian Svc. medal U.S. Army, 1962, 77, Outstanding Civilian Svc. medal Def. Intelligence Agy., 1977, Disting. Pub. Svc. medal Dept. Def., 1980, 81, medal of Achievement Am. Electronic Assn., 1980, Disting. Svc. medal NASA, 1981, James Forrestal Meml. award, 1993, Disting. Alumnus award Pa. State U., 1995, SARNOFF award, 1995; decorated Knight Comdr.'s Cross of Fed. Republic of Germany, grand officer de l'Ordre National du Merute (France). Fellow Am. Acad. Arts and Scis.; mem. Am. Math. Soc., NAE, Sigma Xi. Home: 14 Wolfe St Alexandria VA 22314-3822 Office: Office of Sec Dept Def Pentagon Washington DC 20301-1000

PERRY, WILLIAM JOSEPH, food processing company executive; b. Sacramento, Calif., Nov. 4, 1930; s. Joseph Nasciemeto and Jennie (Nunez) P.; m. Beverly Ann Styles, Dec. 9, 1956 (div. May 1981); children: Katherine, Bill Jr., Kathleen, Barbara; m. Leslie Z. Blumberg, June 30, 1986. BS, U. Calif., Berkeley, 1953; MBA, U. So. Calif., 1995. Quality control supr. Stokely Van Camp, Oakland, Calif., 1953-54; plant mgr. Safeway Stores, Brookside div., Grandview, Wash., 1954-61, Gallo Winery, Modesto, Calif., 1961-62; gen. mgr. Bocca Bella Olive Assoc., Wallace, Calif., 1962-65; v.p. Early Calif. Ind., L.A., 1965-74, Fairmont Foods, Santa Ana, Calif., 1974-75; pres. Cal Agra Ind., Stockton, Calif., 1975-76; exec. v.p. Food Brokers Internat., L.A., 1976—; pres., co-owner G.F.F., Inc., L.A., 1981—; dir. G.F.F., Inc., L.A., 1981—, Food Brokers, Inc., L.A., 1976—, Cozad & Assoc. Ad Agy., Encino, Calif., 1985-87. Wrestling com., dir. protocol, L.A. Olympic Com., 1981-84. Mem. Nat. Food Brokers Assn., Assn. of Dressings and Sauces, Product Mktg. Assn., Nat. Single Svc. Assn., Am. Chem. Soc., U. Calif. Alumni Assn., U. So. Calif. Alumni Assn., Westlake Tennis and Swim Club. Republican. Roman Catholic. Avocations: tennis, photography, bicycling, amateur sports associations. Home: 3700 Brigantine Cir Westlake Vlg CA 91361-3816 Office: GFF Inc 5443 E Washington Blvd Los Angeles CA 90040-2105

PERRYMAN, MARGARET E., hospital executive; b. Sheridan, Wyo., Mar. 15, 1947; d. Ray Eugene and Eileen Juliann Perryman. BA, Carroll Coll., 1969; MBA, U. St. Thomas, 1978. Med. technologist Children's Hosp. L.A., 1969-70; staff med. technician Porter Hosp., Denver, 1970-71, Denver Children's Hosp., 1971-72; lab. mgr. Mpls. Children's Med. Ctr., 1972-79, dir. support svcs., 1979-85, v.p. adminstrn., 1985-87; pres., CEO Gillette Children's Hosp., St. Paul, 1987—, also bd. dirs.; bd. dirs. Pathfinder Resources, St. Paul; bd. dirs., pres. Children's Miracle NEtwork, St. Paul, 1987—; adv. com. Met. HEalthCare Coun., St. Paul, 1994—; bd. dirs. Audubon Ctr. Northwoods, Nat. Assn. Children's Hosps. and Related Instns., 1995—. Author: (book chpt.) Clinic Laboratory Management. Bd. dirs. Audubon Ctr., Sandstone, Minn. Mem. Am. Coll. Healthcare Execs., Minn. Club. Avocations: travel, gardening, reading, bicycling. Office: Gillette Children Hosp 200 University Ave E Saint Paul MN 55101-2507

PERRY-WIDNEY, MARILYN (MARILYN PERRY), international finance and real estate executive, television producer; b. N.Y.C., Feb. 11, 1939; d. Henry William Patrick and Edna May (Bown) Perry; m. Charles Leonidas Widney (dec. Sept. 1981). BA, Mexico City Coll., 1957. Pres. Marilyn Perry TV Prodns., Inc., N.Y.C., 1970—, C.L. Widney Internat., Inc., N.Y.C., 1977—; mng. dir. Donerail Corp., N.Y.C., 1980-88, Lancer, N.Y.C., 1980-88, Assawata, N.Y.C., 1980-88. Prodr., host TV program Internat. Byline, series of more than 90 documentaries on the UN; host radio series Internat. Byline-mem. nations UN for Nat. Pub. Radio satellite, PBS in S.C., N.C., Ga., Tenn., WNYE-FM, N.Y.C., 1996—. Bd. dirs. UN After Sch. Program; ambassadorial candidate Pres. Bush., 1989; mem. Gibbes Mus., S.C. Recipient U.S. Indsl. Film Festival award, CINE Golden Eagle award, Bronze medal Internat. Film & TV Festival of N.Y., Bronzenen Urkinde, Berlin, award for superior quality Intercom-Chgo. Internat. Film Festival, Knights of Malta Trophy award for superior programming from Min. of Tourism, Internationales Tourismus award Filmfestival, Vienna, Manhattan Cable Ten Year award for continuous programming, citations from former pres. Ford and Carter. Mem. Asia Soc., UN Corrs. Assn., Rep. Presdl. Task Force (charter mem.), Rep. Nat. Com., Harbour Club (S.C.), Gibbes Mus. (S.C.). Avocations: music, art and antiques collecting, travel. Home: 211 E 70th St New York NY 10021-5205

PERSAUD, TRIVEDI VIDHYA NANDAN, anatomy educator, researcher, consultant; b. Port Mourant, Berbice, Guyana, Feb. 19, 1940; arrived in Canada, 1972; s. Ram Nandan and Deen (Raggy) P.; m. Gisela Gerda Zehden, Jan. 29, 1965; children: Indrani Uta and Sunita Heidi (twins), Rainer Narendra. MD, Rostock U., Germany, 1965, DSc, 1974; PhD in Anatomy, U. West Indies, Kingston, Jamaica, 1970. Intern Potsdam, Germany, 1965-66; govtl. med. officer Guyana, 1966-67; lectr., sr. lectr. anatomy dept. U. West Indies, 1967-72; assoc. prof. anatomy dept. U. Man., Winnipeg, 1972-75, prof., 1975—, assoc. prof. ob-gyn., reproductive scis., 1979—, prof. pediatrics and child health, 1989—, prof., chmn./head dept. anatomy, 1977-93, dir. Teratology Rsch. Lab., 1972—; cons. in teratology, Children's Centre, Winnipeg, 1973—; mem. sci. staff Health Scis. Centre, Winnipeg, 1973—. Author, editor 22 med. textbooks, including: Early History of Human Anatomy: From Antiquity to the Beginning of the Modern Era, 1984, (with others) Basic Concepts in Teratology, 1985, Environmental Causes of Human Birth Defects, 1991, (with K.L. Moore) The Developing Human, 5th edit., 1993, Before We Are Born, 4th edit., 1993; contbr. numerous chpts. to books, over 150 articles to profl. jours. Recipient Carveth Jr. Scientist award Can. Assn. Pathologists, 1974, Albert Einstein Centennial medal German Acad. Scis., 1975, Dr. & Mrs. H.H. Saunderson award U. Manitoba, 1985, 12th Raymond Truex Disting. Lectureship award Hahnemann U., 1990. Fellow Royal Coll. Pathologists of London, Royal Coll. Physicians of Ireland; mem. Can. Assn. Anatomists (pres. 1981-83, J.C.B. Grant award 1991), Am. Assn. Anatomists, Teratology Soc., European Teratology Soc. Office: U Man, Dept Anatomy, 730 William Ave, Winnipeg, MB Canada R3E OW3

PERSAVICH, WARREN DALE, diversified manufacturing company executive; b. Cleve., Dec. 15, 1952; s. Nick and Sophie (Makris) P.; m. Anita Geraldine Zeleznik, Oct. 12, 1974; children: Nicholas, Katherine. BBA, Kent State U., 1975. CPA, Ohio. Staff acct. Price Water House, Cleve., 1975-76; asst. contr. Banner Industries Inc., Cleve., 1976-79, contr., 1979-86, treas., 1986-88, v.p., treas., 1988-90; sr. v.p., chief fin. officer Banner Aerospace Inc, 1990—. Mem. AICPA, Ohio Soc. CPAs. Republican. Office: Banner Aerospace Inc Washington Dulles Airport PO Box 20260 / 300 W Service Rd Washington DC 20041

PERSCHETZ, MARTIN L., lawyer; b. Bklyn., Sept. 15, 1952; s. Louis and Edith (Sandhaus) P.; m. Babs D. Hanfling, Mar. 23, 1980; children: Monica, Keith, Evan. BA, U. Md., 1974; JD, SUNY, Buffalo, 1977. Bar: N.Y. 1978, U.S. Dist. Ct. (so. dist.) N.Y. 1978, U.S. Dist. Ct. (ea. dist.) N.Y. 1979, U.S. Ct. Appeals (2d cir.) 1984, U.S. Dist. Ct. (no. dist.) N.Y. 1989. Assoc. Obermaier, Morvillo & Abramowitz, N.Y.C., 1977-80; asst. U.S. atty. So. Dist. N.Y., N.Y.C., 1980-86, chief major crimes unit, 1985-86; chief counsel N.Y.C. Spl. Commn. to Investigate City Contracts, N.Y.C., 1986; dep. commr. N.Y.C. Dept. Investigation, N.Y.C., 1986; spl. counsel Schulte, Roth & Zabel, N.Y.C., 1986-87; ptnr. Schulte, Roth & Zabel, 1988—. Contbr. article to profl. jour. Recipient Joseph Halpern award Buffalo Law Rev., 1977. Mem. ABA, N.Y.C. Bar Assn., N.Y. Coun. Def. Lawyers. Home: 271 Clayton Rd Scarsdale NY 10583-1517 Office: Schulte Roth & Zabel 900 3rd Ave New York NY 10022-4728

PERSCHINO, ARTHUR J., elementary school principal. Prin. Columbus Magnet Sch. Recipient Elem. Sch. Recognition award U.S. Dept. Edn., 1989-90; named Young Astronaut Leader of Yr. by Pres. Bush, 1991. Office: Columbus Magnet Sch 46 Concord St Norwalk CT 06854-2904

PERSELL, CAROLINE HODGES, sociologist, educator, author, researcher, consultant; b. Fort Wayne, Ind., Jan. 16, 1941; d. Albert Randolph and Katherine (Rogers) Hodges; m. Charles Bowen Persell, III, June 17, 1967; children: Patricia Emily, Stephen David. BA, Swarthmore Coll., 1962; MA, Columbia U., 1967, PhD, 1971. Sr. assoc., then nat. coordinator Nat. Scholarship Service and Fund for Negro Students, N.Y.C., 1962-66; project dir. Bur. Applied Social Research, N.Y.C., 1968-71; asst. prof. NYU, 1971-76, assoc. prof., 1976-86, prof. 1986—, dir. grad. studies dept. sociology, 1984-87, chair, 1987-93, Robin Williams Disting. Lectr., 1993-94. Author: Education and Inequality, 1977, Understanding Society, 1984, 2d edit., 1987, 3d edit., 1990; co-author: (with Cookson) Preparing for Power, 1985, Making Sense of Society, 1992, (with Maisel) How Sampling Works, 1996; assoc. editor: Teaching Sociology, 1983-85, Sociology of Edn., 1992-95, Gender & Soc., 1992-95; contbr. articles to profl. jours. Recipient Faculty Devel. award NSF, 1978-79, Women Educators' Research award, 1978; grantee Fund for Improvement of Postsecondary Edn., 1989-92, NSF Equipment Fund, 1993-96. Mem. Am. Sociol. Assn. (chair sec. 1983-84, 88-89, chmn. pubs. com. 1987-89), Am. Edn. Rsch. Assn., Author's Guild, Eastern Sociol. Assn. (pres. 1995-96), Internat. Sociol. Assn., Sociologists for Women in Soc. Avocations: violin, gardening, opera, sports. Office: NYU Dept Sociology 269 Mercer St New York NY 10003-6633

PERSELLIN, ROBERT HAROLD, physician; b. Fargo, N.D., July 3, 1930; s. James Harry and Bessie (Hoffman) P.; m. Bonnie Feibleman, June 27, 1957 (dec. 1983); children: Kathleen, Jamie; m. Diane Cummings, June 14, 1986. B.S., Northwestern U., 1952, M.D., 1956, M.S., 1959. Diplomate: Am. Bd. Internal Medicine, Am. Bd. Rheumatology. Intern Charity Hosp., New Orleans, 1956-57; resident in internal medicine Northwestern U. Med. Center, 1957-60; fellow in rheumatology Southwestern Med. Sch., 1962-64; asst. prof. medicine U. Oreg. Med. Sch., 1964-68; prof. medicine, head div. rheumatology U. Tex. Health Sci. Center, San Antonio, 1968-81; prof. family practice U. Tex. Health Sci. Ctr., San Antonio, 1993—; cons. rheumatology VA Hosps., U.S. Army, Coastal Bend Health Plan; vis. prof. rheumatology Kingstown Med. Coll.; vis. scholar Corpus Christi Coll., Cambridge U., 1979-80; vis. scientist Strangeways Rsch. Lab., Cambridge. Contbr chpts. to books, articles to profl. jours. Bd. dirs. San Antonio Chamber Music Soc., 1970-75, 80-96, pres., 1983-85; bd. dirs. Friends of Strings, 1972-75, San Antonio Bot. Soc., 1985-87; Dem. precinct committeeman Washington County, Oreg., 1966-68. Served to capt. M.C. U.S. Army, 1960-62. Fellow ACP, Am. Coll. Rheumatology (exec. com. mem.); mem. Arthritis Found. (chmn. med. and sci. com. South Ctrl. Tex. chpt.), Heberden Soc., Am. Fedn. Clin. Rsch., So. Soc. Clin. Investigation, Tex. Rheumatism Assn. (pres.), Nat. Soc. Clin. Rheumatology, Mex. Rheumatology Soc. (hon.). Office: 635 E Olmos Dr San Antonio TX 78212-2504

PERSHAN, PETER SILAS, physicist, educator; b. Bklyn., Nov. 9, 1934; s. Max J. and Rosa (Bernekow) P.; m. Patricia S. Birke, Aug. 31, 1957; children: Marc, Jill. BS, Poly. Inst. Bklyn., 1956; AM, Harvard U., 1957, PhD, 1960. Rsch. fellow Harvard U., Cambridge, Mass., 1960, asst. prof., 1961-64, assoc. prof., 1964-68, prof., 1968—; mem. lab. tech. Bell Telephone, Murray Hill, N.J., 1963-64; dir. Materials Rsch. Lab., Cambridge, 1974-78; vis. prof. MIT, Cambridge, 1978-79; vis. scientist Brookhaven Nat. Lab., Upton, N.Y., 1985-86, guest scientist, 1986—; cons. Sperry Gyroscope Co., Great Neck, N.Y., 1961-63, RCA Corp., Princeton, N.J., 1966-73, Battelle Meml. Inst. Naval Ordnance Lab., Silver Springs, Md., 1969-71; mem. proposal rev. panel Stanford Synchtotron Radiation Lab., 1989—; mem. adv. bd. Advanced Liquid Crystalline Optical Materials Consortium, 1991-94; guest scientist RISØ Nat. Lab., Denmark, 1993. Author: Structure of Liquid Crystal Phases, 1988; co-editor: Resonances, 1990; contbr. articles to profl. jours. Fellow Am. Phys. Soc. (com. internat. freedom scientists 1984-86). Home: 218 Follen Rd Lexington MA 02173-5825 Office: Harvard U Div Applied Scis 29 Oxford St Cambridge MA 02138-2901

PERSHAN, RICHARD HENRY, lawyer; b. N.Y.C., Jan. 4, 1930; s. Benjamin and Sadie (Aronowsky) P.; m. Kathryn Schaefler, June 11, 1952; children: Lee S., Richard H., Pamela, Julia B. BA, Yale U., 1951, LLB, 1956. Bar: N.Y. 1956, U.S. Supreme Ct.1969. Assoc. Davis, Polk & Wardwell, N.Y.C., 1956-60; ptnr. Finch & Schaefler, N.Y.C., 1960-85; ptnr. LeBoeuf, Lamb, Greene & MacRae, N.Y.C., 1986-94, of counsel, 1995—. Counsel Mcpl. Art Soc., N.Y.C., 1965-70, Fine Arts Fedn., N.Y.C., 1975-80. Served to 1st lt. USAF. Fellow Am. Coll. Trust and Estate Counsel (author, editor, articles and studies 1960—); mem. Assn. of Bar of City of N.Y., Yale Club. Democrat. Avocation: rowing. Home: 1435 Lexington Ave New York NY 10128-1628 Office: LeBoeuf Lamb Greene & MacRae 125 W 55th St New York NY 10019-5389

PERSHING, DAVID WALTER, chemical engineering educator, researcher; b. Anderson, Ind., Oct. 2, 1948; s. Walter L. and Treva B. (Crane) P.; m. Lynn Marie Kennard, Apr. 9, 1977; 1 child, Nicole. BSChemE, Purdue U., 1970; PhDChemE, U. Ariz., 1976. Rsch. asst. Exxon Prodn. Rsch., Houston, 1969; project engr. EPA, 1970-73; asst. prof. chem. engring. U. Utah, Salt Lake City, 1977-82, assoc. prof., 1982-85, prof., 1985—, assoc. dean Grad. Sch., 1983-87, dean Coll. Engring., 1987—; asst. to pres. Reaction Engring. Inc., Salt Lake City, 1990—; vis. scientist Internat. Flame Rsch. Found., Ijmuiden, The Netherlands, 1972-73; vis. assoc. prof. chem. engring. U. Ariz., Tuscon, 1976-77; cons. Energy and Environ. Rsch. Ctr., Irvine, Calif., 1974-90, Acurex Corp., Mountain View, Calif., 1974-79, Kennecott Corp., Salt Lake City, 1979-81, Nat. Bur. Standards, Washington, 1976-78, Geneva Steel, 1989—; assoc. dir. Engring. Rsch. Ctr., NSF, 1986—. Contbr. articles to profl. publs.; patentee in field. Maj. USPHS, 1970-73. Recipient Disting. Teaching award U. Utah, 1982, Disting. Rsch. award U. Utah, 1990; grantee NSF, PYI, 1984-90. Mem. Am. Inst. Chem. Engrs., Combustion Inst. Methodist. Office: U Utah Coll Engring 2202 Merrill Engring Bldg Salt Lake City UT 84112

PERSHING, RICHARD WILSON, communications company executive, consultant; b. L.A., June 14, 1927; s. Howard Louis and Myrtle Edith (Wilson) P.; m. Norma Louise Davis, Aug. 19, 1950; children: Tina Ann Baine, Timothy Alan. BA, Pepperdine U., 1950. Various positions Security Pacific Bank, L.A., 1950-62; sr. v.p. Home Savs. & Loan Assn., L.A., 1962-64; exec. v.p. Hale Bros. Assocs., Inc., San Francisco, 1964-68, Internat. Controls Corp., Fairfield, N.J., 1968-69; pres., CEO Hale Tech. Corp., San Francisco, 1970-84; chmn. bd. Datron Sys. Inc., Escondido, Calif., 1984—. Serves with USNR, 1945-46, PTO. Home: Datron Systems Inc 75-572 Debby Ln Indian Wells CA 92210 Office: Datron Sys Inc 304 Enterprise St Escondido CA 92029-1239

PERSHING, ROBERT GEORGE, telecommunications company executive; b. Battle Creek, Mich., Aug. 10, 1941; s. James Arthur and Beulah Francis P.; BS in Elec. Engring., Tri-State Coll., Angola, Inc., 1961; m. Diana Kay Prill, Sept. 16, 1961 (div. Jan. 1989); children: Carolyn, Robert; m. Charlene Jean Reed Wallis, Mar. 18, 1989 (div. Dec. 1995). Comm. engr. Am. Elec. Power, Ind., N.Y. and Ohio, 1961-69; design supr. Wescom, Inc., Ill., 1969-74; dir. engring. Tellabs, Inc., Lisle, Ill., 1974-78; pres., CEO, bd. dirs. Teltrend, Inc., St. Charles, Ill., 1979-89, chmn. bd., 1979-88; CEO DKP Prodns. Inc., St. Charles, Ill., 1986-89; exec. cons. Teltrend, 1979-93, bd. dirs., 1988-93; asst. treas. Magnekopy Inc., Villa Park, Ill., chmn. bd.; bd. dirs. TI Investors, Inc.; advisor entrepreneurial studies U. Ill.; engring. cons. Recipient Chgo. Area Small Bus. award, 1986, INC 500 awards, 1987, 88. Mem. IEEE. Office: 1519 Kirkwood Dr Geneva IL 60134-1659

PERSICO, JOSEPH EDWARD, author; b. Gloversville, N.Y., July 19, 1930; s. Thomas Louis and Blanche (Perrone) P.; m. Sylvia La Vista, May 23, 1959; children: Vanya, Andrea. B.A., SUNY-Albany, 1952; postgrad., Columbia U., 1955. Writer on staff of gov. N.Y. State, Albany, 1955-59; commd. fgn. service officer USIA, 1959; served in USIA, Buenos Aires, Argentina, Rio de Janeiro, Brazil, 1959-62; exec. asst. to commr. N.Y. State Health Dept., Albany, 1963-66; chief speechwriter for gov. N.Y. State, Albany, 1966-74; speechwriter for v.p., U.S., Washington, 1975-77. Author: My Enemy My Brother: Men and Days of Gettysburg, 1977; (novel) The Spiderweb, 1979, Piercing the Reich: The Penetration of Nazi Germany by American Secret Agents during World War II, 1979 (Nat. Intelligence Study Ctr. prize for best book on intelligence 1979), The Imperial Rockefeller: A Biography of Nelson A. Rockefeller, 1982, Murrow: An American Original, 1988, Casey: William J. Casey, From the OSS to the CIA, 1990, Nuremberg: Infamy on Trial, 1994; collaborator: Colin Powell: My American Journey, 1995. Served to lt. (j.g.) USN, 1952-55. Recipient Disting. Alumnus award SUNY-Albany, 1982. Mem. Authors Guild, Inc. Home and Office: 222 Heritage Rd Guilderland NY 12084-9314

PERSON, CURTIS S., JR., state senator, lawyer; b. Nov. 27, 1934; married; 6 children. BS, Memphis State U., 1956; LLB, U. Miss., 1959. Practice law, Memphis; former mem. Tenn. Ho. of Reps.; mem. Tenn. Senate, 1968—; Senate Rep. whip, 1973-76, minority caucus chmn., 1976-82; chmn. Senate Judiciary com. 95th-99th Gen. Assemblies; chief legal officer Juvenile Ct. of Memphis and Shelby County. Pres., Memphis-Shelby County Mental Health Assn., 1969-73, Handicapped Inc., 1972-74; chmn. Memphis Commn. on Drug Abuse, 1970-71; charter pres. Memphis State Tiger Rebounders; past trustee Memphis State U.; exec. committeeman St. Jude's Memphis Open Golf Classic; co-chmn. Shelby County Legis. Del., 1973-74, vice chmn., 1970, 75, 76, 85-88; chmn. Shelby Rep. Del., 1977, 83-84. Named Memphis and Tenn. Outstanding Young Man of Yr., Jaycees, 1969, Outstanding Legislator of Yr., Government Leader Against Drunk Driving, Tenn. MADD, 1988, Legislator of Yr., Tenn. Alcohol and Drug Assn., 1988; recipient Liberty Bell Freedom award Memphis/Shelby County Bar Assn., 1969, Tenn. Adv. of Year for Handicapped children, 1978, Outstanding Svc to Children award Tenn. Coun. Juvenile Ct. Judges, 1981, Pres'. Svc. award Tenn. Juvenile Ct. Svcs. Assn., 1981, Americanism award Memphis Civitan Club, 1986, Disting. Svc. award County Officials Assn. Tenn., 1989, Community Svc. award Tenn. Med. Assn., 1989, Eagle award Eagle Forum, 1994, Bill Bates Legis. award United Tenn. League, 1994, Champion for Children award Tenn. Assn. Child Care, 1995. Mem. Tenn. Bar Assn., Miss. Bar Assn., Memphis/Shelby County Bar Assn., Memphis State U. Nat. Alumni Assn. (pres. 1970, 71), So. Golf Assn. (past dir.), Nat. Rifle Assn. (life), Phi Alpha Delta, Phi Alpha Theta, Kappa Sigma, Omicron Delta Kappa. Presbyterian. Clubs: Masons, Shriners. Office: War Meml Bldg Rm 308 Nashville TN 37243

PERSON, DONALD AMES, SR., pediatrician, rheumatologist; b. Fargo, N.D., July 17, 1938; s. Ingwald Haldor and Elma Wilhelmenia (Karlstrom) P.; m. Blanche Durand, Apr. 28, 1962; children: Donald Ames Jr., David Wesley. Student, Gustavus Adolphus Coll., 1956-58, U. Minn., 1958-59; BS, U. N.D., 1961; MD, U. Minn., 1963. Intern Mpls.-Hennepin County Gen. Hosp., 1963-64; resident neurol. surgery Mayo Clinic and Mayo Grad. Sch. Medicine, Rochester, Minn., 1967, fellow in microbiology, 1968-70; rsch. assoc. Baylor Coll. Medicine, Houston, 1971, Arthritis Found. fellow, 1972-74, mem. faculty, asst. prof. internal medicine, 1971-78, asst. prof. pediatrics, 1980-87, resident in pediatrics, 1978-80; asst. attending pediatrics Harris County Hosp. Dist., 1980-88; rheumatologist Tex. Children's Hosp., 1980-88, attending pediatrician, 1982-88; cons. Kelsey Seybold Clinic, 1980-88, Houston Shriner's Crippled Children's Hosp., 1983-88 , Houston Meth. Hosp., 1983-88, St. Luke's Episcopal Hosp., 1983-88, Honolulu Shriner's Crippled Children's Hosp., 1988—; prof. clin. pediatrics U. Hawaii Sch. Medicine, Honolulu, 1991—; prof. clin. pediatrics Uniformed Svcs. U. Health Scis., Bethesda, Md., 1993—, chief gen. pediatric svc., 1991-94; chief ambulatory pediatrics, Tripler Army Med. Ctr., Tripler AMC, Hawaii, 1988-94, asst. chief dept. pediatrics, 1988-94, chief dept. pediatrics, 1994—; "A" proficiency designator in pediatrics from Surgeon Gen. of the Army, 1990. Contbr. articles to profl. jours. With AUS, 1964-66, col., 1987—, Arthritis Found. sr. investigator, 1975-77. Fellow Am. Acad. Pediatrics (v.p. chpt. west uniformed svcs. sect. 1994-95, mem. exec. com. uniformed svcs. sect., 1995—, adv. mem. exec. com. Hawaii chpt. 1994—); mem. AAAS, AMA, Am. Fedn. Clin. Rsch., Am. Coll. Rheumatology, Am. Soc. Microbiology, Soc. Pediat. Rsch., Am. Soc. Tropical Medicine and Hygiene, Am. Pediat. Soc., Arthritis Found. (dir., med. adv. bd.), Assn. Mil. Surgeons U.S. (Philip Hench award 1990), Harris County Med. Soc., Houston Acad. Medicine, Houston Pediatric Soc., Internat. Orgn. Mycoplasmologists, N.Y. Acad. Sci., N.D. Acad. Sci., Soc. Exptl. Biology and Medicine, So. Soc. Pediatric Rsch., S.W. Sci. Forum, Tex. Med. Assn., Tex. Pediatric Soc., Tex. Rheumatism Assn., Tissue Culture Assn., Honolulu Pediatric Soc., U.S. Fedn. Culture Collections. Mem. Evang. Luth. Ch. in Am., deacon, 1991-94. Home: 1321 Parks Rd Honolulu HI 96819-2131 Office: Tripler Army Med Ctr Honolulu HI 96859

PERSON, EVERT BERTIL, newspaper and radio executive; b. Berkeley, Calif., Apr. 6, 1914; s. Emil P. and Elida (Swanson) P.; m. Ruth Finley, Jan. 26, 1944 (dec. May 1985); m. 2d, Norma Joan Betz, Mar. 12, 1986. Student, U. Calif., Berkeley, 1937; LHD, Calif. State Univs., 1983, Sonoma State U., 1993. Co-publisher, sec.-treas. Press Democrat Pub. Co., Santa Rosa, Calif., 1945-72, editor, 1972-73, pres., pub., editor-in-chief, 1973-85; sec.-treas. Finley Broadcasting Co., Santa Rosa, 1945-72; pres. Finley Broadcasting Co., 1972-89, Kawana Pubs., 1975-85; pub. Healdsburg Tribune, 1975-85; prin. Evert B. Person Investments, Santa Rosa, 1985—; pres. Person Properties Co., Santa Rosa, 1945-70; v.p. Finley Ranch & Land Co., Santa Rosa, 1947-72, pres., 1972-79; pres. Baker Pub. Co., Oreg., 1957-67, Sebastopol (Calif.) Times, 1978-81, Russian River News, Guerneville, Calif., 1978-81; pres. publ. Kawana Pubs., 1978-85; mem. nominating com. AP, 1982-84, mem. auditing com., 1984-85. Bd. dirs. Empire Coll., Santa Rosa, 1972—, Sonoma County Taxpayers Assn., 1966-69, San Francisco Spring Opera Assn., 1974-79; bd. dirs. San Francisco Opera, 1986—, v.p., 1988—; pres. Calif. Newspaperboy Found., 1957-58; chmn. Santa Rosa Civic Arts Commn., 1961-62; pres. Santa Rosa Sonoma County Symphony Assn., 1966-68, Luther Burbank Meml. Found., 1979, Santa Rosa Symphony Found., 1967-77; adv. bd. Santa Rosa Salvation Army, 1959-67; commodore 12th Coast Guard Dist. Aux., 1969-70; trustee Desert Mus., Palm Springs, 1987-92, v.p. Nat. Bd. Canine Companions, Inc., 1989-92. Mem. Calif. Newspaper Pubs. Assn. (pres. 1981-82), Internat. Newspaper Fin. Execs. (pres. 1961-62), Navy League U.S., Bohemian Club, Sonoma County Press Club, Santa Rosa Golf and Country club, The Springs Club, Santa Rosa Rotary, Masons (33 degree, Legion of Merit), Shriners. Roman Catholic. Home: 1020 Mcdonald Ave Santa Rosa CA 95404-3525 Office: The Oaks 1400 N Dutton Ave Ste 12 Santa Rosa CA 95401-4644

PERSON, ROBERT JOHN, financial management consultant; b. Mpls., Mar. 7, 1927; s. Otto Carl and Alice Kathryn (Kasper) P.; m. Jeanette Haines, Mar. 11, 1948; 1 dau., Julie Ann. BBA, U. Minn., 1947; MS, Columbia u., 1953. Financial analyst Equitable Life Assurance Soc. U.S., N.Y.C., 1947-53; asst. v.p. bus. devel. met. banking dept. Bankers Trust Co., N.Y.C., 1953-64; v.p. bus. devel. div. Union Bank, Los Angeles, 1964-67; v.p., dir. mktg. Bank of Calif., San Francisco, 1967-70; sr. v.p. Central Nat. Bank of Chgo., 1970-72, 1st v.p., 1973-76; 1st v.p. Central Nat. Chgo. Corp., 1973-76; v.p., regional mgr. Lester B. Knight & Assos., Inc., San Francisco, 1976-77; dir. bank cons. Coopers & Lybrand, San Francisco, 1977-80; partner-in-charge, nat. dir. bank cons. Coopers & Lybrand, Chgo., 1980-89; exec. v.p. RJP Assocs., Inc., Stockton, Calif., 1989-92; instr. salesmanship sch. pub. relations N.Y. Bankers Assn., 1960-63; instr. mktg. research Stonier Grad. Sch. Banking, Rutgers U., 1964-65, 73, 75-77, Brown U., 1964; instr. Agrl. Lending Sch., Ill. Bankers Assn., 1973-76, Nat. Comml. Lending Sch., Am. Bankers Assn., 1973-76, Sch. Bank Adminstrn., U. Wis., 1982-85, Nat. Grad. Trust Sch., Northwestern U., 1982-84, Southwestern Grad. Sch. Banking, 1983-84; Vice chmn. mgmt. effectiveness com. Community Fund Chgo. Treas. Sch. Bd., Huntington, N.Y., 1957-59; Bd. dirs. Am. Cancer Soc., Chgo.; chief crusader Crusade of Mercy. Served to lt. comdr. USNR, 1944-46, ret. Recipient Florence McNeil Stanley award Columbia, 1953. Mem. Am. Bankers Assn., Bank Mktg. Assn., Am. Mgmt. Assn. (mktg. planning council), Mgmt. Centre-Europe (fin. mgmt. adv. com. 1971—), Sales and Mktg. Execs. Internat., Stockton Symphony Assn. (bd. dirs. 1989-92), Beta Gamma Sigma. Republican. Presbyn. Clubs: Eastward Ho (Cape Cod); Stockton Golf and Country (Calif.). Lodge: Elks. Home: 14406 W Trading Post Dr Sun City West AZ 85375-5791 also: 81 Joshua Jethro Rd Chatham MA 02633

PERSON, RUTH JANSSEN, academic administrator; b. Washington, Aug. 27, 1945; d. Theodore Armin and Ruth Katherine (Mahoney) Janssen. BA, Gettysburg (Pa.) Coll., 1967; AMLS, U. Mich., 1969, PhD, 1980; MS in Adminstrn., George Washington U., 1974. Head of reference/asst. prof. Thomas Nelson C.C., Hampton, Va., 1971-74; lectr. U. Mich., Ann Arbor, 1975-79, coord. of continuing edn., 1977-79; asst. prof. Cath. U., Washington, 1979-85, assoc. prof., 1985-86, assoc. dean Sch. of Libr. and Info. Sci., 1983-86; dean Coll. Libr. Sci. Clarion (Pa.) U., 1986-88; assoc. vice chancellor U. Mo., St. Louis, 1988-93; v.p. for acad. affairs, prof. bus. adminstrn. Ashland (Ohio) U., 1993-95; v.p. acad. affairs Angelo State U., San Angelo, Tex., 1995—; reviewer U.S. Dept. Edn., Washington, 1987-89, 92; trustee Pitts. Regional Libr. Ctr., 1986-88; chair publs. com. Assn. of Coll. and Rsch. Librs., Chgo., 1986-90; cons. United Way, Alexandria, Va., 1985; cons.-evaluator North Ctrl. Assn., 1993-95. Co-editor: (book) Academic Libraries: Their Role and Rationale in Higher Education, 1995; editor: (book) The Management Process, 1983; editl. bd. Coll. & Rsch. Librs., 1990—; contr. articles to profl. jours. Mem. Strategic Planning Task Force, Ashland C. of C., 1994; bd. dirs. Alternatives for Living in Violent Environs., Inc., St. Louis, 1992-94; commr. Commn. for Women, Anne Arundel County, Md., 1984-86; mem. Citizens Adv. Bd., Clarion, Pa., 1986-88; mem. Olivette, Mo. Human Rels. Commn., 1992-94; mem. San Angelo Bus. and Profl. Women's Club, 1995—, pres.-elect 1996—; mem. bldg. design oversight com. San Angelo Mus. Fine Arts, 1995—. Fellow Am. Coun. Edn., 1990, Harvard Inst. Ednl. Mgmt., 1989, Rackham fellow U. Mich., 1976; ACE fellow Ariz. Bd. Regents, 1990-91; recipient Washington Woman award Washington Woman mag., 1986. Mem. ALA (com. on accreditation 1993—), Am. Assn. Univ. Adminstrs. (bd. dirs. 1993—), Coun. for the Preservation of Anthropol. Records (bd. dirs.), Psi Chi, Beta Phi Mu, Pi Lambda Theta, Kappa Delta Pi, Phi Alpha Theta. Lutheran. Avocations: piano, herb gardening, antiques, cooking, sailing. Home: 5218 N Bentwood Dr San Angelo TX 76904 Office: Angelo State U Box 11008 ASU Station San Angelo TX 76909

PERSON, WILLIS BAGLEY, chemistry educator; b. Salem, Oreg., Apr. 23, 1928; s. Carl Waldo and Grace Cassity (Bagley) P.; m. Krystyna Szczepaniak, 1985. BS, Willamette U., 1947; MS, Oreg. State Coll., Corvallis, 1949; PhD, U. Calif., Berkeley, 1953. Rsch. fellow U. Minn., 1952-54; instr. Harvard U., 1954-55; asst. prof. U. Iowa, 1955-61, assoc. prof., 1961-66; NSF sr. postdoctoral fellow, vis. assoc. prof. U. Chgo., 1965-66; prof. chemistry U. Fla., Gainesville, 1966—; vis. staff Los Alamos (N.Mex.) Nat. Lab., 1975-89; UNESCO cons. state U. Campinas, Brazil, 1980; vis. prof. Royal Holloway Coll., U. London, 1978, Inst. Molecular Sci., Okazaki, Japan, 1984, U. Pierre et Marie Curie, Paris, 1985; assoc. mem. commn. molecular spectroscopy IUPAC, 1982-89; mem. spectroscopy com. IUPAC Commn., 1989—; vis. scientist Lab. Chem. Phys. NIDDK/NIH, Bethesda, Md., 1993. Author: (with R.S. Mulliken) Molecular Complexes, 1969; editor: (with G. Zerbi) Vibrational Intensities in Infrared and Raman Spectroscopy, 1982; contbr. numerous articles to profl. jours. Guggenheim fellow U. Chgo., 1960-61, Chem. Soc. Sr. Postdoctoral fellow, 1978. Mem. AAAS, Am. Chem. Soc., Optical Soc. Am., Royal Soc. Chemists (London), Coblentz Soc., Soc. Applied Spectroscopy. Office: U Fla Dept Chemistry PO Box 117200 Gainesville FL 32611-7200

PERSONICK, STEWART DAVID, electrical engineer; b. Bklyn., Feb. 22, 1947; s. Louis and Mamie (Katz) P.; m. Carol Ann Cooke, Apr. 12, 1986. B.E.E., CCNY, 1967; S.M., MIT, 1968, Sc.D., 1970. Engr. Bell Labs., Holmdel, N.J., 1967-75, engring. supr., 1975-78, dept. head, 1983-84; engring. mgr. Vidar div. TRW, Mountain View, Calif., 1978-81; research mgr. Tech. Research Ctr. TRW, El Segundo, Calif., 1981-83; cons. Pacific Palisades, Calif., 1983-84; com. mem. NRC, Washington, 1983—; div. mgr. Bell Communications Research, Red Bank, N.J., 1984-85, asst. v.p., 1985-95, v.p., gen. mgr., 1995—. Author: Optical Fiber Transmission Systems, 1981, Fiber Optics Technology and Applications, 1985; editor spl. issue on fiber optic systems, IEEE Trans., 1978, 83; IEEE misc. jours., 1975—; patentee fiber optics; contbr. chpts. in books. Fellow IEEE, Optical Soc. Am.; mem. NAE, IEEE Communications Soc. Office: Bell Communications Rsch 445 South St Rm IC-201B Morristown NJ 07960-6454

PERSONS, J. ROBERT, lawyer; b. New Orleans, Dec. 30, 1946; s. Jo R. and Ellen (Martin) P.; m. Ann Coogler, Aug. 10, 1974; children: Rob, Ellen, Margaret. BA with distinction, U. Va., 1969; JD, U. Ga., 1972. Bar: Ga. 1972, U.S. Ct. Appeals (11th cir.) 1972. Assoc. Hurt, Richardson, Garner & Todd, Atlanta, 1972-78; ptnr. Hurt, Richardson, Garner, Todd & Cadenhead, Atlanta, 1978-85; of counsel Lord, Bissell & Brook, Atlanta, 1985-86, ptnr., 1987—. 1st. Lt. USAR, 1972-75. Mem. ABA, Atlanta Bar Assn. (bd. dirs. 1988-90, 92-93), State Bar Ga. (mem. exec. coun. young lawyers sect. 1978-79, Henry Shinn Meml. award 1972), Ga. Defense Lawyers Assn., Alumni Assn. Westminster Schs., Defense Rsch. Inst., Lawyers Club Atlanta. Democrat. Episcopalian. Avocations: golf, boating, fishing. Office: Lord Bissell & Brook One Atlantic Ctr 1201 W Peachtree St NW Ste 3700 Atlanta GA 30309-3400*

PERSONS, OSCAR N., lawyer; b. McCormick, S.C., Jan. 7, 1939; s. Abner Thaddeus and Esther (Dumas) P.; m. Virginia Van Landingham, July 16, 1988; children: Thaddeus William, Anne Laura Lacour. B in Indsl. Engring., Ga. Inst. Tech., 1960; JD, Emory U., 1967. Bar: Ga. Ptnr. Alston & Bird, Atlanta, 1967—. Mem. Ga. Election Bd., 1976-96; gen. counsel Ga. Rep. Com., 1971-93; Ga. chmn. Dole for Pres. campaign, 1987, 95-96; Ga. vice chmn. Bush for Pres. campaign, 1988; gen. co-chmn. Bush-Quayle campaign, 1992; chmn. Coverdell for U.S. Senate campaign, 1992, Senator Coverdell's Citizens' Senate Del., 1993—. Presbyterian. Office: Alston & Bird One Atlantic Ctr 1201 W Peachtree St NW Atlanta GA 30309-3400

PERSONS, STOW SPAULDING, historian, educator; b. Mt. Carmel, Conn., June 15, 1913; s. Frederick Torrell and Florence Isabel (Cummings) P.; m. Dorothy Mae Reuss, Sept. 4, 1943; 1 dau., Catherine. BA, Yale U., 1936, PhD, 1940. Instr. history Princeton U., 1940-45, asst. prof., 1945-50; prof. history U. Iowa, 1950—, rsch. prof., 1956-57, Carver Disting. prof., 1978-81, prof. emeritus, 1981—, acting dean Grad. Coll., 1960-61; sr. rsch. fellow NEH, 1967-68; Vis. prof. Salzburg (Austria) Seminar, 1955, 61, Stetson U., 1957, San Francisco Coll., 1959, U. Wyo., 1960, U. Colo., 1964. Author: Free Religion, 1947, American Minds, 1958, The Decline of American Gentility, 1973, Ethnic Studies at Chicago, 1987, The University of Iowa in the 20th Century, 1990; editor: Evolutionary Thought in America, 1950, (with D. Egbert and T.D.S. Bassett) Socialism and American Life, 1952, Social Darwinism: Selected Essays of William Graham Sumner, 1963, The Cooperative Commonwealth (Laurence Gronlund); mem. editorial bd. Am. Quar., 1958-61, Mississippi Valley Hist. Rev., 1954-57. Fellow Fund Advancement Edn., 1954-55. Mem. Am. Hist. Assn., Orgn. Am. Historians (exec. com. 1960-63). Home: 1433 Oaklawn Ave Iowa City IA 52245-5648

PERSSON, ERLAND KARL, electrical engineer, electrical company executive; b. Soderala, Sweden, Oct. 9, 1923; came to U.S., 1949, naturalized, 1953; m. Elaine Darm; children—Ann Monn, Eric. B.S.E.E., U. Minn., 1955. Registered profl. engr., Minn. Prin. engr. Gen. Mills, Mpls., 1956-61; v.p. engring. Electro-Craft Corp., Hopkins, Minn., 1961-72, v.p. research and devel., 1972-83, sr. v.p., chief tech. officer, 1983-86; pres. Erland Persson Co., Mpls., 1987—. Contbr. articles to profl. jours. Contbr. chpts. to books. Patentee in field. Mem. Mech. Engring. Adv. Com. U. Minn.; bd. dirs. Minn. High Tech. Council, 1984-86, mem., 1987. Fellow IEEE (mem. subcom. electric machines com., indsl. drives com.), Audio Engring. Soc. (founder Midwest chpt. 1974); mem. Eta Kappa Nu. Office: Erland Persson Co Interchange Tower 600 Highway 169 S Ste 1275 Minneapolis MN 55426-1215

PERSYN, MARY GERALDINE, law librarian, law educator; b. Elizabeth, N.J., Feb. 25, 1945; d. Henry Anthony and Geraldine (Sumption) P. AB, Creighton U., 1967; MLS, U. Oreg., 1969; JD, Notre Dame U., 1982. Bar: Ind. 1982, U.S. Dist. Ct. (no. and so. dists.) Ind. 1982, U.S. Supreme Ct. 1995. Social scis. librarian Miami U., Oxford, Ohio, 1969-78; staff law librarian Notre Dame (Ind.) Law Sch., 1982-84; dir. law library Valparaiso (Ind.) U., 1984-87, law librarian, assoc. prof. law, 1987—. Editor Journal of Legislation, 1981-82; mng. editor Third World Legal Studies, 1986—. Mem. ABA, Ind. State Bar Assn., Am. Assn. Law Libraries, Ohio Regopma; Assn. Law Libraries (pres. 1990-91), Ind. State Quilt Guild (pres. 1996-98). Roman Catholic. Home: 1308 Tuckahoe Park Dr Valparaiso IN 46383-4032 Office: Valparaiso U Law Libr Sch Law Valparaiso IN 46383

PERVIN, WILLIAM JOSEPH, computer science educator; b. Pitts., Oct. 31, 1930; s. Abraham and Stella (Greenberger) P.; m. Susan P. Chizeck, 1981; 1 child, Hannah; children by previous marriage: Edward, James, Rachel. B.S., U. Mich., 1952, M.S., 1952; Ph.D., U. Pitts., 1957. Prof. Pa. State U., 1957-63; vis. prof. Heidelberg (Germany) U., 1963-64; prof., chmn. U. Wis.-Milw., 1964-67; dir. Computer Center, prof. math. Drexel U., Phila., 1967-73; dir. Regional Computer Center U. Tex., Dallas, 1973-78, prof. computer scis., 1973—, chmn. computer scis., 1983-85, master sch. engring. and computer scis., 1987-94. Author: Foundations of General Topology, 1964. Mem. Assn. Computing Machinery, Am. Math. Soc., IEEE Computer Soc., Soc. Indsl. and Applied Math., Math. Assn. Am. Office: U Tex Dallas PO Box 830688 M/S EC 32 Richardson TX 75083-0688

PESCE, GAETANO, architectural, interior, industrial and graphic designer; b. La Spezia, Italy, Nov. 8, 1939; m. Francesca Lucco, 1969; children: Tata, Tato. Studied architecture, U. Venice, 1959-65, Inst. Indsl. Design, Venice, 1961-65. Ind. artist, filmaker, also co-founder Gruppo N, Padua, Italy, 1959-67; freelance designer Padua, 1962-67, Venice, 1968—; prof. archtl. planning Inst. d'Architecture et d'Etudes Urbaines, Strasbourg, France, 1975—; vis. prof., lectr. Ohio State U., Columbus, 1974, Cooper Union, N.Y., 1975, 79, 80, 83, 85, 86, Pratt Inst., N.Y., 1979, 80, 84, Ecole des Beaux-Arts, Nancy, France, 1981, U. Tech., Compiègne, 1981, Yale U., New Haven, 1983, U. Que., 1984, U. Montreal, 1984, Poly. of Hong Kong, 1985, Domus Acad., Milan, 1986, 87, U. São Paulo, 1987, others. Exhbns. include Galleria Bevilacqua La Masa, Venice, 1961, Hochschule für Gestaltung, Ulm, Fed. Republic Germany, 1964, Finnish Design Ctr., Helsinki, 1964, Keski Suomen Mu., Jyvsakyla, 1965, Galleria Il Canale, Venice, 1966, Galleria La Carabaga, Genoa, 1966, Galleria La Chiocciola, Padua, 1966, Linea Sud Gallery, Naples, 1967, Atelier d'Urbanisme at Architecture, Paris, 1969, Galleria Luca Palazzoli, Milan, 1974, Mus. Arts Dècoratifs, Paris, 1975, Archtl. Assn., London, 1978, JDC Gallery, Tokyo, 1978, Mus. Modern Art, N.Y.C., 1979, Carnegie-Mellon U., Pitts., 1980, Centro de Arte y Comunicación, Buenos Aires, 1981, Yale U., 1983, Mus. Arts Dècoratifs, Montreal, 1984, Harvard U., Cambridge, Mass., 1985, U. Architecture, Hong Kong, 1985, Mus. d'Art Moderne, Strabourg, 1986, Galerie Leptien 3, Frankfurt, 1988, Deutsches Architekturmuseum, Frankfurt, 1988, Max Protetch Gallery, N.Y.C., 1989, Sapporo Brewery, Tokyo, 1989, U. Que., Montreal, 1989, others; represented in collections Mus. Modern Art, N.Y.C., Met. Mus., N.Y.C., Centre Georges Pompidou, Paris, Mus. Arts Dècoratifs, Paris, Keski Suomen Mus., Helsinki, Mus. d'Arte Moderna, Turin, Centre Canadien d'Architecture, Montreal, Mus. Arts Dècoratifs, Montreal, others; contbr. articles to profl. jours. Recipient Locarno Film Festival award, 1968, Tokyo Lighting Design Competition award, 1973, Parc de la Villette award, Paris, 1983, Office Furniture Competition award, Paris, 1983. Address: San Toma 2775, Venice Italy also: 67 Boulevard Brune, 75014 Paris France also: Pesce Ltd 543 Broadway New York NY 10012-3931

PESCH, LEROY ALLEN, physician, educator, health and hospital consultant, business executive; b. Mt. Pleasant, Iowa, June 22, 1931; s. Herbert Lindsey and Mary Clarissa (Tyner) P.; children from previous marriage: Christopher Allen, Brian Lindsey, Daniel Ethan; m. Donna J. Stone, Dec. 28, 1975 (dec. Feb. 1985); stepchildren: Christopher Scott Kneifel, Linda Suzanne Kneifel; m. Gerri Ann Cotton, Sept. 27, 1986; 1 child, Tyner Ford. Student, State U. Iowa, 1948-49, Iowa State U., 1950-52; MD cum laude, Washington U., St. Louis, 1956. Intern Barnes Hosp., St. Louis, 1956-57; rsch. assoc. NIH, Bethesda, Md., 1957-59; asst. resident medicine Grace-New Haven Hosp., New Haven, 1959-60; clin. fellow Yale Med. Sch., New Haven, 1960-61; instr. medicine Yale Med. Sch., 1961-62, asst. prof. medicine, 1962-63, asst. dir. liver study unit, 1961-63; assoc. physician Grace-New Haven Hosp., 1961-63; assoc. prof. medicine Rutgers U., New Brunswick, N.J., 1963-64, prof., 1964-66, chmn. dept. medicine, 1965-66; assoc. dean, prof. medicine Stanford Sch. Medicine, 1966-68; mem. gen. medicine study sect. NIH, 1965-70, chmn., 1969-70; dean, dir. univ. hosps. SUNY, Buffalo, 1968-71; spl. cons. to sec. for health HEW, 1970-75; prof. div. biol. scis. and medicine U. Chgo., 1972-77; prof. pathology Northwestern U., 1977-79; health and hosp. cons.; chmn., chief exec. officer Health Resources Corp. Am., 1981-84; chmn. bd. dirs. Republic Health Corp., 1985-88; chmn., chief exec. officer The Bora Health Group, Seattle, 1987-92, The Pesch Group Cos., Sun Valley, Idaho, 1989—; chmn., CEO Bora Corp., Ketchum, Idaho, 1992—; pres. Genus Tech. Corp., 1995—. Contbr. articles on internal medicine to profl. jours. Bd. dirs. Buffalo Med. Found., 1969-72, Health Orgn., Western N.Y., 1968-71, Joffrey Ballet, N.Y.C., 1980—; trustee Michael Reese Hosp. and Med. Ctr., Chgo., 1971-76, pres., CEO, 1971-77; mem. exec. bd. Auditorium Theatre Coun., Chgo.; trustee W. Clement and Jessie V. Stone Found.; mem. adv. com. Congressional Awards; pres. Pesch Family Found. Sr. asst. surgeon USPHS, 1957-59. Mem. AAAS, Am. Assn. Study of Liver Diseases, Am. Fedn. Clin. Rsch., Am. Soc. Biol. Chemists, Internat. Quadrangle Club, Mid-Am. Club, Capitol Hill Club, Acapulco Yacht Club, Sigma Xi, Alpha Omega Alpha. Home: 713-715 Fairway Rd Sun Valley ID 83353-0012 Office: PO Box 5748 Ketchum ID 83340-5748

PESCI, JOE, actor; b. Newark, N.J., Feb. 9, 1943. Film appearances include Death Collector, 1976, Raging Bull, 1980, I'm Dancing as Fast as I Can, 1982, Easy Money, 1983, Dear Mr. Wonderful, 1983, Eureka, 1983, Once Upon a Time in America, 1984, Tutti Dentro, 1984, Man On Fire, 1987, Moonwalker, 1988, Backtrack, 1988, Lethal Weapon II, 1989, Goodfellas (Acad. award Best Supporting Actor, 1991, D.W. Griffith Award, 1990), Home Alone, 1990, The Super, 1991, JFK, 1991, Lethal Weapon III, 1992, Home Alone II, 1992, The Public Eye, 1992, My Cousin Vinny, 1992, A Bronx Tale, 1993, With Honors, 1994, Jimmy Hollywood, 1994, Casino, 1995; appeared in TV series Half Nelson, 1985. Office: care CAA 9830 Wilshire Blvd Beverly Hills CA 90212-1804*

PESEC, DAVID JOHN, data systems executive; b. Cleve., Apr. 19, 1956; s. Rudolph J. and Martha C. (Kessler) P. BS, Cleve. State U., 1988. Cons. in pvt. practice Cleve., 1976-78; programmer Champion Svc. Corp., Cleve., 1978; sr. systems programmer United Telephone of Ohio, Mansfield, 1978-89; dir. devel. Broderick Data Systems, Mansfield, 1989—. Bd. dirs. ARC, Mansfield, 1989—, Mansfield Emergency Svc., 1986; assoc. pastor Cornerstone Grace Bapt. Ch., 1995—; life mem. Rep. Nat. com., 1991—, Rep. Senatorial Inner Circle, 1991—. Mem. Am. Mgmt. Assn., Assn. Computing Machinery, Intercity Radio Club (pres. 1987-90), NRA, Gideons (v.p. 1992), Profl. Photographers. Republican. Mem. Grace Brethren Ch. Avocations: flying, auto racing. Home: 1633 Hickory Ln Mansfield OH 44905-2945 Office: Broderick Data Systems 777 Laver Rd Mansfield OH 44905-2307

PESEK, JAMES ROBERT, management consultant; b. Chgo., May 30, 1941; s. James F. and Elizabeth A. (Ord) P.; m. Connie A. Snow, Nov. 1992; children: Becky, Shelly. B.S.M.E. with honors, U. Ill., 1964; M.B.A., U. Nebr., 1966. Cert. mgmt. cons. Adminstrv. services mgr. Cummins Engine Co., Columbus, Ind., 1966-68; cons. div. Arthur Andersen & Co., Milw., 1968-72; mgr. distbn. div. ADG, Indpls., 1972-74; mgr. Mgmt. Adv. Services Wolf & Co., Chgo., 1974-79; pres. Ind. Mgmt. Services, Hinsdale, Ill., 1979—; cons.; spkr., tchr. Mem. Am. Prodn. and Inventory Control Soc., Inst. Mgmt. Cons., Am. Arbitration Assn. Home: RR 1 Box 230 Milltown IN 47145-9749

PESERIK, JAMES E., electrical, controls and computer engineer, consultant, forensics and safety engineer, fire cause and origin investigator; b. Beloit, Wis., Sept. 30, 1945; s. Edward J. and G. Lucille Peserik; m. Elaine L. Peserik, May 6, 1972. BSEE, U. Wis., 1968; MS, St. Joseph's U., 1990. Registered profl. engr., registered profl. land surveyor; cert. fire and explosion investigator, cert. fire investigation instr. Development and instrumentation engr. Square D Co., Milw., 1968-71; product engr. I-T-E Imperial Corp., Ardmore, Pa., 1971-72; project engr. Harris-Intertype Corp., Easton, Pa., 1972-74; elec. engr. Day & Zimmerman, Inc., Phila., 1974-76; pvt. practice Coopersburg, Pa., 1976—; sr. elec. engr. S.T. Hudson Engrs., Inc., Phila., 1980-81; mem. adv. coun. Swenson Skills Ctr., Phila., 1990-95. Treas. Salford-Fraconia Joint Parks Commn., Montgomery County, Pa., 1980-83. Mem. IEEE (sec. indsl. applications group Phila. chpt. 1980, chmn. 1981), NSPE, Pa. Soc. Profl. Engrs., Del. Assn. Profl. Engrs. (external affairs com. 1995—), Nat. Fire Protection Assn., Internat. Assn. Arson Investigators, Nat. Assn. Fire Inveestigators. Office: PO Box 181 Coopersburg PA 18036-0181

PESHKIN, MURRAY, physicist; b. Bklyn., May 17, 1925; s. Jacob and Bella Ruth (Zuckerman) P.; m. Frances Julie Ehrlich, June 12, 1955; children—Michael, Sharon, Joel. B.A., Cornell U., 1947, Ph.D., 1951. Instr., then asst. prof. physics Northwestern U., 1951-59; physicist, then sr. scientist Argonne (Ill.) Nat. Lab., 1959—, assoc. dir. physics div., 1972-83; fellow Weizmann Inst. Sci., Rehovoth, Israel, 1959-60, 68-69; sr. scientist SciTech Mus., Aurora, Ill., 1991—. Served with AUS, 1944-46. Home: 838 Parkside Ave Elmhurst IL 60126-4813 Office: Argonne Nat Lab Argonne IL 60439

PESHKIN, SAMUEL DAVID, lawyer; b. Des Moines, Oct. 6, 1925; s. Louis and Mary (Grund) P.; m. Shirley R. Isenberg, Aug. 17, 1947; children—Lawrence Allen, Linda Ann. B.A., State U. Iowa, 1948, J.D., 1951. Bar: Iowa 1951. Ptnr. Bridges & Peshkin, Des Moines, 1953-66, Peshkin & Robinson, Des Moines, 1966-82; Mem. Iowa Bd. Law Examiners, 1970—. Bd. dirs. State U. Iowa Found., 1957—, Old Gold Devel. Fund, 1956—, Sch. Religion U. Iowa, 1966—. Fellow Am. Bar Found., Internat. Soc. Barristers; mem. ABA (chmn. standing com. membership 1959—, ho. of dels. 1968—, bd. govs. 1973—), Iowa Bar Assn. (bd. govs. 1958—, pres. jr. bar sect. 1958-59, award of merit 1974), Inter-Am. Bar Assn., Internat. Bar Assn., Am. Judicature Soc., State U. Iowa Alumni Assn. (dir., pres. 1957). Home: 3598 Yacht Club Dr Apt 1203 Aventura FL 33180-4011

PESMEN, SANDRA (MRS. HAROLD WILLIAM PESMEN), editor; b. Chgo., Mar. 26, 1931; s. Benjamin S. and Emma (Lipschultz) P.; m. Harold W. Pesmen, Aug. 16, 1952; children: Bethann, Curtis. B.S., U. Ill., 1952. Reporter Radio and Community News Service, Chgo., 1952-53; wire editor Champaign-Urbana (Ill.) Courier, 1953; reporter, feature writer Lerner Chgo. N. Side Newspapers, 1953-55; stringer corr. Wayne (Mich.) Eagle, 1958-61; reporter, feature writer Chgo. Daily News, 1968-78; features editor Crain's Chgo. Business mag., 1978-89; corp. features editor Crain Communications, Inc., 1989-95; tchr. feature writing Northwestern U. Evening Sch., 1972-81. Author: Writing for the Media, 1983, Dr. Job's Complete Career Guide, 1995; editor: Career News Service; author syndicated column Dr. Job, 1985—. Recipient Golden Key award Ill. Mental Health Dept., 1966, 71, award Inst. Psychoanalysis, 1971, Penny Mo. award, 1978, Stick o'Type award Chgo. Newspaper Guild, 1978, award AP, 1975, Peter Lisagor award Soc. Profl. Journalists, 1991. Home: 2811 Fern Ave Northbrook IL 60062-5809

PESNER, CAROLE MANISHIN, art gallery owner; b. Boston, Aug. 5, 1937; m. Robert Pesner (dec. 1983); children: Ben, Jonah; m. Martin Cherkasky, 1995. BA, Smith Coll., 1959. Asst. dir. Kraushaar Galleries, Inc., N.Y.C., 1959-86, dir., 1986-90, pres., 1991—. Author, editor publs., catalogues in field. Mem. Art Dealers Assn. Am., Internat. Fine Print Dealers Assn. Office: Kraushaar Galleries Inc 724 5th Ave New York NY 10019-4106

PESNER, SUSAN M., lawyer; b. Suffern, N.Y., July 17, 1951; d. Leon and Doris (Elias) P.; m. Steven M. Elliott, Sept. 22, 1978. BA, Am. U., Washington, 1973, JD, 1976. Bar: Va. 1980, U.S. Ct. Appeals (4th cir.) 1980, U.S. Dist. Ct. (ea. dist.) Va. 1981, U.S. Supreme Ct. 1993. Paralegal Walstad, Wickwire, Peterson, Gavin & Asselin, Vienna, Va., 1978-80; assoc. Walstad, Wickwire, Peterson, Gavin & Asselin, Vienna, 1980, Peterson & Assocs., Vienna, 1980-83; ptnr. Peterson & Pesner, P.C., Vienna, 1983-90, Peterson, Pesner, Cochran & Basha, P.C., Vienna, 1991—, Gordon, Estabrook & Pesner, P.C., McLean, Va., 1992-95, Gordon & Pesner, McLean, 1995—. Mem. ABA, Va. Bar Assn., Va. State Bar (area rep. 1988-91, gov. 1991—, vice chair 1995-96, bd. govs. real estate sect. 1988—), No. Va. Bldg. Industry Assn. (chmn. regional real estate fin. conf. 1985-87), No. Va. Young Lawyers (v.p. 1983-85), Fairfax Bar Assn. Jewish. Avocations: gardening, photography, hiking. Home: 2008 Wolftrap Oaks Ct Vienna VA 22182-5070 Office: Gordon & Pesner LC 7926 Jones Branch Dr #570 Mc Lean VA 22102

PESOLA, GENE RAYMOND, physician, educator; b. Oct. 21, 1952; s. Raymond Lloyd and Helen Eleanor Pesola; m. Helen Rostata, Jan. 5, 1991; 1 child, Gene Richard. BS in Biology magna cum laude, Mich. Technol. U., Houghton, 1974; MD, Wayne State U., 1979. Diplomate Am. Bd. Internal Medicine, also sub-bds. pulmonary medicine and critical care medicine; cert. BCLS, ACLS, ATLS, PALS. Intern Harlem Hosp., N.Y.C., 1979-80; resident U. Tenn. Affiliated Hosps., Memphis, 1980-82; fellow in pulmonary medicine Mt. Sinai Hosp. and Affiliates, N.Y.C., 1982-84; fellow in critical care medicine Meml. Sloan-Kettering Cancer Ctr., N.Y.C., 1984-85, rsch. fellow, 1985-87; asst. prof. medicine and anesthesia Albert Einstein U., Bronx, N.Y., 1988-89; attending physician Mt. Vernon (N.Y.) Emergency Room, 1989-90; rschr. cell/molecular pharmacology and exptl. therapeutics Med. U. S.C., Charleston, 1991-94; attending physician critical care and emergency medicine N.Y. Cmty. Hosp., Bklyn., 1989—; attending physician dept. emergency medicine St. Vincent's Hosp., N.Y.C., 1994—; asst. prof. emergency medicine N.Y. Med. Coll., 1995—. Contbr. chpts. to books, numerous articles to profl. jours.; reviewer for numerous jours. including CHEST and Intensive Care Medicine. Recipient various awards; grantee Am. Fedn. Clin. Rsch., 1992; Pharm. Mfrs. Found. fellow, 1992-94.

PESQUERA MORALES, CARLOS I., government official; b. Santurce, P.R., Aug. 7, 1956; s. Rafael Pesquera and Rainelda Barbara Morales; m. Irasema Rivera, July 30, 1977; children: Carlitos, Frances. BS in Civil Engring., U. P.R., 1978; MS in Structural Engring., Cornell U., 1982, PhD in

Structural Engring., 1984. Engr. 3D/Eye, Inc., Ithaca, N.Y., 1983-85; assoc. prof. civil engring. U. P.R., Mayaguez, 1986-91, prof. civil engring., 1991-92, dir. Infrastructure Rsch. Ctr., 1992-93; sec. transp. and pub. works P.R., 1993—; cons. in field. Contbr. articles to profl. jours.; devel. software systems. Mem. Am. Concrete Inst., P.R. Engrs. Profl. Assn., Tau Beta Pi. Avocations: computers, basketball. Home: Golden Ct II Arterial Hostos Ave PO Box 275 San Juan PR 00918-2995 Office: Commonwealth of PR Dept Transp & Pub Works PO Box 41269 Minillas St San Juan PR 00940-1269

PESTANA, CARLOS, physician, educator; b. Tacoronte, Tenerife, Canary Islands, Spain, June 10, 1936; came to U.S., 1968, naturalized, 1973; s. Francisco and and Blanca (Suarez) P.; m. Myrna Lorena Serrato, Aug. 25, 1966; children—Becky Elizabeth, George Byron. B.S., Nat. U. Mex., 1952, M.D., 1959; Ph.D. in Surgery, U. Minn., 1965. Intern St. Mary of Nazareth Hosp., Chgo., 1959-60; resident Mayo Clinic, Rochester, Minn., 1961-65; surgeon Hosp. 20 de Noviembre Mexico City; asst. prof. surgery Nat. U. Mex., 1966-67; asst. prof. surgery U. Tex. Med. Sch. at San Antonio, 1968-70, asso. prof., 1970-74, prof., 1974—, asso. dean for acad. devel., 1971-73, asso. dean for student affairs, 1973-86, assoc. dean acad. affairs, 1986—. Recipient Edward John Noble Found. award, 1965, Piper Prof. award Minnie Stevens Piper Founds., 1972. Mem. ACS, AMA, Assn. Acad. Surgery, Nat. Bd. Med. Examiners, Tex. Med. Soc., Bexar County Med. Soc., San Antonio Surg. Soc., Soc. for Surgery Alimentary Tract, Assn. Am. Med. Colls., Priestley Soc., Sigma Xi, Alpha Omega Alpha. Home: 10123 N Manton Ln San Antonio TX 78213-1932 Office: 7703 Floyd Curl Dr San Antonio TX 78284-6200

PESTER, JACK CLOYD, oil company executive; b. Seymour, Iowa, Mar. 12, 1935; s. Cloyd Russell Pester and Esther O. (Long) Marston; m. Patricia Joanne Shay, July 21, 1956 (div. 1979); m. Barbara Dee Brazil, Aug. 13, 1979. BS in Bus. Adminstrn., Drake U. Dealer Pester Corp., Grinnell, Iowa, pres., Corydon, Iowa, CEO, Des Moines; sr. v.p. Coastal Corp., Houston; chief exec. Coastal Mart, Inc., Houston, bd. dirs., Am. Mutual Life Ins. Co., Des Moines. Bd. dirs. KFx Inc., Denver. Bd. govs. Drake U. Served with U.S. Army, 1957. Reciepient Disting. Alumni award Drake U., 1979, One in a Hundred Alumni award Drake U., 1981. Republican. Roman Catholic. Clubs: Houston City. Home: 11 Auburn Pl Houston TX 77005-2162

PESTKA, STANLEY, secondary school principal. Prin. Granby Meml. Mid. Sch. Recipient Blue Ribbon award U.S. Dept. Edn., 1990-91. Office: Granby Meml Mid Sch 321 Salmon Brook St Granby CT 06035-1804

PESTLE, JOHN WILLIAM, lawyer; b. Brattleboro, Vt., Feb. 28, 1948; s. Ray Irving and Annette Adelia (Lilley) P.; m. Penelope Mendenhall, Oct. 11, 1969; children: William Joseph, Sarah Lilley. BA magna cum laude, Harvard U., 1970; MA magna cum laude, Yale U., 1972; JD magna cum laude, U. Mich., 1975. Bar: Mich. 1975, U.S. Dist. Ct. (we. dist.) Mich. 1975, U.S. Dist. Ct (ea. dist.) Mich. 1978, U.S. Ct. Appeals (6th and D.C. cirs.) 1979, U.S. Supreme Ct. 1980. Assoc. Varnum, Riddering, Wierengo & Christenson, Grand Rapids, Mich., 1975-80; ptnr. Varnum, Riddering, Schmidt & Howlett, Grand Rapids, 1980—, co-chmn. energy and telecommunications practice group, 1986—. Contb. articles to profl. jours. Pres. Blodgett Neighborhood Assn., Grand Rapids, 1982-88; bd. dirs. Blodgett Meml. Med. Ctr. Community Rels., 1983-88, Mich. Trails coun. Girl Scouts U.S., 1982-87; trustee Harvard Glee Club Found., 1987—; sec. Nuclear Non-Oper. Owners Group, 1988-93. Mem. ABA, Fed. Energy Bar Assn. (cogeneration and small power prodn. commn.), Mich. State Bar Assn. (chmn. mcpl. utilities commn., chmn. pub. corp. law sect.), State Bar Mich. Found., Grand Rapids Bar Assn., Am. Pub. Power Assn. (vice chmn. legal sect. 1985-86, chmn. 1986-87), Harvard Club Western Mich. (sec. 1976-82). Avocations: skiing, skating, photography, gardening. Home: 515 Plymouth Ave SE Grand Rapids MI 49506-2841

PESTUREAU, PIERRE GILBERT, literature educator, literary critic, editor; b. Civray, Vienne, France, Feb. 8, 1933; came to U.S., 1991; s. Pierre and Madeleine (Bernard) P.; divorced; children: Veronique, Christophe, Charlotte; m. Ann Shepstone Wakefield, July 12, 1980. MA in Lit., U. Poitiers, France, 1955; profl. degree, Paris, 1956; PhD, Sorbonne U., Paris, 1975, SD in Lit., 1981. Prof. Nat. Edn., France, 1956-65, Tahiti, 1966-70; prof. The French Embassy, Madagascar, 1971-73, U. Natal, Durban, South Africa, 1974-80, U. Ocean Indien, La Reunion, France, 1981-83, U. Nantes, France, 1986-91, Loyola U., Chgo., 1991—; lectr. Alliance Francaise, South Africa, U.S., 1976-96; vis. prof. San Diego State U., spring 1990. Author: Boris Vian, 1978, Dictionnaire Vian, 1985, 93; editor: Boris Vian Oeuvres Choisies, 1991, Romans, 1992, 93, 94, Andrè Brink, 1992, Raymond Queneau, 1993, 94, 95, 96. Rep. Prof.'s Union, France, 1956-70. Sgt. Svc. Corps French Mil., 1960-62. Decorated chevalier Palmes Académiques. Office: Loyola U 6525 N Sheridan Rd Chicago IL 60626-5311

PESUT, TIMOTHY S., investment advisor, professional speaker, consultant; b. Gary, Ind., June 30, 1956; s. Anton and Virginia Udean (Carahoff) P.; m. Michelle Angela Durdov, May 25, 1985; children: Ariel Fay, Caitlin Michelle. AAS in Elec. Engring. Tech., Purdue U., 1978, AAS Supervision, BS Elec. Engring. Tech., 1980. CFP Coll. Fin. Planning; cert. funds specialist, trust and estate planning advisor, investment mgmt. cons.; registered investment advisor. Cardiology clin. rsch. assoc. Cordis Corp., Miami, Fla., 1980-82, neurosurg. specialist, 1982; investment broker A. G. Edwards Sons, Merrillville, Ind., 1982-86, Shearson Lehman, Sarasota, Fla., 1986-88; portfolio mgr. Prudential Securities, Inc., Venice, Fla., 1988-91; registered investment advisor First Southeastern & Co., Sarasota, Fla., 1991—; arbitrator Am. Arbitration Assn., 1992—. Columnist Money Talks, 1988—, Money Mgmt., 1991—. Guardian Ad Litem 12th Dist. Ct., Sarasota, 1988—; founding mem. Anthony Robbins Found., 1990; mem. bd. Sarasota County Jr. Achievement; pres. Wilkinson Sch. Adv. Bd. Lc. cpl. USMC, 1974-76. Mem. Divemaster-Profl. Assn. Diving Instrs., Nat. Spkrs. Assn., Toastmasters Internat. (area gov. of yr. 1994, select disting. gulf divsn. gov. 1995, dist. 47 lt. gov. mktg., dist. 47 treas. 1996). Republican. Methodist. Avocations: scuba diving, skiing, sailing, woodworking, fine arts. Office: First Southeastern & Co 1819 Main St Ste 601 Sarasota FL 34236-5984

PESZKE, MICHAEL ALFRED, psychiatrist, educator; b. Deblin, Poland, Dec. 19, 1932; s. Alfred Bartlomiej and Eugenia Halina (Grebocka) P.; m. Alice Margaret Sherman, Sept. 20, 1958; children: Michele Halina Olender, Michael Alexander. BA, Trinity Coll., Dublin, Ireland, 1956; MB, BCh, BAO, Dublin U., 1956. Bd. cert. psychiatrist. Staff psychiatrist Yale Student Health Svc., New Haven, 1961-64; asst. prof. sch. medicine U. Chgo., 1964-68; cons. psychiatrist Wesleyan U., Middletown, Conn., 1968-70; asst. prof. Sch. Medicine U. Conn., Farmington, 1970-73, assoc. prof., 1973-80, prof. psychiatry, 1980-90; clin. prof. U. Md. Sch. Medicine, Balt., 1991—; chief psychiatry Perry Point (Md.) VA Med. Ctr., 1991—; dir. psychiat. clin. svcs. John Dempsey Hosp., U. Conn. Health Ctr., Farmington, 1983-87; chief VA Med. Ctr., Newington, Conn., 1987-90. Author: Involuntary Treatment of the Mentally Ill: The Problem of Autonomy, 1975, Battle for Warsaw, 1939-44, 1995; co-author: (edited by L.A. Pervin, L.R. Reik, W. Dalrymple) The College Drop-out and the Utilization of Talent, 1966, (edited by J. Zusman, E. Bertsch) The Future of Psychiatric State Hospitals, 1975; contbr. articles to profl. jours.; book reviewer Univ. Chgo. Law Rev., 1968, Conn. Law Rev., 1976, Am. Jour. Psychiatry, 1976-93. Mem. Conn.'s Jud. Law Revision Com., 1982-86, Whiting Forensic Adv. Bd., 1975-87; co-chair Commr. Mental Health's Com. to Re-write Conn. Civil Commitment Statutes, 1976-77. WHO travel fellow, United Kingdom, Denmark, Poland, 1977; U. Conn. Research grantee, 1972-87. Fellow APA (life); mem. Am. Coll. Psychiatrists, Soc. for Mil. History. Avocations: World War II military and diplomatic history, sailing. Home: PO Box 165 Perry Point MD 21902-0165

PETACQUE, ARTHUR M., journalist; b. Chgo., July 20, 1924; s. Ralph David and Fay Nora (Brauner) P.; m. Regina Battinus, Dec. 10, 1944; children: Susan Wendy Petacque Leshin, William Scott. Student, U. Ill., 1940-42; PhD (hon.), So. Ill. U., 1987. With Chgo. Sun, 1942-47; with Chgo. Sun-Times, 1947—, investigative reporter, 1957—, columnist, 1974—; crime editor World Book Ency., 1970-75; lectr. various univs. and civic orgns. Recipient Page One awards for outstanding journalism Chgo. Newspaper Guild, 1949, 57, 59, 62, 63, 65, 68; Joseph M. Fay Meml. award Chgo. Newspaper Reporters Assn., 1960; Prof. Jacob Scher-Theta Sigma Phi Daily Newswriting award Chgo. chpt. Theta Sigma Phi, 1964; John Baptist Scalabrini award for leadership Am. Community Italian Ancestry, 1966; awards for investigative reporting and spot news AP, 1963, 66, 68, (2) 74, 76; Marshall Field award for outstanding editorial contbn. in behalf of Chgo. Sun-Times, 1968; Pulitzer Prize for gen. reporting, 1974; State of Israel Prime Minister's medal, 1976; Dante award Civic Com. Italian Americans, 1980; UPI award for best spot news coverage Ill., 1980; Emmy award for ABC-TV local news spot reporting, 1984; Award for Long and Dedicated Newspaper Reporting on Crime and the Criminal Justice System, Ill. Acad. Criminology, 1985; named to Chgo. Journalism Hall of Fame Chgo Headline Club, 1990. Mem. Chgo. Newspaper Guild, Jewish War Vets. (hon.), Sigma Delta Chi, Sigma Alpha Mu. Jewish. Club: B'nai B'rith. Office: 401 N Wabash Ave Chicago IL 60611-3532 *Have tried to be fair, careful and objective in my profession, realizing that what we say about the person we write about has not only an effect on the subject but his family and friends.*

PETAK, WILLIAM JOHN, systems management educator; b. Johnstown, Pa., June 23, 1932; s. Val Andrew and Lola Agatha (Boroski) P.; m. Ramona Janet Cayuela, Dec. 28, 1957; children: Elizabeth Ann Petak-Aaron, William Matthew, Michael David. BS in Mech. Engring., U. Pitts., 1956; MBA, U. So. Calif., 1963, DPA, 1969. Engr. Northrop Corp., Hawthorne, Calif., 1956-59; test engr. Wyle Labs., El Segundo, Calif., 1959-63; we. regional mgr. Instrument div. Budd Co., Phoenixville, Pa., 1963-69; v.p., dir. J.H. Wiggins Co., Redondo Beach, Calif., 1969-81; prof. systems mgmt. U. So. Calif., L.A., 1982—, exec. dir. Inst. Safety and Sys. Mgmt., 1987—; chmn. earthquake mitigation com. Nat. Com. on Property Ins., Boston, 1990-92; mem. com. on natural disasters NRC, Washington, 1985-91, mem. U.S. nat. com. for the decade for natural disaster reduction, 1989-92. Co-author: Natural Hazard Risk Assessment and Public Policy, 1982, Politics and Economics of Earthquake Hazard Reduction, 1986, Disabled Persons and Earthquake Hazards, 1988; editor spl. issue Pub. Adminstrn. Rev., 1985. Commr. County of Los Angeles, 1994—; mem. policy bd. So. Calif. Earthquake Prep. Project, L.A., 1986-92; trustee Marymount Coll., Palos Verdes, Calif., 1974—. Sgt. U.S. Army, 1950-52. Mem. Soc. for Risk Analysis, Earthquake Engring. Rsch. Inst., Am. Soc. for Pub. Adminstrn., Sigma Xi. Republican. Roman Catholic. Avocations: skiing, fishing, hiking. Office: U So Calif MC 0021 Inst Safety and Systems Mgmt Los Angeles CA 90089

PETCHESKY, ROSALIND POLLACK, political science and women's studies educator; b. Bay City, Tex., Aug. 16, 1942. BA, Smith Coll., 1964; MA, Columbia U., 1966, PhD, 1974. Prof. Hunter Coll. CUNY. Author: (books) The Individual's Rights and International Organization, 1966, Abortion and Women's Choice: The State, Sexuality and Reproductive Freedom, 1984, 2d edit. 1990 (Joan Kelly Meml. prize Am. Hist. Assn. 1984). Founder Internat. Reproductive Rights Rsch. Action Group. MacArthur fellow, 1995. Office: CUNY Hunter Coll Dept Polit Sci 695 Park Ave New York NY 10021

PETER See L'HUILLIER, PETER

PETER, ARNOLD PHILIMON, lawyer; b. Karachi, Pakistan, Apr. 3, 1957; came to U.S., 1968; s. Kundan Lal and Irene Primrose (Mall) P. BS, Calif. State U., Long Beach, 1981; JD, Loyola U., L.A., 1984; MS, Calif. State U., Fresno, 1991. Bar: Calif. 1985, U.S. Dist. Ct. (ea., so., no. and cen. dists.) Calif. 1986, U.S. Ct. Appeals (9th cir.) 1989, U.S. Ct. Appeals (11th cir.) 1990. Law clk. appellate dept. Superior Ct., L.A., 1984-85, U.S. Dist. Ct. (ea. dist.) Calif., Fresno, 1986-88; assoc. Pepper, Hamilton & Scheetz, L.A., 1988-89, McDermott, Will & Emery, P.A., L.A., 1989-90, Cadwalader, Wickersham & Taft, L.A., 1990-91; labor and employment counsel City of Fresno, Calif., 1991-94; dir. labor rels. and litigation Universal Studios, Hollywood, Calif.; adj. prof. law San Joaquin (Calif.) Sch. Law, 1993—, Calif. State U., Fresno, 1993—, acad. inquiry officer, 1993—, Calif. State U., Fresno. Contbr. articles to profl. jours. Mem. ABA, L.A. County Bar Assn. (mem. conf. of dels., com. on fed. cts.), Calif. State Bar Assn. (chmn. com. on fed. cts., exec. com. labor and employment law sect.), L.A. Athletic Club. Office: Universal Studios Bldg #SC79 100 Universal City Pl Universal City CA 91608

PETER, FRANCES MARCHBANK, author, editor, publisher, research agency administrator; b. Paterson, N.J.; d. Frederick James Marchbank, Jr. and Frances Grace (Witbeck) Marchbank Filter. BA with honors, Syracuse (N.Y.) U., 1959; postgrad. NYU, U. Md., The Wharton Sch. Tech. writer GE Corp., 1959-60; assoc. producer Met. Opera Broadcasts, 1960-62; treas. Souvaine Assocs., Inc., 1960-62; asst. to music critic Edward Downes, 1962-63; staff program mgmt. Gen. Electric Co., Wiesbaden, W.Ger., 1963-65, Fed. Electric Co., Frankfurt, W.Ger., 1965, Page Communications Engrs., Inc., Saigon, Vietnam and Tripoli, Libya, 1966-70; head publs. dept., mng. editor BioSci., jour. Am. Inst. Biol. Scis., Washington, 1972-75; editor Commn. on Life Scis., NRC-NAS, Washington, 1975-88, dep. dir. food and nutrition bd., 1987-90, dir. long-range planning for adminstrn., 1990-92; v.p. Peter, Marchbank and Palmer, Inc., 1980-92; cons. in field, 1992—. Recipient cert. merit Am. Inst. Biol. Scis., 1975. Mem. Soc. Scholarly Pub. (charter, editor SSP Letter 1982-84, asst. sec.-treas. 1982-84), Washington Ind. Writers, Coun. Biology Editors (publs. com.), Washington Book Pubs., Delta Delta Delta. Editorial bd. Am. Biology Tchr., 1975-76. Home and Office: 2101 Connecticut Ave NW Washington DC 20008-1728

PETER, KENNETH SHANNON, elementary school educator; b. Chgo., Apr. 2, 1945; s. Joseph Francis and Kathleen Daley (Shannon) P.; m. Susan Ann Richardson, Aug. 27, 1977; children: Megan Elyse, Evan Michael. BA in Elem. Edn., Occidental Coll., L.A., 1967; MA in Phys. Edn., U. Laverne, Calif., 1978; MA in Ednl. Adminstrn., Calif. State U., L.A., 1988. Cert. in elem. edn., gifted and talented, ednl. adminstrn., Calif. Elem. tchr. L.A. Unified Sch. Dist., 1968; elem. tchr. Pasadena (Calif.) Unified Sch. Dist., 1969-77, phys. edn. specialist, 1978-90, project tchr., 1990—; cons. in phys. edn.; mem. program quality rev. Pasadena Unified Sch. Dist., 1990—; bd. dirs., presenter Calif. Poly Elem. Workshop Com., 1981-89. Author monographs: Characteristics of Elementary Physical Education Specialists, 1978, Comparison of Specialist and Non-Specialist Taught Studies, 1988. Mem. nat. sch. site com. Am. Heart Assn., Dallas, 1994—, mem. Jump for Heart task force, So. Calif., 1978—; area dir. Dem. Party, Calif., 1963-74; mem. sch. site coun. Washington Sch., Glendora, Calif., 1993—. Named Outstanding Vol., Am. Heart Assn., 1994, Tchr. of the Yr., Pasadena Unified Schs., 1985; recipient Award of Distinction, Calif. Dept. Health Svcs., 1992. Mem. Calif. Acad. Phys. Edn. (sr. assoc.), Calif. Assn. Health, Phys. Edn., Recreation and Dance (elem. phys. edn. chair 1978—), Phi Kappa Phi, Phi Alpha Theta, Delta Phi Epsilon. Democrat. Roman Catholic. Avocations: tennis, fitness. Home: 1665 S Calmgrove Ave Glendora CA 91740-5907 Office: Pasadena Unified Sch Dist 351 S Hudson Ave Pasadena CA 91101-3507

PETER, LAURA ANNE, lawyer; b. Santa Monica, Calif., June 17, 1964; d. Gabriel George and Barbara Joyce (Leomazzi) P. BS, Cornell U., 1986; MA, U. Chgo., 1988; JD, Santa Clara U., 1992; LLM, U. London, U.K., 1994. Bar: U.S. Patent and Trademark Office, 1989, Calif. 1992, U.S. Dist. Ct. (no. dist.) Calif. 1992, U.S. Ct. Appeals (9th cir.) 1992. Assoc. Law Offices of Rafael Chodos, Santa Monca, 1995—; mgr. Rancho de Vino, Monterey, Calif., 1991-93. Contbr. articles to profl. jours. Fellow The UN Grad. Study Programme, Geneva, Switzerland, 1987; recipient Hague (The Netherlands) Acad. Internat., 1993. Mem. ABA, Internat. Bar Assn., Internat. Lit. and Artistic Assn., Licensing Execs. Soc. Office: Law Offices Rafael Chodos Ste 303 233 Wilshire Blvd Santa Monica CA 90401

PETER, PHILLIPS SMITH, lawyer; b. Washington, Jan. 24, 1932; s. Edward Compston and Anita Phillips (Smith) P.; m. Jania Jayne Hutchins, Apr. 8, 1961; children: Phillips Smith Peter Jr., Jania Jayne Hutchins Stone. BA, U. Va., 1954, JD, 1959. Bar: Calif. 1959. Assoc. McCutchen, Doyle, Brown, Enerson, San Francisco, 1959-63; with GE (and subs.), various locations, 1963-94; v.p. corp. bus. devel. GE (and subs.), 1973-76; v.p. GE (and subs.), Washington, 1976-79, v.p. corp. govtl. rels., 1980-94; counsel, head govt. rels. dept. Reed Smith Shaw & McClay, Washington, 1994—; chmn. bd. govs. Bryce Harlow Found., 1990-92, bd. dirs. Mem. editl. bd. Va. Law Rev., 1957-59. Trustee Howard U., 1981-89; v.p. Fed. City Coun., Washington, 1979-85; bd. dirs. Carlton, 1987-90, 95, pres., 1995—. With transp. corps U.S. Army, 1954-56. Mem. Calif. Bar Assn., Order of Coif, Wee Burn Club, Ea. Yacht Club, Farmington Country Club, Ponte Vedra Club, Lago Mar Club, Landmark Club, Congl. Country Club, Georgetown Club, Chevy Chase Club, Pisces Club, F Street Club, Fairfax Club, Club Washington (bd. dirs. 1990—), Coral Beach and Tennis Club, Johns Island Club, Omicron Delta Kappa. Episcopalian. Home: 10805 Tara Rd Potomac MD 20854-1341 also: Johns Island 1000 Beach Rd Vero Beach FL 32963-3429

PETER, RICHARD ECTOR, zoology educator; b. Medicine Hat, Alta., Can., Mar. 7, 1943; s. Arthur E. and Josephine (Wrobleski) P.; m. Leona L. Booth, Dec. 27, 1965; children: Jason E., Matthew T.B. BSc with honors, U. Alta., 1965; PhD, U. Wash., 1969. Postdoctoral fellow U. Bristol, Eng., 1969-70; asst. prof. U. Alta., Edmonton, 1971-74, assoc. prof., 1974-79, prof., 1979—, chmn. dept. zoology, 1983-89, 90-92, dean of sci., 1992—. Contbr. over 270 papers to sci. publs. Recipient Pickford medal Internat. Com. on Comparative Endocrinology, 1985. Fellow AAAS, Royal Soc. Can.; mem. Can. Soc. Zoology (pres. 1991-92), Endocrine Soc., Soc. for Study of Reproduction, Internat. Soc. Neuroendocrinology, Can. Coun. of Univ. Biology Chmn. (pres. 1986-87), Internat. Fedn. Comparative Endocrinol. Socs. (pres. 1989-93), Canadian Conf. of Deans of Sci., 1995-96 (pres.).

PETER, SEBASTIAN AUGUSTINE, endocrinologist; b. St. Georges, Grenada, Jan. 20, 1944; came to U.S., 1975; s. Sidney Augustine and Cisly (Scoon) P.; m. Angela Missouri Sherman, July 18, 1970; children: Sebastian Augustine Jr., Senaka Akalbi. MBBS, U. W.I., 1969. Intern U. W.I., Nassau, 1970; resident in medicine Dalhousie U., Halifax, N.S., Can., 1971-72; resident in medicine U. Ottawa, Ont., Can., 1972-74, resident in endocrinology, 1974-75; fellow in endocrinology SUNY Health Sci. Ctr., Bklyn., 1975-76, assoc. clin. prof. medicine, 1992—; chief of endocrinology St. Mary's Hosp., Bklyn., 1992—. Contbr. articles to profl. jours. Recipient Community award Grenada Ex-Students Assn., 1991. Democrat. Avocations: music, jazz, playing musical instrument, reading. Home and Office: 1717 Ditmas Ave Brooklyn NY 11226-6603

PETER, VAL JOSEPH, elementary and secondary education educator, social welfare administrator, priest; b. Omaha, Nov. 20, 1934. PhB, Gregorian U., Rome, 1956, Licentiate in Sacred Theology, 1960; STD, U. St. Thomas, Rome, 1965; JCD, Lateran U., Rome, 1967; PhD (hon.), Creighton U., 1992, Coll. St. Mary, 1993. Ordained priest Roman Cath. Ch., 1960. Defender of bond Archdiocese of Omaha, 1966—; chmn. dept. theology Coll. of St. Mary, Omaha, 1966-70; prof. theology Creighton U., Omaha, 1970-84; exec. dir. Father Flanagan's Boys Home, Boys Town, Nebr., 1984—. Bd. dirs. St. Joseph Ctr. for Mental Health, 1985—, Boy Scouts Am., 1985—, NCCJ, 1985-93. Recipient Disting. Faculty award Creighton U., 1983, Presdl. citation, 1984, Archbishop Gerald T. Bergan award, 1986, Svc. to Mankind award Sertoma Internat., 1987, Creighton Prep Alumnus of Yr. award, 1988, Douglas County Bd. Commrs. award, 1990, Person of Yr. award U. Notre Dame, 1991, River City Roundup Heritage award, 1992, Toastmasters Internat. Comm. and Leadership award, 1992, Pope John XXIII award Roncalli H.S., 1993, AK-SAR-BEN Excellence in Edn. award, 1993, Nat. Direct Mktg. award Direct Mktg. Assn., 1993, Golden Apple award Met. C.C. Found., 1994, Silver Beaver award Boy Scouts Am., 1995; named Outstanding Humanitarian, Order Sons of Italy, 1987, Raoul Wallenberg Humanitarian of Yr., 1991. Mem. Nat. Assn. Homes and Svcs. for Children (bd. dirs. 1986-95), League Civil Rights (bd. dirs. 1986-92), Am. Our Sunday Visitor Inst. (bd. dirs. 1986—), Greater Omaha C. of C. (exec. com. 1991—), Omaha Cmty. Partnership, Canon Law Soc. Am., Cath. Theol. Soc. Am., Omaha 2000, Equestrian Order of Holy Sepulchre, 1989. Roman Catholic. Home and Office: Father Flanagan's Boy's Home 14100 Crawford St Boys Town NE 68010-7520

PETERING, DAVID HAROLD, chemistry educator; b. Peoria, Ill., Sept. 16, 1942; married, 1966; 2 children. BA, Wabash Coll., 1964; PhD in Biochemistry, U. Mich., 1969. From asst. prof. to assoc. prof. chemistry and biochemistry U. Wis., Milw., 1971-82, prof. chemistry, 1983—; sr. vis. fellow Nat. Inst. Environ. Health Sci., 1981—; dir. Marine and Freshwater Biomed. Scis. Ctr. Fellow Northwestern U., Am. Cancer Soc., 1969-71. Mem. Am. Chem. Soc., Am. Soc. Biochem. Molecular Biology, Sigma Xi. Achievements include research in the metabolism of essential transition metals zinc, iron, and toxic metals and their complexes, role of zinc in normal and tumor cell proliferation, of cadmium in biological toxicity and various metal complexes in cancer chemotherapy, biochemistry of metallothionein. Home: 7229 N Santa Monica Blvd Milwaukee WI 53217-3506 Office: U Wis Marine & Freshwater Biomed Sci PO Box 413 Milwaukee WI 53201-0413

PETERING, JANICE FAYE, hotel executive; b. Covington, Ky., Feb. 10, 1950; d. Edward Charles Petering Sr. and Shirley Ellen (McKenzie) Petering Brancucci. Student, Eastern Ky. U., 1969; cert., Ramada Mgmt. Inst., 1982. Cert. hotel adminstr. Night auditor Caesars Palace Hotel, Las Vegas, Nev., 1970-77; chief rack clk. Caesars Palace Hotel, Las Vegas, 1979-80, supr. accounts receivable, 1980-82, casino comptr., 1982-83, ops. comptr., 1983-85; exec. asst. to hotel mgr. Tropicana Hotel & Country Club, Las Vegas, 1977-79, hotel mgr., 1985-86; hotel mgr. MGM Marina Casino and Hotel, Las Vegas, 1986-87; dir. hotel ops. MGM MArina Casino and Hotel, Las Vegas, 1987-90; hotel mgr. Vacation Village, Las Vegas, Nev., 1991-93; internal controller, fin. analyst Continental Hotel Casino, Las Vegas, 1993—. Mem. Internat. Assn. Hospitality Accts., Las Vegas Hotel-Motel Assn., Las Vegas Hotel Mgrs. Assn., Network of Exec. Women in Hospitality. Roman Catholic. Avocations: bowling, golf, softball, reading. Office: Hotel Continental Inc 4100 Paradise Rd Las Vegas NV 89109-6528

PETERKIN, ALBERT GORDON, retired education educator; b. Phila., May 25, 1915; s. Albert Gordon and Eleanor Frances (Fricke) P.; m. Helen Webster, June 14, 1947; children: Eleanor Fricke, Scott Boddington, Mark Webster. BA, U. Pa., 1936; MAT, Harvard U., 1946; EdD, Columbia U., 1954. Cert. sch. adminstr., N.J., Conn., Ill. Tchr. Arms Acad., Shelburne Falls, Mass., 1938-39, Park Sch. of Buffalo, Snyder, N.Y., 1939-41; asst. prof. Lehigh U., Bethlehem, Pa., 1948-55; founding supt. Watchung Hills Regional H.S., Warren, N.J., 1955-60; supt. Westport (Conn.) Pub. Schs., 1960-70, Winnetka (Ill.) Sch. Dist. 36, 1971-77; prof. edn. Vanderbilt U., Nashville, 1977-81; ret., 1981; cons. Nat. Assn. Sch. Bus. Officers, Washington, 1968-70, Tenn. State U., Nashville, 1980-81; advisor Coun. Basic Edn., Washington, 1975; trustee Country Sch., Madison, Conn., 1985-91; chmn. master's program Iranian Sch. Devel., 1978-80, assessment instrument student devel., 1974; initiator Cooperative Individualized Reading Project, U.S. Office Edn., 1970-73. Initiator Urban Coalition Sch. Study, Bridgeport, Conn., 1969-70; pres. Friends of Libr., Madison, 1984-85; prodr. cmty. TV, Madison, 1984-90; mem. Madison Inland Wetlands Commn., 1985—, chmn., 1990-92. Lt. comdr. USNR, 1941-45. John Hay fellow Greenwood Found., 1965; Kettering Found. fellow, 1966, 69; Whitehead fellow Harvard Sch. Edn., 1970-71; named to Supt.'s Hall of Fame Sch. Mgmt. Study Group, 1973. Mem. Am. Assn. Sch. Adminstrs., Suburban Sch. Supts., Madison Country Club, Madison Beach Club, Phi Delta Kappa. Mem. Religious Soc. of Friends. Avocations: garden design, travel, home video, golf, music. Home: 210 Neck Rd Madison CT 06443-2720

PETERKIN, GEORGE ALEXANDER, JR., marine transportation company executive; b. Baton Rouge, Apr. 12, 1927; s. George Alexander and Genevieve (Favrot) P.; m. Nancy Girling, Jan. 27, 1965; children—George Alexander III, Julie, John Thomas, Susan, Lynn. B.B.A., U. Tex., 1948. With Dixie Carriers, Inc., Galveston, Tex.; soliciting freight agt. Dixie Carriers, Inc., New Orleans, Houston, 1949-50; asst. to pres. Dixie Carriers, Inc., Houston, 1953, pres., 1953-73, chmn. bd., 1973—; pres. Kirby Industries, Inc., Houston, 1973-76; pres. Kirby Corp., 1976-95, chmn. bd., 1995—. Bd. dirs. Tex. Med. Center, 1965—, Living Bank, 1968-86; trustee Tex. Children's Hosp., 1964—. Served with USN, 1945-46. Mem. World Pres. Orgn., Chief Execs. Orgn., Am. Bur. Shipping, Ramada Club, Houston Country Club, Bayou Club, Univ. Club N.Y. Avocations: swimming, running, golf, shooting. Home: 5787 Indian Cir Houston TX 77057-1302 Office: Kirby Corp 1775 Saint James Pl Ste 300 Houston TX 77056-3403

PETERLE, TONY JOHN, zoologist, educator; b. Cleve., July 7, 1925; s. Anton and Anna (Katic) P.; m. Thelma Josephine Coleman, July 30, 1949; children—Ann Faulkner, Tony Scott. BS, Utah State U., 1949; MS, U. Mich., 1950, PhD (univ. scholar), 1954; Fulbright scholar, U. Aberdeen,

Scotland, 1954-55; postgrad., Oak Ridge Inst. Nuclear Studies, 1961. With Niederhauser Lumber Co., 1947-49, Macfarland Tree Svc., 1949-51; rsch. biologist Mich. Dept. Conservation, 1951-54; asst. dir. Rose Lake Expt. Sta., 1955-59; leader Ohio Coop. Wildlife Rsch. unit U.S. Fish and Wildlife Svc., Dept. Interior, 1959-63; asso. prof., then prof. zoology Ohio State U., Columbus, 1959-89, prof. emeritus, 1989; chmn. faculty population and environmental biology Ohio State U., 1968-69, chmn. dept. zoology, 1969-81, dir. program in environ. biology, 1970-71; liaison officer Internat. Union Game Biologists, 1965-93; co-organizer, chmn. internat. affairs com., mem. com. ecotoxicology XIII Internat. Congress Game Biology, 1979-80; proprietor The Iron Works; pvt. cons., 1989—; mem. com. rev. EPA pesticide decision making Nat. Acad. Scis.-NRC; mem. vis. scientists program Am. Inst. Biol. Scis.-ERDA, 1971-77; mem. com. pesticides Nat. Acad. Scis., com. on emerging trends in agr. and effects on fish and wildlife; mem. ecology com. of sci. adv. council EPA, 1979-87; mem. research units coordinating com. Ohio Coop. Wildlife and Fisheries, 1963-89; vis. scientist EPA, Corvallis, 1987. Author: Wildlife Toxicology, 1991; editor: Jour. of Wildlife Mgmt., 1969-70, 84-85, 2020 Vision Meeting the Fish and Wildlife Conservation Challenges of the 21st Century, 1992. Served with AUS, 1943-46. Fellow AAAS, Am. Inst. Biol. Scis., Ohio Acad. Sci.; mem. Wildlife Disease Assn., Wildlife Soc. (regional rep. 1962-67, v.p. 1968, pres. 1972, Leopold award 1990, hon. mem. 1990, Profl. award of merit North Ctrl. sect. 1993), Nat. Audubon Soc. (bd. dirs. 1985-87), Ecol. Soc., INTECOL-NSF panel U.S.-Japan Program, Xi Sigma Pi, Phi Kappa Phi. Home: 4072 Klondike Rd Delaware OH 43015-9513 Office: Ohio State U Dept Zoology 1735 Neil Ave Columbus OH 43210-1220

PETERMAN, BRUCE EDGAR, aircraft company executive; b. Merrill, Wis., Jan. 27, 1931; s. Neton Elmer and Grace Elisabeth (Schroeder) P.; m. Constance Lenore Callsen, Feb. 9, 1952; children: Michael Lee, Jeffrey Dean, Elizabeth Ann. AA in Aero. Engring., Spartan Coll., 1951; BS in Aero. Engring., Wichita State Univ., 1955, MS in Aero. Engring., 1961. With detail design and drafting dept. Beech Aircraft Corp., Wichita, Kans., 1951-53; with design, flight test and tech. engring. depts. Cessna Aircraft Co., Wichita, 1953-72, chief engr. Wallace div., 1972-81, v.p. product engring., 1981-87, v.p. ops., 1987-89, sr. v.p., 1989—; trustee U. Kans. Ctr. for Rsch., Lawrence, 1985-88, Cessna Found., 1987—; mem. industry adv. com. Nat. Inst. Aviation Rsch., Wichita State U., 1985—; mem. aerospace engring. adv. com. U. Kans., Lawrence, 1975-89, engring. dept. adv. com., 1987-91; mem. Kans. Tech. Enterprise Corp. Ctrs. Com., 1929—, bd. dirs., 1994-96. Bd. dirs. Endowment Assn. Wichita State U., 1993—; co-chair Kans. Math. and Sci. Coalition, 1992-96. Assoc. fellow AIAA; mem. Soc. Automotive Engrs. (aerospace coun. 1976-91, tech. bd. 1987-91). Avocations: instrument rated multi-engine pilot. Home: 15606 Moscelyn Ln Goddard KS 67052-9331 Office: Cessna Aircraft Co PO Box 7706 Wichita KS 67277-7706

PETERMAN, DONALD, cinematographer. Cinematographer: (films) When a Stranger Calls, 1979, Rich and Famous, 1981, King of the Mountain, 1981, Young Doctors in Love, 1982, Kiss Me Goodbye, 1982, Flashdance, 1983 (Academy award nomination best cinematography 1983), Splash, 1984, Best Defense, 1984, Mass Appeal, 1984, American Flyer, 1985, Cocoon, 1985, Star Trek IV: The Voyage Home, 1986 (Academy award nomination best cinematography 1986), Gung Ho, 1986, Planes, Trains and Automobiles, 1987, She's Having a Baby, 1988, She's Out of Control, 1989, Point Break, 1991, Mr. Saturday Night, 1992, Addams Family Values, 1993. Office: The Gersh Agency 232 N Canon Dr Beverly Hills CA 90210-5302

PETERS, A. WINNIETT, leaf tobacco merchant, exporter; b. Tarboro, N.C., Mar. 18, 1927; s. A. Winniett and Ethel (Battle) P.; m. Sarah Walston, June 9, 1951; children: Winniett Jr. (dec.), Paxton, Walston, Tom. BS in Commerce, U. N.C., 1950. Chmn. Jas. I. Miller Tobacco Co., Wilson, N.C., also bd. dirs.; v.p. Standard Comml. Tobacco Co., Wilson, also bd. dirs.; bd. dirs. Branch Corp., Wilson, Branch Banking & Trust Co., Wilson. Mem. Wilson (N.C.) City Council, 1960. Served with USN, 1945-47, PTO. Mem. Orderof Gimghoul, Phi Beta Kappa, Phi Eta Sigma. Presbyterian. Avocations: hunting, fishing, golf. Home: 1009 Woodland Dr NW Wilson NC 27893-2121*

PETERS, ALAN, anatomy educator; b. Nottingham, Eng., Dec. 6, 1929; came to U.S., 1966; s. Robert and Mabel (Woplington) P.; m. Verona Muriel Shipman, Sept. 30, 1955; children: Ann Verona, Sally Elizabeth, Susan Clare. BSc, Bristol (Eng.) U., 1951, PhD, 1954. Lectr. anatomy Edinburgh (Scotland) U., 1958-66; vis. lectr. Harvard, 1963-64; prof., chmn. dept. anatomy and neurobiology Boston U., 1966—; anatomy com. Nat. Bd. Med. Examiners, 1971-75; mem. neurology B study sect. NIH, 1975-79, chmn., 1978-79; affiliate scientist Yerkes Regional Primate Rsch. Ctr., 1984—. Author: (with S.L. Palay and H. deF Webster) The Fine Structure of the Nervous System, 1970, 3rd edit., 1991, Myelination, 1970; contbr. (with A.N. Davison) articles profl. jours.; mem. editorial bd. Anat. Record, 1972-81, Jour. Comparative Neurology, Neurocytology, 1972-89, 93—, Cerebral Cortex, 1990—, Studies of Brain Function, Anat. and Embryology, 1989-92; editor book series: (with E.G. Jones) Cerebral Cortex, 1984—. Served to 2d lt. Royal Army Med. Corps, 1955-57. Recipient Javits neurosci. investigator award NIH, 1986. Mem. Anat. Soc. Gt. Britain and Ireland (Symington prize anatomy 1962, overseas mem. coun. 1969), Assn. Anatomy Chmn. (pres. 1976-77), Am. Anat. Assn. (exec. com. 1986-90, pres. 1992-93), Am. Soc. Cell Biology, Soc. Neuroscis., Internat. Primatological Soc., Cajal Club (Harman lectr. 1990, Cortical Discoverer award 1991). Home: 16 High Rock Cir Waltham MA 02154-2207 Office: Boston U Sch Medicine Dept Anatomy and Neurobiology 80 E Concord St Roxbury MA 02118-2307

PETERS, ALTON EMIL, lawyer; b. Albany, N.Y., Mar. 21, 1935; s. Emil and Winifred (Rosch) P.; m. Elizabeth Irving Berlin, Feb. 27, 1970; children: Rachel Canfield, Emily Anstice Fletcher. A.B. cum laude, Harvard U., 1955, Ll.B., 1958. Bar: N.Y. 1958, U.S. Dist. Ct. (so. dist.) N.Y. 1963. Assoc. Bleakley, Platt, Schmidt & Fritz, 1959-65, mem., 1956-81; ptnr. Miller, Montgomery, Sogi & Brady, 1981-83, Kelley Drye & Warren, N.Y.C., 1983—. Bd. dirs. Am. Friends of Covent Garden and the Royal Ballet, N.Y.C., 1971— v.p., 1971—; mem. coun. Am. Mus. in Britain, Bath, Eng., 1970—, chmn. U.S.A., 1975-92; bd. dirs. Brit. Am. Arts Assn., N.Y.C., 1983—, chmn., 1984—;English-Speaking Union U.S., bd. dirs. N.Y. br., 1963—, chmn. 1972-88; bd. dirs. Goodwill Industries of Greater N.Y., 1965—, pres., 1970-82, chmn., 1982—; mng. dir. Met. Opera Assn., N.Y.C., 1966—, sec. 1974-86, v.p., 1986-93, chm. Executive Com., 1993—; bd. dirs. Met. Opera Guild, Inc., N.Y.C., 1965—, chmn. exec. com. 1968-70, 74-79, 1st v.p., 1979-86, pres., 1986—; bd. dirs. Lincoln Ctr. for Performing Arts, N.Y.C., 1986—; trustee Signet Assocs., Cambridge, Mass., 1957-73, treas. 1957-73, hon. trustee, 1973—; fellow Pierpont Morgan Library, Frick Collection; trustee Acad. Am. Poets, N.Y.C., 1988—, treas., 1993—, Cathedral of St. John the Divine, 1991—. Decorated Knight Order of St. John of Jerusalem, Officer Order of Brit. Empire. Mem. ABA, N.Y. State Bar Assn., Assn. of Bar of City of N.Y., Am. Judicature Soc., Am. Coll. Probate Counsel, Century Assn., Church Club, Grolier Club (coun. 1994—), Harvard Club N.Y.C., Knickerbocker Club (bd. govs. 1986-92, 94—), Pilgrims Club of Odd Volumes. Home: 211 Central Park W New York NY 10024-6020 Office: Kelley Drye and Warren 101 Park Ave New York NY 10178

PETERS, ANN LOUISE, accounting manager; b. Knoxville, Tenn., Jan. 26, 1954; d. William Brown and Louise (Emerson) Nixon; m. Raymond Peters, July 11, 1975. BBA, Miami U., Oxford, Ohio, 1976; MBA, Xavier U., 1985. Cert. internal auditor. Acctg. officer Soc. Bank (formerly Citizens Bank), Hamilton, Ohio, 1977-85; internal auditor Procter & Gamble Co., Cin., 1985-86, audit sect. mgr., 1986-88, sr. cost analyst, beauty care, 1988-90; plant fin. mgr. Procter & Gamble Mfg. Co., Phoenix, 1990-92; sr. fin. analyst, beauty care Procter & Gamble Co., Cin., 1992-93, group mgr., gen. acctg., 1993-96, group mgr. R&D fin., 1996—. Mem. Inst. Internal Auditors, Inst. Mgmt. Accts. Republican. Congregationalist. Avocations: golf, swimming. Home: 7889 Ironwood Way West Chester OH 45069-1623 Office: Procter & Gamble Co Sharon Woods Tech Ctr Box 221 HB2J14A 11511 Reed Hartman Hwy Cincinnati OH 45241

PETERS, ARTHUR KING, international trade executive, author, consultant; b. Charleston, W.Va., Oct. 17, 1919; s. Arthur Cushing and Jessie (King) P.; m. Sarah Jebb Whitaker, Oct. 21, 1943; children: Robert Bruce, Margaret Allen, Michael Whitaker. AB, Cornell U., 1940; grad., U.S. Army Command and Gen. Staff Coll., 1945; MA, Columbia U., 1954, PhD, 1969. With W.R. Grace and Co., 1940-50; pres., owner A.K. Peters Co., N.Y.C., 1950—; asst. prof. French lit. Hunter Coll., CUNY, 1971-74; pres., chmn. French-Am. Found., N.Y.C., 1977-83; del. U.S. Trade Mission to Peru, Argentina, 1957. Author: Cocteau and Gide, 1973, Jean Cocteau and the French Scene, 1983, Jean Cocteau and His World, 1987 (Pirx Littèraire Etats-Unis-France 1989), Seven Trails West, 1996; translator, critic French lit.; contbr. articles to profl. jours. Maj. M.I., U.S. Army, 1941-46. Decorated Chevalier de L'ordre des Arts et des Lettres, Govt. France, 1978, Chevalier de la Legion d'Honneur, Govt. France, 1984. Mem. MLA, Coun. Fgn. Rels., Am. Importers Assn. (pres. 1965), Am. Alpine Club, Alpine Club (London), Univ. Club (N.Y.C.), Bronxville Field Club, Cercle de L'Union Interalliee (Paris). Mem. Reformed Ch. (deacon). Avocations: squash, skiing, mountaineering, tennis. Home: 14 Village Ln Bronxville NY 10708-4806 Office: AK Peters Co 230 Park Ave Ste 518 New York NY 10169-1599

PETERS, AULANA LOUISE, government agency commissioner, lawyer; b. Shreveport, La., Nov. 30, 1941; d. Clyde A. and Eula Mae (Faulkner) Pharis; m. Bruce F. Peters, Oct. 6, 1967. BA in Philosophy, Coll. New Rochelle, 1963; JD, U. So. Calif., 1973. Bar: Calif., 1974. Sec., English corr. Publimondial, Spa, Milan, Italy, 1963-64, Fibramianto, Spa, Milan, 1964-65, Turkish del. to Office for Econ. Cooperation & Devel., Paris, 1965-66; adminstrv. asst. Office for Econ. Cooperation & Devel., Paris, 1966-67; assoc. Gibson, Dunn & Crutcher, L.A., 1973-80, ptnr., 1980-84, 88—; commr. SEC, Washington, 1984-88. Recipient Disting. Alumnus award Econs. Club So. Calif., 1984, Washington Achiever award Nat. Assn. Bank Women, 1986. Mem. ABA, State Bar of Calif. (civil litigation cons. group 1983-84), Los Angeles County Bar Assn., Black Women Lawyers Assn. L.A., Assn. Bus. Trial Lawyers (panelist L.A. 1982), Women's Forum, Washington. Office: Gibson Dunn & Crutcher 333 S Grand Ave Los Angeles CA 90071-1504*

PETERS, BARBARA AGNES, assistant principal; b. Lockport, N.Y., Aug. 11, 1952; d. Raymond Charles Betsch and Evelyn Mae (Ehmke) Soulvie; m. Victor Waldorf Baker, June 17, 1978 (div.); children: Alexander, Erik; m. Robert Emerson Peters, Nov. 3, 1990; children: Brian, Jennifer. BS in Edn., SUNY, Fredonia, 1974; MEd, U. Wales, Cardiff, 1979. Cert. tchr. N, K-6, secondary English, reading, CAS-sch. dist. adminstr., N.Y, CAS Ednl. Adminstrn., SAS, SDA. Tchr. English Emmet Belknap Jr. H.S., Lockport, N.Y., 1974-76; exec. dir. Dept. of Youth and Recreation Svcs., Lockport, 1978-89; instr. Empire State Coll., Lockport, 1983—; tchr. English Akron (N.Y.) Cen. Sch. Dist., 1989-95; asst. prin. West Seneca East Middle Sch., 1995—; mem. dist. planning team Akron Sch., 1990-95, mem. tech. long-range planning com., 1992-94. Team owner's mgr. Buffalo Bills Football Club, Orchard Park, N.Y., 1978—; mem. Bd. Performing and Visual Arts, Tonawanda, 1992. Recipient Erie County Youth Best award, 1995; honoree Internat. Women's Decade, 1985; named to Outstanding Young Women of Am., 1986; Western N.Y. Women in Adminstrn. Excellence in Ednl. Leadership award, 1996; Rotary grad. fellow, 1975. Mem. ASCD, N.Y. State Middle Sch. Assn., Swiftwater Power Squadron Advanced Pilot, LaSalle Yacht Club, Phi Delta Kappa (award innovative ednl. program 1996). Avocations: boating, golf. Office: West Seneca East Middle Sch 1445 Center Rd West Seneca NY 14224

PETERS, BERNADETTE (BERNADETTE LAZZARA), actress; b. Queens, N.Y., Feb. 28, 1948; d. Peter and Marguerite (Maltese) Lazzara. Student, Quintano Sch. for Young Profls., N.Y.C. Ind. actress, entertainer, 1957—. Appeared on TV series All's Fair, 1976-77; frequent guest appearances on TV; films include The Longest Yard, 1974, Vigilant Force, 1975, W.C. Fields and Me, 1975, Silent Movie, 1976, The Jerk, 1979, Heart Beeps, 1981, Tulips, 1981, Pennies from Heaven, 1982 (Golden Globe Best Actress award), Annie, 1982, Slaves of NewYork, 1989, Pink Cadillac, 1989, Impromptu, 1990, Alice, 1990; stage appearances include This is Google, 1957, The Most Happy Fella, 1959, Gypsy, 1961, Riverwind, 1966, Curly McDimple, 1967, Johnny No-Trump, 1967, George M!, 1968, Dames at Sea, 1968, La Strada, 1969, On the Town, 1971, Tartuffe, 1972, Mack and Mabel, 1974, Sally and Marsha, 1982, Sunday in the Park with George, 1983-85 (Tony nomination 1983), Song and Dance, 1985-86, Into the Woods, 1987, The Goodbye Girl, 1992-93; TV films David, 1989, Fall From Grace, 1990, The Last Best Year, 1990; rec. artist: (MCA Records) Bernadette Peters, 1980, Now Playing, 1981. Recipient Drama Desk award for Dames and Sea, 1968; Drama Desk award nomination for Into The Woods, 1987, 88, Tony award nominee, 1971, 74, 83, 85, 92, Tony award for Best Actress in Song and Dance, 1986, Theatre World citation for George M!, 1968, Drama Desk award, 1968, 86, Hasty Pudding Theatrical award, 1987 woman of the Yr., Sara Siddons Actress of Yr. award, 1993-94. Office: Judy Katz PR 1790 Broadway Ste 1600 New York NY 10019-1412

PETERS, CAROL BEATTIE TAYLOR (MRS. FRANK ALBERT PETERS), mathematician; b. Washington, May 10, 1932; d. Edwin Lucius and Lois (Beattie) Taylor; B.S., U. Md., 1954, M.A., 1958; m. Frank Albert Peters, Feb. 26, 1955; children—Thomas, June, Erick, Victor. Group mgr. Tech. Operations, Inc., Arlington, Va., 1957-62, sr. staff scientist, 1964-66; supervisory analyst Datatrol Corp., Silver Spring, Md., 1962; project dir. Computer Concept, Inc., Silver Spring, 1963-64; mem. tech. staff, then mem. sr. staff Informatics Inc., Bethesda, Md., 1966-70, mgr. systems projects, 1970-71, tech. dir., 1971-76; sr. tech. dir. Ocean Data Systems, Inc., Rockville, Md., 1976-83; dir. Informatics Gen. Co., 1983-89; pres. Carol Peters Assocs., 1989—. Mem. Assn. Computing Machinery, IEEE Computer Group. Home and Office: 12311 Glen Mill Rd Potomac MD 20854-1928

PETERS, CAROLJEAN NATALIE, elementary education educator; b. Belleville, Ill., Mar. 6, 1931; d. Frederick Henry and Florence Louise (Spies) Zwetschke; m. Arthur Henry Peters, Dec. 26, 1953; children: Julia Lynn, Thomas Arthur, Douglas Frederick. AA, Belleville Area Coll., 1950; AB, BS summa cum laude, Millikin U., 1952; MEd summa cum laude, So. Ill. U., 1984. Cert. elem. tchr. Elem. tchr. Roxana (Ill.) Dist., 1952-53; elem. tchr. Dist. 118, Belleville, 1954-56, substitute tchr., 1969-79; freelance storyteller, book reviewer Belleville, 1966-82, tchr. reading, 1983-87; reading improvement assistance tchr./chpt. 1 tchr. Wolf Br. Dist. 113, Belleville, 1984-94; reading cons. and diagnostician Belleville, 1994—; young authors conf. presenter St. Clair Region & State, Bloomington, Ill., 1986-91; in-service programmer E. St. Louis Schs., 1983, 85, Illini Grant Dist., Fairview Hghts., Ill., 1988, Wolf Br., 1989, 90, regional supts./prins. meeting, 1990; mem. state assessment project, 1991-92; presenter Belleville Area Arts Coun., 1985, Madison County Arts Coun., 1989, St. Clair; in-svc. portfolio presenter Dist. 113, 1992; storyteller & spl. interest programmer for schs., 1985—. Editor, feature writer: (church newsletter) Our St. Paul News, 1984—. Leader, trainer River Bluffs coun. Girl Scouts U.S., Belleville, 1965-69; broadcaster Radio Info. Svc., Belleville, 1973-83; bd. dirs., sec., pres. Call for Help, Inc., Belleville and East St. Louis, 1978-82, 84-88, 89-91; bd. dirs., life mem. Meml. Hosp. Aux., Belleville, 1957—, YMCA Belleville, 1967-72; sec. ch. coun. St. Paul United Ch. of Christ, Belleville, 1981-84, v.p., 1984-85, pres., 1985-86. Recipient St. Clair Sq. Golden Apple award. Mem. Ill. Reading Coun., Internat. Reading Assn., Lewis & Clark Reading Coun., AAUW, Pi Mu Theta, Phi Kappa Phi, Kappa Delta Pi. Republican. Avocations: travel, church conference work, gardening, baking, church activities. Office: Wolf Br Sch 125 Huntwood Rd Belleville IL 62221-1923

PETERS, CHARLES GIVEN, JR., editor; b. Charleston, W.Va., Dec. 22, 1926; s. Charles Given and Esther (Teague) P.; m. Elizabeth Bostwick Hubbell, Aug. 3, 1957; 1 child, Christian Avery. BA in Humanities, Columbia U., 1949, MA in English, 1951; LLB, U. Va., 1957; LLD (hon.), U. Charleston, 1979. Bar: W.Va. 1957, D.C. 1981. Atty. Peters, Merrick, Leslie & Mohler, Charleston, 1957-61; mem. W.Va State Legislature, Charleston, 1960-62; dir. evaluation Peace Corps, Washington, 1962-68; founder, editor in chief The Washington Monthly, 1968—; Author: How Washington Really Works, 4th edit., 1994, Tilting at Windmills, 1988; editor: (with Taylor Branch) Blowing the Whistle, 1972, (with James Fallows) The System, 1975, (with Michael Nelson) The Culture of Bureaucracy, 1977, (with Jonathan Alter) Inside the System, 5th edit., 1985. Author: How Washington Really Works, 1980, Tilting at Windmills, 1988; editor: (with Taylor Branch) Blowing the Whistle, 1972, (with James Fallows) The System, 1975, (with Michael Nelson) The Culture of Bureaucracy, 1977, (with Jonathan Alter) Inside the System, 5th edit., 1985. Mgr. John F. Kennedy campaign, Kanawha County, W.Va., 1960. Served with inf. U.S. Army, 1944-46. Recipient Columbia Journalism award, 1978; named West Virginian of Yr., Charleston Gazette-Mail, 1980; Poynter fellow Yale U., 1980. Democrat. Presbyterian. Office: The Washington Monthly Co 1611 Connecticut Ave NW Washington DC 20009-1033

PETERS, CHARLES WILLIAM, research and development company manager; b. Pierceton, Ind., Dec. 9, 1927; s. Charles Frederick and Zelda May (Line) P.; m. Katharine Louise Schuman, May 29, 1953; 1 child, Susan Kay; m. 2d, Patricia Ann Miles, Jan. 2, 1981; children: Bruce Miles Merkle, Leslie Ann Merkle Sanaie, Philip Frank Merkle, William Macneil Merkle. AB, Ind. U., 1950; postgrad. U. Md., 1952-58. Supervisory rsch. physicist Naval Rsch. Lab., Washington, 1950-71; physicist EPA, Washington, 1971-76; mgr. advanced systems EATON-Consol. Controls Corp., Springfield, Va., 1976-89, v.p. Nuclear Diagnostic Systems, Inc., Springfield, Va, 1989-92, cons. Am. Tech. Inst., 1993—. With U.S. Army, 1945-47. Mem. IEEE, AAAS, Am. Phys. Soc. Home and Office: 5235 N Whispering Hills Ln Tucson AZ 85704-2510

PETERS, DAVID ALLEN, mechanical engineering educator, consultant; b. East St. Louis, Ill., Jan. 31, 1947; s. Bernell Louis and Marian Louise (Blum) P.; m. Linda J. Conley, Jan. 25, 1969; children: Michael H., Laura A., Nathan C. BS in Applied Mechanics, Washington U., St. Louis, 1969, MS in Applied Mechanics, 1970; PhD in Aeros. and Astronautics, Stanford U., 1974. Assoc. engr. McDonnell Astronautics, 1969-70; rsch. scientist Army Aeronautics Lab., 1970-74; asst. prof. Washington U., 1975-77, assoc. prof., 1977-80, prof. mech. engring., 1980-85, chmn. dept., 1982-85; prof. aerospace engring. Ga. Inst Tech., Atlanta, 1985-91; dir. NASA Space Grant Consortium Ga. Inst. Tech., Atlanta, 1989-91; dir. Ctr. for Computational Mechanics Washington U., 1992—; prof. dept. mech. engring. Washington U., St. Louis, 1991—. Contbr. 50 articles to profl. jours. Recipient sci. contbn. award NASA, 1975, 76. Fellow AIAA, ASME; mem. Am. Helicopter Soc. (jour. editor 1987-90), Am. Soc. for Engring. Edn., Internat. Assn. for Computational Mechanics (charter), Am. Acad. Mechs., Pi Tau Sigma (gold medal 1978). Baptist. Home: 7629 Balson Ave Saint Louis MO 63130-2150 Office: Washington U Dept Mech Engring Campus Box 1185 Saint Louis MO 63130

PETERS, DAVID FRANKMAN, lawyer; b. Hagerstown, Md., Aug. 15, 1941; s. Harold E. and Lois (Frankman) P.; m. Jane Catherine Witherspoon, Aug. 21, 1965; children: Catherine, Elizabeth. BA, Washington and Lee U., 1963; LLB, Duke U., 1966. Bar: Va. 1966, U.S. Dist. Ct. (ea. and we. dists.) Va., U.S. Ct. Appeals (2d, 4th, 6th, 7th and D.C. cirs.). Assoc. Hunton & Williams, Richmond, Va., 1966-73, ptnr., 1973—. Pres. Children's Home Soc. Va., Richmond, 1977-78, bd. dirs., 1970-91; trustee Westminster-Canterbury Corp., 1995—; elder, trustee 1st Presbyn. Ch., Richmond. Mem. ABA, Va. Bar Assn. (chmn. adminstrn. law com. 1985-88), Richmond Bar Assn. Lodge: Kiwanis. Avocations: photography, travel. Home: 3 Windsor Way Richmond VA 23221-3232 Office: Hunton & Williams 951 E Byrd St Richmond VA 23219-4074

PETERS, DENNIS GAIL, chemist; b. L.A., Apr. 17, 1937; s. Samuel and Phyllis Dorothy (Pope) P. BS cum laude, Calif. Inst. Tech., 1958; PhD, Harvard U., 1962. Mem. faculty Ind. U., 1962—, prof. chemistry, 1974—, Herman T. Briscoe prof., 1975—. Co-author textbooks, contbr. articles profl. jours. Woodrow Wilson fellow, 1958-59; NIH predoctoral fellow, 1959-62; vis. fellow Japan Soc. for Promotion Sci., 1980; recipient Ulysses G. Weatherly award disting. teaching Ind. U., 1969, Disting. Teaching award Coll. Arts and Scis. Grad. Alumni Assn. Ind. U., 1984, Nat. Catalyst award for Disting. Teaching Chem. Mfrs. Assn., 1988; grantee NSF. Fellow Ind. Acad. Sci., Am. Inst. Chemists; mem. Am. Chem. Soc. (grantee, Div. of Analytical Chemistry award for excellence in teaching 1990), N.Y. Acad. Scis. Home: 1401 S Nancy St Bloomington IN 47401-6051 Office: Dept Chemistry Ind U Bloomington IN 47405

PETERS, DOLORES YVONNE, neonatal clinical nurse specialist; b. Washington, Aug. 9, 1951; d. Lewis Bradford and Thelma Beatrice (Walker) P. BSN cum laude, U. Md., 1975; MSN in Nursing of Developing Families, Catholic U. Am., 1989; BA in Biology cum laude, Western Md. Coll., 1973. RN, Va., D.C., Md.; cert. neonatal nurse practitioner. Obstet. staff nurse Sibley Meml. Hosp., Washington, 1975-76; staff nurse Nat. Naval Med. Ctr., Bethesda, Md., 1976-80, nursery ednl. coord., 1980-82, neonatal clin. nursing specialist, 1982-90; neonatal clin. nurse specialist Washington Hosp. Ctr., 1990—; mem. Resource Applications faculty C.V. Mosby Co., 1990-93. Am. Lung Assn. of Md. nursing rsch. fellow, 1987-88. Mem. Nat. Assn. Neonatal Nurses, Assn. Women's Health, Obstet. and Neonatal Nurses, Nat. Holistic Nurses Assn., Nat. Perinatal Assn., Sigma Theta Tau, Beta Beta Beta. Home: 2337 Massanutten Dr Silver Spring MD 20906-6178

PETERS, DONALD CAMERON, construction company executive; b. Milw., Mar. 25, 1915; s. Simon C. and May (Gnewuch) P.; m. Twila Bingel, Dec. 7, 1940; children: Susan (Mrs. Douglas Ingram), David C., Bruce C., Douglas C. B.S. in Civil Engring, Marquette U., 1938. Registered profl. engr., Wis., Pa. Engr. Siesel Constrn. Co., Milw., 1938-44; v.p., dir. Crump, Inc., Pitts., 1944-51; pres. Mellon-Stuart Co., Pitts., 1951-73, also bd. dirs., chmn., 1973-81; mem. 5 man gen. com. rewriting Pitts. Bldg. Code, 1947; mem., chmn. Pa. Registration Bd. Profl. Engrs., 1962-82; chmn. bd. standards and appeals Pitts. Bur. Bldg. Inspection, 1960-72; past pres. Pitts. Builders Exch.; adv. bd. Liberty Mut. Ins., 1968—. Chmn. bd. suprs. Pine Twp., Allegheny County, 1953-80; chmn. Constrn. Industry Advancement Program We. Pa., 1975-93; trustee La Roche Coll., Pitts., 1967—, chmn., 1983-84; bd. dirs. North Hills Passavant Hosp., 1963-90, chmn., 1983-84. Fellow ASCE; mem. NSPE (nat. dir. 1954-57, chmn. bd. ethical rev. 1978-79), Pa. Soc. Profl. Engrs. (pres. 1953-54), Assn. Gen. Contractors Am. (nat. dir.), Pitts. C. of C. (chmn., dir. 1973-81), Master Builders Assn. Western Pa. (past pres.), SBA, Triangle, Tau Beta Pi, Alpha Sigma Nu. Club: Duquesne (Pitts.). Home: 2803 SE 18th Ct Cape Coral FL 33904-4077

PETERS, DOROTHY MARIE, writer, consultant; b. Sutton, Nebr., Oct. 23, 1913; d. Sylvester and Anna (Olander) Peters; AB with high distinction, Nebr. Wesleyan U., 1941; MA, Northwestern U., 1957; EdD, Ind. U., 1968. Tchr. Nebr. pub. schs., 1931-38; caseworker Douglas County Assistance Bur., Omaha, 1941; hosp. field dir., gen. field rep. ARC, 1941-50; social worker Urban League, Meth. Ch., Washington, 1951-53; asst. prin., dir. guidance, Manlius (Ill.) Community High Sch., 1953-58; dean of girls, guidance dir. Woodruff High Sch., Peoria, Ill., 1958-66; vis. prof. edn. Bradley U., Peoria, 1959-77; coord., dir. Title I programs Peoria Pub. Sch. System, 1966-68, dir. pupil services, 1968-72; dir. counseling and evaluation Title I Programs, 1972-73; vol. dir. youth service programs, vol. program cons. Cen. Ill. chpt. and Heart of Ill. div. ARC, Peoria, 1973-77; owner, operator Ability-Achievement Unlimited Cons. Services, Saratoga Springs, N.Y., 1978-81; spl. cons. Courage Center, Golden Valley, Minn., 1981-84, mem. pub. policy com., bd. dirs., 1985-87; mem. sr. adv. bd. F&M Marquette Nat. Bank, 1981-85; cons. Sister Kenny Inst., Mpls., 1984-86; freelance writer, 1984—; prin. Dorothy M. Peters & Assocs., Roseville, Minn., 1985-87. Bd. dirs, home service com. disaster com. Peoria chpt. ARC, 1958-73; pres., bd. dirs. Ct. Counselor Program; mem. Mayor's Human Resources Coun., City of Peoria; chmn. met. adv. com. transp. for handicapped; ednl. dir., prin., bd. dirs. Catalyst High Sch., 1975-77; hon. life bd. mem. Am. Nat. Red Cross; mem. Saratoga Springs Hosp. Bldg. Rehab. Com.; founder, steering com. Open Sesame, Saratoga Springs, 1978-81; appointee N.Y. State Employment and Tng. Council, 1979-81, Saratoga County Employment and Tng. Com., 1979-81; bd. dirs. Unlimited Potential, 1979-81; mem. Metro Mobility Adv. Task Force, Mpls., 1981-85, mem. policy com., 1984-85 ; mem. vol. action com. United Way, Mpls., 1982-85 ; mem. Minn. State Planning Coun. for Developmentally Disabled and liason to U. Mo. Affiliated Program, 1983-89 (appreciation award 1990); mem. Gov.'s Task Force on Needs of Adults with Brain Impairment, 1985-87; chmn., bd. dirs. Met. Ctr. for Ind. Living, 1986— (svc. appreciation award 1989); mem. sr. ministries coun. United Meth. Ch., 1984-88; mem. dept. rehab. svcs. Minn. Coun. Ind. Living, 1989—; gov.'s appointee Minn. Bd. on Aging, 1989-94; mem. gov.'s sr. agenda for Ind. Living in the 1990's, 1989-94; mem. Nebr. Wesleyan U. Nat. Caucus, Mpls., 1989—; mem. United Way Older Adults Vision Coun., 1993—. Recipient Spl. Congl. Recognition cert., 1994. Mem. Peoria Edn. Assn. (v.p. 1962-64), Ill. Guidance and Pers. Assn. (v.p. Area 8, 1963-64), NEA, Ill. Edn. Assn. (del. 1962-64), Am. Pers. and Guidance Assn., Am. Sch. Counselors Assn., Nat. Assn. Women Deans and Counselors (K-12 task force chmn. 1974—, editorial bd. Jour.), Ill. Vocat.

Guidance Assn. (dir.), Minn. Head Injury Found., Nat. Head Injury Found., Ill. Assn. Women Deans and Counselors, Phi Kappa Phi, Psi Chi, Pi Gamma Mu, Pi Lambda Theta, Delta Kappa Gamma, Alpha Gamma Delta. Home: 6100 Summit Dr N Apt 103 Brooklyn Center MN 55430

PETERS, DOUGLAS DENNISON, Canadian government official, member of Parliament; b. Brandon, Man., Can., Mar. 3, 1930; s. Wilfrid Seymour and Mary Gladys (Dennison) P.; m. Audrey Catherine Clark, June 26, 1954; children: David Wilfrid, Catherine Elaine Peters Gilchrist. B Commerce, Queen's U., Kingston, Ont., Can., 1963; PhD in Fin. and Commerce, U. Pa., 1969. With Bank of Montreal, Winnipeg, Man., 1950-60; chief economist Toronto (Ont., Can.)-Dominion Bank, 1966—, v.p., chief economist, 1971—, sr. v.p., chief economist, 1980-93; M.P. for Scarborough East House of Commons, Ottawa, Ont., 1993—, sec. of state for fin., 1993—. Author: The Monetarist Counterrevolution - A Critique of Canada's Monetary Policy, 1975-1980, 1980; contbr. articles to profl. publs. Scholar Can. Coun., 1963, 64, Ford Found., 1965. Liberal. Avocation: tennis. Home: 151 Bay St # 102, Ottawa, ON Canada K1R 7T2 Office: House of Commons, Parliament Bldg Rm 442N, Wellington St, Ottawa, ON Canada K1A 0A6

PETERS, ELEANOR WHITE, mental health nurse; b. Highland Park, Mich., Aug. 11, 1920; d. Alfred Mortimer and Jane Ann (Evans) White; m. William J. Peters, 1947 (div. 1953); children: Susannah J., William J. (dec.). RN, Christ Hosp. Sch. Nursing, Jersey City, 1941; BA, Jersey City State Coll., 1968; postgrad., U. Del., 1969-70; MS, SUNY, New Paltz, 1983. RN, N.J., N.Y. Mem. staff various area hosps. N.J., 1941-58; indsl. nurse Abex, Mahwah, N.J., 1958-68; sch. nurse Liberty (N.Y.) Ctrl. Sch., 1971-76; coord. practical nurse program Hudson County C.C., Jersey City, 1979-80; community mental health nurse Letchworth Village, Thiells, N.Y., 1981—. Historian, Bishop House Found., Saddle River, N.J. Mem. AAUW (pres. Liberty-Monticello br. 1988-92), Am. Sch. Health Assn., Alpha Delta Kappa (sec. Mu chpt. 1973-75), Sigma Theta Tau (Kappa Eta chpt.). Republican. Lutheran. Avocations: antiques, history, traveling, education of children. Home: PO Box 224 Saddle River NJ 07458-0224 Office: Letchworth Village Main St Devel Disabil Svcs Office PO Box 823 South Fallsburg NY 12779

PETERS, ELIZABETH ANN HAMPTON, nursing educator; b. Detroit, Sept. 27, 1934; d. Grinsfield Taylor and Ida Victoria (Jones) Hampton; m. James Marvin Peters, Dec. 1, 1956; children: Douglas Taylor, Sara Elizabeth. Diploma, Berea Coll. Hosp. Sch. Nursing, 1956; BS in Nursing, Wright State U., Dayton, Ohio, 1975; MS in Nursing, Ohio State U., Columbus, 1978. Therapist-RN Eastway, Inc., Dayton, Ohio, 1979-81; therapist family counseling svc. Good Samaritan-Community Mental Health Ctr., Dayton, Ohio, 1981-83; instr. Wright State U. Sch. Nursing, Dayton, 1983-84; clin. nurse specialist, pain mgmt. svcs., pain mgmt. program UPSA, Inc., Dayton, 1983-86; staff nurse Hospice of Dayton, Inc., 1985-86, dir. vol. svcs., 1986-89, dir. bereavement svcs., 1986-87; asst. prof. Community Hosp. Sch. Nursing, Springfield, Ohio, 1990-93, prof., 1993—. Author: (with others) Oncologic Pain, 1987. Mem. Clark County Mental Health Bd., Springfield, 1986-95; mem. New Carlisle (Ohio) Bd. Health, 1990—. Mem. ANA, Ohio Nurses Assn., Sigma Theta Tau. Home: 402 Flora Ave New Carlisle OH 45344-1329

PETERS, ELLEN ASH, state supreme court chief justice; b. Berlin, Mar. 21, 1930; came to U.S., 1939, naturalized, 1947; d. Ernest Edward and Hildegard (Simon) Ash; m. Phillip I. Blumberg; children: David Bryan Peters, James Douglas Peters, Julie Peters Haden. BA with honors, Swarthmore Coll., 1951, LLD (hon.), 1983; LLB cum laude, Yale U., 1954, MA (hon.), 1964, LLD (hon.), 1985; LLD (hon.), U. Hartford, 1983; Georgetown U., 1984; LLD (hon.), Yale U., 1985, Conn. Coll., 1985, N.Y. Law Sch., 1985; HLD (hon.), St. Joseph Coll., 1986; LLD (hon.), Colgate U., 1986, Trinity Coll., 1987, Bates Coll., 1987, Wesleyan U., 1987, DePaul U., 1988; HLD (hon.), Albertus Magnus Coll., 1990; LLD (hon.), U. Conn., 1992; LLD, U. Rochester, 1994. Bar: Conn. 1957. Law clk. to judge U.S. Circuit Ct., 1954-55; assoc. in law U. Calif., Berkeley, 1955-56; prof. law Yale U., New Haven, 1956-78, adj. prof. law; assoc. justice Conn. Supreme Ct., Hartford, 1978-84; chief justice Conn. Supreme Ct., 1984—. Author: Commercial Transactions: Cases, Texts, and Problems, 1971, Negotiable Instruments Primer, 1974; contbr. articles to profl. jours. Bd. mgrs. Swarthmore Coll., 1970-81; trustee Yale-New Haven Hosp., 1981-85, Yale Corp., 1986-92; mem. conf. Chief Justices, 1984—, pres., 1994; hon. chmn. U.S. Constl. Bicentennial Com., 1986-91; mem. Conn. Permanent Commn. on Status of Women, 1973-74, Conn. Bd. Pardons, 1978-80, Conn. Law Revision Commn., 1978-84; bd. dirs. Nat. Ctr. State Cts., 1992-96, chmn., 1994. Recipient Ella Grasso award, 1982, Jud. award Conn. Trial Lawyers Assn., 1982, citation of merit Yale Law Sch., 1983, Pioneer Woman award Hartford Coll. for Women, 1988, Disting. Svc. award U. Conn. Law Sch. Alumni Assn., 1993, Raymond E. Baldwin Pub. Svc. award Quinnipiac Coll. Law Sch., 1995, Disting. Svc. award Conn. Law Tribune, 1996. Mem. ABA, Conn. Bar Assn. (Jud. award 1992), Am. Law Inst. (coun.), Am. Acad. Arts and Scis., Am. Philos. Soc. Office: Conn Supreme Ct Drawer N Sta A 231 Capitol Ave Hartford CT 06106-1537

PETERS, ERNEST, metallurgy educator, consultant; b. Steinbach, Man., Can., Jan. 27, 1926; s. Franz Isaac Peters and Margaretha (Klassen) MacLachlan; m. Gwynneth Salome Walker, Sept. 21, 1949; children: Charlotte Ann Peters Garcia, Gwynneth Elizabeth Peters Becker. BASc, U. B.C., Can., 1949, MASc, 1951, PhD, 1956. Registered profl. engr., B.C. Metallurgist Geneva Steel Co., Provo, Utah, 1949-50; rsch. engr. Cominco, Ltd., Trail, B.C., Can., 1951-53, Union Carbide Metals Co., Niagara Falls, N.Y., 1956-58; instr. U. B.C., Vancouver, 1955-56, asst. prof., 1958-65, assoc. prof., 1966-68, prof., 1968-91, prof. emeritis, 1991—; cons. Cominco, Ltd., Trail, 1958-92, Kennecott Copper Corp., Salt Lake City, 1969-71, E Z Australasia, Melbourne, Australia, 1977-78, Bacon, Donaldson & Assocs., Vancouver, 1981-90, Westmin Resources Ltd., 1991—; mem. selection com. NRC Can., Ottawa, 1967-68; extractive metallurgy lectr. The Metals Soc. of AIME, Las Vegas, Nev., 1976; keynote lectr. Benelux Metallurgie, Brussels, 1977. Contbr. articles to profl. jours.; patentee in Hydromet. Mem. selection com. Killam fellowships Can. Coun., Ottawa, 1988-91. Sgt. RCAF, 1943-45. Recipient C.I.M.. Alcan award, 1983, James Douglas Gold medal AIME, 1986, Mineral Scis. Edn. award AIME, 1993, Can. Materials Sci. Conf. Metal Chemistry award, 1993; named Indsl. Rsch. chair, 11 Can. cos., 1987-92; Killam fellow Can. Coun., 1983-85. Fellow Royal Soc. Can., The Metall. Soc. of AIME, Can. Inst. Mining & Metallurgy; mem. B.C. Assn. Profl. Engrs. Baptist. Avocations: skiing, windsurfing, radio control model planes. Home: 2708 W 33d Ave, Vancouver, BC Canada V6N 2G1 Office: U BC Dept Metals and Materials Engring, 309-6350 Stores Rd, Vancouver, BC Canada V6T 1Z4

PETERS, FRANK ALBERT, retired chemical engineer; b. Washington, June 3, 1931; s. Charles Albert and Dorothy Lynette (Paine) P.; m. Carol Beattie Taylor, Feb. 25, 1955; children: Thomas, June, Erick, Victor. B-SChemE, U. Md., 1955. Devel. engr. Celanese Corp. Am., Cumberland, Md., 1955-58; chem. Engr. U.S. Bur. Mines, College Park, Md., 1958-66; project leader U.S. Bur. Mines, College Park, 1966-70, rsch. supr., 1970-77; chief process evaluation U.S. Bur. Mines, Washington, 1977-94, ret., 1994. Contbr. over 20 articles to profl. jours. Avocations: photography, model railroading. Home: 12311 Glen Mill Rd Potomac MD 20854-1928

PETERS, FRANK LEWIS, JR., retired arts editor; b. Springfield, Mo., Oct. 19, 1930; s. Frank Lewis and Mary (Frissell) P.; m. Alba Manciani, Jan. 20, 1963; children—Carl Nathaniel, Adrian Frissell. A.B., Drury Coll., 1951; postgrad., State U. Iowa, 1953-55. Copy editor Ark. Gazette, Little Rock, 1958-59, Springfield (Mo.) Leader & Press, 1960-61; mng. editor Rome (Italy) Daily Am., 1962-64; music editor St. Louis Post-Dispatch, 1967-84, arts editor, 1984-88. Co-author: (with George McCue) A Guide to the Architecture of St. Louis, 1989. Served with AUS, 1951-52. Recipient Pulitzer prize distinguished criticism, 1972. Mem. SAR, Lambda Chi Alpha. Episcopalian. Home: 11959 Lombardy Ln Saint Louis MO 63128-1516

PETERS, GORDON BENES, musician; b. Oak Park, Ill., Jan. 4, 1931; s. Arthur George and Julia Anne (Benes) P. Student, Northwestern U., 1949-50; Mus.B., Eastman Sch. Music, 1956, Mus.M., 1962. Percussionist Rochester (N.Y.) Philharmonic Orch., 1955-59; prin. percussionist Grant Park Symphony Orch., Chgo., 1955-58; mem. faculty Rochester Bd. Edn., 1956-57, Geneseo State Tchrs. Coll., 1957-58; acting prin. percussionist Rochester, N.Y., 1958-59; prin. percussionist Chgo. Symphony Orch., 1959—; condr., adminstr. Civic Orch. Chgo., 1966-87; condr. Elmhurst Symphony Orch., 1968-73; instr. percussion instruments Northwestern U., 1963-68, lectr., 1991; guest conductor Bangor (Maine) Symphony, 1993. Author-pub.: The Drummer: Man; arranger-pub. Marimba Ensemble arrangements; composer-pub.: Swords of Moda-Ling; editor: percussion column Instrumentalist mag, 1963-69; contbr. articles to profl. jours. Bd. dirs. Pierre Monteux Sch., Hancock, Maine, 1965-95. With U.S. Mil. Acad. Band, 1950-53. Recipient Pierre Monteux disciple award conducting, 1962. Mem. Percussion Arts Soc. (pres. 1962-66), Am. Symphony Orch. League, Condrs. Guild (treas., exec. com. 1979-82, 86-90). Home: 824 Hinman Ave # 2N Evanston IL 60202-2302 Office: Chgo Symphony Orch 220 S Michigan Ave Chicago IL 60604-2508

PETERS, HENRY AUGUSTUS, neuropsychiatrist; b. Oconomowoc, Wis., Dec. 21, 1920; s. Henry Augustus and Emma N. P.; m. Jean McWilliams, 1950; children—Henry, Kurt, Eric, Mark. BA, MD, U. Wis. Prof. dept. neurology and rehab. medicine U. Wis. Med. Sch., Madison, emeritus prof., 1996—; mem. med. adv. bd. Muscular Dystrophy Assn. Served to lt. M.C. U.S. Navy. Fellow A.C.P.; mem. Wis. Med. Assn., Am. Acad. Neurology, Am. Psychiatric Assn. Club: Rotary. Office: 600 Highland Ave Madison WI 53792-0001

PETERS, HENRY BUCKLAND, optometrist, educator; b. Oakland, Calif., Nov. 2, 1916; s. Thomas Henry and Eleanor Bernice (Hough) P.; m. Anne Zara Ledin, Feb. 3, 1968; children—Lynn, Thomas Henry, James Clifton, Christopher Patrick, Elizabeth Anne. A.B., U. Calif. at. Berkeley, 1938; M.A., U. Nebr., 1939; D.O.S., So. Coll. Optometry, 1971, New England Coll. Optometry, 1985; D.O.S. (hon.), SUNY, 1990. Pvt. practice optometry Chico, Calif., 1939-40, Oakland, 1946-59; instr., asst. prof. U. Calif., Berkeley, 1947-62; assoc. prof., asst. dean U. Calif. (Sch. Optometry), 1962-69; prof., dean (Sch. Optometry), 1969-86; prof. public health Med. Center, U. Ala., Birmingham, 1969-87; dean and prof. emeritus U. Ala., Birmingham, 1988—; exec. dir. Research Found. U. Ala., Birmingham, 1986-89; dir. Nat. Bd. Examiners in Optometry, 1984-91; pres. Nat. Health Council, 1978-79; cons. So. Regional Edn. Bd., S.C. Comm. Higher Edn., Calif. Dept. Public Health, Lawrence Radiation Lab., Aerojet Gen., Nat. Acad. Sci. Inst. Medicine; v.p. Children's Vision Center, Oakland, 1963-69; dir. Calif. Vision Service, 1953-59; mem. optometric rev. com. Bur. Health, Manpower and Edn., HEW, 1970-73, Rev. and Program Council, Medicaid, Calif., 1966-69; dir. Community Service Council, Birmingham, 1969-76; mem. deans com. VA Hosp., Birmingham; bd. dirs. Birmingham Health Services Agy., 1976-79, chmn. manpower com., 1976-79; chmn. optometry services adv. com. VA, 1977-88, chmn. spl. adv. com. on legally blind, 1977; mem. Nat. Rev. Bd. Health Promotion with Elderly, 1980-82; mem. adv. bd. Health Policy Council N.Y., 1980-88; mem. Adv. Council on Phys. Therapy Edn., 1986-89. Author: (with Blum and Bettman) Vision Screening for Elementary Schools, 1959; History of School of Optometry, University of Alabama at Birmingham, 1994; also articles. Served to lt. USNR, 1942-46. Named Optometrist of Year, Calif. Optometric Assn., 1959; Optometrist of South, So. Council Optometrists, 1982; Thomas P. Carpenter award for disting. service Nat. Health Council, 1983. Fellow Am. Public Health Assn. (Vision Care Disting. Achievement award 1982), Am. Acad. Optometry (life, pres. 1973-74, Carel C. Koch medal 1974, diplomate pub. health sect. 1989); mem. Am. Optometric Assn. (Disting. Service award 1981), Ala. Optometric Assn. (Optometrist of Year 1973), Assn. Schs. and Colls. Optometry (pres. 1967-68, dir.), Phi Beta Kappa, Sigma Xi, Phi Delta Kappa, Beta Sigma Kappa. Home: 712 Vestavia Lake Dr Birmingham AL 35216-2063

PETERS, HOWARD NEVIN, foreign language educator; b. Hazleton, Pa., June 29, 1938; s. Howard Eugene and Verna Catherine (Miller) P.; m. Judith Anne Griessel, Aug. 24, 1963; children—Elisabeth Anne, Nevin Edward. B.A., Gettysburg Coll., 1960; Ph.D., U. Colo., 1965. Asst. prof. fgn. langs. Valparaiso (Ind.) U., 1965-69, asso. prof., 1969-75, dir. grad. div., 1967-70; acting dean Valparaiso (Ind.) U. (Coll. Arts and Scis.), 1970-71, asso. dean, 1971-74, dean, 1974-81, prof. fgn. langs., 1975—, chair dept. Fgn. Langs. and Lits., 1994—. NDEA fellow, 1960-63. Mem. Midwest MLA, Phi Beta Kappa, Sigma Delta Pi, Phi Sigma Iota. Lutheran. Home: 860 N Cr 500 E Valparaiso IN 46383 Office: Meier Hall Rm 113 Valparaiso U Valparaiso IN 46383

PETERS, JON, film producer, film company executive; b. Van Nuys, Calif., 1947; m. 2d Lesley Ann Warren; 1 child; m. 3d Christine Peters. Founder hairstyling bus.; founder Jon Peters Orgn., 1980; formed The Boardwalk Co. (with Peter Guber and Neil Bogart), Guber-Peters-Barris Co., 1988; co-chmn. Columbia Pictures Entertainment Inc., 1989-91, head Jon Peters Group, 1991—. Producer films A Star Is Born, 1976, The Eyes of Laura Mars, 1978, The Main Event, 1979, Die Laughing, 1980, Caddyshack, 1980, Six Weeks, 1982, D.C. Cab, 1983, Flashdance, 1983, Visionquest, 1984, The Color Purple, 1985, The Legend of Billie Jean, 1985, The Clan of the Cave Bear, 1986, Youngblood, 1986, The Witches ofEastwick, 1987, Innerspace, 1987, Who's That Girl, 1987, Batman, 1989 Tango andCash, 1989; exec. producer Gorillas in the Mist, 1988, Missing Link, 1989, The Bonfire of the Vanities, 1990, Batman Returns, 1992, This Boy's Life, 1993. Office: Peters Entertainment Inc 433 N Camden Dr Beverly Hills CA 90210-4426 also: Columbia Pictures Industries 10202 Washington Blvd Culver City CA 90232-3119

PETERS, LAURALEE MILBERG, diplomat; b. Monroe, N.C., Jan. 28, 1943; d. Arthur W. and Opal I. (Mueller) Milberg; m. Lee M. Peters, May 30, 1964; children: David, Evelyn, Edward, Matthew. BA with highest honors, U. Kans., 1964, postgrad., 1965-67; student, Fgn Svc. Inst., 1975. Asst. pub. info. officer NAS, Washington, 1967-69; joined Fgn. Svc., Dept. State, 1972, commd. sr. fgn. svc. officer, 1985; chief visa sect. Am. Embassy, Saigon, Vietnam, 1972-74; internat. fin. officer Dept. State, Washington, 1975-79; U.S. rep. to Econ. and Social Commn. for Asia and Pacific, UN, Bangkok, Thailand, 1979-81; devel. fin. officer Dept. State, Washington, 1981-82; econ. officer Israel, West Bank, Gaza, 1982-84; dir. Office Monetary Affairs Dept. State, Washington, 1984-86; econ. counselor Am. Embassy, Islamabad, Pakistan, 1986-88; career devel. officer Dept. State, Washington, 1988-89, dep. asst. sec. for personnel, 1989-91; mem. Sr. Seminar, 1991-92; U.S. Ambassador to Sierra Leone, 1992-95; internat. affairs adviser to pres. Naval War Coll., 1995—. Various leadership positions Boy Scouts Am., 1977-88. Recipient Disting. award of merit Nat. Capitol Area Coun. Boy Scouts Am., 1986. Mem. Am. Fgn. Svc. Protective Assn. (v.p. 1981-84), Consular Officer's Assn. (sec. 1974-75), Phi Beta Kappa. Home: 9 Jackson Rd Newport RI 02840 Office: Naval War Coll Code 002 686 Cushing Rd Newport RI 02841-1207

PETERS, LEO FRANCIS, environmental engineer; b. Melrose, Mass., Aug. 14, 1937; s. Joseph Leander and Mary Gertrude (Phalen) P.; m. Joan Catherine Anderson, May 20, 1961; children: Elizabeth M., Susan J., Carolyn A., Jennifer L. BS in Civil Engring., Northeastern U., Boston, 1960, MS in Civil Engring., 1966; postgrad., Harvard U., 1989. Registered profl. engr., Mass., N.H.; diplomate Am. Acad. Environ. Engrs. Jr. engr. N.Y. Dept. Transp., Albany, 1960-61; chief engr. John M. Cashman, Weymouth, Mass., 1961-62; project engr. Metcalf & Eddy, Inc., Boston, 1962-65; project engr. Weston & Sampson, Boston, 1965-67, assoc., 1967-70, ptnr., 1970-76; exec. v.p. Weston & Sampson Engrs., Inc., Boston, 1976-82; pres. Weston & Sampson Engrs., Inc., Wakefield and Peabody, Mass., 1982—; mem. Northeastern U. Corp., 1992; treas. The Engring. Ctr., 1991-93; pres. The Engring. Ctr. Edn. Trust, 1994-95. Clk., mem. Melrose (Mass.) Planning Bd., 1969-91. Named Young Engr. of Yr. Mass. Soc. Profl. Engrs. Fellow Am. Cons. Engrs. Coun. (v.p. 1995—); mem. Am. Water Works Assn., Am. Pub. Works Assn., Water Environ. Fedn., Am. Cons. Engrs. Coun. New Eng. (pres. 1990-91), New Eng. Water Works Assn. (pres. 1989-90). Roman Catholic. Home: 187 E Emerson St Melrose MA 02176-3534 Office: Weston & Sampson Engrs Inc 5 Centennial Dr Peabody MA 01960-7906

PETERS, LEON, JR., electrical engineering educator, research administrator; b. Columbus, Ohio, May 28, 1923; s. Leon P. and Ethel (Howland) Pierce; m. Mabel Marie Johnson, June 6, 1953; children: Amy T. Peters Thomas, Melinda A. Peters Todaro, Maria C., Patricia D., Lee A., Roberta J. Peters Cameruca, Karen E. Peters Ellingson. B.S.E.E., Ohio State U., 1950, M.S., 1954, Ph.D., 1959. Asst. prof. elec. engring. Ohio State U., Columbus, 1959-63; assoc. prof. Ohio State U., 1963-67, prof., 1967-93, prof. emeritus, 1993—; assoc. dept. chmn. for rsch. Ohio State U., Columbus, 1990-92, dir. electro sci. lab., 1983-94. Contbr. articles to profl. jours. Served to 2d lt. U.S. Army, 1942-46, ETO. Fellow IEEE. Home: 2087 Ellington Rd Columbus OH 43221 Office: Ohio State U Electrosci Lab 1320 Kinnear Rd Columbus OH 43212-1156

PETERS, MERCEDES, psychoanalyst; b. N.Y.C. Student Columbia U., 1944-45; BS, L.I. U., 1945; MS, U. Conn., 1953; tng. in psychotherapy Am. Inst. Psychotherapy and Psychoanalysis, 1960-70; cert. in Psychoanalysis Postgrad. Ctr. For Mental Health, 1976; PhD in Psychoanalysis, Union Inst., 1989. Cert. psychoanalyst Am. Examining Bd. Psychoanalysis; cert. mental health cons. Sr. psychotherapist Cmty. Guidance Svc., 1960-75; staff affiliate Postgrad. Ctr. for Mental Health, 1974-76; pvt. practice psychoanalysis and psychotherapy, Bklyn., 1961—. Contbr. articles to profl. jours. Bd. dirs. Brookwood Child Care Assn.; mem. vestry Grace Ch., Brooklyn Heights. Fellow Am. Orthopsychiat. Assn.; mem. LWV, NAACP, NASW, Postgrad. Psychoanalytic Soc., Wednesday Club. Office: 142 Joralemon St Brooklyn NY 11201-4709

PETERS, R. JONATHAN, lawyer, chemical company executive; b. Janesville, Wis., Sept. 6, 1927; m. Ingrid H. Varvayn, 1953; 1 dau., Christina. B.S. in Chemistry, U. Ill., 1951; J.D., Northwestern U., 1954. Bar: Ill. 1954. Chief patent counsel Englehard Industries, 1972-82, Kimberly-Clark Corp., Neenah, Wis., 1982-85; gen. counsel Lanxide Corp., Newark, Del., 1985-87; pvt. practice Chgo., 1985—. Served with CIC, U.S. Army, 1955-57. Patentee in field. Mem. ABA, Am. Intellectual Property Law Assn., Lic. Execs. Soc., Assn. Corp. Patent Counsel. Clubs: North Shore Golf (Menasha, Wis.), Masons, Scottish Rite, Shriners.

PETERS, RALPH EDGAR, business executive; b. Harrisburg, Pa., Feb. 20, 1923; s. George Edward and Rebecca Flavia (Michener) P.; m. Roberta Jane Shaffer, June 12, 1948; children: Sheila Jane, Gail Marie, Ralph Jr., Bret Edward. Student, U. Pa., 1942; BA in Bus. Adminstrn., Pa. State U., 1948. From payroll supr. to asst. budget supr. Pa. State U., 1948-52; chief acct., pers. officer Haller, Raymond & Brown, State College, Pa., 1952-54; from contr. to CEO and chmn. bd. Benatec Assocs., Inc. (formerly Berger Assocs., Inc.), Camp Hill, Pa., 1954—; bd. dirs. CCNB Bank, New Cumberland, Pa., 1972-93. Chmn. bd. advisors Pa. State U., Harrisburg, 1979—; chmn. bd. dirs. Holy Spirit Hosp., Camp Hill, 1982—; past pres. Tri-County United Way, Harrisburg, from 1978; chmn. Pvt. Industry Coun., Harrisburg, 1982-87. With U.S. Army, 1943-45, ETO, 1952-53, Korea. Recipient Community Svc. award Salvation Army, 1980, Disting. Alumnus award Pa. State U., 1980, Disting. Pennsylvanian award Greater Phila. C. of C., 1981, Catalyst award Capital Region Economic Devel., 1992. Mem. Pa. C. of C. (bd. dir., transp. com. chmn. 1972-90), Harrisburg Area C. of C. (pres., chmn. 1979-83), Ams. for Competitive Enterprise System (pres. 1981-83), Cumberland County Transp. Authority, Susquehanna Valley Regional Airport Authority, Lions, Masons, Pa. Jaycees (pres. 1955-56, nat. v.p. 1956-57), Delta Sigma Pi. Lutheran. Office: Benatec Assocs Inc 101 Erford Rd Camp Hill PA 17011-1808

PETERS, RALPH FREW, investment banker; b. Mineola, N.Y., Mar. 21, 1929; s. Ralph and Helen Louise (Frew) P.; m. Diana Joyce Clayton, Dec. 19, 1969; children: Louise Frew, Jean Reid, Ralph Frew, Melvyn T., Richard Clayton. B.A., Princeton U., 1951; postgrad., Stonier Grad. Sch. Banking, Rutgers U., 1962. With Corn Exchange Bank & Trust Co., 1947-52; chmn. bd., dir. Discount Corp. N.Y., N.Y.C., 1955-93; dir. Internat. Investors Inc., Sun Life Ins. & Annuity of N.Y., U.S. Life Ins. Fund. Served with USNR, 1948-55. Mem. Pub. Securities Assn. (gov.), Anglers Club, Leash Club, Links Club, North Woods Club. Episcopalian.

PETERS, RALPH MARTIN, education educator; b. Knoxville, Tenn., May 9, 1926; s. Tim C. and Alma (Shannon) P.; m. Lorraine Daniel, 1949; children—Teresa, Marta. B.S., Lincoln Meml. U., 1949; M.S., U. Tenn., 1953, Ed.D., 1960. Tchr. pub. schs. Lincoln Meml. U., 1956-63, prof., dept. chmn., v.p., 1956-63, 92-96; prof. edn., dean students, dean Grad. Sch. Tenn. Tech. U., Cookeville, 1963-89; dean emeritus, 1989. Editor publs. Served with Armed Forces, World War II. Mem. Phi Kappa Phi, Phi Delta Kappa, Omicron Delta Kappa. Baptist. Club: Rotary. Home: 927 Mt Vernon Rd Cookeville TN 38501-1576

PETERS, RAYMOND EUGENE, computer systems company executive; b. New Haven, Aug. 24, 1933; s. Raymond and Doris Winthrop (Smith) P.; m. Millie Mather, July 14, 1978 (div. Nov. 1983). Student, San Diego City Coll., 1956-61; cert., Lumbleau Real Estate Sch., 1973, Southwestern Coll., Chula Vista, Calif., 1980. Cert. quality assurance engr. Founder, pub. Silhouette Pub. Co., San Diego, 1960-75; co-founder, news dir. Sta. XEGM, San Diego, 1964-68; news dir. Sta. XERB, Tijuana, Mex., 1973-74; founder, chief exec. officer New World Airways, Inc., San Diego, 1974-75; co-founder, exec. vice chmn. bd. San Cal Rail, Inc.-San Diego Trolley, San Diego, 1974-77; founder, pres. Ansonia Sta., micro systems, San Diego, 1986—; cons. on multimedia and electronic commerce sys., 1995—; co-founder, dir. S.E. Cmty. Theatre, San Diego, 1960-68; commr. New World Aviation Acad., Otay Mesa, Calif., 1971-77; co-founder New World Internat. Trade and Commerce Commn., Inc., 1991—. Author: Black Americans in Aviation, 1971, Profiles in Black American History, 1974, Eagles Don't Cry, 1988; founder, pub., editor Oceanside Lighthouse, 1958-60, San Diego Herald Dispatch, 1959-60. Co-founder, bd. dirs. San Diego County Econ. Opportunity Commn., 1964-67; co-founder Edn. Cultural Complex, San Diego, 1966-75; co-founder, exec. dir. S.E. Anti-Poverty Planning Coun., Inc., 1964-67; mem. U.S. Rep. Senatorial Inner Circle Com., Washington, 1990—; mem. bus. adv. bd. VAR, 1995. With U.S. Army, 1950-53, Korea. Mem. Am. Soc. Quality Control, Nat. City C. of C., Afro-Am. Micro Sys. Soc. (exec. dir. 1987—), Negro Airmen Internat. (Calif. pres. 1970-75, nat. v.p. 1975-77), Tuskegee Airmen (charter, bd. dirs. Benjamin O. Davis chpt. 1995—), Internat. Platform Assn., U.S. C. of C., Greater San Diego Minority C. of C. (bd. dirs. 1974—, past chmn. bd.), Masons (most worshipful grand master, supreme coun.), Shriners (Disting. Cmty. Svc. award 1975). Republican. Avocations: creative writing, golf, world history. Home: Meadowbrook Estates # 245 8301 Mission Gorge Rd Santee CA 92071-3500

PETERS, RICHARD T., lawyer; b. La Mesa, Calif., Sept. 24, 1946. BA, Santa Clara U., 1968; JD, UCLA, 1971. Bar: Calif. 1972. Ptnr. Sidley & Austin, L.A. Fellow Am. Coll. Banking; mem. State Bar Calif. (mem. debtor-creditor rels. and bankruptcy subcom. bus. law sect. 1979-81, chmn. 1981-82, mem. exec. com. bus. law sect. 1982-85, vice chmn. 1984-85), Calif. Continuing Edn. Bar (cons. 1984), L.A. Fin. Lawyers Conf. (bd. govs. 1976-80). Office: Sidley & Austin 555 W 5th St Fl 40 Los Angeles CA 90013-1010

PETERS, ROBERTA, soprano; b. N.Y.C., May 4, 1930; d. Sol and Ruth (Hirsch) P.; m. Bertram Fields, Apr. 10, 1955; children: Paul, Bruce. Ed. privately; Litt.D., Elmira Coll., 1967; Mus. D., Ithaca Coll., 1968, Colby Coll., 1980; L.H.D., Westminster Coll., 1974, Lehigh U., 1977; D.F.A., St. John's U., 1982; LittD, Coll. New Rochelle, 1989. Author: Debut at the Met; Met. Opera debut as Zerlina in Don Giovanni, 1950; recorded numerous operas; appeared motion pictures; frequent appearances radio and TV; sang at Royal Opera House, Covent Garden, London, Vienna State Opera, Munich Opera, West Berlin Opera, Salzburg Festival, debuts at festivals in Vienna and Munich; concert tours in U.S., Soviet Union, Scandinavian countries, Israel, China, Japan, Taiwan, South Korea, debut, Kirov Opera, Leningrad, USSR, sang at Bolshoi Opera, Moscow (1st Am. to receive Bolshoi medal). Trustee Carnegie Hall; dir. Met. Opera Guild; chmn. Nat. Inst. Music Theater, 1991—; apptd. by Pres. Bush to Nat. Coun. Arts, 1992. Named Woman of Yr. Fedn. Women's Clubs, 1964; honored spl. ceremony on 35th anniversary with the Met. Opera Co., 1985; was 1st Am. to receive Bolshoi medal, 1972. Office: ICM Artists Ltd 40 W 57th St New York NY 10019-4001 *I believe that life is a series of just one darn thing after another. If we can learn that, we can expect, meet, and solve our problems.*

PETERS, SARAH WHITAKER, art historian, writer, lecturer; b. Kenosha, Wis., Aug. 17, 1924; d. Robert Burbank and Margaret Jebb (Allen) Whitaker; m. Arthur King Peters, Oct. 21, 1943; children: Robert Bruce, Margaret Allen, Michael Whitaker. BA, Sarah Lawrence Coll., 1954; MA, Columbia U., 1966; student, L'Ecole du Louvre, Paris, 1967-68; diplome,

Ecole des Trois Gourmandes, Paris, 1968; PhD, CUNY, 1987. Freelance critic Art in Am., N.Y.C.; lectr.-in-residence Garrison Forest Sch., Owings Mills, Md.; adj. asst. prof. art history C.W. Post, U. L.I.; lectr. Bronxville (N.Y.) Adult Sch., Internat. Mus. Photography, 1979, Tufts U., 1979, Madison (Wis.) Art Ctr., 1984, Meml. Art Gallery, Rochester, N.Y., 1988, 91, Caramoor Mus., Katonah, N.Y., 1988, Yale U. Art Gallery, New Haven, Conn., 1989, The Cosmopolitan Club, N.Y.C., 1977, 91, Sarah Lawrence Coll., Bronxville, 1992, The Phillips Collection, Washington, 1993, Mpls. Inst. Arts, 1993, Whitney Mus. Am. Art, Champion, 1994, U. Wis., Parkside, 1994, Nat. Mus. Wildlife Art, Jackson Hole, Wyo., 1995. Author: Becoming O'Keeffe: The Early Years, 1991, The Dictionary of Art, 1996; contbr. articles to profl. jours. Mem. Coll. Art Assn., Bronxville Field Club, The Cosmopolitan Club. Avocations: horsemanship, mountaineering, tennis, cooking. Home: 14 Village Ln Bronxville NY 10708-4806

PETERS, STEPHEN JAY, lawyer; b. Jeffersonville, Ind., Apr. 15, 1955; s. Jerome Humphrey and Mildred Mae (Cooper) P.; m. Paula Gail Zaremba, Oct. 12, 1985; 1 child, Kirsten Alexandra. BA cum laude, Amherst Coll., 1977; JD, Ind. U., 1980. Bar: Ind. 1981, U.S. Dist. Ct. (so. dist.) Ind. 1981, U.S. Ct. Appeals (7th cir.) 1982, U.S. Dist. Ct. (no. dist.) Ind. 1983, U.S. Supreme Ct. 1985. Assoc. Stewart, Irwin, Gilliom, Fuller & Meyer, Indpls., 1980-85, Stewart, Irwin, Gilliom, Meyer & Guthrie, Indpls., 1985-87; ptnr. Stewart & Irwin, Indpls., 1987—. Author, editor: (book) Litigating Insurance Claims in Indiana, 1992. Named Outstanding Young Man in Am., U.S. Jaycees, 1984. Mem. ABA, Def. Rsch. Inst., Ind. State Bar Assn., 7th Cir. Bar Assn., Ind. Def. Lawyers Assn., Lawyers Club Indpls. Office: Stewart & Irwin 251 E Ohio St Ste 1100 Indianapolis IN 46204

PETERS, STEPHEN PAUL, pastor; b. Warsaw, Ind., May 25, 1953; s. Jack Klyne and Stellina Maxine (Mustard) P.; m. Susan Christine Jamison Peters, June 28, 1975; children: Suzanne, Stephen Jr., Scott, Stewart, Sarah, Seth. Student, Bob Jones U., 1972-73; BS, Liberty U., 1978; MA, Grace Grad. Sch., 1979. Ordained to ministry Maranatha Brethren Ch., 1984. Youth pastor Maranatha Brethren Ch., Hagerstown, Md., 1979-84; sr. pastor Cmty. Grace Brethren Ch., West Milton, Ohio, 1984—; bd. dirs. Christian Edn. Nat., Winona Lake, Ind., v.p. 1991-93, pres., 1993—; moderator Fellowship of Grace Brethern Ch., Winona Lake, Ind., 1995—, music dir. Nat. Conf., 1987, 89, Focus I Com., 1991-93, rep. Charis I & II, 1994, 96. Editor: The Bridge, 1991. Speaker and hon. inductee Nat. Honor Soc., West Milton, Ohio, 1996. Republican. Office: Cmty Grace Brethren Ch 2261 S Miami St West Milton OH 45383

PETERS, VIRGINIA, actress; b. Los Angeles, July 15, 1924; d. Peter and Tessie (Skiller) Stetzenko. Grad., Pasadena (Calif.) Playhouse, 1944; student, Los Angeles City Coll. Tchr. Burbank (Calif.) Little Theatre, 1978-80, Burbank Acad. Performing Arts, 1979—. TV appearances in Night Strangler, 1972, Love American Style, 1973, Rita Moreno Show, 1977, Laverne and Shirley, 1977, 78, Happy Days, 1977, Dallas, 1980, The Waltons, 1981, House Detective, 1985, Knight Rider, 1985, Murder She Wrote, 1986, Hunter, 1986, Hardcastle and McCormick, 1986, Cavanaughs, 1986, Paper Chase, 1986, also Days of Our Lives, Divorce Court, Grace Under Fire, 1993; film appearances include The Arrangement, 1968, The Cat People, 1981, Fast Times at Ridgemont High, 1982, Rat Boy, 1985, The Deacon Street Deer, 1985, My Demon Lover, Mr. President, The Judge, Stripped to Kill II, 1988, Hero, My Girl II; appeared in: TV movie The 11th Victim, 1979; TV pilot We Got It Made; also numerous commls. Mem. Masquers Club (past dir.), Pasadena Playhouse Alumni Assos. (past dir.). Democrat. Roman Catholic.

PETERS, WILLIAM, author, producer, director; b. San Francisco, July 30, 1921; s. William Ernest and Dorothy Louise (Wright) P.; m. Mercy Ann Miller, Oct. 12, 1942 (div. 1968); children: Suzanne Peters Payne, Geoffrey Wright, Jennifer Peters Johnson, Gretchen Peters Daniel; m. Helene Louise Yager White, May 31, 1987. BS, Northwestern U., 1947. Account exec. pub. relations J. Walter Thompson Co., Chgo., 1947-51; mem. fiction staff Ladies' Home Jour., 1951-52; article editor Woman's Home Companion, N.Y.C., 1952-53; freelance writer, Pelham, N.Y., 1953-62; producer CBS Reports, CBS News, N.Y.C., 1962-66; freelance writer, film dir. and TV producer/exec. producer N.Y.C., 1966-82; dir. Yale U. Films, New Haven, 1982-89; freelance writer, film dir., TV producer/exec. producer Guilford, Conn., 1990—; cons. race relations, 1959—, hist. TV documentaries, 1976—. Author: American Memorial Hospital--Reims, France: A History, 1955, Passport to Friendship--The Story of the Experiment in International Living, 1957, The Southern Temper, 1959, (with Mrs. Medgar Evers) For Us, The Living, 1967, A Class Divided, 1971; A More Perfect Union, 1987, A Class Divided: Then and Now, 1987; producer, writer, dir. documentaries Storm Over the Supreme Court, Parts II and III, 1963 (George F. Peabody award, Golden Gavel award ABA), (co-producer) After Ten Years: The Court and the Schools, 1964 (Nat. Sch. Bell award NEA), The Eye of the Storm, 1970 (George Foster Peabody award, Christopher award, Cine Golden Eagle award), Suddenly an Eagle, 1976 (George Foster Peabody award, Cine Golden Eagle award), Death of a Family, 1979 (Writers Guild Am. award), A Bond of Iron, 1982, A Class Divided, 1985 (Emmy award, Sidney Hillman award, Cine Golden Eagle award), others; exec. producer dramas Boswell's London Journal, 1986, others. Co-founder North Shore Citizens Com., 1946, bd. dirs., 1946-51; co-founder Pelham Com. Human Relations, 1963, vice chmn., 1963-65, chmn., 1965-66. Served to capt. USAAF, 1942-45, ETO. Decorated Air medal with 2 oak leaf clusters, D.F.C.; recipient Benjamin Franklin mag. award, 1954; Peabody TV award, 1963, 70, 76, Golden Gavel award ABA, 1963, Sch. Bell award NEA, 1964, Emmy award, Sidney Hillman award, 1985. Mem. Dirs. Guild Am., Writers Guild Am. Democrat. Home: 3108 Long Hill Rd Guilford CT 06437-3619

PETERS, WILLIAM P., oncologist, science administrator, educator; b. Buffalo, Aug. 26, 1950; m. Elizabeth Zentai; children: Emily, Abigail, James. BS, BS, BA, Pa. State U., 1972; MPhil, PhD, Columbia U., 1976, MD, 1978; postgrad., Harvard U., 1984; MBA, Duke U., 1990. Diplomate Am. Bd. Internal Medicine, Am. Bd. Med. Oncology. Prof. medicine Duke U. Med. Ctr.; assoc. dir. for clin. ops. Duke Comprehensive Cancer Ctr.; dir. bone marrow transplant program Duke U. Med. Ctr., Durham, N.C., 1984-95; pres., CEO Mich. Cancer Found., Detroit, 1995—; assoc. dean Wayne State U., Detroit, 1995—; pres., dir., CEO Karmanos Cancer Inst., Detroit. Office: Presidents Office Karmanos Cancer Inst 110 E Warren Detroit MI 48201

PETERSDORF, ROBERT GEORGE, physician, medical educator; b. Berlin, Feb. 14, 1926; s. Hans H. and Sonja P.; m. Patricia Horton Qua, June 2, 1951; children: Stephen Hans, John Eric. BA, Brown U., 1948, DMS (hon.), 1983; MD cum laude, Yale U., 1952; ScD (hon.), Albany Med. Coll., 1979; MA (hon.), Harvard U., 1980; DMS (hon.), Med. Coll. Pa., 1982, Brown U., 1983; DMS, Bowman-Gray Sch. Medicine, 1986; LHD (hon.), N.Y. Med. Coll., 1986; DSc (hon.), SUNY, Bklyn., 1987, Med. Coll. Ohio, 1987, Univ. Health Scis., The Chgo. Med. Sch., 1987, St. Louis U., 1988; LHD (hon.), Ea. Va. Med. Sch., 1988; DSc (hon.), Sch. Medicine, Georgetown U., 1991, Emory U., 1992, Tufts U., 1993, Mt. Sinai Sch. Medicine, 1993, George Washington U., 1994; other hon. degrees. Diplomate Am. Bd. Internal Medicine. Intern, asst. resident Yale U., New Haven, 1952-54; sr. asst. resident Peter Bent Brigham Hosp., Boston, 1954-55; fellow Johns Hopkins Hosp., Balt., 1955-59; chief resident, instr. medicine Yale U., 1957-58; asst. prof. medicine Johns Hopkins U., 1957-60, physician, 1958-60; assoc. prof. medicine U. Wash., Seattle, 1960-62, prof., 1962-79, chmn. dept. medicine, 1964-79; physician-in-chief U. Wash. Hosp., 1964-79; pres. Brigham and Women's Hosp., Boston, 1979-81; prof. medicine Harvard U. Med. Sch., Boston, 1979-81; dean, vice chancellor health scis. U. Calif.-San Diego Sch. Medicine, 1981-86; clin. prof. infectious diseases Sch. Medicine Georgetown U., 1986-94; pres. Assn. Am. Med. Colls., Washington, 1986-94, pres. emeritus, 1994—; prof. medicine U. Wash., 1994—, disting. prof., 1995; disting. physician Vets. Health Adminstrn., Seattle, 1994—; cons. to surgeon gen. USPHS, 1960-79; cons. USPHS Hosp., Seattle, 1962-79; mem. spl. med. adv. group VA, 1987-94. Editor: Harrison's Priciples of Internal Medicine, 1968-90; contbr. numerous articles to profl. jours. Served with USAAF, 1944-46. Recipient Lilly medal Royal Coll. Physicians, London, 1978, Wiggers award Albany Med. Coll., 1979, Robert H. Williams award Assn. Profs. Medicine, 1983, Keen award Brown U., 1980, Disting. Svc. award Baylor Coll. Medicine, 1989, Scroll of Merit Nat. Med. Assn., 1990, 2d Ann. Founder's award Assn. Program Dirs. in Internal Medicine, 1991, Flexner award Assn. Amer. Med. Coll., 1994; named Disting. Internist of 1987, Am. Soc. Internal Medicine; Disting. Teacher award 1993, Amer. Coll. of Physicians. Felow AAAS, ACP (prs. 1975-76, Stengel award 1980, Disting. Tchr. award 1993), Am. Coll. Physician Execs. (hon.); mem. Inst. Medicine of NAS (councillor 1977-80), Assn. Am. Physicians (pres. 1976-77), Cosmos Club, Rainier Club. Home and Office: 1219 Parkside Dr E Seattle WA 98112-3717

PETERSEN, ANN NEVIN, computer systems administrator, consultant; b. Mexico City, Aug. 7, 1937; parents Am. citizens; d. Thomas Marshall and Gerry (Cox) Nevin; m. Norman William Petersen, Aug. 24, 1956; children: Richard, Robert, Thomas, Anita, David. AS in Electronics, Monterey Peninsula Coll., Monterey, Calif., 1962; student, U. N.Mex., 1956, Las Positas Coll., Livermore, Calif., 1992. Cert. computer profl. CAD mgr. Naval Air Rework Facility, Alameda, Calif., 1979-80; computer systems analyst Space and Naval Warfare System Command, Washington, 1980-84, Facilities Computer Systems Office, Port Hueneme, Calif., 1984-86; systems mgr. Lawrence Livermore Nat. Lab., Livermore, 1986-89; data base mgr. Clayton Environ. Cons., Pleasanton, Calif., 1989-90; computer systems mgr. Waltrip & Assocs., Sacramento, 1990-94; dir. computer systems, CFO Innovative Techs. Inc., Pleasanton, 1992—. Author databases. Bd. dirs. Am. Field Svc., Port Hueneme, 1976-78; mem. various adv. bds. U.S. Navy, 1957-86; mem. adv. bd. Calif. Deaf/Blind Regional Ctr., Sacramento, 1976-80; bd. dirs. ARC Alameda County, Hayward, Calif., 1992—. Recipient Superior Performance award U.S. Navy, 1980, Speaker of Month award Toastmasters, 1985. Mem. Data Processing Mgmt. Assn., bd. dirs., sec.), Assn. for Computing Machinery, Tri Valley MacIntosh Users Group, Inst. for Cert. of Computer Profls. Avocations: astronomy, rockhounding, sewing, tennis, painting. Office: Innovative Techs Inc 5238 Riverdale Ct Pleasanton CA 94588-3759

PETERSEN, ARNE JOAQUIN, chemist; b. L.A., Jan. 27, 1932; s. Hans Marie Theodore and Astrid Maria (Pedersen) P.; m. Sandra Joyce Sharp, Aug. 12, 1961; children: Christina Lynn, Kurt Arne. AA, Compton Coll., 1957; BS, Calif. State U., Long Beach, 1959; BA, U. Calif., Irvine, 1975. Comml. pilots lic. Chemist/scientist Beckman Instruments, Inc., Fullerton, Calif., 1959-62, engr., scientist, 1962-65, project, sr. project engr., 1965-74; project/program mgr. Beckman Clin. Ops., Fullerton/Brea, Calif., 1974-80; ops. mgr. Graphic Controls Corp., Irvine, 1980-82; engr./rsch. and devel. mgr. Carle Instruments, Anaheim, Calif., 1982-84; ops. mgr. Magnaflux/X-Ray Devel., L.A., 1984-85; rsch. and devel. dir., new products Am. Chem. Systems, Irvine, Calif., 1985-86; rsch. assoc. U. Calif., Irvine, 1987-88; ind. cons., contractor, sales real estate investment, 1989—; bus. cons. electronics co. Internat. Exec. Svc. Corps, 1993-94. Author scientific papers in field; patentee in field. Vol. F.I.S.H., Costa Mesa and Newport Beach, Calif.; basketball coach Boys-Girls, Newport Beach, 1975-78, baseball coach Newport Beach Parks, 1975-78; adv. com. Newport/Costa Mesa Sch. Bd., 1974-75. Sgt. USAF, 1951-55. Mem. AAAS, Am. Chem. Soc., Biomed. Engring. Soc., Am. Mgmt. Assn., Internat. Exec. Svc. Corps (exec. svc. with Agy Internat. Devel., 1993, 94), U. Calif. Irvine Club (bd. dirs.), Kappa Sigma. Avocations: flying, photography, surfing, travel, Bridge.

PETERSEN, BENT EDVARD, mathematician, educator; b. Copenhagen, July 31, 1942; came to U.S., 1964; s. Edvard Valdemar and Grethe Julie (Larsen) P.; m. Marguerite Kathleen Anne McCrindle, Aug. 21, 1965; children: Erik, Poul, Kirsten. BS, U. B.C., Vancouver, Can., 1964; PhD, MIT, 1968. Asst. prof. math. Oreg. State U., Corvallis, 1968-74, assoc. prof. math., 1974-80, prof. math., 1980—; vis. mem. Inst. Advanced Study, Princeton, N.J., 1973-74; guest scientist Internat. Atomic Energy Agy., Trieste, Italy, 1975. Author: Introduction to the Fourier Transform and Pseudo-differential Operators, 1983. Mem. Am. Math. Soc., Math. Assn. Am., Oreg. Acad. Sci., Sigma Xi. Office: Oreg State U Dept Math Corvallis OR 97331-4605

PETERSEN, BENTON LAURITZ, paralegal; b. Salt Lake City, Jan. 1, 1942; s. Lauritz George and Arleane (Curtis) P.; m. Sharon Donnette Higgins, Sept. 20, 1974 (div. Aug. 9, 1989); children: Grant Lauritz, Tashya Eileen, Nicholas Robert, Katrina Arleane. AA, Weber State Coll., 1966, BA, 1968; BA, Weber State Coll., 1968; M of Liberal Studies, U. Okla., 1980; diploma, Nat. Radio Inst. Paralegal Sch., 1991. Registered paralegal. Announcer/news dir. KWHO Radio, Salt Lake City, 1968-70, KDXU Radio, St. George, Utah, 1970-73, KSOP Radio, Salt Lake City, 1973-76; case worker/counselor Salvation Army, Midland, Tex., 1976-84; announcer/news dir. KBRS Radio, Springdale, Ark., 1984-86; case worker/counselor Office of Human Concern, Rogers, Ark., 1986-88; announcer KZAM Radio, Sedona, Ariz., 1988-91; paralegal Benton L. Petersen, Manti, Utah, 1991—; cons. Sanpete County Srs., Manti, 1992—. Award judge Manti City Beautification, 1992—; treas. Manti Destiny Com., 1993—; tourism com. Sanpete County Econ. Devel., Ephraim, Utah, 1993—. Served with U.S. Army N.G., 1959-66. Mem. Am. Soc. Notaries, Nat. Assn. Federated Tax Preparers, Nat. Paralegal Assn., Am. Legion. Mem. LDS Ch. Avocations: reading, participating in Doctor Who role playing games. Home: 470 E 120 N Manti UT 84642-0011 Office: Benton L Petersen ND Paralegal Svcs 470 E 120 N Manti UT 84642-0011

PETERSEN, CATHERINE HOLLAND, lawyer; b. Norman, Okla., Apr. 24, 1951; d. John Hays and Helen Ann (Turner) Holland; m. James Frederick Petersen, June 26, 1973 (div.); children: T. Kyle, Lindsay Diane. B.A., Hastings Coll., 1973; J.D., Okla. U., 1976. Bar: Okla. 1976, U.S. Dist. Ct. (we. dist.) Okla. 1978. Legal intern, police legal advisor City of Norman, 1974-76; sole practice, Norman, 1976-81; ptnr. Williams Petersen & Denny, Norman, 1981-82; pres. Petersen Assocs., Inc., Norman, 1982—; adj. prof. Okla. City U. Coll. Law, 1982, U. Okla. Law Ctr., 1987; instr. continuing legal edn. U. Okla. Law Ctr., Norman, 1977, 79, 81, 83, 84, 86, 89-95. Bd. dirs. United Way, Norman, 1978-84, pres., 1981; bd. dirs. Women's Resource Ctr., Norman, 1975-77, 82-84; mem. Jr. League, Norman, 1980-83, Norman Hosp. Aux., Norman, 1982-84; trustee 1st Presbyn. Ch., 1986-87. Named to Outstanding Okla. Women of 1980's, Women's Polit. Caucus, 1980, Outstanding Women Am., 1981, 83. Fellow Am. Acad. Matrimonial Lawyers (pres. Okla. chpt. 1990-91, bd. govs. 1991-95); mem. ABA (seminar instr. 1993, 95, 96), Cleve. County Bar Assn., Okla. Bar Assn. (chmn. family law sect. 1987-88, seminar instr. 1986-93, 95), Phi Delta Phi. Republican. Home: 4716 Sundance Ct Norman OK 73072-3900 Office: PO Box 1243 314 E Comanche St Norman OK 73069-6009

PETERSEN, DAVID L., lawyer. AA, Concordia Jr. Coll., Milw., 1963; BA, Concordia Sr. Coll., Ft. Wayne, Ind., 1965; JD, Valparaiso U., Ind., 1968. Bar: Wis. 1968, U.S. Dist. Ct. (ea. dist.) Wis. 1969, U.S. Ct. Appeals (7th cir.) 1972, U.S. Supreme Ct. 1988, Fla. 1989. Ptnr. Quarles & Brady, Milw. and West Palm Beach, Fla., 1968—. Author: Wisconsin Condominium Law, 1988, 94; editor Valparaiso U. Law Rev., 1967-68; contbr. articles to profl. jours. Mem. Greater Milw. Com. Community Devel., 1983; bd. dirs. Goals for Greater Milw. 2000, 1982, Broward Com. of 100. Lt. col., instr. pilot USAF/Wis. Air N.G., 1970-90. Mem. ABA, Wis. Bar Assn., Milw. Bar Assn., Fla. Bar Assn., Broward County Bar Assn., Palm Beach County Bar, Wis. Mortgage Bankers Assn., Am. Coll. Real Estate Lawyers, Milw. Yacht Club, Palm Beach Yacht Club. Office: Quarles & Brady 222 Lakeview Ave 4th Fl West Palm Beach FL 33401-6145 also: Quarles & Brady 411 E Wisconsin Ave Milwaukee WI 53202-4409

PETERSEN, DONALD SONDERGAARD, lawyer; b. Pontiac, Ill., May 14, 1929; s. Clarence Marius and Esther (Sondergaard) P.; m. Alice Thorup, June 5, 1954; children: Stephen, Susan Petersen Schuh, Sally Petersen Riordan. Student, Grand View Coll., 1946-48; B.A., Augustana Coll., Rock Island, Ill., 1951; J.D., Northwestern U., 1956. Bar: Ill. 1957. Assoc. Norman & Billick and predecessors, Chgo., 1956-64, ptnr., 1965-78; counsel Sidley & Austin, Chgo., 1978-80, ptnr., 1980-93, ret., 1993; pres. Chgo. Exhibitors Corp., Chgo., 1978-85. Bd. dirs. Mount Olive Cemetery Co. Inc., Chgo., 1972-90; bd. dirs. Augustana Hosp., 1983-87, Danish Old People's Home, 1976—; bd. dirs. Luth. Gen. Hosp., Park Ridge, Ill., 1968—, chmn., 1979-81, 89-91; bd. dirs. Luth. Gen. Health System and predecessors, Park Ridge, 1980-95, chmn., 1980-81, 83-85; bd. dirs., chmn. Parkside Health Mgmt. Corp., Parkside Home Health Svcs., 1985-88. With U.S. Army, 1951-53. Mem. Chgo. Bar Assn., Ill. State Bar Assn. Club: Union League (Chgo.). Home: 241 N Aldine Ave Park Ridge IL 60068-3009 Office: 1 First Nat Plz Ste 2550 Chicago IL 60603

PETERSEN, ELLEN ANNE, artist; b. N.Y.C., Dec. 18, 1930; d. William George and Dina (Bochmeier) Heinrich; m. Ralph Lamon Petersen, Dec. 14, 1952; children: William, Bryan. BS, NYU, 1968, MS, 1970. Art educator Paramus (N.J.) High Sch., 1969-85; tchng. artist William Carlos Williams Ctr. for Arts, Rutherford, N.J., 1989-91; studio artist Parrish Mus., Southampton, N.Y., 1988—; artist workshops Guild Hall Mus., East Hampton, N.Y., 1992—; Video interview "Women in the Arts", Fairleigh Dickinson U., Teaneck, N.J., 1977, LTV-local TV, East Hampton, 1991. Represented in permanent collection Guild Hall Mus., East Hampton. Bd. dirs. Jimmy Ernst Artists' Alliance, East Hampton, N.Y., 1985-92; mem. edn. com. Parrish Art Mus., Southampton, 1989—; curator Springs Invitational Art Exhbn., East Hampton, 1994, 95. Recipient hon. mention Guild Hall Mus., 1994, 1st prize N.J. state Exhbn., East Orange, N.J., 1967, award Springs-Ashawagh Hall Invitational, East Hampton, 1993, Juried Exhbn., Parrish Mus., 1992. Mem. Nat. Women's Caucus of Art, Artists' Equity, Jimmy Ernst Artists' Alliance (treas. 1988-90, v.p. 1990-92), Art Students' League (life), Women's Caucus for Art (v.p. Dallas chpt. 1987-88). Avocations: musician/playing the recorder in Greensleeves Consort ensemble. Home and Studio: 7 S Pond Rd East Hampton NY 11937-3719

PETERSEN, EVELYN ANN, education consultant; b. Gary, Ind., July 2, 1936; d. Eric Maxwell and Julia Ann (Kustron) Ivany; m. Ozzie G. Hebert, Feb. 27, 1957 (div. July 1963); children: Heather Lynn Petersen Hewett, Eric Dean Hebert; m. Jon Edwin Petersen, June 13, 1964; children: Karin Patricia, Kristin Shawn. BS, Purdue U., 1964; MA, Cen. Mich. U., 1977. Cert. tchr. elem. edn. with early childhood and vocat. edn. endorsements, Mich. Elem. tchr. Harford Day Sch., Bel Air, Md., 1958-62, Interlochen (Mich.) Elem. Sch., 1964-67; dir., tchr. Traverse City (Mich.) Coop. Presch., 1969-77; off-campus instr. grad. level Cen. Mich. U., Mt. Pleasant, 1977-92; Child Devel. Assoc. nat. rep. Coun. for Early Childhood Profl. Recognition, Washington, 1981—; instr. N.W. Mich. Coll., Traverse City, 1974-75, 78, U. Wis., Sheboygan, 1981-83; project dir., instr. West Shore C.C., Scotville, Mich., 1984-86, 89; ednl. cons., 1980—; parenting columnist Detroit Free Press, Knight Ridder Tribune Wire, 1984—; bd. mem. Children's Trust Fund, Lansing, Mich., 1983-85; mem. ad hoc adv. com. Bd. Edn. State of Mich., Lansing, 1985-86, child care provider trainer Dept. Social Svcs., 1988; chairperson adv. bd. Traverse Bay Vocat. Edn. Child Care Program, 1976-79; panelist Nat. Parenting Ctr., L.A., 1992—. Author: A Practical Guide to Early Childhood Planning, Methods and Materials: The What, Why and How of Lesson Plans, 1996; author, co-prodr. (audio and video cassette series) Parent Talk, 1990, Effective Home Visits: Video Training, 1994. County coord. Week of the Young Child, Traverse City, 1974-78; vol. probate ct. Traverse City, 1973-83; commr. Traverse City Human Rights Commn., 1981-82. Mem. AAUW (chairperson, coord. Touch & Do Exploratorium 1974-76), Nat. Fedn. Press Women, Nat. Assn. for Edn. of Young Children, Children's Trust Fund for Abuse Prevention, Mich. Assn. for Edn. of Young Children, Mich. Mental Health Assn., Assn. for Childhood Edn. Internat., Author's Guild. Avocations: writing, reading, travel, snorkeling. Home and Office: 843 S Long Lake Rd Traverse City MI 49684

PETERSEN, GLADYS, accounting clerk, writer; b. Guayaquil, Ecuador, June 3, 1941; d. Ezio and Rebeca (Ratti) Bellettini; m. Ronald Petersen, July 4, 1965. Grad. in med. secretarial, Nat. Sch, L.A., 1987; student, Los Angeles Valley Coll., 1992. With accounts receivable/accounts payable So. Calif. Wholesales Co., L.A.; acctg. clk. Prudential Ins. Co., L.A. Mem. World of Poets (3 awards). Home: 330 N Cordova St Burbank CA 91505-3412

PETERSEN, JAMES L., lawyer; b. Bloomington, Ill., Feb. 3, 1947; s. Eugene and Cathryn Teresa (Hemmele) P.; m. Helen Louise Moser, Nov. 20, 1971; children: Christine Louise, Margaret Teresa. BA, Ill. State U., 1970; MA, Sangamon State U., 1973; JD magna cum laude, Ind. U., 1976. Bar: Ind. 1976, Fla. 1980, U.S. Dist. Cts. (no. and so. Ind.), U.S. Ct. Appeals (7th cir.), U.S. Supreme Ct. Admissions officer Sangamon State U., Springfield, Ill., 1970-71, asst. to v.p., 1971-72, registrar, 1972-73; assoc. Ice Miller Donadio & Ryan, Indpls., 1976-83, ptnr., 1983—. Pres. United Cerebral Palsy of Ctrl. Ind., 1981-83, pres. Found., 1988-90. Mem. ABA, Fla. Bar Assn., Ind. Bar Assn., Internat. Assn. Def. Counsel, Ill. State U. Alumni Assn. (pres. 1990-92), Ind. U. Law Alumni Assn. (bd. dirs. 1992—). Home: 11827 Sea Star Dr Indianapolis IN 46256-9400 Office: Ice Miller Donadio & Ryan PO Box 82001 One American Sq Indianapolis IN 46282

PETERSEN, JEAN SNYDER, association executive; b. N.Y.C., Oct. 16, 1931; d. Peter Eugene and Helyn Brownell (Parker) Snyder; m. Elton Reed Petersen, Sept. 16, 1954; children—Bruce Brownell, Craig Reed. Student, N.Y. U., 1949-51; degree fgn. banking, Am. Inst. Banking, 1952. Fgn. credit investigator Chase Nat. Bank Hdqrs., N.Y.C., 1952-56; nat. exec. dir. Assn. Children and Adults with Learning Disabilities (name changed to Learning Disabilities Assn. of Am.), Pitts., 1972—. Mem. exec. com., treas. Jr. League, Pitts.; bd. dirs. Found. for Children with Learning Disabilities, N.Y.C., Children's Hosp., Pitts., Music for Mt. Lebanon, Vocat. Rehab. Ctr., Pitts.; bd. dirs., v.p., mem. exec. com. Assn. Retarded Citizens Pa.; ptnr. UN Internat. Yr. of Disabled; ruling elder Presbyn. Ch.Assn. Retarded Citizens Pa.; mem. exec. com. Pat Buckley Moss Nat. Children's Charity Found. Recipient Sustainers award Jr. League, 1977, Recognition award, 1975, Pres.'s award, 1978. Mem. Meeting Planners Internat. (treas.), Am. Soc. Assn. Execs. Republican. Presbyterian. Home: 343 Shadowlawn Ave Pittsburgh PA 15216-1239 Office: 4156 Library Rd Pittsburgh PA 15234-1349

PETERSEN, KENNETH CLARENCE, chemical company executive; b. Chgo., Mar. 17, 1936; s. Clarence and Theresa (Tomazin) P.; m. Gladys Marie Boyte, Jan. 21, 1956; children: Robert, Michael, Karen, William, Eric, John. Student, Crane Jr. Coll., 1956-57, Wright Jr. Coll., 1957-58; BS in Chemistry, Northwestern U., 1960, MS in Organic Chemistry, 1963. Chem. lab. tech. Glidden Paint Co., Chgo., 1956-58; chemist, group leader Acme Resin Co., Forest Pk., Ill., 1958-64; group leader, research coordinator, research mgr. resin div., mgr. chemistry & tech., mgr. chem. div. mfg., v.p. mfg. then exec. v.p. Schenectady (N.Y.) Chems., Inc., 1964-81, pres., 1981-93; pres. Schenectady Internat. Inc. (formerly Schenectady Chems., Inc.), 1993—; bd. dirs. TRUSTCO, Schenectady; mem. The Fifty Group, tri-city area, 1981—. Contbr. articles to profl. jours.; holder 12 patents. bd. dirs. Schenectady Boys and Girls Club, 1980—, Sunnyview Hosp., Schenectady, 1982—, Schenctady Econ. Devel. Council, 1984—, Fund Raising Rev. Bd. Schenectady, 1985—. Mem. Am. Chem. Soc. (chmn. eastern N.Y. sect. 1979). Clubs: Mohawk, Mohawk Golf (Schenectady). Avocations: fishing, golf, bridge, poker. Office: Schenectady Internat Inc Congress And # 10th Sts Schenectady NY 12303

PETERSEN, MARTIN EUGENE, museum curator; b. Grafton, Iowa, Apr. 21, 1931; s. Martin S. and Martha Dorothea (Paulsen) P. B.A., State U. Iowa, 1951, M.A., 1957; postgrad., The Hague (Netherlands), 1964. Curator San Diego Mus. Art, 1957—; extension instr. U. Calif., 1958, lectr., 1960. Author art catalogues, articles in field. Served with AUS, 1952-54. Mem. So. Calif. Art Historians. Home: 4571 Narragansett Ave San Diego CA 92107-2915 Office: San Diego Mus Art PO Box 2107 San Diego CA 92112-2107

PETERSEN, NORMAN RICHARD, JR., religious studies educator; b. Chgo., Aug. 25, 1933; s. Norman Richard and Mildred May (Wilson) P.; m. Antoinette DeRosa, Jan. 28, 1956; children: Kristen, Mark, Joanna. B.F.A., Pratt Inst., 1957; S.T.B., Harvard U., 1961, Ph.D., 1967. Instr., asst. prof. Wellesley Coll., Mass., 1963-69; asst. prof., then assoc. prof. religion Williams Coll., Williamstown, Mass., 1969-77; prof. Williams Coll., 1978-79, Washington Gladden prof. religion, 1980—. Author: Literary Criticism for New Testament Critics, 1978, Rediscovering Paul, The Sociology of Paul's Narrative World, 1985 (Bibl. Archeology Soc. book award 1986, Am. Acad. Religion book award 1987), The Gospel According to John and the Sociology of Light, Language and Characterization in the Fourth Gospel, 1993. Mem. Mt. Greylock Regional High Sch. Com., Williamstown, 1980-85. Served with AUS, 1952-54. Mem. Soc. Bibl. Lit., Studiorum Novi Testamenti Societas. Office: Williams Coll Dept Religion Williamstown MA 01267

PETERSEN, ROBERT E., publisher; b. Los Angeles, Sept. 10, 1926; s. Einar and Bertha (Putera) P.; m. Margie McNally, Jan. 26, 1963. Founder, chmn. bd. Petersen Pub. Co. (pubs. Hot Rod, Motor Trend, Car Craft, Motorcyclist, Photog., Skin Diver, Teen, Hunting, Guns & Ammo, Circle Track, Dirt Rider, Los Angeles, 1948—; founder, chmn. bd. (pubs. 4 Wheel and Off Road mags.), Los Angeles, %; owner Robert E. Petersen Prodns. (producers TV series, commls., auto shows, trade shows), Petersen Galleries, Beverly Hills, Calif., Scandia Restaurant. Mem. Los Angeles Library Commn., 1963-64; Bd. dirs. Boys Club Am., past pres. Hollywood br.; bd. dirs. Thalians. Served with USAF. Clubs: So. Calif Safari, Balboa Bay, Catalina Island Yacht, Confrerie de la Chaine des Rotisseurs. Office: Petersen Publishing Co 6420 Wilshire Blvd Los Angeles CA 90048-5502*

PETERSEN, ROLAND, artist, printmaker; b. Endelave, Horsens, Denmark, 1926; came to U.S., 1928; m. Sharane Havlina, Aug. 12, 1950; children—Dana Mark, Maura Brooke, Julien Conrad, Karena Caia. B.A., U. Calif.-Berkeley, 1949, M.A., 1950; postgrad., Han Hofmann's Sch. Fine Arts, summers 1950-51, S.W. Hayter's Atelier 17, Paris, 1950, 63, 70, Islington Studio, London, 1976, The Print Workshop, London, 1980. Tchr. State Coll. Wash., Pullman, 1952-56; mem. faculty U. Calif., Davis, 1956-91, prof. art, 1991; ret., 1991. Exhibited one-man shows: Gump's Gallery, San Francisco, 1962, Staempfli Gallery, N.Y.C., 1963, 65, 67, Adele Bednarz Gallery, Los Angeles, 1966, 69, 70, 72, 73, 75, 76, Crocker Art Gallery, Sacramento, 1965, de Young Mus., San Francisco, 1968, La Jolla Mus., 1971, Phoenix Mus., 1972, Santa Barbara Mus., 1973, USIS sponsored touring one-man exhbn., Turkey, U. Reading, Eng., 1977, 80, U. Calif., Davis, 1978, 92, Brubaker Gallery, Sarasota, Fla., 1979, Rorick Gallery, San Francisco, 1981, 82, 83, 84, 85, Himovitz-Salomon Gallery, Sacramento, 1987-88, 91, Vanderwoude Tananbaum Gallery, N.Y.C., 1987-89, Harcourts Gallery, San Francisco, 1989, 91, 93, U. Calif., Davis, 1992, Maxwell Galleries, San Francisco, 1995; group shows include Calif. Palace Legion of Honor, San Francisco Art Inst., 1962, Mus. Art, Carnegie Inst., Pitts., 1964, Obelisk Gallery, Washington, John Herron Art Inst., Indpls., 1964, Pa. Acad. Fine Arts, Phila., Crocker Art Gallery, Sacramento, 1965, 81, Art Inst. Chgo., 1965, Va. Mus. Fine Arts, Richmond, 1966, U. Ariz. Art Gallery, Tucson, 1967, Am. Cultural Center, Paris, 1971, Nat. Gallery, Washington, 1972, Otis Art Inst. Gallery, Los Angeles, 1974, Auerbach Fine Art Gallery, London, 1977, U. Wis., Madison, 1977, Bklyn. Mus., 1978, U. Ill., 1978, U. Nev., Las Vegas, 1980, Brubaker Gallery, Sarasota, Fla., 1983, U.S.A. World Print Council, San Francisco, Nat. Mus., Singapore, Nat. Gallery, Bangkok, Thailand, Amerika Haus, Berlin, Malmo Konsthall, Sweden, Museo Carrillo Gil, Mexico City, all 1984-86, Crocker Art Mus., 1991, Fresno Met. Mus., 1992, Hall of Pictures, Uman, Russia, 1992, Calif. State U., L.A., 1992, San Bernardino, 1993 Pence Gallery, Davis, Calif., 1993, Artists Contemporary Gallery, Sacramento, 1994, Andre Milan Gallery, Sao Paulo, Brazil, 1995; represented in permanent collections: de Young Mus., San Francisco, San Francisco Mus. Modern Art, Va. Mus. Fine Arts, Richmond, Mus. Modern Art, N.Y.C., Phila. Mus. Art, Whitney Mus. Am. Art, Phoenix Mus., Santa Barbara Mus., Musée Municipal, Brest, France, Smithsonian Instn. Nat. Collection Fine Arts & Archives of Am. Art, Hirschorn Coll., Washington, others. Served with USN, 1944-46, PTO. Recipient numerous prizes and awards, 1950—; Guggenheim fellow, 1963; U. Calif. creative arts fellow, 1967, 70, 77; Fulbright grantee, 1970. Mem. AAUP, San Francisco Art Assn., Calif. Soc. Printmakers. Home: 6 Lanai Way PO Box 1 Dillon Beach CA 94929-0001

PETERSEN, ULRICH, geology educator; b. Negritos, Peru, Dec. 1, 1927; s. Georg and Harriet (Bluhme) P.; m. Edith Martensen, Apr. 27, 1952 (dec. Aug. 1978); children: Erich, Armin (dec.), Heidi.; m. Eileen Bourque, June 19, 1982. Mining Engr., Escuela Nacional de Ingenieros, Lima, Peru, 1954; M.A., Harvard U., 1955, Ph.D., 1963. Geologist Instituto Geológico del Peru and Instituto Nacional de Investigación y Fomento Mineros, 1946-51; geologist Cerro de Pasco Corp., Peru, 1951-54; asst. chief geologist Cerro de Pasco Corp., 1956-57, chief geologist, 1958-63; lectr. Harvard, 1963-66; assoc. prof. Harvard U., 1966-69, prof. mining geology, 1969-81, Harry C. Dudley prof. econ. geology, 1981-95; cons. geologist, 1963—, prof. emeritus, 1996—. Named comendador de la orden al Merito por Servicios Distinguidos Peru, 1968; recipient A. von Humboldt rsch. award, 1992-93. Mem. Soc. Econ. Geologists (pres. 1988-89), Geol. Soc. Am., Soc. Geologica del Peru, Am. Inst. Mining and Metall. Engrs. Home: 414 Marsh St Belmont MA 02178-1109 Office: 20 Oxford St Cambridge MA 02138-2902

PETERSEN, WILLIAM OTTO, lawyer; b. Chgo., Nov. 28, 1926; s. William Ferdinand and Alma Schmidt P.; m. Jane Browne, Nov. 25, 1978. AB cum laude, Harvard U., 1949, LLB, 1952. Bar: Ill., 1952. Atty. No. Trust. Co., Chgo., 1952-55; ptnr. Vedder, Price, Kaufman & Kamholz, Chgo., 1955—. Mem. exec. bd. Ct. Theatre, 1992—; mem. vis. to U. Chgo. Libr., 1992—; bd. dirs. Chgo. Youth Ctrs., 1958—, pres., 1971, 72; bd. dirs. Taylor Inst., Chgo., 1979—, chmn., 1988—; bd. dirs. Chgo. Commons Corp., 1988—; bd. dirs., v.p. Luther I. Replogle Found., Chgo. and Washington, 1986—. With USN, 1944-46. Mem. ABA, Ill. State Bar Assn., Chgo. Bar Assn. (chmn. corp. law com. 1976), Racquet Club of Chgo. (pres. 1981, 82), Univ. Club, Lake Geneva (Wis.) Country Club, Lake Geneva Yacht Club, Caxton Club. Republican. Lutheran. Home: 1120 N Lake Shore Dr Chicago IL 60611-1042

PETERSEN, WOLFGANG, film director; b. Emden, Germany, Mar. 14, 1941. Asst. state dir. Ernst Deutsch Theatre, Hamburg, Fed. Republic Germany. Dir.: (films) The Consequence, 1977, Black and White Like Day and Night, 1978, Enemy Mine, 1985, In the Line of Fire, 1993, Outbreak, 1995; (TV) Smog (Prix Futura award 1975), For Your Love Only, Scenes of the Crime; dir., screenwriter: Das Boot, 1981 (Acad. award nomination Best Adapted Screenplay 1981), The Neverending Story, 1984, Shattered, 1991. Office: care The Chasin Agy 190 N Canon Dr # 210 Beverly Hills CA 90210 Office: CAA 9830 Wilshire Blvd Beverly Hills CA 90212-1804

PETERSON, ALLEN JAY, lawyer, educator; b. Los Alamos, N.C., Oct. 26, 1949; s. Lyle Jay and Lois May (Richards) P.; m. Beverly White, May 27, 1989; children: Elizabeth Bishop, Adam Bryant. AA, St. Petersburg Jr. Coll., 1969; BA, Davidson Coll., 1971; postgrad., Harvard U., 1972; JD, U. N.C., 1976. Bar: N.C. 1974, U.S. Dist. Ct. (we. dist.) N.C. 1976. Ptnr. James, McElroy & Diehl, Charlotte, N.C., 1976-84, Howell & Peterson, Burnsville, N.C., 1984-87, Norris & Peterson, Burnsville, N.C., 1987-94; v.p., gen. counsel North State Foods, Inc., 1995—; constnl. law instr. U. N.C., Charlotte, 1977-78. Sunday sch. tchr. Higgins Meml. Meth. Ch., Burnsville, 1991-93, mem. adminstrv. bd., 1990-93. Mem. Am. Assn. Trial Lawyers, N.C. Acad. Trial Lawyers. Avocation: trout fishing. Home: RR 6 Box 944 Burnsville NC 28714-9632

PETERSON, AMY, Olympic athlete; b. Maplewood, Minn., 1971. Bronze medalist, women's 500m short-track speedskating Olympic Games, Lillehammer, Norway, 1994; Bronze medalist, women's 3000m short-track speedskating Olympic Games, 1994. Office: US Olympic Committee 1750 E Boulder St Colorado Springs CO 80909-5724*

PETERSON, ANN SULLIVAN, physician, health care consultant; b. Rhinebeck, N.Y., Oct. 11, 1928; A.B., Cornell U., 1950, M.D., 1954; M.S. (Alfred P. Sloan fellow 1979-80), M.I.T., 1980. Diplomate Am. Bd. Internal Medicine. Intern, Cornell Med. Div.-Bellevue Hosp., N.Y.C., 1954-55, resident, 1955-57; fellow in medicine and physiology Meml.-Sloan Kettering Cancer Ctr., Cornell Med. Coll., N.Y.C., 1957-60; instr. medicine Georgetown U. Sch. Medicine, Washington, 1962-65, asst. prof., 1965-69, asst. dir. clin. research unit, 1962-69; assoc. prof. medicine U. Ill., Chgo., 1969-72, asst. dean, 1969-71, assoc. dean, 1971-72; assoc. prof. medicine, assoc. dean Coll. Physicians and Surgeons, Columbia U., N.Y.C., 1972-80; assoc. prof. medicine, assoc. dean Cornell U. Med. Coll., N.Y.C., 1980-83; assoc. dir. div. med. edn. AMA, Chgo., 1983-86, dir. div. grad. med. edn., 1986-89; v.p. Mgmt. Cons. Corp., 1989-93; ind. cons., Chgo., 1993—; mem. bd. regents Uniformed Svcs. U. of Health Scis., 1984-90. John and Mary R. Markle scholar, 1965-70. Fellow ACP; mem. Mortar Board, Alpha Omega Alpha, Alpha Epsilon Delta. Contbr. articles to med. jours.

PETERSON, ARTHUR LAVERNE, former college president; b. Glyndon, Minn., June 27, 1926; s. John M. and Hilda C. (Moline) P.; m. Connie Lucille Harr, June 14, 1952; children: Jon Martin, Rebecca Ruth, Donna Harr, Ingrid Bliss. AB, Yale U., 1947; MSPA, U. So. Calif., 1949; postgrad., U. Chgo., 1949-50; PhD, U. Minn., 1962; LLD, Lebanon Valley Coll., 1988. Mem. Wis. State Legislature, 1951-55; from instr. to assoc. prof. polit. sci. U. Wis., Eau Claire, 1954-60; assoc. prof. to prof. polit. sci. Ohio Wesleyan U., Delaware, 1961-65, 70-80; pres. Am. Grad. Sch. Internat. Mgmt., Phoenix, 1966-70; dean spl. programs Eckerd Coll., St. Petersburg, Fla., 1980-84, dir. Acad. Sr. Profls., 1987-94; pres. Lebanon Valley Coll., Annville, Pa., 1984-87; bd. dirs. Arnold Industries; asst. to chmn. Rep. Nat. Com., Washington, 1960-61; founding dir. Ctr. Internat. Bus., L.A., 1969-70; cons. Novin Inst. Polit. Affairs, Tehran, Iran, 1973; exec. dir. Fla. Assn. Colls. and Univs., 1988—. Author: McCarthyism: Ideology and Foundations, 1962; co-author: Electing the President, 1968; contbr. articles to scholarly jours. Chmn. Ohio Civil Rights Commn., 1963-65; dep. chmn. Republican Nat. Com., 1965-66; mem. Ohio Ethics Commn., 1976-80. Served to capt. USMC, 1951-52; Korea. Citizenship Clearing House Nat. Faculty fellow, 1960; recipient citation for excellence Sigma Phi Epsilon, 1977; Marshall award Ohio Wesleyan Students, 1979. Mem. Am. Polit. Sci. Assn., Am. Judicature Soc. (dir. 1975—), Soc. Polit. Enquiries (pres. 1985—), Acad. Polit. Sci., Pi Sigma Alpha (dir. 1972—), Phi Mu Alpha Sinfonia, Omicron Delta Kappa. Republican. Mem. United Ch. of Christ. Lodges: Rotary, Masons. Avocations: sailing; flying; music. Home: 552 Johns Pass Ave Saint Petersburg FL 33708-2366 *Give the most you can give, of what you are and what you believe, both talent and treasure - where you are - now!.*

PETERSON, BARBARA ANN BENNETT, history educator, television personality; b. Portland, Oreg., Sept. 6, 1942; d. George Wright and Hope (Chatfield) Bennett; m. Frank Lynn Peterson, July 1, 1967. BA, BS, Oreg. State U., 1964; MA, Stanford U., 1965; PhD, U. Hawaii, 1978; PhD (hon.), London Inst. Applied Rsch., 1991, Australian Inst. Coordinated R, 1995. Prof. history U. Hawaii, Honolulu, 1967-96; prof. emeritus history, 1996—; chmn. social scis. dept. U. Hawaii, Honolulu, 1971-73, 75-76, asst. dean, 1973-74; prof. Asian history and European colonial history and world problems Champman Coll. World Campus Afloat, 1974, European overseas exploration, expansion and colonialism U. Colo., Boulder, 1978; assoc. prof. U. Hawaii-Manoa Coll. Continuing Edn., 1981; Fulbright prof. history Wuhan (China) U., 1988-89; Fulbright rsch. prof. Sophia U., Japan, 1978; rsch. assoc. Bishop Mus., 1995—; lectr. Capital Spkrs., Washington, 1987—; tchr. Hawaii State Ednl. Channel, 1993—. Co-author: Women's Place is in the History Books, Her Story, 1962-1980: A Curriculum Guide for American History Teachers, 1980; author: America in British Eyes, 1988; editor: Notable Women of Hawaii, 1984, (with W. Solheim) The Pacific Region, 1990, 91, American History: 17th, 18th and 19th Centuries, 1993, America: 19th and 20th Centuries, 1993, John Bull's Eye on America, 1995; assoc. editor Am. Nat. Biography; contbr. articles to profl. pubis. Participant People-to-People Program, Eng., 1964, Expt. in Internat. Living Program, Nigeria, 1966; chmn. 1st Nat. Women's History Week, Hawaii, 1982; pres. Bishop Mus. Coun., 1993-94; active Hawaii Commn. on Status of Women. Fulbright scholar, Japan, 1967, China, 1988-89; NEH-Woodrow Wilson fellow Princeton U., 1980; recipient state proclamations Gov. of Hawaii, 1982, City of Honolulu, 1982, Outstanding Tchr. of Yr. award Wuhan (China), U., 1988, Medallion of Excellence award Am. Biog. Assn., 1989, Woman of Yr. award, 1991; named Hawaii State Mixed Doubles Tennis Champion, 1985. Fellow World Literacy Acad. (Eng.), Internat. Biog. Assn. (Cambridge, Eng. chpt.); mem. AAUW, Am. Hist. Assn. (mem. numerous coms.), Am. Studies Assn., Am. Studies Assn. (pres. 1984-85), Fulbright Alumni Assn. (founding pres. Hawaii chpt. 1984-88, mem. nat. steering com. chairwomen Fulbright Assn. ann. conf. 1990), Am. Coun. on Edn., Maison Internat. des Intellectuals, France, Hawaii Found. History and Humanities (mem. editl. bd. 1972-73), Hawaii Found. Women's History, Hawaii Hist. Assn., Nat. League Am. Pen Women (contest chairperson 1986), Women in Acad. Adminstrn., Phi Beta Phi, Phi Kappa Phi. Avocation: tennis.

PETERSON, BONNIE LU, mathematics educator; b. Escanaba, Mich., Jan. 19, 1946; d. Herbert Erick and Ruth Alberta (Erickson) P. AA, Bay de Noc C.C., 1966; BS, No. Mich. U., 1968, MA in Math., 1969; EdD, Tenn. State U., 1989. Tchr. Lapeer (Mich.) High Sch., 1969-70, Nova High Sch., Ft. Lauderdale, Fla., 1970-79, Hendersonville (Tenn.) High Sch., 1979—; adj. faculty Vol. State C.C., Gallatin, Tenn., 1989—; chair Sumner County Schs. Tchrs. Insvc., Gallatin, 1990-92; mem. math. specialist team State of Tenn., 1991-93; spkr. in field. Mem. edn. com. Vision 2000-City of Hendersonville, 1993-94. Tenn. State Bd. grantee, 1989-92; Woodrow Wilson fellow, 1993; State-Level Presdl. awardee, 1994, 95; Tandy Scholars award, 1995. Mem. ASCD, Nat. Coun. Tchrs. Math. (chair workshop support com. 1990), Tenn. Math. Tchrs. Assn., Mid. Tenn. Math. Tchrs. Assn. (pres.-elect), Phi Delta Kappa (past pres.). Avocations: cooking, counted cross stitch. Home: 1081 Coon Creek Rd Dickson TN 37055-4014

PETERSON, CARL, professional football team executive; b. Long Beach, Calif.; 1 child, Dawn. BS in Kinesiology, UCLA, 1966, M in Kinesiology, 1967, D in Adminstrn. in Higher Edn., 1970. Asst. coach Wilson High Sch., Calif., 1966, Loyola High Sch., 1967-68, Calif. State U., Somona, 1969-70; head coach Calif. State U., 1970-72; receivers coach UCLA, 1972-74, receivers coach, adminstrv. asst., 1974-76; coach recievers and tight ends Phila. Eagles, 1976, dir. player personnel, 1977-82; pres., gen. mgr. Phila. Stars, 1982-88; pres., gen. mgr., COO Kansas City Chiefs, Mo., 1988—; pres., CEO PhillySport Mag., Phila.; mem. nat. bd. Maxwell Football Club and Pop Warner Little Scholar Orgn. Recipient USFL Exec. of Yr. award Sporting News, 1983, 84. Mem. Young Pres. Orgn. (Kansas City chpt.). Office: Kansas City Chiefs 1 Arrowhead Dr Kansas City MO 64129-1651*

PETERSON, CARL ERIC, banker, metals company executive; b. Wareham, Mass., Apr. 8, 1944; s. E. Gunnar and Ruth (Kramer) P.; m. Frances Harkness, Sept. 7, 1966; children—Robin, Alec Harkness. BA, Brown U., 1966; MA, U. Pa., 1971; grad., Sch. for Internat. Banking, 1974, Stonier Grad. Sch. Banking, 1978. With R.I. Hosp. Trust Nat. Bank, Providence, 1971-82; with Engelhard Corp., Iselin, N.J., 1982-85, Dryvit System, Inc., West Warwick, R.I., 1986, Gerald Metals, Inc., Stamford, Conn., 1987—; lectr. World Gold Markets Conf., London, 1981, Am. Mining Congress, Phoenix, 1984, 12th Internat. Precious Metals Inst. Conf., Boston, 1988. Bd. dirs., mem. adv. coun. Internat. House of R.I., 1974-79; mem. of corp. Woods Hole Oceanographic Instn., 1981-94, audit com., 1988-94; mem. R.I. Pub. Expenditure Coun., 1974-82, Internat. Ctr. New Eng., 1980-81. Episcopalian. Clubs: Hope (Providence); Willow Dell Beach (Matunuck, R.I.). Office: Gerald Metals Inc High Ridge Park Stamford CT 06905-1328

PETERSON, CARL RICHARD, mechanical engineering educator, consultant; b. Detroit, Mar. 6, 1934; s. Signor and Francis Elizabeth (McClure) P.; m. Susan J. Truby, Sept. 2, 1958; children: Laura Lyne, Mark Allan. BS in Mech. Engring., U. Mich., 1956; MS in Mech. Engring., MIT, 1958, DSc in Mech. Engring., 1963. Asst. prof. dept. aeronautics and astronautics MIT, Cambridge, Mass., 1961-63, assoc. prof. dept. mech. engring, 1976-95, prof., 1995—; asst. chief spl. projects Ingersoll-Rand Rsch., Inc., Princeton, N.J., 1963-70; mgr. spl. projects Foster-Miller Assocs., Waltham, Mass., 1970-72; pres., founder RAPIDEX, Inc., Gloucester, Mass., 1972-76; chmn., co-author report Nat. Rsch. Coun., 1994. Co-author: Mechanics and Thermodynamics of Propulsion, 1964; patentee in field. Fellow ASME (founder Mining and Excavation Rsch. Inst., Washington), Tau Beta Pi. Avocations: hunting, fishing. Office: Massachusetts Inst of Technology Dept of Mech Engring 77 Massachusetts Ave Cambridge MA 02139-4301

PETERSON, CHARLES EMIL, architect; b. Madison, Minn., Aug. 23, 1906; s. Charles Emil and Mae (Nisbit) P. BA, U. Minn., 1928. With U.S. Nat. Pk. Svc., 1929-62, architect, landscape architect, San Francisco, 1929-30, resident landscape architect, Yorktown, Va., 1930-33, dep. chief architect, Washington, 1933-35, sr. landscape architect riverfront project, St. Louis, 1936-48, regional architect, Richmond, Va., 1948-49, resident architect Independence, Nat. Hist. Project, Phila., 1950-54, supervising architect historic structures, Ea. U.S., 1954-62; cons. archtl. historian, restorationist, planner, 1962—; adj. prof. architecture Columbia U., 1964-78; pioneered Hist. Am. Bldgs. Survey, 1933; conducted devel. studies, Easter Island for UNESCO, 1966-68; AIA del. II Internat. Congress Architects and Technicians Hist. Monuments, Venice, 1964, 1st-2d assemblies Internat. Coun. Monuments and Sites, Warsaw-Cracow, Poland, 1965, Oxford, Eng., 1969, Budapest, 1972; contbr. to Conf. on Edn. Restorationists, Pistoia, Italy, 1968; organized forums on restoration historic bldgs. Bldg. Research Inst., 1964, Nat. Trust, 1966, A.I.A., 1969; founder St. Louis Hist. Documents Found.; corr. mem. com. Tng. Architects for Conservation, Gt. Britain; founding mem. standing coms. Internat. Centre, Rome and originator, leader travelling summer sch. for restorationists, Europe, 1972; mem. City Phila. Hist. Commn., 1956-64; bd. dirs. Soc. Hill. neighborhood assns., 1957-68; organizer Robert Smith Celebration at Newbattle, Edinburgh and Dalkeith, Scotland, 1982. Pioneered numerous projects including Skyline Drive, Va., Great Smoky Mountains Nat. Park, Colonial Nat. Hist. Park, Williamsburg to Yorktown; restorations include Moore House, Yorktown, Va., Pierce Mill, Washington, Tempe Wicke House, Morristown, N.J., Andrew Johnson Home, Greenville, Tenn., Hampton Mansion, Balt., Independence Hall, Phila., Liberty Hall, Frankfort, Ky.; author: Colonial St. Louis, 1948, 93, Rapa Nui, Paris, 1968, Notes on Hampton Mansion, 1970, The Moore House, 1981; Contbg. author: Historic Philadelphia, 1953, Philadelphia Architecture in the 19th Century, 1953, The French in the Mississippi Valley, 1965, Historic America, 1983; editor: The 1786 Carpenters' Company Rule Book, 1971, Building Early America, 1976; contbr. numerous articles to profl. jours. Served to comdr. C.E. Corps, USNR, 1941-46. Recipient Disting. Svc. award Dept. Interior, 1961, Alumni award Columbia U., 1972, Conservation Svc. award, 1976, Citation City of Phila., 1986, 94, Commendation, Gov. Hawaii, 1992; Benjamin Franklin fellow Royal Soc. of Arts, Joseph Jackson award Atwater Kent Mus., 1992; named Disting. Assoc. Ea. Nat. Pk. and Conservation Assn., 1981. Fellow AIA (medal 1979, Presdl. citation 1990, former mem. nat. com. on historic bldgs.), Athenaeum of Phila., Assn. Preservation Tech. (founder 1968, past pres., Harley J. McKee award 1988), HABS Found.; mem. Soc. Archtl. Historians (dir. 1950-64, past pres., v.p. editor Am. notes 1950-67), Nat. Trust Historic Preservation (charter, Louise du Pont Crowninshield award for superior achievement 1966), Nat. Pk. and Conservation Assn. (hon. mem. nat. adv. com.), McAneny Hist. Preservation medal 1984), Mo. Hist. Soc. (dir.), Assn. Studies in Conservation Historic Bldgs. (Gt. Britain), William Clark Soc. (founder), Independence Hall Assn. (hon. life 1987), Carpenters' Co. of City and County Phila. (co. historian emeritus), Friends of Nicholas More (convenor), Friends of HABS (sec. pro-tem), St. Andrew's Soc. Phila., Newcomen Soc. (G.B.), Phi Kappa Sigma. Address: 332 Spruce St Society Hill Philadelphia PA 19106-4201

PETERSON, CHARLES GORDON, retired lawyer; b. Lansing, Mich., May 21, 1926; s. Russell V. and Edna E. (Jones) P.; m. Clara Elizabeth Parmelee, Mar. 8, 1947; children—Wendy, Pamela, Christopher. B.S., Columbia U. Sch. Gen. Studies, 1954; LL.B., Columbia U. Sch. Law, 1956. Bar: N.Y., 1957. Legal assoc. Beekman & Bogue, N.Y.C., 1956-67; mem. Gaston & Snow, N.Y.C., 1967-91; of counsel Reid & Priest, N.Y.C., 1991-93; ret., 1993. Trustee The Riverside Ch., N.Y.C., 1968-80, 82-89, mem. bd. deacons, 1960-68; pres., bd. dirs. Lincoln Guild Housing Corp., N.Y.C., 1961-62, 84-89; pres. Lincoln Guild Housing Corp., N.Y.C., 1961-62, 84-87, v.p., 1987-89, 94—, bd. dirs., 1961-62, 84-89, 94—. Mem. Phi Beta Kappa. Republican. Baptist. Avocations: flying; swimming; piano; reading. Home: 303 W 66th St Apt 20ee New York NY 10023-6347

PETERSON, CHARLES HAYES, lawyer; b. St. Louis, May 8, 1938; s. Edmund Herbert and Dorothy Marie (Brennan) P.; m. Auli Irene Ahonen, Nov. 28, 1981; children: Mika, Charles, Michael, Katja. BS, U.S. Naval Acad., 1960; MBA, Stanford U., 1971, JD, 1974. Commd. ensign USN, 1956, advanced through grades to capt., resigned, 1969; with USNR, 1969-89; counsel Gen. Electric, San Jose, Calif., 1973-79; div. counsel Syracuse, N.Y., 1980-83; v.p. COGEMA, Inc., Washington, 1983-87; pres. NUEXCO Trading Co., Washington, 1987-95; spl. counsel Morgan, Lewis & Bocklus, LLP, 1995—. Recipient Meritorious Service medal State of Calif., 1986. Mem. Calif. and Washington Bar Assns. Lutheran. Home: 8407 River Rock Ter Bethesda MD 20817-4300 Office: Morgan Lewis & Buckius Ste 500 South 1800 M St NW Washington DC 20006

PETERSON, CHARLES LOREN, agricultural engineer, educator; b. Emmett, Idaho, Dec. 27, 1938; s. Clarence James and Jane (Shelton) P.; m. Julianne Rekow, Sept. 7, 1962; children—Val, Karl, Marianne, Cheryl Ann, Charles Lauritz, Brent. B.S., U. Idaho, 1961, M.S., 1965; Ph.D. in Engring. Sci, Wash. State U., Pullman, 1973. Registered profl. engr., Idaho, Wash. Exptl. engr. Oliver Corp., Charles City, Iowa, 1961; farmer Emmett, 1962-65; instr. math. Emmett High Sch., 1962-63; instr. freshman engring., then extension agrl. engr. U. Idaho, Moscow, 1963-67; prof. agrl. engring. U. Idaho, 1973—; asst. prof. Wash. State U., 1968-73; cons. in field. Contbr. numerous articles profl. jours. Rep. precinct committeeman, 1972-75; sec. 5th legis. dist. Idaho, 1976-79; mem. Latah County Planning and Zoning Commn., 1980-90, 1st counselor Pullman Wash. Stake Presidency, 1989—. Grantee Wash. Potato, 1971-73, U & I, Inc., 1974, Amalgamated Sugar Co., 1974, 1992-95m Nat. Biodiesel Bd. 1994-95, BPA/USDOE 1993-95, Beet Sugar Devel. Found., 1975-85, Phillips Chem. Co., 1976-80, USDA, 1976-95, Idaho Dept. Water Resources, Energy div., 1992-93, Star Found., 1978; Recipient Excellence in Rsch. award U. Idaho, 1992-93, Best in Category award Transp. Tech. U.S. Dept. Energy, 1994, Silver Beaver award Boy Scouts Am., 1996. Fellow Am. Soc. Agrl. Engrs. (chmn. Inland Empire chpt. 1978-79, chmn. nat. environ. stored products com. 1978-80, chmn. biomass energy com. 1985-86, chmn. Pacific N.W. region 1984-85, chmn. T-11 Energy com. 1989-90, dir. dist. 5, 1989-91, Engr. of Year award Inland Empire chpt., 1978, nat. Blue Ribbon award 1975, Engr. of Yr. award Pacific N.W. sect. 1990, Outstanding Paper award 1990); mem. Nat. Soc. Profl. Engrs., Am. Soc. Engring. Edn., Potato Assn. Am., Am. Soc. Sugarbeet Technologists, Idaho Soc. Profl. Engrs., Nat. Assn. Colls. and Tchrs. of Agriculture (Tchr. award 1990), Soc. Automotive Engrs., Phi Kappa Phi, Sigma Xi, Gamma Sigma Delta (Outstanding Rsch. in Agriculture award 1989). Mem. LDS Ch. Office: U Idaho Agrl Engring JML # 81-b Moscow ID 83844-2040

PETERSON, CHASE N., university president; b. Logan, Utah, Dec. 27, 1929; s. E.G. and Phebe (Nebeker) P.; m. Grethe Ballif, 1956; children: Erika Elizabeth, Stuart Ballif, Edward Chase. A.B., Harvard U., 1952, M.D., 1956. Diplomate Am. Bd. Internal Medicine. Asst. prof. medicine U. Utah Med. Sch., 1965-67; assoc. Salt Lake Clinic; dean admissions and fin. aids to students Harvard U., 1967-72, v.p. univ., 1972-78; v.p. health scis. U. Utah, Salt Lake City, 1978-83, prof. medicine, 1983—, pres., 1983-91, clin. prof. medicine, 1991—; pres. emeritus U. Utah, Salt Lake City, 1992—; bd. dirs. First Security Corp., Utah Power & Light Co., D.C. Tanner Co., OEC Med. Systems. Mem. Nat. Assn. State Univs. and Land-Grant Colls. (chmn. 1988-89, chair U.S. Ofc. Tech. Assessment adv. bd. 1990-92). Home: 66 Thaynes Canyon Dr Park City UT 84060-6711 Office: U Utah 1C26 Sch Medicine Salt Lake City UT 84112

PETERSON, COLLIN C., congressman; b. Fargo, N.D., June 29, 1944; children: Sean, Jason, Elliott. BA in Bus. Adminstrn. and Acctg., Moorhead State U., 1966. CPA, Minn. Senator State of Minn., 1976-86; mem. 102nd-104th Congresses from 7th Minn. dist., 1991—; mem. agrl. com., subcoms. gen. farm commodities, specialty crops and natural resources, livestock, environ. credit and rural devel., mem. govt. ops. com., chmn. subcom. employment housing and aviation, chmn. subcom. employment, housing and aviation, mem. 104th Cong. resource conservation com., rsch. and forestry subcom., livestock, dairy and poultry subcom., govt. reform and oversight com., nat. econ. growth com., nat. resources and regulatory affairs com.-ranking minority mem. With U.S. Army N.G., 1963-69. Mem. Am. Legion, Ducks Unltd., Elks, Sportsmen's Club, Rural Caucus, Mainstream Forum, Cormorant Lakes Sportsmen Club, Congl. Sportsmen's Caucus, Mainstream Forum, Congl. Rural Caucus. Democrat. Office: US Ho of Reps 1314 Longworth Bldg Washington DC 20515-0004*

PETERSON, COURTLAND HARRY, law educator; b. Denver, June 28, 1930; s. Harry James and Courtney (Caple) P.; m. Susan Schwab, Gisvold, Jan. 28, 1966; children: Brooke, Linda, Patrick. B.A., U. Colo., 1951, LL.B., 1953; M.C.L., U. Chgo., 1959; J.D., U. Freiburg, Ger., 1964. Bar: Colo. 1953. Mem. faculty U. Colo. Law Sch., 1959—, prof., 1963—, dean, 1974-79, Nicholas Rosenbaum prof., 1991-94, Nicholas Doman prof., 1995—; vis. prof. U. Calif. Law Sch., Los Angeles, 1965, Max Planck Inst., Hamburg, Ger., 1969-70, U. Tex. Law Sch., Austin, 1973-74, Summer Program Tulane U., Rodos, Greece, 1993; bd. dirs. Continuing Legal Edn. in Colo., 1974-77. Author: Die Anerkennung Auslaendischer Urteile, 1964; Translator: (Bauer) An Introduction to German Law, 1965. Served to 1st lt. USAF, 1954-56. Fgn. Law fellow U. Chgo., 1957-59; Ford Found. Law Faculty fellow, 1964; Alexander von Humboldt Stiftun fellow, 1969-70. Mem. ABA, Colo. Bar Assn. (bd. govs. 1974-79), Boulder County Bar Assn., Am. Soc. Comparative

Law (dir., bd. editors, treas. 1978-89), Internat. Acad. Comparative Law, Am. Law Inst. Home: 205 Camden Pl Boulder CO 80302-8032 Office: U Colo Law Sch Boulder CO 80309

PETERSON, DAVID CHARLES, photojournalist; b. Kansas City, Mo., Oct. 22, 1949; s. John Edward and Florence Athene (Hobbs) P.; m. Adele Mae Johnson, Dec. 31, 1952; children: Brian David, Scott Ryun, Anna Victoria. BS in Edn., Kansas State U., 1971; BS in Journalism, U. Kans., 1973, U. Kans., 1974. Staff photographer Topeka Capital-Jour., 1975-77, Des Moines Register, 1977—. Photographer (photo essay) Shattered Dreams-Iowa's Rural Crisis, 1986 (Pulitzer prize 1987); exhibited at Creative Ctr. Photography, Tucson, 1989. Mem. Nat. Press Photographers Assn. (Nikon sabbatical 1986). Democrat. Home: 2024 35th St Des Moines IA 50310-4438 Office: Des Moines Register News Dept 715 Locust St Des Moines IA 50309-3724

PETERSON, DAVID FREDERICK, government agency executive; b. Washington, Apr. 4, 1937; s. Victor Henry and Alice Augusta (Vogle) P.; m. Laurie A. Cadigan, June 11, 1988. A.B., Harvard U., 1959; LL.B., Cornell U., 1962. Bar: D.C. 1963. With Metromedia Inc., N.Y.C. and Los Angeles, 1963-70; exec. dir. consumer info. ctr. GSA, Washington, 1970-76, dir. consumer affairs, 1976-82, assoc. archivist for mgmt. Nat. Archives and Records Service, 1982-83; asst. archivist for Fed. Records Ctrs. Nat. Archives and Records Adminstrn., Washington, 1983—. Served with U.S. Army, 1963. Home: 2315 N Glebe Rd Arlington VA 22207-3410 Office: Nat Archives & Records Admn 8601 Adelphi Rd College Park MD 20740-6001

PETERSON, DAVID MAURICE, plant physiologist, research leader; b. Woodward, Okla., July 3, 1940; s. Maurice Llewellyn and Katharine Anne (Jones) P.; m. Margaret Ingegerd Sundberg, June 18, 1965; children: Mark David, Elise Marie. BS, U. Calif., Davis, 1962; MS, U. Ill., 1964; PhD, Harvard U., 1968. Rsch. biologist Allied Chem. Corp., Morristown, N.J., 1970-71; plant physiologist U.S. Dept. Agr.-Agrl. Rsch. Svc., Madison, Wis., 1971—; from asst. to full prof. U. Wis., Madison, 1971—. Capt. U.S. Army, 1968-70. Fellow AAAS; mem. Am. Soc. Plant Physiologists (editorial bd. 1984-86), Am. Assn. Cereal Chemists (assoc. editor 1988-91), Crop Sci. Soc. Am. (assoc. editor 1975-78). Office: USDA Cereal Crops Rsch Unit 501 Walnut St Madison WI 53705-2334

PETERSON, DAVID R., porfessional basketball team executive. Chmn. Toronto Raptors, 1995—. Office: Cassels Brock & Blackwell, Scotia Plz Ste 2100, 40 King St W, Toronto, Canada M5H 3C2

PETERSON, DAVID ROBERT, lawyer, former Canadian government official; b. Toronto, Dec. 28, 1943; s. Clarence and Laura Marie (Scott) P.; m. Shelley Peterson, Jan. 16, 1974; children—Benjamin David, Chloe Matthews, Adam Drake Scott. BA, U. Western Ont., 1964; LLB, U. Toronto, 1967; LLD (hon.), U. Ottawa, Am. U. of Caribbean, U. Tel Aviv, U. Toronto. Bar: Ont. 1969, Queens counsel 1981. Chmn., pres. C.M. Peterson Co. Ltd., 1969-75, Cambridge Acceptance Corp., 1969-75; M.P. Ontario Parliament, Can., 1975—; leader Ont. Liberal Party, 1982; premier Province of Ont., 1985-90; sr. counsel Cassels Brock & Blackwell, Toronto, 1991—; chmn. Toronto Raptors Basketball Club, Inc.; bd. dirs. Rogers Comms., Ltd., Nat. Life Assurance Co., Industrielle-Alliance Life Assurance Co., Nat. Trust, Banque Nationale de Paris (Can.), Cascades Paperboard Internat. Inc., SHL Systemhouse, Inc., Speedy Muffler King Inc., Quorum Growth Inc., Euro-Nev. Mining Corp. Ltd. Leader of the official opposition party, Liberal Party, Ont., 1982-85; dir. Legal Services, Yorkville; mem. Kidney Found. Can., Ont., Cystic Fibrosis Found. Fellow McLaughlin Coll., 1985. Mem. Law Soc. U.C., Young Pres. Orgn., London C. of C. Mem. United Ch. Christ. Clubs: London Hunt Country, London Racquets; Canadian. Avocations: theatre, riding, jogging, skiing, tennis, reading. Office: Cassels Brock & Blackwell, 40 King St W Ste 2100, Toronto, ON Canada M5H 3C2

PETERSON, DONALD CURTIS, life care executive, consultant; b. Seattle, Feb. 27, 1931; s. Arthur O. and Agnes V. (Erickson) P.; m. Marilyn Jane, June 21, 1952; children: Bruce D., Mark A., Daryl R., Debra L., Joseph J. AA, North Park Coll., 1950; cert. in mgmt., Am. Mgmt. Assn., 1965. With fgn. ops. staff Internat. Harvester Co., Chgo., 1950-54; mktg. exec. UARCO, Inc., Barrington, Ill., 1954-67; group v.p. Victor Comptometer, Lincoln, Nebr., 1967-68; pres. Nationwide Data, Wheeling, Ill., 1968-71, Nationwide Bus. Forms, Wheeling, 1968-71, Ins. Producers Bulletin, Wheeling, 1968-71, Alpha Internat., Sawyer, Mich., 1971-83; exec. dir. Freedom Sq. U.S.A., Seminole, Fla., 1983-92; adminstr., CEO Mount Miguel Covenant Village, Spring Valley, Calif., 1992—; mktg. cons. Balt. Bus. Forms., Hunt Valley, Md., 1974-76. Supr., chmn. water bd., sanitary bd. Chikaming Twp., Lakeside, Mich., 1972-76. Served with U.S. Army, 1952-57. Republican. Baptist. Home: 10405 Pine Grove St Spring Valley CA 91978-1505

PETERSON, DONALD MATTHEW, insurance company executive; b. Mt. Vernon, N.Y., Dec. 22, 1936; s. Cornelius J. and Catherine M. (Carney) P.; m. Patricia A. Frusciante, Sept. 10, 1960; children: Daniel, Linda, David, Debra, James. BA in Econs., LaSalle U., 1958. CLU; ChFC; FSA, MAAA, EA, RHU. Actuarial analyst Met. Life, N.Y.C., 1958-63; actuarial assoc. N.Am. Co. for Life and Health, Chgo., 1963-66; pres., CEO Trustmark Ins. Co., Lake Forest, Ill., 1966—; bd. dirs. Trustmark Ins. Co., Trustmark Life Ins. Co., Star Mktg. and Adminstrs. Bd. dirs. Glenview (Ill.) Pub. Schs., 1973-76, Lake County (Ill.) United Way, 1989—, Glenview Dist. 34 Found., 1990-93, Lake Forest Hosp., 1992—, Ill. Life Ins. Coun., 1990-94, Barat Coll., 1994—, Lake Forest Grad. Sch. Mgmt., 1995—. Mem. NALU, Nat. Assn. Health Underwriters, Am. Acad. Actuaries, Health Inst. Assn. Am. (bd. dirs. 1992—), Am. Coun. Life Ins. (bd. dirs. 1995—), Econ. Club Chgo., North Shore Country Club, Conway Farms Golf Club, Pelican Nest Golf Club. Republican. Roman Catholic. Avocations: golf, curling, swimming, running. Office: Trustmark Ins Co 400 N Field Dr Lake Forest IL 60045-4809

PETERSON, DONALD ROBERT, psychologist, educator, university administrator; b. Pillager, Minn., Sept. 10, 1923; s. Frank Gordon and Ruth (Friedland) P.; m. Jean Hole, Feb. 10, 1952 (div.); children: Wendy, Jeffrey, Roger, Lisa; m. Jane Snyder Salmon., Dec. 21, 1974. BA, U. Minn., 1948, MA, 1950, PhD, 1952. Mem. faculty U. Ill., Urbana, 1952-75, prof. clin. psychology, 1963-75, head div. clin. psychology, 1963-70, dir. Psychol. Clinic, 1961-70, dir. D. Psychology program, 1970-75; dean Grad. Sch. Applied and Profl. Psychology Rutgers U., New Brunswick, 1975-89; pres. Nat. Coun. Schs. of Profl. Psychology, 1981-83. Author: The Clinical Study of Social Behavior, 1968; co-author: Close Relationships, 1983; also articles; editor Jour. Abnormal Psychology, 1970-72. With AUS, 1943-46. Mem. N.J. Psychol. Assn., Am. Psychol. Assn. (awards for disting. contbns. to practice of psychology 1983, disting. contbns. to edn. and tng. 1989). Office: Rutgers U Grad Sch Applied & Profl Psychology New Brunswick NJ 08903

PETERSON, DONALD ROBERT, magazine editor, vintage automobile consultant; b. Sandstone, Minn., Apr. 1, 1929; s. Martin Theodore and Margaret Mildred (Dezell) P.; m. Lois Taylor, Dec. 31, 1951 (div. 1975); children: Wyatt A., Winston B., Whitney C. (dec.), Westley D., Webster E.; m. Edie Tannenbaum, Aug. 31, 1975; 1 child, Ryan Kerry. Student, U. Minn., 1947-50; B.S., Gustavus Adolphus Coll., 1952. Asst. underwriter Prudential Ins. Co. Am., Mpls., 1953-64; chief health underwriter North Central Life, St. Paul, 1964-66; pres. 1st State Bank Murdock, Minn., 1967-73, EDON, Inc., Roswell, Ga., 1974—; editor Car Collector mag., Roswell, 1977-91, editor emeritus, 1992—; v.p., dir. Classic Pub. Inc., Atlanta, 1979—. Contbr. chpt. to book. Councilman, City of Murdock, 1968-72, mayor, 1972-74; del. State Republican Conv., 1970-72; treas. Swift County Rep. Com., 1970-73. Served with U.S. Navy, 1946-47. Recipient citation for disting. service Classic Car Club Am., 1965. Mem. Internat. Soc. Philos. Enquiry, Swift County Bankers Assn. (pres. 1970-73), Soc. Automotive Historians, Am. Legion, Mensa (pres. Ga. chpt. 1976-78), Milestone Car Soc., Atlanta Press Club, Classic Car Club Am. (chpt. pres. 1959, 60, 63), Rolls-Royce Owners Club, Antique Automobile Club, Vet. Motor Car Club Am., Packard Club, Horseless Carriage Club Am. Republican. Avocations: automobile collecting, internat. traveling. Home: 1400 Lake Ridge Ct Roswell GA 30076-2869 Office: 1241 Canton St Roswell GA 30075-3618

PETERSON, DONN NEAL, forensic engineer; b. Northwood, N.D., Jan. 1, 1942; s. Emil H. and Dorothy (Neal) P.; m. Lorna Jean Kappedal, July 8, 1962 (div. July 1966); m. Donna Sue Butts Daiker, Aug. 26, 1967; children: Barbara Daiker, Elizabeth Plamondon, Phoebe, Phaedra, Rosalind Peterson. BSME, U. N.D., 1963; MSME, U. Minn., 1972. Registered profl. engr. Advanced engring. courses student GE, Evendale, Ohio, 1963-66; systems engr. GE Aircraft Engine Group, Evendale, Ohio, 1963-70; prin. Donn N. Peterson & Assocs., Mpls., 1971-74; pres. Donn N. Peterson & Assocs., Inc., Mpls., 1974-85, Peterson Engring., Inc., Mpls., 1985—; instr. GE Edn. Program, 1968-69; seminar presenter State Bd. of Registration, Mpls., 1980; seminar leader Minn. Fedn. Engring. Socs., Mpls., 1990-91; speaker in field; expert witness 100 ct. trials and 100 depositions. Del. Minn. 6th Dist. Rep. Conv., Brooklyn Park, Minn., 1982. Fellow Am. Acad. Forensic Scis. (sect. chmn. 1989-90, Founders award 1991), Nat. Acad. Forensic Engrs. (v.p. 1996); mem. ASME (Young Engr. of Yr. 1976, state chmn. 1979-80), NSPE, Profl. Engrs. in Pvt. Practice (state pres. 1987-88, Svc. award 1988), Soc. of Automotive Engrs., Rotary Club (sec. Brooklyn Park chpt. 1990-93, v.p. 1993-94, pres.-elect 1994-95, pres. 1995-96, Svc. award 1992), Brooklyn Park C. of C. (city hwy. 610 corridor com. 1992-94). Lutheran. Achievements include devel. of successful math. models to simulate jet engine transient performance and wave dynamics in gas flow, computer simulations for vehicle and occupant dynamics during collisions. Home: 15720 15th Pl N Plymouth MN 55447-2405 Office: 4455 Hwy 169N Plymouth MN 55442-2856

PETERSON, DONNA KAY, business consultant; b. Chgo., July 7, 1960; d. Richard Lavern and Donna Kay (Menthe) P. BS in Gen. Engring., U.S. Mil. Acad., 1982. Commd. 2d lt. U.S. Army, 1982, advanced through grades to capt., 1986; helicopter pilot U.S. Army, Ft. Hood, Tex., 1983-86, chief of protocol, 1986-87; resigned U.S. Army, 1987; freelance author, 1988-90; freelance bus. cons. Orange, Tex., 1991—; mem. Svc. Acad. Selection Bd., State of Tex., 1992—. Author: Dress Gray: A Woman at West Point, 1990; contbr. articles to mil. and polit. jours. Maj. USAR, 1987—. Named Outstanding Female Vet. of Tex., Tex. Vet.'s Land Bd., 1988; Capt. Donna Peterson Day proclaimed in Orange County, Tex., 1988. Mem. Am. Legion, Vietnam Vets. Am. (life., hon. award 1990), Houston West Point Soc. (1st female mem.), Women Mil. Pilots, Inc., Tex. Bus. and Profl. Women's Club (Young Careerist award 1987). Republican. Avocations: snow skiing, horseback riding, running, raising dogs, judo. Home: PO Box 158 Orange TX 77631-0158

PETERSON, DOROTHY LULU, artist, writer; b. Venice, Calif., Mar. 10, 1932; d. Marvin Henry and Fay (Brown) Case; m. Leon Albert Peterson, June 21, 1955; 1 child, David. AD, Compton (Calif.) Coll., 1950. Artist Moran Printing Co., Lockport, N.Y., 1955-59; caricature artist West Seneca and Kenmore Creative Artist Socs., 1973-86; commd. artist in pvt. practice, 1986—; comml. artist Boulevard Mall, Kenmore (N.Y.) Arts Soc., 1974—. Works include portraits of Pres. and Mrs. Reagan in Presdl. Libr. Collection, also portraits of Geraldine Ferraro, Presidents Clinton, Bush, Nixon, Ford, also Bette Davis, Lucille Ball, Bing Crosby, Elizabeth Taylor, 1971-94; author articles. Recipient awards West. Seneca Art Soc., 1975, Kenmore Art Soc., 1982, 86. Democrat. Baptist. Home: 55 Raintree Is Tonawanda NY 14150-9516

PETERSON, DOUGLAS ARTHUR, physician; b. Princeton, N.Y., Sept. 13, 1945; s. Arthur Roy William and Marie Hilma (Anderson) P.; m. Virginia Kay Eng., June 24, 1967; children: Rachel, Daniel, Rebecca. BA, St. Olaf, 1966; PhD, U. Minn., 1971, MD, 1975. Postdoctoral fellow U. Pitts., 1971-72; intern Hennepin County Med. Ctr., Mpls., 1975-76, resident in medicine, 1976-78; physician Bloomington Lake Clinic, Mpls., 1978-82; staff physician Mpls. VA Med. Ctr., Mpls., 1992—, chief compensation and pension, 1992—; asst. prof. U. Minn., 1985—. Bd. dirs. Rolling Acres Home, Victoria, Minn., 1985—. Lt. Col. M.C., USAR. Mem. AAAS, Am. Assn. Pathologists, N.Y. Acad. Scis. Achievements include introduction of concept of reductive activation of receptors. Home: 5008 Queen Ave S Minneapolis MN 55410 Office: VA Med Ctr One Veterans Dr Minneapolis MN 55417

PETERSON, DOUGLAS PETE (PETE PETERSON), congressman; b. Omaha, Nebr., June 26, 1935; m. Carlotta Ann Neal; children: Michael, Paula, Douglas. Grad., Nat. War Coll., 1975; BA, U. Tampa, 1976; postgrad., U. Ctrl. Mich., 1977. Commd. USAF, 1954, advanced through grades to col., ret., 1980; exec. CRT Computers, 1984-90; adminstr. Dozier Sch. for Boys, 1985-90; mem. 101st-104th Congresses from 2nd Fla. Dist., 1991—; mem. appropriation com.-energy and water, agrl. Prisoner of war, Vietnam. Mem. DAV, Am. Legion, Elks. Roman Catholic. Office: US Ho of Reps 306 Cannon House Ofc Bldg Washington DC 20515*

PETERSON, DOUGLAS SHURTLEFF, state legislator, packaging company official; b. Ogden, Utah, Dec. 9, 1966; s. Lowell Skeen and Kathleen (Shurtleff) P.; m. Catherine Jolley, July 9, 1994. BS in Polit. Sci. and English, Weber State U., 1994. With UPS, Ogden, 1989—; rep. Utah Ho. of Reps., Salt Lake City, 1993—; cons. Rep. Gov.'s Assn. Pres. Assn. Students Weber State U., Ogden, 1990-91; trustee Weber State U., 1990-91; regent Utah Bd. Regents of Higher Edn., Salt Lake City, 1991-92. Republican. Mem. LDS Ch. Home: 5121 S 1225 W Riverdale UT 84405

PETERSON, EDWARD ADRIAN, lawyer; b. St. Louis, May 19, 1941; s. Adrian J. and Virginia (Hamlin) P.; m. Catherine Frances Younghouse, Dec. 17, 1960; children: Kristin, Kendra. B.S.B.A., Washington U., St. Louis, 1963; LL.B., So. Methodist U., 1966. Bar: Tex. 1966, U.S. Dist. Ct. (no. and so. dists.) Tex. Instr. bus. law and acctg. Midwestern U., Wichita Falls, Tex., 1966-67; assoc. Schenk & Wesbrooks, Wichita Falls, 1966-67, Newman & Pickering, Dallas, 1967-72; ptnr. Moore & Peterson, Dallas, 1972-89, Winstead Sechrest & Minick P.C., Dallas, 1989—; speaker in field. Contbr. articles to legal jours. Bd. dirs. Leukemia Soc., 1970-71, North Tex. Commn., South Dallas/Fair Park Trust Fund, 1992; active No. Tex. Commn. Fellow Tex. Bar Found. (life); mem. ABA, Am. Coll. Real Estate Lawyers (chmn. professionalism and practice com.), State Bar Tex., Coll. State Bar Tex., Tex. Coll. Real Estate Attys., Dallas Bar Assn., Phi Alpha Delta, Sigma Alpha Epsilon. Lutheran. Avocation: snow skiing. Home: 9442 Spring Hollow Dr Dallas TX 75243-7533 Office: Winstead Sechrest & Minick PC 5400 Renaissance Tower Dallas TX 75270

PETERSON, EDWIN J., retired supreme court justice, law educator; b. Gilmanton, Wis., Mar. 30, 1930; s. Edwin A. and Leora Grace (Kitelinger) P.; m. Anna Chadwick, Feb. 7, 1971; children: Patricia, Andrew, Sherry. B.S., U. Oreg., 1951, LL.B., 1957. Bar: Oreg. 1957. Assoc. firm Tooze, Kerr, Peterson, Marshall & Shenker, Portland, 1957-61; mem. firm Tooze, Kerr, Peterson, Marshall & Shenker, 1961-79; assoc. justice Supreme Ct. Oreg., Salem, 1979-83, chief justice, 1983-91; ret., 1993; disting. juror-in-residence, adj. instr. Willamette Coll. of Law, Salem, Oreg., 1994—; chmn. Supreme Ct. Task Force on Racial Issues, 1992-94; mem. standing com. on fed. rules of practice and procedure, 1987-93; bd. dirs. Conf. Chief Justices, 1985-87, 88-91. Chmn. Portland Citizens Sch. Com., 1968-70; vice chmn. Young Republican Fedn. Orgn., 1951; bd. visitors U. Oreg. Law Sch., 1978-83, 87-93, chmn. bd. visitors, 1981-83. Served to 1st lt. USAF, 1952-54. Mem. ABA, Am. Judicature Soc., Oreg. State Bar (bd. examiners 1963-66, gov. 1973-76, vice chmn. profl. liability fund 1977-78), Multnomah County Bar Assn. (pres. 1972-73), Phi Alpha Delta, Lambda Chi Alpha. Episcopalian. Home: 3365 Sunridge Dr S Salem OR 97302-5950 Office: Willamette Univ Coll Law 250 Winter St SE Salem OR 97301-3900

PETERSON, EILEEN M., state agency administrator; b. Trenton, N.J., Sept. 22, 1942; d. Leonard James and Mary (Soganic) Olschewski; m. Lars N. Peterson, Jr., 1970 (div. 1983); children: Leslie, Valerie, Erica. Student, Boise State U. Adminstrv. sec. State Ins. Fund, Boise, 1983-85; legal asst. Bd. Tax Appeals, Boise, 1985-87, exec. asst., 1987-92, dir., 1992—. Vol. Boise Art Mus., Idaho Refugee Svc. Recipient Gov's. Cert. of Recognition for Outstanding Achievement, 1995. Mem. Mensa, Investment Club (pres.), Mountains West Outdoor Club, Idaho Rivers United. Democrat. Avocations: white water rafting, teaching ESL, non-fiction reading. Home: 3317 Mountain View Dr Boise ID 83704-4638 Office: Idaho State Bd Tax Appeals 1109 Main St Boise ID 83702-5640

PETERSON, ELMOR LEE, mathematical scientist, educator; b. McKeesport, Pa., Dec. 6, 1938; s. William James and Emma Elizabeth (Scott) P.; m. Sharon Louise Walker, Aug., 1957 (div. Jan. 1961); 1 child, Lisa Ann Peterson Loop; m. Miriam Drake Mears, Dec. 23, 1966; 1 child, David Scott. BS in Physics, Carnegie Mellon U., 1960, MS in Math., 1961, PhD in Math., 1964. Technician U.S. Steel Rsch. Ctr., Monroeville, Pa., summer 1959; engr. Westinghouse Atomic Power, Forest Hills, Pa., summer 1960; rsch. engr. Atomics Internat., Canoga Park, Calif., summer 1961; physicist Lawrence Radiation Labs., Livermore, Calif., summer 1963; sr. math. Westinghouse R & D, Churchill Boro, Pa., 1963-66; asst. prof. math. U. Mich., Ann Arbor, 1967-69; assoc. prof. math. and mgmt. sci. Northwestern U., Evanston, Ill., 1969-73, prof. math. and mgmt. sci., 1973-77, prof. applied math. and mgmt. sci., 1977-79; prof. math. and ops. rsch. N.C. State U., Raleigh, 1979—; vis. asst. prof. W.Va. U., dept. Math., Morgantown, 1966; vis. assoc. prof. U. Wis. Math. Rsch. Ctr., Madison, 1968-69; vis. prof. Stanford U. Ops. Rsch. Dept., 1976-77. Author: (with others) Geometric Programming, 1967, Russian trans., 1971; contbr. articles to profl. jours. Mobil Found. Rsch. grantee, 1967-69, Air Force Office Sci. Rsch. grantee, 1973-75, 76-78, NSF grantee, 1985-86. Mem. Soc. for Indsl. and Applied Math., Ops. Rsch. Soc. Am., Am. Math. Soc., Math. Assn. Am. Avocations: aerobic exercise, antique furniture. Home: 3717 Williamsborough Ct Raleigh NC 27609-6357 Office: NC State U Hillsborough St Raleigh NC 27695

PETERSON, ERLE VIDAILLET, retired metallurgical engineer; b. Idaho Falls, Idaho, Apr. 29, 1915; s. Vier P. and Marie (Vidaillet) P.; m. Rosemary Sherwood, June 3, 1955; children: Kent Sherwood, Pamela Jo. BS in Mining Engring., U. Idaho, 1940; MS in Mining Engring., U. Utah, 1941. Tech. advisor Remington Arms Co., Salt Lake City, 1941-43; constrn. engr. plutonium plant duPont, Hanford, Wash., 1943-44; R & D engr. exptl. sta. duPont, Wilmington, Del., 1944-51; plant metallurgist heavy water plant duPont, Newport, Ind., 1951-57; rsch. metallurgist metals program duPont, Balt., 1957-62, prin. project engr. USAF contracts, 1962-68; devel. engr. duPont, Wilmington, 1969-80; ret., 1980. Patentee in field; contbr. articles to profl. jours. Candidate for State Senate-Am. Party, Wilmington, 1974; com. chmn. Boy Scouts Am., Wilmington, 1975-78; treas. Local Civic Assn., Wilmington, 1977-79. Rsch. fellow U. Utah, 1940. Mem. Am. Soc. Metallurgists Internat., Del. Assn. Profl. Engrs. Republican. Avocations: lapidary, jewelry making, photography, prospecting, gardening. Home: PO Box 74 Rigby ID 83442-0074 *It matters not that you grow up on homestead and graduate from a country high school in a class of five during a great depression. With persistence and dedication toward your objectives, you can achieve goals that appear impossible.*

PETERSON, ESTHER, secondary school principal. Prin. Orchard Lake Mid. Sch. Recipient Blue Ribbon award U.S. Dept. Edn., 1990-91.

PETERSON, ESTHER, consumer advocate; b. Provo, Utah, Dec. 9, 1906; d. Lars and Annie (Nielsen) Eggertsen; m. Oliver A. Peterson, May 28, 1932; children: Karen Kristine, Eric N., Iver E., Lars E. A.B., Brigham Young U., 1927; M.A., Columbia Tchrs. Coll., 1930; M.A. hon. degrees, Smith Coll., Bryant Coll., Carnegie Inst. Tech., Montclair Coll., Hood Coll., Maryhurst Coll., Simmons Coll., Northeastern U., U South Utah, Western Coll. Women, Oxford, Ohio, Mich. State U., U. Mich., U. Utah, Williams Coll., Georgetown U., Temple U., Goucher Coll., Tufts U. Tchr. Branch Agr. Coll., Cedar City, Utah, 1927-29, Utah State U., Winsor Sch., Boston, 1930-36, Bryn Mawr Summer Sch. for Women Workers in Industry, 1932-39; asst. dir. edn. Amal. Clothing Workers Am., 1939-44, Washington legis. rep., 1945-48; legis. rep. indsl. union dept. AFL-CIO, 1958-61; dir. Women's Bur., U.S. Dept. Labor, 1961-64, asst. sec. labor for labor standards, 1961-69; exec. vice chmn. Pres.'s Commn. on Status of Women, 1961-63, Interdeptl. Com. Status Women, 1963-65; chmn. Pres.'s Com. Consumer Interests, 1964-67, spl. asst. to President for consumer affairs, 1964-67; legis. rep. Amal. Clothing Workers Am., Washington, 1969-70; consumer adviser Giant Food Corp., 1970-77; spl. asst. to Pres. for consumer affairs, 1977-80; chmn. Consumer Affairs Council, 1979-80. Active Internat. Med. Svcs. for Health, 1987, United Srs. Health Coop., 1987, Ctr. Sci. in Pub. Interest, 1964; mem. Women's Nat. Dem. Club; NGO rep. Internat. Orgn. Consumers Union at Econ. and Social Coun. UN, 1985, appointed pub. mem. U.S. Del. to Gen. Assembly, 1993. Decorated Presdl. medal of Freedom, 1981; recipient Food Industry Consumer award, 1986, Mgmt. award Brigham Young U., 1989. Mem. AAUW, Am. Home Econs. Assn. (hon.), Nat. Consumers League (pres. 1974-76, hon. pres. 1981), Cosmos Club, Phi Chi Theta (hon.), Delta Sigma Theta (hon.). Home: 3032 Stephenson Pl Washington DC 20015

PETERSON, ETHEL MARIE, education educator; b. Dodge City, Kans., Oct. 31, 1933; d. Henry Lindberg and Myrtle May (Smith) P. AA, Dodge City C.C., 1955; BS in Edn., Ft. Hays State U., 1960, MS in Edn., 1967, postgrad., 1977. Cert. elem. tchr., sch. counselor. Tchr. 5th & 6th grades Sch. Dist. #1, Kismet, Kans., 1955-57, tchr. 7th grade, 1957-58; tchr. 5th grade Unified Sch. Dsit. 443, Dodge City, Kans., 1958-76, counselor elem. sch., 1976-94, coord. guidance, 1989-94; western Kans. coord. tchr. edn. Kans. Newman Coll., Wichita, 1994—. Sec., bd. dirs. New Chance, Inc., Dodge City, 1988-94; del. nat. conv. Dem. Nat. Conv., N.Y.C., 1992, chair Ford County Dems., Dodge City, 1982-90.; bd. dirs. United West Community Credit Union, Dodge City, 1993—. Named Kans. Master Tchr. Emporia State U., 1992; inducted into Kans. Tchrs. Hall of Fame, 1992. Mem. NEA (nat. bd. dirs. 1975-81, Kans. bd. dirs. 1972-83, Dodge City exec. com. 1968-71, 90-94, pres. 1969-70, Kans. del. 1972-83, 90-94), Bus. and Profl. Women;s Club (parliamentarian 1994—), Phi Delta Kappa (alternate del. 1994—). Avocation: baseball. Home: 2315 Melencamp Ave Dodge City KS 67801-2512 Office: Kans Newman Coll PO Box 1058 Dodge City KS 67801-1058

PETERSON, FRED MCCRAE, librarian; b. Mpls., Dec. 29, 1936. B.A., U. Minn., 1958, M.S., 1960; Ph.D. in L.S., Ind. U., 1974. Asst. to dir. Iowa State U. Library, 1961-64, head catalog dept., 1964-67, asst. dir. library, 1967-69, assoc. dir. library, 1969-70; with Catholic U. Am., Washington, 1970-82, asst. prof., assoc. chairperson, 1973-77, acting dir. libraries, 1977-78, dir., 1978-82; univ. librarian Ill. State U., Normal, 1982—. Mem. ALA (past pres.), Ill. Library Assn. (Librian of Year 1994). Home: RR 2 Box 160 Bloomington IL 61704-9628 Office: Milner Libr 311 Ill State U Normal IL 61761

PETERSON, GALE EUGENE, historian; b. Sioux Rapids, Iowa, May 23, 1944; s. George Edmund and Vergene Elizabeth (Wilson) P. B.S., Iowa State U., 1965; M.A., U. Md., 1968, Ph.D., 1973. Instr. dept. history U. Md., College Park, 1971-72, Cath. U. Am., Washington, 1972-73; prin. investigator Gregory Directory project Orgn. Am. Historians, Bloomington, Ind., 1973-75; instr. dept. history Purdue U., West Lafayette, Ind., 1975-76; dir. U.S. Newspaper Project, Orgn. Am. Historians, Bloomington, Ind., 1976-78; exec. dir. Cin. Hist. Soc., 1978—. Author: (with John T. Schlebecker) Living Historical Farms Handbook, 1970, Harry S Truman and the Independent Regulatory Commissions 1945-52, 1985. Mem. Cin. Bicentennial Commn., 1983-88. Mem. Orgn. Am. Historians (treas. 1993—), Am. Assn. State and Local History, Am. Hist. Assn., Am. Assn. Mus., Midwestern Mus. Conf. (v.p.-at-large 1993-95, exec. v.p. 1996—), Cincinnatus Assn., Nat. Coun. on Pub. History (bd. dirs. 1992-95). Home: 3767 Middleton Ave Cincinnati OH 45220-1143 Office: Cin Hist Soc Cin Mus Ctr Cin Union Terminal Cincinnati OH 45203

PETERSON, GARY ANDREW, agronomics researcher; b. Holdrege, Nebr., Apr. 30, 1940; s. Walter Andrew and Evelyn Christine (Johnson) P.; m. Jacquelyn Charlene Flick, June 18, 1965; children: Kerstin, Ingrid. BS, U. Nebr., 1963, MS, 1965; PhD, Iowa State U., 1967. Research assoc. agronomy Iowa State U., Ames, 1964-67; prof. U. Nebr., Lincoln, 1967-84; prof. soil and crop scis. Colo. State U., Ft. Collins, 1984—. Assoc. editor AGronomy Jour., 1979-81, tech. editor, 1981-83, editor, 1984-89, editor-in-chief, 1991-96; contbr. articles to profl. jours. Fellow Am. Soc. Agronomy (Ciba-Geigy Agr. Achievement award 1974, Agronomic Achievement award-Soils 1990), Soil Sci. Soc. Am. (Applied Rsch. award 1987); mem. Soil Conservation Soc. Am. Republican. Avocations: reading, hiking, skiing. Office: Colo State U Dept Soil Crop Scis Fort Collins CO 80523

PETERSON, GEORGE EMANUEL, JR., lawyer, business executive; b. Mt. Vernon, N.Y., Mar. 8, 1931; s. George E. and Lydia Evelyn (Peterson)

P.; m. Barbara Ritter, Aug. 30, 1957; children—Lisa Manvel, George Emanuel III. B.A., Yale, 1953; LL.B., U. Va., 1958. Bar: N.Y. State 1959, Conn. 1974. Assoc. firm Reid & Priest, N.Y.C., 1958-68, ptnr., 1968-70; v.p., gen. counsel Insilco Corp., Meriden, Conn., 1970-72, v.p. fin., 1972-76, v.p., sec., 1976-79, v.p., gen. counsel, 1976-89; pvt. practice North Haven, Conn., 1989—. Served to lt. USNR, 1953-55. Mem. ABA, N.Y. State Bar Assn. Home and Office: 225 Blue Trl Hamden CT 06518-1601

PETERSON, GERALD ALVIN, physics educator; b. Chesterton, Ind., Apr. 12, 1931; s. Gustaf Albert and Esther Josephine (Carlson) P.; m. Doris Lee DeJonge, Dec. 22, 1953; children—Curtis Mark, Thomas Andrew, Anna Beth. BS, Purdue U., 1953, MS, 1955; PhD, Stanford U., 1962. Lectr. Yale U., New Haven, 1962-64; asst. prof., 1964-67; research scientist Inst. voor Kernphysisch Onderzoek, Amsterdam, 1967-68; assoc. prof. physics U. Mass., Amherst, 1968-73, prof., 1973—; vis. prof. U. Mainz, Fed. Republic Germany, 1975, Japan Soc. Promotion Sci., 1972, 89; U.S.-Israel Binat. Sci. Found. vis. prof. Tel Aviv U., 1983; cons. in field. Contbr. articles to profl. jours. Served with U.S. Army, 1955-57. NATO fellow, 1969, U.K. sr. rsch. fellow, 1970. Fellow Am. Phys. Soc. (chmn. New Eng. sect. 1996); mem. Sigma Xi. Congregationalist. Research in electron scattering and nuclear structure. Home: 10 Old Briggs Rd Leverett MA 01054-9759 Office: U Mass Nuclear Physics Grad Rsch Ctr Amherst MA 01003

PETERSON, GERALD C., lawyer; b. Chgo., Dec. 7, 1948. BA, Loyola U., 1969, JD, 1977. Bar: Ill. 1977. Ptnr. Winston & Strawn, Chgo. With U.S. Army, 1970-71. Decorated Bronze Star. Mem. ABA, Chgo. Bar Assn., Cook County Bar Assn. Office: Winston & Strawn 35 W Wacker Dr Chicago IL 60601-1614*

PETERSON, HARRIES-CLICHY, financial adviser; b. Boston, Sept. 7, 1924; s. Edwin William and Annekathe (Lieske) P. AB, Harvard U., 1946, MBA, 1950; MA in Edn., San Francisco State U., 1993. Sci. officer Ronne Antarctic Expdn., 1947-48; staff asst. Kidder Peabody & Co., N.Y.C., 1952-53, Devel. and Resources Corp., N.Y.C., 1959-61; dir. indsl. devel. W.R. Grace & Co., Lima, Peru, 1953-57; staff asst. Devel. & Resources Corp., N.Y.C., 1959-61; bus. cons. Lima, 1961-65; v.p. internat. div. Foremost Dairies, Inc. (now McKesson Corp.), San Francisco, 1965-67; v.p. H.K. Porter Co., Inc., Pitts., 1967-68; also chmn. and dir. overseas affiliates H.K. Porter Co., Inc., 1967-68; independent fin. adviser San Francisco and Los Angeles, 1968—; cons. investment banking projects for 3d world countries, Brazil, 1981, 82, 84, Nepal, 1987, Ecuador, 1988, Kenya, 1989, Indonesia, 1989, Peru, 1989, 90, 92, 93, 95, Hungary, 1992, Argentina, 1993, Bolivia, 1993; ind. cons. in field. Author: Development of Titanium Metals Industry, 1950, Che Guevara on Guerrilla Warfare, 1961, Petróleo: Hora Céro, 1964, Islamic Banking, 1979; contbr. articles gen. interest, bus., mil. publs. Served to col. USMCR, 1943-45, 51-52, 57-59. Decorated Silver Star. Mem. Colegio de Economistas del Peru (co-founder, past dir.), Am. Mgmt. Assn. (conf. chmn.). Address: PO Box 190002 San Francisco CA 94119-0002 also: Donatello 131, San Borja, Lima 41, Peru *I am grateful to classical education for having shown me truth and beauty. But the challenge to apply ideals and innovation into tradition and hierarchy requires endless self-appraisal and adjustment, sometimes exhilarating, sometimes disheartening, sometimes edifying, sometimes extracting great sacrifices from self and others I might have better served. Yet, the pursuit of uncynical truth and harmonious beauty remains an unshakeable mistress needed to satisfy soul and spirit.*

PETERSON, H(ARRY) WILLIAM, chemicals executive, consultant; b. Yokohama, Honshu Island, Japan, Mar. 9, 1922; came to U.S., 1924; s. Harry William and Alice (Mateer) P.; m. Doris Jane Howe, Apr. 27, 1946; children: Robert, Christine Fitzpatrick, Janet McMillan. BA in Chemistry and Botany, Colgate U., 1946; postgrad., Princeton U., 1949-50, U. Del., 1982-83. Lic. capt. U.S. inland waters U.S. Coast Guard. Researcher, developer ESSO Standard Oil Co., Bayway, N.J., 1946-51; various positions Enjay Chem. Co., N.Y.C., 1951-65; coord. world-wide chem. Gulf Oil Corp., Pitts., 1965-67; gen. mktg. mgr. Gulf Oil-Eastern Hemisphere, London, 1967-71; corp. v.p. chem. mktg., corp. v.p. mktg. Gulf Oil Can. Ltd., Montreal, Que., Can., 1971-77; CEO chems. divsn., corp. v.p. Golfoil Can., Montreal, Quebec, Can., 1971-77; chief operating officer Corpus Christi Chem. Co., Wilmington, Del., 1971—; mng. dir. Food Machinery & Chem. Corp. Internat. Chems., Phila., 1979-80; internat. cons. Bozman, Md., 1980—. Patentee in field. Leader Young Christians Assn., 1st Bapt. Ch., Somerville, N.J., 1948-53; lay speaker, mem. adminstrn. bd. Riverview Charge, United Meth. Ch.; chaplain Mil. Order Purple Heart. With USMC, 1942-46, PTO. Decorated Purple Heart, two battle stars. Fellow Am. Inst. Chemists; mem. Am. Chem. Soc. (emeritus). Avocations: writing, philosophy, religion. Home and Office: Quakerneck Rd Mulberry Pt Bozman MD 21612

PETERSON, HOWARD COOPER, lawyer, accountant; b. Decatur, Ill., Oct. 12, 1939; s. Howard and Lorraine (Cooper) P.; BEE, U. Ill., 1963; MEE, San Diego State Coll., 1967; MBA, Columbia U., 1969; JD, Calif. Western Sch. Law, 1983; LLM in Taxation NYU, 1985. Bar: Calif., cert. fin. planner.; CPA, Tex.; registered profl. Engr., Calif.; cert. neuro-linguistic profl. Elec. engr. Convair div. Gen. Dynamics Corp., San Diego, 1963-67, sr. electronics engr., 1967-68; gen. ptnr. Costumes Characters & Classics Co., San Diego, 1979-86; v.p., dir. Equity Programs Corp., San Diego, 1973-83; pres., dir. Coastal Properties Trust, San Diego, 1979-89, Juno Securities, Inc., 1983—, Juno Real Estate INc., 1974—, Scripps Mortgage Corp., 1987-90, Juno Transport Inc., 1988—; chief fin. officer and dir. Imperial Screens of San Diego, 1977—, Heritage Transp. Mgmt. Inc., 1989-91, A.S.A.P. Ins. Svcs. Inc., 1983-85. Mem. ABA, Interamerican Bar Assn., Nat. Soc. Public Accts., Internat. Assn. Fin. Planning, Assn. Enrolled Agts.

PETERSON, HOWARD GEORGE FINNEMORE, sports executive; b. Presque Isle, Maine, Mar. 23, 1951; s. George Conrad and Valeda (Finnemore) P. Student New Eng. Conservatory of Music, 1967-68, Andrews U., 1968-71, Orson Welles Film Sch., 1971-72, Loma Linda U., 1972-75. Pres., Nat. Ski Touring Operators Assn., 1977-79; exec. v.p. mktg. U.S. Skiing, 1979-81, exec. dir., 1981-85, sec. gen., 1985—; chief exec. officer U.S. Ski Team, 1988—, U.S. Ski Ednl. Found., 1988-92; dir. Mountain Rescue Svc., Inc. Mem. U.S. Ski Coaches Assn. (dir.), Nat. Ski Touring Operators Assn. (dir.), Internat. Ski Fedn. (eligibility com., TV and sponsorship freestyle com., chmn. expert's group for pool questions 1988—), U.S. Olympic Properties Com., Winter Olympic Sports Coun. (sec. 1988—, Olympic Tng. Ctrs. Com. 1988—), U.S. Skiing Found. (exec. dir., trustee), Pan Am. Sports Orgn. (winter games adv. com. 1988—). Author: Cross Country Citizen Racing, 1980; I Hope I Get a Purple Ribbon, 1980; Cross Country Ski Trails, 1979; Cannon: A Climber's Guide, 1972. Office: US Skiing PO Box 100 Park City UT 84060-0100*

PETERSON, JAMES ALGERT, geologist, educator; b. Baroda, Mich., Apr. 17, 1915; s. Djalma Hardaman and Mary Avis (McAnally) P.; m. Gladys Marie Pearson, Aug. 18, 1944; children—James D., Wendy A., Brian H. Student, Northwestern U., 1941-43, U. Wis., 1943; B.S. magna cum laude, St. Louis U., 1948; M.S. (Shell fellow), U. Minn., 1950, Ph.D., 1951. Mem. staff U.S. Geol. Survey, Spokane, Wash., 1949-51; instr. geology Wash. State U., Pullman, 1951; geologist Shell Oil Co., 1952-65; geologist div. stratigrapher, 1958-63, sr. geologist, 1963-65; instr. geology N. Mex. State U., San Juan, (P.R.), br., 1959-65; prof. geology U. Mont., Missoula, 1965—; cons. U.S. Geol. Survey, 1976-82, rsch. geologist, 1982—. Editor: Geology of East Central Utah, 1956, Geometry of Sandstone Bodies, 1960, Rocky Mountain Sedimentary Basins, 1965, (with others) Pacific Geology, Paleotectonics and Sedimentation, 1986; Contbr. (with others) articles to profl. jours. Served to 1st lt. USAAF, 1943-46. Recipient Alumni Merit award St. Louis U., 1960, Outstanding Achievement award U. Minn., 1995. Fellow AAAS, Geol. Soc. Am.; mem. Am. Assn. Petroleum Geologists (pres. Rocky Mountain sec. 1964, Pres.'s award 1988, Disting. Svc. award 1992, hon.), Rocky Mountain Assn. Geologists (Outstanding Scientist award 1987), Four Corners Geol. Soc. (hon., pres. 1962), Am. Inst. Profl. Geologists (pres. Mont. sect. 1971), Soc. Econ. Paleontologists and Mineralogists (hon. 1985, sec.-treas. 1969-71, editor 1976-78, Disting. Pioneer Geologist award 1988), Mont. Geol. Soc. (hon. 1987), Utah Geol. Soc., Explorers Club. Club: Explorers. Home: 301 Pattee Canyon Dr Missoula MT 59803-1624

PETERSON, JAMES KENNETH, manufacturing company executive; b. Sioux City, Iowa, Oct. 17, 1934; s. David Winfield and Beulah Lillian (Johnson) P.; m. Nanette Kay Olin, Feb. 2, 1957; children: Kimberly, Kristin, David. B.A. in Econs, Mich. State U., 1956. Research/devel. engr. Reynolds Metals Co., Richmond, Va., 1957-59, sales rep., 1959-61, dist. sales mgr., 1961-65, regional sales mgr., 1965-67, asst. to exec. v.p., 1968, mktg. dir., 1969-71; dir. nat. account sales The Continental Group, Stamford, Conn., 1971, gen. mgr. sales, 1972-73, div. gen. mgr., 1974-78, v.p., corp. officer, 1974-80, v.p., gen. mgr. global bus. devel., 1979; pres., chief oper. officer Ludlow Corp., Needham, Mass., 1980-82, also bd. dirs.; pres., CEO, dir. Graphic Packaging Corp., Paoli, Pa., 1982-89; pres., CEO Peterson Group, Easton, Md., 1989—; chmn., CEO The Petters Co., Lititz, Pa.; chmn. bd. dirs. Comml. Printers of Conn.; bd. dirs. Graphic Packaging Corp., South Chester Tube Co.; mem. Precision Strip Inc. Served to 1st lt. U.S. Army, 1957. Mem. Merion Golf Club, Merion Cricket Club, Talbot Country Club. Home: 27779 Waverly Rd Easton MD 21601-8121 Office: Peterson Group PO Box 738 Easton MD 21601-0738 also: The Petters Co 2077 Main St Lititz PA 17543-3029

PETERSON, JAMES LINCOLN, museum executive; b. Kewanee, Ill., Nov. 12, 1942; s. Reinold Gustav and Florence Josephine (Kjellgren) P.; m. M. Susan Pepin, Aug. 15, 1964; children: Hans C., Erika C. BA, Gustavus Adolphus Coll., 1964; PhD, U. Nebr., 1972. Sci. tchr. pub. schs. Ill. and Minn., 1964-68; research asst. U. Nebr., Lincoln, 1968-72; research assoc. U. Wis., Madison, 1972-74; staff ecologist Nat. Commn. Water Quality, Washington, 1974-75; v.p. research Acad. Nat. Scis., Phila., 1976-84, v.p. devel., 1982-84; pres. Sci. Mus. Minn., St. Paul, 1984—. Bd. dirs. Ea. Pa. chpt. Nature Conservancy, Phila., 1982-84, Downtown Coun., St. Paul, 1986-93, Keystone (Colo.) Ctr., 1989-93; mem. St. Paul Riverfront Commn., 1987-91; mem. adv. com. U. Minn. Coll. Biol. Scis., 1989-95. Mem. Assn. Sci. Mus. Dirs., Assn. Sci. and Tech. Ctrs. (pres. 1993-95), Sci. Mus. Exhibit Collaborative (pres. 1986-89), St. Paul C. of C. (bd. dirs. 1985-89), Informal Club. Office: Sci Mus Minn 30 10th St E Saint Paul MN 55101-2205

PETERSON, JAMES ROBERT, retired writing instrument manufacturing executive; b. Momence, Ill., Oct. 28, 1927; s. Clyde and Pearl (Deliere) P.; m. Betty Windham, May 12, 1949; children: Richard James, Lynn Peterson Anderson, Susan Peterson Hanske, John Windham. Student, St. Thomas Coll., 1945, Iowa State U., 1945-46, U. Colo., 1946, Northwestern U., 1946; BS in Mktg. cum laude, U. Ill., 1952; grad. exec. MBA program, Stanford U., 1967. With Pillsbury Co., Mpls., 1952-76; brand mgr. grocery products Pillsbury Co., 1953-57, brand supr. flour, 1957-61, dir. mktg., 1961-66, v.p. mktg., 1966-68; v.p., gen. mgr. Grocery Products Co., 1968-71, group v.p. consumer cos., 1971-73, pres., dir., 1973-76; exec. v.p., dir. R.J. Reynolds Industries, Inc., Winston-Salem, N.C., 1976-82; pres., chief exec. officer, dir. Parker Pen Co., Janesville, Wis., 1982-85; dir. Dun & Bradstreet Corp., N.Y.C., 1977, Waste Mgmt., Inc., Oak Brook, Ill., 1980. Former mem. bd. dirs. Boy Scouts Am., past pres. Viking coun.; mem. bd. regents St. Olaf Coll., 1974-91. Lt. USN, 1945-50. Recipient Bronze Tablet award U. Ill. Mem. Pilgrims of U.S., Tequesta Country Club, Janesville Country Club, Bodega Harbour Golf, Links Club, Jupiter Hills Club. Methodist. Address: 19750 Beach Rd 505 Tequesta FL 33469

PETERSON, JAMES ROBERT, retired engineering psychologist; b. St. Paul, Apr. 16, 1932; s. Palmer Elliot and Helen Evelyn (Carlson) P.; BA in Psychology cum laude, U. Minn., 1954; MA in Exptl. Psychology, 1958; PhD in Engring. Psychology, U. Mich., 1965; m. Marianna J. Stockvig, June 26, 1954; 1 child, Anne Christine. Devel. engr. Honeywell Inc., 1961-65, sr. devel. engr., 1965-67, staff engr., 1967-90, sr. project staff engr., 1990-93, ret., 1993; Honeywell sponsor rep. Shuttle Student Involvement Program, 1982, 84. Served with USMC, 1954-57, with Res., 1957-62. Assoc. fellow AIAA; mem. Human Factors and Ergonomics Soc. (life), Air & Space Mus. (charter), Smithsonian Inst. Club: Mason. Contbr. articles to profl. jours. Achievements include invention of Apollo translation hand controller; participation in development work on all U.S. Manned Space Programs (Mercury, Gemini, Apollo, Lunar Excursion Module, Manned Orbiting Laboratory, Space Shuttle and Space Station) as member/manager of associated human factors groups. Home: 3303 San Gabriel St Clearwater FL 34619-3341

PETERSON, JANE WHITE, nursing educator, anthropologist; b. San Juan, P.R., Feb. 15, 1941; d. Jerome Sidney and Vera (Joseph) Peterson; 1 child, Claire Marie. BS, Boston U., 1968; M in Nursing, U. Wash., 1969, PhD, 1981. Staff nurse Visiting Nurse Assn., Boston, 1964-66; prof. Seattle U., 1969—, dir. nursing home project, 1990-92, chair pers. com., 1988-90; chair dept. Community Health and Psychiat. Mental Health Nursing, 1987-89; sec. Coun. on Nursing and Anthropology, 1984-86; pres. Wash. League Nursing, Seattle, 1988-90; pres. bd. Vis. Nurses Svcs., Seattle, 1988-90; contbg. cons. CSI Prodn., Okla., 1987; cons. in nursing WHO/U. Indonesia, Jakarta, fall 1989, Myanmar, Burma, winter 1995, Yengon, 1995, China, Beijing, 1995. Contbr. articles to profl. jours., chptrs. to books. Co-owner (with Robert Colley) North End Train Ctr., Seattle; mem. Seattle Art Mus., 1986—. Fellow: Soc. for Applied Anthropology; mem. Am. Anthropological Assn., Soc. for Med. Anthropology, Nat. League for Nursing, Am. Ethological Soc. Office: Seattle U Sch Nursing Broadway and Madison Seattle WA 98122

PETERSON, JIM LEE, food service executive; b. Kansas City, Mo., Oct. 1, 1935; s. Lee C. and Lucille (Wiss) P.; m. Sue Ann Peterson, Dec. 7, 1956 (div. Jan. 1989); children: Ronald, Gaye, Craig. Student, Ottawa U., 1953-55; BA, U. Mo., Kansas City, 1957. Mgr. floor ops. Montgomery Ward & Co., Chgo., 1955-59; mgr. dist. sales Sinclair Oil Co., N.Y.C., 1959-64; pres. Food Host USA, Lincoln, Nebr., 1964-74, Whataburger, Inc., Corpus Christi, Tex., 1974-94, Bojangles' Restaurants Inc., Charlotte, N.C., 1994—; bd. dirs. 1st City Bank and Mercantile Bank Tex./Corpus Christi, Cen. Power & Light Co., Corpus Christi; mem. adv. bd. U. Nebr. Sch. Bus. and Franchising, Lincoln. Pres., bd. dirs. United Way Coastal Bend, Corpus Christi; chmn. Drug Edn., Law Enforcement and Community Unity Commn., Corpus Christi, Found. for Scis. and Arts, Corpus Christi; founder Corpus Christi Crimestoppers, Inc. Recipient Golden Chain and Operator of Yr. award Nation's Restaurant News, 1980, Silver Plate award Internat. Food Svc. Mfr. Assoc., 1983, Leadership award in food svc. mgmt. Restaurant Bus. mag., 1986, Disting. Citizen award Coastal Bend coun. Boy Scouts Am., 1989, Humanitarian of Yr. award NCCJ, Corpus Christi, 1990. Mem. Internat. Franchise Assn. (chmn. ethical standards com. 1986), Nat. Restaurant Assn. (nat. pres. 1988-89, chmn., bd. dirs. Edn. Found. 1992-93), World Bus. Coun., Corpus Christi C. of C. (pres.), Road Runners Club (Corpus Christi and N.Y.C.). Republican. Episcopalian. Avocations: running marathons, tennis, ranching, poetry, music. Home: PO Box 1338 Goliad TX 77963-1338 Office: Bojangles' Restaurants Inc 9600 Southern Pines Blvd Ste H Charlotte NC 28273-5520*

PETERSON, JOHN DOUGLAS, museum administrator; b. Peshtigo, Wis., July 9, 1939; s. Rubin and Ruth (Erickson) P.; m. Beth L. Lynch, July 22, 1965; children: Marie Storm, Beth Storm. BFA, Layton Sch. Art, 1962, cert. in indsl. design, 1962; MFA, Cranbrook Acad. Art, Bloomfield Hills, Mich., 1966. Asst. dir. Cranbrook Acad. Art Mus., Bloomfield Hills, Mich., 1969-70, assoc. dir., 1970-71, dir., 1971-77; exec. dir. Lakeview Mus. Arts and Scis., Peoria, Ill., 1977-82, The Morris Mus., Inc., Morristown, N.J., 1982-94; v.p. The Morris Mus. Found., Morristown, 1990-94; exec. dir. Scienceport, Rye, N.Y., 1994-95; bd. dirs. Morristown Inf. Ctr., Gill St. Bernard Sch., 1988-94, Mng. Mainstreet, J/B Peterson, Inc.; mem. adv. panel Ill. Arts Coun., Chgo., 1980-82, N.J. State Coun. Arts, Trenton, 1984-85; reviewer Inst. Mus. Svcs., Washington, 1985-87. Bd. dirs. Peoria City Beautiful, 1978-82, Met. Detroit Arts Coun., 1972-77, New Philharmonic Orch., N.J.; chmn. Arts Coun., Triangle, 1972-73; co-chmn. Pub. Arts Com., Peoria, 1977-78. Mem. Am. Assn. Mus., Am. Assn. State and Local History, Advocates for the Arts, Mid-Atlantic Mus. Assn., New England Mus. Assn., N.J. Assn. Mus. (bd. dirs. 1990-94), Somerset Art Assn. (bd. dirs. 1990-94), N.J. Art Pride (bd. dirs. 1990-94), Morris Area Mus. Assn., Park Ave Club, Morristown Club. Home: 165 Lakeshore Dr Oakland NJ 07436-2102

PETERSON, JOHN DWIGHT, investment company executive; b. Indpls., July 20, 1933; s. J. Dwight and Mary Irene (Frisinger) P.; m. Nancy Jane Browning, July 16, 1955; children: Debbra Lee, John Dwight III, Penny Anne. B.S., Ind. U., 1955. With City Securities Corp., Indpls., 1955—; dir. City Securities Corp., 1966—, v.p., 1968-70, pres., 1970—, CEO, now chmn., 1979—; dir. Lilly Indsl. Coatings, Inc., Farm Fans, Inc., Forum Group, Inc., Capital Industries, Duke Realty Investments. Mem. James Whitcomb Riley Meml. Assn., 1965—, Ind. Bd. Vocat. and Tech. Edn., 1973-81; mem. career edn. action com. Indpls. Pub. Schs., 1974-80; mem. Ind. U. Athletic Bd., 1971-74; pres. bd. dirs. Jr. Achievement Central Ind., 1979. Served as capt. U.S. Army, 1956. Mem. Young Pres. Orgn., Nat. Assn. Securities Dealers (dist. com. 8 1975-78), Indpls. Bond Club (pres. 1969), Sigma Chi. Presbyterian (elder). Clubs: Marion County Varsity (chmn. 1961-71); Columbia, University (Indpls.); Highland Golf and Country. Lodges: Masons, Rotary. Office: City Securities Corp 135 N Pennsylvania St Indianapolis IN 46204-2400

PETERSON, JOHN ERIC, physician, educator; b. Norwalk, Ohio, Oct. 26, 1914; s. Charles Augustus and Fannie Helen (Stanford) P.; m. Lodene C. Pruett, Aug. 18, 1938; children—Carol Peterson Haviland, John Eric. Student, Columbia Jr. Coll., 1932-34; M.D., Coll. Med. Evangelists, 1938. Diplomate: Nat. Bd. Med. Examiners, Am. Bd. Internal Medicine. Intern Henry Ford Hosp., Detroit, 1938-39; resident Henry Ford Hosp., 1939-42; practice medicine specializing in internal medicine Los Angeles, 1942-56, Loma Linda, Calif., 1956—; mem. staff Los Angeles County Hosp., Riverside (Calif.) County Gen. Hosp.; mem. faculty Sch. Medicine, Loma Linda U., 1942—, prof. medicine, 1967-88, prof. medicine emeritus, 1988—, chmn. dept., 1969-80; asso. dean Sch. Medicine, Loma Linda U. (Sch. Medicine), 1965-75; mem. staff Loma Linda U. Hosp., 1967—, chief medicine service, 1969-80; rsch. assoc. Harvard Med. Sch., 1960-61; cons. to univs. and fgn. govts. Contbr. articles to various publs. Fellow ACP; mem. AMA, Calif. Med. Assn., San Bernardino County Med. Assn., Calif. Soc. Internal Medicine, Inland Soc. Internal. Medicine, Am. Diabetes Assn., Western Soc. Clin. Investigation, Assn. Profs. of Medicine, L.A. Acad. Medicine, Diabetes Assn. So. Calif., Sigma Xi, Alpha Omega Alpha. Office: Loma Linda U Med Ctr Dept Medicine Rm 1576 Loma Linda CA 92350

PETERSON, JOHN LEONARD, lawyer, judge; b. Butte, Mont., Sept. 11, 1933; s. Roy Victor and Lena Pauline (Umhang) P.; m. Jean Marie Hollingsworth, June 10, 1957; children: Michael R., John Robert, Carol Jean. BA in Bus., U. Mont., 1957, JD, 1957. Bar: Mont. 1957, U.S. Supreme Ct. 1964, U.S. Ct. Appeals (9th cir.) 1974, U.S. Tax Ct. 1978. Assoc., McCaffery, Roe, Kiely & Joyce, 1957-63; ptnr. McCaffery & Peterson, 1963-79; sole practice, Butte, Mont., 1979-85; part-time U.S. bankruptcy judge, 1963-85; U.S. bankruptcy judge, Mont., 1985—. Bd. govs. Nat. Conf. Bankruptcy Judges, 1989-92; mem. Mont. Bd. Regents Higher Edn., 1975-82; del. Democratic Nat. Conv., 1968. Mem. Nat. Conf. Bankruptcy Judges, Assn. Trial Lawyers Am., Mont. Bar Assn., Silver Bow County Bar Assn., Butte Country Club, Butte Town Club, Butte Exch. Club, VASA Order Am., Scandinavia Fraternity of Am. Democrat. Lutheran. Office: US Dist Ct 215 Fed Bldg Butte MT 59701

PETERSON, KAREN IDA, marketing research company executive; b. Rahway, N.J., Dec. 30, 1939; d. Sigurd Thage and Harriet Erma (Pearson) P.; m. Thomas Lea Davidson, Oct. 7, 1978 (dec.). BA, Wellesley Coll., 1961; postgrad., CCNY, 1963-66. Rsch. asst. Opinion Rsch. Corp., Princeton, N.J., 1961-63; rsch. sec. Interpub. Group of Cos., N.Y.C., 1963-65; project dir., account supr., group head, v.p. Oxtoby Smith, Inc., N.Y.C., 1965-74; founder, prin., pres. Davidson-Peterson Assoc., N.Y.C. and York, Maine, 1974—; treas. Coun. Am. Survey Rsch. Orgn., Pt. Jefferson, N.Y., 1978-83, bd. dirs. Maine Publicity Bur., Hallowell. Co-author: Rural Tourism Marketing, 1994; mem. editl. rev. bd. Jour. Travel Rsch. Dir. Seashore Trolley Mus., Kennebunk, Maine, 1994—. Recipient Noah award Acad. of Travel, 1986. Mem. S.E. Tourism Soc., Women Execs. Internat. Tourism Assn. (bd. dirs., pres. 1984-89), Travel & Tourism Rsch. Assn. Internat. (bd. dirs. 1990-92). Avocations: photography, travel, antiques. Office: Davidson-Peterson Assoc Inc PO Box 350 York ME 03909-0350

PETERSON, KENT WRIGHT, physician; b. Portsmouth, Va., Apr. 16, 1943; s. Gerald Milton and Julia Elizabeth (Hoover) P.; m. Virginia Mae Sonne, Dec. 26, 1979; children: Liesl Lynn, Owen Sonne. B.A., U. N.C., Chapel Hill, 1964; M.D., U. Pa., 1968. Diplomate Am. Bd. Gen. Preventive Medicine and Occupational Medicine. Intern U. Wis., 1968-69, resident, 1970-71; Robert Wood Johnson clin. scholar George Washington U., 1975-77; family physician E. Madison Clinic, Madison, Wis., 1969; chief med. officer policy devel. U.S. Cost of Living Council, Washington, 1973-74; assoc. dir. Assn. Univ. Programs in Health Adminstrn., Washington, 1974-77; exec. v.p. Am. Coll. Preventive Medicine, Washington, 1977-81; corp. mgr. preventive and environ. medicine IBM Corp., White Plains, N.Y., 1981-84; corp. med. dir. Am. Standard, N.Y.C., 1984-86; pres. Occupational Health Strategies, Charlottesville, Va., 1984—; clin. asst. prof. Georgetown U. Sch. Medicine, 1979-85; clin. assoc. prof. NYU dept. environ. medicine, 1985—; rep. to Coun. Med. Specialty Socs., 1980-86; mem. Accreditation Coun. for Continuing Med. Edn., 1981-86; treas. Med. Rev. Officer Cert. Coun., 1992—; v.p. Am. Bd. of Ind. Med. Examiners, 1995—. Author books including Directory of Occupational Health and Safety Software, 9th edit., 1996, Handbook of Health Risk Appraisals, 3d edit., 1996; contbr. nuermous articles to profl. jours. and chpts. to books. Pres. Children of the Americas Found., 1979-84. Served to maj. M.C. U.S. Army, 1971-73. Fellow Am. Coll. Preventative Medicine, Am. Coll. Occupl. and Environ. medicine (chmn. computers in occupl. medicine com. 1986-90); mem. AMA, APHA, Assn. Tchrs. Preventive Medicine, N.Y. Acad. Medicine, Ramazzini Soc., Soc. Prospective Medicine (officer) World Future Soc., Coun. for Liveable World, Va. Occupl. Medicine Assn. (pres. 1988-90). Home: 7767 Faber Rd Faber VA 22938-9715 Office: Occupational Health Strategies Inc 901 Preston Ave Ste 400 Charlottesville VA 22903-4491

PETERSON, KEVIN BRUCE, newspaper editor, publishing executive; b. Kitchener, Ont., Can., Feb. 11, 1948; s. Bruce Russell and Marguerite Elizabeth (Hammond) P.; m. Constance Maureen Bailey, Feb. 11, 1975 (dec. May 1975); m. Sheila Helen O'Brien, Jan. 9, 1981. B.A., U. Calgary, Alta., Can., 1968. Chief bur. Calgary Herald, 1972-75, city editor, 1976-77, news editor, 1977-78, bus. editor, 1978, mng. editor, 1978-86, editor, asst. pub., 1986-87, gen. mgr., 1987-88, pub., 1989-96; pres. Canadian Univ. Press, Ottawa, Ont., Can., 1968-69; dir. New Directions for News. Harry Brittain Meml. fellow Commonwealth Press Union, London, 1979. Mem. Can. Mng. Editors (bd. dirs. 1983-87), Am. Soc. Newspaper Editors, Horsemen's Benevolent and Protective Assn., Alta. Legis. Press Gallery Assn. (v.p. 1971-76), Can. Daily Newspaper Assn. (bd. dirs. 1990-96, vice chmn., treas 1992, chmn. 1993-96), Calgary Petroleum Club, Ranchmen's Club, 100-1-1 Club, (Arcadia, Calif.). Avocations: thoroughbred horse racing; art collecting. Office: Calgary Herald, 215 16th St Se, Calgary, AB Canada T2P 0W8

PETERSON, KIRK CHARLES, ballet dancer; b. New Orleans, Dec. 10, 1949; s. John Lawrence and Dorothy Ann (Wagner) P. Student pub. schs.; scholar, Harkness House for Ballet Arts. Charter mem. Harkness Youth Dancers, 1968-69; prin. dancer Harkness Ballet, 1970, Nat. Ballet, Washington, 1971-74, London Festival Ballet, 1973; mem. Am. Ballet Theatre, 1974-80, soloist, 1975-78, prin. dancer, 1978-80; prin. dancer, choreographer, ballet master Ballet Nat. de Venezuela, 1980; prin. dancer, resident choreographer, tchr. San Francisco Ballet, 1981-85; resident tchr. Met. Opera Ballet, Steps Studio; tchr. master classes, condr. lecture demonstrtions; artistic dir. Hartford Ballet, 1993—. Choreographer: The Nutcracker, Floating Weeds, Cloudless Sulphur, Othello, Overlay, Valse Triste; asst. choreographer Anything Goes, Lincoln Ctr., 1987, Anything Goes, Australia and London, 1989, Ballet Metropolitan, Columbus, Ohio, 1989; co-choreographer Shogun, Broadway, 1990; prin. roles include Albrecht in Giselle, James in La Sylphide; co-founder, dir. Omo Dancers, 1985. Recipient Bronze medal Internat. Ballet Competition, Varna, Bulgaria, 1972, Cultural award Dept. State, 1972, key to City of New Orleans, 1965, 66, 67. Mem. Am. Guild Musical Artists, Screen Actors Guild, AFTRA.

PETERSON, KRISTIN, artist; b. Urbana, Ill., May 17, 1954; d. Theodore Bernard and Helen (Clegg) P. BFA, Kansas City Art Inst., 1978; MFA, U. Calif., 1982. Vis. artist Calif. State U., Humbolt, 1990. Solo exhbn. Diablo Valley Community Coll. Art Gallery, 1981, Meml. Union Art Gallery, 1982, Joseph Chowning Gallery, 87, 89; group exhbns. include Ten Video Artists, 1977, Crosby-Kemper Art Gallery, Kansas City, 1978, The Calif. State Fair Exhibit, 1982, cowtown, Chan-Elliot Gallery, 1983, The Show Box Show, The Art Store Gallery, 1986, Rags, San Francisco Art Commn. Gallery, 1989, Functional Fantasy, The Trans-Am. Pyramid, San Francisco, 1990.

Nat. Endowment for the Arts grantee, 1986; Humanities Rsch. grantee, 1981-82. Mem. Emeryville Artists Cooperative.

PETERSON, KRISTINA, publishing company executive. Pres., pub. Fodor's Travel Pub. Inc. subs. Random House Inc. Office: Fodor's Travel Pub Inc 201 E 50th St New York NY 10022-7703

PETERSON, LARRY JAMES, medical educator, oral surgeon; b. Winfield, Kans., Apr. 23, 1942; m. Susan Bartlett; children: Brie, Tucker. BS, U. Kans., 1964; DDS cum laude, U. Mo., Kans. City, 1968; MS, Georgetown U., 1971. Diplomate Am. Bd. Oral and Maxillofacial Surgery. Oral surgery resident Georgetown U. Sch. Dentistry, Washington, 1968-71; active staff Eugene Talmadge Meml. Hosp., Augusta, Ga., 1971-75, John N. Dempsey Hosp., Farmington, Conn., 1975-82, Ohio State U. Hosp., Columbus, 1982—, Children's Hosp., Columbus, 1982—; asst. prof. oral surgery Med. Coll. Ga. Sch. Dentistry, Augusta, 1971-74, assoc. prof. oral surgery, 1974-75; assoc. prof. oral and maxillofacial surgery U. Conn. Sch. Dental Medicine, Farmington, 1975-81; program dir. oral and maxillofacial surgery residency U. Conn. Affiliated Program, Farmington, 1980-82; prof. oral and maxillofacial surgery U. Conn. Sch. Dental Medicine, Farmington, 1981-82; prof., chmn. oral and maxillofacial surgery and pathology Ohio State U. Coll. Dentistry, Columbus, 1982—; adv. com. Am. Bd. Oral and Maxillofacial Surgeons 1980-86, assoc. subject leader 1982-84, subject leader 1984-86. Editor: (textbook) Contemporary Oral and Maxillofacial Surgery, (multi-vol. ref. book) Principles of Oral and Maxillofacial Surgery; contbr. over 40 articles to profl. jours., 25 chpts. to books; editor oral surgery sect. Clinical Dentistry, 1981-87, oral and maxillofacial surgery sect. Oral Surgery, Oral Medicine, Oral Pathology, 1992—, editor-in-chief 1993—; editl. bd. Jour. Oral and Maxillofacial Surgery 1991-92; presenter in field. Recipient awards Am. Coll. Dentists, 1984, Internat. Coll. Dentists, 1992; Mosby scholar 1968. Fellow Am. Dental Soc. of Anesthesiology; mem. ADA (cons., oral and maxillofacial surgery site visitor, commn. on dental accreditation 1985-91, nat. dental bd. test constrn. com. oral and maxillofacial surgery 1985-90, nat. dental bd. part II restructuring com. 1987-92, cons. coun. on dental therapeutics 1980-92), Am. Assn. of Oral and Maxillofacial Surgeons (rsch. adv. com. 1976-79, test constrn. com. 1978-91, com. on scientific sessions 1991-94, com. on residency edn. and tng. 1992—, del. Ho. Dels. 1991-94), Internat. Assn. for Dental Rsch., Am. Assn. Dental Schs., Acad. of Osteointegration, Assn. for Acad. Surgery, Surg. Infection Soc., Alliance for Prudent Use of Antibiotics, Ohio Dental Assn., Ohio Soc. Oral and Maxillofacial Surgeons, Great Lakes Soc. Oral and Maxillofacial Surgeons, Columbus Dental Soc., Sigma Xi, Omicron Kappa Upsilon. Office: Ohio State U Coll Dentistry Dept Oral and Max Surgery 305 West 12th Ave Columbus OH 43210-1241

PETERSON, LAURENCE E., physics educator; b. Grantsburg, Wis., July 26, 1931; m. Joelle Dallancon, 1956; children: Mark L., Daniel F., Lynn M., Julianne. BS, U. Minn., 1954, PhD, 1960. Rsch. assoc. in physics U. Minn., Mpls., 1960-62; from resident physicist to prof. physics U. Calif., San Diego, 1962—; physics subcom. NASA Space Sci. Steering Com., 1964—, assoc. dir. sci. astrophysics divsn., 1986-88; dir. Ctr. Astrophysics & Space Sci., U. Calif., San Diego, 1988—. Fellow NSF, 1958-59, Guggenheim Found., 1973-74. Fellow Am. Phys. Soc.; mem. AIAA (space sci. award 1978), AAAS, Am. Astron. Soc., Internat. Astronomical Union. Office: U Calif-San Diego Ctr. Astrophysics & Space Scis MC 0111 9500 Gilman Dr La Jolla CA 92093*

PETERSON, LESLIE ERNEST, bishop; b. Noranda, Que., Can., Nov. 4, 1928; s. Ernest Victor and Blanch (Marsh) P.; m. Yvonne Hazel Lawton, July 16, 1953; children—Shauna Peterson Van Hoof, Tom, Jennifer Peterson Glage, Kathryn Peterson Scott, Jonathan. B.A., U. Western Ont., London, Ont., Can., 1952; L.T.H., Huron Coll., London, Ont., Can., 1954, D.D. (hon.), 1984; tchr.'s cert., North Bay Tchrs. Coll., Ont., 1970. Ordained to ministry Anglican Ch., 1954. Priest Diocese of Algoma, Coniston, Ont., 1954-58; priest Diocese of Algoma, Elliot Lake, Ont., 1959-63, rural dean, 1961-63; priest Diocese of Algoma, North Bay, 1963-78; priest Diocese of Algoma, Parry Sound, Ont., 1978-83, archdeacon, 1980-83; bishop Diocese of Algoma, Sault Ste. Marie, Ont., 1983-94; tchr. North Bay Elem. Sch., 1970-78; ret., 1994. Avocations: canoeing, woodworking, gardening. Address: 615 Santa Monica Rd, London, ON Canada N6H 3W2

PETERSON, LESLIE RAYMOND, barrister; b. Viking, Alta., Can., Oct. 6, 1923; s. Herman S. and Margaret (Karen) P.; m. Agnes Rose Hine, June 24, 1950; children: Raymond Erik, Karen Isabelle. Student, Camrose Luth. Coll., Alta., McGill. U., Can., London U., Eng.; LLB, U. B.C., Can., 1949; LLD, Simon Fraser U., Can., 1965, U. B.C., 1993; EdD, Notre Dame U., Nelson, Can., 1966; hon. diploma tech., B.C. Inst. Tech., 1994. Bar: B.C. 1949; called to Queens Counsel, 1960. Pvt. practice barrister Vancouver, B.C., 1949-52; with Peterson & Anderson, 1952; then with Boughton & Co. (now Boughton Peterson Yang Anderson).; mem. B.C. Legislature for Vancouver Centre, 1956-63, Vancouver-Little Mountain, 1966; min. of edn., 1956-68, min. of labour, 1960-71, atty. gen., 1968-72; bd. govs. U. B.C., 1979-83, chancellor, 1987-93; bd. dirs. Can. Found. Econ. Edn., Inst. Corp. Dirs. Can., Tordiam Inc., West Vancouver Found., Karay Holdings Ltd., Amaric Prodns. Inc., Rick Hansen Enterprises Inc.; trustee Peter Wall Inst. for Advanced Studies. Bd. dirs. Portland unit Shriners Hosp. for Crippled Children; past bd. dirs. Western Soc. of Rehab., YMCA, Victoria B.C.; past pres. Twenty Club; hon. mem. Vancouver Jr. C. of C.; former v.p. Normanna Old People's Home; founding mem. Convocation, Simon Fraser U. and U. Victoria, pres., 1964-65; hon. dep. French Nat. Assembly, Paris; hon. commr. labor State of Okla.; gov. Downtown Vancouver Assn.; chmn. U. B.C. Found. With Can. Army, 1942-46, ETO. Recipient Disting. Alumnus award Camrose Luth. Coll., 1980. Fellow Royal Soc. Arts; mem. Internat. Bar Assn., Vancouver Bar Assn., Law Soc. B.C., Internat. Assn. of Govt. Labour Ofcls. (chmn. standing com., Can. mins. of edn. 1965-66), Terminal City Club (pres. 1991—), Scandinavian Bus. Men's Club (past pres.), Hazelmere Golf and Tennis Club (bd. dirs.), Union Club (Victoria), Wesbrook Soc. of U. B.C. (chmn. 1987), Order of St. Lazarus (knight comdr.), Freemason (potentate Gizeh Temple Shrine 1988). Avocations: skiing, golf, fishing, hunting. Home: 814 Highland, West Vancouver, BC Canada V7S 2G5 Office: Boughton Peterson Yang Anderson, 1055 Dunsmuir St PO Box 49290, Vancouver, BC Canada V7X 1S8

PETERSON, LINDA H., English language and literature educator; b. Saginaw, Mich., Oct. 11, 1948. BA in Lit. summa cum laude, Wheaton Coll., 1969; MA in English, U. R.I., 1973; PhD in English, Brown U., 1978. From lectr. to assoc. prof. Yale U., New Haven, 1977-92, prof., 1992—, dir. undergrad. studies English, 1990-94, chair, 1994—; dir. Bass writing program Yale Coll., 1979-89, 90—; mem. various departmental and univ. coms. Yale U., 1977—; presenter in field. Author: Victorian Autobiography: The Tradition of Self-Interpretation, 1986; co-author: Writing Prose, 1989, A Struggle for Fame: Victorian Women Artists and Authors, 1994; co-editor: Wuthering Heights: A Case Study in Contemporary Criticism, 1992, The Norton Reader, 9th edit., 1996, Instructor's Guide to the Norton Reader, 1996; mem. editl. bd. Writing Program Adminstrn., 1983-85, Coll. Composition and Comm., 1986-88, Auto/Biography Studies, 1990-96; contbr. articles to profl. jours. Resident fellow Branford Coll., 1979-87, Mellon fellow Whitney Humanities Ctr., 1984-85, fellow NEH, 1989-90. Mem. MLA (del. assembly 1984-86, mem. program com. 1986-89, mem. non-fiction divsn. com. 1988-92, mem. nominating com. 1993-94, mem. teaching of writing divsn. 1993—), Nat. Coun. Writing Program Adminstrs. (mem. cons.-evaluator program 1982—, mem. exec. bd. 1982-84, 89-90, v.p. 1985-86, pres. 1987-88), Nat. Coun. Tchrs. English (mem. CCCC nominating com. 1985, mem. coll. sect. com. 1987-90). Home: 53 Edgehill Rd New Haven CT 06511-1343 Office: Yale U Dept English New Haven CT 06520

PETERSON, LINDA S., lawyer; b. Grand Forks, N.D., Mar. 15, 1952. BA summa cum laude, U. N.D., 1973; JD, Yale U., 1977. Bar: N.D. 1977, D.C. 1978, U.S. Dist. Ct. D.C. 1979, U.S. Ct. Appeals (D.C. cir.) 1979, U.S. Ct. Appeals (9th cir.) 1982, Calif. 1986, U.S. Ct. Appeals (fed. cir.) 1986. Law clk. Ct. of Appeals for D.C., Washington, 1977-78; ptnr. Sidley & Austin, L.A. Dep. counsel Webster Commn., 1992; mem. bd. trustees Southwestern U. Sch. Law, 1995. Mem. State Bar Calif. (rules of ct. com. 1988-91), L.A. County Bar Assn. (conf. dels. 1987-90), Women Lawyers Assn. L.A. (bd. dirs. 1989-95), Phi Beta Kappa. Office: Sidley & Austin 555 W 5th St Ste 4000 Los Angeles CA 90013-3000*

PETERSON, LOUIS ROBERT, retired consumer products company executive; b. Racine, Wis., Nov. 11, 1923; s. Edward J. and Effie (Buenning) P.; m. Marian Francis Barber, Nov. 22, 1947; children: Karen Jean, Kathleen Alice, Jill Ann. Student, Utah State Agrl. Coll., U. Wis.-Racine. With Johnson Wax Co., Racine, Wis., 1947—; sales rep. Johnson Wax Co., 1970-72, v.p. household sales, 1972-76, exec. v.p. U.S. consumer products, ptnr. in office of the chmn., 1976-86, exec. v.p. internat. consumer products, 1980—; bd. dirs. Biltmore Investors Bank, Phoenix. Past pres., bd. dirs. Racine Area United Way.; bd. dirs. St. Mary's Med. Ctr. With U.S. Army, 1943-46. Mem. Northwestern U. Assocs., Conf. Bd. (internat. council), Internat. C. of C. (U.S. Council internat. bus.). Republican. Roman Catholic. Clubs: Somerset (Racine, Wis.); Pinnacle Peak Country (Scottsdale, Ariz.) (bd. dirs.). Home: RR 1 Box 1168 Hayward WI 54843-9727 also: 8723 E Clubhouse Way Scottsdale AZ 85255-4231

PETERSON, M. ROGER, international banker, retired manufacturing executive, retired air force officer; b. Chgo., June 6, 1929; s. Milton Albert and LaVergne Geraldine (Andelin) P.; m. Sally Ann Alder, Apr. 25, 1952; children: Bruce Roger, Dale Alder, Drew Alan. B.S. in Acctg., UCLA, 1955; M.S. in Mgmt., U. Colo., 1964; grad., Air Command and Staff Coll. Air U., Ala., 1965; grad. Exec. Program for Internat. and Nat. Security, J.F. Kennedy Sch. Govt., Harvard U., 1983. Joined USAF, 1955, advanced through grades to maj. gen., 1981, pilot, 1956-61, mgr. tactical missile site constrn., 1961; air officer comdg. 11th Cadet Squadron, Air Force Cadet Wing USAF Acad., 1961-64; asst. sec. Joint Chiefs of Staff and NSC matters for Hdqrs. Pentagon, 1965-68; transport pilot USAF, Vietnam, 1968; asst. chmn. U.S.-Japan Joint Com., Adminstrn. of Status of Forces Agreement USAF, 1968-73, chief program cost, dir. budget, 1973-76, chief plans, comptroller of Air Force, 1976-78, dir. mgmt. analysis, 1978-79, dir. programs, asst. chief of staff for research and devel., 1979-81; asst. dir. plans, policies and programs Def. Logistics Agy., Alexandria, Va., 1981-82, dep. dir., 1982-83; asst. dep. chief staff for logistics and engring. Hdqrs. USAF, Washington, 1983-84; pres., chief exec. officer advanced tech. factory, 1984-85; strategic planner United Techs. Corp., 1985-88; v.p., chief oper. officer Sikorsky Support Svcs. Inc., 1988-90; exec. asst. to mng. ptnr. O'Connor & Assocs., 1990-92; mng. dir. global ops. and svcs. Swiss Bank Corp., Zurich, 1992-96; chief of staff Swiss Bank Corp. N.Am., N.Y., 1996—. Decorated Disting. Service medal; decorated Legion of Merit, Air medal with oak leaf cluster, Joint Service Commendation medal, Air Force Commendation medal with two oak leaf clusters. Mem. Air Force Assn., Beta Gamma Sigma, Sigma Iota Epsilon. Presbyterian. Designed and negotiated consolidation of U.S. Air Force bases in Tokyo, 1970-73; negotiated mil. and civil aviation agreement for return of Okinawa to Japan; created global bus. mgmt. system for Swiss Bank Corp. Home: 175 N Harbor Dr Apt 3902/03 Chicago IL 60601 Office: Swiss Bank Corp 222 Broadway New York NY 10038 also: Swiss Bank Corp c/o Jan Galayda 141 W Jackson Blvd Chicago IL 60604-2904 *Always with honor.*

PETERSON, MARY L., state agency official. BA in English, Carleton Coll., 1972; MA in Tchg. in Edn. and English, Duke U., 1974; postgrad., U. Utah, 1977-80. Tchr. English, New Canaan (Conn.) Sch. Dist., from 1973, Brighton Ctrl. Sch. Dist., Rochester, N.Y., Davis County Sch. Dist., Kaysville, Utah, until 1977; rsch. asst. in cultural founds. and ednl. adminstrn. U. Utah, Salt Lake City, 1977-79; prin. St. Nicholas Elem. Sch., Rupert, Idaho, 1979-81; cons. Nev. Dept. Edn., Carson City, 1981-92, dep. supt. instrnl., rsch. and evaluative svcs., 1992-94, supt. pub. instrn., 1994—; assessor Nev. Assessment Ctr., Nat. Assn. Secondary Sch. Prins.; mem. accreditation team N.W. Assn. Schs. and Colls.; trainer Tchr. Effectiveness for Student Achievement, Correlates Effective Schs.; facilitator Assisting Change in Edn.; mem. state team Nat. Coun. for Accreditation Tchr. Edn. Asst. editor: Work, Family and Careers (C. Brooklyn Derr), 1980; contbr. to profl. publs. Scholar Carleton Coll., Duke U. Mem. Phi Kappa Phi, Delta Kappa Gamma. Office: Nev Dept Edn Capitol Complex 700 E 5th St Carson City NV 89710

PETERSON, MARYBETH A., church administrator. Bd. chmn. Division for Ministry of the Evangelical Lutheran Church in America, Chicago, Ill. Office: Evangelical Lutheran Church Am 8765 W Higgins Rd Chicago IL 60631-4101

PETERSON, MERRILL DANIEL, history educator; b. Manhattan, Kans., Mar. 31, 1921; s. William Oscar and Alice Dwinell (Merrill) P.; m. Jean Hymphrey, May 24, 1944 (dec. Nov. 1995); children: Jeffrey Ward, Kent Merrill. Student, Kans. State U., 1939-41; AB, U. Kans., 1943; PhD in History of Am. Civilization, Harvard U., 1950. Teaching fellow Harvard U., Cambridge, Mass., 1948-49; instr., then asst. prof. history Brandeis U., Waltham, Mass., 1949-55; asst. prof., bicentennial preceptor Princeton U., N.J., 1955-58; mem. faculty Brandeis U., Waltham, Mass., 1958-62, dean students, 1960-62; Thomas Jefferson Found. prof. U. Va., Charlottesville, 1962-87, Thomas Jefferson Found. prof. emeritus, 1987—, chmn. dept. history, 1966-72, dean of faculty Arts and Scis., 1981-85; Mary Ball Washington prof. Am. History University Coll., Dublin, Ireland, 1988-89; scholar in residence Bellagio Study Ctr., 1974; faculty Salzburg Seminar in Am. Studies, 1975; Lamar lectr. Mercer U., 1975; Fleming lectr. La. State U., 1980; lectr. at 15 European univs., 40 Am. colls. and univs. Author: The Jefferson Image in the American Mind, 1960 (Bancroft prize, Gold medal Thomas Jefferson Meml. Found.), Major Crises in American History, 2 vols., 1962, Democracy, Liberty and Property: The State Constitutional Convention Debates of the 1820s, 1966, Thomas Jefferson and the New Nation: A Biography, 1970, James Madison: A Biography in His Own Word, 1974, Adams and Jefferson: A Revolutionary Dialogue, 1976, Olive Branch and Sword: The Compromise of 1933, 1982, The Great Triumvirate: Webster, Clay and Calhoun, 1987; editor: Thomas Jefferson: A Historical Profile, 1966, The Portable Thomas Jefferson, 1975, Thomas Jefferson Writings, 1984, Thomas Jefferson: A Reference Biography, 1986, The Virginia Statute for Religious Freedom: Its Evolution and Consequences in American History, 1988, Visitors to Monticello, 1989, Lincoln in American Memory, 1994 (History finalist, Pulitzer prize, PBK Book award U. Va.). Bd. dirs. Thomas Meml. Found.; chmn. Thomas Jefferson Commemoration Commn., 1993-94. Guggenheim fellow, 1962-63, Ctr. for Advanced Study in Behavioral Scis. fellow, 1968-69, NEH and Nat. Humanities Ctr. fellow, 1980-81; recipient 20th Anniversary award Va. Found. for Humanities, 1994. Fellow Am. Acad. Arts and Scis.; mem. Am. Hist. Assn., So. Hist. Assn., Orgn. Am. Historians, Soc. Am. Historians, Am. Antiquarian Soc., Mass. Hist. Soc., Phi Beta Kappa. Home: # 6 250 Pantops Mountain Rd Charlottesville VA 22911

PETERSON, MILDRED OTHMER (MRS. HOWARD R. PETERSON), lecturer, writer, librarian, civic leader; b. Omaha, Oct. 19, 1902; d. Frederick George and Freda Darling (Snyder) Othmer; m. Howard R. Peterson, Aug. 25, 1923 (dec. Feb. 9, 1970). Student, U. Iowa, 1919, U. Nebr., 1921-23, Northwestern U., 1935, U. Chgo., 1943, Am. U. Switzerland, 1985. Asst. purchasing agt. Met. Utilities Dist., 1920-21; asst. U. Nebr. Library, 1921-23; tchr. piano, dir. choir Harlan, Iowa, 1924-26; dir. pub. relations and gen. asst. Des Moines Pub. Library, 1928-35; broadcaster weekly book programs Sta. WHO, Des Moines, and other Iowa radio stas.; columnist, writer Mid-West News Syndicate, Des Moines Register and Tribune; editor Book Marks, 1929-35; writer for Drug Topics, Drug Trade News, others, No. Ill., 1935; writer, spl. asst. ALA, Chgo., 1935-59, Chgo. Tribune, 1941—; travel writer Hyde Park Herald, 1974—; lectr. SS. Rotterdam of Holland Am. Line, 1971; lectr. tours U.S., Can., Mexico, 1970—; internat. lectr. on travel, fgn. jewelry and internat. relations, 1940—; guest lectr. on Golden Odyssey Ship Royal Cruise Line to Orient, world trip with Purdue U. Alumni, Feb.-Mar., 1988; del. 1st Assembly Librarians Ams., Washington, 1947. Contbr. articles to newspapers, periodicals, encys. and yearbooks. Chmn. India Famine Relief, 1943; a founder Pan Am. Coun., 1939, v.p., 1982-86, numerous other coms.; founder, past pres. Pan Am. Bd. Edn., 1955-58, Internat. Visitors Ctr., 1952-56, a founder, 1st pres. and hon. life dir., 1986; rep. Chgo. at State Dept. Conf. on Cmty. Svcs. to Fgn. Visitors; a founder COSERV (Nat. Coun. Cmty. Svcs. to Internat. Visitors), Washington, 1957; mem. exec. bd., awards com. Mayor's Com. on Chgo. Beautiful; mem. Ill. Gov.'s Com. on Ptnrs. of The Ams., São Paulo, Brazil and Ill. sister states; mem. U.S. Dept. State conf. for Ptnrs. of Am., Dominican Republic, 1985, Little Rock, 1986, Jamaica, 1987 (Superior Svc. award 1987), Miami Beach, Fla., 1988; mem. chancellor's com. U. Nebr., conf. com. U. Chgo., 1990; former bd. dirs. coun., troop leader Girl Scouts U.S., Council Bluffs, Iowa, 1926-28; mem. Women's Soc., coun., stewardship and mission bds. Hyde Pk. Union Ch., also 75th, 100th and 110th anniversary coms.; bd. dirs. YWCA, Chgo. Lung Assn.; women's bd. Camp Brueckner-Farr, Grad. Bapt. Student Ctr.; mem. exec. coun. Friends of Sta. WTTW-TV; chairwoman Hyde Pk. Christmas Seals Campaign, 1985-86, 87-88 (Outstanding Svc. award 1987); bd. dirs. Maridian Hospice; mem. centennial com. U. Chgo. Svc. League, 1995; mem. benefit com. Chgo. Svc. League, 1995, mem. music and travel sects.; v.p. U. Chgo. Internat. House Assn.; mem. Vista Homes Garden Assn., Mus. Sci. and Industry, Chgo. Art Inst. Decorated Uruguayan medal, 1952; Internat. Eloy Alfaro medal, 1952; Order of Carlos Manuel de Cespedes Cuba; Order of Vasco Nuñez de Balboa Panama; cited by Chgo. Sun, Ill. Adult Edn. Council, 1953; recipient scholarship in Latin-Am. field U. Chgo. and Coordinator Inter-Am. Affairs, U.S. Govt., 1943, world understanding merit award Chgo. Council on Fgn. Relations, 1955, Disting. Service award Hospitality Center, 1958, Disting. Service medal U. Nebr., Disting. Service medal U. Nebr. Alumni Assn., 1963, Disting. Achievement award, 1975, Ambassador of Friendship award Am. Friendship Club, 1963, merit award YWCA for 10 yrs. as mem. bd., 1964 and Disting. Service award, 1975; Civic salute WMAQ radio, Chgo., 1965; Disting. Service award Pan-Am. Bd. Edn., 1966; also founders award, 1968; Laura Hughes Lunde Meml. award Citizens Greater Chgo., 1968; Friendship award Philippine Girl Scouts, 1971; Disting. Service award OAS, 1971; named Woman of Yr. Friends of Chgo. Sch. and Workshop for Retarded, 1975; Disting. Service trophy Fedn. Latin Am. Orgns., 1976; Merit Award WTTW-TV, Chgo., 1983; named to Sr. Citizens Hall of Fame, 1992, Chgo. Hall of Fame, 1992. Fellow Am. Internat. Acad. (life mem.); mem. Nat. Council Women U.S., Chgo. Council for USA-USSR Friendship (mem. Leaders Tour of China 1990), English Speaking Union, Japan-Am. Com., U.S.-China Friendship Assn. (bd. dirs. 1987—, Vol. award 1990), Internat. House Assn. (v.p.), Pan-Am. Bd. Edn. (founder, pres., Merit award), U.S. Capitol Hist. Soc., Ill. Hist. Soc., Nebr. Hist. Soc., Chgo. Hist. Soc., Hyde Park Hist. Soc. (charter mem. award 1978), Field Mus. Natural History, Mus. Sci. and Industry, Lincoln Park Zool. Soc., Citizenship Council Met. Chgo., Oriental Inst., Am. Heritage Coun., ALA, Ill. Libr. Assn. (local arrangements com. of nat. conf. 1976, 78, 85, 95), Internat. Fedn. Libr. Assns. (local arrangements com. 1985 Chgo.), Soc. Woman Geographers (pres. Chgo. chpt., v.p. internat. coun. 1987—), Coun. Fgn. Rels. (speakers bur.), Nat. Assn. Travel Ofcls. (Chgo. Tribune rep.), Library Internat. Rels. (ball com. 1969—), U. Nebr. Alumni Assn. (past pres. Des Moines, Rockford and Chgo. chpts.), U. Nebr. Found., U. Chgo. Internat. House Assn. (v.p. 1976—), Art Inst. Chgo., U. Chgo. Svc. League (past bd. mem., now bd. dirs. Camp Brueckner-Farr Aux.), Am. Legion Aux. (mem. state bds. Iowa and Ill.), AAUW, LWV, Children's Benefit League, Woman's Bd. United Negro Coll. Fund, Renaissance Soc., Peruvian Arts Soc., Hispanic Soc. Chgo., Chgo. Acad. Scis. (woman's bd.), Chgo. Chamber Orch. Assn., John G. Shedd Soc., Japan Am. Soc., Friends Chgo. Pub. Library, Chgo. Symphony Soc., Citizens Greater Chgo., Found. for Ill. Archaeology, Cook County Hosp. Aux., Lyric Opera Guild, Crossroads Student Center, Internat. Platform Assn., Exec. Service Corps Chgo., Friends of Grant Park Concerts, Chgo. Council for USA-USSR, Friendship U. Ill., Chgo. Internat. Programs, Friends of Parks, Friends of Downtown, Friends of Chgo. River, Met. Planning Coun., Chgo. Architecture Found., Landmarks Presrvation Coun., Open Lands Project, Women in Arts (charter mem. Washington chpt.), Geographic Soc. Chgo., Alpha Delta Pi (past pres. Omaha, Des Moines and Chgo. alumnae chpts., editor Adephean 1938-39, woman of year award U.S. and Can. 1955), Xi Delta. Clubs: Mem. Order Eastern Star, South Shore Country, College, Quadrangle, Ill. Athletic, University of Chicago Dames, Iowa Authors, Lakeside Lawn Bowling, Hyde Park Neighborhood, Travellers Century (World's Most Travelled Person plaque 1993). Travelled to and lecturer on over 250 countries, including China and Albania; extensive foreign Christmas card collection Exhibited at Museum Scienc and Industry, Chicago Public Library, Chicago Sun Times, Des Moines Public Library, others, given to Chicago Pub Library; donor sheet music, musical records, thousands of colored slides taken during her extensive travels to Chicago Public Library, Egyptian jewelry to University of Chicago Oriental Institute, East Indian rose cut diamonds and other jewels to Smart Gallery, University of Chicago, Cruise of the Americas through Panama Canal from East to West. Address: 5834 S Stony Island Ave Chicago IL 60637-2026

PETERSON, MONICA DOROTHY, actress, singer, model, writer, entrepreneur. Drama cert., Neighborhood Playhouse, N.Y.C., 1963, Jeff Corey Sch. Acting, 1967; student Sch. Music and Dance, Covent Garden, London, 1972; AA, Santa Monica Coll., 1983; BA, U. So. Calif., 1986. Editorial sec., writer Look mag., N.Y.C., 1964-66; asst. mgr. Venture Mag. Advt., N.Y.C., 1965-66; actress, singer, performer William Morris Agy., Hollywood, Calif., 1967-70, also London, Spain, Italy; contract player 20th Century Fox, 1967-70; contract singer, dancer, actress L.A. City Hall Theatre of Arts, 1975-80; staff writer SMC, L.A., 1981-83, newspaper editor, 1983-84; exec. asst., 1986—; script writer Crystal Awards (WIF), 1992, chair, writer, 1993; with Dem. Leadership for 21st Century L.A. Chpt., 1993, asst. p.r. media Mayoral Roundtable Whittle Communications, 1993; jazz singer-actress, 1987—; active in telecom., 1987—; exec. asst., 1987—; comml. agt. Tisherman Agy., L.A.; theatrical agt. Bonnie Allen Talent Agy., Beverly Hills, Calif., Atkins & Assocs. Agy., L.A.; Paris fashion runway model, 1993; scriptwriter, 1993; asst. pub. rels./media Dem. Leadership 21st Century Mayoral Roundtable for Whittle Comm. Raleigh Studios, 1993, working with L.A. chpt., 1993. Editorial and entertainment editor, prodr., writer, reporter Sta. KCRW Radio Programs; extensive travel as a performer (including 2-month concert in Japan), theatre, stage, TV, radio; one-woman shows include Toys for Tots Shows, L.A., Biltmore Jazz Club, other jazz, supper clubs; contbr. articles to mags. Script analyst, editor, asst. casting dir. Inner City Cultural City, L.A., 1974-76; vol. Easter Seals, also vol. work for diabetics, homeless, needy, elderly and sick; v.p. Internat. Coun.; active Bill Clinton for Pres. Campaign, 1992, Voters Revolt Campaign, 1992; mem. Dem. Com., Washington; elected Community Bd. Dirs. Recipient Hollywood Star of Tomorrow award ABC, 1968, Oversees award USO, 1969, Poetry award N.Am. Poetry Contest, 1996, others. Mem. SAG (v.p. minority com. 1969-71, rep. Image award 1969-72), AFTRA, Women in Film (scriptwriter, prodr. Cannes Film Festival, scriptwriter Crystal awards 1992, chair and writer Crystal awards 1993), Equity, Internat. Platform Assn., Women In Comm. (del. Cannes Film Festival 1993), U. So. Calif. Alumni Assn. Democrat. Roman Catholic. Avocations: jogging, reading, softball, music.

PETERSON, MYRA M., special education educator; b. Eagle Bend, Minn., July 1, 1937; children: Randy E., Vicky L. Rholl. Assoc. in Edn., St. Cloud State U., 1957, BS in Elem. Edn., 1963; cert. in learning disabilities, Bemidji State U., 1979. Cert. edn. Elem. instr. Wadena (Minn.) Pub. Sch., 1957-60; supplemental edn. and secondary devel. reading Bertha-Hewitt (Minn.) Sch., 1964-75, learning disabilities instr., 1975—; coord. for local sch. Minn. Basic Skills Program, Bertha-Hewitt (Minn.) Sch., 1980-85; adv. bd. for spl. needs N.W. Tech. Coll., Wadena, 1992—. Mem., edn. com. United Meth. Ch., Wadena; pres. Am. Legion Aux., Wadena, 1990—. Named Tchr. of Yr., Bertha-Hewitt (Minn.) Edn. Assn., 1981. Mem. NEA, Minn. State Edn. Assn., Bertha-Hewitt Edn. Assn., N.W. Reading Coun. (pres. 1987-88), Delta Kappa Gamma Internat. (pres. Alpha Eta chpt. 1993—, Woman of Achievement 1991). Office: Bertha-Hewitt Sch PO Box 8 Bertha MN 56437

PETERSON, N. CURTIS, JR., landscape architect, former state senator; b. Lakeland, Fla., Aug. 23, 1922; s. N. Curtis and Caroline Ellen (Smith) P.; m. Ethel Schultz, Apr. 8, 1944; children: N. Curtis III, Peter Karl. Student, George Washington U., 1941-42, Fla. So. Coll., 1950-53. Registered landscape architect, Fla. Mem. Fla. Senate from Dist. 12, 1972-90; senate pres. pro-tem, 1980-82, senate pres., 1982-84, chmn. appropriations edn. com., 1976-82, 86-90, chmn. edn. com., 1976-78, 84-86, 1988-90, chmn. agr. com., 1974-76, vice chmn. agr. com., 1986-88. Bd. dirs. Awareness in Fla. Govt.; mem. Fla. Gov.'s Commn. on Secondary Schs., 1981-82; del. Democratic Charter Conf., 1974; commr. Edn. Commn. of States, 1973-90, chmn. edn. task force Nat. Conf. State Legislatures, 1987; sponsor achievement in secondary edn. RAISE; mem. platform com. Fla. Dem. Com., 1978-79; bd. dirs. Polk County Assn. Retarded Citizens; commr. So. Regional Edn. Bd. Named Most Effective Senator Fla. Senate, 1977, 80, 81. Mem. Fla. Nurserymen and Growers Assn. (pres. 1961-62, named Nurseryman of Yr.), Agribus Inst. Fla. (pres. 1975-76), Agrl. Tax Coun. (pres. 1967-70), Agrl. Adv. Coun. Fla. (pres. 1970-72), Sigma Nu, Kiwanis. Democrat. Baptist. Home: 1504 S Warren Ave Lakeland FL 33803-2063

PETERSON, NAD A., lawyer, retired corporate executive; b. Mt. Pleasant, Utah, 1926; m. Martha Peterson, 1948; children: Anne Carroll (Mrs.

Stanford P. Darger, Jr.), Christian, Elizabeth (Mrs. Henry G. Ingersoll), Robert and Lane (twins). A.B., George Washington U., 1950, J.D., 1953. Bar: D.C. 1953, Calif. 1960, U.S. Supreme Ct. 1958. Law practice Washington, 1953-60; sec., asst. gen. counsel Dart Industries, Los Angeles, 1960-67; chief counsel, 1967-73; gen. counsel Fluor Corp., 1973-79, v.p. law, 1979-82, sr. v.p. law, 1983-84; sr. v.p., sec. Fluor Corp., Irvine, Calif., 1984-93; sr. v.p., gen. counsel San Diego Gas & Electric Co., 1993-95. Mem. ABA, State Bar Assn., Phi Delta Phi. Home: PO Box 9101 Rancho Rancho Santa Fe CA 92067

PETERSON, NADEEN, advertising agency executive; b. McKeesport, Pa., Dec. 3, 1934; d. Michael James and LaVerna Peal (Long) Powell; m. Robert Glenn Kilzer, Dec. 24, 1966; 1 son, Douglas Robert. Student, U. Fla., 1952-53. Copywriter Ellington & Co., N.Y.C., 1961-64; v.p., assoc. creative dir. Tatham-Laird, N.Y.C., 1964-65, Foote, Cone & Belding, Inc., N.Y.C., 1966-69; v.p., sr. assoc. creative dir. Norman, Craig & Kummell, N.Y.C., 1969-70, sr. v.p., creative dir., 1975-77; sr. v.p., creative dir. Doyle, Dane, Bernbach, Inc., N.Y.C., from 1978; sr. v.p. Saatchi & Saatchi DFS Compton, N.Y.C., exec. v.p., creative dir., exec. v.p., exec. creative dir., 1987-89; vice-chmn., exec. creative dir. Saatchi & Saatchi DFS Compton (now Saatchi & Saatchi Advt.), N.Y.C., 1989—. Recipient Matrix award, 1977; named 100 Best Brightest Women in Advt. Advt. Age, 1988, vice chmn. World Wide Creative dir. advt. Woman of Yr., 1992. Office: Saatchi & Saatchi Advt 375 Hudson St New York NY 10014-3658*

PETERSON, OSCAR EMMANUEL, pianist; b. Montreal, Que., Can., Aug. 15, 1925; s. Daniel and Olivia (John) P. Studied with, Paul deMarky; LL.D. (hon.), Carleton U., 1973, Queen's U., 1976, Concordia U., 1979, McMaster U., 1981, U. of Victoria, 1981, U. Toronto, 1985; D.Mus. (hon.), Sackville U., 1980, U. Laval, 1985; Litt.D. (hon.), York U., 1982; D.F.A. (hon.), Northwestern U., Evanston, Ill., 1983; LLD (hon.), U. Toronto, 1985; MusD (hon.), U. Laval, 1985. Founder Advanced Sch. Contemporary Music, Toronto; former chancellor York U., 1991-94; chancellor York U., 1991. Began music career on weekly radio show, then with Johny Holmes Orchestra, Can., 1944-49; recorded with RCA Victor Records; appeared with Jazz at the Philharmonic, Carnegie Hall, 1949; toured the U.S. and Europe, 1950—; leader trio with Ray Brown, Irving Ashby, later Barney Kessel, Herb Ellis, Ed Thigpen, Sam Jones, Louie Hayes, concert appearances with Ella Fitzgerald, Eng., Scotland, 1955; appeared Stratford (Ont.) Shakespeare Festival, Newport Jazz Festival; recorded and performed solo piano works, 1972—; toured USSR, 1974, recordings with Billie Holiday, Fred Astaire, Benny Carter, Count Basie, Roy Eldridge, Lester Young, Ella Fitzgerald, Niels-Henning, Joe Pass, Orsted Pederson, Dizzy Gillespie, Harry Edison, Clark Terry ; composer: Canadiana Suite, Hymn to Freedom, Fields of Endless Day, City Lights, Begone Dull Care, (with Norman McLaren) salute to Johann Sebastian Bach, music for films Big North and Silent Partner; author: Jazz Exercises and Pieces: Oscar Peterson New Piano Solos; numerous TV specials. Decorated officer Order of Canada, 1972, companion, 1984; recipient award for piano Down Beat mag. 13 times, Metronome mag. award, 1953-54, Edison award, 1962, Award of merit City of Toronto, (1st mention) 1973 (2d mention 1983), Diplome d'honneur Can. Conf. of the Arts, 1975, Grammy award 7 times, Olympic Key to Montreal, The Queen's medal, 1977, Genie Film award for film score The Silent Partner, 1978, Grand-Prix du Disques for Night Child album, 1981, Canadian Band Festival Award, 1982, Juno Hall of Fame award, 1982, George Peabody medal Peabody Conservatory of Music, Balt., 1987, Volunteer award Roy Thompson Hall, Toronto, 1987, Can. Club Arts and Letters award, N.Y.C., 1987, Officer in Order of Arts and Letters, France, 1989, Chevalier Order of Que., 1991, Lifetime Achievement Toronto Arts Award, 1991, appointed Order of Ontario, 1992, Lifetime Achievement Gov. Gens. award, 1992, Glenn Gould prize, 1993, Carnegie Hall Anniversary medal, Charlie Parker bronze medal, Ville de Salon de Provence medal, Award of Thanks, Mexico City; 12-time jazz poll winner Playboy mag.; named number one (piano) Jazz and Pop, Readers Poll 1968, 85; named to U. Calif. at Berkeley Hall of Fame, 1983, Contemporary Keyboard Hall of Fame, 1983; Oscar Peterson Day proclaimed by Baltimore, Oreg., 1981, 83; Oscar Peterson Scholarship founded in his honor Berklee Sch. of Music, Boston, 1982. Avocations: fly fishing, photography, astronomy. Office: Regal Recordings Ltd, 2421 Hammond Rd, Mississauga, ON Canada L5K 1T3

PETERSON, OSCAR JAMES, III, retired utility holding company executive; b. Clinton, N.C., Aug. 26, 1935; s. Oscar James Jr. and Elizabeth Julia (Collins) P.; m. Amanda Louise Wade, Dec. 29, 1962; children: Amanda Leigh, Oscar James, Windley Collins. BSBA, U. N.C., 1962. With Carolina Tel. & Tel. Co., 1962-70; fin. staff asst. Carolina Tel. & Tel. Co., Taboro, N.C., 1966-70; exec. asst. fin., then asst. treas. Va. Electric & Power Co., Richmond, 1970-75, treas., 1975, v.p., chief fin. officer, 1978-85; v.p., chief fin. officer Dominion Resources Inc., Richmond, 1985-88, sr. v.p., 1988-94; cons., pres. O.J. Peterson & Co.; CFO Md. Jockey Club, Laurel; chmn. bd. Thermopress Corp., Richmond. Trustee Sci. Mus. Va., 1987—. With USNR, 1957-59. Mem. Va. C. of C., Commonwealth Club.

PETERSON, PATTI MCGILL, college president; b. Johnstown, Pa., May 20, 1943; d. Earl Frampton and Helen G. McGill; m. Luther D. Peterson, Aug. 31, 1968; 1 son, Lars-Anders. B.A. in Polit. Sci., Pa. State U., 1965; M.A. in Polit. Sci., U. Wis., 1968, Ph.D. in Polit. Sci. and Ednl. Policy, 1974; cert. advance study, Harvard U., 1977; D.Litt (hon.), Le Moyne Coll., 1983. Asst. prof. polit. sci., dean of freshman women Schiller Coll., Ger., 1968-69; asst. prof. polit. sci. SUNY-Oswego, 1971-72, asst. to pres., adj. prof., 1972-77, v.p. acad. services and planning, assoc. prof., 1978-80; pres. Wells Coll., Aurora, N.Y., 1980-87, St. Lawrence U., Canton, N.Y., 1987—; bd. dirs. Nia. Mo. Power Corp., Security Mut. Life Ins. Co., John Hancock Mut. Funds. Author numerous articles in field. Trustee Northwood Sch. Sta.; bd. overseers The Nelson A. Rockefeller Inst. Govt., 1988; trustee Assn. Am. Colls., 1987; chmn. Pub. Leadership Edn. Network, 1983-85; mem. Gov.'s Com. on Vol. Enterprise, 1983-85; pres. Assn. Colls. and Univs., N.Y., 1984-86; chair Women's Coll. Coalition, 1983-85, U.S.-Can. Fulbright Com., 1990—; mem. Com. on Nat. Challenges in Higher Edn., 1986-88. Carnegie fellow Harvard U., 1977. Mem. Am. Coun. Edn. (chmn. com. on leadership devel. and acad. adminstrn. 1982-84), Mid. States Assn. Colls. and Schs. (cons., chmn.). Home: 54 E Main St Canton NY 13617-1419 Office: St Lawrence U Office of the President Canton NY 13617-1455

PETERSON, PAUL QUAYLE, retired university dean, physician; b. Marissa, Ill., June 30, 1912; s. Charles Logan and Phoebe (Lewis) P.; m. Kathryn Lentz, Aug. 1936; children—Philip Lewis, Frances Anne; m. Mildred Cook Allison, Dec. 7, 1957; foster children—Patricia Elaine Allison, Susan Claire Allison. B.S., U. Ill., 1933, M.D., 1937; M.P.H., U. Mich., 1946. Diplomte Am. Bd. Preventive Medicine (service mem., vice chmn. 1976—). Intern Bethesda Hosp., Cin., 1936-37; gen. resident Meml. Hosp., Lima, Ohio, 1937-38; gen. practice medicine McLeansboro, Ill., 1939-40; practice medicine specializing in preventive medicine, 1940-46; health officer Breckenridge, Meade and Hancock counties, Ky., 1940-41, Warren, Simpson and Allen counties, 1942-45; regional cons., div. local health Ky. Health Dept., 1946-47; chief bur. direct services, asst. to dir. Ohio Dept. Health, 1948-51; asst. prof. preventive medicine Ohio State U., 1948-51; chief health div. Mut. Security Mission to China, Taipei, Taiwan, 1952-53; chief health and sanitation div. USOM (asso. states Cambodia, Laos and Vietnam), 1954; chief program services, div. internat. health USPHS, Washington, 1955; chronic disease program USPHS, 1957; asst. dir. Nat. Inst. Allergy and Infectious Diseases, NIH, 1958-61; dep. chief div. pub. health methods Office Surgeon Gen., 1961-62, chief div., 1962-64; asst. surgeon gen. USPHS, 1964, asso. chief bur. state services (community health), 1964-67; dep. dir. Bur. Health Services, 1967-68; asso. adminstr. Health Services and Mental Health Adminstrn., 1968-70; dep. surgeon gen., 1970; dean Grad. Sch. Pub. Health, U. Ill., Chgo., 1971-82, dean emeritus, 1982—; dir. office rsch. Ctr. Study Patient Care, U. Ill. Med. Ctr., 1979-86; dir. Ill. Dept. Pub. Health, 1977-79, Am. Bur. Med. Aid to China; mem. residency rev. com. Liaison Com. Grad. Med. Edn., 1976—; cons. Ctr. for Health Services Research, 1982—. mem. editorial bd. Pub. Health Service World, Mil. Medicine. Commr. USPHS, 1941. Recipient Disting. Service award U. Ill. Alumni Assn., 1984. Fellow Am. Pub. Health Assn. (chmn. program area com. pub. health adminstrn.); mem. Am. Assn. Pub. Health Physicians (pres. 1975-76), AMA (intersplty. adv. bd. 1975-77), Assn. Schs. Pub. Health (exec. com. 1975—), Pub. Health Service Commd. Officers Assn. (sec. D.C. 1959), AAAS, Assn. Mil Surgeons, Am. Coll. Preventive Medicine (regent 1975—), Ill. Hosp. Assn. (exec. bd. 1974-77, cert. correctional health com. of profl. cert. bd. 1990), Nat. Inst. of Health Alumni Assn. bd. dirs., 1993—, Phi Beta Pi (pres. 1935), Delta Omega. Methodist. Home: 1600 N Oak St Arlington VA 22209-2751

PETERSON, PETER G., investment banker; b. Kearney Nebr., June 5, 1926; s. George and Venetia P.; m. Sally H., May 1953 (div. 1979); children: John, Jim, David, Holly, Michael; m. Joan Ganz Cooney, Apr. 26, 1980. BS, Northwestern U., 1947; MBA, U. Chgo. 1951; PhD (hon.) Colgate U., George Washington U., Northwestern U., Georgetown U. Exec. v.p. Market Facts, Chgo., 1948-52; v.p. McCann Erickson, Chgo. 1952-58; pres. Bell and Howell, Chgo., 1958-71, exec. v.p. 1958-61, CEO, 1963-71; asst. to Pres. of U.S. for Internat. Econ. Affairs, Washington, 1961-63; sec. of commerce U.S. Govt., 1972-73; CEO, chmn. bd. Lehman Bros. and Lehman Bros., Kuhn, Loeb, Inc., N.Y.C., 1973-84; chmn. The Blackstone Group, 1985—; bd. dirs. Rockefeller Ctr. Properties, Inc., Sony Corp., Transtar Inc. Author: Facing Up: How to Rescue the Economy from Crushing Debt and Restore the American Dream; editor: Readings in Market Organization and Price Policies; co-author: On Borrowed Time: How The Growth In Entitlement Spending Threatens America's Future. founding mem. Bi-Partisan Budget Appeal; pres. The Concord Coalition; trustee Commn. for Econ. Devel., Mus. Modern Art, N.Y.C. Recipient Outstanding Service award, Phoenix House, N.Y.C., 1976, Stephen Wise award, Am. Jewish Congress, 1981, U. Chgo. Alumni medal, 1983, Man of Vision award, 1994, Nebraskalander award, 1994; named to Pres. Clinton's Bi-Partisan Comm. on Entitlement Refirm, 1994. Mem. Council Fgn. Relations (chmn. bd. 1985—), Inst. Internat. Econs. (chmn. bd.), Nat. Bur. Econ. Research (trustee), Japan Soc. Republican. Clubs: Maidstone (Easthampton, N.Y.); Chgo., River, Links (Chgo.); Augusta Nat.; Burning Tree (Washington), Atlantic. Home: 435 E 52nd St Apt 11G New York NY 10022-6445 Office: The Blackstone Group 345 Park Ave New York NY 10154-0004

PETERSON, PHILIP EVERETT, legal educator; b. Galena, Ill., July 10, 1922; s. Everett Marvin and Marie Isabelle (Gleason) P.; m. Jeanne Rosanna Payette, Nov. 17, 1947; children—Christine Marie, Barbara Ellen, Claudia Ann, Patricia Eileen, Eric Karl, Kurt Kevin. Student, Loras Coll., 1948; B.S., U. Ill., 1950, J.D., 1952; LL.M., Harvard, 1958. Bar: Ill. bar 1951, Idaho bar 1955, U.S. Supreme Ct. bar 1958. Practice in Urbana, Ill., 1951-52; mem. faculty U. Idaho Law Sch., 1952-88, prof. law, 1961—, dean, 1962-67; legal cons., 1955—. Served with AUS, 1942-48. Mem. ABA, Ill. Bar Assn., Idaho Bar Assn., AAUP. Home: 318 5th St Lewiston ID 83501-2408

PETERSON, RALPH, financial executive; b. N.Y.C., Jan. 24, 1924; s. James and Mildred (Lebowitz) P.; m. Patricia Bloom, Mar. 18, 1951; children: Jeffrey, Stacey Peterson Evans, Beth Lisa. B.B.A., CCNY, 1948. CPA, N.Y. Sr. acct. S.D. Leidesdorf Co., N.Y.C., 1948-51; mgr. Peat, Marwick, Mitchell, N.Y.C., 1951-70; sr. v.p., treas. Warner Bros., Inc., N.Y.C., 1970—; v.p., treas. Warner Bros., Inc., Burbank, Calif., 1970—, exec. v.p., treas., 1987—, sr. v.p., treas., 1987-89, exec. v.p., 1989—, also bd. dirs., mem. exec. com. Bd. dirs. Arthritis Found., Los Angeles, 1981—. Served with USAF, 1943-46. Mem. Am. Inst. CPA's, N.Y. Soc. CPA's. Office: Warner Bros Inc 4000 Warner Blvd Burbank CA 91522-0001*

PETERSON, RALPH R., engineering executive; b. 1944. BS in Civil Engring., Oreg. State U., 1969; MS in Environ. Engring., Stanford U., 1970. Engring. aide Johnson, Underkofler & Briggs, Boise, 1962-63; surveyor Smith, Keyes & Blakely, Caldwell, Idaho, 1963-64; with Chrome & Assocs., Boise, 1964-65; with CH2M Hill Cos., Ltd., 1978—, sr. v.p., dir. tech., 1988, pres., CEO, 1990. Office: CH2M Hill Cos Ltd 6060 S Willow Dr Greenwood Village CO 80111*

PETERSON, RICHARD ELTON, publisher; b. Spokane, Wash., Apr. 26, 1941; s. Darrel Emil and Katherine (Millar) P.; m. Ruthanne Hawkins, Aug. 12, 1977; children—Scott Edward, Andrew Richard; stepchildren—Troy Donald Slocum, Sean James Slocum. B.S. in Edn., U. Mo., 1963; M.B.A., U. Chgo., 1975; postgrad., Stanford U. Tchr. high sch. math. Brunswick, Mo.; tchr. Park Ridge, Ill., 1963-65; profl. baseball player N.Y. Mets., 1963-65; with Scott, Foresman & Co., 1965-93, sales rep., 1965-70, market rsch. profl., 1970-73; mktg. coord. Scott, Foresman & Co., Calif., 1973-77; regional v.p., mgr. ea. region Scott, Foresman & Co., Oakland, N.J., 1977-78; sr. v.p. mktg. Scott, Foresman & Co., Glenview, Ill., 1978-84, sr. v.p., gen. mgr. sch. div., 1984-88, pres., CEO, 1988-93, also bd. dirs.; group v.p. Harper/Collins Pub., N.Y.C., 1992-93. Bd. dirs. Evanston Hosp. Corp., 1991—; bd. govs. Northwestern U. Libr., Evanston, Ill., 1993—; bd. dirs. The Youth Campass, Park Ridge, Ill., 1995—. Mem. Assn. Am. Pubs. (chmn. Calif. com. 1980-86, exec. com. sch. divsn. 1985-88, 90-93, chmn. exec. com. 1986-88), Western Golf Assn. (bd. dirs. 1987—). Home: 707 Edgemont Ln Park Ridge IL 60068-2652

PETERSON, RICHARD HAMLIN, utility executive, lawyer; b. Berkeley, Calif., May 6, 1914; s. Otto Wallace and Gladys (Grinstead) P.; m. Marianne Hammond, May 17, 1957; children: John, Stephen, Richard Hamlin. A.B., U. Calif.-Berkeley, 1935, J.D., 1940. Bar: Calif. 1941. Assoc. McCutchen, Olney, Mannon & Greene, Los Angeles, 1940-43, McCutchen, Thomas, Matthews, Griffiths & Greene, San Francisco, 1946-47; atty. law dept. Pacific Gas & Electric Co., San Francisco, 1947-54, asst. gen. counsel, 1954-55, gen. counsel, 1955-69, sr. v.p., gen. counsel, 1965-69, exec. v.p., 1969-72, vice chmn. bd., 1972-76, chmn. bd., 1976-79, past bd. dirs.; chmn. bd. Pacific Gas Transmission Co., 1974-79; dir. ANGUS Chem. Co., ANGUS Petroleum Corp. Trustee San Francisco U. High Sch., Mus. Soc. of San Francisco; chmn. Yosemite Found. Served with USNR, 1943-46; lt. comdr. Res. Mem. ABA, Calif. Bar Assn., Bar Assn. San Francisco, U. Calif. Alumni Assn. (council), Phi Beta Kappa, Order of Coif, Delta Tau Delta, Phi Delta Phi. Clubs: Pacific Union, Bohemian, Commonwealth of California (bd. govs.). Office: Pacific Gas & Electric Co PO Box 770000 123 Mission St Rm 1727-H17F San Francisco CA 94177

PETERSON, RICHARD WILLIAM, lawyer, magistrate judge; b. Council Bluffs, Iowa, Sept. 29, 1925; s. Henry K. and Laura May (Robinson) P.; m. Patricia Mae Fox, Aug. 14, 1949; children: Katherine Ilene Peterson Sherbondy, Jon Eric, Timothy Richard. BA, U. Iowa, 1949, JD with distinction, 1951; postgrad., U. Nebr.-Omaha, 1972-80, 86. Bar: Iowa 1951, U.S. Dist. Ct. (so. dist.) Iowa 1951, U.S. Supreme Ct. 1991. Pvt. practice law Council Bluffs, 1951—; U.S. commr. U.S. Dist. Ct. (so. dist.) Iowa, 1958-70; part-time U.S. magistrate judge U.S. Dist. Ct. (so. dist.) Iowa, 1970—; mem. nat. faculty Fed. Jud. Ctr., Washington, 1972-82; emeritus trustee Children's Square, U.S.A.; verifying ofcl. Internat. Prisoner Transfer Treaties, Mexico City, 1977, La Paz, Bolivia, 1980, 81, Lima, Peru, 1981. Contbr. articles to legal publs. Bd. dirs. Pottawattamie County (Iowa) chpt. ARC, state fund chmn., 1957-58; state chmn. Radio Free Europe, 1960-61; dist. chmn. Trailblazer dist. Boy Scouts Am., 1952-55; mem. exec. coun. Mid-Am. Coun., 1976—. With inf. U.S. Army, 1943-46. Decorated Purple Heart, Bronze Star; named Outstanding Young Man Council Bluffs C. of C., 1959. Fellow Am. Bar Found.; mem. ABA, Am. Judicature Soc., Iowa Bar Assn. (chmn. com. fed. practice 1978-80), Pottawattamie County Bar Assn. (pres. 1979-80), Fed. Bar Assn., Inter-Am. Bar Assn., Supreme Ct. Hist. Soc., Fed. Magistrate Judges Assn. (pres. 1978-79), Iowa Conf. Bar Assn. Pres. (pres. 1985-87), Hist. Soc. of U.S. Cts. Eighth Jud. Cir. (pres. 1989—), Kiwanis (pres. Council Bluffs club 1957), Masons, Phi Delta Phi, Delta Sigma Rho, Omicron Delta Kappa. Republican. Lutheran. Home: 1007 Arbor Ridge Cir Council Bluffs IA 51503-5000 Office: 406 First Bank Iowa Bldg PO Box 1661 Council Bluffs IA 51503

PETERSON, ROBERT ALLEN, marketing educator; b. N.Y.C., Mar. 25, 1944; s. Robert A. and Carrol D. (Collins) P.; m. Diane S. Femrite, June 18, 1966; children: Jeffrey, Jennifer, Matthew. B.S., U. Minn., 1966, M.S., 1968, Ph.D., 1970. Asst. prof. mktg. U. Tex., Austin, 1970-73, assoc. prof., 1973-77, prof., 1977—, John T. Stuart chair, 1985—, chmn. dept. mktg. adminstrn., 1983-85; prin. Group Seven Assocs., Austin. Author: Marketing Research, 1982, 2d edit., 1988; co-author: Modern American Capitalism, 1990, Strategic Marketing, 7th edit., 1995; editor: Jour. Mktg. Rsch., 1985-88, Jour. Acad. Mktg. Sci., 1991-94; mem. editorial bd. Jour. Mktg., Bus. Rev., Internat. Mktg. Rev. Recipient rsch. award AMA, 1988, Charles Hurwitz fellow, 1983—. Fellow Southwestern Mktg. Assn. (pres. 1977-78), Am. Mktg. Assn. (v.p. 1980-81), Acad. Mktg. Sci. (bd. govs. 1982-86, chmn. 1994—, Am. Inst. Decision Scis. (dir. 1974-75). Lutheran. Office: Univ Texas Dept Mktg Austin TX 78712

PETERSON, ROBERT AUSTIN, manufacturing company executive retired; b. Sioux City, Iowa, July 5, 1925; s. Austen W. and Marie (Mueller) P.; m. Carol May Hudy, May 17, 1952; children: Roberta, Richard, Bruce. B.S., U. Minn., 1946, B.B.A., 1947. Credit mgr. New Holland Machine div. Sperry Rand Corp., Mpls., 1952-61, Toro Co., Mpls., 1961-68; treas. Toro Co., 1968-70, v.p. and treas. of internat. fin., 1970-83; v.p. fin., pres. Toro Credit Co., 1983-93; bd. dirs. Tesco, South Miami, Fla., Turf Products Corp., Enfield, Conn., Wesco Turf, Sarasota, Fla., Toro Credit Co. Chmn. Prior Lake Spring Lake Watershed Dist., 1970-80; chmn., bd. dirs. Prior Lake Bd. Edn., 1965-71; chmn. Scott County Republican Party, 1969-70; bd. dirs. Scott Carver Mental Health Center, 1969-73, Minn. Watershed Assn., 1972-76. Served to ensign USNR, 1943-46. Mem. St. Joseph's Bay Country Club, Prior Lake Yacht Club (bd. dirs.). Office: 870 Como Ave Saint Paul MN 55103-1015

PETERSON, ROBERT BYRON, petroleum company executive; b. Regina, Sask., Can., BSc in Chem. Engring., Queen's U., Kingston, Ont., Can., 1959, MSc in Chem. Engring., 1961. Various prodn. positions Imperial Oil Ltd. and affiliates, Can. and U.S., 1960-82; pres., chief exec. officer Esso Resources Can. Ltd., Calgary, Alta., Can., 1982-85; dir. Imperial Oil Ltd., Toronto, Ont., Can., 1984—; exec. v.p., chief operating officer Imperial Oil Ltd., Toronto, 1985-88, pres., COO, 1988-92, chmn., pres., CEO, 1992—; bd. dirs. Royal Bank Can., C.D. Howe Inst., Bus. Coun. Nat. Issues. Gov. Jr. Achievement Can.; chmn. The Conf. Bd. Can. Mem. Assn. Profl. Engrs. Geologists and Geophysicists of Alta. Office: Imperial Oil Ltd, 111 St Clair Ave W, Toronto, ON Canada M5W 1K3*

PETERSON, ROBERT L., meat processing executive; b. Nebr., July 14, 1932; married; children: Mark R., Susan P. Student, U. Nebr., 1950. With Wilson & Co., Jim Boyle Order Buying Co.; cattle buyer R&C Packing Co., 1956-61; cattle buyer, plant mgr., v.p. carcass prodn. Iowa Beef Processors, 1961-69; exec. v.p. ops. Spencer Foods, 1969-71; founder, pres., chmn., chief exec. officer Madison (Nebr.) Foods, 1971-76; group v.p. carcass div. Iowa Beef Processors, Inc. (name now IBP, Inc.) div. Occidental Petroleum Corp., Dakota City, Nebr., 1976-77, pres., chief operating officer, 1977-80, chief exec. officer, 1980-81, co-chmn. bd. dirs., 1981-82, chmn., chief exec. officer, pres., 1981—, also dir.; exec. v.p., dir. Occidental Petroleum Corp., Los Angeles, 1982-87. Served with Q.M.C. U.S. Army, 1952-54. Mem. Sioux City Country Club. Office: IBP Inc IBP Ave PO Box 515 Dakota City NE 68731-0515*

PETERSON, ROBIN TUCKER, marketing educator; b. Casper, Wyo., July 31, 1937; s. Walfred Arthur and Mary Lurene Peterson; m. Marjorie K. Greenwald, June 25, 1963; children: Timothy, Kimberly. BS, U. Wyo., 1959, MS in Bus., 1961; Ph.D., U. Wash., Seattle, 1967. Mem. faculty Idaho State U., Pocatello, 1963-73; prof. mktg., head mktg. dept. St. Cloud (Minn.) State U., 1973-76, N.Mex. State U., Las Cruces, 1976—; Fulbright lectr., Yugoslavia, 1973; vis. scholar Ea. Mont. State Coll., 1985; Sunwest Fin. Svcs. Disting. Centennial prof. N.Mex. State U., 1991, 92. Author: Marketing-A Contemporary Introduction, 1976, Forecasting, 1976, edit., 1983, Personal Selling, 1977, Marketing in Action, 1977, Lernbook Marketing, 1984, Marketing: Concepts and Decision Making, 1987, Principles of Marketing, 1989, Argentina, 1990, Managing the Distributor Sales Network, 1990, Business Forecasting, 1992, Getting New Products to Market Rapidly, 1994; exec. editor Bus. Forecaster, 1993-94; editor: Journal of Business and Entrepreneurship, 1994; also contbr. articles to profl. publs. Served with USAR, 1962-63. Mem. Am. Mktg. Assn., Sales and Mktg. Execs. Internat., Acad. Mktg. Sci. (pres. 1977-78, 80-82), Am. Arbitration Assn. (Outstanding Educators Am. award), S.W. Small Bus. Assn. (pres. 1983-84, Outstanding Mktg. Educators award), S.W. Mktg. Assn., Western Mktg. Educators, Las Cruces C. of C., Las Cruces Sales and Mktg. Club, Beta Gamma Sigma, Phi Kappa Psi, Alpha Kappa Psi, Alpha Mu Alpha. Republican. Presbyterian. Home: 4227 E Winchester Rd Las Cruces NM 88011-7544 Office: Box 5280 New Mexico State U Las Cruces NM 88001

PETERSON, RODERICK WILLIAM, television writer, producer; b. Phoenix, July 7, 1921; s. Paul Culver and Elizabeth (Butler) P.; m. Jewell Nichols, Feb. 28, 1943 (div. 1972); children: Eric, Lisa Peterson Winslow, Sally Peterson Hinson; m. Claire Whitaker, Nov. 18, 1972. Student, Phoenix Community Coll., 1939-41; B.A., U. Ariz., 1949. Program dir., writer Sta. KTAR, Phoenix, 1949-56; program dir. Sta. KGUN-TV, Tucson, 1956-57. Freelance network radio writer NBC, CBS, Mut. Broadcasting Sys.; freelance writer: (TV) Bonanza, Emergency, Black Saddle, Kilpatricks, Combat, The Deputy, Wonderful World of Disney, Laramie, (film) The Chartroose Caboose, 1959, (TV series) Laramie, 1960-64; writer, assoc. prodr. Walt Disney Prodns., 1965-75; writer, prodr.: (TV) The Waltons, 1977-79, exec. prodr., 1980-81; writer, prodr. MTM Studios, 1981-83; exec. supervising prodr., writer: (TV) Falcon Crest, 1984-86; writer: (TV spls.) (with Claire Whitaker) Walton Thanksgiving Reunion, 1993, A Walton Wedding, 1995. Served with USAAF, 1943-46, PTO. Mem. Writers Guild Am., Hollywood TV Acad., Am. Film Inst., ASCAP. Democrat.

PETERSON, RODNEY DELOS, mediator, forensic economist; b. Sioux Falls, S.D., Nov. 10, 1932; s. Severin Ingvald and Vera (Blow) P.; m. Evelyn Koubsky, Dec. 26, 1965; children: Douglas, Russell, Stuart. B.A., Huron (S.D.) Coll., 1958; M.S. in Econs, S.D. State U., 1959; Ph.D. in Econs. and Bus. Orgn, U. Nebr., 1964; J.D., U. Denver, 1982. Instr. U. Nebr., Lincoln, 1959-64; vis. asst. prof. agrl. econs. U. Nebr., summers 1964-66; instr. adult edn. U. Omaha, part-time 1963-64; asst. prof. econs. Cen. Wash. State U., Ellensburg, 1964-65; asst. prof., then assoc. prof. U. Idaho, Moscow, 1965-68; mem. faculty Colo. State U., Ft. Collins, 1968-91; prof. econs. Colo. State U., 1971-91; mediation officer, 1985-91; prof. emeritus Colo. State U., 1991; economist Fla. Dept. Commerce, 1991—; dir. Ctr. Econ. Edn. Colo. State U., 1976-77; vis. prof. Simon Fraser U., Vancouver, B.C., Can., 1974-75, univ. mediation officer, 1985-91. Author: Student Guide to Accompany Our Changing Economy, 1976, Economic Organization in Medical Equipment and Supply, 1973, Political Economy & American Capitalism, 1991; contbr. numerous articles to profl. jours. NSF fellow, summers 1971, 73, expert witness personal injury and antitrust cases. Mem. Am. Econ. Assn., Midwest Econs. Assn., Sigma Xi, Delta Sigma Pi, Beta Gamma Sigma, Omicron Delta Epsilon (regional dir. 1975-76). Home: 5433 Pinderton Way Tallahassee FL 32311-1412 Office: Fla Dept Commerce/BEA W Gaines St Tallahassee FL 32399

PETERSON, ROY JEROME, physics educator; b. Everett, Wash., Oct. 18, 1939; married; four children. BS, U. Wash., 1961, PHD, 1966. Instr. physics Princeton (N.J.) U., 1966-68; rsch. assoc. Yale U., New Haven, 1968-70; from rsch. assoc. to prof. physics & astrophysics U. Colo., Boulder, 1970—; program dir. Intermediate Energy Physics NSF, 1978-79. Fellow Am. Phys. Soc. Office: U Colo Box 446 Nuclear Physics Lab Boulder CO 80309*

PETERSON, RUDOLPH A., banker; b. Svenljunga, Sweden, Dec. 6, 1904; s. Aaron and Anna (Johannson) P.; m. Barbara Welser Lindsay, Dec. 25, 1962; children: Linnea Peterson Bennett, R. Price; stepchildren: Robert I. Lindsay, Lorna Lindsay, Anne Lindsay, Margaret Lindsay. B.S. in Commerce, U. Calif., 1925, LL.D., 1968; L.H.D., U. Redlands, 1967. With Comml. Credit Co., 1925-36; successively asst. mgr. Comml. Credit Co., San Francisco; v.p., gen. mgr. Comml. Credit Co., Mexico City; div. operations mgr. Comml. Credit Co., Chgo.; dist. mgr. Bank Am. Nat. Trust & Savs. Assn., Fresno, Calif., 1936-41; v.p. Bank Am. Nat. Trust & Savs. Assn., San Francisco, 1941-46; vice chmn. bd Bank Am. Nat. Trust & Savs. Assn., 1961-63, pres., CEO, 1963-70, chmn. exec. com., 1970-75, also dir., 1961—; pres., chief exec. officer Allied Bldg. Credits, 1946-52; v.p. Transam. Corp., San Francisco, 1952-55; pres., chief exec. officer Bank of Hawaii, Honolulu, 1956-61; pres., chief exec. officer BankAm. Corp., San Francisco, 1968-70, chmn. exec. com., 1970-76, also dir., 1968—; adminstr. UN Devel. Programme, 1971-76; bd. dirs. Alza Corp., Mcpl. Fund for Calif. Investors, Inc., Asia Found.; chmn. Euro Can. Bank, 1982-94; adminstr. UN Devel. Programme, 1972-76. Mem. adv. coun. Calif. Acad. Scis. Decorated Grand Cross of Civil Merit Spain; Order of Merit Italy; named Swedish-Am. of Year Vasa Order, 1965; U. Calif. Alumnus of Year, 1968; recipient Capt. Robert Dollar Meml. award for contbn. to advancement Am. fgn. trade, 1970, Chancellor's award U. Calif., 1992. Clubs: Bohemian (San Francisco), Pacific-Union (San Francisco), Villa Taverna (San Francisco). Home: 86 Sea

View Ave Piedmont CA 94611-3519 Office: Bank Am Ctr 555 California St Ste 500 San Francisco CA 94104-1507

PETERSON, RUSSELL WILBUR, former association executive, former state governor; b. Portage, Wis., Oct. 3, 1916; s. John Anton and Emma (Anthony) P.; m. E. Lillian Turner, June 30, 1937 (dec. Apr. 28, 1994); children: Russell Glen, Peter Jon, Kristin, Elin; m. June B. Jenkins, Oct. 21, 1995. B.S., U. Wis., 1938, Ph.D., 1942, LL.D. (hon.), 1984; D.Sc. (hon.), Williams Coll., 1975, Butler U., Springfield Coll., Stevens Inst. Tech., 1979, Gettysburg Coll., 1980, Alma Coll., 1981, Ohio State U., SUNY-Syracuse, Northland Coll., Fairleigh Dickinson U., 1981; LL.D. (hon.), Monmouth Coll., 1982, Salisbury State U., 1988; D of Humane Letters, Meadville-Lombard Theol. Sch., 1992. With E. I. DuPont de Nemours & Co., Inc., 1942-69, research dir. textile fibers dept., 1954-55, 56-59, merchandising mgr. textile fibers, 1955-56, dir. new products div. textile fibers, 1959-62, dir. research and devel. div. devel. dept., 1963-69; bd. dirs. Textile Research Inst., Princeton, N.J., 1956-63, chmn. exec. com., 1959-61, chmn. bd. dirs., 1961-63, fellow, 1969; gov. of Del., 1969-73; chmn. exec. com. Nat. Commn. Critical Choices for Am., 1973; chmn. U.S. Council on Environ. Quality, 1973-76; pres. New Directions, 1976-77, Nat. Audubon Soc., 1979-85; mem. Nat. Commn. Critical Choices for Am., 1973-74; dir. Office Tech. Assessment, U.S. Congress, 1978-79; regional v.p. Nat. Mcpl. League, 1968-78; chmn. Edn. Commn. States, 1970; chmn. com. nuclear energy and space tech. So. Govs. Conf., 1970-71; chmn. Nat. Adv. Commn. on Criminal Justice Standards and Goals, 1971-73; chmn. com. law enforcement, justice and pub. safety Nat. Govs. Conf., 1970-73; v.p. Council State Govts., 1970-71; chmn. adv. bd. Solar Energy Research Inst., 1979-83; vis prof. Dartmouth Coll., 1985, Carleton Coll., 1986, U. Wis.-Madison, 1987; chmn. Centennial Internat. Symposium, Nat. Geog. Soc., 1986-88. Chmn. Del. River Basin Commn., 1971-72; founding chmn. Bio-Energy Coun., 1976-78; bd. dirs. World Wildlife Fund, 1976-82, Population Action Internat., 1973—, Alliance to Save Energy, 1979-93; bd. dirs. Global Tomorrow Coalition, 1981-91, chmn., 1981-87; regional councillor Internat. Union Conservation Nature and Natural Resources, 1981-88, v.p., 1984-88; mem. Pres.'s Commn. on Accident at Three Mile Island, 1979; pres. Internat. Coun. Bird Preservation, 1982-90; chmn. Ctr. on Consequences of Nuclear War, 1983-87; vice chmn. Better World Soc., 1985-90, pres., 1985-87; vis. com. John F. Kennedy Sch. Govt., 1979-85; Goodwill amb. UN Environ. Program, 1984—, mem. world environ. prize com., 1989—; mem. Gov. Cuomo's Environ. Adv. Bd., 1985-94; mem. adv. bd. Pace U. Sch. Law, 1988—, Earth Island Inst., 1988—; chmn. bd. Earth Lobby, 1992—; co-chmn. gov.'s task force on rejuvenating Wilmington waterfront, 1992-95; mem. Del. Riverfront Devel. Corp., 1995—. Decorated Order of Golden Ark (The Netherlands); recipient Ann. award NCCJ, 1966, Gold medal World Wildlife Fund, 1971, Ann. award Comml. Devel. Assn., 1971, Gold Plate award Nat. Acad. Achievement, 1971, Parsons award Am. Chem. Soc., 1974, Audubon award Nat. Audubon Soc., 1977, Proctor prize Sigma Xi, 1978, Frances K. Hutchinson medal Garden Club Am., 1980, Robert Marshall award Wilderness Soc., 1984, Nat. Conservation medal DAR, 1989, Human and Civil Rights award Del. Human Rights Commn., 1989, Environ. Law Inst. award, 1990, Ann. award Am. Civil Liberties Found. Del., 1992, Lawrence Solid Waste award Assn. N.Am., 1993, Kiwanis Cmty. Svc. award, 1993, Lifetime Achievement award Global Tomorrow Coalition, 1994, Lifetime Achievement award League of Conservation Voters, 1995; named Conservationist of Yr., Nat. Wildlife Fedn., 1972, Swedish-Am. of Yr., Vasa Order of Am. In Sweden, 1982,. Hon. fellow Am. Inst. Chemists, AAAS (past bd. dirs.); mem. Am. Ornithologists' Union, Linnaean Soc., Fedn. Am. Scientists, Am. Chem. Soc., Del. Acad. Sci., U.S. Assn. for Club of Rome, Cosmos Club, Phi Beta Kappa, Sigma Xi (Proctor prize 1978), Phi Lambda Upsilon, Phi Kappa Phiarian. Address: 11 E Mozart Dr Wilmington DE 19807

PETERSON, SKIP (ORLEY R. PETERSON, III), newspaper photographer; b. Dayton, Ohio, July 6, 1951; s. Orley Ray and Helen Louise (Stafford) P.; m. Jennifer Susan Hinders, Sept. 22, 1990; children from previous marriage: Meredith, Sam, Elizabeth; 1 stepchild, Erin. BS in Journalism, Ohio U., 1973. Staff photographer Dayton Daily News, 1973-82, chief photographer, 1982—; part-time faculty mem. U. Dayton. Contbr. photographs to mags., including Life, Time, Newsweek, Sports Illustrated, also book Photojournalism. Judge ann. contests for White House News Photographers, Ind. News Photographers Assn., Mich. Press Photographers Assn., Ky. News Photographers Assn., Soc. Profl. Journalists. Recipient awards Soc. Profl. Journalists, 1st Place Sports Feature award Pictures of Yr. Competition, 1985, Robert Carson award for outstanding contbn. to photojournalism in Ohio, Ohio Understanding award for documentary. Mem. Ohio News Photographers Assn. (chmn. bd. dirs., past pres., awards), Nat. Press Photographers Assn. (past regional dir., exec. com. bd. rep., awards). Methodist. Avocations: restoring British sports cars, golf, auto racing. Home: 440 Wing View Ln Kettering OH 45429 Office: Dayton Daily News 45 S Ludlow St Dayton OH 45402-1810

PETERSON, STEVEN H., school system administrator. Supt. Washington County Sch. Dist., St. George, Utah. State finalist Nat. Supt. Yr., 1993. Office: Washington County Sch Dist 189 W Tabernacle St Saint George UT 84770-3338

PETERSON, THEODORE BERNARD, retired journalism educator; b. Albert Lea, Minn., June 8, 1918; s. Theodore B. and Emilie (Jensen) P.; m. Helen M. Clegg, Sept. 13, 1946; children: Thane Eric, Kristin, Megan, Daniel Alan. B.A., U. Minn., 1941; M.S., Kans. State Coll., 1948; Ph.D., U. Ill., 1955. Instr., then asst. prof. journalism Kans. State Coll., 1945-48, head coll. news bur., 1945-47; instr. journalism U. Ill., 1948-55, assoc. prof., 1955-57, prof., 1957-87; dean U. Ill. (Coll. Communications), 1957-79; judge Nat. Mag. Awards, 1967-88. Author: Writing Nonfiction for Magazines, 1949, Magazines in the Twentieth Century, 1956, rev., 1964, (with F.S. Siebert, Wilbur Schramm) Four Theories of the Press, 1956, (with J.W. Jensen, Wm. L. Rivers) The Mass Media in Modern Society, 1965, rev., 1971. Recipient award for distinguished research journalism Sigma Delta Chi, Kappa Tau Alpha, 1956, Outstanding Achievement award U. Minn., 1973, Outstanding Undergraduate Teaching award U. Ill., 1987. Mem. Assn. Edn. Journalism (1st v.p. 1962, pres. 1963), Am. Council on Edn. Journalism (accrediting com. 1961-70, 72-81), Am. Assn. Schs. and Depts. Journalism (pres. 1965), Kappa Tau Alpha, Phi Kappa Phi. Home: 103 E George Huff Dr Urbana IL 61801-5807

PETERSON, TRUDY HUSKAMP, national archivist; b. Estherville, Iowa, Jan. 25, 1945. BS, Iowa State U., 1967; MA, U. Iowa, 1972, PhD, 1975. Various positions Nat. Archives, Washington, 1968-87, asst. archivist, 1987-93, dep. archivist of U.S., 1993-95, acting archivist, 1993-95; exec. dir. Open Soc. Archives, Budapest, 1995—; Fulbright lectr. in Am. studies, 1983-84; commr. U.S.-Russia Joint Commn. on MIA/POWs, 1992—; sec. Internat. Conf. on Round Table on Archives, 1992-93, pres., 1993-95; mem. European Bd. on Archives, 1995—. Author: Agricultural Exports, Farm Income and the Eisenhower Administration, 1979, Basic Archival Workshop Exercises, 1982, Archives and Manuscripts: Law, 1985; editor: Farmers, Bureaucrats and Middlemen: Historical Perspectives on American Agriculture, 1980; mem. editl. bd. The Am. Archivist, 1978-81; contbr. articles to profl. jours. Pres. Capitol Hill Restoration Soc., 1987-88. Recipient Order of Arts and Letters Republic of France, 1995, Hancher-Finkbine Medallion, Disting. Alumni award U. Iowa, 1995; named Samuel Lazerow Lectr. Simmons Coll., 1995. Fellow Soc. Am. Archivists (mem. coun. 1984-87, pres. 1990-91, held various offices, Gondos Meml. award 1973, Fellows Posner prize 1987); mem. Agrl. History Soc. (mem. exec. com. 1982-85, pres. 1988-89), Soc. History in Fed. Govt. (mem. exec. com. 1987-89). Office: Open Soc Archives, Veres Palne 14 I/1, H-1053 Budapest Hungary

PETERSON, VICTOR LOWELL, aerospace engineer, management consultant; b. Saskatoon, Sask., Can., June 11, 1934; came to U.S., 1937; s. Edwin Galladet and Ruth Mildred (McKeeby) P.; m. Jacqueline Dianne Hubbard, Dec. 21, 1955; children: Linda Kay Peterson Landrith, Janet Gale, Victor Craig. BS in Aero. Engring., Oreg. State U., 1956; MS in Aerospace Engring., Stanford U., 1964; MS in Mgmt., MIT, 1973. Rsch. scientist NASA-Ames Rsch. Ctr., Moffett Field, Calif., 1956-68, asst. chief hypersonic aerodyns., 1968-71, chief aerodyns. br., 1971-74, chief thermo and gas dynamics div., 1974-84, dir. aerophysics, 1984-90, dep. dir., 1990-94; pvt. mgmt. cons., 1994—; mem. nat. adv. bd. U. Tenn. Space Inst., Tullahoma, 1984-94. Contbr. numerous articles to profl. jours. Treas. Woodland Acres Homeowners Assn., Los Altos, Calif., 1978—. Capt. USAF, 1957-60. Recipient medal for outstanding leadership NASA, 1982; Alfred P. Sloan fellow MIT, 1972-73. Fellow AIAA. Republican. Methodist. Achievements include development of numerical aerodynamic simulation system for aerospace, of method for reconstructing planetary atmosphere structure from accelerations of body entering atmosphere, of theory for motions of tumbling bodies entering planetary atmospheres. Home: 484 Aspen Way Los Altos CA 94024-7126 *Achievements in life are maximized by creating visions of success and focussing relentlessly on successful accomplishment of intermediate objectives.*

PETERSON, WALLACE CARROLL, SR., economics educator; b. Omaha, Mar. 28, 1921; s. Fred Nels and Grace (Brown) P.; m. Eunice V. Peterson, Aug. 16, 1944 (dec. Nov. 24, 1985); children: Wallace Carroll Jr., Shelley Lorraine; m. Bonnie B. Watson, Nov. 11, 1988. Student, U. Omaha, 1939-40, U. Mo., 1940-42; BA in Econs. and European History, U. Nebr., 1947, MA in Econs. and European History, 1948, PhD in Econs. and European History, 1953; postgrad., Handelshochschule, St. Gallen, Switzerland, 1948-49, U. Minn., 1951, London Sch. Econs. and Polit. Sci., 1952. Reporter Lincoln (Nebr.) Jour., 1946; instr. econs. U. Nebr., Lincoln, 1951-54, asst. prof., 1954-57, assoc. prof., 1957-61, prof., 1962—, chmn. dept. econs., 1965-75, George Holmes prof. econs., 1966-92; George Holmes prof. econs. emeritus, 1992—; v.p. faculty senate U. Nebr., Lincoln, 1972-73, pres. faculty senate, 1973-74; S.J. Hall disting. vis. prof. U. Nev., Las Vegas, 1983-84. Author: The Welfare State in France, 1960, Elements of Economics, 1973, Our Overloaded Economy: Inflation, Unemployment and the Crisis in American Capitalism, 1982, Market Power and the Economy, 1988, Transfer Spending, Taxes and the American Welfare State, 1991, Income, Employment and Economic Growth, 8th edit., 1996, Silent Depression: The Fate of the American Dream, 1994; contbr. articles to profl. jours. and columns to newspapers. Mem. Nebr. Dem. Cen. Com., 1968-74, vice-chmn., chmn. Nebr. Polit. Accountability and Disclosure Commn., 1977-80; chmn. Nebr. Coun. Econ. Edn., 1976-77. Capt. USAAF, 1942-46. Recipient Champion Media award for Econ. Understanding, 1981; Fulbright fellow, 1957-58, 64-65; Mid-Am. State Univs. honor scholar, 1982-83. Mem. ACLU, AAUP (pres. Nebr. 1963-64, nat. coun.), Assn. for Evolutionary Econs. (pres. 1976, Veblen-Commons award 1991), Am. Econs. Assn., Midwest Econs. Assn. (pres. 1968-69), Mo. Valley Econ. Assn. (pres. 1989), Assn. Social Econs. (pres. 1992, Thomas F. Devine award 1995), Fedn. Am. Scientists. Home: 4549 South St Lincoln NE 68506-1253 Office: U Nebr Dept Econs CBA Lincoln NE 68588-0489

PETERSON, WALTER FRITIOF, academic administrator; b. Idaho Falls, Idaho, July 15, 1920; s. Walter Fritiof and Florence (Danielson) P.; m. Barbara Mae Kempe, Jan. 13, 1946; children: Walter Fritiof III, Daniel John. BA, State U. Iowa, 1942, MA, 1948, PhD, 1951; HHD (hon.), Loras Coll., 1983; LHD (hon.), Clarke Coll., 1991. Asst. prof. history, chmn. dept. history Milw. Downer Coll., 1952-57, assoc. prof. history, chmn. social sci. div., 1957-64; assoc. prof. history Lawrence U., Appleton, Wis., 1964-67; prof. history, Alice G. Chapman libr. Lawrence U., 1967-70; pres. U. Dubuque, 1970-90, chancellor, 1990—; regional tng. officer Peace Corps, 1965-68; cons. history Allis-Chalmers Mfg. Co., 1959-75, Secura Ins. Group, 1968-92, Wm. C. Brown Pub. Co., 1981-92, bd. dirs. Editor: Transactions of Wis. Acad. Scis., Arts and Letters, 1965-72, The Allis-Chalmers Corporation: An Industrial History, 1977, A History of Wm. C. Brown Cos., 1994, A History of Haukeye Bancorporation, 1996. Recipient Templeton Prize for Progress in Religion, 1986-91; bd. dirs. Finley Hosp., pres., 1983-84; chmn. Finley Health Found., 1986-95; bd. dirs. Dubuque Symphony Orch., Dubuque Art Assn., Jr. Achievement, Nat. River Hall of Fame, 1984; chmn. Iowa Assn. Coll. and Univ. Pres., 1975-76; chmn. Iowa Coll. Found., 1982-83. With USAAF, 1942-45, PTO. Recipient Dubuque Citizen award, 1990, Disting. Civic Svc. award, 1991, Benjamin Franklin award Nat. Soc. Fundraising Execs., 1994, Paul Harris fellowship, 1993; named to Dubuque Bus. Hall of Fame, 1990. Mem. Iowa Assn. Ind. Colls. and Univs. (chmn. 1988-89), Dubuque County Hist. Soc. (bd. dirs.), Phi Alpha Theta, Kappa Delta Pi, Phi Delta Kappa. Office: U Dubuque Office of Chancellor 2000 University Ave Dubuque IA 52001-5050

PETERSON, WAYNE TURNER, composer, pianist; b. Albert Sea, Minn., Sept. 3, 1927; s. Leslie Jules and Irma Thelma (Turner) P.; m. Harriet Christiansen, 1948 (div. 1978); children: Alan, Craig, Drew, Grant. BA, U. Minn., 1951, MA, 1953; postgrad., Royal Acad. Music, London, 1953-54. Instr. music U. Minn., 1955-59; asst. prof. music Chico (Calif.) State U., 1959-60; prof. music San Francisco State U., 1960—; vis. prof. composition U. Ind., Bloomington, 1992, Stanford U., 1992-94; artist in residence Briarcombe Found., Bolinas, Calif., 1983; vis. artist Am. Acad. in Rome, 1990. Composer: Allegro for String Quartet, 1952, Introduction and Allegro, 1953, Free Variations for Orch., 1954-58, Can Death Be Sleep, 1955, Earth, Sweet Earth, 1956, (cappella chorus) Cape Ann, 1957, Three Songs for Soprano and Piano, 1957, (cappella chorus) Psalm 56, 1959, Exaltation, Dithyramb and Caprice, 1959-60, (cappella chorus) An e e Cummings Triptych, 1962, Tangents for flute, clarinet, horn and violin, 1963, An e e Cummings Cantata, 1964, Fantasy Concertante for violin and piano, 1965, Reflections, 1965, Metamorphosis for Wind Quintet, 1967, Phantasmagoria for flute, clarinet, double bass, 1968, Cataclysms, 1968, Clusters and Fragments for string orch., 1969, Ceremony After a Fire Raid, 1969, Sinfonia and Canticle for baritone voice and organ, 1969, Capriccio for Flute and Piano, 1973, Transformations for String Quartet, 1974, Trialogue for violin, cello and piano, 1975, Diatribe for violin and piano, 1975, Encounters, 1976, Rhapsody for Cello and Piano, 1976, An Interrupted Serenade for flute, harp and cello, 1978, Dark Reflections (cycle of four songs for high voice, violin and piano), 1980, Mallets Aforethought (symphony for percussion ensemble), 1981, Sextet for flute, clarinet, percussion, harp, violin and cello, 1982, Doubles for 2 flutes and 2 clarinets, 1982, Debussy Song Cycle, 1983, String Quartet, 1983-84, Ariadne's Thread for harp, flute, clarinet, horn, percussion and violin, 1985, Transformations for chamber orch., 1986, Duo for viola and cello, 1986-87, Trilogy for Orch., 1987, Labyrinth for flute, clarinet, violin and piano, 1987, The Widening Gyre for full orch., 1991, The Face of the Night, the Heart of the Dark for full orch., 1991 (Pulitzer prize for music 1992), Mallets Aforthought, 1991, String Quartet # 2, 1992, Diptych, 1992, Janus, 1993, Duo for Violin and Piano, 1993, And the Winds Shall Blow, a fantasy for saxophone quartet, symphony winds, brass and percussion, 1994; recs. with Mercury Records, Desto Records, Arch Records, Grenadilla Records, Koch Internat.; Recordings commd. Am. Music Ctr., 1959, Virtuosi of San Francisco, 1968, Unitarian Ch., 1969, Paul Mason, Inc., 1974, 87, NEA Consortium Commn., 1982, Charles Wuorinen and San Francisco Symphony, 1985, Am. Composers Symphony, Inc., 1987, San Francisco Symphony, 1991, Gerbode Found., 1990, Koussevitzky Found., 1990, Fromm Music Found., 1992, Philharmonic Orch. of Freiburg in Breisgau, Germany, 1993. Recipient 11th Ann. Norman Fromm Composer's award, 1982, Meritorious Svc. award Calif. State U. System, 1984, Top award Am. Harp Soc., 1985, Composer's award Am. Acad. and Inst. Arts and Letters, 1986, Pulitzer Prize for music, 1992; Fulbright scholar, Royal Acad. Music, 1953-54; NEA grantee, 1976; Guggenheim fellow, 1989-90, Djerassi Found. fellow, 1989-91. Home: 140 S Lake Merced Hls San Francisco CA 94132-2935

PETERSON, WILLARD JAMES, Chinese history educator; b. Oak Park, Aug. 1, 1938; s. Otto Stewart and Catherine (Esin) P.; m. Toby Black, Aug 27, 1960. BA, U. Rochester, 1960; MA, U. London, 1964; PhD, Harvard U., 1970. Asst. prof. Dartmouth Coll., Hanover, N.H., 1970-71; prof. East Asian Studies and History Princeton (N.J.) U., 1971—. Author: Bitter Gourd, 1979, Power of Culture, 1994. Office: Dept of East Asian Studies & Hist Princeton U Princeton NJ 08544

PETERSON, WILLIAM HERBERT, economist; b. N.Y.C., Feb. 26, 1921; s. George C. and Anna (Ericksson) P.; m. Mary Jean Bennett, Feb. 17, 1949; children: Mark, Laura. BS, NYU, 1943, PhD, 1952; MS, Columbia U., 1948; hon. degree, Francisco Marroquin U., Guatemala, 1991. Asst. prof. economics Poly. Inst. Bklyn., 1948-53; prof. econs. NYU, 1953-64; economist U.S. Steel Corp., 1964-71; sr. econ. adviser U.S. Dept. Commerce, Washington, 1972-74; John David Campbell prof. Am. bus. Am. Grad. Sch. Internat. Mgmt., Glendale, Ariz., 1974-76; Burrows T. Lundy prof. philosophy of bus. Campbell U., Buies Creek, N.C., 1976-78, 88-93; Scott L. Probasco Jr. chair free enterprise, dir. Ctr. Econ. Edn. U. Tenn., Chattanooga, 1979-87; mem. Conf. Bd. Econ. Forum, 1964-71. Author: The Great Farm Problem, 1959; also monographs and articles. Mem. nat. campaign staff Nixon for Pres., 1960. Lt. (j.g.) USNR, WWII. Disting. scholar Assn. for Pvt. Enterprise Edn., 1989; recipient George Washington Medal of Honor Freedoms Found. at Valley Forge, 1990. Mem. Am., So. econ. assns., Nat. Assn. Bus. Econs., Am. Statis. Assn., Mont Pelerin Soc., Cosmos Club. Home: 700 New Hampshire Ave NW Washington DC 20037-2406

PETERSON, WILLIS LESTER, economics educator; b. Mpls., Mar. 3, 1932; s. Lester Wilfred and Valeria Leone (Slatoski) P.; m. Dorothy Feiertag, July 5, 1969. BS, U. Minn., 1960, MS, 1962; PhD, U. Chgo., 1966. Rsch. fellow U. Chgo., 1962-65; mem. faculty U. Minn., St. Paul, 1965—, prof. econs., 1972—. Author: Principles of Economics: Macro, 1971, 9th edit., 1994, Principles of Economics: Micro, 1971, 9th edit., 1994, Introduction to Economics, 1977, rev. edit., 1995. With U.S. Army, 1952-54. Home: 500 Constance Blvd Anoka MN 55304 Office: U Minn 337 Cla Ofc Bldg Saint Paul MN 55108

PETHICK, CHRISTOPHER JOHN, physicist; b. Horsham, Sussex, Eng., Feb. 22, 1942; s. Richard Hope and Norah Betty (Hill) P. BA, Magdalen Coll., Oxford (Eng.) U., 1962, PhD, 1965. Fellow Magdalen Coll., Oxford U., 1965-70; research assoc. U. Ill., Urbana, 1966-68, research asst. prof., 1968-69, assoc. prof. physics, 1970-73, prof. physics, 1973-95; prof. physics Nordita, Copenhagen, 1975—. A.P. Sloan research fellow, 1970-72. Fellow Am. Phys. Soc.; mem. Am. Astron. Soc., European Phys. Soc. Home: Niels W Gades Gade 34, DK-2100 Copenhagen Denmark Office: U Ill Dept Physics 1110 W Green St Urbana IL 61801-3003 also: Nordita, Blegdamsvej 17, DK-2100 Copenhagen Denmark

PETICOLAS, WARNER LELAND, physical chemistry educator; b. Lubbock, Tex., July 29, 1929; s. Warner Marion and Beulah Francis (Lowe) P.; m. Virginia Marie Wolf, June 30, 1969; children—Laura M., Alicia B.; children by previous marriage—Cynthia M., Nina P., Phillip W. B.S., Tex. Technol. Coll., 1950; Ph.D., Northwestern U., 1954. Research asso. DuPont Co., Wilmington, Del., 1954-60; research div. IBM, San Jose, Calif., 1960-67; cons. IBM, 1967-69, mgr. chem. physics group, 1965-67; prof. phys. chemistry U. Oreg., 1967—; vis. prof. U. Paris-Pierre and Marie Curie, 1980-81; vis. prof. Weizmann Inst. Sci., Rahovat, Israel, 1991, vis. prof. U. Reims, 1996. Committeeman Democratic party, Eugene, Oreg., 1967-70. Served with USPHS, 1955-57. Recipient Alexander von Humboldt award, W. Ger., 1984-85. Guggenheim fellow Max von Laue-Paul Langevin Inst., Grenoble, France, 1973-74. Fellow Am. Phys. Soc.; mem. Am. Chem. Soc., Am. Phys. Soc., Sigma Xi, Alpha Chi Sigma, Tau Beta Pi. Episcopalian. Home: 2829 Arline Way Eugene OR 97403-2527 Office: U Oregon Dept Of Chemistry Eugene OR 97403

PETILLON, LEE RITCHEY, lawyer; b. Gary, Ind., May 6, 1929; s. Charles Ernest and Blanche Lurene (Mackay) P.; m. Mary Anne Keeton, Feb. 20, 1960; children: Andrew G., Joseph R. BBA, U. Minn., 1952; LLB, U. Calif., Berkeley, 1959. Bar: Calif. 1960, U.S. Dist. Ct. (so. dist.) Calif. 1960. V.p. Creative Investment Capital, Inc., L.A., 1969-70; corp. counsel Harvest Industries, L.A., 1970-71; v.p., gen. counsel, dir. Tech. Svcs. Corp., Santa Monica, Calif., 1971-78; ptnr. Petillon & Davidoff, L.A., 1978-92, Gipson Hoffman & Pancione, 1992-93; pvt. practice, Torrance, Calif., 1993-94; ptnr. Petillon & Hansen, Torrance, Calif., 1994—. Co-author: R&D Partnerships, 2d edit., 1985, Representing Start-Up Companies, 1992, 3d edit., 1995; contbr. chpt. 8 to California Transaction Forms, 1996. Chmn. Neighborhood Justice Ctr. Com., 1983-85, Middle Income Co., 1983085; active Calif. Senate Commn. on Corp. Governance, State Bar Calif. Task Force on Alternative Dispute Resolution, 1984-85; chmn. South Bay Sci. Found., Inc.; vice chmn. Calif. Capital Access Forum, Inc. Recipient Cert. of Appreciation L.A. City Demonstration Agy., 1975, United Indian Devel. Assn., 1981, City of L.A. for Outstanding Vol. Svcs., 1984. Mem. ABA, Calif. State Bar Assn. (pres., Pro Bono Svcs. award 1983), L.A. County Bar Found. (bd. dirs. 1986-89), L.A. County Bar Assn. (chmn. law tech. sect., alt. dispute resolution sect. 1992-94, trustee 1984-85, Griffin Bell Vol. Svc. award 1993). Avocations: backpacking, reading, music, painting. Home: 1636 Via Machado Palos Verdes Estates CA 90274-1930 Office: Petillon & Hansen PC 21515 Hawthorne Blvd # 1260 Torrance CA 90503

PETIT, PARKER HOLMES, health care corporation executive; b. Decatur, Ga., Aug. 4, 1939; s. James Percival and Ethel (Holmes) P.; children: William Wright, Patricia Monique, Meredith Katherine. BS in Mech. Engring., Ga. Inst. Tech., 1962, MS in Engring. Mechanics, 1964; MBA, Ga. State U., 1973. Engr. Gen. Dynamics Corp., Fort Worth, Tex., 1966-67; engring. project mgr. Lockheed-Ga. Co., Marietta, 1967-71; pres., founder, chief exec. officer Healthdyne, Inc., Marietta, 1971—; bd. dirs. Atlantic S.E. Airlines, Atlanta, Healthdyne Technologies, Inc., Atlanta, Healthdyne Info. Enterprises, Inc., Marietta, Ga., Matria Healthcare, Inc., Marietta. Author: Primer on Composite Materials, 1968; patentee in field. Chmn. bd. dirs. Sudden Infant Death Syndrome Alliance, Washington, 1986; active nat. adv. coun. Emory U. Med. Sch., Coun. fellows for the Emory, Ga. Tech. Biomed. Tech. Rsch. Ctr.; bd. dirs. Ga. Rsch. Alliance, 1995. 1st lt. U.S. Army, 1964-67. Recipient Humanitarian award La SocieteFrancaise de Bienfaisance, 1981; mem. Tech. Hall of Fame of Ga.; mem. Ga. Tech. Acad. Disting. Alumni, 1994; Internat. Bus. fellow, 1986. Mem. Health Industry Mfrs. Assn., Cobb County C. of C. (bd. dirs. 1980-82), Pi Kappa Phi. Republican. Methodist. Avocations: flying; oil painting; golf; tennis. Office: Healthdyne Inc 1850 Parkway Pl Marietta GA 30067-8237

PETITO, MARGARET L., public relations executive, consultant; b. Dallas, Sept. 28, 1950; d. Jacob Charles and Eileen (Shank) Loehr; m. John Haven Petito, 1978 (div. 1984); children: John Christian Robert, David Nelson. BA, So. Meth. U., 1972. Mem. Action/Vista Program U.S. Govt., Middlesex, N.Y., 1972-74; dir., curator Oliver House Mus., Penn Yan, N.Y., 1975-77; staff asst. Williams & Jensen, P.C., Washington, 1986-89; dir. fed. affairs DSSI-U.S. Biotech., Washington, 1992-94; cons., dir. pub. affairs Embassy Ecuador, Govt. Ecuador, Washington, 1994—; prin. Petito & Assocs. Dir. Marshall House Mus., Lambertville, N.J., 1980-92; spl. legis. advisor Drugwatch Internat., Chgo., 1993—; bd. dirs., Nyumbani Orphanage for Kenyan Children with AIDS, Africa, Washington, 1989—; mem. Women's Coun. Energy and Environ., Washington, 1990—; mem. task force Women in Govt. Rels., Washington, 1990—; founder, co-chair Forum for the Environ., Washington, 1989-91. Mem. Tex. State Soc., Tex. Breakfast Club. Presbyterian. Avocations: squash, needlepoint, fishing. Home: 3906 Huntington St NW Washington DC 20015-1914 Office: Embassy of Ecuador 2533 15th St NW Washington DC 20009-4102

PETITO, VICTOR THOMAS, JR., credit bureau executive; b. Bklyn., Jan. 29, 1936; s. Victor Sr. and Domenica (DeCarlo) P.; m. Geneva Mae Macom, June 5, 1957 (div. Aug. 1980); children: Victor Bret, Rick Thomas, Gina Lynn; m. Jean Austin, Nov. 22, 1988. Student, Tex. Christian U., 1953-55. Credit mgt. Family Loan, Lubbock, Tex., 1959-62, Goodyear Tire & Rubber, Ft. Worth, 1962-63, Montgomery Wards, Ft. Worth, 1963-68; pres., chief exec. officer The Credit Bur. of Oklahoma City, 1969—; pres. Consumer Credit Counseling, Oklahoma City, 1985-86. Bd. dirs. Okla. Spl. Olympics, Oklahoma City, 1984—; coach track and field Jr. Amateur Athletic Union U.S., Oklahoma City, 1980; deacon Village Christian Ch., Disciples of Christ. With USAF, 1955-57. Mem. Assoc. Credit Burs. (bd. dirs. 1987—, Gemini award 1976, award of excellence 1989), Assoc. Credit Burs. Okla. (pres. 1985-86), Internat. Credit Assn. (exec. dist. 1985—, disting. svc. award 1986, merit award 1987, internat. legis. award 1988), Internat. Soc. Cert. Credit Execs. (chmn. 1987—, Fellow Yr. award 1986), Okla. Soc. Cert. Credit Execs. (founder, pres. 1983-84), Retail Credit Mgrs. Assn. (pres. 1984-85), U.S. C. of C., Oklahoma City C. of C., Del City C. of C., Moore (Okla.) C. of C., Norman (Okla.) C. of C., Edmond (Okla.) C. of C., Moose. Republican. Avocations: golf, fishng, photography. Office: The Credit Bur of Oklahoma City 2519 NW 23rd St Oklahoma City OK 73107-2252

PETITTO, BARBARA BUSCHELL, artist; b. Jersey City; d. John Edward and Anna (Barnaba) Buschell; m. Joseph Bruno Petitto, Feb. 1, 1964; children: Vincent John, Christopher Joseph. Student, Fairleigh Dickinson U., 1969-70; studio art cert., N.J. Ctr. Visual Arts, Summit, 1985; student, Art Students League, N.Y.C., 1980, 89-92, Montclair Art Mus., 1991-93. Represented by Ward-Nasse Gallery, N.Y.C.; artist-in-resident art faculty Acad. St. Elizabeth, Convent Stations, N.J., 1989, 90, 91; art faculty Morris County Art Assn., Morristown, N.J., 1989; curator Olcott Studio Gallery

Art Show, Bernardsville, N.J., 1985; curator Color/Divine Madness Ward-Nasse Gallery, N.Y.C., 1995; demonstrator Acad. St. Elizabeth Convent Station, 1989, 90, DuCret Sch. of the Arts Student Art Exhbn.; organizer for acad. students, 1989; dir. Student's Art Festival WNET/Thirteen, Acad. St. Elizabeth, 1989. One-woman shows include Ariel Gallery, N.Y.C., 1987, 88, Corner Gallery, World Trade Ctr., N.Y.C., 1989, 90, Montserrat Gallery, N.Y.C., 1992; juried shows include N.J. Ctr. Visual Arts, Summit, 1985, 92, Nat. Assn. Women Artists, Meadowlands Cultural Ctr. for Arts, Rutherford, N.J., 1995; exhibited in group shows at Ward-Nasse Gallery, 1989-94, 95, 96, Artworks-Trenton, N.J., 1989, 92, Jain Gallery, N.Y.C., 1989, 91, Blackwell St. Gallery, Dover, N.J., 1993, Ben-Shahn Gallery, William Paterson Coll., 1992, 94, Jain-Marunouchi Gallery, N.Y.C., 1992, 93, Cmty. Arts Assn., Ridgewood, N.J., 1995, Nat. Assn. Women Artists, Inc., Soho, N.Y., 1995, 96, Nat. Soc. Painters in Casein and Acrylic, Salmagundi Gallery, 1996; represented in permanent collections Palisades Amusement Pk. Hist. Soc., Cliffside Pk. Libr., also pvt. collections; contbr. articles to profl. jours. Named Miss Livingston N.J., Livingston C. of C., 1956; recipient Rudolph A. Voelcker Meml. award Art Ctr. N.J., 1982, Excellence award Hunterdon Art Mus., 1988, award for excellence Artists League Ctrl. N.J., 1989, Cornelius Low House, Middlesex County Mus., Montclair Art Mus., 1990, award for mixed media Millburn-Short Hills Art Assn., 1989, 1st Pl. award N.E. Caldwell Arts Festival, 1989, award Nabisco Brands, Inc., East Hanover, N.J., 1990, Excellence award Ann. Tri-State Artists League Ctrl. N.J., 1991, 92, Winsor & Newton plaque, Visual Arts League, Edison, N.J., 1992, Excellence award Manhattan Arts Internat. Cover Art Competition, 1994, Hunterdon Art Ctr. award for mixed media, 1996. Mem. Nat. Soc. Painters in Casein and Acrylic, Nat. Assn. Women Artists, Inc., Artists Equity, N.J. Ctr. Visual Arts, Nat. Mus. Women in Arts, Jersey City Mus., Catherine Lorillaird Wolfe Art Club. Avocations: opera, vocalist, piano, concerts, museums. Office: PO Box 515 Whippany NJ 07981-0515

PETKUS, ALAN FRANCIS, microbiologist; b. Chgo., Feb. 4, 1956; s. Frank Anthony and Valeria (Shimkus) P.; m. Karan Elaine Blakely, Apr. 21, 1990; children: Sabrina Marie, Alexandra Louise. BS, Ill. Benedictine Coll., Lisle, 1979; PhD, Chgo. Med. Sch., North Chicago, 1986. Technologist Palos Community Hosp., Palos Heights, Ill., 1973-79, med. technologist, 1979-86; microbiologist South Bend (Ind.) Med. Found., 1986-91; microbiology dir. Met. Hosp., Grand Rapids, Mich., 1991—. Mem. AAAS, Am. Soc. Clin. Pathologists, Am. Soc. Microbiology, N.Y. Acad. Sci., Ill. Soc. Microbiology, South Ctrl. Assn. Microbiology. Roman Catholic. Avocations: designing computer programs, fishing, skiing. Office: Met Hosp 1919 Boston St SE Grand Rapids MI 49506-4160

PETOK, SAMUEL, retired manufacturing company executive; b. Detroit, Aug. 12, 1922; s. Harry and Jennie (Weingarten) P.; m. Fayne Joyce Myers, June 26, 1952; children—Carol, Seth, Michael. B.A. in History, Wayne State U., Detroit, 1945; postgrad., Medill Sch. Journalism, Northwestern U., 1946. Reporter Detroit Free Press, 1946-50; account exec. McCann Erickson, 1950-52; pub. relations exec. Chrysler Corp., 1952-70; Vice pres. public relations and advt. White Motor Corp., Cleve., 1971-76; dir. communications automotive ops. Rockwell Internat. Co., Troy, Mich., 1976-77; corp. staff v.p. public relations Rockwell Internat. Co., Pitts., 1977-78; v.p. communications Rockwell Internat. Co., 1978-82, sr. v.p. communications, mem. mgmt. com., 1982-88; retired. Former trustee Arthur W. Page Soc. Recipient Page One award Newspaper Guild Detroit, 1948. Mem. Pub. Rels. Soc. Am. (Silver Anvil award 1964, award Cleve. chpt. 1975), Internat. Pub. Rels. Assn., Overseas Press Club Am., The Old Guard of Princeton, Green Acres Country Club.

PETOSA, JASON JOSEPH, publisher; b. Des Moines, Iowa, Apr. 26, 1939; s. Joseph John and Mildred Margaret (Cardamon) P.; m. Theodora Anne Doleski, Aug. 12, 1972; 1 son, Justin James. Student, Marquette U., 1957-59, St. Paul Sem., 1959-63, 65-67, Colegio Paolino Internationale, Rome, 1963-65. Asso. editor Cath. Home Mag., Canfield, Ohio, 1965-67; editor Cath. Home Mag., 1968; dir. Alba House Communications, Canfield, 1968-71; with Office of Radio and TV, Diocese of Youngstown, Ohio, 1969-71; dir. pub. relations, instr. Alice Lloyd Coll., Pippa Passes, Ky., 1971-76; writer, cons. Bethesda, Ohio, 1976-79; pres., pub. Nat. Cath. Reporter, Kansas City, Mo., 1979-85; v.p., gen. mgr. Towsend-Kraft Pub. Co., Liberty, Mo., 1985-86; pres., pub. Steadfast Pub. Co., Kansas City, 1986—; owner CF&E Ptnrs. Bd. dirs. David (Ky.) Sch., 1973-79; mem. Mayor's UN Day Com., Kansas City. Mem. Kansas City Direct Mktg. Assn., UN Assn. (bd. dirs. Met. Kansas City chpt.), Sigma Delta Chi. Roman Catholic. Office: 19 W Linwood Blvd PO Box 410265 Kansas City MO 64141

PETRAIT, BROTHER JAMES ANTHONY, secondary education educator, Roman Catholic brother; b. Phila., May 4, 1937; s. John Joseph and Antonina Frances (Cizek) P. BA, U. Detroit, 1969; MEd, U. Ga., 1971; postgrad. in Scis. and Edn., 8 Univs. and Colls. in U.S., 1971—. Cert. tchr., Mich.; joined Oblates of St Francis de Sales, Roman Cath. Ch., 1957. Sci. tchr. Salesian H.S., Detroit, 1961-70, Judge Meml. H.S., Salt Lake City, 1972-76, Benedictine H.S., Detroit, 1976-82; sci. tchr. St. Joseph H.S., Ogden, Utah, 1983-88, Fredriksted, V.I., 1988—; pres. Mich. Assn. of Biology Tchrs., 1978-82, Utah Biology Tchrs. Assn., 1985-88; bd. dirs. Utah Sci. Tchrs. Assn., 1985-88; presenter at workshops, speaker in Chgo., New Orleans, Las Vegas, Detroit, Phila., Salt Lake City, Layton, Orlando, Purdue U., Anaheim, Australian Nat. Univ., Canberra; participant in 8 NSF-funded programs: U. Ga., Christian Bros. Colls., Vanderbilt U., St. Lawrence U., Ball State U., W. Va. U., No. Ariz. U. Contbr. article to teacher's mags. and ednl. jours. including The Am. Biology Tchr., The Sci. Tchr., The Cath. Digest., Congrl. Record. Anti nuclear weapons activist, founder and leader Nuclear Free Utah, Ogden, 1986-88; led boycott against Morton Salt Co., maker of nuclear weapons.. Recipient Outstanding Biology Tchr. award Nat. Assn. Biology Tchrs., 1975, Nat. Finalist in Presdl. awards for excellence in sci. and math. tchg. Nat. Sci. Tchrs. Assn./NSF/The White House, 1995. Mem. Nat. Sci. Tchrs. Assn. (cert. in biology and gen. sci., Star award 1976, Ohaus awards, 1980, 84), Am. Astron. Soc., Soc. of Amateur Radio Astronomers. Avocations: radio amateur, computers, photography, videography. Home and Office: Saint Joseph H S Plot 3 Rte 2 Frederiksted VI 00840

PETRAKIS, HARRY MARK, author; b. St. Louis, June 5, 1923; s. Mark E. and Stella (Christoulakis) P.; m. Diane Perparos, Sept. 30, 1945; children: Mark, John, Dean. Student, U. Ill., 1940-41, L.H.D., 1971; L.H.D., Governor's State U., 1980, Hellenic Coll., 1984, Roosevelt U., 1987. Freelance writer, tchr., lectr.; tchr. workshop classes in novel, short story; McGuffey vis. lectr. Ohio U., Athens, 1971; writer-in-residence Chgo. Pub. Library, 1976-77, Chgo. Bd. Edn., 1978-79; Kazantzakis Prof. San Francisco State U., 1992. Author: Lion at My Heart, 1959, The Odyssey of Kostas Volakis, 1963, Pericles on 31st Street, 1965 (nominated for Nat. Book award), The Founder's Touch, 1965, A Dream of Kings, 1966 (Nat. Book award nomination), The Waves of Night, 1969, Stelmark: A Family Recollection, 1970, In the Land of Morning, 1973, The Hour of the Bell, 1976, A Petrakis Reader, 28 Stories, 1978, Nick the Greek, 1979, Days of Vengeance, 1983, Reflections on a Writer's Life and Work, 1983, Collected Stories, 1986, Ghost of the Sun, 1990; contbr. short stories to mags. including, Atlantic Monthly, Sat. Eve. Post, Harper's Bazaar, Country Beautiful. (Story included in Prize Stories, also O. Henry Award 1966). Recipient awards Friends of Am. Writers, Friends of Lit., Soc. Midland Authors, Carl Sandburg award, Ellis Island medal of honor, 1995. Mem. Authors Guild, PEN, Writers Guild Am.-West. Address: 80 East Rd Dune Acres Chesterton IN 46304 *"...The older I become, the more clearly I see that there is a stunning purity in the writing of a book that I cannot achieve in my own life with its frailty and desperation. The work takes over with a life of its own. In those moments, I wouldn't trade writing with all its loneliness and sometimes with its pain, for any other profession in the world.*

PETRAKIS, LEONIDAS, research scientist, educator, administrator; b. Sparta, Greece, July 23, 1935; came to U.S., 1951, naturalized, 1956; s. Lina Contos P.; m. Ismene Lempesis, June 21, 1959; children: Ismene L., Alexis L. BS, Northeastern U., 1958; PhD, U. Calif., Berkeley, 1961. Faculty research grantee Nat. Research Council, Can., 1961-62; prof. chemistry U. Md., College Park, 1962-63; researcher DuPont Co., Wilmington, Del., 1963-65; sr. scientist Gulf-Chevron Research Co., Richmond, Calif., 1965-89; sr. scientist Brookhaven Nat. Lab., Upton, N.Y., 1989—, chmn. dept. applied scis., 1989-94; sr. vis. lectr. Carnegie-Mellon U., Pitts., 1972-73; vis. prof. U. Paris, 1985, 91, 95; adj. prof. U. Pitts., 1981-85; mem. Coun. for Chem. Rsch. Author: Free Radicals in Syn Fuels, 1983, NMR for Liquid Fuels, 1986; editor and author four books on chemistry for fossil energy, 1978, 80, 84, 94; contbr. articles to profl. jours. Mem. environ. com. L.I. Assn.; bd. advisors Barnett Inst., Northeastern U.; mem. Organizing Group and Sci. and Bus. Adv. Bd. for L.I. Rsch. Inst. Advanced Study Inst. rsch. grantee Dept. Energy, Nat. Sci. Found, NATO, Washington, 1979-83. Mem. Am. Chem. Soc. (adv. bd. 1979-83, officer 1974-78, Pitts. award 1984), Am. Phys. Soc.(symposium organizer), AAAS, NSF (grantee, Washington 1981-85, also symposium organizer), Sigma Xi. Office: Brookhaven Nat Lab Dept Of Applied Sci Upton NY 11973 *Technological progress has its downside: complexity, obfuscation, lack of depth, alienation; homo sapiens become homo economicus and now auto-sapiens; quantity become quality, although it is clear enough that more, as in cancer, is not always better; and the wrappings are the package. It is time to take time with the poets and listen to the raindrops, time to read again the myth of the Tower of Babel, and to rediscover the lessons of entropy in everyday life.*

PETRAKIS, NICHOLAS LOUIS, physician, medical researcher, educator; b. San Francisco, Feb. 6, 1922; s. Louis Nicholas and Stamatina (Boosalis) P.; m. Patricia Elizabeth Kelly, June 24, 1947; children: Steven John, Susan Lynn, Sandra Kay. BA, Augustana Coll., 1943; BS in Medicine, U. S.D., 1944; MD, Washington U., St. Louis, 1946. Intern Mpls. Gen. Hosp., 1946-47; physician-researcher U.S. Naval Radiol. Def. Lab., San Francisco, 1947-49; resident physician Mpls. Gen. Hosp., 1949-50; sr. asst. surgeon Nat. Cancer Inst., USPHS, San Francisco, 1950-54; asst. research physician Cancer Research Inst., U. Calif., San Francisco, 1954-56; asst. prof. preventive medicine U. Calif. Sch. Medicine, San Francisco, 1956-60, assoc. prof., 1960-66, prof., 1966-91, chmn. dept. epidemiology and internat. health, 1978-88, prof. emeritus, 1991—; prof. epidemiology U. Calif. Sch. Pub. Health, Berkeley, 1981-91; assoc. dir. G.W. Hooper Edn., U. Calif., San Francisco, 1970-74, acting dir., 1974-77, chmn. dept. epidemiology and internat. health, 1979-89; co-dir. Breast Screening Ctr. of No. Calif., Oakland, 1976-81; cons. Breast Cancer Task Force, Nat. Cancer Inst., Bethesda, Md., 1972-76; chmn. Biometry & Epidemiology Contract Rev. Com., Bethesda, 1977-81; mem. bd. sci. counselors, div. cancer etiology Nat. Cancer Inst., Bethesda, 1982-86; mem. scientific adv. com. Calif. State Tobacco-Related Disease Rsch. Program, 1991-93; cons. U. Crete Sch. Medicine, Heraklion, Greece, 1984; bd. dirs. No. Calif. Cancer Ctr., 1991. Contbr. over 200 research papers on breast cancer, med. oncology and hematology. Eleanor Roosevelt Internat. Cancer fellow Am. Cancer Soc., Comitato Reserche Nucleari, Cassacia, Italy, 1962; U.S. Pub. Health Service Spl. fellow Galton Lab., U. London, 1969-70; recipient Alumni Achievement award Augustana Coll., Sioux Falls, S.D., 1979, Axion award Hellenic-Am. Profl. Soc. of Calif., San Francisco, 1984, Lewis C. Robbins award Soc. for Prospective Medicine, Indpls., 1985. Mem. Am. Soc. Preventive Oncology (founding, pres. 1984-85, Disting. Achievement award 1992), Soc. for Prospective Medicine (founding), Am. Assn. Cancer Rsch., Am. Epidemiol. Soc., Am. Soc. Clin. Investigation, Am. Bd. Preventive Medicine (cert.). Home: 335 Juanita Way San Francisco CA 94127-1657 Office: U Calif Sch Medicine Dept Epidemiology and Biostats 1699 HSW San Francisco CA 94143-0560

PETRALIA, RONALD SEBASTIAN, entomologist, neurobiologist; b. Lawrence, Mass., Nov. 7, 1954; s. Samuel and Rosalie (Zanfagna) P.; B.S. summa cum laude in Entomology, U. Mass., 1975; Ph.D. in Entomology and Biology, Tex. A&M U., 1979. Rsch. asst., 1975-79, rsch. assoc. Tex. A&M U., College Station, 1979-80; asst. prof. biology St. Ambrose Coll., Davenport, Iowa, 1980-85; rsch. fellow dept. anatomy George Washington U., Washington, 1985-90; sr. staff fellow Nat. Inst. for Deafness and Other Comm. Disorders., NIH, Bethesda, Md., 1991—; presenter in field. Co-author: (book chpts. with others) Excitatory Amino Acids, 1992, The Mammalian Cochlear Nuclei: Organization and Function, 1993, Excitatory Amino Acids: Their Role in Neuroendocrine Function, 1995; contbr. articles to profl. jours. Mem. AAAS, Chesapeake Soc. for Microscopy (coun. mem., newsletter editor), Soc. for Neurosci., Entomol. Soc. Am., Microscopy Soc. Am., Assn. Rsch. in Otolaryngology, Cambridge Entomol. Club, Sigma Xi. Roman Catholic. Home: 78 Boston St Methuen MA 01844-5359 Office: NIDCD NIH Bldg 36 Rm 5D08 9000 Rockville Pike Bethesda MD 20892

PETRASH, JEFFREY MICHAEL, lawyer; b. Cleve., Dec. 14, 1948; s. Robert Anthony and Naomi Marjorie (Close) P.; m. Patricia Ann Early, May 29, 1971 (div. Mar. 1986); 1 child, Michael Stewart. AB, U. Mich., 1969, JD, 1973. Bar: Mich. 1974, D.C. 1975. Assoc. Dickinson, Wright, McKean, Cudlip & Moon, Detroit, 1973-75, Hamel, Park, McCabe & Saunders, Washington, 1975-78; from assoc. to ptnr. Dickinson, Wright, Moon, Van Dusen & Freeman, Washington, 1978—. Served to capt. U.S. Army, 1973-74. Mem. Soc. Barristers. Episcopalian. Avocation: sailing. Home: 6606 Hillandale Rd Bethesda MD 20815-6406 Office: Dickinson Wright Moon Van Dusen & Freeman 1901 L St NW Washington DC 20036-3506

PETRE, DONNA MARIE, county judge; b. Joliet, Ill., Apr. 21, 1947; d. James Jacob and Catherine (Hedrick) P.; m. Dennis Michael Styne, Sept. 4, 1971; children: Rachel Catherine, Jonathan James, Juliana Claire, Aaron Coopersmith. BA, Clarke Coll., 1969; MA, Northwestern U., 1971; JD, U. Calif., San Francisco, 1976. Bar: Calif. 1976. Jud. clk. Calif. Ct. Appeals, San Francisco, 1976-77; instr. legal rsch. and writing Hastings Coll. Law, U. Calif., San Francisco, 1976; dep. atty. gen. criminal appeals dept. State of Calif., San Francisco, 1977-80, dep. atty. gen. consumer fraud dept., 1980-83; dep. atty. gen. med. fraud dept. State of Calif., Sacramento, 1983-86; judge Yolo County Mcpl. Ct., Woodland, Calif., 1986-89, Yolo County Superior Ct., 1990—; presiding judge Consolidated Superior/Mcpl. Ct., 1993; adj. prof. trial practice U. Calif., Davis; mem. criminal justice commn. Marin County Bd. Suprs., 1982; mem. adv. com. Jud. Coun. on Adminstrv. Justice in Rural Counties, 1988—; mem. adv. com. on ct. consolidation Judicial Coun. Mng. editor Hastings Constl. Law Quar., 1975-76. Bd. dirs. Woodland Literacy Coun., 1986. Mem. AAUW, Calif. Judges Assn. (mem. commn. on studying problems with driving under influence of alcohol and other drugs), Yolo County Bar Assn., Women Lawyers Calif., Sacramento Women Lawyers, Bus. and Profl. Women (co-chairperson legis. 1986—), Davis C. of C., Woodland C. of C. Republican. Office: Yolo County Superior Ct 725 Court St Woodland CA 95695-3436

PETREE, WILLIAM HORTON, lawyer; b. Winston-Salem, N.C., Nov. 4, 1920; s. Elbert Heaton and Ethel (Tucker) P.; m. Lena Morris, Dec. 23, 1943; children: William Horton Jr., Mary Jo. BS, U. N.C., 1944, JD, 1948. Bar: N.C. 1948. Ptnr. Petree Stockton and predecessors, 1956—; past chmn. local bd. dirs. First Union Nat. Bank, Winston-Salem. Past bd. dirs., mem. exec. com. Old Salem, Inc.; past mem. campaign coordinating com. Forsyth County, N.C.; past chmn. found. com. Winston-Salem Found.; past pres. Forsyth County Tb and Health Assn.; trustee, elder, past bd. dirs. Moravian Home; past chmn. fin. bd. Moravian Ch. in Am., South; past trustee, exec. com. Salem Coll., bd. visitors, 1995—. 1st lt. USMCR, 1944-46. Mem. Forsyth County Bar Assn. (past pres.), Forsyth Country Club (past dir.), Piedmont Club, Kiwanis (bd. dirs. Winston-Salem club, pres. 1976-77), Alpha Tau Omega, Phi Delta Phi. Democrat. Mem. Moravian Ch. Home: 144 Muirfield Dr Winston Salem NC 27104-3949 Office: Petree Stockton 1001 W 4th St Winston Salem NC 27101-2410 *Enthusiasm, coupled with proper motivation, contributes most to a successful, happy and fulfilling life.*

PETREK, WILLIAM JOSEPH, college president emeritus; b. Arcadia, Wis., Feb. 26, 1928; s. Roman Casper and Agnes (Jankowski) P.; m. Sandra Lucille Nash, Nov. 24, 1961; children: Michele, Søren. B.A. cum laude, St. John's U., Minn., 1948; S.T.L. magna cum laude, Gregorian U., Rome, 1952; Ph.D. with great distinction, Higher Inst. Philosophy, U. Louvain, Belgium, 1956; DHumLitt, Richmond Coll., London. Asst. prof. philosophy, chmn. dept. philosophy Holy Cross Coll., La Crosse, Wis., 1956-60; from asst. prof. to prof. philosophy and religion DePauw U., Greencastle, Ind., 1961-71; dir. internat. edn., asst. dean internat. edn. and off-campus programs DePauw U., 1966-71; v.p. Gt. Lakes Colls. Assn., Ann Arbor, Mich., 1971-72; dean Coll. Liberal Arts, Hofstra U., Hempstead, N.Y., 1972-74; provost, dean faculties Hofstra U., 1974-76; acad. v.p. Southeast Mo. State U., Cape Girardeau, 1976-80; pres. Richmond Coll., London, 1980-92. Translator, author: introduction (Jean Nabert) Elements for an Ethic, 1969. Trustee Nassau Higher Edn. Consortium, 1973-76; exec. com. bd. Council Intercultural Studies and Programs, 1974-88; bd. nat. cons. Nat. Endowment Humanities, 1974—; bd. dirs. World Univ. Service, 1976-80; mem. Ct. Govs. Mill Hill Sch., London, 1989-94. Danforth asso., 1964; recipient Best Prof. award DePauw U., 1965; Ford Found. humanities grantee, 1970; Gt. Lakes Colls. Assn. Non-Western research grantee, 1965; hon. fellow Inst. Am. Univs., Aix-en-Provence, France, 1973. Mem. Soc. Phenomenology and Existential Philosophy, Assn. Internat. Colls. and Univs. (pres. 1984-89). Office: Richmond Coll, Queens Rd Richmond, Surrey TW10 6JP, England

PETREQUIN, HARRY JOSEPH, JR., foreign service officer; b. Ste. Genevieve, Mo., July 1, 1929; s. Harry Joseph and Crescentia Ellen (Bechter) P.; m. Katharine McDonnell Drouin, Oct. 7, 1980; children: John Andrew, Marc Christopher, Paul Nicholas. AB, Westminster Coll., 1950; B of Fgn. Trade, Am. Grad. Sch. Internat. Mgmt., 1954; postgrad., Johns Hopkins U., 1960; MA, Tufts U., 1970. Joined U.S. Fgn. Svc., 1955; assigned AID and predecessor agys., 1955—; dep. dir. S.E. Asia Regional Econ. Devel. Office, Thailand, 1970-74; U.S. coord. Senegal River Basin Authority, Dakar, 1975-76; dir. ASEAN and South Pacific Affairs, 1977-80; dir. program devel. and evaluation staff Bur. Internat. Orgn. Affairs State Dept., 1980-81; dep. dir. AID Mission, Morocco, 1981-85; coord. AID Sr. Mgmt. Course, 1985-86, Indsl. Coll. of the Armed Forces, 1986-87; faculty dept. nat. security policy Nat. War Coll., Washington, 1987-89; internat. devel. cons. Black Mountain, N.C., 1989—; adj. prof. polit. sci. Warren Wilson Coll., Swannanoa, N.C., 1993—. Lt. (j.g.) USCGR, 1951-53, comdr. Res. Recipient Superior Honor award AID, 1979, State Dept. Superior Honor award, 1981, Comdrs. award for Civilian Svc., Dept. of the Army, 1989. Mem. Soc. Internt. Devel., World Federalist Assn. (nat. bd. dirs.), Am. Fgn. Svc. Assn., UN Assn. U.S., Acad. Polit. Sci., Cousteau Soc., Common Cause, Inst. Noetic Scis., World Future Soc., Amnesty Internat., Coast Guard Combat Vets Assn., Greenpeace, Vets. for Peace, The Land Inst., Phi Alpha Theta.

PETRI, PETER ALEXANDER, economist, educator, director; b. Budapest, Hungary, Oct. 17, 1946; came to U.S., 1959; s. George and Margaret (Fejer) P.; m. Jean H. Lawrence, June 19, 1976; children: Philip, Nicholas. BA, Harvard U., 1968, PhD, 1976. Prof. of Econ. Brandeis U., Waltham, Mass., 1974—; dean Grad. Sch. Internat. Econs. and Fin., Waltham, Mass., 1994—; dir. Lemberg Prog. in Internat. Econ. & Fin., Brandeis U., Waltham, 1986-94; Carl Shapiro prof. of internat. fin. Brandeis U., Waltham, 1989—; Fulbright rsch. scholar Keio U., Tokyo, 1991; cons. World Bank, Washington. Author: The Future of the World Economoy, 1977, Modeling Japanese-American Trade, 1984, East Asia's Trade and Investment, 1994; editor: Wassily Leontief, 1982, The Economics of the Dollar Cycle, 1990, Jour. of Asian Econs., Singapore Econ. Rev. Grantee Study of Japanese Trade, U.S. State Dept., 1980, Study of U.S. Social Security, Social Security Adminstrn., 1982-83, Internat. Bus. Edn., U.S. Dept. Edn., 1989, 92, 94, Ctr. for Global Partnership, 1995—, NSF, 1995; Econ. Policy fellow Brookings Inst., 1979. Mem. Am. Econ. Assn., Acad. Internat. Bus. Office: Grad Sch Internat Econs & Fin Brandeis U Waltham MA 02254

PETRI, THOMAS EVERT, congressman; b. Marinette, Wis., May 28, 1940; s. Robert and Marian (Humleker) P.; m. Anne Neal, Mar. 26, 1983; 1 child, Alexandra. BA in Govt., Harvard U., 1962, JD, 1965. Bar: Wis. 1965. Law clk. to presiding justice U.S. Dist. (we. dist.) Wis., Madison, 1965-66; vol. Peace Corps, Somalia, 1966-67; aide White House, Washington, 1969-70; dir. crime and drug studies Pres.'s Nat. Adv. Coun. on Exec. Orgn., 1969; pvt. practice Fond du Lac, Wis., 1970-79; mem. Wis. State Senate, Madison, 1973-79, 96th-104th Congress from 6th Wis. Dist., Washington, 1979—. Editor: National Industrial Policy: Solution or Illusion, 1984. Republican. Lutheran. Avocations: reading, swimming, hiking, biking, skiing. Office: US Ho of Reps 2262 Rayburn Bldg Washington DC 20515-0005

PETRICK, ALFRED, JR., mineral economics educator, consultant; b. Mt. Vernon, N.Y., Dec. 30, 1926; s. Alfred and Ruth (Updike) P.; m. Ruth Goodridge, Jan. 2, 1956; children: Elizabeth, Andrew Wayne. B.S., B.A., Columbia U., 1952, M.S., 1962; M.B.A., Denver U., 1966; Ph.D., U. Colo., 1969. Registered profl. engr., Colo. Sales engr. Ingersoll Rand Co., N.Y.C., 1953-54; project engr. U.S. AEC, Grand Junction, Colo., 1954-57; mining engr. Reynolds Metals Co., Bauxite, Ark., 1957-61, Guyana, 1957-61; mineral economist U.S. Bur. Mines, Denver, 1963-70; Coulter prof. Colo. Sch. Mines, Golden, 1970-84, emeritus prof., 1984—; dir. Petrick Assocs., Evergreen, Colo. Author: Economics International Development, 1977, Economics of Minerals, 1980, Preparacion y Evaluacion, 1982. Mem. com. tech. aspects strategic materials Nat. Acad. Sci., Washington, 1973-76, mem. com. surface mining and reclamation, 1979. Served with USAF, 1945-47, PTO. Fulbright research scholar U. Otago, Dunedin, New Zealand, 1986; recipient Edn. award Instituto Para Funcionarios De Las Industrias Minera y Siderurgica, Mexico City, 1981; recipient Service award Office Tech. Assessment, U.S. Congress, 1981. Mem. AIME (chmn. council econs. 1977-78, Henry Krumb lectr. 1986, service award), Profl. Engrs. Colo. Presbyterian. Home: 5544 S Hatch Dr Evergreen CO 80439-7233 Office: Colo Sch Mines Golden CO 80401

PETRICK, ERNEST NICHOLAS, mechanical engineer; b. Pa., Apr. 9, 1922; s. Aurelius and Anna (Kaschak) P.; m. Magdalene Simcoe, June 13, 1946; children: Deborah Petrick Healey, Katherine, Denise, Victoria Ann Petrick Kropp. B.S. in Mech. Engring, Carnegie Inst. Tech., 1943; M.S., Purdue U., 1948, Ph.D., 1955. Registered profl. engr., Mich. Faculty Purdue U., 1946-53; dir. heat transfer research Curtiss-Wright Corp., Woodridge, N.J., 1953-56; chief advanced propulson systems Curtiss-Wright Research divsn., Quehanna, Pa., 1957-60; chief research engr. Kelsey-Hayes Co., Detroit, 1960-65; chief scientist, tech. dir. U.S. Army Tank-Automotive Command, Warren, Mich., 1965-82; chief scientist, dir. engring. labs. Gen. Dynamics, 1982-87; engring. cons., 1987—; adj. prof. engring. Wayne State U., U. Mich.; panel mem. combat vehicles NATO, 1973-82; mem. adv. bd. on basic combustion research NSF, 1973; chmn. advanced transp. systems com. White House Energy Project, 1973; mem. vis. adv. com. NSF-RANN research program Drexel U. Coll. Engring., 1976-78; mem. Army Sci. Bd., 1983-89; cons. Air Force Studies Bd. NRC, 1991-93, cons. Def. Sci. Bd., 1994-95. Contbr. articles on transp., ground vehicles, flight propulsion and project mgmt. to profl. jours. Mem. adv. bd. Wayne State U. Engring., Detroit. Served to lt. USN, 1942-46; to lt. comdr. USNR, 1946-54. Recipient certificate of achievement U.S. Army, 1967, Outstanding Performance awards, 1970, 71, 76, 82, Outstanding Mech. Engring. award Purdue U., 1991; named Disting. Engring. Alumnus Purdue U., 1966. Mem. Soc. Automotive Engrs. (nat. dir. 1978-80), Am. Def. Preparedness Assn. (chmn. land warfare survivability divsn. 1990-95, Silver medal 1992), Assn. U.S. Army, Sigma Xi, Pi Tau Sigma. Home: 1540 Stonehaven Rd Ann Arbor MI 48104-4150

PETRICOFF, M. HOWARD, lawyer, educator; b. Cin., Dec. 22, 1949; s. Herman and Neoma P.; m. Hanna Sue, Aug. 11, 1974; children: Nicholas, Eve. BS, Am. U., 1967-71; JD, U. Cin., 1971-74; M in Pub. Adminstrn., Harvard U., 1980-81. Bar: Ohio, U.S. Ct. Appeals (D.C. cir.) 1977, U.S. Ct. Appeals (10th cir.) 1985, U.S. Ct. Appeals (6th cir.) 1989, U.S. Supreme Ct. 1989. Asst. city law dir. City of Toledo (Ohio), 1975-77; asst. atty. gen. Ohio Atty. Gen. Office, Columbus, 1977-82; ptnr. Vorys, Sater, Seymour & Pease, Columbus, 1982—; adj. prof. law Capital U. Law Sch., Columbus, 1991—. Contbr. articles to profl. jours. Reginald Heber Smith Found. fellow Washington, 1974-75. Mem. Ohio Bar Assn., Columbus Bar Assn., Ohio Oil and Gas Assn. Office: Vorys Sater Seymour & Pease PO Box 1008 52 E Gay St Columbus OH 43215-3161

PETRIDES, GEORGE ATHAN, ecologist, educator; b. N.Y.C., Aug. 1, 1916; s. George Athan and Grace Emeline (Ladd) P.; m. Miriam Clarissa Pasma, Nov. 30, 1940; children: George H., Olivia L., Lisa B. B.S., George Washington U., 1938; M.S., Cornell U., 1940; Ph.D., Ohio State U., 1948; postdoctoral fellow, U. Ga., 1963-64. Naturalist Nat. Park Service, Washington and Yosemite, Calif., 1938-43, Glacier Nat. Park, Mont., 1947, Mt. McKinley Nat. Park, Alaska, 1959; game technician W.Va. Conservation Commn., Charleston, 1941; instr. Am. U., 1942-43, Ohio State U., 1946-48; leader Tex. Coop. Wildlife Unit; assoc. prof. wildlife mgmt. Tex. A. and M. Coll., 1948-50; assoc. prof. wildlife mgmt., zool. and African studies Mich. State U., 1950-58, prof., 1958—; research prof. U. Pretoria, S. Africa, 1965; vis. prof. U. Kiel, Germany, 1967; vis. prof. wildlife mgmt. Kanha Nat. Park, India, 1983; del. sci. confs. Warsaw, 1960, Nairobi and Salisbury, 1963, Sao Paulo, Aberdeen, 1965, Lucerne, 1966, Varanasi, India, Nairobi, 1967, Oxford, Eng., Paris, 1968, Durban, 1971, Mexico City, 1971, 73, Banff, 1972,

Nairobi, Moscow, The Hague, 1974, Johannesburg, 1977, Sydney, 1978, Kuala Lumpur, 1979, Cairns, Australia, Mogadishu, Somalia, Peshawar, Pakistan, 1980; participant NSF Expdn., Antarctic, 1972, FAO mission to, Afghanistan, 1972, World Bank mission to, Malaysia, 1975. Author: Field Guide to Trees and Shrubs, 1958, 2d edit., 1972, Field Guide to Eastern Trees, 1988, Field Guide to Western Trees, 1992, First Guide to Trees, 1993, Trees of the California Sierra Nevada, 1996; Editor wildlife mgmt. terrestial sect.: Biol. Abstracts, 1947-72; Contbr. articles to biol. publs. Served to lt. USNR, 1943-46. Fulbright research awards in E. Africa Nat. Parks Kenya, 1953-54; Fulbright research awards in E. Africa Nat. Parks Kenya, Uganda, 1956-57; N.Y. Zool. Soc. grantee Ethiopia, Sudan, 1957; N.Y. Zool. Soc. grantee Thailand, 1977; Mich. State U. grantee Nigeria, 1962; Mich. State U. grantee Zambia, 1966; Mich. State U. grantee Kenya, 1969; Mich. State U. grantee Africa, 1970, 71, 73, 81; Mich. State U. grantee Greece, 1974, 83; Mich. State U. grantee Iran, 1974; Mich. State U. grantee Botswana, 1977; Mich. State U. grantee Papua New Guinea, Thailand, 1979; Iran Dept. Environment grantee, 1977; Smithsonian Instn. grantee India and Nepal, 1967, 68, 75, 77, 83, 85; World Wildlife Fund grantee W. Africa, 1968. Mem. Am. Ornithologists Union, Am. Soc. Mammalogists, Wildlife Soc. (exec. sec. 1953), Wilderness Soc., Am. Comm. Internat. Wildlife Protection, Ecol. Soc., Fauna Preservation Soc., E. African Wildlife Soc., Internat. Union Conservation Nature, Zool. Soc. So. Africa, Sigma Xi. Presbyterian. Home: 4895 Barton Rd Williamston MI 48895-9649 Office: Mich State U Dept Fisheries And Wil East Lansing MI 48824

PETRIE, DANIEL MANNIX, film, theatre and television director; b. Glace Bay, N.S., Can., Nov. 26, 1920; came to U.S., 1945; s. William Mark and Mary (Campbell) P.; m. Dorothea Grundy, Oct. 27, 1946; children: Daniel Mannix, Donald Mark, Mary Susan and June Anne (twins). BA, St. Francis Xavier U., Antigonish, N.S., 1942, LittD (hon.), 1974; MA, Columbia U., 1945; postgrad., Northwestern U., 1947-48; LittD (hon.), St. Francis Xavier U.; LLD (hon.), U. Coll. Cape Breton. chmn. Ctr. for Advanced Film and TV Studies Am. Film Inst. Broadway actor, 1945-46, TV dir., 1950—; TV shows include Eleanor and Franklin, ABC, 1976 (Outstanding Drama award 1976, Emmy award 1976, Critics Circle award 1976, Peabody award 1976), Harry Truman Plain Speaking, Pub. Broadcasting Sta., 1976 (Emmy nomination), Sybil, NBC, 1976 (Emmy award for Outstanding Spl. 1977, Peabody award 1976), Eleanor and Franklin: The White House Years, ABC, 1977 (Emmy award, Dirs. Guild award), Silent Night, Lonely Night, 1969, The Quinns, 1977, The Dollmaker, 1984 (Emmy nomination), The Execution of Raymond Graham, 1985 (Emmy nomination), Half a Lifetime, 1986 (Cable award), film My Name is Bill W. (Emmy and Golden Globe nominations), 1989, (also prodr.) Mark Twain and Me (Emmy award), 1991, A Town Torn Apart (Emmy nomination), 1992; dir. films including. Served as lt. Canadian Army, 1942. Recipient Humanitas award Cannes, DGA award, Christopher award, 1958, 84, 89, 92. Mem. Acad. Motion Picture Arts and Scis., Dir.'s Guild Am. (1st v.p. 1981-95), Am. Film Inst. (chmn.), Acad. TV Arts. Office: care Creative Artists Agy 9830 Wilshire Blvd Beverly Hills CA 90212-1804

PETRIE, DONALD ARCHIBALD, lawyer, investment banker, publisher; b. Charleston, W.Va., Apr. 27, 1921; s. James MacFarlin and Emma (Leunig) P.; m. Ruth Elfrieda Hauser, June 28, 1942 (div. 1971); children: Ann Elizabeth Sauter, James MacFarlin; m. Elizabeth M. Greenfield, Sept. 12, 1973 (div. 1995); m. Mary S. Cook, Dec. 29, 1995. B.A., U. Chgo., 1942, J.D., 1947. Bar: Ill. 1947, N.Y. 1961, D.C. 1970. Partner D'Ancona, Pflaum, Wyatt & Riskind, Chgo., 1947-55; v.p. Hertz Corp., 1955-59, exec. v.p., dir., 1959-60; pres. Hertz Am. Express Internat., Ltd., 1960-61; chmn. exec. com. Avis Rent A Car, 1962-66; ptnr. Lazard Freres & Co., N.Y.C., 1967-71, 78—; of counsel Courdert Bros., Washington, 1973-74; pub. Washington Monitor, 1975-77; chmn., CEO Harper's Mag., 1982-83; chmn. Leadership Directories, Inc. Treas. Democratic Nat. Com., 1972. Mem. Century Assn., Univ. Club. Unitarian.

PETRIE, DONALD JOSEPH, banker; b. N.Y.C., Sept. 2, 1921; s. John and Elizabeth (Thomson) P.; m. Jane Adams, Aug. 27, 1949; children: R. Scott, Anne, Elizabeth, Douglas, Susan. B.B.A., Manhattan Coll., 1950. Personnel mgr. Otis Elevator Co., N.Y.C., 1951-59; personnel dir. Brown Bros. Harriman & Co., N.Y.C., 1959-68; exec. v.p. U.S. Trust Co., N.Y.C., 1968-79; sr. v.p. Marine Midland Bank, N.Y.C., 1979-86, Drake Beam Morin Inc., N.Y.C., 1986-90; chmn., chief exec. officer Webster Corp., N.Y.C., 1990—; lectr. Baruch Sch. Bus., Coll. City N.Y., 1955-58; pres., chmn. exec. and fin. coms., dir. Webster Apts., N.Y.C., 1973—; adj. prof. mgmt. Hofstra U., Hempstead, N.Y., 1986-93. Author: Explaining Pay Policy, 1969, Handling Employee Questions About Pay, 1976. Capt. USAAF, 1942-46. Mem. N.Y. Chamber Commerce and Industry (chmn. mgmt. edn. and adv. com. 1964—). Home: 11 Fairview Ave Great Neck NY 11023-1462 Office: 419 W 34th St New York NY 10001-1596

PETRIE, FERDINAND RALPH, illustrator, artist; b. Hackensack, N.J., Sept. 17, 1925; s. Archibald John and Bessie (Rutherford) P.; m. Phyllis C. Haddow, Oct. 19, 1951; children: Beth, David. Advt. cert., Parson's Sch. Design, N.Y.C., 1949; student, Art Students League, 1947-49, Famous Artists Course in Illustration, 1958-59. Illustrator J. Gans Assos., N.Y.C., 1950-69. Free lance illustrator, artist, 1969—, owner, Petrie Gallery, Rockport, Mass., 1971-95; represented in permanent collections, U.S. Supreme Ct., Smithsonian Instn., Washington, Indpls. Mus. Art; designer U.S. commemorative stamp design, 2 Zaire commemorative stamps, 1980; Author: Drawing Landscapes in Pencil, 1979; illustrator: The Drawing Book, 1980, The Color Book, 1981, The Alkyd Book, 1982, The Watercolorists Guide to Painting Trees, 1983, The Watercolorists Guide to Painting Skies, 1984; The Watercolorists Guide to Painting Water, 1985, Painting Nature in Watercolor, 1990. Served with U.S. Maritime Service, 1943-46. Mem. Artists Fellowship, Rockport Art Assn., Am. Artists Profl. League, N.J. Watercolor Soc. Presbyterian. Address: 51 Vreeland Ave Rutherford NJ 07070-2227

PETRIE, GEOFF, professional basketball team executive. Grad., Princeton U., 1970. Guard Portland Trail Blazers, 1970-76, exec., 1976-93; v.p. basketball ops. Sacramento Kings, 1994—. Named NBA Rookie of the Yr., 1970; selected to NBA All-Star Team, 1971, 74. Avocations: working out, golfing. Office: Sacramento Kings One Sports Parkway Sacramento CA 95834*

PETRIE, GREGORY STEVEN, lawyer; b. Seattle, Feb. 25, 1951; s. George C. and Pauline (Majers) P.; m. Margaret Fuhrman, Oct. 6, 1979; children: Kathryn Jean, Thomas George. AB in Polit. Sci and Econs., UCLA, 1973; JD, Boston U., 1976. Bar: Wash. 1976, U.S. Dist. Ct. (we. dist.) Wash. 1976. Adminstr. Action/Peace Corps, Washington, 1973, Fed. Power Commn., Washington, 1974; assoc. Oles Morrison et al, Seattle, 1976-80; ptnr. Schwabe Williamson Ferguson & Burdell, Seattle, 1981-94; of counsel Krutch, Lindell, Housh, Bingham, Keller & Jones, Seattle, 1994—. Mem. ABA, Seattle-King County Bar Assn., Profl. Liability Architects and Engrs. Club: Washington Athletic (Seattle). Avocations: woodworking, skiing. Office: Krutch Lindell Housh Bingham Keller & Jones 1201 3rd Ave # 3100 Seattle WA 98101

PETRIE, HUGH GILBERT, university dean, philosophy of education educator; b. Lamar, Colo., Sept. 21, 1937; s. Charles Albert and Mary Madeleine (Ocsay) P.; m. Patricia Donahoe Bradasich, June 3, 1959 (div. 1978); children: Trent Anthony, Ragan Andrea, Brock Asher; m. Carol Ann Hodges, Aug. 26, 1978; stepchildren: Lara Wardrop, Amy Wardrop. BS in Bus., BS in Applied Math., U. Colo., 1960; Phd in Philosophy, Stanford U., 1965. Asst. prof. Northwestern U., Evanston, Ill., 1965-71; assoc. prof. U. Ill., Champaign/Urbana, 1971-75, prof., 1975-81, assoc. vice chancellor for academic affairs, 1977-80; dean Grad. Sch. Edn. SUNY, Buffalo, 1981—; coord. N.E. region Holmes Group, 1986-90, bd. dirs.; mem. bd. overseers N.E. Regional Lab., 1986-92, chmn., 1986-87; co-chmn. N.Y. State Task Force on Preparation and Licensure Sch. Adminstrs., 1988-89; mem. N.Y. State Spl. Commn. on Edn., Structure, Policies, and Practices, 1993; bd. dirs. Orgn. Internat. Affiliates, Am. Edn. Rsch. Assn., 1991-93; pres. Tchr. Edn. Conf. Bd., N.Y., 1991-95. Author: The Dilemma of Enquiry and Learning, 1981; editor jour. Ednl. Theory, 1980-81; founding mem. bd. editors jour. Ednl. Policy, 1986—; contbr. numerous articles to profl. jours. Mem. commn. on teaching Nat. Assn. State Univs. and Land Grant Colls., 1988-92. Resident assoc. Ctr. for Advanced Study, U. Ill., 1980-81. Fellow Philosophy of Edn. Soc. (pres. 1984-85, mem. exec. com. 1974-76, 82-83); mem. Am. Ednl. Rsch. Assn., Am. Philos. Assn. Office: SUNY 367 Baldy Hall Buffalo NY 14260

PETRIE, MICHAEL JEROME, clergyman; b. New Holstein, Wis., Apr. 17, 1960; s. Francis Joseph and Cecilia Helen (Baus) P. MDiv, St. Francis Sem., Milw., 1987. Ordained priest Roman Cath. Ch., 1987. Mem. pastoral team St. Alphonsus Congregation, Greendale, Wis., 1987-92; assoc. pastor Mary Queen of Heaven Congregation, West Allis, Wis., 1992-94; pastor St. Kilian Congregation, Hartford, Wis., 1994—; mem. Meth.-Cath. Dialogue, Milw., 1988—. Mem. Kettle Moraine Chorus, 1995—. Mem. Sheboygan County Hist. Rsch. Ctr., We Believe, Rotary. Democrat. Avocations: music, local history, genealogy, hiking. Office: St Kilian Congregation 264 W State St Hartford WI 53027

PETRIE, MILTON J., retail company executive; b. 1902. With JL Hudson Co., 1923-27; sales mgr. Bernard and Schwartz Cigar Co.; with Red Robin Hosiery Shops, 1927; chmn., pres., chief exec. officer Petrie Stores Corp., Seacuacus, N.J., 1932-94. Died Nov. 6, 1994.

PETRIE, WILLIAM, physicist; b. Victoria, B.C., Can., Dec. 30, 1912; s. James and Amelia (Robertson) P.; m. Isabelle Ruth Chodat, May 8, 1944; children: Heather Louise (dec.), Douglas Bruce. B.A., U. B.C., Vancouver, Can., 1938; A.M., Harvard U., 1941, Ph.D., 1944. Assoc. prof. U. Sask., Saskatoon, Can., 1945-51; chief ops. research Def. Research Bd., Ottawa, Ont., Can., 1954-60, dep. chmn., 1966-68; chief Can. def. research staff Def. Research Bd., London, 1968-71; sci. advisor Apollo Energy, Victoria, 1981-83; mem. numerous sci. bds. and coms. Author: The Story of the Aurora Borealis, 1963, Guide to Orchids of North America, 1981; also numerous articles. Recipient Centennial medal Govt. of Can., 1967, numerous research grants and contracts. Fellow Royal Soc. Can. Avocations: gardening; fishing. Home: 52-1255 Wain Rd, Rural Rt 4, Sidney, BC Canada V8L 4R4

PETRILLO, ANTHONY R., grocery store executive. Pres., chief operating officer Mayfair Supermarkets Inc., Elizabeth, N.J., also bd. dirs. Office: Kash N Karry Food Stores Inc 6422 Harney Rd Tampa FL 33610

PETRILLO, CARL EDWARD, construction company executive; b. Mount Vernon, N.Y., Nov. 14, 1940; s. Edward Joseph and Mary Helene (Pagliaro) P.; m. Kathryn Mary Smith, Aug. 28, 1965 (div. Dec. 1977); children—Carl Edward, Christina Elizabeth, Gregory Joseph; m. Dian A. Tomassetti, Nov. 24, 1979; 1 child Mathew John. Degree in Bus. Adminstrn., Lehigh U., 1962. Project engr. Yonkers Contracting Co., N.Y., 1964-68, supt., 1968-70, asst. to v.p., 1970-72, v.p., 1972-78, pres., 1978—; pres. Petmar Builders Co., Yonkers, 1973—; chmn., trustee Internat. Brotherhood Teamsters and Chauffers Union; mem. Pres.' Forum Constrn. Industry, 1987—. Mem. Anti-Defamation League, chmn. disting. communtiy svc. award dinner of Westchester, Putnam and Rockland Counties., N.Y., 1992, Nat. Conf. Christians and Jews, vice chmn., 1991, Am. Jewish Com., co-chmn. community svc. dinner Westchester chpt., 1992, Pvt. Industry Council, Yonkers, 1983—, Indsl. Devel. Agy., Yonkers, 1983—; bd. dirs. St. Joseph's Med. Ctr., Yonkers, Westchester County Assn., White Plains, N.Y., Am. Diabetes Assn., White Plains, Westchester-Putnam Affirmative Action Program; mem. pres.' adv. coun. Westchester Med. Ctr., 1988—; mem. Cardinal's com. laity for Most Rev. John J. O'Connor, Archbishop of N.Y. Recipient Westchester Leadership award Am. Diabetes Assn., 1984, Man of Yr. award Dominican Coll. of Blauvelt, Orangeburg, N.Y., 1985; honored by Yonkers C. of C., 1984, Westchester chpt. NCCJ for disting. svcs. in advancement of human rels., 1989; award Pvt. Sector, Westchester Minority Contractors Assn., 1984, Outstanding Svc. award St. Joseph's Med. Ctr., Yonkers, 1987, Good Scout award Boy Scouts of Am., 1990, Humanitarian award Boys Town of Italy, 1991. Mem. Moles, Gen. Contractors Assn., Yonkers C. of C. (bd. dirs. 1986). Roman Catholic. Avocations: tennis; boating; reading; photography. Office: Yonkers Contracting Co Inc PO Box 39 969 Midland Ave Yonkers NY 10704

PETRILLO, LEONARD PHILIP, corporate securities executive, lawyer; b. Toronto, June 20, 1941; s. Philip Ralph and Bernice (Kowalski) P.; children: Larissa, Matthew. BSc, U. Toronto, 1964; LLB, Osgoode Hall Law Sch., Toronto, 1967. Bar: Ont. 1969. Ptnr. Robinson & Petrillo, 1969-79; corp. counsel Seel Enterprises Ltd., 1979-81; gen. counsel Toronto Stock Exch., 1981, corp. sec., sec. to bd. govs., 1984, v.p., 1985, v.p., corp. affairs, gen. counsel, sec., 1988—. Office: Toronto Stock Exch, 2 First Canadian Pl, Toronto, ON Canada M5X 1J2

PETRIN, HELEN FITE, lawyer, consultant; b. Bklyn., June 22, 1940; d. Clyde David and Connie Marie Keaton; m. Michael Richard Petrin, June 29, 1963; children: Jennifer Lee, Michael James, Daniel John. BS, Rider Coll. (now Rider U.), 1962, MA, 1980; postgrad., Glassboro (N.J.) Coll. (now Rowan Coll.), 1981; JD, Widener U., 1987. Bar: Pa. 1989, N.J. 1990, U.S. Dist. N.J. 1990. Tchr. bus. edn. Pennsville (N.J.) Meml. High Sch., 1962-66; asst. prof. Salem Community Coll., Carney's Point, N.J., 1977-81; asst. prof. Brandywine Coll. Widener U., Wilmington, Del., 1981-87, asst. prof., adminstr., dir. paralegal program, 1987-88; dir. continuing legal edn. Widener U. Sch. Law, Brandywine, 1987-88; pvt. practice computer cons. Phila., N.J. and Del., Del., Pa., N.J., 1988—; pvt. practice law Salem, N.J., 1989—; prosecutor Pilesgrove Township, N.J., 1990-91; dep. surrogate Salem County, N.J., 1991—; word processing cons. New Castle County (Del.) Pers. Dept., 1983; mem. dist. I ethics com. N.J. Supreme Ct., 1993—; instr. N.J. Inst. for CLE, 1995—. Pres. bd. Salem County YMCA, 1983, bd. dirs., 1980—; dir. mediator Salem County YMCA Mediation Svcs., 1995—; col. atty. Phila. Vols. for Indigent Program, 1990-95, Camden Legal Svcs., Inc. for Salem County, 1990—; bd. dirs. United Way Salem County, 1991—, treas., 1994-95; bd. dirs. United Ways of Pa. & N.J., 1994—; mem. III com. (Home Ownership and Opportunity for People Everywhere) HOPE, Salem, N.J., 1992—. Mem. ABA (chmn. young lawyers econs. com. 1990-93, vice chmn. mktg. legal svcs. com. gen. practice sect. 1993—), ATLA, N.J. Bar Assn. (exec. com. 1990-93), Pa. Bar Assn., Phila. Bar Assn. (probate adv. panel 1992-94), Salem County Bar Assn. (treas. 1991-92, sec. 1992-93, v.p., pres.-elect 1993-94, pres. 1994-95, dir. of Salem County, N.J. YMCA Family Ct. Mediation program 1995—), Delta Pi Epsilon (sec. bd. dirs. 1980-82). Avocations: swimming, music, walking, reading. Home: 99 Marlton Rd Woodstown NJ 08098-1260 Office: 51 Market St Salem NJ 08079-1909

PETRINA, ANTHONY J., mining executive, retired. Formerly sr. v.p., chief oper. officer Placer Devel. Ltd., Vancouver, B.C., Can., exec. v.p., chief oper. officer, until 1988, pres., chief exec. officer, 1988-93; ret., 1993; bd. dirs. Miramar Mining Corp., Vancouver, Arequipa Resources Ltd., Vancouver, Metall. Mining Corp. (now Inmet Mining Corp.), Toronto, Pegasus Gold Corp., Vancouver, Wajax Inc., Vancouver. Mem. Mining Assn. B.C. (bd. dirs.), Mining Assn. Can. (past chmn.). Office: 8 Sunset Beach, West Vancouver, BC Canada V7W 1R8

PETRINOVICH, LEWIS F., psychology educator; b. Wallace, Idaho, June 12, 1930; s. John F. and Ollie (Steward) P. BS, U. Idaho, 1952; PhD, U. Calif., Berkeley, 1962. Asst. prof. San Francisco State Coll., 1957-63; from assoc. to prof. SUNY, Stony Brook, 1963-68; prof. U. Calif., Riverside, 1968-91, chmn. psychology, 1968-71, 86-89, prof. emeritus, 1991—. Author: Understanding Research in Social Sciences, 1975, Introduction to Statistics, 1976, Human Evolution, Reproduction and Mortality, 1995, Living and Dying Well, 1996; editor: Behavioral Development, 1981, Habituation, Sensitization and Behavior, 1984; cons. editor Behavioral and Neural Biology, 1972-90, Jour. Physiol. and Comparative Psychology, 1980-82, Jour. Comparative Psychology, 1983-90. Fellow Am. Psychol. Assn., Am. Psychol. Soc., Calif. Acad. Scis., Human Behavior and Evolution Soc., Western Psychol. Assn.; mem. Am. Ornithological Union (elected), Animal Behavior Soc., Sigma Xi. Home: 415 Boynton Ave Berkeley CA 94707 Office: U Calif Riverside Dept of Psychology Riverside CA 92521

PETROCELLI, ANTHONY JOSEPH, management executive, consultant; b. Bklyn., Sept. 25, 1937; s. Lucio and Carmela (Carrione) P.; m. Antoinette Cassata, May 25, 1963; 1 child, Serena Ann. BS in Mgmt., Fairleigh Dickinson, Madison, N.J., 1969, MBA, 1972. Pres. Met. Consolidated Inc., N.Y.C., 1978-84; pvt. practice mgmt. cons., 1984-88; ptnr., mng. dir. D. George Harris & Assocs., N.Y.C., 1984—, vice chmn., 1989—; vice chmn. Salt Union Ltd., U.K., 1992—, Societa Chimica Larderello SpA, Italy, 1993—, Harris Chem. Group, 1993—, Harris Specialty Chemicals, Inc., 1994—, Matthes & Weber GmbH, Germany, 1994—. Trustee Italian Am. Club, North Brunswick, N.J. With U.S. Army, 1956-58, Germany. Office: D George Harris & Assocs 399 Park Ave New York NY 10022-4614*

PETRONI, DONALD VICTOR, lawyer; b. Reno, Nev., Apr. 22, 1931; s. Victor and Mary (Ceresola) P.; m. Abby Williams Richmond, June 16, 1956 (div. 1973); children: Victor, Lisa; m. Ann Gelston King, Sept. 7, 1973; stepchildren: Chisholm, Pamela, Samuel, Michael Halle. B.A., U. Nev., 1952; postgrad., Stanford U., 1953, J.D., 1958. Bar: Calif. 1959. Assoc. firm O'Melveny & Myers, Los Angeles, 1958-65; ptnr. O'Melveny & Myers, 1965—. Served with U.S. Army, 1953-55. Mem. ABA, Calif. Bar Assn., Los Angeles County Bar Assn. Democrat. Club: Regency. Home: 10770 Chalon Rd Los Angeles CA 90077-3315 Office: O'Melveny & Myers 1999 Avenue Of The Stars Los Angeles CA 90067-6022 also: O'Melveny & Myers 400 S Hope St Los Angeles CA 90071-2801

PETROS, RAYMOND LOUIS, JR., lawyer; b. Pueblo, Colo., Sept. 19, 1950. BS, Colo. Coll., 1972; JD, U. Colo., 1975. Bar: Colo. 1975. Jud. clk. to Justice Paul V. Hodges Colo. Supreme Ct., Denver, 1975-77; assoc. Bermingham, White, Burke & Ipsen, Denver, 1977-78; from assoc. to ptnr. Hall & Evans, Denver, 1978-81; ptnr. Kirkland & Ellis, Denver, 1981-86; mem. Holme, Roberts & Owen, Denver, 1986-96, Petros & White, LLC, 1996—. Contbr. articles to profl. jours. Bd. dirs. Rocky Mountain Poison Control Found., Denver, 1988-94. Office: Petros & White LLC Ste 820 730 Seventeenth St Denver CO 80202-3518

PETROSIAN, VAHÉ, astrophysicist, educator; b. Arak, Iran, Sept. 13, 1938; came to U.S., 1958; s. Armenak and Chnarik (Beglarian) P.; m. Maude Denney Voegeli, Aug. 21, 1965 (div. 1992); children: Gabrielle Elane, Meline Chnar. B.E.E., Cornell U., 1962, M.S., 1963, Ph.D., 1967. Research fellow Calif. Inst. Tech., Pasadena, Calif., 1967-69; vis. scientist Inst. Theoretical Astronomy, Cambridge, Eng., summer 1969; asst.prof. Stanford U., (Calif.), 1969-71; assoc. prof. Stanford U., 1972-79, prof., 1980—, chmn. astronomy program; vis. cons. Kitt Peak Nat. Obs., Tucson. Alfred P. Sloan fellow, 1972-74; NASA grantee, 1983; NSF grantee, 1983. Fellow Royal Astron. Soc.; mem. Internat. Astron. Union, Am. Astron. Soc., U.S. Volleyball Assn. Home: 4114 Willmar Dr Palo Alto CA 94306 Office: Stanford U Astronomy Program Varian 302C Stanford CA 94305

PETROZZINO, JANE A., learning consultant; b. Newark, Oct. 5, 1947; d. Anthony Frank and Janet Louise Petrozzino. BA, William Paterson Coll., 1969, MEd, 1974; PhD, Fordham U., 1982. Elem. tchr. Wayne (N.J.) Pub. Schs., 1969-74, learning disabilities specialist, 1974-75, learning cons., 1975-84; pvt. practice as learning cons. Kinnelon and Wayne, N.J., 1981—; supr. spl. edn. Ramapo Ctrl. Sch. Dist., Hillburn, N.Y., 1984-87; prin./asst. to regional exec. dir. spl. edn. Region VII Coun. Spl. Edn., Bergen County, N.J., 1987-88; supr. instrn./asst. to supt. Moonachie Bd. Edn., Bergen County, N.J., 1987-88; supr. spl. svcs. Totowa (N.J.) Bd. Edn., 1988-89; adj. prof. William Paterson Coll., Wayne, 1978—: panelist/cons. U.S. Dept. Edn., Washington, 1982—; lectr., in-svc. staff trainer various bds. edn., N.Y., N.J., 1982—; mem. U.S. world team in field of dyslexia Orton Dyslexia Soc./Pres.'s Com. U.S. Amb. Program, 1993. Mem. N.J. Assn. Learning Cons., N.Y. State Adminstrs. Assn., Orton-Dyslexia Soc., Assn. Children with Learning Disabilities, Fordham U. Sch. Adminstrs. Assn., Phi Delta Kappa. Roman Catholic. Avocations: piano, dance, foreign languages, skating. Home: 77 Old Cow Pasture Ln Kinnelon NJ 07405-2413

PETRU, SUZANNE MITTON, health care finance executive; b. Shawano, Wis., Sept. 26, 1947; d. William Wallace and Gertrude Priscilla (Humphrey) Mitton; m. W. James Petru, Jan. 2, 1987. BSBA, Northwestern U., 1970, MBA, 1971. CPA, Ill., Wis. Sr. acct. Arthur Andersen & Co., Chgo., 1971-77; v.p. fin. Thorek Hosp. and Med. Ctr., Chgo., 1977-82; sec./treas. La Grange (Ill.) Meml. Health Sys., 1982-85; v.p. fin. La Grange Meml. Hosp., 1982-85; audit prin. Deloitte & Touche (formerly Touche Ross & Co.), Chgo., 1985-88; sr. v.p. fin., treas. SSM Health Care Sys., St. Louis, 1988-95; pres. healthcare divsn. Am. Home Assurance Co. (subs. Am. Internat. Group, Inc.), 1995—. Mem. investment com. Sisters of Charity Healthcare Sys., Cin., 1993—, mem. fin. com., 1994—; mem. assoc. bd. La Grange Meml. Hosp., 1988—; advisor Jr. Achievement, 1971-76. Fellow Healthcare Fin. Mgmt. Assn. (bd. dirs. 1989-91, principles and practices bd. 1992-95, nat. matrix, 1985-86, 88-89, pres., pres.-elect, sec., bd. First Ill. chpt. 1979-86, Follmer Bronze award 1982, Reeves Silver award 1985, Muncie Gold award 1988, Alice V. Runyan chpt. achievement award First Ill. chpt. 1988); mem. Am. Coll. Healthcare Execs. (diplomate), Fin. Execs. Inst., Country Club at Legends (adv. bd. 1991-93), St. Louis Club (house com. 1991-95). Republican. Presbyterian. Avocations: golf, travel. Home: 12033 Tindall Dr Saint Louis MO 63131-3135 Office: Am Home Assurance Co 70 Pine St New York NY 10270

PETRUCELLI, JAMES MICHAEL, lawyer; b. Fresno, Calif., Dec. 28, 1949; s. Gene Vincent and Josephine Marie (Frediani) P.; m. Kathleen Jean Rose, June 2, 1990; 1 child, Vincent Michael. BS, Fresno State Coll., 1972; JD, San Joaquin Coll., 1989. Bar: Calif. 1989, U.S. Dist. Ct. (ea. dist.) Calif. 1989, U.S. Dist. Ct. (no. dist.) Calif. 1990, U.S. Ct. Appeals (9th cir.) 1990, U.S. Supreme Ct., 1993. Dep. sheriff Fresno County Sheriff's Dept., 1974-89; pvt. practice Fresno, 1989—; del. State Bar Conf. of Dels., Fresno, 1990—; State Bar Law Practice Mgmt. Sect., 1994—, dir. Commn. For Adv. Calif. Paralegal Specialation Inc., 1995—. Pres. San Joaquin Coll. Law Alumni Assn., Fresno, 1990—; mem. exec. com. San Joaquin Coll. Law, 1990-91, 20th anniversary com., 1990-91; trustee Kerman (Calif.) Unified Sch. Dist., 1982-88; bd. dirs. North Cen. Fire Protection Dist., Kerman, 1990—. Mem. ABA, Am. Trial Lawyers Assn., Consumer Attorney of Calif., Calif. Bar Assn., Fresno County Bar Assn., Inns of Ct. Office: 2350 W Shaw St Ste 137 Fresno CA 93711

PETRUCELLI, R(OCCO) JOSEPH, II, nephrologist; b. Meriden, Conn., Sept. 20, 1943; s. Rocco Joseph and Marguerite Robena (Colwell) P. BA, Yale U., 1965; MD, Harvard U., 1969. Diplomate Am. Bd. Internal Medicine, Am. Bd. Nephrology. Intern, then resident Mt. Sinai Hosp., N.Y.C., 1969-72; fellow in nephrology U. Calif. San Francisco Med. Ctr., San Francisco, 1972-74; asst. prof. Mt. Sinai Sch. Medicine, 1978-92; assoc. prof. N.Y. Med. Coll., 1992—; vis. rschr. Karolinska Inst., Stockholm, 1970-71; exec. com. End Stage Renal Disease, N.Y.C., 1980-90, pres. 1985. Author: Medicine: An Illustrated History, 1978, transl. into fgn. langs., 1978-95. Pres. Bklyn. Opera Soc.; mem. med. adv. bd. Nat. Kidney Found., 1987-94, v.p., 1994; treas. Friends of Rare Book Rm. of N.Y. Acad. Medicine, 1993, sec., 1994. Recipient Richard Cabot prize Harvard Med. Sch., 1969, Boylston prize Boylston Med. Soc., 1969, John P. McGovern prize Baylor Coll. Medicine, Houston, 1993. Fellow N.Y. Acad. Medicine (libr. com. 1975—), Am. Soc. Nephrology, Internat. Soc. Nephrology. Democrat. Episcopalian. Home: 19 Fulton Ave Rye NY 10580-2515 Office: Chief Nephrology New Rochelle Med Ctr 16 Guion Pl New Rochelle NY 10801-5503

PETRUSKI, JENNIFER ANDREA, speech-language pathologist; b. Kingston, N.Y., Jan. 28, 1968; d. Andrew Francis and Judith (Cruger) P. BS, SUNY, Buffalo, 1990; MSEd, SUNY, 1992. Cert. tchr. speech-hearing handicapped, N.Y.; cert. clin. competence; lic. speech-lang. pathology, N.Y. Speech-lang. pathologist Kingston (N.Y.) City Schs., 1992—; cooperating tchr. SUNY, New Paltz, 1995-96, student clinician supr., 1996. Mem. Am. Speech and Hearing Assn., N.Y. State Speech-Lang. and Hearing Assn., Speech and Hearing Assn. Hudson Valley (corr. sec. 1995-96, membership com. 1995-96, editor newsletter 1995-96). Home: 235 Millbrook Ave Hurley NY 12443-5614 Office: Kingston City Schs 61 Crown St Kingston NY 12401

PETRUSKY, JOHN W., banker, consultant; b. Johnstown, Pa.; children: John T., Dianna L., James W. B.S. in Acctg., Pa. State U., 1961. With Bank of N.Y., N.Y.C., 1961-64; asst. v.p. Dry Dock Savs. Bank, N.Y.C., 1964-68, Leasco Systems Internat., N.Y.C., 1968-69; sr. v.p. Phoenix Systems Internat., N.Y.C., 1969-70; (with Dollar Dry Dock Savs. Bank, N.Y.C., 1970-87, pres., 1985-87; founder, pres. The Petrusky Group, Inc., 1987—. Internat. rep. for banking standards The Am. Banker's Assn.; chmn. Am. Nat. Standards Inst., 1979-81; chmn. Internat. Standards Orgn. 68, Geneva, 1979-86; trustee Waldorf Sch., Garden City, N.Y., 1986; bd. dirs. Am. Nat.

Standards Inst., 1979-81; mem. ch. coun. St. James Luth. Ch., Stewart Manor, N.Y. Served with USAF, 1955-59. Recipient IBM Point of Sale award, 1976; Electronic Funds Transfer award Mutual Inst. Nat. Transfer System, 1980. Copyright computer software for tele-mktg. system, 1989, mortgage systems, 1992. Republican. Home and Office: 111 Chester Ave Garden City NY 11530-4124

PETRY, THOMAS EDWIN, manufacturing company executive; b. Cin., Nov. 20, 1939; s. Edwin Nicholas and Leonora Amelia (Zimpelman) P.; m. Mary Helen Gardner, Aug. 25, 1962; children: Thomas Richard, Stephen Nicholas, Daniel Gardner, Michael David. B.S., U. Cin., 1962; M.B.A., Harvard, 1964. Group v.p., treas. Eagle-Picher Industries, Inc., Cin., 1968-81; pres. Eagle-Picher Industries, Inc., 1981-89, COO, 1981—, CEO, 1982—, chmn. bd., 1989—. Republican. Clubs: Queen City, Terrace Park (Ohio) Country, Cin. Country. Office: Eagle-Picher Industries Inc 580 Walnut St Cincinnati OH 45202-3110*

PETSCHEK, ALBERT GEORGE, physicist, consultant; b. Prague, Bohemia, Czechoslovakia, Jan. 31, 1928; came to U.S., 1938; s. Hans Petschek and Eva (Epler) Petschek-Newman; m. Marilyn Adiene Poth, June 25, 1948; children: Evelyn A., Rolfe G., Elaine L., Mark A. BS, MIT, 1947; MS, U. Mich., 1948; PhD, U. Rochester, 1953. Jr. physicist Carter Oil Co., Tulsa, 1948-49; sr. rsch. scientist Systems, Science and Software, San Diego, Calif., 1968-71; staff mem., group leader, fellow, cons. Los Alamos (N. Mex.) Nat. Lab., 1953—; prof. of physics N. Mex. Inst. Mining and Tech., Socorro, 1966-68, 71—, prof. emeritus, 1994—; vis. asst. prof. Cornell U., Ithaca, N.Y., 1960-61; vis. prof. Tel Aviv U., Israel, 1978; cons. Sandia Corp., Albuquerque, N. Mex., 1966-70. Editor: (book) Supernovae, 1990; contbr. more than 50 articles to profl. jours. Fellow AAAS; mem. AAUP, Am. Phys. Soc., Am. Astron. Soc. Republican. Unitarian. Avocations: bicycling, skiing. Home: 122 Piedra Loop White Rock NM 87544 Office: Los Alamos Nat Lab Box 1663 Los Alamos NM 87545

PETSKO, GREGORY ANTHONY, chemistry and biochemistry educator; b. Washington, Aug. 7, 1948; s. John and Mary (Santoro) P.; m. Carol Bannister Chamberlain, July 3, 1971 (div. 1982). BA, Princeton U., 1970; DPhil, Oxford U., 1973. Instr. Wayne State U. Med. Sch., Detroit, 1973-75, asst. prof., 1975-78; assoc. prof. MIT, 1979-85, prof. chemistry, 1985-90; Lucille P. Markey prof. biochemistry and chemistry Brandeis U., Waltham, Mass., 1990—, dir. Rosenstiel Basic Med. Scis. Rsch. Ctr., 1994—; cons. Arqule, Inc., Medford, 1993—. Editor. Jour. Protein Engring., 1988—. Recipient Max Planck prize Mack Planck Gesellschaft, 1992; Rhodes scholar Oxford U., 1970, Danforth fellow, 1980; Alfred P. Sloan fellow MIT, 1978; elected to NAS, 1995. Mem. NAS, Am. Crystallographic Assn. (Siddhu award 1981), Am. Chem. Soc. (Pfizer award 1987), Biophys. Soc., Am. Soc. Biochemistry and Molecular Biology. Avocations: writing poetry and fiction, hiking, basketball, old movies, sports cars. Home: 8 Jason Rd Belmont MA 02178-3129 Office: Brandeis U Rosenstiel Ctr Waltham MA 02254-9110

PETT, JOHN LYMAN, banker; b. Erie, Pa., Dec. 7, 1948; s. Peter Paul and Dorothy (Rhoades) P. BS, Gannon U., 1971; MBA, DePaul U., 1977; postgrad., Harvard Bus. Sch., 1989. Asst dir. acctg. and adminstrn. Constrn. Engring. div. Continental Can Co., Chgo., 1974-77; comml. v.p. and lending officer Mfrs. & Traders Trust Co., Buffalo, 1977-79, unit mgr. Mid. Market Lending, 1979-84, sr. v.p., chief credit officer, 1984—. Mem., cons. Erie County Fiscal Res. Com., Buffalo, 1984-86. Capt. USMC, 1971-74. Mem. Robert Morris Assocs., Am. Bankers Assocs., Wanakah Country Club (Hamburg, N.Y.). Republican. Roman Catholic. Avocations: golf, running, reading. Office: First Empire State Corp MFT Ctr Buffalo NY 14203

PETTEE, DANIEL STARR, neurologist; b. N.Y.C., Feb. 15, 1925; s. Allen Danforth and Helen Marien (Starr) P.; m. Dimetra Marie Peters, June 24, 1961; children: William, Margaret, Allen. BA, Yale U., 1951; MD, Columbia U., 1955. Diplomate Am. Bd. Psychiatry and Neurology, 1965, Am. Bd. Clin. Neurophysiology, 1984. Rotating internship Strong Meml. Hosp. U. Rochester, N.Y., 1955-57, residency neurology, 1957-62; neurologist pvt. practice, Rochester, N.Y., 1962—; clinic dir. Rochester (N.Y.) Area Multiple Sclerosis Chpt., Rochester, N.Y., 1962-76; assoc. prof. neurology U. Rochester (N.Y.) Sch. Medicine, 1978—; clin. assoc. Dept Neurology Strong Meml. Hosp., Rochester, N.Y., 1978—; head neurology Div. Dept. Medicine The Genesee Hosp., Rochester, N.Y., 1972—; pres. Genesee Neurological Assocs., Rochester, 1974—; mem. bd. dirs. Rochester (N.Y.) Area Multiple Sclerosis Chpt., 1970-76. Contbr. articles to profl. jours. Mem. bd. dirs., singer Rochester (N.Y.) Oratorio Soc., 1960-61, 1955-78. Recipient Purple Heart, Bronze Star U.S. Army, 1944, Bronze Hope Chest for Svc. award Rochester (N.Y.) Area Multiple Sclerosis Chpt., 1976. Mem. N.Y. Acad. Sci., Rochester Acad. Sci. (astronomy sect. 1989—, bd. dirs. astronomy sect. 1993-94). Home: 150 Summit Dr Rochester NY 14620-3130 Office: Genesee Neurol Assocs 222 Alexander St Rochester NY 14607-4005

PETTENGILL, GORDON H(EMENWAY), physicist, educator; b. Providence, Feb. 10, 1926; s. Rodney Gordon and Frances (Hemenway) P.; m. Pamela Anne Wolfenden, Oct. 28, 1967; children—Mark Robert, Rebecca Jane. B.S., MIT, 1948; Ph.D., U. Calif., Berkeley, 1955. Staff mem. Lincoln Lab. MIT, Lexington, 1954-63, 65-68; prof. planetary physics, dept. earth, atmospheric and planetary scis. MIT, Cambridge, 1971—, dir. Ctr. Space Rsch., 1984-90; assoc. dir. Arecibo (P.R.) Obs., 1963-65, dir., 1968-71. Served with inf., Signal Corps AUS, 1944-46. Decorated Combat Inf. badge; recipient Magellanic Premium, Am. Philos. Soc., 1994. Fellow Am. Geophys. Union (Whipple award 1995); mem. AAAS, Am. Phys. Soc., Am. Astron. Soc., Internat. Astron. Union, Internat. Radio Sci. Union, Nat. Acad. Sci., Am. Acad. Arts and Sci. Pioneer several techniques in radar astronomy for describing properties of planets and satellites; discovered 59-day rotational period of planet Mercury. Office: MIT 77 Massachusetts Ave Rm 37-641 Cambridge MA 02139-4301

PETTENGILL, HARRY JUNIOR, federal agency administrator; b. Lock Haven, Pa., Apr. 16, 1946; s. Harry Blair and Bertha Irene (Quigg) P.; m. Sandra Kaye Conway, Sept. 3, 1970; children: Keri-Beth Irene, Justin Matthew, Rebekah Ann Louise. BA, Lock Haven U., 1968; MS, Temple U., 1971; PhD, U. Mich., 1974. Dep. mgr. waste environ. studies project U.S. EPA, Washington, 1975-80; chief uranium mills licensing NRC, Washington, 1980-83; chief uranium recovery licensing NRC, Denver, 1983-88; dir. nuclear safety tech. div. Dept. Energy, Washington, 1988-90, dep. asst. sec. for health, 1990—. U.S. AEC fellow Temple U., 1968, USPHS fellow U. Mich., 1971. Mem. OECD-NEA (com. radiology protection and pub. health), Health Physics Soc. Lt. comdr. USPHS, 1977-79. Office: US Dept Energy 1000 Independence Ave SW Washington DC 20585-0001

PETTERCHAK, JANICE A., library director, researcher, writer; b. Springfield, Ill., Sept. 15, 1942; d. Emil H. and Vera C. (Einhoff) Stukenberg; m. John J. Petterchak, Oct. 5, 1963; children: John A., Julie Gilmour, James. AA, Springfield Coll., 1962; BS, Sangamon State U., 1972, MA, 1982. Supr. hist. markers Ill. State Hist. Soc., Springfield, 1973-74, asst. exec. dir., 1985-87; curator photographs Ill. State Hist. Libr., Springfield, 1974-79, assoc. editor, 1979-83, rep. local history svcs., 1983-85, libr. dir., 1987-95; project dir. NEH/Ill. newspaper cataloging project. Author: Mapping a Life's Journey: The Legacy of Andrew McNally III, 1995, Jack Brickhouse: A Voice for All Seasons, 1996, (booklets) Researching and Writing Local History in Illinois: A Guide to the Sources, 1987; editor: Illinois History: An Annotated Bibliography, 1995; assoc. editor Illinois Historical Jour.; contbr. articles to profl. jours. Grantee NEH, 1987-95. Mem. Ill. State History Soc., Abraham Lincoln Assn. (co-editor Papers Abraham Lincoln Assn. 1981-82), Stephen A. Douglas Assn., Sangamon County Hist. Soc. (bd. dirs. 1991-94, v.p. 1994-95, pres. 1995-96). Home: 11381 Mallard Dr Rochester IL 62563-9753

PETTERSEN, KEVIN WILL, investment company executive; b. Yonkers, N.Y., July 4, 1956; s. Kjell Will and Marilyn Ann (Stevens) P.; m. Mary Elizabeth Murphy, Aug. 30, 1981; children: Kelly, Elizabeth, Erin. Diploma academia, Chaminade, Mineola, N.Y., 1974; BA in Econs., SUNY at Stony Brook, 1978. Buyer JC Penney Co., Inc., N.Y.C., 1979-82; nat. sales mgr. Randa Corp., Inc., N.Y.C., 1982-83; dir. sales Wemco, Inc., N.Y.C., 1983-86; mng. dir., sr. v.p. D.H. Blair & Co., Inc., N.Y.C., 1986-89; exec. v.p. Brean Murray, Foster Securities, Inc., N.Y.C., 1989-90; v.p., br. mgr., corp. officer A.G. Edwards and Sons, Inc., Huntington, N.Y., 1990—; cons. Oncor Inc., Gaithersburg, Md., 1987-93, Wedding Info. Network, Inc., Omaha, 1987-91; fin. adviser European banking, ins. and investment industry, 1987—; mem. Pres. Coun. A.G. Edwards, Million Dollar Club A.G. Edwards; mem. pres.'s adv. coun. The Rochester Funds, exec. coun. The Oppenheimer Funds Group; mem. All-Am. team The Am. Funds Group. Bd. dirs. Harbour Green L.I. Assn., 1990-94, pres., 1991; mem. Oyster Bay Supr.'s Adv. Com. on Crime, 1993—. Recipient Outstanding Character award Chaminade, 1974. Mem. ASPCA, U.S. Golf. Assn., Sons of Norway, Chaminade Wall St. Assn., SUNYStony Brook Alumni Assn., Green Harbour Green Beach Club (bd. dirs. 1994—), Swan Lake Country Club, Southward Ho Country Club, Chaminade Torch Club. Republican. Roman Catholic. Avocations: golf. skiing, swimming. Home: 122 Exeter Rd Massapequa NY 11758-8128 Office: AG Edwards and Sons Inc 24 W Carver St Huntington NY 11743-3309

PETTERSEN, KJELL WILL, stockbroker, consultant; b. Oslo, Norway, June 19, 1927; came to U.S., 1946, naturalized, 1957; s. Jens Will and Ragna O. (Wickstrom) P.; m. Marilyn Ann Stevens, Aug. 16, 1952; children: Thomas W., Maureen, Kevin W., Maryann, Kathleen. Student, Zion Theol. Sch., 1945-49, N.Y. Inst. Finance, 1955-56. Mgr. A.M. Kidder & Co., N.Y.C., 1954-64; sr. v.p., sec., dir. Halle & Stieglitz, Fillor Bullard Co., Inc., 1964-73; sr. v.p., dir. mktg. Parrish Securities, Inc., N.Y.C., 1973-74; cons. Loeb, Rhoades & Co., N.Y.C., 1974-79; mng. dir. Prudential Securities, N.Y.C., 1979-89; pres. Arbitration Recovery Cons., Marco, Fla., 1992-93; vice chmn. Noddings Investment Group, Inc., Oakbrook Terrace, Ill., 1993-95, cons., 1996—; dir. Ski for Light Inc., Mpls., Creative Arts Rehab. Ctr. Inc., N.Y.C. Dem. candidate N.Y. State Assembly, Nassau County, 1962; past dir. Guadalupe Ctr., Marco, YMCA; pres. Quest for Peace Internat. Mem. Security Industry Assn., Nat. Assn. Security Dealers (bd. arbitrators), N.Y. C. of C. (past dir.), Norwegian-Am. C. of C. (dir. Guadalupe Ctr.), Scandinavian Found., Bankers Club of Am., Norwegian Club (N.Y.C.), Rotary (dir.). Mem. Security Industry Assn., Nat. Assn. Security Dealers (bd. arbitrators), N.Y. C. of C., Norwegian-Am. C. of C. (dir. Guadalope Ctr.), Scandinavian Found., Bankers Club of Am., Norwegian Club (N.Y.C.), Marco Bay Yacht Club, Rotary. Home: 350 Rockhill Ct Marco Island FL 33937-3860

PETTEWAY, SAMUEL BRUCE, college president; b. Fayetteville, N.C., July 18, 1924; s. Walter Bernard and Margaret Maysie (Cole) P.; m. Eleanor Glenn Sugg, Nov. 27, 1948; children—Margaret Petteway Small, Samuel Bruce. B.S., N.C. State U., 1949, M.Ed., 1966, Ed.D., 1968. Gen. mgr. Homeowners Ins. and Realty Co., 1960-63; engring. tech. dept. chmn., dean occupational and transfer programs, dir. evening programs Lenoir County Community Coll., 1963-68; pres. Coll. of the Albemarie, Elizabeth City, N.C., 1968-75, N.C. Wesleyan Coll., Rocky Mount, 1975-86; prof. Va. Poly. Inst. and State U., 1973-75, East Carolina U., 1994—; pres. Philanthropic Cons., Inc., Kinston, N.C., 1986—; sec. Coll. Mgmt. Svcs., Inc., Raleigh, N.C., 1989; lic. amateur radio operator, 1992—. Pres. chpt. Am. Cancer Soc., 1960-61, Boys' Club Lenoir County, 1987-91; bd. dirs. Rocky Mount Acad., 1979-80, Triangle East, Inc., 1985-86, Meth. Home for Children, Cypress Glen Retirement Home, chmn. 1996; chmn. deferred giving com. N.C. Meth. Found., 1979-86; chmn. coun. on ministries 1st United Meth. Ch., Rocky Mount, 1980-81, Westminster United Meth. Ch., 1989-90, chmn. bd. trustees, 1994—; chmn. bd. trustees Art Edn. Found., 1980; mem. Nash County Bd. Health, 1985-86; bd. trustees United Meth. Retirement Homes, Inc., 1996—. Named Tar Heel of Week News and Observer, 1975, Today's Outstanding N.C. Citizen WNCT-TV, 1975; NSF fellow U. Ill., 1963. Mem. Nat. Assn. for Hosp. Devel., N.C. Assn. Colls. and Univs., N.C. Conf. United Meth. Ch. (chmn. bd. trustees 1973-79), Nat. Soc. Fund Raising Execs. (cert.), Rocky Mount C. of C. (bd. dirs. 1980-84), Phi Kappa Phi, Theta Alpha Phi. Democrat. Clubs: Benvenue Country, Galaxy Social; Kinston Country. Lodge: Rotary (pres. 1980-81, bd. dirs. Kinston chpt. 1988-92). Office: 708 Westminster Ln Kinston NC 28501-2770

PETTEY, WALTER GRAVES, III, lawyer; b. Bessemer, Ala., Aug. 24, 1949; s. Walter Graves Jr. and Mildred Louise (Nebrig) P.; m. Virginia McWherter Lott, Feb. 28, 1976; 1 child, Stephen Blacksher. BA, Washington & Lee U., 1971; JD, U. Ala., 1976. Bar: Ala. 1976, Tex. 1977. Law clk. to Hon. Walter P. Gewin U.S. Ct. Appeals (5th cir.), Tuscaloosa, Ala., 1976-77; assoc. Hughes & Hill, Dallas, 1977-82; assoc. Pettit & Martin, Dallas, 1983-84, ptnr., 1985-92; ptnr. Hughes & Luce, L.L.P., Dallas, 1992—. 1st lt. U.S. Army, 1971-73. Office: Hughes & Luce L L P 1717 Main St Ste 2800 Dallas TX 75201-7342

PETTEY, WILLIAM HALL, lawyer; b. New Orleans, Apr. 22, 1958; s. William Hall and Jeanie Nelson (Hewes) P.; m. Kimberly Ann Mosley, Apr. 25, 1992; 1 child, William Hall III. BS, U. So. Miss., 1980; JD, U. Miss., Oxford, 1983. Bar: Miss. 1983, U.S. Dist. Ct. (no. dist.) Miss. 1983, U.S. Ct. Appeals (5th cir.) 1984, U.S. Dist. Ct. (so. dist.) Miss. 1984. Lawyer Dukes Dukes Keating & Faneca, Gulfport, Miss., 1984—. V.p. Miss. Railway Mus., Hattiesburg, 1983-87; elder Westminster Presbyn. Ch., Gulfport, 1992, ch. sch. steering com., 1994—. Mem. Miss. Bar Assn., Harrison County Bar Assn., Louisville & Nashville Hist. Soc., Ill. Ctrl. Hist. Soc., Trinity United Meth. Ch., Nat. Railway Hist. Soc. Avocations: railroading, model railroading, photography. Home: 323 2d St Gulfport MS 39607 Office: Dukes Dukes Keating Faneca 2308 E Beach Blvd Gulfport MS 39607

PETTIBONE, PETER JOHN, lawyer; b. Schenectady, N.Y., Dec. 11, 1939; s. George Howard and Caryl Grey (Ketchum) P.; m. Jean Kellogg, Apr. 23, 1966; children: Stephen, Victoria. AB summa cum laude, Princeton U., 1961; JD, Harvard U., 1964; LLM, NYU, 1971. Bar: Pa. 1965, D.C. 1965, N.Y. 1968, U.S. Supreme Ct. 1974, Russia (fgn. legal cons.), 1995. Lectr. Heidelberg (Fed. Republic Germany) U., 1965-67; assoc. Cravath, Swaine & Moore, N.Y.C., 1967-74, Lord Day & Lord, Barrett Smith, N.Y.C., 1974-76; ptnr. Lord Day & Lord, Barrett Smith, N.Y.C. and Washington, 1976-94, Patterson, Belknap, Webb & Tyler LLP, N.Y.C. and Washington, 1994—; pres. 1158 Fifth Ave. Corp., N.Y.C., 1991-94; pres. North Ferry Co., Shelter Island, N.Y., 1987-90; bd. dirs., vice-chmn. N.Y. State Facilities Devel. Corp., N.Y.C., 1983-89. Editor USSR Legal Materials, 1990-92. Trustee, treas. Hosp. Chaplaincy Inc., N.Y.C., 1980-86, Civitas, N.Y.C., 1984-92; mem. N.Y. State Gov.'s World Trade Coun., 1989—; mem. Coun. Fgn. Rels., 1993—; trustee Union Chapel, Shelter Island, N.Y., 1990—, CEC Internat. Ptnrs., 1996—; bd. dirs., vice chmn. Geonomics Inst., Middlebury, Vt., 1991—; mem. vestry Ch. of Heavenly Rest, N.Y.C., 1987-93. Capt. U.S. Army, 1965-67, Heidelberg, Germany. Mem. ABA, Assn. Bar City N.Y. (chmn. com. on CIS affairs 1991-94), U.S.-USSR Trade and Econ. Coun. Inc. (U.S. co-chmn. legal com. 1980-92), U.S.-Russia Bus. Coun. (bd. dirs.), Soc. of Cin., Anglers Club N.Y.C., Shelter Island Yacht Club, Amateur Ski Club N.Y. (pres. 1980-82), Canterbury Choral Soc. (pres. 1983-84), Phi Beta Kappa. Episcopalian. Home: 1158 Fifth Ave New York NY 10029-6917 also: 10 Wesley Ave Shelter Island Heights NY 11965 Office: Patterson Belknap et al LLP 1133 Ave of the Americas New York NY 10036

PETTIGREW, CLAIRE RUDOLPH, music educator; b. Chambersburg, Pa., Aug. 3, 1961; d. Herman Leon and Helen Frances (Tobey) Rudolph; m. Daniel Pettigrew III, Mar. 10, 1991; stepchildren: Christine, Sara. BS in Edn. in Music, West Chester U., 1983, MEd in Elem. Edn., 1991. Tchr. music West Chester (Pa.) Area Sch. Dist., 1989—; co-dir. summer music program West Chester Cmty. Ctr., 1986. Mem. West Chester Cmty. Band, 1987—, sec., 1993—; active Gilbert and Sullivan Soc. Chester County. Mem. NEA, Pa. Sch. Edn. Assn., Music Educator Nat. Conf., Am. ORFF-Schulwerk Assn., Phi Delta Kappa, Sigma Alpha Iota (Coll. Honor award 1983). Avocations: counted cross-stitch, playing flute and piccolo. Office: Starkweather Elem Sch 1050 Wilmington Pike West Chester PA 19382-7368

PETTIGREW, JOHNNIE DELONIA, educational diagnostician; b. Electra, Tex., July 2, 1948; d. John Drew and Dolly Marie (Watkins) Chester; divorced; 1 child, Jan Elise. B Elem. Edn., U. North Tex., 1970, MEd, 1982; postgrad., Tex. Woman's U., 1993—. Cert. elem., kindergarten, learning disabilities, spl. edn. early childhood, gifted edn. tchr., ednl. diagnostician, adminstr., Tex. 2d grade tchr. Azle (Tex.) Ind. Sch. Dist., 1969-70; 3d grade tchr. Decatur (Tex.) Ind. Sch. Dist., 1970-72; kindergarten, spl. edn. tchr. Boyd (Tex.) Ind. Sch. Dist., 1972-74, kindergarten, gifted edn., spl. edn. tchr., 1981-93; spl. edn. tchr. Springtown (Tex.) Ind. Sch. Dist., 1977-81; gifted edn. tchr. Denton (Tex.) Ind. Sch. Dist., 1993-94, ednl. diagnostician, 1994—; cons. in gifted edn., early childhood and drama to various sch. dists., Tex.; adj. prof. U. North Tex., Denton, 1993. Author: (play) The Monks Tale: Romeo and Juliet, 1990, also ednl. materials. Co-founder children's story hour Decatur Pub. Libr., 1970; dir. Wise County Little Theatre, Decatur; life mem. Boyd Ind. Sch. Dist. PTA, 1989, Tex. PTA. Mem. Am. Assn. for Tchg. and Curriculum, Assn. for Childhood Edn. Internat., Am. Edn. Rsch. Assn., Tex. Assn. for Gifted and Talented, Nat. Assn. for the Edn. of Young Children, So. Early Childhood Assn., Phi Delta Kappa, Phi Kappa Phi. Avocations: theater, needlecraft, sewing. Home: PO Box 91 Decatur TX 76234-0091 Office: Denton Ind Sch Spl Edn Svcs 1117 Riney Rd Denton TX 76208

PETTIGREW, L. EUDORA, academic administrator; b. Hopkinsville, Ky., Mar. 1, 1928; d. Warren Cicero and Corrye Lee (Newell) Williams; children: Peter W. Woodard, Jonathan R. (dec.). MusB, W.Va. State Coll., 1950; MA, So. Ill. U., 1964, PhD, 1966. Music/English instr. Swift Meml. Jr. Coll., Rogersville, Tenn., 1950-51; music instr., libraian Western Ky. Vocat. Sch., Paducah, 1951-52; music/English instr. Voorhees Coll., Denmark, S.C., 1954-55; dir. music and recreation therapy W.Ky. State Psychiatric Hosp., Hopkinsville, 1956-61; research fellow Rehab. Inst., So. Ill. U., Carbondale, 1961-63, instr., resident counselor, 1963-66, coordinator undergrad. ednl. psychology, 1963-66, acting chmn. ednl. psychology, tchr. corps instr., 1966; asst. prof. to assoc. prof. dept. psychology U. Bridgeport, Conn., 1966-70; prof., chmn. dept. urban and met. studies Coll. Urban Devel. Mich. State U., East Lansing, 1974-80; assoc. provost, prof. U. Del., Newark, 1981-86; pres. SUNY Coll. at Old Westbury, 1986—; cons. for rsch. and evaluation Hall Neighborhood House Day Care Tng. Project, Bridgeport, 1966-68, U.S. Ea. Regional Lab., Edn. Devel. Ctr., Newton, Mass., 1967-69; coordinator for edn. devel., 1968-69; cons. Bridgeport Public Schs. lang. devel. project, 1967-68, 70; Lansing Model Cities Agy., Day Care Program, 1971; U. Pitts., 1973, 74, Leadership Program, U. Mich. and Wayne State U., 1975, Wayne County Pub. Health Nurses Assn., 1976, Ill. State Bd. Edn., 1976-77; assoc. prof. U. Bridgeport, 1970, Ctr. for Urban Affairs and Coll. of Edn., Mich. State U., East Lansing, 1970-73; trustee L.I. Community Found.; program devel. specialist Lansing Public Schs. Tchr. Corps program, 1971-73; chair commn. SUNY Higher Edn. in Africa, 1994—; lectr. in field; condr. workshops in field; cons. in field. Tv/radio appearances on: Black Women in Edn, Channel 23, WKAR, East Lansing, 1973, Black Women and Equality, Channel 2, Detroit, 1974, Women and Careers, Channel 7, Detroit, 1974, Black Women and Work: Integration in Schools, WITL Radio, Lansing, 1974, others.; Contbr. articles to profl. jours. Recipient Diana award Lansing YWCA, 1977, Outstanding Profl. Achievement award, 1987, award L.I. Ctr. for Bus. and Profl. Women, 1988, Educator of Yr. 100 Black Men of L.I., 1988, Black Women's Agenda award, 1988, Woman of Yr. Nassau/Suffolk Coun. of Adminstrv. Women in Edn., 1989, Disting. Ednl. Leadership award L.I. Women's Coun. for Equal Edn. Tng. and Employment, 1989, L.I. Disting. Leadership award L.I. Bus. News, 1990, Disting. Black Women in Edn. award Nat. Coun. Negro Women, 1991; named Outstanding Black Educator, NAACP, 1968, Oustanding Woman Educator, Mich. Women's Lawyers Assn. and Mich. Trial Lawyers Assn., 1975, Disting. Alumna, Nat. Assn. for Equal Opportunity in Higher Edn., 1990, Woman of Yr., Nassau County League of Women Voters, 1991. Mem. AAAS, Nat. Assn. Acad. Affairs Adminstrs., Internat. Assn. Univ. Pres. (exec. com.), Phi Delta Kappa. Office: SUNY-Old Westbury PO Box 210 Old Westbury NY 11568-0210

PETTIGREW, THOMAS FRASER, social psychologist, educator; b. Richmond, Va., Mar. 14, 1931; s. Joseph Crane and Janet (Gibb) P.; m. Ann Hallman, Feb. 25, 1956; 1 son, Mark Fraser. A.B. in Psychology, U. Va., 1952; M.A. in Social Psychology, Harvard U., 1955, Ph.D., 1956; D.H.L. (hon.), Governor's State U., 1979. Rsch. assoc. Inst. Social Rsch., U. Natal, Republic South Africa, 1956; asst. prof. psychology U. N.C., 1956-57; asst. prof. social psychology Harvard U., Cambridge, Mass., 1957-62, lectr., 1962-64, assoc. prof., 1964-68, prof., 1968-74, prof. social psychology and sociology, 1974-80; prof. social psychology U. Calif., Santa Cruz, 1980-94, rsch. prof. social psychology, 1994—; prof. social psychology U. Amsterdam, 1986-91; mem. com. status black Ams. NRC, 1985-88; adj. fellow Joint Ctr. Polit. and Econ. Studies, Washington, 1982—; mem. adv. bd. women's studies program Princeton (N.J.) U., 1985—. Author: (with E.Q. Campbell) Christians in Racial Crisis: A Study of the Little Rock Ministry, 1959, A Profile of the Negro American, 1964, Racially Separate or Together?, 1971, (with Frederickson, Knobol, Glazer and Veda) Prejudice, 1982, (with Alston) Tom Bradley's Campaigns for Governor: The Dilemma of Race and Political Strategies, 1988, How to Think Like a Social Scientist, 1995; editor: Racial Discrimination in the United States, 1975, The Sociology of Race Relations: Reflection and Reform, 1980, (with C. Stephan & W. Stephan) The Future of Social Psychology: Defining the Relationship Between Sociology and Psychology, 1991; mem. editorial bd. Jour. Social Issues, 1959-64, Social Psychology Quarterly, 1977-80; assoc. editor Am. Sociol. Rev, 1963-65; mem. adv. bd. Integrated Edn, 1963-84, Phylon, 1965-93, Edn. and Urban Society, 1968-90, Race, 1972-74, Ethnic and Racial Studies, 1978-95, Rev. of Personality and Social Psychology, 1980-85, Community and Applied Social Psychology, 1989—, Individual and Politics, 1989-93, New Cmty., 1994—; contbr. articles to profl. publs. Chmn. Episcopal presiding Bishop's Adv. Com. on Race Relations, 1961-63; v.p. Episcopal Soc. Cultural and Racial Unity, 1962-63; mem. Mass. Gov.'s Adv. Com. on Civil Rights, 1962-64; social sci. cons. U.S. Commn. Civil Rights, 1966-71; mem. White House Task Force on Edn., 1967; mem. nat. task force on desegregation policies Edn. Commn. of States, 1977-79; trustee Ella Lyman Cabot Trust, Boston, 1977-79; mem. Emerson Book Award com. United Chpts. Phi Beta Kappa, 1971-73. Guggenheim fellow, 1967-68; NATO sr. scientist fellow, 1974; fellow Center Advanced Study in Behavioral Scis., 1975-76; Sydney Spivack fellow in intergroup relations Am. Sociol. Assn., 1978; Netherlands Inst. Advanced Study fellow, 1984-85; recipient Kurt Lewin Meml. award Soc. for Psychological Study of Social Issues, 1987, (with Martin) Gordon Allport Intergroup Rels. Rsch. prize, 1988, Faculty Rsch. award U. Calif., Santa Cruz, 1988; Bellagio (Italy) Study Ctr. resident fellow, Rockefeller Found., 1991. Fellow Am. Psychol. Assn., Am. Sociol. Assn. (council 1979-82); mem. Soc. Psychol. Study Social Issues (council 1962-66, pres. 1967-68), NRC (com. status black Ams. 1985-88), European Assn. Social Psychology. Home: 524 Van Ness Ave Santa Cruz CA 95060-3556

PETTIJOHN, FRANCIS JOHN, geology educator; b. Waterford, Wis., June 20, 1904; m. Dorothy Bracken, 1930 (dec.); children: Norma Pettijohn Friedemann, Clare Pettijohn Maher, Loren; m. Virginia Romberger, 1990 (dec.). A.B., U. Minn., 1924, A.M., 1925, Ph.D., 1930; D.H.L. (hon.), Johns Hopkins U., 1978; Sc.D. (hon.), U. Minn., 1986. Instr. Macalester Coll., 1924-25, Oberlin Coll., 1925-29, U. Minn., 1928-29; instr. U. Chgo., 1929-31, asst. prof., 1931-39, assoc. prof., 1939-46, prof., 1946-52; prof. Johns Hopkins U., Balt., 1952-73; prof. emeritus Johns Hopkins U., 1973—, chmn. dept. geology, 1963-68, acting chmn. dept. earth and planetary scis., 1970; geologist U.S. Geol. Survey, 1943-53; cons. Shell Oil Co., 1953-63; mem. adv. panel for earth scis. NSF, 1959-62; mem. adv. bd. Petroleum Research Fund., 1963-65. Author: numerous books in field including Sedimentary Rocks, 1949, 3d edit., 1973, (with P.E. Potter) Paleocurrents and Basin Analysis, 1963, 2d edit., 1977, (with P.E. Potter, R. Siever) Sand and Sandstone, 1987, 2d edit.; contbr. articles to profl. jours.; editor: Jour. Geology, 1947-52. Recipient Sorby medal Internat. Assn. Sedimentologists, 1982. Fellow AAAS, Geol. Soc. London (Wollaston medal 1974), Geol. Soc. Am. (Penrose medal 1975); mem. Soc. Econ. Paleontologists and Mineralogists (hon., pres. 1955-56, Twenhofel medal 1974), Geol. Soc. India (hon.), Geol. Soc. Finland (corr.), Soc. for Sedimentary Geology (established Francis J. Pettijohn medal 1992), Am. Assn. Petroleum Geologists, Am. Acad. Arts and Scis., Nat. Acad. Scis., Explorers Club (life), Phi Beta Kappa, Sigma Xi. Home: U38 11630 Glen Arm Rd Glen Arm MD 21057-9448 Office: Johns Hopkins U Dept Earth And Scis Baltimore MD 21218

PETTIJOHN, FRED PHILLIPS, retired newspaper executive, consultant; b. Balt., May 11, 1917; s. Fred and Adelaide Josephine (Phillips) P.; m. Elaine Wilson, Dec. 7, 1946; children: Fred Phillips, Mark Clay. B.A.E., U. Fla., 1941. Sports editor Tallahassee Democrat, 1946-53; with Fort Lauderdale (Fla.) News, 1953-82, exec. editor, 1960-68, gen. mgr., 1968-77, editorial dir., from 1977; 1st v.p. Gore Newspapers Co., from 1960; now cons. Bd. dirs. Salvation Army, 1975-79, v.p., 1979; bd. dirs. Fla. Council 100, 1976-78. Served with AUS, 1943-45. Recipient Disting. Service award Fla. Press Assn., 1976, Disting. Alumnus award U. Fla., 1977; inducted into Fla. Newspaper Hall of Fame, 1990. Mem. Fla. Press Assn. (pres. 1963-64, 69-70), AP Mng. Editors (bd. dirs. 1964-66), So. Newspaper Pubs. Assn.,

Lauderdale Yacht Club, Tower Club, Sigma Delta Chi, Theta Chi. Democrat. Presbyterian. Home: 911 N Rio Vista Blvd Fort Lauderdale FL 33301-3037

PETTINELLA, NICHOLAS ANTHONY, financial executive; b. Little Falls, N.Y., Sept. 9, 1942; s. Nicholas and Rose (Zuccaro) P.; m. Nancy C. Whitehouse, Oct. 28, 1978; children: Albert J., Michael A. BS, Bentley Coll., 1968; MBA, Babson Coll., 1975; postgrad. Harvard U., 1979, Stanford U., 1983. CPA, Mass. Auditor, Coopers & Lybrand, Boston, 1970-76; treas. Courier Corp., Lowell, Mass., 1976-80; controller corp. ops. Digital Equipment Corp., Maynard, Mass., 1980-81; dir. fin. Intermetrics, Inc., Cambridge, Mass., 1981-83; v.p. fin., chief fin. officer, treas., 1983—; bd. dirs. The Computer Mus., Boston, 1986—, treas. 1988—. Chmn. fin. com. Town of Ashland, Mass., 1980-82. Served with U.S. Army, 1964-66. Mem. Fin. Execs. Inst., AICPA, Inst. Mgmt. Accts., Mass. Soc. CPAs, Treas. Club Boston, Pacioli Soc. Roman Catholic. Home: 141 South St Ashland MA 01721-2263 Office: Intermetrics Inc 733 Concord Ave Cambridge MA 02138-1002

PETTINGA, CORNELIUS WESLEY, pharmaceutical company executive; b. Mille Lacs, Minn., Nov. 10, 1921; s. R.C. and Adrianna (Landaal) P.; m. Yvonne Imogene Svoboda, Dec. 22, 1943; children—Julie, Steven, Mark, Tom, Jennifer. A.B., Hope Coll., 1942; postgrad., Syracuse U., 1943; Ph.D. in Chemistry, Iowa State Coll., 1949; DSc with honors, Hope Coll., 1985; DSc (hon.), Ind. U., 1988. With Eli Lilly & Co., Indpls., 1949-86, v.p. research, devel. and control, 1964-70, v.p., asst. to pres., 1970-72, exec. v.p., 1972-86, bd. dirs., 1966-86, cons. bus. & tech., 1987—; pres. Elizabeth Arden, Inc., 1971-72, now bd. dirs.; bd. dirs. Eli Lilly Internat. Corp., IVAC, Cardiac Pacemakers Inc., Physio-Control, Ind. Corp. for Sci. and Tech., Indpls., Collagen Corp., Palo Alto, Calif., Atrix Labs Inc., Ft. Collins, Colo., Wyckoff Chem. Co., South Haven, Mich., Celtrix Corp., Palo Alto, Integrated Biotech. Corp., Indpls. Contbr. articles to profl. jours. Bd. overseers Sweet Briar Coll.; trustee, bd. govs., fin. com., exec. com. Indpls. Mus. Art; bd. dirs. Hanover Coll.; trustee Park-Tudor Sch., Coe Coll.; mem. corp. vis. com. dept. nutrition and food sci. M.I.T.; mem. Purdue Rsch. Found. With USNR, 1943-45. Fellow Nat. Cancer Inst., 1949; recipient Charles H. Best award ADA, 1986. Mem. Am. Chem. Soc., AAAS, Ind. Acad. Sci., Bus. Com. for Arts, Indpls. C. of C. (new bus. devel. com.), Sigma Xi. Clubs: Lambs (Indpls.), University (Indpls.), Woodstock (Indpls.), Meridian Hills Country (Indpls.); Piedmont (Lynchburg, Va.); John's Island (Vero Beach, Fla.). Home: 445 Somerset Dr W Indianapolis IN 46260-2919 Office: 44 Winterton 1010 E 86th St Indianapolis IN 46240-1801

PETTIS-ROBERSON, SHIRLEY MCCUMBER, former congresswoman; b. Mountain View, Calif.; d. Harold Oliver and Dorothy Susan (O'Neil) McCumber; m. John J. McNulty (dec.); m. Jerry L. Pettis (dec. Feb. 1975); m. Ben Roberson, Feb. 6, 1988; children: Peter Dwight Pettis, Deborah Neil Pettis Moyer. Student, Andrews U., U. Calif., Berkeley. Mgr. Audio-Digest Found., L.A., Glendale; sec.-treas. Pettis, Inc., Hollywood, 1958-68; mem. 94th-95th Congresses from 37th Calif. Dist., mem. coms. on interior, internat. rels., edn. and labor; pres. Women's Rsch. and Edn. Inst., 1979-80; bd. dirs. Kemper Nat. Ins. Cos., 1979—, Lumbermines Mut. Ins. Co. Mem. Pres.'s Commn. on Arms Control and Disarmament, 1980-83, Commn. on Presdl. Scholars, 1990-92; trustee U. Redlands, Calif., 1980-83, Loma Linda (Calif.) U. and Med. Ctr., 1990-95; chair Loma Linda U. Children's Hosp. Found.; bd. dirs. Former Mems. Congress. Mem. Morningside Country Club (Rancho Mirage, Calif.), Capitol Hill Club (Washington).

PETTIT, FREDERICK SIDNEY, metallurgical engineering educator, researcher; b. Wilkes Barre, Pa., Mar. 10, 1930; s. Edwin Humes and Edith Mae (Barnecut) P.; m. Lou-Jean Mary Corso, Aug. 30, 1958; children: Frederick N., Theodore E., John C., Charles A. B in Engring., Yale U., 1952, M in Engring., 1960, D in Engring., 1962. Jr. engr. Westinghouse Electric Corp., Pitts., 1952-54; engr. Avco-Lycoming, Stratford, Conn., 1957-58; postdoctoral student Max Planck Inst. Phys. Chemistry, Gottingen, Fed. Republic Germany, 1962-63; sr. staff scientist Pratt & Whitney Aircraft Co., East Hartford, Conn., 1963-79; prof. metall.-material engring. dept., chmn. U. Pitts., Pa., 1979-88; prof. U. Pitts., 1988—, Harry S. Tack prof. materials engring., 1992—; mem. adv. bd. Jour. Oxidation of Metals, Plenum Press, N.Y., 1975—. 1st lt USMC, 1954-57. NSF fellow, 1962-63. Mem. Metall. Soc. (program dir. 1982-83), Electrochem. Soc. (sec.-treas. high temperature materials div. 1979-83), Am. Soc. Metals, Materials Rsch. Soc. Roman Catholic. Home: 201 Ennerdale Dr Pittsburgh PA 15237-4026 Office: U Pitts 848 Benedum Hall Pittsburgh PA 15261-2208

PETTIT, GEORGE ROBERT, chemistry educator, cancer researcher; b. Long Branch, N.J., June 8, 1929; s. George Robert and Florence Elizabeth (Seymour) P.; m. Margaret Jean Benger, June 20, 1953; children: William Edward, Margaret Sharon, Robin Kathleen, Lynn Benger, George Robert III. B.S., Wash. State U., 1952; M.S. Wayne State U., 1954, Ph.D., 1956. Teaching asst. Wash. State U., 1950-52, lecture demonstrator, 1952; rsch. chemist E.I. duPont de Nemours and Co., 1953; grad. teaching asst. Wayne State U., 1952-53, rsch. fellow, 1954-56; sr. rsch. chemist Norwich Eaton Pharms., Inc., 1956-57; asst. prof. chemistry U. Maine, 1957-61, assoc. prof. chemistry, 1961-65, prof. chemistry, 1965; vis. prof. chemistry Stanford U., 1965; chmn. organic div. Ariz. State U., 1966-68, prof. chemistry, 1965—; vis. prof. So. African, Univs., 1978; dir. Cancer Rsch. Lab., 1974-75, Cancer Rsch. Inst., 1975—; lectr. various colls. and univs.; cons. in field. Contbr. articles to profl. jours. Mem. adv. bd. Wash. State U. Found., 1981-85. Served with USAFR, 1951-54. Recipient Disting. Rsch. Professorship award Ariz. State U., 1978-79, Alumni Achievement award Wash. State U., 1984; recipient Rsch. Achievement award Am. Soc. Pharmacolgnosy, 1995; named Dalton Prof. Medicinal Chemistry and Cancer Rsch., 1986—, Regents Prof. Chemistry, 1990—. Fellow Am. Inst. Chemists (Pioneer award 1989, Ariz. Gov.'s Excellence award 1993); mem. Am. Chem. Soc. (awards com. 1968-71, 78-81), Chem. Soc. (London), Pharmacognosy Soc., Am. Assn. Cancer Rsch., Sigma Xi, Phi Lambda Upsilon. Office: Ariz State U Cancer Rsch Inst Tempe AZ 85287

PETTIT, GHERY DEWITT, retired veterinary medicine educator; b. Oakland, Calif., Sept. 6, 1926; s. Hermon DeWitt Pettit and Marion Esther (St. John) Menzies; m. Frances Marie Seitz, July 5, 1948; children: Ghery St. John, Paul Michael. BS in Animal Sci., U. Calif., Davis, 1948, BS in Vet. Sci., 1951, DVM, 1953. Diplomate Am. Coll. Vet. Surgeons (recorder 1970-77, pres., chmn. bd. dirs. 1978-80). Asst. prof. vet. surgery U. Calif., Davis, 1953-61; prof. vet. surgery Wash. State U., Pullman, 1961-91, prof. emeritus, 1991—; mem. Wash. State Vet. Bd. Govs., 1981-88, chmn., 1987; vis. fellow Sydney (Australia) U., 1977. Author/editor: Intervertebral Disc Protrusion in the Dog, 1966; cons. editoral bd. Jour. Small Animal Practice, Eng., 1970-88; mem. editoral bd. Compendium on C.E., Lawrenceville, N.J., 1983-86, editoral rev. bd. Jour. Vet. Surgery, Phila., 1984-86, editor 1987-92; contbr. articles to profl. jours., chpts. to books. Elder Presbyn. Ch., Pullman, 1967—. Served with USN, 1944-46. Recipient Norden Disting. Tchr. award Wash. State U. Class 1971, Faculty of Yr. award Wash. State U. Student Com., 1985. Mem. AVMA, Am. Legion, Kiwanis Internat., Sigma Xi, Phi Zeta, Phi Kappa Sigma (chpt. advisor 1981-93, 2d v.p. 1993—). Republican. Avocations: camping, small boat sailing.

PETTIT, GHERY ST. JOHN, electronics engineer; b. Woodland, Calif., Apr. 6, 1952; s. Ghery DeWitt and Frances Marie (Seitz) P.; m. Marilyn Jo Van Hoose, July 28, 1973; children: Ghery Christopher, Heather Kathleen. BS in Electrical Engring., Wash. State U., 1975. Nuclear engr. Mare Island Naval Shipyard, Vallejo, Calif., 1975-76; electronics engr. Naval Electronic Systems Engring. Ctr., Vallejo, 1976-79; sr. engr. Martin Marietta Denver Aerospace, 1979-83; staff engr. Tandem Computers Inc., Santa Clara, Calif., 1983-90; mgr. electromagnetic capability Tandem Computers Inc., Cupertino, Calif., 1990-91, electromagnetic compatibility lead engr., 1991-95; EMC engr. Intel Corp., Hillsboro, Oreg., 1995—. Asst. cubmaster Boy Scouts Am., San Jose, Calif., 1985-86, cubmaster, 1986-88, ast. scoutmaster, 1988-90, scoutmaster, 1990-93. Mem. IEEE (sr.), Electromagnetic Capability Soc. (sec.-treas. Littleton, Colo. chpt. 1983, sec. Santa Clara Valley chpt. 1985-87, vice chmn. 1987-89, chmn. 1989-91, sec. Santa Clara Valley sect. 1991-92, treas. 1992-93, vice chmn. 1993-94, chmn. 1994-95). Republican. Presbyterian. Avocations: target shooting, hiking, camping, amateur radio. Office: Intel Corp 5200 NE Elam Young Pky Hillsboro OR 97124

PETTIT, JOHN W., administrator; b. Detroit, Mar. 6, 1942; s. John W. and Clara (Schartz) P.; m. Kathleen Endres, Aug. 8, 1970; children: Julie, Andrew, Michael. BBA, U. Notre Dame, 1964; MBA, Mich. State U., 1974. CPA, Mich. Acct. Ernst & Ernst, Detroit, 1964-67; chief acct. Detroit Inst. Tech., Detroit, 1967-69; controller, dir. adminstrn. & fin. Mich. Cancer Found., Detroit, 1969-80; chief adminstrv. officer Dana-Farber Cancer Inst., Boston, 1980-94; exec. v.p., chief oper. officer John Wayne Cancer Inst., Santa Monica, Calif., 1995—; grant reviewer Nat. Cancer Inst., Bethesda, Md., 1979—. Pres. advanced mgmt. program Mich. State U., 1978-79. Mem. Am. Inst. CPA's. Avocations: sailing, woodworking, photography, music. Office: John Wayne Cancer Inst 2200 Santa Monica Blvd Santa Monica CA 90404-2301

PETTIT, JOHN WHITNEY, lawyer; b. Washington, Mar. 20, 1935; s. Manson Bowers and Dagny Bernice (Rudback) P.; m. Anne McCullough, Jan. 20, 1939; children: John Whitney, Jennifer Read. BA, Duke U., 1957; JD, Georgetown U., 1960. Bar: D.C. 1960, U.S. Supreme Ct. 1965. Gen. counsel FCC, 1972-74; assoc. Hamel & Park, Washington, 1963-67, ptnr., 1967-72; gen. counsel FCC, Washington, 1972-74; ptnr. Hamel & Park, Washington, 1974-88, mng. ptnr., 1978-80, 86-88; mng. ptnr. Hopkins & Sutter, Washington, 1988-94; ptnr. Drinker Biddle & Reath, Washington, 1994—, ptnr.-in-charge, 1995—, mng. ptnr., 1996—. Fellow Am. Bar Found.; mem. ABA, Fed. Comms. Bar Assn., Vis. Nurse Assn. Washington (chair, bd. dirs. 1990-95), Met. Club, Chevy Chase (Md.) Club. Office: Drinker Biddle & Reath 901 15th St NW Washington DC 20005-2327

PETTIT, LAWRENCE KAY, university president; b. Lewistown, Mont., May 2, 1937; s. George Edwin and Dorothy Bertha (Brown) P.; m. Sharon Lee Anderson, June 21, 1961 (div. Oct. 1976); children: Jennifer Anna, Matthew Anderson, Allison Carol, Edward McLean; m. Elizabeth DuBois Medley, July 11, 1980; 3 stepchildren. BA cum laude, U. Mont., 1959; AM, Washington U., St. Louis, 1962; PhD, U. Wis., 1965. Legis. asst. U.S. Senate, 1959-60, 62; asst. & assoc. prof. dept. polit. sci. Pa. State U., 1964-67; assoc. dir. fed. rels. Am. Council Edn., Washington, 1967-69; prof., chmn. dept. polit. sci. Mont. State U., 1969-72; adminstrv. asst. to gov. State of Mont., 1973; chancellor Mont. Univ. System, Helena, 1973-79; pvt. practice ednl. cons. Mont., 1979-81; dep. commr. for acad. affairs Tex. Coordinating Bd. for Higher Edn., 1981-83; chancellor Univ. System of South Tex., 1983-86; chancellor So. Ill. U., Carbondale and Edwardsville, 1986-91, Disting. svc. prof., 1991-92; pres. Indiana U. Pa., 1992—; mem. various nat. and regional bds. and coms. on higher edn. Author: (with H. Albinski) European Political Processes, 2d edit., 1974, (with E. Keynes) Legislative Process in the U.S. Senate, 1969, (with S. Kirkpatrick) Social Psychology of Political Life, 1972, (with J. Goetz and S. Thomas) Legislative Process in Montana, 1975; mem. editorial bd. Ednl. Record, 1985—. Mem. adv. bd. Leadership Ctr. Ams., 1988-90, Ill. Coalition, 1989-92; candidate for 2d dist. U.S. Ho. of Reps., Mont., 1980; mem. Ill. Gov.'s Com. on Sci. and Tech., 1986-90; bd. dirs. Tex. Guaranteed Student Loan Corp., 1985-86; chmn. Ill.-Niigata Commn. on Edn. and Econ. Devel., 1990-92; chair bd. dirs. Nat. Environ. Edn. and Tng. Ctr., 1994—. U. Wis. fellow 1962-63, Vilas fellow U. Wis., 1963-64. Mem. AAUP (pres. Mont. conf. 1971-72), Nat. Assn. Sys. Heads (pres. 1989), Am. Coun. on Edn. (chmn. leadership commn. 1989-90, sr. fellow 1991-92), Am. Assn. Higher Edn., Am. Assn. State Colls. and Univs. (Disting. Svc. award 1991), Newcomen Soc., Duquesne Club Pitts., Allegheny Club Pitts., World Affairs Coun. Pitts., Univ. Club Pitts., Pa. Soc., Ind. Country Club, Rotary, Sigma Chi (Significant Sig award 1988), Phi Kappa Phi. Episcopalian. Office: Indiana U President's Office 201 John Sutton Hall Indiana PA 15705

PETTIT, THOMAS HENRY, ophthalmologist; b. Salt Lake City, Jan. 20, 1929; s. William A. and Laura M. (Tanner) P.; m. Betty Ann Dain, June 12, 1953; children: Thomas H., Heather, Daina Lee, Drucilla, Elizabeth, Kristen. AB, UCLA, 1949; MD, U. Pa., 1955. Diplomate Am. Bd. Ophthalmology (bd. dirs. 1983-90, chmn. 1990). Intern Los Angeles County Gen. Hosp., 1955-56; resident ophthalmology Washington U., Barnes Hosp., St. Louis, 1958-61; trainee Nat. Insts. Neurol. Diseases and Blindness, St. Louis, 1959-61, spl. fellow, 1961-62; spl. fellow U. Calif. Sch. Medicine, San Francisco, 1962-63; rsch. fellow ophthalmology Sch. Medicine, UCLA, 1962-63, asst. prof. in residence, 1963-65, asst. prof. surgery-ophthalmology, 1965-67, assoc. prof., 1967-69, prof. ophthalmology, 1969-91, prof. emeritus, 1991—; mem. staff Jules Stein Eye Inst., L.A., 1965—, assoc. dir., 1971-91; cons. ophthalmology VA Hosp., Long Beach, Calif., 1963-70, Sepulveda (Calif.) VA Hosp., 1969-91; mem. staff UCLA Hosp.; attending physician Wadsworth VA Hosp., L.A., 1963-70; vis. prof. ophthalmology Washington U., St. Louis, 1969, 78, 83, U. W.Va., 1985; Zanvyl Krieger lectr. Mt. Sinai Hosp., Johns Hopkins U., 1985; guest of honor Ann. Proctor Fellows meeting U. Calif. Med. Ctr., San Francisco, 1978, Ralph Heintz lectr., 1988; mem. vision rsch. com. Nat. Eye Inst., USPHS, 1971-75. Contbr. articles to profl. jours.; mem. editorial bd.: Investigative Ophthalmology, 1969-73, Am. Jour. Ophthalmology, 1985-87. Trustee Estelle Doheny Eye Found., L.A., 1968—, v.p., 1971-75. Lt. M.C., USN, 1956-63. Fellow Am. Acad. Ophthalmology and Otolaryngology (assoc. sec. continuing edn. in ophthalmology 1978-82, Honor award 1969, Sr. Honor award 1984); mem. AMA, Assn. for Rsch. in Vision and Ophthalmology, Pan-Am. Assn. Ophthalmology, L.A. Soc. Ophthalmology, Ocular Microbiology and Immunology Group, Contact Lens Assn. Ophthalmologists, Calif. Cornea Club, Am. Intraocular Implant Soc., Rsch. Study Club in Ophthalmology, Calif. Med. Soc., Los Angeles County Med. Soc., Phi Beta Kappa, Alpha Omega Alpha. Mem. LDS Ch. (bishop 1980-86). Office: UCLA Med Ctr Jules Stein Eye Instit Los Angeles CA 90024

PETTITE, WILLIAM CLINTON, public affairs consultant; b. Reno, Nev.; s. Sidney Clinton and Wilma (Stibal) P.; m. Charlotte Denise Fryer; children: Patrick Keane, William Ellis, Joseph Clinton. Owner, Market Lake Citizen & Clark County Enterprise Newspapers, Roberts, Idaho, 1959-70, pub., 1959-61; publicity dir. Golden Days World Boxing Champs, Reno, 1970; pub. Virginia City (Nev.) Legend newspaper, 1970; public affairs cons., Fair Oaks, Calif., 1966—, owner PT Cattle Co., Firth, Idaho; cons. in Ireland, Wales, Korea, Japan, France, Czech Republic, Alberta, British Columbia, New Brunswick, Prince Edward Island, Nova Scotia, Can., Channel Islands, Costa Rica, Macau, Hong Kong, 1984—. County probate judge, Idaho, 1959-61; acting county coroner, 1960-61; sec., trustee Fair Oaks Cemetery Dist., 1963-72; bd. dir. Fair Oaks Water Dist., 1964-72, v.p., 1967-68, pres., 1968-70; dir., v.p. San Juan Cmty. Svcs. Dist., 1962-66, 68-72; exec. sec. Calif. Bd. Landscape Archs., 1976-78, Calif. Assn. Collectors, 1966-68. Cons. Senate-Assembly Joint Audit Com. Calif. Legislature, 1971-73; exec. officer Occupational Safety and Health Appeals Bd., 1981-83; mem. regulatory rev. commn. Calif. FabricCare Bd., 1981-82; mem. Sacramento County Grand Jury, 1981-82, cons. bd. supvs. Sacramento County, 1985-86; chmn. bus. adv. bd. East Lawn Corp, 1991—. Election campaign coord. for E.S. Wright, majority leader Idaho Senate, 1968, Henry Dworshak, U.S. Senator, 1960, Hamer Budge, U.S. Rep., 1960, Charles C. Gossett, former Gov. Idaho, 1959-74; asst. sgt. at arms Rep. Nat. Conv., 1956; chmn. Rep. County Cen. Com., 1959-61; del. Rep. State Conv., 1960. Chmn. Idaho County Centennial Commn., 1959-61. Recipient Idaho Centennial award, 1968, 69. Mem. Assn. Sacramento County Water Dists. (bd. dir. 1967-72, pres. 1970-72), No. Calif. Peace Officers Assn., Nat. Coun. Juvenile Ct. Judges (com. 1959-61). Club. Author: Memories of Market Lake, Vol. I, 1965; A History of Southeastern Idaho, Vol. II, 1977, Vol. III, 1983, Vol. IV, 1990; contbr. articles to newspapers, profl. jours. Home: PO Box 2127 Fair Oaks CA 95628-2127 Office: 2631 K St Sacramento CA 95816-5103 *Personal philosophy: Proverbs 3:3 "Never forget to be truthful and kind. Hold these virtues tightly. Write them deep within your heart."*

PETTITT, JAY S., architect, consultant; b. Redford, Mich., Jan. 6, 1926; s. Jay S. and Florence Marian (Newman) P.; m. Ruth Elizabeth Voigt, June 21, 1947; children—J. Stuart, Laura Ellen, Patricia Lynn, Carol Ann. B.Arch., U. Mich., 1951. Registered architect, Mich. Draftsman Frank J. Stepnoski and Son, Fond du Lac, Wis., 1951; project architect Albert Kahn Assocs., Inc., Detroit, 1951-62; chief archtl. devel. Albert Kahn Assocs., Inc., 1962-67, v.p., 1967-88, dir. architecture, 1975-88; archtl. cons. Beulah, Mich., 1988—. Active Jr. Athletic Assn., Redford, Mich., 1959-63; com. chmn. Boy Scouts Am., 1960-65; supr. Benzonia Twp. Served with U.S. Army, 1943-46, ETO. Fellow AIA; mem. Mich. Soc. Architects (pres. 1967), Am. Arbitration Assn., Am. Assn. Hosp. Planning, Engring. Soc. Detroit, U. Mich. Pres.' Club. Avocations: sailing; skiing.

PETTY, CHARLES SUTHERLAND, pathologist; b. Lewistown, Mont., Apr. 16, 1920; s. Charles Frederic and Mae (Reichert) P.; m. Lois Muriel Swenson, Dec. 14, 1957; children—Heather Ann, Charles Sutherland II; children by previous marriage—Daniel S., Carol L. B.S., U. Wash., 1941, M.S., 1946; M.D., Harvard U., 1950. Intern Mary Imogene Bassett Hosp., Coopertown, N.Y., 1950-52; resident in pathology Peter Bent Brigham Hosp., Children's Med. Center, New Eng. Deaconness Hosp., Boston, 1952-55; instr. pathology La. State U. Sch. Medicine, 1955-56, asst. prof., 1956-58; asst. med. examiner State of Md., 1958-67; asst. prof. forensic pathology U. Md. Sch. Medicine, 1958-64, asso. prof., 1964-67; lectr., then asso. Johns Hopkins U. Sch. Hygiene and Public Health, 1959-67; adj. prof. police adminstrn. U. Louisville, 1978—; dir. Balt. Regional ARC Blood Program, 1959-67; prof. forensic pathology Ind. U. Sch. Medicine, Indpls., 1967-69; dir. lab. Ind. Commn. on Forensic Scis., 1967-69; chief med. examiner Dallas County, 1969-91; prof. forensic scis., pathology U. Tex. Southwestern Med. Sch., Dallas, 1969—; dir. Southwestern Inst. Forensic Scis., 1969-91. Served from ensign to lt. comdr. USNR, 1941-45. Fellow Coll. Am. Pathologists, Am. Soc. Clin. Pathologists, A.C.P., Am. Acad. Forensic Scis. (pres. 1967-68); mem. Sigma Xi. Episcopalian. Home: 3964 Goodfellow Dr Dallas TX 75229-2722 Office: 5601 Med Ctr Dr Dallas TX 75235-7200

PETTY, GEORGE OLIVER, lawyer; b. L.A., Mar. 31, 1939; s. Hugh Morton and May (Johnson) P.; m. Sandra Diane Kilpatrick, July 14, 1962; children: Ross Morton, Alison Lee, Christopher Henry. AB, U. Calif., Berkeley, 1961; LLB, U. Calif., 1964. Bar: Calif. 1965, Eng. and Wales 1986, U.S. Supreme Ct. 1976. Atty. Huovinen & White, Oakland, Calif., 1967-69; counsel Bechtel Power Corp., San Francisco, 1969-83; prin. counsel Bechtel Ltd., London, 1983-86; gen. counsel Sun-Diamond Growers of Calif., Pleasanton, Calif., 1987-95; pvt. practice, 1995—. Capt. U.S. Army, 1965-67. Mem. Calif. State Bar Assn., Alameda County Bar Assn., Eng. and Wales Bar Assn., Bar Assn. for Commerce, Fin. & Industry (Eng.), Middle Temple Inn. Office: 843 Arlington Ave Berkeley CA 94707

PETTY, JOHN ROBERT, banker; b. Chgo., Apr. 16, 1930; s. Dewitt Talmage and Beatrice (Worthington) P.; children: L. Talmage, Robert D., George M., Victoria Lee. AB, Brown U., 1951; postgrad., NYU, 1953-54. With Chase Manhattan Bank, N.Y.C. and Paris, 1953-66; v.p. Chase Manhattan Bank, 1964-66; dep. asst. sec. Dept. Treasury, Washington, 1966-68, asst. sec. for internat. affairs, 1968-72; partner Lehman Bros., N.Y.C., 1972-76; pres., dir., chmn. exec. com. Marine Midland Banks, Inc., from 1976, chmn., chief exec. officer, 1976-88; mng. gen. ptnr. Petty-FBW Assocs., Washington, 1989-91; chmn. Fed. Nat. Payables Inc. Washington, 1992—, Fed. Nat. Svcs. Inc., 1992—; chmn. Nippon Credit Trust Co., N.Y.C.; chmn. Hydro-Icona, Inc., Czech & Slovak Am. Enterprise Fund, 1991-95; bd. dirs. Antec Corp., Magnetic Analysis Corp., Anixter Internat. Corp.; trustee Am. Univ. With USNR, 1951-53. Mem. Council Fgn. Relations, Fgn. Bondholders Protective Council (pres.). Office: 7315 Wisconsin Ave Ste 322E Bethesda MD 20814

PETTY, KYLE, professional stock car driver; s. Richard and Lynda P. 5th in NASCAR money leaders, 1992. Winner Champion Spark Plug 500, 1993. Office: c/o NASCAR PO Box 2875 Daytona Beach FL 32120-2875*

PETTY, RICHARD, retired professional race car driver; s. Lee and Elizabeth T. P.; m. Lynda Owens; children: Kyle, Sharon, Lisa, Rebecca. Auto racer, 35 years, ret., 1992; owner Car # 43. Mem. Pres.'s Council Fitness and Sport. Recipient Myers Bros. award Nat. Motorsports Press Assn., 1961, 67, 71, Excellence award NASCAR, 1987; named Grand Nat. Rookie of Year, 1959; Most Popular Driver in Grand Nat., 1962, 64, 68, 70, 74, 75, 76, 77, 78; Martini & Rossi Am. Driver of Year, 1971; Driver of Year Nat. Motorsport Press Assn., 1974-75; Driver of Quarter Century, 1991; inducted into N.C. Athletic Hall of Fame, 1973. Mem. Nat. Assn. Stock Car Auto Racing (7 time champion; Winston Cup grand nat. champion 1964, 67, 71, 72, 74, 75, 79). Entered 1015 Grand Nat. Races, winner 200, 1958-86, with 55 Superspeedway wins; winner Daytona 500, 1964, 66, 71, 73, 74, 79, 81; 1000th career Winston Cup start June 15, 1986 at Mich. Internat. Speedway; 500th consecutive start on Aug. 21, 1988 in Champion Spark Plug 500. Address: 311 Branson Mill Rd Randleman NC 27317-8008*

PETTY, RICHARD EDWARD, psychologist, educator, researcher; b. Garden City, N.Y., May 22, 1951; s. Edmund and Josephine (Serzo) P.; m. Virginia Lynn Oliver, Aug. 29, 1978. BA, U. Va., 1973; PhD, Ohio State U., 1977. Asst. prof. psychology U. Mo., Columbia, 1977-80, assoc. prof. psychology, 1981-83, Middlebush prof. psychology, 1984-85; vis. fellow Yale U., New Haven, Conn., 1986; prof. psychology Ohio State U., Columbus, 1987—; vis. prof. Princeton U., 1995; advisor com. on dietary guidelines implementation NAS, 1989-91; chair NIMH Social and Group Processes Panel. Author: Attitudes and Persuasion, 1981, Communication and Persuasion, 1986, Attitude Strength, 1995; editor Personality and Social Psychology Bull., 1988-92; mem. editl. bd. of 6 jours.; contbr. articles to profl. jours. Grantee NIMH, 1978-79, NSF, 1984-88, 90-94, 95—. Fellow AAAS, APA, Am. Psychol. Soc. Achievements include origination of the elaboration likelihood model of persuasion. Home: 2955 Scioto Pl Columbus OH 43221-4753 Office: Ohio State U 1885 Neil Ave Columbus OH 43210-1222

PETTY, THOMAS LEE, physician, educator; b. Boulder, Colo., Dec. 24, 1932; s. Roy Stone and Eleanor Marie (Kudrna) P.; m. Carol Lee Piepho, Aug. 7, 1954; children: Caryn, Thomas, John. B.A., U. Colo., 1955, M.D., 1958. Intern Phila. Gen. Hosp., 1958-59; resident U. Mich., 1959-60, U. Colo., Denver, 1960-62; pulmonary fellow U. Colo., 1962-63, chief resident medicine, 1963-64, instr. medicine, 1962-64, asst. prof., 1964-68, assoc. prof., 1968-74, prof. medicine, 1974—; pres. Presbyn./St. Luke's Ctr. for Health Scis. Edn., 1989-95; practice medicine, specializing in internal medicine, pulmonary medicine Denver, 1962—; prof. medicine Rush Univ., 1992—; Cons. Fitzsimmons Army Hosp., 1970—. Author: For Those Who Live and Breathe, 1967, 2d edit., 1972, Intensive and Rehabilitative Respiratory Care, 1971, 3d edit., 1982, Chronic Obstructive Pulmonary Disease, 1978, 2d edit., 1985, Principles and Practice of Pulmonary Rehabilitation, 1993, Enjoying Life With COPD, 1995, 3d edit., others; contbr. articles to profl. jours. NIH and Found. grantee, 1966-88. Mem. Am. Lung Assn. (Colo. chpt. pres. 1975), Am. Coll. Chest Physicians (pres. 1982), Assn. Am. Physicians, Assn. of Pulmonary Program Dirs. (founding pres. 1983-84), Am. Bd. Internal Medicine (bd. govs. 1986-92), Phi Beta Kappa, Phi Delta Theta, Alpha Omega Alpha, Phi Rho Sigma (pres. 1976-78). Home: 1940 Grape St Denver CO 80220-1353 Office: Presbyn Hosp Dept Internal Medicine Denver CO 80218

PETTY, TOM, rock guitarist, band leader, composer; b. Gainesville, Fla., Oct. 20, 1950; s. Earl Petty. Rock guitarist, 1969—; leader Tom Petty and the Heartbreakers, 1975—. Played in local bands The Epics, Mudcrutch while in Gainesville; songwriter, musician for Leon Russell, 1974; rec. and touring artist with the Heartbreakers, albums include Tom Petty and the Heartbreakers, 1976, You're Gonna Get It, 1978, Damn the Torpedoes, 1979, Hard Promises, 1981, Long After Dark, 1982, Southern Accents, 1985, Pack Up the Plantation, 1986, Let Me Up (I've Had Enough), 1987, Full Moon Fever, 1989, Into the Great Wide Open, 1991, Tom Petty and the Heartbreakers' Greatest Hits, 1993, Wildflowers, 1994; (with The Traveling Wilburys) Traveling Wilburys Vol. 1, 1989, Traveling Wilburys Vol. 3, 1990; hit singles include Breakdown, 1978, Here Comes My Girl, 1979, Refugee, 1979, The Waiting, 1981, You Got Lucky, 1982, Don't Come Around Here No More, 1985, Jammin' Me, 1987, Free Fallin', 1989 (solo album) Wildflowers, 1995; toured the world with Bob Dylan, 1986, toured America with Georgia Satellites and Del Fuegos (Rock 'n' Roll Caravan tour), 1987. Grammy nomination (Best Rock Duo or Group Performance, 1994) for My Back Pages (with Bob Dylan, Roger McGuinn, Neil Young, Eric Clapton, and George Harrison); MTV Best Male Video (with the Heartbreakers) for Mary Jane's Last Dance; recipient MTV Video Vanguard award. Address: 433 N Camden Dr Beverly Hills CA 90210-4426

PETYKIEWICZ, SANDRA DICKEY, editor; b. Detroit, Sept. 23, 1953; d. James Fulton and Alice Diane (Nowak) Dickey; m. Edward W. Petykiewicz,

Oct. 17, 1981; 1 child, Kendall Lee. BA, Cen. Mich. U., Mt. Pleasant, 1975. Reporter Big Rapids (Mich.) Pioneer, 1975, Midland (Mich.) Daily News, 1975-77; reporter Saginaw (Mich.) News, 1977-79, feature editor, 1979-80, asst. metro editor, 1980-81; copy editor Washington Post, 1981-82; asst. city editor Balt. News Am., 1982-83; metro editor Jackson (Mich.) Citizen Patriot, 1983-87, editor, 1987—; bd. dirs. Mich. AP, 1987-93, pres., 1990, 1991-92; bd. dirs. Mid Am. Press Inst., 1992—; mem. alumni bd. Ctrl. Mich. U., 1992-96, mem. journalism adv. bd., 1992—. Pulitzer Prize juror, 1990-92. Mem. Jackson Area Quality Initiative, 1990—. Mem. Am. Soc. Newspaper Editors, Soc. Profl. Journalists, Bus. and Profl. Women's Club (editor newsletter 1985-86, Young Career Woman of Yr. award 1984), Rotary Club, Jackson Eocn. Club (chairwoman 1992), Sigma Delta Chi. Avocations: golf, writing, reading, travel.

PETZ, EDWIN V., real estate executive, lawyer; b. Beatrice, Nebr., May 14, 1935; s. Virgil Leonard and Ruth Elenor (Thomsen) P.; m. Daphne Cross, May 17, 1958 (div. June 1964); 1 dau., Katherine J.; m. Anne Higgins, Dec. 3, 1964 (div. Sept. 1993); 1 son, W. Christopher. B.A., Principia Coll., Elsah, Ill., 1955; J.D., Harvard U., 1958. Bar: N.Y. 1959, Mass. 1976. Assoc. Chadbourne, Parke, Whiteside & Wolff, N.Y.C., 1958-62; asst. gen. counsel Martin Marietta Corp., Bethesda, Md., 1963-64, 1965-75; gen. atty. sec. Bunker-Ramo Corp., Oakbrook, Ill., 1964-65; asst. gen. counsel United Brands Co., N.Y.C., 1975-82, v.p., gen. counsel, sec., 1982-84; sr. v.p., gen. counsel Milstein Properties Corp., 1985—; sr. v.p., gen counsel The Milstein Group Inc., 1992—. Mem. ABA, Assn. of Bar of City N.Y. Republican. Episcopalian. Club: University (N.Y.C.). Office: Milstein Properties Corp 1271 Avenue Of The Americas New York NY 10020

PETZAL, DAVID ELIAS, editor, writer; b. N.Y.C., Oct. 21, 1941; s. Henry and Aline Born (Bixer) P.; m. Arlene Anne Taylor, May 29, 1974. B.A., Colgate U., 1963. Editor Maco Publs., N.Y.C., 1964-69; mng. editor Davis Publs., N.Y.C., 1969-70; features editor Hearst Publs., N.Y.C., 1970-72; mng. editor CBS Publs., N.Y.C., 1972-79, editor, 1979-83, exec. editor, 1983-87; exec. editor Times-Mirror Mags., N.Y.C., 1987—. Author: The .22 Rifle, 1972; editor: The Experts Book of the Shooting Sports, 1972, The Experts Book of Upland Game and Waterfowl Hunting, 1975, The Experts Book of Big-Game Hunting in North America, 1976, The Ency. of Sporting Firearms, 1991. Home: PO Box 219 Bedford NY 10506-0219 Office: Times Mirror Mags 2 Park Ave New York NY 10016-5603

PETZEL, FLORENCE ELOISE, textiles educator; b. Crosbyton, Tex., Apr. 1, 1911; d. William D. and A. Eloise (Punchard) P. PhB, U. Chgo., 1931, AM, 1934; PhD, U. Minn., 1954. Instr., Judson Coll., 1936-38; asst. prof. textiles Ohio State U., 1938-48; assoc. prof. U. Ala., 1950-54; prof. Oreg. State U., 1954-61, 67-75, 77, prof. emeritus, 1975—, dept. head, 1954-61, 67-75; prof., div. head U. Tex., 1961-63; prof. Tex. Tech U., 1963-67; vis. instr. Tex. State Coll. for Women, 1937; vis. prof. Wash. State U., 1967. Effie I. Raitt fellow, 1949-50. Mem. Met. Opera Guild, High Mus. Art, Sigma Xi, Phi Kappa Phi, Omicron Nu, Iota Sigma Pi, Sigma Delta Epsilon. Author Textiles of Ancient Mesopotamia, Persia and Egypt, 1987; contbr. articles to profl. jours. Home: 150 Downs Blvd Apt D205 Clemson SC 29631-2049

PETZOLD, ANITA MARIE, psychotherapist; b. Princeton, N.J., June 2, 1957; d. Charles Bernard and Kathleen Marie (McDonald) P. AS in Bus., Indian River C.C., Ft. Pierce, Fla., 1986; BS in Liberal Studies, Barry U., 1988; MS in Human Svcs. Adminstrn., Nova U., 1989, postgrad., 1989-91; PhD in Human Svcs. Adminstrn., LaSalle U., 1994. Lic. mental health counselor, Fla.; cert. addictions profl.; internat. cert. alcohol and drug abuse counselor; nat. cert. counselor; cert. employee assistance counselor; nat. cert. clin. mental health counselor; nat. cert. addictions counselor; cert. DUI instr. Admissions asst. The Palm Beach Inst., West Palm Beach, Fla., 1985-86; dir. admissions Heritage Health Corp., Jensen Beach, Fla., 1986-89; drug abuse strategy coord. Martin County Bd. of County Commrs., Stuart, Fla., 1989—; mem. Drug Resource Team for the 12th Congl. Dist., Fla., 1990—, Juvenile Justice Assn. of the 19th Jud. Ct., Fla., 1993—; grant writer in field. Vol. Hist. Soc. Martin County, Stuart, 1986—; mem. United Way Martin County, Stuart, 1993; mem. bd. dirs. Cmty. AIDS Adv. Project, Stuart, 1993; chmn. treatment com. Martin County Task Force on Substance Abused Children, Stuart, 1993—. Recipient Outstanding Cmty. Svc. award United Way Martin County, Stuart, 1993. Mem. NASW, Am. Mental Health Counselors Assn., Nat. Criminal Justice Assn., Nat. Assn. Alcoholism and Drug Abuse Counselors, Nat. Consortium Treatment Alternatives to St. Crime Programs, Am. Coll. Addiction Treatment Adminstrs., Am. Labor-Mgmt. Adminstrs., Fla. Alcohol and Drug Abuse Assn. Republican. Roman Catholic. Avocations: walking, reading. Office: Martin County Bd County Commrs 400 SE Osceola St Stuart FL 34994-2577

PETZOLD, CAROL STOKER, state legislator; b. St. Louis, July 28; d. Harold William and Mabel Lucille (Wilson) Stoker; m. Walter John Petzold, June 27, 1959; children: Ann, Ruth, David. BS, Valparaiso U., 1959. Tchr. John Muir Elem. Sch., Alameda, Calif., 1959-60, Parkwood Elem. Sch., Kensington, Md., 1960-62; legis. aide Md. Gen. Assembly, Annapolis, 1975-79; legis. asst. Montgomery County Bd. Edn., Rockville, Md., 1980; community sch. coordinator Parkland Jr. High Sch., Rockville, 1981-87; mem. judiciary com. Md. Ho. of Dels., Annapolis, 1987—; mem. transp. planning bd. Nat. Capitol Region, 1989—; vice chair energy and transp. com. Nat. Conf. State Legislatures; exec. com. Montgomery United Way Coun., 1981—. Editor Child Care Sampler, 1974, Stoker Family Cookbook, 1976. Pres. Montgomery Child Care Assn., 1976-78; mem. Md. State Scholarship Bd., 1978-87, chmn. 1985-87; chmn. Legis. Com. Montgomery County Commn. for Children and Youth, 1979-84; mem., v.p. Luth. Social Services Nat. Capitol Area, Washington, 1980-86. Recipient Statewide award Gov.'s Adv. Bd. on Homelessness; recognized for outstanding commitment to children U.S. Dept. HEW, 1980. Mem. AAUW (honoree Kensington br. 1971, honoree Md. div. 1981), Women's Polit. Caucus (chmn. Montgomery County 1981-83), Women's Caucus Md. Legislature. Democrat. Lutheran. Home: 14113 Chadwick Ln Rockville MD 20853-2103

PEUGEOT, PATRICK, insurance executive; b. Paris, Aug. 3, 1937; s. Jacques Louis and Edith (Genoyer) P.; m. Catherine Dupont, 1963; children: Hubert, Thomas, Camille. Degree, Ecole Poly., Paris, 1959, Ecol Nat. D'Adminstrn., Paris, 1965. Ins. auditor Ministry of Fin., Paris, 1962-65; auditor Cour des Comptes, Paris, 1965-83; spl. asst. Bur. Planning, Paris, 1966-70; sr. v.p. EMC, Toulouse, France, 1970-72, Hachette Inc., Paris, 1972-74; exec. v.p. ops. AGF Life, Paris, 1974-78; exec. v.p. AGF Reins., Paris, 1979-82; pres. Caisse Cen. de Reassurance, Paris, 1983-85; chmn. Scor S.A., Paris, 1984-94, hon. chmn., 1994, 1994—; vice chmn., CEO La Mondiale, Paris; dir. SCOR U.S., 1994—; chmn., CEO La Mondiale, 1996—. Home: 82 rue Notre Dame Champs, 75006 Paris France Office: Scor US Corp 2 World Trade Ctr New York NY 10048-0178

PEURA, ROBERT ALLAN, electrical and biomedical engineering educator; b. Worcester, Mass., Jan. 26, 1943; married; four children. BS, Worcester Poly. Inst., 1964; MS, Iowa State U., 1967, PhD, 1969. From asst. prof. to assoc. prof. elec./biomed. engring. Worcester (Mass.) Poly. Inst., 1968—; sir. dir. St. Vincent Hosp. Internship Ctr., Worcester, 1972—; lectr. biomed. engring. Med. Sch. U. Mass., 1974—; vis. assoc. prof. health sci. & technol. divsn. Mass. Inst. Tech., Cambridge, 1981-82. Mem. IEEE, Am. Heart Assn., Am. Soc. Engring. Edn., Assn. Advanced Med. Instrumentation. Office: Worcester Polytechnic Inst Applied Bioengineering Ctr 100 Institute Rd Worcester MA 01609*

PEVEC, ANTHONY EDWARD, bishop; b. Cleve., Apr. 16, 1925; s. Anton and Frances (Darovec) P. MA, John Carroll U., Cleve., 1956; PhD, Western Res. U., Cleve., 1964. Ordained priest Roman Catholic Ch., 1950. Assoc. pastor St. Mary Church, Elyria, Ohio, 1950-52, St. Lawrence Ch., Cleve., 1952-53; rector-prin. Borromeo Sem. High Sch., Wickliffe, Ohio, 1953-75; adminstrv. bd. Nat. Cath. Edn. Assn., 1972-75; pastor St. Vitus Ch., Cleve., 1975-79; rector-pres. Borromeo Coll., Wickliffe, 1979-82; aux. bishop Diocese of Cleve., 1982—; cons. Nat. Conf. Cath. Bishops Com. on Pro-Life Activities, 1990-92; mem. U.S. Cath. Conf., 1982—, Ohio Cath. Conf., 1982—, Papal Visitation Team, 1982-87, Bishops' Com. on Vocations, 1984-86, Bishops' Com. on Sci. and Human Values, 1993—, Bishops' Com. on Priestly Formation, 1993—. Mem. v.p. Slovenian-Am. Heritage Found., Cleve., 1975—. Honoree, Heritage Found., Cleve., 1982; named Man of Yr., Fedn. Slovenian Nat. Homes, Cleve., 1985; inducted into Hall of Fame, St. Vitus Alumni Assn., 1989. Democrat. Roman Catholic. Avocations: reading; music. Home and Office: Diocese of Cleve 28700 Euclid Ave Wickliffe OH 44092-2527 *Ultimately I must always remember that the Lord is totally in control of my life, no matter how complicated it may seem to be. I am here to do the Lord's will,, and wherever I go I come to do His will.*

PEW, JOHN GLENN, JR., lawyer; b. Dallas, Apr. 18, 1932; s. John Glenn Sr. and Roberta (Haughton) P. BA, U. Tex., 1954. LLB, 1955. Bar: Tex. 1955, U.S. Dist. Ct. (no. dist.) Tex. 1959, U.S. Supreme Ct. 1959, U.S. Ct. Appeals (5th cir.) 1961, U.S. Ct. Appeals (10th cir.) 1982. Ptnr., Jackson & Walker, L.L.P., Dallas, 1964—. With USNR, 1955-58. Mem. Order of Coif, Phi Beta Kappa. Republican. Presbyterian. Office: Jackson & Walker LLP 901 Main St Ste 6000 Dallas TX 75202-3797

PEW, ROBERT ANDERSON, retired real estate corporation officer; b. Phila., Aug. 22, 1936; s. Arthur Edmund and Mary Elizabeth (Elliott) P.; children from previous marriage: Robert Anderson (dec.), James Cunningham, Glenn Edgar, Joan Elliott; m. Daria S. Decerio, June 19, 1993. Student, Princeton U., 1954-56; B.S., Temple U., 1959; M.S. in Mgmt. (Alfred P. Sloan fellow), MIT, 1970; LL.D. (hon.), Widener U., 1982; D.P.S. (hon.), Temple U., 1983; L.H.D. (hon.), Gettysburg Coll., 1984. Ops. asst. prodn. div. Sun Oil Co., Premont, Tex., 1959-60; ops. asst. prodn. div. Sun Oil Co., Morgan City, La.; auditor internal audit dept. Sun Oil Co., Phila., 1960-65, staff asst. treasury dept., 1965-69, asst. to exec. v.p. corp. projects group, 1970-71, sec.-treas., mgr. financial control of products group, 1971-74, corp. sec., 1974-77; bd. dirs. Sun Co., Inc., Phila., Glenmede Corp., Phila., Pew Charitable Trusts, Phila., Glenmede Trust Co., Phila., Brown & Glenemede Holdings, Inc., Balt., Alex Brown Adv. & Trust Co., Balt. Trustee Children's Hosp. Phila., vice chmn. 1991—, Bryn Mawr (Pa.) Coll., vice chmn., 1991—, Curtis Inst. Music, 1993—. Served Pa. Air N.G., 1956-59. Recipient R. Kelso Carter award Widener U., 1971. Mem. Aircraft Owners and Pilots Assn. (trustee, chmn. 1974-77, 85—, vice-chmn. 1979-85), Am. Hosp. Assn. (hon.), Union League Club, Seal Harbor Club (pres. 1992-96), Phila. Aviation Country Club, Merion Cricket Club, N.E. Harbor Fleet Club. Republican. Presbyterian. Home: 916 Muirfield Rd Bryn Mawr PA 19010-1921 Office: Sun Co Ten Penn Ctr 17th Flr 1801 Market St Philadelphia PA 19103-1699

PEW, ROBERT CUNNINGHAM, II, office equipment manufacturing company executive; b. Syracuse, N.Y., June 4, 1923; s. Robert Carroll and Bernice (Evans) P.; m. Mary Bonnell Idema, Aug. 23, 1947; children: Robert Cunningham, John Evans, Kate Bonnell. B.A., Wesleyan U., Middletown Conn.; HHD (hon.), Aquinas Coll., LLD (hon.). Labor relations exec. Doehler-Jarvis Corp., Grand Rapids, Mich., 1948-51; with Steelcase Inc., Grand Rapids, 1952—; exec. v.p. Steelcase Inc., 1964-66, pres., 1966-75, chmn. bd., pres., from 1975, formerly chmn., chief exec. officer, now chmn. bd.; dir. Old Kent Financial Corp., Foremost Corp. Am. Bd. control Grand Valley State Coll.; bd. dirs. Econ. Devel. Corp. Grand Rapids, Mich. Strategic Fund, Nat. Orgn. on Disability; mem. Gov.'s Commn. on Jobs and Econ. Devel. Served to 1st lt. USAAF, 1942-45; to capt. USAF, 1951-52. Decorated Purple Heart, Air medal with 2 oak leaf clusters. Mem. Grand Rapids C. of C. (dir.), Grand Rapids Employers Assn. (dir.), Chi Psi. Episcopalian. Clubs: Lost Tree (North Palm Beach Fla.); Peninsular; University, Kent Country (Grand Rapids). Home: 11307 Old Harbour Rd No Palm Beach FL 33408-3406 Office: PO Box 1967 Grand Rapids MI 49501-1967 Office: Steelcase Inc 901 44th St SE Grand Rapids MI 49508-7575*

PEW, THOMAS W., JR., advertising executive; b. Houston, Sept. 14, 1938; s. Thomas William and Floranz (Leebove) P.; m. Laura Rice Neuhaus, June 10, 1964; children—Katherine, William, David. B.A., Cornell U., 1961. Editor, assoc. pub. Troy Daily News, Ohio, 1965-72; freelance writer, 1972-80; editor, pres. Am. West mag. Am. West Pub. Co., Tucson, 1981-89; pres. Hawkeye West, Tucson, 1986—; advt. dir. Sturm Ruger & Co., 1986—; pres. Merlin Inc., Advt. Agy., Inc., 1991—. Contbr. articles to Smithsonian Mag., Am. Heritage Mag., numerous others. Served with inf. U.S. Army, 1961-63. Avocations: skiing; guitar; backpacking.

PÉWÉ, TROY LEWIS, geologist, educator; b. Rock Island, Ill., June 28, 1918; s. Richard E. and Olga (Pomrank) P.; m. Mary Jean Hill, Dec. 21, 1944; children: David Lee, Richard Hill, Elizabeth Anne. AB in Geology, Augustana Coll., 1940; MS, State U. Iowa, 1942; PhD, Stanford U., 1952; DSc (hon.), U. Alaska, 1991. Head dept. geology Augustana Coll., 1942-46; civilian instr. USAAC, 1943-44; instr. geomorphology Stanford, 1946; geologist Alaskan br. U.S. Geol. Survey, 1946-93; chief glacial geologist U.S. Nat. Com. Internat. Geophys. Year, Antarctica, 1958; prof. geology, head dept. U. Alaska, 1958-65; prof. geology Ariz. State U., 1965-88, prof. emeritus, 1988—, chmn. dept., 1965-76; dir. Mus. Geology, 1976—; lectr. in field, 1942—; mem. organizing com. 1st Internat. Permafrost Conf. Nat. Acad. Sci., 1962-63, chmn. U.S. planning com. 2d Internat. Permafrost Conf., 1972-74, chmn. U.S. del. 3d Internat. Permafrost Conf., 1978, chmn. U.S. organizing com. 4th Internat. Permafrost Conf., 1979-83; com. to study Good Friday Alaska Earthquake Nat. Acad. Scis., 1964-70, mem. glaciological com. polar research bd., 1971-73, founding chmn. permafrost com., mem. polar research bd., 1975-81; organizing chmn. Internat. Assn. Quarternary Research Symposium and Internat. Field Trip Alaska, 1965; mem. Internat. Commn. Periglacial Morophology, 1964-71, 80-88 ; mem. polar research bd. NRC, 1975-78, late Cenozoic study group, sci. com. Antarctic research, 1977-80. Contbr. numerous papers to profl. lit. Recipient U.S. Antarctic Svc. medal, 1966, Outstanding Achievement award Augustana Coll., 1969, Disting. Alumnus award U. Iowa, 1994, Internat. Geophysics medal USSR Nat. Acad. Sci., 1985; named 2d hon. internat. fellow Chinese Soc. Glaciology and Geocryology, 1985. Fellow AAAS (pres. Alaska div. 1956, com. on arid lands 1972-79), Geol. Soc. Am. (editorial bd. 1975-82, chmn. cordilleran sect. 1979-80, chmn. geomorphology div. 1981-82), Arctic Inst. N.Am. (bd. govs. 1969-74, exec. bd. 1972-73), Iowa Acad. Sci., Ariz. Acad. Sci. (pres. 1982-83); mem. Assn. Geology Tchrs., Glaciological Soc., N.Z. Antarctic Soc., Am. Soc. Engring. Geologists, Internat. Permafrost Assn. (founding v.p. 1983, pres. 1988-93), Am. Quaternary Assn. (pres. 1984-86), Internat. Geog. Union. Club: Cosmos. Home: 538 E Fairmont Dr Tempe AZ 85282-3723

PEYGHAMBARIAN, NASSER, optical science educator; b. Mar. 26, 1954. MS in Physics, Ind. U., 1979, PhD in Physics, 1982. Rsch. asst. prof. Optical Sci. Ctr. U. Ariz., Tucson, 1983-85, asst. prof. Optical Sci. Ctr., 1985-88, assoc. prof. Optical Sci. Ctr., 1988-91, prof. Optical Sci. Ctr., 1991—, chair lasers and photonic, 1994—. Author: Introduction to Semiconductor Optics, 1993; editor: Nonlinear Optical Materials and Devices for Photonic Switching IV, 1988, Nonlinear Photonics, 1990, Optical Bistability, 1988, (jour.) Optics Letters, 1992—; contbr. articles to prof. jours. Recipient TRW Young Faculty award, 1989-90, 3M Co.'s Young Faculty award, 1987-89. Fellow Optical Soc. Am., Am. Phys. Soc. Office: U Ariz Optical Scis Ctr Tucson AZ 85721

PEYSER, JOSEPH LEONARD, historical researcher, translator, author; b. N.Y.C., Oct. 19, 1925; s. Samuel and Sadye (Quinto) P.; m. Julia Boxer, May 30, 1948; children: Jay Randall, Jan Ellen. B.A., Duke U., 1947, M.A., 1949; profl. diploma, Columbia U., 1955; postgrad., U. Nancy, France, 1949-50; Ed.D., NYU, 1965. Prof., chmn. fgn. langs. Nancy (France) Pub. Schs., 1949-50; Tchr., chmn. fgn. langs. Monroe (N.Y.) Pub. Schs., 1951-54, Uniondale (N.Y.) Pub. Schs., 1954-61; asst. high sch. prin. Plainview, N.Y., 1961-63; mem. faculty Hofstra U., Hempstead, N.Y., 1963-68; assoc. prof. edn. Hofstra U., 1966-68; asst. dean, then asso. dean Hofstra U. (Sch. Edn.), 1964-66; interim dean Sch. Edn. Hofstra U., 1966-68; dean acad. affairs, prof. French and edn. Dowling Coll., Oakdale, N.Y., 1968-70; v.p. acad. affairs, dean faculty Dowling Coll., 1970-73; prof. French and edn. Ind. U., South Bend, 1973-94, prof. emeritus French, 1994—; dean faculties Ind. U., 1973-75, chmn. fgn. lang. dept., 1987-89; vis. asst. prof. NYU, 1964-66; adj. asst. prof. L.I. U., 1961-63; prin. researcher, translator French Michilimackinac Rsch. Project, Mich., 1991—. Author: Letters from New France, 1981, rev. edit. Letters from France: The Upper Country, 1686-1783, 1992; co-author: The Fox Wars: The Mesquakie Challenge to New France, 1993, Jacques Legardeur de Saint-Pierre: Officer, Gentleman, Entrepreneur, 1996; translator Fort St. Joseph Manuscripts, 1978, William Henry Harrison's French Correspondence, 1994; contbr. profl. publs. Bd. dirs. South Bend Symphony, 1979-86. Served with USNR, 1943-46. Recipient Founders Day award NYU, 1966, State Hist. Soc. of Wis. Hesseltine award, 1991, French Colonial Hist. Soc. Heggoy Book prize, 1994; tchg. fellow French Ministry Edn., 1949-50, Lilly Endowment faculty fellow, 1985-86, NEH fellow, 1988, 94-95, Lundquist faculty fellow, 1989-90; Newberry Libr. rsch. assoc., 1985-86. Mem. AAUP, NEA, Ind. Hist. Soc., Ind. Assn. Historians, Hist. Soc. Mich., French Colonial Hist. Soc. (v.p. 1988-91, exec. com. 1988-94).

PEYSER, ROXANE D., lawyer; b. Queens, N.Y., June 17, 1959; m. Ted Ross Peyser; children: Rachel Renee, Natasha Tovah, Samuel Aaron. BA in Middle Eastern Studies, George Washington U., 1981; JD, U. Houston, 1987. Bar: Tex., Ala., U.S. Dist. Ct. (so., no. dists.) Tex., U.S. Ct. Appeals (5th cir.). Intern Harris County Dist. Atty's. Office, Houston, 1987; atty. Saccomanno & Clegg, Houston, 1988-90, Graham, Bright & Smith, Dallas, 1990-92; sr. legal counsel Compass Bancshares, Inc., Birmingham, 1992-94; atty. Sirote & Permutt, P.C., Birmingham, Ala., 1994—; participant grad. Project Corp. Leadership, Birmingham, 1993-94. Contbr. numerous articles to profl. jours. Mem. bd. dirs. Am. Jewish Congress, Dallas, 1990-91; tchr. Temple Emanu El, Birmingham, 1993—; mem., contbr. Israel Bonds Bd., 1994—, Nat. Coun. Jewish Women, 1993—; mem. steering com. bus. & profl. women section Jewish Fedn., 1994—. Mem. ABA, Am. Corp. Counsel Assn., Tex. Bar Assn., Ala. Bar Assn., Tex. Assn. Bank Counsel, Internat. Platform Assn. Avocations: scuba diving, music, writing, reading, theatre. Office: Sirote & Permutt PC 2222 Arlington Ave S Birmingham AL 35205-4004

PEYTON, DONALD LEON, retired standards association executive; b. Portland, Oreg., May 5, 1925; s. Bernard Thomas and Nelle (Moses) P.; m. Jane Frances Kirkman, Aug. 26, 1950; children: Patrick Philip, James Allen. Student, Mont. State U., 1946-47; BA, No. Colo. U., 1950. Civilian edn. specialist USAF, 1951-56; engaged in real estate Cheyenne, Wyo., 1956-57; adminstrv. asst. to congressman, 1957-60; with U.S. C. of C., 1960-66, gen. mgr. govt. relations, 1965-66; pres. Am. Nat. Standards Inst., Inc., 1966-89, ret., 1989, Peyton Assocs., Standards Cons., White Plains, N.Y., 1989—; Lectr. govt. bus. relations Am. U., 1965-66, Amos Tuck Sch., Dartmouth, 1965—. Author: Standards and Trade in the 1990's; author monographs. Pres., Cheyenne Jr. C. of C., 1955-56. Mem. Am. Soc. Assn. Execs., Old Guard of White Plains. Home and Office: 2 Beverly Rd White Plains NY 10605-3306 *My personal philosophy of life parallels that of my philosophy regarding voluntary organizations. In personal and professional life there is no hope for the self-satisfied individual or the self-satisfied organization.*

PEYTON, WILLIAM MAUPIN, transportation executive, educator; b. Richmond, Ky., Jan. 5, 1932; s. Russell Page and Amanda Thomas (Bogie) P.; m. Margaret Christine Dahl, Sept. 8, 1956; children: Michael William, Stephen Todd, John Patrick. B.S. in Bus. Adminstrn., UCLA, 1957; M.B.A. in Fin., U. So. Calif., 1967; postgrad., Harvard U., 1980. Office mgr., cost acct. Ralphs Grocery Co., Los Angeles, 1957-62; cost acctg. supr. Lockheed Air Terminal, Burbank, Calif., 1962-69; chief acct. Lockheed Air Terminal, Burbank, Calif, 1969-72, treas., 1972-80, exec. v.p., 1980-86, also dir.; treas. Lockheed Air Terminal, Panama City, 1976—; pres. Peyco, Inc., Burbank, 1986—; asst. prof. Glendale (Calif.) Coll., 1969—. Served with USAF, 1951-55. Mem. Inst. Mgmt. Accts. (dir. 1963). Republican. Episcopalian. Home: 12525 E Lupine Ave Scottsdale AZ 85259-3447

PEZ, GUIDO PETER, research chemist; b. Fiume, Italy, Feb. 10, 1941; married, 1966; 3 children. BSc, U. NSW, 1962; PhD in Chemistry, Monash U., Australia, 1967. Fellow McMaster U., 1967-69; rsch. chemist Allied Chem. Corp., 1969-74, sr. rsch. chemist, 1974-78, rsch. assoc., 1978-81; sr. rsch. assoc. Air Products & Chems., Inc., 1981-93, chief scientist, 1993—. Recipient award in Inorganic Chem. Am. Chem. Soc., 1995. Mem. Am. Chem. Soc. (Award in Inorganic Chemistry 1995). Achievements include research in synthetic inorganic and organometallic chemistry applied to catalysis, selective gas absorption materials, gas separation membranes, organofluorine chemistry, fluorinating reagents for synthesizing bio-active compounds. Office: Air Products & Chemicals Inc 7201 Hamilton Blvd Allentown PA 18195-1526

PEZZELLA, JERRY JAMES, JR., investment and real estate corporation executive; b. Chesapeake, Va., Sept. 30, 1937; s. Jerry James Sr. and Mabel (Aydlett) P.; m. Carolyn Blades; children: James M., Stanley J., Julie Pezzella Scanlon. BS, U. Richmond, 1963; MBA, U. Pa., 1964. Asst. v.p. Va. Nat. Bank (now Nations Bank), Norfolk, 1964-68; chmn. bd., pres. First Am. Investment Corp., First Ga. Investment Corp., Atlanta, 1968-74; v.p. Great Am. Investment Corp., Atlanta, 1974-78; sr. exec. v.p., 1984-85; exec. v.p. Equity Fin. & Mgmt. Co., Chgo., 1978—; pres., chmn. bd. First Capital Fin. Corp., Chgo., 1983-85; pres. GAFGI Holdings Inc., Chgo., 1983—; chmn. bd. 1st Property Mgmt. Corp., 1990-92; bd. dirs. Great Am. Mgmt. and Investment, Inc., Chgo., Nat. Multi Housing coun., 1992-94, mem. exec. com. Bd. dirs., exec. com. Nat. Multi-Housing Coun., 1991-93. Mem. River Club (Chgo.), Met. Club (Chgo.), Cherokee Golf and Country Club (Murphy, N.C.). Office: 2 N Riverside Plaza Ste 700 Chicago IL 60606

PFAELZER, MARIANA R., federal judge; b. L.A., Feb. 4, 1926. AB, U. Calif., 1947; LLB, UCLA, 1957. Bar: Calif. 1958. Assoc. Wyman, Bautzer, Rothman & Kuchel, 1957-69, ptnr., 1969-78; judge U.S. Dist. Ct. (ctrl. dist.) Calif., 1978—. pres., v.p., dir. Bd. Police Commrs. City of L.A., 1974-78; bd. vis. Loyola Law Sch. Named Alumna of Yr. by UCLA Law Sch., 1980. Mem. ABA, Calif. Bar Assn. (local adminstrv. com., spl. com. study rules procedure 1972, joint subcom. profl. ethics and computers and the law coms. 1972, profl. ethics com. 1972-74, spl. com. juvenile justice, women's rights subcom. human rights sect.), L.A. County Bar Assn. (spl. com. study rules procedure state bar 1974). Office: US Dist Ct 312 N Spring St Los Angeles CA 90012-4701

PFAFF, DONALD W., neurobiology and behavior educator; b. Rochester, N.Y., Dec. 9, 1939; s. Norman J. and Eleanor W. (Blakeslee) P.; married Stephanie Pfaff; children: Robin W., Alexander S., Douglas B. AB magna cum laude, Harvard U., 1961; PhD, MIT, 1965. Rsch. assoc. dept. psychology MIT, Cambridge, 1965-66; trainee Marine Biol. Lab., Woods Hole, Mass., 1966; postdoctoral fellow Rockefeller U., N.Y.C., 1966-68, staff scientist biomed. div. population coun., 1968-69, asst. prof., 1969-71, assoc. prof., 1971-78, prof., 1978—. Author: Estrogens and Brain Function, 1980; editor: The Physiological Mechanisms of Motivation, 1982, Ethical Questions in Brain and Behavior, 1983, Molecular Neurobiology: Endocrine Approaches, 1987. Recipient Pres.'s award MIT, 1962-63; Woodrow Wilson fellow, 1961-62, fellow Neuroscis. Rsch. Program, 1969. Fellow Am. Acad. Arts and Scis.; mem. NAS, Am. Physiol. Soc., Soc. for Neurosci., Endocrine Soc., Sigma Xi. Office: Rockefeller U 1230 York Ave New York NY 10021-6307

PFAFF, WILLIAM WALLACE, physician, educator; b. Rochester, N.Y., Aug. 14, 1930; s. Norman Joseph and Eleanor Blakesley (Wells) P.; m. Patricia Ann Clark, June 25, 1960; children—Nancy, Karen, Margaret, Mary Catherine. A.B., Harvard U., 1952; M.D., U. Buffalo, 1956. Intern U. Chgo., 1956-57, resident, 1957-58; resident in surgery Stanford U. Med. Center, 1960-65, instr. surgery, 1965; faculty U. Fla., Gainesville, 1965—; prof. surgery U. Fla., 1971—. Contbr. numerous articles to profl. jours. Served with USPHS, 1958-60. Mem. ACS, Am. Surg. Assn., Transplantation Soc., Am. Soc. Transplant Surgery, Southeastern Surg. Congress, So. Surg. Assn., Fla. Kidney Found., Alachua County Med. Soc. (pres. 1977-78), Alpha Omega Alpha. Home: 2445 NW 15th Pl Gainesville FL 32605-5148 Office: U Fla Dept Surgery PO Box 100286 Gainesville FL 32610-0286

PFAFFMAN, WILLIAM SCOTT, sculptor; b. Albany, Ga., July 10, 1954; s. Roy Alton and Corabel (Scales) P. BFA, Auburn U., 1976; postgrad., U. Ala., Huntsville, 1976; MA, CUNY, 1978. Curator Bklyn. Waterfront Artists Coalition, 1980-92; dir. Kentler Internat. Drawing Space, Bklyn., 1989-92, artist-in-residence, 1983; vis. artist Reed Deer (Alta., Can.) Coll., 1985, N.Y. State Coll. Ceramics, Alfred, 1985, Wayne State U., Detroit, 1985, Edinborough (Pa.) Coll., 1987, Erie (Pa.) Art Mus., 1987, John F. Kennedy H.S., Bronx, N.Y., 1987. One-man show CUNY Grad. Ctr. Mall, 1982; exhibited in group shows, 1976—, including Birmingham (Ala.) Mus. Art, 1976, The Clocktower, N.Y.C., 1984, SUNY, Purchase, 1984, Am. Acad. and Nat. Inst. Arts and Letters, N.Y.C., 1985, Queens Mus., 1985, Sculpture Space, Utica, N.Y., 1986, Erie (Pa.) Art Mus., 1987, Willis Gallery, Detroit, 1988, Sander Gallery, N.Y.C., 1988, München Gladbach, Fed. Republic

Germany, 1991, Picnic Mass, Bklyn., 1993, The Drawing Room, Amsterdam, Holland, 1994, Galerie Seghaier, Vienna, Austria, 1994; commns. include Artpark Sculpture Commn., 1984, N.Y.C. Dept. Gen. Svcs., 1988; one-person installation Roermond, Holland, 1992. Project developer N.Y.C. Artist Housing Program, Bklyn., 1986-91; dir. Shell Found., 1995—. Recipient award Nat. Studio Program, 1983, ann. award in art AAAL, 1985; resident Sculpture Space, 1986; fellow Pollack Krasner Found., 1987; grantee N.Y. State Coun. on Arts, 1987. Home: 190 Coffey St Brooklyn NY 11231-1026 Studio: 353 Van Brunt St Brooklyn NY 11231-1245

PFALMER, CHARLES ELDEN, secondary school educator; b. Trinidad, Colo., Aug. 9, 1937; s. Arthur Joseph and Nettie Mildred (Powell) P.; m. Margaret Christine La Duke, June 25, 1964; children: Betholyn Ann, Garret. AA, Trinidad State Jr. Coll., 1957; BA, Adams State Coll., 1959, MA, 1962. Cert. tchr., Colo. Tchr. Olathe (Colo.) H.S., 1959-60, Yuma (Colo.) H.S., 1960—; instr. Northeastern Jr. Coll., Sterling, Colo., 1990-94. Precinct chmn. Dem. Orgn., Yuma, 1992-96, del. to state conv., 1984-86, 88-90, 92-94, 96; ch. treas. Yuma Episcopal Ch., 1985—; v.p. Citizens Action Com., Yuma, 1994. Recipient Outstanding Educator award West Yuma Sch. Dist., 1987, Colo. State Ho. of Reps., 1987, Local Disting. Svc. award Colo. H.S. Activities Assn., 1991, Outstanding Cmty. Svc. award Colo. Athletic Dirs. Assn., 1990. Mem. NEA, Am. Polit. Collectors, Nat. Coun. for the Social Studies, Colo. Edn. Assn., Phi Delta Kappa. Avocations: collecting political buttons, antiques, sports. Home: 321 E 10th Ave Yuma CO 80759-3001 Office: Yuma HS 1000 S Albany St Yuma CO 80759-3001

PFALTZGRAFF, ROBERT LOUIS, JR., political scientist, educator; b. Phila., June 1, 1934; s. Robert L. and Mary (Warriner) P.; m. Diane A. Kressler, May 20, 1967; children: Suzanne Diane, Robert Louis III. B.A. with honors, Swarthmore Coll., 1956; M.B.A., U. Pa., 1958, Ph.D. in Polit. Sci. (Penfield fellow), 1964; M.A. in Internat. Relations, 1959. Research assoc. Fgn. Policy Research Inst., 1964-71; asst. prof. polit. sci. U. Pa., Phila., 1964-70; dep. dir. Fgn. Policy Research Inst., 1971-73; assoc. prof. internat. politics Fletcher Sch. Law and Diplomacy, Tufts U., Medford, Mass., 1971-78, prof. internat. politics, 1978-83, Shelby Cullom Davis prof. internat. security studies, 1983—; vis. lectr. Fgn. Service Inst. Dept. State, 1970-71; George C. Marshall prof. Coll. of Europe, Bruges, Belgium, 1970-71; pres. Inst. for Fgn. Policy Analysis, Cambridge, Mass., 1976—; short term acad. guest prof. Nat. Defense Coll., Tokyo, Japan, 1981; pres. U.S. Strategic Inst., Washington, 1977-79. Author: Britain Faces Europe, 1957-1967, 1969, Politics and the International System, 1969, The Atlantic Community: A Complex Balance, 1969, The Study of International Relations, 1977, The Cruise Missile: Bargaining Chip or Defense Bargain, 1977, Power Projection and the Long Range Combat Aircraft: Missions, Capabilities and Alternative Designs, 1981, Contending Theories of International Relations: A Comprehensive Survey, 1981; co-editor: Contrasting Approaches to Strategic Arms Control, 1974, SALT: Implications for Arms Control in the 1970s, 1973, The Other Arms Race: New Technologies and Non Nuclear Conflict, 1975, Arms Transfers to the Third World: The Military Build-up in Less Industrial Countries, 1978, Intelligence Policy and National Security, 1981, Projection of Power: Perspectives, Perceptions and Problems, 1982, (with Ra'anan) The U.S. Defense Mobilization Infrastructure: Problems and Priorities, 1983, International Dimensions of Space, 1984, National Security Policy: The Decision-Making Process, 1984, The Peace Movements in Europe and the United States, 1985, co-author: American Foreign Policy: FDR to Reagan, 1986, co-editor: Selling the Rope to Hang Capitalism? The Debate on West-East Trade and Technology Transfer, 1987, Emerging Doctrines and Technologies: Implications for Global and Regional Political-Military Balance, 1987, Protracted Warfare--The Third World Arena: A Dimension of U.S.-Soviet Conflict, 1988, Guerrilla Warfare and Counter-Insurgency: U.S.-Soviet Policy in the third World, 1988, U.S. Defense Policy in an Era of Constrained Resources, 1989; co-author: Contending Theories of International Relations: A Comprehensive Study, 1990; co-editor: National Security Decisions: The Participants Speak, 1990, The United States Army: Challenges and Missions for the 1990s, 1991, The Future of Air Power in the Aftermath of the Gulf War, 1992, Naval Forward Presence and the National Military Strategy, 1993, Ethnic Conflict and Regional Instability: Implications for U.S. Policy and Army Roles and Missions, 1994, Naval Expeditionary Forces and Power Projection: Into the 21st Century, 1994, Long-Range Bombers and the Role of Airpower in the New Century, 1995, Roles and Missions of Special Operations Forces in the Aftermath of the Cold War, 1995, others; contbr. articles to scholarly jours. Guggenheim fellow, 1968-69; Relm Found. grantee, 1969. Mem. Internat. Studies Assn., Coun. Fgn. Rels., Internat. Inst. Strategic Studies, Capitol Hill Club, Army and Navy Club (Washington). Home: 663 Wallace Dr Wayne PA 19087-1911 Office: Inst Fgn Policy Analysis 675 Massachusetts Ave Cambridge MA 02139-3309

PFAU, GEORGE HAROLD, JR., stockbroker; b. Milw., May 7, 1924; s. George Harold and Elisabeth C. (Hunter) P.; m. Anne Elizabeth Mayhew; 1 child, George Harold III; children by previous marriage: Mary D., Peter W., Elizabeth C. B.S., Yale U., 1948. Tchr., 1948-49; with Fleishhacker Paper Box Co., San Francisco, 1952-54; salesman A.G. Becker & Co., San Francisco, 1954-55; v.p., sec., dir. Carl W. Stern & Co., San Francisco, 1955-57; with White Weld & Co. Inc., San Francisco, 1957-78; 1st v.p. corp. fin. dept. Blyth Eastman Dillon, San Francisco, 1978-79; sr. v.p. Paine Webber, San Francisco, 1979—; bd. dirs. IA Dist. Argl. Assn. Bd. dirs. The Guardsmen, 1966-67, Pathfinder Fund, 1974-82, San Francisco Zool. Soc., 1979-80; trustee Thacher Sch., Ojai, Calif., 1967-76, Town Sch., San Francisco, 1966-70; pres. Planned Parenthood San Francisco-Alameda County, 1968-69, bd. dirs., 1965—; chmn. Lincoln Club of No. Calif, 1993-95, mem., 1982—; chmn. Citizens for Better San Francisco. With C.E. AUS, 1942-44; with Am. Field Svc., 1944-45. Mem. Kappa Beta Phi, San Francisco (Calif.) Bond Club, Bohemian Club (San Francisco), Calif. Tennis Club. Office: Paine Webber 32d Fl 555 California St San Francisco CA 94104

PFAU, RICHARD ANTHONY, college president; b. N.Y.C., Feb. 19, 1942; s. Hugo and Irene Beatrice P.; m. Nancy Ann DiPace, Sept. 12, 1964; children: Bradley Madison, Aleksandra Nicole. AB, Hamilton Coll., 1964; MA, U. Va., 1973, PhD, 1975. Systems analyst Equitable Life Ins. Co., N.Y.C., 1964-66; asst. prof. history Dickinson Coll., Carlisle, Pa., 1975-80; assoc. prof., assoc. dean U. Miami, Coral Gables, Fla., 1980-85; dean of faculty, provost Emory (Va.) and Henry Coll., 1985-93; pres. Ill. Coll., Jacksonville, Ill., 1993—. Author: No Sacrifice Too Great: The Life of Lewis L. Strauss, 1985. Contbr. articles, book revs. to profl. publs. Vestryman St. Thomas Episc. Ch., Abingdon, Va.; chmn., sec.-treas., exec. com., bd. dirs. Va. Found. for Humanities and Pub. Policy, Exec. Com. Fedn. Ind. Ill. Colls. and Univs. Capt. USAF, 1966-71. DuPont fellow, 1974-75; Hoover fellow, 1982. Mem. Omicron Delta Kappa, Alpha Psi Omega, Pi Delta Epsilon. Home: Barnes House 310 Lockwood Pl Jacksonville IL 62650-2225 Office: Ill Coll Pres Office Jacksonville IL 62650

PFEFFER, DAVID H., lawyer; b. N.Y.C., Mar. 15, 1935. B. Chem. Engring., CCNY, 1956; J.D., NYU, 1961, LL.M. in Trade Regulation, 1967. Bar: N.Y. 1961. With patent dept. U.S. Rubber Co., Wayne, N.J., 1957-61; assoc. Watson, Leavenworth, Kelton & Taggart, N.Y.C., 1961-63; assoc. Morgan & Finnegan, N.Y.C., 1963-70, ptnr., 1971—; village prosecutor Roslyn Harbor, N.Y., 1976-78, village justice, 1979—; panel of arbitrators Am. Arbitration Assn. Mem. ABA (litigation sect.), N.Y. State Bar Assn., Assn. Bar City N.Y., Nassau County Bar Assn. (coms. on patent and trademarks, fed. practice), Am. Intellectual Property Law Assn. (com. alt. dispute resolution), N.Y. Patent Trademark and Copyright Law Assn., N.Y. State Magistrates Assn., Nassau County Magistrates Assn., Order of Coif. Office: Morgan & Finnegan 345 Park Ave New York NY 10154-0004

PFEFFER, EDWARD ISRAEL, educational administrator; b. Newark, July 1, 1914; s. Jacob and Fannie Bessie (Fisher) P.; m. Anna Chinich, July 14, 1940; children—Cynthia Roberta, Bruce Paul. B.S., N.Y. U., 1937; M.A., N.J. State Tchrs. Coll., Montclair, 1942; Ed.D., Rutgers U., 1954. Tchr. Abington Ave. Sch., Newark, 1937-46; vice prin. Warren St. Sch., 1946-53; prin. Monmouth St. and Coes Pl. schs., 1953-57, Robert Treat Jr. High and Elem. Sch., 1957-64; asst. supt. spl. services Newark Dist. Pub. Schs., 1964-67, dep. supt., 1967-72, 73—, acting supt., 1972-73. Contbr. articles profl. publs. Commr. Newark Sr. Citizens Commn., 1967—; mem. Newark Juvenile Problems Commn., 1958-62; chmn. Children's Resources Commn., Council Social Agys., 1955-60; mem. exec. bd. Family and Children's Div., 1955-62; mem. Newark Commn. for UN Week, 1962—, Newark Disaster Com., 1967—, Bd. Edn., Temple B'nai Abraham, Essex County, N.J., 1964-65; Mem. exec. bd. Newark Central Community Council; mem. adv. bd. Essex County Tech. Sch. Recipient citations Newark Assn. Dirs. and Suprs., 1973, citations Newark Title I Central Parents Council, 1973. Mem. Newark Pub. Sch. Prins. Assn. (pres. 1963-64), N.J. Elementary Sch. Prest Assn. (pres.), Congress Parents and Tchrs. (life), NEA (life), Am., N.J. assns. sch. adminstrs., Newark Schoolmens Assn. (bd. govs., named Outstanding Schoolman of Year 1972-73), Columbia Scholastic Press Assn. (v.p., Gold Key 1948), Urban League, NAACP, Phi Delta Kappa. Home: 507 Clinton Pl Newark NJ 07112-1703 Office: 2 Cedar St Newark NJ 07102-3015

PFEFFER, JEFFREY, business educator; b. St. Louis, July 23, 1946; s. Newton Stuart and Shirlee (Krisman) P.; m. Kathleen Frances Fowler, July 23, 1986. BS, MS, Carnegie Mellon U., 1968; PhD, Stanford U., 1972. Mem. tech. staff Research Analysis Corp., McLean, Va., 1968-69; asst. prof. U. Ill., Champaign, 1971-73; from asst. prof. to assoc. prof. U. Calif., Berkeley, 1973-79; prof. Grad. Sch. Bus., Stanford U., Calif., 1979—; vis. prof. Harvard U. Sch. Bus., Boston, 1981-82; dir., mem. compensation com. Portola Packaging, Inc. Author: The External Control of Organizations, 1978, Organizational Design, 1978, Power in Organizations, 1981, Organizations and Organization Theory, 1982 (Terry Book award 1984), Managing with Power, 1992, Competitive Advantage Through People, 1994. Fellow Acad. Mgmt. (bd. govs. 1984-86, New Concept award 1979, Richard D. Irwin award for scholarly contbns. to mgmt. 1989); mem. Am. Sociol. Assn., Indsl. Rels. Rsch. Assn. Jewish. Avocations: cooking, music. Home: 5 Burnett Ave San Francisco CA 94131-3317 Office: Stanford U Grad Sch of Bus Stanford CA 94305

PFEFFER, PHILIP ELLIOT, biophysicist; b. N.Y.C., Apr. 8, 1941; s. Charles and Della (Smith) P.; m. Judith Stadlen, Dec. 22, 1962; children: Charles, Ari, Shira. AB, Hunter Coll., 1962; MS, Rutgers U., 1964, PhD, 1966. Rsch. asst. dept. chemistry Rutgers U., New Brunswick, N.J., 1964-66; rsch. fellow dept. chemistry U. Chgo., 1966-68; rsch. scientist Ea. Regional Rsch. Ctr. USDA, Phila., 1968-88, rsch. leader Ea. Regional Rsch. Ctr., 1976-88, lead scientist Ea. Regional Rsch. Ctr., 1988—; editor-at-large Marcel Dekker, N.Y.C., 1990—; adj. prof. dept. biosci. and biotech. Drexel U., Phila., 1996—. Editor: Nuclear Magnetic Resonance in Agriculture, 1989, Nuclear Magnetic Resonance in Plant Biology, 1996; mem. editl. bd. Jour. Carbohydrate Chemistry, 1985—, Jour. Magnetic Resonance Analysis; contbr. articles to profl. jours. including Plant Physiology, Carbohydrate Rsch., Biochemica Acta, Biophysica. Recipient Bond award Am. Oil Chemists Soc., 1976, Fed. Svcs. award Phila. Fed. Assn., 1979, Science and Edn. award USDA, 1982; fellow Orgn. for Econ. Cooperation and Devel., 1989; Agrl. Rsch. Svc. rsch. fellow, 1989; vis. scientist grantee Centre d'Etudes Nucleaires de Grenoble, 1986, Oxford U., 1989. Mem. AAAS, Internat. Soc. for Magnetic Resonance, Am. Chem. Soc. (Phila. sect. Scientist of Yr. 1982), Soc. for Applied Spectroscopy. Achievements include patents and publs. concerning use of alpha-anions; discovery of deuterium isotope shift NMR method for determining carbohydrate structures; development of P-31 NMR in vivo methodology for studying metal ion transport and C-13 NMR for studying plant/microbe interactions in nitrogen fixing plant nodules and symbiotic mycorrhizae. Office: USDA 600 W Mermaid Ln Glenside PA 19038

PFEFFER, PHILIP MAURICE, distribution company executive; b. St. Louis, Jan. 20, 1945; s. Philip McRae and Jeanne (Kaufman) P.; m. Pamela Jean Korte, Aug. 28, 1965; children: John-Lindell Philip, James Howard, David Maurice. B.A. in Math. and Chemistry, So. Ill. U., 1965, M.A. in Econs., 1966; postgrad., Vanderbilt U., 1966-68. Economist Genesco, Inc., Nashville, 1968, mgr. internat. fin., 1969, asst. treas.; pres. Genesco Export Co., Nashville, 1970-75; dir. fin. planning Ingram Distribution Group, Inc., Nashville, 1976-77, v.p. fin. and adminstrn., 1977-78, exec. v.p., 1978, pres. and chief exec. officer, 1978-81, chmn. bd. and chief exec. officer, 1981—, dir., 1978—; exec. v.p. Ingram Industries, Inc., Nashville, 1981—, dir., 1981—; bd. dirs. Ingram Barge Co., Ingram Micro Inc., Ingram Coal Co., Tenn. Ins. Co.; instr. fin. and econs. U. Tenn., Nashville, 1968-77; lectr. corp. fin. Vanderbilt U., 1972-77. Bd. dirs. So. Ill. U. Found., 1982—. Nashville Area YMCA, 1982—. Recipient Long Rifle and Silver Beaver award Boy Scouts Am., Nashville, 1981, also Disting. Eagle from Nat. Coun.; Benjamin Gomez award for Disting. Contbns. to the Art of Book Pub. Mem. Fin. Execs. Inst. (pres. 1978-79), Nat. Eagle Scout Assn. (bd. dirs., Silver Wreath award), Nashville Area C. of C. (vice chmn.), Am. Wholesale Booksellers Assn. (past v.p., trustee), So. Ill. U. Alumni Assn. (past bd. dirs.), Young Pres.'s Orgn., Tenn. Assn. Bus., Rotary, Percy Priest Yacht Club (Nashville). Avocations: scouting, sailing, water sports, landscaping. Home: 836 Treemont Ct Nashville TN 37220-1536 Office: Ingram Distbn Group Inc 1 Ingram Blvd La Vergne TN 37086-3629

PFEFFER, RICHARD LAWRENCE, geophysics educator; b. Bklyn., Nov. 26, 1930; s. Lester Robert and Anna (Newman) P.; m. Roslyn Ziegler, Aug. 30, 1953; children—Bruce, Lloyd, Scott, Glenn. B.S. cum laude, CCNY, 1952; M.S., Mass. Inst. Tech., 1954, Ph.D., 1957. Research asst. MIT, 1952-55, guest lectr., 1956; atmospheric physicist Air Force Cambridge Research Center, Boston, 1955-59; sr. scientist Columbia U., 1959-61, lectr., 1961-62, asst. prof. geophysics, 1962-64; assoc. prof. meteorology Fla. State U., Tallahassee, 1964-67, prof. meteorology, 1967—; dir. Geophys. Fluid Dynamics Inst., 1967-93; cons. NASA, 1961-64, N.W. Ayer & Son, Inc., 1962, Ednl. Testing Service, Princeton, N.J., 1963, Voice of Am., 1963, Grolier, Inc., 1963, Naval Research Labs., 1971-76; Mem. Internat. Commn. for Dynamical Meteorology, 1972-76. Editor: Dynamics of Climate, 1960; Contbr. articles to profl. jours. Bd. dirs. B'nai B'rith Anti-Defamation League; chmn. religious concern and social action com. Temple Israel, Tallahassee, 1971-72. Fellow Am. Meterol. Soc. (program chmn. ann. meeting 1963); mem. Am. Geophys. Union, N.Y. Acad. Scis. (chmn. planetary scis. sect. 1961-63), Sigma Xi, Chi Epsilon Pi, Sigma Alpha. Home: 926 Waverly Rd Tallahassee FL 32312-2813

PFEFFER, ROBERT, chemical engineer, academic administrator, educator; b. Vienna, Austria, Nov. 26, 1935; came to U.S., 1938, naturalized, 1944; s. Joseph and Gisela (Aberbach) P.; m. Marcia Borenstein, Dec. 24, 1960; children—Michael, Jacqueline. B.Ch.E., N.Y. U., 1956, M.Ch.E., 1958, D.Eng.Sc., 1962. Mem. faculty CCNY, 1957-92, asst. prof. chem. engring., 1962-66, assoc. prof., 1966-71, prof., 1971-92, chmn. dept. chem. engring., 1973-87, Herbert Kayser prof., 1980-92, dean grad. studies and research, dep. provost, 1987-88, provost, v.p. acad. affairs, 1988-92; v.p. rsch. and grad. studies, prof. chem. engring. N.J. Int. Tech., Newark, 1992—; vis. prof. Imperial Coll., London, 1969; Fulbright scholar Technion-Israel Inst. Tech., 1976-77; cons. in field. Contbr. articles to tech. publs. Fulbright Hays awardee, 1976-77; DuPont faculty fellow, 1962; NASA faculty fellow, 1964-65. Mem. AIChE (Particle Tech. Forum Nat. award 1995), Am. Soc. Engring. Edn., Sigma Xi, Tau Beta Pi, Phi Lambda Upsilon. Jewish. Office: NJ Inst Tech 323 Dr Martin Luther King Jr Blvd Newark NJ 07102

PFEFFER, RUBIN HARRY, publishing executive; b. Bklyn., Oct. 9, 1951; s. Martie and Idell (Treiber) P.; m. Lurie Horns; children: Stephanie, Ian, Rebecca, Vaughn. BFA in Graphic Design, Carnegie-Mellon U., 1973. Dir. art Harcourt Brace Jovanovich, San Diego, 1979-84; corp. art dir. Harcourt Brace Jovanovich, Orlando, Fla., 1984—; dir. children's books Harcourt Brace Jovanovich, San Diego, 1984-85; pres. Harcourt Brace & Co. Trade Books, San Diego, 1985—. Bd. dirs. Calif. Ballet Co., San Diego, 1986-87, Easter Seal Soc., San Diego, 1988—. Avocation: painting. Office: HB Trade Divsn 525 B St San Diego CA 92101-4403

PFEFFERKORN, LAURA BIGGER, middle school educator; b. Spartanburg, S.C., May 24, 1963; d. Samuel Patrick Jr. and Laura Christine (Smith) Bigger; m. James W. Pfefferkorn, June 1, 1982. BS in Banking and Fin., U. S.C., Aiken, 1987; MAT in Health Edn., U. S.C., Columbia, 1993. Account rep. NCR Corp., Charleston, S.C., 1988; grad. asst. U. S.C. Sch. Pub. Health, Columbia, 1990-93; tchr. sci. Dent Mid. Sch., Columbia, 1993—, team leader, 1994—; forum on quality edn. mem. Richland Dist. 2, Columbia, 1993-94; tchr. grad. courses Sch. Pub. Health/U. S.C. Contbr. chpt. to textbook. Roper Mountain Sci. Ctr. scholar, 1994. Mem. APHA, AAHPERD, S.C. Alliance for Health, Phys. Edn., Recreation and Dance, S.C. Mid. Sch. Assn., S.C. Assn. for Health Edn., Phi Delta Kappa. Avocations: mountain biking, running, weight training, reading. Home: 2500 Wilmot Ave Columbia SC 29205-2355 Office: Dent Mid Sch 2719 Decker Blvd Columbia SC 29206-1704

PFEIFER, LARRY ALAN, public health service coordinator; b. Rock Springs, Wyo., July 20, 1958; s. Jack Albert and Betty Lee (Ethington) P.; m. Sandra Lynn, June 20, 1986. BS cum laude, So. Oreg. State Coll., 1983, MS in Health Edn., 1989; paramedic diploma, Rogue Community Coll., 1984; postgrad., Columbia Pacific U. Cert. paramedic, Oreg. Lt., paramedic Tualatin Valley Fire and Rescue, Portland, Oreg., 1991—; adj. faculty Oreg. Health Scis. U. Sch. of Medicine, Dept. of Emergency Medicine, 1995; lectr. in field. Author (text) Non-Verbal Pre-Hospital Assessment of the Trauma Patient. Mem. Oreg. Paramedic Assn., Phi Kappa Phi, Kappa Delta Pi. Home: 5156 NW 173rd Pl Portland OR 97229-7325

PFEIFER, MICHAEL DAVID, bishop; b. Alamo, Tex., May 18, 1937; s. Frank and Alice (Savage) P. Student, Oblate Sch. Theology. Ordained priest Roman Cath. Ch., 1965, consecrated bishop, 1985; mem. Missionary Oblates of Mary Immaculate. Priest Roman Cath. Ch., Mexico City, 1964-1981; provincial-superior of Oblate So. U.S. Province Roman Cath. Ch., San Antonio, 1981-85; bishop Roman Cath. Ch., San Angelo, Tex., 1985—. Address: PO Box 1829 804 Ford St San Angelo TX 76902*

PFEIFER, PAUL E., state supreme court justice; b. Bucyrus, Ohio, Oct. 15, 1942; m. Julia Pfeifer; children: Lisa, Beth, Kurt. BA, Ohio State U., 1963, JD, 1966. Asst. atty. gen. State of Ohio, 1967-70; mem. Ohio Ho. of Reps., 1971-72; asst. prosecuting atty. Crawford County, 1973-76; mem. Ohio Senate, 1976-92, minority floor leader, 1983-84, asst. pres. pro-tempore, 1985-86; ptnr. Cory, Brown & Pfeifer, 1973-92; justice Ohio Supreme Ct., 1992—; chmn. jud. com. Ohio Senate, 10 yrs. Mem. Grace United Meth. Ch., Bucyrus. Mem. Bucyrus Rotary Club. Office: 30 E Broad St Fl 3 Columbus OH 43215-3414

PFEIFER, PETER M., physics educator; b. Zurich, Switzerland, Apr. 19, 1946; came to U.S., 1986; s. Max and Eva (Korrodi) P.; m. Therese M. Abgottspon, June 13, 1980; children: Anne, Helen. MS in Chemistry, Swiss Fed. Inst. Tech., 1969, PhD in Natural Scis., 1980. Rsch. and tchg. asst. Swiss Fed. Inst. Tech., Zurich, 1970-75, rsch. assoc., instr., 1975-80; rsch. fellow Hebrew U. Jerusalem, 1981-82; asst. prof. chemistry U. Bielefeld, West Germany, 1982-86, habilitation, 1986; assoc. prof. physics U. Mo., Columbia, 1986-95; vis. prof. physics Swiss Fed. Inst. Tech., 1993-94; vis. scientist Ecole Poly., Palaiseau, France, 1994; prof. physics U. Mo., Columbia, 1995—; mem. adv. bd. Symposium on Probability Methods in Physics, Bielefeld, 1984, Symposium on Small Irregular Particles, Cuernavaca, Mex., 1988, Conf. on Fractals in Natural Scis., Budapest, Hungary, 1993, 22d Midwest Solid-State Theory Symposium, Columbia, 1994, 2d Internat. Symposium on Surface Heterogeneity, Zakopane, Poland, 1995; spkr. in field. Mem. editl. bd. Internat. Jour. Fractals, 1992—, Heterogeneous Chemistry Reviews, 1992—; contbr. over 75 articles to profl. jours. Recipient Gränacher Grad. fellowship Found. of Swiss Chem. Industry, 1970-71, fellowship for jr. scientists Swiss Nat. Sci. Found., 1981-82, Outstanding Rsch. prize U.Bielefeld, 1986, Rsch. Coun. fellowship U. Mo., 1986, Rsch. grant Petroleum Rsch. Fund, 1987-90, 90-93, 94—, Rsch. Leave award U. Mo., 1993-94. Mem. Am. Phys. Soc., Materials Rsch. Soc. Achievements include development of fractal analysis in surface science; discovery of first fractal materials and of numerous structure-function relationships (diffusion, scattering, wetting and transport properties); fundamental research in quantum theory: discovery of chiral superselection rule in molecules, unified framework for reduced quantum dynamics, generalized time-energy uncertainty relations. Office: Univ Mo Dept Physics Columbia MO 65211

PFEIFFER, ALICE RANDEL, comptroller; b. New York, N.Y., Jan. 4, 1954; d. Wilmer Henry Jr. and Lucy (Scognamilo) R.; m. Peter F. Pfeiffer, June 24, 1989; 1 child, Kevin William Pfeiffer. BA in Psychology, Ithaca Coll., 1975; MS in Counseling and Guidance, Syracuse U., 1977, MBA in Accounting, 1986. Counselor Syracuse (N.Y.) Boy's Club, 1978-79; psychiat. aide SUNY Upstate Med. Ctr., Syracuse, 1980-85; computer operator, test supr. Syracuse U. Test Svcs., Syracuse, 1985-86; acct. Syracuse U. Press, Syracuse, 1987-90, comptroller, 1990—; acct. TJ's Big Boy, Syracuse, N.Y., 1987. Avocations: dancing, reading, art, theater, music. Office: Syracuse U Press 1600 Jamesville Ave Syracuse NY 13244

PFEIFFER, ECKHARD, computer company executive. BA, Nuremberg Business, 1963; MBA, SMU, 1983. Pres. & CEO Compaq Computer, 1991—. Office: Compaq Computer Corp 20555 State Hwy Houston TX 77070*

PFEIFFER, ERIC ARMIN, psychiatrist, gerontologist; b. Rauental, Germany, Sept. 15, 1935; came to U.S., 1952; naturalized, 1957; s. Fritz and Emma (Saborowski) P.; m. Natasha Maria Emerson, Mar. 21, 1964; children: Eric Alexander, Michael David, Mark Armin. AB, Washington U., 1956, MD, 1960. Intern Albert Einstein Coll. Medicine, Bronx, N.Y., 1960-61; resident in psychiatry U. Rochester, N.Y., 1961-64; practice medicine specializing in psychiatry Durham, N.C., 1966-76, Denver, 1976-78; asst. prof. Duke U., Durham, 1966-69, assoc. prof., 1969-72, prof., 1973-76, project dir., 1971-76, assoc. dir., 1974-76; dir. Davis Inst. Care and Study Aging, Denver, 1976-77; prof. psychiatry U. Colo., Denver, 1976-78; prof. psychiatry, chief div. geriatric psychiatry U. South Fla. Coll. Medicine, Tampa, 1978—; dir. Suncoast Gerontology Ctr. U. South Fla. Coll. Medicine, 1980—; chief psychiatry svc. Tampa VA Med. Ctr., 1979-80; cons. in field; chmn. bd. Social Systems, Inc., 1975-76; chmn. com. on mental health and mental illness of elderly HEW, 1976-77. Author: Disordered Behavior, 1968, (with E.W. Busse) Behavior and Adaptation in Late Life, 1970, 3d edit., 1977, Successful Aging, 1974, Multidimensional Functional Assessment, 1977, Alzheimer's Disease, 1989. With USPHS, 1964-66. Markle Found. scholar acad. medicine, 1968-73; Eric Pfeiffer Chair in Alzheimer's Disease Rsch. named in his honor, U. S. Fla., 1985. Fellow Gerontol. Soc. (chmn. clin. medicine sect. 1975-76), Am. Psychiat. Assn.; mem. Am. Geriatrics Soc. (Allen Gold medal 1977), So. Psychiat. Soc., Phi Beta Kappa. Home: 5140 W Longfellow Ave Tampa FL 33629-7534 Office: 12901 Bruce B Downs Blvd Tampa FL 33612-4742

PFEIFFER, JANE CAHILL, former broadcasting company executive, consultant; b. Washington, Sept. 29, 1932; d. John Joseph and Helen (Reilly) Cahill; B.A., U. Md., 1954; postgrad., Cath. U. Am., 1956-57; LHD (hon.), Pace Coll., 1978, U. Md., 1979, Manhattanville Coll., 1979, Amherst U., 1980, Babson Coll., 1981, U. Notre Dame, 1991; m. Ralph A. Pfeiffer, Jr., June 3, 1975. With IBM Corp., Armonk, N.Y., 1955-76, sec. mgmt. rev. com., 1970, dir. communications, 1971, v.p. communications and govt. relations, 1972-76, bus. cons., 1976-78; chmn. NBC, Inc., N.Y.C., 1978-80; bus. cons., 1980—; dir. Ashland Oil Co., Mony Fin. Svcs., Internat. Paper Co., J.C. Penney Co.; trustee The Conf. Bd., 1991. Mem. pres.'s adv. com. White House Fellows, 1966, Pres.'s Gen. Adv. Commn. on Arms Control and Disarmament, 1977-80, Pres.'s Commn. Mil. Compensation, trustee Rockefeller Found., U. Md., Carnegie Hall, U. Notre Dame. White House fellow, Washington, 1966; recipient Achievement award Kappa Kappa Gamma, 1974-80, Eleanor Roosevelt Humanitarian award N.Y. League for Hard of Hearing, 1980, Disting. Alumna award U. Md., 1975, Humanitarian award NOW, 1980, Centennial Alumna Medallion U. Md., 1988. Mem. Council on Fgn. Relations, Overseas Devel. Council. Club: Econ. of N.Y. Office: 90 Field Point Cir Greenwich CT 06830-7011

PFEIFFER, JOHN EDWARD, author; b. N.Y.C., Sept. 27, 1914; s. Edward Heyman and Jeannette (Gross) P.; m. Naomi Ranson, Sept. 9, 1939; 1 son, Anthony John. B.A., Yale U., 1936. Sci. editor Newsweek mag., N.Y.C., 1936-42; sci. dir. CBS, N.Y.C., 1946-48; mem. editorial bd. Sci. Am., N.Y.C., 1948-50; free-lance writer, editor, 1950—; prof. anthropology Livingston Coll., Rutgers U., 1968—; cons. NSF, U. Chgo., Princeton U. Adv. Council for Anthropology, Tulane U., Ednl. Testing Svc. Princeton, N.J., Harvard U. Negotiation Project, Pacific Gas and Electric Co., Berkeley Study of High Risk Orgns., Harper's mag., others; mem. adv. council on anthropology Princeton U. Author: Science in Your Life, 1939, The Human Brain, 1955, The Changing Universe, 1956, From Galaxies to Man, 1959, The Thinking Machine, 1962, The Search For Early Man, 1963, The Cell, 1964, New Look at Education, 1968, The Emergence of Man, 1969, 4th edit., 1985, The Emergence of Society...A Prehistory of the Establishment, 1977, The Creative Explosion....An Inquiry into the Origins of Art and Religion,

1982; reviewer, cons. N.Y. Times Book Rev., 1982—; cons., contbg. editor Smithsonian mag. Trustee Solebury Sch., New Hope, Pa. Recipient CBS TV Writing award, 1959, Wenner-Gren Found. grant, 1961, Carnegie Corp. of N.Y. grants, 1965, 69; John Simon Guggenheim fellow, 1952, 54; Fulbright fellow, 1958; Harry Frank Guggenheim fellow, 1979-80, 80-81. Mem. AAAS, Am. Anthrop. Assn., Acad. Mgmt., Prehistoric Soc. of Eng., Soc. Am. Archeologists, Soc. Am. Anthropology, Antarctic Archaeol. Inst., Nat. Assn. Sci. Writers (past pres.), Prehistoric Soc. London. Home: 331 Lower Dolington Rd Newtown PA 18940-1696

PFEIFFER, JOHN WILLIAM, publisher, management consultant; b. Wallace, Idaho, July 10, 1937; s. John William and Mary Loretta (Schmidt) P.; children: Heidi Erika, Charles Wilson. BA, U. Md., 1962; PhD (fellow), U. Iowa, 1968; JD, Western State U., 1982; DABS (hon.), Calif. Am. U., Escondido, 1980. Instr. U. Md., 1965-67; dir. adult edn. Kirkwood (Iowa) Community Coll., 1967-69; dir. ednl. resources Ind. Higher Edn. Telecommunications Systems, Indpls., 1969-72; pres. Univ. Assocs., San Diego, 1972-90, Pfeiffer & Co., San Diego, 1991—; adj. tchr. Ind. U., 1969-72, Purdue U., 1971-72. Author: Instrumentation in Human Relations Training, 1973, 2d edit. 1976, Reference Guide to Handbooks and Annuals, 1975, 2d edit. 1977, 3d. edit. 1981, (With Goodstein and Nolan) Applied Strategic Planning, 1986, 2d edit. 1988, (with Judith A. Pfeiffer) LBP, 1990; editor: A Handbook of Structured Experiences for Human Relations Training, 10 vols., 1969-85, The Annual Handbook for Facilitators, 10 vols. 1972-81, Group and Orgns. Studies Internat. Jour. for Group Facilitators, 1976-79, The Annual for Facilitators, Trainers and Consultants, 1982-91, Strategic Planning: Selected Readings, 1986, The Instrumentation Kit, 1988, Shaping Strategic Planning, 1988, Training Technology, 7 vols., 1988, Theories and Models, 4 vols., 1992, Plan or Die, 1993, Pfeiffer Library, 28 vols., 1993. Served with U.S. Army, 1958-62. Office: Pfeiffer & Co 8517 Production Ave San Diego CA 92121-2204

PFEIFFER, LEONARD, IV, executive recruiter, consultant; s. Leonard Jr. and Felicia Pfeiffer; m. Anna Gunnarsson. BA, Harvard U., MBA. Mktg. mgr. Am. Express, N.Y.C., 1970-72; project dir. S.T.I., N.Y.C. and San Francisco, 1972-74; v.p. R. Olivier & Assocs., N.Y.C., 1974-76, A. Kane & Assoc., N.Y.C., 1976-78; v.p., ptnr. Korn/Ferry Internat., Washington and N.Y.C., 1978—. Bd. dirs. Cmty. Found., Washington, 1982-84, Nat. Ctr. for Missing Children, 1989—, Nat. Blood Found., 1995—; founding mem. jr. bd. dirs. Washington Opera, 1983-93; mem. men's com. Project Hope; devel. com. Nat. Head Injury Found. and Nat. Symphony Orchestra. Lt. U.S. Army, 1968-70. Schepp Found. scholar, 1968-70. Mem. Am. Soc. Assn. Execs., Greater Washington Soc. Assn. Execs., Nat. Club Assn., Harvard Club (activities com., admissions com. N.Y.C. chpt. 1975-81, 1st v.p. bd. dirs. Washington chpt. 1985-87), City Club. Avocations: water and snow skiing, power and sail boating, tennis. Office: Korn Ferry Internat 900 19th St NW Washington DC 20006-2105

PFEIFFER, MARGARET KOLODNY, lawyer; b. Elkin, N.C., Oct. 7, 1944; d. Isadore Harold and Mary Elizabeth (Brody) K.; m. Carl Frederick Pfeiffer II, Sept. 2, 1968. BA, Duke U., 1967; JD, Rutgers U., 1974. Bar: N.J. 1974, N.Y. 1976, D.C. 1981, U.S. Supreme Ct. 1979. Law clk. to Hon. F.L. Van Dusen U.S. Ct. Appeals 3d cir., Phila., 1974-75; assoc. Sullivan & Cromwell, N.Y.C. and Washington, 1975-82, ptnr., 1982—. Contbr. articles to profl. jours. Mem. ABA, Internat. Bar Assn., D.C. Bar Assn., N.Y. State Bar Assn., Assn. of Bar of City of N.Y. Avocations: hiking, reading, music. Office: Sullivan & Cromwell 1701 Pennsylvania Ave NW Washington DC 20006-5805

PFEIFFER, MICHELLE, actress; b. Santa Ana, Calif., Apr. 29, 1957; d. Dick and Donna P.; m. Peter Horton (div.); 1 adopted child, Claudia Rose; m. David Kelley, Nov. 13, 1993. Student, Golden West Coll., Whitley Coll. Actress: (feature films) Falling in Love Again, 1980, Hollywood Knights, 1980, Charlie Chan and the Curse of the Dragon Queen, 1981, Grease II, 1982, Scarface, 1983, Ladyhawke, 1985, Into the Night, 1985, Sweet Liberty, 1986, Amazon Women on the Moon, 1987, Witches of Eastwick, 1987, Married to the Mob, 1988, Tequila Sunrise, 1988, Dangerous Liaisons, 1988 (Acad. award nominee 1989), The Fabulous Baker Boys, 1989 (Achievement award L.A. Film Critics Assn. 1989, D.W. Griffith award Nat. Bd. Rev. 1989, N.Y. Film Critics award 1989, Nat. Soc. Film Critics award 1990, Golden Globe award 1990, Acad. award nominee 1990), The Russia House, 1990,Frankie & Johnny, 1991, Love Field, 1992 (Acad. award nominee 1993), Batman Returns, 1992, The Age of Innocence, 1993, Wolf, 1994, Dangerous Minds, 1995; (TV movies) The Solitary Man,1979, Callie and Son, 1981, The Children Nobody Wanted, 1981, Splendor in the Grass, 1981, (TV series) Delta House, 1979, B.A.D. Cats, 1980. Named Woman of the Yr., Harvard's Hasty Pudding Theater Club, 1995. Office: care ICM 8942 Wilshire Blvd Beverly Hills CA 90211-1934*

PFEIFFER, PHYLLIS KRAMER, publisher; b. N.Y.C., Feb. 11, 1949; d. Jacob N. and Estelle G. Rosenbaum-Pfeiffer. B.S., Cornell U., 1970; postgrad. U. San Diego, 1976-78; m. Stephen M. Pfeiffer, Dec. 21, 1969; children: Andrew Kramer, Elise Kramer. Instr., Miss Porter's Sch., Farmington, Conn., 1970; tchr. N.Y.C. Bd. Edn., Dewey Jr. High Sch., 1970-73; research Hunter Coll., N.Y., 1971-72; account exec. La Jolla (Calif.) Light, 1973-75, advt. dir., 1975-77, gen. mgr., 1977-78, pub., 1978-87 ; exec. v.p. Harte Hanks So. Calif. Newspapers, 1985-87; gen. mgr. San Diego edit. L.A. Times, 1987-93; pres., pub. Marin Ind. Jour., Novato, Calif., 1993—; dir. communications center San Diego State U., 1980-93. Bd. dirs. La Jolla Cancer Research Found., 1979-82; bd. dirs. Alvarado Hosp., 1981-88, chmn. fin. com., 1986, sec. bd., 1986; co-chmn. Operation USS La Jolla, U.S. Navy, 1980—; mem. mktg. com. United Way, 1979-81, chmn., 1983; bd. dirs. YMCA, San Diego Ballet, 1980; trustee La Jollan's Inc., 1975-78; mem. Conv. and Visitors Bur. Blue Ribbon Com. on Future, 1983, resource panel Child Abuse Prevention Found., 1983—; bd. overseers U. Calif., San Diego; mem. violent crimes task force San Diego Police Dept.; bd. dirs. Dominican Coll., San Rafael, Calif., 1994—. N.Y. Bd. Edn. grantee, 1971-72. Mem. Newspaper Assn. Am., Calif. Newspaper Pubs. Assn. (bd. dirs., exec. com.), Chancellor's Assn. U. Calif.-San Diego., Tiburon Peninsula Club. Home: 198 Stewart Dr Belvedere Tiburon CA 94920-1313 Office: Marin Ind Jour 150 Alameda Del Prado Novato CA 94949-6665

PFEIFFER, ROBERT JOHN, business executive; b. Suva, Fiji Islands, Mar. 7, 1920; came to U.S., 1921, naturalized, 1927; s. William Albert and Nina (MacDonald) P.; m. Mary Elizabeth Worts, Nov. 29, 1945; children—Elizabeth Pfeiffer Tumbas, Margaret Pfeiffer Hughes, George, Kathleen. Grad. high sch., Honolulu, 1937; DSc (hon.), Maine Maritime Acad.; HHD (hon.), U. Hawaii; DHL (hon.), Hawaii Loa Coll. With Inter-Island Steam Navigation Co., Ltd., Honolulu, (re-organized to Overseas Terminal Ltd. 1950); with (merged into Oahu Ry. & Land Co. 1954), 1937-55, v.p., gen. mgr., 1950-54, mgr. ship agy. dept., 1954-55; v.p., gen. mgr. Pacific Cut Stone & Granite Co., Inc., Alhambra, Calif., 1955-56, Matcinal Corp., Alameda, Calif., 1956-58; mgr. div. Pacific Far East Line, Inc., San Francisco, 1958-60; with Matson Nav. Co., San Francisco, 1960—, v.p., 1966-70, sr. v.p., 1970-71, exec. v.p., 1971-73, pres., 1973-79, 84-85, 89-90, CEO, 1979-92, chmn. bd., bd.dirs., 1979-95, chmn. emeritus, 1995—; v.p. The Matson Co., San Francisco, 1968-70; pres. The Matson Co., 1970-82; v.p., gen. mgr. Matson Terminals, Inc., San Francisco, 1960-62; pres. Matson Terminals, Inc., 1962-70, chmn. bd., 1970-79; chmn. bd. Matson Svcs. Co., 1973-79, Matson Agys., Inc., 1973-78; sr. v.p. Alexander & Baldwin, Inc., Honolulu, 1973-77; exec. v.p. Alexander & Baldwin, Inc., 1977-79, chmn. bd., 1980-95; chmn. emeritus Alexander & Baldwin, Inc., Honolulu, 1995—; CEO Alexander & Baldwin, Inc., 1980-92, pres., 1979-84, 89-91; chmn. bd., pres., dir. A&B-Hawaii, Inc., 1988-89, chmn. bd., 1989-95; chmn. emeritus A&B Hawaii, Honolulu, 1995—; former mem. Gov.'s commn. on exec. salaries State of Hawaii, com. on jud. salaries. Past chmn. maritime transp. rsch. bd. NAS; former mem. select com. for Am. Mcht. Marine Seamanship Trophy Award; mem. commn. sociotech. systems NRC; mem. adv. com. Joint Maritime Congress; trustee Pacific Tropical Bot. Garden, Pacific Aerospace Mus., also bd. dirs.; vice-chmn. Hawaii Maritime Ctr.; former chmn. A. Com. on Excellence (ACE), Hawaii; bd. govs. Japanese Cultural Ctr. Hawaii; hon. co-chmn. McKinley H.S. Found. Lt. USNR, WWII; comdr. Res. ret. Mem. VFW (life), Nat. Assn. Stevedores (past pres.), Internat. Cargo Handling Coord. Assn. (past pres. U.S. Com.), Propeller Club U.S. (past pres. Honolulu chpt.), Nat. Def. Transp. Assn., Containerization & Intermodal Inst. (hon. bd. advisors), 200 Club, Aircraft Owners and Pilots Assn., Pacific Club, Outrigger Club, Oahu Country Club, Maui Country Club, Pacific Union Club, Bohemian Club, World Trade Club (San Francisco), Masons, Shriners. Republican. Home: 535 Miner Rd Orinda CA 94563-1429 Office: Alexander & Baldwin Inc 822 Bishop St Honolulu HI 96813-3924

PFEIFFER, SOPHIA DOUGLASS, state legislator, lawyer; b. N.Y.C., Aug. 10, 1918; d. Franklin Chamberlin and Sophie Douglass (White) Wells; m. Timothy Adams Pfeiffer, June 7, 1941; children: Timothy Franklin, Penelope Mersereau Keenan, Sophie Douglass. AB, Vassar Coll., 1939; JD, Northeastern U., 1975. Bar: R.I. 1975, U.S. Ct. Apls. (1st cir.) 1980, U.S. Supreme Ct. 1979. Editl. rschr. Time, Inc., N.Y.C., 1940-41; writer Office War Info., Washington, 1941-43, N.Y.C., 1943-45; editl. staff Nat. Geog. Mag., Washington, 1958-59, 68-70; editor Turkish Jour. Pediatrics, Ankara, 1961-63; staff atty. R.I. Supreme Ct., Providence, 1975-76, chief staff atty., 1977-86; mem. Maine Ho. Reps., 1990-94; lectr. U. So. Maine, 1995; bd. dirs. Death and Dying project. Chair bioethics study League Women Voters. Contbr. in field. Pres., Karachi Am. Sch. (Pakistan), 1955-56; chair, Brunswick Village Review Bd., 1986-89. Home: 15 Franklin St Brunswick ME 04011-2101

PFEIFFER, STEVEN BERNARD, lawyer; b. Orange, N.J., Jan. 19, 1947; s. Bernard Victor and Elizabeth Sophia (Bissell) P.; m. Kristin Reagan, June 27, 1970; children: Victoria Elizabeth, Rachel Catherine, Emily Dorothea, Stephanie Kristin Bissell, Andrew Steven Bernard. BA in Govt., Wesleyan U., 1969; BA in Jurisprudence, Oxford U., 1971, MA, 1983; MA in African Studies, U. London, 1973; JD, Yale U., 1976. Bar: N.J. 1976, D.C. 1978. Assoc. Fulbright & Jaworski, Houston, London, 1976-83; ptnr. Fulbright & Jaworski, London, Washington, 1983—; ptnr.-in-charge Fulbright & Jaworski, London, 1983-86; head internat. dept. Fulbright & Jaworski, Washington, 1989—; bd. dirs. Riggs Nat. Corp., Washington, Riggs Nat. Bank, Washington, Riggs AP Bank, London, Halston Borghese, Inc., N.Y.C., U. Cape Town Fund, N.Y.C. Contbr. articles to profl. jours. Alumni-elected trustee Wesleyan U., Middletown, Conn., 1976-79, charter trustee, 1980-92, vice chmn. bd. trustees, 1986-87, chmn. bd. trustees, 1987-92, chmn. emeritus, 1992—. With USN, 1969, 72-74; asst. cinceur plans officer, Office of CNO, Washington, 1972-73; spl. asst. to Sec. of Navy, Washington, 1973-74. Rhodes scholar, 1969-72; Thomas Watson Travel fellow, The Watson Found., 1969. Mem. ABA, N.J. State Bar Assn., Am. Soc. Internat. Law, Internat. Bar Assn. (immediate past chmn. sect. energy and natural resources law), Naval Res. Assn., Internat. Inst. Strategic Studies, Coun. Fgn. Rels. Avocations: tennis, history, fishing, books. Home: 301 N View Ter Alexandria VA 22301-2609 Office: Fulbright & Jaworski LLP 801 Pennsylvania Ave NW Washington DC 20004-2604

PFEIFFER, WERNER BERNHARD, artist, educator; b. Stuttgart, Germany, Oct. 1, 1937; came to U.S., 1961; s. Jakob and Emilie (Nufer) P.; children: Jan-Stephen, Michaela Veronica. Diploma, Grafische Fachschule, Stuttgart, Akademie Fine Arts, Stuttgart. Instr. Pratt Inst., Bklyn., 1961-64, prof., 1968-75, adj. prof., 1976—; asst. prof. N.Y. Inst. Tech., Westbury, 1965-67; dir. Pratt Adlib Press, Bklyn., 1968-75. Exhibited in over 50 one-man shows. Mem. Soc. Am. Graphic Artists. Avocations: skiing, travel, music. Address: Flat Rock Rd Cornwall Bridge CT 06754

PFENDER, EMIL, mechanical engineering educator; b. Stuttgart, Germany, May 25, 1925; came to U.S., 1964, naturalized, 1969; s. Vinzenz and Anna Maria (Dreher) P.; m. Maria Katharina Staiger, Oct. 22, 1954; children: Roland, Norbert, Corinne. Student U. Tuebingen, Germany, 1947-49; Diploma in Physics, U. Stuttgart, 1953, D. Ing. in Elec. Engring., 1959. Assoc. prof. mech. engring. U. Minn., Mpls., 1964-67, prof., 1967—. Contbr. articles to profl. jours. Patentee in field. Fellow ASME, ASM; mem. IEEE (assoc.), NAE, ASM Internat. Home: 1947 Bidwell St Saint Paul MN 55118-4417 Office: U Minn Dept of Mech Engrg 111 Church St SE Minneapolis MN 55455-0150

PFENING, FREDERIC DENVER, III, manufacturing company executive; b. Columbus, Ohio, July 28, 1949; s. Frederic Denver Jr. and Lelia (Bucher) P.; m. Cynthia Gordon, July 1, 1978; children: Lesley, Frederic Denver IV. BA, Ohio Wesleyan U., 1971; MA, Ohio State U., Columbus, 1976. Various positions Fred. D. Pfening Co., Columbus, 1976-88, pres., 1988—. Bd. dirs. Friends of Ohio State U. Librs., 1988-94, Columbus State C.C. Devel. Found., 1991—, Hist. Sites Found., Baraboo, Wis., 1984—, pres., 1987-91. Mem. Am. Soc. Bakery Engrs., Orgn. Am. Historians, Bakery Equipment Mfrs. Assn. (bd. dirs. 1985-91), Young Pres.'s Orgn., Circus Hist. Soc. (pres. 1986-89, mng. editor Bandwagon Jour.), Rotary. Office: 1075 W 5th Ave Columbus OH 43212-2629

PFENNIGER, RICHARD CHARLES, JR., lawyer; b. Akron, Ohio, July 26, 1955; s. Richard Charles Pfenniger and Phyllis Irene (Rutan) Gatto. BBA, Fla. Atlantic U., 1977; JD, U. Fla., 1982. Bar: Fla. 1982; CPA, Fla. Acct. Price Waterhouse & Co., Ft. Lauderdale, Fla., 1977-79; assoc. Stearns, Weaver, Miller, Weisller, Alhadeff & Sitterson, P.A., Miami, Fla., 1982-86, Greer, Homer, Cope & Bonner P.A., Miami, 1986-89; sr. v.p. legal affairs and gen. counsel IVAX Corp., Miami, 1989-94, COO, 1994—. Mem. ABA, AICPA. Office: IVAX Corp 4400 Biscayne Blvd Miami FL 33137-3227

PFENNIGSTORF, WERNER, lawyer; b. Hamburg, Germany, Sept. 28, 1934; s. Walter and Ilse (Schroeter) P.; m. Heika Helene Droenner, Apr. 6, 1963. Habilitation, U. Hamburg, Germany, 1974; JD, 1960; MCL, U. Mich. 1961. Bar: Germany 1962. Wissenschaftl asst. U. Hamburg, 1963-66; staff atty. Ins. Laws Rev. Commn., State Wis., Madison, 1967-70; rsch. fellow U. Hamburg, 1970-72; project dir. Am. Bar Found., Chgo., 1973-86; pvt. practice, 1986— . Author: Legal Expense Insurance, 1975, German Insurance Laws, 3rd edit., 1995, A Comparative Study of Liability Law and Compensation Schemes in Ten Countries and the U.S., 1991, Public Law of Insurance, 1996; co-editor: Legal Service Plans, 1977; editor: Personal Injury Compensation, 1993, Pollution Insurance, 1993. Mem. Deutscher Verein für Versicherungswissenschaft, ABA (assoc.), Internat. Assn. Ins. Law. Lutheran. Office: Roethkampstr 3, 21709 Duedenbuettel Germany

PFENNINGER, KARL H., cell biology and neuroscience educator; b. Stafa, Switzerland, Dec. 17, 1944; came to U.S., 1971, naturalized, 1993; s. Hans Rudolf and Delie Maria (Zahn) P.; m. Marie-France Maylié, July 12, 1974; children—Jan Patrick, Alexandra Christina. M.D., U. Zurich, 1971. Research instr. dept. anatomy Washington U., St. Louis, 1971-73; research assoc. sect. cell biology Yale U., New Haven, 1973-76; assoc. prof. dept. anatomy and cell biology Columbia U., N.Y.C., 1976-81, prof., 1981-86; prof., chmn. dept. cellular and structural biology U. Colo. Sch. Medicine, Denver, 1986—; dir. interdeptmental program in cell and molecular biology Columbia U. Coll. Physicians and Surgeons, N.Y.C., 1980-85; chmn. Given Biomed. Inst., Aspen, Colo., 1992-93. Author: Essential Cell Biology, 1990; contbr. articles to profl. jours. Recipient C.J. Herrick award Am. Assn. Anatomists, 1977; I.T. Hirschl Career Scientist award, 1977; Javits neurosci. investigator awards NIH, 1984, 91. Mem. AAAS, Am. Soc. for Cell Biology, Am. Soc. for Biochemistry and Molecular Biology, Toxicology Forum (bd. dirs. 1995—), Harvey Soc., Soc. for Neurosci., Internat. Brain Rsch. Orgn., Internat. Soc. for Neurochemistry. Office: U Colo Health Scis Ctr Dept Cellular and Structural Biology B-111 4200 E 9th Ave Denver CO 80262

PFEUFFER, ROBERT JOHN, musician; b. Cleve., Dec. 25, 1925; s. Henry Vincent and Elmo Alice (Burger) P.; m. Betty June Weller, Sept. 21, 1946; children—Barbara (Mrs. Steven Mosley), Jeanne, Susan, Catherine. B.Mus. in Edn, U. Mich., 1950, M.Mus. in Edn, 1951. Contrabassoonist, bassoonist Detroit Symphony Orch., 1951-61, Phila. Orch., 1962-91; instr. bassoon Wayne State U., 1957-61, New Sch. Music, Phila., 1969—; prin. bassoon Lynchburg Symphony, 1994—. Served with AUS, 1942-44. Mem. U.S. Power Squadron, Kappa Kappa Psi, Pi Mu Alpha. Roman Catholic. Home: RR 1 Box 481F Moneta VA 24121-9801

PFISTER, CLOYD HARRY, consultant, former career officer; b. State College, Pa., Dec. 20, 1936; s. Rudolf John Pfister and June Ruth (Braun) Pfister Gray; m. Rita Askerc Kracht, Aug. 17, 1962 (div. Mar. 1982); m. Gail Williams, Apr. 24, 1982; children, Gabriele, Catherine, Michael, Romi, Eric Williams, Lori Williams. BA in Philosophy, Oberlin Coll., 1957; MA in Internat. Rels., Am. U., 1964, postgrad., 1964-67. Enlisted U.S. Army, 1957, advanced through grades to maj. gen., 1989; staff officer Nat. Security Agy., Fort Meade, Md., 1965-68; S3 (Ops.) 303d Radio Rsch. Bn., Plantation, Vietnam, 1968-69; instr. JFK Ctr. and Sch., Fort Bragg, N.C., 1969-72; politico-mil. officer, Office Dep. Chief of Staff for Ops. Hdqrs. Dept. Army, Washington, 1972-75; comdr. 307th U.S. Army Security Agy. Bn., VII U.S. Corps, Ludwigsburg, Fed. Republic Germany, 1975-77; asst. chief of staff intelligence 8th Mech. Inf. Div., Bad Kreuznach, Fed. Republic Germany, 1977-79; Mid. East staff officer Office Sec. Def., The Pentagon, 1979-82; comdr. U.S. Army Field Sta., Berlin, 1982-84; chief of staff U.S. Army Intelligence Ctr. and Sch., Fort Huachuca, Ariz., 1984-85, dep. comdt., 1985-86; dir. intelligence (J2), Hdqrs., U.S. Cen. Command, MacDill AFB, Fla., 1986-88; dep. chief of staff intelligence Hdqrs., U.S. Army Europe and 7th Army, Heidelberg, Fed. Republic Germany, 1988-91; asst. dep. chief of staff Intelligence Hdqrs., Dept. Army, Pentagon, 1991—; cons. Def. Sci. Bd. Decorated Def. D.S.M., D.S.M. Def. Superior Svc. medal, Legion of Merit with two oak leaf clusters, Nat. Intelligence D.S.M.; Ehrenkreutz der Bundeswehr (gold) (Fed. Republic Germany); other awards. Mem. Internat. Inst. for Strategic Studies, Middle East Inst., Security Affairs Support Assn., Assn. U.S. Army. Avocations: tennis, photography, gardening, computers. Office: Tech Strategies & Alliances 5242 Lyngate Ct Burke VA 22015-1631

PFISTER, DONALD HENRY, biology educator; b. Kenton, Ohio, Feb. 17, 1945; s. William A. and Dorothy C. (Kurtz) P.; m. Cathleen C. Kennedy, July 1, 1971; children: Meghan, Brigid, Edith. AB, Miami U., Oxford, Ohio, 1967; PhD, Cornell U., 1971; AM (hon.), Harvard U., 1980. Asst. prof. biology U. P.R., Mayaguez, 1971-74; asst. prof. biology, asst. curator Farlow Herbarium Harvard U., Cambridge, Mass., 1974-77, assoc. prof. biology, assoc. curator Farlow Herbarium, 1977-80, prof. biology, curator Farlow Herbarium, 1980—, dir. univ. herbaria, 1983-95; vis. mycologist U. Copenhagen, 1978; vis. prof. field station U. Minn., Itasca, 1979; master Kirkland House Harvard U., 1982—. Contbr. over 80 articles to profl. jours. Grantee NSF, 1973-75, 81-85, 85—, Am. Philos. Soc., 1975-76, Whiting Found., 1986. Fellow Linnean Soc. London; mem. Mycol. Soc. Am. (sec. 1988-91, v.p. 1993-94, pres.-elect 1994-95), Am. Phytopath. Soc., Am. Microbiol. Soc., New Eng. Bot. Club, Sigma Xi. Office: Harvard U Herbarium 22 Divinity Ave Cambridge MA 02138

PFISTER, KARL ANTON, industrial company executive; b. Ernetschwil St. Gallen, Switzerland, Oct. 17, 1941; came to U.S., 1966; s. Josef Anton and Paula (Hobi) P.; m. Karen Antonie Sievers; children: Kirsten, Marc, Theodore, Alexandra. Student trade sch., Rapperswil, Switzerland, 1957-61; student bus. sch., Zuerich, Switzerland, 1964-65. Tool and die maker H. Schmid, Rapperswil, Switzerland, 1957-61, Neher AG, Ebnat-Kappel, Switzerland, 1962-63; process engr. NCR, Buelach, Switzerland, 1964-66, Gretag, Regensdorf, Switzerland, 1966; tool and die maker Stoffel Fineflow Corp., White Plains, N.Y., 1966-67; mgr. mfg. Finetool Corp., Detroit, 1968; pres. Mich. Precision Ind., Inc., Detroit, 1969—; chmn. bd., pres. Kautex N.Am., Inc., 1994; pres. Kloeckner Automotive, Inc., Rochester Hills, Mich., 1996; dir. Kloeckner Capital Corp., Gordonsville, Va., MPI Internat., Inc., Kautex N.Am., Inc., Kloeckner Automotive, Inc. Consul, consulate Switzerland, Detroit, 1984—. Mem. Plum Hollow Club, Fairlane Club. Republican. Roman Catholic. Office: MPI Internat Inc 2129 Austin Ave Rochester Hls MI 48309-3668

PFISTER, PETER J., lawyer; b. Mar. 29, 1948. AB in Econs. and German, U. Calif., Santa Barbara, 1970; JD, Yale U., 1973. Bar: Calif. 1975. Law clk. to Hon. Samuel Conti U.S. Dist. Ct. (no. dist.) Calif., 1974; assoc. Morrison & Foerster, San Francisco, 1975-79, ptnr., 1979-93, chmn. litigation dept., 1987-90, mng. ptnr. practice, 1990-93, chmn., 1993—. Mem. ABA (antitrust sect., litigation sect.). Office: Morrison & Foerster 345 California St San Francisco CA 94104-2635*

PFISTER, RICHARD CHARLES, physician, radiology educator; b. Ypsilanti, Mich., Nov. 27, 1933; s. Emil Robert and Francis Josephine (LeForge) P.; m. Sally DeAnn Haight, Dec. 31, 1956 (div. 1980); children: Kirk Alan, Gary Raymond, Karen Dawn, James Kevin, William Charles. BS, Ctrl. Mich. U., 1958; MD, Wayne State U., 1962. Assoc. prof. radiology Harvard Med. Sch. and Mass. Gen. Hosp., Boston, 1966-89; med. officer FDA, Washington, 1989-90; prof. radiology U. South Ala., Mobile, 1990-92, La. State U., New Orleans, 1993—. Editor, author: Interventional Radiology, 1982. With U.S. Army Med. Corps, 1953-55. Recipient Investigator award NIH, Washington, 1972. Fellow Am. Coll. Radiology; mem. AMA, Soc. Uroradiology (pres. 1984-85), Radiologic Soc. N.Am., Am. Roentgen Ray Soc., Soc. Cardiovascular Interventional. Avocation: sailing (Trans-Atlantic passages). Office: LSU Med Ctr 1542 Tulane Ave New Orleans LA 70112-2825

PFISTER, ROSWELL ROBERT, ophthalmologist; b. Buffalo, Jan. 19, 1938; s. Milton Albert and Florence P. Student, U. Buffalo, 1955-58; M.D., U. Mich., 1962, M.S., 1969. Diplomate Am. Bd. Ophthalmology. Intern Los Angeles County Hosp., 1962-63; resident in ophthalmology U. Mich., Ann Arbor, 1965-69; research fellow dept. cornea research Retina Found., Boston, 1969-71; clin. fellow cornea service Mass. Eye and Ear Infirmary, 1969-71; assoc. prof. U. Colo. Med. Center, Denver, 1971-75; prof., chmn. dept. ophthalmology Combined Program in Ophthalmology, U. Ala. in Birmingham-The Eye Found. Hosp., 1976-81; head research dept. ophthalmology Ellen Gregg Ingalls Eye Research Instn., 1976-81; dir. eye research labs. Brookwood Med. Ctr. (Birmingham), 1982—. Served with USAF, 1963-65. Mem. Med. Assn. Ala., Jefferson County Med. Soc., Assn. Univ. Profs. in Opthalmology, Research to Prevent Blindness, Am. Acad. Ophthalmology, Assn. Research in Vision and Opthalmology, Ala. Acad. Ophthalmology, AMA, Colo. Ophthalmology Soc., Mich. State Med. Soc., Mass. Eye and Ear Infirmary Alumnus Soc., Corneal Soc., Colo. Soc. Prevention of Blindness (mem. med. adv. bd. 1974-76), Colo. Eye Bank (med. dir. 1974-76), Kerato-Refractave Soc. Office: Brookwood Med Ctr Ste 504 513 Brookwood Blvd Birmingham AL 35209

PFLANZE, OTTO PAUL, history educator; b. Maryville, Tenn., Apr. 2, 1918; s. Otto Paul and Katrine (Mills) P.; m. Hertha Maria Haberlander, Feb. 20, 1951; children: Stephen, Charles, Katrine. B.A., Maryville Coll., 1940; M.A., Yale U., 1942, Ph.D., 1950. Historian Dept. State, 1948-49; instr. N.Y. U., 1950-51; asst. prof. U. Mass., 1952-58, U. Ill., 1958-61; prof. history U. Minn., 1961-76; prof. history Ind. U., 1977-86, emeritus, 1986; Stevenson Prof. of History Bard Coll., Annandale On Hudson, N.Y., 1987-92, emeritus, 1992; chmn. Conf. Group Central European History, 1978; mem. exam. bd., grad. record exam Ednl. Testing Service, 1972-76; mem. Inst. Advanced Study, 1970-71, mem. Historisches Kolleg, Munich, 1980-81. Author: Bismarck and the Development of Germany: Vol. 1.-The Period of Unification, 1815-1871, 1963 (Biennal Book award Phi Alpha Theta), rev. edit., 1990, Vol. 2-The Period of Consolidation, 1871-1880, 1990, Vol. 3-The Period of Fortification, 1880-1898, 1990 (3 vols. collectively named Most Outstanding Book in History, Govt. & Polit. Sci. by Assn. Am. Pubs., 1991); co-author: A History of the Western World: Modern Times, 3d edit, 1975; editor: Innenpolitische Probleme des Bismarck-Reiches, 1983; co-editor: Documents on German Foreign Policy, 1918-1945, Vols. I-III, 1949-50; editor Am. Hist. Rev., 1976-85; mem. editorial bd. Jour. Modern History, 1971-73, Central European History, 1972-74. Served to 1st It. U.S. Army, 1942-46. Fulbright research fellow, 1955-57; fellow Am. Council Learned Socs., 1951-52; fellow Guggenheim Found., 1966-67; fellow Nat. Endowment Humanities, 1975-76; fellow Internat. Research and Exchanges Bd., 1976; fellow Thyssen Stiftung, Essen, 1986; recipient Humanities award McKnight Found., 1962. Mem. Am. Hist. Assn., German Studies Assn.

PFLAUM, SUSANNA WHITNEY, college dean; b. Boston, Dec. 7, 1937; d. William T. and Ann. (Van Bibber) Whitney; m. Peter E. Pflaum, Apr. 10, 1963 (div. Mar. 1973); children: Melanie Ann, William E.; m. Joseph C. Grannis, Jan. 30, 1987; stepchildren: Eric Grannis, Alexander Grannis. AB cum laude, Radcliffe Coll., 1959; MEd, Harvard U., 1960; PhD, Fla. State U., 1971. Tchr. Newton (Mass.) Pub. Schs., 1960-63, Inter-Am. U., San German and Hato Rey, P.R., 1963-66; instr. Mankato (Minn.) State Coll., 1970-71; from asst. prof. to prof. U. Ill., Chgo., 1971-85, dean Honors Coll., 1982-85; dean Sch. Edn. CUNY Queens Coll., Flushing, N.Y., 1985-90; dean Bank St. Coll., N.Y.C., 1990—. Author: Development of Language and Literacy in Young Children, 3d edit., 1986; editor: Aspects of Reading

Education, 1978; co-editor: Celebrating Diverse Voices: Progressive Education and Equity, 1993, Experiencing Diversity: Toward Educational Equity, 1994; contbr. articles to profl. jours., 1973-92. Mem. Am. Edn. Rsch. Assn., Nat. Reading Conf., Internat. Reading Assn. (Harris Rsch. award 1981). Democrat. Episcopalian. Office: Bank Street Coll New York NY 10025

PFLUEGER, M(ELBA) LEE, academic administrator; b. St. Louis, Sept. 2, 1942; d. Pless and Edna Mae (Russell) Counts; m. Raymond Allen Pflueger, Sept. 14, 1963 (div. June 1972); children: Salem Allen, Russell Counts. BS in Home Econs., Univ. Mo., 1969; MEd in Guidance and Counseling, Washington Univ., St. Louis, 1973. Ednl. psychologist Ozark Regional Mental Health Ctr., Harrison, Ark., 1974-75; from account mgr. to mgr. pers. Enterprise Leasing Co., St. Louis, 1977-79; mgr. employee rels. Eaton Corp., Houston, 1979-80; owner Nature's Nuggets Fresh Granola, St. Louis, 1980-83; dir. corp. ednl. svcs. Maryville Coll., St. Louis, 1983-84; adminstr. mgmt. skills devel. McDonnell Douglas, St. Louis, 1984-85, mgr. employee involvement, 1985-86, prin. specialist human resources mgmt., 1988-89; mgr. human resources McDonnell Douglas, Houston, 1986-88; dir. devel. sch. engring. U. Mo., Rolla, 1989-93, dir. devel., corp. and found. rels., 1992-93; regional dir. devel., assoc. dir. maj. gifts and capital projects Washington U., St. Louis, 1994—; part-time leader trainer Maritz Motivation, St. Louis, 1984-89. Chair United Fund Campaign for U. Mo., Rolla, 1991. Mem. PEO. Avocations: reading, theatre, yoga. Office: Washington U Office Maj Gifts and Capital Projects Campus Box 1228 One Brookings Dr Saint Louis MO 63130-4899

PFLUG, DONALD RALPH, electrical engineer; b. Shreveport, La., May 22, 1941; s. Donald Ralph and Yullee Estelle (Yarborough) P.; m. Andrea Garza, Oct. 28, 1967; children; Mark David, Paul Eric. BA in Math., Rice U., 1966; MSEE, Syracuse U., 1985; PhD in Chem. Physics, U. Calif., Santa Barbara, 1975. Sr. engr. Atlantic Rsch. Corp., Rome, N.Y., 1976-84, prin. engr., 1987-92; mem. tech. staff Mitre Corp., Griffiss AFB, N.Y., 1984-85; sr. scientist Kaman Scis. Corp., Utica, N.Y., 1985-87; electronics engr. Rome lab. rome Lab., Griffiss AFB, 1993—. Judge sci. fair, Syracuse, N.Y., 1995. With U.S. Army, 1966-68. Mem. IEEE (sr. mem., reviewer Transactions on Antennas), IEEE Electromagnetic Compatibility Soc. (chpt. chmn. 1994—, reviewer 1994—), Applied Computational Electromagnetics Soc. (com. chmn. 1994—), Am. Phys. Soc., Electromagnetics Soc. Avocations: golf, jogging, weightlifting. Office: Rome Lab ERST 525 Brooks Rd Rome NY 13441

PFLUM, WILLIAM JOHN, physician; b. N.Y.C., July 30, 1924; s. Peter Arthur and Caroline (Schmidt) P.; BS, Georgetown U., 1947; MD, Loyola U., Chgo., 1951; m. Roseann Sarah Stubing, Oct. 13, 1956; children: Carol Jean, Jeannine, Suzanne, Denise, Peter. Intern, St. Vincent's Hosp., N.Y.C., 1951-52, resident in internal medicine, 1954-55; resident in internal medicine NYU div. Goldwater Meml. Hosp., N.Y.C., 1952-53; resident in allergy Inst. Allergy, Roosevelt Hosp., N.Y.C., 1956; attending internal medicine (allergy and immunology) Overlook Hosp., Summit, N.J., 1958—; assoc. attending Inst. Allergy, Immunology and Infectious Diseases, Roosevelt Hosp., N.Y.C., 1957-92; pvt. practice medicine, specializing in allergy and immunology, Summit, 1957-92; ret.; cons. in field. Served with USAAF, 1943-45; ETO. Decorated Purple Heart, Air medal with two clusters, POW medal. Diplomate Am. Bd. Allergy and Immunology. Fellow Am. Acad. Allergy, Am. Coll. Allergists, Am. Assn. Clin. Immunology and Allergy; mem. Summit Med. Soc., Am. Assn. Clin. Immunology and Allergy (pres. Mid-Atlantic region 1975-76), Disabled Am. Vets., Mil. Order Purple Heart, Am. Ex-Prisoners of War, 8th Air Force Hist. Soc., World Marathon Runners Assn., Robert A. Cooke Allergy Alumni Assn. Roman Catholic. Home: 16 Packer Ave Rumson NJ 07760-2028

PFNISTER, ALLAN OREL, humanities educator; b. Mason, Ill., July 23, 1925; s. Ardon Orel and Rose Margaret (Sandtner) P.; m. Helen Edith Klobes, Dec. 18, 1948; children: Alicia Ann, Jonathan Karl, Susan Elaine. AB summa cum laude, Augustana Coll., 1945; MDiv summa cum laude, Augustana Theol. Sem., 1949; AM with honors, U. Chgo., 1951, PhD, 1955; LLD (hon.), U. Denver, 1978. Instr. in religion Augustana Coll., 1946-47; instr. in philosophy and German Luther Coll., Wahoo, Nebr., 1949-52; dean Luther Coll., 1953-54; research asst., univ. fellow U. Chgo., 1952-53, instr., 1954-57, asst. prof., 1957-58; dir. research joint bds. parish edn. Lutheran Ch. Am., 1958-59; vis. asso. prof. U. Mich., 1959-62, asso. prof., 1962-63; dean Coll. Liberal Arts, prof. philosophy Wittenberg (Ohio) U., 1963-67, provost, prof., 1967-69, acting pres., 1968-69; prof. higher edn. U. Denver, 1969-77, 78-90, exec. vice chancellor and acting chancellor, 1977-78, vice chancellor acad. affairs, 1984-87, assoc. provost, 1988-89, prof. emeritus, 1990—; dir. study fgn. study programs Fedn. Regional Accrediting Commns. Higher Edn., 1970-72; cons. in field; bd. dirs. Nat. Ctr. for Higher Edn. Mgmt. Systems Mgmt. Svcs.; trustee Capital U., Columbus, Ohio, 1983, vice chmn. bd., 1987-89, 91-94. Author: Teaching Adults, 1967, Trends in Higher Education, 1975, Planning for Higher Education, 1976; contbr. numerous articles on higher edn. to profl. jours. Bd. visitors Air Force Inst. Tech., 1978-83, chmn. bd. visitors, 1981-83. Recipient Outstanding Achievement Alumni award Augustana Coll., 1963, Outstanding Contributions to the Univ. award Univ. Denver, 1995. Mem. Am. Am. Assn. Higher Edn., Assn. for Study Higher Edn., Comparative and Internat. Edn. Soc., Blue Key, Phi Beta Kappa (alumnus mem.). Democrat. Home: 7231 W Linvale Pl Denver CO 80227-3556

PFOUTS, RALPH WILLIAM, economist, consultant; b. Atchison, Kans., Sept. 9, 1920; s. Ralph Ulysses and Alice (Oldham) P.; m. Jane Hoyer, Jan. 31, 1945 (dec. Nov. 1982); children: James William, Susan Jane Pfouts Portman, Thomas Robert (dec.), Elizabeth Ann Pfouts Klenowski; m. Lois Bateson, Dec. 21, 1984 (div.); m. Felicia Sprincenatu, 1993. B.A., U. Kans., 1942, M.A., 1947; Ph.D., U. N.C., 1952. Rsch. asst., instr. econs. U. Kans., Lawrence, 1946-47; instr. U. N.C., Chapel Hill, 1947-50, lectr. econs., 1950-52, assoc. prof. econs., 1952-58, prof. econs., 1958-87, chmn. grad. studies dept. econs. Sch. Bus. Adminstrn., 1957-62, chmn. dept. econs. Sch. Bus. Adminstrn., 1962-68; cons. econs. Chapel Hill, 1987—; vis. prof. U. Leeds, 1983; vis. rsch. scholar Internat. Inst. for Applied Systems Analysis, Laxenberg, Austria, 1983; prof. Cen. European U., Prague, 1991. Author: Elementary Economics-A Mathematical Approach, 1972; editor: So. Econ. Jour, 1955-75; editor, contbr.: Techniques of Urban Economic Analysis, 1960, Essays in Economics and Econometrics, 1960; editorial bd.: Metroeconomica, 1961-80, Atlantic Econ. Jour, 1973—; contbr. articles to profl. jours. Served as deck officer USNR, 1943-46. Social Sci. Research Council fellow U. Cambridge, 1953-54; Ford Found. Faculty Research fellow, 1962-63. Mem. AAAS, Am. Statis. Assn., N.C. Statis. Assn. (past pres.), Am. Econ. Assn., So. Econ. Assn. (past pres.), Atlantic Econ. Soc. (v.p. 1973-76, pres. 1977-78), Population Assn. Am., Econometric Soc., Math. Assn. Am., Phi Beta Kappa, Pi Sigma Alpha, Alpha Kappa Psi, Omicron Delta Epsilon. Home and Office: 127 Summerlin Dr Chapel Hill NC 27514-1925

PFRIEM, BERNARD ALDINE, artist; b. Cleve., Sept. 7, 1914; s. Charles and Amanda (Ketterer) P. Student, John Huntington Poly., 1934-36; diploma, Cleve. Inst. Art, 1940. Tchr. Mus. Modern Art, N.Y.C., 1946-51; chief design U.S. Govt. Program Trade Fairs and World Fairs in Europe, 1953-56; tchr. Cooper Union Sch. Art and Architecture, N.Y.C., 1963-69, Sarah Lawrence Coll., 1969-75; founder, dir. Lacoste Sch. of the Arts, France, 1971-91, dir. emeritus, 1991—. Represented in permanent collections: Mus. of Modern Art, N.Y.C., Met. Mus., N.Y.C., Ark. Art Ctr., Little Rock, Bklyn. Mus., Utah Mus., Salt Lake City, Finch Mus., N.Y.C., Worcester (Mass.) Mus., Corcoran Gallery, Washington, Chase Manhattan Bank, N.Y.C., Columbia Banking, Savs. and Loan Assn., Rochester, N.Y., Atlantic Richfield Corp., Los Angeles, Chgo. Art Inst. Served with USAF, 1942-46. William Copley grantee, 1959; Agnes Gund travelling scholar, 1940; Mary Sugget Ranney travelling scholar. Club: Century. Office: 84710 Lacoste, Vaucluse France

PHAIR, JOSEPH BASCHON, lawyer; b. N.Y.C., Apr. 29, 1947; s. James Francis and Mary Elizabeth (Baschon) P.; m. Bonnie Jean Hobbs, Sept. 04, 1971; children: Kelly I., Joseph B., Sean P. BA, U. San Francisco, 1970, JD, 1973. Bar: Calif., U.S. Dist. Ct. (no. dist.) Calif., U.S. Ct. Appeals (9th cir.). Assoc. Berry, Davis & McInerney, Oakland, Calif., 1974-76, Bronson, Bronson & McKinnon, San Francisco, 1976-79; staff atty. Varian Assocs., Inc., Palo Alto, Calif., 1979-83, corp. counsel, 1983-86, sr. corp. counsel, 1986-87, assoc. gen. counsel, 1987-90, v.p., gen. counsel, 1990-91, v.p., gen. counsel, sec., 1991—. Mem. devel. bd. St. Vincent de Paul Devel. Coun., San Francisco, 1992—. Mem. Bay Area Gen. Counsel, Peninsula Assn. Gen. Counsel, The Olympic Culb. Roman Catholic. Office: Varian Assoc Inc M/S V-250 3050 Hansen Way Palo Alto CA 94304-1000

PHALEN, ROBERT FRANKLYNN, environmental scientist; b. Fairview, Okla., Oct. 18, 1940; married, 1966; 2 children. B in Physics, San Diego State U., 1964, M in Physics, 1966; PhD in Biophysics, U. Rochester, 1971. Engring. aide advanced space systems dept. Gen. Dynamics/Astronautics, San Diego, 1962-63; asst. to radiation safety officer, lab. teaching asst. San Diego State U., 1964-66, instr. physics dept., 1966; mem. summer faculty biology dept. Rochester (N.Y.) Inst. Tech., 1970-72; rsch. assoc. aerosol physics dept. Lovelace Found. for Med. Edn. and Rsch., Albuquerque, 1972-74; from adj. asst. prof. to assoc. prof. in residence dept. community and environ. medicine U. Calif., Irvine, 1974-84, prof. in residence, dir. Air Pollution Health Effects Lab., 1985—, faculty Ctr. for Occupl. Environ. Health, 1985—; reviewer Am. Review of Respiratory Disease, Applied Indsl. Hygiene, Bulletin of Math. Biology, Exptl. Lung Rsch., Jour. Toxicology and Environ. Health, Jour. Toxicology and Applied Pharmacology, Jour. Aerosol Sci., Sci.; reviewer, mem. editorial bd. Fundamental and Applied Toxicology, 1986-92, Inhalation Toxicology, Jour. Aerosol Medicine; mem. safety and occupational health study sect. NIH, 1988-90, mem. spl. study sects., 1980, 81, chmn. spl. study sects., 1982, 83, 84, 87, 88, 92, mem. site visit teams., 1980, 81, 82, 83, 84, 88; mem. expert panel on sulfur oxides EPA, mem. inhalation toxicology divsn. peer rev. panel, 1982, session chmn., 1983, participant workshop on non-oncogenic lung disease, 1984, mem. grants rsch. sci. rev. panel on health rsch., 1985-88; mem. task group on respiratory tract kinetic model Nat. Coun. Radiation Protection, 1978—; mem. adv. panel on asbestos Am. Pub. Health Assn., 1978; chmn. atmospheric sampling com. Am. Coun. Govtl. Indsl. Hygienists, 1982—; chmn. NIOSH spl. study sect., 1983; panelist workshop Nat. Heart, Lung and Blood Inst., 1982; sci. advisor Prentice Day Sch., 1986—. Author: Inhalation Studies: Foundations and Techniques, 1984; author: (with others Advances in Air Sampling, 1988, Concepts in Inhalation Toxicology, 1989; contbr. numerous articles to profl. jours. Am. Legion scholar. Mem. AAAS, Am. Assn. Aerosol Rsch. (charter, chmn. ann. meeting 1985), Am. Conf. Govtl. Indsl. Hygienists, Am. Indsl. Hygiene Assn. (jour. reviewer, chmn. ann. conf. 1981, 85, 86), Brit. Occupational Hygiene Soc., Fine Particle Soc., Soc. for Aerosol Rsch., Health Physics Soc., Soc. Toxicology (chmn. 20th ann. meeting 1981). Achievements include research in nasal, tracheobronchial and pulmonary transport of inhaled deposited particles and effects of pollutant exposure on transport kinetcs, laboratory simulation and characterization of airborne environmental pollutants, respiratory tract deposition and clearance models for inhaled particles, including species comparisons and body size effects, behavior of highly-concentrated aerosols with respect to deposition in the respiratory tract. Office: University of California Air Pollution Health Effects Lab Dept of Community & Environ Irvine CA 92717-1825

PHAM, SI MAI, cardiothoracic surgeon, medical educator; b. Ninh Hoa, Khanh Hoa, Vietnam, Oct. 6, 1955; came to U.S. 1975; s. Tro Pham and Nhung Thi Mai; m. Marie Christine Pham, Sept. 9, 1987; children: Benjamin Bartley, Anthony Ninh. Student, U. Saigon, Sch. Pharmacy, Vietnam, 1973-75; BS in Chem. magna cum laude, Lebanon Valley Coll., Annville, Pa., 1979; MD, U. Pitts., 1983. Diplomate Am. Bd. Surgery, Am. Bd. Thoracic Surgery. Intern, resident gen. surgery U. Pitts., Pitts., Pa., 1983-86, rsch. fellow, cardiothoracic surgery, 1986-87, sr. and chief resident, gen. surgery, 1987-89, resident cardiothoracic surgery, 1989-92, asst. prof. surgery, Sch. of Medicine, 1992—, dir. adult cardiac transplant program, Sch. of Medicine, 1993—; dir. extracorporeal membrane oxygenation svc. Presbyterian U. Hosp., Pitts., Pa., 1993—. Contbr. chpts. to books, articles to profl. jours. Recipient Am. Chem. award, 1979, Radiology award U. Pitts., 1983; ACS Faculty fellowship award, 1994—; grantee Children's Hosp. Pitts., 1987, Am. Heart Assn., 1987-88, 94—, Presbyn. U. Hosp., 1987-89. Fellow Am. Coll. Surgeons (assoc.); mem. AMA, Am. Soc. Artificial Internal Organs, Internat. Soc. Heart and Lung Transplantation, Soc. Critical Care Medicine, Am. Assn. Advancement of Sci., Am. Soc. Transplant Surgeons, Soc. Thoracic Surgeons, Extracorporeal Life Support Organization, Phi Alpha Epsilon. Home: 305 Marberry Dr Pittsburgh PA 15215-1437 Office: U Pitts Med Ctr Divsn CTS 200 Lothrop St Rm C-700 Pittsburgh PA 15213-2546

PHARES, ALAIN JOSEPH, physicist, educator; b. Beirut, Apr. 20, 1942; came to U.S., 1975, naturalized, 1982; s. Joseph Michel and Renee Cecile (Dommar) P.; m. Claude Tawa, July 27, 1968; children—Caroline, Denis, Pascal. B.S. in Engring., St. Joseph U., 1964; Docteur-es-Sciences, U. Paris, 1971; Ph.D., Harvard U., 1973. Research fellow Nat. Council Sci. Research, Lebanon, 1973-75; assoc. prof. Lebanese U., 1973-75; research fellow Internat. Centre Theoretical Physics, Trieste, Italy, 1974, Harvard U., 1975-76; vis. asst. prof. U. Mont., 1976-77; asst. prof. physics Villanova U., Pa., 1977-79, assoc. prof., 1979-82, prof., 1982—, chmn. dept., 1981-91, dir. secondary sch. sci., 1981-94. Contbr. articles to profl. jours. French Govt. fellwo, 1964-66, IAEA fellow, 1974; grantee Villanova Rsch., 1978, NSF, 1991—; recipient Outstanding Faculty Rsch. award Villanova U., 1986;. Mem. Am. Phys. Soc., Internat. Assn. Math. and Computers in Simulation, Sigma Xi. Office: Villanova U Dept Physics Villanova PA 19085

PHARES, E. JERRY, psychology educator; b. Glendale, Ohio, July 21, 1928; s. Bruce and Gladys (West) P.; m. Betty L. Knost, Aug. 6, 1955; 1 dau., Lisa M. B.A., U. Cin., 1951; M.A., Ohio State U., 1953, Ph.D., 1955. Faculty Kans. State U., Manhattan, 1955—, prof. psychology, 1964-91, prof. emeritus, 1991—, head dept., 1967-89; Vis. asso. prof. Ohio State U., Columbus, Ohio Wesleyan U., 1961-62. Author, co-author books.; Contbr. articles to profl. jours. Research grantee NIMH, 1960, 80; Research grantee NSF, 1964-76; Research grantee Population Council, 1971. Fellow Am. Psychol. Assn., Am. Psychol. Soc. Office: Psychology Dept Kan State U Manhattan KS 66506

PHARES, LYNN LEVISAY, public relations communications executive; b. Brownwood, Tex., Aug. 6, 1947; m. C. Kirk Phares, Aug. 22, 1971; children: Laura, Margaret, Adele, Jessica. BA, La. State U., 1970; MA, U. Nebr., 1987. Asst. to advt. mgr. La. Nat. Bank, 1970-71; writer, producer, asst. v.p., account exec. Smith, Kaplan, Allen & Reynolds, Inc., Omaha, 1971-80; assoc. dir. pub. affairs U. Nebr. Med. Ctr., 1980-83; dir. pub. rels. ConAgra, Inc., Omaha, 1985-87, 1985-87, v.p. pub. rels., 1987-90, v.p. pub. rels. and cmty. affairs, 1990—; pres. ConAgra Found. Office: ConAgra Inc 1 Conagra Dr Omaha NE 68102-5094

PHARIS, RUTH MCCALISTER, retired banker; b. San Diego, Feb. 13, 1934; d. William L. and Mary E. (Beuk) McC.; grad. Del Mar Coll., Corpus Christi, Tex., 1975-79; m. E. Edwin Pharis, Mar. 14, 1953; children—Beth, Tracey, Todd. Asst. cashier Parkdale State Bank, Corpus Christi, 1970-72, asst. v.p., 1972-76, v.p., 1976-79: v.p. Cullen Center Bank & Trust, Houston, 1979-81, sr. v.p., 1982-93; instr. Am. Inst. Banking, 1977-79. Mem. adv. council Houston Community Colls. Mem. Human Resource Mgmt. Assn., Bank Adminstrn. Inst. (v.p. Coastal Bend chpt. 1979), Nat. Assn. Bank Women (ednl. chmn. Coastal Bend group), Am. Inst. Banking (rep.), Tex. Bankers Assn. (council 1983-84, instr.), Coastal Bend Personnel Soc. (v.p.), Houston Personnel Assn., Corpus Christi C. of C. (mem. women's com. 1976-79). Republican. Baptist. Club: Order Eastern Star. Home: 2750 Laurel Cliff Dr New Braunfels TX 78132-3256

PHARR, JACQUELINE ANITA, biology educator; b. Charlotte, N.C., July 18, 1931; d. Sidney Marion and Gladys Zenobia (Graves) P. BS, Johnson C. Smith U., 1954; MEd, Columbia U., 1961. Tchr., chmn. sci. dept. Mecklenburg Coll., Charlotte, N.C., 1954-64; tchr., chmn. sci. dept. West Charlotte-Charlotte-Mecklenburg Schs., 1964-87, ret., 1987. Mem. Phi Delta Kappa, Alpha Kappa Alpha. Democrat. Methodist. Home: 2501 Senior Dr Charlotte NC 28216-4349

PHELAN, ARTHUR JOSEPH, financial executive; b. N.Y.C., Oct. 26, 1915; s. Arthur Joseph and Josephine Adelaide (Barrett) P.; m. Mary Frances Ryan, Feb. 11, 1939; children—Jane Carolee, Leslie Diane, Sandra Christine. Student, Am. Inst. Banking, 1934-35, NYU, 1935-36. With Guaranty Trust Co. of N.Y., 1933-37; accountant N.Y. Post, 1937-38; accountant Webb & Knapp, Inc., N.Y.C., 1938-41, asst. sec., 1941, comptroller, 1942-44, treas., 1944-53, v.p., treas., 1953-55, sr. v.p., dir., 1955-65; also trustee employees profit sharing plan, exec. v.p. David Greenewald Assocs., Inc., 1965-66; sr. v.p. Lefrak Orgn., Inc., Forest Hills, N.Y., 1966-92; exec. v.p., dir. LOGO Inc., Tulsa, Okla., 1976-92. Roman Catholic. Club: North Hempstead Country. Home: 88 Summit Rd Port Washington NY 11050-3341

PHELAN, CHARLOTTE ROBERTSON, journalist, book critic; b. Vernon, Tex., May 12, 1917; d. Macum and Bonita (Robertson) P. BA, Tex. Wesleyan U., 1940. City editor Daily News, Lufkin, Tex., 1941-43; an editor Tex. bur. AP, Dallas, 1943-45; publicity dir., program editor, annotator San Antonio Symphony and Grand Opera, 1945-55; staff writer Houston Post, 1955-70, film and drama critic, 1970-73, book editor, 1973-82; leader workshops, panelist in field. Dir. Guadalupe Valley Telephone Cooperative, Inc.; bd. durs. G.V. Communication Systems, Inc.; past mem. Bishop's com. St. Francis by the Lake Episcopal Ch. Recipient 1st pl. feature writing Headliners Club, Austin, Tex., 1964, 1st pl. women's page series, 1968. Mem. Nat. Book Critics Cir., Pilot Internat., Canyon Lake Golf and Country Club. Democrat. Episcopalian. Home: 679 Irene Dr Canyon Lake TX 78133-5293

PHELAN, ELLEN, artist; b. Detroit, Nov. 3, 1943; d. Thomas Edward and Katherine Louise (Gojlewicz) P; m. Joel Elias Shapiro, Nov. 22, 1978. BFA, Wayne State U., 1969, MFA, 1971. Instr. Wayne State U., Detroit, 1969-72, Fairleigh Dickinson U., 1974, Mich. State U., East Lansing, 1974-75, Calif. Inst. Arts, 1978-79, Bard Coll., 1980, NYU, 1981, Sch. of Visual Arts, 1981-83, Calif. Inst. Arts, 1983; prof. of practice of studio art Harvard U., Cambridge, Mass., 1995—; Milton Avery vis. lectr. Bard Coll., 1994. One-woman exhbns. include Willis Gallery, Detroit, 1972, 74, Artist's Space, N.Y.C., 1975, Susanne Hilberry Gallery, Birmingham, Mich., 1977, 79, 81, 82, 84, 86, 88, 90, 92, 94, Wadsworth Athenaeum, Hartford, Conn., 1979, Ruth Schaffner Gallery, L.A., 1979, The Clocktower, N.Y.C., 1980, Hansen-Fuller-Goldeen Gallery, San Francisco, 1980, 82, Dart Gallery, Chgo., 1981, Barbara Toll Fine Arts, N.Y.C., 1982, 85, 86, 87-88, 89, 90, 92, 93, Asher/Faure, L.A., 1989, 92, 94, Balt. Mus. Art, 1989, Albright-Knox Art Gallery, Buffalo, 1991, U. Mass. Amherst Fine Arts Ctr., 1992, Saidye Bronfman Ctr., Montreal, Que., 1993, Contemporary Mus., Honolulu, 1993, John Stoller, Inc., Mpls., 1993, Cin. Art Mus., 1994; exhibited in group shows at Detroit Inst. Arts, 1970, 80, Willis Gallery, Detroit, 1971, 79, J.L. Hudson Gallery, Detroit, 1972, Cranbrook Acad. Art, Bloomfield Hills, Mich., 1972, 79, 84, Grand Rapids (Mich.) Art Mus., 1974, Paula Cooper Gallery, N.Y.C., 1975, 76, 77, 78, 79, 90, Fine Arts Bldg., N.Y.C., 1976, Acad. der Kunste, Berlin, 1976, Susanne Hilberry Gallery, Birmingham, 1976-77, 83, 85, 91, Willard Gallery, N.Y.C., 1977, Kansas City (Mo.) Art Inst., 1977, N.A.M.E. Gallery, Chgo., 1977, Hallwalls, Buffalo, 1977, Mus. Modern Art, N.Y.C., 1978, 89, 92, Weatherspoon Art Gallery U. N.C., Greensboro, 1979, 92, Albright-Knox Gallery, Buffalo, 1979, Brown U., Providence, 1980, XIII Olympic Winter Games, Lake Placid, N.Y., 1980, Jeffrey Fuller Fine Art, Phila., 1980, Portland (Oreg.) Ctr. for Visual Arts, 1980, The Drawing Ctr., N.Y.C., 1980, 82, Brooke Alexander Gallery, N.Y.C., 1980, Mus. Contemporary Art, Chgo., 1980, 81, P.S. 1 Mus., N.Y.C., 1981, 92, Art Latitude Gallery, N.Y.C., 1981, Leo Castelli Gallery, N.Y.C., 1981, Sutton Place, Guildford, Eng., 1982, Gallerie d'Arte Moderna di Ca'Pesaro, Venice, Italy, 1982, Inst. Contemporary Art of Virgini Mus., Richmond, Va., 1982, Galerie Biedermann, Munich, 1982, Thomas Segal Gallery, Boston, 1983, Fuller-Goldeen Gallery, San Francisco, 1983, 86, William Paterson Coll., Wayne, N.J., 1983, 89, Artist's Space, N.Y.C., 1983, 84, Harborside Indsl. Ctr., Bklyn., 1983, Orgn. Ind. Artists, N.Y.C., 1984, Bernice Steinbaum Gallery, N.Y.C., 1984, Brentwood Gallery, St. Louis, 1984, U. Calif., Irvine, 1984, U. No. Iowa Gallery Art, Cedar Falls, 1984, Hudson River Mus., N.Y.C., 1984, Barbara Toll Fine Arts, N.Y.C., 1984, 85, 86, 87, Detroit Focus Gallery, 1984, Cable Gallery, N.Y.C., 1984, Wayne State U., Detroit, 1984, Matthews Hamilton Gallery, Phila., 1984, Barbara Krakow Gallery, Boston, 1984, BlumHelman Warehouse, N.Y.C., 1984, Pam Adler Gallery, N.Y.C., 1985, Daniel Weinberg Gallery, L.A., 1985, 89, Knight Gallery, Charlotte, N.C., 1985, Bank of Boston, 1986, Whitney Mus. Am. Art, Stamford, Conn., 1987, 89, Scott Hansen Gallery, N.Y.C., 1987, Saxon-Lee Gallery, L.A., 1987, Parrish Art Mus., East Hampton, N.Y., 1987, Curt Marcus Gallery, N.Y., 1988, Loughelton Gallery, N.Y.C., 1988, 90, Whitney Mus. Am. Art, N.Y.C., 1988, 91, Hillwood Art Gallery C.W. Post Campus, Brookville, N.Y., 1989, USIA traveling exbhn., 1989, Edward Thorp Gallery, N.Y.C., 1989, Pine Street Lobby Gallery, San Francisco, 1989, Fuller Gross Gallery, San Francisco, 1989, Solo Press/Soho Gallery, N.Y.C., 1989, Maxwell Davidson Gallery, N.Y.C., 1989, Blum Helman Gallery, N.Y.C., 1989, R.I.S.D., Providence, 1989, Graham Modern, N.Y.C., 1990, Hood Mus. Art Dartmouth Coll., Hanover, N.H., 1990, 92, New Britain Mus. Am. Art, Hartfor, Conn., 1991, Asher-Faure, L.A., 1991, Annina Nosei Gallery, N.Y.C., 1991, Lintas Worldwide, N.Y.C., 1991, Nina Fredenheim Gallery, Buffalo, 1991, Molica Guidarte Gallery, N.Y.C., 1991, Squibb Gallery, Princeton, N.J., 1991, Cleve. State U. Gallery, 1992, Ind. Curators Inc., N.Y.C., 1992, Wexner Ctr. for the Arts, Columbus, Ohio, 1992, Transamerica Corp., San Francisco, 1992, The Gallery Three Zero, N.Y.C., 1992, Haggerty Mus. Art, Milw., Barbara Methes Gallery, N.Y.C., Asher Fauve Gallery, L.A., Hillwood Art Mus., Brookville, N.Y., Pamela Auchincloss Gallery, N.Y.C., Leo Castelli Gallery, N.Y.C.; represented in permanent collections Mus. Modern Art, N.Y.C., Whitney Mus. Am. Art, N.Y.C., Bklyn. Mus., Walker Art Ctr., Mpls., Balt. Mus., Toledo Mus. Art, Hood Mus. Dartmouth Coll., High Mus. Art, Albright-Knox Art Gallery, Moderna Museet, Stockholm, Mus. Contemporary Art, Mexico City, Detroit Inst. Arts, MIT, Whitehead Inst., Philip Morris, Inc., Volvo Corp., Chase Manhattan Bank, Chem. Bank, BankAm., Bank of Am., Prudential Ins. Co., U.S. Trust & Co., Inter Metro Industries, Lannan Found., numerous pvt. collections. Nat. Endowment for Arts grantee, 1978-79; recipient Am. Acad. Arts and Letters award, 1995, Arts Achievement award Wayne State U., 1989.

PHELAN, JOHN DENSMORE, insurance executive, consultant; b. Kalamazoo, Aug. 31, 1914; s. John and Ida (Densmore) P.; m. Isabel McLaughlin, July 31, 1937; children: John Walter, William Paul, Daniel Joseph. BA magna cum laude, Carleton Coll., 1935. Reporter New Bedford (Mass.) Standard-Times, 1935-36; with Hardware Mut. Ins. Co. (name now Sentry Ins. Co.), Stevens Point, Wis., 1936-45; with Am. States Ins. Co., Indpls., 1945-90, pres., 1963-76, chmn., 1976-79, also dir. numerous subs.; bd. govs. Internat. Ins. Soc. Author: Business Interruption Primer, 1949, also later edits.; contbr. articles to profl. jours. Past pres. Marion County Assn. Mental Health; chmn. emeritus. CPCU-Harry J. Loman Found.; adv. bd. ins. dept. Ball State U. Sch. Bus. Named to Honorable Order of Ky. Colonels, Sagamore of the Wabash. Mem. CPCU Soc. (past nat pres.), CLU Soc., Woodland Country Club (Indpls.), El Conquistador Country Club (Bradenton, Fla.), Phi Beta Kappa. Presbyterian. Home: 6501 17th Ave W W-206 Bradenton FL 34209 also: 307 Woodland Ln Carmel IN 46032-3570

PHELAN, JOHN J., JR., former stock exchange executive, corporate director; b. N.Y.C., May 7, 1931. BBA magna cum laude, Adelphi U., 1970, LLD (hon.), 1987; LLD (hon.), Hamilton Coll., 1980, Niagara U., 1985; hon. doctorate, U. Notre Dame, 1986, Tulane U., Brooklyn Polytech. Joined Nash & Co., N.Y.C., 1955, ptnr., 1957-62; sr. ptnr. Phelan & Co., N.Y.C., 1962-72, Phelan, Silver, N.Y.C., 1972-77, Phelan, Silver, Vesce, Barry & Co., N.Y.C., 1977-80; mem. N.Y. Stock Exch., N.Y.C., 1957—, bd. govs., 1971-72, bd. dirs., 1974-80, vice chmn., 1975-80, pres., COO, 1980-84, chmn., CEO, 1984-91; sr. advisor Boston Cons. Group, 1992—; chmn. N.Y. Futures Exch., 1979-85; chmn. Presdl. Bd. Advisors on Pvt. Sector Initiatives, 1986-89; bd. dirs. Met. Life Ins. Co., Eastman Kodak Co., Merrill Lynch, Sonat, Cold Spring Harbor Labs.; bd. dirs. Bus. Coun. N.Y. State, vice chmn. bd., chmn. fin. com., 1988-90; trustee Com. for Econ. Devel., 1985-90; mem. N.Y. State Temp. Com. on Banking, Ins. and Fin. Svcs., 1983-84; leader del. to symposium N.Y. Stock Exch.-Peoples Bank China, Beijing, 1986; head symposium on Russian economy. Mem. cardinal's com. on laity Archdiocese of N.Y., 1968—, mem. fin. coun., 1986-92; chmn. Wall Street divsn. NCCJ, 1973, 76; bd. dirs. Mercy Hosp., Rockville Centre, N.Y., 1976-81, N.Y. Heart Assn., 1979-84; chmn. campaigns N.Y.C. Heart Fund, 1982-83; trustee Adelphi Coll., 1980-85, chmn. bd. trustees, 1981-85; mem. coun. Rockefeller U.; trustee Tulane U., 1983-87, N.Y. Med. Coll., 1984-91, Cath. Charities, 1985—, Asia Soc., 1987-93; mem. bd. advisors Boston U. Ctr. for Banking Law Studies, 1981-90; chmn. fin. svcs. div. United Way N.Y., 1985-86; bd. govs. United Way Am., 1988-91; mem. bd. councillors Holy Sepulcher, 1985—; mem. adv. bd. Bus. Higher Edn. Forum, 1985-91; bd. dirs. Aspen Inst., past chmn. With USMC, 1951-54. Decorated knight Sovereign Mil. Order of Malta, knight Holy Sepulchre of Jerusalem; Medal of Arts and Letters (France); recipient Brotherhood award NCCJ, 1974, Disting. Alumni award Adelphi U., 1979, Nat. Youth Services award B'nai B'rith Found., Wall St. Man of Yr. award B'nai B'rith, 1980, Stephen S. Wise award Am. Jewish Congress, 1981, Good Scout award Greater N.Y. coun. Boy Scouts Am., 1983, Man of Yr. award Nat. Found. for Ileities and Colitis, 1985, Chancellor's Medal award Molloy Coll., 1987, Disting. Service award Investment Edn. Inst., 1987, award of merit for disting. entrepreneurship The Wharton Sch., U. Pa., 1987, Silver Ambrosiana award Commune of Milan, 1987, Lion of Venice award City of Venice, 1987, Medal of Veneto Veneto region Govt. of Italy, 1987, Albert Schweitzer Leadership award Hugh O'Brien Youth Found., 1987, Torch of Learning award NYU Ctr. for Ednl. Rsch., 1987, C. Walter Nichols award Stern Sch. Bus. NYU, Vetty award Vietnam Vets. Ensemble Theatre Co., Gold medal 100 Yr. Assn. N.Y., Founders' award N.Y. chpt. Arthitis Found., others. Mem. Internat. Fedn. Bourses (pres.), Nat. Audubon Soc. (bd. dirs. 1989-92), Econ. Club N.Y. (trustee 1989-92).

PHELAN, KATHLEEN MCGRATH, public relations executive; b. Bethesda, Md., Oct. 18, 1956. BSBA, Am. U., 1979. Account exec. E.F. Hutton, 1983-85, Drexel Burnham, 1985-87; account exec. FRB, 1987-88, sr. assoc., 1988-89; v.p. Fin. Rels. Bd., N.Y.C., 1989-90, ptnr., dir. east coast ops., 1990—. Mem. Pub. Rels. Soc. Am. Office: Fin Rels Bd 675 3rd Ave New York NY 10017-5704*

PHELAN, MARTIN DUPONT, retired film company executive; b. Chgo., Dec. 25, 1913; s. Martin Anthony and Margaret Crespo (DuPont) P.; m. Mary Katharine Harris, Aug. 14, 1937; children—Richard H., Jeremy D. A.B., DePauw U., 1934. Mdse. exec. Montgomery Ward, Chgo., 1934-42, Butler Bros., Chgo., 1946-47; corporate officer Eastin-Phelan Corp., Davenport, Iowa, 1947-77. Served to col. U.S. Army, 1942-46. Mem. Iowa Libr. Trustee Assn. (pres. 1980), Ponte Vedra Club, Rotary. Republican. Episcopalian. Home: Guildford 207 Vicar's Landing Ponte Vedra Beach FL 32082

PHELAN, RICHARD MAGRUDER, mechanical engineer; b. Moberly, Mo., Sept. 20, 1921; s. Frederick William and Ethel Ray (Magruder) P.; m. Olive Bernice McIntosh, May 25, 1951; children—William James, Susan Ray. Student, Moberly Jr. Coll., 1939-41; B.S. in Mech. Engring. U. Mo., Columbia, 1943; M.M.E., Cornell U., 1950; postgrad., U. Mich., 1956-57. Instr. Cornell U., 1947-50, asst. prof. mech. engring., 1950-56, assoc. prof., 1956-62, prof., 1962-87, prof. emeritus, 1988—. Author: Fundamentals of Mechanical Design, 1957, 3d rev. edit., 1970, Dynamics of Machinery, 1967, Automatic Control Systems, 1977. Served with USNR, 1943-46. Mem. ASME, Am. Soc. Engring. Edn., Soc. Exptl. Stress Analysis, Am. Gear Mfrs. Assn., AAUP, AAAS, N.Y. Acad. Scis., Soc. Exptl. Mechanics, Sigma Xi, Phi Kappa Phi, Pi Tau Sigma, Tau Beta Pi. Home: 4 Cornell Walk Ithaca NY 14850-6145 Office: Cornell U Upson Hall Ithaca NY 14853

PHELAN, RICHARD PAUL, trust company executive; b. N.Y.C., Oct. 26, 1939; s. Peter James and Florence (Leary) P.; m. Bridget Burke, Sept. 17, 1966; children: Richard Matthew, Peter Michael, Robert William. Student, CCNY, 1957-58; Diploma, Am. Inst. Banking, N.Y.C., 1962; BS, NYU, 1967, MBA, 1969; MA, Columbia U., 1992. Sr. v.p. Chem. Bank (formerly Mfrs. Hanover Trust Co.), N.Y.C., 1957—. Mem. Union League Club. Republican. Roman Catholic. Home: 564 Dutch Neck Rd East Windsor NJ 08520-1124

PHELAN, ROBIN ERIC, lawyer; b. Steubenville, Ohio, Dec. 28, 1945; s. Edward John and Dorothy (Borkowski) P.; m. Melinda Jo Ricketts, May 27, 1995; children: Travis McCoy, Tiffany Marie, Trevor Monroe. BSBA, Ohio State U., 1967, JD, 1970. Bar: Tex. 1971, U.S. Ct. Appeals (5th cir.) 1981, U.S. Ct. Appeals (11th cir.) 1981, U.S. Ct. Appeals (6th cir.) 1986, U.S. Ct. Appeals (10th cir.) 1988, U.S. Supreme Ct. Ptnr. Haynes and Boone, Dallas, 1970—; bd. dirs. Am. Bankruptcy Inst., Washington, pres., 1994; regent Am. Coll. Bankruptcy. Co-author: Bankruptcy Practice and Strategy, 1987, Cowans Bankruptcy Law and Practice, 1987, Annual Survey of Bankruptcy Law, 1988, Bankruptcy Litigation Manual; contbr. articles to profl. jours. Mem. ABA (chmn. bankruptcy litigation subcom. 1990-95), State Bar Tex. (chmn. bankruptcy law com. sect. bus. law 1989-91), Dallas Bar Assn. Roman Catholic. Avocation: athletics. Home: 4214 Woodfin St Dallas TX 75220-6416

PHELAN, THOMAS, clergyman, academic administrator, educator; b. Albany, N.Y., Apr. 11, 1925; s. Thomas William and Helen (Rausch) P. A.B. (N.Y. State Regents scholar 1942, President's medal 1945), Coll. Holy Cross, Worcester, Mass., 1945; S.T.L., Catholic U. Am., 1951; postgrad., Oxford (Eng.) U., 1958-59, 69-70. Ordained priest Roman Cath. Ch., 1951; pastor, tchr., adminstr. Diocese of Albany, 1951-58; resident Cath. chaplain Rensselaer Poly. Inst., Troy, N.Y., 1959-72, prof. history, 1972—, dean Sch. Humanities and Social Scis., 1972-95, inst. historian, inst. dean, sr. adviser to pres., 1995—; chmn. architecture and bldg. commn. Diocese Albany, 1968—; cons. in field. Author: Hudson Mohawk Gateway, 1985, Achieving the Impossible, 1995; author monographs, articles, revs. in field. Treas. The Rensselaer Newman Found., 1962—; pres. Hudson-Mohawk Indsl. Gateway, 1971-84, bd. dirs. exec. com. 1984—; mem. WMHT Ednl. Telecomm. Bd., 1966-77, 84-90, chmn. 1973-77; chmn. Troy Hist. Dist. and Landmarks Rev. Commn., 1975-86, chmn. hist. adv. com., 1987—; v.p. Preservation League N.Y. State, 1979-82, mem. trustees coun., 1982-87, 89—, pres. 1987-89; sec. and bd. dirs. Ptnrs. for Sacred Places, 1989—; bd. dirs. Hall of History Found., 1983-87; trustee Troy Pub. Libr., 1992—, bd. dirs.; mem. Pres.' Coun. Sage Colls. With USN, 1943-46. Recipient Paul J. Hallinan award Nat. Newman Chaplains Assn., 1967; ann. award Albany Arts League, 1977; Disting. Community Service award Rensselaer Poly. Inst., 1979; Edward Fox Demers medal Alumni Assn. Rensselaer Poly. Inst., 1986; Disting. Service award Hudson-Mohawk Consortium of Colls. and Univs., 1988; named Citizen Laureate of the State Univ. N.Y. Found. at Albany, 1988; Danforth Found. fellow, 1969-70; grantee Homeland Found., 1958-59; grantee Dorothy Thomas Found., 1969-70. Fellow Soc. Arts, Religion and Contemporary Culture; mem. Ch. Soc. Coll. Work (dir., exec. com. 1970—), Am. Conf. Acad. Deans, Liturgical Conf., Soc. Indsl. Archaeology, Assn. Internat. pour l'Etudes des Religions Prehistoriques et Ethnologiques, Cath. Campus Ministry Assn., Cath. Art Assn., Assn. for Religion and the Intellectual Life (bd. dirs. 1987—), Soc. History of Tech. Clubs: Ft. Orange, Troy Country; Squadron A (N.Y.C.). Home: 5 Whitman Ct Troy NY 12180-4732 Office: Rensselaer Poly Inst Troy NY 12180 *Service and community building have motivated most of my business and personal actions. I received these values from my parents and from the church. I work to make positive contributions towards a world in which there is more justice and consequent hope of peace.*

PHELPS, ARTHUR VAN RENSSELAER, physicist, consultant; b. Dover, N.H., July 20, 1923; s. George Osborne and Helen (Ketchum) P.; m. Gertrude Kanzius, July 21, 1956; children: Wayne Edward, Joan Susan. ScD in Physics, MIT, 1951. Cons. physicist rsch. labs. Westinghouse Elec. Corp., Pitts., 1951-70; sr. rsch. scientist Nat. Bur. Standards, Boulder, Colo., 1970-88; fellow Joint Inst. Lab. Astrophysics U. Colo., Boulder, 1970-88, adjoint fellow, 1988—, chmn., 1979-81; chmn. Gordon Rsch. Conf., Plasma Chemistry, 1990. Recipient Silver Medal award Dept. Commerce, 1978. Fellow Am. Phys. Soc. (Will Allis prize 1990). Achievements include patent for Schulz-Phelps ionization gauge; research on electron and atomic collision processes involving low energy electrons, molecules, ions, metastable atoms and resonance radiation; on laser processes and modeling; on gaseous electronics. Home: 3405 Endicott Dr Boulder CO 80303-6908 Office: U Colo Joint Inst Lab Astrophysics Campus Box 440 Boulder CO 80309-0440

PHELPS, ASHTON, JR., newspaper publisher; b. New Orleans, Nov. 4, 1945; s. Ashton Sr. and Jane Cary (George) P.; m. Mary Ella Sanders, Apr. 10, 1976; children—Cary Clifton, Mary Louise, Sanders. BA, Yale U., 1967; JD, Tulane U., 1970. Trainee Times-Picayune Pub. Corp., New Orleans, 1970-71; asst. to pub. Times-Picayune Pub. Corp., 1971-79, pres., pub., 1979—. Bd. dirs. Bur. Govtl. Rsch., New Orleans, 1973-89, Xavier U. of La., New Orleans, 1974-82, Coun. for Better La., 1982-85, Met. Area Com., New Orleans, Ochsner Found. Hosp., New Orleans, 1982—, Internat. House, New Orleans, 1981-83, Pub. Affairs Rsch., New Orleans, 1982-85, La. Children's Mus., New Orleans, 1983-90, Yale Alumni Assn. of La., 1985, Newspaper Advt. Bur. Future of Advt. Com., 1986-89; chmn. Audit Com. of Associated Press, 1986-90. Mem. So. Newspaper Pubs. Assn. (bd. dirs. 1982-85, found. bd. dirs. 1982-83, pres. 1990-91), La. Press Assn. (bd. dirs. 1984-93, v.p. 1989-90, pres. 1991-92). Avocation: tennis. Office: The Times-Picayune 3800 Howard Ave New Orleans LA 70140-1002

PHELPS, BARTON CHASE, architect, educator; b. Bklyn., June 27, 1946; s. Julian Orville and Elizabeth Willis (Faulk) P.; m. Karen Joy Simonson; 1 child, Charlotte Simonson Phelps. BA in Art with honors, Williams Coll., 1968; MArch, Yale U., 1973. Registered architect, Calif. With Colin St. John Wilson & Ptnrs., London, 1972-73, Frank O. Gehry and Assocs., Inc., Santa Monica, Calif., 1973-76, Charles Moore/Urban Innovations Group, L.A., 1976-78; dir. architecture Urban Innovations Group, L.A., 1980-84; prin. Barton Phelps & Assocs., L.A., 1984—; asst. prof. architecture Rice U. Sch. of Architecture, Houston, 1977-79; asst. dean Grad. Sch. Architecture and Urban Planning, UCLA, 1980-83; prof. architecture Sch. Arts and Architecture UCLA; faculty mem. Nat. Endowment Arts, Mayor's Inst. for City Design, 1990, 92. Author, editor: Architecture California, 1988-92. Fellow Graham Found. for advanced Studies in Fine Art, 1989, Nat. Endowment for the Arts, 1988. Mem. AIA (Coll. of Fellows, chair nat. com. on design, recipient design awards for Arroyo House, Kranz House, North Range Clark Libr. UCLA, L.A. Dept. Water and Power Ctrl. Dist. Hdqrs., No. Hollywood Pump Sta., East Bldg. Seeds U. Elem. Sch., UCLA, Inst. Honor for Collaborative Design, Games XXIII Olympiad L.A. 1984). Democrat. Home: 10256 Lelia Ln Los Angeles CA 90077-3144 Office: Barton Phelps & Assocs 5514 Wilshire Blvd Los Angeles CA 90036-3829

PHELPS, CATHERINE, elementary school principal. Prin. Trinity Sch. Recipient Elem. Sch. Recognition award U.S. Dept. Edn., 1989-90. Office: Trinity Sch 4985 Ilchester Rd Ellicott City MD 21043-6837

PHELPS, EDMUND STROTHER, economics educator; b. Evanston, Ill., July 26, 1933; s. Edmund Strother and Florence Esther (Stone) P.; m. Viviana Regina Montdor, Oct. 1, 1974. BA, Amherst Coll., 1955, DLitt (hon.), 1985; MA, Yale U., 1956, PhD, 1959. Economist Rand Corp., Santa Monica, Calif., 1959-60; asst. prof. Yale U., Cowles Found., 1960-62, assoc. prof., 1963-66; vis. assoc. prof. M.I.T., 1962-63; prof. econs. U. Pa., Phila., 1966-71; prof. econs. Columbia U., 1971-78, 79-82, McVickar prof. polit. economy, 1982—; scholar Russell Sage Found., 1993-94; prof. NYU, 1978-79; fellow Ctr. for Advanced Study in Behavioiral Scis., 1969-70; sr. advisor Brookings Inst., 1976—; econ. advisor European Bank for Reconstrn. and Devel., 1991-94; mem. econ. policy panel Observatoire Francais des Conjonctures Economiques, 1991—. Author: numerous books including Golden Rules of Economic Growth, 1966, Microeconomic Foundations of Employment and Inflation Theory, 1970, Economic Justice, 1973, Studies in Macroeconomic Theory, Vol. I, 1979, Vol. II, 1980, Political Economy, 1985, The Slump in Europe, 1988, Structural Slumps, 1994. Guggenheim fellow, 1978; Social Sci. Research Council fellow, 1966. Mem., NAS, Fellow Econometric Soc.; Fellow Am. Acad. Arts and Scis.; mem. Am. Econ. Assn. (mem. exec. com. 1976-78, v.p. 1983, Kenan Enterprise award 1996), Phi Beta Kappa. Home: 45 E 89th St New York NY 10128-1251 Office: Columbia Univ Dept Economics New York NY 10027

PHELPS, FLORA L(OUISE) LEWIS, editor, anthropologist, photographer; b. San Francisco, July 28, 1917; d. George Chase and Louise (Manning) Lewis; m. C(lement) Russell Phelps, Jan. 15, 1944; children: Andrew Russell, Carol Lewis, Gail Bransford. Student, U. Mich.; AB cum laude, Bryn Mawr Coll., 1938; AM, Columbia U., 1954. Acting dean Cape Cod Inst. Music, East Brewster, Mass., summer 1940; assoc. social sci. analyst U.S. Govt., 1942-44; co-adj. staff instr. anthropology Univ. Coll., Rutgers U., 1954-55; mem. editorial bd. Américas mag. OAS, Washington, 1960-82; mng. editor, 1974-82, contbg. editor, 1982-89; N.J. vice chmn. Ams. Dem. Action, 1950; mem. Dem. County Com. N.J., 1948-49. Author articles in fields of anthropology, art, architecture, edn., travel; contbr. Latin Am. newspapers. Mem. AAAS, Am. Anthrop. Assn., Archaeological Inst. Am., Latin Am. Studies Assn., Soc. for Am. Archaeology, Soc. Woman Geographers. Home: Collington # 2212 10450 Lottsford Rd Mitchellville MD 20721-2748

PHELPS, JUDSON HEWETT, marketing sales executive; b. Evanston, Ill., Oct. 18, 1942; s. Sidney Norman and Mary Schyler (Coons) P.; m. Barbara Ann Ray, Dec. 21, 1963; children: Wyeth Hewett, Christopher Ashley, Whitney Magee. BA, Williams Coll., 1964; MS, Springfield Coll., 1993. Asst. brand mgr. Procter & Gamble Co., Cin., 1968-70; brand mgr. Memorex, Santa Clara, Calif., 1970-72; product mgr. Chesebrough Ponds Inc., Greenwich, Conn., 1972-76; v.p. mktg. L'Oreal subs. Cosmair, Inc., N.Y.C., 1976-77; v.p. sales Bio Products, Inc., Norwalk, Conn., 1978, exec. v.p., 1979, pres., 1980-86, corp. v.p. Ketchum & Co. parent co. Bio Products, Norwalk, 1982-86; mng. dir. Dameon Ptnrs. Inc., Wilton, Conn., 1987-88, pres. Theracom Corp., Rye, N.Y., 1988-89; v.p. Promotion Info. Bur., Norwalk, 1990; prin. Daniel Adams Co., Danbury, Conn., 1991-92; clin. coord., addictions therapist, counselor The Ctr., Bridgeport, Conn., 1993—. Pres. Camp Dudley (YMCA) Alumni Assn., Westport, N.Y., 1974-79; family counselor Caregivers, Assn. Religious Communities, Danbury, 1975-79; leader, treas. Ridgefield Emmaus Teenage Christian Retreats, Ridgefield, Conn., 1983-92; chmn. Ridgefield Alcohol and Drug Use Commn., 1992—. Lt. USNR, 1964-68. Home: 5 Wooster Heights Dr Ridgefield CT 06877-3109

PHELPS, KATHRYN ANNETTE, mental health counseling executive, consultant; b. Creswell, Oreg., Aug. 1, 1940; d. Henry Wilbur and Lake Ilene (Wall) M.; children: David Bryan (dec.), Derek Alan, Darla Ailene. BS in edn., Western Oreg. State Coll., 1962; MSW, Columbia State U., 1992, PhD, 1993. Tchr. Germany, Thailand, U.S., 1962-88; acct. exec. ins. industry; weight-loss counselor, alchohol/drug abuse prevention/intervention counselor teens, 1990-93; counselor Eugene, 1989-94; sr. exec. v.p., edn. dir. Light Streams, Inc., Eugene, 1993—; sr. exec. v.p., therapist Comprehensive Assessment Svcs./The Focus Inst., Inc., Eugene, 1994—; mental health counselor in pvt. practice; ednl. cons. specializing in learning testing Comprehensive Assessment Svcs., Eugene, 1996—; cons. consumer edn. Author: Easy Does It, books 1 & 2; hosted weekly TV cooking segment, Portland and U.S. Guardian Jobs Daughters, 1980-82; bd. dirs., den mother Cub Scouts, Boy Scouts, Kansas, Oreg., 1974-82; coach girls volleyball, 1974-80; vol. in orphanages, elderly nursing homes, Thailand, Germany, U.S., 1954-95; sunday sch. tchr., 1956-90; sponsored exchange student, 1984-88. Mem. Eastern Star, Nat. Assn. Social Workers, Am. Counseling Assn., Columbia State U. Alumni Assn., Women's Internat. Bowling Conf. Avocations: cooking, gardening, reading, walking, car races, bowling. Home: 3838 Kendra St Eugene OR 97404 Office: Comprehensive Assessment Sv The Focus Inst Inc 400 E 2d St Ste 103 Eugene OR 97401

PHELPS, MICHAEL EDWARD, biophysics educator; b. Cleve., Aug. 24, 1939; s. Earl E. and Regina Bridget (Hines) P.; m. Patricia Emroy, May 15, 1969; children: Patrick, Kaitlin. B.A., Western Wash. State U., 1965; Ph.D., Washington U., St. Louis, 1970. Asst. prof. Washington U. Sch. Medicine and Engring., 1970-73, assoc. prof., 1973-75; assoc. prof. dept. radiology U. Pa., Phila., 1975-76; prof. biomath. UCLA, 1976—, prof., chief div. nuclear medicine and biophysics, 1980—, dir. Crump Inst. for Biol. Imaging; mem. study sect. NIH, Bethesda, Md., 1974-78. Author: Reconstruction Tomography in Diagnostic Radiology and Nuclear Medicine, 1977, Physics in Nuclear Medicine, 1980, Principles of Tracer Kinetics, 1983; contbr. articles to profl. jours. Recipient Von Hersey Found. award, 1975, Von Hersey Found. award, 1982, Von Heresy prize Von Heresy Found., Zurich, 1978, 82, E.O. Lawrence award Dept. Energy, 1983, Rosenthal award Am. Coll. Physicians, 1987; holder Jennifer Jones Simon endowed chair, 1983; named Disting. Alumnus Western Wash. State U., 1980. Fellow Am. Heart Assn.; mem. Inst. Medicine NAS (elected), Soc. Nuclear Medicine (Aebersold award 1983), Internat. Soc. Cerebral Blood Flow and Metabolism (Excellence award 1979), N.Y. Acad. Scis. (Sarah L. Poiley award 1984), Soc. Neuroscis., Am. Coll. Physicians (Rosenthal award). Roman Catholic. Home: 16720 Huerta Rd Encino CA 91436-3544

PHELPS, ORME WHEELOCK, economics educator emeritus; b. Hobart, Okla., July 5, 1906; s. William Andrews and Kate Mae (Forman) P.; m. Jean Wright, Aug. 18, 1940; children—John Jackson, Sarah Hamilton; m. Barbara C. Green, July 25, 1981. A.B., U. Chgo., 1937, M.B.A., 1939, Ph.D., 1945. Asst. prof. bus. adminstrn. U. Chgo., 1942-47; prof. econs. Claremont (Calif.) Men's Coll. and Grad. Sch., 1947-63, sr. prof., 1963-76, emeritus, 1976—, dean faculty, 1970-74; vis. prof. UCLA, 1950, State U. N.Y. at Brockport, 1968-69; Fulbright research prof. Univ. Coll. of W.I., Kingston, Jamaica, 1957-58; Brookings research prof., Washington, 1962-63. Author: Introduction to Labor Economics, 4th edit, 1967, Discipline and Discharge in the Unionized Firm, 1959, Union Security, 1954, Legislative Background of the Fair Labor Standards Act, 1939. Contbr. articles, book revs. to profl. jours. Pub. mem., regional vice-chmn. Wage Stblzn. Bd., 1951-53; labor arbitrator, mem. various govt. bds. Ford found. fellow, 1953-54. Mem. Indsl. Relations Research Assn., Am., Western econ. assns., Am. Assn. U. Profs. Democrat. Episcopalian. Home: 1421 Rust Ct Claremont CA 91711-2732

PHELPS, PAUL MICHAEL, lawyer; b. Lake Forest, Ill., Sept. 19, 1933; s. Paul and Elizabeth Anne (Wilson) P.; m. Laura Elaine Pepe, Dec. 26, 1966; stepchildren: Kimberly A. Springer, Wendy L. Field, Gregory L. Field. BA, Wesleyan U., Middletown, Conn., 1955; LLB, Harvard U., 1958. Bar: Ill. 1958, U.S. Ct. Mil. Appeals 1959. Assoc. atty. Keck Mahin & Cate, Chgo., 1958, 63-65; atty. Ekco Products Co., Chgo., 1965-67, E. J. Brach & Sons, Chgo., 1967-69; asst. corp. sec. R. R. Donnelley & Sons Co., Chgo., 1969-73; asst. counsel Marsh & McLennan, Chgo., 1973-74; corp. sec. Morton-Norwich Products, Inc. (name changed to Morton Thiokol Inc., 1982, and to Thiokol Corp., 1989), Chgo., 1974-89; v.p., corp. sec. Morton Internat. Inc., Chgo., 1989—. Trustee Wanger Advisors Trust, 1994—. Served to capt. JAGC, U.S. Army, 1959-63. Mem. Am. Soc. Corp. Secs. (bd. dirs. 1987-93, chmn. 1991-92), Univ. Club, Chikaming Club (Lakeside, Mich.), Phi Beta Kappa, Psi Upsilon. Home: 222 E Chestnut St Apt 10B Chicago IL 60611-2351 Office: Morton Internat Inc 100 N Riverside Plz Chicago IL 60606-1596

PHELPS, TIMOTHY MILLER, reporter; b. Newport, R.I., May 18, 1947; s. Walter Kane and Constance (Miller) P.; m. Helen Watson Winternitz; children: Constance, Paul. BA, U. Pa., Phila., 1969. Reporter Providence Jour., 1968-69, St. Petersburg (Fla.) Times, 1972-76, N.Y. Times, N.Y.C., 1980-81; freelance reporter Cairo, 1976-77; reporter Balt. Sun, 1977-80, state editor, 1981-85; Mid. East bur. chief Newsday, Cairo, 1985-91; Washington corr. Newsday, 1991-95, fgn. editor, 1996—. Contbr. to book: Capitol Games: The Inside Story of Clarence Thomas, Anita Hill and a Supreme Court Nomination, 1992. With U.S. Army, 1969-72. Recipient Barnet Novelz award White House Correspondents Assn., 1992. Office: Newsday Fgn Desk 235 Pinelawn Rd Melville NY 11747

PHEMISTER, ROBERT DAVID, veterinary pathology educator; b. Framingham, Mass., July 15, 1936; s. Robert Irving and Georgia Nora (Savignac) P.; m. Ann Christine Lyon, June 14, 1960; children: Katherine, David, Susan. D.V.M., Cornell U., 1960; Ph.D., Colo. State U., Ft. Collins, 1967. Diplomate: Am. Coll. Vet. Pathologists. Research assoc. U. Calif., Davis, 1960-61, vis. rsch. pathologist, 1974-75; staff scientist Armed Forces Inst. Pathology, Washington, 1962-64; sect. leader to dir. collaborative radiol. health lab. Colo. State U., 1964-77; mem. faculty Coll. Vet. Medicine and Biomed. Scis., 1968-85, prof. vet. pathology, 1973-85, assoc. dean, 1976-77, assoc. dir. expt. sta., 1977-85, dean, 1977-85, interim acad. v.p. Univ., 1982, interim pres. Univ., 1983-84, spl. counselor to pres., 1984-85; vis. prof. Colo. State U., 1995-96; prof. vet. pathology Cornell U., 1985—, dean Coll. Vet. Medicine, 1985-95; cons. Miss. State U., 1977-81; commr. Colo. Advanced Tech. Inst., 1983-84; mem. governing bd. N.Y. Sea Grant Inst., 1985-95, vice chmn., 1990-92; mem. vet. medicine adv. com. FDA, 1984-88; mem. joint coun. on food and agrl. scis. USDA, 1988-92, mem. exec. com., 1989-92; chmn. Zweig Meml. Fund for Equine Rsch., 1985-95; mem. adv. panel for vet. medicine Pew Health Professions Commn., 1991-93. Author papers in field. Served to comdr. USPHS, 1960-68. Recipient Charles A. Lory award and Disting. Univ. Leadership award Colo. State U., 1984, Disting. Practitioner award Nat. Acad. Practice, 1985, Regional Health Adminstr.'s award, 1985; named Honor Alumnus, Colo. State U., 1989. Mem. AVMA (coun. on edn. 1985-91), Assn. Am. Vet. Med. Colls. (pres. 1982-83), Colo. Vet. Med. Assn. (Disting. Svc. award 1985), N.Y. State Vet. Med. Soc. (Centennial award 1990), Sigma Xi, Phi Zeta, Phi Kappa Phi, Gamma Sigma Delta. Home: 5110 Hogan Ct Fort Collins CO 80525 Office: Coll Vet Medicine Cornell U Ithaca NY 14853

PHEMISTER, THOMAS ALEXANDER, lawyer; b. Framingham, Mass., June 2, 1940; s. Robert Irving and Georgia Nora (Savignac) P.; m. Lois Ann Devol, Dec. 28, 1963; children: Michael Anderson, Elizabeth Lynn, Mary Nicole, Virginia Noel. B.A., Carleton Coll., 1962; J.D., U. Chgo., 1965. Bar: Ill., Colo. 1965. Pvt. practice law Chgo., 1965-69; gen. atty. Western R.R. Assn., Chgo., 1969-71; in law practice with Richard J. Hardy, Washington, 1972-73; gen. atty. Assn. Am. R.R.s, Washington, 1973-79; dir. Bur. Explosives Assn. Am. Railroads, 1979-85; sole practice Washington, 1985-87; lead hazardous materials atty. Office Chief Counsel Fed. R.R. Adminstrn., Washington, 1987—; mem. dept. of transp. intermodal hazardous materials attys. group, 1989—; mem. com. on transp. of hazardous materials Transp. Rsch. Bd., 1980-86; mem. nat. motor carrier adv. com. Fed. Hwy. Adminstrn., 1982-86; mem. Can. Nat. Rail Task Force for Movements of Dangerous Commodities, 1985; mem. hazardous materials control course oversight com. Tex. A&M U., 1981-87. Pub.: Emergency Handling of Hazardous Materials in Surface Transportation, 1981, Hazardous Materials Regulations Excerpted for Railroad Employees, 1981, Emergency Action Guides, 1983; author: A Report on Tank Cars: Federal Oversight of Design Construction and Repair, 1990, Forward through the 90s: A Report on Selected Issues in the Transportation by Rail of Hazardous Materials, 1994. Treas. Ill. Lawyers for McCarthy, 1968; trustee First Congregational Ch., Western Springs, Ill., 1970-71; mem. program ministries council United Christian Parish of Reston, Va., 1980-82, mem. South Lakes vestry, 1984-87, mem. parish bd., 1 deacon, ministries com., 1987-93; bd. dirs. Upper Room Emmaus of nat. capital area, 1989-90, lay leader, 1990; mem. Fairfax County Drug Task Force chpt. Parents Alliance to Neutralize Drug and Alcohol Abuse (PANDAA), 1987-89; adult advisor Fairfax County 4-H Horse Forum. Mem. Hunters Valley Riding Club (bd. dirs., v.p. 1993-94). Home: 10802 Dayflower Ct Reston VA 22091-5110 Office: 400 7th St SW Washington DC 20590-0001 *Integrity is an absolute essential - both preserving my own and dealing with other people so that they, too, do not have to compromise on matters of principle.*

PHENIS, NANCY SUE, educational administrator; b. Anderson, Ind., Oct. 29, 1943; d. Wilma (Anderson) Baker; m. Richard W. Phenis, June 11, 1966; 1 child, Heidi L. BA, Ind. State U., 1965; MA, Ball State U., 1974, postgrad., 1985. Elem. tchr. Highland Park (N.J.) Schs., 1966-68, Anderson City Schs., 1969-71; elem. tchr., tchr. gifted and talented South Madison Schs., Pendleton, Ind., 1974-85, elem. prin., 1985—. Bd. dirs. South Madison Community Found., Pendleton, 1991, First Am. Bank FirstGrant. Recipient Outstanding Contbn. award Internat. Reading Assn., 1991. Mem. NAEPS, AAUW (pres. 1985-87), Ind. Assn. Sch. Prins. (bd. dirs. 1994—), First Am. (bd. dirs. 1992-95), Phi Delta Kappa (historian 1987, Leadership award 1994), Delta Kappa Gamma (sec. 1990-92, pres. 1992-94, Leadership/Adminstr. award 1993). Office: East Elem Sch 893 E US Highway 36 Pendleton IN 46064-9580

PHENIX, GLORIA GAYLE, educational association administrator; b. Dallas, Mar. 4, 1956; m. Douglas William Phenix, Aug. 8, 1987; children: David William, Duncan Kenneth. BA, U. North Tex., 1979, postgrad., 1979-81; PhD, ABD, U. Minn., 1981-89. Dean Jordan Coll., Benton Harbor, Mich., 1990; pres. Phenix & Assocs. Tng. Cons., St. Joseph, Mich., 1991—, Topeka, Kans., 1993—; bd. dirs. Cornerstone, Inc. Mem. allocation com. United Way, 1990-92, Literacy Coun., 1991-93; mem. Topeka Race Rels. Task Force, 1994; mayor's commn. status women, 1996—; bd. dirs. Cmty. Youth Homes, 1996—, Cornerstone, Inc. Fulbright-Hayes fellow Africa, 1990; Hewlett Mellon Found. grantee, 1987, Benton Found. grantee, 1988. Mem. Am. Polit. Sci. Assn., Minn. Polit. Sci. Assn. (bd. dirs. 1989-90), Midwest Polit. Sci. Assn., Am. Assn. Trainers and Developers, Am. Soc. for Quality Control. Presbyterian. Office: Phenix & Assocs 505 Pleasant St # 200 Saint Joseph MI 49085-1269 also: Phenix Assocs 530 S Kansas Topeka KS 66604

PHIBBS, CLIFFORD MATTHEW, surgeon, educator; b. Bemidji, Minn., Feb. 20, 1930; s. Clifford Matthew and Dorothy Jean (Wright) P.; m. Patricia Jean Palmer, June 27, 1953; children—Wayne Robert, Marc Stuart,

Nancy Louise. B.S., Wash. State U., 1952; M.D., U. Wash., 1955; M.S., U. Minn., 1960. Diplomate Am. Bd. Surgery. Intern Ancker Hosp., St. Paul, 1955-56; resident in surgery U. Minn. Hosps., 1956-60; practice medicine specializing in surgery Oxboro Clinic, Mpls., 1962—, pres., 1985—; cons. to health risk mgmt. corps., 1994—; mem. Children's Hosp. Ctr., Northwestern-Abbott Hosp., Fairview-Southdale Hosp., Fairview Ridges Hosp.; clin. asst. prof. U. Minn., Mpls., 1975-78, clin. assoc. prof. surgery, 1978—; med. dir. Minn. Protective Life Ins. Co. Contbr. articles to med. jours. Bd. dirs. Bloomington Bd. Edn., Minn., 1974—, treas., 1976, sec., 1977-78, chmn., 1981-83; mem. adv. com. jr. coll. study City of Bloomington, 1964-66, mem. community facilities com., 1966-67, advisor youth study commn., 1966-68; vice chmn. bd. Hillcrest Meth. Ch., 1970-71; mem. Bloomington Adv. and Rsch. Coun., 1969-71; bd. dirs. Bloomington Symphony Orch., 1976—, Wash. State U. Found., trustee, 1990—; dir. bd. mgmt. Minnesota Valley YMCA, 1970-75; bd. govs. Mpls. Met. YMCA, 1970—; bd. dirs. Bloomington Heart-Health Found., 1989—, Martin Luther Manor, 1989; pres. Oxboro Clinics, 1985—; bd. dirs. Bloomington History Clock Tower Assn., 1990—; bd. dirs. Fairview Hosp. Clinic, 1994—. Capt. M.C., U.S. Army, 1960-62. Mem. ACS, AMA (Physician Recognition awards 1969, 73, 76, 79, 82, 85, 88, 91, 94), Assn. Surg. Edn., Royal Soc. Medicine, Am. Coll. Sports Medicine, Minn. Med. Assn. (del. 1991-94), Minn. Surg. Soc., Mpls. Surg. Soc., Hennepin County Med. Soc., Pan-Pacific Surg. Assn., Jaycees, Bloomington C. of C. (chmn. bd. 1984, chmn. 1985-86). Home: 9613 Upton Rd Minneapolis MN 55431-2454 Office: 600 W 98th St Minneapolis MN 55420-4773

PHIBBS, HARRY ALBERT, interior designer, professional speaker, lecturer; b. Denver, Jan. 9, 1933; s. Harry Andrew and Mary May (Perriam) P.; m. Alice Conners Glynn, Oct. 23, 1957 (div. Jan. 1988); children: Kathleen Ann, Paul Robert, Mary Alice, Michael John, Peter James, Daniel Edward; m. Nevelle Haley Jones, Feb. 1988. B.A., U. Colo., 1954, B.F.A., 1957. Interior designer Howard Lorton, Inc., Denver, 1957-68; interior designer, v.p. Ronald Ansay Inc., Wheatridge, Colo., 1969-71; interior designer, pres. Phibbs Design Assos., Inc., Denver, 1972-78; interior designer, mgr. Howard Lorton, Inc., Colorado Springs, Colo., 1979-93; prin. Phibbs Design, Colorado Springs, 1993—; pres. Interior Designers Housing Devel. Corp., 1969-72. V.p. Arvada (Colo.) Hist. Soc., 1973; bd. dirs. Colo. Opera Festival, also pres., 1986; bd. dirs. Downtown Colorado Springs, Inc., also pres., 1984; chmn. bd. trustees Interior Design Inst. Denver, 1991-94. With U.S. Army, 1954-56. Fellow Am. Soc. Interior Designers (nat. pres. 1977); mem. Am. Arbitration Assn., Theta Xi (pres. Denver Area alumni club 1958-64). Democrat. Roman Catholic. Home: 91 W Boulder St Colorado Springs CO 80903-3371 Office: 10 Boulder Crescent St Colorado Springs CO 80903-3344 *Each of God's infinite creations was carefully placed on earth with the same responsibility....to grow. Man has the unique role in that plan in that he can help other things and the people around him to grow. This process is contingent upon "loving your neighbor as yourself." Transposing the equation therefore requires that you love yourself. I wish I had learned at an earlier age to take what you do seriously, but not to take yourself too seriously.*

PHILBIN, REGIS, television personality; b. N.Y.C.; s. Frank and Florence P.; m. Kay Faylan, 1957 (div.); children: Amy, Danny; m. Joy Senese, Mar. 1, 1970; children: Joanna, Jennifer. Student, U. Notre Dame. Hollywood stagehand, NBC page The Tonight Show; truck driver, newswriter, sportscaster. Co-host The Joey Bishop Show, 1967-69, host Sta. KABC Am. L.A., Sta. WABC TV Morning Show, 1983-88 (with Kathy Lee Gifford in 1985); co-host (syndicated show) Live! With Regis and Kathie Lee, 1988—, Miss Am. Pageant, 1991, 92, 95; co-author: Cooking with Regis and Kathie Lee, 1993, Entertaining with Regis and Kathie Lee, 1994; author: I'm Only One Man, 1995. Office: Regis & Kathie Lee ABC-TV 77 W 66th St New York NY 10023-6201

PHILBRICK, DONALD LOCKEY, lawyer; b. Portland, Maine, May 3, 1923; s. Donald Ward and Ruth (Lockey) P.; children: Deborah Palmer, Sarah Peyton; adopted children: Paul Sloat, Mark Whitfield, Andrew Hunter; m. Janet Mitchell Poole, Aug. 7, 1982. A.B., Bowdoin Coll., 1944; J.D., Harvard U., 1948. Bar: Maine 1948. Pvt. practice Portland; ptnr. Verrill & Dana, 1951-82. Selectman, Cape Elizabeth, Maine, 1957-63. Served with AUS, 1943-45; with USAF, 1951-53. Mem. Maine Hist. Soc. (past pres.), N.E. Hist. Gen. Soc., Delta Kappa Epsilon. Republican. Congregationalist. Club: Portland Country. Home: 39 Wildwood Dr Cape Eliz ME 04107-1160 Office: 80 Exchange St Portland ME 04101-5035

PHILBRICK, MARGARET ELDER, artist; b. Northampton, Mass., July 4, 1914; d. David and Mildred (Pattison) Elder; m. Otis Philbrick, May 23, 1941 (dec. Apr. 1973); 1 child, Otis. Grad., Mass. Sch. Art, Boston, 1937; student, De Cordova Mus., Lincoln, Mass., 1966-67. Juror art shows; exhibited one woman show, Bare Cove Gallery, Hingham, Mass., 1979, Greenwich Garden Ctr., Cos Cob, Conn., 1981; retrospective exhbn. graphics, Ainsworth Gallery, Boston, 1972; exhibited 40 yr. retrospective, Westenhook Gallery, Sheffield, Mass., 1977, 50 yr. retrospective, 1985; group shows, Boston Printmakers, 1948—, USIA tour to Far East, 1958-59, Boston Watercolor Soc., 1956—, Pratt Graphic Art Ctr., N.Y.C., 1966, New Eng. Watercolor Soc., 1982—; represented in permanent collections Nat. Mus. Fine Arts, Hanoi, Library of Congress, Washington, Boston Pub. Library, Nat. Bezalel Mus., Jerusalem; artist, designer: Wedgwood Commemorative Plates, Stoke-on-Trent, Eng., 1944-55, Nat. Mus. of Women in the Arts, Washington, Wiggin Collection Boston Pub. Library, The Margaret Philbrick Collection Westwood (Mass.) Pub. Libr.; illustrator books; exhibited "The Book as Art" Nat. Mus. of Women in the Arts, 1987, "The Book as Art II", 1989. Recipient purchase Libr. of Congress, 1948; recipient 1st graphics Acad. Artist, Springfield, Mass., 1957, Multum in Parvo Pratt-2d Internat. Miniature Print Exhbn., 1966, 1st prize in floral Miniature Art Soc. Fla., 1986, Ralph Fabri award. Mem. NAD (Ralph Fabri 1977), Boston Printmakers Presentation Print (exec. bd. 1951—), Acad. Artists, New Eng. Watercolor Soc., Miniature Painters, Washington Sculptors and Gravers Soc. (Founders award), Miniature Art Soc. N.J., Miniature Art Soc. Home and Office: 47 Westwood Glen Rd Westwood MA 02090-1614

PHILBRICK, RALPH, botanist; b. San Francisco, Jan. 1, 1934; s. Howard R. and Elizabeth (Jauckens) P.; children—Lauren P. Lester, Winston H., Edward W. B.A., Pomona Coll., 1956; M.A., UCLA, 1958; Ph.D., Cornell U., 1963. Research assoc. Cornell U., 1957-63; assoc. in botany U. Calif., Santa Barbara, 1963-64; biosystematist Santa Barbara Botanic Garden, 1964-73, dir., 1974-87, biol. cons., 1987—; research assoc. U. Calif., Santa Barbara, 1964-82. Mem. Santa Barbara County Planning Commn., 1981-85. Mem. Sigma Xi, Phi Kappa Phi. Office: 29 San Marcos Trout Clb Santa Barbara CA 93105-9726

PHILIP, JAMES (PATE PHILIP), state senator; b. May 26, 1930; married; 4 children. Student, Kansas City Jr. Coll., Kans. State Coll. Ret. dist. sales mgr. Pepperidge Farm, Inc.; rep. State of Ill., 1967-74, senator, 1975—; asst. senate minority leader, 1979, senate minority leader, 1981-93, senate pres., 1993—; chmn. DuPage County Rep. Ctrl. Com.; committeeman Addison Twp. Precinct 52; past Jr. Nat. Rep. Committeeman. Past dir. Nat. Found. March of Dimes; past gen. chmn. Elmhurst March of Dimes; spl. events chmn. DuPage Heart Assn.; mem. DuPage Meml. Hosp. Century Club; dir. Ray Graham Assn. Handicapped Children; mem. bd. sponsors Easter Seal Treatment Ctr.; active Lombard YMCA; bd. dirs. Danada Sculpture Garden. With USMC, 1950-53. Recipient Ill. Coun. on Aging award, 1989, Leaders of 90's award Downers Grove Twp., 1989, Man of Yr. award United Hellenic Voters Am., 1989, Legis. of Yr. award Ill. County Treas.'s Assn., 1990, Tax$avers award Ill. Assn. County Auditors, 1990, Statesman of Yr. award Internat. Union of Operating Engrs. Local 150, 1991, Friend of Youth award Assn. Ill. Twp. Com. on Youth, 1991, Spl. Svc. award Serenity House, 1991, Recognition award DuPage Ctr. Independent Living, 1991. Mem. Am. Legion, Ill. Young Reps. (past pres.), DuPage County Young Rep. Fedn. (past chmn.), DuPage County Marine Corps League (life), DuPage Indsl. and Mfg. Assn. (past dir.), Suburban Bus. Mgmt. Coun. (past v.p.), Mil. Order Devil Dogs, Gocery Mgmt. and Sales Exec. Club Chgo., Exec. Club DuPage County, Shriners, Elks, Masons, Order of DeMolay (life), Moose. Office: Ill State Senate 327 State Capitol Bldg Springfield IL 62706

PHILIP, PETER VAN NESS, former trust company executive; b. N.Y.C., Feb. 23, 1925; s. Van Ness and Lilian (Davis) P.; m. Sabina FitzGibbon, May 3, 1952; children: William Van Ness, Thomas Winslow, Peter Sandys. AB, Yale U., 1945W; MBA, NYU, 1950. With Price, Waterhouse & Co., N.Y.C., 1947-52; W.H. Morton & Co., Inc., N.Y.C., 1952-73; pres., CEO Equitable Securities, Morton & Co., Inc., 1970-73; sr. v.p., dir. White Weld & Co., Inc., N.Y.C., 1974-76; v.p. Morgan Guaranty Trust Co., N.Y.C., 1977-88, ret. With 86th inf. div. AUS, 1943-45. Decorated Purple Heart, Bronze Star. Clubs: Racquet and Tennis (N.Y.C.); Links; Yale (N.Y.C.), Downtown Assn. (N.Y.C.), Bond (N.Y.C.); Bedford ((N.Y.); Golf and Tennis; Ekwanok (Manchester, Vt.). Home: Guard Hill Rd Bedford NY 10506

PHILIPP, WALTER VIKTOR, mathematician, educator; b. Vienna, Dec. 14, 1936; came to U.S., 1963, naturalized, 1974; s. Oskar and Anna Julie (Krasucky) P.; m. Ariane Randell, Dec. 10, 1984; children: Petra, Robert, Anthony, Andre. MS in Math. and Physics, PhD in Math., U. Vienna, 1960. Asst. U. Vienna, 1960-63, 65-67, dozent, 1967; asst. prof. U. Mont., 1963-64; vis. asst. prof. U. Ill., Urbana, 1964-65; mem. faculty U. Ill., 1967—, prof. math., 1973—, prof. stats., 1988—, chmn. dept. stats., 1990-95; vis. prof. U. N.C., Chapel Hill, 1972, 88, MIT, 1980, Tufts U., 1981, U. Göttingen, 1982, 85, Imperial Coll., London, 1985; adv. bd. Monatshefte für Mathmatik, 1994—. Assoc. editor Annals of Probability, 1976-81. Fellow Inst. Math. Stats.; mem. Am. Math. Soc., Austrian Math. Soc., Internat. Statis. Inst., Am. Statis. Assn., Austrian Acad. Scis. (corr. mem.). Avocations: mountaineering. Home: 1922 Maynard Dr Champaign IL 61821-5265 Office: U Ill Dept Math Champaign IL 61821

PHILIPPI, DIETER RUDOLPH, academic administrator; b. Frankfurt, Germany, July 26, 1929; came to U.S., 1956, naturalized, 1961; s. Alfred and Ellen Marguerite (Glatzel) P.; BBA, Johann Wolfgang Goethe U., 1952; postgrad. Sorbonne, summers 1951, 52, U. Omaha, U. Tex.; MBA, Canadian Inst. Banking, 1953-55; children: Bianca Maria, Christopher Thomas; m. 2d, Helga Philippi, May 29, 1982; children: Stephan Andreas, Michael Joachim. With Toronto-Dominion Bank, Calgary, Edmonton, Alta., Can., 1953-56; chief acct. Baylor U. Coll. Medicine, Houston, 1956-63; contr. Wittenberg U., Springfield, Ohio, 1963-68; bus. mgr. Park Coll., Kansas City, Mo., 1968-70; bus. mgr., treas. Lone Mountain Coll., San Francisco, 1970-75; v.p. bus. affairs Findlay (Ohio) Coll., 1975-76; bus. mgr. Bologna (Italy) Ctr., The Johns Hopkins U., Balt., 1976-78; dir. bus. and fin. Mt. St. Mary's Coll., Los Angeles, 1978-81; asst. to v.p. overseas programs Boston U., Mannheim, Germany, 1981-85, dir. adminstrn. and finance, 1985-93; bus. mgr., controller Schiller Internat. U., Ingersheim, Germany, 1993—. lectr., Laurence U., Santa Barbara, Calif., 1973-75; fin. cons. various charitable orgns. Pres., German Sch. of East Bay, 1970-75; campaign coord. United Appeals Fund, 1968, recipient Disting. Svc. award, 1970; active Boy Scouts, Germany, 1948-52, Can., 1952-56, U.S., 1956-86, exec. bd. Tecumseh council, 1967-68, recipient Silver Beaver award, Wood badge, 1968. Bd. dirs. Bellaire Gen. Hosp., Greenland Hills Sch., Chaminade Coll. Prep. Sch. Mem. Am. Acctg. Assn., Am., Eastern Fin. Assns., Am. Mgmt. Assn., Am. Assn. Univ. Adminstrs., Nat. Coll. and Univ. Bus. Officers Assn., Western Coll. and Univ. Bus. Officers Assn., Nat. Assn. Accts., Am. Assn. Higher Edn., Coll. and Univ. Personnel Assn., San Francisco Consortium, Alpha Phi Omega. Clubs: Commonwealth of Calif. (San Francisco); Univ. (Kansas City). Office: Schiller Internat Univ, Im Schloss, D-74379 Ingersheim Germany

PHILIPPI, ERVIN WILLIAM, mortician; b. Lodi, Calif., June 4, 1922; s. William and Rebecca (Steinert) P.; m. Emma Grace Mosely, May 8, 1958 (div. Mar. 1979); m. Helen Jo Hunt, June 3, 1979. Grad., Calif. Coll. Motuary Sci., 1948. Embalmer, mortician, mgr. Salas Bros. Chapel, Modesto, Calif., 1946-92; dep. coroner Stanislaus County, Calif., 1955-75. With U.S. Army, 1942-46. Avocations: old car restoration, travel.

PHILIPPS, EDWARD WILLIAM, banker, real estate appraiser; b. N.Y.C., Dec. 19, 1938; s. Edward Charles and Eleanor Elizabeth (Eisenger) P.; m. Diane Rose DiCuffa, June 12, 1960; children: James Michael, Robert Christopher. Appraiser Dry Dock Savs., N.Y.C., 1956-70, Nat. Bank of West, White Plains, N.Y., 1970-72, Aires Real Estate, Yonkers, N.Y., 1972-74; sr. v.p. Am. Savs. Bank (merger Empire Savs. Bank), N.Y.C., 1974-92; self employed real estate appraiser Yonkers, 1992-93; sr. v.p., chief lending officer Stamford (Conn.) Fed. Savs., 1993—; mem. mortgage com. Cmty. Preservation Corp., N.Y.C., 1990-92. Mem. Am. Inst. Real Estate Appraisers, Homebuilders Assn. Fairfield County (bd. dirs.). Avocations: wood working, fishing. Home: 261 Kimball Ave Yonkers NY 10704-3030 Office: 999 Bedford St Stamford CT 06905-5609

PHILIPPS, LOUIS EDWARD, data systems manufacturing company executive; b. Duluth, Minn., Feb. 7, 1906; s. Carl Frederick Ferdin and Sarah Marguerithe (Mortenson) P.; m. Gladys Victoria Monsen, Nov. 13, 1930. Student pub. schs., Duluth. Engr. Cleve. Radioelectric Co., 1946-48; v.p., gen. mgr. Radio Systems, Inc., Cleve., 1948-50, Royal Communications, Inc., Cleve., 1950-56; dir. engring. Auth Electric Co., N.Y.C., 1956-59; chief engr. hosp. products div. Motorola-Dahlberg Co., Mpls., 1959-63; founder, pres., chmn. bd. Medelco Inc., Schiller Park, Ill., 1964-74; founder, 1975; since chmn. bd., dir. Datx Corp., Chgo.; dir. sales, chmn. bd. Smart Controllers, Inc., Skokie, Ill., 1985—; cons. to health care industry. Contbr. to profl. jours. Named Father of Hosp. Systems Industry Am. Hosp. Assn., 1974. Sr. mem. IEEE. Republican. Presbyterian. Clubs: Anvil (E. Dundee, Ill.); Order Eastern Star (Robbinsdale, Minn.), Masons (Robbinsdale, Minn.); Masons (Chgo.), Shriners (Chgo.). Patentee pulsed audio signaling, radio nurse system, data handling system. Home: 31 W Diversey Ave Addison IL 60101-3527 Office: Datx Corp 303 E Ohio St Chicago IL 60611-3317 *My wife's faith and encouragement to use defeat as a stepping stone to success made it possible for me to reach my goals. Encouraging and teaching employees also played an important part.*

PHILIPPUS, AL A., protective services official; b. San Antonio, Mar. 18, 1951; m. Jeanne Theresa Philippus; children: Dawn Michelle, Jason Allen, Mary Lamm. A. in Law Enforcement, San Antonio Coll., 1977; BS in Criminal Justice magna cum laude, S.W. Tex. State U., 1979; MS in Criminal Justice Mgmt./Adminstrn., Sam Houston State U., 1992, PhD in Criminal Justice Mgmt./Adminstrn., 1994adr. Patrol officer City of San Antonio Police Dept., 1975-81, detective homicide unit, 1981-84, sgt. patrol divsn., 1984-86, sgt. internal affairs, 1986-88, lt., dir. rsch. and planning, 1988-89, capt., comdr. fiscal mgmt. and rsch. divs., 1989-94, dep. police chief, comdr. uniform divsn., 1994-95, chief of police, 1995—; adj. prof. St. Mary's U., San Antonio, 1993—. Adv. bd. Police Found. Law Enforcement; law enforcement adv. bd. Alamo Area Coun. Govts.; mem. law enforcement coord. com. U.S. Western Dist. Tex.; bd. dirs. Tex. Ctr. for Legal Ethics and Professionalism. Sgt. USAF, 1969-73. Named Officer of the Yr., Greater San Antonio Builder's Assn., 1979, Optimist Club, 1993. Mem. Internat. City Mgmt. Assn., Nat. Assn. Rschrs. and Planners, Internat. Assn. Law Enforcement Planners, Internat. Assn. Chiefs of Police, Police Exec. Rsch. Found., Am. Pub. Welfare Assn., Assn. of Police Planning and Rsch. Officers, Combined Law Enforcement Assn. of Tex., San Antonio Police Officers Assn. Office: PO Box 839948 214 W Nueva St San Antonio TX 78283

PHILIPS, DAVID EVAN, English language educator; b. Wilkes-Barre, Pa., Aug. 30, 1926; s. Jesse Evan and Edith Kathleen (Stone) P.; m. Janet Briggs Walker, Aug. 19, 1950; children: Evan Walker, Donald David, Kimberly Anne. B.A., Haverford Coll, 1950; M.A., Johns Hopkins U., 1952; postgrad., U. Pa., 1953-56. Instr. English Tufts U., 1956-62; asst. prof. English Ea. Conn. State U., Willimantic, 1962-68, assoc. prof., 1968-80, prof., 1980-90, prof. emeritus, 1990—, head dept., 1966-68, 81-83, dir. Office Pub. Affairs, 1965-67, dir. freshman writing program, 1978-79; profl. storyteller, 1984—. Co-author: A Guide to College Writing Skills, 1979; author: Legendary Connecticut: Traditional Tales from the Nutmeg State, 1984, paperback reprint, 1992; book and author citation Conn. Gen. Assembly, 1994; book rev. columnist: Down East, 1956-87, contbg. editor, 1979-87; assoc. editor: Conn. History, 1972-75, 82-85, editor, 1986-87. Chmn. Windham (Conn.) Devel. and Indsl. Commn., 1965-68; bd. dirs. Conn. Assn. Mcpl. Devel. Commns., 1965-68, Vis. Nurse Assn., Windham, 1968-72; mem. Windham Dem. Town Com., 1968-85, 90—, rec. sec., 1972-74, 82-84, sec. 1978-82; mem. Windham Charter Commn., 1969-71, vice chmn., 1970-71; bd. dirs. Windham Sch. Dist., 1971-79, vice chmn., 1975-79; mem. Windham Zoning Commn., 1982-83; mem. Windham Planning Commn., 1983—, chmn., 1988—; mem. Windham Hist. Soc., 1985—, bd. dirs., 1991-94. With U.S. Merchant Marine, 1944-51, lic. Third Mate, 1946-51; lt. USNR, 1951-53. Danforth Found. Tchr. Study grantee, 1960-61, summer 1963. Mem. AAUP (sec.-treas. Conn. State conf. 1963-65, sec. 1966-68, Emeritus Assembly 1990—, treas. 1991-95), Conn. State Employees Assn. (sr. v.p. 1971-73), Conn. Hist. Soc. Democrat. Unitarian. Home: 7 Antrim Rd RFD 1 Willimantic CT 06226

PHILIPS, MALCOLM H., lawyer; b. Alexandria, La., Sept. 20, 1945. BS, U.S. Military Acad., 1967; MS, Iowa State U., 1971; JD, Georgetown U., 1978. Bar: D.C. 1978, Md. 1979; registered profl. engr. Tex., 1974. Plant mgr. SM-1 Nuclear Power Plant, 1973-74; mgr. program devel. dept. NUS Corp., 1974-78; ptnr. Winston & Strawn, Washington, 1978—; coun. govts. Transp. adv. com., 1976-77. With U.S. Army, 1967-74. Office: Winston & Strawn 1400 L St NW Washington DC 20005*

PHILIPSON, HERMAN LOUIS, JR., investment banker; b. Dallas, May 14, 1924; s. Herman Louis and Lillian (Adler) P.; m. Sonia Topletz, July 20, 1955; children: Cynthia Ann, Leslie, Nancy, Julie. B.S., Tex. A&M U., 1946; postgrad., Harvard Sch. Bus. Adminstrn., 1947-48. Pres. Philipson's, Inc., 1946-56; pres. Nat. Data Processing Corp., 1957-60, chmn. bd., 1960-61; chmn. bd. Techno-Growth Capital Corp., 1962-72; pres. Recognition Internat. Inc., Dallas, 1961-73; chmn. exec. com. Recognition Internat. Inc., 1973-76; vice chmn. Recognition Equipment Inc., 1976-83; pres. Internat. Bus. Devel. Ltd., Dallas, 1973—, IBDL, Inc., Dallas, 1979—. Mem. Dallas Citizens Coun., also v.p., mem. exec. com.; bd. dirs. Dallas County Camp Fire Girls; trustee So. Meth. U. Found. for Sci. and Engring.; mem. engring. adv. and devel. coun. Tex. A&M U. 1st Lt. AUS, 1943-46. Decorated Bronze Star, Purple Heart with cluster; recipient Dallas Exporter of Yr. award, 1970, Ernest Thompson Seton award, 1975; named to Tex. A&M U. Acad. Disting. Mech. Engring. Grads. Mem. Dallas C. of C. (world trade com.), Japan-Tex. Assn. Lodges: Masons, Shriners. Patentee in field. Home: 9100 Rockbrook Dr Dallas TX 75220-3907 Office: Internat Bus Devel Ltd 1545 W Mockingbird Ln Dallas TX 75235-5014

PHILIPSON, WILLARD DALE, curriculum and instructional educator; b. Sleepy Eye, Minn., Mar. 18, 1930; s. Walter and Alice Anna (Rasmussen) P.; m. Sylvia Eileen Olson, Sept. 26, 1953; children: Andrew Will, Jennifer Dale, Pamela Elizabeth. B.S., U. Minn., 1953, M.A., 1959, Ph.D., 1967. Instr. agrl. engring. U. Minn., Morris, 1959; audio visual materials adv. Audio Visual Edn. Service, Mpls., 1960-63; assoc. prof., head ednl. film library No. Ill. U., DeKalb, 1963-66; mem. faculty U. Minn., Mpls., 1966-95, prof. emeritus, 1995—; prof. curriculum and instrn. systems U. Minn., 1978-94, dir. audio visual library services, 1966-78, architect microcomputer info. systems network, 1978-88; spl. projects dir. U. Minn., Mpls., 1988-93; mem. Minn. Civil Service Exec. Mgmt. Tng. Commn., 1969-71; mem. legis. com. Minn. Citizens for Libraries, 1976-91. Editor: Audi0-Visual Jour, 1966-78. Trustee Ramsey County Pub. Libr., 1992-95; active local Boy Scouts Am., 1972-75, chmn. fund dr., 1974-75. Capt. USNR, 1953-85. Recipient Gov. of Minn. Service award, 1969; Adult Educator of Yr. award Minn. Adult Edn., 1973; Silver Reel award Consortium U. Film Centers, 1979; Sears, Roebuck & Co. scholar, 1952. Mem. ASCD, Assn. Ednl. Comms. and Tech., Adult Edn. Assn., Minn. Ednl. Media Orgn., Naval Res. Assn., Am. Legion (vice comdr., comdr. local post 1991-95), Alpha Tau Alpha. Home: 1960 10th St Saint Paul MN 55110-6636 Office: U Minn Wesbrook Hall 77 Pleasant St SE Minneapolis MN 55455-0216

PHILLABAUM, LESLIE ERVIN, publisher; b. Cortland, N.Y., June 1, 1936; s. Vern Arthur and Beatrice Elizabeth (Butterfield) P.; m. Roberta Kimbrough Swarr, Mar. 17, 1962; children—Diane Melissa, Scott Christopher. B.S., Pa. State U., 1958, M.A., 1963. Editor Pa. State U. Press, 1961-63; editor-in-chief U. N.C. Press, 1963-70; assoc. dir., editor La. State U. Press, Baton Rouge, 1970-75; dir. La. State U. Press, 1975—. Served to 1st lt. AUS, 1959-61. Mem. Assn. Am. Univ. Presses (dir. 1978-80, 83-86, pres. 1984-85), So. Hist. Assn., Acacia, Omicron Delta Kappa, Alpha Kappa Psi. Democrat. Home: 769 Castle Kirk Dr Baton Rouge LA 70808 Office: La State U Press Baton Rouge LA 70893

PHILLIPPI, WENDELL CRANE, editor; b. Zionsville, Ind., July 4, 1918; s. Jesse F. and Bernice (Brock) P.; m. Georgiana Pittman, Jan. 10, 1942 (dec. July 10, 1978); children—Frank, Ann; m. Barbara Jean Caniff Howden, Oct. 30, 1980. A.B., Ind. U., 1940. Copy editor Indpls. News, 1940-46, state editor, 1946-47, city editor, 1947-52, asst. mng. editor, 1952-62, mng. editor, 1962-84; Pres. Ind. A.P., 1957; dir. Mid-Am. Press Inst., 1969-84; bd. dirs. A.P. Mng. Editors Assn., 1963-66, 69-72, v.p., 1971, pres., 1972; mem. Pulitzer Prize in Journalism Jury, 1971, 75, 76. Author: Dear Ike, 1991. Pres. Ind. Armory Bd., 1968-73; bd. dirs. 500 Festival, v.p. 1963-65; mem. Ind. U. Daily Student Bd., 1968-77; sr. warden Episcopal Ch., 1966, 69, 71. Maj. AUS, 1941-45; commanding gen., 38th divsn., 1959-63; maj. gen. Res. Decorated Silver Star, Bronze Star with cluster, Purple Heart. Mem. VFW, NG Assn., U.S. and Ind. (pres. 1953-55), Army Assn. Ind. (pres. 1957-58), Assn. U.S. Army, Indpls. C. of C. Am. Soc. Newspaper Editors, Am. Legion, Ind. U. Alumni Assn. (mag. bd. 1967-81), Econ. Club of Indpls., Indpls. Columbia Club, Blue Key, Sigma Nu, Sigma Delta Chi. Episcopalian. Home: 2244 Rome Dr Indianapolis IN 46208-3240

PHILLIPS, ADRAN ABNER (ABE PHILLIPS), geologist, oil and gas exploration consultant; b. Sugden, Okla., Feb. 6, 1924; s. James M. and Jennie Elizabeth (Norman) P.; m. Carmel Darlene Pesterfield, Aug. 20, 1949 (div.); 1 son, John David. B.S. in Geology, U. Okla., 1949. With Exxon Corp. and affiliates, 1949-79, dist. geologist, Chico, Calif., 1959-64, ops. geologist, Sydney, Australia, 1964-67, exploration coordinator North Slope Alaska, Houston, 1968-70, div. geologist, Denver, 1970-71, exploration mgr. P.T. Inc., Stanvac, Jakarta, Indonesia, 1971-73, exploration mgr. ESSO exploration, Singapore, 1973-76; div. mgr. Exxon U.S.A., Denver, 1976-79; v.p. Coors Energy div., Golden, Colo., 1979-80, pres., 1980-92; oil and gas exploration cons., 1992—. Bd. dirs. Mountain States Legal Found., 1991—. Mem. Am. Assn. Petroleum Geologists, Ind. Petroleum Assn. Mountain States (past pres.), Ind. Petroleum Assn. Am. (dir.), Nat. Coal Council. Home and Office: 2194 S Augusta Dr Evergreen CO 80439-8923

PHILLIPS, ALMARIN, economics educator, consultant; b. Port Jervis, N.Y., Mar. 13, 1925; s. Wendell Edgar and Hazel (Billett) P.; m. Dorothy Kathryn Burns, June 14, 1947 (div. 1976); children: Almarin Paul, Frederick Peter, Thomas Rock, David John, Elizabeth Linett, Charles Samuel; m. Carole Cherry Greenberg, Dec. 19, 1976. B.S., U. Pa., 1948, M.A., 1949; Ph.D., Harvard, 1953. Instr. econs. U. Pa., 1948-50, 51-53, asst. prof. econs., 1953-56, prof. econs. and law, 1963-91; Hower prof. pub. policy U. Pa. 1983-91; chmn. dept. econs. U. Pa., 1968-71, 72-73, assoc. dean Wharton Sch., 1973-74, dean Sch. Pub. and Urban Policy, 1974-77, chair faculty senate, 1990-91; teaching fellow Harvard, 1950-51; assoc. prof. U. Va, 1956-61, prof., 1961-63; vis. prof. U. Hawaii, summer 1968, U. Warwick, London Grad. Sch. Bus. Studies, 1972, Ohio State U., McGill U., 1978, Calif. Inst. Tech, Northwestern U., 1980, Ariz. Coll. Law, 1987, Inst. Europeén d'Adminstrn. des Affairs (INSEAD), France, spring 1990; co-dir. Pres.'s Commn. Fin. Structure and Regulation, 1970-71; mem. Nat. Commn. Electronic Fund Transfers, 1976-77; chmn. bd. Econsult Corp., 1990—. Author: (with R.W. Cabell) Problems in Basic Operations Research Methods for Management, 1961, Market Structure, Organization and Performance, 1962, Technology and Market Structure: A Study of the Aircraft Industry, 1971, (with P. Phillips and T.R. Phillips) Biz Jets: Technology and Market Structure in the Corporate Jet Aircraft Industry, 1994; Editor: Perspectives on Antitrust Policy, 1965, (with O.E. Williamson) Prices: Issues in Theory, Practice and Policy, 1968, Promoting Competition in Regulated Markets, 1975 ; editor Jour. Indsl. Econs., 1974-90; Contbr. articles to tech. lit. Served with AUS, 1943-45. Decorated Purple Heart, Bronze Star. Fellow Am. Statis. Assn., AAAS; mem. Am. Econ. Assn., Econometric Soc., European Econ. Assn., Internat. Telecommunications Soc. (bd. dirs. 1990—). Home: 1115 Remington Rd Wynnewood PA 19096-4021

PHILLIPS, ANTHONY FRANCIS, lawyer; b. Hartford, Conn., May 18, 1937; s. Frank and Lena Phillips; m. Rosemary Karran McGowan, Jan. 28, 1967; children: Karran, Antonia, Justin. BA, U. Conn., 1959; JD, Cornell U., 1962. Bar: N.Y. 1964, U.S. Dist. Ct. (so. dist., ea. dist.) N.Y. 1965, (ctrl. dist.) Calif. 1980, U.S. Tax Ct. 1981, U.S. Ct. Appeals (2nd cir.) 1967, (3d cir.) 1985, (4th cir.) 1983, (5th cir.) 1972, (7th cir.) 1987, (9th cir.) 1983,

(10th cir.) 1983, U.S. Supreme Ct. 1971. Assoc. Willkie, Farr & Gallagher, N.Y.C., 1963-69, ptnr., 1969—. Mem. adv. com. Cornell U. Law Sch., 1994—. Fellow Am. Bar Found.; mem. ABA, N.Y. State Bar Assn., N.Y. County Bar Assn. (bd. dirs. 1989-95), Assn. of Bar of City of N.Y. Home: 3 Elm Rock Rd Bronxville NY 10708-4202 Office: Willkie Farr & Gallagher 1 Citicorp Ctr 153 E 53rd St New York NY 10022-4602

PHILLIPS, ANTHONY GEORGE, neurobiology educator; b. Barrow, Cumbria, Eng., Jan. 30, 1943; came to Can., 1953; s. George William and Mabel Lilian (Wood) P. BA (hon.), U. Western Ont., London, Can., 1966, MA, 1967, PhD, 1970. Asst. prof. psychobiology U. British Columbia, Vancouver, Can., 1970-75, assoc. prof., 1975-80, prof., 1980—; head dept. psychology, 1994—; founder Quadra Logic Tech., Inc., Vancouver. Contbr. numerous papers to sci. jours. Chmn. Can.-India Village Aid, Vancouver, 1981-86, bd. dirs. 1987—; bd. dirs. Tibetian Refuge Aid Soc., Vancouver, 1980—. Recipient Killam rsch. prize Can. Coun., 1977, Killam Rsch. prize U. B.C., 1986, D.O. Hebb award Can. Psychol. Assn.; Steacie fellow Nat. Scis. and Engring. Rsch. Coun. (Can.), 1980. Fellow Royal Soc. Can.; mem. Soc. Neurosci., Can. Soc. for Neurosci., Can. Coll. Neuropsychopharmacology. Office: U BC Dept Psychology, 2136 W Mall, Vancouver, BC Canada V6T 1Z4

PHILLIPS, ARTHUR WILLIAM, JR., biology educator; b. Claremont, N.H., Sept. 25, 1915; s. Arthur William and Jane Helen (Daley) P.; m. Mary Catherine Mich, Oct. 21, 1950; children: Marilynn, William (dec.). BS, U. Notre Dame, 1939, MS, 1941; DSc, MIT, 1947. Rsch. asst. Lobund lab. U. Notre Dame, Ind., 1937-41, rsch. scientist, 1943-45; rsch. assoc. MIT, 1947-49; rsch. assoc. prof., head div. bioengring. Lobund lab. U. Notre Dame, Ind., 1949-54; rsch. scientist dept. biology and bioengring. MIT, Cambridge, 1942-43, rsch. fellow dept. food tech., 1945-47, rsch. assoc. dept. food tech., 1947-49; rsch. assoc. prof. dept. bacteriology Syracuse (N.Y.) U., 1954-58, prof. microbiology, 1959-86, prof. emeritus, 1986—, founder, dir. biol. rsch. labs., 1955-65, head radiation and isotope lab., 1956-63, dir. germ-free life rsch. lab., 1956-84; mem. Internat. Congress on Nutrition, Washington, 1960, Internat. Congress for Microbiology, Montreal, Can., 1962, Moscow, 1966, Internat. Congress for Germ-Free Life Rsch., Nagoya, Japan, 1967; mem. com. on nutrition NAS-NRC, Washington, 1964-66; mem. Conf. on Germ-Free Life and Gnobiotics, Madison, Wis., 1986, Internat. Conf. on Gnotobiology, Versailles, France, 1987; cons. NSF, Washington, Cradle Soc. Inc., Evanston, Ill., GE, Syracuse, Am. Cyanamid, Pearl River, N.Y., Carnation Co., L.A., C.V. Mosby, St. Louis, Can. Dry Corp., Greenwich, Conn., Chocolate Mfrs. Assn., Washington, Continental Can Co., Syracuse. Contbr. articles to profl. jours., chpts. to books. Refrigeration Rsch. Found. fellow, 1945-47; NIH grantee, 1956-80. Mem. Am. Soc. for Microbiology (placement com. 1968-78), Gnotobiotics Assn., Soc. for Gen. Microbiology. Avocations: history, genealogy, hiking. Home: Clark Hollow Rd East Poultney VT 05741-0604 Office: Syracuse U Dept Biology 108 College Pl Syracuse NY 13244-1270

PHILLIPS, BARNET, IV, lawyer; b. New York, N.Y., July 5, 1948; s. Barnet III and Isabelle (Auriema) P.; m. Sharon Walsted Packey, Jan. 2, 1981; children: Victoria Ilonka, Caroline Walsted. BA, Yale U., 1970; JD, Fordham U., 1973; LLM, NYU, 1977. Bar: N.Y. 1974. Assoc. Hughes Hubbard & Reed, N.Y.C., 1973-76; assoc. Skadden, Arps, Slate, Meagher & Flom, N.Y.C., 1977-81, ptnr., 1981—; adj. assoc. prof. Forham U., N.Y.C., 1987-88; articles editor The Tax Lawyer, 1989-91. Co-author: Structuring Corporate Acquisition - Tax Aspects. Bd. dirs Student/Sponsor Partnership, N.Y.C.; bd. cons. Portsmouth (R.I.) Abbey Sch. Republican. Avocations: skiing, opera, triathlons. Home: 6 Hycliff Rd Greenwich CT 06831-3223 Office: Skadden Arps Slate Meagher & Flom 919 3rd Ave New York NY 10022

PHILLIPS, BARRY, lawyer; b. Valdosta, Ga., Feb. 16, 1929; s. W. Otis and Gypsy (Mercer) P.; m. Grace Greer, Aug. 3, 1957; children: Mary Grace, Barry Jr., Greer, Quinton. AB, U. Ga., 1949, LLB, 1954. Bar: Ga. 1951, D.C. 1977. Assoc. Kilpatrick & Cody, Atlanta, 1954-60, ptnr., 1960—; bd. dirs., mem. exec. com., credit com. Bank South Corp., 1978-96. Mem. bd. regents Univ. Sys. Ga., 1988-94, vice chmn., 1991-93, chmn., 1993-94; trustee U. Ga. Found., Atlanta, 1983-87, treas., 1985-87; mem. bd. visitors U. Ga. Law Sch., 1983-87, chmn., 1995; dir. Ctrl. Atlanta Progress, 1985-86; dir. USA-ROC Econ. Coun., 1985-91; bd. dirs. Ga. Coun. Internat. Visitors, Atlanta, 1986-93, sec., 1986-87, pres., 1987-88; bd. dirs. Atlanta Conv. and Visitor's Bur., 1986-91, sec., 1986-87, v.p., 1987-88; bd. dirs. Ga. Region NCCJ, 1980—, co-chair, 1982-83; chmn. Met. Atlanta Olympic Games Authority, 1990-91; bd. dirs. Nat. H.S. Football Hall of Fame, 1994—, Ga. Sports Hall of Fame, 1990, vice chmn., 1993-95, chmn., 1995-96; attache Can. Olympic Team for 1996 Olympics, 1995-96. 1st lt. U.S. Army, 1951-53, Korea. Decorated Air medal; recipient Brotherhood-Sisterhood award Ga. Regional NCCJ, 1993. Fellow Am. Coll. Investment Counsel (bd. dirs. 1986-88), ABA, Ga. Bar Found., Soc. Internat. Bus. Fellows; mem. Ga. Bar Assn. (chmn. corp. and banking law sect. 1977-78), Atlanta Bar Assn., D.C. Bar Assn., Lawyers Club Atlanta, U. Ga. Law Sch. Alumni Assn. (trustee 1979-84, pres. 1982-83), Can. Am. Soc. (bd. dirs. 1981-90, pres. 1981-83), Brit. Am. Bus. Group (bd. dirs. 1985-95), Sphinx, Gridiron, Phi Beta Kappa, Phi Kappa Phi, Omicron Delta Kappa. Democrat. Methodist. Avocations: reading, travel. Home: 4850 Tanglewood Ct NW Atlanta GA 30327-4558 Office: Kilpatrick & Cody Ste 2800 1100 Peachtree St NE Atlanta GA 30309-4530

PHILLIPS, BERNICE CECILE GOLDEN, retired vocational education educator; b. Galveston, Tex., June 30, 1920; d. Walter Lee and Minnie (Rothsprack) Golden; m. O. Phillips, Mar. 1950 (dec.); children: Dorian Lee, Loren Francis. BBA cum laude, U. Tex., 1945; MEd, U. Houston, 1968. cert. tchr., tchr. coord., vocat. tchr., Tex. Dir. Delphian Soc., Houston, 1955-60; bus. tchr. various private schs., Houston area, 1960-65; vocat. tchr. coord. office edn. program Pasadena (Tex.) Ind. Sch. Dist., 1965-68, Houston Ind. Sch. Dist., John H. Reagan High Sch., 1968-85. Bd. dirs. Regency House Condominium Assn., 1991-93. Recipient numerous awards and recognitions for vocat. bus. work at local and state levels. Mem. AAUW (life, Houston Br. v.p. ednl. found. 1987-90, pres. 1992-94, bd. dirs. 1987-96), NEA, Nat. Bus. Edn. Assn. Am. Vocat. Assn. (life), Tex. State Tchrs. Assn. (life), Tex. Classroom Tchrs. Assn. (life), Tex. Bus. Edn. Assn. (emeritus), Vocat. Office Edn. Tchrs. Assn. Tex. (past bd. dirs.), Greater Houston Bus. Edn. Assn. (reporter), Houston Assn. Ret. Tchrs., Tex. Assn. Ret. Tchrs., Delta Pi Epsilon (emeritus), Beta Gamma Sigma. Avocations: bridge, reading, arts, crafts, travel, theater. Home: 2701 Westheimer Rd Apt 8H Houston TX 77098-1235

PHILLIPS, BETTY LOU (ELIZABETH LOUISE PHILLIPS), author, interior designer; b. Cleve.; d. Michael N. and Elizabeth D. (Materna) Suvak; m. John S. Phillips, Jan. 27, 1963 (div. Jan. 1981); children: Bruce, Bryce, Brian; m. John D.C. Roach, Aug. 28, 1982. BS, Syracuse U., 1960; postgrad. in English, Case Western Res. U., 1963-64. Cert. elem. and spl. edn. tchr., N.Y. Tchr. pub. schs. Shaker Heights, Ohio, 1960-66; sportswriter Cleve. Press, 1976-77; spl. features editor Pro Quarterback Mag., N.Y.C., 1976-79; freelance writer specializing in books for young people, 1976—; interior designer residential and comml.; bd. dirs. Cast Specialties Inc., Cleve. Author: Chris Evert: First Lady of Tennis, 1977; Picture Story of Dorothy Hamill (ALA Booklist selection), 1978; American Quarter Horse, 1979; Earl Campbell: Houston Oiler Superstar, 1979; Picture Story of Nancy Lopez, (ALA Notable book), 1980; Go! Fight! Win! The NCA Guide for Cheerleaders (ALA Booklist), 1981; Something for Nothing, 1981; Brush Up on Your Hair (ALA Booklist), 1981; Texas ... The Lone Star State, 1989, Who Needs Friends? We All Do!, 1989; also contbr. articles to young adult and sports mags. Bd. dirs. The Children's Mus., Denver; mem. Friends of Fine Arts Found., Denver Art Mus., Cen. City Opera Guild, Alameda County Cancer League. Mem. Soc. Children's Book Writers, Internat. Interior Design Assn. (profl. mem.), Am. Soc. Interior Designers (profl. mem., cert.), Delta Delta Delta. Republican. Roman Catholic. Home: 4278 Bordeaux Ave Dallas TX 75205

PHILLIPS, BRUCE HAROLD, lawyer; b. Little Rock, Feb. 5, 1962; s. Philip Kirkland and Jayne (Jack) L.; m. Nancy Lee Williams, Nov. 12, 1994. BA in Bus. Adminstrn., U. Ark., Little Rock, 1988; JD, U. Ark., Fayetteville, 1993. Bar: Ark. 1993, Tenn. 1994, U.S. Dist. Ct. (mid. dist.) Tenn. 1994, U.S. Ct. Appeals (6th cir.) 1995. Golf profl. Internat. Golf, Little Rock, 1982-85, Tee-to-Green Golf, Little Rock, 1985-89; assoc. Jack, Lyon & Jones, P.A., Nashville, 1993—. Mem. Phi Alpha Delta. Avocation: golf. Office: Jack Lyon & Jones PA 11 Music Circle S Nashville TN 37203

PHILLIPS, CARLA, county official; b. Balt., Nov. 14, 1963; d. Paulo Pereira de Mendonca and June Ann (Lewis) Cortese; m. Wayne Shriver Phillips, Mar. 24, 1990. BS, East Carolina U., 1985; MPA, U. Balt., 1993. Program dir. YMCA of Met. Washington, Alexandria, Va., 1985-86; ctr. supr. Balt. County Govt., Towson, Md., 1986-90, community supr., 1990-92, sr. community supr., 1992-94, asst. therapeutic recreation coord., 1994—. Water safety instr. YMCA of Greater Balt., 1986—, Rosedale Recreation Coun., Balt., 1991, 93; asst. basketball coach Md. Spl. Olympics, Towson, 1994—, soccer coach, dir. track and field; mem. 6th Dist. Substance Abuse Adv. Coun., Towson, 1990-92, Villa Cresta PTA, Parkville, Md., 1988-92; ski instr. Ski Roundtop, Lewisberry, Pa., 1996—. Mem. ASPA, Nat. Recreation and Park Assn. (cert. leisure profl.), Md. Recreation and Parks Assn., Soc. for Pub. Affairs and Adminstrn., Kappa Delta Pi, Phi Sigma Pi, Pi Alpha Alpha. Avocations: Alpine skiing, bicycling. Home: 1000 Harris Mill Rd PO Box 306 Parkton MD 21120-0306 Office: Balt County Govt Parks and Recreation 301 Washington Ave Baltimore MD 21204-4715

PHILLIPS, CARTER GLASGOW, lawyer; b. Canton, Ohio, Sept. 11, 1952; s. Max Dean and Virginia Scott (Carter) P.; m. Sue Jane Henry, June 5, 1976; children: Jessica, Ryan. BA, Ohio State U., 1973; MA, Northwestern U., 1975, JD, 1977. Bar: Ill. 1977, D.C. 1979, U.S. Dist. Ct. (no. dist.) Ill., U.S. Dist. Ct. (D.C. dist.), U.S. Ct. Appeals (2d, 3d, 4th, 5th, 6th, 7th, 8th, 9th, 10th, 11th, D.C. and fed. cirs.). Law clk. U.S. Ct. Appeals (7th cir.), Chgo., 1977-78; law clk. to chief Justice Warren E. Burger U.S. Supreme Ct., Washington, 1978-79; asst. prof. law U. Ill., Champaign, 1979-81; asst. solicitor gen. U.S. Dept. Justice, Washington, 1981-84; ptnr. Sidley & Austin, Washington, 1984—, mng. ptnr., 1995—. Contbr. articles to profl. jours. Chief counsel Spina Bifida Assn. Am., Rockville, Md., 1987—; mem. bd. advisors state and local legal ctrs., Washington, 1985-91. Mem. Am. Law Inst. Republican. Episcopalian. Office: Sidley & Austin 1722 I St NW Washington DC 20006-3705

PHILLIPS, CHARLES ALAN, accounting firm executive; b. Cin., Aug. 12, 1939; s. Charles Stanley and Mary Lucile (Kirkpatrick) P. BS in Bus. Adminstrn., Northwestern U., 1960, MBA, 1961. Cert. systems profl. Investment adviser Continental Ill. Bank, Chgo., 1960-65; asst. to pres. A.S. Hansen, Chgo., 1965-67; investment adviser Francis I. du Pont, N.Y.C., 1967-70; prof. North Central Coll., Mansfield, Ohio, 1970-73; prin. Peat, Marwick, Mitchell (now KPMG Peat Marwick), Cleve., Tulsa, Houston, 1973-88. Presbyterian. Avocations: classical music; natural history; gardening.

PHILLIPS, CHARLES FRANKLIN, economic consultant; b. Nelson, Pa., May 25, 1910; s. Frank G. and Emily Catherine (Stevens) P.; m. Evelyn Minard, June 22, 1932; children—Charles Franklin Jr., Carol Ann. A.B., Colgate U., 1931, LL.D., 1945; Ph.D., Harvard U., 1934; LL.D., Colby Coll., 1949, Bowdoin Coll., 1952, Northeastern U., 1953, Shaw U., 1966, Bates Coll., 1967; L.H.D., U. Maine, 1954; Litt.D., Western New Eng. Coll., 1959, Nasson Coll., 1959, Morehouse Coll., Atlanta, 1963. Asst. econs. Hobart Coll., Geneva, N.Y., 1933-34; instr. econs. Colgate U., 1934-36, asst. prof., 1936-39, prof., 1939-44; on leave of absence, 1941-44; to serve as cons. counsumers div. Nat. Def. Adv. Com., 1941; asst. price exec. OPA, 1941-42, chief tire rationing div., 1942-43, dir. automotive supply rationing div., 1943-44, dep. adminstr. charge rationing dept., 1944; pres. Bates Coll., 1944-67, pres. emeritus, 1967—; former pub. gov. Am. Stock Exch.; ret. dir. several corps. Author: Marketing, 1938, (with Jasper V. Garland) Government Spending and Economic Recovery, 1938, Discussion Methods, 1938, The American Neutrality Problem, 1939, (with Delbert J. Duncan and Stanley C. Hollander) Modern Retailing Management, rev. edit, 1972, (with others) Marketing Principles and Methods, rev. edit, 1973, Marketing by Manufacturers, rev. edit, 1951, A Tax Program to Encourage the Economic Growth of Puerto Rico, 1958; contbr. articles to acad., trade jours. Pres. New Eng. Colls. Fund, 1954. Mem. Phi Beta Kappa, Phi Delta Theta. Address: 117 Maple Hill Rd Auburn ME 04210-8728

PHILLIPS, CHARLES FRANKLIN, JR., economist, educator; b. Geneva, N.Y., Nov. 5, 1934; s. Charles Franklin and Evelyn (Minard) P.; m. Marjorie Hancock, June 22, 1957; children: Charles Franklin, Susan Hancock, Anne Davis. B.A., U. N.H., 1956; Ph.D., Harvard U., 1960. Asst. prof. econs. Washington and Lee U., Lexington, Va., 1959-63; asso. prof. Washington and Lee U., 1963-66, prof., 1966—; mem. adv. bd. Lexington-Covington area, First Union, 1971—; econ. cons. pub. utilities. Author: Competition in the Synthetic Rubber Industry, 1963, The Economics of Regulation, 1965, rev. edit., 1969, The Regulation of Public Utilities, 1984, 3d edit., 1993; editor: Competition and Monopoly in the Domestic Telecommunications Industry, 1974, Competition and Regulation-Some Economic Concepts, 1976, Expanding Economic Concepts of Regulation in Health, Postal and Telecommunications Services, 1977, Regulation, Competition and Deregulation-An Economic Grab Bag, 1978, Regulation and the Future Economic Environment-Air to Ground, 1980. Mem. city coun. Lexington, 1969-71, mayor, 1971-88; trustee Hebron Acad., Maine, 1971-82, Presbyn. Ch., 1991—, elder, 1993—; mem. Commn. on Rev. of Nat. Policy Toward Gambling, 1972-76; chmn. Valley Program for Aging Svcs., 1993-95, treas., 1996—; bd. dirs. Rockbridge Area Presbyn. Home, 1973—, Nat. Regulatory Rsch. Inst., 1992-95; pres. United Way of Lexington-Rockbridge County, 1996—. Recipient McKinsey Found. award, 1962; Outstanding Regional Dir. award Omicron Delta Epsilon, 1971. Mem. Am. Econ. Assn., So. Econ. Assn., Am. Mktg. Assn., Phi Beta Kappa, Omicron Delta Epsilon (pres. 1976-77, 78-79, 96—). Republican (mem. Va. central com. 1974-76, 77—). Home: 414 Morningside Dr Lexington VA 24450-2739 Office: Washington and Lee U Dept Economics Lexington VA 24450

PHILLIPS, CHARLES GORHAM, lawyer; b. Glen Ridge, N.J., Apr. 27, 1921; s. Charles Swayne and Margaret Cook (Atwell) P.; m. Martha Hall Belden, Dec. 19, 1942; children: Webster B., Charles G. Jr., Tacey P. Carroll, Tyler A. AB magna cum laude, Williams Coll., 1943; JD cum laude, Harvard U., 1948. Bar: N.Y. 1949. Assoc. Cadwalader, Wickersham & Taft, N.Y.C., 1948-51; assoc. Dewey Ballantine and predecessor firm, N.Y.C., 1951-57, ptnr., 1958—, chmn. mgmt. com., 1984-88. Assoc. trustee Montclair (N.J.) Art Mus., 1988—. Cpl. USAAF, 1943-46. Mem. ABA, Montclair Golf Club, Riomar Bay Yacht Club, Riomar Country Club (Vero Beach, Fla.). Republican. Congregationalist. Avocations: golfing, bridge, needlepoint. Home: 746 Riomar Dr Vero Beach FL 32963-2013 also: 10 Crestmont Rd Montclair NJ 07042-1930 Office: Dewey Ballantine 1301 Avenue Of The Americas New York NY 10019-6022

PHILLIPS, CHRISTOPHER HALLOWELL, diplomat; b. The Hague, The Netherlands, Dec. 6, 1920; s. William and Caroline A. (Drayton) P.; m. Mabel B. Olsen, May 11, 1943 (dec. May 1995); children: Victoria A. Phillips Corbett, Miriam O. Phillips Eley, David W. A.B., Harvard U., 1943. Reporter, Beverly (Mass.) Evening Times, 1947-48; mem. Mass. Senate, 1948-53; spl. asst. to asst. sec. UN affairs Dept. State, 1953; later dep. asst. sec. of state for internat. orgn. affairs; apptd. U.S. Civil Service commr.; vice chmn. U.S. Civil Service Commn., 1957; U.S. rep. on UN Econ. and Social Council, 1958-61; Chase Manhattan Bank rep. for UN affairs, 2d v.p., mgr. Canadian div., 1961-65; pres. U.S. council Internat. C. of C., 1965-69; ambassador, dep. U.S. rep. UN Security Council, 1969-70; ambassador, dep. permanent U.S. rep. to UN, 1970-73; pres. Nat. Council for U.S.-China Trade, Washington, 1973-86, now hon. mem. bd. dirs.; U.S. ambassador to Brunei Darussalam, 1989-91; presdl. appointee to bd. U.S. Inst. Peace, 1992—; trustee Am. Inst. in Taiwan, 1995—; mem. adv. coun. Sch. Advanced Internat. Studies, Johns Hopkins U. Mass. dist. del. Rep. Nat. Conv., 1952, 60. Served to capt. USAAF, 1942-46. Fellow Am. Acad. Arts and Scis.; mem. UN Assn. U.S.A., Coun. Fgn. Rels., Asia Soc., Coun. Am. Ambassadors (bd. dirs.), Met. Club Washington. Episcopalian. Home: 2801 New Mexico Ave NW Washington DC 20007-3921

PHILLIPS, CLIFTON J., history educator; b. Olean, N.Y., Apr. 11, 1919; s. Charles Clifton and Edith (Grey) P.; m. Rachel Jacqueline Martin, July 19, 1952; children: Peter Martin, Elaine Abigail, Alexis Anne, Patience Cecily. B.A., Hiram Coll., 1941; Th.B., Starr King Sch. Religious Leadership, 1944; M.A., Harvard U., 1950, Ph.D., 1954. Civil edn. officer Dept. Def., Kobe, Japan, 1946-49; faculty history De Pauw U., 1954—, prof., 1965-85, sr. prof., 1985—, chmn. dept. history, 1969-72, 78—; lectr. Am. Studies, Korea, 1968-69. Author: Indiana in Transition: The Emergence of an Industrial Commonwealth, 1880-1920, 1968, Protestant America and the Pagan World: The First Half Century of the American Board of Commissioners for Foreign Missions, 1810-1860, 1969, (with others) The Missionary Enterprise in China and America, 1974, Missionary Ideologies in the Imperialist Era, 1880-1920, 1982; DePauw: A Pictorial History, 1987, From Frontier Circuit to Urban Church: The History of Greencastle Methodism, 1989. Served with inf. AUS, 1944-46, PTO. Fulbright-Hays fellow Chinese civilization Taiwan, summer 1962. Mem. Am. Hist. Assn., Assn. Asian Studies, Orgn. Am. Historians, Ind. Hist. Soc., Ind. Assn. Historians (past pres.). Home: 111 S Spring St Greencastle IN 46135-1727

PHILLIPS, DANIEL ANTHONY, trust company executive; b. Boston, Feb. 24, 1938; s. Lyman Waldo and Harriet Anthony (Carlow) P.; m. Diana Walcott, Aug. 18, 1962; children: Lisa Walcott Phillips, Bradford Lyman, Phillips. AB cum laude, Harvard U., 1960, MBA, 1963. From v.p. to dir. to mem. exec. com. Fiduciary Trust Co., Boston, 1963-92, exec. v.p., dir., trust com. sec., trust officer, 1992—, exec. v.p., dir., trust com., trust officer, 1993-94, pres., CEO, 1993—. Bd. dirs. Family Svc. Am., chair fin. comn., 1993-95, treas., chair bd. dirs., 1995—; pres., bd. dirs. Am. Meml. Hosp., Reims, France; bd. dirs. Family Found., N.Am., 1993—, Grimes-King Found. for the Elderly, Inc.; v.p., treas. Frederick E. Weber Charities Corp. Mem. Boston Soc. Security Analysts, Harvard U. Alumni Assn. (1st v.p. 1996—, Harvard Alumni Assn. award 1995), Boston Econ. Club, Comml. Club. Home: 975 Memorial Dr Cambridge MA 02138-5753 Office: Fiduciary Trust Co 175 Federal St Boston MA 02110-2210

PHILLIPS, DANIEL MILLER, lawyer; b. Cleve., Mar. 21, 1933; s. Clovis H. and Lillian (Miller) P.; m. Joyce C. Hamilton, July 26, 1958; children: Meegan M., Sarah H., Anthony J. Student, Wesleyan U., Middletown, Conn., 1951-53; B.S., Ohio State U., 1958, J.D., 1961. Bar: Ohio 1961. Since practiced in Toledo; mem. firm Robison, Curphey & O'Connell, 1961-77, ptnr., 1967-77; dir. litigation Owens-Corning Fiberglas Corp., Toledo, 1977-86; spl. cons. Asbestos Claim Facility, Princeton, N.J., 1986-87, dir. adminstrn. and human resources, 1987-89, pres., 1990-92, trustee, 1985-86; cons. UNR Asbestos-Disease Claims Trust, 1991—; lectr. Ohio Legal Ctr. Inst., 1969-70, 73; pres. Found. for Practice Law in Pub. Interest, Toledo, 1976; legal rep. for unknown and future asbestos bodily injury persons Chpt. II Procs. Nat. Gypsum Co., 1992—; designated trustee Eagle-Pitcher Industries Chpt. II Procs. Pres. Toledo Florence Crittenton Services, 1971-72; mem. Lucas County Mental Health and Retardation Bd., 1975-76; trustee Toledo Legal Aid Soc., 1977-82, Community Planning Council of Northwestern Ohio, 1978-82; mem. working group on asbestos litigation Nat. Ctr. for State Cts. Jud. Adminstrn., 1982-83. Served with AUS, 1953-55. Mem. ABA, Ohio Bar Assn. (chmn. negligence law com. 1971-73, mem. ins. law com. 1974-79), Toledo Bar Assn. (exec. com. 1971-80, sec. 1974, pres. 1978-79), Toledo Jr. Bar Assn. (pres. 1970-71), Fedn. Ins. Counsel, Def. Rsch. Inst., Ohio Assn. Civil Trial Lawyers (pres. 1971-72), U.S. Jud. Conf. 6th Cir. (life). Home and Office: 2049 Delaware Dr Ann Arbor MI 48103-6014

PHILLIPS, DONALD WRIGHT, investment company executive; b. Streator, Ill., Apr. 24, 1948; s. Dale W. and Betty (Cronk) P.; m. Karen Phillips; children: David, Ryan. BA, Western Ill. U., 1970; MBA, No. Ill. U., 1974. Dir. employee benefits Beatrice Cos., Inc., Chgo., 1974-84; chief investment officer Ameritech, Chgo., 1984-90; pres. Nucorp, Inc., 1990-92; chmn. Consol. Fibres Co., 1991-93, Equity Instnl. Investors, Inc., Chgo., 1991—; exec. v.p. Equity Fin. and Mgmt. Co., Chgo., 1990—; bd. dirs. Capsure Holdings Corp. (formerly Nucorp), United Capitol Ins. Co., Sit New Beginning Mut. Fund Group, Mpls., Larimer and Co., Denver. With U.S. Army, 1970-72. Office: Equity Instnl Investors Inc 2 N Riverside Plz Ste 600 Chicago IL 60606-2609*

PHILLIPS, DOROTHY ORMES, elementary education educator; b. Denver, July 26, 1922; d. Jesse Edward and Belle (Noisette) Ormes; m. James Kermit Phillips, Apr. 28, 1945; children: William K., Dorothy E., Valerie A. BBA, Case Western Res. U., 1946, MA, 1959; PhD, U. Akron, 1989. Cert. tchr., adminstr., Ohio. Tchr. Cleve. Pub. Schs., 1955-68, math. cons., 1968-83, adminstrv. intern, 1970-73; grad. asst. U. Akron, Ohio, 1983-85, lectr. elem. edn., supr. student tchrs., 1985—; math. workshop presenter Norton (Ohio) Pub. Schs., 1986. Presenter Career Day, Cleve. Pub. Schs., 1992. Grantee NDEA, 1960, NSF, 1966. Mem. ASCD, Nat. Coun. Tchrs. Math., Ednl. Computer Consortium Ohio, Cleve. Pub. Schs. Math. Cons. (assoc.), Alpha Kappa Alpha, Pi Lambda Theta. Avocations: swimming, camping, reading. Home: 8746 Crackel Rd Chagrin Falls OH 44023-1807

PHILLIPS, EARL NORFLEET, JR., financial services executive; b. High Point, N.C., May 5, 1940; s. Earl Norfleet Phillips and Lillian Jordan; m. Sarah Boyle, Oct. 19, 1971; children: Courtney Dorsett, Jordan Norfleet. BSBA, U. N.C., 1962; MBA, Harvard U., 1965. Security analyst Wertheim & Co., N.Y.C., 1965-67; exec. v.p. Factors Inc., High Point, N.C., 1967-71, exec. v.p. First Factors Corp., High Point, 1972-81, pres., 1982—; bd. dirs. Oakdale Cotton Mills, First Union Nat. Bank N.C.; bd. dirs., sec. N.C. Enterprise Corp. Bd. dirs. Culp, Inc. Trustee U. N.C., Chapel Hill, 1983-91, chmn. bd., 1989-91, chmn. endowment bd. U. N.C., 1989-91, U. N.C. Found., 1989-91, bd. govs., 1995—; bd. dirs. N.C. Bus. Found., N.C. Citizens for Bus. and Industry; mem. N.C. Econ. Devel. Bd., Raleigh, N.C., 1984-91; mem. nat. adv. coun. SBA, 1988-91; trustee High Point Regional Hosp., Asian Inst. Tech., Bangkok, Thailand, 1993—; mem. Piedmont Triad Airport Authority. Named Young Man of Yr., High Point Jaycees, 1971; named One of Five Outstanding Young Men, N.C. Jaycees, 1971. Mem. Nat. Comml. Fin. Assn. (bd. dirs.). Clubs: The Brook (N.Y.C.), Country of N.C. (Pinehurst), Willow Creek, String and Splinter (High Point), Linville (N.C.) Golf. Lodge: Gorgons Head. Office: First Factors Corp PO Box 2730 101 S Main St High Point NC 27261-2730

PHILLIPS, EDWARD JOHN, consulting firm executive; b. Phila., Sept. 8, 1940; s. Harold E. and Mary C. P.; m. Kathleen A. Everett, July 23, 1960; children: Elizabeth J., Edward J. B of Mech. Engring., Villanova U., 1973; MBA, Widener U., 1975. Registered profl. engr., Ill., Kans., Mo., Pa., Ohio; chartered engr., U.K. Tech. ops. mgr. Motorola, Inc., Franklin Park, Ill., 1976-81; v.p. engring. Rival Mfg. Co., Kansas City, Mo., 1981-82; prin., sr. cons. Richard Muther & Assocs., Kansas City, 1982-85; chmn. KANDE, Inc., Overland Park, Kans., 1983-86; pres., CEO Sims Cons. Group Inc., Lancaster, Ohio, 1986—; chmn. bd. dirs. Sims Consulting Group, Lancaster, Ohio; bd. dirs. KANDE, Inc., Wilmington, Del. Contbr. articles to profl. jours. Mem. NSPE, ASME (chmn. material handling divsn. 1989-91, mem. internat. mgmt. com. 1977), MIMechE, Tau Beta Pi, Pi Tau Sigma. Office: Sims Cons Group Inc PO Box 968 111 N Broad St Lancaster OH 43130-0968

PHILLIPS, EDWIN CHARLES, gas transmission company executive; b. Saskatoon, Sask., Can., Oct. 19, 1917; s. Charles Henry and Beatrice Grace (Johnson) P.; m. Elizabeth Winnifred Johnston, June 27, 1942; children: Diane, Carol, Glen, Earl, Jane, Sue. Student, Lethbridge Collegiate Inst., 1931-35. Asst. buyer Loblaw Groceries Co. Ltd., Toronto, 1938-42; advt. mgr. Can. and Dominion Sugar Co., Chatham, Ont., 1945-47; asst. to gen. mgr. Consumers Gas Co., Toronto, 1947-52; with Trane Co. Can., Ltd., 1952-68, exec. v.p., gen. mgr., 1964-65, pres., 1966-68; group v.p. Westcoast Energy Inc., Vancouver, 1968-70, exec. v.p., 1971-72, pres., 1972-82, chief exec. officer, 1976-83, chmn. bd., 1980-83, also dir.; dir. emeritus, 1989; bd. dirs. Balaclava Enterprises Ltd., Cheni Resources, Inc., Cambridge Resources Ltd., Future Shop Ltd., Pe Ben Oilfield Svcs. Ltd., Weiser Inc. Served with RCAF, World War II. Home: 4458 W 2nd Ave, Vancouver, BC Canada V6R 1K5 also: 5125 C Renaissance Ave San Diego CA 92122-5575

PHILLIPS, ELIZABETH JOAN, marketing executive; b. Cleve., July 8, 1938; d. Joseph Tinl and Helen Walter; m. Erwin Phillips, June 1956 (div. 1960); 1 child, Michael A. B.A., Fordham U., 1980. Account exec. David Cogan Mgmt., N.Y.C., 1969-77; account exec. N.F.L. Films, N.Y.C., 1977-78; mgr. sports programs Avon Products, N.Y.C., 1978-83; v.p. Needham, Harper & Steers (now Needham, Harper Worldwide), N.Y.C., 1983-86; v.p. Ted Bates Event Mktg., N.Y.C., 1986-87; pres. Custom Event Mktg. 1987—. adj. prof. NYU, N.Y.C., 1987—. Mem. exec. com. Vanderbilt YMCA,

N.Y.C., 1976-84; ofcl. 1984 Olympic Games, L.A.; referee Women's Olympic Marathon, L.A., 1984; pres. Met. Athletics Congress, N.Y.C., 1980-83. Mem. Women's Sports Found. (bd. advisors 1983—), N.Y. Road Runners Club (v.p., mem. exec. com. 1976—, pres. 1970—, bd. dirs. 1992—), Road Runners Club of Am. (bd. dirs. 1992—). Office: Custom Event Mktg Inc 19 W 44th St Ste 1506 New York NY 10036

PHILLIPS, ELLIOTT HUNTER, lawyer; b. Birmingham, Mich., Feb. 14, 1919; s. Frank Elliott and Gertrude (Zacharias) P.; m. Gail Carolyn Isbey, Apr. 22, 1950; children—Elliott Hunter, Alexandra. A.B. cum laude, Harvard U., 1940, J.D., 1947. Bar: Mich. 1948. Since practiced in Detroit; ptnr. Hill Lewis (formerly Hill, Lewis, Adams, Goodrich & Tait), 1953-89, of counsel, 1989-96; of counsel Clark Hill, 1996—; chmn. bd. dirs. Detroit & Can. Tunnel Corp.; pres., dir. Detroit and Windsor Subway Co.; mem. Mich. Bd. Accountancy, 1965-73. Contbr. to legal and accounting jours. Chmn. bd. dirs. Southeastern Mich. chpt. ARC; pres., trustee McGregor Fund; trustee Boys Republic, Detroit Inst. for Children, United Way Southeastern Mich., Univ. Liggett Sch.; mem. nat. maj. gifts com. Harvard U., Harvard Pres.'s Assocs., 1974—; Pres.'s Coun., 1990, mem. overseers com. to visit Law Sch., overseers com. unbiv. resouces, Mich. chmn. Harvard Coll. Fund; trustee, pres. Ch. Youth Svc.; mem. Detroit Area coun. Boy Scouts Am. Lt. comdr. USNR, 1946. Recipient Spitzley award Detroit Inst. for Children, 1986, Harvard Alumni Assn. Disting. Svc. award, 1991. Fellow Mich. State Bar Found. (life), Am. Bar Found. (life); mem. ABA, State Bar Mich., Detroit Bar Assn., Lincoln's Inn Soc., Soc. Colonial Wars in Mich. and Fla., Country Club Detroit, Detroit Club (pres. 1988-89), Yondotega Club, Leland Country Club, Grosse Pointe Club, Harvard Ea. Mich. Club (pres. 1955-56, Disting. Alumnus award 1992), Harvard Club N.Y.C., John's Island Club. Episcopalian (vestryman, sr. warden). Home: 193 Ridge Rd Grosse Pointe MI 48236-3554 Office: 333 W Fort St Detroit MI 48226-3134

PHILLIPS, ELLIS LAURIMORE, JR., foundation executive; b. N.Y.C., Feb. 26, 1921; s. Ellis Laurimore and Kathryn (Sisson) P.; m. Marion Grumman, June 13, 1942; children: Valerie Phillips Parsegian, Elise Phillips Watts, Ellis Laurimore III, Kathryn Noel Phillips Zimmermann, Cynthia. AB, Princeton U., 1942; LLB, Columbia U., 1948; LLD, Keuka Coll., N.Y., 1956; LLD (hon.), Adelphi U., 1979; LL.D. (hon.), L.I. U., 1980, Ithaca Coll., 1986. Bar: N.Y. 1948. With firm Burke & Burke, N.Y.C., 1948-53; mem. staff Pres.'s Com. Internat. Info. Activities, 1953; asst. dean Columbia Sch. Law, 1953-61, assoc. prof. law, 1953-56, prof., 1956-70, dir. univ. budget, 1961-64; pres. Ithaca (N.Y.) Coll., 1970-75; spl. asst. to U.S. amb. to Eng. Ct. St. James, 1957-58. Author: (with others) Cases and Materials in Accounting for Lawyers, 1964, The Legal Profession, 1970, Information Services for Academic Administration, 1971, Look Back from Forty, 1967, A New Approach to Academic Administration, 1969, Accounting and the Law: Cases and Materials, 1978. Pres. Bd. Edn. Union Free Sch. Dist. 15, Jericho, L.I., 1950-53, Ellis L. Phillips Found., 1959-93, v.p., 1993—; pres. Action Com. for L.I., Inc., 1978-81; trustee Inc. Village Brookville, L.I., 1958-64, Bangor Theol. Sem. With AUS, USAF, 1942-45. Republican. Home: 1855 Bay Rd # 302 Vero Beach FL 32963

PHILLIPS, ETHEL C. (MRS. LLOYD J. PHILLIPS), writer; b. N.Y.C.; d. Henry and Minnie (Hirshfeld) Cohen; m. Lloyd Jay Phillips, 1930; children: Lloyd James, Anne. B.A., Vassar Coll.; M.A. in Pub. Law, Columbia U. Publs. dir. Am. Jewish Com., Inst. Human Relations, N.Y.C., 1939-65; bd. dirs., mem. exec. com. Nat. Charities Info. Bur., N.Y.C., 1966-90, vice-chmn., 1982-90. Author: Mind Your World, 1964, Record and the Vision, 1965, You in Human Rights, 1968; also pamphlets and media features on civil rights, internat. cooperation, human rights, volunteerism. Mem. N.Y. Soc. for Ethical Culture (trustee 1977-83), Nat. Coun. Women U.S. (pres. 1972-74, hon. pres. 1974-76, UN rep. 1976—), Vassar Club (N.Y.C.), Harvard Club (N.Y.C.), Harvard Club of N.Y. Clubs: Vassar (N.Y.C.), Women's City (N.Y.C.). Home: 201 E 69th St Apt 15G New York NY 10021-5465

PHILLIPS, EUAN HYWEL, publishing executive; b. Chipstead, Surrey, Eng., Mar. 31, 1928; s. Edgar Aneurin and Elsie Llewella (Davies) P.; m. Margaret June Savage, June 12, 1954; children: David John, Janet Margaret. B.A., Emmanuel Coll., Cambridge, Eng., 1949, M.A., 1965. Cost acct. J. Lyons & Co. Ltd., London, 1950-53; dispatch mgr. Pickerings Produce Canners Ltd., Manchester, Eng., 1953-56; mgmt. cons. P.A. Mgmt. Cons. Ltd., London, 1956-65; mng. dir. Unwin Bros. Ltd., Old Woking, Eng., 1965-73; univ. printer designate Cambridge (Eng.) U. Press, 1973-74, univ. printer, 1974-76; dir. Cambridge (Eng.) U. Press (Am. br.), N.Y.C., 1977-82; owner New Canaan Bibles and Manx Knitwear, Stamford, Conn., 1982-87; exec. dir. Assn. Am. Univ. Presses, 1987-90; gov. Guildford Sch. Art, 1966-69, Cambridge Coll. Arts and Tech., 1974-76; dir. East Asian History of Sci., Inc., 1978-81. Contbr. Scholarly Pub. Served with Royal Navy, 1946-48. Mem. Brit. Printing Industries Fedn. (mem. coun. 1966-73, pres. Home Counties Alliance 1970-71), Troupers Light Opera Co. Home: 289 Connestee Trl Brevard NC 28712-9009

PHILLIPS, FRANCES MARIE, history educator; b. Hale Center, Tex., Nov. 8, 1918; d. Clyde C. and Ada (Stutzman) P. B.A., West Tex. State Coll., 1940, M.A., 1946; Ph.D. (Univ. fellow), U. N.Mex., 1956; postgrad. (Fulbright scholar), U. London, 1954-55. Tchr. public schs. Channing, Tex., Miami, Tex., Palisade, Colo., Tucumcari, N.Mex., 1940-46; supr. State Tchrs. Coll. Campus High Sch., Wayne, Nebr., 1947-51; instr. U. Md. Overseas Program, Eng., 1955; grad. asst. U. N.Mex., 1955-56; asst., assoc. prof. history Sul Ross State Coll., Alpine, Tex., 1956-60; prof. history, dean grad. div. Sul Ross State Coll., 1962-71; program dir. sr. colls. Coordinating Bd. Tex. Coll. and Univ. System, Austin, 1971-85; asst. prof. Mankato (Minn.) State Coll., 1960-62; lectr. Lifetime Learning Ins. of Austin, 1994—. Editor: Dear Mother and Folks at Home: Iowa Farm to Clermont-Ferrand, 1917-1918, 1988. Chmn. bd. Carlsbad dist. Wesley Found., 1962-66; mem. Adv. Council for Ednl. Personnel Devel., 1972—, State Bd. Examiners for Tchr. Edn., 1972-79, Tex. Com. on Early Childhood Devel. Careers, 1976—. Mem. AAUW, N.Mex. Hist. Soc., Am. Assn. Higher Edn., Assn. Tex. Grad. Schs. (v.p. 1967-69, pres. 1969-70), Alpha Chi, Phi Kappa Phi, Phi Alpha Theta, Delta Kappa Gamma. Democrat. Methodist (past mem. N.Mex. Conf. Bd. Edn., mem. ofcl. bd.). Research in Anglo-Am. relations, 1954-56, 1962. Home: 8700 Millway Dr Austin TX 78757-6832

PHILLIPS, FREDERICK FALLEY, architect; b. Evanston, Ill., June 18, 1946; s. David Cook and Katharine Edith (Falley) P.; m. Gay Fraker, Feb. 26, 1983 (div. Dec. 1993). BA, Lake Forest Coll., 1969; MArch, U. Pa., 1973. Registered architect, Ill., Wis. Draftsman, Harry Weese & Assocs., 1974, 75; pvt. practice architecture Frederick F. Phillips, Architect, Chgo., 1976-81; pres. Frederick Phillips and Assocs., Chgo., 1981—. Bd. dirs. Landmarks Preservation Coun., 1981-85, Chgo. Acad. Sci., 1988—, Friends of Ceuros de Escazu, Costa Rica, 1992—; mem. aux. bd. Chgo. Architecture Found., 1975-89; chmn. Task Group on Manufactured Housing, AIA Nat. Com. on Design, 1994—. Recipient award Townhouse for Logan Square Competition, AIA and Econ. Redevel. Corp. Logan Square, 1980, Gold medal award Willow St. Houses, Ill. Ind. Masonry Coun., 1981, Silver award for pvt. residence, 1989, Gold medal award for private residence Archtl. Record, 1994, Three Record Houses awards Archtl. Record, 1990, 95, award 2d Compact House Design Competition, 1990, award of exellence for pvt. residence AIA/Nat. Concrete Masonry Assn., 1992, award for pvt. residence Am. Wood Coun., 1993, Honorable mention-Best in Am. Living award Profl. Builders Mag., 1995, Jury's Choice award for pvt. residence Chgo. Athenaeum, 1996 . Fellow AIA (Disting. Bldg. award for Willow St. Houses, Chgo. chpt. 1982, for Pinewood Farm 1983, for Pvt. Residences 1990, 92); mem. Chgo. Archtl. Club, Racquet Club (bd. govs. 1983-89), Arts Club, Cliff Dwellers Club (bd. govs. 1985-88). Office: Frederick F Phillips & Assocs 53 W Jackson Blvd Ste 1752 Chicago IL 60604-3705

PHILLIPS, GABRIEL, travel marketing executive; b. North Vandergrift, Pa., Aug. 3, 1933; s. Samuel and Margaret (Solomon) P.; m. Margaret Mednis, Sept. 5, 1965 (div. 1970). BS, U. Md., 1956; JD, George Washington U., 1962. Various positions CAB, Washington, 1956-66; dir. internat. programs Air Transport Assn., Washington, 1966-69, exec. sec. fin. and acctg., 1970, v.p. internat. programs, 1970-76, v.p. traffic svcs., 1976-79, sr. v.p. industry svcs., 1979-86, exec. v.p., 1986-91, acting pres., 1988-89, ret., 1991; chmn. Holiday Mktg. Inc., Herndon, Va., 1991—; bd. dirs. Phillips Corp., Columbia, Md. Contbr. articles to profl. jours. Bd. dirs. Nat. Alliance of Sr. Citizens. With U.S. Army, 1956-58. Mem. Travel Industry Assn. Am. (bd. dirs., nat. chmn. 1985-86), Nat. Assn. Arab Ams. (bd. dirs., treas. 1985—, pres. 1990-92). Republican. Roman Catholic.

PHILLIPS, GAIL, state legislator; b. Juneau, Alaska; m. Walt Phillips; children: Robin, Kim. BA in Bus. Edn., U. Alaska. Mem. Homer (Alaska) City Coun., 1981-84, Kenai Peninsula Borough Assembly, 1986-87; chmn. legis. com. Alaska Mcpl. League; mem. Alaska Ho. of Reps., 1990, 92, 94, house majority leader, 1993-94, speaker, 1995—; owner, mgr. Quiet Sporting Goods; ptnr. Lindphil Mining Co.; pub. rels. cons. Active Homer United Meth. Ch., Rep. Ctrl. Com. Alaska, Kenai Peninsula Coll. Coun.; past mem. com. bd. and race coord. Iditarod Trail Dog Sled Race. Mem. Western States Legis. Coun. (exec. com.), Am. Legis. Exch. Coun. (state chmn.), Resource Devel. Coun. Alaska, Western Legis. Conf. (exec. bd.), Western States Coalition (co-founder), The Energy Coun. Home: PO Box 3304 Homer AK 99603-3304 Office: 126 W Pioneer Ave Homer AK 99603-7564 also: Alaska House of Reps State Capitol Juneau AK 99801-1182

PHILLIPS, GENEVA FICKER, editor; b. Staunton, Ill., Aug. 1, 1920; d. Arthur Edwin and Lillian Agnes (Woods) Ficker; m. James Emerson Phillips, Jr., June 6, 1955 (dec. 1979). B.S. in Journalism, U. Ill., 1942; M.A. in English Lit., UCLA, 1953. Copy desk Chgo. Jour. Commerce, 1942-43; editorial asst. patents Radio Research Lab., Harvard U., Cambridge, Mass., 1943-45; asst. editor adminstrv. publs. U. Ill., Urbana, 1946-47; editorial asst. Quar. of Film, Radio and TV, UCLA, 1952-53; mng. editor The Works of John Dryden, Dept. English, UCLA, 1964—. Bd. dirs. Univ. Religious Conf., Los Angeles, 1979—. UCLA teaching fellow, 1950-53, grad. fellow 1954-55. Mem. Assn. Acad. Women UCLA, Dean's Coun., Coll. Letters and Scis. UCLA, Friends of Huntington Library, Friends of UCLA Library, Friends of Ctr. for Medieval and Renaissance Studies, Samuel Johnson Soc. of So. Calif., Assocs. of U. Calif. Press., Conf. Christianity and Lit., Soc. Mayflower Descs. Lutheran. Home: 213 1st Anita Dr Los Angeles CA 90049-3815 Office: UCLA Dept English 2225 Rolfe Hall Los Angeles CA 90024

PHILLIPS, GEORGE LANDON, prosecutor; b. Fulton, Miss., May 24, 1949; s. Gilbert L. and Grace (Staker) P. BS, U. So. Miss., 1971; JD, U. Miss., 1973. Bar: Miss. 1973. Assoc. Johnson, Pittman & Pittman, Hattiesburg, Miss., 1980-94; ptnr. Norris & Phillips, 1975-76; county pros. atty. Forrest County, Miss., 1976-80; U.S. atty. So. Dist. Miss., Jackson, Miss., 1980-94; chmn. investigative agys. subcom. U.S. Atty. Gen.'s Adv. Com., 1983-86, mem. law enforcement coordination subcom. and budget subcom., 1986-88; spl. coun. U.S. Senator T. Cochran, 1995—; chmn. AGAC subcom. law enforcement cooperation and victim/witness assistance, 1989-94; instr. Hattiesburg Police Acad., 1977. Bd. dirs. Forrest County Youth Ct.; pres. South Ctrl. chpt. ARC, 1980-81; bd. dirs. Pine Burr Area coun. Boy Scouts Am.; mem. Atty. Gen.'s Adv. Com., 1981-82, 89-91; bd. dirs. Jackson Zoo, 1989-91. Mem. Miss. Prosecutors Assn. (pres.), Fed. Bar Assn., Miss. Bar Assn. (v.p. southern region), Am. Criminal Justice Assn., Nat. Dist. Attys. Assn., Miss. Trial Lawyers, Miss. Quarter Horse Assn. (pres.), Kiwanis. Baptist. Office: Spl Counsel Office of US Sen T Cochran 188 E Capital Ste 614 Jackson MS 39201-2125

PHILLIPS, GEORGE MICHAEL, food manufacturing company executive; b. New Kensington, Pa., Nov. 6, 1947; s. Samuel and Margaret (Solomon) P.; m. Juliana Marie Orkwis, Nov. 8, 1969; children: Christopher Michael, Kimberly Ann, Jill Michelle. BS in Acctg., U. Md., 1969; MBA, Suffolk U., 1973. Cert. investment adviser. Cost analyst Polaroid Corp., Cambridge, Mass., 1969-73; mgr. fin. analysis Clorox Co., Oakland, Calif., 1973-75; pres., chief operating officer, dir. Acton (Mass.) Corp., 1975-85; chmn., chief exec. officer W.P. Ihrie and Sons, Inc., 1983-92, Chimill Corp., 1983—, Condor Corp., 1985—, Vesper Corp., 1988—. Bd. vis. U. Md. Served with U.S. Army, 1969-70. Republican. Roman Catholic. Club: Pres.'s U. Md.

PHILLIPS, GERALD BAER, internal medicine educator, scientist; b. Bethlehem, Pa., Mar. 20, 1925; s. Abel H. and Cecilia (Blum) P.; m. Maria Bonzi Lewis, July 15, 1970; children: Abigail, Elizabeth. AB, Princeton U., 1948; MD, Harvard U., 1948. Diplomate Am. Bd. Internal Medicine. Intern Presbyn. Hosp., N.Y.C., 1948-50; rsch. fellow Thorndike Meml. Lab., Med. Sch. Harvard U., Boston, 1950-53; vis. fellow biochemistry Columbia U. Coll. Physicians and Surgeons, N.Y.C., 1954-56, from assoc. in medicine to assoc. prof., 1956-73, prof., 1973—; sr. attending physician Roosevelt Hosp.; attending physician Presbyn. Hosp. Sr. asst. surgeon USPHS, 1952-54. Recipient Lederle Med. Faculty award, 1963-66. Mem. Am. Fedn. for Clin. Rsch., Am. Soc. for Clin. Investigation, Am. Soc. for Biochemistry and Molecular Biology, Alpha Omega Alpha. Home: 196 E 75th St New York NY 10021-3257 Office: 428 W 59th St New York NY 10019-1105 *I attribute any success I may have had to heredity and luck.*

PHILLIPS, GLYNDA ANN, editor; b. Riverside, Calif.; d. Henry Grady and Patricia (Loflin) P. BA in English, Millsaps Coll., 1977; postgrad., Miss. Coll. News editor The Magee (Miss.) Courier, 1981-84; editor Miss. Farm Bur. Country and Miss. Farm Bur. Producer Edition, Jackson, 1984—. Contbr. articles to profl. jours. Recipient first place personal column Nat. Fedn. Press Women, 1984, first place personal column Miss. Press Women's Assn., 1984, first place feature articles Miss. Press Women's Assn., 1984. Mem. Soc. Profl. Journalists. Avocation: church organist.

PHILLIPS, GRAHAM HOLMES, retired advertising executive; b. London, Jan. 30, 1939; emigrated to U.S., 1965, naturalized, 1974; s. Leonard George and Mary Marjorie (Holmes) P.; m. Laurel Gilbert; 1 child, Debra Ann. Student, RAF Coll. Cranwell, 1957-58; M.B.A., London U., 1962. Mgmt. trainee Shell Internat. Petroleum, Ltd., London, 1957-59; aviation sales rep., 1960-63; aviation sales mgr. Shell Philippines, 1964; with Ogilvy & Mather (U.S.), N.Y.C., 1965—, account mgr., 1965-73; dep. mgr., account supr. Ogilvy & Mather (U.S.), Houston, 1970, v.p., 1971-72, sr. v.p., mgmt. supr., 1972-73; mng. dir. Ogilvy & Mather Inc., Amsterdam, 1973-75; former pres., then chief exec. officer Ogilvy & Mather (Can.) Ltd., Toronto, from 1975, former chmn., from 1979; dir. Ogilvy & Mather, 1978—; former chief fin. officer Ogilvy & Mather Internat., from 1983; former exec. v.p. Ogilvy & Mather (U.S.), N.Y.C., from 1979, former gen. mgr., from 1980, former mng. dir., chief fin. officer, from 1981; former chmn., CEO Ogilvy & Mather Worldwide. Episcopalian. Office: Ogilvy & Mather Worldwide Inc Worldwide Plz 309 W 49th St # 12 New York NY 10019-7316

PHILLIPS, GRETCHEN, clinical social worker; b. Erie, Pa., July 14, 1941; life ptnr. Beverly Campbell, June 10, 1989. BA, Mercyhurst Coll., 1966; MSW, Yeshiva U., 1972; postgrad., Advanced Ctr. Psychotherapy, 1972-73, Washington Sq. Inst., 1973-77. Bd. cert. diplomate clin. social work; cert. social worker, N.Y. Psychiat. social worker, forensic social worker Creedmoor Psychiat. Ctr., Queens Village, N.Y., 1972-80; Med. social worker Bellevue Hosp. Ctr., N.Y.C., 1980-83; intake probation officer N.Y.C. Probation, Family Court, Bklyn., 1983—. Mem. NASW, Am. Group Psychotherapy Assn., Internat. Soc. Traumatic Stress Studies. Home: 125 Radford St # 3C Yonkers NY 10705-3049 Office: Probation Intake Kings Family Ct 283 Adams St Brooklyn NY 11201-2898

PHILLIPS, HARVEY, musician, music educator, arts consultant; b. Aurora, Mo., Dec. 2, 1929; s. Jesse E. and Lottie A. (Chapman) P.; m. Carol A. Dorvel, Feb. 22, 1954; children: Jesse E., Harvey G., Thomas A. Student, U. Mo., 1947-48, Juilliard Sch. Music, 1950-54, Manhattan Sch. Music, 1956-58; Mus.D. (hon.), New Eng. Conservatory of Music, 1971; HHD (hon.), U. Mo., Columbia, 1987. Founder, v.p. Mentor Music, Inc., N.Y.C., 1958-79; v.p. Wilder Music, Inc., N.Y.C., 1964-77, Magellan Music, Inc., N.Y.C., 1971—, Peaslee Music Inc., 1971—; mem. faculty Aspen Sch. Music, summer 1962, U. Wis., summer 1963, Hartt Sch. Music, Hartford, Conn., 1962-64, Mannes Sch. Music, N.Y.C., 1964-65; exec. v.p. Orchestra USA, N.Y.C., 1962-65; exec. v.p., personnel mgr., tubist Symphony of the Air N.Y.C., 1957-66; v.p. Brass Artists, Inc., N.Y.C., 1964—; adminstrv. asst. to Julius Bloom, Rutgers U., New Brunswick, N.J., 1966-67; v.p. fin. affairs New Eng. Conservatory of Music, Boston, 1967-71; mem. faculty dept. music Ind. U., Bloomington, 1971-94; disting. prof. music, trustee, 1979; disting. prof. emeritus Ind. U., Bloomington, 1994; adv. bd. Am. Brass Chamber Music, Inc., 1971—; chmn. bd. Summit Brass/Keystone Brass Inst., 1986-92, Rafael Mendez Brass Inst., 1993—; cons. Margun Music, Inc., 1977—. Brass coach Festival at Sandpoint, Idaho, 1986-94; mem. faculty Joven Orch., Spain, Festival Casal Orch., San Juan, P.R., 1964-76; dir. 1st Internat. Tuba Symposium Workshop, 1973, Brass-Wind Music Studios, Carnegie Hall, N.Y.C., 1961-67; tubist, King Bros. Circus Band, 1947, Ringling Bros. & Barnum & Bailey Circus Band, 1948-50, N.Y.C. Ballet Orch., 1951-71, N.Y.C. Opera Orch., 1951-62, Voice of Firestone Orch., 1951-53, Sauter-Finegan Orch., 1952-53, Band of Am., 1952-54, NBC Opera Orch., 1956-65, Bell Tel. Hour Orch., 1956-66, Goldman Band, 1957-62; founding mem., tubist N.Y. Brass Quintet, 1954-67; condr., co-prodr. Burke-Phillips All Star Concert Band, 1960-62; co-founder, tubist Matteson-Phillips Tubajazz Consort, 1976—; founding mem. TubaShop Quartet, 1996—; rec. artist Crest Records, 1958—; originator Octubafest, TubaChristmas, Tubasantas, Tuba Jazz, Tubaeaster; exec. editor Instrumentalist mag. Founder, pres. Harvey Phillips Found., Inc., N.Y.C., 1977—; bd. dirs. Mid-Am. Festival of the Arts, 1982—, Bloomington Area Arts Coun., 1983—; judge 1st Internat. tuba competition of CIEM Internat. Competition for Musical Performers, Geneva, 1991. Served with U.S. Army Field Band, 1955-56. Recipient Disting. Svc. to Music award Kappa Kappa Psi, 1978, Cmty. Svc. award City of Bloomington, 1978, Nat. Assn. Jazz Educators award, 1977, 78, Nat. Music Conf. award, 1977, T.U.B.A. award, 1978, MI Hummel The Tuba Player award, 1990, Disting. Achievement award Ednl. Press Assn. Am., 1991, Mentor Ideal award Assn. Concert Bands, 1994, Lifetime Achievement award United Music Instruments, 1995, Sudler award medal of the Order of Merit Sousa Found., 1995, Summit Brass Outstanding Svc. and Support Internat. Brassfest, 1995; elected to Acad. Wind and Percussion Arts Nat. Band Assn., 1995; Harvey Phillips Day proclaimed New Eng. Conservatory Music, 1971, Edwin Franko Goldman citation Am. Bandmasters Assn., 1996; Harvey Phillips Day proclaimed Marionville, Mo. Bicentennial, 1976. Mem. Am. Fedn. Musicians, Tubists Universal Brotherhood Assn. (bd. advs. 1973—, pres. 1984-87, hon.), Hoagy Carmichael Jazz Soc. (founder, acting pres. 1983—), Tau Beta Sigma, Phi Mu Alpha Sinfonia, Kappa Gamma Psi. Home and Office: Tubaranch 4769 S Harrell Rd Bloomington IN 47401-9028 Office: Sch of Music Ind U Bloomington IN 47405 *The role of a performer and teacher is to give, to share skills and knowledge. My primary goal in life is to create new opportunities in the music profession, to develop, expand, and preserve the music arts.*

PHILLIPS, HOWARD WILLIAM, investment banker; b. N.Y.C., May 16, 1930; s. Louis and Helen (Klein) P.; children: Jan Davis, Richard Louis; m. Carol Napack, June 9, 1985. B.A., Dartmouth Coll., 1951, M.B.A., 1952; J.D., Harvard U., 1957. Bar: N.Y. 1957. Asso. Cahill, Gordon, Reindel & Ohl, N.Y.C., 1957-64; v.p., gen. counsel McCall Corp., N.Y.C., 1964-68; sr. v.p. McCall Corp., 1968-69; partner Oppenheimer & Co., N.Y.C., 1969-81; chmn. Holmes, Phillips & Co., N.Y.C., 1981-83; dir. corp. fin. D.H. Blair & Co., Inc., 1983—; bd. dirs. Monaco Fin., Denver, Food Ct. Entertainment Network, Inc., N.Y.C., Telechips Corp., Reno. Served to lt. (j.g.) USNR, 1952-54. Mem. Easthampton (N.Y.) Tennis Club, Longboat Key Club (Sarasota, Fla.). Home: 885 Park Ave New York NY 10021-0325 Office: 435 L'Ambiance Dr Longboat Key FL 34228

PHILLIPS, JACK CARTER, educational administrator; b. Scottsboro, Ala., Jan. 27, 1935; s. Howard E. and Marie (Carter) P.; m. Frances Juanita Fortham, May 17, 1967; 1 dau., Annette. A.B., Birmingham So. Coll., 1960; M.Div., Vanderbilt U., 1963; LL.D., Union Coll. Ky., 1981. Dir. ch. relations Birmingham So. Coll., Ala., 1968-70, Fla. So. Coll., Lakeland, 1970-73; asst. to pres. U. Ala., Huntsville, 1973-75; exec. dir. Marshall U. Found., Huntington, W.Va., 1975-77; pres. Nat. Methodist Found., Nashville, 1977-83, Union Coll., Barbourville, Ky., 1983—; dir. funding Bach Festival, Carmel, Calif., 1977-82; mem. estate planning commn. Vanderbilt U. Sch. Religion, Nashville, 1980—; cons., pres. J. Phillips & Assocs., Nashville, 1981—. Author: National TV Presence Program and Ministry for United Methodist Church, 1980. Served with USMC, 1954-57. Apptd. Ambassador of Goodwill Gov. of Ky., 1983; apptd. hon. Ky. Col., 1983. Mem. Council for Support Edn., C. of C. Republican. Clubs: Lafayette (Lexington, Ky.); Richland Country (Nashville). Lodges: Rotary; Kiwanis. Office: Union College Office of Pres Barbourville KY 40906

PHILLIPS, JAMES CHARLES, physicist, educator; b. New Orleans, Mar. 9, 1933; s. William D. and Juanita (Hahn) P.; m. Joanna Vandenberg, July 4, 1993. B.A., U. Chgo., 1952, B.S., 1953, M.S., 1955, Ph.D., 1956. Mem. tech. staff Bell Labs., 1956-58; NSF fellow U. Calif. at Berkeley, 1958-59, Cambridge (Eng.) U., 1959-60; faculty U. Chgo., 1960-68, prof. physics, 1965-68; mem. tech. staff Bell Labs., 1968—. Sloan fellow, 1962-66; Guggenheim fellow, 1967. Fellow Am. Phys. Soc. (Buckley prize 1972), Minerals, Metals and Materials Soc. (William Hume-Rothery award 1992); mem. NAS. Home: 204 Springfield Ave Summit NJ 07901-3909

PHILLIPS, JAMES D., retired diplomat; b. Peoria, Ill., Feb. 23, 1933; s. James D. and Ehila (Hardy) P.; m. Rosemary Leeds, Mar. 30, 1957 (div. Dec. 1981); children: Michael, Madolyn, Catherine; m. Lucie Gallistel, Jan. 7, 1984; stepchildren: Charles, David. B.A., Wichita State U., 1956, M.A., 1957; cert., U. Vienna, Austria, 1956; postgrad., Cornell U., 1958-61. Joined fgn. svc. Dept. State, 1961; served at Am. embassy Paris, before 1975; Am. Consulate Zaire, before 1975; Dept. State Washington, before 1975; dep. chief of mission Am. Embassy, Luxembourg, 1975-78; charge d'affaires Am. Embassy, Banjul, The Gambia, 1978-80; student Nat. War Coll., Washington, 1980-81; office dir. Dept. State, Washington, 1981-84; consul gen. Am. Consulate, Casablanca, Morocco, 1984-86; U.S. amb. to Burundi, 1986-90; U.S. amb. Republic of the Congo, 1990-93; diplomat in residence The Carter Ctr., Atlanta, 1993-94; ret., 1994; pres. Dan Phillips & Assocs., Arlington, Va., 1994—; bd. dirs. Gulf Resources, H.M. Salaam Found.; pres. Ctrl. Africa Found. Contbr. articles to Fgn. Svc. Jour. Bd. dirs. Jane Goodall Inst., 1994—. Avocations: golf; tennis; skiing. Home: 3607 Military Rd Arlington VA 22207-4829 Office: 1101 30th St NW Ste 200 Washington DC 20007

PHILLIPS, JAMES DICKSON, JR., federal judge; b. Scotland County, N.C., Sept. 23, 1922; s. James Dickson and Helen (Shepherd) P.; m. Jean Duff Nunalee, July 16, 1960; children: Evelyn, James Dickson, III, Elizabeth Duff, Ida Wills. BS cum laude, Davidson Coll., 1943; JD, U. N.C., 1948. Bar: N.C. 1948. Asst. dir. Inst. Govt., Chapel Hill, N.C., 1948-49; ptnr. firm Phillips & McCoy, Laurinburg, N.C., 1949-55, Sanford, Phillips, McCoy & Weaver, Fayetteville, N.C., 1955-60; from asst. prof. to prof. law U. N.C., 1960-78, dean Sch. Law, 1964-74; circuit judge U.S. Ct. Appeals (4th cir.), 1978—; Mem. N.C. Wildlife Resources Commn., 1961-63; mem. N.C. Cts. Commn., 1963-75; also vice chmn.; chmn. N.C. Bd. Ethics, 1977-78. Served with parachute inf. U.S. Army, 1943-46. Decorated Bronze Arrowhead, Bronze Star, Purple Heart; recipient John J. Parker Meml. award, Thomas Jefferson award, Disting. Alumnus award U. N.C., 1993. Mem. Am. Law Inst. Democrat. Presbyterian.

PHILLIPS, JAMES EDGAR, lawyer; b. N.Y.C., Aug. 30, 1947; s. Jack Louis Phillips and Jacqueline (Kasper) Ehrman; children: Zachary J., Mark H. BA, Boston U., 1971; JD, Case Western Reserve U., 1975. Bar: Ohio 1975, U.S. Supreme Ct. 1977, U.S. Dist. Ct. (so. dist.) 1978, U.S. Ct. Appeals (6th cir.) 1981, U.S. Dist. Ct. (no. dist.) 1982. Asst. prosecutor Franklin County Prosecutor Office, Columbus, Ohio, 1975-77; sr. asst. prosecutor Franklin County Prosecutor Office, Columbus, 1977-79; assoc. Vorys, Sater, Seymour & Pease, Columbus, 1979-84, ptnr., 1984—; spl. prosecutor State of Ohio, 1993—; gen. counsel Nat. Fraternal Order of Police, Washington, 1987—, Conrail Police #1, U.S. Postal Police #2; mem. Bd. Profl. Law Enforcement Certification; pres. Ohio Ctr. for Law-Related Edn., 1985-95. Author: Civil Recovery in Ohio, 1986, Collective Bargaining in the Pub. Sector, 1988; editor Bar Briefs; contbr. articles Jours., 1987-89. Fellow Ohio Bar Found., Columbus Bar Found., Ohio Bar Assn. (chmn. com. law-related edn. 1982-86), Columbus Bar Assn., Am. Judicature Soc., Sixth Cir. Jud. Conf. (life). Office: Vorys Sater Seymour & Pease PO Box 1008 52 E Gay St Columbus OH 43215-3161

PHILLIPS, JAMES MACILDUFF, material handling company executive, engineering and manufacturing executive; b. Carrick, Pa., June 13, 1916; s. John MacFarlane and Harriet (Duff) P.; m., Majorie Watson, June 1940 (div. 1964); children: James M. Jr., William W.; m. Regina Leininger, Apr. 1964 (dec.); children: Jeffrey M., Molly M., Becky J., Thomas S. BSME, Carnegie Inst. of Tech., 1938; grad., Pitts. Inst. Aeronautics, 1939; ME refresher, Pa. State U. State Coll., 1960; grad., Internat. Corespondence Sch., Scranton,

Pa., 1988. Profl. engr. Pa. Draftsmen, engr. Phillips Mine & Mill Supply Co., Pitts., 1933-40, v.p., 1941-77; v.p. engring. Salem Brosius, Inc., Carnegie, Pa., 1956-64; pres. Phillips Corp., Bridgeville, Pa., 1977-83, Phillips Jet Flight, Bridgeville, Pa., 1977-83, Phillips Mine & Mill Inc., Pitts., 1964—; also chmn. bd. Phillips Mine & Mill Inc. Inventor in field; contbr. articles to profl. mags. Bd. dirs. Brashear Assn., Pitts. Mem. Air Force Assn., Aero Club of Pitts., Pa. Pilots Coun. (pres.), Quiet Birdmen (pres.), Early Bird Pilots (bd. dirs.), Exptl. Aircraft Assn. Aircraft Owners and Pilots Assn. (founding), OX-5 Pioneer Airmen (pres. 1987, nat. bd. dirs. 1995), St. Clair County Club. Methodist. Avocations: airline transport pilot, flight instructor, golf, tennis. Office: Phillips Mine & Mill Inc 1738 N Highland Rd Pittsburgh PA 15241-1200

PHILLIPS, JAMES OSCAR, minister; b. Greenville, S.C., Sept. 9, 1920; s. James Henry and Ida Louise (Fortner) P.; m. Marie Burns, Jan. 31, 1943; children: Martha Phillips Henderson, Gwendolyn Phillips Mullinax, Linda Phillips Richey. Grad. bible langs., Missionary Bapt. Sem., 1948, M in bible langs., 1949, D in bible langs., 1961; DDiv (hon.), Carolina Missionary Bapt. Theol. Sem., 1959. Pastor Vilonia (Ark.) Bapt. Ch., 1946-48, Harmony Missionary Bapt. Ch., Stephens, Ark., 1948-50, Corinth Missionary Bapt. Ch., Stephens, Ark., 1948-50, East Union Missionary Bapt. Ch., Hensley, Ark., 1950-52, Glendale Bapt. Ch., Mauldin, S.C., 1952—; pres. Landmark Missionary Inst., Mauldin, 1954—. Sgt. USMC, 1942-45. Mem. Am. Bapt. Assn. (pres. 1992-94, v.p. 1990-91, mem. Bapt. Suncay Sch. com. 1955—). Office: Glendale Bapt Ch 212 E Butler Ave Mauldin SC 29662-2129

PHILLIPS, JANE BANNING, aviatrix, pilot examiner and flight instructor. BA, U. Calif., Irvine, 1972; AAS in Flight Tech., Lane C.C., Eugene, Oreg., 1988. Cert. multi-engine airline transport pilot, DC-3 Type Rating; FAA designated pilot examiner. Flight instr. Lane C.C., 1988-90; pilot McKenzie Flying Svc., Eugene, 1990-93; asst. chief flight instr. Lane C.C., 1990—; FAA pilot examiner Eugene, 1992—; guest lectr. C. of C., AAUW, sch. and ch. groups, Eugene, 1990—. ESL instr. Lane County Literacy Coun., Eugene, 1993. Amelia Earhart scholar, 1993; Santa Rosa Ninety-Nines scholar, 1987. Mem. Internat. Ninety-Nines, Willamette Valley Ninety-Nines (treas. 1990-91, chmn. 1993-94), Nat. Assn. Flight Instrs., Assn. Ind. Airmen, Airplane Operators and Pilots Assn., Exptl. Aircraft Assn. Avocations: restoration of antique airplanes, including 1941 Interstate Cadet S1A; gardening, camping, travel. Office: PO Box 40635 Eugene OR 97404-0104

PHILLIPS, JANET COLLEEN, educational association executive, editor; b. Pittsfield, Ill., Apr. 29, 1933; d. Roy Lynn and Catherine Amelia (Wills) Barker; m. David Lee Phillips, Feb 7, 1954; children—Clay Cullen, Sean Vincent. B.S., U. Ill, 1954. Reporter Quincy (Ill.) Herald Whig, 1951, 52, soc. editor, 1953; editorial asst. Pub. Info. Office U. Ill.-Urbana, 1953-54, asst. editor libr., 1954-61; asst. editor Assn. for Libr. and Info. Sci. Edn., State College, Pa., 1960-61, mng. editor, 1961-89, exec. sec., 1970-89; adminstrv. dir. Interlibr. Delivery Svc. of Pa., 1990—. Mem. AAUW, Assn. for Libr. and Info. Sci. Edn., Embroiderer's Guild Am., Pa. State Blue Course Club, Pa. State U. Women's Club, Theta Sigma Phi, Delta Zeta. Presbyterian. Avocations: travel; golf; sewing; needlecraft. Address: 471 Park Ln State College PA 16803-3208

PHILLIPS, JERRY JUAN, law educator; b. Charlotte, N.C., June 16, 1935; s. Vergil Ernest and Mary Blanche (Wade) P.; m. Anne Butler Colville, June 6, 1959; children: Sherman Wade, Dorothy Colville. B.A., Yale U., 1956, J.D., 1961; B.A., Cambridge (Eng.) U., 1958, M.A. (hon.), 1964. Bar: Tenn. bar 1961. Assoc. firm Miller, Martin, Hitching, Tipton & Lenihan, Chattanooga, 1961-67; asst. prof. law U. Tenn., 1967-72, assoc. prof., 1972-73, prof., 1973—, W.P. Toms prof., 1980—; advisor Tenn. Law Revision Commn., 1968-70; mem. Tenn. Jud. Council, 1970-74; adv. Fed. Interagy. Task Force on Products Liability, 1976-77; lectr. in field. Author: Products Liability in a Nutshell, 4th edit., 1993, Products Liability Cases and Materials on Torts and Related Law, 1980, Products Liability Treatise, 3 vols., 1986, Cases and Materials on Tort Law, 1992, Products Liability-Cases, Materials, Problems, 1994; advisor Tenn. U. Law Rev., 1977—. U. Tenn. grantee, 1978. Mem. ABA, Am. Law Inst., Knoxville Bar Assn., Am. Assn. Law Schs., Order of Coif, Phi Beta Kappa. Democrat. Episcopalian. Club: Knoxville Racquet. Office: 1505 Cumberland Ave Knoxville TN 37916-3199

PHILLIPS, JILL META, novelist, critic, astrologer; b. Detroit, Oct. 22, 1952; d. Leyson Kirk and Leona Anna (Rasmussen) P. Student pub. schs., Calif. Lit. counselor Book Builders, Charter Oak, Calif., 1966-77; pres. Moon Dance Astro Graphics, Covina, Calif., 1994—. Author: (with Leona Phillips) A Directory of American Film Scholars, 1975, The Good Morning Cookbook, 1976, G.B. Shaw: A Review of the Literature, 1976, T.E. Lawrence: Portrait of the Artist as Hero, 1977, The Archaeology of the Collective East, 1977, The Occult, 1977, D.H. Lawrence: A Review of the Literature and Biographies, 1978, Film Appreciation: A College Guide Book, 1979, Annus Mirabilis: Europe in the Dark and Middle Centuries, 1979, (with Leona Rasmussen Phillips) The Dark Frame: Occult Cinema, 1979, Misfit: The Films of Montgomery Clift, 1979, Butterflies in the Mind: A Précis of Dreams and Dreamers, 1980; The Rain Maiden: A Novel of History, 1987, Walford's Oak: A Novel, 1990, The Fate Weaver: A Novel in Two Centuries, 1991, Saturn Falls: A Novel of the Apocalypse, 1993; contbr. book revs. to New Guard mag., 1974-76; contbr. numerous articles to profl. jours. Mem. Young Ams. for Freedom, Am. Conservative Union, Elmer Bernstein's Film Music Collection, Ghost Club London, Count Dracula Soc., Dracula Soc. London, Richard III Soc. Republican. Home: 851 N Garsden Ave Covina CA 91724-2636 Office: Moon Dancer Astro Graphics 1037 N Grand Ave Ste 202 Covina CA 91724-2048

PHILLIPS, JOHN A(TLAS), III, geneticist, educator; b. Sanford, N.C., Jan. 24, 1944; s. John A. and Rachael (Sloan) P.; m. Gretchen Lynch, Aug. 1, 1965; children: Jennifer Allene, John Atlas IV, Charles Andrew, James William. Student, U. N.C., 1962-65; MD, Wake Forest U., 1969. Diplomate Am. Bd. Pediatrics, Am. Bd. Med. Genetics. Intern Children's Hosp. Med. Ctr., Boston, 1969-70, jr. resident, 1970-71, sr. resident, 1973-74, chief resident, 1974-75; asst. prof. Johns Hopkins U., Balt., 1978-82, assoc. prof., 1982-84; prof. pediatrics Vanderbilt U., Nashville, 1984—, prof. biochemistry, 1986—, David T. Karzon chair genetics, 1992—; bd. sci. counselors Nat. Inst. Child Health, Washington, 1984-88; counsilor Ctr. Study Polymorphisme Humain, Paris, 1988—; mem. adv. com. Ctr. Reproductive Biology, Nashville, 1990—; bd. dirs. March of Dimes Birth Defects Found., Nashville, 1986—; mem. adv. bd. Nat. Neurofibromatosis Found., Tenn., 1990—; mem. Tenn. Genetics Adv. Com., Nashville, 1984—. Contbr. to profl. publs. Lt. comdr. USNR, 1971-73. Recipient Sidney Farber award Children's Hosp., Boston, 1975, E Mead Johnson award Mead Johnson Co., 1984; Pediatric Postdoctoral fellow Johns Hopkins U. Sch. Medicine, 1975-77. Mem. Am. Soc. Clin. Investigation, Soc. Pediatric Rsch., Am. Coll. Med. Genetics (founding, bd. dirs. 1995—), Phi Beta Kappa, Alpha Omega Alpha. Achievements include discovery of cause of hemoglobin H disease in Black Americans, chromosomal location of multiple genes in humans, improved diagnoses of cystic fibrosis, hemophilia, inborn metabolic errors, familial neurodegenerative diseases. Office: Vanderbilt U Dept Genetics DD 2205 Med Ctr N Nashville TN 37232

PHILLIPS, JOHN DAVID, management consultant; b. Exeland, Wis., June 29, 1920; s. Mathew Frank and Iva (Bryant) P.; m. Estelle Margaret Pautsch, July 19, 1941; 1 son, John David. B.S., U. Wis., 1937. Partner Miss Wis. Cheese, 1946-56; dir. marketing Armour & Co., 1956-60; v.p. Am. Home Corp., 1960-66; founder, pres. R.J. Reynolds Foods, Inc., 1966-72; pres., dir. CBS/Columbia Group, N.Y.C., 1973-81; vice chmn. Nat. Exec. Service Corp., N.Y.C., 1981-94, dir., 1981—; ptnr. Edjon Ltd., Ft. Washington, Pa., 1990—; pres. Intercity Oil & Gas Corp., 1980—; bd. dirs. Glenmore Distillers Co., Airwick Industries, Inc., subs. of Ciba-Geigy Corp., Tex. Internat. Co.; founder, chmn. Sr. Careers Planning and Placement Svc., 1987-94. Past trustee N.Y.C. Pub. Libr., Juniata Coll., Mt. Senario Coll., Greenwich Coun. Boy Scouts Am.; adv. bd. Howard U.; trustee Safe Streets, Washington, 1992—. With USAAF, 1944-46; adminstr. Am. Armenian Diocese, 1994—. Mem. Assn. Corp. Growth (past pres. N.Y.C.), Hamilton Coll. Parents Assn. Conglist. (past pres., trustee). Clubs: Greenwich Country, Riverside Yacht, N.Y. Yacht; Links (N.Y.C.); Petroleum (Corpus Christi, Tex.). Home: Pilot Rock Riverside CT 06878 Office: 630 2nd Ave New York NY 10016-4806

PHILLIPS, JOHN DAVID, communications executive; b. Charlotte, N.C., Nov. 27, 1942; s. Louis and A. Viola (Pack) P.; m. Cheryl Helen Rudd; children: Hunter, Scott, Andrew, Lauren. Student, U. Va., 1962-63. Pres. RMS Distbg., Frankfurt, West Germany, 1965-66, NGK Spark Plugs, Atlanta, 1967-82; pres., chief exec. officer Advanced Telecommunication, Atlanta, 1982-88, also bd. dirs., 1982-88; owner Specialized Hauling Trucking Co., 1987-89; pres., CEO Resurgens Comm. Group, Inc., Atlanta, 1989-93; pres., CEO, bd. dirs. Actava Group, Inc., Atlanta, 1994-95; pres., CEO Metromedia Group Internat. Inc., 1995—. Served to capt. USMC, 1963-64. Republican. Methodist. Avocations: fishing, automobiles, flying, boating.

PHILLIPS, JOHN DAVISSON, retired lawyer; b. Clarksburg, W.Va., Aug. 21, 1906; s. Robert Bruce and Lela (Davisson) P.; m. Virginia Maxwell, Nov. 12, 1932; children: John Davisson, Julia Anne. Student, Washington and Lee U., 1924-25; A.B., W.Va. U., 1928, LL.B., 1930; postgrad., Oxford U., 1930-32. Bar: W.Va. 1932. Gen. practice law Wheeling, W.Va., 1932-91; of counsel Phillips, Gardill, Kaiser & Altmeyer; ret., 1991; asst. pros. atty. Ohio County, 1937-40; city solicitor City of Wheeling, 1942-47. Past mem. W.Va. State Bd. Law Examiners. Served as capt. USMCR, World War II. Fellow Am. Bar Founds.; mem. ABA, W.Va. Bar Assn. (pres. 1955-56), Am. Judicature Soc., Phi Kappa Psi, Phi Delta Phi, Fort Henry Club. Episcopalian. Home: 4 Arlington Dr Howard Pl Wheeling WV 26003 Office: 61 14th St Wheeling WV 26003-3426

PHILLIPS, JOHN EDWARD, zoologist, educator; b. Montréal, Que., Can., Dec. 20, 1934; s. William Charles and Violet Mildred (Lewis) P.; m. Eleanor Mae Richardson, Sept. 8, 1956; children: Heather Anne, Jayne Elizabeth, Jonathan David, Catherine Melinda, Wendy Susannah. BSc with honors, Dalhousie U., Halifax, N.S., 1956, MSc, 1957; PhD, Cambridge U., Eng., 1961. Asst. prof. Dalhousie U., Halifax, N.S., 1960-64; assoc. prof. U. B.C., Vancouver, Can., 1964-71, prof., 1971—, head dept. zoology, 1991—; vis. rschr. Cambridge (Eng.) U., 1972, 76, 81; chair grant selection com. Nat. Rsch. Coun. Can., Ottawa, Ont., 1969-71; mem. coun. Nat. Sci. and Engring. Rsch. Coun., Ottawa, 1983-87. Mem. editorial bd.: Can. Jour. Zoology, 1971-75, Am. Jour. Physiology, 1978-93, Jour. Experimental Biology, 1981-85; contbr. articles to profl. jours. Mem. grant selection com. Can. Cystic Fibrosis Found., Toronto, 1989-91; active Vancouver Bach Choir. Named to James chair St. Francis Xavier U., Antigonish, N.S., 1993. Fellow Royal Soc. Can.; mem. Can. Soc. Zoologists (sec. 1972-76, v.p. 1976-78, pres. 1979), Am. Soc. Zoologists (exec. 1983-85, chair divsn. comp. physiol. biochemistry 1983-85). Avocations: music, choir. Home: 12908-22 B Ave, White Rock, BC Canada V4A 6Z3 Office: U BC, Dept Zoology, Vancouver, BC Canada V6T 1Z4

PHILLIPS, JOHN RICHARD, engineering educator; b. Albany, Calif., Jan. 30, 1934; s. Eric Lester and Adele Catherine (Rengel) P.; m. Joan Elizabeth Soyster, Mar. 23, 1957; children: Elizabeth Huntley, Sarah Rengel, Catherine Hale. BS, U. Calif., Berkeley, 1956; M in Engring., Yale U., 1958, PhD in Engring., 1960. Registered profl. engr., Calif. Chem. engr. Stanford Rsch. Inst., Menlo Park, Calif., 1960; rsch. engr. Chevron Rsch. Co., Richmond, Calif., 1962-66; mem. faculty Harvey Mudd Coll., Claremont, Calif., 1966—, prof. engring., 1974—, James Howard Kindleberger prof. engring., 1991—, dir. engring. clinic, 1977-93, chmn. engring. dept., 1993—; vis. prof. U. Edinburgh, Scotland, 1975, Cambridge (Eng.) U., 1981, ESIEE, France, 1981, Naval Postgrad. Sch., 1984-85, Calif. Poly. U., San Luis Obispo, 1992; vis. scientist So. Calif. Edison Co., 1980; founder Claremont Engring., 1973; cons. in field. Contbr. articles to profl. jours. 1st lt. AUS, 1960-62. Mem. Am. Inst. Chem. Engrs., Sigma Xi, Alpha Delta Phi, Tau Beta Pi. Home: 911 W Maryhurst Dr Claremont CA 91711-3320

PHILLIPS, JOHN ROBERT, college dean, political scientist; b. Henderson, Ky., Dec. 16, 1942; s. Leander Armstead and Ann Reid (Brown) P. Diploma, Lang. Inst., Chateauroux, France, 1966; BA, Centre Coll., Danville, Ky., 1969; MA, Western Ky. U., Bowling Green, 1973. Instr. Drury Coll., Springfield, Mo., 1971-73, Western Ky. U., Bowling Green, 1975-79; asst. prof. Thiel Coll., Greenville, Pa., 1979-83, scholar-in-residence, 1983-85; pvt. cons. Henderson, Ky., 1985-87; adj. prof. Lockyear Coll., Evansville, Ind., 1987-88, acad. dean, 1988-90, v.p. acad. affairs, dean coll., 1990-91; exec. dir. human rels. commn. Henderson (Ky.) Mcpl. Ctr., 1991-93; dean acad. affairs, prof. political studies/govt. Springfield (Ill.) Coll., 1993—; adj. prof. pub. adminstrn. Ind. State U., Terre Haute; field investigator on religion and culture in ancient city of Taxila, 1968, on indsl. pollution of hist. bldgs. and monuments, France, Italy, Austria, 1969; rschr. on nationalism, Scotland, 1972, on local govt. and urban deves., 1993; participant in internat. confs. on The Future of a United Germany, 1991; mem. adv. coun. St. John's Hosp. Sch. respiratory Therapy, 1993, Ursuline Acad Sch. Bd., v.p., 1995-96, fin. com., 1993-96, Cen. Ill. Fgn. Lang. and Internat. Studies Consortium, 1993—, chmn., 1994-95. Mem. editorial bd. Jour. Urban Affairs, 1985-89; manuscript referee Pub. Adminstrn. Rev., 1985-87; contbr. chpts. to multi-vol. reference series The Small City and Regional Cmty. 1981, 85, 87, 95; contbr. articles on urban affairs, policy planning and federalism/intergovtl. rels. to profl. jours. Policy advisor Lt. Gov.'s Office, Frankfort, Ky., 1985-86; cons. Commn. on Ky.'s Future, Frankfort, 1985-87; mem. Bd. Cath. Edn., Diocese of Springfield, 1994—. With USAF, 1963-68. Mem. Am. Polit. Sci. Assn. (Leon Weaver Disting. Rsch. Award com. 1990-93), Am. Soc. Pub. Adminstrn. (publs. com. 1984-88, 92-95), Urban Affairs Assn. (publs. com. 1985-89, nominating com. 1984-85, 88-89), Am. Philatelic Soc., Am. Guild Organists, Pi Sigma Alpha. Democrat. Episcopalian. Avocations: reading, classical music, philately. Home: 2605 Delaware Dr Springfield IL 62702-1213

PHILLIPS, J(OHN) TAYLOR, judge; b. Greenville, S.C., Aug. 20, 1923; s. Walter Dixon and Mattie Sue (Taylor) P.; m. Mary Elizabeth Parrish, Dec. 18, 1954; children: John Allen, Susan, Linda-Lea, Julia. AA, Glenville State Coll., 1952; JD, Mercer U., 1955; LLD, Asbury Coll., 1992. Bar: Ga. 1954, U.S. Supreme Ct. 1969. Mem. Ho. of Reps. State of Ga., Atlanta, 1959-62, Senate, 1962-64. With USMC, 1942-51. Methodist. Home: 1735 Winston Dr Macon GA 31206 Office: State Ct Bibb County PO Box 5086 Macon GA 31213

PHILLIPS, JOSEF CLAYTON, insurance and investment company executive; b. Seattle, June 27, 1908; s. Joseph Clinton and Margaret Janet (Branlund) P.; m. Ada May Gummer, Sept. 24, 1931; 1 dau., Barbara Lee (Mrs. Richard Angus). Student, U. Wash., 1925-28, U. Paris, France, 1928-29. With Merrill, Lynch, Pierce, Fenner & Bean, Seattle, 1930-35; with United Pacific Corp., 1936—, pres., 1960-63, chmn. bd., 1963-67; dir., chmn. exec. com. United Pacific Ins. Co., 1957-72, N.W. Bldg. Co., M.G. Norton Corp., Pelican Seafoods. Clubs: Seattle Golf (Seattle); Wailea Golf (Maui, Hawaii). Home: 12523 Greenwood Ave N Apt 2 Seattle WA 98133-8001

PHILLIPS, JOSEPH ROBERT, museum director; b. Utica, N.Y., Mar. 14, 1950; m. Dixie Anne Stedman, 1988. BS in Marine Transp., SUNY, 1972; MA in History, SUNY, Cooperstown, 1981; MBA, New Hampshire Coll., 1990. Capt., exec. dir. Hudson River Sloop Clearwater, Poughkeepsie, N.Y., 1972-75; capt., assoc. project dir. N.Y. Bicentennial Barge, Albany, 1975-76; mgr. hist. shipyard Maine Maritime Mus., Bath, 1978-81; various program mgmt. positions Bath Iron Works Corp., 1982-86, various mktg. positions, 1986-92; mus. dir. Maine State Mus., Augusta, 1992—; mktg. cons. Australian Warships Systems, Sydney, 1988; chmn. indsl. engring. panel Soc. Naval Architects Marine Engrs., 1984-86, chmn. shipbuilding standards panel, 1984-86. Bd. dirs. Maine Cmty. Cultural Alliance, Friends of Maine State Mus.; mem. Maine Cultural Affairs Coun., 1992—, State House and Capital Park Commn., 1992—, Blaine House Commn., 1994—; treas. Maine Assn. Mus.; mem. bd. advisors Damariscotta River Assn. Office: Maine State Mus 83 State House Station Augusta ME 04333-0083

PHILLIPS, JOYCE MARTHA, human resources executive; b. Bridgeport, Conn., Dec. 18, 1952; d. Stephen and Shirley B. (Howard) Tabory; m. Glenn L. Phillips, July 14, 1974. BA in English, Fairfield (Conn.) U., 1974; MS in Indsl. Rels., U. New Haven, 1982. Tchr. English and Reading Fairfield Woods Jr. High Sch., 1975; asst. to v.p. mktg. Bunker Ramo Corp., Trumbull, Conn., 1975-76; rep. in investor rels. Gen. Electric Co., Fairfield, 1976-77, specialist in manpower rels., 1977-79; specialist in employee benefits Gen. Electric Co., Bridgeport, Conn., 1979-80, specialist in employee rels., orgn. and staffing, 1980-84; mgr. hdqrs. personnel and office svcs. Armtek Corp., New Haven, 1984-87, dir. compensation and benefits, 1987-89; v.p. human resources (div. sr. human resources officer) Citibank, N.Y.C., 1989-91, v.p. compensation global fin., 1991-95; sr. v.p. human resources Barclays Bank/BZW, N.Y.C., 1995—. Counsel Fairfield U. Alumni Adv. Coun. Avocations: tennis, piano, dance, boating. Office: Barclays Bank/BZW 222 Broadway New York NY 10038

PHILLIPS, JULIA MILLER, film producer; b. N.Y.C., Apr. 7, 1944; d. Adolph and Tanya Miller; m. Michael Phillips (div.); 1 dau., Kate Elizabeth. B.A., Mt. Holyoke Coll., 1965. Former prodn. asst. McCall's Mag.; later advt. copywriter Macmillan Publs.; editorial asst. Ladies Home Journal, 1966-67; later assoc. editor; East Coast story editor Paramount Pictures, N.Y.C., 1969; head Mirisch Prodns., N.Y., 1970; creative exec. First Artists Prodns., N.Y.C., 1971; founded (with Tony Bill and Michael Phillips) Bill/Phillips Prodns., 1971; founder, producer Ruthless Prodns., Los Angeles, 1971—. Author: You'll Never Eat Lunch in This Town Again, 1991, Driving Under the Affluence, 1995; films include Steelyard Blues, 1972, The Sting, 1973 (Acad. award for Best Picture of Yr.), Taxi Driver, 1976 (Palme d'or for best picture), The Big Bus, 1976, Close Encounters of the Third Kind, 1977, The Beat, 1988; dir. The Estate of Billy Buckner, for Women Dirs. Workshop, Am. Film Inst., 1974. Recipient Katherine McFarland Short Story award, 1963, Short Story award Phi Beta Kappa, 1964. Mem. Acad. Motion Picture Arts and Scis., Writers Guild. Office: care Writers Guild 8955 Beverly Blvd Los Angeles CA 90048-2420

PHILLIPS, KAREN BORLAUG, economist, association executive; b. Long Beach, Calif., Oct. 1, 1956; d. Paul Vincent and Wilma (Tish) Borlaug. Student Cath. U. P.R., 1973-74; B.A., U. N.D., 1977, B.S., 1977; postgrad. George Washington U., 1978-80. Research asst. research and spl. programs adminstrn. U.S. Dept. Transp., Washington, 1977-78, economist, office of sec., Washington, 1978-82; profl. staff mem. (majority) Com. Commerce, Sci., Transp., U.S. Senate, Washington, 1982-85, tax economist (majority) com. on fin., 1985-87, chief economist (minority) senate com. on fin., 1987-88; commr. Interstate Commerce Commn., 1988-94; v.p. legislation Assn. Am. Railroads, Washington, 1994-95, sr. v.p. policy, legis. & econ., 1995—. Contbg. author studies, publs. in field. Recipient award for Meritorious Achievement, Sec. Transp., 1980, Spl. Achievement awards, 1978, 80, Outstanding Performance awards, 1978, 80, 81. Mem. Am. Econ. Assn., Women's Transp. Seminar (Woman of Yr. award 1994), Transp. Research Forum, Assn. Transp. Law, Logistics & Policy, Tax Coalition, Blue Key, Phi Beta Kappa, Omicron Delta Epsilon. Republican. Lutheran. Office: Assn Am Railroads 50 F St NW Washington DC 20001-1530

PHILLIPS, KEITH WENDALL, minister; b. Portland, Oreg., Oct. 21, 1946; s. Frank Clark and Velma Georgina (Black) P.; m. Mary Katherine Garland, July 16, 1973; children: Joshua, Paul, David. BA, UCLA, 1968; MDiv, Fuller Theology Sem., 1971, D. of Ministries, 1972; LHD (hon.), John Brown U., 1990. Dir. Youth For Christ Clubs, L.A., 1965-71; pres. World Impact, L.A., 1971—; mem. urban ministries resources svcs. editorial adv. bd. Zondervan Pub. House; commencement speaker Tabor Coll., 1969, 91, John Brown U., 1990. Author: Everybody's Afraid in the Ghetto, 1973, They Dare to Love the Ghetto, 1975, The Making of a Disciple, 1981, No Quick Fix, 1985. Chmn. L.A. Mayor's Prayer Breakfast Com., 1985—. Named Disting. Staley lectr., 1969. Mem. Evangelistic Com. of Newark (pres. 1976—), World Impact of Can. (pres. 1978—), The Oaks (pres. 1985—), Faith Works (pres. 1987—). Baptist. Office: World Impact 2001 S Vermont Ave Los Angeles CA 90007-1256 *Our knowledge of God's Word outruns our obedience. The challenge for Christians is to live what we know.*

PHILLIPS, KEVIN PRICE, columnist, author; b. N.Y.C., Nov. 30, 1940; s. William Edward and Dorothy Virginia (Price) P.; m. Martha Eleanor Henderson, Sept. 28, 1968; children: Andrew, Alexander. A.B., Colgate U., 1961; postgrad., U. Edinburgh, Scotland, 1959-60; LL.B., Harvard U., 1964. Bar: N.Y. 1965, D.C. 1965. Adminstrv. asst. to Congressman Paul Fino, 1964-68; spl. asst. atty. gen. U.S., 1969-70; newspaper columnist syndicated King Features, 1970-83; pres. Am. Polit. Rsch. Corp., 1971; commentator Nat. Pub. Radio, 1984—; spl. asst. to campaign mgr. Nixon for Pres. Com., 1968. Author: The Emerging Republican Majority, 1969, Electoral Reform and Voter Participation, 1975, Mediacracy, 1975, Post-Conservative America, 1982, The Business Case for a National Industrial Strategy, 1984, The Politics of Rich and Poor, 1990, Boiling Point: Democrats, Republicans and the Decline of Middle-Class Prosperity, 1993, Arrogant Capital: Washington, Wall Street and The Frustration of American Politics, 1994; editor, pub.: The American Political Report, 1971—; contbg. columnist L.A. Tim. Mem. N.Y., D.C. bars, Phi Beta Kappa. Home: 5115 Moorland Ln Bethesda MD 20814-6117 Office: 7316 Wisconsin Ave Bethesda MD 20814-2925

PHILLIPS, LARRY EDWARD, lawyer; b. Pitts., July 5, 1942; s. Jack F. and Jean H. (Houghtelin) P.; m. Karla Ann Hennings, June 5, 1976; 1 son, Andrew H.; 1 stepson, John W. Dean IV. BA, Hamilton Coll., 1964; JD, U. Mich., 1967. Bars: Pa. 1967, U.S. Dist. Ct. (we. dist.) Pa. 1967, U.S. Tax Ct. 1969. Assoc. Buchanan, Ingersoll, Rodewald, Kyle & Buerger, P.C. (now Buchanan Ingersoll P.C.), Pitts., 1967-73, mem., 1973—. Mem. Am. Coll. Tax Counsel, Tax Mgmt. Inc. (adv. bd.), Pitts. Tax Club, ABA (sect. taxation, com. on corp. tax and sect. real property, probate and trust law), Allegheny County Bar Assn., Pa. Bar Assn. Republican. Presbyterian. Clubs: Duquesne, St. Clair County. Contbr. articles to profl. jours. Office: Buchanan Ingersoll PC One Oxford Ctr 301 Grant St 20th Fl Pittsburgh PA 15219-1410

PHILLIPS, LAUGHLIN, museum president, former magazine editor; b. Washington, Oct. 20, 1924; s. Duncan and Marjorie Grant (Acker) P.; m. Elizabeth Hood, 1956 (div. 1975); children: Duncan Vance, Elizabeth Laughlin; m. Jennifer Stats Cafritz, 1975. Student, Yale U., 1942-43; M.A., U. Chgo., 1949. Fgn. service officer, 1949-64; vice consul Hanoi, Vietnam, 1950-53; 2d sec. Tehran, Iran, 1957-59; co-founder Washingtonian mag., 1965, editor, 1965-74, editor-in-chief, 1974-79; pres. Washington Mag., Inc., 1965-79; dir. Phillips Collection, 1972-92, pres., chmn. of bd., 1967—; bd. dirs. Nat. Capital Area div. UN Assn. Am. (nat. coun. mem.). Bd. trustees MacDowell Colony, 1977-79, Nat. Com. for an Effective Congress, 1966—, Pax World Svc., 1995—. Served with AUS, 1943-46, PTO. Decorated Bronze Star; comendador Orden de Mayo al Mérito (Argentina); chevalier de l'Ordre de la Couronne (Belgium), knight's cross 1st class Order of Danebrog (Denmark); officier Arts et Lettres (France). Mem. Nat. Coun., UN Assn. Am. Clubs: Cosmos (Washington), Metropolitan (Washington), Rolling Rock (Ligonier, Pa.). Home: 3044 O St NW Washington DC 20007-3107

PHILLIPS, LAWRENCE H., II, neurologist, educator; b. Clarksburg, W.Va., Dec. 30, 1947; m. Elayne K. Phillips, 1985; children: Joshua, Melanie. AB, Princeton U., 1970; MD, U. W.Va., 1974. Diplomate Am. Bd. Psychiatry and Neurology. Intern U. Wis. Hosps., Madison, 1974-75; resident in neurology Mayo Clinic, Rochester, Minn., 1975-78, rsch. fellow neurophysiology, 1978-79; instr. neurology Mayo Med. Sch./U. Minn., 1979-80; asst. prof. U. Va. Med. Ctr., Charlottesville, 1981-87, dir. electromyography lab., 1981—, assoc. prof., 1987—; dir. neuromuscular ctr. Muscular Dystrophy Assn. Clinic, Charlottesville, 1983—; mem. med. adv. com. Diabetes Rsch. and Tng. Ctr., U. Va., 1981-88; cons. neurologist Mayo Clinic, 1979-80, VA Hosp., Salem, 1983—; cons. panel AMA Diagnostic and Therapeutic Tech. Assessment, 1989—, arbitrator panel, 1990—; expert panel mem. NIH, 1991. Recipient Young Investigator Travel award Internat. Congress Electromyography, 1979. Mem. Am. Neurol. Assn., Am. Acad. Neurology, Am. Assn. Electrodiagnostic Medicine, Assn. Univ. Profs. Neurology, Sigma Xi. Office: Univ VA Neuromuscular Ctr UVA Medical Ctr Dept Neurology Box 394 Charlottesville VA 22908

PHILLIPS, LAYN R., lawyer; b. Oklahoma City, Jan. 2, 1952; s. James Arthur Cole and Eloise (Gulick) P.; m. Kathryn Hale, Aug. 17, 1986; children: Amanda, Parker, Graham. BS, U. Tulsa, 1974, JD, 1977; postgrad., Georgetown U., 1978-79. Bar: Okla. 1977, D.C. 1978, Calif. 1981, Tex. 1991. Asst. U.S. atty. Miami, 1980-81, L.A., 1980-83; trial atty. Bur. of Competition, Washington, 1977-80; U.S. atty. U.S. Dist. Ct. (no. dist.) Okla., Tulsa, 1983-87; judge U.S. Dist. Ct. (we. dist.) Okla., Oklahoma City, 1987-91; litigation ptnr. Irell & Manella, Newport Beach, Calif., 1991—; tchr. trial practice U. Tulsa Coll. Law, Okla. City U. Law Sch.; lectr. Attys. Gen's.

Adv. Inst., Washington. Pres. Am. Inn of Ct. XXIII, Sch. Law, Okla. U., 1989-90; pres. Am. Inn. of Ct. CVIII, Sch. Law., Okla. City U. 1990-91. Named one of Outstanding Young Ams., U.S. Jaycees, 1989. Office: Irell & Manella 840 Newport Center Dr Newport Beach CA 92660-6310*

PHILLIPS, LEO HAROLD, JR., lawyer; b. Detroit, Jan. 10, 1945; s. Leo Harold and Martha C. (Oberg) P.; m. Patricia Margaret Halcomb, Sept. 3, 1983. BA summa cum laude, Hillsdale Coll., 1967; MA, U. Mich., 1968; JD cum laude, 1973; LLM magna cum laude, Free Univ. of Brussels, 1974. Bar: Mich. 1974, N.Y. 1975, U.S. Supreme Ct. 1977, D.C. 1979. Fgn. lectr. Pusan Nat. U. (Korea), 1969-70; assoc. Alexander & Green, N.Y.C., 1974-77; counsel Overseas Pvt. Investment Corp., Washington, 1977-80, sr. counsel, 1980-82, asst. gen. counsel, 1982-85; asst. gen. counsel Manor Care, Inc., Silver Spring, Md., 1985-91 asst. sec. 1988—, assoc. gen. counsel, 1991—; vol. Peace Corps, Pusan, 1968-71; mem. program for sr. mgrs. in govt. Harvard U., Cambridge, Mass., 1982. Contbr. articles to legal jours. Chmn. legal affairs com. Essex Condominium Assn., Washington, 1979-81; deacon Chevy Chase Presbyn. Ch., Washington, 1984-87, moderator, 1985-87, supt. ch. sch., elder, trustee, 1987-90, pres., 1988-90, mem. nominating com., 1995-96. Recipient Alumni Achievement award Hillsdale Coll., 1980; Meritorious Honor award Overseas Pvt. Investment Corp., 1981, Superior Achievement award, 1984. Mem. ABA (internat. fin. transactions com., vice chmn. com. internat. ins. law), Am. Soc. Internat. Law (Jessup Internat. Law moot ct. judge semi-final rounds 1978-83, chair corp. counsel com. 1993—), Internat. Law Assn. (Am. br.; com. sec. 1982), D.C. Bar, N.Y. State Bar Assn., Royal Asiatic Soc. (Korea br.), State Bar Mich., Washington Fgn. Law Soc. (sec.-treas. 1980-81, bd. dirs., program coordinator 1981-82, v.p. 1982-83, pres.-elect 1983-84, pres. 1984-85, chmn. nominating com. 1986, 88), Washington Internat. Trade Assn. (bd. dirs. 1984-87), Assn. Bar City N.Y., Hillsdale Coll. Alumni Assn. (co-chmn. Washington area 1977-90). Club: University (N.Y.C.). Home: 4740 Connecticut Ave NW Apt 702 Washington DC 20008-5632 Office: Manor Care Inc 10750 Columbia Pike Silver Spring MD 20901-4427

PHILLIPS, LORELEI, nursing administrator; b. Doddridge County, W.Va., Aug. 16, 1933; d. Hadsal Mansfield and Thelma Louise (Smith) Ford; m. Robert G. Phillips, Mar. 21, 1954; children: Roberta Sue (dec.), Mark Lane, Eric, Timothy. AS, Salem Coll., 1973. Charge nurse United Hosp. Ctr., Clarksburg, W.Va.; coord., dir. nurses Doddridge County Bd. of Health, West Union, W.Va., adminstr., 1978-88; nursing surveyor W.Va. State Div. Health, Charleston; DON Clarksburg (W.Va.) Continuios Care Ctr., AM/FM Corp.; Mem. Region VI Health Adv. Coun. Mem. ANA, NADON, WVADON. Home: 302 Front St West Union WV 26456-1014

PHILLIPS, LOYAL, newspaper executive; b. Cullman, Ala., Apr. 11, 1905; s. Monroe and Lucy Ann (Bailey) P.; m. Evelyn Caldwell, Apr. 8, 1928; children: Sharon Kay, Terry Lynn. B.A., Howard Coll. (now Samford U.), 1928. Promotion mgr. Atlanta Georgian-Am., 1929; classified advt. mgr. Birmingham (Ala.) Post, 1930, Nashville Banner, 1931-32, Omaha World-Herald, 1933-34; classified advt. mgr. Washington Daily News, 1936, acting advt. dir., 1937-38; co-founder, partner, editor Parish-Phillips Newspaper Advt. Syndicate, Miami, Fla., 1939-43; also spl. cons. Tampa Times, Miami News, Washington Post; columnist Editor and Pub. mag., N.Y.C., 1940; advt. dir. New Orleans Item, 1945-49; gen. mgr., treas. St. Petersburg Ind., Inc., 1950-59, editor, pub., sec., treas., 1952-59, pres., 1959-62; pres. Petersburg (Va.) Newspaper Corp., 1959-62; sec.-treas. Punta Gorda Herald and Clewiston News, 1953—; gen. mgr. Southwest Citizen; pres. Laurel (Miss.) Leader-Call, 1959-62, Independent, Inc., 1962—, WCCF radio sta., 1960; pub., v.p. Ocala (Fla.) Star-Banner, 1963-67; gen. mgr. Elizabeth City (N.C.) Daily Advance, 1967—, co-pub., 1970—; asst. to pres. Dear Publ. & Radio, Inc., 1971-72; gen. mgr. Seabag Newspaper for Norfolk Navy Base, 1967—; roving columnist Gannett Fla. Newspapers, 1973; dir. Citizens Pub. Co. Author: Newspaper Advertising, 1946, Fifty Successful Advertising Ideas, 1948. Active ARC, Goodwill Industries, Childrens Service Bur., Salvation Army, Boy Scouts Am.; treas. New Orleans Art Acad.; chmn. Gov.'s Traffic Safety Adv. Com. State Fla., 1956; chmn. Elizabeth City United Fund, 1969, pres., 1970; Bd. dirs. Greater New Orleans. Served as lt. (j.g.) USNR, 1943-47. Named VFW Man of Yr., Elizabeth City (N.C.), 1971, Man of Yr. City of Fort Walton Beach (Fla.), 1981, Cullman, 1982, Alumnus of Yr. Samford U., 1981. Mem. Nat. Assn. Newspaper Classified Advt. Mgrs. (v.p. 1933—), So. Newspaper Pubs. Assn. (dir., chmn. pub. relations), Sales Exec. Council, Assn. Commerce, Newspaper Advt. Execs. Assn., Internat. House, Elizabeth City C. of C. (pres. 1971), Lambda Chi Alpha. Clubs: Metairie Country, Quarterback, New Orleans Advertising (pres. 1945-46). Lodge: Rotary. Home: 102 4th Ave NE Fort Walton Beach FL 32547-2507

PHILLIPS, MARRISE MASON, clinical research coordinator; b. York, S.C., Sept. 28, 1946; d. George T.C. and Terether Ella Mae (Stowe) Mason; m. George Ray Phillips, Sept. 5, 1970; children: Adrian Masonray, Persephone Dionne. ADN, Ctrl. Piedmont C.C., 1969; BSN, Wingate Coll., 1988. RN, N.C.; cert. clin. rsch. coord. Staff nurse pediat. ICU Carolinas Med. Ctr., Charlotte, N.C., 1969-70, staff nurse gen. pediat., 1970-73, nurse mgr. gen. pediat., 1973-82, nurse mgr. adolescent unit, 1982-85, nurse mgr. adult med. surg., 1985-91, diagnostics and therapeutics, 1985-91, clin. rsch. coord., 1991—; Author: (manual) Diagnostics & Therapeutics Patient Education, 1990; co-author: (manual) CMC Nursing Quality Assurance Program, 1991. Mem. Dermatology Nurses Assn. (pres. N.C. chpt. S.E. region 1995—), Soc. for Clin. Trials, Rsch. Coords. Network, Assn. Clin. Pharmacology, HPC Support Group, Chi Eta Phi. Democrat. Baptist. Avocations: reading, walking, sewing, cross stitching, crocheting. Home: 5111 Caravel Ct Charlotte NC 28215-1501

PHILLIPS, OLIVER, tropical biodiversity scientist. Scientist U. Leeds, Eng. Recipient Edmund H. Fulling award Soc. Econ. Botany, 1992. Office: Geography Sch, U Leeds, Leeds LS2 9JT, England

PHILLIPS, OLIVER CLYDE, classics educator; b. Kansas City, Mo., Oct. 23, 1929; s. Oliver Clyde and Blanche (Campbell) P.; m. Shirley Ann Liese, June 6, 1954; children—Stephen Oliver, Mark Clyde. Student, Kansas City Jr. Coll., 1946-48; B.S. in Edn., U. Kans., 1950; postgrad., Perkins Sch. Theology, So. Meth. U., 1951-53; M.A., U. Mo., 1954; Ph.D., U. Chgo., 1962. Tchr. Great Bend High Sch., Kans., 1950; tchr. Southeast High Sch., Kansas City, Mo., 1951, Northeast Jr. High Sch., Kansas City, Mo., 1954-55; from assoc. prof. to prof. William Jewell Coll., Liberty, Mo., 1955-64; dir. corr. study, prof. classics U. Kans., Lawrence, 1964-93; ret.; vis. prof. U. Cologne, Fed. Republic of Germany, 1983. Named Mortar Bd. Outstanding Educator, U. Kans., Lawrence, 1978; U. Chgo. Shorey fellow, 1958-59. Mem. Classical Assn. of Mid. West and South (Ovatio award 1993), Am. Philol. Assn., Am. Classical League, Vergilian Soc. Episcopalian. Home: 2235 Westchester Rd Lawrence KS 66049-1635

PHILLIPS, OWEN MARTIN, oceanographer, geophysicist, educator; b. Parramatta, Australia, Dec. 30, 1930; s. Richard Keith and Madeline (Lofts) P.; m. Merle Winifred Simons, Aug. 8, 1953; children: Lynette Michelle, Christopher Ian, Bronwyn Ann, Michael Stuart. B.Sc., Sydney (Australia) U., 1952; Ph.D., U. Cambridge (Eng.), 1955. Rsch. fellow Imperial Chem. Industries, U. Cambridge, 1955-57; asst. prof., then assoc. prof. Johns Hopkins, 1957-61; asst. dir. rsch. U. Cambridge, 1961-64; prof. geophys. mechanics Johns Hopkins, 1964—, chmn. dept. earth and planetary scis., 1971-77, 88-89, Decker prof. sci. and engring., 1975—; Cons. to industry, 1960—; Mem. council mems. Nat. Center Atmospheric Research, 1964-67, chmn. rev. and goals, 1965-67; mem. com. global atmospheric research project Nat. Acad. Sci., 1967-69; mem. Waterman award com. NSF, 1975-77. Author: The Dynamics of the Upper Ocean, 1966, 2d edit., 1968, 3d edit., 1977, Russian edit., 1969, 2d Russian edit., 1980, Chinese edit., 1986, The Heart of the Earth, 1968, Italian edit., 1970, 74, 77, The Last Chance Energy Book, 1979, 2d edit., 1980, Japanese edit., 1986; editor: Wave Dynamics and Radio Probing of the Ocean Surface, 1986, Flow and Reactions in Permeable Rocks, 1991; assoc. editor Jour. Fluid Mechanics, 1964-95; regional editor Proc. Royal Soc., 1990—; mem. editl. adv. com. Ann. Rev. Fluid Mechanics, 1994—; contbr. numerous articles to profl. jours. Trustee Roland Park Country Sch., 1974-81; trustee Chesapeake Research Consortium, 1972-76, sec., 1972. Recipient Adams prize U. Cambridge, 1965, Sverdrup Gold medal Am. Meteorol. Soc., 1974. Fellow Royal Soc. (London), Am. Meteorol. Soc. (publs. commn. 1971-77, planning com. 1983-84); mem. Nat. Acad. Engring., Am. Geophys. Union, Md. Acad. Sci. (sci. coun. 1974-85, pres. 1979-85, trustee 1985-87), Phi Beta Kappa, Sigma Xi, Pi Tau Sigma. Home: 23 Merrymount Rd Baltimore MD 21210-1908

PHILLIPS, PATRICIA JEANNE, retired school administrator, consultant; b. Amarillo, Miss., Jan. 13, 1935; d. William Macon and Mary Ann (Cawthon) Patrick; m. William Henry Phillips, June 22, 1962; 1 child, Mary Jeanne. BA, Millsaps Coll., 1954; MA, Vanderbilt/Peabody U., 1957; EdD, U. So. Miss., 1978. Tchr. Jackson (Miss.) Pub. Schs., 1954-73, prin., 1973-75, asst. prin., 1975-77; dir. ednl. program Eden Prairie (Minn.) # 272, 1977-80; dir. elem. edn. Meridian (Miss.) Pub. Schs., 1980-91, asst. supt. curriculum, 1991, ret., 1991; prof. Miss. Coll., Clinton, part-time 1977, Miss. State U., Meridian, 1981-95; ednl. cons. in field. Co-author: (testing practice) Test Taking Tactics, 1987; contbr. articles to profl. jours. pres. Meridian Symphony Orch., 1987; v.p. Meridian Coun. Arts, 1986; bd. dirs. Meridian Art Mus. Named Boss of Yr., Meridian Secretarial Assn., 1985, Arts Education of Yr., Meridian Coun. Arts, 1991; recipient Excellence award Pub. Edn. Form, 1993. Mem. ASCD, Miss. ASCD, Miss. Assn. Women (pres.), Rotary, Phi Kappa Alpha, Phi Delta Kappa (pres. 1986-87), Alpha Delta Kappa Gamma (pres. 1962). Republican. Methodist. Avocations: grant writing, computers, sewing. Home: 322 51st St Meridian MS 39305-2013 Office: Miss State Univ Meridian Campus 1000 Highway 19 S Meridian MS 39301-8205

PHILLIPS, PETER CHARLES BONEST, economist, educator, researcher; b. Weymouth, Dorset, Eng., Mar. 23, 1948; came to U.S., 1980; s. Charles Bonest and Gladys Eileen (Lade) P.; m. Emily Dowdell Birdling, Feb. 10, 1971 (div. 1980); 1 child, Daniel Lade; m. Deborah Jane Blood, June 13, 1981; children: Justin Bonest, Lara Kimberley. BA, Auckland (New Zealand) U., 1969, MA, 1971; PhD, London U., 1974; MA (hon.), Yale U., 1979. Teaching fellow U. Auckland, 1969-70, jr. lectr., 1970-71; lectr. in econs. U. Essex, Colchester, Eng., 1972-76; prof. econs. U. Birmingham, Eng., 1976-79; prof. econs. Yale U., New Haven, Conn., 1979-85, Stanley Resor prof. econs., 1985-89, Sterling prof. econs., 1989—; Alumni disting. prof. econs. U. Auckland, 1991—; pres. Predicta Software Inc., Madison, Conn., 1994—; vis. scholar Ecole Polytechnique, Paris, 1977; univ. vis. prof. Monash U., Melbourne, Australia, 1986; vis. prof. Inst. Advanced Studes, Vienna, Austria, 1989; disting. visitor London Sch. Econs., 1989. Editor Econometric Theory jour., 1985; contbr. over 150 articles, book revs., notes to profl. jours. Recipient award for promotion of sci. Japan Soc., 1983; Commonwealth Grants Com. scholar, Eng., 1971, Guggenheim fellow, N.Y., 1984-85. Fellow Am. Acad. Arts & Scis., Royal Soc. New Zealand (hon.), Econometric Soc., Jour. Econometrics, Am. Statis. Soc.; mem. Inst. Math. Stats. Avocations: building, poetry, reading, tennis. Home: 133 Concord Dr Madison CT 06443-1814 Office: Cowles Found PO Box 208281 New Haven CT 06520-8281

PHILLIPS, RALPH SAUL, mathematics educator; b. Oakland, Calif., June 23, 1913; s. Isadore and Mary (Shaw) P.; m. Jean Adair, Oct. 11, 1942; 1 child, Xanthippe. A.B., UCLA, 1935; Ph.D., U. Mich., 1939. Instr. U. Wash., 1940-41, Harvard U., 1941-42; group leader Radiation Lab., Mass. Inst. Tech., 1942-46; asst. prof. math. NYU, 1946-47; assoc. prof. U. So. Calif., 1947-53, prof., 1953-58; prof. UCLA, 1958-60, Stanford U., 1960—; Rackham fellow Inst. Advanced Study, 1939-40, mem., 1950-51; research assoc. Yale U., 1953-54; Guggenheim fellow, 1954, 74; research asso. N.Y. U., 1958; vis. prof. U. Aarhus, 1968; mem. interacad. exchange program mission to USSR, 1975. Co-author: Theory of Servomechanisms, 1947, Functional Analysis and Semigroups, 1957, Scattering Theory, 1967, Scattering Theory for Automorphic Functions, 1976; co-editor Jour. Functional Analysis. Mem. Am. Acad. Arts and Scis. Home: 1076 Cathcart Way Palo Alto CA 94305-1047 Office: Stanford U Dept Math Stanford CA 94305

PHILLIPS, RENEÉ, magazine editor, writer, public speaker; b. Freeport, N.Y.. Student, Art Students League, 1979, Am. Art Sch., 1979, Fashion Inst. Tech., 1980, New Sch. for Social Rsch., 1980. Dir., founder Artopia, not-for-profit art orgn., N.Y.C., 1980-84; pub., editor-in-chief Manhattan Arts Internat., N.Y.C., 1983—; condr. seminars at mus. and galleries, including Katonah Art Mus., N.Y. Artists Equity, Salmagundi Club; instr. Learning Annex, Marymount Manhattan Coll., N.Y.C.; juror Excellence in Arts Awards, 1988, N.Y. Lung Assn. Ann. Exhbn., 1990, Manhattan Arts Internat. Ann. Internat. Cover Art Competition, 1992-95; juror, co-curator Redefining Visionary ARt, Doma Gallery, N.Y.C., 1989; curator Synthesis of Painting and Sculpture exhbn., 1st Women's Bank, N.Y.C., 1984, Salute to Liberty internat. art exhbn., N.Y.C., 1986; organizer over 40 art and cultural events. Author: New York Contempoary Art Galleries, 1995; editor-in-chief Success Now!, 1991—. Recipient award of merit Muscular Dystrophy Assn., 1986, award for outstanding contbns. to arts Mayor of N.Y.C., 1987. Mem. Internat. Assn. Art Critics, N.Y. Artists Equity (former bd. dirs.). Office: Manhattan Arts Internat 200 E 72d St New York NY 10021

PHILLIPS, RICHARD HART, psychiatrist; b. Atlanta, June 23, 1922; s. Wendell Brooks and Margaret (Hart) P.; married Mar. 10, 1945; children: Valerie, Richard Jr., Hugh, Nancy, Mark. BS, U. N.C., 1943; MD, NYU, 1945. Intern U.S. Naval Hosp., Camp Lejeune, N.C., 1945-46; resident med.-surg. Harrisburg Hosp., Harrisburg, Pa., 1948; resident, chief resident psychiatry Duke U. Hosp., Durham, N.C., 1949-51; instr. psychiatry U. Pa., Phila., 1952-53; sr. psychiat. cons. Consolidated Industries Greater Syracuse, Syracuse, N.Y., 1976-89; from asst. prof. to prof. health sci. ctr. SUNY, Syracuse, 1953-92, prof. emeritus, 1992—; dir. adult psychiat. clinic health sci. ctr. SUNY, 1981-92. Author: (poetry) Bindweed, 1988; contbr. sci. and popular articles on psychology to jours. Pres. bd. dirs. Marcellus (N.Y.) Free Libr., 1968-75. Lt. (j.g.) USNR, 1943-48. Fellow Am. Psychiat. Assn. (life); mem. Soc. Children's Book Writers, Thursday Night Club. Republican. Avocations: poetry writing, sculpture, nature photography, bees, goats. Home: 4149 Bishop Hill Rd Marcellus NY 13108-9613 Office: SUNY Health Sci Ctr 750 E Adams St Syracuse NY 13210-2306

PHILLIPS, RICHARD L(OVERIDGE), marine corps officer; b. Sacramento, Nov. 27, 1939; s. Will D. and Lorraine (Richardson) P.; m. Linda Shughart; children: Rebecca, Richard. BS in Engring., Calif. Poly. Coll., 1961; MS in Computer Sci., Naval Postgrad. Sch., Monterey, Calif., 1973. Commd. 2d lt. USMC, 1961, advanced through grades to maj. gen., 1991; served in combat as squadron pilot and ground co. comdr. Vietnam, 1966-67, 70-71; project team leader Marine Corps Tactical Systems Support Activity, 1973-76; comdg. officer Marine Aircraft Group 39 and Marine Amphibious Units 11 and 17, Camp Pendleton and San Diego; dep. comdr. Naval Space Command, 1985-87; dep. asst. chief of staff, command, control, communications and computer, intelligence and interoperability Hdqrs. Marine Corps, Washington, 1987-89; dep. comdr. Fleet Marine Force, Pacific, Marine Corps Bases, Pacific, 1990-91; comdg. gen. 1st Marine Expeditionary Brig., Kaneohe Bay, Hawaii, 1989-91; comdr. U.S. Joint Task Force Cobra Gold, Thailand, 1990; dep. asst. sec. Navy Expeditionary Force Programs, Washington, 1992-93; insp. gen. USMC, Washington, 1993-95; ret., 1995; v.p. Wheat Internat. Comm. Corp., Vienna, Va., 1995—. Decorated D.S.M., Legion of Merit, Meritorious Svc. medal, Air medal (26), numerous others. Republican. Presbyterian. Office: Wheat Internat Comm Corp 8229 Boone Blvd Vienna VA 22182

PHILLIPS, RICHARD WENDELL, JR., air force officer; b. Harrisburg, Pa., Nov. 6, 1929; s. Richard Wendell Sr. and Mary Viola (Myers) P.; m. Betty Jo Teel, Mar. 7, 1954; children—David Wendell, Karen Marie, Terry Lee Phillips Woods. B.S. in Engring., U.S. Mil. Acad., 1953; grad., U.S. Air Force Exptl. Test Pilot Sch., Edwards AFB, Calif., 1960, Air Command and Staff Coll., Maxwell AFB, Ala., 1967, Air War Coll., Maxwell AFB, Ala., 1972; M.S. in Pub. Adminstrn., George Washington U., 1967. Commd. 2d lt. U.S. Air Force, 1953, advanced through grades to maj. gen., 1983; fighter pilot 51st Fighter Interceptor Wing, Naha Air Base,Okinawa, Japan, 1954-57; instr. pilot Laredo AFB, Tex., 1958-60; test pilot Eglin AFB, Fla., 1960-64; exchange officer to U.S. Navy Air Devel. Squadron Four/Point Mugu Naval Air Sta., Calif., 1964-66; chief of tactics 366th Tactical Fighter Wing, Da Nang AB, Vietnam, 1967-68; chief of fighter test 4950th Test Wing, Wright-Patterson AFB, Ohio, 1968-71; chief of operational test and eval. div. Hdqrs. U.S. Air Force, Washington, 1972-75; vice comdr. 51st Composite Wing (tactical), Osan AB, Korea, 1975-76; chief aero. systems div. Hdqrs. U.S. Air Force, Washington, 1977-78, dep. dir. requirements - gen. purpose forces, 1978-80; dir. electronic warfare during close air support joint test force Nellis AFB, Nev., 1980-82; comdr. Air Force Operational Test and Evaluation Ctr., Kirtland AFB, N.Mex., 1982-85; comdr. Sheppard Tech. Tng. Ctr., Sheppard AFB, Tex., 1985-87, ret., 1987. Mem. Soc. Exptl. Test Pilots. Avocations: sailing; golf; skiing. Home: 816 Weeden Island Dr Niceville FL 32578-3708

PHILLIPS, ROBERT JAMES, JR., banking and real estate corporation executive; b. Houston, Aug. 4, 1955; s. Robert James and Mary Josephine (Bass) P.; m. Nancy Norris, Apr. 24, 1982; 1 child, Mary Ashton. BBA, So. Meth. U., 1976, JD, 1980. Bar: Tex. 1980. Vp., gen. counsel Aegis Shipping Ltd., London, 1980-81; assoc. Bishop, Larrimore, Lamsens & Brown, 1981-82; pres. Phillips Devel. Corp., Ft. Worth, Tex., 1982—; pvt. practice Ft. Worth, 1982-87, 89—; assoc. Haynes and Boone, Ft. Worth, 1988-89; sr. v.p. Am. Real Estate Group, 1989-93, Am. Savs. Bank, N.A., New West Fed. Savs. and Loan Assn., 1989-93, Am. Savs. Bank, Ft. Worth, 1991-92; chmn., CEO, CRC CRC Environ. Risk Mgmt. Inc., Ft. Worth, 1993—; bd. dirs. Tex. Heritage, Inc. Bd. dirs., exec. com. Ft. Worth Ballet Assn., 1984-85, Van Cliburn Found.; v.p. planning, bd. dirs., exec. com. Ft. Worth Symphony Orch., 1984-85; bd. dirs. Mus. Modern Art, 1986—; bd. dirs., exec. com., chmn. investment com. Tex. Boys Choir, 1983-85. Mem. ABA, Tex. Bar Assn., Ft. Worth Bd. Realtors, Crescent Club, Phi Delta Phi, Kappa Sigma, Beta Gamma Sigma. Clubs: River Crest Country, Ft. Worth. Avocations: hunting, fishing, photography. Home and Office: PO Box 470099 Fort Worth TX 76147-0099

PHILLIPS, ROGER, steel company executive; b. Ottawa, Ont., Can., Dec. 17, 1939; s. Norman William Frederick and Elizabeth (Marshall) P.; m. Katherine Ann Wilson, June 9, 1962; 1 child, Andrée Claire. B.Sc., McGill U., Montreal, 1960. Vice pres. mill products Alcan Can. Products Ltd., Toronto, Ont., Can., 1969-70, exec. v.p., 1971-75; pres. Alcan Smelters and Chems. Ltd., Montreal, Que., Can., 1976-79; v.p. tech. Alcan Aluminium Ltd., Montreal, Que., Can., 1980-81; pres. Alcan Internat. Ltd., Montreal, Que., Can., 1980-81; pres., chief exec. officer IPSCO Inc., Regina, Sask., Can., 1982—; sr. mem. Conf. Bd. Inc., N.Y., 1987—; bd. dirs. Toronto Dominion Bank. Dir. Coun. for Can. Unity, Montreal, 1987—; bd. dirs. Conf. Bd. of Can., 1984-87, Inst. for Polit. Involvement, Toronto, 1982-88. Mem. Can. Assn. Physicists, Bus. Coun. on Nat. Issues, Am. Iron and Steel Inst. (bd. dirs. 1984—), Inst. of Physics U.K. (chartered physicist), Sask. C. of C. (bd. dirs. 1984—), Que. C. of C. (pres. 1981), Pub. Policy Forum (bd. dirs.), Assiniboia Club (Regina), St. Denis Club, Univ. Club (Montreal). Home: 3220 Albert St, Regina, SK Canada S4S 3N9 Office: IPSCO Inc, Armour Rd, Regina, SK Canada S4P 3C7

PHILLIPS, RONALD EDWARD, artist, sales executive; b. Clovis, N.Mex., Apr. 10, 1937; s. Rodney Vernon and Ethel Edna (Huff) P.; m. May Frances Willingham, Aug. 27, 1957; children: Rhonda Louise, Russell Kent, Teresa Gail; m. Janet Irene Johnsonbaugh Smith, July 4, 1938; stepchildren: Steven, Gregg, Laura. Student, Ea. N.Mex. U., 1955-56, U. N.Mex., 1957, Famous Artist Schs., 1963-64, North Light Art Sch., 1989-90. Group merchandiser women's fashions J.C. Penney Inc., Albuquerque, 1957-64; chem. salesman Take Over Products, Clovis, N.Mex., 1964-65; with International Auto Leasing, Albuquerque, 1965; salesman Pennsalt Chems., N.Mex. div., Albuquerque, 1965-67; N.Mex. sales rep. W.W. Grainger Inc., Chgo., 1967-72; founder Pueblo Arts, Inc., Albuquerque, 1972—; mgr. Dairy Queen, Santa Rosa and Lovington, N.Mex., 1982-85; owner, mgr. Western Pit n Grill & Food Gallery, Lovington, 1985-88; owner Pueblo Arts Inc./Trailwest Gallery, Albuquerque, 1988—; tchr. quick draw, continuous line drawing, 1990; artist, guide Pueblo Arts Inc. Trailwest Paintouts, Guide for Artists, 1990-92; ind. sales cons. SWEPCO Bldg. Projects, 1993—. Artist, author sketchbooks Traveling Man's Old Town Sketchbook, 1990, The Shooting of Wyatt Earp, 1994, others; movie extra Whitesands, 1991, Next Fire on Earth, 1992, Wyatt Earp, 1993, Desperate Trails, 1993, Buffalo Girls, 1995, East Meets West, 1995, Lazarus Man Premier, 1995-96. Pres. Albuquerque Wildlife and Conservation, 1963-64; active Albuquerque Conf. & Vis. Bur., 1988—, Albuquerque Arts Alliance, 1994-95, Tourism Assoc. of N.Mex., Albuquerque Film Commn. With N.Mex. Air Nat. Guard, 1955-61. Mem. N.Mex. Art League (hon. life, pres. 1964-65, instr., bd. arts after sch. project 1995-96), Indian Arts and Crafts Assn. (ethics com. 1973-74), Albuquerque Arts Alliance, Guild of Albuquerque Artist Models (advisor, bd. dirs. 1994-95). Republican. Avocations: art, sales and marketing. Office: Pueblo Arts Inc 5555 Zuni Rd SE # 154 Albuquerque NM 87108-2935

PHILLIPS, RONALD FRANK, legal educator, academic administrator, dean; b. Houston, Nov. 25, 1934; s. Franklin Jackson and Maudie Ethel (Merrill) P.; m. Jamie Jo Bottoms, Apr. 5, 1957; children: Barbara Celeste Phillips Oliveira, Joel Jackson, Phil Edward. B.S., Abilene Christian U., 1955; J.D., U. Tex., 1965. Bar: Tex. 1965, Calif. 1972. Bldg. contractor Phillips Homes, Abilene, Tex., 1955-56; br. mgr. Phillips Weatherstripping Co., Midland and Austin, Tex., 1957-65; corp. staff atty. McWood Corp., Abilene, 1965-67; sole practice law Abilene, 1967-70; mem. adj. faculty Abilene Christian U., 1967-70; prof. law Pepperdine U., Malibu, Calif., 1970—, dean Sch. Law, 1970—, vice chancellor, 1995—. Deacon North A and Tenn. Ch. of Christ, Midland, 1959-62; deacon Highland Ch. of Christ, Abilene, 1965-70; elder Malibu Ch. of Christ, 1978-95; mgr., coach Little League Baseball, Abilene, Huntington Beach and Malibu, 1968-78, 90-95; coach Youth Soccer, Huntington Beach, Westlake Village and Malibu, 1972-80, 85-86, 91. Recipient Alumni citation Abilene Christian U., 1974. Fellow Am. Bar Found. (life); mem. ABA, State Bar Tex., State Bar Calif., Christian Legal Soc., L.A. Bar Assn., Assn. Am. Law Schs. (chmn. sect. on adminstrn. law schs. 1982, com. on cts. 1985-87), Am. Law Inst., Nat. Conf. Commrs. on Uniform State Laws. Republican. Office: Pepperdine U Sch Law 24255 Pacific Coast Hwy Malibu CA 90263-0001

PHILLIPS, RONALD LEWIS, plant geneticist, educator; b. Huntington County, Ind., Jan. 1, 1940; s. Philemon Lewis and Louise Alpha (Walker) P.; m. Judith Lee Lind, Aug. 19, 1962; children: Brett, Angela. B.S. in Crop Sci., Purdue U., 1961, M.S. in Plant Breeding and Genetics, 1963; Ph.D. in Genetics, U. Minn., 1966; postgrad., Cornell U., 1966-67. Research and teaching asst. Purdue U., 1961-62; research and teaching asst. U. Minn., St. Paul, 1962-66; research assoc. U. Minn., 1967-68, asst. prof., 1968-72, assoc. prof., 1972-76, prof. genetics and plant breeding, 1976-93, Regents prof., 1993—; program dir. Competitive Rsch. Grants Office, USDA, Washington, 1979; mem. adv. grant panels NSF, USDA, AID; chmn. Gordon Conf. on Plant Cell and Tissue Culture, 1985; mem. sci. adv. coun. U. Calif. Plant Gene Expression Ctr., Berkeley, 1986-93; vis. prof., Italy, 1981, Can., 1983, China, 1986, Japan, 1990; dir. Plant Molecular Genetics Inst., 1991-94; chief scientist USDA, 1996—; trustee Biol. Stain Commn.; mem. Nat. Plant Genetic Resources Bd.; mem. editorial procs. Nat. Acad. Sci., 1996—. Co-editor: Cytogenetics, 1977, Molecular Genetic Modification of Eucaryotes, 1977, Molecular Biology of Plants, 1979, The Plant Seed: Development, Preservation and Germination, 1979, Genetic Improvement of Crops: Emergent Techniques, 1980, DNA-Based Markers in Plants, 1994; assoc. editor: Genetics, 1978-81, Can. Jour. Genetics and Cytology and Genome, 1985-90; mem. edit. bd. Maydica, 1978—, In Vitro Cellular and Developmental Biology, 1988-92, Cell Culture and Somatic Cell Genetics of Plants, 1983-91, Elaeis, 1994—; contbr. chpts. to Maize Breeding and Genetics, 1978, Staining Procedures, 1981, Cell Culture and Somatic Cell Genetics of Plants, 1984, Chromosome Structure and Function, 1987, Corn and Corn Improvement, 1988, Plant Transposable Elements, 1988, Chromosome Engring. in Plants, 1991, Maize Handbook, 1994; contbr. sci. articles to profl. jours. Mem. chmn. coun. on ministries, lay leader United Meth. Ch., 1968, dir. Project AgGrad, 1983—; Cub Scout Pack co-chmn. Boy Scouts Am., 1976-77; judge Minn. Regional and State Sci. Fair, 1970-80. Recipient Purdue Agrl. Alumni Achievement award, 1961, Purdue Disting. Agrl. Alumni award, 1993; NSF fellow, 1961; NIH fellow, 1966-67, Northrup King Oustanding Faculty Performance award, 1985, Crop Sci. Rsch. award, 1988. Fellow AAAS, Am. Soc. Agronomy, Crop Sci. Soc. Am. (awards com., div. chmn., bd. rep. 1988-91, rsch. award 1988); mem. NAS, Genetics Soc. Am., Am. Soc. Agronomy (award student sect., Caleb-Dorr award), Sigma Xi, Gamma Alpha (nat. treas.), Gamma Sigma Delta (award of merit 1994), Alpha Zeta. Office: U Minn Dept Agronomy & Plant Genetics Saint Paul MN 55108

PHILLIPS, RUSSELL ALEXANDER, JR., foundation executive; b. Charlotte, N.C., Sept. 19, 1937; s. Russell Alexander and Robmae (Black) P. A.B., Duke U., 1959; LL.B. (Edward John Noble fellow), Yale U., 1962.

Bar: N.C. 1962, D.C. 1966. Clk. to Sr. Judge, U.S. Ct. Appeals, 4th Circuit, 1962-63; legal adv. Ministry of Fin., Govt. No. Nigeria, 1963-65; asst. commr. income tax (legal) East African Common Services Orgn., Nairobi, Kenya, 1965-66; assoc. firm Wilmer, Cutler & Pickering, Washington, 1966-68; program officer Rockefeller Bros. Fund, N.Y.C., 1968-73, corp. sec., 1973-81; v.p. Rockefeller Bros. Fund, 1979-81, exec. v.p., 1982—, acting pres., 1987-88. Trustee Lingnan Found.; trustee, v.p., sec. Asian Cultural Coun. Mem. N.C. Bar Assn., D.C. Bar, Council Fgn. Relations, Phi Beta Kappa. Democrat. Presbyterian. Club:; University (N.Y.C.), Century Assn. (N.Y.C.). Home: 40 E 88th St Apt 5D New York NY 10128-1176 Office: Rm 3450 1290 Avenue Of the Americas New York NY 10104-0012

PHILLIPS, SANDRA ALLEN, primary school educator; b. Newport News, Va., Mar. 10, 1943; d. Cecil Lamar and Mary (Schenk) Allen. BS, Appalachian State U., Boone, N.C., 1965; MEd, U. N.C., Charlotte, 1990. Tchr. Rockwell (N.C.) Elem. Sch., 1964-65, Granite Quarry (N.C.) Elem. Sch., 1965-68, Lillian Black Elem. Sch., Spring Lake, N.C., 1970, Berryhill Elem. Sch., Charlotte, N.C., 1970-71, 77—, J.C. Roe Sch., Wilmington, N.C., 1974-76; elected to tchr.'s adv. coun., 1995-96. Named Tchr. of Yr., Berryhill Elem. Sch., 1989. Mem. Profl. Educators N.C., Classroom Tchrs. Assn. Office: Berryhill Elem Sch 10501 Walkers Ferry Rd Charlotte NC 28208-9721

PHILLIPS, SIDNEY FREDERICK, gastroenterologist; b. Melbourne, Australia, Sept. 4, 1933; s. Clifford and Eileen Frances (Fitch) P.; m. Decima Honora Jones, Mar. 29, 1957; children: Penelope Jane, Nichola Margaret, David Sidney. M.B.B.S., U. Melbourne, 1956, M.D., 1961. Resident med. officer Royal Melbourne Hosp., 1957-61, asst. sub-dean clin. sch., 1961-62; research asso. Central Middlesex Hosp., London, 1962-63, Mayo Clinic, Rochester, Minn., 1963-66; cons. in gastroenterology Mayo Clinic, 1966—; prof. medicine Mayo Med. Sch., 1976—, dir. gastroenterology research unit, 1977-94; program dir. Mayo Gen. Clin. Research Ctr., 1974-87; dir. Mayo Digestive Diseases Core Ctr., 1984-90; Karl F. and Marjory Hasselman prof. rsch., 1994—. Editor: Digestive Diseases and Sciences, 1977-82, Gastroenterology International, 1990-95; sr. assoc. editor: Gastroenterology, 1991-96; contbr. chpts. to books, articles to profl. jours. Fellow ACP, Royal Coll. Physicians, Royal Australian Coll. Physicians; mem. Am. Motility Soc. (pres. 1994-96), Am. Soc. Clin. Investigation (emeritus), Gastroenterology Soc. Australia, Am. Gastroenterology Assn. Assn. Am. Physicians, Brit. Soc. Gastroenterology (hon.). Home: 524 14th Ave SW Rochester MN 55902-1956 Office: St Mary's Hosp Gastroenterology Unit 200 1st St SW Rochester MN 55905-0001

PHILLIPS, SUSAN DIANE, secondary school educator; b. Shelbyville, Ky., Aug. 28, 1955; d. James William and Catherine Elizabeth (Jones) P. B of Music Edn., Eastern Ky. U., 1977; postgrad., U. Ky., 1987. Tchr. music Breckinridge County Schs., Hardinsburg, Ky., 1978, Perry County Schs., Hazard, Ky., 1980-83, Music on the Move, Louisville, 1985-86, Cooter (Mo.) R-4 Sch., 1987-90, Lewis County High Sch., Vanceburg, Ky., 1990—; staff-cavalcade of bands Ky. Derby Festival, Louisville, 1984-86. Dir. Simpsonville (Ky.) United Meth. Ch. Handbell Choirs, 1985-86. Named Ky. Colonel Gov. Commonwealth of Ky., 1979. Mem. Nat. Band Assn., Am. Choral Dirs. Assn., Ky. Educators Assn., Ky. Music Educators Assn., Music Educators Nat. Conf. Office: Lewis County High Sch Lions Ln Vanceburg KY 41179

PHILLIPS, SUSAN MEREDITH, financial economist, former university administrator; b. Richmond, Va., Dec. 23, 1944; d. William G. and Nancy (Meredith) P. BA in Math., Agnes Scott Coll., 1967; MS in Fin. and Ins., La. State U., 1971, PhD in Fin. and Economics, 1973. Asst. prof. La. State U., 1973-74, U. Iowa, 1974-78; Brookings Econ. Policy fellow, 1976-77; econ. fellow Directorate of Econ. and Policy Rsch., SEC, 1977-78; assoc. prof. fin. dept. U. Iowa, 1978-83, assoc. v.p. fin. and univ. svcs., 1979-81; commr. Commodity Futures Trading Commn., 1981-83, chmn., 1983-87; prof. fin. dept., v.p. fin. and univ. svcs. U. Iowa, Iowa City, 1987-91; bd. govs. Fed. Res. Bd., Washington, 1991—. Author (with J. Richard Zecher): The SEC and the Public Interest; contbr. articles in field to profl. jours. Office: Fed Res System 20th Constitution St NW Washington DC 20551

PHILLIPS, T. STEPHEN, lawyer; b. Tennyson, Ind., Oct. 1, 1941. AB, DePauw U., 1963; LLB, Duke U., 1966. Bar: Ohio 1966, Ind. 1967. Assoc. Frost & Jacobs, Cin., 1966-72, ptnr., 1972—; adj. prof. North Ky. U. Chase Coll. Law, Highland Hights, 1983—. Contbg. editor: Ohio Probate Practice (Addams and Hosford), Page on Wills. Trustee Spring Grove Cemetery, Cin. Methodist. Office: Frost & Jacobs 2500 PNC Ct 201 E 5th St Cincinnati OH 45202-4117

PHILLIPS, TED RAY, advertising agency executive; b. American Falls, Idaho, Oct. 27, 1948; s. Virn E. and Jessie N. (Aldous) P.; m. Dianne Jacqulynne Walker, May 28, 1971; children: Scott, Russell, Stephen, Michael. BA, Brigham Young U., 1972, MA, 1975. Account exec. David W. Evans, Inc., Salt Lake City, 1972-75; dir. advt. Div. Continuing Edn., U. Utah, Salt Lake City, 1975-78; sr. v.p. Evans/Lowe & Stevens, Inc., Atlanta, 1978, exec. v.p., 1979; pres., CEO David W. Evans/Atlanta, Inc., 1979-80; dir. advt. O.C. Tanner Co., Salt Lake City, 1980-82; pres. Thomas/Phillips/Clawson Advt., Inc., Salt Lake City, 1982-86; pres. Hurst & Phillips, Salt Lake City, 1986-94; CEO, chmn. Phillips Twede & Spencer Advt., Salt Lake City, 1994—; advt. instr. div. continuing edn. Brigham Young U., 1983-85. Dir. publicity, promotion Western States Republican Con., 1976. Recipient Silver Beaver award Boy Scouts Am., 1994, Spurgeon award, 1995. Mem. Am. Advt. Fedn. (8 Best-in-West awards, 2 nat. Addy awards, Clio finalist 1984, Telly award 1991, 92), Utah Advt. Fedn. (bd. dirs. 1976-78, 80-87, pres. 1984-85). Mormon. Home: 1792 Cornwall Ct Sandy UT 84092-5436 Office: Phillips Twede Spencer Advt Inc 428 E 6400 S Salt Lake City UT 84107-7500

PHILLIPS, THEODORE LOCKE, radiation oncologist, educator; b. Phila., June 4, 1933; s. Harry Webster and Margaret Amy (Locke) P.; m. Joan Cappello, June 23, 1956; children: Margaret, John, Sally. BSc, Dickinson Coll., 1955; MD, U. Pa., 1959. Intern Western Res. U., Cleve., 1960; resident in therapeutic radiology U. Calif., San Francisco, 1963, clin. instr., 1963-65, asst. prof. radiation oncology, 1965-68, assoc. prof., 1968-70, prof., 1970—, chmn. dept. radiation oncology, 1973—; rsch. radiobiologist U.S. Naval Radiologic Def. Lab., San Francisco, 1963-65; rsch. assoc. Cancer Rsch. Inst. and Lab. Radiobiology; rsch. physician Lawrence Berkeley Lab. and Donner Lab., U. Calif., Berkeley. Contbr. numerous articles to profl. publs. With USNR, 1963-65. Nat. Cancer Inst. grantee, 1970-96. Mem. Am. Soc. Therapeutic Radiologists (pres. 1984), Am. Soc. Clin. Oncology, Radiol. Soc. N.Am., Hyperthermia Soc. (pres.-elect 1993, pres. 1994), Am. Assn. Cancer Rsch., Calif. Med. Assn., Am. Coll. Radiology Radium Soc., No. Calif. Radiation Oncology Assn., Inst. Medicine, Phi Beta Kappa, Alpha Omega Alpha. Democrat. Office: U Calif San Francisco Dept Radiation Oncology L-75 Box 0226 San Francisco CA 94143

PHILLIPS, THOMAS EDWORTH, JR., investment executive, senior consultant; b. Danville, Va., July 7, 1944; s. Thomas Edworth Sr. and Jean (Worley) P.; m. Claudia Mitchell, July 23, 1966; children: Kelly Marie, Melissa Joyce. BS in Econs., Va. Tech., 1966; cert. in investments, N.Y. Inst. Fin., 1969; MS in Bus., Va. Commonwealth U., 1973; postgrad., U. Pa., 1989. Cert. investment analyst; registered prin. NYSE and NASD. Edn. coord. Prince William County Schs., Manassas, Va., 1966-67; investment broker Conrad and Co., Richmond, Va., 1967-68; investment exec. Paine Webber, Inc., Richmond, 1968—, divisional v.p., 1980—; registered prin. NYSE, NASD, 1987—; mem. access program nat. com. PaineWebber, N.Y.C., 1989-90, mem. dir.'s coun., 1987-88, mem. managed accounts nat. adv. bd., 1991-93; bd. dirs. Madison Group, Inc., Richmond, Meadowbrook Assocs., Inc., Richmond; speaker in field. Bd. dirs. Va. Non-Profit Housing Coalition, pres., 1992—; chmn. bd. deacons. Mt. Olivet Ch., Hanover, Va., 1984-85; trustee Hanover Acad., Ashland, Va., 1980-84. Rotary Found. fellow, 1989. Mem. Investment Mgmt. Cons. Assn., Capital Soc., Melody Hills Property Owners Assn. (bd. dirs. 1980—), Va. Tech. Alumni Assn., Rotary, Bull and Bear Club, Omicron Delta Epsilon. Baptist. Avocations: horses, tennis, golf. Home: 15058 Melody Hills Dr Doswell VA 23047-2075 Office: PaineWebber Inc 1021 E Cary St Ste 1800 Richmond VA 23219-4000

PHILLIPS, THOMAS H., writer, journalism educator; b. Montclair, N.J., Jan. 18, 1942; s. William Louis and Josephine (Hoornbeek) P.; m. Mary Jo Dolembo, June 15, 1963 (div. 1975); children: Jennifer, Luke, Django; m. Debra Given, July 7, 1979; children: Talitha, Cassia, Zoey. BA, Grinnell (Iowa) Coll., 1964; MA, New Sch., 1981. Writer N.Y. Times, N.Y.C., 1965-69; writer, producer Sta. WPIX-TV News, N.Y.C., 1969-73; editor CBS Evening News, N.Y.C., 1974-77, writer, 1986—; asst. prof. Columbia U., N.Y.C., 1979-87. Contbr. numerous articles and revs. to N.Y. Times, Rolling Stone mag., Village Voice, others. Mem. Writers Guild Am. (Outstanding Achievement award 1987-90). Presbyterian. Avocation: fiddle. Office: CBS News 524 W 57th St New York NY 10019-2902

PHILLIPS, THOMAS JOHN, lawyer; b. Mpls., Nov. 24, 1948. BA, U. Minn., 1970; JD, U. Utah, 1973; LLM in Taxation, NYU, 1974. Bar: Wis. 1974. Assoc. Whyte & Hirschboeck, S.C., Milw., 1974-78, Minahan & Peterson, S.C., Milw., 1978-91, Quarles & Brady, Milw., 1991—; law clk. Utah Supreme Ct., Salt Lake City, 1972-73. Mem. ABA, Wis. Bar Assn., Profl. Inst. Taxation, North Shore Country Club, Order of Coif. Avocations: gardening, golf, hockey, jogging, racquetball. Office: Quarles & Brady 411 E Wisconsin Ave Milwaukee WI 53202-4409

PHILLIPS, THOMAS ROYAL, judge; b. Dallas, Oct. 23, 1949; s. George S. and Marguerite (Andrews) P.; m. Lyn Bracewell, June 26, 1982; 1 son, Daniel Austin Philips; 1 stepson, Thomas R. Kirkham. BA, Baylor U., 1971; JD, Harvard U., 1974. Bar: Tex. 1974; cert. in civil trial law Tex. Bd. Legal Specialization. Briefing atty. Supreme Ct. Tex., Austin, 1974-75; assoc. Baker & Botts, Houston, 1975-81; judge 280th Dist. Ct., Houston, 1981-88; chief justice Supreme Ct. Tex., Austin, 1988—; mem. com. on fed.-state rels. Jud. Conf. U.S., 1990-96; chair Tex. Jud. Dists. Bd., 1988—; mem. State Judges Mass Tort Litig. Com., 1991-96; bd. dirs. Elmo B. Hunter Citizens Ctr. for Jud. Selection, 1992-94, Southwestern Legal Found.; dir. Nat. Conf. Chief Justices, 1989-95, 1st v.p., 1995—; adv. dir. Rev. of Litigation, U. Tex. Law Sch., 1990—; chair Nat. Mass Tort Conf. Planning Com., 1993-94. Bd. advisors Ctr. for Pub. Policy Dispute Resolution, U. Tex. Law Sch., 1993—; mem. planning com. South Tex. Coll. of Law Ctr. for Creative Legal Solutions, 1993—. Recipient Outstanding Young Lawyer award Houston Young Lawyers Assn., 1986, award of excellence in govt. Tex. C. of C., 1992; named Appellate Judge of Yr., Tex. Assn. Civil Trial and Appellate Specialists, 1992-93. Mem. ABA, Am. Law Inst., State Bar Tex. (chmn. pattern jury charges IV com. 1985-87, vice chmn. adminstrn. justice com. 1986-87), Am. Judicature Soc. (bd. dirs. 1989-95, exec. bd. 1995-96), Conf. Chief Justices (bd. dirs. 1993-95), Tex. Philol. Soc., Houston Philol. Soc., Houston Bar Assn., Travis County Bar Assn. Republican. Methodist. Office: Tex Supreme Ct PO Box 12248 Austin TX 78711-2248

PHILLIPS, THOMAS WADE, judge, lawyer; b. Oneida, Tenn., July 6, 1943; s. W.T. and Lucille (Lewallen) P.; m. Dorothy Mills, Jan. 2, 1971; children: Lori Ann, Wade Thomas. BA, Berea (Ky.) Coll., 1965; JD, Vanderbilt U., 1969; LLM in Labor Law, George Washington U., 1973. Bar: Tenn. 1969, U.S. Supreme Ct. 1972, U.S. Ct. Appeals (6th cir.) 1980. Assoc., ptnr. Baker, Worthington, Crosley, Stansberry & Wolfe, Huntsville, Tenn., 1973-77; ptnr. Phillips & Williams, P.C., Oneida, Tenn., 1977-91; U.S. magistrate judge ea. dist., Tenn., 1991—; county atty. Scott County, Huntsville, 1976-91; city atty. Town of Oneida, 1978-91. Capt. JAGC, U.S. Army, 1969-73. Mem. ABA, Tenn. Bar Assn. (ho. of dels. 1989-91), Scott County Bar Assn. Office: US District Court Howard H Baker Jr Courtho 800 Market St Knoxville TN 37902

PHILLIPS, WALTER RAY, lawyer, educator; b. Democrat, N.C., Mar. 19, 1932; s. Walter Yancey and Bonnie (Wilson) P.; m. Patricia Ann Jones, Aug. 28, 1954; children: Bonnie Ann, Rebecca Lee. A.B., U. N.C., 1954; LL.B., Emory U., 1957, LL.M., 1962, J.D., 1970; postgrad., Yale U., 1965-66. Bar: Ga. 1957, Fla. 1958, U.S. Supreme Ct. 1962, Tex. 1969. With firm Jones, Adams, Paine & Foster, West Palm Beach, Fla., 1957-58; law clk. to chief judge U.S. Dist. Ct., Atlanta, 1958-59; with firm Powell, Goldstein, Frazer & Murphy, Atlanta, 1959-60; bankruptcy judge U.S. Cts., Atlanta, 1960-64; prof. law U. N.D., 1964-65; teaching fellow Yale U., 1965-66; prof. law Fla. State U., 1966-68, Tex. Tech. U., Lubbock, 1968-71; Disting. vis. prof. law Baylor U., 1971; atty. Commn. on Bankruptcy Laws of U.S., Washington, 1971-72; dep. dir., adminstrv. officer, 1972-73; prof. Sch. Law, U. Ga., 1973—, assoc. dean, 1975-83, acting dean, 1976, Joseph Henry Lumpkin prof., 1977-94, also dir. univ's self. study, 1978, Herman E. Talmadge prof., 1994—; Chapman disting. vis. prof. law U. Okla., 1985-86; vis. prof. law U. Okla., 1990, U. Mo., Columbia, 1993, 94; reporter Gov.'s Legislation for Ga., 1973; v.p., dir. Killearn Estates, Inc.; mem. Conf. on Consumer Fin. Law. Author: Florida Law and Practice, 1960, Encyclopedia of Georgia Law, 1962, Seminar for Newly Appointed Referees in Bankruptcy, 1964, Damages: Cases and Materials, 1967, (with James William Moore) Debtors' and Creditors' Rights, Cases and Material, 1966, 5th edit., 1979, The Law of Debtor Relief, 1969, 2d edit., 1972, supplement, 1975, (with James William Moore) Rule 6, Moore's Federal Practice, 1969, Adjustment of Debts for Individuals, 1979, 2d edit., 1981, supplement, 1982, 84, 85, Liquidation Under the Bankruptcy Code, 3d edit., 1988, supplement, 1989, 90, 91, 92, 93, 94, Cases and Materials on Corporate Reorganization, 1983, 3d edit., 1986, 4th edit., 1988, 5th edit., 1990, 7th edit., 1996, Family Farmer and Adjustment of Individual Debts, 1987, supplement, 1988, 89, 90, 91, 92, 93, 94, A Primer of Chapters 12 and 13 of the Bankruptcy Code, 1995. Bd. dirs. Lubbock Day Nurseries, 1969, pres., 1970-71. Served with USAF, 1950. Mem. ABA (consumer bankruptcy com. 1973—, chmn. 1986-90), Fed. Bar Assn., Fla. Bar Assn., Tex. Bar Assn., Western Circuit Bar Assn., Ga. Bar Assn. (vice chmn. publs. com. 1977-89, com. on profl. responsibility 1983—), Am. Judicature Soc., Am. Trial Lawyers Assn., Phi Alpha Delta (chief tribune). Baptist. Home: 310 Red Fox Run Athens GA 30605-4409

PHILLIPS, WARREN HENRY, publisher; b. June 28, 1926; s. Abraham and Juliette (Rosenberg) P.; m. Barbara Anne Thomas, June 16, 1951; children: Lisa, Leslie, Nina. AB, Queens Coll., 1947, LHD (hon.), 1987; JD (hon.), U. Portland, 1973; LHD (hon.), Pace U., 1982, L.I. U., 1987. Copyreader Wall St. Jour., 1947-48; fgn. corr. Wall St. Jour., Germany, 1949-50; chief London bur. Wall St. Jour., 1950-51, fgn. editor, 1951-53, news editor, 1953-54, mng. editor Midwest edit., 1954-57, mng. editor, 1957-65, pub., 1975-88; exec. editor Dow Jones & Co., 1965-70, v.p., gen. mgr., 1970-71, exec. v.p., 1972, editl. dir., 1971-88, pres., 1972-79, CEO, 1975-90, also bd. dirs., past chmn.; co-pub. Bridge Works Pub. Co., 1992—; bd. dirs. PBS; copyreader European edit. Stars and Stripes, 1949; pres. Am. Coun. Edn. for Journalism, 1971-73; mem. Pulitzer Prize Bd., 1977-87; adj. faculty Grad. Sch. Journalism, Columbia U., 1992—, John F. Kennedy Sch. Govt., Harvard Coll., 1992. Author: (with Robert Keatley) China: Behind the Mask, 1973. Trustee Columbia U., 1980-93, trustee emeritus, 1993—; mem. vis. com. John F. Kennedy Sch. Govt., Harvard U., 1984-90, 92—; corp. adv. bd. Queens Coll., 1986-90, found. bd. trustees, 1990—. Named one of 10 Outstanding Young Men in U.S., U.S. Jaycees, 1958; inductee Info. Industry Assn.'s Hall of Fame, 1984. Mem. Am. Newspaper Pubs. Assn. (bd. dirs. 1976-84), Am. Soc. Newspaper Editors (pres. 1975-76), Bridgehampton Club, River Club. Office: Bridge Works Publ PO Box 1798 Bridgehampton NY 11932-1798

PHILLIPS, WILLIAM, English language educator, editor, author; b. N.Y.C.; s. Edward and Marie (Berman) P.; m. Edna M. Greenblatt (dec.). BS, CCNY; MA, NYU; postgrad., Columbia U.; DHL, Adelphi U., 1991. Instr. Columbia U., N.Y.C., 1945; lectr. New Sch. Social Rsch., N.Y.C.; vis. lectr. Sarah Lawrence Coll., N.Y., 1951-54, 56-57, U. Minn., 1953; assoc. prof. NYU, 1960, 61-63; prof. English Rutgers U., New Jersey, 1963-78; prof. Boston U., 1978—. Author: A Sense of the Present, 1967, A Partisan View: Five Decades of the Literary Life, 1983; editor-in-chief Partisan Review, 1934—; editor Short Stories of Dostoyevsky; co-editor The Partisan Review Anthology, Literature and Psychoanalysis, 1983, Writers and Politics, 1983; former cons. editor Dial Press, Criterion Books, Random House, Chilmark Press; editor: Our Country, Our Culture: The Politics of Political Correctness, 1994. Mem. Gov. N.J. Com. Arts, 1964-66, Pres. Carter Task Force Arts and Humanities, arts adv. group Bus. Com. Arts. Rockefeller Found. grantee, 1977-78; NEH fellow, 1978-79, Guggenheim Found. fellow, 1977. Mem. PEN, Assn. Lit. Mags. Am., Author's League, Coord. Coun. Lit. Mags. Am. (chmn. 1967-75, hon. pres., chmn. 1975). Office: Partisan Review 236 Bay State Rd Boston MA 02215-1403

PHILLIPS, WILLIAM A., research animal scientist; b. Sept. 23, 1948; m. Barbara Moore, 1969; children: Jeffrey, Bradley, Jennifer. BS in Agr., Mid. Tenn. State U., 1971; MS in Animal Nutrition, Va. Poly. Inst. and State U., 1974, PhD in Animal Nutrition, 1976. Rsch. animal scientist Grazinglands Rsch. Lab., Agrl. Rsch. Svc., USDA, El Reno, Okla., 1976-85, 93—, rsch. leader, animal scientist, 1985-93; mem. adv. com. for agr. Redlands C.C. Mem. Maple Sch. Bd.; fundraiser, basebalal coach YMCA; lay leader, pres. Men's Fellowship, Sunday sch. tchr., mem. fin., missions, long range planning, bldg. and pers. coms. Wesley United Meth. Ch. 2d lt. USAR, 1971-77. Mem. Am. Soc. Animala Sci. (program com., editl. bd.), Coun. for Agrl. Sci. and Tech., Okla. Grain and Stocker Prodrs., Am. Registry Profl. Animal Scientists, El Reno C. of C. (bd. dirs., exec. bd., v.p. for orgn.). Office: USDA Agrl Rsch Svc Grazinglands Rsch Lab El Reno OK 73036

PHILLIPS, WILLIAM E., advertising agency executive; b. Chgo., Jan. 7, 1930; s. William E. and Alice P.; children: Michael, Tom, Sarah. B.S., Cornell U., 1951; M.B.A., Northwestern U., 1955. Brand mgr. Procter & Gamble, Cin., 1955-59; with Ogilvy & Mather, N.Y.C., 1959-90; chief exec. officer Ogilvy Group, 1981-88; exec. in residence, prof. Johnson Grad. Sch. Mgmt. Cornell U., 1989-90; bd. dirs. Lillian Vernon, Inc., Sun Glass Hut, Inc., D.S.M. Internat. Exec. Office Group. chmn. internat. adv. bd. Outward Bound; trustee Cornell U., Achilles Track Club, N.Y.C., Florence Griswold Mus., Old Lyme, Conn.; bd. dirs. Internat. Tennis Hall of Fame, Newport, R.I. Lt. (j.g.) USN, 1951-54. Mem. Old Lyme Country Cub, Am. Alpine Club, Explorers Club, Cornell Club, Naval Mil. Club. Home: 200 N Cove Rd Old Saybrook CT 06475-2537

PHILLIPS, WILLIAM RAY, JR., retired shipbuilding executive; b. West Point, Va., Feb. 23, 1931; s. William Ray and Marjorie Evelyn (Treat) P.; m. Marian Belle Culbreth, Nov. 7, 1953; children: William Ray III, Dana Louise. Attended, Newport News (Va.) Shipbuilding Apprentice Sch., 1949-54; BS, Va. Poly. Inst., 1960; student advanced mgmt. program, Harvard U., 1975. Foreman machine shops and tool rm. Newport News (Va.) Shipbuilding Co., 1964-66, asst. supt. machine shops div., 1966-67, mgr. nuclear constrn., 1967-72, dir. waterfront ops., 1972-75, v.p. yard ops., 1975-79, v.p. mktg., 1979-83, v.p. engring., 1983-84, sr. v.p. engring., 1984-87, exec. v.p., 1987-92, pres., CEO, 1992-94, chmn., CEO, 1994-95; ret., 1995; bd. dirs. Newport News Reactor Svcs., Idaho Falls, Idaho, pres.; bd. dirs. Newport News Indsl. Ohio, North Perry, Ohio, chmn., 1992—. Sgt. U.S. Army, 1955-57. Named Engr. of Yr., Peninsula Engrs. Com., 1986. Mem. Soc. Naval Architects and Marine Engrs. (pres.), Navy League U.S. (life), Naval Submarine League, Am. Soc. Naval Engrs., Propeller Club U.S., Seaford Yacht Club (Yorktown, Va., trustee). Republican. Presbyterian.

PHILLIPS, WINFRED MARSHALL, dean, mechanical engineer; b. Richmond, Va., Oct. 7, 1940; s. Claude Marshall and Gladys Marian (Barden) P.; children—Stephen, Sean. B.S.M.E., Va. Poly. Inst., 1963; M.A.E., U. Va., 1966, D.Sc., 1968. Mech. engr. U.S. Naval Weapons Lab., Dahlgren, Va., 1963; NSF trainee, teaching, research asst. dept. aerospace engring. U. Va., Charlottesville, 1963-67; research scientist, 1966-67; asst. prof. dept. aerospace engring. Pa. State U., University Park, 1968-74, from assoc. prof. to prof., 1974-80, assoc. dean research Coll. Engring., 1979-80; head Sch. Mech. Engring. Purdue U., West Lafayette, Ind., 1980-88; dean Coll. Engring. U. Fla., Gainesville, 1988—, assoc. v.p. engr. rsch., 1989—; chmn. bd. dirs. North Fla. Tech. Innovation Corp., 1995—; vis. prof. U. Paris, 1976-77; bd. dirs. Tokheim Corp., Fla., Innovation Partnership; adv. com. Nimbus Corp., 1985-90, Hong Kong U. Sci. and Tech., 1990-93, Fla. Bd. Profl. Regulation, 1992—; co-founder, v.p., CEO Inc., 1990—; mem. acad. adv. coun. Indsl. Rsch. Inst., 1990-93; mem. sci. adv. com. electric Power Rsch. Inst., 1994—; bd. dirs. Southeastern Coalition for Minorities in Engring. Sect. editor Am. Soc. Artificial Internal Organs Jour.; contbr. more than 130 articles to profl. jours., chpts. to books. Bd. dirs. Ctrl. Pa. Heart Assn., 1974-80, U. Fla. Found., 1989-91, 95—; mem. Ind. Boiler and Pressure Vessel Code Bd., 1981-88. Named Disting. Hoosier Engr., 1987, Sagamore of the Wabash, 1988; recipient Career Rsch. award NIH, 1974-78, Surgery and Bioengring. Study sect., 1988-91, Fla. High Tech. and Industry Coun., 1990-94, So. Tech. Coun., 1991—. Fellow AAAS, AIAA (assoc.), ASME (sr. v.p. edn. 1986-88, bd. dirs. 1995—), N.Y. Acad. Scis., Am. Astron. Soc., Am. Inst. Med. and Biol. Engring. (founding fellow, chair coll. fellows 1994-95, pres.-elect 1995-96, pres. 1996—), Am. Soc. Engring. Edn. (past chmn. long range planning soc. awards 1990—, vice chmn. engring. deans coun. 1991-93, chair 1993—, bd. dirs. 1994—, 1st v.p. 1994-95, pres.-elect 1995-96), Royal Soc. Arts; mem. Am. Soc. Artificial Internal Organs (trustee 1982-90, sec.-treas. 1986-87, pres. 1988-89), Nat. Assn. State Univs. and Land-Grant Colls. (com. quality of engring. edn.), Accreditation Bd. on Engring. and Tech. (bd. dirs. 1989—, exec. com. 1991—, mem. internat. revs. for univs. in Saudi Arabia, USSR, The Netherlands, Kuwait, pres.-elect 1994-95, pres. 1996—), Univ. Programs in Computer-Aided Engring., Design and Mfg. (bd. dirs. 1985-91), Am. Phys. Soc., Biomed. Engring. Soc., Internat. Soc. Biorheology, Fla. Engring. Soc., Cosmos Club, Fla. Blue Key, Rotary (pres. Lafayette chpt. 1987-88), Sigma Xi, Phi Kappa Phi, Phi Tau Sigma, Sigma Gamma Tau, Tau Beta Pi (eminent engr.). Achievements include development of artificial heart pumps; research on reentry aerodynamics, on blood rheology, on modelling blood flow, on fluid dynamics of artificial hearts, on the use of smooth blood contacting surfaces, on prosthetic valve fluid dynamics and on laser Doppler studies of unsteady biofluid dynamics. Home: 4140 NW 44th Ave Gainesville FL 32606-4518 Office: U Fla Coll Engineering 300 Weil Hall Gainesville FL 32611-2083

PHILLIPS, ZAIGA ALKSNIS, pediatrician; b. Riga, Latvia, Sept. 13, 1934; came to U.S., 1949; d. Adolfs and Alma (Ozols) Alksnis; (div. 1972); children: Albert L., Lisa K., Sintija. BS, U. Wash., 1956, MD, 1959. Fellow Colo. Med. Ctr., Denver, 1961-62; sch. physician Bellevue and Issaquah (Wash.) Sch. Dists., 1970-77; pvt. practice Bellevue, 1977—; staff pediatrician Swedish Overlake Ctr., 1977—, Childrens Hosp. and Med. Ctr., Seattle, 1977—, Evergreen Med. Ctr., 1977—; cons. physician Allergy Clinic, Childrens Hosp., Seattle, 1988—; cons. and contact to pediatricians in Latvia, 1988—; team mem. to Latvia, Healing the Children Contact with Latvia, 1993—; bd. mem. Bellevue's Stay in Sch. Program, 1994—. Mem. Am. Latvian Assn., 1972—, Wash. Latvian Assn., Seattle, 1972—; pres. Latvian Sorority Gundega, Seattle, 1990-93; bd. dirs. Sister Cities Assn., Bellevue, 1992—. Fellow Am. Acad. Pediatricians; mem. Am. Latvian Physicians Assn., Wash. State and Puget Sound Pediatric Assn. Office: Pediatric Assn 2700 Northup Way Bellevue WA 98004-1461

PHILLIPS-MICHELSEN, OLIVERIO, chemical engineer, consultant; b. Fusagasuga, Colombia, June 6, 1928; s. Oliverio Phillips and Carmen Michelsen; m. Yolanda Villaveces, Mar. 25, 1950; children: Jorge, Gustavo, Yolanda, Roberto, Alberto, Jose Maria, Carolina. BSc in Chemistry, MIT, 1948, MSChemE, 1950, ScD in Chem. Engring., 1957. Registered chem. engr., Colombia. Prodn. mgr. Planta Col. de Soda, Bogota, Colombia, 1950-54; asst. dir., dir. Inst. Invest. Tecnol., Bogota, 1957-64; pres. Maderas y Chapas de Nariño, Bogota, 1972-77, Corp. de Invest. Forestal, Bogota, 1978-81; project mgr., mgr. ARINCO S.A., Bogota, 1982-91; indsl. cons., Bogota, 1964-72, 92—; mem. UN Commn. for Sci. and Tech., N.Y.C., 1964-71; mem. comn. on sci. and tech. OAS, Washington, 1972-76. Contbr. articles to Jour. Am. Chem. Soc., Chem. Engring. Progress. Recipient medal of merit Inst. Investigative Tech., 1975. Mem. Colombian Soc. Chem. Scis. (pres. 1963—), Colombian Standards Inst. (hon.), N.Y. Acad. Scis., MIT Club Colombia (pres. 1966-68). Roman Catholic. Avocations: music, horseback riding, walking.

PHILLIS, JOHN WHITFIELD, physiologist, educator; b. Port of Spain, Trinidad, Apr. 1, 1936; came to U.S., 1981; s. Ernest and Sarah Anne (Glover) P.; m. Pamela Julie Popple, 1958 (div. 1968); children: David, Simon, Susan; m. Shane Beverly Wright, Jan. 24, 1969. B in Vet. Sci., Sydney (Australia) U., 1958, D in Vet. Sci., 1976; PhD, Australian Nat. U., Canberra, 1961; DSc, Monash U., Melbourne, Australia, 1970. Lectr./sr. Monash U., 1963-69; vis. prof. Ind. U., Indpls., 1969; prof. physiology, assoc. dean rsch. U. Man., Winnipeg, Can., 1970-73; prof., chmn. dept. physiology U. Sask., Saskatoon, Can., 1973-81, asst. dean rsch., 1973-75; prof. physiology, chmn. dept. physiology Wayne State U., Detroit, 1981—; Wellcome vis. prof. Tulane U., 1986; mem. scholarship and grants com. Can. Med. Rsch. Coun., Ottawa, Ont., 1973-79; mem. sci. adv. bd. Dystonia Med. Rsch. Found., Beverly Hills, Calif., 1980-85; mem. sci. adv. panel World Soc. for Protection of Animals, 1982—. Author: Pharmacology of Synapses,

1970; editor: Veterinary Physiology, 1976, Physiology and Pharmacology of Adenosine Derivatives, 1983, Adenosine and Adenine Nucleotides as Regulators of Cellular Function, 1991, The Regulation of Cerebral Blood Flow, 1993, Novel Therapies for CNS Injuries: Rationales and Results, 1996; editor Can. Jour. Physiology and Pharmacology, 1978-81, Progress in Neurobiology, 1973—. Mem. grants com. Am. Heart Assn. of Mich., 1985-90, mem. rsch. coun., 1991-92, mem. rsch. forum com., 1991—, chair, 1992-93. Wellcome fellow London, 1961-62; Can. Med. Rsch. Found. grantee, 1970-81, rsch. prof., 1980; NIH grantee, 1983—. Mem. Brit. Pharmacol. Soc., Physiol. Soc., Can. Physiol. Soc. (pres. 1979-80), Am. Physiol. Soc., Soc. Neurosci., Internat. Brain Rsch. Orgn. Office: Wayne State U Dept Physiology 540 E Canfield St Detroit MI 48201-1928

PHILLIS, MARILYN HUGHEY, artist; b. Kent, Ohio, Feb. 1, 1927; d. Paul Jones and Helen Margaret (Miller) Hughey; m. Richard Waring Phillis, Mar. 19, 1949; children: Diane E., Hugh R., Randall W. Student, Kent State U., 1945; BS, Ohio State U., 1949. Chemist Battelle Meml. Inst., Columbus, Ohio, 1949-53; sec. Lakewood Park Cemetery, Rocky River, Ohio, 1972-75; illustrator periodical Western Res. Hist. Mag., Garrettsville, Ohio, 1974-78; illustrator book AAUW, Piqua, Ohio, 1976; art instr. Edison State C.C., Piqua, 1976; watermedia instr. Springfield (Ohio) Mus. Art, 1976-84; juror art exhbns. state and nat. art group, 1980—; painting instr. state and nat. orgns., 1980—; dir. Nat. Creativity Seminars, Ohio Watercolor Soc., Fairborn, 1993, 95, 97; lectr. art and healing Wheeling (W.Va.) Jesuit Coll., 1994, 95, 96. Author: Watermedia Techniques for Releasing the Creative Spirit, 1992; contbr. articles and illustrations to profl. jours.; one-woman shows include Stifel Fine Art Ctr., Wheeling, W.Va., Springfield (Ohio) Art Mus., Zanesville (Ohio) ARt Ctr., Cleve. Inst. Music, Columbus Mus. Art, Cheekwood Mus. of Art, Bot. Hall, Nashville; exhibited in group shows at No. Ariz. U. Art Mus., Flagstaff, 1993, Taiwan Art Edn. Inst., Taipei, 1994; represented in permanent collections at Springfield Mus. Art, Ohio Watercolor Soc., also corp. collections. Gallery dir. Green St. United Meth. Ch., Piqua, 1972-75; pres. Rocky River (Ohio) H.S. PTA, 1971; chmn. Cmty. Health and Humor Program, Wheeling, 1992. Recipient First awards Watercolor West, riverside, Calif., 1990, W.Va. Watercolor Soc., Morgantown, 1993, Hudson Soc. award Nat. Collage Soc., 1995, Art Masters award Am. Artist mag., 1996. Mem. Internat. Soc. Study of Subtle Energies and Energy Medicine (art cons. sci. jour. 1992—, art and healing workshop 1995), Am. Watercolor Soc. (dir. 1991-93, newsletter editor 1992—, Osborne award 1975), Soc. Layerists in Multi-Media (nat. v.p. 1988-93), Ohio Watercolor Soc. (sec. 1979-82, v.p. 1982-89, pres. 1990—, Gold medal, Best of Show 1993), Nat. Watercolor Soc., Int. Noetic Sci., We. Ohio Watercolor Soc. (pres. 1979-80, 2d award 1982), Allied Artists N.Y., W.Va. Watercolor Soc., Ky. Watercolor Soc., Ga. Watercolor Soc. Avocations: hiking, reading, genealogy, music, travel. Home and Office: Phillis Studio 72 Stamm Cir Wheeling WV 26003-5549

PHILLS, BOBBY RAY, dean, agricultural research director. BS in Horticulture, So. U. and A&M Coll., 1968; MS in Horticulture/Vegetable Crops, La. State U., 1972, PhD in Horticulture/Plant Breeding, 1975. Postdoctoral fellow Cornell U., 1975-76; from asst. prof. plant and soil scis. to prof. plant and soil scis. Tuskegee (Ala.) U., 1976-82, assoc. dir. Carver Rsch. Found., 1982-85, dir. George Washington Carver Agrl. Expt. Sta., 1982-85; dean, rsch. dir. Coll. Agriculture So. U. and A&M Coll., Baton Rouge, 1985-86, prof. plant and soil scis., 1985—, interim dir. Small Farm and Family Resource Devel. Ctr., 1989—, dean, rsch. dir. Coll. Agriculture and Home Econs., 1986—; bd. dirs. Baton Rouge Green, Allegation Bd.; chmn.-elect So. Ariculture Dean's Coun.; mem. U.S. Dept. Agriculture/1890 Task Force, Nat. Urban Forestry Task Force on Minority Recruitement; chmn. 1890 Land-grant Legis. Com.; bd. regents La. Taskforce Agriculture, 1991; mem. La.-Nigerian Agriculture Commn., 1988; chmn. Nat. 1890 Centennial Com., 1989-90; co-chmn. SCS/1890 Symposium Com., 1987; mem. rsch. adv. com. US/AID, 1988-92; mem. joint coun. food and agrl. scis. U.S. Dept. Agriculture, 1990-92; team leader worldwide; presenter at numerous sci. meetings. U.S. Dept. Agriculture-CSRS grantee. Mem. Agrl. Rsch. Inst., Am. Soc. Horticultural Sci., Assn. 1890 Agrl. Adminstrs., Assn. Rsch. Dirs. (chmn. long-range planning com. 1986-90, chmn. 9th bi-annual rsch. symposium com. 1987, chmn. small-scale agriculture com. 1987-88, chmn. human capital devel., legis. com., com. chmn. 1988-90), Coun. 1890 Deans Resident Instrn. (chmn.), Nat. Assn. State Land-grant Colls. and Univs. (bd. dirs. divsn. agriculture 1989-90, legis. com. divsn. agriculture 1988-92, program planning com. 1989, budget com. divsn. agriculture 1989), Resident Instrn. Com. Orgn. and Policy, Sigma Xi, Alpha Phi Alpha, Beta Kappa Chi. Office: Southern Univ-Agr & Mech College Coop St Research Service Program Southern Branch PO Baton Rouge LA 70813

PHILOGENE, BERNARD J. R., academic administrator, science educator; b. Beau-Bassin, Mauritius, May 4, 1940; came to Can., 1961; s. Raymond Pierre and Simone Marie (Ruffier) P.; m. Hélène Marie Lebreux, July 7, 1964; children: Simone, Catherine. BS, U. Montreal, 1964; MS, McGill U., 1966; PhD, U. Wis., 1970; DSc (hon.), Compiègne, 1995. Research officer Can. Forestry Service, Que., 1966-70, research scientist, 1970-71; asst. prof. U. B.C., Vancouver, 1971-74; asst. prof., assoc. prof., then prof. entomology U. Ottawa, Can., 1974—, vice dean sci. and enging., 1982-85, acting dean, 1985-86, dean faculty of sci., 1986-90, acad. vice rector, 1990—; pres. Can. Consortium of Sci. Socs., 1992-94; cons. OAS, Washington, 1979-80, Agence de Coop. Culture & Tech., Paris, 1982-83, Can. Internat. Devel. Agy., Ottawa, 1983-85, UN Environ. Program, Geneva, Switzerland, 1985-86, Internat. Devel. Research Ctr., Ottawa, 1985—. Mem. Ont. Pesticide Adv. Com., 1987-91. Decorated officier de l'Ordre des Palmes Académiques (France); knight of merit Order of St. John of Jerusalem. Fellow Entomol. Soc. Can. (bd. dirs. 1977-80); mem. Am. Inst. Biol. Scis., Entomol. Soc. Am., Can. Pest Mgmt. Soc., Assn. Can.-Française Advancement Sci. (bd. dirs. 1984-86). Office: U Ottawa, 550 Cumberland, Ottawa, ON Canada K1N 6N5

PHILON, JAMES LEON, retired hotel executive; b. La Porte, Ind., June 10, 1928; s. Leon John and Leontine (Pol) P.; m. Margareet Metoyer, July 1, 1960; children: Christi, Anthony, Bryan. PhB, U. Chgo., 1948. Various operating positions Stevens/Conrad Hilton Hotel unit Hilton Hotels Corp., Chgo., 1951-60; asst. to v.p. Hilton Hotels Corp., Beverly Hills, Calif., 1960-65, asst. v.p., 1965-72, v.p. real estate and devel., 1972-80, sr. v.p. real estate and devel. and real estate and constrn., 1980-91, sr. v.p. real estate, 1991-94; ret., 1994. Mem. Urban Land Inst. (coun. 1980-94), Internat. Assn. Assessing Officers. Republican. Office: Hilton Hotels Corp 9336 Civic Center Dr Beverly Hills CA 90210-3604

PHILPOTT, HARRY MELVIN, former university president; b. Bassett, Va., May 6, 1917; s. Benjamin Cabell and Daisy (Hundley) P.; m. Pauline Breck Moran, Sept. 15, 1943; children: Harry Melvin, Jean Todd, Benjamin Cabell II, Virginia Lee. A.B., Washington and Lee U., 1938, LL.D., 1966; Ph.D., Yale U., 1947; D.D., Stetson U., 1960; LL.D., U. Fla., 1969, U. Ala., 1970; H.H.D., Samford U., 1978, Montevallo U., 1980, Auburn U., 1981. Ordained to ministry Bapt. Ch., 1942; dir. religious activities Washington and Lee U., 1938-40; prof. religion U. Fla., 1947-52, v.p., 1957-65; dean, head dept. religion and philosophy Stephens Coll., 1952-57; pres. Auburn U., 1965-80. Mem. Regional Edn. Bd., 1966-82, vice chmn., 1973-75; chmn. Ala. Edn. Study Commn., 1967-69; pres. Southeastern Conf., 1972-74. Served to 1st lt. Chaplains Corps., USNR, 1943-46. Mem. Nat. Assn. State Univs. and Land-Grant Colls. (chmn. council presidents 1972-73, exec. com. 1973-78, pres. 1976-77), Fla. Blue Key, Kappa Alpha, Omicron Delta Kappa, Kappa Delta Pi, Phi Kappa Phi. Home: PO Box 3037 Auburn AL 36831-3037

PHILPOTT, JAMES ALVIN, JR., lawyer; b. Lexington, Va., Apr. 26, 1947; s. James Alvin and Helen (Gibbs) P.; m. Judy Mauze, June 10, 1968; children: John Harman, Jean Cameron, James Hundley. BS in Commerce, Washington & Lee U., 1969, JD summa cum laude, 1972. Bar: N.Y. 1974, KY. 1980, U.S. Dist. Ct. (so. dist.) N.Y. 1975, U.S. Dist. Ct. (ea. dist.) Ky. 1991, U.S. Ct. Appeals (4th cir.) 1973, (U.S. Ct. Appeals (6th cir.) 1993. Law clk. to justice U.S. Ct. Appeals (4th cir.), Asheville, N.C., 1972-73; assoc. Cravath, Swaine & Moore, N.Y.C., 1974-79; exec. v.p., gen. counsel Gainesway Farm, Lexington, Ky., 1980-85; dir., mem. exec. com., sec. Breeders' Cup Ltd., 1983—. Editor-in chief Washington & Lee U. Law Rev., 1972. Trustee The Lexington Sch., 1984-91. Served to capt. U.S. Army, 1972-73. Mem. ABA (corp., banking and bus. law sect.), Ky. Bar Assn., Ky. Thoroughbred Assn., Washington & Lee U. Law Sch. Assn. (mem. coun. 1986-91), Idle Hour Country Club, The Lexington Club, Omicron Delta Kappa. Presbyterian. Office: PO Box 54350 Lexington KY 40555-4350

PHILPOTT, LARRY LA FAYETTE, horn player; b. Alma, Ark., Apr. 5, 1937; s. Lester and Rena (Owens) P.; m. Elise Robichaud, Nov. 24, 1962 (div. June 1975); children: Daniel, Stacy; m. Anne Sokol, Feb. 14, 1984. B.S., Ga. So. Coll., 1962; Mus.M., Butler U., 1972. Instr. in horn Butler U., De Pauw U.; dir. music Cedarcrest Sch., Marysville, Wash., 1991—; instr. horn Western Wash. U., Dept Music, Bellingham, 1995—. Mem., N.C. Symphony, 1960, Savannah (Ga.) Symphony, L'Orchestre Symphonique de Quebec, Que., Can., 1962-64, prin. horn player, Indpls. Symphony Orch., 1964-89, Flagstaff Summer Festival, 1968—; artist in-residence Ind.-Purdue Indpls.; appeared with, Am. Shakespeare Theatre, summer 1965, Charlottetown Festival, summers 1967-68, Flagstaff Summer Festival, 1968-85, Marrowstone Music Festival, 1985—. Served with USN, 1956-60. Mem. Music Educators Nat. Conf., Am. Fedn. Musicians, Internat. Conf. Symphony and Opera Musicians, Internat. Horn Soc., Coll. Music Soc., Phi Mu Alpha Sinfonia. Home: 14925 63rd Ave SE Snohomish WA 98290-5277 Office: Cedarcrest Sch 6400 88th St NE Marysville WA 98270-2800 also: Western Wash U Dept Music Bellingham WA 98225-9107

PHILPOTT, LINDSEY, civil engineer, researcher, educator; b. Bridestowe, Devonshire, Eng., Aug. 2, 1948; came to U.S., 1983; s. George Anthony and Joyce Thirza (Teeling) P.; m. Christine May Pembury, Aug. 20, 1974 (div.); children: David, Elizabeth; m. Kathleen Linda Matson, Feb. 17, 1982 (div.); children: Nicholas, Benjamin; m. Kim Elaine Moore, Nov. 24, 1991. Higher Nat. Cert. in Civil Engring., Bristol (Eng.) Poly., 1973; BSCE, U. Ariz., 1986, MSCE, 1987. Registered profl. engr., Calif. Area structural engr. Dept. Environment (Property Svcs. Agy.), Bristol, 1971-73; civil engr. Webco Civil Engring., Exeter, Eng., 1973-75; tech. mgr. Devon & Cornwall Housing Assn., Plymouth, Eng., 1975-79; prin., architect S.W. Design, Plymouth, 1979-81; archtl. engr. United Bldg. Factories, Bahrain, 1981-83; jr. engr. Cheyne Owen, Tucson, 1983-87; civil engr. Engring. Sci. Inc., Pasadena, Calif., 1987-89; project engr. Black & Veatch, Santa Ana, Calif., 1989-90; sr. engr. Brown & Caldwell, Irvine, Calif., 1990-91; environ. engr. Met. Water Dist. So. Calif., San Dimas, 1991—; adj. prof. hydraulics and instrumentation, San Antonio Coll., Walnut, Calif., 1995—. Foster parent Foster Parents Plan, Tucson, 1985-87; vol. reader tech. books Recording for the Blind, Hollywood, Calif., 1988-89, South Bay, Calif., 1990-91, Pomona, Calif., 1991—; vol. sailor/tchr. L.A. Maritime Inst. Topsail Youth Program, 1994—. Mem. ASCE, Am. Water Works Assn., Am. Water Resources Assn. (water quality com. 1990—), Water Environment Fedn., Engrs. Soc. (pres. 1985-96), Mensa, South Bay Yacht Racing Club (Marina del Rey, Calif., vice commodore 1995, commodore 1996). Avocations: hiking, cycling, sailing, crosswords. Office: Met Water Dist Environ Compliance Divsn PO Box 699 San Dimas CA 91773

PHINAZEE, HENRY CHARLES, systems analyst, educator; b. Birdnest, Va., Oct. 26, 1956; s. Charlie Phinazee and Johnnie Belle (Harris) Brice. BEd, Fort Hays State U., 1978, B of Psychology, 1979, M of Psychology, 1980; MEd, Wichita State U., 1985. Cert. tchr., Kans., Tex. Minority advisor Fort Hays State U., 1978-80; tchr. Wichita Pub. Schs., 1980—; tchr. Wichita State U., 1988-92, dorm coord. coll. of health profession, 1986-92, work coord. coll. of health profession, 1988-91; computer analyst Beech Aircraft Corp., Wichita, 1992—. Author: (software) Dayreq, 1989. Mentor Grow Your Own Tchrs., Wichita Pub. Schs., 1990; liaison Com. on Polit. Edn., Wichita, 1988—. Recipient Svc. award Big Bros./Big Sisters, 1987. Mem. Am. Amature Racquetball, Wichita Assn. of Black Educators (treas. 1991-92), Wichita Fedn. of Tchrs. (2d v.p. 1988-92, Svc. award 1991), Kans. Assn. of Black Educators (com. head 1991-92), Phi Delta Kappa, Kappa Alpha Psi (polemark 1988-92, Svc. award). Democrat. Baptist. Avocations: racquetball, running, bicycling, reading, church. Home: 4400 Horizon Hill # 4807 San Antonio TX 78229 Office: Brackenridge HS 400 Eagleland Dr San Antonio TX 78210

PHINIZY, ROBERT BURCHALL, electronics executive; b. Ben Hill, Ga., June 30, 1926; BS, U. Ariz., 1951; postgrad. U. So. Calif., 1952-55, UCLA, 1956-62; children: Robert B., William, David. Pres., LB Products, Santa Monica, Calif., 1954-68, IMC Magnetics Western, South Gate, Calif., 1968-69, Am. Electronics, Fullerton, Calif., 1969-71; gen. mgr. electronics div. Eaton Co., Anaheim, Calif., 1971-82; pres., CEO Genisco Tech. Corp., Compton, Calif., 1972-83; chmn. bd., CEO Genisco Computers Corp., Costa Mesa, Calif., 1983—, Trans Tech. Alliances, Calif., 1986—; bd. dirs. Microsemi Corp., Santa Ana, Calif., 1992—, Biosonics Inc., Seattle, 1989—. Contbr. articles to tech. jours.; patentee in field. Bd. dirs. U. Calif., Dominguez Hills, 1975-89; mem. L.A. Town Hall; chmn. bd. dirs. Calif. State U. Found., 1986. Served to capt. USN, 1943-47, USNR, 1947-80. Fellow Coll. Engrs. L.A.; mem. IEEE, Communication and Computers Indsl. Assn., Electronics Assn. Calif. (treas. 1986), Am. Electronics Assn. (chmn. small bus. com. Orange County, Calif. 1989-90). Democrat. Home: PO Box 65351 Port Ludlow WA 98365-0351 Office: 20 Bluebird Ln Port Ludlow WA 98365

PHINNEY, JEAN SWIFT, psychology educator; b. Princeton, N.J., Mar. 12, 1933; d. Emerson H. and Anne (Davis) Swift; m. Bernard O. Phinney, Dec. 11, 1965; children: Peter, David. BA, Mass. Wellesley Coll., 1955; MA, UCLA, 1969, PhD, 1973. Asst. prof. psychology Calif. State U., L.A., 1977-81, assoc. prof. psychology, 1981-86, prof. psychology, 1986—. Editor: Children's Ethnic Socialization, 1987; asst. editor Jour. Adolescence; contbr. articles to profl. jours. NIH grantee. Mem. Am. Psychol. Assn., Soc. for Rsch. in Child Devel., Soc. for Rsch. in Adolescence. Avocations: skiing, hiking, travel, chamber music. Office: Calif State U Dept Psychology 5151 State University Dr Los Angeles CA 90032

PHINNEY, WILLIAM CHARLES, retired geologist; b. South Portland, Maine, Nov. 16, 1930; s. Clement Woodbridge and Margaret Florence (Foster) P.; m. Colleen Dorothy Murphy, May 31, 1953; children—Glenn, Duane, John, Marla. B.S., MIT, 1953, M.S., 1956, Ph.D., 1959. Faculty geology U. Minn., 1959-70; chief geology br. NASA Lyndon B. Johnson Space Center, Houston, 1970-82; chief planetology br. NASA Lyndon B. Johnson Space Center, 1982-89, ret., 1994; NASA prin. investigator lunar samples. Contbr. articles to profl. jours. Served with C.E. AUS, 1953-55. Recipient NASA Exceptional Sci. Achievement medal, 1972, NASA Cert. of Commendation, 1987; NASA rsch. grantee, 1972-94, NSF rsch. grantee, 1960-70. Mem. Am. Geophys. Union, AAAS, Mineral. Soc. Am., Geol. Soc. Am., Minn. Acad. Sci. (dir.), Sigma Xi. Home: 18063 Judicial Way S Lakeville MN 55044-8839

PHIPPS, ALLEN MAYHEW, management consultant; b. Seattle, Oct. 3, 1938; s. Donald Mayhew and Virginia (McGinn) P.; B.A. in Econs., U. Calif., Berkeley, 1961; M.B.A. with honors, Stanford U., 1969; m. Joyce Elisabeth Alberti, Aug. 21, 1971; children—Ramsey Mayhew, Justin Beckwith. Security analyst Morgan Guaranty Trust Co., 1968; with Boston Cons. Group, Inc., 1969—, mgr. 1971-74, mem. sr. team, Calif., 1974-77, corp. v.p., dir., 1975—; mgr. Boston Cons. Group, G.mb.H, Munich. W. Ger., 1978-82, partner-in-charge West Coast client devel., Menlo Park, Calif., 1982-84; pres. Techno Digital Systems, Inc., 1984-86; pres., chief exec. officer, Techno Digital System (Sellectek, Inc.), 1984-85; exec. v.p., Regis McKenna Inc., Palo Alto, Calif., 1985-87; pvt. practice mgmt. cons., Menlo Pk., 1987-95; chief exec. officer Bio Electro Systems, Palo Alto, 1989-92; mng. dir., Bus. Engring. Inc., Menlo Park, Calif., 1992-95; sr. v.p. bus. and policy group SRI Internat., Menlo Park, Calif., 1995-96; pres., CEO SRI Consulting, Menlo Park, 1996—. Served to capt. U.S. Army, 1961-67. Decorated Bronze Star, Army Commendation medal with 2 oak leaf clusters. Mem. Alpha Delta Phi. Republican. Presbyterian. Clubs: Bohemian (San Francisco); Sharon Heights Golf and Country (Menlo Park). Home: 33 Prado Secoya St Atherton CA 94027-4126 Office: SRI Consulting 333 Ravenswood Ave Menlo Park CA 94025-3453

PHIPPS, JOHN RANDOLPH, retired army officer; b. Kansas, Ill, May 16, 1919; s. Charles Winslow and Kelsey Ethel (Torrence) P.; m. Pauline M. Prunty, Feb. 8, 1946; children: Charles W., Kelsey J. Phipps-Selander. B.S. in Econs. with honors, U. Ill., 1941; M.P.A., Sangamon State U., 1976; assoc. course, Command and Gen. Staff Coll., 1959, nuclear weapons employment course, 1962; course, U.S. Army War Coll., 1973, U.S. Nat. Def. U., 1978. Owner, operator chain shoe stores in Eastern Ill., 1946-70; commd. 2d lt. F.A. U.S. Army, 1941, advanced through grades to capt., 1943; service in Philippines and Japan; discharged as maj., 1946; organizer, comdr. Co. E, 130th Inf., Ill.; N.G., Mattoon, 1947; comdg. officer 2d Bn., 130th Inf. N.G., 1951, lt. col. 2d Bn., 130th Inf., 1951; called to fed. service, 1952; adv. (29th Regt., 9th Republic of Korea Div.), 1952-53; comdr. officer 1st Bn., 130th Inf., Ill. N.G., 1954, col., 1959; comdg. officer 2d Brigade, 33d Div., 1963-67; asst. div. comdr. 33d Inf. Div., 1967, brig. gen., 1967; comdr. 33d Inf. Brigade, Chgo., 1967-70; comdr. Ill. Emergency Ops. Hdqrs., 1970, asst. adj. gen. Ill., 1970-77, acting adj. gen., 1977-78, adj. gen., 1978, promoted to maj. gen., 1978, now maj. gen. ret. Decorated Silver Star, Bronze Star, Disting. Service medal, Combat Infantry Badge, Army Disting. Service medal Ill., various Philippine and Korean decorations; State of Ill. Long and Honorable Service medal. Mem. VFW, Adj. Gens. Assn. U.S., N.G. Assn. U.S., N.G. Assn. Ill., Am. Legion, Amvets. Home: 100 Wabash Ave Mattoon IL 61938-4524 Office: Phipps 100 Wabash Ave Mattoon IL 61938-4524

PHIPPS, LYNNE BRYAN, interior architect, clergywoman, parent educator; b. Chapel Hill, N.C., Sept. 23, 1964; d. Floyd Talmadge and Sandra Patricia (McLester) Bryan; m. Thomas Otey Phipps, July 18, 1985. BFA, RISD, 1986, B Interior Architecture, 1987; cert. in parent edn., Wheelock Coll., Boston, 1989; postgrad., Andover Newton Theol. Sem., 1991—. Nat. cert. interior arch. Apprentice Thompson Ventulett Stainback, Atlanta, 1983-85; jr. designer Flansberg & Assocs., Boston, 1986-87; sr. designer, prin. Innovative Designs, Duxbury, Mass., 1986—; parent educator, pres. Parenting Puzzle, 1990—; parent educator Families First, Cambridge, Mass.; youth min. St. Andrew's Episcopal Ch., Hanover, Mass., 1992-95; youth and family min. St. Stephen's Episcopal Ch., Cohasset, Mass., 1993—; guest lectr., jurist Auburn (Ala.) U., 1988, RISD, Providence, 1990; assoc. prof. Mass. Bay C.C., Wellesley, 1987-88; guest jurist Wentworth U., Boston, 1988-89; guest lectr. Architectural and Family Issues; guest jurist U. Memphis, 1995. Designer furniture. Mem. Internat. Interior Design Assn., Assn. Parent Educators, Jr. League Boston. Avocations: sailing, tennis, antique boats. Office: Innovative Designs The Parenting Puzzle 18 Bayview Rd Duxbury MA 02332-5009

PHIPPS, WILMA J., nursing educator, author; b. Detroit, Jan. 24, 1925; d. Walter and Inez M. (Steele) P. Diploma, Harper Hosp. Sch. Nursing, 1946; BSN, Wayne U., 1954; AM, U. Chgo., 1956, PhD, 1977. Assoc. prof. med./surg. nursing Case Western Res. U., Cleve., 1970-76, prof. med./surg. nursing, 1976-87, prof. emeritus, 1987—. Editor: Medical-Surgical Nursing, Concepts and Clinical Practice, 1995, Medical-Surgical Nursing, A Nursing Process Approach, 1993. Mem. ANA, APHA, Am. Acad. Nursing, Nat. League Nursing, Sigma Theta Tau, Pi Lambda Theta. Home: 3701 Mayfield Rd Apt 302 Cleveland OH 44121-1750

PHISTER, MONTGOMERY, JR., computer engineering consultant, writer; b. San Pedro, Calif., Feb. 26, 1926; s. Montgomery and Helga Laurena (Winther) P.; m. Melinda Miles, Mar. 29, 1974; children—Montgomery, Julia Elizabeth, Roger Benjamin. Student, Stanford U., 1943-44, B.S., 1949, M.S., 1950; Ph.D., Cambridge (Eng.) U., 1953. Mem. tech. staff Hughes Aircraft Co., Culver City, Calif., 1953-55; dir. engring. TRW Products Co., Los Angeles, 1955-60; v.p. engring. Scantlin Electronics Inc. (later Quotron Systems), Los Angeles, 1960-66; v.p. devel. Xerox Data Systems, Los Angeles, 1966-72; pvt. practice cons., writer Santa Fe, 1972—; instr. UCLA, 1954-64, Harvard U., 1974, U. Sydney, Australia, 1975. Author: Logical Design of Digital Computers, 1958, Data Processing Technology and Economics, 1976. Served with USMCR, 1944-46. Fellow IEEE; mem. Assn. for Computing Machinery. Republican. Patentee. Home and Office: 414 Camino De Las Animas Santa Fe NM 87501-4535

PHLEGAR, BENJAMIN FOCHT, retired magazine editor; b. Salina, Kans., Nov. 21, 1921; s. Benjamin Gray and Frances Lucile (Focht) P.; m. Jane Fulton, Sept. 19, 1945 (dec. Sept. 1983); children: Janet Margaret, Benjamin Fulton. B.J., U. Mo., 1943. Reporter St. Louis Star-Times, 1943-44; with AP, 1944-63; newsman, then automotive editor AP, Detroit, 1955-63; Detroit bur. chief, asso. editor, then asst. mng. editor U.S. News & World Report, Washington, 1963-78; exec. editor U.S. News & World Report, 1979-85. Mem. Am. Soc. Mag. Editors. Home: 4740 Connecticut Ave NW Washington DC 20008-5632

PHOCAS, GEORGE JOHN, international lawyer, business executive; b. N.Y.C., Dec. 1, 1927; m. Katrin Gorny, Feb. 26, 1966; 1 child, George Alexander. A.B., U. Chgo., 1950, J.D., 1953. Bar: N.Y. 1955, U.S. Supreme Ct. 1962. Assoc. Sullivan & Cromwell, N.Y.C., 1953-56; counsel Creole Petroleum Corp., Caracas, Venezuela, 1956-60; internat. negotiator Standard Oil Co. N.J. (Exxon), 1960-63; sr. ptnr. Casey, Lane & Mittendorf, London, 1963-72, counsel, 1972-76; exec. v.p. Occidental Petroleumm Corp., Los Angeles, 1972-74; adv., U.S. del. UN, ECAFE, Teheran, 1963. Trustee Assn. Naval Aviation, Washington, Owl's Head Aviation Mus., Maine; mem. vis. bd. U. Chgo. Law Sch.; bd. visitors U. Chgo. Law Sch. Capt. U.S. Army. Mem. ABA, Law Soc. London, Brit. Inst. Comparative Law, Am. Soc. Internat. Law, Assn. Bar City N.Y., Boodles Club, Met. Club (N.Y.C.). Home: 28 Aubrey Walk, London W87JG, England also: 1605 Middle Gulf Dr 102 Sanibel FL 33957

PHOENIX, ANTOINETTE DAVIS, fundraiser; b. Clarksville, Tex., July 26, 1959; d. Robert and Addie (Wilson) Davis; m. Donnell Phoenix, Apr. 25, 1986; 1 child, Brittanie Dionne. AA in Social Sci., Wichita State U., 1989, B of Gen. Studies, 1989. Sales assoc. Henry's Inc., Wichita, 1981-84; with Wichita State U., 1981-90; accounts mgr. United Way of the Plains, Wichita, 1990—; panel spkr. numerous confs. Wichita State U., 1989, 92, 93-94; spkr. Wichita Metro Family Preservation Agy., Inc. Allocation vol. United Way of the Plains, 1990. Mem. NAFE, Wichita Area C. of C. (com. mem. 1991-92), The Chamber, Small Bus. Coun., 1992—, Nat. Assn. for Advancement of Colored People, 1990, Bus. and Profl. Women, Tabernacle Bapt. Ch., 1991—. Democrat. Baptist. Avocations: creative writing, reading, aerobics. Office: United Way of the Plains 212 N Market St Ste 200 Wichita KS 67202-2015

PHULÉ, PRADEEP PRABHAKAR, engineering educator; b. Pune, India, Mar. 14, 1960; s. Prabhakar P. and Pratibha P. (Joshi) Fulay; m. Jyotsna D. Pangrekar, Dec. 28, 1990; children: Aarohee, Suyash. B in Tech. with honors, IIT Bombay, 1983, M in Tech. with honors, 1984; PhD, U. Ariz., 1989. Trainee engr. Sandvik Asia, India, 1980-81; trainee engr. Mahindra Sintered Products, India, 1981-82; rsch. asst., dept. metallurgical enging. IIT, Bombay, 1983-84; teaching asst., dept. chemistry Brigham Young U., Provo, Utah, 1985; grad. rsch. and teaching asst, dept. materials sci. enging. U. Ariz., Tucson, 1985-89; asst. prof. materials sci. and engring. U. Pitts., 1989-92, William Kepler Whiteford faculty fellow, asst. prof., 1992-94, assoc. prof. materials sci. and enging., 1994—. Contbr. numerous articles to profl. jours. Presenter in field. Recipient NSF, Alcoa Found., Am. Chem. Soc., U. Pitts. Ctrl. Rsch. Devel. Fund, Internat. Soc. for Hybrid Microelectronics, Ben Franklin Tech. Ctr., Air Force Office Scientific Rsch. grants. Mem. AAAS, Materials Rsch. Soc. (v.p. Greater Pitts. sect. 1990-91, bd. dirs. 1992-93, sec. 1990), Am. Ceramic Soc. (assoc. editor jour. 1995—, electronics divsn.-edn. com. 1992-93, 93-94), Am. Soc. for Engring. Edn., Internat. Soc. for Hybrid Microelectronics, Am. Chem. Soc. Achievements include rsch. in chem. synthesis of advanced electronic and optical ceramic materials. Avocations: tennis, swimming. Office: U Pitts 848 Benedum Hall Pittsburgh PA 15261

PHYPERS, DEAN PINNEY, retired computer company executive; b. Cleve., Jan. 13, 1929; s. Fordham S. and Grace Ellen (Pinney) P.; children: Dean A., Toni T., William C., Jonathan W., Katharine L. B.A. in Physics, Harvard U., 1950; postgrad., U. Mich. Sch. Bus., 1952. With IBM, 1955-87; v.p. bus. plans IBM, Armonk, N.Y., 1972-74; v.p. fin. and planning IBM, 1974-79, sr. v.p. fin. and planning, dir., 1979-82, sr. v.p., dir., 1982-87; bd. dirs. Bethlehem Steel, Am. Internat. Group, Church and Dwight Co., Inc., Cambrex Inc. Trustee Com. for Econ. Devel. Served with USNR, 1952-55. Home: 220 Rosebrook Rd New Canaan CT 06840-3727

PIAKER, PHILIP MARTIN, accountant, educator; b. N.Y.C., Oct. 26, 1921; s. Jacob and Sarah (Schloss) P.; m. Pauline Strum, Sept. 22, 1946;

children: Susan, Alan, Matthew. BA, CCNY, 1943, MBA, 1949. Lectr. CCNY, 1949-52; asst. prof. acctg. SUNY, Binghamton, 1952-57, assoc. prof., 1957-62, prof., 1962—, Disting. Svc. prof. acctg., 1980—, chmn. dept. acctg., 1970-76, 77-89; chmn. bd. Endicott Rsch. Group, Inc., Johnson City, N.Y., 1983—; adv. dir. Endicott Bank N.Y.; mem. N.Y. State Bd. for Pub. Accountancy, 1973-83, chmn., 1982-83; v.p. Piaker, Lyons, P.C., CPA's; mem. Nat. Bd. to Evaluate CPA Exams., 1979-83; Danforth Seminar on Bus. Morality fellow Harvard U., 1959; Summer Study on Ethics in Bus. fellow U. So. Calif., 1982. Mem. editorial bd. Binghamton Reporter, 1975—. Bd. dirs. Broome chpt. Am. Cancer Soc., 1974-79, Tri-Cities Opera; trustee Temple Israel Binghamton, 1978—. With U.S. Army, 1943-46. SUNY SWANA fellow Jerusalem, 1966, Am. Profs. for Peace in Middle East fellow Jerusalem, 1974; recipient Chancellors award for teaching excellence, 1975, David Ben Gurion award State of Israel, 1979, Outstanding Contbn. to Acctg. award Found. for Acctg., 1979, Outstanding Educator award Found. for Acctg. Rsch., 1986. Mem. AICPA, N.Y. State Soc. CPA's (pres. Binghamton chpt. 1963-65), Am. Acctg. Assn., Acctg. Rsch. Assn., Nat. Assn. Accts., Bus. Ethics Soc., SUNY Alumni Assn. (Disting. Svc. award 1989), CHABAD (pres. 1989-92). Home: 301 Manchester Rd Vestal NY 13850-3604 also: 7421 Hearth Stone Ave Boynton Beach FL 33437

PIAN, RULAN CHAO, musicologist, scholar; b. Cambridge, Mass., Apr. 20, 1922; d. Yuen Ren and Buwei (Yang) Chao; m. Theodore Hsueh-huang Pian, Oct. 3, 1945; 1 child, Canta Chao-po. BA, Radcliffe Coll., 1944, MA, 1946, PhD, 1960. Teaching asst., instr. in modern Chinese Harvard U., 1947-60, lectr. Chinese and Chinese music, 1961-74, prof. Ea. Asian langs. and civilizations, prof. music, 1974-92; prof. emerita, 1992—; coordinator modern Chinese lang. instrn. Harvard U., 1962-68, mem. council E. Asian studies, 1975-92, faculty mem. Com. on Degrees in Folklore and Mythology, 1976-92, master of South House, 1975-78; vis. prof. dept. music The Chinese U. Hong Kong, 1975, 78-79, 82, 94, inst. humanities Nat. Tsing Hua U., Taiwan, 1990, Sch. Humanities, Nat. Cen. U., Taiwan, 1992; hon. prof. Cen. China U. of Sci. and Tech., Wuhan, 1990, Chengdu, China, 1994; hon. rsch. fellow Shanghai Conservatory Music, China, 1991; hon. guest rschr. Inst. Music Rsch., China Acad. of Arts, Beijing, 1993; academician Academia Sinica, Taiwan, 1990. Author: A Syllabus for the Mandarin Primer, 1961, Sonq Dynasty Musical Sources and Their Interpretation, 1967; compiler: Complete Musical Works of Yuen Ren Chao, 1987; contbr. articles to scholarly jours. Recipient Caroline Wilby dissertation prize Radcliffe Coll., 1960, Radcliffe Grad. Soc. medal, 1980; NDEA Fulbright-Hayes research grantee Chinese Music Taiwan, 1964; NEH grantee Hong Kong, 1978-79. Mem. Am. Musicological Soc. (coun. 1993—, Otto Kindeldey book award 1968), Internat. Musicological Soc., Soc. Ethnomusicology (coun. 1968-75, 87-90), Conf. Chinese Oral and Performing Lit. (co-founder, pres. 1983-90, permanent hon. pres. 1995—), Assn. for Chinese Mus. Rsch. (co-founder). Home: 14 Brattle Cir Cambridge MA 02138-4625 Office: 2 Divinity Ave Cambridge MA 02138-2020

PIAN, THEODORE HSUEH-HUANG, engineering educator, consultant; b. Shanghai, China, Jan. 18, 1919; came to U.S., 1943; s. Chao-Hsin Shu-Cheng and Chih-Chuan (Yen) P.; m. Rulan Chao, Oct. 3, 1945; 1 child, Canta Chao-Po. B in Engring., Tsing Hua U., Kunming, China, 1940; MS, MIT, 1944, DSc, 1948; DSc (hon.), Beijing U. Aeros. and Astronautics, 1990; PhD (hon.), Shanghai U., 1991. Engr. Cen. Aircraft Mfg. Co., Loiwing, China, 1940-42, Chengtu Glider Mfg. Factory, 1942-43; tchg. asst. MIT, Cambridge, 1946-47, rsch. assoc., 1947-52, asst. prof., 1952-59, assoc. prof., 1959-66, prof., 1966-89, prof. emeritus, 1989—; vis. assoc. Calif. Inst. Tech., Pasadena, 1965-66; vis. prof. U. Tokyo, 1974, Tech. U., Berlin, 1975; vis. chair prof. Nat. Tsing Hua U., Hsin Chu, Taiwan, 1990, Nat. Ctrl. U., ChungLi, Taiwan, 1992; hon. prof. Beijing U. Aero. and Astronautics, Beijing Inst. Tech., Southwestern Jaiotong U., Dalian U. Tech., Huazhong U. Sci. and Tech., Changsha Rwy. U., Ctrl.-South U. Tech., Hohai U., Nanjing U. of Aero. and Astronautics, Dalian Rwy. U. Recipient von Karman Meml. prize TRE Corp., Beverly Hills, Calif., 1974. Fellow AAAS, AIAA (assoc. editor jour. 1973-75, Structures, Structural Dynamics and Materials award 1975), U.S. Assn. Computational Mechanics (founding mem.); mem. ASME (hon.), Nat. Acad. Engring., Am. Soc. Engring. Edn., Internat. Assn. for Computational Mechanics (hon. mem. gen. coun.). Home: 14 Brattle Cir Cambridge MA 02138-4625 Office: MIT Dept Aeronautics and Astronautics 77 Massachusetts Ave Cambridge MA 02139-4301

PIANALTO, SANDRA, bank executive; b. Vicenza, Italy, 1954. Graduate, U. Akron, 1976; Post graduate, George Washington U., 1985. First v.p., coo Fed. Reserve bank of Cleve. Office: Fed Reserve Bank Cleveland PO Box 6387 Cleveland OH 44101-2021*

PIANKO, THEODORE A., lawyer; b. Dennville, N.J., Sept. 5, 1955; s. Theodore and Pasqualina (Liguori) P.; m. Beatriz Maria Olivera (div. Dec. 1985); m. Kathryn Anne Lindley, Feb. 18, 1990; children: Matthew James, Samuel Wahoo. BA, SUNY, 1975; JD, U. Mich., 1978. Bar: Mich. 1978, Ill. 1979, Calif. 1980. Atty. Ford Motor Co., Dearborn, Mich., 1978-80; assoc. Lillick McHose & Charles, L.A., 1980-83; ptnr. Sidley & Austin, L.A., 1983-94, Christie, Parker & Hale, Pasadena, Calif., 1994—. Office: Christie Parker & Hale 350 Colorado Blvd Fl 5 Pasadena CA 91109-7068

PIANTINI, CARLOS, conductor; b. Santo Domingo, Dominican Republic, May 9, 1927; s. Alberto and Marina (Espinal) P.; m. Marianne Piantini (div. 1977); children: Susan, Vivian, Albert, Frank; m. Yolanda Trujillo, Dec. 5, 1982. MusB, NYU, 1968. Violinist 1st Recital, Santo Domingo, 1937-44, Mex. Symphony, 1944-47, Juilliard Sch., N.Y.C., 1947-50, N.Y. Philharm. Orch., N.Y.C., 1956-71; condr. Vienna (Austria) Acad. Music, 1971-73; artistic dir. Nat. Theatre, Santo Domingo, 1973-78; condr. Caracas (Venezuela) Philharm., 1979-83, Nat. Symphonic Orch., Santo Domingo, 1983—; Domican amb. to UN; head cultural affairs Dominican Rep. Govt., 1950-56. Contbr. articles to profl. jours. Cons. V Centennial Commemorative, Santo Domingo, 1988. Avocation: stamp collecting. Office: Nat Symphonic Orch, Palacio de Bellas Artes, Santo Domingo Dominican Republic

PIASSICK, JOEL BERNARD, lawyer; b. Atlanta, June 2, 1940; s. Louis S. and Sarah (Freeman) P.; m. Karen Pevow, Aug. 11, 1963; children: Joan, Louis. BA in Polit. Sci., Tulane U., 1962; LLB, U. Va., 1965. Bar: Va. 1965, Ga. 1966. Ptnr. Smith, Gambrell & Russell, Atlanta, 1967-90, Kilpatrick & Cody, Atlanta, 1990—; bd. dirs. Southeastern Bankruptcy Law Inst., Inc. Fellow Am. Coll. Bankruptcy. Office: Kilpatrick & Cody 1100 Peachtree St NE Ste 2800 Atlanta GA 30309-4528

PIATT, JACK BOYD, manufacturing executive; b. Washington, Pa., Jan. 8, 1928; s. Harold Boyd and Violet Marie (Amos) P.; m. Thelma Jean Ritchie, Mar. 15, 1948 (div. 1974); children: Jack Boyd, Rod L., Rebecca, Regina; m. Kathleen Mary Shattuck, May 4, 1975. Student schs. Washington, Pa. Chmn. Millcraft Industries, Washington, Pa., 1957—; bd. dirs. Pitts. br. Fed. Res. Bank Cleve. Pres., bd. dirs. Meadowcroft Found., Avella, Pa.; bd. dirs. Southeastern Found., Miami, Fla., 1983-84. Recipient Disting. Svc. award Greater Washington Area Jaycees, 1980; named Tri-State Entrepreneur of Yr. Arthur Young and INC. mag., 1989. Mem. Am. Iron and Steel Inst., Eastern States Blast Furnace Assn., Assn. Iron and Steel Engrs., Duquesne Club (Pitts.) Republican. Home: PO Box 396 Meadow Lands PA 15347-0396 Office: Millcraft Industries 90 W Chestnut St Washington PA 15301-4524

PIAZZA, MARGUERITE, opera singer, actress, entertainer; b. New Orleans, May 6, 1926; d. Albert William and Michaela (Piazza) Luft; m. William J. Condon, July 15, 1953 (dec. Mar. 1968); children: Gregory, James (dec.), Shirley, William J., Marguerite P., Anna Becky; m. Francis Harrison Bergtholdt, Nov. 8, 1970. MusB, Loyola U., New Orleans; MusM, La. State U.; MusD (hon.), Christian Bros. Coll., 1973; LHD honoris causa, Loyola U., Chgo., 1975. Singer N.Y.C. Ctr. Opera, 1948, Met. Opera Co., 1950; TV artist, regular singing star Your Show of Shows NBC, 1950-54; entertainer various supper clubs Cotillion Room, Hotel Pierre, N.Y.C., 1954, Las Vegas, Los Angeles, New Orleans, San Francisco, 1956—; ptnr. Sound Express Music Pub. Co., Memphis, 1987—; bd. dirs. Cemrel, Inc. Appeared as guest performer on numerous mus. TV shows. Nat. crusade chmn. Am. Cancer Soc., 1971; founder, bd. dirs. Marguerite Piazza Gala for the Benefit of St. Jude's Hosp., 1976; bd. dirs. Memphis Opera Co., World Literacy Found., NCCJ; v.p., life bd. dirs. Memphis Symphony Orch.; nat. chmn. Soc. for Cure Epilepsy. Decorated Mil. and Hospittaler Order of St. Lazarus of Jerusalem; recipient svc. award Chgo. Heart Assn., 1956, svc. award Fedn. Jewish Philanthropies of N.Y., 1956, Sesquicentennial medal Carnegie Hall, St. Martin De Porres award So. Dominicans, 1994; named Queen of Memphis, Memphis Cotton Carnival, 1973, Person of Yr., La. Coun. for Performing Arts, 1975, Woman of Yr., Nat. Am. Legion, Woman of Yr., Italian-Am. Soc. Mem. Nat. Speakers Assn., Woman's Exchange, Memphis Country Club, Memphis Hunt and Polo Club, New Orleans Country Club, Summit Club, Beta Sigma Omicron, Phi Beta. Roman Catholic. Home: #301 Park Pl 5400 Park Ave Apt 301 Memphis TN 38119-3639

PIAZZA, MICHAEL JOSEPH, professional baseball player; b. Norristown, Pa., Sept. 4, 1968. Student, Miami (Fla.)-Dade C.C. Player L.A. Dodgers, 1988—; mem. Nat. League All-Star Team, 1994. Named Nat. League Rookie Player of Yr., Sporting News, 1993, Catcher on the Sporting News N.L. All-Star Team, 1993-94, N.L. Silver Slugger Team, 1993-94, named to Nat. League Slugger Team, 1993; named Nat. League Rookie of Yr., Baseball Writers Assn., 1993. Office: LA Dodgers Dodger Stadium 100 Elysian Park Ave Los Angeles CA 90012*

PICARD, DENNIS J., electronics company executive; b. 1932. BBA, Northeastern Univ., 1962. With RCA, 1954-55; elec. engr. Raytheon Co., 1955-59, design engr., 1959-61, sect. mgr., 1961-69, dir. equipment div., data acquisition systems directorate, 1969-76, asst. gen. mgr. ops., equipment div., 1976-77, asst. gen. mgr. ops., equipment div., also corp. v.p., 1977-81, v.p. equipment div., 1981-1985, sr. v.p., gen. mgr. missile systems div., 1985-89, pres., 1989-90, chmn. bd., CEO, 1990—, also bd. dirs. Served USAF 1951-53. Mem. NAE. Office: Raytheon Co 141 Spring St Lexington MA 02173-7899*

PICARD, LAURENT A(UGUSTIN), management educator, administrator, consultant; b. Quebec, Que., Can., Oct. 27, 1927; s. Edouard and Alice (Gingras) P.; m. Therese Picard; children: Andre, Marc, Robert (dec.), Denys, Jean-Louis, François (dec.). BA, Laval U., Quebec, 1947, BS, 1954; DBA, Harvard U., 1964. Prof. U. Montreal, Que., Can., 1962-68, dir. bus. adminstrn. dept., 1964-68; exec. v.p. Can. Broadcasting Corp., Ottawa, Ont., 1968-72, pres., chief exec. officer, 1972-75; joint prof. McGill U. and U. Montreal, 1977-78; dean faculty mgmt. McGill U., Montreal, 1978-86, prof., 1986—; mem. Royal Commn. on Newspapers, Royal Commn. on Econ. Union and Devel. Prospects for Can.; conciliation commr. Maritime Employers Assn., Prot of Montreal; bd. dirs. Lombard-Odier Trust Co., Jean Coutu Group, Dorel Ind. Inc.; chmn. Bonsecours Market; cons. to industry; guest speaker at internat. meetings. Contbr. articles to profl. jours. Chmn. Nat. Book Festival, 1978-79; chmn. jury Prix Gerin Lajoie, Ministry Cultural Affairs, 1982. Recipient 125th Anniversary medal Can., 1992; decorated companion Order of Can., 1977. Mem. Commonwealth Broadcasting Assn. (1st pres.). Home: 5602 Wilderton Ave, Montreal, PQ Canada H3T 1R9 Office: McGill U Faculty Mgmt, 1001 Sherbrooke St W, Montreal, PQ Canada H3A 1G5

PICCILLO, JOSEPH, artist; b. Buffalo, Jan. 9, 1941. B.S., Buffalo State U., 1961, M.S., 1964. Faculty Buffalo State U. Coll., 1967—, prof. art edn., 1980—. One-man shows include Banfer Gallery, N.Y.C., 1966, 68, 70, Krasner Gallery, N.Y.C., 1971-79, Housitanic (Conn.) Mus., 1977, Galerie Loyse Oppenheim, Geneva, 1978, 79, Monique Knowlton Gallery, N.Y.C., 1980, 81, 83, 84, Betsy Rosenfeld Gallery, Chgo., 1980, 83, 85, 87, 89, 91, 94, Albright-Knox Art Gallery, Buffalo, 1981, Galleria Forni, Bologna, Italy, 1983, Barbara Fendrick Gallery, N.Y.C., 1988, Brendan Walter Gallery, Santa Monica, Calif., 1990, 92, Fay Gold Gallery, Atlanta, 1994, Monique Knowlton Gallery, N.Y.C., 1995; group shows include Fischer Fine Arts Ltd., London, 1977, 78, Galerie Isy Brachot, Brussels, 1977, Art 9'78, Basle, Switzerland, 1978, 79; represented in permanent collections, Mus. Modern Art, N.Y.C., Chgo. Art Inst., Albright-Knox Gallery, Bklyn. Mus., Rochester (N.Y.) Meml. Art Center, Minn. Mus. Art, Mpls., Little Rock Mus., Met. Mus. Art, N.Y.C., Butler Mus. Art, Youngstown, Ohio, San Francisco Mus. Modern Art, Ball State U., Muncie, Ind., So. Ill. U., Carbondale, SUNY, Buffalo, Fredonia, Alfred (N.Y.) U., St. Lawrence U., Canton, N.Y., Kutztown (Pa.) State Coll., Hamline U., St. Paul, 1st Nat. Bank Chgo., others; panelist, Visual Arts Panel, N.Y. State Council on Arts, 1976-78. SUNY fellow, 1968, 69, 72, 76, 79, 80; Creative Artists Pub. Service Program grantee, 1972, grantee Nat. Endowment Arts fellow, 1979. Home: 461 West Ave Buffalo NY 14213-2501

PICCININI, ROBERT M., grocery store chain executive. CEO, chmn. Save Mart Supermarkets, Modesto, Calif. Office: Save Mart Supermarkets 1800 Standiford Ave Modesto CA 95350-0180*

PICCININO, ROCCO MICHAEL, librarian; b. Phila., Aug. 21, 1949; s. Rocco Anthony and Ida Marie (Minicozzi) P. BA in History magna cum laude, LaSalle Coll., 1971; postgrad., U. N.C., 1971-73; MSLS, Drexel U., 1981. Edn!. resources specialist C.C. of Phila., 1973-74; asst./assoc. libr. United Engrs. & Constructors Inc. (A Raytheon Co.) Libr., Phila., 1974-81; head libr. United Engrs. & Constructors Inc. (A Raytheon Co.) Libr., Boston, 1981-84; asst/assoc. dir. Wentworth Inst. of Tech. Libr., Boston, 1984-89; sci. libr. Smith Coll. Librs., Northampton, Mass., 1989-91, coord. br. and media svcs., sci. libr., 1991—. Mem. ALA (Assn. Coll. Rsch. Librs. divsn., Libr. Adminstrn. and Mgmt. Assn. divsn., Libr. and Info. Tech. Assn. divsn), Spl. Librs. Assn., Beta Phi Mu. Democrat. Roman Catholic. Avocations: travel, biking, reading, films. Home: 104 Woods Rd Northampton MA 01060-3507 Office: Smith Coll Young Sci Libr Northampton MA 01063

PICCOLO, C. A. LANCE, healthcare company executive; b. 1940. BS, Boston U., 1962; postgrad., Calif. State U. Pharm. rep. Riker Labs. Inc., 1965-68; territory mgr. parenteral products divsn., regional field asst., dist. mgr., ctrl. regional mgr., field sales mgr. Baxter Internat. Inc., Deerfield, Ill., 1968-77, dir. sales parenteral products divsn., 1977-78, v.p. sales parenteral products divsn., 1978-79, v.p. parenteral products divsn., 1979, pres. parenteral products divsn., 1979-81, v.p., 1981-85, group v.p., 1985-87, exec. v.p., 1987; dir. Crompton & Knowles Corp. & Orthomet Inc.; chmn., CEO, dir. Caremark Internat., Northbrook, Ill. Capt. USMC, 1962-65. Office: Caremark Internat 2215 Sanders Rd Northbrook IL 60062-6126*

PICCOLO, RICHARD ANDREW, artist, educator; b. Hartford, Conn., Sept. 17, 1943; S. John D. and Lenore (Pasqual) P. BID, Pratt Inst., 1966; MFA, Bklyn. Coll., 1968. Instr. Pratt Inst., Bklyn., 1966-68, Rome, 1969—; dir. Pratt Inst., 1980—; instr. U. Notre Dame Rome Program, 1984—. Artist: solo exhibitions include: Robert Schoelkopf Gallery, N.Y.C., 1975, 79, 83, 89, Suffolk C.C., Long Island, N.Y., 1976, Am. Acad. in Rome, 1977, Galleria Temple, Rome 1979, Galleria Il Gabbiano, Rome. 1985, Contemporary Realist Gallery, San Francisco, 1989, 95; exhibited in group shows Six Americans in Italy, 1973, Metaphor in Painting, Fed. Hall Meml., N.Y., 1978, Realism and Metaphor, U. S. Fla. (traveling), 1980, Contemporary Figure Drawings, Robert Schoelkopf Gallery, 1981, Contemporary Arcadian Painting, 1982, Moravian Coll. Invitational, Bethlehem, Pa., 1981, Art on Paper, Weatherspoon Gallery of Art, N.C., 1981, Out of N.Y., Hamilton Coll., Clinton, N.Y., 1981, Galleria Gabbiano, Rome, FIAC, Paris, 1982, Contemporary Arts Mus., Houston, 1984, Umbria: Americans Painting in Italy, Gallery North, Setauket, N.Y., 1985, Storytellers, Contemporary Realist Gallery, San Francisco, Painted from Life, Bayly Mus., Charlottesville, Va., 1987; work in permanent collections Crown Am. Corp., Johnstown, Pa., Grosvenor Internat., Sacramento, Calif., Mrs. Lillian Cole, Sherman Oaks, Calif., Mr and Mrs. Robert Emery, San Francisco, Mr. Graham Gund, Boston, Dr. Robert Gutterman, San Francisco, Mr and Mrs. Joseph Jennings, San Francisco, Dr. and Mrs. Donald Innes, Jr., Charlottesville, Va., Mr. and Mrs. Alan Ovson, San Francisco, Mr. Frank Pasquerilla, Johnstown, Pa., Mr. Jon Roberts and Mr. John Boccardo, L.A. Recipient E. A. Abbey Meml. scholarship for mural painting, 1973-75; grantee NEA, 1989; mural commn. Simplicity Inspiring Invention: An Allegory of the Arts, Crown Am. Corp., Johnstown, Pa., 1989, Aer, Ignis, Terra, Aqua, U.S. Bank Plaz., Sacramento, Calif., 1991-94. Home: Piazza S Apollonia 3, Rome 00153, Italy Office: Contemporary Realist Gallery 250 Sutter St Fl 4 San Francisco CA 94108-4403

PICHARDO PAGAZA, IGNACIO, Mexican government official; b. Toluca, Mex., Nov. 13, 1935; s. Carlos Pichardo and Carmen Pagaza Varela; m. Juleta Lechuga Manternach. Degree in Indsl. Rels., Latin Am. U.; MA in Adminstrn. and Pub. Fin., U. London. Fed. dep. dist 4 State of Mex., 1967-70, pres. budget com., fed. dep. dist. 27, 1979-82; pres. Programming, Budgeting and Pub. Accts. Com.; dir. dept. utilities Secretariat of Treasury, subdir. income tax dept.; dir. treasury State of Mex., 1969-71, sec. gen. govt., 1971-75, subsec. of revenues, 1976-78, subsec. A of contr. Gen. Mex., 1983-87, contr. Gen. of Mex., 1987—; dir. dept. publs. Nat. Fgn. Trade Bank, 1964-67; mem. tech. coun. CNC, 1966; v.p. Consultoria Externa de Mex., S.A., 1978-79. Editor PRI Youth Sector newspaper, 1958, Comercio Exterior, 1964-67. Office: Sec of Energy Mines & Parastatal Ind, Avenida Insurgentes Sur 552 3 Piso, Mexico City 06769, Mexico

PICHETTE, CLAUDE, former banking executive, university rector, research executive; b. Sherbrooke, Que., Can., June 13, 1936; s. Donat and Juliette (Morin) P.; m. Renée Provencher, Sept. 5, 1959 (dec. 1994); children: Anne-Marie, Martin, Philippe. B.A., U. Sherbrooke, 1956; M.Sc.Soc. (Econ.), U. Laval, 1960; Doct. d'Etat es Sc. Econ, U. D'Aix-Marseille, France, 1970. Prof. U. Sherbrooke, 1960-70; civil servant Govt. Que., 1970-75; vice rector adminstrn. and fins. U. Que., Montreal, 1975-77; rector U. Que., 1977-86; pres., chief exec. officer La Financière prêts-épargne, 1986-90, La Financière Entraide-Cooperants (holding co.), 1987-90; pres. Que. Found. Econ. Edn., 1979-81; CEO Institut Armand-Frappier Rsch. Inst.; chmn. bd. La Financière Entraide-Cooperants (holding co.), 1987-90; pres. Que. Found. Econ. Edn., 1979-81; CEO Institut Armand-Frappier Rsch. Inst.; chmn. bd. La Financière Credit-Bail, 1989-90; bd. dirs. Shermag, Rona-Dismat, Montreal Stock Exch. Author: Analyse micro-economique et cooperative, 1972. Can. Council grantee, 1958; Federation nationale des cooperatives de consommation de France grantee, 1973. Mem. Que. Assn. Econs. (pres. 1977-78). Club: St.-Denis (Montreal). Home: 745 Hartland, Outremont, PQ Canada H2V 2X5 Office: Armand-Frappier Institute, 531 Blvd des Praires, Laval, PQ Canada H7N 4Z3

PICHLER, JOSEPH ANTON, food products executive; b. St. Louis, Oct. 3, 1939; s. Anton Dominick and Anita Marie (Hughes) P.; m. Susan Ellen Eyerly, Dec. 27, 1962; children: Gretchen, Christopher, Rebecca, Josh. JBA, U. Notre Dame, 1961; MBA, U. Chgo., 1963, PhD, 1966. Asst. prof. bus. U. Kans., 1964-68, assoc. prof., 1968-73, prof., 1973-80; dean U. Kans. (Sch. Bus.), 1974-80; exec. v.p. Dillon Cos. Inc., 1980-82, pres., 1982-86; exec. v.p. Kroger Co., 1985-86, pres., COO, 1986—, also bd. dirs., 1986-90, pres., CEO, 1990, chmn., CEO, 1990—, also dir.; spl. asst. to asst. sec. for manpower U.S. Dept. Labor, 1968-70; chmn. Kans. Manpower Svcs. Coun., 1974-78; bd. dirs. B.F. Goodrich Co.; indsl. cons. Author: (with Joseph McGuire) Inequality: The Poor and the Rich in America, 1969; contbg. author: Creativity and Innovation in Manpower Research and Action Programs, 1970, Contemporary Management: Issues and Viewpoints, 1973, Institutional Issues in Public Accounting, 1974, Co-Creation and Capitalism: John Paul II's Laborem Exercens, 1983; Co-editor, contbg. author: Ethics, Free Enterprise, and Public Policy, 1978; Contbr. articles to profl. jours. Bd. dirs. Kans. Charities, 1973-75, Benedictine Coll., Atchison, Kans., 1979-83, Cin. Opera; nat. bd. dirs. Boys Hope, 1983—, Tougaloo Coll., 1986—; chmn. nat. bd. Nat. Alliance of Bus. Recipient Performance award U.S. Dept. Labor Manpower Adminstrn., 1969, Disting. Svc. citation U. Kans., 1992; Woodrow Wilson fellow, Ford Found. fellow, Standard Oil Indsl. Rels. fellow, 1966, Woodrow Wilson fellow adv. com., 1990-93; named Disting. Alumnus U. Chgo., 1994. Mem. Bus. Roundtable, Queen City Club, Comml. Club of Cin. Office: Kroger Co 1014 Vine St Cincinnati OH 45202-1100

PICHOIS, CLAUDE P., classical studies educator; b. Paris, July 21, 1925; s. Léon and Renée (Baudoi) P.; m. Vincenette Rey, Oct. 26, 1961. D ès L, U. Paris, 1963; D (hon.), U. Neuchâtel, Switzerland, 1983, Trinity Coll., Dublin, Ireland, 1984. Asst. prof. U. Aix-en-Provence, France, 1958-61; prof. U., Basel, Switzerland, 1961-70; vis. rsch. prof. U. Wis., Madison, 1968; prof. Vanderbilt U., Nashville, 1970-73, disting. prof., 1973—; prof. Sorbonne Nouvelle, Paris, 1979-84; bd. dirs. W.T. Bandy Ctr. for Baudelaire Studies, Vanderbilt U., Nashville, Centre de recherches Nerval/Baudelaire, Namur, Belgium, Paris. Author: L'Image de Jean-Paul Richter dans les Lettres Francaise, 1963, Ph. Chasles et la vie litteraire au temps du Romantisme, 1965, Baudelaire, 1987, Gérard de Nerval, 1995, Auguste Poulet-Malassis, 1996; editor: Baudelaire, Complete Works, 1975-76, Baudelaire, Correspondence, 1973, 93, Nerval, Complete Works, 1984, 89, 93, Collette, Works, 1984, 86, 91, Littrature Francaise (16 vols.), 1968-79. Recipient Prix de la critique Académie Française; Guggenheim fellow, 1978. Mem. MLA (hon.), Societe Hist. litt. de la France (v.p.), Societe Etudes Romantiques, Nineteenth-Century French Studies (bd. dirs.), Lettres Romanes, Bull. Baudelairien, Annee Baudelaire. Avocation: bibliophilia. Office: Vanderbilt U Station B Nashville TN 37235

PICIRILLI, ROBERT EUGENE, clergyman, college dean, writer; b. High Point, N.C., Oct. 6, 1932; s. Eugene and Lena (Harrell) P.; m. Clara Mae Lee, June 14, 1953; children: Annina Jean, Myra Jane, Mary June, Celina Joy, Roberta Jill. B.A., Free Will Bapt. Bible Coll., Nashville, 1953; M.A., Bob Jones U., 1955, Ph.D., 1963, D.D., 1967. Ordained to ministry Free Will Bapt. Ch., 1952; grad. asst. Bob Jones U., 1954-55; prof. N.T., Free Will Bapt. Bible Coll., 1955—, registrar, 1960-79, dean, 1979—, dean grad. sch., 1982-86; clk. Nat. Assn. Free Will Baptists, 1961-65, moderator, 1966-71, treas. hist. commn., 1974—, mem. bd. of retirement and ins., 1978-89, sec., 1979-89; mem. testing com. Am. Assn. Bible Colls., 1959-72, research commn., 1982-91, chmn., 1989-91; sec.-treas. So. region Evang. Theol. Soc., 1964-68, vice chmn., 1972-73, 84-85 chmn., 1973-74, 85-86. Author: Paul, the Apostle, 1986, 1, 2 Corinthians, 1987; co-author: The NKJV Greek English Interlinear New Testament, 1993. Pres. Ransom Elementary Sch. P.T.A., 1965-67. Fellow Inst. for Bibl. Rsch.; mem. AAHE, Am. Assn. Bible Colls. (v.p. 1992-94, pres. 1994—), Nashville Philatelic Soc. (treas. 1980-81, 92—, pres. 1981-82, 1st v.p. 1982-88), Delta Epsilon Chil. Home: 301 Greenway Ave Nashville TN 37205-2307

PICK, ARTHUR JOSEPH, JR., chamber of commerce executive; b. Louisville, Mar. 22, 1931. BS, U. Calif., Riverside, 1959; grad., Coro Found., L.A., 1960; MA in Urban Studies, Occidental Coll., 1969. Pres. Greater Riverside C. of C., 1972—. Mem. Riverside Monday Morning Group, 1978-96; pres. Riverside Symphony Orch. Soc., 1966-69; elected Riverside City Coun., 1967, 71; founder Friends of Calif. Bapt. Coll., 1978, Friends of La Sierra U., Riverside, 1978, Friends of Sherman Indian H.S., Calif. Sch. for the Deaf, Riverside, 1988; trustee La Sierra U., 1992—; mem. Calif.-Nev. Super Speed Train Commn., 1992—; treas. Calif. State Citrus Heritage Park Bd.; co-chair Mayor's Vision Com.; chair City/Univ. Task Force Com.; founding chair adv. bd. U. Calif.-Riverside Ext.; founding chair Riverside Festival of Lights. With U.S. Army, 1953-55. Recipient Disting. Svc. award Riverside Jaycees, 1966, Patron of Arts award Cultural Arts Coun., 1977, Vernon Jordan Humanitarian award Riverside Area Urban League, 1989, Citizen of Yr. award Riverside Police Officers Assn., 1990, Atlas award Riverside YWCA, 1990, Community Svc. award, 1990; named Young Man of Yr. Riverside Jaycees, 1966, Citizen of Yr. Internat. Rels. Coun., 1992. Mem. Inland Area Urban League (founder, bd. dirs., Pacesetter award 1982), U. Calif. Riverside Alumni Assn. (bd. dirs. 1981-87), Riverside Jaycees (life), Riverside Raincross Club. Office: Greater Riverside C of C 3685 Main St Ste 350 Riverside CA 92501-2804

PICK, JAMES BLOCK, management and sociology educator; b. Chgo., July 29, 1943; s. Grant Julius and Helen (Block) P. BA, Northwestern U., 1966; MS in Edn., No. Ill. U., 1969; PhD, U. Calif., Irvine, 1974. Cert. computer profl. Asst. rsch. statistician, lectr. Grad. Sch. Mgmt. U. Calif., Riverside, 1975-91, dir. computing, 1984-91; co-dir. U.S.-Mex. Database Project, 1988-91; assoc. prof. mgmt. and bus., dir. info. mgmt. program U. Redlands, Calif., 1991-95, prof. mgmt. and bus., chair dept. mgmt. and bus., 1995—; cons. U.S. Census Bur. Internat. Div., 1978; mem. Univ. Commons Bd., 1982-86; mem. bd. govs. PCCLAS, Assn. Borderlands Studies, 1989-92. Trustee Newport Harbor Art Mus., 1981-87, 88—, chmn. permanent collection com., 1987-91, v.p., 1991—. Recipient Thunderbird award Bus. Assn. Latin Am. Studies, 1993. Mem. AAAS, Assn. Computing Machinery, Assn. Systems Mgmt. (pres. Orange County chpt. 1978-79), Am. Statis. Assn., Population Assn. Am., Internat. Union for Sci. Study of Population, Soc. Info. Mgmt. Club, Standard (Chgo.). Author: Geothermal Energy Development, 1982, Computer Systems in Business, 1986, Atlas of Mexico,

1989, The Mexico Handbook, 1994; condr. research in info. systems, population, environ. studies; contbr. sci. articles to publs. in fields.

PICK, MICHAEL CLAUDE, international exploration consultant; b. Stuttgart, Fed. Republic Germany, Sept. 17, 1931; came to Can., 1963; s. Manfred and Berti (Baer) P.; m. Jeanette Patrucia Zaharko, Mar. 13, 1965; children—David, Christopher. B.A., U. New Zealand, Wellington, 1952, M.A. with honors, 1954; Ph.D., U. Bristol, Eng., 1963. Sr. geologist Todd Bros. Ltd., Wellington, 1954-58; research assoc. Stanford U., Calif., 1958-60; geologist Chevron Standard Ltd., Calgary, Alta., Can., 1963-68; regional geologist BP Oil & Gas Ltd., Calgary, 1968-71; chief geologist, acting exploration mgr. Columbia Gas, Calgary, 1971-80; sr. v.p. Asamera, Inc., Calgary, 1980-87; pres. Torwood Assocs. Ltd. Contbr. articles to profl. jours. Mem. Am. Assn. Petroleum Geologists, Can. Soc. Petroleum Geologists. Avocations: music; reading; model railroading. Home: 3359 Varna Crescent NW, Calgary, AB Canada T3A 0E4

PICK, ROBERT YEHUDA, orthopedic surgeon, consultant; b. Haifa, Israel, 1945; came to U.S., 1957; s. Andre B. and Hanna (Gross) P.; m. Roni L. Kestenbaum, Sept. 25, 1977; children: Benjamin A., Joseph E., Jennifer L., Abigail I. BA, B in Hebrew Lit., Yeshiva U., 1967; MD, Albert Einstein Coll. Med., 1971; MPH, Harvard U., 1979. Diplomate Nat. Bd. Med. Examiners, Am. Bd. Orthopaedic Surgery. Intern Brookdale Hosp., Bklyn., 1971-72; resident in orthopedic surgery Albert Einstein-Bronx (N.Y.) Mcpl. Hosp. Ctr., 1972-74; resident in orthopedic surgery USPHS Hosp., Staten Island, N.Y., 1974-75, asst. chief orthopedic surgery, 1975-77; asst. chief orthopedic surgery USPHS Hosp., Boston, 1977-78; fellow orthopedic trauma Boston City Hosp., 1979-80, assoc. dir. orthopedic surgery, 1980-84, dir. pediatric orthopedics, 1981-83; practice medicine specializing in orthopedic surgery Newton Ctr., Mass., 1984—; instr. orthopedic surgery Boston U., 1980-82, asst. prof., 1982—; adj. asst. prof. health scis. and orthopedics Touro Coll., N.Y.C., 1976-78; dir. spinal screening program Dept. Health and Hosps., Boston, 1979-82; dist. med. advisor U.S. Dept. Labor, Boston, 1984—; cons. Boston Retirement Bd., 1983-84, New Eng. Telephone, Boston, 1985—, Commonwealth of Mass. Pub. Employee Retirement Adminstrn., Boston, 1985-90. Contbr. articles on med. issues to profl. jours. Trustee Young Israel Jackson Heights, Queens, N.Y., 1969-76, pres., 1976-77; sec. Young Israel Brookline, Mass., 1978-79; trustee Maimonides Sch., Brookline, 1990—. Served to lt. comdr. USPHS, 1975-78. Fellow Am. Acad. Orthopedic Surgeons; mem. Am. Physicians Fellowship for Medicine in Israel (trustee 1975—, exec. com. 1976—, asst. treas. 1987-90, treas. 1990—, Man of Yr. award 1977), Nat. Inst. Occupational Safety and Health (traineeship 1978-79), Mensa.

PICK, RUTH, research scientist, physician, educator; b. Carlsbad, Bohemia, Czechoslovakia, Nov. 13, 1913; came to U.S., 1949; d. Arthur and Paula (Lenk) Holub; m. Alfred Pick, May 28, 1938 (dec. Jan. 1982). M.D., German U., 1938. Resident in medicine Priessnitz Hosp., Graefenberg, Czechoslovakia, 1938; resident in psychiatry Hosp. Veleslavin, Prague, Czechoslovakia, 1945-47; extern in pathology State Hosp. Motol, Prague, 1948; research fellow cardiovascular dept. Michael Reese Hosp. & Med. Ctr., Chgo., 1949-50, research assoc., 1950-58, asst. dir., 1958-66, sr. investigator, 1966-71, chief exptl. atherosclerosis lab., 1971-83, attending physician div. cardiovascular diseases dept. medicine, 1964—; chief cardiac morphology lab. Cardiovascular Inst. Michael Reese Hosp. & Med. Ctr., 1983—; prof. emeritus medicine and pathology U. Chgo., 1973—; mem. research council Chgo. Heart Assn., 1979-84, bd. govs., 1983, pres., 1985-86. Fellow Am. Heart Assn. (coun. on arteriosclerosis, coun. on circulation, established investigator), AAAS; mem. Am. Assn. Pathologists and Bacteriologists, Chgo. Heart Assn. (past pres. 1985-86), Am. Fedn. Clin. rsch., Am. Physiol. Soc., Ctrl. Soc. Clin. Rsch. Home: 400 E Randolph St Chicago IL 60601-7329 Office: Michael Reese Hosp and Med Ctr 2929 S Ellis Ave Chicago IL 60616-3302

PICKARD, CAROLYN ROGERS, secondary school educator; b. Steubenville, Ohio, Dec. 13, 1945; d. Thomas Orlando and Alice Marie (Romick) Rogers; 1 child, Carri Alyce. BA, Fla. State U., 1967; AA, Stephens Coll., Columbia, Mo., 1965. Cert. English tchr., Fla. Tchr. English, chair dept. New World Sch. Arts, Dade County Pub. Schs., Miami, Fla., 1969—; sponsor jr. class; advisor yearbook; liason New World Sch. Arts. Vol. Shores Performing Arts Theater Soc. Recipient Tchr. of Yr. award North Miami Beach High Sch., 1982, Presdl. Scholars Tchr. of Excellence award, 1984. Mem. Nat. Coun. Tchrs. English, United Tchrs. Dade County, Delta Kappa Gamma. Home: 539 Catalonia Ave Coral Gables FL 33134-6532

PICKARD, DEAN, philosophy and humanities educator; b. Geneva, N.Y., Mar. 12, 1947; s. William Otis and Frances (Dean) P.; chidlren: Justin Matthew, Christopher Dean. BA cum laude, U. Calif., Riverside, 1973; MA, Calif. State U., Long Beach, 1976-77; PhD, Claremont (Calif.) Grad. Sch., 1992. Instr. phys. edn. Pomona Coll., Claremont, 1975-82; instr. philosophy, humanities, and phys. edn. Moorpark (Calif.) Coll., 1978-82; assoc. prof. philosophy, humanities, and phys. edn. Mission Coll., Sylmar, Calif., 1979-83; instr. philosophy Calif. State U., Northridge, 1988-94; prof. philosophy and humanities Pierce Coll., Woodland Hills, Calif., 1983—. Author: Nietzsche, Transformation and Postmodernism; contbr. articles to profl. jours. Marious De Brabent & Henry Carter scholar, 1973; fellow Claremont Grad. Sch., 1988-89. Mem. Am. Philos. Assn., Am. Fedn. Tchrs., N.Am. Nietzsche Soc., L.A. Area Nietzsche Soc. (bd. dirs. 1994-96), Phi Beta Kappa. Avocations: guitar, snow skiing, wind surfing, golfing, martial arts (5th degree black belt). Office: Pierce Coll 6201 Winnetka Ave Woodland Hills CA 91371-0001

PICKARD, FRANKLIN GEORGE THOMAS, mining company executive; b. Sudbury, Ont., Can., Sept. 10, 1933; s. Chester William and Margaret Christine (Downes) P.; m. Audrey Elaine Bull, Apr. 27, 1967; children: Barbara, Beverly. BA, Queen's U., Kingston, Ont., 1958. With Falconbridge Ltd., Toronto, Ont., 1957—, concentrator supt., 1967-75, chief metall. engr., 1975-82, v.p., 1982-89, sr. v.p., 1989-90, pres., chief exec. officer, 1991—; also, bd. dirs.; bd. dirs. Falconbridge Ltd., Falconbridge Nikkelverk A/S (Norway), Falconbridge Dominicana C por A (Dominican Republic). Mem. AIME, Can. Inst. Mining and Metall. Engrs., Mining Assn. Can. (bd. dirs.), Assn. Profl. Engrs. Ont., Nickel Devel. Inst. (bd. dirs., chmn. 1988-90), Ont. Club, Toronto Club, Thornhill Country Club, Keowee Key Golf and Country Club. Avocations: fishing, golf, sports cars. Office: Falconbridge Ltd, 95 Wellington St W Ste 1200, Toronto, ON Canada M5J 2V4

PICKARD, GEORGE LAWSON, physics educator; b. Cardiff, Wales, July 5, 1913; came to Can., 1947; s. Harry Lawson and Phoebe P.; m. Lilian May Perry; children—Rosemary Ann, Andrew Lawson. B.A., Oxford U., 1935, M.A., 1947, D.Phil., 1937; D.M.S. (hon.), Royal Roads Mil. Coll., Victoria, B.C., Can., 1980. Sci. officer Royal Aircraft Establishment, Farnborough, Eng., 1937-42; sr. sci. officer ops. research sect. Coastal Command, RAF, 1942-46, prin. sci. officer ops. research sect., 1947; assoc. prof. dept. physics U. B.C., Vancouver, Can., 1947-54, prof. dept. physics, 1954-70, prof. emeritus, 1979—, dir. Inst. Oceanography, 1958-79; cons. Seaconsult Marine Research, Vancouver, Can., 1979—. Author: Descriptive Physical Oceanography, 1964, 5th edit., 1990; (with S. Pond) Introductory Dynamical Oceanography, 1978, 2d edit., 1983. Served with RAF, 1942-47. Decorated mem. Order Brit. Empire; recipient J.P. Tully medal Can. Meteorol. and Oceanographic Soc., 1987. Fellow AAAS, Royal Soc. Can. Avocations: aviation; diving; coral reef oceanography. Home: 4546 W 5th Ave, Vancouver, BC Canada V6R 1S7

PICKARD, JOHN ALLAN, lawyer; b. White Plains, N.Y., Sept. 4, 1940; s. Victor and Rhoda (Walinshinsky) P. BA, The Am. U., 1963; JD, Washington Coll. Law, 1966. Bar: N.Y. 1987, Oreg. 1969, U.S. Ct. Appeals (9th cir.) 1970, U.S. Ct. Appeals (2d cir.) 1988, U.S. Dist. Ct. Oreg. Dep. dist. atty., 1970, criminal appeals atty., 1967-71; tax law specialist IRS, Washington, 1966-67; dep. dist. atty. Clachamus County, Oregon City, Oreg.; atty. pvt. practice Oreg., 1972—; mem. Arnold, Fortan & Porter, 1964-65. Advisor Mental Health Law Project, N.Y.C., 1984—, ACCESS Inc. Homeless. Appt. to Lawyers Conf. on Appellate Cts. ABA. Fellow Roscoe Pound Found.; mem. ABA (jud. adminstrv. sec., health law forum, legal edn. and bar admissions, tort ins. practice), ATLA, Am. Jud. Soc. Democrat. Avocation: politics. Home: 90 Bryant Ave Apt 3B White Plains NY 10605-1922 Office: PO Box 1907 White Plains NY 10602-1907

PICKARD, MYRNA RAE, dean; b. Sulphur Springs, Tex., Oct. 10, 1935; d. George Wallace and Ellie (Williams) Swindell; m. Bobby Ray Pickard, May 17, 1957; 1 child, Bobby Dale. B.S. summa cum laude, Tex. Wesleyan Coll., 1957, M.Ed., 1964; M.S., Tex. Women's U., 1974; EdD, Nova U., 1976. Instr. John Peter Smith Hosp., Fort Worth, 1956-58; pub. health nurse Forest County Health Dept., Hattiesburg, Miss., 1958-60; asst. nurse adminstrn. John Peter Smith Hosp. Sch. Nursing, Fort Worth, 1960-70, nurse adminstr., 1970-73; assoc. dean, dean U. Tex. System Sch. Nursing, Fort Worth, 1971-76; dean U. Tex. Sch. Nursing, Arlington, 1976-95; prof. nursing, 1976—; cons. in field; adv. com. Rural Health Rsch. Ctr., U. N.D., 1990. Mem. editorial bd. Jour. Rural Health, 1985-92, 94; contbr. articles to profl. jours., chpt. in book. Pres. Tex. League for Nursing, 1986-89. Fellow Am. Acad. Nursing; mem. ANA, Nat. League Nursing, Nat. Rural Health Assn. (bd. dirs., treas. 1990-92), Sigma Theta Tau. Methodist. Avocations: jogging; gardening. Home: 8301 Anglin Dr Fort Worth TX 76140-4213 Office: U Tex Box 19407 Arlington TX 76019

PICKEN, HARRY BELFRAGE, aerospace engineer; b. Grimsby, Ont., Can., Jan. 8, 1916; s. John Belfrage and Leila Lucinda (Jarvis) P.; m. Florence Elizabeth Runciman, July 7, 1945; children: Roger Belfrage, Donald William, Wendy Elizabeth. BSc in Aero. Engring., U. Mich., 1940. Registered profl. engr., Ont., Can. Chief engr. White Can. Aircraft Ltd., Hamilton, Ont., 1940-45, Weston Aircraft Ltd., Oshawa, Ont., 1946-47, Field Aviation Ltd., Oshawa, 1947-51; pres., chief engr. Genaire Ltd. (Aerospace), St. Catharines, 1951-81; v.p., tech. dir. Ardrox Ltd. (Chems.), Niagara on the Lake, 1968-75, Avionics Ltd. (Electronics), Niagara on the Lake, 1953-67; v.p. Rotaire Ltd. (Helicopters), St. Catharines, Ont., 1958-63; design approval rep. acting on behalf of Dept. of Transport Can., Ottawa, 1948-78; mem. bd. govs. Niagara Coll., Welland, Ont., 1974-80. Editor, pub.: Early Architecture Town and Township of Niagara, 1968, architecture student edit., 1991, Map of the Colonial Town of Niagara-on-the-Lake, 1981; composer (music book) Calgary Song Suite, 1983, Chacun a son Goût, 1991;. Chmn. Planning Bd. of Niagara-on-the Lake, 1963-65; pres. Niagara-on-the-Lake C. of C., 1961-62; bd. dirs., v.p. Niagara Found., Niagara-on-the-Lake, 1963-80; mem. tech. adv. bd. Niagara Coll., 1966-74; vice chmn. bd. govs. Niagara Coll. Applied Arts and Tech., 1979-81; mem. Ont. Coun. of Regents, 1987-93. Named Citizen of Yr. Niagara-on-the-Lake C. of C., 1968; recipient Award of Merit, Mohawk Community Coll., Hamilton, Ont., 1990, Medal-Community Svc., Profl. Engrs. Ont., 1981, Citation for Outstanding and Meritorious Work, Transport Can. Civil Aviation Ont. Region, 1978, Caring and Sharing award Niagara Regional Govt., 1992, Citation from Premier Ont., 1993. Fellow Can. Aero. and Space Inst. (assoc.); mem. AIAA, Am. Helicopter Soc., Assn. Profl. Engrs. Ont. (lic. profl. engr.), Composers, Authors and Music Pubs. of Can. (assoc.), Am. Fedn. Musicians (bd. dirs. local 298 Niagara Falls, Ont.). Achievements include patent for developing an entirely new type of honeycomb primary structure and beams fabricated using staples and acrylic adhesives; research in thermal electric modules independently used in cooling and refrigeration techniques. Home: 494 Glenwood Dr, Ridgeway, ON Canada L05 IN0 Office: Genaire Ltd, Niagara Dist Airport Box 84, Saint Catharines, ON Canada L2R 6R4

PICKENPAUGH, THOMAS EDWARD, archaeologist; b. St. Clairsville, Ohio, Feb. 8, 1945; s. Douglas Giffin and Betty June (Brown) P. BA, Kent State U., 1970, MA, 1971; ABD, Cath. U., 1980. Anthropologist, instr. sociology and anthropology Wheeling (W.Va.) Coll., 1972-73; anthropologist, instr., asst. prof. anthropology Ohio U.-Eastern, 1972-74, 78; archaeologist, asst. prof. anthropology Ohio U.-Eastern, St. Clairsville, 1986-95; mus. technician U.S. Dept. Interior, Nat. Pk. Svc., Washington, 1983; mus. technican Nat. Mus. Natural History, Smithsonian Instn., Washington, 1984-87; mus. specialist, loan officer USN, Naval Hist. Ctr., Washington, 1987—; dir. archaeol. excavations Brokaw Village Site, St. Clairsville, Ohio, 1972-74, 76-78, 82, 86-94; mem. archaeol. staff Thunderbird Site, Front Royal, Va., Savannah River, Ga., S.C., Richard B. Russell Dam Project, 1980, El Mirador Site, Guatemala, 1980, Louis Berger Internat. Project, Trenton, N.J., 1983-84, Sully Plantation, Loudon County, Va., 1984, Fells Point Project, Balt., 1984; others. Contbr. articles to profl. publs. Rsch. grantee U.S. Dept. Interior, Nat. Pk. Svc., 1978-79, Nat. Geog. Soc., 1992-93. Mem. Washington Assn. Profl. Anthropologists, Anthropol. Soc. Washington, Am. Assn. Museums, Internat. Platform Assn. Home: # 201 12512 Village Sq Ter Rockville MD 20852 Home: 12512 Village Square Ter Rockville MD 20852 Office: Naval Hist Ctr Washington Navy Yard 9th And M St SE Washington DC 20374

PICKENS, ALEXANDER LEGRAND, education educator; b. Waco, Tex., Aug. 31, 1921; s. Alex LeGrand and Elma L. (Johnson) P.; m. Frances M. Jenkins, Aug. 20, 1955. B.A., So. Methodist U., 1950; M.A., North Tex. State U., Denton, 1952; Ed.D., Columbia U., 1959. Tchr. art public schs. Dallas, 1950-53, Elizabeth, N.J., 1953-54; instr. Coll. Architecture and Design U. Mich., 1954-59; assoc. prof. dept. art U. Ga., Athens, 1959-62; assoc. prof. Coll. Edn. U. Hawaii, Honolulu, 1962-68, prof. edn., 1968—; U. Hawaii; chmn. doctoral studies curriculum instrn. Coll. Edn. U. Hawaii, Honolulu, 1984-89, asst. to dean for coll. devel., 1989—; dir. children's classes Ft. Worth Children's Mus., 1951-53; head art Nat. Music Camp, Interlochen, Mich., summers, 1957-58, U. Oreg., Portland, summers 1959-60, 62; cons. youth art activities Foremost Dairies, 1964-74; cons. art films United World Films, 1970-75; art edn. cons. Honolulu Paper Co., 1970-76, Kamehameha Sch., Bishop Estate, 1978-95. Exhibited ceramics, Wichita Internat. Exhbn., Syracuse (N.Y.) Nat. Exhbn., St. Louis Mus., Dallas Mus., San Antonio Mus., Detroit Art Inst., Hawaii Craftsmen, also others; editorial bd.: Arts and Activities mag, 1955-82; editor: U. Hawaii Ednl. Perspectives, 1964—; contbr. articles to profl. jours. Memm. adult com. Dallas County chpt. Jr. ARC, 1951-53; exec. com. Dallas Crafts Guild, 1950-53; v.p., publicity chmn. U. Ga. Community Concert Assn., 1960-62, mem., program chmn. Gov.'s Commn. Observing 150 Yrs. Pub. Edn. in Hawaii, 1990-91. Served with USAAF. Recipient award merit, Tex. State Fair, 1957, All-Am. award, Ednl. Press Assn. Am., 1968, 70, 72, 75, 79, Regents' medal for excellence in teaching, U. Hawaii, 1989, Gov.'s Commn. Observance of 150 Yrs. Pub. Edn., 1990-91. Mem. AAUP, NEA, Internat. Soc. Edn., Nat. Art Edn. Assn., Coun. for Advancement and Support of Edn., Nat. Soc. Fundraising Execs., Hawaii Planned Giving Coun., Phi Delta Kappa, Kappa Delta Pi. Address: 1471 Kalaepohaku St Honolulu HI 96816

PICKENS, FRANKLIN ACE, lawyer; b. Borger, Texas, Aug. 19, 1936; s. A.O. and Rhoda (Shaw) P.; m. Dianna Barnard, Dec. 17, 1966. BBA, U. Tex., 1958, JD, 1962. Bar: Tex. 1962, U.S. Dist. Ct. (we. dist.) Tex. 1964, U.S. Dist. Ct. (ea. dist.) Tex. 1983, U.S. Dist. Ct. (so. dist.) Tex. 1989; cert. adminstrv. law Tex. Bd. Legal Specialization. Pvt. practice Odessa, Tex., 1962-63; ptnr. McDonald and Pickens, Odessa, Tex., 1963-69; atty. Shafer, Gilliland, Davis, Bunton & McCollum, Odessa, Tex., 1969-71; rep. State of Texas, Odessa, 1964-73; pvt. practice Austin, Texas, 1973-76; ptnr. Brown McCarroll & Oaks Hartline, Austin, Texas, 1976—; state bd. Ins. Adv. Com. HMOs; former gen. counsel Tex. State Bd. Nurse Examiners; former Washington counsel Tex. R.R.; mem. state bar com. Liason with Med. Profession, 1975-82; spkr. in field. Listed Naifeh and Smith, 1993-94; contbr. articles to profl. jours. Chmn. bd. trustees Shoal Creek Hosp., Austin, 1981-96; former mem. strategic planning task force Brackenridge Hosp., Austin; former mem. coun. advisors Austin Children's Cancer Ctr. Lt. comdr. USNR, 1958-60. Mem. ABA, Nat. Health Lawyers Assn., Am. Soc. Law and Medicine, State Bar Tex. (coll., coun., health law sect. 1980-82, legis. com. 1989), Travis County Bar Assn. (adminstrv. law sect., health law sect.). Episcopalian. Home: 713 Windsong Trl Austin TX 78746-3539 Office: Brown McCarroll & Oaks Hartline 1400 Franklin Plz 111 Congress Ave Austin TX 78701-4043

PICKENS, ROBERT BRUCE, accountant; b. Uniontown, Pa., May 20, 1926; s. Joseph Abraham and Margaret Gertrude (Brown) P.; m. Mary Ellen Evans, Sept. 9, 1950; children: Laura Gail Martin, Rachel Diane Rosen, David Bruce. B.S. in Bus. Adminstrn, Waynesburg Coll., 1950. C.P.A., Pa., Ill., Ind. Vice pres. Home Bottle Gas Corp., Uniontown, 1950-51; jr. accountant to sr. accountant Tenney & Co., Uniontown, 1951-56; mgr. Hosp. Service Assn. Western Pa., Pitts., 1956-57; auditor U. Pitts., 1957-58; sr. accountant Eugene A. Conniff Co., Pitts., 1958-59; mgr. Sheppard & Co., Pitts., 1959-63; supr. Alexander Grant & Co., Chgo., 1963-65; asst. to treas. CTS Corp., Elkhart, Ind., 1965, gen. auditor, controller, 1966-81; self-employed as acct., 1981-86; sec., controller, chief acctg. officer SEA Group, Inc. and SEA-ILAN, Inc., 1987-88; pvt. cons., 1989—. Mem. Bower Hill Civic League, 1956-62; active Boy Scouts Am., 1938-62. Served to cpl. USAAF, 1944-45. Mem. AICPA, Pa. Inst. CPAs, Ill. CPA Soc., Ind. CPA Soc. Republican. Presbyn. (elder, trustee 1959-61, treas. 1960-61). Home and Office: 73 Rogers Rd Carmel IN 46032-1467

PICKERELL, JAMES HOWARD, photojournalist; b. Dayton, Ohio, June 9, 1936; s. Howard and Frances (Harrison) P.; m. Mary Louise Fisher, June 26, 1965; children: Cheryl Elizabeth, Stacy Rae. Student, Ohio U., 1954-56; BA, UCLA, 1963. Comml. photographer, 1963—; ind. photographer Vietnam, 1963-67. Author: Vietnam in the Mud, 1966, Marketing Photography in the Digital Evnironment, 1994, Negotiating Stock Photo Prices, 3d edit., 1995; writer, pub. newsletter Taking Stock. With USNR, 1956-60. Mem. Nat. Press Photographers Assn. (1st Pl. Spot News award 1965), Am. Soc. Mag. Photographers (nat. bd. 1987-89), Beta Theta Pi. Address: 8104 Cindy Ln Bethesda MD 20817-6915

PICKERING, CHARLES W., federal judge; b. 1937. BA, U. Miss., 1959, JD, 1968; Hon. Doctorate, William Carey Coll. Ptnr. Gartin, Hester and Pickering, Laurel, Miss., 1961-71; judge Laurel Mcpl. Ct., 1969; pvt. practice Laurel, 1971-72, 80; ptnr. Pickering and McKenzie, Laurel, 1973-80, Pickering and Williamson, Laurel, 1981-90; judge U.S. Dist. Ct. (so. dist.) Miss., Hattiesburg, 1990—. Contbr. articles to Mississippi Law Journal. Mem. ABA, Miss. Bar Assn., Jones County Bar. Assn., State 4-H Adv. Coun., Assn. Trial Lawyers in Am., Miss. Trial Lawyers Assn., U. Miss. Alumni Assn., Jones County Jr. Coll., Jones County Farm Bur., Kiwanis Club. Office: US Courthouse 701 N Main St Ste 228 Hattiesburg MS 39401-3471

PICKERING, HOWARD WILLIAM, metallurgy engineer, educator; b. Cleve., Dec. 15, 1935; s. Howard William and Marian (Vittes) P.; m. Judith Anne Burch, Apr. 20, 1963; children: John, Kim, Scott, Carolyn. BS in Metall. Engring., U. Cin., 1958; MS, Ohio State U., 1959, PhD, 1961. Scientist U.S. Steel Corp., Monroeville, Pa., 1962-69, sr. scientist, 1969-72; postdoctoral U.S. Steel fellow Max-Planck Inst., Gottingen, Fed. Republic Germany, 1964-65; assoc. prof. metall. engring. Pa. State U., University Park, 1972-76, chmn., 1975-80, prof., 1976-90, disting. prof., 1990—; cons. Ga. Pacific Corp., Newark, 1983-88, Argonne Nat. Lab., 1986-88, Allegheny Ludlum Corp., 1992—; mem. external adv. panel Corrosion Research Ctr., U. Minn., 1980-86. Co-author: Atom Probe Field Ion Microscopy and Its Applications, 1988; editor Corrosion Sci. Jour., 1975-95; contbr. numerous articles to profl. jours. Recipient Disting. Alumnus award Coll. Engring. U. Cin., 1988, Coll. Rsch. award Pa. State U., 1989, Disting. Alumnus award Coll. Engring. Ohio State U., 1990; numerous rsch. grants. Fellow Nat. Assn. Corrosion Engrs. (rsch. com. 1980-89, A.B. Campbell award 1964, Willis Rodney Whitney award 1985), Electrochem. Soc. (chmn. edn. com. 1979, Young Author award 1967, H.H. Uhlig award 1987); mem. AAAS, Metall. Soc. (edn. and profl. affairs com. 1979-83, corrosion resistant metals com. 1974—), Sigma Xi, Tau Beta Pi, Phi Lambda Upsilon.

PICKERING, JAMES HENRY, III, academic administrator; b. N.Y.C., July 11, 1937; s. James H. and Anita (Felber) P.; m. Patricia Paterson, Aug. 18, 1962; children: David Scott, Susan Elizabeth. BA, Williams Coll., 1959; MA, Northwestern U., 1960, PhD, 1964. Instr. English Northwestern U., 1963-65; mem. faculty Mich. State U., East Lansing, 1965-81; prof. English Mich. State U., 1972-81, grad. and asso. chmn. dept., 1968-75, dir. Honors Coll., 1975-81; dean Coll. Humanities and Fine Arts U. Houston, 1981-90, sr. v.p., provost, 1990-92, pres., 1992-95. Author: Fiction 100, 1974, 78, 82, 85, 88, 92, 95, The World Turned Upside Down: Prose and Poetry of the American Revolution, 1975, The Spy Unmasked, 1975, The City in American Literature, 1977, Concise Companion to Literature, 1981, Literature, 1982, 86, 90, 94, Mountaineering in Colorado, 1987, Wild Life on the Rockies, 1988, A Mountain Boyhood, 1988, The Spell of the Rockies, 1989, Purpose and Process, 1989, Poetry, 1990, In Beaver World, 1990, Rocky Mountain Wonderland, 1991, A Summer Vacation in the Parks and Mountains of Colorado, 1992, Fiction 50, 1993, Knocking Round the Rockies, 1994, Drama, 1994, Fredrick Chapin's Colorado, 1995. Mem. Coll. English Assn. (pres. 1980-81), Phi Beta Kappa, Phi Kappa Phi, Omicron Delta Kappa. Office: U Houston-University Park Office of the President Houston TX 77204

PICKERING, JOHN HAROLD, lawyer; b. Harrisburg, Ill., Feb. 27, 1916; s. John Leslie and Virginia Lee (Morris) P.; m. Elsa Victoria Mueller, Aug. 23, 1941 (dec. Nov., 1988); children: Leslie Ann, Victoria Lee; m. Helen Patton Wright, Feb. 3, 1990. AB, U. Mich., 1938, JD, 1940; LLD, D.C. Sch. Law, 1995. Bar: N.Y. 1941, D.C. 1947. Practiced in N.Y.C., 1941, practiced in Washington, 1946—; assoc. Cravath, de Gersdorff, Swaine & Wood, 1941; law clk. to Justice Murphy, Supreme Ct. U.S., 1941-43; assoc. Wilmer & Broun, 1946-48, ptnr., 1949-62; ptnr. Wilmer, Cutler & Pickering, 1962-79, Wilmer & Pickering, 1979-81; ptnr. Wilmer, Cutler & Pickering, 1981-88, sr. counsel, 1989—; vis. lectr. U. Va. Law Sch., 1958; mem. com. visitors U. Mich. Law Sch., 1962-68, chmn. devel. com., 1973-81; mem. com. on adminstrn. of justice U.S. Ct. Appeals (D.C. cir.), 1966-72, chmn. adv. com. on procedures, 1976-82, chmn. mediation project, 1988—; bd. govs. D.C. Bar, 1975-78, pres., 1979-80; dir. Nat. Ctr. for State Cts., 1987-93. Lt. comdr. USNR, 1943-46. Recipient Outstanding Achievement award U. Mich., 1978, Disting. Svc. award Nat. Ctr. for State Cts., 1985, 50 Yr. award from fellows Am. Bar Found., 1993, Paul. C. Reardon award, 1994, Pro Bono award NAACP Legal Def. Fund, 1990, numerous other awards. Mem. ABA (state del. 1984-93, chmn. commn. on legal problems of elderly 1985-93, sr. advisor 1993-95, chmn. 1995—, chmn.-elect sr. lawyers divsn. 1995—), D.C. Bar Assn., Am. Law Inst., Barristers Washington, Lawyers Club, Met. Club, Chevy Chase Club, Wianno Club, Order of Coif, Phi Beta Kappa, Phi Kappa Phi. Democrat. Mem. United Ch. Christ. Home: 5317 Blackistone Rd Bethesda MD 20816-1822 Office: 2445 M St NW Ste 8 Washington DC 20037-1435

PICKERING, THOMAS REEVE, diplomat; b. Orange, N.J., Nov. 5, 1931; s. Hamilton R. and Sarah C. (Chasteney) P.; m. Alice J. Stover, Nov. 24, 1955; children: Timothy R., Margaret S. A.B., Bowdoin Coll., 1953; M.A., Fletcher Sch. Law and Diplomacy, 1954, U. Melbourne, Australia, 1956. Joined U.S. Fgn. Svc., 1959; fgn. affairs officer ACDA, 1961; polit. adviser U.S. del. 18 Nation Disarmament Conf., Geneva, 1962-64; consul Zanzibar, 1965-67; counselor of embassy, dep. chief mission Am. embassy, Dar es Salaam, Tanzania, 1967-69; dep. dir. Bur. Politico-Mil. Affairs, State Dept., 1969-73; spl. asst. to Sec. of State; exec. sec. Dept. State, 1973-74; U.S. amb. to Jordan, 1974-78; asst. sec. for Bur. Oceans, Internat. Environ. and Sci. Affairs, Washington, 1978-81; U.S. amb. to Nigeria, 1981-83, U.S. amb. to El Salvador, 1983-85, U.S. amb. to Israel, 1985-88, U.S. permanent rep. to UN, 1989-92, U.S. amb. to India, 1992-93, U.S. amb. to Russia, 1993—. Served to lt. comdr. USNR, 1956-59. Mem. Council Fgn. Relations, Internat. Inst. Strategic Studies, Phi Beta Kappa. Office: American Embassy APO AE 09721

PICKERING, WILLIAM HAYWARD, physics educator, scientist; b. Wellington, N.Z., Dec. 24, 1910; s. Albert William and Elizabeth (Hayward) P.; m. Muriel Bowler, Dec. 30, 1932 (dec. Mar. 1992); children: William B., Anne E.; m. Inez Chapman, July 28, 1994. B.S., Calif. Inst. Tech., 1932, M.S., 1933, Ph.D. in Physics, 1936; hon. degrees, Clark U., 1966, Occidental Coll., 1966, U. Bologna, 1974. Mem. Cosmic Ray Expdn. to, India, 1939, Mexico, 1941; faculty Calif. Inst. Tech., 1940—, prof. elec. engring., 1946-80, prof. emeritus, 1980—, dir. jet propulsion lab., 1954-76; Mem. sci. adv. bd. USAF, 1945-48; chmn. panel on test range instrumentation (Research and Devel. Bd.), 1948-49; mem. U.S. nat. com. tech. panel Earth Satellite Program, 1955-60; mem. Army Sci. Adv. Panel, 1960-64; dir. rsch. inst. U. Petroleum and Minerals, Dharan, Saudi Arabia, 1977-79; pres. Pickering Rsch. Corp., 1980-91, Lignetics, Inc., 1983—. Decorated Order of Merit Italy, 1966, knight comdr. Order Brit. Empire, 1975; recipient James Wyld Meml. award Am. Rocket Soc., 1957, Columbus medal Genoa, 1964, Prix Galabert for Astronautics; Goddary trophy Nat. Space Club, 1965, NASA Disting. Svc. medal, 1965, Army Disting. Civilian Svc. award, 1959, Spirit of St. Louis medal, 1965, Crozier medal Am. Ordnance Assn., 1965, Man of Yr. award Indsl. Rsch. Inst., 1968, Interprofl. Coop. award Soc. Mfg. Engrs., 1970, Marconi medal Marconi Found., 1974, Nat. Medal of Sci., 1976, Fahrney medal Franklin Inst., 1976, award of merit Am. Cons. Engrs. Coun., 1976, Francoix-Xavier Bagnoud Internat. award, 1994, Japan prize

Sci. and Tech. Found. of Japan, 1994. Fellow AIAA (pres. 1963, Louis W. Hill Transp. award 1968, Aerospace Pioneer award 1986), AAAS, IEEE (Edison medal 1972); mem. NAS, Am. Geophys. Union, Internat. Astronautical Fedn. (pres. 1965-66), Am. Assn. Engring. Scis. Home: 294 St Katherine Dr Flintridge CA 91011 Office: Lignetics Inc 1150 Foothill Blvd Ste E La Canada Flintridge CA 91011

PICKETT, BETTY HORENSTEIN, psychologist; b. Providence, R.I., Feb. 15, 1926; d. Isadore Samuel and Etta Lillian (Morrison) Horenstein; m. James McPherson Pickett, Mar. 10, 1952. A.B. magna cum laude, Brown U., 1945, Sc.M., 1947, Ph.D., 1949. Asst. prof. psychology U. Minn., Duluth, 1949-51; asst. prof. U. Nebr., 1951; lectr. U. Conn., 1952; profl. assoc. psychol. scis. Bio-Scis. Info. Exchange, Smithsonian Instn., Washington, 1953-58; exec. sec. behavioral scis. study sect. exptl. psychology study sect. div. research grants NIH, Washington, 1958-61; research cons. to mental health unit HEW, Boston, 1962-63; exec. sec. research career program NIMH, 1963-66, chief cognition and learning sect. div. extramural research program, 1966-68, dep. dir., 1968-74, dir. div. spl. mental health programs, 1974-75, acting dir. div. extramural research program, 1975-77; assoc. dir. for extramural and collaborative research program Nat. Inst. Aging, 1977-79; dep. dir. Nat. Inst. Child Health and Human Devel., Bethesda, Md., 1979-81; acting dir. Nat. Inst. Child Health and Human Devel., 1981-82, dir. Div. Rsch. Resources, 1982-88; mem. health scientist adminstr. panel CSC Bd. Examiners, 1970-76, 81-88; mem. coun. on grad. edn. Brown U. Grad. Sch., 1989-91. Contbr. articles to profl. jours. Mem. APA, Am. Psychol Soc., Psychonomic Soc., Assn. Women in Sci., AAAS, Phi Beta Kappa, Sigma Xi. Home: Morgan Bay Rd PO Box 198 Surry ME 04684-0198

PICKETT, CALDER MARCUS, retired journalism educator; b. Providence, Utah, July 26, 1921; s. Leland M. and Julia (Gessel) P.; m. Nola Agricola, Mar. 20, 1947; children: Carolyn Zeligman, Kathleen Jenson. BS, Utah State U., 1944; MS in Journalism, Northwestern U., 1948; PhD, U. Minn., 1959. Copy editor Salt Lake (City) Tribune, 1946, Deseret News, Salt Lake City, 1948-49; instr. Utah State U., Logan, 1946-48, U. Denver, 1949-51; prof. U. Kans., Lawrence, 1951—, Oscar Stauffer prof. Journalism, 1973-77, Clyde M. Reed prof. Journalism, 1985-88, ret., 1988. Author: Ed Howe: Country Town Philosopher, 1968; author, editor: Voices of the Past, 1977; columnist Lawrence Jour.-World; writer, producer, narrator radio program The Am. Past; contbr. articles to profl. jours. Recipient Disting. Teaching award Standard Oil Found., 1967, Frank Luther Mott award, 1969, George Foster Peabody award, 1974, HOPE award U. Kans., 1975, Mortar Bd. award U. Kans., 1983, Armstrong Broadcasting award, 1983, Chancellor's Club Career Teaching award, 1987. Avocations: history, music. Home: 712 Lawrence Ave Lawrence KS 66049-4521

PICKETT, DOYLE CLAY, employment and training counselor, consultant; b. Greencastle, Ind., July 15, 1930; s. Joseph Virgil and Lora Clay (Phillips) P.; m. Judith Ann Marshall, 1956 (div. 1961); children: Brian Doyle, Marsha Ann; m. Dorothy Newgent McGinnis, 1964. AB, Wabash Coll., 1952; MBA, Ind. U., 1953. Exec. trainee, various staff and line exec. positions, asst. store mgr. L.S. Ayres & Co., Lafayette and Indpls., Ind., 1953-64; mgmt. analyst Cummins Engine Co., Columbus, Ind., 1964-67; adminstrv. asst. to pres., other exec. positions Baker & Taylor Co., 1967-80; v.p. mktg. Baker & Taylor Co. subs. W.R. Grace Co., N.Y.C., Somerville, N.J., 1980-82; pres. UNIPUB subs. Xerox Co., N.Y.C., 1982-86; mem. exec. com. R.R. Bowker Co., N.Y.C., 1982-86; pres. D.C. Pickett Assocs., 1986-93; counselor Work Force Devel. Program N.J. Dept. Labor, Somerville, 1993-94, counselor Project Reemployment Opportunities Sys., 1994-96; counselor, facilitator Career Transition Ctr., Somerville, 1996—. Co-author: Approval Plans and Academic Libraries, 1977; mem. editorial adv. bd. Technicalities, 1980-81; contbr. articles to profl. jours. Mem. Dean's Assocs., Ind. U. Sch. of Bus., Bloomington, 1983-90. Mem. Assn. Coll. and Rsch. Librs. (publs. com. 1983-87), Soc. Logistics Engrs. (adv. bd. 1981-91), Nat. Assn. Wabash Men (bd. dirs. 1983-90), Logistics Edn. Found., Caleb Mills Soc., Kiwanis (charter pres. N.W. Indpls. club 1958-59), Masons, Blue Key, Alpha Phi Omega, Delta Tau Delta (ednl. found.). Mem. Christian Ch. Home: 240 Great Hills Rd Bridgewater NJ 08807-1516

PICKETT, EDWIN GERALD, financial executive; b. Washington, Aug. 12, 1946; s. Clarence Edwin and Katherine (Molesworth) P.; m. Nancy Johnson, May 30, 1970; children: Karen, Andrew, Allison. BBA, W.Va. U., 1969; MBA, Loyola Coll. Balt., 1981. CPA, Md. Staff acct. Haskins and Sells CPA's, Balt., 1969-73; dir. internal audit Sun Life Ins. of Am., Balt., 1973-77; v.p., treas. Sun Life Group, Atlanta, 1977-80; v.p., treas. Md. Casualty Co., Balt., 1980-82, sr. v.p. fin., 1982-84; sr. v.p., exec. v.p. Am. Gen. Corp., Houston, 1984-86, CFO, 1986-89; exec. v.p., CFO USF&G Corp., Balt., 1990-93, TIG Holdings, Inc., Irving, Tex., 1993—. Treas. Poplar Springs (Md.) Meth. Ch., 1978-84; trustee Poplar Springs Meth. Ch., 1989-93, Hood Coll., 1990-95, Glenelg Country Sch., 1991-93. Mem. Am. Inst. CPA's, Fin. Execs. Inst., Caves Valley Golf Club (bd. dirs. 1991-93). Republican. Methodist. Avocations: golf, outdoor activities. Office: TIG Holdings Inc Ste N1624 5205 N O Connor Blvd Irving TX 75039-3712

PICKETT, GEORGE BIBB, JR., retired military officer; b. Montgomery, Ala., Mar. 20, 1918; s. George B. and Marie (Dow) P.; BS, U.S. Mil. Acad., 1941; student Nat. War Coll., 1959-60; m. Beryl Arlene Robinson, Dec. 27, 1941; children: Barbara Pickett Harrell, James, Kathleen, Thomas; m. 2d, Rachel Copeland Peeples, July 1981. Commd. 2d lt. U.S. Army, 1941, advanced through grades to maj. gen., 1966; instr. Inf. Sch., Fort Benning, Ga., 1947-50, instr. Armed Forces Staff Coll., Norfolk, Va., 1956-59; comdg. officer 2d Armored Cav. Regt., 1961-63; chief of staff Combat Devel. Command, 1963-66; comdg. gen. 2d inf. div., Korea, 1966-67; ret., 1973; field rep. Nat. Rifle Assn., 1973-85. Decorated Purple Heart with oak leaf cluster, D.S.M. with two oak leaf clusters, Bronze Star with two oak leaf clusters and V device, Silver Star, Legion of Merit with two oak leaf clusters, Commendation medal with two oak leaf clusters. Mem. SAR (pres. Ala. Soc. 1984), Old South Hist. Assn. Episcopalian. Club: Kiwanis. Author: (with others) Joint and Combined Staff Officers Manual, 1959; contbr. articles on mil. affairs to profl. jours. Home: 3525 Flowers Dr Montgomery AL 36109-4719 Office: PO Box 4 Montgomery AL 36101-0004

PICKETT, LAWRENCE KIMBALL, physician, educator; b. Balt., Nov. 10, 1919; s. Herbert E. and Emily (Ames) P.; m. Pauline Ferguson, Dec. 17, 1943; children: Lawrence Kimball, Nancy Lee, Paul F., Stephen B. B.A., Yale U., 1941, M.D., 1944. Intern Peter Bent Brigham Hosp., Boston, 1945-46; resident surgery Boston Childrens Hosp., 1946-50; practice medicine specializing in pediatrics and surgery Syracuse, N.Y., 1950-64, New Haven, 1964-84; clin. assoc. prof. surgery Upstate Med. Center, 1953-64; prof. surgery and pediatrics Yale U. Sch. Medicine, 1964-84, prof. emeritus, 1984—, asso. dean, 1973-84; chief of staff Yale-New Haven Hosp., 1973-83; med. dir. Welch Allen Co., Inc., Skaneateles, N.Y., 1983-95. Served to capt. M.C. AUS, 1951-53. Fellow ACS, Am. Acad. Pediatrics (past sect. chmn.); mem. Am. Surg. Assn. Home and Office: 386 Savage Farm Dr Ithaca NY 14850-6505

PICKETT, OWEN B., congressman; b. Richmond, Va., Aug. 31, 1930. BS, Va. Poly. Inst., 1952; LLB, U. Richmond, 1955. Bar: Va. 1955; CPA. Lawyer, acct. Virginia Beach, Va., 1955-72; mem. Va. Ho. of Dels., Richmond, 1972-86, 100th-103rd Congresses from 2d Va. dist., Washington, D.C., 1987—; chmn. Va. Dem. State Cen. Com., 1980-82; ranking minority mem. Nat. Security Subcom. on mil. personnel. Mem. Va. Bar Assn., Virginia Beach Bar Assn. Office: US Ho of Reps 2430 Rayburn Bldg Washington DC 20515-0005*

PICKETT, WILLIAM LEE, academic administrator; b. Kansas City, Mo., Jan. 28, 1941; s. William L. and Ruth Marie (Platt) P.; m. Patricia Jean Vincent, Dec. 26, 1964; children: Sean, Brian, Galen, Amy, Liam, Brendan, Erin. AB, Rockhurst Coll., 1962; MA, Duke U., 1963; MPA, U. Mo., 1973; PhD, U. Denver, 1977. Tchr. various high schs., 1963-66; dir. planning Rockhurst Coll., Kansas City, 1966-72; sr. analyst Midwest Research Inst., Kansas City, 1972-73; dir. devel. Regis Coll., Denver, 1973-77; v.p. U. Detroit, 1977-79, U. San Diego, 1979-86; pres. St. John Fisher Coll., Rochester, N.Y., 1986—. Democrat. Roman Catholic. Office: St John Fisher Coll 3690 East Ave Rochester NY 14618-3537

PICKHARDT, CARL EMILE, JR., artist; b. Westwood, Mass., May 28, 1908; s. Carl Emile and Louise (Fowler) P.; m. Marjorie Sachs, June 15, 1935 (div. 1952); children: Nancy Louise Arnold, Carl Emile III, Sally Anne Duncan; m. Rosamond Forbes Wyman, Mar. 28, 1953. BA, Harvard U., 1931; studied with Harold Zimmerman, 1931-37. Tchr. Fitchburg Art Mus., 1951-62, Worcester Mus. Sch., 1949-50, Sturbridge Art Sch., 1952-60. Author: Portfolio of Etchings, 1942; one-man shows, Berkshire Art Mus., 1941, Doris Meltzer Gallery, N.Y.C., 1961, 68, 70, 71, 72, Jacques Seligmann Gallery, N.Y.C., 1935, 51, 52, 54, Stuart Gallery, Boston, 1946, Margaret Brown Gallery, Boston, 1951, Fitchburg Art Mus., 1951, 91, Lawrence Gallery, Kansas City, Mo., 1955, Artek Gallery, Helsinki, Finland, 1959, Laguna Gloria Art Mus., Austin, Tex., 1966, Radcliffe Coll., 1983, Providence Art Club, 1986, Fitchburg Art Mus., 1991; exhibited in group shows at Carnegie Internat., 1951, Mus. Modern Art, N.Y.C., 1940, 63, 64, Whitney Mus., 1936, Nat. Acad., 1942, 49, Boston Inst. Contemporary Art, 1941, Internat. Exhbn., Japan., 1952, Exhbn. Am. Drawings, France, 1955, Art Inst. Chgo., Calif. Palace of Legion of Honor, 1953, Boston Arts Festival, 1950, Am. Drawing Biennial, Norfolk, 1964, Pa. Acad. Fine Arts, 1968, Laguna Gloria Art Mus., 1973, Fitchburg Art Mus., 1974, 91; represented in permanent collections, Mus. Modern Art, N.Y.C., Boston Mus. Fine Arts, Bklyn. Art Mus., Worcester Art Mus., Library of Congress, N.Y. Pub. Library, Newark Art Mus., Fogg Art Mus., Addison Gallery, Finch Coll. Art Mus., Pa. Acad. Fine Arts, Boston Pub. Library, Fitchburg Art Mus., Wadsworth Athenaeum, De Cordova Mus. Served with USNR, 1942-45. Ford Found. and Am. Fedn. Arts artist-in-residence Laguna Gloria Art Mus. 1966; recipient Shope prize Nat. Acad. 1942. Address: 66 Forest St Sherborn MA 01770-1618 *My life-long purpose has been to create in visual images a new language and to express order in asymetrical terms.*

PICKHOLTZ, RAYMOND LEE, electrical engineering educator, consultant; b. N.Y.C., Apr. 12, 1932; s. Isidore and Rose (Turkish) P.; m. Eda Rebecca Mittler, June 30, 1957. BEE, CUNY, 1954, MEE, 1958; Ph.D., Poly. Inst. N.Y., 1966. Research engr. RCA Labs., Princeton, N.J., 1954-57, ITT Labs., Nutley, N.J., 1957-61; assoc. prof. Poly. Inst. Bklyn., 1962-71; prof. elec. engring., chmn. dept. George Washington U., Washington, 1977-80, prof., 1971—; pres. Telecommunication Assocs., Fairfax, Va., 1963—; cons. Inst. Def. Analyses, 1971-90, IBM Research, Yorktown Heights, N.Y., 1968-72; del. Union Radio Scientifique, Geneva, 1979—, vice chmn., 1987; del. NRC, Washington, 1980-83; vis. prof. U. Que., 1977; vis. scholar U. Calif., 1983; chmn. U.S. Nat. Commn. C, Union Radio Sci. Internat., 1990-92; mem. sci. and indsl. adv. bd. Telecom. Inst. Ont., Can. and Inst. Nacionale de la Recherches Scientique. Editor: book series Computer Science Press, 1979—; IEEE Trans., 1975-80; author: Local Area and Multiple Access Networks, 1986; contbr. articles to profl. jours.; patentee in field. Recipient rsch. award RCA Labs., 1955; rsch. grantee Office of Naval Research, Washington, 1982, E-Systems, Falls Church, Va., 1983, MCI, Falls Church, Va., Instelsat, Washington. Fellow IEEE (bd. govs. 1979-82, digital comm. com., Centennial medal 1984), AAAS, Washington Acad. Scis.; mem. IEEE Comm. Soc. (v.p. 1986-88, pres. 1990-92, Donald W. McLellan award, 1994), Math. Assn. Am., Cosmos Club, Sigma Xi, Eta Kappa Nu. Home: 3613 Glenbrook Rd Fairfax VA 22031-3210 Office: George Washington U Dept Elec Engring Washington DC 20052

PICKHOLZ, JEROME WALTER, advertising agency executive; b. N.Y.C., Sept. 11, 1932; s. Solomon and Miriam (Schussler) P.; m. Phyllis Rachelle Plump, July 11, 1954; children: Keith, Michelle. BBA, CCNY, 1953. CPA, N.Y. Sr. acct. Eisner & Lubin (CPAs), 1957-60; contr. Hodes-Daniel Co., Elmsford, N.Y., 1960-65; v.p. Hodes-Daniel Co., 1965-70; pres., mgr. direct mail ops. Cordura Corp. div. Hodes Daniel Co., Elmsford, 1970-74; exec. v.p. Ogilvy & Mather Direct Response, Inc., N.Y.C., 1974-79, pres., 1979-86, chmn., chief exec. officer, 1986-95, chmn. emeritus, 1995—; vice chmn. Ogilvy & Mather Worldwide, N.Y.C., 1991-95; founding prin. Pickholz, Tweedy, Cowan, N.Y.C., 1996—; bd. dirs. Ogilvy & Mather U.S., Ogilvy & mather Worldwide, Mail-Well, Inc. Bd. dirs. ARC Greater N.Y., 1987—. Lt. (j.g.) USN, 1954-56. Recipient Eddy award Mail Advt. Svcs. Assn., 1988, Silver Apple award Direct Mktg. Club N.Y., 1989, Direct Marketer of Yr., 1992, Malcolm F. Dunn Leadership award, 1994. Mem. Direct Mktg. Assn. (bd. dirs. 1985—, mem. exec. com. 1986-88, chmn. 1991—). Office: Pickholz, Tweedy, Cowan 520 Madison Ave New York NY 10020

PICKHOLZ, MARVIN G., lawyer; b. N.Y.C., Apr. 18, 1942; children—Jason, Michael. A.B., NYU, 1963, LL.B., 1966, LL.M., 1968. Bar: N.Y., D.C.; trial atty. SEC, N.Y.C., 1967-69, chief atty. br. enforcement, 1969-72, spl. counsel div. enforcement, Washington, 1975-76, asst. chief trial atty., 1976-78, asst. dir., 1978-79; ptnr. Camhy Karlinsky & Stein, N.Y.C., 1995—; lectr. numerous legal assns., univs., profl. orgns. Author: (book) Securities Crimes, 1993. Mem. ABA (chmn. subcom. on legal compliance programs and preventive law 1981-82, chmn. govt. litigation com. 1982-84, chmn. com. on white collar crime 1984-89, coun. mem. criminal justice sect. 1985-89, mem. com. criminal laws and procedures, chmn. 1992-95, chair com. corp. compiance, mem. coord. com. on RICO, task force on SEC practice, task force on insider trading), Nat. Assn. Criminal Def. Lawyers (chmn. com. white collar crime), Assn. of Securities and Exchg. Commn. Alumni Inc. (founder, pres.). Mem. various editorial adv. bds.; contbr. articles to legal jours. Office: Camhy Karlinsky & Stein 1740 Broadway New York NY 10019

PICKLE, JAMES C., hospital administrator; b. Memphis, June 8, 1943; s. John Lott and Sarah Elizabeth (Adams) P.; m. Peggy Jean Massey, Dec. 18, 1965; children—Jeff, Matt. B.S. in Liberal Arts, Memphis State U., 1967, M.P.A., 1977. Asst. to pres. Store Devel. Corp., Memphis, 1967-69; investment analyst First Tenn. Adv. Corp., Memphis, 1972-73; v.p., dir. Care Inns Inc., Memphis, 1973-76; dir. shared services Meth. Hosps., Memphis, 1978, v.p. adminstrn., 1978-83, sr. v.p., 1983-84, exec. v.p., 1985-87. Mem. health and welfare ministry bd. Memphis Conf., United Meth. Ch., 1983-87; chief oper. officer Meth. Hosps., Memphis, 1983-87; pres., chief exec. officer Erlanger Med. Ctr., Chattanooga, Tenn., 1987-94; pres. Ky. divsn. Columbia/HCA Healthcare Corp., 1994—; mem. health adv. bd. Memphis State U., 1984-87; chmn. bd. dirs. Dogwood Village of Memphis and Shelby County Inc., 1984-87. Recipient Humanitarian award Am. Lung Assn., 1991, Mgr. of the Yr award Chattanooga Area Mgr. Assn., 1993. Mem. Am. Coll. Hosp. Adminstrs., Nat. Assn. Pub. Hosps. (bd. dirs., exec. com. 1991-94), Tenn. Hosp. Assn. (bd. dirs., numerous coms.), Memphis Hosp. Council (sec.-treas. 1985, pres. 1987), Tenn. Pub. and Teaching Hosp. Assn. (chmn. 1989-94). Republican. Methodist. Avocations: snow skiing; sailing. Home: 22 Brownsboro Hill Rd Louisville KY 40207-2009 Office: Columbia/HCA Healthcare Corp 201 W Main St Louisville KY 40202

PICKLE, JERRY RICHARD, lawyer; b. Paris, Tex., Feb. 2, 1947; s. Joseph Rambert and Martha Marie (Biggers) P.; m. Helen Leigh Russell, May 3, 1975; children: Jonathan Russell, Sarah Elizabeth. BA in History, U. Houston, 1969, JD, 1971. Bar: Tex. 1972, U.S. Dist. Ct. (no. dist.) Tex. 1974, U.S. Dist. Ct. (we. dist.) Tex. 1989. Mem. Luna, Ballard & Pickle, Garland, Tex., 1972-74; assoc. Hightower & Alexander, Dallas, 1974-76, Cuba & Johnson, Temple, Tex., 1976-77; assoc. gen. counsel Scott & White Clinic, Temple, 1977—; assoc. prof. Tex. A&M U. Coll. of Medicine, Temple, 1986—. Contbr. articles to profl. jours. V.p. The Caring House, Temple, 1989, Tex. divsn. Am. Cancer Soc., Temple, 1976-77; adv. bd. R.R. & Pioneer Mus., Temple, 1982-84; hist. preservation bd. City of Temple, 1979-90; chmn. Bell County Hist. Commn., 1980-82; bd. dirs. Bell County Mus., 1992—, Temple Coord. Child Care Coun., 1991-93, Sr. Citizens Activites Ctr., Temple, 1993-94, pres., 1994-95; bd. dirs. Temple Cultural Activities Ctr., 1992—, pres., 1994-95; chair Heart o'Tex. Coun., Chisholm Trail Dist., Boy Scouts Am., 1987-88. Mem. ABA, Am. Acad. Hosp. Attys., State Bar Tex. (health law sect. councilman 1980-84, 85-87, chmn. 1983-84), Tex. Young Lawyers Assn., State Bar Coll., Bell-Lampasas-Mills Counties Bar Assn. (bd. dirs. 1985-90, pres. 1988-89), Bell-Lampasas-Mills Counties Young Lawyers Assn. (pres. 1980-81), Nat. Health Lawyers Assn., Am. Acad. Healthcare Attys., Temple C. of C. (bd. dirs. 1983-85, 88-90), Rotary (chpt. dir. 1981-85, 86-87), Jaycees (chpt. dir. 1977-78). Democrat. Episcopalian. Avocations: reading, golf, music. Office: Scott & White Clinic 2401 S 31st St Temple TX 76508-0001

PICKLE, JOSEPH WESLEY, JR., religion educator; b. Denver, Apr. 8, 1935; s. Joseph Wesley and Wilhelmina (Blacketor) P.; m. Judith Ann Siebert, June 28, 1958; children: David E., Kathryn E., Steven J. BA, Carleton Coll., 1957; B.D., Chgo. Theol. Sem., 1961; MA, U. Chgo., 1962, PhD, 1969. Ordained to ministry Am. Bapt. Conv., 1962. Asst. pastor Judson Meml. Ch., N.Y.C., 1959-60; acting dean summer session Colo. Coll., Colorado Springs, 1969-70, from asst. prof. to prof. religion, 1964—, faculty dir. internat. studies, 1994—; vis. prof. theology Iliff Sch. Theology, Denver, 1984; vis. prof. religious studies U. Zimbabwe, Harare, 1989; cons. Colo. Humanities Program, Denver, 1975-89; coord. Sheffer Meml. Fund, Colo. Coll., Colorado Springs, 1983—. Co-editor Papers of the 19th Century Theology Group, 1978, 88, 93. Pres. bd. dirs. Pikes Peak Mental Health Ctr., Colorado Springs, 1975; chmn. Colo. Health Facilities Rev. Coun., Denver, 1979-84; mem. Colo. Health Facilities Rev. Coun., Denver, 1976-84, Colo. Bd. Health, Denver, 1986-91. Am. Bapt. Conv. scholar, 1953-59; Fulbright Hays Grad. fellow U. Tübingen, Fed. Republic Germany, 1963-64, Danforth fellow, 1957-63, Joseph Malone fellow, 1987. Fellow Soc. for Values in Higher Edn.; mem. Am. Theol. Soc. (pres. 1996—), Am. Acad. Religion (regional pres. 1983-84, 92-93), Cath. Theol. Soc. Am., Fulbright Assn., Phi Beta Kappa. Democrat. Home: 20 W Caramillo St Colorado Springs CO 80907-7314 Office: Colo Coll 14 E Cache La Poudre St Colorado Springs CO 80903-3243

PICKLE, ROBERT DOUGLAS, lawyer, footwear industry executive; b. Knoxville, Tenn., May 22, 1937; s. Robert Lee and Beatrice Jewel (Douglas) P.; m. Rosemary Elaine Noser, May 9, 1964. AA, Schreiner Mil. Coll., Kerrville, Tex., 1957; BSBA, U. Tenn., 1959, JD, 1961; honor grad. seminar, Nat. Def. U., 1979. Bar: Tenn. 1961, Mo. 1964, U.S. Ct. Mil. Appeals 1962, U.S. Supreme Ct. 1970. Atty. Brown Shoe Co., Inc., St. Louis, 1963-69, asst. sec., atty., 1969-74; sec., gen. counsel Brown Group, Inc., St. Louis, 1974-85, v.p., gen. counsel, corp. sec., 1985—; indiv. mobilization augmentee, asst. army judge adv. gen. civil law The Pentagon, Washington, 1984-89. Provisional judge Municipal Ct., Clayton, Mo., summer 1972; chmn. Clayton Region attys. sect., profl. div. United Fund Greater St. Louis Campaign, 1972-73, team capt., 1974-78; chmn. City of Clayton Parks and Recreation Commn., 1985-87; liaison admissions officer, regional and state coordinator U.S. Mil. Acad., 1980—. Col. JAGC, U.S. Army, 1961-63. Fellow Harry S. Truman Meml. Library; mem. ABA, Tenn. Bar Assn., Mo. Bar Assn., St. Louis County Bar Assn., Bar Assn. Met. St. Louis, St. Louis Bar Found. (bd. dirs. 1979-81), Am. Corp. Counsel Assn., Am. Soc. Corp. Secs. (treas. St. Louis regional group 1976-77, sec. 1977-78, v.p. 1978-79, pres. 1979-80), U. Tenn. Gen. Alumni Assn. (pres., bd. dirs. St. Louis chpt. 1974-76, 80-84, bd. govs. 1982-89), U.S. Trademark Assn. (bd. dirs. 1978-82), Tenn. Soc. St. Louis (bd. dirs. 1980-88, treas., sec., v.p. 1984-87, pres. 1987-88), Smithsonian Nat. Assocs., World Affairs Coun. St. Louis, Inc., Am. Legion, University Club (v.p., sec. St. Louis chpt. 1976-81, bd. dirs. 1976-81), Stadium Club, West Point Soc. St. Louis (hon. mem., bd. dirs. 1992—), Scabbard and Blade, Kappa Sigma, Phi Delta Phi, Phi Theta Kappa, Beta Gamma Sigma, Phi Kappa Phi. Republican. Presbyterian. Avocations: reading, spectator sports. Home: 214 Topton Way Saint Louis MO 63105-3638 Office: Brown Group Inc 8300 Maryland Ave Saint Louis MO 63105-3645

PICKLE BEATTIE, KATHERINE HAMNER, real estate agent; b. Henrico County, Va., Sept. 30, 1936; d. Laurance Davis and Susan (Mooers) Hamner; widowed 1969; children: Katherine Carter Beattie, Harry Canfield Beattie IV, Margaret Spotswood Beattie; m. Timothy L. Pickle, III, Dec. 29, 1989. Attended, Va. Commonwealth U. Pres. Varina Wood Products, Inc., Gloucester-Mathews County, 1969-75; real estate agt. Nat. Assn. Bd. Realtors, Gloucester-Mathews County, Richmond, Va., 1975—; pres. Varina Wood Products, Inc., 1969-75. Pres. George F. Baker PTA, 1970; v.p. Varina Women's Club, Henrico, Va., 1969-70; sec. Mathews Women's Club, 1992-94; mem. Rep. Women's Club; mem. Va. Mus. Fine Arts, Naples, Fla. Philharm. Ctr. for Arts com. of a thousand. Mem. DAR (Cricket Hill chpt.), Raleigh Tavern Soc., Va. Lions Club. Episcopalian. Avocations: tennis, bridge, reading, swimming, fishing. Home: PO Box 317 Gwynn VA 23066-0317

PICKLEMANN, JACK R., surgeon. MD, McGill U., Montreal, Que., Can., 1964. Intern Royal Victoria Hosp., Montreal, Que., Can., 1964-65; resident in surgery U. Chgo. Med. Ctr., 1967-73; prof. surgery Loyola U., Chgo.; attending physician Loyola Med. Ctr., Maywood, Ill. Mem. ACS. Office: Loyola U Med Ctr 2160 S 1st Ave Maywood IL 60153*

PICKOVER, BETTY ABRAVANEL, retired executive legal secretary, civic volunteer; b. N.Y.C., Apr. 20, 1920; d. Albert and Sultana (Rousso) Abravanel; m. Bernard Builder, Apr. 6, 1941 (div. 1962); children: Ronald, Stuart; m. William Pickover, Aug. 23, 1970 (dec. Nov. 1983). Student, Taft Evening Ctr., 1961-70. Sec. U.S. Treasury Dept., Washington, 1942-43; exec. legal sec. various attys., Bronx, N.Y., 1956-70; exec. legal sec. various attys., Yonkers, N.Y., 1971-83, ret., 1983. Chair Uniongram Sisterhood of Temple Emanu-El, Yonkers, N.Y., 1975—, Honor Roll, 1975—, v.p. 1995-96; sr. citizen cmty. leader Yonkers Officer for Aging, 1984—, Westchester County Sr. Adv. Bd., White Plains, N.Y., 1989-92; mem. Mayor's Cmty. Rels. Com. of Yonkers, 1985—, historian, photographer, 1988—; v.p. Mayor's cmty. Rels. com. Yonkers, 1995; mem. adv. coun. Westchester County Office Aging Sr., 1993—; bd. legislators task force sr. citizens Westchester County, 1995-96; Mayor Silver City Coun. Yonkers, 1989; mem. Mayor's adv. coun. sr. citizens, 1990. Recipient Appreciation cert. Westchester County, 1992, Pres. Coun., City of Yonkers, 1992, Merit cert., 1993, Cmty. Svc. award Mayor, City of Yonkers, 1995, John E. Andrus Meml. Vol. award, 1995, Appreciation cert. Westchester County Exec., 1993, 94, Merit cert. N.Y. State Senator, 1995, Merit cert. N.Y. State Senator, 1994; nominee Pres.'s Svc. award, 1995. Democrat. Jewish. Avocations: writing, photography, entertaining at all nursing homes in Yonkers, history, public relations. Home: 200 Valentine Ln Yonkers NY 10705-3608

PICKREL, PAUL, English educator; b. Gilson, Ill., Feb. 2, 1917; s. Clayton and Inez (Murphy) P. A.B., Knox Coll., 1938; M.A., Yale U., 1942, Ph.D., 1944. Instr. English Lafayette Coll., 1941-42; instr. Yale U., 1943-45, asst. prof., 1945-50, lectr. English, 1954-66, chmn. Scholar of House Program, 1959-60, 61-66; fellow Morse Coll., 1962-66; adviser John Hay fellows, 1959-66; vis. prof. English Smith Coll., Northampton, Mass., 1966-67, prof., 1967-87, prof. emeritus, 1987—, chmn. dept., 1972-75, 81-82. Author: (novel) The Moving Stairs, 1948; also essays on fiction, numerous book revs.; mng. editor: Yale Rev., 1949-66; chief book critic: Harper's mag., 1954-65. Mem. Aurelian Honor Soc., Phi Beta Kappa. Clubs: Elizabethan (New Haven), Faculty (Northampton); Yale (N.Y.C.). Office: Smith Coll Wright Hall Northampton MA 01063

PICKRELL, THOMAS RICHARD, retired oil company executive; b. Jermyn, Tex., Dec. 30, 1926; s. Mont Bolt and Martha Alice (Dodson) P.; m. M. Earline Bowen, Sept. 9, 1950; children—Thomas Wayne, Michael Bowen, Kent Richard, Paul Keith. B.S., North Tex. State U., 1951, M.B.A., 1952; postgrad., Ohio State U., 1954-55; advanced mgmt. program, Harvard U., 1979. CPA, Tex. Auditor, acct. Conoco, Inc., Ponca City, Okla., 1955-62; mgr. acctg. Conoco, Inc., Houston, 1965-67; asst. controller Conoco, Inc., Ponca City, 1967-81; v.p., controller Conoco, Inc., Stamford, Conn., 1982-83, Wilmington, Del., 1983-85; asst. prof. Okla. State U., Stillwater, Okla., 1962-63; controller Douglas Oil Co., Los Angeles, 1963-65; mem. adv. bd. dept. acctg. North Tex. State U., Denton, 1978-85; mem. adv. bd. Coll. Bus., Kansas State U., Manhattan, 1979-81. Bd. dirs. YMCA, Ponca City, 1976-78, Kay Guidance Clinic, Ponca City, 1971-74, United Way, Ponca City, 1979-81; chmn. Charter Rev. Com., Ponca City, 1971-72. Served to sgt. U.S. Army, 1944-46; ETO. Mem. AICPA, Fin. Execs. Inst. (pres. Okla. chpt. 1972), Am. Petroleum Inst. (acctg. com., gen. com.), Ponca City Country Club (pres. 1980-81), Rotary (pres. Ponca City club 1973-74), Beta Gamma Sigma, Beta Alpha Psi. Republican. Presbyterian. Home: 10 San Juan Ranch Rd Santa Fe NM 87501-9804

PICON-WAGONER, DORA AMALIA, neurologist; b. San Juan, P.R., Mar. 20, 1950; d. Guido F. Picon and Rosa L. Ramirez; children: Dora, Daphne, Dariush; m. Kent A. Wagoner, June 10, 1995. BA, U. P.R., 1970; MD, U. Central del Este, San Pedro, R.D., 1982; postgrad., Wayne State U., Detroit, 1986, Wayne State U., 1987. From neurology resident to EEG fellow Wayne State U., Detroit, 1982-87; neurologist pvt. practice, Richmond, Ky., 1995—; ethics com. Holy Cross Hosp., Detroit 1988—, South Macomb Hosp. Mem. AMA, American Acad. Neurology. Avocations: camping, canoeing, scuba. Office: Med Arts Bldg 527 West Main St Richmond KY 40475

PICOTTE, LEONARD FRANCIS, naval officer; b. Calumet, Mich., Dec. 8, 1939; s. Irving René and Maria (Tamborino) P.; m. Sandra Lees Whiteley, July 14, 1984; children from previous marriage: Mary Elizabeth, Lance, Michael. BS in Econs. cum laude, U. No. Mich., 1963; MA in Polit. Sci., San Diego State U., 1975; grad. with distinction, Armed Forces Staff Coll., Norfolk, Va., 1976; M in Strategic Studies, Naval War Coll., Newport, R.I., 1985. Commd. ensign USN, 1963, advanced through grades to rear adm., 1991; comdg. officer USS Marathon, Vietnam, 1971-73; exec. officer USS Point Defiance, San Diego, 1976-78; exec. officer, officer in charge Surface Warfare Officers' Sch., Coronado, Calif., 1978-80; exec. officer Naval Sta., San Diego, 1980; comdg. officer USS Alamo, San Diego, 1980-82; surface warfare detailer Bur. Naval Pers., Washington, 1982-84; comdg. officer USS Duluth, San Diego, 1986-88; 1st comdg. officer USS Wasp, 1988-90; insp. gen. Comdr. in Chief, U.S. Atlantic Command, Comdr. in Chief, U.S. Atlantic Fleet, Norfolk, 1990-92; comdr. Amphibious Group Two, Norfolk, 1992-95; ret., 1995; lead analyst expeditionary warfare Am. Systems Corp., Chesapeake, Va., 1995—. Decorated Legion of Merit (2); recipient Disting. Svc. medal. Mem. Surface Navy Assn., USS Wasp Assn. (hon.), Army and Navy Club, Town Point Club, Hampton Roads Coun. Navy League (bd. dirs.). Republican. Roman Catholic. Avocations: jogging, hunting, reading, gardening, chess. Home: 119 Northgate Ln Suffolk VA 23434 Office: Am Systems Corp Greenbriar Cir Chesapeake VA 23320

PICOTTE, MICHAEL BERNARD, real estate developer; b. Albany, N.Y., Sept. 22, 1947; s. Bernard Francis and Kathleen (McManus) P.; m. Margaret Nelson Lindsay; children: Nicole Lindsay, Joseph McManus, Michelle Harrison. BBA, Villanova U., 1969; owner's and pres.'s mgmt. program, Harvard U., 1982. Exec. v.p. West Bradford Corp., Albany, N.Y., 1975-82; mng. ptnr. Picotte Cos., Albany, 1982-90, pres., chief exec. officer, 1990—; bd. dirs. Fleet Fin. Group. Trustee Coll. St. Rose, 1983-89, Albany Inst. History and Art, 1988—; former chmn., trustee St. Peter's Hosp., Albany, 1986—; cir. Ctr. for Econ. Growth, 1992. With USNG, 1969-74. Trustee Coll. St. Rose, 1983-89, Albany Inst. History & Art, 1988—; chmn. St. Peter's Hosp., Albany, 1986—; cir. Ctr. for Econ. Growth, 1992. With USNG, 1969-74. Mem. Young Pres.'s Orgn., Schuyler Meadows Club, Ft. Orange Club (Albany). Avocations: skiing, golf, tennis. Office: Picotte Cos 20 Corporate Woods Blvd Albany NY 12211-2370

PICOWER, WARREN MICHAEL, magazine editor; b. N.Y.C., Aug. 21, 1934; s. Abraham and Nell (Bloom) P.; divorced; children: Jenny Emelia, Eve Julie. BA, Queens Coll., 1956; MA, New Sch. for Social Rsch., 1978; PsyD in Psychology, Heed U., L.A., 1982. Editorial asst. Newsweek mag., N.Y.C., 1956-59; assoc. editor SM Pub. Co., N.Y.C., 1961-63; assoc., mng. editor Fawcett Pubs., N.Y.C., 1963, 64-65; mng. editor Tuesday Publs., N.Y.C., 1965-67, exec. editor, v.p., 1967-73; sr. editor King Features Syndicate, N.Y.C., 1974-78; mng. editor Food & Wine Mag., N.Y.C., 1978-93; consulting editor Travel Holiday Mag., N.Y., 1993-94; mng. editor Zagat Survey restaurant and hotel guides, N.Y.C., 1994—; cons. in field. Contbr. articles to profl. jours. Mem. Am. Soc. Mag. Editors, Assn. of Food Journalists. Office: Zagat Survey 4 Columbus Cir New York NY 10019-1100

PICOZZI, ANTHONY, dentistry educator, educational administrator; b. Bklyn., Dec. 24, 1917; s. Louis and Ida (DeRosa) P.; m. Gloria Margaret Patinella, Feb. 9, 1952; children—Kathryn, Lori. B.S., Columbia U., 1939; D.D.S., NYU, 1944. Section chief Lever Bros. Research, Edgewater, N.J., 1955-68; prof. dentistry NYU, N.Y.C., 1968-74; adminstr., researcher Fairleigh Dickinson U., Hackensack, N.J., 1974-89; rsch. cons. Warner Lambert Co., Morris Plains, N.J., 1989—; cons. Lever Research, Edgewater, 1968-74, W.R. Grace, Balt., 1979-81. Contbr. articles to profl. jours. Served to lt. col. USAR. Mem. ADA (mem. coun. on dental rsch. 1987-91), Am. Assn. Dental Research (councillor 1981, bd. dirs. 1988-90), Am. Assn. Dental Schs. (sect. chmn. 1980-81). Home: 21 Ridge Rd Ridgewood NJ 07450-3159 Office: Warner Lambert Co 170 Tabor Rd Morris Plains NJ 07950-2536

PIDERIT, JOHN J., university educator; b. N.Y.C., Feb. 26, 1944. BA in Math. and Philosophy magna cum laude, Fordham U., 1967; Lic. in Sacred Theology cum laude, Philosophische und Theologische Hochschule Sankt Georgen, Frankfurt, West Germany, 1971; MPhil, Oxford U., 1974; MA, PhD in Econ., Princeton U., 1979. Ordained Jesuit priest Roman Cath. Ch., 1971. Tchr. math. Regis H.S., N.Y.C., 1967-68; asst. campus minister Fordham U., 1971-72; asst. campus minister Princeton U., 1975-78, preceptor, 1976-77; asst. chairperson grad. studies Fordham U., 1984-88, dir. program internat. polit. econ. and devel., 1981-83, 87-88, asst. chairperson dept. econs., 1979-82, 88-89, asst. prof. econs., 1978-89, assoc. prof. econs., 1989-90; corp. v.p. Marquette U., 1990-93; pres. Loyola U. Chgo., 1993—; vis. fellow Woodstock Theol. Ctr., Washington, summer 1982; sabbatical Santa Clara U., 1989-90; master Queen's Ct. Residential Coll., 1987-90; chmn. responsible investment com. N.Y. province SJ, 1986-88, mem. fin. com., 1986-88; mem. joint commn. govtl. rels. of Am. Coun. Edn., 1994—; mem. exec. com. Nat. Planning Com. Jesuit Assembly '89, 1988-90. Contbr. articles to profl. jours. Founder, moderator Friends of Loyola, 1987-90; pres. Univ. Neighborhood Housing Corp., 1986-90, Maroon Enterprises, Inc., 1986-90; trustee Canisius Coll., Buffalo, 1983-88, 89-94; bd. dirs. Corp. Cmty. Schs. of Am., 1993—; promoter PIVOT H.S. and Middle Sch. with Milw. Pub. Schs., 1990-93; mem. Greater Milw. Edn. Trust, 1990-93; mem. steering com., chair edn. task force Milw. Cmty. Traffic Safety Com., 1991-93; mem. steering com. Libr. Literacy Soc. Milw., 1991-93; mem. scholarship com. Knitworkers Union Local 155, N.Y.C., 1982-90; mem. Princeton Schs. Com. N.Y. Region, 1985-88. Mellon grantee Fordham U., summer 1983, summer grantee Fordham U., 1979, Princeton U. fellow, 1974-78. Office: Loyola U Chgo 820 N Michigan Ave Chicago IL 60611-2103

PIDGEON, JOHN ANDERSON, headmaster; b. Lawrence, Mass., Dec. 20, 1924; s. Alfred H. and Nora (Regan) P.; children: John Anderson, Regan S., Kelly; m. Barbara Hafer, May 1986. Grad., Phillips Acad., 1943; B.A., Bowdoin Coll., 1949; Ed.D., Bethany Coll., 1973; D.Litt., Washington and Jefferson Coll., 1979. Instr. Latin, adminstrv. asst. to headmaster Deerfield Acad., 1949-57; headmaster Kiskiminetas Springs Sch., Saltsburg, Pa., 1957—; dir. Saltsburg Savs. & Trust. Served as ensign USNR, 1943-46. Mem. New Eng. Swimming Coaches Assn. (pres. 1956-57), Cum Laude Soc., Delta Upsilon. Home and Office: Kiski Sch 1888 Brett Ln Saltsburg PA 15681-8951

PIDOT, WHITNEY DEAN, lawyer; b. N.Y.C., Mar. 2, 1944; s. George B. and Virginia (Ulrich) P.; m. Jeanne Stoddard, April 23, 1973; children: Whitney Dean Jr., Philip Martin, Seth Thayer. AB, Harvard U., 1966; JD, Columbia U., 1970, MBA, 1970. Bar: N.Y. 1971. Ptnr. Shearman & Sterling, N.Y.C., 1970—; adv. bd. Barclays Bank N.Y., 1989-92, Molecular Tool, Inc. (biotech.) Balt., 1991-96, Equine Genetic Rsch. Ptnrs., Balt., 1991-95; trustee Winthrop Univ. Hosp., Mineola, N.Y., 1989—; bd. dirs. Oneida Ltd., R.I. Corp., North Ctrl. Oil Corp., Houston, Cold Spring Harbor Labs., N.Y. Mayor, Village of Matinecock, Locust Valley, N.Y., 1977-92; vice chmn. North Shore Mayors Com., Long Island, N.Y., 1980-92; bd. dirs. Nassau County (N.Y.) Village Officials Assn., 1978-80; commr. Locust Valley Fire Dist., 1979-93. Republican. Home: Piping Rock Rd Locust Valley NY 11560 Office: c/o Shearman & Sterling 599 Lexington Ave Ste C-2 New York NY 10022-6030

PIECEWICZ, WALTER MICHAEL, lawyer; b. Concord, Mass., Jan. 27, 1948; s. Benjamin Michael and Cecelia (Makuc) P.; A.B. magna cum laude, Colgate U., 1970; J.D., Columbia U., 1973; m. Anne T. Mikolajczyk, Oct. 28, 1978; children—Tiffany Anne, Stephanie Marie. Admitted to Ill. bar, 1973; mem. firm Levenfeld, Kanter, Baskes & Lippitz, Chgo., 1973-78, Boodell, Sears, Giambalvo & Crowley, Chgo., 1978-87, Peterson & Ross, Chgo., 1987—; bd. dirs. No. Data Systems, Inc., Steiner Co., Inc., Arrow Pattern & Foundry Co., Inc. Mem. ABA, Ill. Bar Assn., Chgo. Bar Assn., Chgo. Estate Planning Coun., Internat. Bus. Coun. Midwest, Phi Beta Kappa. Democrat. Roman Catholic. Office: Peterson & Ross 200 E Randolph St Ste 7300 Chicago IL 60601-6436

PIECH, MARGARET ANN, mathematics educator; b. Bridgewater, N.S., Can., Apr. 6, 1942; d. Frederick Cecil and Margaret Florence (Laschinger) Garrett; m. Kenneth Robert Piech, June 19, 1965; children: Garrett Andrew, Marjorie Ann. BA, Mt. Allison U., Sackville, N.B., Can., 1962; PhD, Cornell U., 1967. Asst. prof. SUNY, Buffalo, 1967-72, assoc. prof., 1972-78, prof. math., 1978—; cons. NSF, Washington, 1980-81, Aspen Analytics, Buffalo, 1986—; v.p. Seventy Niagara Svcs., 1990—. Contbr. articles to profl. jours. Woodrow Wilson fellow, 1962-63; grantee NSF, 1976-85, U.S. Army Rsch. Office, 1985-89. Mem. IEEE, Am. Math. Soc., Assn. Computing Machinery, Greater Yellowstone Coalition, Henry's Fork Found. Avocation: fly fishing. Office: SUNY Diefendorf Hall Buffalo NY 14214

PIECUCH, JOHN M., manufacturing company executive; b. South Bend, Ind., 1949. BS, U. Notre Dame, 1965; postgrad., U. Chgo., 1983. Past pres., bd. dirs. Sun Metal Products, Warsaw, Ind., Sun Wheels Ltd., Warsaw; sr. v.p., pres. Great Lakes region LaFarge Corp., Reston, Va., 1987-89, exec. v.p., pres. Cement group, 1989-92, sr. v.p., now dir., 1992—; exec. v.p. LaFarge Group. Office: LaFarge Corp 11130 Sunrise Valley Dr Reston VA 22091-4329*

PIEHL, DONALD HERBERT, chemist, consultant; b. Chgo., Jan. 18, 1939; s. Herbert Herman and Faye L. (Pentti) P.; m. Ann Elizabeth Guildner; children: Mark Donald, Jennifer Ann. BA in Chemistry, Carthage Coll., 1961; MS in Chemistry, U. Iowa, 1964, PhD in Chemistry, 1966; postgrad. Young Exec. Inst., U. N.C., 1974. Quality control chemist Bowey's, Inc., Chgo., 1961; polymer chemist Borg-Warner Corp., Des Plaines, Ill., 1962; sr. rsch. chemist R.J. Reynolds Tobacco Co., Winston-Salem, N.C., 1965-70, group leader, 1969-70; section head R.J. Reynolds Industries, Winston-Salem, 1970-76, rsch. mgr., 1976-80, dir. applied R & D, 1980-83; dir. tech. svcs. RJR Nabisco, Winston-Salem, 1983-85; v.p. R & D Heublein Inc., Hartford, Conn., 1985-89, v.p. tech. and brand devel., 1989-94; tchr. mgmt. of tech. and total quality mgmt., quality cons., 1994—; head rsch. and devel. PTHM, Sampoerna, Indonesia, 1995—; instr. Am. Mgmt. Assn., organizer, chmn. Pub. Symposium on Energy and Environ, Greensboro, N.C., 1974; mem. adv. com. mgmt. of tech. program U. N.C., Chapel Hill, 1982-84; tchr. bus. inst. Mgmt. Devel., Inc., Chapel Hill, 1975-85. Contbr. articles to profl. jours. Bd. dirs. Sci. and Tech. Inst. of New Eng., Storrs, Conn., 1988—, Sci. Mus. Conn., Hartford, 1989—, Indsl. Rsch. Inst., 1993—, chmn. precoll. edn. com., 1993-94; pres. Optimist CLub, Winston-Salem, 1971. Recipient Outstanding Young Man of Am. award, 1970, Optimist of Yr. award Optimist Club, 1971, Spl. Teaching award U. N.C. Sch. Bus., 1984; fellow Ethyl Corp., 1964-65. Fellow Conn. Acad. Edn.; mem. World Assn. of Alcohol Beverage Industry (v.p. and com. chair Conn. chpt. 1992-94), Am. Chem. Soc. (chmn. local sect. 1962—, Outstanding Svc. award 1974), Inst. Food Technologists, Conn. Quality Coun. (co-founder 1989—), N.C. Acad. Scis., Hartford C. of C. (chmn. bd. tech. coun. 1986-89), Sigma Xi, Alpha Chi Sigma. Republican. Avocations: tennis, golf, skiing, photography.

PIEKARSKI, VICTOR J., lawyer; b. Lawrence, Mass., Feb. 20, 1950. BA cum laude, Boston Coll., 1971; MBA, U. Chgo., 1978; JD cum laude, Northwestern U., 1974. Bar: Ill. 1974, U.S. Ct. Appeals (7th cir.) 1977, U.S. Supreme Ct. 1978. Ptnr. Querrey & Harrow Ltd., Chgo. Mem. ABA, Ill. State Bar Assn., Chgo. Bar Assn., Ill. Assn. Def. Trial Counsel, Trial Lawyers Club Chgo., Def. Rsch. Inst. Office: Querrey & Harrow Ltd 180 N Stetson Ave Chicago IL 60601-6710*

PIEL, CAROLYN FORMAN, pediatrician, educator; b. Birmingham, Ala., Oct. 18, 1918; d. James R. and Mary Elizabeth (Dortch) Forman; m. John Joseph Piel, Aug. 3, 1951; children: John Joseph, Mary Dortch, Elizabeth Forman, William Scott. BA, Agnes Scott Coll., 1940; MS, Emory U., 1943; MD, Washington U., St. Louis, 1946. Diplomate Am. Bd. Pediatrics (examiner 1973-88, pres. 1986-87); diplomate Am. Bd. Pediatric Nephrology. Intern Phila. Gen. Hosp., 1946-47; resident Phila. Children's Hosp., 1947-49; fellow Cornell U. Med. Sch., N.Y.C., 1949-51; from instr. to assoc. clin. prof. Stanford U. Sch. Medicine, San Francisco, 1951-59; from asst. prof. to prof. Sch. Medicine, U. Calif., San Francisco, 1959-89, emeritus prof., 1989—. Author, co-author research articles in field. Bd. mem. San Francisco Home Health Service, 1977-83. Emeritus mem. Soc. for Pediatric Research, Am. Pediatric Soc., Am. Soc. for Pediatric Nephrology, Am. Soc. Nephrology, Western Soc. for Pediatric Nephrology (pres. 1960). Democrat. Presbyterian. Home: 2164 Hyde St San Francisco CA 94109-1701 Office: U Calif PO Box 748 San Francisco CA 94143

PIEL, GERARD, editor, publisher; b. Woodmere, L.I., N.Y., Mar. 1, 1915; s. William F.J. and Loretto (Scott) P.; m. Mary Tapp Bird, Feb. 4, 1938; children: Jonathan Bird, Samuel Bird (dec.); m. Eleanor Virden Jackson, June 24, 1955; child, Eleanor Jackson. A.B. magna cum laude, Harvard U., 1937; D.Sc., Lawrence Coll., 1956, Colby Coll., 1960; U. B.C., Brandeis U., 1965, Lebanon Valley Coll., 1977, L.I. U., 1978, Bard Coll., 1979, CUNY, 1979, U. Mo., 1985, Blackburn Coll., 1985; Litt.D., Rutgers U., 1961, Bates Coll., 1974; L.H.D., Columbia, 1962, Williams Coll., 1966, Rush U., 1979, Hahnemann Med. Coll., 1981, Mt. Sinai Med. Sch., 1985; LL.D., Tuskegee Inst., 1963, U. Bridgeport, 1964, Bklyn. Poly. Inst., 1965, Carnegie-Mellon U., 1968, Lowell U., 1986; Dr. (honoris causa), Moscow State (Lomonosov) U., 1985. Sci. editor Life mag., 1938-44; asst. to pres. Henry J. Kaiser Co. (and assoc. cos.), 1945-46; organizer (with Dennis Flanagan, Donald H. Miller, Jr.), pres. Sci. Am., Inc., 1946-84, chmn., 1984-87, chmn. emeritus, 1987—; pub. mag. Sci. Am., 1947-84. Translated editions: Le Scienze, 1968, Saiensu, 1971, Investigacion y Ciencia, 1976, Pour la Science, 1977, Spektrum der Wissenschaft, 1978, KeXue, 1979, V Mire Nauki, 1983, Tudomany, 1985, Majallat Al Oloom, 1986, Erde im Gleichgewicht, 1994; author: Science in the Cause of Man, 1961, The Acceleration of History, 1972, Only One World, 1992. Chmn. Commn. Delivery Personal Health Services City N.Y., 1967-68; trustee Am. Mus. Nat. History, N.Y. Bot. Garden, René Dubos Ctr.; trustee emeritus Radcliffe Coll., Phillips Acad., Mayo Clinic, Henry J. Kaiser Family Found., Found. for Child Devel.; pub. mem. Am. Bd. Med. Specialities; bd. overseers Harvard U., 1966-68, 73-79. Recipient George Polk award, 1961, Kalinga prize, 1962, Bradford Washburn award, 1966, Arches of Sci. award, 1969; Rosenberger medal U. Chgo., 1973, A.I. Djavakhishvili medal U. Tbilisi, 1985; named Pub. of Yr. Mag. Pubs. Assn., 1980. Fellow Am. Acad. Arts and Scis., AAAS (pres. 1985, chmn. 1986); mem. Coun. Fgn. Rels., Am. Philos. Soc., Nat. Acad. Sci. Inst. Medicine, Harvard Club, Century Club, Met. Opera Club, Cosmos Club, Somerset Club, Phi Beta Kappa, Sigma Xi. Home: 1115 5th Ave New York NY 10128-0100

PIEL, WILLIAM, JR., retired lawyer; b. N.Y.C., Nov. 28, 1989; s. William and Loretto (Scott) P.; m. Eleanor Green, Dec. 1, 1951; children by former marriage: Michael, Anthony, Thomas. AB, Princeton U., 1932; LLB, Harvard U., 1935. Bar: N.Y. 1935. Practiced in N.Y.C.; partner Sullivan & Cromwell, 1945-80; expert cons. mil. intelligence service War Dept. Gen. Staff, 1944-45; dir. emeritus Campbell Soup Co., Phillips Petroleum Co. Hon. dir. Greater N.Y.. coun. Girl Scouts Am.; hon. trustee Cancer Rsch. Inst.; trustee Internat. Crane Found., Baraboo, Wis. Fellow Am. Coll. Trial Lawyers, N.Y. State Bar Found.; mem. ABA, Assn. Bar City N.Y., Am. Judicature Soc., Fed. Bar Coun., Squadron A Assn., Century Assn., Princeton Club (N.Y.C.). Home: Tree House 44 Briggs Hill Rd Sherman CT 06784

PIELE, PHILIP KERN, education infosystems educator; b. Portland, Oreg., May 14, 1935; s. Theodore R. and Helen D. (Hanson) P.; m. Sandra Jean Wright, Aug. 10, 1963; children: Melissa, Kathryn. BA, Wash. State U., 1957; student, U. Wash., 1960, San Jose State U., 1964; MS, U. Oreg., 1963, PhD, 1968. Prof. dept. ednl. policy and mgmt. U. Oreg., Eugene, 1979—, mem. faculty applied info. mgmt. program, 1989—, dir. numerous ednl. orgns. and coms. Coll. Edn., 1968—, dir. Edn. Resources Info. Ctr. (ERIC) clearinghouse on ednl. mgmt., 1969—, assoc. dir. Ctr. for Ednl. Policy and Mgmt., 1973-76; vis. lectr. U. Western Australia, Monashe U., U. New S. Wales, and several other Australian Univs., 1973; vis. prof. Ontario Inst. for Studies in Edn., U. Toronto, 1974; vis. scholar Stanford U., 1984; exec. sec. Oreg. Sch. Study Coun., 1980—; dir. Networks and Comms. Ctr. for Advanced Tech. in Edn., 1984-92. Author numerous books, chpts., monographs; editor numerous books; contbr. articles to profl. jours. Bd. dirs. Oreg. Bach Festival, Eugene, 1980-83, Oreg. Mozart Players, Eugene, 1995—. Mem. Nat. Orgn. in Legal Problems in Edn. (pres. 1977-78), Nat. Sch. Devel. Coun. (pres. 1985-86), Am. Ednl. Rsch. Assn. (sec. adminstrn. divsn. 1991-93). Home: 2026 Morning View Dr Eugene OR 97405-1632 Office: U Oreg ERIC Clearinghouse on Ednl Mgmt 1787 Agate St Eugene OR 97403-1923

PIELOU, EVELYN C., biologist; m. Patrick Pielou, June 22, 1944; 3 children. B.Sc., U. London, 1950, Ph.D., 1962, DSc, 1975; LLD (hon.), Dalhousie U., 1993. Research scientist Can. Govt., 1963-67; vis. prof. N.C. State U., 1968, Yale, New Haven, 1969; prof. biology Queen's U., Kingston, Ont., 1969-71, Dalhousie U., Halifax, N.S., 1971-84; vis. prof. U. Sydney, Australia, 1975; oil sands environ. vis. research prof. U. Lethbridge, Alta., 1981-86. Author: Introduction to Mathematical Ecology, 1969, Population and Community Ecology, 1974, Ecological Diversity, 1975, Mathematical Ecology, 1977, Biogeography, 1979, Interpretation of Ecological Data, 1984, World of Northern Evergreens, 1988, After the Ice Age, 1991, Naturalist's Guide to the Arctic, 1994; contbr. articles to profl. jours. Recipient Lawson medal Can. Bot. Assn., 1984, Eminent Ecologist award Ecol. Soc. Am., 1986, Disting. Statis. Ecologist award Internat. Congress Ecology, Commemorative medal for 125th Anniversary of Confedn. of Can., 1992. Mem. Brit. Ecol. Soc. (hon. life), Am. Acad. Arts and Scis. (fgn. hon. mem.).

PIEMME, THOMAS E., medical educator. BS with high honors, U. Pitts., 1954, MD, 1958; postgrad., Ohio State U., 1964-65. Diplomate Nat. Bd. Med. Examiners; cert. Am. Bd. Family Practice. Intern Health Ctr. Hosps., Pitts., 1958-59, asst. resident in medicine, 1959-60; jr. asst. resident in medicine Peter Bent Brigham Hosp., Boston, 1960-61, fellow/AHA, asst. in medicine, 1961-63; rsch. cardiologist, chief bioanalysis br. Envrion. Med. Div. USAF, Wright-Patterson AFB, Ohio, 1964-66; asst. prof. medicine U. Pitts. Sch. of Medicine, 1966-69; asst. chief of medicine Presbyn. U. Hosp., Pitts., 1966-69; prof. medicine, dir. Divsn. Gen. Medicine George Washington U. Sch. of Medicine, 1969-74; various to prof. health care scis. and medicine, assoc. dean George Washington U. Sch. Medicine, 1977—, 1987—. Contbr. articles to profl. jours. and publs. Maj. USAF. Scholar of John and Mary Markle Found., 1966-71; recipient Disting. Svc. award Nat. Bd. Med. Examiners, 1984, others. Mem. AAAS, AMA, AAUP, Am. Fedn. Clin. Rsch., Aerospace Med. Assn., Assn. Am. Med. Colls., Am. Soc. Internal Medicine, Am. Heart Assn., Soc. Tchrs. of Family Medicine, Assn. Phys. Asst. Programs, Am. Acad. Family Physicians, Alliance for Continuing Med. Edn., Soc. for Med. Decision Making (adminstrv. dir.), Phi Beta Kappa, Alpha Omega Alpha, others. Office: George Washington U Office Continuing Med Edn 2300 K St NW Washington DC 20037

PIEMONTE, ROBERT VICTOR, association executive; b. N.Y.C., July 28, 1934; s. Rosario and Carmela (Santoro) P. BS, L.I. U., 1967; MA, Columbia U., 1968, MEd, 1970, EdD, 1976; DSc (hon.), L.I. U., Bklyn., 1993. Asst. dir. nursing svc. ANA, N.Y.C., 1968-69, dir. nursing svc., 1971-72, divsn. dir., 1983-85; asst. dir. nursing Univ. Hosp.-NYU, N.Y.C., 1970-71; assoc. dir. ops. N.Y.C. Health and Hosps. Corp., N.Y.C., 1972-76; assoc. prof. Tchr.'s Coll. Columbia U., N.Y.C., 1976-78; exec. dir. N.J. State Nurses Assn., Montclair, 1978-80; dep. exec. dir. Nat. Student Nurses Assn., N.Y.C., 1980-83, exec. dir., 1985—; adj. prof. nursing Tchr.'s Coll. Columbia U., 1990—; cons. Consensus Mgmt., N.Y.C., 1992—. Contbr. articles to profl. publs.; mem. editl. adv. bd. Nursing and Health Care, 1985—. Area-wide chair nursing Greater N.Y. chpt. ARC, N.Y.C., 1990-93. Col. U.S. Army, 1987-94, ret. Recipient Disting. Alumni award L.I. U., 1984, Hon. Recognition award N.Y. State Nurses Assn., 1992. Fellow Am. Acad. Nursing (treas. 1993—); mem. Am. Soc. Assn. Execs. (cert., bd. dirs. 1993—), Am. Nurses Found. (trustee 1994—), Nursing House, Inc. (pres. 1993—), Nat. Adv. Coun. on Nurse Edn. and Practice, N.Y. Soc. Assn. Execs. (Outstanding Assn. Exec. 1991, pres. 1989-90). Democrat. Roman Catholic. Avocations: theatre, reading, travel. Home: 76 W 86th St New York NY 10024-3607 Office: Nat Student Nurses Assn 555 W 57th St New York NY 10019-2925

PIEMONTESE, DAVID STEFANO, pharmaceutical scientist; b. Paterson, N.J., July 9, 1965; s. Gennarino and Alba (Reis) P. BS in Biology, William Paterson Coll., 1988; MS in Pharm. Sci., St. John's U., Jamaica, N.Y., 1995. Asst. scientist Hoffmann-LaRoche, Inc., Nutley, N.J., 1988-95; presenter in field. Contbr. chpts. to books and articles to profl. jours. Mem. Am. Assn. Pharm. Scientists. Avocations: travel, bicycling, music, reading. Home: 152-18 Union Trnpk Bldg 2 Apt 4F Flushing NY 11367

PIEN, FRANCIS D., internist, microbiologist; b. Detroit, Apr. 7, 1945; s. Chung Ling and Nung Chung (Lee) P.; m. Harriet Ho, Dec. 27, 1967; children: Brian, Ethan, Kevin. BA, Johns Hopkins U., Balt., 1965, MPH, 1971; MD, U. Chgo., 1969; MS in Microbiology, U. Minn., 1973. Diplomate Nat. Bd. Med. Examiners, Am. Bd. Internal Medicine, subspecialty in infectious disease, Am. Bd. Med. Microbiology. Intern U. Ill., 1969-70; fellow in microbiology, resident in internal medicine Mayo Grad. Sch. Medicine, Rochester, Minn., 1970-73; fellow in infectious disease Stanford (Calif.) U., 1973-74; assoc. program dir. integrated med. residency program U. Hawaii, Honolulu, 1977-90, assoc. prof. medicine, 1977-88, prof. medicine, 1988-93, chief infectious diseases, 1987-93, clin. prof. tropical medicine and med. microbiology, 1983—; infectious disease cons. Straub Clinic, Honolulu, 1974—; exchange prof. U. Osaka (Japan) Sch. Medicine, 1990; cons. in infeciton control Leahi Hosp., 1993—; bd. dirs. Rehab. Hosp. of Pacific, Honolulu, 1989-93, Interfaith Hosp. Chaplaincy Ministry, 1990-94, Samaritan Counseling Ctr., 1992-95, Straub Clinic and Hosp., 1990-93. Reviewer Hawaii Med. Jour., Reviews of Infectious Diseases, Western Jour. Medicine, Straub Clinic Proceedings; contbr. over 150 articles to profl. jours. Fellow ACP, Am. Acad. Microbiology, Infectious Disease Soc. Am., Royal Soc. Tropical Medicine and Hygiene; mem. AMA, Hawaii Med. Soc. (chmn. communicable disease com. 1979-83), Am. Soc. Tropical Medicine and Hygiene (mem. delegation to Mainland China 1978), Am. Soc. Microbiology (Hawaii br. pres. 1982-83), Christian Med. Soc., Assn. for Practitioners for Infection Control, Internat. Soc. Travel Medicine, Am. Soc. Sexually Transmitted Diseases, Soc. of Hosp. Epidemiologists of Am., European Soc. Clin. Microbiology. Republican. Presbyterian. Avocations: medical missions, research, travel. Office: Straub Clinic 888 S King St Honolulu HI 96813-3009

PIENE, OTTO, artist, educator; b. Laasphe, Westphalia, Germany, Apr. 18, 1928; s. Otto and Anne (Niemeyer) P.; children—Annette, Herbert, Claudia, Chloe. Student, Acad. Fine Arts, Munich, Germany, 1949-50, Acad. Fine Arts, Dusseldorf, Germany, 1950-52; Staatsexamen in Philosophy, U. Cologne, Germany, 1957; DFA, U. Md., Balt., 1995. Co-founder Group Zero, Dusseldorf, Germany, 1957; vis. prof. Grad. Sch. Art, U. Pa., Phila., 1964; prof. environ. art Sch. Architecture and Planning, MIT, Cambridge, Mass., 1972-93, dir. Ctr. for Advanced Visual Studies, MIT, 1974-94; dir. emeritus Ctr. for Advanced Visual Studies MIT, 1994—; dir. Sky Art Conf. MIT, 1981, 82, 83, 86; vis. artist, guest prof. numerous univs.; prin. artist, designer numerous archtl. and environ. art commns. and pub. celebrations. Author: (with Heinz Mack) Zero 1, 2, 3, 1958, 61, More Sky, 1973, Sky Art Conf. Proc., 1981, 82, 83, Feuerbilder und Texte, 1988; one man exhbns. include, Howard Wise Gallery, N.Y.C., 1965, 69, 70, Galerie Heseler, Munich, 1971, 72, 75, 77, 78, 79, 83, 86, MIT, 1975, 93, Galerie Schoeller, Düsseldorf, Fed. Republic Germany, 1977, 79, 83, 87, 91, 95, Fitchburg (Mass.) Art Mus., 1977, Galerie Watari, Tokyo, 1983, Pat Hearn Gallery, N.Y.C., 1985, Gallery 360, Tokyo, 1991, 92, Galèrie d'Art International, Paris, 1993, Städt Kunstmuseum, Düsseldorf, 1996; numerous group exhbns. U.S. and abroad including, Guggenheim Mus., N.Y.C., 1964, 66, 84, Albright-Knox Gallery Buffalo, 1968, Nat. Mus. Modern Art, Tokyo, 1969, Tate Gallery, London, 1974, Smithsonian Instn., Washington, 1978, Royal Acad. Art, London, 1985, National Gallery, Berlin, 1986, Statsgalerie, Stuttgart, 1986, Berlinische Galerie, Berlin, 1988-89, 91-92, MIT, 1994, Haus der Kunst, Munich, 1995, Bundeskunsthalle, Bonn, 1995, others; also represented in numerous permanent collections. Recipient award Internat. Exhibition Graphic Art, Ljubljana, Yugoslavia 1967, 69, prize 8th Internat. Biennial Prints Nat. Mus. Modern Art, Tokyo, Japan 1972, Kohler-Maxwell prize 1987). Recipient Sculpture prize Am. Acad. Arts and Letters, N.Y.C., 1996. Mem. Deutscher Kunstlerbund. Office: MIT Ctr Advanced Visual Studies 265 Massachusetts Ave Cambridge MA 02139-4312

PIEPER, DAROLD D., lawyer; b. Vallejo, Calif., Dec. 30, 1944; s. Walter A. H. and Vera Mae (Ellis) P.; m. Barbara Gillis, Dec. 20, 1969; 1 child, Christopher Radcliffe. AB, UCLA, 1967; JD, USC, 1970. Bar: Calif. 1971.

Ops. rsch. analyst Naval Weapons Ctr., China Lake, Calif., 1966-69; assoc. Richards, Watson & Gershon, L.A., 1970-76, ptnr., 1976—; spl. counsel L.A. County Transp. Commn., 1984-93, L.A. County Met. Transp. Authority, 1993-94; commr. L.A. County Delinquency and Crime Commn., 1983—, pres., 1987—; chmn. L.A. County Delinquency Prevention Planning Coun., 1987-90. Contbr. articles to profl. jours. Peace officer Pasadena (Calif.) Police Res. Unit, 1972-87, dep. comdr., 1979-81, comdr., 1982-84; chmn. pub. safety commn. City of La Canada Flintridge, Calif., 1977-82, commr. 1977-88; bd. dirs. La Canada Flintridge Coordinating Council, 1975-82, pres. 1977-78; exec. dir. Cityhood Action Com., 1975-76; active Calif. Rep. Party, Appellate Circle of Legion Lex U. So. Calif.; chmn. Youth Opportunities United, Inc., 1990—, vice-chmn. 1988-89, bd. dirs. 1988—; mem. L.A. County Justice Systems Adv. Group, 1987-92; trustee Lanterman Hist. Mus. Found., 1989-94, Calif. City Mgmt. Found., 1992—. Recipient commendation for Community Service, L.A. County Bd. Suprs., 1978. Mem. La Canada Flintridge C. of C. and Cmty. Assn. (pres. 1981, bd. dirs. 1976-83), Navy League U.S., Pacific Legal Found., Peace Officers Assn., L.A. County, UCLA Alumni Assn. (life), U. So. Calif. Alumni Assn. (life), L.A. County Bar Assn., Calif. Bar Assn., ABA, U. So. Calif. Law Alumni Assn. Office: Richards Watson & Gershon 333 S Hope St Fl 38 Los Angeles CA 90071-1406

PIEPER, HEINZ PAUL, physiology educator; b. Wuppertal, Germany, Mar. 24, 1920; came to U.S., 1957, naturalized, 1963; s. Heinrich Ludwig and Agnes Marie (Koehler) P.; m. Rose Irmgard Hackl, Apr. 23, 1945. M.D., U. Munich, Germany, 1948. Resident 2d Med. Clinic, U. Munich, 1948-50, asst. prof. dept. physiology, 1950-57; asst. prof. dept. physiology Coll. Medicine, Ohio State U., Columbus, 1957-60; assoc. prof. Coll. Medicine, Ohio State U., 1960-68, prof., 1968—, chmn. dept. physiology, 1974-85, prof. emeritus, 1985—; established investigator Am. Heart Assn., 1962-67. Mem. editorial bd.: Am. Jour. Physiology, 1973-82; contbr. articles on cardiovascular physiology to profl. jours. Mem. Am. Physiol. Soc., German Physiol. Soc., Ohio Acad. Scis., Biophys. Soc., Sigma Xi. Home: 2206 SE 36th St Cape Coral FL 33904-4434 Office: Ohio State U Coll Medicine 333 W 10th Ave Columbus OH 43210-1239

PIEPER, PATRICIA RITA, artist, photographer; b. Paterson, N.J., Jan. 28, 1923; d. Francis William and Barbara Margareth (Ludwig) Farabaugh. Student, Baron von Palm, 1937-39, Deal (N.J.) Conservatory, 1939, 40, Utah State U., 1950-52; m. George F. Pieper, July 1, 1941 (dec. May 3, 1981); 1 child, Patricia Lynn; m. Russell W. Watson, Dec., 9, 1989. One-woman shows include Charles Russell Mus., Great Falls, Mont., 1955, Fisher Gallery, Washington, 1966, Tampa City Libr., 1977-81, 83, 84, Ctr. Pl. Art Ctr., Brandon, Fla., 1985; exhibited in group shows Davidson Art Gallery, Middletown, Conn., 1968, Helena (Mont.) Hist. Mus., 1955, Dept. Commerce Alaska Statehood Show, 1959, Joslyn Mus., Omaha, 1961, Denver Mus. Natural History, 1955, St. Joseph's Hosp. Gallery, 1980, 82, 84-86; represented in pvt. collections. Pres. Bell Lake Assn., 1976-78, 79. Winner photog. competition Gen. Tel. Co. of Fla., 1979; recipient Outstanding Svc. award Bell Lake Assn., 1987, Meml. award Land O' Lake Bd. of Realtors, 1989, Appreciation award Southwest Fla. Water Mgmt. Dist., 1993; photography winner in top 100 out of 8,000 Nat. Wildlife Fedn. competition, 1986; 1st place photography MacDill AFB, 1991. Mem. Pasco County (Fla.) Water Adv. Coun., 1978—, chmn., 1979-82, 83-84, 86-88, 92—; gov.'s appointee to S.W. Fla. Water Mgmt. Dist., Hillsborough River Basin Bd., 1981-82, 84-87, sec., 1988-91, vice chmn. 1992; active Save Our Rivers program, 1982-84, 85-86, 92—; ad hoc chmn., 1991-92; mem. adv. bd. Fla. Suncoast Expwy., 1988-90; pres. Bell Lake Assn., 1986, 87; mem. adv. bd. Tampa YMCA, 1979-80. Mem. Nat. League Am. Pen Women (v.p. Tampa 1976-78, Woman of Yr. award 1977-78), Tampa Art Mus., Ret. Officer's Wives Assn., Land O' Lakes C. of C. (bd. dir. 1981-82, Outstanding Svc. award 1980), Fla. Geneal. Soc., West State Archaeol. Soc. (distaff mem.), Ret. Officer's Assn., MacDill AFB, 1982—, Lutz Club, Land O' Lakes Women's Club, Moose. Home and Studio: 3304 E Derry Dr Sebastian FL 32958-8577 *I believe that those of us born with the gift of creativity are truly blessed. It is our duty to make the most of, and be worthy of that gift. And if we work hard and sincerely apply ourselves a chosen few will become immortal through the beauty we leave behind for others to enjoy. As an artist and photographer I am truly blessed.*

PIEPHO, (EDWARD) LEE, humanities educator; b. Detroit, Jan. 10, 1942; s. Edward Ernest and Dolores Faye (Dowis) P.; m. Susan Brand, June 13, 1964. AB, Kenyon Coll., 1964; MA, Columbia U., 1966; PhD, U. Va., 1972. Instr. Sweet Briar (Va.) Coll., 1969-72, asst. prof., 1972-78, assoc. prof., 1978-83, prof., 1983-94, Shallenberger Brown prof., 1994—, dept. chmn., 1983-86, coord. European civilization program, 1986-89. Translator, editor: Adulescentia: The Eclogues of Mantuan, 1989; contbr. articles to profl. jours. SIMRS fellow, 1979, Dulin fellow Folger Shakespeare Libr., 1989-90. Mem. Internat. Assn. for Neo-Latin Studies, Modern Lang. Assn. Am., Renaissance Soc. Am. Avocations: tennis, scuba diving. Home: Woodland Rd Sweet Briar VA 24595-9999 Office: Sweet Briar Coll Dept English Sweet Briar VA 24595

PIEPHO, ROBERT WALTER, pharmacy educator, researcher; b. Chgo., July 31, 1942; s. Walter August and Irene Elizabeth (Huybrecht) Apfel; m. Mary Lee Wilson, Dec. 10, 1981. BS in Pharmacy, U. Ill.-Chgo., 1965; PhD in Pharmacology, Loyola U., Maywood, Ill., 1972. Registered pharmacist, Ill., Colo. Assoc. prof. U. Nebr. Med. Ctr., Omaha, 1970-78; prof. pharmacy, assoc. dean Sch. Pharmacy U. Colo., Denver, 1978-86; prof. pharmacol., dean U. Mo. Sch. Pharmacy, Kansas City, 1987—. Contbr. articles to profl. jours., chpts. to books. Pres. Club Monaco Homeowners Assn., Denver, 1980-82. Named Outstanding Tchr. U. Nebr. Coll. Pharmacy, 1975; recipient Arthur Hassan Colo. Pharmacal Assn., 1983, Excellence in Teaching U. Colo. Med. Sch., 1983. Fellow Am. Coll. Clin. Pharmacology (regent 1983-88, 91-96), Am. Coll. Apothecaries; mem. Am. Soc. Hosp. Pharmacists, Am. Soc. Pharmacology and Exptl. Therapeutics, Rho Chi. Roman Catholic. Office: U Mo Sch Pharmacy 5005 Rockhill Rd Kansas City MO 64110-2239

PIERAS, JAIME, JR., federal judge; b. San Juan, P.R., May 19, 1924; s. Jaime Pieras and Ines Lopez-Cepero; m. Elsie Castaner, June 6, 1953; 1 child, Jaime Pieras Castaner. AB in Econs., Catholic U. Am., 1945; JD, Georgetown U., 1948. Bar: P.R. Pvt. practice San Juan, 1949-82; judge U.S. Dist. Ct. for P.R., San Juan, 1982—; mem. Com. on the Bicentennial of the Constitution, Judicial Conf. U.S.; mem. Puerto Rico Commn. on the Bicentennial of the U.S. Constituion. Contbr. article to Cath. U. Law Rev., 1986. Chmn. fin. Statehood Republican Party, San Juan, 1963-64; Rep. nat. committeeman for P.R., San Juan 1967-80. 2nd Lt. U.S. Army (Mediterranean) 1946-47, MTO; Res., 1949. Mem. ABA (exec. bd., Nat. Conf. Fed. Trial Judges), P.R. Bar Assn., D.C. Bar Assn. Lodge: Rotary. Office: US Dist Ct CH-111 Fed Bldg 150 Carlos Chardon Ave Hato Rey San Juan PR 00918-1761*

PIERCE, ALLAN DALE, engineering educator, researcher; b. Clarinda, Iowa, Dec. 18, 1936; s. Franklin Dale and Ruth Pauline (Wright) P.; m. Penelope Claffey, Oct. 27, 1961; children: Jennifer Irene, Bradford Loren. BS, N.Mex. Coll. Agrl. and Mechanic Arts, 1957; PhD, MIT, 1962. Registered profl. engr., Mass. Staff researcher Rand Corp., Santa Monica, Calif., 1961-63; sr. staff scientist Avco Corp., Wilmington, Mass., 1963-66; asst. prof. MIT, Cambridge, 1966-68, assoc. prof., 1968-73; prof. mech. engring. Ga. Inst. Tech., Atlanta, 1973-76, Regent's prof., 1976-88; Leonhard chair in engring. Pa. State U., University Park, 1988-93; chmn. dept aerospace and mech. engring. Boston U., 1993—; vis. prof. Max Planck Inst., Goettingen, Fed. Republic Germany, 1976-77; cons. in field. Author: Acoustics: An Introduction to Its Physical Principles and Applications, 1981; editor phys. acoustics monograph series, 1988—; editor Jour. Computation Acoustics, 1992—; contbr. articles on acoustics, wave propagation, vibrations, solid and fluid mechanics to profl. jours. Recipient Sr. U.S. Scientist award Alexander von Humboldt Found., 1976, Cert. of Recognition Nat. Aeronautics and Space Adminstrn., 1984, Per Bruel Gold medal for noise control and acoustics ASME, 1995; NSF fellow, 1957-60, Shell Oil fellow, 1960-61, U.S. Dept. Transp. faculty fellow, 1979-80. Fellow Acoustical Soc. Am. (silver medal 1991), ASME (Rayleigh lectr. 1992, Per Bruel gold medal 1995); mem. IEEE, AIAA. Home: PO Box 339 East Sandwich MA 02537 Office: Boston U Dept Aerospace & Mech Engring 110 Cummington St Boston MA 02215-2407

PIERCE, ANNE-MARIE BERNHEIM, private school administrator; b. Grenoble, Isere, France, Sept. 9, 1943; came to U.S., 1961; d. Joseph and Andree Georgette (Haguenauer) Bernheim; m. Robert L. Pierce, Mar. 21, 1964; 1 child, Eric. BA, U. Calif., Berkeley, 1965; MA, Hayward State U., 1973. Head fgn. lang. dept. Head-Royce Sch., Oakland, Calif., 1965-75; head fgn. lang. dept. San Francisco U. High Sch., 1975-80, dir. pub. events, 1979-80; headmistress Ecole Bilingue, Berkeley, 1980-89; cons. A.M.P. and Assocs., San Francisco, 1989-91; head Washington Internat. Sch., 1991—. Co-author radio instrn. A Touch of France, 1980—. Bd. dirs. Mid-Atlantic Multi-Cultural Alliance. Named to Cum Laude Soc. Head-Royce Schs., 1982. Mem. Assn. French Schs. in Am. (founder, pres. 1985-86, 87-88), Calif. Assn. Ind. Schs. (exec. bd. dirs. 1985-88, v.p. 1987-88), Internat. Sch. Assn. (exec. bd. dirs.), Assn. Ind. Schs. Greater Washington. Democrat. Avocation: skiing.

PIERCE, CHARLES EARL, software engineer; b. Edenton, N.C., July 13, 1955; s. Charles William and Carrie (Rankins) P.; m. Jan Saunders, Nov. 16, 1991. BS in Math., L.I. U., 1977. Rsch. analyst Equitable Life, N.Y.C., 1977-80; systems analyst CTEK Software, N.Y.C., 1980-83; asst. v.p. Bank N.Y., N.Y.C., 1987—; cons. Nibor Assocs., N.Y.C., 1983-85, Vital Cons., N.Y.C., 1985-87. Mem. IEEE, N.Y. Acad. Scis., Data Processing Mgmt. Assn., Assn. for Computing Machinery, Math. Assn. Am. Mem. Pentecostal Ch. Mem. Pentecostal Ch. Achievements include development of English test interpreter/command processing for mainframe at CTEK Software; automated phased conversion of DMS system.

PIERCE, CHARLES ELIOT, JR., library director, educator; b. Springfield, Mass., Dec. 25, 1941; s. C. Eliot and Dora Mason (Redway) P.; m. Barbara G. Hanson, Oct. 18, 1969; children: Sheila H., Charles Eliot III. B.A., Harvard U., 1964, M.A.T., 1966, Ph.D., 1970. Prof. English Vassar Coll., Poughkeepsie, N.Y., 1970-87; dir. Pierpont Morgan Library, N.Y.C., 1987—. Author: (literary criticism) The Religious Life of Samuel Johnson, 1983. Mem. Johnsonians, Century Assn., Grolier Club, Walpole Soc., Knickerbocker Club. Episcopalian. Home: Clinton Corners Rd Salt Point NY 12578 Office: Pierpont Morgan Libr 29 E 36th St New York NY 10016-3403

PIERCE, CHARLES R., electric company consultant; b. Bar Harbor, Maine, 1922. AB, Hofstra Coll., 1947; LLB, Columbia U., 1949. Bar: N.Y. 1950, U.S. Ct. Appeals (2nd cir.) 1951. Ret. chmn., chief exec. officer L.I. Lighting Co. Mem. Nassau County Bar Assn., Suffolk County Bar Assn., Nat. Assn. Securities Dealers N.Y. Stock Exch., Am. Arbitration Assn. Bds. of Arbitration. Office: 33 Walt Whitman Rd Huntington Station NY 11746-3627

PIERCE, CHESTER MIDDLEBROOK, psychiatrist, educator; b. Glen Cove, N.Y., Mar. 4, 1927; s. Samuel Riley and Hettie Elenor (Armstrong) P.; m. Jocelyn Patricia Blanchet, June 15, 1949; children: Diane Blanchet, Deirdre Anona. AB, Harvard U., 1948, MD, 1952; ScD (hon.), Westfield Coll., 1977, Tufts U., 1984. Instr. psychiatry U. Cin., 1957-60; asst. prof. psychiatry U. Okla., 1960-62, prof., 1965-69; prof. edn. and psychiatry Harvard U., 1969—; pres. Am. Bd. Psychiatry and Neurology, 1977-78; mem. Polar Research Bd.; cons. USAF. Author publs. on sleep disturbances, media, polar medicine, sports medicine, racism; mem. editorial bds. Advisor Children's TV Workshop; chmn. Child Devel. Assn. Consortium; bd. dirs. Action Children's TV. With M.C. USNR, 1953-55. Fellow Royal Australian and N.Z. Coll. Psychiatrists (hon.), Gt. Britain Royal Coll. Psychiatrists (hon.); mem. Inst. Medicine, Black Psychiatrists Am. (chmn.), Am. Orthopsychiat. Assn. (pres. 1983-84). Democrat. Home: 17 Prince St Jamaica Plain MA 02130-2725

PIERCE, DANIEL THORNTON, physicist; b. L.A., July 16, 1940; s. Daniel Gordon Pierce and Celia Francis Thornton Thayer; m. Barbara Harrison, Nov. 19, 1988; children: Jed, Maia, Stephen. BS, Stanford U., 1962, PhD in Applied Physics, 1970; MA, Wesleyan U., Middletown, Conn., 1966. NSF rsch. asst. materials sci. dept. Stanford U., 1961; lectr in physics U.S. Peace Corps, Kathmandu, Nepal, 1962-64; rsch. asst. Wesleyan U., 1964-66; rsch. asst. Stanford Electronics Lab., 1966-70, rsch. assoc., 1970-71; rsch. staff Solid State Physics Lab., Swiss Fed. Inst. Tech., 1971-75; physicist Nat. Inst. Standards and Tech. (formerly Nat. Bur Standards), Gaithersburg, Md., 1975—. Contbr. chpts. to books, more than 150 articles to profl. jours. Trustee Unitarian Ch. of Rockville, Md., 1994—. Recipient IR-100 award R&D Mag., 1980, 85, Gold medal Dept. Commerce, 1987, William P. Schlichter award Nat. Inst. Standards and Tech., 1992. Gaede-Langmuir Award, 1994; American Vacuum Society. Fellow Am. Phys. Soc., Am. Vacuum Soc. (chair surface sci. exec. com. 1984-88, Gaede-Langmuir prize 1994). Achievements include patents for source of spin polarized electrons, absorbed current and low energy spin polarization detectors; development of scanning electron microscopy with polarization analysis. Office: Nat Inst Standards and Tech Bldg 220 Rm B206 Gaithersburg MD 20899

PIERCE, DANNY PARCEL, artist, educator; b. Woodlake, Calif., Sept. 10, 1920; s. Frank Lester and Letitia Frances (Parcel) P.; m. Julia Ann Rasmussen, July 19, 1943; children: Julia Ann, Mary L., Danny L., Duane Nels. Student, Art Ctr. Sch., L.A., 1939, Chouinards Art Inst., L.A., 1940-41, 46-47, Am. Art Sch., N.Y.C., 1947-48, Bklyn. Mus. Art Sch., 1950-53; BFA, U. Alaska, 1963. Instr. Hunter Coll., N.Y.C., 1952-53, Burnley Sch. Art, Seattle, 1954-58, Seattle U., 1956-59; publ. Red Door Studio Press, Kent, Wash., 1959—; artist-in-res. U. Alaska, College, 1959-63; asst. prof. U. Wisc., Milw., 1964; head art dept. Cornish Sch. Allied Arts, Seattle, 1964-65; prof. art U. Wisc., Milw., 1965-84, prof. emeritus, 1984—. One person exhibition shows include Contemporaries Gallery, N.Y.C., 1953, Handforth Gallery, Tacoma, Washington, 1958, U. Alaska, College, 1959, 63, 73, 74, Gonzaga U., Bradley Galleries, Milw., 1966, 68, 70, 72, 74, 76, 78-80, 82; represented in permanent collections Bibliothèque Nationale, Paris, Mus. Modern Art, N.Y.C., Libr. Congress, Washington, Smithsonian Instn., Washington, Seattle Art Mus., U. Washington Henry Art Gallery, Bklyn. Mus., Princeton U., U. Alaska, U. So. Calif., William and Mary Coll., Oostduinkerke (Belgium) Nat. Fishing Mus., Nat. Mus. Sweden, Stockholm, Johnson Wax Found., Racine, Wisc., Gen. Mills Collection Art, Mpls., Huntington Libr., San Marino, Calif., various pvt. collections. Recipient Best Oil Landscape award Conn. Acad. Fine Arts, Hartford, 1st Prize oil Kohler Gallery, Seattle, 1974, others; chosen one of twelve artists to represent State Wash. Expo 70, Osaka, Japan, rep. U.S. Internat. São Paulo Biannual Art Exhbn.; established archives at Golda Meier Libr., U. Wis.-Mils. Mem. Artist Equity Assn. (charter, pres. Seattle chpt. 1958), Am. Colorprint Soc., Internat. Arts and Letters (life). Office: Red Door Studio 330 Summit Ave N Kent WA 98031-4714

PIERCE, DAVID R., educational administrator. AA in Math., Fullerton Coll., 1958; BA in Math., Long Beach State U., 1960, MA in Edn., 1961; MS in Math., Purdue U., 1965, PhD in Math. Edn., 1969. Math. instr. Orange Coast Coll., Costa Mesa, Calif., 1962-65; supr. math. student teaching Purdue U., Lafayette, Ind., 1965-66; chmn. natural scis. & math. divsn. Golden West Coll., Huntington Beach, Calif., 1966-67; dean instrn. Waubonsee C.C., Sugar Grove, Ill., 1967-70; supt., pres. North Iowa Area C.C., Mason City, 1970-80; exec. dir. Ill. C.C. Bd., Springfield, 1980-90; chancellor Va. C. C. Sys., Richmond, 1990-91; pres., chief exec. officer Am. Assn. C.C., Washington, 1991—; also joint Am. Assn. C.C./ACCT Comm. Fed. Rels. mem., 1984-86, 88-91; also bd. mem. Am. Assn. C.C., 1988-91, vice-chmn., 1990-91, chmn. task force on allied health, 1989-91, chmn. com. on fed. rels., 1990-91; mem. Nat. Coun. State Dirs. Cmty. and Jr. Colls., 1981-91 (chmn. 1984-85), Ill. Employment & Edn. Subcabinet, 1980-90; cons., evaluator North Ctrl. Assn. Commn. Insts. Higher Edn. (commr.-at-large 1977-83). mem. Ill. Econ. Devel. Subcabinet, 1980-90. Named Person of Yr. Nat. Coun. Cmty. Svcs. & Continuing Edn. Region 5, 1982, Nat. Person of Yr. Nat. Coun. Cmty. Svcs. & Continuing Edn., 1990; recipient Meritorious Svc. award Ill. C.C. Trustee Assn., 1988, Outstanding Ill. Citizen award Coll. Lake County, 1989, Outstanding Alumnus award Calif. C.C. League, 1991, Outstanding Alumnus award Fullerton Coll., 1992, B. Lamar Johnson Leadership award League for Innovation in the C.C., 1993. Mem. Nat. Policy Bd. Higher Edn. Instl. Accreditation, Washington Higher Edn. Secretariat, Nat. Alliance of Bus. Coun. on Workforce Excellence. Office: Am Assn Cmty Colls 1 Dupont Cir NW Ste 410 Washington DC 20036-1110

PIERCE, EDWARD FRANKLIN, academic administrator; b. Cambridge, Mass., July 15, 1927; s. John and Kathleen (McCue) P.; m. Sandra Lea, June 8, 1958; children—Valerie, Marc, Adrienne. B.S., Boston Coll., 1949, M.A., 1950; Ph.D., Columbia U., 1959, Ed.D., 1959. Research chemist AEC, 1950-51; mem. faculty Skagit Valley Coll., Mt. Vernon, Wash., 1954; instr. chemistry SUNY, Geneseo, 1959-66; chmn. dept. SUNY, 1962, dean, 1964; dean U. N.H. System, Keene, 1966-72; pres. Quincy (Mass.) Sr. Coll., 1972-82, Mt. Aloysius Coll., 1982—; mem. New Eng. Dist. Scholarship Com.; cons. in field, seminar lectr. Author: Selected Quantitative Studies in Physical Science, 1962, Modern Chemistry, 1960, Historical Perspectives in the Physical Sciences, 1964, also articles. Chmn. United Fund, 1968; dist. com. Boy Scouts Am., 1951-54, Council for Children, Quincy, 1972-82; pres., treas. South Shore Day Care Services, 1972-76. Served to ensign USNR, 1944-46. Fellow Am. Inst. Chemists; mem. AAAS, N.Y. Acad. Sci. Club: Quincy Kiwanis (past pres.). Lodge: Rotary (Altoona, Pa.). Home: 79 Circle Dr Hollidaysburg PA 16648-9234 Office: Mt Aloysius Sr Coll Office of Pres Cresson PA 02169

PIERCE, FRANCIS CASIMIR, civil engineer; b. Warren, R.I., May 19, 1924; s. Frank J. and Eva (Soltys) Pierce; student U. Conn., 1943-44; B.S., U. R.I., 1948; M.S., Harvard U., 1950; postgrad. Northeastern U., 1951-52; Reg. profl. engr. Conn., N.H., Mass., R.I., Vt.; reg. profl. land surveyor R.I.; m. Helen Lynette Steinouer, Apr. 24, 1954; children—Paul F., Kenneth J., Nancy L., Karen H., Charles E. Instr. civil engring. U. R.I., Kingston, 1948-49, U. Conn., Storrs, 1950-51; design engr. Praeger-Maguire & Ole Singstad, Boston, 1951-52; chief found. engr. C.A. Maguire & Assocs., Providence, 1952-59, assoc., 1959-69, v.p., 1969-72; sr. v.p. C.E. Maguire, Inc., 1972-76, officer-in-charge Honolulu office, 1976-78, exec. v.p., corp. dir. ops., 1975-87; dir. The Maguire Group, Inc., 1979—, gen. mgr. East Atlantic Casualty Co., Ltd., 1987-88; also dir.; pres. Magma, Inc., tech. ops. service co., 1986-88; lectr. found. engring. U. R.I., 1968-69, trustee, 1987—; mem. Coll. Engring. adv. council, 1986—, U.S. com. Internat. Commn. on Large Dams; mem. register of expert witnesses in the construction industry ABA. Vice chmn. Planning Bd. East Providence, R.I., 1960-73; bd. dirs. R.I. Civic Chorale and Orch., 1986-90. Served with AUS, 1942-46. Mem. ASCE (chpt. past pres., dir.), Am. Arbitration Assn., R.I. Soc. Profl. Engrs. (nat. dir., engr. of year award 1973), Am. Soc. Engring. Edn., Soc. Am. Mil. Engrs., ASTM, Soc. Marine Engrs. and Naval Architects, Am. Soc. Planning Ofcls., Harvard Soc. Engrs., Scientists, Providence Engrs. Soc., R.I. Soc. Planning Agys. (past pres.). Contbr. articles to profl. jours. Recipient Commendation Min. of Pub. Works Rep. Venezuela, 1970, Geotechnical award ASCE sect. Boston Soc. Civil Engrs., 1979, USCG Meritorious Pub. Service award, 1987, Chester H. Kirk Disting. Engr. award U. R.I. Coll. Engring., 1987. Home: 3830 St Girons Dr Punta Gorda FL 33950-7870 Office: 225 Foxborough Blvd Foxboro MA 02035

PIERCE, GEORGE ADAMS, university administrator, educator; b. Carlsbad, N.Mex., May 21, 1943; s. Jack Colwell and Shirley (Adams) P.; m. Margaret Mary Brakel, Feb. 10, 1980; children: Christopher, Catherine Rose. BA in Polit. Sci., Fairleigh Dickinson U., 1969; MA in Polit. Sci., New Sch. Social Rsch., 1971; PhD in Higher Edn., Claremont Grad. Sch., 1976. Asst. dir. promotion Afco, N.Y.C., 1969-71; dir. spl. programs U. Calif., Riverside, 1971-73; asst. to pres. Claremont (Calif.) Grad. Sch., 1973-75; asst. to pres. Seattle U., 1975-78, dir. planning, 1978-83, v.p. adminstrn., 1983-87, v.p. planning, 1987-89; v.p. bus. and fin. affairs Western Wash. U., Bellingham, 1989—; chmn. regional rev. panel Truman Scholarship Found., 1977-90. Chmn. Seattle Ctr. Adv. Commn., 1977-83; bd. dirs. N.W. Kidney Found., Seattle, 1986—, YMCA, Bellingham, 1990—; chmn. pack 41 Boy Scouts Am., Bellingham, 1992-94. With USAF, 1963-65. Recipient Cert. Merit Riverside County Comprehensive Health Planning, 1972, Cert. Appreciation Office Mayor City of Seattle, 1983, Nat. Truman Scholarship Found., 1986. Mem. Am. Assn. Higher Edn., Assn. Instnl. Rsch. (regional pres. 1977), Nat. Assn. Coll. and Univ. Bus. Officers (chmn. pers. and benefits com. 1992-94), Rotary. Democrat. Roman Catholic. Avocations: backpacking, canoeing, swimming, tennis. Home: 421 Morey Ave Bellingham WA 98225-6344 Office: Western Wash U Old Main 300 Bellingham WA 98225

PIERCE, GEORGE EMORY, surgeon, researcher; b. Washington, Iowa, July 15, 1933; s. George Owens and Jessie (Culver) P.; m. Carolyn Bell, Oct. 6, 1962; children: Cathryn Lynn Pollinger, William Brooks. Student, U. Utah, 1951-52; BS, U. Wyo., 1955; postgrad., Johns Hopkins U., 1955-56, MD, 1960. Diplomate Am. Bd. Surgery, Am. Bd. Thoracic Surgery, Am. Sub-Bd. Vascular Surgery. Intern Johns Hopkins Hosp., Balt., 1960-61, resident in surgery, 1961-62, 64-65; resident in gen. and thoracic surgery U. Wash., Seattle, 1965-69, asst. prof. surgery, 197--71; asst. prof. surgery U. Colo., Denver, 1971-72; assoc. prof. surgery U. Kans., Kansas City, 1972-77, prof.surgery, 1978—; attending surgeon, chief surg. svc. VA Med. Ctr., Kansas City, Mo., 1979—; attending surgeon U. Kans. Med. Ctr.; mem. med. adv. bd. Nat. Kidney Found. Kans. and We. Mo., 1976—; bd. dirs. Midwest Organ Bank, Kansas City, Kans., 1974—, pres., 1980-81. Contbr. numerous articles to profl. jours. Lt. col. USPHS, 192-64. Mem. AMA, ACS, Am. Assn. Cancer Rsch., Am. Assn. Immunologists, Am. Coll. Cardiology, Am. Soc. Transplant Surgeons, Am. Surg. Assn., Assn. for Acad. Surgery, Assn. VA Surgeons, Ctrl. Surg. Assn., Halsted Soc., Internat. Surg. Soc., Midwestern Vascular Surg. Soc., Reticuloendothelial Soc., Soc. for Surg. Oncology, Soc. Univ. Surgeons, Soc. for Vascular Surgery, Southwestern Surg. Congress, Transplantation Soc., Western Surg. Assn., Western Trauma Assn., Wyandotte County Med. Soc., Phi Beta Kappa, Sigma Xi. Achievements include studies of the immune responses to tumors in both humans and experimental models; studies of the mechanism of tolerance induction to allografts. Office: U Kans Med Ctr Dept Surgery 3901 Rainbow Blvd Kansas City KS 66160-0001

PIERCE, GEORGE FOSTER, JR., architect; b. Dallas, June 22, 1919; s. George Foster and Hallie Louise (Crutchfield) P.; m. Betty Jean Reistle, Oct. 17, 1942; children: Ann Louise Pierce Arnett, George Foster III, Nancy Reistle Pierce Brumback. Student, So. Meth. U., 1937-39; BA, Rice U., 1942, BS in Architecture, 1943; diplome d'architecture, Ecole des Beaux-Arts, Fontainebleau, 1958. Pvt. practice architecture, 1946—; founding ptnr. Pierce, Goodwin, Alexander & Linville (architects, engrs. and planners), 1946-96, of counsel, 1987—; design cons. Dept. Army, 1966-70; instr. archtl. design Rice U., 1945, preceptor dept. architecture, 1962-67; past trustee, mem. exec. com. Rice Ctr. for Community Design and Rsch.; bd. dirs. Billboards Ltd. Prin. works include projects 8 bldgs., Rice U. Campus, Exxon Brook Hollow Bldg. Complex, Houston Mus. Natural Sci. and Planetarium, Michael Debakey Center Biomed. Edn. and Research, Baylor Coll. Medicine; 4 terminal bldgs., master plan Houston Intercontinental Airport; S.W. Bell Telephone Co. office bldg.; U. Tex. Med. Sch. Hosp., Galveston, U. Houston Conrad Hilton Sch. Hotel & Club Mgmt., U. Houston Univ. Center; 40 story office bldg. for Tex. Eastern Transmission Corp.; outpatient facility U. Tex. M.D. Anderson Cancer Hosp.; 44 story Marathon Oil Tower, others; contbr. articles to profl. jours. Mem. exec. adv. bd. Sam Houston Area Coun. Boy Scouts Am.; past mem. grad. coun. Rice U.; adv. coun. Rice Sch. Architecture, chmn. Houston Mcpl. Sign Control Bd.; past chmn. bd. trustee Contemporary Arts Mus., Houston; past trustee Houston Mus. Natural Sci.; trustee emeritus, past pres. Tex. Archtl. Found. With USNR, WWII. Recipient numerous nat., state, local archtl. awards for design, Silver Beaver award Boy Scouts Am.; named one of five Outstanding Young Texans Tex. Jr. C. of C., 1954; named Disting. R Man Rice U., 1992. Fellow AIA (past nat. chmn. com. on aesthetics, student affairs and chpt. affairs, Golden award, 1990), La Soc. Arquitectos Mexicanos (hon.); mem. Tex. Soc. Archs. (past pres., L.W. Pitts award 1985), Houston C. of C. (past chmn. future studies), Rice U. Pres.'s Club (founding chmn. 1970-72), Rice U. Assocs., SAR, Tex. Golf Assn. (bd. dirs.), Kappa Alpha. Methodist. Home: 5555 Del Monte Dr Apt 1103 Houston TX 77056-4118 Office: 5555 San Felipe St Ste 1000 Houston TX 77056-2726 *I am pleased to have chosen architecture as my profession, whereby I have been able to influence the quality of life of my community and my country, not only in its physical form through building design and planning, but also toward its cultural, educational and political well being.*

PIERCE, HARVEY R., Insurance company executive. Pres. Am. Family Ins. Group, Madison, Wis. Office: Am Family Ins Group 6000 American Pky Madison WI 53783-0001*

PIERCE, HILDA (HILDA HERTA HARMEL), painter; b. Vienna, Austria; came to U.S., 1940; 1 child, Diana Rubin Daly. Student, Art Inst. of Chgo.; studied with Oskar Kokoschka, Salzburg, Austria. Art tchr. Highland Park (Ill.) Art Ctr., Sandburg Village Art Workshop, Chgo., Old Town Art Center, Chgo.; owner, operator Hilda Pierce Art Gallery, Laguna Beach, Calif., 1981-85; guest lectr. major art mus. and Art Tours in France, Switzerland, Austria, Italy; guest lectr. Russian river cruise and major art mus. St. Petersburg and Moscow, 1994. One-woman shows include Fairweather Hardin Gallery, Chgo., Sherman Art Gallery, Chgo., Marshall Field Gallery , Chgo.; exhibited in group shows at Old Orchard Art Festival, Skokie, Ill., Union League Club (awards), North Shore Art League (awards), ARS Gallery of Art Inst. of Chgo.; represented in numerous private and corporate collections; commissioned for all art work including monoprints, oils, and murals for Carnival Cruise Lines megaliner M.S. Fantasy, 1990, 17 murals for megaliner M.S. Imagination, 1995, 49 paintings for megaliner M.S. Imagination, 1995; contbr. articles to Chgo. Tribune Mag., American Artist Mag., Southwest Art Mag., SRA publs., others. Recipient Outstanding Achievement award in Field of Art for Citizen Foreign Birth Chgo. Immigrant's Svc. League. Mem. Arts Club of Chgo. Studio: PO Box 7390 Laguna Niguel CA 92607-7390 *An artist's most precious quality is curiosity. It has kept me young for many years, kept me searching, experimenting and never being complacent, in my life and my work.*

PIERCE, JACK, Olympic athlete, track and field. Olympic track and field participant Barcelona, Spain, 1992. Recipient 110m Hurdles Bronze medal Olympics, Barcelona, 1992. Office: US Olympic Com 1750 E Boulder St Colorado Springs CO 80909-5724*

PIERCE, JAMES CLARENCE, surgeon; b. Huron, S.D., Aug. 5, 1929; s. Henry Montraville and Carrie Bernice (Matson) P.; m. Carol Sue Wilson, 1967; children: Henry MacDonald, Richard Matson, Elizabeth Gail. B.A., Carleton Coll., 1951; M.D., Harvard U., 1955; M.S., U. Minn., 1963, Ph.D. in Surgery, 1966. Diplomate: Am. Bd. Surgery. Surg. intern Peter Bent Brigham Hosp., Boston, 1955-56; surg. fellow U. Minn., 1959-66; instr. surgery Med. Coll. Va., Richmond, 1966; prof. surgery and microbiology Med. Coll. Va., 1972-75; dir. Tissue Typing Lab., 1969-75; attending surgeon, dir. surg. research, dir. transplantation service St. Luke's Hosp. Center, N.Y.C., 1975-78; prof. surgery Columbia U., 1976, Ailsa Mellon Bruce prof. surgery, 1977-78; clin. prof. surgery Pa. State U. and, 1979-88; chmn. dept. surgery Geisinger Med. Center, Danville, Pa., 1979-90, chmn. emeritus, 1990—; clin. prof. surgery Jefferson U., 1990—. Contbr. articles to profl. jours. Elder Presbyn. Ch. With M.C., USAF, 1957-59. NIH fellow, 1963-65; Royal Soc. Medicine Found. travelling fellow, 1971; James IV Assn. Surg. traveller, 1978. Mem. ACS (pres. Ctrl. Pa. chpt. 1981-82), Am. Assn. Pathologists, Transplant Soc., Am. Soc. Transplant Surgeons, Ea. Surg. Assn., N.Y. Clin. Soc., Soc. Univ. Surgeons, Sigma Xi. Republican. Home: 1906 Red Ln Danville PA 17821-8415

PIERCE, JAMES ROBERT, magazine executive; b. Stockton, Ill., Apr. 15, 1933; s. Ellsworth B. and Mayme (Smythe) P.; m. Patricia Curran, May 14, 1960; children: Stacy, John Kelly, Shannon. B.A., U. Ill., 1955. Dist. mgr. McGraw Hill Publs., N.Y.C., 1960-75; computer category mgr. Bus. Week mag., N.Y.C., 1976-79; pub. Aviation Week & Space Tech. mag., N.Y.C., 1979-82; v.p., pub. Bus. Week, 1982, sr. v.p., pub., 1983-84, exec. v.p., pub., 1984; pres., chief exec. officer James R. Pierce, Inc., 1985—; chief oper. officer Lotus Pub. Corp, 1986-88; pub. Investment Vision Mag. Fidelity Pub. Corp., 1988-91; pres., chief oper. officer Hunter Pub., Elk Grove Village, Ill., 1991-94; vice chmn. Adams Trade Press, Inc., 1995—; bd. dirs. Adams Trader Press, City Media, Inc. Served to 1st lt. SAC USAF, 1956-59. Mem. Bus. and Profl. Advt. Assn., Worthington Country Club, LBS Golf Club. Roman Catholic.

PIERCE, JOHN ROBINSON, electrical engineer, educator; b. Des Moines, Mar. 27, 1910; s. John Starr and Harriet Anne (Robinson) P.; m. Martha Peacock, Nov. 5, 1938 (div. Mar. 1964); children: John Jeremy, Elizabeth Anne; m. Ellen R. McKown, Apr. 1, 1964 (dec. Sept. 1986); m. Brenda K. Woodard, Oct. 17, 1987. BS, Calif. Inst. Tech., 1933, MS, 1934, PhD, 1936; D Engring., Newark Coll. Engring., 1961; DSc, Northwestern U., 1961, Poly. Inst. Bklyn, 1963, Yale U., 1963, Columbia U., 1965, U. Nev., 1970, UCLA, 1977; D. Engring., Carnegie Inst. Tech., 1964; D. Elec. Engring., U. Bologna, Italy, 1974; LLD, U. Pa., 1974; DSc, U. So. Calif., 1978. With Bell Telephone Labs., Inc., Murray Hill, N.J., 1936-71; mem. tech. staff, dir. electronics research, 1952-55, dir. research, communication principles, 1958-62, exec. dir. research, communications principles and systems div., 1963-65, exec. dir. research, communications scis. div., 1965-71; prof. engring. Calif. Inst. Tech., Pasadena, 1971-80; chief technologist Jet Propulsion Lab., 1979-82; vis. prof. music emeritus Stanford U., Calif., 1983—; past mem. Pres.'s Sci. Adv. Com., Pres.'s Com. of Nat. Medal of Sci. Author: Theory and Design of Electron Beams, rev. edit., 1954, Traveling Wave Tubes, 1950, Electrons, Waves and Messages, 1956, Man's World of Sound, 1958, Symbols, Signals and Noise, 1961, (with A.G. Tressler) The Research State: A History of Science in New Jersey, 1964, The Beginnings of Satellite Communications, 1968, Science, Art and Communication, 1968, Almost All About Waves, 1973; (with E.C. Posner) Introduction to Communication Science and Systems, 1980, Signals: The Telephone and Beyond, 1981, The Science of Musical Sound, 1983, rev. edit., 1992, (with Hiroshi Inose) Information Technology and Civilization, 1984, (with A. Michael Noll) Signals, The Science of Telecommunications, 1990; editor: (with M.V. Mathews) Current Directions in Computer Music Research, 1989; articles on popular sci.; short stories. Recipient Morris Liebmann meml. prize Inst. Radio Engrs., 1947; Stuart Ballantine medal 1960, Man of Yr., Air Force Assn., 1962; Golden Plate award Acad. Achievement, 1962; General Hoyt S. Vandenberg trophy Arnold Air Soc., 1963; Nat. Medal of Sci., 1963; Edison medal AIEE, 1963; Valdemar Poulsen Gold medal, 1963; H.T. Cedergren medal, 1964; Marconi award, 1974; John C. Scott award, 1975; Japan Prize, 1985; Arthur C. Clarke award, 1987; Pioneer award Internat. Telemetering Conf., 1990, Charles Stark Draper prize Nat. Acad. of Engring., 1995; Marconi Internat. fellow, 1979. Fellow IEEE (medal of honor 1976), Acoustical Soc. Am., Am. Phys. Soc.; mem. NAS, NAE (Founders award 1977, Charles Stark Draper Prize, 1995), Am. Acad. Arts and Scis., Royal Acad. Sci. (Sweden), Inst. Electronics, Info. and Communication Engrs. of Japan (hon.), Inst. TV Engrs. Japan (hon.), Acad. Engring. of Japan (fgn. assoc.), Am. Philos. Soc. Home: 4008 El Cerrito Rd Palo Alto CA 94306-3114 Office: Stanford U Ctr for Computer Rsch in Music and Accoustics Stanford CA 94305

PIERCE, KENNETH RAY, veterinary medicine educator; b. Snyder, Tex., May 21, 1934; s. Clois Vernon and Ellen (Goolsby) P.; m. Anne Stasney, Aug. 31, 1956; children: Cynthia Cae, Mindy Rae. D.V.M., Tex. A&M U., 1957, M.S., 1962, Ph.D. (NSF fellow), 1965. Diplomate Am. Coll. Vet. Pathologists (pres. 1984). Instr. vet. anatomy Tex. A. and M. U., College Station, 1957-59; asst. prof. vet. pathology Tex. A. and M. U., 1961-65, assoc. prof., 1965-69, prof., 1969—, head dept., 1978-89, chief sect. vet. clin. pathology, 1967-75, 94—; comparative pathologist Inst. Comparative Medicine, Tex. A. and M. U.-Baylor Coll. Medicine, Houston, 1976-79; pvt. vet. practice San Angelo (Tex.) Vet. Hosp., 1959-61; adj. prof. dept. vet. medicine and surgery M.D. Anderson Tumor Inst. and Hosp., Houston, 1971-92; program dir continuing edn. C.L. Davis, D.V.M. Found., 1981-88; vis. scientist Nat. Inst. Environ. Health Scis., 1985. Co-editor: Vet. Pathology Jour, 1971-81; contbr. articles to profl. jours. Mem. AVMA, AAAS, Am. Soc. Vet. Clin. Pathologists, Am. Assn. of Avian Pathologists, U.S.-Can. Acad. Pathology, Tex. Vet. Med. Assn., Am. Assn. Vet. Med. Colls., N.Y. Acad. Scis., Sigma Xi, Phi Kappa Phi, Phi Zeta, Gamma Sigma Delta. Presbyterian (deacon, elder). Home: 12777 Hopes Creek Rd College Station TX 77845-9297 Office: Dept Vet Pathobiology Tex A&M U College Station TX 77843

PIERCE, LAWRENCE WARREN, retired federal judge; b. Phila., Dec. 31, 1924; s. Harold Ernest and Leora (Bellinger) P.; m. Wilma Taylor (dec.); m. Cynthia Straker, July 8, 1979; children: Warren Wood, Michael Lawrence, Mark Taylor. BS, St. Joseph's U., Phila., 1948, DHL, 1967; JD, Fordham U., 1951, LLD, 1982; LLD, Fairfield U., 1972, Hamilton Coll., 1987, St. John's U., 1990. Bar: N.Y. State 1951, U.S. Supreme Ct. 1968. Civil law practice N.Y.C., 1951-61; asst. dist. atty. Kings County, N.Y., 1954-61; dep. police commr. N.Y.C., 1961-63; dir. N.Y. State Div. for Youth, Albany, 1963-66; chmn. N.Y. State Narcotic Addiction Control Commn., 1966-70; vis. prof. criminal justice SUNY, Albany, 1970-71; U.S. dist. judge So. dist. N.Y., 1971-81; judge U.S. Fgn. Intelligence Surveillance Ct., 1979-81; apptd. U.S. cir. judge for 2d Cir., 1981-89, sr. U.S. cir. judge for 2d Cir., 1990-95; dir. Cambodian Ct. Tng. project Internat. Human Rights Law Group, 1995—; apptd. dir. Cambodian Ct. Tng. Project Internat. Human Rights Law Group, 1995—; ret., 1995; former mem., bd. fellows Inst. Jud. Adminstrn.; former trustee Practising Law Inst.; former mem. Am. Law Inst. Former mem. bd. mgrs. Lincoln Hall for Boys; past trustee Fordham U., St. Joseph's U., Phila. With AUS, 1943-46, MTO. Mem. ABA (former alt. observer U.S.mission to UN), Nat. Bar Assn., Assn. Bar of City of N.Y. (past mem. com. on 2d century). Roman Catholic.

PIERCE, LISA MARGARET, lecturer, product and market development manager; b. Nyack, N.Y., June 2, 1957; d. William Twining and Elizabeth P. BA with honors, Gordon Coll., Wenham, Mass., 1978; MBA, Atkinson Sch., Salem, Oreg., 1982. Campaign mgr. Carter/Mondale, Manchester, Mass., 1976; investigator Dept. Social Svcs., Nyack, 1977-78; paralegal Beverly, Mass., 1978-79; campaign mgr. Reagan Presdl. Primary, Rockland County, N.Y., 1980; cons. Sidereal, Portland, Oreg., 1981-82; performance analyst Dept. Social Svcs., Pomona, N.Y., 1982; market analyst Momentum Techs., Parsippany, N.J., 1983; cons. Booz Allen & Hamilton, Florham Park, N.J., 1984, Deloitte-Touche, Morristown, N.J., 1985; market researcher, forecaster AT&T, Bedminster, N.J., 1985-87, asst. pvt. line product mgr., 1987-89, Integrated Svcs. Digital Network product mgr., 1989-93; cons., dir. Telecomms. Rsch. Assocs., St. Marys, Kans., 1993—; panelist, contbr. TeleComms. Assn., San Diego, 1992, Internat. Comm. Assn., Atlanta, Ea. Comm. Forum, N.Y., Nat. Engring. Consortium, Chgo.; contbr. N.Y.C. ISDN/Internat User's Group. Tutor Literacy Vols. Am., Somerville, N.J., 1989-91; mem. Jr. League Am., Morristown, N.J., 1987-90; mem. Internat. Oceanographic Found., Washington. Grantee in field. Mem. Am. Mgmt. Assn. (profl.), Humane Soc. U.S., Internat. Platform Assn., W. Wilson Internat. Ctr. for Scholars, Environ. Def. Fund, Nat. Audubon Soc., Wilderness Soc., Nature Conservancy. Republican. Avocations: swimming, sailing, reading, music, poetry.

PIERCE, MARGARET HUNTER, government official; b. Weedsport, N.Y., June 30, 1910; d. Thomas Murray and Ruby (Sanders) Hunter; m. John R. Pierce, Nov. 4, 1950 (div. May 1959); 1 dau., Barbara Hunter. B.A., Mt. Holyoke Coll., 1932; J.D., N.Y. U., 1939. Bar: N.Y. bar 1941, D.C. bar 1958. Atty. Office Alien Property Custodian, Washington, 1942-43, 45, Office Solicitor, Dept. Labor, 1943-45, NLRB, 1946, 47-48; atty.-adviser U.S. Ct. Claims, 1947-48, 48-59, reporter decisions, 1959-68; commr. U.S. Indian Claims Commn., 1968-78; pvt. practice Washington, 1978—. Pres. Monday Night Musicales, Inc., 1995—. Mem. D.C. Bar Assn. (ct. claims com. 1958—, mil. law com. 1967), Fed. Bar Assn. (Indian law com. 1955—), ABA (sec. adminstrv. law-vets. com., mil. law com., immigration and nationality com.), Women's Bar Assn., Nat. Assn. Women Lawyers, Exec. Women in Govt., Bus. and Profl. Women (Cosmopolitan br.), Am. Women Composers, Zonta (Washington pres. 1977-78), Harvard Club (D.C.). Home: 3829 Garfield St NW Washington DC 20007-1319

PIERCE, MARTIN E., JR., fire commissioner; b. Boston, Nov. 13, 1940. Student, Boston Coll., 1958-60; cert. fire sci. program, Mass. Bay C.C., 1974. Fire fighter Boston Fire Dept., 1969-73, fire lt., 1973-76, fire capt., 1976-82, dist. fire chief, 1982-86, dep. fire chief, 1986-91, fire commr., chief dept., 1991—. Mem. Hyde Park Adv. Com.; coach varsity hockey Matignon High Sch., Cambridge, Mass., 1964—. With U.S. Army, 1962, with Res. 1962-68. Mem. Internat. Assn. of Fire Chiefs, Internat. Soc. for Respiratory Protection, Nat. Fire Protection Assn., Met. Fire Chiefs Assn., Urban Fire Forum, Fire Chiefs Assn. of Mass., Inc., Hundred Club of Mass., Inc. Avocation: golf. Office: Fire Dept 115 Southampton St Boston MA 02118-2713

PIERCE, MORTON ALLEN, lawyer; b. Liberec, Czechoslovakia, June 25, 1948; m. Nancy Washor, Dec. 14, 1975; children: Matthew J., Nicholas L. BA, Yale Coll., 1970; JD, U. Pa., 1974; postgrad. Oxford U., 1974-75. Bar: N.Y. 1975. Assoc. Reid & Priest, N.Y.C., 1975-83, ptnr., 1983-86; ptnr. Dewey Ballantine, N.Y.C., 1986—. Contbr. articles to profl. jours. Mem. Internat. Bar Assn., ABA (chairman subcom. internat. securities matters 1986-91), Assn. Bar City of N.Y. Home: 161 E 79th St New York NY 10021-0421 Office: Dewey Ballantine 1301 Ave Of The Americas New York NY 10019-6022

PIERCE, PONCHITTA ANNE, television host, producer, journalist; b. Chgo., Aug. 5, 1942; d. Alfred Leonard and Nora (Vincent) P. Student, Cambridge (Eng.) U., summer 1962; BA cum laude, U. So. Calif., 1964. Asst. editor Ebony mag., 1964-65, assoc. editor, 1965-67; editor Ebony mag. (N.Y.C. office), 1967-68; chief N.Y.C. editl. bur. Johnson Pub. Co., 1967-68; corr. news divsn. CBS, N.Y.C., 1968-71; contbg. editor McCall's mag., 1971-77; editl. cons. Philips Stokes Fund, 1971-78; staff writer Reader's Digest, 1976-77, roving editor, 1977-80; co-prodr., host Today in New York, Sta. WNBC-TV, N.Y.C., 1982-87; freelance writer, TV broadcaster; bd. govs. Overseas Press Club. WNBC-TV co-host: Sunday, 1973-77, The Prime of Your Life, 1976-80; author: Status of American Women Journalists on Magazines, 1968, History of the Phelps Stokes Fund 1911-1972; contbg. editor: Parade mag., 1993. Del. to WHO Conf., Geneva, 1973; bd. dirs. Dance Theatre of Harlem, Voice Found., Third St. Music Sch. Settlement, Big Sisters, Inc., Unward, Inc., Inner-City Scholarship Fund, Sta. WNET-TV; mem. women's bd. Madison Sq. Boys and Girls Club; mem. Columbia U. Health Scis. Adv. Coun. Recipient Penney-Mo. mag. award excellence women's journalism, 1967; John Russwurm award N.Y.C. Urban League, 1968; AMITA Nat. Achievement award in communications, 1974. Mem. NATAS, Women in Comm. (Woman Behind the News award 1969, Nat. Headliner award 1970), Fgn. Policy Assn. (mem. bd. govs., bd. dirs.), Coun. on Fgn. Rels., Calif. Scholarship Fedn. (life), Econs. Club N.Y., Lotos Club, Nat. Honor Soc., Mortar Bd.

PIERCE, RHONDA YVETTE, criminologist; b. Tampa, Fla., Dec. 4, 1959; d. Howard Jr. and Olivia (Powell) P. AA in Criminal Justice, Hillsboro C.C., Tampa, 1979; BS in Criminology, Fla. State U., Tallahassee, 1981. Cert. mgr. of housing. With Tampa Housing Authority, 1982-85, mgmt. coord., 1988-90, lease enforcement officer, exec. asst., 1991, dir. ops., 1992-94, dir. human resources, 1994-95; exec. dir. Sarasota (Fla.) Housing Authority, 1996—. Area youth dir. 11th Episcopal dist. A.M.E. Ch., Tampa, 1991-93; local youth dir. Mt. Olive A.M.E. Ch., Tampa, 1989-91. Recipient Dedicated Christian Svc. award Mt. Olive A.M.E. Ch., 1983. Mem. Nat. Assn. Housing and Redevel. Ofcls. Methodist. Avocations: sewing, reading, collecting Black art. Office: Sarasota Housing Authority 1300 6th St Sarasota FL 34236

PIERCE, RICHARD HILTON, lawyer; b. Westerly, R.I., May 2, 1935; s. Ralph Wilson and Mildred (Clark) P.; m. Cynthia Nanian, Sept. 8, 1962; children: Stacey, Andrew, Hilary. AB cum laude, Bates Coll., 1957; JD, NYU, 1960. Bar: R.I. 1961, U.S. Dist. Ct. R.I. 1961, Mass. 1985. Assoc. Hinckley, Allen, Salisbury & Parsons, Providence, 1960-66; ptnr. Hinckley, Allen, & Snyder, Providence, 1966—. Councilman City of Cranston, R.I., 1967-68; libr. trustee Cranston Pub. Libr., 1969-85; mem. sch. com., Cranston, 1985-86; pres. St. Andrews Sch. Fellow Am. Coll. Trust and Estate coun.; mem. ABA, Mass. Bar Assn., R.I. Bar Assn. Office: Hinckley Allen Snyder 1500 Fleet Ctr Providence RI 02903

PIERCE, RICKLIN RAY, lawyer; b. Waukegan, Ill., Sept. 16, 1953; s. Forest Ellsworth and Mildred Colleen (Cole) P. BBA in Acctg., Washburn U., 1975; BA in Econs., 1978, JD, 1978. Bar: Kans. 1978, U.S. Dist. Ct. Kans. 1978, U.S. Ct. Appeals (10th cir.) 1981, U.S. Supreme Ct. 1986. Assoc. Law Firm of C. C. Whittaker, Jr., Eureka, Kans., 1978-79; trust officer Smith County State Bank & Trust Co., Smith Center, Kans., 1979-80; staff atty. Northwest Kans. Legal Aid Soc., Goodland, 1980-81; assoc. Jochems, Sargent & Blaes, Wichita, Kans., 1981-82, Garden City, Kans., 1982-83; pvt. practice, Garden City, 1983-88; atty. County of Finney, 1988-93; pvt. practice, Garden City, 1993—. Pres., chmn. bd. dirs. Volunteers, Inc. of Finney County. Mem. Western Kans. Coun. Estate Planning & Giving. Mem. ABA, Assn. Trial Lawyers Am., Kans. Bar Assn., Southwest Kans. Bar Assn., Kans. Trial Lawyer Assn., Finney County Bar Assn. (treas.). Republican. Methodist. Home: 2015 Campus Dr Garden City KS 67846-3706 Office: 206 W Pine St Garden City KS 67846-5347

PIERCE, RICKY CHARLES, professional basketball player; b. Dallas, Aug. 19, 1959; m. Joyce Wright. Student, Walla Walla (Wash.) Community Coll., 1978-79, Rice U., 1979-82. Player Detroit Pistons, 1982-83, San Diego (now L.A.) Clippers, 1983-84, Milw. Bucks, 1984-91, Seattle Super Sonics, 1991-94, Golden State Warriors, 1994—; player NBA All-Star Game, 1991. Recipient Sixth Man award NBA, 1987, 90.

PIERCE, ROBERT LORNE, petrochemical, oil and gas company executive. Chmn. and chief exec. officer Foothills Pipe Lines Ltd., Calgary, Alta., Can.; bd. dirs. NOVA Corp. of Alta., Bank of N.S. Mem. Internstate Natural Gas Assn. Am. (bd. dirs.). Office: Foothills Pipe Lines Ltd, 3100 707 8th Ave SW, Calgary, AB Canada T2P 3W8

PIERCE, ROBERT NASH, writer; b. Greenville, Miss., Dec. 5, 1931. Student, U. Mo., 1950; BA, Ark. State U., 1951; MJ, U. Tex., Austin, 1955; PhD, U. Minn., 1968. Reporter, asst. state editor, acting state editor Ark. Democrat, Little Rock, 1953-55; reporter, real estate editor San Angelo (Tex.) Standard-Times, 1955-56; news editor, assoc. editor Sarasota (Fla.) News, 1956-60; dir. public relations Fla. Presbyn. Coll., St. Petersburg, 1960-62; asst. city editor St. Petersburg Evening Independent, 1962-63; asst. prof. La. State U., 1965-70; assoc. prof. U. Fla., Gainesville, 1970-76; legis. corr. La. Legislature Shreveport Jour., summer 1970; copy editor Miami Herald, 1972; prof. U. Fla., 1976-85, prof. emeritus, 1985—, dir. journalism grad. studies, 1978-83; Fulbright-Hays lectr. journalism U. Argentina de la Empresa, 1973; vis. lectr. Cath. U. Minas Gerais, Belo Horizonte, Brazil, 1973; vis. prof. Autonomous U., Barcelona, Spain, 1982-83, U. Yaounde, Cameroon, 1988. Author: Keeping the Flame: Media and Government in Latin America, 1979, A Sacred Trust: Nelson Poynter and the St. Petersburg Times, 1993; contbr. chpts. to Internat. Communication as a Field of Study, 1970, Mass Communication in Mexico, 1975, World Press Ency., 1981, Handbook of Latin Am. Popular Culture, 1985; contbr. monograph, articles to profl. publs. Research grantee Fulbright-Hays Faculty Research Abroad Program.

PIERCE, ROBERT RAYMOND, materials engineer, consultant; b. Helena, Mont., Feb. 17, 1914; s. Raymond Everett and Daisy Mae (Brown) P.; m. Stella Florence Kankos, June 12, 1938; children: Keith R., Patricia L., Diana L. BS in Chem. Engring., Oreg. State U., 1937. Process supr. Pennwalt Corp., Portland, Oreg., 1941-45, asst. tech. svc. mgr., Tacoma, 1945-47, gen. mgr., Phila., 1947-58, Natrona, Pa., 1958-65, tech. mgr., Phila., 1965-78, sr. tech. cons., Phila., 1978-80; self-employed cons., also Ohio State U., 1980—; former pres. Pierce CorMat Svcs., Inc. Contbr. articles to prof. jours. Patentee in field. Vice chmn. Phila. Air Pollution Control Bd., Phila., 1969-79, chmn. Ad Hoc # 1, 1974-79; Ky. Colonel, Louisville 1975—; mem. People to People del. on corrosion, People's Republic China, 1986. Recipient Phila. award City of Phila., 1973, Resolution award, City of Phila., 1979, World Decoration of Excellence for Exceptional Contributions to World Communities award, 1980-90. Mem. AIChE (Spl. Half-Century Membership and Contbrns. to the Advancement of Chem. Engring. award 1992), Nat. Assn. of Corrosion Engr. (bd. dirs.), Inter Soc. Corrosion Com. (world chmn. 1960-61), Internat. Com. for Industrial Chimneys (recipient best paper award Dusseldorf, Germany 1970), Rotary (Paul Harris fellow 1988). Lutheran.

PIERCE, ROY, political science educator; b. N.Y.C., June 24, 1923; s. Roy Alexander and Elizabeth (Scott) P.; m. Winnifred Poland, July 19, 1947. Ph.D., Cornell U., 1950. Instr. govt. Smith Coll., Northampton, Mass., 1950-51, asst. prof., 1951-56; asst. prof. polit. sci. U. Mich., Ann Arbor, 1956-59, assoc. prof., 1959-64, prof., 1964-94, prof. emeritus, 1993—; vis. prof. Columbia U., 1959, Stanford U., 1966, U. Oslo, 1976, Ecole des Hautes Etudes en Sciences Sociales, Paris, 1978. Author: Contemporary French Political Thought, 1966, French Politics and Political Institutions, 1968, 2d edit., 1973, (with Philip E. Converse) Political Representation in France, 1986, Choosing the Chief: Presidential Elections in France and the United States, 1995. Served with USAF, 1943-46. Mem. Am. Polit. Sci. Assn. (co-winner Woodrow Wilson Found. award 1987). Office: Inst for Social Rsch U Mich Ann Arbor MI 48109

PIERCE, RUTH A., federal agency administrator. BS in English and History, U. Wis., 1962. Fin. mgmt. br. chief Bur. Retirement and Survivors Ins. Social Security Adminstrn., Balt., 1974-77, asst. dir. fgn. ops., 1977-78, dep. assoc. commr. for ctrl. ops., 1981-83, acting assoc. commr. for retirement and survivors ins., 1983, exec. staff dir. to acting commr., 1983-84, assoc. commr. for ctrl. ops., 1984-88, assoc. dep. commr. for regional ops., 1988-90, dep. commr. for human resources, 1990—; asst. dir. for program mgmt. Office Program Mgmt., Washington, 1978-80; instr. Office Program Mgmt. Seminars, Oak Ridge, Tenn. Mem. pastor's planning com. Queen's Chapel United Meth. Ch.; mem. human resources conf. Conf. Bd.; active NAACP, Pub. Employees Roundtable, Fed. Exec. Bd., Md. chpt. Balt., Black Human Resources Network, Washington. Mem. Sr. Exec. Assn., Profl. Black Women's Assn., Forsgate Neighborhood Assn. Office: Social Security Adminstrn 6401 Security Blvd Baltimore MD 21235

PIERCE, SAMUEL RILEY, JR., government official, lawyer; b. Glen Cove, L.I., N.Y., Sept. 8, 1922; s. Samuel R. and Hettie E. (Armstrong) P.; m. Barbara Penn Wright, Apr. 1, 1948; 1 child, Victoria Wright. AB with honors, Cornell U., 1947, JD, 1949; postgrad. (Ford Found. fellow), Yale U., 1957-58; LLM in Taxation, NYU, 1952, LLD, 1972; various other hon. degrees including LL.D., L.H.D., D.C.L., Litt.D. Bar: N.Y. 1949, Supreme Ct. 1956. Asst. dist. atty. County N.Y., 1949-53; asst. U.S. atty. So. Dist. N.Y., 1953-55; asst. to under sec. Dept. Labor, Washington, 1955-56; assoc. counsel, counsel Jud. Subcom. on Antitrust U.S. Ho. Reps., 1956-57; pvt. practice law, 1957-59, 61-70, 73-81, 89—; sec. HUD, 1981-89; faculty N.Y. U. Sch. Law, 1958-70; guest speaker colls., univs.; judge N.Y. Ct. Gen. Sessions, 1959-61; gen. counsel, head legal div. U.S. Treasury, Washington, 1970-73; cons. Fund Internat. Social and Econ. Edn., 1961-67; chmn. impartial disciplinary rev. bd. N.Y.C. Transit System, 1968-81; chmn. N.Y. State Minimum Wage Bd. Hotel Industry, 1961; mem. N.Y. State Banking Bd., 1961-70, N.Y.C. Bd. Edn., 1961, Adminstrv. Conf. U.S., 1968-70, Battery Park City Authority, 1968-70, N.Y.C. Spl. Commn. Inquiry into Energy Failures, 1977; mem. nat. adv. com. Comptroller of Currency, 1975-80; adv. group commr. IRS, 1974-76; mem. Nat. Wiretapping Commn., 1973-76; dir. N.Y. 1964-65 World's Fair Corp. Contbr. articles to profl. jours. Trustee Inst. Civil Justice, Mt. Holyoke Coll., 1965-75, Hampton Inst., Inst. Internat. Edn., Cornell U., Howard U., 1976-81; bd. dirs. Tax Found. U.S. del. Conf. on Coops., Georgetown, Brit. Guiana, 1956; mem. panel symposium Mil.-Indsl. Conf. on Atomic Energy, Chgo., 1956; fraternal del. All-African People's Conf., Accra, Ghana, 1958; mem. Nat. Def. Exec. Res., 1957-70; mem. nat. exec. bd. Boy Scouts Am., 1969-75; mem. N.Y.C. U.S.O. Com., 1959-61; mem. panel arbitrators Am. Arbitration Assn. and Fed. Mediation and Conciliation Service, 1957—; Bd. dirs. Louis T. Wright Meml. Fund, Inc., Nat. Parkinson Found., Inc., 1959-61; sec., dir. YMCA Greater N.Y., 1960-70; Mem. N.Y. State Republican Campaign Hdqrs. Staff, 1952, 58; gov. N.Y. Young Rep. Club, 1951-53. With AUS, 1943-46; as 1st lt. J.A.G.C. Res., 1950-52. Recipient N.Y.C. Jr. C. of C. Ann. Disting. Svc. award, 1958, Alexander Hamilton award Treasury Dept., 1973, Disting. Alumnus award Cornell Law Sch., 1988, Disting. Svc. Medallion Nassau County Bar Assn., 1988, Reagan Revolution Medal of Honor, 1989, Presdl. Citizens medal, 1989, Salute to Greatness award Martin Luther King Jr. Ctr., 1989; selected mem. of L.I. Sports Hall of Fame, 1988. Fellow Am. Coll. Trial Lawyers; mem. ABA, Assn. of Bar of City of N.Y., Cornell Assn. Class Secs., Telluride Assn. Alumni, Cornell U. Alumni Assn. N.Y.C. (gov.), C.I.D. Agts. Assn. (gov.), N.Y. County Lawyers Assn., Inst. Jud. Adminstrn., Phi Beta Kappa, Phi Kappa Phi, Alpha Phi Alpha, Alpha Phi Omega. Methodist (former mem. commn. on interjurisdictional relations United Meth. Ch.).

PIERCE, SUSAN RESNECK, academic administrator, English educator; b. Janesville, Wis., Feb. 6, 1943; d. Elliott Jack and Dory (Block) Resneck; m. Kenneth H. Pierce; 1 child, Alexandra Parr. AB, Wellesley Coll., 1965; MA, U. Chgo., 1966; PhD, U. Wis., 1972. Lectr. U. Wis., Rock County, 1970-71; from asst. prof. to prof. English Ithaca (N.Y.) Coll., 1973-83, chmn. dept., 1976-79, 81-82; dean Henry Kendall Coll. Arts and Scis., prof. English U. Tulsa, 1984-90; v.p. acad. affairs, prof. English Lewis and Clark Coll., Portland, Oreg., 1990-92; pres. U. of Puget Sound, Tacoma, 1992—; vis. assoc. prof. Princeton (N.J.) U., 1979; program officer div. ednl. programs NEH, 1982-83, asst. dir., 1983-84; bd. dirs. Janet Elson Scholarship Fund, 1984-

1990, Tulsa Edn. Fund, Phillips Petroleum Scholarship Fund, 1985-90, Okla. Math. & Sci. High Sch., 1984-90, Hillcrest Med. Ctr., 1988-90, Portland Opera, 1990-92, St. Joseph's Hosp., 1992—, Seattle Symphony, 1993—; cons. U. Oreg., 1985, Drury Coll., Springfield, Mo., 1986; mem. Middle States and N. Cen. Accreditation Bds.; mem. adv. com. Fed. Women's Program, NEH, 1982-83; participant Summit Meeting on Higher Edn., Dept. Edn., Washington, 1985; speaker, participant numerous ednl. meetings, sems., commencements; chair Frederick Ness Book Award Com. Assn. Am. Colls., 1986; mem. award selection com. Dana Found., 1986, 87; mem. Acad. Affairs Council, Univ. Senate, dir. tchr. edn., chmn. adv. group for tchr. preparation, ex-officio mem. all Coll. Arts and Scis. coms. and Faculty Council on Internat. Studies, all U. Tulsa; bd. dirs. Am. Conf. Acad. Deans; bd. trustees Hillcrest Med. Ctr. Author: The Moral of the Story, 1982, also numerous essays, jour. articles, book sects., book revs.; co-editor: Approaches to Teaching "Invisible Man"; reader profl. jours. Bd. dirs. Arts and Humanities Coun., Tulsa, 1984-90; trustee Hillcrest Hosp., Tulsa, 1986-90; mem. cultural series com., community rels. com. Jewish Fedn., Tulsa, 1986-90; bd. dirs. Tulsa chpt. NCCJ, 1986-90. Recipient Best Essay award Arix. Quar., 1979, Excellence in Teaching award N.Y. State Edn. Council, 1982, Superior Group Service award NEH, 1984, other teaching awards; Dana scholar, Ithaca Coll., 1980-81; Dana Research fellow, Ithaca Coll., 82-83; grantee Inst. for Ednl. Affairs, 1980, Ford Found., 1987, NEH, 1989. Mem. MLA (adv. com. on job market 1973-74), South Ctrl. MLA, Soc. for Values in Higher Edn., Assn. Am. Colls. (bd. dirs.), Am. Conf. Acad. Deans (bd. dirs. 1988-91), Coun. of Presidents, Assn. Governing Bds., Phi Beta Kappa, Phi Kappa Phi, Phi Gamma Kappa. Office: U of Puget Sound 1500 N Warner St Tacoma WA 98416-0005

PIERCE, WILLIAM SCHULER, cardiac surgeon, educator; b. Wilkes-Barre, Pa., Jan. 12, 1937; s. William Harold and Doris Louis (Schuler) P.; m. Peggy Jayne Stone, June 12, 1965; children: William Stone, Jonathan Drew. B.S., Lehigh U., 1958; M.D., U. Pa., 1962. Intern U. Pa., 1962-63; resident in surgery Hosp. U. Pa., 1963-70; asst. prof. M.S. Hershey Med. Ctr., Pa. State U. Coll. Medicine, Hershey, 1970-73, assoc. prof., 1973-77, prof. surgery, 1977—, chief divsn. cardiothoracic surgery, 1991-95; assoc. chmn. dept. surgery, dir. rsch., dept. surgery, 1995—. Contbr. over 300 articles to profl. jours.; inventor cardiac valve, blood pump. Served with USPHS, 1965-67. Fellow ACS; mem. AMA, AAAS, Internat. Cardiovascular Soc., Am. Soc. Artificial Internal Organs, Soc. Vascular Surgery, Am. Heart Assn., Assn. Acad. Surgery, Inst. Medicine, So. Pa. Assn. Thoracic Surgery, Soc. Univ. Surgeons, Am. Surg. Assn., Soc. Clin. Surgery. Office: Milton S Hershey Med Ctr PO Box 850 Hershey PA 17033-0850

PIERCE-ROBERTS, TONY, cinematographer. Cinematographer: (TV movies) Tinker, Tailor, Soldier, Spy, 1979, Caught on a Train, 1980, A Voyage Round My Father, 1983, The Good Soldier, 1983, The Cold Room, 1984, (films) Moonlighting, 1982, Kipperbang, 1984, A Private Function, 1985, A Room with a View, 1986 (Academy award nomination best cinematography 1986), A Tiger's Tale, 1988, Slaves of New York, 1989, Out Cold, 1989, Mr. & Mrs. Bridge, 1990, White Fang, 1991, The Dark Half, 1993, The Remains of the Day, 1993, The Client, 1994. Office: Treetops 11 Croft Rd, Chalfront St Peter Gerrards Crossing, Buckinghamshire England

PIERCY, GORDON CLAYTON, bank executive; b. Takoma Park, Md., Nov. 23, 1944; s. Gordon Clayton and Dorothy Florence (Brummer) P.; m. Roberta Margaret Walton, 1985; children: Elizabeth Anne, Kenneth Charles, Virginia Walton, Zachary Taylor Walton. BS, Syracuse U., 1966; MBA, Pace U., 1973. Mgmt. trainee Suburban Bank, Bethesda, Md., 1962-66; mktg. planning assoc. Chem. Bank, N.Y.C., 1966-70; sr. market devel. officer Seattle-First Nat. Bank, 1970-74; product expansion adminstr., mktg. planning mgr. VISA, Inc., San Francisco, 1974-76; v.p., dir. mktg. Wash. Mut. Savs. Bank, Seattle, 1976-82; v.p., mktg. dir. First Interstate Bank of Wash. N.A., 1983-86; sr. v.p. mktg., dir. Puget Sound Nat. Bank, Tacoma, 1986-92; sr. v.p., dir. mktg. and sales Key Bank, 1993-94, dir. corp. sales Kiro Inc., 1994—; dir. mktg., sales InterWest Bancorp, Oak Harbor, Wash., Seattle Aquarium Soc., Concerts on the Cove. Mem. Am. Mktg. Assn., Bank Mktg. Assn., Mktg. Communications Execs. Internat., Seattle Advt. Fedn., Ctrl. Whidbey Lions, Island County United Way (allocations com.), Sigma Nu, Alpha Kappa Psi, Delta Mu Delta. Episcopalian. Home: 750 Snowberry Ln Coupeville WA 98239 Office: InterWest Bancorp PO Box 1649 Oak Harbor WA 98277

PIERCY, MARGE, poet, novelist, essayist; b. Detroit, Mar. 31, 1936; d. Robert Douglas and Bert Bernice (Bunnin) P.; m. Ira Wood, 1982. AB, U. Mich., 1957; MA, Northwestern U., 1958. Instr. Gary extension Ind. U., 1960-62; poet-in-residence U. Kans., 1971; disting. vis. lectr. Thomas Jefferson Coll., Grand Valley State Colls., fall 1975, 76, 78, 80; vis. faculty Women's Writers Conf., Cazenovia (N.Y.) Coll.; Elliston poetry fellow U. Cin., 1986; DeRoy Disting. vis. prof. U. Mich., 1992. Author: Breaking Camp, 1968, Hard Loving, 1969, Going Down Fast, 1969, Dance the Eagle to Sleep, 1970, Small Changes, 1973, To Be of Use, 1973, Living in the Open, 1976, Woman on the Edge of Time, 1976, The High Cost of Living, 1978, Vida, 1980, The Moon is Always Female, 1980, Braided Lives, 1982, Circles on the Water, 1982, Stone, Paper, Knife, 1983, My Mother's Body, 1985, Gone to Soldiers, 1988, Available Light, 1988 (May Sarton award 1991), Summer People, 1989, He, She and It, 1991, Body of Glass, 1991 (Arthur C. Clarke award 1993), Mars and Her Children, 1992, The Longings of Women, 1994, Eight Chambers of the Heart, 1995. Cons. N.Y. State Coun. on Arts, 1971, Mass. Found. for Humanities and Coun. on Arts, 1974; mem. Writer Bd., 1985-86; bd. dirs. Transition House, Mass. Found. Humanities and Pub. Policy, 1978-85, Am. ha-Yam, 1988—, v.p., 1995-96; gov.'s appointee to Mass. Cultural Coun., 1990-91, Mass. Coun. on Arts and Humanities, 1986-89; artistic adv. bd. ALEPH Alliance for Jewish Renewal, Am. Poetry Ctr., 1988—; lit. adv. panel poetry NEA, 1989. Recipient Borenstone Mountain Poetry award, 1968, 74, Lit. award Gov. Mass. Commn. on Status of Women, 1974, Nat. Endowment of Arts award, 1978, Carolyn Kizer Poetry prize, 1986, 90, Shaeffer-Eaton-PEN New Eng. award, 1989, Golden Rose Poetry prize, 1990, Brit ha-Dorot award The Shalom Ctr., 1992. Mem. PEN, NOW, Authors Guild, Authors League, Writers Union, Am. Poetry Soc., Nat. Audubon Soc., Mass. Audubon Soc., New Eng. Poetry Club. Address: PO Box 1473 Wellfleet MA 02667-1473

PIERESON, JAMES EUGENE, foundation administrator; b. Grand Rapids, Mich., Oct. 4, 1946; s. Lloyd Eugene and Katherine Louise (Graham) P.; Patricia Giles Leeds, Aug. 28, 1983; 1 child, James William. BA cum laude Polit. Sci., Mich. State U., 1968, PhD in Polit. Sci., 1973. Vis. faculty polit. sci. Ind. U., Bloomington, 1974-75; asst. prof. polit. sci. U. Pa., Phila., 1976-82; vis. faculty polit. sci. U. Minn., Mpls., 1979; program officer John M. Olin Found., N.Y.C., 1982-85; exec. dir. John M. Olin Found., 1986—; trustee John M. Olin Found., N.Y.C., 1987—; mem. adv. com. Simon Grad. Sch. Bus. Adminstrn., U. Rochester, Rochester, N.Y., 1986—. Co-author: Political Tolerance and American Democracy, 1981; contbr. articles to profl. jours. Trustee Adelphi U., 1991—. Evans scholar Evans Scholars Found., 1964-68; NDEA Grad. fellow, 1968-71, NSF Research fellow, 1978-79, U.S. Govt. Mem. Phila. Soc., Am. Hist. Assn., Union League Club. Republican. Roman Catholic. Office: John M Olin Found 300 Madison Ave New York NY 10017

PIERGALLINI, ALFRED A., food products executive; b. Easton, Pa., Aug. 1, 1946. BA, Lafayette Coll., 1968; MBA, U. Chgo., 1970. Regional dir. Beverage Mgmt. Inc.; sales mgr. Procter & Gamble Co., then brand mgr.; pres. Shasta Beverages Inc., Hayward, Calif., 1985-90; chmn., pres., chief exec. officer Gerber Prods. Co., Fremont, Mich., from 1985, also COO, dir. •

PIERGIES, BARBARA ALICE, computer scientist; b. Cleve., June 7, 1958; d. Robert William and Mildred Eileene (Fowler) Homan; m. James Douglas Piergies, Jan. 9, 1988; children: Robert James, Mary Catherine. BA, Cleve. State U., 1983, M.Computer and Info. Sci., 1985. Instr. Cleve. State U., 1984-85, Lorain County Community Coll., Elyria, Ohio, 1984; cons. Booz-Allen & Hamilton, Dayton, Ohio, 1985-88; sr. computer scientist Sci. Applications Internat. Corp., Dayton, Ohio, 1988—, instr., 1988-91; configuration control expert Suppressor Simulation System. Co-author computer program: User Friendly Interface, 1992, Information Analysis System, 1988. Asst. Germantown (Ohio) Area Concerned Citizens Assn., 1991; team walk leader March of Dimes, Dayton, 1988-91. Mem. Am. Def. Preparedness Assn., Internat. Test and Evaluation Assn., Phi Eta Sigma, Beta Gamma Sigma. Lutheran. Avocations: walking, cross stitch, cake decorating, tap dancing. Home: 12701 Air Hill Rd Brookville OH 45309-9304 Office: Sci Applications Internat 101 Woodman Dr Ste 103 Dayton OH 45431-1482

PIERLUISI, PEDRO RAFAEL, attorney general; b. San Juan, P.R., Apr. 26, 1959; s. Jorge A. and Doris (Urrutia) P.; m. Maria E. Rojo, June 20, 1981; children: Anthony, Michael, Jacqueline, Rafael. BA, Tulane U., 1981; JD, George Washington U., 1984. Bar: D.C. 1984, U.S. Dist. Ct. D.C. 1985, U.S. Ct. Appeals (D.C. cir.) 1985, P.R. 1990, U.S. Supreme Ct. 1990. Assoc. Verner, Liipfert, Bernhard, McPherson & Hand, Washington, 1984-85, Cole, Corette & Abrutyn, Washington, 1985-90; ptnr. Pierluisi & Pierluisi, San Juan, 1990-93; atty. gen. Govt. of P.R., 1993—; chmn. exec. bd. Forensic Scis. Inst., 1993—, Criminal Justice Info. System, 1993—; chmn. confiscations bd. Govt. of P.R., 1993—. Mem. ABA (mem. ho. of dels., mem. standing com. on substance abuse), Nat. Assn. Attys. Gen. (vice chair eastern region), Fed. Bar Assn., George Washington U. Internat. Law Soc. (pres. 1982-83), Rotary, Phi Alpha Delta (hon., Munoz chpt.). Avocations: tennis, jogging. Office: Puerto Rico Dept Justice PO Box 192 San Juan PR 00902

PIEROTTI, JOHN WILLIAM, prosecutor; b. Memphis, Dec. 29, 1936; s. Harry C. and Alma (Folis) P.; m. Barbara Anne Dixon, Jan. 6, 1957; children: John Jr., Andrew, Thomas, Marianne. BS, Spring Hill Coll., 1958; JD, Memphis State U., 1968. Bar: Tenn. 1968. Asst. dist. atty. Dist. Atty.'s Office Shelby County, Memphis, 1968-90, dist. atty., 1990—. 1st lt. U.S. Army, 1958-60. Roman Catholic. Avocation: breeding, raising and racing thoroughbred horses. Office: Dist Atty Gen's Office 201 Poplar Ave Ste 301 Memphis TN 38103-1947

PIERPOINT, POWELL, lawyer; b. Phila., Apr. 30, 1922; s. James Reynolds and Ruth (Powell) P.; m. Margaret Shaw Sagar, Mar. 24, 1950; 1 child, Harriet Pierpoint Bos. B.A., Yale, 1944, LL.B., 1948. Bar: N.Y. bar 1949. Assoc. Hughes, Hubbard & Reed (and predecessors), N.Y.C., 1948-53; ptnr. Hughes, Hubbard & Reed (and predecessors), 1955-61, 63-93, of counsel, 1993—; asst. U.S. atty. So. Dist. N.Y., 1953-55; gen. counsel Dept. Army, 1961-63; dir. Legal Aid Soc., 1968-90, pres., 1979-81; mem. N.Y.C. Bd. Ethics, 1972-89, chmn. 1983-89; spl. master appellate divsn. 1st Dept., 1992. Served with USNR, 1943-46. Fellow Am. Coll. Trial Lawyers; mem. ABA, N.Y. State Bar Assn., Assn. Bar City of N.Y. Home: 155 E 72nd St New York NY 10021-4371 Office: Hughes Hubbard & Reed 1 Battery Park Plz New York NY 10004-1405

PIERPONT, ROBERT, fund raising executive, consultant; b. Somers Point, N.J., Jan. 27, 1932; s. Robert E. and Elise D. (White) P.; m. Marion J. Welde, Oct. 11, 1958; children: Linda J. Staropoli, Nancy P. Oler, Robert W., Richard F. B.S. in Bus. Adminstrn, Pa. Mil. Coll., 1954; postgrad. Inst. Ednl. Mgmt, Harvard Grad. Sch. Bus. Adminstrn., 1970. Comml. sales rep. Atlantic City (N.J.) Electric Co., 1956-58; asst. dir. devel. Widener U. (formerly Pa. Mil. Coll.), Chester, 1958-61, asst. to pres., 1961-62, dir. devel., 1962-68, v.p. for devel., 1968-70; sr. cons. v.p. and dir. Brakeley, John Price Jones, Inc., N.Y.C., 1970-79; v.p. devel. Mt. Sinai Med. Center, N.Y.C., 1979-85; ptnr. Pierpont & Wilkerson, 1986—; guest faculty mem. Big 10 Fund Raisers Inst., Mackinac Island, Mich., 1971; mem. adv. com. on application of standards Philanthropic Adv. Service, Council of Better Bus. Burs., Washington, 1978-81; faculty The Fund Raising Sch., Ctr. on Philanthropy, Ind. U., 1989—. Mem. bishops adv. com. on stewardship Diocese of Pa., 1968-69; vestryman Trinity Episcopal Ch., Swarthmore, 1970-72; trustee Putnam Valley Free Libr., 1986-92; pres. Roaring Brook Lake Property Owners Assn., 1995—. Recipient Alumni Svc. award Widener U., 1989; named Disting. Alumnus in Econs., Widener U., 1986. Mem. Nat. Soc. Fund Raising Execs. (dir.-at-large 1970-78, pres. found. 1977-79, chmn. bd. 1979-82, chmn. cert. bd. 1982-87, presdl. search com. 1989, chmn. ethics com. 1993-95). Office: The Stone House PO Box 179 Rt 9 Garrison NY 10524

PIERPONT, WILBUR K., retired administrator, accounting educator; b. Winn, Mich., Mar. 15, 1914; s. Clarence N. and Ethel (Kent) P.; m. Maxine Sponseller, Feb. 7, 1941; children: Ann Pierpont Mack, James. AB, Central Mich. U., 1934; MBA (Univ. scholar), U. Mich., 1938, PhD, 1942; LLD, Central Mich. U., 1958, Hope Coll., 1977. Brookings Instn. fellow, 1941; price analyst Ordnance Dept., Washington, 1942-44; teaching fellow U. Mich., 1938-40, instr. Sch. Bus. Adminstrn., 1941-42, asst. prof., 1946-51, controller, 1947-51, v.p., chief fin. officer, prof., 1951-76, prof. acctg., 1977-81; bd. dirs. R and B Machine Tool Co., Chelsea Milling Co. Contbr. articles to numerous jours. Trustee Buhr Found. Served as lt. Bur. Ordnance, USNR, 1944-46. Recipient Outstanding Achievement award U. Mich., Alumni award U. Mich., Alumni award Cen. Mich. U. Mem. Delta Sigma Pi, Beta Gamma Sigma, Phi Kappa Phi. Methodist. Clubs: Golf and Outing (Ann Arbor), Rotary (Ann Arbor). Home: 2125 Nature Cove Ct Ann Arbor MI 48104-8325

PIERRE, CHARLES BERNARD, mathematician, statistician, educator; b. Houston, Dec. 2, 1946; s. Rufus and Charles (Ellis) P.; m. Patsy Randle, Aug. 28, 1970 (div. 1971); m. Cynthia Gilliam, June 28, 1980 (div. 1994); 1 child, Kimberly Keri. BS, Tex. So. U., 1970, MS in Edn., 1974; PhD in Math. Edn., Am. U., 1992. Cert. tchr., Tex., D.C. Comml. photographer Photographics Labs., Houston, 1968-69; elec. engr., mathematician Sta. KPRC-TV, Houston, 1970-71; instr. math. Houston Ind. Sch. Dist., 1971-72, Meth. Secondary Sch., Kailahun, Sierra Leone, West Africa, 1972-73; math. researcher West African Regional Math Program, Freetown, Sierra Leona, West Africa, 1973-77; instr. math. Houston Ind. Sch. Dist., 1977-80, 81-87, Episcopal Acad., Merion, Pa., 1980-81, D.C. Pub. Schs., Washington, 1987-91; instr. math. Houston C.C., 1985-87; asst. prof. math. and computer sci. San Jose State U., 1992-94; assoc. prof. math. scis. Clark Atlanta U., 1994—; African cons. Peace Corps, Phila., 1977, Sierra Leone, West Africa; lectr. math. Tex. So. U., U. Sierra Leone, U. Liberia, Bunambu Tchrs. Coll., Port Loko Tchrs. Coll., Inst. Edn., West Africa; assessment coord. Calif. State U. Alliance for Minority Participation, San Jose, 1994; advisor design team SKYMATH Project, Boulder, Colo., 1994—; assoc. dir. Park City/IAS Math. Inst. Clark Atlanta U., 1995—; participant Inst. History Math., 1995—; cons. in field. Author: Introduction to Coordinate Analytic Geometry, 1974, Mathematics for Elementary School Teachers, 1976; co-author: The Modern Approach to Trigonometry, 1975, A Resource Book for Teachers, 1975, Picture Book for the West African Regional Math. Program, 1975, textbook 6th grade STEM project U. Mont., 1996. Vol. Peace Corps., Sierra Leone. NSF fellow. Mem. ASCD, NAM, Am. Soc. for Quality Control, Nat. Coll. Tchrs. Math., Am. Math. Soc., Math. Assn. Am. Democrat. Baptist. Avocations: reading, writing, tennis, chess, French horn, Photography, computers, collecting pipes, travel, surfing the web. Home: 3360 Penny Ln Apt C East Point GA 30344-5557

PIERRE, JOSEPH HORACE, JR., commercial artist; b. Salem, Oreg., Oct. 3, 1929; s. Joseph Horace and Miriam Elisabeth (Holder) P.; m. June Anne Rice, Dec. 20, 1952; children: Joseph Horace III, Thomas E., Laurie E., Mark R., Ruth A. Grad., Advt. Art Sch., Portland, Oreg., 1954, Inst. Comml. Art, 1951-52. Lithographic printer Your Town Press, Inc., Salem, Oreg., 1955-58; correctional officer Oreg. State Correctional Instn., 1958-60; owner Illustrators Workshop, Inc., Salem, 1960-61; advt. mgr. North Pacific Lumber Co., Portland, 1961-63; vocat. instr. graphic arts Oreg. Correctional Instn., 1963-70; lithographic printer Lloyd's Printing, Monterey, Calif., 1971-72; illustrator McGraw Hill, 1972-73; owner Publishers Art Svc., Monterey, 1972-81; correctional officer Oreg. State Penitentiary, 1982-90; ret.; owner Northwest Syndicate, 1993—. Editor/publisher: The Pro Cartoonist & Gagwriter; author: The Road to Damascus, 1981, The Descendants of Thomas Pier, 1992, The Origin and History of the Callaway and Holder Families, 1992; author numerous OpEd cols. in Salem, Oreg. Statesman Jour., others; pub. cartoons nat. mags.; mural Mardi Gras Restaurant, Salem; cartoon strip Fabu, Oreg. Agr. mo. Mem. Rep. Nat. Com., Citizens Com. for Right to Keep and Bear Arms. Served with USN, 1946-51. Decorated victory medal WWII, China svc. medal, Korea medal, Navy occupation medal. Mem. U.S. Power Squadron, Nat. Rifle Assn., Acad. of Model Aeronautics, Oreg. Correctional Officers Assn. (co-founder, hon. mem.), Four Corners Rod and Gun Club. Republican. Avocations: sailing, flying, scuba, model aircraft building and flying. Home: 4822 Oak Park Dr NE Salem OR 97305-2931

PIERRE, PERCY ANTHONY, university president; b. nr. Donaldsville, La., Jan. 3, 1939; s. Percy John and Rosa (Villavaso) P.; m. Olga A. Markham, Aug. 8, 1965; children: Kristin Clare, Allison Celeste. BSEE, U. Notre Dame, 1961, MSEE, 1963, D of Engring. (hon.), 1977; PhD in Elec. Engring, Johns Hopkins U., 1967; postgrad., U. Mich., 1968; DSc (hon.), Rensselear Poly. Inst. Asst. prof. elec. engring. So. U., 1963; instr. Johns Hopkins U., Balt., 1963-64; instr. physics Morgan State Coll., 1964-66; instr. info. and control engring. U. Mich., Ann Arbor, 1967-68; instr. systems engring. UCLA, 1968-69; research engr. in communications RAND Corp., 1968-71; White House fellow, spl. asst. Office of Pres., 1969-70; dean Sch. Engring., Howard U., Washington, 1971-77; program officer for engring. edn. Alfred P. Sloan Found., 1973-75; asst. sec. for research, devel. and acquisition U.S. Dept. Army, 1977-81; engring. mgmt. cons., 1981-83; pres. Prairie View (Tex.) Agrl. and Mech. U. System, 1983-89, Honeywell prof. elec. engring., 1989-90; v.p. rsch. and grad. studies Mich. State U., East Lansing, 1990-95, prof. elec. enging., 1995—; dir. engring. coll. council Am. Soc. for Engring. Edn., 1973-75; mem. sci. adv. group Def. Communications Agy., 1974-75; mem. adv. panel Office Exptl. Research and Devel. Incentives, NSF, 1973-74; mem. Commn. Scholars To Rev. Grad. Programs, Ill. Bd. Higher Edn., 1972-74; mem. panel on role U.S. engring. sch. in fgn. tech. assistance, 1972, co-chmn. symposium on minorities in engring., 1973; mem. rev. panel for Inst. for Applied Tech., Nat. Bur. Standards, 1973-77; chmn. com. on minorities Nat. Acad. Engring., 1976-77; cons. to dir. Energy Rsch. and Devel. Adminstrn., 1976-77; mem. Army Sci. Bd., 1984; mem. adv. bd. Sch. Engring., Johns Hopkins U., 1981-84; cons. Office Sec. Def., 1981-84; mem. adv. bd. Lincoln Labs., MIT. Contbr. articles on communications theory to profl. publs. Trustee U. Notre Dame, 1974-77, 81—; trustee, mem. exec. com. Nat. Fund for Minority Engring. Students, 1976-77; bd. dirs. The Hitachi Found., 1987, Ctr. for Naval Analysis, 1986, Assn. Tex. Colls. and Univs.; pres. Southwest Athletic Conf., 1985-87, bd. dirs. CMS Corp., 1990—, Defense Sci., 1992-94, Old Kent Fin. Corp., 1993—, bd. trustee Aerospace Corp., 1991—. Recipient Disting. Civilian Service award Dept. Army, 1981; award of merit from Senator Proxmire, 1979. Mem. IEEE (sr. mem.; Edison award com. 1978-80), Sigma Xi, Tau Beta Pi. Home: 2445 Emerald Lake Dr East Lansing MI 48823-7256 Office: Mich State U 357 Engineering Blvd East Lansing MI 48824-1226

PIERRO, GRACE EDNA, mechanical engineer; b. New Brunswick, N.J., Sept. 2, 1960; d. Joseph Laurence Jr. and Elissa Anne (Lucadamo) Kish; m. Gerald Pierro, June 30, 1990; 1 child, Alexis. BSME, N.J. Inst. Tech., 1986. Drafter, designer Brown, Boveri Co., Inc. (BBC), North Brunswick, N.J., 1984-86; prodn. engr. Singer-Kearfott Divsn., Little Falls, N.J., 1986-88; sr. prodn. engr. White Tool Co., Kenilworth, N.J., 1988-89; from application engr. to mgr. prodns. Miniflow Sys., Inc., Watertown, Mass., 1991-94; from process engr. to ISO9000 mgmt. rep./corp. engr. Shawmut Mills, West Bridgewater, Mass., 1994—. Mem. ASME. Roman Catholic. Home: PO Box 825 Onset MA 02558-0825

PIERSKALLA, WILLIAM PETER, university dean, management-engineering educator; b. St. Cloud, Minn., Oct. 22, 1934; s. Aloys R. and Hilda A. P.; m. Carol Spargo, Children: Nicholas, William, Michael. A.B. in Econs., Harvard U., 1956, M.B.A., 1958; M.S. in Math., U. Pitts., 1962; Ph.D. in Ops. Research, Stanford U., 1965; M.A., U. Pa., 1978. Assoc. prof. Case Western Res. U., Cleve., 1965-68, So. Meth. U., Dallas, 1968-70; prof. dept. indsl. engring. and mgmt. scis. Northwestern U., Evanston, Ill., 1970-78; exec. dir. Leonard Davis Inst., U. Pa., Phila., 1978-83; prof., chmn. health care systems dept. U. Pa., Phila., 1982-90, prof. decision sci. and systems engring., dep. dean acad. affairs Wharton Sch., 1983-89, Ronald A. Rosenfield prof., 1986-93; dir. Huntsman Ctr. Global Competition and Leadership Wharton Sch., U. Pa., 1989-91; John E. Anderson prof. UCLA, 1993—, dean of John E. Anderson Grad Sch. of Mgmt., 1993—; cons. HHS, Bethesda, Md., 1974-87, MDAX, Chgo., 1985-91, MEDICUS, Evanston, 1970-75, Sisters of Charity, Dayton, Ohio, 1982-83, Project Hope, 1990—; bd. dirs. Huntsman Ctr. for Global Competition and Leadership, 1989-93, No. Wilderness Adventures, Griffin Funds, Inc., 1993-95, No. Trust Corp. Calif. Contbr. articles to various publs. Mem. adv. bd. Lehigh U., 1986-93, U. So. Calif. Bus. Sch., 1987-93. Recipient Harold Larnder Meml. prize Can. Oper. Rsch. Soc., 1993; grantee NSF, 1970-83, HHS, Washington, 1973-82, Office Naval Rsch., Arlington, Va., 1974-77. Mem. Ops. Rsch. Soc. Am. (pres. 1982-83, editor 1979-82, Kimball Disting. Svc. medal 1989), Inst. Mgmt. Scis. (assoc. editor 1970-77), Internat. Fedn. Operational Rsch. Socs. (pres. 1989-91). Office: UCLA Anderson Grad Sch Mgmt 110 Westwood Plz Box 951481 Los Angeles CA 90095-1481

PIERSOL, LAWRENCE L., federal judge; b. Vermillion, S.D., Oct. 21, 1940; s. Ralph Nelson and Mildred Alice (Millette) P.; m. Catherine Anne Vogt, June 30, 1962; children: Leah C., William M., Elizabeth J. BA, U. S.D., 1962, JD summa cum laude, 1965. Bar: S.D. 1965, U.S. Ct. Mil. Appeals, 1965, U.S. Dist. Ct. S.D. 1968, U.S. Supreme Ct. 1972, U.S. Dist. Ct. Wyo. 1980, U.S. Dist. Ct. Nebr. 1986, U.S. Dist. Ct. Mont. 1988. Ptnr. Davenport, Evans, Hurwitz & Smith, Sioux Falls, S.D., 1968-93; judge U.S. Dist. Ct., Sioux Falls, 1993—. Majority leader S.D. Ho. of Reps., Pierre, 1973-74, minority whip, 1971-72; del. Dem. Nat. Conv., 1972, 76, 80; S.D. mem. del. select commn. Dem. Nat. Com., 1971-75. Capt. U.S. Army, 1965-68. Mem. ABA, State Bar S.D. Roman Catholic. Avocations: reading, running, sailing, mountaineering. Office: US Dist Ct 400 S Phillips Ave Sioux Falls SD 57102-0961

PIERSON, ALBERT CHADWICK, business management educator; b. Pierson, Ill., Jan. 3, 1914; s. Charles Clevel and Gertrude Fannie (Gale) P.; m. Evelyn Matilda Swanson, Sept. 13, 1952; 1 stepson, Jay F. Lynch. B.A. in Liberal Arts and Scis, U. Ill., 1935; M.B.A. with distinction, Harvard U., 1947; Ph.D., Columbia U., 1963. Merchandiser Montgomery Ward & Co., Chgo., 1935-41; mgmt. cons. N.Y.C., 1947-53; prof. mgmt. San Diego State U., 1954—; cons. in field; pub. accountant, Calif.; research editor Jour. Travel Research, 1967—. Author: Trends in Lodging Enterprises, 1939-1963, 1963. Chmn. bd. Nat. Arts Found., N.Y.C.; mem. accreditation vis. teams Am. Assembly Collegiate Schs. Bus., 1977—. Served to col. AUS, 1941-46. Decorated Bronze Star. Fellow Soc. Applied Anthropology; mem. Acad. Mgmt. (pres. Western div. 1974-75), Western Council Travel Research (dir. 1965-67), Acad. Internat. Mgmt., Mil. Logistics Soc., James Joyce Soc., Beta Gamma Sigma, Sigma Iota Epsilon, Tau Sigma. Democrat. Methodist. Clubs: Harvard (Chgo.); Columbia (N.Y.C.); Marine Corps Officers (San Diego). Home: 1245 Park Row La Jolla CA 92037-3706 Office: Coll Bus San Diego State U San Diego CA 92182-0096

PIERSON, ANNE BINGHAM, physician; b. N.Y.C., June 9, 1929; d. Woodbridge and Ursula Wolcott (Griswold) Bingham; m. Richard N. Pierson Jr., July 10, 1954 (div. Aug. 1974); children: Richard N. III, Olivia Tiffany Jacobs, Alexandra deForest Griffin, Cordelia Stewart Comfort Smela; m. Richard Taliaferro Wright, Nov. 25, 1978. Student, Katharine Branson Sch., Ross, Calif., 1943-47; BA, Vassar Coll., 1951; MD, Columbia U., 1955, MPH, 1972. Intern Lenox Hill Hosp., N.Y.C., 1955-56; substitute internship AUH, Beruit, Lebanon, 1955; mem. staff 7th Day Adventist Hosp., Taipei, Taiwan, 1957; clinic physician, med. dir. Planned Parenthood of Bergen County, Hackensack, N.J., 1960-74, also bd. dirs.; asst. clin. prof. dept. ob-gyn. Columbia U. Coll. Physicians and Surgeons, Internat. Inst. Study of Human Reproduction, 1972-74; med. dir. Memphis Assn. for Planned Parenthood, Inc., 1974-75; staff physician N.Y. Telephone Co., 1976-87; med. dir. Planned Parenthood Assn. Hudson County, 1976-79; physician Sonalysts, Waterford, Conn., 1988—; mem. nat. med. adv. com. Planned Parenthood-World Population, 1966-69. Pres. Vassar Class 1951, 1986-91; artist mem. Clinton Art Soc., 1989—, East Lyme Art League, 1991—; active Jr. League, 1964—. Mem. AMA (Physicians Recognition award 1973—), Am. Occupational Med. Assn., Occupational Med. Assn. Conn., Am. Assn. Planned Parenthood Physicians (exec. com. 1969-71), Nat. Soc. Colonial Dames (life, asst. sec. 1991-94, 2d v.p. 1994—), Cosmopolitan Club. Home: Griswold Pt Old Lyme CT 06731 Office: Sonalysts 215 Parkway N Waterford CT 06385-1209

PIERSON, DON, sports columnist. Tribune Pro Football columnist Chicago Tribune. Recipient Dick McCann Mem. Award, 1994. Office: Chicago Tribune Sports Dept 435 N Michigan Ave Chicago IL 60611-4001

PIERSON, EDWARD SAMUEL, engineering educator, consultant; b. Syracuse, N.Y., June 27, 1937; s. Theodore and Marjorie O. (Bronner) P.; m.

Elaine M. Grauer, June 6, 1971; 1 child, Alan. BS in Elec. Engring., Syracuse U., 1958; SM, MIT, 1960, ScD, 1964. Asst. prof., fellow MIT, 1965-66; assoc. prof., assoc. dept. head U. Ill., Chgo., 1966-75; program mgr. Argonne Nat. Labs., Ill., 1975-82; head dept. engring. Purdue U. Calumet, Hammond, Ind., 1982-95, spl. asst to chancellor for environ. programs, 1995—; cons. Argonne Nat. Lab., 1972-75, 82—, Solmecs Corp., 1982-88, HMJ Corp., Washington, 1983-88, LM Mfg., 1994—. Contbr. numerous articles to profl. jours. NSF fellow, 1958-60. Mem. IEEE, Am. Soc. Engring. Edn., Am. Soc. Mech. Engrs. Office: Purdue U Calumet Hammond IN 46323

PIERSON, FRANK ROMER, screenwriter, director; b. Chappaqua, N.Y., May 12, 1925; s. Harold C. and Louise (Randall) P.; m. Polly Stokes, 1948 (div.); m. Dori Derfner, 1978 (div.); m. Helene Szamet, June 24, 1990; children: Michael, Eve. BS, Harvard U., 1946. Writer, corr. Time/Life mags., 1950-58; bd. trustees Los Angeles Theatre Ctr., 1984—. Screenwriter: (television) Naked City, 1962, Route 66, 1963, Nichols, 1971, Haywire, 1979, (feature films) Cat Ballou, 1965 (Academy award nomination best adapted screenplay 1965), The Happening, 1967, Cool Hand Luke, 1967 (Academy award nomination best adapted screenplay 1967), The Anderson Tapes, 1970, Dog Day Afternoon, 1975 (Academy award best original screenplay 1975), In Country, 1989, Presumed Innocent, 1990; screenwriter, dir.: The Looking Glass Wars, 1970, A Star is Born, 1976, King ofthe Gypsies, 1978; dir.: (television) The Neon Ceiling, 1972 (San Francisco Film Festival award 1972), Alfred Hitchcock Presents, 1985, Somebody Has to Shoot the Picture, HBO, 1990 (Cable ACE award for best direction 1990), Citizen Cohn, HBO, 1992 (Cable ACE award for best direction 1992, Emmy award nomination for direction 1993); dir., prodr.: (television series) Have Gun Will Travel, 1960-62. Served with U.S. Army, 1943-46. Mem. Writers Guild Am. West (v.p. 1980-81, pres. 1981-83), Humanities Found. (pres. 1994).

PIERSON, JOHN HERMAN GROESBECK, economist, writer; b. N.Y.C., Mar. 28, 1906; s. Charles Wheeler and Elizabeth Granville (Groesbeck) P.; m. Gertrude Trumbull Robinson, 1930 (div. 1942); children: Elizabeth P. Friend, John Trumbull Robinson Pierson; m. Sherleigh Elizabeth Glad, June 16, 1948 (dec. 1991); m. Harriet-Anne Duell, Feb. 22, 1992. BA, Yale Coll., 1927, PhD in Econ., 1938. Tchr. St. Bernard's Sch., N.Y.C., 1928-29; spl. asst. to v.p. Consol. Gas Co. of N.Y., N.Y.C., 1929-33; instr. econ. Yale Coll., New Haven, 1933-38, Sterling rsch. fellow, 1938-39; assoc. dir. Inst. for Applied Social Analysis, N.Y.C., 1939-41; asst. chief, then chief of Postwar Labor Problems div. Bur. Labor Statistics, Washington, 1941-45, adviser to acting commr., 1945-46; econ. adviser, spl. asst. to asst. and Under Sec. of Labor Washington, 1946-48; econ. adviser to asst. to adminstr. Econ. Cooperation Adminstrn., Washington, 1949-50; econ. adviser, policy adviser Asia/Far East Aid in Econ. Cooperation Adminstrn. and Mutual Security Agy., 1950-53; founder, pres. Voices to Am., Inc., N.Y.C., 1953-54; dir. rsch., planning div. U.N. Econ. Commn. for Asia and the Far East, Bangkok, 1955-59; spl. cons. Bur. Social Affairs U.N., N.Y.C., 1959-61, spl. adviser to Under-Sec. for Econ. and Social Affairs, 1961-66, sec. adv. com. on application of sci. & tech. to devel., 1964-66; free-lance writer, 1966—; chmn. U.S. Govt. interdepartmental com. on full employment and econ. fgn. policy, 1944-46; U.S. del. 3 internat. confs. to draft "Havana Charter", 1946-48; adviser various other internat. meetings; active Nat. Environ. Leadership Coun., 1990-91. Author: (poems) The Circling Beast, 1941, (books) Full Employment, 1941, Full Employment and Free Enterprise, 1947, Insuring Full Employment: A United States Policy for Domestic Prosperity and World Development, 1964, Essays on Full Employment, 1942-72, Island in Greece, 1973, Hubert Benoit's Reasoned Formulation of Zen, 1975, Full Employment Without Inflation: Papers on the Economic Performance Insurance Proposal, 1980, Full Employment: Why We Need It; How to Guarantee It; One Man's Journey, 1996; co-author: Guaranteed Full Employment: A Proposal for Achieving Continuous Work Opportunity for All, Without Inflation, through "Economic Performance Insurance", 1985; contbr. numerous articles to profl. jours. Mem. Am. Econ. Assn., Athens Soc. of the Friends of the Trees, Century Assn., Phi Beta Kappa. Home: 235 Walker St Lenox MA 01240-2762

PIERSON, JOHN THEODORE, JR., manufacturer; b. Kansas City, Mo., Oct. 13, 1931; s. John Theodore and Helen Marguerite (Sherman) P.; m. Susan K. Chadwick, Apr. 16, 1977; children by previous marriage—Merrill Sherman Pierson, Karen Louise, Kimberly Ann. B.S.E., Princeton U., 1953; M.B.A., Harvard U., 1958. With Vendo Co., Kansas City, Mo., 1960—, gen. automatic products salesman, 1960-61, mgr. new products, 1961-63; v.p. sales equipment for Coca-Cola, 1963-66; pres. Vendo Internat., 1966-69, exec. v.p., chief operating officer, 1969-71, pres., chief exec. officer, 1971-74; pres. Preco Industries, Inc., 1976-95; chmn. Internat. Trade and Exhbn. Ctr. Co-author: Linear Polyethylene and Polypropylene: Problems and Opportunities, 1958. Trustee Midwest Rsch. Inst.; bd. dirs. and chmn. MidAm. Mfg. Tech. Ctr.; bd. dirs. Johnson County Bus. Tech. Ctr., Youth Symphony Kansas City, 1965-69; past trustee Pembroke-Country Day Sch., Barstow Sch.; past mem. adv. coun. U.S.-Japan Econ. Rels. Coun.; mem. coun. chmn. for exploring Boy Scouts Am., mem. Nat. coun. Lt. M.I. USNR, 1953-56. Mem. Kansas City C. of C. (v.p. interna.), U.S. C. of C. (dir. 1970-74), River Club (pres. 1994-96), Kansas City Country Club. Home: 2801 W 63rd St Shawnee Mission KS 66208-1866 Office: 9501 Dice Ln Shawnee Mission KS 66215-1158

PIERSON, RICHARD ALLEN, hospital administrator; b. Emporia, Kans., Dec. 17, 1944; s. Lea Ross and Irene (Loren) P.; m. LuJean Hiatt, June 24, 1967; children: Lindsey, Alyssa, Jedd, Amanda, Adam, Aaron, Spencer. BS, Kans. State Tchrs. Coll., 1966; MBA, U. Utah, 1971; MHA, U. Minn., 1974. Adminstrv. resident U. Minn. Hosp., Mpls., 1973-74, asst. dir., 1974-77, assoc. dir., 1977-81; hosp. dir. Univ. Hosp. Ark., Little Rock, 1981-86, exec. dir., 1986—; bd. dirs. Univ. Hosp. Consortium, Chgo. Vice chmn., mem. Ark. Kidney Disease Commn., Little Rock, 1982-92, chmn., 1992-95. Capt. USAF, 1966-70. Mem. Am. Hosp. Assn. (governing coun. met. hosps. sect. 1988-90), Am. Coll. Healthcare Execs. (nominee). Mem. LDS Ch. Office: U Hosp Ark 4301 W Markham St Little Rock AR 72205-7101

PIERSON, RICHARD NORRIS, JR., medical educator; b. N.Y.C., Sept. 22, 1929; s. Richard Norris and Dorothy (Stewart) P.; m. Alice Roberts, Aug. 26, 1974; children by previous marriage: Richard N., Olivia Tiffany, Alexandra de Forest, Cordelia S.C.; stepchildren: Alice W. Dunn, Eric C.W. Dunn. BA, Princeton U., 1951; MD, Columbia U., 1955. Diplomate Am. Bd. Internal Medicine, Am. Bd. Nuclear Medicine. Resident St. Luke's Roosevelt Hosp., N.Y.C., 1955-61, assoc. dir., 1961-65, dir. div. nuclear medicine, 1965-89, dir. body composition unit, 1965—, attending physician, 1975—; prof. clin. medicine Columbia U., 1980—; dir. medicine Hackensack Hosp., 1973-74; staff assoc. Brookhaven Nat. Lab., 1970—; research scholar Lawrence Radiation Lab., Berkeley, Calif., 1970-71, bioengring. inst. Columbia U., 1976—, chmn., 1989—. Editor: Quantitative Radiocardiography, 1975. Contbr. articles to profl. jours. Bd. dirs. Englewood Health Dept., N.J., 1966-74; warden St. Paul's Ch., 1980-82, bd. dirs. Empire Blue Cross/Blue Shield, N.Y., 1978-91, v.p., 1990-91. Lt. USNR, 1956-58. NIH grantee, 1973-76, 86—; John A. Hartford Found. grantee, 1967-70. Fellow N.Y. Acad. Medicine, ACP; mem. N.Y. County Med. Soc. (pres. 1978-79), N.Y. County Health Svc. Rev. Orgn. (chmn. 1980-82), Am. Bur. Med. Advancement in China (pres. 1979-87), Am. Med. Rev. Rsch. Ctr. (pres. 1985-89, N.Y. State del. to AMA 1978-90), Alliance for Continuing Med. Edn. (pres. 1985-89), Soc. Nuclear Medicine (greater N.Y. area pres. 1982-83, trustee 1991—, del. to AMA 1991-95), P&S Alumni Assn. (pres. 1989-91), Century Club, Englewood Field Club. Home: 60 Lincoln St Englewood NJ 07631-3117 Office: St Lukes Roosevelt Hosp Ctr 1111 Amsterdam Ave New York NY 10025-1716

PIERSON, ROBERT DAVID, banker; b. Orange, N.J., Mar. 5, 1935; s. Carleton Wellington and Muriel Browning (Potter) P.; BA, Lehigh U., 1957; m. Virginia Duncan Knight, Apr. 30, 1960; children: Lisa Boles, Alexandra Mead, Robert Wellington. Exec. asst. 1st Nat. City Bank N.Y., N.Y.C., 1958-61; asst. to pres. Cooper Labs. Inc., N.Y.C., 1961-65; dir. mktg. svcs. Arbrook div. Johnson & Johnson, Somerville, N.J., 1965-69; v.p. Klemtner Advt. Inc., N.Y.C., 1969-71; sr. v.p. Bowery Savs. Bank, N.Y.C., 1972-80; vice chmn., dir. Carteret Bancorp, Inc. Wilmington, Del., 1980-90 , Carteret Savs. Bank, F.A., Morristown, N.J., 1980-90; pres. Collective Fin. Svcs., Inc., Harbor Mortgage Co., (divsns. of Collective Bank, Montclair, N.J.), 1990—. Mayor Township of Mendham, N.J., 1995—. With USCG, 1958-59. Republican. Presbyterian. Clubs: Morris County Golf, Morristown. Home: Green Hills Rd Mendham NJ 07945-3305 Office: Collective Bank 560 Valley Rd Montclair NJ 07042

PIERSON, WILLIAM ROY, chemist; b. Charleston, W.Va., Oct. 21, 1930; s. Roy H. Pierson and Gay Harris; m. Juliet T. Strong, May 20, 1961; children: Elizabeth T., Anne H. Veis. BSE, Princeton U., 1952; PhD, MIT, 1959. Rsch. assoc. Enrico Fermi Inst. for Nuclear Studies U. Chgo., 1959-62; rsch. scientist Ford Motor Co., Dearborn, Mich., 1962-87; exec dir. Energy and Environ. Engring. Ctr. Desert Rsch. Inst., Reno, 1987-95, rsch. prof., 1996—. Contbr. over 100 articles to profl. jours. Bd. dirs Reno Chamber Orch., 1992-92. Lt. USN, 1952-55. Fellow Air and Waste Mgmt. Assn.; mem. AAAS, Am. Phys. Soc., Am. Chem. Soc., Am. Assn. for Aerosol Rsch. (bd. dirs. 1982-85). Office: Desert Rsch Inst 5625 Fox Ave PO Box 60220 Reno NV 89506

PIETAK, RAYMOND ADAM, academic administrator; b. North Tonawanda, N.Y., June 3, 1933; s. Adam Stanley and Josephine Mary (Piwowarczyk) P.; m. Marie Alice Dettmer, Dec. 26, 1959; children: Lynn Marie, Raymond Jr., Scott Dettmer. AB, Niagara U., 1955; EdM, U. Buffalo, 1958; EdD, SUNY, Buffalo, 1966; PhD (hon.), Lewis U. Tchr. history Starpoint Cen. Sch., Pendleton, N.Y., 1958-60; dir. admissions Niagara County C.C., Niagara Falls, N.Y., 1963-65; assoc. dean, then dean Forest Park C.C., St. Louis, 1965-68; pres. Southwestern Mich. Coll., Dowagiac, 1968-69; provost C.C. Phila., 1969-85; pres. Joliet (Ill.) Jr. Coll., 1985-95, pres. emeritus, 1995—; bd. dirs. COMBASE; chmn. Mid. States Assn. Commn. Higher Edn. Accrediting Teams; cons. to community colls. Contbr. articles to ednl. publs. Bd. dirs. Joliet/Will County Coun. Econ. devel., 1986-90; adv. bd. St. Joseph's Hosp., Joliet, 1987-90. 1st lt. U.S. Army, 1955-57. Mem. Am. Assn. Higher Edn., Am. Assn. Community and Jr. Colls., Am. Coun. Edn., Nat. Coun. Occupational Edn. (past pres.), Ill. Coun. Pub. C.C. Pres. (past pres.), Rotary Internat., Joliet Region C. of C. (bd. dirs. 1988-94), Phi Delta Kappa. Home: 2033 Woodland Rd Abington PA 19001

PIETERS, C.M., geology educator, astrophysicist, researcher; b. Ft. Sill, Okla., Nov. 11, 1943; widower. BA, Antioch Coll., 1966; BS, MIT, 1971, MS, 1972, PhD, 1977. Tchr. math. Somerville (Mass.) H.S., 1966-67; tchr. sci. Peace Corps, Sarawak, Malaysia, 1967-69; staff scientist rschr. Planetary Astron. Lab. MIT, 1972-75; space scientist Johnson Space Ctr. NASA, 1977-80; asst. prof. Brown U., Providence, R.I., 1980-83, assoc. prof. geology, 1983—. Asteroid named in honor, Pieters. Mem. AAAS, Am. Geophys. Union, Am. Astron. Soc., Meteoritical Soc. Office: Dept Geol Sci Brown University Providence RI 02912*

PIETRA, GIUSEPPE GIOVANNI, pathology educator; b. Piacenza, Italy, Dec. 30, 1930; came to U.S., 1957; s. Angelo and Emilia (Veratti) P.; m. Kathy Leuzinger, Nov. 23, 1957; children: Peter A., Philipp J. MD, U. Milan, 1955; BA (hon.), U. Pa., 1976. Diplomate Am. Bd. Pathology. Oncology fellow Chgo. Med. Sch., 1957-60; resident pathology Mass. Gen. Hosp., Boston, 1962-63; prosector pathology U. Zurich, Switzerlaand, 1963-64; asst. prof. pathology Chgo. Med. Sch., 1965-66, U. Ill., Chgo., 1966-69; asst. prof. pathology U. Pa., Phila., 1969-72, assoc. prof., 1972-76, prof., 1976-96, prof. emeritus, 1996—; staff pathologist U. Pa. Hosp., 1969-76, dir. med. pathology, 1976-82, dir. anatomic pathology, 1982-94. Lt. M.C., Italian Army, 1955-57. Fellow ACP; mem. Internat. Acad. Pathology, Microscopy Soc. Am. Office: U Pa Sch Medicine HUP 34th and Spruce Sts Philadelphia PA 19104-1999

PIETRINI, ANDREW GABRIEL, automotive aftermarket executive; b. Bryn Mawr, Pa., Feb. 27, 1937; s. Bernard and Irene (Norcini) P.; m. Pam Mari, Sept. 29, 1962; children: Darrin, Wayne. B.S., Villanova U., 1958. C.P.A., Pa. Jr. acct. Fernald & Co., Phila., 1958-60; sr. acct. O & W Audit Co., Narberth, Pa., 1960-62; asst. sec. James Talcott, Inc., N.Y.C., 1962-68; pres. UIS, Inc., N.Y.C., 1968—, dir., 1972—, now dir., chief oper. officer, chmn bd. dirs. Bd. dirs. Lebensfeld Found., N.Y.C., 1979—. Mem. Am. Inst. C.P.A.s, Fin. Execs. Inst. Republican. Roman Catholic. Avocations: sailing; golf. Office: UIS Inc 15 Exchange Place Ste 1120 Jersey City NJ 07302-2302*

PIETROWSKI, ROBERT FRANK, JR., lawyer; b. Pasadena, Calif., Feb. 7, 1945; s. Robert Frank Sr. and Annabelle (Johnson) P.; m. Barbara Holly Himel, June 25, 1966; children: Robert Frank III, Michael Scott. BS in Petroleum Engring., Stanford U., 1970; JD, U. Va., 1973. Bar: D.C. 1974, U.S. Supreme Ct. 1978. Assoc. Law Offices of Northcutt Ely, Washington, 1973-77, ptnr., 1977-84; ptnr. Bracewell & Patterson, Washington, 1984-89, Bryan, Cave, Washington and London, 1989-94, Coudert Bros., Washington and London, 1994—; mem. U.S. panel of arbitrators Internat. Ctr. for Settlement of Investment Disputes, 1988-94; chief counsel to Govt. Rep. of Guinea in Guinea-Bissau case, The Hague, 1984-85; arbitrator Pyramids Oasis case, 1984; legal advisor Ministry of Oil and Mineral Resources, Republic of Yemen, 1988—. Contbr. articles to profl. jours. Served to 1st lt. U.S. Army, 1966-69. Fellow Am. Bar Found.; mem. ABA, Am. Soc. Internat. Law, Internat. Bar Assn., Internat. Law Assn., Comml. Bar of U.K. (hon. overseas mem.), Assn. Internat. Petroleum Negotiators, Union Internationale Des Avocats, Sigma Chi. Republican. Episcopalian. Clubs: Metropolitan, Cosmos (Washington); Farmington Country (Charlottesville, Va.); Guards Polo (Windsor, Eng.). Office: Coudert Brothers 1627 I St NW Ste 1200 Washington DC 20006-4007

PIETRUSKA, STANLEY ROBERT, lawyer, jury consultant; b. Bayonne, N.J., Dec. 11, 1963; s. Stanley Thomas and Maureen Margaret (Warren) P.; m. Tracey Anne Connors, May 16, 1993. BA, Jersey City State Coll., 1985; JD, Okla. State U., 1993. Bar: N.J. 1994, U.S. Dist. Ct. N.J. 1994, U.S. Ct. Appeals (3d cir.) 1994. Law clk. Legal Aid We. Okla., Oklahoma City, 1992-93, Okla. Indian Legal Svcs., Oklahoma City, 1993-94; sole practice law Jersey City, 1994—; Law Office of Anthony Bufano, 1995—; price guide analyst Sports Collectors Digest, Iola, Wis., 1990—. Co-author: Legal Aid of Western Oklahoma Guide to Garnishments, 1993; columnist Collectors Sportslook, 1993-94, Baseball Card News, 1991-92, Sports Card Price Guide, 1992-93; contbr. articles to profl. jours. Fundraiser, organizer Okla. Children's Hosp., Oklahoma City, 1992, 93. Recognized as one of Top 50 Most Influential People in Sports Memorabilia, Autograph News, 1992. Mem. ABA, ATLA, Phi Alpha Delta. Avocations: ice hockey, travel, golf, sports memorabilia, writing. Office: 580 Newark Ave Jersey City NJ 07306

PIETRUSKI, JOHN MICHAEL, JR., biotechnology company executive, pharmaceuticals executive; b. Sayreville, N.J., Mar. 12, 1933; m. Roberta Jeanne Talbot, July 3, 1954; children: Glenn David, Clifford John, Susan Jane. BS with honors, Rutgers U., 1954; LLD (hon.), Concordia Coll., 1993. With Proctor and Gamble Co., 1954-63; pres. med. products div. C.R. Bard, Inc., 1963-77; with Sterling Drug, Inc., N.Y.C., 1977-88; pres. Pharm. Group, 1977-81, corp. exec. v.p., 1981-83, pres., chief operating officer, 1983-85, chmn., chief exec. officer, 1985-88, ret., 1988; pres. Dansara Cons., 1988—; chmn. Tex. Biotech. Corp., 1990—; bd. dirs. Hershey Foods Corp., Gen. Pub. Utilities Corp., Lincoln Nat. Corp., McKesson Corp. Regent Concordia Coll. 1st lt. U.S. Army, 1955-57. Mem. Phi Beta Kappa. Club: Union League (N.Y.C.). Home: 27 Paddock Ln Colts Neck NJ 07722-1266 Office: One Penn Plaza Ste 3408 New York NY 10119

PIETRZAK, ALFRED ROBERT, lawyer; b. Glen Cove, N.Y., June 26, 1949; s. Alfred S. and Wanda M. (Wapniarski) P.; m. Sharon Esther Chizek, July 9, 1978; children: Eric A., Daniel J. BA, Fordham U., 1971; JD, Columbia U., 1974. Bar: N.Y. 1975, U.S. Dist. Ct. (so., ea., we. and no. dists.) N.Y. 1975, U.S. Dist. Ct. (no. dist.) Calif. 1983, U.S. Ct. Appeals (2d cir.) 1975, U.S. Ct. Appeals (9th cir.) 1983, U.S. Ct. Appeals (11th cir.) 1985, U.S. Supreme Ct. 1985. Assoc. Brown & Wood (formerly Brown, Wood, Ivey, Mitchell & Petty), N.Y.C., 1974-82, ptnr., 1983—, mem. policy com.; mem. fin. products adv. com. Commodity Futures Trading Commn.; mem. C.L.E. faculty Fordham U. Sch. Law.; Bd. editors Futures Internat. Law Letter; adv. bd. Fordham Internat. Law Jour.; contbr. articles to legal jours. Mem. ABA (litigation, bus law sect.), Assn. of Bar of City of N.Y. (securities regulation com., chair futures regulation com.), Am. Law Inst. (lectr.), Securities Industry Assn., Futures Industry Assn., Univ. Glee Club. Democrat. Roman Catholic. Home: 525 Monterey Ave Pelham NY 10803 Office: Brown & Wood 1 World Trade Ctr Fl 58 New York NY 10048-5899

PIETRZAK, LEONARD WALTER, accountant; b. Phila., Dec. 6, 1939; s. Walter Chester and Estelle Anne (Libucha) P.; m. Patricia Ann Cole, June 17, 1961; children: Stephen L., Diana L., Jeffrey S., Kristen M. BS, St. Joseph's U., Phila., 1961. Commd. officer USAF, Washington, 1961-64; audit mgr. Ernst & Young, Phila., 1964-77; corp. contr. Kleinert's Inc., Plymouth Meeting, Pa., 1977-81; v.p. fin. Jetronic Industries, Inc., Phila., 1981—; pres. NAA, So. Jersey, 1975-76. Mem. AICPA, Pa. Inst. CPA. Home: 60 Surrey Dr Southampton PA 18966-1224

PIETRZAK, TED S., art gallery director; b. Kitchener, Ont., Can., Sept. 18, 1952; m. Marlene C. Longdon, Aug. 25, 1990; 1 child, Christina. BA in Arts Mgmt., U. Guelph, Banff, Alta., Can.; attended, Mus. Mgmt. Inst., Berkeley, Calif. Asst. to dir. Art Gallery Hamilton, Ont., 1976-80; dir. Burlington Cultural Ctr., 1980-91, Art Gallery Hamilton, 1992—. Mem. Ont. Assn. Art Galleries (pres. 1983-84), Can. Art Mus. Dirs. Orgn. (chair govt. and arts com., treas. 1991-95). Office: Art Gallery of Hamilton, 123 King St W, Hamilton, ON Canada L8P 4S8

PIFER, ALAN (JAY PARRISH), former foundation executive; b. Boston, May 4, 1921; s. Claude Albert and Elizabeth (Parrish) P.; m. Erica Pringle, June 20, 1953 (div. 1994); children: Matthew, Nicholas, Daniel. AB, Harvard U., 1947; Lionel de Jersey Harvard student Emmanuel Coll., Cambridge (Eng.) U., 1947-48; LLD (hon.), Mich. State U., 1971, Hofstra U., 1974, Notre Dame U., 1975; DHL (hon.), Marymount Coll., 1983, Millsaps Coll., 1986; D of Univ. (hon.), Open U., Eng., 1974; JD (hon.), Atlanta U., 1980; DEd (hon.), U. Cape Town, South Africa, 1984. Exec. sec. U.S. Ednl. Commn. in U.K., London, 1948-53; program officer Carnegie Corp. N.Y., 1953-63, v.p., 1963-65, acting pres., 1965-67, pres., 1967-82, pres. emeritus, sr. cons., 1982-87; chmn., pres. Southport Inst. for Policy Analysis, 1987-91, chmn., 1991-94; v.p. Carnegie Found. for Advancement of Teaching, 1963-65, acting pres., 1965-67, pres., 1967-79, trustee, 1979-87; bd. dirs. Technoserve, Inc. Author: (with others) Our Aging Society, 1986, (with others) Women on the Front Lines: Meeting the Challenge of an Aging America, 1993; Government for the People, 1987. Mem. mgmt. com. U.S.-South Africa Leader Exch. Program, 1957—, pub. policy com. Advt. Coun., 1987-91, adv. coun. Columbia U. Sch. Social Work, 1963-69, R & D ctr. panel U.S. Office Edn., 1963-65, adv. com. higher edn. U.S. Dept. Health Edn. and Welfare, 1967-68, bd. of overseers Harvard U., 1969-75, Charles Stark Draper Lab. bd. MIT, 1970-76, Commn. Pvt. Philanthropy and Pub. Needs, 1973-75; chmn. Consortium Advancement Pvt. Higher Edn., 1983-92, mayor's adv. com. Bd. Higher Edn. N.Y.C., 1966-69, Pres.'s Task Force on Edn., 1968, Aging Soc. Project, 1982-87, Nat. Conf. on Social Welfare Project, 1983-87; co-chmn. N.Y. State Nutrition Watch com., 1982; trustee U. Bridgeport, Conn., 1973—, Assn. Governing Bds. Colls. and Univs., 1985-91, African Am. Inst., 1957-71, Found. Libr. Ctr., 1967-71, Am. Ditchley Found., 1973-81; bd. dirs. Bus. Coun. Effective Literacy Inc., 1984-93, N.Y. Urban Coalition, 1967-71, Nat. Assembly for Social Policy and Devel., 1967-71, Coun. on Founds., Inc., 1970-76, Fed. Reserve Bank N.Y., 1970-76, Harry Frank Guggenheim Found., 1989—. Capt. U.S. Army, 1942-46, ETO. Recipient Barnard Coll. medal of distinction, 1980, Cleveland E. Dodge medal of distinction Tchrs. Coll., Columbia U., 1982. Fellow Am. Acad. of Arts and Scis., African Studies Assn. (founding), Royal Soc. Arts (London); mem. Am. Assn. for Higher Edn. (bd. dirs. 1982-90), Council Fgn. Relations, Century Assn. Democrat. Episcopalian. Clubs: Harvard (N.Y.C.). Avocation: gardening.

PIGA, STEPHEN MULRY, lawyer; b. Bklyn., Apr. 9, 1929; s. Stephen Paul and Ella (Mulry) P.; married, Feb. 23, 1952 (div.); children: Maureen, Stephen, Susan, Elizabeth; m. Emilie Halliday, Aug. 1, 1975; 1 dau., Margaret. A.B., Princeton U., 1950; LL.B., Columbia U., 1955. Bar: N.J. 1955, N.Y. 1956. Assoc. White & Case, N.Y.C., 1955-63, ptnr., 1964-92; ret., 1992; lectr. Practicing Law Inst. N.Y. and various insts., bar assns. Served to capt. USMCR, 1951-53. Mem. ABA, N.Y. State Bar Assn. (exec. com. tax sect. 1981-89, chmn. employee benefits com.), Assn. of Bar of City N.Y., N.J. Bar Assn., Am. Contract Bridge League (life master), Profl. Bowlers' Assn. Am. Republican. Clubs: High Mt. Golf (Franklin Lakes, N.J.), Princeton (N.Y.C.). Avocations: fishing, golf, bowling.

PIGFORD, THOMAS HARRINGTON, nuclear engineering educator; b. Meridian, Miss., Apr. 21, 1922; s. Lamar and Zula Vivian (Harrington) P.; m. Catherine Kennedy Cathey, Dec. 31, 1948 (dec. 1992); children: Cynthia Pigford Naylor, Julie Pigford Brink; m. Elizabeth Hood Weekes, Nov. 12, 1994. B.S. in Chem. Engring., Ga. Inst. Tech., 1943; S.M. in Chem. Engring., M.I.T., 1948, Sc.D. in Chem. Engring., 1952. Asst. prof. chem. engring., dir. Sch. Engring. Practice, M.I.T., 1950-52, asst. prof. nuclear and chem. engring., 1952-55, assoc. prof., 1955-57; head engring., dir. nuclear reactor projects and asst. dir. research lab. Gen. Atomic Co., La Jolla, Calif., 1957-59; prof. nuclear engring., chmn. dept. nuclear engring. U. Calif., Berkeley, 1959—; sr. rsch. scientist Lawrence Berkeley Lab., 1959—; mem. panel Nat. Atomic Safety Licensing Bd. AEC-Nuclear Regulatory Commn., 1963-77; mem. Pres.'s Commn. on accident at 3-Mile Island, 1979; mem. bd. radioactive waste mgmt. and energy engring. bd., NAS-NAE, chmn. waste isolation systems panel, waste isolation pilot plant panel, fusion hybrid panel, separations and transmutations panel, transmutation of military plutonium panel, panel on health standard for radioactive waste disposal, chmn. adv. coun. Inst. Nuclear Power Op.; mem. Sec. of Energy's expert cons. group on Chernobyl accident; chmn. nuclear oversight com. Sacramento Mcpl. Utility Dist.; chmn. nuclear safety com. Gulf States Utilities Co.; mem. expert cons. group Swedish Nuclear Power Inspectorate; mem. peer rev. group for waste isolation pilot plant; mem. corp. rev. com. Oak Ridge Nat. Lab.; lectr. Taiwan Nat. Sci. Found., 1990; vis. prof. Kyoto U., 1975, Kuwait U., 1976; cons. in field. Author: (with Manson Benedict) Nuclear Chemical Engineering, 1958, 2d edit., 1981; contbr. numerous articles to profl. jours. Served with USNR, 1944-46. Recipient John Wesley Powell award U.S. Geol. Survey, 1981; named Outstanding Young Man of Greater Boston, Boston Jaycees, 1955; E. I. DuPont DeNemours rsch. fellow, 1948-50; Berkeley citation U. Calif., 1987; Japan Soc. for Promotion Sci. fellow, 1974-75; grantee NSF, 1960-75, EPA, 1973-78, Dept. Energy, 1979—, Ford Found., 1974-75, Electric Power Rsch. Inst., 1974-75, Mitsubishi Metals Corp., 1989—; named to Ga. Hall of Fame, 1995. Fellow Am. Nuclear Soc. (bd. dirs., Arthur H. Compton award 1971); mem. AIME, NAE, Am. Chem. Soc., Am. Inst. Chem. Engrs. (Robert E. Wilson award 1980, Service to Society award 1985), Atomic Indsl. Forum (dir.), Sigma Xi, Phi Kappa Phi, Tau Beta Pi. Patentee in field. Home: 166 Alpine Ter Oakland CA 94618-1823 Office: U Calif Dept Nuclear Engring Berkeley CA 94720

PIGGFORD, ROLAND RAYBURN, library and information services consultant; b. Monongahela, Pa., Jan. 28, 1926; s. Roland Rayburn and Emily Frances (Sanders) P.; m. Carole Meanor, Aug. 10, 1965; children—Eric, Susan. B.A., W.Va. Wesleyan Coll., Buckhannon, 1948; M.L.S., U. Pitts, 1964. Research assoc. Internat. Studies U. Pitts, 1964-66; librarian Internat. Studies Documentation Ctr., Oyster Bay, N.Y., 1966-67; asst. prof. SUNY, Albany, 1967-73; head planning and research Mass. Bd. Library Commrs., Boston, 1974-80, dir., 1980-91; cons. libr. and info. svcs., 1991—; cons. AID, Washington, 1967-70; bd. dirs. N.E. Document Conservation Ctr., Andover, Mass. 1980-89. Co-author: Book and Library Activities in Developing Countries, 1971; contbr. articles to profl. jours. Served to ensign USN, 1943-46; ETO. Mem. ALA, Mass. Libr. Assn. Home: 180 Oak St Shrewsbury MA 01545-5810

PIGNATARO, LOUIS JAMES, engineering educator; b. Bklyn., Nov. 30, 1923; s. Joseph and Rose (Capi) P.; m. Edith Hoffmann, Sept. 12, 1954; 1 child, Thea. B.C.E., Poly. Inst. Bklyn., 1951; M.S., Columbia U., 1954; Dr. Tech. Sci., Tech. U. Graz, Austria, 1961. Registered profl. engr., N.Y., Calif., Fla. Faculty Poly. Inst. N.Y., 1951-85, prof. civil engring., 1965—, dir. div. transp. planning, 1967—, head dept. transp. planning and engring., 1970, dir. Transp. Tng. and Research Center, 1975; Kayser prof. transp. engring. CCNY, N.Y.C., 1985-88; assoc. dir. Inst. for Transp. CCNY, 1985-88; mem. faculty N.J. Inst. Tech., 1988—, disting. prof. transp. engring., 1988—, dir. ctr. transp. studies and research, 1988-93; exec. dir. Inst. for Transp., 1994—; cons. govtl. agys., pvt. firms. Mem. Gov.'s Task Force Advisers on Transp. Problems, Gov.'s Task Force on Alcohol and Hwy. Safety; commr.'s council advisers N.Y. State Dept. Transp.; mem. adv. bd.

freight services improvement conf. Port Authority N.Y. and N.J.; mem. adv. com. N.Y.C. Dept. Transp.; mem. rev. com. N.Y.C. Dept. City Planning; mem. Mayor's Transp. Commn., City of Newark. Sr. author: Traffic Engineering-Theory and Practice, 1973; contbr. over 70 papers to profl. jours. Served with AUS, 1943-46. Recipient Distinguished Tchr. citation Poly. Inst. Bklyn., 1965, Dedicated Alumnus award, 1971, Distinguished Alumnus award, 1972; citation for distinguished research Poly. chpt. Sigma Xi, 1975; named Engr. of Year N.Y. State Soc. Profl. Engrs., 1974. Fellow ASCE (dir.), Inst. Transp. Engrs. (Transp. Engr. of Yr. Met. sect. N.Y. and N.J. 1982); mem. Am. Rd. and Transp. Builders Assn. (div. dir.), Transp. Research Bd. (univ. liaison rep., Outstanding Paper award 1980 ann. meeting), Transp. Research Forum, Nat. Soc. Profl. Engrs., Sigma Xi, Chi Epsilon, Tau Beta Pi. Home: 230 Jay St Brooklyn NY 11201-1948 Office: NJ Inst Tech Inst for Transp 323 Martin Luther King Jr Blvd Newark NJ 07102-1824

PIGNATELLI, DEBORA BECKER, state legislator; b. Weehawken, N.J., Oct. 25, 1947; d. Edward and Frances (Fishman) Becker; m. Michael Albert Pignatelli, Aug. 22, 1971; children: Adam Becker, Benjamin Becker. AA, Vt. Coll., 1967; BA, U. Denver, 1969. Exec. dir. Girl's Club Greater Nashua, N.H., 1975-77; dir. tenant svcs. Nashua Housing Authority, 1979-80; vocat. counselor Comprehensive Rehab. Assocs., Bedford, N.H., 1982-85; specialist job placement Crawford & Co., Bedford, 1985-87; mem. appropriations com. N.H. Ho. of Reps., Concord, 1986-91, asst. minority leader, 1989-92; mem. N.H. State Senate, 1992—; Senate Dem. Whip; mem. environ., vice chmn., econ. devel., judiciary coms., fish and game com., interstate coop. com.; del. Am. Coun. Young Polit. Leaders, Germany, 1987. Mem. Nashua Peace Ctr., 1980—; asst. coach Little League Baseball, Nashua, 1987-90; mem. steering com. Gephardt for Pres. Campaign, N.H., 1987-88; del. Dem. Nat. Conv., 1988; mem. Gov.'s Commn. on Domestic Violence. Mem. N.H. Children's Lobby, Women's Lobby. Jewish. Avocations: skiing, children, swimming, boating. Home: 22 Appletree Grn Nashua NH 03062-2252 Office: NH State Senate State House Rm 115 Concord NH 03301

PIGOTT, CHARLES MCGEE, transportation equipment manufacturing executive; b. Seattle, Apr. 21, 1929; s. Paul and Theiline (McGee) P.; m. Yvonne Flood, Apr. 18, 1953. B.S., Stanford U., 1951. With PACCAR Inc, Seattle, 1959—, exec. v.p., 1962-65, pres., 1965-86, chmn., pres., 1986-87, chmn., chief exec. officer, 1987—, also bd. dirs.; dir. The Seattle Times, Chevron Corp., The Boeing Co. Pres. Nat. Boy Scouts Am., 1986-88, mem. exec. bd. Mem. Bus. Council. Office: Paccar Inc 777 106th Ave NE Bellevue WA 98004-5001*

PIGOTT, GEORGE MORRIS, food engineering educator, consulting engineer; b. Vancouver, Wash., Oct. 25, 1928; s. Alexander William and Moreita (Howard) P.; m. Joyce Burroughs (div. 1980); children: George Jr., Roy K., Randall E., Julie M., Becky P.; m. Barbee W. Tucker. BS in Chem. Engring., U. Wash., 1950, MS in Chem. Engring., 1955, PhD in Food Sci. and Chemistry, 1962. Field engr. Continental Can Co., Seattle, 1951-53; rsch. engr. Fish and Wildlife Svc., Seattle, 1947-51, Nat. Canners Assn., Seattle, 1953-55, Boeing Corp., Seattle, 1957-60; cons. engr., 1960-62; prof. food engring. Inst. Food Sci. and Tech. U. Wash., Seattle, 1962—, dir. Inst. Food Sci. and Tech., 1990—; pres. Sea Resources Engring. Inc., Bellevue, Wash., 1965—; bd. dirs. various cos. Author: Pathway to a Healthy Heart, 1983, Fish and Shellfish in Human Nutrition, 1988, Seafood: The Effect of Technology on Nutrition, 1990; contbr. more than 200 tech. papers; patentee in field. Served to lt. U.S. Army, 1951-53. Mem. NSPE, Am. Inst. Chem. Engrs., Am. Inst. Nutrition, Am. Chem. Soc., Inst. Food Technologists, Am. Inst. Chemistry, Am. Dietetic Assn., Am. Soc. Agrl. Engrs. Avocations: skiing, fishing, boating, scuba diving. Office: U Wash Inst for Food Sci and Tech Box 355680/3707 Brooklyn NE Seattle WA 98105-6715 Address: 4525-105 NE Kirkland WA 98033

PIGOTT, IRINA VSEVOLODOVNA, educational administrator; b. Blagoveschensk, Russia, Dec. 4, 1917; came to U.S., 1939, naturalized, 1947; d. Vsevolod V. and Sophia (Reprev) Obolianinoff; m. Nicholas Prischepenko, Feb. 1945 (dec. Nov. 1964); children: George, Helen. Grad. YMCA Jr. Coll., Manchuria, 1937; BA, Mills Coll., 1942; cert. social work U. Calif.-Berkeley, 1944; MA in Early Childhood Edn., NYU, 1951. Dir.-owner Parsons Nursery, Flushing, N.Y., 1951-59; dir. Montessori Sch., N.Y.C., 1966-67; dir., tchr. Day Care Ctr., Harlem, 1967-68; dir.-owner East Manhattan Sch. for Bright and Gifted, N.Y.C., 1968—; dir.-founder The House for Bright and Gifted Children, Flushing, N.Y., 1988-93; organizer, pres., exec. dir. Non-Profl. Children's Performing Arts Guild, Inc., N.Y.C., 1961-65, 87—. Organizer Back Yard Theatre, Bayside, N.Y., 1959-61. Democrat. Greek Orthodox. Avocations: music, dance, theatre, art, sports. Home and Office: East Manhattan Sch 208-210 E 18th St New York NY 10003

PIGOTT, JOHN DOWLING, geologist, geophysicist, geochemist, educator, consultant; b. Gorman, Tex., Feb. 2, 1951; s. Edwin Albert and Emma Jane (Poe) P.; m. Kulwadee Lawwongngam, May 28, 1994. BA in Zoology, U. Tex., 1974, BS in Geology, 1974, MA in Geology, 1977; PhD in Geology, Northwestern U., 1981. Geologist Amoco Internat., Chgo., 1978-80; sr. petroleum geologist Amoco Internat., Houston, 1980-81; asst., then assoc. prof. U. Okla., Norman, 1981—; vis. prof. Mus. Natural History, Paris, 1988, Sun Yat Sen U., Kaohsiung, Taiwan, 1991; rsch. dir. 5 nation Red Sea-Gulf of Aden seismic stratigraphy and basis analysis industry consortium, 1992—; internat. energy cons., 1981—; instr. I.H.R.D.C., Boston, 1987-91, O.G.C.I., Tulsa, 1991—. Mem. editl. bd. Geotectonica et Metallogenin Jour., 1992—. Mem. Am. Assn. Petroleum Geologists, Soc. Exploration Geophysicists, Soc. Petroleum Engrs., Geol. Soc. Am., Indonesian Petroleum Assn., Sigma Xi. Roman Catholic; Buddhist. Achievements include discovering relationship between global CO2 and natural tectonic cycles on the scale of millions of years showing previous greenhouse times, during the Phanerozoic, processing first three-dimensional amplitude variation with offset seismic survey to quantify rocks, fluids, and pressures in rocks, processing and displaying first ground penetrating radar survey as a seismic section for ultrahigh resolution sequence stratigraphy, practical developing tectonic subsidence analysis as a tool for investigating the comparative anatomy of a sedimentary basins, their tectonic history, and evolving hydrocarbon potential, and constructed first paleo-heatflow maps for the Red Sea for the past 25 ma. Office: U Okla Sch Geology & Geophysics 100 E Boyd St Norman OK 73019-1000

PIGOTT, KAREN GRAY, community health nurse, geriatrics nurse; b. Utica, N.Y., May 15, 1956; d. Charles Philip and Pauline (Nelson) Gray; m. James H. Pigott, Apr. 30, 1977; children: William Charles, Christopher McCabe. Diploma, Albany Med. Ctr. Sch. Nursing, 1978; diploma nurse practitioner, SUNY, Syracuse, 1982. Cert. adult nurse practitioner. Staff nurse Albany (N.Y.) Med. Ctr., 1978-79, St. Elizabeth's Hosp., Utica, 1979-80; staff nurse RN Community Meml. Hosp., Hamilton, N.Y., 1980-81; nurse practitioner pvt. office, Waterville, N.Y., 1982-87, VA Med. Ctr., Gainesville, Fla., 1987-90; nurse practitioner pvt. office Balt., 1990—; cons. in field; preceptor for grad. students U. Fla., 1988-90, U. South Fla., 1989-90, U. Md., Johns Hopkins U. Vol. health care provider Salvation Army Homeless Clinic, Gainesville, 1989-90, Spl. Olympics Events, Gainesville, 1990. Mem. ANA, Fla. Nurses Assn. (Expert in Clin. Practice award 1990). Presbyterian. Home: 115 Wakely Ter Bel Air MD 21014-5439 Office: 301 St Paul Pl Baltimore MD 21202-2102

PIGOTT, RICHARD J., food company executive; b. Chgo., May 26, 1940; s. Charles Francis and Mary Barbara (Amberg) P.; m. Karen Victoria Nahigian, Aug. 22, 1964; children: Alicia, Christopher. B.B.A., U. Notre Dame, 1961; J.D., U. Wis., 1966. Law ptnr. Winston & Strawn, 1966-77; with Beatrice Foods Co., Chgo., 1977-88, sr. v.p., gen. counsel, 1977-80, exec. v.p., chief adminstrv. officer, 1981-88; merger and acquisition advisor, investor, atty., 1988—; bd. dirs. Rodman & Renshaw Capital Group, Inc., Chgo., Ameriwood Industries, Grand Rapids, Mich. Trustee Chgo. Symphony Orch., 1983—; mem. bus. adv. coun. U. Ill., Chgo., 1983—. 1st lt., U.S. Army, 1961-63. Home: 1038 Longvalley Rd Glenview IL 60025-3414 Office: Three First Nat Plz 70 W Dearborn St Ste 3100 Chicago IL 60602

PIGOZZI, RAYMOND ANTHONY, architect; b. Chgo., Feb. 29, 1928; s. Mario and Milena (Kervin) P.; m. Judith M. Hays, Feb. 12, 1955; children: Raymond J., Thomas M., Robert J., Ellen A., Andrew H. BS in Architecture, U. Ill., 1951. Registered architect, Ill., Iowa, Wis., Mich., Ind., N.C. Designer Ganster & Henninghausen, Waukegan, Ill., 1954-58; prin. designer O'Donnell Wicklund Pigozzi & Peterson Architects, Inc., Deerfield, Ill., 1958—; juror Coun. Ednl. Facility Planners Internat., Chgo., 1977-78, Am. Assn. Sch. Adminstrs., Washington, 1982-83, honor awards program Masonry Inst. Mich., 1987, Am. Sch. and Univ. Award Winning Ednl. Bldg., 1989, Metal Constrn. Assn. Merit awards, 1993; cons. Ednl. Facilities Lab., N.Y.C., 1972-75; Ednl. Environ. Exhbn. Jury, Ill. Assn. Sch. Bds., 1993. Prin. works include Fairview South Elem. Sch. Auditorium and Learning Ctr., Skokie, Ill. (Chgo. Chpt. AIA Disting. Bldg. award 1968), Onwentsia Country Club Tennis and Squash Facility, Lake Forest, Ill. (Chgo. Chpt. AIA Disting. bldg. award 1971), Berkeley Elem. Sch., Arlington Heights, Ill. (Am. Assn. Sch. Adminstrs. citation 1971), Field Elem. Sch. Remodeling, Chgo. (Coun. Ednl. Facility Planners Modernization award 1973), Von Humboldt Child-Parent Ctr. (Assn. Sch. Bus. Ofcls. award of Merit 1981, Met. Chgo. Masonry Coun. Honor award for excellence in masonry 1981), Robert Crown Community Ctr., Evanston, Ill., Loyola U. Humanities Bldg., 1983, Crystal Lake Village Hall, 1987, Frank C. Whiteley Sch. Hoffman Estates, Ill., 1989, Arthur Anderson & Co. Campus Ctr. Expansion, St. Charles, Ill., 1990 (Gold medal Excellence in Masonry Awards), Science Wing Niles H.S., Skokie, Il., 1993 (Disting. Bldg. award, Silver medal Execllence in Masonry AIA, 1994). mem. ednl. adv. com. Evanston Twp. High Sch., 1979-83; chmn. profl. svc. Evanston United Way, 1982; mem. state's fine arts rev. com. Northeastern Ill. U., 1987. Recipient Metal Construction Assn. Merit award, 1993, Ill. Assn. Sch. Bd. Award of Distinction, Homewood Floosmoor High Sch., 1993. Fellow AIA (mem. nat. com. on architecture for edn. 1980—, juror N.E. chpt. bldg. honor awards program 1989, Disting. Svc. award 1990, Disting. Svc. award Chgo. chpt. 1990); mem. Ill. Sch. Bus. Ofcls., Ill. Libr. Assn., Ill. Assn. Sch. Bus. Ednl. Environments (juror 1992), Coun. Ednl. Facility Planners (pres. Great Lakes region 1988-90), Landmarks Preservation Coun. Ill. Democrat. Roman Catholic. Home: 200 Lee St Evanston IL 60202-1450 Office: O'Donnell Wicklund Pigozzi and Peterson Architecs Inc 570 Lake Cook Rd Deerfield IL 60015-5612 also: 1 N Franklin St Chicago IL 60606-3421

PIHL, JAMES MELVIN, electrical engineer; b. Seattle, May 29, 1943; s. Melvin Charles and Carrie Josephine (Cummings) P.; divorced; 1 child, Christopher James. AASEE, Seattle, 1971; BSA, City Univ., Bellevue, Wash., 1996. 1st class operators lic., FCC; lic. in real estate sales. Journeyman machinist Svc. Exch. Corp., Seattle, 1964-67; design engr. P.M. Electronics, Seattle, 1970-73, Physio Control Corp., Redmond, Wash., 1973-79; project engr. SeaMed Corp., Redmond, 1979-83; sr. design engr. Internat. Submarine Tech., Redmond, 1983-85; engring. mgr. First Med. Devices, Bellevue, Wash., 1985-89; rsch. engr. Pentco Products, Bothell, Wash., 1989—. Inventor, patentee protection system for preventing defibrillation with incorrect or improperly connected electrodes, impedance measurement circuit. With U.S. Army., 1961-64. Mem. N.Y. Acad. Scis. Avocations: boating, target shooting, violin. Home: 14303 82nd Ave NE Bothell WA 98011-5016 Office: Pentco Products PO Box 403 Kenmore WA 98028-9999

PIHLAJA, MAXINE MURIEL MEAD, orchestra executive; b. Windom, Minn., July 19, 1935; d. Julian Wright and Mildred Eleanor (Ray) Mead; m. Donald Francis Pihlaja, Jan. 4, 1963; children: Geoffrey Blake, Kirsten Louise, Jocelyn Erika. BA, Hamline U., 1957; postgrad., Columbia U., 1957-58. Group worker Fedn. of Chs., L.A., 1956; case worker St. John's Guild Floating Hosp. Ship, N.Y.C., 1957-59; Y-Teen program dir. YWCA, Elizabeth, N.J., 1957-60, Boulder, Colo., 1964-65; spl. svcs. program and club dir. U.S. Army, Ingrandes and Nancy, France, 1960-62; music buyer, salesperson Guinn's Music, Billings, Mont., 1977-78, N.W. Music, Billings, 1978-79; office adminstr. Am. Luth. Ch., Billings, 1979-84; gen. mgr. Billings Symphony Orchestra, 1984—; substitute tchr. Community Day Care and Enrichment Ctr., Billings, 1971-76. Dir. Handbell choir 1st Presybn. Ch., Billings, 1972—, Am. Luth. Ch., 1981-84, 1st English Luth. Ch., 1982—; mem. Billings Symphony Chorale, 1965-91, Bellissimo!, 1983-93. Mem. Nat. Soc. Fund Raising Execs. (sec. Mont. 1988), Mont. Assn. Female Execs. (mem. membership com. 1994—), Am. Guild English Handbell Ringers (state chmn. 1988-89, treas. Area X bd. dirs. 1990-94, membership chmn. 1994—), Mont .Assn. Symphony Orchs. (treas. 1987-92, sec. 1995—). Lutheran. Office: Billings Symphony Orch Box 7055 401 N 31st St Ste 530 Billings MT 59103

PIIPPO, STEVE, educator. Dir. math. sci. tech. program Richland (Wash.) High Sch. Creator, author Materials Sci.Tech. Recipient A Sites Recognition award U.S. Dept. Edn. Office: Richland High Sch Math Sci Tech Program 930 Long Ave Richland WA 99352-3311

PIIRTO, DOUGLAS DONALD, forester, educator; b. Reno, Nev., Sept. 25, 1948; s. Rueben Arvid and Martha Hilma (Giebel) P.; BS, U. Nev., 1970; MS, Colo. State U., 1971; PhD, U. Calif., Berkeley, 1977; m. Mary Louise Cruz, Oct. 28, 1978. Rsch. asst. Colo. State U., 1970-71, U. Calif., Berkeley, 1972-77; forester, silviculturist U.S. Dept. Agr., Forest Svc., Sierra Nat. Forest, Trimmer and Shaver Lake, Calif., 1977-85; assoc. prof. natural resources mgmt. dept. Calif. Poly. State U., San Luis Obispo, 1985-90, prof. 1990—; researcher in field; instr. part-time Kings River Community Coll., Reedley, Calif.; forestry cons., expert witness. Registered profl. forester, Calif.; cert. silviculturist USDA Forest Svc. Recipient Meritorious Performance and Profl. Promise award CalPoly, 1989, CalPoly Coll. Agr. Outstanding Tchg. award Dole Food Co., 1995. Mem. Soc. Am. Foresters, Am. Forestry Assn., Forest Products Rsch. Soc., Soc. Wood Sci. and Tech., Alpha Zeta, Xi Sigma Pi, Sigma Xi, Beta Beta Beta, Phi Sigma Kappa. Lutheran. Contbr. articles to sci. and forestry jours. Home: 7605 El Retiro Ave Atascadero CA 93422-3722 Office: Calif Poly State U Dept Natural Resources Mgmt San Luis Obispo CA 93710

PIKE, CHARLES JAMES, employee benefits consultant, financial planner; b. Montreal, Apr. 9, 1914; s. Andrew and Frances Alicia (Webster) P.; m. Lois R. Bennet, Dec. 26, 1953 (dec. Aug. 1963); m. Marjorie H. Murdoch, Nov. 25, 1977. Grad. high sch., Montreal. CLU, chartered ins. broker, CFP, registered fin. planner, chartered adminstr. Subscription sales mgr. Hearst Orgn., then Maclean Hunter, Can., 1932-39; sales mgr. Hires Root Beer, Que., 1939-41; from group rep. to group mgr. Sun Life Can., 1941-48; asst. br. mgr. Sun Life Can., Edmonton, Montreal, 1948-54; pvt. group welfare cons. Montreal, 1955—; pres. Fin. and Estate Planning Coun., Montreal, 1954, Life Underwriters Assn. Montreal, 1955; founding pres. Que. chpt. Can. Assn. Fin. Planners, 1982. Ins. editor, weekly columnist Fin. Times Can., 1950-56. Co-founder mktg. execs. course U. Western Ont., London, 1952; pres. Montreal (Que.) Boys' and Girls' Assn., 1960-63; coun. mem. The Montreal (Que.) Bd. Trade, 1970-72. Mem. Life Underwriters Assn. Can. (life), Million Dollar Round Table (life), Montreal Bd. Trade (life), Que. Assn. Fin. Planners (planner emeritus), Can. Alpine Masters Racing Group (life), JB Ski Club Inc. (past pres.), Beaconsfield Golf Club (life), Montreal Hunt Club (past pres.), Montreal Amateur Athletic Assn. (past coun. mem.). Avocations: skiing, horseback fox hunting, roller blading, golfing. Office: Pike Vezina Assurance, 800 Blvd Rene-Levesque O, Montreal, PQ Canada H3B 1X9

PIKE, DOUGLAS EUGENE, university program director; b. Cass Lake, Minn., July 27, 1924; s. Clarence Eugene and Esther (Jensen) P.; m. Myrna Louise Johnson, Sept. 15, 1956; children: Andrew Jefferson, Victoria Louise, Ethan Edward. BA, U. Calif., 1953; MA, Am. U., 1961; postgrad., MIT, 1963-64. Writer UN, Korea, 1950-52; fgn. service officer U.S. Govt. State Dept., Washington, Saigon, Hong Kong, Tokyo, and Taipei, Taiwan., 1958-82; dir. Indochina Studies Program, U. Calif., Berkeley, 1982—. Author: Viet Cong: The Organizational Techniques of the National Liberation Front of South Vietnam, 1965, War, Peace and the Viet Cong, 1969, History of Vietnamese Communism, 1978, PAVN: People's Army of Vietnam, 1986, Vietnam and the USSR: Anatomy of an Alliance, 1987, The Bunker Papers: Reports to the President from Vietnam, 1991; editor: Indochina Chronology, 1983—; contbr. numerous articles to profl. jours. Served to sgt. Signal Corps, U.S. Army, 1943-46, PTO. Recipient Superior Honor award U.S. Info. Agy., 1976, Sec. Def. medal, U.S. Dept. Def., 1981. Mem. Author's Guild, Army-Navy Club (Washington), Fgn. Svc. Club, Faculty Club U. Calif. Methodist. Avocation: philately. Home: 2265 Alva Ave El Cerrito CA 94530-1857 Office: U Calif 6701 San Pablo Ave Oakland CA 94608

PIKE, GEORGE HAROLD, JR., religious organization executive, clergyman; b. Summit, N.J., Jan. 14, 1933; s. George Harold and Ann Aurelia (Brewer) P.; m. Pauline Elizabeth Blair, Aug. 27, 1955; children: Elizabeth, George 3d, James. BA, Trinity Coll., Hartford, Conn., 1954; MDiv, Dubuque (Iowa) Theolog. Sch., 1957. Ordained to ministry Presbyn. Ch. USA., 1957. Pastor 1st PResbyn. Ch., Kasson, Minn., 1956-59, 3d Presbyn. Ch., Dubuque, 1959-64; sr. pastor Presbyn. Ch., Bettendorf, Iowa, 1964-68; sr. pastor 1st Presbyn. Ch., Vancouver, Wash., 1968-78, Cranford, N.J., 1978-88; exec. chair Presbyn. Ch. USA, Louisville, 1988-93; interim pastor 2d Presbyn. Ch., Kansas City, Mo., 1993-95; dir. sem. devel. U. Dubuque, Iowa, 1995—; mem. exec. com. Consultation on Ch. Union, Princeton, 1980-89, pres., 1984-88. Dir. Bettendorf Bd. Edn., 1964-68, pres. 1967-68; bd. dirs. Southwest Wash. Hosps., Vancouver, 1969-78. Named Citizen of Yr., Jaycees, Bettendorf, 1967, Citizen of Yr., B'nai B'rith, Cranford, 1988; named to Honorable Order of Ky. Cols., 1989. Avocations: golf, photography. Home: 3650 Keystone Dr Dubuque IA 52002 Office: U Dubuque 2000 University Dubuque IA 52001-5050

PIKE, JOHN NAZARIAN, optical engineering consultant; b. Boston, Feb. 13, 1929; s. Arthur Thorndike and Sarah Lucy (Nazarian) P.; m. Margaretta May Horner, Dec. 28, 1957; children: Sally Katharine, Susan Horner. AB, Princeton U., 1951; PhD in Physics and Optics, U. Rochester, 1958. Staff scientist Parma (Ohio) Rsch. Ctr., Union Carbide Corp., 1956-63; mem. physics faculty Baldwin-Wallace Coll., Berea, Ohio, 1961-63; sr. scientist Tarrytown (N.Y.) Tech. Ctr., Union Carbide Corp., 1963-85; pres. J.J. Pike & Co., Inc., Pleasantville, N.Y., 1986—. Patentee in applied indsl. optics; contbr. numerous articles to profl. jours. Bd. dirs. United Way Westchester, N.Y., 1979-85, 95—, chmn. planning com., 1989-95, chmn. planned giving, 1995—. Recipient Harold J. Marshall Citation for Cmty. Svc., United Way No. Westchester, 1976, Cmty. Svc. award Union Carbide Corp., 1982. Mem. Optical Soc. Am., Soc. Photo-Optical Instrument Engrs., Internat. Soc. for Optical Engring., Phi Beta Kappa, Sigma Xi. Home: 71 Cedar Ave Pleasantville NY 10570-1932 Office: JJ Pike & Co Inc PO Box 186 Pleasantville NY 10570-0186

PIKE, KENNETH LEE, linguist, educator; b. Conn., June 9, 1912; s. Ernest R. and Hattie (Granniss) P.; m. Evelyn Griset, Oct. 20, 1938; children: Judith, Barbara, Stephen. BTh, Gordon Coll., 1933, LHD (hon.), 1982; PhD, U. Mich., 1942; PhD (hon.), Huntington Coll., 1967, Wheaton Coll., Irian Jaya, 1975, René Descartes U., Sorbonne, 1978, Monterrey, Mex.; LHD (hon.), U. Chgo., 1974, Georgetown U., 1984. Assoc. prof. U. Mich., Ann Arbor, 1948-55, prof., 1955-79; adj. prof. U. Tex., Arlington, 1979—; researcher, cons. Summer Inst. Linguistics, Dallas; researcher, lectr. in Mex., Ecuador, Peru, Guatemala, Papua New Guinea, Ghana, Nigeria, Philippines, Irian Jaya, Nepal, Thailand, Chile, Brazil, Singapore, others. Author: Phonetics, 1943, Intonation of American English, 1945, Phonemics, 1947, Tone Languages, 1948, Language in Relation to a Unified Theory of the Structure of Human Behavior, 1954, 2d edit., 1967, (with R. Young and A. Becker) Rhetoric, Discovery and Change, 1971, (with Evelyn G. Pike) Grammatical Analysis, 1977, 2d edit., 1982, Linguistics Concepts--An Introduction to Tagmemics, 1982, (with Evelyn G. Pike) Text and Tagmeme, 1983, (with D. Stark and Angel Merecias) Translator: New Testament Mixtec, With Heart and Mind, 1962, Stir, Change, Create: Poems and Essays, 1961; editor: (with Thomas N. Headland, Marvin Harris) Emics and Etics—The Insider/Outsider Debate, 1990, Talk, Thought and Thing—The Emic Road Toward Conscious Knowledge, 1993. Bd. dirs. Wycliffe Bible Translators, Huntington Beach, Calif., 1942-79. Recipient Presdl. Medal Merit, Govt. of Philippines, 1974; named Hon. Prof., U. Trujillo, 1987. Mem. Summer Inst. Linguistics (pres. 1979), Linguistic Soc. Am. (pres. 1961), Linguistic Assn. Can. and U.S. (pres. 1978), Am. Anthrop. Assn., Internat. Phonetic Soc., Am. Acad. Arts and Sci., Nat. Acad. Sci. Republican. Presbyterian. Avocation: water polo. Home and Office: Summer Inst Linguistics 7500 W Camp Wisdom Rd Dallas TX 75236-5628

PIKE, KERMIT JEROME, library director; b. East Cleveland, June 19, 1941; s. Frank James and Pauline Frances (Prijatel) P.; m. Joyce Rita Massillo, June 27, 1964; children: Christopher James, Laura Elizabeth. BA, Case Western Res. U., 1963, MA, 1965. Rsch. asst. Western Res. Hist. Soc., Cleve., 1965-66, curator manuscripts, 1966-72, chief libr., 1969-75, dir. libr., 1976—; adj. prof. history, libr. sci. Case Western Res. U., 1975-84. Author: Guide to the Manuscripts and Archives, 1972, Guide to Shaker Manuscripts, 1974; editor: Guide to Jewish History Sources, 1983; Compiler: Guide to Major Manuscript Collections, 1987. Mem. Super Sesquicentennial Com., Cleve., 1971, Cleve. Bicentennial History Com., 1992—, Family Heritage adv. bd., Numa Corp., 1995—; trustee Nationalities Svc. Ctr., Cleve., 1979-86; chmn. vis. com. on humanities and arts, Cleve. State U., 1980-82. Recipient Achievement award No. Ohio Live, Cleve., 1987; Spl. Recognition award Gov. Richard F. Celeste of Ohio, 1990. Mem. Soc. Ohio Archivists (co-founder 1968, pres. 1971-72), Black History Archives (founder 1970), Orgn. Am. Historians, Soc. Am. Archivists, Manuscripts Soc., Midwest Archives Conf., Ohio Geneal. Soc., Early Settlers Assn. of the Western Res., Rowfant Club, Lake County Farmers' Conservation Club, Lambda Chi Alpha. Roman Catholic. Home: 3985 Orchard Rd Cleveland OH 44121-2411 Office: Western Res Hist Soc 10825 East Blvd Cleveland OH 44106-1777

PIKE, (JOHN) KEVIN, special effects expert; b. Hartford, Conn., May 9, 1951. Spl. effects expert (films) Heartbeeps, 1981, The Return of the Jedi, 1983, Twilight Zone: The Movie, 1983, Indiana Jones and the Temple of Doom, 1984, The Cast Starfighter, 1984, Mrs. Soffel, 1984, Back to the Future, 1985, City Limits, 1985, Warning Sign, 1985, La Bamba, 1987, Everybody's All-American, 1988, Little Monsters, 1989, (TV) Earth 2 (Emmy award for Outstanding Ind. Achievement in Sple Visual Effects 1995). Office: Filmtrix Inc PO Box 715 North Hollywood CA 91603*

PIKE, LARRY ROSS, insurance executive; b. Harrisburg, Pa., Aug. 14, 1935; m. Sandra Marie Thomas; children: Karen Lynn Aungst, Christine Elaine Frain. AB in Econs., Franklin & Marshall Coll., 1958; MBA, U. Del., 1974. CLU. Sr. life and health underwriter Provident Mutual Life Ins. Co., 1958-68; v.p. underwriting/issue Continental Life Ins. Co., 1968-79, Bankers Nat. Life Ins. Co., 1979-80; v.p. underwriting/issue Home Life Ins. Co., 1980-81, sr. v.p. ins. svcs., 1981-84, sr. v.p. corp. fin. info., 1984-87; exec. v.p. ind. ins. and annuities Union Cen. Life Ins. Co., Cin., 1987-89, pres., chief oper. officer, 1989-90, pres., chief exec. officer, chmn. bd. dirs., 1990—; chmn. bd. dirs., pres., chief exec. officer Manhattan Nat. Corp., Cin.; bd. dirs. Manhattan Life Ins. Co., Manhattan Nat. Pension Svc., Inc., Carillon Advisors, Inc., Carillon Investments, Inc., Carillon Mktg. Agy., Carillon Life Ins. Co. Fellow Life Mgmt. Inst.; mem. Cert. Life Underwriters, Bankers Club, Masons. Avocations: travel, Civil War history, walking. Home: 3598 Carpenters Creek Dr Cincinnati OH 45241-3819 Office: Union Cen Life Ins Co 1876 Waycross Rd Cincinnati OH 45240-2825*

PIKE, LARRY SAMUEL, lawyer; b. Savannah, Ga., Feb. 23, 1939; s. Abram and Ida (Feinberg) P.; m. Bonnie Jo Haykin, June 21, 1959; children: Douglas, Stacey, Scott. BA, Emory U., 1960, LLB, 1963; postgrad., Leeds (Eng.) U., 1960-61. Assoc. L. Jack Swertfeger Jr. Atty., Decatur, Ga., 1963-65; ptnr. Swertfeger, Scott, Pike & Simmons, Decatur, 1966-75, Simmons, Pike & Warren, Decatur, 1975-76, Lefkoff, Pike & Sims, Atlanta, 1976-85, Branch, Pike & Ganz, Atlanta, 1985-95, Holland & Knight, Atlanta, 1995—; Pres. Ansley Park Civic Assn., Atlanta, 1977-79, Northshore Homeowners Assn., Tybee Island, Ga., 1992-95, The Temple, Atlanta, 1979-81, trustee, 1977—, Am. Cancer Soc., DeKalb County, Ga. unit, 1970-71, crusade chmn., 1969-70; trustee Ansley Park Beautification Found., Inc., Atlanta, 1984—, The Temple Endowment Fund, Atlanta, 1979-87, Atlanta Jewish Cmty. Ctr., 1973-76; bd. overseers Hebrew Union Coll., Cin., 1987-93; alumni coun. Emory U., Atlanta, 1966-72; bd. trustees Union of Am. Hebrew Congregations, 1991—; mem. Rabbinical Placement Commn., 1994—. Editor-in-chief law jour. and newspaper; contbr. numerous articles to profl. jours. Fulbright fellow, 1960-61; named Outstanding Young Man of Yr. North DeKalb Jaycees, 1968. Mem. ABA, State Bar Ga. (exec. coun. Young Lawyers sect. 1968-72), Atlanta Bar Assn., Decatur-DeKalb Bar Assn. (sec. 1965-66), Atlanta Legal Aid Soc. (pres. 1974-75, past bd. dirs.), Atlanta Tax Forum, Lawyers Club Atlanta, B'nai B'rith (pres. Atlanta lodge 1970-71, Ga. pres. 1974-75, dist. 5 bd. govs. 1973-76, chair Youth Orgn. Bd.

1971-73), Phi Beta Kappa, Omicron Delta Kappa. Office: Holland and Knight 2 Midtown Plz Fl 15 Atlanta GA 30309

PIKE, LAURENCE BRUCE, retired lawyer; b. Brattleboro, Vt., Sept. 11, 1927; s. Lee Ernest and Alice Louise (Temple) P.; m. Norma I. Ecklund, Sept. 2, 1950; children: Barbara L., William T., Jeffrey O., Alan B. B.A., U. Iowa, 1951; J.D., Columbia U., 1954. Bar: N.Y. 1955. Assoc. firm Simpson Thacher & Bartlett, N.Y.C., 1954-64, ptnr., 1964-87. Mem. Scarsdale Town Club, N.Y., 1964-68; mem. capt. Scarsdale Aux. Police, 1960-72. Served with USN, 1945-48. Mem. ABA, Bar Assn. City N.Y., N.Y. State Bar Assn., Ardsley Curling Club (N.Y., dir., sec. 1974-77), Phi Beta Kappa. Congregationalist. Home: 7 Guilford St Brattleboro VT 05301-2607 Office: Simpson Thacher & Bartlett 425 Lexington Ave New York NY 10017-3903

PIKE, RALPH WEBSTER, chemical engineer, educator, university administrator; b. Tampa, Fla., Nov. 10, 1935; s. Ralph Webster and Macey (Adams) P.; m. Patricia Jennings, Aug. 23, 1958. B Chem. Engring., Ga. Inst. Tech., 1957, PhD, 1962. Rsch. chem. engr. Exxon R & D Co., Baytown, Tex., 1962-64; Paul M. Horton prof. chem. engring. and sys. sci. La. State U., Baton Rouge, 1964—, assoc. vice chancellor for rsch., 1975—, dir. La. Mineral Inst., 1979—; cons. to chem. and petroleum refining industry, fed. govt. and State of La., 1964—. Author: Formulation and Optimization of Mathematical Models, 1970, Optimization for Engineering Systems, 1986, Optimizacion en Ingenieria, 1989. Active various civic, ch. and community orgns., Baton Rouge, 1964—. 2d lt. U.S. Army, 1958-60. Recipient over 60 rsch. grants, including NASA, NSF, Dept. Interior, EPA, NOAA, state agys. and pvt. industry, 1964—. Fellow Am. Inst. Chem. Engrs. (chmn. nat. program com. 1984, local sect. 1985); mem. Am. Chem. Soc. (Charles E. Coates Mem. Award, 1994, univ. and profl.), Sigma Xi. Democrat. Methodist. Avocation: skiing. Home: 6063 Hibiscus Dr Baton Rouge LA 70808-8844 Office: La State U 210 Ctr Energy Studies Baton Rouge LA 70803

PIKE, ROBERT WILLIAM, insurance company executive, lawyer; b. Lorain, Ohio, July 25, 1941; s. Edward and Catherine (Stack) P.; m. Linda L. Feitz, Dec. 26, 1964; children: Catherine, Robert, Richard. BA, Bowling Green State U., 1963; JD, U. Toledo, 1966. Bar: Ohio 1966, Ill. 1973. Ptnr. Cubbon & Rice Law Firm, Toledo, 1968-72; asst. counsel Allstate Ins. Co., Northbrook, Ill., 1972-74, assoc. counsel, 1974-76, asst. sec., asst. gen. counsel, 1976-77, asst. v.p., asst. gen. counsel, 1977-78, v.p., asst. gen. counsel, 1978-86, sr. v.p., sec., gen. counsel, 1987—, also bd. dirs.; bd. dirs. Allstate subs., including the Northbrook Group of Cos. Bd. dirs., exec. com. Assn. Calif. Ins. Cos., Nat. Assn. Ind. Insurers. Served to capt. inf. U.S. Army, 1966-68. Mem. ABA, Ill. Bar Assn., Ohio Bar Assn., Ivanhoe (Ill.) Club. Roman Catholic. Home: 811 Hawthorne Pl Lake Forest IL 60045-2210 Office: Allstate Ins Co 2775 Sanders Rd Ste F8 Northbrook IL 60062

PIKE, WILLIAM EDWARD, business executive; b. Ft. Collins, Colo., Jan. 25, 1929; s. Harry H. and Alice Francis (Swinscoe) P.; m. Catherine Broward Crawford, June 26, 1965; children: Elizabeth Catherine, Robert Crawford, Daniel William. Student, U. Colo., 1947-48; B.S., U.S. Naval Acad., 1952; M.B.A., Harvard, 1960. Commd. ensign USN, 1952, advanced through grades to lt., 1958; ret., 1958; asst. treas. Morgan Guaranty Trust Co., N.Y.C., 1962-64; asst. v.p. Morgan Guaranty Trust Co., 1964-66, v.p., 1966-71, sr. v.p., 1971-74, chmn. credit policy com., 1974-86; exec. v.p. J.P. Morgan & Co. Inc., 1986-89; bd. dirs. VF Corp., Somat Corp., Am. States Ins. Co.; corp. dir., trustee, pvt. investor. Episcopalian. Club: Country (New Canaan, Conn.). Home: Indian Waters Dr New Canaan CT 06840 Office: 36 Grove St New Canaan CT 06840-5329

PIKLER, CHARLES, musician. Student violin, Norwich, Conn.; student, U. Conn., violin studies with Bronislaw Gimpel; BA in math., U. Minn. Violin soloist Chgo. Symphony Orch., 1987—. Appeared in summer festivals including Tanglewood Young Artist Program, Berkshire Music Ctr., 1965-71; prin. appearances include Hartford Symphony Orch., Ea. Conn. Symphony Orch. and Manchester Civic Orch.; substitute in Chgo. Symphony Orch. viola sect., violin soloist, solo performer on violin and viola; concertmaster of Chgo. Chamber Orch. Office: care Chgo Symphony Orch Orch Hall 220 S Michigan Ave Chicago IL 60604-2508

PILARCZYK, DANIEL EDWARD, archbishop; b. Dayton, Ohio, Aug. 12, 1934; s. Daniel Joseph and Frieda S. (Hilgefort) P. Student, St. Gregory Sem., Cin., 1948-53; PhB, Pontifical Urban U., Rome, 1955, PhL, 1956, STB, 1958, STL, 1960, STD, 1961; MA, Xavier U., 1965; PhD, U. Cin., 1969; LLD (hon.), Xavier U., 1975, Calumet Coll., 1982, U. Dayton, 1990, Marquette U., 1990, Thomas More Coll., 1991. Ordained priest Roman Catholic Ch., 1959; asst. chancellor Archdiocese of Cin., 1961-63; synodal judge Archdiocesan Tribunal, 1971-82; mem. faculty Athenaeum of Ohio, St. Gregory Sem., 1963-74; v.p. Athenaeum of Ohio, 1968-74, trustee, 1974—; also rector St. Gregory Sem., 1968-74; archdiocesan dir. ednl. services, 1974-82, aux. bishop of Cin., 1974-82, vicar gen., 1974-82, archbishop of Cin., 1982—; bd. dirs. Pope John Ctr., 1978-85; trustee Cath. Health Assn., 1982-85, Cath. U. Am., 1983-91, Pontifical Coll. Josephinum, 1983-92; v.p. Nat. Conf. Cath. Bishops, 1986-89, pres., 1989-92; U.S. rep. Episc. Bd. Internat. Commn. on English in Liturgy 1987-97; chmn., 1991-97. Author: Praepositini Cancellarii de Sacramentis et de Novissimis, 1964-65, Twelve Tough Issues, 1988, We Believe, 1989, Living in the Lord, 1990, The Parish: Where God's People Live, 1991, Forgiveness, 1992, What Must I Do?, 1993, Out Priests: Who They Are and What They Do, 1994, Sacraments, 1994, Lenten Lunches, 1995, Bringing Forth Justice, 1996. Ohio Classical Conf. scholar to Athens, 1966. Mem. Am. Philol. Assn. Home and Office: 100 E 8th St Cincinnati OH 45202-2129

PILCHER, ELLEN LOUISE, rehabilitation counselor; b. Washington, Feb. 5, 1949; d. Donald Everett and Edna Lois (Walker) P.; m. Adam J. Buzon Jr., July 27, 1974 (div. Apr. 1991). BA in Psychology, So. Ill. U., 1971, MA in Rehab. Counseling, 1973. Social svcs. asst. Dept. Army, Ft. Huachuca, Ariz., 1973-74, New Ulm, Germany, 1974-75, Ft. Sill, Okla., 1977-87; counselor Goodwill Industries, Lawton, Okla., 1976-77; ind. living specialist Ariz. Bridge to Ind. Living, Phoenix, 1984-87; disability specialist Samaritan Rehab. Inst., Phoenix, 1987-89; disability cons. Peoria, Ariz., 1989—; founder Problems of Architecture and Transp. to Handicapped, Lawton, Okla., 1976-79; founder, past pres. Polio Echo Support Group, Phoenix, 1985—; co-founder, bd. mem. Disability Network of Ariz., Phoenix, 1986—; disability speaker Easter Seal Soc. and free lance, Phoenix, 1984—; producer, host Cable Community Svc. TV Show, Glendale, Ariz., 1987-91; mem. nat. adv. bd. Polio Support Groups, St. Louis, 1987. Named Ms. Wheelchair Ariz. Good Samaritan Med. Ctr., Phoenix, 1986, Second Runner-Up Ms. Wheelchair Am., Ms. Wheelchair Am. Assn., Richmond, Va., 1986, Outstanding Bus. Person Ariz. Parks/Recreation, 1987; recipient Celebration of Success award Impact for Enterprising Women, Phoenix, 1989, Extraordinary Personal Achievement award Lions Club Found., Phoenix, 1987. Mem. NOW (co-founder Lawton chpt. 1982, Glendale, Ariz. chpt. 1984), Nat. Rehab. Assn., Nat. Rehab. Counselors Assn., Ariz. Rehab. Assn., Ariz. Rehab. Counselors Assn. Democrat. Unitarian. Avocations: animal rescue and welfare, wheelchair dancing, acting, community activities.

PILCHIK, ELY EMANUEL, rabbi, writer; b. Russia, June 12, 1913; came to U.S., 1920, naturalized, 1920; s. Abraham and Rebecca (Lipovitch) P.; m. Ruth Schuchat, Nov. 20, 1941 (dec. 1977); children: Susan Pilchik Rosenbaum, Judith Pilchik Zucker; m. Harriet Krichman Perlmutter, June, 1981. A.B., U. Cin., 1935; M.Hebrew Lit., Hebrew Union Coll., 1936, D.D., 1964. Ordained rabbi, 1939; founder, dir. Hillel Found. at U. Md., 1939-40; asst. rabbi Har Sinai Temple, Balt., 1940-41; rabbi Temple Israel, Tulsa, 1942-47, Temple B'nai Jeshurun, Short Hills, N.J., 1947-81; prof. Jewish Thought Upsala Coll., 1969—; pres. Jewish Book Council Am., 1957-58. Author: books, including Hillel, 1951, From the Beginning, 1956, Judaism Outside the Holy Land, 1964, Jeshurun Essays, 1967, A Psalm of David, 1967, Talmud Thought, 1983, Midrash Memoir, 1984, Touches of Einstein, 1987, Luzzatto on Loving Kindness, 1987, Prayer in History, 1989; author: play Toby, 1968; lyricist 6 cantatas; contbr. articles to profl. and gen. jours. Bd. dirs. Newark Mus.; mem. ethics com. N.J. Bar Assn. Served as chaplain USNR, 1944-46. Mem. N.J. Bd. Rabbis (pres. 1955-57), Central Conf. Am. Rabbis (pres. 1977-79). Office: 1025 S Orange Ave Short Hills NJ 07078-3135 *I have been influenced by the teaching of the 1st sage Hillel who said: "If I am not for myself, who will be for me? And if I am for myself only, what am I? And if not now, when?".*

PILDER, RICHARD JOSEPH, management consultant; b. Cin., Mar. 25, 1940; s. Frank William and Marie Ann (Kamp) P.; m. Mary Louise Donoghue, Aug. 31, 1976; children: Kathy, Christopher, Chrissy, Kerry. BA, U. Dayton, 1964; MA, St. Louis U., 1971; PhD, Calif. Western U., 1973. Tchr. St. Joseph High Sch., Cleve., 1965-69; pvt. practice as therapist Greenwich, Conn., 1974-78; pres. Mainstream Access, Inc., N.Y.C., 1978—. Author: How to Find Your Life's Work, 1979. Active PTA, local youth shelter, Greenwich, 1980. Mem. Innis Arden. Home: Mainstream Access Inc 7 Bryon Rd Old Greenwich CT 06870 Office: Mainstream Access Inc 210 Signal Rd Stamford CT 06901

PILE, ROBERT BENNETT, advertising executive, writer, consultant; b. Pierre, S.D., May 27, 1918; s. Homer Bennett and Ruth (Gleckler) P.; m. Cynthia Way, Feb. 28, 1953; children: Timothy, Benjamin, Robert, Michael, Cynthia, Anthony. BA, U. Minn., 1941. Asst. advt. mgr. Red Owl Stores, Mpls., 1946-47; advt. mgr. Lactona, St. Paul, 1947-48; acct., ptnr. Olmsted & Foley Advt. Agy., Mpls., 1948-55; account exec. Campbell-Mithun, Inc., Mpls., 1955-59; v.p., group head Campbell-Mithun, Inc., 1960-69, sr. v.p., mgmt. rep., 1969-80; founder, pres., dir., mem. exec. com., chief exec. officer Bob's Wide World of Golf, 1980—; bd. dirs. Roberts-Hamilton Co., 1992; cons. in field; instr. St. Thomas Coll., St. Paul, 1980-86; mgr. 4-A Inst. Advt. Studies, 1981-87. Author: Letters from French Windmill, 1986, Panic in the Morning Mail, 1986, Crisis Every Fifteen Minutes, 1988, Top Entrepreneurs and Their Business, 1993, Women Business Leaders, 1995, For the Love of Rose, 1995; contbg. editor Active Lifestyles Mag.; writer Mpls. Tribune, T.C. Mag.; columnist Format mag., Skyway News. Bd. dirs. Big Bros. Mpls., Minn. Heart Assn., St. Mary's Hosp.; bd. dirs., chmn. 4-A's of Twin Cities, bd. govs. Ctrl. Region. Capt. USAAF, 1941-46. Recipient spl. award Mpls. Spruce Up Drive, 1965; named Alumnus of Notable Achievement, U. Minn., 1994. Mem. Northwest Advt. Golf Assn. (pres. 1977-78, gov.), Am. Assn. ADvt. Agys. (chmn. Twin City coun.), Interlachen Country Club (bd. govs., chmn. house com. & food and beverage com., editor monthly newsletter Interocutor), Ham and Eggs Breakfast Club, Mpls. Club, Yo Yo's Club, Phi Kappa Psi. Home: 4315 E Lake Harriet Blvd Minneapolis MN 55409-1725

PILECKI, PAUL STEVEN, lawyer; b. Norristown, Pa., Sept. 12, 1950; m. Barbara Derrickson; children: Derek Steven, Christopher Drew. AB, St. Joseph's Coll., Phila., 1972; JD, Temple U., 1978. Bar: Pa. 1978, D.C. 1985. Sr. counsel Fed. Res. Bd., Washington, 1978-84; ptnr. Shaw, Pittman, Potts & Trowbridge, Washington, 1984—. Mem. ABA (banking law com.). Home: 11108 Deville Estates Dr Oakton VA 22124-1002 Office: Shaw Pittman Potts et al 2300 N St NW Washington DC 20037-1122

PILETTE, PATRICIA CHEHY, health care organizational/management consultant; b. Rutland, Vt., June 28, 1945; d. John Edward and Mary T. (McNamara) Chehy; m. Wilfrid Pilette, July 22, 1972; 1 child, Patrick John. Diploma, Jeanne Mance Sch. Nursing, 1966; BSN magna cum laude, St. Anselm Coll., 1971; MS summa cum laude, Boston U., 1974, EdD in Counseling and Human Svcs. Adminstrn. summa cum laude, 1984. RN, Mass. Clin. specialist adult psychiatry mgmt. and counseling practice Framingham, Mass.; employee assistance counselor St. Elizabeth's Med. Ctr., 1984—. Contbr. articles to profl. publs., chpts. to books. Mem. Mass. Soc. Nurse Execs., N.E. Assn. for Specialists in Group Work, N.E. Soc. Group Psychotherapists, Mass. Assn., Women Deans, Adminstrs. and Counselors, Assn. for Humanistic Psychologists, N.E. Assn. Soc. Employee Assistance, Am. Mental Health Counselors Assn., Pi Lambda Theta, Sigma Theta Tau.

PILGRIM, DIANNE HAUSERMAN, art museum director; b. Cleve., July 8, 1941; d. John Martin and Norma Hauserman; divorced. BA, Pa. State U., 1963; MA, Inst. Fine Arts, NYU, 1965; postgrad., CUNY, 1971-74; LHD (hon.), Amherst Coll., 1991, Pratt Inst., 1994. Chester Dale fellow Am. wing. Met. Mus. Art, N.Y.C., 1966-68, rsch. cons. Am. paintings and sculpture, 1971-73; asst. to dirs. Pyramid Galleries, Ltd., Washington, 1969-71, Finch Coll. Mus. Art, Washington, 1971; curator dept. decorative arts Bklyn. Mus., 1973-88, chmn. dept., 1988; dir. Cooper-Hewitt Nat. Design Mus., N.Y.C., 1988—; mem. adv. com. Gracie Mansion, N.Y.C., 1980; mem. design adv. com. Art Inst. Chgo., 1988; mem. Hist. House Trust N.Y.C., Mayor's Office, 1989-94. Co-author, curator: (book and exhbn. catalogue) Mr. and Mrs. Raymond Horowitz Collection of American Impressionist and Realist Paintings, 1973, The American Renaissance 1876-1917, 1979; (book) The Machine Age in America 1918-1941, 1986 (Charles F. Montgomery prize Decorative Arts Soc.). Bd. dirs. Nat. Multiple Sclerosis Soc., 1989. Recipient Disting. Alumni award Pa. State U., 1991. Mem. Decorative Arts Soc. (pres. 1977-79), Art Deco Soc., Victorian Soc., Art Table. Office: Smithsonian Instn Cooper-Hewitt Nat Design Mus 2 E 91st St New York NY 10128-0606

PILGRIM, LONNIE (BO PILGRIM), poultry production company executive; b. 1928; married. Ptnr. Pilgrims Pride Corp., Pittsburg, Tex., 1953-68, chmn., CEO, 1968—; chmn. First State Bank Pitts. Served with U.S. Armed Forces, 1951-53. Office: Pilgrim's Pride Corp 110 S Texas St Pittsburg TX 75686-1532*

PILIAVIN, JANE ALLYN, social psychologist; b. Montclair, N.J., Feb. 21, 1937; d. Horace Warren and Mary Elizabeth (Young) Allyn; m. Curtis Dale Hardyck, Jan. 20, 1962 (div.); 1 child, Allyn Henry Hardyck; m. Irving Morris Piliavin, Dec. 27, 1968; 1 child, Elizabeth Elaine Piliavin. BA in Psychology with high honors, U. Rochester, 1958; PhD in Social Psychology, Stanford U., 1962. Acting instr. Stanford U., 1960-62; rsch. psychologist Survey Rsch. Ctr. U. Calif., Berkeley, 1962-66, lectr. in psychology, 1964-66; asst. prof. psychology U. Pa., 1967-70; assoc. prof. Sch. Family Resources and Consumer Scis. U. Wis., Madison, 1970-73, prof. Sch. Family Resources and Consumer Scis., 1973-76, prof. dept. sociology, 1976—; vis. asst. prof. psychology Mills Coll., 1966-67; reviewer Am. Found. for AIDS Rsch., 19 87—; mem. blood products adv. com. FDA, 1993—. Author: (with others) Adolescent Prejudice, 1975, Emergency Intervention, 1981, Giving Blood: The Development of an Altruistic Identity, 1991, The Psychology of Helping and Altruism: Problems and Puzzles, 1995; assoc. editor Personality and Social Psychology Bull., 1975-77; cons. editor Jour. Personality and Social Psychology, 1974-77, 84-86, European Jour. Social Psychology, 1982—, Jour. Applied Social Psychology, 1982—, Social Psychology Quar., 1988-90, 94—; hon. mem. editorial bd. Polish Psychol. Bull., 1989—; contbr. chpts. to books, articles to profl. jours. Fellow Am. Psychol. Soc.; mem. AAAS, Soc. Exptl. Social Psychology, European Assn. Exptl. Social Psychology, Am. Sociol. Assn. (coun. sect. on social psychology 1983-86, chair 1990-91, mem. profl. affairs com. 1993—), Phi Beta Kappa, Sigma Xi. Democrat. Office: U Wis 8128 Social Sci Bldg Madison WI 53706

PILISUK, MARC, community psychology educator; b. N.Y.C., Jan. 19, 1934; s. Louis and Charlotte (Feferholtz) P.; m. Phyllis E. Kamen, June 16, 1956; children: Tammy, Jeff. BA, Queens Coll., 1955; MA, U. Mich., 1956, PhD, 1961. Asst. prof., assoc. rsch. psychologist U. Mich., Ann Arbor, 1961-65, founder teach-in, 1965; assoc. prof. Purdue U., West Lafayette, Ind., 1965-67; prof.-in-residence U. Calif., Berkeley, 1967-77; prof. community psychology U. Calif., Davis, 1977—; vis. prof. U. Calif., Wright Inst., 1991—; cons. Ctr. for Self Help Rsch., Berkeley, Calif., 1991-93; prof. psychology Saybrook Inst. and Grad. Ctr., San Francisco, 1993—. Author: International Conflict and Social Policy, 1972, The Healing Web: Social Networks and Human Survival, 1986; editor: The Triple Revolution, 1969; Poor Americans, 1970; Triple Revolution Emerging, 1972; How We Lost the War on Poverty, 1973. NIMH fellow, 1959-60; NSF grantee, 1962-66; Nat. Inst. Alcoholism and Drug Abuse tng. grantee, 1973-77. Fellow Soc. for Community Rsch. and Action, Soc. for Psychol. Study Social Issues (council), APA (pres.-elect divsn. peace psychology 1996), Am. Orthopsychiat. Assn.; mem. ACLU, Am. Soc. on Aging, Am. Pub. Health Assn., Psychologists for Social Responsibility, Faculty for Human Rights in C.Am.

PILLA, ANTHONY MICHAEL, bishop; b. Cleve., Nov. 12, 1932; s. George and Libera (Nista) P. Student, St. Gregory Coll. Sem., 1952-53, Borromeo Coll. Sem., 1955, St. Mary Sem., 1954, 56-59; B.A. in Philosophy, John Carroll U., Cleve., 1961, M.A. in History, 1967. Ordained priest Roman Cath. Ch., 1959. Assoc. St. Bartholomew Parish, Middleburg Hts., Ohio, 1959-60; prof. Borromeo Sem., Wickliffe, Ohio, 1960-72; rector-pres. Borromeo Sem., 1972-75; mem. Diocese Cleve. Liturgical Commn., 1964-69, asst. dir., 1969-72; sec. for services to clergy and religious personnel Diocese Cleve., 1975-79; titular bishop Scardona; and aux. bishop of Cleve. and vicar Eastern region Diocese of Cleve., 1979-80, apostolic adminstr., from 1980; bishop of Cleve., from 1981; trustee Borromeo Sem., 1975-79, Cath. U., 1981-84; trustee, mem. bd. overseers St. Mary Sem., 1975-79; mem. adv. bd. permanent diaconate program Diocese of Cleve., 1975-79, hospitalization and ins. bd., 1979; bd dirs. Cath. Communications Found., 1981—. Bd. dirs. NCCJ, 1986—. Mem. Nat. Cath. Edn. Assn. (dir. 1972-75), U.S. Cath. Conf., Nat. Conf. Cath. Bishops, Cath. Conf. Ohio., Greater Cleve. Roundtable (trustee from 1981). Home and Office: Chancery Office 350 Chancery Bldg 1027 Superior Ave E Cleveland OH 44114-2503*

PILLA, FELIX MARIO, hospital administrator; b. Phila., Sept. 22, 1932; s. Domenick and Carmela (DiPalma) P.; m. Sally Irene Bixler, Oct. 2, 1953; children: Mark, Beth Ann, Michael, Matthew. Diploma profl. nursing, Pa. Hosp. Sch. Nursing, 1956; B.S. in Bus. Adminstrn, LaSalle Coll., Phila., 1959; M.S. in Hosp. Adminstrn, Columbia U., 1961. Various progressively responsible positions in health care field, 1957-70; exec. dir. Monmouth Med. Center, 1970-80; adminstrv. dir. U. Ariz. Health Scis. Center, Tucson, 1980-82; pres. Newton-Wellesley Hosp., Newton, Mass., 1982-85, Abington Meml. Hosp., Pa., 1985—; chmn. N.J. State Health Planning Council, 1976-77. USPHS tng. grantee, 1961. Fellow Am. Coll. Hosp. Adminstrs., Am. Pub. Health Assn.; mem. Am. Hosp. Assn. (life, mem. Ho. of Dels., governing coun. met. hosps. 1991-94), N.J. Hosp. Assn. (chmn. 1979-80), Hosp. Assn. of Pa. (trustee 1988-94), Del. Valley Hosp. Coun. (bd. dirs. 1986-94, chmn. bd. 1990-92). Office: Abington Meml Hosp 1200 Old York Rd Abington PA 19001-3720

PILLA, MARK DOMENICK, hospital administrator; b. Phila., July 2, 1954; married;. BA, LaSalle U., 1976; MA, Temple U., 1978. Adm. res. Frankford Hosp., Phila., 1977-78; asst. to v.p. West Jersey Hosp.-Voorhees, 1978-79, adminstrv. dir., 1979-80; v.p. adminstrn. Community Med. Ctr., Toms River, N.J., 1980-82, sr. v.p., 1982-87, pres., CEO, 1987-94; pres., CEO Cmty.-Kimball Health Care System, Toms River, 1994—. Mem. Am. Coll. Healthcare Execs. (com. serv. community svc.). Office: Community Med Ctr 99 Route 37 W Toms River NJ 08755-6423

PILLAERT, E(DNA) ELIZABETH, museum curator; b. Baytown, Tex., Nov. 19, 1931; d. Albert Jacob and Nettie Roseline (Kelley) P. B.A., U. St. Thomas, 1953; M.A., U. Okla., 1963; postgrad., U. Wis., 1969-67, 70-73. Asst. curator archaeology Stovall Mus., Norman, Okla., 1959-60, ednl. liaison officer, 1960-62; research asst. U. Okla., Norman, Okla., 1962; research asst. U. Wis., Madison, 1962-65, cons. archaeol. faunal analysis, 1965—; curator osteology Zool. Mus., Madison, 1965—, chief curator, 1967-92, assoc. dir., 1992—. Bd. dirs. Lysistrata Feminist Coop., Madison, 1977-81, Univ. YMCA, Madison, 1974-77. Mem. Soc. Vertebrate Paleontology, Wis. Archaeol. Soc., Okla. Anthrop. Soc., Am. Assn. Mus., NOW, Stoughton Hist. Soc., Am. Ornithological Union, Friends of Stoughton Libr., Friends of Stoughton Auditorium. Home: 216 N Prairie St Stoughton WI 53589-1647 Office: U Wis Zool Mus 434 Noland Bldg 250 N Mills St Madison WI 53706-1708

PILLAI, A(RRACKAL) K(ESAVA) B(ALAKRISHNA), integral development therapist, anthropology educator; b. Changanacherry, Kerala, India, May 9, 1930; came to U.S., 1966; s. V. Potti and Amma (Narayani) P.; children: Gita, Prita; m. Donna Pompa, 1995. MA, Kerala (India) U., 1955, East Carolina U., 1968; MPhil, Columbia U., 1972, PhD, 1975. Cert. Am. Bd. Med. Psychotherapists. Prof., chair dept. English Sri Sankara Coll., Kalady, India, 1955-66; dir. Asian Studies, Hollywood Coll., Fla., 1966-67; prof., chair anthropology Ramapo Coll. of N.J., Mahwah, 1972—; co-chair East Asian studies Ramapo Coll. of N.J., 1988—; pvt. practice psychotherapist Riverdale, N.Y., 1986—; trainer psychotherapists, social workers, 1986—; founder Integral Devel. Therapy, Integral Devel. Social Work, Integral Human Devel.; assoc. univ. seminar Columbia U., N.Y.C., 1972—; co-chair nat. com. Anthropology and Social Work, 1988—; founder, chair N.Y. Inst. Integral Human Devel., Riverdale, 1987—. Author: (English) King Lear: A Study of Human Order, 1985, Transcendental Self, 1987, Culture of Social Stratification and Sexism: The Nayars, 1987; (Malayalam) five volumes of short stories, two volumes of travelogues, two novels.s. Founder, chairperson Devel. Projects, India, 1955-66. Predoctoral fellowship NIMH, 1972-75. Fellow Am. Anthropol. Assn.; mem. Met. Med. Anthropology Assn. (subcom. chair 1980-83), Am. Assn. Counseling and Human Devel., Soc. Indian Academics Am. (chair ad hoc com.), Internat. Assn. Marriage and Family Counselors, World Malayalee Convention (exec. v.p.), World Malayalee Coun. (chair ad hoc com.), Assn. Multicultural Counseling and Devel., Assn. Asian Studies, Ramapo Anthropology Soc. (founder, dir.), India Devel. Inst. (chair). Avocations: travel field study, horticulture, bridge, poetry/music.

PILLAI, RAVIRAJ SUKUMAR, chemical engineer, researcher; b. Bombay, July 29, 1961; came to U.S., 1986; s. Sukumar and Ratnavalli Pillai; m. Bina Menon, Jan. 4, 1995; 1 child, Amit. BS, U. Mysore, India, 1984; MS, U. Ill., Chgo., 1991, PhD, 1993. Rsch. asst. U. Ill., Chgo., 1989-93; postdoctoral scientist Eli Lilly and Co., Indpls., 1993-94; rsch. chem. engr. SRI Internat., Menlo Park, Calif., 1995; sr. scientist GeneMedicine, Inc., The Woodlands, Tex., 1995—. Sci. reviewer Aerosol Sci. and Tech., 1994, Jour. Pharm. Scis.; contbr. articles to profl. jours. Mem. Am. Assn. for Aerosol Rsch., Am. Assn. Pharm. Scientists, Internat. Soc. for Aerosols in Medicine, Sigma Xi. Hindu. Achievements include development of novel approaches for delivery of aerosolized drugs to the lungs for local and systemic effect. Avocations: reading, traveling. Home: Apt 2203 333 Holy Creek Ct The Woodlands TX 77381

PILLARELLA, DEBORAH ANN, elementary education educator, consultant; b. Chgo., Oct. 2, 1960; d. Richard J. and Josephine A. (Miceli) Ban; m. James J. Pillarella, Sept. 1, 1989. BA in Edn., U. Ill., 1983, MEd in Ednl. Leadership, 1992. Tchr. elem. sch. Chgo. Bd. Edn., 1983—; youth and adult cons. Bodyworks, Chgo., 1982—; sec. Profl. PPAC, Chgo., 1990-94; cons. IDEA, San Diego, 1989—; mem. adv. bd. Spl. Devel. Com., Whiting, Ind., 1993—, Am. Coun. on Exercise, 1995. Author: Healthy Choices for Kids, 1993, Step Fitness, 1995, Adventures in Fitness, 1995. Vol. activist City of Hope, Chgo., 1990—; side coord. Cystic Fiborsis Found., Chgo., 1988; vol. Chgo. Heart Assn., 1989. Mem. AAHPERD, Am. Coll. Sports Medicine, Chgo. Tchrs. Union, Internat. Assn. Fitness Profls., Internat. Fitness Assn. Am., Phi Kappa Phi. Avocations: biking, hiking, swimming, walking, reading, piano, sewing. Home: 12916 S Commercial Ave Chicago IL 60633-1209 Office: Chgo Bd Edn Taylor Sch 9912 S Avenue H Chicago IL 60617-5548

PILLIAR, ROBERT MATHEWS, metallurgy educator, materials scientist; b. Beamsville, Ont., Can., Dec. 13, 1939; married; two children. BS, U. Toronto, 1961; PhD in Metall. Engring., U. Leeds, 1965. Univ. grant metall. McMaster U., Can., 1965-67; rsch. engr. Internat. Nickel, Inc., 1967-68; rsch. scientist Ont. Rsch. Found., 1968-78; adj. prof. metall. and material sci., U. Toronto, 1977-78; adj. prof. mech. engring. dept. U. Waterloo, 1976-77; vis. fellow Dental Biomats., Liverpool U., 1984-85. Mem. ASTM, Can. Soc. Biomats (sec./treas. 1977-78, 80-82, pres. 1982-84), Soc. Biomats, Inst. Assn. Dental Rsch. Orthopedic Rsch. Soc. Office: Univ Toronto/Ctr Biomaterials, Mining Bldg/170 College St, Toronto, ON Canada M5S 1A1*

PILLOT, GENE MERRILL, retired school system administrator; b. Canton, Ohio, Apr. 13, 1930; s. John D. Pillot and Vera R. Granstaff; m. Beverly Ann Shaw, June 4, 1982; children: Vera Kathleen Martin, Michael Gene, Patrick Merrill. BS in Math., Ohio State U., 1952; MEd in Adminstrn. and Supvervision, Kent State U., 1957; EdD in Adminstrn. and Supervision, U. Fla., 1970. Asst. prin. North Royalton (Ohio) High Sch., 1959-61, prin., 1961-63; asst. prin. Sarasota (Fla.) Sr. High Sch., 1963-64, prin., 1964-68; dir. staff development Sarasota Dist. Schs., 1968-70, asst. supt., 1970-71, supt., 1971-80; dir. human resources Sarasota Meml Hosp., 1980-83; owner, broker Pillot Realty, Sarasota, 1986-90; commr. Sarasota City, 1989—, vice mayor, 1992-93, 96-97, mayor, 1993-94; prof. Am. Assn. Sch. Adminstrn., Nat. Acad. Sch. Execs., 1969-73; adj. prof. U. South Fla., Tampa, 1978-81; pvt. cons. edn. orgns., 1969-76. Author (chpt.) Differentiated Staffing, Strategies for D.S., 1971; contbr. articles to profl. jours.

Trustee Fla. Sch. Deaf/Blind, St. Augustine, 1989-90, chmn. bd. dirs., 1986-89; bd. dirs. Riverview Found., 1985-94, Girls Club, Sarasota, 1985-89, Hospice Found., Sarasota Opera Assn., Hispanic Am. Alliance; mem. Civil Svc. Bd. Sarasota, 1984-89; mem. adv. bd. Cath. Social Svcs., 1987-89. Mem. Sara Bay Country Club (Sarasota), Phi Delta Kappa (Educator of Yr. 1980). Republican. Roman Catholic. Avocations: writing, Spanish language, ballroom dancing. Home: 1212 Hillview Dr Sarasota FL 34239-2020

PILLSBURY, EDMUND PENNINGTON, museum director; b. San Francisco, Apr. 28, 1943; s. Edmund Pennington and Priscilla Keator (Giesen) P.; m. Mireille Marie-Christine Bernard, Aug. 30, 1969; children: Christine Bullitt, Edmund Pennington III. BA, Yale U., 1965; MA, U. London, 1967, PhD, 1973; DFA, U. North Tex., 1996. Curator European art Yale U. Art Gallery, New Haven, 1972-76; asst. dir. Yale U. Gallery, New Haven, 1975-76; dir. Yale Ctr. Brit. Art, New Haven, 1976-80; chief exec. officer Paul Mellon Ctr. Studies in Brit. Art, London, 1976-80; dir. Kimbell Art Mus., Ft. Worth, 1980—; founding chmn. Villa I Tatti Coun., Harvard U., 1979-84; adj. prof. Yale U., 1976-80, lectr., 1972-76; internat. adv. bd. State Hermitage Mus., 1995—. Author: Florence and the Arts, 1971, Sixteenth-Century Italian Drawings: Form and Function, 1974, David Hockney: Travels with Pen, Pencil and Ink, 1978, The Graphic Art of Federico Barocci, 1978. Trustee Ft. Worth Country Day Sch., 1982-87, 88-94, St. Paul's Sch., Concord, N.H., 1985—, Burlington Mag. Found., London, 1987—; bd. govs. Yale U. Art Gallery, 1990—; chmn. art adv. panel indemnity program Nat. Endowment Arts, 1984-87; mem. vis. com. Sherman Fairchild Paintings Conservation Ctr., Met. Mus. Art, N.Y.C., 1982—; mem. bd. advisors art dept. U. North Tex., Denton, 1990—; mem. art adv. panel IRS, 1982-84. Decorated chevalier Ordre des Arts et des Lettres, 1985; David E. Finley fellow Nat. Gallery Art, Washington, 1970, Ford Found. fellow Cleve. Mus. Art, 1970-71, Nat. Endowment Arts rsch. fellow, 1974, Morse fellow Yale U., 1975. Mem. Assn. Art Mus. Dirs. (trustee 1989-90), Master Drawings Assn. (bd. dirs. 1987—), Coll. Art Assn., Century Club, Ft. Worth Club, Rivercrest Club, City Club. Episcopalian. Home: 1110 Broad Ave Fort Worth TX 76107-1529 Office: Kimbell Art Mus 3333 Camp Bowie Blvd Fort Worth TX 76107-2744

PILLSBURY, GEORGE STURGIS, investment adviser; b. Crystal Bay, Minn., July 17, 1921; s. John S. and Eleanor (Lawler) P.; m. Sally Whitney, Jan. 4, 1947; children: Charles Alfred, George Sturgis, Sarah Kimball, Katharine Whitney. BA, Yale U., 1943. Chmn. Sargent Mgmt. Co. Clubs: Seminole Golf (Juno beach, Fla.), Woodhill, Minnetonka Yacht, Mpls. Athletic, Mpls. Club, River (N.Y.C.), Bath and Tennis, Everglades (Palm Beach, Fla.). Home: 1300 Bracketts Point Rd Wayzata MN 55391-9393 Office: 4800 First Bank Pl Minneapolis MN 55402

PILLSBURY, HAROLD CROCKETT, otolaryngologist; b. Balt., 1947. MD, George Washington U., 1972. Intern U. N.C., Chapel Hill, 1972-73, resident in surgery, 1973, prof.; resident in otolaryngology N.C. Meml. Hosp., Chapel Hill, 1973-76, mem. staff, 1976—. Mem. ACS, AMA, AAFPRS, AAO-NHS, Alpha Omega Alpha. Office: U NC Womack Bldg CB7070 610 Burnett Chapel Hill NC 27599*

PILOUS, BETTY SCHEIBEL, nurse; b. Cleve., July 30, 1948; d. Raymond W. and Dorothy E. (Groth) S.; m. Lee Alan Pilous, Sept. 11, 1970; 1 child. Diploma in nursing, Huron Rd. Hosp., Cleve., 1970; BSBA, St. Joseph's Coll., 1989, MHSA, 1995. RN, Ohio; cert. med.-surg. nurse, nursing adminstr. Nurse Huron Rd. Hosp., Cleve., 1970-71, Hillcrest Hosp., Cleve., 1974-77; head nurse, relief supr. Oak Park Hosp., Oakwood, Ohio, 1977-81; head nurse med.-surg. Bedford Hosp., Ohio, 1981-87; dir. inpatient svcs. Meridia Euclid Hosp., Euclid, Ohio, 1987-93, coord. hosp. info. system for nursing, chair nurse practice com., los com. nursing liason; DON, Manor Care, Willoughby, Ohio; team leader referral/assessment Hospice Western Res. Former instr. ARC; chair nurse practice com. Am. Heart Assn.; mem. nursing standards com. Cmty. Hosp. of Bedford; mem. health and safety com. Twinsburg Schs., Ohio, 1984, mem. curriculum com., 1981-83; chairperson standards com. Cmty. Hosp. of Bedford; former counselor jr. high youth 1st Congl. Ch., Twinsburg; past chair adv. bd. chairperson Brecksville Rainbow Assembly for Girls, 1992; mem. Twinsburg Libr. Levy Com., 1991. Recipient Paradiam award, 1991. Mem. Ohio Citizen League Nursing Nurse Execs. Network (former sec.), Ohio Hosp. Assn., Ohio Orgn. Nurse Execs., Ohio Directors of Nursing Assocs. Long Term Care, Nat. League Nursing, Southeast Cleve. Mid Mgrs. Ohio Orgn. Nurse Exec., Acad. Med.-Surg. Nursing (charter mem.), Networking Group Nurse Mgrs. (initiated), Order Eastern Star, Sigma Theta Tau, Iota Psi. Avocation: hiking.

PILSON, MICHAEL EDWARD QUINTON, oceanography educator; b. Ottawa, Ont., Can., Oct. 25, 1933; came to U.S., 1958; s. Edward Charles and Frances Amelia (Ferguson) P.; m. Joan Elaine Johnstone, July 6, 1957; children: Diana Jane, John Edward Quinton. BSc, Bishops U., Lennoxville, Que., Can.; MSc, McGill U., Montreal, Que., Can., 1958; PhD, U. Calif., San Diego, 1964. Chemist Windsor Mills (Can.) Paper Co., 1954-55; asst. chemist Macdonald Coll. of McGill U., 1955-58; biologist Zool. Soc. San Diego, 1963-66; asst. prof. U. R.I., Narragansett, 1966-71, assoc. prof., 1971-78, prof., 1978—; dir. Marine Ecosystems Rsch. Lab., Narragansett, 1976—. Contbr. articles to profl. and popular jours.; author chpts. for 5 books. Grantee NSF, NOAA, EPA, NIH. Mem. AAAS, AGU, ASLO, Oceanography Soc., Am. Soc. Mammalogists, Saunderstown Yacht Club (bd. govs. 1974-87, commodore 1985-87). Home: PO Box 27 Saunderstown RI 02874-0027 Office: U RI Grad Sch Oceanography Narragansett RI 02882

PILZ, ALFRED NORMAN, manufacturing company executive; b. Evergreen Park, Ill., Oct. 12, 1931; s. Alfred and Erma Louise (Deane) P.; m. Constance Ney, Nov. 1957; children: Kerry, Kurt, Stephen, Matthew. B.S., Ill. Inst. Tech., 1953; M.B.A., Harvard U., 1960. Registered profl. engr., Mass. Indsl. engr. Harnischfeger Corp., Milw., 1956-58; cons. Arthur D. Little Co., Cambridge, Mass., 1959-60; asst. to exec. v.p., mgr. prodn. engring. Nat. Forge Co., Irvine, Pa., 1960-62; mgmt. cons. McKinsey & Co., N.Y.C. and Cleve., 1962-67; pres., gen. mgr. Ajax Iron Works div. Cooper Industries, Corry, Pa., 1967-72; pres., chief exec. officer WDP, Inc., 1972-79, Swank Refractories Co., Johnstown, Pa., 1972-77, Hyde Park (Pa.) Foundry & Machine Co., 1974-79, Shepard-Niles Corp., Montour Falls, N.Y., 1979-82, Acco Babcock Materials Handling, Frederick, Md., 1982-85; ptnr. Fagan and Co., Ligonier, Pa.; bd. dirs. Acco Babcock, Inc., Babcock Internat., Chemung Foundry, Parnell Precision Products Co., Carre-Orban and Partners, Liberty Mut. Ins. Co., Ind. Steel and Engring. Corp., Bedford Crane Co., Shepard Niles Corp., Marine Bank, WDP, Inc.; chmn. Parnell Precision Products, 1980-82, Ind. Steeland Engring., Bedford Crane Co., 1981-82, pres., chmn., chief exec. officer, Greenway Products. Served with USN, 1953-56, Korea. Mem. Crane Mfrs. Assn., Hoist Mfrs. Assn., Conveyor Equipment Mfg. Assn., Nat. Trust Soc. Clubs: HYP (Pitts.). Auburn-Cord-Duesenberg. Home: 139 Ramsey Rd Ligonier PA 15658-0244 Office: 223 E Main St Ligonier PA 15658-1347

PIMENTEL, DAVID, entomologist, educator; b. Fresno, Calif., May 24, 1925; s. Frank and Marion V. (Sylva) P.; m. Marcia R. Hutchins, July, 16, 1949; children: Christina, Susan, Mark David. Student, St. John's U., Collegeville, Minn., 1943, Clark U., summer 1946; BS, U. Mass., 1948; PhD, Cornell U., 1951. Chief tropical rsch. lab. USPHS, San Juan; chief tropical research lab. USPHS, P.R., 1951-54; project leader tech. devel. lab USPHS, Savannah, Ga., 1954-55; postdoctoral investigator U. Chgo., winters 1954-55; postdoctoral investigator, OEEC rsch. fellow Oxford (Eng.) U., 1961; postdoctoral investigator, NSF computer scholar MIT, Cambridge, summer 1961; mem. faculty Cornell U., 1955—, prof. insect ecology, 1963—, head dept. entomology and limnology, 1963-69, prof. entomology, ecology and systematics, 1969-76, prof. insect ecology and agrl. scis., 1976—; prof., core faculty Center Environ. Quality Mgmt., 1973-74; cons. Office Sci. and Tech., Exec. Office Pres., 1964-67, 69-70, EPA, 1971; co-chmn. Commn. on Mosquito Control for Developing Countries, Nat. Acad. Scis., 1972-73; mem. commn. on pesticides and pest mgmt. in Inter-Am., 1973-77; mem. Nat. Adv. Coun. on Environ. Edn., 1973-74; chmn. panel on environ. impact of herbicides EPA, 1972-74, pesticide adv. coun., 1975-78; nat. adv. coun. environ. edn. Office Edn., HEW, 1975-78, chmn., 1975; chmn. study team on interdependence of food, population, health, energy, and environment World Food and Nutrition Study, Nat. Acad. Scis., 1976-77, chmn. environ. studies bd., 1980-83; mem. energy rsch. adv. bd. Dept. Energy, 1979-85; mem. rsch. adv. com. USAID, 1979-82, chmn. panel on land productivity; mem. Office of Tech. Assessment, U.S. Congress, 1979-80; hon. prof. Inst. Applied Ecology, Shengang, China, 1995—. Assoc. editor: Am. Midland Naturalist; contbr. articles to profl. jours. Trustee Village of Cayuga Heights, 1974—. Served to 2d lt., pilot USAAF, 1943-45. Recipient Disting. Svc. award Rural Sociol. Coun., 1992. Mem. AAAS (climate com. 1979-82, population, resource and environ. com. 1985-91, chmn. subcom. on food, population, and resources 1986-87), NAS (chmn. panel on biology and renewable resources, exec. bd. com. on life scis. 1966-68, com. on world food, health and population 1974-75, chmn. panel on econ. and environ. aspects of pest mgmt. in Ctrl. Am. 1974-76, chmn. bd. on sci. and tech. for internat. devel. 1975-79, com. on food and food prodn. 1974-76, alt. agr. com. 1985-89, com. on role of alt. farming methods in modern productive agr. 1985-89), Entomol. Soc. Am. (gov. bd., chmn. editl. bd., pres. Eastern br. 1974-75), Ecol. Soc. Am., Am. Soc. Naturalists, Soc. Study of Evolution, Entomol. Soc. Can., Am. Soc. Zoologists, Nat. Geog. Soc. (com. on rsch. and explorations 1993—), Internat. Union for Conservation of Nature and Natural Resources (commn. on ecology 1981-90), Royal Swedish Acad. Scis. (bd. dirs. Beijer Inst. 1994—), Chinese Acad. Scis. (hon. prof., acad. com. Inst. Applied Ecology 1994—), Sigma Xi, Phi Kappa Phi, Gamma Alpha (nat. recorder 1960-62). Office: Cornell U Dept Entomology Comstock Hall Ithaca NY 14853

PIMLEY, KIM JENSEN, financial training consultant; b. Abington, Pa., Apr. 29, 1960; d. Alvin Christian Jensen and Helen Marie (Kairis) Meinken; m. Michael St. John Pimley, Nov. 10, 1988; 1 child, Oliver Jensen Pimley. BA, Emory U., 1982, MA magna cum laude, 1982; postgrad., U. Chgo., 1985—. Mgr. tng. ops. Continental Bank, Chgo., 1986-88, mgr. coll. rels., 1988-90; mgr. client svcs. The Globecon Group, N.Y.C., 1990-92; prin. Pimley & Pimley, Inc., Glencoe, Ill., 1992-93; pres. P&P Tng. Resources, Inc., Glencoe, 1993—. Contbr. poetry to various jours. Mem. Chgo. Coun. on Fgn. Affairs, 1990—. Scholarship U. Chgo., 1984. Mem. ACLU, NOW, Oxford and Cambridge Club, Poetry Soc. Am. Office: P&P Tng Resources Inc 117 Library Pl Princeton NJ 08540

PINARD, GILBERT DANIEL, psychiatrist, educator; b. Montréal, Que., Can., July 19, 1940; s. Roland and Gabrielle (Laurendeau) P.; children by previous marriage: Eric, Marc. BA, U. Montréal, 1961, MD, 1965, Spl. diploma in psychiatry, 1970. Intern Hôpital Maisonneuve, Montreal, 1965-66, resident in psychiatry, 1967-68; resident in psychiatry Hôpital Ste-Justine, Montreal, 1968-69, Hôpital St-Jean-de-Dieu, Montreal, 1969-70; asst. prof. research U. Montréal, 1975-76, assoc. prof., 1975-76; assoc. prof. U. Sherbrooke, Que., 1976-78, chmn. dept. psychiatry, 1976-82, prof., 1978, assoc. dean edn. and medicine, 1983-85; prof., chmn. dept. psychiatry McGill U., Montréal, 1986—; vis. prof. dept. psychiatry, U. Tex., Dallas, South Western Med. Sch., 1982-83; councillor, mem. nominating com. Can. Coll. Neuropsychopharmacology; mem. planning com. Fonds de la Recherche en Santé du Que.; vis. prof. Sultan Qabous U., Muscat, Oman, 1996. Contbr. numerous articles to profl. jours. and chpts. to books. Fellow Royal Coll. Physicians Can. (evaluation com. 1989—), Am. Psychiat. Assn. (Que. br. counsellor, chmn. pres.); mem. Can. Psychiat. Assn. (bd. adminstrs., liaison, edn. com., chmn. sci. program com., nominating com., R.O. Jones meml. vis. prof.), Que. Psychiat. Assn. (adv. com. dean medicine), Internat. Children's Found. (acad. planning com.). Home: 3430 Peel Apt 11C, Montreal, PQ Canada H3A 3K8 Office: McGill U Dept Psychiatry, 1033 Pine Ave W, Montreal, PQ Canada H3A 1A1

PINARD, RAYMOND R., pulp and paper consultant; b. Trois-Rivieres, Que., Can., May 13, 1930; s. Albert and Mariette (Dufresne) P.; m. Estelle Frechette, Nov. 5, 1965; children: Robert, Andree. B.A., U. Laval, (Que., Can.), 1951; B.Eng., McGill U., Montreal, 1955. Registered profl. engr., Que. Process engring. plant mgr. Domtar Inc., East Augus, Que., 1955-68; gen. mgr. Domtar Kraft & Bd. Domtar Inc., Montreal, 1968-73, v.p., gen. mgr. Domtar Newspring & Pulp, 1974-79, pres. Domtar Pulp & Paper, 1979-81, exec. v.p., chief operating officer, 1981-90, also dir.; bd. dirs. South Shore Industries, E.F. Walter Ltd., United Auto Parts, Gen. Accident; bd. dirs., chmn. Centre Canadien de Fusion Magnetique; chmn. St. Laurent Paperboard Inc.; mem. Montreal adv. bd. Nat. Trust. Bd. dirs., past chmn. PPRIC; bd. dirs. Fondation de l'Universite' du Que., Montreal, 1979-92. Mem. TAPPI, Can. Pulp and Paper Assn. (chmn. 1982, bd. dirs.), Corp. Profl. Engrs. Que., Can. Mfrs. Assn. (chmn. 1988-89), Can. Pulp and Paper Tech. Assn. Office: R Pinard Cons Inc Ste 3000, 630 René-Lévesque Blvd W, Montreal, PQ Canada H3B 5C7

PINCAY, LAFFIT, JR., jockey; b. Panama City, Panama, 1946; s. Laffit and Rosario P.; m. Linda Pincay (dec.); children: Lisa, Laffit III. Jockey, 1964—. Winner Belmont Stakes, 1982, 84, 85, Ky. Derby, 1984, Preakness; leading money winner in thoroughbred horse racing, 1970-74, 79, 84; named Jockey of Yr., 1971, 72, 73, 79, 84, 85; inducted into Racing Hall of Fame.

PINCH, JOHN G., radio executive; b. Milw., Oct. 28, 1948; s. Ken and Gwen Maud (Watkins) P.; m. Linda Diane Postles; children: Jodi, Lori, Michelle. BA, U. Wis., 1972. Sales mgr. Sta. WOKY, Milw., 1978-82; gen. mgr. Sta. WXJY, Milw., 1981-82, Sta. WFMR, Milw., 1982-83; pres., gen. mgr. Stas. WMTX & WHBO, Tampa, Fla., 1983—. Office: Sta WMTX-FM 18167 Us Highway 19 N Ste 500 Clearwater FL 34624-6573

PINCHOT, BRONSON, actor; b. N.Y.C., 1959; s. Rosina Pinchot. BA with honors, Yale U., 1981. Ind. actor, 1981—. appeared in television series including Sara, 1985, Perfect Strangers, 1986-93, The Trouble With Larry, 1993; other TV appearances include George Burns Comedy Week, Amazing Stories, Saturday Night Live; films include Risky Business, 1983, The Flamingo Kid, 1984, Beverly Hills Cop, 1984, After Hours, 1985, Hot Resort, 1986, Second Sight, 1989, Blame It on the Bellboy, 1992, True Romance, 1993, Beverly Hills Cop III, 1994; television film Jury Duty, 1989, The Langoliers, 1995; appeared in Broadway play Zoya's Apartment, 1990; appeared in off-Broadway prodn. Poor Little Lambs. Office: ICM care Corey Weisman 8942 Wilshire Blvd Beverly Hills CA 90211*

PINCKNEY, C. COTESWORTH, lawyer; b. Richmond, Va., Oct. 23, 1939; s. Thomas and Charlotte (Kent) P.; m. Helen Raney, Aug. 13, 1966; children: Sarah Whitley, Thomas. BA, Yale U., 1961; LLB, U. Va., 1967. Bar: Va. 1967. Assoc. Mays, Valentine, Davenport & Moore, Richmond, 1967-72; ptnr. Mays & Valentine, Richmond, 1972—; pres Bd. dir., Sweet Briar Coll., 96—. Bd. dirs. Sweet Briar Coll., 1996—; pres. Sheltering Arms Hosp., Richmond, 1986-87, bd. dirs., 1972—; trustee William H.-John G.-Fmma Scott Found., 1974—. Mem. ABA, Va. Bar Assn., Richmond Bar Assn., Phila. Quarry Club (pres. 1985-91), Country Club of Va., Commonwealth Club (bd. govs.), Soc. of Cin.1995-91,. Republican. Episcopalian. Home: 2 Roslyn Rd Richmond VA 23226-1610 Office: Mays & Valentine 1111 E Main St PO Box 1122 Richmond VA 23218-1122

PINCKNEY, NEAL THEODORE, psychologist, educator; b. N.Y.C., July 26, 1935; s. Leo Allen and Jean (Wiener) P.; children: Andrew Allen, Jennifer Elizabeth, Matthew Ian. Cert. polit. social and hist. issues, King's Coll., U. Durham, Eng., 1957; A.B., U. So. Calif., 1958, postgrad., 1958-61; Ph.D., Oxford U., 1966; postgrad., U. Vienna, U. Hiroshima, Stanford U. Mem. Pub. Welfare Commn., Los Angeles County, 1958-60; tchr. pub. schs., Los Angeles, 1960-61; tchr., counselor Las Vegas, 1961-62, admninstr. therapist psychiat. clinic, 1962-63; educator, dir. guidance service Dept. Def. Overseas Dependent Schs., England and Japan, 1963-67; pvt. practice clin. psychology, 1967-87; lectr. Calif. State U., Sacramento, 1967-68, asst. prof., 1968-71, assoc. prof., 1971-77, prof. psychology and edn., 1977-87, prof. emeritus, 1987—, chmn. dept. behavioral scis., 1980-82, prof. counseling psychology, coordinator grad. studies, dept. adminstrn., counseling and policy studies, 1982—; founder, clin. dir. A Healing Heart, 1993—; vis. prof. U. Calif.-Davis, 1979—; psychologist, instr. enforcement psychology and human rels. Calif. Hwy. Patrol, 1967-80; dir. Univ. Software Evaluation Project, 1987; tech. cons., adv. Ministry Edn. and Culture, Goft. Brazil, Brasilia, 1974-76; cons. psychologist Calif. Med. Facility, Vacaville, various law enforcement agys.; prof. U. Hawaii, lectr. U. Hawaii Leeward C.C., 1992-93; founder, clin. dir. Healing Heart Found., 1993—. Author: Healthy Heart Handbook, 1994, Law and Ethics in Counseling and Psychotherapy, A Casebook, 1961, 86; pub. USER, a Software Report Card, 1987; editor: Incite Newsletter of Hawii Portable Computer Users Assn., 1987-88; editor: Ency. of Psychology, 2d edit. Served with 3d Armored Div. U.S. Army, 1954-55. Queen's scholar Eng., 1956-57; scholar Dept. State Fgn. Service Inst., 1964; fellow Ford Found., 1960-61. Mem. Am. Psychol. Assn., Brit. Psychol. Assn., Japanese Psychol. Assn., Brazilian Psychol. Assn., Am. Ednl. Research Assn., Am. Assn. Counseling and Devel., Am. Radio Relay League (life), Hawaii Portable Computer Users Assn., Hawaii Personal Computer Users Group (pres. 1989-91, system operator Electronic Bulletin Bd. Svc.), Quarter Century Wireless Assn. (life), Vegetarian Soc. Honolulu, No. Calif. DX Club, Hawaii DX Assn., Phi Delta Kappa, Delta Phi Epsilon. Clubs: Commonwealth (San Francisco); Oxonian (Tokyo); Toastmasters (area gov. 1962-63). Lodge: Masons. Home: 84-683 Upena St Waianae HI 96792-1935 *Those who rush through life are merely hurrying toward their death. When one pauses to savor its many subtle varieties one begins to gain some insight and to be in awe of the wonder of it all. Then we begin to place ourselves in perspective and everything has meaning.*

PINCO, ROBERT G., lawyer; b. L.A., Feb. 9, 1944. BS Pharmacy, U. Conn., 1966; JD, Georgetown U., 1969. Bar: Md. 1969, D.C. 1970, U.S. Claims Ct. 1971, U.S. Supreme Ct. 1973; registered pharmacist D.C. Atty. Dept. Justice, 1969-72; asst. gen. counsel spl. action office drug abuse prevention Exec. Office Pres., 1972-74; dir. over-the-counter drugs FDA, 1977—; ptnr. Akin, Gump, Strauss, Hauer & Feld, Washington, 1993—; adj. assoc. prof. pharmacy U. Md., 1978—; mem. bd. advisors U. Md. Sch. Pharmacy, 1994—. Contbr. articles to profl. jours. Mem. ABA, D.C. Bar Assn., Md. State Bar Assn., Fed. Bar Assn. (vice chair food and drug com 1977), Am. Soc. Pharmacy Law (Pres'. award 1986). Office: Akin Gump Strauss Hauer & Feld 1333 New Hampshire Ave NW Washington DC 20036-1511

PINCOCK, DOUGLAS GEORGE, electronics company executive; b. Vancouver, B.C., Can., Sept. 29, 1940; s. George Leyland and Sadie McElvenna (Boyle) P.; m. Gloria Dawn Werth, Sept. 5, 1964 (div. 1985); children: Barrt, James, David, Lisa; m. Marilyn Marie Spearns, Oct. 28, 1990. BSEE, Man. (Winnipeg, Can.) U., 1963, MSEE, 1967; PhD, New Brunswick U., Fredericton, 1971. Registered profl. engr., N.S. Asst. prof. St. Francis Xavier U., Antigonish, N.S., 1969-70; from lectr. to asst. prof. to assoc. prof. U. N.B., 1970-75, 76-79; maitre de conf. U. Paris, 1975-76; prof. Tech. U. N.S., Halifax, 1979-82; pres., founder Applied Microelectronics Inc., Halifax, 1982—; bd. dirs. Can. Microelectronics Corp., Kingston, Ont., VEMCO, Shad Bay, N.S.; pres., bd. dirs. AMI Techs., Halifax, 1992—; mem. adv. bd. Can. Intellectual Property Orgn. Contbr. 25 papers to profl. jours. Head coach basketball Tech. U. N.S., 1989-95. With Can. Air Force, 1963-66. Achievements include co-invention weatherstar 4000, other inventions in underwater telemetry products. Office: Microelectronics Inc, 1046 Barrington St, Halifax, NS Canada B3H 2R1

PINCOCK, RICHARD EARL, chemistry educator; b. Ogden, Utah, Sept. 14, 1935; s. Earl Samuel and Virginia (Christenson) P.; m. Elke Gertrud Hermann, Aug. 20, 1960; children—Christina, Gordon, Jennifer. B.S., U. Utah, 1956; A.M., Harvard U., 1957, Ph.D., 1960. Postdoctoral research fellow Calif. Inst. Tech., 1959-60; faculty U. B.C., Vancouver, Can., 1960—; prof. U. B.C., 1969—. Mem. Phi Beta Kappa, Sigma Pi. Office: U BC, Chemistry Dept, Vancouver, BC Canada V6T 1Y6

PINCUS, ANN TERRY, federal agency administrator; b. Little Rock, Sept. 12, 1937; d. Fred William and Cornelia (Witsell) Terry; m. Walter Haskell Pincus, May 1, 1965; children: Ward, Adam, Cornelia Battle. BA, Vassar Coll., 1959. Editorial asst., writer Glamour Mag., 1963; reporter Ridder Pubs., Washington, 1963-66; freelance writer Washington, 1966-76; dir. info. select com. on U.S. population U.S. Ho. Reps., Washington, 1977-79; nat. publicist Nat. Pub. Radio, Washington, 1979-83; press sec. U.S. Sen. Charles Mathias, Washington, 1983-87; profl. staff mem. Senate Com. on Rules, Washington, 1983-87; v.p. communications Stas. WETA-TV/Radio, Washington, 1987-93; dir. Office of Rsch., U.S. Info. Agy., Washington, 1993—; bd. dirs. Fgn. Student Svcs. Coun., Washington, Woodley House. Editor: Kennedy Center Cookbook, 1977; contbr. articles to profl. jours. Avocations: politics, reading, walking, tennis. Home: 3202 Klingle Rd NW Washington DC 20008-3403 Office: Office of Rsch US Info Agy 301 4th St SW Rm 352 Washington DC 20547-0009

PINCUS, GEORGE, engineering educator; b. Havana, Cuba, July 5, 1935; came to U.S., 1957, naturalized, 1966; s. Max and Ana (Slutzkaya) P.; m. Dora Dzubquevich, June 8, 1958; children: Cynthia Judith, David Nathan, Karen Joy. BSCE, Ga. Inst. Tech., 1959, MSCE, 1960; PhD, Cornell U., 1963; MBA, U. Houston, 1974. Registered profl. engr., Ky., Tex., Fla., Calif., N.J. Teaching asst. Cornell U., Ithaca, N.Y., 1959-61; rsch. asst. Cornell U., Ithaca, 1961-63; asst. prof. structural engring. U. Ky., Lexington, 1963-66; assoc. prof. civil engring. U. Ky., 1968-69; prof. civil engring. U. Houston, 1969-86, chmn. dept., 1976-80; prof. civil engring. N.J. Inst. Tech., Newark, 1986—, dean engring., 1986-94; chief party grad. engring. program AID, Rio de Janeiro, Brazil, also prof. Fed. U., Rio de Janeiro, 1967-68. Author: Design of Structures and Foundations for Vibrating Machines, 1979, other books; contbr. articles to profl. jours. Recipient W.T. Kittinger Tchg. Excellence award U. Houston, 1975, Silver medal 4th World Congress on Engring. Edn., 1995. Fellow ASCE (D.V. Terrel award dist. 9, 1959); mem. AAUP, Am. Soc. for Engring. Edn., NSPE, N.J. Soc. Profl. Engrs. (N.J. Engr. of Yr. award 1990), Soc. Mfg. Engrs. (sr.), Order of Engr., Phi Kappa Phi, Omicron Delta Kappa, Tau Beta Pi, Chi Epsilon. Avocations: music, art. *It is surprising to find some who underestimate the value of living in this country with its principles of reward for hard work, full equal opportunity for all, personal liberty, and its tradition for world moral leadership. My primary goals have been: to show continued improvement and growth in my academic career and to prepare myself for greater administrative responsibilities in higher education. I hope that these goals will result in tangible benefits for my adopted country and in some way, repay my debt of gratitude to the United States of America.*

PINCUS, HOWARD JONAH, geologist, engineer, educator; b. N.Y.C., June 24, 1922; s. Otto Max and Gertrude (Jankowsky) P.; m. Maud Lydia Roback, Sept. 6, 1953; children: Glenn David, Philip E. BS, CCNY, 1942; PhD, Columbia U., 1949. Mem. faculty Ohio State U., 1949-67, successively instr., asst. prof., assoc. prof., 1949-59, prof., 1959-67, chmn. dept. geology, 1960-65; rsch. geologist U. S. Bur. Mines, summers 1963-67; geologist, rsch. supr. U.S. Bur. Mines, 1967-68; prof. geol. sci. and civil engring. U. Wis., Milw., 1968-87, prof. emeritus, 1987—, dean Coll. Letters and Sci., 1969-72; rsch. assoc. Lamont Geol. Obs., Columbia, 1949, 50, 51; geologist Ohio Dept. Natural Resources, summers 1950-61; cons. geology and rock mechanics, 1954-67, 68—; mem. U.S. nat. com. on tunnelling tech. NAE, 1972-74, mem. U.S. nat. com. on rock mechanics NAS/NAE, 1975-78, 80-89, chmn., 1985-87; mem. U.S. com. Internat. Assn. Engring. Geology/NAS, chmn., 1987-90; sr. postdoctoral fellow NSF, 1962. Tech. editor: Geotech. Testing Jour., 1992-95. Served to 1st lt. C.E. AUS, 1942-46. Recipient award for teaching excellence U. Wis.-Milw. Alumni Assn., 1978. Fellow ASTM (Reinhart award 1987, Award of Merit 1989), AAAS, Geol. Soc. Am.; mem. NSPE, AAUP (pres. Ohio State U. chpt. 1955-56, mem. coun. 1965-67, pres. U. Wis.-Milw. chpt. 1976-77), Am. Geophys. Union, Geol. Soc. Am. (chmn. engring. geology divsn. 1973-74), Soc. Mining Engrs., Internat. Assn. Engring. Geology, Internat. Soc. Rock Mechanics, Assn. Engring. Geologists, Am. Inst. Profl. Geologists (pres. Ohio sect. 1965-66), Computer Oriented Geol. Soc., Phi Beta Kappa (pres. Ohio State U. chpt. 1959-60, pres. U. Wis.-Milw. chpt. 1976-77), Sigma Xi. Home: 17523 Plaza Marlena San Diego CA 92128-1807 Office: PO Box 27598 San Diego CA 92198-1598

PINCUS, JILLIAN RUTH, physician; b. Bklyn., May 26, 1947; d. William and Elsa Bronson Pincus. BA, Radcliffe Coll., 1969; MD, Med. Coll. Pa., 1974. Cert. Am. Bd. Internal Medicine, Am. Bd. Nephrology. Intern, resident U. Medicine and Dentistry of N.J.-Robert Wood Johnson Med. Sch., 1974-77, nephrology fellow, 1978-79; nephrology fellow U. Miami Sch. Medicine, 1977-78; attending physician Jewish Inst. Geriatric Care, New Hyde Park, N.Y., 1979-80, L.I. Jewish Hosp.-Hillside Med. Ctr., New Hyde Park, 1980-82; from asst. to assoc. med. dir. Sandoz Pharm., East Hanover, N.J., 1982-88; med. dir. CIBA-Geigy Corp., Summit, N.J., 1988-90, exec. med. dir., 1990-92, clin. head, 1992-93, head, 1993—. Active Nat. Kidney Found. Mem. AMA, Am. Soc. Nephrology, Am. Med. Women's Assn., Women in Nephrology. Avocations: sports, reading, arts. Home: 1 Plymouth Rd Chatham NJ 07928-1814 Office: CIBA-Geigy Corp 556 Morris Ave Summit NJ 07901-1330

PINCUS, JONATHAN HENRY, neurologist, educator; b. Bklyn., May 4, 1935; s. Joseph Bernhard and Hannah Martha (Palestine) P.; m. Cynthia Sterling Deery, Jan., 1961 (div. 1983); children: Daniel, Jeremy, Adam; m. Fortuna Mizrahi Fries, Nov. 1983 (div. 1995). AB, Amherst Coll., Mass., 1956; MD, Columbia U., 1960; MA, Yale U., 1973. Asst. prof. neurology Yale U., New Haven, 1965-69, assoc. prof. neurology, 1969-73, prof. neurology, 1973-86; prof., chmn. neurology Sch. Medicine Georgetown U., Washington, 1987-95, prof. neurology, 1987—. Author: Behavioral Neurology, 1974, 3d edit., 1986. Fellow Am. Acad. Neurology (v.p. 1991—); mem. Am. Neurol. Assns. (counselor 1984-86). Achievements include linkage of anticonvulsant properties of phenytoin to reduction of Ca influx; introduction of protein redistribution diet to restore 1-dopa responsiveness in end stage Parkinsonism; correlation of neurologic deficits, the experience of abuse and paranoia with episodic violence in delinquents and criminals; proposition of defect in thiamine triphosphate as cause of Leigh's encephalomyelopathy. Office: Georgetown Univ Hosp Dept Neurology 1st Fl Bles Bldg 3800 Reservoir Rd NW Washington DC 20007-2196

PINCUS, JOSEPH, economist, educator; b. N.Y.C., Apr. 17, 1919; s. Samuel and Lillian (Sirotkin) P.; m. Ethel Frances London, July 6, 1952; children: Terri Ellen Pincus Forman, Sally Neila, Robert Alan. BSS, CCNY, 1941; MA, Am. U., 1947, PhD, 1953. Internat. economist Latin Am. studies project U.S. Tariff Commn., Washington, 1946-47, 61-62; economist, fgn. affairs analyst Div. Research Am. Republics, Dept. State, Washington, 1949-58; tariff adviser ICA, USOM, Honduras, 1958-60; rep. with Continental Allied Co. to study indsl. devel., 1961; program officer, econ. adviser AID, Costa Rica, 1962-64; acting dir. mission AID, 1964; econ. adviser, pvt. enterprise adviser Am. Embassy, Asuncion, Paraguay, 1964-66, acting embassy econ. officer, 1967; pvt. enterprise devel. officer Am. Embassy, San Salvador, El Salvador, 1967-69, acting program officer, 1968, loan economist, 1968-69; dir. research Brokers Internat. Ltd., Miami, Fla., 1972-73; adj. prof. econs. Fla. Internat. U., also Embry-Riddle Aero. U., 1974-75; vis. prof. econs. U. Miami, 1974, 79, Fla. Meml. Coll., 1975; pres. Common Market Devel. Corp., Miami, 1975-86; ptnr., chief economist Brown and Pincus Assocs.; hon. fellow U. Asuncion Sch. Advanced Econ. Studies, 1966-67; dir. enterprise devel. program Ctr. for Advanced Internat. Studies, U. Miami; mem. Fla.-Colombia Ptnrs. Program. Mem. indsl. devel., promotion and retention task force Dade County Overall Econ. Devel. Program Com., 1983-85; senator Fla. Silver-Haired Legislature; mem. internat. bus. and commerce task force Beacon Council; founder South Dade-Kendall Rep. Club, Dade County, Fla. Mem. Am. Fgn. Svc. Assn., Nat. Assn. Ret. Fed. Employees, Latin Am. Studies Assn., Soc. Internat. Devel., Acad. for Internat. Bus., Caribbean Studies Assn., U. Miami Consortium on Hunger and Poverty, Omicron Delta Epsilon, Beta Gamma Sigma. Avocations: amateur radio at Sta. KD6TCE. Home and Office: 50 Chumasero Dr San Francisco CA 94132-2338 *To those involved in corporate or governmental bureaucracies, my advice is to exercise initiative, go as far as you can on your own, and then seek advice. If you're wrong, someone in authority will stop you eventually. But you could be RIGHT.*

PINCUS, LIONEL IRWIN, venture banker; b. Phila., Mar. 2, 1931; s. Henry and Theresa Celia (Levit) P.; m. Suzanne Storrs Poulton (dec.). BA, U. Pa., 1953; MBA, Columbia U., 1956. Assoc. gen. ptnr. Ladenburg, Thalmann & Co., N.Y.C., 1955-63; pres. Lionel I. Pincus & Co., Inc., N.Y.C., 1964-66; pres., chief exec. officer E.M. Warburg & Co., Inc., N.Y.C., 1966-70; chmn., chief exec. officer E.M. Warburg, Pincus & Co., Inc., N.Y.C., 1970—. Bd. trustees Montefiore Hosp., N.Y.C.; trustee Ittleson Found., Inc., Columbia U., co-chmn.; trustee Sch. Am. Ballet, Citizens Budget Commn., German Marshall Fund USA, 1982-88; mem. bd. overseers Columbia Grad. Sch. Bus.; mem. bd. Nat. Park Found. Mem. Council Fgn. Rels., N.Y.C. Partnership, Nat. Golf Links Am. Club, Meadow Club. Office: EM Warburg Pincus Co Inc 466 Lexington Ave New York NY 10017-3140

PINCUS, ROBERT LAWRENCE, art critic, cultural historian; b. Bridgeport, Conn., June 5, 1953; s. Jules Robert and Carol Sylvia (Rosen) P.; m. Georgianna Manly, June 20, 1981; 1 child, Matthew Manly. BA, U. Calif., Irvine, 1976; MA, U. So. Calif., 1980, PhD, 1987. Instr. U. So. Calif., L.A., 1978-83; art critic L.A. Times, 1981-85, San Diego Union, 1985-92, San Diego Union-Tribune, 1992—; vis. prof. San Diego State U., 1985-86, 92. Author: On A Scale That Competes with the World: The Art of Edward and Nancy Reddin Kienholz, 1990, (with others) West Coast Duchamp, 1991, But Is It Art: The Spirit of Art as Activism, 1994, Paradise, 1994; author introduction to W.D.'s Midnight Carnival, 1988, Manuel Neri Early Work, 1953-78. Recipient Chem. Bank award, 1994, Best Critical Writing award San Diego Press Club, 1994. Mem. Internat. Assn. Art Critics, Coll. Art Assn. Democrat. Office: San Diego Union-Tribune 350 Camino De La Reina San Diego CA 92108-3003

PINCUS, STEPHANIE HOYER, dermatologist, educator; b. Lakehurst, N.J., Feb. 28, 1944; d. Ernest Carl and Aviva (Silbert) Hoyer; m. David Frank Pincus, Aug. 22, 1965 (div. Dec. 1984); children: Matthew Jonah, Tamara Hope; m. Allan Roy Oseroff, Mar. 24, 1985; 1 child, Benjamin Henry Oseroff. BA, Reed Coll., 1964; MD cum laude, Harvard U., 1968. Diplomate Am. Bd. Dermatology, Am. Bd. Internal Medicine. Intern Boston City Hosp., 1968-69; rsch. fellow U. Wash., 1969-71; resident internal medicine U. WN, 1971-72, resident-fellow dermatology, 1972-74; fellow instr. dept. dermatology Harvard Med. Sch., 1974-75; asst. prof. medicine U. Wash., Seattle, 1975-77; lectr. Sch. Medicine Boston U., 1977-89; asst. prof. medicine Sch. Medicine Tufts U., Boston, 1977-82, mem. dept. immunology, 1977-89, asst. prof. dermatology, 1979-82, assoc. prof. dermatology and medicine, vice chairperson dermatology, 1982-89; prof. medicine and dermatology, chairperson dermatology SUNY, Buffalo, 1989—. Mem. majority coun. Emily's List. Dermatology Found. fellow, Evanston, Ill., 1974-75, 77-78; Vets. Adminstrn. rsch. assoc., 1975-77; recipient Clin. Investigator award NIH, Bethesda, Md., 1979-81. Mem. Am. Contact Dermatitis Soc. (mem. liaison com. 1993—), Women's Dermatologic Soc. (bd. dirs. 1992—), Soc. Investigative Dermatology (chmn. com. on govt. and pub. rels. 1992—), Profs. of Dermatology (mem. program com. 1993—), Internat. Soc. for Study of Vulvar Diseas (mem. exec. com. 1993—), Harvard Med. Alumni (pres.-elect 1993—), Phi Beta Kappa, Alpha Omega Alpha. Office: SUNY 100 High St Ste C319 Buffalo NY 14203-1126

PINCUS, THEODORE, microbiologist, rheumatologist, educator. AB, Columbia U., 1961; MD, Harvard U., 1966. Assoc. Sloan-Kettering Inst., N.Y.C., 1973-75; asst. prof. medicine/immunology, dir. clin. immunology lab. Stanford (Calif.) U., 1975-76; prof. Wistar Inst., Phila., 1976-80; adj. assoc. prof. medicine-rheumatology U. Pa., Phila., 1976-80; prof. medicine and microbiology Vanderbilt U., Nashville, 1980—. Fellow ACP, Am. Rheumatism Assn., Am. Soc. Microbiology. Achievements include description of morbidity and mortility of rheumatoid arthritis; analyses of host genetic and psychosocial variables in chronic diseases; description of host genetic control of experimental retrovirus infection; description of psychological and economic consequences of chronic disease; analysis of "mind body" explanations of associations between socioeconomic status and chronic disease. Office: Vanderbilt U Divsn Rheumatology & Immunology 230 Oxford House Nashville TN 37232

PINCUS, THEODORE HENRY, public relations executive; b. Chgo., Sept. 15, 1933; s. Jacob T. and J. (Engel) P.; m. Sharon Barr, Jan. 16, 1988; children: Laura, Mark, Susan, Anne, Jennifer. BS in Journalism, Ind. U., 1955. Free-lance bus. writer, 1955-58; sr. exec. Harshe Rotman & Druck, Chgo., 1958-62; dir. comm. Maremont Corp., Chgo., 1962-64; chmn., CEO, majority owner The Fin. Rels. Bd. Inc., N.Y.C., Chgo., L.A., San Francisco, Boston, Washington, 1964—; pub. affairs advisor to Nelson Rockefeller, N.Y.C., 1960, 68; advisor U.S. Info. Agy., 1993—. Author: Giveaway Day, 1977; contbr. articles to profl. jours. Active presdl. nomination campaigns; vice-chmn. Midwest region Am. Jewish Com.; mem. adv. bd. Ind. U. Bus. Sch. With USAF, 1955-57. Recipient numerous nat. awards for profl. excellence in investor rels. and corp.pub. rels. including Silver Anvil award Pub. Rels. Soc. Am., 1966, Civic Achievement award Am. Jewish Com., 1993. Mem. Young Pres.'s Orgn., Nat. Investor Relations Inst. (founding). Club: Union League. Office: The Financial Relations John Hancock Ctr 875 N Michigan Ave Chicago IL 60611-1803

PINCUS, WALTER HASKELL, editor; b. Bklyn., Dec. 24, 1932; s. Jonas and Clare (Glassman) P.; m. Betty Meskin, Sept. 12, 1954; 1 son, Andrew John; m. Ann Witsell Terry, May 1, 1965; children: Ward Haskell, Adam Witsell, Cornelia Battle Terry. B.A., Yale, 1954; postgrad., Georgetown U., 1995—. Cons. Senate Fgn. Relations Com., 1962-63; spl. writer Washington Evening Star, 1963-66; editor, reporter Washington Post, 1966-69; chief cons. Symington subcom. Senate Fgn. Relations Com., 1969-70; asso. editor New Republic, 1972-74, exec. editor, 1974-75; spl. writer Washington Post, 1975—; Cons. NBC News, 1971-79, CBS News, 1979-86, NBC News, 1987-88, Washington Post Co., 1989—; vis. lectr. Yale U., Fall 1988; dir. N.Y. Rev. Corp., 1979-85. Trustee Shakespeare Theater at the Folger, 1988—, co-chmn. edn. com., 1989-91, chmn. nominating com., 1992—. Served with AUS, 1955-57. Recipient Page One award, 1960, George Orwell award, 1977, George Polk award, 1978, Emmy award, 1981. Mem. Council Fgn. Relations. Clubs: Federal City (Washington), Yale (Washington). Home: 3202 Klingle Rd NW Washington DC 20008-3403 Office: Washington Post 1150 15th St NW Washington DC 20071-0001

PINCUS-WITTEN, ROBERT A., art history educator, art gallery director, critic; b. N.Y.C., Apr. 5, 1935. Diploma, The Cooper Union, N.Y.C., 1956; MA, U. Chgo., 1962, PhD, 1968. Prof. art history CUNY, 1964-90, prof. art history, doctoral faculty, 1970-90; sr. editor Artforum, N.Y.C., 1966-76; assoc. editor Arts Magazine, N.Y.C., 1976-89; dir. The Gagosian Gallery, N.Y.C., 1990—. Author: Postminimalism into Maximalism: American Art 1966-1986, 1987, Eye to Eye: Twenty Years of Art Criticism, 1984; Occult Symbolism in France: Joséphin Peladan and the Salons de la Rose-Croix; catalogues for The Mus. of Modern Art, N.Y., The Whitney Mus. of Am. art, N.Y., The New Mus., N.Y., The Inst. of Contemporary Art, Phila., The Milw. Art Ctr., numerous others; contbr. numerous articles to profl. jours.

PINCZUK, ARON, physicist; b. San Martin, Argentina, Feb. 15, 1939; s. Faiwel and Ester (Wejeman) P.; m. Gladys Norma Teitelman, June 14, 1962; children: Ana Gabriela, Guillermo Fabian. Licenciado, U. Buenos Aires, Argentina, 1962; PhD, U. Pa., 1969. Staff mem. Nat. Rsch. Coun., Argentina, 1971-76; head physics dept. Faculty of Scis., U. Buenos Aires, Argentina, 1974; vis. scientist Max Planck Inst., Stuttgart, Germany, 1976, IBM Rsch., Yorktown Heights, N.Y., 1976-77; staff mem. AT&T Bell Labs., Murray Hill, N.J., 1978—; sec. Argentina Phys. Soc., Buenos Aires, 1972-75; editor Solid State Communications, 1989-92, assoc. editor in chief, 1992—. Contbr. over 180 articles to profl. jours. and numerous chpts. to books. Recipient Oliver E. Buckley Condensed-Matter Physics prize Am. Physical Soc., 1994. Fellow Am. Phys. Soc. (Oliver E. Buckley prize 1994); mem. AAAS. Achievements include use and devel. novel optical methods in studies of structural phase transitions, semiconductor interfaces and interactions of free electrons in semiconductors; discovered novel phenomena in studies of quantum electron fluids. Office: Bell Labs Lucent Techs 600 Mountain Ave Rm 1d-433 New Providence NJ 07974

PINDELL, HOWARDENA DOREEN, artist; b. Phila., Apr. 14, 1943; s. Howard Douglas and Mildred Edith (Lewis) P. B.F.A., Boston U., 1965; M.F.A., Yale U., 1967. Curatorial asst. Mus. Modern Art, N.Y.C., 1969-71; asst. curator Mus. Modern Art, 1971-77, asso. curator dept. prints and illus. books, 1977-79; asso. prof. art SUNY, Stony Brook, 1979-84, prof. art, 1984—. Contbr. articles to profl. jours.; exhbns. include, Mus. Modern Art, Stockholm and 5 European mus., 1973, Fogg Art Mus., Cambridge, Mass., 1973, Indpls. Mus., Taft Mus., Cin., 1974, Gerald Piltzer Gallery, Paris, 1975, 9th Paris Biennale, Mus. Modern Art, Paris, 1975, Vassar Coll. Art Gallery, 1977; represented in permanent collections, Mus. Modern Art, N.Y.C., Fogg Art Mus., Met. Mus., N.Y.C., Whitney Mus. Am. Art; represented in travelling exhbns. Brandeis U., U. Calif. at Riverside, Cleve. Inst. Arts, SUNY, Potsdam, New Paltz, Wesleyan U., Davison Art Ctr., others. Recipient Artist award Studio Mus. of Harlem, 1994, Joan Mitchell Painting award Joan Mitchell Found., 1994/95; N.Y.C. Nat. Endowment Arts grantee, 1972-73, 83-84; Japan/U.S. Friendship fellow, 1981-82; recipient Boston U. Alumni award, 1983, Ariana Found. grant, 1984-85, Guggenheim fellowship, 1987-88. Mem. ACASA, Coll. Art Assn. (Best Exhbn./Performance award 1990), Internat. Assn. Art Critics, Internat. Hous of Japan (acad.). Office: SUNY Art Dept Stony Brook NY 11794

PINDER, GEORGE FRANCIS, engineering educator, scientist; b. Windsor, Ont., Can., Feb. 6, 1942; s. Percy Samuel and Stella Marie P.; m. Phyllis Marie Charlton, Sept. 14, 1963; children—Wendy Marie, Justin George. B.Sc., U. Western Ont., 1965; Ph.D., U. Ill., 1968. Research hydrologist U.S. Geol. Survey, 1968-72; mem. faculty dept. civil engring. Princeton U., 1972-89, prof., 1972-89, chmn. dept., from 1980, dir. water resources program, 1972-80; dean Coll. Engring. and Math. U. Vt., Burlington, 1989—. Recipient O.E. Meinzer award Geol. Soc. Am., 1975, WUC medal, 1992; U. Vt. Univ. scholar, 1993. Fellow Am. Geophys. Union (Robert E. Horton award 1969); mem. ASCE, Soc. Petroleum Engrs. Home: 7 Bishop Rd Shelburne VT 05482-7351 Office: U Vt Coll Engring and Math Burlington VT 05405

PINDERA, JERZY TADEUSZ, mechanical and aeronautical engineer; b. Czchow, Poland, Dec. 4, 1914; immigrated to Can., 1965, naturalized, 1975; s. Jan Stanislaw and Natalia Lucia (Knapik) P.; m. Aleksandra-Anna Szal, Oct. 29, 1949; children: Marek Jerzy, Maciej Zenon. BS in Mech. Engring, Tech. U., Warsaw, 1936; MS in Aero. Engring, Tech. U., Warsaw and Lodz, 1947; D in Applied Scis., Polish Acad. Scis., 1959; DS in Applied Mechanics, Tech. U., Cracow, 1962. Registered profl. engr., Ont. Asst. Lot Polish Airlines, Warsaw, 1947; head lab. Aero. Inst., Warsaw, 1947-52, Inst. Metallography, Warsaw, 1952-54; dep. prof., head lab. Polish Acad. Scis., 1954-59; head lab. Bldg. Research Inst., Warsaw, 1959-62; vis. prof. mechanics Mich. State U., East Lansing, 1963-65; prof. mechanics U. Waterloo (Ont. Can.), 1965-83, adj. prof., 1983-86, Disting. prof. emeritus, 1987—; pres. J.T. Pindera & Sons Engring. Services, Inc., Waterloo, 1980—; chmn. Internat. Symposium Exptl. Mechanics, U. Waterloo, 1972, dir. Inst. for Exptl. Mechanics, 1983-86; chmn. 10th Can. Fracture Conf., 1983; hon. adv. prof. Chongqing (Sichuan, China) U., 1988—; hon. prof. Shanghai (China) Coll. Archtl. and Mcpl. Engring., 1988—; hon. chmn. Internat. Conf. on Advanced Exptl. Mechanics, U. Tianjin, People's Republic of China, 1988; co-chmn. Second Internat. Conf. on Composites Engring., New Orleans, 1995; vis. prof. in France, Fed. Republic Germany, Slovenia, U.S.A., China; cons. in field. Bd. editors Mechanics Rsch. Comm., 1974—, Theoretical and Applied Fracture Mechanics, 1984—; mem. editl. adv. bd. Acta Mechanica Sinica, 1990—; guest editor spl. issue Birefringence Methods, Jour. Optics and Lasers in Engring., 1995; patentee in field; contbr. tech. books, articles, and chpts. in books. Served with Polish Army, 1939. Decorated Def. War 1939 medal (Poland), Cross of Oswiecim (Poland),; Comdr.'s Cross of Order of Merit (Fed. Republic Germany). Fellow Soc. Exptl. Mechanics (M.M. Frocht award 1978), Can. Soc. for Mech. Engring. (H.G. Duggan medal 1986); mem. Gesellschaft Angewandte Mathematik und Mechanik, N.Y. Acad. Scis., Soc. Engring. Sci., ASME, Assn. Profl. Engrs. Ont. Home: 310 Grant Crescent, Waterloo, ON Canada N2K 2A2 Office: U Waterloo Dept Civil Engring, 200 University Ave, Waterloo, ON Canada N2L 3G1 *It is true that "Nothing is more practical than a theory," provided however, that the assumptions on which the theory is founded are well understood. But, indeed, nothing can be more disastrous than a theory when applied to a real problem outside of the practical limits of the assumptions made, simply because of an homonymous identity with the problem under consideration!.*

PINDYCK, BRUCE EBEN, lawyer, corporate executive; b. N.Y.C., Sept. 21, 1945; s. Sylvester and Lillian (Breslow) P.; m. Mary Ellen Schwartz, Aug. 18, 1968; children: Ashley Beth, Eben Spencer, Blake Michael Lawrence. AB, Columbia U., 1967, JD, 1970, MBA, 1971. Bar: N.Y. 1971, Wis. 1987. Assoc. Olwine, Connelly, Chase, O'Donnell & Weyher, N.Y.C., 1971-80; asst. gen. counsel Peat, Marwick, Mitchell & Co., N.Y.C., 1980-82; ptnr. Hollyer, Jones, Pindyck, Brady & Chira, N.Y.C., 1983-87; pres., chief exec. officer Meridian Industries, Inc., Milw., 1985—; also chmn. bd. dirs. Meridian Industries, Inc.; chief exec. officer Majilite Corp., Dracut, Mass., 1987—; also chmn. bd. dirs. Majilite Corp.; mem. capital campaign com. Columbia U., 1984-87. Bd. dirs. Harambee Community Sch., 1991—, Milw. Ballet Co., 1993—, Milw. Pub. Mus., 1994—. Mem. Columbia Coll. Alumni Assn. (regional dir. 1988-94, v.p. 1994—, exec. com.), Young Pres.'s Orgn. Office: 100 E Wisconsin Ave Milwaukee WI 53202-4107

PINE, CHARLES JOSEPH, clinical psychologist; b. Excelsior Springs, Mo., July 13, 1951; s. Charles E. and LaVern (Upton) P.; m. Mary Day, Dec. 30, 1979; children: Charles Andrew, Joseph Scott, Carolyn Marie. BA in Psychology, U. Redlands, 1973; MA, Calif. State U.-L.A., 1975; PhD, U. Wash., 1979; postdoctoral UCLA, 1980-81. Diplomate in Clinical Psych. Am. Bd. Profl. Psych. Lic. psychologist, Calif., Fla. Psychology technician Seattle Indian Health Bd., USPHS Hosp., 1977-78; psychology intern VA Outpatient Clinic, L.A., 1978-79; instr. psychology Okla. State U., 1979-80, asst. prof., 1980; asst. prof. psychology and native Am. studies program Wash. State U., 1981-82; dir. behavioral health services Riverside-San Bernardino County Indian Health Inc., Banning, Calif., 1982-84; clin. psychologist, clin. co-dir. Inland Empire Behavioral Assocs., Colton, Calif., 1982-84; clin. psychologist VA Med. Ctr., Long Beach, Calif., 1984-85; clin. psychologist, psychology coordinator Psychiatry div. VA Med. Ctr., Sepulveda, Calif., 1985-93; clin. dir. Traumatic Stress Treatment Ctr., Thousand Oaks, Calif., 1985-93; assoc. clin. prof. UCLA Sch. Medicine, 1985—, Fuller Grad. Sch. Psychology, Pasadena, Calif., 1985-93, indep. practitioner Orlando, 1993-94; adj. assoc. prof. Calif. Sch. Profl. Psychology, L.A., 1989—; mem. adj. faculty, psychologist, administv. coord. alcohol and drug abuse U. Ctrl. Fla.; rsch. assoc. Nat. Ctr. for Am. Indian and Alaska Native Mental Health Rsch., U. Col. Health Sci. Ctr., Denver, 1989—; psychologist alcohol and drug abuse treatment program, Orlando VA Outpatient divsn. Tampa VA Med. Ctr., 1993—; cons. NIH, 1993—; mem. L.A. County Am. Indian Mental Health task force, 1987-92. Editorial cons. White Cloud Jour., 1982-85; cons. Dept. Health and Human Services, USPHS, NIMH, 1980. Vol. worker Variety Boys Clubs Am., 1973-75; coach Rialto Jr. All-Am. Football League, 1974, Conejo Youth Flag Football Assn., pres., 1990, coach, bd. dirs. Westlake Youth Football, 1991-92; coach, Conejo Valley Little League, Dr. Phillips Little League, 1993—; co-commr., coach Dr. Phillips Pop Warner Football, 1993—. U. Wash. Inst. Indian Studies grantee, 1975-76, UCLA Inst. Am. Cultures grantee, 1981-82. Fellow Am. Psychol. Assn. (chair task force on service delivery to ethnic minority populations bd. ethnic minority affairs 1988—, bd. ethnic minority affairs 1985-87), Acad. Clin. Psychology; mem. Soc. Indian Psychologists (pres. 1981-83), Nat. Register Health Svc. Providers in Psychology, Calif. Psychol. Assn. Found. (bd. dirs. 1990-92), N.Y. Acad. Sci., Soc. for Psychol. Study Ethnic Minority Issues (exec. com. 1987-88), Sigma Alpha Epsilon. Republican. Roman Catholic. Contbr. psychol. articles to profl. lit.

PINE, JEFFREY BARRY, state attorney general; b. N.Y.C., Jan. 10, 1955; s. Henry F. Pine and Irma (Goldberg) Nass; m. Faith Marcia Scavitti, May 20, 1984; children: Bethany Arielle, Jonathan Ian Lee. BA in Polit. Sci., Haverford Coll., 1976; JD, George Washington U., 1979. Bar: R.I. 1979, Mass. 1979, U.S. Dist. Ct. R.I. 1979. Asst. atty. gen., dep. chief criminal prosecution R.I. Dept. Atty. Gen., Providence, 1979-89; assoc. atty. Decof & Grimm, Providence, 1990-93; atty. gen. State of R.I., 1993—. Bd. dirs. Camp Jori, Providence, 1989—, Jewish Family Svcs., Providence, 1989-92; trustee Temple Beth El, Providence, 1990-92; mem. R.I. Criminal Bench Bar Com., 1979-90, MADD, 1987—, Bd. Bar Overseers Mass. Recipient Beta Rho Sigma award; named top prosecutor by R.I. Monthly. Mem. ABA, R.I. Bar Assn., Assn. Am. Trial Lawyers, R.I. Trial Lawyers Assn., Ledgemont Country Club. Home: 15 Westford Rd Providence RI 02906-4943 Office: Office of Attorney General 72 Pine St Providence RI 02903-2836*

PINEDA, MARIANNA, sculptor, educator; b. Evanston, Ill., May 10, 1925; d. George and Marianna (Dickinson) Packard; m. Harold Tovish, Jan. 14, 1946; children: Margo, Aaron, Nina. Student, Cranbrook Acad. Art, summer 1942, Bennington Coll., 1942-43, U. Calif.-Berkeley, 1943-45, Columbia U., 1945-46, Ossip Zadkine Sch. Drawing and Sculpture, Paris, 1949-50. instr. sculpture Newton Coll. Sacred Heart, 1972-75, Boston Coll., 1975-77; vis. assoc. prof. Boston U., 1974, 78, annually 83-87, 89-90; vis. sculptor Sch. of Mus. Fine Arts, Boston, 1990-91; vis. critic Boston U., 1992. One-woman shows include Slaughter Gallery, San Francisco, 1951, Walker Art Ctr., Mpls., 1952, Currier Gallery, Manchester, N.H., 1954, De Cordova Mus., Lincoln, Mass., 1954, Premier Gallery, Mpls., 1963, Swetzoff Gallery, Boston, 1953, 56, 64, Honolulu Acad. Art, 1970, Alpha Gallery, Boston, 1972, Newton Coll., (Mass.), 1972, Bumpus Gallery, Duxbury, Mass., 1972, Contemporary Art Ctr., Honolulu, 1982, Hanalei Palace, Kona, Hawaii, 1982, Lyman House Mus., Hilo, Hawaii, 1982, Pine Manor Coll., Mass., 1984, Rotenberg Gallery, Boston, 1990, 93, 94, Coll. of William and Mary, 1992, Wiggin Gallery, Boston Libr., 1993 ; group shows include Oakland (Calif.) Civic Mus., 1944, Village Art Ctr., N.Y.C., 1944, Albright Art Gallery, Buffalo, 1947, Bklyn. Mus., 1947, Galerie 8 Paris, 1950, Met. Mus. Art, N.Y.C., 1951, Art Gallery U. Nebr., 1953, San Francisco Mus. of Art, 1955, Inst. Contemporary Art, Boston, 1958, 59, 61, Whitney Mus. Am. Art, N.Y.C., 1953, 54, 55, 57, 59, Boston Arts Festival, 1957, 58, 60, 62, 63, 65, 85, Silvermine Annual Exhibit, Conn., 1957, Art Inst. Chgo., 1957, 61, Pitts. Internat., 1958, Mus. Modern Art., N.Y.C., 1960 (traveling), Addison Gallery Am. Art, 1959, Dallas Mus. Art, 1961, Nat. Inst. Arts & Letters, 1961, N.Y. World's Fair, 1964, De Cordova Mus., 1963, 64, 1972, 75, 87, Sculptors Guild, N.Y.C., 1967-95, Pine Manor Coll., Mass., Pa. State U., 1974, The Women's Bldg., L.A., 1976, Simmons Coll., Mass., 1980, Helen Schlein Gallery, Boston, 1982, SUNY-Buffalo, 1983, Fitchburg Mus. Art, Mass., 1984, Newton Art Ctr., Mass., 1985, Boston U. Art Gallery, 1986, Shulman Sculpture Pk., White Plains, N.Y., 1986, 87, 88, Alchemie Gallery, Boston, 1987, 93, Nat. Acad. Design, N.Y.C., 1985-89, 91, 92, 93, 94-95, Boston Visual Artist Union Invitational, 1986, Bunting Inst., Fed. Reserve Gallery, Boston, 1986, Port of History, Phila., 1987, Brockton Art Ctr., Mass., 1987, Judi Rotenberg Gallery, Boston, ann. 1987—, A.I.R. Gallery, N.Y.C., 1988, Boston Pub. Libr., 1988, Nat. Sculpture Soc., N.Y.C., 1986-89, 90-95, Holyoke Mus., Mass., 1989, Washington Art Assn., Conn., 1989, Bumpus Art Gallery, Duxbury, 1989, Page St. Gallery, San Francisco, 1989, Louis Ross Gallery, N.Y.C., 1990, Shidoni Galleries, Santa Fe, N. Mex., 1990, The Contemporary Mus., Honolulu, 1990, Cast Iron Gallery, 1993, Kyoto (Japan) Civic Gallery, 1993, Walsh Art Gallery, Fairfield, Conn., 1991, Wingspread Gallery, Northeast Harbor, Maine, 1991, World Fin. Ctr. Gallery, 1992, Phila. Sculptors Guild, 1992, Kingsborough C.C., Bklyn., 1994, Womens Caucus for Arts, Staten Island, N.Y., 1995, FSS Gallery, N.Y.C., 1995, Danforth Mus., Framingham, Mass., 1995, Rose Art Mus. Brandeis U., Mass., George Washington U., 1996; represented permanent collections, Walker Art Ctr., Mus. Fine Arts, Boston Williams Coll., (Mass.), Dartmouth coll., Hanover, N.H., Addison Gallery, Andover, Mass., Munson-Williams-Proctor Inst., Ithaca, N.Y., Fogg Art Mus., Cambridge, Mass., Radcliff Coll., Boston Pub. Library, Wadsworth Athenaeum, Hartford, Conn. State of Hawaii, NAD, 1983, 84, 85, 87, 88, 90, 91, 92, 93, 94, Muscarelle Mus., Williamsburg, Va., Walker Art Ctr., Mpls., Bowdoin Coll., Lewiston, Me., U. Mass., Perseus Collection, Honolulu, Nat. Acad. Design, N.Y.C., Boston Conservatory Music, Boston U.; commd. work, Twirling, Bronze figure group, East Boston Housing for Elderly, The Spirit of Lili'uokalani bronze, Hawaii Stat Capitol. Recipient award Oakland Civic Mus., 1944, Mather prize Chgo. Art Inst., 1944, Best of Show award Minn. State Fair, 1954, Margaret Brown award Ins. Contemporary Art, Boston, 1957, Grand prize Boston Arts Festival, 1960, Lampston prize Nat. Sculpture Soc., N.Y.C., 1986, Gold medal Nat. Sculpture Soc., 1988, Herbert Adams Meml. medal, 1996, Taillex award, 1991, Lifetime Achievement award Nat. Womens Caucus Art, 1996; grantee Florsheim Art Fund, 1995, Mass. Found. for Humanities, 1995, Thanks to Grandmother Winnefred Found., 1995; Bunting Inst., Radcliffe Coll. fellow, 1962, 63. Fellow NAD (Gold medal 1987, Artists award 1988, 93). Home: 380 Marlborough St Boston MA 02115-1502 Office: care Judi Rotenberg 130 Newbury St Boston MA 02116-2904 *In a period of history such as ours where trend overtakes trend, the artist must somehow be true to her inner vision without shutting out the world or denying the human dilemma.*

PINEDA, MAURICIO HERNAN, reproductive physiologist, educator; b. Santiago, Chile, Oct. 17, 1930; came to U.S., 1970, naturalized, 1982; s. Teofilo Pineda-Garcia and Bertila Pinto-Bouvret; m. Rosa A. Gomez, July 26, 1956; children—Anamaria, George H., Monserrat. D.V.M., U. Chile, 1955; M.S., Colo. State U., 1965, Ph.D., 1968. Prof. Coll. Vet. Medicine, Austral U. Chile, Valdivia, 1958-63, prof., head animal reprodn. lab., 1968-70; postdoctoral trainee U. Wis., Madison, 1970-72; postdoctoral fellow Colo. State U., Ft. Collins, 1972-74, research assoc., 1972-78; assoc. prof. physiology, dept. physiology and pharmacology Coll. Vet. Medicine, Iowa State U., Ames, 1979-84, prof., 1984—. Assoc. editor: Veterinary Endocrinology and Reproduction, 4th edit., 1989; contbr. chpts. to books, articles to profl. jours.; mem. editl. bds. sci. jours. Recipient Best Student award U.

Chile Coll. Vet. Medicine, 1954; Rockefeller Found. scholar, 1963; Morris Animal Found. fellow, 1974. Mem. Chilean Vet. Med. Assn. (Disting. Services award 1987), Soc. for Study of Fertility (Eng.), Sigma Xi, Beta Beta Beta, Phi Kappa Phi, Gamma Sigma Delta. Office: Dept Physiology and Pharmacology Vet Med Iowa State U Ames IA 50011

PINEDO, MYRNA ELAINE, psychotherapist, educator; b. Riverton, Wyo., Apr. 28, 1944; d. Pedro Berumen and Ruth Jama (Kuriyama) P.; m. Alan P. Schiesel, Sept. 9, 1964 (div. July 1973); 1 child, Elaine Marie (Schiesel) Thompson; m. Wallace Vern Calkins, Aug. 31, 1990. BA in Psychology, Calif. State U., Northridge, 1980; MA in Cmty. Clin. Psychology, Calif. Sch. Profl. Psychology, 1982; PhD in Cmty. Clin. Psychology, Calif. Sch. Profl. Psychiatry, 1987. Lic. marriage, family and child counselor, Calif.; cert. mental health counselor, Wash.; cert. marriage and family therapist, Wash. Pychiat. asst. William Newton, M.D., Marine del Rey, Calif., 1983-84; psychologist forensic svcs. dept. Kern County Mental Health, Bakersfield, Calif., 1984-88; alcohol counselor Spl. Treatment Edn. Program Svcs., Bakersfield, 1985-87; marriage and family therapist Jay Fisher & Assocs., Bakersfield, 1986-87; therapist program devel. Correctional Specialties, Bellevue, Wash., 1988-90; pvt. practice HAP Counseling Svcs., Bellevue, 1990—; adj. faculty Calif. State U., Bakersfield, 1986, Kern County Mental Health, 1987, Bellevue C.C., 1989, Antioch U., 1992, 93; instituted various treatment programs for adolescents, Spanish speaking adults and Spanish speaking sex offenders; spkr. in field; expert witness in ct. Panelist EastSide Domestic Violence Com., 1991-93; bd. dirs. Kern County Child Abuse Coun., 1986-88; mem. treatment com. Kern County Child Abuse Task Force, 1985-88; mem. Stop-Abuse by Counselors, 1993—. Mem. Am. Counseling Assn., Am. Assn. Christian Counselors, Assn. Orthopsychiatry, Wash. Assn. Mental Health Counselors, Assn. Marriage and Family Therapists. Avocations: gardening, hiking, cooking. Office: HAP Counseling Svcs 515 116th Ave NE Ste 165 Bellevue WA 98004-5204

PINES, ALEXANDER, chemistry educator, researcher, consultant; b. Tel Aviv, June 22, 1945; came to U.S., 1968.; s. Michael and Neima (Ratner) P.; m. Ayala Malach, Aug. 31, 1967 (div. 1983); children: Itai, Shani; m. Ditsa Kafry, May 5, 1983; children: Noami, Jonathan, Talia. BS, Hebrew U., Jerusalem, 1967; PhD, MIT, 1972. Asst. prof. chemistry U. Calif., Berkeley, 1972-75, assoc. prof., 1975-80, prof., 1980—, Pres.'s chair, 1993; faculty sr. scientist materials scis. div. Lawrence Berkeley Lab., 1975—; cons. Mobil Oil Co., Princeton, N.J., 1980-84, Shell Oil Co., Houston, 1981—; chmn. Bytel Corp., Berkeley, Calif., 1981-85; vis. prof. Weizmann Inst. Sci., 1982; adv. prof. East China Normal U., Shanghai, People's Rep. of China, 1985; sci. dir. Nalorac, Martinez, Calif., 1986—; Joliot-Curie prof. Ecole Superieure de Physique et Chemie, Paris, 1987; Walter J. Chute Disting. lectr. Dalhousie U., 1989, Charles A. McDowell lectr. U. B.C., 1989, E. Leon Watkins lectr. Wichita State U., 1990; Hinshelwood lectr., U. Oxford, 1990, A.R. Gordon Disting. lectr. U. Toronto, 1990, Venable lectr. U. N.C., 1990, Max Born lectr. Hebrew U. of Jerusalem, 1990; William Draper Harkins lectr. U. Chgo., 1991, Kolthoff lectr. U. Minn., 1991; Md.-Grace lectr. U. Md., 1992; mem. adv bd. Nat. High Magnetic Field Lab., Inst. Theoretical Physics, U. Calif. Santa Barbara; mem. adv. panel chem. Nat. Sci. Found.; Randolph T. Major Disting. Lectr. U. Conn., 1992; Peter Smith lectr. Duke U., 1993, Arthur William Davidson lect. U. Kansas, 1992, Arthur Birch lect. Australian Nat. U., 1993, Richard C. Lord Meml. lectr. MIT, 1993, Steacie lectr. Nat. Rsch. Coun. Can., 1993, Centenary lectr. Royal Soc. Chemistry, 1994, Morris Loeb lectr. Harvard U., 1994, Jesse Boot Found. Lectr., U. Nottingham, 1994. Editor Molecular Physics, 1987-91; mem. bd. editors Chem. Physics, Chem. Physics Letters, Nmr: Basic Principles and Progress, Advances in Magnetic Resonance; adv. editor Oxford U. Press; contbr. articles to profl. jours.; patentee in field. Recipient Strait award North Calif. Spectroscopy Soc., Outstanding Achievement award U.S. Dept. of Energy, 1983, 87, 89, R & D 100 awards, 1987, 89, Disting. Teaching award U. Calif., E.O. Lawrence award, 1988, Pitts. Spectroscopy award, 1989, Wolf Prize for chemistry, 1991, Donald Noyce Undergrad. Teaching award U. Calif., 1992, Robert Foster Cherry award for Great Tchrs. Baylor U., Pres.'s Chair for undergrad. edn. U. Calif., 1993; Guggenheim fellow, 1988, Christensen fellow St. Catherine's Coll., Oxford, 1990. Fellow Am. Phys. Soc. (chmn. divsn. chem. physics), Inst. Physics; mem. NAS, Am. Chem. soc. (mem. exec. com. divsn. phys. chemistry, Signature award, Baekeland medal, Harrison Howe award 1991), Royal soc. Chemistry (Bourke lectr.), Internat. Soc. Magnetic Resonance (v.p., pres.). Office: U Calif Chemistry Dept D 64 Hildebrand Hall Berkeley CA 94720

PINES, BURTON YALE, broadcasting executive; b. Chgo., Apr. 6, 1940; s. Hyman and Mary Pines; m. Helene Brenner, May 21, 1972. B.A., U. Wis., 1961, M.A., 1963. Instr. U. Wis., Madison, 1962-65; corr. Time mag., Bonn, Saigon and Vienna, 1966-73, editor, N.Y.C., 1973-81; sr. v.p. Heritage Found., Washington, 1981-92; chmn. Nat. Ctr. for Pub. Policy Rsch., Washington, 1982-94; co-founder, exec. v.p., COO NET Polit. Newstalk Network, Washington, 1992-95; pres. BookNet Cable TV Network, N.Y.C., 1995—. Author: Back to Basics, 1982, Out of Focus, 1994; editor: Mandate for Leadership II, 1984, Mandate for Leadership III, 1988. Recipient Page One award N.Y. Newspaper Guild, 1976, 77, 78, Freedom's Found. award, 1983. Jewish. Office: BookNet 30 Rockefeller Plz 29th Fl New York NY 10112

PINES, WAYNE LLOYD, public relations counselor; b. Washington, Dec. 31, 1943; s. Jerome Martin and Ethel (Schnall) P.; B.A., Rutgers U., 1965; postgrad. George Washington U., 1969-71; m. Nancy Freitag, Apr. 16, 1966; children—Noah Morris, Jesse Mireth. Reporter, city editor Middletown (N.Y.) Times Herald-Record, 1965-68; copy editor Reuters News, 1968-69; assoc. editor FDC Reports, Washington, 1969-72; chief Consumer Edn. and Info., FDA, also editor FDA Consumer, 1972-74; exec. editor Product Safety Letter and Devices and Diagnostics Letter, Washington, 1974-75; dep. asst. commr. for pub. affairs, chief press relations FDA, Rockville, Md., 1975-78, assoc. commr. public affairs, 1978-82; adj. prof. Washington Public Affairs Center, U. So. Calif., 1980-81; instr. N.Y.U. Sch. Continuing Edn., 1982-84; instr. Profl. Devel. Inst., 1983-85; spl. asst. to dir. NIMH, 1982-83; sr. v.p., sr. counselor Burson-Marsteller, 1983-87; exec. v.p., dir. med. issues, 1987-93; pres. healthcare practice APCO Assocs., Washington, 1993—, dir. crisis com.; sr. counselor Gross, Townsend, Frank, Hoffman, 1993—; bd. dirs. Transcell Techs., Inc.; columnist Med. Advt. News., 1985-90; mem. adv. bd. Nat. Orgn. Rare Disorders, Orphan Med.; mem. corp. adv. bd. ANA. Author: The Sermons of Jerome Martin Pines, FDA Advertising and Promotional Manual, When Lightning Strikes: A How-to Crisis Manual; contbr. numerous articles in field to profl. jours. Home: 5821 Nevada Ave NW Washington DC 20015-2547 Office: APCO Assocs 1615 L St NW Washington DC 20036-5610

PINET, FRANK SAMUEL, former university dean; b. Topeka, Nov. 8, 1920; s. Frank Leo and Hattie Blanche (McClure) P.; m. Winifred Sarann Meyer, Jan. 27, 1956 (dec. Jan. 1995); children: Christopher Paul, Nancy Ann, Rosemary, Winifred Suzanne, Caroline Michele. B.S., U. Kans., 1942, M.B.A., 1947, Ph.D., 1955. Mem. faculty U. Kans., Lawrence, 1946—; prof. bus. adminstrn. U. Kans., 1970-80, Telecommunications Industry disting. teaching prof., 1980-85, prof. emeritus, 1986—; asso. dean U. Kans. (Sch. Bus.), 1969-80; vis. prof. OEC, Italy, 1959-60; dir. Dold Foods, Inc.; cons. to industry, 1955—. Author: Probated Estates in Kansas, 3d edit, 1956. Served to lt. comdr. USNR, 1942-46, 50-52. Recipient Standard Oil Co. (Ind.) Outstanding Teaching award, 1973, Henry A. Bubb Outstanding Teaching award, 1972, 84, Pacesetter award U.S. Ind. Telephone Assn., 1982; named Outstanding Educator Mortar Board, 1980; Ford Found. fellow, 1961-62. Mem. Am. Econ. Assn., Indsl. Relations Research Assn. Home: 704 W 12th St Lawrence KS 66044-3212 Office: Univ Kans 202 Summerfield Hall Lawrence KS 66044-7522

PING, CHARLES JACKSON, academic administrator, educator; b. Phila., June 15, 1930; s. Cloudy J. and Mary M. (Marion) P.; m. Claire Oates, June 5, 1951; children: Andrew, Ann Shelton. B.A., Rhodes Coll., 1951; B.D., Louisville Presbyn. Theol. Sem., 1954; Ph.D., Duke, 1961. Asso. prof. philosophy Alma Coll., 1962-66; prof. philosophy Tusculum Coll., 1966-69, v.p., dean faculty, 1967-68, acting pres., 1968-69; provost Central Mich. U., Mt. Pleasant, 1969-75; pres. Ohio U., Athens, 1975-94, pres. emeritus, trustee, prof. philosophy and edn., 1994—; dir. Ping Inst. for Teaching of the Humanities; bd. dirs. Nationwide Corp.; bd. dirs. Wing Lung Bank Internat. Inst. for Bus. Devel., Hong Kong; trustee Louisville Presbyn. Theol. Sem.; mem. adv. bd. Ind. Coll. Program N.W. Area Found., Inst. Ednl. Mgmt. of Harvard U.; chair Commn. Planning for Future of Higher Edn., Kingdom of Swaziland, Internat. Edn. Exch.; mem. Commn. on Higher Edn. Republic of Namibia; exec. dir. Manasseh Cutler Scholars Program. Author: Ohio University in Perspective, 1985, Meaningful Nonsense, 1966, also articles. Fulbright Sr. Rsch. scholar for So. Africa, 1995. Mem. Am. Assn. Higher Edn., Nat. Assn. State Univs. and Land-Grant Colls., Coun. on Internat. Ednl. Exch. (chair bd.), David C. Lam Inst. for East-West Studies (bd. dirs.), Coun. Internat. Exch. Scholars (bd. dirs., chair Africa com.). Office: Ohio U Office of Pres Emeritus Athens OH 45701

PINGEL, JOHN SPENCER, advertising executive; b. Mt. Clemens, Mich., Nov. 6, 1916; s. George F. and Margaret (Dalby) P.; m. Isabel Hardy, Dec. 12, 1939; children—John S., Roy Hardy. Student, U.S. Mil. Acad., 1936; B.A., Mich. State U., 1939. Asst. dir. truck merchandising Dodge div. Chrysler Corp., 1940-41, fleet sales rep., 1949; adminstrv. asst. Mich. State U., 1945-46; dir. advt. Reo Motors, Inc., 1947-48; with mdsg. dept. Brooke, Smith, French & Dorrance, Inc., 1949-55, v.p., account supr., 1955-57, v.p., asst. to pres., 1957-60, exec. v.p., 1960; exec. v.p. Ross Roy-BSF & D, Inc., Detroit, 1960-62; exec. v.p. Ross Roy, Inc., 1962-64, pres., 1964—, vice-chmn., 1979—. Exec. bd., pres., chmn. orgn. and extension com. Detroit area council Boy Scouts Am.; pres. Inst. for Econ. Edn., 1971; mem. adv. bd. United Found., 1970-71; mem. Pres.'s Council on Phys. Fitness and Sports, 1975—; Trustee Alma Coll., New Detroit, Inc., Harper Grace Hosp., Oakland U. Found.; mem. exec. com. Grosse Pointe U. Sch., 1957-58, trustee, 1959—; bd. dirs. Boys Republic, Inc., Greater Met. Detroit Project Hope, Greater Mich. Found.; trustee emeritus Mich. State U. Served from 2d lt. to lt. col. 95th Inf. Div. AUS, 1941-45. Decorated Bronze Star, Purple Heart; named to Nat. Football Hall of Fame, 1968, to Mich. Sports Hall of Fame, 1973, Mich. State U. Sports Hall of Fame, 1993. Mem. Detroit Sales Execs. Club (v.p. 1951), Am. Assn. Advt. Agys. (chmn. Mich. 1960, nat. chmn. 1978-79), Mich. C. of C. (dir.), Greater Detroit C. of C. (dir. 1970-71, chmn. 1977-78). Presbyterian (elder). Clubs: Detroit Athletic, Country of Detroit, Adcraft (pres. 1960-61), Detroit, Economic, Yondotega (Detroit); Seminole Golf, Everglades (Palm Beach, Fla.); Jupiter Hills. Home: 582 Peachtree Ln Grosse Pointe MI 48236-2717 also: 80 Celestial Way Juno Beach FL 33408-2371 Office: Ross Roy Inc 100 Bloomfield Hills Pky Bloomfield Hills MI 48304-2949

PINGREE, BRUCE DOUGLAS, lawyer; b. Salt Lake City, June 6, 1947; s. Howard W. and Lois (Ivie) P.; m. Lorraine Bertelli, Oct. 11, 1981; children: Christian James, Matthew David, Alexandra Elizabeth, Meredith Gillian, Lauren Ashley, Geoffrey Nicholas. BA in Philosophy, U. Utah, 1970, JD, 1973. Bar: Ariz. 1973, Tex. 1990. Ptnr. Snell & Wilmer, Phoenix, 1973-89; shareholder Johnson & Gibbs, Dallas, 1989-93; ptnr. Gardere & Wynne, Dallas, 1993-95; ptnr. Baker & Botts, L.L.P., Dallas, 1995—; lectr. in field of taxation. Contbr. articles to profl. jours. Served to capt. USAR. Mem. ABA (tax sect., past chair employee benefits com., past vice chair, past chmn. various sub-coms., 1993-94, chair joint com. on employee benefits 1994-95), Western Pension Conf., Southwest Benefits Conf., Order of Coif. Episcopalian. Home: 4065 Bryn Mawr Dr Dallas TX 75225-7032 Office: Baker & Botts LLP 2001 Ross Ave Dallas TX 75201-2980

PINGREE, DAVID EDWIN, ancient languages educator; b. New Haven, Conn., Jan. 2, 1933; s. Daniel and Elizabeth (Maconi) P.; m. Isabelle Sanchirico, June 20, 1963; 1 child, Amanda. AB, Harvard U., 1954, PhD, 1960; LittD (hon.), U. Chgo., 1992. Jr. fellow Harvard U., Cambridge, Mass., 1960-63; from asst. prof. to prof. U. Chgo., 1963-71; prof. history of math. Brown U., Providence, R.I., 1971—. Author: Census of the Exact Sciences in Sanskrit, series A, vols. 1-5, 1970-94, The Latin Picatrix, 1986. Recipient Abhinavavarahamihira award Gov. Uttar Pradesh, 1976. Fellow AAAS; mem. Am. Philos. Soc. Office: Brown U PO Box 1900 Providence RI 02912-1900

PINGS, ANTHONY CLAUDE, architect; b. Fresno, Calif., Dec. 16, 1951; s. Clarence Hubert and Mary (Murray) P.; m. Carole Clements, June 25, 1983; children, Adam Reed, Rebecca Mary. AA, Fresno City Coll., 1972; BArch, Calif. Poly. State U., San Luis Obispo, 1976. Lic. architect, Calif.; cert. Nat. Council Archtl. Registration Bds. Architect Aubrey Moore Jr., Fresno, 1976-81; architect, prin. Pings & Assocs., Fresno, 1981-83, 86—, Pings-Taylor Assocs., Fresno, 1983-85. Prin. works include Gollaher Profl. Office (Masonry Merit award 1985, Best Office Bldg. award 1986), Fresno Imaging Ctr. (Best Instnl. Project award 1986, Nat. Healthcare award Modern Health Care mag. 1986), Orthopedic Facility (award of honor Masonry Inst. 1987, award of merit San Joaquin chpt. AIA 1987), Modesto Imaging Ctr. (award of merit San Joaquin chpt. AIA 1991), Peachwood Med. Ctr. (award of merit San Joaquin chpt. AIA). Mem. Calif. Indsl. Tech. Edn. Consortium Calif. State Dept. Edn., 1983, 84. Mem. AIA (bd. dirs. Calif. chpt. 1983-84, v.p. San Joaquin chpt. 1982, pres. 1983, Calif. Coun. evaluation team 1983, team leader Coalinga Emergency Design Assistance team), Fresno Arts (bd. dirs., counsel 1989—, pres. 1990-93), Fig Gardens Home Owners Assn. (bd. dir. 1991—, pres. 1994—). Republican. Home: 4350 N Safford Ave Fresno CA 93704-3509 Office: 1640 W Shaw Ave Ste 107 Fresno CA 93711-3506

PINGS, CORNELIUS JOHN, educational association administrator; b. Conrad, Mont., Mar. 15, 1929; s. Cornelius John and Marjorie (O'Loughlin) P.; m. Marjorie Anna Cheney, June 25, 1960; children: John, Anne, Mary. B.S., Calif. Inst. Tech., 1951, M.S., 1952, Ph.D., 1955. Inst. chem. engrng. Stanford U., 1955-56, asst. prof., 1956-59; assoc. prof. chem. engrng. Calif. Inst. Tech., 1959-64, prof., 1964-81, exec. officer chem. engrng., 1969-73, vice-provost, dean grad. studies, 1970-81; provost, sr. v.p. acad. affairs U. So. Calif., 1981-93; pres. Assn. Am. Univs., Washington, 1993—; mem., dir. Nat. Commn. on Rsch., 1978-80; mem. bd. mgmt. Coun. on Govtl. Rels., 1980-83; bd. dirs. and chmn. Pacific Horizon Funds; mem. bd. dirs. Farmers Group, Inc., L.A.; pres. Assn. Grad. Schs., 1977-78; pres. Western Coll. Assn., 1988-90; mem. sci. engrng. and pub. policy com. NAS, 1987-92, chmn., 1988-92; pres., Assn. Amer. Universities, 1993—. Contbr. articles to tech. jours. Mem., chmn. bd. trustees Mayfield Sr. Sch. Bd., 1979-85; mem. Pasadena Redevel. Agy., 1968-81, chmn., 1974-81; bd. dirs. Huntington Meml. Hosp., Pasadena; chmn. L.A. Ctrl. City Assn. Recipient Arthur Nobel medal, City of Pasadena, 198l, Disting. Alumni award Calif. Inst. Tech., 1989, Presdl. medallion U. So. Calif., 1993. Fellow AIChE, Am. Acad. Arts and Scis.; mem. NAE, Calif. Club, Twilight Club, Bohemian Club, Cosmos Club, Valley Hunt Club. Roman Catholic. Home: 2330 Massachusetts Ave NW Washington DC 20008-2801 Office: Assn of Am Univs One Dupont Circle Ste 730 Washington DC 20036

PINIELLA, LOUIS VICTOR, professional baseball team manager; b. Tampa, Fla., Aug. 28, 1943; m. Anita Garcia, Apr. 12, 1967; children: Lou, Kristi, Derrick. Student, U. Tampa. Baseball player various minor-league teams, 1962-68, Cleve. Indians, 1968, Kansas City Royals, 1969-73; baseball player N.Y. Yankees, 1974-84, coach, 1984-85, mgr., 1985-87, 1988, gen. mgr., 1987-88, spl. advisor, TV announcer, 1989; mgr. Cin. Reds, 1990-92, Seattle Mariners, 1992—. Named to Am. League All-Star Team, 1972; recipient Ellis Island Medal of Honor, 1990; Named A.L. Rookie of the Yr Baseball Writers Assoc of Amer, 1969, Named A.L. Manager of the Yr, 1995. Office: Seattle Mariners PO Box 4100 83 S King St Seattle WA 98104-2875*

PINKEL, DONALD PAUL, pediatrician; b. Buffalo, Sept. 7, 1926; s. Lawrence William and Ann (Richardson) P.; m. Marita Donovan, Dec. 26, 1949 (div. 1981); children: Rebecca, Nancy, Christopher, Mary, Thomas, Anne, Sara, John, Ruth; m. Cathryn Barbara Howarth, May 16, 1981; 1 child, Michael. BS, Canisius Coll., 1947; MD, U. Buffalo, 1951. Diplomate Am. Bd. Pediatrics, Pediatric Hematology and Oncology, Nat. Bd. Med. Examiners. From intern to resident to chief resident Children's Hosp., Buffalo, 1951-54; research fellow Children's Hosp. Med. Ctr., Boston, 1955-56; chief. of pediatrics Roswell Park Meml. Inst., Buffalo, 1956-61; med. dir. St. Jude Children's Research Hosp., Memphis, 1961-73; chmn. pediatrics Med. Coll. Wis., Milw., 1974-78; pediatrician-in-chief Milw. Children's Hosp., 1974-78; chief. of pediatrics City of Hope Med. Ctr., Duarte, Calif., 1978-82; chmn. pediatrics Temple U. Sch. Medicine, Phila., 1982-85; prof., Kana Research chmn., dir. pediatric leukemia program U. Tex. System Cancer Ctr., M.D. Anderson Hosp. and Tumor Inst., Houston, 1985-93; prof. emeritus U. Tex.-M.D. Anderson Cancer Ctr., Houston, 1994—. Contbr. numerous articles to profl. jours. Bd. dirs. Lee County Coop. Clinic, Mariana, Ark., 1972-74. Served with USN, 1944-45, served to 1st lt. U.S. Army, 1954-55. Recipient Albert Lasker award for Med. Research Lasker Found., 1972, Windermere Lectureship Brit. Pediatric Assn., 1974, David Karnofsky award Am. Soc. Clin. Oncology, 1978, Zimmerman prize for Cancer Research Zimmerman Found., 1979, Charles Kettering prize Gen. Motors Cancer Research, 1986, Clin. Rsch. award Am. Cancer Soc., 1988, Return of the Child award Leukemia Soc. Am., 1992. Mem. Am. Pediat. Soc., Am. Assn. Cancer Rsch., Soc. Exptl. Biology and Medicine, Am. Soc. Hematology. Democrat. Roman Catholic. Avocations: swimming, sailing. Home: 2501 Addison Rd Houston TX 77030-1811 Office: Driscoll Children's Hosp 3533 South Alameda Corpus Christi TX 78411

PINKER, STEVEN A., cognitive science educator; b. Montreal, Que., Can., Sept. 18, 1954; came to U.S., 1976; s. Harry and Roslyn (Wiesenfeld) P. BA, McGill U., Montreal, 1976; PhD, Harvard U., 1979. Asst. prof. Harvard U., Cambridge, Mass., 1980-81, Stanford U., Palo Alto, Calif., 1981-82; prof. cognitive sci. MIT, Cambridge, 1982—. Author: Language Learnability and Language Development, 1984, Learnability and Cognition, 1989, The Language Instinct, 1994; assoc. editor Cognition, 1984—. Recipient grad. teaching award MIT, 1986, Troland Rsch. award NAS, 1993. Fellow AAAS; mem. APA (Disting. Early Career award 1984, Boyd McCandless award 1986). Office: MIT Dept Brain-Cognitive Scis E10-016 Cambridge MA 02139

PINKERT, DOROTHY MINNA, chemist; b. N.Y.C., June 2, 1921; d. Harry and Frieda Dorothy (Pinkert) Klein. A.B., Bklyn. Coll., 1944; M.S., Bklyn. Poly. Inst., 1952. Creep lab. technician Am. Brakeshoe Co., Mahwah, N.J., 1942-44; rsch. and quality control chemist Reed and Carnrick, Jersey City, 1944-48; chief quality control chemist Gold Leaf Pharmacal Co., New Rochelle, N.Y., 1948-56; rsch. chemist Internat. Salt Co., Watkins Glen, N.Y. and N.Y.C., 1957-61; sr. assoc. drug regulatory affairs Hoffmann-LaRoche Inc., Nutley, N.J., 1962-83. Mem. AAAS, Am. Chem. Soc., Am. Inst. Chemists, Am. Soc. Quality Control, Poly. U. Alumni Assn. (life dir.), N.Y. Acad. Scis. Republican.

PINKERTON, GUY CALVIN, savings and loan executive; b. Seattle, Aug. 1, 1934; s. John L. and Dorothy V. (Kock) P.; children: Deborah, Lisa. BA, U. Wash., 1959. CPA, Wash. Supr. Touche Ross & Co., Seattle, 1959-65; pres., CEO Wash. Fed. Savs., Seattle, 1965—; bd. dirs., vice chair Fed. Home Loan Bank of Seattle. With USN, 1956-58. Mem. Fin. Mgrs. Soc. (dist. gov.), Fin. Execs. Inst. (sec.). Republican. Presbyterian. Office: Wash Fed Savs 425 Pike St Seattle WA 98101-2334*

PINKERTON, HELEN JEANETTE, health care executive; b. Chattanooga, Mar. 17, 1956; d. Jesse Robert and Irene Louise (Boyd) Pinkerton. BS, U. Tenn.-Knoxville, 1979, MPH, 1980. Dir. Hypertension/Diabetes Program Alton Park Health Ctr., Chattanooga, 1981—. Contbr. to Tenn. Hypertension Control Manual, 1984. Dir. Choirs for First Baptist Ch., Hixson; Community Services Club, 1986— (sec.); mem. Chattanooga Jaycees, Chattanooga Hunger Coalition (chairperson cmty. outreach com.). Doak scholar, 1977. Mem. Tenn. Soc. Pub. Health, Nat. Assn. Female Execs., Hypertension Coalition (chmn. 1984—), Am. Cancer Soc. (bd. dirs.), Neighbors for Life (chairperson, Am. Cancer Soc.), Am. Heart Assn. (bd. dirs., correspondent, sec.) Alton Park C. of C. (council mem. 1982-86), Alpha Kappa Alpha. Democrat. Avocations: walking, reading, singing, jogging. Home: 5419 Moody Sawyer Rd Hixson TN 37343 Office: Alton Park Health Ctr 100 E 37th St Chattanooga TN 37410-1401

PINKERTON, LINDA F., lawyer; b. Phila., Dec. 4, 1949; d. Vicotr M. and Callie (Noland) Ferreri; m. Michael S. Foster, June 5, 1984. BA, Duke U., 1971; MA, NYU, 1973; JD, U. Tulsa, 1980. Bar: Calif. 1981, N.C. 1991, N.Y. 1996, U.S. Dist. Ct. (all dists.) Calif., U.S. Ct. Appeals (9th and 10th cirs., U.S. Supreme Ct. Atty. Exxon, Los Angeles, 1980-85; assoc. Pillsbury, Madison & Sutro, San Francisco, Calif., 1985-88; sec., gen. counsel J. Paul Getty Trust, L.A., 1988-94; gen. counsel Christie's Inc., N.Y.C., 1995-96. Mem. Internat. Bar Assn. Office: Christies Inc 11 N Market St Asheville NC 28801

PINKERTON, RICHARD LADOYT, management educator; b. Huron, S.D., Mar. 5, 1933; s. Abner Pyle and Orral Claudine (Arneson) P.; m. Sandra Louise Lee, Aug. 28, 1965 (div. 1992); children—Elizabeth, Patricia. B.A. (La Verne Noyes scholar 1952-55), U. Mich., 1955; M.B.A., Case Western Res. U., 1962; Ph.D. (Nat. Assn. Purchasing Mgmt. fellow 1967-68), U. Wis., 1969. Sr. market research analyst Harris-Intertype Corp., Cleve., 1957-61; mgr. sales devel. Triax Corp., Cleve., 1962-64; coordinator mktg. program Mgmt. Inst., U. Wis., 1964-67; dir. exec. programs Mgmt. Inst., U. Wis. (Grad. Sch. Bus.), also asst. prof. mktg., 1969-74; prof. mgmt., dean Grad. Sch. Adminstrn., Capital U., Columbus, Ohio, 1974-86; prof. mgmt., dir. Univ. Bus. Ctr., Craig Sch. of Bus. Calif. State U., Fresno, 1986-89, prof. mktg., 1989—, chair mktg. and logistics dept., 1996—; trustee Ohio Coun. Econ. Edn., 1976-87; bd. dirs. Univ. Bus. Ctr.; cons. to govt. and industry, 1960—. Co-author: The Purchasing Manager's Guide to Strategic Proactive Procurement, 1996; contbr. articles to profl. jours. Bd. dirs. The Fresno Townhouse Assn.; bd. govs. Hannah Neil Home for Children, Columbus, 1975-78. Served as officer USAF, 1955-57, lt. col. USAFR, 1957-78. Mem. Nat. Assn. Contract Mgmt. (chmn. validation cert. com. 1990), Nat. Assn. Purchasing Mgmt. (chmn. acad. planning 1979-84, rsch. symposium 1992), Am. Mktg. Assn. (chpt. pres. 1972-73), Res. Officers Assn., Air Forces Assn., Ft. Washington Golf and Country Club, Beta Gamma Sigma, Alpha Kappa Psi, Phi Gamma Delta, Rotary (Paul Harris fellow). Home: 4721 N Cedar Ave Apt 111 Fresno CA 93726-1007 Office: Calif State U Dept of Mktg Fresno CA 93740-0007

PINKERTON, ROBERT BRUCE, mechanical engineer; b. Detroit, Feb. 10, 1941; s. George Fulwell and Janet Lois (Hedke) P.; m. Barbara Ann Bandfield, Aug. 13, 1966; 1 child, Robert Brent. BSME, Detroit Inst. Tech., 1965; MA in Engring., Chrysler Inst. Engring., 1967; JD, Wayne State U., 1976. From mech. engr. to emissions and fuel economy planning specialist Chrysler Engring. Office Chrysler Corp., Highland Park, Mich., 1967-80; dir. engring. Replacement div. TRW, Inc., Cleve., 1980-83; v.p. engring. TRW Automotive Aftermarket Group, 1983-86; v.p. engring. and rsch. Blackstone Corp., Jamestown, N.Y., 1986-89; pres., CEO Blackstone Corp., Jamestown, 1989-90, Athena Corp., Beaufort, S.C., 1990—, Cedar Crest Corp., Beaufort, S.C., 1990—. Active oper. audit com. Beaufort County; bd. dirs. Village Renaissance, Inc., 1994—; exec. com. Greater Beaufort Com., 1994—, Beaufort Schs. Oversight Com., 1995—. Mem. Rotary. Presbyterian. Home: PO Box 2417 Beaufort SC 29901-2417 Office: PO Box 2115 128 Castle Rock Rd Beaufort SC 29401-2115

PINKHAM, DANIEL, composer; b. Lynn, Mass., June 5, 1923; s. Daniel R. and Olive C. (White) P. A.B., M.A., Harvard, 1944; Litt.D. (hon.), Nebr. Wesleyan U., 1976; Mus.D. (hon.), Adrian Coll., 1977, Westminster Choir Coll., 1979, New Eng. Conservatory, 1993, Ithaca Coll., 1994. Mem. faculty New Eng. Conservatory Music, 1959—; music dir. King's Chapel, Boston, 1958—; co-founder Cambridge Festival Orch., 1948. Composer: Sonatas for Organ and Strings, 1943, 54, 86, Piano Concertino, 1950, Concerto for Celesta and Harpsichord, 1954, Wedding Cantata, 1956, Christmas Cantata, 1958, Easter Cantata, 1961, Symphonies, 1961, 64, 85, Signs of the Zodiac, 1964, St. Mark Passion, 1965, Jonah, 1966, In the Beginning of Creation, 1970, Ascension Cantata, 1970, Organ Concerto, 1970, When the Morning Stars Sang Together, 1971, the Other Voices of the Trumpet, 1971, Safe in Their Alabaster Chambers, 1972, To Troubled Friends, 1972, Daniel in the Lions' Den, 1973, The Seven Deadly Sins, 1974, Four Elegies, 1974, The Passion of Judas, 1975, Garden Party, 1976, Blessings, 1977, Company at the Creche, 1977, Miracles, 1978, Epiphanies, 1978, Serenades, 1979, Proverbs, 1979, Diversions for Organ and Harp, 1980, Descent Into Hell, 1980, Before the Dust Returns, 1981, The Death of the Witch of Endor, 1981, Prelude and Scherzo for Wind Quintet, 1981, The Dreadful Dining Car, 1982, Brass Quintet, 1983, In Heaven Soaring Up, 1985, The Left-Behind Beasts, 1985, A Biblical Book of Beasts, 1985, Versets, 1985, A Mast for the Unicorn, 1986, A Crimson Flourish, 1986, Winter Nights, 1986, De Profundis, 1986, In the Isles of the Sea, 1986, Antiphons, 1987, Getting To Heaven, 1987, Angels Are Everywhere, 1987, Heav'n Must Go Home, 1988, Four Marian Antiphons, 1988, Alleluias, 1988, Sonata da Chiesa, 1988, Sonata da Camera, 1988, Petitions, 1988, Pedals, 1988, The Seasons Pass, 1988, Reeds, 1988,

Concerto Piccolo, 1989, The Small Passion, 1989, Requiem Collects, 1989, The Saints Preserve Us!, 1989, String Quartet, 1989, Stabat Mater, 1990, Symphony Number 4, 1990, The Book of Hours, 1990, Carols and Cries, 1990, The Dryden Te Deum, 1990, Pentecost Cantata, 1991, Three Canticles from Luke, 1991, For Solace in Solitude, 1991, Advent Cantata, 1991, Smart Set, 1991, First Organbook, 1991, The Small Requiem, 1991, Second Organbook, 1992, Christmas Symphonies, 1992, Overture Concertante, 1992, Nocturnes for Flute and Guitar, 1992, Vowels, 1993, Adagietto for Organ and Strings, 1993, Wondrous Love, 1993, When Love Was Gone, 1993, Missa Domestica, 1993, Miserere mei Deus, 1993, The Guiding Star, 1994, The Creation of the World, 1994, Reed Trio, 1994, Morning Music, 1994, Organ Concerto Number Two, 1995, Preludes for Piano, 1995, Passion Music, 1995, The Tenth Muse, 1995, The Inner Room of the Soul, 1995, Festive Processional, 1995, The White Raven, 1996, O Come, Emanuel, 1996, Called Home, 1996. Fellow Am. Acad. Arts and Scis.; mem. Am. Guild Organists (past dean Boston chpt.). Home: 150 Chilton St Cambridge MA 02138-1227

PINKHAM, ELEANOR HUMPHREY, retired university librarian; b. Chgo., May 7, 1926; d. Edward Lemuel and Grace Eleanor (Cushing) Humphrey; m. James Hansen Pinkham, July 10, 1948; children: Laurie Sue, Carol Lynn. AB, Kalamazoo Coll., 1948; MS in Library Sci. (Alice Louise LeFevre scholar), Western Mich. U., 1967. Pub. svcs. libr. Kalamazoo Coll., 1967-68, asst. libr., 1969-70, libr. dir., 1971-93, ret. 1993; vis. lectr. Western Mich. U. Sch. Librarianship, 1970-84; mem. adv. bd., 1977-81, also adv. bd. Inst. Cistercian Studies Libr., 1975-80. Mem. ALA, AAUP, ACRL (chmn. coll. libr. sect. 1988-89), Mich. Libr. Assn. (pres. 1983-84, chmn. acad. div. 1977-78), Mich. Libr. Consortium (exec. coun. 1974-82, chmn. 1977-78, Mich. Libr. of Yr 1986), OCLC Users Coun., Beta Phi Mu. Home: 2519 Glenwood Dr Kalamazoo MI 49008-2405

PINKHAM, FREDERICK OLIVER, foundation executive, consultant; b. Ann Arbor, Mich., June 16, 1920; s. Frederick Oliver and Leah Winifred (Hallett) P.; m. Helen Kostia, June 20, 1943; children: Peter James, Gail Louise, Steven Howard. AB, Kalamazoo Coll., 1942, LLD (hon.), 1958; MA, Stanford U., 1947, EdD, 1950; LLD (hon.), Lawrence Coll., 1957; DSc (hon.), Ripon Coll., 1990. Tchr., counselor Sequoia Union High Sch., Redwood City, Calif., 1947-49; researcher Stanford (Calif.) Consultation Service, 1949-50; asst. to pres. George Washington U., 1950-51; exec. sec. Nat. Commn. on Accrediting, 1951-55; pres. Ripon (Wis.) Coll., 1955-66; dir. The Yardstick Project, Cleve., 1966-67; v.p., dir. Western Pub. Co., 1967-70; founder, pres. Edn. Mgmt. Services, Inc., 1970-76; asst. adminstr. for population and humanitarian affairs AID, Dept. State, 1976-77; chmn., pres. Population Crisis Com., 1977-87; assoc. dir. Inst. for Population and Resource Studies, Stanford U., 1987-90; program officer David and Lucile Packard Found., 1988-92; cons. for population David and Lucile Packard Found., Los Altos, Calif., 1993—; cons. True North Found., Portland, Oreg., 1993—, Compton Found., Menlo Park, Calif., 1996—, Mgmt. Scis. for Health, 1994—, Poptech, Washington, 1995; v.p., dir. rsch. Ednl. Recs. Bur., Darien, Conn., 1970-72; founder, pres. Edn. Mgmt. Svcs., Inc., 1970-76; v.p., co-founder World Bus. Coun., 1970-77; pres. Capital Higher Edn. Svc., 1975-76; pres., dir. The Omni Group, 1977-83; treas., co-founder Monterey Peninsula Coll. Found., 1994—. Chmn. Wisconsin adv. com. Nat. Commn. on Civil Rights.; bd. visitors Air U.; pres. Wis. Found of Ind. Colls.; chmn. Assn. Colls. Midwest, Midwest Coll. Council; sec., trustee, mem. exec. com. Young Pres.'s Found.; chmn. task force on fgn. assistance Pres.'s Pvt. Sector Survey on Cost Control (Grace Commn.); chmn. bd. Global Tomorrow Coalition, 1985-89; bd. dirs. Internat. Human Assistance Programs, N.Y.C., 1984-87, Mineral Fibre Internat. and Kings Mills Internat., 1986-90; v.p. Big Sur Land Trust, 1990—. Served with AUS, 1942-45, ETO. Decorated Bronze Star, Purple Heart. Mem. Young Pres. Orgn. (nat. sec., dir., exec. com.), Soc. Internat. Devel., Nat. Heritage Soc. (watchkeeper, bd. dirs.), Old Capital Club Monterey, Calif. (gov.). Home and Office: 25715 Rio Vista Dr Carmel CA 93923-8811

PINKNEY, D. TIMOTHY, investment company executive; b. Long Beach, Calif., June 6, 1948; s. Robert Patten and Mary (Chernus) P.; m. Nancy Dianne Fisher, Aug. 21, 1971; 1 child, Heather Anne. BA, Calif. Luth. U., 1970; MA, Pepperdine U., 1976. CFP. Membership mgr. Seattle C. of C., 1977-79; v.p. mktg. John L. Scott Investment, Bellevue, Wash., 1980-81, SRH Fin., Bellevue, 1981-82, Foster Investment Co., Bellevue, 1982-83; pres., CEO Footprint Fin. Planning, Bellevue, 1983-88, Sheppard & Assocs. Personal Fin. Advs., Bellevue, 1988-91; mgr. and v.p. asset mgmt. div. U.S. Bank, Tacoma, Wash., 1991-92; v.p., Calif. mgr. trust and investment mgmt. U.S. Bank of Calif., Sacramento, 1992—; founder, chief exec. officer Wealth Link Enterprises. Author: book, video and cassete series Pathways to Wealth, Yes IRA's Still Make Cent$?, 1988. Co-chmn. Fin. Independence Week, Western Wash., 1987; bd. dirs. Traveler's Aid Soc., A United Way Agy., Seattle, 1988, pacesetter United Way, 1988-91; alumni class steward Calif. Luth. U., 1992, 93; chmn., bd. dirs. Friends Scouting, Golden Empire council Boy Scouts Am.. Lt. USN, 1970-77, comdr. USNR, ret., 1992. Selected as Jr. Officer of Yr., USNR, 1984, 85. Mem. Nat. Spkrs. Assn. (bd. dirs. N.W. chpt. 1992), Internat. Assn. Fin. Planning (chmn. West Region 1987-90, pres. Western Wash. chpt. 1986-87), Seattle Soc. (CPFs (bd. dirs. 1985-86), Inst. CFPs, Real Estate Securities and Syndication Inst. (v.p. 1980-83), East King County and Pierce County Estate Planning Coun., Seattle Res. Officer Assn. (pres., v.p. 1983-85), Puget Sound Naval Res. Assn. (v.p. 1985-90), Sacramento Rotary (chmn. edn. com. 1994), Sacramento Rotary Found. (bd. dirs. 1996), Seattle Rotary (bd. dirs., chmn. membership devel. com.). Avocations: flying gliders, giant pumpkin growing and sculpting, photography.

PINKNEY, JERRY, artist, educator; b. Phila., Dec. 22, 1939; s. James H. and Willemae (Landers) P.; m. Gloria Jean Maultsby, Mar. 19, 1959; children: Troy Bernardette, Jerry Brian, Scott Cannon, Myles Carter. Student, U. of the Arts, 1957-59. Designer, illustrator Rustcraft Pub. Co., Dedham, Mass., 1959-63, Barker/Black Studio, Boston, 1963-65, Kaleidoscope Studio, Boston, 1965-67, Jerry Pinkney Studio, Boston, 1967-70; illustrator, pres. Jerry Pinkney, Inc., Croton, N.Y., 1970—; assoc. prof. art U. Del., Newark, 1988-92; vis. critic R.I. Sch. Design, Providence, 1969-70; assoc. prof. Pratt Inst., Bklyn., 1986-87; disting. vis. prof. U. Del., 1986-88; vis. prof. art U. Buffalo, 1991. One-man retrospective shows include Northeastern U., Boston, 1983, Mass. Coll. Art, Boston, 1987, Mus. Nat. Ctr. African Am. Artists, Boston, 1987, U. Del., Newark, 1987, Phila. Afro-Am. Hist. and Cultural Mus., 1988, Johnson Mus. Art, Cornell U., Ithaca, N.Y., 1988, Schomburg Ctr. for Rsch. in Black Culture, N.Y., 1990, Bethume Hall, U. Buffalo, 1991, Indpls. Mus. Art, 1991, Every Picture Tells a Story, L.A., 1991, Md. Inst. Art, Balt., 1992, ARt Inst. Chgo., 1993; internat. group shows Biennale Bratislace, Czechoslovakia, 1989, 91; illustrator Turtle in Julu, 1989 (award N.Y. Times 1989, Time mag. 1989); included in Caldecott honor boof Mirandy and Brother Wind, 1989, The Talking Eggs, 1990, The Man Who Kept His Heart in a Bucket (Gold medal Soc. of Ill., N.Y. 1991), Homeplace, 1991 (Golden Kite award 1991), Caidecott Honor Book "John Henry", 1995. Mem. U.S. Citizens Stamp Adv. Com., Washington, 1982-92, U.S. Postal Svc. Quality Assurance Com., Washington, 1986-92. Recipient Alumni award Phila. Sch. Art & Design-U. Arts, 1992. Mem. N.Y. Soc. Illustrators (Hamilton King award 1993, gold medal 1993, 94). Avocation: music.

PIN-MEI, IGNATIUS KUNG (GONG) CARDINAL See KUNG (GONG) PIN-MEI, IGNATIUS CARDINAL

PINNELL, SHELDON RICHARD, physician, medical educator; b. Dayton, Ohio, Feb. 3, 1937; s. Jacob and Nevella P.; m. Doren Madey; children: Kevin, Alden, Tyson. AB, Duke U., 1959; MD, Yale U., 1963. Intern in medicine U. Minn. Hosp., 1963-65; resident in dermatology Harvard U., 1968-71; prof. medicine Duke U. Med. Ctr., Durham, N.C., 1978—, chief div. dermatology, 1982—; asst. prof. of biochemistry, 1988—, J. Lamar Callaway prof. dermatology, 1989—; med. dir. Fibrogen, 1994—. Contbr. over 100 articles to profl. jours.; four patents in field. Office: Duke U Med Ctr PO Box 3135 Durham NC 27715-3135

PINNEY, FRANCES BAILEY, art therapist, artist, consultant; b. Newton, Mass., July 18, 1935; d. Gage and Ellen (Nealley) Bailey; m. Peter T. McKinney, June 7, 1957 (div. Nov. 1981); children: Peter, Karen, David; m. Edward Lowell Pinney, Nov. 24, 1988. A.B., Vassar Coll., 1957; M.A., U. Houston-Clear Lake, 1979. Social worker State Bd. Child Welfare, Elizabeth, N.J., 1957-58; art therapist Mental Health and Mental Retardation Authority, Houston, 1979-81; exec. dir. Creative Alternatives, Houston, 1982-87. Bd. dirs. Citizens Alliance for Mentally Ill, Houston, 1983, 84, 85; pres. Berkeley County League of Women Voters, 1993-94. Mem. Am. Art Therapy Assn., Nat. Art Edn. Assn., Am. Group Psychotherapy Assn., Am. Assn. Counseling and Devel., Artist's Equity. Episcopalian. Avocation: scuba diving. Home: PO Box 2210 Martinsburg WV 25401-7210 Office: 404 W Burke St Martinsburg WV 25401-2732

PINNEY, SIDNEY DILLINGHAM, JR., lawyer; b. Hartford, Conn., Nov. 17, 1924; s. Sydney Dillingham and Louisa (Griswold) Wells P.; m. Judith Munch, Sept. 30, 1990; children from previous marriage: William Griswold, David Rees. Student, Amherst Coll., 1941-43, Brown U., 1943; also, M.I.T., 1943-44; BA cum laude, Amherst Coll., 1947; LLB, Harvard U., 1950. Bar: Conn. 1950. Pvt. practice Hartford, 1950; assoc. Shepherd, Murtha and Merritt, Hartford, 1950-53; ptnr. Shepherd, Murtha and Merritt (name changed to Murtha, Cullina, Richter and Pinney 1967), 1953-92, of counsel, 1993—; lectr. on estate planning. Contbr. to: Estate Planning mag. Bd. dirs. Greater Hartford Area TB and Respiratory Diseases Health Soc., 1956-69, pres., 1966-67; mem. Wethersfield (Conn.) Town Coun., 1958-62; trustee Hartford Conservatory Music, 1967-71, 75-81; trustee, pres. Historic Wethersfield Found., 1961-81; bd. dirs. Hartford Hosp., 1971-80, adv. bd., 1980—; mem. adv. com. Jefferso House, 1978-82; mem. Mortensen Libr. Bd. of Visitors U. Hartford, 1984—; corporator Hartford Pub. Libr., 1969—, Renbrook Sch., West Hartford, Conn., 1970-75. 1st lt. USAF, 1943-46. Fellow Am. Coll. Trust and Estate Counsel; mem. ABA, Nat. Acad. Elder Law Attys., Conn. Bar Assn. (exec. com. elder law sect.), Hartford County Bar Assn. Republican. Congregationalist. Office: City Place 185 Asylum St Hartford CT 06103-3402

PINNEY, THOMAS CLIVE, English language educator; b. Ottawa, Kans., Apr. 23, 1932; s. John James and Lorene Maude (Owen) P.; m. Sherrill Marie Ohman, Sept. 1, 1956; children—Anne, Jane, Sarah. B.A., Beloit Coll., Wis., 1954; Ph.D., Yale U., New Haven, 1960. Instr. Hamilton Coll., Clinton, N.Y., 1957-61; instr. English Yale U., New Haven, 1961-62; asst. prof. to prof., chmn. dept. English Pomona Coll., Claremont, Calif., 1962—. Editor: Essays of George Eliot, 1963, Selected Writings of Thomas Babington Macaulay, 1972, Letters of Macaulay, 1974-81, Kipling's India, 1986, A History of Wine in America, 1989, Kipling's Something of Myself, 1990, Letters of Rudyard Kipling, 1990, The Vineyards and Wine Cellars of California, 1994, The Wine of Santa Cruz Island, 1994. Guggenheim fellow, 1966, 84,Recipient Disting. Svc. citation Beloit Coll., 1984; fellow NEH, 1980; grantee Am. Coun. Learned Socs., 1974, 84, Am. Philos. Soc., 1968, 82, 94. Mem. MLA, Elizabethan Club (New Haven), Zamorano Club (L.A.), Phi Beta Kappa. Home: 228 W Harrison Ave Claremont CA 91711-4323 Office: Pomona Coll Dept English Claremont CA 91711

PINOLA, RICHARD J., management consultant; b. Pa., Jan. 16, 1946; m. Shirley A. Pinola, Sept. 23, 1946; children: Jennifer L., Richard J. Jr. BS in Acctg., Kings Coll., 1967. CPA, Pa. Acct. Price Waterhouse, Phila., 1967-69; various positions Penn Mut. Life Ins. Co., Phila., 1969-88, pres., COO, 1988-91; pres., CEO Right Assocs., Phila., 1992-94, chmn., CEO, 1994—; bd. dirs. Yardley Holdings, Jenkintown, Pa., K-Tron, Internat., Cherry Hill, N.J., Robec, Inc., Horsham, Pa.; mem. adv. bd. Micro Diagnostics, Bethlehem, Pa., 1993—. Bd. dirs. Vis. Nurse Assn., Phila., 1995—. Avocations: tennis, golf. Office: Right Assocs 1818 Market St Ste 14 Philadelphia PA 19103-3602

PINSKER, WALTER, allergist, immunologist; b. Bay Shore, N.Y., Mar. 27, 1933; s. Albert and Irene (Kuchlick) P.; m. Tillene Giller, June 15, 1958; children: Neil, Andrew, Susann. BA, U. Rochester, 1954; MD, Chgo. Med. Sch. U. Health Sci., 1958. Diplomate Am. Bd. Allergy and Immunology. Intern L.I. Jewish Hosp., New Hyde Park, N.Y., 1958-59; resident internal medicine Bklyn. VA Hosp., 1959-60; resident internal medicine Long Beach (Calif.) VA Hosp., 1960-61, resident allergy and immunology, 1961-62; chief of allergy Letterman Army Hosp., San Francisco, 1962-64; pres. Bay Shore Allergy Group, 1964-94; attending physician Mather Hosp., Port Jefferson, N.Y., St. Charles Hosp., Port Jefferson, 1981, Southside Hosp., Bay Shore, 1964—, Good Samaritan Hosp., West Islip, N.Y., 1964—, asst. clin. prof. medicine SUNY, Stony Brook, 1968—. Contbr. articles to profl. jours. Bd. visitors Pilgrim State Hosp., Brentwood, N.Y., 1974-77; pres. Suffolk Assn. Children with Learning Difficulties, N.Y., 1972-74; trustee Leeway Sch., Stony Brook, 1974-75, Bay Shore Jewish Ctr., 1974-84; com. for handicapped West Islip Schs., 1971—. Capt. U.S. Army, 1962-64. Named Co-Humanitarian of Yr. L.I. Adults and Children with Learning and Developmental Disabilities, 1994; recipient Physician's Recognition award AMA, 1969—. Fellow Am. Acad. Allergy and Immunology, Am. Coll. Allergy and Immunology, Am. Assn. Certified Allergists, Am. Coll. Chest Physicians, Am. Assn.- Study of Headaches, N.Y. Acad. Scis., Suffolk Acad. Medicine, Nassau-Suffolk Allergy Soc. (officer, bd. dirs. 1970—, pres. 1980-82). Avocations: golf, boating, photography. Office: Bay Shore Allergy Group P C 649 W Montauk Hwy Bay Shore NY 11706-8222

PINSKY, ROBERT NEAL, poet, educator; b. Long Branch, N.J., Oct. 20, 1940; s. Milford Simon and Sylvia (Eisenberg) P.; m. EllenJane Bailey, Dec. 30, 1961; children: Nicole, Caroline, Elizabeth. B.A., Rutgers U., 1962; Ph.D., Stanford U., 1966. Mem. English faculty U. Chgo., 1967-68, Wellesley Coll., 1968-80; prof. English U. Calif., Berkeley, 1980-89; prof. Boston U., 1980-89, prof. creative writing, 1989—; poetry editor New Republic mag., 1978; vis. lectr. Harvard U.; Hurst prof. Washington U., St. Louis. Author: Landor's Poetry, 1968, Sadness and Happiness, 1975, The Situation of Poetry, 1977, An Explanation of America, 1980, History of My Heart, 1984, Poetry and the World, 1988, The Want Bone, 1990, The Inferno of Dante, 1994, The Figured Wheel: New and Collected Poems 1966-1996, 1996. Recipient Artists award Am. Acad. Arts and Letters, 1979; Saxifrage prize, 1980; William Carlos Williams prize, 1984; Guggenheim fellow, 1980. Mem. AAAS, PEN. Office: Boston U English Dept 236 Bay State Rd Boston MA 02215-1403

PINSKY, STEVEN MICHAEL, radiologist, educator; b. Milw., Feb. 2, 1942; s. Leo Donald and Louise Miriam (Faldberg) P.; m. Sue Brona Rosenzweig, June 12, 1966; children—Mark Burton, Lisa Rachel. BS, U. Wis., 1964; MD, Loyola U., Chgo., 1967. Resident in radiology and nuclear medicine U. Chgo., 1968-70, chief resident in diagnostic radiology, 1970-71, asst. prof., 1973-77, then assoc. prof. radiology and medicine, 1977-84, prof., 1984-89; prof., chmn. dept. radiology U. Ill., 1989— ; dir. nuclear medicine Michael Reese Med. Ctr., Chgo., 1973-87, vice-chmn. radiology, 1984-87, chmn. radiology, 1987-93, v.p. med. staff, 1986-87, pres., 1988-89, trustee, 1984-86, 90-93; dir. nuclear medicine tech. program Triton Coll., River Grove, Ill., 1974-87. Contbr. chpts. to books, articles to med. jours. Rsch. fellow Am. Cancer Soc., 1969-70. Maj., M.C., U.S. Army, 1971-73. Fellow Am. Coll. Nuclear Physicians (Ill. del., treas. 1982-84), Am. Coll. Radiology (alt. councilor 1986-92, councilor 1993—); mem. Soc. Nuclear Medicine (trustee 1979-87, pres. central chpt. 1980-81), Radiologic Soc. N.Am. (councilor 1994—, chmn. tech. exhibits com. 1994—, edn. coun. 1994—), Ill. Radiologic Soc. (sec./treas. 1992-94, pres.-elect 1994-95, pres. 1995-96). Home: 1821 Lawrence Ln Highland Park IL 60035-4326 Office: U Ill Hosp 1740 W Taylor St Chicago IL 60612-7232

PINSOF, NATHAN, retired advertising executive; b. Havana, Cuba, July 16, 1926; came to U.S., 1928, naturalized, 1952; s. Oscar and Rose (Newman) P.; m. Barbara Cohn, Oct. 28, 1956; children—Ellen, Diane. Student, City Jr. Coll., Chgo., 1944-46; M.B.A., U. Chgo., 1949. Asst. controller Stineway Drugs, 1949-51; mgr. media dept. Weiss & Geller, 1953-60; sr. v.p., media dir. Edward H. Weiss & Co., 1960-67; v.p., mgr. media dept. J. Walter Thompson, 1967-69; sr. v.p., dir. media and fin. Grey-Chgo., Inc., Chgo., 1969-75; exec. v.p. Grey-Chgo., Inc., 1975-88, Lois/USA, Chgo., 1989-92; ret., 1992. Bd. dirs. Off The Street Club; trustee North Shore Cong. Israel.; Bd. dirs. Jewish Children's Bur.; chmn. communications div. Jewish United Fund, 1978-79. Served with U.S. Army, 1951-53. Clubs: B'nai B'rith, The Arts of Chicago. Home: 3900 Mission Hills Rd Apt 101 Northbrook IL 60062-5721

PINSON, ARTIE FRANCES, elementary school educator; b. Rusk, Tex., June 20, 1933; d. Tom and Minerva (McDuff) Neeley; m. Robert H. Pinson, Dec. 14, 1963 (div. Nov. 1967); 1 child, Deidre R. BA magna cum laude, Tex. Coll., 1953; postgrad., U. Tex., 1956, North Tex. U., 1958, 63, New Eng. Conservatory, 1955, 57, 59, 62, Tex. So. U., 1971-72; MEd, U. Houston, 1970. Music tchr. Bullock High Sch., LaRue, Tex., 1953-59; music tchr., 9th grade English tchr. Story High Sch., Palestine, Tex., 1959-64; 3d to 6th grade gifted and talented math. tchr. Turner Elem. Sch., Houston, 1964-66; 3d, 5th and 6th grade tchr. Kay Elem. Sch., Houston, 1966-70; 6th grade tchr. Pilgrim Elem. Sch., Houston, 1970-75; 3d to 6th grade math. tchr. Pleasantville Elem. Sch., Houston, 1975-79; kindergarten to 5th grade computer/math. tchr. Betsy Ross Elem. Sch., Houston, 1979—, instrnl. coord., tchr. technologist; instrnl. coord.; lead tchr. math./sci. program Shell/Houston Ind. Sch. Dist., 1986-87, Say "Yes" program, 1988-89; math. tchr. summer potpourri St. Francis Xavier Cath. Ch., 1991; math. tchr. sci. and engring. awareness and coll. prep. program Tex. So. U., 1993, 94, 95; presenter confs. in field; condr. tchr. tng. workshops. Author computer software in field; contbr. articles to mags. Musician New Hope Bapt. Ch., Houston, 1991—, Sunday sch. tchr.; pianist Buckner Bapt. Haven Nursing Home, Houston, 1990-91; mem. N.E. Concerned Citizens Civic League. Recipient Excellence in Math. Teaching award Exxon Corp., 1990. Mem. Assn. African Am. Math. Educators (Salute to Math. Tchrs. award 1991, treas. 1991-93, sec. 1993—), Nat. Coun. Tchrs. Math., Tex. Coun. Tchrs. Math. (Excellence in Math. Tchg. award 1988), Houston Coun. Tchrs. of Math. (Excellence in Math. Tchg. award 1993), Heoines of Jericho, Palestine Negro Bus. and Profl. Women (charter mem.). Avocations: needlework, number puzzles, piano, photography, gardening. Home: 5524 Makeig St Houston TX 77026-4021 Office: Betsy Ross Elem Sch 2819 Bay St Houston TX 77026

PINSON, CHARLES WRIGHT, medical educator; b. May 29, 1952. Student, Miami U., 1970-72; BA, U. Colo., 1974, MBA, 1976; MD, Vanderbilt U., 1980. Intern Oreg. Health Sci. U., 1980-81, resident, 1981-85, chief resident, 1985-86; staff surgeon Portland Vets Affairs Med. Ctr., 1988-90; asst. prof. physiology Oreg. Health Scis. U., 1988-90, asst. prof. surgery, 1988-90, assoc. prof. surgery, 1990; staff surgeon Nashville Vets. Affairs Med. Ctr., 1990—; prof. surgery, mem. divsn. surg. oncology Vanderbilt U., Nashville, 1990—; presenter in field. Contbr. articles to profl. jours., chpts. to books. Gastrointestinal Surgery fellow Lahey Clinic Med. Ctr., 1986-87, Harvard U., 1987-88, Oreg. Am. Heart Assn. Postdoctoral fellow, 1983-84; Good Samaritan Hosp. Martin A. Howard scholar, 1985, St. Vincent Hosp. and Med. Ctr. Resident scholar, 1986; recipient Culler Physics prize, 1972, John and Julia Sawyers Rsch. award, 1995. Fellow Am. Coll. Surgeons; mem. Am. Assn. Study Liver Disease, Am. Gastroenterological Assn., Am. HEart Assn., Am. Hepatopancreatobiliary Assn. (mem. com. 1994—), Am. Inst. Phusics, Am. Liver Found., Am. Physiologic Soc., Am. Soc. Transplant Surgeons, Assn. Acad. Surgery, Assn. Surg. Edn., Assn. Program Dirs. in Surgery, Internat. Fedn. Surg. Colls., Internat. Liver Transplantation Soc., Internat. HEpato Pancreato Biliary Assn., Mass. Med. Soc., Nashville Surg. Soc. (mem. com. 1993-94), North Pacific Surg. Assn. (scientific progra, 1990-92, chmn. 1991), Pacific Northwest Transplantation Soc., The Pancreas Club, Portland Surg. Soc., Royal Soc. Medicine, Soc. Surgery Alimentary Tract, Soc. Surg. Chmn., Soc. Surg. Oncology, So. Med. Assn., Southeastern Surg. Congress, Tenn. Transplant Soc., Western Assn. Transplant Surgeons, Western Surg. Assn., World Assn. Hepaticopancreaticobiliary Surgery (founder), Alpha Omega ALpha, Phi Beta Kappa, Sigma Pi Sigma. Office: Vanderbilt U Med Ctr Oxford House Ste 801 Nashville TN 37232

PINSON, ELLIS REX, JR., chemist, consultant; b. Wichita, Kans., Oct. 23, 1925; s. Ellis Rex and Vivian (Neal) P.; m. Betty Ann Hogarth, Dec. 4, 1954; children: Matthew, Martha Pinson Salander, Thomas. B.Sc., U. of South, 1948; Ph.D., U. Rochester, 1951. Research chemist Pfizer Inc., Groton, Conn., 1951-59; project leader Pfizer Inc., 1959-61, sect. mgr., 1961-65, asst. dir. pharmacology research, 1965-67, dir. pharmacology research, 1967-71, dir. research, 1971-72, v.p. medicinal products research and devel., 1972-81; exec. v.p. Pfizer Cen. Research, 1981-86; cons., 1986—. Contbr. articles to profl. jours. Trustee Waterford Pub. Libr., 1980—, pres., 1988-93; bd. dirs., exec. com. Am. Indsl. Health Coun., 1980-86; bd. dirs. S.E. Area Tech. Devel. Ctr., 1992—. With USNR, 1943-46. Fellow N.Y. Acad. Scis.; mem. Am. Chem. Soc., AAAS, Am. Soc. Pharmacology and Exptl. Therapeutics, Phi Beta Kappa, Sigma Xi. Club: Baker Street Irregulars. Patentee in field. Office: Pfizer Inc Eastern Point Rd Groton CT 06340

PINSON, LARRY LEE, pharmacist; b. Van Nuys, Calif., Dec. 5, 1947; s. Leland J. and Audrey M. (Frett) P.; m. Margaret K. Pinson, Mar. 18, 1972; children: Scott C., Kelly E. Student, U. Calif., Davis, 1967-69; AA, Am. River Coll., Sacramento, 1969; PharmD, U. Calif., San Francisco, 1973. Staff pharmacist/asst. dir. pharm. svcs. St. Mary's Hosp., Reno, 1973-77; chief pharmacist May Ang Base USAF, 1973-77; owner/chief pharmacist Silverada Pharmacy, Reno, 1979—; adj. prof. Idaho State U., Pocatello, 1989—; cons. pharmacist Physicians Hosp., 1974-93, Reno Med. Plaza, 1973—; pharmacist coordinator Intensive Pharm. Svcs., 1986-87; cons. Calif. Dept. Health & Corrections, Susanville, 1975-76, Nev. Med. Care Adv. Bd., Carson City, 1984-87; provider and reviewer Nev. State Bd. Pharmacy, Reno, 1975-84; instr. we. Nev. Cmty. Coll., 1974-76; cons. Rural Calif. Hosp. Assn., 1973-74. Co-author: Care of Hickman Catheter, 1984. Apptd. by Gov. Bob Miller, Nev. State Bd. Pharmacy, 1995—; mem. Nev. Arthritis Found.; bd. dirs. Am. Cancer Soc., 1986—; softball coach Reno/Sparks Recreation Dept., 1973—; cubmaster Pack 153, Verdi, nev.; scoutmaster com. chmn. Reno troop 1, Boy Scouts Am., 1988-92. Recipient Bow of Hygeia award (Pharmacist of the Year), 1984. Mem. Nat. Assn. Bds. of Pharmacy, Am. Pharm. Assn., Nev. Pharmacists Assn. (pres. 1981-82), Nev. Profl. Stds. Rev. Orgn., Greater Nev. Health Sys. Agy., Kappa Psi. Avocations: skiing, fishing, backpacking, softball, golf. Home: PO Box 478 Verdi NV 89439-0478 Office: Silverada Pharmacy 2005 Silverada Blvd Ste 160 Reno NV 89512-2057

PINSON, WILLIAM MEREDITH, JR., pastor, writer; b. Ft. Worth, Aug. 3, 1934; s. William Meredith and Ila Lee (Jones) P.; m. Bobbie Ruth Judd, June 4, 1955; children: Meredith Pinson Creasey, Allison Pinson Hopgood. BA, U. N. Tex., 1955; BD, Southwestern Bapt. Theol. Sem., Ft. Worth, 1959, ThD, 1963, MDiv, 1973; LittD (hon.), Calif. Bapt. Coll., Riverside, 1978; DD (hon.), U. Mary Hardin-Baylor, Belton, Tex., 1984; LHD (hon.), Howard Payne U., Brownwood, Tex., 1986; LittD (hon.), Dallas Bapt. U., 1990. Ordained to ministry Bapt. Ch., 1955. Assoc. sec. Christian Life Commn., Dallas, 1957-63; prof. Christian ethics Southwestern Bapt. Theol. Sem., Ft. Worth, 1963-75; pastor First Bapt. Ch., Wichita Falls, Tex., 1975-77; pres. Golden Gate Bapt. Theol. Sem., Mill Valley, Calif., 1977-82; exec. dir. Bapt. Gen. Conv. Tex., 1982—; chmn. program com. Christian Life Commn., So. Bapt. Conv., spl. rschr. for home mission bd., mem. nat. task force planned growth in giving, 1984—, mem. stewardship commn., 1986-96; bd. dirs. T.B. Maston Found., 1991—; adj. prof. Southwestern Bapt. Theol. Sem., 1976-77; chmn. study commn. freedom, justice and peace Bapt. World Alliance, 1975-80, mem. study commn. on ethics, 1990—, mem. commmn. on racism, 1992—; v.p. Bapt. Gen. Conv. Tex., 1972-73, mem. state missions commn., 1976-77, vice chmn. urban strategy com., chmn. order of bus. com., 1976, chmn. steering com. Good News Tex., 1976-77, chnmn. resolutions com., exec. dir., 1982—; author, spkr. in field. Contbr. articles to numerous theological publs. Named Lilly Found. scholar Southwestern Bapt. Theol. Sem., 1960-62; Recipient Disting. Alumni award Southwestern Bapt. Theol. Sem., 1979, U. North Tex., 1980, Mosaic Missions award Home Mission Bd., 1984. Avocations: travel, reading. Office: Bapt Gen Conv Tex 333 N Washington Ave Dallas TX 75246-1754

PINSTRUP-ANDERSEN, PER, educational administrator; b. Bislev, Denmark, Apr. 7, 1939; came to U.S., 1965; s. Marinus and Alma (Pinstrup) Andersen; m. Birgit Lund, June 19, 1965; children: Charlotte, Tina. BS, Royal Vet. & Agrl. U., Copenhagen, 1965; MS, Okla. State U., 1967, PhD, 1969. Agrl. economist Centro Internacional de Agricultura Tropical, Cali, Colombia, 1969-72, head econ. unit, 1972-76; dir. agro.-econ. div. Internat. Fertilizer Devel. Ctr., Florence, Ala., 1976-77; sr. rsch. fellow, assoc. prof. Econ. Inst. Royal Vet. & Agr. U., 1977-80; rsch. fellow Internat. Food Policy Rsch. Inst., Washington, 1980, dir. food consumption and nutrition divsn., 1980-87, dir. gen., 1992—; dir. food and nutrition policy program, prof. food econs. Cornell U., Ithaca, N.Y., 1987-92; cons. The World Bank, Washington, 1978-92, Can. Internat. Devel. Agy., 1982-83, 86, UNICEF, N.Y.C.; cons. subcom. on nutrition UN, Rome, 1980-87. Author: The World Food and Agricultural Situation, 1978, Agricultural Research and Economic

Development, 1979, The Role of Fertilizer in World Food Supply, 1980, Agricultural Research and Technology in Economic Development, 1982; editor: (with Magaret Biswas) Nutrition and Development, 1985, Food Subsidies in Developing Countries: Costs, Benefits, and Policy Options, 1988, Macroeconomic Policy Reforms, Poverty, and Nutrition: Analytical Methodologies, 1990, The Political Economy of Food and Nutrition Policies, 1993, (with David Pelletier and Harold Alderman) Child Growth and Nutrition in Developing Countries: Priorities for Action, 1995. With Danish Army, 1958-59. Recipient Ford Internat. fellowship, 1965-66, People to People Cert. of Appreciation, 1967, Kellogg Travel fellowship, 1979, Competition prize Nordic Soc. Agrl. Rschrs. and Norsk Hydro, 1979, Cert. Merit, Gamma Sigma Delta, 1991, Disting. Alumnus award U. Colo., 1993. Mem. Am. Assn. Agrl. Econs. (PhD Thesis award 1970, Outstanding Jour. Article award 1977), Internat. Assn. Agrl. Econs., Columbian Nat. Orgn. Profls. in Agr. (hon.). Home: 1451 Highwood Dr Mc Lean VA 22101-2516 Office: Internat Food Policy Rsch Inst 1200 17th St NW Washington DC 20036-3006

PINTER, GABRIEL GEORGE, physiology educator; b. Bekes, Hungary, June 23, 1925; came to U.S., 1958; s. Lajos and Regina (Szilagyi-Farkas) P.; m. Berit Helgesen, Dec. 19, 1958 (dec. May 1980); children: Renee Astrid, Eva Ingelill; m. Vera Lederer Dallos, May 23, 1984. M.D., U. Sch. of Medicine, Budapest, Hungary, 1951. Asst. prof. U. Sch. Medicine, Budapest, 1951-56; rsch. assoc. U. Inst. Med. Rsch., Oslo, Norway, 1957-58; asst. prof. U. Tenn., Memphis, 1958-61; from asst. prof. to prof. U. Md., Balt., 1961-92, ret.; vis. prof. King's Coll., London, 1990-94. Contbr. articles to profl. jours. Recipient A.V. Humbolt prize Fed. Republic of Germany, 1980; Swedish Royal Med. Soc. fellow, Uppsala, Sweden, 1972. Mem. Am. Physiol. Soc., Physiol. Soc. Great Britain, Scandinavian Physiol. Soc., European Soc. Microcirculation.

PINTER, HAROLD, playwright; b. London, Oct. 10, 1930; s. Hyman and Frances (Mann) P.; m. Vivien Merchant, Sept. 14, 1956 (div. 1980); 1 son, Daniel; m. Antonia Fraser, Nov. 1980. Student, Brit. schs.; D.Litt. (hon.), U. Reading, 1970, U. Birmingham, 1971, U. Glasgow, 1974, U. East Anglia, 1974, U. Stirling, 1979, Brown U., 1982, U. Hull, 1986, U. Sussex, 1990, U. East London, London, 1994, U. Sofia, Bulgaria, 1995; hon. fellow, Queen Mary Coll., London, 1987. Actor in repertory theatres, 1949-57; dir. plays and films, 1970—; assoc. dir. Nat. Theatre, 1973-83; author (plays) The Dumb Waiter, 1957, A Slight Ache, 1958, The Hothouse, 1958, A Night Out, 1959, The Caretaker, 1959, Night School, 1960, The Dwarfs, 1960 (pub. 1990), The Collection, 1961, The Lover, 1962 (Italia prize 1963), Tea Party, 1964, The Homecoming, 1964, The Basement, 1966, Landscape, 1967, Silence, 1968, Night, 1969, Old Times, 1970, Monologue, 1972, No Man's Land, 1974, Betrayal, 1978 (screenplay 1981), Family Voices, 1980, A Kind of Alaska, 1982, Victoria Station, 1982, One for the Road, 1984, Mountain Language, 1988, The New World Order, 1991, Party Time, 1991, Moonlight, 1993, others; (screenplays) The Caretaker, 1962, The Servant, 1962, The Pumpkin Eater, 1963, The Quiller Memorandum, 1965, Accident, 1966, The Birthday Party, 1967, The Go-Between, 1969, The Homecoming, 1969, Langrishe Go Down, 1970, A la Recherche du Temps Perdu, 1972, The Last Tycoon, 1974, The French Lieutenant's Woman, 1980, Betrayal, 1981, Victory, 1982, Turtle Diary, 1984, The Handmaid's Tale, 1987, Reunion, 1988, The Heat of the Day, 1988, The Comfort of Strangers, 1989, The Trial, 1989; (pub.); (novel) Collected Poems and Prose, 1990. Decorated Comdr. Order Brit. Empire; recipient Shakespeare prize Hamburg, Germany, 1970, Austrian prize lit., 1973, Pirandello prize, 1980, Commonwealth award, 1981, Donatello prize, 1982, Elmer H. Bobst award, 1984, David Cohen Brit. Lit. prize, 1995. Office: care Judy Daish Assocs Ltd, 2 St Charles Pl, London W10 6EG, England

PINTO, ROSALIND, retired educator, civic volunteer; b. N.Y.C.; d. Barney and Jenny Abrams; m. Jesse E. Pinto (dec.); children: Francine, Jerry, Evelyn. BA in Polit. Sci. cum laude, Hunter Coll.; MA in Polit. Sci., History, Columbia U.; postgrad., Queens Coll., LaGuardia Community Coll. Lic. social studies tchr. jr. high sch., N.Y., per diem lifetime substitute; cert. N.Y. State secondary sch. social studies grades 7-12. Substitute tchr., 1966-69, 90, 91—; tchr. social studies I.S. 126Q, L.I. City, N.Y., 1969-88, Jr. High Sch. 217 Briarwood, N.Y.C., 1988-89; ret., 1989; part-time cluster tchr. social studies and communication arts Pub. Sch. 140, Bronx, N.Y., 1990-91, 92; substitute tchr. I.S. 227Q, 1992-93; participant numerous personal and profl. devel. seminars and workshops. Author curriculum materials; contbr. study guide for regent's competency test, 1990; contbr. poems to anthologies; recorded poem for The Sound of Poetry, Nat. Libr. Poetry (Editor's Choice award 1993, 94). Enrollment asst. Insight Heart Team, 1989; vol. receptionist Whitney Mus., N.Y.C.; mem. com. on pub. transp. Cmty. Bd. 6, Queens, 1990—, mem. com. on history, 1990—, chmn. beautification com., 1992—; active Great Smokies Song Chase Warren-Wilson Coll., N.C., 1992; vol. local polit. campaigns; mem. Queens Hist. Soc., Forest Hills Van Ct. Homeowners Assn., Ctrl. Queens Hist. Soc., bd. dirs.; mem. Rego Park Coalition Against Violence, Forest Hills Civic Assn., Neighbors Against Graffiti. Recipient cert. of appreciation for participation in workside sponsor program Dept. Probate Cmty. Svc. Project, 1993, for participation in Make a Difference Day, 1994, 95, Beautification Com., 1995, 96. Fellow Mcpl. Art Soc. (hon. mention design 2000 award); mem. NAFE, Internat. Soc. Poets (life mem. adv. panel, Internat. Poet of Merit award 1993), N.Y. Insight Alumni Assn., Columbia U. Grad. Sch. Arts and Scis. Alumni Assn., Hunter Coll. Alumni Assn., Robert F. Kennedy Dem. Assn. (bd. dirs.), Ctr. for Sci. in the Pub. Interest. Avocations: poetry and poetry contests, reading, long distance walking, art shows, plays. Home: 97-04 70th Ave Forest Hills NY 11375-5808 *Loving people and having faith in them and the possibility of happy outcomes is the greatest motivation toward achievement of goals.*

PINTO, WILLIAM A., construction executive; b. 1947. B in Bldg. Cons., U. Fla., M in Bldg. Cons. With The Hardin Co., Inc., 1974—, group pres., exec. com., 1988—. Office: Hardin Constrn Group Inc 1380 W Paces Ferry Rd NW Atlanta GA 30327-2439*

PINTOZZI, CHESTALENE, librarian; b. Macomb, Okla., Apr. 4, 1947; d. Otis William and Edith Marie (Jordan) Bowerman; m. Nicola Francis Xavier Pintozzi, Aug. 2, 1967. Student, U. Okla., 1965-67; BA in English, No. Ill. U., 1969; MLS, U. Tex., 1981. Geology libr. U. Tex., Austin, 1982-84; environ. libr., Ann Marbut Environ. Libr. Sarasota (Fla.) County Pub. Libr. Sys., 1985-87; temporary reference libr. Sci.-Engring. Libr. U. Ariz., Tuscon, 1989-90, reference libr. Sci.-Engring. Libr., 1990—. Mem. ALA (Whitney-Carnegie award 1993), N.Am. Serials Interest Group, Beta Phi Mu, Phi Kappa Phi. Democrat. Office: U Ariz Bldg 54 Rm 216 Tucson AZ 85720

PINZLER, ISABELLE KATZ, lawyer; b. New York, N.Y., May 2, 1945; d. Leon Sidney and Jeanne Eleanor (Sprung) K.; m. William Michael Pinzler, Mar. 29, 1970 (div. Dec. 5, 1985); children: Johanna Elisabeth, Andrew Howard; m. James Brook, Sept. 2, 1990. AB in History, Goucher Coll., 1967; JD, Boston U., 1970. Bar: Mass. 1970, Ohio 1971, N.Y. 1974, U.S. Dist. Ct. Mass. 1971, (no. dist.) Ohio 1971, (so. dist.) N.Y. 1974, U.S. Ct. Appeals (6th cir.) 1973, (2nd cir.) 1975, (9th cir.) 1987, (11th cir.) 1992, U.S. Supreme Ct. 1977. Cons. staff atty. Lawyers Com. for Civil Rights Under Law, Boston, 1970-71; staff atty. Housing Svcs. Ctr., Fair Housing, Inc., Boston, 1970-71; staff atty. Law Reform Unit Legal Aid Soc. Cleveland, 1971-73; sr. staff atty. Nat. Employment Law Project, N.Y.C., 1973-78, dep. dir., 1977-78; dir.Women's Rights Project Am. Civil Liberties Union Found., N.Y.C., 1978-94; dep. asst. atty. gen.Civil Rights Divsn. U.S. Dept. of Justice, Washington, 1994—; adv. com. Women's Rsch. and Edn. Inst. project on women and the mil., 1991-94. Author: (with others) The Rights of Women, 1993; contbr. articles to profl. jours. Mem. Assn. of the Bar of the City of N.Y. (Com. on Sex and Law, 1984-87, Edn. and Law, 1989-92). Office: US Dept Justice Civil Rights Divsn 9th & Pennsylvania Ave Washington DC 20530

PIONKE, HARRY BERNHARD, research leader and soil scientist; b. Bklyn.. BS, U. Wis., 1963, MS, 1966, PhD in Soils, 1967. Asst. prof. soils U. Wis., Madison, 1967-68. Mem. Soil Sci. Soc. Am., Am. Geophys. Union, Am. Soc. Agron., Nat. Water Well Assn.

PIORE, EMANUEL RUBEN, physicist; b. Wilno, Russia, July 19, 1908; came to U.S., 1917; s. Ruben and Olga (Gegusin) P.; m. Nora Kahn, Aug. 26, 1931; children—Michael Joseph, Margot Deborah, Jane Ann. A.B., U. Wis., 1930, Ph.D., 1935, D.Sc. (hon.), 1966; D.Sc. (hon.), Union U., 1962. Asst. instr. U. Wis., 1930-35; research physicist RCA, 1935-38; engr.-in-charge TV lab. CBS, 1938-42; head spl. weapons group, bur. ships U.S. Navy, 1942-44; head electronics br. Office Naval Research, 1946-47, dir. phys. sci., 1947-48, dep. for natural sci., 1949-51, chief sci., 1951-55; v.p., dir. Avco Mfg. Corp., 1955-56; dir. research IBM Corp., 1956-61, v.p. research and engring., 1961-63, v.p., group exec., 1963-65, v.p., chief scientist, 1965—; also dir.; physicist research lab. electronics MIT, 1948-49; dir. Sci. Research Assocs., Inc., Health Advancement, Inc., Paul Revere Investors, Guardian Mut. Fund.; adj. prof. Rockefeller U., 1974—. Mem. Pres.'s Sci. Adv. Com., 1959-62; mem. Nat. Sci. Bd., 1961—; bd. dirs. N.Y. State Found. for Sci.; past bd. dirs. NSF; chmn. vis. com. Nat. Bur. Standards; chmn. bd. Hall of Science, N.Y.C.; mem. corp. Woods Hole Oceanographic Instn.; mem. exec. com. Resources for Future; bd. dirs. Stark Draper Lab., Nat. Info. Bur., Meml. Cancer Hosp.; mem. vis. com. to elec. engring. dept. Mass. Inst. Tech., 1956-57; vis. com. Harvard Coll., 1958-70; trustee Sloan-Kettering Inst. Cancer Research; mem. N.Y.C. Bd. Higher Edn., 1976—. Served to lt. comdr. USNR, 1944-46. Recipient Indsl. Research Inst. award, 1967; Distinguished Civilian medal Dept. Navy; Kaplun award Hebrew U., 1975. Fellow AAAS, Royal Soc. Arts (London, Eng.), Am. Phys. Soc., IEEE, Am. Acad. Arts Scis.; mem. Sci. Research Soc. Am., Sci. Research Assn. (dir.), Nat. Acad. Sci., Nat. Acad. Engring., Am. Inst. Physics (dir.), Am. Philos. Soc. (sec. 1985—), Sigma Xi. Clubs: University (N.Y.C.), Cosmos (Washington), Century (N.Y.C.). Home: 2 Fifth Ave New York NY 10011

PIORE, MICHAEL JOSEPH, educator; b. N.Y.C., Aug. 14, 1940. BA magna cum laude, Harvard U., 1962, PhD in Econs., 1966. Asst. prof. labor econs. MIT, 1966-70, assoc. prof., 1970-75, prof. econs., 1975—, Mitsui prof. of Comtemporary Tech., 1981-86; David W. Skinner prof. polit. economy, 1991—; cons. NAACP Legal Def. and Edn. Fund, Inc., 1966-68, Boston Model Cities Adminstrn., 1960, Dept. Labor, 1968-70, Labor, Manpower and Income Maintenance, Commonwealth of P.R., 1970-72, rsch. coord., acting exec. dir., 1970-71, cons., 1977-86; mem. Nat. Manpower Policy Task Force Assocs., 1968-70; mem. Nat. Coun. on Employment Policy, 1977-79; cons. v.p. task force on youth employment; mem. gov. bd. Inst. for Labour Studies, Internat. Labour Orgn., 1990—. Author: Birds of Passage, Migrant Labor and Industrial Societies, 1979, Beyond Individualism, 1995, (with B. Doeringer) Internal Labor Markets and Manpower Adjustment, 1981, (with Charles Sabel) The Second Industrial Divide, 1984; editor: Unemployment and Inflation: Institutionalist and Structuralist Views, 1979, (with Thomas Kochen and Richard Locke) Employment Relations in a Changing World Economy; contbr. articles to profl. jours. and publs. Recipient Harvard Coll. scholarship, 1959-60, Detur Prize, 1960, John Harvard scholarship, 1960-61; Honorary Woodrow Wilson fellowship, 1962-63, MacArthur Found. fellow, 1984-89. Mem. Am. Econ. Assn. (exec. com. 1991-94), Indsl. Rels. Rsch. Assn. Union of Radical Polit. Economists. Home: 295 Beacon St Apt 62 Boston MA 02116-1238 Office: MIT Dept Ecos Rm E52-271C Cambridge MA 02139

PIORE, NORA KAHN, economist, health policy analyst; b. N.Y.C., N.Y., Nov. 28, 1912; d. Alexander and Sara (Rosenbaum) Kahn; m. Emanuel R. Piore, Aug. 26, 1931; children: Michael Joseph, Margot Deborah, Jane Anne. B.A., U. Wis., 1933, MA, 1934. Research economist health legislation subcom. U.S. Senate, Washington, 1950-53; spl. asst. to commr. N.Y.C. Dept. Health, 1957-68; adj. prof. urban affairs Hunter Coll., N.Y.C., 1962-72; dir. N.Y.C. Urban Med. Econs. Research Ctr., 1960-68; vis. scientist Assn. Aid of Crippled Children, N.Y.C., 1968-72, study dir. hosp. ambulatory care svcs. in U.S., 1968-72; prof. pub. health econs. Columbia U. Sch. Pub. Health, N.Y.C., 1972-82; assoc. dir. Columbia U. Ctr. Community Health Systems, N.Y.C., 1971-82, cons. Health Services Research, 1982—; sr. program cons. Commonwealth Fund, N.Y.C., 1982-88; sr. fellow United Hosp. Fund, N.Y.C., 1982-90; dir. Health Svcs. Improvement Fund (Blue Cross-Blue Shield), 1984—, Sun Valley Health Forum, Boise, Idaho, 1978-88; active numerous coms., founds., task forces, funds in field; cons. Carnegie Corp. N.Y., R.I. Health Svcs. Rsch. Corp., Robert Wood Johnson Found., Pew Meml. Trust; mem. N.Y. State Hosp. Rev. and Planning Coun., 1976-84. Contbr. chpts. to books, articles to profl. jours. Recipient Merit award N.Y. Pub. Health Assn., 1977 Career Scientist award N.Y. Health Rsch. Coun., 1961-65, 66-71; Belding scholar Assn. Aid Crippled Children, 1968; grantee USPHS, 1980. Fellow Am. Pub. Health Assn., N.Y. Acad. Medicine; mem. Am. Econs. Assn., AAAS, Health Services Research Assn., Assn. Social Scientists in Health, Inst. Medicine, Nat. Acad. Sci., Phi Beta Kappa. Clubs: Cosmopolitan, Women's City (N.Y.C.).

PIOTROW, PHYLLIS TILSON, public health educator, international development specialist; b. N.Y.C., Mar. 16, 1933; d. Paul and Phyllis Tilson; children: Diana, Stephen. BA in History summa cum laude, Bryn Mawr Coll., 1954; BA in Modern History first class, Oxford U., England, 1956, MA, 1959; PhD in Pol. Sci. and Population Dynamics, Johns Hopkins U., 1971. Social sci. analyst history and govt. dvsn., legis. reference svc. Libr. Congress, 1956-57; writer Editorial Rsch. Reports (Congresl. quarterly), Washington, 1957-58; instr. St. Anne's Coll. Oxford (England) U., 1958-59; legis. asst. Senator Kenneth B. Keating of N.Y., Washington, 1960-64, Senator G. McGovern of S.D., Washington, 1965; first exec. dir. Population Crisis Com. Population Action Internat., Washington, 1965-69, 71-72, 75-78; adminstr. population info. program Dept. Med. and Pub. Affairs, George Washington U. Med. Ctr., Washington, 1972-75; prin. investigator Population Communication Svcs., Johns Hopkins U., Washington, 1982—; dir. Population Info. Program, Balt., 1978—, Ctr. Communication Programs, Johns Hopkins U., Balt., 1988—; bd. dirs., sec. Population Action Internat., 1969—, mem. exec. com., 1978—; bd. dirs. Ctr. Devel. and Population Activities, Washington, 1975-92, exec. com., 1978-92, sec., 1979-84, chmn., 1984-86; internat. cons. and presenter in field. Author: World Population Crisis: The United States Response, 1972, World Population: The Present and Future Crisis, 1980; (with G. Tapinos) Six Billion People: Demographic Dilemmas and World Politics, 1978; contbr. numerous articles to profl. jours. Advisor U.S. Del. to UN Population Comsn., 1969, 71, 73, 77, U.S. Del. to World Population Conf., Bucharest, 1974; mem. Internat. Adv. Coun. Bryn Mawr Coll., 1972-76, nat. adv. coun. Marshall Scholarship Comsn., 1972-80, Brit. Adv. Coun., 1973-84; mem. adv. com. UN POPIN database, 1982—; bd. dirs. New Directions, 1977-79; chmn. Informed Choice Task Force, 1988-91. European fellow Bryn Mawr Coll., 1954; Marshall scholar Oxford U., 1954-56; Ford mid-career fellow, 1969-71; recipient Charles A. Dana Found. award, 1991; U.S. AID grantee, 1978-84, 82-87, 84-87, 85-89, 86-91, 87-92, 88-92, 90—; POPLINE database grantee UN Population Fund, 1988. Mem. APHA (chair population and family planning sect. 1979-80, Carl Schultz award 1989), Population Assn. Am., Cosmos Club. Avocations: tennis, gardening, hiking. Office: Johns Hopkins Univ Ctr for Comm Programs 111 Market Pl Ste 310 Baltimore MD 21202-4012

PIOTROWSKI, RICHARD FRANCIS, state agency administrator, council chairman; b. Manchester, N.H., Mar. 13, 1945; s. Stanley J. and Marion G. (Rubino) P.; m. Claudia H. Rund, Aug. 28, 1971; children: Richard Jr., Courtney. AAS in Civil Tech., Hartford (Conn.) State Tech. Coll., 1965; student, U. Conn., 1965-69. Registered profl. engr., Conn. Sr. engr. Henry N. Loomis and Assoc., New Hartford, Conn., 1970-77; quality control engr. Atlantic Pipe Corp., Plainville, Conn., 1977; sr. civil engr. C.E. Maguire, New Britain, Conn., 1977-80; chief civil engr. Anderson-Nichols and Co., Newington, Conn., 1980-83; project engr. Cahn Co., Wallingford, Conn., 1983-84; asst. chief engr. State of Conn. Dept. Pub. Works, Hartford, 1984-85, asst. dir. facilities, design and constrn., 1985-87; dep. commr. dept. pub. works State of Conn., Hartford, 1987—. Councilor Plainville Town Council, 1975-81, 85-87, council chmn./mayor, 1979-81, 1985-87; mem. adv. bd. Colonial Bank, Plainville, 1980-86; pres. Plainville Pre-Sch. Assn., 1984-85; corporator New Britain Gen. Hosp. Recipient Disting. Svc. award Plainville Jaycees, 1980, Conn. Engr. Recognition award, 1991, Dist. Mgr. Svc. award State of Conn., 1994. Mem. Nat. League of Cities (transp. and communications policy com. 1981, 87), Conn. Conf. Municipalities, Conn. Assn. Street and Hwy. Ofcls. Democrat. Roman Catholic. Home: 14 Peace Ct Plainville CT 06062-2836 Office: State of Conn Dept Pub Works 165 Capitol Ave Hartford CT 06106-1630

PIPAL, GEORGE HENRY, journalist; b. Lafayette, Ind., Oct. 14, 1916; s. Francis John and Belle (Kadavy) P.; m. Caroline Dunsmore, Aug. 17, 1946; children—John, Susan, Philip, Frank. B.A., U. Nebr., 1937; M.S., Columbia, 1939. Corr. various bureaus UPI, 1937-41; bur. mgr. UPI, Prague, 1946; mgr. for UPI, Eastern Europe, 1947, Germany, 1948; dir. European Services, 1949-51; gen. bus. mgr. Europe, Middle East, Africa, 1952-65; gen. sales exec. computer svcs. N.Y.C., 1966-68; gen. mgr. internat. features div., 1968-78; mng. dir. UPI (U.K.), Ltd., 1964-65; v.p. United Feature Syndicate, 1978-84, United Media Enterprises, 1985—. Served as lt. USNR, 1942-46. Office: United Media 1 Snoopy Pl Santa Rosa CA 95403-2665

PIPER, A. COLEMAN, retail executive; b. 1947. Exec. v.p. ops. Proffitt's Inc., 1972-93; exec. v.p. ops. & real estate Proffitt's Inc., Alcoa, Tenn., 1994—; tchr. Pa. Office: Proffitt's Inc Midland Shopping Ctr PO Box 388 Alcoa TN 37701-0388*

PIPER, ADDISON LEWIS, securities executive; b. Mpls., Oct. 10, 1946; s. Harry Cushing and Virginia (Lewis) P.; m. Louise Wakefield (div.); children: Gretchen, Tad, William; m. Cynthia Schuneman, Nov. 14, 1979; children: Elisabeth LaBelle, Richard LaBelle. BA in Econs., Williams Coll., 1968; MBA, Stanford U., 1972. Mktg. cons. Earl Savage and Co., Mpls., 1968-69; mem. capital market dept. Piper and Jaffray, Mpls., 1969-70; asst. syndicate mgr. Piper, Jaffray and Hopwood, Mpls., 1972-73, v.p., 1973-79, dir. trading, 1973-77, dir. sales, 1977-79, exec. v.p., dir. mktg., 1979-83, chief exec. officer, chmn. mgmt. com., 1983—, chmn. bd. dirs., 1988—; adv. com. N.Y. Stock Exch., 1966-90; bd. dirs. Allina Health Systems, Greenspring Corp., Mpls., Minn. Bus. Partnership, Mpls.; vice chair Abbott Northwestern Hosp., Mpls.; trustee CARE Found., Mpls. Fin. chmn. Senator Durenberger Fin. Com., Mpls., 1980-88; chmn. Minn. Pub. Radio, 1985-95. Mem. Securities Industry Assn. (bd. govs. 1986-90, tax policy com.), Country Club of the Rockies (Colo.), Mpls. Club. Republican. Episcopalian. Clubs: Woodhill Country (Wayzata); Minneapolis. Avocations: skiing, golfing, hunting, tennis, horses. Office: Piper Jaffray Cos. PO Box 28 222 S 9th St Minneapolis MN 55440

PIPER, ADRIAN MARGARET SMITH, philosopher, artist, educator; b. N.Y.C., Sept. 20, 1948; d. Daniel Robert and Olive Xavier (Smith) P.; m. Jeffrey Ernest Evans, June 27, 1982 (div. 1987). AA, Sch. Visual Arts, 1969; BA in Philosophy, CCNY, 1974; MA, Harvard U., 1977, PhD, 1981; student, U. Heidelberg, Germany, 1977-78; LHD (hon.), Calif. Inst. Arts, 1992, Mass. Coll. Art, 1994. Asst. prof. U. Mich., Ann Arbor, 1979-86; Mellon rsch. fellow Stanford (Calif.) U., 1982-83; assoc. prof. Georgetown U., Washington, 1986-88, U. Calif., San Diego, 1988; prof. philosophy Wellesley (Mass.) Coll., 1990—; speaker, lectr. on both philosophy and art. Artist: one-woman exhbns. include N.Y. Cultural Ctr., N.Y.C., 1971, Montclair (N.J.) State Coll., 1976, Wadsworth Atheneum, Hartford, Conn., 1980, Nexus COntemporary Art Ctr., Atlanta, 1987, The Alternative Mus., N.Y.C., 1987, Goldie Paley Gallery, Phila., 1989, Power Plant Gallery, Toronto, 1990, Lowe Art Mus., Coral Gables, Fla., 1990-91, Santa Monica (Calif.) Mus. Contemporary Art, 1991, John Weber Gallery, N.Y.C., 1989, 90, 91, 92, Whitney Mus. Am. Art, N.Y.C., 1990, Hirschorn Mus., Washington, 1991, Ikon Gallery, Birmingham, Eng., 1991, Cornerhouse, Manchester, Eng., 1992, Cartwright Hall, Bradford, Eng., 1992, Kunstverein, Munich, Germany, 1992, Indpls. Ctr. Contemporary Art, 1992, Manasterio de Santa Clara, Moguer, Spain, 1992, Grey Art Gallery, N.Y.C., 1992, Paula Cooper Art Galler, 1992, 94; group exhbns. include Paula Cooper Gallery, 1969, Dwan Gallery, N.Y.C., 1969, 70, Seattle Art Mus., 1969, Stadtisches Mus., Leverkusen, Germany, 1969, Kunsthalle Berne, Berne, Switzerland, 1969, N.Y. Cultural Ctr., 1970, Allen Mus., Oberlin, Ohio, 1970, Mus. Modern Art, N.Y.C., 1970, 88, 91, Musee d'Art Moderne, Paris, 1971, 77, 89, Inhibodress Gallery, New South Wales, Australia, 1972, Calif. Inst. Arts, Valencia, 1973, Samuel S. Fleischer Art Meml., Phila., 1974, Mus. Contemporary Art, Chgo., 1975, Newberger Mus., Purchase, N.Y., 1978, Mass. Coll. Art, Boston, 1979, Artemesia Gallery, Chgo., 1979, A.I.R. Gallery, N.Y.C., 1980, Inst. Contemporary Arts, London, 1980, The New Mus., N.Y.C., 1981, 83, 85, Kenkeleba Gallery, N.Y.C., 1983, The Studio Mus. Harlem, N.Y.C., 1985, 89, Mus. Moderner Kunst, Vienna, Austria, 1985, Intar Gallery, N.Y.C., 1988, Whitney Mus. Downtown, N.Y.C., 1988, Art Gallery Ont., Toronto, 1988, Long Beach (Calif.) Art Mus., 1989, Simon Watson Gallery, N.Y.C., 1990, Feigen Gallery, Chgo., 1990, Barbara Krakow Gallery, Boston, 1990, Milw. Art Mus., 1990, Contemporary Arts Ctr., Houston, 1991, John Weber Gallery, 1991, Anne Plumb Gallery, N.Y.C., 1991, Hirschorn Mus., 1991, The Albuquerque Mus. Art, 1991, The Toledo Mus. Art, 1991, Denver Art Mus., Fukui Fine Arts Mus., Fukyuiken, Japan, 1992-93, N.J. State Mus., Trenton, 1992-93, Philippe Staib Gallery, N.Y.C., 1992, New Loom House, London, 1992, Espace-Lyonnais D'Art Contemporain, Lyon, France, 1993, Am. Acad. Inst. Arts and Letters, N.Y.C., 1993; permanent collections include The Bklyn. Mus., Denver Art Mus., Kunstmuseum Berne, Musee d'Art Moderne, The Mus. Contemporary Art, Chgo., The Wadsworth Atheneum, Met. Mus. Art; art performances include RISD, 1973, The Whitney Mus. Am. Art, 1975, Kurfurstendamm, Berlin, 1977, Hauptstrasse, Heidelburg, Germany, 1978, Allen Meml. Mus., Oberlin, Ohio, 1980, Contemporary Art Inst. Detroit, 1980, San Francisco Art Inst., 1985, Calif. Inst. Art, 1984, The Studio Mus. Harlem, 1988; performances on video, 1987—; contbr. articles to profl. jours. Recipient N.Y. State Coun. on Arts award, 1989, Visual Arts award, 1990, Skowhegan medal for sculptural installation, 1995; NEH Travel fellow, 1979, NEA Visual Artists' fellow, 1979, 82, Andrew Mellon Postdoctoral fellow, 1982-84, Woodrow Wilson Internat. Scholars fellow, 1988-89, Guggenheim Meml. fellow, 1989, non-resident fellow N.Y. Inst. for Humanities, NYU, 1996—; NEA Artists Forums grantee, 1987. Mem. AAUP, Am. Philos. Assn. (mem. ea. divsn.), Am. Soc. Polit. and Legal losophy, N.Am. Kant. Soc. Avocations: medieval and renaissance music, fiction, poetry, yoga, German. Office: Wellesley Coll 106 Central St Wellesley MA 02181-8209

PIPER, DON COURTNEY, political science educator; b. Washington, July 29, 1932; s. Don Carlos and Alice (Courtney) P.; m. Rowena Inez Wise, July 6, 1956; children: Sharon, Valarie. B.A., U. Md., 1954, M.A., 1958; Ph.D. (James B. Duke fellow), Duke U., 1961. Research assoc. Duke U., 1961-62; exec. sec. Commonwealth-Studies Center, 1962-64; asst. prof. dept. govt. and politics U. Md., College Park, 1964-67; assoc. prof. U. Md., 1967-69, prof., 1969—, head dept. govt. and politics, 1968-74, dir. grad. studies dept., 1982-95, mem. coun. of system faculty, 1989-90; chmn. faculty council College Park Faculty Assembly, 1974-75, chmn. campus senate, 1975-77, 89-90, univ. marshal, 1981—, mem. Athletic Council, 1986-93, mem. senate ad hoc com. on undergrad. edn., 1986-88, chmn. chancellor's ad hoc com. on campus ceremonies, 1986-87, chmn. acad. com. of Athletic Council, 1986-89; chmn. campaign for College Park, 1988-89; chmn. retention review com. U. Md., 1990-91, chmn. budget and facilities com. athletic coun., 1991-93, chmn. senate com. on programs courses and curriculi, 1991-93, co-chair Mid. States self-study exec. com., 1995—; teaching fellow Lilly Ctr. for Teaching Excellence, 1994-95; rsch. asst. Am. Coun. on Edn., 1966-68; faculty adv. com., planning adv. com. Md. State Bd. Higher Edn., 1977-82; chmn. com. on dept. chairmen Am. Polit. Sci. Assn., 1973-75; mem. coun. So. Polit. Sci. Assn., 1970-72, chmn. Chastain award com., 1973-75. Author: International Law of Great Lakes, 1967; contbg. author: International Law Standard and Commonwealth Developments, 1966, De Lege Pactorum, 1970, Foreign Policy Analysis, 1975; editor: (with R. Taylor Cole) Post-primary Education and Political and Economic Development, 1964; co-editor, contbg. author: (with Ronald Terchek) Interaction: Foreign Policy and Public Policy, 1983; bd. editors: World Affairs, 1971-94; editl. adv. com.: Internat. Legal Materials, 1977-78. Served to 1st lt. USAF, 1955-58. Recipient U. Md. Regents award for excellence in teaching, 1966, Teaching Excellence award Div. Behavioral and Social Scis., 1982-83, Outstanding Tchr. award Greek System, U. Md., 1982, Pres.'s medal, U. Md., 1992. Mem. Am. Soc. Internat. Law, Internat. Law Assn., Internat. Studies Assn. (chmn. internat. law sect. 1981-83), Am. Peace Soc. (bd. dirs. 1972-94), UN Assn./USA, Phi Beta Kappa (pres. Gamma chpt. 1978-79), Phi Kappa Phi (chpt. pres. 1982-83), Omicron Delta Kappa (faculty adviser 1990—), Pi Sigma Alpha. Methodist. Home: 4323 Woodberry St Hyattsville MD 20782-1174 Office: U Md Dept Govt & Politics College Park MD 20742

PIPER, MARGARITA SHERERTZ, retired school administrator; b. Petersburg, Va., Dec. 20, 1926; d. Guy Lucas and Olga Doan (Akers) Sherertz; m. Glenn Clair Piper, Feb. 3, 1950; children: Mark Stephen, Susan Leslie Piper Weathersbee. BA in Edn., Mary Washington Coll. of Fredericksburg, 1948; MEd, U. Va., 1973, EdS, 1976. Svc. rep. C&P Telephone, Washington, 1948-55, adminstrv. asst., 1955-56, svc. supr., 1956-62; tchr. Culpeper (Va.) County Pub. Schs., 1970-75, reading lab dir., 1975-80; asst. prin. Rappahannock (Va.) County Pub. Schs., 1980-81, prin., 1981-88, dir.

pupil pers., spl. programs, 1988-95; ret., 1995; chair PD 9 regional transition adv. bd. Culpeper, Fauquier, Madison, Orange and Rappahannock Counties, Va., 1991-94; vice chair Family Assessment and Planning Team, Washington, 1992-95. Recipient Va. Gov. Schs. Commendation cert. Commonwealth of Va., 1989-93. Mem. NEA, Va. Edn. Assn., Va. Coun. Adminstrs. Spl. Edn., Va. Assn. Edn. for Gifted, Rappahannock Edn. Assn. Democrat. Episcopalian. Avocations: creative writing, music, walking, crosstitch, knitting.

PIPER, MARK HARRY, retired banker; b. Flint, Mich., Apr. 17, 1931; s. James U. and Dorothy (Weed) P.; m. Wanda L. Hubbard, June 20, 1953; children: Mark T., Kathryn L. BS, St. John's Mil. Acad., 1949; AB with distinction and honors in Econs, U. Mich., 1953, JD cum laude, 1956. Bar: Mich. 1956. With Clark, Klein, Winter, Parsons & Prewitt, Detroit, 1956-57; with Genesee Mchts. Bank & Trust Co., Flint, 1957-88, v.p., sr. trust officer, 1966-72, sr. v.p., 1972-88; sr. v.p. NBD Genesee Bank (formerly United Mich. Corp.), 1985-88, cashier, sec. bd. dirs., 1985-88; adj. instr. bus. adminstrn. U. Mich., Flint, 1976-80; pres. Flint Estate Planning Coun., 1969-70; mem. Flint citizens adv. coun. U. Mich., 1974-82; vice chmn., 1975-82. Bd. dir. Retirement Homes of Detroit Ann. Conf. Meth. Ch., 1968-76, vice chmn. profl. ministry and support, 1975, mem. bd. support systems, 1975, coun. fin. and adminstrn., 1976-84, chmn. coun. fin. and adminstrn., 1980-84; bd. dirs. United Meth. Devel. Fund, 1986-90; gen. bd. pensions United Meth. Ch., 1988—; trustee Flint YMCA Boysfarm Found., 1964-78, chmn., 1976-78; bd. mgmt. Flint YMCA Boysfarm, 1964-74; mem. Detroit Conf. Bd. P. United Meth. Ch., 1968-76, chmn., 1972-75, 88—, mem., 1986—; bd. dirs. U. Mich. Devel. Coun., 1980-82; bd. dirs., asst. treas., sec.-treas. Flint Area Young Life Found., 1979—, Mich. Area Young Life Com., 1980-88; bd. dirs., vice chmn. The Crim Road Race Inc., 1985-87. Mem. ABA, Mich. Bar Assn., Genesee County Bar Assn., Inst. Continuing Legal Edn., U. Mich.-Flint Club (bd. dirs., pres. 1973-74). Home: 1378 Ox Yoke Dr Flint MI 48532-2352 also: PO Box 3121 Estes Park CO 80517

PIPER, ROBERT JOHNSTON, architect, urban planner; b. Byron, Ill., Feb. 2, 1926; s. Leo Edward and Helen Anna (Johnston) P.; m. Carol Jane White, June 23, 1951; children—Christopher White, Brian Douglas, Eric Johnston. B.S. in Archtl. Engring, U. Ill., 1951; M. City and Regional Planning, Cornell U., 1953. Architect, planner Orput & Assos., Rockford, Ill., 1953-61; dir. profl. services AIA, Washington, 1961-67; partner, v.p. Perkins & Will, Chgo., 1967-74; dep. dir. Northeastern Ill. Planning Commn., Chgo., 1974-76; asso. Metz, Train, Olson & Youngren, Inc., Chgo., 1976-79; dir. community devel. City of Highland Park, Ill., 1980-91; ret. City of Highland Park, 1991; coord. various programs Chgo. Cultural Ctr., 1992—; pres. Landmarks Preservation Council Ill., Chgo., 1976-80. Author: Careers in Architecture, vocat. guidance manuals, 1967, 71, 75, 80, 85, 93; author, editor: Architect's Handbook of Professional Practice, 7th edit., 1963; prin. works include Regional Open Space Plan, Northeastern Ill., Spring Valley Operations Breakthrough Housing Complex, Kalamazoo, CBD Streetscape and Skokie Corridor Master Plan, Highland Park. Trustee Village of Winnetka, Ill., 1978-83; mem. Potomac Planning Task Force Dept. Interior, 1967-68, Commn. on Fed. Procurement, Washington, 1970-71; mem. nat. advisory bd. community characteristics HEW, 1970-78. Served with USNR, 1944-46, PTO. Fellow AIA (mem. Task Force Future of Inst. 1974-75, various coms., pres. AIA Ill. coun. 1986, Disting. Achievement awards AIA Ill., AIA Chgo. 1993); mem. Am. Inst. Cert. Planners (metro chpt. pres. 1971-72), Lambda Alpha. Episcopalian. Home: 972 Elm St Winnetka IL 60093-2207

PIPER, THOMAS LAURENCE, III, investment banker; b. Washington, June 20, 1941; s. Thomas Laurence and Edna (Milewski) P.; m. Ann Runnette, Apr. 8, 1967; children: Thomas Laurence IV, Andrew Kerr. Student, U. Va., 1959-61. Asso. Hodgdon & Co., Inc., Washington, 1962-65; sr. v.p., dir. Hayden Stone Inc., N.Y.C., 1966-73; mng. dir. New Court Securities Corp., N.Y.C., 1974-81, Dillon, Read & Co., Inc., N.Y.C., 1981—. Chmn. fund dir. New Canaan chpg. ARC, 1978; bd. dirs. Manhattan coun. Boy Scouts Am., Waveny Care Ctr., New Canaan, Our Lady Queen of Angels, Manhattan. Mem. Investment Assn. N.Y. (pres. 1974), Bond Club N.Y. Clubs: Racquet and Tennis, Brook (N.Y.C.); Country of New Canaan. Home: Windrow Ln New Canaan CT 06840 Office: Dillon Read & Co Inc 535 Madison Ave New York NY 10022-4212

PIPERNO, SHERRY LYNN, psychotherapist; b. La Crosse, Wis., Sept. 22, 1953; d. Morris and Leona Jennie (Shelmadine-Hanson) Piperno. BA in Fine Arts, U. N.Mex., 1982, MA in Counseling, 1989. Nat. cert. counselor; lic. clin. mental health counselor; cert. criminal justice specialist. Mental health counselor Bernalillo County Detention Ctr., Albuquerque, 1990—; group facilitator and youth authority Juveinile Probation dept. 2d Jud. Dist. Ct., Albuquerque, 1990-92; program therapist Heights Psychiatric Hosp., Albuquerque, 1990-91; cons. Albuquerque Fire Dept. Mem. ACA, Nat. Assn. Forensic Counselors, Am. Mental Health Counselors Assn., Internat. Assn. Addictions and Offender Counseling, Fraternal Order of Police. Democrat. Lutheran. Avocations: rock climbing, nordic skiing, horse-back riding, animal rescue.

PIPES, DANIEL, writer, editor; b. Boston, Sept. 9, 1949; s. Richard and Irene (Roth) P.; children: Sarah, Anna. Student, U. Tunis, Institut Bourguiba des Langues Vivantes, 1970; BA in History Sci., Harvard U., 1971; student, U. Cairo, 1971-72, Al-Azhâr U., Cairo, 1971-72, U. Calif. (Berkeley) Ctr. for Arabic Studies Abroad, Cairo, 1971, 1972-73; reader, Orientalisches Sem., Freiburg U., 1976; PhD in Mid. Ea. Studies, Harvard U., 1978; hon. degree, Am. Coll. of Switzerland, 1988. Vis. fellow Princeton U., 1977-78; Harper instr., rsch. assoc. U. Chgo., 1978-82; mem. policy planning staff, spl. advisor U.S. Dept. State, 1982-83; lectr. history Harvard U., 1983-84; prof. U.S. Naval War Coll., 1984-86; dir. Fgn. Policy Rsch. Inst., Phila., 1986-93, Mid. East Forum, 1994—. Author: Slave Soldiers and Islam, 1981, In the Path of God: Islam and Political Power, 1983, An Arabist's Guide to Egyptian Colloquial, 1983, The Long Shadow: Culture and Politics in the Middle East, 1988, Greater Syria, 1990, The Rushdie Affair, 1990; co-editor: Friendly Tyrants: An American Dilemma, 1991, Damascus Courts the West, 1991, Syria Beyond the Peace Process, 1996; editor: Sandstorm, 1993, Orbis: Jour. World Affairs, 1986-90, Mid. East Quar., 1994—. Vice chmn. J. William Fulbright Scholarship Bd., 1992-95; mem. adv. com. Internat. Rep. Inst., 1993. Woodrow Wilson nat. fellow, 1971-72, fellow NDEA Title VI, 1974-76, Am. Rsch. Ctr. in Egypt, 1979, vis. fellow Heritage Found., 1984, Japan Soc., Nat. Inst. for Rsch. Advancement, Tokyo, 1985, Washington Inst. for Near East Policy, 1986, 91, 94-95; rsch. grantee Israel Inter-Univ., 1979, Smith Richardson Found., 1980-82, 95-96, Schumann Found., 1990-91, U.S. Inst. Peace, 1990-91, Ford Found., 1992-93, Scaife Found., 1995-97, Bradley Found., 1995—. Mem. Coun. on Fgn. Rels. (internat. affairs fellow 1982-83), Internat. Ho. of Japan. Office: Mid East Quar 1920 Chestnut St Ste 600 Philadelphia PA 19103-4634

PIPES, RICHARD, historian, educator; b. Cieszyn, Poland, July 11, 1923; came to U.S., 1940, naturalized, 1943; s. Mark and Sophia (Haskelberg) P.; m. Irene Eugenia Roth, Sept. 1, 1946; children—Daniel, Steven. Student, Muskingum (Ohio) Coll., 1940-43; AB, Cornell U., 1945; PhD, Harvard U., 1950; LLD (hon.), Muskingum Coll., 1988; LHD (hon.), Adelphi U., 1991; Doctor honoris causa, U. Silesia, Poland, 1994. Mem. faculty Harvard U., 1950—, prof. history, 1958-75, Frank B. Baird Jr. prof. history, 1975-96, Baird prof. emeritus, 1996—; assoc. dir. Russian Rsch. Ctr., 1962-64, dir., 1968-73; sr. cons. Stanford Research Inst., 1973-78; dir. East European and Soviet affairs NSC, 1981-82; cons. Ency. Britannica;. Author: Formation of the Soviet Union, rev. edit., 1964, Karamzin's Memoir on Ancient and Modern Russia, 1959, Social Democracy and the St. Petersburg Labor Movement, 1963, Europe Since 1815, 1970, Struve: Liberal on the Left, 1870-1905, 1970, Russia Under the Old Regime, 1974, Struve: Liberal on the Right, 1905-1944, 1980, U.S.-Soviet Relations in the Era of Detente, 1981, Survival Is Not Enough, 1984, Russia Observed, 1989, The Russian Revolution, 1990, Communism: The Vanished Specter, 1993, Russia Under the Bolshevik Regime, 1994, A Concise History of the Russian Revolution, 1995, Three "Whys" of the Russian Revolution, 1996; editor: Russian Intelligentsia, 1961; (with John Fine) Of the Russe Commonwealth (Giles Fletcher), 1966, Revolutionary Russia, 1968, Collected Works in Fifteen Volumes (P.B. Struve), 1970, Soviet Strategy in Europe, 1976, The Unknown Lenin, 1996; mem. editl. bd. Strategic Rev., Orbis, Comparative Strategy, Jour. Strategic Studies, Continuity, Arka. Mem. exec. com. Com. on Present Danger, 1977-92; chmn. Govt. Team B to Rev. Intelligence Estimates, 1976; mem. Reagan transition team Dept. State, 1980. Served with USAAF, 1943-46. Guggenheim fellow, 1956, 65; fellow Am. Coun. Learned Socs., 1965; fellow Ctr. for Advanced Study in Behavioral Scis., Stanford, Calif., 1969-70; lectr. Spring lecture Nobel Inst., Oslo, 1993; recipient Comdr.'s Cross of Merit, Republic of Poland, 1996. Fellow Am. Acad. Arts and Scis.; mem. Coun. Fgn. Rels., Polish Acad. (fgn. mem.). Home: 17 Berkeley St Cambridge MA 02138-3409

PIPES, ROBERT BYRON, academic administrator, mechanical engineer; b. Shreveport, La., Aug. 14, 1941; s. Walter H. and Mattye Mae (Wilson) P.; B.S., La. Poly. Inst., 1964, M.S., 1965; M.S.E., M.A., Princeton U., 1969; Ph.D., U. Tex., 1972; m. Ruth Ellen Franz, June 27, 1964; children: Christopher Franz, Mark Robert. Sr. structures engr. Gen. Dynamics Corp., 1969-72; asst. prof. mech. engring. Drexel U., 1972-74; assoc. prof. mech. and aerospace engring. U. Del., 1974-80, prof., 1980—, also dir. Center Composite Materials, 1978-85, dean Coll. Engring., 1985-91, provost, v.p. acad. affairs, 1991-93; pres. Rensselaer Polytech. Inst., N.Y., 1993—; dir. Nat. Ctr. Composites Mfg. Sci. and Engring., 1985; cons. in field; mem. com. NRC. Mem. ASME (Gustus Larson award 1983), Soc. Mfg. Engrs., Soc. Advancement of Material and Processing Engring., Nat. Acad. Engring. (elected 1987), Soc. Exptl. Stress Analysis (chaire Francqui-Belgium), Swedish Acad. Engring., Am. Soc. Composites (tech. rev. com. Air Force Composite Materials Design Guide—Analytical Methods), ASTM, Sigma Xi, Tau Beta Pi, Pi Tau Sigma, Omicron Delta Kappa. Methodist. Author: Experimental Mechanics of Fiber Reinforced Composite Materials, 1982, Characterization of Advanced Composite Materials, 1987; series editor 10 vols. Composite Materials; contbr. numerous articles to tech. jours. Home: 2005 Tibbits Ave Troy NY 12180-7016 Office: Rensselaer Polytech Inst Office of Pres Pittsburg Bldg Troy NY 12180-3590

PIPES, WESLEY O'FERAL, civil engineering educator; b. Dallas, Jan. 28, 1932; s. Wesley O'Feral and Lunnette (Waller) P.; children—Phylis, Victoria (dec.), Wesley, Susan, Gordon. B.S., N. Tex. State U., 1953, M.S., 1955; Ph.D., Northwestern U., 1959. Research engr. U. Calif.-Berkeley, 1955-57; asst. prof. Northwestern U., 1959-62, assoc. prof., 1962-67, prof. civil enging., 1967-74, prof. biol. scis., 1969-74; L. Drew Betz prof. ecology Drexel U., 1975-83, prof. civil engring., 1983—, head civil engring. dept., 1983-87; cons. water pollution and wastewater treatment Office of Drinking Water, EPA, 1986-91, P.R. Aquaduct and Sewer Authority, 1991, Malcolm Pirnie, Inc., 1991-92, Delaware County (Pa.) Regional Authority, 1992, environ. enforcement divsn. U.S. Dept. Justice, 1993-95, Ductile Iron Pipe Rsch. Assn., 1994, Smith & Loveless, Inc., 1994-95. Mem. tech. adv. com. on water resources Northeastern Ill. Planning Commn., 1968-74. Named one of 10 Outstanding Young Men of Chgo. Chgo. Jr. Assn. Commerce and Industry, 1963; recipient Rsch. award Pa. Water Pollution Control Assn., 1989. Mem. ASCE, Assn. Environ. Engring. Profs. (dir. 1970-76, v.p. 1974, pres. 1975), Am. Water Works Assn., Water Pollution Control Fedn., Am. Soc. Microbiology, The Internat. Environmetrics Soc. (dir. 1994—), Sigma Xi, Tau Beta Pi. Research and publs. on microbiology of water and wastewater. Office: Drexel U Dept Civil Engring Philadelphia PA 19104

PIPKIN, JAMES HAROLD, JR., lawyer; b. Houston, Jan. 3, 1939; s. James Harold and Zenda Marie (Lewis) P. BA, Princeton U., 1960; JD, Harvard U., 1963; Diploma in Law, Oxford (Eng.) U., 1965. Bar: D.C. 1964, U.S. Supreme Ct. 1969, D.C. Ct. Appeals, 1972. Law ck. to assoc. justice U.S. Supreme Ct., Washington, 1963-64; assoc. Steptoe and Johnson, Washington, 1965-70, ptnr., 1971-93; counselor to The Sec. of the Interior U.S. Dept. of the Interior, 1993—; U.S. spl. negotiator for Pacific Salmon, Dept. of State, 1994—; rank of amb. Dept. of State, 1995—; counsel Friends of Music, Smithsonian Inst., Washington, 1984-88; mem. Nat. Arbitration Panel, 1983-94. Author or co-author: The English Country House: A Grand Tour, 1985, The Country House Garden: A Grand Tour, 1987, Places of Tranquility, 1990; contbr. photographs and articles to mags. including House & Garden, Smithsonian mag., The Mag. Antiques, Archtl. Digest. Grand officier Confrérie des Chevaliers du Tastevin, 1989. Mem. ABA, D.C. Bar Assn., Met. Club. Home: 6109 Davenport Ter Bethesda MD 20817-5827 Office: Office of The Secretary 1849 C St NW Washington DC 20240-0001

PIPPEL, GERANE GODDARD, volunteer; b. Long Beach, Calif., Jan. 16, 1929; d. Philip Hubbard and Ethlyn (Bradley) Goddard; m. John Richard Lawson, Jan. 30, 1946 (dec. 1969); children: Kathleen Lynd Hodges, Dawn Elizabeth Lawson, Susan Doreen Lawson; m. William Harold Pippel Jr., Apr. 4, 1979; children: Mary Ellen Leopard, Dulcy Murchison, Cecilia Anne Andrzewski. AA, Santa Ana Jr. Coll., Calif.; student, Del. State U., 1992—. Adminstrv. sec. Paint Branch Unitarian Ch., Adelphi, Md., 1966-73; asst. dir. field svcs. Americans United for Ch. and State, Silver Spring, Md., 1973-76; exec. sec. to dir. edn. Chemical Mfg. Assn., Washington, 1976-79; sec. Lighthouse Realty, Ocean City, Md., 1981-82; asst. town clk. Fenwick Island Town Hall, Fenwick Island, Del., 1983-84; coun. mem. Persons with Disabilities Dover, Del., 1992—; mem. Universal Health Care Reform, Dover, 1993—, Nat. Assn. Social Workers, Dover, 1994—; co-chair adv. bd. Crossroads Milford, Del., 1994—. Mem. Gov. adv. coun. Svcs. for Aging and Adults with Physical Disabilities, New Castle, Del., 1992—; medicare/medicaid counselor Elderinfo, Dover, Del., 1993—. Mem. World Clown Assn., Del. Agenda for Women (health com.), Ret. Sr. Vol. Program (knitter), Health Care Providers (vol.), Nat. Orgn. for Women (vol.). Democrat. Methodist. Avocations: knitting, reading, cross stitching, sewing. Home: 58 Keenwick Rd Selbyville DE 19975-9738

PIPPEN, SCOTTIE, professional basketball player; b. Hamburg, Ark., Sept. 25, 1965. Student, U. Cen. Ark., 1983-87. With Seattle Super Sonics, 1987; guard/forward Chgo. Bulls, 1987—; player NBA Championship Team, 1991, 92, 93, U.S. Olympic Basketball Team, 1992. Named to All-Star team, 1990, 92-93, NBA All-Defensive First team, 1992, 93, 94, All-Defensive second team, 1991, NBA All-Star Team, 1992-94, NBA All-Star MVP, 1994, All-NBA First Team, 1994; mem. NBA championship team, 1991-93, 96. Office: Chgo Bulls United Ctr 1901 W Madison St Chicago IL 60612*

PIPPIN, JOHN ELDON, electronics engineer, electronics company executive; b. Kinard, Fla., Oct. 7, 1927; s. Festus and Mary Elvie (Scott) P.; m. Barbara A. Pippin, June 15, 1952; children: Carol Jean Pippin Franklin, John F., Mary Christine Pippin Mobley. B.E.E., Ga. Inst. Tech., 1951, M.S.E.E., 1953; Ph.D. in Applied Physics, Harvard U., 1958. Research. engr. Ga. Inst. Tech. Expt. Sta., Atlanta, 1951-53; head research dept. Sperry Microwave Electronics Co., Clearwater, Fla., 1958-64; v.p., dir. research Scientific-Atlanta, Inc., 1964-68; pres. Electromagnetic Scis., Inc., Norcross, Ga., 1968—; adj. prof. U. Fla., 1962-64; cons. Cascade Research Corp., 1953-58. Contbr. articles to profl. jours. Served in USN, 1945-46. NSF fellow; Gen. Commns. fellow. Fellow IEEE (Outstanding Engr. Region III 1972, Engr. of Yr. 1972); mem. Briarean Soc., Am. Phys. Soc., Microwave Theory and Techniques Soc. (adminstrv. com.), Sigma Xi, Tau Beta Pi, Phi Kappa Phi, Eta Kappa Nu. Achievements include research in microwave physics; radar tracking problems. Home: 3760 River Summit Trl Duluth GA 30136-2278 Office: Electromagnetic Sci Inc 660 Engineering Dr Norcross GA 30092-2821*

PIRANI, CONRAD LEVI, pathologist, educator; b. Pisa, Italy, July 29, 1914; came to U.S., 1939, naturalized, 1945; s. Mario Giacomo Levi and Adriana P.; m. Luciana Nahmias, Mar. 12, 1955; children: Barbara, Sylvia, Robert. Diploma, Ginnasio-Liceo Beccaria, 1932; M.D., U. Milano, Italy, 1938. Intern Columbus Meml. Hosp., Chgo., 1940-42; resident Michael Reese Hosp., Chgo., 1942-45; instr. pathology U. Ill., Chgo., 1945-48; asst. prof. U. Ill., 1948-52, asso. prof., 1952-55, prof., 1955-70; chmn. dept. pathology Michael Reese Hosp., Chgo., 1965-72; prof. pathology Coll. Physicians and Surgeons, Columbia U., N.Y.C., 1972-85; prof. emeritus Coll. Physicians and Surgeons, Columbia U., 1985—; dir. Renal Pathology Lab., 1972-84; cons. Armed Forces Inst. Pathology; mem. sci. com. Kidney Found., N.Y., 1973-80. Contbg. author various books.; assoc. editor Lab. Investigation, 1972-82, Nephron, 1975-92, Clin. Nephrology, 1989-92; contbr. numerous articles to profl. jours. USPHS, NIH grantee. Mem. Am. Assn. Pathologists, AAAS, Internat. Acad. Pathology (counselor 1966-69), Am. Soc. Nephrology (John P. Peters award 1987), Internat. Soc. Nephrology. Home: 28 Bradford St Glen Rock NJ 07452-2102 Office: 630 W 168th St New York NY 10032-3702

PIRCHER, LEO JOSEPH, lawyer; b. Berkeley, Calif., Jan. 4, 1933; s. Leo Charles and Christine (Moore) P.; m. Phyllis McConnell, Aug. 4, 1956 (div. April 1981); children: Christopher, David, Eric; m. Nina Silverman, June 14, 1987; B.S., U. Calif.-Berkeley, 1954, J.D., 1957. Bar: Calif. 1958, N.Y. 1985; cert. specialist taxation law Calif. Bd. Legal Specialization. Assoc. Lawler, Felix & Hall, L.A., 1957-62, ptnr., 1962-65, sr. ptnr., 1965-83; sr. ptnr. Pircher, Nichols & Meeks, L.A., 1983—; adj. prof. Loyola U. Law Sch., L.A., 1959-61; corp. sec. Am. Metal Bearing Co., Gardena, Calif., 1975—, dir. Varco Internat. Inc., Orange, Calif.; speaker various law schs. and bar assns. edn. programs. Author: (with others) Definition and Utility of Leases, 1968. Chmn. pub. fin. and taxation sect. Calif. Town Hall, Los Angeles, 1970-71. Mem. Calif. State Bar, N.Y. State Bar, Los Angeles County Bar Assn. (exec. com. comml. law secton), ABA, Nat. Assn. Real Estate Investment Trusts Inc. (cert. specialist taxation law). Republican. Club: Regency (L.A.). Office: Pircher Nichols & Meeks 1999 Avenue Of The Stars Los Angeles CA 90067-6022

PIRES, MARY ANN, public relations consultant; b. Saginaw, Mich., May 6, 1944; d. Vincent Paul and Ann Catherine (Mainolfi) Kingry; m. Edward A. Pires, Oct. 21, 1973; 1 dau., Carrie Ann. BA in Sociology Nazareth Coll., 1966; MS in Pub. Rels., Boston U., 1973. Asst. to pres. Boston City Coun., 1970-71; speechwriter Gov.'s Press Office, Boston, 1971-72; asst. editor John Hancock Ins. Co., Boston, 1970-72; pub. rels. dir. Greater Boston C. of C., 1972-77; staff coord. pub. rels. Texaco Inc., White Plains, N.Y., 1977-79, mgr. planning, pub. rels., 1980-84; dir. corp. comm. program Combustion Engring., Stamford, Conn., 1984-85; pub. rels. cons., Armonk, N.Y., 1985—. Contbr. articles to profl. jours., newspapers. Mem. nat. alumni coun., Boston U., 1977—; dir. Pub. Affairs Coun., Found. for Pub. Affairs. Recipient Young Am. medal for svc. Pres. John F. Kennedy, 1962. Fellow Pub. Rels. Soc. Am. (nat. dir. 1983—, accredited). Roman Catholic. Office: The Pires Group Inc 400 King St Chappaqua NY 10514-3544

PIRET, MARGUERITE ALICE, investment banker; b. St. Paul, May 10, 1948; d. E.L. and Alice P.; children: Andrew, Anne. AB, Radcliffe Coll., 1969; MBA, Harvard U., 1974. Comml. loan officer Bank New Eng. (now Fleet Bank), Boston, 1974-79; mng. dir. Kridel Securities, N.Y.C., 1979-81; pres., founder, dir. Newbury, Piret & Co., Inc., Boston, 1981—; trustee, chmn. audit com. Pioneer Mutual Funds, Boston. Vis. com. mem. Am. decorative arts and sculpture Mus. Fine Arts, Boston, 1982—; mem. nominating com. for candidates for overseer of Harvard U. and for candidates for dir. of Harvard Alumni Assn.; adv. com. on shareholder responsibility Harvard U., 1986-87; trustee, mem. exec. com. Boston U. Med. Ctr. Hosp., 1979—, chmn. fin. com.; trustee Mass. Hosp. Assn., 1983-86, Boston Ballet Ctr. for Dance Edn., 1989-93. Mem. Harvard Club. Office: Newbury Piret & Co Inc One Boston Pl Boston MA 02108

PIRIE, ROBERT BURNS, JR., defense analyst; b. San Diego, Sept. 10, 1933; s. Robert Burns and Gertrude May (Freeman) P.; m. Joan Adams, Dec. 23, 1960; children: John Winthrop, Carl Joseph Emil, Susan Gilman. Student, Princeton U., 1950-51; B.S., U.S. Naval Acad., 1955; B.A., Magdalen Coll., Oxford U., 1959, M.A., 1963. Commd. ensign U.S. Navy, 1955, advanced through grades to comdr., 1969; comdg. officer (U.S.S. Skipjack), 1969-72; dep. asst. dir. Congl. Budget Office, 1975-77; prin. dep. asst. sec. for manpower, res. affairs and logistics Dept. Def., Washington, 1977-79; asst. sec. Dept. Def., 1979-81; mgmt. cons., 1981—; def. analyst Ctr. for Naval Analyses, Alexandria, Va., 1981-83; asst. v.p. Inst. for Def. Analyses, Alexandria, Va., 1983-86, v.p., 1986-87; exec. v.p. Essex Corp., Alexandria, Va., 1987, pres., 1987-88; sr. economist Rand Corp., Washington, 1989; dir. strategic studies group U.S. Naval War Coll., 1989-92; v.p. Ctr. Naval Analyses, Alexandria, Va., 1992-94; asst. sec. of Navy for Installations and Environ. USN, Washington, 1994—. Vestryman St. John's Episcopal Ch., Chevy Chase, Md., 1973-76, 81, jr. warden, 1982-84, sr. warden, 1984-87; trustee U.S. Naval Acad. Found., 1980-94. Rhodes scholar, 1956. Mem. U.S. Naval Inst., Internat. Inst. Strategic Studies, U.S. Naval Acad. Alumni Assn. (trustee 1967-70). Club: Vincent's. Office: 1000 Navy Pentagon Washington DC 20350-1000

PIRKL, JAMES JOSEPH, industrial designer, educator, writer; b. Nyack, N.Y., Dec. 27, 1930; s. James and Ida Bertha (Gigrich) P.; m. Sarah B. W. Woolsey, June 8, 1974; children: Theo, James, Philip. Cert. Advt. Design, Pratt Inst., 1951, B of Indsl. Design cum laude, 1958. With design staff Gen. Motors Corp., Warren, Mich., 1958-65; sr. designer Gen. Motors Corp., 1961-64, asst. chief designer, 1964-65; instr. indsl. design Center for Creative Studies, Detroit, 1963-65; faculty dept. design Syracuse (N.Y.) U., 1965-92, assoc. prof., 1969-73, prof. indsl. design, 1974-92, prof. emeritus, 1992—, coord. indsl. design program, 1979-84, chmn. dept. design, 1985-91; exec. council chmn. Sch. Art, 1976-78, 80-81; sr. rsch. fellow All-U. Gerontology Ctr., 1990—; prin. James J. Pirkl/Design, 1965—; cons. Brownlie Design, Inc., 1972—, Rolland Co., 1993, Arthritis Found., 1993—, GE Appliances, 1994, Prince Corp., 1991, Ford Motor Design Ctr., 1992, Loretto Geriatric Ctr., Sage Marcom Inc., 1988-90, Hazard Mgmt. Co., 1985, Marcom Switches Inc., 1977-82, Cazenovia Abroad Ltd., 1973-81, Holistic Mgmt. Group, Inc., 1981, Pulos Design Assocs., 1972-80, Beck Assocs., 1976, Fed. Prison Industries, 1974, Gen. Electric Co., 1967-70, Genesee Labs., Inc., 1968, N.Y. State Council on Arts, 1968-69, Stettner-Trush, Inc., 1972-78, Strathmore Chem. Coatings, Inc., 1969, 72, Village of Cazenovia, 1979-93, Xerox Corp., 1975, Age Wave, Inc., 1993—; chmn. accreditation council Design Found., 1982-84; interviewed on Nat. Pub. Radio. Author: Transgenerational Design: Products for an Aging Population, 1994; co-author: Guidelines and Strategies for Designing Transgenerational Products, 1988; co-editor: State of Art and Science of Design, 1971; co-designer: Gen. Motors Futurama Exhbn., N.Y. World's Fair, 1964-65; contbr. articles to profl. jours. including Design Mgmt. Jour., Jour. Indsl. Designers Soc. Am., Bus. Adminstrn. Jour., Design News, Design Perspectives, Indsl. Design. Mem. Everson Mus. Art, 1977-85; chmn. planning commn. Town of Cazenovia, N.Y., 1988-93; mem. senate Syracuse U., 1973-80; mem. adv. bd. SEARS Project, 1989-91; chmn. chancellor's citation com., 1988-92; mem. exhbns. com. Syracuse Cultural Resources Coun., 1992-93; coord. Tylenol/Arthritis Found. Student Design Awards Program, 1993—. With SeaBees USN, 1951-55. Recipient Gold Indsl. Design Excellence award Indsl. Designers Soc. Am. and Bus. Week Mag., 1994. Fellow Indsl. Designers Soc. Am. (chmn. universal design com. 1991-94, chmn. NASAD liaison com. 1984-88, mem. archives com. 1988-92, nat. bd. dirs. 1977-81, chmn. Cen. N.Y. chpt. 1977-78, v.p. Mid-East region 1978-80, dir., chmn. edn. com. 1980-81, U.S. rep., del. Internat. Congress Socs. Indsl. Design 1989, mem. edn. com. 1989); mem. The Design Found. (chmn. accreditation coun. 1982), Nat. Assn. Schs. Art and Design (accreditation evaluator 1985-95), Nat. Ctr. for a Barrier Free Environment (adv. task force 1981), Human Factors Soc. (life mem.), Am. Soc. Aging (contbr. articles to jour.), Author's Guild. Achievements include patent for 4-way handle. Home: 66 Camino Barranca Placitas NM 87043-9314

PIRKLE, EARL CHARNELL, geologist, educator; b. nr. Buckhead, Ga., Jan. 8, 1922; s. Early Charnell and Eva Lee (Collins) P.; m. Valda Nell Armistead, July 9, 1942; children: Betty Jean, William A., Fredric L. AB, Emory U., 1943; MS, 1947; postgrad., U. Tenn., 1947-50; PhD, U. Cin., 1956. Certified profl. geologist. Prodn. coordinator, research crystallographer Pan-Electronics Labs., Inc., Atlanta, 1942-45; instr. geology U. Tenn., 1947-50; mem. faculty dept. phys. scis. and geology U. Fla., Gainesville, 1950-93, prof. emeritus, 1993—; prof. U. Fla., 1963—, chmn. dept. phys. scis., 1972-79; dir. Phys. Scis., 1979-82; cons. in field; vis. prof. geology Emory U., summers 1959-65; rsch. cons. Fla. Dept. Nat. Resources Bur. Geology, 1950-70. Author: Natural Regions of the United States, 1977, 4th edit., 1985; Editor: Physical Science- Our Environment, 1968, Our Physical Environment, 1980; Contbr. articles to profl. jours. Served with AUS, 1945-46. Fellow Geol. Soc. Am., Soc. Econ. Geologists; mem. Am. Assn. Petroleum Geologists, Am. Soc. Mining, Metall. and Petroleum Engrs., Fla. Acad. Scis., Southeastern Geol. Soc., Phi Beta Kappa, Sigma Gamma Epsilon, Gamma Theta Epsilon, Sigma Chi. Democrat. Methodist.

PIRKLE, ESTUS WASHINGTON, minister; b. Vienna, Ga., Mar. 12, 1930; s. Grover Washington and Bessie Nora (Jones) P.; m. Annie Catherine Gregory, Aug. 18, 1955; children: Letha Dianne, Gregory Don. BA cum laude, Mercer U., 1951; BD, MRE, Southwestern Bapt. Sem., 1956, ThM, 1958; DD, Covington Theol. Sem., 1982. Ordained to ministry So. Bapt. Conv., 1949. Pastor Locust Grove Bapt. Ch., New Albany, Miss.; speaker

Camp Zion, Myrtle, Miss. Author: Wintertime, 1968, Preachers in Space, 1969, Sermon Outlines Book, 1969, Are Horoskopes All Right?, 1971, I Believe God, 1973, Who Will Build Your House?,1978, The 1611 King James Bible: A Study by Dr. Estus Pirkle, 1994; producer religious films: If Footmen Tire You, What Will Horses Do?, 1973, The Burning Hell, 1975, Believer's Heaven, 1977. Home and Office: PO Box 80 Myrtle MS 38650-0080

PIRKLE, GEORGE EMORY, television and film actor, director; b. Atlanta, Sept. 3, 1947; s. George Washington and Glanna Adeline (Palmer) P.; m. Karen Leigh Horn, Oct. 20, 1973; 1 child, Charity Caroline. Student North Ga. Coll., 1965-66; BA in Journalism, U. Ga., 1969, MA, 1971. Radio announcer, sportscaster for various radio stas., North Ga. area, 1968-70; TV producer, dir. Instructional Resources Ctr., Athens, Ga., 1969-70; info. officer, Southeastern Signal Sch., U.S. Army, 1971; producer, dir. DA MoPic Svc., Continental Army Command Network and Signal Corps TV Div., 1972-73; pub. info. officer Ga. Dept. Revenue, Atlanta, 1973-78; coord. TV prodn. svcs. So. Co. Svcs., Inc., Birmingham, Ala., 1978-88; exec. v.p. Mgmt. and Human Devel. Assocs., Inc., Birmingham, 1984-86; producer Prodn. Works, Birmingham, 1984-88; actor for various radio and TV commercials, corp. TV programs, radio dramas, stage plays, 1968—; owner Talking Rock Prodns., Cumming, Ga., 1989—. Editor monthly newsletter Ga. Revenews, 1973-78; editor, dir. Bankers TV Network, 1990-92; writer, producer, dir., exec. producer more than 500 corp. and pub. svc. TV and film programs. Recipient So. Superlative outstanding employee award, So. Co. Svcs., 1986. Mem. communications com. Birmingham Area Coun. Boy Scouts Am., 1983-85; Master of ceremonies gov.'s vet. awards presentation World Peace Luncheon, Birmingham, 1981, 82, 84; dir. campaign film Pensacola United Way, 1989; exec. producer videotape for Birmingham Film Coun., 1985; producer, dir. Highway in Crisis, 1986; writer, producer, dir. campaign film Birmingham Area United Way. 1981, 86, 87; writer, producer, narrator, 1987 campaign film; bd. dirs. Birmingham Internat. Ednl. Film Festival, 1987-91; chmn. Sadie award com., student video competition dir.; comml. acting instr. elan/Casablancas Modeling/Career Ctr., 1988-92; instr. Cliff Osmond Acting Program, 1989-92; anchor This Week in Banking, 1990-92; mem. tech. steering com. Forsyth Bd. Edn., 1995—; dir. City Pks. & Recreation Bd., 1996—. 1st lt. U.S. Army, 1971-73. Recipient Battles award, 1988, various others. Mem. Internat. TV Assn. (charter pres. Birmingham chpt. 1984-85, pres. pro tem 1984, editor newsletter Freeze Frame), So. Electric System Visual Communications Subcom. (founding), Ga. Hist. Soc., United Way of Forsyth County (bd. dirs., 1995—), Hist. Soc. Forsyth County (pres. 1996—). Methodist. Avocations: photography, music, genealogy, hist. rsch., archaeology. Home and Office: 105 Brooks Farm Dr Cumming GA 30130

PIRKLE, WILLIAM H., chemistry educator; b. Shreveport, La., May 2, 1934; married, 1956; 4 children. BS, U. Calif., Berkeley, 1959; PhD in Chemistry, U. Rochester, 1963. NSF fellow Harvard U., 1963-64; asst. prof., 1964-69; assoc. prof. chemistry U. Ill., Urbana, 1969-80, prof. chemistry, 1980—; vis. prof. U. Wis., Madison, 1971. Assoc. editor Enantiomer; mem. editl. bd. Jour. Liquid Chromatogrpahy, Chirality, HRC, Supramolecular Chemistry. Recipient A.J.P. Martin medal Chromatographic Soc. Gt. Britain, 1990, Merit award Chgo. Chromatography Discussion Group, 1991, Chirality medal Swedish Assn. Pharm. Scis., 1994; Alfred P. Sloan fellow, 1971-72. Mem. Am. Chem. Soc. (Chromatography award 1994), Am. Chem. Soc. Office: U Illinois 161 Roger Adam Lab 600 S Mathews Urbana IL 61801-3731

PIRO, ANTHONY JOHN, radiologist; b. Boston, May 28, 1930; s. John Anthony and Josephine (Pepe) P.; m. Marian Giallombardo, Sept. 5, 1955; children—Anthony John, Janet, Jacquelyn. A.B., Boston U., 1952, M.D., 1956. Diplomate: Am. Bd. Internal Medicine, Am. Bd. Radiology. Intern Mass. Meml. Hosp., Boston, 1956-57; resident Boston VA Hosp., 1959-62; practice medicine specializing in internal medicine Framingham, Mass., 1962-63; staff physician Boston VA Hosp., 1963-66; sr. assoc. Children's Cancer Research Found., 1966-70; radiotherapist Harvard Joint Center for Radiation Therapy, 1970-77; prof. therapeutic radiology, chmn. dept. therapeutic radiology Tufts-New Eng. Med. Center Hosp., 1977-79; radiation oncologist Salem (Mass.) Hosp., 1979—. Contbr. articles to profl. jours. Served with USAF, 1957-59. Nat. Cancer Inst. grantee, 1977-79. Fellow ACP, Am. Coll. Radiology; mem. Am. Soc. Clin. Oncologists, Am. Soc. Therapeutic Radiologists, Am. Assn. Cancer Rsch., Phi Beta Kappa, Alpha Omega Alpha. Unitarian. Home: 6 Cider Mill Rd Lynnfield MA 01940-1132 Office: 81 Highland Ave Salem MA 01970-2768

PIRONE, THOMAS PASCAL, plant pathology educator; b. Ithaca, N.Y., Jan. 3, 1936; s. Pascal Pompey and Loretta Muriel (Kelly) P.; m. Sherrill Sevier, Aug. 1, 1961; children—John Sevier, Catherine Sherrill. B.S., Cornell U., 1957; Ph.D., U. Wis., 1960. Asst. prof. La. State U., Baton Rouge, 1960-63; asso. prof. La. State U., 1963-67, U. Ky., Lexington, 1967-71; prof. U. Ky., 1971—, chmn. plant pathology, 1978-86; mem. recombinant DNA adv. com. NIH, 1984-87. Contbr. articles on plant virology to profl. jours.; mem. editorial bd.: Virology, 1974-76, Phytopathology, 1971-73, sr. editor, 1977-78, Ann. Rev. Phytopathology, 1985-90. Sr. Fulbright research fellow U.K., 1974-75. Fellow Am. Phytopathol. Soc. (Ruth Allen award 1989); mem. AAAS, Internat. Soc. Plant Pathology, Am. Soc. Virology. Office: U Ky Dept Plant Pathology Lexington KY 40546

PIRONTI, LAVONNE DE LAERE, developer fundraiser; b. L.A., Jan. 11, 1946; d. Emil Joseph and Pearl Mary (Vilmur) De Laere; m. Aldo Pironti, May 21, 1977. BA in Internat. Rels., U. So. Calif., L.A., 1967. Commd. ensign USN, 1968-91, advanced through grades to comdr., 1979; pers. officer Lemoore (Calif.) Naval Air Sta., 1972-74; human rels. mgmt. specialist Human Resource Mgmt. Detachment, Naples, Italy, 1975-78; comms. staff officer Supreme Hdqrs. Allied Powers Europe, Shape, Belgium, 1979-83; dir. Navy Family Svc. Ctr. Sigonella Naval Air Sta., Sicily, 1983-85; exec. officer Naval Sta. Guam, Apra Harbor, 1985-87; comms. staff officer NATO Comm. and Info. Sys. Agy., Brussels, Belgium, 1987-89; polit. officer for Guam, trust Territories Pacific Islands Comdr. Naval Forces Marianas, Agana, Guam, 1989-91; store mgr. Sandal Tree, Lihue, Hawaii, 1991-92; CEO, exec. dir. YWCA of Kauai County, Lihue, 1992—. Mem. Kauai Children's Justice com., Lihue, 1993—; co-chair Kauai Human Svcs. Coun., Lihue; bd. dirs. Hawaii Health and Human Svcs. Alliance, Lihue, 1993—; chair Kauai County Family Self Sufficiency Program Adv. Bd., Lihue, 1993—. Decorated Navy Commendation medal, Meritorious Svc. Medal with 1 star, Def. Meritorious Svc. Medal with 2 stars, others; named Fed. Woman of the Yr. Comdr. Naval Forces Marianas, 1986-87. Roman Catholic. Avocations: racquetball, reading, aquacise. Office: YWCA of Kauai 3094 Elua St Lihue HI 96766-1209

PIROZZI, MILDRED JEAN, nursing administrator; b. Syracuse, N.Y., Jan. 22, 1943; d. Alfred George and Mildred Erma (Tripp) Farmer; m. Robert T. Pirozzi, Jan. 25, 1969; children: Matthew Robert, Michael Thomas. Diploma, Gen. Hosp. Syracuse, 1963; BS, SUNY, Utica, 1983. RN, N.Y. Med., surg. staff nurse Gen. Hosp. Syracuse, 1963-64; staff nurse ICU U. Rochester Strong Meml. Hosp., N.Y., 1964-65; nurse ICU Upstate Med. Ctr. U. Hosp., Syracuse, 1965-69, rschr. anesthesia Upstate Med. Ctr., 1969-70; nurse recovery room Highland Hosp., Rochester, 1970-71; nurse orthopedic unit Auburn (N.Y.) Meml. Hosp., 1978-80; home dialysis tng. unit nurse SUNY Health Sci. Ctr., Syracuse, 1980-88; with home dialysis tng. unit U. Dialysis Ctr., Syracuse, 1988-91, home program coord., 1991—; chmn. com. profl. edn. Ctrl. N.Y. chpt. Nat. Kidney Found., Syracuse, 1986-91. Co-author: Hemodialysis Training Manual for Patients and Partners, 1981, CAPD Training Manual for Patients, 1982. Mem. folk ensemble St. Joseph's Ch., 1984—. Recipient Above and Beyond award Nat. Kidney Found., 1991. Mem. Am. Nephrology Nurses Assn. (pub. rels. com. 1988-91, sec., treas., pres. ctrl. N.Y. chpt. 1984-93, 96—, N.E. regional sec. 1987-89, legis. rep. 1991-95). Roman Catholic. Avocations: sewing, crafts, gardening, sports, music. Home: 4699 Howlett Hill Rd Marcellus NY 13108-9701 Office: U Dialysis Ctr/DCI 1127 E Genesee St Syracuse NY 13210-1911

PIRSCH, CAROL MCBRIDE, state senator, community relations administrator; b. Omaha, Dec. 27, 1936; d. Lyle Erwin and Hilfrie Louise (Lebeck) McBride; student U. Miami, Oxford, Ohio, U. Nebr., Omaha; m. Allen I. Pirsch, Mar. 28, 1954; children: Pennie Elizabeth, Pamela Elaine, Patrice Eileen, Phyllis Erika, Peter Allen, Perry Andrew. Former mem. data processing staff Omaha Public Schs.; former mem. wage practices dept. Western Electric Co., Omaha; former legal sec., Omaha; former office mgr. Pirsch Food Brokerage Co., Inc., Omaha; former employment supr. U.S. West Communications, Omaha, now mgr. pub. policy; mem. Nebr. Senate, 1979—. mem. Omaha Pers. Bd.; founder, past pres., bd. dirs. Nebr. Coalition for Victims of Crime. Recipient Golden Elephant award; Outstanding Legis. Efforts award YWCA, Breaking the Rule of Thumb award Nebr. Domestic Violence Sexual Assault Coalition, Cert. of Appreciation award U.S. Dept. Justice, Partnership award NE Credit Union League, 1995, Wings award League of Women Voters of Greater Omaha, 1995, NE VFW Spl. Recognition award for Exceptional Svc., 1995. Mem. VASA, Nat. Orgn. Victim Assistance (Outstanding Legis. Leadership award), Freedom Found., Orgn. U.S. West Women, Nat. Order Women Legislators, Tangier Women's Aux., Footprinters Internat., Nebr. Hist. Soc., Nebr. Taxpayers Assn., Gretna Optimists, Springfield Boosters, Keystone Citizen Patrol (Keystoner of the Month award), Audubon Soc., Rotary Internat., N.W. Community Club, Benson Rep. Women's Club, Bus. and Profl. Rep. Women Club. Office: State Capitol Lincoln NE 68509

PIRSIG, ROBERT MAYNARD, author; b. Mpls., Sept. 6, 1928; s. Maynard Ernest and Harriet Marie (Sjobeck) P.; m. Nancy Ann James, May 10, 1954 (div. Aug. 1978); children—Christopher (dec. Nov. 17, 1979), Theodore; m. Wendy L. Kimball, Dec. 28, 1978; 1 dau., Nell. B.A., U. Minn., 1950, M.A., 1958. Author: Zen And The Art of Motorcycle Maintenance, 1974, Lila, 1991. Served with AUS, 1946-48. Recipient Award AAAL, 1979; Guggenheim fellow, 1974—. Mem. Soc. Tech. Communicators (sec. Minn. chpt. 1970-71, treas. 1971-72). Office: care Bantam Books 1540 Broadway New York NY 10036-4039

PIRTLE, H(AROLD) EDWARD, lawyer; b. Detroit, Apr. 6, 1948; s. Edward Bensen Pirtle and Lorraine Virginia (La Pointe) Schwartz; m. Maxine Mary Stencel, June 10, 1971 (div. May 1981); children: Kimberly, Jeffrey, Michelle; m. Betsy Yvonne Mark, Sept. 1, 1984. AS, Macomb County Cmty. Coll., Warren, Mich., 1977; B in applied sci., Siena Heights Coll., 1983; JD, U. Toldeo, 1990. Bar: Mich. 1990, U.S. Dist. Ct. (ea. dist.) Mich. 1990. Assoc. Beaman & Beaman, Jackson, Mich., 1990-91; solo practitioner H. Edward Pirtle, Atty. at Law, Detroit, 1991—. With U.S. Navy, 1967-72. Mem. ABA, Criminal Def. Attys. of Mich., Washtenaw County Bar Assn., Detroit Bar Assn., Am. Mensa (gen. rep. 1984-85). Avocations: camping, hunting, fishing. Office: 407 E Fort St Ste 110 Detroit MI 48226-2940

PISANI, JOSEPH MICHAEL, physician; b. N.Y.C., Mar. 22, 1919; s. Antonio David and Josephine Catherine (Walsh) P.; m. Agatha Rita Evaskitis, Nov. 11, 1942; children: Michael, Robert, Richard. A.B., Fordham Coll., 1938; M.D., N.Y.U., 1942; grad., Army Sch. Tropical Medicine, 1943. Intern Bellevue Hosp., 1942-43; resident medicine Bronx (N.Y.) VA Hosp., 1946-48, asst. chief chest service, 1948-49; dep. exec. dir. Com. on Med. Scis., Research and Devel. Bd., Washington, 1949-50; exec. dir. Com. on Med. Scis., Research and Devel. Bd., 1950-51; asst. dean and instr. medicine State U. Coll. of Medicine at N.Y., Bklyn., 1951-54; asst. dean, asst. prof. medicine State U. Coll. of Medicine at N.Y., 1954-57; asst. vis. physician Kings County Hosp., 1951-57; med. dir. Bankers Trust Co., N.Y.C., 1957-60, Union Family Med. Fund of Hotel Industry of N.Y.C., 1960-64; dep. med. dir. FDA, Dept. Health, Edn. and Welfare, Washington, 1964-66; industry liaison rep. FDA-OTC rev. panels, 1972-76; v.p. for med.-sci. affairs and med. dir. Proprietary Assn., Washington, 1966-84; clin. instr. medicine George Washington U. Sch. Medicine; asso. in medicine George Washington U. Hosp., 1949-51; adj. asso. prof. adminstrv. medicine Columbia U., N.Y.C., 1960-64; asso. clin. prof. adminstrv. medicine George Washington U., 1964-67, asso. clin. prof. medicine, 1968-84, assoc. professorial lectr. medicine, 1984-92, assoc. prof. emeritus clin. medicine, 1992—; domestic and internat. cons. on health affairs, 1984—; exec. sec. Spl. Com. on Med. Rsch., NSF, 1955, cons. on med. rsch., 1956; Del. U.S. Pharmacopeial Convs., 1970, 75, 80; mem. adv. bd. Physicians Desk Reference for Non-Prescription Drugs, 1979-88; mem. instl. rev. bd. Hill Top Rsch., Inc., West Palm Beach, Fla., 1989—. Contbr. articles on adminstrv. aspects med. care, med. edn. and med. research, drug evaluation. Served as capt. M.C. U.S. Army, 1943-46; NATOUSA and MTO with 5th Army, Field and Hosp. Med. Service. Recipient Alumni Achievement award in medicine Fordham U., 1959. Fellow Am. Pub. Health Assn., Indsl. Med. Assn.; mem. A.M.A., Am. Soc. Clin Pharmacology and Therapeutics, D.C. Med. Soc., N.Y. Acad. Scis., Soc. Alumni of Bellevue Hosp., Alumni Assn. N.Y. Univ. Coll Medicine, Celtic Med. Soc., Soc. Med. Cons. to Armed Forces., Am. Med. Tennis Assn. (bd. dirs. 1986-89). Roman Catholic. Home: 484 NE Plantation Rd Apt 4108 Stuart FL 34996-1751 *Whatever small success I may have thus far achieved can be completely attributed to my good fortune in being blessed by a fine heritage, both past and present. The principles of conduct, discipline, ideals and goals in life to which my dear wife and I were exposed in our respective families, have guided us in our own family. No matter how trite it may seem to some, our basic philosophy of life is centered on the golden rule. This involves a fundamental interest in people and trust in them despite disappointments in this regard from time to time.*

PISANKO, HENRY JONATHAN, command and control communications company executive; b. Trenton, N.J., Mar. 14, 1925; s. Isadore Stephen and Victoria (Gula) P.; m. Sophia Emily Zudnak, May 29, 1949; children: Barbara, Henry Jonathan, Jr., Michael. B in Naval Sci., U. Notre Dame, 1945, BA, 1947; cert. in Japanese, U. Colo. and Okla. State U., 1945; postgrad. Woodrow Wilson Sch., Columbia U., 1948-50. Constrn. reporter ea. div. F.W. Dodge div. McGraw-Hill, N.Y.C. and Phila., 1950-52; internat. affairs analyst Dept. Def., Washington, 1953-59; ops. officer Dept. Def., Pacific Rim, Japan and Hong Kong, 1960-63; sr. intelligence officer Internat. Security Affairs, Dept. Def., Washington, 1964-70; overseas adminstr. diplomatic telecommunications Dept. State, Asia, Africa, 1971-73; spl. advisor Def. Intelligence Coll., Washington, 1974-75; ctr. dep. chief, adminstrn. dir. Intelligence Community, Washington, 1976-82; exec. officer USA-EIGO Svcs. Co., Rockville, Md., 1983-87; exec. officer USA-EIGO Svcs. Co., Princeton, N.J., 1983-87, now bd. dirs.; pres. P.K. Co. Ltd., Bethesda, 1987—; chmn. bd. dirs. emeritus P.K. Co. Ltd., Hong Kong; bd. dirs. Asia Mgmt. Internat., Princeton; assoc. Bi-Lingual U.S.A. Corp., Bethesda, Md., 1984, Mgmt. Logistics Internat., Arlington, Va., 1983-86. Editor, translator: Yoshio Kodama, 1952; author: (monographs) Items of Inquiry Far East, 1983, Japanese Technology-Ancient Culture, 1985, Augur, 1994 (pamphlet) Fiber Optics Across the Pacific, 1989; editor (handbook) Japanese-English Proprietary Business Lexicon for Command Control Communications Intelligence, 1990-93. Sponsor, contbr. Pisanko-Kikan, 1982, Hotel Okura, Japan, 1983, Bungei Shunju, Japan, 1988. Lt. J.G., USN, 1942-46. Trenton Times scholar, 1942; recipient Moe Berg award Pub. Security Investigation Agy.-Japan, Tokyo, 1961, Telecommunications award Thai Gen. Staff, Bangkok, 1972, Shimoda Diplomatic award, Japan. Mem. Asian Rsch. Svc., Bus. Devel. Africa, Internat. Inst. Japan, Bus. Execs. for Internat. Security, Internat. Platform Assn., Info. Processing Soc. Japan, Naval Res. Officers Tng. Corps, Unit Alumni Club, Boulder Boys-Japanese Club, Shek-O Club. Avocations: rare book collecting, cryptology, desert safaris. Office: PK Co Ltd Far East Hdqs, Peninsula New Business Ctr, Hong Kong Hong Kong *"I seek no other man's shoes. If I've misdirected my priorities, and I'm confident this is not so, I've had a fair time in lost country. There are no regrets."Moe Berg Pr #23.*

PISANO, A. ROBERT, entertainment company executive, lawyer; b. San Jose, Calif., Mar. 3, 1943; s. Anthony Edward and Carmen Jeanne (Morisoli) P.; m. Carolyn Joan Pollock, May 5, 1979; children: Catherine J., Anthony Daniel, Elizabeth A., Alexandra N. B.A. in Pub. Administrn., San Jose State U., 1965; J.D., U. Calif.-Berkeley, 1968. Bar: Calif. Assoc. O'Melveny & Myers, Los Angeles, 1968-75, ptnr., 1976-85, 92-93; exec. v.p. office of chmn., gen. counsel Paramount Pictures, Los Angeles, 1985-91; exec. v.p. Metro-Goldwyn-Mayer, Inc., Santa Monica, Calif., 1993—. Bd. dirs. Info. for Pub. Affairs, Sacramento, 1983—. Mem. Motion Picture Assn. Am. (bd. dirs. 1989-91, 93—), Acad. Motion Picture Arts and Scis. Office: Metro Goldwyn Mayer Inc 2500 Broadway St Santa Monica CA 90404-3061

PISANO, RONALD GEORGE, art consultant; b. N.Y.C., Dec. 19, 1948; s. Robert Louis and Mildred Jan Pisano. BA, Adelphi U., 1971; postgrad., U. Del., 1971-73. Dir. exhbns. Baruch Coll. City U., N.Y., 1974-76; assoc. curator William Merritt Chase collection and archives Parrish Art Mus., Southampton, N.Y., 1976; curator mus. William Merritt Chase collection and archives Parrish Art Mus., 1977-78, dir., 1978-82; art cons., 1981—; guest curator Mus. at Stony Brook, N.Y., 1977-79, 85, 90, Henry Art Gallery U. Wash., 1982-83; cons. curator Am. art Heckscher Mus., Huntington, N.Y., 1977-77, guest curator, 1985, 90.. Author: William Merritt Chase, 1979, The Heckscher Mus. Catalogue of the Am. Collection, 1979, An Am. Pl. Exhbn. Catalogue, 1981, A Leading Spirit in American Art: William Merritt Chase, 1849-1916, 1983, The Long Island Landscape, 1820-1920, 1985, The Art Students League; Selections from the Permanent Collection, 1987, A Centennial Celebration of the National Association of Women Artists, 1988, Idle Hours: Americans at Leisure, 1865-1914, 1989, Long Island Landscape Painting in the 20th Century, 1990, Summer Afternoons: Landscape Paintings by William Merritt Chase, 1993, The League at the Cape, 1993, Parodying the American Masters: The Society of Fakirs, 1993, Gifford Beal; Picture Maker, 1993, Photographs from the William Merritt Chase Archives, 1993, William M. Chase and Irving R. Wiles: The Artist as Teacher, 1994, Henry and Edith Prellwitz and the Peconic Art Colony, 1995. Recipient A. Conger Goodyear award, 1971; Disting. Art Historian award Grand Central Art Galleries, 1979; Stebbins Family grantee, 1972-73. Mem. Coll. Art Assn., Am. Assn. Museums. Home: 6 Lakeview Trl Salisbury Mills NY 12577-5408 Office: Ronald G Pisano Inc 375 Riverside Dr Apt 13-b New York NY 10025-2180

PISCHL, ADOLPH JOHN, school administrator; b. East Orange, N.J., Mar. 28, 1920; s. Adolph and Anna (Ellerman) P.; m. Tennessee Wild, Sept. 9, 1947; 1 child, Sallyann. Certificate, Drake Coll., 1940. With Juilliard Sch. of Music, N.Y.C., 1962-86, asst. to concert mgr., 1962-66, dir. pub. relations, 1966-68, concert mgr., 1966-86; adminstr. The Sch. for Strings, N.Y.C., 1987-88; with The Dance Mart, N.Y.C., 1950—, pub. dir. Am. Dance Festival, Conn. Coll., 1964-68; mgr. Betty Jones Dances I Dance, 1966-68, Ruth Currier Dance Co., 1966-68, Anna Sokolow Dance Co., 1966-68, Julliard Sch. Bookstore, 1971-86. Founder, editor: Dance Perspectives, 1958-64, Dance Data, 1977; editor: Juilliard News Bull. and Rev. Ann, 1964-85; pub.: Dance Horizons, 1965-86; Contbr. articles to dance mags. Bd. dirs. Dance Notation Bur.; sec. bd. dirs. Walter W. Naumburg Found., Inc. Served with AUS, 1940-46. Home: 878 Warren Pky Teaneck NJ 07666-5640

PISCIOTTA, ANTHONY VITO, physician, educator; b. N.Y.C., Mar. 3, 1921; s. Andrew and Mary (Zinnanti) P.; m. Lorraine Gault, June 15, 1951; children: Robert Andrew, Nancy Marie, Anthony Vito. B.S., Fordham U., 1941; M.D., Marquette U., 1944, M.S., 1952. Diplomate: Am. Bd. Internal Medicine. Intern Jersey City Med. Center, 1944-45; resident pathology Fordham Hosp., N.Y.C., 1947-48; resident medicine Milwaukee County Gen. Hosp., 1948-51; rsch. fellow hematology New Eng. Center Hosp., 1951-52; instr. medicine Tufts U., 1951-52; mem. faculty Marquette U., 1952-81, prof., 1966-81; vice chmn. Radiation Effects Rsch. Found., Hiroshima, Japan, 1981-83; prof. medicine Med. Coll. Wis., Milw., 1983—, Robert A. Uihlein, Jr. prof. Hematologic Rsch., 1983—; dir. blood rsch. lab., staff hematologist John L. Doyne Hosp. (now Froedtert Meml. Hosp.), 1952-95. Mem. adv. editl. bd. of: Transfusion, 1960-67; mem. editl. bd. of: Jour. Lab. and Clin. Medicine, 1967-70. Served to capt. M.C. AUS, 1945-47. Named Alumnus of Yr. Med. Coll. Wis. Alumni Assn., 1977. Fellow A.C.P.; mem. AMA, Wis., Milw. County med. socs., Assn. Am. Physicians, AAAS, Am. Assn. Immunologists, Am. Soc. for Exptl. Pathology, Am. Soc. Hematology, Central Soc. Clin. Research, Internat. Soc. Hematology, Milw. Acad. Medicine (Achievement award 1987)), Milw. Soc. Internal Medicine, N.Y. Acad. Sci., Soc. Exptl. Biology and Medicine, Nat. Blood Club (sec. 1970-71), Alpha Omega Alpha. Home: 12550 W Grove Ter Elm Grove WI 53122-1973 Office: Med Coll Wis 9200 W Wisconsin Ave Milwaukee WI 53226-3512

PISCIOTTA, VIVIAN VIRGINIA, psychotherapist; b. Chgo., Dec. 7; d. Vito and Mary Lamia; m. Vincent Diago Pisciotta, Apr. 1, 1951; children: E. Christopher, Vittorio, V. Charles, Mary A. Pisciotta Higley, Thomas Sansone. BA in Clin. Psychology, Antioch U., 1974; MSW, George Williams Coll., 1984; postgrad., Erickson Inst. of No. Ill., 1990. Lic. clin. social worker; diplomate in clin. social work. Short-term therapist Woman Line, Dayton, Ohio, 1976-79; psychotherapist Cicero (Ill.) Family Svcs., 1982-83, Maywood (Ill.) - Proviso Family Svcs., 1983-84, Maple Ave. Med. Ctr., Brookfield, Ill., 1985-88, Met. Med. Clinic, Naperville, Ill., 1986-88; allied staff Riveredge Psychiat. Hosp., Forest Park, Ill., 1986—, Linden Oaks Hosp., Naperville, Ill., 1990—; psychotherapist, pvt. practice Oakbrook, Ill., 1988—; psychotherapist, co-founder Archer Austin Counseling Ctr., Chgo., 1988-89; psychotherapist, founder Archer Counseling Ctr., Chgo., 1989—; allied staff Linden Oaks Psychiat. Hosp., Naperville, 1990—; substitute tchr. Chgo. Pub. High Sch., 1981. Author treatment prog., workshops in field. Co-founder Co-op Nursery Sch., Rockford, Ill., 1956; leader Great Books of the Western World series, Piqua, Ohio, 1977, Rockford, 1960-65; leader Girl Scouts U.S., St. Bridget Sch., Rockford, 1968-71. Mem. Assn. Labor-Mgmt. and Cons. on Alcoholism, Soc. Clin. Exptl. Hypnosis, Nat. Assn. Social Workers, Acad. Cert. Social Workers, Nat. social Wk. Register, Antioch Univ. Alumnus Assn. Rockford Coll. Alumnae Orgn. (newsletter contbr. 1972-73), Soc. for Clin. and Exptl. Hypnosis (assoc. mem.), Internat. Soc. for Clin. and Exptl. Hypnosis (assoc. mem.). Republican. Roman Catholic. Avocations: reading, travel, study/rsch., music, religion. Office: Archer Counseling Ctr 7002 W Archer Ave Ste 2B Chicago IL 60638-2202

PISHKIN, VLADIMIR, psychologist, educator; b. Belgrade, Yugoslavia, Mar. 12, 1931; came to U.S., 1946, naturalized, 1951; s. Vasili and Olga (Bartosh) P.; m. Dorothy Louise Martin, Sept. 12, 1953; children—Gayle Ann, Mark Vladimir. B.A., Mont. State U., 1951, M.A., 1955; Ph.D., U. Utah, 1958. Dir. neuropsychiat. research labs. VA Hosp., Tomah, Wis., 1959-62; chief research psychologist Behavioral Sci. Labs.., Oklahoma City, 1962-75; prof. psychiatry Coll. Medicine, U. Okla. Health Scis. Ctr., Oklahoma City, 1973-93, prof. emeritus, 1994; chmn. rsch. coun. dept. psychiatry and behavioral scis., 1972-75; bd. dirs. VA Med Ctr, Oklahoma City; dir. clin rsch. Willow View Hosp., Oklahoma City, 1987—. Author: (with Mathis and Pierce) Basic Psychiatry, rev. 3d edit, 1977; editor in chief: Jour. Clin. Psychology, 1974—; contbr. numerous articles to profl. jours. Served with USAF, 1952-54. Recipient Disting. Service award Jr. C. of C. Fellow Am. Psychol. Assn., Am. Psychol. Soc.; mem. Southwestern Psychol. Assn. (pres. 1973-74), Okla. Psychol. Assn.(Disting. Psychologist award 1986), Midwestern Psychol. Assn., AAAS, Psychonomics Soc. Clubs: Masons, Shriners. Home: 3113 NW 62nd St Oklahoma City OK 73112-4224 Office: 2601 Spencer Rd PO Box 11137 Oklahoma City OK 73136-0137

PISIGAN, RODOLFO ARIAS, JR., environmental chemist; b. Agdangan, Quezon, The Philippines, June 4, 1948; came to U.S., 1975; s. Rodolfo M. and Crispiniana (Arias) P.; m. Portia Ortiz, June 26, 1979; children: Cherry, Jeremy. BS in Agrl. Chemistry cum laude, U. Philippines, Los Baños, 1970, MS in Agrl. Chemistry, 1975; MS in Environ. Chemistry, U. Fla., 1980, PhD in Environ. Chemistry, 1981. Environ. chemist environ. engring. div. Environ. Sci. & Engring., Inc., Gainesville, Fla., 1983-86, environ. chemist environ. assessment and toxicology div., 1986-92, sr. scientist geosics. divsn., 1992-95. Contbr. articles to Jour. Am. Water Works Assn., Materials Performance and Phytochemistry. Lectr., judge sci. fair cmty. resource vol. program Sch. Bd. Alachua County, Gainesville, 1991—; sec.-treas. Filipino Cultural Assn., Gainesville, 1993, treas., 1994. Fellow Ford Found., 1976. Mem. Nat. Ground Water Assn., Am. Water Works Assn., Water Environment Fedn., Soc. Environ. Toxicology and Chemistry (pres. southeastern regional chpt. 1994-95), Sigma Xi. Achievements include development of equations for predicting $CaCO_3$ saturation and corrosion rate through computerized multivariate regression analyses; applications of environmental chemistry concepts to solve chemical contamination problems; showed that traditional methods of evaluating water corrosivity are inadequate and unreliable using laboratory and field experiments; isolated and characterized a key enzyme involved in starch biosynthesis. Avocations: reading, travel, basketball, science movies, listening to music. Home and Office: 421 SW 75th Ter Gainesville FL 32607-1556

PISNEY, RAYMOND FRANK, international consulting services executive; b. Lime Springs, Iowa, June 2, 1940; s. Frank A. and Cora H. P. BA, Loras Coll., 1963; postgrad., Cath. U. Am., 1963; MA, U. Del., 1965. Asst. adminstrn. and rsch. Mt. Vernon, Va., 1965-69; historic sites adminstr. N.C. Archives and Hist. Dept., Raleigh, 1969; asst. adminstr. div. historic sites and museums N.C. Dept. Art, Culture and History, Raleigh, 1969-72; cons.

Cannon Mills Co., Kannapolis, N.C., 1972-73; exec. dir. Woodrow Wilson Birthplace Found., Staunton, Va., 1973-78, Mo. Hist. Soc., St. Louis, 1978-87; sr. v.p., cons. svcs. ETI Internat., Washington, 1987—; pres. Va. History and Museums Fedn., 1977-78; pres. Mo. Museums Assoc., 1982-84; cons. assoc. Battelle, Washington, 1994. Author: Historical Markers: A Bibliography, 1977, Historic Markers: Planning Local Programs, 1978, A Preview to Historical Marking, 1976, Old Buildings: New Resources for Work and Play, 1976; editor: Virginians Remember Woodrow Wilson, 1978, Woodrow Wilson in Retrospect, 1978, Woodrow Wilson: Idealism and Realty, 1977, Historic Preservation and Public Policy in Virginia, 1978. Bd. trustees James Clerk Maxwell Mus. and Found., Edinburgh, Scotland, 1993—, Internat. Human Rights Monument and Mus., Moscow, 1991—; sec., trustee Scotland WorldWide Heritage, Glasgow, 1993—; mem. internat. com. Charles A. Lindbergh Anniversary, Paris, 1987. Recipient Bertha Black Rhoda award NAACP, 1985; Hagley fellow U. Del., 1963-65; Seminar for Hist. Adminstrs. fellow, 1965. Mem. Internat. Assn. Consulting Firms, Washington Ind. Writers, Am. Assn. Museums, Nat. Trust Hist. Preservation U.S., Am. Assn. State and Local History, Can. Museums Assn., Brit. Museums Assn., Internat. Coun. Monuments and Sites, Internat. Coun. Museums, Lindbergh Anniversary Assn. (internat. com. 1987), Phi Alpha Theta. Roman Catholic. *Words that have guided my career were written more than two millenia ago by Marcus Tullius Cicero (106-43 B.C.); the highest level of effort by a man is to 'critcize by creating, rather than by finding fault."*

PISTELLA, CHRISTINE LEY, public health educator; b. Pitts., July 11, 1949; d. David Adam and Mary Louise (Barrett) Ley; m. Frank Joseph Pistella; 1 child, Lauren Nicole. BA in Edn., U. Pitts., 1970, MSW, 1972, MPH, 1977, PhD with distinction, 1979. Lic. social worker, Pa. Program counselor/supr. Transitional Svcs., Inc., Pitts., 1972-74; mental health profl. St. Francis Med. Ctr., Pitts., 1974-75; sr. rsch. social worker Magee-Women's Hosp., Pitts., 1976-78; rsch. assoc. Sch. Pub. Health U. Pitts., 1976-80, rsch. coord. Sch. Social Wk., 1978-79; asst. prof. pub. health U. Pitts. Sch. Pub. Health, 1980—; rsch. cons. USPHS Region V, Chgo., 1985-88, Washington-Greens Human Svcs., 1982-84, Southwestern Pa. Area on Aging, Monessen, 1980-83; rsch. dir. Family Health Coun. of Western Pa., Pitts., 1982-87. Contbr. articles to profl. jours., chpts. to books; editor/co-editor more than 10 rsch. monographs on family health, social wk. Active Mayors Commn. on Families, Pitts., 1988-94, Infant Mortality Rev. Team, Pa. Perinatal Assn., Pitts., 1990-93, Injury Prevention Adv. Bd. Allegheny County, Pitts., 1989—, Venango-Forest Cmty. Health Action Com., 1992-95; steering com. Pa. Area Health Edn. Ctr., 1994—. Mem. NASW, APHA, Nat. Rural Health Assn., Pa. Forum for Primary Health Care, Pa. Pub. Health Assn., Assn. of Tchrs. of Maternal and Child Health, Assn. Cert. Social Workers, Greater Pitts. C. of C. (alumni bd. of leadership Pitts. 1991-94), Delta Omega. Democrat. Roman Catholic. Avocations: photography, travel, art appreciation, genealogy, antiques, history of Western Pa. Office: U Pitts Grad Sch Pub Health 216 Parran Hall Pittsburgh PA 15261

PISTER, KARL STARK, engineering educator; b. Stockton, Calif., June 27, 1925; s. Edwin LeRoy and Mary Kimball (Smith) P.; m. Rita Olsen, Nov. 18, 1950; children: Francis, Therese, Anita, Jacinta, Claire, Kristofer. BS with honors, U. Calif., Berkeley, 1945, MS, 1948; PhD, U. Ill., 1952. Instr. theoretical and applied mechanics U. Ill., 1949-52; mem. faculty U. Calif., Berkeley, 1952-91, prof. engring. scis., 1962—, Roy W. Carlson prof. engring., 1985-90, dean Coll. Engring., 1980-90; chancellor U. Calif., Santa Cruz, 1991—, now pres., chancellor; Richard Merton guest prof. U. Stuttgart, W. Ger., 1978; cons. to govt. and industry; bd. dirs. Monterey Bay Aquarium Rsch. Inst.; bd. trustees Monterey Inst. Internat. Studies; chmn. bd. Calif. Coun. Sci. and Tech. Author research papers in field; assoc. editor: Computer Methods in Applied Mechanics and Engring, 1972, Jour. Optimization Theory and Applications, 1982; editorial adv. bd. Encyclopedia Phys. Sci. and Tech. Served with USNR, World War II. Recipient Wason rsch. medal Am. Concrete Inst., 1960, Vincent Bendix Minorities in Engring. award Am. Soc. for Engring. Edn., 1988, Lamme medal, 1993, Alumni Honor award U. Ill. Coll. Engring., 1982, Disting. Engring. Alumnus award U. Calif. Coll. Engring., 1992. Fellow ASME, AAAS, Am. Acad. Mechanics, Am. Acad. Arts and Scis., Calif. Acad. Scis. (hon.); mem. NAE, ASCE, Soc. Engring. Sci. Office: U Calif Santa Cruz Office of Chancellor 1156 High St Santa Cruz CA 95064-1077

PISTOLE, THOMAS GORDON, microbiology educator, researcher; b. Detroit, Sept. 17, 1942; s. Leotis Merton Pistole and Lillian Nell (Bosley) Besser; m. Donna Dulcie Straw, Sept. 11, 1965; children: James Alexander, Jennifer Katharine. PhB, Wayne State U., 1964, MS, 1966; PhD, U. Utah, 1969. Postdoctoral fellow U.S. Army, Frederick, Md., 1969-70; research assoc. U. Minn., Mpls., 1970-71; asst. prof. U. N.H., Durham, 1971-77, assoc. prof., 1977-83, prof., 1983—, chmn., 1983-92; vis. scientist Weizmann Inst., Rehovot, Israel, 1979; vis. prof. U. Edinburgh, Scotland, 1986. Co-editor: Biomedical Application of the Horseshoe Crab, 1979; mem. editorial bd. Jour. Invertebrate Pathology, 1988-90. NRC fellow, 1969-70, NIH sr. internat. fellow, 1986; grantee NIH, 1975-77, 89-93, 96—, NSF, 1981-84. Mem. Am. Soc. for Microbiology, Am. Assn. Immunologists, Internat. Soc. Devel. and Comparative Immunology, Soc. for Leukocyte Biology. Avocations: singing, collecting old sheet music, walking, cooking. Office: U NH Dept Microbiology Durham NH 03824

PISTOR, CHARLES HERMAN, JR., former banker, academic administrator; b. St. Louis, Aug. 26, 1930; s. Charles Herman and Virginia (Brown) P.; m. Regina Prikryl, Sept. 20, 1952; children: Lori Ellen, Charles Herman III, Jeffrey Glenn. BBA, U. Tex., 1952; MBA, Harvard U., 1956, So. Meth. U., 1961. Chmn., chief exec. officer First RepublicBank Dallas, 1980-88, also bd. dirs.; chief exec. officer, chmn. bd. dirs. Northpark Nat. Bank, Dallas, 1988-90; vice chair So. Meth. U., Dallas, 1990—; bd. dirs. Am. Brands, AMR, Centex Corp., Oryx Corp. Trustee So. Meth. U., Dallas; elder Presbyn. Ch. Served to lt. USNR, 1952-54. Mem. Am. Bankers Assn. (past pres., bd. dirs.). Club: Dallas Country. Home: 4200 Belclaire Ave Dallas TX 75205-3033 Office: So Meth U Dallas TX 75275-0224

PISTORIUS, GEORGE, language educator; b. Prague, Czechoslovakia, Mar. 19, 1922; came to U.S., 1958, naturalized, 1964; s. Theodor and Blazena (Jiranek) P.; m. Marie Skokan, June 30, 1945; 1 dau., Erika. Student, Charles U., Prague, 1945-48; postgrad., Université de Paris, 1948-50; certificats d'etudes superieures, Université de Strasbourg, France, 1950, 1951; Ph.D., U. Pa., 1963. Asst. dept. comparative lit. Charles U., 1946-48; instr. Lafayette Coll., Easton, Pa., 1958-61; asst. prof. French Lafayette Coll., 1961-63; asso. prof. Williams Coll., 1963-68, prof. Romanic langs., 1968-92, chmn. dept., 1971-82, prof. emeritus, 1992—; instr. French, Colby Coll. Summer Sch. Lang., 1959-65. Author: Bibliography of the works of F.X. Salda, 1948, Destin de la culture francaise dans une democratie populaire, 1957, L'Image de l'Allemagne dans le roman francais entre les deux guerres (1919-1939), 1964, Marcel Proust und Deutschland, Eine Bibliographie, 1981, André Gide und Deutschland: Eine internationale Bibliographie, 1990. Mem. MLA, Am. Assn. Tchrs. of French, Assn. Internationale des Etudes Francaises. Home: 54 Cluett Dr Williamstown MA 01267-2805

PI-SUNYER, F. XAVIER, medical educator, medical investigator; b. Barcelona, Catalonia, Spain, Dec. 3, 1933; came to U.S., 1942; s. James and Mercedes (Diaz) Pi-S.; m. Penelope Wheeler; children: Andrea, Olivia, Joanna. BA, Oberlin (Ohio) Coll., 1955; MD, Columbia U., 1959; MPH, Harvard U., 1963. From instr. to asst. prof. Coll. of Physicians & Surgeons, Columbia U., N.Y.C., 1965-76, assoc. prof., 1976-85, prof. clin. medicine, 1985-91; prof. St. Luke's-Roosevelt Hosp. Ctr., N.Y.C., 1991—; from asst. to assoc. attending physician St. Luke's Hosp., N.Y.C., 1965-75; attending physician St. Luke's-Roosevelt Hosp. Ctr., N.Y.C., 1975—, chief div. endocrinology, diabetes and nutrition, 1988—, dir. Obesity Rsch. Ctr., 1988—; dir. Joslin Diabetes Ctr. at St. Luke's Hosp., 1994—, Van Itallie Ctr. for Nutrition and Weight Mgmt., 1994—; mem. adj. faculty Rockefeller U., 1984—; vis. physician Rockefeller U. Hosp., 1984—; attending physician Presbyn. Hosp., 1985—; sr. investigator N.Y. Heart Assn., 1968-73; Hsien Wu investigator St. Luke's-Roosevelt Hosp., 1982-90; Sigma Xi lectr. Pa. State U., 1989; Howard Heinz vis. prof. Med. Coll. Pa., 1987; pfizer vis. prof. in diabetes Boston U./Tufts U./Harvard U., 1995; mem. C study sect. NIDDKD, 1988-92, mem. task force on obesity, 1990—, mem. nutrition study sect., 1983-87; v.p. Am. Bd. Nutrition, 1987-88. Contbr. numerous articles to profl. jours. Fogarty Internat. fellow NIH, 1979-80. Mem. Am. Soc. for Clin. Nutrition (coun. 1987-90, pres. 1989-90), Am. Diabetes Assn. (exec. com. 1990-93, pres. 1992-93), N.Am. Assn. Study Obesity (v.p. 1992-93, pres. 1994-95), N.Y. State Health Rsch. Coun., N.Y. Acad. Medicine (com. on pub. health 1983—). Avocations: tennis, skiing, hiking, theater. Home: 305 Riverside Dr New York NY 10025-5286 Office: St Luke's-Roosevelt Hosp Ctr Dept Medicine 1111 Amsterdam Ave New York NY 10025-1716

PITCHELL, ROBERT J., business executive; b. N.Y.C.; m. Louise Clark, Oct. 26, 1974; 1 dau. A.B., Fordham U., 1939; Ph.D., U. Calif., 1955. Mem. faculty Purdue U.; lectr. polit. sci. Butler U.; prof. Ind. U., to 1963; pres. Roosevelt U., 1963-65; formerly dep. adminstr. Fed. Extension Service, Dept. Agr.; later exec. dir. Nat. U. Extension Assn., Washington; pres. Hamden Enterprises Inc., Fairfax, Va.; cons., past dir. Ind. Tax Study Commn. Author books on taxation and continuing edn. Assisted senatorial campaign Birch Bayh, 1962. Home and Office: 3134 Prosperity Ave Fairfax VA 22031-2820

PITCHER, GRIFFITH FONTAINE, lawyer; b. Balt., Nov. 1, 1937; s. William Henry and Virginia Griffith (Stein) P.; m. Sandra E. Barnett, Dec. 16, 1994; children: Virginia T. Pitcher Ballinger, L. Brooke Pitcher Fick, William T. B., Margaret W. Pitcher Lombino. B.A., Johns Hopkins U., 1960; J.D., U. Va., 1963. Bar: Ala. 1963, Fla. 1971. Assoc. Bradley, Arant, Rose & White, Birmingham, Ala., 1963-71; mem. Van den Berg, Gay & Burke, P.A., Orlando, Fla., 1971-76, Mahoney, Hadlow & Adams, P.A., Jacksonville, Fla., 1976-82; ptnr. Squire, Sanders & Dempsey, Miami, Fla., 1982-93; of counsel Mershon, Sawyer, Johnston, Dunwoody & Cole, Miami, 1994-95; of counsel Chamberlain, Hrdlicka, White, Williams & Martin, Atlanta, 1996—. Vice-chmn. Winter Park (Fla.) Planning and Zoning Bd., 1974-75. Served with Army N.G., 1961-64. Fellow Am. Coll. Bond Counsel (dir.); mem. ABA, Nat. Assn. Bond Lawyers, The Fla. Bar, Fla. Econ. Devel. Coun., Fla. Mcpl. Attys. Assn., Fla. Acad. Hosp. Attys., Ala. State Bar Assn., Order of Coif, Delta Phi. Republican. Contbr. articles on law to profl. jours.

PITCHER, TONY JOHN, fishery science educator, author; b. Banbury, Eng., Oct. 23, 1944; arrived in Can., 1994; s. Ernest William and Winifred Nellie (Harris) P.; m. Marguerite Elizabeth Tinsey; children: Susannah Jane, Tamsin Charlotte Lucy; m. Valerie Marie Gray, May 20, 1994. BA, Oxford (Eng.) U., 1966, DPhil, MA (hon.), 1970. Lectr. biology U. Ulster, Coleraine, Ireland, 1970-78; lectr. zoology U. Wales, Bangor, 1978-84, sr. lectr., 1984-87, reader, 1988-90; prof. fisheries Inst. fü4 Meereskunde, Kiel, Germany, 1987; spl. rsch. fellow renewal resources assessment group Imperial Coll., London, 1990-93; prof., dir. Fisheries Ctr., U. B.C., Vancouver, Can., 1994—; cons. Marine Resources Assessment Ltd., London, 1990-93; hon. prof. U. Concepcion, Chile, 1994—; participant internat. devel. aid projects in fisheries in Angola, Cameroon, Chile, Ecuador, Shana, Indonesia, Kenya, Malawi, Mex., The Philippines, Sri Lanka, Tanzania, Thailand, Uganda, Zambia, Zimbabwe, Australia, Iceland, Italy, Norway, U.K., South Africa. Co-author: Fisheries Ecology, 1982; co-editor: Control Processes in Fish Physiology, 1983, The Behavior of Fishes, 1986, Collected Reports on Fisheries Research in Malawi, vol. 1, 1990, Hake: Fisheries Ecology and Markets, 1994, Molecular Genetics in Fisheries, 1994, The Impact of Species Changes in the African Lakes, 1995; editor: The Behaviour of Teleost Fishes, 1986, 2d edit., 1992; asst. editor Jour. Fish Biology, 1981-87; series editor Fish and Fisheries, 1990; founding editor Revs. in Fish Biology and Fisheries, 1991—; contbr. over 110 articles to sci. jours. Achievements include laboratory field and theoretical research on schooling behavior of fishes and its implications for human harvest. Office: U of British Columbia, Fisheries Ctr, Vancouver, BC Canada V6T 1Z4

PITCHUMONI, CAPECOMORIN SANKAR, gastroenterologist, educator; b. Madura, India, Jan. 20, 1938; came to U.S., 1967; s. Sankara and Jaya (Lekshmi) Iyer; m. Prema Iyer, Nov. 11, 1964; children: Sheila, Shoba, Suresh. Student, St. Xavier Coll., India, 1953-55; M.B. B.S., Trivandrum Med. Coll., India, 1959, M.D., 1965. Intern Med. Coll., Trivandurm, India, 1961-63; resident in gastroenterology Yale U., 1967-69; N.Y. Med. Coll., 1969-72; practice medicine specializing in gastroenterology N.Y.C., 1972—; asst. prof. medicine Kottayam Med. Coll., India, 1967; asst. prof. medicine N.Y. Med. Coll., 1972-75, assoc. prof., 1975-80, prof. clin. medicine, 1980-85, prof. medicine, 1985—, assoc. prof. preventive and social medicine, 1975-86, prof. community and preventive medicine, 1986—; chief sect. gastroenterology Our Lady of Mercy Med. Ctr., N.Y., 1980—; assoc. dir. medicine Our Lady of Mercy Med. Ctr., N.Y.C., 1985—, program dir. internal medicine, 1987—; dir. medicine, 1992. Contbg. author med. textbooks; contbr. articles to profl. jours. Recipient Om Prakash award Indian Soc. Gastroenterology, 1976, Outstanding Scientist of Yr. award MV Spltys., Madras, 1994, Oration award Thangavelu Endowment, 1994. Fellow Royal Coll. Physicians and Surgeons Can., ACP, Am. Coll. Gastroenterology, Am. Coll. Nutrition; mem. Am. Soc. for Gastrointestinal Endoscopy, Assn. Physicians India, Am. Coll. Nuitrition, Am. Gastroent. Assn., India Soc. Gastroenterology (life), Am. Inst. Nutrition, N.Y. Gastroent. Assn., N.Y. Acad. Scis., N.Y. Soc. Gastrointestinal Endoscopy, Am. Soc. for Clin. Nutrition. Hindu. Home: 178 Fairmount Ave Glen Rock NJ 07452-3014 Office: 600 E 233rd St Bronx NY 10466-2697

PITCOCK, JAMES KENT, head and neck surgical oncologist; b. Tachikawa AFB, Japan, Nov. 18, 1951; s. James Kenneth and Helen (Robertson) P.; m. Cynthia H. Zipperly. Student, U. Houston, 1974; MD, Baylor U., 1979. Diplomate Am. Bd. Otolaryngology. Resident in gen. surgery Baylor Coll. Medicine, Houston, 1979-81, resident in otolaryngology, head and neck surgery, 1981-84; clinician Kelsey-Seybold Clinic, P.A., Houston, 1984-85; lectr. head and neck surgery Inst. Laryngology and Otology, U. London, 1985-86; instr., fellow head and neck surgery U. Chgo., 1986-88; asst. prof. dept. otolaryngology, head and neck surgery, chief div. head and neck surgical oncology U. Calif.-Irvine Med. Ctr., Orange, 1988-92; dir. head and neck oncology clin. & rsch. program Clin. Cancer Ctr. U. Calif., Irvine. Author: Oral and Maxillofacial Trauma, 1989, Musculocutaneous Flap Reconstruction of the Head and Neck, 1989, Surgery of the Skull Base, 1989. Fellow Am. Acad. Otolaryngology, Head and Neck Surgery; mem. ACS. Office: Dauphin W EENT Specialists 3701 Dauphin St Mobile AL 36608-1756

PITEGOFF, PETER ROBERT, lawyer, educator; b. N.Y.C., Mar. 6, 1953; s. Joseph and Libbie (Shapiro) P.; m. Ann Casady, Mar. 22, 1986; children: Maxwell Jacob, Elias Samuel. AB, Brown U., 1975; JD, NYU, 1981. Bar: Mass 1981, N.Y. 1988; cert. tchr., R.I. Tchr. Hope High Sch., Providence, 1974-75; community organizer Nat. Assn. for So. Poor, Petersburg, Va., 1975-76, Citizens Action League, Oakland, Calif., 1976-78; gen. counsel ICA Group, Boston, 1981-88; ptnr. Arrington & Pitegoff, Somerville, Mass., 1986-88; prof. law SUNY, Buffalo, 1988—; adj. asst. prof. law NYU, 1986-88; cons. in field, 1978—; legal counsel cmty. devel. worker purchases of bus. corp. fin. dem. corp. structures child care policy and welfare reform. Contbr. to profl. publs. Root-Tilden scholarship NYU, 1978; grantee Pub. Interest Law Found., N.Y.C., 1981. Democrat. Jewish. Avocations: athletics, travel, music. Office: SUNY Sch of Law 507 O'Brian Hall Buffalo NY 14260

PITELKA, FRANK ALOIS, zoologist, educator; b. Chgo., Mar. 27, 1916; s. Frank Joseph and Frances (Laga) P.; m. Dorothy Getchell Riggs, Feb. 5, 1943; children: Louis Frank, Wenzel Karl, Vlasta Kazi Helen. B.S. with highest honors, U. Ill., 1939; summer student, U. Mich., 1938, U. Wash., 1940; Ph.D., U. Calif. at Berkeley, 1946. Mem. faculty U. Calif. at Berkeley, 1944—, prof. zoology, 1958—, chmn. dept., 1963-66, 69-71, Miller research prof., 1965-66; curator birds Mus. Vertebrate Zoology, 1945-63, assoc. dir., 1982—; exec. com. Miller Inst. Basic Rsch. in Sci., 1967-71, chmn., 1967-70; Panel environ. biology NSF, 1959-62, panel polar programs, 1978-80; mem. panel biol. and med. scis., com. polar research Nat. Acad. Scis., 1960-65; research assoc. Naval Arctic Research Lab., Barrow, Alaska, 1951-80; ecol. adv. com. AEC, 1956-1958; adv. coms. U.S. Internat. Biol. Program, 1965-69; mem. adv. com. U. Colo. Inst. Arctic and Alpine Research, 1968-73; mem. U.S. Tundra Biome Program, 1968-73, dir., 1968-69; vis. prof. U. Wash. Friday Harbor Labs, summer 1968; mem. U.S. Commn. for UNESCO, 1970-72. Contbr. research papers in field.; Editorial bd.: Ecology, 1949-51, 60-62, editor, 1962-64; mem. editorial bd. U. Calif. Press, 1953-62, chmn., 1959-62; mem. editorial bd. Pacific Coast Avifauna, 1947-60, Ecol. Monographs, 1957-60, Systematic Zoology, 1961-64, The Veliger, 1961-85, Studies in Ecology, 1972-84, Current Ornithology, 1980-85; asst. editor Condor, 1943-45, assoc. editor, 1945-62; mem. editorial bd. Studies in Avian Biology, 1979-84, editor, 1984-87. Guggenheim fellow, 1949-50; NSF sr. postdoctoral fellow Oxford (Eng.) U., 1957-58; Research fellow Ctr. for Advanced Study in Behavioral Scis., Stanford, 1971; recipient Disting. Teaching award U. Calif.-Berkeley, 1984; The Berkeley citation, 1985, Alumnus Achievement award, U. Ill., 1993. Fellow Arctic Inst. N.Am., Am. Ornithologists Union (Brewster award 1980), Calif. Acad. Scis., AAAS, Animal Behavior Soc.; mem. Ecol. Soc. Am. (Mercer award 1953, Eminent Ecologist award 1992), Soc. Study Evolution, Cooper Ornithol. Soc. (hon. mem.; pres. 1948-50), Brit. Ecol. Soc., Am. Soc. Mammalogists, Am. Soc. Naturalists, Am. Inst. Biol. Scis., Western Soc. Naturalists (pres. 1963-64), Nat. Audubon Soc., Sierra Club, Phi Beta Kappa, Sigma Xi. Home: PO Box 9278 Berkeley CA 94709-0278 *My ideas and goals reflect three important sources of influence: strong university teachers; the excellence of colleagues and the setting of my university base; and, most importantly, the unremitting stimulus and challenge of my graduate students to grow with them over years of dramatic changes in biology.*

PITERNICK, ANNE BREARLEY, librarian, educator; b. Blackburn, Eng.; emigrated to Can., 1956, naturalized, 1965; d. Walter and Ellen (Harris) Clayton; m. George Piternick, May 6, 1971. B.A., U. Manchester (Eng.), 1948, F.L.A., 1983. Mem. library staff U. B.C., Vancouver, Can., 1956-66; head sci. div. U. B.C., 1960-61, head social scis. div., 1965-66, prof. Sch. Library, Archival and Info. Studies, 1966-91, prof. emerita, 1991—, assoc. dean Faculty of Arts, 1985-90; mem. Nat. Com. Bibliog. Svcs. Can., 1975-80, chmn. com. on bibliography and info. services for social scis. and humanities, 1981-84; mem. adv. acad. panel Social Scis. and Humanities Research Council, 1981-84; mem. adv. bd. Nat. Libr. Can., 1978-84; mem. Nat. Adv. Com. Culture Stats., 1985-90; organizer Confs. on Can. Bibliography, 1974, 81; pres. Can. Assn. Spl. Librs. Info. Svcs., 1969-70, Can. Libr. Assn., 1976-77. Author articles on electronic info. svcs. and scholarly communication. Recipient Queen's Silver Jubilee medal, 1977, award for Spl. Librarianship Can. Assn. Spl. Librs. and Info. Svcs., 1987, 75th Anniversary medal U.B.C., 1990, Can. 125 medal, 1993. Fellow Council on Library Resources (1980). Home: 1849 W 63rd Ave, Vancouver, BC Canada V6P 2H9

PITINO, RICHARD, college basketball coach; b. N.Y.C., Sept. 18, 1952. Student, U. Mass. Asst. coach U. Hawaii, 1975-76, Syracuse U., 1976-78; coach Boston U., 1978-83; asst. coach N.Y. Knicks, 1983-85, coach, 1987-89; coach Providence U., 1986-87; basketball coach U. Ky., Lexington, 1989—. Author: (with Dick Weiss) Full Court Pressure: A Year in Kentucky Basketball, 1992. Named Coll. Coach of Yr., Sporting News, 1987. Office: U Ky Athletics Dept Basketball Office Lexington KY 40506*

PITKIN, EDWARD THADDEUS, aerospace engineer, consultant; b. Putnam, Conn., Dec. 14, 1930; s. Thaddeus Eugene and Florence Mabel (Brown) P.; m. Clara Lucy Modliszewski, June 13, 1953; children—Gayle Linda, Dale Edward. B.S., U. Conn., 1952; M.S. (Guggenheim fellow), Princeton, 1953; Ph.D. (NASA fellow), UCLA, 1964. Project engr. Astro Div. Marquardt Co., Los Angeles, 1956-59; mgr. space propulsion Astro Div. Marquardt Co., 1959-61; engring. cons. Los Angeles, 1961-64; asso. prof. aerospace engring. U. Conn., Storrs, 1964-70, prof. mech. and aerospace engring., 1970-90, prof. emeritus, 1990—; cons. engr., 1990—; asst. dean U. Conn., Storrs, 1977-87. Contbr. articles to tech. publs. Served as lt. USAF, 1953-55. Asso. fellow AIAA. Mem. Solar Energy Soc. Home: 115 Brookside Ln Mansfield Center CT 06250-1001 Office: U Conn Dep Mech Engring U-139 191 Auditorium Rd Storrs CT 06269

PITKIN, ROY MACBETH, physician, educator; b. Anthon, Iowa, May 24, 1934; s. Roy and Pauline Allie (McBeath) P.; m. Marcia Alice Jenkins, Aug. 17, 1957; children: Barbara, Robert Macbeth, Kathryn, William Charles. B.A. with highest distinction, U. Iowa, 1956, M.D., 1959. Diplomate Am. Bd. Obstetrics & Gynecology, 1967. Intern King County Hosp., Seattle, 1959-60; resident in ob-gyn U. Iowa Hosps. and Clinics, Iowa City, 1960-63; asst. prof. ob-gyn U. Ill., 1965-68; assoc. prof. ob-gyn U. Iowa, Iowa City, 1968-72; prof. U. Iowa, 1972-87, head dept. ob-gyn, 1977-87; prof. UCLA, 1987—, head dept. ob-gyn., 1987-95; mem. residency rev. com. ob-gyn, 1981-87, chmn. 1985-87. Editor-in-chief: Year Book of Obstetrics and Gynecology, 1975-86; editor-in-chief: Clinical Obstetrics and Gynecology, 1979; editor: Obstetrics and Gynecology, 1985. Contbr. articles to med. jours. Served to lt. comdr. M.C. USNR, 1963-65. NIH career awardee, 1972-77. Fellow Royal Obstetricians and Gynecologists (ad eundem); mem. AMA (Goldberger award in clin. nutrition 1982), Am. Coll. Obstetricians and Gynecologists, Am. Gynecol. and Obstet. Soc. (pres. 1994-95), German Soc. Gynecology and Obstetrics (hon. 1992), Ctrl. Assn. Obstetricians and Gynecologists, Soc. Gynecologic Investigation (pres. 1985-86), Soc. Perinatal Obstetricians (pres. 1978-79), NAS, Inst. of Medicine. Presbyterian. Office: UCLA Sch Med Dept Ob-Gyn Los Angeles CA 90024-1740

PITOFSKY, ROBERT, federal agency administrator, law educator; b. Paterson, N.J., Dec. 27, 1929; s. Morris and Sadye (Katz) P.; m. Sally Levy, June 4, 1961; children: Alexander, David, Elizabeth. BA, NYU, 1951; LLB, Columbia U., 1954; LLD (hon.), Georgetown U., 1989. Bar: N.Y. 1956, D.C. 1973, U.S. Supreme Ct. 1972. Atty. Dept. Justice, Washington, 1956-57; assoc. Dewey, Ballantine, Bushby, Palmer & Wood, N.Y.C., 1957-63; prof. law NYU, 1963-70; dir. Bur. Consumer Protection, FTC, 1970-73; prof. law Georgetown U. Law Ctr., Washington, 1973-83, 89—, dean, exec. v.p. law ctr. affairs, 1983-89; commr. FTC, Washington, 1978-81, chmn., 1995—; of counsel Arnold & Porter, Washington, 1973-78, 81-95; guest scholar Brookings Instn., Washington, 1989-90; vis. prof. law Harvard Law Sch., 1975-76; faculty mem. Salzburg (Austria) Seminar in Am. Studies, 1975; chmn. Def. Sci. Bd. task force on antitrust aspects of def. industry downsizing, 1994. Co-author: Cases on Antitrust Law, 1967, Cases on Trade Regulation, 3d edit., 1990; co-editor: Revitalizing Antitrust in Its Second Century, 1991; contbr. articles on consumer protection and antitrust to profl. publs. Served with U.S. Army, 1954-56. Recipient Disting. Service award FTC, 1972; named One of Ten Outstanding Mid-Career Law Profs. Time Mag., 1977. Mem. ABA (coun. antitrust sect. 1986-89), Am. Law Inst., Assn. Am. Law Schs., Columbia U. Ctr. for Law Econ. Studies (adv. bd. 1975-95). Democrat. Jewish. Home: 3809 Blackthorn St Bethesda MD 20815-4905

PITONIAK, GREGORY EDWARD, state representative; b. Detroit, Mich., Aug. 12, 1954; s. Anthony Edward and Constance Elizabeth (Matuszak) P.; m. Denise Ruth Kadi, Apr. 21, 1979; children: Gregory, Mallory. BA, U. Mich., 1976; Masters, U. N.C., 1980. Adminstrv. asst. Taylor (Mich.) Neighborhood Devel. Com., 1977-78; pers. analyst Downriver Community Conf., Southgate, Mich., 1978-79; dir. client svcs. Econ. Devel. Corp. Wayne County, Dearborn, Mich., 1979-84; exec. dir. Econ. Devel. Corp. Wayne County, Livonia, Mich., 1984-88; dir. econ. dev. Downriver Community Conf., Southgate, Mich., 1988; state rep. Mich. Ho. Reps., Lansing, 1989—. Councilman Taylor City Coun., 1981-88, chmn., 1983-85, 87-88; pres. Mich. Young Dems., 1982-84; treas. 15th Congl. Dist. Dem. Orgn., Taylor, 1988-90. Named Outstanding Young Person, Taylor Jaycees, 1987, State Legislator of Yr., Mich. Credit Union League, 1993. Mem. Am. Econ. Devel. Coun. (cert. econ. developer 1984), Am. Soc. Pub. Adminstrn., Polish Am. Congress, Dem. Club Taylor, KC. Roman Catholic. Home: 9686 Rose St Taylor MI 48180-3046 Office: Mich Ho Rep PO Box 30014 Lansing MI 48909-7514

PITOT, HENRY CLEMENT, III, physician, educator; b. N.Y.C., May 12, 1930; s. Henry Clement and Bertha (Lowe) P.; m. Julie S. Schutten, July 29, 1954; children: Bertha, Anita, Jeanne, Catherine, Henry, Michelle, Lisa, Patrice. BS in Chemistry, Va. Mil. Inst., 1951; MD, Tulane U., 1955, PhD in Biochemistry, 1959, DSc (hon.), 1995. Instr. pathology Med. Sch. Tulane U., New Orleans, 1955-59; postdoctoral fellow McArdle Lab. U. Wis., Madison, 1959-60, mem. faculty Med. Sch., 1960—, prof. pathology and oncology, 1966—, chmn. dept. pathology, 1968-71, acting dean Med. Sch., 1971-73, dir. McArdle Lab., 1973-91. Recipient Borden undergrad. rsch. award, 1955, Lederle Faculty award, 1962, Career Devel. award Nat. Cancer Inst., NIH, 1965, Parke-Davis award in exptl. pathology, 1968, Noble Found. Rsch. award, 1984, Esther Langer award U. Chgo., 1984, Disting.

Svc. award Am. Cancer Soc., 1989, Hilldale award U. Wis., 1991, Founders award Chem. Industry Inst. Toxicology, 1993. Fellow AAAS, N.Y. Acad. Scis.; mem. Am. Soc. Cell Biology, Am. Assn. Cancer Rsch., Am. Soc. Biochemistry and Molecular Biology, Am. Chem. Soc., Am. Soc. Investigative Pathology (pres. 1976-77), Soc. Exptl. Biology and Medicine (pres. 1991-93), Soc. Surg. Oncology (Lucy J. Wortham award 1981), Am. Soc. Preventive Oncology, Soc. Toxicology, Soc. Toxicologic Pathologists, Japanese Cancer Soc. (hon.). Roman Catholic. Home: 314 Robin Pky Madison WI 53705-4931 Office: U Wis McArdle Lab Cancer Rsch 1400 University Ave Madison WI 53706-1526 *Where and who we are today is the result of those whom we have met and known and loved until now.*

PITRELLA, FRANCIS DONALD, human factors professional; b. Seneca Falls, N.Y., Jan. 23, 1934; s. Frank and Minnie Lee (Buchanan) P.; m. Narcissa Voluntad, July 1, 1956 (div. Apr. 1964); children: Paolo, Jason; m. Anke Elly Hofmeyer, Feb. 13, 1970. BA, Bklyn. Coll., 1960; Drs., Tilburg (Netherlands) U., 1981. Cert. human factors profl. Human factors analyst ITT Fed. Labs., Nutley, N.J., 1961-64; systems analysis engr. Grumman Aircraft engring. Corp., Bethpage, N.Y., 1964-65; human factors engr. Loral Electronics, Inc., Bronx, 1965; rsch. scientist Matrix Corp., Alexandria, Va., 1966; sr. scientist Dunlap and Assocs., Inc., Santa Monica, Calif., 1967-71; rsch. assoc. traffic safety rsch. group Psychology Dept., Uppsala (Sweden) Univ., 1972; human factors engr. Royal Inst. of Tech., Stockholm, Sweden, 1972; rsch. scientist Rsch. Inst. Human Engring. Forschungs Inst. Anthropotechnik, Wachtberg, Germany, 1972—. Contbr. articles to profl. jours. and books. With USN, 1951-55. Mem. Human Factors and Ergonomics Soc. (Europe chpt., founding mem., pres. 1991-93, past pres. 1994—). Democrat. Achievements include contributions to the ergonomic design of current military systems, design of a performance test to form matched experimental groups, design of the two-level, sequential judgment rating scale, and design of a cognitive rating model. Office: FGAN/FAT, Neuenahrer Strasse 20, 53343 Wachtberg Germany

PITSTICK, LESLIE JAMES, food products company executive; b. Jamestown, Ohio, Feb. 10, 1935; s. Harold B. and Helen L. (Gray) P.; m. Sharon N. Berg, Nov. 17, 1956; childern: Michele, John. BS in Indsl. Mgmt., Miami U., Oxford, Ohio, 1957; MBA in Bus., Xavier U., Cin., 1970. Systems analyst IBM, Cin., 1957-59; data processing mgr. U.S. Shoe Corp., Cin., 1959-68, Dayco Corp., Dayton, Ohio, 1968-82; owner, mgr. CDCI, Dayton, 1982-83; corp. indsl. systems planner NCR Corp., Dayton, 1983-84; v.p. adminstrn. IAMS Co., Dayton, 1984-85, v.p. mktg. and adminstrn., 1986-87, sr. v.p. ops., 1988-90, sr. v.p. internat., 1991—.

PITT, BERTRAM, cardiologist, educator, consultant; b. Kew Gardens, N.Y., Apr. 27, 1932; s. David and Shirley (Blum) P., m. Elaine Liberstein, Aug. 10, 1962; children—Geoffrey, Jessica, Jillian. BA, Cornell U., 1953; MD, U. Basel, Switzerland, 1959. Diplomate Am. Bd. Internal Medicine, Am. Bd. Cardiology. Intern Beth Israel Hosp., N.Y.C., 1959-60; resident Beth Israel Hosp., Boston, 1960-63; fellow in cardiology Johns Hopkins U., Balt., 1966-67; from instr. to prof. Johns Hopkins U., 1967-77; prof. medicine, dir. div. cardiology U. Mich., Ann Arbor, 1977-91, assoc. chmn. dept. medicine, 1991—. Author: Atlas of Cardiovascular Nuclear Medicine, 1977; editor: Cardiovascular Nuclear Medicine, 1974. Served to capt. U.S. Army, 1963-65. Mem. ACP, Am. Coll. Cardiology, Am. Soc. Clin. Investigation, Assn. Am. Physicians, Am. Physiol. Soc., Am. Heart Assn., Assn. Univ. Cardiologists, Am. Coll. Chest Physicians, Royal Soc. Mich. Home: 24 Ridgeway St Ann Arbor MI 48104-1739 Office: U Mich Divsn Cardiology 1500 E Medical Center Dr Ann Arbor MI 48109-0999

PITT, BRAD, actor; b. Okla., Dec. 18, 1963; s. Bill and Jane P. Appearences include: (TV series) Dallas, Another World, Growing Pains, The Image(HBO), Glory Days, Two-Fisted Tales; (TV movie) Too Young To Die?, 1989; (films)Cutting Glass, Happy Together, 1989, Across the Tracks, 1990, Contact, Thelma and Louise, 1991, The Favor, 1992, Johnny Suede, 1992, Cool World, 1992, A River Runs Through It, 1992, Kalifornia, 1993, True Romance, 1993, Interview with the Vampire, 1994, Legends of the Fall, 1994, 12 Monkeys, 1995 (Golden Globe award for best supporting actor in film 1996, Acad. award nominee for best supporting actor 1996). Office: Creative Artists Agy 9830 Wilshire Blvd Beverly Hills CA 90212-1804*

PITT, GEORGE, lawyer; b. Chgo., July 21, 1938; s. Cornelius George and Anastasia (Geocaris) P.; m. Barbara Lynn Goodrich, Dec. 21, 1963 (div. Apr. 1990); children: Elizabeth Nanette, Margaret Leigh; m. Pamela Ann Pittsford, May 19,1990. BA, Northwestern U., 1960, JD, 1963. Bar: Ill. 1963. Assoc. Chapman and Cutler, Chgo., 1963-67; ptnr. Borge and Pitt, and predecessor, 1968-87; ptnr. Katten Muchin & Zavis, Chgo., 1987—. Notes and Comments editor Northwestern U. Law Rev., 1962-63. Served to 1st lt. AUS, 1964. Fellow Am. Coll. of Bond Counsel; mem. Ill. State Bar Assn., The Monroe Club, Univ. Club Chgo., Michigan City Yacht Club, Ind. Soc. of Chgo., Eta Sigma Phi, Phi Delta Phi, Phi Gamma Delta. Home: 600 N McClurg Ct Chicago IL 60611-3044 Office: Katten Muchin & Zavis 525 W Monroe St Ste 1600 Chicago IL 60661-3693

PITT, HARVEY LLOYD, lawyer; b. Bklyn., Feb. 28, 1945; s. Morris Jacob and Sara (Sapir) P.; m. Saree Ruffin, Jan. 7, 1984; children: Robert Garrett, Sara Dillard; children from previous marriage: Emily Laura, Jonathan Bradley. BA, CUNY, 1965; JD with honors (Univ. scholar), St. John's U., N.Y.C., 1968. Bar: N.Y. 1969, U.S. Supreme Ct. 1972, D.C. 1979. With SEC, Washington, 1968-78; legal asst. to commr. SEC, 1969; editor Instl. Investor Study, 1970-71; spl. counsel Office Gen. Counsel, 1971-72, chief counsel div. market regulation, 1972-73, exec. asst. to chmn., 1973-75, gen. counsel, 1975-78; mng. ptnr. Fried, Frank, Harris, Shriver & Jacobson, Washington, 1978—; adj. prof. law George Washington U. Nat. Law Ctr., 1974-82, U. Pa. Law Sch., 1983-84, vis. practitioner, 1984, Georgetown U. Law Ctr., 1976-84; comml. arbitrator Am. Arbitration Assn. Contbr. articles to profl. jours. V.p. Glen Haven Civic Assn., Silver Spring, Md., 1972-73, pres., 1974. Recipient Learned Hand award Inst. for Human Rels., 1988. Mem. ABA (past chmn. subcom. SEC practice and enforcement, past co-chmn. subcom. state takeover laws), Fed. Bar Assn. (Outstanding Young Lawyer award 1975), Adminstrv. Conf. U.S., Am. Law Inst. (project advisor on restatement law on corp. governance 1981—), Eldwick Homes Assn. (sec. bd. dirs.), Delta Sigma Rho, Tau Kappa Alpha, Phi Delta Phi. Home: 2404 Wyoming Ave NW Washington DC 20008-1643 Office: Fried Frank Harris Shriver & Jacobson 1001 Pennsylvania Ave NW Washington DC 20004-2505 also: Fried Frank Harris Shriver 1 New York Plz New York NY 10004

PITT, JOSEPH CHARLES, philosophy educator; b. Hempstead, N.Y., Sept. 12, 1944; fs. Louis Antony and Miriam (Baumstein) P.; m. Donna Hanlon Smith, Feb. 25, 1946. AB in Philosophy, Coll. William and Mary, 1966; MA in Philosophy, U. We. Ont., London, Ont., Can., 1970; PhD, U. We. Ont., 1972. Instr. Va. Poly. Inst. and State U., Blacksburg, 1971-72; asst. prof. Va. Poly. Inst. and State U., 1972-78; vis. asst. prof. U. Pitts., 1974; assoc. prof. Va. Poly. Inst. and State U., 1978-83, prof. philosophy, 1983—; founding dir. Ctr. for Study of Sci. in Soc., Va. Poly. Inst. and State U., 1980-81, dir. humanities, sci. and tech. program, 1979-89, head dept. philosophy, 1992—. Author: Pictures, Images and Conceptual Change, 1981, Galileo, Human Knowledge and the Book of Nature, 1992; editor: New Perspectives on Galileo, 1978, Theories of Explanation, 1988; editor-in-chief Perspectives on Sci.; mem. bd. editors Philosophy and Tech., 1985-94, Behaviorism, 1985—, History of Philosophy Quar., 1990—, Sci. and Edn., 1992—; contbr. articles to profl. jours. U. Pitts. Ctr. for Philosophy of Sci. vis. sr. fellow, 1984. Mem. Philosophy of Sci. Assn., Soc. for Philosophy and Tech. (v.p., pres.-elect 1989-91, pres. 1991-93), History of Sci. Soc., Soc. for History of Tech., Am. Philos. Assn., Irish Wolfhound Club Am. (bd. dirs. 1987-95), Sigma Xi. Home: Gavagai Hollow Farm Newport VA 24128 Office: Va Poly Inst and State U Dept Philosophy Blacksburg VA 24061

PITT, ROBERT ERVIN, environmental engineer, educator; b. San Francisco, Apr. 25, 1948; s. Wallace and Marjorie (Peterson) P.; m. Kathryn Jay, Mar. 18, 1967; children: Gwendolyn, Brady. BS in Engring. Sci., Humboldt State U., 1970; MSCE, San Jose State U., 1971; PhD in Civil and Environ. Engring., U. Wis., 1987. Registered profl. engr., Wis.; diplomate Am. Acad. Environ. Engrs. Environ. engr. URS Rsch. Co., San Mateo, Calif., 1971-74; sr. engr. Woodward-Clyde Cons., San Francisco, 1974-79; cons. environ. engr. Blue Mounds, Wis., 1979-84; environ. engr. Wis. Dept. Natural Resources, Madison, 1984-87; assoc. prof. depts. civil and environ. engring. and environ. health scis. U. Ala., Birmingham, 1987—; mem. Resource Conservation and Devel. Coun., Jefferson County, Ala., 1992-94; mem. com. on augmenting natural recharge of groundwater with reclaimed wastewater NRC, 1991-94; Ala. state dir. for energy and environment U.S. DOE EPSCOR, 1992-94; guest lectr. U. Gesamthochschule, Essen, Germany, 1994. Author: Small Storm Urban Flow and Particulate Washoff Contributions to Outfall Discharges, 1987, Stormwater Quality Management, 1996, Groundwater Contamination from Stormwater Infiltration, 1996; co-author: Manual for Evaluating Stormwater Runoff Effects in Receiving Waters, 1995; author software in field. Asst. scoutmaster Boy Scouts Am., Birmingham, 1988-94. Recipient 1st Pl. Nat. award U.S. Soil Conservation Svc. Earth Team, 1989, 94, award of recognition USDA, 1990, 1st Pl. Vol. award Take Pride in Am., 1991; Fed. Water Pollution Control Adminstrn. fellow, 1970-71, GE Engring. Edn. fellow, 1984-86. Mem. ASCE, Soc. for Environ. Toxicology and Chemistry, N.Am. Lake Mgmt. Soc. (Profl. Speakers award 1992), Water Environ. Fedn. (1st Pl. Nat. award 1992), Am. Water Resources Assn., Ala. Acad. Sci., Sigma Xi. Achievements include development of small storm urban hydrology prediction methods, toxicant control devices for stormwater source flows, methods to identify and correct inappropriate discharges to storm drain systems. Office: U Ala Birmingham Dept Civil/Environ Engring 1150 10th Ave S Birmingham AL 35294-4461

PITTARD, WILLIAM BLACKBURN (BILLY PITTARD), television graphic designer; b. Murfreesboro, Tenn., May 8, 1954; s. Samuel G. and Annette (Batey) P.; m. Linda C. Rheinstein; 1 child, Colby. BS, Middle Tenn. State U., 1978. Art dir. Sta. WKRN-TV, Nashville, 1978-84; design mgr. Sta. KCBS-TV, Los Angeles, 1984-86; pres. Pittard Design, Hollywood, Calif., 1986—. Mem. Broadcast Designer's Assn. (bd. dirs. 1984—, Outstanding Service award, 1986), Nat. Acad. TV Arts and Scis. Office: Pittard Design Inc 6430 W Sunset Blvd Ste 200 Los Angeles CA 90028-7905*

PITTAWAY, DAVID BRUCE, investment banker, lawyer; b. Kansas City, Mo., Oct. 4, 1951; s. Alan Ralph and Joanne (Kenney) P. BA with highest distinction, U. Kans., 1972; JD, Harvard U., 1975, MBA with high distinction, 1982. Bar: Md., D.C., Pa. Assoc. Morgan, Lewis and Bockius, Washington, 1975-80; cons. Bain and Co., Boston, 1982-85; v.p. strategic planning, asst. to pres. Donaldson, Lufkin and Jenrette, N.Y.C., 1985-86; mng. dir. Castle Harlan, Inc., N.Y.C., 1986—; adj. prof. Columbia U., N.Y.C., 1986—; CFO Branford Chain, Inc., N.Y.C., 1987—, bd. dirs., Morton's Restaurant Group, Inc., New Hyde Park, N.Y., McCormich & Schmick Holdings, Inc., Portland, Oreg. Summerfield scholar, 1972, Baker scholar, 1982. Mem. Harvard Club N.Y., Harvard Club Boston, Phi Beta Kappa. Office: Castle Harlan Inc 150 E 58th St New York NY 10155-0001

PITTELKO, ROGER DEAN, clergyman; b. Elk Reno, Okla., Aug. 18, 1932; s. Elmer Henry and Lydia Caroline (Nieman) P.; A.A., Concordia Coll., 1952; B.A., Concordia Sem., St. Louis, 1954, M.Div., 1957, S.T.M., 1958; postgrad. Chgo. Luth. Theol. Sem., 1959-61; Th.D., Am. Div. Sch., Pineland, Fla., 1968; D.Min., Faith Evang. Luth. Sem., Tacoma, 1983; m. Beverly A. Moellendorf, July 6, 1957; children—Dean, Susan. Ordained to ministry, Lutheran Ch.-Mo. Synod, 1958; vicar St. John Luth. Ch., S.I., N.Y., 1955-56; asst. pastor St. John Luth. Ch., New Orleans, 1958-59; pastor Concordia Luth. Ch., Berwyn, Ill., 1959-63; pastor Luth. Ch. of the Holy Spirit, Elk Grove Village, Ill., 1963-87; chmn. Commn. on Worship, Luth. Ch.-Mo. Synod; asst. bishop Midwest region English dist., 1983; pres. and bishop English dist., 1987—. Mem. Luth. Acad. for Scholarship, Concordia Hist. Inst. Republican. Clubs: Maywood (Ill.) Sportsman; Itasca (Ill.) Country. Author: Guide to Introducing Lutheran Worship. Contbr. articles to jours. Home: 19405 Stamford Dr Livonia MI 48152-1240 Office: 23001 Grand River Ave Detroit MI 48219-3130

PITTELKOW, MARK ROBERT, physician, dermatology educator, researcher; b. Milw., Dec. 16, 1952; s. Robert Bernard and Barbara Jean (Thomas) P.; m. Gail L. Gamble, Nov. 26, 1977; children: Thomas, Cameron, Robert. BA, Northwestern U., 1975; MD, Mayo Med. Sch., 1979. Intern then resident Mayo Grad. Sch., 1979-84, post-doctoral exptl. pathology, 1981-83; from asst. to assoc. prof. dermatology Mayo Med. Sch., Rochester, Minn., 1984-95, prof. dermatology, 1995—, assoc. prof. biochemistry and molecular biology, 1992—; cons. Mayo Clinic/Found., Rochester, 1984—. Fellow Am. Acad. Dermatology; mem. AAAS, Am. Dermatol. Assn., Soc. Investigative Dermatology, Am. Burn Assn., Am. Soc. Cell Biology, N.Y. Acad. Scis., Chi Psi. Home: 721 12th Ave SW Rochester MN 55902-2027 Office: Mayo Clinic 200 1st St SW Rochester MN 55905-0001

PITTI, DONALD ROBERT, financial planner, consultant; b. N.Y.C., Sept. 15, 1929; s. August and Mary (Vitaglione) P.; m. Grace Allen Curtis, Aug. 14, 1954; children: Gail, Robert. BA, NYU, 1959; postgrad., Adelphi U., 1963-65. Asst. v.p. Standard & Poor's Corp., N.Y.C., 1959-65; v.p. Quotron, Inc., N.Y.C., 1965-67; pres. Wiesenberger & Co., N.Y.C., 1967-76; v.p. John Nuveen & Co., Inc., N.Y.C., 1976-87; pres. Monarch Resources, Inc., N.Y.C., 1987-88; chmn., chief exec. officer Monarch Fin. Svcs., Inc., N.Y.C., 1988-89; pres., chief exec. officer Seligman Fin. Svcs. Inc., N.Y.C., 1989-95; pres. Graydon Consulting Corp., Manhasset, N.Y., 1996—; chmn. Found. Fin. Planning, Atlanta, 1986—. Editor: Handbook of Financial Planning, 1988; contbr. articles to profl. publs. With USN, 1948-49, 50-52. Mem. Internat. Assn. Fin. Planning (pres.), Union League, Manhasset Bay Yacht Club, Met. Opera Club. Avocations: gardening, reading, swimming. Home: 169 Kensett Rd Manhasset NY 11030-2140

PITTMAN, CONSTANCE SHEN, physician, educator; b. Nanking, China, Jan. 2, 1929; came to U.S., 1946; d. Leo F.-Z. and Pao Kong (Yang) Shen; m. James Allen Pittman, Jr., Feb. 19, 1955; children: James Clinton, John Merrill. AB in Chemistry, Wellesley Coll., 1951; MD, Harvard U., 1955. Diplomate Am. Bd. Internal Medicine, sub-bd. Endocrinology. Intern Baltimore City Hosp., 1955-56; resident U. Ala., Birmingham, 1956-57; instr. in medicine U. Ala. Med. Ctr., Birmingham, 1956-59, fellow dept. pharmacology, 1957-59, from asst. prof. to assoc. prof., 1959-70, prof., 1970—; prof. medicine Georgetown U., Washington, 1972-73; mem. diabetes and metabolism tng. com. NIH, Bethesda, Md., 1972-76, mem. nat. arthritis, metabolism and digestive disease coun., 1975-78, mem. gen. clin. rsch. ctrs. com., 1979-83, 87-90; dir. internat. coun. for the control of iodine deficiency diseases, 1994—. Fellow ACP (master); mem. Assn. Am. Physicians, Am. Soc. for Clin. Investigation, Endocrine Soc. (coun., 1978-79, pres. women's caucus 1978-79), Am. Thyroid Assn. (pres. 1990-91). Achievements include research in activation and metabolism of thyroid hormone; kinetics of thyroxine conversion to triiodothyrine in healthy and disease states; control of iodine deficiency disorders. Office: U Ala Div Endocrinology/Metab Univ Sta Birmingham AL 35294-0012

PITTMAN, DAVID JOSHUA, sociologist, educator, researcher, consultant; b. Rocky Mount, N.C., Sept. 18, 1927; s. Jay Washington and Laura Frances (Edwards) P. BA, U. N.C., 1949, MA, 1950; postgrad., Columbia U., 1953; PhD, U. Chgo., 1956. Asst. prof. sociology Washington U., St. Louis, 1958-60, assoc. prof., 1960-64, prof., 1964-91, prof. sociology in psychology, 1991-92, prof. psychology, 1992-93, prof. emeritus, 1993—, chmn. dept. sociology, 1976-86, dir. Social Sci. Inst., 1963-76; cons. Jellinek Clinic, Amsterdam, The Netherlands, 1965-68, HEW, Washington, 1977-85, Wine Inst., 1985-94; mem. sci. adv. com. Distilled Spirits Coun., Washington, 1976-86; field editor social scis. Jour. Study Alcoholism, 1985-92, mem. editorial bd., 1992—; Dent Meml. lectr. U. London, 1989. Author: Revolving Door: A Study of Chronic Police Case Inebriates, 1958, The Drug Scene in Great Britain, 1967, Primary Prevention of Alcoholism, 1980; editor: Society, Culture and Drinking Patterns, 1962, Alcoholism, 1967, Society, Culture and Drinking Patterns Reexamined, 1991; mem. editl. bd. Internat. Jour. Advt., 1990—. Bd. dirs. Nat. Gay and Lesbian Task Force, 1993—; pres. N.Am. Assn. Alcoholism Programs, 1965-67; chmn. 28th Internat. Congress on Alcohol and Alcoholism, Washington, 1968, Mo. Adv. Coun. on Alcoholism and Drug Abuse, Jefferson City, 1972-75, 87-91; mem. Mo. Mental Health Commn., Jefferson City, 1975-78. Recipient Page One Civic award St. Louis Newspaper Guild, 1967, Bronze Key St. Louis Coun. on Alcoholism, 1976, Silver Key Nat. Coun. on Alcoholism, N.Y.C., 1978, Biennal Rsch. award Soc. of the Med. Friends of Wine, 1992; spl. fellow NIMH, 1966. Fellow Am. Sociol. Soc.; mem. Soc. Study Social Problems (chmn. alcoholism com. 1957-59, Disting. Sr. Scholar award 1993), Internat. Coun. on Alcohol and Addictions (exec. com. 1968-84), Am. Sociol. Assn. (chmn. alcohol and drugs sect. 1992), Phi Beta Kappa, Sigma Xi, Omicron Delta Kappa. Episcopalian. Avocations: collecting elephant replicas, collecting political memorabilia. Office: Washington U Psychol Dept Box 1125 One Brookings Dr Saint Louis MO 63130

PITTMAN, JAMES ALLEN, JR., physician, educator; b. Orlando, Fla., Apr. 12, 1927; s. James Allen and Jean C. (Garretson) P.; m. Constance Ming-Chung Shen, Feb. 19, 1955; children—James Clinton, John Merrill. BS, Davidson Coll., 1948; MD, Harvard, 1952; DSc (hon.), Davidson Coll., 1980, U. Ala., Birmingham, 1984. Intern, asst. resident medicine Mass. Gen. Hosp., Boston, 1952-54; tchg. fellow medicine Harvard U., 1953-54; clin. assoc. NIH, Bethesda, Md., 1954-56; instr. medicine George Washington U., 1955-56; chief resident U. Ala. Med. Ctr., Birmingham, 1956-58, instr. medicine, 1956-59, asst. prof., 1959-62, assoc. prof., 1962-64, prof. medicine, 1964—, dir. endocrinology and metabolism div., 1962-71, co-chmn. dept. medicine, 1969-71, also prof., physiology and biophysics, 1967-92; dean U. Ala. Med. Ctr. (Sch. Medicine), 1973-92; asst. chief med. dir. rsch. and edn. in medicine U.S. VA, 1971-73; prof. medicine Georgetown U. Med. Sch., Washington, 1971-73; mem. endocrinology study sect. NIH, 1963-67; mem. pharmacology and endocrinology fellowships rev. coms., 1967-68; mem. grad. med. edn. nat. adv. com. HEW; mem. HHS coun. on Grad. Med. Edn., 1986-90; mem. nat. adv. rsch. resources coun. NIH, 1991-95; hon. prof. Chung Shan Med. and Dental Coll., Taiwan, 1995; sr. advisor Internat. Coun. on Control of Iodine Deficiency Diseases, 1994-95. Author: Diagnosis and Treatment of Thyroid Diseases, 1963; Contbr. articles in field to profl. jours. Master ACP; fellow Am. Coll. Endocrinology; mem. Assn. Am. Physicians, Endocrine Soc., Am. Assn. Clin. Endocrinologists, Am. Thyroid Assn., N.Y. Acad. Scis. (life), Soc. Nuclear Medicine, Am. Diabetes Assn., Am. Chem. Soc., Wilson Ornithol. Club (life), Am. Ornithologists Union (life), Am. Fedn. Clin. Rsch. (pres. So. sect., nat. coun. 1952-66), So. Soc. Clin. Investigation (Founder's medal 1993), Harvard U. Med. Alumni Assn. (pres. 1986-88), Phi Beta Kappa, Alpha Omega Alpha, Omicron Delta Kappa. Office: U Ala Sch of Med CAMS 75 SDB Birmingham AL 35294-0007 *I hope that each person I meet leaves the encounter better for it.*

PITTMAN, ROBERT TURNER, retired newspaper editor; b. Gates, N.C., Sept. 24, 1929; s. Thomas Everett and Lillian (Turner) P.; m. Ruth Fike, Aug. 25, 1956; children—Laura Emily, Mary Ann, Lillian Elizabeth. B.A., Washington and Lee U., 1951; M.A., U. N.C., 1957. Reporter Times Dispatch, Richmond, Va., 1951; editor, pub. Daily Ranger, Glendive, Mont., 1957-58; writer editorials Times Union, Jacksonville, Fla., 1958-63; editorial editor Times, St. Petersburg, Fla., 1963-92; dir. Times Pub. Co., 1968-92; trustee Poynter Inst. Media Studies, St. Petersburg, 1978-92. Editor: (jour.) Masthead, 1980, 81. Active St. Petersburg Charter Revision Com., 1992-93; dir. Fla. Bar Found., 1994-96; Lt. (j.g.) USNR, 1951-55. Recipient Pinellas Civil Liberties award, 1993; U. N.C.-Chapel Hill scholarship established in honor, 1994. Mem. Am. Soc. Newspaper Editors, Nat. Conf. Editorial Writers (pres. 1978, life), Nat. Conf. Editorial Writers Found. Inc. (pres. 1984). Methodist. Home: 736 18th Ave NE Saint Petersburg FL 33704-4608

PITTMAN, STEUART LANSING, lawyer; b. Albany, N.Y., June 6, 1919; s. Ernest Wetmore and Estelle Young (Romeyn) P.; children by previous marriage—Andrew Pinchot, Nancy Steuart, Rosamond Pinchot, Tamara Pickering; m. Barbara Milburn White, Mar. 29, 1958; children—Patricia Milburn, Steuart Lansing, Anne Romeyn. Grad., St. Paul's Sch., Concord, N.H., 1937; B.A., Yale U., 1941, LL.B., 1948. Bar: N.Y. 1948, D.C. 1954. With Pan Am. Airways Africa Ltd., Cairo, 1941-42, China Nat. Aviation Co., Calcutta, India, 1942; with firm Cravath, Swaine & Moore, N.Y.C., 1948-50; with govt. agys. ECA, Mut. Security Agy. and FOA, 1950-54; founder Shaw, Pittman, Potts & Trowbridge (and predecessors), Washington, 1954-61, 64—; asst. sec. of def., 1961-64; cons. 2d Hoover Commn., 1954-55, Dept. State, 1955, Devel. Loan Fund, 1958-59; sr. fellow Inst. Def. Analysis. Bd. dirs. Hudson Inst., Chesapeake Environ. Protection Assn.; mem. Atlantic Coun. 1st lt. USMCR, WWII, CBI. Decorated Silver Star. Mem. Met. Club (Washington). Office: Shaw Pittman Potts & Trowbridge 2300 N St NW Washington DC 20037-1122

PITTMAN, VIRGIL, federal judge; b. Enterprise, Ala., Mar. 28, 1916; s. Walter Oscar and Annie Lee (Logan) P.; m. Floy Lasseter, 1944; children—Karen Pittman Gordy, Walter Lee. B.S., U. Ala., 1939, LL.B., 1940. Bar: Ala. bar 1940. Spl. agt. FBI, 1940-44; practice law Gadsden, Ala., 1946-51; judge Ala. Circuit Ct., Circuit 16, 1951-66; U.S. dist. judge Middle and So. Dist. Ala., 1966-71; chief judge U.S. Dist. Ct. for Ala. So. Dist., 1971-81, sr. judge, 1981—; periodically sits as judge U.S. Ct. Appeals 11th Cir., 1981—; lectr. bus. law, econs. and polit. sci. U. Ala. Center, Gadsden, 1948-66. Author: Circuit Court Proceedings in Acquisition of a Tract of Right of Way, 1959, A Judge Looks at Right of Way Condemnation Proceedings, 1960, Technical Pitfalls in Right of Way Proceedings, 1961. Mem. Ala. Bd. Edn., 1951; trustee Samford U., 1974-90, 92—. Lt. (j.g.) USN, 1944-46. Mem. Ala. State Bar, Etowah County Bar Assn. (pres. 1949), Omicron Delta Kappa. Democrat. Baptist. Office: US Dist Ct PO Box 465 Mobile AL 36601-0465

PITTMAN, WILLIAM CLAUDE, electrical engineer; b. Pontotoc, Miss., Apr. 22, 1921; s. William Claude and Maude Ella (Bennett) P.; m. Eloise Savage, Apr. 20, 1952; children: Patricia A. Pittman Ready, William Claude III, Thomas Allen. BSEE, Miss. State Coll., 1951, MSEE, 1957. From electronic engr. to supr. elec. engring. dept. U.S. Army Labs., Redstone Arsenal, Ala., 1951-59; supr. electronic engr. to aero. engring. supr. NASA/Marshall Space Flight Ctr., 1960; electronic engr. Army Missile Labs., 1962-82; program mgr. Army Labs. and R&D Ctr., Redstone Arsenal, 1982—; organizer numerous sci. and tech. confs. Author patents, reports, papers. Sgt. USMC, 1940-46, PTO. Recipient Medal of Honor, DAR, Meritorious Civilian Svc. award Dept. Army, 1993. Fellow AIAA (assoc.; chmn. Miss.-Ala. chpt. 1981-82, Martin Schilling award 1980); mem. IEEE (sr.), NSPE, First Marine Div. Assn., DAV, IRE (chmn. Huntsville sect. 1957-58), Madison Hist. Soc., SAR (pres. Tenn. Valley chpt. 1984-85, Ala. Soc. 1990-91, Cert. 1991, Patriot medal), Tau Beta Pi, Phi Kappa Phi, Kappa Mu Epsilon. Avocations: history, genealogy. Home: 704 Desoto Rd SE Huntsville AL 35801-2032 Office: US Army Missile Command Huntsville AL 35809

PITTS, BARBARA TOWLE, accountant; b. St. Paul, Minn., Nov. 8, 1944; d. James Francis and Helen (Gorman) Towle; m. E.R. Pitts, Oct. 19, 1965; 1 child, Paris Tucker Pitts. BSBA, U. Ala., 1980. CPA, Wash., Tenn. Prin. Barbara M. Pitts Assocs., Fayetteville, Tenn., 1982-90, Barbara M. Pitts CPA, Seattle, 1990—. Bd. dirs. United Way Lincoln County, Fayetteville, 1989, Lincoln County Bd. Edn., Fayetteville, 1988-90; mem. planning com. Tenn. Hist. Soc., Nashville, 1989. Recipient Cert. of Recognition Tenn. Main St. Program, 1989; named Woman of Yr. Fayetteville Bus. and Profl. Women, 1988. Mem. AICPA, Wash. Soc. CPA, N.W. Watercolor Soc. (treas.), Group Health Coop. Puget Sound (ctrl. regional coun.). Home: 3515 E Marion St Seattle WA 98122-5258

PITTS, BILL, museum director; b. Castleton, Kans., Jan. 7, 1934. BA, Northwestern State Coll., Alva, Okla., 1957; postgrad., Northwestern State Coll., We. Wash. Coll. Edn., Portland (Oreg.) State Coll. Curator Northwestrn State Coll. Mus., Alva, Okla., 1964-74; dir., curator Santa Fe Trail Ctr., Larned, Kans., 1974-83; dir. State Mus. of Okla. Hist. Soc., Oklahoma City, 1983—; adj. instr. Emporia (Kans.) State U., 1978-83; grant evaluator Inst. Mus. Services, 1980—. Mem. coordinating com. Promotion of Kans. History, 1979-83; mem. council Kans. Com. for Humanities, 1980-83; panel mem. Okla. Arts and Humanities Council, 1966-73; mem. Okla. Hist. Soc. Mem. Am. Assn. Mus. (past Okla. rep.), Am. Assn. State and Local History, Mountain-Plains Mus. Conf., Okla. Mus. Assn. (regional rep. 1984-85, past pres.), Kans. Mus. Assn. (past pres.), Santa Fe Trail Assn. (pres. 1991-95), Westerners Internat., Toastmasters Internat. Home: 2600 NW 16th St Oklahoma City OK 73107-3004 Office: Okla Hist Soc Hist Bldg 2100 N Lincoln Blvd Oklahoma City OK 73105-4915

PITTS, JAMES ATWATER, financial executive; b. Greenwich, Conn., Apr. 8, 1940; s. Jeremiah Patrick and Mary Louise (McGregor) P.; m. Noreen Mary Kiggins, July 20, 1963; children: Paul, Andrew, Sarah. BBA with honors, Niagara U., 1962; MBA, U. Conn., 1971. CPA, N.Y. Staff acct. Price Waterhouse, Stamford, Conn., 1962; tax specialist Deloitte Haskins &

Sells, Rochester, N.Y., 1965-68; div. contr. Xerox Corp., Stamford, 1968-76; asst. corp. contr. Digital Equipment Corp., Maynard, Mass., 1976-81; v.p., corp. contr. Data Gen. Corp., Westboro, Mass., 1981-86; exec. v.p. fin. adminstrn. and strategic planning Cullinet Software, Inc., Westwood, 1986-88; v.p., chief fin. officer Bain & Co. Inc., Boston, 1988-91; sr. v.p. fin. and adminstrn., treas., CFO Clean Harbors Inc., 1992-96; pres. The Pitts Group, Boston, 1996—. Chmn. Sudbury (Mass.) Town Fin. Com., 1984; v.p., mem. exec. com. Children's Mus. Boston, 1984-96; bd. dirs. Mus. Wharf Inc., 1988-96, Lake Winniepesaukee Assn., Wolfeboro, N.H.; chmn. Sudbury Long Range Capital Expenditures Com., 1981; trustee Lake Regional Conservation Trust, Meridith, N.H. With U.S. Army, 1963-64, USAR, 1965-90, Desert Storm, 1991. Decorated Meritorious Svc. medal, 1991; recipient Internat. Exec. Mgmt. award Internat. Mgmt. Inst. U. Geneva, 1980. Mem. AICPAs, Conn. CPA Soc., N.Y. Soc. CPAs, Fin. Execs. Inst., Harvard Bus. Sch. Assn. Boston (bd. govs. 1992, pres.), Res. Officers Assn. (life), Soc. Mil. Compts., Algonquin Club, Bald Peak Colony Club, Officers Club. Home and Office: 282 Beacon St Boston MA 02116-1152

PITTS, JOE W., III (CHIP PITTS), lawyer, law educator; b. Baton Rouge, Nov. 24, 1960; s. Joe Wise Pitts Jr. and Bobbie (Chachere) Edwards. Cert., Cambridge (Eng.) U., 1980; spl. diploma, Oxford (Eng.) U., 1981; BA, Tulane U., 1982; JD, Stanford U., 1985. Bar: Tex. 1986. Assoc. Legal Resources Ctr., Johannesburg, Republic South Africa, 1984, Carrington Coleman Sloman & Blumenthal, Dallas, 1985-88; vis. asst. prof. law So. Meth. U., Dallas, 1988-89; ptnr. Baker and McKenzie, Dallas, 1989-96; v.p. transactions, gen. counsel Nokia Telecomm. Inc., Helsinki, 1996—; del. UN Commn. on Human Rights, Geneva, 1989, 92-96; U.S. del. to internat. conf. on European security NATO, Rome, 1990. Author numerous articles in field. Bd. dirs. Shakespeare Festival Dallas, 1987-94, pres., 1990-91, chmn., 1991-93; bd. dirs. Proyecto Adelante, 1988—; bd. dirs. Dallas Dem. Forum, 1989-93, sec., 1991-92; chmn. pub. awareness effort Dallas Young Lawyers Constl. Bicentennial Program, 1985-87, bd. dirs., 1987-91; vol. Cath. Charities Dallas, 1987—, North Ctrl. Tex. Legal Svcs., 1985—. Recipient cert. of appreciation Lawyers Against Domestic Violence, Dallas, 1985-87, cert. of recognition North Cen. Tex. Legal Svcs., 1985-87. Fellow Tex. Bar Found.; mem. ABA (vice chmn. sect. of bus. law, young lawyers div. 1986-88, exec. com., internat. law com. 1990—, vice-chair 1991-92, chair 1993—, editor-in-chief law practice notes Barrister Mag. 1988-91, commn. on pub. understanding about law 1989-91), Dallas Bar Assn. (Disting. Pro Bono Svc. award, 1986, 87, 88, 91, coord. immigration amnesty appeals com. 1987-88, chair, minority participation com. 1988-89, Pro Bono Vol. of Yr. 1989, spl. recognition 1990, 92), Tex. Assn. Young Lawyers (internat. law, editorial coms. 1985-91, chair refugee com. 1988-90, co-chmn. internat. law com. 1991-93), Dallas Assn. Young Lawyers (co-chair internat. law com. 1990-92, chair membership com. 1987-88, chair bill of rights com. 1988-89, treas. 1989, v.p. 1989-90), Tex. Accts. and Lawyers for Arts, Dallas Com. Fgn. Rels. (gen. counsel 1987—), Council on Fgn. Relations N.Y. (term mem.), Dallas Council on World Affairs, Dallas Assembly, Crescent Spa Club, Phi Beta Kappa, Pi Sigma Alpha, Omicron Delta Kappa. Democrat. Roman Catholic. Avocations: tennis, piano. Office: Nokia Telecomm Inc 7 Village Cir Ste 100 Westlake TX 76262

PITTS, LEONARD GARVEY, JR., columnist, writer; b. Orange, Calif., Oct. 11, 1957; s. Leonard Garvey and Agnes (Rowan) P.; m. Marilyn Vernice Pickens, June 27, 1981; children: Markise Pickens, Monique Pickens; (stepchildren) Marlon, Leonard, Onjél. BA English, U. So. Calif., 1977. Editor, writer Soul Mag., L.A., 1976-80; writer KFWB Radio, L.A., 1980-83; editor Radioscope, L.A., 1983-86; writer Westwood One Inc., Culver City, Calif., 1989-91; columnist, writer Miami (Fla.) Herald, 1991—. Writer, co-producer (broadcast) King: From Atlanta to the Mountaintop, 1986 (CEBA award 1987), (documentary) Young Black Men: A Lost Generation?, 1990 (Armstrong award 1991); writer, producer (documentary) Who We Are, 1988 (CEBA award 1989). Recipient Internat. Radio Festival award, 1991, Nat. Headliner award Arts criticism, 1991. Mem. Fla. Soc. Newspaper Editors (award arts criticism), Nat. Headliners, Am. Assn. Sunday and Feature Editors (award arts criticism 1991), Nat. Assn. of Black Journalists (Award of Excellence in commentary 1994, 95). Democrat. Baptist. Avocations: computer strategy games, reading. Office: Miami Herald One Herald Plaza Miami FL 33132

PITTS, ROBERT EUGENE, JR., marketing educator, consultant; b. Griffin, Ga., Feb. 12, 1948; s. Robert Eugene and Oree Francis (Brown) P.; m. Cheryl Ann Belew, May 31, 1968. BBA, Ga. State U., 1970, M in Bus. Info. Systems, 1972; PhD, U. S.C., 1977. Account sect. leader Gen. Electric Corp., Atlanta, 1970-72; instr. mktg. Jacksonville (Ala.) State U., 1972-74; assoc. dir. consumer panel U. S.C., Columbia, 1974-77; asst. prof. mktg. U. Notre Dame, South Bend, Ind., 1977-82; assoc. prof. mktg. U. Miss., Oxford, 1982-83, dir. bur. bus. and econ. research, 1983-85; prof., chmn. dept. mktg. DePaul U., Chgo., 1985—, dir. Kellstadt Ctr. Mktg. Analysis and Planning; cons. in mktg. strategy; expert legal witness in mktg. Author books on bank mktg.; contbr. articles on personal values in mktg. and pub. policy issues to profl. jours. Fellow Am. Mktg. Assn., Assn. Mktg. Sci.; mem. Decision Sci. Inst., So. Mktg. Assn. Avocations: running, akido. Office: DePaul U 243 S Wabash Ave Chicago IL 60604-2302

PITTS, ROBERT LYNN, automotive company executive; b. Los Angeles, Feb. 7, 1948; s. Leo Willard and Jane Ann (Rawson) P.; m. Helen Frances Donohoe, May 3, 1969; children: Brian M., Laura D. BBA, Calif. State U., Long Beach, 1970, MBA, 1973. Fin. mgr. Toyota Motor Sales, USA, Inc., Torrance, Calif., 1971-84; gen. mgr., now group v.p. fin. and adminstrn. Toyota Motor Credit Corp., Torrance, 1984—. Mem. Nat. Assn. Accts., Beta Gamma Sigma. Republican. Roman Catholic. Avocations: camping, skiing, motorcycling, windsurfing. Home: 4123 Quinlin Dr Palos Verdes Peninsula CA 90274-3945 Office: Toyota Motor Sales USA Inc 19001 S Western Ave Torrance CA 90501-1106*

PITTS, TERENCE RANDOLPH, curator, museum director; b. St. Louis, Feb. 5, 1950; s. Benjamin Randolph and Barbara Avalon (Gilliam) P.; m. Judith Ellen Brown, Oct. 21, 1979; children: Jacob Richard, Rebecca Suzanne. BA, U. Ill., 1972, MLS, 1974, MA in Art History U. Ariz., 1986. Registrar Ctr. for Creative Photography, Tucson, 1976-77, curator, 1978-88, dir., 1989—; cons. Art and Architecture Thesaurus, Getty Mus., 1984—. Author: (with others) George Fiske: Yosemite Photographer, 1981, Edward Weston: Color Photography; author: exhbn. catalogs: Four Spanish Photographers, 100 Years of Photography in the American West, Photography in the American Grain; contbr. reviews to mags. NEA fellow, 1983; travel grantee Nat. Mus. Act, 1979, rsch. grantee U. Ariz., 1983.

PITTS, THOMAS E., lawyer; b. Providence, R.I., May 21, 1947. BA magna cum laude, Yale U., 1969; JD magna cum laude, U. Pa., 1976. Bar: R.I. 1976, U.S. Dist. Ct. R.I., 1976, U.S. Ct. Appeals (1st cir.) 1978, N.Y. 1984, U.S. Dist. Ct. (so. dist.) N.Y. 1985. Ptnr. Sidley & Austin, N.Y.C. Contbr. articles to profl. jours. Mem. N.Y. County Lawyers Assn. (com. bankruptcy 1985—), R.I. Bar Assn. (debtor's and creditor's rights com. 1984—), Order of Coif, Phi Beta Kappa. Office: Sidley & Austin 875 3rd Ave New York NY 10022-6225*

PITTS, VIRGINIA M., human resources executive; b. Boston, Nov. 22, 1953; d. Harold Francis and Connie (Caico) Cummings; m. Daniel J. Pitts, Mar. 12, 1977. Student, Northeastern U., 1982-85, Lesley Coll. Adminstrv. asst. J. Baker Inc., Hyde Park, Mass., 1980-82, fin. adminstr., 1982-84, dir. human resources, 1984—, 1st sr. v.p., 1991—; trustee New Eng. Joint Bd. AFL-CIO, Quincy, Mass., 1984-89; guest lectr. Aquinas Jr. Coll.; mem. bd. dirs. Boston Crusaders, Drum & Bugle Corps. Instr. Boston Crusaders Drum and Bugle Corps, other marching bands, Mass., R.I., Maine, N.H., 1973-85; regional v.p. 210 Central Assn., Watertown, Mass., 1989-90; bd. dirs. Handi-Kids, Boston Crusaders Drum and Bugle Corps; guest lectr. Aquinas Jr. Coll., Milton, Mass. Mem. Am. Mgmt. Assn., Am. Compensation Assn. (cert. profl.), Soc. Human Resource Mgrs. Avocations: competitive horseback riding, gardening. Office: J Baker Inc 555 Turnpike St Canton MA 02021-2724

PITYNSKI, ANDRZEJ PIOTR, sculptor; b. Ulanow, Poland, Mar. 15, 1947; naturalized citizen, 1987; s. Aleksander and Stefania (Krupa) P.; m. Christina Teresa Gacek, Aug. 6, 1976; 1 child, Alexander Mark. MFA in Sculpture, Acad. Fine Arts, Cracow, Poland, 1974; postgrad., Art Students League, N.Y., 1975. Cert. tchr., N.J.; supr. modeling, mold, enlarging, resin crafts. Supr. and instr. sculpture Tech. Inst. of Sculpture - Johnson Atelier, Mercerville, N.J., 1979—; instr. sculpture Rider Coll., Trenton, N.J., 1992—; asst. to sculptor Alexander Ettl, Sculpture House, N.Y., 1975-79;. Bronze/granite monumental sculptures include Katyn-1940, Jersey City, N.J., 1991-92, Pope John Paul II, Manhattan, N.Y., 1991, Ulanow, Poland, 1989, General Anders, Doylestown, Pa., 1995, Father J. Popieluszko, Trenton, N.J., 1987, Avenger, Doylestown, Pa., 1987, Portrait Bust M Curie, 1986, Bayonne, N.J.; aluminum sculpture Partisans, Boston, 1983, Ignacy Paderewski, Cracow, Poland, 1973; exhbn. Mus. of Polish Army, Warsaw, 1995, Contemporary Artists Guild, Lever House, N.Y., 1991, Zacheta Nat. Art Gallery, Warsaw, 1991, Fedn. Internat. De La Medaille/Brit. Mus., London, 1992, Cast Iron Gallery, Soho, N.Y., 1992, Alt. Ext. Gallery, Phila., 1992, others. Recipient Polonia Restituta Cross, R.P. London, 1989, Gold Order of Merit, Rep. of Poland, 1990, Cultural award Am. Inst. Polish Culture, Washington, 1992. Fellow Nat. Sculpture Soc.; mem. Allied Artists of Am. (Silver medal of honor 1985, Elliot Liskin Meml. award 1989, Mems. and Assocs. award 1994), Audubon Artists, Contemporary Artists Guild, Am. Medallic Sculpture Assn. Republican. Roman Catholic. Avocations: horse jumping, hunting, judo. Office: Johnson Atelier Tech Inst Sculpture 60 Ward Ave Mercerville NJ 08619

PITZER, KENNETH SANBORN, chemist, educator; b. Pomona, Calif., Jan. 6, 1914; s. Russell K. and Flora (Sanborn) P.; m. Jean Mosher, July 1935; children—Ann, Russell, John. B.S., Calif. Inst. Tech., 1935; Ph.D., U. Calif., 1937; D.Sc., Wesleyan U., 1962; LL.D., U. Calif. at Berkeley, 1963, Mills Coll., 1969. Instr. chemistry U. Calif., 1937-39, asst. prof., 1939-42, asso. prof., 1942-45, prof., 1945-61, asst. dean letters and sci., 1947-48, dean coll. chemistry, 1951-60; pres., prof. chemistry Rice U., Houston, 1961-68, Stanford, Calif., 1968-70; prof. chemistry U. Calif. at Berkeley, 1971—; tech. dir. Md. Rsch. Lab. for OSRD, 1943-44; dir. research U.S. AEC, 1949-51, mem. gen. adv. com., 1958-65, chmn., 1960-62; Centenary lectr. Chem. Soc. Gt. Britain, 1978; mem. adv. bd. U.S. Naval Ordnance Test Sta., 1956-59, chmn., 1958-59; mem. commn. chem. thermo-dynamics Internat. Union Pure and Applied Chemistry, 1953-61; mem. Pres.'s Sci. Adv. Com., 1965-68; dir. Owens-Ill., Inc., 1967-86. Author: (with others) Selected Values of Properties of Hydrocarbons, 1947, Quantum Chemistry, 1953, (with L. Brewer) Thermodynamics, 2d edit., 1961, Activity Coefficients in Electrolyte Solutions, 2d ecit., 1992, Molecular Structure and Statistical Thermodynamics, 1993, Thermodynamics, 3d edit., 1995; editor: Prentice-Hall Chemistry series, 1955-61; contbr. articles to profl. jours. Trustee Pitzer Coll., 1966—; Mem. program com. for phys. scis. Sloan Found., 1955-60. Recipient Precision Sci. Co. award in petroleum chemistry, 1950, Clayton prize Instn. Mech. Engrs., London, 1958, Priestley medal Am. Chem. Soc., 1969, Nat. medal for sci., 1975, Robert A. Welch award, 1984, Clark Kerr award U. Calif., Berkeley, 1991; named to Outstanding Young Men, U.S. Jaycees, 1950; named to Hall of Fame of Alpha Chi Sigma, 1994; Guggenheim fellow, 1951. Fellow Am. Nuclear Soc., Am. Inst. Chemists (Gold Medal award 1976), Am. Acad. Arts and Scis., Am. Phys. Soc.; mem. AAAS, NAS (councilor 1964-67, 73-76), Am. Chem. Soc. (award pure chemistry 1943, Gilbert N. Lewis medal 1965, Williard Gibbs medal 1976), Faraday Soc., Geochem. Soc., Am. Philos. Soc., Chem. Soc. (London), Am. Coun. Edn., Chemists Club (hon.), Bohemian Club, Cosmos Club of Washington. Clubs: Chemists (hon.), Bohemian; Cosmos (Washington). Home: 12 Eagle Hl Kensington CA 94707-1408 Office: U Calif Dept Chemistry Berkeley CA 94720

PITZER, RUSSELL M., chemistry educator; b. Berkeley, Calif., May 10, 1938; s. Kenneth Sanborn and Jean Elizabeth (Mosher) P.; m. Martha Ann Seares, Sept. 3, 1959; children: Susan M., Kenneth R., David S. BS, Calif. Inst. Tech., 1959; AM, Harvard U., 1961, PhD, 1963. Instr. Calif. Inst. Tech., Pasadena, 1963-66, asst. prof., 1966-68, assoc. prof., 1968-79; prof. Ohio State U., Columbus, 1979—, chmn. dept. chemistry, 1989-94; acting assoc. dir. Ohio Superconducter Ctr., Columbus, 1986-87; cons. Lawrence Livermore (Calif.) Nat. Lab., 1981—; trustee Pitzer Coll., Claremont, Calif., 1988—. Contbr. articles to profl. jours. Mem. AAUP, Am. Chem. Soc., Am. Phys. Soc. Office: Ohio State U Dept Chemistry 120 W 18th Ave Columbus OH 43210

PIVEN, FRANCES FOX, political scientist, educator; b. Calgary, Alta., Can., Oct. 10, 1932; came to U.S., 1933, naturalized, 1953; d. Albert and Rachel (Paperny) F.; 1 dau., Sarah. B.A., U. Chgo., 1953, M.A., 1956, Ph.D., 1962; L.H.D. (hon.), Adelphi U., 1985. Mem. faculty Columbia, 1966-72; prof. polit. sci. Boston U., 1972-82, Grad. Ctr., CUNY, 1982—. Co-author: Regulating the Poor: The Functions of Public Welfare, 1971, 2d edit., 1993, The Politics of Turmoil: Essays on Poverty, Race and the Urban Crisis, 1974, Poor People's Movements, 1977, New Class War, 1982, The Mean Season, 1987, Why Americans Don't Vote, 1988; editor: Labor Parties in Post Industrial Societies, 1992. Recipient C. Wright Mills award Soc. Study Social Problems, 1971, Fulbright Disting. Lectureship award U. Bologna, 1990, President's award APHA, 1993, Annual award Nat. Assn. Sec. of State, 1994, Lifetime Achievement award Pol. Sociology Am. Sociological Assn., 1995; Guggenheim fellow, 1973-74; Am. Council Learned Socs. awardee, 1982. Mem. Am. Polit. Sci. Assn. (v.p. 1981-82), Soc. Study Social Problems (pres. 1980-81, Lee founders award 1992), ACLU (dir.). Home: PO Box N Millerton NY 12546 Office: 33 W 42nd St New York NY 10036-8003

PIVEN, PETER ANTHONY, architect, management consultant; b. Bklyn., Jan. 3, 1939; s. William Meyer and Sylvia Lee (Greenberg) P.; m. Caroline Cooper, July 9, 1961; children: Leslie Ann, Joshua Lawrence. A.B., Colgate U., 1960; M.Arch., U. Pa., 1963; M.S., Columbia U., 1964. Diplomate: cert. Nat. Council Archtl. Registration Bds.; registered architect, N.Y., Pa., N.J. Architect Westermann-Miller Assocs., N.Y.C., 1964-66, Bernard Rothzeid, A.I.A., N.Y.C., 1967-68; v.p. Caudill Rowlett Scott, N.Y.C., 1968-72; prin. Geddes Brecher Qualls Cunningham, Phila., 1972-87; pres. The Coxe Group, Inc., Phila., 1980-90, dir., prin. cons., 1980—; adj. prof. U. Pa. Grad. Sch. Fine Arts, 1989—, Rensselaer Poly. Inst. Sch. Architecture, 1994—. Author: Compensation Management: A Guideline for Small Firms, 1982; co-author: Success Strategies for Design Professionals, 1987; contbr. editor Archtl. Record and Design Intelligence; contbg. author: Architects Handbook of Professional Practice, 1994. Mem. N.Y.C. Community Planning Bd., 1969-72. Fellow AIA (chmn. fin. mgmt. com. 1976-80, pres. Phila. chpt. 1980); mem. Phila. C. of C. (dir. 1980-81), The Carpenters Co. of City and County of Phila. (mng. com. 1989-91). Home: 112 N Lambert St Philadelphia PA 19103-1107 Office: The Coxe Group Inc 1218 3rd Ave Seattle WA 98101-3021

PIVER, M. STEVEN, gynecologic oncologist; b. Washington, Sept. 29, 1934; s. Harry Samuel and Sonia (Bard) P.; m. Susan Myers, June 25, 1958; children: Debra Ellen, Carolyn Jan, Kenneth Stuart. BS, Gettysburg Coll., 1957; MD, Temple U., 1961. Diplomate Am. Bd. Ob-Gyn, Am. Coll. Surgeons. Intern Nazareth Hosp., Phila., 1961-62; resident Johns Hopkins U. Hosp., Balt., 1962; resident ob-gyn. Pa. Hosp., U. Pa., Phila., 1965-68; fellow gynecologic oncology U. Tex., Hosp. and Tumor Inst., Houston, 1968-70; asst. prof. gynecologic oncology U. N.C. Sch. Medicine, 1970-71; assoc. chief gynecologic oncology Roswell Park Cancer Inst., Buffalo, 1972-83, founder, dir. Gilda Radner Familial Ovarian Cancer Registry, 1981—, chief gynecologic oncology, 1984—; clin. prof., dir. div. gynecologic oncology SUNY, Buffalo, 1986—. Cons., editor Yearbook of Cancer, 1972-88; assoc. editor Nat. Cancer Inst., PDQ, 1984—; mem. editl. bd. The Female Patient, 1989—, Oncology Reports, 193—; author: Ovarian Malignancies: Clinical Care of Adults and Adolescents, 1983; editor: Ovarian Malignancies: Diagnostic and Therapeutic Advances, 1987, Manual of Gynecologic Oncology/Gynecology, 1989, Conversations About Cancer, Handbook of Gynecologic Oncology, 1995, Gilda's Disease: Sharing Personal Experiences and a Medical Perspective on Ovarian Cancer, 1996; contbr. 292 articles to profl. jours. Bd. dirs. United Way of Buffalo and Erie County, 1986-91; trustee D'Youville Coll., Buffalo, 1989—, chmn. bd. trustees. Hon. fellow Phi Beta Kappa, Gettysburg Coll., 1956, Tex. Assn. Obstetricians and Gynecologists, 1983, Alpha Omega Alpha, Temple U. Sch. Medicine, 1995; named Citizen of Yr., Buffalo News, 1989; recipient YMCA Leadership award Buffalo YMCA, 1990, Brotherhood/Sisterhood Award in Medicine (Western N.Y. Region), NCCJ, 1991, St. Marguerite D'Youville Coll. Community Svc. award, 1992. Fellow ACS, Am. Coll. Obstetricians and Gynecologists; mem. Am. Soc. Clin. Oncology, Soc. Gynecologic Oncologists, Soc. Surg. Oncology, Am. Radium Soc., Phi Beta Kappa, Alpha Omega Alpha. Achievements include documentation of hydroxyurea as a radiation sensitizer in cervix cancer that significantly improves cure rate and that ovarian cancer can be inherited. Home: 315 Lincoln Pky Buffalo NY 14216-3127 Office: Roswell Park Cancer Inst Elm And Carlton St Buffalo NY 14263-0001

PIVIK, ROBERT WILLIAM, accounting executive; b. Renton, Pa., Oct. 29, 1937; s. George and Amelia (Kern) P.; m. Yvonne C. Pivik, Aug. 6, 1960; children: Keith, Sharon, Tracey. BS, Pa. State U., 1959. CPA, D.C. Staff acct. Deloitte Haskins & Sells, Pitts., 1959-67; mgr. Deloitte Haskins & Sells, N.Y.C., 1967-72, ptnr., 1972, various positions, 1967-83; ptnr.-in-charge Deloitte Haskins & Sells, Washington, 1983-86; area mng. ptnr. Deloitte Haskins & Sells, Md., Va. and Washington, 1986-89; group mng. ptnr. Deloitte and Touche, Md., Va., Pa., Washington, 1989—; also bd. dirs. Deloitte Haskins & Sells; chief fin. officer Deloitte & Touche, 1993—; mem. Greater Washington bd. Trade, 1983, tax policy task force, 1985, chmn. mktg. com., 1989-90. Legacy com. Md. civ. Am. Cancer Soc., Silver Spring, 1984; adv. com. DeSales Sch. Theology, Washington, 1986; trustee Fed. City Coun., 1990—; adv. com. mayor of Washington, 1991, mem. subcom. Mgmt. System. & Tech. Mem. AICPA, Columbia Inst. CPAs, Washington-Balt. Regional Assn. (bd. dirs.), Econ. Club Washington, Tournament Players Club, Univ. Club, City Club, Beta Gamma Sigma, Phi Kappa Phi, Alpha Psi. Republican. Roman Catholic. Avocation: golf. Office: Deloitte and Touche 10 Westport Rd PO Box 820 Wilton CT 06897

PIVIROTTO, RICHARD ROY, former retail executive; b. Youngstown, Ohio, May 26, 1930; s. Arthur M. and Ruth (Erhardt) P.; m. Mary Burchfield, June 27, 1953; children: Mary B., Richard Roy, Susan W., Nancy P., David H., Jennifer P. A.B., Princeton U., 1952; M.B.A., Harvard U., 1954. Pres. Joseph Horne Co., Pitts., 1954-70; vice chmn. Associated Dry Goods Corp., N.Y.C., 1970-72; pres. Associated Dry Goods Corp., 1972-76, chmn. bd., 1976-81, also dir.; bd. dirs. Westinghouse Electric Corp., Pitts., Gen. Am. Investors Co., N.Y.C., N.Y. Life Ins. Co., Gillette Corp., Immunomedics Inc., Morris Plains, N.J. Trustee Princeton U., 1977—; chmn. bd., trustee Greenwich Hosp.; bd. dirs. Gen. Theol. Sem., N.Y.C. Served with AUS, 1955-56. Mem. Am. Retail Fedn. (dir. 1968-81). Clubs: Union League, Princeton (N.Y.C.); Duquesne, Rolling Rock, Fox Chapel Golf (Pitts.); Greenwich, Country, Field of Greenwich; Bald Peak Colony (Melvin Village, N.H.). Office: 111 Clapboard Ridge Rd Greenwich CT 06830-3405

PIVONKA, LEONARD DANIEL, priest; b. Bryan, Tex., Oct. 19, 1951; s. Herbert Daniel and Geraldine (Schoppe) P. Student, Tex. A&M U., 1969-70, Del Mar Coll., 1970-71; BA, Pontifical Coll. Josephinum, Columbus, Ohio, 1973; MDiv, Josephinum Sch. Theology, Columbus, 1977; JCD, Cath. U. Am., 1982. Ordained priest Roman Cath. Ch., 1977, named monsignor, 1985. Mem. faculty Corpus Christi (Tex.) Minor Sem., 1982-84; adminstr. St. Philip the Apostle Parish, Corpus Christi, 1983-85, pastor, 1985-91; adj. jud. vicar Diocesan Tribunal, Corpus Christi, 1984-88, bishop's sec. for canonical affairs, 1983—; episcopal vicar for synod and coun. Chancery, Corpus Christi, 1985-88, chancellor, 1987-88, jud. vicar Diocesan Tribunal, 1988—; rector Corpus Christi Cathedral, 1991—; mem. adminstrv. coun. Diocese of Corpus Christi, 1985—, Coll. of Consultors, 1985—; chaplain Natural Family Planning Office, Corpus Christi, 1991—; bishop's rep. Spohn Hosp. Coun. on Human Values; treas. Corpus Christi Ministerial Alliance, 1983-84; diocesan chaplain Legion of Mary, 1993—. Avocations: golf, tennis, cycling. Office: Diocese of Corpus Christi 620 Lipan St Corpus Christi TX 78401-2434

PIZER, DONALD, author, educator; b. N.Y.C., Apr. 5, 1929; s. Morris and Helen (Rosenfeld) P.; m. Carol Hart, Apr. 7, 1966; children—Karin, Ann, Margaret. B.A., UCLA, 1951, M.A., 1952, Ph.D., 1955. Mem. faculty Tulane U., 1957—, prof. English, 1964-72, Pierce Butler prof. English, 1972—, Mellon prof. humanities, 1978-79. Author: Hamlin Garland's Early Work and Career, 1960, Realism and Naturalism in Nineteenth-Century American Literature, 1966, The Novels of Frank Norris, 1966, The Novels of Theodore Dreiser, 1976, Twentieth-Century American Literary Naturalism: An Interpretation, 1982, Dos Passos "USA": A Critical Study, 1988, The Theory and Practice of American Literary Naturalism, 1993, American Expatriate Writing and the Paris Moment, 1996. Served with AUS, 1955-57. Guggenheim fellow, 1962; Am. Council Learned Socs. fellow, 1971-72; Nat. Endowment Humanities fellow, 1978-79. Mem. MLA. Home: 6320 Story St New Orleans LA 70118-6340

PIZER, HOWARD CHARLES, sports and entertainment executive; b. Chgo., Oct. 23, 1941; s. Edwin and Estyr (Seeder) P.; m. Sheila Graff, June 14, 1964; children: Jacqueline, Rachel. B.B.A., U. Wis., 1963; J.D. magna cum laude, Northwestern U., 1966. Assoc. McDermott, Will & Emery, Chgo., 1966-72; ptnr. Katten, Muchin, Zavis, Chgo., 1972-74; exec. v.p., gen. counsel Balcor Co., Skokie, Ill., 1975-80; exec. v.p. Chgo. White Sox, Chgo., 1981—; exec. v.p. United Ctr. Joint Venture. Bd. dirs. Chgo. Conv. and Tourism Bur., Inc., 1983—, Spl. Children's Charities, 1984—, Chgo. Baseball Cancer Charities, 1983—, Near West Side Cmty. Devel. Corp. Mem. Chgo. Bar Assn., Standard Club Chgo., Briarwood County. Home: 300 Euclid Ave Winnetka IL 60093 Office: Chgo White Sox 333 W 35th St Chicago IL 60616-3621

PIZITZ, RICHARD ALAN, retail and real estate group executive; b. Birmingham, Ala., Feb. 24, 1930; s. Isadore and Hortense (Hirsch) P.; m. Joan Black; children: Richard Alan Jr., Jill Carole, Susan Lyn. BA, Washington & Lee U., 1951; MBA, Harvard U., 1953. Mdse. mgr. Pizitz Dept. Stores, Birmingham, 1953-59, v.p., 1959-66, pres., 1966-86, chmn. bd., 1986-87; chmn. Pizitz Mgmt. Group, Birmingham, 1987—. Pres. United Way, Birmingham, 1988, Ala. Commn. on Higher Edn., 1987-95; pres. Better Bus. Bur., Birmingham, 1962; mem. Ala adv. commn. U.S. Commn. on Civil Rights, 1985. Recipient Erskine Ramsay award, 1974; named Mktg. Man of Yr., Am. Mktg. Assn., 1966, Man of Yr., Young Men's Bus. Club, 1970. Mem. Ala. Commn. on Higher Edn., Birmingham C. of C. (pres. 1970), Ala. Retail Assn. (pres. 1965). Avocations: pvt. pilot, skiing, tennis, scuba diving. Home: 2716 Hanover Cir S Birmingham AL 35205-1733 Office: Pizitz Mgmt Group 2140 11th Ave S Birmingham AL 35205-2832

PIZZAGALLI, ANGELO, construction company executive; b. Lugano, Switzerland, July 1, 1934; came to U.S., 1937; s. Angelo and Theresa Pizzagalli; m. Patricia Haron, Jan 19, 1935; children: Lisa, Mia, Jon. BSBA, U. Vt., 1956. Pres. Pizzagalli Constrn. Co., South Burlington, Vt., 1958—; bd. dirs. The Howard Bank, Burlington, Vt., Cen. Vt. Ry., Detroit. Past chmn. bd. trustees U. Vt.; active Vt. Indsl. Devel. Authority; past gov. Med. Ctr. Hosp. Vt., past trustee. Served to capt. USAF. Mem. Chief Execs. Orgn. Home: PO Box 2009 South Burlington VT 05407 Office: Pizzagalli Constrn Co 50 Joy Dr South Burlington VT 05407*

PIZZAGALLI, JAMES, construction executive; b. Burlington, Vt., Nov. 23, 1944; s. Angelo and Theresa (Moalli) P.; m. Judy Rock, June 21, 1969; 1 child, Michael. BS, U. Vt., 1966; JD, Boston U., 1969. Treas. Pizzagalli Constrn. Co., Burlington, Vt., 1969-76, v.p., 1976-91, chmn., chief exec. officer, 1991—; dir. Chittenden Corp., Burlington, 1982—, AGC Edn. Found., Washington, 1992—, Shelburne (Vt.) Mus., 1983-92; life dir. Assn. Gen. Contractors, Washington, 1976—, atty.-at law. Mem. TheMoles, Ethan Allen Club. Republican. Roman Catholic. Home: 158 Harbor Rd Shelburne VT 05482 Office: Pizzagalli Constrn Co PO Box 2009 South Burlington VT 05407

PIZZI, CHARLES PETER, association president; b. Phila., Oct. 1, 1950; s. Charles Ralph and Philomena Ritz (Martella) P.; m. Elise Kathleen Robinson, Aug. 14, 1976; children: Justin, Gabriel, Christian, Keith. BSBA, LaSalle U., 1972; student, Temple U., 1976-78. Client relation rep. Phila. Indsl. Devel. Corp., 1975-77, mktg. dir., 1978-80, v.p., 1981-83; from dep. to dir. commerce City of Philadelphia, 1984-88; v.p. spl. projects Richard I. Rubin & Co., Inc., Phila., 1988-89; pres. Greater Phila. C. of C., 1989—; bd. dirs. Airport Adv. Com., Blue Shield Med. Review Com., Cen. Phila. Devel. Corp., Delaware Valley Indsl. Rsch. Coun., Private Industry Coun., Temple U. Sch. Bus. Mgmt., Southeastern Pa. Transportation Authority, Nat. Constitution Ctr., Maritime Exch., Independence Blue Cross, Internat. Visitors Ctr. Phila. and various others. Bd. dirs. YMCA of Roxborough, Phila., Boy Scouts Am., Phila., Police Athletic League, Phila., United Way, Phila. Sports Congress, Urban League of Phila., Corp. Alliance for Drug Edn., Fairmont Park Hist. Houses Project, Mayoral Residence Com; mem. rep. com.

Chmn's. Club Montgomery County, Norristown, Pa., 1990—. Mem. African-Am. Hist. and Cultural Mus. (bd. dirs.), Jaycees, Union League Phila. Office: Greater Phila C of C 1234 Market St Fl 1800 Philadelphia PA 19107-3721

PIZZO, SALVATORE VINCENT, pathologist; b. Phila., June 22, 1944; s. George J. P. and Aida (Alcaro) Lepore; m. Carol Ann Kurkowski, Dec. 28, 1968 (div. 1987); children: Steven, David, Susan. PhD, Duke U., 1972; BS, St. Joseph's Coll., 1966; MD, Duke U., 1973. Asst. prof. Duke U. Med. Ctr., Durham, N.C., 1976-80, assoc. prof., 1980-85, prof., 1985—, dir. med. scientist tng. program, 1987—, chmn., 1991—; mem., chmn. program rev. com. NIH, Bethesda, Md., 1986-90; vice chmn. Gordon Conf. Proteases, Holderness, N.H., 1990, chmn., 1992—; cons. in field, 1980—; mem. Cellular and Molecular Basis of Disease Rev. Com., 1992—. Contbr. articles to profl. jours. Grantee NIH, 1976—, Am. Cancer Soc., 1976—. Mem. Am. Heart Assn. (exec. com. Thrombosis coun. 1990, 92), Am. Chem. Soc., Am. Assn. Pathologists (program com. 1985-88, long range planning com. 1990—), Am. Soc. Biological Chemists, Alpha Sigma Nu, Phi Beta Kappa, Alpha Omega Alpha, Sigma Xi. Achievements include patents in field; research in lipoproteins in coagulation and fibronolysis, a link to atherosclerosis, anticoagulation drug development. Office: Duke U Med Ctr PO Box 3712 Durham NC 27710

PIZZURO, SALVATORE NICHOLAS, special education educator; b. Passaic, N.J., Jan. 25, 1945; s. John G. and Mary F. (Interdonato) P. BA, Jersey City State Coll., 1970, MA, 1973; profl. diploma, Fordham U., 1980; EdD, Columbia U., 1991. Tchr. spl. edn. Garfield (N.J.) Pub. Schs., 1970-71, Lodi (N.J.) Pub. Schs., 1971-75, 76-78; learning cons. Mt. Carmel Guild, Newark, 1976-76; instr. Columbia U., N.Y.C., 1988-91; asst. prof. spl. edn. Jersey City State Coll., 1990—; post-doctoral fellow U. Ky., 1993-94; dir. Learning Consultation Svcs., N.Y.C., 1990—; coord. pre-svcs. program in mental retardation Tchrs. Coll., Columbia U., 1990-91; rsch. assoc. U. Ill., 1991-92; chmn. Early Childhood Inclusion Conf., Phila., 1993; dir. United Learning Consultants, 1994—; chmn. conf. "Assessment: Impact on Svc. Delivery", N.J., 1995; cons. Independent Child Study Teams, Inc., 1995—. Editor: Learning Consultant Journal, 1995. Chmn. Walk for Hunger, 1979, NE Regional Legis. Coalition, 1984-86, Nat. AD HOC Comm. on the Reauthorization of the Individuals with Disabilities Edn. Act, chmn. Nat. Forum on Reauthorization, 1996. Recipient award for dedication to mentally retarded Mt. Carmel Guild, 1972. Mem. Coun. for Exceptional Children, N.J. Coun. for Exceptional Children (pres. 1984-85), N.J. Divsn. on Mental Retardation (pres. 1986-87), Jersey City State Coll. Alumni Assn. (pres. 1974-75), Tchrs. Coll. Christian Fellowship (pres. 1988-90), Rehab. Engring. Soc. N.Am. Roman Catholic. Avocations: writing nonfiction, jogging.

PLAA, GABRIEL LEON, toxicologist, educator; b. San Francisco, May 15, 1930; arrived in Can., 1968; s. Jean and Lucienne (Chalopin) P.; m. Colleen Neva Brasefield, May 19, 1951; children: Ernest (dec.), Steven, Kenneth, Gregory, Andrew, John, Denise, David. BS, U. Calif., Berkeley, 1952; PhD, U. Calif., San Francisco, 1958. Diplomate Am. Bd. Toxicology. Asst. toxicologist City/County San Francisco, 1954-58; asst. prof. Sch. Medicine Tulane U., New Orleans, 1958-61; assoc. prof. U. Iowa, Iowa City, 1961-68; prof. U. Montreal, 1968-95, chmn. dept. pharmacology, 1968-80, vice-dean Faculty Medicine, 1982-89, dir. Interuniv. Ctr. Rsch. in Toxicology, 1991-95; ret., 1995, prof. emeritus, 1996; Dorothy Snider disting. lectr. U. Ark., 1995; chmn. Can. Coun. Animal Care, Ottawa, Ont., Can., 1985-86. Editor Toxicology and Applied Pharmacology, 1972-80; contbr. over 200 articles to profl. jours. 1st lt. U.S. Army, 1952-53, Korea. Recipient Thienes award Am. Acad. Clin. Toxicology, 1977. Mem. Am. Soc. Pharmacology, Soc. Toxicology Can. (pres. 1981-83, Henderson award 1969, award of distinction 1994), Pharm. Soc. Can. (pres. 1973-74), Soc. Toxicology (pres. 1983-84, Achievement award 1967, Lehman award 1977, Edn. award 1987, Amb. award 1987, Merit award 1996), Acad. Toxicological Scis. Roman Catholic. Home: 236 Meredith Ave, Dorval, PQ Canada H9S 2Y7 Office: U Montreal Dept Pharmacology, PO Box 6128 Sta A, Montreal, PQ Canada H3C 3J7

PLACHTA, LEONARD E., academic administrator. Pres. Ctrl. Mich. U., Mt. Pleasant, Mich. Office: Ctrl Mich U Office of Pres Mount Pleasant MI 48859

PLACIER, PHILIP R., lawyer; b. Chillicothe, Ohio, Mar. 7, 1933; s. Don Harold and Ruth (Hartmann) P.; m. Nancy Kay Young, July 27, 1963; children—David Lane, Thomas Alan, Elizabeth Ann. A.B., Ohio Wesleyan U., 1955; LL.B., U. Mich., 1958. Bar: Calif. 1959. Assoc. Thelen, Marrin, Johnson & Bridges, San Francisco, 1962-69, ptnr., 1970—, chmn. mgmt. com., 1984-92. Contbr. chpt. to book. Elder United Presbyterian Ch., Lafayette, Calif.; trustee San Francisco Theological Seminary. Served to lt. JAGC, USN, 1958-62. Mem. ABA, Calif. State Bar Assn., Orinda County Club (Calif.), World Trade Club (San Francisco). Republican. Avocations: golf; skiing. Office: Thelen Marrin Johnson & Bridges 2 Embarcadero Ctr San Francisco CA 94111-3823

PLACKE, ANN CATHERINE, oncology nurse; b. Batesville, Ind., May 6, 1946; d. Malcolm M. and Edith Marie (Drockelman) Lightner; m. Daniel Oscar Placke, July 20, 1968; children: Max Daniel, Andrea Lynn. Diploma, Meth. Hosp., 1968. Staff nurse Meth. Hosp., Indpls., 1968-70, asst. head nurse, 1970-72, staff nurse, 1980-92, mgr. patient care, 1992—. Mem. Ctrl. Ind. Oncology Nursing Soc. (edn. com. 1995), Oncology Nursing Soc. (cert. oncology), Meth. Hosp. Ind. Sch. Nursing Nursing Alumni (treas. 1993-94). Republican. Methodist.

PLACKE, JAMES A(NTHONY), foreign service officer, international affairs consultant; b. Grand Island, Nebr., June 14, 1935; s. Gerhard F. and Florence E. (McCormick) P.; m. Mary Sabina Shea, July 25, 1959; children—Elizabeth, Stephen, Carolyn. B.Sc., U. Nebr., 1957, M.A., 1959. Commd. fgn. service officer Dept. State, 1958; econ. counselor Am. embassy, Tripoli, Libya, 1970-71; fgn. service insp. Dept. State, Washington, 1971-73, dir. office food policy, 1974-76; econ. counselor Am. embassy, Ottawa, Ont., Can., 1977-79; minister Am. embassy, Jidda, Saudi Arabia, 1979-82; dep. asst. sec. Nr. Eastern and South Asian Affairs Bur., Dept. State, Washington, 1982-85, ret., 1986; internat. affairs cons., 1986-90; dir. Cambridge Energy Rsch. Assoc., 1991; del. UN World Food Conf., 1974. Recipient Meritorious Honor award Dept. State, 1969, 71; Presdl. Meritorious Service award, 1985. Office: Ste 1000W 1299 Pennsylvania Ave NW Washington DC 20004-2400

PLACZEK, ADOLF KURT, librarian; b. Vienna, Austria, Mar. 9, 1913; came to U.S., 1940, naturalized, 1943; s. Oswald and Pauline (Selinko) P.; m. Jan Struther, Mar. 1, 1948 (dec. July 1953); m. Laura Beverley Robinson, Jan. 5, 1957. Student, U. Vienna Med. Sch., 1931-34, Inst. Fine Arts, U. Vienna, 1934-38; B.L.S., Columbia U., 1942; diploma of honor, U. Vienna, 1993. Asst. librarian Avery Archtl. Library, Columbia U., 1948-60; Avery librarian Avery Archtl. Library, 1960-80, emeritus, 1980—, adj. prof. architecture, 1971-80, prof. emeritus, 1980—; commr. N.Y.C. Landmarks Preservation Commn., 1984-93. Editor in chief Macmillan Ency. Architects, 1982, Bldgs. of the U.S., Oxford Press, 1984-90; contbr. articles to Columbia Ency., Ency. Brit., also to books and mags. Served with AUS, 1943-46. Decorated Austrian Cross of Honor for Sci. and Art 1st class, 1993; recipient Honor award AIA, 1986. Mem. Soc. Archtl. Historians (sec. 1963-67, dir. 1968-71, 2d v.p. 1974-75, 1st v.p. 1976-77, pres. 1978-80), Am. Council Learned Socs. (del. 1971-74). Home: 176 W 87th St New York NY 10024-2902

PLAEGER, FREDERICK JOSEPH, II, lawyer; b. New Orleans, Sept. 10, 1953; s. Edgar Leonard and Bernice Virginia (Schiwetz) P.; m. Kathleen Helen Dickson, Nov. 19, 1977; children: Douglas A., Catherine E. BS, La. State U., 1976, JD, 1977. Bar: La. 1978, U.S. Dist. Ct. (ea. dist.) La. 1978, U.S. Ct. Appeals (5th cir.) 1981, U.S. Supreme Ct. 1989. Law clk. U.S. Dist. Ct. (ea. dist.) La., New Orleans, 1977-79; assoc. Milling, Benson, Woodward, Hillyer, Pierson & Miller, New Orleans, 1979-85, ptnr., 1985-89; v.p., gen. counsel, corp. sec. La. Land and Exploration Co., New Orleans, 1989—. Bd. dirs. New Orleans Speech and Hearing Ctr., 1985-91, pres., 1988-90; bd. dirs. Children's Oncology Svcs. La. (Ronald McDonald House of New Orleans), 1987-90; selected mem. Met. Area Com. Leadership Forum, 1986; bd. dirs. Soc. Environ. Edn., La. Nature and Sci. Ctr., 1992-94. Recipient Service to Mankind award Sertoma, 1989. Mem. ABA, La. Bar Assn., Am. Corp. Counsel Assn. (bd. dirs. New Orleans chpt. 1995—), Am. Soc. Corp. Secs., Am. Petroleum Inst. (mem. gen. commn. law), Pickwick Club. Republican. Avocations: golf, hunting, fishing. Home: 4632 Neyrey Dr Metairie LA 70002-1423 Office: La Land & Exploration Co 909 Poydras St Ste 3600 New Orleans LA 70112-4000

PLAGENZ, GEORGE RICHARD, minister, journalist, columnist; b. Lakewood, Ohio, Dec. 11, 1923; s. George William and Edith Louise (Fenner) P.; m. Faith Hanna, Sept. 12, 1953 (div.); children—Joel, George William II, Nicole, Sarah. B.A. cum laude, Western Res. U., 1945; S.T.B., Harvard, 1949. Ordained to ministry Unitarian Ch., 1951. Sports writer Cleve. Press, 1943-46; asst. minister King's Chapel, Boston, 1951-54; news broadcaster Radio Sta. WEEI, Boston, 1955-63; writer Boston Sunday Advertiser, 1963-70; religion editor Cleve. Press, 1970-82; syndicated columnist Scripps-Howard Newspapers, 1974-80, Newspaper Enterprise Assn., 1980—. Mem. Beta Theta Pi. Club: Harvard (Boston). Home: 239B E Beck St Columbus OH 43206-1210

PLAGER, S. JAY, federal judge; b. Long Branch, N.J., May 16, 1931; s. A.L. and Clara L. (Matross) P.; m. Ilene H. Nagel; children—Anna Katherine, David Alan, Daniel Tyler. A.B., U. N.C., 1952; J.D., U. Fla., 1958; LL.M., Columbia U., 1961. Bar: Fla. 1958, Ill. 1964. Asst. prof. law U. Fla., 1958-62; assoc. prof., 1962-64; assoc. prof. law U. Ill., Champaign-Urbana, 1964-65, prof., 1965-77; dir. Office Environ. and Planning Studies, 1972-74, 75-77; dean, prof. law Ind. U. Sch. Law, Bloomington, 1977-84; prof. law Ind. U. Sch. Law, 1984-90; counselor to undersec. U.S. Dept. Health and Human Svcs., 1986-87; assoc. dir. Office of Mgmt. and Budget Office of Mgmt. and Budget, 1987-88; adminstr. info. and regulatory affairs Exec. Office of the Pres., 1988-89; cir. judge U.S. Ct. Appeals (fed. cir.), 1989—; vis. research prof. law U. Wis., 1967-68; vis. scholar Stanford U., 1984-85. Author: (with others) Water Law and Administration, 1968, Social Justice Through Law-New Approaches in the Law of Property, 1970, (with others) Florida Water Law, 1980. Chmn. Gainesville (Fla.) Planning Commn., 1962-63; mem. Urbana Plan Commn., 1966-70; mem. nat. air pollution manpower devel. adv. com., 1971-75; cons. Ill. Inst. for Environ. Quality, U.S. EPA; chmn. Ill. Task Force on Noise, 1972-76; vice chmn. Nat. Commn. on Jud. Discipline and Removal, 1991-93. With USN, 1952-55. Office: US Ct Appeals for Fed Cir The National Courts Bldg 717 Madison Pl NW Washington DC 20439-0001

PLAGMAN, RALPH, principal. Prin. George Washington High Sch., Cedar Rapids, Iowa. Recipient Blue Ribbon Sch. award Dept. Edn., 1990-91. Office: George Washington High Sch 2205 Forest Dr SE Cedar Rapids IA 52403-1653

PLAIN, BELVA, writer; b. N.Y.C., Oct. 9, 1919; d. Oscar and Eleanor Offenberg; m. Irving Plain, June 14, 1941 (dec. 1982); 3 children. Grad., Barnard Coll. Author: Evergreen, 1978, Random Winds, 1980, Eden Burning, 1982, Crescent City, 1984, The Golden Cup, 1987, Tapestry, 1988, Blessings, 1989, Harvest, 1990, Treasures, 1992, Whispers, 1993, Daybreak, 1994, The Carousel, 1995. Office: care Delacorte Press 1540 Broadway New York NY 10036-4039

PLAINE, DANIEL J., lawyer; b. Washington, Aug. 23, 1943; s. Herzel H.E. and Norma (Stein) P.; m. Susan Ambrose, Oct. 5, 1985; children: Caroline, Meredith. BA magna cum laude, Williams Coll., 1965; LLB, Cambridge U., Eng., 1967; JD, Yale U., 1970. Bar: D.C. 1970, U.S. Dist. Ct. DC 1970, U.S. Ct. Appeals (D.C. cir.) 1970, U.S. Ct. Appeals (fed. cir.), 1985, U.S. Supreme Ct., 1974. Ptnr. Steptoe & Johnson, Washington, 1970—. Marshall scholar, 1967. Mem. ABA, Am. Soc. Internat. Law, Washington Inst. Internat. Law. Office: 1330 Connecticut Ave NW Washington DC 20036-1795

PLAINE, LLOYD LEVA, lawyer; b. Washington, Nov. 3, 1947. BA, U. Pa., 1969; postgrad., Harvard U.; JD, Georgetown U., 1975. Bar: D.C. 1975. Legis. asst. to U.S. Rep. Sidney Yates, 1971-72; with Sutherland, Asbill & Brennan, Washington, 1975-82, ptnr., 1982—. Fellow Am. Bar Found., Am. Coll. Trust and Estate Counsel, Am. Coll. of Tax Counsel; mem. ABA (chmn. elect real property, probate and trust law sect.). Office: Sutherland Asbill & Brennan 1275 Pennsylvania Ave NW Washington DC 20004-2404

PLAIR, WENDELL SAMUEL, psychologist; b. Charlotte, N.C., Aug. 31, 1921; s. William Samuel and Alice Geneva (Oglesby) P.; BS, Johnson C. Smith U., 1942; MS, Howard U., 1967, PhD, 1994; m. Willa Mae Vaught, Mar. 6, 1950; 1 dau., Barbara Ann. With Airway Sales and Services, Inc., Washington, 1951-63; research asst. NIH, Bethesda, Md., 1963-66; staff psychologist DC Dept. Corrections, Lorton facility, 1967-69, research psychologist, rsch. and planning div., 1970-72; mental health coordinator, mental health svcs. D.C. Detention Center, 1973-87; group therapist Georgetown U. Clinic, 1970-71; mem. adv. bd. Parental Imprisonment and Child Socialization Project, Howard U., 1974-76. Served with USNR, 1945-46. Recipient Outstanding Performance awards D.C. Govt., 1976, 80, Quality Service award, 1982. Mem. D.C. Psychol. Assn., Am. Psychol. Assn., Assn. Black Psychologists, Am. Assn. Correctional Psychologists, Soc. Psychol. Study Social Issues, Omega Psi Phi. Clubs: Pigskin of Washington, Masons. Home: 1314 Nicholson St Hyattsville MD 20782-1512

PLAISTED, HARRIS MERRILL, III, real estate executive; b. Portland, Maine, June 3, 1935; s. Harris Merrill and Elizabeth Parsons (Hatch) P.; m. Patricia Walker, Feb. 20, 1982; children: Frederick William II, Parker Bennett; stepchildren: William H. Nau Jr., Mary Beth Nau. BA in Econs., Washington and Lee U., 1957. With Morton G. Thalhimer, Inc., Richmond, Va., 1960-66, v.p., 1966-80, sr. v.p., 1980-86, pres., 1986-92, vice chmn., 1992—; bd. dirs. Morton G. Thalhimer Realty Adivosrs, Inc., Richmond, Excel Svcs., Inc., Richmond. Pres. Ridgetop Recreation Assn., 1967, Big Bros. of Richmond, Inc., 1970; bd. dirs. Robert E. Lee coun. Boy Scouts Am., 1981; state dir. Internat. Coun. Shopping Ctrs., 1974-77. Capt. U.S. Army, 1957-59. Mem. Va. Assn. Realtors (bd. dirs. 1973-82), Richmond Bd. Realtors (pres. 1975, Realtor of Yr. 1975), Richmond Real Estate Group (pres. 1987), Richmond Jaycees (life, Key Man Club), Soc. Indsl. and Office Realtors (dist. v.p. 1979-80, regional v.p. 1984-85, Howell H. Watson Disting. Svc. award 1995), Sons of the Revolution (sec. 1994, 2d v.p. 1995), Ships Watch Assn. (bd. dirs. 1994, pres. 1995), Kiwanis Club Richmond (bd. dirs. 1978-79). Episcopalian. Avocations: golf, sailing. Home: 9013 Wood Sorrel Ct Richmond VA 23229-7072 Office: Morton G Thalhimer Inc 1313 E Main St Richmond VA 23219-3600

PLAISTED, JOAN M., diplomat; b. St. Peter, Minn., Aug. 29, 1945; d. Gerald A. and Lola May (Peters) P. Student, U. Grenoble, France, 1965-66, U. Calif., Berkeley, 1966; BA in Internat. Rels., Am. U., 1967, MA in Asian Studies, 1969; graduate, Nat. War Coll., 1988. Korea desk officer Commerce Dept., Washington, 1969-72, Japan desk officer, 1972-73; commercial officer Am. Embassy, Paris, 1973-78; internat. economist Orgn. Econ. Cooperation & Devel., Paris, 1978-80; econ. officer Am. Consulate Gen., Hong Kong, 1980-83; trade negotiator White House Office of Spl. Trade Rep., Geneva, 1983-85; deputy dir. China desk State Dept., Washington, 1985-87; acting dep. dir., chief econ./comml. sect. Am. Inst. in Taiwan, Taipei, 1988-91; chargé d'affaires, deputy chief of mission Am. Embassy, Rabat, Morocco, 1991-94; dir. Thai and Burma affairs Dept. of State, Washington, 1994-95; sr. advisor U.S. Mission to UN Dept. of State, 1995; amb. to Republic of Marshall Islands and Republic of Kiribati, 1996—; sr. advisor U.S. Mission to the UN, 1995. Recipient Lodestar award Am. U., 1993. Mem. Am. Fgn. Svc. Assn., Hong Kong Wine Soc. (founding). Avocations: wine tasting, gastronomy, history, skiing, travelling. Address: PO Box 1379, Majuro 96960-1379, Marshall Islands

PLAISTED, ROBERT LEROY, plant breeder, educator; b. Hornell, N.Y., Jan. 1, 1929; s. Robert A. and Eva B. (Gitchell) P.; m. Ellen B. Overbaugh, Feb. 10, 1951; children: Deborah (dec.), Kathleen, Thomas, Diane. B.S., Cornell U., 1950; M.S., La. State U., 1954, Ph.D., 1956. Grad. asst. la. State U., 1953-56; asst. prof. Cornell U., 1956-60, assoc. prof., 1960-64, prof., 1964-95, prof. emeritus, 1995—. Served with AUS, 1951-53. Mem. European Assn. Potato Research, Potato Assn. Am. (pres. 1971). Home: 536 Ellis Hollow Creek Rd Ithaca NY 14850-9623

PLAMONDON, WILLIAM N., rental company executive. Sr. v.p. mktg. Budget Rent A Car Corp., Lisle, Ill., 1982-89, 1989-91, exec. v.p., gen. mgr. N.Am., 1991—. Office: Budget Rent A Car 4225 Naperville Rd Lisle IL 60532*

PLANCHER, ROBERT LAWRENCE, manufacturing company executive; b. N.Y.C., Feb. 21, 1932; s. Murray Leon and Pearl P.; m. Ellen Roslyn, Feb. 14, 1954; children: Kevin, Daryn. B.B.A., CCNY, 1954. With American Brands, Inc., N.Y.C., 1963—; asst. tax dir. American Brands, Inc., 1967, tax dir., 1971, controller, 1978, dir., v.p., controller, 1981-86, sr. v.p., chief acctg. officer, 1986—; bd. dirs. ACCO World Corp., Acushnet Co., Am. Brands Internat. Corp., Am. Tobacco Internat. Corp., Jim Beam Brands Co., Gallaher Ltd., MasterBrand Industries, Inc.; chmn. bd. 1700 Ins. Co. Ltd., dir. JBB Worldwide, Inc.; mem. Mid Atlantic Metro regional adv. bd. Arkwright Mut. Ins. Co. Served with U.S. Army, 1954-56. Mem. Fin. Execs. Inst., Tax Execs. Inst., Inst. Mgmt. Accts. Office: Am Brands Inc 1700 E Putnam Ave Old Greenwich CT 06870-1321

PLANE, DONALD RAY, management science educator; b. Evansville, Ind., July 17, 1938; s. Edward L. and Margaret I. (Downen) P.; m. Rosemary Bieber, Sept. 4, 1961; children: Brian Russell, Dennis Lowell, Margaret Diane. ME, U. Cin., 1961; M.B.A. (NDEA fellow), Ind. U., 1963, D.B.A. (NDEA fellow), 1965. Instr. econs. U.S. Air Force Acad., 1965-67, asst. prof. econs., 1967-68; assoc. prof. mgmt. sci. U. Colo., Boulder, 1968-72; prof. mgmt. sci. and info. systems U. Colo., 1972-84, head div. mgmt. sci., 1976-84; prof. mgmt. sci. Crummer Grad. Sch. Bus., Rollins Coll., Winter Park, Fla., 1984—, pres. Crummer grad. faculty, 1992-93; vis. Fulbright prof. mgmt. sci. U. Nairobi, 1978-79; cons. in field. Co-author: (with E.B. Oppermann) Business and Economic Statistics, 3d edit., 1986; (with J. Dinkel, G. Kochenberger) Management Science: Text and Applications, 1978, Quantitative Tools for Decision Support Using IFPS, 1986, Management Science: A Spreadsheet Approach for Windows, 1996. Served with USAF, 1965-68. Ford Found. fellow, 1965. Research, publs. in field. Home: 980 S Lake Sybelia Dr Maitland FL 32751-5403 Office: Rollins College Crummer Grad Sch Bus Winter Park FL 32789

PLANE, ROBERT ALLEN, academic administrator, chemistry educator, author; b. Evansville, Ill., Sept. 30, 1927; s. Allen george and Altha Margaret (Warren) P.; m. Georia Louise Ames, Dec. 30, 1950 (dec. Oct. 1961); children: David Allen, Martha Lu Plane Deblasio; m. Mary Moore, July 2, 1963; children: Ann Marie, Jennifer Plane Hartman. BA, Evansville Coll., 1948; SM, U. Chgo., 1949, PhD, 1951; DSc (hon.), U. Evansville, 1968, Clarkson U., 1985; LHD, St. Lawrence U., Canton, N.Y., 1986; LLD, Hobart Coll., 1990. Rsch. chemist Oak Ridge Nat. Lab., Tenn., 1951-52; prof. and provost Cornell U., Ithaca, N.Y., 1952-74; pres. Clarkson U., Potsdam, N.Y., 1974-85; dir. N.Y. Agr. Expt. Sta., Geneva, N.Y., 1986-90; pres. Wells Coll., Aurora, N.Y., 1991-95. Author: (with M. Sienko) Chemistry, 1957, Physical Inorganic Chemistry, 1963, Chemistry: Principles and Properties; (with R. Hester) Elements of Inorganic Chemistry, 1965. Decorated Outstanding Civilian Svc. medal, US Army. Fellow AAAS; mem. Assn. Ind. Engring. Colls. (pres. 1982-84), Commn. Ind. Coll. U. (chmn. 1976-78). Avocations: wine making, trumpet playing.

PLANGERE, JULES L., III, newspaper company executive; b. Neptune, N.J., Nov. 4, 1944; s. Jules L. and Virginia May (Polhemus) P.; m. Nona Helen Chadwick, Nov. 20, 1971 (div. Mar. 25, 1985). B.A., Lafayette Coll., 1966. Reporter, photographer Asbury Park Press, Asbury Park, N.J., 1970-72, account exec., 1972-74, asst. prodn. mgr., 1974-80, dir. ops., 1980-82, v.p. ops., 1982-85, v.p. pub., 1986-89, exec. v.p., 1989—. Served to lt. comdr. USNR, 1966-69. Mem. N.J. Press Assn. Methodist. Home: 2805 Williamsburg Dr Wall NJ 07719-9516 Office: Asbury Pk Press 3601 Hwy 66 PO Box 1550 Neptune NJ 07754

PLANGERE, JULES LEON, JR., media company executive; b. Spring Lake, N.J., Dec. 30, 1920; s. Jules Leon and Jesse Alene (Davidson) P.; student Rutgers U., 1942; m. Jane Wallhauser, Feb. 5, 1978; 1 son, Jules L. III; stepchildren: Mrs. John Bickart, John C. Conover III, Jeffrey Conover. With Asbury Park (N.J.) Press, 1947—, pub., 1977-91, chief exec. officer, 1980-91, chmn. bd., 1980—; former dir. N.J. Bell Telephone Co. Former chmn. bd. trustees Monmouth Coll., West Long Branch, N.J.; past pres. Welfare Council Monmouth County. Lt. U.S. Army, 1942-46. Mem. Asbury Park C. of C. (past pres.), N.J. Press Assn. (past pres.), Am. Newspaper Pubs. Assn., N.J. State C. of C. (bd. dirs.). Clubs: Spring Lake Bath and Tennis, Nassau, Quail Ridge Country, Metedeconk Nat. Golf.

PLANK, BETSY ANN (MRS. SHERMAN V. ROSENFIELD), public relations counsel; b. Tuscaloosa, Ala., Apr. 3, 1924; d. Richard Jeremiah and Bettye (Hood) P.; m. Sherman V. Rosenfield, Apr. 10, 1954. Student, Bethany (W.Va.) Coll., 1940-43; A.B., U. Ala., 1944. Continuity dir. radio sta. KQV, Pitts., 1944-47; account exec. Mitchell McKeown Orgn., Chgo., 1947-54; pub. relations counsel Chgo. chpt. A.R.C., 1954-57; dir. pub. relations Chgo. Council on Fgn. Relations, 1957-58; v.p. Ronald Goodman Pub. Relations Counsel, Chgo., 1958-61; exec. v.p., treas., dir. Daniel J. Edelman, Inc., Chgo., 1961-73; dir. pub. relations planning Am. Tel. & Tel. Co., N.Y.C., 1973-74; asst. v.p. corp. communications Ill. Bell, Chgo., 1974-90; prin. Betsy Plank Pub. Rels., Chgo., 1990—; dep. chmn. VII World Congress on Pub. Rels., 1976; co-chmn. nat. commn. on Pub. Rels. Edn., 1984-86; mem. adv. bd. Ill. Issues. Bd. dirs. United Way Chgo., 1986-90; chmn. Citizenship Coun. Met. Chgo., Betsy Plank chpt. Pub. Rels. Students Soc. Am., No. Ill. U.; trustee Found. for Pub. Rels. Rsch. and Edn., 1975-80; nat. bd. dirs. Girl Scouts U.S.A., 1975-85. Recipient medal of merit Pi Delta Epsilon; named One of World's 40 Leading Pub. Relations Profls., 1984. Fellow Pub. Rels. Soc. Am. (accredited, nat. pres. 1973, chmn. pub. utilities sect. 1977, Outstanding Profl. award 1977, Outstanding Community Svc. award 1989); mem. Pub. Rels. Clinic (pres. 1979), Publicity Club Chgo. (pres. 1963-64, Outstanding Profl. award 1961), Ill. Coun. on Econ. Edn. (past chmn. bd. trustees), Welfare Pub. Rels. Forum Chgo. (pres. 1966-67), Internat. Pub. Rels. Assn., Chgo. Network (chmn. 1980-81), Nat. Pub. Rels. Coun. (bd. dirs. 1973-75), Union League Club of Chgo., Bon Vivant Soc., Econ. Club Chgo., Zeta Tau Alpha. Presbyterian. Home and Office: 421 W Melrose St Chicago IL 60657-3848

PLANK, WILLIAM BRANDT, minister; b. Fond du Lac, Wis., Apr. 17, 1941; s. Lloyd Thomsen Plank and Helen Frances (Brandt) Plank Moersch; m. Susan Jane Hawthorne, June 29, 1963; children: David Hawthorne, Stephen Brandt, Elizabeth Anne. BA, Carleton Coll., 1963; MDiv, McCormick Theol. Seminary, Chgo., 1966; DMin, McCormick Theol. Seminary, 1986. Ordained minister Presbyn. Ch. Assoc. pastor Glen Avon Presbyn. Ch., Duluth, Minn., 1966-71, Highland Park (Ill.) Presbyterian Ch., 1971-76; pastor First Presbyn. Ch., Kankakee, Ill., 1976-81, Manitowoc, Wis., 1981—; staffing, nominating, evangelism coms., Winnebago Presbytery, N.E. Wis., 1994—, coun. mem., 1994—, moderator, 1986-87. Bd. dirs. Family Svc. Assn., Manitowoc, 1994—; sec./treas. Fairweather Lodge for Mentally Ill, Manitowoc, Wis., 1981—; founding bd. dirs. Peter's Pantry, Manitowoc, 1987-93. Mem. Rotary, Manitowoc County Clergy Assn. Avocations: sailing, travel, reading, cross-country skiing. Home: 715 New York Ave Manitowoc WI 54220 Office: First Presbyterian Ch 502 N 8th St Manitowoc WI 54220

PLANO, RICHARD JAMES, physicist, educator; b. Merrill, Wis., Apr. 15, 1929; s. Victor James and Minnie (Hass) P.; m. Louise Sylvia Grevillius, July 3, 1956; children—Linda Sylvia, Robert James. A.B., U. Chgo., 1949, B.S., 1951, M.S., 1953, Ph.D., 1956. Faculty Columbia, 1956-60; faculty Rutgers U., New Brunswick, N.J., 1960—; prof. physics Rutgers U., 1962-81, prof. II, 1981—. Mem. Am. Inst. Physics, Am. Assn. Physics Tchrs., AAUP. Studies on properties of elementary particles. Home: PO Box 5306 Somerset NJ 08875-5306 Office: Physics Dept Rutgers U New Brunswick NJ 08903

PLANT, ALBIN MACDONOUGH, lawyer; b. Balt., July 30, 1937; s. Albin Joseph and Ruth E. (Frech) P.; m. Anne Warwick Brown, June 17, 1961; children: Katherine, Albin MacDonough Jr., Elizabeth Ashby. BA, Princeton U., 1959; LLB, U. Va., 1963; MLA, Johns Hopkins U., 1975.

Bar: Md. 1963, U.S. Dist. Ct. Md. 1963, U.S. Ct. Appeals 1970. Assoc. Semmes, Bowen & Semmes, Balt., 1963-71, ptnr., 1971-91; ptnr. Stewart, Plant & Blumenthal, Balt., 1991—; adj. prof. law U. Balt., 1979, U. Md., 1979-83, 84-85. Co-author Md. Estate Planning, Will Drafting and Estate Administn. Forms Practice Ann. Bd. dirs. Ctr. Stage, T. Rowe Price Renaissance Fund, Ltd., T. Rowe Price Spectrum Fund, New Age Media Fund. Mem. Am. Coll. Probate Counsel (regent), Lawyers Roundtable, Md. Club, Wednesday Law Club. Democrat. Office: 7 St Paul St Baltimore MD 21202-1626

PLANT, DAVID WILLIAM, lawyer; b. Ottawa, Ill., Apr. 22, 1931; s. Arthur Percival and Margery Elmina (Flick) P.; children: Susan W. BME, Cornell U., 1953, LLB, 1957. Bar: N.Y. 1957, U.S. Dist. Ct. (ea. and so. dists.) N.Y., U.S. Supreme Ct., 1968, U.S. Patent Office 1982. Assoc. Fish & Neave, N.Y.C., 1957-70; ptnr. Fish & Neave, 1970—, mng. ptnr., 1981-84; panel mem., arbitration cons. com. World Intellectual Property Orgn., 1994—; mem. panels of neutrals Internat. C. of C., 1992—, London Ct. Internat. Arbitration, 1992—, ea. dist. N.Y., so. dist. N.Y.; lectr. in field. Contbr. articles to profl. jours. Bd. dirs. Cornell Rsch. Found. Mem. ABA, Assn. of Bar of City of N.Y. (com. on patents 1980-83, chmn. 1983-86, com. on arbitration and alternative dispute resolution 1987-90, 91-94, chmn. 1994—), Am. Arbitration Assn. (various coms.), N.Y. Intellectual Property Law Assn. (chmn. arbitration com. 1989-91, bd. dirs. 1994—), Am. Intellectual Property Law Assn. (chmn. alternative dispute resolution com. 1993-95), Ctr. Pub. Resources (bd. dirs., co-chmn. tech. com. 1995—, licensing com., exec. sec., mem. panels), Cornell Law Assn. (exec. com., pres. 1994-96). Home: 7 George Langeloh Ct Rye NY 10580-4150 Office: Fish & Neave 49th Flr 1251 Ave of the Americas New York NY 10020

PLANT, FORREST ALBERT, lawyer; b. Sacramento, Dec. 17, 1924; s. Forrest A. and Marie (Phleger) P.; m. Shirley J. Boles, Oct. 15, 1949; children: Forrest Albert, Jr., Randall B., Gregory M., Brian J. AB, U. Calif., Berkeley, 1944, JD, 1949. Bar: Calif. 1950. Ptnr. Diepenbrock, Wulff, Plant & Hannegan, Sacramento, 1950—; prof. law McGeorge Coll. Law, 1952-61; mem. Jud. Coun. State Calif., 1972-76; mem. Calif. Law Revision Commn., 1988-94, chmn., 1988-89. Chmn. bd. editors: Calif. Lawyer, 1981-82. Trustee, dir. Golden Empire coun. Boy Scouts Am., 1963-67; pres. Legal Aid Soc. Sacramento County, 1961-62; former bd. dirs. Sacramento Children's Home; former trustee and mem. exec. com. Sutter Comty. Hosps., Sutter Health Sys.; trustee, pres. Crocker Art Mus. Found., 1994-95, Sacramento Symphony Found., U. Calif.-Berkeley Found., 1980-86; former bd. dirs., v.p. exec. com. Sacramento Symphony Assn.; trustee Calif. Mus. Assn., pres., 1968-69, Sacramento Regional Found., treas., 1993—; bd. visitors Stanford Law Sch., 1971-74; bd. regents U. Calif., 1978-79. With USNR, WWII. Recipient Disting. Svc. award, Boalt Law Sch. Alumni, 1989, Citation award, 1995; U. Calif.-Berkeley fellow. Fellow Am. Bar Found., Am. Coll. Trust and Estate Counsel, Am. Coll. Trial Lawyers (bd. regents 1977-81); mem. State Bar of Calif. (bd. govs. 1968-71, pres. 1970-71), Sacramento County Bar Assn. (pres. 1966, mem. coun.), U. Calif. Alumni Assn. (pres. 1977-79, Alumni citation 1980), Sutter club (past bd. dirs.), Del Paso Country Club, Rotary (past pres., bd. dirs. Sacramento Club, Paul Harris fellow), Phi Beta Kappa. Home: 1515 13th Ave Sacramento CA 95818-4148 Office: 455 Capitol Mall Sacramento CA 95814-4404

PLANT, MARETTA MOORE, public relations and marketing executive; b. Washington, Sept. 4, 1937; d. Henry Edwards and Lucy (Connell) Moore; m. William Voorhees Plant, June 14, 1959; children: Scott Voorhees, Craig Culver, Suzannah Holliday. BS in Bus. Adminstrn., U. Ark., 1959. Owner, mgr. Handcrafts by Maretta, Westfield, N.J., 1966-73; photographer M-R Pictures, Inc., Allendale, N.J., 1973-77; communications asst. United Way-Union County, Elizabeth, N.J., 1977-79; pub. rels. cons. Creative Arts Workshop, Westfield, 1977-81, Coll. Adv. Cons., 1983-89; community rels. coord. Raritan Bay Health Svcs. Corp., Perth Amboy, N.J., 1979-81; dir. pub. rels. St. Elizabeth Hosp., Elizabeth, N.J., 1981-86; dir. mkgt./communications Somerset Med. Ctr., Somerville, N.J., 1986-90; v.p. mktg. and pub. rels. Somerset Med. Ctr., Somerville, 1990—. Trustee Bridgeway House, Elizabeth, 1982-86, Far Hills Race Meeting Assn., N.J., 1989—, pub. rels com. N.J. Hosp. Assn., Princeton, 1982-83, 89-92, coun. auxs., 1988-92, pub. rels. com., 1989-92; committeewoman Union County Rep. Com., Westfield, 1983-85; bd. dirs. pub. affairs com. Morris Mus., Morristown; bd. dirs. communications com. Somerset County United Way, 1992—. Mem. Pub. Rels. Soc. Am., Nat. Fedn. Press Women, N.J. Press Women (chmn. communications contest 1990-92), Am. Soc. Hosp. Mktg. and Pub. Rels. (coun. mem. Region II, membership com.), N.J. Hosp. Mktg. and Pub. Rels. Assn. (corr. sec. 1984-86, pres. 1986-88), Somerset County C. of C. (mag. com. 1988-93), U. Ark. Alumni Assn., Summit-Westfield Assn., Delta Gamma, Coll. Women's (Westfield) Club, Soroptomists (internat., charter). Home: 118 Effingham Pl Westfield NJ 07090-3926 Office: Somerset Med Ctr Rehill Ave Somerville NJ 08876-2546

PLANTS, WALTER DALE, elementary education educator, minister; b. Middlefield, Ohio, June 8, 1942; s. William E. and Hazel A. Plants; m. Sarah A. Gaddis, July 5, 1962; children: Dale Anthony, Jeanette Marie. BD, Azusa Pacific U., 1967; MEd, U. Nev., 1970. Cert. elem. tchr., ednl. adminstr. Elem. tchr. Churchill County Sch. Dist., Fallon, Nev., 1967-69, 70-72, 81—; grad. asst. U. Nev., Reno, 1969-70; tchr. Kingman (Ariz.) Elem. Sch. Dist. #4, 1972-77; head sci. program E. C. Best Elem. Sch., Fallon, 1988—; adj. instr. Ariz. State U., Tempe, 1973-77; cons. sci. Ariz. State Dept. Edn., 1975-77. Bd. dirs. Solar Energy Commn. Mohave County, Ariz., 1974; coord. County Sci. Fair, 1988-93; active Western Regional Sci. Fair Com.; sci. fair coord. Churchill County, 1989-94; mem. com. Regional Sci. Fair, 1992-94. HEW fellow, 1969; NSF grantee, 1973; AIMS Found. scholar, 1988; recipient Ariz. State PTA award, 1977, Ruth Neldon award Ariz. State Dept., 1977, Conservation award Big Sandy Natural Resources Conservation Dist. Ariz., 1976, Community Builder Svc. award Masons, Fallon, 1991, Disting. Leadership award, 1991, 92, 93; named State Tchr. of Yr. Nev. PTA, 1991, Conservation Tchr. of Yr., 1991; named to Congl. Select Edn. panel U.S. Congress, 1993. Mem. NEA, AAAS, Nat. Sci. Tchrs. Assn., Nat. Coun. Tchrs. Math., Internat. Reading Assn., Churchill County Edn. Assn. (Tchr. of Yr. 1989), Internat. Platform Assn., Nat. Arbor Day Found., World Wildlife Fund, Nat. Parks and Conservation Assn., Nat. Audubon Soc., Nev. State Tchrs. of Yr. Assn. (pres. 1994-95), Phi Delta Kappa. Office: EC Best Elem Sch 750 E Williams Ave Fallon NV 89406-3022

PLAPP, BRYCE VERNON, biochemistry educator; b. DeKalb, Ill., Sept. 11, 1939; s. Vernon Edgar and Eleanor Barbara (Kautz) P.; m. Rosemary Kuhn, June 13, 1962; children—Brendan Bryce, Laurel Andrea. B.S., Mich. State U., East Lansing, 1961; Ph.D., U. Calif.-Berkeley, 1966. Research assoc. J.W. Goethe U., Frankfurt/Main, Fed. Republic Germany, 1966-68; research assoc. Rockefeller U., N.Y.C., 1968-70; faculty U. Iowa, Iowa City, 1970—, prof. biochemistry, 1979—. Contbr. articles to profl. jours.; mem. editorial bd. Jour. Biol. Chemistry, Archives Biochemistry and Biophysics. Am. Cancer Soc. fellow, 1966-68. Mem. Am. Soc. for Biochemistry and Molecular Biology, Am. Chem. Soc., Sigma Xi. Avocations: travel; sports. Office: U Iowa Dept Biochemistry 4-370 BSB Iowa City IA 52242

PLASIL, FRANZ, physicist; b. Prague, Czechoslovakia, May 17, 1939; came to U.S., 1960; s, Frank and Eva (Wenger) P.; m. Catherine Logan, Feb. 15, 1964 (div. Sept. 1979); 1 child, Maia; m. Carol Baratz, Apr. 12, 1980. BS, Queen Mary Coll., U. London, 1960; PhD, U. Calif., Berkeley, 1964. Chemist Lawrence Berkeley (Calif.) Lab., 1964-65; rsch. assoc. Brookhaven Nat. Lab., Upton, N.Y., 1965-67; rsch. staff physics div. Oak Ridge (Tenn.) Nat. Lab., 1967-78, group leader physics div., 1978-86, sect. head physics div., 1986—. Contbr. articles to Annals of Physics, Phys. Rev., Phys. Rev. Letters. Recipient Alexander von Humboldt award 1985. Fellow Am. Phys. Soc. Achievements include definition of angular-momentum-imposed limits on the stability of rotating nuclei. Home: 964 W Outer Dr Oak Ridge TN 37830-8607 Office: Oak Ridge Nat Lab PO Box 2008 Oak Ridge TN 37831-6372

PLASKETT, THOMAS G., transportation company executive; b. Raytown, Mo., Dec. 24, 1943; s. Warren E. and Frances S. (Winegar) P.; m. Linda Lee Maxey, June 8, 1968; children—Kimberly, Keith. B.I.E., Gen. Motors Inst.; M.B.A., Harvard U. Supr. indsl. engring. Gen. Motors, Flint, Mich., 1968, supt. indsl. engring., 1969-73; sr. staff asst., treas Gen. Motors, N.Y.C., 1973; asst. controller Am. Airlines, N.Y.C., 1974, v.p. mktg. adminstrn., 1975-76, sr. v.p. fin., 1976-80; sr. v.p. mktg. Am. Airlines, Dallas, from 1980; pres., chief exec. officer Continental Airlines Inc., Houston, Tex., until 1988; chmn., chief exec. officer, pres. Pan Am Corp., N.Y.C., 1988-91; mng. dir. Fox Run Capital Assocs., 1991—; dir., interim pres., CEO, acting CFO Greyhound Lines, Inc., Dallas, 1994-95, chmn., dir., 1995—; bd. dirs. Tandy Corp., Ft. Worth, Neostar Retail Group, Dallas, Smart & Final, Inc., L.A. Mem. bus. adv. com. Northwestern U. Transp. Ctr.; trustee GMI Engring. and Mgmt. Inst., Flint, Mich. Avocations: golf, skiing, squash. Office: 5215 N O'Connor Ste 1070 Irving TX 75039

PLASKONOS, ANNE, school nurse; b. McAdoo, Pa., June 10, 1917; d. Theodore and Martha (Snihur) P. Diploma in nursing, St. Agnes Hosp., 1939; postgrad., Willis Eye Hosp., Phila., 1948; BS in Edn., U. Pa., 1954; M in Health Edn., Temple U., 1964, postgrad., 1940, 50. RN, Pa. Staff Comty. Disease Hosp., Phila., 1940, Fitzgerald Hosp., Phila., N.D., 1941-44; ensign USNR, Phila., N.C., 1944; staff Vis. Nurse Soc. Phila., 1954-57, U.S. Pub. Health Svc., Whapeton, N.D., 1957-58, Nazareth Hosp., Phila., 1958; retired, 1993. Ensign USN, 1944. Mem. ANA (life), Am. Sch. Health Assn., Temple U. Alumni Assn. (life), St. Agnes Hosp. Alumni Assn. (life), Women in Edn.

PLAT, RICHARD VERTIN, corporate finance executive; b. San Jose, Calif., July 14, 1929; s. Gaston and Frances (Vertin) P.; children from previous marriage: Julie, Carl, Marsha; m. Janet Toll Davidson, Dec. 19, 1992. BEE, U. Santa Clara, 1951; MBA, Washington U., St. Louis, 1957. Sr. ind. econ. Stanford Rsch. Inst., Menlo Park, Calif., 1959-65; dir. planning Litton Industries, Inc., Beverly Hills, Calif., 1965-70; v.p. Waltham Industries, N.Y.C., 1970-71, Computer Machinery Corp., L.A., 1971-77; exec. v.p. Pacific Scientific Co., Newport Beach, Calif., 1978—; bd. dirs. Powertec Indsl. Corp., Rock Hill, S.C., Automation Intelligence, Inc., Duluth, Ga., High Yield Tech., Inc., Sunnyvale, Calif., Helisys, Inc., Torrance, Calif., Pacific Sci. Ltd., Royce Thompson Ltd., Eng., Pacific Sci. S.A.R.L., France, Pacific Sci. GmbH, Eduard Bautz GmbH, Fed. Republic of Germany, Pacific Sci. Internat., Inc., U.S., V.I. 1st lt. U.S. Army, 1951-54. Mem. Fin. Execs. Inst. (bd. dirs., v.p. 1984—). Republican. Club: Jonathan (L.A.), Balboa Bay (Newport Beach, Calif.). Home: 2027 Bayside Dr Corona Del Mar CA 92625-1847 Office: Pacific Scientific Co 620 Newport Center Dr Newport Beach CA 92660-6420

PLATE, THOMAS GORDON, newspaper columnist, educator; b. N.Y.C., May 17, 1944; s. John William and Irene (Henry) P.; m. Andrea I. Margolis, Sept. 22, 1979; 1 child, Ashley Alexandra. AB, Amherst Coll., 1966; MPA, Princeton U., 1968. Writer Newsweek, N.Y.C., 1968-70; editor Newsday, L.I., N.Y., 1970-72; sr. editor N.Y. Mag., N.Y.C., 1972-75; editor edit. page L.A. Herald Examiner, 1978-82; sr. editor Time Mag., N.Y.C., 1982-83; editor in chief Family Weekly, N.Y.C., 1984-85; editor edit. pages N.Y. Newsday, N.Y.C., 1986-89; editor edit. pages L.A. Times, 1989-95, Times Op-Ed Page columnist, 1995—; vis. prof. UCLA Pub. Policy Sch. and Letters and Scis.; mem. founders bd. UCLA Sch. Pub. Policy. Author: Understanding Doomsday, 1971, Crime Pays!, 1975, Secret Police, 1981; co-author: Commissioner, 1978. Recipient Best Deadline Writing award Am. Soc. Newspaper Editors, 1981, Best Edit. awards L.A. Press Club, 1979, 80, 81, Best Edit. award Calif. Newspaper Pubs. Assn., 1991, 92, 94. Mem. Pacific Coun. on Internat. Rels., Century Assn. (N.Y.C.), Phi Beta Kappa. Avocations: tennis, fiction writing, computer games. Office: LA Times Times Mirror Sq Los Angeles CA 90053

PLATER, WILLIAM MARMADUKE, English language educator, academic administrator; b. East St. Louis, Ill., July 26, 1945; s. Everett Marmaduke and Marguerite (McBride) P.; m. Gail Maxwell, Oct. 16, 1971; children: Elizabeth Rachel, David Matthew. BA, U. Ill., 1967, MA in English, 1969, PhD in English, 1973. Asst. dir. Unit One, asst. to dean Coll. Liberal Arts and Scis. U. Ill., Urbana, 1971-72, acting dir. Unit One, 1972-73, asst. dean Coll. Arts and Scis., 1973-74, asst. dir. Sch. Humanities, 1974-77, dir., 1977-83, assoc. coordinator interdisciplinary programs, 1977-83; prof. English, dean Sch. Liberal Arts Ind. U., Indpls., 1983-87; dean of faculties Ind. U.-Purdue U., Indpls., 1987—, exec. vice chancellor, 1988—; cons. in field. Author: The Grim Phoenix: Reconstructing Thomas Pynchon, 1978, also articles, revs., poetry. Bd. dirs. Ind. Com. for Humanities, 1986-92, Ind. Repertory Theatre, 1987-93, Children's Mus., 1992—, U. Ill. YMCA, Urbana, 1982-83, Herron Gallery Contemporary Art, 1987—. Recipient Program Innovation prize Am. Acad. Ednl. Devel., 1982. Mem. MLA, Midwest MLA. Home: 3919 Cooper Ln Indianapolis IN 46208-3136 Office: Ind U-Purdue U Adminstrn Bldg Indianapolis IN 46202

PLATER-ZYBERK, ELIZABETH MARIA, architectural educator; b. Bryn Mawr, Pa., Dec. 20, 1950; d. Josaphat and Maria (Meysztowicz) P.-Z.; m. Andres M. Duany, June 12, 1976. BA in Architecture, Princeton U., 1972; MArch, Yale U., 1974. Registered architect, Fla. Architect, prin. Andres Duany & Elizabeth Plater-Zyberk, Architects, Miami, Fla., 1979—; prof. U. Miami, 1979—; dean Sch. Architecture U. Miami, 1995—. Contbr. numerous articles to profl. jours. and popular publs. Mem. adv. coun. Princeton (N.J.) U. Sch. Architecture, 1982—, trustee 1987-91, 93-2003; mem. vis. com. MIT Sch. Architecture, 1990—. Mem. AIA, Archtl. Club Miami (pres. 1982-87). Office: 1023 SW 25th Ave Miami FL 33135-4824

PLATIS, JAMES G., secondary school educator; b. Detroit, Mar. 23, 1927; s. Sam and Myra (Theodore) P.; m. Mary Lou Campbell, Aug. 16, 1974. BS in Physical Edn., Ind. U., 1955, MS in Edn., 1965; postgrad., Ind. State U., 1967. Cert. physical edn. tchr., Ind. Foreman Cast Armor, Inc., East Chicago, Ind., 1951-53, Youngstown Sheet & Tube, East Chicago, 1953-54; dir., tchr. East Chicago Pub. Schs., 1955—; sports editor East Chicago Globe/Calumet News, 1973-78, Herald Newspapers, Merrillville, Ind., 1973-78. Contbr. articles to newspapers, jours. Founder East Chicago Hall of Fame, 1975, Little Olympics, East Chicago, 1956; pres. Ind. Am. Amateur Baseball Congress, 1954-57, commr., 1984-96; dir. No. Ind. State Sports Mus., 1988-96. Cpl. AUS, 1945-47, ETO. Named to Ind. Amateur Baseball Hall of Fame, 1962, East Chicago Hall of Fame, 1976, All-Am. Amateur Baseball Congress, 1955, 56, The Athletic Congress Masters All-Am., 1986, 87, 88, 89, 90, 91, 92, 93, 94, 95, 96; selected to 90 Yr. Greatest Athletes in East Chicago History, Nat. Athletic Congress, 1990; named Amateur Coach of Yr., U.S. Baseball Fedn. Ind., 1990, Amateur Runner-up Coach of Yr., 1988; recipient 19 World and 27 Nat. No. 1 track rankings, Athletic Congress Masters, 1989, 90, 91, 92, 93, 94, 95, 96, 14 League Batting Titles, 12 MV League Players awards; 18 times Ind. all-state team; mem. team won 52 League Championships, 53 Playoff championships, 39 Ind. State Baseball Championships, 7 World Regional Titles, 5 World Finalists, 2 runner-up World Champions, Nat. C.I.O. Baseball Championship. Fellow Nat. Assn. Basketball Coaches, Am. Assn. Health, Phys. Edn. and Recreation; mem. Athletic Dirs. Assn. Sportswriters Guild, VFW, Am. Legion. Republican. Avocations: reading, running, baseball, writing. Home: 427 Fisher St Munster IN 46321-2330 Office: E Chgo Pub Schs 2700 Cardinal Dr East Chicago IN 46312-3150

PLATIS, TOM GUST, lawyer, oil company executive; b. Price, Utah, Dec. 8, 1939; s. Gust Nick and Matilda (Hvala) P.; m. Helen J. Rasmussen, July 3, 1964; children: Tiffany, Christopher, John, Andrea. AS, Coll. Ea. Utah, 1960; JD, U. Utah, 1964. Bar: Utah 1964, Calif. 1975, Kans. 1978. Law clk. to presiding justice Utah Supreme Ct., Salt Lake City, 1963-65; pvt. practice law Salt Lake City, 1965-68; asst. atty. gen. State of Utah, 1964-68; judge City of Price, 1968-72; adminstrv. law judge Calif. Bd. of Unemployment and Appeals, Sacramento and Fresno, Calif., 1972-77; sr. adminstrv. law judge Calif. Bd. of Unemployment and Appeals, Fresno, 1977-78; pres., gen. counsel Hiway, Inc., Topeka, 1978-90. Mem. Crimestoppers of Kans., Inc. Mem. ABA, Topeka Bar Assn., California State Bar, Utah State Bar. Office: Hiway Inc 534 S Kansas Ave Ste 1200 Topeka KS 66603-3434

PLATNER, JOHN LELAND, process equipment company executive; b. Palmyra, Wis., Oct. 13, 1932; s. Lyle K. and Irma Amelia (Mundshau) P. m. Mary Lois Singer, June 19, 1954; children: Teresa Ann, Karen Jean, Susan Marie, Thomas Charles, Jean Marie, Patricia Ann. BSME, U. Wis., Madison, 1954; postgrad., U. Wis., Milw. Registered profl. engr., Wis. Corp. v.p. Allis-Chalmers Corp., Milw., 1976-88, v.p. strategic planning and bus. devel., 1982-83, v.p. tech., 1983-84, pres. Allis. Chalmers Energy and Minerals Co., 1984-88, pres. Allis-Chalmers Solids Process Equipment Co., 1986-88; pres. Boliden Allis, Inc., Milw., 1988-90, Svedala Inc., Milw., 1991—; also bd. dirs. Svedala Inc., Waukesha, Wis. Served to capt. USAF, 1954-57. Mem. Am. Mining Congress (bd. govs. mfrs. div.), Am. Mgmt. Assn., Am. So. Mech. Engrs., Soc. Mining Engrs. Republican. Avocation: commercial instrument pilot. Office: Svedala Inc 20965 Crossroads Cir Waukesha WI 53186*

PLATNER, WARREN, architect; b. Balt., June 18, 1919; s. Warren Kelly and Alice Darling (Chapman) P.; m. Joan Payne, 1945; children: Bronson, Joan, Sharon, Madeleine. B.Arch., Cornell U., 1941. Assoc. Eero Saarinen and Assocs. (architects), 1950-65; propr. Warren Platner Assocs. (architects), New Haven, 1965—; vis. lectr. archtl. schs. Prin. works include Kent Meml. Library, Suffield, Conn., 1972, Princeton U. Prospect Center, 1970, MGIC Hdqrs, Milw., 1973, Am. Restaurant, Kansas City, Mo., 1974; malls at Water Tower Pl., Chgo., 1975, Windows on the World, N.Y.C., 1976, Standard Brands Research Center, Wilton, Conn., 1979, Providence Athenaeum, 1980; Sea Containers Hdqrs., London, 1983, Wildflower Restaurant Lodge, Vail, Colo., 1985, Porter, Wright, Morris & Arthur Headqrs., Columbus, Ohio, 1986, Pan Am Bldg. additions, N.Y.C., 1987, ships Fantasia and Fiesta, 1990, Carlyle Hotel additions, 1990, Fair Residence, 1990, Friedman Residence, 1993. Recipient Rome prize architecture, 1955; advanced research Fulbright award architecture, 1955; Graham Found. award advanced studies fine arts, 1962; 1st ann. award Designers Lighting Forum, 1975; Pres.'s fellow R.I. Sch. Design, 1980; Interior Design Hall of Fame award, 1985; also several internat. design awards. Fellow AIA, Am. Acad. in Rome. Address: 18 Mitchell Dr New Haven CT 06511-2516

PLATNICK, NORMAN I., curator, arachnologist; b. Bluefield, W.Va., Dec. 30, 1951; s. Philip and Fannie (Kascenewsky) P.; m. Nancy Stewart Price, June 14, 1970; 1 child, William Durin. BS in Biology, Concord Coll., 1968; MS in Zoology, Mich. State U., 1970; PhD in Biology, Harvard U., 1973. Asst. curator Am. Mus. Natural History, N.Y.C., 1973-77, assoc. curator, 1977-82, curator, 1982—, chmn. dept. entomology, 1987-94; sci. attaché Consulate of Gondwana, N.Y.C., 1976—. Author: Advances in Spider Taxonomy, 1989, 93; co-author: Systematics and Biogeography, 1981; co-editor: Advances in Cladistics, 1983. V.p. Ctr. Internat. de Documentation Arachnologie, 1986-89 (pres. 1995-98). Fellow Willi Hennig Soc. (founder, pres. 1990-92); mem. Am. Arachnological Soc. (charter, membership sec. 1976—). Office: Am Mus Natural History Central Pk W At 79th St W New York NY 10024

PLATOU, JOANNE (DODE), museum director; b. Mpls., Jan. 6, 1919; d. Wesley Richmond and Catherine Harriet (Fisher) Pierson; m. Ralph Victor Platou, Jan. 23, 1942 (dec. Sept. 1968); children: Peter Erling, Thomas Stoud, Mary Kirk Platou Marloff. BS, U. Minn., 1939; MFA, Tulane U., 1959. Columnist Mpls. Tribune, 1939-42; med. photographer Ochsner Clinic, New Orleans, 1943-46; tchr. photography Metairie (La.) Pk. Country Day Sch., 1946-51; free lance artist New Orleans, 1953-68; curator edn. New Orleans Mus. Art, 1969-75; chief curator Historic New Orleans Collection, 1976-86, dir., 1986-92, dir. emerita, 1992—; bd. dirs. Arts Coun. New Orleans, 1972-88, Long Vue House and Gardens, New Orleans, 1982-88; tchr. mus. career course Tulane U., New Orleans, 1983-87. Curator exhbns. The Wit of It, 1972, The Art Works, 1972, The Camera, 1974; author catalogue, curator exhbn. Alfred R. Waud, 1979. NEH grantee, New Orleans Mus. Art, 1975. Mem. Am. Mus. Assn., Friends of the Cabildo, Coll. Art Assn., Am. Assn. State and Local History. Avocations: travel, gardening.

PLATSIS, GEORGE JAMES, lawyer; b. Khaniá, Crete, Nov. 8, 1937; came to U.S., 1938; s. Artemi and Marika (Siradakis) Platsidakis; m. Barbara Jean Spor, Aug. 16, 1964; children: Christina Mary, Maria Elizabeth. BA, U. Mich., 1962, JD, 1967. Bar: D.C. 1969, Mich. 1969, U.S. Ct. Appeals, U.S. Ct. Appeals (6th cir.), U.S. Dist. Ct. (we. dist.) Mich. Atty. FTC, Washington, 1967-69; asst. atty. gen. Mich. Dept. Atty. Gen., Lansing, 1969-75; spl. asst. atty. gen. Mich. Dept. Atty. Gen., Okemos, 1975-89; pvt. practice, Okemos, 1975—. Bd. dirs., v.p., treas. Holy Trinity Greek Orthodox Ch., Lansing, 1980-84, 94-95. With U.S. Army, 1963-65. Mem. Am. Hellenic Ednl. and Progressive Assn. (local officer 1975—, dist. gov. 1980—, supreme counsellor 1989-90), Pancretau Assn. Am. (legal advisor 1984-86), Kiwanis. Avocations: sailing, travel, archaeology. Office: 2019 Shagbark Ln Okemos MI 48864-3631

PLATSOUCAS, CHRIS DIMITRIOS, immunologist; b. Athens, Greece, Apr. 17, 1951; came to U.S., 1973; s. Dimitrios Evagelos and Maria (Tsonidis) P.; m. Emilia L. Oleszak, Oct. 18, 1985. BS, U. Patras (Greece), 1973; postgrad., Purdue U., 1974; PhD, MIT, 1978. Rsch. fellow/assoc. Meml. Sloan-Kettering Cancer Ctr., N.Y.C., 1978-80, asst. mem., 1980-85, asst. prof., 1981-85, head lab. biol. response modifiers, 1981-85; assoc. prof. dept. immunology M.D. Anderson Cancer Ctr., Houston, 1985-89, prof., dep. chmn., 1989-93, Ashbel Smith professorship, 1991-92, H.L. and O. Stringer professorship in cancer rsch., 1992-93; L.H. Carnell prof. and chmn. dept. microbiology, immunology Temple U. Sch. Medicine, Phila., 1993—; biotech. cons., sci. renewer study sects. NIH, Bethesda, 1982—. Contbr. numerous articles to profl. jours. Nat. Rsch. Svc. award NIH, 1978-79; NIH grantee, 1982—, Am. Cancer Soc. grantee, 1980-91. Mem. Am. Assn. Immunologists, Am. Soc. Hematology, Am. Assn. Biochem & Molecular Biology, Am. Assn. Pathologists. Greek Orthodox. Achievements include patents in field; research on human T cell immunology, on T-cell antigen receptors, on tumor-infiltrating lymphocytes in malignant melanoma and ovarian carcinoma, on lymphoproliferative disorders, on immunoregulatory factors. Office: Temple U Sch Medicine Dept Microbiology and Immunology 3400 N Broad St Philadelphia PA 19140-5196

PLATT, CHARLES ADAMS, architect, planner; b. N.Y.C., May 16, 1932; s. William and Margaret (Littell) P.; m. Joan Mathieson, June 20, 1958; children: Sylvia, Ethan, Virginia L. A.B., Harvard, 1954, M.Arch., 1960. Gen. ptnr. Smotrich & Platt, N.Y.C., 1965-85, Charles A. Platt Ptnrs., N.Y.C., 1985-89; ptnr. Platt Byard Dovell, 1989—; assoc. prof. Columbia U. Grad. Sch. Architecture and Planning, 1985-86. Mem. nat. panel arbitrators Am. Aribitration Assn.; bd. dirs. Pub. Health Research Inst., N.Y.C., 1982-92, The New 42nd Street, 1990—, Municipal Art Soc., N.Y.C., 1966-78, 85—; pres. bd. trustees Augustus St.-Gaudens Meml., 1977-91; commr. N.Y.C. Landmarks Preservation Commn., 1979-84. Recipient Nat. Honor award for excellence in architecture AIA, 1969, Bard award for civic architecture and urban design, 1969, 85, Record Interiors award, 1970, 73, 75, Record House awards, 1971, 78, Et Alia. Mem. AIA, Century Club (N.Y.C.). Home: 1261 Madison Ave New York NY 10128-0569 Office: Platt Byard Dovell Archs 19 Union Sq W New York NY 10003-3307

PLATT, FRANKLIN DEWITT, history educator; b. Marion, La., Nov. 15, 1932; s. Robert Baxter and Ethel Estelle (White) P.; m. Dixie Ferguson, Aug. 4, 1956; 1 dau. Dixie. B.A., La. State U., 1955; Rockefeller Bros. Theol. fellow, Union Theol. Sem., 1955-56; A.M., Washington U., St. Louis, 1963, Ph.D., 1969. Instr. dept. humanities Mich. State U., 1964-69, asst. prof., 1969-72, assoc. prof., 1972-77, prof., 1977-89, asst. chmn. dept. humanities, 1971-78, chmn., 1978-80, prof. dept. history, 1989—. Co-author: The Western Humanities, 1991 (named Best Coll. Textbook Bookbuilders West 1991), Readings in the Western Humanities, 1994. Served with USNR, 1956-60. Home: 1134 Southlawn Ave East Lansing MI 48823-3041 Office: Mich State U Dept History East Lansing MI 48824

PLATT, JAN KAMINIS, former county official; b. St. Petersburg, Fla., Sept. 27, 1936; d. Peter Clifton and Adele (Diamond) Kaminis; m. William R. Platt, Feb. 8, 1962; 1 son, Kevin Peter. B.A., Fla. State U., 1958; postgrad. U. Fla. Law Sch., 1958-59, U. Va., 1962, Vanderbilt U., 1964. Pub. sch. tchr. Hillsborough County, Tampa, Fla., 1959-60; field dir. Girl Scouts Suncoast Coun., Tampa, 1960-62; city councilman Tampa City Council, 1974-78; county commr. Hillsborough County, 1978-94; chmn. Hillsborough County Bd. County commrs., 1980-81, 83-84, ret., 1994; chmn. Tampa Bay Regional Planning Council, 1982; chmn. West Coast Regional Water Supply Authority, Tampa, 1985; chmn. Hillsborough County Council of Govts., 1976, 79; chmn. Sunshine Amendment Drive 7th Congrl. Dist., Tampa, 1976; chmn. Community Action Agy., Tampa, 1980-81, 83-84; chmn. pro tem Tampa Charter Revision Commn., 1975; chmn. Prison Sitting Task Force, Tampa, 1983, Tampa Housing Study Com., 1983, Met. Planning

Orgn., Tampa, 1984, Bd. Tax Adjustment, Tampa, 1984; appointee Constitution Revision Commn., Fla., 1977, HRS Dist. IV Adv. Council, Fla.; mem. Hillsborough County Expressway Authority, Taxicab Commn.; vice chmn. steering com. Nat. Assn. Counties Environ. Task Force; Bd. dirs. March of Dimes, Tampa, The Fla. Orchestra, Tampa; trustee Hillsborough County Hosp. Authority, Tampa, 1984-94; pres. Suncoast Girl Scout Council, Citizens Alert, Tampa, Bay View Garden Club; v.p. Hillsborough County Bar Aux.; mem. adv. bd. Northside Community Mental Health Ctr.; Access House, Tampa; active mem. Arts Council of Tampa-Hillsborough County, 1983-85, Drug Abuse Coordinating Council Orgn., Tampa, Bd. Criminal Justice, Tampa, Fla. Council on Aging, Inebriate Task Force, Tampa, Tampa Downtown Devel. Authority Task Force, Tampa Sports Authority, Tampa Area Mental Health Bd., Children's Study Commn., Manahill Area Agy. on Aging, Tampa, Athena Soc., Tampa Area Com. Fgn. Affairs, LWV. Recipient Athena award Women in Comm., 1976, First Annual Humanitarian award Nat. Orgn. for Prevention of Animal Suffering, 1981, Spessard Holland Meml. award Tampa Bay Com. for Good Govt., 1979, First Lady of Yr. award Beta Sigma Phi, 1980, Women Helping Women award Soroptimist Internat. Tampa, 1983, Eliza Wolff award Tampa United Methodist Ctrs., 1982, Good Govt. award Tampa Jaycees, 1983, Good Govt. award League of Women Voters, 1983. Mem. Am. Judicature Soc., State Assn. County Commrs. Fla. (at-large dir.), AAUW (bd. dirs.), Mortar Bd., Garnet Key, Phi Beta Kappa, Phi Kappa Phi. Democrat. Episcopalian. Home and Office: 3531 Village Way Tampa FL 33629-8950

PLATT, JOSEPH BEAVEN, former college president; b. Portland, Oreg., Aug. 12, 1915; s. William Bradbury and Mary (Beaven) P.; m. Jean Ferguson Rusk, Feb. 9, 1946; children: Ann Ferguson Walker, Elizabeth Beaven Garrow. BA, U. Rochester, 1937; PhD, Cornell U., 1942; LLD, U. So. Calif., 1969, Claremont McKenna Coll., 1982; DSc, Harvey Mudd Coll., 1981. Instr. physics U. Rochester, N.Y., 1941-43, from asst. prof. to prof., 1946-56, assoc. chmn. dept. physics, 1954-56; staff mem. radiation lab. MIT, Cambridge, 1943-46; pres. Harvey Mudd Coll., Claremont, Calif., 1956-76, now part-time sr. prof. physics; pres. Claremont U. Ctr., 1976-81; trustee Aerospace Corp., 1972-85, Consortium for Advancement of Pvt. Higher Edn., 1985-92; chief physics br. AEC, 1949-51; cons. U.S. Office Ordnance Rsch., NSF, 1953-56; mem. com. on sci. in UNESCO, Nat. Acad. Scis.-NRC, 1960-62, mem. com. on internat. orgns. and programs, 1962-64; sci. advisor U.S. Del., UNESCO Gen. Conf., Paris, 1960, alt. del., 1962; mem. panel on internat. sci. Pres.'s Sci. Adv. Com., 1961; chmn. Subcom. on Sino-Am. Sci. Cooperation, 1965-79; trustee Analytic Svcs., Inc., 1958-89, chmn., 1961-89; mem. adv. com. on sci. edn. NSF, 1965-70, 72-76, chmn., 1969-70, 73-74, 74-75; bd. dirs. Lincoln Found., 1979-85, Bell & Howell Corp., 1978-88, Am. Mut. Fund, 1981-88, DeVry, Inc., 1984-87, Sigma Rsch., 1983-87, Jacobs Engring. Co., 1978-86. Author: Harvey Mudd College: The First Twenty YEars, 1994. Trustee China Found. for Promotion of Edn. and Culture, 1966—, Carnegie Found. for Advancement Tchg., 1970-78; chmn. select com. Master Plan for Higher Edn. Calif., 1971-73; mem. Carnegie Coun. for Policy Studies in Higher Edn., 1975-80. Fellow Am. Phys. Soc.; mem. IEEE, Automobile Club So. Calif. (bd. dirs. 1973-90, chmn. bd. dirs. 1986-87), Calif. Club, Sunset Club, Twilight Club, Cosmos Club, Bohemian Club, Phi Beta Kappa, Sigma Xi, Phi Kappa Phi. Home: 452 W 11th St Claremont CA 91711-3833

PLATT, LEWIS EMMETT, electronics company executive; b. Johnson City, N.Y., Apr. 11, 1941; s. Norval Lewis and Margaret Dora (Williams) P.; m. Joan Ellen Redmund, Jan. 15, 1983; children: Caryn, Laura, Amanda, Hillary. BME, Cornell U., 1964; MBA, U. Pa., 1966. With Hewlett Packard, Waltham, Mass., 1966-71, engring. mgr., 1971-74, ops. mgr., 1976-77, div. gen. mgr., 1974-80, group gen. mgr., Palo Alto, Calif., 1980-84, v.p., 1983-85, exec. v.p., 1987-92, pres., CEO, chmn., 1993—; dir. Molex Inc., Lisle, Ill.; dir. Pacific Telesis. Trustee Waltham Hosp., 1978-80, Wharton Sch. Bd. Overseers, 1993; mem. Mid-Peninsula YMCA, 1980—, Cornell U. Coun., 1992, Computer Sys. Policy Project, 1993, Calif. Bus. Roundtable, 1993, Bus. Coun., 1993, Bay Area Coun., 1993, Bus. Roundtable, 1993; vice chmn. Y Coun., 1989. Recipient Red Triangle award Min-Peninsula YMCA, 1992, Internat. Citizens award World Forum Silicon Valley, San Jose, Calif., 1994. Mem. IEEE, Sci. Apparatus Mfg. Assn. (dir. 1978-80). Office: Hewlett Packard Co 3000 Hanover St Palo Alto CA 94303-1112

PLATT, MARK E., motion picture company executive. Pres. Orion Pictures Prodns., L.A. Office: Orion Pictures Prodns 1888 Century Park E Los Angeles CA 90067-1702

PLATT, NICHOLAS, Asian affairs specialist, retired ambassador; b. N.Y.C., Mar. 10, 1936; s. Geoffrey and Helen (Choate) P.; m. Sheila Maynard, June 28, 1957; children: Adam, Oliver, Nicholas. B.A. cum laude, Harvard U., 1957; M.A., Johns Hopkins U., 1959. Commd. fgn. service officer Dept. State, 1959; vice consul Windsor, Ont., Can., 1959-61; Chinese lang. trainee, 1962-63; polit. officer consulate gen. Hong Kong, 1964-68; chief Asian Communist areas div. Bur. Intelligence and Research, Dept. State, Washington, 1969, chief North Asia div., 1970, dept. dir. Exec. Secretariat staff, 1971, dir. staff, 1972-73; chief polit. sect. U.S. Liaison Office, Peking, China, 1973-74; 1st sec. Am. embassy, Tokyo, 1974-77; dir. Office of Japanese Affairs, Dept. State, 1977-78; mem. staff Nat. Security Council, White House, 1978-79; dep. asst. sec. for internat. security affairs Dept. Def., 1980-81; dep. asst. sec. for internat. orgn. affairs Dept. State, 1981-82; amb. Lusaka, Zambia, 1982-84; exec. sec., psl. asst. to sec. state Dept. State, 1985-87; amb. Manila, The Philippines, 1987-91, Pakistan, 1991-92; pres. Asia Soc., N.Y.C., 1992—. Recipient Meritorious award exemplary achievement pub. adminstrn. William A. Jump Found., 1973, Disting. Civilian Svc. medal Dept. Def., 1981, Presdl. Merit award, 1985, 87, Disting. Honor award U.S. Dept. State, 1987, 91, Wilbur Carr award, 1992. Mem. N.Y. Council Fgn. Relations. Clubs: Metropolitan (Washington); Century (N.Y.C.). Home: 131 E 69th St New York NY 10021-5158

PLATT, OLIVER, actor. Films include: Crusoe, 1988, Married to the Mob, 1988, Working Girl, 1988, Flatliners, 1990, Postcards from the Edge, 1990, Beethoven, 1992, Diggstown, 1992, Benny & Joon, 1993, Indecent Proposal, 1993, The Temp, 1993, The Three Musketeers, 1993, Tall Tale, 1995, Funny Bones, 1995, Executive Decision, 1996, A Time to Kill, 1996. Office: c/o William Morris Agy 151 El Camino Beverly Hills CA 90212

PLATT, PETER GODFREY, lawyer; b. Battle Creek, Mich., May 11, 1937; s. Frank Kenneth and Louise Joy (Godfrey) P.; m. Kristine Koch; children: Peter G. Jr., Geoffrey B. BA, Yale U., 1959, JD, 1962. Bar: Calif. 1962. Assoc. Brobeck, Phleger & Harrison, San Francisco, 1962-68, ptnr., 1969-90; ptnr. Coudert Bros., San Francisco, 1990-95, Bangkok, Thailand, 1995—. Trustee Grace Cathedral, San Francisco, 1976—, chmn. bd. trustees, 1985-89; mem. bd. govs. San Francisco Symphony, 1981—, v.p., 1993—; bd. dirs. Arthritis Found., San Francisco, 1983-86; chancellor Episcopal Diocese of Calif., 1989—. Mem. Calif. Bar Assn., San Francisco Bar Assn. Republican. Episcopalian. Clubs: San Francisco Golf, Pacific Union (San Francisco), Burlingame Country (Hillsborough, Calif.) (sec. 1980), Links (N.Y.C.). Avocation: golf. Office: Coudert Bros Ste 3300 Four Embarcadero Ctr San Francisco CA 94111

PLATT, SHERMAN PHELPS, JR., publishing consultant; b. N.Y.C., Mar. 29, 1918; s. Sherman Phelps and Penelope (Sears) P.; m. Leila Bronson, Jan. 11, 1941 (div. 1968); children: Sherman Phelps III, John, Bronson; m. Margaret McClure Smithers, 1968. Grad., Taft Sch., 1936; B.A., Yale, 1940. With Dodd, Mead & Co., N.Y.C., 1940-82, beginning as editor, successively salesman, prodn. mgr., sec., dir., exec. v.p., then pres., until 1982; v.p., dir. Apollo Edits., Inc., N.Y.C., 1962-72; pub. cons., 1982—. Served as 1st lt. inf. U.S. Army, 1943-46. Mem. Yale Club (N.Y.C.). Home: 38 Aylesbury Circle Madison CT 06443-3434

PLATT, THOMAS COLLIER, JR., federal judge; b. N.Y.C., N.Y., May 29, 1925; s. Thomas Collier and Louise Platt; m. Ann Byrd Symington, June 25, 1948; children: Ann Byrd, Charles Collier, Thomas Collier, III, Elizabeth Louise. B.A., Yale U., 1947, LL.B., 1950. Bar: N.Y. 1950. Assoc. Root, Ballantine, Harlan, Bushby & Palmer, N.Y.C., 1950-53; asst. U.S. atty. Bklyn., 1953-56; assoc. Bleakley, Platt, Schmidt, Hart & Fritz, N.Y.C., 1956-60, ptnr., 1960-74; judge U.S. Dist. Ct. (ea. dist.) N.Y., Bklyn., 1974—, chief judge, 1988-95; former dir. Phoenix Mut. Life Ins. Co., RAC Corp., McIntyre Aviation, Inc.; atty. Village of Laurel Hollow, N.Y., 1958-74; acting police justice Village of Lloyd Harbor, N.Y., 1958-63. Alt. del. Republican Nat. Conv., 1964, 68, 72; del. N.Y. State Rep. Conv., 1966; trustee Brooks Sch., North Andover, Mass., 1968-82, pres., 1970-74. Served with USN, 1943-46. Mem. Fed. Judges Assn. (sec., bd. dirs. 1982-91). Episcopalian. Clubs: Phelps Assn. (New Haven) (bd. govs. 1960—); Cold Spring Harbor Beach (N.Y.) (bd. mgrs. 1964-70); Yale of N.Y.C. Office: US Dist Ct Uniondale Ave at Hempstead Tpke Uniondale NY 11553

PLATT, TREVOR CHARLES, oceanographer, scientist; b. Salford, Eng., Aug. 12, 1942; arrived in Can., 1963; s. John and Lily (Hibbert) P.; m. Shubha Sathyendranath, Feb. 24, 1988. BSc, U. Nottingham, U.K., 1963; MA, U. Toronto, Ont., Can., 1965; PhD, Dalhousie U., Halifax, N.S., Can., 1970. Rsch. scientist Bedford Inst. Oceanography, Dartmouth, N.S., 1965-72, chief biol. oceanography, 1972—; chmn. Joint Global Ocean Flux Study, 1991-93. Recipient Rosenstiel medal U. Miami, 1984, A.G. Huntsman medal A.G. Huntsman Found., 1992. Fellow Royal Soc. Can., Acad. Sci. Can.; mem. Am. Soc. Limnology and Oceanography (pres. 1990-92, G.E. Hutchinson medal 1988). Home: 33 Crichton Park Rd, Dartmouth, NS Canada B3A 2N9 Office: Bedford Inst Oceanography, Dartmouth, NS Canada B2Y 4A2

PLATT, WILLIAM HENRY, judge; b. Allentown, Pa., Jan. 25, 1940; s. Henry and Genevieve (McElroy) P.; m. Maureen Hart, Nov. 29, 1969; children: Meredith H., William H., James H. AB, Dickinson Coll., 1961; JD, U. Pa., 1964. Bar: Pa. 1967, U.S. Supreme Ct. 1971. Ptnr. Yarus and Platt, Allentown, 1967-77; asst. pub. defender Lehigh County (Pa.), 1972-75, chief pub. defender, 1975-76, dist. atty., 1976-91; ptnr. Eckert, Seamans, Cherin & Mellott, 1991-95; judge Ct. Common Pleas of Lehigh County, Allentown, 1996—; mem. criminal procedural rules com. Supreme Ct. Pa., 1982-92, chmn., 1986-92. Mem. Gov.'s Trial Ct. Nominating Commn. Lehigh County, 1984-87; mem. Pa. Commn. on Crime and Delinquency Victim Services Adv. Com., 1983-91. Served with M.P., U.S. Army, 1964-66. Mem. ABA, Pa. Bar Assn., Lehigh County Bar Assn., Nat. Assn. Dist. Attys. (state dir. 1982-84), Pa. Assn. Dist. Attys. (pres. 1983-84, exec. com. 1980-86, tng. inst. chmn. 1986-91), Pa. Bar Inst. (bd. dirs. 1989—, treas. 1994-95, sec. 1995—). Office: Lehigh County Courthouse PO Box 1548 Allentown PA 18105

PLATT, WILLIAM RADY, pathology educator; b. Balt., July 25, 1915; s. Louis Abraham and Ida Selma (Rady) P.; m. Shirley Ades, June 26, 1949 (dec. 1972); children: Karen J., Lois A., James R.; m. Jeanette Krulevitz Fineman, Mar. 4, 1979. BS in Pharmacy, U. Md., 1936, MD, 1940. Diplomate Am. Bd. Pathology. Intern St. Joseph's Hosp., Lexington, Ky., 1940-41; resident in pathology Emory U. Hosp., Atlanta, 1941-44; instr. in pathology Yale U. Sch. Medicine, New Haven, 1944-45, Washington U., St. Louis, 1945-46, U. Pa., Phila., 1948-52; dir. lab. Norton Meml. Hosp., Louisville, 1946-48, West Jersey Hosp., Camden, N.J., 1948-52, Mo. Bapt. Hosp., St. Louis, 1952-76, U.S. Pub. Health Service Hosp., Balt., 1977-81; profl. Southwestern Med. Sch., Dallas, 1976-77, prof., 1976-77; lectr. Johns Hopkins U., Balt., 1977—; profl. Chinese U., Hong Kong, 1985-86. Author: Color Atlas and Textbook of Hematology, 1975, 2d edit., 1979; editor-in-chief Pathology Update, 1972-87. Fellow cytology Cornell U. 1946, radioisotope research AEC, 1947, tropical diseases Tulane U., 1943. Fellow ACP; mem., Coll. Am. Pathologist, Am. Soc. Hematology, Am. Soc. Clin. Pathology, Internat. Acad. Pathology, Rho Chi., Johns Hopkins Club, U. Club. Clubs: Johns Hopkins; Univ. (Balt.). Home and Office: 12 Hamlet Hill Rd Baltimore MD 21210-1501

PLATTEN, PETER MICHAEL, III, bank holding company executive; b. Green Bay, Wis., July 25, 1939; s. Peter M. and Helen V. (Brown) P.; m. Bonnie Anna Lipps, June 27, 1964; children: Carolyn, Peter, Christopher. BBA in Acctg. and Fin., U. Wis., Green Bay, 1962; postgrad., Northwestern U., 1970. Mgmt. trainee Continental Bank, Chgo., 1964-65; with West Side State Bank, Green Bay, 1965-67, asst. v.p., 1967-73; exec. v.p. West Bank and Trust, Green Bay, 1973-80, pres., chief exec. officer, 1980-83; pres. United Bankshares, Inc. (merged with Valley Bancorp), Green Bay, 1973-83; chmn., CEO M&I Bank Northeast (formerly West Bank and Trust), Green Bay, 1983-94; also bd. dirs. Valley Bank, N.E. (formerly West Bank and Trust), Green Bay; vice chmn., dir. Marshall & Isley Corp., Milw., Wis., 1989-94; chief oper. officer Valley Bancorp., Appleton, Wis., 1983-89, chief exec. officer, 1989-94, also bd. dirs.; chmn. Valley Bank Northeast(now MI Bank Northeast), Green Bay, 1993—; bd. dirs. Pro-Drive, Inc., Green Bay; mem. Carter Golembe Assocs., mgmt. seminars; vice chmn. Marshall & Isley Corp., 1994—, also bd. dirs. Bd. dirs. U. Wis. Found.; capital campaign chmn., adv. dir. St. Mary's Hosp., adv. dir. and profl. care com. St Vincent Hosp., vp., dir. Ft. Howard Cemetery Assn.; treas., bd. dirs. Tri-High Sch. Found., Assn. for Retarded Children; mem. Gov.'s Task Force on Edn., Taxation; mem. Green Bay Park Bd., bus. adv. bd. St. Norbert Coll., Chmn. Town of Hobart Planning Com.; bd. dirs. St. Joseph Acad., co-chmn. capital fund campaign; bd. dirs. Jr. Achievement, Green Bay Comty. Found.; bd. visitors U. Wis. Mem. Wis. Taxpayers Alliance (bd. dirs.), World Bus. Coun., The Bankers Roundtable Emerging Issues Com., Chief Exec. Orgn., Bascom Hill Soc. Avocations: sailing, skiing, football, fitness, manufacturing maple syrup. Home: 1555 Arapahoe Trl Green Bay WI 54313-6759 Office: MI Bank Northeast PO Box 2427 Appleton WI 54306-2427*

PLATTHY, JENO, cultural association executive; b. Dunapataj, Hungary, Aug. 13, 1920; s. Joseph K. and Maria (Dobor) P.; m. Carol Louise Abell, Sept. 25, 1976. Diploma, Peter Pazmany U., Budapest, Hungary, 1942; PhD, Ferencz J. U., Kolozsvar, Hungary, 1944; MS, Cath. U., 1965; PhD (hon.), Yangmingshan U., Taiwan, 1975; DLitt (hon.), U. Libre Asie, Philippines, 1977. Lectr. various univs., 1956-59; sec. Internat. Inst. Boston, 1959-62; adminstrv. asst. Trustees of Harvard U., Washington, 1962-85; exec. dir. Fedn. Internat. Poetry Assns., UNESCO, 1976—; pub. New Muses Quar., 1976—. Author: Winter Tunes, 1974, Ch'u Yuan, His Life and Works, 1975, Springtide (opera), 1976, Bamboo, Collected Poems, 1981, The Poems of Jesus, 1982, Holiness in a Worldly Garment, 1984, Ut Pictures Poeta, 1984, European Odes, 1985, The Mythical Poets of Greece, 1985, Book of Dithyrambs, 1986, Asian Elegies, 1987, Space Ecologues, 1988, Cosmograms, 1988, Nova Comoedia, 1988, vols. II-III, 1992, Bartok: A Critical Biography, 1988, Plato: A Critical Biography, 1990, Near-Death Experiences in Antiquity, 1992, Celebration of Life, 1992, Idylls, 1992, Elegies Asiatiques, 1992, Paeans, 1993, Rhapsodies, 1994, Prosodia, 1994, Visions, 1994, Prophecies, 1994, Epyllia, 1994, Budapesttol Tokyoig, 1994, 2d edit., 1995, Walking Two Feet Above the Earth, 1995, Dictionarium Cumanico Hungaricum, 1996, Emblems, 1996, Epodes, 1996, Aeolian Lilts, 1996, Transformations, 1996, Inexpressions, 1996, Songs of the Soul, 1996, Sacrifices, 1996, numerous others, also translations; editor-in-chief Monumenta Classica Perennia, 1967-84. Named Poet Laureate 2d World Congress of Poets, 1973; recipient Confucius award Chinese Poetry Soc., 1974, Yunus Emre award 12th Internat. Congress of Poets, Istanbul, Turkey, 1991, Jacques Raphael-Leygues prize Société des Poètes Français, 1992, French Ordre des Arts et des Lettres (officer), 1992. Mem. PEN, ASCAP, Internat. Soc. Lit., Die Literarische Union, Internat. Poetry Soc., Acad. Am. Poets, Assn. Lit. Scholars and Critics, 3d Internat. Congress Poets (pres. 1976, poet laureate 1976). Office: UNESCO Fedn Internat Poetry Assns PO Box 579 Santa Claus IN 47579-0579

PLATTS, FRANCIS HOLBROOK, plastics engineer; b. Brunson, S.C., Sept. 15, 1939; s. Holbrook Trowbridge and Mildred Ruth (Thomar) P.; m. Martha Ann Price, July 1963; children: Martha Susan Platts Gilliam, David Holbrook. BS in Chem. Engring., U. S.C., 1962. Chem. engr. U.S. Naval Weapons Lab., Dahlgren, Va., 1962-64; engr. Westinghouse Electric Corp., Hampton, S.C., 1964-74, sr. engr., 1974-89, mgr. engring. and quality assurance, 1989-91, mgr. design and mktg. svcs., 1991-93, div. engr. mgr., 1993-95; engr. mgr. Internat. Paper Co., Hampton, S.C., 1995—; chmn. NEMA DLATC Engring. Com., Washington, 1991—; mem., chair Color Mktg. Group, Alexandria, Va., 1991—. Pres., mem. Hampton Jaycees, 1964-74; chmn., bd. dirs. Hampton County Watermelon Festival, 1965-76; mem., chmn. blood bank bd. South Atlantic region ARC, Savannah, Ga., 1974—; mem. Western Carolina Higher Edn. Com., Allendale, 1982—. Mem. ASTM (E-5 com. 1972—), Hampton Rotary (sr. mem., pres. 1981, Outstanding Mem. award 1982), Hampton Gamecock Club (pres. 1966—). Methodist. Achievements include development of decorative high-pressure laminate specialty product, research on color and design treands for interior finish applications; research and development on composites. Office: Internat Paper Co PO Box 248 Hampton SC 29924-0248

PLATTS, HOWARD GREGORY, scientific/educational organization executive; b. N.Y.C., Aug. 14, 1947; s. Thayer Horton and Anne Elizabeth (Gregory) P.; m. Elizabeth Hertzler Murray, June 7, 1969; children—James Thayer, Christopher Wilke. A.B., Harvard U., 1969; M. Pub. and Pvt. Mgmt., Yale U., 1980. Tchr., Potomac Sch., McLean, Va., 1969-72; investment officer First Am. Bank, Washington, 1972-78; fin. analyst Yale U., New Haven, 1979; fin. asst. to pres. Nat. Geog. Soc., Washington, 1980-82, asst. treas., 1982-91, v.p., treas., 1992—. Treas., bd. dirs. Edes Home Found., Washington, 1975-78; bd. trustees Nat. Presbyn. Sch., Washington, 1988-91; treas., bd. trustees regional blood svcs. ARC, Balt., 1992. Mem. Washington Soc. Investment Analysts (pres., bd. dirs. 1985-91), Assn. Investment Mgmt. and Rsch. Clubs: Alfalfa (treas., bd. dirs. 1992—), Alibi (Washington), Bulldog Hockey (treas., bd. dirs. 1993—), Metropolitan (Washington, bd. govs.); Chevy Chase (Md.), Congregational (trustee 1988-91). Home: 5302 Portsmouth Rd Bethesda MD 20816-2929 Office: Nat Geog Soc 1145 17th St NW Washington DC 20036-4688

PLATTS-MILLS, THOMAS ALEXANDER E., immunologist, educator, researcher; b. Colchester, Essex, Eng., Nov. 22, 1941; came to U.S., 1982; s. John Faithful F. and Janet Katherine (Cree) P.-M.; m. Roberta Rosenstock, Apr. 9, 1970; children: Eliza, Timothy, James, Oliver. BA, Balliol Coll., Oxford (Eng.) U., 1963; MB, BChir, Oxford U., 1967; PhD, London U., 1982. Registrar in medicine Bury St. Edmunds, and New Market, Suffolk, Eng., 1968-71; fellow in medicine Johns Hopkins U., Balt., 1971-74; staff mem. Med. Rsch. Coun., U.K., 1976-82; hon. cons. physician Northwick Park Hosp., London, 1978-82; prof. medicine, head div. allergy and clin. immunology U. Va., Charlottesville, 1982—, dir. Asthma and Allergic Diseases Ctr., 1994; mem. immunological scis. study sect. NIH, 1988. Editl. bd. Am. Jour. Respiratory Critical Care Medicine, Clin. and Exptl. Immunology, Clin. Allergy, Jour. Immunological Methods; contbr. articles to profl. jours. Grantee NIH. Fellow Royal Coll. Physicians, Am. Acad. Allergy; mem. Assn. Am. Physicians, Am. Acad. Allergy, Asthma & Immunology (bd. dirs. 1995—), Southeastern Allergy Assn. (Hal Davidson award 1986, pres. 1987-88), Brit. Soc. Allergy and Clin. Immunology. Office: U Va Dept Medicine PO Box 225 Charlottesville VA 22902-0225

PLATZ, GEORGE ARTHUR, III, lawyer; b. Safford, Ariz., Sept. 12, 1939; s. George Arthur and Dickey Azalea (Slagle) P.; m. Mary Condon, Sept. 20, 1963; m. Andrea Maxwell, Oct. 25, 1979; children—Susan, Stephanie. B.S., Northwestern U., 1960; LL.B., Harvard U., 1963. Bar: Ill. 1964, U.S. Dist. Ct. (no. dist.) Ill. 1964, U.S. Ct. Appeals (7th cir.) 1964, U.S. Tax Ct. 1981, U.S. Supreme Ct. 1981. Assoc. Sidley & Austin, Chgo., 1964-71, ptnr., 1972—. Mem. ABA, Chgo. Bar Assn., Chikaming Country Club, Mid-Day Club.

PLATZMAN, GEORGE WILLIAM, geophysicist, educator; b. Chgo., Apr. 19, 1920; s. Alfred and Rose I. (Kaufman) P.; m. Harriet M. Herschberger, Feb. 19, 1945 (dec. 1985). B.S., U. Chgo., 1940, Ph.D., 1948; M.S., U. Ariz., 1941. Instr. U. Chgo., 1942-45, research asso., 1947-48, mem. faculty, 1949—, head phys. scis. in coll., 1959-60, prof. meteorology, 1960-90, chmn. dept. geophys. scis., 1971-74, emeritus prof., 1990—; cons. Inst. Advanced Study, Princeton, 1950-53. Contbr. articles to profl. jours. Hydrologic engr. C.E., U.S. Army, 1945-46. Guggenheim fellow, 1967-68. Fellow AAAS, Am. Geophys. Union, Am. Meteorol. Soc. (editor jour. 1948-49, chmn. publs. com. 1966-70, Meisinger award 1966). Office: Dept Geophys Scis U Chgo 5734 Ellis Ave Chicago IL 60637

PLAUD, JOSEPH JULIAN, psychology educator; b. Worcester, Mass., Mar. 25, 1965; s. Henry Emile and Barbara Ann (Perry) P.; m. Christine Marie Therlault, Mar. 14, 1987 (div. Mar. 1990); 1 child, Brianna Marie; m. Nancy Denise Vogeltanz, Nov. 25, 1994. BA summa cum laude, Clark U., 1987; PhD in Psychology, U. Maine, 1993. Lic. clin. psychologist, N.D. Psychology resident U. Miss. Med. Ctr., Jackson, 1992-93; asst. prof. psychology U. N.D., Grand Forks, 1993—; cons. N.D. Devel. Ctr., Grafton, 1994—. Author: From Behavior Theory to Behavior Therapy, 1995; contbr. articles to profl. jours. Fellow Behavior Therapy and Rsch. Soc. (clin.); mem. AAAS, Assn. for Advancement of Behavior Therapy, Am. Psychol. Soc., Am. Psychol. Assn., Phi Beta Kappa, Psi Chi. Democrat. Roman Catholic. Home: 1606 S 15th St Grand Forks ND 58201-5326 Office: U ND Dept Psychology PO Box 8380 Grand Forks ND 58202

PLAUT, ERIC ALFRED, psychiatrist, educator; b. N.Y.C., Nov. 16, 1927; s. Alfred and Margaret (Blumenfeld) P.; m. Eloine Raab, Sept. 5, 1976. B.S., Columbia U., 1949, M.D., 1953. Diplomate: Am. Bd. Psychiatry and Neurology. Intern Montefiore Hosp., Bronx, N.Y., 1953-54; psychiat. resident State Hosp., Worcester, Mass., 1954-55, Mass. Meml. Hosp., Boston, 1956-57; cons. psychiatrist Mass. Dept. Corrections, 1957; fellow student health psychiatry U. Calif., Berkeley, 1957-58; practice medicine specializing in psychiatry Berkeley, 1958-74; staff psychiatrist Kaiser Hosp., Oakland, Calif., 1958-62, Cowell Meml. Hosp., U. Calif., Berkeley, 1958-62; cons. psychiatrist Bur. Indian Affairs, Dept. Interior, 1967-68; program chief Berkeley Mental Health Services, 1968-71; dep. commr. Ind. Dept. Mental Health, Indpls., 1974-76; commr. Conn. Dept. Mental Health, Hartford, 1976-81; prof. Northwestern U. Med. Sch., Chgo., 1981-93, prof. emeritus, 1994—; asst. clin. prof. psychiatry U. Calif. Med. Sch., San Francisco, 1958-74; asso. clin. prof. psychiatry U. Ind. Med. Sch., Indpls., 1975-76; clin. prof. psychiatry U. Conn. Med. Sch., Farmington, 1978-81, Yale U. Med. Sch., 1979-81; cons. Assembly Sci. Adv. Coun., Calif. Legislature, 1970; chmn. Bay Area region Calif. Conf. Local Mental Health Dirs., 1970-71; gen. ptnr. Vanguard Investments, Berkeley, 1971-78. Author: Grand Opera: Mirror of the Western Mind, 1993; mem. editl. bd. Yale Psychiat. Quar., 1976-81; sect. editor Northeast Univ. Press, 1991—; contbr. articles to profl. jours. Bd. dirs. ACLU, Berkeley, 1960-65; mem. task force on access and barrier Pres.'s Commn. on Mental Health, 1977; mem. psychiatry panel Grad. Med. Edn. Nat. Adv. Com., 1979-81. With USN, 1944-46. Fellow Am. Psychiat. Assn. (cons. task force on govt. rels. 1973-76, chmn. com. public info. 1975-76, mem. com. cert. in adminstrv. psychiatry 1979-82, chmn. task force on problems of Americans overseas 1984-88, chmn. task force on joint meeting with German Psychiat. Soc., 1989-90); mem. com. Chron. Ment. Ill; mem. No. Calif. Psychiat. Soc. (chmn. com. law and legis. 1968-72, fed. legis. rep. 1972-74, councillor 1972-73, pres.-elect 1973-74), Calif. Med. Assn. (alt. del. 1968-71), Alameda-Contra Costa Med. Assn. (chmn. mental health com. 1972), Conn. Med. Soc., Nat. Assn. State Mental Health Program Dirs. (dir.). Address: 912 Michigan Ave Evanston IL 60202-1425 Office: Rm 203 2530 Ridge Ave Ste 203 Evanston IL 60201-5400

PLAUT, JONATHAN VICTOR, rabbi; b. Chgo., Oct. 7, 1942; s. W. Gunther and Elizabeth (Strauss) P.; m. Carol Ann Fainstein, July 5, 1965; children: Daniel Abraham, Deborah Maxine. BA, Macalester Coll., 1964; postgrad., Hebrew Union Coll., Jerusalem, 1967-68; BHL, Hebrew Union Coll., Cin., 1968, MA, 1970, DHL, 1995; DD, Hebrew Union Coll., 1995. Ordained rabbi, 1970. Rabbi Congregation Beth-El, Windsor, Ont., Can., 1970-84; sr. rabbi Temple Emanu-El, San Jose, Calif., 1985-93; dir. comty. outreach and involvement Jewish Fed. of Met. Detroit, 1993-95; vis. Rabbinic scholar Temple Beth El, Bloomfield Hills, Mich., 1993-96; pres. JUP Fund Raising Cons., Inc., Farmington Hills, Mich., 1994—; lectr. Assumption Coll. Sch., 1972-84, St. Clair Coll., 1982-84, U. Windsor, Ont., Can., 1984; adj. asst. prof. Santa Clara U., 1985-93; vis. Rabbinic scholar Temple Beth El, 1993—; pres. JVP Fund Raising Cons., 1994—. Contbg. author: Reform Judaism in America: A Biographical Dictionary and Sourcebook, 1993; editor: Through the Sound of Many Voices, 1982, Jour. Can. Jewish Hist. Soc., 1976-83; also articles; host weekly program Religious Scope, Sta. CBET-TV, Religion in News, Sta. CKWW, 1971-84. Pres. Jewish Nat. Fund Windsor, 1978-81, chmn. bd. dirs., 1981-84; chmn. United Jewish Appeal Windsor, 1981-83, State of Israel Bonds, Windsor, 1980; nat. bd. dirs. Jewish Nat. Fund Can., 1972-84; pres. Reform Rabbis of Can., 1982-84; bd. dirs. Can. Jewish Congress, 1978-84, Jewish Family Svc. Santa Clara County, 1987-90, Jewish Fedn. Greater San Jose, 1986-93; chaplain San Jose Fire Dept., 1987-93; mem. exec. cabinet United Jewish Appeal, Windsor, 1971-84, mem. nat. rabbinic cabinet, 1993—; mem. exec. com. Windsor Jewish Community Coun., 1970-84, chmn. 1975-84; mem. adv. coun. Riverview unit Windsor Hosp. Ctr., 1972-81; pres. Credit Counselling Svc. Met. Windsor, 1977-79. Mem. NCCJ, Can. Jewish Congress (nat. exec. bd. 1978-84), Can. Jewish Hist. Soc. (nat. v.p. 1974-84), Calif. Bd. Rabbis, Rabbinic Assn. Greater San Jose (chmn. 1986-87), Ctrl. Conf. Am. Rabbis, Nat. Assn.

Temple Educators. Home & Office: 30208 Kingsway Dr Farmington Hills MI 48331

PLAUT, SHARON EVERT, psychiatric nurse; b. Buffalo, Nov. 6, 1941; d. Kenneth Eugene and Marie Therese (O'Connor) Evert-Densmore; m. Martin Edward Plaut, Sept. 10, 1965; children: Benjamin Bogart, Anne, Susan. BSN, SUNY, Buffalo, 1981. Cert. emergency nurse; BLS, ACLS, TNCC, TNCI. Staff to head nurse surg. unit Buffalo Gen. Hosp., 1962-65; staff/charge nurse psychiatry Mass. Gen. Hosp., Boston, 1965-67; staff/charge nurse med./surg. unit Millard Fillmore Hosp., Buffalo, 1967-68; staff/charge nurse ICU/CCU St. Joseph Intercmty. Hosp., Buffalo, 1981-83; staff/charge nurse emergency dept. Erie County Med. Ctr., Buffalo, 1983-91, staff/charge nurse emergency psychiatry, 1991-93; supr. admissions and customer svc. Brylin Hosp., Buffalo, 1993; rsch./program coord. U. Buffalo Clin. Ctr., 1994—. Recipient Top Gun award Erie County, Buffalo, 1991, Emergency Svc. Appreciation award, 1990. Mem. Emergency Nurses Assn., N.Y. State Nurses Assn. (dist. I), SUNY-Buffalo Alumnae Assn., Buffalo Gen. Hosp. Alumnae Assn., Am. Psychiat. Nurses Assn. Democrat. Avocations: travel, fine dining, jazz, reading, movies. Home: 135 Parkwood Dr Snyder NY 14226-4068 Office: SUNY Clin Ctr Dept Psychiat Erie County Med Ctr 462 Grider St Buffalo NY 14215-3075

PLAUT, WOLF GUNTHER, minister, author; b. Muenster, Germany, Nov. 1, 1912; emigrated to U.S., 1935, arrived in Canada, 1961; s. Jonas and Selma (Gumprich) P.; m. Elizabeth Strauss, Nov. 10, 1938; children: Jonathan, Judith. LLB, U. Berlin, 1933, JD, 1934; MHL, Hebrew Union Coll., Cin., 1939, DD, 1964; LLD, U. Toronto, 1978; DLitt, Cleve. Coll. Jewish Studies, 1979; LLD, York U., 1987. Ordained rabbi, 1939. Rabbi B'nai Abraham Zion, Chgo., 1939-48, Mt. Zion Temple, St. Paul, 1948-61; sr. rabbi Holy Blossom Temple, Toronto, Ont., Can., 1961-77; sr. scholar Holy Blossom Temple, 1978—; adj. prof. York U., 1991—. Author: Mount Zion, 1956, The Jews in Minnesota, 1959, The Book of Proverbs: A Commentary, 1961, Judaism and the Scientific Spirit, 1962, The Rise of Reform Judaism, 1963, The Growth of Reform Judaism, 1964, The Case for the chosen People, 1965, Your Neighbour Is a Jew, 1967, Page 2, 1971, Genesis: A Modern Commentary, 1974, Time to Think, 1977, Hanging Threads, 1978, (U.S. title) The Man in the Blue vest, 1980, Numbers: A Modern Commentary, 1979; editor, chief author: The Torah: A Modern Commentary, 1981, 10th edit., 1995, Unfinished Business (autobiography), 1981, Refugee Determination in Canada, 1985, The Letter, 1986, The Magen David: How the Six Pointed Star Became the Jewish Symbol, 1991, The Man Who Would be Messiah, 1988, 2d edit., 1990, Asylum--A Moral Dilemma, 1995, The Haftorah Commentary, 1996; co-author: The Rabbi's Manual, 1988; editor: Affirmation, 1981-87; editl. contbr. Toronto Globe and Mail, 1962-94, Can. Jewish News; bibliography pub. in Through the Sound of Many Voices, 1982; contbr. to encys., anthologies, other books, articles to mags., newspapers. Chmn. Minn. Gov.'s Commn. on Ethics in Govt., 1958-61 ; pres. St. Paul Gallery and Sch. Art (name changed to Minn. Mus.), 1953-59, World Federalists Can., 1966-68; nat. pres. Can. Jewish Congress, 1977-80; vice chmn. Ont. Human Rights Commn., 1978-85; bd. govs. World Union for Progressive Judaism, 1970— pres. Central Conf. Am. Rabbis, 1983-85, bd. inquiry human rights cases, 1987—. Capt. AUS, 1943-46. Decorated Bronze Star; named officer Order of Can.; awarded Order of Ont.; Plaut Chair for Project Mgmt. established in his honor at Ben-Gurion U., Israel, 1991, Plaut Manor (pub.-assisted housing project) named in his and his wife's honor, Toronto. Clubs: York Racquets, Oakdale Golf and Country. Office: 1950 Bathurst St, Toronto, ON Canada M5P 3K9

PLAVOUKOS, SPENCER, advertising executive; b. N.Y.C., May 30, 1936; s. George and Elva (Murzi) P.; m. Harriet Phylis Gladstone, Jan. 9, 1964; children: Stacy, Matthew. B.S., Syracuse U., 1961. Account exec. SSC&B, Inc., N.Y.C., 1961-64; account exec. Grey Advt., 1964-67; exec. v.p., dir. account service Manoff Advt., N.Y.C., 1967-79; exec. v.p. SSC&B, N.Y.C., 1979; chmn., chief exec. officer Lintas: N.Y. (formerly SSC&B), N.Y.C., until 1991; formerly vice chmn. Lintas: USA; pres., Lintas: Worldwide, chmn., Lintas: Americas, 1991—. Clubs: Country of New Canaan, Marco Polo (N.Y.C.), St. James (London). Office: Lintas Worldwide 1 Dag Hammarskjold Plz New York NY 10017*

PLAWECKI, JUDITH ANN, nursing educator; b. East Chicago, Ind., June 5, 1943; d. Joseph Lawrence and Anne Marilyn (Hamnik) Curosh; m. Henry Martin Plawecki, June 10, 1967; children: Martin H., Lawrence H. BS, St. Xavier Coll., Chgo., 1965; MA, U. Iowa, 1971; PhD, 1974. Asst. prof. Mt. Mercy Coll., Cedar Rapids, Iowa, 1971-73; asst. dept. chmn., assoc. prof., 1974-75; assoc. prof. U. Iowa, 1975-76; asst. dean, assoc. prof. U. Minn., 1976-81; acting dean, assoc. dean and prof. U. N.D., Grand Forks, 1981-82, dean and prof. nursing, 1982-83; dean and prof. nursing Lewis U., Romeoville, Ill., 1983-87; dean U. South Fla., Tampa, 1987-95, prof. nursing, 1987—. Univ. Iowa Fellow, 1973. Mem. ANA, AHNA, Nat. League for Nursing, Older Women's League, Sigma Xi, Sigma Phi Omega, Sigma Theta Tau, Phi Lambda Theta. Office: U South Fla Coll Nursing MDC 22 12901 Bruce B Downs Blvd Tampa FL 33612-4742

PLAYER, GARY JIM, professional golfer; b. Johannesburg, South Africa, Nov. 1, 1935; s. Francis Harry Audley and Muriel (Ferguson) P; m. Vivienne Verwey, 1955; children: Jennifer, Marc, Wayne, Michele, Theresa, Amanda. Ed., King Edward Sch., Johannesburg; LLD (hon.), St. Andrews U., Scotland, 1995. Profl. golfer, 1953—; joined PGA, 1957—; winner East Rand Open, Republic of South Africa, 1955-56, Egyptian Matchplay, 1955, South African Open, 1956, 60, 65-69, 72, 75-77, 79, 81, Dunlop Tournament, Eng., 1956, Ampol Tournament, Australia, 1956, 58, 61, Australian PGA, 1957, Coughs Harbour Tournament, Australia, 1957-58, Natal Open, South Africa, 1958-60, 62, 66, 68, Ky. Derby Open, 1958, Australian Open, 1958, 62-63, 65, 69-70, 74, Transvaal Open, South Africa, 1959, 60, 62, 63, 66, South African PGA, 1959-60, 69, 79, 82, Western Province Open, South Africa, 1959-60, 68, 71-72, Dunlop Masters, South Africa, 1959-60, 63-64, 67, 71-74, 76-77, Brit. Open, 1959, 68, 74, Victoria Open, Australia, 1959, Masters Tournament, U.S., 1961, 74, 78, Lucky Internat. Open, U.S., 1961, Sunshine Open, U.S., 1961, Yomiuri Open, Japan, 1961, PGA Championship, U.S., 1962, 72, Sponsored 5000, South Africa, 1963, Liquid Air Tournament, South Africa, 1963; winner Richelieu Grand Prix, Capetown, 1963, Johannesburg, 1963; winner San Diego Open, 1963, Pensacola Open, 1964, 500 Festival Open, U.S., 1964, U.S. Open (1st foreigner to win in 45 yrs.), 1965, Piccadilly World Match Play, Eng., 1965, 66, 68, 71, 73, NTL Challenge Cup, Can., 1965, World Series of Golf, U.S., 1965, 68, 72, World Cup Internat., 1965, Australian Wills Masters, 1968, 69, Tournament of Champions, U.S., 1969, 78, Greater Greensboro Open, 1970, Dunlop Internat., Australia, 1970, Gen. Motors Open, South Africa, 1971, 73, 74, 75, 76, Jacksonville Open, 1971, Nat. Airlines Open, U.S., 1971, New Orleans Open, 1972, Japan Airlines Open, 1972, Brazilian Open, 1972, 74, So. Open, U.S., 1973, Rand Internat. Open, South Africa, 1974, Gen. Motors Internat. Classic, South Africa, 1974, Memphis Classic, 1974, Ibergolf Tournament, Spain, 1974, La Manga Tournament, Spain, 1974, Gen. Motors Classic, 1975, ICL Transvaal, South Africa, 1977, World Cup Individual, Philippines, 1977, Houston Open, 1978, Kronenbrau Masters, South Africa, 1979, Sun City, S. Am., 1979, Trophee Boigny, Ivory Coast, 1980, Chilean Open, S. Am., 1980, Australian Tooth Gold Coast Classic, 1981, Johnnie Walker Trophy, Spain, 1984, Quadel Srs. Classic, 1985, PGA Srs. Championship, 1986, 1990, Northville Srs., 1987, Sr. Tournament, 1987, U.S. Sr. Open, 1987; PGA Srs. Championship, 1988, Aetna Challenge, 1988, Southwestern Bell Classic, 1988, USGA Srs., 1988, Sr. British Open, 1988. Named Christian Athlete of Yr. So. Bapt. Conv., 1967, Sportsman of the Year in South Africa, 1955, 56, 59, 61, 63, 65, 72, 74, 78; Richardson award Golf Writers Assn. Am., 1975; named to World Golf Hall of Fame, 1974; hon. mem. R&A, 1994, Skills Challenge, 1994. Avocations: fitness, health, diet, music, gardening. Office: Gary Player Group 3930 RCA Blvd Ste 3001 West Palm Beach FL 33410 Office: PO Box 785629, Sandton 2146, South Africa

PLAYER, GERALDINE (JERI PLAYER), small business executive; b. Cleve., Mar. 26, 1952; d. Cornelius Millsape and Ola Mae (Maxie) Fisher; m. Van O. Player, Aug. 27, 1970 (dec. Mar. 1975); children—Ricardo T., Van O., Michelle. Student Sawyer Coll. Bus., Mayfield, Ohio, Virginia Marti Sch. Design, Lakewood, Ohio, Inst. Children's Lit., Conn., Case Western Res. U., Fall 1988. Owner, Jeri's Designs, Inc., Cleve., 1970—, Success Writers, Cleve., 1986—; freelance scriptwriter, 1990—; fashion cons. Active adoptive parenting orgn. Mem. Nat. Assn. Female Execs. Club: Back Wall (Beachwood, Ohio). Lodge: Brotherhood (Bklyn.). Avocations: aerobics; photography; theatre; speech. Home: PO Box 12471 Cleveland OH 44112-0471 Office: 1605 N Cahuenga Blvd Ste 211 Los Angeles CA 90028-6276

PLAYER, THELMA B., librarian; b. Owosso, Mich.; d. Walter B. and Grace (Willoughby) Player; B.A., Western Mich. U., 1954. Reference asst. USAF Aero. Chart & Info. Center, Washington, 1954-57; reference librarian U.S. Navy Hydrographic Office, Suitland, Md., 1957-58; asst. librarian, 1958-59; tech. library br. head U.S. Navy Spl. Project Office, Washington, 1959-68, Strategic Systems Project Office, 1969-76. Mem. Spl. Libraries Assn., D.C. Library Assn., AAUW, Canterbury Cathedral Trust in Am., Nat. Geneal. Soc., Internat. Soc. Brit. Genealogy and Family History, Ohio Geneal. Soc., Royal Oak Found., Daus. of Union Vets. of Civil War. Episcopalian. Home: 730 24th St NW Washington DC 20037-2543

PLEASANT, JAMES SCOTT, lawyer; b. Anniston, Ala., July 14, 1943; s. James C. and Barbara (Scott) P.; m. Susan M. Pleasant, May 17, 1966; children: Deborah Kaye, Carol Ann, Julie Ruth. BS, Oreg. State U., 1965; JD summa cum laude, Williamette U., 1972. Bar: Tex. 1972, U.S. Dist. Ct. (no. dist.) Tex. 1973, U.S. Ct. Appeals (5th cir.) 1975, U.S. Supreme Ct. 1977. Ptnr. Gardere & Wynne LLP, Dallas, 1972—. Mem. Smithsonian Assn., Washington, 1985—, Dallas Mus. of Art, 1987—. Capt. U.S. Army, 1966-69, Vietnam. Mem. ABA (partnership law sect. 1969—), Tex. Bar Assn. (partnership law sect. 1989—), Vietnam Pilots Assn., Dustoff Assn. Office: Gardere & Wynne LLP 1601 Elm St Ste 3000 Dallas TX 75201-4757

PLEASANT, ROBERT DALE, manufacturing executive; b. Port Arthur, Tex., Nov. 1, 1946; s. Ned Earl and Mary Jeanne (Royalty) P.; children: Angela M. (dec.), Richard D. Student, W. Liberty State Coll. Maintenance, process technician Mammoth Plastics, Wellsburg, W.Va., 1969-72; field svc. engr. Van Dorn Plastic Machinery, Cleve., 1972-73, mgr. process devel., 1973-75; sales engr. Van Dorn Plastic Machinery, Phila., 1975-76; nat. sales mgr. Lester Engring., Cleve., 1976-77; pres. Torval, Wauconda, Ill., 1977-80; regional mgr. Improved Plastic Machinery, Chgo., 1980-83, Hayssen Mfg., Sheboygan, Wis., 1983-84; v.p. Improved Blow Molding Equipment Co. Inc., Chgo., 1985-92; pres. Dale Pleasant & Assocs., Charlotte, N.C., 1993—, Dale Pleasant and Assocs., Charlotte, N.C., 1992—, Select Plastic Sys., Inc., Charlotte, 1994—, Select Investigations, Inc., Charlotte, 1995—. With USCG, 1964-68. Mem. Soc. Plastic Engrs. (sr.). Republican. Methodist. Avocations: flying, golf, skiing, sport fishing, hunting, scuba diving.

PLEASANTS, HENRY, music critic; b. Wayne, Penn., May 12, 1910; s. Henry and Elizabeth Washington (Smith) P.; m. Virginia V. Duffey, Aug. 31, 1940. Student, Phila. Music Acad., Curtis Inst. Music; D.M. (hon.), Curtis Inst. Music, 1977. Music critic Phila. Evening Bulletin, 1930-42; Central European music corr. N.Y. Times, 1945-55; with U.S. Fgn. Service, Munich, 1950-52, Bern, 1952-56, Bonn, 1956-64; London music critic Internat. Herald Tribune, Paris, 1967—; London editor Stereo Review, N.Y.C., 1967—; lectr. in field. Appearances on T.V., U.K., U.S.A., Europe.; Author: The Agony of Modern Music, 1955, Death of a Music?, 1961, The Great Singers, 1966, Serious Music-And All That Jazz!, 1969, The Great American Popular Singers, 1974; translator, editor various books in field; contbr. articles to musical, lit. jours. Served in U.S. Army, 1942-50, Alaska, ETO, NATOUSA. Decorated Bronze Star (twice). Mem. Authors Guild. Home: 95 Roebuck House, Palace St, London SW1E 5BE, England

PLENTY, ROYAL HOMER, writer; b. Phila., Aug. 28, 1918; s. Royal Homer and Florence (Gehman) P.; m. Evelyn Treaster, Dec. 15, 1945 (dec. 1958); 1 dau., Evelyn Ann; m. Mildred Craig, Sept. 12, 1959 (div. 1970); m. Gladys Ann Muller, Nov. 14, 1970. B.S. in Econs, U. Pa., 1941. Clk. H.M. Byllesby & Co. (investment bankers), 1941; jr. underwriter New Amsterdam Casualty Co., 1941-42; reporter Phila. office Wall St. Jour., 1942-46; mem. staff Phila. Inquirer, 1946-72, financial editor, 1957-72; dir. pub. relations Levitz Furniture Corp., 1972-73; pub. relations account exec. Aitkin-Kynett Co., Inc., Phila., 1973-75; dir. pub. info. Securities Industry Assn., N.Y.C., 1975-77; corporate relations Merrill Lynch & Co., 1977-78; free-lance editor, writer, 1978—. Mem. Phila. Econ. Assn., Phila. Press Assn., Phila. Investment Traders Assn., Sigma Delta Chi. Unitarian. Home: Harrison Towers Apt 7P Somerset NJ 08873

PLESEC, WILLIAM THOMAS, lawyer; b. Cleve., June 14, 1942. AB, John Carroll U., 1966; JD, Cleve. State U., 1971. Bar: Ohio 1971, D.C. 1981. Trial atty. Antitrust divsn., U.S. Dept. Justice, 1971-75; ptnr. Jones, Day, Reavis & Pogue, Cleve. Office: Jones Day Reavis & Pogue North Point 901 Lakeside Ave E Cleveland OH 44114-1116

PLESHETTE, SUZANNE, actress, writer; b. N.Y.C., Jan. 31; d. Eugene and Geraldine; m. Thomas Joseph Gallagher III, Mar. 16, 1968. Student, Sch. Performing Arts, Syracuse U., Finch Coll., Neighborhood Playhouse Sch. of Theatre. Founder, prin. The Bedside Manor (later div. of J.P. Stevens). Theatre debut in Truckline Cafe; star in Broadway prodns. Compulsion, The Cold Wind and the Warm, The Golden Fleecing, The Miracle Worker, Special Occasions; star TV series Bob Newhart Show, 1972-78, Suzanne Pleshette is Maggie Briggs, 1984; starred in TV series Bridges to Cross, 1986-87, Nightingales, 1988-89, The Boys Are Back, 1994-95; star 30 feature films including The Birds, Forty Pounds of Trouble, If It's Tuesday This Must Be Belgium, Nevada Smith, Support Your Local Gunfighter, Hot Stuff, Oh God! Book II; TV movies include Flesh and Blood, Starmaker, Fantasies, If Things Were Different, Help-Wanted Male, Dixie Changing Habits, One Cooks, The Other Doesn't, For Love or Money, Kojak, The Belarus File, A Stranger Waits, Alone In The Neon Jungle, Leona Helmsley: The Queen of Mean, 1990, Battling for Baby, 1991-92, A Twist of the Knife, 1993; writer, co-creator, producer two TV series; published author.

PLESKOW, ERIC ROY, motion picture company executive; b. Vienna, Austria; came to U.S., 1939; Film officer U.S. War Dept., 1946-48; asst. gen. mgr. Motion Picture Export Assn., Germany, 1948-50; continental rep. for Sol Lesser Prodns., 1950-51; with United Artists Corp., Far Eastern sales mgr., 1951-52, South African mgr., 1952-53, German mgr., 1953-58, exec. asst. to continental mgr., 1958-59, asst. continental mgr., 1959-60, continental mgr., 1960-62, v.p. in charge fgn. distbn., 1962, exec. v.p., chief operating officer, 1973, pres., chief exec. officer, 1973-78; pres., chief exec. officer Orion Pictures Co., N.Y.C., 1978-82; pres., chief exec. officer Orion Pictures Corp., N.Y.C., 1982-92, also chmn. bd. dirs., until 1992; ptnr. Pleskow/Spikings Partnership, Beverly Hills, Calif., 1992-95; prin. Pleskow Entertainment Inc., Santa Monica, Calif., 1995—. Office: Pleskow Entertainment Inc. 201 Ocean Ave Ste 1501-B Santa Monica CA 90402

PLESS, JOHN EDWARD, forensic pathologist, educator; b. Bedford, Ind., 1938. BA, Ind. U., 1960, MD, 1963. Intern South Bend (Ind.) Med. Found. Hosps., 1963-64, resident in anatomic and clin. pathology, 1966-70; instr. pathology Ind. U. Sch. Medicine, South Bend, 1967-70; fellow Forensic Pathology Oka U. Med. Ctr., 1970-71; asst. prof. Ind. U. Sch. Medicine, Bloomington, 1973-83, prof. pathology, 1983—, now Culbertson prof. pathology. Capt. USMC, 1964-66. Mem. Am. Soc. Forensic Sci., Am. Soc. Clin. Pathologist, Coll. Am. Pathologist, Nat. Assn. Med. Examiners. Office: Ind U Med Ctr Pathology Med Sci Bldg 157 Indianapolis IN 46202

PLESS, LAURANCE DAVIDSON, lawyer; b. Jacksonville, Fla., Dec. 22, 1952; s. James William Pless III and Anne (Dodson) Martin; m. Dana Halberg, June 20, 1980; children: Anna Amesbury, William Davidson, Deane Ahlgren. AB with distinction, Duke U., 1975; JD, U. N.C., Chapel Hill, 1980. Assoc. Neely & Player, P.C., Atlanta, 1980-86, ptnr., 1986-92; ptnr. Welch, Spell, Reemsnyder & Pless, P.C., Atlanta, 1992—. Contbr. articles to profl. jours. Vol. Saturday Vol. Lawyer's Found., Atlanta, 1980—. Mem. ABA, Lawyer's Club of Atlanta, Atlanta Bar Assn., Capital City Club. Democrat. Episcopalian. Avocations: hiking, tennis, coaching kid's sports, canoeing. Home: 25 Palisades Rd NE Atlanta GA 30309-1530 Office: Welch Spell Reemsnyder & Pless Ste 2020 400 Colony Sq Atlanta GA 30361-6305

PLESS, VERA, mathematics and computer science educator; b. Chgo., Mar. 5, 1931; d. Lyman and Helen (Blinder) Stepen; m. Irwin Pless, June 15, 1952 (div. 1980); children: Naomi, Benjamin, Daniel. PhD, U. Chgo., 1949, MS, 1952; PhD, Northwestern U., 1957. Mathematician USAF, Lincoln, Mass., 1962-72; rsch. assoc. MIT, Cambridge, Mass., 1972-75; prof. math. U. Ill., Chgo., 1975—. Author: The Theory of Error Correcting Codes, 1989; contbr. articles to profl. publs. U. Ill. scholar, 1989-92; recipient Tempo All-Professor Team, Sciences, Chicago Tribune, 1993. Mem. Am. Math. Soc. (chair nominating com. 1984), Math. Assn. Am., IEEE (bd. govs. 1985-89), Assn. Women in Math. Office: UIC MSCS (M/C 249) 851 S Morgan 322 SEO Chicago IL 60607-7045

PLETCHER, DAVID MITCHELL, history educator; b. Faribault, Minn., June 14, 1920; s. Nuba Mitchel and Jean (Hutchinson) P. B.A., U. Chgo., 1941, MA, 1941, PhD, 1946. Asst. U. Chgo., 1943; instr. history U. Iowa, 1944-46; asso. prof. Knox Coll., Galesburg, Ill., 1946-56; asso. prof., then prof. Hamline U., St. Paul, 1956-65; prof. history Ind. U., 1965-90, prof. emeritus, 1990—. Author: Rails, Mines and Progress, Seven American Promoters in Mexico, 1867-1911, 1958, The Awkward Years, American Foreign Relations Under Garfield and Arthur, 1962, The Diplomacy of Annexation, Texas, Oregon and the Mexican War, 1973. Recipient McKnight Found. award, 1962; grantee Social Sci. Research Found., 1950-51, 62-63; grantee Nat. Archives, 1972; Fulbright sr. research fellow, 1953-54. Mem. Orgn. Am. Historians, Am. Hist. Assn. (Albert J. Beveridge award 1957), Soc. Historians Am. Fgn. Relations (v.p. 1979, pres. 1980). Home: 509 N Fess Ave Bloomington IN 47408-3821 Office: Indiana Univ Dept History Ballantine Hall Bloomington IN 47405

PLETCHER, ELDON, editorial cartoonist; b. Goshen, Ind., Sept. 10, 1922; s. Arthur and Dora (Cripe) P.; m. Barbara Jeanne Jones, Jan. 29, 1948; children—Thomas Lee, Ellen Irene. Student, Chgo. Acad. Fine Arts, 1941-42, U. Aberdeen, Scotland, 1945, John Herron Art Sch., Indpls., 1946-47. Editorial cartoonist Sioux City (Iowa) Jour., 1949-66; editorial cartoonist The Times-Picayune, 1966-85; free-lance gag cartoonist Sat. Eve. Post, Rotarian, Nat. Enquirer, other publs. Rep. permanent exhbns., Syracuse U., U. South Miss., U. Cin., Boston Mus. Art, Harry S. Truman Library, Lyndon B. Johnson Library, Wichita State U., John F. Kennedy Libr., Richard M. Nixon Libr. Served with AUS, 1943-46. Recipient Christopher award, 1955, Freedoms Found. award, 12 years. Mem. Assn. Am. Editorial Cartoonists. Democrat. Presbyterian.

PLETCHER, JOHN HAROLD, JR., career officer; b. Findlay, Ohio, May 26, 1945; s. John H. and Bernadette (Gerschutz) P.; m. Phyllis G. Morrin, Jun. 7, 1968; children: Eric, Mary. BS in Aerospace Engring., USAF Acad., 1967; MS in Aerospace Engring., Ill. Inst. Tech., 1969; PhD in Mech. and Aerospace Engring., AF Inst. Tech., 1979. Registered prof. engr., Colo. Commd. 2d lt. USAF, 1967, advanced through grades to col., 1988; pilot 39th Rescue and Recovery Squadron, Cam Ranh AB, Vietnam, 1970-71; pilot and wing air ops. officer 41st Rescue and Recovery Wing, Hickam AFB, Hawaii, 1971-75; assoc. prof. aero., dir. academic ops. USAF Acad., Colorado Springs, Colo., 1978-82; chief systems engr. Aero. Systems Div., Wright Patterson AFB, Ohio, 1982-85; comdr. Frank J. Seiler Rsch. Lab., Colorado Springs, 1985-87; asst. dep. engring. Strategic Def. Initiative, Washington, 1987-90; dir. Armament Directorate, Eglin AFB, Fla., 1990-94; comdr. European Office of Aerospace Rsch. and Devel., London, 1994—. Youth soccer, T-ball coach Dayton, 1982-85. Mem. AIAA, AF Assn., AF Acad. Assn. of Grads. Roman Catholic. Avocations: squash, tennis, chess, gardening, fishing. Home: 7 Manor House Marylebone Rd, London NW1 5NP, England

PLETZ, THOMAS GREGORY, lawyer; b. Toledo, Oct. 3, 1943; s. Francis G. and Virginia (Connell) P.; m. Carol Elizabeth Connolly, June 27, 1969; children: Anne M., John F. BA, U. Notre Dame, 1965; JD, U. Toledo, 1971. Bar: Ohio 1971, U.S. Ct. Appeals (6th cir.) 1978, U.S. Supreme Ct. 1985. Ct. bailiff Lucas County Common Pleas Ct., Toledo, 1967-71; jud. clk. U.S. Dist. Ct. (no. dist.) Ohio, Toledo, 1971-72; assoc. Shumaker, Loop & Kendrick, Toledo, 1972-76, litigation ptnr., 1976—; acting judge Sylvania (Ohio) Mcpl. Ct., 1990—; mem. Ohio Bar Bd. Examiners, 1993—, chair, 1996. mem. Toledo Parish Coun., 1987-93; chmn., trustee Kiroff Trial Adv. Com., Toledo, 1982-91. With USNR, 1965-92; ret. CDR. Recipient Toledo Jr. Bar award, 1995. Mem. ABA, Ohio State Bar Assn., Toledo Bar Assn. (trustee 1981-93), Diocesan Attys. Bar Assn., 6th Cir. Jud. Conf. (life). Roman Catholic. Office: Shumaker Loop & Kendrick 1000 Jackson St Toledo OH 43624-1515

PLEWES, THOMAS JEFFREY, economic statistician, government executive; b. Zeeland, Mich., Dec. 15, 1940; s. Lloyd Angus and Joyce (Wicht) P.; m. Elizabeth Marie Hall Feb. 20, 1971; children: Jeffrey Charles, Melissa Joy. BA, Hope Coll., Holland, Mich., 1962; MA in Econs., George Washington U., 1972. Economist U.S. Dept. Labor, Washington, 1962-66, Bur. Labor Standards, Washington, 1969-81; assoc. commr. Bur. Labor Stats., Washington, 1981—. Pres. Sr. Army Res. Commdrs. Assn. Served to U.S. Army, 1966-69, maj. gen. Res., 1993—. Decorated Legion of Merit. Fellow Am. Statis. Assn.; mem. Assn. U.S. Army, Res. Officers Assn. Home: 4510 Banff St Annandale VA 22003-4513 Office: Dept of Labor Employment & Unemployment Stats 2 Massachusetts Ave NE Washington DC 20212-4225

PLIMPTON, CALVIN HASTINGS, physician, university president; b. Boston, Oct. 7, 1918; s. George Arthur and Fanny (Hastings) P.; m. Ruth Talbot, Sept. 6, 1941; children: David, Thomas, George (dec.), Anne, Edward. B.A. cum laude, Amherst Coll., 1939; M.D. cum laude, Harvard, 1943, M.A., 1947; Med. Sci.D., Columbia, 1951; LL.D., Williams Coll., 1960, Wesleyan U., 1961, Doshisha U., Kyoto, Japan, 1962, St. Lawrence U., 1963, Amherst U., 1971; L.H.D., U. Mass., 1962; D.Sc., Rockford Coll., 1962, St. Mary's, 1963, Trinity Coll., 1966, Grinnell (Iowa) Coll., 1967; Litt.D., Am. Internat. Coll., 1965, Mich. State Coll., 1969; DSc, N.Y. Med. Coll., 1986. Diplomate: Nat. Bd. Med. Examiners, Am. Bd. Internal Medicine. Intern, asst. resident, resident medicine Presbyn. Hosp., N.Y.C., 1947-50; asst. attending physician Columbia-Presbyn. Med. Center, 1950-60; asso. medicine (Coll. Phys. and Surg.), 1950-59, asst. prof. clin. medicine, 1959-60; prof. medicine, chmn. dept. Am. U. Beirut, Am. U. Hosp., Beirut, Lebanon, 1957-59; pres. Amherst Coll., 1960-71; pres. Downstate Med. Center, SUNY, 1971-79, dean med. sch., 1971-74, 76-79, prof. medicine, 1971-82, prof. emeritus, 1982—; pres. Am. U., Beirut, 1984-87; vis. prof. Columbia Presbyn. Med. Center, 1976-77. Trustee Am. U., Beirut, 1960-90, trustee emeritus, 1990—, chmn. bd., 1965-82; trustee World Peace Found., 1962-77, Phillips Exeter Acad., 1963-76, Commonwealth Fund, 1962-83, Hampshire Coll., 1963-71, U. Mass., 1962-70, L.I. U., 1972-82, N.Y. Law Sch., 1976-84; mem. Harvard Bd. Overseers, 1969-75. Capt. U.S. Army, 1944-46, ETO. Decorated comdr. Order of Cedars Lebanon; recipient award Nat. Geog. Soc., award New Eng. Soc., John Phillips award Phillip Exeter Acad. Fellow ACP; mem. Am. Acad. Arts and Scis., Coun. Fgn. Rels., Soc. Mayflower Descs., Harvey Soc., Alpha Omega Alpha, Sigma Xi. Clubs: Century, Univ. (N.Y.C.), Charaka (N.Y.C.), Riverdale Yacht (N.Y.C.), Pilgrims (N.Y.C.); Tavern Boston. Home and office: 4600 Palisade Ave Bronx NY 10471-3508

PLIMPTON, GEORGE AMES, writer, editor, television host; b. N.Y.C., Mar. 18, 1927; s. Francis T.P. and Pauline (Ames) P.; m. Freddy Medora Espy, 1968 (div. 1988); children: Medora Ames, Taylor Ames; m. Sarah Whitehead Dudley, 1991; children: Olivia Hartley, Laura Dudley. Student, Phillips Exeter Acad., 1944; A.B., Harvard U., 1948; M.A., Cambridge (Eng.) U., 1952; L.H.D. (hon.), Franklin Pierce Coll., 1968; Litt.D. (hon.), Hobart Smith Coll., 1978, Stonehill Coll., 1982, L.I.U., 1984, U. S.C., 1986, Pine Manor Coll., 1988. Editor in chief Paris Rev., 1953—, Paris Rev. Edits. (subs. Doubleday and Co.), 1965-72; editor-in-chief Paris Rev. Edits. (subs. Brit. Am. Publs.), 1987—; instr. Barnard Coll., 1956-58; assoc. editor Horizon mag., 1959-61; dir. Am. Lit. Anthology program, 1967-71; assoc. editor Harper's mag., 1972-81; contbg. editor Food and Wine Mag., 1978; editorial adv. bd. Realities, 1978; TV host Dupont Plimpton Spls., 1967-69, Greatest Sports Legends, 1979-81, The Ultimate High, 1980, Survival Anglia, 1980—, Writers' Workshop, 1982, Mousterpiece Theater, 1983—, Challenge, 1987; spl. contbr. Sports Illustrated, 1968—; bd. dirs. Int. Film Investors, 1979-82, Leisure Dynamics, 1983-85; curator Tennis Week, 1990—. Author: Rabbit's Umbrella, 1956, Out of My League, 1961, Paper Lion, 1966, The Bogey Man, 1968, Mad Ducks and Bears, 1973, One for the Record, 1974, Shadow-Box, 1976, One More July, 1976, (with Neil Leifer) Sports!, 1978, (with Arnold Roth) A Sports Bestiary, 1982, Fireworks, 1984, Open Net, 1985, The Curious Case of Sidd Finch, 1987, The X-Factor, 1990, The Best of Plimpton, 1990; also numerous articles.; editor; Writers at Work,

Vol. 1, 1957, Vol. 11, 1963, Vol. 111, 1967, Vol. IV, 1976, Vol. V, 1981, Vol. VI, 1984, Vol. VII, 1987, Vol. VIII, 1989, Vol. IX, 1992, (with Jean Stein) American Journey: The Times of Robert Kennedy, 1970, Pierre's Book, 1971, The Fancy, 1973, (with Jean Stein) Edie, An American Biography, 1982, (with Christopher Hemphill) D.V., 1984; The Paris Review Anthology, 1989, The Writer's Chapbook, 1989, Women Writers at Work, 1989, Poets at Work, 1989, The Norton Book of Sports, 1992, (with Jean Kennedy Smith) Chronicles of Courage, 1992; contbg. editor Gentlemen's Quar., 1983-85, Smart mag., 1988-90, Esquire mag., 1990. Commr. fireworks, N.Y.C., 1973—; trustee WNET, 1973-81, Nat. Art Mus. Sport, 1967—, Police Athletic League, 1976-90, African Wildlife Leadership Found., 1980—, Guild Hall, East Hampton, 1980—, N.Y. Zool. Soc., 1985—; bd. dirs. Dynamite Mus., Nat. Tennis Found., 1979—, Squaw Valley Center for Written and Dramatic Arts, 1979—, Authors Trust Am., 1979, Friends of the Masai Mara, 1986, Friends of Conservation, 1988—, Roger Tory Peterson Inst., The Carnegie Cook Ctr. for the Arts; chmn. Books Across the Sea, English Speaking Union, 1988—; bd. dirs., pres. N.Y. Philomusica, Pen/Faulkner, 1995; mem. adv. bd. Coordinating Council Lit. Mags., 1979, Yoknapatawpha Press, Am. Chess Found., East Harlem Tutorial, Boy's Harbor. Served to 2d lt. AUS, 1945-48. Assoc. fellow Trumbull Coll., Yale, 1967; recipient Disting. Achievement award U. So. Calif., 1967, Blue Pencil award Columbia Spectator, 1981, Mark Twain award Internat. Platform Assn., 1982, Chancellor's award L.I. U., 1986, l'Ordre des Arts et des Lettres, France, 1994. Mem. NFL Alumni Assn., Am. Pyrotechnics Assn., Pyrotechnics Guild Internat., Explorers Club., Linnean Soc., PEN, Mayflower Descendants Soc. Clubs: Century Assn, Racquet and Tennis, Brook, Piping Rock, Dutch Treat, River, Coffee House, Devon Yacht; Travellers (Paris). Address: Paris Review Inc 541 E 72nd St New York NY 10021-4010

PLIMPTON, PEGGY LUCAS, trustee; b. Nov. 3, 1931; d. David Nicholson and Margaret (MacMillan) Lucas; m. Hollis Winslow Plimpton, June 11, 1955; children: Victoria P. Babcock, Priscilla P. Morphy, Hollis Winslow Plimpton III. AB, Duke U., 1954. Trustee Cape Cod Conservatory of Music, 1989—. Bd. trustees Carleton Williard Retirement Home, Bedford, Mass., 1968—, Cape Cod Conservatory Music, 1990—; bd. dirs. Episcopal Ch. Women, 1968-78, Brigham & Women's Hosp., Boston, 1975—; pres. Boston Lying-In Hosp., 1970-72; chmn. Mass. Nat. Cathedral Assn., Boston, 1978-80, 1985-88; pres. bd. trustees Women's Ednl. and Indsl., Boston, 1980-83. mem. New Eng. Farm and Garden Club (bd. dirs. 1965—, pres. 1995—), Chestnut Hill Garden Club (bd. dirs. 1970-74), Jr. League Garden Club (pres. 1981-83), Colonial Dames (bd. mgrs. 1983-89, v.p. 1993—), Vincent Club, Chilton Club. Republican. Episcopalian. Avocations: gardening, golf, bridge, grandchildren.

PLISCHKE, ELMER, political science educator; b. Milw., July 15, 1914; s. Louis and Louise (Peterleus) P.; m. Audrey Alice Siehr, May 30, 1941; children: Lowell Robert, Julianne. Ph.B. cum laude, Marquette U., 1937; M.A., Am. U., 1938; certificate Carnegie summer session internat. law, U. Mich., 1938; Ph.D. (fellow), Clark U., 1943; certificate, Naval Sch. Mil. Govt. and Civil Affairs, Columbia, 1944. Instr. Springfield Coll., 1940; dist. supr., state dir. Wis. Hist. Records Survey, 1940-42; exec. sec. War Records Commn., Wis. Council Def., 1942; asst. prof. DePauw U., 1946-48, U. Md., College Park, 1948-49; assoc. prof. U. Md., 1949-52, prof., 1952-79, prof. emeritus, 1979—, head dept. govt. and politics, 1954-68; adj. prof. Gettysburg (Pa.) Coll., 1979-85; spl. historian Office U.S. High Commr. for Germany, 1950-52; cons. Dept. State, summer 1952; adj. scholar Am. Enterprise Inst. Pub. Policy Research, 1978—; lectr. Air War Coll., Armed Forces Staff Coll., Army War Coll., Def. Intelligence Sch., Indsl. Coll. Armed Forces, Inter-Am. Def. Coll., Nat. War Coll.; lectr. Sr. Officers Seminar Fgn. Service Inst. Dept. State; lectr. Instituto de Altos Estudios Nacionales, Quito, Ecuador.; mem. adv. com. fgn. relations of U.S. Dept. State, 1967-72, chmn., 1969-70; assoc. fellow Gettysburg Coll., 1993—. Author 28 books and monographs including: Conduct of American Diplomacy, 3d edit, 1967, reissued, 1974, (with Robert G. Dixon, Jr.) American Government: Basic Documents and Materials, 1950, reissued, 1971, Berlin: Development of Its Government and Administration, 1952, reissued, 1970, The Allied High Commission for Germany, 1953, International Relations: Basic Documents, rev. 1962, American Foreign Relations: A Bibliography of Official Sources, 1955, reissued, 1966, American Diplomacy: A Bibliography of Biographies, Autobiographies, and Commentaries, 1957, Summit Diplomacy: Personal Diplomacy of the President of the United States, 1958, reissued, 1974, Contemporary Governments of Germany, 1961, rev. edit., 1969, Government and Politics of Contemporary Berlin, 1963, Foreign Relations Decisionmaking: Options Analysis, 1973, United States Diplomats and Their Missions: A Profile of American Diplomatic Emissaries Since 1778, 1975, Microstates in World Affairs: Policy Problems and Options, 1977, Neutralization as an American Strategic Option, 1978, Modern Diplomacy: The Art and the Artisans, 1979, U.S. Foreign Relations: A Guide to Information Sources, 1980, Presidential Diplomacy: A Chronology of Summit Visits, Trips and Meetings, 1986, Diplomat in Chief: The President at the Summit, 1986, Foreign Relations: Analysis of Its Anatomy, 1988, Contemporary United States Foreign Policy: Documents and Commentary, 1991, others; contbr. more than 80 articles to profl. and lit. jours., and encyclopaedias; Americana Ann., 1972-83; also editorials in newspapers; editor, contbr. Systems of Integrating the International Community, 1964; mem. bd. editors Jour. Politics, 1966-68. Served from ensign to lt. USNR, 1943-46; exec. asst., then exec. officer Civil Affairs div., comdr. U.S. Naval Forces for Europe, London, 1944-45; charge de- Nazification policy coordination Office Dir. Polit. Affairs, Office Mil. Govt. for Germany 1945. Recipient research awards U. Md. Gen. Research Bd., 1956, 58, 69; research grantee Earhart Found., 1982-83, 86-87; book Interaction: Foreign Policy and Public Policy (Piper and Terchek) dedicated in honor, 1983; elected knight Mark Twain, Mark Twain Jour., 1970. Mem. AAUP, Am. Soc. Internat. Law, Am. Polit. Sci. Assn. (coun.), D.C. Polit. Sci. Assn. (coun. pres. 1961), So. Polit. Sci. Assn. (coun.), Internat. Studies Assn., Com. Study Diplomacy, Inst. Study Diplomacy, Internat. Torch Club (sec. Gettysburg club 1985-91, archivist 1991—, bd. mem. 1995-96), Eclectic Club, Phi Beta kappa, Phi Kappa Phi, Pi Sigma Alpha, Sigma Tau Delta. Home: 227 Ewell Ave Gettysburg PA 17325-3108

PLISCHKE, LE MOYNE WILFRED, research chemist; b. Greensburg, Pa., Dec. 11, 1922; s. Fred and Ruth Naomi (Rumbaugh) P.; m. Joan Harper, Mar. 11, 1966. BS, Waynesburg Coll., 1948; MS, W.Va. U., 1952. Rsch. chemist U.S. Naval Ordinance Test Sta., China Lake, Calif., 1952-53; asst. prof. chemistry Commonwealth U., Richmond, Va., 1953-54; rsch. chemist E.I. du Pont, Gibbstown, N.J., 1955-57, Monsanto Chem. Co., Pensacola, Fla., 1957—. Mem. Am. Chem. Soc. Achievements include 16 U.S. patents and 48 foreign patents in field. Home: 2100 Club House Dr Lillian AL 36549-5402 Office: Monsanto Co The Chem Group PO Box 97 Gonzalez FL 32560-0097

PLISHNER, MICHAEL JON, lawyer; b. Rockville Centre, N.Y., Jan. 22, 1948; s. Meyer J. and Lillian (Gold) P.; m. Rosalind F. Schein, Jan. 26, 1969; children: Aaron, Alexander, Elias. BA summa cum laude, Yale U., 1969, JD, 1972. Bar: Calif. 1972, U.S. Dist. Ct. (no. dist.) Calif. 1972, U.S. Ct. Appeals (9th cir.) 1972. Assoc. McCutchen, Doyle, Brown & Enersen, San Francisco, 1972-79, ptnr., 1979—. Mem. Phi Beta Kappa. Home: 114 St Albans Rd Kensington CA 94708-1035 Office: McCutchen Doyle Brown & Enersen 3 Embarcadero Ctr San Francisco CA 94111-4003

PLISKA, EDWARD WILLIAM, lawyer; b. Rockville, Conn., Apr. 13, 1935; s. Louis Boleslaw and Constance (Dombrowski) P.; m. Luisa Anne Crotti, Nov. 29, 1958; children: Gregory, John, Thomas, Laura. AB, Princeton (N.J.) U., 1956; LLB, U. Conn., 1964; LLD (hon.), San Mateo (Calif.) U., 1975. Bar: Calif. 1965. Dep. dist. atty. Santa Barbara (Calif.) County, 1965; dep. dist. atty. San Mateo County Dist. Atty., Redwood City, Calif., 1965-71, chief trial dep., 1970-71; pvt. practice San Mateo, 1971-72; judge San Mateo County Mcpl. Ct., 1973-86; ptnr. Corey, Luzaich, Gemello, Manos & Pliska, Millbrae, Calif., 1986—; officer Am. Judges Assn., 1983-86; prodr. and host (TV and Radio show) Justice Forum, 1973-78; prof. criminal and constitutional law San Mateo Law Sch., 1971-76; leader People to People legal delegations to Europe, India, Nepal, 1985, 87, 91. Editor Ct. Rev., 1981-88. Leader People to People Legal Delegations, Europe, India, Nepal, 1985, 87, 91; trustee Belmont (Calif.) Sch. Dist., 1987-91, pres., 1990; chmn. San Mateo County Cultural Arts Commn., 1987-90; mem. Peninsula Comty. Found. Arts Fund, 1988—; v.p. Hillbarn Theatre, 1989-92. With U.S. Army, 1957. NEH grantee, 1975, 80. Mem. Calif. Judges Assn., Calif. State Bar Assn., Nat. Assn. Criminal Def. Lawyers, Calif. Attys. for Criminal Justice, San Mateo County Bar Assn., San Mateo County Trial Lawyers (bd. dirs. 1990-91), Bohemian Club. Democrat. Roman Catholic. Avocations: acting and directing plays, reading, running, sports spectator. Home: 1567 Escondido Way Belmont CA 94002-3634 Office: Corey Luzaich Gemello Manos Pliska PO Box 669 700 El Camino Real Millbrae CA 94030-2009

PLISKIN, MARVIN ROBERT, lawyer; b. Akron, Ohio, Nov. 7, 1938; s. Abraham David and Roselle (Cohen) P.; m. Suzanne Schreiber, Aug. 27, 1961; children: Daniel, Lawrence. BS, Ohio State U., 1960, JD, 1963. Bar: Ohio 1963. Assoc. Murphey, Young & Smith, Columbus, Ohio, 1963-69; ptnr. Murphey, Young & Smith, Columbus, 1970-88, Squire, Sanders & Dempsey, Columbus, 1988-90, Porter, Wright, Morris & Arthur, Columbus, 1990—. Contbr. articles to profl. jours. Active Columbus Jewish Found. Legal and Tax Adv. Com., 1982—, Columbus Found. Legal Adv. Com., 1991—; mem. planning com. Columbus Estate Planning Coun. II, 1975—. Fellow Am. Coll. Trust & Estate Coun. (state chmn. Ohio 1991-95); mem. ABA, Ohio State Bar Assn. (bd. govs. probate and trust sect. 1979—, state chmn. 1987-88), Columbus Bar Assn. (mem. probate law com. 1971—, chmn. 1975-76, mem. estate and gift tax com. 1975—), Columbus Met. Club (mem. nominating com. 1991-94). Avocations: music, sports, travel. Home: 255 S Roosevelt Ave Columbus OH 43209-1827 Office: Porter Wright Morris & Arthur 41 S High St Columbus OH 43215-6101

PLISKIN, WILLIAM AARON, physicist; b. Akron, Ohio, Aug. 9, 1920; s. Max and Lena (Slavin) P.; m. Miriam Jaffee, Mar. 15, 1944; children: Karen, Michael, Bina. B.S., Kent State U., 1941; M.S., Ohio U., 1943; Ph.D., Ohio State U., 1949. Rsch. physicist Texaco Rsch. Ctr., Beacon, N.Y., 1949-59; staff physicist IBM, Poughkeepsie, N.Y., 1959-60; adv. physicist IBM, 1960-63; sr. physicist, mgr. IBM, East Fishkill, N.Y., 1964-79; sr. staff mem. IBM, 1979-82, mgr., sr. tech. staff mem., 1982-87, sr. tech. staff mem., 1987-90; cons. characterization and measurement of dielectric films, 1990—. Contbr. numerous articles to profl. jours., chpts. in books; patentee in field. Served to 1st lt. U.S. Army, 1943-46, PTO. Fellow IEEE, Electrochem Soc. (ann. award electronics div. 1973); mem. Am. Phys. Soc., Am. Chem. Soc. (ann. award Mid Hudson sect. 1964), Sigma Xi, Pi Mu Epsilon, Sigma Pi Sigma. Jewish. Home: 31 Greenvale Farms Rd Poughkeepsie NY 12603-4201

PLISKOW, VITA SARI, anesthesiologist; b. Tel Aviv, Israel, Sept. 13, 1942; arrived in Can., 1951; came to U.S., 1967; d. Henry Norman and Renee (Mushkatel) Stahl; m. Raymond Joel Pliskow, June 30, 1968; children: Tia, Kami. MD, U. B.C., Vancouver, 1967. Diplomate Am. Bd. Anesthesiology. Ptnr. Olympic Anesthesia, Bremerton, Wash., 1971-74, pres., anesthesiologist, 1974-84; co-founder Olympic Ambulatory Surgery Ctr., Bremerton, 1977-83; ptnr., anesthesiologist Allenmore Anesthesia Assocs., Tacoma, 1983—; staff anesthesiologist Harrison Meml. Hosp., Bremerton, 1971-95, Allenmore Hosp., Tacoma, 1983—. Trustee Tacoma Youth Symphony Assn., 1994—; active Nat. Coun. Jewish Women, 1972—. Fellow Am. Coll. Anesthesiologists, Am. Coll. Chest Physicians; mem. Am. Soc. Anesthesiologists (del. Wash. State 1987—), Wash. State Med. Assn. (del. Pierce County 1993-94), Wash. State Soc. Anesthesiologists (pres. 1985-87), Pierce County Med. Soc. (sec.-treas. 1992). Avocations: classical music, opera, singing (mezzo soprano). Office: # 109 900 Sheridan Rd Bremerton WA 98310-2701

PLOGER, ROBERT RIIS, retired military officer, engineer; b. Mackay, Idaho, Aug. 12, 1915; s. Robert and Elfrieda (Riis) P.; m. Marguerite Anne Fiehrer, June 13, 1939 (dec. Feb. 1982); children: Wayne David, Robert Riis III, Daniel Bruce, Marguerite Anne, Marianne Ploger Hill, Gregory Fiehrer; m. Jeanne Allys Pray, Nov. 20, 1982. BS, U.S. Mil. Acad., 1939; MS in Engring., Cornell U., 1947; MBA, George Washington U., 1963. Registered civil engr., D.C. Commd. 2d lt. U.S. Army, 1939; served in corps of engrs. U.S. Army, ETO, Okinawa, 1939-65; advanced through grades to maj. gen. U.S. Army, 1966, div. engr. New England div., 1965, comdg. gen. 18th engr. brigade, 1965-66, comdg. gen. engr. command, Vietnam, 1966-67; dir. topography and mil. engring., Office Chief Engrs. U.S. Army, Washington, 1967-70; comdg. gen. Ft. Belvoir and commandant U.S. Army Engr. Sch. Va., 1970-73; ret. U.S. Army, 1973; engr. specialist Bechtel Power Corp., Ann Arbor, 1974-80, mgr. adminstrv. services, 1980-81; counselor SCORE, Ann Arbor, Mich., 1984—; lectr. Indsl. Coll. Armed Forces, 1962-65. Author: Vietnam Studies, U.S. Army Engineers 1965-70; contbr. numerous articles on war and mil. engring. to profl. jours. Chmn. gift com. Class of 1939 50th Reunion of U.S. Mil. Acad., 1985-89. Decorated DSM with oak leaf cluster, Legion of Merit, Silver Star with oak leaf cluster, Bronze Star with oak leaf cluster, Air medal, Purple Heart, Korean Order Mil. Merit Chung Mu, Nat. Order 5th Class Republic of Vietnam; recipient George Washington medal ICAF, 1965, Wheeler medal Soc. Am. Mil. Engrs., 1966, Silver Beaver award Boy Scouts Am., 1973, Médaille du Jubilé, Vire, France, 1994. Fellow Soc. Am. Mil. Engrs.; mem. NSPE (priviliged; chpt. pres. 1979-80), 29th Inf. Divsn. Assn. (Phila. award 1985), West Point Soc. Mich. (pres. 1981-84), SCORE (at-large exec. com. 1991, counselor chpt. 18), Ann Arbor C. of C. (counselor svc. corps ret. execs.), Army Engr. Assn. (life, Silver Order de Fleury medal 1995), SHAPE Officers Assn. (life). Baptist. Avocations: tennis, skiing, sailboarding. Home: 2475 Adare Rd Ann Arbor MI 48104-4021

PLOMGREN, RONALD ARTHUR, retail executive; b. Oakland, Calif., Apr. 1, 1934; s. Arthur Ivar and Augusta W. (Nelson) P.; m. Sharon Jensen, May 15, 1959; children: David, Susan, Karen. B.S., U. Calif.-Berkeley, 1956. Clk. Longs Drug Stores, Walnut Creek, Calif., 1948-56; clk. to store mgr. Long Drug Stores, Walnut Creek, Calif., 1957-68; property supr., constrn. mgr. Longs Drug Stores, Walnut Creek, Calif., 1968-74, v.p., 1974-76, sr. v.p., 1976—, dir., 1972—; dir. APS, Oakland. Vice chmn. Orinda Parks and Recreation Dist., Calif., 1974-78; vice chmn. Orinda Found., 1978-83; chmn. Orinda Planning Commn.; co-chmn. U. Calif.-Berkeley Engring. Fund. Office: Longs Drug Stores Inc 141 N Civic Dr Walnut Creek CA 94596-3815

PLOMP, TEUNIS (TONY PLOMP), minister; b. Rotterdam, The Netherlands, Jan. 28, 1938; arrived in Can., 1951; s. Teunis and Cornelia (Pietersma) P.; m. Margaret Louise Bone, July 21, 1962; children: Jennifer Anne, Deborah Adele. BA, U. B.C. (Can.), Vancouver, 1960; BD, Knox Coll., Toronto, Ont., Can., 1963, DD (hon.), 1988. Ordained to ministry Presbyn. Ch., 1963. Minister Goforth Meml. Presbyn. Ch., Saskatoon, Sask., Can., 1963-68, Richmond (B.C.) Presbyn. Ch., 1968—; clerk Presbytery of Westminster, Vancouver, 1969—; moderator 113th Gen. Assembly Presbyn. Ch. Can., 1987-88, dep. clk., 1987—; chaplain New Haven Correctional Centre, Burnaby, B.C. Contbr. mag. column You Were Asking, 1982-89. Avocations: record collecting, audiophile, biking, swimming. Office: Richmond Presbyn Ch, 7111 #2 Rd, Richmond, BC Canada V7C 3L7

PLONSEY, ROBERT, electrical and biomedical engineer; b. N.Y.C., July 17, 1924; s. Louis B. and Betty (Vinograd) P.; m. Vivian V. Vucker, Oct. 1, 1948; 1 child, Daniel. BEE, Cooper Union, 1943; MSEE, NYU, 1948; PhD, U. Calif., Berkeley, 1955; postgrad. med. sch., Case Western Res. U., 1969-71; D of Technol. Scis., Slovak Acad. Scis., 1995. Registered profl. engr., Ohio. Asst. prof. elec. engring. U. Calif., Berkeley, 1955-57; asst. prof. elec. engring. Case Inst. Tech., Cleve., 1957-60, assoc. prof., 1960-66, prof., 1966-68, dir. bioengring. group, 1962-68; prof. biomed. engring. Sch. Engring. and Sch. Medicine Case Western Res. U., 1968-83, chmn. dept., 1976-80; vis. prof. biomed. engring. Duke U., Durham, N.C., 1980-81, prof., 1983—, prof. biomed. engring., Hudson prof. engring., 1990-93, Pfizer-Inc.-Edmond T. Pratt Jr. Univ. prof. biomed. engring., 1993—; mem. biomed. fellowships rev. com. NIH, 1966-70; mem. tng. com. Engrs. in Medicine and Biology, 1972-73, cons., 1974—; cons. NSF, 1973-93; mem. internat. sci. adv. com. Ragnar Granit Inst., Tampere (Finland) U. Tech., 1992—; ad hoc mem. sci. adv. com. Whitaker Found., 1989-91. Author: (with R. Collin) Principles and Applications of Electromagnetic Fields, 1961, Bioelectric Phenomena, 1969, (with J. Liebman and P. Gillette) Pediatric Electrocardiography, 1982, (with T. Pilkington) Engineering Contributions to Biophysical Electrocardiography, 1982, (with J. Liebman and Y. Rudy) Pediatric and Fundamental Electrocardiography, (with R.C. Barr) Bioelectricity: A Quantitative Approach, 1988, (with J. Malmivuo) Bioelectromagnetism, 1995; mem. editorial bd. Trans. IEEE, Biomed. Engring, 1965-70; assoc. editor, 1977-79, editorial bd. TIT Jour. 1971-81, Electrocardiology Jour., 1974—, Medical and Biological Engineering and Computing, 1987—; proc. editor Engring. in Medicine and Biology, 17th Ann., Conf., 1965. Mem. com. on electrocardiography Am. Heart Assn., 1976-82; v.p. Your Schs., Cleveland Heights, ohio, 1968-69, 73-75; provisional trustee Am. Bd. Clin. Engrs., 1973-74, pres. 1975, trustee, 1976-85. With AUS, 1944-46. Recipient sr. postdoctoral award NIH, 1980-81. Fellow AAAS, IEEE (chmn. Cleve. chpt. group on biomed. electronics 1962-63, chmn. publs. com. group on engring. in medicine and biology 1968-70, v.p. adminstr. com. 1970-72, pres. 1973-74, chmn. fellows com. Engring. in Medicine and Biology Soc. 1986-88, v.p. tech. and conf. activities 1991, William S. Morlock award 1979, Centennial medal 1984, co-program chair annual conf. Paris 1992); mem. AAUP, NAE (bioengring. peer com. 1988-91, chair, 1990-91, nominating com. 1991-92, mem. com. 1992-94, program adv. com. 1995—, NRC postdoctoral rsch. associateships evaluation panel 1987-90), Am. Inst. Med. and Biological Engring. (founding fellow 1992—), Alliance for Engring. in Medicine and Biology (treas. 1976-78), Biomed. Engring. Soc. (bd. dir. 1975-78, 79-89, ALZA Disting. lectr. 1988), Am. Physiol. Soc., Am. Soc. Engring. Edn. (bd. dir. biomed. engring. divsn. 1978-83, chmn. 1982-83), Acad. Medical Biological Engring. (foundig fellow, membership com. 1995—), Internat. Soc. Bioelectromagnetism (hon. pres. 1995—). Office: Duke U Dept Biomed Engring Durham NC 27706 *External recognition of success is not nearly so important as the inner awareness of coming to full grips with life, to be fully involved, bending all strengths to fulfill one's goals and philosophies. And of all involvements, those with people are most meaningful (to be aware of and share the feelings of colleagues, students, friends, and family—and to enrich these relationships)—and for me most difficult.*

PLOPPER, CHARLES GEORGE, anatomist, cell biologist; b. Oakland, Calif., June 16, 1944; s. George Eli and Josephine Viola (Gates) P.; m. Suzanne May, Nov. 9, 1969. AB, U. Calif., Davis, 1967, PhD, 1972. Chief. electron microscopy br. U.S. Army Med. Research Nutrition Lab., Denver, 1972-73; vis. scientist Calif. Primate Research Ctr., Davis, 1974-75; chief. electron microscopy div. Letterman Army Inst. Research, San Francisco, 1974-75; asst. prof. U. Hawaii Sch. Medicine, Honolulu, 1975-77; assoc. prof. Kuwait U. Sch. Medicine, 1977-78; sr. staff fellow Nat. Inst. Environ. Health Sci. Research, Triangle Park, N.C., 1978-79; from asst. to assoc. prof. U. Calif. Sch. Vet. Medicine, Davis, 1979-86, dept. chmn., 1984-88; prof. anatomy, physiology and cell biology, Sch. Vet. Medicine U. Calif., Davis, 1986—; mem. study sect. NIH div. Research Grants, Bethesda, Md., 1986-90; Paley vis. prof. Boston U. Sch. Medicine, 1985; vis. pulmonary scholar Duke U., U. N.C., N.C. State U., 1991. Served to capt. U.S. Army, 1972-75. Mem. Am. Soc. Cell Biology, Am. Thoracic Soc., Am. Assn. Antomists, Am. Assn. Pathologists, Anat. Soc. Great Britain and Ireland, Davis Aquatic Masters (bd. dirs. 1993-95). Democrat. Avocations: swimming, hiking, tennis. Home: 511 Hubble St Davis CA 95616-2720 Office: Univ Calif Sch Vet Medicine Dept Anatomy Physiol Cell Biology Davis CA 95616

PLOSSER, CHARLES IRVING, university dean, economics educator; b. Birmingham, Ala., Sept. 19, 1948; s. George Gray and Dorothy (Irving) P.; m. Janet Schwert, June 26, 1976; children: Matthew, Kevin, Allison. B.E. cum laude, Vanderbilt U., 1970; MBA, U. Chgo., 1972, PhD, 1976. Cons. Citicorp Realty Cons., N.Y.C., 1972-73; lectr. Grad. Sch. Bus., U. Chgo., 1975-76; asst. prof. Grad. Sch. Bus. Stanford (Calif.) U., 1976-78; asst. prof. econs. W.E. Simon Grad. Sch. Bus., U. Rochester (N.Y.), 1978-82, assoc. prof., 1982-86, prof., 1986-89; Fred H. Gowen prof. econs. U. Rochester, N.Y., 1989-92, John M. Olin Disting. prof. econs. and pub. policy, 1992—, acting dean W.E. Simon Grad. Sch. Bus., 1990-91, 92-93; dean W.E. Simon Grad. Sch. Bus., 1993—; mem. Consortium for Grad. Study in Mgmt.; chmn. bd. Consortium for Grad. Study in Mgmt., 1995—; bd. dirs. Greater Rochester Health Sys., Inc. Editor, Jour. Monetary Econs., 1983—, Carnegie-Rochester Conference Series on Public Policy, 1989—; contbr. articles to profl. jours. 1st lt., U.S. Army, 1972-73. NSF research grantee, 1982, 84. Mem. Am. Econs. Assn., Econometrics Soc., Am. Fin. Assn., Am. Statis. Assn., Tau Beta Pi, Beta Gamma Sigma. Home: 95 Ambassador Dr Rochester NY 14610-3402 Office: U Rochester Dean Of Simon Grad Sch Rochester NY 14627

PLOSZAJ, STEPHEN CHARLES, lawyer; b. Hartford, Conn., Aug. 16, 1949; s. John Francis and Irene (Duval) P.; m. Faith Marion Margolis, May 21, 1972; children: Sara Lynne, Laura Beth. BS, USCG Acad., New London, Conn., 1971; JD with honors, George Washington U., 1978; LLM in Taxation, Boston U., 1984. Bar: Md. 1978, Mass. 1984. Commd. ensign USCG, 1971, advanced through grades to lt. comdr., 1980; dept. head USCGC Vigilant (WMEC-617), New Bedford, Mass., 1971-73; commdg. officer Loran Sta., Pt. Clarence, Alaska, 1973-74, Commandant (G-PO), Washington, 1974-75, Commandant (G-PTE), Washington, 1975-78, Commandant (GL) CGHQ, Washington, 1978-80, Commander (dist. legal) 1st CG Dist., Boston, 1980-84; ptnr. Hale and Dorr, Boston, 1984-91, McDermott, Will & Emery, Boston, 1992—; mil. magistrate 1st Coast Guard Dist., Boston, 1980-84. Mem. ABA, Boston Bar Assn. Avocations: golf, racquetball, scuba diving. Office: McDermott Will & Emery 75 State St Ste 1700 Boston MA 02109-1807

PLOTCH, WALTER, management consultant, fund-raising counselor; b. N.Y.C., July 19, 1932; s. Harry and Belle (Lebowsky) P.; AB, Queens Coll., 1957; MA, Harvard U., 1959, postgrad., 1959-61; m. Yvette Gabrielle Lambert, Mar. 15, 1957; children: Allison, Jennifer, Adrienne. Instr. history Pine Manor Jr. Coll., Wellesley, Mass., 1960-62; analyst L.F. Rothschild & Co., N.Y.C. and Boston, 1962-64; community cons., 1964-65; edn. dir. for New Eng., Anti-Defamation League of B'nai B'rith, 1965-68, nat. edn. dir., 1968-76; v.p. Brakeley, John Price Jones Inc., N.Y.C., 1976-79, sr. v.p., dir., 1979-89; sr. v.p. The Oram Group, Inc., N.Y.C., 1989-92, exec. v.p.; pres. and CEO Walter Plotch Assocs., Inc., Croton-On-Hudson, N.Y., 1992—; mem. faculty Grad. Sch. Mgmt. and Urban Affairs, New Sch. Social Rsch.; lectr. Harvard U. Grad. Sch. Edn.; cons. Harcourt, Brace, Plenum Pubs. Bd. dirs. Schizophrenia Found., 1975-90; nat. bd. dirs. NCCJ, 1980-84, Nat. Charitable Info. Bur., mem. exec. com., 1986-94. Served with USCGR, 1953-55; Korea. Grantee, U.S. Office Edn., Dept. Labor, N.Y. Council Humanities; teaching fellow Harvard U., 1959-61. Mem. Princeton Club, U. Washington Club, Phi Alpha Theta. Democrat. Jewish. Co-editor: Pluralism in a Democratic Society, 1977; gen. editor: The Job Corps Intergroup Relations Series, 1974; author articles in field, contbg. editor Grants mag., Jour. Sponsored Research 1978-82. Office: 39 Furnace Dock Rd Croton On Hudson NY 10520-1406

PLOTHOW, ROGER HENRY, college official, consultant; b. Peru, Ind., Nov. 21, 1934; s. Anthony Fredrick Jr. and Wilma Lavon (Henry) P.; m. Lenora Dean Damron, May 24, 1957; children: Roger D., Phillip A., Kathleen L., Melissa A., Amy L. BS, Purdue U., 1956, MS, 1965; EdD, Brigham Young U., 1974. Tchr. vocat. agr. Gilead (Ind.) High Sch., 1956-58; tchr. vocat. agr. Lewis Cass High Sch., Walton, Ind., 1958-62, dir. counseling, 1962-65, asst. prin., 1965-66; state exec. dir. Agrl. Stblzn. and Conservation Svc., USDA, Indpls., 1966-68; asst. to pres. Indpls. Campus, Purdue U., 1968-70; adult edn. cons. Utah Office Edn., Salt Lake City, 1970-72; dean continuing edn. Utah Valley C.C., Provo, 1972-84, dir. devel., 1984—; cons., owner Henry Dean Pub., Provo, 1989—. Author: Philanthropic Foundations of Utah, 1989, 2d edit., 1991, (software) Proposal Writing, 1991-92. Bd. dirs. Utah County Fair, Provo, 1974-78; cons. USA Volkschule Evaluation Team, Germany, 1982; scoutmaster Boy Scouts Am., Provo, 1974-80. Capt. USAR, 1957-66. Scholar Purdue U., 1952, Manchester (Ind.) Coll., 1962. Mem. Nat. Coun. for Resource Devel. (nat. bd. dirs. 1988—), Adult Edn. Assn. U.S.A. (nat. bd. dirs. 1978-82), Kiwanis (pres. 1990-91). Democrat. Mem. LDS Ch. Avocations: gardening, reading, travel, family history. Home: 1254 N 1200 W Provo UT 84604-6058 Office: Utah Valley CC 800 W 1200 S Orem UT 84058-5999

PLOTKIN, HARRY MORRIS, lawyer; b. Athol, Mass., May 18, 1913; s. Louis and Fannie (Coffman) P.; m. Esther Lipsez, Dec. 25, 1937; children—Ira L., Judith Deborah (Mrs. Jonathan Wilkenfeld). A.B. magna cum laude, Harvard, 1934, LL.B. magna cum laude, 1937. Bar: Ill. 1937, D.C. 1951. Assoc. firm Topliff & Horween, Chgo., 1937-39; atty. FCC, 1940-51, asst. gen. counsel, 1943-51; ptnr. Arnold, Fortas & Porter, Washington, 1951-56, Arent, Fox, Kintner, Plotkin & Kahn, Washington, 1956-82; of counsel Arent, Fox, Kintner, Plotkin & Kahn, 1983—. Trustee Washington United Jewish Appeal Fedn., Mem. ABA, Fed. Bar Assn., Fed. Communications Bar Assn., D.C. Bar Assn., Phi Beta Kappa. Clubs: Harvard, Nat.

Lawyers (Washington). Home: 3719 Harrison St NW Washington DC 20015-1815 Office: 1050 Connecticut Ave NW Washington DC 20036-5303

PLOTKIN, IRVING H(ERMAN), economist, consultant; b. Bklyn., July 19, 1941; s. Samuel H. and Dorothy (Falick) P.; BS in Econs., U. Pa., 1963; PhD in Math. Econs., Mass. Inst. Tech., 1968; m. Janet V. Bufe, July 26, 1969; children: Aaron Jacob, Joshua Benjamin. Corp. planning analyst Mobil Oil Co., N.Y.C., 1962-63, Mobil Oil Italiana, Genoa, Italy, 1965; ind. cons. econs. and ops. rsch. to banks, mut. funds, ins. cos. govt. agys., Cambridge, Mass., 1965-68; sr. economist Arthur D. Little, Inc., Cambridge, 1968—; dir. regulation and econs., 1974—, v.p., 1979—; bd. dir. Arthur D. Little Valuation, Inc., 1980—; trustee Arthur D. Little, Inc., ESOP, 1988—; instr. fin. and computer scis. Mass. Inst. Tech., 1965-68; lectr. maj. univs. U.S. and abroad; expert witness U.S. Ho. of Reps. and Senate coms., U.S. Ct. Claims, U.S. Tax Ct. I.C.C., FTC, Fed. Maritime Commn., Fed. Dist. Cts., Fed. Res. Bd., other fed. and state govt. agys., 1967—. NASA fellow, 1963-66, NSF fellow, 1967, Am. Bankers Assn. fellow, 1968. Mem. Am. Econ. Assn., Econometric Soc., Am. Fin. Assn., Beta Gamma Sigma, Pi Gamma Mu, Tau Delta Phi (chpt. pres. 1962-63). Editorial reviewer Jour. Am. Statis. Assn., 1968, Jour. Indsl. Econs., 1968—, Jour. Risk and Ins., 1980—; author: Prices and Profits in the Property and Liability Insurance Industry, 1967, The Consequences of Industrial Regulation on Profitability, Risk Taking, and Innovation, 1969, National Policy, Technology, and Economic Forces Affecting the Industrial Organization of Marine Transportation, 1970, Government Regulation of the Air Freight Industry, 1971, The Private Mortgage Insurance Industry, 1975, On The Theory and Practice of Rate Review and Profit Measurement in Title Insurance, 1978, Torrens in the United States, 1978, Total Rate of Return and the Regulation of Insurance Profits, 1979, Studies on the Impact of Sophisticated Manufacturing Industries on the Economic Development of Puerto Rico, 1981, The Economic Consequences of Controlled Business in the Real Estate Industry, 1981, On the Nature of Captive Insurance, 1984, Economic Foundations of Limited Liability for Nuclear Reactor Accidents, 1985, Transfer Prices, Royalties, and Adam Smith, 1987, Guide to Transfer Pricing Compliance, 1994; contbr. numerous articles to profl. jours. Home: 55 Baskin Rd Lexington MA 02173-6928 Office: 35 Acorn Park Cambridge MA 02140-2301

PLOTKIN, MANUEL D., management consultant, educator, former corporate executive and government official; s. Jacob and Bella (Katz) P.; m. Diane Fern Weiss, Dec. 17, 1967; 1 child, Lori Ann. B.S. with honors, Northwestern U., 1948; M.B.A., U. Chgo., 1949. Price economist, survey coordinator U.S. Bur. Labor Statistics, Washington, 1949-51, Chgo., 1951-53; sr. economist Sears Roebuck & Co., Chgo., 1953-61; mgr. market research Sears Roebuck & Co., 1961-66, chief economist, mgr. mktg. rsch., 1966-73, dir. corp. planning and research, 1973-77, exec. corp. planner, 1979-80; dir. U.S. Bur. Census, Washington, 1977-79; v.p., dir. group practice Divsn. Mgmt. Cons. Austin Co., Evanston, Ill., 1981-85; pres. M.D. Plotkin Research & Planning Co., Chgo., 1985—; tchr. statistics Ind. U., 1953-54; tchr. econs. Wilson Jr. Coll., Chgo., 1954-55; tchr. quantitative methods and managerial econs. Northwestern U., 1955-63; tchr. contemporary mktg. and mktg. mgmt. DePaul U., Chgo., 1992—; mem. Conf. Bd. Mktg. Rsch. Adv. Coun., 1968-77, chmn.-elect, 1977; chmn. adv. com. U.S. Census Bur., 1974-75; trustee Mktg. Sci. Inst., 1968-77; mem. Nat. Commn. Employment and Unemployment Stats., 1978-79, Adv. Coun. Edn. Stats., 1977-79, Interagy. Com. Population Rsch., 1977-79; mem. adv. coun. Kellstadt Ctr., DePaul U., 1987-92; trustee U.S. Travel Data Ctr., 1977-79. Contbr. articles to profl. jours. Served with AUS, 1943-46, ETO. Decorated Bronze Star medal with oak leaf cluster. Mem. Am. Mktg. Assn. (pres. Chgo. 1968-69, nat. dir. 1969-70, nat. v.p. mktg. rsch. 1970-72, nat. v.p. mktg. mgmt. 1981-83, pres., CEO 1985-86), Am. Statis. Assn. (pres. Chgo. 1966-67, Forecasting award 1963), Am. Econ. Assn., Nat. Assn. Bus. Economists, Planning Execs. Inst., World Future Soc., Midwest Planning Assn., U. Ill. Businessmen Rsch. Adv. Group, Chgo. Assn. Commerce and Industry, Beta Gamma Sigma, Alpha Sigma Lambda, Delta Mu Delta. Office: Ste 3910 2650 N Lakeview Ave Chicago IL 60614-1831

PLOTKIN, MARTIN, retired electrical engineer; b. Bklyn., July 22, 1922; s. David and Tessie (Esris) P.; m. Beverly Ferber, July 2, 1949; 1 child, George Michael. BEE, CCNY, 1943; MEE, Poly. Inst. Bklyn., 1951. Electronic engr. Bendix Aviation Corp., Bklyn., 1943-44; sr. elec. engr. Brookhaven Nat. Lab., Upton, N.Y., 1946-84, ret., 1984, cons., 1986—. Inventor alternating gradient synchrotron radio frequency system, 1960. Lt. (j.g.) USNR, 1944-46. Fellow IEEE; mem. Nuclear and Plasma Scis. Soc. (pres. 1977-78), Trans. on Med. Imaging (mem. steering com. 1981-90, chmn. steering com. 1981-84, 86-90). Avocations: mineralogy; philately. Home: 117 Clover Dr Massapequa Park NY 11762

PLOTNICK, HARVEY BARRY, publishing executive; b. Detroit, Aug. 5, 1941; s. Isadore and Esther (Sher) P.; m. Susan Regnery, Aug. 16, 1964 (div. Apr. 1977); children: Andrew, Alice; m. Elizabeth Allen, May 2, 1982; children: Teresa, Samuel. B.A., U. Chgo., 1963. Editor Contemporary Books, Inc., Chgo., 1964-66; pres. Contemporary Books, Inc., 1966-94; with Paradigm Holdings, Inc., Chgo., 1994—. Trustee U. Chgo., 1994—. Office: Paradigm Holdings Inc 2 Prudential Plz Ste 1550 Chicago IL 60601-6790

PLOTNICK, ROBERT DAVID, educator, economic consultant; b. Washington, Aug. 3, 1949; s. Theodore and Jean (Hirshfeld) P.; m. Gay Lee Jensen, Dec. 22, 1972. BA, Princeton U., 1971; MA, U. Calif., Berkeley, 1973, PhD, 1976. Research assoc. Inst. Research on Poverty, Madison, Wis., 1973-75; asst. prof. Bates Coll., Lewiston, Maine, 1975-77, Dartmouth Coll., Hanover, N.H., 1977-84; assoc. prof. U. Wash., Seattle, 1984-90, prof., 1990—; assoc. dean, 1990-95, acting dean, 1994-95; vis. scholar Russell Sage Found., 1990; rsch. affiliate Inst. for Rsch. on Poverty, 1989—; cons. Wash. Dept. Social and Health Svcs., Olympia, 1984-86, 90-96; cons. numerous pub. and non-profit orgns. Author: Progress Against Poverty, 1975; also numerous articles. Recipient Teaching Excellence award U. Wash., 1985, 89. Mem. Am. Econ. Assn., Assn. Policy Analysis and Mgmt., Population Assn. Am. Avocations: tennis, hiking, bird watching, scuba. Office: U Wash Grad Sch Pub Affairs Box 353055 Seattle WA 98195-3055

PLOTNICKI, STEVEN JOEL, record company executive; b. Bklyn., May 22, 1954; s. Harry and Lillian (Jones) P.; m. Linda Sherry Sokoloff; children: Noah Issac, Gideon Maxwell (twins). Grad. high sch., Bayside, N.Y. Freelance songwriter, musician N.Y.C.X, 1969-79; sales rep. Musical Maze, N.Y.C.X, 1979-80, Win Inc., Long Island City, N.Y., 1980-81; v.p., co-owner Profile Records, Inc., N.Y.C., 1981—. Composer: Love Insurance, 1979. Mem. ASCAP. Democrat. Jewish. Office: Profile Records Inc 740 Broadway # 7flr New York NY 10003-9518

PLOTNIK, ARTHUR, publishing executive, writer; b. White Plains, N.Y., Oct. 1, 1937; s. Michael and Annabelle (Taub) P.; m. Meta Von Borstel, Sept. 6, 1960 (div. 1979); children: Julia Nicole, Katya Michelle.; m. Mary Phelan, Dec. 2, 1983. B.A., State U. N.Y., Binghamton, 1960; M.A., U. Iowa, 1961; M.S. in L.S, Columbia U., 1966. Gen. reporter, reviewer Albany (N.Y.) Times Union, 1963-64; freelance writer, 1964-66; editor Librarians Office, Library of Congress, 1966-69; assoc. editor Wilson Library Bull., Bronx, N.Y., 1969-74; editor-in-chief Am. Libraries, Chgo., 1975-89; assoc. pub. ALA, 1989—; editl. dir. ALA Editions, 1993—; adj. instr. journalism Columbia Coll., Chgo., 1988-89; speaker in field. Author: The Elements of Editing: A Modern Guide for Editors and Journalists, 1982, Jacob Shallus, Calligrapher of the Constitution, 1987, Honk If You're a Writer, 1992, The Elements of Expression, 1996; also fiction, articles, video scripts, photography; exec. producer Libr. Video mag., 1986-91. Bd. dirs. Am. Book Awards, 1979-82; bd. advs. Univ. Press of Am., 1982—. Served with USAR, 1962-67. Fellow Iowa Writers Workshop Creative Writing, 1961; recipient award Ednl. Press Assn. Am., 1973 (3), 77, 82, 83; cert. of excellence Internat. Reading Assn., 1970, First Pl. award Verbatim essay competition, 1986, award Am. Soc. Bus. Press Editors, 1987. Mem. ALA. Home: 2120 W Pensacola Ave Chicago IL 60618-1718 Office: ALA 50 E Huron St Chicago IL 60611-2729 also: N E Pub Assocs Literary Agents PO Box 5 Chester CT 06412

PLOTT, CHARLES R., economics educator; b. Frederick, Okla., July 8, 1938; s. James Charles and Flossie Ann (Bowman) P.; m. Marianna Brown Cloninger, May 30, 1961; children: Rebecca Ann, Charles Hugh. BS, Okla. State U., 1961, MS, 1964; PhD, U. Va., 1965; LittD, Purdue U., 1995. Asst. prof. econs. Purdue U., 1965-68, assoc. prof., 1968-70; vis. prof. econs. Stanford U., 1968-69; Edward S. Harkness prof. econs. and polit. sci. Calif. Inst. Tech., Pasadena, 1970—, dir. Program for Study of Enterprise and Public Policy, 1979—, dir. Lab. for Exptl. Econs. and Polit. Sci., 1987—; vis. prof. law U. So. Calif. Law Center, 1976; vis. prof. U. Chgo., 1980; dir. Lee Pharms. Author works in fields of econs., polit. sci., philosophy, exptl. methods, math. methods; contbr. articles to profl. jours.; bd. editors: Social Sci. Research, 1976-77, Public Choice, 1973—, Jour. Econ. Behavior, 1983—. Named to Coll. Bus. Hall of Fame Okla. State U.; Ford Found. fellow, 1968, Guggenheim fellow, 1981, fellow Ctr. for Advanced Studies in Behavioral Scis., 1981; NSF grantee, 1972, 74, 78, 79, 80, 83, 86, 88, 92, 95. Fellow Am. Acad. Arts and Scis., Econometric Soc., Huntington Library and Art Gallery; mem. Am. Econ. Assn., Econ. Sci. Assn. (pres. 1987), So. Econ. Assn. (exec. com. 1978-79, v.p. 1985-87, pres. 1989-90), Pub. Choice Soc. (pres. 1977-78), Royal Econ. Assn., Am. Polit. Sci. Assn., Econs. Sci. Assn. (pres. 1987-88). Clubs: Cosmos, Mont Pelerin Soc. Home: 881 El Campo Dr Pasadena CA 91107-5565 Office: Calif Inst Tech Divsn Humanities & Social Scis Pasadena CA 91125

PLOTTEL, JEANINE PARISIER, foreign language educator; b. Paris, Sept. 21, 1934; came to U.S., 1943; m. Roland Plottel, 1956; children: Claudia S., Michael E., Philip B. Baccalauréat lettres, Lycée Français de N.Y., 1952; BA with honors, Barnard Coll., 1954; MA, Columbia U., 1955, PhD with distinction, 1959. Lectr. dept. French and Romance philology Columbia U., N.Y.C., 1955-59; rsch. assoc. fgn. lang. program MLA of Am., N.Y.C., 1959-60; lectr. dept. romance langs. CUNY, N.Y.C., 1960; asst. prof. div. humanities Julliard Sch. Music, N.Y.C., 1960-65; dir. lang. labs. Hunter Coll. CUNY, N.Y.C., 1965-69; asst. prof. dept. romance langs. Hunter Coll. CUNY, N.Y.C., 1965-69, assoc. prof. dept. romance langs., 1969-81, prof. dept. romance langs., 1981—, assoc. prof. French doctoral program grad. sch., univ. ctr., 1980-81, prof. French doctoral program grad. sch., univ. ctr., 1981—; extensive adminstrv. experience in CUNY including chairperson Dept. Romance Langs. Author: Les Dialogues de Paul Valéry, 1960; pub., editor N.Y. Literary Forum, 1978-88; contbr. articles to profl. jours., chpts. to books. Pres. Maurice I. Parisier Found., Inc. Named Chevalier des Palmes Acad., 1982; recipient NEH fellowship, 1979; grantee N.Y. Coun. for the Humanities, 1986, Helena Rubenstein Found., 1986, Florence J. Gould Found., 1986, N.Y. Times Found., 1986. Mem. Maison Française (bd. dirs. Columbia U.). Home: 50 E 77th St Apt 14a New York NY 10021-1836

PLOTZ, CHARLES MINDELL, physician; b. N.Y.C., Dec. 6, 1921; s. Isaac and Rose (Bluestone) P.; m. Lucille Weckstein, Aug. 5, 1945; children: Richard, Thomas, Robert. B.A., Columbia U., 1941, D.Sc., 1951; M.D., L.I. Coll. Medicine, 1944. Diplomate: Am. Bd. Internal Medicine. Intern New Haven Hosp., 1944-45; resident internal medicine Kings County Hosp., 1945-46, Maimonides Hosp., 1948-49; postdoctoral research fellow USPHS, Columbia Coll. Phys. and Surgs., 1949-50; practice medicine, specializing in internal medicine Bklyn., 1950—; chief Arthritis Clinic, attending physician Kings County Hosp. Center, 1950-85; chief L.I. Coll. Hosp. (Arthritis Clinic), 1950-65; asst. attending physician Mt. Sinai Hosp., 1955—; chief Mt. Sinai Hosp. (Arthritis Clinic), 1955-65, Arthritis Clinic, State U., Hosp., 1967-85; asst. physician Columbia-Presbyn. Med. Center, 1949-71; attending physician Bklyn. State Hosp.; dir. ambulatory care Bklyn. Hosp.Ctr., 1991-93; emeritus prof. medicine SUNY, 1991—; professorial lectr. Mt. Sinai Sch. Medicine, 1992—; emeritus prof. in medicine SUNY, 1991—; cons. physician Peninsula Gen. Hosp., Jamaica Hosp.; cons. on rheumatology VA Hosp., Bklyn., L.I. Coll. Hosp.; cons. family practice Luth. Med. Ctr.; vis. cons. internal medicine Jewish Gen. Hosp., Mont., Que., Can., 1965; cons. internal medicine Avicenna Hosp. and Wazir Akbar Hosp., Kabul, Afganistan, 1965; prof. medicine, dir. continuing edn., chmn. dept. family practice SUNY Downstate Med. Ctr., 1967-91, prof. emeritus medicine and family practice, 1991—; Fulbright lectr. U. Paris, 1984, 91; professorial lectr. Mt. Sinai Sch. Medicine, 1992—. Editorial adv. bd.: Pakistan Med. Forum; editor-in-chief: Clin. Rheumatology in Practice, 1981—; editor-in-chief: Advances in Rheumatology, 1986—. Mem. nat. bd. govs. Arthritis Found., 1964-82, bd. govs. N.Y. chpt., 1965—, v.p., 1971-83, trustee, 1977-82, N.Y. chpt. sr. v.p., 1977-82, vice chmn. bd. trustees, 1983-85, 87—, pres., 1985-87; trustee Leo N. Levi Meml. Nat. Arthritis Hosp., Alumni Fund-Alumni Assn. SUNY Downstate Med. Center, Bklyn. Inst. Arts and Scis., Bklyn. Bot. Garden; mem. adv. bd. MEDICO, corp. mem., 1977—; treas. Internat. League Against Rheumatism, 1981-89; trustee Internat. League Against Rheumatism Trust, 1981-89. Served to capt. AUS, 1946-48. WHO fellow U. Negev, 1974; master Am. Coll. Rheumatology, 1991—; recipient Gold medal Am. Coll. Rheumatology, 1992. Master Am. Coll. Rheumatology (Gold medal 1992), fellow ACP, Am. Acad. Family Physicians (charter), N.Y. Acad. Medicine (chmn. edn. com. 1976-78); mem. AMA, (N.Y. chpt.), AAUP, Internat. Soc. for Rheumatic Therapy (chmn. 1987-89), Am. Fedn. Clin. Rsch., Am. Rheumatism Assn. (past sec.-treas.), N.Y. Rheumatism Assn. (past pres., exec. com.), Harvey Soc., (N.Y. chpt.), Kings County med. socs., Bklyn. socs. internal medicine, Soc. Tchrs. Family Medicine, N.Y. State Acads. Family Physicians, Soc. Urban Physicians, Mystery Writers Am., Sigma Xi, Alpha Omega Alpha; hon. mem. Rheumatology Soc. France, Rheumatology Soc. Japan, Rheumatology Soc. Mex., Rheumatology Soc. Brazil, Rheumatology Soc. Yugoslavia, Rheumatology Soc. Norway, Rheumatology Soc. Egypt, Med. Soc. Czechoslovakia. Club: Heights Casino. Home: 184 Columbia Hts Brooklyn NY 11201-2186 also: 450 Clarkson Ave Brooklyn NY 11203-2012

PLOUFFE, JEAN-LOUIS, bishop. Address: Bishop's Residence, 480 McIntyre StW, PO Box 510, North Bay, ON Canada P1B 8J1

PLOUGH, CHARLES TOBIAS, JR., retired electronics engineering executive; b. Oakland, Calif., Sept. 7, 1926; s. Charles Tobias Sr. and Miriam Lucille (Miller) P.; m. Jean Elizabeth Rose, June 13, 1950 (div. May 1969); children: Charles III, Cathleen, Mark, Barbara; m. Janet Mary Ansell Lumley, July 5, 1969; children: Mark Ansell Lumley, Simon John Lumley. AB with honors, Amherst Coll., 1950; BSEE with honors, U. Calif., Berkeley, 1953. Mgr. tech. devel. Fairchild Semiconductor, Palo Alto, Calif., 1958-71; v.p. Multi-State Devices, Montreal, Can., 1971-78; mgr. research and devel. Dale Electronics, Norfolk, Nebr., 1978-89, ret., 1989. Patentee in field. Mem. Lions (sec. Norfolk 1982-86); Leader Albuquerque Interfaith 1993—. Avocation: golf. Home: 2030 Quail Run Dr NE Albuquerque NM 87122-1100

PLOURDE, GERARD, company executive; b. Joliette, Que., Can., Feb. 12, 1916; s. Louis-George and Rose de Lima (Jolicoeur) P.; m. Jeannine Martineau, Dec. 4, 1943; children: Monique, Pierre, Marc-André. BA, Brébeuf Coll., 1936; M in Commerce, U. Montreal, Que., 1939, D. Honoris Causa, 1971. Accountant UAP Inc., Montreal, from 1941; pres., gen. mgr. UAP Inc., 1951-70, chmn. bd., chief exec. officer, 1970-80, chmn. bd., 1980-86, hon. dir., 1986—; hon. dir. Molson Cos., Northern Telecom; vice-chmn. bd. Cambior, Inc. Decorated Order of Can. Mem. Soc. Automotive Engrs., Laval-sur-le-Lac Club, Saint Denis Club, Mt. Bruno Country Club. Office: 1010 Sherbrooke W #2012, Montreal, PQ Canada H3A 2R7

PLOWDEN, DAVID, photographer; b. Boston, Oct. 9, 1932; s. Roger and Mary Russell (Butler) P.; m. Pleasance Coggeshall, June 20, 1962 (div. 1976); children: John, Daniel; m. Sandra Oakes Schoellkopf, July 8th, 1977; children: Philip, Karen. BA Econs., Yale U., 1955; pvt. study with Minor White, Rochester, N.Y., 1959-60. Asst. O. Winston Link Studio, N.Y.C., 1958-59, George Meluso Studio, N.Y.C., 1960-62; photographer, writer, 1962—; assoc. prof. Inst. Design, Ill. Inst. Tech., Chgo., 1978-86; lectr. U. Iowa Sch. Journalism, 1985-88; vis. prof. Grand Valley State Univ., 1988-90, 91—; artist-in-residence U. Balt., 1990-91. Author and photographer: Farewell to Steam, 1968, Lincoln and His America, 1970 (Benjamin Barondess award 1971), The Hand of Man on America, 1971, 2d edit, 1974, The Floor of the Sky: the Great Plains, 1972, Bridges: the Spans of North America, 1974, 2d edit. 1984, Commonplace, 1974, Tugboat, 1976 (notable Children's books ALA 1976, Children's Book Showcase 1976), Steel, 1981, An American Chronology, 1982 (Notable Books ALA 1982, Booklist's Best of the 80s 1989), Industrial Landscape, 1985, A Time of Trains, 1987, A Sense of Place, 1988, End of an Era: The Last of the Great Lakes Steamboats, 1992, Small Town America, 1994; co-author, photographer, Nantucket, 1970, Cape May to Montauk, 1973, Desert and Plains, the Mountains and the River, 1975, The Iron Road, 1978 (notable children's books 1978, Honor list Horn Books 1979), Wayne County: the Aesthetic Heritage of a Rural Area, 1979; introduction The Gallery of World Photography/the Country, 1983; commd. illustrator Gems, 1967, The Freeway in the City, 1968, America the Vanishing, 1969, New Jersey, 1977, North Dakota, 1977, Vermont, 1979, New York, 1981, A Place of Sense, 1988; contbr. articles to numerous jours. including Time, Newsweek, Life, Audubon, Fortune; one-man shows include Columbia U., 1965, Smithsonian Instn., 1970, 71, 75, 76, 81, 89, Internat. Ctr. Photography, N.Y., 1976, Witkin Gallery, N.Y.C., 1979, Cin. Art Acad., 1979, The Gilbert Gallery, Chgo., 1980, 81, Chgo. Ctr. Contemporary Photography, 1982, Fed. Hall Mus., N.Y.C., 1982, Calif. Mus. Photography, Riverside, 1982-83, Chgo. Hist. Soc., 1985, Martin Gallery, Washington, 1987, Kunstmuseum, Luzern, Switzerland, 1987, Burchfield Ctr., Buffalo, 1987-88, Iowa State Mus., Des Moines, 1988-89, Catherine Edelman Gallery, Chgo., 1990, Grand Valley State U., 1993, Ewing Gallery, Washington, 1994; exhibited in group shows at Met. Mus. Art, N.Y.C., 1967, Kodak Gallery, N.Y.C., 1976, Currier Gallery Art, Manchester, N.H., 1978, Whitney Mus., 1979, Art Inst. Chgo., 1983-86, 87, Witkin Gallery, N.Y.C., 1988, Davenport (Iowa) Mus. Art, 1992; represented in permanent collections Art Inst. Chgo., Calif. Mus. Photography, Ctr. Creative Photography, Chgo. Hist. Soc., Libr. Congress, Smithsonian Instn., U. Md., J.B. Speed Mus., Iowa Humanities Bd., Iowa State Hist. Dept., Burchfield Art Ctr., Buffalo and Erie County Hist. Soc., Am. Soc. Media Photographers Archives Internat. Mus. Photography George Eastman House, Internat. Ctr. Photography, Ekstrom Libr. U. Louisville, Beinecke Rare Book and Mauscript Library, Yale U., 1995—. John Simon Guggenheim fellow, 1968; grantee N.Y. State Coun. Arts, 1966, 87, Smithsonian Inst., 1970-71, Dept. Transp. and Smithsonian Inst., 1975-76, H. E. Butt Found., 1977, United Bd. Homeland Ministries, 1976, Chgo. Hist. Soc., 1980-84, Seymour H. Knox Found., 1987, Baird Found., 1987, State Hist. Soc. Iowa, 1987-88, Iowa Humanities Bd., 1987-88; recipient Railroad History award, 1989. Mem. Am. Soc. Media Photographers. Home and Office: 609 Cherry St Winnetka IL 60093-2614

PLOWMAN, JACK WESLEY, lawyer; b. Blairsville, Pa., Sept. 12, 1929; s. Ralph Waldo, Sr., and Ethel Beatrice (Nicely) P.; m. Barbara Ellen Brown, Apr. 5, 1952; children—Linda Ellen, Judith Lynn. A.B., U. Pitts., 1951, LL.B. with honors, 1956. Bar: Pa. 1956, U.S. Dist. Ct. (we. dist.) Pa. 1956, U.S. Ct. Appeals 1960, U.S. Supreme Ct. 1978. Assoc. Campbell, Houck & Thomas, Pitts., 1956-57; ptnr. Rose, Houston, Cooper & Schmidt, Pitts., 1957-63, Plowman, Spiegel & Lewis, Pitts., 1963—; adj. prof. Duquesne U. Sch. Law, 1963-70, 83-96. Editor-in-chief Pitts. Legal Jour., 1971-81, U. Pitts. Law Rev., 1955-56. Trustee, sec. Allegheny County Bar Found.; bd. dirs. United Meth. Pub. House, 1984-96, Ward Home for Children, United Meth. Ch. Union, 1977-83, Wesley Inst., 1977-81, Neighborhood Legal Svcs. Assn., 1969-74; chancellor Western Pa. Ann. Conf., United Meth. Ch. Capt. USAF, 1951-53. Fellow Am. Bar Found. (life mem.), Am. Coll. Trial Lawyers; mem. ABA, Pa. Bar Assn., Allegheny County Bar Assn. (pres. 1982), Pa. Bar Inst. (bd. dirs. 1988-92), Supreme Ct. Pa. Hist. Soc. (trustee, pres.). Republican. Home: 1025 Lakemont Dr Pittsburgh PA 15243-1817 Office: Grant Bldg 2d floor Pittsburgh PA 15219-2200

PLOWRIGHT, JOAN ANNE, actress; b. Brigg, Lancashire, Eng., Oct. 28, 1929; d. William and Daisy (Burton) P.; m. Roger Gage, 1953 (div.); m. Sir Laurence Olivier, 1961 (dec.); 3 children. Student Old Vic Theatre Sch. Mem. Old Vic Co., toured South Africa, 1952-53; 1st leading role in The Country Wife, London, 1956; mem. English Stage Co., 1956, Nat. Theatre, 1963-74. Appearences include (plays) The Chairs, 1957, The Entertainer, 1958, Major Barbara and Roots, 1959, A Taste of Honey, 1960 (Tony Best Actress award 1960), Uncle Vanya, 1962-64, St. Joan, 1963 (London Evening Standard Best Actress award 1964), Hobson's Choice, 1964, The Master Builder, 1965, Much Ado About Nothing, 1967, Tartuffe, 1967, Three Sisters, 1967, 69, The Advertisement, 1968, 69, Love's Labour's Lost, 1968, 69, The Merchant of Venice, 1970, 71-72, Rules of the Game, 1971-72, Woman Killed with Kindness, 1971-72, Taming of the Shrew, 1972, Doctor's Dilemma, 1972, Rosmersholm, 1973, Saturday Sunday Monday 1973, Eden's End, 1974, The Sea Gull, 1975, The Bed Before Yesterday, 1975 (Variety award 1976), Filumena, 1977 (Soc. West End Theatres Best Actress award 1978), Enjoy, 1980, Who's Afraid of Virginia Woolf?, 1981, Cavell, 1982, The Cherry Orchard, 1983; The Way of the World, 1985, The House of Bernada Alba, 1986-87, Uncle Vanya, 1988, Time and The Conways, 1991, (films) Much Ado About Nothing, 1969, Equus, 1976, Richard Wagner, 1982, Brimstone and Treacle, 1982, Brittania Hospital, 1983, Revolution, 1985, The Dressmaker, 1987, Drowning By Numbers, 1987, The Divider, Conquest of the South Pole, 1989, I Love You To Death, 1990, Avalon, 1990, Enchanted April, 1991, Dennis the Menace, 1993, Last Action Hero, 1993, The Summer House, 1993, Widows' Peak, 1994, Pyromaniacs: A Love Story, 1995, The Grass Harp, 1995, Hotel Sorrento, 1995; (TV films) Merchant of Venice, 1973, Daphne, Laureola, 1977, Saturday Sunday Monday, 1977, The Importance of Being Earnest, 1988, The Birthday Party, 1987, House of Bernarda Alba, A Nightingale Sang, 1989, Stalin, 1992 (Emmy nomination, Supporting Actress - Miniseries, 1993), A Place for Annie, 1994, On Promised Land, 1994.*

PLUCIENNIK, THOMAS CASIMIR, lawyer, former assistant county prosecutor; b. Irvington, N.J., Apr. 8, 1947; s. Casimir Stanley and Helen Victoria (Sienicki) P.; m. Maria Anne Soriano, June 16, 1974. BS in Acctg., Seton Hall U., 1969, JD, 1983; MA in Criminal Justice, CUNY, 1976. Bar: N.J. 1983, U.S. Dist. Ct. N.J. 1983, D.C. 1994, U.S. Supreme Ct. 1995, N.Y. 1996; cert. criminal trial atty. Mng. ptnr. Joe Bell's Tavern & Restaurant, Newark, 1979; police officer City of Newark, 1972-79; criminal investigator Essex County Prosecutor, Newark, 1980-84, asst. prosecutor, 1984-88; sr. asst. prosecutor, Warren County, N.J., 1988-89; atty. Voorhees & Acciavatti, Esq., Morristown, N.J., 1989-94; defense atty. Picillo Caruso, 1994—. certified instr. N.J. State Police Tng. Commn., Trenton, 1984; mil. instr. N.J. Mil. Acad., Sea Girt, N.J., 1979-81. Committeeman South Orange Republican Club, N.J., 1978-83; treas., founder Tuxedo Park Neighborhood Assn., South Orange, 1977; fin. sec. J. T. Kosciusko Assn., Irvington, N.J., 1979. Served to 1st lt. U.S. Army, 1969-71, maj. JAGC, 1985-90. Recipient Class C Commendations, Newark Police Dept., 1973, 74, 75, Command Citations, 1973, 74, 75, 77, 78. Mem. Worrall F. Mountain Inn of Ct. (master), N.J. State Bar Assn., Morris County Bar Assn., Am. Legion. Republican. Roman Catholic. Clubs: Officers (Sea Girt, N.J.) (pres. 1979-81). Home: 11 Laurel Ln Morris Plains NJ 07950-3216 Office: Picillo Caruso 300 Executive Dr Ste 200 West Orange NJ 07052

PLUFF, STEARNS CHARLES, III, investment banker; b. Biloxi, Miss., Jan. 30, 1953; s. Stearns Charles Jr. and Patricia Elizabeth (Diaz) P.; m. Joan Marie Jay Jones, May 28, 1987; children: Micleah Frances, Ashleigh Nicole. BA, U. Miss., 1975. Supr. Host Internat., New Orleans, 1975-77; contractor Greg Edwards & Co., Falls Church, Va., 1977-80; registered rep. Donald Sheldon & Co., Houston, 1982-85; sr. v.p. GMS Group Inc., Houston, 1985—; dir., v.p. MMP Investments, Inc., Cary, Ill., 1989—; pres. R.P. Telekom U.S.A., Warsaw, 1993—. Vol. Petrosky Elem. Sch., Alief, Tex., 1991—, Girl Scouts U.S., Houston, 1991—. Mem. Chi Psi. Avocations: world travel, hiking, camping, gardening. Home: GMS Group Inc 15210 La Mancha Houston TX 77083 Office: 5075 Westheimer Rd Ste 1175 Houston TX 77056-5606

PLUIMER, EDWARD J., lawyer; b. Rapid City, S.D., 1949. BA cum laude, U. S.D., 1971; JD cum laude, NYU, 1974. Bar: Minn. 1975. Law clk. to Hon. Robert A. Ainsworth, Jr. U.S. Ct. Appeals (5th cir.), 1974-75; ptnr. Dorsey & Whitney, Mpls.; mem. Minn. Supreme Ct. ADR Task Force, 1988-92. Editor N.Y. U. Law Rev. Mem. Order of the Coif. Office: Dorsey & Whitney LLP 220 S 6th St Minneapolis MN 55402-4502

PLUM, CHARLES WALDEN, retired business executive and educator; b. Circleville, Ohio, Apr. 13, 1914; s. Horace Walden and Anna Frances (Eaton) P.; m. Margaret E. McCollister, Sept. 17, 1939; children: David Walden, Donald Alan (dec.). B.S., Ohio State U., 1936; M.B.A., Case Western Res. U., 1951; postgrad., Advanced Mgmt. Program, Harvard, 1954. CPA, N.Y., Tex. Sr. accountant Coopers and Lybrand, N.Y.C., 1936-42; supr. acctg. Amertorp Corp., Naval Ordnance Plant, St. Louis, 1942-45; various positions to v.p. acctg. and mgmt. systems Standard Oil Co. (Ohio), Cleve., 1945-78; prof. bus. adminstrn. Tex. A&M, College Station, 1978-89; dir., chmn. audit com. Hospitality Motor Inns, Inc., Cleve., 1976-79; sec.-treas., dir., mem. mgmt. com. Am. Assembly Collegiate Schs. Bus., 1977-78; lectr. acctg. Western Res. U., 1946-54; bus. exec. in residence, disting. lectr.

Tex. A. and M. U., 1976; Mem. bus. adv. council Kent State U., 1967-77. Mem. AICPA, Fin. Execs. Inst., Am. Petroleum Inst. (chmn. com. on cooperation with AICPA 1955-68), Tex. Soc. CPAs, Sigma Phi Epsilon, Beta Gamma Sigma, Beta Alpha Psi. Home: 5 Forest Dr College Station TX 77840-2321

PLUM, FRED, neurologist; b. Atlantic City, Jan. 10, 1924; s. Fred and Frances (Alexander) P.; children—Michael, Christopher, Carol; m. Susan Butler, Apr. 23, 1990. BA, Dartmouth Coll., 1944, postgrad., 1944-45; MD, Cornell U., 1947; MD (hon.), Karolinska Inst., Stockholm, 1982; DSc (hon.), L.I. U., 1990. Resident N.Y. Hosp., 1947-50, physician to outpatients, 1950-53, neurologist-in-chief, 1963—; instr. neurology Sch. Medicine Cornell U., 1950-53, Anne Parrish Titzell prof. neurology, 1963—, chmn. dept. neurology, 1963—; head neurology sect. U.S. Naval Hosp., St. Albans, N.Y., 1951-53; from asst. prof. to prof. neurology Sch. Medicine U. Wash., 1953-63; vis. scientist U. Lund, Sweden, 1970-71; vis. physician Rockefeller U. Hosp., 1975-85; assoc. neurosci. research program MIT and Rockefeller U., 1977-87; mem. neurology study sect. , 1964-68, grad. tng. com., 1959-63, 71, nat. adv. council, 1977-81, Nat. Inst. Neurol., Communicative Disorders and Stroke, 84-86; past pres. McKnight Endowment Fund for Neurosci., 1986-90. Author: Diagnosis of Stupor and Coma, 1966, 3d edit., 1980, Clinical Management of Seizures, 1976, 2d edit., 1983, (with others) Cecil Essentials of Medicine, 1986, 3d edit., 1995; editor, contbg. author: Cecil's Textbook of Medicine, 1968, 2d edit., 1996; chief editor neurology sect. Contemporary Neurology series; editor: Recent Trends in Neurology, 1969, 2d edit., 1989, Brain Dysfunction in Metabolic Disorders, 1974; mem. editorial bd. Archives Neurology, 1958-68; chief editor, 1972-76; founding editor Annals of Neurology, 1977—; contbr. articles to scientific and profl. jours. Mem. Inst. of Medicine, Nat. Acad. Sci., Am. Neurol. Assn. (v.p. 1974-75, pres. 1976-77, Jacoby award 1984), Am. Acad. Neurology (past mem. council), Soc. Neurosci., Am. Soc. Clin. Investigation, Assn. Rsch. Nervous Mental Diseases (pres. 1973, 87), Assn. Am. Physicians, Alpha Omega Alpha; hon. mem. Can., Brit., French, Italian, Swiss neurol. socs. Rsch. in consciousness, coma and stroke. Office: Cornell U Medical Coll 1300 York Ave New York NY 10021-4805

PLUMB, PAMELA PELTON, consulting company executive, former mayor and councilwoman; b. St. Louis, Oct. 26, 1943; d. Frank E. and Dorothey-Lee (Culver) Pelton; m. Peter Scott Plumb, June 11, 1966; children: Jessica Culver, David Scott. BA, Smith Coll., 1965; MA, NYU, 1967. Tchr., Master's Sch., Dobbs Ferry, N.Y., 1967-69; exec. dir. Greater Portland (Maine) Landmarks, 1969-71; engaged in civic and vol. work, 1971-79; mem. Portland City Council, 1979-90, mayor, 1981-82; prin. Pamela Plumb & Assocs., 1990—; vice chmn. Peoples Heritage Fin. Group. Bd. dirs. Tom's of Maine; pres. Nat. League Cities, 1987-88. Recipient Doric Dames's Bullfinch award for preservation, 1979, Greater Portland Landmark's Preservation award, 1980, Deborah Morton award Westbrook Coll., Portland, 1982, Neal W. Allen award Greater Portland C. of C., 1982, Disting. Svc. award Kiwanis Club of Portland, 1990; named Portland and Maine Outstanding Young Woman, Jaycees, 1979. Democrat.

PLUMEZ, JEAN PAUL, advertising agency executive, consultant; b. N.Y.C., Oct. 31, 1939; s. Jean Paul and Marie Antoinette (Compagne) P.; m. Jacqueline Hornor, Feb. 20, 1965; children: Jean Paul, Nicole. B.S. in Chem. Enging., Bucknell U., 1962, B.A. in Chemistry, 1962; M.B.A., U. Pa., 1968. Product engr. Mobil Oil Co., Paulsboro, N.J., 1965-66; account mgr. Dancer Fitzgerald, Sample, Inc., N.Y.C., 1968-86, exec. v.p., 1979-86; pres. Leadership on Paper, Larchmont, N.Y., 1986—; founding ptnr. The Right Direction, 1987—. Served to capt. Signal Corps U.S. Army, 1962-64. Mem. Alpha Chi Sigma, Beta Gamma Sigma, Kappa Delta Rho. Clubs: Larchmont Yacht, Wharton of N.Y., Princeton of N.Y. Home and Office: 90 Beechtree Dr Larchmont NY 10538-1202

PLUMMER, AMANDA, actress; b. N.Y.C., Mar. 23, 1957; d. Christopher and Tammy (Grimes) Plummer. Student, Middlebury Coll. Has appeared in theatre roles: A Taste of Honey, 1981; A Month in the Country, 1980; N.Y.C. debut: Artichoke, 1979; The Glass Menagarie, 1983-84; motion picture debut: Cattle Annie and Little Britches, 1981, The World According to Garp, 1982, Daniel, 1983, Hotel New Hampshire, 1984, The Fisher King, 1991, Freejack, 1991, Pulp Fiction, 1994, Search and Destroy, 1995; other theatre roles include: Agnes of God (Tony, Drama Desk award, Outer Circle Critics award), 1982; A Lie of the Mind, 1985; TV appearances include Hallmark Hall of Fame: Miss Rose White (Emmy award supporting actress, 1992). Office: The Gersh Agency 232 N Canon Dr Beverly Hills CA 90210*

PLUMMER, (ARTHUR) CHRISTOPHER (ORME), actor; b. Toronto, Ont., Can., Dec. 13, 1929; s. John and Isabella Mary (Abbott) P.; m. Tammy Grimes (div.); 1 child, Amanda; m. Particia Audrew Lewis, May 4, 1962 (div.); m. Elaine Taylor. Ed. pub. and pvt. schs., Can.; pupil, Iris Warren, C. Herbertcasari. Stage debut in The Rivals with Can. Repertory Theatre, 1950; Broadway debut in Starcross Story, 1954; London debut in Becket, 1961; leading actor Am. Shakespeare Theatre, Stratford, Conn., 1955, Royal Shakespeare Co., London and Stratford, Avon, Eng., 1961-62, Stratford (Ont.) Shakespeare Festival, 1956, 57, 58, 60, 62, 67, Nat. Theatre Co., London; radio roles include Shakespeare, Canada; plays include Home is the Hero, 1954, Twelfth Night, 1954, 70-71, Dark is Light Enough, The Lark, Julius Caesar, The Tempest, 1955, Henry VI, 1956, Hamlet, 1957, Winter's Tale, 1958, Much Ado About Nothing, 1958, J.B., 1958, King John, 1960, Romeo and Juliet, 1960, Richard III, 1961, Arturo Ui, 1963, The Royal Hunt of the Sun, 1965, Antony and Cleopatra, 1967, Danton's Death, 1971, Amphitryon 38, 1971; (musicals) Cyrano, 1973, The Good Doctor, 1973, Love and Master Will, 1975; Othello, 1982, Macbeth, 1988, No Man's Land, 1993; made TV debut 1953; TV prodns. include Little Moon of Alban, Johnny Belinda, 1958, Cyrano de Bergerac, 1962, Oedipus Rex, After the Fall, 1974, The Doll's House, The Prince and the Pauper, Prisoner of Zenda, Hamlet at Elsinore, BBC, 1964, Time Remembered, Capt. Brassbound's Conversion, The Shadow Box, 1981, The Thorn Birds, 1983, Little Gloria-Happy at Last, A Hazard of Hearts, 1987, Crossings, 1986, Danielle Steele's Secrets, 1992, Liar's Edge, 1992; star TV series The Moneychangers, 1977; made film debut in 1957; films include Stage Struck, 1957, Wind Across the Everglades, 1958, The Fall of the Roman Empire, 1963, Inside Daisy Clover, 1965, Sound of Music, 1965, Triple Cross, 1967, Nobody Runs Forever, 1969, The Battle of Britain, 1969, The Royal Hunt of the Sun, 1969, Lock up your Daughters, 1969, The Phyx, 1970, Waterloo, 1971, The Man Who Would Be King, 1975, The Return of the Pink Panther, 1975, Conduct Unbecoming, 1975, International Velvet, 1978, Murder By Decree, 1979, Starcrash, 1979, The Silent Partner, 1979, Hanover Street, 1979, Somewhere in Time, 1980, Eye witness, 1981, The Disappearance, 1981, The Amateur, 1982, Dreamscape, 1984, Ordeal by Innocence, 1984, Lily in Love, 1985, The Boss' Wife, 1986, The Boy In Blue, 1986, An American Tail, 1986 (voice), Souvenir, 1987, Dragnet, 1987, Light Years (voice), 1988, Where the Heart Is, 1989, Fire Head, 1991, Star Trek: VI: The Undiscovered Country, 1991, Rock a Doodle, 1992 (voice), Malcolm X, 1992, Wolf, 1994, Dolores Claiborne, 1994. Decorated companion Order of Can., 1968; recipient Theatre World award, 1955, Evening Standard award, 1961, Delia Austrian medal, 1973, 2 Drama Desk awards, 1973, 82, Antoinette Perry award, 1974, Emmy award Nat. Acad. TV Arts and Scis., 1977, Genie award, Can., 1980, Golden Badge of Honor, Austria, 1982, Maple Leaf award Nat. Acad. Arts and Letters. Mem. Theatre's Hall of Fame. Office: ICM care Lou Pitt 8942 Wilshire Blvd Beverly Hills CA 90211*

PLUMMER, DANIEL CLARENCE, III, insurance consultant; b. Chgo., Apr. 30, 1927; s. Daniel C. and Ida May (Hayden) P.; m. Margaret Louise Marshall, Apr. 30, 1955; children: Daniel C., Judith Ann, David Marshall. B.S., Northwestern U., 1950. C.P.A., Ill. Sales rep. Sunbeam Corp., Chgo. and Phila., 1950-51; sr. acct. Touche Ross & Co., Chgo., 1952-56; adminstrv. mgr. Consol. Foundries & Mfg. Corp., Rockford, Ill., 1956-59; dir. internal audit Continental Casualty Co., Chgo., 1959-63; sec.-treas. Moline Malleable Iron Co., St. Charles, Ill., 1963-64; v.p. Allstate Ins. Cos., Northbrook, Ill., 1964-90, ret.; cons. re fin. regulation and mgmt. of insurers Lake Forest, Ill., 1990—; mem. acctg. com. Nat. Assn. Ind. Insurers, 1966-89, chmn., 1984-85; mem. acctg. prins. adv. com. Nat. Assn. Ins. Commrs., 1983-85, emerging acctg. issues com., 1985-93, chmn. data sys. adv. com., 1986-90. Co-author: Property-Liability Insurance Accounting, 1991. Bd. dirs. Chgo. coun. Boy Scouts Am., 1979-87, mem. fin. com., 1979-87, chmn. audit com., 1983-87, mem. exec. com., 1979-81, asst. treas., 1979-81, chmn. ins. com. 1986, adv. bd., 1987-90. With USN, 1945-46. Mem. Ill. Soc. CPAs (chmn. ins. industry com. 1976-77), Torch Lake Yacht Club Mich. Avocations: tennis; sailing; fishing.

PLUMMER, DIRK ARNOLD, electrical engineer; b. Stamford, Conn., Apr. 18, 1930; s. Charles Arnold Plummer and Edwina Woodling Johnson; m. Janis Susan Lowery Stuart, Feb. 18, 1967 (div. 1973); 1 child, Julie. B-SChEngr, MIT, 1952; BSEE, U. Calif., Berkeley, 1961; MSEE, Monmouth Coll., 1985. Cert. nondestructive test examiner of inspectors for radiography, magnetic particle, liquid penetrant and ultrasonic testing methods; cert. comml. pilot. Chem. engr. Foster Wheeler Corp., N.Y.C., 1952; engr. The M.W. Kellogg Co., N.Y.C., 1954; project engr. Am. Machine & Fdry. Co., Greenwich, Conn., 1955-56; devel. engr. Aerojet-Gen. Corp., Azusa, Sacramento, San Ramon, Calif., 1956-61; sr. mem. tech. staff Aerospace Comm. & Controls Divsn. RCA, Burlington, Mass., 1961-62; engr. Elec. Boat Div. Gen. Dynamics Corp., Groton, Conn., 1963; electronics engr. U.S. Civil Svc., various locations, 1963-88; pvt. practice profl. engring. Sea Bright, N.J., 1988—. Contbr. articles to profl. jours. Archtl. control officer Sea Bright Village Assn., 1991. 1st lt. U.S. Army, 1952-54. Recipient Meritorious Svc. medal Pres. of U.S., 1982, Cert. for Commendable Svc. Def. Supply Agy., 1972. Mem. AAAS, ASCE, NSPE, Soc. Logistics Engrs., Am. Cons. Engrs. Coun., AICE (profl. devel. officer 1990), IEEE (chmn. nuclear and plasma sci. chpt. 1990), Am. Cons. Engrs. Coun., Am. Phys. Soc., Am. Math. Soc., Math. Assn. Am. Home and Office: 45 Village Rd Sea Bright NJ 07760-2233

PLUMMER, EDWARD BRUCE, college librarian; b. Toledo, Feb. 27, 1938; s. Paul Abel and Mabel Bernardine (Wert) P.; m. Mary Louise Girsch, Sept. 9, 1967; children: Andrew Brooks, Jonathan Tad. BA, Ohio Wesleyan U., 1960; MLS, Kent State U., 1967. Tchr., adult tutor Cin. Pub. Schs., 1960-65; dir. br. libr. Kent (Ohio) State U., 1967-70; assoc. dir. Worcester (Mass.) State Coll., 1971-80, dir., libr., 1980—; bd. dirs. Citizens for Edn. Resources, Worcester, 1994; pres. Cen./Western Mass. Automated Resource Sharing, Paxton, Mass., 1991-92; treas. Mass. Coun. Chief Librs. of Pub. Higher Edn. Instn., Amherst, Mass., 1991-93. Author: (book of poetry) Innovations, 1993. Bd. dirs. Talking Books, Worcester, 1991-94, Unitarian Universalist Ch., Worcester, 1991-94; mem. Libr. Pub. Sch. Power Group, Worcester, 1994—; bd. dirs., tutor Literacy Vols. of Am., Worcester, 1989—, del. to nat. conf., 1991; pres. Friends of the Worcester Pub. Libr. Club, 1989-91. Mem. Mass. Libr. Assn., Life Info. for Edn., Ferry Beach Park Assn. (bd. dirs. 1993-96), New England Libr. Assn., Assoc. of Coll. and Rsch. Libr., New Eng. (city commr. 1995—), Worcester Cult. Commn. Avocations: photography, gardening, painting. Home: 66 Navasota Ave Worcester MA 01602-1119 Office: Worcester State Coll Learning Resources Ctr 486 Chandler St Worcester MA 01602-2832

PLUMMER, MARCIE STERN, real estate broker; b. Plymouth, Mass., Oct. 28, 1950; d. Jacob and Rosalie (Adelman) Stern; m. John Dillon McHugh II, Oct. 8, 1974 (div.); 1 child, Joshua Stern; m. Louis Freeman Plummer Jr., Sept. 25, 1982; children: Jessica Price, Denelle Boothe. BA, Am. Internat. Coll., 1972, MAT in English, 1973, postgrad., 1974; postgrad., U. Conn., 1974; lic. real estate broker, Anthony Sch. Real Estate, Walnut Creek, Calif., 1985. Educator, chair dept. Windsor Locks (Conn.) Sch. Dist., 1972-74; educator, placement dir. Heald Bus. Coll., San Francisco, 1974-77; educator evening and day divs. Diablo Valley Coll., Pleasant Hill, Calif., 1975-77; real estate agt. Morrison Homes, Pleasant Hill, Calif., 1977-78; real estate agt., tract mgr. Dividend Devel., Santa Clara, Calif., 1978-81; real estate agt. Valley Realty, 1981-84; broker, owner Better Homes Realty, 1984-89; real estate broker, owner The Presád Co. Inc. subs. Better Homes Realty, Danville, Calif., 1984-90; owner The Mktg. Group, 1989—; v.p., treas. Realty Resource Group, 1996. Better Homes Realty rep. for orgn. of Danville 4th of July Parade, City of Danville, 1984-88; publicist San Ramon Valley Little League, Alamo, Calif., 1986—; active Battered Women's Found., Contra Costa County, Calif., 1986—, Yosemite Fund, 1992—, Safe Home Teen Program, 1991—; active rep. voter registration, Walnut Creek, Calif., 1987—; mem. Civic Arts Coun., Walnut Creek, 1988—; drama coach, dir. Advanced Drama Ensemble, 1993-94. Recipient numerous nat., state and regional awards in field, $400 million closed vol. in real estate sales achievement award, 1991. Mem. AAUW, Bldg. Industry Assn. (Sales vol. award 1978-89), Sales & Mktg. Coun. (sponsor MAME awards banquet 1978-89, Gold sponsor 1986-88), Calif. Assn. Realtors, Contra Costa Bd. Realtors. Jewish. Avocations: playing piano, horseback riding, writing poetry and prose. Home: 123 Erselia Trl Alamo CA 94507-1311 Office: Better Homes Realty PO Box 939 Danville CA 94526-0939

PLUMMER, ORA BEATRICE, nursing educator, trainer; b. Mexia, Tex., May 25, 1940; d. Macie Idella (Echols); B.S. in Nursing, U. N.Mex., 1961; M.S. in Nursing Edn., UCLA, 1966; children—Kimberly, Kevin, Cheryl. Nurses aide Bataan Meml. Meth. Hosp., Albuquerque, 1958-60, staff nurse, 1961-62, 67-68; staff nurse, charge nurse, relief supr. Hollywood (Calif.) Community Hosp., 1962-64; instr. U. N.Mex. Coll. of Nursing, Albuquerque, 1968-69; sr. instr. U. Colo. Sch. Nursing, Denver, 1971-74; asst. prof. U. Colo. Sch. Nursing, Denver, 1974-76; staff assoc. III Western Interstate Commn. for Higher Edn., Boulder, Colo., 1976-78; dir. nursing Garden Manor Nursing Home, Lakewood, Colo., 1978-79; ednl. coordination Colo. Dept. Health, Denver, 1987—. Active Colo. Cluster of Schs.-faculty devel.; mem. adv. bd. Affiliated Children's and Family Services, 1977; mem. state instl. child abuse and neglect adv. com., 1984—; mem. bd. trustee Colo. Acad., 1990—; mem. planning com. State Wide Conf. on Black Health Concerns, 1977; mem. staff devel. com. Western Interstate Commn. for Higher Edn., 1978, minority affairs com., 1978, coordinating com. for baccalaureate program, 1971-76; active minority affairs U. Colo. Med. Center, 1971-72; mem. ednl. resources com. public relations com., rev. com. for reappointment, promotion, and tenure U. Colo. Sch. Nursing, 1971-76; regulatory tng. com., 1989—, gerontol. adv. com., Met. State Coll., 1989-93; expert panel mem. Long Term Care Training Manual, HCFA, Balt., 1989; mem. EDAC com. Colo. Dept. of Health, 1989-96. Mem. NAFE, Am. Soc. Tng. and Devel., Am. Nurses Assn., Colo. Nurses Assn. (affirmative action comm. 1977, 78, 79, 93-96), Phi Delta Kappa. Avocation: pub. speaking, training. Contbr. articles in field to profl. jours. Office: 4300 Cherry Creek South Dr Denver CO 80222-1523

PLUMMER, RISQUE WILSON, lawyer; b. Mobile, Ala., Oct. 13, 1910; s. Frederick Harvey and Caroline (Wilson) P.; m. Constance M. Burch, Feb. 21, 1939; children: Risque Wilson Jr., Richard Randolph. J.D., U. Va., 1933. Bar: Va. 1932, Md. 1938. Atty. in charge of litigation HOLC, 1933-38; pvt. practice law, 1938—; counsel U.S. Maritime Commn., 1942; partner firm Griffin & Plummer, 1951-73; counsel O'Connor, Preston, Glenn & Smith, Balt., 1979—; prof. law Am. Inst. Banking, 1948-52. Contbr. articles to profl. jours. Exec. sec. Md. Commn. on Anti-Subversive Activities, 1949-50; co-founder, pres. Roland Park Baseball Leagues, Inc., 1956-57; co-founder, pres. Wyndhurst Improvement Assn., Inc., 1957-59; mem. Selective Service Adv. Bd., 1940-42. Served to lt. USNR, 1943-46, ATO, PTO. Fellow Internat. Acad. Law and Sci.; mem. Am. Judicature Soc., ABA (council sect. of family law 1966-70), Md. Bar Assn. (council sect. of family and juvenile law 1968-70), Md. Assn. Trial Lawyers (gov. 1966-67), Bar Assn. Baltimore City (com. on grievances 1966-69, chmn. com. on profl. ethics 1969-70, exec. com. 1969-70), Am. Contract Bridge League (Bronze life master, cert. dir., author The Small Club), Soc. Colonial Wars, Delta Tau Delta (pres. U. Va. chpt.), Phi Delta Phi. Episcopalian. Home: Highfield House Unit 512 4000 N Charles St Baltimore MD 21218 Office: Law Bldg 425 St Paul Pl Baltimore MD 21202-2107

PLUMMER, STEVEN TSOSIE, bishop; b. Coalmine, N. Mex., Aug. 14, 1944; m. Catherine B. Tso; children: Brian Tso, Byron Tso, Steven, Jr., Cathlena. Student, San Juan Community Coll., Farmington, N. Mex., Phoenix (Ariz.) Jr. Coll., Ch. Divinity Sch. of the Pacific, San Francisco. Ordained deacon, The Episc. Ch., 1975, priest, 1976. Deacon, priest Good Shepherd Mission, Fort Defiance, Ariz., 1976-77; vicar St. John the Baptizer, Montezuma Creek, Utah, 1977-83; regional vicar for Utah Bluff, Utah, from 1983; consecrated bishop Episc. Ch. in Navajoland, Farmington, N. Mex., 1990; mem. Episc. Council of Indian Ministries. Office: The Episcopal Ch Navajoland Area Mission PO Box 720 Farmington NM 87499-0720*

PLUMSTEAD, WILLIAM CHARLES, quality engineer, consultant; b. Two Rivers, Wis., Nov. 2, 1938; m. Peggy Bass, July 19, 1959 (div. July 1968); children: William Jr., Jennifer; m. Vicki Newton, June 27, 1981. Student, U. Fla., 1956-58, Temple U., 1966-72, Albright Coll., 1973-75; BSBA, Calif. Coast U., 1985, MBA, 1989. Registered profl. engr., Calif. V.p. U.S. Testing Co., Inc., Hoboken, N.J., 1963-76; div. mgr. Daniel Internat., Inc., Greenville, S.C., 1976-83; group mgr. Bechtel Group, Inc., San Francisco, 1983-89; prin. engr. Fluor Daniel, Inc., Greenville, 1989-94; pres. Plumstead Quality and Tech. Svcs., Greenville, S.C., 1994—. Author: (with others) Code/Specification Syndrome, 1976, NDT Laboratories Update, 1991, NDT in Construction, 1991, NDT-A Partner in Excellence, 1994; contbr. articles to profl. jours. Bd. dirs. Piedmont Food Bank, 1994-97. Fellow Am. Soc. Nondestructive Testing (coun. chmn. 1985-88, nat. sec., treas. 1992-93, nat. v.p. 1993-94, pres. 1994-95, chmn. bd. dirs. 1995-96); mem. ASTM (sec. 1989-93, vice chmn. 1994-96, chmn. 1996—), Toastmasters Internat. (pres. local chpt. 1990-91, Competent Toastmaster award 1986, Able Toastmaster award 1993). Avocations: sports, wine tasting. Home and Office: Plumstead Quality Tech Svcs 806 Botany Rd Greenville SC 29615-1608

PLUNK, ROBERT MALCOME, insurance company executive; b. Bethel Springs, Tenn., Oct. 12, 1932; s. William E. and Pearl (Wilkes) P.; m. Carolyn Elizabeth Garland; children: Kathy, Sharon. BA, MA, Memphis State U., 1962; JD, Western State U., Fullerton, Calif., 1973. Agt. Preferred Risk Ins. Co., Tenn., 1962-63; career agy. mgr. Tenn., 1963-65; sales mgr. Atlanta, 1965-68; asst. regional mgr. Calif., 1968-71, regional mgr., 1971-73; mgr. preferred abstrs. West Des Moines, 1973-78, dir. corp. responsibilities, 1978-82, v.p., 1982-85, exec. v.p., 1985-87, pres., chief exec. officer, 1987—, also bd. dirs.; bd. dirs. Midwest Mut. Ins. Co., West Des Moines, Preferred Risk Life, West Des Moines. Founding dir. Mothers Against Drunk Driving, Dallas. Mem. ABA, Calif. Bar Assn. Office: Preferred Risk Ins Co 1111 Ashworth Rd West Des Moines IA 50265-3544*

PLUNKERT, DONNA MAE, business owner; b. Pa., Apr. 26, 1951; d. Norman Francis and Rada Mae (Snyder) Dickensheets; m. Bruce Herbert Plunkert, Nov. 2, 1975; 1 child, Gabriel Bruce. Grad., Littlestown (Pa.) H.S., 1969. Sales clk. Colonial Fair, Hanover, Pa., 1970-72, sec., 1972-75; full-time sec. Norm's Auction, Hanover, 1975-79, part-time sec., 1979-84; owner Old Buttermould Patterns Products, Littlestown, 1989—. Reproduced antique buttermolds for gift shops Carroll County Farm Mus., Westminster, Md., Historic Michie Tavern, Charlottesville, Va. Mem. U.S. C. of C., Mus. Store Assn. (assoc.). Mem. Brethren Ch. Avocations: collecting antique buttermoulds presses, country music, playing pool. Home: 315 N Queen St Littlestown PA 17340-1221

PLUNKET, DANIEL CLARK, pediatrician; b. Birmingham, Ala., May 7, 1929; s. Henry Clark and Carolyn Clark (Langford) P.; m. Lillian C. Barrington, Dec. 31, 1971; children: Dennis, Beth, Ann, Brenda, Scott. B.S., Emory U., 1949, M.D., 1952. Diplomate Am. Bd. Pediatrics. Intern Med. Coll. Va. Hosp., Richmond, 1952-53; resident in pediatrics Med. Coll. Va. Hosp., 1953-54, Tripler Army Med. Center, Honolulu, 1958-59, Walter Reed Army Inst., 1962-64; pediatrician, pediatric hematologist/oncologist acad. medicine, chief pediatric service William Beaumont Gen. Hosp., El Paso, Tex., 1959-62; commd. 1st lt. U.S. Army, 1955, advanced through grades to col., 1967; asst. chief dept. pediatrics Letterman Army Med. Center, San Francisco, 1964-65; chmn. dept. pediatrics Fitzsimons Army Med. Center, Denver, 1965-75; prof., chmn. dept. pediatrics U. Okla. Coll. Medicine, Tulsa, 1975—; sr. assoc. dean for clin. affairs U. Okla. Health Scis. Ctr., Tulsa, 1993—; clin. prof. pediatrics U. Colo., Denver, 1974-75. Mem. adv. chmn. March of Dimes, Tulsa chpt., 1975-92; bd. dirs. ARC, Tulsa chpt., 1981—. Decorated Legion of Merit; Walter Reed Inst. Research fellow hematology and research, 1962-64. Mem. Am. Acad. Pediatrics, Am. Pediatric Soc., Am. Soc. Hematology, AMA, So. Soc. Pediatric Rsch. Episcopalian. Home: 2436 E 33rd St Tulsa OK 74105-2316 Office: 2815 S Sheridan Rd Tulsa OK 74129-1013

PLUNKETT, MARYANN, actress; b. Lowell, Mass., 1953; m. Jay O. Sanders; 1 child, James Plunkett. Student, U. N.H. Co-founder Portland (Maine) Stage Co. Broadway debut in Agnes of God, 1983; other Broadway appearances include Sunday in the Park with George, Me and My Girl (Tony award for best actress in a mus. 1987), (off Broadway) Aristocrats, (stage) The Crucible (Belasco Theatre, N.Y.), 1991, Little Hotel on the Side (Belasco Theatre, N.Y.) 1992, The Seagull, 1992, St. Joan, 1993 (nominated Best Actress Drama Desk). *

PLUNKETT, PAUL EDWARD, federal judge; b. Boston, July 9, 1935; s. Paul M. and Mary Cecilia (Erbacher) P.; m. Martha Milan, Sept. 30, 1958; children: Paul Scott, Steven, Andrew, Kevin. BA, Harvard U., 1957, LLB, 1960. Asst. atty. U.S. Atty.'s Office, Chgo., 1963-66; ptnr. Plunkett Nisin et al, Chgo., 1966-78, Mayer Brown & Platt, Chgo., 1960-63, 78-83; judge U.S. Dist. Ct. (no. dist.) Ill., Chgo., 1983—; adj. faculty John Marshall Law Sch., Chgo., 1964-76, 82—, Loyola U. Law Sch., Chgo., 1977-82. Mem. Fed. Bar Assn. Clubs: Legal, Law, Union League (Chgo.). Office: US Dist Ct 219 S Dearborn St Chicago IL 60604-1702*

PLUSK, RONALD FRANK, manufacturing company executive; b. Chgo., Mar. 30, 1933; s. Frank and Ann (Petrauskas) P.; m. Rose Marie Pawlikowski, May 25, 1957; children—Frank A., Ronald S., Cynthia Marie. B.S.C., Loyola U., Chgo., 1954; postgrad., Northwestern U., 1957-59. Mgmt. cons. Peat, Marwick, Mitchell & Co., Chgo., 1963-66; corp. controller Varo, Inc., Garland, Tex., 1966-69; dir. planning and mgmt. systems Rucker Co., Oakland, Calif., 1969-72; dir. ops., audit and systems Rucker Co., 1972-76, v.p. ops., audit and systems, 1976-77; v.p. fin. adminstrn. Rucker Co. (merged with NL Petroleum Svcs. Co.), Houston, 1977-79; v.p. fin., treas. Cobe Labs., Inc., Lakewood, Colo., 1979-92. Contbr. articles to profl. jours. Served to 1st lt. AUS, 1954-56, ETO. Mem. Am. Mgmt. Assn., Planning Execs. Inst., Fin. Execs. Inst. Roman Catholic. Home: 6151 Middlefield Rd Littleton CO 80123-6620

PLUSS, JACQUES ANTHONY, historian, educator; b. Zurich, May 29, 1953; came to U.S., 1954; s. Jacques Miro and Nina Elizabeth (Bucalo) P.; divorced; 1 child, Rebecca Anne. BA with honors, Lafayette Coll., Easton, Pa., 1975; MA, U. Chgo., 1978, PhD, 1983; postgrad., U. Cambridge, Eng., 1980. Instr. history U. Chgo., 1982-84; assoc. prof. history William Paterson Coll., Wayne, N.J., 1984—; lay minister. Contbr. articles to The Historian, Thought, Am. Jour. Legal History. Dir. edn. Christ Episcopal Ch., Ridgewood, N.J., 1990-94, vestryman, 1992-96. NEH summer seminar fellow, 1987, 90. Mem. Medieval Acad. Am., Nat. Assn. Scholars. Avocations: volunteering, archaeology, equitation. Home: 9 Brighton Pl Fair Lawn NJ 07410 Office: William Paterson Coll 300 Pompton Rd Wayne NJ 07470-2103

PLYLER, JOHN LANEY, JR., healthcare management professional; b. Greenville, S.C., Jan. 31, 1934; s. John Laney and Beatrice Elizabeth (Dennis) P.; m. Caroline Raysor Williams, June 26, 1959; children: Sharon, John III, James (dec.). Student, U.S. Naval Acad., 1953-54; BA, Furman U., 1956; MHA, Duke U., 1970. Prodn. planner J. P. Stevens & Co., Greenville, 1958-65; mgmt. engr., outpatient mgr. Greenville Hosp. Sys., 1967-68; assoc. dir. Cleveland Meml. Hosp., Shelby, N.C., 1970-79; exec. v.p., COO Bapt. Med. Ctr., Oklahoma City, 1979-85; group v.p. SunHealth Alliance, Charlotte, N.C., 1985-86, sr. v.p., 1986-96. 2d lt. U.S. Army, 1957, capt. USAR, 1957-65. Fellow Am. Coll. Healthcare Execs. (mem. ethics com. 1990-93, chair 1992-93), Okla. Hosp. Assn. (mem. coun. on edn.), N.C. Hosp. Assn. (coun. on pers.). Avocations: travel, sailing, photography. Home: PO Box 909 Davidson NC 28036

POCH, STEPHEN, metallurgical engineer, consultant; b. Homestead, Pa., June 17, 1909; s. George and Mary (Banyas) P.; m. Elizabeth Alberta Mrasko, Feb. 1, 1941 (dec. Sept. 1994); 1 child, Pamela Elizabeth. Student, Geneva Coll., Beaver Falls, Pa., 1930-31; BS in Metall. Enging., U. Pitts., 1939, postgrad., 1942-44, 46-47. Registered profl. engr., N.J., Pa., Conn. Metall. observer Carnegie-Ill. Steel Corp., Homestead, 1936-39; devel. engr. Irvin (Pa.) Works, U.S. Steel Corp., 1940-41; commentator N.Y. World's Fair, U.S. Steel, Homestead, 1941; chief metall. observer Farrell (Pa.) Works, U.S. Steel, 1942; rsch. engr. Acid Open Hearth Rsch., U. Pitts., 1942-44, 46-47; supt. metall. processes Driver Harris Co., Harrison, N.J., 1947-58; v.p., dir. R&D Molecu Wire Corp., Farmingdale, N.J., 1958-69; asst. prof. N.Y.C. Tech. Coll., Bklyn., 1969-74; metall. cons. in pvt. practice, 1974—; fine wire cons. C.O. Jelliff Co., Southport, Conn., 1970-72; cons. Kanthal Corp., Bethel, Conn., 1972-75, Marcal Paper Mills, Inc., Elmwood Park, N.J., 1979-80. Co-author monographs; patentee in field. Judge of elections Republican Party, Homestead, 1935-39; bd. dirs. Whitaker Depression Coll., Munhall, Pa., 1934-35. Lt. (s.g.) USN, 1944-46, PTO. Mem. AIME (sr.), IEEE (sr., life), NSPE, ASTM (chmn. com. B-4, 1953-54), Metal Sci. Club, Am. Soc. for Metals.

POCHI, PETER ERNEST, physician; b. Boston, Mar. 8, 1929; s. Anesti and Alice (Peterson) P.; m. Barbara Orlob, June 11, 1955; children: Alan, Rena. A.B. cum laude, Harvard Coll., 1950; M.D., Boston U., 1955. Diplomate Am. Bd. Dermatology. Intern Boston City Hosp., 1955-56, vis. dermatologist, 1978-91, assoc. dir., 1967-74, 78-84, acting chief dermatology, 1984-85; resident in dermatology Boston U. Hosp., 1958-61, vis. dermatologist, 1977-91, acting chief dermatology, 1984-85; assoc. in medicine Peter Bent Brigham Hosp., Boston, 1972-78; sr. cons. in dermatology Lemuel Shattuck Hosp., Boston, 1975-91; Herbert Mescon prof. dermatology Sch. Medicine, Boston U., 1988-91, prof. emeritus, 1991—, interim chmn. dept. dermatology, 1984-85; cons. med. service in dermatology Boston VA Hosp., 1978-82; lectr. dermatology Sch. Medicine, Tufts U., 1980-91; assoc. staff New Eng. Med. Ctr. Hosp., 1981-91. Assoc. editor: Jour. Investigative Dermatology, 1968-73; contbg. editor: Year Book of Dermatology, 1983-90; mem. editorial bd.: Archives of Dermatology, 1979-84, Jour. Am. Acad. Dermatology, 1981-90; contbr. articles to med. jours. Bd. dirs. Cmty. Music Ctr., 1973-77, corp. mem., 1994—. With USN, 1956-58. USPHS fellow, 1960-62, 62-63; USPHS grantee, 1965-84. Fellow Am. Acad. Dermatology (bd. dirs. 1981-85); mem. Am. Fedn. Clin. Research, AMA, Boston Dermatological Club (sec.-treas. 1967-69), Boston U. Sch. Medicine Alumni Assn. (pres. 1979-80), Boston U. Nat. Alumni Council, Dermatology Found., Evans Med. Found. (dir., sec.), Internat. Soc. Dermatology, Mass. Acad. Dermatology, Mass. Med. Soc. (chmn. sect. dermatology 1977-78), New Eng. Dermatol. Soc., Soc. Investigative Dermatology (bd. dirs. 1976-81, v.p. 1986-87). Home: 333 Commonwealth Ave Boston MA 02115-1931

POCHYLY, DONALD FREDERICK, physician, hospital administrator; b. Chgo., June 3, 1934; s. Frank J. and Vlasta (Bezdek) P.; m. Diane Dilelio, May 11, 1957; children: Christopher, Jonathan, David. M.D., Loyola U., 1959; M.Ed., U. Ill., 1971. Diplomate Am. Bd. Internal Medicine, Am. Bd. Geriatrics. Fellow ACP, 1966-67; asst. prof. med. edn. U. Ill., 1967-72, asso. prof., 1972-74; chmn. dept. health scis. edn. U. of Health Scis., Chgo. Med. Sch., 1975-77, provost, acting pres., 1977-79; prof. clin. medicine Loyola U., Chgo., 1980—; v.p. med. affairs N.W. Community Hosp., Arlington Heights, Ill.; chmn. com. rev. and recognition Am. Coun. Continuing Med. Edn., 1993; cons. Nat. Libr. Medicine, WHO. Contbr. articles to med. jours. Mem. AMA, Ill. Geriatrics Soc. (pres. Chgo. chpt. 1988-89), Ill. Med. Soc., Chgo. Med. Soc., Alpha Omega Alpha. Roman Catholic. Office: Northwest Community Hosp 800 W Central Rd Arlington Heights IL 60005-2349

POCKELL, LESLIE M., publishing company executive; b. Norwalk, Conn., June 19, 1942; s. Abe and Mildred (Shapiro) P.; m. Noriko Maejima, June 23, 1967. A.B., Columbia Coll., 1964. Articles editor Avant-Garde Mag., N.Y.C., 1967-70; dir. trade dept. St. Martin's Press, N.Y.C., 1970-84; exec. editor, dir. spl. interest group Doubleday & Co. Inc., N.Y.C., 1984-88; editorial dir. Kodansha Internat., 1988-94; dir. book devel. Book-Of-The-Month Club, Inc., N.Y.C., 1994—; adj. lectr. NYU, 1984-86. Served with U.S. Army, 1964-67.

POCKER, YESHAYAU, chemistry, biochemistry educator; b. Kishinev, Romania, Oct. 10, 1928; came to U.S., 1961; naturalized, 1967.; s. Benzion Israel and Esther Sarah (Sudit) P.; m. Anna Goldenberg, Aug. 8, 1950; children: Rona, Elon I. MSc, Hebrew U., Jerusalem, 1949; PhD, Univ. Coll., London, Eng., 1953; DSc, U. London, 1960. Rsch. assoc. Weizmann Inst. Sci., Rehovot, Israel, 1949-50; humanitarian trust fellow Univ. Coll., 1951-52, asst. lectr., 1952-54, lectr., 1954-61; vis. assoc. prof. Ind. U., Bloomington, 1960-61; prof. U. Washington, Seattle, 1961—; bicentennial lectr. Mont. State U., Bozeman, 1976; Horizons in Chemistry lectr. U. N.C., Chapel Hill, 1977, guest lectr. U. Kyoto, Japan, 1984; Edward A. Doisy vis. prof. biochemistry St. Louis U. Med. Sch., 1990; plenary lectr. N.Y. Acad. Sci., 1983, Fast Reactions in Biol. Systems, Kyoto, Japan, 1984, NATO, 1989, Consiglio nat. delle Richerche, U. Bari, Italy, 1989, Sigma Tau, Spoleto, Italy, 1990; Internat. lectr. Purdue U., 1990; cons. NIH, 1984, 86, 88; Spl. Topic lectr. on photosynthesis, Leibniz House, Hanover, Fed. Republic Germany, 1991; enzymology, molecular biology lectr., Dublin, Ireland, 1992. Mem. editorial adv. bd. Inorganica Chimica Acta-Bioinorganic Chemistry, 1981-89; bd. reviewing editors Sci., 1985—; contbr. numerous articles to profl. jours.; pub. over 220 papers and 12 revs. Numerous awards worldwide, 1983-90. Mem. Royal Soc. Chemistry, Am. Chem. Soc. (nat. spkr. 1970, 74, 84, chmn. Pauling award com. 1978, plaque awards 1970, 74, 84, Outstanding Svc. award 1979), Soc. Exptl. Biology, Am. Soc. Biol. Chemists, N.Y. Acad. Scis., Sigma Xi (nat. lectr. 1971). Avocations: Aramaic, etymology, history, philology, poetry. Office: U Wash Dept Chemistry Campus Box 351700 Seattle WA 98195-1700

POCOCK, FREDERICK JAMES, scientist, consultant; b. Canton, Ohio, May 28, 1923; s. Frederick Stanley and Mary Elizabeth (Tinker) P.; m. Lois Jean Rice, Jan. 12, 1952; children—Kathleen Jean, David Walter. B.S. in Chemistry, Mt. Union Coll., 1950; grad., Lincoln Aero Inst., 1942; postgrad., Akron U., 1953. Registered profl. engr., Calif. Aircraft insp. Bell Aircraft Corp., 1942; in tech. sales Republic Steel Corp., 1949-50; with Babcock & Wilcox Co., Alliance, Ohio, 1950-88; sr. scientist Alliance Research Center, 1974-88; cons. water technology. Contbr. articles to profl jours. Past precinct committeeman Louisville Republican Com., Ohio. Served with USAAF, 1943-46. Recipient recognition for 30 yrs. rsch. Ohio Ho. of Reps., 1980, award of merit Internat. Water Conf., 1985; co-recipient Paul Cohen Meml. award, 1993, Engrs. award for disting. svc. Soc. Profl. Engrs., 1987. Fellow ASME (co-recipient Prime Movers award 1962, Disting. Svc. award 1987, Dedicated Svc. award 1987); mem. ASTM, Am. Chem. Soc. (Cert. of Merit 1967), Nat. Assn. Corrosion Engrs. (accredited corrosion specialist).

POCOSKI, DAVID JOHN, cardiologist; b. Waterbury, Conn., July 15, 1945; s. Edward J. and Stella E. (Kolpa) P.; m. Madelyn M. Pocoski, Sept. 25, 1971; 1 child, Sarah C. BA, U. Conn., 1967; MD magna cum laude, Upstate Med. Ctr., Syracuse, N.Y., 1971. From intern to fellow in cardiology U. Rochester, N.Y.; pres. Osler Clinic of Medicine, Melbourne, Fla. Maj. USAF, 1974-76. Mem. AMA; Fellow Am. Coll. Cardiologists. Republican. Roman Catholic. Avocations: music, art, running. Office: 930 S Harbor City Blvd Melbourne FL 32901-1963

POCSIK, ROBERT ALAN, engineering consulting company executive; b. N.Y.C., Sept. 24, 1941; s. Valentine and Josephine (Ragno) P.; m. Elaine A. Piantosi, Oct. 24, 1964; children: Darren Bret, Erica P. Pocsik Lahn. BS, NYU, 1964; postgrad., N.Y. Law Sch., 1967. Dir. adminstr. and human resources Western Union Telegraph Co., N.Y.C., 1968-72, Childrens TV Workshop, N.Y.C., 1972-77; v.p. ops. Coventry Agy., Inc., N.Y.C., 1977-79; dir. ops. and human resources Allied-Signal, Melville, N.Y., 1979-84; exec. v.p. Lundy Electronics and Sys., Inc., Glenhead, N.Y., 1984-88; v.p. ops. Gibbs & Hill, Inc., N.Y.C., 1988-91; chmn. bd., pres. Hayden-Wegman, Inc., N.Y.C., 1991—; bd. dirs., v.p. ORB Mgmt. Assocs., N.Y.C.; pres. Paridon House Corp., N.Y.C. Author: Creative Advertising, 1975. Appointed chmns. advisor U.S. Congress, Washington, 1989, N.Y. State chairperson N.Y. State Dem. Party, Albany, 1991; patron N.Y. Met. Mus. Art. Mem. Uptown C. of C. Office: Hayden Wegman Inc 330 W 42d St 20 Fl New York NY 10036

PODBERESKY, SAMUEL, lawyer; b. Cremona, Italy, Mar. 16, 1946; came to U.S., 1947; s. Noah and Mina (Milikowsky) P.; m. Rosita Rubinstein, March 8, 1970; children: Daniel J., Michael J. BS in Aeronautical Engring., U. Md., 1967; JD, U. Md., Balt., 1971. Bar: Md. 1972. Flight test engr. Vertol div. Boeing Co., Phila., 1967-68; regulatory atty. FAA, Washington, 1971-78; dep. asst. gen. counsel U.S. Dept. Transp., Washington, 1978-86, asst. gen. counsel aviation enforcement and proceedings, 1986—. Office: US Dept Transp 400 7th St SW Washington DC 20590-0001

PODBOY, ALVIN MICHAEL, JR., lawyer, law library director; b. Cleve., Feb. 10, 1947; s. Alvin Michael and Josephine Esther (Nagode) P.; m. Mary Ann Gloria Esposito, Aug. 21, 1971; children: Allison Marie, Melissa Ann. AB cum laude, Ohio U., 1969; JD, Case Western Res. U., 1972, MLS, 1977. Bar: Ohio 1972, U.S. Dist. Ct. (no. dist.) Ohio 1973, U.S. Supreme Ct. 1992. Assoc. Joseph T. Svete Co. LPA, Chardon, Ohio, 1972-76; dir. pub. services Case Western Res. Sch. Law Libr., Cleve., 1974-77, assoc. law libr., 1977-78; libr. Baker & Hostetler, Cleve., 1978-88, dir. librs., 1988—; instr. Notre Dame Coll. of Ohio, Cleve., 1991—, Am. Inst. Paralegal Studies, Cleve., 1991-96. Bd. overseers Case Western Res. U., 1981-87, mem. vis. com. sch. libr. sci., 1980-86, mem. Westlaw adv. bd., 1987-92, bd. govs. law sch. alumni assn., 1992-95, West's Legal Directory Ohio Adv. Panel, 1990-91; mem. adv. com. West's Info. Innovators Inst., 1995—; chmn. Case Western Res. Libr. Sch. Alumni Fund, 1979-80. Rep. precinct committeeman Cuyahoga County, Cleve., 1981-95, mem. exec. com., 1984-87. 1st lt. USAF, 1972. Mem. ABA, Ohio State Bar Assn. (chmn. libraries com. 1989-91), Cleve. Bar Assn., Am. Assn. Law Librs. (cert., chmn. pvt. law librs. spl. interest sect. 1994-95), Ohio Regional Assn. Law Librs. (pres. 1985), Case Western Res. U. Libr. Sch. Alumni Assn. (pres. 1981), Arnold Air Soc., Am. Legion, Pi Gamma Mu, Phi Alpha Theta. Roman Catholic. Lodge: K.C. Avocations: alpine skiing, boating. Home: 5705 Deercreek Dr Willoughby OH 44094 Office: Baker & Hostetler 3200 National City Ctr Cleveland OH 44114-3485

PODD, ANN, newspaper editor; b. Buffalo, Jan. 15, 1954; d. Edward and Florence (Bojan) P.; m. Timothy Murray, 1980; children: Laura, Gregory. AB, Syracuse U., 1976; MBA, SUNY, Buffalo, 1981. Reporter AP, 1977; reporter Buffalo Courier-Express, 1977-80, bus. editor, 1980-82; bus. editor Bergen (N.J.) Record, 1982-88; bus. editor New York Daily News, 1988-90, assoc. editor, 1990-92, assoc. editor, dir. human resources, 1992-93; dep. spot news editor Wall St. Jour., N.Y.C., 1994, spot news editor, 1994—. Office: Wall St Journal 200 Liberty St New York NY 10281-1003

PODGORNY, GEORGE, emergency physician; b. Tehran, Iran, Mar. 17, 1934; s. Emanuel and Helen (Parsian) P.; came to U.S., 1954, naturalized, 1973. B.S., Maryville Coll., 1958; postgrad. Bowman Gray Sch. Medicine, 1958; M.D., Wake Forest U., 1962; m. Ernestine Koury, Oct. 20, 1962; children: Adele, Emanuel II, George, Gregory. Intern in surgery N.C. Bapt. Hosp., Winston-Salem, 1962-63, chief resident in gen. surgery, 1966-67, in cardiothoracic surgery, 1967-69; sr. med. examiner Forsyth County, N.C., 1972—; dir. dept. emergency medicine Forsyth Meml. Hosp., Winston-Salem, 1974-80; sec.-treas. Forsyth Emergency Services, Winston-Salem, 1970-80; clin. prof. emergency medicine East Carolina U. Sch. Medicine, Greenville, 1984—, chmn. residency rev. com. on emergency medicine, 1980-88; mem. Accreditation Coun. for Grad. Med. Edn. Dir. Emergency Med. Svcs. Project Region II of N.C., 1975—; chmn. bd. trustees Emergency Medicine Found.; chmn. residency rev. com. emergency medicine Accreditation Coun. Grad. Med. Edn.; founder Western Piedmont Emergency Med. Svcs. Coun., 1973; mem. N.C. Emergency Med. Svcs. Adv. Coun., 1976-81; assoc. prof. clin. surgery Bowman Gray Sch. Medicine, Wake Forest U., Winston-Salem, 1979—. Bd. dirs. Piedmont Health Systems Agy., 1975-84; trustee Forsyth County Hosp., Authority, 1974-75; bd. dirs. N.C. Health Coordinating Coun., 1975-82, Medic Alert Found. Internat. Fellow Internat. Coll. Surgeons, Internat. Coll. Angiology, Royal Soc. Health (Great Britain), Royal Soc. Medicine, Southeastern Surg. Congress; mem. Am. Coll. Emergency Physicians (charter, pres. 1978-79), AMA, (chmn. coun. of sect. emergency medicine 1978-90, alt. del. for Am. Coll. Emergency Physicians, 1990—), Am. Bd. Emergency Medicine (pres. 1976-81). Contbr. articles to profl. publs. on trauma, snake bite and history of medicine; editorial bd. Annals of Emergency Medicine, Med. Meetings. Home and Office: 2115 Georgia Ave Winston Salem NC 27104-1917

PODGORNY, RICHARD JOSEPH, biologist, science administrator; b. Chgo., Jan. 27, 1944; s. Leon and Mary Agatha (Gryzik) P.; m. Dorothy Mary Dorece, June 11, 1966; 1 child, Nicole Marie. BA, St. Mary's Coll., 1966; MS, Am. U., 1971; PhD, Georgetown U., 1975; postgrad., Fed. Exec. Inst., 1989. Quality control supr. Capital Aerosol Packaging Co., Melrose Park, Ill., 1965-66; Peace Corps vol., Adi Teclesan, Ethiopia, 1966-68; sci. dept. chmn. and tchr. Western Sr. High Sch., Washington, 1968-76; dir. marine scis. D.C. Pub. Sch. Systems, 1976-79; mgr. nat. sanctuaries programs U.S. Dept. Commerce, NOAA, Washington, 1979-82, chief user affairs/mktg. unit, external affairs staff, 1983-86, chief internat. affairs Nat. Ocean Service, 1986-94, sr. advisor, pres. Coun. Sustainable Devel., 1994—; U.S. del. to Intergovtl. Oceanographic Commn., 1986—, South Pacific Commn., 1989—; bd. dirs. Pacific Congress Internat., 1987—; lectr. in field; cons. in field. Author: Introduction to Marine Science, 1977; Ocean Ecology, 1978; contbr. articles to profl. jours. Vice pres., bd. dirs. Friends of Arlington County Parks, 1982-86; chmn. bd. dirs. planning com. Burgundy Farm Country Day Sch., Inc., 1980-86. NSF scholar, 1969-71; Georgetown U. fellow, 1972-75; recipient service commendation Emperor Haile Sallassie, 1967. Mem. AAAS, Oceanography Soc., Marine Tech. Soc., Sigma Xi. Roman Catholic. Clubs: Capital Yacht, Skyline Health and Racquet. Home: 4858 28th St S Arlington VA 22206-1370 Office: US Dept Commerce NOAA Office Sustainable Devel Rm 5222 14th St & Constitution Ave NW Washington DC 20011-6930

PODGORSAK, ERVIN B., medical physicist, educator, administrator; b. Vienna, Austria, Sept. 28, 1943; arrived in Slovenia, 1946, came to U.S., 1968, Can., 1973; s. Franc and Gabriella (Cukale) P.; m. Marjana Ambrozic, Oct. 23, 1965; children: Matthew, Gregor. Dipl.Ing. in Physics, U. Ljubljana, Slovenia, 1968; MSc in Physics, U. Wis., 1970, PhD in Physics, 1973. Diplomate Am. Bd. Med. Physics. Rsch. asst. U. Ljubljana, 1965-68, U. Wis., Madison, 1968-73; postdoctoral fellow U. Toronto, Ont., Can., 1973-74; asst. prof. McGill U., Montreal, Que., Can., 1975-79, assoc. prof., 1980-84, prof. med. physics, 1985—, dir. med. physics unit, 1991—; dir. dept. med. physics Montreal Gen. Hosp., 1979—; presenter in field. Contbr. over 130 articles to sci. jours., chpts. to books. Fellow Can. Coll. Physicists in Medicine (bd. dirs. 1981-89, v.p. 1984-87, pres. 1987-89); mem. Am. Assn. Physicists in Medicine (bd. dirs. 1990-93, assoc. editor Med. Physics Jour. 1989—, radiother. com. 1994—), Am. Coll. Med. Physics, Am. Soc. Ther. Radiology and Oncology, Can. Orgn. Med. Physics, Can. Assn. Radiation Oncologists, Can. Radiation Protection Assn., Internat. Stereotactic Radiosurgery Soc. (bd. dirs. 1991-95). Home: 1540 croissant Seville, Brossard, PQ Canada J4X 1J4 Office: Montreal Gen Hosp Dept Med Physics, 1650 Cedar Ave, Montreal, PQ Canada H3G 1A4

PODGORSKY, ARNOLD BRUCE, lawyer; b. Glen Cove, N.Y., Feb. 8, 1951; s. Stanley Morton and Lillian (Cantor) P.; m. Jean Carol Levine, June 17, 1972; children: Anna, Carolyn. BA, Alfred (N.Y.) U., 1972; JD, Syracuse (N.Y.) U., 1975. Bar: D.C. 1975, U.S. Ct. Appeals (7th and 8th cirs.) 1977, U.S. Ct. Appeals (2d, 4th and 9th cirs.) 1978, U.S. Supreme Ct. 1979, U.S. Ct. Appeals (5th cir.) 1980, U.S. Dist. Ct. D.C. 1980. Atty. NLRB, Washington, 1975-79; with Cadwalader, Wickersham & Taft, Washington, 1979-86, Gerst, Heffner, Carpenter & Podgorsky, Washington, 1986-92, Wright & Talisman, P.C., Washington, 1992—. Mem. ABA, Pi Gamma Mu. Avocations: horseback riding, youth pony club. Office: Wright & Talisman PC 1200 G St NW Ste 600 Washington DC 20005-3814

PODHAJSKI, BLANCHE RITA, language foundation administrator; b. New Britain, Conn., Sept. 4, 1945; d. Charles Anthony and Blanche Margaret (Poplawski) P.; m. Kenneth R. Kreiling, June 22, 1990. BS in Speech and Hearing, Boston U., 1967; MS in Speech Pathology, U. Vt., 1969; PhD in Learning Disabilities, Northwestern U., 1980. Speech/lang. pathologist Ctr. Disorders of Comm. Med. Ctr. Hosp. of Vt., Burlington, 1968-70, acting dir. Ctr. Disorders of Comm., 1970-71, dir. Ctr. Disorders of Comm., 1971-78; asst. prof. learning disabilities Northwestern U., Evanston, Ill., 1980-81; pvt. practice as lang. and learning disabilities specialist Aesculapius Med. Ctr., South Burlington, Vt., 1981-83; founder, dir. Stern Ctr. for Lang. and Learning, Williston, Vt., 1983—; clin. assoc. prof. neurology dept. neurology U. Vt. Med. Sch., Burlington, 1971—; field faculty Goddard Coll., Plainfield, Vt., 1973-76, summer vis. prof., 1980; adj. faculty Johnson (Vt.) State Coll., 1975-79; adj. faculty dept. comm. sci. and disorders, 1983—; mem. Vt. State Dept. Edn. Task Force, Vt. Spl. Edn. Evaluation Project, 1985; exec. bd. dirs. Vt. New Eng. br. Orton Dyslexia Soc., 1986; presenter in field. Contbr. articles to profl. jours. Commencement speaker Pine Ridge Sch., Williston, 1991, bd. dirs., edn. com. chair, 1989. Grantee Found. for Children with Learning Disabilities, 1985, Vt. Dept. Spl. Edn., 1986, Vt. Dept. Vocat. Rehab., 1992, Kresge Found., 1994, Freeman Found., 1994, Alma Gibbs Donchian Found., 1995; Turrell scholar, 1994-95. Mem. Am. Speech Lang. and Hearing Assn. (cert. clin. competence), Coun. for Exceptional Children (divsn. for children with learning disabilities), Vt. Speech and Hearing Assn. (pres.-elect 1977-78, clin. achievement award 1989), Vt. Assn. for Learning Disabilities (lifetime hon., outstanding leadership award for contbns. to learning disabled 1976, lamp of knowledge award 1983), Orton Soc. Office: Stern Ctr Language & Learning 20 Allen Brook Ln Williston VT 05495

PODHORETZ, JOHN, writer, editor; b. N.Y.C., Apr. 18, 1961; s. Norman and Midge (Rosenthal) P. BA, U. Chgo., 1982. Exec. editor news Insight Mag., Washington, 1985-87; contbg. editor U.S. News and World Report, Washington, 1987-88; speechwriter to Pres. of U.S. White House, Washington, 1988-89; asst. mng. editor Washington Times, 1989-91; sr. fellow Hudson Inst., 1991—. Recipient Gen. Excellence in Feature Sects. award J.C. Penney, 1990, Best Living Pages award Nat. Better Newspapers, 1990. Jewish. Home and Office: 1200 N Veitch St Arlington VA 22201-5818

PODHORETZ, NORMAN, magazine editor, writer; b. Bklyn., Jan. 16, 1930; s. Julius and Helen (Woliner) P.; m. Midge Rosenthal Decter, Oct. 21, 1956; children: Rachel, Naomi, Ruth, John. A.B., Columbia, 1950; B.H.L., Jewish Theol. Sem., 1950, LL.D. (hon.), 1980; B.A. (Kellett fellow), Cambridge (Eng.) U., 1952, M.A., 1957; LHD (hon.), Hamilton Coll., 1969, Yeshiva U., 1991, Boston U., 1995. Assoc. editor Commentary, 1956-58, editor in chief, 1960-95, editor-at-large, 1995—; editor in chief Looking Glass Library, 1959-60; sr. fellow Hudson Inst., 1995—; LHD (hon.) Adelphi U., 1996; Mem. U. Seminar Am. Civilization, Columbia, 1958. Author: Doings and Undoings, The Fifties and After in American Writing, 1964, Making It, 1968, Breaking Ranks, 1979, The Present Danger, 1980, Why We Were in Vietnam, 1982, The Bloody Crossroads, 1986; editor: The Commentary Reader, 1966. Chmn. new directions adv. com. USIA, 1981-87. Served with AUS, 1953-55. Fulbright fellow, 1950-51. Mem. Coun. on Fgn. Rels.

PODLES, ELEANOR PAULINE, state senator; b. Dudley, Mass., June 6, 1920; d. Francis and Pauline Magiera; student U. N.H.; m. Francis J. Podles, June 28, 1941; children: L. Patricia Podles Barrett Fogleman, Elizabeth Lee Podles Keegan. Mem. N.H. Ho. of Reps., Concord, 1976-80; selectman City of Manchester, N.H., 1976-81, v.p., 1978—; mem. N.H. State Senate, Concord, 1980—; asst. majority whip, mem. fin. com., chmn. public affairs com., public instns. health and welfare com. Del., N.H. Republican Conv., 1976, 78, N.H. Constl. Conv., 1984; pres. pro tem N.H. Senate, 1986—, chair jud. com., vice chair exec. com., senate fin. com., senate edn. com., health and human services for pub. insts. com.; pres. Manchester Rep. Women's Club, 1979—; bd. dirs. St. Joseph's Community Service, Manchester Vis. Nurse Assn., Mental Health Ctr. Manchester, Senate Edn. Com.; state chmn. Am. Legis. Exchange Council; mem. sen. fin. com., 1995—; sen. pres. pro tem, 1995—. Bd. dirs. Mental Health Ctr. Greater Manchester; mem. N.H. Childrens Trust Fund, 1986—. Mem. Am. Legis. Exch. Coun. (state chmn.), Orgn. Women Legislators, Manchester Vis. Nurse Assn., Manchester Country Club. Club: Manchester Country. Home: 185 Walnut Hill Ave Manchester NH 03104-2136 Office: N H State Senate State Capitol Concord NH 03301

PODOS-UNTERMEYER, SALLE, lawyer; b. Bklyn., Oct. 1, 1938; d. David Meyer and Rose (Ifshin) Garber; m. Steven Maurice Podos, June 20, 1959 (div. Dec. 1978); children: Richard Lance Podos, Lisa Beth Podos; m. Walter Untermeyer, Jr., May 2, 1982. BA, Vassar Coll., 1959; MA, Brandeis U., 1960; JD, Columbia U., 1977. Bar: N.Y. 1978. Assoc. Paul, Weiss, Rifkind, Wharton & Garrison, N.Y.C., 1977-79; gen. counsel, v.p., sec. MacAndrews & Forbes Group, Inc., N.Y.C., 1979-81; sr. assoc. Sage Gray Todd & Sims, N.Y.C., 1981-84, Proskauer Rose Goetz & Mendelsohn, N.Y.C., 1984-87; pres., gen. counsel Untermeyer Mace Ptnrs., 1987-89; of counsel Mazur Carp & Rubin, 1989-91; mem. fin. com. Congresswoman Carolyn Maloney, 1994-96; founder, bd. dirs. Hamptons Music Festival, 1995—. Class fund-raising chmn. Vassar Coll., 1977-80; bd. dirs. Vassar Club N.Y., 1978-80; chmn. women's div. U.S. Senate Campaign, 1970; regional chmn. U.S. Presdl. Campaign, 1972; chmn. State Rep.'s Campaign, 1973; del.-elect Interim Dem. Conv., 1974, Lawyers Com. for Gov. Carey, 1978; chmn. Mo. state legis. Nat. Coun. Jewish Women, 1969-75, mem. nat. affairs com., 1969-77, chmn. Mo. juvenile justice project, 1970-75, mem. legis. coordinating com. Midwestern region, 1971-75, mem. nat. task force on constl. rights, 1974-77; v.p., bd. dirs. St. Louis Jewish Community Rels. Coun., 1970-75, chmn. ch.-state and Black Jack Amicus Curiae coms.; v.p., bd. dirs. St. Louis chpt. Am. Jewish Com., 1969-75, chmn. urban affairs and placement for ex-offenders coms., mem. com. on status of women, 1974-77; mem. legis. liaison Coalition for Environment, St. Louis, 1970-74; bd. dirs. St. Louis Jewish Community Ctrs. Assn., 1970-74, chmn. urban affairs and legis. affairs coms.; bd. dirs. St. Louis Jewish Family and Children's Svc., 1972-74, chmn. welfare rights and health svcs. coms.; bd. dirs. Glaucoma Found., 1986—; vol. coord. Poor People's Campaign, 1968; founder, bd. dirs. Consumer's Assn., 1967-69; founder, chmn. Urban Corps program St. Louis Mayor's Com. on Youth, 1969-72; panelist White House Conf. on Children and Youth, 1970, 72, White House Conf. on Aging, 1974; founder, bd. dirs. Mo. chpt. PEARL (Pub. Edn. and Religious Liberty), 1972-75; fundraising chmn. N.Y. Found. Arts, 1992-94; bd. dirs. N.Y. Found. Sr. Citizens. Woodrow Wilson Found. fellow, 1959, NDEA fellow, 1959. Mem. ABA, Assn. of Bar of City of N.Y. (mem. continuing legal edn. com., com. on lecture), N.Y. State Bar Assn., Womens Prison Assn. (bd. dirs.). Home: 950 Park Ave New York NY 10028-0320

PODUSKA, JOHN WILLIAM, SR., computer company executive; b. Memphis, Dec. 30, 1937; s. Ben F. and Lily Mae (Reid) P.; m. Susan McElaney, Oct. 1, 1983; 1 child, Lily; children by previous marriage: Alice Casey, Margaret Kay, John Jr., Mary Beth Pandiscio. BS, MS, MIT, 1960, ScD, 1962; LHD (hon.), U. Lowell, 1986. Dir. Honeywell Info. Systems, Cambridge, Mass., 1970-72; v.p. research and devel. Prime Computer, Framingham, Mass., 1972-79; chmn., chief exec. officer, pres. Apollo Computer, Chelmsford, Mass., 1980-85; chmn., chief exec. officer, founder Stellar Computer Inc., Newton, Mass., 1986-89; CEO Stardent Computer, Inc., Newton, 1989-92; chmn. bd. dirs., founder Advanced Visual Systems Inc., Waltham, Mass., 1992—; dir. Safeguard Sci., Pa., Cambridge Tech. Ptnrs., Mass., XLvision, Melbourne, Fla., Union Pacific Resources, Ft. Worth. Trustee Bentley Coll., U. Mass., Rice U., Boston Ballet; ind. advisor. Recipient Ah Wang award C. of C., North Middlesex, Mass., 1985; named Man of Yr., Boy Scouts Am., 1983. Fellow IEEE; mem. Nat. Acad. Engrs. Office: Advanced Visual Systems Inc 300 5th Ave Waltham MA 02154-8705

PODWALL, KATHRYN STANLEY, biology educator; b. Chgo., Oct. 14; d. Frank and Marie C. Stanley. BS, U. Ill.; MA, NYU. Prof. biology Nassau C.C., Garden City, N.Y.; developmental reviewer West Ednl. Pub., Amesbury, Mass. and Highland Park, Ill., 1989, 91-92; reviewer AAAS, Washington, 1970-96; exec. bd., advisor Women's Faculty Assn., Nassau C.C., 1990—; lectr. in field. Author: Tested Studies for Laboratory Teaching, vol. 5, 1993; editor: (books and cassettes) Rhyming Simon Books and Cassettes, 1990. Mem. AAUW, Nat. SSn. Biology Tchrs., Nat. Sci. Tchrs. Assn., Soc. for Coll. Sci. Tchrs., Am. Women in Sci., Met. Assn. Coll. and Univ. Biologists, LaSalle County Hist. Soc. (life), Garden City Hist. Soc. (life), Soroptimist Internat. (Dist. 1 dir. 1994-96, club pres. 1992-94). Avocations: travel, gardening, zoological pursuits. Office: Nassau Community College One Education Dr Garden City NY 11530

POE, DAVID RUSSELL, lawyer; b. Columbia, Mo., Sept. 4, 1948; s. Russell Warren and Chloe Ardith (Prichard) P.; m. Constance Elizabeth Vaught, Aug. 3, 1974; children: Meghan Elizabeth, Michael Lewis. BS in Mechanical and Aerospace Engring., U. Mo., 1970; JD, Duke U., 1974. Bar: N.Y. 1975, N.C. 1977, U.S. Supreme Ct. 1985, D.C. 1991, U.S. Ct. Appeals (1st, 2d, 4th, 6th and D.C. cirs.), U.S. Dist. Ct. (so., ea. dists.) N.Y., U.S. Dist. Ct. (ea. dist.) N.C. Network engr. Southwestern Bell Telephone Co., St. Louis, 1970-71; assoc. LeBoeuf, Lamb, Leiby & MacRae, N.Y.C., 1974-82, ptnr., 1983-89; ptnr. LeBoeuf, Lamb, Leiby & MacRae, Washington, 1989-93, LeBoeuf, Lamb, Greene & MacRae, Washington, 1994—; adj. faculty Columbus Sch. Law, Cath. U. Am., 1992—. Vestry St. Paul's Ch., Englewood, N.J., 1986-89; legal advisor First Presbyn. Pre-Sch. and Kindergarten, Englewood, 1984-88. Mem. ABA (pub. utility sect., chmn. adminstrv. law com. 1988-89, chmn. cable TV com. 1989-92, mem. coun. 1990-93, chmn. publs. com. 1993-95), Fed. Comm. Bar Assn., Fed. Energy Bar

Assn. (vice chmn. jud. rev. com. 1994-95, chmn. 1995-96). Home: 1017 Galium Ct Mc Lean VA 22102-1106 Office: LeBoeuf Lamb Greene MacRae 1875 Connecticut Ave NW Washington DC 20009-5728

POE, DOUGLAS ALLAN, lawyer; b. Chicago Heights, Ill., Nov. 14, 1942; s. Armand Leslie and Marcella Elizabeth (Grote) P. BA, DePauw U., 1964; JD, Duke U., 1967; LLM, Yale U., 1968. Bar: Ill. 1967, U.S. Ct. Appeals (4th cir.) 1968, U.S. Supreme Ct. 1972, U.S. Ct. Appeals (7th cir.) 1973. Clk. U.S. Ct. Appeals (4th cir.), Balt., 1968-69; law clk. to Chief Justice Warren E. Burger U.S. Supreme Ct., 1969, to Hon. William J. Brennan, Jr., 1970; assoc. Mayer, Brown & Platt, Chgo., 1970-74, ptnr., 1974—. Mem. ABA, Am. Law Inst., Chgo. Council Lawyers, Order of Coif. Office: Mayer Brown & Platt 190 S La Salle St Chicago IL 60603-3410

POE, H. SADLER, lawyer; b. Rock Hill, S.C., Oct. 17, 1944; s. Alvis Bynum and Frances Guy (Sadler) P.; m. Justina Lasley, Aug. 12, 1972; children: Justina Lasley, Julia Rives, Abigail Sadler. AB, Princeton U., 1967; LLB, U. Va., 1971. Bar: Ga. 1971, U.S. Dist. Ct. (no. dist.) Ga. 1976. Assoc. Alston, Miller & Gaines, Atlanta, 1971-77, ptnr., 1977-82; ptnr. Alston & Bird, Atlanta, 1982—, chmn. bus. and fin. dept., 1988-93; bd. dirs., pres. Hillside, Inc., Atlanta. Presenter in field. Elder Trinity Presbyn. Ch., Atlanta, 1977-80, 92-95; active Leadership Atlanta, 1988, mem. exec. com., 1991-92, 93-94; trustee Ga. Assn. Pastoral Care, Atlanta, 1991—. Mem. State Bar Ga. (chmn. securities com. 1981-88, chmn. bus. and banking law sect. 1991-92), Am. Coll. Investment Counsel. Avocations: woodworking, water skiing. Office: Alston & Bird One Atlantic Ctr 1201 W Peachtree St NW Atlanta GA 30309-3400

POE, JERRY B., financial educator; b. Springfield, Mo., Oct. 3, 1931; s. Carlyle and Eunice P.; m. Carol J. Mussler, Sept. 9, 1959; children: Cheryl Marie, Jennifer Brenna. A.B., Drury Coll., 1953; M.B.A. (Weinheimer fellow), Washington U., St. Louis, 1957; D.B.A. (Ford Found. fellow), Harvard U., 1963. Instr. U. Ark., spring 1957; indsl. engr. McDonnell Aircraft Corp., St. Louis, 1957; lectr. on fin. Boston U., 1959-61; asst. prof. bus. adminstrn. Drury Coll., 1961-64, assoc. prof., 1964-68, prof., 1968-74; dir. Breech Sch. Bus. Adminstrn., 1968-74; prof. fin. Ariz. State U., 1974—, chmn. dept. fin., 1974-82; vis. prof. Fla. Tech. U., 1971; examiner, commr. North Central Assn. Colls. and Schs.; dir. NDEA Inst. Econs.; cons. in field. Author: Essentials of Finance: An Integrated Approach, 1995, An Introduction to the American Business Enterprise, 1969, 7th rev. edit., 1989, Cases in Financial Management, 1977, 3d rev. edit., 1987. Mem. Regional Manpower Adv. Com.; mem. bus. and profl. adv. council Empire Bank. Served to lt. comdr. USNR, 1953-55. Mem. Fin. Mgmt. Assn., Kappa Alpha, Beta Gamma Sigma, Omicron Delta Kappa. Methodist. Office: Ariz State U Coll Bus Dept Fin Tempe AZ 85287-3906

POE, LENORA MADISON, psychotherapist and author; b. New Bern, Ala., Jan. 3, 1934; d. Tommy and Carrie (Norfleet) Madison; m. Levi Mathis Poe, June 21, 1957; children: Michael DeWayne, Michaelle DaNita Burke. BS, Stillman Coll., Tuscaloosa, Ala., 1956; MA, Calif. State U., Hayward, 1972, MS, 1980; PhD, Ctr. for Psychol. Studies, Albany, Calif., 1991. Lic. marriage, family and child therapist. Classroom tchr. Perry County Schs., Uniontown, Ala., 1956-59, Richmond (Calif.) Unified Schs., 1962-69; guidance counselor Berkeley (Calif.) Unified Schs., 1969-79; psychotherapist in pvt. practice Berkeley, 1982—, West Coast Children's Ctr., El Cerrito, Calif., 1982—; lectr. Grandparents as Parents, 1992—; part-time prof. J.F.K. U., Orinda, Calif., 1993; del. White House Conf. on Aging, Washington, 1995; cons. in field; staff cons. Cmty. Adult Day Health Svcs., Highland Gen. Hosp., Oakland. Author: Black Grandparents as Parents, 1992. Pres. nat. bd. dirs. Stillman Coll., 1992—; mentor cons. Black Women Organized for Ednl. Devel., Oakland, Calif., 1994—; mem. adv. bd. Nat. Black Aging Network, Oakland, 1992—; founding mem., advisor Realmindcas Civic Club, Richmond, 1976—; mem. Families United Against Crack Cocaine, Oakland; bd. dirs. Ctr. for Elders for Independence, Oakland; trustee Ctr. for Psychol. Studies, Albany; chairperson Grandparents Caregivers Advocacy Task Force, Oakland, Calif.; mem. bd. edn. Ministry of Ch. by Side of Road, Berkeley; also others. Recipient cert. of Appreciation African Am. Hist. and Cultural Soc., San Francisco, 1992, President's citation for Excellence Nat. Assn. for Equal Opportunity in Higher Edn., 1993, award Excellence in Edn. Nat. Coun. Negro Women, 1993, S award Stillman Coll., Appreciation award for Excellence Nystrom Elem. Sch., Richmond, 1994, Outstanding Alumna of the Yr. award Ctr. for Psychological Studies, 1995. Mem. Nat. Coalition Grandparents as Parents (adv. com. 1992—), No. Coalition Grandparents as Parents (co-chmn. 1991-93), Stillman Coll. Nat. Alumni Assn. (pres.). Home: 940 Arlington Ave Berkeley CA 94707-1929 Office: 2034 Blake St Ste 1 Berkeley CA 94704-2604

POE, LUKE HARVEY, JR., lawyer; b. Richmond, Va., Jan. 29, 1916; s. Luke Harvey and Alice Colburn (Reddy) P. BS in Math, U. Va., 1938, JD, 1941; postgrad. (Rhodes scholar), Oxford (Eng.) U., 1939; D.Phil., Christ Ch., 1957. Bar: Va. bar 1940, D.C. bar and D.C. Ct. Appeals bar 1967, U.S. Supreme Ct. bar 1969, Md. bar 1974. Asso. firm Cravath, Swaine & Moore, N.Y.C., 1941-42; tutor St. John's Coll., Annapolis, Md., 1946-50; asst. dean St. John's Coll., 1947-49, tenure tutor, 1953-60, dir. physics and chemistry lab., 1959-60; asst. chmn. Nat. Citizens Com. for Kennedy and Johnson and chmn. Citizens Com., Pres.'s Inaugural Com., 1960-61; asst. to chmn. bd. Aerojet-Gen. Corp., El Monte, Calif., 1961-63; div. pres. Internat. Tech. Assistance and Devel. Co., Washington, 1963-66; ptnr. Howard, Poe & Bastian, Washington, 1966-83; pvt. practice law, 1983—; bd. dirs. First Am. Bank of Md.; cons. Dept. Transp., Dept. State, NEH; lectr. War Coll. of USAF, Gen. Studies program U. Va.; seminar leader Aspen Inst. Humanistic Studies; guest panelist Panel on Sci. and Tech. of Com. on Sci. and Astronautics, U.S. Ho. of Reps., 1970; pres. bd. dirs. Watergate East, Inc., 1976-79, 90-92; organizer U. Va. Unified Liberal Arts Program, 1988—. Author: The Combat History of the Battleship U.S.S. Mississippi, 1947, The Transition From Natural Law to Natural Rights, 1957; (with others) lab. manuals Einstein's Theory of Relativity, 1957, Electro-Magnetic Theory, 1959; editor: (with others) Va. Mag., 1936-38, U. Va. Law Rev., 1940-41. Dean's adv. coun. Lehigh U., 1962-65, mem. Seminar on Sci., Tech. and Pub. Policy, Brookings Instn., 1964-66; coun. on trends and perspectives U.S. C. of C., 1966-69; chmn. bd. Bristol Property Mgmt. and Svcs., Inc., 1967-88; chmn. Annapolis Bd. Zoning Appeals, 1966-75; mem. Annapolis Mayor's Task Force, 1967-74, Md. Gov.'s Commn. on Capital City, 1970-76. Lt. comdr. USNR, 1942-46. Decorated Jhalvada Order Durbargadh. Mem. Am. Law Inst., AAUP, Raven Soc. (pres.), Soc. Cin., Phi Beta Kappa, Phi Delta Phi, Met. Club (Washington), Travellers Club (London), Brook Club (N.Y.C.), New Providence Club (Annapolis), Vincent's Club (Oxford). Episcopalian. Home: 139 Market St Annapolis MD 21401-2628 also: 2500 Virginia Ave NW Washington DC 20037-1901 Office: 2600 Virginia Ave NW Washington DC 20037-1905

POE, WILLIAM FREDERICK, insurance agency executive, former mayor; b. Tampa, Fla., July 22, 1931; s. Fred Holland and Zula Blanche (Willoughby) P.; m. Elizabeth Ann Blackburn, June 21, 1954; children—William, Keren, Janice, Marilyn, Charles. Student, Duke U., 1950; B.S., U. Fla., 1953. Founder, pres. Poe & Assocs. (Ins. Agency), Tampa, 1956-74, chmn., 1979-87, chmn. bd., 1987-93; bd. Poe and Brown, Inc. (formerly Poe & Assocs.), Tampa, 1993—; mayor City of Tampa, 1974-79. Mem. Hillsborough County Port Authority, 1961, chmn., 1963; pres. chpt. ARC, United Way of Greater Tampa. Served with USAF, 1955-56. Mem. Tampa Assn. Ins. Agents, Chief Execs. Orgn. Democrat. Baptist. Club: Yacht. Office: Poe Investments Inc 1901 N 13th St Tampa FL 33605

POE-BORDEN, AUDREY, writer, business educator; b. Memphis, May 15, 1926; d. William Arthur and Ethel Lula (Mincey) Poe; m. Arthur Murray Borden, Aug. 5, 1955 (div. Oct. 1975); children: Erica, Ross, Mark, Lindsay, Andrew, Anthony. BS in English and Edn., U. Memphis, 1947; MS in Journalism, Columbia U., 1950; PhD, Columbia Pacific U., 1995. Photojournalist Comml. Appeal-Scripps Howard newspapers, Memphis, 1948-55; writer Gen. Features Corp., N.Y.C., 1950-55; writer, broadcaster Turkish Radio, Ankara, Turkey, 1952-55; spl. edn. tchr. Perry County Schs., Linden, Tenn., 1982-84; spl. edn. tchr. CDC Lewis County Schs., Hohenwald, Tenn., 1985-87, spl. edn. tchr. TAG, 1994—; spl. edn. tchr. Memphis City Schs., 1987-91; cons., writer Inst. for War and Peace Reporting, London, 1991—; bd. dirs. Lewis County Edn. Found., Analytix, Inc., Solytix, Inc., Vesta Svcs., Inc., Software Constrn. Co., Inc. Avocations: painting, sculpture. Home: Buffalo River Farm Box 459 Hohenwald TN 38462 Office: Inst War & Peace Reporting, 33 Islington High St, London N19LH, England

POEHLEIN, GARY WAYNE, chemical engineering educator; b. Tell City, Ind., Oct. 17, 1936; s. Oscar Raymond and Eva Lee (Dickman) P.; m. Sharon Eileen Wood., Jan. 1, 1958; children: Steven Ray, Timothy Wayne, Valorie Ann, Sandra Lee. BSChemE, Purdue U., 1958, MSChemE, 1961, PhD, 1966. Design engr. Proctor & Gamble, Cin., 1958-61; from asst. prof. to assoc. prof. Lehigh U., Bethlehem, Pa., 1965-75, prof. chem. engring., 1975-78, co-dir. emulsion polymers inst., 1973-78; dir. sch. chem. engring. Ga. Inst. Tech., Atlanta, 1978-86, assoc. v.p. rsch., dean grad. studies, 1986-91, v.p. interdisciplinary programs, prof. chem. engring., 1991-95; prof. chem. engring., 1978—; bd. dirs. Flexible Products Co., Marietta, Ga. Contbr. over 100 articles to tech. publs. Mem. sch. bd. Bethlehem Area Sch. Dist., 1969-75. Recipient Honor Scroll award Phila. br. Am. Inst. Chemists, 1977, Mac Pruitt award Coun. for Chem. Rsch., 1989. Fellow AICE; mem. Am. Chem. Soc., Sigma Xi. Avocations: woodworking, beekeeping. Home: 3147 Habersham Rd NW Atlanta GA 30305-2060 Office: Ga Inst Tech Sch Chem Engrs Atlanta GA 30332-0100

POEHLING, ROBERT EDWARD, plumbing supply company executive; b. LaCrosse, Wis., May 6, 1944; s. Gerhard George and Anne Elizabeth (Schwartz) P. BA, Marquette U., 1968. Mgr. data processing LaCrosse Plumbing, 1968-74, v.p., 1974-80, pres., 1980-90, vice chair, 1990—; dir. Norwest Bank-La Crosse. Pres. LaCrosse Symphony Orch., 1984-90; bd. dirs. United Fund for the Arts, LaCrosse, 1983-90, Viterbo Coll., LaCrosse; mem. LaCrosse County Harbor Commn., 1986—. Republican. Roman Catholic. Home: 1900 La Salle Ave Minneapolis MN 55403 Office: La Crosse Plumbing Supply Co 1904 La Salle Ave Minneapolis MN 55403

POEHLMANN, CARL JOHN, agronomist, researcher; b. Calif., Mo., Jan. 29, 1950; s. Edwin William and Lucille Albina (Neu) P.; m. Linda Kay Garner, Dec. 29, 1973; children: Anthony, Kimberly. BS, U. Mo., 1972, MS, 1978. Farmer Jamestown, Mo., 1972-73; vocat. agrl. tchr. Linn (Mo.) Pub. Schs., 1973-75, Columbia (Mo.) Pub. Schs., 1975-78; dir., mgr. agronomy rsch. ctr. U. Mo., Columbia, 1978—. Mem. Am. Soc. Agronomy (div. A-7 chair 1985-86, bd. mem. 1991-94, cert. crop advisor 1993), Crop Sci. Soc. Am., Soil Sci. Soc. Am. Mem. Christian Ch. (Disciples of Christ). Office: U Mo 4968 S Rangeline Rd Columbia MO 65201-8973

POEHLMANN, JOANNA, artist, illustrator, designer; b. Milw., Sept. 5, 1932; d. Herbert Emil and Lucille (Conover) P. Attended, Layton Sch. Art, 1950-54, K.C. (Mo.) Art Inst., 1954, Marquette U., 1958, U. Wis., 1965, 1985. Solo exhbns. include St. James Gallery, Milw., 1963, (retrospective) Milw. Art Mus., 1966, Bradley Galleries, Milw., 1982, Signature Gallery, John Michael Kohler Art Ctr., Sheboygan, Wis., 1979, 84, Woodland Pattern Book Ctr., Milw., 1988, The Cell Gallery, Rochester, N.Y., 1988, 89, Charles Allis Art Mus., Milw., 1991, Layton Gallery at Cardinal Stritch Coll, Milw., 1993, Univ. Meml. Libr., Madison, Wis., 1993, Wustum Mus. Fine Arts, Racine, Wis., 1994; two-man shows include Bradley Galleries, 1964, 69, 80, 91, Cardinal Stritch Coll., Milw., 1980; invitational group shows include Cudahy Gallery of Wis. Art, Milw. Art Mus., 1962-85, 92, Bradley Galleries, 1967-79, Lakefront Festival of Art, Milw. Art Mus., 1962-63, 70-72, 76-79, Country Art Gallery, Long Island, N.Y., 1963-71, Mount Mary Coll., Milw., 1979, 83, Chosy Gallery, 1980, 81, 86, U. Dallas, 1987, Frick Gallery, Germany, 1991, Spertus Mus. Judaica, Chgo., 1986, World Fin. Ctr., N.Y.C., 1992, Istvan Kiraly Muzeum, Budapest, Hungary, 1992, Artspace, Richmond, Va., 1994, Va. Ctr. For Craft Arts, Richmond, 1994, many others; juried group shows include Milw. Art Mus., 1963, 75, 78, Chgo. Art Inst., 1978, 81, Milw. Fine Arts Gallery, 1980, U. Wis. Fine Arts Gallery, Milw., 1980, The West Pub. Co., St. Paul, 1982, Auburn U., 1983, Zaner Gallery, Rochester, N.Y., 1984, Pratt Graphics Ctr., N.Y.C., 1985, Art 54 Gallery, N.Y.C., 1987, Boston Art Inst., 1987, Bradley U., Peoria, Ill., 1989, Wustum Mus. Fine Arts, 1989, 1992, Trenton State Coll., 1991, numerous others; represented in collections including Victoria & Albert Mus., London, N.Y. Pub. Libr., Mus. Kunsthandwerk, Frankfurt, Germany, Milw. Art Mus., Milw. Pub. Libr., U. Dallas, Orchard Corp. Am., St. Louis, McDonald's Corp., GE Med. Systems Bldgs., Waukesha, Goldhirsh Group, Boston, Marquette U.-Haggerty Mus. Art, others; subject of articles; author: Love Letters, Food for Thought, Cancelling Out. Recipient Merit award Art Dir.'s Club, Milw., 1962, 100 Best award, 1967, 100 Best award Milw. Soc. Communicating Arts, 1973, 76, MGIC award Wis. Painters & Sculptors, 1981, Merit award Illustration Milw. Advt. Club, 1983, 2d award Wustum Mus. Fine Arts, 1983, 4th Purchase Prize award McDonald's Fine Art Collection Competition, 1983, Juror's award Zaner Gallery, 1984, Hopper/Koch award Wustum Mus. Fine Arts, 1985, spl. mention, Purchase award Bradley U., 1985, Purchase award Moravian Coll., 1985, Jack Richeson award Wustum Mus. Fine Arts, 1985, Purchase award U. Del., 1986, Strathmore Paper Co. award Wustum Mus. Fine Arts, 1986, Purchase award U. N.Dak., 1987, Award of Excellence miniature art Metro Internat. Competition, N.Y.C., 1987, 3d award Wustum Mus. Fine Arts, 1987, Purchase award U. Dallas, 1988, Award of Excellence Wustum Mus. Fine Arts, 1992, Individual Art fellowship Milw. County, 1993; Arts Midwest/NEA Regional Visual Artist fellow, 1994—. Roman Catholic. Home and Studio: 1231 N Prospect Ave Milwaukee WI 53202-3013

POE-JACKSON, GERTIE LAVERNE, sales executive; b. Chgo., Feb. 7, 1949; d. L.C. and Gertrude (Winfrey) Poe. BSBA, Roosevelt U., 1978, MBA, 1984. Policy analyst Continental Bank, Chgo., 1971-87; fin. planner IDS/Am. Express, Merrillville, Ind., 1987-89; sales rep. Valic, Chgo., 1990-94, Invest Fin. Svcs., Bridgeview, IL, 1994—. Mem. Sigma Gamma Rho. Baptist. Home: PO Box 19201 Chicago IL 60619-0201 Office: Invest Fin Svcs Bridgeview Bank & Trust 7940 S Harlem Ave Bridgeview IL 60455-1500

POEL, ROBERT WALTER, air force officer, physician; b. Muskegon, Mich., July 24, 1934; s. Abel John and Fannie M. (Vanderwall) P.; m. Carol Anne Noordeloos, June 24, 1960; children: Kathryn Anne Poel Engle, James Robert, Sharon Kay Poel Thompson. BS, Calvin Coll., 1957; MD, U. Mich., 1959. Diplomate Am. Bd. Surgery. Commd. capt. USAF, 1962, advanced through grades to brig. gen., 1988, ret., 1993; comdr. Hosp. Malmstrom AFB, Great Falls, Mont., 1971-73; dir. profl. svcs. Hdqrs. Tactical Air Command Command Surgeon's Office, Langley AFB, Va., 1973-74; div. chief, med. plans Office of Air Force Surgeon Gen., Wash., 1974-78; comdr. regional hosp. Sheppard AFB, Wichita Falls, Tex., 1978-83; dir. profl. svcs. Office of Air Force Logistics Command Surgeon, Wright-Patterson AFB, Ohio, 1983-85; vice-comdr. Wilford Hall USAF Med. Ctr., San Antonio, 1985-87; chief, quality assurance, dir. plans and resources Air Force Surgeon Gen., Bolling AFB, Washington, 1987-89; hosp. comdr. Malcolm Grow Med. Ctr., Andrews AFB, Washington, 1989-93; v.p. med. affairs, med. dir. Burdette Tomlin Meml. Hosp., Cape May Court House, N.J., 1993-95; acting med. dir. North Capitol office Meth. Occupational Healthctrs. Inc., Indpls., 1995—; dir. Andrews Fed. Credit Union, 1991-95, vice chmn. bd. dirs., 1992-95. Advisor, bd. regents Uniformed Svcs. U. the Health Scis., Bethesda, Md., 1989-93; mem. pres. coun. Calvin Coll., 1990. Named Disting. alumnus, Calvin Coll., 1990; Paul Harris fellow Rotary Club of Wichita Falls, 1982. Mem. AMA, Air Force Soc. Clin. Surgeons (sr.), Assn. Mil. Surgeons of U.S., Am. Coll. Physician Execs. Republican. Mem. Christian Reformed Ch. Home: 12085 Waterford Ln Carmel IN 46033-5501 Office: 1919 N Capitol Ave Indianapolis IN 46202

POEN, MONTE M., history educator, researcher; b. Lake city, Iowa, Nov. 25, 1930; s. John and Garnette (Montgomery) P.; m. Bonnie L. Diehl, July 15, 1952 (div. Feb. 1972); children: John M., Gregory E., Mark A.; m. Kathryn Lomen, May 22, 1982. AA, San Jose (Calif.) City Coll., 1959; BA, San Jose State U., 1961; MA, U. Mo., 1963, PhD, 1967. Instr. U. Mo., Columbia, 1964-66; with No. Ariz. U., Flagstaff, 1966—, prof., 1979-90, regents prof., 1990-96, regents prof. emeritus, 1996—; cons. McFarland papers Earnest W. McFarland Estate, Florence, Ariz., 1987. Author: Harry S. Truman Versus the Medical Lobby, 1979; editor: Strictly Personal & Confidential: Letters Harry Truman Never Mailed, 1982, Letters Home by Harry Truman, 1984. Mem. Coccnino County Dem. Cen. Com., Flagstaff, 1988—. Sgt. USAF, 1950-54, PTO. Truman Libr. Inst. scholar, 1987. Fellow Harry S. Truman Libr. Inst.; mem. Orgn. Am. Historians, Oral History Assn., Ariz. Humanities Coun., Ctr. for Study of the Presidency. Democrat. Avocations: camping, fishing, travel, gardening, hiking. Home: 3703 N Grandview Dr Flagstaff AZ 86004-1601 Office: Dept History Dept of History No Ariz U Flagstaff AZ 86011

POEPPELMEIER, KENNETH REINHARD, chemistry educator; b. St. Louis, Mo., Oct. 6, 1949. BS in Chemistry, U. Mo., 1971; PhD in Inorganic Chemistry, Iowa State U., 1978. Rsch. chemist, corp. rsch. sci. labs. Exxon Rsch. & Engring. Co., Annandale, N.J., 1978-80, sr. chemist, corp. rsch. sci. labs., 1980-81, staff chemist, corp. rsch. sci. labs., 1981-84, sr. staff chemist, corp. rsch. sci. labs., 1984; assoc. prof. chemistry Northwestern U., Evanston, Ill., 1984-88, assoc. dir. sci. and tech. ctr. for superconductivity, 1989—, prof., 1988—, Dow prof. chemistry, 1992-94; lectr., cons. in field; organizer, chmn. nat. symposium on solid state chemistry of heterogeneous oxide catalysis including new microporous solids ACS, New Orleans, 1987; cons. Exxon Chemicals, Air Products and Chemicals, Inc., Shell, FMC Corp.; assoc. dir. NSF Sci. and Tech. Ctr. for Superconductivity; vice-chair, chair-elect, Gordon Conf. on Solid State Chem. Contbr. articles to numerous chemistry publications; patentee in field. Iowa State U. fellow, 1977-78; Iowa State scholar, 1975-76. Mem. Am. Assn. for the Advancement of Sci., ACS (chmn. Solid State Subdiv. of Div. Inorganic Chemistry 1988-89), AAAS, Am. Phys. Soc., Materials Rsch. Soc., Catalysis Club (Chgo.), Sigma Xi. Office: Northwestern U Dept Chemistry 2145 Sheridan Rd Evanston IL 60208-3113

POESCH, JESSIE JEAN, art historian; b. Postville, Iowa, May 19, 1922; parents: Edward H. and Vina (Meier) P. BA, Antioch Coll., 1944; MA, U. Del., 1956; PhD, U. Pa., 1966. Relief worker Am. Friends Svc. Com., Phila., also, France, Germany, 1946-54; curatorial asst. H.F. DuPont Winterthur (Del.) Mus., 1956-58; from asst. prof. to prof. art history Tulane U., New Orleans, 1963-92, Maxine and Ford Graham chair in fine arts, 1988-92; guest curator "Painting in the South", Va. Mus. Fine Arts, Richmond, 1980-84; curator "Newcomb Pottery: An Enterprise for So. Women, 1895-1940", Newcomb Coll. Tulane U. and Smithsonian Instn. traveling exhbn. svc., 1980-87. Author: Titian Ramsay Peale, 1799-1885, and His Journals of the Wilkes Expedition, 1961, The Art of the Old South: Painting, Sculpture, Architecture and the Products of Craftsmen, 1560-1860, 1983; (book/exhbn. catalogue) The Early Furniture of Louisiana, 1972, Newcomb Pottery: An Enterprise for Southern Women 1895-1940, 1984, Will Henry Stevens, 1987; also numerous articles and book revs. Fellow U. Del., 1954-56; Fulbright scholar U. London, 1960-62; NEH grantee, London, 1969-70. Mem. Soc. Archtl. Historians (bd. dirs. 1986-89), Coll. Art Assn., Am. Antiquarian Soc., La. Endowment for the Humanities (bd. dirs. 1984-90, La. Humanist of Yr. 1992), Victorian Soc. Am. (bd. dirs. 1988-92). Office: Tulane U Newcomb Art Dept New Orleans LA 70118

POETTCKER, HENRY, retired seminary president; b. Rudnerweide, Russia, Mar. 27, 1925; s. John and Margaretha (Voth) P.; m. Aganetha Baergen, July 4, 1946; children: Victoria, Ronald, Martin. A.B., Bethel Coll., North Newton, Kans., 1950; B.D., Mennonite Bibl. Sem., Chgo., 1953; Th.D., Princeton Theol. Sem., 1961, converted Ph.D., 1973. Ordained to ministry Mennonite Ch., 1948; instr. Can. Mennonite Bible Coll., Winnipeg, Man., 1954-59; pres. Can. Mennonite Bible Coll., 1959-78; pres. Mennonite Bibl. Sem., Elkhart, Ind., 1978-90, assoc. for devel., 1991-93; 1993; interim dean Bluffton (Ohio) Coll., 1965-66; vis. lectr. Taiwan Theol. Coll. and Tainan Theol. Coll., Taiwan, 1973-74. Editor: (with Rudy A. Regehr) Call to Faithfulness, 1972, Alumni Bull. Can. Mennonite Bible Coll., 1960-73. Pres. Gen. Conf. Mennonite Ch., Newton, Kans., 1968-74. Mem. Soc. Bibl. Lit. and Exegesis. Home: 80 Plaza Dr Ste 2502, Winnipeg, MB Canada R3T 5S2 *The secret of happiness lies not in doing what one likes, but in liking what one does.*

POFF, RICHARD HARDING, state supreme court justice; b. Radford, Va., Oct. 19, 1923; s. Beecher David and Irene Louise (Nunley) P.; m. Jo Ann R. Topper, June 24, 1945 (dec. Jan. 1978); children: Rebecca, Thomas, Richard Harding; m. Jean Murphy, Oct. 26, 1980. Student, Roanoke Coll., 1941-43; LL.B., U. Va., 1948, LL.D., 1969. Bar: Va. 1947. Partner law firm Dalton, Poff, Turk & Stone, Radford, 1949-70; mem. 83d-92d congresses, 6th Dist. Va.; justice Supreme Ct. Va., 1972-89, sr. justice, 1989—; Vice chmn. Nat. Commn. on Reform Fed. Crime Laws; chmn. Republican Task Force on Crime; sec. Rep. Conf., House Rep. Leadership. Named Va.'s Outstanding Young Man of Year Jr. C. of C., 1954; recipient Nat. Collegiate Athletic Assn. award, 1966, Roanoke Coll. medal, 1967, Distinguished Virginian award Va. Dist. Exchange Clubs, 1970, Presdl. certificate of appreciation for legislative contbn., 1971, legislative citation Assn. Fed. Investigators, 1969, Thomas Jefferson Pub. Sesquicentennial award U. Va., 1969, Japanese Am. Citizens League award, 1972; named to Hall of Fame, Am. Legion Boys State, 1985. Mem. Bar Assn., VFW, Am. Legion, Pi Kappa Phi, Sigma Nu Phi. Clubs: Mason, Moose, Lion. Office: Va Supreme Ct 100 N 9th St Richmond VA 23219-2335 *When you know you are right, fight. When you are in doubt, wait. When you know you are wrong, admit your mistake and correct it.*

POGO, BEATRIZ TERESA GARCIA-TUNON, cell biologist, virologist, educator; b. Buenos Aires, Argentina, Dec. 24, 1932; came to U.S., 1964, naturalized, 1976; d. Dario and Maria Teresa (Vergnory) Garcia-Tunon; m. Angel Oscar Pogo, Jan. 13, 1956; children: Gustavo, Gabriela. B.S., Lycee No. 1, Buenos Aires, 1950; M.D., Sch. Medicine, Buenos Aires, 1956; D.M.Sci., 1961. Intern Univ. Hosp., Buenos Aires, 1956-57; asst. Inst. Histology and Embryology, Buenos Aires U., 1957-59; fellow Sloan Kettering Meml. Hosp., N.Y.C., 1959-60, Rockefeller U., N.Y.C., 1960-61; asst. prof. cell biology Inst. Cell Biology, Cordoba U., Argentina, 1962-64; research assoc. Rockefeller U., N.Y.C., 1964-67; asst. Pub. Health Research Inst., N.Y.C., 1967-69, assoc., 1969-73, assoc. mem. 1973-78; prof. exptl. cell biology and microbiology Mt. Sinai Sch. Medicine, CUNY, 1978—, acting dir. ctr. for exptl. cell biology, 1987-89, prof. neoplastic diseases, 1989—. Contbr. articles to profl. jours. Damon Runyon Fund fellow, 1964-65; grantee Am. Cancer Soc., 1970-73, 79-80, 84-85, 94-95, NIH, 1975—. Fellow N.Y. Acad. Scis.; mem. Am. Assn. for Cancer Rsch., N.Y. Acad. Sci., Am. Soc. Cell Biology, Harvey Soc., Am. Soc. Virology, Assn. for Women in Sci. (v.p. met. N.Y. chpt. 1981-83, pres. 1984-86), Am. Microbiol. Soc., Sigma Xi. Home: 237 Nyac Ave Pelham NY 10803-1907 Office: Mt Sinai Sch Medicine 1 Gustave L Levy Pl New York NY 10029-6504

POGORELEC, STEVEN MARTIN, fraternal organization administrator; b. Passaic, N.J., Nov. 9, 1946; s. Albert Joseph and Anna (Paciga) P.; m. Anne G. Boyle, Sept. 18, 1971; children: Jennifer Anne, Steven Martin, Scott Thomas. Air traffic controller FAA, Washington, 1970-81; custodian Slovak Cath. Sokol, Passaic, N.J., 1981-83; bookkeeper Slovak Cath. Sch., Passaic, N.J., 1983-86, office mgr., 1986-91, CEO, 1992—. Staff Sgt. USAF, 1965-69. Roman Catholic. Avocations: bowling, golf, softball, track & field. Office: Slovak Cath Sokol 205 Madison St PO Box 899 Passaic NJ 07055

POGREBIN, LETTY COTTIN, writer, lecturer; b. N.Y.C., June 9, 1939; d. Jacob and Cyral (Halpern) Cottin; m. Bertrand B. Pogrebin, Dec. 8, 1963; children: Abigail and Robin (twins), David. A.B. cum laude with spl. distinction in English and Am. Lit, Brandeis U., 1959. V.p. Bernard Geis Assocs. (book pubs.), N.Y.C., 1960-70; columnist The Working Woman column Ladies Home Jour., 1971-81; editor Ms mag., N.Y.C., 1971-87, columnist, editor at large, 1987-89, contbg. editor, 1990—; columnist The N.Y. Times, Newsday, Washington Post, Moment Mag., Washington, 1990—, Moment Mag., Washington, 1990—; contbg. editor Family Circle, Ms. mag., Tikkun mag.; cons. Free to Be, You and Me projects, 1972—; lectr. women's issues and family politics, changing roles of men and women, friendship in Am., non-sexist child rearing and edn., Judaism and feminism, Mid-East politics. Author: How to Make It in a Man's World, 1970, Getting Yours: How to Make the System Work for the Working Woman, 1975, Growing Up Free, 1980, Stories for Free Children, 1982, Family Politics, 1983, Among Friends, 1986, Deborah, Golda, and Me: Being Female and Jewish in America, 1991, Getting Over Getting Older: An Intimate Journey, 1996; mem. editl. bd. Tikkun Mag.; contbr. articles to N.Y. Times, Washington Post, Boston Globe, The Nation, TV Guide, also other mags., newspapers. Sec. bd. Author's Guild; bd. dirs. Ms. Found., Ams. for Peace Now, New Israel Fund, Jewish Fund for Justice, Commn. on Women's Equality, Am. Jewish Congress, PEN Am.; mem. Task Force on Women Fedn. Jewish Philanthropies, Women's Forum. Pointer fellow Yale U., 1982, MacDowell Colony fellow, 1979, 89, 94, Cummington Colony Arts fellow

1985, Edna St. Vincent Millay Colony fellow, 1985. Address: 33 W 67th St New York NY 10023-6224

POGUE, FORREST CARLISLE, retired historian; b. Eddyville, Ky., Sept. 17, 1912; s. Forrest Carlisle and Frances (Carter) P.; m. Christine Brown, Sept. 4, 1954. AB, Murray (Ky.) State Coll., 1931, LLD, 1970; MA, U. Ky., 1932, LittD, 1983; PhD, Clark U., 1939, LHD, 1975; LittD, Washington and Lee U., 1970. Instr. history Western Ky. State Coll., 1933; instr. to assoc. prof. Murray State Coll., 1933-42, prof., 1954-56; with Office Chief Mil. History U.S. Dept. Army, 1946-52; ops. rsch. analyst Johns Hopkins U., U.S. Army Hdqrs., Heidelberg, Fed. Republic of Germany, 1952-54; dir. George C. Marshall Rsch. Ctr., Lexington, Va., 1956-64, George C. Marshall Rsch. Libr., Lexington, 1964-74; Harmon Meml. lectr. U.S. Air Acad., 1968; disting. Bicentennial lectr. U.S. Mil. Acad., 1974; disting. vis. prof. Va. Mil. Inst., 1972; professorial lectr. George Washington U., 1948, 49, 50; past chmn. Am. Com. on History 2d World War; former mem. adv. groups U.S. Army, USAF and Navy Hist. Office; chmn. adv. com. Senate Hist. Office; mem. adv. bd. Former Mems. Congress, Ky. Oral History Commn.; mem. adv. com. on Eisenhower papers; adj. fellow Woodrow Wilson Internat. Ctr. Scholars, 1974-77; mem. Hist. Found., Centennial Adv. Com. on the History of the Eisenhower Era; dir. Dwight D. Eisenhower Inst. Hist. Rsch., Nat. Mus. Am. History, Smithsonian Inst., 1974-84; mem. Marine Corps Hist. Found. Author: The Supreme Command, 1954, George C. Marshall: Education of a General, Vol. 1, 1963, Ordeal and Hope, 1939-42, Vol. 2, 1966, Organizer of Victory, 1943-45, Vol. 3, 1973, Statesman, 1945-59, Vol. 4, 1987; author: (with others) The Meaning of Yalta, 1956; contbr. to books including Command Decisions, 1960, Total War and Cold War, 1962, D Day: The Normandy Invasion in Retrospect, 1970, America's Continuing Revolution, 1975, The War Lords, 1976, Bicentennial History of the United States, 1976, (with others) The Marshall Plan in Germany, 1991; contbg. editor: Guide to American Foreign Relations Since 1700, 1983. Trustee Harry S. Truman Inst. Libr.; mem. adv. com. Nat. Hist. Soc. With U.S. Army, 1942-45, ETO. Decorated Bronze Star, Croix de Guerre, France; recipient Disting. Alumni Centennial award U. Ky., 1965, Samuel Eliot Morison award Am. Mil. Inst., 1988; U. Paris Inst. des Hautes Etudes Internationales Am. Exchange fellow, 1937-38. Fellow U.S. Army History Rsch. Inst. (adv. group), Am. Mil. Inst. (past pres.); mem. Assn. U.S. Army (Disting. Svc. award 1990), Oral History Assn. (past pres.), U.S. Commn. on Mil. History (trustee), Am. Hist. Assn., So. Hist. Assn., Orgn. Am. Historians, Soc. Am. Historians (Francis Parkman medal 1988), NEA (life), English Speaking Union, Am. Legion, Murray State U. Alumni Assn. (past pres.), Cosmos Club. Democrat. Presbyterian.

POGUE, LLOYD WELCH, lawyer; b. Grant, Iowa, Oct. 21, 1899; s. Leander Welch and Myrtle Viola (Casey) P.; m. Mary Ellen Edgerton, Sept. 8, 1926; children: Richard Welch, William Lloyd, John Marshall. A.B., U. Nebr., 1924; LL.B., U. Mich., 1926; S.J.D., Harvard Law Sch., 1927. Bar: Mass., N.Y., D.C., Ohio, U.S. Supreme Ct. bars. Assoc. Ropes, Gray, Boyden and Perkins, 1927-33; ptnr. firm Searle, James and Crawford, N.Y.C., 1933-38; asst. gen. counsel CAB, 1938-39, gen. counsel, through 1941, chmn. bd., 1942-46; mng. ptnr. Pogue & Neal, Washington, 1946-67; Washington mng. ptnr. Jones, Day, Reavis & Pogue, Washington, 1967-79, ret., 1981; Lindbergh Meml. lectr. Nat. Air and Space Mus., 1991; presenter essay 50th Ann. Internat. Civil Aviation Orgn., Montreal, 1994; spkr. in field. Author: International Civil Air Transport Transition Following WW II, 1979, Pogue/Pollack/Polk Genealogy as Mirrored in History, 1990 (1st pl. in Anna Ford Family history book contest 1991, Nat. Genealogical Soc. award for excellence genealogy and family history 1992, William H. and Banjamin Harrison Book award Coun. Ohio Genealogists, Outstanding Achievement award County and Regional History category Ohio Assn. Hist. Socs. and Mus., 1st pl. award Iowa Washington County Geneal. Soc. 1994, cert. commendation Am. Assn. State and Local History 1994). Mem. U.S. dels. Chgo. Internat. Civil Aviation Conf., 1944; mem. U.S. dels., vice chmn., del. Bermuda United Kingdom-U.S. Conf., 1946; vice chmn., del. Provisional Assembly PICAO, 1996. With AUS, 1918. Recipient Elder Statesman of Aviation award Nat. Aeronautic Assn., Golden Eagle award Soc. Sr. Aerospace Execs.; fellow Am. Helicopter Soc., Benjamin Franklin fellow Royal Soc. Arts. Fellow Royal Aero. Soc.; mem. AIAA (hon.), Can. Aeronautics and Space Inst., Nat. Geneal. Soc., New Eng. Hist. Geneal. Soc. (life, former trustee), Ohio Geneal. Soc. (life), Md. Geneal. Soc. (life), First Families of Ohio, Halicopter Assn. Internat. (hon. mem. for life), Met. Club, Univ. Club, Wings Club (hon., N.Y.C.), Bohemian Club (San Francisco), Cosmos Club, Masons. Home: 5204 Kenwood Ave Bethesda MD 20815-6604 Office: Metropolitan Sq 1450 G St NW Washington DC 20005-2001

POGUE, MARY ELLEN E. (MRS. L. WELCH POGUE), youth and community worker; b. Fremont, Nebr., Oct. 27, 1904; d. Frank E. and Mary (Coe) Edgerton; m. L. Welch Pogue, Sept. 8, 1926; children: Richard Welch, William Lloyd, John Marshall. BFA, U. Nebr., 1926; studied violin with Harrison Keller, Boston, 1926-28, Kemp Stillings Master Class, N.Y.C., 1935-37. Mem. Potomac String Ensemble, 1939-80. Historian, Gov. William Bradford Compact, 1966—; vice chmn. Montgomery County (Md.) Victory Garden Ctr., 1946-47; pres. Bethesda Community Garden Club, 1947-48; founder Montgomery County YWCA, bd. dirs., 1946-50, 52-55; founder Welcome to Washington Music Group, 1947—; co-founder Group Piano in Montgomery County, Md. schs., 1954. Recipient Outstanding Service award Bethesda United Meth. Ch., 1984, Bethesda Cmty. Garden Club, 1985, 93, Devoted Svc. award D.C. Mayflower Soc., 1985, 89, Welcome to Washington Internat. Club award, 1986. Mem. Soc. Mayflower Descs. D.C. (dir. D.C. 1954—, elder 1971-91, elder emeritus), PEO Sisterhood (pres. 1957-59, charter mem. chpt. R, PEO), Mortar Bd. Alumnae (pres. 1965-67, Mortar Bd. award, 1986), Nat. Cap. Area Fedn. Garden Clubs, Bethesda United Meth. Women, Nat. Geneal. Soc., New Eng. Historic Geneal. Soc. (life), Ohio Geneal. Soc. (life), Md. Geneal. Soc., Md. Hist. Soc., Conn. Soc. Genealogists, Pilgrim Soc. (life), Plimoth Plantation, Hereditary Order of Descs. Colonial Govs., Nat. Soc. Magna Charta Dames, Colonial Order of Crown, Sovereign Colonial Soc. Ams. Royal Descent, Order of Descs. Colonial Physicians and Chirurgiens, Nat. Soc. Women Descs. Ancient and Hon. Arty. Co., First Families of Ohio, Sons and Daughters of the Colonial and Antebellum Bench and Bar 1565-1861 (charter mem.), Welcome to Washington Internat. Club, Ind. Agy. Women (assoc.), Capital Speakers Club, The Plantagenet Soc., Soc. Descs. of Knights of the Most Noble Order of the Garter, DAR, Order Ams. Armorial Ancestry, Saybrook Colony Founders Assn., Soc. Founders of Norwich, Conn., Kenwood Country Club, Delta Omicron Music (life). Methodist. Compiler, editor: Favorite Menus and Recipes of Mary Edgerton of Aurora, Nebraska, 1963, Edgerton-Coe History, 1965. Home: 5204 Kenwood Ave Bethesda MD 20815-6604

POGUE, RICHARD WELCH, lawyer; b. Cambridge, Mass., Apr. 26, 1928; s. Lloyd Welch and Mary Ellen (Edgerton) P.; m. Patricia Ruth Raney, July 10, 1954; children: Mark, Tracy, David. B.A., Cornell U., 1950; J.D., Mich. Law Sch., 1953. Bar: Mich. 1953, Ohio 1957, U.S. Dist. Ct. (no. dist.) Ohio 1960, U.S. Ct. Appeals (6th cir.) 1972, U.S. Ct. Appeals (D.C. and 9th cirs.) 1979. Assoc. Jones, Day, Reavis & Pogue, Cleve., 1957-60, ptnr., 1961—, mng. ptnr., 1984-92, sr. ptnr., 1993-94; sr. advisor Dix & Eaton, Cleve., 1994—; vis. prof. Mich. Law Sch., 1993-95; bd. dirs. Derlan Industries, Toronto, Continental Airlines, Inc., Houston, OHM Corp., Findlay, Ohio, M.A. Hanna Co., Cleve., Redland PLC, Reigate, Eng., Rotek Inc., Aurora, Ohio, Key Corp., Cleve, TRW Inc. Cleve. Chmn. Cleve. Found. 1985-89, Greater Cleve. Roundtable, 1986-89, Greater Cleve. Growth Assn., 1991-93, Univ. Hosps., 1994—, truste 1975—, Cleve. Ballet, 1983-85, United Negro Coll. Fund, Cleve., 1979; mem. Adminstrv. Conf. U.S., 1974-80; vice chmn. Cleve. Tomorrow, 1988-93, 50 Club Cleve., 1988-89; trustee Case Western Res. U.; gen. campaign chmn. United Way, Cleve., 1989; active Coun. Fgn. Rels., 1989—, Am./EC Assn. Bus. Adv. Coun., 1988-93; trustee Rock and Roll Hall of Fame and Mus., 1986—; co-chmn 1996 Cleve. Bicentennial Commn., interim chmn. Cleve. Inst. Music, 1994. Army, 1954-57. Recipient Outstanding Alumnus award U. Mich. Club, Cleve., 1983, Torch of Liberty award Anti-Defamation League, 1989, Leadership Cleve. Vol. of Yr. award, 1990, 1st Econ. Devel. Workshop award Nat. Coun. on Urban Econ. Devel., 1992, Humanitarian award Nat. Conf. Christians and Jews, 1992. Mem. ABA (chmn. antitrust sect. 1983-84), Ohio State Bar Assn. (chmn. antitrust sect. 1969-73). Republican. Mem. United Ch. of Christ. Clubs: Bohemian (San Francisco), Soc., Union (Cleve.), Metropolitan (Washington), Links (N.Y.C.).

POGUE, WILLIAM REID, former astronaut, foundation executive, business and aerospace consultant; b. Okemah, Okla., Jan. 23, 1930; s. Alex W. and Margaret (McDow) P.; m. Jean Ann Pogue; children: William Richard, Layna Sue, Thomas Reid. B.S. in Secondary Edn., Okla. Bapt. U., 1951, D.Sc. (hon.), 1974; M.S. in Math., Okla. State U., 1960. Commd. 2d lt. USAF, 1952, advanced through grades to col., 1973; combat fighter pilot Korea, 1953; gunnery instr. Luke AFB, Ariz., 1954; mem. acrobatic team USAF Thunderbirds, Luke AFB and Nellis AFB, Nev., 1955-57; asst. prof. math. USAF Acad., 1960-63; exchange test pilot Brit. Royal Aircraft Establishment, Ministry Aviation, Farnborough, Eng., 1964-65; instr. USAF Aerospace Research Pilots Sch., Edwards AFB, Calif., 1965-66; astronaut NASA Manned Spacecraft Center, Houston, 1966-75; pilot 3d manned visit to Skylab space sta.; now with Vutara Services of Springdale, Ark. Decorated Air medal with oak leaf cluster, Air Force Commendation medal, D.S.M. USAF; named to Five Civilized Tribes Hall of Fame, Choctaw descent; recipient Distinguished Service medal NASA, Collier trophy Nat. Aero. Assn.; Robert H. Goddard medal Nat. Space Club; Gen. Thomas D. White USAF Space Trophy Nat. Geog. Soc.; Halley Astronautics award, 1975; de la Vaalx medal Fedn. Aeronautique Internat., 1974; V.M. Komarov diploma, 1974. Fellow Acad. Arts and Scis. of Okla. State U., Am. Astron. Soc.; mem. Soc. Exptl. Test Pilots, Explorers Club, Sigma Xi, Pi Mu Epsilon. Baptist (deacon). Home: RR 3 Huntsville AR 72740-9803 Office: Vutara Services PO Box 150 Hindsville AR 72738

POHL, ADOLF LEOPOLD, clinical chemist; b. St. Poelten, Austria, Dec. 14, 1936; s. Adolf Theodor and Cornelia Maria Anna (Moerth) P.; m. Ingrid Maria Antonia Payer, Feb. 24, 1962 (div. Dec. 1975); children: Martin, Ulrike; m. Nanako Tanaka, Mar. 14, 1989; 1 child, Anna Yumi. BSc, U. Vienna, 1957, MSc, 1965, DPhil, 1968. Rsch. asst. med. dept. I U. Vienna Med. Sch., 1967-69, asst. prof., 1969-85, head erythrocyte enzyme lab. med. dept. I, 1969-85, assoc. prof. med. dept. I, dept. chemotherapy, 1985-87, assoc. prof. dept. chem. labs., 1987—; quality assurance cons. Med. Pharm. Rsch. Ctr., Vienna, 1993—. Mem. editl. bd. Cancer Molecular Biology Jour., 1994—; contbr. articles to profl. jours. Mem. Am. Assn. for Clin. Chemistry, Internat. Soc. for Oncodevel. Biology and Medicine, N.Y. Acad. Scis., IEEE Computer Soc., Drug Info. Assn. Achievements include discovery in human blood serum of a new ADP-ribosyltransferase, implementation of advanced data analysis in clinical chemistry, detection by new micromethods of phospholipid metabolism in red blood cell membranes and study of its abnormalities in hemolytic anemia; research on serum glycosyltransferases as possible cancer markers and critical analysis of galactosyltransferase heterogeneity. Home: Lambrechtgasse 3/10, A-1040 Vienna Austria Office: U Hosp Labs, Rummelhardtgasse 4/3, A-1090 Vienna Austria

POHL, FREDERIK, writer; b. N.Y.C., Nov. 26, 1919; s. Fred George and Anna Jane (Mason) P.; m. Carol Ulf, Sept. 15, 1953 (div. 1981); children—Ann, Karen, Frederik, Kathy; m. Elizabeth Anne Hull, July 27, 1984. Editor Popular Pubs., N.Y.C., 1939-43; editor Popular Sci., N.Y.C., 1946-49; freelance writer N.Y.C., 1950-60, 80—; editor Galaxy Pubs., N.Y.C., 1961-69, Bantam Books, N.Y.C., 1973-80. Author: Man Plus, 1977 (Nebula award), Gateway, 1978 (Nebula, Hugo, Campbell awards, Prix Apollo award), Jem, 1979 (Am. Book award), The Years of the City (Campbell award 1985). Served to sgt. USAAF, 1943-45; Italy. Recipient Popular Culture Assn. award, 1982. Fellow AAAS, Brit. Interplanetary Soc.; mem. Sci. Fiction Writers of Am. (pres. 1974-76, Grand Master award 1993), World Sci. Fiction (pres. 1980-82), Authors Guild, N.Y. Acad. Scis., Astron. Soc. Pacific. Democrat. Unitarian. Home: 855 Harvard Dr Palatine IL 60067-7026

POHL, GUNTHER ERICH, retired library administrator; b. Berlin, July 22, 1925; came to U.S., 1927; s. Erich Ernst and Martha (Seidel) P.; m. Dorothy Edna Beck, Aug. 21, 1949; children: Christine, Louise, Elizabeth, Ronald. BA, NYU, 1947, MA, 1950; MLS., Columbia U., 1951. Librarian local history and genealogy div. N.Y. Pub. Library, N.Y.C., 1948-69, chief local history and genealogy div., 1969-80, chief U.S. history and local history and genealogy div., 1980-85; ret. Compiler: N.Y. State Biographical, Genealogical and Portrait Index. Fellow N.Y. Geneal. and Biog. Soc.; mem. ALA (chmn. genealogy com. 1971-73, 76-78), N.Y. Geneal. and Biog. Soc. (libr., trustee 1982-92), Sigma Phi Epsilon (trustee local chpt. 1978—). Republican. Avocations: stamps, opera; collecting New Yorkiana. Home: 24 Walden Pl Great Neck NY 11020

POHL, JOHN HENNING, chemical engineer, consultant; b. Ft. Riley, Kans., May 29, 1944; s. Herbert Otto and Ellen Irene (Henning) P.; m. Judith Lynn Sykes, Aug. 10, 1968; children: J. Otto, Clint. AA, Sacramento City Coll., 1964; BS, U. Calif., Berkeley, 1966; SM, MIT, 1973, DSci, 1976. Inspector constrn. C.O. Henning Cons. Engrs., Sacramento, 1965; engr. E.I. du Pont Nemours, Wilmington, Del., 1966-70; rsch. asst. MIT, Cambridge, 1971-75, lectr., 1975-76; mem. tech. staff Sandia Nat. Labs., Livermore, Calif., 1976-81; dir. fossil fuels Energy and Environ. Rsch., Irvine, Calif., 1981-86; dir. R & D Energy Systems Assocs., Tustin, Calif., 1986-89; sr. scientist energy W.J. Schafer Assocs., Irvine, 1989-91; pres. Energy Internat., Laguna Hills, Calif., 1988—; sr. cons. ESA Engring., Laguna Hills, 1989—; v.p. Advanced Combustion Tech. Co., Hsinchu, Taiwan, 1993-95; v.p. tech. Energeo, Inc., San Mateo, Calif., 1995-96; prof. chem. engring., dir. Coal Utilization Rsch. Ctr. U. Queensland, Brisbane, Australia, 1996—. Contbr. articles to profl. jours.; patentee in field. Treas. Headstart, Cambridge, 1975-76. Recipient Sci. and Tech. Achievement award U.S. EPA, 1987, Best Energy Projects award Energy Commn., Taiwan, coal evaluation, 1989, Low NOx Burner, 1992. Mem. ASME (advisor corrosion and deposits com. 1989—, rsch. project subcom. 1994—), AIChE (combustion advisor 1988-92), Am. Flame Rsch. Com., Am. Chem. Soc., Combustion Inst. Western States (mem. exec. com. 1988-95), Combustion Inst. (mem. program subcom. 1976—), Engring. Found. (mem. steering com. on ash deposits 1989—). Home: 26632 Cortina Dr Mission Viejo CA 92691-5429

POHL, PAUL MICHAEL, lawyer; b. Erie, Pa., July 17, 1948; s. Joseph Paul and Mary (Strenio) P.; m. Kaya Lynn Gavriloff, Aug. 13, 1970; children: Thomas Michael, Mary Elizabeth, Michael David. AB, Princeton U., 1970; JD, U. Pitts., 1975. Bar: Pa. 1975, Ohio 1976, U.S. Dist. Ct. (we. dist.) Pa. 1975, U.S. Dist. Ct. (no. dist.) Ohio 1976, U.S. Ct. Appeals (5th cir.) 1980, U.S. Ct. Appeals (11th cir.) 1983, U.S. Ct. Appeals (1st, 3d and 6th cir.) 1993, U.S. Ct. Appeals (D.C. cir.) 1995. Reporter Erie Daily Times, 1970-71; law clk. to presiding justice Pa. Supreme Ct., 1975-76; assoc. Jones, Day, Reavis & Pogue, Cleve., 1976-82, ptnr., 1982—; ptnr.-in-charge Jones, Day, Reavis & Pogue, Pitts., 1989—; guest mem. faculty Sch. Law, Hofstra U., Hempstead, N.Y., 1982, 84; mem. trial advocacy program Sch. Law, Emory U., Atlanta, 1983—; bd. dirs. JURA Corp., Erie, Lord Corp., Cary, N.C. Co-author: Conflicts of Interest—A Trial Lawyers Guide, 1984. Bd. dirs. Franciscan U., Steubenville, Ohio, 1991—, vice chmn., 1994—; bd. dirs. Gannon U., Erie, Cath. Charities, Diocese of Pits., Inc. With USMC, 1971-72. Named one of Cleve.'s 78 Most Interesting People, Cleve. mag., 1978. Mem. Cleve. Bar Assn. (mem. com. task force on violent crime 1983). Roman Catholic. Office: Jones Day Reavis & Pogue 500 Grant St Pittsburgh PA 15219-2502 also: Jones Day Reavis & Pogue 901 Lakeside Ave E Cleveland OH 44114-1116

POHL, ROBERT OTTO, physics educator; b. Gottingen, Germany, Dec. 17, 1929; came to U.S., 1958; s. Robert Wichard and Auguste Eleonore (Madelung) P.; m. Karin Ursula Koehler, May 6, 1961; children: Helen M., Robert S., Otto C. Vordiplom, U. Freiburg, Fed. Rep. Germany, 1951; diploma, U. Erlangen, Fed. Rep. Germany, 1955, Dr. rer. nat., 1957. Asst. U. Erlangen, 1957-58; research assoc. Cornell U., Ithaca, NY, 1958-60, asst. prof., 1960-63, assoc. prof., 1963-68, prof., 1968—; vis. prof. Tech. Hochschule Stuttgart, 1966-67, Tech. U. Munchen, 1973-74, Konstanz U., Regensburg U., 1987-88, all Fed. Republic Germany; vis. scientist Nuc. Research Ctr., Juelich, Fed. Rep. Germany, 1980-81, Hahn-Meitner Inst., Berlin, 1995. Contbr. articles on solid state physics to profl. jours. Recipient Sr. Scientist award Alexander von Humboldt Found., 1980; Guggenheim Found. fellow, 1973, Erskine fellow U. Canterbury, New Zealand, 1988. Fellow AAAS, Am. Inst. Physics (O.E. Buckley award 1985), Internat. Thermal Conductivity Confs. Office: Cornell U Physics Dept Ithaca NY 14853-2501

POHLAD, CARL R., professional baseball team executive, bottling company executive; b. West Des Moines, Iowa. Ed., Gonzaga U. With MEI Diversified, Inc., Mpls., 1959—, chmn. bd., 1976—; pres. Marquette Bank Mpls., N.A., pres., dir.; pres., dir. Bank Shares, Inc.; owner Minn. Twins, 1985—; dir. Meth. Hosp. Adminstrv. Group, T.G.I. Friday's, Tex. Air Corp., Ea. Airlines, Continental Air Lines, Inc., Carlson Cos. Inc. Address: Minnesota Twins 501 Chicago Ave S Minneapolis MN 55415*

POHLAND, FREDERICK GEORGE, environmental engineering educator, researcher; b. Oconomowoc, Wis., May 3, 1931; s. Arnold Ernest and Eda Karoline (Petermann) P.; m. Virginia Ruth Simmons, Sept. 10, 1966; 1 child, Elizabeth Eda. BS in Civil Engring., Valparaiso U., 1953; MS in Civil Engring., Purdue U., 1958, PhD, 1961. Profl. engr.; diplomate Am. Acad. Environ. Engrs. Civil engr. Erie Railroad Co., Huntington, Ind., 1953; preventive medicine specialist U.S. Army, Ft. Bragg, N.C., 1953-56; grad. rsch. asst. Purdue U., West Lafayette, Ind., 1956-61; asst. prof. Ga. Inst. Tech., Atlanta, 1961-64, assoc. prof., 1964-71, prof., 1971-88; Weidlein prof. U. Pitts., 1989—; vis. scholar U. Mich., Ann Arbor, 1967-68; guest prof. Delft U. Tech., Netherlands, 1976-77; mem. sci. adv. bd. EPA, Washington, 1989—, Nat. Inst. for Environ. Renewal, 1995—; mem. sci. adv. com. Gulf Coast Hazardous Substance Rsch. Ctr., Beaumont, Tex., 1989-92, EPRI, Palo Alto, Calif., 1990-94; mem. adv. coun. Purdue U., 1990-94; mem. com. on water rsch. and on innovative techs. NRC, 1993—; mem. indsl. adv. com. DOD Advanced Applied Tech. Demonstration Facility, 1994—; co-dir. EPA Ctr. for Groundwater Remediation Tech. Analysis, 1995—. Author: Emerging Technologies in Hazardous Waste Management, 1990, 91, 93, 94, 95, Design of Anaerobic Processes for the Treatment of Industrial and Municipal Waste, 1992; regional editor (jour.) Water Rsch., 1983—, hon. exec. editor Water Rsch., 1994—; author over 130 publs. in field. Served with U.S. Army, 1953-56. Recipient Harrison Prescott Eddy medal Water Pollution Control Fedn., 1964, Charles Alvin Emerson medal, 1983, Gordon Maskew Fair medal, 1989; recipient Rsch. award Water Pollution Control Assn. Pa., 1991. Fellow ASCE; mem. AIChE, NSPE, Am. Acad. Environ. Engrs. (diplomate, pres. 1992-93, Stanley E. Kappe award 1995), Assn. Environ. Engring. Profs. (sec.-treas. 1970-71, disting. lectr. 1992), Solid Waste Assn. N.Am. (Lawrence lectr. 1992), Am. Water Works Assn. (life), Nat. Acad. Engring., Am. Chem. Soc., Am. Soc. Microbiology, Am. Acad. Microbiology, Ga. Soc. Profl. Engrs., Internat. Assn. on Water Quality, Pa. Soc. Profl. Engrs., Pa. Water and Pollution Control Assn., Sigma Xi, Tau Beta Pi, Chi Epsilon, others. Achievements include major contributions to phase separation in anaerobic treatment processes; originated concept of leachate recirculation for accelerated stabilization in landfill bioreactors. Home: 118 Millstone Dr Pittsburgh PA 15238-1624 Office: U Pitts Dept Civil and Environ Engring Pittsburgh PA 15261

POHLMAN, JAMES ERWIN, lawyer; b. Iowa City, Apr. 10, 1932; s. Erwin Christian and Agnes Freda (Johanns) P.; m. Patricia Anne Likert, Sept. 6, 1958; children: William James, John David, Bruce Likert. AB, Oberlin Coll., 1954; LLB, U. Mich., 1957. Bar: Ohio 1957. Assoc. Wright, Harlor, Purpus, Morris & Arnold, Columbus, Ohio, 1957-62; ptnr. Wright, Harlor, Morris & Arnold, Columbus, 1962-77; ptnr. Porter, Wright, Morris & Arthur, Columbus, 1977—, chmn. litigation dept., 1986—; bd. dirs. Physicians Ins. Co. Ohio, Pickerington. Trustee Oberlin (Ohio) Coll., 1986—, Columbus Children's Hosp., 1976-91; pres. John Frederick Oberlin Soc., 1983-86. Served with Air N.G., 1957-60. Fellow NEH seminar Yale U., summer 1977. Fellow Am. Coll. Trial Lawyers; mem. Am. Soc. Med. Assn. Counsel (pres. 1982-85), Internat. Assn. Def. Counsel (exec. com. 1984-87, sec.-treas. 1993—), Barristers Soc. (pres Columbus club 1963-64). Republican. Congregationalist. Clubs: Golf (New Albany, Ohio); Rocky Fork Country (Gahanna, Ohio) (trustee 1980-83). Office: Porter Wright Morris & Arthur 2900 Huntington Ctr Columbus OH 43215

POHLMAN, RANDOLPH A., business administration educator, dean; b. Topeka, Jan. 25, 1944; s. Clarence Alvin and Martha Melissa (McElheny) P.; m. Jeanne Lucille Gebhart, Aug. 22, 1965; children—Kristina, Lisa. B.S., Kans. State U., 1967, M.S., 1969; Ph.D., Okla. State U., 1976. Asst. prof., assoc. prof. fin. Kans. State U., Manhattan, 1976-82, assoc. prof., head dept. fin., 1982-84, prof., dean Coll. Bus. Administrn., 1984-90; dir. employee devel. Koch Industries, 1990-91, dir. human resources, 1991-95; dean sch. bus. and entrepreneurship Nova Southeastern Univ., Ft. Laud, Fla., 1995—; vis. rsch. scholar UCLA, 1983; holder L.L. McAninch Chair of Entrepreneurship, 1988-90; bd. dirs. Union Nat. Bank, Manhattan, mem. investment com., 1986-87, mem. trust mgmt. com., 1988. Author: International Investment, 1977, Financial Statement Analysis and Forecasting for the Non-Financial Executive, 1990, Understanding the Bottom Line: Finance for Non-financial Managers and Supervisors. Chmn. Kans. State U., United Way, 1982; trustee Meml. Hosp., Manhattan, 1984-90; treas. Kans. State U. Found., 1980-90, mem. investments com., 1988; mem. steering com. Ctr. for Workforce Mgmt.; mem. cost containment roundtable Sedgwick County med. Soc.; mem. bd. dirs. Wichita/Sedgwick County Partnership for Growth Employment and Tng.; mem. Broward Econ. Devel. Coun., 1995; mem. exec. edn. adv. bd. Wharton Sch. Univ. Pa., 1995. With USAF, 1971-73. Recipient Outstanding Tchr. award Coll. of Bus., Kans. State U., 1977, All-Univ. Disting. Tchg. award Kans. State U., 1977, Cutting Edge award selection com. Miami C. of C., 1995-96; investments rsch. grantee Kans. State U., 1978. Mem. Fin. Execs. Inst., Am. Fin. Assn., Am. Econ. Assn., Fin. Mgmt. Assn., Midwest Fin. Assn., Kans. State U. Alumni Assn. (treas. 1980-90, trustee 1983-90, bd. dirs.), Manhattan C. of C. (bd. dirs. 1987-90). Republican. Club: Manhattan Country (bd. dirs. 1983-85). Lodge: Rotary (bd. dirs. Manhattan club, 1986—, pres.-elect Manhattan chpt.). Avocations: golf; guitar playing; reading. Office: Nova Southeastern Univ Sch Bus & Entrepreneurship 3100 SW 9 Ave Ft Laud FL 33315

POHLSANDER, HANS ACHIM, classics educator; b. Celle, Germany, Oct. 10, 1927, came to U.S., 1947, naturalized, 1953; m. Navee Newby, Aug. 20, 1956; children—Dianne, Eileen, Margaret. B.A. with high honors, U. Utah, 1954; M.A., U. Calif.-Berkeley, 1955; Ph.D., U. Mich., 1961. Tchr. Carmel High Sch., Calif., 1956-58; asst. prof. Washington U., St. Louis, 1961-62; asst. to assoc. prof. SUNY, Albany, 1962-71, prof. classics, 1971-95, prof. religious studies, 1991-95, chmn. dept. classics, 1972-78, prof. emeritus, 1995—; vis. assoc. prof. Am. U. Beirut, 1968-69; vis. prof. Ohio State U., Columbus, 1983-84; lectr. Aegean Inst., Greece, summers 1969, 72, 75, 78, 83, Anatolia Coll., Greece, summer 1981. Contbr. articles to profl. jours. Served to cpl. U.S. Army, 1950-52. Grantee NEH, 1979, German Acad. Exchange Service, 1982, Am. Philos. Soc., 1983, 88, Am. Coun. Learned Socs., 1963. Mem. Archaeol. Inst. Am., Am. Philol. Assn., Hagiographic Soc. Home: 52 Wellington Rd Delmar NY 12054-3322 Office: SUNY at Albany Dept Classics 1400 Washington Ave Albany NY 12222-0100

POHOST, GERALD MICHAEL, cardiologist, medical educator; b. Washington, Oct. 27, 1941; married; 3 children. BS, George Washington U., 1963; MD, U. Md., 1967. Diplomate Am. Bd. Internal Medicine, Am. Bd. Cardiovascular Disease, Am. Bd. Nuclear Medicine. Intern Montefiore Hosp. & Med. Ctr., Bronx, N.Y., 1967-68, asst. resident, 1968-69; sr. resident Jacobi Hosp. Albert Einstein Coll. Medicine, Bronx, 1969-70; cardiology resident Montefiore Hosp. & Med. Ctr.; clin. & rsch. fellow in medicine Mass. Gen. Hosp., Boston, 1971-73; rsch. fellow in medicine Harvard Med. Sch., Boston, 1971-73; instr. medicine Harvard Med. Sch., 1974-77, asst. prof., assoc. prof. medicine, 1977-83; with dept. radiology Mass. Gen. Hosp., Boston, 1977-83, asst. gen. med. svcs., 1978-82; prof. medicine, radiology U. Ala., Birmingham, 1983—, dir. divsn. cardiovascular disease doctors, 1983, Mary Gertrude Waters chair cardiovascular medicine divsn. cardiovascular disease, 1991—; cons. nuclear medicine radiology dept. Mass. Gen. Hosp., 1977-83; dir. ctr. NMR R&D U. Ala. Hosp., Birmingham, 1986—. Sr. editor: Noninvasive Cardiac Imaging, 1983, New Concepts in Cardiac Imaging, 1985, 86, 87, 88, 89, The Principles and Practice of Cardiovascular Imaging, 1991; contbr. more than 400 articles, reviews, book chpts., editls. to profl. jours.; nat. and internat. spkr. in field; mem. editl. bd. Circulation, Jour. Magnetic Resonance in Medicine, Internat. Jour. Cardiology, NMR in BioMedicine, Coronary Artery Disease, others; rsch. interests in radionuclide and nuclear magnetic resonance studies of the heart, myocardial metabolism, cardiac pathophysiology. SCOR grant NIH, 1990—, tng. grant, 1992—, Dept. Energy grant, 1992—, Nat. Ctr. Rsch. Resources, 1992—. Fellow Am. Coll. Cardiology (editl. bd. jour., chmn. cardiac imaging com. 1982-88, current procedural terminology com. 1988—, gov. rels. com. 1989—, trustee 1994—); mem. AMA (chmn. panel nuclear magnetic resonance imaging 1985-88), Am. Fedn. Clin. Rsch., Am. Soc. Clin. Investigations, Am. Assn. Profs., Am. Heart Assn. (fellow coun. clin. cardiology 1975—, Mass. affiliate 1975-83, established investigator 1979-84, Richard and Hinda Rosenthal award for excellence in clin. investigation 1985, chmn. advanced cardiac tech. com. of coun. on clin. cardiology 1981-86, exec. com. 1981—, Ala. affiliate 1983—, long range planning com. 1986-89, chmn. 1989-91, vice chmn. exec. com. coun. clin. cardiology 1988—, nominating com. 1989-91, chmn. 1993—, budget com. 1989-91, chmn. exec. com. 1991-93, immediate past chmn. 1994—, rsch. com. fellow subgroup A 1988-91), Soc. Nuclear Medicine (coun. nuclear Cardiology 1990—), Soc. Magnetic Resonance in Medicine (exec. com. 1987, sci. program com. 1988-89), Nat. Heart, Lung and Blood Inst. (program project rev. com. A 1984-88, cardiovascular and renal study sect. 1991—), So. Med. Assn., NIH Reviewers Res., U.S. Nuclear Regulatory Commn. (adv. com. 1984—), Assn. Univ. Cardiologists, Assn. Profs. Cardiology (sec. treas. 1994—), Sigma Xi. Home: 4301 Kennesaw Dr Birmingham AL 35213-3311 Office: U Ala Med Ctr THT 311 1900 University Blvd Birmingham AL 35294-0006

POIANI, EILEEN LOUISE, mathematics educator, college administrator, higher education planner; b. Newark, Dec. 17, 1943; d. Hugo Francis and Eileen Louise (Crecca) P. BA in Math., Douglass Coll., 1965; MS in Math., Rutgers U., 1967, PhD in Math., 1971. Teaching asst., grad. preceptor Rutgers U., New Brunswick, N.J., 1966-67; asst. counselor Douglass Coll., New Brunswick, 1967, 69-70; instr. math. St. Peter's Coll., Jersey City, 1967-70, asst. prof., 1970-74, dir. of self-study, 1974-76, assoc. prof., 1974-80, prof., 1980—, asst. to pres., 1976-80; asst. to pres. for planning St. Peter's Coll., 1980—; chairwoman U.S. Commn. on Math. Instrn., NRC of NAS, Washington, 1983-90; founding nat. dir. Women and Math. Lectureship Program, Washington, 1975-81, mem. adv. bd., 1981—; project dir. Consortium for Advancement of Pvt. Higher Edn., Washington, 1986-88; mem. N.J. Math. Coalition, 1991—, Nat. Seminar on Jesuit Higher Edn., 1990-94, mem. strategic planning com. N.J. Assn. Ind. Colls. and Univs., 1990-92; charter trustee Rutgers U., 1992—. Author: (with others) Mathematics Tomorrow, 1981; contbr. articles to profl. jours. Mem. Newark Mus., Nutley (N.J.) Hist. Soc., Friends of Newark Libr.; trustee Nutley Free Pub. Libr., 1974-77, St. Peter's Prep. Sch., Jersey City, 1986-92; active fee arbitration commn. N.J. Supreme Ct., 1983-86, ct. ethics com., 1986-90; U.S. nat. rep. Internat. Congress Math. Edn., Budapest, Hungary, 1988; mem. statewide planning com. NCCJ, 1988-92; chair evaluation teams Mid. States Assn. Coll. and Schs.; mem. U.S. delegation to Internat. Congress on Math; trustee The Cath. Advocate, 1993—. Recipient Douglass Soc. award Douglass Coll., 1982, Outstanding Cmty. Svc. award Christopher Columbus Found., N.J., 1994, Outstanding Svc. award Middle States Assn. Colls. and Schs., 1994, Cert. of Appreciation in Reconition of Outstanding Contbns. as Nat. Dir. of Women and Math. Program, 1993; named Danforth Assoc., Danforth Found., 1972-86. Mem. AAUP, Math. Assn. Am. (bd. dirs. lectureship program, gov. N.J. chpt. 1972-79, chair human resources coun. 1991—, Outstanding Coll. Tchg. award 1993), Am. Math. Soc., Nat. Coun. Tchrs. Math. (spkr. 1974—), Soc. Coll. and Univ. Planning (program com. 1989—, spkr. nat. conf. 1986, 88, 89, 90, judge grad. paper competition), Pi Mu Epsilon (1st woman pres. in 75 yrs. 1987-90, C.C. MacDuffee award for disting. svc. and to math. 1995). Roman Catholic. Avocations: gourmet cook, traveling, biking. Office: St Peter's Coll 2641 Kennedy Blvd Jersey City NJ 07306

POILE, DAVID ROBERT, professional hockey team executive; b. Toronto, Ont., Can., Feb. 14, 1949; s. Norman Robert and Margaret (Elizabeth) P.; m. Elizabeth Ramey, July 4, 1971; children: Brian Robert, Lauren Elizabeth. B.S., Northeastern U., 1971. Asst. mgr. Atlanta Flames, 1971-80, Calgary Flames, Alta., Can., 1980-82; gen. mgr., v.p. Washington Capitals, Landover, Md., 1982—. Office: Washington Capitals Usair Arena Landover MD 20785*

POINDEXTER, BEVERLY KAY, media and communications professional; b. Noblesville, Ind., Nov. 12, 1949; d. Wayne Francis and Rosalie Christine (Nightenhelser) Hunter; m. Jerry Roger Poindexter, Dec. 7, 1969; children: Nick Ashley, Tracy Lynne, Wendy Dawn, Cory Matthew. Student, Purdue U. Editor Tri Town Topics Newspaper, 1965-69; reporter, photographer Noblesville Daily Ledger, 1969-70; asst. mgr., sales mgr., sports dir. Sta. WHYT Radio, Noblesville, Ind., 1973-79; sales mgr., music dir., DJ, news Sta. WBMP Radio, Elwood, Ind., 1979-88; acct. exec. Sta. WAXT-WHBU Radio, Anderson, Ind., 1988-89; gen. mgr., sales mgr. Sta. WEWZ, Elwood, Ind., 1989-90; now news stringer Sta. WRTV-6, Indpls., Sta. WTHR TV-13, Indpls.; acct. exec. Sta. WLHN Radio, Elwood, Ind.; real estate broker Booker Realty, Cicero, Ind., 1990—. Area rep. Am. Field Svc., Hamilton County, Ind.; pres. bd. dirs. Hamilton Heights Elem. Football, Arcadia, Ind., 1981-83; founder, chmn. Hamilton Heights Elem. Cheerleaders, Arcadia, 1981-87; youth leader, counselor Ch. of the Brethren, Arcadia, 1991-94; active Ch. of Brethren Women's Fellowship. Mem. Nat. Assn. Realtors, Ind. Assn. Realtors, Met. Indpls. Bd. Realtors. Republican. Avocations: horseback riding, canoeing, swimming, singing, dancing. Home: 14645 E 281st St Atlanta IN 46031-9722 Office: Booker Realty PO Box 437 99 S Peru Cicero IN 46034

POINDEXTER, BUSTER See JOHANSEN, DAVID

POINDEXTER, CHRISTIAN HERNDON, utility company executive; b. Evansville, Ind., Sept. 20, 1938; s. Marlan Glenn and Ellen Mabelle (Sommers) P.; m. Marilyn Ann Mills, June 12, 1960; children: Scott H., Todd S. B.S. in Engring., U.S. Naval Acad., 1960; M.B.A. in Fin., Loyola Coll., Balt., 1976. With Balt. Gas & Electric Co., 1967—, gen. supr. fin. dept., 1976-78, treas., asst. sec., 1978-79, v.p. engring. and constrn., 1980-85; pres., chief exec. officer, dir. Constellation Holdings, Inc. subs. Balt. Gas & Electric Co., 1985-89; vice chmn. bd. Balt. Gas & Electric Co., 1989-93, chmn., CEO, 1993—; chmn. bd., chief exec. officer Constellation Biogas Inc., Constellation Investments Inc., Constellation Properties Inc.; bd. dirs. The KMS Group, Inc., 1986—. Bd. dirs., sec. YMCA of Anne Arundel County, Md., 1985—; bd. dirs., pres. Scholarships for Scholars, Inc.; exec. bd. Balt. Area council Boy Scouts Am.; trustee Md. Acad. Scis., 1984—, Villa Julie Coll., 1986—. Served to lt. USN, 1960-67. Mem. Engring. Soc. Balt., IEEE. Republican. Office: Balt Gas & Electric Co Charles Ctr Baltimore MD 21201*

POINDEXTER, JOHN BRUCE, entrepreneur; b. Houston, Oct. 7, 1944; s. George Emerson and Rose Ellen (McDowell) P.; B.S.B.A. with honors, U. Ark., 1966; M.B.A., N.Y. U., 1971, Ph.D. in Econs. and Fin., 1976. Assoc., Salomon Bros., N.Y.C., 1971-72; v.p. Lombard, Nelson & McKenna, N.Y.C., 1972-73; v.p., registered prin. Dominick & Dominick, Inc., N.Y.C., 1973-76; sr. v.p. Smith Barney Venture Corp., N.Y.C., 1976-83; gen. partner First Century Partnership, N.Y.C., 1980-83; mng. partner KD/P Equities, ptnr. Kellner, DiLeo & Co., N.Y.C., 1983-85; mng. ptnr., J.B. Poindexter and Co., L.P., 1985-94; chmn. bd. dirs. J.B. Poindexter & Co., Inc., 1994—; chmn. bd. dirs. EFP Corp., Truck Accessories Group, Morgan Trailer Mfg. Co., Southwestern Holdings, Inc., Lowy Group, Inc., Magnetic Instruments Inc., Gem Top, Inc., Raider Industries, Inc.; adj. assoc. prof. L.I. U. Author various monographs. Served to capt. U.S. Army, 1966-70; Vietnam. Decorated Silver Star, Bronze Star (2), Purple Heart (2), Soldier's medal, others. Mem. Beta Gamma Sigma, Alpha Kappa Psi. Club: Metropolitan, N.Y.C., Argyle (San Antonio), Coronado (Houston). Office: 1100 Louisiana St Houston TX 77002

POINDEXTER, WILLIAM MERSEREAU, lawyer; b. Los Angeles, June 16, 1925; s. Robert Wade and Irene M. (Mersereau) P.; m. Cynthia Converse Pastushin, Nov. 10, 1979; children: James Wade, David Graham, Honour Hêlenê, Timothy John. B.A., Yale U., 1946; postgrad., U. Chgo., 1946-47; LL.B., U. Calif., Berkeley, 1949. Bar: Calif. 1952. Practiced in San Francisco, 1952-54, Los Angeles, 1954—; mem. firm Poindexter & Doutre, Inc., 1964—; Pres. Consol. Brazing & Mfg. Co., Riverside, Calif., 1949-52. Pres. South Pasadena-San Marino (Calif.) YMCA, 1963; Mem. San Marino Sch. Bd., 1965-69, pres., 1967; pres. Conf. of Ins. Counsel, 1975. Served with USMCR, 1943. Fellow Am. Coll. Probate Counsel; mem. Am., Los Angeles County bar assns., State Bar Calif. Republican. Presbyterian. Clubs: Yale of So. Calif. (pres. 1961), California. Office: 1 Wilshire Bldg Suite 2420 Los Angeles CA 90017

POINTER, SAM CLYDE, JR., federal judge; b. Birmingham, Ala., Nov. 15, 1934; s. Sam Clyde and Elizabeth Inzer (Brown) P.; m. Paula Purse, Oct. 18, 1958; children: Minge, Sam Clyde III. A.B., Vanderbilt U., 1955; J.D., U. Ala., 1957; LL.M., NYU, 1958. Bar: Ala. 1957. Ptnr. Brown, Pointer & Pointer, 1958-70; judge U.S. Dist. Ct. (no. dist.) Ala., Birmingham, 1970-82, chief judge, 1982—; judge Temp. Emergency Ct. Appeals, 1980-87; mem. Jud. Panel Multi-dist. Litigation, 1980-87; mem. Jud. Conf. U.S., 1987-90; mem. Jud. Coun. 11th Cir., 1987-90, mem. standing com. on rules, 1988-90, chmn. adv. com. on civil rules, 1990-93. Bd. editors: Manual for Complex Litigation, 1979-91. Mem. ABA, Ala. Bar Asn., Birmingham Bar Assn., Am. Law Inst., Am. Judicature Soc., Farrah Order of Jurisprudence, Phi Beta Kappa. Episcopalian. Office: US Dist Ct 882 US Courthouse 1729 5th Ave N Birmingham AL 35203-2000

POINTON, MARY LOU, special education educator; b. Ft. Smith, Ark., Aug. 1, 1933; d. Clyde Morgan and Rilla Belle (Prater) Dollar; m. Vernie Rodney Pointon, Oct. 24, 1954; children: Pamela Kaye Pointon McDonald, Susan Gail Pointon Friberg. Assoc. BA, Ft. Smith Jr. Coll., 1953; BS Ed in Speech and English, Tex. Tech U., 1962; MEd in Spl. Edn., East Tex. U., 1989. Cert. real estate agt., appraiser Tex. Real Estate Commn. English and drama tchr. Wolforth (Tex.) H.S., 1962-63; drama tchr. Monterrey H.S., Lubbock, Tex., 1963-64; English and history tchr. Meml. Cath. H.S., Enid, Okla., 1964-66; reading and drama tchr., libr. Covington (Okla.) H.S., 1966-68; spl. edn. tchr. drug abuse unit Mercer Island (Wash.) H.S., 1968-69; English, bus. and drama tchr. LaConner (Wash.) H.S., 1969-72; English tchr. Tehran (Iran) Am. Sch., 1972; v.p., dir. tng. and devel. Mary Lou English Tng. Ctr., Tehran, 1972-78; spl. edn. tchr. Mills Elem. Sch., Midlothian, Tex., 1987-88; tchr. learning difference students Fairhill Sch., Dallas, 1988-93; tutor learning difference students Masterpiece Co., Plano, Tex., 1993—; owner, v.p. Masterpiece Real Estate Co., Duncanville, Tex., 1978-89, Masterpiece Co., Plano, Tex., 1993—. Author: Teacher Training Manual/Individual English Training, 1973, also lang. program, 1972-78. V.p. Duncanville C. of C., 1983-85; mem. polit. action com. Dallas Assn. Realtors, 1982-84. Named Outstanding Mem. of Yr. Duncanville C. of C., 1983. Mem. DAR (v.p., founding mem. Duncanville chpt. 1980-88), NAFE, Nat. Safety Assn. Dallas Coop. (outstanding sales team 1994), Nat. Chrysanthemum Soc., N.W. Ark. Chrysanthemum Club (v.p., founding mem. 1988—). Avocations: plants, flowers, music, reading. Home and Office: 3700 Interlaken Plano TX 75075

POINTS, ROY WILSON, municipal official; b. Quincy, Ill., Oct. 21, 1940; s. Jess C. and Gladys (Wilson) P.; m. Karen Lee Olsen, July 23, 1966; children: Eric, Holly. BBA, Culver Stockton Coll., 1968. Tchr., coach Lewis County C-1, Ewing, Mo., 1968-69, Community Unit 3, Camp Point, Ill., 1969-78; real estate salesman Landmark, Quincy, 1978-80; supr. of assessment County of Adams, Quincy, 1980-90; assessor City Twp. of Quincy, 1990—; mem., chmn. Adams County Bd. Rev., 1977-80. Bd. dirs., 1st v.p., sec. Quincy Jaycees, 1970-76, Quincy Rotary East, 1980. Mem. Cert. Ill. Assessing Officers, Internat. Assn. Assessing Officers (cert. ednl. recognition 1988), Ill. Assessors Assn. (bd. dirs. 1992—), Tri-Twp. Ofcls. Ill. Democrat. Avocations: fishing, hunting, jogging, raising cattle. Office: Quincy Twp Assessor City Hall Annex 706 Maine St Quincy IL 62301-4042

POIRIER, FRANK EUGENE, physical anthropology educator; b. Paterson, N.J., Aug. 7, 1940; s. Frank Eugene and Alice (Apelian) P.; m. Darlene Matsko, July 6, 1963; children—Alyson, Sevanne Cara. B.A., Paterson State Coll., Wayne, N.J., 1962; M.A., U. Oreg., 1964, Ph.D., 1967. Asst. prof. dept. psychiatry U. Fla., 1967-68; prof., chair anthropology Ohio State U., Columbus, 1968—. Co-author: Human Evolution in China, 1995, In Search of Ourselves, 5th edit., 1993, An Introduction to Physical Anthropology and the Archaelogical Record, 1982, Understanding Human Evolution, 3d edit., 1993; editor: Primate Socialization, 1972, (with others) Primate Bio-Social Development, 1977; contbr. articles to profl. jours., chpts. to books. Fellow NIH, 1963-67, NIMH, 1969-70, Fulbright, 1986. Mem. AAAS, Internat. Primatological Soc., Am. Assn. Phys. Anthropologists, Current Anthropology, Am. Soc. Primatologists, Internat. Soc. Cryptozoology, Explorers Club, Sigma Xi. Democrat. Home: 420 Greenglade Ave Columbus OH 43085-2206 Office: Ohio State U Dept Anthropology 124 W 17th Ave Columbus OH 43210-1316

POIRIER, HELEN VIRGINIA LEONARD, elementary education educator; b. Worcester, Mass., Oct. 2, 1954; d. Robert O'Donnell and Rose C. (Pepper) Leonard; m. Paul Nelson Poirier, Aug. 3, 1985. BS, Worcester State Coll., 1976. Cert. tchr. K-6, reading supr. K-12, adminstrn. K-8. Tchr. grade 5-6 reading and social studies Quabbin Regional Sch. Dist., Oakham, Mass., 1980—. Sec. Local Cable Access Com., Auburn, 1985-92. NEH grantee, 1986; town history grantee Oakham Hist. Soc., 1986, Oakham Hist. Commn., 1986. Mem. Cen. Mass. Coun. Social Studies (bd. dirs., sec. 1986-90, treas. 1990—), Hodges Village Environ. Edn. Assn., Tanheath Hunt Club (pres. 1995—, sec./newsletter editor 1988-95). Avocations: horseback riding, fox hunting. Office: Oakham Center Sch Deacon Allen Dr Oakham MA 01068

POIRIER, LOUIS JOSEPH, neurology educator; b. Montreal, Que., Can., Dec. 30, 1918; s. Gustave Joseph and Calixta (Brault) P.; m. Liliane Archambault, June 11, 1947; children—Guy, Michel, Louise, Esther. B.Sc., U. Montreal, 1942, M.D., 1947; Ph.D., U. Mich., 1950; D. (hon.), U. Rennes, France, 1973. Asst. prof. U. Montreal, 1950-55, assoc. prof., 1955-58, prof., faculty of medicine, 1958-65; chmn. dept. anatomy Faculty of Medicine, Laval U., Cité Universitaire, Que., 1970-78; prof. exptl. neurology Faculty of Medicine, Laval U., Cité Universitaire, 1970-83; dir. Centre de Research in Neurobiology, Laval U. and Hosp. de l'Enfant-Jesus, 1977-85, prof. emeritus, 1985—. Contbr. articles to profl. jours.; editor the extrapyramidal system and its disorders in: Advances in Neurology, vol. 24, 1979. Pres. Que. Health Scis. Research Council, 1978-81. Decorated officer Order of Can.; recipient Que. sci. award, 1975; Killam commemorative scholar, 1977, 78. Mem. Royal Soc. Belgium (hon.), Neurol. Soc. France (hon.), AAAS, Am. Assn. Anatomists, Am. Physiol. Soc., Soc. for Neuroscis., Internat. Brain Research Orgn. Address: 603 Chemin Caron, Lac Simon, Montpellier, PQ Canada J0V 1M0

POIROT, JAMES WESLEY, engineering company executive; b. Douglas, Wyo., 1931; m. Raeda Poirot. BCE, Oreg. State U., 1953. With various constrn. firms, Alaska and Oreg.; with CH2M Hill Inc., 1955, v.p., Seattle and Atlanta, from 1967; chmn. bd. CH2M Hill Ltd., Englewood, Colo., 1983-93; former chmn. Western Regional Coun., Design Profls. Coalition, Accreditation Bd. Engring. and Tech., Indsl. Adv. Coun.; former mem. Oreg. Joint Grad. Schs. Engring., Engring. Coun. Named ENR Constrn. Man of Yr., 1988. Fellow ASCE (pres. 1993-94); mem. Am. Cons. Engrs. Coun. (pres. 1989-90), Am. Acad. Environ. Engrs. (diplomate), Am. Assn. Engring Socs. (vice chmn. 1995), Nat. Acad. Engring. (nat. chmn. engrs. week 1994), World Engring. Partnership for Sustainable Devel. (founding dir.), World Fedn. Engring. Orgns. (com. on tech. transfer, pres. 1995-96). Office: CH2M Hill Inc PO Box 22508 Denver CO 80222-0508

POIS, JOSEPH, lawyer, educator; b. N.Y.C., Dec. 25, 1905; s. Adolph and Augusta (Lesser) P.; m. Rose Tomarkin, June 24, 1928 (dec. May 1981); children: Richard Adolph (dec.), Robert August, Marc Howard.; m. Ruth Livingston, Nov. 27, 1983 (div. 1984). A.B., U. Wis., 1926; M.A., U. Chgo., 1927, Ph.D., 1929; J.D., Chgo.-Kent Coll. Law, 1934. Bar: Ill. 1934, Pa. 1978. Staff mem. J.L. Jacobs & Co., Chgo., 1929-35; jr. partner J.L. Jacobs & Co., 1946-47; gen. field supr. Pub. Adminstrn. Service, Chgo., 1935-38; chief adminstrv. studies sect. U.S. Bur. Old Age and Survivors Ins., 1938-39; chief adminstrv. and fiscal reorgn. sect. U.S. Bur. Budget Exec. Office of Pres., 1939-42; dir. finance State of Ill., 1951-53; counsel, asst. to pres., v.p., treas., dir. Signode Corp., 1947-61; prof. U. Pitts., 1961-76, emeritus, 1976—, chmn. dept. pub. adminstrn., 1961-71, assoc. dean, 1973-75; dir. Vision Service Plan of Pa., 1984-85; cons. ECA, 1948, Dept. State, 1949, 62-65, U.S. Dept. Def., 1954, Brookings Instn., 1962-63, AID, 1965, Indian Inst. Pub. Adminstrn., 1972, Commn. on Operation Senate, 1976, Pitts. Citizens' Task Force on Refuse Disposal, 1976-78; mem. cons. panel Comptroller Gen. of U.S., 1967-75. Author: The School Board Crisis: a Chicago Case Study, 1964, Financial Administration in the Michigan State Government, 1938, Kentucky, Handbook of Financial Administration, 1937, Public Personnel Administration in the City of Cincinnati, 1936, (with Edward M. Martin and Lyman S. Moore) The Merit System in Illinois, 1935, Watchdog on the Potomac: A Study of the Comptroller General of the United States, 1979; contbg. author: The New Political Economy, 1975, State Audit-Developments in Public Accountability, 1979. Mem. Chgo. Bd. Edn., 1956-61; pres. Chgo. Met. Housing and Planning Council, 1956-57, Immigrants Service League, Chgo., 1960-61; dir. Pitts. Council Pub. Edn., 1965-67; mem. citizens bd. U. Chgo., 1958-78; mem. Pitts. Bd. Pub. Edn., 1973-76; bd. dirs. Pitts. Center for Arts, 1977-85, World Federalist Assn. Pitts., 1984—, Pitts. dist. Zionist Orgn. Am., 1979-81, mem. Hunger Action Coalition, Pitts., 1985-86; mem. Allegheny County Bd. Assistance, 1981-90, chmn. 1981-87. Served from comdr. to capt. USCGR, 1942-46. Decorated Navy Commendation medal; recipient alumni citation for pub. service U. Chgo., 1960; award for pub. service U.S. Gen. Accounting Office, 1971. Mem. ABA, FBA, ASPA (award for pub. svc. Pitts. area chpt. 1995), Am. Polit. Sci. Assn., Ctr. for Study of the Presidency, Govt. Fin. Officers Assn., Fin. Execs. Inst., Inst. Mgmt. Accts., Chgo. Bar Assn., U. Chgo. Alumni Club (pres. Pitts. chpt. 1981-84), Army and Navy Club, Allegheny County Bar Assn., Phi Beta Kappa, Pi Lambda Phi, Phi Delta Phi. Home: 825 Morewood Ave Pittsburgh PA 15213-2950

POISSANT, CHARLES-ALBERT, paper manufacturing company executive; b. Montreal, Sept. 13, 1925; m. Florence Drouin, June 12, 1951; children: Louise, Marc-André Hélène, Isabelle. Chartered acct., U. Montreal, 1953. Chartered acct, Que. Ptnr., pres. Poissant Thibault affiliate Peat Marwick Thorne, Montreal, 1947-87; chmn., CEO Donohue, Inc., Québec City, Que., 1987-92, chmn. bd., 1992—; bd. dirs., mem. exec. com. Quebecor, Inc., Montreal, Premier Choix: TVEC, Inc., Orchestre Metropolitain, Hopital du Sane-Coeur de Montreal; bd. dirs. Found. de l'Universite de Que., Montreal, Can. Pulp and Paper Assn. Author: Taxation in Canada of Non-residents, 1976, Commentary on Canada-Germany Tax Agreement, 1976, How to Think Like a Millionaire, 1985 (transl. into 7 langs.). Mem. Can. Pulp and Paaper assn. (bd. dirs., mem. exec. com.), Club St. Denis, Laval sur-le-Lac. Roman Catholic. Avocations: golf, downhill skiing. Home: 333 Somerville, Ahuntsic, PQ Canada H3L 1A4 Office: Donohue Inc, 612 St-Jacques, Montreal, PQ Canada H3C 4M8

POIST, WILLIAM G., diversified financial service company executive; b. 1933. BA in Bus. & Indsl. Mgmt., Johns Hopkins U., 1955; MBA in Mktg., Boston U., 1965. Active with parent cos. and subsidiaries COM/Energy Svcs. Co., Cambridge, Mass., 1971-92, pres., CEO, 1992—. Office: COM / Energy Svcs Co PO Box 9150 Cambridge MA 02142

POITEVENT, EDWARD BUTTS, II, lawyer; b. New Orleans, Oct. 19, 1949; s. Eads and Elizabeth (Schramm) P.; m. Julia Dunbar Baños, Dec. 29, 1972; children: Sarah Dunbar,Elizabeth Grehan, Edward Scott, Mary McCutchen. BA, Tulane U., 1971, JD, 1974. Assoc. Jones, Walker, Waechter, Poitevent, Carrere & Denegre, New Orleans, 1974-79, ptnr., 1979-91; ptnr. Phelps Dunbar, New Orleans, 1991—; mem. ad hoc com. Pipeline div. La. Office of Conservation; mem. adv. coun. La. Mineral Law Inst. Mem. editorial bd. Oil and Gas Law and Taxation Rev.; contbr. articles to profl. jours.; presenter in field. Pres. La. chpt. Leukemia Soc. Am., Inc., New Orleans, 1991; trustee Ea. Mineral Law Found., 1988-93; co-chmn. oil and gas sect. Rocky Mountain Mineral Law Found. 36th Ann. Inst., Santa Fe; trustee-at-large Rocky Mountain Mineral Law Found., 1995—. Mem. ABA (sect. on natural resources, energy and environ. law natural gas and oil coms., litigation sect. energy litigation com., chair program com., editor energy litigation com. newsletter, chair energy litigation com. natural gas mktg. and trans. com., mem. coun. 1994—, mem. nominating com. 1995—), La. State Bar Assn., Fed. Energy Bar Assn., Am. Assn. Petroleum Landmen (chair ad hoc com. on model form gas Balancing Agreement). Republican. Roman Catholic. Office: Phelps Dunbar 28th Fl 400 Poydras St Fl 28 New Orleans LA 70130-3245

POITIER, SIDNEY, actor, director; b. Miami, Fla., Feb. 20, 1927; s. Reginald and Evelyn (Outten) P.; m. Juanita Hardy (div.); children: Beverly, Pamela, Sherri, Gina; m. Joanna Shimkus; children: Anika, Sydney. Ed. pub. schs., The Bahamas. Ind. stage, screen, TV actor, 1948—; bd. dirs. Walt Disney Co. Appeared at Am. Negro Theater in numerous prodns. including: Days of Our Youth, Strivers Road, You Can't Take It With You; various roles in Broadway prodns. including: Anna Lucasta, 1948, A Raisin in the Sun, 1959; films include: No Way Out, 1950, Cry, the Beloved Country, 1951, Red Ball Express, 1952, Blackboard Jungle, 1955, Something of Value, 1957, Edge of the City, Band of Angels, 1958, The Defiant Ones, 1958; film adaptation of Porgy and Bess, 1959, A Raisin in Sun, 1960, Paris Blues, 1960, Pressure Point, 1962, The Long Ships, 1964, Lilies of the Field, 1963 (Acad. award Best Actor), The Greatest Story Ever Told, 1965, Slender Thread, 1965, Duel of Diablo, To Sir With Love, 1967, In the Heat of the Night, 1967, Guess Who's Coming to Dinner, 1967, The Lost Man, 1968, For the Love of Ivy, 1968, They Call Me Mr. Tibbs, 1969, The Organization, 1971, Brother John, 1971, The Wilby Conspiracy, 1975, Little Nikita, 1987, Shoot to Kill, 1988, Sneakers, 1992; star, dir.: Buck and the Preacher, 1972, A Warm December, 1973, Uptown Saturday Night, 1974, Let's Do It Again, 1975, A Piece of the Action, 1977; dir.: Stir Crazy, 1980, Hanky Panky, 1982, Fast Forward 1984, Ghost Dad, 1990; TV mini series Separate But Equal, 1991, Children of the Dust, 1995; TV movie To Sir With Love II, 1996; author: This Life, 1981. Served with 1267th Med. Detachment AUS, 1944-45. Decorated knight comdr. Order Brit. Empire; recipient Silver Bear award Berlin Film Festival, 1958, N.Y. Film Critics award and Acad. award nomination for The Defiant Ones, 1958, Best Actor award For Love of Ivy, San Sebastian Film Festival, 1968, Am. Film Inst. Lifetime Achievement award, 1992, Kennedy Ctr. Honors, 1995. Office: CAA 9830 Wilshire Blvd Beverly Hills CA 90212-1804

POJETA, JOHN, JR., geologist; b. N.Y.C., Sept. 9, 1935; s. John and Emilie (Pilat) P.; m. Mary Louise Eberz, June 23, 1957; children: Kim Louise, John Martin. B.S., Capital U., Columbus, Ohio, 1957; M.S., U. Cin., 1961, Ph.D., 1963. Teaching fellow U. Cin., 1957-63; geologist U.S. Geol. Survey, 1963—, chief lower paleozoic studies unit, 1969-74, chief br. paleontology and stratigraphy, 1989-94; assoc. prof., lectr. George Washington U., 1965-74; research assoc. Smithsonian Instn., 1969—; U.S. Geol. Survey-Australian Bur. Mineral Resources exchange scientist, 1974-75. Author papers in field. Pres. Potomac Woods Citizens Assn.; mem. area 4 council Montgomery County (Md.) Bd. Edn.; mem. bd. Citizens for Good Govt.; trustee Paleontol. Research Instn., 1976-85, v.p., 1978-79, pres., 1980-82. Fellow Geol. Soc. Am., AAAS (coun.); mem. Paleontol. Soc. (sec. 1982-88, pres. 1989-90), Assn. Australasian Paleontologists. Home: 1492 Dunster Ln Rockville MD 20854-6119 Office: US Geol Survey Rm E-308 MRC137 Mus Natural History Washington DC 20560

POKELWALDT, ROBERT N., manufacturing company executive; b. North Tonawanda, N.Y.. BS, SUNY, Buffalo, 1960. With York Internat. Corp., 1983—, pres., chief exec. officer, 1991—, now also chmn., dir. Office: York Internat Corp 631 S Richland Ave York PA 17403-3445*

POKEMPNER, JOSEPH KRES, lawyer; b. Monessen, Pa., June 11, 1936; s. Leonard and Ethel Lee (Kres) P.; m. Judith Montague Stephens, Aug. 23, 1970; children: Elizabeth, Jennifer, Amy. AB, Johns Hopkins U., 1957; LLB, U. Md., 1962. Bar: Md. 1962. Law clk. to judge Supreme Bench Balt., 1960-62; field atty. 5th region NLRB, 1962-64; pvt. practice labor law Balt., 1964—; ptnr. Wolf, Pokempner & Hillman, Balt., 1972-86, Whiteford, Taylor & Preston, Balt., 1986—. Contbr. articles to legal jours. Capt. AUS, 1969-74. Mem. ABA, Fed. Bar Assn. (pres. Balt. chpt. 1979-80), Md. Bar Assn., Balt. Bar Assn. (pres. 1984-85), Serjeant's Inn Law Club. Jewish. Home: 1500 Willow Ave Baltimore MD 21204

POKORNY, JAN HIRD, architect; b. Brno, Czechoslovakia, May 25, 1914; came to U.S., 1940, naturalized, 1945; s. Jaroslav and Theresia (Harrer) P.; m. Marise Angelucci, 1967; 1 son, Stefan Alexander. Engr.-Architect, Tech. U., Prague, 1937; M.S. in Architecture, Columbia U., 1941. Gen. practice architecture Prague, 1938-39; designer Winn-Roensch & Brezner, Detroit, 1942, Leo Bauer, Detroit, 1942-44, Skidmore, Owings & Merrill, N.Y.C., 1944-45; owner firm Jan Hird Pokorny (architect), N.Y.C., 1945-71, 77—; partner Pokorny & Pertz, 1971-77; Assoc. prof. Columbia Sch. Architecture, 1958-74, dir. evening program in architecture, 1957-73, prof. architecture Grad. Sch. Architecture, Planning and Preservation, 1974-82, prof. emeritus, 1982—; architect mem. Art Commn. City N.Y., 1973-77, James William Kideney award N.Y. State Assn. of Architects, 1992. Contbr. articles to profl. jours.; prin. works include: Taylor Meml. Library and Reeves Student Union Bldg. at Centenary Coll. for Women, Hackettstown, N.J., Lewisohn

Hall at Columbia U., (with Damaz and Weigel) Student Union Bldg., Adminstrn. Bldg., Library and Fine Arts Bldg. at N.Y. State U., Stony Brook, (with David Todd Assts.) master plan Library, Auditorium and renovated Music Bldg., Speech and Theatre Bldg., Lehman Coll.-City U. N.Y.; housing at Grasslands Westchester Med. Ctr. and housing for Urban Devel. Corp., in Middletown, Elmira and Wayne County, N.Y., Corp. offices for Samuel H. Kress Found., Ambassador's Offices U.S. Mission to UN, Offices John and Marry R. Markle Found.; restoration of: Schermerhorn Row Block, South St., Seaport, N.Y.C., Monsignor McGolrick Park Shelter, Bklyn., Sloppy Louie's Restaurant, South St., Seaport, N.Y.C., Shellens Gallery of Bklyn. History, Bklyn. Hist. Soc., Firemen's Meml., N.Y.C., Church of Incarnation, N.Y.C., Morris-Jumel Mansion, N.Y.C., Century Club Facade, N.Y.C. Bd. dirs. Am. Fund for Czechoslovak Refugees, 1959—, sec., 1964-71, chmn., 1971—; trustee Grand Central Terminal Trust Fund, N.Y.C.; v.p. of Fine Arts Fedn. of N.Y.C., pres. Bohemian Benevolent and Literary Assn., N.Y.C., 1987—. Recipient Ethnic New Yorker award by Mayor of N.Y., 1985, Lifetime Preservation award Columbia Alumni, 1990, Felber Gold medal Czech Tech. U., 1991, award for Morris-Jumel restoration N.Y.C. Landmarks Commn., 1993. Fellow AIA (awards of merit 1955, 61,74, N.Y. state assn. award 1975, Bard award 1985, Arthur Ross award); mem. Nat. Acad. Design. Club: Century Assn. Home and Office: 306 E 51st St New York NY 10022-7803

POKOTILOW, MANNY DAVID, lawyer; b. Patterson, N.J., June 26, 1938; s. Samuel Morris and Ruth (Fuchs) P.; children: Mali, Charyse, Mona, Andrew. BEE, Newark Coll. Engring., 1960; LLB, Am. U., 1964. Bar: Pa. 1964, U.S. Supreme Ct. 1969. Examiner Patent Office, Washington, 1960-64; ptnr. Caesar, Rivise, Bernstein, Cohen & Pokotilow Ltd., Phila., 1965—; lectr. Dickinson Law Sch., various trade assns., expert witness on protection of computer software, patents, trademarks, trade secrets and copyrights; faculty Temple U. Sch. Law, 1985-94. Vol. Support Ctr. for Child Advs., Phila., 1979—; bd. dir., organizer Phila. Bar Assn. 10k Race, Phila., 1980—, Packard Press Road Run Grand Prix, 1986; bd. dirs. Hist. Soc. U.S. Dist. Ct. (ea. dist.) Pa., 1989—. Recipient Chair award for vol. excellence Am. Diabetes Assn., 1991; honored by Support Ctr. for Child Advocates, 1992. Mem. ABA (chmn. proprietary rights in software com., coun. sci. and tech. sect. 1989—), IEEE, Assn. Trial Lawyers Am., Phila. Bar Assn. (bd. govs. 1982-84, chmn. sports and recreation com. 1977—, hon. trustee campaign for qualified judges 1993), Phila. Patent Law Assn. (bd. govs. 1982-84, chmn. fed. practice and procedure com. 1983-88), Phila. Trial Lawyers (chmn. fed. cts. com. 1986-90), Lawyers Club Phila. (bd. govs. 1984-94, chmn. publicity 1994—), Pa. Trial Lawyers, Tau Epsilon Rho (vice chancellor Phila. grad. chpt. 1986-88, chancellor 1988-90). Office: Caesar Rivise Bernstein Cohen & Pokotilow Ltd 1635 Market St Philadelphia PA 19103-2217

POLACCO, PATRICIA, children's author, illustrator. Works include (juevniles) Meteor!, 1987, Rechenka's Eggs, 1988, The Keeping Quilt, 1988, Uncle Vova's Tree, 1989, Boatride with Lillian Two-Blossom, 1989, Thunder Cake, 1990, Just Plain Fancy, 1990, Babushka's Doll, 1990, Some Birthday!, 1991, Appelemando's Dreams, 1991, Picnic at Mudsock Meadow, 1992, Mrs. Katz & Tush, 1992, Chicken Sunday, 1992, The Bee Tree, 1993, Babushka Baba Yaga, 1993, Tikvah Means Hope, 1994, Pink & Say, 1994, My Rotten Readheaded, Older Brother, 1994, Firetalking, 1994, My Ol' Man, 1995, Babushka's Mother Goose, Aunt Chip and the Great Triple Creek Dam Affair, 1995; illustrator: Casey at the Bat, 1992. Office: Putnam Pub Group 200 Madison Ave New York NY 10016-3903

POLAK, ELIJAH, engineering educator, computer scientist; b. Bialystok, Poland, Aug. 11, 1931; came to U.S., 1957, naturalized, 1977; s. Isaac and Fruma (Friedman) P.; m. Virginia Ann Gray, June 11, 1961; children: Oren, Sharon. B.S.E.E., U. Melbourne, Australia, 1957; M.S.E.E., U. Calif., Berkeley, 1959, Ph.D., 1961. Instrument engr. ICIANZ, Melbourne, Australia, 1956-57; summer student IBM Research Labs., San Jose, Calif., 1959-60; vis. asst. prof. M.I.T., fall 1964; asso. dept elec. engring. and computer scis. U. Calif., Berkeley, 1958-61; asst. prof. elec. engring. and computer scis. U. Calif., 1961-66, asso. prof., 1966-69, prof., 1969-94, prof. Grad. Sch., 1994—. Author: (with L.A. Zadeh) System Theory, 1969, (with E. Wong) Notes for a First Course on Linear Systems, 1970, (with others) Theory of Optimal Control and Mathematical Programming, 1970, Computational Methods in Optimization, 1971. Guggenheim fellow, 1968; U.K. Sci. Research Council sr. fellow, 1972, 76, 79, 82. Fellow IEEE; mem. Soc. Indsl. and Applied Math. (asso. editor Jour. Theory and Applications Optimization 1972—), Soc. Math. Programming. Home: 38 Fairlawn Dr Berkeley CA 94708-2106 Office: U Calif Dept Elec Engring Comp S Berkeley CA 94720

POLAK, JACQUES JACOBUS, economist, foundation administrator; b. Rotterdam, The Netherlands, Apr. 25, 1914; came to U.S., 1940; s. James and Elisabeth F. Polak; m. Josephine Weening, Dec. 21, 1937; children: H. Joost, Willem L. MA in Econs., U. Amsterdam, 1936, PhD in Econs., 1937; PhD in Econs. (hon.), Erasmus U., Rotterdam, 1972. Economist League of Nations, Geneva, Switzerland and Princeton, N.J., 1937-43, Netherlands Embassy, Washington, 1943-44; advisor UN Relief & Rehab. Adminstrn., Washington, 1943-44; from div. chief, asst. dir. to dir. rsch. dept. IMF, Washington, 1947-80, exec. dir., 1981-86; fin. cons. World Bank, Washington, 1987-89, Orgn. Econ. Coop. and Devel., Paris, 1987-89; pres. Per Jacobsson Found., Washington, 1987—; profl. lectr. Johns Hopkins U., Balt., 1949-50, George Washington U., 1950-55. Author: (with J. Tinbergen) The Dynamics of Business Cycles, 1950; author: An International Economic System, 1953, Finanical Policies and Development, 1989, Economic Theory and Financial Policy-The Selected Essays of Jacques J. Polak, 1994; contbr. articles to profl. jours. Fellow Econometric Soc., Royal Netherlands Acad. Sci. (corr.); mem. Cosmos Club (Washington). Home: 3420 Porter St NW Washington DC 20016-3126 Office: care Internat Monetary Fund Washington DC 20431

POLAK, VIVIAN LOUISE, lawyer; b. N.Y.C., Nov. 1, 1952; d. Henri and Greta Etty (Querido) P. BA, Barnard Coll., 1974; JD, Harvard U., 1977. Bar: N.Y. 1978, D.C. 1978, U.S. Dist. Ct. (ea. and so. dists.) N.Y. 1978. Assoc. Donovan, Leisure, Newton and Irvine, N.Y.C., 1977-86; ptnr. LeBoeuf, Lamb, Greene & MacRae, N.Y.C., 1986—. Mem. N.Y. Bar Assn. (sec. antitrust sect. 1991-92, mem. exec. com. 1993-95, chmn. internat. trade com. 1985-90). Office: LeBoeuf Lamb Greene and MacRae 125 W 55th St New York NY 10019-5369

POLAK, WERNER L., lawyer; b. Bremen, Germany, May 19, 1936; came to U.S., 1946, naturalized, 1955; s. Ludwig and Hilde (Schultz) P.; m. Evelyn F. Ruhmann, June 21, 1959; children—Douglas H., Deborah L. B.A., Columbia U., 1960, LL.B., 1963. Bar: N.Y. 1963. Assoc., Shearman & Sterling, N.Y.C., 1963-72, ptnr., 1972—. Served with U.S. Army, 1954-56. Mem. Trustee Practicing Law Inst. Office: 153 E 53rd St New York NY 10022-4602

POLAKIEWICZ, LEONARD ANTHONY, foreign language and literature educator; b. Kiev, Ukraine, Mar. 30, 1938; came to the U.S., 1950; s. Wladyslaw and Aniela (Ossowska) P.; m. Marianne Helen Swanson, Sept. 7, 1963; children: Barbara, Kathryn, Janet. BS in Russian with distinction, U. Minn., 1964, BA in Internat. Rels., 1964; MA in Russian, U. Wis., 1968; cert. Russian area studies, 1969; PhD in Slavic Langs./Lit., U. Wis., 1978; diploma in Polish Curriculum and Instrn., Curie-Sklodowska U., Lublin, Poland, 1981. Instr. U. Minn., Mpls., 1970-78, asst. prof., 1978-90, assoc. prof., 1990—, dir. Inst. Langs., 1991-93, chair Slavic dept., 1993—; vis. asst. prof. U. London, Eng., fall 1984; dir. U. Minn. Polish Lang. Program, Curie-Sklodowska U., Lublin, Poland, summers 1984-89, dir. Polish Faculty Exch., 1988—; dir. Russian Faculty Exch., Herzen Pedagogical U., St. Petersburg, Russia, 1993—; adv. bd. mem. Studia Sienkiewiczowskie, Lublin, 1986—; mem. exec. com. Coun. on Internat. Edn., N.Y.C., 1991-94; mem. Russian Lang. Program Acad. Policy Com. CIEE, N.Y.C., 1994—; mem. nat. task force Polish Studies in Am., Ind. U., 1995—; project dir. Nat. Coun. Orgns. of Less Commonly Taught Langs. Polish Lang. Learning Framework, 1995—. Author: Supplemental Materials for First Year Polish, 1991, Supplemental Materials for Fifteen Modern Polish Short Stories, 1994; assoc. editor Slavic and East European Jour., 1988-94. Bd. dirs. Immigration Hist. Rsch. Ctr., Mpls., 1984-89; co-founder Polish-Am. Cultural Inst., Mpls., 1986; mem. gov.'s Commn. on Ea. Europe, St. Paul, 1991. With U.S. Army, 1961-63. Grantee Kościuszko Found., 1981, Coun. for European Studies grantee Columbia U., 1981, 84, 86, Wasie Found. grantee, 1983, IREX Collaborative Activities and New Exchs. grantee, 1984, Ireland Travel grantee Trinity Coll., Dublin, 1984, Bush Found. Rsch. grantee, 1986-87, grantee U.S. Dept. Edn., 1988-91; Fulbright-Hays Group Projects Abroad grantee for Poland, 1989, USIA U. Linkage grantee for Poland, 1989-93, IREX Short Term Travel grantee, 1995, USIA Coll. & U. Affiliations grantee for Poland, 1995—; recipient Polanie Club of the Twin Cities Merit award, 1982, Curie-Sklodowska U. medal for acad. linkage devel., 1992. Mem. Am. Assn. for the Advancement Slavic Studies, Am. Assn. Tchrs. Slavic and East European Langs. and Lits. (Excellence in Tchg. in U.S. award 1994), Internat. Czeslaw Milosz Soc. (pres. 1984-85), N.Am. Chekhov Soc., Am. Coun. Tchrs. of Russian, Polish Inst. Arts & Scis. Am. (N.Y.C.), Assn. Literary Scholars & Critics. Democrat. Roman Catholic. Avocations: reading, philatelics, genealogy, touring, gardening. Home: 466 Oak St Drive South Vadnais Heights MN 55127

POLAKOFF, ABE, baritone; b. Bucharest, Rumania; s. Sam and Mary P. Ousherenkova; children: David Fred, Mark Evan, Robert Ira; m. Judyth Kanner, Dec. 5, 1992. Civil engring. student, CCNY; profl. tng. program, Am. Theater Wing, 1952-54; student, N.Y. Coll. Music, 1955-57. Dir. Island Opera Players; opera lectr. Arts Couns. (municipalities and schs.); cantor Progressive Shaari Zedek synagogue, Bklyn., 1972-77, Temple Emanuel, Denver, 1984-94. Debuts include Marcello in La Boheme, Milan, Florence, 1960; leading baritone Zurich Opera, 1961-63, numerous appearances with N.Y. Met. Opera, City Opera N.Y., Phila. Lyric Opera, Pitts. Opera, Seattle Opera, Berlin Deutsche Opera, Frankfurt Opera, Cinn. Opera, Hamburg, Munich Staatsoper, Stuttgart Staatsoper, The Netherlands Opera, Cin. Opera, Kansas City Lyric Opera, Canadian Opera Co., others; soloist with Mex. State Symphony Orch., Kalamazoo Symphony Orch., Winston-Salem (N.C.) Symphony, numerous concert and recital appearances. 1st prize winner Am. Theatre Wing Vocal Profl. Scholarship award, 1954, 1st prize winner Am. Opera Auditions, 1960, Silver medal Vercelli (Italy) Internat. singing contest, 1960; Rockefeller Found. grantee, 1961-62; Bayreuth Festival Masterclass scholar. Mem. Cen. Opera Service, Am. Guild Musical Artists (bd. govs.), Actors Equity Assn. Address: 11132 76th Ave Apt 7H Forest Hills NY 11375-6409

POLAKOFF, MURRAY EMANUEL, university dean, economics and finance educator; b. N.Y.C., Dec. 18, 1922; s. Joseph and Elizabeth (Zimmerman) P.; m. Sheila Doreen Brazil, Dec. 23, 1951; children: Michael Anton, Toni. BA summa cum laude, NYU, 1946; MA, Columbia U., 1951, PhD, 1955. Asst. prof. econs. U. Tex., Austin, 1951-57, assoc. prof. econs., 1957-61; prof. econs. and fin. U. Rochester, N.Y., 1961-63; prof., chmn., vice dean Grad. Sch. Bus. Adminstrn. NYU, 1968-71; leading prof., dean Sch. Mgmt. SUNY, Binghamton, 1971-77; prof. econs. and fin., provost U. Md., College Park, 1977-86, dean, 1986-91, dir. internat. devel. and conflict mgmt., 1991-92, prof. emeritus, 1993—; cons. U.S. House Com. on Banking and Currency, Washington, 1964; lectr. and cons. Brazilian Central Banking, Dept. State, São Paulo, 1966-68; chmn. bd. advisors of joint ventures Cen. Inst. Mathematical and Econ. Modelling of Soviet Acad. Scis., USSR and U. Md., College Park, 1989. Editor, contbg. author: Financial Institutions and Markets, 2d edit., 1981; contbr. articles to profl. jours. Scholar Sch. Law Columbia U., N.Y.C., 1946; Fund for Advancement Edn. faculty grantee, 1955-56; Found. Econ. Edn. fellow, summer 1956; Social Sci. Research Council fellow, 1957; Ford Found. faculty research grantee, 1961-62. Mem. Fin. Mgmt. Assn., Phi Beta Kappa. Jewish. Avocations: squash, theater. Office: Ctr Intl Dev & Conflict Mgmt Univ MD Tydings Hall College Park MD 20742

POLAN, ANNETTE LEWIS, artist, educator; b. Huntington, W.Va., Dec. 8, 1944; d. Lake and Dorothy (Lewis) P.; m. Arthur Lowell Fox Jr., Aug. 31, 1969 (div. 1994); children: Courtney Van Winkle Fox, Arthur Lowell Fox III. 1st degree, Inst. des Profs. de Francaise, Paris, 1965; BA, Hollins Coll., 1967; postgrad., Corcoran Sch. Art, 1968-69. Vis. artist Art Therapy Italia, Vignale, Italy, 1986; dir. summer program La Napoule Art Found., Chateau de la Napoule, France, 1987, 88, 90; guest lectr. China, Japan, 1989, Australia, 1996; prof. Corcoran Sch. Art, Washington, 1974—; chmn. painting dept. Corcoran Coll. Art, Washington, 1991—; dir. Washington Project for the Arts. Illustrator: Say What I Am, 1989, Relearning the Dark, 1991; cover designer Doers of the Word, 1995; portrait commns. include Sandra Day O'Connor, Va. Gov. Gaston Caperton. Bd. dirs. Washington Project for the Arts, 1994—. Mem. Corcoran Faculty Assn. (pres. 1988-89). Avocations: equitation, skiing. Office: Corcoran Sch Art 1680 Wisconsin Ave NW Washington DC 20007-2707

POLAN, MARY LAKE, obstetrics and gynecology educator; b. July 17, 1943. Student, Smith Coll., Paris, 1963-64; BA cum laude, Conn. Coll., 1965; PhD in Biophysics and Biochemistry, Yale U., 1970, MD, 1975. Diplomate Am. Bd. Ob-Gyn., Am. Bd. Reproductive Endocrinology, Nat. Bd. Med. Examiners. Postdoctoral fellow dept. biology, NIH postdoctoral fellow Yale U., New Haven, 1970-72, resident dept. ob-gyn. Sch. Medicine, 1975-78, fellow in oncology, then fellow in endocrinology-infertility, 1978-80, asst. instr., then lectr. molecular biophysics-biochemistry, 1970-72, instr., then asst. prof. ob-gyn., 1978-79, 80-85, assoc. prof., 1985-90; clin. clk. in ob-gyn. and pediat. Radcliffe Infirmary, Oxford (Eng.) U. Med. Sch., 1974; instr. Pahlavi U., Shiraz, Iran, 1978; Katharine Dexter McCormick and Stanley McCormick Meml. prof. Stanford (Calif.) Sch. Medicine, 1990—, chmn. dept. gynecology and obstetrics, 1990—; vis. prof. Hunan Med. Coll., Changsha, China, 1986; mem. med. bd. Yale-China Assn., 1987-90; liaison com. on ethics in modern world Conn. Coll., New London, 1988-90; mem. med. adv. bd. Ova-Med Corp., Palo Alto, Calif., 1992—, Vivus, Menlo Park, Calif., 1993—; bd. dirs. Metra Biosys., Palo Alto, Quidel, San Diego, LipoMatrix, Palo Alto, Stanford Health Svcs., 1994—; mem. reproductive endocrinology study sect. NIH, 1989-90, co-chmn. task force on opportunities for rsch. on woman's health, 1991. Author: Second Seed, 1987; guest editor: Seminars in Reproductive Endocrinology, 1984, Infertility and Reproductive Medicine Clinics of North America: GnRH Analogues, Vol. 4, 1993; editor; (with A.H. DeCherney) Surgery in Reproductive Endocrinology, 1987, (with DeCherney, S. Boyers and R. Lee) Decision Making in Infertility; ad hoc reviewer Jour. Clin. Endocrinology and Metabolism, Fertility and Sterility, Ob-Gyn., also others; contbr. numerous articles to med. jours., chpts. to books. Fellow NRSA, 1981-82; grantee NIRA, 1082-85, HD, 1985-90, NRSA, 1987-88, Johnson & Johnson, 1993-96; scholar Assn. Acad. Health Ctrs., 1993—. Fellow ACOG (PROLOG task force for reproductive endocrinology and infertility 1988-89, rep. to CREOG coun. 1994-97); mem. Am. Fertility Soc., Soc. for Gynecologic Investigation, Soc. for Reproductive Endocrinologists, Am. Gynecologic and Obstetric Soc., Inst. Medicine (com. on rsch. capabilities of acad. depts. ob-gyn. 1990-91, bd. on health scis. policy 1992—), San Francisco Gynecologic Soc., Bay Area Reproductive Endocrine Soc., Phi Beta Kappa. Home: 4251 Manuela Ct Palo Alto CA 94306-3731 Office: Stanford U Sch Medicine 300 Pasteur Dr Rm Hh333 Stanford CA 94305-2203*

POLAN, MORRIS, librarian; b. St. Louis, Jan. 24, 1924; s. Jacob and Fannie (Poe) P.; m. Cecelia Hassan, Nov. 16, 1947 (div. 1974); children: Miriam, Ruth. Student, So. Ill. U., 1941-42; B.A., UCLA, 1949; postgrad., 1949-50; M.S. in L.S, U. So. Calif., 1951. Libr. Mcpl. Reference Libr., L.A., 1951-52; serials and reference libr. Hancock Libr. of Biology and Oceanography, U. So. Calif., L.A., 1952-55; periodicals libr. Calif. State U., L.A., 1955, supervising reference libr., 1956-57, chief reader svcs., 1958-64, acting coll. libr., 1965, univ. libr., 1966-89, univ. libr. emeritus, 1989—; libr. and media resources cons., 1990—; publs. coord. Edmund G. "Pat" Brown Inst. Pub. Affairs, 1992-94, pub. affairs and publs. coord., 1995—; univ. adminstr. Ctr. Pub. Resources Calif. State U., 1980-86, mem. chancellor's library adv. com., 1984; lectr. library sci. U. So. Calif., 1967; mem. chancellor's library personnel study com. Calif. State Univs. and Colls., 1969, mem. adv. com. library devel., 1974; chmn. Council Calif. State Univ. and Colls. Library Dirs., 1967-68, 70, 74; Mem. adv. bd. U. So. Calif. Library Sch., 1966-69, Productivity Council of Southwest, 1981-84; mem. library edn. adv. com. U. Calif. System, 1966-70; mem. U. Calif.-Calif. State Univ. and Colls. Task Force on Library Co-op., 1974-76; co-founder Los Angeles Coop. Library Consortium, 1983. Editor: California Librarian, 1971-74. Mem. Com. to Advise Gov. on State Librarian, 1972; mem. planning com. Calif. Library Authority for Systems and Services, 1973-75, adv. council, 1977-80, long range planning group, 1979-81, pres. congress of mems., 1979; mem. adv. bd. Arnold Schoenberg Ins., U. So. Calif., 1974-86, 89-92, Edmund G. (Pat) Brown Inst. Pub. Affairs, 1987-89; exec. com. Roy Harris Archive, 1978-86; mem. Mayor's Blue Ribbon Com. on L.A. Pub. Libr., 1976-77; mem. bd. scholars El Pueblo State Hist. Park, 1978-91; chmn. Calif. del. White House Conf. on Libraries and Info. Services, 1979; bd. dirs. ETHIKON: Inst. Study Ethical Diversity, 1981-88; Calif. state coord. Ctr. for the Book in Library of Congress, 1986-89; mem. adv. com. Ctr. for Study of Media and Values, 1988-90; treas. Frank Casado Meml. Scholarship Fund, 1992-95. With USAF, 1943-46. Mem. ALA, Calif. Library Assn. (pres. 1975, chmn. govt. relations com. 1977). Office: Calif State U 5151 State University Dr Los Angeles CA 90032-4221

POLAN, NANCY MOORE, artist; b. Newark, Ohio; d. William Tracy and Francis (Flesher) Moore; m. Lincoln Milton Polan, Mar. 28, 1934; children: Charles Edwin, William Joseph Marion. AB, Marshall U., 1936. One-man shows include Charleston Art Gallery, 1961, 67, 73, Greenbrier, 1963, Huntington Mus. Art, 1963, 66, 71, N.Y. World's Fair, 1965, W.Va. U., 1966, Carroll Reese Mus., 1967; exhibited in group shows Am. Watercolor Soc., Allied Artists of Am., Nat. Arts Club, 1968-74, 76-77, 86, 87, 91-95, Pa. Acad. Fine Arts, Opening of Creative Arts Center W.Va. U., 1969, Internat. Platform Assn. Art Exhibit, 1968-69, 72-74, 74, 79, 85-86, 88-90, (Gold medal Best of Show 1991, 2d award painting 1994, 1st award watercolor), Allied Artists W.Va., 1968-69, 86, Joan Miro Graphic Traveling Exhbn., Barcelona, Spain, 1970-71, XXI Exhibit Contemporary Art, La Scala, Florence, Italy, 1971, Rassegna Internazionale d'Arte Grafica, Siena, Italy, 1973, 79, 82, Opening of Parkersburg (W.Va.) Art Center, 1975, Art Club Washington, 1992, Pen & Brush, 1992-93, others. Hon. v.p. Centro Studie Scambi Internazionale, Rome, Italy, 1977. Recipient Acad. of Italy with Gold medal, 1979, 86, Norton Meml. award 3d Nat. Jury Show Am. Art, Chautauqua, N.Y., 1960; Purchase prize, Jurors award, Watercolor award Huntington Galleries, 1960, 61; Nat. Arts Club for watercolor, 1969; Gold medal Masters of Modern Art exhbn., La Scala Gallery, Florence, 1975, gold medal Accademia Italia, 1984, 1986, diploma Internat. Com. for World Culture and Arts, 1987, Philip Isenberg Watercolor award Pen & Brush, 1995, many others. Mem. AAUW, DAR, Nat. Mus. Women Artists (charter), Allied Artists W.Va., Internat. Platform Assn. (3rd award-painting in ann. art exhbn. 1977, Gold medal for Best of Show 1991, 1st award for painting 1994), Huntington Mus. Fine Arts (life), Tri-State Arts Assn. (Equal Merit award 1978), Sunrise Found., Composers, Authors, Artists Am., Inc., Pen and Brush (Watercolor exhbn. 1993, Grumbacher golden palette mem., Grumbacher award 1978), W.Va. Watercolor Soc. (charter mem.), Nat. Arts Club, Leonardo da Vinci Acad. (Rome), Accademia Italia, Vero Beach Arts Club, Riomar Bay Yacht Club, Guyan Golf and Country Club, Huntington Cotillion (charter mem.), Mass. Hist. Soc. (hon.), Sigma Kappa. Episcopalian. Address: 2106 Club Dr Vero Beach FL 32963-2154 also: 2 Prospect Dr Huntington WV 25701

POLAND, DONNA LEE, elementary education educator; b. Appleton City, Mo.; d. Earnest Loyd and Evon Gladys (Medearis) Reed; m. Gary Keel Poland, May 24, 1969; children: Christina Lynn Wilkerson, Matthew Keel, Gari Dawn Jackson. BA in Bus. Edn., S.W. Bapt. U., 1967; elem. cert., Ottawa (Kans.) U., 1992. Cert. secondary bus., Mo., Kans.; cert. elem., Kans. Bus. edn. tchr. Butler (Mo.) H.S., 1967-72; substitute tchr. USD 368 Schs., Lakemary Ctr. for Exceptional Students, Paola, Kans., 1974-90; part-time libr. Paola (Kans.) Free Libr., 1993-94; chpt. one math tchr. 3rd and 4th grade Osawatomie (Kans.) East Elem., 1994-95, title one math and comms. tchr. 3rd and 5th grade, 1995-96. Mem. Nat. Coun. Tchrs. Math., East Ctrl. Kans. Reading Assn. Baptist. Avocations: genealogy, reading, knitting, gardening. Home: 1009 N Pearl St Paola KS 66071-1141 Office: East Elem Sch Fifth and Pacific Osawatomie KS 66064

POLAND, PHYLLIS ELAINE, secondary school educator, consultant; b. Norwood, Mass., May 10, 1941; d. Kenneth Gould Vale and Mildred Eloise (Fisk) Arnold; m. Thomas Charles Poland, June 6, 1968 (div. Nov. 1991); 1 child, Sherilyn Ann Poland Colon. AB in Math., Ea. Nazarene Coll., 1963; BS in Math., Nova U., 1986. Cert. secondary tchr., Fla. H.S. math. tchr. Burrillville, R.I., 1963-64; jr. H.S. math. tchr. Quincy, Mass., 1964-65; math. tchr. Seekonk (Mass.) H.S., 1965-68, Howard Jr. H.S., Orlando, Fla., 1968-74, Lake Highland Prep. Sch., Orlando, Fla., 1977-81, Lake Brantley H.S., Altamonte Springs, Fla., 1981—. Mem. coun. Joy Club Ctrl. Nazarene Ch., 1988—, adult edn. sec., 1990—, mem. choir, 1986—. Grantee NSF, 1969, 70, 71, 72. Mem. NEA. Home: 401 Navarre Way Altamonte Springs FL 32714-2224

POLAND, ROBERT PAUL, business educator, consultant; b. Bowling Green, Ohio, July 11, 1925; s. Donovan and Florence (Buck) P. BS, Bowling Green State U., 1949; MA, Columbia U., 1956; PhD, Mich. State U., 1962. Tchr. Mt. Edgecumbe Vocat. Sch., Alaska, 1949-53, Perrysburg High Sch., Ohio, 1954-58; prof. bus. edn. Mich. State U., East Lansing, 1960-92; cons. in field; leader seminars, presentations, workshops and confs. Author: (textbooks) Processing Medical Documents Using WordPerfect, 1995, Gregg Coll. Typing, 1979, 5th edit., 1984, 6th edit., 1989, Gregg College Keyboarding & Document Processing for Microcomputers, 7th edit., 1994, Gregg College Keyboarding & Document Processing for Electronic Typewriters, 7th edit., 1994, A Teaching-Learning System for Business Education, 1986, College Keyboarding and Document Processing for Windows, 8th edit., 1996, (audiovisual programs) Gregg Typing IPM, 1975, 2d edit., 1985; contbr. numerous articles to profl. jours. Served with USN, 1943-46; PTO. Recipient numerous grants in field; recipient John Robert Gregg award, 1986. Mem. Nat. Bus. Edn. Assn. (pres. 1978-79, exec. bd. dirs. 1969-70, 75-76, 77-80, Outstanding Teaching award 1981, Disting. Svc. award 1980), North-Central Bus. Edn. Assn. (pres. 1975, Disting. Svc. award 1972), Internat. Soc. Bus. Edn. (v.p. 1970-74, pres. U.S. chpt. 1967-69, Recognition of Significant Contbns. to internat. bus. edn. U.S. chpt. 1969), Mich. Bus. Edn. Assn. (pres. 1965-66, Recognition award 1970, Disting. Svc. award 1980), Delta Pi Epsilon , Phi Delta Kappa, Pi Omega Pi. Home: 901 N Harrison Rd East Lansing MI 48823-3020

POLANSKI, ROMAN, film director, writer, actor; b. Paris, Aug. 18, 1933; s. Ryszard and Bule (Katz-Przedborska) P.; m. Barbara Lass (div.); m. Sharon Tate (dec.); m. Emmanuelle Seigner. Student, Art Sch., Cracow, State Film Coll., Lodz. Appeared in children's radio show The Merry Gang, stage prodn. Son of the Regiment; dir. films Two Men and a Wardrobe, 1958, When Angels Fall, 1958, Le Gros et le Maigre, 1960, Knife in the Water, 1962 (Venice Film Festival award), The Mammals, 1963 (Tours Film Festival award), Repulsion, 1965 (Berlin Film Festival award), Cul-de-Sac, 1966 (Berlin Film Festival award), The Vampire Killers, 1967, Rosemary's Baby, 1968, Macbeth, 1971, What?, 1972, Chinatown, 1974 (Best dir. award Soc. film and TV Arts, Prix Raoul-Levy 1975), The Tenant, 1976, Tess, 1980, Pirates, 1986, Frantic (also co-writer), 1988, Bitter Moon, 1994, Death and the Maiden, 1994; actor: on stage The Metamorphosis, 1988, in films A Generation, The End of the Night, See You Tomorrow, The Innocent Sorcerers, Two Men and a Wardrobe, The Vampire Killers, What?, The Magic Christian and Andy Warhol's Dracula, Back in the U.S.S.R., A Pure Formality, Chinatown, The Tennant; star, dir. play Amadeus, Warsaw, 1981, Paris, 1982; dir. operas Lulu (Spoleto Festival), 1974, Rigoletto, 1976; author (autobiography): Roman, 1984. also: ICM 8942 Wilshire Blvd Beverly Hills CA 90211

POLANSKY, LARRY PAUL, court administrator, consultant; b. Blkyn., July 24, 1932; s. Harry and Ida (Gershengoren) P.; m. Eunice Kathryn Neun; children: Steven, Harriet, Bruce. BS in Acctg., Temple U., 1958, JD, 1973. Bar: Pa. 1973, U.S. Dist. Ct. (ea. dist.) Pa. 1973, U.S. Ct. Appeals (3d cir.) 1973, D.C. 1978, U.S. Supreme Ct. 1980. Acct., systems analyst City of Phila., 1956-63; data processing mgr. Jefferson Med. Coll. and Hosp., Phila., 1963-65; systems engr. IBM Corp., Phila., 1965-67; dep. ct. adminstr. Common Pleas Cts. of Phila., 1967-76; dep. state ct. adminstr. Pa. Supreme Ct., Phila., 1976-78; exec. officer D.C. Cts., Washington, 1979-90; presdl. appt. to bd. dirs. State Justice Inst., 1985-89; bd. dirs. Search Group, Inc. Author: A Primer for the Technologically Challenged Judge, 1995; contbr. articles to profl. jours. Served as cpl. U.S. Army, 1951-53, Korea. Fellow Inst. for Ct. Mgmt., Denver, 1984; recipient Reardon award Nat. Ctr. for State Cts., 1982, Disting. Svc. award Nat. Ctr. for State Cts., 1986, Justice Tom C. Clark award Nat. Conf. of Metro. Cts., 1991. Mem. ABA (jud. adminstrn. divsn., chmn. tech. com. 1991-93, 95, exec. com. lawyers conf. 1985—, chmn. 1991-92, JAD coun. 1994—), Conf. State Ct. Adminstrn. (bd. dirs. 1980-86, pres. 1984-85). Republican. Jewish. Avocations: tennis, skiing, computers. Home and Office: PO Box 752 Lake Harmony PA 18624-0752

POLANYI, JOHN CHARLES, chemist, educator; b. Jan. 23, 1929; m. Anne Ferrar Davidson, 1958; 2 children. BSc, Manchester (Eng.) U., 1949, MSc, 1950, PhD, 1952, DSc, 1964; DSc (hon.), U. Waterloo, 1970, Meml. U., 1976, McMaster U., 1977, Carleton U., 1981, Harvard U., 1982, Rensselaer U., Brock U., 1984, Lethbridge U., Sherbrooke U., Laval U., Victoria U., Ottawa U., 1987, Manchester U. and York U., Eng., 1988, U. Montreal, Acadia U., 1989, Weizmann Inst., Israel, 1989, U. Bari, Italy, 1990, U. B.C., 1990, McGill U., 1990, Queen's U., 1992, Free U. Berlin, 1993, Laurentian U., 1995, U. Toronto, 1995, U. Liverpool, 1995; LLD (hon.), Trent U., 1977, Dalhousie U., 1983, St. Francis-Xavier U., 1984; LLD (hon.), Concordia U., 1990; LLD (hon.), Calgary U., 1994. Mem. faculty dept. chemistry U. Toronto, Ont., Can., 1956—; prof. U. Toronto, 1962—; William D. Harkins lectr. U. Chgo., 1970; Reilly lectr. U. Notre Dame, 1970; Purves lectr. McGill U., 1971; F.J. Toole lectr. U. N.B., 1974; Philips lectr. Haverford Coll., 1974; Kistiakowsky lectr. Harvard U., 1975; Camille and Henry Dreyfus lectr. U. Kans., 1975; J.W.T. Spinks lectr. U. Sask., Can., 1976; Laird lectr. U. Western Ont., 1976; CIL Disting. lectr. Simon Fraser U., 1977; Gucker lectr. Ind. U., 1977; Jacob Bronowski meml. lectr. U. Toronto, 1978; Hutchinson lectr. U. Rochester, N.Y., 1979; Priestley lectr. Pa. State U., 1980; Barré lectr. U. Montreal, 1982; Sherman Fairchild disting. scholar Calif. Inst. Tech., 1982; Chute lectr. Dalhousie U., 1983; Redman lectr. McMaster U., 1983; Wiegand lectr. U. Toronto, 1984; Edward U. Condon lectr. U. Colo., 1984; John A. Allan lectr. U. Alta., 1984; John E. Willard lectr. U. Wis.; 1984, Owen Holmes lectr. U. Lethbridge, 1985; Walker-Ames prof. U. Wash., 1986, John W. Cowper disting. vis. lectr. U. Buffalo, SUNY, 1986; vis. prof. chemistry Tex. A&M U., 1986; Disting. vis. spkr. U. Calgary, 1987; Morino lectr. U. Japan, 1987; J.T. Wilson lectr. Ontario Sci. Ctr., 1987; Welsh lectr. U. Toronto, 1987; Spiers Meml. lectr. Faraday div. Royal Soc. Chemistry, 1987; Polanyi lectr. Internat. Union Pure & Applied Chemistry, 1988; W.B. Lewis lectr. Atomic Energy of Can. Ltd., 1988; Consol. Bathurst vis. lectr. Concordia U., 1988; Priestman lectr. U. N.B., 1988; Killam lectr. U. Windsor, 1988; Herzberg lectr. Carleton U., 1988; Falconbridge lectr. Laurentian U., 1988; DuPont lectr. Ind. U., 1989, C.R. Mueller lectr. Purdue U., 1989; Luther lectr. U. Regina, 1989; Franklin lectr. Rice U., 1990; Laurier lectr. Wilfred Laurier U., 1990; Pratt lectr. U. Va., 1990; Goodrich lectr. Case Western Res. U., 1990; Phillips lectr. U. Pitts., 1991; Albert Noyes lectr. U. Tex., 1992; John and Lois Dove Meml. lectr. U. Toronto, 1992, Fritz London lectr. Duke U., 1993; Castle lectr. U. South Fla., 1993; Linus Pauling lectr. Calif. Inst. Tech., 1994; Hagey lectr. U. Waterloo, 1995; Larkin Stuart lectr. U. Toronto, 1995; Hungerford lectr., 1995, York Club, 1995; disting. lectr. ser. Meml. U., 1995, John C. Polanyi nobel laureate lectr. U. Toronto, 1995, Floyd E. Bartell Meml. lectr. U. Mich., 1996, Christian Culture award lectr. Assumption U., 1996, Liversidge lectr. U. Sidney, Australia, 1996; mem. sci. adv. bd. Max Plank Inst. for Quantum Optics, Fed. Republic Germany, 1982-92; mem. nat. adv. bd. on Sci. and Tech., 1987-89; hon. cons. Inst. Molecular Sci., Okazaki, Japan, 1989-94; bd. dirs. Steacie Inst. Molecular Scis., Ottawa, Can., 1991—; founding mem., pres. Can. Com. of Sci. and Scholars; Beam Disting. vis. prof. U. Iowa, 1992, Charles M. & Martha Hitchcock prof. U. Calif., Berkeley, 1994; Young Meml. visitor Royal Mil. Coll., 1994. Co-editor: (with F.G. Griffiths) The Dangers of Nuclear War, 1979; contbr. articles to jours., mags., newspapers; producer: film Concepts in Reaction Dynamics, 1970. Mem. Queen's Privy Coun. for Can., 1992; bd. dirs. Can. Ctr. for Arms Control and Disarmament; founding mem. Can. Pugwash Com., 1960. Decorated officer Order of Can., companion Order of Can., knight grand cross Order St. John of Jerusalem; recipient Marlow medal Faraday Soc., 1962, Centenary medal Chem. Soc. Gt. Brit., 1965, Noranda award Chem. Inst. Can., 1967, award Brit. Chem. Soc., 1971, Mack award and lectureship Ohio State U., 1969, medal Chem. Inst. Can., 1976, Remsen award and lectureship Am. Chem. Soc., 1978, Nobel Prize in Chemistry, 1986, Izaak Walton Killam Meml. prize, 1988, John C. Polanyi award Can. Soc. Chemistry, 1992, Floyd E. Bartell Meml. lectureship U. Mich., 1996, Liversidge lectureship U. Sydney, Australia, 1996, Christian Culture award and lectureship Assumption U., 1996; co-recipient (with N. Bartlett) Steacie prize, 1965, Wolf prize in chemistry, 1982; named Sloan Found. fellow, 1959-63, Guggenheim fellow, 1979-80 Geoffrey Frew fellow, 1996. Fellow Royal Soc. Can. (founding mem., pres., com. on scholarly freedom, Marshall Tory medal 1977), Royal Soc. London (Royal medal 1989, Bakerian Lectr. and award 1994), Royal Soc. Edinburgh, Royal Soc. Chemistry (hon., Michael Polanyi medal 1989), Chem. Inst. Can. (hon.); mem. NAS (fgn.), Am. Acad. Arts and Sci. (hon. fgn., mem. com. on internat. security studies), Pontifical Acad. Scis., Rome. Office: U Toronto Dept Chemistry, 80 St George St, Toronto, ON Canada M5S 1A1

POLASCIK, MARY ANN, ophthalmologist; b. Elkhorn, W.Va., Dec. 28, 1940; d. Michael and Elizabeth (Halko) Polascik; BA, Rutgers U., 1967; MD, Pritzker Sch. Medicine, 1971; m. Joseph Elie, Oct. 2, 1973; 1 dau., Laura Elizabeth Polascik. Jr. pharmacologist Ciba Pharm. Co., Summit, N.J., 1961-67; intern Billings Hosp., Chgo., 1971-72; resident in ophthalmology U. Chgo. Hosp., 1972-75; practice medicine specializing in ophthalmology, Dixon, Ill., 1975—; pres. McNichols Clinic, Ltd.; cons. ophthalmology, Jack Mabley Devel. Ctr., 1976-93; mem. staff Katherine Shaw Bethea Hosp. Bd. dirs. Sinnissippi Mental Health Ctr., 1977-82, Dixon Cmty. Trust Mental Health Ctr., 1989—. Mem. AMA, Ill. Med. Soc., Ill. Assn. Ophthalmology, Am. Assn. Ophthalmology, Alpha Sigma Lambda. Roman Catholic. Club: Galena Territory. Office: 1700 S Galena Ave Dixon IL 61021-9600

POLASEK, EDWARD JOHN, electrical engineer, consultant; b. Cudahy, Wis., Oct. 12, 1927; s. John Vincent and Mary Ann (Totka) P.; m. Alice S. Nee (Harnecki), Aug. 18, 1948. BSEE, Marquette U., 1948. Registered profl. engr., Wis., Fla. Cons. engr. Eau Claire, Wis., Gainesville, Fla., 1955-60, various countries, Korea, Vietnam, Nicaragua, 1960-72; v.p., dir. Finley Engrng. Co., Eau Claire, 1972-78; pres. Chippewa Devel. Co., Eau Claire, 1978-82; planning engr. Harza Engrng. Co. in Cairo, Egypt and Dominican Rep., 1982-86; cons. engr. Gainesville, 1986—; cons. Lake Altoona Rehab. Dist., Eau Claire, 1974. Author: Planning Methods, 1982, Feasibility Study, 1984; editor: Field Engineer's Handbook, 1982. Chmn. Eau Claire chpt. Am. Cancer Soc.; master gardner U. Fla. Ext. Svc., Gainesville, 1990. With USN, 1944-46, PTO. Mem. Nat. Soc. Profl. Engrs. (pres. 1956), IEEE, Audobon Soc., Tau Beta Pi, Eta Kappa Nu. Avocations: mycology, fishing, arts. Home: 8620 NW 13th St #350 Gainesville FL 32653

POLAYES, IRVING MARVIN, plastic surgeon; b. New Haven, Sept. 2, 1927; s. Abraham Noah and Ida (Stern) P.; m. Marcia Kresel, July 1, 1951 (dec. Apr. 1985); children: Roy Peter, Amy Lynn. BA, Duke U., 1948; DDS, Columbia U., 1953; MD, Albany Med. Coll., 1959. Diplomate Am. Bd. Plastic Surgery. Intern Albany (N.Y.) Med. Ctr., 1959-60, fellow plastic surgery, 1963-65; pvt. practice medicine specializing in plastic and reconstructive surgery Albany (N.Y.) Med. Ctr., New Haven, 1965—; attending plastic surgeon Yale New Haven Med. Ctr., 1965—, assoc. chief plastic surgery, 1969—; attending plastic surgeon St. Raphael's Hosp., New Haven; cons. plastic surgeon West Haven (Conn.) VA Hosp., Gaylord Hosp., Wallingford; clin. prof. plastic and reconstructive surgery Yale Med. Sch., 1977-86. Co-author: Diseases of the Salivary Glands, 1976. Concertmaster, violinist New Haven Civic Symphony Orch., 1970-84—; v.p. New Haven Symphony Orch., 1977—. Lt. comdr. USNR, 1954-56. Fellow ACS; mem. N.E. Soc. Plastic Surgeons (founding mem.), Am. Assn. Plastic Surgeons, Am. Soc. Plastic and Reconstructive Surgeons, Am. Trauma Soc., N.Y. Regional Soc. Plastic and Reconstructive Surgeons (bd. dirs.), New Eng. Soc. Plastic and Reconstructive Surgeons (pres. 1979-80), Am. Soc. Maxillofacial Surgeons (pres. 1979-80, lectr. syllabus-maxillofacial basic course), Soc. Head and Neck Surgeons, Am. Soc. Aesthetic Plastic Surgery, Conn. Med. Soc., New Haven County Med. Soc., Alpha Omega Alpha. Home: 49 N Racebrook Rd Woodbridge CT 06525-1407

POLEBAUM, ELLIOT EDWARD, lawyer; b. Lowell, Mass., Sept. 8, 1950; s. Eugene Harvey and Phyllis Diane (Sherman) P.; m. Gilda Brancato, June 24, 1979; children: Danielle, David. BA, Middlebury Coll., 1972; MPA, Harvard U., 1975; JD, NYU, 1977. Bar: Mass. 1978, N.Y. 1978, D.C. 1981. Law clk. to Judge James L. Oakes, U.S. Ct. Ct., Brattleboro, Vt., 1977-78; assoc. Goodwin, Procter & Hoar, Boston, 1979-80; law clk. to Justice William J. Brennan, Jr., U.S. Supreme Ct., Washington, 1980-81; assoc. Cleary Gottlieb Steen & Hamilton, Washington, 1981-82, 85-86, Brussels, 1982-85; assoc. Fried, Frank, Harris, Shriver, Washington, 1986-89; ptnr. Fried, Frank, Harris, Shriver & Jacobson, Washington, 1989—; arbitrator Am. Arbitration Assn.; speaker on internat. litigation and arbitration issues to profl. programs throughout U.S. and fgn. countries. Contbr. articles to legal jours. Mem. ABA, Internat. Bar Assn. Office: Fried Frank Harris Shriver & Jacobson 1001 Pennsylvania Ave NW Washington DC 20004*

POLEBAUM, MARK NEAL, lawyer; b. Lowell, Mass., May 1, 1952; s. Eugene Harvey and Phyllis Diane (Sherman) P.; m. Diane M. Buhl, June 6, 1982; children: Katherine Elizabeth, Jessica Leigh, Michael William. BA, Middlebury Coll., 1974; JD, NYU, 1978. Bar: Mass. 1979, U.S. Dist. Ct. Mass. 1979. Law clk. to chief judge U.S. Ct. Appeals (5th cir.), Montgomery, Ala., 1978-79; assoc. Hale and Dorr, Boston, 1979-83, jr. ptnr., 1983-86, sr. ptnr., 1986—; counsel bondholders com. in out of ct. restructuring of Swan Brewery, Inc.; counsel bondholders com. in chpt. 11 reorgn. of EUA Power Corp. Mem. appropriations com., City of Lexington, Mass., 1984-88. Watson Found. fellow, 1974-75. Mem ABA (corp., banking and bus. law sects., ad hoc subcom. on scope of uniform comml. code), Mass. Bar Assn., Order of Coif, Phi Beta Kappa. Office: Hale & Dorr 60 State St Boston MA 02109-1803

POLEDOURIS, BASIL K., composer; b. Kansas City, Mo., Aug. 21, 1945; s. Konstantine John and Helen Poledouris; m. Barbara Renée Godfrey, Aug. 15, 1969; children: Zoë Renée, Alexis Elene. BA in Music and Cinema, U. So. Calif., 1967, postgrad., 1967-69. Intern Am. Film Inst., L.A., 1969; freelance composer Hollywood, Calif., 1970—; pres. Basil Poledouris, Inc., Encino, Calif., 1987—; bd. dirs. Blowtorch Flats, Venice, Calif.; mem. adv. bd. Soc. for Preservation Film Music, L.A., 1985—. Composer music for films 90028, 1971, Extreme Close-Up, 1973, Tintorerra, 1977, Bid Wednesday, 1979, Defiance, 1979, The Blue Lagoon, 1980, The House of God, 1980, Conan the Barbarian, 1981, Summer Lovers, 1982, Making the Grade, 1984, Conan the Destroyer, 1984, Red Dawn, 1984, Protocol, 1984, Flesh and Blood, 1985, Cherry 2000, 1986, Iron Eagle, 1986, Robocop, 1987 (BMI award 1988), No Man's Land, 1987, Split Decisions, 1988, Spellbinder, 1988, Farewell to the King, 1989, Wired, 1989, Hunt for Red October, 1990 (BMI award 1991), Quigley Down Under, 1990, Flight of the Intruder, 1991, White Fang, 1992, Return to the Blue Lagoon, 1991, Harley Davidson and the Marlboro Man, 1991, Robocop III, 1992, Free Willy, 1992 (BMI award 1994, gold record 1994), Hot Shots! Part Deux, 1993, Serial Mom, 1993, On Deadly Ground, 1994, Lassie, 1994, Jungle Book, 1994, Free Willy II, 1995, Under Seige II, 1995; composer music for TV films Congratulations It's A Boy, 1973, A Whale for the Killing, 1981, Fire on the Mountain, 1981, Amazons, 1984, Single Women, Single Bars, 1984, Amerika, 1987, Intrigue, 1988, Lonesome Dove, 1989 (Emmy award 1988, BMI award 1989), Nasty Boys, 1989, Lone Justice, 1990, Return to Lonesome Dove, 1993, TV pilots Alfred Hitchcock Presents, 1985, Misfits of Science, 1986, Island Sons, 1987, Murphy's Law, L.A. Takedown, 1989, The Life and Times of Ned Blessing, 1991. Recipient resolution Calif. Legislature, 1990, Orange County Bd. Suprs., 1990, Key to City, Garden Grove City Coun., 1990, Disting. Artist award Calif. State U., Long Beach, 1992. Mem. NARAS, BMI, Am. Fedn. Musicians, Acad. Motion Picture Arts and Scis., Soc. Lyricists and Composers. Avocations: sailing, surfing.

POLEMITOU, OLGA ANDREA, accountant; b. Nicosia, Cyprus, June 28, 1950; d. Takis and Georgia (Nicolaou) Chrysanthou. BA with honors, U. London, 1971; PhD, Ind. U., Bloomington, 1981. CPA, Ind. Asst. productivity officer Internat. Labor Office/Cyprus Productivity Ctr., Nicosia, 1971-74; cons. Arthur Young & Co., N.Y.C., 1981; mgr. Coopers & Lybrand, Newark, 1981-83; dir. Bell Atlantic, Reston, Va., 1983—; chairperson adv. coun. Extended Day Care Community Edn., West Windsor Plainsboro, 1987-88. Contbr. articles to profl. jours. Bus. cons. project bus. Jr. Achievement, Indpls., 1984-85. Mem. NAFE, AICPAs, Nat. Trust for Hist. Preservation, Ind. CPA Soc., N.J. Soc. CPAs (sec. mems. in industry com.), Princeton Network of Profl. Women. Avocations: water skiing, tennis. Home: PO Box 2744 Reston VA 22090-0744 Office: Bell Atlantic Video Svcs Co 1880 Campus Commons Dr Reston VA 22091-1512

POLENSKE, KAREN ROSEL, economics educator; b. Lewiston, Idaho, Mar. 20, 1937; d. Albert T. and Helen M. Polenske. BA in Home Econs., Oreg. State U., 1959; MA in Pub. Adminstrn. and Econs., Syracuse U., 1961; PhD in Econs., Harvard U., 1966. Instr., lectr. Harvard U., Cambridge, Mass., 1966-70, rsch. assoc. econ. rsch. project, 1966-72; sr. visitor faculty of econs. King's Coll., Cambridge U., Cambridge, Eng., 1970-71; assoc. prof. dept. urban studies and planning MIT, Cambridge, Mass., 1972-81, prof. dept. urban studies and planning, 1981—; sr. econs. cons. World Bank (in China), Washington, 1988-90, CMT (in Kuwait), Cambridge, 1987-88, Devel. Alternatives Inc. (in Pakistan), Washington, 1987-88, Asian Devel. Bank (in China), Manila, 1988, 92, Boston Inst. for Developing Econs., Washington, 1990-91, UN Devel. Programme (in India), 1993; del. System of Nat. Accounts Revisions, UN, Vienna, Austria, 1988; vis. scholar exch. program NAS, Beijing, 1986; vis. prof. U. Queensland, Brisbane, Australia, 1983, U. Montpellier, France, 1985, Chinese Acad. Scis., 1988, 90-92, 94; dir. Spl. Program in Urban and Regional Studies (SPURS), 1991—. Co-author: (with mem. of rsch. staff) State Estimates of the Gross National Product, 1947, 58, 63, State Estimates of Technology, 1963; author: The U.S. Multiregional Input-Output Accounts and Model, 1980; editor: Multiregional Input-Output Analysis, 1972, 73; co-editor: (with Jiri V. Skolka) Advances in Input-Output Analysis, 1976, (with Ronald E. Miller, Adam Z. Rose), Frontiers of Input-Output Analysis, 1989, (with Chen Xi Kang) Chinese Economic Planning and Input-Output Analysis, 1991. Mem. Cambridge (Mass.) Com. on the Status of Women, 1978-80. Netherlands Inst. for Advanced Study fellow, 1980. Mem. Am. Econ. Assn., Regional Sci. Assn. (councillor at large 1990-93), Internat. Assn. for Rsch. in Income and Wealth, Internat. Input-Output Assn. (v.p. 1992—). Avocations: birding, photography. Office: MIT 77 Massachusetts Ave Rm 9-535 Cambridge MA 02139-4301

POLER, ARIEL, communications executive; b. Caracas, Venezuela, 1968. BA, Mass. Inst. Tech., 1987; MBA, Stanford U., 1994. Computer programmer Shimizu Constrn., 1988-89; project mgr. Aventura Hotels, 1989-91; pres. Internet Profiles Corp., San Francisco, 1994—. Office: Internet Profiles 785 Market St 13th Fl San Francisco CA 94103

POLESKIE, STEPHEN FRANCIS, artist, educator, writer; b. Pringle, Pa., June 3, 1938; s. Stephen Francis and Antoinette Elizabeth (Chludzinski) P.; m. Jeanne Mackin, 1979. B.S., Wilkes Coll., 1959; postgrad., New Sch. for Social Research, 1961. Owner Chiron Press, N.Y.C., 1961-68; instr. Sch. Visual Arts, N.Y.C., 1968; prof. art Cornell U., Ithaca, N.Y., 1969—; vis. critic Pratt Graphic Arts Center, N.Y.C., 1965-68; vis. artist Colgate U., Hamilton, N.Y., 1973, USSR, 1979, Escuela de Bellas Artes, Honduras, 1980, Loughborough Coll. Art and Design, Eng., 1989; vis. prof. U. Calif., Berkeley, 1976. Contbr. short stories to mags.; one-man shows include Louis K. Meisel Gallery, N.Y.C., 1978-80, Galerie Kupinski, Stuttgart, Germany, 1979, Palace of Culture and Sci., Warsaw, Poland, 1979, Sky Art Presentation, MIT, 1981, Am. Ctr., Belgrade, 1981, William and Mary Coll., 1983, McPherson Art Gallery, Victoria, B.C., Can., 1984, Studio D'Ars, Milan, 1985, Gallery Flaviana, Locarno, Switzerland, 1985, Il Salatto Gallery, Como, Italy, 1985, Galleria Schneider, Rome, 1987, Mus. Sztuki Lodz, Poland, 1987, Alternative Mus., Lido di Spina, Italy, 1987, Galerie Klaus Lea, Munich, 1987, Patricia Correga Gallery, Washington, 1988, Nine Columns Gallery, Palermo, Italy, 1988, John Hansard Gallery, Southampton, Eng., 1989, Quai Art Gallery, Isle of Wight, Eng., 1989, Lee Art Gallery, Clemson (S.C.) U., 1990, Apogeeairway, N.Y.C., 1991, Nine Columns Gallery, Brescia, Italy, 1991, Glenn Curtiss Mus., Hammondsport, N.Y., 1993, Caproni Mus., Trento, Italy, 1995, Temple U., Rome, 1995, Gallery of Modern Art, Maribor, Slovenia, 1995, Palazzo Communale, Todi, Italy, 1995, Palazzo Della Pretura, Piacenza, Italy; works represented in collections at Met. Mus., N.Y.C., Mus. Modern Art, N.Y.C., Victoria and Albert Mus., London, Whitney Mus., N.Y.C., Walker Art Center, Mpls., Tate Gallery, London, Fort Worth Art Center, Nat. Collection, Washington, others. Am. Fedn. of Arts grantee, 1965; Carnegie Found. grantee, 1967; Nat. Endowment for Arts grantee, 1973; N.Y. State Council on Arts grantee, 1973; Creative Artists Public Service Program grantee, 1978; Best Found. grantee, 1985. Mem. Exptl. Aircraft Assn., Aircraft Owners and Pilots Assn., Polish Acad. Sci. and Art, Internat. Aerobatic Club. Home: 306 Stone Quarry Rd Ithaca NY 14850-5308 Office: Cornell U Tjaden Hall Ithaca NY 14853 also: care Richard Curtis Assocs Inc 171 E 74th St New York NY 10021 *I have taken my artwork out of the museums and galleries into the sky. I use an aerobatic bi-plane which I build and fly to make large works in space. The airplane is flown through a series of complex maneuvers while trailing smoke in order to make a four-dimensional piece visible to the spectators for only a few short moments. The work of art has no existence other than in the memory or in documentation.*

POLEVOY, NANCY TALLY, lawyer, social worker, genealogist; b. N.Y.C., May 27, 1944; d. Charles H. and Bernice M. (Gang) Tally; m. Martin D. Polevoy, Mar. 19, 1967; children: Jason Tally, John Gerald. Student, Mt. Holyoke Coll., 1962-64; BA, Barnard Coll., 1966; MS in Social Work, Columbia U., 1968, JD, 1986. Bar: N.Y. 1987. Caseworker unmarried mothers' svc. Louise Wise Svcs., N.Y.C., 1967, caseworker adoption dept., 1969-71; caseworker Youth Consultation Svc., N.Y.C., 1968-69; asst. rsch. scientist, psychiat. social worker dept. child psychiatry NYU Med. Ctr., N.Y.C., 1973-81; adv. ct. apptd. spl. advs. Manhattan Family Ct., N.Y.C., 1981-82; cons. social work, 1981-86; matrimonial assoc. Ballon, Stoll & Itzler, 1987, Herzfeld & Rubin, P.C., 1987-88; pvt. practice, N.Y.C. Contbr. articles on early infantile autism and genealogy to profl. jours. Mem. Parents' Adv. Bd. Riverdale Country Sch., 1988-93; mem. outreach bd. Manhattan divsn. United Jewish Appeal Fedn., 1990-94, exec. bd. Manhattan divsn., 1992-94, mem. met. campaign cabinet, 1994-95; mem. archives com. Cen. Synagogue, 1991—, chmn. 1994—; trustee Am. Jewish Hist. Soc., 1992—, asst. treas., 1995—. Recipient French Govt. prize, 1963. Mem. NASW, Bar Assn. of City of N.Y., N.Y. State Bar Assn., Acad. Cert. Social Workers, Barnard Coll. Alumni Assn. (v.p. 1966, class pres. of 1966 1996—). Home and Office: 1155 Park Ave New York NY 10128-1209

POLI, KENNETH JOSEPH, editor; b. Bklyn., June 8, 1921; s. Joseph H. and Irene (Seeman) P.; m. Virginia Osk, Dec. 14, 1946; 1 child, Bruce. Student, Goddard Coll., 1938-40. Writer, photographer North Atlantic Area Office ARC, N.Y.C., 1946-49; Editorial cons., 1965—. Author Critical Focus Column, 1972-83; editor: External House Mags., Internat. Nickel Co., N.Y.C., 1949-53, Leica Photography mag., E. Leitz, Inc., N.Y.C., 1953-65; assoc. editor Popular Photography mag., Ziff-Davis Pub. Co., N.Y.C., 1965-69, sr. editor, 1969-70, editor, 1970-83, cons. editor, 1983-87; cons. editor Photography Ann., 35-mm Photography, Photography Directory and Buying Guide, 1970-83; contbr. articles to photog. jours. and encys. With inf. U.S. Army, 1942-45, PTO. Decorated Purple Heart medal. Mem. Am. Photog. Hist. Soc., Photographic Adminstrs., Circle of Confusion, Mensa. Home & Office: 362 Middle Rd Bayport NY 11705-1904

POLI, RINALDO, chemist, researcher and educator; b. Barga, Italy, Aug. 17, 1956; s. Luciano and Ivana (Tognocchi) P.; m. Bénédicte Leurent, Aug. 31, 1985; children: Clementina, Arianna. Laurea, U. Pisa, Italy, 1981; PhD, Scuola Normale Superiore, Pisa, 1985; Dottore di Ricerca, Italian Ministry Edn., Rome, 1987. Rsch. assoc. Tex. A&M U., College Station, 1985-87; asst. prof. U. Md., College Park, 1987-92, assoc. prof., 1992-95, prof., 1995—; vis. prof. Technische U. Munich, Garching, Germany, 1993-94, Tokyo Met. U., 1995; cons. W.R. Grace, Columbia, Md., 1991, Shell, Houston, 1995. Contbr. chpts. to books, articles to profl. jours. Recipient Disting. New Faculty award Camille and Henry Dreyfus Found., 1987, Presdl. Young Investigator award NSF, 1990, award Exxon Edn. Found., 1991, Medaglia Nasini, Soc. Chimica Italiana; rsch. fellow Alfred P. Sloan Found., 1992, rsch. fellow Alexander von Humboldt Stiftung, 1993. Office: U Md Dept Chemistry/Biochemistry College Park MD 20742

POLICANO, ANDREW J., university dean; b. July 4, 1949; m. Susanne Policano; children: Emily, Keith. BS in Math., SUNY, Stony Brook, 1971; MA in Econs., Brown U., 1973, PhD in Econs., 1976. Asst. prof. U. Iowa, Iowa City, 1975-79, assoc. prof. dept. econs., 1979-81, prof., chair dept. econs., 1984-87, sr. assoc. dean academic affairs, 1987-88; prof. dept. econs. Fordham U., N.Y.C., 1981-84, asst. chair, dir. grad. studies, 1982-83; rsch. assoc. Ctr. for Study of Futures Markets Columbia U., N.Y.C., 1982-86; dean divsn. social & behavioral sci. SUNY, 1988-91; dean Sch. Bus. U. Wis., Madison, 1991—; guest prof. Inst. Advanced Studies, Vienna, Austria, 1985; dir. Nat. Guardian Life, Madison, 1991—; mem. Nat. Total Quality Forum Steering Com., Schaumburg, Ill., 1992—, Am. Assembly Collegiate Sch. Bus. Diversity Com., St. Louis, 1993—. Contbr. articles profl. jours. Recipient Disting. Alumnus award SUNY, Stony Brook, 1994. Mem. Rotary. Office: U Wis Sch Bus Grainger Hall 975 University Ave Madison WI 53706-1324

POLICH, JAMES W., environmental services consultant; b. 1941. Degree, Purdue U., 1966. With USPHS, Washington, 1966-68; ind. civil engr. Detroit, 1968-72; with Gen. Motors Co., Detroit, 1972-82, Environ, Deerfield, Ill., 1982—; now pres. Environ. Office: Environ 540 Lake Cook Rd Ste 300 Deerfield IL 60015*

POLICINSKI, EUGENE FRANCIS, author, newspaper editor; b. South Bend, Ind., Aug. 31, 1950; s. E.T. and Margaret C. (O'Neill) P.; m. Kathleen Beta O'Donnell Powell, Aug. 19, 1972; children: Ryan, David. Degree in journalism and polit. sci., Ball State U., 1972. Corr. Gannett News Svc., Washington, 1979-82; Washington editor USA Today, Arlington, Va., 1982-83, page one editor, 1983-89, mng. editor sports, 1989-96; host, commentator USA Today Sky Radio, Arlington, 1992-95. Founding editor USA Today Baseball Weekly, 1991. Named one of 100 Most Important People in Sports Sporting News, 1992, 93, 95; inducted into Ball State U. Journalism Hall of Fame, 1989. Mem. Am. Soc. Newspaper Editors (com. chmn. 1989—), Associated Press Sports Editors (com. chmn. 1989-96). Avocations: sailing, tennis, bicycling.

POLICOFF, LEONARD DAVID, physician, educator; b. Wilmington, Del., Apr. 22, 1918; s. David and Rosalie (Rockkind) P.; m. Naomi Lewis, June 25, 1942; children: Susan, Stephen. B.S., U. Richmond, 1938; M.D., Med. Coll. Va., 1942. Diplomate Am. Bd. Internal Medicine, Am. Bd. Phys. Medicine and Rehab. (mem. 1968-80). Asst. prof. Med. Coll. Va., 1948-55; prof., chmn. dept. phys. medicine and rehab. Albany Med. Coll., Union U., 1955-67, Temple U., Phila., 1967-70; prof., chmn. Hahnemann Med. Coll., Phila., 1970-71; prof. clin. phys. medicine U. Pa.; chmn. dept. rehab. medicine Princeton (N.J.) Hosp., 1971-75, cons., 1975-78; dir. rehab. medicine Somerset Hosp., Somerville, N.J., 1975-78; acting chmn., prof. clin. phys. medicine Rutgers Med. Sch., 1976-78; clin. prof. phys. medicine and rehab. U. Calif.-Davis Sch. Medicine, 1980-86; chmn. dept. rehab. medicine Pacific Med. Center, San Francisco, 1978-81; med. cons. Dept. Health Svcs., State of Calif., 1987-91; chief rehab. medicine svc. VA Med. Ctr., Martinez, Calif., 1983-85; med. dir. Rehab. Ctr., John Muir Meml. Hosp., Walnut Creek, Calif., 1985-87; mem. Bd. Med. Examiners, N.Y. State, 1962-67; chief of staff VA Hosp., Livermore, Calif., 1987-88. Contbr. articles to profl. jours., textbooks. Bd. dirs. Commn. on Edn. in Phys. Medicine and Rehab., 1968-80, com. for Handicapped People-to-People Program, 1967-75. Served to maj. M.C., AUS, 1943-46. Nat. Inst. Neurologic Diseases fellow, 1953-55. Fellow ACP, Am. Acad. Phys. Medicine and Rehab., Am. Acad. Cerebral Palsy; mem. Am. Congress Rehab. Medicine (pres. 1971), Assn. Acad. Physiatrists, AMA (chmn. phys. medicine sect. 1965-66), Phi Beta Kappa, Alpha Omega Alpha, Sigma Zeta. Home: 1304 Henry St Berkeley CA 94709-1929

POLIKOFF, BENET, JR., lawyer; b. Winston-Salem, N.C., Nov. 25, 1936; s. Benet and Margaret (New) P.; m. Jean Troubh, June 26, 1959 (div. Mar. 1971); children—Elisabeth, Benet Steven, Lee; m. Florence Davis, June 11, 1971. BA, Yale U., 1959; LLB, Harvard U., 1962. Ptnr. Marshall, Bratter, Greene, Allison & Tucker, N.Y.C., 1969-82; Ptnr. Rosenman and Colin, N.Y.C., 1982-90, of counsel, 1990—. Mem. Assn. Bar City N.Y. (chmn. real property law com. 1981-84), N.Y. State Bar Assn., Am. Coll. Real Estate Lawyers.

POLIMENO, LAWRENCE A., computer softwear company executive. P-res., COO Med. Info. Tech., Westwood, Mass. Office: Medical Info Tech Meditech Cir Westwood MA 02090*

POLING, HAROLD ARTHUR, retired automobile company executive; b. Troy, Mich., Oct. 14, 1925; s. Plesant Arthur and Laura Elizabeth (Thompson) P.; m. Marian Sarita Lee, 1957; children—Pamela Lee, Kathryn Lynn, Douglas Lee. BA, Monmouth (Ill.) Coll., 1949, LHD (hon.), 1981; MBA,

Ind. U., 1951, LHD (hon.), 1990; LHD (hon.), Hofstra U., 1986, U. Detroit, 1990, Mich. State U., 1992. Cost analyst, supr. steel divsn. Ford Motor Co., Deaborn, Mich., 1951-59, fin. analyst, mgr. transmission and chassis divsn., 1960-64; asst. contr. transmission and chassis divsn. Ford Motor Co., Dearborn, Mich., 1964-66, contr. transmission and chassis divsn., 1966-67, contr. engine and foundry divsn., 1967-68, contr. product devel. group, 1968-72; v.p. fin. Ford of Europe, Inc., 1972-75; pres. Ford of Europe, Inc., Brentwood, Eng., 1975-77; chmn. bd. Ford of Europe, Inc., 1977-79; exec. v.p. Ford Motor Co., Dearborn, Mich., 1979, exec. v.p. N.Am. automotive ops., 1980-85, mem. office of chief exec., 1984, pres., COO, 1985-87, vice-chmn., COO, 1987-90, chmn., CEO, 1990-93, chmn., 1993-94, also bd. dirs.; retired Chmn. Ford Motor Co., 1995; mem. Pres.' Commn. on Environ. Quality, The Bus. Coun., The Conf. Bd., The Bus. Roundtable, BHP Minerals Internat. Adv. Coun.; bd. dirs. Shell Oil Co., Detroit Renaissance Inc. Bd. dirs. Monmouth (Ill.) Coll. Senate; mem. dean's adv. coun. Ind. U. Sch. Bus.; mem. Nat. 4-H Coun.; bd. visitors Sch. Econs. and Mgmt. Oakland (Mich.) U., Grad. Sch. Bus., U. Pitts.; v.p. Boys and Girls Club S.E. Mich.; chmn.-elect Bus.-Higher Edn. Forum, The Brookings Coun. With USNR, 1943-45. Recipient Disting. Svc. Citation award Auto. Hall Fame, 1986, Leadership award Engring. Soc. Detroit, 1987, Horatio Alger award, 1991. Mem. Am. Auto Mfg. Assn., Hwy. Users Fedn. Office: Ford Motor Co 16800 Executive Plaza Dr Dearborn MI 48126*

POLING, KERMIT WILLIAM, minister; b. Elkins, W.Va., Oct. 1, 1941; s. Durward Willis and Della Mae (Boyles) P.; m. Patricia Ann Groves, June 12, 1965; children: David Edward Elson, Mikael Erik. Diploma in Bible, Am. Bible Sch., 1966; BRE, Am. Bible Coll., 1991; BA in Bible, Reed Coll. Religion, 1968; AA, W.Va. U., 1970; ThD, Zion Theol. Sem., 1971; post-grad., Wesley Theol. Sem., 1974; LLD, Geneva Theol. Coll., 1980; DSL (hon.), Berean Christian Coll., 1981; postgrad., Mansfield Coll., U. Oxford, Eng., 1986, 90, 91; D Ecumenical Rsch., St. Ephrem's Inst. for Oriental Studies, 1989; M of Herbology, Emerson Coll., 1994. Ordained to ministry United Meth. Ch., 1967. Pastor Parkersburg-Crossroads (W.Va.) Cir., 1967-70; asst. sec. W.Va. Ann. Conf., 1967-69; pastor Hope-Halleck Morgantown Cir., 1970-76, Trinity-Warren Grafton (W.Va.) Charge, 1976-83, 1st Trinity Pennsboro (W.Va.) Charge, 1983—; editor local ch. news; instr. Bible Bodkin Bible Inst., 1975-75, United Meth. Lay Acad., 1992—; mem. staff Taylor County Coop. Parish, 1976-83; coord. Hughes River Coop. Parish, 19836; mem. chaplains com. Grafton City Hosp., 1976-82; mem. coun. Ctr. d'Etudes et d'Action Oecumeniques, 1972-74. Author: A Crown of Thorns, 1963, A Silver Message, 1964, History of the Halleck Church, 1970, Eastern Rite Catholicism, 1971, From Brahmin to Bishop, 1976, Cult and Occult: Data and Doctrine, 1978, The Value of Religious Education in Ancient Traditional Churches, 1993; editor: Jane's Heirs; contbr. articles and poems to religious jours. Decorated Royal Afghanistan Order of Crown of Amanullah, Byzantine Order of Leo the Armenian, Order of Polonia Presituta, Mystical Order of St. Peter, knight Grand Cross of the Order of St. Dennis of Zante, 1990; recipient Good Citizenship award Doddridge County, 1954, Silver medal Ordre Universel du Merit Humain, Geneva, 1973, Commendation for Outstanding Achievement in Ministry, Ohio Ho. of Reps., 1988; named Chief of Dynastic Ho. of Polanie-Patrikios, 1988. Mem. SAR, Assn. Bible Tchrs. (founder), Internat. Platform Assn., Sovereign Order St. John Jerusalem, Ritchie County Ministerial Assn. (pres. 1984—), Order Sacred Cup, Knights of Malta, Order of the Crown of Lauriers. Home: 118 Ray Ave Pennsboro WV 26415-1155

POLING, WESLEY HENRY, college president; b. Akron, Ohio, May 22, 1945; s. Elmer Francis and Norma May (Flickinger) P.; m. Carol Ann Young, Aug. 17, 1968; children: Jason Alder, Todd Wesley. BA, Ohio Wesleyan U., 1968; MDiv, Yale U., 1971; PhD, U. Conn., 1983. Dir. parents program Yale U., New Haven, 1971-73, dir. alumni records, 1973-86; v.p. for devel. and alumni rels. Goucher Coll., Towson, Md., 1986-94; pres. Ky. Wesleyan Coll., Owensboro, 1994—; treas. Dist. I CASE, 1985-86, program chair Conf., 1984-85. Chmn. bd. mgr. Ctrl. br. YMCA of New Haven, 1976-83; v.p., treas. Balt. Choral Arts Soc., 1989-93, pres., 1993-94; bd. dirs. Roland Park Place, Balt., 1991-94; mem. Citizens Com. on Edn., Owensboro, 1994—. Berkeley Coll., Yale U. fellow. Mem. Owensboro C. of C. (bd. dirs. 1994-95), Williams Club, Rotary, Phi Delta Kappa. Avocations: squash, running, music. Home: 3100 Frederica St Owensboro KY 42301-6059 Office: Ky Wesleyan Coll PO Box 1039 Owensboro KY 42302-1039

POLINGER, IRIS SANDRA, dermatologist; b. N.Y.C., Feb. 10, 1943; m. Harvey I. Hyman, Feb. 6, 1972. AB, Barnard Coll., 1964; PhD, Johns Hopkins U., 1969; MD, SUNY Downstate, Bklyn., 1975. Diplomate Am. Bd. Dermatology. Teaching positions various schs. including NYU Coll. Dentistry and Harvard Med. Sch., 1969-73; med. intern Baylor Coll. Medicine, 1975-76, resident in dermatology, 1976-79; pvt. practice dermatology Houston, 1979—. Bd. dirs. Ft. Bend County Women's Ctr., Richmond, Tex., 1993—. Mem. Am. Bus. Women's Assn. (chair scholarship com. 1992, 96, chair scholarship event com. 1993—). Office: 4915 S Main St Ste 104 Stafford TX 77477-4601

POLINSKY, JANET NABOICHECK, state official, former state legislator; b. Hartford, Conn., Dec. 6, 1930; d. Louis H. and Lillian S. Naboicheck; BA, U. Conn., 1953; postgrad. Harvard U., 1954; m. Hubert N. Polinsky, Sept. 21, 1958; children: Gerald, David, Beth. Mem. Waterford 2d Charter Commn. (Conn.), 1967-68, Waterford Conservation Commn., 1968-69; Waterford rep. Town Meeting, 1969-71, SE Conn. Regional Planning Agy., 1971-73; mem. Waterford Planning and Zoning Commn., 1970-76, chmn., 1973-76; mem. Waterford Dem. Town Com., 1976-92, del. State Dem. Conv., 1976, 78, 80, 82, 84, 86, 90, 92; mem. Conn. Ho. of Reps. from 38th Dist., 1977-92, asst. majority leader, 1981-83, chmn. appropriations com., 1983-85, 87-89, ranking mem., 1985-87, minority whip, 1985-86, dep. speaker, 1989-92; dep. commr. dept. adminstrv. svcs., State of Conn., 1993-94, commr., 1994-95, asst. sec. of state, 1995; commr. utilities ctrl. auth. State of Conn., 1995—. Trustee Eugene O'Neill Meml. Theatre Ctr., 1973-76, 81-92; corporator, Lawrence and Meml. Hosps., 1987—; mem. New Eng. Bd. Higher Edn., 1981-83; mem. fiscal affairs com. Eastern Conf. Council of State Govts., 1983-88. Named Woman of Yr., Waterford Jr. Women's Club, 1977, Nehantic Women's Bus. and Profl. Club, 1979, Legislator of Yr., Conn. Library Assn., 1980. Mem. Order Women Legislators, Delta Kappa Gamma (hon.). Home: 15 Gardner Cir New London CT 06320-4314 Office: 30 Trinity St Hartford CT 06106-1629

POLIRER, DEBRA JOYCE, accountant; b. Mt. Kisco, N.Y., June 13, 1962; d. Frank Mathew and Cynthia Claire (Wertheimer) Gasthalter; m. Peter Ian Polirer, June 26, 1988. Student, Georgetown U., 1980-82; BS in Acctg., Mercy Coll., 1987. CPA, N.Y. Sr. proofreader Pennysaver Corp., Yorktown Heights, N.Y., 1983-87; sr. staff acct. Combe Inc., White Plains, N.Y., 1987-94; tax editor H & R Block, Poughkeepsie, N.Y., 1994—. Contbg. author: Hearts on Fire, 1987, The Poetry of Life: A Treasury of Moments, 1987, Best New Poets of 1987, Editor's Choice, 1988. Mem. Inst. Mgmt. Accts., Delta Mu Delta. Jewish. Avocations: classical piano, music, creative writing, foreign languages. Home: 186 Spackenkill Rd Poughkeepsie NY 12603-5135

POLIS, MICHAEL PHILIP, university dean; b. N.Y.C., Oct. 24, 1943; s. Max and Sylvia (Goldner) P.; m. Claudette Martin, May 28, 1966; children: Melanie Bobby, Martin Pascal, Karine Melissa. BSEE, U. Fla., 1966; MSEE, Purdue U., West Lafayette, Ind., 1968, PhD, 1972. Grad. instr. elec. engring. Purdue U., West Lafayette, 1966-71; postdoctoral fellow Ecole Polytechnique, Montreal, 1972-73, asst. prof. elec. engring., 1973-74, assoc. prof., 1974-82, prof., 1982-83; program dir. sys. theory NSF, Washington, 1983-87; chmn. dept. elec. and computer engring. Wayne State U., Detroit, 1987-93; dean Sch. Engring. and Computer Sci. Oakland U., Rochester, Mich., 1993—; expert witness various law firms, 1989—; cons. Mich. Bell-Ameritech, Detroit, 1989-95, ICAM Technologies, Inc., Montreal, 1981-83; vis. rsch. assoc. LAAS, Toulouse, France, 1978. Contbr. articles to profl. jours. Mem. IEEE (sr.), IEEE Control Sys. Soc. (bd. govs. 1993-95, Best Paper Trans. on Automatic Control 1974-75, Disting. Mem. 1993, v.p. mem. activities 1990-91, assoc. editor 1981-82). Office: Oakland Univ Sch Engring & Computer Sci Rochester MI 48309

POLISAR, LEONARD MYERS, lawyer; b. Bklyn., Oct. 25, 1929; s. Aaron and Anna (Myers) P.; m. Judith Sarah Weisstein, Aug. 16, 1959; children: Mark Joseph, Daniel Aaron. BA, Bklyn. Coll., 1950; LLB, Yale U., 1953; LLM in Taxation, NYU, 1959. Bar: N.Y. 1954. Assoc. Hays, Podell, Algase, Crum & Feuer, N.Y.C., 1955-63; asst. to gen. counsel CIT Fin. Corp., N.Y.C., 1963-65; v.p. law and pub. affairs Mgmt. Assistance Inc., N.Y.C., 1966-72; v.p., gen. counsel Internat. Controls Corp., Fairfield, N.J., 1972-73; v.p., sec., gen. counsel Baker Industries Inc., Parsippany, N.J., 1973-80; ptnr. Herzfeld & Rubin, P.C., N.Y.C., 1980—; arbitrator N.Y. Stock Exch., 1987—; speaker at computer, securities and corp. seminars. Editor Yale Law Jour., 1953. Bd. dirs. Mental Health Assn. N.Y. and Bronx counties, 1960—, chmn., 1985—; trustee, v.p. Union Temple Bklyn. Mem. ABA, Assn. of Bar of City of N.Y., Am. Soc. Corp. Secs. (chmn. audit com. 1989-92), Bus. Coun. for UN (bus. adv. com.), Bus. Execs. for Nat. Security (exec. com. N.Y.C. chpt.), Computer Law Assn., Citizens Union, Yale Club of N.Y., Yale Club of Montclair, Phi Beta Kappa. Jewish. Avocations: skiing, sailing, spectator sports, music, drama. Home: 63 Briarcliff Rd Mountain Lakes NJ 07046-1304 Office: Herzfeld & Rubin PC 40 Wall St New York NY 10005

POLISI, JOSEPH W(ILLIAM), academic administrator; b. N.Y.C., Dec. 30, 1947; s. William Charles and Pauline (Kaplan) P.; m. Elizabeth Marlowe. BA in Polit. Sci., U. Conn., 1969; MA in Internat. Relations, Tufts U., 1970, MusM, 1973, M of Mus. Arts, 1975; DMA, Yale U., 1980; DHL (hon.), Ursinus Coll., Collegetown, Pa., 1986; MusD (hon.), Curtis Inst. Music, 1990. Exec. officer Yale Sch. of Music, New Haven, 1976-80; dean of faculty Manhattan Sch. of Music, N.Y.C., 1980-83; dean Coll. Conservatory of Music U. Cin., 1983-84; pres. The Juilliard Sch., N.Y.C., 1984—. Performances as bassoonist throughout the U.S.; contbr. articles to various publs. in U.S. and France. Office: Juilliard Sch Office of the Pres 60 Lincoln Center Plz New York NY 10023-6500

POLITAN, NICHOLAS H., federal judge; b. Newark, Nov. 13, 1935; m. Marian E. Politan; children: Nicholas H. Jr., Vincent J. Bar: N.J. 1961, U.S. Dist. Ct. N.J. 1961, U.S. Ct. Appeals (2d cir.) 1969, U.S. Ct. Appeals (3d cir.) 1971, U.S. Tax Ct. 1972, U.S. Supreme Ct. 1973. Law clk. to Hon. Gerald McLaughlin U.S. Ct. Appeals (3d cir.), Newark, 1960-61; sr. ptnr. Cecchi and Politan, Lyndhurst, N.J., 1961-64, 72-87; litigation ptnr. Krieger, Chodash & Politan, Jersey City, 1964-72; dir., chmn. exec. com. County Trust Co., Lyndhurst, 1980-87; judge U.S. Dist. Ct. N.J., 1987—; instr. legal rsch. and writing Rutgers U. Law Sch., 1963. Mng. editor Rutgers Law Rev., 1959; contbr. articles to profl. jours. Office: US Dist Ct Box 999 King Bldg Newark NJ 07101-0999

POLITANO, VICTOR ANTHONY, urology educator, physician; b. Point Marion, Pa., Jan. 13, 1919; s. Anthony and Elizabeth (Parco) P.; m. Aida Mishkin, June 20, 1969; children: Victor, Michael, Rebecca, Betty Frances, Jonathan. B.S., Marshall U., 1940; M.D., Duke U., 1944. Asso. urologist Mass. Gen. Hosp.; instr. surgery Harvard U., 1955-58; asso. prof. surgery div. urology Duke U., 1958-62; prof., chmn. dept. urology U. Miami, 1962—, chmn. emeritus Dept. Urology, 1992. Served with USN, 1945-47, 53-55. Recipient Disting. Faculty scholar award U. Miami, 1995, Pediat. Urology medal Am. Acad. Pediat., 1995; Victor A. Politano chair in urology established at U. Miami Sch. Medicine, 1982. Mem. Am. Urol. Assn. (pres.-elect 1984-85, pres. 1985-86), Soc. Univ. Urologists (pres.), Pediatric Urol. Soc. (pres.), Fla. Urol. Soc. (pres.), AMA, ACS (internat. relations com.), Am. Assn. Genito-urinary Surgeons, Clin. Soc. Genito-urinary Surgeons, Internat. Soc. Urology, Confederacion Americana de Urologia (pres. 1986-87), Fla. Med. Assn., Dade County Med. Assn., Greater Miami Urol. Soc. Developed technique for anti-reflux ureteral reimplantation, technique for teflon injection to correct urinary incontinence; developed periureteral Polytef paste injection for vesicoureteral reflux. Office: U Miami Jackson Meml Med Ctr 1611 NW 12th Ave Miami FL 33136-1005

POLITES, MICHAEL EDWARD, aerospace engineer; b. Belleville, Ill., Mar. 19, 1944; s. Matthew Charles and Edith Louise (Schwarz) P. BS in Sys. and Automatic Controls, Washington U., St. Louis, 1967; MSEE, U. Ala., 1971; PhD in Elec. Engring., Vanderbilt U., 1986. Aerospace rsch. engr. guidance, navigation and control sys. NASA/Marshall Space Flt. Ctr. Structures & Dynamics Lab, Huntsville, Ala., 1967-95; chief instrumentation and control divsn. Astrionics Lab. NASA/Marshall Space Flight Ctr., Huntsville, Ala., 1995—. 4 patents in field. Fellow AIAA (assoc. guidance navigation and control tech. com. 1990—, digital avionics tech. com. 1995—); mem. IEEE (sr. Outstanding Engr. Huntsville sect. 1995), ASME, Am. Astronautical Soc. (session co-chmn. 1995 Guidance and Control Conf.), Mensa, Tau Beta Pi, Eta Kappa Nu, Pi Tau Sigma. Office: NASA/ Marshall Space Flight Ctr Astronics Lab Huntsville AL 35812

POLITIS, TIMOTHY JUDE, insurance company executive; b. Manchester, Eng., Nov. 21, 1944; came to U.S. 1946; s. Joseph Paul and Dorothy (McGurk) P.; m. Deborah Dyer, Dec. 23, 1967 (div. 1975); children: Wendy Ellen, Holly Lynn; m. Elaine Bishop, Mar. 10, 1979; children: John Joseph, Alexandra Marjory, Daphne Earl. BS, Castleton (Vt.) Coll., 1967; student, Siena Coll., Loudenville, N.Y., 1962-63, Dartmouth Coll., 1963-65. CLU. Agt. Conn. Mutual Life, Rutland, Vt., 1971-74; mktg. cons. Conn. Mutual Life, Hartford, Conn., 1974-76; agy. supr. Conn. Mutual Life, Portland, Maine, 1976-78; dir. tng. Union Mutual Life Ins. Co., Portland, 1978-82; chartered life underwriter Mass. Mutual Life, Portland, 1982—. Vice chmn. Scarborough Rep. Town Com., 1989—; mem. Maine Estate Planning Coun., 1982—, Waterfowl Adv. Com., Maine, 1986-88, Com. on Fgn. Rels., Portland, 1979—, Maine State Rep. Com., 1992—; regional dir. Nat. Ski Patrol Sys., Maine, 1984-88, 1993-94; mem. Maine State Rep. coms., 1992—. Capt. USMC, 1967-71. Recipient Disting. Svc. award, Ducks Unltd., Inc., Long Grove, Ill., 1984, 88, Carl Horner award, 1987. Mem. Atlantic Salmon Fedn., Purpoodock Country Club, Auburn Skeet Club, Scarborough Rod and Gun Club, Sugarloaf/USA Ski Patrol, Shawnee Peak Ski Patrol. Republican. Avocations: skiing, bird and duck hunting, salmon and trout fishing. Home: 1 Milliken Rd Scarborough ME 04074-8989 Office: Massachusetts Mutual Life 93 Exchange St Portland ME 04101-5001

POLITZ, HENRY ANTHONY, federal judge; b. Napoleonville, La., May 9, 1932; s. Anthony and Virginia (Russo) P.; m. Jane Marie Simoneaux, Apr. 29, 1952; children: Nyle, Bennett, Mark, Angela, Scott, Jane, Michael, Henry, Alisa, John, Nina. B.A., La. State U., 1958, J.D., 1959. Bar: La. 1959. Assoc., then ptnr. firm Booth, Lockard, Jack, Pleasant & LeSage, Shreveport, 1959-79; judge U.S. Ct. Appeals (5th cir.), Shreveport, 1979—, chief judge, 1992—; vis. prof. La. State U. Law Center; bd. dirs. Am. Prepaid Legal Services Inst., 1975—; mem. La. Judiciary Commn., 1978-79. Mem. editorial bd. La. State U. Law Rev., 1958-59. Mem. Shreveport Airport Authority, 1973-79, chmn., 1977; bd. dirs. Rutherford House, Shreveport, 1975—, pres., 1978; pres. Caddo Parish Bd. Election Suprs., 1975-79; mem. Electoral Coll., 1976. Served with USAF, 1951-55. Named Outstanding Young Lawyer in La., 1971, Outstanding Alumnus La. State U. Law Sch., 1991; inducted in La. State U. Hall of Distinction, 1992. Mem. Am. Bar Assn., Am. Judicature Soc., Internat. Soc. Barristers, La. Bar Assn., La. Trial Lawyers Assn., Shreveport Bar Assn., Justinian Soc., Omicron Delta Kappa. Democrat. Roman Catholic. Club: K.C. Office: US Ct Appeals 300 Fannin St Rm 2B04 Shreveport LA 71101-3074

POLITZER, HUGH DAVID, physicist, educator; b. N.Y.C., Aug. 31, 1949; s. Alan A. and Valerie T. (Diamant) P. B.S., U. Mich., 1969; Ph.D., Harvard U., 1974. Jr. fellow Harvard U. Soc. Fellows, 1974-77; mem. faculty Calif. Inst. Tech., 1977—, prof. theoretical physics, 1979—, exec. officer for physics, 1986-88. Recipient J.J. Sakurai prize, 1986. Fellow NSF, 1969-74; Sloan Found., 1977-81; Woodrow Wilson grad. fellow, 1969-74. Mem. Phi Beta Kappa. Address: 452-48 Calif Inst Tech Pasadena CA 91125

POLIVNICK, PAUL, conductor, music director; b. Atlantic City, N.J., July 7, 1947; s. Sidney and Beatrice Ann (Craven) P.; m. Kathleen Lenski, Jan. 19, 1970 (div. 1976); m. Marsha Hooks, June 20, 1980. MusB, Juilliard Sch., N.Y.C., 1969; MusD (hon.), U. Montevallo, 1987. Condr. Debut Orch., L.A., 1969-73; mem. faculty UCLA, 1973-76; assoc. condr. Indpls. Symphony, 1977-80, Milw. Symphony, 1981-85; dir. music Ala. Symphony, Birmingham, 1985-93; music dir. N.H. Music Festival, 1993—; guest condr. various symphony and opera cos., worldwide. Avocations: backpacking, working out, traveling, cooking. Address: care Maxim Gershunoff Attractions Inc PO Box 224055 Hollywood FL 33022

POLJAK, ROBERTO J(UAN), research director, biotechnology educator; b. Buenos Aires, Argentina, Sept. 17, 1932; s. Giovanni P. and Josephine (Zorzut) P.; m. Mabel Amelia Iglesias, Dec. 28, 1956; children: Leonora, Gustavo. BSc, Coll. Nat. Quilmes, Argentina, 1949; PhD, U. de la Plata, Argentina, 1956. Teaching assoc. Instituto de Fisica, Bariloche, Argentina, 1957; fellow Sch. for Advanced Studies MIT, Boston, 1958-60; postdoctoral fellow Davy Faraday Rsch. Lab., Royal Instn., London, 1960-62; postdoctoral flelow MRC Unit for Molecular Biology, Cambridge, Eng., 1962; asst. prof. biophysics Johns Hopkins Sch. Medicine, Balt., 1962, assoc. prof. biophysics, 1966, prof. biophysics, 1972-81; prof. Institut Pasteur, Paris, 1981-92; dir. rsch. CNRS, Paris, 1981-92; prof., dir. Ctr. Advanced Rsch. in Biotech. U. Md./Nat. Inst. Stds. and Tech., Balt., 1992—; W.H. Elkins prof. U. Md., 1994—. Contbr. about 150 rsch. papers to sci. jours. Recipient Rsch. Career Devel. award USPHS, 1972-77, gold medal Soc. d'Encouragement au Progres, Paris, 1986, Jacques Monod prize Fondation de France, 1986, Disting. Scientist award S.W. Found. for Biomed. Rsch., 1987, Louis Jeantet Found. Medicine prize, Geneva, 1989, Gold medal Jimenez Diaz Found., 1991; Macy Faculty scholar, 1977-78. Mem. European Molecular Biology Orgn., Am. Assn. Immunologists. Office: Ctr for Advanced Rsch Biotech 9600 Gudelsky Dr Rockville MD 20850-3479

POLK, BENJAMIN KAUFFMAN, retired architect, composer, educator; b. Des Moines, May 18, 1916; s. Harry Herndon and Alice (Kauffman) P.; m. Emily Despain Isaacs, Aug. 23, 1946. Student, Amherst Coll., 1933-35, U. Chgo., 1935-36, Iowa State Coll., 1936-38. Ptnr. Polk and Malone, San Francisco, 1948-53; propr. Benjamin Polk, Architect & Planner, New Delhi, Calcutta, Karachi, 1952-64; assoc. W.R. Ewald Jr., Regional Planning, Washington, 1965-66; mem. architecture & planning faculty Calif. Poly. State U., San Luis Obispo, 1966-80; ret., 1980. Author: Architecture and the Spirit of the Place, 1961, Building for South Asia, An Architectural Autobiography, 1992, (with Emily Polk) India Notebook, 1986, (with Seneviratna) Buddhist Monastic Architecture, 1992, A Figure in a Landscape, 1992, Christchurch Priory, Dorset, 1994; Structure for Music and Synthesized Orchestrations, 1995; also booklets, articles; prin. works include Am. Libr., Times of India Press, New Delhi, Jallian Wala Bagh Amritsar India, Utkal U., Orissa, Gwalior Rayons Factories and Town Calicut, Birla Mus., Rajasthan, Woodlands, Calcutta, Palace for the King of Nepal, Buddhist Libr., Rangoon. Vice-pres. Service Civile Internat., East India, 1957-63; advisor Small Wilderness Area Preservation, Calif., 1970-80. Tech. sgt. U.S. Army, 1942-46. Recipient Gold medal Prime Min. of Burma, 1961. Republican. Presbyterian. Avocations: writing, sketching, hiking. Home: 2361 Claranita Ave Los Osos CA 93402-4013 Office: Quaker Gardens 12151 Dale St Stanton CA 90680

POLK, CHARLES, electrical engineer, educator, biophysicist; b. Vienna, Austria, Jan. 15, 1920; came to U.S., 1940, naturalized, 1943; s. Heinrich and Amalie (Canar) P.; m. Dorothy R. Lemp, Apr. 27, 1946; children: Dean F., Gerald W. Student, U. Paris-Sorbonne, 1939; BS, Washington U., 1948; MS, U. Pa., 1953, PhD, 1956. Engr. RCA Victor div., Camden, N.J., 1948-52; rsch. and teaching assoc. U. Pa., 1952-57; prof. elec. engring. Drexel Inst. Tech., Phila., 1957-59; tech. staff RCA Labs., Princeton, N.J., 1957-59; prof. elec. engring. U. R.I., 1959-90, prof. emeritus, 1990—, chmn. dept., 1959-79; head elec. scis. and analysis sect. engring. div. NSF, Washington, 1975-76; acting dir. engring. div. NSF, 1976-77; vis. prof. elec. engring. Stanford U., 1968-69, U. Wis., Madison, 1983-84; cons. Oak Ridge Nat. Lab., 1993—. Editor Handbook of Biologial Effects of Electromagnetic Fields; contbr. articles to profl. publs. Mem. R.I. Legis. Commn. on Electricity Rates, 1974-75. With AUS, 1943-46. NSF Superior Accomplishment award, 1977. Fellow IEEE (chmn. Phila. chpt. profl. group antennas and propagation 1954-55, chmn. Providence sect. 1964-65, mem. adminstrn. com., com. on man and radiation 1987—, chair subcom. biol. effects of power frequency fields 1989—, engring. in med. and biology soc.); mem. AAAS, AAUP, Am. Geophys. Union (nat. com. on space electricity 1974-75), Am. Soc. for Engring. Edn., N.Y. Acad. Scis., Internat. Sci. Radio Union, Bioelectromagnetics Soc. (pres. 1988-89), Bioelec. Repair and Growth Soc. (coun. mem. 1990-92), Sigma Xi, Tau Beta Pi. Organized 1st microwave closed circuit television link for grad. edn. in U.S., 1962. Home: 53 Springhill Rd Kingston RI 02881-1805

POLK, HIRAM CAREY, JR., surgeon, educator; b. Jackson, Miss., Mar. 23, 1936; s. Hiram Carey and Dorris (Hemby) P.; m. Susan Galandiuk; children: Susan Elizabeth, Hiram Cary. BS, Millsaps Coll., 1956; MD, Harvard U., 1960. Intern Barnes Hosp., St. Louis, 1960-61; resident Barnes Hosp., 1961-65; instr. in surgery Washington U., St. Louis, 1964-65; asst. prof. surgery U. Miami, Fla., 1965-69; assoc. prof. U. Miami, 1969-71; prof. chmn. dept. surgery U. Louisville, 1971—; pres., chmn. bd. Univ. Surg. Assocs., P.S.C., 1971—; chmn. bd. Clin. Services Assn., Inc.; mem. merit rev. bd. for surgery VA, 1983-85. Author: (with H.H. Stone) Contemporary Burn Management, 1971, Hospital-Acquired Infections in Surgery, 1977; (with B. Gardner, H.H. Stone and W.L. Sugg) Basic Surgery, 1978, (with H.H. Stone and B. Gardner) 2d edit., 1983, 3d edit., 1987, 4th edit., 1992, 5th edit., 1995; (with D.C. Carter) Trauma, 1982; (with J.E. Conte Jr. and L.S. Jacob) Antibiotic Prophylaxis in Surgery: A Comprehensive Review, 1984; (with J.D. Richardson and L.M. Flint Jr.) Trauma: Clinical Care and Pathophysiology, 1987; contbr. numerous articles to profl. publs.; mem. editl. bd. So. Med. Jour., 1970-72, Jour. Surg. Rsch., 1970-72, 75-77, 78-80, Current Problems in Surgery, 1973—, Surgery, 1975-85, Current Surgery, 1977—, Current Surg. Techniques, 1977—, Emergency Surgery: A Weekly Update, 1977—, Collected Letters in Surgery, 1978—, Brit. Jour. Surgery, 1981-94; chief editor Am. Jour. Surgery, 1986—. Bd. govs. Trover Clinic Found., Madisonville, Ky. Mem. ACS (gov. 1972-80, commn. on cancer 1975-80), AMA, Allen O. Whipple Soc. (exec. coun. 1977-80), Am. Assn. Cancer Edn. (exec. coun. 1968-72), Am. Assn. Surgery of Trauma, Am. Burn Assn., Am. Cancer Soc. (pres. Ky. div. 1989-90, nat. del. dir. 1989-92, 93-95), Am. Surg. Assn. (sec. 1984-89), Acad. Surgery (pres. 1975-76), Cen. Surg. Assn., Assn. Am. Med. Colls. (chmn. ad hoc com. on Medicare and Medicaid 1978-79), Collegium Internationale Chirurgiae Digestivae (sec.-treas. 1981-86, pres. 1986-87), Council on Public Higher Edn. (task group on health scis.), Halsted Soc., Jefferson County Med. Soc., Ky. Med. Assn., Ky. Surg. Soc. (pres. 1982-83), Louisville Surg. Soc. (pres. 1989-90), Residency Rev. Com. for Surgery (vice chmn. 1981-83, chmn. 1983-85), Société Internationale de Chirurgie, Soc. Surgery Alimentary Tract (treas. 1975-78, pres. 1985-86), Soc. Clin. Surgery, Soc. Surg. Chairmen, Soc. Surg. Oncology (pres. 1984-85), Soc. Univ. Surgeons (treas. 1971-74, pres. 1979-80), Southeastern Surg. Congress (exec. coun. for Ky. 1985-86, pres. 1994-95), So. Med. Assn. (vice chmn. sect. on surgery 1969-70, chmn. sect. 1972-73, sec. 1970-72, exec. coun. for Ky. 1971-77, 89-90), So. Surg. Assn. (pres. 1988-89), Alpha Omega Alpha. Home: 5609 River Knolls Dr Louisville KY 40222 Office: U Louisville Dept Surgery Louisville KY 40292

POLK, JAMES RAY, journalist; b. Oaktown, Ind., Sept. 12, 1937; s. Raymond S. and Oeta (Fleener) P.; m. Bonnie Becker, Nov. 4, 1962; children: Geoffrey, Amy; m. Cara Bryn Saylor, June 21, 1980; 1 child, Abigail. B.A., Ind. U., 1962. With A.P., Indpls., 1962-65, Milw., 1965, Madison, Wis., 1966-67, Washington, 1967-71; investigative reporter Washington Star, 1971-75; correspondent NBC News, Washington, 1975-92; sr. producer CNN Spl. Assignment, 1992—; pres. Investigative Reporters and Editors, Inc., 1978-80, chmn. bd., 1980-82, nat. coll. chmn., 1983-90. Recipient Raymond Clapper Meml. award, 1972, 74, Pulitzer prize for nat. reporting, 1974, Sigma Delta Chi award, 1974, Nat. Headliner award 2d place, 1994, 96, Ind. U. Disting. Alumni award. Mem. Phi Kappa Psi.

POLK, ROBERT FORREST, banker; b. Oshkosh, Wis., Jan. 14, 1947; s. Robert R. and Mary Ann (Witzel) P.; m. Joyce Elaine Peterson, Aug. 28, 1969; children: Sandra L., Jeremy R. BEE, U. Wis., Madison, 1969; MBA in Fin., U. Wis., Whitewater, 1973. Design engr. Honeywell Inc., St. Petersburg, Fla., 1969-71; sales rep. T&T Tech. Inc., McFarland, Wis., 1971-72; lending officer, asst. v.p. Firstar Bank Madison, N.A., 1973-81; dept. mgr., sr. v.p. 1st City Nat. Bank Houston, 1981-87; exec. v.p., chief lending officer Altus Bank, Mobile, Ala., 1987-89; v.p. Firstar Bank Milw., N.A., 1989-91; 1st v.p. Firstar Bank Oshkosh N.A., 1991-94; v.p. Firstar Bank Milw. N.A., 1994—. Avocations: travel, electronics, music, hiking, bicycling.

POLK, WILLIAM ROE, historian; b. Ft. Worth, Tex., Mar. 7, 1929; m. Joan Alison Cooledge, Dec. 1950; children: Milbry Catherine Polk Bauman, Alison Elizabeth Polk Hoffman; m. Ann Borders Cross, June 9, 1962 (div.

Oct. 1979); children: George Washington, Eliza Polk Spence; m. Baroness Elisabeth von Oppenheimer, Dec. 29, 1981. BA with honors, Harvard U., 1951, PhD, 1958; BA with honors, Oxford, Eng., 1955, MA, 1959; LLD (hon.), Lake Forest Coll., 1967. Asst. prof. Harvard Univ., 1956-62; fgn. svc. res. officer class 1, mem. policy planning coun. U.S. State Dept., 1961-65; prof. U. Chgo., 1965-73; pres. Adlai Stevenson Inst., Chgo., 1967-72, Naftex Ltd., Switzerland, 1972-94; chmn. EP Systems, N.Y.C., 1990-93, Chaika Oil Co., London and Moscow, 1993-95; bd. dirs. Hyde Park Bank, Chgo., Microform Data Systems, Arlington Books, Cambridge, Naftex Ltd., Harris & Harris, EP Systems, Chaika Corp., Morrison Internat. Ltd.; cons. Aetna Life and Casualty, Time Inc., TWA, Crocker Nat. Bank, Wheelabrator Frye Inc., Fuller Petroleum, GTE, Teledyne, J. Henry Schroder, U.K., Power Corp., Can., Allianz Versicherungs A.G., Germany, Louis Féraud & Cie, France, UN Stockholm and Vancouver Confs. on the Environment; lectr. in field. Author: What the Arabs Think, 1952, Backdrop to Tragedy, 1957, The Opening of South Lebanon, 1963, The United States and the Arab World, 1965, 2d edit., 1969, 3rd edit., 1975, Passing Brave, 1973, 74, The Golden Ode, 1974, 77, 93, The Elusive Peace, 1979, The Arab World, 1980, The Arab World Today, 1991, Neighbors and Strangers: The Beginnings of Foreign Affairs, 1990, The Vence Partitas, 1992; editor: The Developmental Revolution, 1963, The Beginnnings of Modernization in the Middle East, 1968; contbr. over 100 articles to books and profl. jours. including Fgn. Affairs, The Atlantic, etc. Dir. YMCA C.C., The Middle East Inst., The Adlai Stevenson Inst. Recipient Medal of Honor, Kingdom of Afghanistan, 1967; fellow Rockefeller Found., 1951-55, Ford Found., 1954, Guggenheim Found., 1961. Mem. The Century Assn., Coun. on Fgn. Rels., Middle East Studies Assn. (bd. dirs.), Fed. City Club, The Arts Club, The Cosmos Club, Soc. of the Cin. Democrat. Avocations: exploration, tennis, sailing, gardening. Home: 669 Chemin de la Sine, 06140 Vence France

POLKA, WALTERS S., schools superintendent; b. Niagara Falls, N.Y., Nov. 5, 1945; s. Frank W. and Josephine B. (Ziblut) P.; m. Victoria M. Homiszczak, Aug. 3, 1968; children: Jennifer Marie, Monica Jo. BA, U. Buffalo, 1968; MA, Niagara U., 1970, MS, 1971; EdD, U. Buffalo, 1977; postgrad., Harvard U., 1989-95, Fla. State U., 1993. Cert. sch. dist. adminstr., tchr. social studies, N.Y. Asst. supt. Lewiston-Porter Cen. Schs., Youngstown, N.Y., 1986-90; curriculum coord. Williamsville (N.Y.) Cen. Schs., 1973-86; tchr., high sch. Lewiston-Porter Cen. Schs., 1968-73; supt. Lewiston-Porter Sch. Dist., 1990—; adj. prof. Niagara U., Buffalo State Coll., Medaille Coll., U. Buffalo; curriculum advisor Hudson Inst., 1981-84. Scholar Niagara U. Grad. Sch., 1968-70; Filene Found. fellow Harvard U., summer 1989. Mem. ASCD, Am. Assn. Sch. Adminstrs., Am. Mgmt. Assn., Internat. Soc. Ednl. Planning (pres.), Phi Delta Kappa, Phi Alpha Theta, Pi Lambda Theta. Office: Lewiston-Porter Cen Schs 4061 Creek Rd Youngstown NY 14174-9707

POLKINGHORNE, PATRICIA ANN, hotel executive; b. Galveston, Tex., Aug. 17, 1948; d. C.L. and Barbara Ann (Rathke) Hughes; children: Pamela, Christopher. Student, Sam Houston State Tchrs. Coll., Huntville, Tex. Catering mgr. Rodeway Inn, Denver; office mgr. sales dept. Hyatt Regency, Phoenix; asst. to v.p., treas., controller Continental Drilling, Okla. City; asst. to v.p. resort food and beverage The Pointe Resorts Inc., Phoenix; dir. adminstrn. S.W. Audio Visual, Inc.; asst. to dir. and mgr. catering Phoenician Resort, 1991-92, asst. to dir. of travel industry sales, 1992-93, exec. adminstrv. asst. to dir. of food and beverage divsn., 1993—. Mem. NAFE, Assn. for Info. Systems Profls. Republican. Episcopalian. Avocations: reading, ceramics, gardening, computers, law. Office: 6000 E Camelback Rd Scottsdale AZ 85251-1949

POLK-MATTHEWS, JOSEPHINE ELSEY, school psychologist; b. Roselle, N.J., Sept. 24, 1930; d. Charles Carrington and Olive Mae (Bond) Polk; m. Donald Roger Matthews, Aug. 29, 1959 (div. 1974); children: John Roger, Alison Olivia; m. William Y. Delaney, Sept. 17, 1994. AB, Mt. Holyoke Coll., 1952; credential in occupational therapy, Columbia U., 1954; MA, U. So. Calif., L.A., 1957; Cert. Advanced Study, Harvard U., 1979, MS, 1980; postgrad., Coll. William & Mary, 1995-96. Cert. elem. edn. life teaching credential, Calif; cert. ednl. adminstrn. life credential, Calif.; cert. pupil personnel svcs., counseling life credential, sch. psychology credential, Calif.; sch. psychology credential, Nev. Occupational therapist VA Hosp., Northport, N.Y., 1953-55, L.A., 1955-57; health svcs. adminstr. John Wesley County Hosp., L.A., 1957-59; elem. tchr. L.A. (Calif.) City Schs., 1959-60, Santa Clara (Calif.) Unified Sch. Dist., 1960-65, 71-74; asst. prof. Sch. Edn., San Jose (Calif.) State U., 1971; asst. prin. Berryessa Union Sch. Dist., San Jose, Calif., 1974-77, 85-86; ednl. cons. Boston (Mass.) U. Sch. Medicine, 1981-83; asst. prin. Inglewood (Calif.) Unified Sch. Dist., 1986-90; sch. psychologist Clark County Sch. Dist., Las Vegas, 1990-94; contract sch. psychologist Newport News (Va.) Sch. Dist., 1995—; med. facility developer Commonwealth Mass., Dept. Mental Health, Boston, 1980-81, ednl. liaison, Roxbury Juvenile Ct., 1979. Author: (with others) The New Our Bodies Ourselves, 1983; prodr.: (video) Individualized Rsch., 1971. Commr. Commn. on the Status of Women, Cambridge, Mass., 1981-83; hostess Ctr. for Internat. Visitors, Boston, 1983-84; pers. recruiter L.A. (Calif.) Olympic Organizing Com., 1984; vol. tutor Las Vegas (Nev.) Libr., 1992. Mem. Nat. Assn. Sch. Psychologists, Calif. Assn. Sch. Psychologists, Nev. Assn. Sch. Psychologists, Clark County Assn. Sch. Psychologists, Assn. Black Psychologists, Phi Delta Kappa, Alpha Kappa Alpha. Office: Sch Edn Spl Edn PO Box 8795 Williamsburg VA 23187-8795

POLL, HEINZ, choreographer, artistic director; b. Oberhausen, Germany, Mar. 18, 1926; came to U.S., 1964, naturalized, 1975; s. Heinrich and Anna Margareta (Winkels) P. Co-founder, dir. The Dance Inst., U. Akron, 1967-77; founder, artistic dir., choreographer Ohio Ballet, Akron, 1968—; tchr. Chilean Instituto de Extension Musical, 1951-61, N.Y. Nat. Acad., 1965-66. Dancer Göttingen Mcpl. Theatre, 1947-49, Deutsches Theatre Konstanz, 1949-50, East Berlin State Opera, 1950-51, Nat. Ballet Chile, 1951-62, Ballet de la Jeunesse Musicales de France, 1963-64; guest appearances with Nat. Ballet Chile, 1964, Am. Dance Festival, 1965; choreographer works for Nat. Ballet Chile, Paris Festival Ballet, Ballet Jeunesse de la Musicales de France, Nat. Ballet Can., Pa. Ballet, Ohio Ballet, Limon Dance Co. Recipient Ohio Dance award, 1983, 88-89, Achievement Dance award No. Ohio Live Mag., 1985-86, 88-89, 93-94, 94-95, Cleve. Arts prize, 1995; Nat. Endowment for Arts grantee, 1974-75. Mem. NEA (dance panelist 1987-89, 92-93). Office: Ohio Ballet U Akron Akron OH 44325-2501

POLL, MARTIN HARVEY, film producer; b. N.Y.C.; s. David and Fay (Tamber) P.; m. Lee Lindenberg, May 21, 1954 (div. Oct. 10, 1967); children: Mark, Jonathan; m. Gladys Peltz Jaffe, Oct. 31, 1976; 1 son, Anthony. B.S., Wharton Sch. Bus. U. Pa., 1943. Pres. Inter-Continental TV Films Inc., N.Y.C., 1952; exec. producer Theatre Network TV Inc., N.Y.C., 1953; pres. Gold Medal Studios, Bronx, N.Y., 1954-62; ind. producer, 1962—. (Named Hon. Commr. Motion Picture Arts N.Y.C. 1958, recipient David Di Donatello Best Film Producer award Pres. Italy 1968, N.Y. Film Critics award 1968, Hollywood Fgn. Press Assn. Golden Globe award 1968, Brit. Acad. award 1968); films include Love is a Ball, 1962, Sylvia, 1964, The Appointment, 1968, The Lion in Winter, 1968 (Best Picture award), The Magic Garden of Stanley Sweetheart, 1970, Night Watch, 1972, The Man Who Loved Cat Dancing, 1973, Love and Death, 1975, The Sailor Who Fell From Grace with The Sea, 1976, The Dain Curse, Somebody Killed Her Husband, 1978, Nighthawks, 1981, Arthur the King, 1984, Gimme An F, 1984, Haunted Summer, 1987, My Heroes Have Always Been Cowboys, 1991, (TV miniseries) Diana—Her True Story, 1993. Served with AUS, 1944-47. Mem. Producers Guild of Am., Acad. Motion Picture Arts and Scis., Cinema Circulus, Friends of Library U. So. Calif.

POLL, ROBERT EUGENE, JR., bank executive; b. Urbana, Ill., Apr. 16, 1948; s. Robert E. Sr. and Dorothy (Baker) P.; m. Leslie Tompkins, Aug. 8, 1970 (div. Mar. 1980); m. Virginia O'Donnell, July 17, 1982; children: Alexandra, Bianca, Paulo Felipe Kos. BA, Kenyon Coll., 1970; MBA, Ind. U., 1972. V.p. Chase Manhattan Bank, N.Y.C., 1970-78; assoc. Lazard Freres & Co., N.Y.C., 1978-82, mng. dir., mgr. mcpl. divsn., 1985—; gen. ptnr. William Blair & Co., Chgo., 1982-84; mem. adv. bd. Ind. Small Bus. Assistance Corp., Bloomington, 1971, Pub. Fin. Inst., N.Y.C., 1976; adv. bd. Worldvest. Mem. Am. Mktg. Assn., N.Y. Acad. Sci., Am. Assn. Polit. and Social Scis., Acad. Polit. Sci., Chgo. Econ. Forum. Clubs: Tavern (Chgo.); N.Y. Athletic. Office: Lazard Freres & Co 30 Rockefeller Plz New York NY 10020

POLLACK, DANIEL, concert pianist; b. Los Angeles, Jan. 23, 1935. MS in Music, Juilliard Sch., 1957, Acad. Musik, Vienna, Austria, 1958. Asst. prof. U. Hartford, Conn., 1966-70; prof. piano U. So. Calif., Los Angeles, 1971—. Concert performances in U.S., USSR, Europe, Far East, South Am. Recipient prize Internat. Tschaikowsky Piano Competition, Moscow, USSR, 1958; Fulbright grantee, 1957-58; Martha Baird Rockefeller Found. grantee, 1963. Mem. Am. Fedn. Musicians, Kosciuszko Found., Chopin Found., Music Tchrs. Nat. Assn. (nat. exec. bd.). Office: U So Calif Dept Music Los Angeles CA 90089

POLLACK, FLORENCE K.Z., management consultant; b. Washington, Pa.; d. Charles and Ruth (Isaacson) Zaks; divorced; children: Melissa, Stephanie. BA, Flora Stone Mather Coll., Western Res. U., 1961. Pres., CEO Exec. Arrangements, Inc., Cleve., 1978—. Lobbyist Ohio Citizens Com. for Arts, Columbus, 1975-83; mem. Leadership Cleve., 1978-79; trustee jr. com. Cleve. Orch., mem. pub. rels. adv. com.; trustee Great Lakes Theatre Festival, 1989-90; mem. pub. rels. adv. com., Cleve. Ballet, Dance Cleve., Jr. Com. of No. Ohio Opera Assn., Cleve. Opera, Shakers Lakes Regional Nature Ctr., Cleve. Music Sch. Settlement, Playhouse Sq. Cabinet, Cleve. Ctr. Econ. Edn., ARC, Cleve. Conv. and Visitors Bur., domed stadium adv. com. Named Idea Woman of Yr. Cleve. Plain Dealer, 1975, to Au Courrant list Cleve. Mag., 1979, one of Cleve.'s 100 Most Influential Women, 1985, one of 1988 Trendsetters Cleve. Woman mag. Mem. Cleve. Area Meeting Planning, Skating Club, Univ. Club, Women's City Club, Playhouse Club, Shoreby Club. Avocations: arts, travel, reading. Office: Exec Arrangements Inc 13221 Shaker Sq Cleveland OH 44120

POLLACK, GERALD ALEXANDER, economist, government official; b. Vienna, Austria, Jan. 14, 1929; came to U.S. 1938; s. Stephen J. and Tini (Herschel) P.; m. Patricia S. Sisterson; children: Nora S., Carol A. BA, Swarthmore (Pa.) Coll., 1951; MA, MPA, Princeton U., 1953, PhD, 1958. Corp. economist Leeds & Northrup Co., Phila., 1958-62; officer in charge internat. payments U.S. Dept. State, Washington, 1962-63; internat. economist Joint Econ. Com. of Congress, Washington, 1963-65; chief economist Office Spl. Rep. for Trade Negotiations, 1964; dep. asst. sec. U.S. Dept. Commerce, Washington, 1965-68; v.p. Loeb, Rhoades & Co., N.Y.C., 1968-69, Bendix Corp., Southfield, Mich., 1969-70, Citibank, N.Y.C., 1970-71; internat. economist Exxon Corp., N.Y.C., 1971-86; v.p., chief economist Overseas Shipholding Group, N.Y.C., 1986-89; assoc. prof. fin. Pace U., N.Y.C., 1990-94; assoc. dir. for internat. econs. Bur. Econ. Analysis, U.S. Dept. Commerce, 1994—. Contbr. articles to profl. jours. Bd. dirs. Jamaica Estates Assn., 1976-80, Oakwood Sch., Poughkeepsie, N.Y., 1979-89; trustee Lindley Murray Fund, 1990-94; mem. Greenwich Dem. Town Com., 1992-94; clk. Flushing Friends monthly meeting Soc. of Friends, 1990-94. With U.S. Army, 1953-55. Mem. Am. Econ. Assn., Nat. Assn. Bus. Economists, Coun. on Fgn. Rels., Forecasters Club N.Y., Downtown Economists Club, The Nat. Economists Club, Soc. of Friends, Phi Beta Kappa. Soc. of Friends. Avocations: cello, classical music, photography, hiking, bicycling.

POLLACK, GERALD HARVEY, bioengineering educator; b. Bklyn., May 20, 1940; s. Max and Helen (Solomon) P.; m. Sylvia A. Byrne, Aug. 12, 1966 (div. 1982); children: Seth Benjamin, Ethan David, Mia Raphaella. BS, Poly. Inst. Bklyn., 1961; PhD, U. Pa., 1968. Mem. faculty U. Wash. Med. Sch., Seattle, 1968—; prof. bioengring. U. Wash. Med. Sch., 1977—. Author: Muscles and Molecules: Uncovering the Principles of Biological Motion, 1990 (Excellence award Soc. for Tech. Communication 1992); co-editor: Ballistocardiography and Cardiac Performance, 1967, Cross-bridge Mechanism of Muscle Contraction, 1979, Contractile Mechanisms in Muscle, 1983, Molecular Mechanism of Muscle Contraction, 1988, Mechanism of Sliding in Muscle Contraction, 1993; mem. editorial bd. Jour. Molecular and Cellular Cardiology, 1975-80, Am. Jour. Physiology, 1976-80, Circulation Rsch., 1982-89; contbr. articles to profl. jours. Established investigator Am. Heart Assn., 1974-79. Recipient Kulka award Poly. Inst. Bklyn., 1961; grantee NIH, 1970—; grantee Am. Heart Assn., 1973—; grantee Muscular Dystrophy Assn. Am., 1980. Fellow Am. Inst. Med. and Biol. Engring. (founding); mem. Bioengring. Soc. (dir. 1976-79), Biophys. Soc., Am. Heart Assn. (exec. com. Basic Sci. Coun. 1982-86), Eta Kappa Nu, Tau Beta Pi, Alpha Epsilon Pi. Address: 3714 48th Ave NE Seattle WA 98105-5250

POLLACK, GERALD J., financial executive; b. N.Y.C., Jan. 20, 1942; s. Charles and Reba P.; m. Diane Pollack, Aug. 30, 1964; children: Suzanne, Jennifer, John. BS in Physics, Rensselaer Poly Inst., 1963; MBA, Dartmouth Coll., 1965. Comptroller trainee Exxon Corp., N.Y.C., 1965-67; asst. ops. comptroller Amerada Hess, Woodbridge, N.J., 1967-68; mgr. customer svc. Arthur Young & Co., N.Y.C., 1969-73; dir. mgmt. svc. Arthur Young & Co., Stamford, Conn., 1973-74; v.p., controller Avis Inc., Garden City, L.I., 1975-81; sr. v.p., chief fin. officer Rayonier, Stamford, 1982—. Mem. N.Y. Adv. Bd. Allendale Ins. Co., Fin. Exec. Inst. Office: Rayonier Inc 1177 Summer St Stamford CT 06905-5522

POLLACK, GERALD LESLIE, physicist, educator; b. Bklyn., July 8, 1933; s. Herman and Jennie (Tenenbaum) P.; m. Antoinette Amparo Velasquez, Dec. 22, 1958; children: Harvey Anton, Samuela Juliet, Margolita Mia, Violet Amata. BS, Bklyn. Coll., 1954; Fulbright scholar, U. Gottingen, 1954-55; MS, Calif. Inst. Tech., 1957, PhD, 1962. Physics student trainee Nat. Bur. Standards, Washington, 1954-58, solid state physicist, 1961-65; cons. Nat. Bur. Standards, Boulder, Colo., 1965-70; assoc. prof. dept. physics Mich. State U., East Lansing, 1965-69, prof., 1969—; cons. NRC, Ill. Dept. Nuclear Safety; physicist Naval Med. Rsch. Inst., Bethesda, Md., summer 1979; physicist USAF Sch. Aerospace Medicine, San Antonio, Tex., summer 1987. Contbr. articles to profl. jours. Fellow Am. Phys. Soc.; mem. AAAS, Am. Assn. Physics Tchrs. Office: Mich State U Dept Physics and Astronomy East Lansing MI 48824-1116

POLLACK, HENRY NATHAN, geophysics educator; b. Omaha, July 13, 1936; s. Harold Myron and Sylvia (Chait) P.; m. Lana Beth Schoenberger, Jan. 29, 1963; children—Sara Beth (dec.), John David. A.B., Cornell U., 1958; M.S., U. Nebr., 1960; Ph.D., U. Mich., 1963. Lectr. U. Mich., 1962, asst. prof., assoc. prof., prof. geophysics, 1964—, assoc. dean for research, 1982-85, chmn. dept. geol. scis., 1988-91; rsch. fellow Harvard U., 1963-64; sr. lectr. U. Zambia, 1970-71; vis. scientist U. Durham, U. Newcastle-on-Tyne, Eng., 1977-78, U. Western Ont., 1985-86; chmn. Internat. Heat Flow Commn., 1991-95. Fellow AAAS, Geol. Soc. Am.; mem. Am. Geophys. Union. Achievements include research on thermal evolution of the earth, recent climate change. Office: U Mich Dept Geol Scis Ann Arbor MI 48109

POLLACK, HERBERT WILLIAM, electronics executive; b. N.Y.C., Mar. 27, 1927; s. Benjamin and Shirley (Fine) P.; m. Sandra Rowe, March 26, 1950; children: Jill C., Mindy L. BEE, CCNY, 1950; MEE, NYU, 1953. Electronic engr. A.B. Dumont Co., Clifton, N.J., 1950-51; rsch. assoc. NYU, N.Y.C., 1951-54; electronic engr. CBS - Columbia, N.Y.C., 1954-55; v.p., dir. Polarad Electronics Inc., N.Y.C., 1955-65; group div. mgr. Sanders Assocs., Nashua, N.H., 1965-70; chmn., pres. Parlex Corp., Methuen, Mass., 1970—; pres., dir. Inst. for Interconnecting and Packaging Electronic Cirs., Lincolnwood, Ill., 1984-86. With USN, 1945-46. Fellow IEEE; mem. Tau beta Pi, Eta Kappa Nu. Avocations: reading, music, tennis. Office: Parlex Corp 145 Milk St Methuen MA 01844-4664

POLLACK, HOWARD JAY, lawyer; b. Cheltenham, Pa., Oct. 31, 1965; s. Barry Allen and Karen Elizabeth (Plone) P.; m. Lisa Marie Fitzgerald, Oct. 24, 1993. BA in Economics, U. Del., 1987; JD cum laude, Syracuse U., 1991. Bar: Del. 1991, U.S. Dist. Ct. Del. 1991, Pa. 1992. Atty. Richards, Layton & Finger, Wilmington, Del., 1990-94, Brownstein Hyatt Farber & Strickland, P.C., Denver, 1994—. Contbr. articles to profl. jours. Bd. dirs. Del. Jewish Cmty. Ctr., Wilmington, 1993-94; active Del. Rep. Party, Wilmington, 1991-94. Recipient Robert Anderson Writing award, 1991. Mem. ABA (planning bd. Young Lawyers Divsn. real estate law divsn., com. on law and tech., com. on joint ventures, partnerships, 1993—), Del. Bar Assn., Order of Coif. Republican. Jewish. Avocations: skiing, mountaineering, reading, squash. Home: 1583 S Columbine St Denver CO 80210 Office: Brownstein Hyatt Farber & Stickland 410 17th St Ste 2200 Denver CO 80202

POLLACK, IRWIN WILLIAM, psychiatrist, educator; b. Phila., Aug. 14, 1927; s. Nathan and Rose (Bergman) P.; m. Barbara Jean Callaway, Oct. 9, 1988; children from previous marriage: Nathaniel Edward, Joshua Frank, Jonathan Daniel. A.B., Temple U., 1950; M.A., Columbia, 1951; student, U. Pa., 1951-52; M.D., U. Vt., 1956. Diplomate: Am. Bd. Psychiatry and Neurology. Intern Grad. Hosp. U. Pa., 1956-57; asst. resident psychiatry Henry Phipps Psychiat. Clinic (John Hopkins Hosp.), 1957-60; chief resident psychiatry Johns Hopkins Hosp., 1960-61, adminstr. psychosomatic clinic, psychiat. liaison service, 1961-64; psychiatrist-in-chief Sinai Hosp., Balt., 1964-68; mem. faculty psychiatry Coll. Medicine and Dentistry N.J. (Rutgers Med. Sch.), 1968-87, U. Medicine and Dentistry N.J., Robert Wood Johnson Med. Sch., 1987—; asso. prof. psychiatry, 1968-70, prof. psychiatry, 1970—; chmn. dept. Univ. Medicine and Dentistry, prof. neurology, dir. Ctr. for Cognitive Rehab.; exec. dir. Coll. Medicine and Dentistry (Community Mental Health Ctr.), 1970-77. Served with USNR, 1945-46. Fellow Am. Psychiat. Assn. (life); mem. N.J. Psychiat. Assn., Am. Psychosomatic Soc., Am. Congress Rehab. Medicine, Alpha Omega Alpha. Spl. research or problems of time and space perception, psychology of phys. disability, doctor-patient relationships, cognitive retraining of brain-injured persons. Home: 238 Sayre Dr Princeton NJ 08540 Office: Robert Wood Johnson Med Sch U Medicine and Dentistry NJ Hoes Ln Piscataway NJ 08854

POLLACK, JOE, retired newspaper critic and columnist, writer; b. Bklyn., Feb. 3, 1931; s. Samuel H. and Anna (Weisman) P.; m. Joan S., Mar. 6, 1952 (div. 1964); children: Wendy, Dara, Sharon; m. Carol Atchison, Dec. 1, 1964 (dec. 1993); m. Ann Lemons, Nov. 20, 1994. BJ, U. Mo., 1952. Sports writer St. Louis Globe-Democrat, 1955-61; dir. pub. rels. St. Louis Football Cardinals, 1961-72; critic, columnist St. Louis Post-Dispatch, 1972-95; critic Sta. KSDK-TV, St. Louis, 1973-88, Sta. KMOV-TV, St. Louis, 1988-92; commentator Sta. KMOX, St. Louis, 1960-85, Sta. KWMU, St. Louis, 1994—. Author: Joe Pollack's Guide to St. Louis Restaurants, 1988, updated, 1992; contbr. numerous articles to mags. Mem. Am. Theatre Critics Assn., Profl. Football Writers Assn., Am. Soc. Profl. Journalists, Internat. Writers Ctr. (adv. bd. St. Louis). Home: 7417 Oxford Dr Saint Louis MO 63105

POLLACK, JORDAN ELLIS, pharmaceutical company executive; b. N.Y.C., June 16, 1934; s. Irving and Ann Pollack; m. Francine Hornstein, Aug. 23, 1959; children: Robert, Randi. BS in Pharmacy, Columbia U., 1956; MBA in Mktg., Iona Coll., 1971. Registered pharmacist, N.Y., N.J., Fla. Med. rep./market researcher Geigy Pharm., Ardsley, N.Y., 1959-70; account exec. William Douglas McAdams, N.Y.C., 1970-71; account supr. Grey Advt., N.Y.C., 1971-75; account dir. Carrafiello-Diehl Advt., Irvington, N.Y., 1975-79; sr. product mgr. Knoll Pharms., Whippany, N.J., 1979-85, mgr. new product planning, 1985-88, dir. new bus. devel., 1988—. Chmn. Florham Park (N.J.) Airport Adv. Com., 1989—; apptd. to Florham Park Zoning Bd. of Adjustment. With U.S. Army, 1957-59. Mem. Pharm. Advt. Coun., Am. Soc. Hosp. Pharmacists, Lic. Exec. Soc. Avocations: walking, softball, swimming. Home: 4 Partridge Ln Florham Park NJ 07932-1728 Office: Knoll Pharm Co 3000 Continental Dr N Budd Lake NJ 07828-1234

POLLACK, LOUIS, telecommunications company executive; b. N.Y.C., Nov. 4, 1920; s. Benjamin and Lena (Woloshen) P.; m. Dorothy Silverman, Feb. 4, 1945; children: Annette Pollack Rachlin, Barbara Pollack Held, Lawrence. BEE, CCNY, 1953; postgrad., Stevens Inst. Tech., 1954-55. Registered profl. engr. Dir. transmission system ops. ITT Fed. Labs., Nutley, N.J., 1943-67; exec. dir. Comsat Labs., Clarksburg, Md., 1967-80; v.p. world systems div. Communications Satellite Corp., Washington, 1980-84; cons. Satellite System design, 1984—; del. XVIII Gen. Assembly Nat. Acad. Sci. Contbr. articles to profl. jours.; patentee in field. Fellow IEEE; mem. AIAA (asso. fellow), Nat. Soc. Profl. Engrs., Sigma Xi. Office: 15321 Delphinium Ln Rockville MD 20853-1725

POLLACK, MICHAEL, lawyer; b. N.Y.C., July 14, 1946; s. Irving and Bertha (Horowitz) P.; m. Barbara Linda Shore, Aug. 23, 1970; children: Matthew, Ilana. BEng, Cooper Union, 1967; MS, U. Pa., 1970; JD, Temple U., 1974. Bar: Pa. 1974, U.S. Dist. Ct. (ea. dist.) Pa. 1974. Rsch. scientist Pa. Rsch. Assocs., Phila., 1968-69; engr. GE Co., Valley Forge, Pa., 1969-70, Burroughs Corp., Great Valley, Pa., 1970-71; assoc. Blank, Rome, Comisky & McCauley, Phila., Pa., 1974-82; ptnr. Blank, Rome, Comisky & McCauley, Phila., 1982—; lectr., course planner Pa. Bar Inst., Phila., chmn. legal edn. com. for R.E. Dept. Mem. ABA, Pa. Bar Assn., Phila. Bar Assn., Internat. Assn. Attys. and Execs. in Corp. Real Estate, Eta Kappa Nu, Tau Beta Pi. Republican. Avocations: music, tennis. Office: Blank Rome Comisky & McCauley 4 Penn Center Plz Philadelphia PA 19103-2521

POLLACK, MILTON, federal judge; b. N.Y.C., Sept. 29, 1906; s. Julius and Betty (Schwartz) P.; m. Lillian Klein, Dec. 18, 1932 (dec. July 1967); children—Stephanie Pollack Singer, Daniel A.; m. Moselle Baum Erlich, Oct. 24, 1971. A.B., Columbia U., 1927, J.D., 1929. Bar: N.Y. 1930. Assoc. Gilman & Unger, N.Y.C., 1929-38; ptnr. Unger & Pollack, N.Y.C., 1938-44; propr. Milton Pollack, N.Y.C., 1945-67; dist. judge U.S. Dist. Ct. (so. dist.) N.Y., 1967—, sr. status, 1983; mem. com. on ct. adminstrn. Jud. Conf., 1968-87, mem. Jud. Panel on Multi-dist. Litigation, 1983-95. Mem. Prospect Park So. Assn., Bklyn., pres., 1948-50, counsel, 1950-60, bd. dirs., 1945-60; mem. local SSS, 1952-60; chmn. lawyers div. Fedn. Jewish Philanthropies, 1957-61, vice chmn., 1954-57; chmn. lawyers div. Am. Jewish Com., 1964-66, bd. dirs., from 1967; hon. dir. Beth Isreal Hosp.; trustee Temple Emanu-El, from 1977, v.p., from 1978. Recipient Learned Hand award Am. Jewish Com., 1967, Proskauer medal lawyers divsn. Fedn. Jewish Philanthropies, 1968, Disting. Svc. medal N.Y. County Lawyers Assn., 1991, Fordham-Stein Prize award, 1994, Devitt award Disting. Svc. to Justice, 1995; decorated chevalier Legion of Honor (France). Mem. ABA, N.Y. State Bar Assn., Assn. of Bar of City of N.Y., Columbia Law Sch. Alumni Assn. (pres. 1970-72), Harmonie Club (bd. trustees). Office: US Dist Ct US Courthouse Foley Sq New York NY 10007-1501

POLLACK, NORMAN, history educator; b. Bridgeport, Conn., May 29, 1933; s. Benjamin and Mary (Beimel) P.; m. Nancy Bassing, Feb. 2, 1957; 1 son, Peter Franklin. B.A., U. Fla., 1954; M.A., Harvard U., 1957, Ph.D., 1961. Instr. history Yale, 1961-62, asst. prof., 1962-65; asso. prof. Wayne State U., 1965-68; prof. Mich. State U., 1968—. Author: The Populist Response to Industrial America, 1962, The Populist Mind, 1967, The Just Polity, 1987, The Humane Economy, 1990. Guggenheim fellow, 1968-69. Home: 929 Roxburgh Ave East Lansing MI 48823-3130 Office: Dept of History Mich State U East Lansing MI 48824

POLLACK, PAUL ROBERT, airline service company executive; b. N.Y.C., Nov. 17, 1941; s. Harry and Hilda (Tepper) P.; m. Linda Weinstein, Aug. 14, 1965; children: Mark, Melissa. BBA, CCNY, 1962; MBA, L.I. U., Greenvale, N.Y., 1993. CPA, N.Y. Staff acct. Seidman & Seidman, N.Y.C., 1962-68; with Hudson Gen. Corp., Great Neck, N.Y., 1968—, exec. v.p., chief oper. officer, 1990—. With U.S. Army, 1962. Mem. AICPA, N.Y. State Soc. CPAs (Haskins award 1966). Office: Hudson Gen Corp 111 Great Neck Rd Great Neck NY 11021-5402

POLLACK, REGINALD MURRAY, painter, sculptor; b. Middle Village, L.I., N.Y., July 29, 1924; m. Kerstin Birgitta Soederlund; children by previous marriage: Jane Olivia, Maia Jaquine. Grad., High Sch. Music and Art, N.Y.C., 1941; student with, Wallace Harrison, Moses Soyer, Boardman Robinson; student, Academie de la Grande Chaumiere, 1948-52. Occasional asst. to Constantin Brancusi; vis. critic Yale U., 1962-63, Cooper Union, 1963-64; mem. staff Human Rels. Tng. Ctr., UCLA, 1966; artistic dir. The Gallery, Washington Collection Fine Arts, Leesburg, Va., 1991—; chmn. artists adv. com. Loudon Arts Coun., Va., 1990-93. One-man shows include Charles Fourth Gallery, N.Y.C., 1948, Peridot Gallery, 1949, 52, 55-57, 59, 60, 62, 63, 65, 67, 69, Galerie Saint-Placide, Paris, 1952, Dwan Gallery, 1960, Jefferson Gallery, LaJolla, Calif., 1963, 68, 69, Goldwach Gallery, Chgo., 1964, 65, 66, Gallery Z, Beverly Hills, Calif., 1973, David Alexander Gallery, 1974, Washington Gallery Arts, 1974, Cosmos Club, Washington, 1976, Washington Project for Arts, 1976, Everhart Mus., Scranton, Pa., 1977, Pa. State U., 1977, Jack Rasmussen gallery, 1978, 79, 80, 81, 82, Art Washington, 1979, 81, Corcoran Mus., 1980, Zenith Gallery, Washington, 1982, Summit Gallery, N.Y., 1982, Tartt Gallery, Washington, 1986, Arctic Images Gallery, Aspen, Colo., 1987, Loudoun County Adminstrn. Bldg.,

1988, Susan Conway Carroll Gallery, Washington, 1990, The Gallery, Leesburg, 1992, Loudoun Valley Vineyard, Waterford, Va., 1992-93, Sondoni Art Gallery, Wilkes U., Pa., 1994, The Natural Light Art School Gallery, Leesburg, Va., 1995, George Washington U., Va. Campus, Leesburg; exhibited group shows including Whitney Mus. Am. Art, 1953, 55, 56, 58, 62, U. Nebr., 1951, 56, 57, 60, 63, Chgo. Art Inst., Carnegie, Pitts., Salon du Mai, Paris, U. Ill., Salon des Artistes Independants, Paris, 1955-58, NAS, 1990, NIH, 1990, Elaine Benson Gallery, Bridgehampton, L.I., 1991, numerous others; multi-media theatrical prodns. The War of The Angels, 1974; The Twelve Gifts of Christmas, 1974; commns. include Jacob's Ladder painting, Washington Cathedral, bronze sculpture, The World Bank, awarded to King of Thailand; represented in permanent collections, Bezalel Mus., Bklyn. Mus., Collection de L'Etat, France, U. Glasgow, Haifa, Mus. Modern Art, U. Nebr., Newark Mus., Rockefeller Inst., Whitney Mus. Am. Art, Worcester Art Mus., Nat. Mus. Am. Art, Ft. Lauderdale (Fla.) Mus., Loew Mus. U. Miami, Fla., Met. Mus., N.Y., numerous other pub. and pvt. collections.; author and illustrator: The Magician and the Child, 1971; illustrator: Get a Horse (Steven Price), 1974, Visions from the Ramble (John Hollander), 1964, The Quest of the Gole (John Hollander), 1966, O is for Overkill, A Survival Alphabet (Merrill Pollack), 1968, The Blessed Ones (Ulla Isaksson), 1970, Oedipus (Seneca, transl. Ted Hughes), 1973, The Enjoyment of Music (Joseph Machlis). Instr. Quaker Half-way House, Los Angeles, 1968; cons. staff Lighthouse Child Guidance Center Presbyn. Hosp., 1966-69; pvt. instr., 1966-69; vis. artist Materials Research Lab., Pa. State U., 1977; trustee Washington Project for Arts, 1976-80. Served with AUS, 1941-45. Recipient Prix Neumann Paris, 1952, Prix Othon Friesz Paris, mention, 1954, 57, Prix de Peintres Etrangeres, 2d prize Paris Moderne, 1958; Ingram-Merrill Found. grantee, 1964, 70-71. Address: RR 1 Box 955 Waterford VA 22190-9700

POLLACK, ROBERT ELLIOT, biologist, educator; b. Bklyn., Sept. 2, 1940; s. Hyman Ephraim and Molly (Pollack) P.; m. Amy Louise Steinberg, Dec. 23, 1961; 1 child, Marya. BA in Physics, Columbia U., 1961; PhD in Biology, Brandeis U., 1966. Asst. prof. pathology Med. Sch. NYU, N.Y.C., 1969-70; sr. scientist Cold Spring Harbor Lab., N.Y., 1971-75; prof. microbiology Med. Sch., SUNY-Stony Brook, 1975-78; prof. biol. sci. Columbia U., N.Y.C., 1978—; dean Columbia Coll., N.Y.C., 1982-89; bd. dirs. Applied Microbiology, Inc.; instr. Pratt Archtl. Sch., Bklyn., 1970; vis. prof. pharmacology Albert Einstein Coll. Medicine, Bronx, N.Y., 1977-92; lectr. Rosenthal Colloquium, March of Dimes, 1989; McGregory lectr. Colgate U., 1979; du Vigneaud lectr. Med. Sch., Cornell U., 1983. Co-editor: Readings in Mammalian Cell Culture, 1973, 3d rev. edit., 1981, Signs of Life, 1984 (translations in 7 langs., Lionel Trilling award 1995); mng. editor BBA Revs. on Cancer, 1980-86; contbr. numerous rsch. articles on molecular cell biology to profl. jours. Trustee N.Y. Found., 1986—, Brandeis U., 1989-94, Solomon Schechter Sch. of N.Y.C., 1996—; mem. World Econ. Forum, 1995—. Recipient Rsch. Career Devel. award NIH, 1974, Alexander Hamilton medal, 1989, Lionel Trilling award Columbia U., 1995; NIH spl. fellow Weizmann Inst., Rehovot, Israel, 1970-71; grantee Nat. Cancer Inst., NIH, 1968-92, Am. Cancer Soc., 1985-94; John Simon Guggenheim fellow, 1993. Fellow AAAS; mem. N.Y. Acad. Scis., Am. Soc. Microbiology. Jewish. Office: Columbia U Dept Biol Scis 749 Fairchild Hall New York NY 10027

POLLACK, RONALD F(RANK), foundation executive, lawyer; b. N.Y.C., Feb. 21, 1944; s. Max Louis and Hanna Esther (Borchardt) Pollack Baruch; m. Rebecca Lucy Bolling, Jan. 8, 1972; children: Sarah Shoshana, Abraham Max, Martin Landrum. B.A., Queens Coll., 1965; J.D., NYU, 1968. Bar: N.Y. 1968, D.C. 1978, U.S. Ct. Appeals (D.C. cir) 1970, U.S. Ct. Appeals (5th cir.) 1971, U.S. Ct. Appeals (6th cir.) 1974, U.S. Supreme Ct. 1973. Atty. Ctr. on Social Welfare Policy and Law, N.Y.C., 1968-73; founder, exec. dir. Food Research and Action Ctr., N.Y.C., 1970-80; dean Antioch Sch. Law, Washington, 1980-83; exec. dir. Families U.S.A., Washington, 1983—, Families U.S.A. Found., Washington, 1983—; sec. treas., bd. dirs. Food Research and Action Ctr., Washington, 1980—; mem. civil legal services D.C. Jud. Conf. Com., 1980-83. Author: If We Had Ham, We Could Have Ham and Eggs...If We Had Eggs: A Study of the National School Breakfast Program, 1972, Out to Lunch: A Study of USDA's Child Care Feeding and Summer Feeding Programs, 1974; co-author: On the Other Side of Easy Street: Myths and Facts About the Economics of Old Age, 1987. Treas. Jewish Fund for Justice, 1985-88, bd. dirs., 1985-93; bd. dirs. Am. Jewish World Service, Self-Help Community Services, 1974-77; mem. domestic adv. bd., project rev. bd. U.S.A. for Africa/Hands Across Am., 1986-88; v.p. of bd. dirs. Burgundy Farm Country Day Sch., 1988-90, pres. 1990-91; bd. dirs. Americans for Health, 1986-81. Arthur Garfield Hays Civil Liberties fellow, 1967; research fellow Legal Services Corp., Washington, 1978-80.

POLLACK, SEYMOUR VICTOR, computer science educator; b. Bklyn., Aug. 3, 1933; s. Max and Sylvia (Harrison) P.; m. Sydell Altman, Jan. 23, 1955; children: Mark, Sherie. BChemE, Pratt Inst., 1954; MChemE, Bklyn. Poly. Inst., 1960. Lic. chem. engr., Ohio. Engr. Schwarz Labs., Mt. Vernon, N.Y., 1954-55; design engr. Curtiss-Wright, Wood-Ridge, N.J., 1955-57, Fairchild Engines, Deer Park, N.Y., 1957-59, GE, Evendale, Ohio, 1959-62; rsch. assoc. U. Cin., 1962-66; prof. computer sci. Washington U., St. Louis, 1966—; cons. Mo. Auto Club, St. Louis, 1969-82, United Van Lines, Fenton, Mo., 1984-86, Computer Sci. Accreditation Bd., N.Y.C., 1985—. Author: Structured Fortran, 1982, UCSD Pascal, 1984, Studies in Computer Science, 1983, The DOS Book, 1985, Turbo Pascal Programming, 1991; cons. editor Holt Rinehart & Winston, N.Y.C., 1979-86. Bd. dirs. Hillel orgn., Washington U., 1983-84. Recipient Alumni Achievement award Pratt Inst., 1966, Outstanding Teaching award Burlington Northern Found., 1987. Mem. Assn. for Computing Machinery, Am. Assn. for Engring. Edn. Jewish. Avocations: classical and jazz piano, jogging. Office: Campus Box 1045 Washington U Saint Louis MO 63130

POLLACK, SOLOMON ROBERT, bioengineering educator; b. Phila., May 7, 1934; s. Henry and Hannah (Segal) P.; married; children: Michael, Andrea, Carolyn. A.B. in Physics, U. Pa., 1955, M.S., 1957, Ph.D., 1961. Rsch. scientist Univac (div. Sperry Rand), Blue Bell, Pa., 1960-64; asst. prof. dept. materials sci. and engring. U. Pa., Phila., 1964-67; assoc. prof. U. Pa., 1967-75, prof., 1975—, prof., chmn. dept. bioengring., 1977-81, assoc. dean grad. edn. and rsch. (Sch. Engring and Applied Sci.), 1981-86; pres. Cara Corp., Phila., 1971-85, chmn. bd., 1986-90. Editor: (with C. Brighton and J. Black) Electrical Properties of Bone and Cartilage, 1979; editor, contbr. to Ency. of Materials Sci. and Engring, 1981—; contbr. articles to profl. jours. Recipient Lindback award for disting. teaching, 1968, award for disting. rsch. Kappa Delta, 1985, bronze medal in honor of Luigi Galvani for disting. rsch. U. Bologna, 1989, S. Reid Warren award for disting. rsch., 1991, Clemson award for applied rsch., 1993. Fellow Am. Inst. Med. and Biol. Engring (pres. 1st World Congress in Electricity and Magnetism); mem. Soc. for Biomaterials (pres. 1981), Bioelectric Repair and Growth Soc. (pres. 1985), Orthopaedic Rsch. Soc., Bioelectromagnetics Soc., Engring. in Medicine and Biology, Sigma Xi. Jewish. Patentee in field. Home: 115 Westminster Dr North Wales PA 19454-1221 Office: 116 Hayden Hall U Pa Philadelphia PA 19104

POLLACK, STANLEY P., lawyer; b. N.Y.C., Apr. 23, 1928; s. Isidor and Anna (Shulman) P.; m. Susan Aronowitz, June 16, 1974; 1 child, Jane. BA, NYU, 1948; JD, Harvard U., 1951; LLM in Taxation, NYU, 1959. Bar: N.Y. 1951, U.S. Dist. Ct. (so. dist.) N.Y. 1955. Sole practice N.Y.C., 1955-61; v.p., gen. counsel James Talcott, Inc., N.Y.C., 1961-73; exec. v.p., gen. counsel Rosenthal & Rosenthal Inc., N.Y.C., 1973—. Served to j.g. lt. USNR, 1951-54. Mem. Bklyn. Bar Assn. (banking com., bankruptcy com.), Fed. Bar Council, Assn. Comml. Fin. Atty.'s (pres. 1968), Factors Chain Internat. (legal com.). Club: Harvard (N.Y.C.). Home: 6 Peter Cooper Rd New York NY 10010-6701 Office: Rosenthal & Rosenthal Inc 1370 Broadway # 2 New York NY 10018-7302

POLLACK, STEPHEN J., stockbroker; b. N.Y.C., Aug. 25, 1937; s. Harold S. and Gladys H. Pollack; m. Barbara Jane Podgur, May, 1992; B.S. in Econs., U. Pa., 1960. Vice pres. retail sales Drexel Burnham Lambert, N.Y.C., 1960-77; v.p. retail sales, Drexel Burnham Lambert, N.Y.C., 1960-77, 1st v.p. investments Dean Witter Reynolds Inc., N.Y.C., 1978—. pres. Bnai Brith Gothem, N.Y.C.; exec. v.p. Cosmopolitan League of City of Hope; v.p., circle mem. Whitney Mus., N.Y.C.; treas. Sutton Pl. Synagogue, pres. Havurah Group. Served with USAR, 1966. Recipient Double Chai Citation, State of Israel Bonds, 1984; Appreciation award City of Hope, 1984, Kiter Key Club award Franklin Funds, Million Dollar Club Svc. award City of Hope, Bnai Brith Internat. award. Mem. Internat. Assn. Fin. Planners, Assn. Investment Brokers (dir.), Youngmen's Philanthropic League (bd. dirs.), Am. Biog. Inst. (life), Internat. Study & Research Inst, Dean Witter Pres. Club. Jewish. Clubs: Town, Atrium, Schuylkill Country, Wharton Sch., U. Pa., Yale, East River Tennis, Schuylkill Country, Matterhorn Sports, East Side Republican, Knickerbocker Republican, Friars, Penn (charter). Home: 245 E 40th St Apt 14E New York NY 10016-1714 Office: Dean Witter Reynolds Inc 900 3rd Ave New York NY 10022-4728

POLLACK, SYDNEY, film director; b. Lafayette, Ind., July 1, 1934; s. David and Rebecca (Miller) P.; m. Claire Griswold, Sept. 22, 1958; children: Steven, Rebecca, Rachel. Grad., Neighborhood Playhouse Theatre Sch., N.Y.C., 1954. Asst. to Sanford Meisner, Neighborhood Playhouse Theatre, 1954, instr. acting, 1954-60; exec. dir. West Coast br. The Actors Studio. Appeared in Broadway prodns.: The Dark Is Light Enough, 1954, A Stone For Danny Fisher, 1955; appeared on live TV programs: Alcoa Presents, others; toured in Stalag 17; dir. TV programs: The Chrysler Theatre, Ben Casey, 1962-63, Something About Lee Wiley, 1963-64; Films include: (dir.) The Slender Thread, 1965, This Property is Condemned, 1966, The Scalphunters, 1968, Castle Keep, 1969, Jeremiah Johnson, 1972, Three Days of the Condor, 1975, The Electric Horseman, 1979, The Firm, 1993; (exec. prodr.) Sense and Sensibility, 1995; (dir., prodr.) They Shoot Horses, Don't They?, 1969, The Way We Were, 1973, The Yakuza, 1975, Bobby Deerfield, 1977, Absence of Malice, 1981, Tootsie, 1982 (also actor), Out of Africa, 1985 (Academy Award for Best Picture and Dir.), Havana, 1990, Sabrina, 1995; (prodr.) Songwriter, 1984, Bright Lights, Big City, 1988, The Fabulous Baker Boys, 1989, Presumed Innocent, 1990, The Firm, 1993; (exec. prodr.) Honeysuckle Rose, 1980, White Palace, 1990, King Ralph, 1991, Dead Again, 1991, Leaving Normal, 1992, Searching for Bobby Fischer, 1993; (actor) The Player, 1992, Death Becomes Her, 1992, Husbands and Wives, 1992, The Firm, 1993. Served with U.S. Army, 1957-59. Recipient Acad. award for best dir. and best picture, 1986. Office: Mirage Enterprises De Mille Bldg # 110 5555 Melrose Ave Los Angeles CA 90038-3149 also: CAA 9830 Wilshire Blvd Beverly Hills CA 90212-1804*

POLLACK, SYLVIA BYRNE, educator, researcher, counselor; b. Ithaca, N.Y., Oct. 18, 1940; d. Raymond Tandy and Elsie Frances (Snell) Byrne; divorced; children: Seth Benjamin, Ethan David. BA, Syracuse U., 1962; PhD, U. Pa., 1967; MA, Antioch U., 1993. Instr. Women's Med. Coll. Pa., Phila., 1967-68; rsch. assoc. U. Wash., Seattle, 1968-73, rsch. asst. prof., 1973-77, rsch. assoc. prof., 1977-85, rsch. prof., 1985—, counselor Sch. Nursing, 1993—; asst. mem. Fred Hutchinson Cancer Ctr., Seattle, 1975-79, assoc. mem., 1979-81; mem. study sect. NIH, Washington, 1978-79, 83-85. Contbr. numerous articles to profl. jours.; reviewer for profl. jours. Recipient rsch. grants Am. Cancer Soc., 1969-79, Nat. Cancer Inst., 1973—, Chugai Pharm. Co., Japan, 1985-91. Mem. Am. Counsel Assn., Am. Assn. Immunologists, Soc. Devel. Biology. Office: U Wash Box 357261 Seattle WA 98195-7261

POLLAK, BARTH, mathematics educator; b. Chgo., Aug. 14, 1928; s. Samuel and Esther (Hirschberg) P.; m. Helen Charlotte Schiller, Aug. 22, 1954; children: Martin Russell, Eleanor Susan. BS, Ill. Inst. Tech., 1950, MS, 1951; PhD, Princeton U., 1957. Instr. math. Ill. Inst. Tech., Chgo., 1956-58; asst. prof. Syracuse (N.Y.) U., 1958-63; assoc. prof. U. Notre Dame, Ind., 1963-67, prof., 1967—. Office: U Notre Dame Dept Math Notre Dame IN 46556

POLLAK, CATHY JANE, lawyer; b. Newark, Nov. 15, 1951; d. Seymour and Ruth Norma (Seidler) P.; m. Steven Michael Rosner, Aug. 12, 1976; children: Jessica Dori, Elizabeth Meryl. BA magna cum laude, Cedar Crest Coll., 1973; JD, Rutgers U., 1976. Bar: N.J. 1976, U.S. Dist. Ct. N.J. 1976, N.Y. 1990. Law clk., assoc. atty. O'Brien Daaleman & Liotta, Elizabeth, N.J., 1974-78; assoc. atty., ptnr. Feinberg, Dee & Feinberg, Bayonne, N.J., 1978-84; sr. assoc. Stoldt & Horan, Hackensack, N.J., 1984-93; atty. pvt. practice, Hillsdale, N.J., 1993—; mem. bd. trustees, sec. Bergen County Task Force on Women and Addictions, Paramus, N.J., 1993—; mem. Bergen County Dist. Domestic Violence Legal Advocacy Project, Hackensack, 1993—. Mem. Hebrew sch. exec. com. Temple Beth Or, Washington Twp., N.J., 1993—. mem. sisterhood. Mem. N.J. State Bar Assn. (family law com.), Bergen County Bar Assn. (family law com.). Avocations: reading, dancing. Office: 188 Broadway Woodcliff Lake NJ 07675

POLLAK, EDWARD BARRY, chemical manufacturing company executive; b. N.Y.C., Sept. 6, 1934; s. Ben N. and Harriet E. (Springer) P.; m. Marianne E. Modi, Feb. 27, 1960; children: David, Anne, Kari. BChemE, Cornell U., 1956, MBA, 1957. With Olin Corp., Stamford, Conn., 1957-94, bus. mgr. splty. and consumer products, 1970-72, v.p. Internat. Chems. Group, 1973-76, v.p., gen. mgr. designed products dept., 1976-80, corp. v.p., internat., 1980-86; pres., CEO Olin Hunt Splty. Products, Inc., 1986-93; chmn. OCG Microelectronic Materials Inc., 1991-93; v.p. internat. OSI Spltys. Inc., 1994—; dir. Etoxyl C.A., Venezuela, Asahi-Olin Ltd., Japan; mem. steering com. internat. affairs group Chem. Mfrs. Assn. 1979-81, SRI adv. coun., 1994—. Bd. dirs. Stamford Symphony, U. Wyo. Inst. for Environment and Natural Resources. Mem. Synthetic Organic Chem. Mfrs. Assn. (gov. 1977-81, v.p. 1978, pres. 1979-80, steering com. internat. affairs group 1979-81), Internat. Isocyanate Inst. (bd. dirs. 1979-81), Cornell Soc. Engrs. (bd. dirs. 1967-72, v.p. 1971-72), Cornell Club For Fairfield County, Japan Soc. Office: OSI Spltys Inc 39 Old Ridgebury Rd. Danbury CT 06810-5124

POLLAK, HENRY OTTO, retired utility research executive, educator; b. Vienna, Austria, Dec. 13, 1927; came to U.S., 1940, naturalized, 1945; s. Ludwig and Olga (Weil) P.; m. Ida Jeanne Tobias, May 7, 1949; children: Katherine, James. BA, Yale, 1947; MA, Harvard U., 1948, PhD, 1951; DSc, Rose Poly. Inst., 1964; DSc (hon.), Monmouth Coll., 1975, Bowdoin Coll., 1977, Technol. U., Eindhoven, 1981; LLD (hon.), Montclair State Coll., 1984; DSc (hon.), Laval U., Que., 1992. With Bell Telephone Labs., Murray Hill, N.J., 1951-83; mem. tech. staff Bell Telephone Labs., 1951-59, head dept. communications fundamentals II, 1959-61, acting dir. math. and mechanics research center, 1961-62, dir. math. and statistics research center, 1962-83; asst. v.p. math., communications, computer scis. research Bell Communications Research, Morristown, N.J., 1984-86; mem. sch. math. study group, com. on undergrad. program in math. Internat. Commn. on Math. Instrn., 1970-74, 82-86, mem. adv. bd. Unified Sci. and Maths. for Elem. Schs., 1969-77; mem. adv. com. for sci. edn. NSF, 1977-80, 85-89, chmn., 1978-80; program chmn. 4th Internat. Congress Math. edn., 1980; bd. dirs. Math. Inst. Woodrow Wilson Found.; vis. prof. Tchrs. Coll., Columbia U., 1987—. Trustee N.C. Sch. for Sci. and Math, Durham, 1979-89; bd. dirs. COMAP, 1987-96. Mem. Am. Math. Soc., Math. Assn. Am. (pres. 1975-76, Yueh-Gin Gung & Dr. Charles Y. Hu award for Disting. Svc. to Math. 1993), Nat. Coun. Tchrs. Math., Phi Beta Kappa, Sigma Xi. Mem. Christ Ch. Home: 40 Edgewood Rd Summit NJ 07901-3988

POLLAK, LOUIS HEILPRIN, judge, educator; b. N.Y.C., Dec. 7, 1922; s. Walter and Marion (Heilprin) P.; m. Katherine Weiss, July 25, 1952; children: Nancy, Elizabeth, Susan, Sarah, Deborah. A.B., Harvard, 1943; LL.B., Yale, 1948. Bar: N.Y. bar 1949, Conn. bar 1956, Pa. bar 1976. Law clk. to Justice Rutledge U.S. Supreme Ct., 1948-49; with Paul, Weiss, Rifkind, Wharton & Garrison, N.Y.C., 1949-51; spl. asst. to Amb. Philip C. Jessup State Dept., 1951-53; asst. counsel Amalgmated Clothing Workers Am., 1954-55; mem. faculty Yale Law Sch., 1955-74, dean, 1965-70; Greenfield prof. U. Pa., 1974-78, dean Law Sch., 1975-78, lectr., 1980—; judge U.S. Dist Ct. (ea. dist.), Pa., 1978—; vis. lectr. Howard U. Sch. Law, 1953; vis. prof. U. Mich. Law Sch., 1961, Columbia Law Sch., 1962. Author: The Constitution and the Supreme Court: A Documentary History, 1966. Mem. New Haven Bd. Edn., 1962-68; chmn. Conn. adv. com. U.S. Civil Rights Commn., 1962-63; mem. bd. NAACP Legal Def. Fund, 1960-78, v.p., 1971-78; chmn. New Haven Human Rights Com., 1963-64. Served with AUS, 1943-46. Mem. ABA (chmn. sec. individual rights 1970-71), Assn. Bar City N.Y., Fed. Bar Assn., Phila. Bar Assn., Am. Law Inst. (coun. 1978—). Office: US Dist Ct 13613 US Courthouse 601 Market St Philadelphia PA 19106-1510

POLLAK, MARK, lawyer; b. Paris, July 16, 1947; came to U.S., 1955; s. Joseph and Zofia (Berkowitz) P.; m. Joanne Elizabeth Harris, Dec. 26, 1976; children: Joshua David, Jonathan Stephen, Benjamin Eric, Rebecca Lynn. BA, Bklyn. Coll., 1968; MA in City Planning, U. Pa., 1972, JD, 1972. Bar: Md. 1972. Assoc. Piper & Marbury, Balt., 1972-81, ptnr., 1981—; pres. Balt. Corp. for Housing Partnerships; bd. dirs. Balt. Regional Community Devel. Corp. Bd. dirs. Balt. Children's Mus., Downtown Partnership of Balt., Inc. Mem. ABA, Md. Bar Assn., Am. Coll. Real Estate Lawyers, Am. Planning Assn., Nat. Assn. Bond Lawyers. Office: Piper & Marbury 36 S Charles St Baltimore MD 21201-3020

POLLAK, MARTIN MARSHALL, lawyer, patent development company executive; b. N.Y.C., July 31, 1927; s. Edward and Jennie (Horowitz) P.; m. Ellen R. Spiegel, Sept. 16, 1929; children: David W., Richard M., Barbara S. AB, Syracuse U., 1950; LLB, St. John's U., Bklyn., 1953. Bar: N.Y. 1953, U.S. Dist. Ct. (ea. and so. dists.) N.Y. 1957, U.S. Supreme Ct. 1959. Ptnr. Feldman & Pollak, Attys., N.Y.C., 1953-59; atty. N.Y. State, 1953—; founder, exec. v.p., treas. Nat. Patent Devel. Corp., N.Y.C., 1959—; pres. Internat. Hydron Corp., Woodbury, N.Y., 1981-88; chmn. bd. Interferon Scis. Corp., New Brunswick, N.J., 1981—, Gen. Physics Corp., Columbia, Md., 1987—; trustee Worcester Found. for Exptl. Rsch., Shrewsbury, Mass., 1977—; bd. dirs. Duratek Corp., Silver Spring, Md., Brandon Corp., Secaucus, N.J.; cons. Allergan Optical Corp., Irvine, Calif., 1988-89; chmn. bd. Czechoslovak-U.S. Econ. Coun., Washington, 1987—; pres. NPO Trading USA, Inc., N.Y.C., Washington, Prague, Czechoslovakia, 1990—, Am. Drug Co., Washington, N.Y., Moscow, 1993—. With USN, 1945-47. Recipient gold medal Czechoslovakian Rep. C. of C., 1984. Office: Nat Patent Devel Corp 9 W 57th St New York NY 10019 also: Gen Physics Corp 6700 Alexander Bell Dr Columbia MD 21046-2100

POLLAK, NORMAN L., retired accountant; b. Chgo., Aug. 16, 1931; s. Emery and Helen P.; m. Barbara Zeff, Aug. 21, 1955 (div. 1980); m. Sharon Levin, Nov. 12, 1995; children: Martin Joel, Elise Susan McNeal, Rhonda Louise Wilder. BS, Northwestern U., 1955. CPA, Calif.; lic. real estate agt. Calif. Sr. acct., staff acct., 1952-58, pvt. practice, 1958-86; ret. acct., fin. and mgmt. cons., pres. Norman L. Pollak Accountancy Corp., Westlake Village, 1958-86; expert witness on domestic dissolution, 1984-86; lectr. profl. orgns.; bus. mgr. for Steven Martin, Nitty Gritty Dirt Band, 1967-77; acct. for Gregg and Howard Allman, 1967, Marion Ross. Former pres. Ventura County Estate Planning Coun., 1975-78, 78-79); founder San Fernando Valley Estate Planning Coun., 1962, chpt. pres., 1964-65; founder Ventura Co. Estate Planning Coun.; chmn. Comm. Contest for Hearing Impaired Optimist Club, emergency com. Disaster Preparedness, Oak Forest Mobile Estates Assn.; compiled disaster preparedness plan; coach Braile Olympics for Blind; mem. Conejo Future Found.; bd. dirs. Oak Forest Homeowners Assn., Honokowai Palms Homeowners Assn.; bd. trustees Westlake Cultural Found.; active sponsor Code 3 for Homeless Children, 1993. Mem. AICPA, Calif. Soc. CPAs (former chmn. San Fernando tech. discussion group 1960-61, former mem. com. on cooperation with credit grantors), Nat. Assn. Accts., Westlake Village C. of C., Northwestern U. Alumni Club. Home and Office: 143 Sherwood Dr Westlake Village CA 91361-4814

POLLAK, RAYMOND, general and transplant surgeon; b. Johannesburg, South Africa, Nov. 12, 1950; came to U.S., 1977; MB BCh, U. Witwatersrand, Johannesburg, 1973. Diplomate Am. Bd. Surgery. Rotating intern Gen. Hosp., Johannesburg, 1974; intern in surgery U. Ill. Hosps. and Clinics, Chgo., 1977-78, resident in surgery; immunology and transplant fellow U. Ill., Chgo., 1982-84, assoc. prof. surgery, chief div. transplant dept. surgery, 1988—; prof. surgery, 1995—. Office: U Ill Dept Surgery 801 S Paulina St # C 960 Chicago IL 60612-7210

POLLAK, RICHARD, writer, editor; b. Chgo., Apr. 5, 1934; s. Robert and Janet (Spitzer) P.; m. Merle Ann Winer, Mar. 26, 1961 (div. 1979); 1 dau., Amanda.; m. Diane Walsh, Mar. 6, 1982. Student, Knox Coll., 1952-54; B.A. in English, Amherst Coll., 1957. Reporter Worcester (Mass.) Telegram & Gazette, 1957; polit. reporter Evening Sun, Balt., 1959-64; assoc. editor Newsweek, N.Y.C., 1964-67; asst. editor Honolulu Star Bull., 1967-68; freelance writer N.Y.C., 1968-71; co-founder, editor More mag., N.Y.C., 1971-76; lit. editor The Nation, 1980-81, exec. editor, 1988-89; editor-at-large, 1989-95; tchr. Yale U., spring 1977, NYU, fall 1977, 82-86; cons. Ford Found., 1970-72. Author: Up Against Apartheid, 1981, The Episode, 1986; editor: Stop The Presses, I Want To Get Off!, 1975. Served with AUS, 1957-59. Poynter fellow Yale U., 1977. Mem. Authors Guild. Home and Office: 404 Riverside Dr New York NY 10025-1861

POLLAK, SAM, editor, columnist; b. Queens, N.Y., May 18, 1950; s. Harry Jacob and Hannah (Brodsky) P.; m. Julie Ann Anderson, Aug. 27, 1978; children: Rachel, Deborah, Sarah, Joseph. Attended, U. Tex., El Paso. Reporter/slot Hollywood (Fla.) Sun-Tattler, 1976-77; slot/desk Miami (Fla.) News, 1977-78, Dallas Times Herald, 1978-80; sports editor The Ariz. Daily Star, Tucson, 1980-85; sports copy desk chief Dallas Morning News, 1985-86; sports mng. editor New Orleans Times-Picayune, 1986-90; dep. sports editor The Plain Dealer, Cleve., 1990-91; sports editor The Fresno (Calif.) Bee, 1991-93; asst. mng. editor Thomson L.A. News Group, West Covina, Calif., 1993-95; editor Portsmouth (N.H.) Herald, 1995—. Mem. AP Sports Editors. Democrat. Jewish. Avocations: reading, sports, politics, history. Office: Portsmouth Herald 111 Maplewood Ave Portsmouth NH 03801-3715

POLLAK, TIM, advertising agency executive. Exec. v.p. Young & Rubicam N.Y., 1987; pres., CEO D.Y&R Worldwide (formerly HDM Worldwide), 1987—; corp. CEO HDM Worldwide; pres., CEO HDM USA, N.Y.C., 1987-90, Young & Rubicam NY, N.Y.C., 1990-91; vice chmn. Young & Rubicam Advt., N.Y.C., 1991—; mem. exec. com., bd. dirs. Young & Rubicam, Inc.; mem. exec. com., bd. dirs. Dentsu, Young & Rubicam. Mem. Internat. Advt. Assn. (pres. N.Y. chpt. 1988-90, mem. worldwide bd. dirs.). Office: Young & Rubicam NY 285 Madison Ave New York NY 10017-6401

POLLAK, WILLIAM L., newspaper publishing executive. Exec. v.p. sales The New York Times, N.Y.C. Office: The New York Times 229 W 43rd St New York NY 10036-3913

POLLAN, CAROLYN JOAN, state legislator; b. Houston, July 12, 1937; d. Rex and Faith (Basye) Clark; B.S. in Radio and TV, John Brown U., 1959; postgrad. NYU, 1959; PhD in Edn., Walden U., 1993. m. George A. Pollan, Jan. 6, 1962; children—Cee Cee, Todd (dec.), Robert. Mem. Ark. Ho. of Reps., 1974—, now sr. Republican mem., asst. speaker pro-tempore, 1993; apptd. by Gov. numerous coms., commns.; ex-officio mem. Workplace Literacy Project Adv. Bd. U.S. Dept. Labor & Ednl. Testing Svc., 1990-93, Nat. Adult Literacy Survey, 1990-93; del. Am. Soviet Seminar, Am. Council Young Polit. Leaders, Exeter, N.H., 1976; co-developer Total Touch Test; owner Patent Model Mus.. Vice chmn. Ark. Rep. Com., 1972-76; del. Rep. Nat. Conv., 1976; bd. dirs. Ark. Cancer Soc., Ark. Easter Seals Soc.; bd. dirs. Greg Kistler Treatment Center for Physically Handicapped, Ark. Found. Assoc. Colls., 4-H Found. for Sebastian County; trustee John Brown U.; mem. legis. adv. com. So. Regional Edn. Bd. Recipient Conservation Legislator of Yr. award Ark. Wildlife Fedn., Nat. Wildlife Fedn., Sears Roebuck & Co., 1976, Outstanding State Legislator of Yr. award Ark. Pub. Employees Assn., 1979, Lifetime Mem. award Ark. PTA, 1994, many others; named 1 of 10 Outstanding Legislators, Assembly of Govtl. Employees, 1980, Legislator of Yr., Ark. Human Service Providers Assn., 1982, Citizen of Yr. by Ark. Social Workers, 1993, Outstanding Women in Ark. Politics by Ark. Dem., 1990, One of 10 Top Legislators in 1993 Ark. Dem. Gazette, 1993, one of Top 100 Women in Ark., Ark. Bus. Publ., 1995, 96; voted 1 of Ft. Smith's 10 Most Influential Citizens, S.W. Times Record Readers, 1979. Mem. Ark. Internat. Woman's Forum (founding mem.), Ft. Smith Car Restoration Assn. Baptist.

POLLAND, REBECCA ROBBINS, foundation executive; b. Phila., Jan. 11, 1922; d. Louis Aron Jonah and Edith Frances (Kapnek) Robbins; B.A., Bryn Mawr Coll., 1942; M.A., U. Calif., Berkeley, 1957, Ph.D., 1971; m. Harry L. Polland, July 14, 1946 (div. 1979); children: Louise, Margaret, Jonathan. Analyst, cons., commission mem., local and nat. govt., 1942-82; cons. U.S. Dept. Agr., 1977; lectr. Polit. sci. Sacramento State U., 1975-76; asst. prof. Sonoma State U. (Calif.), 1976-78; asst. prof. Rutgers U., Camden, N.J., 1978-86. Chmn. bd. Frogmore Tobacco Estates Ltd., Zimbabwe; Presdl. appointee Bd. Internat. Food and Agrl. Devel., 1979-82. Exec. trustee J.F. Kapnek Charitable Trust, Phila., 1980—; mem. Berkeley City Commn.

on Recreation and Parks, 1970-75; v.p.; mem. White House Conf. Food, Nutrition, Health, 1969, World Food Conf., Rome, 1974. Mem. Am. Polit. Sci. Assn., AAUP, Am. Soc. Public Adminstrn., Am. Soc. Tropical Medicine and Hygiene, Assn. Dirs. Internat. Agrl. Programs Assn. Women in Devel. (founding). Contbr. articles to profl. jours. Home: 220 Locust St Apt 30E Philadelphia PA 19106-3933 also: 1308 Portal Dr Bellingham WA 98226-2447

POLLARA, BERNARD, immunologist, educator, pediatrician; b. Chgo.; s. Joseph and Mamie P. PhB, Northwestern U., 1951, MS, 1954; MD, U. Minn., 1960, PhD, 1963. Intern USPHS Hosp., Seattle, 1960; resident in pediatrics U. Minn. Hosps., 1968-69; rsch. assoc. pediatrics U. Minn., 1960-63, assoc. prof. biochemistry and pediatrics, 1969; prof. pediatrics Albany (N.Y.) Med. Coll., 1969-94, chmn. dept., 1979-93; pediatrician in chief Albany Med. Ctr. Hosp., 1979-93; sabbatical leave, pediatrician Yukon Kuskokwim Regional Hosp., 1992-93; John and Aliese prof. pediatrics and adolescent medicine U. South Fla., Tampa, 1994—, head divsn. gen. pediatrics, dept. pediatrics, 1995—; v.p. for rsch. affairs Albany Med. Ctr., 1986-89. Dir. N.Y. State Kidney Disease Inst., 1969-79. With USN, 1945-46. Recipient Acad. Laureate award SUNY, Albany, 1991; Arthritis and Rheumatism Found. fellow, 1961-64. Fellow Am. Acad. Pediats.; mem. AAAS, Am. Assn. Immunologists, Am. Pediat. Soc., Am. Soc. Cell Biology, Clin. Immunology Soc., Sigma Xi, Phi Lambda Upsilon, Alpha Omega Alpha. Office: U South Fla Sch Medicine Dept Pediatrics 17 Davis Blvd Fl 2 Tampa FL 33606-3475

POLLARD, CARL F., health insurance company executive; b. Lancaster, Ky., 1938. Grad., Univ. Ky., 1960. With Yeager Ford & Warren, Louisville, 1960-68; sr. exec. v.p. Humana Inc., Louisville; now owner Hermitage Farm, Goshen, KY. Office: Hermitage Farm PO Box 9 Goshen KY 40026*

POLLARD, CHARLES W., transportation services executive; b. 1957. Student, 1977-83. With Skadden, Arps, Slate, Meagher & Flom, Washington, 1983-87; sec., gen. counsel World Airways, Inc., Herndon, Va., pres. Office: World Airways Inc 13873 Park Center Rd Herndon VA 22071-3223*

POLLARD, CHARLES WILLIAM, airline company executive, lawyer; b. St. Mary's City, Md., June 1, 1957; s. Lyle H. and Teresa V. (Lavelle) P.; m. Lynna P. Maidman, Aug. 14, 1983; children: Louisa Ray, Katherine Allissa. AB magna cum laude, St. Anselm Coll., 1979; MPA, Syracuse U., 1980; JD, George Washington U., 1983. Bar: D.C. 1983, U.S. Dist. Ct. D.C. 1983. Law clk. Am. Petroleum Inst., Washington, 1981-83; assoc. Skadden, Arps, Slate, Meagher & Flom, Washington, 1983-87; gen. counsel WorldCorp, Herndon, Va., 1987-90, v.p. adminstrn. and legal affairs, 1990-92; pres. World Airways, Inc., 1992-95, pres., CEO, 1995—; chmn. bd. trustees The Kingsbury Ctr., Washington, 1992—; bd. dirs. Found. Capital Ptnrs., Inc., Nat. Air Carrier Assn. Vol. counsel Reagan-Bush Campaign, Washington, 1984. Grad. fellow Maxwell Sch., Syracuse U., 1979-80. Mem. ABA, St. Anselm Coll. Alumni Assn. (pres. Washington chpt. 1988), Chesapeake Bay Yacht Racing Assn., So. Md. Sailing Assn. Republican. Avocations: sailing, skeet shooting, backpacking. Office: World Airways Washington Dulles Internat Airport 13873 Park Center Rd Ste 400 Herndon VA 22071-3223

POLLARD, CHARLES WILLIAM, diversified services company executive; b. Chgo., June 8, 1938; s. Charles W. and Ruth Ann (Humphrey) P.; m. Judith Ann, June 8, 1959; children: Julie Ann, Charles W., Brian, Amy. A.B., Wheaton Coll., 1960; J.D., Northwestern U., 1963. Bar: Ill. 1963. Mem. firm Wilson and McIlvaine, 1963-67, Vescelus, Perry & Pollard, Wheaton, Ill., 1968-72; prof., v.p. fin. Wheaton Coll., 1972-77; sr. v.p. ServiceMaster Industries, Downers Grove, Ill., 1977-80, exec. v.p., 1980-81, pres., 1981-83; pres., COO ServiceMaster Industries, 1981-83; pres., CEO ServiceMaster Co., Downers Grove, Ill., 1983-93, chmn. bd. dirs., mem. exec. com., 1994—; bd. dirs. Wheaton Coll., Herman Miller, Inc., Provident Life and Accident Ins. Co. Office: Servicemaster LP 1 ServiceMaster Way 2300 Warrenville Rd Downers Grove IL 60515-1765

POLLARD, DAVID EDWARD, editor; b. Columbus, Ohio, Oct. 7, 1927; s. James Edward and Marjorie Olive (Pearson) P.; m. Ilse Knack, Dec. 24, 1960; children: Walter Thomas, Marcus Andreas, Michael David, Christopher James. B.S., Ohio State U., 1950; postgrad. in cotton econs, Memphis State U., 1967. With Columbus Citizen, 1943-50; with Army Times Pub. Co., 1952-60; mng. editor U.S. Coast Guard Mag., Washington, 1956-57; asso. editor Am. Weekend, Washington, also Frankfurt, Ger., 1957-60; info. specialist Air Forces Europe Exchange, Wiesbaden, Ger., 1961-63; reporter Comml. Appeal, Memphis, 1963-66; fin. writer Comml. Appeal, 1967-68; news-desk editor U.S. News & World Report, Washington, 1968-76; chief news desk U.S. News & World Report, 1976-91; pres. U.S. Moose Co., Inc., Boothbay Harbor, Maine, 1993—. Patentee garden implement. Served with USMC, 1945-46, 51-52. Mem. Sigma Delta Chi, Alpha Delta Sigma, Alpha Tau Omega. Roman Catholic. Home: 8405 Tobin Rd Annandale VA 22003-1103 and: Capitol Island ME 04538

POLLARD, DENNIS BERNARD, lawyer, educator; b. Phila., May 12, 1968. BS in Psychology, Pa. State U., 1990; JD, Ohio State U., 1993. Bar: Ohio 1993, U.S. Dist. Ct. (no. dist.) Ohio 1994, U.S. Ct. Appeals (6th cir.) 1994. Staff atty. The Legal Aid Soc. Cleve., 1993-95; atty. student affairs, student life Pa. State U., 1995—. Mem. ABA, Ohio State Bar Assn., Cleve. Bar Assn., Phi Delta Phi. Avocation: biking. Home: 801-C Southgate Dr # 3 State College PA 16801 Office: 135 Boucke Bldg University Park PA 16802

POLLARD, FRANKLIN DAWES, minister, seminary president; b. Olney, Tex., Feb. 25, 1934; s. Daniel Spurgeon and Ova Roena (Boone) P.; m. Jane Shepard, Sept. 1, 1955; children—Brent, Suzanne. BBA, Tex. A&M U., 1955; BD, Southwestern Bapt. Theol. Sem., Fort Worth, 1959; D.Min., New Orleans Bapt. Theol. Sem., 1983; D.D. (hon.), Miss. Coll., Clinton, 1977; L.H.D., Calif. Bapt. Coll., Riverside, 1983. Ordained to ministry So. Bapt. Conv., 1956. Pastor First Bapt. Ch., Seagraves, Tex., 1961-64; pastor First Bapt. Ch., Dimmitt, Tex., 1964-66, Tulia, Tex., 1966-70; pastor Shiloh Terr. Bapt. Ch., Dallas, 1970-74; pastor First Bapt. Ch., Jackson, Miss., 1974-80, San Antonio, 1980-83; pres. Golden Gate Bapt. Theol. Sem., Mill Valley, Calif., 1983-86; preacher The Bapt. Hour radio show, Fort Worth, 1976-86, 91—; pastor 1st Bapt. Ch., Jackson, Miss., 1986—; host, Bible tchr. At Home with the Bible, radio and TV show, 1978-83; nat. TV preacher nat. The Bapt. Hour, So. Bapt. Conv., 1990—; v.p., exec. bd. Bapt. Gen. Conv., Tex., 1973; exec. bd. Miss. Bapt. Conv., 1977-80. Author: How to Know When You're a Success, 1973; The Bible In Your Life, 1978; After You've Said I'm Sorry, 1982; Keeping Free, 1983. Recipient Disting. Service award Jaycees, 1966, Valley Forge Freedom Found. award, 1982; named one of Seven Outstanding Preachers, Time mag., 1979. Lodge: Rotary. Home: 2332 Southwood Rd Jackson MS 39211-6212

POLLARD, FRED DON, finance company executive; b. Proctorsville, Vt., Sept. 15, 1931; s. Bryant Frank and Millie Viola (Brobst) P.; m. Sandra Jean Norton, Oct. 19, 1957; children: Fred Don, Bruce Gardiner, Mark Bryant. BA, Dartmouth Coll., 1953, MBA, 1954. CPA, N.Y. Staff auditor Touche, Niven, Bailey & Smart, Chgo., 1954-55, 57-58; with Hertz Corp., Chgo., 1958-60, London, 1960-62, Paris, France, 1962-64, N.Y.C., 1964-65; European controller Avis Rent A Car, London, 1965-69; internat. treas. Avis Rent A Car, 1969-71; asst. v.p., dir. fin. Avis Rent A Car, Garden City, N.Y., 1971-72; asst. treas. Avis Rent A Car, 1972-75; treas. Garcia Corp., Teaneck, N.J., 1975-78; v.p. fin., treas. Augsburg Orgn., Inc., Ogdensburg, N.Y., 1978-79; sr. v.p. fin., treas. Augsburg Orgn., Inc., 1979-83, also dir.; pres. Corp. Fin. Assocs. No. N.Y., Canton, 1983—, Agrl. Processing Corp., Canton, 1983—; dir. Augsburg Corp., Halco Inc., Montreal, Que., Can., 1978-83, Carlton Holding Co./N.Y. Casualty, Watertown, N.Y., 1978-82, Creg System Inc., Watertown, Whalen, Daley & Looney (CPAs), Ogdenburg, N.Y., 1989—; Mem. adv. bd. Clarkson Sch. Mgmt., Potsdam, N.Y., 1979-83; vis. lectr. sch. of mgmt. Clarkson U., Potsdam, 1986-87; vis. lectr. dept. econs. St. Lawrence U., Canton, N.Y., 1987-88. Exec. bd. Seaway Valley coun. Boy Scouts Am., 1980-86, adv. bd., 1986-95. Served with U.S. Army, 1955-57. Mem. N.Y. State Soc. CPAs, Am. Inst. CPAs. Presbyterian. Lodges: Masons; Shriners. Home: Old Stone House 1129 County Route 25 Canton NY 13617-6539 Office: Russell Rd Canton NY 13617

POLLARD, GEORGE MARVIN, economist; b. St. Joseph, Mo., Oct. 5, 1909; s. James Coleman and Ethel (Mallory) P.; m. Jean Mary Campion, Apr. 15, 1939; 1 child, Elizabeth G. A.B., George Washington U., 1934, A.M., 1939; student, Columbia, 1940-41, sch. mil. govt. U. Va., 1944, Stanford, 1944-45. Mem. staff U.S. Dept. Agr., 1928-41, WPB, 1941-43; sr. economist U.S. Dept. Army, 1946-49; internat. economist, 1949-51; fgn. service officer Dept. State, 1955-64, internat. economist, 1951-55, 64—; consul, chief polit. and econ. affairs Am. Consulate Gen., Düsseldorf, Fed. Republic Germany, 1956-58; 1st sec. econ. affairs U.S. Mission to European Communities, Luxembourg, 1958-61; supervisory officer econ. affairs Bur. Internat. Orgn. Affairs, Dept. State, Washington, 1961-63; assigned to Bur. Internat. Commerce, U.S. Dept. Commerce, Washington, 1964-76; Mem. planning and zoning commn., Vienna, Va., 1953-56. Served as lt. USNR, 1943-46; mil. govt. officer Occupation of Japan 1945-46; mem. U.S. rep. Far Eastern Commn. 1947-49, Washington; lt. col. U.S. Army Res., 1949-63; ret. Mem. Phi Theta Kappa, Phi Sigma Kappa, Alpha Kappa Psi. Club: DACOR. Home: 2017 Dundee Rd Rockville MD 20850-3066

POLLARD, HARVEY B., physician, neuroscientist; b. San Antonio, May 26, 1943. BA in Biology, Rice U., 1964; MS in Biochemistry, U. Chgo., 1969, MD, 1969, PhD, 1973. Rsch. assoc. NIH-Nat. Inst. Arthritis and Metabolic Diseases, Bethesda, Md., 1969-71, sr. investigator, 1972-74, 1977-79, sect. chief, 1979-81; lab. chief Nat. Inst. Diabetes, Digestive and Kidney Diseases, Bethesda, 1981—. Contbr. over 200 articles to profl. jours. With USPHS, 1969—. Recipient Commendation medal USPHS, 1982, Alumni award for Disting. Svc., U. Chigo. Alumni Assn., 1989, NIH Inventor's award, 1991. Mem. Biophys. Soc., Soc. for Neurosci., Am. Soc. for Pharmacology and Exptl. Therapeutics, Soc. for Cell Biology. Office: Nat Inst Diabetes Digestive & Kidney Disease 9000 Rockville Pike Blg 8 Rm 403 Bethesda MD 20892

POLLARD, HENRY, lawyer; b. N.Y.C., Jan. 10, 1931; s. Charles and Sarah (Lanster) P.; m. Adele Ruth Brodie, June 16, 1954; children: Paul A., Lydia S. AB, CCNY, 1953; JD, Columbia U., 1954. Bar: N.Y. 1954, Calif. 1962. Assoc. Sullivan & Cromwell, N.Y.C., 1954, 56-61; ptnr. Kaplan, LIvingston, Goodwin, Berkowitz & Selvin, Beverly Hills, 1962-81, Pollard, Bauman, Slome & McIntosh, Beverly Hills, Calif., 1981-87, Seyfarth, Shaw, Fairweather & Geraldson, L.A., 1987-95; of counsel Oberstein, Kibre & Horwitz, L.A., 1995—; judge pro tem L.A. County Mcpl. Ct.; arbitrator/mediator, mem. large complex case program Am. Arbitration Assn.; arbitrator/mediator Nat. Assn. Securities Dealers, N.Y. Stock Exch., Am. Stock Exch., Pacific Stick Exch., L.A. County Dispute Resolution Svcs. Editor Columbia U. Law Rev., 1953-54. Served with U.S. Army, 1954-56. Harlan Fiske Stone scholar, 1953-54. Mem. ABA, Calif. Bar Assn., Los Angeles County Bar Assn., Beverly Hills Bar Assn.

POLLARD, JOSEPH AUGUSTINE, advertising and public relations consultant; b. N.Y.C., June 22, 1924; s. Joseph Michael and Mary Theresa (Sheerin) P.; m. Helen Frances O'Neill, Jan. 18, 1947 (dec.); children: Christopher (dec.), Kenneth, Eugene, Daniel, Theresa, Michael; m. 2d, Lee Sharon Rivkins, Jan. 1, 1981. Student Pratt Inst., 1946-50. Advt. mgr. Boston Store, Utica, N.Y., 1951-53; sales promotion dir. Interstate Stores, N.Y., 1954-60, 67-70; v.p. sales Community Discount Stores, Chgo., 1960-63; dir. sales S. Klein, N.Y., 1964-66; v.p. advt. and pub. relations Peoples Drug Stores, Alexandria, Va., 1970-89; ret. Bd. dirs. Nat. Am. Cancer Soc., 1992-95, trustee D.C. div., pres. 1985-86, nat. del., 1991-92; pres. Modern Retailers Ill., 1962. With USAF, 1943-46, 50-51. Recipient Am. Advt. Fedn. Silver medal award, 1982, St. George's medal Am. Cancer Soc., 1984. Mem. Advt. Club Met. Washington (pres. 1975-76), Country Club of Fairfax (pres. 1994, bd. dirs. 1992-95). Home and Office: 173 Clubhouse Dr SW Supply NC 28462

POLLARD, MORRIS, microbiologist, educator; b. Hartford, Conn., May 24, 1916; s. Harry and Sarah (Hoffman) P.; m. Mildred Klein, Dec. 29, 1938; children: Harvey, Carol, Jonathan. D.V.M., Ohio State U., 1938; M.S., Va. Poly. Inst., 1939; Ph.D. (Nat. Found. Infantile Paralysis fellow), U. Calif.-Berkeley, 1950; D.Sc. (hon.) Miami U., Ohio, 1981. Mem. staff Animal Disease Sta., Nat. Agrl. Research Center, Beltsville, Md., 1939-42; asst. prof. preventive medicine Med. br. U. Tex., Galveston, 1946-48; assoc. prof. U. Tex., 1948-50, prof., 1950-61; prof. biology U. Notre Dame, Ind., 1961-66; prof., chmn. microbiology U. Notre Dame, 1966-81, prof. emeritus, 1981—, dir. Lobund Lab., 1961-85, Coleman dir. Lobund Lab., 1985—; vis. prof. Fed. U. Rio de Janeiro, Brazil, 1977; vis. prof. Katholieke U., Leuven, Belgium, 1981; mem. tng. grant com. NIH, 1965-70; mem. adv. bd. Inst. Lab. Animal Resources NRC, 1965-68; mem. adv. com. microbiology Office Naval Research, 1966-68, chmn., 1968-70; mem. sci. adv. com. United Health Found., 1966-70; cons. U. Tex., M.D. Anderson Hosp. and Tumor Inst., 1958-66; mem. colon cancer com. Nat. Cancer Inst., 1972-76, chmn. tumor immunology com., 1976-79; mem. com. cancer cause and prevention NIH, 1979-81; program rev. com. Argonne Nat. Lab, 1979-85, chmn., 1983-84; lectr. Found. Microbiology, 1978. Editor: Perspectives in Virology Vol. I to XI, 1959-80; contbr. articles to profl. jours. Served from 1st lt. to lt. col. Vet. Corps, AUS, 1942-46. Recipient Disting. Alumnus award Ohio State U., 1979, Army Commendation medal, Presdl. citation; named Hon. Alumnus U. Notre Dame, 1989; McLaughlin Faculty fellow Cambridge U., 1956; Raine Found. prof. U. Western Australia, 1975; vis. scientist Chinese Acad. Med. Scis., 1979, 81; hon. prof. Chinese Acad. Med. Scis., 1982. Mem. Am. Acad. Microbiology (charter), Brazilian Acad. Scis., Soc. Exptl. Biology and Medicine, Am. Soc. Microbiology (Acad. Sci. Achievement award 1990), Am. Assn. Pathologists, Am. Assn. Cancer Rsch., Am. Soc. Lab. Animal Sci., Assn. Gnotobiotics (pres.), Internat. Commn. Lab. Animal Sci., AAAS, Internat. Assn. Gnotobiology (pres.), Internat. Assn. Gnotobiotics (hon. pres. 1987), Sigma Xi, Phi Delta Epsilon (hon.), Phi Zeta (hon.). Home: 3540 Hanover Ct South Bend IN 46614-2331 Office: Lobund Lab Notre Dame IN 46556

POLLARD, OVERTON PRICE, state agency executive, lawyer; b. Ashland, Va., Mar. 26, 1933; s. James Madison and Annie Elizabeth (Hutchinson) P.; m. Anne Aloysia Meyer, Oct. 1, 1960; children—Mary O., Price, John, Anne, Charles, Andrew, David. AB in Econs., Washington and Lee U., 1954, JD, 1957. Bar: Va. Claims supr. Travelers Ins. Co., Richmond, Va., 1964-67; asst. atty. gen. State of Va., Richmond, 1967, 70-72; spl. asst. Va. Supreme Ct., Richmond, 1968-70; exec. dir. Pub. Defender Commn., Richmond, 1972—; ptnr. Pollard & Boice and predecessor firms, Richmond, 1972-87; bd. govs. Va. Criminal Law Sect., Richmond, 1970-72, 91-93; chmn. prepaid legal services com. Va. State Bar, Richmond, 1982-85; pres. Met. Legal Aid, Richmond, 1978. Del. to State Dem. Cong., Richmond, 1985; mem. Va. Commn. on Family Violence Prevention, 1995. With USN, 1957-59. Recipient service award Criminal Law Bd. of Govs. for Pub. Defender Study, 1971. Mem. ABA, Va. Bar Assn. (chmn. criminal law sect. 1991-93), Richmond Bar Assn., Nat. Legal Aid and Defender Assn. (Reginald Heber Smith award 1991), Va. Bar Assn. (Pro Bono Publico award 1995). Democrat. Baptist. Avocation: fishing. Home: 7726 Sweetbriar Rd Richmond VA 23229 Office: Pub Defender Commn 701 E Franklin St Ste 1416 Richmond VA 23219-2510

POLLARD, SHIRLEY, employment training director, consultant; b. Brunswick City, Va., July 8, 1939; 1 child, Darryl. Degree in bus. adminstrn., Upper Iowa U., 1978. Adminstr. East. Balt. Community Corp.; tng. coord. Balt. County Concentrated Employment Tng. Program; exec. dir. Park Heights Community Corp., Balt.; dir. Linkages, Inc., Balt.; mem. women's and children's adv. coun. Sinai Hosp. Contbr. articles to Afro Am. newspaper. Pres. Park Hts. Cmty. Devel. Corp., United Black Fund, Balt., 1989—, Presdl. Task Force, 1992; active Balt. Urban League, Balt. Welfare Rights Orgn.; founder, pres. Balt. County Polit. Action Coalition, 1982—; founder, dir. Linkages, Inc., 1980; founder, dir. Tng. and Placement Svcs., 1989; active United Svc. Orgn., Md. Minority Contractors Assn., U.S. Civil Rights Mus. and Hall of Fame, Smithsonian Instn.; founder African Am. Culture Ctr.; co-founder Project Lou, Inc.; founder The Afro Fund, Inc.; active Fund for a Free South Africa's Founding Assocs. Leadership Coun., Nat. Women's Hall of Fame, Nat. Abortion Rights Action League, Srs. Coalition, Md. Edn. Coalition, CORE, So. Christian Leadership Conf., Nat. Trust for Hist. Preservation; presdl. appointment Md. Selective Svc. Bd., 1993, Exec. Com. of Am. Friends Svc. Com.; mem. women's adv. coun. Sinai Hosp., 1994—. Recipient Outstanding Achievement award Md. Minority Contractors Assn., Mayor's Citation, Martin Luther King Civil Rights award, 1987, Md. State Dept. Edn. award, 1987, congl. Achievement award, Kool Achiever awards, 1990, Nat. Black Caucus Spl. award, 1990, Congressional Achievement award, 1988, Svc. award The Writers Club, 1991, USO Meritorious Svc. award, 1991, Gov.'s Vol. award, 1992, Acad. of Excellence award, 1992, Signs of Hope award, 1995, Mayor's citation, 1984, Gov.'s citation, 1995, Senatorial award, 1995. Mem. Am. Soc. Pers. Adminstrn., Am. Soc. Health/Manpower/Edn./Tng., Assn. for Providers Employment and Tng., NAACP (founder, pres. Randallstown chpt. 1988-95, Signs of Hope award), Balt. Coun. on Fgn. Affairs, Transafrica, USO, Md. Minority Contractors Assn. (Achievement award 1986, bd. dirs. 1984-89), Smithsonian Assoc., Md. C. of C. (greater Balt. com. 1985). Office: PO Box 32051 Baltimore MD 21208-8051

POLLARD, THOMAS DEAN, biologist, educator; b. Pasadena, Calif., July 7, 1942; s. Dean Randall and Florence Alma (Dierker) P.; m. Patricia Elizabeth Snowden, Feb. 7, 1964; children: Katherine, Daniel. BA, Pomona Coll., Claremont, Calif., 1964; MD, Harvard U., 1968. Intern Mass. Gen. Hosp., Boston, 1968-69; staff assoc. NIH, Bethesda, Md., 1969-72; from asst. prof. to assoc. prof. Harvard Med. Sch., Boston, 1972-78; prof., dir. dept. cell biology and anatomy Johns Hopkins Sch. Medicine, Balt., 1977—; mem. Commn. on Life Sci., NRC, 1990—, chair, 1993—; mem. coun. Nat. Inst. Gen. Med. Scis., NIH. Guggenheim fellow, 1984. Fellow AAAS, Am. Acad. Arts and Scis.; mem. NAS, Am. Soc. Cell Biology (pres. 1987-88, K. R. Porter lectr. 1989), Biophys. Soc. (pres. 1992-93), Marine Biol. Lab. (trustee 1991—). Office: Johns Hopkins Med Sch Dept Cell Biology-Anatomy 725 N Wolfe St Baltimore MD 21205-2105

POLLARD, WILLIAM SHERMAN, JR., civil engineer, educator; b. Oak Grove, La., Jan. 1, 1925; s. William Sherman and Carrie Lois (Hornor) P.; m. Gloria Louise Ponder, June 29, 1946; children: William Sherman, III, Katherine Lynn. B.S. in Civil Engring, Purdue U., 1946, M.S., 1948. Instr. civil engring. Purdue U., 1948-49; instr. U. Ill., 1949-51, assoc. prof., 1951-55; with Harland Bartholomew & Assos., St. Louis, 1955-71; assoc. partner, chief civil engr. Harland Bartholomew & Assos., 1956-58; partner Harland Bartholomew & Assos., Memphis, 1958-71; head ops. Harland Bartholomew & Assos., 1958-60; head Harland Bartholomew & Assos. (Memphis office), 1960-71; pres. William S. Pollard Cons., Inc., Memphis, 1971-81; prof. civil engring. U. Colo., Denver, 1981—; adj. prof. urban planning Memphis State U., 1973-81; dir. Ctr. Urban Transp. Studies, U. Colo.; chmn. WKNO-TV, Memphis. Served with USMC, 1942-46. Named Distinguished Engring. Alumnus Purdue U., 1969. Fellow Am. Cons. Engrs. Council, ASCE (state of the art award 1970), Inst. Transp. Engrs.; mem. Am. Rd. Builders Assn., Nat. Soc. Profl. Engrs., Soc. Am. Mil. Engrs., Urban Land Inst., Transp. Research Bd., Lambda Alpha. Presbyterian. Lodge: Rotary (pres. 1979-80). Office: U Colo PO Box 173364 Denver CO 80217-3364

POLLART, DALE F(LAVIAN), petroleum company research executive; b. Holly, Colo., Jan. 7, 1932; s. Flavian J. and Agnes E. (Reedy) P.; m. Mary Galvin, Aug. 14, 1954; children: John, Susan, Daniel, Eileen, James. BS, Regis Coll., 1952; PhD in Organic Chemistry, Northwestern U., 1956. Research chemist, group leader, assoc. dir., tech. mgr. Union Carbide Corp., 1956-74, product mgr., 1974-76, dir. research and devel., 1976-79, bus. mgr., 1979-81; v.p. tech. Occidental Chem. Co., 1981-82; dir. strategic research Texaco Inc., Beacon, N.Y., 1982-85, dir. research and environ. affairs, 1985-89, gen. mgr. R&D, 1989—; Texaco rep. Indsl. Rsch. Inst., Washington, 1985—, bd. dirs., 1989-92. Contbr. articles to profl. jours.; patentee in field. Bd. dirs. United Way, Poughkeepsie, N.Y., 1985-89, Vassar Bros. Hosp. Found., Poughkeepsie, 1985—. Recipient Forrestal award Regis Coll., 1952, Phi Lambda Upsilon award Northwestern U., 1956. Mem. AAAS, Am. Chem. Soc., Chemist's Club, Dirs. Indsl. Rsch., Darien Boat Club (Conn.), Ischoda Yacht Club (Conn.), Sigma Xi. Roman Catholic. Avocations: tennis, boating. Office: Texaco Inc R & D PO Box 509 Beacon NY 12508-0509

POLLAZZI, ROGER G., transportation executive; b. 1937. BS, Lawrence Inst. Tech.; MBA, Mich. Rackum Meml. Campus, 1972. With ExCello Corp., Houston, 1964-70; with Joy Mfg. Co., Pitts., 1970-83, pres., 1983-88; founder Atlantic Products and Fa-Presto, Pitts., 1988-91; pres., CEO Pullman Co., Lebanon, N.J., 1990—. Office: Pullman Co 3 Werner WaySte 200 Lebanon NJ 08833-2223*

POLLEY, DALE WHITCOMB, bank executive; b. Madisonville, Ky., May 5, 1949; s. Carl Mason and Sarah (Beazley) P.; m. Nancy Jo Weeks, Dec. 27, 1970; children: Lucinda Lynn, Dale Whitcomb Jr. B.B.A., Memphis State U., 1971. C.P.A., Tenn., Ky. Auditor Touche Ross & Co., Memphis, Tenn., 1971-73; auditor Schotte & Taylor, Paducah, Ky., 1973; acct. Commerce Union Corp., Nashville, 1973-78, contr., 1978-84, exec. v.p., chief fin. officer, 1984-87; exec. v.p., chief adminstrv. and fin. officer Sovran Fin. Corp./Cen. South, 1987; chief fin. officer, treas. Sovran Fin. Corp., Norfolk, Va., 1988, exec. v.p., CFO, 1989-91; vice chmn., chief adminstrv. officer First Am., Nashville, 1991-94; pres. First Am. Nat. Bank, Nashville, 1994—. Pres., U. Ky. Alumni Assn., Nashville, 1984—; vice chmn. United Way-Allocations Panel 10, Nashville, 1984—. Mem. Fin. Execs. Inst. (v.p. 1984—), Am. Inst. C.P.A.s, Tenn. Soc. C.P.A.s. Republican. Methodist. Office: First American Corp 1 American Ctr, 6th Fl Nashville TN 37237*

POLLEY, EDWARD HERMAN, anatomist, educator; b. Chgo., Sept. 20, 1923; s. Sam and Anna (Revzin) P.; m. Jo Ann Welsh, Aug. 11, 1953; children: Lisa, Eric. B.A., DePauw U., Greencastle, Ind., 1947; M.S., St. Louis U., 1949, Ph.D., 1951. USPHS postdoctoral research fellow Washington U., St. Louis, 1951-53; Instr., then asst. prof. anatomy Hahnemann Med. Coll., Phila., 1953-59; asst. prof., then assoc. prof. U. Md. Med. Sch., 1964-70; research biologist Edgewood (Md.) Arsenal, 1959-70; prof. anatomy, neurosurgery and ophthalmology U. Ill. Med. Sch., Chgo., 1970—; vis. prof. dept. pharm. and physiol. scis. U. Chgo., 1979-80. Served to lt. (j.g.) USNR, 1942-46. Mem. Am. Assn. Anatomists, Assn. for Research in Vision and Ophthalmology, AAAS, Am. Soc. Neurosci., Sigma Xi. Club: Cajal. Office: U Ill Dept Anat Cell Biol M/C 512 808 S Wood St Chicago IL 60612-7300

POLLEY, HARVEY LEE, retired missionary and educator; b. Wapato, Wash., Aug. 14, 1924; s. Edward Prestley and Alda June Polley; m. Corinne Weber; children: Catherine, David, Corinne, Robert. BA, Whitworth Coll., Spokane, Wash., 1951; postgrad., East Wash. Coll., 1953, Berkeley Bapt. Div. Sch., 1958-59; MEd, Cen. Wash. Coll., 1958; postgrad., Ecole d'Adminstrn. des Affaires Africaines, Brussels, 1959-60. Tchr. Quincy (Wash.) Pub. Schs., 1953-57, N.W. Christian Schs., Spokane, 1958; missionary Am. Bapt. Fgn. Missionary Soc., Zaire, 1958-89; tchr. Evang. Pedagogical Inst., Kimpese, Zaire, 1961-69, asst. legal rep., dir., prin., supt., 1969-72; dir. BIM Hostel, Kinshasa, Zaire, 1972-73; mem. staff Ctr. for Agrl. Devel. Lusekele, Zaire, 1975-85, dir., 1976-79, 83-85; dir. Plateau Bateke Devel. Program, Kinshasa, 1985-89; ret., 1989. Author: Mpila Kele, a rural development guide written in the Kituba lang., 1989. Mem. Coun. Elders, Kimpese, 1969-72; pres. bd. adminstrn. Vanga (Zaire) Hosp., 1981-83; mem. exec. com. Nat. Human Nutrition Planning Coun. Govt. Zaire-USAID, Kikwit, 1983-85. Home: W2405 W Johansen Rd Spokane WA 99208-9616

POLLEY, HOWARD FREEMAN, physician; b. Columbus, Ohio, Nov. 12, 1913; s. David William Latimer and Mary Ann (Lakin) P.; m. Georgiana Alice Redrup, June 5, 1938 (dec. Feb. 1981); children: Alice Lynne, Mary Ann (Mrs. Dale McCoy), William Redrup. A.B., Ohio Wesleyan U., 1934, Sc.D., 1965; M.D., Ohio State U., 1938; M.S., U. Minn., 1945. Intern St. Luke's Hosp., Chgo., 1938-39; resident medicine St. Luke's Hosp., 1939-40; fellow medicine Mayo Grad. Sch. Medicine, 1940-43; cons. in medicine Mayo Clinic, 1943-83, emeritus, 1983—, head sect., 1962-66, chmn. div. rheumatology and internal medicine, 1966-76, sr. cons., 1976-83; instr. U. Minn., 1946-50, asst. prof. medicine, 1950-54, assoc. prof. medicine, 1954-60, prof. medicine, 1960-83; prof. medicine Ind. U. Sch. Medicine, 1983-89; asso. Doctors Hench, Kendall and Slocumb (in original clin. research cortisone and ACTH for rheumatoid arthritis, rheumatic fever.); Bd. dirs. Arthritis Found., 1963-69, exec. com., 1963-68, v.p., 1966-68; trustee Ohio Wesleyan U., 1967—, exec. bd., 1970-72. Sr. author: Rheumatologic Interviewing and Physical Examination of Joints, 2d edit., 1978; assoc. editor: Arthritis and Rheumatism, 1960-64; co-author: Physical Examinations of Joints, 1965; internat. adv. bd. Japanese Jour. Rheumatology, 1985-94; contbr. articles to profl. jours. Mem. adv. council Nat. Inst. Arthritis, Metabolism and Digestive Diseases, NIH, 1972-76; mem. Nat. Arthritis Commn., 1975-76, Nat. Arthritis Adv. Bd., 1981-85; sec. gen. Internat. League Against Rheumatism, 1981-85. Recipient Alumni Achievement award Ohio State U., 1958; Fellow A.C.P. Mem. AMA (spl. cons. council phys. medicine and rehab. 1946-50), Central Soc. Clin. Research, Am. Rheumatism Assn. (v.p. 1962-64, pres. 1964-65, master charter group 1987—), Uruguay Soc. Rheumatology (hon. mem.), All-Union (USSR) Rheumatol. Soc. (hon.), Indian Rheumatism Assn. (hon. mem.), Japan Rheumatism Assn., (hon. mem.), French Rheumatism Assn. (hon. mem.), Sigma Xi, Alpha Omega Alpha, Omicron Delta Kappa, Phi Mu Alpha, Pi Delta Epsilon, Phi Delta Theta, Alpha Kappa Kappa. Home: 211 2nd St NW Rochester MN 55901 Office: Mayo Clinic 200 1st St SW Rochester MN 55905-0001

POLLEY, MICHAEL GLEN, secondary school educator; b. Mattoon, Ill., Feb. 23, 1964; s. George Warren Polley and Judith Maxine (Yarger) Hull; m. Janet Jorene Gray, June 20, 1987; children: Thias Jorene, Aaron Michael, Jessica Connie, Benjamin Ray. BS, Iowa State U., 1986, M in Sch. Math., 1994. Cert. tchr., Tex., Iowa. Tchr. Porter H.S. Brownsville (Tex.) Ind. Sch. Dist., 1986-91; tchr., dept. chair Wapello (Iowa) Comm. Schs. H.S., 1991—; adj. tchr. Southeastern C.C., Burlington, Iowa, 1995—. Author: Geometry: A Lab Approach, 1994. Mem., sound engr., Sunday sch. tchr. Grandview Comm. Bible Ch., 1991-95; mem. Brownsville Bapt. Ch., 1988-91, sound engr., 1989-91; founding mem. Solid Rock Chapel, 1995—. Mem. Nat. Coun. Tchrs. Math. Evangelical. Avocations: sports, photography, music. Home: 310 S Main St Wapello IA 52653-1544 Office: Wapello HS 500 Buchanan Ave Wapello IA 52653-1302

POLLICINO, JOSEPH ANTHONY, investment company executive; b. N.Y.C., Dec. 22, 1939; s. Paul and Carmela (Iudici) P.; m. Margaret Ryan, Nov. 29, 1957; children: Joseph, John, Kerry. Cert., Am. Inst. Banking, 1967; exec. cert. Grad. Sch. Credit & Fin. Mgmt., Dartmouth Coll., 1977. Various tng. and mgmt. positions Mfrs. Hanover Trust, N.Y.C., 1957-73, v.p., officer in charge, 1973-77; sr. v.p. Mfrs. Hanover Comml. Corp., N.Y.C., 1980-82, exec. v.p., 1982-84; pres. CIT Group, Inc. subs. Mfrs. Hanover Corp., N.Y.C., 1984-88; vice chmn. CIT Group Holdings, Inc., N.Y.C., 1988—; bd. dirs. CIT Group, Inc., Livingston, N.J. Recipient Community Leadership award Am. Jewish Congress, N.Y.C., 1982, Disting. Community Service award Brandeis U., 1986. Republican. Roman Catholic. Clubs: 475; Esquire Credit; Plandome (N.Y.) Country. Office: The CIT Group Holdings Inc 1211 Ave of the Americas New York NY 10036*

POLLICK, G. DAVID, academic administrator, philosopher; b. Kansas City, Mo., Oct. 13, 1947; m. Janice Pollick, 1975; 2 children, Dayna, Landon. BA, philosophy, U. San Diego, 1971; Ph.L., philosophy, St. Paul U., Ont., Can., 1973; MA, philosophy, U. Ottawa, Can., 1973, Ph.D., philosophy, 1981. Lecturer, philosophy U. San Diego, San Diego, Calif., 1972-73; tchr.-counselor, neurologically and physically handicapped Aseltine Sch. Neurol. Handicapped, 1972-73; dir. heroin rehab. ctr. Imperial County Diversion Program, El Centro, Calif., 1973-74; tchr.-counselor, emotionally handicapped Finley Elem Sch, Holtville, Calif., 1974-75; lecturer, philosophy U. Ottawa, Ottawa, ON, Canada, 1975-77; asst. prof. philosophy, dept. chrm., acad. coordinator St. John's U., Collegeville, Minn., 1977-84; assoc. prof., dean coll. arts and scis. Seattle U., 1984-89; provost, v.p. for acad. affairs SUNY, Cortland, 1989-93; acting pres., 1991-93; co-CEO, pres. Art Inst. Chgo., Sch. of Art Inst. of Chgo., 1993—. Author: The Work of Roman Ingarden, 1977, (with others) The Aesthetics of Roman Ingarden, 1982; co-editor Supplementary Volume on Aesthetics, 1977. Served with USN. Fellow philosophy and fine arts, Inst. Ecumenical and Culture Rsch., 1976-77; Koscjusko Foundation awd., 1978. Avocations: sculpture, art history, archaeology. Office: Sch of Art Inst Chicago Office of the President 37 S Wabash Ave Chicago IL 60603-3103

POLLICOVE, HARVEY MYLES, manufacturing executive; b. Utica, N.Y., May 28, 1944; s. Maxwell Hymen and Carolyn (Vogel) P.; m. Catherine Mary Keady, Aug. 3, 1968; children: Carolyn, Sarah. AAS, Monroe Community Coll., 1968; BS, U. Rochester, 1973. Sr. engr. supr. optics Eastman Kodak Co., Rochester, 1978-82; engring. mgr. optics Eastman Kodak Co., 1982-84, mfg. mgr., 1984-86, mgr. tech. mkts. (internat.), 1986-89; dir. Ctr. for Optics Mfg. U. Rochester, 1989—; U.S. del. (optics) to Internat. Stds. Orgn., 1995—; lectr. in field. Editorial adv. bd. (optics mag. for mfg.) Laser Focus World, 1990—; contbr. articles to profl. jours. Advisor High Tech. of Rochester, 1988-89; advisor tech. applications rev. bd. Strategic Def. Initiative Orgn., 1990-92, Ballistic Missile Def. Orgn., 1993—; industry advisor Monroe C.C., 1986—. Recipient Dept. of Def. Mfg. Tech. Achievement award, 1992. Mem. Am. Precision Optics Mfrs. Assn. (exec. com. 1987—, elected to bd. dirs. 1990-93), Internat. Soc. for Optical Engring., Optical Soc. Am. Home: 177 Georgian Court Rd Rochester NY 14610-3416 Office: U Rochester Ctr for Optics Mfg 240 E River Rd Rochester NY 14623-1212

POLLIHAN, THOMAS HENRY, lawyer; b. St. Louis, Nov. 15, 1949; s. C.H. and Patricia Ann (O'Brien) P.; m. Donna M. Bickhaus, Aug. 25, 1973; 1 child, Emily Christine. BA in Sociology, Quincy U., 1972; JD, U. Notre Dame, 1975; Exec. Masters in Internat. Bus., St. Louis U., 1992. Bar: Mo. 1975, U.S. Dist. Ct. (ea. dist.) Mo. 1975, Ill. 1976, U.S. Dist. (so. dist.) Ill. 1976. Jud. law clk. to judge Mo. Ct. of Appeals, St. Louis, 1975-76; from assoc. to ptnr. Greenfield, Davidson, Mandelstamm & Voorhees, St. Louis, 1976-82; asst. gen. counsel Kellwood Co., St. Louis, 1982-89, gen. counsel, sec., 1989-93, v.p., sec., gen. counsel, 1993—. Trustee Quincy (Ill.) U., 1987-93, pres. alumni bd., 1986-87; pres. S.W. Neighborhood Improvement Assn., St. Louis, 1984. Mem. Bar Assn. Met. St. Louis. Roman Catholic. Avocations: soccer, cycling. Home: 4934 Magnolia Ave Saint Louis MO 63139-1026 Office: Kellwood Co 600 Kellwood Pky Chesterfield MO 63017-5800

POLLIN, ABE, professional basketball team executive, builder; b. Phila., Dec. 3, 1923; s. Morris and Jennie (Sack) P.; m. Irene S. Kerchek, May 27, 1945; children: Robert Norman, James Edward. B.A., George Washington U., 1945; student, U. Md., 1941-44. Engaged in home bldg. bus., 1945—; pres. Abe Pollin Inc., Balt., 1962—; chmn. Balt. Bullets Basketball Club, Inc. (now Washington Bullets), 1964—; dir. County Fed. Savs. & Loan Assn., Rockville, Md. Bd. dirs. United Jewish Appeal, Nat. Jewish Hosp., Jewish Community Center; bd. dirs., adv. com. John F. Kennedy Cultural Center. Mem. Nat. Assn. Home Builders, Asso. Builders and Contractors Md., Washington Bd. Trade. Jewish. Office: Washington Bullets US Air Arena Landover MD 20785 also: Washington Capitals US Air Arena Landover MD 20785*

POLLINI, FRANCIS, author; b. West Wyoming, Pa., Sept. 9, 1930; s. Sem and Assunta (Ciani) P.; m. Gloria Ann Swann, Sept. 12, 1959; children: Susanne, Lisa. BA in Psychology, Pa. State U., 1951. Author: Night, 1959, Glover, 1965, Excursion, 1966, The Crown, 1967, Three Plays, 1967, Pretty Maids All In a Row, 1968, Dubonnet, 1973, The Hall, 1975. 1st lt. USAF, 1952-57. Home: 14 Oak Ln, Hingham NR9 4JY Norfolk, England

POLLINI, JOHN, archaeology and art educator, dean; b. Boston, Oct. 15, 1945; s. Frederick and Isabell Pollini; m. Phyllis Marie Van Neste, Feb. 1, 1946; children: Gaius, Drusus. BA magna cum laude, U. Wash., 1968; MA, U. Calif., Berkeley, 1973, PhD, 1978. Asst. prof. classics, curator archaeol. mus. Johns Hopkins U., Balt., 1979-87; prof. art and archaeology U. So. Calif., L.A., 1987—, dean sch. fine arts, 1993-96; mem. Comitato di Collaborazione Culturale to the Consul Gen. of Italy at L.A., 1995—; lectr. in field. Author: The Portraiture of Gaius and Lucius Caesar, 1987, (manuals) Greek Art and Archaeology, 1990, Roman Art and Archaeology, 1990; author, editor: Roman Portraiture, 1990; editl. asst. Jour. Classical Studies, 1968-69, assoc. editor, 1969-70; editl. bd. Am. Jour. Philology, 1982-87; co-dir. exhbn. Fisher Gallery, 1989. Faculty fellow U. Calif., 1973-77, Fulbright fellow, 1975-76, Mabelle McLeod Lewis Meml. Fund fellow, 1975-76, Mellon fellow, 1978-79, NEH fellow, 1983-84, 95-96, Am. Coun. Learned Socs. fellow, 1987-88; U. So. Calif. grantee, 1988. Mem. Am. Acad. in Rome (adv. coun. 1993—), Am. Philol. Assn., Archaeol. Inst. Am., Classical Archaeol. Soc. So. Calif. (pres. 1989—), Coll. Art Assn., Assn. Ancient Historians, Soc. for Promotion of Roman Studies, Assn. Study of Marble and other Stones in Antiquity, Phi Beta Kappa. Achievements include research in Greek and Roman art and archaeology. Home: 4028 Midway Ave Culver City CA 90232-3715 Office: U Southern California Sch Fine Arts Watt Hall 104 Los Angeles CA 90089-0292

POLLIO, RALPH THOMAS, editor, writer, magazine publishing consultant; b. Bronx, N.Y., Nov. 1, 1948; s. Thomas and Dolores (Miccioli) P.; m. Rita Lucia Napolitano, Sept. 29, 1974; 1 child, Christopher. BCE, Manhattan Coll., 1978; postgrad., Columbia U., 1988—. Founding pub., editor, owner Ea. Basketball Publs., Franklin Square, N.Y., 1975-88; cons., ptnr., founder Ea. Basketball Mag., Rochester, Mich., 1988—; founding pub., owner, editor High School News, 1984, EB News, 1981. Contbr. articles to mags. and profl. jours., 1985—. Sgt. U.S. Army N.G., 1969-74. Mem. U.S. Basketball Writers Assn. (1st Place award for best mag. feature 1984), ASCE, Soc. Profl. Journalists, Sigma Delta Chi, Internat. Soc. Philos. Enquiry, World Lit. Acad., Mag. Pubs. Assn., Am. Soc. Mag. Editors, Mensa, and numerous other high IQ socs. Roman Catholic. Clubs: N.Y. Road Runners (N.Y.C.), Dix Hills Runners. Avocations: running, listening to jazz, gourmet cooking, reading, film. Home: 201 Oak St West Hempstead NY 11552

POLLITT, JEROME JORDAN, art history educator; b. Fair Lawn, N.J., Nov. 26, 1934; s. John Kendall and Doris B. (Jordan) P.; m. Susan Baker Matheson, Feb. 10, 1977. B.A., Yale U., 1957; Ph.D., Columbia U., 1963. Instr. history of art Yale U., New Haven, 1962-64; asst. prof. Yale U., 1964-68, assoc. prof., 1969-73, prof., 1973—, chmn. dept. classics, 1975-77, chmn. dept. history of art, 1981-84, dean, 1986-91. Author: Art and Experience in Classical Greece, 1972, The Ancient View of Greek Art, 1975, Art in the Hellenistic Age, 1986; editor-in-chief: Am. Jour. Archaeology, 1973-77; contbr. articles to profl. jours. Mem. Archaeol. Inst. Am., Coll. Art Assn. Home: 48 Dillon Rd Woodbridge CT 06525-1219 Office: Dept History of Art Yale U PO Box 208272 New Haven CT 06520-8272

POLLITT, KATHA, writer, poet, educator; b. N.Y.C., Oct. 14, 1949; d. Basil Riddiford and Leanora (Levine) P.; div.; 1 child, Sophie Pollitt-Cohen. BA, Harvard U., 1972; MFA, Columbia U., 1975. Lit. editor The Nation, N.Y.C., 1982-84, contbg. editor, 1986-92, assoc. editor, 1992—; jr. fellow council of humanities Princeton (N.J.) U., 1984; lectr. The New Sch., N.Y.C., 1986-90, Poetry Ctr. 92d St. YMHA and YWHA, N.Y.C., 1986-95; bd. dirs. Am. PEN Club. Author: Antarctic Traveller, 1982 (Circle award Nat. Book Critics 1983), Reasonable Creatures: Essays on Women and Feminism, 1994; poetry appeared in The New Yorker, The New Republic, Poetry, and others; contbr. articles to jours. Whiting fellow, 1993; recipient I.B. Lavan Younger Poet's award Acad. Am. Poets, 1984; Fulbright grantee, 1985; grantee N.Y. Found. of the Arts, 1987, Nat. Endowment for Arts, 1984; Guggenheim fellow, 1987. Fellow N.Y. Inst. Humanities. Democrat. Home: 317 W 93rd St New York NY 10025-7236

POLLITZER, WILLIAM SPROTT, anatomy educator; b. Charleston, S.C., May 6, 1923; s. Richard Morris and Cora (Sprott) P.; m. Margaret Buhlig, Aug. 29, 1955; children—Virginia, Patricia. A.B., Emory U., 1944, M.A., 1947; Ph.D., Columbia U., 1957. Instr. anatomy U. N.C., Chapel Hill, 1957-59, asst. prof., 1959-67, assoc. prof., 1967-73, prof., 1973-87, emeritus prof., 1987—. Contbr. articles to profl. jours. Served with U.S. Army, 1944-47. Mem. Am. Assn. Phys. Anthropologists (v.p. 1978-79, pres. 1979-81, editor jour. 1970-77), Human Biology Council (pres. 1986-88). Democrat. Avocations: tennis; cycling. Home: 513 Morgan Creek Rd Chapel Hill NC 27514-4931 Office: U NC Dept Cell Biology & Anatomy Chapel Hill NC 27599-7090

POLLOCK, ALEXANDER JOHN, banker; b. Indpls., Jan. 28, 1943; s. Alex S. and Doris L. (VanHorn) P.; m. Anne M. Fryfogle, Jan. 27, 1968; children: Elizabeth, Alexander, Evelyn, James. B.A., Williams Coll., 1965; M.A., U. Chgo., 1966; M.P.A., Princeton U., 1969. Instr. philosophy Lake Forest Coll., (Ill.), 1967; with internat. banking dept. Continental Ill. Nat. Bank, Chgo., 1969-77, v.p., 1977-82, sr. v.p., 1982-85; prin. Nolan Norton & Co., Chgo., 1985-86; chief fin. officer The Marine Corp., Milw., 1986-87; pres. Marine Bank N.A., Milw., 1987; pres., chief exec. officer Community Fed. Savs., St. Louis, 1988-90; vis. scholar Fed. Res. Bank of St. Louis, 1991; pres., CEO Fed. Home Loan Bank Chgo., 1991—; bd. advisors Banking Rsch. Ctr.; bd. dirs. Gt. Lakes Higher Edn. Corp., Gt. Books Found.; exec. com. Internat. Union of Housing Fin. Instns. Bd. dirs. Great Books Found., Success Lab Inc. Mem. Union League Club, Phi Beta Kappa. Office: Fed Home Loan Bank Chgo 111 E Wacker Dr Chicago IL 60601-4208 *Omnia superans vi rationis et arte loquendi.*

POLLOCK, DAVID, television writer and producer. Writer TV series That's My Mama, 1974-75, Paul Sands Friends and Lovers, 1975, Hot L Baltimore, 1975, Hollywood High, 1977, The Carol Burnett Show, 1978, Delta House, 1979, One Day at a Time, 1981, Goodnight Beantown, 1983, M*A*S*H, 1980-83, Chicken Soup, 1989, Cheers, 1989, Bagdad Cafe, 1990, Growing Pains, 1990-91, Full House, 1991-92; prodr. TV series Frasier, 1992— (Emmy award for outstanding comedy series 1995). Office: care Broder Kurland Webb Offner Agy 9242 Beverly Blvd Ste 200 Beverly Hills CA 90210

POLLOCK, EARL EDWARD, lawyer; b. Decatur, Nebr., Feb. 24, 1928; s. Herman and Della (Rosenthal) P.; m. Betty Sokol, Sept. 8, 1951; children: Stephen, Della, Naomi. B.A., U. Minn., 1948; J.D., Northwestern U., 1953; LLD (hon.), Morningside Coll., 1995. Bar: D.C. 1955, Va. 1955, Ill. 1959, U.S. Supreme Ct. 1960. Law clk., chief justices Vinson and Warren, U.S. Supreme Ct. Washington, 1953-55; atty. antitrust div. Dept. Justice, Washington, 1955-56, asst. to solicitor gen., 1956-59; ptnr. Sonnenschein Carlin Nath & Rosenthal, Chgo., 1959—. Trustee Loyola U., Chgo., 1983-92; life trustee Northwestern Meml. Hosp. Mem. Chgo. Bar Assn. (chmn. antitrust law com. 1967-68), ABA (chmn. antitrust law sect. 1979-80), Alumni Assn. Northwestern U. Sch. Law (pres. 1974-75, svc. award 1976). Office: Sonnenschein Nath 233 S Wacker Dr Ste 8000 Chicago IL 60606-6404

POLLOCK, GEORGE HOWARD, psychiatrist, psychoanalyst; b. Chgo., June 19, 1923; s. Harry J. and Belle (Lurie) P.; m. Beverly Yufit, July 3, 1946; children: Beth L. Pollock Ungar, Raphael E., Daniel A., Benjamin B., Naomi R. Pollock Sneider. B.S., U. Ill., 1944, M.D. cum laude, 1945, M.S., 1948, Ph.D., 1951. Diplomate Am. Bd. Psychiatry and Neurology. Intern Cook County Hosp., Chgo., 1945-46; resident Ill. Neuropsychiat. Inst., Chgo., 1948-51; practice medicine, specializing in psychiatry Chgo., 1948-91; clin. assoc. prof. dept. psychiatry Coll. Medicine, U. Ill., 1955-64, clin. prof., 1964-72; prof. psychiatry Northwestern U., 1972-93, Dunbar prof. psychiatry and behavioral scis. emeritus, 1993—, dir. rsch. dept. psychiatry/behavioral scis.m 1988-93, emeritus, 1993—; faculty Inst. for Psychoanalysis, Chgo., 1956-92, asst. dean edn., 1960-67, tng. analyst 1961-92, supervising analyst, 1962-92, dir. rsch., 1963-71, pres., 1971-89; exch. program participant Hampstead Child Therapy Clinic, 1962-63; pres. Ctr. Psychosocial Studies, 1972-90. Chmn. bd. editors Ann. of Psychoanalysis, 1971-89; mem. editorial bd. Jour. Am. Psychoanalytic Assn., 1971-74; mem. editorial bd. sect. psychoanalysis Psychiat. Jour. U. Ottawa Faculty Medicine, 1976—; corr. editor Jour. Geriatric Psychiatry, 1975—; Med. Problems of Performing Artists, Psychoanalytic Edn., Psychoanalytic Psychology, Internat. Forum for Psychoanalysis, Internat. Jour. Behavioral Scis. and the Law, Internat. Psychogeriatrics, Depression and Stress. Mem. med. adv. com. Planned Parenthood Assn., 1966-70; pres. governing bd. Parents Assn. Lab. Schs., U. Chgo., 1966-70; mem. med. adv. coun. Asthma and Allergy Found. for Greater Chgo. Capt. U.S. Army, 1946-48. Commonwealth fellow, 1951; research grantee Founds. Fund for Research in Psychiatry, 1960-65. Fellow Am. Coll. Psychiatrists, Am. Orthopsychiat. Assn., Am. Psychiat. Assn. (treas. 1980-86, pres. 1987-88), Am. Coll. Psychoanalysts (pres. 1985-86); mem. Internat. Psychogeriatrics (mem. editorial bds.), Am. Acad. Polit. and Social Sci., Am. Anthrop. Assn., Nat. Council on Family Relations, AAAS, AAUP, Profs., Am. Electroencephalographic Soc., Am. Heart Assn., Assn. for Research in Nervous and Mental Disease, Soc. for Exptl. Biology and Medicine, Ill., N.Y. acads. scis., Chgo. Psychoanalytic Soc. (pres. 1984-85), Soc. for Gen. Systems Research, AMA, World Med. Assn., Am. Name Soc., Am. Psychoanalytic Assn. (pres. 1974-75), Am. Psychol. Assn., Am. Psychosomatic Soc., Am. Pub. Health Assn., Am. Sociol. Assn., Assn. Am. Med. Colls., Ill. Psychiat. Soc. (pres. 1973-74), Sigma Xi, Alpha Omega Alpha, numerous others. Home: 5759 S Dorchester Ave Chicago IL 60637-1726 Office: 30 N Michigan Ave Chicago IL 60602-3400

POLLOCK, JOHN ALBON, broadcasting and manufacturing company executive; b. Kitchener, Ont., Can., Jan. 18, 1936; s. Carl Arthur and Helen Isabel (Chestnut) P.; m. Joyce Mary Smethurst, Apr. 13, 1963; children—Kimberlee, Kristen, Nichola, Graham. B.A.Sc., U. Toronto, Can., 1959; M.B.A., Harvard U., 1962. Tng. positions Electrohome Ltd., Kitchener, 1962-69, v.p., 1969-71, exec. v.p., 1971-74, pres., 1974-80, chmn., pres., CEO, 1980-92, chmn., CEO, 1992—; bd. dirs. Budd Can. Inc., S.C. Johnson & Sons, Ltd., Can. Gen. Tower, Waterloo Sci. Inc.; dir. Electrohome Ltd., CAP Comm. Ltd., CTV; past mem. Sci. Coun. Can.. Past chmn. adv. bd. U. Western Ont.; bd. dirs. Trillium Found., Can. Clay and Glass Gallery, Jr. Achievement; past pres. K-W Art Gallery; past mem. bd. govs. U. Waterloo; past chmn. bd. govs. St. John's Sch., Elora; bd. govs. Grand Valley Conservation Found., Freeport Hosp. Mem. XPO Forum Group, Muskoka Lakes Golf and Country Club, Univ. Club Toronto, K-W Gyro Club, Rotary. Office: Electrohome Ltd, 809 Wellington St N, Kitchener, ON Canada N2G 4J6

POLLOCK, JOHN GLENNON, facilities management services company executive; b. St. Louis, Aug. 7, 1943; s. Joseph A. and Eleanor K. (Donahue) P.; m. Susan M. Weber, July 10, 1965; children: Jennifer, John Jr., Rebecca, Donna, Nancy. BS, St. Louis U., 1965. Sales rep. Proctor & Gamble, Cin., 1965-68; coordinating mgr. ServiceMaster, Downers Grove, Ill., regional mgr., area mgr., div. mgr., sales rep., div. v.p., group pres., 1968-89; pres. subs. co. ServiceMaster, Downers Grove, 1989-91, exec. v.p. mgmt. svc., 1992-94; pres. bus. & industry group, 1994—; chmn. ClassiCare Inc., Chgo., 1992—, Exec. Touch., Inc., Naples, Fla., 1994—. Bd. dirs. St. Andrews Mgmt. Svcs., Inc., St. Louis, 1987—. Republican. Roman Catholic. Office: ServiceMaster Co One ServiceMaster Way Downers Grove IL 60515

POLLOCK, JOHN PHLEGER, lawyer; b. Sacramento, Apr. 28, 1920; s. George Gordon and Irma (Phleger) P.; m. Juanita Irene Gossman, Oct. 26, 1945; children: Linda Pollock Harrison, Madeline Pollock Chiotti, John, Gordon. A.B., Stanford U., 1942; J.D., Harvard U., 1948. Bar: Calif. 1949, U.S. Supreme Ct. 1954. Ptnr. Musick, Peeler & Garrett, L.A., 1953-60, Pollock, Williams & Berwanger, L.A., 1960-80; ptnr. Rodi, Pollock, Pettker, Galbraith & Phillips, L.A., 1980-89, of counsel, 1989—. Contbr. articles to profl. publs. Active Boy Scouts Am.; trustee Pitzer Coll., Claremont, Calif., 1968-76, Pacific Legal Found., 1981-91, Fletcher Jones Found., Good Hope Med. Found. With AUS, 1942-45. Fellow Am. Coll. Trial Lawyers; mem. ABA, L.A. County Bar Assn. (trustee 1964-66). Home: 30602 Paseo Del Valle Laguna Niguel CA 92677-2317 Office: 801 S Grand Ave Los Angeles CA 90017-4613

POLLOCK, KAREN ANNE, computer analyst; b. Elmhurst, Ill., Sept. 6, 1961; d. Michael Paul and Dorothy Rosella (Foskett) P. BS, Elmhurst Coll., 1984; MS, North Cen. Coll., 1993. Formatter Nat. Data Corp., Lombard, Ill., 1985; computer specialist Dept. VA, Hines, Ill., 1985—. Lutheran. Avocations: cross-stitch, mystery books, bowling, bicycling, softball.

POLLOCK, MARC, educational media administrator, consultant; b. Pitts., Mar. 27, 1945; s. Hyman Disney and Beatrice (Berman) P.; m. Marjorie Ann Ginsburg, Dec. 16, 1967; 1 child, Brian Seth Ginsburg-Pollock. ABD in Eng., U. Pitts., 1973; BA in Eng. and Chemistry, Washington & Jefferson, 1966; MA in Eng., U. Pitts., 1969. Teaching fellow Eng. U. Pitts., 1968-74; instr. Eng. Chatham Coll., Pitts., 1972-79; exec. asst. to pres. WQED/Pitts., 1979-81, mgr. ednl. project devel., 1981-86; dir. edn. Sta. WQED/Pitts., 1986-93; WQED/Pitts., cons. media and devel., 1993-95, dir. found. and govt. support, 1995—. Lectr., presenter in field. Vol. March of Dimes, Pitts., 1990-92; cons. Am. Heart Assn., 1992-95, Nat. Kidney Assn., 1995. Recipient Gold Screen award, Nat. Assn. Govt. Comm., 1991, 93, 2 CINE Golden Eagle awards, 1994. Mem. Acad. of TV Arts and Scis. (Emmy award Info. Series 1986), Modern Lang. Assn., Am. Assn. for Tng. and Devel., Melville Soc., Phi Beta Kappa. Avocations: tennis, skiing. Office: WQED 4802 fifth Ave Pittsburgh PA 15213

POLLOCK, MARGARET LANDAU, elementary school educator; b. Jefferson City, Mo., Oct. 18, 1936; d. William Wold and Grace Elizabeth (Creamer) Anderson; m. Charles Walker Nichols, Aug. 10, 1958 (div. Sept. 1970); children: Elizabeth, Charles, Christopher, Jeffrey; m. William Whalen Pollock, Jan. 30, 1993. AA, Stephens Coll., 1956; BS in Elem. Edn., U. Mo., Columbia, 1958; MA in Reading Edn., U. Mo., Kansas City, 1987. Cert. elem. tchr., Mo. Kindergarten tchr. Columbia Schs., 1958-59, Moberly (Mo.) Schs., 1960-62; 1st grade tchr. Kansas City Schs., 1962-63; kindergarten tchr. Independence (Mo.) Schs., 1966-75; chpt. I reading specialist Thomas Hart Benton Elem. Sch., Independence, 1975-93; book reviewer Corpus Christi (Tex.) Caller Times, 1994—; children's libr. Corpus Christi Pub. Libr., 1995—; cons., presenter in field. Bd. dirs. Boys and Girls Club, Independence, 1990-93; coord. Independence Reading Fair, 1989-93; coord. books and tutoring Salvation Army, Kansas City, 1990-92. Mem. AAUW, ASCD, Internat. Reading Assn. (People to People del. to USSR 1991, local v.p. 1990-91, pres. 1991-92), Internat. Platform Assn., Austin Writer's League, Archeol. Inst. Am., Earthwatch, Nature Conservancy, Sierra Club, Phi Kappa Phi, Pi Lambda Theta (pres. Beta Upsilon chpt. 1992-93). Avocations: native American history, rights and education, archeology, reading, travel, conservation. Home: 3535 Santa Fe St # 3 Corpus Christi TX 78411-1346

POLLOCK, ROBERT ELWOOD, nuclear physicist; b. Regina, Sask., Can., Mar. 2, 1936; s. Elwood Thomas and Harriet Lillian (Rooney) P.; m. Jean Elizabeth Virtue, Sept. 12, 1959; children—Bryan Thomas, Heather Lynn, Jeffrey Parker, Jennifer Lee. B.Sc. (Hons.), U. Man., Can., 1957; M.A., Princeton U., 1959, Ph.D., 1963. Instr. Princeton U., 1961-63; Nat. Research Council Can. postdoctoral fellow Harwell, Eng., 1963-64; asst. prof. Princeton U., 1964-69, research physicist, 1969-70; assoc. prof. Ind. U., 1970-73, prof., 1973-84, disting. prof., 1984—, dir. Cyclotron Facility, 1973-79, mem. Nuclear Sci. Adv. Com., 1977-80; Recipient Alexander von Humboldt sr. U.S. scientist award, 1985-87. Fellow Am. Phys. Soc. (Bonner prize 1992); mem. Can. Assn. Physicists. Home: 1261 Winfield Rd Bloomington IN 47401-6147 Office: West Ind U Swain Hall Dept of Physics Bloomington IN 47405

POLLOCK, ROY VAN HORN, pharmaceutical company animal health researcher; b. Detroit, Dec. 23, 1949; s. Alexander Samuel and Doris Louise (Van Horn) P.; m. Barbara Kathleen James, Aug. 22, 1970; children: Roy Alexander, Irene Eva, Sarah Helen. BA, Williams Coll., 1972; DVM, Cornell U., 1978, PhD, 1981. Asst. dean Coll. Vet. Medicine, Cornell U., Ithaca, N.Y., 1981-85, dir. med. informatics, 1985-89; dir. tech. svcs. SmithKline Beecham Animal Health, Exton, Pa., 1989-93; v.p. strategic product devel. SmithKline Beecham Animal Health, West Chester, Pa., 1993-94; v.p. companion animal divsn. Pfizer Animal Health, West Chester, Pa., 1995—; adj. prof. vet. pathobiology Purdue U., 1990—; cons. Impromed Computer Sys., Oshkosh, Wis., 1989-93; mem. adv. bd. Cornell Feline Health Ctr., 1990—. Author: (with others) Provides Computer Aided Diagnosis, 1987; also articles; editor: (computer program) Active Learning, 1989; editor: Cornell Animal Health Newsletter, 1985-89. Cubmaster local chpt. Boy Scouts Am., Ithaca, 1988-89. Recipient Small Animal Rsch. award Ralston-Purina, 1981; Kellogg Nat. fellow, 1987-90. Mem. AVMA (student advisor 1987-89, Gaines award 1989), N.Y. Acad. Sci., Am. Animal Hosp. Assn. (Veterinarian of Yr. award 1987), Phi Beta Kappa, Phi Zeta. Avocations: photography, creative writing. Office: Pfizer Animal Health 812 Springdale Dr Exton PA 19341-2801

POLLOCK, SHELDON IVAN, language professional, educator; b. Cleve., Feb. 16, 1948; s. Abraham and Elsie (Russ) P.; m. Estera Milman, Dec. 21, 1968 (div. May 1985); children: Nira, Mica; m. Ute Gregorius, 1991. AB, Harvard U., 1971, AM, 1973, PhD, 1975. Instr. Harvard U., Cambridge, Mass., 1974-75; asst. prof. U. Iowa, Iowa City, 1975-79, assoc. prof., 1979-85, prof., 1985-89; George V. Bobrinskoy prof. Sanskrit and Indic Studies U. Chgo., 1989—, chmn. Dept. S. Asian Langs. and Civilizations, 1991—; vis. prof. Collège de France, Paris, 1991; prin. investigator NEH collaborative rsch. project Literay Cultures in History, 1995-98. Author: Aspects of Versification in Sanskrit Lyric Poetry, 1977, Ramayana of Valmiki, Vol. II, 1986, Vol. III, 1991; regional editor: Harper Collins World Reader; contbr. articles to profl. jours. Am. Inst. Indian Studies sr. and short-term fellow, 1979, 84, 87, 94; Maharaja of Cochin Meml. lectr., Sanskrit Coll., Tripunithura, Kerala, 1989. Mem. Am. Oriental Soc., Assn. Asian Studies, Social Sci. Rsch. Coun. (Joint Com. on South Asia 1990-96). Home: 5532 S South Shore Dr Chicago IL 60637-1922 Office: U Chgo Dept South Asian Langs 1130 E 59th St Chicago IL 60637-1543

POLLOCK, STEPHEN MICHAEL, industrial engineering educator, consultant; b. N.Y.C., Feb. 15, 1936; s. Meyer and Frances R. Pollock; m. Bettina Dorn, Nov. 22, 1962; children: Joshua, Aaron, Ethan. B in Engring. Physics, Cornell U., 1958; SM, MIT, 1960, PhD in Physics and Ops. Research, 1964. Mem. tech. staff Arthur D. Little Inc., Cambridge, Mass., 1964-65; asst. prof. Naval Postgrad. Sch., Monterey, Calif., 1965-68, assoc. prof., 1968-69; assoc. prof. U. Mich., Ann Arbor, 1969-73, prof., dept. indsl. and ops. engring., 1974—, chmn. dept., 1980-90; research scientist Inst. Pub. Policy Studies, Ann Arbor, 1972—; cons. to over 25 orgns. Area editor Ops. Rsch. Jour., 1977-82; sr. editor Inst. Indsl. Engrs. Trans., 1985-89, Army Sci. Bd., 1994—; contbr. more than 60 tech. papers to profl. jours. Fellow, Space Tech. Labs., 1960; sr. fellow NSF, 1975. Fellow AAAS; mem. Inst. Mgmt. Scis., Ops. Research Soc. Am. (pres. 1986-87). Home: 2694 Wayside Dr Ann Arbor MI 48103 Office: U of Mich Dept Indsl Ops Engring Ann Arbor MI 48109-2117

POLLOCK, STEWART GLASSON, state supreme court justice; b. East Orange, N.J., Dec. 21, 1932. BA, Hamilton Coll., 1954, LLD (hon.), 1995; LLB, NYU, 1957; LLM, U. Va., 1988. Bar: N.J. 1958. Asst. U.S. atty. Newark, 1958-60; ptnr. Schenck, Price, Smith & King, Morristown, N.J., 1960-74, 76-78; commr. N.J. Dept. Pub. Utilities; counsel to gov. State of N.J., Trenton, 1978-79; assoc. justice N.J. Supreme Ct., Morristown, 1979—; mem. N.J. Commn. on Investigation, 1976-78; chmn. coordinating coun. on life-sustaining med. treatment decision making Nat. Ctr. for State Cts., 1994—; bd. dirs. Law Ctr. Found., Inst. of Jud. Adminstrn. Assoc. editor N.J. Law Jour.; contbr. articles to legal jours. Trustee Coll. Medicine and Dentistry, N.J., 1976. Mem. ABA (chmn. appellate judges conf. 1991-92), N.J. Bar Assn. (trustee 1973-78), Am. Judicature Soc. (dir. 1984-88), Morris County Bar Assn. (pres. 1973). Office: NJ Supreme Ct Morris County Courthouse Morristown NJ 07963-0900

POLLOCK, WILLIAM JOHN, secondary school administrator; b. N.Y.C., Nov. 25, 1943; s. Edward and Rose (Favero) P.; m. Jennie Ann Taccetta, Jan. 28, 1967; children: John-Paul, Elizabeth. BSEd, CCNY, 1967; MSEd, Trenton State Coll., 1985; EdD, Nova U., 1993; postgrad., Harvard Graduate Sch., 1992. Tchr. N.Y.C. Pub. Schs., 1967-69; tchr. electronics Howell High Sch., Farmingdale, N.J., 1970-85, dept. supr., 1985-89; vice-prin. Monmouth County Vocat. Schs., Middletown, N.J., 1989-90; prin. High Tech. High Sch., Brookdale Community Coll. Campus, Lincroft, N.J., 1990—; pres. suprs.' assn. Freehold (N.J.) Regional High Sch. Dist., 1988-89; pres. exec. bd. Region V Libr. Coop., Freehold, 1989-92. Asst. scout master Jackson (N.J.) area Boy Scouts Am., 1987-92; pres. exec. bd. St. Mary Acad., Lakewood, N.J., 1987-89; mem. Ocean County Agrl. Devel. Bd., Toms River, N.J., 1989—. 1st lt. U.S. Army, 1969-70, Vietnam. Decorated Bronze Star; recipient Geraldine R. Dodge Found. "Dodge Fellow principal award, 1993", N.J.Star Sch.award N.J. State Dept. Edn., 1995, Best Practices award N.J. State Dept. Edn., 1995. Mem. ASCD, N.J. ASCD (Outstanding Curriculum award 1995), Nat. Assn. Secondary Sch. Prins., Internat. Tech. Edn. Assn., Am. Vocat. Edn. Assn., Prins. and Suprs. Assn., Garden State Prin.'s Ctr. (charter mem.), KC. Avocations: farming, growing Christmas trees, photography, pottery, solar energy. Office: High Tech High Sch PO Box 119 Lincroft NJ 07738-0119

POLLOCK, WILSON F., architectural firm executive. BArch, Pa. State U.; MS in Architecture, Columbia U. Cert. Nat. Coun. Archtl. Registration Bds.; registered architect, 15 states. Formerly with Sert, Jackson Assocs., Cambridge, Mass., Cambridge Seven Assocs., Eshback Pullinger, Phila., Emo Goldfinger, London; founder, pres. ADD Inc., Cambridge; lectr. in field. Prin. works include One Federal Street Renovation, Boston, Hewlett Packard's Med. Products Group Expansion, Andover, Mass., 404 Wyman Street, Waltham, Mass. Bd. trustees Boston Found. for Architects; bd. dirs. Newton Community Devel. Found., Jackson Homestead Mus.; frequent sem. leader Build Boston. Recipient Alumni Achievement award Pa. State U., 1991. Fellow AIA; mem. I.D.R.C., Nat. Assn. Indsl. and Office Parks (assoc.), Boston Soc. Architects (past pres.), Urban Land Inst. Office: ADD Inc 80 Prospect St Cambridge MA 02139-2503

POLO, RICHARD JOSEPH, nuclear engineering executive; b. Barranquilla, Colombia, Oct. 14, 1936; s. Pedro Pastor and Clotilde (Verano) P.; m. Ana Isabel Cepeda, Feb. 1, 1958; children: Richard J. Jr., James Alan. BCE, NYU, 1957; MS in Structural Engring., Iowa State U., 1963, PhD in Structural and Nuclear Engring., 1971; disting. grad., Command and Gen. Staff Coll., Ft. Leavenworth, Kans., 1970; grad., Inter-Am. Def. Coll., Ft. McNair, Washington, 1977; MBA, Marymount U., 1986. Registered profl. engr., Md., Iowa, Fla., Pa., Conn., N.Y. Commd. 2d lt. U.S. Army, 1957, advanced through grades to col., 1979, various positions, 1957-79; asst. dir. civil works Pacific U.S. Army Office Chief of Engrs., 1979-80; corps engr., engr. brigade comdr. U.S. Army, Ludwigsburg, Fed. Republic Germany, 1980-83; dep. study dir. U.S. Army Office Chief of Staff, Washington, 1984-85; ret. U.S. Army, 1985; v.p. constrn. inspection Kidde Cons. Inc., Balt., 1985, sr. v.p. constrn. inspection, 1986, exec. v.p., 1986-89, corp. sec., 1988-89, also bd. dirs.; v.p. Fla. region CRSS, Miami, 1989-90; CEO, program dir. CRSS/WRJ joint venture, 1989-90; assoc. v.p., dep. divsn. dir. fed. programs Greiner, Inc., Miami, 1991-92; dir. engring. & project ops. CKC (OSC), Miami, 1993-94; dir. L.Am. ops., dir. engring. devel. GeoSyntec Cons., Boca Raton, 1994-95; dir. Miami ops. ICF Kaiser Engrs., Inc., 1995—; pres. Amerint, Miami, 1994—, Am. Enterprises Internat., Inc., Polo Mortgage-Plus, Miami, 1993—; dir. ops. ICF Kaiser Engrs., Inc., Miami, 1995—; bd. dirs. KCI Holdings, 1988-90. Contbr. articles on mil. and structural engring. to profl. jours. Inventor arcuate space frame. Cmty. comdr. and sr. U.S. rep. Ludwigsburg Mil. Cmty., 1980-83. Decorated Legion of Merit with bronze oak leaf cluster, Bronze Star, others; Brookings Institution Fed. Exec. fellow, 1983-84. Fellow Soc. Am. Mil. Engrs. (bd. dirs. El Paso chpt. 1967-68, pres. Stuttgart chpt. 1980-82); mem. ASCE, NSPE, Md. Soc. Profl. Engrs., Va. Soc. Profl. Engrs. (dir. no. Va. chpt. 1985-89, pres. elect 1988-89), Assn. U.S. Army (pres. Ludwigsburg chpt. 1980-83), Fla. Engring. Soc., Army-Navy Club Coral Gables (dir. 1994—, sec. 1994—), Greater Miami C. of C. (trustee 1989-92), Country Club Coral Gables, Rotary, Sigma Xi, Phi Kappa Phi, Tau Beta Pi, Chi Epsilon, Psi Upsilon (pres. local chpt. 1956-57). Republican. Roman Catholic. Avocations: model airplanes, racquetball. Home: 430 Sunset Rd Miami FL 33143-6339 Office: ICF Kaiser Engrs Inc 2nd Fl 3750 NW 87th Ave 2d Fl Miami FL 33178

POLOMÉ, EDGAR CHARLES, foreign language educator; b. Brussels, Belgium, July 31, 1920; came to U.S., 1961, naturalized, 1966; s. Marcel Félicien and Berthe (Henry) P.; m. Julia Joséphine Schwindt, June 22, 1944 (dec. May 1975); children: Monique Laure (Mrs. John Ellsworth), André Robert; m. Barbara Baker Harris, July 11, 1980 (div. Jan. 1991); m. Sharon Looper Rankin, Feb. 8, 1991. B.A., Université Libre de Bruxelles, 1941, Ph.D., 1949; M.A., Cath. U. Louvain, 1943. Prof. Germanic lang. Athénée, 1942-56; prof. Dutch Belgian Nat. Broadcasting Corp., Brussels, 1954-56; prof. linguistics U. Belgian Congo (now Zaire), 1956-61; prof. Germanic, Oriental, African langs. and lits. U. Tex., Austin, 1961—, dir. Ctr. for Asian Studies, 1962-72, Christie and Stanley Adams Jr. Centennial prof. liberal arts, 1984—; chmn. dept. U. Tex., 1969-76. Author: Swahili Language Handbook, 1967, Language in Tanzania, 1980, Language, Society and Paleoculture: Essays, 1982, Essays on Germanic Religion, 1989; editor: Old Norse Literature and Mythology, 1969, The Indo-Europeans in the 4th and 3rd Millennia, 1982, Guide to Language Change, 1990, Reconstructing Languages and Cultures, 1992; co-editor The Jour. Indo-European Studies, 1973—, mng. editor, 1987—; co-editor: The Mankind Quar., 1980—. Served with Belgian Aux. Aerodrome Police, 1945. Fulbright prof. U. Kiel, 1968; Ford Found. team dir. Tanzania survey, 1969-70. Mem. MLA, Linguistics Soc. Am., Am. Oriental Soc., Am. Anthrop. Assn., Indogermanische Gesellschaft, Societas Linguistica Europea, Société de Linguistique de Paris, Am. Inst. Indian Studies (chmn. lang. com. 1972-78). Home: 2701 Rock Terrace Dr Austin TX 78704-3843 Office: U Tex Dept Germanic Langs EPS 3 102 Austin TX 78712 *Having taught and done research on four continents—Europe, Africa, America and Asia—I feel gratitude that my experience has enabled me to discover the richness of man's intellectual and artistic heritage. It has especially allowed better appreciation of the perennial aesthetic, ethical and social values that make us all part of the great human brotherhood, whatever our language, creed or ethnic background.*

POLONIS, DOUGLAS HUGH, engineering educator; b. North Vancouver, B.C., Can., Sept. 2, 1928; came to U.S., 1955, naturalized, 1963; s. William and Ada (Burrows) P.; m. Vera Christine Brown, Jan. 30, 1953; children: Steven Philip, Malcolm Eric, Douglas Hugh, Christine Virginia. B.A.Sc., U. B.C., 1951, Ph.D., 1955; M.A.Sc., U. Toronto, 1953. Metall. engr. Steel Co. Can., Hamilton, Ont., 1951-52; mem. faculty U. Wash., Seattle, 1955—; prof. metall. engring., materials sci. & engring. U. Wash., 1962-95, chmn. dept. mining, metall. and ceramic engring., 1969-71, 73-82, prof. emeritus, 1995—; metall. cons., 1955—. Contbr. articles to profl. jours. Fellow Am. Soc. Metals; mem. AIME, Sigma Xi, Tau Beta Pi, Alpha Sigma Mu, Sigma Phi Delta. Home: 19227 46th Ave NE Seattle WA 98155-2909

POLONSKY, ARTHUR, artist, educator; b. Lynn, Mass., June 6, 1925; s. Benjamin and Celia (Hurwitz) P.; children: Eli, D.L., Gabriel. Diploma with highest honors, Sch. of Mus. Fine Arts, Boston, 1948. Instr. painting dept. Sch. Mus. Fine Arts, Boston, 1950-60; asst. prof. dept. fine arts Brandeis U., 1954-65; assoc. prof. Boston U., 1965-90, prof. emeritus, 1990—. One-man shows include Boris Mirski Gallery, Boston, 1950, 54, 56, 64, Boston Pub. Libr., 1969, 90, 93, 96, Durlacher Gallery, N.Y.C., 1965, Mickelson Gallery, Washington, 1966, 74, Boston Ctr. for Arts, 1983, Starr Gallery, Boston, 1987, Fitchburg Art Mus., 1990; exhibited in group shows including Met. Mus., N.Y.C., 1950, Stedelijk Mus., Amsterdam, The Netherlands, 1950, Carnegie Internat. Expn., 1951, Inst. Contemporary Art, Boston, 1960, Mus. Fine Arts, Boston, 1976, Boston Arts Festival, 1985, Expressionism in Boston, Decordova Mus., Lincoln, Mass., 1986, Decordova Mus., 1987, Palais Univ. de Strasbourg, France, 1992, Boston's Honored Artists, Danforth Mus., Framingham, Mass., 1995; represented in permanent collections Mus. Fine Arts, Boston, Fogg Mus., Harvard U., Addison Gallery of Am. Art, Andover, Mass., Stedelijk Mus., Walker Art Ctr., Mpls. Recipient Louis Comfort Tiffany award for painting, 1951, 1st prize Boston Arts Festival, 1954; European travelling fellow Sch. Mus. Fine Art, Boston, 1948-50. Mem. AAUP, Artists Equity Assn., Inc. (founding, former dir. New Eng. chpt.). Address: 364 Cabot St Newtonville MA 02160-2252

POLOUJADOFF, MICHEL EUGENE, electrical engineering educator; b. Asnières, France, Apr. 2, 1932; s. Léon and Marguerite Blanche (Guillot) P.; m. Jacqueline Suatton, Mar. 21, 1964; children: Muriel, Marie-Pierre. Degree, Ecole Superieure d'Electricity, Paris; MS, Harvard U.; DSc in Physics, U. Paris; Doct.h.c., Liége (Paris) U., 1983. Prof. U. Grenoble, France, 1961-83, 84-85, U. Pierre et Marie Curie, Paris, 1985—; prof., chair Ecole Centrale, Paris, 1985—; disting. Hooker vis. prof. McMaster U., Hamiton, Ont., Can., 1983-84. Author: The Theory of Linear Induction Machinery, 1980, Chinese translation, 1985, also 3 tutorial books, 1970, Spanish translations, 1974; mem. editl. bd. 2 internat. revs. in field. Sous lt. Armée de l'Air, France, 1960-61. Recipient prix Charles Saulces de Freycinet, Acad. Sci. Paris, 1987. Fellow IEEE (Lamme medal 1994, Nikola Tesla award 1991), N.Y. Acad. Scis.; mem. Soc. Electriciens et Electr. (emérite). Roman Catholic. Avocations: skiing, photography. Home: 2 Rue de Paris, 75013 Paris France Office: U Paris, 4 Place Jussieu, 75252 Paris France

POLOVETS, ALEXANDER, editor, publisher; b. Moscow, USSR, July 12, 1935; came to the U.S., 1976; naturalized U.S. citizen, 1983; s. Boris and Dina (Tsank) P.; widower; 1 child, Stanislav. Grad., Stanford Poligraphical Coll. of Moscow, 1951-55; M in Pub., Moscow Pub. Poligraphical Inst., 1958-64; M in Patent Info., Cen. Inst. Patent Studies, 1968-71. With All-Union Pub. Svcs., 1965-76; supr. quality control Western Lithograph, 1976-80; founder, publisher Alamanac Press Russian-Am. Pub. Co., 1977—; pres. Almanac Enterprises, Inc., 1983—. Author: Fugitive Pachikhin, and Other Stories, 1987, It is My Destiny, 1992, There Where We Are, 1994; pub. Russian Underground Jokes (2 vol. anthology Soviet humor), Russian lang. suppliment for Isreal Today mag., 1978-80, and numerous others in Russian and English; pub., editor-in-chief Panorama (internat. Russian lang. newspaper), 1980—, ann. Russian Community Ref. Guide (Russian Yellow Pages); author 32 books; contbr. numerous articles in USSR and Am. Recipient Resolutions for contbns. to Almanac Panorama from mems. of Cong. and Senate, V.P. and Pres. U.S.A., Gov. Calif. Mem. Press Club Greater L.A. Office: Almanac Press 501 S Fairfax Ave Los Angeles CA 90036-3179

POLOZOLA, FRANK JOSEPH, federal judge; b. Baton Rouge, Jan. 15, 1942; s. Steve A. Sr. and Caroline C. (Lucito) P.; m. Linda Kay White, June 9, 1962; children: Gregory Dean, Sheri Elizabeth, Gordon Damian. Student bus. adminstrn., La. State U., 1959-62, JD, 1965. Bar: La. 1965. Law clk. to U.S. Dist. Ct. Judge E. Gordon West, 1965-66; assoc. Seale, Smith & Phelps, Baton Rouge, 1966-68, ptnr., 1968-73; part-time magistrate U.S. Dist. Ct. (mid. dist.) La., Baton Rouge, 1972-73, magistrate, 1973-80, judge, 1980—; adj. prof. Law Ctr., La. State U., 1977—. Bd. dirs. Cath. High Sch. Mem. FBA, La. Bar Assn., Baton Rouge Bar Assn., Fed. Judges Assn., 5th Cir. Dist. Judges Assn., La. State U. L Club, KC, Omicron Delta Kappa. Roman Catholic. Office: US Dist Ct Russell B Long Fed Bldg & US Courthouse 777 Florida St Ste 313 Baton Rouge LA 70801-1717

POLSELLI, LINDA MARIE, elementary education educator; b. Providence, R.I., June 13, 1958; d. Anthony Natale and Helen Marie (Magnan) P. BS, R.I. Coll., 1982; MEd, Providence Coll., 1986. Spl. edn. educator Wyman Elem., Warwick, R.I., 1986-91; elem. edn. educator Holliman Elem., Warwick, 1991—; computer software com. Warwick Sch. Dept., mem. math./curriculum revisions com., 1992, report card com., 1995—. Adminstr. Warwick Citizens Vol. Assn., Warwick Police Dept., 1983—. Mem. ASCD, Nat. Coun. Tchrs. English, Nat. Coun. Tchrs. Math., Internat. Reading Assn., R.I. Math. Tchrs. Assn., Tchrs. Applying Whole Lang. Roman Catholic. Avocations: travel, guitarist. Home: 128 Cove Ave Warwick RI 02886-5402

POLSKY, DONALD PERRY, architect; b. Milw., Sept. 30, 1928; s. Lew and Dorothy (Geisenfeld) P.; m. Corinne Shirley Neer, Aug. 25, 1957; children: Jeffrey David, Debra Lynn. BArch, U. Nebr., Lincoln, 1951; postgrad., U. So. Calif., 1956, U. Calif., Los Angeles, 1957, U. Nebr., Omaha, 1964, U. Ill., 1965. Project architect Richard Neutra, Architect, Los Angeles, 1953-56, Daniel Dworsky, Architect, Los Angeles, 1956; prin. Polsky, AIA & Assocs., Los Angeles, 1956-62, Omaha, 1964—; dir. dept. architecture MCA, Inc., Universal City, Calif., 1962-64. Prin. works include Mills residence, 1958, apt. bldgs., 1960, Polsky residence, 1961, Milder residence, 1965. Chmn. Design Control 1480 Study Mayor's Riverfront Devel., Omaha, 1969, 71; pres. Swanson Sch. Community Club, Omaha, 1972; mem. Mayor's Adv. Panel Design Services, Omaha, 1974; vice chmn. Omaha Zoning Bd. Appeals, 1976. Recipient archtl. awards Canyon Crier Newspaper, Los Angeles, 1960, House and Home Mag., Santa Barbara, Calif., 1960. Mem. AIA (pres. Omaha chpt. 1968, numerous awards 1956-95), Nebr. Soc. Architects (pres. 1975, award 1965, 87). Office: Donald P Polsky AIA & Assocs 8723 Oak St Omaha NE 68124-3051

POLSON, LAURA LAMKIN, nurse administrator; b. Louisville, Dec. 4, 1962; d. Robert Dane and Martha Louise (Penick) Lamkin; m. Louis Scott Heimann, Dec. 15, 1978 (div. Apr. 1979); m. James Howard Polson, Aug. 25, 1984; children: Amanda Brooke, Morgan Elizabeth, Joshua Dane. AS in Nursing, U. Louisville, 1982; postgrad., Bellarmine Coll., 1994—. RN, Ky.; CCRN, ACLS, RCVT. Staff nurse Sts. Mary & Elizabeth Hosp., Louisville, 1982-85, charge nurse, 1985-87; staff nurse Homecare Ptnrs., Louisville, 1985-86; staff nurse Humana Hosp. Audubon, Louisville, 1987-90, lab. mgr., 1990-91, dir. cardiovascular svcs., 1991-93; dir. invasive cardiovascular svcs. Audubon Regional Med. Ctr., Louisville, 1993—; mem. Columbia Cardiovascular Mgmt. Network, Columbia Healthcare Corp., 1993—. Mem. Nat. Soc. Profl. Cardiovascular Technologists. Democrat. Home: 5350 Highway 62 NE Corydon IN 47112-8382 Office: Audubon Regional Med Ctr 1 Audubon Plaza Dr Louisville KY 40217-1318

POLSTON, BARBARA, principal, educational psychologist; b. Litchfield, Ill., Oct. 9, 1943; d. Wilbur Lee and Frances (Leitschuh) P.; children: Charles, Beth, Ann. B of Music Edn., Webster Coll., 1965; MA, St. Louis U., 1985. Cert. elem. tchr., Prin., Mo., Wash. Prin. Archdiocese St. Louis, Our Lady of the Presentation, St Martin de Porres, Corpus Christi, St. Louis; archdiocesan coord. alternative sch. practices, sch. calendars, multi media and tech., accelerative learning interventions. Mem. Mo. Lead Program, Nat. Yr. Round Edn., Danforth Found. Mem. ASCD, NCEA, Prins. Acad. Mo., Nat. Cath. Prins. Acad., Inst. Responsive Edn., Consortium Responsive Schs.

POLSTON, MARK FRANKLIN, minister; b. Indpls., Feb. 9, 1960; s. Albert Franklin and Mildred (Wiggington) P.; m. Lisa Kaye Polston, July 21, 1984; 1 child, Jordan Franklin. AS, Somerset (Ky.) C. C., 1981; BS, Campbellsville Coll., 1984; JD, Ind. Sch. Law, 1995. Real estate agt. Homestead Real Estate, Somerset, 1978-89; pastor Trace Fork Separate Bapt. Ch., Liberty, Ky., 1979-81, Calvary Separate Bapt. Ch., Nancy, Ky., 1980-84, Harmony Separate Bapt. Ch., Jacksonville, Fla., 1984-85, Fairview Separate Bapt. Ch., Russell Springs, Ky., 1985-89, Calvary Separate Bapt. Ch., Nancy, Ky., 1989-91, Edinburgh (Ind.) Separate Bapt. Ch., 1992—; sales rep. Sentry Ins., Somerset, 1989-91; law clk. Ind. Atty. Gen., Indpls., 1992—; clk. Gen. Assn. Separate Bapt., 1988—; bd. dirs. Separate Bapt. Missions., Inc., 1988-92; adj. prof. Ind. Vocat. Tech. Coll., Indpls., 1993—. Home: 787 Kitchen Rd Mooresville IN 46158-8057 Office: Ind Atty Gen 402 W Washington St Indianapolis IN 46204-2739 also: Edinburgh Separate Bapt Ch 1010 S Main St Edinburgh IN 46124-1377

POLSTON, RONALD WAYNE, law educator; b. Raymond, Ill., Nov. 1, 1931; s. Joseph M. and Minnie V. (Wilson) P.; m. Mary Ann Campbell, Aug. 5, 1961; children—Anne Campbell, Joseph Harrison. B.S., Eastern Ill. U., 1953; LL.B., U. Ill., 1958. Bar: Ill. 1959, Ind., 1967, U.S. Supreme Ct. 1964. Assoc. Craig & Craig, Mt. Vernon, Ill., 1958-64; ptnr., 1964-65; asst. prof. Ind. U. Sch. Law, Indpls., 1965-68, assoc. prof., 1968-71, asst. dean, 1968-71, prof. 1971-95, prof. emeritus, 1995—; vis. prof. Monash U., Melbourne, Australia, 1972-73. Trustee Eastern Mineral Law Found., 1985—. Served to cpl. U.S. Army, 1953-55. Democrat. Methodist. Home: 311 S McGown Raymond Raymond IL 62560 Office: Indiana Univ Sch Law 735 W New York St Indianapolis IN 46202-5222

POLSTRA, LARRY JOHN, lawyer; b. Lafayette, Ind., June 28, 1945; s. John Edward and Elizabeth (Vandergraff) P.; m. Joan Marie Blair Rozier, Sept. 2, 1972 (dec.); 1 stepchild, Shawn M. Rozier; m. Barbara Dominy, Mar. 18, 1988; stepchildren: Tobi Shawn Porter, Teri Lane Kelly. BS in Bus. Mgmt., Bob Jones U., 1968; JD, Atlanta Law Sch., 1976, LLM, 1977. Bar: Ga. 1976, U.S. Dist. Ct. (no. dist.) Ga. 1976, U.S. Ct. Appeals (11th cir.) 1990, U.S. Supreme Ct. 1994. Mktg. dir. N.Am. Security, Atlanta, 1972-73; acctg. supr. Allstate Ins. Co., Atlanta, 1973-76; sole practice Atlanta, 1976-77; ptnr. Law Smith (formerly Smith & Polstra), Atlanta, 1977-94, of counsel, 1995; of counsel England & McKnight, 1996—; arbitrator Fulton County Superior Ct., Atlanta, 1986. Served to 1st lt. USMC, 1968-71, Vietnam. Mem. ATLA, Atlanta Bar Assn., Ga. Assn. Trial Lawyers, Ga. Assn. Criminal Def. Lawyers, Marine Corps Assn. Ga. Lawyers. Avocation: golf. Home: 2081 Hampton Tr Conyers GA 30208

POLUNIN, NICHOLAS, environmentalist, author, editor; b. Checkendon, Oxfordshire, Eng.; s. Vladimir and Elizabeth Violet (Hart) P.; m. Helen Lovat Fraser, 1939 (dec.); 1 child, Michael; m. Helen Eugenie Campbell, Jan. 3, 1948; children: April Xenia, Nicholas V. C., Douglas H. H. Open scholar, Christ Ch., 1928-32; BA (1st class honors), U. Oxford, 1932, MA, 1935, DPhil, 1935, DSc, 1942; MS, Yale U., 1934. Participant or leader numerous sci. expdns., 1930-65, primarily in arctic regions, including Spitsbergen, Greenland, Alaska, Can., Arctic, North Pole; curator, tutor, demonstrator, lectr. various instns., especially Oxford U., 1933-47; vis. prof. botany McGill U., 1946-47, Macdonald prof. botany, 1947-52; Guggenheim fellow, rsch. assoc. Harvard U., 1950-53; earlier fgn. research asso., USAF botanical Ice-island research project dir., lectr. plant sci. Yale, also biology Brandeis U., 1953-55; prof. plant ecology and taxonomy, head dept. botany, dir. U. Herbarium and Botanic Garden, Baghdad, Iraq, 1955-58; guest prof. U. Geneva, 1959-61, 75-76; adviser establishment, founding prof. botany, dean faculty sci. U. Ife, Nigeria, 1962-66; founding editor Plant Sci. Monographs and World Crops Books, 1954-78, Biol. Conservation, 1967-74, Environ. Conservation, 1974-95; chmn. internat. steering com., organizer, editor procs. Internat. Conf. on Environ. Future, Finland, 1971; chmn. internat. steering com., sec. gen., editor procs. 2d Internat. Conf. on Environ. Future, Reykjavik, Iceland, 1977, 3d Internat. Conf. on Environ. Future, Edinburgh, Scotland, 1987; sec.-gen., joint editor procs. 4th Internat. Conf. Environ. Future, Budapest, Hungary, 1990; pres., CEO Found. for Environ. Conservation, 1975—; participant Internat. Bot. Congresses, Stockholm, 1950, Paris, 1954, Edinburgh, 1964, Seattle, 1969, Leningrad, 1975, Sydney, 1981; councillor (pres., CAO) World Council For The Biosphere, 1984—. Author: Russian Waters, 1931, The Isle of Auks, 1932, Botany of the Canadian Eastern Arctic, 3 vols., 1940-48, Arctic Unfolding, 1949, Circumpolar Arctic Flora, 1959, Introduction to Plant Geography and Some Related Sciences, 1960 (various fgn. edits.), Eléments de Géographie Botanique, 1967; editor: The Environmental Future, 1972, Environmental Monographs and Symposia (series), 1979-88, Growth Without Ecodisasters?, 1980, Ecosystem Theory and Application, 1986, (with Sir John Burnett) Maintenance of the Biosphere, 1990, Surviving with the Biosphere, 1993; (with Mohammad Nazim) Environmental Challenges I: From Stockholm to Rio and Beyond, 1993, II: Population and Global Security, 1994, 97; founding chmn. editl. bd. Cambridge Studies in Environ. Policy, 1984—; contbr. articles to various jours. Decorated comdr. of Order Brit. Empire, 1975; recipient undergrad., grad. student scholarships, fellowships, rsch. associateships Yale U., 1933-34, Harvard U., 1936-37, 50-53; Rolleston Meml. prize, 1938; D.S.I.R. spl. investigator, 1938; Leverhulme Rsch. award, 1941; from sr. scholar to sr. rsch. fellow New Coll., Oxford, 1934-47; Guggenheim fellow, 1950-52; recipient Ford Found. award Scandinavia, USSR, 1966-67, Can. Marie-Victorin medal, 1957, Indian Ramdeo medal, 1986, Internat. Sasakawa Environ. prize, 1987, USSR Vernadsky commemoration, 1988, Chinese Academia Sinica medal, 1988, Vernadsky medal USSR Acad. Scis., 1988, 89, Founder's (Zéchenyi) medal Hungarian Acad. Scis., 1990; named to Netherlands Order of the Golden Ark, 1990 (officer), UN Environ. Programme Global 500 Roll of Honour, 1991. Fellow AAAS, Royal Geog. Soc. (life), Royal Hort. Soc. (life), Linnean Soc. London (life), Arctic Inst. N.Am. (life), INSONA (v.p.), NECA (India), Pierson Coll., Yale U. (assoc.); mem. Internat. Soc. Environ. Edn. (life), Internat. Acad. Environment Geneva (conseil de fondation), Torrey Bot. Club (life), Bot. Soc. Am. (life), N.Am. Assn. Environ. Edn. (life), Asian Soc. Environ. Protection (life), Sigma Xi, various fgn. and nat. profl. and sci. socs., Harvard Club (N.Y.C.) (life), Field Naturalists' Club (Ottawa) (life), Reform (London) (life), Oxford U. Exploration Club (v.p.). Achievements include confirming existence of Spicer Islands in Foxe Basin and making world's last major land discovery, Can. Arctic, 1946; past rsch. plant life and ecology of arctic, subarctic, and high-altitude regions; present occupation environ. conservation at the global level; initiator of ann. worldwide Biosphere Day, 1991, plans and seeking funds for major Biosphere Fund and Prizes, 1992, Biosphere Clubs, 1993 and plans for planetary econetwork of environmental/conservational watchdogs colllated by World Coun. for Biosphere; initiating and editing World Who is Who and Does What in Environment Conservation, 1996. Address: Found Environ Conservation, 7 Chemin Taverney, 1218 Grand-Saconnex, 1218 Grand-Saconnex Geneva Switzerland

POLUNSKY, BOB A., movie critic, talk show host; b. San Antonio, Dec. 3, 1931; s. Maurice Bernard and Ethel (Mazur) P.; m. Paulina Norman, June 12, 1960; children: Julianne, Laurianne, Adrianne. BFA, U. Tex., 1953. Traffic mgr. KABC Radio, San Antonio, 1953-55; Yellow Pages sales S.W. Bell Telephone, 1957-60; sales svc. mgr. KONO/KSAT, San Antonio, 1960-68; sales mgr. KENS-TV, San Antonio, 1968-85; movie critic San Antonio Express-News, 1968—, KENS-TV and WDAI RAdio, San Antonio, 1968—. With U.S. Army, 1950-57. Home: 619 Briar Oak St San Antonio TX 78216-3006 Office: The Express News Corp Ave E & 3rd St PO Box 2171-7297 # 3rd St San Antonio TX 78205

POLZIN, JOHN THEODORE, lawyer; b. Rock Island, Ill., Dec. 23, 1919; s. Max August and Charlotte Barbara (Trenkenschuh) P.; m. Helen Louise Hosford, Nov. 27, 1969. A.B., U. Ill., 1941, J.D., 1943. Bar: Ill. 1943. Sole practice, Galva, Ill., 1946-55, Chgo., 1975—; city atty., Galva, 1950-54; assoc. Langner, Parry, Card & Langner, Chgo., 1955-75; lectr. Ill. Inst. for Continuing Legal Edn., 1978. Served to lt. USNR, 1943-46. Mem. ABA, Ill. State Bar Assn. (chmn. patent, trademark and copyright law sect. 1981-82), Patent Law Assn. Chgo. (chmn. fgn. trademark com. 1972, 74). Republican. Home and Office: 1503 Oak Ave Evanston IL 60201-4260

POMBO, RICHARD, congressman, rancher, farmer; b. Tracy, Calif., 1961; m. Annette, 1983; children: Richard Jr., Rena. Student, Calif. State U., Pomona, 1981-83. Councilman City of Tracy, 1991-92; mayor pro-tem Tracy City Coun., 1992; mem. 103rd-104th Congresses from 11th Calif. dist., 1993—; mem. Agrl. Com., Resources Com.; chmn. Pvt. Property Rights Task Force, 1993-94, Endangered Species Act Task Force, 1995-96; co-chmn. Spkr.'s Environ. Task Force, 1996. Co-founder San Joaquin County Citizen's Land Alliance, Calif., 1986—; active San Joaquin County Econ. Devel. Assn., Tracy Bus. Improvement Dist., City Coun. (vice chmn. Cmty. Devel. Agy., Cmty. Parks Com., and Waste Mgmt. Com.), San Joaquin County Rep. Ctrl. Com. Mem. Rotary Club. Roman Catholic. Office: US Ho of Reps 1519 Longworth HOB Washington DC 20515-0511

POMERANCE, NORMAN, publishing company executive; b. Greensburg, Pa., June 24, 1926; s. Isaac and Esther (Cohen) P.; m. Paula Diamond, Aug. 2, 1985; children—John, Jane, Jason. BS (Evan Pugh scholar), Pa. State U., 1950; MS, Ohio State U., 1951; JD, Yeshiva U., 1990. Dir. planning and analysis Gen. Precision, Inc., Tarrytown, N.Y., 1954-66; dir. bus. planning IT&T, N.Y.C., 1966-69; sr. v.p. Macmillan, Inc.; pres., dir. Macmillan Pub. Co., N.Y.C., 1969-74; group v.p. Arlen Realty and Devel. Corp., N.Y.C., 1974-76; v.p., dir. Am. Optical Corp., Southbridge, Mass., 1976-79; pres. internat. div. Am. Optical Corp., 1976-79; group v.p. Harper & Row (Pubs., Inc.), 1980-87; ret.; strategic planning advisor CARE, N.Y.C., 1991—. Served with USNR, 1944-46. Mem. Tau Beta Pi, Eta Kappa Nu, Pi Mu Epsilon, Phi Kappa Phi, Phi Eta Sigma. Home: 60 Gramercy Park N Apt 4A New York NY 10010-5435

POMERANTZ, CHARLOTTE, writer; b. Bklyn., July 24, 1930; d. Abraham L. and Phyllis (Cohen) P.; m. Carl Marzani, Nov. 12, 1966; children: Gabrielle Rose, Daniel Avram. B.A., Sarah Lawrence Coll., 1953. Children's books include The Bear Who Couldn't Sleep, 1965, The Moon Pony, 1967, Ask the Windy Sea, 1968, Why You Look Like You Whereas I Look Like Me, 1968, The Day They Parachuted Cats on Borneo, 1971 (chosen for Internat. Year of the Child 1977-78), The Princess and the Admiral, 1974 (Jane Addams Children's Book award), The Piggy in the Puddle, 1974 (Featured on Reading Rainbow in Claymation, 1992, NYT Outstanding Picture Book of the Year award 1974), The Ballad of the Long Tailed Rat, 1975, Detective Poufy's First Case, 1976, The Mango Tooth, 1977 (Jr. Literary Guild Selection), The Downtown Fairy Godmother, 1978, The Tamarindo Puppy and Other Poems, 1980 (an ALA Notable Book), Noah's and Namah's Ark, 1980, If I Had a Paka, 1982 (Jane Addams Honor award 1983), Buffy and Albert, 1982, Posy, 1983 (1984 Christopher award), Whiff, Sniff, Nibble and Chew, 1984, Where's the Bear?, 1984, The Half-Birthday Party (Jr. Literary Guild Selection), 1984, All Asleep, 1984, One Duck, Another Duck, 1984, How Many Trucks Can a Tow Truck Tow? (Children's Book of the Year Libr. of Congress 1991) 1987, Timothy Tall Feather, 1987, The Chalk Doll (Top 10 Picture Books of 1989 Boston Globe, Parents Choice award, 1990) 1989, Flap Your Wings and Try, 1989, Serena Katz, 1992, The Outside Dog (One of 100 Books Recommended by the N.Y. Pub. Libr., 1993, ALA Notable) 1993, Halfway to Your House, 1993, Mangaboom, 1994, You're Not My Friend Any More, 1994, Here Comes Henny, 1994; Lyricist: (children's musical) Eureka!, 1994; contbr. stories to mags.; spl. editorial asst.: Einstein on Peace, 1960; editor: A Quarter Century of Un-Americana, 1963. Address: 260 W 21st St New York NY 10011-3447

POMERANTZ, JAMES ROBERT, psychology educator, academic administrator; b. N.Y.C., Aug. 21, 1946; s. Mihiel Charles and Elizabeth (Solheim) P.; divorced; children: Andrew Emil, William James. BA, U. Mich., 1968; PhD, Yale U., 1974. Prize teaching fellow Yale U., New Haven, 1973-74; asst. prof. psychology Johns Hopkins U., Balt., 1974-77; assoc. prof. SUNY, Buffalo, 1977-83, prof., 1983-88, chmn. dept. psychology, 1986-88, assoc. dean, 1983-86; dean social scis., Elma W. Schneider prof. psychology Rice U., Houston, 1988-95; provost, prof. cognitive and linguistic scis. Brown U., Providence, 1995—; adj. prof. Baylor Coll. Medicine, 1992—. Editor: Perceptual Organization, 1981, The Perception of Structure, 1991. Fellow APA, Am. Psychol. Soc.; mem. Psychonomic Soc. Office: Brown U Provosts Office Box 1892 Providence RI 02912

POMERANTZ, LAURA, apparel company executive; b. 1948. V.p. Leslie Fay Cos., N.Y.C. Office: Leslie Fay Cos 1412 Broadway New York NY 10018*

POMERANTZ, MARTIN, chemistry educator, researcher; b. N.Y.C., May 3, 1939; s. Harry and Pauline (Sietz) P.; m. Maxine Miller, June 4, 1961; children: Lee Allan, Wendy Jane, Heidi Lauren. B.S., CCNY, 1959; M.S., Yale U., 1961, Ph.D., 1964. NSF postdoctoral fellow U. Wis.-Madison, 1963-64; asst. prof. Case Western Res. U., Cleve., 1964-69; assoc. prof. chemistry Yeshiva U., N.Y.C., 1969-74; prof. Yeshiva U., 1974-76, chmn. dept., 1971-72, 73-76; prof. chemistry U. Tex.-Arlington, 1976—; co-dir. Ctr. for Advanced Polymer Rsch., 1988-91, dir. Ctr. for Advanced Polymer Rsch., 1991—; vis. assoc. prof. U. Wis.-Madison, 1972; vis. prof. Columbia U., N.Y.C., 1970-75, Ben Gurion U. of the Negev, Beer Sheva, Israel, summers 1981, 85. Contbr. articles to sci. jours. Fellow Alfred P. Sloan Found., 1971-76m, NSF and Sterling, 1962-63, Leeds and Northrup Found., 1960-62, Woodrow Wilson fellow, 1959-60; grantee NSF, Robert A. Welch Found., Def. Adv. Rsch. Projects Agy., Air Force Office Sci. Rsch., Dept. Energy, Petroleum Rsch. Fund, Tex. Advanced Tech. program, Tex. Advanced Rsch. program, also others. Mem. Am. Chem. Soc., Royal Soc. Chemistry, Phi Beta Kappa, Sigma Xi. Home: 5521 Williamstown Rd Dallas TX 75230-2127 Office: U Tex Dept Chemistry & Biochemistry Box 19065 Arlington TX 76019

POMERANTZ, MARVIN, thoracic surgeon; b. Suffern, N.Y., June 16, 1934; s. Julius and Sophie (Luksin) P.; m. Margaret Twigg, Feb. 26, 1966; children: Ben, Julie. AB, Colgate U., 1955; MD, U. Rochester, 1959. Diplomate Nat. Bd. Med. Examiners, Am. Bd. Surgery, Am. Bd. Thoracic Surgery (dir. 1989—). Intern Duke U. Med. Ctr., Durham, N.C., 1959-60, resident, 1960-61, 63-67, instr. surgery, 1966-67; asst. prof. surgery U. Colo. Med. Sch., Denver, 1967-71, assoc. prof. surgery, 1971-74, assoc. clin. prof. surgery, 1974-93, prof. surgery, chief gen. thoracic surgery, 1992—; chief thoracic and cardiovascular surgery Denver Gen. Hosp., 1967-73, asst. dir. surgery, 1967-70, assoc.dir. surgery, 1970-73; pvt. practice Arapahoe CV Assocs., Denver, 1974-92; clin. assoc. surgery br. Nat. Cancer Inst., 1961-63; mem.staff Univ. Hosp., Denver, Denver Gen. Hosp., Rose Med. Ctr., Denvr, St. Joseph's Hosp., Denver, Englewood, Colo., Porter Meml. Hosp., Denver, Swedish Med. Ctr., Englewood, Denver VA Med. Ctr., Children's Hosp., Denver, U. Coll. Health Sci. Ctr., 1992—, bd. dirs., 1995-97. chmn., 1997, Am. Bd. Thoracic Surgery. Guest editor Chest Surgery Clinics N.Am., 1993; contbr. numerous articles to profl. publs., chpts. to books. Fellow ACS, Am. Coll. Chest Surgeons; mem. AMA, Western Thoracic Surg. Assn. (v.p. 1992, pres. 1993-94, counselor-at-large 1988-90), Am. Assn. Thoracic Surgeons (program com. 1991), Am. Heart Assn. (bd. dirs. Colo. chpt. 1993), Arapahoe Med. Soc., Colo. Med. Soc., Denver Acad. Surgery (pres. 1980), Internat. Cardiovascular Soc., Rocky Mtn. Cardiac Surgery Soc., Rocky Mtn. Traumatologic Soc., Soc. Thoracic Surgeons (nomenclature/coding com. 1991-95, standards and ethics com., govt. rels. com., chmn. program com. 1994-95), Soc. Vascular Surgeons, Am. Bd. Thoracic Surgery (vice chmn. 1996—). Office: UCHSC Divsn CTS 4200 E 9th Ave # C310 Denver CO 80220-3706

POMERANTZ, MARVIN ALVIN, container corporation executive; b. Des Moines, Aug. 6, 1930; s. Alex and Minnie (Landy) P.; m. Rose Lee Lipsey, Nov. 12, 1950; children: Sandy, Marcy Kuperman, Vickie Ginsberg, Lori Wolnerman. BS in Commerce, U. Iowa, 1952. Exec. v.p. Midwest Bag Co., Des Moines, 1952-60; founder, pres., gen. mgr. Gt. Plains Bag Corp., Des Moines, 1961-75; v.p. Continental Can Co. Inc., Greenwich, Conn., 1971-75; v.p., gen. mgr. Forest Products Brown Systems Operation (div. Continental Can Co. Inc.), Greenwich, Conn., 1975-77; pres. Diversified Group Internat. Harvester, Chgo., 1980-81, ex. v.p., 1981-82; pres., chmn., chief exec. officer The Mid-Am. Group, Des Moines, 1981—; chmn., chief exec. officer Gaylord Container Corp., Deerfield, Ill., 1986—. Mem. Greater Des Moines Commn.; trustee Drake U., 1978—; pres. Iowa State Bd. Regents, 1987-93, 95—; mem. U.S. Olympic Budget and Audit Commn., Colorado Springs., Colo., 1989-92. Republican. Avocations: golf, tennis. Office: Gaylord Container Corp 4700 Westown Pky Ste 303 West Des Moines IA 50266-6718

POMERANZ, FELIX, accounting educator; b. Vienna, Austria, Mar. 28, 1926; s. Joseph and Irene (Meninger) P.; m. Rita Lewin, June 14, 1953; children: Jeffry Arthur, Andrew Joseph. BBA, CCNY, 1948; MS, Columbia U., 1949; PhD, U. Birmingham, Eng., 1992. CPA, N.Y., Va., La., N.C.; cert. computer profl., fraud examiner, govt. fin. mgr. Audit staff Coopers & Lybrand, CPAs, N.Y.C., 1949-56; mgr. Marks, Grey & Shron (now Ernst & Young, CPA's), N.Y.C., 1956-58; asst. chief auditor Am.-Standard, N.Y.C., 1958-62; mgr. systems Westvaco Corp., N.Y.C., 1962-66; dir. operational auditing Coopers & Lybrand, CPAs, N.Y.C., 1966-68, ptnr., 1968-85; disting. lectr./dir. Ctr. for Acctg., Auditing, Tax Studies U. Miami, Miami, 1985-93; prof. acctg. Fla. Internat. U., Miami, 1993—, assoc. dir. sch. acctg., 1993—; affil. faculty dept. religious studies U. Miami, 1996—. Author: Managing Capital Budget Projects, 1984; The Successful Audit: New Ways to Reduce Risk Exposure and Increase Efficiency, 1992; co-author: Pensions-An Accounting and Management Guide, 1976; Auditing in the Public Sector: Efficiency, Economy, and Program Results, 1976; Comparative International Auditing Standards, 1985; contbr. articles to profl. jours. Emeritus trustee Nat. Ctr. for Automated Info. Rsch. 1st lt. AUS, 1944-46, 51-52. Recipient Spear Safer Harmon faculty fellow, 1987. Mem. AICPAs, N.Y. State Soc. CPAs, Assn. Systems Mgmt., Acad. Acctg. Historians, Assn. Govt. Accts., N.Y. Acad. Scis., Am. Acctg. Assn., Inter-Am. Acctg. Assn., Assn. Cert. Fraud Examiners, Beta Gamma Sigma, Beta Alpha Psi (Most Disting. and Most Outstanding Prof. awards 1993), Alpha Kappa Psi. Home: 250 Jacaranda Dr Apt 406 Plantation FL 33324-2532 Office: Fla Internat U Sch Acctg University Park Miami FL 33199

POMERENE, JAMES HERBERT, retired computer engineer; b. Yonkers, N.Y., June 22, 1920; s. Joel Pomerene and Elsie Bower; m. Edythe R. Schwenn, Dec. 1, 1944; children: James Bennett, Katherine Ellen, Andrew Thomas Stewart. BSEE, Northwestern U., 1942; postgrad., Princeton U., 1950. Elec. engr. Hazeltine Corp., Little Neck, N.Y., 1942-46; mem. staff electronic computer project Inst. for Advanced Study, Princeton, N.J., 1946-51; chief engr. Inst. for Advanced Study, Princeton, 1951-56; sr. engr. IBM Corp., Poughkeepsie, N.Y., 1956-67; sr. staff mem. IBM Corp., Armonk, N.Y., 1967-76; cons. in field. Patentee in field. IBM fellow T.J. Watson Rsch. Ctr., 1976—. Fellow IEEE (Computer Pioneer award Computer Soc. 1986, Edison medal 1993); mem. NAE, Sigma Xi, Tau Beta Pi. Episcopalian. Home: 403 Bedford Rd N Chappaqua NY 10514-2207

POMEROY, BENJAMIN SHERWOOD, veterinary medicine educator; b. St. Paul, Apr. 24, 1911; s. Benjamin A. and Florence A. (Sherwood) P.; D.V.M., Iowa State U., 1933; M.S., Cornell U., 1934; Ph.D., U. Minn., 1944; m. L. Margaret Lyon, June 25, 1938; children—Benjamin A., Sherwood R., Catherine A., Margaret D. Diagnostician, U. Minn., 1934-38, faculty, 1938-81, prof., 1948-81, prof. emeritus, 1981—, head dept. vet. microbiology and pub. health, 1953-73, assoc. dean, 1970-74, acting dean, 1979-80. Mem. adv. com. FDA; cons. animal scis. div. and animal health div., meat insp. service, animal health service USDA. Republican precinct officer, 1958-60, chmn., 1960-61; chmn. Ramsey County (Minn.) Rep. Com., 1961-65, 4th Congl. Dist., 1961-63, 67-69; mem. Minn. Rep. Central Com., 1961-71; del. Minn. Rep. Conv., 1960-71, 92, 94, 96, Rep. Nat. Conv., 1964. Named Veterinarian of Year in Minn., 1970; recipient Eminent Citizen award St. Anthony Park Legion Post and Aux., 1955, Alumni Merit award, 1975, Stange award, 1977, Disting. Achievement citation, 1981 (all Iowa State U.), Centennial Merit award U. Pa., 1984, Animal Health award USDA, 1986; named to Am. Poultry Hall of Fame, 1977. Fellow Poultry Sci. Assn.; mem. Nat. Turkey Fedn. (life; Research award 1950), Tex. Poultry Assn. (life), Minn. Turkey Growers Assn. (life), Soc. Exptl. Biology and Medicine, Am. Assn. Avian Pathologists (life), Am. Coll. Vet. Microbiologists, Am. Acad. Microbiology, Am. Soc. Microbiology, AVMA (council research 1961-73, Pub. Service award 1980), U.S. Animal Health Assn. (life), Nat. Acad. of Practice, Minn. Vet. Med. Assn. (sec.-treas. 1950-75, pres. 1978-79, Disting. Service award 1980, presdl. award 1992), Sigma Xi, Phi Kappa Phi, Alpha Gamma Rho, Phi Zeta, Gamma Sigma Delta. Presbyterian (elder). Co-author: Diseases and Parasites of Poultry, 1958; contbg. author: Diseases of Poultry, 1972, 78, 84, 91. Home: 1443 Raymond Ave Saint Paul MN 55108-1430

POMEROY, EARL R., congressman, former state insurance commissioner; b. Valley City, N.D., Sept. 2, 1952; s. Ralph and Myrtle Pomeroy; m. Laurie Kirby, Dec. 26, 1986. BA, U. N.D., 1974, JD, 1979. Atty. Sproul, Lenaburg, Fitzner and Walker, Valley City, 1979-84; commr. of ins. State of N.D., Valley City, 1984-92; mem. 103rd Congress from N.D. (at large), Washington, D.C., 1993—; mem. coms.: budget, agriculture. State rep. N.D. Legis. Assembly, 1980-84. Recipient Found. award Rotary, 1975; named Outstanding Young North Dakotan N.D. Jaycees, 1982. Mem. Nat. Assn. of Ins. Commrs. (chmn. midwest zone 1987-88, exec. com. 1987-88), Phi Beta Kappa. Democrat. Presbyterian. Office: US Ho Rep 1533 Longworth Washington DC 20515-3401*

POMEROY, HARLAN, lawyer; b. Cleve., May 7, 1923; s. Lawrence Alson and Frances (Macdonald) P.; m. Barbara Lesser, Aug. 24, 1962; children: Robert Charles, Caroline Macdonald, Harlan III. BS, Yale U., 1944; LLB, Harvard U., 1948. Bar: Conn. 1949, U.S. Supreme Ct. 1954, U.S. Ct. Appeals (fed. cir.) 1954, Ohio 1958, U.S. Dist. Ct. (no. dist.) Ohio 1958, U.S. Claims Ct. 1958, U.S. Ct. Appeals (6th cir.) 1958, U.S. Tax Ct. 1958, D.C. 1975, Md. 1981, U.S. Dist. Ct. (D.C. dist.) 1984, U.S. Ct. Internat. Trade 1984, U.S. Ct. Appeals (D.C. cir.) 1986. Atty. trial sect. tax div. Dept. Justice, Washington, 1952-58; assoc. Baker & Hostetler, Cleve., 1958-62, ptnr., 1962-75; ptnr. Baker & Hostetler, Washington, 1975-92; gen. chmn. Cleve. Tax Inst., 1971; lectr. in field. Author: (monographs) The Privatization Process in Bulgaria; Bulgarian Government Structure and Operation-An Overview; contbr. articles to profl. jours. Treas. Shaker Heights (Ohio) Dem. Club, 1960-62; trustee, mem. exec. com. 1st Unitarian Ch. Cleve., 1965-68; trustee River Road Unitarian Ch., 1988-90; gen. counsel, former asst. treas. John Glenn Presdl. Com., 1983-87; participant Vol. Lawyers Project, Legal Counsel for Elderly, Washington, 1983-92; vol. Guardian Ad Litem Program, Sarasota, Fla., 1990-92, GED-H.S. Equivalency Program, Sarasota, 1990-92; vol. exec. fgn. legal advisor Internat. Exec. Svc. Corps. with Privatization Ministry, Prague, Czech Republic, 1994-95; mem. spl. mission to Bulgarian Ministry of Fin., U.S. Dept. Treasury, 1995. Mem. ABA (resident liaison Bulgaria for Ctrl. and Eastern European Law Initiative 1992-93), Am. Arbitration Assn. (arbitrator 1992—), Nat. Assn. of Securities Dealers (arbitrator 1992—), D.C. Bar Assn., Columbia Country Club (Bethesda, Md.), Yale Club, Harvard Club, Ivy League Club, Oaks Club of Sarasota. Home: 7336 Villa D Este Dr Sarasota FL 34238-5648 Office: Baker & Hostetler 11th Fl 1050 Connecticut Ave NW Washington DC 20036-5304 also: 3200 National City Ctr 3200 National City Ctr Cleveland OH 44414

POMEROY, HORACE BURTON, III, accountant, corporate executive; b. Bronxville, N.Y., July 11, 1937; s. Horace Burton Jr. and Juhn (McCalla) P.; m. Margarita Maria Benavidez, July 14, 1973; children: Josephine, Emily. BS in Bus Adminstrn., U. Ariz., 1964; MBA, Boise State U., 1982. Comml. bank officer Continental Bank, Chgo., 1964-67; cons. Morgan Olmstead Kennedy Gardner, L.A., 1967-74; mgr. cash and banking Morrison Knudsen Corp., Boise, Idaho, 1974-88; rep. Idaho State Legistature Dist. 16, 1988—. With U.S. Army, 1959-60. Mem. NRA, Nat. Assn. Accts., Nat. Corp. Cash Mgrs. Assn., Nat. Philatelic Assn. Republican. Episcopalian. Avocations: stamp collecting, fishing, golf, tennis. Home: 6822 Kingsdale Dr Boise ID 83704-7343 Office: Statehouse Boise ID 83720

POMEROY, LEE HARRIS, architect; b. N.Y.C., Nov. 19, 1932; s. Alfred and Florence Pomeroy; m. Sarah Pomeroy; children: Jordana, Jeremy, Alexandra. BArch, Rensselaer Poly. Inst., 1955; MArch, Yale U., 1961. Registered architect, N.Y., Conn., Mass., Vt., N.J., Fla., Pa., Maine. Architect William Tabler, N.Y.C., 1958-59, The Architects Collaborative, Cambridge, Mass., 1959-60; asst. prof. CCNY, 1962-64; pres. Lee Harris Pomeroy Assocs., N.Y.C., 1965-87; adj. prof. Sch. Architecture, CUNY, 1964-87; prin. solar rsch. group ECOSOL, Conn., Eng., Spain, 1965-84; dir. Project for Pub. Spaces, Inc., N.Y.C., 1982-88; dean's adv. coun. Sch. Architecture, Resselaer Poly, Inst., 1991—, adv. to pres., 1994—. Prin. works include Swiss Bank Tower and Saks Fifth Ave. extension, N.Y.C., restoration of Plaza Hotel, N.Y., Sch. Art and Dance City Coll., N.Y.C., 1989, New Rochelle Pub. Libr., 1980 (AIA-ALA design award 1980, N.Y. State AIA and Urban Design awards 1980), Dutchess County Jail, Poughkeepsie, N.Y. (AIA-ACA design award 1981), HBO Satellite Comm. Ctr., 1983 (N.Y. State AIA design award 1984), Manitou Sta. planned cmty., 1973 (AIA and Progressive Architecture awards 1973), Henry St. studios artists housing (Progressive Architecture mag. design award 1963, AIA design award 1975), Bedford Mews housing (AIA, Owens Corning energy conservation and Record Homes design awards 1980), Fulton Mall, Bklyn., 1985 (City Club N.Y.C. Bard award for design 1985), Trinity Ch. Bridge (AIA design award 1991), Hotel Usixtu, Prague, Czech Republic, Teda Hotel, Tanjin, China. Mem. Cmty. Bd. 5, Midtown Manhattan, N.Y.C., 1980-91; bd. dirs. Bellview Assn.; bd. dirs. Bellview Hosp., N.Y.C., 1992—, chmn. strategic planning com. Recipient Mcpl. Arts Soc. award, N.Y.C., 1982; Nat. Endowment for Arts grantee, N.Y.C., 1983. Fellow AIA (bd. dirs. 1979-81); mem. Mcpl. Arts Soc., Regional Plan Assn., Yale Club, Century Club, City Club N.Y. (co-chmn. Bard award program for excellence in urban design 1988-90, 94). Avocations: tennis, photography, travel. Home: 285 Central Park W New York NY 10024-3006 Office: 462 Broadway New York NY 10013-2618

POMEROY, ROBERT CORTTIS, lawyer; b. Syracuse, N.Y., Sept. 17, 1943; s. Stuart E. and Elizabeth (Corttis) P.; m. Sandra Campbell; children: Lisa, Robert Jr., Heather. AB, Hamilton Coll., 1965; LLB, Harvard U., 1968. Bar: Mass. 1968, Fla. 1981. Assoc. Goodwin, Procter & Hoar, Boston, 1968-76, ptnr., 1977—. Mem. Am. Coll. Trust & Estate Counsel. Avocations: skiing, golf, sailing. Home: 3 Pier 7 Charlestown MA 02129 Office: Goodwin Procter & Hoar LLP Exchange Pl Boston MA 02109-2881

POMEROY, THOMAS WILSON, JR., lawyer, former state supreme court justice; b. Crafton, Pa., Nov. 20, 1908; s. Thomas Wilson and Marion Elizabeth (Bradbury) P.; m. Maria Frances Whitten, July 6, 1935 (dec. Dec. 1994); children: Anne Whitten Pomeroy Martin, George Robinson, Helen F. Pomeroy Hopkins, Benjamin Bradbury. A.B., Lafayette Coll., 1929; LL.B., Harvard U., 1933; LLD (hon.), Lafayette Coll., 1962, Wilson Coll., 1988. Bar: Pa. 1933. Instr. pub. speaking Lafayette Coll., 1929-30; practiced in (Pitts.); ptnr. Kirkpatrick, Pomeroy, Lockhart & Johnson, 1946-68; gen. counsel Pitts. & W.Va. Ry. Co., 1946-65; justice Supreme Ct., Pa., 1968-78; of counsel firm Kirkpatrick & Lockhart, Pitts., 1979—; chmn. Pa. Joint Council's Com. to Study Unified Jud. System in Pa., 1980-85. Pres. Pitts. Council Intercultural Edn., 1943-44; pres. Pitts. YMCA, 1964-66, now emeritus dir.; chmn. Pa. Gov.'s Commn. to Investigate Charges of Excessive Use of Force by Police in Chester, Pa., 1964; mem. Pa. Gov.'s Commn. on Three Mile Island, 1979, Commonwealth Commn. on Bicentennial of U.S. Constn., 1986-88; former mem. bd. Christian edn. United Presbyn. Ch. U.S.A.; trustee emeritus Lafayette Coll. Served to lt. comdr. USNR, 1944-46. Fellow Am. Bar Found., Pa. Bar Found.; mem. ABA, Pa. Bar Assn. (pres. 1961), Allegheny County Bar Assn. (pres. 1959), Am. Law Inst., Am. Judicature Soc., Inst. Jud. Adminstrn., World Affairs Coun. Pitts. (pres. 1940-44), Scotch-Irish Soc. U.S. (pres. 1962-64), Phi Kappa Psi, Tau Kappa Alpha. Clubs: Harvard-Yale-Princeton (Pitts.), Duquesne (Pitts.). Office: 1500 Oliver Building Bldg Pittsburgh PA 15222-2300

POMORSKI, STANISLAW, lawyer, educator; b. Lwow, Poland, Nov. 23, 1934; came to U.S., 1972, naturalized, 1983; s. Juliusz and Maria (Ziemba) P.; m. Patricia Smith; children—Lukasz, Christopher, Maria. M.Law, U. Warsaw, 1956, D.Law, 1968. Law clk., 1958-61; pvt. practice law Warsaw, 1961-64; vis. scholar Harvard U. Law Sch., 1964-66; rsch. assoc. Polish Acad. Scis., 1966-72; mem. faculty Rutgers U. Law Sch., Camden, N.J., 1973—; prof. law Rutgers U. Law Sch., 1977-81, Disting. prof. law, 1981—; fellow Soviet law U., Leyden, Netherlands, 1980-81; trustee Nat. Coun. Soviet and East European Rsch., Washington, 1988-94. Author: American Common Law and the Principle Nullum Crimen Sine Lege, 2d edit, 1975, Restructuring the System of Ownership in the USSR, 1991; co-author: A Profile of the Soviet Constitution of 1977, 1979. Ford Found. fellow, 1972-73. Office: Rutgers U Law Sch 5th And Penn St Camden NJ 08102

POMPADUR, I. MARTIN, communications executive; b. Bklyn., June 25, 1935; s. Jack and Florence (Raitbord) P.; m. Joan Lynn Krassner, Dec. 18, 1960 (div. 1986); children: F. Douglas (dec.), Jana Sue; m. Marian Hackett, Dec. 23, 1987; 1 child, Chelsea Rae. BA, Williams Coll., 1955; LLB, U. Mich., 1958. Bar: Conn. 1958, N.Y. 1961. Atty. ABC-TV Network, N.Y.C., 1960-61, 61-66, chief adminstrv. officer, 1966-68, gen. mgr., 1968-70, v.p. broadcast div., 1970-72, corp. v.p., 1972; pres. ABC Leisure Group I, 1973-75, asst. to pres. parent co., 1975-76; also dir. parent co.; sr. v.p. Ziff Corp., 1977-78, pres., 1978-82; chmn., chief exec. officer GP Sta. Ptnrs., 1982-96; mng. gen. ptnr. TV Sta. Ptnrs., 1982-96; chmn., chief exec. officer PBTV, Inc., 1984—; mng. gen. ptnr. Northeastern TV Investors Ltd. Partnership, 1984—; prin. owner, sec. Caribbean Internat. News Corp., 1985—, also bd. dirs.; CEO, COO RP Media Mgmt., Inc., 1986-93; chief exec. officer ML Media Ptnrs., L.P., 1986—; chief exec. officer, chief oper. officer RP Opportunity Mgmt.; chief exec. officer ML Media Opportunity Ptnrs., L.P., 1988—; prin. shareholder Hispanic Media Inc., 1986-90; prin. shareholder, vice-chmn. Hunter Pub. L.P., 1986-94; co-trustee Lidan Trust, 1983—; atty. Young & Rubicam, Inc., advt. agy., N.Y.C., summer 1961. Mem. Stamford bd. reps., chmn. legis. and rules com., 1959-60. Home: 10 Highland Farm Rd Greenwich CT 06831-2606 Office: RP Cos Inc 350 Park Ave Fl 16 New York NY 10022-6022

POMPER, PHILIP, history educator; b. Chgo., Apr. 18, 1936; s. Solomon and Rebecca (Fenigstein) P.; m. Alice N. Epstein, Aug. 27, 1961 (div.); children: Erica, Stephen, Karen; m. Emily Meyer, June 26, 1994. B.A., U. Chgo., 1959, M.A., 1961, Ph.D., 1965. Instr. history Wesleyan U., Middletown, Conn., 1964-65, asst. prof., 1965-71, assoc. prof., 1971-76, prof., 1976—, chmn. dept. history, 1981-84; William F. Armstrong prof. history, 1992—. Author: The Russian Revolutionary Intelligentsia, 1970, 2nd edit., 1993, Peter Lavrov and the Russian Revolutionary Movement, 1972, Sergei Nechaev, 1979 (Choice award 1979), The Structure of Mind in History: Five Major Figures in Psychohistory, 1985, Trotsky's Notebooks, 1933-35: Writings on Lenin, Dialectics and Evolutionism, 1986, Lenin, Trotsky, and Stalin: The Intelligentsia and Power, 1990; assoc. editor History and Theory, 1991—; contbr. articles on Russian history and theory of history to profl. jours. Fellow, Ford Found., 1963-64, Social Scis. Rsch. Coun., 1968, Hoover Instn., 1987, Wilson Ctr., 1988; Russian Rsch. Ctr. scholar, 1987—. Mem. Am. Hist. Assn., Am. Assn. for Advancement Slavic Studies, Conn. Acad. Arts and Scis. Home: 13 Red Orange Rd Middletown CT 06457-4916 Office: History Dept Wesleyan U Middletown CT 06457

POMRANING, GERALD CARLTON, engineering educator; b. Oshkosh, Wis., Feb. 23, 1936; s. Carlton Chester and Lorraine Helen (Volkman) P.; m. Gayle Ann Burkitt, May 27, 1961 (div. 1983); children: Linda Marie, Sandra Lee. BS, U. Wis., 1957; cert., Technische Hogeschool, Delft, Holland, 1958; Ph.D. (NSF fellow), MIT, 1962. Mgr. GE, Pleasanton, Calif., 1962-64; group leader Gen. Atomic Co., La Jolla, Calif., 1964-69; v.p. Sci. Applications, La Jolla, 1969-76; prof. engring. UCLA, 1976—; cons. to govt. and industry. Author: Radiation Hydrodynamics, 1973, Transport in Stochastic Mixtures, 1991; editor: Reactor Physics, 1966; contbr. articles to profl. jours. Fulbright fellow, 1957-58. Fellow AAAS, Am. Nuclear Soc. (Mark Mills award 1963), Am. Phys. Soc.; mem. Math. Assn. Am., Soc. Indsl. Applied Math., Am. Math. Soc., Sigma Xi, Alpha Xi Sigma, Phi Eta Sigma, Phi Kappa Phi, Tau Beta Pi, Phi Lambda Upsilon.

POND, BYRON O., manufacturing company executive; b. 1936. BSBA, Wayne State U. With Fed. Mogul Corp., Detroit, 1958-68; with Maremont Corp., Chgo., 1968—, dir. sales exhaust systems div., 1970-74, corp. v.p., 1974-76, sr. v.p. nat. accounts, 1976-78, exec. v.p., 1978-79, pres., chief exec. officer, from 1979, now pres., chmn. bd. dirs., chief exec. officer; chmn. bd. of dirs., chief exec. officer Arvin Industries, Columbus, IN. Also: Arvin Industries Inc PO Box 3000 Columbus IN 47202-3000*

POND, LINDA RAE, senior research scientist, administrator; b. Flint, Mich., Aug. 22, 1944; d. Frederick Lewis and Orle Darlene (Fairbanks) Smith; m. Joseph M. Wood, Aug. 31, 1964 (div. 1979); children: Timothy Joseph, Melissa Jill; m. Daniel James Pond, June 18, 1983; children: David Alan, Steven Douglas. BS in Orgnl. Comm., U. Ctrl. Fla., 1983; MS in Human Resource Mgmt., Fla. Inst. Tech., 1985. System engring. specialist Harris Corp., Melbourne, Fla., 1984-90; sr. rsch. scientist Pacific N.W. Lab., Richland, Wash., 1990-94, mgr. operational effectiveness, 1994—. Mem. Acad. Mgmt., Phi Kappa Phi. Home: RR 3 Box 3885 Prosser WA 99350-9541 Office: Battelle Pacific NW Lab Battelle Blvd Richland WA 99352

POND, PATRICIA BROWN, library science educator, university administrator; b. Mankato, Minn., Jan. 17, 1930; d. Patrick H. and Florence M. (Ruehle) Brown; m. Judson S. Pond, Aug. 24, 1959. BA, Coll. St. Catherine, St. Paul, 1952; MA, U. Minn., 1955; PhD, U. Chgo., 1982. Sch. libr. Minn., N.Y., 1952-62; asst. prof. libr. sci. U. Minn., 1962-63; reference libr. U. Mont., 1963-65; asst. prof. U. Oreg., 1967-72, assoc. prof., 1972-77; prof., dept. chair, assoc. dean Sch. Libr. and Info. Sci. U. Pitts., 1977-85. Mem. ALA (life), Phi Beta Kappa, Beta Phi Mu, Delta Phi Lambda, Kappa Gamma Pi. Home: 14740 SW Forest Dr Beaverton OR 97007-5117

POND, THOMAS ALEXANDER, physics educator; b. L.A., Dec. 4, 1924; s. Arthur Francis and Florence (Alexander) P.; m. Barbara Eileen Newman, Sept. 6, 1958; children: Arthur Phillip Ward, Florence Alexandra. A.B., Princeton U., 1947, A.M., 1949, Ph.D., 1953. Instr. physics Princeton U., 1951-53; asst. prof., then assoc. prof. physics Washington U., St. Louis, 1953-62; prof. physics SUNY, Stony Brook, 1962-81, chmn. dept., 1962-68, exec. v.p., 1967-79, acting pres., 1970, 75, 78; prof. physics Rutgers U., New Brunswick, N.J., exec. v.p., chief acad. officer, 1982-91, acting pres., 1990, univ. prof., 1991—; Bd. dirs. Action Com. for L.I., 1978-80, Tri-State Regional Planning Commn., 1979-82; trustee Univs. Research Assn., 1985-87; bd. dirs. Fermilab, 1987-89. Served to ensign USNR, 1943-46. Mem. Am. Phys. Soc., Phi Beta Kappa, Sigma Xi. Home: 8 Campbells Brook Rd White House Station NJ 08889-9469 Office: Rutgers Univ Dept Physics and Astronomy Piscataway NJ 08855-0849

PONDER, ALONZA, church administrator. Vice-chief bishop Ch. of the Living God Exec. Bd. Officež: Church of The Living God 5609 N Terry Ave Oklahoma City OK 73111-6866

PONDER, HERMAN, geologist; b. Light, Ark., Jan. 31, 1928; s. Herman Cook and Sylvia Adell (Cameron) P.; m. Barbara Elaine Sando, May 10, 1947; children: Teresa Elaine, David Mark. BA, U. Mo., 1955, PhD, 1959. Rsch. engr. A.P. Green Refractories Co., Mexico, Mo., 1959-61, lab mgr., 1961-63; project engr., then mgr. mining div. Colo. Sch. Mines Rsch. Inst., Golden, 1963-67, dir. rsch., 1967-70, pres., 1970-85; pres. ATI Exploration, Golden, Colo., 1985-90; chmn. bd. dirs. Analytica, Inc.; v.p. Copper Range Co., White Pine, Mich., 1985-89. Served with USN, 1946-47. Recipient Disting. Alumnus award U. Mo., 1993. Home: PO Box 23268 Silverthorne CO 80498

PONDER, LESTER MCCONNICO, lawyer, educator; b. Walnut Ridge, Ark., Dec. 10, 1912; s. Harry Lee and Clyde (Gant) P.; m. Sallie Mowry Clover, Nov. 7, 1942; children—Melinda, Constance; m. Phyllis Gretchen Harting, Oct. 14, 1978. B.S. summa cum laude in Commerce, Northwestern U., 1934; J.D. with honors, George Washington U., 1938. Bar: Ark. 1937, Ind. 1948. Atty. Ark. Dept. Revenue, Little Rock, 1939-41; atty. IRS, Chgo. and Indpls., 1941-51; ptnr. Barnes & Thornburg and predecessor Barnes, Hickam, Pantzer & Boyd, Indpls., 1952—; adj. prof. Sch. Law, Ind. U., Bloomington, 1951-54, Sch. Law, Ind. U., Indpls., 1954-63; lectr. polit. sci. Ind. U., Indpls., 1982-85. Author: United States Tax Court Practice & Procedure, 1976. Bd. dirs., vice chmn., chmn. Ind. chpt. The Nature Conservancy, 1981-89; mem. adv. coun. Ind. Dept. Natural Resources, 1986—; past bd. mem. Sigma Chi Found. Served with USN, 1942. Fellow Am. Bar Found., Ind. State Bar Found., Ind. Bar Found., Am. Coll. Tax Counsel; mem. ABA (coun., taxation sect. 1970-73, chair sr. lawyers div. 1993-94, adv. coun. Commr. Internal Revenue 1964—), Ind. State Bar Assn., Indpls. Bar Assn., Assn. of Seventh Fed. Cir. Republican. Presbyterian. Club: Meridian Hills Country (Indpls.). Lodge: Rotary (past bd. dirs.). Office: Barnes & Thornburg Merchants Bank Bldg Ste 1313 Indianapolis IN 46204-3506

PONEMAN, DANIEL BRUCE, federal official; b. Toledo, Mar. 12, 1956; s. Meyer and Delores Suzanne (Shapiro) P.; m. Susan Anne Danoff, Aug. 12, 1984; children: Claire Gillian, Michael Bruder, William Meyer. AB in Govt. and Econs. magna cum laude, Harvard Coll., 1978; MLitt in Politics, Lincoln Coll., Oxford, Eng., 1981; JD cum laude, Harvard U., 1984. Bar: D.C. 1985. Vis. fellow Internat. Inst. Strategic Studies, London, 1980-81; rsch. fellow ctr. sci. and internat. affairs Kennedy sch. govt. Harvard U., 1981-84; assoc. Covington & Burling, 1985-89; White House fellow Dept. of Energy, 1989-90; dir. def. policy and arms control Nat. Security Coun., Washington, 1990-93, spl. asst. to the Pres., sr. dir. nonproliferation and export controls, 1993—. Author: Nuclear Power in the Developing World, 1982, Argentina: Democracy on Trial, 1987; contbr. articles to profl. jours. and newspapers including N.Y. Times, Washington Post, L.A. Times, Boston Globe. Grantee Corp. Pub. Broadcasting; Lord Crewe scholar. Mem. D.C. Bar, Coun. Fgn. Rels., Phi Beta Kappa. Home: 2109 Mason Hill Dr Alexandria VA 22306-2416 Office: Nat Security Coun 1600 Pennsylvania Ave NW Washington DC 20506

PONITZ, DAVID H., academic administrator; b. Royal Oak, Mich., Jan. 21, 1931; s. Henry John and Jeanette (Bouwman) P.; m. Doris Jean Humes, Aug. 5, 1956; children: Catherine Anne, David Robinson. BA, U. Mich., 1952, MA, 1954; EdD, Harvard U., 1964. Prin. Waldron (Mich.) Area Schs., 1956-58, supt., 1958-60; cons. Harvard U., Boston Sch. Survey, 1961-63; supt. Freeport (Ill.) Pub. Schs., 1962-65; pres. Freeport C.C., 1962-65, Washtenaw C.C., 1965-75, Sinclair C.C., 1975—; cons. to community colls.; chmn., pres. Ohi Advanced Tech. Ctr. Mem. editorial adv. bd. Nations Schs, 1963-70; chmn. adv. bd. Community Coll. Rev, 1978-89. Past chmn. Dayton Mayor's Coun. on Econ. Devel., 1977-85; mem. Nat. Adv. Coun. on Nursing; former co-chair Performing Arts Edn. Task Force; bd. dirs. Alliance for Edn.; former campaign chmn. Ann Arbor and Dayton United Way; past vice chmn. Dayton Citizens Adv. Coun. for Desegregation Implementation; v.p. Miami Valley Rsch. Park; mem., past chmn. Area Progress Coun., Dayton; bd. dirs. Dayton Devel. Coun.; mem. F.S.B. bd. Citizens Fed. Banks, Universal Energy Systems Bd.; past chmn. Miami Valley Joint Labor/Mgmt. Profls., Area Progress Coun.; bd. dirs Ctr. Occupational R & D; chmn. Human Svcs. Levy, Tech-Prep Coll. H.S. Consortium; vice chair Miami Valley Rsch. Found.; bd. dirs. League Innovation C.C., Miami Valley Regional Planning Commn. Served with U.S. Army, 1954-56. Named Outstanding Alumnus U. Mich., One of Top 100 Pres. in U.S. Council for Advancement and Support of Edn., Exec. of Yr., Bd. Realtors, Presdl. medallion Patron emeritus Horry-Georgetown Tech. Coll.; recipient Bogie Buster Red Jacket award, 1987, Thomas J. Peters award for Excellence Assn. Community and Jr. Colls. 1988, Marie N. Martin Chief Exec. Officer award, ACCT, 1989, The Living Legend award Martin Luther King Jr. Holiday Celebration Com., 1991, Sinclair Hon. Alumnus award, 1991, India Found. Honor, 1992, Disting. Eagle Scout award Nat. Eagle Scout Assn., 1993. Mem. Am. Assn. Community and Jr. Colls. (nat. future commn., bd. dirs., chmn. 1988-89), Ohio Tech. and Community Coll. Assn. (pres. 1979-80), Rotary. Methodist. Office: Sinclair Community Coll 444 W 3rd St Dayton OH 45417

PONITZ, JOHN ALLAN, lawyer; b. Battle Creek, Mich., Sept. 7, 1949; m. Nancy J. Roberts, Aug. 14, 1971; children: Amy, Matthew, Julie. BA, Albion Coll., 1971; JD, Wayne State U., 1974. Bar: Mich. 1974, U.S. Dist. Ct. (ea. dist.) Mich. 1975, (we. dist.) Mich. 1986, U.S. Ct. Appeals (6th cir.) Mich. 1981, U.S. Supreme Ct. 1992. Assoc. McMachan & Kaichen, Birmingham, Mich., 1973-75; atty. Grand Trunk Western R.R., Detroit, 1975-80, sr. trial atty., 1980-89; gen. counsel, 1990-95; ptnr. Hopkins & Sutter, Detroit, 1995—. V.p. Beverly Hills (Mich.) Jaycees, 1981. Served to capt. USAR, 1974-82. Mem. Mich. Bar Assn., Detroit Bar Assn., Nat. Assn. R.R. Trial Counsel, Oakland County Bar Assn. Lutheran. Avocations: golf, sailing. Office: Hopkins & Sutter Ste 101 1333 Brewery Park Blvd Detroit MI 48207-2635

PONKO, WILLIAM REUBEN, architect; b. Wausau, Wis., Apr. 4, 1948; s. Reuben Harrison and Ora Marie (Ranke) P.; m. Kathleen Ann Hilt, May 5, 1973; children: William Benjamin, Sarah Elizabeth. B.Arch. magna cum laude, U. Notre Dame, 1971. Cert. Nat. Council Archl. Registration Bds. V.p., architect, dir. ednl./instl. specialty LeRoy Troyer & Assocs. (now The Troyer Group), Mishawaka, Ind., 1971—; design instr. dept. architecture U. Notre Dame, 1976; mem. Ind. State Bd. Registration for Architects, 1990—; mem. registration exam com. Nat. Coun. Archtl. Registration Bds., 1992—, vice chair 1996, chair 1997. Leonard M. Anson Meml. scholar, 1966-70. Mem. AIA (gold medal for excellence in archtl. edn. 1971), Ind. Soc. Architects (design excellence award 1978, chpt. pres. 1985). Prin. archtl. works include: St. Peter Luth. Ch., Mishawaka, Ind., 1979, 4 brs. for South Bend Pub. Library, 1983; Edward J. Funk & Sons office bldg., Kentland, Ind., 1976; Music Edn. bldg. Taylor U., Upland, Ind., 1982, Taylor U. Library, carillon tower, 1985, Early Childhood Devel. Ctr. U. Notre Dame, 1994, Convents for Sisters of Holy Cross St. Mary's, Notre Dame, Ind., 1995. Office: The Troyer Group Inc 415 Lincoln Way E Mishawaka IN 46544-2213

PONNEMAN, DANIEL, federal official. Spl. asst. to pres. Non-Proliferation & Export Controls NSC, Washington. Office: Non-Proliferation Export Controls NSC 1600 Pennsylvania Ave NW Washington DC 20500

PONSETI, IGNACIO VIVES, orthopaedic surgery educator; b. Cuidadela, Balearic Islands, Spain, June 3, 1914; s. Miguel and Margarita (Vives) P.; 1 child, William Edward; m. Helena Percas, 1961. BS, U. Barcelona, 1930, MD, 1936, D honoris causa, 1984. Instr. dept. orthopaedic surgery State U. Iowa, 1944-57, prof., 1957—. Author papers on cogenital and developmental skeletal deformities. Capt. M.C. Spanish Army, 1936-39. Recipient Kappa Delta award for orthopaedic rsch., 1955. Mem. Assn. Bone and Joint Surgeons, Am. Acad. Cerebral Palsy, Soc. Exptl. Biology and Medicine, Internat. Coll. Surgeons, N.Y. Acad. Sci., AMA (Ketoen gold medal 1960), Am. Acad. Orthopedic Surgeons, ACS, Am. Orthopedic Assn., Pediatric Orthopaedic Soc. (hon.), Iowa Med. Soc., Orthopedic Rsch. Soc. (Shands award 1975), Sigma Xi, Asociacion Argentina de Cirugia (hon.), Asociacion Balear de Cirugia (hon.), Sociedad de Cirujanos de Chile (hon.), Sociedad Espanola de Cirugia Ortopedica (hon.), Sociedad Brasilera de Ortopedia e Traumatologia (hon.). Home: 110 Oakridge Ave Iowa City IA 52246-2935 Office: Carver Pavilion U Iowa Hosps Iowa City IA 52242

PONSOLDT, WILLIAM RAYMOND, JR., lawyer; b. Westwood, N.J., July 6, 1966; s. William Raymond and Marriane (Kannegeiger) P.; m. Kimberly Rae Waller, Sept. 4, 1993. BS, U. Fla., 1988, JD, 1992. Bar: Fla. 1993, U.S. Dist. Ct. (all dists.) Fla. 1993. Assoc. Kohl, Bobko, McKey, McManus et al., Stuart, Fla., 1992-93, Kohl, Metzger, Spotts, PA, Stuart, 1993—; bd. dirs. Regency Affiliates, Denver. V.p. Treas. Coast Leaders, Stuart, 1992—; active Leadership Martin County, Stuart, 1993—; mem. bd. adjustments Stuart County, 1993—; chmn. Stuart Law Libr. Com., 1994—. mem. Mem. Martin County Bar Assn. Avocations: sports, reading. Office: Kohl Metzger Spotts PA 50 Kindred St Stuart FL 34994-3040

PONSOR, MICHAEL ADRIAN, federal judge; b. Chgo., Aug. 13, 1946; s. Frederick Ward and Helen Yvonne (Richardson) P.; children from previous marriage, Anne, Joseph; 1 stepchild, Christian Walker; m. Nancy L. Coiner, June 30, 1996. BA magna cum laude, Harvard Coll., 1969; BA second class honors, Oxford U., 1971, MA, 1979; JD, Yale U., 1975. Bar: Mass., U.S. Dist. Ct. Mass., U.S. Ct. Appeals (1st cir.), U.S. Supreme Ct. Tchr. Kenya Inst. Administrn., Nairobi, 1967-68; law clk. U.S. Dist. Ct., Boston, 1975-76; assoc. Homans, Hamilton, Dahmen & Lamson, Boston, 1976-78; ptnr. Brown, Hart & Ponsor, Amherst, Mass., 1978-83; U.S. magistrate judge U.S. Dist. Ct., Springfield, Mass., 1984-94, U.S. dist. judge, 1994—; adj. prof. Western N.E. Coll. Sch. Law, Springfield, 1988—, Yale Law Sch., New Haven, 1989-91; presenter in field. Rhodes scholar Oxford U., 1969. Mem. Mass. Bar Assn., Hampshire County Bar Assn., Boston Bar Assn. Office: US Dist Ct 1550 Main St Springfield MA 01103-1422

PONT, JOHN, football coach, educator; b. Canton, Ohio, Nov. 13, 1927; s. Bautista and Susie (Sikurinec) P.; m. H. Sandra Stoutt, June 23, 1956; children: John W., Jennifer Ann, Jeffrey David. BS, Miami U., Oxford, Ohio, 1952, MS, 1956. Profl. football player Can., 1952-53; instr., freshman football and basketball coach Miami U., 1953-55, asst. prof., head football coach, 1955-62; head football coach Yale U., 1963-65; prof., head football coach Ind. U., Bloomington, 1965-73; head coach Northwestern U., Evanston, Ill., 1973-77, athletic dir., 1974-79; head football coach, athletic dir. Hamilton, Ohio; head football coach, tennis coach, asst. athletic dir. Coll. Mt. St. Joseph, Mt. St. Joseph, Ohio; now head football coach Gakusei-Engo-Kai Inc., Tokyo, Japan; agt. Equitable Assurance Soc., U.S., 1981-82; v.p. Fin. Leasing Corp., 1983-85, Splty. Brush, Inc.; athletic dir. Jewish Community Center, Canton, 1953; v.p. NCAA Coun., 1979-80; mem. bd. dirs. Cin. chpt. Nat. Football Found. Hall Of Fame. Mem. Pres.'s Coun. on Phys. Fitness; chmn. Ind. Easter Seal, 1968-69, Ind. div. Cancer Crusade, 1969; bd. dirs. Multiple Sclerosis, N.E. Ill. counc. Boy Scouts Am., Boys Hope. Served with USN, 1945-47. Named Coach of Year Coaches Assn., 1967, Coach of Year Football Writers, 1967, Coach of Yr. Washington Touchdown Club, 1968, Coach of Yr. Walter Camp Found.; recipient Significant Sig award, 1968, Disting. Am. award Nat. Football Found., 1987; charter mem. Miami U. Hall of Fame, 1968; elected Ind. Football Hall of Fame, 1984, Butler County Hall of Fame, 1986, Mid-Am. Conf. Hall of Fame, 1992, Ind. U. Sports Hall of Fame, 1992. Mem. Am. Football Coaches Assn. (chmn. ethics com.), Kusatsu City Football Assn. Japan (hon. chmn.), Am. Legion, Blue Key, Sigma Chi, Phi Epsilon Kappa, Omicron Delta Kappa. Republican. Home: 482 White Oak Dr Oxford OH 45056-9272

PONTIKES, WILLIAM N., computer rental and leasing company executive; b. 1941. BA, So. Ill. U., 1968. With Ill. Police Dept., 1963-65; with Comdisco, DesPlaines, Ill., 1973—, v.p. ops., 1975-76, sr. v.p. ops., 1976-77, dir., 1977—; exec. v.p. Comdisco, Des Plaines, I.L. With U.S. Army, 1963-65. Office: Comdisco Inc 6111 N River Rd Des Plaines IL 60018*

PÖNTINEN, PEKKA JUHANI, anesthesiologist, consultant; b. Tampere, Finland, Apr. 5, 1932; s. Otto Edvard and Ellen Margareta (Heiniö) P.; m. Anja Anita Kuukankorpi; children: Anna-Katriina, Juha-Pekka, Riikka-Leena, Hanna-Maaria; m. Irja Tuulikki Ketovuori, Jan. 8, 1976; 1 child, Mika Juhani. B in med., Helsinki U., Finland, 1953; MD, Turku U., Finland, 1957; PhD, Kuopio U., Finland, 1977. Diplomate Finnish Bd. Health Legitimation, Finnish Bd. Anesthesiology. Chief dept. anesthesiology Savonlinna Cen. Hosp., Finland, 1965-69, Kainuu Cen. Hosp., Finland, 1969-75; asst. prof. neurophysiology Kuopio U., Finland, 1974-75; med. dir. Kankaanpää Rehabilitation Ctr., Finland, 1989-92; assoc. prof. anesthesiology Kuopio U., 1978—, Tampere U., Finland, 1980—; chief acupuncture rsch. project Kuopio U., 1976—; cons. dept. neurology Tampere U. Hosp., 1976-93, adv. Ministry of Health & Social Affairs, Helsinki,. 1975—, WHO Com. Standardisation Acupuncture Nomenclature, Geneva, Switzerland, 1989-95uropean Coun. Subcom. Higher Edn., Strassbourg, France, 1990-95. Author: Acupuncture as a Medical Treatment Modality (in Finnish), 1983, Laser as a Medical Treatment Modality (in Finnish), 1988, Low Level Laser as a Medical Treatment Modality (in Swedish), 1991, Low Level Laser Therapy as a Medical Treatment Modality, 1992, Laseracupuncture (in German), 1993; editor-in-chief Scandinavian Jour. Acupuncture and Electrotherapy, 1987—; editor Acupuncture & Electrotherapeutics Rsch. Internat. Jour., 1981—, AKU, Akupunktur, Theorie und Praxis, 1991—; mem. sci. com. Internat. Jour. Pain Therapy, 1991-95. Recipient German Promotion award Pain Rsch. and Therapy, 1988. Fellow Internat. Coll. Acupuncture & Electro-Therapeutics Rsch. (vice chmn. coun. 1987—), Acupuncture Found. of India (hon.), Am. Acad. Acupuncture (hon.), Am. Coll. Acupuncture (charter); mem. Am. Pain Soc., Am. Soc. Laser Medicine & Surgery, Brit. Med. Acupuncture Soc. (hon.), German Med. Acupuncture Soc. (hon.), Can. Acupuncture Assn. Can. (hon.), Nordic Acupuncture Soc. (pres. 1980-87, 89—, founding), Internat. Assn. Study of Pain (founding), Phys. Medicine Rsch. Found. (intermultidisciplinary bd. dirs. 1995—), N.Y. Acad. Scis., Società Internazionale di Laserterapia Medico Chirugica (v.p. for Finland 1989—), Finnish Soc. Anesthesiologists (v.p. 1970-71, pres. 1972-73), Finnish Med. Acupuncture Soc. (hon.). Avocations: classical music, fishing, gardening, skiing, ice hockey. Home: Pikkusaarenkuja 4B 77, 33410 Tampere Finland

PONTIUS, STANLEY N., bank holding company executive; b. Auburn, Ind., Aug. 26, 1946; s. Clayton and Frances (Beuret) P.; m. Cheryl Ann Dawson, Aug. 3, 1968; children: Jarrod B., Dorian K. BS, Ind. U., 1968. Mgmt. trainee Bank One Corp., 1968-73; asst. to v.p. Bank One Corp., Cambridge, Ohio, 1973-75; v.p. Bank One Corp., Fremont, Ohio, 1975-79, dir., pres., CEO, 1979-83; pres. Bank One Corp., Marion, Ohio, 1983-84, dir., CEO, 1984-88; dir., CEO Bank One Corp., Mansfield, Ohio, 1988-91; dir., pres., COO 1st Fin. Bancorp, Hamilton, Ohio, 1991, dir., pres., CEO, 1992—; dir., pres., CEO 1st Nat. Banl of Southwestern Ohio, Hamilton, 1991—. bd. trustee, exec. com. Fort Hamilton-Hughes Meml. Hosp., fin. com. Fitton Ctr. for Creatice Arts, voting com. Butler County United Way, adv. com. Hamilton City Schs., Hamilton C. of C., bd. dirs. Inroads of Greater Cin.-Cayton, Inc., Ohio Casualty Corp., Fort Hamiliton Health Network. With U.S. Army, 1968-70. Mem. Am. Bankers Coun., Ohio Bankers Assn., Home Builders Assn. of Greater Cin., Hamilton-Fairfield Arts Assn. Office: 1st Fin Bancorp 300 High St Hamilton OH 45011-6037

PONTY, JEAN-LUC, violinist, composer, producer; b. Avranches, Normandy, France, Sept. 29, 1942; came to U.S., 1973; Grad., Conservatoire National Superieur de Musique, Paris, 1960. Classical violinist to 1964, played with Concerts Lamoureux Symphony Orch.; jazz violinist, Europe, 1964-69, night club and music festivals with George Duke Trio, U.S., 1969, toured with own group, Europe, 1970-72, recorded with Elton John, Honky Chateau, 1972; with Frank Zappa and the Mothers of Invention, 1973, Mahavishnu Orch., 1974-75, pioneer of electric violin, Jazz innovator, headlining internat. concerts with own group since 1975; appearances at music festivals in the U.S. including Meadowbrook, Artpark, Wolf Trap, and in Europe Montreux, North Sea Festival, Paris Jazz Festival; spl. appearance as guest soloist with Montreal Symphony Orch., 1984, Toronto Symphony Orch., 1986, New Japan Philharm., 1987; European tour with Stanley Clarke and Al DiMeola The Rite of Strings, 1994; own-produced albums include: Upon the Wings of Music, Aurora, Imaginary Voyage, Enigmatic Ocean, Cosmic Messenger, Jean-Luc Ponty: Live, Civilized Evil, A Taste for Passion, Mystical Adventures, Individual Choice, Open Mind, Fables, The Gift of Time, Storytelling, Tchokola (with African musicians), No Absolute Time; television appearances include: (with Doug Kershaw and Itzhak Perlman) Fiddlers Three, Soundstage, Rock Concert, The Tonight Show, The Merv Griffin Show, Solid Gold, Pat Sajak Show CNN Entertainment; TV show appearances throughout Europe, Brazil, Chile and Venezuela. Recipient numerous internat. awards. Office: care Bob Zievers ICM 8942 Wilshire Blvd Beverly Hills CA 90211-1934

POOL, MARY JANE, design consultant, writer; d. Earl Lee Pool and Dorothy (Matthews) Evans. Grad., St. de Chantal Acad., 1942; BA in Art with honors, Drury Coll., 1946. Mem. staff Vogue mag., N.Y.C., 1946-68; assoc. merchandising editor Vogue mag., 1948-57, promotion dir., 1958-66, exec. editor, 1966-68; editor House and Garden mag., 1969, editor-in-chief, 1970-80; cons. Baker Furniture Co., 1981-94, Aves Advt., Inc., 1981-94, bd. dirs.; mem. bd. govs. Decorative Arts Trust; past mem. bd. govs. Fashion Group, Inc., N.Y.C. Co-author: The Angel Tree, 1984, The Gardens of Venice, 1989, The Gardens of Florence, 1992, The Angel Tree-A Christmas Celebration, 1993; editor: 20th Century Decorating, Architecture, Gardens, Billy Baldwin Decorates, 26 Easy Little Gardens. Mem. bus. com. N.Y. Zool. Soc., 1979-86; trustee Drury Coll., 1971—; bd. dirs. Isabel O'Neil Found., 1978—. Recipient award Nat. Soc. Interior Designers, Disting. Alumni award Drury Coll., 1961. Address: 1 E 66th St New York NY 10021-5852

POOL, PHILIP BEMIS, JR., investment banker; b. N.Y.C., Apr. 11, 1954; s. Philip B. and Virginia Middleton (French) P.; m. Joan H. Barnes, May 19, 1978; children: Elliott Livingston, Victoria Middleton. BS in Commerce, U. Va., 1976; MBA, Columbia U., 1980. Asst. treas. The Bank of N.Y., N.Y.C., 1976-78; v.p. Kidder Peabody & Co., Inc., N.Y.C., 1980-85; mng. dir. Merrill Lynch & Co., N.Y.C., 1985-94, Donaldson, Lufkin & Jenrette, N.Y.C., 1994—. Mem. Piping Rock Club (gov. 1989—), Meadow Brook Club, Lyford Cay Club, Racquet and Tennis Club. Republican. Episcopalian. Avocations: golf, squash.

POOLE, CALVERT KING, elementary school educator; b. Richmond, Va., July 17, 1935; d. Marion Hardaway and Elise (Phillips) King; m. Arnold Travis Poole Jr., Dec. 27, 1959; children: Arnold Travis III, Steven Ware. BS in Elem. Edn., Longwood Coll., 1959, BS in Libr. Sci., 1979. Cert. k-7 tchr., libr. sci. tchr., Va. Tchr. Roanoke County Sch. Bd., Salem, Va., 1959-60, Northumberland County Schs., Reedville, Va., 1962-63, West Point (Va.) Schs., 1964-66, Pulaski County Schs., Dublin, Va., 1966-68, Appomattox (Va.) Schs., 1968-77, 80-81, Montgomery County Schs., Radford, Va., 1992—; libr. Upper Arlington (Ohio) Pub. Libr., 1978-79, Newman Libr., Blacksburg, Va. Pres. Country Lane Home Demonstration Club, Appomattox, 1970-72, Appomattox Garden Club, 1975-77; treas. Blacksburg Intermediate Woman's Club, 1983-95; sec. United Meth. Women Meml. Meth. Ch., Appomattox. Named One of Outstanding Young Women Am., 1970. Mem. NEA, PTA (life), Va. Edn. Assn., Montgomery Edn. Assn., Va. State Rading Assn., New River Valley Reading Coun., Internat. Reading Assn., Alpha Delta Kappa (sec. Rho chpt. 1983-95, mem. membership-pledge com., pres. southwest dist.). Methodist. Home: 4510 Preston Forest Dr Blacksburg VA 24060-8660

POOLE, CECIL F., federal judge; b. Birmingham, Ala., 1914; children: Gayle, Patricia. LL.B., U. Mich.; LL.M., Harvard U., 1939. Practice of law San Francisco, former asst. dist. atty., 1951-58; clemency sec. to Gov. Brown of Calif., 1958-61; U.S. atty. No. Dist. Calif., 1961-70; Regents prof. Law U. Calif., Berkeley, 1970; counsel firm Jacobs, Sills & Coblentz, San Francisco, 1970-76; judge U.S. Dist. Ct., No. Dist. Calif., 1976-79, U.S. Ct. of Appeals for 9th Circuit, 1979—; adj. prof. Golden Gate U. Sch. Law, 1953-58; mem. adv. com. Nat. Commn. for Reform Fed. Criminal Laws, 1968-70. Served to 2d lt. AUS, World War II. Mem. ABA (chmn. sect. individual rights 1971-72, ho. of dels. 1972-74), San Francisco Bar Assn. (dir. 1975-76). Office: US Ct Appeals 9th Cir PO Box 547 San Francisco CA 94101*

POOLE, D. BRUCE, lawyer; b. Hagerstown, Md., June 17, 1959; s. David Kreigh Jr. and Janice Marie (Zaiser) P. BA, Washington & Lee U., 1981, JD, 1985. Bar: Md. 1985. Ptnr. Poole & Poole, P.A., Hagerstown, 1985-89, Snyder & Poole, P.A., Hagerstown and Frederick, Md., 1989-95, Poole & Poole, P.A., Hagerstown, Md., 1995—; mem. Md. Ho. of Dels., Annapolis, 1987—, house majority leader, 1991-93, mem. commerce and govt. matters com., chmn. procurement subcom. Assoc. mem., bd. dirs. March of Dimes of Washington County, Hagerstown, 1986-91; pres. United Dems. Washington County, Hagerstown, 1985-86; mem. Gov.'s Commn. on Drug & Alcohol Abuse and Truck Safety, Annapolis, 1989-93. Mem. Sons of American Legion, Jaycees (named one of Ten Outstanding Marylanders 1991), Elks, Rotary (fellow U. Melbourne, Australia 1981). Lutheran. Avocations: tennis, travel, history, hunting. Office: Poole & Poole PA 92 W Washington St Hagerstown MD 21740-4804

POOLE, DARRYL VERNON, financial and management consultant; b. Springfield, Mass., Aug. 18, 1946; s. Edward Saxon and Dorothea Vivian (Collins) P. BS in Acctg., Bentley Coll., Waltham, Mass., 1968; SM in Mgmt., MIT, Cambridge, 1973; postgrad., Columbia U. Sr. Exec. Program, 1982. Cert. internal auditor. Cost acct. Westvaco, Springfield, 1968-69; fin. analyst Polaroid Corp., Cambridge, 1969-72; dir. spl. audits Am. Can Co., Greenwich, Conn., 1974-82; sr. v.p. Opportunity Funding Corp., Washington, 1982-88; v.p., CFO Endispute Inc., Washington, 1988-94; chief exec., founder Cambridge Inst. for Applied Rsch., Inc., Washington, 1973—; chmn. Poole Bros. Fund, Amherst, Mass., 1988—; bd. dirs. Youth Svcs. Am., Washington, 1992-95. Pub.: Wishard's A World in Search of Meaning, 1988. Trustee Bentley Coll., Waltham, Mass., 1978—. Mem. Inst. Internal Auditors, Black Alumni of MIT. Home: 5736 Prince Cv Memphis TN 38115-3130 Office: The Cambridge Inst Applied Rsch Inc 1725 Desales St NW Ste 700 Washington DC 20036-4406

POOLE, EVA DURAINE, librarian; b. Farrell, Pa., Dec. 20, 1952; d. Leonard Milton and Polly Mae (Flint) Harris; m. Tommy Lynn Cole, May 15, 1970 (div. Sept. 1984); 1 child, Tommy Lynn Cole; m. Earnest Theodore Poole, Sept. 22, 1990; 1 child, Aleece Remelle Poole. BA in LS, Tex. Woman's U., 1974, MLS, 1976; postgrad., U. Houston, 1989. Libr. asst. Emily Fowler Pub. Libr., Denton, Tex., 1970-74; children's libr. Houston Pub. Libr., 1974-75, 1st asst. libr., 1976-77; children's libr. Ector County Libr., Odessa, Tex., 1977-80; head pub. svcs. Lee Davis Libr. San Jacinto Coll., Pasadena, Tex., 1980-84; libr. dir. San Jacinto Coll. South, Houston, 1984-90; libr. svcs. mgr. Emily Fowler Pub. Libr., Denton, 1990-93, interim dir., 1993; dir. libr. svcs. Denton Pub. Librs., Denton, 1993—. Named to Outstanding Young Women of Am., 1991. Mem. ALA (conf. program com. 1994—), Pub. Libr. Assn., Libr. Administrn. and Mgmt. Assn. (program com. 1994—), Tex. Libr. assn. (pub. libr. divsn. sec. 1995-96, leadership devel. com. 1995—, ad hoc leadership inst. com. 1995, alumnae 1st class Tex. Accelerated Libr. Leaders 1994, chair-elect pub. libr. divsn. 1996—), Pub.

Libr. Adminstrs. North Tex. (vice chair 1994-95, chair 1995—, pres. 1994-95), Tex. Mcpl. Libr. Dirs. Assn. (pres. 1995-96, grantee 1993), Denton Rotary Club. Office: Denton Pub Libr 502 Oakland St Denton TX 76201-3102

POOLE, GORDON LEICESTER, lawyer; b. Mpls., Dec. 25, 1926; s. Arthur Bensell and Mildred Loyal (Wood) P.; m. Lois Claire Teasdale, Oct. 30, 1954; children—David Wilson, Edward Gray, Elisabeth Claire. A.B., Harvard U., 1949, LL.B., 1952. Assoc. Treadwell & Laughlin, San Francisco, 1953-54; assoc. Lillick, McHose & Charles, San Francisco, 1955-63, ptnr., 1963—, mem. exec. com., 1977-81, chmn. mgmt. com., 1981-84, chmn., 1984—. Contbr. articles to profl. jours. Pres. Young Republicans, San Mateo County, Calif., 1958-59; vestryman Trinity Episcopal Parish, Menlo Park, Calif., 1968, 70, 76-78, sr. warden, 1970. Served as sgt. U.S. Army, 1944-47, Korea. Mem. Calif. Bar Assn., San Francisco Bar Assn., Maritime Law Assn. (com. on marine financing), Maritime Adminstrv. Bar Assn., ABA, Mng. Ptnrs. Assn. Clubs: Bohemian, World Trade (San Francisco); Ladera Oaks (Menlo Park). Avocations: stamp collecting; marine paintings, prints and memorabilia. Home: 2280 Stockbridge Ave Redwood City CA 94062-1130 Office: Lillick & Charles 2 Embarcadero Ctr Ste 2600 San Francisco CA 94111-3823

POOLE, MONTE LARUE, sports columnist, consultant; b. Oakland, Calif., Nov. 30, 1955. AA, Chabot Coll., 1983; BA, San Jose State U., 1985. Dist. mgr. Mervyn's, Hayward, Calif., 1979-81; sports writer Oakland Tribune, 1982-91, Oakland Tribune/Alameda Newspaper Group, Oakland, 1991—; host talk show Sta. KSFO, San Francisco, 1992; instr. New Coll. Calif., 1994. Mem. com. U. Calif. Hall of Fame, Berkeley, 1993—. Mem. Nat. Assn. Black Journalists, Baseball Writers' Assn. Am. Avocations: reading, exercise, jazz music. Office: Oakland Tribune PO Box 28884 66 Jack London Sq Oakland CA 94607

POOLE, NANCY GEDDES, art gallery curator; b. London, Ont., Can., May 10, 1930; d. John Hardy and Kathleen Edwards (Robinson) G.; m. William Robert Poole, Aug. 15, 1952; 1 child, Andrea Mary. BA, U. Western Ont., 1956, LLD, 1990. Owner, dir. Nancy Poole's Studio, Toronto, Ont., Can., 1969-78; acting dir. London Regional Art Gallery, Ont., Can., 1981—, exec. dir., 1985-89; dir. London Regional Art and Hist. Museums, Ont., Can., 1989-95; chair governing coun. Ont. Coll. Art, 1972-73. Author: The Art of London 1939-1980, 1984; editor Jack Chambers, 1978, The Collection, 1990. Bd. govs. U. Western Ont., 1974-85. Fellow Ont. Coll. Art. Office: 420 Fanshawe Park Rd, London, ON Canada N5X 2S9

POOLE, RICHARD WILLIAM, economics educator; b. Oklahoma City, Dec. 4, 1927; s. William Robert and Lois (Spicer) P.; m. Bertha Lynn Mehr, July 28, 1950; children: Richard William, Laura Lynne, Mark Stephen. B.S., U. Okla., 1951, M.B.A., 1952; postgrad., George Washington U., 1957-58; Ph.D., Okla. State U., 1960. Research analyst Okla. Gas & Electric Co., Oklahoma City, 1952- 54; mgr. sci. and mfg. devel. dept. Oklahoma City C. of C., 1954-57; mgr. Office of J.E. Webb, Washington, 1957-58; instr., asst. prof., assoc. prof., prof. econs. Okla. State U., Stillwater, 1960-65; prof. econs., dean Coll. Bus. Adminstrn. Okla. State U., 1965-72, v.p., prof. econs., 1972-88, Regents Disting. Svc. prof., prof. econs., 1988-93, emeritus v.p., dean, Regents Disting. Svc. prof./prof. econ., 1993—; cons. to adminstr. NASA, Washington, 1961-69; adviser subcom. on govt. rsch. U.S. Senate, 1966-69; lectr. Intermediate Sch. Banking, Ops. Mgmt. Sch., Okla. Bankers Assn., 1968-89; lectr. internat. off-campus programs, Okla. City U., 1994-96. Author: (with others) The Oklahoma Economy, 1963, County Building Block Data for Regional Analysis, 1965. Mem. Gov.' Com. on Devel. Ark.-Verdigris Waterway, 1970-71, Gov.'s Five-Yr. Econ. Devel. Plan, 1993; past v.p., bd. dirs., past chmn. Mid-Continent Rsch. and Devel. Coun. 2d lt., arty. U.S. Army, 1946-48. Recipient Delta Sigma Pi Gold Key award Coll. Bus. Adminstrn., U. Okla., 1951, Merrick Found. Tchg. award on Am. Free Enterprise Sys., 1992, Disting. Alumni award Okla. State U., 1995; inductee Coll. Bus. Adminstrn. Hall of Fame, Okla. State U., 1993. Mem. Southwestern Econ. Assn. (past pres.), Am. Assembly Collegiate Schs. Bus. (past bd. dirs.), Nat. Assn. State Univs. and Land Grant Colls. (past chmn. commn. on edn. for bus. professions), Southwestern Bus. Adminstrn. Assn. (past pres.), Okla. C. of C. (past bd. dirs.), Stillwater C. of C. (past bd. dirs. and pres.), Beta Gamma Sigma (past bd. dirs.), Phi Kappa Phi, Phi Eta Sigma, Omicron Delta Kappa. Home: 815 S Shumard Dr Stillwater OK 74074-1136

POOLE, RICHARD WILLIAM, JR., secondary school educator; b. Norman, Okla., Apr. 13, 1951; s. Richrad W. and Lynn (Mehr) P.; m. Sonya Lee, Mar. 20, 1982; 1 child, Amanda Lee. BS in Social Studies, Okla. State U., Stillwater, 1976. Tchr., coach West Jr. H.S., Ponca City, Okla., 1976-80; tchr., coach Ponca City Sr. H.S., 1980-92, Am. history tchr., supr. jr. high athletics, 1992—. Served with USNR, 1969-71, Viet Nam. Mem. Lions Club (tail twister 1992, v.p. 1993, pres. After 5 club 1994), Elks. Democrat. Methodist. Avocations: golf, fishing, country music, reading history books. Home: 1306 El Camino St Ponca City OK 74604-4011

POOLE, ROBERT ANTHONY, journalist; b. St. Austell, Cornwall, Eng., Dec. 17, 1944; arrived in Can., 1977; m. Valerie Avril Taggart, Apr. 14, 1973; children—Claire Lucy, Emma Louise. Irish editor Press Assn., Belfast, Northern Ireland, 1970-77; gen. reporter Calgary Herald, Alta., Can., 1977-79; city editor Calgary Albertan, 1979-80; city editor Calgary Sun, 1980-81, mng. editor, 1981-84, editor-in-chief, 1984—. Office: Calgary Sun, 2615 12th St NE, Calgary, AB Canada T2E 7W9

POOLE, ROBERT WILLIAM, JR., foundation executive; b. Englewood, N.J., July 4, 1944; s. Robert William and Frances Ann (Giese) P.; m. Lou Villadsen, May 28, 1983; m. Marilyn V Kinsky, June 1968 (div. 1974). B.S., MIT, 1966, M.S., 1967. Systems analyst Sikorsky Aircraft, Stratford, Conn., 1967-70; criminal justice analyst Gen. Research Co., Santa Barbara, Calif., 1970-74; cons. local govt. mgmt. Santa Barbara, 1974-76; pres. Local Govt. Ctr., Santa Barbara, 1976-78; pres. Reason Found., Santa Monica, 1978—. Author: Cutting Back City Hall, 1980. Editor: Instead of Regulation, 1982; Defending a Free Society, 1984, Unnatural Monopolies, 1985; editor, publisher mag. Reason, 1971—. NSF fellow, 1966-67. Mem. AAAS, Sigma Xi. Libertarian. Bd. dirs. Mission Canyon Assn., Santa Barbara, 1984-85, Santa Barbara Futures Found., 1982-83. Home: 2801B Ocean Park Blvd Santa Monica CA 90405-2905 Office: Reason Found 3415 S Sepulveda Blvd # 400 Los Angeles CA 90034-6060

POOLE, RONALD WILLIAM, training specialist, industrial education educator; b. Pitts., June 29, 1948; s. William Rufus and Angie (Lorenzi) P.; m. Karyol Kay Kniffen, July 9, 1980; children: Sundee, Matthew, Bryan. Cert. indsl. edn. tchr., U. Md., 1992; student, Frederick (Md.) C.C., 1994—. Owner, mgr. R&L Refrigeration Svc., Dickerson, Md., 1972-76; refrigeration technician div. engring. svcs. NIH, Bethesda, Md., 1976-90, facilitator and tng. specialist, 1990—, program mgr. apprenticeship and tech. tech., 1992—; instr. indsl. end. Frederick C.C., 1986—, bd. dirs. focus group, 1992—; mem. curriculum rev. com. Montgomery C.C., Rockville, Md., 1994; mem. Inter-Agy. Tng. Coun., Washington, 1992—. Author: (manuals) Heat Pump Basics, 1991, Heat Pump Repair, 1992, (instr.'s guide) Heat Pump Basics and Repair, 1992. Pres. Lewistown (Md.) Youth Assn., 1991-93. Sgt. USMC, 1966-70, Vietnam. Recipient spl. recognition award NIH Div. Engring. Svcs., 1988, outstanding performance award, 1993, 94. Mem. Air Conditioning Contractors Am. Home: 13416 Moser Rd Thurmont MD 21788-2233 Office: NIH Div Engring Svcs 13 South Dr Bldg 13 Rm 2E43 Bethesda MD 20892-5758

POOLE, WILLIAM, economics educator, consultant; b. Wilmington, Del., June 19, 1937; s. William and Louise (Hiller) P.; m. Mary Lynne Ahroon, June 26, 1960; children—William, Lester Allen, Jonathan Carl. AB, Swarthmore Coll., 1959, LLD (hon.), 1989; MBA, U. Chgo., 1963, PhD, 1966. Asst. prof. polit. economy Johns Hopkins U., Balt., 1963-69; professorial lectr. Am. U., Washington, 1970-71; assoc. professorial lectr. George Washington U., Washington, 1971-73; lectr. Georgetown U., Washington, 1972, Harvard U., Cambridge, Mass., 1973; vis. lectr. MIT, Cambridge, 1974, 77; Bank Mees and Hope vis. prof. econs. Erasmus U. Rotterdam, 1991; prof. econs. Brown U., Providence, R.I., 1974, 85—, dir. ctr. for the study fin. markets and insts., 1987-92, prof., chmn. econs. dept., 1981-82, 85-86; economist Bd. Govs. of FRS, Washington, 1964, 1969-70, sr. economist, 1970-74; vis. scholar Fed. Res. Bank, San Francisco, 1977; adviser Fed. Res. Bank, Boston, 1973-74, cons., 1974-81; vis. economist Res. Bank of Australia, 1980-81; mem. Council Econ. Advisers, 1982-85; adj. scholar Cato Inst., 1985—. Mem. Am. Econ. Assn., Am. Fin. Assn. (mem. nominating com. 1979), Western Econ. Assn. (mem. internat. exec. com. 1986-89, mem. nominating com. 1995). Office: Brown U Dept Econs 64 Waterman St Providence RI 02912-9029

POOLER, ROSEMARY S., federal judge; b. 1938. BA, Brooklyn Coll., 1959; MA, Univ. of Conn., 1961; JD, Univ. of Mich. Law Sch., 1965. With Crystal, Manes & Rifken, Syracuse, 1966-69, Michaels and Michaels, Syracuse, 1969-72; asst. corp. counsel Dir. of Consumer Affairs Unit, Syracuse, 1972-73; common counsel City of Syracuse N.Y. Public Interest Rsch. Group, 1974-75; chmn., exec. dir. Consumer Protection Bd., 1975-80; commr. N.Y. State Public Services Commn., 1981-86; staff dir. N.Y. State Assembly, Com. on Corps., Authorities and Commns., 1987-94; judge Supreme Ct., 5th Judicial Dist., 1991-94; district judge U.S. Dist. Ct. (N.Y. no. dist.), 2nd circuit, Syracuse, 1994—; vis. prof. of law Syracuse Univ. Coll. of Law, 1987-88; v.p. legal affairs Atlantic States Legal Found., 1989-90. Mem. Onondaga County Bar Assn., N.Y. State Bar Assn., Women's Bar Assn. of the State of N.Y., Assn. of Supreme Ct. Justices of the State of N.Y. Office: Federal Bldg PO Box 7395 100 S Clinton St Rm 1240 Syracuse NY 13261

POOLEY, BEVERLEY JOHN, law educator, librarian; b. London, Eng., Apr. 4, 1934; came to U.S., 1957; U.S. citizen, 1993; s. William Vincent and Christine Beatrice (Coleman) P.; m. Patricia Joan Ray, June 8, 1958; children—Christopher Jonathan, Rachel Vanessa. BA, Cambridge U., Eng., 1956, LLB, 1957; LLM, U. Mich., Ann Arbor, 1958, SJD, 1961, MLS, 1964. Legis. analyst U. Mich. Law Sch., Ann Arbor, 1958-60; lectr. U. Ghana Law Sch., 1960-62; instr. U. Mich. Law Sch., Ann Arbor, 1962-63, asst. prof., 1963-66, assoc. prof., 1966-70, dir. law library, 1966-84, prof., 1970—, assoc. dean law library, 1984-94. Author: The Evolution of British Planning Legislation, 1960; Planning and Zoning in the United States, 1961. Scholar, King's Coll., Cambridge, Eng., 1956; Blackstone Scholar, Middle Temple, London, 1957. Democrat. Avocations: Acting; musical comedy; food preparation.

POOLEY, JAMES HENRY ANDERSON, lawyer, author; b. Dayton, Ohio, Oct. 4, 1948; s. Howard Carl and Daisy Frances (Lindsley) P.; children by previous marriage: Jefferson Douglas, Christopher James; m. Laura Jean Anderson, Oct. 13, 1984; 1 child, Catherine Lindsley. BA, Lafayette Coll., 1970; JD, Columbia U., 1973. Bar: Calif. 1973, U.S. Dist. Ct. (no. dist.) Calif. 1973, U.S. Ct. Appeals (9th cir.) 1974, U.S. Supreme Ct. 1977, U.S. Dist. Ct. (cen. dist.) Calif. 1978. Assoc. Wilson, Mosher & Sonsini, Palo Alto, Calif., 1973-78; ptnr. Mosher, Pooley & Sullivan, Palo Alto, 1978-88, Graham and James, 1988-93, Fish & Richardson, Menlo Park, 1993—; lectr. Practicing Law Inst., N.Y.C., 1983, 85-86, 88, 95, Santa Clara U. Sch. Law, 1985-87. Author: Trade Secrets, 1982, Protecting Technology, 1983, Trying the High Technology Case, 1984, Trade Secrets: A Guide to Protecting Proprietary Business Information, 1989; contbr. articles to profl. jours.; editor-in-chief Trade Secret Law Reporter, 1984-85; bd. advisors Santa Clara Computer and High Tech. Law Jour., 1984—; chair Nat. Trade Secret Law Inst., 1994. Arbitrator, spl. master U.S. Dist. Ct. (no. dist.) Calif., Santa Clara County Superior Ct., San Jose, 1979—. Mem. Am. Intellectual Property Lawyers' Assn., Am. Electronics Assn. (chmn. lawyers' com. 1981-82), Internat. Bar Assn., Union Internationale de Avocats. Republican. Office: Fish & Richardson 2200 Sand Hill Rd Ste 100 Menlo Park CA 94025-6936

POOLMAN, JIM, state legislator; b. Fargo, N.D., May 15, 1970; s. Robert Francis and Susan Faye (Brown) P. BBA, U. N.D., 1992, postgrad., 1994—. Sales cons. Straus Co., Grand Forks, N.D., 1987-95; state representative N.D. State Ho. of Reps., 1992—; trust officer First Am. Bank, 1995—. Task force State of N.D., Grand Forks, 1992; mem. United Hosp. Corp. United Health, Grand Forks, 1992—, Presdl. Search Com., U. N.D., 1992; bd. dirs. Red River Red Cross, 1995—. Mem. Toastmasters Internat. (sec.), Phi Delta Theta Alumni (varsity bachelors club scholarship ednl. found. 1992). Republican. Lutheran. Avocations: fishing, water sports, golf. Home: 529 Oxford St # 4 Grand Forks ND 58203-2846

POON, PETER TIN-YAU, engineer, physicist; b. Hengyang, Hunan, China, May 31, 1944; came to U.S., 1967; s. Sam. Chak-Kwong and Lai (Yiu) P.; m. Mable Tsang, Apr. 13, 1974; children: Amy Wei-Ling, Brian Wing-Yan. BS, U. Hong Kong, 1965; MA, Calif. State U., Long Beach, 1969; PhD, U. So. Calif., L.A., 1974. Sr. engr. gasdynamics, planetary probe heat shield design, sys. simulation Jet Propulsion Lab./Calif. Inst. Tech., Pasadena, 1974-77, tech. mgr. advanced solar receiver, task leader advanced solar concentrator, 1978-80, systems engr. mission control and computing ctr. devel., 1981-83; advisor Space Sta. Ada Task, staff mem, task leader software mgmt. and assurance program NASA, 1984-85; mission control ctr. devel. telemetry systems engr. software mgmt. stds., element mgr. NASA software info. sys. Jet Propulsion Lab./Calif. Inst. Tech., Pasadena, 1986-88, systems mgr. for missions to Mars, Comet/Asteroid/Saturn, flight projects interface office, 1988-91, multimission ground systems office mgr. Mission to Mars, 1991-93, telecomm. and mission svcs. mgr. Cassini Mission to Saturn, 1993—; U.S.A. chmn., program com. 2nd Internat. Software Engring. Stds. Symposium, Montreal, Can., 1994-95; program com. session chair Software Engring. Stds. Symposium, Brighton, Eng., 1992-93; mem. program mgmt. com. 3rd Internat. Software Engring. Stds. Symposium, 1995-97; session chair, mem. program com. 2nd IEEE Internat. Conf. on Engring. of Complex Computer Systems, 1995-96; mem. Internat. Orgn. for Standardization/Internat. Electrotech. Com./Joint Tech. Com. in Info. Tech. Subcom. Working Group and U.S. Technical Adv. Group, 1995—; U.S. del., Prague, Czech Republic, 1996; program com. mem. 5th Ann. Conf. on Artificial Intelligence and Ada, 1989, 6th Ann. Conf. on Artificial Intelligence and Ada, 1990. Author numerous profl. publs. Recipient numerous group awards in field, NASA, 1977-93. Mem. IEEE Software Engring. Stds. (exec. com. 1993—, co-author long range plans and stds. survey 1993), Arcadia Music Club (pres. 1994-95, 1st v.p. 1993-94), Sigma Xi, Eta Kappa Nu, Phi Kappa Phi, Athenaeum. Avocations: music appreciation, hiking, theatre arts, choreography. Office: Jet Propulsion Lab Calif Inst Tech 4800 Oak Grove Dr Pasadena CA 91109

POONS, LARRY, artist; b. Tokyo, Oct. 1, 1937; came to U.S., 1938; Student, New Eng. Conservatory Music, 1955-57, Boston Mus. Fine Arts Sch., 1958. Mem. vis. faculty N.Y. Studio Sch., 1967. Author: The Structure of Color, 1971; exhbns. include, Green Gallery, N.Y.C., 1963-65, Art Inst. Chgo., 1966, Corcoran Gallery Art, Carnegie Inst., 1967, Leo Castelli Gallery, 1967-68, Documenta IV, Kassel, W. Ger., 1968, Whitney Mus. Am. Art Ann., 1968, 72, Lawrence Rubin Gallery, 1970-73, Whitney Biennial, 1973, Knoedler & Co., 1973-78, Knoedler Contemporary Art, N.Y.C., 1974-78, Andre Emmerlich Gallery, N.Y.C., 1979-87, Albright-Knox Art Gallery, Buffalo, 1968, 70, Pasadena Art Mus., 1969, Gallery 99, Bar Harbor Islands, Fla., 1981, Mus. Fine Arts, Boston, 1981-82, Galerie Montaigne, Paris, 1990, Helander Gallery, Palm Beach, Fla., 1990, Salander-O'Reilly Galleries, N.Y.C., 1990, Beverly Hills, Calif., 1990, Berlin, 1990, Gallery Afinsa, Madrid, 1991; represented in permanent collection, Mus. Modern Art, N.Y.C., Allen Meml. Art Mus., Oberlin Coll., Cleve. Mus. Art, Hirschhorn Mus. and Sculpture Garden, Washington, Milw. Art Ctr., Solomon R. Guggenheim Mus., N.Y.C., Tate Gallery, London, Whitney Mus. Am. Art, Met. Mus. Art, Chgo. Art Inst., Denver Mus., Boston Mus. Fine Arts, Albright-Knox Art Gallery, Stedelijk Mus., Amsterdam, Woodward Found., Washington, David Mirvish Gallery, Toronto; artist-in-residence, Inst. Humanistic Studies, Aspen, Colo., 1966-67. Address: PO Box 115 Islamorada FL 33036

POOR, ANNE, artist; b. N.Y.C., Jan. 2, 1918; d. Henry Varnum and Bessie (Breuer) P. Student, Bennington Coll., 1936, 38, Art Students League, 1935, Acad. Julien, Paris. trustee, gov. Skowhegan Sch. Painting and Sculpture, 1947-61, 89, 96; artist corr. WAC, 1943-45. Illustrator: Greece, 1964; works exhibited Am. Brit. Art Ctr., 1944, 45, 48, Maynard Walker Gallery, 1950, Graham Gallery, 1957-59, 62, 68-71, 85, Rockland Ctr. for Arts, West Nyack, N.Y., 1982, 83, Terry Dintenfass Gallery, N.Y.C.; executed murals, P.O., Gleason, Tenn., DePew, N.Y., South Solon, Maine, Free Mtg. House, 1957, others; represented permanent collections Whitney Mus., Bklyn. Mus., Wichita Mus., Art Inst. Chgo. Edwin Austin Abbey Meml. fellow, 1948; grantee Nat. Inst. Arts and Letters, 1957; recipient Benjamin Altman 1st prize landscape painting N.A.D., 1971, 86, Childe Hassam award, 1972, 77. Mem. Artists Equity Assn., Nat. Inst. Arts and Letters. Office: Terry Dintenfass Gallery 20 E 79th St New York NY 10021

POOR, CLARENCE ALEXANDER, physician; b. Ashland, Oreg., Oct. 29, 1911; s. Lester Clarence and Matilda Ellen (Doty) P.; AB, Willamette U., 1932; MD, U. Oreg., 1936. Diplomate Am. Bd. Internal Medicine. Intern U. Wis., Madison, 1936-37, resident in internal medicine, 1937-40, instr. dept. pathology Med. Sch., 1940-41, clin. instr., clin. asst. dept. internal medicine, 1942-44; pvt. practice medicine specializing in internal medicine, Oakland, Calif., 1944—; mem. emeritus staff Highland Alameda County Hosp., Oakland, 1949—; mem. staff Providence Hosp., Oakland, 1947—, pres. staff, 1968-69; staff mem. Samuel Merritt Hosp., Oakland, 1958—; staff mem. Summit Med. Ctr. (merger Providence Hosp. and Samuel Merritt Hosp.), 1991—. Mem. Nat. Coun. on Alcoholism, 1974—, bd. dirs. Bay Area, 1977—. Mem. Am., Calif., Alameda-Contra Costa med. assns., Alameda County Heart Assn. (trustee 1955-62, 72-82, pres. 1960-61), Calif. Heart Assn. (dir. 1962-72), Soc. for Clin. and Exptl. Hypnosis, Am. Soc. Clin. Hypnosis, San Francisco Acad. Hypnosis (dir. 1966—, pres. 1973). Home: 1241 Westview Dr Berkeley CA 94705-1650 Office: 400 29th St Ste 201 Oakland CA 94609-3547 *Personal philosophy: No matter how easy or how hard the task, the goal is that it be an enjoyment on final review.*

POOR, HAROLD VINCENT, electrical engineering educator; b. Columbus, Ga., Oct. 2, 1951; s. Harold Edgar and Virginia (Hardin) P.; m. Connie Irene Hazelwood, Sept. 1, 1973; children: Kristin Elizabeth, Lauren Alissa. BEE with highest honors, Auburn U., 1972; PhD, Princeton U., 1977. Asst. prof. U. Ill., Urbana, 1977-81, assoc. prof., 1981-84, prof., 1984-90; prof. dept. elec. engring. Princeton (N.J.) U., 1990—; acad. visitor Imperial Coll. London U., 1985; vis. prof. Newcastle (Australia) U., 1987; sr. visiting fellow Imperial Coll., London U., 1993; cons. numerous orgns., 1978—. Author: An Introduction to Signal Detection and Estimation, 1988, 2d edit., 1994; contbr. numerous articles to profl. jours. Grantee NSF, Office of Naval Rsch., Army Rsch. Office, 1978—; recipient Terman award Am. Soc. Engring. Edn., 1992, Centennial certificate Am. Soc. for Engring. Edn., 1993. Fellow IEEE (bd. dirs. 1991-92), AAAS, Acoustical Soc. Am.; mem. Info. Theory Soc. of IEEE (pres. 1990), IEEE Control Sys. Soc. (Disting. Mem. award 1994). Office: Princeton Univ Dept Elec Engring Princeton NJ 08544

POOR, JANET MEAKIN, landscape designer; b. Cin., Nov. 27, 1929; d. Cyrus Lee and Helen Keats (Meakin) Lee-Hofer; m. Edward King Poor III, June 23, 1951; children: Edward King IV, Thomas Meakin. Student, Stephens Coll., 1947-48, U. Cinn., 1949-51, Triton Coll., 1973-76. Pres. Janet Meakin Poor Landscape Design, Winnetka, Ill., 1975—; chmn. bd. dirs. Cgho. Horticultural Soc., Chgo. Botanic Garden. Author, editor: Plants That Merit Attention Vol. I: Trees, 1984; contbr. articles to profl. jours. Participant in long range planning City of Winnetka, 1978-82, archtl. and environ. bd., 1980-84, beautification commn., 1978-84, garden coun., 1978-82; adv. coun., sec. of agr. Nat. Arboretum, Washington; nat. adv. bd. Filoli, San Francisco; trustee Ctr. Plant Conservation at Mo. Botanical Garden, St. Louis, also mem. exec. com.; mem. adv. coun. The Garden Conservancy, 1989—; trustee Winnetka Congl. Ch., 1978-80. Recipient merit award Hadley Sch. Blind, 1972; named Vol. of Yr. Hadley Sch. Blind. Mem. Chgo. Hort. Soc. (chmn. bd. dirs. 1987-93, medal 1984, gold medal garden design, exec. com., chmn. rsch. com., women's bd., designer herb garden Farwell Gardens at Chgo. Botanic Garden, Hutchinson medal 1994), Am. Hort. Soc. (bd. dirs., Catherine H. Sweeney award 1985), Garden Club Am. (chmn. nat. plant exchange 1980-81, chmn. hort. com. 1981-83, bd. dirs., 1983-85, corresponding sec. 1985-87, Horticulture award Zone XI 1981, Creative Leadership award 1986), Fortnightly Club, Garden Guild (bd. dirs.), Garden Club Am. (v.p. 1987-89, medal awards chmn. 1991-93, Honor medal 1994). Republican. Avocations: gardening, writing, music, hort. rsch., lecturing.

POOR, PETER VARNUM, producer, director; b. N.Y.C., May 17, 1926; s. Henry Varnum and Bessie Breuer (Freedman) P.; m. Eloise Marcovicci Miller, Sept. 27, 1950; children: Candida Eustacia, Anna Maria, Graham Varnum. BA, Harvard U., 1947; postgrad., Centro Sperimentale di Cinematografia, Rome, 1951-52. Prodn. asst. New World Films, N.Y.C., 1948; editor, dir. Willard Pictures, N.Y.C., 1948-51; film editor, dir. and producer CBS News-Airpower, 1954-57, 7 Lively Arts, 1957-58, Twentieth Century, 1958-66, 21st Century, 1966-69, 60 Minutes, 1970-71, CBS Reports, 1971-75; sr. producer NBC News, Monitor, First Camera, White Paper, 1977-87; freelance producer and dir. Crow House Prodns., N.Y.C., 1988—; instr. in TV journalism Fordham U., 1976-78; mem. Screening Com. for Fulbright Grants in Film, TV and Radio, 1965-67, chmn., 1967, 70; adj. assoc. history of documentary Columbia U. Grad. Sch. Journalism, 1987; adj. asst. prof. visual arts NYU, 1991-92. Producer-dir.: (TV documentary films) What's New at School, 1972, The IQ Myth, 1975, The Biggest Lump of Money in the World, 1985, The Japan They Don't Talk About, 1986, Nuclear Power in France, 1987, The Cronkite Report, 1993. Served with USAF, 1944-45. Recipient Emmy award Acad. TV Arts and Sci., 1961, 62, 67, Lasker TV award Lasker Found., 1968, 69, U.S. CEA Forum award, 1967, 87; hon. mention Robert Kennedy Journalism Award in TV, 1976; Fulbright scholar, 1951-52. Mem. Dirs. Guild Am. (coun. 1980-90), Film Editors Union, Writers Guild Am. East. Club: Phoenix S-K (Cambridge, Mass.). Avocations: bicycling, reading, photography, gardening. Home and Office: 1150 5th Ave New York NY 10128-0724

POORE, JAMES ALBERT, III, lawyer; b. Butte, Mont., June 28, 1943; s. James A. Jr. and Jesse (Wild) P.; m. Shelley A. Borgstede, Feb. 12, 1989; children: James IV, Jeffrey. AB, Stanford U., 1965; JD with honors, U. Mont., 1968. Bar: Mont. 1968, U.S. Dist. Ct. Mont. 1968, U.S. Ct. Appeals (9th cir.) 1972, U.S. Supreme Ct. 1973. Assoc. Poore, Poore, McKenzie & Roth, Butte, 1968-74; prin., v.p. Poore, Roth & Robinson, P.C., Butte, 1974—; speaker in field. Assoc. editor U. Mont. Law Rev., 1967-68; contbg. editor Product Liability Desk Reference, 1996; contbr. articles to profl. publs. Dist. dir. Boy Scouts Am., S.W. Mont., 1969; dir. YMCA, Butte, 1981-83; founding bd. dirs. Hospice of Butte, 1982-85, Butte Community Theater, 1977-80; pres. Butte Uptown Assn., 1974; dir. Butte Silverbow Am. Cancer Soc. Bd., 1992—. Fellow Am. Bar Found.; mem. ABA, State Bar Mont., Am. Judicature Soc., Silver Bow Bar Assn., Phi Delta Phi. Home: 6 Cedar Lake Dr Butte MT 59701-4338 Office: Poore Roth & Robinson PC 1341 Harrison Ave Butte MT 59701-4801

POORE, RALPH EZRA, JR., editorial page editor; b. Mobile, Ala., Mar. 21, 1951; s. Ralph Ezra Sr. and Beatrice Valara (Pierce) P.; m. Carron Lynn Walker, May 26, 1979 (div. Apr. 1987); 1 child, Ralph Ezra III. BA, U. So. Ala., 1973; MA, U. Ala., Tuscaloosa, 1974. Reporter Fairhope (Ala.) Courier, 1973, George County Times, Lucedale, Miss., 1975; journalism instr. Spring Hill Coll., Mobile, 1975-78; assoc. editor The News-Herald, Chickasaw, Ala., 1978-79; reporter The Mobile Press Register, 1979-84, editorial page editor, 1984-94; editorial page editor The Idaho Statesman, Boise, 1994-96, bus. editor, 1996—. Mem. exec. com. Mobile Community Orgn., 1975; bd. dirs. Friends of Mus., Mobile, 1976-78; mem. Mobile Historic Devel. Commn., 1977-79; chmn. bd. dirs. John M. Will Meml. Scholarship Found., Mobile, 1982-84. Recipient Newswriting award Ala. AP, 1981, 83, 90, Community Svc. award, Press Club Mobile, 1979, Commendation award, 1981. Mem. Nat. Conf. Editorial Writers, Soc. Profl. Journalists (pres. Mobile chpt. 1982-83). Methodist. Avocations: triathlete, writing history. Home: 3725 Gekeler Lane # 54 Boise ID 83706 Office: The Idaho Statesman 1200 North Curtis Rd Boise ID 83706

POORMAN, PAUL ARTHUR, educator, media consultant; b. Lock Haven, Pa., Aug. 29, 1930; s. Wilson Paul and Margaret (Heylmun) P.; m. Sylvia Elizabeth Powers, Nov. 22, 1952; children: Pamela (Mrs. Robert Phillips), Cynthia (Mrs. Donald Paul), Peter, Stephen, Thomas, Andrew, Robert, William. B.A., Pa. State U., 1952. Reporter State College (Pa.) Centre Daily Times, 1953-57, news editor, 1957-62; news editor Harrisburg (Pa.) Patriot, 1962-63, Phila. Bulletin, 1963-66; asst. mng. editor Detroit News, 1966-69, mng. editor, 1969-75; vis. prof. Northwestern U., Evanston, Ill., 1975-76; editor Akron (Ohio) Beacon Jour., 1976-86; prof. journalism, spl. asst. to pres. Kent (Ohio) State U., 1986—. Served with USAF 1951-53. Mem. Am. Soc. Newspaper Editors, AP Mng. Editors (regent). Office: Kent State U 2D Fl Libr Kent OH 44242

POORMAN, ROBERT LEWIS, education educator, consultant, academic administrator; b. Germantown, Ohio, Dec. 9, 1926; s. Dale Lowell and Bernice Velma (Krick) P.; m. Lois May Romer, Dec. 26, 1949; children: Paula Beth, Janice Marie, Mark Leon, John Alex, Lisa Ann, Daniel Romer. Student, Ohio Wesleyan U., 1944-45, U. Va., 1945-46; B.S.Ed., Ohio State U., 1948, M.A., 1950; postgrad., U. So. Calif., 1951-53; Ed.D. (Kellogg fellow 1960-62, Disting. Scholar Tuition grantee 1960-62), UCLA, 1964. Tchr., counselor, adminstr., secondary schs. Colo., Mo., Ariz., 1948-57; registrar Phoenix Coll., 1957-60; intern Bakersfield Coll., 1960-63, asst. to pres., 1963-64, asso. dean instrn., 1964-65, dean students, 1965-67; founding pres. Lincoln Land Community Coll., 1967-88, pres. emeritus; edn. cons. MARA of Malaysia, 1983; higher edn. cons. Springfield, Ill., 1988—; interim pres. Parkland Coll., Champaign, Ill., 1989-90; Fulbright lectr., cons. to Lithuania, 1993; vis. assoc. prof. Fla. Internat. U., 1994-95. Contbr. articles to profl. jours. Bd. dirs. (past) United Way of Springfield, bd. dirs. Urban League of Springfield, Good Will Industries of Springfield, Springfield (Ill.) Symphony, Catholic Youth Orgn., Springfield, Gov.'s Prayer Breakfast, Springfield Mental Health, Griffin H.S. Bd., Diocesan Sem.; mem. adv. bd. Sacred Heart Acad., Springfield Commn. on Internat. Visitors, Sisters Cities Assn. Served with USNR, 1944-46. Recipient Midwest region Chief Exec. Officer of Yr. Assn. Community Coll. Trustees, 1988, recognition Ill. Community Coll. Trustees Assn., 1988; named an Outstanding Chief Exec. Officer for Ill. Community Colls. U. Tex. Leadership Program, 1987; Phi Theta Kappa fellow, 1981. Mem. Am. Assn. Community and Jr. Colls., Ill. Council Public Community Coll. Pres. (sec. 1973-74, vice chmn. 1974-75, chmn. 1975-76), Council North Central Community and Jr. Colls. (exec. bd. 1979-81), North Central Assn. (cons., evaluator 1984-88). Republican. Roman Catholic. Home and Office: 2324 Willemoore Ave Springfield IL 62704-4362

POP, IGGY (JAMES NEWELL OSTERBERG), composer, singer, musician; b. Muskegon, Mich., Apr. 21, 1947; s. James Newell and Louella Kristine (Christensen) Osterberg. Student, U. Mich., 1963-64. Drummer, lead singer, composer The Iguanas, 1966-67; lead singer, composer The Stooges, 1967-74; solo artist, 1975—, toured extensively with David Bowie and others. composer music and lyrics for over 90 songs including China Girl (recorded by David Bowie); rec. artist, albums include The Stooges, 1970, Funhouse, 1972, Raw Power, 1973, Kill City, 1976, The Idiot, 1977, Lust for Life, 1977, TV Eye, 1977, New Values, 1979, Soldier, 1980, Party, 1982, Zombie Birdhouse, 1983, Blah, Blah, Blah, 1986, Instinct (Grammy nomination 1988), 1988, BrickXBricks, 1990, ArizonaDream, 1992, American Caesar, 1993; has recorded for Elektra, Columbia; RCA, solo albums for Arista, Chrysallis, A&M; guest appearances on television and prodns.; known as Godfather of Punk; appeared in films The Color of Money, Cry-Baby, 1990, Coffey and Cigarettes (Palme d'Or 1993). Named Punk of the Yr. Creem Mag. Office: care Floyd Peluce 449 S Beverly Dr # 102 Beverly Hills CA 90212-4428

POPCHRISTOV, DAMYAN CHRISTOV, theater director and educator; b. Sofia, Bulgaria, June 25, 1956; came to U.S., 1990; s. Christo Damyanov and Antoinette Ivanova (Popova) P.; m. Olga Lebedeva-Popchristova; 1 child, Antoinette Damyanova. BFA in Acting, Theater Acad. Sofia, 1979, MFA in Directing, 1981. Resident dir. City Theater Haskovo, Bulgaria, 1981-85, City Theater Plovdiv, Bulgaria, 1985-89, Nat. Youth Theater Bulgaria, Sofia, 1989-90; asst. prof. theater Arts Acad. Sofia, 1987-89, assoc. prof., 1989-91; mem. adj. faculty NYU Tisch Sch. Arts, N.Y.C., 1991—; dir. Trinity/LaMaMa N.Y.C. Performing Arts Program, 1994—; guest dir. several theaters, Sofia, Vidin, St. Petersburg, 1981-90; founder, dir. Magic Voices, exptl. theater co., Sofia, 1989-91; vis. prof. U. Tenn., 1990, Columbia U., 1991; vis. prof., theater dir. Trinity Coll., Hartford, Conn., 1992; participant Knoxville (Tenn.) World Theater Festival, 1990, Edmonton (Alta., Can.) Fringe Festival, 1990, Maison des Cultures du Monde, Paris, 1991; mem. bd. new theater com. Internat. Theater Inst., 1985—, pres., 1989—, gen. sec. Bulgarian Ctr., 1987-91. Guest dir. The Last Night of Socrates, 1988, Tale for the Four Hats, 1989, Lattice and Lavage, 1990, The Murderer, 1990, The Underground Man, 1990; founder, dir. internat. festival Theater in a Suitcase, Sofia, 1987—. Office: NYU Tisch Sch Arts 721 Broadway Fl 3 New York NY 10003-6807

POPE, ALEXANDER H., lawyer, former county official; b. N.Y.C., June 4, 1929; s. Clifford H. and and Sarah H. (Davis) P.; m. Katherine Mackinlay, Sept. 14, 1985; children by previous marriage: Stephen C., Virginia L., Daniel M. A.B. with honors, U. Chgo., 1948, J.D., 1952. Bar: Ill. 1952, Republic of Korea 1953, Calif. 1955, U.S. Supreme Ct. 1970. Pvt. practice L.A., 1955-77, 87—; assoc. David Ziskind, L.A., 1955; ptnr. Shadle, Kennedy & Pope, L.A., 1956, Fine & Pope, L.A., 1957-59, 61-77; legis. sec. to gov. State of Calif., 1959-61; county assessor Los Angeles County, L.A., 1978-86; ptnr. Mayer, Brown & Platt, L.A., 1987-88, Barash & Hill, L.A., 1989-92; of counsel Seyforth, Shaw, Fairweather & Geraldson, L.A., 1993—. Pres. Westchester Mental Health Clinic, 1963; nat. bd. mem. Vols. for Stevenson, 1952; vice-chmn. L.A. County Dem. Cen. Com., 1958-59; mem. Calif. Hwy. Commn., 1966-70; mem. L.A. Bd. Airport Commrs., 1973-77, v.p., 1973-75, pres., 1975-76; trustee, sec. L.A. Theatre Ctr., 1984-89. With U.S. Army, 1952-54, Korea. Mem. ACLU, Calif. State Bar Assn. (state and local tax com. 1991—, chair 1993-94), L.A. County Bar Assn. (state and local tax com. 1987—, chair 1995—), U. Chgo. Alumni Club Greater L.A. (pres. 1970-71), Zero Population Growth, Ams. United, Common Cause, Order of Coif, Phi Beta Kappa. Democrat. Unitarian. Home: Unit 2205 800 W 1st St Los Angeles CA 90012-2430 Office: Seyforth Shaw Fairweather & Geraldson 2029 Century Park East #3300 Los Angeles CA 90067

POPE, ANDREW JACKSON, JR. (JACK POPE), retired judge; b. Abilene, Tex., Apr. 18, 1913; s. Andrew Jackson and Ruth Adelia (Taylor) P.; m. Allene Esther Nichols, June 11, 1938; children: Andrew Jackson III, Walter Allen. BA, Abilene Christian U., 1934, LLD (hon.), 1980; LLB, U. Tex., 1937; LLD (hon.), Pepperdine U., 1981, St. Mary's U., San Antonio, 1982, Okla. Christian U., 1983. Bar: Tex. 1937. Practice law Corpus Christi, 1937-46; judge 94th Dist. Ct., Corpus Christi, 1946-50; justice Ct. Civil Appeals, San Antonio, 1950-65; justice Supreme Ct. of Tex., Austin, 1965-82, chief justice, 1982-85. Author: John Berry & His Children, 1988; chmn. bd. editors Appellate Procedure in Tex., 1974; author numerous articles in law revs. and profl. jours. Pres. Met. YMCA, San Antonio, 1956-57; chmn. Tex. State Law Libr. Bd., 1973-80; trustee Abilene Christian U., 1958—. Seaman USNR, 1944-46. Recipient Silver Beaver award Alamo council Boy Scouts Am., 1961, Distinguished Eagle award, 1983; Rosewood Gavel award, 1962, St. Thomas More award, St. Mary's U., San Antonio, 1982; Outstanding Alumnus award Abilene Christian U., 1965; Greenhill Jud. award Mcpl. Judges Assn., 1980; Houston Bar Found. citation, 1985; San Antonio Bar Found. award, 1985; Disting. Jurist award Jefferson County Bar, 1985; Outstanding Alumnus award U. Tex. Law Alumni Assn., 1988; George Washington Honor medal Freedom Found., 1988; Disting. Lawyer award Travis County, 1992. Fellow Tex. Bar Found. (Law Rev. award 1979, 80, 81); mem. ABA, State Bar Tex. (pres. jud. sect. 1962, Outstanding Fifty Years Lawyer award 1994), Order of Coif, Nueces County (pres. 1946), Travis County Bar Assn., Bexar County Bar Assn., Tex. Philos. Soc., Austin Knife and Fork (pres. 1980), Am. Judicature Soc., Tex. State Hist. Assn., Tex. Supreme Ct. Hist. Soc. (v.p.), Sons of Republic of Tex., Christian Chronicle Coun. (chmn.), Masons, K.P. (grand chancellor 1946), Alpha Chi, Phi Delta Phi, Pi Sigma Alpha. Mem. Ch. of Christ. Home: 2803 Stratford Dr Austin TX 78746-4626

POPE, BILL JORDAN, chemical engineering educator, business executive; b. Salt Lake City, Sept. 12, 1922; s. Louis Albert and Ruth (Jordan) P.; m. Margaret McConkie, Sept. 10, 1943; children: Louis, Leslie (Mrs. Alan S. Layton), Kathryn (Mrs. Richard D. Hoopes), Patrice (Mrs. Wayne L. Tew). B.S. in Chem. Engring., U. Utah, 1947; M.S., U. Wash., 1949, Ph.D., 1959. Project chem. engr. Utah Oil Refining Co., 1951-58; mem. faculty Brigham Young U., 1958-59, 62-78, prof. chem. engring., 1962-78, prof. emeritus, 1978—, chmn. dept., 1966-78; prof. chem. engring., acting pres. Abadan (Iran) Inst. Tech., 1959-62; founder, v.p. Megadiamond Corp., Provo, 1966-70, exec. v.p., 1970-73, pres. 1973-78; pres. Megadiamond Industries N.Y., 1976-78; pres. U.S. Synthetic Corp., 1978-92, chmn. bd., 1988—; cons. to industry; specialist in ultra high pressure processes and equipment, diamond synthesis, diamond sintering. Del. Utah Republican Conv., 1958, 74. Served to 1st lt., C.E. AUS, 1942-46. Research fellow U. Wash., 1947-49; Keysor Chem. Research grantee, 1964-70. Mem. Am. Inst. Chem. Engrs., Am. Chem. Soc., Am. Soc. Profl. Engrs., Am. Soc. Engring. Edn., Utah Acad. Arts and Scis., Utah Soc. Profl. Engrs., Sigma Xi, Tau Beta Pi. Mem. Ch. of Jesus Christ of Latter Day Saints (bishop 1965-72, stake pres., counsellor 1972-76, stake pres. 1976-81, regional rep. 1981-87). Home: 1866 N 1450th E Provo UT 84604

POPE, DALE ALLEN, investment company executive; b. Racine, Wis., Apr. 11, 1953; s. Warren Edward and Ruth Ann (Adams) P.; m. Colleen Ranee Esson, Aug. 6, 1976; children: Shayna Ranee, Justin Daniel, Evan Hunter. BBA, U. Wis., Eau Claire, 1975, postgrad., 1976-77. V.p. Am. Bankers Life, Miami, Fla., 1981-82; pres., COO IFS Capital Corp., North Palm Beach, Fla., 1982-87; founder, pres., CEO Am. Capital Corp., King of Prussia, Pa., 1987—; bus. ins. cons., 1978-81. Mem. Internat. Assn. for Fin. Planning, Internat. Assn. of Registered Fin. Cons., Inc. (charter mem.), Inst. CFPs, Am. Soc. CLU and ChFC, Nat. Assn. Securities Dealers, Inc. (mem. dist. bus. conduct com. 1990-92, bd. arbitrators), Rotary Internat. (dist. gov.'s rep. 1994-95, Paul Harris fellow 1989), Rotary Club of Wayne (past pres., dir. 1993). Avocations: golf, tennis, hunting, fishing. Office: Am Capital Corp Ste 900 1150 1st Ave King Of Prussia PA 19406

POPE, DANIEL JAMES, lawyer; b. Chgo., Nov. 22, 1948. BA, Loyola U., Chgo., 1972; JD cum laude, John Marshall Law Sch., 1975; postgrad., U. Chgo., 1977-78. Bar: Ill. 1975, U.S. Dist. Ct. (no. dist.) Ill. 1982, N.Y. 1983, U.S. Tax Ct. 1985, Tex. 1995, U.S. Supreme Ct. 1995. Corp. trust adminstr. Continental Bank, Chgo., 1972-74; assoc. Haskell & Perrin, Chgo., 1975-77; assoc. Coffield, Ungaretti, Harris & Slavin, Chgo., 1977-81, ptnr., 1981-90, head litigation dept., 1988-90; ptnr. Seyfarth Shaw Fairweather & Geraldson, Chgo., 1990-95, Bell, Boyd & Lloyd, 1996; adj. prof. John Marshall Law Sch., Chgo., 1978-79; appointed panel atty. Fed. Defender Program, Chgo., 1983. Mem. ABA, Ill. Bar Assn., Chgo. Bar Assn. (chmn. aviation law com. 1979, jud. evaluation com. 1982-87), Pub. Interest Law Initiative (dir. 1989-91), Chgo. Athletic Club, Tavern Club, Oak Park Country Club. Home: 146 N Taylor Ave Oak Park IL 60302-2524 Office: Bell Boyd & LLoyd 70 W Madison St Ste 3300 Chicago IL 60602-4207

POPE, DAVID E., geologist, micropaleontologist; b. Forrest City, Ark., Dec. 20, 1920; s. Jesse Ellis and Mary Ruth (Remley) P.; m. Dorothy Angeline Salario, June 8, 1947 (dec. Jan. 1982); children: David Brian, Mark Alan; m. Alice Duke Akins, June 1, 1990. BS, La. State U., 1947, MS, 1948; grad. U.S. Army Command and Gen. Staff Coll., 1967. Paleontologist, Union Producing Co., Houston, 1948-49, New Orleans, 1949-55, dist. paleontologist, New Orleans, 1955-63, Lafayette, La., 1963-67; cons., Lafayette, La., 1967-75; sr. rsch. geologist, La. Geol. Survey, Baton Rouge, 1975—; lectr. La. State U., 1979, 80, N.E. La. U., 1983. Mem. nat. adv. bd. Am. Security Coun., 1983—; bd. dirs. La. State U. Mus. Geosci. Assocs., 1980—, pres. 1981-82, 1987—. Capt. U.S. Army, 1942-46, to lt. col. USAR, 1945-70. Contbr. articles to profl. jours. Decorated Silver Star medal with oak leaf cluster, Purple Heart, Combat Inf. badge. Mem. Am. Assn. Petroleum Geologists (cert., mem. ho. of dels. 1981—), Am. Inst. Profl. Geologists, Gulf Coast sect. SEPM (pres. 1959-60, hon. mem., 1987), New Orleans Geol. Soc. (v.p. 1962-63), Lafayette Geol. Soc., Baton Rouge Geol. Soc. (pres. 1980-81, hon. mem. 1989), Gulf Coast Assn. Geol. Socs. (bd. dirs. 1980-87, historian 1983—, pres. 1985-86), Res. Officers Assn. (life), Mil. Order World Wars, La. State U. Sch. Geology Alumni Assn. (pres. 1958-59, 84-85), La. Petroleum Coun. Home: 12026 Pecan Grove Ct Baton Rouge LA 70810-4835 Office: La Geol Survey Univ Sta PO Box G Baton Rouge LA 70893

POPE, DEANNA L. T., music educator; b. Frederick, Md., July 27, 1959; d. Donald Thomas and Nadia Simone (Wheatley) Taylor; m. James Henry Pope; children: Gregory James, Brian Nathaniel, Emily Amanda. BA in Music Edn., Western Md. Coll., 1981, MS in Curriculum and Instrn., 1992. Cert. advanced profl. music tchr. grades 7-12. Tchr. mid. sch. choral & gen. music Middletown (Md.) Mid. Sch., 1982-83; tchr. gen. music Brunswick (Md.) Mid. Sch., 1983, 84; tchr. choral and gen. music Middletown Mid. Sch., 1984, 85-86; tchr. piano Gov. Thomas Johnson H.S., Frederick, 1986—; tchr. piano Visual and Performing Arts Sch., Frederick, 1988-95, instr. adv. musical studies, 1995—; instr. grad. edn. Western Md. Coll./Performance Learning Sys., Inc., Westminster, Md., 1992—; wellness contact for staff Gov. Thomas Johnson H.S., Frederick, 1989-91, mem. sch. improvement team, 1991-93, staff devel. contact, 1991—. Deacon consistory Christ Reformed Ch., Middletown, 1989-92, mem. missions bd., 1989-92, sec. consistory, 1990-91, dir. children's choirs, 1990—, supr. music summer camp, summer 1992—. Mem. NEA, Md. Music Educators Assn., Music Educators Nat. Conf., Md. State Tchrs. Assn., Assn. for Supr. and Curriculum Devel., Frederick County Tchrs. Assn., Tri-M Music Honor Soc. (life mem., advisor chpt. 2329 1992—, Letter of Commendation 1992). Republican. United Ch. of Christ. Avocations: water exercise, reading, Computers, classical music. Office: Gov Thomas Johnson H S 1501 N Market St Frederick MD 21701-4430

POPE, G. PHILLIP, insurance company executive. Sr. v.p. fin., cfo Blue Cross Blue Shield of Ala., Birmingham, 1970—. Office: Blue Cross Blue Shield of Ala 450 Riverchase Pky E Birmingham AL 35298*

POPE, HARRISON GRAHAM, JR., psychiatrist, educator; b. Lynn, Mass., Dec. 26, 1947; s. H. Graham and Alice (Rider) P.; m. Mary M. Quinn, June 7, 1974; children: Kimberly, Hilary, Courtney. AB summa cum laude, Harvard U., 1969, MPH, 1972, MD, 1974. Diplomate Am. Bd. Psychiatry and Neurology. Resident in psychiatry McLean Hosp., Belmont, Mass., 1974-77, clin. rsch. fellow Mailman Rsch. Ctr., 1977-79, asst. psychiatrist, 1979-84, assoc. psychiatrist, 1984-92, psychiatrist, 1992—, chief biol. psychiatry lab., 1984—; Dupont-Warren rsch. fellow Harvard Med. Sch., Boston, 1976-77; instr. psychiatry Harvard Med. Sch., Boston, 1977-82, asst. prof., 1982-85, assoc. prof., 1985—; staff psychiatrist Hampstead (N.H.) Hosp., 1976-80; vis. fellow The Maudsley Hosp., London, 1977, Hôp. Ste. Anne, Paris, 1977; mem. Am. Psychiat. Assn., 1976-80, adv. com. on schizophrenic, paranoid and affective disorders, 1979, adv. com. on preparation of DSM-III-R, 1984, task force on nomenclature and stats., 1979, 84. Author: Voices from the Drug Culture, 1971, The Road East, 1974, (with J.I. Hudson) New Hope for Binge Eaters: Advances in the Understanding and Treatment of Bulimia, 1984; co-editor: The Psychobiology of Bulimia, 1987, Use of Anticonvulsants in Psychiatry: Recent Advances, 1988; contbr. over 250 papers on biol. psychiatry, with particulary emphasis on diagnosis of psychotic disorders, treatment of mood disorders and eating disorders, and substance abuse, particularly abuse of anabolic steroids by athletes; mem. editl. bd. European Psychiatry, Paris, 1984—, Internat. Jour. of Eating Disorders, 1984—, Jour. Clin. Psychiatry, 1993—. Named one of Outstanding Americans under 40 Esquire mag., 1984; fellow Scottish Rite Schizophrenia Program, No. Masonic Jurisdiction, 1977-81, Charles A. King Trust, Boston, 1977-79. Avocation: weightlifting. Office: McLean Hosp 115 Mill St Belmont MA 02178-1041

POPE, INGRID BLOOMQUIST, sculptor, lecturer, poet; b. Arvika, Sweden, Apr. 2, 1918; came to U.S., 1928; father U.S. citizen.; d. Oscar Emanuel and Gerda (Henningson) Brostrom; m. Howard Richard Bloomquist, Feb. 14, 1941 (dec. Nov. 1982); children: Dennis Howard, Diane Cecile Connelly, Laurel Ann Shields; m. Marvin Hoyle Pope, Mar. 9, 1985. BA cum laude, Manhattanville Coll., 1979, MA in Humanities, 1981; MA in Religion, Yale Div. Sch. Yale U., 1984. lectr. Nat. Assn. Am. Pen Women, Greenwich, Soroptimist Club, Greenwich, Greenwich Travel Club, Ch. Women United Greenwich, 1st Congl. Ch., Scarsdale, N.Y., 2d Congl. Ch., Greenwich, 1st Congl. Ch., Stamford, Conn., 1st Ch. of Round Hill, St. Mary Ch., Greenwich. Exhbns. include Manhattanville Coll., Purchase, N.Y., Yale Div. Sch., Ch. of Sweden in N.Y.C., Greenwich Arts Coun., Greenwich Arts Soc., First Ch. of Round Hill; author: (poems) Musings, 1994. Past bd. dirs. N.Y.C. Mission Soc., Greenwich YWCA, Greenwich Acad. Mother's Assn.; past trustee First Ch. Round Hill, Greenwich, mem.; pres. Ch. Women United, Greenwich, 1989-91; bd. dirs. Greenwich Chaplaincy. Mem. AAUW, Nat. Assn. Pen Women (v.p.), English Speaking Union, Yale Club N.Y.C. and Greenwich, Stanwich Club, Acad. Am. Poets, Nat. Mus. of Women in the Arts. Home: 704 Cutlass Austin TX 78734 also: 704 Cutlass Austin TX 78734 *I need to share my feelings deep inside be it in verse or prose or form or line. I need to say it, do it, show, or write and so creatively I try to do my best. I lift up brush and paint a scene, I struggle with a stone or paint in clay or write my verse just as I do today.*

POPE, JEROME W., lawyer; b. Chgo., July 30, 1951. BS summa cum laude, Bradley U., 1973; JD with honors, DePaul U., 1976. Bar: Ill. 1976, U.S. Dist. Ct. (no. dist.) Ill. 1977, U.S. Ct. Appeals (7th cir.) 1978. Ptnr. Winston & Strawn, Chgo. Mem. ABA, Ill. State Bar Assn., Chgo. Bar Assn. Office: Winston & Strawn 35 W Wacker Dr Chicago IL 60601-1614*

POPE, JOHN CHARLES, airline company executive; b. Newark, Mar. 30, 1949; s. John Aris Coutant and Eleanor Laura (Hillman) P. BA, Yale U., 1971; MBA, Harvard U., 1973. Dir. profit analysis and capital analysis GM, N.Y.C., 1973-77; sr. v.p. fin., treas., chief fin. officer Am. Airlines, Inc., AMR Corp., Dallas-Fort Worth, 1977-88; exec. v.p., chief fin. officer UAL Corp., United Airlines (subs.), Chgo., 1988-91, pres., COO, 1991-94; bd. dirs. Fed. Mogul Corp., Detroit; trustee Sta. WTTW, Chgo. Mem. Air Transport Assn. (chmn. fin. com.). Home: 810 S Ridge Rd Lake Forest IL 60045-2756 Office: United Airlines Inc PO Box 66100 AMF Ohare IL 60666*

POPE, JOHN EDWIN, III, newspaper sports editor; b. Athens, Ga., Apr. 11, 1928; s. Henry Louis and Rose (McAfee) P. B.A. in Journalism, U. Ga., 1948. Sports editor Banner-Herald, Athens, Ga., 1944-48; So. sports editor UPI, Atlanta, 1948-50; sports writer Atlanta Constn., 1950-54; exec. sports editor Atlanta Jour., 1954-56; asst. sports editor Miami (Fla.) Herald, 1956-67, sports editor, 1967—. Author: Football's Greatest Coaches, 1956, Baseball's Greatest Managers, 1960, Encyclopedia of American Greyhound Racing, 1963, Ted Williams: The Golden Year, 1970, (with Norm Evans) On the Line, 1976, The Edwin Pope Collection, 1988; contbr. articles to popular mags. and Ency. Brittanica, World Book. Recipient Bill Corum Meml. award Thoroughbred Racing Assn., 1962, top sports column award Nat. Headliners Club, 1962, 79, 86, eclipse award Thoroughbred Racing Assn., 1986, 82, 86, Red Smith award AP Sports Editors, 1989; named to Internat. Churchmen's Sports Hall of Fame, 1976, nat. Sportswriters and Sportscasters Assn. Hall of Fame, 1994, Fla. Sports Hall of Fame, 1996. Mem. Profl. Football Writers Am. (pres. 1968-69), Football Writers Assn. Am., Golf Writers Am., U.S. Basketball Writers, Basketball Writers Am., Nat. Turf Writers, U.S. Tennis Writers. Presbyterian. Office: Miami Herald 1 Herald Plz Miami FL 33132-1693

POPE, JOHN M., journalist; b. Hattiesburg, Miss., Nov. 5, 1948; s. Paul M. Jr. and Mary Lee (Scott) P.; m. Diana Pinckley, May 19, 1984. BA cum laude, U. Tex., 1970, MA, 1972. Copy editor The States-Item, New Orleans, 1972-73, reporter, 1973-80; reporter The Times-Picayune, New Orleans, 1980-86, med.-health reporter, 1986—. Co-author: American First Ladies: Their Lives and Their Legacy, 1996. Recipient Frank Allen award La.-Miss. AP, 1989, Med. Writing award La. State Med. Soc., 1990. Mem. Soc. Profl. Journalists, Nat. Assn. Sci. Writers, Press Club New Orleans (4 1st pl. awards 1978-87, Alex Waller award 1987), Phi Beta Kappa. Avocations: running, travel, aerobics. Office: The Times-Picayune 3800 Howard Ave New Orleans LA 70140-1097

POPE, JOHN W., retail executive; b. 1924. With Pope's 5$5 Stores, 1944-57; with Variety Wholesalers, Inc., Raleigh, N.C., pres. Office: Variety Wholesalers Inc 3401 Gresham Lake Rd Raleigh NC 27615-4111*

POPE, KERIG RODGERS, magazine executive; b. Waukesha, Wis., Sept. 30, 1935; s. Kerig James Pope and Mildred (Offerman) Troemel; m. Claudia T. Koralewski, Nov. 1961 (div. 1975); children—Kerig William, Giles Thomas; m. Beth Leslie Kasik, May 24, 1980; children: Kolin Jared, Zoe Alissa. Grad., Art Inst. Chgo., 1958. Designer Jack Denst Wallpaper Designs, Chgo., 1958-60; designer Continental Casualty Ins. Co., Chgo., 1960-62, Leo Burnett Advt. Agy., Chgo., 1962-63; art dir. Mercury Records Corp., Chgo., 1963-66; mng. art dir. Playboy mag., Chgo., 1966—. Exhibited in group shows Whitney Mus. Am. Art, N.Y.C., 1969, Mus. Contemporary Art, Chgo., 1972, Bienal de Sao Paulo, Brazil, 1973, Museo de Arte Moderno, Mexico City, 1974, Nat. Collection Fine Arts, Washington, 1979, Moderno, Mexico City, 1974; represented in permanent collections Nat. Collection Fine Arts, Washington, Mus. Contemporary Art, Chgo., Smart Mus., U. Chgo. Recipient silver medal Communigraphics, N.Y.C., 1971, gold medal, 1971, 72; award of excellence Soc. Publ. Designers, 1979, 4 awards of excellence Design Ann., 1984, Silver medal Illustrators 29, 1986, Silver medal Soc. of Illustrators, 1988. Mem. Soc. Illustrators (gold medal 1981, 84, 91), Art Dirs. Club N.Y., Soc. Typog. Arts, Soc. Publ. Arts (3 Silver awards 1987). Club: Arts (Chgo.). Office: Playboy Enterprises Inc 680 N Lake Shore Dr Chicago IL 60611-4402

POPE, LAURENCE E., II, ambassador; b. New Haven, Conn., Sept. 24, 1945; m. Elizabeth Harris; 2 children. BA, Bowdoin Coll. Joined Fgn. Svc., Dept. State, 1969; vice consul Fgn. Svc., Dept. State, Saigon, Vietnam, 1970-72; polit. officer Fgn. Svc., Dept. State, Rabat, 1973, Tripoli, 1973-76; desk officer Fgn. Svc., Dept. State, Lebanon, 1977-78; Mid. East specialist Bur. Internat. Orgn. Affairs Dept. State, 1979-81; polit. counselor Dept. State, Tunis, 1981; dep. chief of mission Dept. State, Manama, 1985-86; dir. office No. Gulf affairs Dept. State, 1987-90, assoc. coordinator for counterterrorism, 1991-93; U.S. amb. to Chad N'Djamena, 1993-96. Contbr. articles on Mid. East policy to profl. jours. Una Chapman Cox fellow. Mem. Am. Fgn. Svc. Assn. Office: Ave Felix Eboue BP 413, N'Djamena Chad

POPE, LISTON, JR., writer, journalist; b. New Haven, Dec. 26, 1943; s. Liston and Bennie (Purvis) P. BA in English, Duke U., 1965; postgrad., Sorbonne, Paris, 1965-70, U. Vienna, 1966-67. Probation officer Bronx (N.Y.) Supreme Ct., 1972-73; freelance journalist, 1972—; war correspondent World Coun. of Chs., Beirut, 1978-79, Nat. Cath. News Svc., Managua, Nicaragua, 1983-84; radio prodr. Pacifica Radio, N.Y.C., 1983-90; critic art/lit. Pacifica News, N.Y.C., 1984-89; press agent Liston Pope & Assocs., N.Y.C., 1983-90; media dir. Casa Nicaragua, N.Y.C., 1983-90. Author: Redemption: A Novel of War in Lebanon, 1994, Living Like the Saints: A Novel of Nicaragua, 1996, (plays) Somoza's Niece, 1987, Oratorio, 1987, Canto Epico, 1989. Vis., supporting vol. Meml. Sloan-Kettering, 1972-78; recreation dir., tutor Cath. Guardian Group Home, 1975-90; life skills tchr. Harlem I Men's Shelter, N.Y.C., 1991-93; AIDS support worker St. Vincent's Supportive Care, Bellevue Visitation Program, Bellevue Pediatrics. Recipient Narrative Poetry award N.Y. Poetry Soc., 1972, Grand prize Am. Poetry Assn., 1986, Poetry award Nat. Libr. of Poetry, 1993. Home and Office: 126 W 73rd St Apt 11A New York NY 10023-3031

POPE, MARVIN HOYLE, language educator, writer; b. Durham, N.C., June 23, 1916; s. Charles Edgar and Bessie Cleveland Sorrell Pope; m. Helen Thompson, Sept. 4, 1948 (dec. Feb. 1979); m. Ingrid Brostrom Bloomquist, Mar. 9, 1985. AB, Duke U., 1938, AM, 1939; PhD, Yale U., 1949. Instr. dept. religion Duke U., Durham, 1947-49; asst. prof. Hebrew Yale U., New Haven, 1949-55, assoc. prof., 1955-64, prof. Semitic langs. and lit., 1964-86, prof. emeritus, sr. rsch. scholar, 1986—; Haskell lectr. Oberlin Coll., 1971, vis. lectr. Cath. U. Lublin, Poland, 1977, Fulbright lectr. U. Aleppo, Syria, 1980; Wickenden lectrs. Miami U., Oxford, Ohio, 1982; Fulbright Rsch. scholar Inst. Ugaritforschung U. Muenster, Germany, 1986, 90; Hooker disting. vis. prof. McMaster U., Hamilton, Ont. Can., 1986; dir. Hebrew Union Coll. Bibl. and Archeol. Sch., Jerusalem, 1966-67; trustee Albright Inst. Archeol. Rsch., Jerusalem; fellow Pierson Coll. Yale U. Author: El in the Ugaritic Texts, 1955; The Book of Job, 1973, Song of Songs, 1977 (Nat. Religious Book award 1978), Syrien Die Mythologie der Ugariter und Phoenizier, 1962, Collected Essays, 1994; contbr. articles to scholarly jours. and dictionaries. Mem. Revised Standard Version Bible com. Nat. Coun. Chs., 1960—; mem. First Ch. Round Hill. With USAF, 1941-45, PTO. Nat. Endowment for Humanities Rsch. grantee, 1980—. Mem. Am. Oriental Soc., Am. Schs. Oriental Rsch., Soc. Bibl. Lit., Am. Soc. Study Religions, Columbia U. Seminar for Study of Hebrew Bible, Yale Club, Oriental Club New Haven, Mory's Club, Stanwich Country Club, Phi Beta Kappa. Home: 538 Round Hill Rd Greenwich CT 06831-2641

POPE, MICHAEL THOR, chemistry educator; b. Exeter, Devon, Eng., Apr. 14, 1933; came to U.S. 1962; naturalized, 1992; s. Hector Maurice and Edith Mary (Hewett) P.; m. Ann Mavis Potter, July 12, 1957; children—Gregory, Lucy. B.A., Oxford U., 1954, D.Phil., 1957. Postdoctoral, Boston U., Mass., 1957-59; research chemist Laporte Chems., Luton, Eng., 1959-62; asst. prof. Georgetown U., Washington, 1962-67, assoc. prof., 1967-73, prof., 1973—, dept. chair, 1990—; vis. prof. Tech. U., Vienna, Austria, 1970-71, Free U. of Berlin, 1979, Northeast Normal U., Changchun, China,

1985, U. Umeå, U. Bielefeld, Germany; prof. associé U. Pierre et Marie Curie, Paris, 1979. Author: Heteropoly and Isopoly Oxometalates, 1983, Polyoxometalates: From Platonic Solids to Anti-Retroviral Activity, 1994; contbr. articles to profl. publs. Recipient Sr. U.S. Scientist award Alexander von Humboldt Found., 1989-90; Petroleum Research Fund Internat. award fellow, 1970-71; Research grantee NSF, NIH, Petroleum Research Fund, Office Naval Research, Army Research Office, Air Force Office of Sci. Research. Mem. Royal Soc. Chemistry (London), Am. Chem. Soc., Sigma Xi (chpt. pres. 1969-70). Episcopalian. Avocations: music, art. Office: Georgetown Univ Chemistry Dept Washington DC 20057-1227

POPE, RANDALL RAY, retired national park superintendent; b. Durham, Kans., Oct. 15, 1932; s. Reuben S. and Enid Lillian (Powers) P.; m. Kathleen V. Higer, Feb. 23, 1958; children: Mark Randall, Renee Lynn Pope Polenske. BS in Landscape Architecture, Kans. State U., 1959. Cert. landscape arch., Nebr. State Bd. Landscape Archs., 1968. Landscape architect Midwest regional office Nat. Pk. Svc., Omaha, 1959-61, 65-69; pk. landscape architect Grand Teton Nat. Pk. Nat. Pk. Svc., Moose, Wyo., 1961-65; supt. Herbert Hoover Nat. Hist. Site Nat. Pk. Svc., West Branch, Iowa, 1969-71; supt. Ozark Nat. Scenic Riverway Nat. Pk. Svc., Van Buren, Mo., 1971-76; dep. regional dir. Midwest regional office Nat. Pk. Svc., Omaha, 1976-87; supt. Great Smoky Mountains Nat. Pk. Nat. Pk. Svc., Gatlinburg, Tenn., 1987-93; ret., 1993. Counselor Boy Scouts Am., West Branch, Van Buren, 1970-76; bd. dirs. Foothills Land Conservancy, 1994—. With USN, 1951-55. Mem. Am. Soc. Landscape Archs., Rotary (Gatlinburg), Lions (instl. rep. 1970-71, 1st, 2d, 3d v.p., pres. Sunrise club 1986-87), Gamma Sigma Delta. Avocations: hiking, photography, gardening, fishing. Home: 845 Vixen Run Gatlinburg TN 37738-6345

POPE, RICHARD M., rheumatologist; b. Chgo., Jan. 10, 1946. Student, Procopius Coll., 1963-65, U. Ill., 1965-66; MD, Loyola U., 1970. Diplomate Am. Bd. Internal Medicine. Intern in medicine Med. Ctr. Michael Reese Hosp., Chgo., 1970-71, resident in internal medicine, 1971-72; fellow in rheumatology U. Wash., Seattle, 1972-74; asst. clin. prof. medicine U. Hawaii, 1974-77; asst. prof. medicine U. Tex. Health Sci. Ctr., San Antonio, 1976-81, assoc. prof. medicine, 1981-85; assoc. prof. medicine Northwestern U. Med. Sch., 1985-88, prof. medicine, 1988—; attending physician Northwestern Meml. Hosp., Chgo., 1985—, VA Lakeside Med. Ctr., Chgo., 1985—, Rehab. Inst. Chgo., 1985—; chief divsn. rheumatology VA Lakeside Med. Ctr., 1985-91, divsn. arthritis-connective tissue diseases Northwestern U. and Northwestern Meml. Hosp., 1989—, Northwestern Med. Faculty Found., 1989—; mem. program com. Ctrl. Soc. Clin. Rsch., 1987, ctrl. region Am. Rheumatism Assn., 1987; mem. sci. com. Ill. chpt. Arthritis Found., 1988-1992, bd. dirs., 1990—, mem. chpt. review grants subcom., 1983-88, chmn. chpt. rsch. grant subcom., 1986-88, mem. rsch. com., 1986-88; mem. site visit teams NIH, 1986, 87, 89; cons. reviewer VA Merit Review Bd., 1984, 87, 91; cons. reviewer Arthritis Soc. Can., 1986, 87; mem. editorial adv. bd. Arthritis and Rheumatism Jour. Lab. and Clin. Medicine, 1992—. Author: (with others) The Science and Practice of Clinical Medicine, 1979, Proceedings of the University of South Florida International Symposium in the Biomedical Sciences, 1984, Concepts in Immunopathology, 1985, Biology Based Immunomodulators in the Therapy of Rheumatic Diseases, 1986, Primer on the Rheumatic Diseases, 1988; contbr. numerous articles to profl. jours. With U.S. Army, 1974-76. Anglo-Am. Rheumatology fellow, 1983. Mem. Am. Coll. Physicians, Am. Coll. Rheumatology (councillor ctrl. region coun. 1990—, program com. 1983-86, 91), Am. Assn. Immunologists, Am. Fedn. Clin. Rsch., Am. Soc. Clin. Investigation, Lupus Found. Ill. (mem. adv. bd. 1990-93), Chgo. Rheumatism Assn. (pres. 1991-93), Ctrl. Soc. Clin. Investigation, Soc. Irish and Am. Rheumatologists (sec., treas. 1989-93), Univ. Rheumatology Coun. Chgo., Alpha Omega Alpha. Achievements include research in pathophysiology of rheumatoid arthritis, T cell activation, T cell receptor, macrophage gene expression. Office: Northwestern U Multipurpose Arthritis Ctr 303 E Chicago Ave Chicago IL 60611-3008

POPE, ROBERT DANIEL, lawyer; b. Screven, Ga., Nov. 29, 1948; s. Robert Verlyn and Mae (McKey) P.; m. Teresa Ann Mullis, Jan. 26, 1981; children: Robert Daniel Jr., Veronica Teres, Jonathan Chase, Byron Christopher, Jessica Victoria. BS in Criminal Justice magna cum laude, Valdosta (Ga.) State Coll., 1975; JD, John Marshall Law Sch., Savannah, Ga., 1980. Bar: Ga. 1981, U.S. Dist. Ct. (no., mid. and so. dist.) Ga. 1983, U.S. Ct. Appeals Ga. 1982. Pvt. practice Cartersville, 1981—; mem. Valdosta Indigent Def. Atty. Panel, 1981-83, Bartow County Indigent Def. Panel, Cartersville, 1987-91, So. Dist. of Ga. Indigent Def. Panel, Brunswick, 1982-84; mem. Cobb County Cir. Defender's Panel for Indigent Criminal Def., Marietta, Ga., 1986—. Recognized as one of most successful criminal def. lawyers Cobb County Cir. Defenders Office, 1994. Mem. Ga. Assn. Criminal Def. Lawyers, Ga. Bar Assn. (criminal law sect.), Am. Criminal Justice Orgn. (Valdosta chpt. pres. 1974-75). Home: 74 Spruce Ln Cartersville GA 30120 Office: 140 W Cherokee Ave Cartersville GA 30120

POPE, ROBERT DEAN, lawyer; b. Memphis, Mar. 10, 1945; s. Ben Duncan and Phyllis (Drenner) P.; m. Elizabeth Dante Cohen, June 26, 1971; 1 child, Justin Nicholas Nathanson. AB, Princeton U., 1967; Diploma in Hist. Studies, Cambridge U., 1971; JD, Yale U., 1972, PhD, 1976. Bar: Va. 1974, D.C. 1980. Assoc. Hunton & Williams, Richmond, Va., 1974-80; ptnr. Hunton & Williams, Richmond, 1980—. Contbg. author: Disclosure Rules of Counsel in State and Local Government Securities Offerings, 2d edit., 1994. Mem. adv. com. Va. Sec. of Health and Human Svcs. on Continuing Care Legislation, 1992—; mem. Anthony Commn. on Pub. Fin.; adv. coun. dept. history Princeton U., 1987-91. Mem. Govt. Fin. Officers Assn. (com. on govtl. debt and fiscal policy), Va. Bar Assn. (chmn. legal problems of elderly 1982-88), Nat. Assn. Bond Lawyers (treas. 1984-85, sec. 1985-86, pres. 1987-88, bd. dirs. 1982-89, Bernard P. Friel medal for contbns. to pub. fin. 1994), Am. Acad. Hosp. Attys., Yale Law Sch. Assn. (exec. com. 1985-88), Bond Club Va. (bd. dirs. 1990—, v.p. 1993-94, pres. 1994-95), NCCJ (Richmond area bd.), Phi Beta Kappa. Republican. Episcopalian. Avocations: history, golf, music, book reviews. Home: 8707 Ruggles Rd Richmond VA 23229-7918 Office: Hunton & Williams PO Box 1535 951 E Byrd St Richmond VA 23219-4040

POPE, ROBERT E(UGENE), fraternal organization administrator; b. Wellington, Kans., Sept. 10, 1931; s. Samuel E. and Opal Irene (Davis) P. BSChemE with honors, U. Kans., 1952, MS, 1958. Registered profl. engr., Kans. Asst. instr. U. Kans., Lawrence, 1952-56; lab. technician Monsanto Co., St. Louis, 1952; project engr. Mallinckrodt, Inc., St. Louis, 1953-59; traveling sec. Theta Tau, St. Louis, 1959-62, exec. sec., 1963-84, exec. dir., 1984—. Author: Years of Progress, 1995; (with C.E. Wales) Designing a Rush Program, 3d edit., 1996; mem. bd. editors (mag.) The Gear of Theta Tau, 1993—. Carillonneur, Grace United Meth. Ch., St. Louis, 1985—, chmn. adminstrv. coun., 1991-95. Mem. Am. Soc. Assn. Execs., Am. Soc. Engring. Edn., St. Louis Soc. Assn. Execs., Profl. Fraternity Execs. Assn. (charter), Profl. Fraternity Assn. (exec. sec. 1977-86, Disting. Svc. award 1995), Engrs. Club St. Louis, Creve Coeur Country Club, Tau Beta Pi, Phi Lambda Upsilon, Omicron Delta Kappa. Democrat. United Methodist. Avocations: physical fitness, sports, photography. Home: 13 Sona Ln Saint Louis MO 63141-7742 Office: Theta Tau Ctrl Office 655 Craig Rd Ste 128 Saint Louis MO 63141-7168

POPE, ROBERT GLYNN, telecommunications executive; b. Greenville, Tex., Dec. 5, 1935; s. Edwin R. P.; m. Shirley Hall, Dec. 30, 1958; children: Kenneth, Richard, David. BSME, So. Meth. U., 1958. Registered profl. engr. Chief engr. Southwestern Bell Telephone Co., Houston, 1973-77; v.p. staff Tex. Southwestern Bell Telephone Co., Dallas, 1977-78, v.p. centralized svcs., 1978-80; v.p. residence and pub. svcs. Southwestern Bell Telephone Co., St. Louis, 1980-81, v.p. transition, 1981-83, v.p. strategic planning, 1983; v.p. corp. devel. Southwestern Bell Corp., St. Louis, 1984-86, vice-chmn. corp. devel., 1986-88, vice chmn. corp. devel., chief fin. officer, 1988-90, vice chmn., chief fin. officer, 1990-94, now vice chmn., bd. dirs.; mem. Adv. Bd. Battery Ventures; bd. dirs. Boatmen's Bancshares Corp., Cullen/Frost Bankers, Inc. Trustee Maryville U.; mem. governing bd. Luth. Med. Ctr. With U.S. Army, 1959. Mem. NSPE, Mo. Soc. Profl. Engrs., Media Club St. Louis, Univ. Club, Golf Club Okla., Old Warson Country Club, St. Louis Club. Avocations: golf, coin collecting, fishing. Office: Southwestern Bell Corp PO Box 2933 175 E Houston 6th Fl San Antonio TX 78299-2933*

POPE, STEPHEN BAILEY, engineering educator; b. Nottingham, England, Nov. 26, 1949; came to U.S., 1977; s. Joseph Albert and Evelyn Alice (Gallagher) P.; m. Linda Ann Syatt, Aug. 16, 1979; children: Sarah Evelyn, Samuel Joseph. BS in Engring., Imperial Coll., London, 1971; MS, Imperial Coll., 1972, PhD, 1976; DSc in Engring., U. London, 1986. Rsch. asst. Imperial Coll., London, 1972-77; rsch. fellow Calif. Inst. Tech., Pasadena, 1977-78; asst. prof. MIT, Cambridge, Mass., 1978-81; assoc. prof. MIT, 1981, Cornell U., Ithaca, N.Y., 1982-87; prof. engring. Cornell U., 1987—; cons. GE, Schenectady, N.Y., 1984—, GM, Warren, Mich., 1985—, Allison Engine Co., Indpls., 1986—. Assoc. editor Physics of Fluids A; contbr. articles to profl. jours. Overseas fellow Churchill Coll, Cambridge, Eng., 1989; awards NSF, Army Rsch. Office, Air Force Office Sci. Rsch., U.S. Dept. Energy. Fellow Am. Phys. Soc., Combustion Inst. Office: Cornell U Upson Hall Ithaca NY 14853

POPE, THEODORE CAMPBELL, JR., utilities executive, consultant; b. Sanford, Fla., Oct. 28, 1932; s. Theodore Campbell and Mary (Cook) P.; m. Edith L. Carlton; children: Theodore, Jeffrey, Laura; m. Jeris Julia Dawson, Nov. 21, 1973. BSME, U. Fla., 1954, MBA, 1959. Registered profl. engr., Fla.; diplomate Am. Acad. Environ. Engrs. Chief mech. engr. Orlando Utilities, 1959-64, plant supt., 1964-67, dir. elec. generation, 1967-70, asst. mgr. elec. ops., 1970-72, mgr water ops., 1972-84, asst. gen. mgr., 1984-86, gen. mgr., 1986-92; pres. Ted Pope Enterprises, Orlando, 1992—. Contbr. articles to profl. jours.; patentee water treatment process. Bd. dirs. United Fund Brevard County; bd. dirs. Econ. Devel. Commn. of Mid-Fla., Orlando; bd. dirs., pres. Ctrl. Fla. Fair; trustee United Arts of Ctrl. Fla. 1st lt. U.S. Army, 1955-57. Recipient Abel Waldman award InterAm. Assn. San. Engrs., 1982. Mem. Am. Water Works Assn. (hon.; Disting. Pub. Svc. award 1991, George Warren Fuller award, chair emeritus Rsch. Found.), Greater Orlando Area C. of C. (pres. 1990-91), Fla. Engring. Soc. (Engr. of Yr.), Fla. Conservation Assn., Rotary Club of Orlando, Smyrna Yacht Club, Country Club of Orlando, Univ. Club, Delta Sigma Pi. Democrat. Avocations: sailing, golfing, travel, hunting, fishing. Home and Office: 39605 Swift Rd Eustis FL 32736-9510

POPE, THOMAS HARRINGTON, JR., lawyer; b. Kinards, S.C., July 28, 1913; s. Thomas H. and Marie (Gary) P.; m. Mary Waties Lumpkin, Jan. 3, 1940; children: Mary Waties (Mrs. Robert H. Kennedy Jr.), Thomas Harrington III, Gary Tusten. A.B., The Citadel, 1935, LL.D., 1977; LL.B., U. S.C., 1938; grad., Command and Gen. Staff Coll., 1951; LL.D., Newberry Coll., 1969. Bar: S.C. 1938, U.S. Supreme Ct. 1962. Practice in Newberry, 1938—; sr. ptnr. Pope and Hudgens, P.A.; spl. circuit judge Richland and Lexington counties, 1955-56; dir. emeritus the Citizens and So. Nat. Bank S.C., Carolina Motor Club; dir. Newberry Fed. Savs. Bank; mem. S.C. Ports Authority, 1957-65; mem. Jud. Coun. S.C., 1957—, chmn., 1979-83; mem. S.C. Archives Commn., 1965-75, vice chmn., 1974-75. Author: The History of Newberry County, South Carolina, Vol. 1, 1973, Vol. 2, 1992; co-author: The History of the 107th Separate Coast Artillery Battalion (AA), 1982. Chmn. Newberry County Sesqui-Centennial Commn., 1939; Mem. S.C. Ho. of Reps. from Newberry County, 1936-40, 45-50, speaker, 1949-50; chmn. S.C. Democratic Party, 1958-60; del. at large Dem. Nat. Conv., 1956, 60; pres. S.C. Dem. Conv., 1958, 62; Mem. S.C. Tricentennial Commn., 1966-71; Trustee U. of South, 1965-70, Newberry Coll., 1965-75; chmn. S.C. Found. Ind. Colls.; bd. visitors The Citadel, 1939-40, 46. Served to lt. col. AUS, 1941-45, ETO; brig. gen. ret. S.C. N.G. Recipient Algernon Sydney Sullivan award Newberry Coll., 1976, Durant Disting. Pub. Svc. award S.C. Bar Found., 1983, The Compleat Lawyer award Law Sch., U. S.C., 1992, U. S.C. Disting. Alumnus, 1994. Fellow Am. Coll. Trial Lawyers, Am. Bar Found., S.C. Bar Found.; mem. ABA, S.C. Bar Assn. (pres. 1964, chmn. exec. com. 1956-58), Newberry County Bar Assn. (pres. 1951), Am. Law Inst. (life), John Belton O'Neall Inn of Ct., So. Hist. Assn., Soc. Colonial Wars, Nat. Trust Historic Preservation (adv. bd. 1967-72), U. S.C. Soc. (curator 1968-72), S.C. Hist. Soc. (curator 1968-74), Newberry County Hist. Soc. (pres. 1966), Mason (grand master S.C. 1958-60, Albert Gallatin Mackey medal Grand Lodge S.C. 1965, Henry Price medal Grand Lodge Mass. 1960), Newberry Country Club, Palmetto Club (Columbia), Pine Tree Hunt Club (Columbia), Phi Beta Kappa, Omicron Delta Kappa, Phi Delta Phi, Phi Kappa Phi, Alpha Tau Omega. Episcopalian (sr. warden 1963-65, 70). Home: 1700 Boundary St Newberry SC 29108-3912 Office: 1508 College St Newberry SC 29108-2749

POPE, TIM L., state legislator, consultant; b. Mooresville, Ind., Oct. 2, 1957; s. Eugene L. and Mary L. (Clark) P.; m. LaDonna K. Freeman, Aug. 6, 1976; children: Melissa, Andrea, Erica. Sales mgr. Generay Sales, Martinsville, Ind., 1976-80, Royal Mobile Homes, Oklahoma City, 1980-86; counselor Draughon Coll., Oklahoma City, 1986-88; mem. Okla. Ho. of Reps., Oklahoma City, 1988—. County chmn. Canadian County (Okla.) Reps., 1992; bd. dirs. Mustang (Okla.) Handicapped Assn., 1989—. Recipient Taxpayers Friend award Okla. Taxpayers Union, 1993. Mem. Mustang Kiwanis. Home: 11503 Belle Blvd Mustang OK 73064-9795 Office: 504 State Capital Bldg Oklahoma City OK 73105

POPE, WILLIAM L., lawyer, judge; b. Brownsville, Tex., Nov. 5, 1960; s. William E. and Maria Antonieta P. AA, Tex. Southmost Coll., 1980; postgrad., U. Tex., 1980-81, Tex. Christian U., 1982, Tex. Coll. Osteo. Medicine, 1982-83; JD, Baylor U., 1986. Bar: Tex. 1986, U.S. Dist. Ct. (so. dist.) Tex. 1988, U.S. Supreme Ct. 1990. Assoc. Adams & Graham, Harlingen, Tex., 1986-91, ptnr., 1991—; mcpl. ct. judge City of La Feria, Tex., 1987—. Mem. ABA, Tex. State Bar Assn., Cameron County Bar Assn. Mem. Ch. of Christ. Office: Adams & Graham L L P PO Box 1429 Harlingen TX 78551-1429

POPEIL, RON, consumer products company executive; b. Chgo., 1936; s. Sam and Julia P.; children: Kathryn, Shannon, Lauren. Owner Ronco, Inc.; bd. dirs. Mirage Hotel & Casino, Las Vegas; Golden Nugget, Las Vegas. Office: Mirage Resort Inc PO Box 7777 Las Vegas NV 89177*

POPEL, ALEKSANDER S., engineering educator; b. Moscow, Oct. 8, 1945; came to U.S., 1975; s. Samson Popel and Mary Gellershtein; m. Natalya Kalnitskaya, Sept. 17, 1966; 1 child, Julie. MS, Moscow State U., 1967, PhD, 1972. Rsch. scientist Inst. Mechanics, Moscow State U., 1970-75; asst. prof. Tulane U., New Orleans, 1976; rsch. assoc. prof. U. Ariz., Tucson, 1976-80; assoc. prof. U. Houston, 1980-84; assoc. prof. Johns Hopkins U., Balt., 1984-88, prof., 1988—. Editor 2 books; contbr. articles to profl. jours. NIH, NSF grantee. Fellow ASME, Am. Inst. Med. & Biol. Engring.; mem AAAS, Biomed. Engring. Soc. (sr.), Am. Physiol. Soc., Soc. for Indsl. and Applied Math. Office: Johns Hopkins U Sch Medicine Dept Biomed Engring Baltimore MD 21205

POPENOE, HUGH LLYWELYN, soils educator; b. Tela, Honduras, Aug. 28, 1929; s. Frederick Wilson and Dorothy (Hughes) P. BS, U. Calif., Davis, 1951; PhD, U. Fla., 1960. Mem. faculty U. Fla., Gainesville, 1960—, dir. ctr. tropical agr., 1965—, dir. internat. programs, 1966-92, dir. Fla. Sea Grant Coll., 1971-81; bd. dirs. Escuela Agricola Panamericana, Zamorano, Honduras, Orgn. Tropical Studies. Contbr. numerous articles to profl. jours. Chari Assn. U.S. Univ. Dirs. Internat. Agrl. Programs, 1969-70, Joint Rsch. Com. Bd. Internat. Food and Agrl. Devel., 1977-82, Joint Com. Agrl. Rsch. and Devel., 1982-86; chair numerous reports Bd. Sci. and Tech. in Devel., 1979-84; trustee Internat. Found. for Sci., Stockholm, 1984-87; mem. sci. liaison officer Internat. Inst. for Tropical Agr., Nigeria, 1983-88; mem. adv. com. internat. programs NSF, 1985-87; bd. dirs. League for Internat. Food Edn., 1976-87. With U.S. Army, 1952-54. Recipient Sci. Pioneer prize Egyptian Vet. Assn. for Buffalo Devel., 1985. Fellow AAAS, Am. Soc. Agronomy, Am. Geog. Soc., Internat. Soil Sci. Soc., Am. Water Buffalo Assn. (pres. 1988—), Cosmos Club. Office: U Fla 3028 McCarty Gainesville FL 32611

POPENOE, JOHN, horticultural consultant, retired botanical garden administrator; b. L.A., Jan. 24, 1929; s. Paul and Betty (Stankowitch) P.; m. Geraldine V. Mann, June 29, 1952; children: Deborah Irene, Natalie, Juanita, Jennifer. B.S., UCLA, 1950; M.S., U. Md., 1952, Ph.D., 1955. Asst. horticulturist U.S. Dept. Agr., Miami, 1955-58; asso. prof. horticulture Ala. Poly. Inst., 1958-59; assoc. horticulturist U. Fla. Subtropical Experiment Sta., 1960-63; dir. Fairchild Tropical Garden, Miami, 1963-91; horticultural cons., 1991—. Served with U.S. Army, 1952-54. Home: 113 Washington St Hancock MD 21750-1127

POPHAM, ARTHUR COBB, JR., lawyer; b. Louisville, Mar. 31, 1915; s. Arthur C. and Ethel (Estes) P.; m. Mary Corzine, July 6, 1939; children: Carole Popham McKnight, Melinda Popham Benton, Arthur C. III; m. Phoebe T. Kennedy, Nov. 13, 1969. BA, U. Ariz., 1937; JD, U. Mo., 1939. Bar: Mo. 1939, U.S. Dist. Ct. (we. dist.) Mo. 1940. Assoc. Cowgill & Popham, Kansas City, Mo., 1939-40; ptnr. in successive firms to Popham Law Firm, P.C., Kansas City, 1940—, also bd. dirs. Author: Stalking Game From Desert to Tundra, 1986.; contbr. articles on various topics to outdoor mags. Collector, planner Natural History Habitat Groups, Kansas City Mus., 1951-63; pres., bd. dirs. Kansas City Mus. History and Sci., 1952-85. 1st lt., pilot USAAFA, 1942-45. Mem. ABA, Mo. Bar Assn., Kansas City Bar Assn., Boone and Crockett Club (v.p 1970-86) (Missoula, Mont.), Shikar Safari Internat. Club, Camp Fire Club of America (Chappaqua, N.Y.), Sigma Nu, Phi Delta Phi. Avocations: hunting, conservation groups. Home: 5521 Mission Dr Mission Hills KS 66208 Office: Commerce Trust Bldg 922 Walnut St Kansas City MO 64106-1809

POPKIN, DAVID R., academic dean, obstetrician, gynocologist; m. Linda Popkin, 1964; 4 children. Dean U. Saskatchewan Coll. Medicine, Can. Office: Coll Medicine, Health Scis Bldg 107, Wiggins Rd Rm B103, Saskatoon, SK Canada S7N 5E5*

POPKIN, GERRI CHAPPELL, county official; b. Long Branch, N.J., Nov. 21, 1949; d. Percival Henry and Cecelia Lydia (Biertuempfel) Chappell; m. Joel Popkin, Oct. 11, 1970 (div. 1993); children: David Joel, Michael Lee, Jamie Danielle. AA, Monmouth Coll., 1973; BA, Thomas Edison State Coll., 1985. Registered pub. purchasing ofcl.; cert. profl. pub. buyer, county purchasing ofcl., pub. mgr. Dir. consumer affairs County of Monmouth, Freehold, N.J., 1983, 86, dir. purchasing, 1987—; sr. field rep. N.J. State Lottery Dept. Treasury, Trenton, N.J., 1984-85. Councilwoman Boro of Neptune City, N.J., 1982-88; candidate N.J. State Senate, 1987; teamwalker March of Dimes Walkathon, 1984, 85, 94; rep. mcpl. chairperson Neptune City Reps., 1989—; pres. Monmouth County Fedn. Rep. Women, Monmouth, N.J., 1987-89; bd. dir. Women's Political Caucus of N.J., 1993—; legis. chair WPC-N.J., Monmouth-Ocean County Devel. Coun. Mem. Nat. Inst. Govtl. Purchasing, N.J. Legis. Agenda for Women (trustee 1993), Thomas Edison Alumni Assn., Monmouth Coll. Alumni Assn. Methodist. Avocations: reading, writing, theatre, movies, walking. Home: 50 Sylvania Ave Neptune City NJ 07753-6764 Office: County of Monmouth Hall of Records Freehold NJ 07728

POPLE, JOHN ANTHONY, chemistry educator; b. Burnham, Somerset, Eng., Oct. 31, 1925; s. Herbert Keith and Mary Frances (Jones) P.; m. Joy Cynthia, Sept. 22, 1952; children: Hilary Jane, Adrian John, Mark Stephen, Andrew Keith. BA in Math., Cambridge U., Eng., 1946, MA in Math., 1950; PhD in Math., Cambridge U., 1951. Research fellow Trinity Coll., Cambridge U., Eng., 1951-54, lectr. in math., 1954-58; Ford vis. prof. chemistry Carnegie Inst. Tech., Pitts., 1961-62; Carnegie prof. chem. physics Carnegie-Mellon U., Pitts., 1964-74, J.C. Warner prof., 1974-91; prof. Northwestern U., Evanston, Ill., 1986—. Recipient Wolf Found. Chemistry prize, 1992, Kirkwood medal Am. Chem. Soc., 1994, J.O. Herschfelder Prize in Theoretical Chemistry, Univ. of Wis., Theoretical Chemistry Inst., 1994. Fellow AAAS, Royal Soc. London; mem. NAS (fgn.). Office: Northwestern U Dept Chemistry 2145 Sheridan Rd Evanston IL 60208

POPLER, KENNETH, behavioral healthcare executive, psychologist; b. Bklyn., Nov. 7, 1945; s. Irving and Mildred P.; m. Lois L., Aug. 31, 1969; children: Jonathan, Emily. BA in Psychology, CUNY, 1967; MA in Psychology, New Sch. Social Rsch., N.Y.C., 1969, PhD in Psychology, 1974; MBA, Wagner Coll., 1994. Diplomate Am. Bd. Profl. Psychology. Case worker N.Y.C. Dept. Social Svcs., 1967-70; intern Bklyn. Psychiat. Ctrs., 1970-72; sch. psychologist N.Y.C. Bd. Edn., 1972-73; psychologist Mid Nassau Community Guidance Ctr., Hicksville, N.Y., 1973-77; dir. St. Mary Community Mental Health Ctr., Hoboken, N.J., 1978-81; exec. dir. Staten Island (N.Y.) Mental Health Soc., Inc., 1981—; psychometrician L.I. Hillside Jewish Med. Ctr., Queens, N.Y., 1972-73; sr. psychologist, dir. psychol. svcs. HHC Gouverneur Hosp., N.Y.C., 1973-78; asst. rsch. scientist N.Y. State Psychiat. Inst., N.Y.C., 1971; vol. rsch. Manhattan Sch. for Seriously Disturbed Children, N.Y.C., 1972-73; instr. CUNY Bklyn. Coll. grad. divsn., 1972-73; pvt. practice, N.Y.C., 1976-85; asst. clin. prof. psychiatry Mt. Sinai Med. Sch., N.Y.C., 1978-94. Apptd. N.Y.C. Cmty. Svcs. Bd., 1984—, alcoholism subcom., 1987-91; pres. Coalition of Voluntary Mental Health Agys., Inc., 1991-94; sec. Head Start Sponsoring Bd. Coun. N.Y.C., 1985-92; chmn. Mental Health Coun. S.I., 1987-89, S.I. United Way Execs. Com., 1985. Mem. Rotary Club of Staten Island, Inc. Office: SI Mental Health Soc Inc 669 Castleton Ave Staten Island NY 10301-2028

POPOFF, FRANK PETER, chemical company executive; b. Sofia, Bulgaria, Oct. 27, 1935; came to U.S., 1940; s. Eftim and Stoyanka (Kossoroff) P.; m. Jean Urse; children: John V., Thomas F., Steven M. B.S. in Chemistry, Ind. U., 1957, M.B.A., 1959. With The Dow Chem. Co., Midland, Mich., 1959—, exec. v.p., 1985-87, dir., pres., chief executive officer, 1987-92; chmn., CEO, dir. Dow Chemical Corp., Midland, Mich., 1992—; exec. v.p., then pres. Dow Chem. Europe subs., Horgen, Switzerland, 1976-85; bd. dirs. Dow Corning Corp., Am. Express, Chem. Bank & Trust Co., Chem. Fin. Corp., Midland. Mem. dean's adv. coun. Ind. U.; mem. vis. com. U. Mich. Sch. Bus.; mem. Pres.' Commn. Environ. Quality. Recipient Internat. Palladium medal, 1994, Société de Chimie Industrielle (Am. Section). Mem. Chem. Mfrs. Assn. (bd. dirs.), U.S. Coun. for Internat. Bus., Bus. Roundtable, Conf. Bd., Am. Chem. Soc. Office: Dow Chem Co 2030 Dow Ctr Midland MI 48674*

POPOFSKY, MELVIN LAURENCE, lawyer; b. Oskaloosa, Iowa, Feb. 16, 1936; s. Samuel and Fannye Charlotte (Rosenthal) P.; m. Linda Jane Seltzer, Nov. 25, 1962; children: Mark Samuel, Kaye Sylvia. BA in History summa cum laude, U. Iowa, 1958; BA in Jurisprudence (first class honors), Oxford U., Eng., 1960; LLB cum laude, Harvard U., 1962. Bar: Calif. 1962. Assoc. Heller, Ehrman, White & McAuliffe, San Francisco, 1962-69, ptnr., 1969—, mem. exec. com., 1980-93, co-chair, 1988-93. Contbr. articles to law jours. Bd. dirs. Mt. Zion Hosp., San Francisco, 1982-88, U.S. Dist. Ct. (no. dist.) Calif. Hist. Soc., 1988—, Jewish Home for Aged, San Francisco, 1989—. Rhodes scholar, 1958. Fellow Am. Bar Found., Am. Coll. Trial Lawyers; mem. ABA, Calif. Bar Assn., San Francisco Bar Assn., Bur. Nat. Affairs (adv. bd. antitrust sect.), Calif. Acad. Appellate Lawyers. Democrat. Jewish. Home: 1940 Broadway Apt 10 San Francisco CA 94109-2216 Office: Heller Ehrman 333 Bush St San Francisco CA 94104-2806

POPOV, EGOR PAUL, engineering educator; b. Kiev, Russia, Feb. 19, 1913; s. Paul T. and Zoe (Derabin) P.; m. Irene Zofia Jozefowski, Feb. 18, 1939; children—Katherine, Alexander. B.S., U. Calif., 1933; M.S., Mass. Inst. Tech., 1934; Ph.D., Stanford, 1946. Registered civil, structural and mech. engr., Calif. Structural engr., bldg. designer Los Angeles, 1935-39; asst. prodn. engr. Southwestern Portland Cement Co., Los Angeles, 1939-42; machine designer Goodyear Tire & Rubber Co., Los Angeles, 1942-43; design engr. Aerojet Corp., Calif., 1943-45; asst. prof. civil engring. U. Calif. at Berkeley, 1946-48, assoc. prof., 1948-53, prof., 1953-83, prof. emeritus, 1983—, chmn. structural engring. and structural mechanics div., dir. structural engring. lab., 1956-60; Miller rsch. prof. Miller Inst. Basic Rsch. in Sci., 1968-69. Author: Mechanics of Materials, 1952, 2d edit., 1976, Introduction to Mechanics of Solids, 1968, Engineering Mechanics of Solids, 1990; Contbr. articles profl. jours. Recipient Disting. Tchr. award U. Calif.-Berkeley, 1976-77, Berkeley citation U. Calif.-Berkeley, 1983, Disting. Lectr. award Earthquake Engring. Rsch. Inst., 1993. Fellow AAAS (assoc.), Am. Concrete Inst.; mem. NAE, Am. Soc. Metals, Internat. Assn. Shell Structures (hon. mem.), ASCE (hon. mem., Ernest E. Howard award 1976, J. James R. Cross medal 1979, 82, Nathan M. Newmark medal 1981, Raymond C. Reese rsch. prize 1986, Norman medal 1987, von Karman medal 1989), Soc. Exptl. Stress Analysis (Hetenyi award 1967, William M. Murray medallion 1986), Am. Soc. Engring. Edn. (Western Electric Fund award 1976-77, Disting. Educator award 1979), Soc. Engring. Sci., Internat. Assn. Bridge and Structural Engring., Am. Inst. Steel Constrn. (adv. com. specifications, chmn. subcom. on seismic design), Sigma Xi, Chi Epsilon, Tau Beta Pi. Home: 2600 Virginia St Berkeley CA 94709-1045

POPOVA, NINA, dancer, choreographer, director; b. Novorossisk, USSR, 1922. Ed. in Paris, studied ballet with Olga Preobrajenska, Lubov Egorova,

Anatole Vilzak, Anatole Oboukhov, Igor Schwezoff. Ballet debut with Ballet de la Jeunesse, Paris, London, 1937-39; soloist Original Ballet Russe, 1939-41, Ballet Theatre (now Am. Ballet), 1941-42, Ballet Russe de Monte Carlo, 1943, 47, Ballet Alicia Alonso, Cuba; mem. faculty Sch. Performing Arts, N.Y.C., from 1954; later artistic dir. Houston Ballet, 1975; tchr. Nat. Acad. Arts, Champaign, Ill., also N.Y.C., 1975—, now Eglevsky Ballet Sch., L.I.; tchr. ballet Mexico City, Mex.; asst. choreographer mus. comedy Birmingham So. Coll., Ala., 1960; numerous appearances on Broadway stage, TV; former mem. regular cast Your Show of Shows; currently teaching N.Y.C. Address: 33 Adams St Sea Cliff NY 11579-1614

POPOVICH, PETER STEPHEN, lawyer, former state supreme court chief justice; b. Crosby, Minn., Nov. 27, 1920; s. Peter and Rose Mary (Mehelich) P.; children: Victoria, Dorothy, Stephen, Susan Jane; stepchildren: Michelle, Paul, Stephen; m. Gail Prince Javorina, July 5, 1985. AA, Hibbing (Minn.) Jr. Coll., 1940; BA, U. Minn., 1942; LLB, St. Paul Coll. of Law, 1947; LLD (hon.), William Mitchell Coll. Law, 1991. Bar: Minn. 1947, U.S. Dist. Ct. Minn. 1947, U.S. Supreme Ct. 1956, U.S. Ct. Appeals (8th cir.) 1975. Sr. ptnr. Peterson & Popovich, St. Paul, 1947-83; chief judge Minn. Ct. Appeals, St. Paul, 1983-87; assoc. justice Minn. Supreme Ct., St. Paul, 1987-89, chief justice, 1989-90; ptnr. Briggs & Morgan, St. Paul, 1991—. Chmn. Minn. Statehood Centennial Com., 1955-59; rep. Minn. State Legis., St. Paul, 1953-63. Named Outstanding Minnesotan, Minn. Broadcasters Assn., 1983; recipient Dist. Svc. to Journalism award Minn. Newspaper Assn., 1991, John Finnegan Freedom of Info. award, 1991. Mem. ABA, Minn. Bar Assn. Minn. Hist. Soc. (hon. council). Roman Catholic. Avocations: boating, reading. Home: 2301 River Rd S Lakeland MN 55043-9777 Office: Briggs & Morgan 2200 1st Nat Bank Bldg Saint Paul MN 55101

POPOVICI, ADRIAN, law educator; b. Bucharest, Rumania, Sept. 6, 1942; came to Can., 1951; s. Adrian and Alice (Moruzi) P.; children—Adrian, Alexandra. B.A., Stanislas Coll., Montreal, 1959; B.C.L., McGill U., 1962; D.E.S., U. Paris, 1965. Bar: Que. 1963. Prof. law U. Montreal, Que., Can., 1968—. Author: L'Outrage au Tribunal, 1977, La Couleur du Mandat, 1985; editor: Problèmes de Droit Contemporain, 1974. Roman Catholic. Home: 5589 Canterbury, Montreal, PQ Canada H3T 1S8 Office: U Montreal Faculte de Droit, CP 6128 Succursale A, Montreal, PQ Canada H3C 3J7

POPOVICS, SANDOR, civil engineer, educator, researcher; b. Budapest, Hungary, Dec. 24, 1921; came to U.S., 1957; s. Milan and Erzsebet (Droppa) P.; m. Lea M. Virtanen, Aug. 29, 1960; children: John, Lisa. 1st Degree in Civil Engring., Poly. U., Budapest, Hungary, 1944; Advanced Degree in Civil Engring., Poly. U., 1956; PhD, Purdue U., 1961. Registered profl. engr., Ala., Ariz., Pa. Rsch. engr. Met. Lab., Budapest, 1944-48; adj. prof. Tech. Coll., Budapest, 1949-52; rsch. engr., mgr. Inst. for Bldg. Scis., Budapest, 1949-56; grad. asst. Purdue U., Lafayette, Ind., 1957-59; prof. engring. Auburn (Ala.) U., 1959-69; prof. civil engring. No. Ariz. U., Flagstaff, 1968-76; prof. engring. King Abdulazziz U., Jeddah, Saudi Arabia, 1977-78; Samuel S. Baxter prof. civil engring. Drexel U., Phila., 1979-92, rsch. prof., 1992—; pres. Optimum Engring. Rsch. Author: Fundamentals of Pc Concrete, 1982, Concrete Materials, 1992, others; author more than 200 tech. papers in various langs. Recipient numerous grants and awards. Fellow ASCE (life), Am. Concrete Inst.; mem. ASTM, Ala. Acad. Scis., Ariz. Acad. Scis., Sigma Xi, Chi Epsilon. Avocations: jogging, music, fine art. Home and Office: 283 Congress Ave Lansdowne PA 19050-1206 Office: Drexel U Dept Civil Engring 32d and Chestnut Philadelphia PA 19104

POPP, JAMES ALAN, toxicologist, toxicology executive; b. Salem, Ohio, Mar. 13, 1945; s. John W. and Florence H. (Rowley) P.; m. Gloria Jean Paxton, Aug. 20, 1966; 1 child, Candice Renee. DVM summa cum laude, Ohio State U., 1968; PhD, U. Calif., Davis, 1972. Postdoctoral rsch. fellow Temple U. Sch. Medicine, Phila., 1972-74; asst. prof. U. Fla., Gainesville, 1974-78; scientist Chem. Industry Inst. Toxicology, Research Triangle Park, N.C., 1978-84, dept. head, 1984-93, v.p., 1989-93; v.p. Sterling Winthrop Inc., Collegeville, Pa., 1993-94, Sanofi Winthrop Inc., Collegeville, Pa., 1994—; mem. bd. sci. counselors Nat. Inst. Environ. Health Scis., Research Triangle Park. Editor mouse liver neoplasia Current Perspectives, 1984, mouse liver carcinogenesis Mechanisms and Species Comparisons, 1990. Recipient George H. Scott award Toxicology Forum, 1992; Borden scholar. Mem. Am. Soc. for Investigative Pathology, Am. Assn. Cancer Rsch., Am. Coll. Vet. Pathologists, Soc. for Toxicology, Phi Eta Sigma, Phi Zeta, Phi Kappa Phi. Office: Sanofi Winthrop Inc PO Box 3026 9 Great Valley Pkwy Malvern PA 19355

POPP, NATHANIEL, bishop; b. Aurora, Ill., June 12, 1940; s. Joseph and Vera (Boytor) P. BA, Ill. Benedictine U., 1962; ThM, Pontifical Gregorian U., 1966. Ordained priest, 1966, bishop, 1980. Asst. priest St. Michael Byz Cath. Ch., Aurora, Ill., 1967; parish priest Holy Cross Romanian Orthodox Ch., Hermitage, Pa., 1975-80; aux. bishop Romanian Orthodox Episcopate of Am., Orthodox Ch. in Am., Jackson, Mich., 1980-84, ruling bishop, 1984—; mem. Holy Synod, Orthodox Ch. in Am., Syosset, N.Y., 1980—; participant Monastic Consultation World Coun. Chs., Cairo, 1979, 7th Assembly, Vancouver, Can., 1983. Author: Holy Icons, 1969; working editor: (monthly newspaper) Solia. Trustee Romanian-Am. Heritage Ctr., Grass Lake, Mich.; chmn. bd. dirs. Congress of Romanian Ams., 1990. Mem. Mineral and Rock Soc. Mich. Home: 2522 Grey Tower Rd Jackson MI 49201-9120 Address: PO Box 309 Grass Lake MI 49240-0309

POPPA, RYAL ROBERT, manufacturing company executive; b. Wahpeton, N.D., Nov. 7, 1933; s. Ray Edward and Annabelle (Phillips) P.; m. Ruth Ann Curry, June 21, 1952; children: Sheryl Lynn, Kimberly Marie. BBA, Claremont Men's Coll., 1957. Sales trainee IBM, L.A., 1957-59, sales rep., 1959-62, product mktg. rep., 1963, sales mgr., 1964-66; v.p., gen. mgr. Comml. Computers Inc., L.A., 1966-67; v.p. Greyhound Computer Corp., Chgo., 1967-68, pres., chief exec. officer, bd. dirs., 1969-70; pres., chief exec. officer, bd. dirs., mem. exec. com. Data Processing Fin. & Gen., Hartsdale, N.Y., 1970-72; exec. v.p., chief fin. officer, bd. dirs., mem. exec. com. Mohawk Data Sci. Corp., Utica, N.Y., 1972-73; chmn., pres., chief exec. officer Pertec Computer Corp., L.A., 1973-81, BMC Industries, Inc., St. Paul, 1982-85; pres., chmn., chief exec. officer Storage Tech. Corp., Louisville, Colo., 1985—; founder Charles Babbage Inst. Trustee Claremont Men's Coll.; mem. Chmn.'s Circle Colo. Reps.; past mem. Pres. Com. Nat. Medal of Sci. Recipient Exec. of Yr. award U. Colo. MBA Alum Assn., 1986, Community Svc. award Inst. Human Rels. Am. Jewish Com., 1980, Colo. Bus. Leader of Yr. award CACI, 1991. Mem. Computer and Comm. Industry Assn. (chmn., past bd. dirs., mem. exec. com., vice chmn.), Am. Electronics Assn. (past bd. dirs., mem. exec. com. Colo. chpt.), Electronic Mfrs. Club, Boulder Country Club. Office: Storage Tech Corp 2270 S 88th St Louisville CO 80028-4315

POPPE, FRED CHRISTOPH, advertising agency executive; b. Bklyn., Dec. 26, 1923; s. Fred G. and Laura (Funk) P.; m. Inez Hanssen, Oct. 2, 1952; children: Steven Hammond, Ellen Jane. Student, Adm. Farragut Acad., Toms River, N.J., 1940-41, Bklyn. Poly. Inst., 1941-42; AB, Princeton U., 1948. Copywriter Fuller & Smith & Ross, Inc., N.Y.C., 1948-51; advt. mgr. Yale & Towne Mfg. Co., 1951-53; group account supr. G.M. Basford Co., N.Y.C., 1953-59; mgr. account devel. Donahue & Coe, Inc., N.Y.C., 1959-60; exec. v.p. T.N. Palmer, Inc., N.Y.C., 1960-63; pres. Complan, Inc., N.Y.C., 1963-74; chmn. Poppe Tepon Inc., 1974-86; pres., chmn. emeritus Poppe Tyson Inc., N.Y.C., 1986—; bd. dirs. Inter-Ad Ltd., Skills Unlimited Inc. Author: The Hundred Greatest Corporate and Industrial Ads, 1983, 50 Rules to Keep a Client Happy, 1987, 100 New Greatest Corporate Ads, 1993. Served with USNR, 1941-46. Named Advt. Agy. Man of Yr., N.Y. Bus./Mktg. Assn., 1966-67. Mem. Bus./Mktg. Assn. (past pres., G.C. Crain award, Advt. Hall of Fame 1981, Communicator of Yr. 1983), Gt. South Bay Yacht Racing Assn., Princeton Club (N.Y.C.), Stuart Yacht and Country Club (Fla.), Elm Club (Princeton, N.J.), Southward Ho Country Club (Bay Shore, N.Y.), Magoun Landing Yacht Club (West Islip, N.Y.). Republican. Home: 3713 SE Fairway E Stuart FL 34997-6117 also: 133 Tahlulah Ln West Islip New York NY 11795 Office: Poppe Tyson 40 W 23rd St New York NY 10010-5200

POPPE, KENNETH C., school system administrator. Supt. Wall (S.D.) Sch. Dist. 51-5; del. Am. Assn. Sch. Adminstrs. Nat. Conf., 1995. State finalist Nat. Supt. Yr., 1993. Mem. S.D. Sch. Supts. Assn. (pres. 1994-95). Office: Wall Sch Dist 51-5 512 Norris St Wall SD 57790

POPPEL, HARVEY LEE, management consultant; b. Bklyn., Dec. 18, 1937; s. Frank M. and Fannie (Axenzow) P.; m. Emily A. Daigneault, Jan. 2, 1959; children: Marc F., Clinton S. BS, Rensselaer Poly. Inst., 1958, MS, 1959. Sr. info. systems analyst Westinghouse Electric Corp., Pitts., 1959-65; mgr. industry systems Western Union, Paramus, N.J., 1965-67; assoc., cons. Booz, Allen & Hamilton, N.Y.C., 1967-69, v.p., 1969-72, sr. v.p., 1972-84, mem. operating council, 1973-84; pres. Poptech, Inc., Sarasota, Fla., 1984—; mng. dir. Broadview Assocs., Ft. Lee, 1984—; mem. panel, lectr. on computers, comms. and info. industry; judge Entrepreneur of Yr., 1991, 93, 94, 95, 96. Co-author: Information Technology: The Trillion Dollar Opportunity, 1987; contbr. articles to profl. jours. Mem. Aspen Inst. Fellows, Inst. Mgmt. Cons., Soc. Mgmt. Info. Systems (exec. council), Zeta Psi. Club: Road Runners. Office: 1875 S Grant St San Mateo CA 94402

POPPEL, SETH RAPHAEL, business executive; b. Bklyn., Mar. 17, 1944; s. Frank M. and Fritzi R. (Axenzow) P.; BS magna cum laude, L.I. U., 1965; MBA, Columbia U., 1967; m. Danine Vokt, Jan. 5, 1974; children: Clarysa, Jared, Stacy. Asst. prof. L.I. U., Greenvale, N.Y., 1967-68; v.p. Synergistic Systems Corp., N.Y.C., 1968-77; v.p., dir. corp. planning Chase Manhattan Corp., N.Y.C., 1977-90; chmn., pres. Am. Vision Ctrs., N.Y.C., 1990-96; owner, pres. Poppel Enterprises, Merrick, N.Y., 1995—; owner harness horses Seth Poppel Stables, 1983—; founder, owner, operator Seth Poppel Yearbook Archives, 1986—. E.I. DuPont fellow, 1965-67, Downie Muir fellow, 1965-66; recipient Claire F. Adler award in math., 1964-65, Mepham High Sch. Hall of Fame award, 1993. Mem. Am. Statis. Assn., Ops. Research Soc. Am., Inst. Mgmt. Sci., Nat. Assn. Bus. Economy, N.Am. Soc. Corp. Planning, U.S. Trotting Assn., Beta Gamma Sigma, Psi Chi, Omega Epsilon. Home and Office: 38 Range Dr Merrick NY 11566-3233

POPPELIERS, JOHN CHARLES, architectural historian; b. Binghamton, N.Y., Oct. 5, 1935; s. Johannes Marinus and Irene (Marx) P.; m. Julia Margaret Tatnell, Dec. 16, 1967. AB, Hamilton Coll., 1957; MA, U. Pa., 1962; PhD, Cath. U. of Am., 1975. Instr. history and English various high schs., Binghamton, Johnson City, 1957-58, 60-62; sr. editor, architectural historian Historic Am. Bldgs. Survey, Dept. Interior, 1962-72, chief, 1972-80; chief ops. and tng. Divsn. Cultural Heritage, Unesco, 1980-86; internat. liaison Officer for Cultural Resources, U.S. Nat. Park Svc., 1986—; rep. for exec. and consultative coms. for internat. campaigns to safeguard Moonjodaro, Pakistan, Göreme and Istanbul, Turkey, Tyr (Lebanon) UNESCO; rep. Christopher Columbus Quincentenary Commn., U.s. Dept. Interior, 1987-92; curator Smithsonian Traveling Exhbns. on Archtl. History. Author: HABS Massachusetts Catalog, 1965; author: (with Nancy B. Schwartz and S. Allen Chambers) What Style Is It?; contbr. articles to profl. jour.; editor many tech. reports. Fulbright-Hays rsch. grantee, U. Vienna, 1968-69; grad. fellow U. Pa., 1960-62, Catholic U. Am., 1966-68; recipient History Dept. award Hamilton Coll., 1957. Fellow Internat. Coun. on Monuments and Sites (U.S. com. 1990, bd. trustees, asst. sec.-treas.); mem. AIA (cons. mem. com. on historic resources), Nat. Trust for Hist. Preservation, Fulbright Assn., Cosmos Club, Soc. of Arch. Historians (com. on arch. preservation, former pres. Latrobe chpt.), Com. for the Preservation of Architectural Records, Nat. Preservation Inst. (dir. for edn. 1988-92), Nat. Trust Libr. (bd. advisors 1988—), Secular Franciscan Order. Roman Catholic. Avocations: vol. charitable causes, ecology, painting, music. Home: 2939 Van Ness St NW Apt 606 Washington DC 20008-4622 Office: US Nat Park Svc PO Box 37127 Washington DC 20013-7127

POPPEN, ALVIN J., religious organization administrator. Dir., office ministry and pers. svcs. Reformed Ch. in Am., N.Y.C. Office: Reformed Church in Am 475 Riverside Dr Ste 1811 New York NY 10115-0122

POPPENHAGEN, RONALD WILLIAM, newspaper editor, publishing executive; b. Chgo., Feb. 23, 1948; s. Andrew Charles and Elaine Edith (Larson) P.; m. Judy Diane Wagenblast, July 25, 1981. BA. in History and Lit., Augustana Coll., 1970. Reporter Sta. KBUR, Burlington, Iowa, 1970-71, Sta. KROS, Clinton, Iowa, 1971-72; reporter Sta. WDWS, Champaign, Ill., 1972-73, news dir., 1973-77; reporter The Morning Courier, Urbana, Ill., 1977-79; mng. editor The Daily Journal, Wheaton, Ill., 1979-80; met. editor The Southern Illinoisan, Carbondale, Ill., 1980-83; editor Green Bay (Wis.) News Chronicle, 1983-86, editor, general mgr., 1986—. Recipient Best Editls. award Wis. Newspaper Assn., 1985, 86, 93, UPI, 1983-86, Best Local Column award, 1993. Avocation: railroads. Office: Green Bay News Chronicle 133 S Monroe Ave Green Bay WI 54301-4056

POPPENSIEK, GEORGE CHARLES, veterinary scientist, educator; b. N.Y.C., June 18, 1918; s. George Frederick and Emily Amelia (Miller) P.; m. Edith M. Wallace, July 3, 1943; children: Neil Allen, Leslie Marion. Student, Cornell U., 1936-37, M.S., 1951; student, U. Pa., 1937-42, V.M.D., 1942. Diplomate Am. Bd. Microbiology, Am. Coll. Vet. Microbiology (charter), Am. Coll. Vet. Preventive Medicine (hon.). Asst. instr. medicine U. Pa. Sch. Vet. Medicine, 1943; asst. prof. vet. sci. U. Md., 1943-44; head dept. vet. virus vaccine prodn. Lederle Labs. div. Am. Cyanamid Co., 1944-49; dir. diagnostic lab. N.Y. State Coll. Vet. Medicine Cornell U., 1949-51, research assoc. Vet. Virus Research Inst., 1951-55; veterinarian Plum Island Animal Disease Ctr., animal disease and parasite research div. Agrl. Research Service, U.S. Dept. Agr., 1955-56, acting-in-charge diagnostic investigations, 1956-58, charge immunological investigations, 1958-59; dean and prof. microbiology N.Y. State Coll. Vet. Medicine, Cornell U., 1959-74, James Law prof. comparative medicine, 1974-88, dean emeritus, James Law prof. comparative medicine emeritus, 1988—; guest prof. U. Bern, Switzerland, 1975; mem. exam. com. Nat. Bd. Vet. Med. Examiners, 1976-79; bd. dirs. Cornell Research Found., 1963-74; chmn. bd. dirs. Cornell Veterinarian, Inc., 1976-86. Recipient Certificate of Merit award U.S. Dept. Agr., 1958; citation Sch. Vet. Med., U. Pa., 1978, Centennial medals U. Pa., 1984, Ohio State U., 1985; others. Charter fellow Am. Acad. Microbiology; fellow AAAS; charter mem. Am. Soc. Virology; mem. AVMA, N.Y. State Vet. Med. Soc. (disting. life), Am. Bd. Microbiology, U.S. Animal Health Assn., Assn. Am. Vet. Med. Colls. (pres. 1970-71), So. Tier Vet. Med. Assn., Am. Vet. Radiology Soc., Am. Soc. for Microbiology, N.Y. Agrl. Soc. (life), Argentine Nat. Acad. Agronomy and Vet. Medicine (hon.), Societas Polona Medicinae Veterinariae (hon.), Sigma Xi, Phi Kappa Phi, Alpha Psi, Omega Tau Sigma, Phi Zeta. Congregationalist. Home: 122 E Remington Rd Ithaca NY 14850-1456

POPPER, ARTHUR N., zoology educator; b. N.Y.C., May 9, 1943; s. Martin and Evelyn (Levine) P.; m. Helen Apfel, Nov. 30, 1968; children: Michelle, Melissa. BA, NYU, 1964; PhD, CUNY, 1969. Asst. prof. zoology U. Hawaii, Honolulu, 1969-72; assoc. prof. zoology U. Hawaii, 1972-78; assoc. prof. dept. anatomy & cell biology Georgetown U., Washington, 1978-83; prof. dept. anatomy & cell biology Georgetown U., 1983-87; prof., chmn. dept. zoology U. Md., College Park, 1987—. Editor: Comparative Studies of Hearing in Vertebrates, 1980, Hearing and Sound Communication in Fishes, 1981, Sensory Biology of Aquatic Animals, 1988, Evolutionary Biology of Hearing, 1992, Springer Handbook of Auditory Research, 1992. Recipient Research Career Devel. award NIH, 1978-83. Fellow AAAS, Acoustical Soc.; mem. Soc. for Neurosci., Am. Assn. for Rsch. in Otolaryngology, Internat. Soc. Neurothology, Sigma Xi. Office: U Md Dept Zoology College Park MD 20742

POPPER, BRETTE, publishing executive. Pres., publ. USA Weekend, N.Y.C., 1989—. Office: USA Weekend Gannett Co 535 Madison Ave 21st Fl New York NY 10022*

POPPER, ROBERT, law educator, former dean; b. N.Y.C., May 22, 1932; s. Walter G. and Dorothy B. (Kluger) P.; m. Mary Ann Schaefer, July 12, 1963; children: Julianne, Robert Gregory. BS, U. Wis., 1953; LLB, Harvard U., 1956; LLM, NYU, 1963. Bar: N.Y. 1957, U.S. Dist. Ct. (so. dist.) N.Y. 1962, U.S. Ct. Appeals (2d cir.) 1962, U.S. Supreme Ct. 1962, U.S. Dist. Ct. (ea. dist.) N.Y. 1969, U.S. Ct. Appeals (7th cir.) 1970, U.S. Ct. Appeals (8th cir.) 1971, Mo. 1971, U.S. Dist. Ct. (we. dist.) Mo. 1973. Trial atty. criminal br. N.Y.C. Legal Aid Soc., 1960-61; asst. dist. atty. N.Y. County, 1961-64; assoc. Seligson & Morris, N.Y.C., 1964-69; mem. faculty School of Law, U. Mo., Kansas City, 1969—, prof., 1973—, acting dean, 1983-84, dean, 1984-93, cons. and lectr. in field. Author: Post Conviction Remedies in a Nutshell, 1978, De-Nationalizing the Bill of Rights, 1979; contbr. articles to profl. jours. Mem. N.Y. State Bar Assn., Mo. Bar Assn., Kansas City Met. Bar Assn., Mo. Inst. of Justice. Office: U Mo Kansas City Sch Law 500 E 52nd St Kansas City MO 64110-2467

POPPERS, PAUL JULES, anesthesiologist, educator; b. Enschede, Netherlands, June 30, 1929; came to U.S., 1958; naturalized, 1963; s. Meyer and Minca (Ginsburg) P.; m. Ann Feinberg, June 3, 1969; children: David Matthew, Jeremy Samuel. MD, U. Amsterdam, 1955. Diplomate Am. Bd. Anesthesiology. Instr. anesthesiology Columbia U., N.Y.C., 1962-63, assoc., 1963-65, asst. prof. anesthesiology, 1965-71, assoc. prof. anesthesiology, 1971-74; prof., vice chmn. dept. anesthesiology NYU, 1974-79; prof., chmn. dept. anesthesiology SUNY, Stony Brook, 1979—; cons. Brookdale Med. Ctr., Bklyn., 1975—, VA Med. Ctr., Northport, N.Y., 1979—, The N.Y. Hosp. Med. Ctr. of Queens (formerly Booth Meml. Hosp.), Flushing, N.Y., 1979—, L.I. Jewish Med. Ctr., New Hyde Pk., N.Y., 1980—, Ea. L.I. Hosp., Greenport, N.Y., 1995—, Am. Hosp. Paris, 1989-93; cons., lectr. Author: Regional Anesthesia, 1977; editor: Beta Blockade and Anaesthesia, 1979; sect. editor Jour. Clin. Anesthesia, 1990—; mem. editorial bd. Internat. Jour. Clin. Monitoring and Computing, 1990—, Gynecologic and Obstetric Investigation, 1996—; internat. bd. editors Anaesthesiology Digest, 1991-94; contbr. numerous articles to profl. jours. NIH postdoctoral rsch. fellow, 1961; recipient medal Polish Acad. Scis., Poland, 1987, Univ. medal Jagiellonian U., Krakow, Poland, 1987, 1st Sci. award Post-grad. Assembly in Anesthesiology; named Hon. Prof. Anesthesiology, U. Leiden, The Netherlands, 1977. Fellow Am. Coll. Anesthesiology, Am. Coll. Ob-gyns., Royal Soc. Medicine, Post-grad. Assembly in Anesthesiology (hon. chmn. 1989—); mem. Am. Soc. Anesthesiologists, Assn. Univ. Anesthesiologists, Soc. Acad. Anesthesia Chmn., Internat. Anesthesia Rsch. Soc., Soc. Obstetric Anesthesia and Perinatology, Am. Soc. Regional Anesthesia, Jerusalem Acad. Medicine, Am. Soc. Pharmacology and Exptl. Therapeutics, Fedn. Am. Soc. Exptl. Biology, Sigma Xi. Office: SUNY Sch Medicine Health Scis Ctr Stony Brook NY 11794-8480

POPPLER, DORIS SWORDS, lawyer; b. Billings, Mont., Nov. 10, 1924; d. Lloyd William and Edna (Mowre) Swords; m. Louis E. Poppler, June 11, 1949; children: Louis William, Kristine, Mark J., Blaine, Claire, Arminda. Student, U. Minn., 1942-44; JD, Mont. State U., 1948. Bar: Mont. 1948, U.S. Dist. Ct. Mont. 1948, U.S. Ct. Appeals (9th cir.) 1990. Pvt. practice law Billings, 1948-49; sec., treas. Wonderpark Corp., Billings, 1959-62; atty. Yellowstone County Attys. Office, Billings, 1972-75; ptnr. Poppler and Barz, Billings, 1972-79, Davidson, Veeder, Baugh, Broeder and Poppler, Billings, 1979-84, Davidson and Poppler, P.C., Billings, 1984-90; U.S. atty. Dist. of Mont., Billings, 1990-93; field rep. Nat. Indian Gaming Commn., Washington, 1993—. Pres. Jr. League, 1964-65; bd. dirs., pres. Yellowstone County Metre Bd., 1982; trustee Rocky Mt. Coll., 1984-90, mem. nat. adv. bd., 1993—; mem. Mont. Human Rights Commn., 1988-90; bd. dirs. Miss Mont. Pageant, 1995—. Recipient Mont. Salute to Women award, Mont. Woman of Achievent award, 1975, Disting. Svc. award Rocky Mt. Coll., 1990. Mem. AAUW, Mont. Bar Assn., Nat. Assn. Former U.S. Attys., Nat. Rep. Lawyers Assn., Internat. Women's Forum, Yellowstone County Bar Assn. (pres. 1990), Alpha Chi Omega. Republican. Office: Nat Indian Gaming Commn 1441 L St NW 9th Fl Washington DC 20005

PORAY, JOHN LAWRENCE, professional association executive; b. Rochester, N.Y., Nov. 9, 1955; s. Jack Loysen and Jane Ann (Williams) P.; m. Rebecca Sue Wells, June 16, 1979 (div. Jan. 1993); children: John Lawrence Jr., David Scott. AA in Liberal Arts, Monroe C.C., Rochester, 1975; BA in Human Rels., Salem (W.Va.) Coll., 1977. Sr. dist. exec. Ctrl. Ohio Coun. Boy Scouts Am., Columbus, 1977-83; asst. exec. dir. Columbus Apt. Assn., 1983-88, Apt. Assn. Ind., Indpls., 1988-92; exec. dir. Soc. Broadcast Engrs., Indpls., 1992—. Youth coach Plainfield (Ind.) Optimist Club, 1988-96; moderator 1st Bapt. Ch., Plainfield, 1995—. Mem. Am. Soc. Assn. Execs. (cert.), Ind. Soc. Assn. Execs. Office: Soc Broadcast Engrs Inc 8445 Keystone Crossing Ste 140 Indianapolis IN 46240

PORCARO, MICHAEL FRANCIS, advertising agency executive; b. N.Y.C., Apr. 3, 1948; s. Girolamo M. and Marianna (DePasquale) P.; m. Bonnie Kerr, Apr. 7, 1972; children: Sabrina, Jon. BA in English, Rockford (Ill.) Coll., 1969. Broadcaster Sta. KFQD, Anchorage, 1970-71, Sta. KENI, Anchorage, 1972-73; v.p. ops. Cook Inlet Broadcasters, Anchorage, 1973-74; owner Audio Enterprises, Anchorage, 1974-75; asst. Alaska Pub. Broadcasting Commn., Anchorage, 1975-76; exec. dir. Alaska Pub. Broadcasting Commn., 1976-81; chief exec. officer, ptnr. Porcaro Blankenship Advt. Corp., Anchorage, 1981—; cons. Arco Alaska TV sta., Anchorage, 1981; expert witness U.S. Senate Subcom. on Telecomms., Washington, 1978; chmn. citizens adv. com. dept. journalism U. Alaska, 1995-96. Chmn. Municipality of Anchorage Urban Design Commn., 1990-93; mem. mayor's transition team Municipality of Anchorage, 1987-88; bd. dirs. Anchorage Glacier Polits Baseball Club, 1987-88, Anchorage Mus. History and Art, Anchorage C. of C., Anchorage Symphony Orch.; chmn. bd. dirs. Bro. Francis Shelter for the Homeless, Anchorage; mem. mktg. com. gov.'s transition team, 1995; mem. United Way Anchorage Cabinet, 1996; bd. dirs. Alaska Ctr. Internat. Bus., 1996. Recipient Silver Mike award Billboard mag., 1974, Bronze award N.Y. Film Critics, 1981, Best of North award Ad. Fedn. Alaska, 1982—, Addy award, 1985, 91, Grand Addy award 1990, Cable TV Mktg. award 1986; Paul Harris fellow. Mem. Advt. Fedn. Alaska, Anchorage C. of C. (bd. dirs.). Republican. Roman Catholic. Avocations: softball, hockey, travel, fitness. Office: Porcaro Blankenship Advt 433 W 9th Ave Anchorage AK 99501-3519

PORCELLO, LEONARD JOSEPH, engineering research and development executive; b. N.Y.C., Mar. 1, 1934; s. Savior James and Mary Josephine (Bacchi) P.; m. Patricia Lucille Berger, July 7, 1962 (dec. Sept. 1991); children—John Joseph, Thomas Gregory. B.A. in Physics, Cornell U., 1955; M.S. in Physics, U. Mich., 1957, M.S. in Elec. Engring, 1959, Ph.D. in Elec. Engring, 1963. Research asst. U. Mich., Ann Arbor, 1955-58; instr. elec. engring. U. Mich., 1958-61; research engr. Radar & Optics Lab., 1968-72; asso. dir. Willow Run Labs., 1970-72, asso. prof., 1969-72, prof., 1972-73, adj. prof., 1973-75; dir. radar and optics divsn. Environ. Rsch. Inst. of Mich., Ann Arbor, 1973-76, v.p., 1973-76, trustee, 1975; asst. v.p., mgr. sensor sys. operation Sci. Applications Internat. Corp., Tucson, 1976-79, v.p., 1979-85, corp. v.p., 1985-87, mgr. def. sys. group, 1986-95, sr. v.p., 1987—, dep. mgr. tech. and advanced sys. sector, 1993—, mgr. applied sys. group, 1995—. Bd. dirs. Tucson Jr. Strings, 1977-79, chmn., 1978-79. Fellow IEEE; mem. Optical Soc. Am., AAAS, Sigma Xi, Eta Kappa Nu. Roman Catholic. Research on imaging radar, synthetic aperture radar systems and radar remote sensing. Home: PO Box 13106 Tucson AZ 85732-3106 Office: Sci Applications Internat Corp 5151 E Broadway Blvd Ste 900 Tucson AZ 85711-3713

PORCHÉ-BURKE, LISA MARIE, chancellor; b. L.A., Nov. 9, 1954; d. Ralph Antoine and June Yvonne (James) P.; m. Peter A. Burke, Oct. 27, 1984; children: Mallory, Dominique, Lauren. BA in Psychology magna cum laude, U. So. Calif., 1976; MA in Counseling Psychology, U. Notre Dame, 1981, PhD in Psychology, 1983; LLD (hon.), Chgo. Sch. Profl. Psychology, 1994. Tchr. Spanish Pius X High Sch., Downey, Calif., 1976-77; assoc. AVENUES of South Bend (Ind.), Inc., 1981-82; clin. psychology intern Boston U. Sch. Medicine, 1983-84; sch. psychologist Pierce Sch., Brookline, Mass., 1983-84; asst. prof., profl. tng. faculty Calif. Sch. Profl. Psychology, L.A., 1985-87, asst. prof., 1987-90, coord. ethnic minority mental health proficiency, 1987-90, assoc. prof., 1987-90, coord. multicultural cmty./proficiency clin. psychology, 1990-91, chancellor, 1992—; guest lectr. Ind. U., South Bend, 1981; adj. faculty Calif. Sch. Profl. Psychology, 1985, acting provost, 1991-92; cons. Clarke-Porche Constrn. Co., Inc., 1981, Adolscent Sch. Health Program Boston City Hosp., 1983-84, Calif. State Dept. Edn., 1987, The Feilding Inst., Santa Barbara, Calif., 1991; workshop leader Personnel Dept. City of South Bend, 1979; rsch. asst. U. Notre Dame, 1980-81; presenter in field. Contbr. articles to profl. jours. Minority fellow U. Notre Dame, 1977; grad. scholar U. Notre Dame, 1979; recipient Outstanding Young Women Am. award, 1983, Exemplary Profl. Svc. award, 1991. Fellow APA (pub. info. com., 1993-95, mem.-at-large 1987-90, 92-95, treas. 1990—, chair 1985-86, chair fundraising com. 1988-90, midwinter program com. 1989-93, bd. ethnic minority affairs 1987-88, Jack B. Krasner award 1991); mem. Nat. Coun. Sch. Profl. Psychology (nominating com. 1989-90, chair nominating subcom. 1989-90, chair ethnic racial diversity com. 1990-92), Calif. Psuchol. Assn. Found. (bd. dirs. 1992, treas./CEO 1993—), Women Psychology for Legislative Action (bd. dirs. 1992—), Assn. Black

Psychologists. Office: Calif Sch Profl Psychology 1000 S Fremont Ave Alhambra CA 91803-1360

PORENSKI, HARRY STEPHEN, material engineer; b. Louisville, June 23, 1945; s. Harry Stephen Sr. and Nellie Adelade (Jeffries) P.; m. Geraldine Crawford, Aug. 1967; 1 child, Lisa Marie. BA in Edn., U. Ky., 1968; MS in Physics, U. Louisville, 1977. Sci., math. tchr. Jefferson County Bd. Edn., Louisville, 1969-71; mfg. supr. Brown & Williamson Tobacco Co., Louisville, 1972-74, rsch. physicist, 1974-89; sr. material engr. Brown & Williamson Tobacco Co., Macon, Ga., 1989—. Mem. Am. Physical Soc. Republican. Baptist. Achievements include 10 patents, most recent patent for smokeless cigarette. Home: 100 Wexford Circle Bonaire GA 31005 Office: Brown & Williamson Tobacco 2600 Weaver Rd PO Box 1056 Macon GA 31298

PORFELI, JOSEPH J., computer and software development company, computer leasing company executive; b. 1947. BS in Bus. Administrn. and Mktg., Point Park Coll., 1969. With sales dept. Comshare, Inc., Bala Cymwyd, Pa., 1969-73; v.p. comms. svcs. Compuserve, Inc., Pitts., 1973-83; v.p. sales and mktg. Telenet Comms. Corp.-US Sprint, Plymouth Meeting, Pa., 1983-87; exec. v.p. Centex Telemanagement Corp., Pitts., 1987-89; with Electronic Info. Syss., Inc., Stamford, Conn., 1989—; now pres., CEO, chmn. bd. EIS Internat., Stamford, Conn. Office: EIS Internat Inc 1351 Washington Blvd Stamford CT 06902*

PORFILIO, JOHN CARBONE, federal judge; b. Denver, Oct. 14, 1934; s. Edward Alphonso Porfilio and Caroline (Carbone) Moore; m. Joan West, Aug. 1, 1959 (div. 1983); children: Edward Miles, Joseph Arthur, Jeanne Kathrine; m. Theresa Louise Berger, Dec. 28, 1983; 1 stepchild, Katrina Ann Smith. Student, Stanford U., 1952-54; BA, U. Denver, 1956, LLB, 1959. Bar: Colo. 1959, U.S. Supreme Ct. 1965. Asst. atty. gen. State of Colo., Denver, 1962-68, dep. atty. gen., 1968-72, atty. gen., 1972-74; U.S. bankruptcy judge Dist. of Colo., Denver, 1975-82; judge U.S. Dist. Ct. Colo., Denver, 1982-85, U.S. Ct. Appeals (10th cir.), Denver, 1985—; instr. Colo. Law Enforcement Acad., Denver, 1965-70, State Patrol Acad., Denver, 1968-70; guest lectr. U. Denver Coll. Law, 1978. Committeeman Arapahoe County Republican Com., Aurora, Colo., 1968; mgr. Dunbar for Atty. Gen., Denver, 1970. Mem. ABA. Roman Catholic. Office: US Ct Appeals Byron White US Courthouse 1823 Stout St Denver CO 80257-0001

PORGES, WALTER RUDOLF, television news executive; b. Vienna, Nov. 26, 1931; s. Paul and Charlotte (Posamentier) P.; m. Jean Belle Mlotok, Dec. 22, 1953; children: Donald F., Marian E., Lawrence M. B.A., CCNY, 1953. News writer radio sta. WOR, N.Y.C., 1955-56, WCBS Radio and TV, N.Y.C., 1956-57; news writer ABC Radio Network, N.Y.C., 1958-60; news editor ABC Radio Network, 1960-63, asst. dir. radio news, 1963-65; asst. assignment mgr. ABC-TV, 1965-68; asso. producer ABC-TV Evening News, 1968-70, sr. producer, 1973-75; European producer ABC News, London, 1970-73; producer ABC-TV spl. events, N.Y.C., 1975-76; coordinating producer ABC News (Republican Nat. Conv.), 1976; editorial producer, chief writer ABC Evening News, 1976-77, sr. producer, 1977-80; sr. producer ABC World News Tonight, 1978-83; fgn. news dir. ABC News, N.Y.C., 1983-89, v.p. news practices, 1989-93; assoc. Exec. TV, 1993. Served with U.S. Army, 1953-55.

PORIES, WALTER JULIUS, surgeon, educator; b. Munich, Germany, Jan. 18, 1930; came to U.S., 1940; s. Theodore Francis and Frances (Lowin) P.; m. Muriel Helen Aronson, Aug. 18, 1951; children: Susan E., Mary Jane, Carolyn A., Kathy G.; m. Mary Ann Rose McCarthy, June 4, 1977; children: Mary Lisa, Michael McCarthy. BA, Wesleyan U., Middletown, Conn., 1952; MD with honors, U. Rochester, 1955. Diplomate: Am. Bd. Surgery, Am. Bd. Thoracic Surgery. Intern Strong Meml. Hosp., Rochester, N.Y., 1955-56, resident, 1958-62; chmn. dept. surgery Wright-Patterson AFB, Ohio, 1952-67; asst. prof. surgery and oncology U. Rochester, 1967-69; prof. surgery and assoc. chmn. dept. surgery U. Cleve., 1969-77; prof. surgery East Carolina U., Greenville, N.C., 1977—, chmn. dept. surgery, 1977—; chief surgery Pitt County Meml. Hosp., 1977—; prof. surgery U. Health Scis. of Uniformed Svcs., 1982—; founder, assoc. dir. Rochester Cancer Ctr., 1967-69; founder, dir. Cleve. Cancer Ctr., 1972-77, Hospice of Cleve., 1975; founder, chmn. bd. Hospice of Greenville, 1981; med. dir. Home Health Care of Greenville, 1978-83; founder, chmn. bd. Ctr. for Creative Living, 1985-91. Author: Clinical Applications of Zinc Metabolism, 1974; editor: Operative Surgery series, vols. 1-4, 1979-83, Office Surgery for Family Physicians, 1985; editor in chief Current Surgery, 1990—; editor Nat. Curriculum for Residency in Surgery, 1988—, mem. residency rev. com., 1992—; contbr. articles to profl. jours. Bd. dirs. Boy Scouts Am., Cleve., 1974-77, Greenville Arts Mus., 1980-82; pres., CEO, chmn. bd. dirs. Ea. Carolina Health Orgn. Maj. USAF, 1955-67; col. USAR, 1979-91, comdr. USAF Hosp., Durham, N.C.; activated Desert Shield, 1990. Decorated Legion of Merit; Thorndyke scholar, 1948-51; recipient McLester award USAF, 1966, Miss. Magnolia Cross, 1989, Presdl. citation for Desert Shield, 1994; named to Hon. Order of Ky. Cols., 1965. Fellow ACS, Am. Coll. Cardiology, Am. Coll. Chest Physicians; mem. Soc. for Vascular Surgery, Soc. Surg. Oncology, Soc. Univ. Surgeons, Am. Surg. Assn., Soc. Environ. Geochemistry (past pres.), Residency Rev. Com. for Surgery, So. Surg. Assn., Soc. for Thoracic Surgery, Ea. Carolina Health Orgn. (pres., chmn. bd. 1994—), Assn. Programs Dirs. in Surgery (pres. 1995-96), N.C. Surg. Assn. (pres. 1995-96), Greenville Country Club, Phi Kappa Phi. Republican. Roman Catholic. Home: Deep Sun Farm 7464 NE Hwy 43 N Macclesfield NC 27852 Office: East Carolina U Dept Surgery Greenville NC 27858

PORILE, NORBERT THOMAS, chemistry educator; b. Vienna, Austria, May 18, 1932; came to U.S., 1947, naturalized, 1952; s. Irving and Emma (Intrator) P.; m. Miriam Eisen, June 16, 1957; 1 son, James. B.A., U. Chgo., 1952, M.S., 1954, Ph.D., 1957. Rsch. assoc. Brookhaven Nat. Lab., Upton, N.Y., 1957-59; assoc. chemist Brookhaven Nat. Lab., 1959-63, chemist, 1963-64; vis. prof. chemistry McGill U., 1963-65; assoc. prof. chemistry Purdue U., West Lafayette, Ind., 1965-69; prof. chemistry Purdue U., 1969—; rsch. collaborator Brookhaven Nat. Lab., Argonne Nat. Lab., Los Alamos Sci. Lab., Lawrence Berkeley Lab.; vis. prof. Facultes des Scis., Orsay, France; fellow Soc. Promotion of Sci. in Japan, Inst. Nuclear Study, U. Kyoto, 1961. Editor: Radiochemistry of the Elements and Radiochemical Techniques, 1986-90. John Simon Guggenheim meml. fellow Institut de Physique Nucleaire Orsay, 1971-72; recipient F.D. Martin Undergrad. Teaching award, 1977; Von Humboldt Sr. U.S. Scientist award Philipps U., Marburg, W. Ger., 1982. Mem. Am. Chem. Soc., Am. Phys. Soc. Office: Purdue U Dept Chemistry Chemistry Bldg Lafayette IN 47907

PORITZ, DEBORAH T., state attorney general. Atty. gen. State of N.J. Office: Law & Pub Safety Dept Justice Complex CN 080 Trenton NJ 08625-0080*

PORIZKOVA, PAULINA, model, actress; b. Czechoslovakia, Apr. 9, 1965; came to U.S., 1982; m. Ric Ocasek; 1 child. Ind. model Europe and U.S., 1980-88; became model for Estee Lauder, 1988. Cover girl for numerous mags. including Cosmopolitan, Vogue, Women's Day, Sports Illustrated, Playboy; film acting debut: Anna, 1987, also appeared in Portfolio, 1987, Her Alibi, 1989. Office: Elite Model Management Corp 111 E 22nd St Fl 2 New York NY 10010-5400

POROSOFF, HAROLD, chemist, research and development director; b. Bklyn., Apr. 3, 1946; s. Solomon and Ruth (Goldberg) P.; m. Leslie Pamela Freiman, May 19, 1948; children: Lauren, Stephen, Marc. BS, MIT, 1966; PhD, Brown U., 1970. Various rsch. and mgmt. positions fibers div. Am. Cyanamid Co., Stamford, Conn. and Milton, Fla., 1970-78; various mgmt. positions Shulton Rsch. div. Am. Cyanamid Co., Clifton, N.J., 1978-83, dir., 1983-88; v.p. R & D chem. rsch. divsn. Am. Cyanamid Co., Stamford, 1989-93; v.p. R & D Cytec Industries Inc., Stamford, 1993-95; v.p., chief tech. officer Cytec Industries, Inc., Stamford, 1995—. Patentee in field. Mem. AAAS, Am. Chem. Soc., N.Y. Acad. Scis. Office: Cytec Industries Inc PO Box 60 Stamford CT 06904-0060

PORRETTA, EMANUELE PETER, retired bank executive; b. N.Y.C., Aug. 4, 1942; s. Joseph Edward and Italia (Sesti) P.; m. Mary Valanzano, Apr. 18, 1964; children: Denise, Robert, Janice. Student, N.Y. Tech. Coll., 1960-61. Transfer clk. Mfrs. Trust Co., N.Y.C., 1961; sr. v.p. U.S. Trust Co. N.Y., N.Y.C., 1984—, sr. v.p., dir. adminstrv. svcs., instn. asst. svcs. divsn., ret., 1996; mem. payment system com. N.Y. Clearing House, 1978-80, chmn. Bank Ops. Conf., 1981-82. Treas. Manalapan, N.J. Rep. campaign, 1980; mem. adv. com. Williams Coll. Exec. Program. Mem. Am. Mgmt. Assn., Am. Bankers Assn. Roman Catholic. Avocations: running, reading, golf.

PORT, SIDNEY CHARLES, mathematician, educator; b. Chgo., Nov. 27, 1935; s. Isadore and Sarah (Landy) P.; m. Idelle Jackson, Mar. 24, 1957; children—Ethan, Jonathan, Daniel. A.B., Northwestern U., 1957, M.S., 1958, Ph.D., 1962. Staff mathematician Rand Corp., 1962-66; asso. prof. math. U. Calif. at Los Angeles, 1966-69, prof., 1969—. Author: (with P. Hoel and C. Stone) Probability, Statistics and Stochastic Processes, 1971, (with C. Stone) Brownian Motion and Classical Potential Theory, 1978, Theoretical Probability for Applications, 1993; contbr. articles to profl. jours. Fellow Inst. Math. Statistics; mem. Am. Math. Soc. Home: 680 Kingman Ave Santa Monica CA 90402-1334 Office: Math Dept Univ Calif Los Angeles Los Angeles CA 90024

PORTAL, GILBERT MARCEL ADRIEN, oil company executive; b. Paris, Aug. 2, 1930; came to U.S., 1982; s. Emmanuel Jules and Henriette Josephine (Bonnard) P.; m. Monique Janine Adam, July 12, 1951; children: Dominique, Veronique, Marc-Emmanuel. Baccalaureate, Lycee Charlemagne U., Paris, 1949; Ingenieur Civil des Mines, Sch. of Mines, St. Etienne, 1955; diplome du C.P.A., Ctr. Advanced Bus., Paris, 1969; auditeur 30 eme session IHEDN, Higher Studies Nat. Defense, Paris, 1978. Geophysicist Societe Nationale Elf Aquitaine, Sahara, Algeria, 1957-63; exploration mgr. north sea Societe Nationale Elf Aquitaine, 1963-65, dep. exec. v.p. Europe, 1965-68, dep. exec. v.p. North and South Am., 1968-70; chief exec. officer Societe Nationale Elf Aquitaine, Iraq, 1970-72; dir., chief exec. officer Societe Nationale Elf Aquitaine, Gabon, Africa, 1972-76; dep. exec. v.p. hydrocarbons Societe Nationale Elf Aquitaine, 1976-78, exec. v.p. North Africa, Mid. East, Far East, 1978-82; pres. Elf Aquitaine Petroleum, Houston, 1982-89; chmn., chief exec. officer Elf Exploration, Inc., Houston, 1989-90; sec.-gen. European Petroleum Industry Assn., 1990-95; ptnr. G.M.H. Internat. Oil and Gas Consulting, Paris, 1995—; bd. dirs. Sterling Chems., Houston, Sonat Offshore, Inc., Houston. Served to lt. French Army, 1955-57. Decorated Legion of Honor (France), Nat. Merit Order (France); Equatorial Star (Gabon). Mem. Cercle Royal Gaulois Artistique et Littéraire. Roman Catholic.

PORTALE, CARL, publishing executive. Pub. Elle-Machette Filipacchi Mags., Inc., N.Y.C. Office: ELLE HACHETTE FILIPACCHI MAGAZINES 1633 Broadway, 44th FL. New York NY 10019

PORTAS, JOSE, oil industry executive. Sec., treas., exsc. mgr. PDV Am. Inc., N.Y.C. Office: PDV Am Inc 750 Lexington Ave Fl 10 New York NY 10022-1200*

PORTE, JOEL MILES, English educator; b. Bklyn., Nov. 13, 1933; s. Jacob I. and Frances (Derison) P.; m. Ilana D'Ancona, June 17, 1962 (div. 1977); 1 child, Susanna Maria; m. Helene Sophrin, Oct. 18, 1985. A.B. magna cum laude, CCNY, 1957; A.M., Harvard U., 1958, Ph.D., 1962. Instr. English Harvard U., Cambridge, Mass., 1962-64, asst. prof., 1964-68, assoc. prof., 1968-69, prof., 1969-82, Bernbaum prof. of lit., 1982-87, chmn. English and Am. Lit. Dept., 1985-87; Frederic J. Whiton prof. of English Cornell U., Ithaca, N.Y., 1987-89, Ernest I. White prof. Am. Studies and Humane Letters, 1989—; vis. lectr. Am. Studies Research Ctr., Hyderabad, India, spring 1976. Author: Emerson and Thoreau: Transcendentalists in Conflict, 1966, The Romance in America: Studies in Cooper, Poe, Hawthorne, Melville and James, 1969, Representative Man: Ralph Waldo Emerson in His Time, 1979, In Respect to Egotism: Studies in American Romantic Writing, 1991; editor: Emerson in His Journals, 1982, Emerson: Prospect and Retrospect, 1982, Emerson: Essays and Lectures, 1983, New Essays on Portrait of a Lady, 1990. Scholar in Residence, Rockefeller Found., Bellagio, Italy, 1979; fellow John Simon Guggenheim Found., 1981-82. Mem. Am. Studies Assn., Am. Lit. Assn., Phi Beta Kappa. Home: 1405 Hanshaw Rd Ithaca NY 14850-2730 Office: Cornell U Dept Eng Rockefeller Hall Ithaca NY 14853

PORTELLI, VINCENT GEORGE, business executive, consultant; b. Detroit, Jan. 6, 1932; s. Camillo and Mary (Borg) P.; B.S., U. Detroit, 1953, tchr. cert., 1961; M.A., U. Mich., 1965; postgrad. Harvard Grad. Sch. Bus. Adminstrn., summer 1971; m. Eugenia A. Naruc, Feb. 7, 1959; children: Debra, Mark, David, Anne, James. Mgmt. trainee, cost acct., cost analyst, sr. internal auditor, sr. cost acct. Ford Motor Co., Dearborn, Mich., 1953-60; tchr. Bedford Sch., Dearborn Heights, Mich., 1960-62; bus. mgr., adminstrv. asst. to dir. Wayne State U. Center For Adult Edn., 1962-64; controller, dir. bus. affairs Mercy Coll. of Detroit, 1964-73; sec.-treas. Am. Sunroof Corp., v.p., corp. sec., 1977-81; sec.-treas. Automobile Splty. Corp., Southgate, Mich., 1973-81; pres., dir. Servia, Inc., cons. to mgmt., Livonia, Mich., 1980-81; corp. v.p. ops. Crown Group, Inc., 1981-83; v.p., gen. mgr. Mktg. Displays, Inc., 1983-85; chief exec. officer Physicians Health Plan (United Health Care), Lansing, Mich., 1985-86, Physicians Choice Northwest, Ind. (Unted Healthcare), Merrillville, 1986-87; exec. dir. Capital Dist. Physician's Health Plan, Albany, N.Y., 1987-92; exec. v.p. Emerald Health Network, Inc., Cleve., 1992-94; pres., CEO Emerald HMO, Inc., 1994-95; gen. mgr. Genesis Health Plans of Ohio, Inc., 1996—; cons. Managed Health Care, 1995-96. Rep. adv. council Livonia Bd. Edn., 1968-71; v.p. Country Homes Estates Civic Assn., 1971-73; commr. Econ. Devel. Corp.; mem. U. Albany Found. Mem. Employers Assn. Detroit, Am. Soc. Tng. Dirs., Am. Arbitration Assn. (mem. nat. panel), Am. Managed Care and Rev. Assn. (founder exec. leadership program), Nat. Found. for Ileitis and Colitis (bd. dir. capital dist. chpt.), Albany Execs. Assn., Group Health Assn. Am., Delta Sigma Pi, Beta Gamma Sigma. Republican. Roman Catholic. Home: 29642 Washington Way Westlake OH 44145-6400 Office: Genesis Health Plans of Ohio Inc 2 Summit Park Dr Ste 340 Cleveland OH 44131

PORTER, ALAN LESLIE, industrial and systems engineering educator; b. Jersey City, June 22, 1945; s. Leslie Frank and Alice Mae (Kaufman) P.; m. Claudia Loy Ferrey, June 14, 1968; children: Brett, Doug, Lynn. BSChemE, Calif. Inst. Tech., 1967; MS, UCLA, 1968, PhD in Psychology, 1972. Research assoc., asst. prof. program social mgmt. tech. U. Wash., Seattle, 1972-74; asst. prof. indsl. and systems engring. Ga. Inst. Tech., Atlanta, 1975-78, assoc. prof., 1979-85, prof., 1986—, dir., tech. policy and assessment ctr., 1989—; cons. Dept. Commerce, State of Md., Search Tech., IBM, Coca Cola. Author, editor: (with others) A Guidebook for Technology Assessment and Impact Analysis, 1980, (with T.J. Kuehn) Science Technology and National Policy, 1981, (with F.A. Rossini) Integrated Impact Assessment, Impact Assessment Bull., 1981-84, Methods and Experience in Impact Assessment, 1986, Interdisciplinarity, 1986, Impact of Office Automation on Clerical Employment, 1985, Forecasting and Management of Technology, 1991. NIH fellow, 1968; NSF grantee, 1974-75, 78-86, 89—, Dept. Transp. grantee, 1977-79, Fund for Improvement Post Secondary Edn. grantee, 1977-79, Dept. Labor grantee, 1973-74. Mem. Internat. Assn. Impact Assessment (co-founder, sec. 1981-87, exec. dir. 1987-90, pres. 1995-96), IEEE Systems Man and Cybernetics Soc. (chmn. tech. forecasting com.), Am. Soc. Engr. Edn. (chmn. engrs. and pub. policy div. 1982-83, Bellcore adv. coun.). Home: 110 Lake Top Ct Roswell GA 30076-3017 Office: Sch Indsl and Systems Engring Ga Tech Atlanta GA 30332

PORTER, ANDREW CALVIN, educational administrator, psychology educator; b. Huntington, Pa., July 10, 1942; s. Rutherford and Grace (Johnson) P.; m. Susan Porter, June 5, 1967; children: Matthew, Anna, John, Joe, Kate. BS, Ind. State U., 1963; MS, U. Wis., 1965, PhD, 1967. Prof., co-dir. inst. rsch. on teaching Mich. State U., East Lansing, 1967-88; assoc. dir. basic skills group Nat. Inst. Edn., Washington, 1975-76; prof. ednl. psychology, dir. Wis. Ctr. Edn. Rsch. U. Wis., Madison, 1988—; vis. asst. prof. Ind. State U., Terre Haute, 1967; mem. adv. bd. Am. Jour. Edn., 1988—; mem. bd. Internat. Studies, Nat. Acad. Scis., Nat. Rsch. Coun., 1993—; chmn. U.S. Dept. Edn., adv. coun. on edn. stats., 1994—. Author: Creating a System of School Process Indicators, 1991. Bd. dirs. Madison Urban League, 1992—. Recipient award Inst. for Sci. Edn., NSF, Ctr. for Policy Rsch. in Edn., Disting. Alumni award Ind. U., 1994. Mem. Am. Ednl. Rsch. Assn. (mem.-at-large), Nat. Coun. Edn. Measurement, Nat. Coun. Tchrs. Math., Psychometric Soc., Nat. Acad. Edn., Phi Delta Kappa (life). Office: U Wis Madison Wis Ctr Edn Rsch 1025 W Johnson St Madison WI 53706-1706

PORTER, ARTHUR T., oncologist, educator; b. June 11, 1956; m. Pamela Porter; 4 children. Student, U. Sierra Leone, 1974-75; BA in Anatomy, Cambridge U., 1978, M.B.B.Chir./M.D., 1980, MA, 1984; DMRT, Royal Coll. Radiologists, Eng., 1985; postgrad., U. Alta., 1984-86; FRCPC, Royal Coll. Physicians and Surgeons, Can., 1986; cert. for physicians mgr. program, U. Toronto, 1990; postgrad., LaSalle U. Lic., bd. cert., Mich., Can., Eng. House physician gen. medicine Norfolk and Norwich Hosp., Eng., 1981; house sugeon gen. surgery New Addenbrookes Hosp., Cambridge, Eng., 1981-82; sr. house officer clin. hematology No. Gen. Hosp., Sheffield, Eng., 1982; sr. house officer gen. medicine Huntington County Hosp., Hinchingbrooke Hosp., Eng., 1982-83; sr. house officer radiotherapy and oncology Norfolk and Norwich Hosp., Norwich, 1983-84; chief resident radiation oncology Cross Cancer Inst., Edmonton, Alta., Can., 1984-86, radiation oncologist, 1986-87, sr. radiation oncologist, 1987; asst. prof. faculty medicine U. Alta., Edmonton, 1987, assoc. clin. prof. dept. surgery faculty medicine, 1988; head divsn. radiation oncology U. Western Ont., London, Can., 1988; cons. radiation oncologist, chief dept. radiation oncology London Regional Cancer Ctr., 1988, program dir. radiation oncology, 1989-91; chmn. dept. oncology Victoria Hosp. Corp., London, 1990; assoc. prof. dept. oncology U. Western Ont., 1990; program dir. radiation oncology Wayne State U., Detroit, 1991-92, prof., chmn. dept. radiation oncology Sch. Medicine, 1991—; chief Gershenson Radiation Oncology Ctr. Harper Hosp., Detroit, 1991—; radiation oncologist-in-chief Detroit Med. Ctr., 1991—; pres., CEO Radiation Oncology R & D Ctr., Detroit, 1991—; dir. multidisciplinary svcs. Meyer L. Prentice Comprehensive Cancer Ctr., Detroit, 1992—; chmn. radiation oncology Grace Hosp., Detroit, 1993—; vis. prof. U. London, Eng., 1990, U. Mich., 1991, U. Ky., 1992, U. Rochester, 1992, U. So. Calif., 1995; cons. neutron therapy Dept. Health Govt. of U.K., 1990; mem. editorial bd. Endocurietherapy/Hyperthermia Oncology, 1991—, Cambridge Cancer Series, 1991—, Baxter Adminstrv. Manual, 1991—, Oncore, 1989-91, Internat. Monitor Oncology, 1992—; mem. genito-urinary com. Radiation Therapy Oncology Group, 1986—, new investigators com., 1986-87, bladder task force, 1986-88, time dose and fractionation, 1987—, large field working group, 1987—, full mem. com., 1987-91, exec. com., 1991; mem. radiation oncology com. Nat. Cancer Inst. Can., 1987-90, radiation quality assurance subcom., 1987-90, G.U. com., 1987-90; prin. investigator Radiation Therapy Oncology Group, U. Alta., 1987-88, U. Western Ont., 1989-91; mem. working group on bladder cancer Internat. Consensus, 1988, working group on prostate cancer, 1988; mem. Can. Uro-Oncology Group, 1990; chmn. brachytherapy subcom. Radiation Therapy Oncology Group, 1990-92, spl. populations com., 1991, systemic radionucleides com., 1991; mem. G.U. com. Southwest Oncology Group, 1991, selection com. Windsor Cancer Ctr., 1992; mem. cancer grant review conf. Nat. Cancer Inst., 1992; mem. NIH Sub-Saharan African Health Rsch. Initiative, 1993; chmn. South Western Ont. Uro-Oncology Group, 1988-91, Profl. Adv. Com. Radiation Oncology, 1990-91, Site Com. for Prostate Cancer, 1990-91; mem. Ont. Commn. Radiation Oncology, 1989-91, Cancer 2000 Com., 1990-91, PET com. Children's Hosp. Mich., 1991—, adv. com. dept. radiology Detroit Receiving Hosp., 1991—; dir. Univ. Physicians, Inc., 1991—; bd. dirs. MLPCCCMD, Biomide Corp., Vetrogen Corp., MedCyc, Med. Knowledge Systems, Am. Cancer Soc.; bd. trustees Fund Med. Rsch. Edn., 1991—, Meyer L. Prentice Comprehensive Cancer Ctr., 1992—; mem. exec. com. Am. Cancer Soc., Wayne County, 1992—; mem. Amersham Internat. Adv. Bd., 1992—; co-chmn. regional adv. bd. Am. Cancer Soc., 1992—, pres., 1994—; mem. Medi-Pysics Adv. Bd., 1992—; pres. Biomide Corp. Bd., 1993—; lectr. in field. Author: (with others) Fundamental Problems in Breastic Progress in Urological Cancers, 1988, Proceedings of the Consensus Meeting of the Treatment of Bladder Cancer-1987, 1988, Brachytherapy, 1989, High and Low Dose Rate Brachytherapy, 1989, Brachytherapy of Prostate Cancer, 1991; co-editor Treatment of Cancer, 1991—; assoc. editor Can. Jour. Oncology, 1990—, Antibody and Radiopharmaceuticals, 1992—; contbr. articles to profl. jours. Recipient Nat. award Sierra Leone, 1975-80, Commonwealth Found. scholarship, 1980, Best Doctor in Am. award, 1992, 93, 94, 95, Testimonial Resolution, City of Detroit, 1993. Fellow Am. Coll. Angiology, Detroit Acad. Medicine, Royal Soc. Medicine; mem. AMA (Physicians Recognition award 1986), Am. Soc. Therapeutic Radiation Oncology, Am. Radium Soc., Am. Soc. Clin. Oncology, Am. Coll. Radiation Oncology (chancellor 1994-97), Am. Coll. Oncol. Adminstrs. (pres. 1994-96), Am. Acad. Med. Adminstrs., Am. Endocurietherapy Soc. (pres. 1994-95), Mich. State Med. Soc., Mich. Soc. Therapeutic Radiation Oncology, Mich. Radiol. Soc., Detroit Med. Soc. (Ann. award for Excellence 1993), Wayne County Med. Soc., European Soc. Therapeutic Radiation Oncology, Brit. Inst. Radiology, Can. Oncology Soc., Can. Assn. Radiation Oncology, Royal Coll. Radiologists, Sierra Leone Med. and Dental Assn., Greater Detroit C. of C., Sigma Xi. Achievements include patent in a perineal applicator; research in novel methods in delivery dose, brachytherapy, intraoperative therapy, unsealed source therapy, verification and dosimetry, real time portal imaging, three-dimensional and planning, unsealed source dosimetry, the design of perineal applicators. Office: Radiation Oncology Rsch & Dev Ctr 4201 Saint Antoine St Detroit MI 48201-2153

PORTER, BARBARA, anchorwoman, writer, educator; m. Henry Stroud Elms III; children: Tommy, Dorian. Anchorwoman NBC Radio; tchr. in dramatics and journalism; writer cable TV children's programming. Office: Westwood One 1775 S Jefferson Davis Hwy Arlington VA 22202

PORTER, BERNARD HARDEN, consulting physicist, author, publisher; b. Porter Settlement, Maine, Feb. 14, 1911; s. Lewis Harden and Etta Flora (Rogers) P.; m. Helen Elaine Hendron, July 15, 1946 (div. Aug. 1947); m. Margaret Eudine Preston, Aug. 27, 1955 (dec. April 1975); m. Lula Mae Blom, Sept. 9, 1976 (div. Nov. 1986). BS, Colby Coll., 1932; MS, Brown U., 1933; DSc (hon.), Inst. Advanced Thinking, Calais, Maine, 1959. Physicist Acheson Colloids Corp., Port Huron, Mich., 1935-40; rsch. physicist Manhattan Dist. Engrs., Princeton, N.J., Berkeley, Calif. and Oak Ridge, 1940-45; cons. physicist San Francisco and Pasadena, Calif., Waldwick, N.J., Rockland, Belfast, Maine, 1945—; chmn. bd. Bern Porter Inc., Pasadena, Rockland, Belfast, 1945—; pres. Bern Porter Books, Pasadena, Rockland, Belfast, 1929—, Bern Porter Internat., Belfast, 1974—; cons. Internat. Exec. Service Corps, 1968, SBA, 1968-88. Author: The 14th of February, 1971, I've Left, 1971, Founds, 1972, Hand Coated Chocolates, 1972, Contemporary Italian Painters, 1973, Trattoria Due Forni, 1973, The Book of Do's, 1974, The Manhattan Telephone Book, 1975, Run-On, 1975, Where, 1975, Selected Founds, 1975, Gee-Whizzles, 1976, Don't Book, 1981, Last Acts, 1985, My, My, 1985, Left Leg, 1988, Neverends, 1988, Numbers, 1989, Sweetend, 1989, Bern Porter and Fa Gaga, 1990, Sounds That Arouse Me, 1992, Less Than Overweight, 1992, Mothering Time, 1993; contbr. numerous articles to profl. jours. Rep. candidate for gov. Maine, 1969; bd. dirs. Inst. Advanced Thinking, Belfast, chmn. bd., 1959—. Recipient awards PEN, 1975, 76, 77, Authors League, 1977; Carnegie author, 1975; diploma merit Centro Studi E Scambi Internazionale, Rome, 1976; Nat. Endowment for Arts lit. award, 1979. Fellow Am. Astronautical Soc., Tech. Pub. Soc., Am. Rocket Soc. (assoc.), Soc. Tech. Writers and Pubs. (assoc.), Internat. Acad. Poets (London, founding); mem. Am. Phys. Soc., Soc. Internat. Devel., Nat. Soc. Programmed Instrn., Fenway Club (Boston), Algonquin Club, St. Andrews Club (N.B., Can.), Phi Beta Kappa, Sigma Xi, Kappa Phi Kappa, Chi Gamma Sigma. Methodist. Address: 50 Salmond St Belfast ME 04915-1316

PORTER, BLAINE ROBERT MILTON, psychology and sociology educator; b. Morgan, Utah, Feb. 24, 1922; s. Brigham Ernest and Edna (Brough) P.; m. Elizabeth Taylor, Sept 27, 1943 (dec.); children: Claudia Black, Roger B., David T., Patricia A. Hintze, Corinna; m. Myrna Katherine Kennedy, Feb. 26, 1988. Student, Utah State U., 1940-41; BS, Brigham Young U., 1947, MA, 1949; PhD (Grant Found. fellow family life edn. 1951-52), Cornell U., 1952. Instr. sociology Iowa State Coll., 1949-51; asst. prof. sociology and child devel. Iowa State U., 1952-55; prof., chmn. dept. human devel. and family relationships Brigham Young U., 1955-65, dean Coll. Family Living, 1966-80, Univ. prof., 1980-87; vis. prof. Fulbright rsch. scholar U. London, 1965-66; vis. prof. U. Wurzberg, 1980, 81, 83; facilitator human rels. workshops for the Human Devel. Inst., Denver, 1988-90. Editor: The Latter-day Saint Family, 1963, rev. edit., 1966; editor quar. jour.: Family Perspective, 1966-82; contbr. articles to profl. jours. Pres. elect Iowa Coun. Family Rels., 1954-55; pres. Utah Coun. Family Rels., 1957-58; chmn. sect. marriage counseling Nat. Coun. Family Rels., 1958-59, bd. dirs., 1957-60, exec. com., 1958-72, pres., 1963-64; bd. dirs. Am. Family Soc.,

1975-85. Pilot USAAF, 1942-45. Recipient Prof. of Yr. award Brigham Young U., 1964. Mem. Am. Home Econs. Assn. (vice chmn. sect. family relations and child devel. 1955-56), Am. Sociol. Assn. (sec. sect. on family 1964-67), Am. Assn. Marriage and Family Therapy, Am. Psychol. Assn., Soc. Research in Child Devel., Sigma Xi, Phi Kappa Phi (chpt. pres. 1969-71). Home: 1675 Pine Ln Provo UT 84604-2163 Office: Brigham Young U 4505 Hbll Provo UT 84602-1035

PORTER, BRUCE DOUGLAS, educator, federal agency administrator, writer; b. Albuquerque, Sept. 18, 1952; s. Lyle Kay and Wilma (Holmes) P.; m. Susan Elizabeth Holland, Feb. 2, 1977; children: David William, Christopher Jonathan, Lisa Jeanette, Jennifer Rachel. BA in History, Brigham Young U., 1976; AM in Soviet Studies, Harvard U., 1978, PhD in Polit. Sci., 1979. Sr. rsch. analyst Radio Free Europe/Radio Liberty, Inc., Munich, 1980-83; profl. staff mem. armed svcs. com. U.S. Senate, Washington, 1983-84; sr. analyst Northrop Corp. Analysis Ctr., Washington, 1984-86; exec. dir. Bd. for Internat. Broadcasting, Washington, 1986-90; Bradley sr. rsch. assoc. Harvard U., Cambridge, Mass., 1990-93; assoc. prof. Brigham Young U., Provo, Utah, 1993-95; min. LDS Ch., 1995—. Author: The USSR in Third World Conflicts, 1976, Red Armies in Crisis, 1991, War and the Rise of the State, 1993; co-author: The Polish Drama: 1980-82, 1983; contbr. articles to profl. jours. Lay min. Ch. Jesus Christ Latter-day Saints, bishop, 1985-90, missionary, Düsseldorf, Fed. Republic Germany, 1971-73. Post doctoral fellow Harvard Ctr. for Internat. Affairs, 1979-80, Danforth fellow, 1976-79, David O. McKay scholar Brigham Young U., 1970-71, 74-76; recipient Meritorious Svc. award Pres. of U.S., 1990. Mem. Am. Polit. Sci. Assn., Am. Assn. Advancement Slavic Studies, Internat. Studies Assn. Avocations: swimming, creative writing. Office: Brigham Young U 784 Swkt Provo UT 84602-1130

PORTER, BURTON FREDERICK, philosophy educator, author, dean; b. N.Y.C., June 22, 1936; s. John and Doris (Neloway) P.; m. Susan Jane Porter, May 10, 1966 (div. 1974); 1 child, Anastasia; m. Barbara Taylor Metcalf, Dec. 31, 1980; 1 child, Mark Graham. BA Philosophy cum laude, spl. lit. hons., U. Md., 1959; PhD, St. Andrews U., Scotland, 1968; post-grad., Oxford (Eng.) U. Asst. prof. philosophy U. Md., London, 1966-69; assoc. prof. philosophy King's Coll., Wilkes-Barre, Pa., 1969-71; prof. philosophy, chmn. dept. Russell Sage Coll., Troy, N.Y., 1971-87; prof. philosophy, head dept. humanities-comm. Drexel U., Phila., 1987-91; dean arts and scis. Western New England Coll., Springfield, Mass., 1991—. Author: Deity and Morality, 1968, Philosophy, A Literary and Conceptual Approach, 1974, 80, 95, Personal Philosophy: Perspectives on Living, 1976, The Good Life, Alternatives in Ethics, 1980, 91, 94, Reasons for Living: A Basic Ethics, 1988, Religion and Reason, 1993; also articles and book revs. Named Outstanding Educator of Am., NEA, 1975. Mem. Am. Philos. Assn., MLA. Home: 30 Fearing St Amherst MA 01002-1912 Office: Western New Eng Coll Arts & Scis Dean's Office Springfield MA 01119

PORTER, CHARLES KING, advertising executive; b. Mpls., Oct. 10, 1945; s. King E. and Bernetta Porter Andrews; m. Margit Gammeltoft, Feb. 26, 1972; children: Kristin, Catherine, James. BS in Journalism, U. Minn., 1967. Ptnr. Breen & Porter Co., Miami, Fla., 1974-85; pres. Porter Creative Svcs., Miami, 1985-88, Crispin & Porter Advt., Miami, 1988—; dir. Miami Ad Sch. Trustee Beacon Coun., Miami, 1988—. Recipient Nat. Addy award Am. Advt. Fedn., 1991, 92, Andy award Advt. Club N.Y., 1993, 94. Mem. Am. Assn. Advt Agys. (forum, Nat. A Plus award 1991, 94, 95, 96). Presbyterian. Avocations: skiing, travel, history. Office: Crispin & Porter Advt 2699 S Bayshore Dr Miami FL 33133-5408

PORTER, CLOYD ALLEN, state representative; b. Huntley, Ill., May 22, 1935; s. Cecil and Myrtle (Fischer) P.; m. Joan Hawkins, July 25, 1959; children: Ellen, LeeAnn, Jay, Joli. Grad. high sch., Burlington, Wis. Ptnr. Cecil W. Porter & Son Trucking, 1955-70; treas. Burlington Sand and Gravel, 1964-70; owner Cloyd A. Porter Trucking, Burlington, 1970-72; state rep. 43d dist. Wis. State Assembly, Madison, 1972-82; state rep. 66th dist. Wis. State Assembly, 1982—; mem. coun. on recycling, Wis., 1991—, fire svc. legis. adv. com., 1987—, legis. coun. com. on fire inspections and fire dues, 1991, legis. coun. spl. com. on emergency med. svcs., 1992-93. Contbr. articles to profl. jours. Chmn. Town of Burlington, 1971-75; state and met. affairs chmn. Jaycees, Wis., 1963, state v.p., 1969, adminstrv. asst., 1970, exec. v.p., 1971; mem. Wis. Conservation Congress for Natural Resources Leadership and Support in the State Assembly, 1994. Recipient many awards and honors including being named hon. mem. State Fire Chiefs Assn., Wis., 1992, Guardian of Small Bus., NFIB, Wis., 1991, Friend of Agr., Farm Bur. of Wis., 1992, 94, Friend of Edn. Fair Aid Coalition, 1995; recipient Mission Impossible award Consumer Packaging Coun. Wis., 1990, Cert. of Appreciation, Wis. Counties Assn., 1993, award Wis. Sate Fire Chiefs Assn., 1995, others. Mem. Wis. Alliance for Fire Safety. Republican. Roman Catholic. Home: 28322 Durand Ave Burlington WI 53105-9408 Office: State Capitol PO Box 8953 309 North Madison WI 53708

PORTER, DANIEL REED, III, museum director; b. Northampton, Mass., July 2, 1930; s. Daniel Reed and Eleanor (Parsons) P.; m. Joan Joyce Dornfeld, Nov. 22, 1958; children: Leslie Marie, Andrew Gregory. BA, U. Mass., 1952; MA, U. Mich., 1956. Asst. to dir. State Hist. Soc. Wis., Madison, 1956-58; dir. Hist. Soc. York County, Pa., 1958-61; asst. dir., dir. Ohio Hist. Soc., Columbus, 1961-74; exec. dir. Preservation Soc. Newport County, R.I., 1974-78; dir., prof. Cooperstown (N.Y.) Grad. Programs, 1978-82; dir. N.Y. State Hist. Assn. Farmer's Mus. Cooperstown, Cooperstown, 1982-92; hist. preservation officer State of Ohio, Columbus, 1967-74. Editor: N.Y. Heritage, 1984-92; contbr. articles to publs. in field. With U.S. Army, 1952-54, Korea. Recipient Spl. award of Merit Ohio Assn. Hist. Socs., 1970. Mem. Am. Assn. Mus. (accreditation commn. 1982-88, councillor-at-large 1981-84), Am. Assn. State and Local History (coun., Nashville 1971-73, councillor 1985-87). Congregationalist.

PORTER, DARWIN FRED, writer; b. Greensboro, N.C., Sept. 13, 1937; s. Numie Rowan and Hazel Lee (Phillips) P. B.A., U. Miami, 1959. Bur. chief Miami Herald, 1959-60; v.p. Haggart Assocs., N.Y.C., 1961-64; editor, author Arthur Frommer Inc., N.Y.C., 1964-67, Frommer/Pasmantier Pub. Corp., N.Y.C., 1967-86, Prentice Hall Press, N.Y.C., 1987-90, Simon & Schuster, N.Y.C., 1991—. Author: Frommer Travel Guides to: England, 1964, Spain, 1966, Scandinavia, 1967, Los Angeles, 1969, London, 1970, Lisbon/Madrid, 1972, Paris, 1972, Morocco, 1974, Rome, 1974, Portugal, 1968, England, 1969, Italy, 1969, Germany, 1970, France, 1970, Caribbean, Bermuda, the Bahamas, 1980, Switzerland, 1984, Austria and Hungary, 1984, Bermuda and the Bahamas, 1985, Scotland and Wales, 1985, the Virgin Islands, 1991, Scotland, 1992, Jamaica/Barbados, 1992, Puerto Rico, 1992, the Caribbean, 1993, Bermuda, 1993, the Bahamas, 1993, Austria, 1993, Madrid & the Costa del Sol, 1993, San Francisco, 1996, California, 1996; author: (novels) Butterflies in Heat, 1976, Marika, 1977, Venus, 1982. Recipient Silver award Internat. Film and TV Festival N.Y., 1977. Mem. Soc. Am. Travel Writers, Smithsonian Assocs., Nat. Trust for Historic Preservation, Sigma Delta Chi. Home: 75 St Marks Pl Staten Island NY 10301-1606

PORTER, DAVID BRUCE, air force officer, behavioral scientist, educator; b. Lexington, Ky., June 17, 1949; m. Sharon Jo Mahood, June 9, 1971; children: David Damien, Kristin Gillian. BS, USAF Acad., 1971; MS, UCLA, 1972; DPhil, Oxford U., 1986. Commd. 2d lt. USAF, 1967, advanced through grades to col., 1993; chief orgnl. maintenance, functional check flight pilot USAF, Hickam AFB, Hawaii, 1973-79; exec. officer USAF, RAF Woodbridge, U.K., 1981-83; instr. behavioral sci., leadership USAF Acad. USAF, Colorado Springs, Colo., 1979-81, assoc. prof., sr. milit. prof., dept. head USAF Acad., 1986—; cons., examiner N. Ctrl. Assn. Colls. and Univs., 1996—. Contbr. to profl. publs. including Jour. Coll. Reading and Learning, Current Psychology Rsch. and Revs., Counseling and Values, Jour. Adolescent Assessment. Bd. dirs. Citizens Project, Colorado Springs, 1993-95; pres. All Souls Unitarian Ch., 1989-91. Home: 1402 N Weber St Colorado Springs CO 80907-7516 Office: USAF Acad Dept Behavioral Sci 6L67 Fairchild Hall U S A F Academy CO 80840

PORTER, DAVID HUGH, pianist, classicist, academic administrator, liberal arts educator; b. N.Y.C., Oct. 29, 1935; s. Hugh B. and Ethel K. (Flentye) P.; m. Laudie Ernestine Dimmette, June 21, 1958 (dec. Nov., 1986); children: Hugh, Everett, Helen, David; m. Helen Louise Nelson, Aug. 24, 1987. BA with highest honors, Swarthmore Coll., 1958; PhD (Danforth Grad. fellow, Woodrow Wilson Grad. fellow), Princeton U., 1962; student, Phila. Conservatory Music, 1953-56. Instr. in classics and music Carleton Coll., Northfield, Minn., 1962-63, asst. prof., 1963-68, assoc. prof., 1968-73, prof., 1973-87, William H. Laird prof. liberal arts, 1974-87, pres. faculty, 1980-82, coll. pres., 1986-87; pres. Skidmore Coll., Saratoga Springs, N.Y., 1987—, prof. classics, 1987—; Phi Beta Kappa vis. lectr., 1979-92, vis. scholar, 1994-95; vis. prof. classics Princeton U., 1986; recitalist, lectr., especially on contemporary music, at colls., univs. throughout U.S., Europe, on radio and TV; bd. dirs. Adirondack Trust Co.; chmn. Hudson-Mohawk Assn., 1990-92. Author: Only Connect: Three Studies in Greek Tragedy, 1987, Horace's Poetic Journey: A Reading of Odes I-III, 1987; editor: Carleton Remembered, 1909-86, 1987, The Not Quite Innocent Bystander: Writings of Edward Steuermann, 1989; contbr. articles on classics, music and edn. to profl. jours. NEH research fellow, 1969-70, 83-84; Am. Council Learned Socs. research fellow, 1976-77. Mem. Am. Philological Assn., Classical Assn. Atlantic States. Democrat. Mem. United Ch. Christ. Avocations: hiking, fishing, reading, collecting rugs and books. Home: 791 N Broadway Saratoga Springs NY 12866-1601 Office: Skidmore Coll Office of Pres Saratoga Springs NY 12866

PORTER, DAVID LINDSEY, history and political science educator, author; b. Holyoke, Mass., Feb. 18, 1941; s. Willis Hubert and Lora Frances (Bowen) P.; m. Marilyn Esther Platt, Nov. 28, 1970; children: Kevin, Andrea. BA magna cum laude, Franklin Coll., 1963; MA, Ohio U., 1965; PhD, Pa. State U., 1970. Asst. prof. history Rensselaer Poly. Inst., Troy, N.Y., 1970-75, co-dir. Am. studies program, 1972-74; ednl. adminstrv. asst. Civil Svc. Office State of N.Y., Troy, 1975-76; asst. prof. history William Penn Coll., Oskaloosa, Iowa, 1976-77, assoc. prof. history, 1977-82, prof. history and polit. sci., 1982-86, Louis Tuttle Shangle prof. history and polit. sci., 1986—, chmn. Sperry & Hutchinson Found. lectureship series, 1980-82; supr. legis. internship program Iowa Gen. Assembly, 1978—, records inventory project Mahaska County, 1978-79, internship program Washington Ctr., 1985—; active Franklin D. Roosevelt Meml. Commn. Author: The Seventy-sixth Congress and World War II, 1939-40, 1979, Congress and the Waning of the New Deal, 1980; contbr. to Dictionary of American Biography, 1981, 88, 94, 95, Directory of Teaching Innovations in History, 1981, The Book of Lists #3, 1983, Biographical Dictionary of Internationalists, 1983, The Hero in Transition, 1983, Herbert Hoover and the Republican Era: A Reconsideration, 1984, The History of Mahaska County, Iowa, 1984, Franklin D. Roosevelt, His Life and Times: An Encyclopedic View, 1985, The Rating Game in American Politics: An Interdisciplinary Approach, 1987, Sport History, 1987, Book of Days, 1988, Sports Encyclopedia North America, 1988, The Harry S. Truman Encyclopedia, 1989, Encyclopedia of Major League Baseball Team Histories: The National League, 1991, Twentieth Century Sports Champions, 1992, Statesmen Who Changed the World, 1993; editor, contbr.: Biographical Dictionary of American Sports: vols. Baseball, 1987, Football, 1987, Outdoor Sports, 1988, Basketball and Other Indoor Sports, 1989, 1989-92 Supplement for Baseball, Football, Basketball and Other Sports, 1992, 1992-95, Supplement for Baseball, Football, Basketball and Other Sports, 1995, African-American Sports Greats, 1995; compiler, A Cumulative Index to the Biographical Dictionary of American Sports, 1993; assoc. editor: (with others) American National Biography, 20 vols.; contbr. weekly column to Oskaloosa Herald, 1994—, numerous articles to various dictionaries, directories, encys., jours., revs., newspapers, commentary to Nat. Pub. Radio. Mem. Franklin D. Roosevelt Meml. Commn. Grantee NSF, 1967, NEH, 1974, Rensselaer Poly. Inst., 1974, Eleanor Roosevelt Inst., 1981, William Penn Coll., 1986, 89, 92; recipient Choice Outstanding Acad. Book awards, 1989. Mem. AAUP, Am. Hist. Assn., Orgn. Am. Historians, N.Am. Soc. for Sport History, Soc. History Am. Fgn. Rels., Ctr. for Study of the Presidency, Soc. Am. Baseball Rsch., Popular Culture Assn., Profl. Football Researchers Assn., Coll. Football Rschrs. Assn., Coll. Football Hist. Soc., State Hist. Soc. Iowa, Mahaska County Hist. Soc., Iowa State UN Assn. (chmn. ann. assembly 1982, nat. soc. Disting. Svc. award 1981), Mahaska County UN Assn., Oskaloosa Babe Ruth League (bd. dirs.), Oskaloosa Community Choir, Friends of Oskaloosa Pub. Libr. (nominating com.), Phi Alpha Theta, Kappa Delta Pi. Mem. United Meth. Ch. Home: 2314 Ridgeway Ave Oskaloosa IA 52577-9109 Office: William Penn Coll Dept Social Sci 201 Trueblood Ave Oskaloosa IA 52577-1757

PORTER, DEAN ALLEN, art museum director, art historian, educator; b. Gouverneur, N.Y., June 13, 1939; s. Arnold W. and Gertrude V. Porter; m. Carol DuBrava, July 27, 1963; children: Kellie Ann, Tracie Ann. BA, Harpur Coll., 1961; MA in Art History, SUNY, Binghamton, 1966, PhD in Art History, 1974. curator Art Gallery, U. Notre Dame, 1966-74, dir. Snite Mus. Art, 1974—, prof. art history, 1994—; bd. dirs. Southwest Art History Coun.; mem. mus. coun. Harwood Found., U. N.Mex.; mem. adv. bd. Ind. U. Art Mus.; mem. nat. adv. coun. Valparaiso (Ind.) U. Mus. Art. Samuel H. Kress fellow. Mem. Coll. Art Assn., Am. Assn. Mus., Assn. Art Mus. Dirs. Author exhbn. catalogues, including: Janos Scholz, Musician and Collector, 1980, A Guide to The Snite Museum of Art, 1980, Selected Works from the Snite Museum of Art, 1987, Victor Higgins: An Am. Master, 1990, The Univ. Notre Dame Friends and Alumni Collect: A Sesquicentennial Celebration, 1992. Office: Snite Mus of Art PO Box 368 Notre Dame IN 46556-0368

PORTER, DON E., sports adiministrator; b. Oklahoma City, Okla.. Exec. dir. Amateur Softball Assn., 1963; sec. gen. Internat. Softball Fedn., 1965-87; officiator Big Eight Conf., 1970-75; NFL, 1976-79; pres. Internat. Softball Fedn., 1987—; bd. dirs. U.S. Olympic Com., chmn. Transp. Com., 1985, Olympic Festival Com., 1989, 93, U.S. Olympic Congress Site Selection Com., 1991, Sooner State Games Com., Okla., 1983-89, Gov's. Coun. on Physical Fitness and Sports, 1988, 91, pres., 1995; co-chmn. U.S. Olympic Com. Games Site and Nat. Tng. Ctrs. Com., 1980; sec. gen. World Games I, 1981; sec. Assn. Internat. Olympic Com. Recognized Sports Fedns., 1984; rep. U.S. Olympic Com. Nat. Governing Bodies Hall of Fame Oversight Com., 1987, Special Ethics Oversight Com., 1992; apptd. U.S. State Dept. Adv. Com. Internat. Athletics, 1975, Gov's. Task Force on Physical Fitness and Sports,Okla., 1980, U.S. Olympic Com. Internat. Rels. Com., 1980, 95, Eligibility Com., 1986, Task Force Olympic Festivals, 1990, Internat. Olympic Com. Press Commn., 1994. Hearing panel Ethics Commn., Okla., 1979; Mayor's adv. coun., Okla. City, 1985; Riverfront Devel. Authority, 1985, 91. With U.S. Army, 1950-52. Recipient Medal of Honor Italian Olympic Com., 1977, Chinese Taipei Olympic Com., 1991; named Hall of Fame, Internat. Softball Assn., 1982. Office: Nat Softball Hall of Fame & Mus 2801 NE 50th St Oklahoma City OK 73111-7203

PORTER, DOUGLAS TAYLOR, athletic administrator; b. Fayetteville, Tenn., Aug. 15, 1928; s. Waudell Phillip and Sophia Mae (Taylor) P.; m. Jean Butcher, Apr. 18, 1953; children: Daria C., Blanche E., Douglas V. BS, Xavier U., 1952; MS, Ind. U., 1960. Asst. football coach St. Augustine High Sch., Memphis, 1955, Xavier U., New Orleans, 1956-60; dir. athletics, head football coach Miss. Vocat. Coll., Itta Bena, Miss., 1960-65; assoc. dir. athletics, coach Grambling (La.) State U., 1966-73; head football coach Howard U., Washington, 1974-78; dir. athletics, head football coach Ft. Valley (Ga.) State Coll., 1979—; pres. Nat. Athletic Steering Com., Ft. Valley, 1990—. Lt. U.S. Army, 1951-54. Mem. Am. Alliance of Health, Phys. Edn. and Dance, Nat. Assn. of Collegiate Dirs. of Athletics, Sigma Pi Phi, Alpha Phi Alpha (pres. 1983-87), Phi Delta Kappa. Democrat. Roman Catholic. Avocations: reading, listening to jazz. Home: 107 College Ct Fort Valley GA 31030-3216 Office: Ft Valley State Coll 1005 State College Dr Fort Valley GA 31030-3262

PORTER, DUDLEY, JR., environmentalist, foundation executive, lawyer; b. Paris, Tenn., May 10, 1915; s. Dudley and Mary (Bolling) P.; m. Mary Rhoda Montague, Oct. 21, 1950. Student, Murray (Ky.) State Coll., 1933-34; LL.B., Cumberland U., 1936. Bar: Tenn. 1937. Asst. atty. gen. Tenn., 1937-40; mem. firm Tyne, Peebles, Henry & Tyne, Nashville, 1940-49; with law dept. Nat. Life & Accident Ins. Co., Nasvhille, 1940-49; asso. gen. counsel Nat. Life & Accident Ins. Co., 1948; with Provident Life & Accident Ins. Co., Chattanooga, 1949—; gen. counsel Provident Life & Accident Ins. Co., 1954-72, sr. v.p., 1958-72, sec., 1965-72, vice chmn., sr. counsel, 1972-76; of counsel Chambliss, Bahner, Crutchfield, Gaston & Irvine, Chattanooga, 1977—. Mem. Hamilton County Juvenile Ct. Commn., 1958-64, chmn., 1964; mem. Tenn. Health Planning Council, 1968-76, Tenn. Hist. Commn., 1976-86; trustee Hermitage Assn., Nashville, 1983-90; an incorporator, mem. bd. Sr. Neighbors Chattanooga, 1960-66; vice chmn., trustee Maclellan Charitable Trust. With AUS, 1942-46; judge adv. 100th Inf. Div. ETO. Mem. Am., Tenn., Chattanooga bar assns., Am. Life Conv. (chmn. legal sect. 1958), Assn. Life Ins. Counsel (exec. com. 1970—, pres. 1974-75), Nature Conservancy (life, co-founder and trustee Tenn. chpt.), Sigma Alpha Epsilon. Presbyterian. Clubs: Mountain City (Chattanooga); Belle Meade Country (Nashville). Home: 1125 Healing Springs Rd Elder Mountain Chattanooga TN 37419 Office: 1125 Healing Springs Rd Chattanooga TN 37419-1043 *My environmentalist credo: O Lord, how manifold are thy works! In wisdom hast thou made them all: the earth is full of thy riches. (Psalm 104, verse 24).*

PORTER, DWIGHT JOHNSON, former electric company executive, foreign affairs consultant; b. Shawnee, Okla., Apr. 12, 1916; s. Dwight Ernest and Gertrude (Johnson) P.; m. Adele Ritchie, Oct. 6, 1942; children—Dwight A., James G., Ellen Jean, Barbara Adele, Joan Anne. Ritchie Johnson. A.B., Grinnell Coll., 1938, LL.D., 1968; student, Am. U., 1938-40, 46-48, Nat. War Coll., 1957-58. Govt. intern Nat. Inst. Pub. Affairs, Washington, 1938-39; personnel officer U.S. Housing Authority, 1939-41; exec. officer Dept. Agr., San Francisco, 1941-42; asst. personnel dir. Bd. Econ. Warfare, 1942; dir. adminstrv. services Rural Electrification Adminstrn., 1946-48; mgmt. officer Dept. State, 1948; dep. dir. Displaced Persons Commn., 1949; adminstrv. officer U.S. High Commn., Germany, 1949-54; 1st sec. Am. embassy, London, 1954-56; exec. officer econ. area Dept. State, 1956-57; coordinator Hungarian Refugee Relief, 1957, spl. asst. to dep. under-sec., and under-sec. state, 1958-59; counsellor Am. embassy, Vienna, 1959-62; minister Am. embassy, 1962, dep. chief of mission, 1962-63; asst. sec. of state for adminstrn., 1963-65; ambassador to Lebanon, 1965-70; permanent U.S. rep. IAEA, Vienna, 1970-75; v.p. internat. affairs Westinghouse Electric Corp., Washington, 1975-85; fgn. affairs cons., 1986—. Served to capt. USMCR, 1942-45. Recipient alumni award Grinnell Coll., 1958. Home: 15100 Interlachen Dr Apt 526 Silver Spring MD 20906-5606

PORTER, ELSA ALLGOOD, writer, lecturer; b. Amoy, China, Dec. 19, 1928; d. Roy and Petra (Johnsen) Allgood; m. Raeford B. Liles, Mar. 19, 1949 (div. 1959); children: Barbara, Janet; m. G. Hinckley Porter, Nov. 22, 1962; children: David, Brian, Wendy. BA, Birmingham-So. Coll., 1949; MA, U. Ala., 1959; M in Pub. Adminstrn., Harvard U., 1971; LHD (hon.), U. Ala., 1986. With HEW, Washington, 1960-73; with U.S. CSC, Washington, 1973-77; asst. sec. Dept. Commerce, Washington, 1977-81; disting. practitioner in residence Washington Pub. Affairs Ctr., U. So. Calif., Washington, 1982-84; sr. mgmt. assoc. The Prodn. Group, Alexandria, Va., 1985-87; project dir. Cathedral Coll. of the Laity, Washington, 1987-89; v.p. R & D The Maccoby Group, Washington, 1990-96. Bd. dirs. Delphi Internat. Group, 1981—. Fellow Nat. Acad. Pub. Adminstrs.; mem. Women's Nat. Dem. Club. Home: # 742 2309 S W First Ave Portland OR 97201

PORTER, GERALD JOSEPH, mathematician, educator; b. Elizabeth, N.J., Feb. 27, 1937; s. Fred and Tillie Florence (Friedman) P.; m. Judith Deborah Revitch, June 26, 1960; children: Daniel, Rebecca, Michael. AB, Princeton U., 1958; PhD, Cornell U., 1963; MA (hon.), U. Pa., 1971. Instr. MIT, 1963-65; asst. prof. math. U. Pa., Phila., 1965-69; assoc. prof. U. Pa., 1969-75, prof., 1975—, chmn. undergrad. affairs dept. math., 1971-73, assoc. dean computing Sch. Arts and Scis., 1981-91, dir. Interactive Math. Text Project, 1991-96; bd. dirs. Com. Concerned Scientists; chair-elect faculty senate U. Pa., 1992-93, chair, 1993-94, past chair, 1994-95. Mem. Dem. Com., Haverford Twp., Pa., 1976-82, ward leader, 1980-84, treas., 1984-87. Postdoctoral fellow Office Naval Rsch., 1965-66. Mem. AAUP, Am. Math. Soc., Math. Assn. Am. (chmn. com. computers in math. edn. 1983-86, chmn. investment com. 1986—, bd. govs. 1980-83, 86—, mem. fin. com. 1986—, exec. com. 1992—, chmn. audit and budget com. 1988-90, 92, treas. 1992—, chair com. on profl. devel. 1995—), Assn. for Women in Math., AAAS, Nat. Assn. Mathematicians, Nat. Coun. Tchrs. Math., Joint Policy Bd. for Math., Am. Math. Assn. of Two Year Colls. Democrat. Jewish. Home: 161 Whitemarsh Rd Ardmore PA 19003-1698 Office: U Pa 4N69 DRL 209 S 33rd St Philadelphia PA 19104

PORTER, GLENN, museum and library administrator; b. New Boston, Tex., Apr. 2, 1944; s. Pat Paul and Mary Lee (Sanders) P.; m. K.T. Wimberly, June 1, 1968 (div. 1986); m. Barbara H. Butler, Dec. 18, 1987. BA, Rice U., 1966; MA, Johns Hopkins U., 1968, PhD, 1970. Asst. prof. bus. history Harvard Bus. Sch., Boston, 1970-76; dir. regional econ. history research ctr. Hagley Mus. & Library, Wilmington, Del., 1976-83, dir., 1984—. Editor Bus. History Rev., 1970-76; editorial bd. Jour. Am. History, 1977-80, Del. History, 1982—, Bus. History Rev., 1983-92; author: (with Harold C. Livesay) Merchants and Manufacturers, 1971; Rise of Big Business, 1860-1910, 1973, rev. edit., 1992, The Workers World at Hagley, 1981; gen. editor: Ency. of Am. Econ. History, 1980, The Papers of John D. Rockefeller, 1991. Mem. cons. com. Nat. Survey of Historic Sites and Bldgs., Washington, 1976-79; council mem. Del. Humanities Council, 1981-83; trustee Worldesign Found., 1993-95, Andalusia Found., 1994—. pres., Ind. Rsch. Librs. Assn, 1994—. bd. dirs., Nat. Humanities Alliance, 1994—. Recipient Cultural Achievement award, U.S. Dept. Interior, 1979; NEH grantee, 1977-82, 81-83, 85-92, 93—. Mem. Bus. History Conf. (pres.1987), Soc. for History of Tech., Soc. Archtl. Historians, Independent Rsch. Librs. Assn. (pres.1994—), Nat. Humanities Alliance (bd. dirs. 1994—), Am. Assn. Mus., Mid-Atlantic Assn. Mus., Phi Beta Kappa. Office: Hagley Mus & Libr PO Box 3630 Wilmington DE 19807-0630

PORTER, HELEN VINEY (MRS. LEWIS M. PORTER, JR.), lawyer; b. Logansport, Ind., Sept. 7, 1935; d. Charles Lowry Viney and Florence Helen (Kunkel) V.; m. Lewis Morgan Porter, Jr., Dec. 26, 1966; children: Alicia Michelle, Andrew Morgan. A.B., Ind. U., 1957; J.D., U. Louisville, 1961. Bar: Ind. and Ill. 1961, U.S. Supreme Ct. 1971. Atty. office chief counsel Midwest regional office IRS, Chgo., 1961-73; assoc. regional atty. litigation center Equal Employment Opportunity Commn., Chgo., 1973-74; practice in Northbrook, Ill., 1974-79, 80-86; ptnr. Porter & Andersen, Chgo., 1979-80, Porter & Porter, Northfield, Ill., 1986—; lectr. Law in Am. Found., Chgo., summer, 1973, 74; assoc. prof. No Ill Coll Law (formerly Lewis U. Coll. Law), Glen Ellyn, Ill., 1975-79. Lectr. women's rights and fed. taxation to bar assns., civic groups. Recipient Disting. Alumni award U. Louisville Sch. of Law, 1986, President's award Nat. Assn. of Women Lawyers, 1985. Fellow Am. Bar Found., Ill. State Bar Found.; mem. Women's Bar Assn. Ill. (pres. 1972-73), ABA (chmn. standing com. gavel awards 1983-85, bd. editors jour. 1984-90, mem. standing com. assn. comm. 1990-93), Fed. Bar Assn. (pres. Chgo. chpt. 1974-75), Ill. Bar Assn. (assembly del. 1972-78), Nat. Assn. Women Lawyers (pres. 1973-74). Home and Office: 225 Maple Row Northfield IL 60093-1037

PORTER, HENRY HOMES, JR., investor; b. Chgo., Nov. 13, 1934; s. Henry H. and Mary (Kinney) P.; m. Louisa Catherine Perkins, June 10, 1961; children: Mary Porter Johnson, Catherine. A.B., Yale U., 1956; M.B.A., Harvard U., 1962. With Gen. Mills, Inc., Mpls., 1962-76; asst. treas. Gen. Mills, Inc., 1964-67, treas., 1967-76, v.p. fin., treas., 1969-76; sr. v.p., chief fin. officer, dir. Brown & Williamson Industries, Inc., 1977-79, Batus, Inc., 1980; pres., dir. Pormain Holdings, Inc., 1980—; chmn. bd. Active Ankle Systems, Inc.; bd. dirs. SEI Corp., Dame Inc., Droll Inc., Caldwell & Orkin Funds, Inc. Lt. (j.g.) USNR, 1957-60. Home and Office: 5806 River Knoll Dr Louisville KY 40222-5863

PORTER, IVAN, company executive; b. U.K., 1947. Acct. trainee, fin. Brit. Rys., 1963-68; mgmt. acct. Geest Industries Ltd., 1971-72; with Massey-Ferguson Ltd., 1969-71, 72—; with Perkins Engines, 1969-71, 72-80, comptroller, 1978-79, dir. group fin., 1979-80; corp. v.p. and comptroller Massey Ferguson Ltd, Toronto, Ont., Can., 1980-81, corp. v.p. fin. comptroller, 1981-83, pres. combines div., 1983-88; pres. diversified products group Jarrock Ltd., 1988-89; chief exec. officer Canron Inc., Rexdale, 1989—. Office: Canron Inc, 100 Disco Rd, Rexdale, ON Canada M9W 1M1*

PORTER, JACK NUSAN, writer, sociologist; b. Rovno, Ukraine, USSR, Dec. 2, 1944; came to U.S., 1946; s. Irving Puchtik and Faye (Merin) P.; m. Miriam Almuly, Sept. 18, 1977; children: Gabriel, Danielle. Cert., Machon Inst., Jerusalem, 1963; BAS cum laude, U. Wis., Milw., 1967; MA, PhD, Northwestern U., 1971; lic.real estate, Lee Inst., Brookline, Mass., 1982. Rsch. assoc. Harvard U. Ukrainian Rsch. Inst., Cambridge, Mass., 1982-84; pres. The Spencer Group (Real Estate Devel. and Cons.), Newton, Mass.,

1984—; exec. dir. The Spencer Sch. Real Estate, Newton, 1986—; dir. The Spencer Inst. for Bus. and Soc., Newton, 1984—; asst. prof. Coll. of Basic Studies Boston U., 1989-90; vis. lectr. Boston U. Met. Coll., 1987, 88, Bryant Coll., Smithfield, R.I., 1991; adj. lectr. U. Mass., Lowell, 1994—; presenter White House Conf. on Family, 1980; mem. Gov. Dukakis' Adv. Coun., 1982-84; panelist on Comparative Genocide, The Oxford (Eng.) Conf., 1988; sr. rsch. assoc. Ctr. for Atomic Rsch. Studies, Brookline. Author or editor 25 books and anthologies including Confronting History and Holocaust, Sexual Politics in Nazi Germany, Kids in Cults, Jews and the Cults, Genocide and Human Rights, Conflict and Conflict Resolution, Jewish Partisans (2 vols.), The Jew as Outsider, The Sociology of Business, The Sociology of Jewry, An Historical Bibliography , Forclosed Property (with George Glazer), The Agunah: A Sourcebook, Handbook on Cults and Sects, curriculum guides in various fields; contbr. over 300 articles and revs. to jours. in field; founder, editor Jour. of the History of Sociology, 1977-85, The Sociology of Bus. Newsletter, 1977-79. Founder Holocaust Survival Video Project, Newton, Mass., 1992—; judge Nat. Jewish Book Awards, 1993-95; mem. Jewish Radical Edn. Project. John Atherton fellow Breadloaf Writers Conf., Middlebury, Vt., 1976; recipient Spl. award Boston Police Dept., 1986. Mem. PEN (newsletter com. 1992-95), Am. Sociol. Assn., Ea. Sociol. Soc., Am. Philos. Soc., New Eng. Soc., Tikkun. Avocations: collecting Jewish baseball cards and memorabilia, reading, spiritual thinking. Home and Office: 8 Burnside Rd Newton Highlands MA 02161-1401 *The older I get the important things in life are my wife, my children, good health, a few good friends, my brother and sister and Mom, of course, a good meal, and lastly - some money and fame.*

PORTER, JAMES H., chemical engineering executive; b. Port Chester, N.Y., Nov. 11, 1933; s. George James and Josephine (Hall) P.; m. Sandra Adrienne Knox, Sept. 8, 1958 (div. Dec. 1969); children: Michael Brandon, Adrienne Michelle, Lynn Sharon; m. Jennifer Anne Waterhouse, Feb. 26, 1978. BSChemE, Rensselaer Poly. Inst., 1955; ScD, MIT, 1963. Tech. svc. engr. Exxon, Linden, N.J., 1955-58; rsch. engr. Chevron Rsch. Corp., Richmond, Calif., 1963-67; mgr. process design Abcor Inc., Cambridge, Mass., 1967-71; assoc. prof. MIT, Cambridge, 1971-76; v.p. energy div. Energy Resources Co. Inc., Cambridge, 1976-79; pres. Energy and Environ. Engring. Inc., Somerville, Mass., 1979-94; chmn., CEO, 1994—, UV Technologies Inc., 1994—; sci. adv. bd. U.S. EPA, Washington, 1976-83. Author: Chemical Equilibria in C.H.O. Systems, 1976; patentee in field. Bd. dirs. Tisbury Waterways Inc., Vineyard Haven, Mass., 1990, Trustees of Reservation, Boston, 1991, Cambridge Adult Edn. Ctr., Cambridge, 1988, sec., 1991. Mem. Am. Inst. Chem. Engrs., Nat. Orgn. Black Chemists and Chem. Engrs. (pres. 1978-79, bd. dirs., Founders award 1983, Henry Hill lectr. 1995), Sigma Xi, Pi Delta Epsilon. Avocations: sportsfishing, bridge. Home: PO BOX 1131 Vineyard Haven MA 02568

PORTER, JAMES MORRIS, judge; b. Cleve., Sept. 14, 1931; s. Emmett Thomas and Mary (Connell) P.; m. Helen Marie Adams, May 31, 1952; children: James E., Thomas W., William M., Daniel J. A.B., John Carroll U., 1953; J.D., U. Mich., 1957. Bar: Ohio 1957. Assoc. firm M.B. & H.H. Johnson, Cleve., 1957-62, McAfee, Hanning, Newcomer, Hazlett & Wheeler, Cleve., 1962-67; ptnr. firm Squire, Sanders & Dempsey, Cleve., 1967-92; judge Ohio Ct. Appeals, 8th Dist., Cleve., 1993—. 1st lt. U.S. Army, 1953-55. Fellow Am. Coll. Trial Lawyers; mem. Best Lawyers in Am., Union Club, The Club, The Country Club (Cleve.). Republican. Roman Catholic. Office: Lakeside Courthouse Ct Appeals Lakeside Ave Cleveland OH 44113-1082

PORTER, JAMES R., computer company executive; b. 1936. With IBM Corp., 1961-68, Tracor Computer, 1968-70, United Sys., 1970-72, Informatics Gen. Corp., 1972-85; with Triad Sys. Corp., Livermore, Calif., 1985—, pres., chief exec. officer. With USAF, 1958-61. Office: Triad Systems Corp 3055 Triad Dr Livermore CA 94550-9559*

PORTER, JEANNETTE UPTON, elementary education educator; b. Mpls., Mar. 5, 1938; d. Robert Livingston and Ruby Jeannette (Thomas) Upton; divorced; children: Steven, Fritz, Susan Porter Powell. BS, U. Minn., 1960, Mankato State U., 1968; postgrad., St. Thomas U., 1991. Camp dir. St. Paul's Epsicopal Ch., Mpls., 1956-66; tchr. elem. sch. Bloomington (Minn.) Pub. Schs., 1967—, dir. title I, 1975-82, tchr. spl. assignment of rsch. and devel., 1990-91; team cons. Hillcrest Cmty. Sch., Bloomington, 1990-95. Tutor Telephone Hot Line Minn. Fedn. Tchrs., Mpls., 1988-92; crisis counselor Neighborhood Improvement Programs, Mpls., 1988-93; adult literacy counselor Right to Read, Mpls., 1987-89; vol. Abbott Northwestern Hosp. Recipient 1st Bank award Mpls., Red Apple award, Mpls., 1988; named Minn. Tchr. of Excellence, 1988, 89. Mem. Assn. Early Childhood Edn. (treas. 1990-94), Bloomington Edn. Found., Delta Kappa Gamma (1st v.p. 1992-93), PEO (past pres. A.C. chpt.). Avocations: fishing, photography, back packing, pottery, music. Home: 4400 West 44th St Saint Louis Park MN 55424

PORTER, JENNIFER MADELEINE, producer, director; b. Milw., Oct. 3, 1962; d. John Hamlin and Helen Meak (Smith) P. BA in Comm., Bowling Green State U., 1984. Audio visual supr. Liberty Mutual Ins. Group, Berwyn, Pa., 1985-88; sr. prodr. audio visual Prudential Ins. Co., Mpls., 1988-93; proprietor Shoot The Moon Prodns., Mound, Minn., 1993—. Prodr., dir., writer: (audio visual program) Phantom Lake... A Lifetime of Memories, 1991 (Best of Show 1991, Script award Assn. for Multi-Image, Internat. 1991), Vision... The Gamma Phi Beta Foundation, 1992 (First Place award 1993). Mentor U. Minn., Mpls., 1989—; fund raiser Gamma Phi Beta Found. Philanthropy-Spl. Camping for Girls, Minn., Wis., 1991—; chairperson 100th Celebration, Phantom Lake YMCA Camp, Mukwonago, Wis., 1994—. Mem. Assn. for Multi-Image Internat. (exec. bd. local 1986-88), Gamma Phi Beta (internat. officer, pub. rels. speaker/prodr. 1991—). Avocations: travel, music, sports, camping, canoeing. Home and Office: Shoot The Moon Prodns 1764 Heron Ln Mound MN 55364-1252

PORTER, JILL, journalist; b. Phila., Aug. 5, 1946; d. Sidney and Mae (Merion) Chalfin; m. Eric Porter, Mar. 7, 1970 (div. 1975); m. Fred Hamilton, Oct. 28, 1983; 1 child, Zachary. BA, Temple U., 1968. Pub. rels. Manning Smith P.R., Phila., 1968-69; reporter Norristown Times Herald, Norristown, Pa., 1969-72, The Trentonian, Trenton, N.J., 1972-75; reporter The Phila. Daily News, Phila., 1975-79, columnist, 1979—; instr. Temple U., 1976-80. Contbr. articles to numerous mags. Vol. Phila. Futures, 1994, 95, 96. Recipient numerous journalism awards. Avocations: reading, gardening. Home: 715 Stradone Rd Bala Cynwyd PA 19004-2113 Office: Phila Newspapers Inc Phila Daily News 400 N Broad St Philadelphia PA 19130-4015

PORTER, JOAN MARGARET, elementary education educator; b. Vernon, Tex., Dec. 25, 1937; d. Elton Lonnie and Clara Pearl (Yeager) Smith; m. Claude Walker Porter, Feb. 13, 1960; children: Jolene Porter Mohindroo, Richard Euin, Vonda Sue, Darla Ailese Porter Blomquist. BA, Wayland Bapt. U., 1960; M in Elem. Edn., Ea. N.Mex. U., 1981, bilingual endorsement, 1982. cert. classroom tchr., N.Mex. ESL tchr. Jefferson Elem. Sch., Lovington, N.Mex., 1979-81, tchr. first grade, 1981-82; tchr. bilingual first grade Jefferson Elem. Sch., Lovington, 1982-89; tchr. bilingual first grade Highland Elem. Sch., Plainview, Tex., 1989-91, 1992—, tchr. first grade, 1991-92, tchr. bilingual first grade, 1992-95, tchr. bilingual second grade, 1995-96; vol. tchr. Cert. Adult Literacy, Lovington. Mem. PTA, Assn. Tex. Profl. Educators, Delta Kappa Gamma (profl. affairs com. chmn. 1991), Phi Kappa Phi. Southern Baptist. Home: 101 Juanita St Plainview TX 79072-7625 Office: Highland Elem Sch 1707 W 11th St Plainview TX 79072-6439

PORTER, JOHN EDWARD, congressman; b. Evanston, Ill., June 1, 1935; s. Harry H. and Beatrice V. P.; m. Kathryn Cameron; 5 children. Attended, MIT; BSBA, Northwestern U., 1958; JD with distinction, U. Mich., 1961; DHL, Barat Coll., 1988; LLD (hon.), Kendall Coll., 1992. Bar: Ill. 1961, U.S. Supreme Ct. 1968. Former honor law grad. atty., appellate div. Dept. Justice, Washington; mem. Ill. Ho. of Reps., 1973-79; mem. house appropriations com., subcoms. on labor, health & human svcs., edn., fgn. ops. 96-103rd Congresses from 10th Ill. Dist., Ill., 1980—; mem. legis. select com. on aging, 1980-92; founder, co-chmn. Congl. Human Rights Caucus; founder Congl. Coalition on Population and Devel. Past editor: Mich. Law Rev. Recipient Best Legislator award League of Conservation Voters, 1973, Ind. Voters Ill., 1974, Chgo. Crime Commn., 1976, Lorax award Global Tomorrow Coalition, 1989, Spirit of Enterprise award U.S. C. of C., 1988, 89, 90, Golden Bulldog award Watchdogs of the Treasury, 12 times, Taxpayer's Friend award Nat. Taxpayers Union, Taxpayer Superhero award Grace Commn.'s Citizens Against Government Waste. Republican. Office: US Ho of Reps 2373 Rayburn House Bldg Washington DC 20515-1310

PORTER, JOHN FINLEY, JR., physicst, conservationist, retired educator; b. Birmingham, Ala., Aug. 22, 1927; s. John Finley and Janice (Nowell) P.; m. Jacqueline Christine Harbin, Dec. 27, 1949; children: Gayle P. Barnett, John Finley III, Paul William, Adam Michael, David Wade. BS, U. Ala., 1950, MS, 1956; PhD, Johns Hopkins U., 1966. Rsch. staff asst. Radiation Lab., Johns Hopkins U., 1956-59; rsch. assoc. Carlyle Barton Lab. Johns Hopkins U., 1959-66, rsch. scientist, 1966, lectr. elec. engring., 1965-66; assoc. prof. physics U. Ala., Huntsville, 1966-69, chmn. physics faculty, 1968-69, prof., 1969-72; dean faculty U Ala., Hunstville, 1969-70, dean grad. programs and rsch., 1970-72; dep. exec. dir. Ala. Commn. on Higher Edn., 1972-73, exec. dir., 1973-81; vis. prof. adminstrn. and higher edn. U. Ala. Coll. Edn., 1981-83, prof., 1983-92, acting dir. Office Instl. Rsch., 1984-91, dir. Office Instl. Rsch., 1991-92, prof. emeritus, 1992—; cons. Catalyst Rsch. Corp., Balt., Environ. Sci. Svc. Adminstrn., Washington; chmn. State Coun. Grad. Deans, 1971-72; mem. planning bd. Edn. Commn. of States, 1975-77; mem. adv. coun. Ala. Right to Read, 1974-76; mem. Ala. Post Secondary Edn. Planning Commn., 1974-76, Gov.'s Budget Adv. Com., 1976-77. Contbr. articles to profl. jours. Bd. dirs., v.p. Tuscaloosa County Preservation Soc., 1988-89, pres., 1990-91; v.p. Ala. Ornithol. Soc., 1990-91, pres., 1991-93; bd. dirs. Tuscaloosa Audubon Soc., 1989-92, Ala. Coastal Found., 1994—, Mobile Bay Audubon Soc., 1993—; mem. Ala. Audobon Coun., 1990—; pres. Friends of Dauphin Island Audubon Sanctuary Inc., 1992—. Methodist. Home: 1404 Cadillac Ave PO Box 848 Dauphin Island AL 36528-0848

PORTER, JOHN FRANCIS, III, banker; b. Wilmington, Del., Sept. 17, 1934; s. John Francis, Jr. and Eloise Wilhelmina (Berlinger) P.; m. Ann Mayfield, Sept. 8, 1956; children: Leslie Gibson, Nina Porter Winfield, Sophie Porter Rohrer. BA, U. Va., 1956; MBA, U. Del., 1965. With Del. Trust Co., Wilmington, 1958—; asst. treas. Del. Trust Co., 1960-66, sec., 1966-68, v.p., sec., 1968-72, sr. v.p., sec., 1972-75, exec. v.p., 1975-79, pres., 1979-88, chmn., chief exec. officer, 1988—; vice chmn. BANKPAC, 1982-86, chmn., 1986-88; mem. Ct. on Judiciary Preliminary Investigatory Com., 1991—. Mem. bank adv. bd. State of Del., 1969-71; mem. Council on Banking for State of Del., 1970—, chmn., 1976—; trustee Alfred I. duPont Testamentary Trust, 1995—, Alfred I. duPont Inst. Nemours Found., 1971—, chmn. bd. mgrs., 1990-94; chmn. exec. coun. Thomas Jefferson U. Med. Ctr., Del./AIDI Affiliation , 1990-92, mem., 1990—; pres. Wilmington and Brandywine Cemetery, 1974—; bd. dirs., trustee, mem. fin. com. mem. exec. com. Med. Ctr. Del., 1985—; bd. dirs. Penjerdel, 1989—, State v.p., 1990—; bd. gov. Winterthur Corp. Coun., 1989—, chmn., 1993-95. Capt. arty., U.S. Army, 1957. Mem. Am. Bankers Assn. (govt. rels. coun. 1984-88), Del. Bankers Assn. (pres. 1984-85, bd. dirs. 1981-87), Del. Bus. Roundtable (vice chmn. exec. coun. 1989-92, chmn. 1993-94), Wilmington Country Club (bd. dirs.), Wilmington Club (bd. govs. 1980-89), Vicmead Hunt Club, Nassau Club (Princeton, N.J.). Clubs: Wilmington Country (bd. dir.), Wilmington (bd. govs. 1980-89), Vicmead Hunt; Nassau (Princeton, N.J.). Home: 4821 Kennett Pike Wilmington DE 19807-1813 Office: Del Trust Co 900 N Market St Wilmington DE 19801-3030

PORTER, JOHN ROBERT, art history educator, curator, writer; b. Lévis, Que., Can., Apr. 28, 1949; s. John William and Irène (Bernier) P.; m. Martine Tremblay, July 26, 1975; children: Isabelle, Jean-Olivier. LèsL, Laval U., 1971, Ma, 1972; PhD, U. Montreal, 1982. Asst. curator Can. art Nat. Gallery Can., 1972-78; prof. art history Laval U., 1978—; chief curator Montreal Mus. Fine Arts, 1990-93; dir. Musée du Que., 1993—; mem. programming and acquisition coms. for various mus. Author various books, catalogues and articles in field. Office: Musée du Que, Parc des Champs-de-Bataille, Quebec, PQ Canada G1R 5H3

PORTER, JOHN STEPHEN, television executive; b. Avoca, N.Y., Sept. 2, 1932; s. Frank R. and Margaret H. (McGreel) P.; m. Marie C. Eiffert, Sept. 6, 1958; children: Stephen, David, Mark, Kevin, Matthew. B.A. in English, St. John Fisher U., 1958; M.S. in Radio/TV, Syracuse U., 1959; postgrad. in Edn, U. Rochester, 1960-61. Producer, broadcaster weekly news analysis N.Y. State Empire State FM Sch. of Air, 1962-64; producer, narrator weekly series sta. WROC-FM, Rochester, N.Y., 1964-65; pres., gen. mgr. sta. WXXI-TV, Rochester, 1966-69; trustee Eastern Ednl. TV Network, Boston, 1966-68, mem. exec. com., 1967-68, exec. dir., 1969-89, pres., mem. exec. com., 1989-92; pres., mem. exec. com. Am. Program Svc. (formerly Ea. Ednl. TV Network), Boston, 1992—. Served to 1st lt. AUS, 1952-56. Mem. N.Y. State Ednl. Radio/TV Assn. (treas. 1962-64), Pub. TV Sta. Mgrs. New York State (chmn. 1968-69), Nat. Assn. Ednl. Broadcasters (adv. com.). Home: 100 Pond St Apt 82 Cohasset MA 02025

PORTER, JOHN T., health facility administrator; b. 1948. Grad., U. S.D. With Presentation Health Sys., Sioux Falls, S.D., 1980—, pres.; pvt. practice as lawyer, Yankton, S.D., 1973-80. Office: Presentation Health System PO Box 38 Yankton SD 57078*

PORTER, JOHN WILSON, education executive; b. Ft. Wayne, Ind., Aug. 13, 1931; s. James Richard and Ola (Phillips) P.; m. Lois Helen French, May 27, 1961; children: Stephen James, Donna Agnes. BA, Albion Coll., 1953; MA, Mich. State U., 1957, PhD, 1962; D in Pub. Adminstrn. (hon.), Albion Coll., 1973; LLD (hon.), Mich. State U., 1977, Cleary Coll., 1987; LHD, Adrian Coll., 1970, U. Detroit, 1979; LLD, Western Mich. U., 1971, Eastern Mich. U., 1975; HHD, Kalamazoo Coll., 1973, Detroit Coll. Bus., 1975, Madonna Coll., Livonia, Mich., 1977; DEd, Detroit Inst. Tech., 1978; AA, Schoolcraft Coll., Livonia, Mich., 1979; DBA, Lawrence Inst. Tech., 1988; LLD, Cleary Coll., 1989. Counselor Lansing (Mich.) Pub. Schs., 1953-58; cons. Mich. Dept. Pub. Instrn., 1958-61; dir. Mich. Higher Edn. Assistance Authority, 1961-65; assoc. supt. for higher edn. Mich. Dept. Edn., 1966-69, state supt. schs., 1969-79; pres. Ea. Mich. U., Ypsilanti, 1979-89; CEO Urban Edn. Alliance Inc., Ann Arbor, Mich., 1988—; v.p. Nat. Bd. for Profl. Teaching Standards, 1989; gen. supt. Detroit Pub. Schs., 1989-91; CEO Urban Edn. Alliance, Inc., Ypsilanti, Mich., 1991—; mem. numerous profl. commns. and bds., 1959—, including; Commn. on Financing Post-secondary Edn., 1972-74, Commn. for Reform Secondary Edn., Kettering Found., 1972-75, Edn. Commn. of States, 1973-79, Nat. Commn. on Performance-Based Edn., 1974-76, Nat. Commn. on Manpower Policy, 1974-79, Mich. Employment and Tng. Svcs. Coun., 1976-79, Nat. Adv. Coun. on Social Security, 1977-79, Commn. on Ednl. Credit, Am. Coun. on Edn., 1977-80; task panel on mental health of family Commn. on Mental Health, 1977-80; mem. Nat. Coun. for Career Edn. (HEW), 1974-76; pres. bd. dirs. Chief State Sch. Officers, 1974-79; pres. Coun. Chief State Sch. Officers, 1977-78; bd. dirs. Comerica Bank; former chmn. bd. Coll. Entrance Exam. Bd., 1984-86. Trustee Nat. Urban League, 1973-79, Charles Stewart Mott Found., 1981—, Albion Coll., 1989—; bd. dirs. Mich. Internat. Council, 1977—, Mich. Congress Parents and Tchrs.; mem. bd. overseers com. for Grad. Sch., Harvard U., 1980-88; mem. edn. com. NAACP; convener goal 6 Nat. Edn. Goals Panel, 1990—; mem. East Lansing Human Relations Commn.; chmn. Am. Assn. State Colls. and U.'s Task Force on Excellence in Edn.; mem. Mich. Martin Luther King, Jr. Holiday Commn., Gov.'s Blue Ribbon Commn. on Welfare Reform; trustee East Lansing Edgewood United Ch.; mem. Catherine McAuley Health Systems Bd., 1990—. Recipient numerous awards including Disting. Svc. award Mich. Congress Parents and Tchrs., 1963, Disting. Svc. award NAACP, Lansing, 1968; cert. of outstanding achievement Delta Kappa chpt. Phi Beta Sigma, 1970; award for disting. svc. Assn. Ind. Colls. and Univs. Mich., 1974; Disting. Alumni award Coll. Edn., Mich. State U., 1974; award for disting. svc. to edn Mich. State U., 1974; Disting. Alumni award, 1979; award for disting. svc. to edn. in Mich. Mich. Assn. Secondary Sch. Prins., 1974; President's award as disting. educator Nat. Alliance Black Sch. Educators, 1977; Marcus Foster Disting. Educator award, 1979; recognition award Mich. Ednl. Rsch. Assn., 1978; recognition award Mich. Assn. Secondary Sch. Prins., 1978; recognition award Mich. Assn. Intermediate Sch. Adminstrs., 1979; recognition award Mich. Assn. Sch. Adminstrs., 1979; Mich. Sch. Bus. Ofcls., 1979; resolution Mich. State Legislature, 1978; Anthony Wayne award Coll. Edn., Wayne State U., 1979; Educator of Decade award Mich. Assn. State and Fed. Program Specialists, 1979; Spirit of Detroit award Detroit City Coun., 1981; Disting. Svc. award Ypsilanti Area C. of C., 1988; Philip A. Hart award Mich. Women's Hall of Fame, 1988; Summit award Greater Detroit C. of C., 1991; Mich. State C. of C. award 1991; inducted Mich. Edn. Hall of Fame, 1992. Mem. Am. Assn. Sch. Adminstrs., Am. Assn. State Colls. and Univs. (president's council, chmn. task force on excellence in edn.), Nat. Measurement Council, NAACP (life), Greater Detroit C. of C. (Summit 1991), Mich. State C. of C. (Disting. Svc. and Leadership award 1991), Tuskeegee Airmen (Disting. Svc. award 1991), Mich. PTA (hon. life), Econ. Club (dir. 1979), Sigma Pi Phi, Phi Delta Kappa. Office: Urban Edn Alliance Inc 900 Victors Way Ste 210 Ann Arbor MI 48108-1779

PORTER, JUDITH DEBORAH REVITCH, sociologist, educator; b. Phila., Mar. 26, 1940; d. Eugene and Esther (Tulchinsky) Revitch; m. Gerald Joseph Porter, June 26, 1960; children—Daniel, Rebecca, Michael. Student, Vassar Coll., 1958-60; BA, Cornell U., 1962, MA, 1963; PhD, Harvard U., 1967. Lectr. Bryn Mawr (Pa.) Coll., 1966-67, asst. prof., 1967-73, assoc. prof., 1973-79, prof. sociology, 1979—, chair dept. sociology, 1987-93. Author: Black Child, White Child: The Development of Racial Attitudes, 1971; contbr. articles to profl. jours. Committeeperson Haverford Twp. Dem. Party, 1976—; bd. dirs. Phila. AIDS Walk; vol. Prevention Point Needle Exch. Program, Congreso de Latinos Unidos, Inc. Recipient Shannon award NIMH, 1992-94; Ford Found. fellow, 1973-74; NSF fellow, 1967. Mem. APHA, Am. Sociol. Assn., Phi Beta Kappa, Phi Kappa Phi. Jewish. Address: 161 Whitemarsh Rd Ardmore PA 19003-1634 Office: Bryn Mawr Coll Dept Sociology Bryn Mawr PA 19010

PORTER, KARL HAMPTON, orchestra musical director, conductor; b. Pitts., Apr. 25, 1939; s. Reginald and Naomi Arzetta (Mitchell) P. Student, Carnegie-Mellon U., 1957-60, Peabody Conservatory, 1960-62, Juilliard Sch. Music, 1962-63, Domaine Sch. Condrs., 1961-63, Am. Symphony Orch. League, Tanglewood, 1962-72; student Polit. Sci., Fordham U., 1978; student Bus. Computer Tng., SUNY, 1986. judge for Congress of Strings, BMI Composers Competition, 1970-74; instr. theory Mt. Morris Park, 1969-73; instr. woodwind L.I. Inst. Music, 1969-75, U. Denver, 1963-64, Coll. New Rochelle, 1980; tchr. bassoon Newark Community Arts Center, 1969-71; instr. music N.Y.C. Tech. Coll., 1972-90; pres. Finale Prodns. Mem. Denver Symphony Orch., 1963-64, Met. Opera Nat. Co., 1965-67, Gil Evans Band, 1967-69, formed, Harlem Youth Symphony, 1968, Harlem Philharmonic Orch., 1969—, New Breed Brass Ensemble, Harlem String Quartet, Harlem Woodwind Quintet, 1970, condr., Balt, Symphony, 1970, mus. dir., condr., Harlem Philharmonic Orch., 1970—, N.Y.C. Housing Authority Orch., 1972-86, Massapequa (N.Y.) Symphony Soc., 1974-80, condr., Park West Symphony, Northeastern Philharmonic of Pa., Scranton Philharmonic, Ridgefield Symphonette, 1971, mus. dir. for Josephine Baker, 1972-75, free lance bassoonist, Am. Symphony, Bklyn. Philharmonic, N.J. Symphony, 1967—; min. of music St. Thomas the Apostle, 1989—; dir. Independence Community Ctr., 1993—; dir. counselor Elmcor Youth Ctr., 1991-93. Mem. nat. adv. bd. Dance Theatre of Harlem, Air Force Assn., Mental Health Assn.; bd. dirs. Empire Trust; hon. bd. dirs. Sickle Cell, Baton Rouge, La.; performing arts coord. Afro-Acad. Cultural Tech. Sci. Olympics; cons. N.Y. State Coun. Arts; dir. Ind. Cmty. Ctr., 1993—; field ops. supr.; U.S. Bur. Census. Recipient Martha Baird Rockefeller Found. grant, 1969, Nat. Endowment grant, 1970. Mem. NAACP, Nat. Soc. Lit. and Arts, N.Y. State Assn. Jr. Colls., Am. Symphony Orch. League, Performing Arts Assn. N.Y., Soc. Black Composers, Nat. Soc. Symphony Condrs. Club: The Bohemians. Home: 425 Central Park W New York NY 10025-4324 Office: PO Box 445 New York NY 10025-0445

PORTER, LILIANA ALICIA, artist, printmaker; b. Buenos Aires, Argentina, Oct. 6, 1941; came to U.S., 1964, naturalized, 1982; d. Julio and Margarita (Galetar) P.; m. Luis Camnitzer, 1965 (div. 1978); m. Alan B. Wiener, May 28, 1980 (div. 1991). Grad., Nat. Sch. Fine Arts, Argentina, 1963. Co-dir. and instr. Studio Camnitzer-Porter summer workshops, Lucca, Italy, 1974, 75, 76, 77; assoc. prof. art Queens Coll., N.Y.C., 1991—; adj. lectr. SUNY Coll., Old Westbury, N.Y., 1974-76, Purchase br., 1987; co-dir. Studio Porter-Wiener, N.Y.C., 1979-87. One-woman shows of prints and/or paintings include Galeria Artemultiple, Buenos Aires, Argentina, 1977, 78, Galleria Arte Comunale, Adro, Brescia, Italy, 1977, Hundred Acres Gallery, N.Y.C., 1977, Mus. Modern Art, Cali, Colombia, 1978, Center for Inter-american Relations, N.Y.C., 1980, Galeria Arte Nuevo, Buenos Aires, 1980, Barbara Toll Fine Arts, N.Y.C., 1979, 81, 82, 84, Galerie Jolliet, Montreal, 1983, Museo de Arte Contemporaneo, Panama City, Panama, 1984, Dolan/Maxwell Gallery, Phila., 1985, U. Alta., Edmonton, 1985, Dolan/Maxwell Gallery, Phila., 1985, Galería Luigi Marrozzini, San Juan, P.R., 1986, Galería-Taller, Museo de Arte Moderno, Cali, Colombia, 1987, The Space, Boston, 1988, Syracuse U., N.Y., 1990, retrospective exhibit 1968-90 Fundacion San Telmo, Buenos Aires, 1990, Museo Nacional de Artes Plasticas, Montevideo, Uruguay, 1991, Centro de Recepciones del Gobierno, San Juan, P.R., 1991, Bronx Mus. Art, N.Y.C., 1992, retrospective exhibit Archer Huntington Art Gallery U. Tex. Austin, 1993, Steinbaum-Krauss Gallery, N.Y.C., 1993, Galeria Ruth Benzacar, Buenos Aires, 1994; numerous group shows, 1963—, latest being Center for Interamerican Relations, N.Y.C., 1978, Chateau de L'Hermitage, Belgium, 1978, Mus. Fine Arts, Buenos Aires, 1978, Alternative Center for Internat. Arts, N.Y.C., 1978, Ben Shah Gallery, N.J., 1979, Everson Mus., Syracuse, N.Y., 1979, Alternative Mus., N.Y.C., 1980, Bronx Mus. Fine Arts, 1982, Musee d'Art Contemporain, Montreal, 1983, Queens Coll., Flushing, N.Y., 1983, Mus. Modern Art, San Francisco, 1983, Galeria Epoca, Santiago, Chile, 1986, Centro Wilfredo Lam, Cuba, 1986, Mus. Contemporary Spanish Art, N.Y.C., 1987, MOMA, N.Y.C., 1993; represented in permanent collections Mus. Phila., Mus. Modern Art, N.Y.C., RCA Corp., N.Y.C., N.Y. Public Library, N.Y.C., La Biblioteque Nationale, Paris, France, Museo del Grabado, Buenos Aires, Museo Universitario, Mexico City, Mexico, Museo de Art Moderno, Cali, Colombia, Museo de Bellas Artes, Caracas, Venezuela, Met. Mus. Art, N.Y.C. Recipient 1st prize Argentinian Art 78 Mus. Fine Arts, Buenos Aires, 1978, Grand Prix XI, Internat. Print Biennial, Cracow, Poland, 1986, 1st prize VII Latin Am. Print Biennial, San Juan, Puerto Rico, 1986; fellow Guggenheim Found., 1980-81, N.Y. Found. for the Arts, 1985. Address: 178 Franklin St 5th Floor New York NY 10013

PORTER, MARSHA KAY, Language professional and educator, English; b. Sacramento, Feb. 7, 1954; d. Charles H. and Eileen J. (Miller) P. BA in English and Edn., Calif. State U., Sacramento, 1976, traffic safety credential, 1979, MA in Ednl. Adminstrn., 1982. Cert. lang. devel. specialist, Calif.; cert. first aid instr. ARC. Bookkeeper Chuck's Parts House, Sacramento, 1969-76; substitute tchr. Sacramento City Unified Sch. Dist., 1976-78; coord. Title I, Joaquin Miller Mid. Sch., Sacramento, 1978-81; tchr. ESL and driver's edn. Hiram Johnson H.S., Sacramento, 1981-85, C.K. McClatchy H.S., Sacramento, 1985—; freelance editor, 1981-87; guest lectr. Nat. U., Sacramento, 1992-93. Co-author video movie guide film reference book, pub. annually; contbr. movie revs., short stories and articles to publs. Vol. instr. CPR and first aid ARC, Sacramento, 1986-92; guest writer United We Stand Calif., Sacramento, 1993-94. Gov.'s scholar State of Calif., 1972. Mem. NEA, Calif. Tchrs. Assn., Calif. Assn. Safety Educators, Calif. Writers, Calif. Writers Assn. (sec. 1987-94, pres. 1996), Delta Kappa Gamma. Roman Catholic. Avocations: swimming, helping wounded and/or abandoned animals, acting.

PORTER, MICHAEL PELL, lawyer; b. Indpls., Mar. 31, 1940; s. Harold Troxel and Mildred Maxine (Pell) P.; m. Alliene Laura Jenkins, Sept. 23, 1967 (div.); 1 child, Genevieve Natalie, Porter Eason; m. Janet Kay Smith Hayes, Feb. 13, 1983 (div.). Student, DePauw U., 1957-58; BA, Tulane U., 1961, LLB, 1963. Bar: La. 1963, U.S. Ct. Mil. Appeals 1964, N.Y. 1969, Hawaii 1971. Clk. U.S. Ct. Appeals (5th cir.), New Orleans, 1963; assoc. Sullivan & Cromwell, N.Y.C., 1968-71, Cades Schutte Fleming & Wright, Honolulu, 1971-74, ptnr., 1975-94; mem. faculty Addis Ababa (Ethiopia) U. Sch Law, 1995—; legal advisor St. Matthews Anglican Ch. Addis Ababa, 1995—; mem. deans coun. Law Sch. Tulane U., 1981-88; dep. vice chancellor Episcopal Diocese Hawaii, 1980-88, chancellor, 1988-94; chancellor Episcopal Ch., Micronesia, 1988-95. Author: Hawaii Corporation Law & Practice, 1989, Nat. Corp. Law Series, 1989; Hawaii reporter: State Limited Partnership Laws, 1992-94. Bd. dirs. Jr. Achievement Hawaii, Inc., 1974-84, Inst. Human Svcs., Inc., 1980-88; donor Michael P. Porter Dean's Scholastic award U. Hawaii Law Sch., 1977—; lectorship named in his honor, Addis Abba, Ethiopia, 1994—; established Michael P. Porter Prizes on Ethnic Harmony and Religious Tolerance in a Dem. Soc. at Addis Ababa, 1995. With JAGC, U.S. Army, 1963-66, Vietnam. Tulane U. fellow, 1981. Mem. ABA, Assn. of Bar of City of N.Y., Hawaii State Bar Assn. Republican.

PORTER, MILTON, investment executive; b. Charleroi, Pa., Mar. 2, 1911; s. Harry S. and Jennie (Mitnick) P.; m. Adrienne Foster, Nov. 11, 1938. B.A. in Bus. Adminstrn., U. Pitts., 1932. With L.B. Foster Co., Pitts., 1945-89, v.p., 1955, bd. dirs., 1958, pres., CEO, 1968, chmn. bd., CEO, 1981-84, now bd. dirs.; chmn. bd., CEO Foster Industries, Inc., Pitts. Past pres., life bd. dirs. Jewish Health Care Found. of Pitts.; bd. dirs. Pitts. Symphony; dir. United Jewish Fedn., United Way Southwestern Pa.; chmn. emeritus Health Edn. Ctr., Pitts.; trustee emeritus The Carnegie Inst.; dir. emeritus Carnegie-Mellon U. Recipient Benjamin Rush award Pa. Med. Soc., 1984; recognition award N. Am. Soc. for Corp. Planning, Inc. Mem. Duquesne Club, Westmoreland Country Club (life dir.), Concordia Club, Rivers Club (Pitts.) (dir.). Home: Gateway Towers 320 Fort Duquesne Blvd Pittsburgh PA 15222-1102 Office: Foster Industries Inc 681 Andersen Dr Pittsburgh PA 15220-2747

PORTER, PHILIP THOMAS, retired electrical engineer; b. Clinton, Ky., Mar. 18, 1930; s. Philip Henry and Ruth Frances (Pennebaker) P.; m. Louise Monroe Jett, July 3, 1957; children: Philip C., Sara Shelby Porter Taylor. BA in Physics, Vanderbilt U., 1952, MA in Physics, 1953. Mem. tech. staff Bell Telephone Labs., Murray Hill, N.J., 1953-62; mem. tech. staff Bell Telephone Labs., Holmdel, N.J., 1962-70, supr., 1971-78; supr. Bell Telephone Labs., West Long Branch, N.J., 1979-83; dir. wireless and wireline network compatiblity studies Bell Communications Rsch., Red Bank, N.J., 1984-94; ret., 1994; U.S. del. Consultative Com. for Internat. Radio, Geneva, 1984-93. Contbg. author: Electronics Engineers' Handbook, 1982, History of Science and Technology in the Bell System, 1985, Digital Communications, 1986; patentee in field. Fellow IEEE. Unitarian. Avocations: group singing, bridge, sailing.

PORTER, PHILIP WAYLAND, geography educator; b. Hanover, N.H., July 9, 1928; s. Wayland Robinson and Bertha Maria (LaPlante) P.; m. Patricia Elizabeth Garrigus, Sept. 5, 1950; children: Janet Elizabeth, Sara Louise, Alice Catherine. A.B., Middlebury Coll., 1950; M.A., Syracuse U., 1955; Ph.D., U. London, 1957. Instr. geography U. Minn., Mpls., 1957-58; asst. prof. U. Minn., 1958-64, asso. prof., 1964-66, prof., 1966—, chmn. dept., 1969-71; asso. to v.p. acad. affairs, also dir. Office Internat. Programs, 1979-83; Mem. geography panel Com. on Space Programs for Earth Observations Nat. Acad. Scis., 1967-71; bd. dirs., liaison officer Midwest Univs. Consortium for Internat. Activities, 1979-83. Contbr. articles, monographs to profl. lit. Served with AUS, 1952-54. Ctrl. Rsch. Fund (London) grantee, 1955-56, NSF grantee, 1961-62, 78-80, 92-93, Social Sci. Rsch. Coun. grantee, 1966-67, Rockfeller Found. grantee, 1969, 71-73, Gen. Svc. Found. grantee, 1981-83, Exxon Edn. Found. grantee, 1983-84, Fulbright grantee, 1992-93; Bush Sabbatical fellow, 1985-86. Mem. Assn. Am. Geographers, Am. Anthrop. Assn., African Studies Assn. Home: 86 Arthur Ave SE Minneapolis MN 55414-3410 Office: U Minn Dept Geography Minneapolis MN 55455

PORTER, RHONDA DAVIS, critical care, emergency nurse; b. Cabarrus County, N.C., July 31, 1956; d. Donald Matthew and Margaret Louise (Cauble) Davis; m. Allen Lovejoy Porter, Dec. 15, 1979; children: Jeffrey Allen, Matthew Glenn. Diploma, Mercy Sch. Nursing, Charlotte, N.C., 1977; BSN, U. N.C., Charlotte, 1979. Cert. mobile intensive care nurse, trauma nurse, ACLS. Staff nurse Wesley Long Community Hosp., Greensboro, N.C.; nurse cons. Aetna Life Ins., 1990-92, clin. nurse specialist, 1992—; case mgr. Aetna Health Plans, 1992—, trainer, auditor, 1995—. Mem. Boy Scouts Am., coord. Tiger Cub, 1994-95, asst. den leader pack 17, Greensboro, N.C., 1995-96. Home: 5506 Cobble Glen Ct Greensboro NC 27407-6351

PORTER, RICHARD STERLING, retired metal processing company executive, lawyer; b. Newton, Mass., May 14, 1929; s. William Edwin Jr. and Mabel Elizabeth (Saunders) P.; m. Sara Patten McCrum, June 15, 1955; children: Edwin Ross, John Sterling. AB, Princeton U., 1952; LLB, U. Va., 1957. Various positions Alcan Aluminium Ltd., Montreal, Que. and Cleve., 1957-85; sec., corp. counsel Alcan Aluminium Ltd., Montreal, 1985-88. Served to 1st lt. U.S. Army, 1952-54, Korea. Home: 206 Woodside Rd Brunswick ME 04011-7442

PORTER, ROBERT HUGH, economics educator; b. London, Ont., Can., Jan. 25, 1955; came to U.S., 1976; s. Hugh Donald and Olive Marie (Anderson) P.; m. Therese Jane McGuire, June 20, 1981. BA with honors, U. Western Ont., London, 1976; PhD, Princeton U., 1981. Asst. prof. econs. U. Minn., Mpls., 1980-84; post doctoral fellow Bell Labs., Murray Hill, N.J., 1982-83; assoc. prof. SUNY, Stony Brook, 1984-87; mem. tech. staff Bell Communications Rsch., Morristown, N.J., 1986-88; prof. Northwestern U., Evanston, Ill., 1987—. Mem. bd. editors Am. Econ. Rev., 1987-88, 94—; assoc. editor Internat. Jour. Indsl. Orgn., 1989—; co-editor Econometrica, 1988-93, Rand Jour. Econs., 1995—; contbr. articles to profl. jours. NSF grantee, 1985, 88, 93. Fellow Econometric Soc.; mem. Am. Econ. Assn., Can. Econs. Assn. Home: 904 Michiagn Ave # 1 Evanston IL 60202-1416 Office: Northwestern U Dept Econs 2003 Sheridan Rd Evanston IL 60208-0826

PORTER, ROGER BLAINE, government official, educator; b. Provo, Utah, June 19, 1946; s. Blaine Robert and Elizabeth M. (Taylor) P.; m. Ann Robinson, Jan. 6, 1972; children: Robert Roger, Stacy Ann, David R., Rachel Elizabeth. B.A. in History and Polit. Sci., Brigham Young U., 1969; B.Phil, Oxford U., 1971; M.A., Harvard U., 1978, Ph.D., 1978. Asst. dean, tutor in politics Queen's Coll., Oxford U., 1971-72; spl. asst. to pres. The White House, 1974-77; research assoc. Kennedy Sch. Govt. and Grad. Sch. Bus., Harvard U., 1977-79, asst. prof. pub. policy, 1979-81, assoc. prof., 1981, prof. govt. and bus., 1985—; spl. asst. to Pres. of U.S., 1981-82, dep. asst. to Pres., 1982-85; dir. White Ho. Office of Policy Devel., Washington, 1982-85; counselor to sec. U.S. Treasury, 1981-85; exec. sec. Nat. Productivity Adv. Com., 1981-85, Cabinet Coun. on Econ. Affairs, 1981-85, Econ. Policy Coun., 1985; asst. to Pres. for Econ. and Domestic Policy, 1989-93; exec. sec. Pres.'s Econ. Policy Bd., 1974-77; sr. scholar Woodrow Wilson Internat. Ctr. for Scholars, 1993—; dir. Ctr. for Bus. and Govt. Harvard U., 1995—; mem. Pres.'s Commn. on White House Fellowships, 1976—. Author: Presidential Decision Making, 1980, U.S.-U.S.S.R. Grain Agreement, 1984; asst. editor: Public Policy, 1979-81. Mem. Utahns for Effective Govt., Salt Lake City, 1971-72; mem. Republican Nat. Com. Econ. Adv. Com., 1977-81. Rhodes scholar, 1969; Woodrow Wilson fellow, 1969; White House fellow, 1974; recipient spl. citation U.S. Sec. Treasury, 1977; named One of 10 Outstanding Young Men in Am., 1981. Fellow Nat. Acad. Pub. Adminstrn.; mem. Phi Kappa Phi, Pi Sigma Alpha, Phi Eta Sigma, Phi Alpha Theta. Mem. LDS Ch. Avocations: classical music, basketball, tennis, travel. Home: 12 Clifton St Belmont MA 02178-3363 Office: Harvard U Kennedy Sch Govt 79 Jfk St Cambridge MA 02138-5801

PORTER, ROGER JOHN, medical research administrator, neurologist, pharmacologist; b. Pitts., Apr. 4, 1942; s. John Keaggy and Margaret (Parker) P.; m. Candace Marie Leland, Feb. 17, 1968; children: David, Stacey. BS, Eckerd Coll., 1964; MD, Duke U., 1968. Diplomate Nat. Bd. Med. Examiners, Am. Bd. Neurology, Am. Bd. Electroencephalography. Intern U. Calif. at San Diego, 1968-69; resident in neurology U. Calif. at San Francisco, 1971-74; fellow Rsch. Tng. Program Duke U., Durham, N.C., 1966-67; staff assoc. sect. epilepsy Nat. Inst. Neurol. Diseases and Stroke, NIH, Bethesda, Md., 1969-71; investigator U. Calif., San Francisco, 1972-73; sr. rsch. assoc. epilepsy br., Neurol. Disorders Program Nat. Inst. Neurol. and Communicative Disorders and Stroke, NIH, Bethesda, 1974-78, asst. chief epilepsy br., 1977-79, acting chief, 1979-80, acting chief clin. epilepsy sect., IRP, 1979-84, chief epilepsy br., Neurol. Disorders Program, 1980-84, chief med. neurology br. and clin. epilepsy sect. IRP, 1984-87; dep. dir. Nat. Inst. Neurol. Disorders and Stroke, NIH, Bethesda, 1987-92; v.p., clin. pharmacology Wyeth-Ayerst Rsch., Radnor, Pa., 1992—; adj. prof. neurology U. Pa., 1993—; prof. neurology Uniformed Svcs. U. Health Scis., Bethesda, 1980-93, adj. prof. pharmacology, 1982—; cons.-lectr. neurology Nat. Naval Med. Ctr., Bethesda, 1978-93; chmn. White House Subcom. on Brain and Behavioral Scis., 1990-92; scholar-in-residence Assn. Am. Med. Colls., Washington, 1989-90; mem. NIMH/Nat. Inst. Neurol. Disorders and Stroke Coun. of Assembly of Scientists, 1983-86, pres., 1985-86; mem. pharmacy and therapeutics com. NIH, 1977-86, chmn., 1978; mem. instnl. rev. bd. human subjects Nat. Inst. Neurol. Disorders and Stroke, 1984-87, chmn., 1986-87. Author/editor 10 books; mem. editl. bd. Acta Neurologica Scandanavica, Annals of Neurology, Epilepsia; contbr. numerous papers, book chpts., abstracts to profl. publs.; writer, contbr. 5 motion pictures, 1 exhibit. Bd. trustees Eckerd Coll., 1994—. With USPHS, 1969-92. Recipient USPHS Commendation medal, 1977, MacArthur Outstanding Alumnus award Eckerd Coll., 1977, Fulbright Disting. Prof. award, 1985, USPHS Meritorious Svc. medal, 1986, Dept. Def. Meritorious Svc. medal, 1989, Disting. Alumnus award Duke Duke U. Med. Ctr., 1989, USN Commendation medal, 1991, USPHS Disting. Svc. medal, 1991; scholar in residence Assn. Am. Med. Colls., Washington, 1989-90. Fellow Am. Acad. Neurology, Am. Neurol. Assn.; mem. Am. Electroencephalographic Soc., Am. Epilepsy Soc. (pres. 1989-90), Soc. Neurosci., Am. Soc. Clin. Pharmacology and Therapeutics, Am. Soc. Neurologic Investigation (hon.), Internat. League Against Epilepsy (sec.-gen. 1989-93). Home: 461 Timber Ln Devon PA 19333-1232 Office: Wyeth-Ayerst Rsch PO Box 8299 Philadelphia PA 19101

PORTER, ROGER STEPHEN, chemistry educator; b. Windom, Minn., June 2, 1928; s. Sherman Clarence and Cora Ruth (Rogers) P.; m. Catharine Crow, Aug. 3, 1968; children: Margaret Davis, Stephen Cady; children by previous marriage: Laura Jean, Ruth Anne. BS in Chemistry, UCLA, 1950; PhD, U. Wash., 1956; DSc (hon.), U. Mass., 1996. Sr. rsch. assoc. Chevron Rsch. Co., Richmond, Calif., 1956-66; prof., dept. polymer sci. and engring. U. Mass., Amherst, 1966—, head dept., 1966-76, asst. to pres. for rsch., 1979-81; plastics cons. in field; co-dir. NSF Materials Lab., 1972-82; study group head U.S./USSR Commn. on Sci.; com. mem. Nat. Acad. Scis., 1969—; adv. panel NSF; adv. bd. various sci. jours.; lectr. Russian, Brazilian and Romanian acads.; bd. dirs. Plastics Inst. Am.; trustee Gordon Rsch. Conf., chmn. Editor: Polymer Engineering and Science, Polymer Composites; co-editor 14 books. Recipient Polyolefins award Internat. Plastics Edn. award Soc. Plastics Engring., 1977, Internat. award in plastics sci. and engring. Soc. Plastics Engring., 1981, Disting. mem. award Soc. Plastics Engring., 1993, Mettler award, 1983, Bingham medal Soc. Rheology, 1985; named to Plastics Hall of Fame, 1991. Fellow Am. Phys. Soc., N.Am. Thermal Analysis Soc. (pres. 1987); mem. Am. Chem. Soc. (award in plastics 1979), Plastics Acad. (bd. dirs.), Sigma Xi, Alpha Chi Sigma, Phi Gamma Delta. Home: 220 Rolling Ridge Rd Amherst MA 01002-1423 Office: Univ Mass Polymer Rsch Ctr Amherst MA 01003

PORTER, STEPHEN CUMMINGS, geologist, educator; b. Santa Barbara, Calif., Apr. 18, 1934; s. Lawrence Johnson Porter Jr. and Frances (Cummings) Seger; m. Anne Mary Higgins, Apr. 2, 1959; children: John, Maria, Susannah. BS, Yale U., 1955, MS, 1958, PhD, 1962. Asst. prof. geology U. Wash., Seattle, 1962-66, assoc. prof., 1966-71, prof., 1971—, dir. Quaternary Research Ctr., 1982—; mem. bd. earth scis. Nat. Acad. Sci., Washington, 1983-85; mem. adv. com. divsn. polar programs NSF, Washington, 1983-84; vis. fellow Clare Hall Cambridge (Eng.) U., 1980-81; guest prof. Academia Sinica, People's Republic of China, 1987—; v.p. Internat. Union Quaternary Rsch., 1992-95, pres., 1995—. Co-author: Physical Geology, 1987, The Dynamic Earth, 1989, 92, 95, The Blue Planet, 1995, Environmental Geology, 1996; editor: Late Quaternary Environments of the United States, 1983; editor Quaternary Rsch., 1976—; assoc. editor Radiocarbon Jour. 1982-89; mem. editorial bd. Quaternary Sci. Revs., 1988—, Quaternary International, 1989—, Quaternary of South African and Antarctic Peninsula, 1995—. Served to lt. USNR, 1955-57. Recipient Benjamin Silliman prize Yale U., 1962; Willis M. Tale lectr. So. Meth. U., 1984, S.F. Emmons lectr. Colo. Sci. Soc., 1996; Fulbright Hays sr. rsch. fellow, New Zealand, 1973-74. Fellow Geol. Soc. Am., Arctic Inst. N.Am. (bd. govs.); mem. Am. Quaternary Assn. (coun., pres. 1992-94). Avocations: photography, mountaineering. Home: 18034 15th Ave NW Seattle WA 98177-3305 Office: U Wash Quaternary Rsch Ctr PO Box 351360 Seattle WA 98192-1360

PORTER, STEPHEN WINTHROP, stage director; b. Ogdensburg, N.Y., July 24, 1925; s. Charles T. and Anna (Newton) P. B.A., Yale U., 1945, M.F.A., 1948. Asst. prof. English in charge of drama McGill U., Montreal, 1949-56. Stage dir. plays on Broadway Right You Are, Wild Duck, 1966, The Show Off, 1967, The Misanthrope, 1968, 83, The Wrong Way Light Bulb, Private Lives, 1969, Harvey, 1970, The School for Wives, 1971, Captain Brassbound's Conversion, 1972, Don Juan, 1973, Chemin de Fer, 1974, Rules of the Game, 1975, They Knew What They Wanted, 1976, Days in the Trees, 1976, The Importance of Being Earnest, 1977, Tartuffe, 1977, Man and Superman, 1978, Major Barbara, The Man Who Came to Dinner, 1980, You Never Can Tell, 1986, The Devil's Disciple, 1988, The Miser, 1990, Getting Married, 1991. Address: 25 W 54th St New York NY 10019-5411

PORTER, STUART WILLIAMS, investment company executive; b. Detroit, Jan. 11, 1937; s. Stuart Perlee and Alma Bernice (Williams) P.; m. Myrna Marlene Denham, June 27, 1964; children: Stuart, Randall. BS, U. Mich., 1960; MBA, U. Chgo., 1967, postgrad., 1967-68. Investment mgr., ptnr. Weiss Peck & Greer, 1978—. Chmn. Crusade of Mercy, 1973; chmn. investment com. Presbytery of Chgo. Served with USAF, 1961-62. Recipient Excellence in Bus. and Acctg. award Fin. Exec. Inst., 1966; Am. Acctg. Assn. fellow, 1967. Mem. Midwest Pension Conf., Investment Analysts Soc. Chgo., Fin. Analysts Fedn., Inst. Quantitative Rsch. in Fin., Turnberry Country Club, Econ. Club, Haig Point Country Club, Avondale Country Club, Wynstone Golf Club, Beta Gamma Sigma Home: 130 Wyngate Dr Barrington IL 60010-4839 Office: 311 S Wacker Dr Fl 52 Chicago IL 60606-6618

PORTER, TERRY, professional basketball player; b. Milw., Apr. 8, 1963. Student, U. Wis., Stevens Point, 1981-85. With Portland Trail Blazers, 1985—; now with Minnesota Timberwolves, Minneapolis. Recipient Citizenship award, 1993; named to NBA All-Star team, 1991, 93. Holds single game record for most three point field goals without a miss-7, 1992. Office: Minnesota Timberwolves 600 1st Ave N Minneapolis MN 55403*

PORTER, VERNA LOUISE, lawyer; b. L.A., May 31, 1941. B.A., Calif. State U., 1963; JD, Southwestern U., 1977. Bar: Calif. 1977, U.S. Dist. Ct. (cen. dist.) Calif. 1978, U.S. Ct. Appeals (9th cir.) 1978. Ptnr. Eisler & Porter, L.A., 1978-79, mng. ptnr., 1979-86, pvt. practice law, 1986—; judge pro-tempore L.A. Mcpl. Ct., 1983—, L.A. Superior Ct., 1989—, Beverly Hills Mcpl. Ct., 1992—; mem. state of Calif. subcom. on landlord tenant law, panelist conv., mem. real property law sect. Calif. State Bar, 1983; speaker on landlord-tenant law to real estate profls., including San Fernando Bd. Realtors; vol. atty. L.A. County Bar Dispute Resolution, mem. client rels. panel, fee arbitrator. Mem. adv. coun. Freddie Mac Vendor, 1995—. Editl. asst., contbr. Apt. Owner Builder; contbr. to Apt. Bus. Outlook, Real Property News, Apt. Age; mem. World Affairs Coun. Fre Mem. ABA, L.A. County Bar Assn. (client-rels. vol. dispute resolution and fee arbitration, 1981—), L.A. Trial Lawyers Assn., Wilshire Bar Assn., Women Lawyer's Assn., Landlord Trial Lawyers Assn. (founding mem., pres.), Freddie Mac Vendor Adv. Coun., da Camera Soc. Republican. Office: 2500 Wilshire Blvd Fl 1226 Los Angeles CA 90057-4317

PORTER, W. L., bishop. Bishop of Cen. Tenn., Ch. of God in Christ, Memphis. Office: Ch of God in Christ 1235 E Parkway S Memphis TN 38114-6728

PORTER, WALTER ARTHUR, retired judge; b. Dayton, Ohio, June 6, 1924; s. Claude and Estella (Raymond) P.; m. Patricia Reeves Higdon, Dec. 3, 1947; children—Scott Paul, David Bryant. B.S. in Engring, U. Cin., 1948, LL.B., 1949. Bar: Ohio 1949. Legal dep. Montgomery County Probate Ct., 1949-51; asst. pros. atty. Montgomery County, 1951-56; with Albert H. Scharrer (atty.), Dayton, 1956-61; mem. firm Smith & Schnacke, Dayton, 1962-85; pres. Smith & Schnacke, 1980-85; judge Montgomery County Common Pleas Ct., 1985-95; ret., 1995. Served with inf. U.S. Army, 1943-45, ETO. Mem. ABA, Ohio Bar Assn. (pres. 1973-74), Dayton Bar Assn., Am. Coll. Trial Lawyers, Am. Coll. Probate Counsel, Phi Alpha Delta, Omicron Delta Kappa. Democrat. Presbyterian. Club: Mason. Home: 785 E Schantz Ave Dayton OH 45419-3818

PORTER, WALTER THOMAS, JR., bank executive; b. Corning, N.Y., Jan. 8, 1934; s. Walter Thomas and Mary Rebecca (Brookes) P.; m. Dixie Jo Thompson, Apr. 3, 1959; children: Kimberlee Paige, Douglas Thompson, Jane-Amy Elizabeth. BS, Rutgers U., 1954; MBA, U. Wash., 1959; PhD, Columbia U., 1964. CPA, Wash., N.Y. Staff cons. Touche Ross & Co., Seattle, 1959-61; NDEA fellow Columbia U., 1961-64; dir. edn. Touche Ross & Co., N.Y.C., 1964-66; assoc. prof. U. Wash., 1966-70, prof., 1970-74; vis. prof. N. European Mgmt. Inst., Oslo, Norway, 1974-75; nat. dir. planning Touche Ross & Co., Seattle, 1975-78, dir. exec. fin. counseling, 1978-84, exec. v.p., mgr. pvt. banking, Rainier Nat. Bank, 1984-87, exec. v.p., mgr. capital mgmt. and pvt. banking, 1987-88, vice chmn. 1988-89; vice chmn. Security Pacific Bank Washington, 1989-92; exec. v.p., mgr. capital mgmt. group Seafirst Bank, Seattle, 1992—; vis. lectr. taxation U. Wash., 1978-85; bd. dirs. AEI, Inc. Mem. Seattle adv. bd. Salvation Army, 1975-83, 89—, pres. 1993-95; trustee Ryther Child Ctr., 1975-85, pres., 1979-81; trustee Lakeside Sch., 1977-87, pres. 1984-86; trustee Va. Mason Med. Ctr., 1986—, chair, bd. govs. 1994—; Va. Mason Med. Ctr. 1986—, chair, bd. govs. 1994—, Mus. History and Industry, 1982-83. Served with U.S. Army, 1955-57. Author: Auditing Electronic System, 1966; (with William Perry) EDP: Controls and Auditing, 1970, 5th edit., 1987; (with John Burton) Auditing A Conceptual Approach, 1974; (with D. Alkire) Wealth: How to Achieve It, 1976; Touche Ross Guide to Personal Financial Management, 1984, 3d edit., 1989; (with D. Porter) The Personal Financial Planner's Practice Sourcebook, 1986. Mem. Am. Inst. CPA's. Congregationalist. Club: Wash. Athletic, Sand Point Country, Rainer Club, Sand Point Golf Club. Office: Seafirst Bank PO Box 3586 701 5th Ave 56th Fl Seattle WA 98124

PORTER, WILLIAM LYMAN, architect, educator; b. Poughkeepsie, N.Y., Feb. 19, 1934; s. William Quincy and Lois (Brown) P.; m. Lynn Rogers Porter; children: Quayny Lyman, Zoe Lynn, Eve Lyman. B.A., Yale U., 1955, M.Arch., 1957; Ph.D., MIT, 1969. Designer, job capt. Louis I. Kahn (architect), Phila., 1960-62; urban designer, asst. chief of design Ciudad Guayana project Joint Center for Urban Studies of Harvard and MIT, Caracas, Venezuela, 1962-64; Mellon fellow dept. urban studies and planning MIT, 1964-65; Samuel Stouffer fellow Joint Center for Urban Studies, Harvard and MIT, 1966-67; asst. prof. urban design, depts. architecture and urban studies and planning MIT, 1968-70, assoc. prof. urban design, 1970-71, prof. architecture and planning, 1971—, Norman B. and Muriel Leventhal prof. architecture and planning, 1988—, head. dept. architecture, 1987-91, dean Sch. Architecture and Planning, 1971-81; co-dir. Aga Khan Program for Islamic Architecture Harvard U.-MIT, 1979-85; cons. in field; mem. Nat. Archtl. Accrediting Bd., 1978-80, pres., 1979; mem. Mass. Designer Selection Bd., 1978-79, chmn., 1979; mem. steering com. Aga Khan Award for Architecture, 1977-86, mem. master jury, 1989. Co-founder, co-editor Places: A Quarterly Jour. Environ. Design, 1982-88. Trustee Milton (Mass.) Acad., 1989—; mem. bd. overseers Coll. Fine Arts, U. Pa., 1984-90, Mus. Fine Arts, Boston, 1992-94. Fellow AIA; mem. Boston Soc. Architects (dir. 1969-73, 77-81). Clubs: Harvard Musical Assn. (Boston). Home: 17 Concord Ave Cambridge MA 02138-2321 Office: MIT Sch Architecture & Planning 77 Massachusetts Ave Cambridge MA 02139-4301

PORTER, WILMA JEAN, university director; b. Sylacauga, Ala., May 30, 1931; d. Harrison Samuel and Blanche Leonard Butcher; m. Douglas Taylor Porter, Apr. 18, 1953; children: Daria Cecile, Blanche Evette, Douglas Vincent. BS, Tuskegee U., 1951; MS, Mich. State U., 1966; PhD, Iowa State U., 1980. Asst. dietitian Miss. State Tb Sanatorium, 1951-52; therapeutic dietitian dept. of hosp. City of N.Y., S.I., 1952-53; libr. asst. Mississippi Valley State Coll., Itta Bena, Miss., 1963-65; asst. prof. Grambling (La.) State U., 1966-75, Howard U., Washington, 1976-80; country dir. U.S. Peace Corps, Tonga, 1980-82; asst. dir. internat. programs Ft. Valley (Ga.) Coll., 1983-84, dir. Inst. Advancement, 1984-88; dir. Sch. Home Econs., Tenn. Technol. U., Cookeville, 1989—; project dir. Capitol Hill Health and Homemaker, Washington, 1982-83; interim dir. Inst. Advancement Alcorn State U., Lorman, Miss., 1988-89. Author lab. manual for quantity foods, 1977; editor: (cookbook) Some Christmas Foods and Their Origins from Around the World, 1983. Convenor Nat. Issues Forums, Ga. and Tenn., 1985—; citizen participant Nat. Issues Forums Soviet Dialogue, Newport Beach, Calif., 1988; bd. dirs. Leadership Putnam, Cookeville, 1990-94; chmn. Tenn. Technol. U. campaign United Way, 1989; mem. devel. and planning com. Peach County Ft. Valley, 1985-87; mem. Peach County Heart Fund Dr., 1986-88; participant People to People Citizens Amb. program U.S./China Women's Issues Program, 1995. Title III grantee U.S. Dept. Edn., 1986, 87; Tenn. Dept. Human Svcs. grantee, 1993, 94. Mem. AAUW (program chair 1991-92, pres. Cookeville br. 1993-94), Am. Home Econs. Assn., Am. Dietetic Assn., Nat. Coun. Adminstrs. Home Econs., Tenn. Home Econs. Assn., Tenn. Dietetic Assn. Democrat. Roman Catholic. Avocations: writing, vegetable and flower gardening. Home: 512 Fisk Rd Cookeville TN 38501-2925

PORTERFIELD, CHRISTOPHER, magazine editor, writer; b. Weston, W.Va., Apr. 3, 1937; s. James Herman and Irene (Smith) P.; m. Stephanie Brown, Jan. 20, 1962; children: Christopher Brown, Tessa Louise, Kevin Stephenson. BA, Yale U., 1958; MA, Columbia U., 1965. Music critic Time mag., N.Y.C., 1967-69; cultural correspondent Time mag., London, 1969-72; exec. producer Daphne Prodns., N.Y.C., 1974-79; sr. editor Time mag., N.Y.C., 1980-93, asst. mng. editor, 1993—. Co-Author: (with Dick Cavett) (books) Cavett, 1973, Eye on Cavett, 1983; contbr. articles to popular mags. and periodicals, 1975—. Mem. Writer's Guild of Am. Avocations: reading, music, tennis. Home: 315 Central Park W New York NY 10025-7664 Office: Time mag 1271 Avenue Of The Americas New York NY 10020

PORTERFIELD, JAMES TEMPLE STARKE, business administration educator; b. Annapolis, Md., July 7, 1920; s. Lewis Broughton and Maud Paxton (Starke) P.; m. Betty Gold, Apr. 23, 1949 (dec. 1985); m. Janet Patricia Gardiner Roggeveen, Oct. 5, 1986. AB, U. Calif., Berkeley, 1942; MBA, Stanford U., 1948, PhD, 1955. From asst. to assoc. prof. Harvard U. Bus. Sch., Boston, 1955-59; prof. fin. Stanford (Calif.) U. Grad. Sch. Bus., 1959-79, James Irvin Miller Prof. fin., 1979-90, prof. emeritus, 1990—; prof. IMEDE Mgmt. Devel. Inst., Lausanne, Switzerland, 1962-63. Author: Life Insurance Stocks as Investments, 1955, Investment Decisions and Capital Costs, 1965; co-author: Case Problems in Finance, 1959. Served as lt. USNR, 1941-46. Recipient Salgo Noren award Stanford U., 1966, Richard W. Lyman award Stanford U. Alumni Assn., 1995. Home: 295 Golden Oak Dr Portola Vally CA 94028-7730 Office: Stanford U Grad Sch Bus Stanford CA 94305

PORTERFIELD, NEIL HARRY, landscape architect, educator; b. Murrysville, Pa., Aug. 15, 1936; s. Phil Frank and Alvira Clare (Rea) P.; m. Sandra Jean Beswarick, Aug. 9, 1958; children: Eric Jon, Jennifer Jane, Garrett Andrew. BS in Landscape Architecture, Pa. State U., 1958; M in Landscape Architecture, U. Pa., 1964. Landscape architect Pitts. Dept. Parks and Recreation, 1958-59; land planner Neil H. Porterfield & Assocs., Murrysville, 1961-64; dir. landscape architecture and planning Hellmuth, Obata & Kassabaum, Inc., St. Louis, 1964-70; exec. v.p. HOK Assocs., St. Louis, 1970-72, pres., 1972-85; prin., v.p., dir. Hellmuth, Obata & Kassabaum, Inc., 1977-80, corp. dir. planning, sr. v.p., dir., 1980-85; prof., head dept. landscape architecture Pa. State U., University Park, 1985-93, dean Coll. Arts and Architecture, 1993—; lectr. in field; prof. Washington U., 1979; chmn. Landscape Archtl. Accreditation Bd. Contbr. articles to profl. orgns., anthologies. Bd. dirs. Landscape Architecture Found., 1983-85; adv. coun. Coll. Architecture and Urban Studies, Va. Poly. Inst. and State U., Blacksburg, 1984-86; vice-chmn. The Commn. Fine Arts, Washington, 1985-93. Recipient honor award Married Student Housing, U. Mich., honor award Am. Soc. Landscape Architects, 1969, Merit award Parkside Campus Study U. Wis. at Kenosha, Merit award Am. Soc. Landscape Architects, 1969, Outstanding Alumnus award Coll. Arts and Architecture, Pa. State U., 1983, others. Fellow Am. Soc. Landscape Architects (v.p. 1985-87); mem. Coun. of Edn. Presbyterian. Home: RR 1 Centre Hall PA 16828-9801 Office: Pa State U Coll Arts and Architecture 111 Arts Bldg University Park PA 16802-2900

PORTERFIELD, WILLIAM WENDELL, chemist, educator; b. Winchester, Va., Aug. 24, 1936; s. Donald Kennedy and Adelyn (Miller) P.; m. Dorothy Elizabeth Dail, Aug. 24, 1957; children—Allan Kennedy, Douglas Hunter. B.S., U. N.C., 1957, Ph.D., 1962; M.S., Calif. Inst. Tech., 1960. Sr. research chemist Hercules, Inc., Cumberland, Md., 1962-64; asst. prof. chemistry Hampden-Sydney (Va.) Coll., 1964-65, assoc. prof., 1965-68, prof. chemistry, 1968—, Charles Scott Venable prof. chemistry, 1989—, chmn. natural sci. div., 1973-77, chmn. dept. chemistry, 1982-85, 93—; vis. fellow U. Durham (U.K.), 1984. Author: Concepts of Chemistry, 1972, Inorganic Chemistry, 1984, 2d edit., 1993; contbr. articles to profl. jours.

Mem. Am. Chem. Soc., Royal Chem. Soc. (London, Eng.), Phi Beta Kappa. Home: PO Box 697 Hampden Sydney VA 23943

PORTES, ALEJANDRO, sociologist, educator; b. Havana, Cuba, Oct. 13, 1944; came to U.S., 1960; s. Helio B. Portes and Eulalia Cordtada; m. Nancy Brazie, Jan. 28, 1966 (div. Dec. 1974); children: Elizabeth, Charles A., Andrea; m. Patricia Fernandez Kelly, Mar. 31, 1985. BA summa cum laude, Creighton U., 1965; MA, U. Wis., 1967, PhD, 1970. Lectr. U. Wis., Madison, 1969-70; asst. prof. U. Ill., Urbana, 1970-71; assoc. prof. U. Tex., Austin, 1971-75; prof. Duke U., Durham, N.C., 1975-80; prof. Johns Hopkins U., Balt., 1980-87, John Dewey prof., 1987—; chair sociology dept., 1993-96; Frost disting. vis. prof. Fla. Internat. U., Miami, 1988-90; cons. Ford Found., 1977, 79, 89, U.S. Congress Com. for Study of Immigration, 1988-90, Ministries of Labor and Social Welfare of Spain, Immigration Policy, 1990—; fellow Russell Sage Found., 1992-93. Author: Urban Latin America, 1976, Labor, Class and the International System, 1981, Latin Journey, 1985, Immigrant America, a Portrait, 1990, City on the Edge, the Transformation of Miami, 1993 (Robert Park award, Anthony Leeds award); bd. dirs. Ethnic and Racial Studies. Guest Witness U.S. Congress Sub-com. on Immigration, 1983, 86; del. Internat. Sociol. Assn., Madrid, Spain, 1990—. Mem. Am. Sociol. Assn. (coun. mem.), Latin Am. Studies Assn. (mem. jt. com. Social Sci. Rsch. Coun. 1985-88). Avocations: sailing, motor boating. Office: Johns Hopkins U Dept Sociol Baltimore MD 21218

PORTIS, ALAN MARK, physicist, educator; b. Chgo., July 17, 1926; s. Lyon and Ruth (Libman) P.; m. Beverly Aline Levin, Sept. 5, 1948; children: Jonathan Marc, Stephen Compagni, Lori Ann, Eliyahu Shlomo Cohn. Ph.B., U. Chgo., 1948; A.B., U. Calif., Berkeley, 1949, Ph.D., 1953. Mem. faculty U. Pitts., 1953-56; Mem. faculty U. Calif.-Berkeley, 1956—, prof. physics, 1964-95, prof. emeritus, 1995—, asst. to chancellor for research, 1966-67, asso. dean grad. div., 1967-68, dir. Lawrence Hall Sci., 1969-72, univ. ombudsman, 1981-83, 92-94, assoc. dean Coll. Engring., 1983-87, 94-95. Author: Electromagnetic Fields/Sources and Media, 1978, Electrodynamics of High-Temperature Superconductors, 1993; contbg. author: Berkeley Physics Laboratory, 1964, 65, 66, 71. Fulbright fellow, 1961, 67, Guggenheim fellow, 1965, SERC sr. fellow, U.K., 1991-92. Fellow Am. Phys. Soc.; mem. Am. Assn. Physics Tchrs. (Robert Andrews Millikan award 1966).

PORTIS, CHARLES MCCOLL, reporter, writer; b. El Dorado, Ark., Dec. 28, 1933; s. Samuel Palmer and Alice (Waddell) P. BA, U. Ark., 1958. Reporter The Comml. Appeal, Memphis, 1958, Ark. Gazette, Little Rock, 1959-60, N.Y. Herald Tribune, N.Y.C., 1960-64. Author: Norwood, 1966, True Grit, 1968, The Dog of the South, 1979, Masters of Atlantis, 1985, Gringos, 1991. Sgt. USMC, 1952-55, Korea. Presbyterian. Home: 7417 Kingwood Rd Little Rock AR 72207-1734

PORTLAND, CHARLES DENIS, finance and marketing professional; b. N.Y.C., July 11, 1952; s. William and Berta Portela. AAS, CUNY, N.Y.C., 1974; AA, U. Md., 1978, BS, 1979; M in Accounting, U. Okla., 1982; postgrad., Nova U. CPA, Fla. Sr. auditor Arthur Anderson & Co., Oklahoma City, 1982-86; sr. fin. analyst Knight Ridder, Inc., Miami, Fla., 1986-88; special project Miami Herald, Miami, Fla., 1988-89; prin. Denis Portela, CPA, Miami Beach, Fla., 1989-93; founder, pres. Grove Mktg. (dba Charlden Consulting), 1990-95; cons. Carlson Travel Network, MGM Grand Hotel & Casino, City of Miami, Fla., Microsoft. Author: Portland's Computer Guide, 1996. With U.S. Army, 1974-80, Germany, Korea. Mem. AICPA's, Fla. Inst. CPA's, Am. Mgmt. Assn., Governor's Indsl. Dev. Bds. Subcomm. on Computing and Data Communications. Lutheran. Avocation: horticulture. Home: PO Box 267 Stamford NY 12167

PORTLAND, RENE, university athletic coach. Head coach Pa. State U., University Park, 1980—. Office: Pa State U University Park PA 16802

PORTMAN, GLENN ARTHUR, lawyer; b. Cleve., Dec. 26, 1949; s. Alvin B. and Lenore (Marsh) P.; m. Katherine Seaborn, Aug. 3, 1974 (div. 1984); m. Susan Newell, Jan. 3, 1987. BA in History, Case Western Res. U., 1968; JD, So. Meth. U., 1975. Bar: Tex. 1975, U.S. Dist. Ct. (no. dist.) Tex. 1975, U.S. Dist. Ct. (so. dist.) Tex. 1983, U.S. Dist. Ct. (we. and ea. dists.) Tex. 1988. Assoc. Johnson, Bromberg & Leeds, Dallas, 1975-80, ptnr., 1980-92; ptnr. Arter, Hadden, Johnson & Bromberg, Dallas, 1992-95, Arter & Hadden, Dallas, 1996—; chmn. bd. dirs. Physicians Regional Hosp., 1994-96; mem. exec. bd. So. Meth. U. Sch. Law, 1994—; lectr. bankruptcy topics South Tex. Coll. Law, State Bar Tex. Asst. editor-in-chief Southwestern Law Jour., 1974-75; contbr. articles to profl. jours. Firm rep. United Way Met. Dallas, 1982-92; treas. Lake Highlands Square Homeowners Assn., 1990-93. Mem. ABA, Am. Bankruptcy Inst., State Bar Tex. Assn., Dallas Bar Assn., So. Meth. U. Law Alumni Assn. (council bd. dirs., v.p. 1980-86, chmn. admissions com., chmn. class agt. program 1986-89, chmn. fund raising 1989-91), 500 Club Inc., Assemblage Club. Republican. Methodist. Home: 9503 Winding Ridge Dr Dallas TX 75238-1451 Office: Arter & Hadden 1717 Main St Ste 4100 Dallas TX 75201-7302

PORTMAN, RACHEL MARY BERKELEY, composer; b. Eng., Dec. 11, 1960. BA, Oxford Univ. Scores include (films) Sharma and Beyond, 1986, Antonia and Jane, 1991, Life Is Sweet, 1991, Where Angels Fear to Tread, 1991, Rebecca's Daughters, 1992, Used People, 1992, Ethan Frome, 1993, Benny and Joon, 1993, Friends, 1993, The Joy Luck Club, 1993, (TV movies) Young Charlie Chaplin, 1989, The Cloning of Joanna May, 1992, (documentaries) Elizabeth R: A Year In the Life of the Queen, 1992; compositions include Fantasy for Cello and Piano, 1985. Named Composer of Yr. British Film Inst., 1988. Office: The Kraft-Benjamin Agency 8491 W Sunset Blvd Ste 492 West Hollywood CA 90069-1911

PORTMAN, ROB, congressman; b. Cin., Dec. 19, 1955; m. Jane Portman; children: Jed, Will. BA, Dartmouth Coll., 1979; JD, U. Mich., 1984. Ptnr. Head & Ritchey, Cin., 1986-89; assoc. counsel to President of U.S., then dep. asst. to President, dir. Office Legis. Affairs White House, Washington, 1989-92; mem. U.S. Del. to UN Subcom. on Human Rights, 1992, 103d-104th Congresses from 2nd Ohio dist., 1993—; mem. ways and means com., mem. Leaders' Econ. Task Force; asst. whip U.S. Ho. of Reps. Bd. trustees Springer Sch., The United Way, Hyde Park Community United Meth. Ch.; founding trustee Cin.-China Sister City Com.; former bd. dirs. United Home Care; vice chmn. Hamilton County George Bush for Pres. Campaign, 1988, 92; chmn. Rep. Early Bird Campaign com., 1992; del. Rep. Nat. Conv., 1988, 92; active Hamilton County Rep. Party Exec. com., Hamilton County Rep. Party Fin. Com. Mem. Cin. World Trade Assn. Office: US Ho of Reps 238 Cannon HOB Washington DC 20515-0509*

PORTNEY, JOSEPH NATHANIEL, aerospace executive; b. L.A., Aug. 15, 1927; s. Marcus and Sarah (Pilson) P.; m. Ina Mae Leibson, June 20, 1959; children: Philip, Jeffrey. BS, U.S. Naval Acad., 1952. Commd. 2d lt. USAF, 1952, advanced through grades to capt., 1956, resigned, 1960; with Litton Systems, Inc., Woodland Hills, Calif., 1960—; project engr. Litton Aero Products, 1967-68; program mgr. Litton Aero Products Litton Systems, Inc., Woodland Hills, 1968-72, advanced program mgr. Guidance and Control Sys., 1972-85, mgr. advanced programs Guidance and Control Sys., 1985—; navigator engr. on 3 historic inertial crossings of the North Pole. Creator solar compass, pilot and navigator calendar. Mem. Inst. of Navigation (v.p. 1988-89, pres. 1989-90), U.S. Naval Acad. Alumni Assn. (trustee 1980-83). Jewish. Avocation: classical piano. Home: 4981 Amigo Ave Tarzana CA 91356-4505 Office: Litton Systems Inc 5500 Canoga Ave Woodland Hills CA 91367-6621

PORTNOY, IAN KARL, lawyer; b. Phila., Aug. 27, 1943; s. Joseph and Florence Portnoy; m. Judith Kobak; children: Michael, Beth. BA, U. Mich., 1965; JD, Villanova U., 1968. Bar: Pa. 1969, D.C. 1970, U.S. Supreme Ct. 1973. Corp. counsel Villager Industries, Phila.; assoc. Danzansky, Dickey, Tydings, Quint and Gordon, Washington, 1970-88; ptnr. Laxalt, Washington, Perito & Dubuc, Washington, 1988-90, Proskauer, Rose, Goetz & Mendelsohn, Washington, 1991—. Dr. editor Digest Environ. Law, Nat. Property Law Digests, Nat. Financing Law Digest; bd. dirs. The Dial Mag., WETA pub. TV and radio sta.; author numerous legal articles. Chmn. bd. dirs. Dumbarton Concert Series, Washington, Live Music Now; devel. bd. Capitol campaign steering and auction com. Georgetown Day Sch.; bd. dirs. Big Brothers, Washington, chmn. annual gourmet dinner. Mem. Am. Arbitration Assn. (comml. com.), Leadership Washington. Home: 6018 Onondaga Rd Bethesda MD 20816-2152 Office: Proskauer Rose Goetz & Mendelsohn LLP 1233 20th St NW Ste 800 Washington DC 20036*

PORTNOY, MERI, nurse; b. Afula, Israel, May 8, 1950; came to the U.S., 1974; d. Chaim Giladi and Ruth (Feit) Giladi-Meron; m. Yoav Portnoy, Dec. 26, 1972; 1 child, Edan. RN diploma, Hasharon Hosp., Petach-Tikva, Israel, 1972; B in Liberal Studies, Lesley Coll., 1994. Sec. Israel Legetion, South Africa, 1973-74, Israeli Embassy, Washington, 1974-75; nurse Dr. Evrett Gordon, Washington, 1975-76; nurse Dialysis Clinic Renal Treatment Ctr., Rockville, Md., 1986—; nurse dialysis dept. Shady Grove Adventist Hosp., Rockville, 1991—; nurse Dialysis Clinic, Biomed. Application, Bethesda, Md., 1976-84; cardiac critical care unit nurse George Washington U. Hosp., Washington, 1980; kidney transplant nurse Georgetown U. Hosp., Washington, 1984-86; real estate sales agt. Long and Foster Real Estate, 1986-87. Mem. Jewish Cmty. Ctr., 1975—, Hadassa-Women Orgn. Hebrew Speaking Br., 1992—; sec. Weizman Inst. Funds Raising Office, Washington, 1989; dir. asst., actress Jewish Repertory Theatre, Md., 1994—. Democrat. Avocations: writing, theatre, music, art, travel. Home: 6328 Montrose Rd Rockville MD 20852-4153

PORTNOY, SARA S., lawyer; b. N.Y.C., Jan. 11, 1926; d. Marcus and Gussie (Raphael) Spiro; m. Alexander Portnoy, Dec. 13, 1959 (dec. 1976); children—William, Lawrence. B.A., Radcliffe Coll., 1946; LL.B., Columbia U., 1949. Bar: N.Y. 1949, U.S. Dist. Ct. (so. dist.) N.Y. 1952, U.S. Dist. Ct. (ea. dist.) N.Y. 1975, U.S. Ct. Appeals (2d cir.) 1975, U.S. Supreme Ct. 1975. Assoc. Seligsberg, Friedman & Berliner, N.Y.C., 1949-51; atty. AT & T, N.Y.C., 1951-61; assoc. Proskauer Rose Goetz & Mendelsohn, N.Y.C., 1974-78, ptnr., 1978-94, retired 1994. Mem. Commn. on Human Rights, White Plains, N.Y., 1973-78; bd. dirs. Legal Aid Soc. of Westchester County, N.Y., 1975-83, Columbia Law Sch. Assn., 1990-94; mem. Pres.'s Coun. Yaddo. Mem. Assn. of Bar of City of N.Y. (chair com. legal support staff 1994). Democrat.

PORTNOY, WILLIAM MANOS, electrical engineering educator; b. Chgo., Oct. 28, 1930; s. Joseph and Bella (Saltzman) P.; m. Alice Catherine Walker, Sept. 9, 1956; children: Catherine Anne, Michael Benjamin. B.S., U. Ill., 1952, M.S., 1952; Ph.D., 1959. Registered profl. engr., Tex. Mem. tech. staff Hughes Aircraft Co., Newport Beach, Calif., 1959-61, Tex. Instruments Inc., Dallas, 1961-67; mem. faculty Tex. Tech. U., Lubbock, 1967—, prof. biomed. engring., 1973-85, prof. physics, 1985—, prof. elec. engring., 1972; adj. assoc. prof. Baylor Coll. Medicine and Inst. Health Svcs. Rsch., Houston, 1969-73; cons. Hughes Rsch. Labs., Malibu, Calif., 1972, NDM Corp., 1974-76, Los Alamos Nat. Lab., 1980-81, 91, Battelle Rsch. Inst., 1980-81, Westinghouse, 1984, SRI Internat., 1986-88, Lawrence Livermore Nat. Lab., 1986-93, W.J. Shafer Assocs., 1988-91, Sandia Nat. Lab., 1989—, Gen. Rsch. Corp., 1990-92, STI Optronics, 1991-92. Contbr. articles to profl. jours.; patentee in field. Bd. dirs. Am. Heart Assn., Lubbock County, 1972-75. Nat. Heart Inst. postdoctoral trainee, 1969; NASA sr. postdoctoral resident, research assoc. Manned Spacecraft Center, Houston, 1968; Fulbright prof., 1975; recipient Abell faculty award, 1984. Fellow IEEE; mem. Am. Soc. Engring. Edn. (Western Electric Fund award for excellence in instrn. engring. students 1980), Am. Phys. Soc., Sigma Xi. Office: Tex Tech U Dept Elec Engring Lubbock TX 79409

PORTOGHESE, PHILIP SALVATORE, medicinal chemist, educator; b. N.Y.C., June 4, 1931; s. Philip A. and Constance (Antonelli) P.; m. Christine L. Phillips, June 11, 1960; children—Stephen, Stuart, Philip. B.S., Columbia U., 1953, M.S., 1958; Ph.D., U. Wis., 1961; Dr. honoris causa, U. Catania, Italy, 1986, Royal Danish Sch. Pharmacy, Copenhagen, 1992. Asst. prof. Coll. Pharmacy, U. Minn., Mpls., 1961-64; assoc. prof. Coll. Pharmacy, U. Minn., 1964-69, prof. medicinal chemistry, 1969—, prof. pharmacology, 1987—, dir. grad. study in medicinal chemistry, 1974-86, head dept., 1974-83; cons. NIMH., 1971-72; mem. med. chemistry B sect. NIH, 1972-76; mem. pharmacology, substance abuse and environ. toxicology interdisciplinary cluster President's Biomed. Research Panel, 1975; mem. expert panel of Flavor and Extract Mfrs. Assn. of U.S., 1984—. Mem. editorial adv. bd. Jour. Med. Chemistry, 1969-71; editor-in-chief, 1972—; mem. editorial adv. bd. Med. Chem. series, 1972—. Served with U.S. Army, 1954-56. Recipient Research Achievement award in med. chemistry Am. Pharm. Assn. Found./Acad. Pharm. Sci., 1980; Ernest H. Volwiler award for outstanding contbns. to pharm. scis. Am. Assn. Colls. of Pharmacy, 1984, N.B. Eddy Meml. award Coll. on Problems of Drug Dependence-NAS NRC, 1991. Fellow AAAS, Acad. Pharm. Scis., Am. Assn. Pharm. Scientists (Rsch. Achievement award 1990); mem. Am. Chem. Soc. (Medicinal Chemistry award 1990, E.E. Smissman-Bristol-Meyers-Squibb award 1991), Am. Soc. Pharm. Exptl. Therapeutics, Internat. Union Pure and Applied Chemistry (commn. on medicinal chemistry 1978-82, internat. com. med. chemistry 1982-85), Soc. Neurosci., Sigma Xi, Rho Chi, Phi Lambda Upsilon. Home: 17 Oriole Ln Saint Paul MN 55127-6334 Office: U Minn Coll of Pharmacy 308 Harvard St SE Minneapolis MN 55455-0353

PORTWAY, PATRICK STEPHEN, telecommunications consulting company executive, telecommunications educator; b. June 18, 1939; s. Christopher Leo and Ceciala (King) P.; m. Malle M. Portway; children by previous marriage: Shawn, Pam, Vicki. BA, U. Cin., 1963; MA, U. Md., 1973; postgrad., Columbia U. Regional ADP coordinator GSA, Washington, 1963-68; mgr. strategic mkt. planning Xerox Corp., 1969-74; mgr. plans and programs System Devel. Corp., 1974-78; fin. indsl. mktg. exec. Satellite Bus. Systems, 1978-80; western regional mgr. Am. Satellite Co., 1980-81; pres. Applied Bus. Telecomm., San Ramon, Calif., 1981—; prof., lectr. Golden Gate U. Grad. Sch., San Francisco, 1983—; pub. mag. Teleconference, 1981—; pub. (newspapers) Discovery Bay, Delta Clippers; prodr. Telecon & Ioccon Confs., 1981—. Author: (with others) Teleconferencing and Distance Learning, 1992, 2d edit. 1994. Presdl. elector Electoral Coll., Va., 1976; candidate Va. State Legislature from 19th Dist., 1971; chmn. Discovery Bay Mcpl. Adv. Coun., 1992-93; mem adv. coun. Discovery Bay Mcpl., 1992-96, chmn. 1992. Served to 1st lt. U.S. Army, 1963-65. Mem. Internat. Teleconferencing Assn. (founder, bd. dirs. 1983-88), Nat. Univ. Teleconferencing Networdk (mem. adv. bd., bd. dirs. 1986-89), U.S. Distance Learning Assn. (founder, exec. dir. 1987—) Electronic Funds Transfer Assn. (founder, bd. dirs. 1980), Satellite Profls., Jaycees charter pres. Chantilly, VA., Disting. Service award Dale City, VA. Club: Commonwealth. Home: 1908 Windward Pt Discovery Bay CA 94514-9510 Office: Applied Bus Telecomm 2600 Kitty Hawk Rd Ste 110 Livermore CA 94550-9625

PORZAK, GLENN E., lawyer; b. Ill., Aug. 22, 1948; m. Judy Lea McGinnis, Dec. 19, 1970; children: Lindsay and Austin. BA with distinction, U. Colo., 1970, JD, 1973. Bar: Colo. 1973. Assoc. Holme Roberts & Owen, Denver, 1973-80, ptnr., 1980-85, mng. ptnr. Boulder office, 1985-95; mng. ptnr. Porzak Browning & Johnson LLP, Boulder, 1996—; bd. dirs. Norwest Bank Boulder, 1993—. Contbr. articles to profl. jours. 1st Lt. U.S. Army, 1970-78. Named Disting. Alumnus U. Colo., 1991. Fellow Explorers Club (bd. dirs. 1995—); mem. Am. Alpine Club (pres. 1988-91), Colo. Mtn. Club (pres. 1983, hon. mem. 1983—), Colo. Outward Bound (trustee 1992—), Phi Beta Kappa. Achievements include reaching summit of Mt. Everest, climbing highest peak on all seven continents. Home: 771 7th St Boulder CO 80302-7402 Office: Porzak Browning & Johnson Ste 100 1300 Walnut St Boulder CO 80302

POSAMENTIER, ALFRED STEVEN, mathematics educator, university administrator; b. N.Y.C., N.Y., Oct. 18, 1942; s. Ernest and Alice (Pisk) P.; children—Lisa Joan, David Richard. A.B., Hunter Coll., 1964; M.A., CCNY, 1966; postgrad., Yeshiva U., N.Y.C., 1967-69; Ph.D., Fordham U., 1973; Nostrifizierung of Doctorate, U. Vienna, Austria, 1992. Tchr. math Theodore Roosevelt High Sch., Bronx, 1964-70; asst. prof. math. edn. CCNY, N.Y.C., 1970-76, assoc. prof., 1977-80, prof., 1981—, dept. chmn. dept. secondary and continuing edn., 1974-80, chmn., 1980-86; assoc. dean Sch. Edn. CCNY, 1986-95; dean Sch. Edn., CCNY, 1995—; dir. select program in sci. and engring. CCNY, 1978—; dir. CCNY, U.K., iniatives program dir., 1983—; dir. Germany/CCNY Exch. Program CCNY, 1985—, dir. Austria/CCNY Exch. Program, 1987—, dir. Czech Republic/CCNY Exch. Program, 1989—, dir. sci. lectr. program, 1981—, dir. Ctr. for Sci. and Maths. Edn., 1986—; chmn. bd. dirs. Salvadori Ednl. Ctr. on Built Environ., 1988—; dir. Exxon sponsored early childhood math. specialist tng. program at City Coll., 1988-92; supr. math. and sci. Mamaroneck H.S., N.Y., 1976-79; project dir. Math Proficiency Workshop, Ossining, N.Y., 1976-79, NSF math. devel. program for secondary sch. tchrs. math., 1978-82, N.Y.C., Porf. Preparation of Math. and Sci. Tchrs., 1978-79; project dir. numerous NSF sponsored math./sci. tchr. devel. insts., 1976—; cons. Croft Ednl. Svcs., New London, 1971, N.Y.C. Bd. Edn., 1973-75, N.Y.C. Bd. Edn. Office of Evaluation, 1974-80, N.Y.C. Bd. Edn. Examiners, 1979-92, Ossining Bd. Edn., 1975-83, numerous others; coord. NSF N.E. Resource Ctr. Sci. and Engring., 1980-90; lectr. various convs. and meetings; vis. prof. U. Vienna, Austria, 1985, 87, 88, 90, Tech. U., Berlin, 1989, Tech. U., Vienna, 1993, Pedgogical Inst., Vienna, 1993—. Author: Geometric Constructions, 1973, Geometry, Its Elements and Structure, 1972, rev. edit., 1977, Challenging Problems in Geometry, 2 vols., 1970, Challenging Problems in Algebra, 2 vols., 1970, A Study Guide for the Scholastic Aptitude Test in Math., 1969, 83, Excursions in Advanced Euclidean Geometry, 1980, 2d edit., 1984, Teaching Secondary School Mathematics: Techniques and Enrichment Units, 1981, 3d edit., 1990, 4th edit., 1995, Uncommon Problems for Common Topics in Algebra, 1981, Unusual Problems for Usual Topics in Algebra, 1981, Using Computers in Mathematics, 1983, 2d edit., 1986, Math Motivators: Investigations in Pre-Algebra, 1982, Math Motivators: Investigations in Algebra, 1983, Using Computers: Programming and Problem Solving, 1984, 2d edit., 1989, Advanced Geometric Constructions, 1988, Challenging Problems in Algebra, 1988, 96, Challenging Problems in Geometry, 1988, 96, The Art of Problem Solving: A Resource for the Mathematics Teacher, 1996, Students! Get Ready for Mathematics for SAT-I: Problem Solving Strategies and Practice Tests, 1996, Teachers! Prepare Your Students for Mathematics for SAT-I: Methods and Problem-Solving Strategies, 1996, Deutch-English Mathematik Wörtenbuch, 1996. Trustee Demarest Bd. Edn., 1977-80. Decorated Medal of Honor, Austria, 1994; named Tchr. of Yr. CCNY Alumni Assn., 1993; hon. fellow U. South Bank, London, 1988; Fulbright scholar U. Vienna, 1990. Mem. Math. Assn. Am., Sch. Sci. and Math. Assn., Nat. Council Tchrs. Math., (reviewer new publs., referee articles Math. Tchr. Jour.), Assn. Tchrs. Math. N.Y.C. (exec. bd. 1966-67, referee articles assn. jour.), Assn. Tchrs. of Math. of N.Y. State, Assn. Tchrs. Math. N.J. (editorial bd. N.J. Math. Tchr. Jour. 1981-84), Nat. Council of Suprs. of Maths. Home: 634 Caruso Ln River Vale NJ 07675-6210 Office: CCNY New York NY 10031

POSCH, ROBERT JOHN, JR., lawyer; b. Levittown, N.Y., Feb. 24, 1950; s. Robert John and Maryrose (Finnegan) P.; m. Mary Lou Collins, July 28, 1974; children: Judith Ann, Robert III, Eric. BA, Manhattan Coll., 1972; JD, Hofstra U., 1975, MBA, 1981. Bar: N.Y. 1977, U.S. Ct. Appeals (2d cir.) 1977. Legal asst. Doubleday & Co., Inc., Garden City, N.Y., 1975-77; staff counsel Doubleday & Co., Inc., Garden City, 1977-82, assoc. counsel, 1982-87; sec., counsel Doubleday Book & Music Clubs, Inc., Garden City, 1987-89, v.p. legal affairs, 1989—; instr. Nassau Community Coll., Hempstead, N.Y., 1984—; mem. adv. bd. real estate symposium Hofstra U. Author: Direct Marketer's Legal Adviser, 1983, What Every Manager Needs to Know About Marketing and the Law, 1984, Marketing and the Law, 1988, Cumulative Supplement, 1989, 90, (with others) The Direct Marketing Handbook, 1984, 91; columnist: Direct Marketing, 1981—; contbr. articles to profl. jours.; speaker in field. Mem. ABA, Am. Corp. Counsel Assn. (newsletter editor 1988-92, bd. dirs. Greater N.Y. chpt.), Third Class Mail Assn. (bd. dirs.), Direct Mktg. Assn. (privacy, use tax and legal lobbying groups, various coms. 1986—), Christian Legal Soc., Nassau Bar Assn. (various coms. 1977—, AAP Postal Affairs), L.I. Assn., N.Y. State Bus. Coun., Alpha Mu Alpha, Beta Gamma Sigma. Republican. Home: 3151 Grand Blvd Baldwin NY 11510-4826 Office: Doubleday Book/Music Clubs 401 Franklin Ave Garden City NY 11530-5943

POSCOVER, MAURY B., lawyer; b. St. Louis, Jan. 13, 1944; s. Edward and Ann (Chapnick) P.; m. Lorraine Wexler, Aug. 14, 1966; children: Michael, Daniel, Joanna. BA, Lehigh U., 1966; JD, Washington U., 1969. Bar: Mo. 1969. Assoc. Husch & Eppenberger, St. Louis, 1969-75, ptnr., 1975—; lectr. Washington U., St. Louis, 1972-79. Editor-in-chief: Business Lawyer; contbr. articles to profl. jours. Bd. dirs. Childhaven, St. Louis, 1978-92, pres. 1986; pres. Jewish Community Rels. Coun., 1990-92. Mem. ABA (chmn. comml. fin. svcs. com. bus. law sect. coun., chair-elect bus. law sect., editor-in-chief jour.), Bar Assn. Met. St. Louis (pres. 1983-84), Mo. Bar Assn. (bd. govs. 1979-81), Am. Judicature Soc. (dir. 1981-87), Washington U. Alumni Law Assn. (pres. 1980-81), Mo. Athletic Club. Jewish. Office: Husch & Eppenberger 100 N Broadway Ste 1300 Saint Louis MO 63102-2706

POSEN, SUSAN ORZACK, lawyer; b. N.Y.C., Nov. 5, 1945. BA, Sarah Lawrence Coll., 1967; JD, Bklyn. Law Sch., 1978. Bar: N.Y. 1979. Assoc. Stroock & Stroock & Lavan, N.Y.C., 1978-83, 84-86; ptnr. Stroock, Stroock & Lavan, N.Y.C., 1987—; asst. gen. counsel Cablevision Systems Corp., Woodbury, N.Y., 1983-84. Office: Stroock & Stroock & Lavan 7 Hanover Sq New York NY 10004-2616

POSER, CHARLES MARCEL, neurology educator; b. Antwerp, Belgium, Dec. 30, 1923; s. Maurice and Sadye (Gleitsman) P.; m. Joan Doris Crawford, Sept. 3, 1950; children: William John, Nicholas Charles. B.S., CCNY, 1947; M.D., Columbia U., 1951. Diplomate Am. Bd. Psychiatry and Neurology. Resident in neurology Neurol. Inst. Columbia-Presbyn. Med. Center, N.Y., 1952-55; Fulbright scholar Neuropathology Inst. Bunge, Antwerp, Belgium, 1955-56; instr. through assoc. prof. neurology U. Kans. Sch. Medicine, 1955-64; prof., head div. neurology U. Mo. Sch. Medicine, Kansas City, 1964-68; prof., chmn. dept. neurology U. Vt. Coll. Medicine, 1968-81; prof. neurology Boston U. Sch. Medicine, 1981-84, lectr., 1984—; sr. neurologist Beth Israel Hosp.; cons. prof. Tex. Tech. U. Sch. Medicine, Lubbock, 1981-90; lectr. on neurology Harvard Med. Sch., 1982, Tufts U. Sch. Medicine, 1982-90; cons. in neurology U.S. Army and U.S. Navy, 1963—; Cross lectr. U. Witwatersrand, Johannesburg, Republic of South Africa, 1990. Editor-in-chief Jour. Tropical and Geog. Neurology, 1989-92, Neurol. Infections and Epidemiology, 1995—; contbr. numerous articles to med. jours. Served with U.S. Army, 1943-46. Decorated officer Order of Leopold II Belgium; recipient Silver Bicentennial medal Coll. of Physicians and Surgeons, 1967; named Luis Guerrero Meml. lectr. U. Santo Tomás, Manila, 1979, Wilder Penfield lectr. Am. U., Beirut, 1983, Salmon James lectr. London Med. Soc., 1987, Kroc lectr. Rush Med. Coll., Chgo., 1987; Wu Ho-Su Meml. Lectr., Taipei, Taiwan, 1994. Fellow ACP, Am. Acad. Neurology, Am. Acad. Pediat., Royal Soc. Medicine (London), Royal Soc. Tropical Medicine and Hygiene (London), Royal Coll. Physicians (Glasgow); hon. fellow Japanese, Belgian, Cuban, French, Icelandic, Filipino, and Columbian socs. neurology, All-Russian Soc. Neurol. Sci., Neurol. Soc. India, Assn. Brit. Neurologists; mem. Am. Neurol. Assn. (sr.), Am. Assn. Neuropathologists, Assn. for Rsch. in Nervous and Mental Diseases, Nat. Acad. Medicine Colombia (hon.). Home: 11 Rutland Sq Boston MA 02118-3105 Office: Beth Israel Hosp Dept Neurology Harvard Med Sch 330 Brookline Ave Boston MA 02215-5400

POSER, ERNEST GEORGE, psychologist, educator; b. Vienna, Austria, Mar. 2, 1921; emigrated to Can., 1942, naturalized, 1946; s. Paul and Blanche (Furst) P.; m. Maria Jutta Cahn, July 3, 1953; children: Yvonne, Carol, Michael. B.A., Queen's U., Kingston, Ont., 1946, M.A., 1949; Ph.D., U. London, 1952. Diplomate: Am. Bd. Profl. Psychologists; registered psychologist, B.C. Asst. prof. U. N.B., 1946-48; chief psychologist N.B. Dept. Health, 1952-54; prof. psychology McGill U., Montreal, 1954-83; assoc. prof. psychiatry Faculty Medicine McGill U., 1963-83; adj. prof. dept. psychology U. B.C., 1984—; dir. behavior therapy unit Douglas Hosp. Center, Montreal, 1966-83. Author: Adaptive Learning: Behavior Modification with Children, 1973, Behavior Therapy in Clinical Practice, 1977. hon. fellow Middlesex Hosp., London, 1964. Fellow Canadian Psychol. Assn., Am. Psychol. Assn.

POSER, NORMAN STANLEY, law educator; b. London, May 28, 1928; came to U.S., 1939, naturalized, 1946; s. Jack and Margaret (Salomon) P.; m. Miriam Kugelman, Sept. 1, 1957 (div. 1979); children: Samuel Marc, Susan; m. Judith Eiseman Cohn, Aug. 11, 1985. A.B. cum laude, Harvard U., 1948, LL.B. cum laude, 1958. Bar: N.Y. 1958. Asso. Greenbaum, Wolff & Ernst, N.Y.C., 1958-61; atty. SEC, Washington, 1961-64; asst. dir. div. trading and markets SEC, 1964-67; asso. Rosenman, Colin, Kaye, Petschek, Freund & Emil, N.Y.C., 1967-68; v.p. Am. Stock Exchange, N.Y.C., 1968-72; sr. v.p. Am. Stock Exchange, 1972-75, exec. v.p., 1975-80; adj. prof. law NYU, 1975-80; prof. law Bklyn. Law Sch., 1980—; cons. World Bank, SEC,

OAS, various stock exchs.; spl. counsel N.Y. Stock Exch., 1987—. Mem. adv. bd.: BNA Securities Regulation & Law Report, 1979—, Rev. Securities and Commodities Regulation, 1975—; author: International Securities Regulation: London's "Big Bang" and the European Securities Markets, 1991, Broker-Dealer Law and Regulation: Private Rights of Action, 1995. Served with U.S. Army, 1951-53. Mem. Am. Law Inst., ABA, N.Y.C. Bar Assn., Nat. Futures Assn. (arbitrator 1987—). Club: Harvard (N.Y.C.). Office: 250 Joralemon St Brooklyn NY 11201-3798

POSEY, CLYDE LEE, business administration and accounting educator; b. Tucumcari, New Mex., Dec. 27, 1940; s. Rollah P. and Opal (Patterson) P.; m. Dora Diane Vassar; children: Amanda Fox, Julia Forsyth, Rebecca; m. Judith James Jerry, July 31, 1991; stepchildren: David Jerry, Georgia Kenyan. BBA, U. Tex., El Paso, 1963; MBA, U. Tex., 1965; postgrad., U. So. Calif., 1968; PhD, Okla. State U., 1978. CPA, Calif., La., Tex. Lab. aide FBI, Washington, 1959-60; acct. Lipson, Cox & Colton (now Deloitte & Touche), El Paso, Tex., 1962; auditor Main & Co. (now KPMG Peat Marwick), El Paso, 1963; teaching asst. U. Tex., Austin, 1963-65; tax cons. Peat, Marwick, Mitchell & Co., Dallas, 1965-66; cons. Roberson, Martin, Horg and Ryckman, Fresno, Calif., 1967; CPA pvt. practice Fresno, Ruston, Calif., La, 1966—; asst. prof. Calif. State U., Fresno, 1966-76; assoc. prof. La. Tech. U., Ruston, 1978-84, prof., 1984—; vis. asst. prof. Ctrl. State U., Edmond, Okla., 1971-72, U. Okla., Norman, 1976-78; cons. J. David Spence Accountancy Corp., Fresno, 1974-76; many coms. at La. Tech. U. including acad. senator, new faculty welcoming com., acctg. scholarship chmn.; faculty senate rep.; Faculty Consortium, St. Charles, Ill., 1993; expert witness Superior Ct. Calif. Contbr. numerous articles to profl. jours., bus. mags., newspapers, also book reviews; presentations to profl. meetings. Past bd. dirs. Goodwill, Inc., Ctrl. Calif.; ch. deacon and mem. many coms.; pres., treas., state scripture coord. Gideons Internat. Ruston Camp; rep. United Way La. Tech. U., Ruston. With USCG, 1965. Recipient El Paso CPA's Outstanding Jr. scholarship, Standard Oil scholarship, Price Waterhouse scholarship, Outstanding Educator award Gamma Beta Phi, 1986. Mem. AICPA, Am. Acctg. Assn. (La. membership com. chmn.), Am. Inst. for Decision Scis. (program com. chmn. acctg. track), Tex. Soc. CPAs, Am. Tax Assn. (internat. tax policy subcom.), Beta Gamma Sigma (pres.), Beta Alpha Psi. Baptist. Avocations: triathlons, bicycle racing, golf, tennis, gardening. Home: 2700 Foxxwood Dr Ruston LA 71270-2509 Office: La Tech U CAB 129A Ruston LA 71272

POSEY, ELDON EUGENE, mathematician, educator; b. Oneida, Tenn., Jan. 25, 1921; s. Daniel M. and Eva (Owens) P.; m. Christine K. Johnson, Dec. 25, 1943; children—Margaret Posey McQuain, Daniel Marion. B.S., East Tenn. State U., 1947; M.A., U. Tenn., 1949, Ph.D., 1954. Instr. W.Va. U., 1954-55, asst. prof., 1955-59; asso. prof. Va. Poly. Inst., 1959-61, prof., 1961-64; prof. math. U. N.C., Greensboro, 1964-88, prof. emeritus, 1988—; head dept. math. U. N.C., 1964-80. Served to capt. USAAF, 1941-46. Decorated Air medal with 18 oak leaf clusters, D.F.C., Silver Star, Purple Heart. Mem. Am. Math. Soc., Math. Assn. Am., Sigma Xi, Pi Mu Epsilon. Home: 4311 Dogwood Dr Greensboro NC 27410-5611

POSHARD, GLENN W., congressman; b. Herald, Ill., Oct. 31, 1945. BA, So. Ill. U., 1970, MS, 1974, PhD, 1984. Tchr. high sch.; asst. dir. then dir. Ill. State Regional Edn. Svc. Ctr.; mem. Ill. State Senate, 1984-88, 101st-104th Congresses from 22nd (now 19th) Ill. Dist., 1989—; ranking minority mem. small bus. subcom. on govt. programs, mem. transp. and infrastructure com. Served with U.S. Army. Democrat. Office: US Ho of Reps 2334 Rayburn HOB Washington DC 20515*

POSIN, DANIEL Q., physics educator, television lecturer; b. Turkestan, Aug. 13, 1909; came to U.S., 1918, naturalized, 1927; s. Abram and Anna (Izritz) P.; m. Frances Schweitzer, 1934; children: Dan, Kathryn. A.B., U. Cal., 1932, A.M., 1934, Ph.D., 1935. Instr. U. Cal., 1932-37; prof. U. Panama, 1937-41; dean natural scis. U. Mont., prof., 1941-44, chmn. dept. physics and math., 1942-44; staff Mass. Inst. Tech., 1944-46; prof. physics, chmn. dept. N.D. State Coll., Fargo, 1946-55; prof. dept. physics DePaul U., 1956-67; prof. phys. sci. dept. Calif. State U., San Francisco, 1967—; chmn. dept. interdisciplinary scis. Calif. State U., 1969—; dir. Schwab Sci. Lecture Series, Atoms for Peace exhibit Mus. Sci. and Industry, Chgo.; Chief cons. Borg Warner Sci. Hall and Allied Chem. Sci. Hall, Times Square; scientific cons. CBS-TV. (Recipient 6 Emmy awards for best educator on TV in Chgo., and best ednl. TV programs). Author: Trigonometria, 1937-41, Fisica Experimental, Fisica, 1937-41, Mendeleyev—The Story of a Great Scientist, 1948, I Have Been to the Village, with Introduction by Einstein, 1948, rev. edit., 1974, Out of This World, 1959, What is a Star, 1961, What is Chemistry, 1961, What is a Dinosaur, 1961, The Marvels of Physics, 1961, Find Out, 1961, Chemistry for the Space Age, 1961, Experiments and Exercises in Chemistry, 1961, What is Matter, 1962, What is Electronic Communication, 1962, What is Energy, Dr. Posin's Giants, 1962, Life Beyond our Planet, 1962, Man and the Sea, 1962, Man and the Earth, 1962, Man and the Jungle, 1962, Man and the Desert, 1962, Science in the Age of Space, 1965, Rockets and Satellites, Our Solar System, The Next Billion Years, 1973; contbr. to: Today's Health; sci. cons.: Compton's Yearbook; contbr. to: feature articles Chgo. Tribune, (book) After Einstein-Remembering Einstein, 1981; co-contbr. to book The Courage to Grow Old, 1989; appearances, CBS Radio-TV, WTTW-WGN-TV, 1956-67, NET; ABC TV series Dr. Posin's Universe. Chmn. edn. com. Chgo. Heart Assn., 1963-67; Trustee Leukemia Soc. James T. Grady award Am. Chem. Soc., 1972. Fellow Am. Phys. Soc.; mem. A.A.A.S., Phi Beta Kappa, Sigma Xi. Office: Calif State Univ Dept Phys Sci San Francisco CA 94132

POSIN, KATHRYN OLIVE, choreographer; b. Butte, Mont., Mar. 23, 1943; d. Daniel Q. and Frances (Schweitzer) P. BA in Dance, Bennington Coll., 1965; MFA in Interdisciplinary and World Dance, NYU, 1994; studies in composition, 1965-78, studies in ballet, 1965-90, studies in modern dance, 1967-80, studies in Alexander, Feldenkreis Techs., 1989-91; physiotherapy tng. with Marika Molnar, West Side Sports Medicine, 1994. Mem. dance co. Am. Dance Theater at Lincoln Ctr., 1965; dancer Anna Sokolow Dance Co., 1965-73; artistic dir. Kathryn Posin Dance Co., N.Y.C., 1972-91; choreographer Eliot Feld Ballet, N.Y.C., 1978, Netherlands Dance Theater, Den Hague, Switzerland, 1980, Alvin Ailey Am. Dance Theater, N.Y.C., 1980; mem. dance faculty U. Wis., Milw., 1984-86, choreographer, 1984-88; tchr., choreographer UCLA, 1988-90, Trinity Coll., Hartford, Conn., 1990-91; mem. dance faculty, choreographer U. Calif., Santa Barbara, 1986; tchr. dance technique and performance Tchr.'s Coll. Columbia U., spring 1990; tchr. composition and technique Nat. Inst. of Arts, Taiwan, 1991; tchr. ballet Hofstra, U., Hempstead, L.I., 1992; tchr. improvisation and repertory CCNY, 1994; guest educator various univs. and performing cos., 1969-94; participant or spkr. profl. confs. Choreographer (performing cos./orgns.) Cherry Orchard, Lincoln Ctr., N.Y.C., 1978, Ballet West, Salt Lake City, 1981, Ohio Ballet, Akron, 1982, Ballet Pacifica, Laguna Beach, Calif., 1993, others, including The Netherlands Dance Theater, Alvin Ailey Am. Dance Theater, Eliot Feld Ballet, Ohio Ballet, Repertory Dance Theater Utah, Extemporary Dance Co. London, Balletmet, Columbus, Ohio, Milw. Ballet, 1996; (prin. works) Salvation, Off-Broadway, N.Y.C., 1969, Waves, 1975 (Am. Dance Festival commn.), Lotta, N.Y. Shakespeare Festival, 1979, The Cherry Orchard, N.Y. Shakespeare Festival, 1979, Mary Stuart, Acting Co., 1980, Shady Grove (grantee joint program of Ohio Arts and Humanities Couns. 1991), Later That Day, 1980, The Tempest, Am. Shakespeare Festival, Strratford, Conn., 1982, Midsummer Night's Dream, Arena Stage, Washington, 1982, Boys From Syracuse, Am. Repertory Theater, Harvard U., 1983, The Paper Gramophone, Hartford Stage, 1989, Of Rage and Remembrance, 1990 (Premiere of Yr. in Music and Dance, Milw. Jour.), Stepping Stones, 1993 (co-recipient Meet the Composer/Choreographer award Milw. Ballet 1993), many others; subject of documentary Kathy's Dance. Grantee Guggenheim Found., 1978, N.Y. State Coun. on Arts, 1977, 79, 80, Jerome Robbins Found., 1972; grantee Nat. Endowment for Arts 1981, 82, 85-87, choreography fellow, 1995-96; Doris Humphrey fellow Am. Dance Festival, New London, Conn., 1968; co-recipient Meet the Composer award for Alvin Ailey Repertory Co., 1994. Office: Kathryn Posin Dance Co 20 Bond St New York NY 10012-2406

POSLER, GERRY LYNN, agronomist, educator; b. Cainsville, Mo., July 24, 1942; s. Glen L. and Helen R. (Maroney) P.; m. O. Shirley Weeda, June 23, 1963; children: Mark L., Steven C., Brian D. BS, U. Mo., 1964, MS, 1966; PhD, Iowa State U., 1969. Asst. prof. Western (Macomb) Ill. U., 1969-74; assoc. prof. Kans. State U., Manhattan, 1974-80, prof., 1980—, asst. dept. head, 1982-90, dept. head, 1990—. Contbr. articles to profl. jours. and popular publs., abstracts, book reviews. Fellow Am. Soc. Agronomy, Crop Sci. Soc. Am.; mem. Am. Forage Grassland Coun., Crop Science Soc. Am. (C-3 div. chmn. 1991), Coun. Agrl. Science Tech. (Cornerstone club), Nat. Assn. Colls. Tchrs. Agr. (tchr. fellow award 1978, ensminger interstate dist. teaching award, 1987, north cen. region dir. 1989, v.p. 1990, pres. 1991; life mem.), Kans. Assn. Colls. Tchrs. Agr. (pres. 1983-85), Kans. Forage Grassland Coun. (bd. dirs. 1989-92), Gamma Sigma Delta (Outstanding Faculty award 1991, pres. 1987). Home: 3001 Montana Ct Manhattan KS 66502-2300 Office: Kans State U Dept Agronomy Throckmorton Hall Manhattan KS 66506

POSLUNS, WILFRED M., manufacturing and retailing company executive; b. Toronto, Ont., Can., Apr. 4, 1932; s. Louis H. and Leah (Granatstein) P.; m. Joyce Eleanor Cohen, June 16, 1953; children: Wendy Carol, Lynn Susan, David Howard. B.Com., U. Toronto, 1955. With Superior Fin. Co. Ltd., Toronto, 1955; customs man Burns Bros. & Denton, 1955-59; dir. R. A. Daly & Co., 1959-61; fin. mgr. Irving Posluns Sportswear and Jack Posluns & Co., Toronto, 1961-67; sec.-treas. Dylex Ltd., Toronto, 1967-76, dir., 1967—, pres., CEO, 1976-88, chmn. bd. dirs., CEO, 1988—, chmn. bd., dir., 1972—; mng. dir. Cedar Point Inv., Inc., 1995; sec.-treas. WET Seal, Pacific Linen. Pres. Jewish Community Ctr., Toronto, 1974-78, chmn. bd. dirs., 1978-82; pres. Can. Friends Hebrew U., 1977—; asst. sec. Toronto Jewish congress; bd. govs. Mount Sinai Hosp.; trustee United Community Fund of Greater Toronto; bd. dirs. United Jewish Appeal Toronto, Nat. Jewish Welfare Bd., Baycrest Centre Geriatric Care, Jewish Camp Council YMHA, Can.-Israel Cultural Found. Mem. Oakdale Golf and Country Club. Office: Cedar Point Inv Inc, 30 St Claire Ave West Ste 900, Toronto, ON Canada M4V 3A1*

POSNER, DONALD, art historian; b. N.Y.C., Aug. 30, 1931; s. Murray and Frances (Teitel) P.; 1 dau., Anne Tyre. A.B., Queens Coll., 1956; M.A., Harvard U., 1957; Ph.D., NYU, 1962. Lectr. Queens Coll., 1957; asst. prof. art history Columbia U., 1961-62; mem. faculty Inst. Fine Arts, NYU, 1962—, Ailsa Mellon Bruce prof. fine arts, 1975—, acting dir. Inst. Fine Arts, 1978-79, now dep. dir.; Robert Sterling Clark prof. Williams Coll., 1973; William R. Kenan, Jr. prof. U. Va., 1976-77; vis. prof. U. Wash., 1991. Author: Annibale Carracci, 1971, Watteau: A Lady at Her Toilet, 1973, Seventeenth and Eighteenth Century Art, 1971, Antoine Watteau, 1984; editor-in-chief: The Art Bull, 1968-71. Served with USAF, 1951-55. Am. Acad. in Rome fellow, 1959-61; Inst. for Advanced Study fellow, 1976; recipient Charles Rufus Morey award, 1972. Mem. Coll. Art Assn. Am. (dir. 1970-74), Am. Soc. 18th Century Studies. Office: Inst Fine Arts 1 E 78th St New York NY 10021-0102

POSNER, EDWARD MARTIN, lawyer; b. Phila., Oct. 20, 1946. BA, Amherst Coll., 1968; JD, Harvard U., 1974. Bar: Pa. 1974. Exec. asst. to sec. of pub. welfare Commonwealth of Pa., Harrisburg, 1971-72; assoc. Drinker, Biddle & Reath, Phila., 1974-80, ptnr., 1980—. Democrat. Avocation: fly fishing. Office: Drinker Biddle & Reath 1345 Chestnut St Philadelphia PA 19107-3496

POSNER, ERNEST GARY, lawyer; b. Nashville, July 2, 1937; s. Alvin Joseph and Bertha (Halpern) P.; m. Gretel Roberta Tishler, Dec. 22, 1963; children: Suzanne Lyn, Deborah Ariel. BChE, Vanderbilt U., 1959; postgrad., Suffolk U., 1963-64; JD, Am. U., 1967. Bar: Va. 1967, Pa. 1968, U.S. Dist. Ct. (ea. dist.) Pa. 1969, U.S. Patent Office 1970, U.S. Supreme Ct. 1975. Advanced through grades to lt. comdr., 1967; commd. U.S. Navy, 1959, ret., 1967; staff Interagy. Com. Oceanography, Washington, 1967-68; patent lawyer Atlantic Richfield Co., Phila., 1968-72; v.p., gen. counsel, corp. sec. PQ Corp., Valley Forge, Pa., 1972—. Commr., vice chmn. Govt. Study Commn., Upper Merion, Pa., 1975-76. Served to capt. USNR. Mem. ABA, Soap & Detergent Assn. (legal com. 1974—), Am. Intellectual Property Law Assn., Internat. Bus. Forum (spkr.), Lic. Exec. Soc. (trustee 1993—), Am. Corp. Counsel Assn., Masons, B'nai B'rith (sec. 1974-76, chpt. founder). Office: PQ Corp Swedesford Rd PO Box 840 Valley Forge PA 19482-0840

POSNER, GARY HERBERT, chemist, educator; b. N.Y.C., June 2, 1943; s. Joseph M. and Rose (Klein) P.; children: Joseph, Michael. BA, Brandeis U., 1965; MA, Harvard U., 1965, PhD, 1968. Asst. prof. Johns Hopkins U., Balt., 1969-74, assoc. prof., 1974-79, prof. dept. chemistry, 1979—, Scowe prof. chemistry, 1989—; prof. dept. environ. chemistry Johns Hopkins U., 1982—, chmn. dept. of chemistry, 1987-90; cons. Batelle Meml. Inst., Columbus, Ohio, 1983, S.W. Rsch. Inst., San Antonio, Nova Pharm. Co., Balt.; mem. Fulbright-Hays Adv. Screening Com. in Chemistry, 1978-81; Fulbright lectr. U. Paris, 1976; Michael vis. prof. Weizmann Inst. Sci., Rehovot, Israel, 1983; leader Round Table discussion Welch Found. Conf. Chem. Rsch., Houston, 1973, 83; Plenary lectr. Nobel Symposium on Asymmetric Synthesis, Sweden, 1984. Author: Introduction to Organic Synthesis Using Organocopper Reagents, 1980; mem. editl. bd. Organic Reactions, 1976-89; exec. editor Tetrahedron Reports, 1996. Named Chemist of Yr., State of Md., 1987; fellow Japan Soc. for Promotion Sci., 1991; recipient Johns Hopkins U. Disting. Tchng. award, 1994. Mem. AAAS, Am. Chem. Soc., AAUP, NIH (medicinal chemistry study sect. 1986-89), Phi Beta Kappa. Office: Johns Hopkins U Dept Chemistry 3300 N Charles St Baltimore MD 21218

POSNER, JEROME BEEBE, neurologist, educator; b. Cin., Mar. 20, 1932; s. Philip and Rose (Goldberg) P.; m. Gerta Grunen, Aug. 29, 1954; children: Roslyn, Joel, P.J. BS, U. Wash., 1951, MD, 1955. Intern King County Hosp., Seattle, 1955-56; asst. resident in neurology U. Wash. Affiliated Hosps., Seattle, 1956-59; fellow in neurology U. Wash. Affiliated Hosps., 1958-59; spl. fellow NIH, U. Wash., 1961-63; instr. medicine U. Louisville Sch. Medicine, 1959-61; attending neurologist King County Hosp., 1962-63; asst. prof. neurology Cornell U. Med. Coll., N.Y.C., 1963-67; assoc. prof. Cornell U. Med. Coll., 1967-70, prof., 1970—, vice chmn. dept. neurology, 1978-87; asst. attending neurologist N.Y. Hosp., 1963-67, asso. attending neurologist, 1967-70, attending neurologist, 1970—; asso. Cotzias Lab. of Neuro-Oncology, Sloan Kettering Inst. Cancer Research, N.Y.C., 1967-76; mem. Cotzias Lab. of Neuro-Oncology, Sloan Kettering Inst. Cancer Research, 1976—; chief neuropsychiat. service, attending physician dept. medicine Meml. Hosp. for Cancer and Allied Diseases, 1967-75, attending physician, 1975—, chmn. dept. neurology, 1975-87, 89—, Cotzias chair neuro-oncology, 1986; mem. med. adv. bd. Burke Rehab. Ctr., White Plains, N.Y., 1973—; adj. prof., vis. physician Rockefeller U. and Hosp., N.Y.C., 1973-75; mem. neurology B study sect. NIH, 1972-76. Author: (with F. Plum) Diagnosis of Stupor and Coma, 3d edit., 1980, (with H. Gilbert and L. Weiss) Brain Metastasis, 1980, Neurologic Complications of Cancer, 1995; mem. editorial bd. Archives of Neurology, 1971-76, Annals of Neurology, 1976-80, Am. Jour. Medicine, 1978-93, Neurology, 1992—; contbr. articles to med. jours. Served with M.C. U.S. Army, 1959-61. Fellow AAAS; mem. AMA, Am. Acad. Neurology (Farber Brain Tumor award 1988), Am. Assn. Cancer Rsch., Am. Fedn. Clin. Rsch., Am. Neurol. Assn., Am. Physiol. Soc., Assn. Am. Physicians, Harvey Soc., N.Y. Acad. Sci. Inst. of Medicine, Soc. Neuroscis., Can. Neurol. Soc. (hon.), Alpha Omega Alpha. Office: Meml Sloan-Kettering Cancer Ctr 1275 York Ave New York NY 10021-6007

POSNER, MARTIN LOUIS, lawyer; b. N.Y.C., June 8, 1948; s. Carl and Evelyn Rachel P.; m. Jane Yvonne Kaplowitz, June 7, 1970. BA in Biology, CCNY, 1970, MA in Environ. Edn., 1975; JD, Pace U., 1984, LLM in Environ. Law, 1993. Bar: N.Y. 1985, U.S. Dist. Ct. (ea. and so. dists.) N.Y. 1991. Tchr. N.Y. Pub. Sch. Sys., N.Y.C., 1970-84; assoc. Law Offices of Henry Greenburg, White Plains, N.Y., 1984-85; ptnr. Greenburg & Posner, White Plains, N.Y., 1985—. Commr. Patterson (N.Y.) Environ. Conservation Commn., 1989-93; councilman Putnam County Environ. Mgmt. Coun., Carmel, N.Y., 1990-93. Mem. ABA, N.Y. State Bar Assn., White Plains Bar Assn., Westchester Bar Assn. Office: Greenburg & Posner 399 Knollwood Rd White Plains NY 10603-1900

POSNER, RICHARD ALLEN, federal judge; b. N.Y.C., Jan. 11, 1939; s. Max and Blanche Posner; m. Charlene Ruth Horn, Aug. 13, 1962; children: Kenneth A., Eric A. AB, Yale U., 1959; LLB, Harvard U., 1962; LLD (hon.), Syracuse U., 1986, Duquesne U., 1987, Georgetown U., 1992; Dr. honoris causa, U. Ghent, 1995. Bar: N.Y. 1963, U.S. Supreme Ct. 1966. Law clk. Justice William J. Brennan Jr. U.S. Supreme Ct., Washington, 1962-63; asst. to commr. FTC, Washington, 1963-65; asst. to solicitor gen. U.S. Dept. Justice, Washington, 1965-67; gen. counsel Pres.'s Task Force on Communications Policy, Washington, 1967-68; assoc. prof. Stanford U. Law Sch., Calif., 1968-69; prof. U. Chgo. Law Sch., 1969-78, Lee and Brena Freeman prof., 1978-81, sr. lectr., 1981—; circuit judge U.S. Ct. Appeals (7th cir.), Chgo., 1981—, chief judge, 1993—; research assoc. Nat. Bur. Econ. Research, Cambridge, Mass., 1971-81; pres. Lexecon Inc., Chgo., 1977-81. Author: Antitrust Law: An Economic Perspective, 1976, Economic Analysis of Law, 4th edit., 1992, The Economics of Justice, 1981, The Federal Courts: Crisis and Reform, 1985 (with William M. Landes) The Economic Structure of Tort Law, 1987, Law and Literature: A Misunderstood Relation, 1988, The Problems of Jurisprudence, 1990, Cardozo: A Study in Reputation, 1990, Sex and Reason, 1992, The Essential Holmes, 1992, (with Tomas J. Philipson) Private Choices and Public Health: The AIDS Epidemic in Economic Perspective, 1993, Overcoming Law, 1995, Aging and Old Age, 1995; pres. Harvard Law Rev., 1961-62; editor Jour. Legal Studies, 1972-81. Fellow AAAS, Am. Law Inst., Brit. Acad.; mem. Am. Econ. Assn., Am. Law and econ. Assn. (pres. 1995-96), Am. Philos. Assn. Office: US Ct Appeals 7th Cir 219 S Dearborn St Chicago IL 60604-1702

POSNER, ROY EDWARD, finance executive; b. Chgo., Aug. 24, 1933; s. Lew and Julia (Cvetan) P.; m. Donna Lea Williams, June 9, 1956 (div. May 1991); children: Karen Lee, Sheryl Lynn. Student, U. Ill., 1951-53, Internat. Accountants Soc., 1956-59, Loyola U., Chgo., 1959; grad., Advanced Mgmt. Program, Harvard U., 1976. CPA, Ill. Pub. acct. Frank W. Dibble Co., Chgo., 1956-61; supr. Harris, Kerr, Forster & Co. (C.P.A.s), Chgo., 1961-66; with Loews Corp., N.Y.C., 1966—; v.p. fin. svcs., chief fin. officer Loews Corp., 1973-86, sr. v.p., chief fin. officer, 1986—; find. cons. N.Y. Football Giants, Inc., Rutherford, N.J.; bd. dirs. Bulova Italy S.P.A., Milan, Bulova Systems and Instruments Corp., N.Y.C., Loews Hotels Monaco S.A.M., Monte Carlo, Monaco, Loews Internat. Svcs. S.A., Switzerland, G F Corp., Youngstown, Ohio, Taj Mahal Holding Corp., Atlantic City. Mem. editorial com.: Uniform System of Accounting for Hotels, 7th edit. Pres. No. Regional Valley High Sch. Music Parents Assn., 1978-79; trustee Loews Found., N.Y.C. With U.S. Army, 1953-55. Mem. AICPA, Fin. Execs. Inst., Ins. Acctg. and Stats. Assn., Internat. Hospitality Accts. Assn., Am. Hotel and Motel Assn., Ill. Soc. CPAs, N.Y. State CPAs (chmn. com. on hotel restaurant and club acctg. 1980-82), Tri-County Golf Assn. (treas. 1985-88, v.p. 1988-89), Alpine Country Club (bd. govs. 1982-94, exec. com. 1982-90, pres. 1988-90), Delta Tau Delta. Home: 273 Whitman St Haworth NJ 07641-1315 Office: Loews Corp 667 Madison Ave New York NY 10021-8029

POSNER, SIDNEY, advertising executive; b. Syracuse, N.Y., Jan. 14, 1924; s. Harry and Fannie (Hoffman) P.; m. Miriam Frances Kaplowitz, June 8, 1952; children: Steven Charles, Peter Scott, Robert Keith. BS, Syracuse U., 1947. Asst. advt. mgr. Rudolph Bros., Syracuse, 1947-48; copy chief Kaletski Advt. Agy., Syracuse, 1948-50; promotion mgr. Photo Trade News, N.Y.C., 1950-53; asst. to pres. Dobin Advt. Agy., N.Y.C.; pres. S. Posner & Co. Advt. Agy., N.Y.C., 1955-59, Constellation Art Corp., 1959-76, Communicorp, N.Y.C., 1959-76, Bus. Counselors Corp., N.Y.C., 1959-76, Newmark, Posner & Mitchell Inc., N.Y.C., 1959-92, Posner Comm. Inc., Boca Raton, Fla., 1993-94. Office: Posner Comm Assocs Inc 17547 Bocaire Way Boca Raton FL 33487-1109

POSNER, WILLIAM, federal government official. BS in Acctg., U. Md.; JD, Am. U. Bar: Md. From agt. to spl. asst. for employee plans matters IRS, Washington, 1961-93; exec. dir., COO Pension Benefit Guaranty Corp., Washington, 1993—. Office: Pension Benefist Guaranty 1200 K St NW Washington DC 20005-4026

POSOKHOV, IOURI, ballet dancer, educator; b. Lougansk, Ukraine, July 20, 1964; came to U.S., 1994; s. Mikail and Alla (Korotkova) P.; m. Anna Yurievna Titova, July 9, 1988; 1 child, Danila Yurievich. Student, Choreographic Acad. Bolshoi, Moscow, 1982. Dancer Bolshoi Ballet, 1982-92, mem. corps de ballet, soloist, 1982-87, prin. dancer, 1987-92; prin. dancer Royal Danish Ballet, Copenhagen, 1992-94, San Francisco Ballet, 1994—. Dancer performing in Sleeping Beauty, Swan Lake, Nutcracker, Bayadera, Raymonda,Romeo and Juliet, La Sylphide, Les Sylphicles, Prodigal Son, Sirano de Berjerak, Violin Concerto, Mahler, 5th Symphony, Somnambula, Sonata, Polaka, Kindertottenlieder, Divertimento # 15, Gizelle, Handel a Celebration. Home: 435 9th Ave # 4 San Francisco CA 94118 Office: San Francisco Ballet 455 Franklin St San Francisco CA 94102-4438

POSPISIL, GEORGE CURTIS, biomedical research administrator; b. Thomas, Okla., Aug. 8, 1945; s. George Frank and Zelpha Earline (Hensley) P.; children: Heather Elizabeth, Derek Curtis. Student Wheaton Coll., 1963-64; BA, U. Okla., 1968, MA, 1971. Peace Corps tchr., Maseru, Lesotho, Southern Africa, 1973-74; dir. health services fin. project State of Wis., Madison, 1975-76; pub. health advisor USPHS, Rockville, Md., 1972-73, program/policy analyst, 1977-81, contract mgr., 1982-84, program/policy analyst, 1984-86; dir. Services Crime Victims/Witnesses Project, Tioga County, N.Y., 1986—; guest lectr. U. Wis., Summer Inst., Carthage Coll.; analyst biomed. rsch.PROGRAM nih, 1989—; sci. editor The Johns Hopkins U. Krieger Mind/Brain Inst., 1993-95; exec. coun. NIH Recreation and Welfare Assn. Mem. Rockville Humanities Commn., 1981-83; spokesperson Neighborhood Planning Com., 1980-82; coordinator mental health svcs. Cuban Refugee Project, Ft. McCoy, Wis., 1980; sec. cmty. adv. com. mental health program Montgomery House, 1982-86; rsch. and tng. adminstr. Cornell U., Ithaca, N.Y., 1986-89; bd. dirs. Family Svc. Montgomery County, 1984-86; legis. fellow U.S. Senate Labor and Human Resources Com./Health Office, 1991; mem. county Spl. Olympics Com., 1982-86; mem. Citizens' Planning Subcom. Carroll County, Md., 1992-93, dep. comdr. civil air patrol squadron; mem. adv. com. Boy Scouts Am. troop 321; bd. dirs. Shepherd's Staff Cmty. Svc. program; mem. Am. Friends Svc. Com.; bd. dirs. Westminster Ch. of the Brethren. Mem. Soc. Rsch. Adminstrs. Editor: Decade of the Brain, 1990, Maximizing Human Potential: Decade of the Brain, 1991. Office: Nat Inst Neurol Disorders NIH 9000 Rockville Pike Rm 8a03 Bethesda MD 20892-0001 *The highest purpose of your business or position is to provide a base to allow you to serve others. When providing basic service, always try to add value to it for the benefit of your client.*

POSPISIL, LEOPOLD JAROSLAV, anthropology educator; b. Olomouc, Czechoslovakia, Apr. 26, 1923; came to U.S., 1949, naturalized, 1954; s. Leopold and Ludmila (Petrlak) P.; m. Zdenka Smyd, Jan. 31, 1945; children: Zdenka, Mira. Juris Universae Candidatus, Charles U., Prague, Czechoslovakia, 1947, Juris Universae Dr., 1991; BA in Sociology, Willamette U., Salem, Oreg., 1950; MA in Anthropology, U. Oreg., 1952; PhD, Yale U., 1956; ScD (hon), Willamette U., 1969; PhD (hon.), Charles U., Prague, Czech Rep., 1994. Instr. Yale U., New Haven, 1956-57, asst. prof., 1957-60; asst. curator Peabody Mus., 1956-60, assoc. prof., 1960-65, prof., curator, 1965-93, dir. divsn. anthropology, 1966-93; prof. anthropology, 1965-93, prof. and curator emeritus, 1993—. Author: Kapauku Papuans and Their Law, 1958, Kapauku Papuan Economy, 1963, Kapauk Papuans of West New Guinea, 1963, Anthropology of Law, 1971, Ethnology of Law, 1972, Anthropologie des Rechts, 1981, Obernberg: Quantitative Analysis of a Tyrolean Economy, 1995; contbr. articles to profl. jours. Guggenheim fellow, 1962, NSF fellow, 1962, 64-65, 67-71, NIMH fellow, 1973-79; Social Sci. Rsch. Coun. grantee, 1966. Fellow AAAS, N.Y. Acad. Scis., Am. Anthrop. Assn.; mem. NAS, Explorers Club, Czechoslovakian Acad. Arts and Scis. (past pres.), Coun. Free Czechoslovakia, Assn. for Polit. and Legal Anthropology (pres.-at-large), Assn. for Social Anthropology in Oceania, Soc. for Econ. Anthropology, Sigma Xi. Home: 554 Orange St New Haven CT 06511-3819 Office: Yale U Dept Anthropology 51 Hillhouse Ave New Haven CT 06520-3703

POSS, JEFFERY SCOTT, architect, educator; b. Harvey, Ill., May 20, 1956. BAS, U. Ill., 1978, MArch, 1980. Intern architect Charles Kober Assocs., Chgo., 1980-81, Skidmore, Owings and Merrill, Chgo., 1981; designer Newman/Lustig and Assocs., Chgo., 1983-84; design assoc. Kevin Roche John Dinkeloo and Assocs., Hamden, Conn., 1985-87; project architect and designer Tai Soo Kim Assocs., Hartford, Conn., 1987-89; pvt. practice architect Urbana, Ill., 1989—; assoc. prof. U. Ill., Champaign-Urbana, 1989—; invited juror, design work exhibited widely; lectr. in field. Contbr. articles to profl. jours. Recipient First Alt. prize Nat. Inst. for Archtl. Edn., 1981, First Place award Champaign Park Dist./AIA, 1989,

Nat. Design award Concrete Steel Reinforcing Inst./AIA, 1992. Mem. AIA (Corp. Ill., Ctrl. Ill. and Champaign-Urbana chpts., Excellence in Edn. Honors award 1993, Ctrl. Ill. award for design excellence, 1993), Am. Soc. Archtl. Perspectives (Excellence in Graphic Representation Architecture award 1990, 93). Office: 909 E Water St Urbana IL 61801-2841

POST, AUGUST ALAN, economist, artist; b. Alhambra, Calif., Sept. 17, 1914; s. Edwin R. and Edna (Stickney) P.; m. Helen E. Wills, Nov. 21, 1940; 1 child, David Wills. AB, Occidental Coll., 1938; student Chouinard Inst. Art, 1938; MA, Princeton, 1940; LLD, Golden Gate U., 1972, Occidental Coll., 1974, Claremont Grad. Sch., 1978. In banking bus., 1933-36; instr. econs. Occidental Coll., 1940-42; asst. prof. Am. U., 1943; economist Dept. State, 1944-45; rsch. dir. Utah Found., 1945-46; chief economist, adminstrv. analyst State of Calif., 1946-50, state legis. analyst, 1950-77; cons. Com. Higher Edn. and State, 1964; mem. Nat. Com. Support of Public Schs., 1967; mem. nat. adv. panel Nat. Center Higher Edn. Mgmt. Systems, 1971-72; chmn. Calif. Gov.'s Commn. on Govt. Reform, 1978; mem. faculty U. So. Calif. Grad. Sch. Pub. Adminstrn., 1978-80; Regents' prof. U. Calif., Davis, 1983, vis. prof., 1984-85; spl. cons. Touche Ross and Co., 1977-87; cons., interim exec. dir. Calif. Commn. for Rev. of Master Plan for Higher Edn., 1985 ; mem. adv. bd. Calif. Tomorrow nat. shows and one-man shows; dir. Crocker Art Gallery Assn., pres., 1966-67. Trustee U. Calif., Berkeley, Art Mus., 1986-91; mem. adv. com. on future ops. Coun. State Govts., 1965; bd. mgrs., pres. YMCA; bd. dirs. Sacramento Civic Ballet Assn.; trustee Calif. Coll. Arts and Crafts, 1982-86; chmn. Calif. State Task Force on Water Future, 1981-82, Sacramento Regional Found., bd. dirs., 1983-91; bd. dirs. Calif. Mus. Assn., pres., 1976-77, Policy Analysis for Calif. Edn., 1985—, Senate Adv. Commn. on Control of Cost of State Govt., 1986—, Pub. Policy Inst. Calif., 1994—; co-chmn. Calif. Citizen's Budget Commn., 1992; chmn. Citizens Commn. on Ballot Initiatives, 1992—, Catalonia Sister State Task Force, 1988—, Commn. on Innovation, Calif. Community Colls., 1992, Judicial Coun. Select com. on Judicial Retirement, 1993—; mem. Supreme Ct. Select com. Judicial Ethics, 1995-96; bd. dirs. Central Valley Found., 1994—, Pub. Policy Inst. Calif., 1994—. With USNR, 1943-44. Mem. Nat. Acad. Public Adminstrn., Phi Beta Kappa, Kappa Sigma. Home: 1900 Rockwood Dr Sacramento CA 95864-1527

POST, AVERY DENISON, retired church official; b. Norwich, Conn., July 29, 1924; s. John Palmer and Dorothy (Church) P.; m. Margaret Jane Rowland, June 8, 1946; children: Susan Macalister Post Ross, Jennifer Campbell, Elizabeth Post Elliott, Anne Denison Post Roy. B.A., Ohio Wesleyan U., 1946; B.D., Yale U., 1949, S.T.M., 1952; L.H.D. (hon.), Lakeland Coll., Sheboygan, Wis., 1977; D.D. (hon.), Chgo. Theol. Sem., 1978, Middlebury Coll. (Vt.), 1978, Defiance Coll. (Ohio), 1979; LL.D. (hon.), Heidelberg Coll. (Ohio), 1982, Chapman Coll.; Litt.D. (hon.), Elmhurst Coll. Ordained to ministry, 1949; pastor chs. in Vt., Ohio, Conn. and N.Y., 1946-63; sr. minister Scarsdale (N.Y.) Congl. Ch., 1963-70; minister, pres. Mass. conf. United Ch. Christ, 1970-77; pres. United Ch. Christ, N.Y.C., 1977-89; mem. central com. World Council Chs., 1978-91; exec. com., bd. govs. Nat. Council Chs., 1977-89; moderator, planning com. 7th Gen. Assembly World Coun. Chs.; lectr. Bible Adelphi Coll., Garden City, N.Y., 1958-59; Luccock lectr. Yale U. Div. Sch., 1961; lectr. homiletics Union Sem., N.Y.C., 1967-69, bd. dirs., 1967-77; trustee Andover Newton Theol. Sem., 1970-80; del. numerous internat. ch. meetings; sr. fellow Hartford Sem., 1989-93. Bd. dirs. Bridges for Peace, 1990-94; exec. dir. Bangor Theol. Sem., Hanover, N.H., 1991-93. With USNR, 1943-45. Decorated Comdr.'s Cross (Federal Republic Germany), 1990; recipient 1st Ecumenical award Mass. Coun. Chs., 1976; Disting. Achievement award Ohio Wesleyan U., 1983. Mem. PTA (life), Randolph Mountain Club (N.H.), Phi Beta Kappa, Omicron Delta Kappa. Democrat. Home: PO Box 344 124 Beaver Meadow Rd Norwich VT 05055

POST, BOYD WALLACE, forester; b. Glouster, Ohio, Oct. 5, 1928; s. Herbert Dwight and Fern Hazel (Wallace) P.; m. Vivian Joan Baker, July 19, 1952; children: Rebecca Jane, Martha Eleanor, Boyd Wallace, Charles Christopher. BS, Ohio U., 1950; M in Forestry, Duke U., 1958, D in Forestry, 1962. Weather observer US Weather Bur., 1948; soil conservationist trainee, Soil Conservation Service USDA, 1948, firefighting laborer Forest Service, 1949; weather observer USAF, 1950, pers. officer, 1952; asst. ranger Ohio Div. Forestry, 1953; asst. prof., asst. forester U. Vermont, Burlington, 1959-67, assoc. prof., assoc. forester, 1967-69; forest biologist CSRS USDA, Washington, 1969-80, 80-81, asst. dept. adminstr., 1981-82, program coordinator, 1982-83, forest biologist, 1984-96; ret., 1996; group leader nat. resources USDA Sci. & Edn. Adminstrn., Washington, 1980; asst. dir. Hawaii Inst. Tropical Agr. & Human Resources, Honolulu, 1983-84. Contbr. articles to profl. jours.; editorial bd. Internat. Jour. Forest Ecology & Mgmt., 1976-90. Co-pres. Juvenile Diabetes Found., N.Va. chpt., 1984-86; scoutmaster Boy Scouts Am., Vienna, Va., 1978-83, asst., 1984—, mem. camping com. Nat. Capital Area Coun., 1987—. Fellow AAAS, Soc. Am. Foresters; mem. Internat. Union Foresty Research Orgns., Internat. Soc. Tropical Foresters, Sigma Xi. Lodge: Masons. Avocations: fishing, canoeing, gardening, acting, singing.

POST, DAVID ALAN, broadcast executive, producer; b. N.Y.C., Oct. 20, 1941; s. Emil R. and Ruth (Rosen) P.; m. Arline Goldbrum, June 10, 1962 (div. 1981); children: Randee, Lori, Jill; m. Katlean de Monchy, Dec. 13, 1984. Student, CCNY, 1959-61; grad., Fleigenheimer Ins. Inst., 1961, N.Y. Inst. Fin., 1968. Sales rep. Aetna Life Ins. Casualty, Hartford, Conn., 1961-63; sales mgr. Globe Rubber Products, Phila., 1963-67; ptnr. Zuckerman Smith and Co., N.Y.C., 1968-71; dir. corp. fin. Andersen and Co., N.Y.C., 1971-72; exec. v.p., dir. R.K. Pace Post Investment Bankers, N.Y.C., 1973-76; chmn., chief exec. officer, founder Page Am. Group, Inc., Hackensack, N.J., 1976-86, also bd. dirs.; chmn., founder Channel Am. TV Network, N.Y.C., 1986—; founder, chmn. Can Do America, 1996—. Contbr. articles to INC. mag.; creator several TV series. Mem. Nat. Assn. TV Programming Execs. Republican. Jewish. Avocation: writing. Home: 400 E 57th St New York NY 10022-3019 Office: Channel Am TV Network 397 Boston Post Rd Darien CT 06820-3647

POST, EMILY (ELIZABETH LINDLEY POST), author; b. Englewood, N.J., May 7, 1920; d. Allen L. and Elizabeth (Ellsworth) Lindley; m. George E. Cookman, 1941 (dec. 1943); 1 child, Allen C.; m. William G. Post, Aug. 5, 1944; children: William G., Lucinda Post Senning, Peter L. Grad. high sch. Dir. Emily Post Inst., 1965—. Author: Emily Post's Book of Etiquette for Young People, 1968, Wonderful World of Weddings, 1970, Please Say Please, 1972, Emily Post's Etiquette, 1965, rev. edit. 1992, The Complete Book of Entertaining, 1981, Emily Post's Complete Book of Wedding Etiquette, 1982, rev. edit., 1991, Emily Post Talks with Teens about Manners and Etiquette, 1986, Emily Post on Weddings, 1987, Emily Post on Entertaining, 1987, Emily Post on Etiquette, 1987, Emily Post on Invitations and Letters, 1990, Emily Post on Business Etiquette, 1990, Emily Post on Second Weddings, 1991, Emily Post's Wedding Planner, rev. edit., 1991, Emily Post's Table Manners For Today: Advice For Every Dining Occasion, 1994, Emily Post on Guests and Hosts, 1994; contbg. editor: Good Housekeeping Mag. Republican. Episcopalian. Office: Good Housekeeping Hearst Corp 959 8th Ave New York NY 10019-3767

POST, GAINES, JR., history educator, dean, administrator; b. Madison, Wis., Sept. 22, 1937; s. Gaines and Katherine (Rike) P.; m. Jean Wetherbee Bowers, July 19, 1969; children—Katherine Doris, Daniel Lawrence. B.A., Cornell U., 1959; B.A., Oxford U., 1963; M.A., Stanford U., 1964, Ph.D., 1969. Instr. Stanford U., 1966-69; asst. prof. history U. Tex., Austin, 1969-74, assoc. prof., 1974-83; dean faculty, sr. v.p. Claremont McKenna Coll., Calif., 1983-88, prof., 1988—; exec dir. Rockefeller Found. Commn. on Humanities, 1978-81; fellow Interuniv. Seminar on Armed Forces and Society. Author: The Civil Military Fabric of Weimar Foreign Policy, 1973; (with others) The Humanities in American Life, 1980, Dilemmas of Appeasement: British Deterrence and Defense, 1934-37, 1993; Editor: German Unification: Problems and Prospects, 1992. Mem. exec. com. Forming the Future Project, Austin Ind. Sch. Dist., 1982; mem. Tex. Com. for Humanities, 1981-83; mem. council Calif. Congl. Recognition Program, 1984-88, Calif. Coun. Humanities, 1995—. Rhodes scholar, 1961-63; Am. Council Learned Socs. fellow, 1982-83; Am. Philos. Soc. grantee, 1974. Mem. Community Coll. Humanities Assn. (bd. dirs. 1981-89), Am. Hist. Assn. Home: 2254 N Navarro Dr Claremont CA 91711-1758 Office: Claremont McKenna Coll Dept History 850 Columbia Ave Claremont CA 91711-3901

POST, GERALD JOSEPH, retired banker, retired air force officer; b. Braintree, Mass., Sept. 27, 1925; s. Robert Z. and Marjorie F. (Dunn) P.; m. Jane Stewart Curry, May 4, 1945; children: Sharyn, Gerald, J., Steven M., Richard J., Sean C., David D., Tracy Post Krupa. M.B.A., U. Chgo., 1958. Commd. 2d lt. U.S. Air Force, 1945, advanced through grades to lt. gen., 1978; comptroller, dir. materiel mgmt. San Antonio Air Materiel Area, 1970-73; dep. chief of Staff for Materiel Mgmt., Wright-Patterson AFB, Ohio, 1973-75; chief of staff Air Force Logistics Command, Wright-Patterson AFB, 1975-77; asst. dep. chief of staff for systems and logistics Hdqrs. USAF, 1977-78, dir. Def. Logistics Agy., 1978-81; ret., 1981; pres. Lackland Nat. Bank, 1981-82. Decorated Def. Disting. Service medal, Legion of Merit with oak leaf cluster, D.F.C., Air medal with 2 oak leaf clusters, others. Mem. Am. Soc. Mil. Comptrollers, Air Force Assn., Am. Inst. Aeros. and Astronautics, Am. Def. Preparedness Assn., Phi Beta Kappa, Beta Gamma Sigma. Home: 12534 Misty Crk San Antonio TX 78232-4629

POST, HOWARD ALLEN, forest industry specialist; b. Mpls., June 14, 1916; s. William Noble and Eva Victoria (Hanson) P.; m. Doloras Clair Nordland, Dec. 6, 1941; children: Philip Noble, Stephen Edward, William Noble, Peter Bentley. BS in Forestry, U. Minn., 1939; MF in Forest Mgmt. and Silviculture, Harvard U., 1942. Forester Colville Indian Reservation, Washington, 1937; with U.S. Forest Svc., various locations, 1939, 64; civil svc. examiner in agriculture and forestry State of Minn., 1939-41; chief materials div. position classifications system War Prodn. Bd., 1942-43; chief China pers. recruitment UN Relief and Rehab. Adminstrn., 1946-47; asst. sec. Soc. Am. Foresters, 1947; adminstrv. forester Minn. and Ont. Paper Co., 1947-57; forester and nat. resources specialist U.S. C. of C., 1957-63; forest industries specialist and team leader Bus. and Def. Svcs. Adminstrn./ Internat. Trade Adminstrn. U.S. Dept. Commerce, Washington, 1965-84; forest industries cons. forest Industries com. on timber valuation and taxation, other Nat. Lumber Mfrs. Assn., 1984—; owner Post Enterprises, Forest Industry Cons.; lectr. in field various univs. U.S. editor World Paper jour. (Britain), Wood Based Panels Internat. column Keeping Posted, 1984—, Xilon Internat. and Perini Jour. (Italy), 1991—; contbr. articles to profl. jours. Com. chmn., scoutmaster, counselor Boy Scouts Am., 1958-80; mem. vestry Episcopal Ch., 1949-57, others. With USAAF, 1943-46, ret., USAFR, 1976. Decorated Air Force Commendation medal; recipient Bronze medal U.S. Dept. Commerce, 1976; named Boy Scouts of Am. Scouter of Yr., 1973. Mem. Tech. Assn. Pulp and Paper Industry, Soc. Am. Foresters, Assn. Cons. Foresters, Ret. Officers Assn., Forest Products Rsch. Soc., Harvard Club (Washington), Mil. Dist. of Washington Club, Nat. Press Club (Harvard group), Am. Legion, Alpha Zeta. Republican. Home: 6203 Colmac Dr Falls Church VA 22044-1811

POST, MARKIE, actress; b. Palo Alto, Calif., Nov. 4, 1950; d. Richard and Marylee Post; m. Michael Ross; 1 child, Kate. BA, Lewis and Clark Coll. Researcher TV game show Split Second; assoc. producer game show Double Dare, 1976-77; actress, 1977—. Actress: (stage prodns.) Joe Egg, The Fantastiks, The Hairy Ape, Guys and Dolls, (TV shows) Masquerade Party, Frankie and Annette - the Second Time Around, (TV series) Semi-Tough, 1980, The Gangster Chronicles, 1981, The Fall Guy, 1982-85, Night Court, 1985-92, Hearts Afire, 1992-95, (TV movies) Not Just Another Affair, 1982, Triple Cross, 1986, Glitz, 1988, Tricks of the Trade, 1988. Mem. AFTRA, Screen Actors Guild. Office: care Jon Carrasco 4044 Melrose Ave Fl 3 Los Angeles CA 90029-3608*

POST, MIKE, composer; b. San Fernando Valley, Calif.; children: Jennifer, Aaron. Founder Wellingbrook Singers, First Edition; backup guitar for Dick and Dee, Sammy Davis Jr., Dean Martin; played in Sonny and Cher's band; producer single I Just Dropped In (To See What Condition My Condition Was In); producer/arranger The Mason Williams Phonograph Album (Grammy award); mus. dir. The Andy Williams Show; producer Mac Davis Show; designer various stage shows; composer numerous music scores for TV including (with Pete Carpenter) Toma, The Rockford Files (Grammy award), Baa Baa Black Sheep, Hunter and Magnum P.I., 1968-87, also composer scores for L.A. Law (Grammy award), Doogie Howser, M.D., Wiseguy, Law and Order, Quantum Leap, The-A-Team, The White Shadow, Riptide, Hardcastle & McCormick, Hill Street Blues (Grammy award), Hooperman, Sonny Spoon, The Joan Rivers Show, The Hat Squad, NYPD Blue, NewsRadio; composer TV movies Gidget Gets Married, 1972, The Morning After, 1974, Locusts, 1974, The Invasion of Johnson County, 1976, Scott Free, 1976, Richie Brockelman: Missing 24 Hours, 1976, Dr. Scorpion, 1978, Captain America, 1979, The Night Rider, 1979, Captain America II, 1979, Scouts Honor, 1980, Coach of the Year, 1980, Willi G. Gordon Liddy, 1982, Adam, 1982, Hard Knox, 1984, No Man's Land, 1984, Heart of a Champion, 1985, Stingray, 1985, The Last Precinct, 1986, Adam: His Song Continues, 1986, Destination: America, 1987, Wiseguy, 1987, J.J. Starbuck, 1987, The Ryan White Story, 1989, B.L. Stryker: The Dancer's Touch, 1989, Unspeakable Acts, 1990, Without Her Consent, 1990, The Great Pretender, 1991; (motion pictures) Rabbit Test, 1978, Deep in the Heart, 1981, Running Brave, 1983, Hadley's Rebellion, 1984, Rhinestone, 1984, The River Rat, 1984; producer, arranger, co-writer (with Stephen Geyer) the theme from The Greatest American Hero (Grammy award); music producer, songwriter TV series Cop Rock; arranger various Ray Charles LP's; record producer Dolly Parton's Nine To Five, Peter Allen's I Could've Been A Sailor; album releases include Music from L.A., Law & Otherwise. Established with BMI Found. Pete Carpenter Meml. Fund, 1989. Avocations: golf, running, arm wrestling. Office: c/o Gorfaine Schwartz Agy 3301 Barham Blvd Ste 201 Los Angeles CA 90068-1477 also: Mike Post Prodns 1007 W Olive Ave Burbank CA 91506-2211

POST, PETER DAVID, lawyer; b. Reading, Pa., Jan. 2, 1947; s. Carl B. and Frances (Gaughan) P.; m. Anne Gage, Feb. 5, 1972; children: Michael, Elizabeth. BS, Pa. State U., 1968; JD, Harvard U., 1971. Bar: Pa. 1971, La. 1974. Assoc. Reed, Smith, Shaw & McClay, Pitts., 1975-81, ptnr., 1982—, dept. head, 1992—. Commr. Upper St. Clair (Pa.) Twp., 1989—. Lt. USN, 1971-75. Avocations: golf, skiing. Office: Reed Smith Shaw & McClay 435 6th Ave Pittsburgh PA 15219-1809*

POST, RICHARD BENNETT, retired human resources executive; b. Clyde, Ohio, July 5, 1936; s. Robert Irving and Elinor May (Bennett) P.; m. Nancy Jane Wardlow, Aug. 31, 1956; children: David Bennett, Todd McKinley, Amy Ellen, Brett Richard, Brina Marie. BS in Psychology, Iowa State U., 1958; student, Ohio U., Athens, 1954-56; postgrad., George Washington U., 1959-60, So. Ill. U., Edwardsville, 1972-74. With U.S. Civil Svc. Commn., 1958-79; chief evaluation div. U.S. Civil Svc. Commn., St. Louis, 1967-71; chief staffing div. U.S. Civil Svc. Commn., 1971-74, dep. reg. dir., 1974-79; dep. assoc. dir. staffing U.S. Office Pers. Mgmt., Washington, 1979-81, assoc. dir. staffing, 1982-86; dir. Washington area svc. ctr. U.S. Office Pers. Mgmt., 1986-94; retired, 1994. Recipient Dirs.' Disting. Svc. award U.S. Office Pers. Mgmt., 1986, Dirs.' citation for Exemplary Pub. Svc., 1994. Mem. ASPA, Sr. Execs. Assn. (life), Fed. Exec. Inst. Alumni Assn., Vienna Choral Soc. (pres. 1987-89), Assn. Quality and Participation. Avocations: woodworking, singing, gardening, photography, stamp collecting.

POST, ROBERT CHARLES, law educator; b. Bklyn., Oct. 17, 1947; s. Ted and Thelma (Feifel) P.; m. Fran Layton, Jan. 22, 1981; children: Alexander, Amelia. AB, Harvard U., 1969, PhD, 1980; JD, Yale U., 1977. Bar: D.C. 1979, Calif. 1983. Law clk. to chief judge U.S. Ct. Appeals (D.C. cir.), 1977-78; law clk. to justice William Brennen Jr. U.S. Supreme Ct. D.C., 1978-79; assoc. Williams & Connelly, Washington, 1980-82; acting prof. law U. Calif., Berkeley, 1983-87, prof. law, 1987-94, Alexander F. and May T. Morrison prof. law, 1994—. Editor: Law and the Order of Culture, 1991; author: Constitutional Domains, 1995. Gen. counsel AAUP, 1992-94. Fellow Guggenheim Found., 1990-91, Am. Coun. Gen. Socs., 1990-91. Mem. AAUP, Am. Acad. Arts and Scis., Law & Soc. Assn. Office: U Calif Sch Law Boalt Hall Berkeley CA 94720

POSTAC, EDWARD P., management consultant. Sr. v.p. Wyatt Corp.

POSTAL, EDWARD DAVID, accountant, corporate executive; b. Washington, Sept. 15, 1955; s. Joseph Lewis and Flora Paula (Gottlieb) P.; m. Marjorie Beth Mayer, Mar. 22, 1987; 1 child, Steven William. BS in Acctg. magna cum laude, U. Md., 1977. CPA, D.C., Md. Asst. to sr. acct. Touche Ross & Co., Washington, 1977-81; sr. acct., mgr. fin. reporting and taxes, mgr. acctg. and taxes Satellite Bus. Systems, McLean, Va., 1981-85; controller Wyatt Co., Washington; 1985—. Mem. AICPA, Md. Assn. CPAs, D.C. Inst. CPAs, Fin. Exec. Inst. (bd. dirs. local chpt.). Office: Wyatt Co 601 13th St NW Washington DC 20005

POSTE, GEORGE HENRY, pharmaceutical company executive; b. Polegate, Sussex, Eng., Apr. 30, 1944; came to U.S., 1972; s. John H. and Kathleen B. (Brooke) P.; m. Mary E. Mudge, Mar. 9, 1968 (div. 1992); 1 child, Eleanor Kathy; m. Linda C. Suhler Lopez, Nov. 21, 1992; stepchildren: John Robert, Lisa Carolyn. DVM, U. Bristol, 1966, PhD, 1969, DSc, 1987. Lectr. Univ. London, 1969-72; assoc. prof. SUNY, Buffalo, 1972-76; prof. pathology Roswell Park Meml. Inst., Buffalo, 1976-80; v.p. rsch. SmithKline Beckman, Phila., 1980-82, v.p. rsch. and devel., 1982-86, v.p. worldwide rsch. and pre-clin. devel., 1987-88, pres. rsch. and devel., 1988-89; pres. rsch. and devel. techs. SmithKline Beecham, King of Prussia, Pa., 1989-90, vice chmn., exec. v.p. rsch. and devel., 1990-91, pres. and chmn. rsch. and devel., 1992—; also bd. dirs. SmithKline Beecham Corp. PLC, King of Prussia, Pa.; mem. pathology B study sect. NIH, Bethesda, Md., 1978-82; chairperson Gordon Conf., N.H., 1985, 86; pres. coun. U. Tex. M.D. Anderson Cancer Ctr.; mem. adv. coun. Beckman Ctr. for Molecular and Genetic Medicine, Stanford U.; mem. coun. Oxford Internat. Biomedical Centre. Editor: Cell Surface Revs., New Horizons in Therapeutics, Cancer Metastasis Revs., Advanced Drug Delivery Revs., 15 books; contbr. numerous articles to profl. jours. Mem. governing bd. UCLA Symposia, Life Sci. Rsch. Found.; mem. bd. Overseers Sch. Vet. Medicine, U. Penn., Gov.'s adv. com. Sci. and Tech., Pa.; mem. adv. bd. Natural Sci. Assn., U. Pa. Fellow Royal Coll. Veterinary Surgeons, Royal Coll. Pathologists; mem. AAAS, Am. Soc. Cell Biology, Pathol. Soc., Nat. Assn. Biomed. Rsch. (bd. govs. 1984), Univ. Assn. Space Rsch. (mem. coun. 1984), Pharm. Mfrs. Assn. (former chmn. rsch. and devel. section 1988). Avocations: military history, foreign affairs, photography, auto racing. Office: SmithKline Beecham Pharms PO Box 1539 King Of Prussia PA 19406

POSTER, JUNE, performing company executive; b. New York, May 6, 1949. BFA, SUNY, Buffalo, 1970; MA, U. Calif., Berkeley, 1975. Exec. dir. San Francisco Camerawork, 1981-87; dir. devel. Meredith Monk/The House, N.Y.C., 1984-87; dir. fin., domestic booking Merce Cunningham Dance Found., N.Y.C., 1987-90; mng. dir. David Gordon Pick Up co., N.Y.C., 1991—; devel. con. various ind. film projects, N.Y.C., 1991. Office: Pick Up Co 131 Varick St Rm 901 New York NY 10013-1410

POSTER, STEVEN BARRY, cinematographer, photgrapher, publisher, digital imaging consultant; b. Chgo., Mar. 1, 1944; s. David and Lillian Violet (Diamondstone) P. Student, So. Ill. U., 1962-64, L.A. Art Ctr. Coll. Design, 1964-66; BS, Ill. Inst. Tech., 1967. Pres. Posters Internat. Ltd., L.A., 1980. Dir. photography (films) Strange Brew, 1983, Testament, 1984, Heavenly Kid, 1985, Blue City, 1986, The Boy Who Could Fly, 1986, Someone to Watch Over Me, 1986, (Am. Soc. Cinematographers nomination 1987), Big Top Pee Wee, 1987, Next of Kin, 1988, Opportunity Knocks, 1989, Rocky V, 1990, Life Stinks, 1991, Cemetery Club, 1993, Roswell, 1994, Strangers on a Train, 1996. Mem. Am. Soc. Cinematographers (1st v.p.), Leica Hist. Soc. Am., Acad. Motion Picture Arts and Scis., Can. Soc. Cinematographers, Internat. Assn. Panoramic Photographers, Behind the Lens (assoc.), Internat. Alliance of Theatrical and Stage Employees. Democrat. Jewish. Avocations: still photography, computers, bicycles.

POSTLEWAITE, PHILIP FREDERICK, law educator. JD, U. Calif., Berkeley, 1970; LLM in Taxation, NYU, 1971. Bar: Wis. 1970, Wash. 1973. Assoc. Foley & Lardner, Milw., 1970-71; instr. in taxation NYU, N.Y.C., 1971-73; assoc. Bogle & Gates, Seattle, 1973-76; assoc. prof. law U. Notre Dame, South Bend, Ind., 1976-81; prof. law Northwestern U., Chgo., 1981—. Author: Policy Readings in Individual Taxation, 1980, International Corporate Taxation, 1980; co-author: Partnership Taxation, 3d ed., vols. I, II and III, 1981, Partnership Taxation Problems and Answers, 1982, International Individual Taxation, 1982, Problems and Materials in Federal Income Taxation, 1986; contbr. articles to profl. jours. Home: 417 Abbotsford Rd Kenilworth IL 60043-1106 Office: Northwestern U Sch Law 375 E Chicago Ave Chicago IL 60611*

POSTMA, HERMAN, physicist, consultant; b. Wilmington, N.C., Mar. 29, 1933; s. Gilbert and Sophia Postma; m. Patricia Dunigan, Nov. 25, 1960; children: Peter, Pamela. BS summa cum laude, Duke U., 1955; MS, Harvard U., 1957, PhD, 1959. Registered profl. engr., Calif. Summer staff Oak Ridge Nat. Lab., 1954-57, physicist thermonuclear div., 1959-62, co-leader DCX-1 group, 1962-66, asst. dir. thermonuclear div., 1966, assoc. dir. div., 1967, dir. div., 1967-73, dir. nat. lab., from 1974; v.p. Martin Marietta, 1984-88, sr. v.p., 1988-91; vis. scientist FOM-Inst. for Plasma Physics, The Netherlands, 1963; cons. Lab. Laser Energetics, U. Rochester; mem. energy rsch. adv. bd. spl. panel Dept. Energy; bd. dirs. Nashville br. Fed. Res. Bank Atlanta, ICS Corp., PAI Corp., ORAS, Inc., M4 Corp. Mem. editorial bd. Nuclear Fusion, 1968-74; contbr. numerous articles to profl. jours. Bd. dirs. The Nucleus; chmn. bd. trustees Hosp. of Meth. Ch.; mem. adv. bd. Coll. Bus. Adminstrn., U. Tenn., 1976-84, Energy Inst., State of N.C.; bd. dirs., exec. com. Tenn. Tech. Found., 1982-88, Venture Capital Fund; vice chmn., commr. Tenn. Higher Edn. Commn., 1984-92; trustee Duke U., 1987—, Pellissippi State Coll., 1991—; chmn. Meth. Hosp. Found., 1990; mem. adv. bd. Inst. Pub. Policy Vanderbilt U., 1986-88, conf. chmn. 1987. Fellow Am. Phys. Soc. (exec. com. div. plasma physics), AAAS, Am. Nuclear Soc. (dir.); mem. C. of C. (v.p. 1981-83, chmn. 1987), Indsl. Rsch. Inst., Gas Rsch. Inst. (adv. bd. 1986-88), Phi Beta Kappa, Beta Gamma Sigma, Sigma Pi Sigma, Omicron Delta Kappa, Sigma Xi, Pi Mu Epsilon, Phi Eta Sigma. Home: 104 Berea Rd Oak Ridge TN 37830-7829

POSTOL, LAWRENCE PHILIP, lawyer; b. Bridgeport, Conn., Oct. 18, 1951; s. Sidney Samuel and Eunice Ruth (Schine) P.; m. Ellen Margaret Russell, Mar. 22, 1975; children: Raymond Russell, Stephen Russell, Carolyn Russell. BS, Cornell U., 1973, JD, 1976. Bar: Conn. 1976, D.C. 1977, U.S. Dist. Ct. D.C. 1977, U.S. Ct. Appeals (D.C. cir.) 1977, U.S. Supreme Ct. 1980, Va. 1982, U.S. Ct. Appeals (4th cir.) 1982, U.S. Dist. Ct. (ea. dist.) Va. 1985, U.S. Dist. Ct. Md. 1989, U.S. Dist. Ct. Conn. 1990. Assoc. Arent, Fox, Kintner & Plotkin, Washington, 1976-80; assoc. Seyfarth, Shaw, Fairweather & Geraldson, Washington, 1980-83, ptnr., 1985—; assoc. Jones, Day, Reavis and Pogue, Washington, 1983-85; lectr. Loyola U., New Orleans, 1983—, U. Cin., 1987—; bd. advisers The Environ. Counselor Jour.; spl. counsel Greater Washington Bd. Trade, 1991-93. Author: Legal Guide to Handling Toxic Substances in the Workplace, 1990, Americans with Disabilities Act - A Compliance Manual for Employers, 1993. Jewish. Avocation: sports. Home: 6340 Chowning Pl Mc Lean VA 22101-4129 Office: Seyfarth Shaw Fairweather & Geraldson 815 Connecticut Ave NW Washington DC 20006-4004

POSTON, FREDDIE LEE, entomologist; b. Jacksonville, Fla., Nov. 19, 1946; m. Charlotte Eller, Mar. 17, 1967; children—Erin E., Lindsay. B.S. in Biology, W. Tex. State U., 1971; M.S. in Entomology, Iowa State U., 1973, Ph.D., 1975. Research assoc. Iowa State U., Ames, 1973-75; asst. prof. Kans. State U., Manhattan, 1975-80, assoc. prof., 1980-84, prof., 1985—, assoc. dir. extension, 1984—; entomologist Coop. State Research Service, USDA, Washington, 1980-81. Contbr. articles to profl. jours. Grantee in field. Mem. Entomol. Soc. Am., Central States Entomol. Soc. (pres. 1979). Avocation: flying. Office: Kans State U Umberger Hall Manhattan KS 66506

POSTON, TOM, actor; b. Columbus, Ohio, Oct. 17, 1927; s. George and Margaret P.; m. Jean Sullivan, 1955; m. Kay Hudson, June 8, 1968; children: Francesca, Hudson, Jason. Student, Bethany Coll., 1938-40. First appeared on stage as a tumbler with The Flying Zebleys; acting and Broadway debuts in Cyrano de Bergerac, 1947; appeared on Broadway, regional theaters, and summer stock; stage appearances include: The Insect Comedy, King Lear, Will Success Spoil Rock Hunter?, Goodbye Again, Best of Burlesque, Romanoff and Juliet, Drink to Me Only, Golden Fleecing, The Conquering Hero, Come Blow Your Horn, Mary, Mary, Forty Carats, But Seriously..., A Funny Thing Happened on the Way to the Forum, The Odd Couple, Bye Bye Birdie, Mother Courage, host WABC-TV series Entertainment, 1955; regular on TV show The Steve Allen Show, 1956-58 (Emmy award for best supporting actor in comedy series 1959); host TV show Split Personality, 1959-60; panelist TV show To Tell the Truth; appeared in TV series On the Rocks, 1975-76, We've Got Each Other, 1977, Mork and Mindy, 1978-82, Newhart, 1982-90, Grace Under Fire, 1993—; numerous TV appearances include The Bob Newhart Show; film appearances include: The Tempest, The City That Never Sleeps, 1953, Zotz, 1962, Soldier in the Rain, 1963, The Old Dark House, 1963, Cold Turkey, 1970, The Happy Hooker, 1975, Rabbit Test, 1978, Up the Academy, 1980, Carbon Copy, 1981. Served with USAAF, World War II. *

POSTON, WALKER S., medical educator. BA in Biol. Scis., U. Calif., Davis, 1983, PhD, 1990. Intern, resident USAF Med. Ctr., Wright-PAtterson AFB, Ohio, 1989-90; dir. psychology svcs., asst. chief mental health svcs. 9th Med. Group, Beale AFB, 1990-92; chief health and rehab. psychology svc. Malcolm Grow Med. Ctr., 1993-95, faculty, 1993-95; clin. asst. prof. dept. med. and clin. psychology F. Edward Herbert Sch. Medicine, Bethesda, Md., 1993-95; asst. prof. medicine Baylor Coll. Medicine, Houston, 1995—. Contbr. articles to profl. jours. U. Calif. Doctoral scholars fellow, 1984-85, 85-86, 86-87, 88-89, Clin. fellow Wilford Hall Med. Ctr., Lackland AFB, 1992-93; Nat. Merit scholar, 1979-80. Office: Baylor Coll Medicine Behavior Medicine Rsch Ctr 6535 Fannin MS F-700 Houston TX 77030

POSUNKO, BARBARA, retired elementary education educator; b. Newark, July 17, 1938; d. Joseph and Mary (Prystauk) P. BA, Rutgers U., Newark, 1960; MA, Kean Coll., Union, N.J., 1973; teaching cert., Seton Hall U., Newark, 1966. Cert. elem. tchr., reading specialist, N.J. Social case worker Newark City Hosp., 1960-65; elem. tchr. Plainfield (N.J.) Bd. Edn., 1966; elem., jr. and sr. high sch. tchr. minimum basic skills and reading Sayreville (N.J.) Bd. Edn., 1966-82; tchr. Chpt. I and minimum basic skills Sayreville (N.J.) Bd. Edn., Parlin, 1982-95, cooperating tchr. to student tchrs., 1983-95, coord. testing, 1984-95; ret., 1995; sch. coord. for congressionally mandated study of ednl. growth and opportunity, 1991-95; mem. numerous reading coms. Recipient Outstanding Tchr. award N.J. Gov.'s Tchr. Recognition Program, 1988. Mem. NEA, Internat. Reading Assn., N.J. Reading Assn., N.J. Edn. Assn. Home: 17 Drake Rd Mendham NJ 07945-1805

POSUNKO, LINDA MARY, retired elementary education educator; b. Newark, Dec. 24, 1942; d. Joseph and Mary (Prystauk) P. BA, Newark State Coll., Union, N.J., 1964; MA, Kean Coll., Union, 1974. Cert. permanent elem. tchr., supr., prin., N.J. Elem. tchr. Roselle (N.J.) Bd. Edn., 1964-65; elem. tchr. Garwood (N.J.) Bd. Edn., 1965-92, head tchr., 1974-76, 79-81, head tchr. elem. and early childhood edn., tchr. 1st grade, 1992-95; ret., 1995; cooperating tchr. to student tchrs.; instr. non-English speaking students and children with learning problems; mem. affirmative action, sch. resource coms.; conductor in-svc. workshops on early childhood devel. practices, 1993. Recipient honor cert. Union County Conf. Tchrs. Assn., 1972-73, Outstanding Tchr. award N.J. Gov.'s Tchr. Recognition Program, 1988; nominee Gov.'s Tchr. Recognition award, 1993-94. Mem. ASCD, NEA, Internat. Reading Assn. (bd. dirs. suburban coun.), N.J. Edn. Assn., Garwood Tchrs. Assn. (sec., v.p., pres.), High/Scope Ednl. Found. Home: 17 Drake Rd Mendham NJ 07945-1805

POTAMKIN, MEYER P., mortgage banker; b. Phila., Nov. 11, 1909; s. Jacob and Ida (Soloman) P.; m. Vivian Orleans, July 27, 1940; children—Macy Ann Potamkin Lasky, Marshall F. Ph.B., Dickinson Coll., 1932; Ed.M., Temple U., 1941; D.F.A., Dickinson Coll., 1972. Social worker, dir. agy. Crime Prevention Assn., Phila., 1935-40; ptnr. Orleans Constrn. Co., Phila., 1940-54; pres. Blvd. Mortgage Co., Phila., 1954—. Pres. Phila. coun. Boys Clubs Am., 1962-82; nat. assoc. Boys Clubs Am., 1972-80; chmn. bd. trustees Camp William Penn, 1964-82; bd. dirs. Glen Mills Sch. for Delinquent Boys, 1960-77, v.p., 1976-77; bd. dirs. Phila. Coll. Art, 1970-75, Phila. Art Commn., 1974-82; mem. Juvenile Task Force Gov.'s Justice Commn. and L.E.A.A. Coun., 1974-80; bd. dirs. Mann Music Ctr., 1982—, Settlement Music Sch., 1962—; trustee Bklyn. Mus., Crime Prevention Assn. (pres., chmn. bd. trustees 1977-87), Phila. Mus. Art, 1960-75, 1981—, Richmond Coll., Eng., 1982-87; bd. dirs., co-founder Sarah Allen Nursing Home for Blacks; mem. adv. coun. to bd. trustees Dickinson Coll., 1976—; trustee, mem. exec. com. Middle States Assn., 1977-82; bd. dirs. Phila. Ctr. for Older People, 1980-83; pres. Phila. Art Alliance, 1991-92. Recipient AME Mother Bethel award, 1977, Silver Keystone award Boys Clubs Am., 1986, Jewish Basketball League award, 1990, Achievement award Perkiomen Sch., 1990, Alumni award Perkiomen Sch., 1990, Alumni Achievement award Dickinson Coll., 1991, Jewish Basketball Honorable Fenkel award, 1994; Israel Bond honoree, 1973. Mem. Home Builders Assn., Mortgage Bankers Assn. Am., Phila. Mortgage Bankers Assn. (pres. 1985-86), Pa. Mortgage Bankers Assn. (pres. 1985-86, award 1990), Locust Club, Union League, Bala Golf Club, Squires Golf Club, Friendly Sons of St. Patrick (hon.), Phi Epsilon Pi (bd. trustees found., Achievement award 1967), Zeta Beta Tau (grand coun. v.p. 1978). Office: Blvd Mortgage Co 111 Presidential Blvd Ste 135 Bala Cynwyd PA 19004

POTAMKIN, ROBERT, automotive executive; b. 1946. Grad., U. Pa., 1970, JD, 1972. CEO Potamkin Cos., Miami, Fla., 1972—. Office: 4675 SW 74th St Miami FL 33143

POTASH, JANE, artist; b. Phila., May 3, 1937; d. Norval and Mary (Fox) Levy; m. Charles Potash, Jan. 21, 1962; children: Andrew Samuel, Dorothy Frances. BA, U. Pa., 1959. One-woman shows include Storelli Gallery, Phila., 1979, Langman Gallery, Jenkintown, Pa., 1979, 81, Phoenix Gallery, N.Y., 1981, A.R.T. Beasley Gallery, San Diego, 1986, Vorpal, N.Y., 1987; exhibited in group shows at Wayne Art Ctr., 1971, Lancaster Summer Arts Festival, 1971, 72, 74, Cooperstown (N.Y.) Nat. Juried Show, 1971, Abington Art Ctr., 1972-74, Phila. Art Alliance, 1975, Allentown Art Mus., 1976, Pa. Acad. Fine Arts, 1978, 80, Butcher and More Gallery, Phila., 1981, Wachs Davis Gallery, Washington, Shayne Gallery, Montreal, Can., 1982, Montreal Mus. Fine Arts, 1982, Source Gallery, San Francisco, 1983, Langman Gallery, 1987, Virginia Miller Gallery, Coral Gables, Fla., 1990; represented in collections at Fox Companies, Blue Cross, Blue Shield of Pa., Subaru, N.J., Nordstrom Stores, Calif., Beaver Ins. Co., San Francisco; represented in pvt. collections in U.S. and Can. Recipient Best of Show award Old York Rd. Avocations: reading, flower arranging, knitting, swimming, opera. Studio: 220 Old York Rd Jenkintown PA 19046-3244

POTASH, JEREMY WARNER, public relations executive; b. Monrovia, Calif., June 30, 1946; d. Fenwick Bryson and Jean Antony (Blair) Warner; m. Stephen Jon Potash, Oct. 19, 1969; 1 child, Aaron Warner. AA, Citrus Coll., 1965; BA, Pomona Coll., 1967. With Forbes Mag., N.Y.C., 1967-69, Japan External Trade Orgn., San Francisco, 1970-75; v.p., co-founder Potash & Co. Pub. Rels., Oakland, Calif., 1980-87; pres. Potash & Co. Pub. Rels., San Francisco, 1987—; founding exec. dir. Calif.-S.E. Asia Bus. Coun., Oakland, 1991—; exec. dir. Customs Brokers and Forwarders Assn., San Francisco, 1990—. Editor: Southeast Asia Environmental Directory, 1994; editor: Southeast Asia Infrastructure Directory, 1995-96. Bd. dirs. Judah L. Magnes Mus., Berkeley, 1981-94, co-founder docent program, 1980, pres. Women's Guild, 1980-81; bd. dirs. Temple Sinai, Oakland, 1984-86; pres. East Bay region Women's Am. Orgn. for Rehab. Through Tng., 1985-86. Mem. Am. Soc. Assn. Execs., World Trade Club San Francisco, Oakland Women's Lit. Soc., Book Club Calif. Office: Potash & Co Pub Rels 1946 Embarcadero Oakland CA 94606-5213

POTASH, STEPHEN JON, international public relations practitioner; b. Houston, Feb. 25, 1945; s. Melvin L. and Petrice (Edelstein) P.; m. Jeremy Warner, Oct. 19, 1969; 1 son, Aaron Warner. BA in Internat. Rels., Pomona Coll., 1967. Account exec. Charles von Loewenfeldt, Inc., San Francisco, 1969-74, v.p., 1974-80; founder, pres. Potash & Co., Pub. Rels., Oakland, Calif., 1980-87; cons. Am. Pres. Lines and Am. Pres. Cos., 1979-87, 90—; exec. dir. Calif. Coun. Internat. Trade, 1970-87; v.p. corp. communications Am. Pres. Cos., Oakland, 1987-90; chmn. Potash & Co., Oakland, 1990—. Bd. dirs. Calif. Coun. Internat. Trade, 1987-94, Calif.-Southeast Asia Bus. Coun., 1992—, Temple Sinai, Oakland, 1979-81. Mem. Pub. Rels. Soc. Am., Commonwealth Club of Calif., World Trade Club San Francisco. Office: Potash & Co 1946 Embarcadero Oakland CA 94606-5213

POTATE, JOHN SPENCER, SR., engineering company executive, consultant; b. Temple, Ga., Mar. 19, 1934; s. Harold Clyde and Eugenia Marie (McClung) P.; m. Barbara Jean Moorefield; children: Pamela, Vivian, Brenda, John Jr. BS in Indsl. Engring., Ga. Inst. Tech., 1959; MS in Aerospace Engring., Fla. Inst. Tech., 1965; MS in Mgmt., MIT, 1975. Program mgr. NASA, Cape Kennedy, Fla., 1961-70; exec. NASA, Washington, 1970-72; exec. Marshall Space Flight Ctr. NASA, Huntsville, Ala., 1973-82; v.p. System Devel. Corp. (now subs. Unisys), Santa Monica, Calif., 1982-84, Unisys, Camarillo, Calif., 1984-89; pres. AC Engring., Huntsville, Ala., 1989-92, ret., 1993; prin. John Potate Assocs., Huntsville, Ala., 1993—. With USCG, 1951-54; engr. USAF, 1959-61. Sloan fellow, MIT, 1972; recipient NASA Exceptional Svc. medal, 1969 (Apollo), NASA Leadership medal, 1980 (shuttle). Home: 1319 Blevins Gap Rd SE Huntsville AL 35802-2709

POTCHEN, E. JAMES, radiology educator; b. Queens County, N.Y., Dec. 12, 1932; s. Joseph Anton and Eleanore Joyce P.; children: Michelle, Kathleen, Michael, Joseph. BS, Mich. State U., East Lansing, 1954; MD, Wayne State U., 1958; MS, MIT, 1973; JD U. Mich., 1984. Diplomate Am. Bd. Nuclear Medicine, Am. Bd. Radiology (examiner 1968-78). Intern Butterworth Hosp., Grand Rapids, Mich., 1958-59; resident Peter Bent Brigham Hosp., Boston, 1961-64; gen. practice medicine, Grand Rapids, 1959-61; chief resident radiologist Peter Bent Brigham Hosp., Children's Hosp., Pondville State Cancer Hosp., 1964; jr. assoc. radiology Peter Bent Brigham Hosp., 1965; dir. div. Nuclear Medicine, Harvard Med. Sch., dept. radiology, Peter Bent Brigham Hosp., 1965-66; dir. nuclear medicine div. Mallinckrodt Inst. Radiology, Washington U. Sch. Medicine, 1966-73, chief diagnostic radiology, 1971-72; asst. prof. radiology Washington U., St. Louis, 1966, assoc. prof. radiology, 1967-70, prof. radiology, 1970-73; prof. radiology, dean mgmt. resources Johns Hopkins U., Balt., 1973-75; mem. faculty Mich. State U., East Lansing, 1975—, prof. radiology Coll. Human Medicine, prof. mgmt. Coll. Bus., Univ. Disting. prof., 1990, chmn. radiology; chmn. faculty group practice Mich. State U.; chmn. Liaison Com. Med. Edn., 1980-86; mem. Bur. Radiologic Health-Med. Radiation Adv. Com. FDA, 1982-85; mem. med. necessity in diagnostic imaging adv. com. Nat. Blue Cross/Blue Shield, 1981. Assoc. editor Investigative Radiology, 1968-72, Jour. Nuclear Medicine, 1969-74, Jour. Microvascular Rsch., 1970-78, Radiology, 1970-90, Internat. Jour. Radiation Oncology, 1977-86, Biology and Physics, Continuing Edn. Radiology; mem. editorial bd. Radiology, 1970-71; editor-in-chief The Radiology Resident, 1992-94. Contbr. articles to various publs. Recipient awards including Dist. Alumni award Wayne State U., 1970; Scholar in Radiologic Rsch. James Picker Found., 1967-68; Advanced fellow Academic Radiology, James Picker Found., Nat. Acad. Scis.-NRC, 1965-66; John J. Larkin award for basic med. research, 1963, Disting. Alumnus award Brigham Women's Hosp., 1993. Fellow ACP, Am. Coll. Chest Physicians; mem. Acad. Mgmt. (div. sec. 1977-78), Am. Cancer Soc. (div. bd. trustees 1977-78), AMA (council med. edn. 1979-88), ABA, Am. Physiologic Soc., Am. Radium Soc., Am. Roentgen Ray Soc., Am. Soc. Clin. Investigation, Assn. Am. Med. Colls., Assn. U. Radiologists (mem. exec. com. 1970-72; mem. com. 1971-72), Central Soc. Clin. Rsch., Fleischner Soc. (pres. 1993), Interam. Coll. Radiology, Ingham County Med. Soc. (mem. com. 1977—), Mich. State Med. Soc. (mem. adv. com. med. edn. 1980—), Nat. Inst. Health Found. Advanced Edn. Scis., Radiologic Soc. N.Am., Soc. Chmn. of Acad. Radiology Depts. (mem. exec. com.), Soc. Nuclear Medicine (nat. pres. 1975-76), Soc. Health and Human Values, Soc. Med. Decision Making (founding mem. 1979), Soc. Thoracic Radiology (founding mem., 1982—), Sigma Xi, Alpha Omega Alpha. Office: Mich State U Dept Radiology B-220 Clinical Ctr East Lansing MI 48824

POTEAT, JAMES DONALD, diaconal minister; b. Spindale, N.C., Feb. 27, 1935; s. Albert Carl and Daliah Elizabeth (Freeman) P.; m. Clara Walker Yelton, Oct. 12, 1957; children: Deborah Poteat Emmons, Clara Poteat Frederick, James Donald Jr., Teresa Poteat Morris. BA disting. mil. graduate, The Citadel, Charleston, S.C., 1957; MA, Kans. State U., 1973; graduate, U.S. Army War Coll., 1980, Indsl. Coll. Armed Forces, 1990. Ordained to ministry United Meth. Ch. Commd. 2nd lt. U.S. Army, 1957, advanced through grades to col., 1979, ret., 1983; pastor's adminstrv. asst. Prospect United Meth. Ch., Covington, Ga., 1988-95. Author: Long Range Planning, Prospect United Methodist Church, 1990, Presidential Decision-Making: Presidents Lincoln and Polk, 1973, others. Decorated Bronze Star medal, three Air medals, Vietnam Cross of Gallantry, three Army Commendation medals with v. Mem. Ret. Officers Assn., Army Aviation Assn. Am., United Meth. Ch. Bus. Adminstrs. Assn. (cert.). Office: Prospect United Meth Ch 6752 Hwy 212 N Covington GA 30209-9132

POTEET, DANIEL P(OWELL), II, college provost; b. Dallas, Dec. 22, 1940; s. Daniel Powell and Helene (Van der Veer) P.; m. Nancy Heusinkveld, Mar. 13, 1971; 1 child, Daniel C. BA, Harvard U., 1963; MA, U. Ill., 1965, PhD, 1969. Asst. prof. U. Del., Newark, 1969-76, West Chester (Pa.) State Coll., 1976-77; dean faculty Hampden-Sydney (Va.) Coll., 1978-81, provost, 1981-85; provost Albion (Mich.) Coll., 1985-91, Guilford (N.C.) Coll., 1991—. Co-author: Rise of the Realists, 1979; also articles and revs. Mem. AAUP, Am. Conf. Acad. Deans, Am. Assn. Higher Edn. Episcopalian. Avocation: sailing. Office: Guilford Coll Office of Provost 5800 W Friendly Ave Greensboro NC 27410-4108

POTEET, MARY JANE, computer scientist; b. Raleigh, N.C., May 26, 1946; d. Charles William and Geraldine Lucile (Adams) Hampton; m. William Walter Schubert, Dec. 30, 1967 (div. June 1979); children: Kristen, Stephen, Betsy, Kathryn; m. H. Wesley Poteet, Mar. 21, 1991 (div. Mar. 1996). BA in Math., Park Coll., 1967. Programmer U. Mo. Med. Ctr., Columbia, 1968-72, City and County of Denver, 1979-80; sr. sys. programmer Citicorp Person to Person, Denver, 1980-82; sys. support rep. Software AG, NA, Denver, 1982-83; prin. info. sysm. specialist Idaho Nat. Engring. Lab., EG&G, Idaho Falls, 1983-89; adv. svcs. specialist IBM Profl. Svcs., Albuquerque, 1989-91; field mgr. IBM Svc., Boulder, Colo., 1991-93; project mgr. IBM Cons. & Svcs. SW, Denver, 1993—; presenter career workshop for girls No. Colo. U., Greeley, 1993. Leader Girl Scout Am., Pocatello, Idaho, Columbia, Mo., 1969-79, Idaho Falls, 1986-89, cluster leader, Rigby, Idaho, 1988-89; active Albuquerque Civic Chorus, 1990-91, Ch. Coun., 1994; bd. dirs. LWV, Pocatello, 1977-79, 84-85, pres., 1978-79; bd. dirs. Luth. Ch. Women, Pocatello, 1978-79; youth advisor Luth. Ch., Idaho Falls, 1984-89; tchr. Sunday sch. local ch., Albuquerque, 1990-91; youth com. chair local ch., Boulder, Colo., 1994-96; tchr., 7th and 8th grade Sunday sch., 1993-96, mem. ch. choir, 1995-96. Mem. AAUW. Lutheran. Avocations: youth work, reading, choir, photography. Home: 3916 W 104th Pl Westminster CO 80030-2402

POTEETE, ROBERT ARTHUR, editor; b. Perry, Ark., Aug. 29, 1926; s. Arthur and Ruby (Farish) P.; m. Frances Reynolds, Feb. 15, 1951 (dec. Mar. 1969); children: Anthony R., Julia Anne, Richard A.R. (dec. Sept. 1973). B.A., U. Central Ark., 1948; postgrad., Medill Sch. Journalism, Northwestern U., 1948-49. Reporter Ark. Gazette, 1949; reporter, day city editor, asst. news editor, asst. Sunday editor N.Y. Herald Tribune, 1950-66; mng. editor N.Y. Herald Tribune (European edit.), Paris, 1963-65; sr. editor Saturday Evening Post, N.Y.C., 1966-69; mng. editor, editor Psychology Today, Del Mar, Calif., 1969-73; mng. editor New Publs., Playboy Enterprises, Inc., Chgo., 1973-74; sr. editor Money mag., 1974-76; editor in chief Am. Illustrated mag. USIA, Washington, 1976-91; free-lance editor, writer, 1991—; editorial cons. Episcopal Diocese L.I., Garden City, N.Y., 1967-68. Contbr. articles popular mags. Mem. bd. United Youth Ministry, La Jolla, Cal., 1971-72. Served with U.S. Army, PTO, 1945-46. Recipient Citizens Budget Commn. citation for articles on N.Y.C. govt. purchase of real estate, 1958; named Disting. Alumnus, U. Ctrl. Ark., 1993. Mem. Am. Soc. Mag. Editors, Inner Circle. Home: 30 Julio Dr Apt 509 Shrewsbury MA 01545-3046

POTENTE, EUGENE, JR., interior designer; b. Kenosha, Wis., July 24, 1921; s. Eugene and Suzanne Marie (Schmit) P.; Ph.B., Marquette U., 1943; postgrad. Stanford U., 1943, N.Y. Sch. Interior Design, 1947; m. Joan Ciofe, Jan. 29, 1946; children: Eugene J., Peter Michael, John Francis, Suzanne Marie. Founder, pres. Studios of Potente, Inc., Kenosha, Wis., 1949—; pres., founder Archtl. Services Assos., Kenosha, 1978—, Bus. Leasing Services of Wis. Inc., 1978—; past nat. pres. Inter-Faith Forum on Religion, Art and Architecture; vice chmn. Wis. State Capitol and Exec. Residence Bd., 1981—. Sec., Kenosha Symphony Assn., 1968-74. Bd. dirs. Ctr. for Religion and the Arts, Wesley Theol. Sem., Washington, 1983-84. Served with AUS, 1943-46. Mem. Am. Soc. Interior Designers (treas., pres. Wis. chpt. 1985-86, 94-95, chmn. nat. pub. svc. 1986), Illuminating Engring. Soc. N.Am., Internat. Inst. Interior Designers, Sigma Delta Chi. Roman Catholic. Lodge: Elks. Home: 8609 2nd Ave Kenosha WI 53143-6511 Office: 914 60th St Kenosha WI 53140-4041

POTENZA, DAISY MCKASKLE, newspaper executive; b. Houston, Mar. 5, 1906; d. George Washington and Dora Amy (Crump) McKaskle; student Sinclair Bus. Coll., 1925, Massey's Bus. Coll., 1924-26, U. Houston; m. Julius Orian Potenza, Sept. 26, 1928; 1 dau., Marjorie Ann (Mrs. William L. Hale) (dec.). With Houston Chronicle, 1926-87, adminstrv. asst. to editor-in-chief, 1930-79, adminstrv. asst. to sr. v.p. and cons., 1979-87, apptd. cons., 1994—. Exec. sec. Houston Endowment, Inc., 1968-69; bd. dirs. Pin Oak Charity Horse Show, 1978, 79, 80, 81, 82, 83, 84. Recipient award United Fund, 1967—; tribute for exec. service to Chronicle, 1983; outstanding ticket sales awardee Pin Oak Charity Horse Show, Tex. Children's Hosp., 1975-83, 84. Mem. Nat., Tex. press women, Women in Communications, Press Club Houston (hon. life). Methodist. Club: Farm and Ranch. Home: 2405 San Felipe St Houston TX 77019-3403 Office: 801 Texas St Houston TX 77002-2906

POTERBA, JAMES MICHAEL, economist, educator; b. Flushing, N.Y., July 13, 1958; s. William Samuel and Margaret Mary (Toale) P.; m. Nancy Lin Rose, June 23, 1984; children: Matthew Robert, Timothy James, Margaret Rose. AB, Harvard U., 1980; MPhil, Oxford U., Eng., 1982, DPhil, 1983. From asst. to assoc. prof. MIT, Cambridge, Mass., 1983-88, prof., 1988—; dir. pub. econs. rsch. program Nat. Bur. Econ. Rsch., Cambridge, 1990—; fellow Ctr. Advanced Study in Behavioral Scis., 1993-94. Editor: Economic Policy Responses to Global Warning, 1991, International Comparisons of Household Saving, 1994; co-editor: Jour. Pub. Econs.; contbr. articles to profl. jours. Marshall scholar, 1980-83. Fellow Am. Acad. Arts and Scis., Econometric Soc.; mem. Am. Fin. Assn. (bd. dirs.), Phi Beta Kappa. Office: MIT 50 Memorial Dr Rm E52-350 Cambridge MA 02139-4307

POTH, EDWARD CORNELIUS, construction company executive; b. Chgo., Aug. 19, 1927; s. John Henry and Cecelia Kathryn (Kuijer) P.; m. Eve Elsie Kaisto, June 25, 1953; children: Susan, Sharon, Cathy. BSCE, Bradley U., 1951. Project mgr. Paschen Contractors, Inc., Chgo., 1955-65, v.p., 1965-70, exec. v.p., 1970-80, pres., 1980-83, also bd. dirs.; exec. v.p. Mellon Stuart Co., Pitts., 1984-85, pres., 1986-88; vice chmn. Case Group, J. H. Pomeroy & Co. Inc., and Pomco, Inc., 1988—, also bd. dirs.; pres., bd. dirs. PCI Ins. Co., Chgo., 1978-83; pres. PCI Aviation Co., Chgo., 1978-83; treas., bd. dirs. Mid Am. Elevator Co., Chgo., 1976-83. Bd. dirs. Dist. 89 Sch. System, Glen Ellyn, Ill., 1970-76, Chgo. Builders Assn., 1978-83; mem. Econ. Devel. Bd., Glen Ellyn, 1991—. Served to sgt. C.E. U.S. Army, 1945-47. Recipient Value Engring. award Gen. Service Adminstrn., Chgo., 1971. Episcopalian. Clubs: Medinah Golf, Mid Am., Ground Hog Club (v.p), Beavers (Chgo.); Duquesne (Pitts.). Avocations: tennis, golf, skiing, fishing, hunting. Home: 591 Hill Ave Glen Ellyn IL 60137-5033*

POTH, STEFAN MICHAEL, retired sales financing company executive; b. Detroit, Dec. 9, 1933; s. Stefan and Anna (Mayer) P.; m. Eileen T. McClimon, May 28, 1966; 1 child, Stefan Michael Jr. Cert. in acctg., Walsh Inst., Detroit, 1954. CPA, Mich.; cert. consumer credit exec. Sr. acct. Lybrand, Ross Bros. & Montgomery, Detroit, 1953-56, 58-61; with Ford Motor Credit Co., Dearborn, Mich., 1961-91; v.p. leasing truck and recreational products and tractor financing Ford Motor Credit Co., Dearborn, 1973-77; v.p. cen. and western U.S. ops. Ford Motor Credit Co., Dearborn, 1977-79; v.p. mktg. and ops. svcs. Ford Motor Credit Co., Dearborn, 1979-85, v.p. bus. planning, 1985-90, v.p. credit policy, 1990-91; bd. dirs. GE Credit Auto Resale Svcs., Inc.; adv. coun. Credit Rsch. Ctr., Krannert Grad. Sch. Mgmt., Purdue U., 1984-91. Chmn. adv. coun. Credit Rsch. Ctr. Krannert Grad. Sch. Mgmt., Purdue U., 1989-90; mem. bd. dirs. Internat. Credit Assoc., 1989-91. With AUS, 1956-58. Roman Catholic. Home: 7230 Mohansic Dr Bloomfield Hills MI 48301-3550

POTOCKI, JOSEPH EDMUND, marketing company executive; b. Jersey City, Jan. 31, 1936; s. Joseph and Estelle (Bielski) P.; m. Margaret Mary Shine, May 21, 1960; children: Joseph, Meg, David. BS, Seton Hall U., 1957. Asst. regional sales mgr. Gen. Mills Inc., Valley Stream, N.Y., 1960-67; group mgr. merchandising Warner Lambert Co., Morris Plains, N.J., 1967-74; dir. merchandising svcs. Beatrice Hunt/Wesson, Fullerton, Calif., 1974-81; pres., chief exec. officer Joseph Potocki & Assocs., Irvine, Calif., 1981-92; pres. Mktg. Fulfillment Svcs., Tustin, Calif., 1985-87; chmn. Clarke Hooper Am., 1987-92; sr. exec. Gage Mktg., Newport Beach, 1992—; instr. nat. bus. seminars. Bd. dirs. L.A. Parent Inst. Quality Edn., 1994—. Recipient Mktg. Motivator award L.A. Mktg. Exhbn., 1981, Mktg. Gold medal Am. Mktg. Assn. 1957. Mem. Promotion Mktg. Assn. (chmn. bd. dirs. 1977-79, v.p. West sect. 1980-87, bd. dirs. 1990, chmn. edn. com., Reggie award 1984, 85, 87), Promotion Mktg. Assn. Am. (bd. dirs. exec. com. 1978-87, Chmn.'s Bowl 1979, Named to Chmn.'s Cir. 1986, chmn. basics and advanced edn.), Nat. Premium Sales Execs. (sec. 1985-86, Pres. award 1985, Cert. Incentive Profl. Republican. Roman Catholic. Avocations: sailing, golf, woodworking, travel. Home: Monarch Pointe 22772 Azure Sea Laguna Niguel CA 92677-5439 Office: Gage Mktg Group 3620 Birch St Newport Beach CA 92660-2619

POTOK, CHAIM, author, artist, editor; b. N.Y.C., Feb. 17, 1929; s. Benjamin Max and Mollie (Friedman) P.; m. Adena S. Mosevitzky, June 8, 1958; children: Rena, Naama, Akiva. BA summa cum laude, Yeshiva Coll., 1950; MHL, Jewish Theol. Sem., 1954; PhD, U. Pa., 1965. Ordained rabbi, 1954. Nat. dir. Leaders Tng. Fellowship, 1954-55; dir. Camp Ramah, Ojai, Cal., 1957-59; scholar-in-residence Har Zion Temple, Phila., 1959-63; mem. faculty Tchrs. Inst., Jewish Theol. Sem., 1963-64; editor Jewish Publ. Soc., 1965-74, spl. projects editor, 1974—; vis. prof. U. Pa., 1992, 93, 94, 95, Johns Hopkins U., 1994, 96; vis. lectr. Bryn Mawr Coll., 1985. Author: The Chosen, 1967 (Edward Lewis Wallant award), The Promise, 1969 (Athenaeum award), My Name is Asher Lev, 1972, In The Beginning, 1975, Wanderings, 1975, The Book of Lights, 1981, Davita's Harp, 1985, Tobiasse: Artist in Exile, 1986, The Gift of Asher Lev, 1990 (Nat. Jewish Book award), I Am the Clay, 1992, The Gates of November, 1996, (children's books with Tony Auth) The Tree of Here, 1993, The Sky of Now, 1995, (plays) Out of the Depths, 1990, Sins of the Father, 1991, The Play of Lights, 1992, also short stories; works translated into more than a dozen fgn. langs. Served as chaplain AUS, 1955-57, Korea. Mem. P.E.N., Artists' Equity, Author's Guild, Dramatists Guild, Rabbinical Assembly.

POTRA, FLORIAN ALEXANDER, mathematics educator; b. Cluj, Romania, Dec. 7, 1950; came to the U.S., 1982; s. Ioan and Ana (Popa) P.; m. ELena Lavric, Nov. 15, 1973; 1 child, Valentin. MS, Babes-Bolyai U., Cluj, 1973; PhD, U. Bucharest, 1980. Analyst IPGGH, Bucharest, Romania, 1974-78; researcher INCREST, Bucharest, 1978-82; postdoctoral researcher U. Pitts., 1982-83, asst. prof., 1983-84; assoc. prof. U. Iowa, Iowa City, 1984-90, prof., 1990—; vis. rschr. Lawrence Livermore Nat. Lab., Rice U., U. Catania, Italy, Konrad Zuse Zentrum, Berlin, U. Darmstadt, Germany, 1990, U. Karlsruhe, Germany, 1987-91, Argonne Nat. Lab., 1991, U. Geneva, 1993, U. NSW, Sydney, 1995. Assoc. editor: SIAM Jour. on Optimization, 1991—, Jour. Optimization Theory and Applications, 1991—; co-author: Research Notes in Mathematics 103, 1984; contbr. articles to profl. jours. Andrew Mellon fellow, 1982, Old Gold fellow, 1984, James Van Allen fellow in natural scis., 1991; NSF grantee, 1985-87., 94—. Home: 4029 W Overlook Rd NE Iowa City IA 52240-7942 Office: U Iowa Mathematics Iowa City IA 52242

POTSIC, WILLIAM PAUL, physician, educator; b. Berwyn, Ill., May 22, 1943; s. Andrew M. and Estella (Buschak) P.; m. Roberta I. Kite; children: Amie, Jordan. B.S., U. Ill., 1965; M.D. cum laude, Emory U., 1969; postgrad., U. Pa. Intern, resident U. Chgo., 1969-74; practice medicine specializing in pediatric otolaryngology Phila., 1974—; mem. staff Presbyn. Hosp., Pa. Hosp., Children's Seashore House; assoc. prof. otorhinolaryngology and human communication U. Pa., 1974-93, prof. otorhinolaryngology and human communication, 1993—; dir. div. otorhinolaryngology and human communication Children's Hosp., Phila., 1975—; sec.-treas. med. staff Children's Hosp., 1980—, pres. med. staff, 1982-84; vice-chmn. clin. affairs dept. surgery, 1995—. Author book on pediatric otolaryngology; contbr. articles to profl. jours. Recipient 1st prize for clin. research Am. Acad. Ophthalmology and Otolaryngology, 1977; NIH grantee. Mem. AMA, Am. Acad. Otolaryngology Head and Neck Surgery, Am. Laryngology, Otolgy and Rhinology Soc., Am. Coll. Physician Execs., Internat. Acad. Cosmetic Surgery, Pa. Med. Soc., Phila. Coll. Physicians, Phila. County Med. Soc., Phila. Laryngol. Soc. (treas. 1983), Phila. Pediatric Soc., Phila Laryngol. Soc.

(pres. 1984), Phila. Soc. Facial Plastic Surgeons, Politzer Soc., Soc. Ear, Nose and Throat Advances in Children (pres. 1983), Am. Soc. Pediatric Otolaryngology (pres. 1991), Soc. Univ. Otolarungologists, Am. Acad. Pediatrics, Alpha Omega Alpha, Phi Chi. Home: 1057 Beaumont Rd Berwyn PA 19312-2007 Office: Children's Hosp Phila 34th And Civic Center Blvd Philadelphia PA 19104-4343

POTT, SANDRA KAY, finance company executive; b. Denver, Apr. 1, 1946; d. Sanford N. and Mary Helen (Davis) Groendyke; m. Joel Frederic Pott, Mar. 7, 1970; children: Eric Christopher, Jessica Elizabeth. BA in English, Ea. Mich. U., 1969. CFP, Mich. Account exec. Dean Witter Reynolds, Troy, Mich., 1984-93, assoc. v.p., 1993—. Mem. AAUW (bd. dirs. 1977-83), Nat. Assn. Women Bus. Owners (bd. dirs. 1994—), Royal Oak C. of C. (edn. com. 1991—, econ. devel. com. 1991—), Royal Oak League Women Voters (bd. dirs. 1977-83). Office: Dean Witter Reynolds 100 W Big Beaver Ste 500 Troy MI 48099

POTTASH, A. CARTER, psychiatrist, hospital executive; b. Phila., Nov. 30, 1948; s. R. Robert and Elizabeth (Braunschweig) P. BS with high honors, Trinity Coll., Hartford, Conn., 1970; MD, Yale U., 1974. Intern in internal medicine Tufts U. Sch. Medicine, Springfield, Mass., 1974-75; clin. fellow Yale-New Haven Hosp., 1977-78; postdoctoral fellow Yale U., New Haven, 1975-78; med. dir. Psychiatric Diagnostic Labs. Am., Summit, N.J., 1979-83; lectr. in field; cons. in field; vis. prof. St. Elizabeth Med. Ctr., Northeastern Ohio U. Coll Medicine, 1979; clin. prof. NYU, 1989—; pres. Fla. Consultation Svcs., P.A., West Palm Beach, 1992—, Psychiatric Assocs. N.J., P.A., Summit, N.J., 1978-93, Met. Med. Group P.C., N.Y.C., 1981—, So. Fla. Med. Group P.A., Delray Beach, 1984-93, Stony Lodge Hosp., Inc., Briarcliff Manor, N.Y., 1985—, Hampton Med. Group, P.A., Rancocas, N.J., 1986—; exec. med. dir. Fair Oaks Hosp., Summit, 1978-92, The Regent Hosp., N.Y.C., 1981-92, Lake Hosp of the Palm Beaches, Lake Worth, Fla., 1984-92, Fair Oaks Hosp. at Boca/Delray, Fla., 1984-92, Hampton Hosp., Rancocas, N.J., 1986-95—; chmn. Stony Lodge Hosp., Briarcliff Manor, N.Y., 1985—. Editor Psychiatry Letter, 1980-91; mem. editl. bd. Internat. Jour. Psychiatry in Medicine, 1978-87, The Psychiatric Hosp., 1982—, Jour. Nat. Assn. Pvt. Psychiatric Hosps., 1980-81, Fla. Psychiatry Newsletter, 1992—; reviewer Jour. Nervous and Mental Disorders, Alcoholism, Clin. and Exptl. Rsch., JAMA, Hosp. and Cmty. Psychiatry; contbr. numerous articles to profl. jours. Mem. adv. bd. Mothers for More Halfway Houses, N.Y.C., 1986—; cons. com. on women and alcoholism Jr. League of N.Y.C., 1987; bd. dirs. Met. Soc. Arts, N.Y.C., 1984-87. Fellow Am. Coll. Clin. Pharmacology, Assn. Clin. Scientists, Nat. Acad. Clin. Biochemistry, Am. Psychiat. Assn., The Acad. Medicine N.J.; mem. AMA, Soc. Neurosci., Nat. Acad. Clin. Biochemistry, Palm Beach County Med. Soc., Am. Acad. Clin. Psychiatrists, British Brain Research Assn. (hon.), European Brain and Behavioral Soc. (hon.), Am. Soc. of Addiction Medicine, Am. Academy of Addiction Psychiatry (founding mem. 1987), Am. Psychiatric Assn., Fla. Med. Soc., Palm Beach County Psychiatric Soc., Med. Soc. State N.Y., Med. Soc. N.J., Union County Med. Soc., N.Y. Athletic Club, Canoe Brook Country Club, Beacon Hill Club, Phi Beta Kappa, Delta Phi Alpha. Office: PO Box 511 West Palm Beach FL 33402-0511

POTTER, BARRETT GEORGE, historian, educator; b. Cortland, N.Y., Oct. 28, 1929; s. Leo Barrett and Charlotte May (Hazen) P.; B.A., Hobart Coll., 1952, M.S. in Edn., 1955; M.A., Cornell U. 1959; Ph.D. in History, SUNY, Buffalo, 1973; postgrad. SUNY, Cortland, 1952, Syracuse U., 1962; m. Beverly Ann Platts, Aug. 6, 1961; children—Barrett George, Heather Gaye. Instr., Hobart Coll., Geneva, N.Y., 1952-54; lectr. SUNY, New Paltz, 1955-57, summer 1960; high sch. tchr., Bayport, N.Y., 1957-58; asst. mgr. 1000 Acres Ranch Resort, Stony Creek, N.Y., 1958-59; asst. prof. history SUNY Tech. Coll., Alfred, 1959-64, prof., 1965-92, prof. emeritus, 1992—, chmn. dept., 1965-71; teaching asst. SUNY, Buffalo, 1964-65; adj. prof. Elmira Coll., 1978, Rochester Inst. Tech., 1979, Alfred U., 1985; tutor Empire State Coll., 1985. Mem. Alfred-Almond Central Sch. Bd. Edn., 1971-74, pres., 1973; trustee Alfred Rural Cemetery Assn., 1973-81, pres., 1979-80; trustee Alfred Hist. Soc., 1974-76, 85-88, Union U. Ch., Alfred, 1977-80, Alfred Village, 1987—; acting mayor City of Alfred, 1990-92; vice chmn. Alfred Community Chest, 1983-90. Coe Found. fellow in Am. Studies, 1961. Mem. Am. Fedn. Musicians, Phi Beta Kappa. Republican. Episcopalian. Clubs: Elks, Masons, Foster Lake (exec. com. 1972-74). Contbr. articles to profl. jours. Home: 76 S Main St Alfred NY 14802-1323 Office: Social Science Dept SUNY Alfred NY 14802

POTTER, BLAIR BURNS, editor; b. Spartanburg, S.C., Mar. 11, 1946; d. Leonard Hill and Nancy Milner (Vaughan) Burns; m. Robert Arthur Potter, May 24, 1974; children: Lillian Howard, Gordon Leonard. BA, Hollins Coll., Roanoke, Va., 1968; MA, U. N.C., 1971. Editl. asst. Professional Engineer, Washington, 1968-69; manuscript editor Science, Washington, 1970-74; freelance editor, 1974-85; assoc. editor Health Adminstrn. Press/U. Mich., Ann Arbor, 1985-87; freelance editor NAS, Inst. Medicine, Office Tech. Assessment, Washington, 1987-92; assoc. editor Science News, Washington, 1992, mng. editor, 1992—; editl. cons. White House Task Force on Infant Mortality, Washington, 1990, Nat. Commn. on Orphan Diseases, Washington, 1988-89, Nat. Comm. on Children, Washington, 1992-93; lay mem. protocol com. Nat. Heart, Lung and Blood Inst., Bethesda, Md., 1973. Whittaker fellow, 1969-70; Hollins Coll. scholar, 1964-68, English-Speaking Union scholar, 1967. Mem. Nat. Press Club. Avocations: gardening, historic preservation, antique American furniture, sailing. Home: 12 Revell St Annapolis MD 21401 Office: Science News 1719 N St NW Washington DC 20036

POTTER, CLARKSON NOTT, publishing consultant; b. Mendham, N.J., May 17, 1928; s. John Howard Nott and Margaretta (Wood) P.; m. Ruth Delafield, June 14, 1949 (div. Aug. 1965); children—Howard Alonzo, Christian, Margaretta, Edward Eliphalet; m. Pamela Howard, Nov. 26, 1973 (div. Apr. 1976); 1 son, Jack Rohe Howard-Potter; m. Helga Maass, Oct. 31, 1981. B.A., Union Coll., 1950. With Doubleday & Co., N.Y.C., 1950-57; sr. editor, advt. mgr., mng. editor Dial Press, N.Y.C., 1958-59; founder, editor-in-chief Clarkson N. Potter Inc., N.Y.C., 1959-76; dir., editor-in-chief Barre Pub. Co. Inc., Mass., 1974-76; pres. The Brandywine Press, N.Y.C., 1976-80; lit. agt., publishing cons. Jamestown, R.I., 1980-86; pres. The Kestrel Press, Inc., 1992—; bd. dirs. Beckham House Pubs., Inc., Hampton, Va.; trustee Newport (R.I.) Art Mus., 1994—. Author: Writing for Publication, 1990, Who Does What and Why in Book Publishing, 1990. Mem. Century Club (N.Y.C.), Newport Reading Room. Home and Office: 5 Westwood Rd Jamestown RI 02835-1165

POTTER, CLEMENT DALE, public defender; b. McMinnville, Tenn., Dec. 22, 1955; s. Johnnie H. and Elnora (Harvey) P.; children: Cory, Sarah, John Warren. BS, Middle Tenn. State U., 1984; JD, U. Tenn., 1987; cert., Tenn. Law Enforcement Acad., 1980. Bar: Tenn. 1987, U.S. Dist. Ct. (ea. dist.) Tenn. 1989. Pvt. practice law McMinnville, 1987-89; city judge City of McMinnville, Tenn., 1988-89; pub. defender 31st Dist. State Tenn., McMinnville, 1989—. Asst. to gen. editor Tools for the Ultimate Trial, 1st edit., 1985. Mem. Warren County Kiwanis Club, McMinnville, 1984-89, pres., 1986-87; mem. Leadership McMinnville, 1989, chmn., 1995-96; TSSAA H.S. Football referee. Staff sgt. USAF, 1974-80. Named McMinnville Warren County C. of C. Vol. of Yr., 1995; recipient D. Porter Henegar & Fred L. Hoover Sr. Bell Ringer award, 1995. Mem. ABA, Cheer Mental Health Assn. (dir. 1988—, pres. 1991-96), Harmony House Inc. (dir. 1993-95), Noon Exch. Club McMinnville (dir. 1992—, sec. 1994, pres. 1996—). Avocations: computers, gardening, coaching youth softball. Office: Pub Defender 31st Dist PO Box 510 314 W Main St Mc Minnville TN 37110

POTTER, CORINNE JEAN, librarian; b. Edmonton, Alta., Can., Feb. 2, 1930; d. Vernon Harcourt and Beatrice A. (Demaray) MacNeill; m. William B. Potter, Aug. 11, 1951 (div. Jan. 1978); children—Caroline, Melanie, Theodore, William, Ellen. B.A., Augustana Coll., 1952; M.S., U. Ill., 1976. Br. librarian Rock Island (Ill.) Pub. Library, 1967-73, children's work supr., 1973-74; dir. St. Ambrose U. Library, Davenport, Iowa, 1978—; chairperson Quad City Library Dir.'s Publicity Com., 1984-88. Chairperson Com. of the Whole for Local Automated Circulation and Online Catalog System, 1989-90. Mem. ALA, Assn. Coll. and Research Libraries (sec., v.p., pres. Iowa chpt. 1979-82), Iowa Library Assn. (com. chmn. 1983-84), Iowa Pvt. Academic Libraries Consortium (sec.-treas. 1986-89), Iowa Oline Computer Libr. Ctr. Users Group (v.p.-pres. elect 1988-89, pres. 1989-90). Office: St Ambrose U Libr McMullen Libr 518 W Locust St Davenport IA 52803-2829

POTTER, DAVID SAMUEL, former automotive company executive; b. Seattle, Jan. 16, 1925; children: Diana (Mrs. Paul Bankston), Janice (Mrs. Robert Meadows), Tom, Bill; m. Nancy Shaar, Dec. 1979. B.S., Yale U., 1945; Ph.D., U. Wash., 1951. Mem. staff Applied Physics Lab., U. Wash., 1946-60, asst. dir., 1955-60; with Gen. Motors Corp., 1960-73; chief engr. Milw. ops. GM Delco Electronics div., 1970-73; dir. research and devel. Detroit Diesel Allison div., 1973; asst. sec. for research and devel. Dept. Navy, 1973-74, under sec., 1974-76; v.p. environ. activities staff Gen. Motors Corp., Detroit, 1976-78; v.p. and group exec. public affairs group Gen. Motors Corp., 1978-83, v.p. in charge power products and def. ops. group, 1983-85; ret., 1985; mem. Gov. Calif. Adv. Commn. Ocean Resources, 1964-68; mem. adv. panel Nat. Sea Grant Program, 1966; adv. bd. Naval Postgrad. Sch., Dept. Energy; bd. dirs. Sanders Assocs. Inc., Sci. Applications Internat. Co., John Fluke Mfg. Co., Lockheed Martin Corp. Served to ensign USNR, 1943-46. Mem. Nat. Acad. Engring., NSF, Marine Tech. Soc., Am. Phys. Soc., AIAA, Am. Acoustical Soc., Nat. Oceanographic Assn. (v.p. 1966), Soc. Automotive Engrs. (chmn. tech. bd. 1978-79, dir. 1981-83), Cosmos Club (Washington), Detroit Club, Birmingham Athletic Club (Mich.), Birnam Wood Country Club (Montecito, Calif.), Santa Barbara Club. Research cosmic rays, magnetics, underwater acoustics. Home: 877 Lilac Dr Santa Barbara CA 93108-1438

POTTER, DEBORAH ANN, news correspondent, educator; b. Hagerstown, Md., June 10, 1951; d. Peter R. and H. Louise (McDevitt) P.; m. Robert H. Witten, May 1, 1982; children: Cameron, Evan. BA, U. N.C., 1972; MA, Am. U., 1977. Assignment editor Sta. WMAL-TV, Washington, 1972-73, prodr., 1973-74; reporter Voice of Am., Washington, 1974-77; anchor Sta. KYW, Phila., 1977-78, CBS Radio, N.Y.C., 1978-81; White House corr. CBS News, Washington, 1981-85, state dept. corr., 1985-87, congl. corr., 1987-89, environ. corr., 1989-91; contbg. corr. 48 Hours, 1989-90; host Nightwatch CBS News, Washington, 1991; Washington corr. Cable News Network, Washington, 1991-94; asst. prof. Sch. Comm. Am. U., Washington, 1994-95; dir. Poynter Election Project, St. Petersburg, Fla., 1995—; faculty mem. Poynter Inst. Media Studies. Co-author: Poynter Election Handbook; host (video prodn.) Beyond the Spotted Owl, 1993, Health Beat, 1994, Risk Reporting, 1995. Mem. adv. coun. Environ. Journalism Ctr., Radio and TV News Dirs. Found., Washington, 1994—; lay reader St. Alban's Episc. Ch., Washington, 1988-89. Mem. Radio TV News Dirs. Assn., Soc. of Environ. Journalists, Investigative Reporters and Editors, Assn. for Edn. in Journalism and Mass Comm., U. N.C. Alumni Assn. (bd. dirs. 1990-93, Disting. Young Alumna award 1990). Office: Poynter Institute 801 3rd St S Saint Petersburg FL 33701

POTTER, DELCOUR S., finance company executive; b. 1935. AB, Bowdoin Coll., 1957. With Gen. Electric Corp., N.Y.C., 1957-65, asst. treas., 1965-72; v.p. fin. Chase Manhattan Mortgage and Realty Trust, N.Y.C., 1972-75, resigned; sec.-treas. Pvt. Export Funding Corp., N.Y.C., 1975—, pres., chief exec. officer. With U.S. Army, 1958. Office: Private Export Funding Corp 280 Park Ave New York NY 10017

POTTER, ELIZABETH STONE, academic administrator; b. Mount Kisco, N.Y., Oct. 18, 1931; d. Ralph Emerson and Elizabeth (Fleming) Stone; m. Harold David Potter, Aug. 1, 1953; children: David Stone, Nicholas Fleming. BA, Wellesley Coll., 1953. Tchr. Spence Sch., N.Y.C., 1960-62; from audiovisual head to asst. mid. sch. head, sci. coord. Chapin Sch., N.Y.C., 1970—; evaluator NYSAIS, N.Y.C., 1994-95. Mem. NSTA, ATIS. Avocations: reading, skiing, tennis, swimming, gardening. Home: 1160 5th Ave New York NY 10029-6936 Office: Chapin Sch 100 E End Ave New York NY 10028

POTTER, EMMA JOSEPHINE HILL, language educator; b. Hackensack, N.J., July 18, 1921; d. James Silas and Martha Loretta (Pyle) Hill; m. James H. Potter, Mar. 26, 1949. AB cum laude with honors in Classics (scholar), Alfred (N.Y.) U., 1943; AM, Johns Hopkins U., 1946. Tchr. Latin, Balt. County Pub. Schs., 1943-44; instr. French, Spanish, Balt. Poly. Inst., 1950-83; instr. Spanish adult edn. classes, 1946-48; treas. Bruno-Potter Inc., acctg. Trustee James Harry Potter Gold Medal, ASME. Mem. Johns Hopkins U., Alfred U. alumni assns., Internat. Platform Assn., Johns Hopkins U. Faculty Club. Democrat. Home: 419 3rd Ave Avon By The Sea NJ 07717-1244

POTTER, ERNEST LUTHER, lawyer; b. Anniston, Ala., Apr. 30, 1940; s. Ernest Luther and Dorothy (Stamps) P.; m. Gwyn Johnston, June 28, 1958; children: Bradley S., Lauren D. A.B., U. Ala., 1961, LL.B., 1963, LL.M., 1979. Bar: Ala. 1963, U.S. Dist. Ct. (no. dist.) Ala. 1964, U.S. Ct. Appeals (5th cir.) 1965, U.S. Supreme Ct. 1972, U.S. Ct. Appeals (11th cir.) 1982. Assoc. Burnham & Klinefelter, Anniston, Ala., 1963-64; assoc. Bell, Richardson, Cleary, McLain & Tucker, Huntsville, Ala., 1964-66, ptnr., 1967-70; ptnr. Butler & Potter, Huntsville, 1971-82; pvt. practice, Huntsville, 1983—; bd. dirs. VME Microsystems Internat. Corp., Inc.; mem. faculty Inst. Bus. Law and Polit. Sci., U. Ala.-Huntsville, 1965-67. Contbg. author: Marital Law, 1976, 2d edit. 1985. V.p. No. Ala. Kidney Found., 1976-77; treas. Madison County Dem. Exec. Com., 1974-78; bd. dirs. United Way Madison County, 1982-87, Girls Inc., Huntsville, 1988—, pres., 1991. Mem. Ala. Law Inst., ABA, Ala. Bar Assn., Madison County Bar Assn., Phi Beta Kappa, Order of Coif. Episcopalian. Home: 1284 Becket Dr SE Huntsville AL 35801-1670 Office: 200 Clinton Ave W Huntsville AL 35801-4918

POTTER, GLENN EDWARD, hospital administrator; b. Canton, Ill., July 4, 1943; married. BA, Ottowa U., 1965; MA, Washington U., 1972. Bus. mgr. Graham Hosp., Canton, 1966-70; adm. res. Samaritan Health Svc., Phoenix, 1971-72; asst. adminstr. Desert Samaritan Hosp., Mesa, Ariz., 1972-73; dir. profl. svcs. N.C. Meml. Hosp., Chapel Hill, 1973-77; sr. v.p. Iowa Methodist Med. Ctr., Des Moines, 1982; v.p. ops. Cuyahoga County Hosp., Cleve., 1977-82; exec. v.p. adminstr. Iowa Methodist Med. Ctr., Des Moines, 1983-90; vice chancelor Kans. U. Med. Ctr., Kansas City, 1990—, now consultant; adj. prof. in field. Fellow HF Med. Assn., Kans. Hosp. Assn. (bd. dirs.). Office: U of Kansas Hospital 3901 Rainbow Blvd Kansas City KS 66160*

POTTER, HAMILTON FISH, JR., lawyer, consultant, author; b. Bklyn., Dec. 21, 1928; s. Hamilton Fish and Alma Virginia (Murray) P.; m. Virginia Fox Patterson, Sept. 17, 1953 (div. May 1979); children: Virginia Patterson, Hamilton Fish III, Robert Burnside, Elizabeth Stuyvesant; m. Maureen Ellen Cotter, Nov. 28, 1981; children: Nicholas Fish, Warwick Alonzo. B.A., Harvard U., 1950, LL.B., 1956. Bar: N.Y. 1957, U.S. Supreme Ct. 1961. Assoc. Sullivan & Cromwell, N.Y.C., 1956-65, ptnr., 1965-91. Bd. dirs. Berkshire Farm for Boys, N.Y.C., 1962-71, Alice and Hamilton Fish Libr., Garrison-on-Hudson, N.Y., 1980—; mem. Bd. Correction, N.Y.C., 1963-71; warden Ch. of Resurrection, 1972-74; trustee Episcopal Sch. of N.Y., 1969-76, Chapin Sch., 1975-81, Knox Sch., 1985—; warden All Saints Episcopal Ch., 1982-90; bd. dirs. Dutch Am. West Indies Found., 1984-89, The Netherlands Am. Found., 1989-92. Lt. (j.g.) USN, 1950-53, Korea. Mem. ABA (chmn. banking law com. 1975-80), Am. Bar Found., N.Y. State Bar Assn. (ho. of dels. 1978-80), N.Y. Bar Found., Assn. of Bar of City of N.Y. (chmn. banking law com. 1972-74), Am. Law Inst. (3-4-8 com. 1975-83), Mystery Writers Am. (assoc.). Home: 325 E 65th St New York NY 10021-6863 Office: c/o Sullivan and Cromwell 125 Broad St New York NY 10004-2498

POTTER, JAMES DOUGLAS, pharmacology educator; b. Waterbury, Conn., Sept. 26, 1944; s. Herbert Eugene and Jean Gladys (Troske) P.; m. Priscilla F. Strang, Aug. 9, 1985; children: Liesse, Andrew, Ian Brown. BS, George Washington U., 1965; PhD, U. Conn., 1970; postgrad. (fellow) Boston Biomed. Rsch. Inst., 1970-74. Staff scientist Boston Biomed. Research Inst., 1974-75; assoc. in neurology Harvard U. Med. Sch., 1974-75; asst. prof. cell biophysics Baylor Coll. Medicine, 1975-77; assoc. prof. pharmacology U. Cin., 1977-81, prof., 1981-83; chmn., prof. dept. molecular and cellular pharmacology U. Miami, 1983—; grant reviewer in field. Grantee NIH, 1978-81, 83—, Nat. Heart Lung and Blood Inst., 1978— (Merit award 1989—), Muscular Dystrophy Assn., 1983-94. Fellow Muscular Dystrophy Assn.; mem. AAAS, Am. Chem. Soc., Am. Soc. Pharmacology and Exptl. Therapeutics, Assn. for Med. Sch. Pharmacology (chmn.), Internat. Soc. Heart Rsch., Am. Heart Assn. (established investigator 1974-79), Am. Soc. Biochem. and Molecular Biologists, Cardiac Muscle Soc. (sec.-treas. 1992-94, pres. 1994-96), Biophys. Soc., Sigma Xi. Contbr. articles to profl. jours. Home: 7240 SW 127th St Miami FL 33156-5336 Office: U Miami Sch Medicine Dept of Molecular & Cellular Pharm 1600 NW 10th Ave Miami FL 33136

POTTER, JAMES EARL, retired international hotel management company executive; b. Utica, N.Y., July 25, 1933; s. Earl Moses and Helen May (Cruikshank) P. BS in Hotel Mgmt. with distinction, Cornell U., 1954, postgrad., 1955-56. Owner, propr. Old Drovers Inn, Dover Plains, N.Y., 1956-89; various acctg. positions Inter-Continental Hotels Corp., N.Y.C., 1960-62, fin. dir. for Asia and Pacific, 1963-69; v.p. Overseas Nat. Airways Hotels, N.Y.C., 1969-71; sr. v.p. Inter-Continental Hotels Corp., N.Y.C., 1972-89, London, 1990-92; instr. acctg. Cornell U., Ithaca, N.Y., 1957-59. Author: A Room with a World View, 1996. Trustee Opera Co. Boston, 1978-85; mem. coun. Cornell U., 1988-91. Mem. Culinary Inst. Am. (trustees com. on acad. policy 1980-90), Met. Opera Club (N.Y.C., house com.), Cornell Soc. Hotelmen, Cornell Club (N.Y.C.). Presbyterian. Avocation: opera.

POTTER, J(EFFREY) STEWART, property manager; b. Ft. Worth, July 8, 1943; s. Gerald Robert Potter and Marion June (Mustain) Tombler; m. Dianne Eileen Roberb, Dec. 31, 1970 (div. Aug. 1983); 1 child, Christopher Stewart; m. Deborah Ann Blevins, Oct. 20, 1991. AA, San Diego Mesa Coll., 1967. Cert. apartment mgr., apartment property supr., housing adminstr. Sales mgr. Sta. KJLM, La Jolla, Calif., 1964-67; mgr. inflight catering Host Internat., San Diego, 1967-69; lead aircraft refueler Lockheed Co., San Diego, 1969-70; property mgr. Internat. Devel. and Fin Corp., La Jolla, 1970-72; mgr. bus. property BWY Constn. Co., San Diego, 1972-73; mgr. residents Coldwell Banker, San Diego, 1973-74; mgr. Grove Investments, Carlsbad, Calif., 1974-76, Villa Granada, Villa Seville Properties Ltd., Don Cohn, Chula Vista, Calif., 1976-83; gen. mgr. AFL-CIO Bldg. Trades Corp., National City, Calif., 1983—; instr., Cert. Apt. Mgmt. San Diego Apt. Assn. Bd. dirs. San Diego County Apt. Assn., 1995—. Fellow Internat. Platform Assn., Nat. City C. of C., Toastmasters, Founding Families San Diego Hist. Soc., Am. Assn. Retired Persons, San Diego County Apt. Assn. (bd. dirs.), La Jolla Monday Night Club (treas. 1984-89). Roman Catholic. Avocations: golf, tennis, snow skiing. Home: 2550 5th Ave Ste 401 San Diego CA 92103-6622 Office: AFL-CIO Bldg Trades Corp 2323 D Ave National City CA 91950-6730

POTTER, JOHN FRANCIS, surgical oncologist, educator; b. N.Y.C., July 26, 1925; s. John Albert and Isabelle Cecelia (Sullivan) P.; m. Tanya Agnes Kristof, Nov. 19, 1955; children: Tanya Jean, Miriam Isabelle, John Mark. Student, Holy Cross Coll., 1943-45; MD, Georgetown Med. Sch., 1949. Intern Grasslands Hosp., Valhalla, N.Y., 1949-50; resident in surgery Grasslands Hosp., Valhalla, 1949-50, Georgetown U. Hosp., Washington, 1953-56; sr. investigator Nat. Cancer Inst., Bethesda, Md., 1957-60; chief divsn. surg. oncology Georgetown Med. Ctr., Washington, 1960-85; instr, asst.prof., then assoc. prof. surgery Georgetown U. Sch. Medicine, 1957-64, prof., 1969—; dir. Vincent T. Lombardi Cancer Rsch. Ctr., Washington, 1967-87; mem. U.S. Mil. Health Adv. Com. hon. prof. Universidad Cayetano Heredia, Lima, Peru, 1980. Lt. (j.g.) USNR, 1951-53. Recipient Pres.'s medal Georgetown U., 1991. Mem. Soc. Surg. Oncology (rep. adv. bd.), ACS, Assn. Am. Cancer Insts. (v.p. 1985-86, pres. 1986-87, bd. dirs. 1982, chmn. bd. dirs. 1987-88), So. Surg. Assn., Peruvian Cancer Soc. (hon.), Knights of Malta. Office: Georgetown U Med Ctr 3800 Reservoir Rd NW Washington DC 20007-2196

POTTER, JOHN LEITH, mechanical and aerospace engineer, educator, consultant; b. Metz, Mo., Feb. 5, 1923; s. Jay Francis Lee and Pearl Delores (Leeth) P.; m. Dorothy Jean Williams, Dec. 15, 1957; children: Stephen, Anne, Carol. BS in Aerospace Engring., U. Ala., Tuscaloosa, 1944, MS in Engring., 1949; MS in Engring. Mgmt., Vanderbilt U., 1976, PhD in Mech. Engring., 1974. Engr., educator various indsl., ednl. and govt. orgns., 1944-52; chief, flight and aerodyns. lab. Redstone Arsenal, Ala., 1952-56; mgr., div. chief, dep. tech. dir., sr. staff scientist Sverdrup Tech., Inc., Tullahoma, Tenn., 1956-83; research prof. Vanderbilt U., Nashville, 1983-92, prof. emeritus, 1992—; cons. engr. Nashville, 1983—; convener NATO-AGARD, U.S. and Eng., 1980-82, mem. working group, 1984-88; mem. adv. com. Internat. Symposium on Rarefied Gasdynamics, 1970—; invited lectr. USSR Acad. Scis., 1967; mem. NRC com. on assessment nat. aeronautical wind tunnel facilities, 1987-88; mem. NASA working groups, 1987—; mem. Engring. Accreditation Commn., 1985-90. Editor: Rarefied Gas Dynamics, 1977. Contbr. articles to profl. publs., chpts. to books. Chmn. bd. dirs. Coffee County Hist. Soc., Tenn., 1971-72; bd. dirs. Southeastern Amateur Athletic Union, 1972-73; pres. Tullahoma Swim Club, 1972-73, Sheffield Homeowners Assn., Nashville, 1983—. Recipient Outstanding Fellow award U. Ala. Aerospace Engring. Dept., 1987; elected 150th Anniversary Disting. Engring. Fellow U. Ala. Coll. Engring., 1988; USAF Arnold Engring. Devel. Ctr. fellow, 1993. Fellow AIAA (assoc. editor jour. 1970-73, publs. com. 1973-78, assoc. editor Progress in Astronautics and Aeronautics 1981-85, Gen. H.H. Arnold award Tenn. chpt. 1964); mem. Capstone Engring. Soc. (regional bd. dirs. 1972-77), Sigma Xi, Tau Beta Pi, Theta Tau, Pi Tau Sigma, Sigma Gamma Tau. Home: 200 Sheffield Pl Nashville TN 37215-3235 Office: Vanderbilt U Box 1592 Sta B Nashville TN 37235

POTTER, JOHN WILLIAM, federal judge; b. Toledo, Ohio, Oct. 25, 1918; s. Charles and Mary Elizabeth (Baker) P.; m. Phyllis May Bihn, Apr. 14, 1944; children: John William, Carolyn Diane, Kathryn Susan. PhB cum laude, U. Toledo, 1940; JD, U. Mich., 1946. Bar: Ohio 1947. Assoc. Zachman, Boxell, Schroeder & Torbet, Toledo, 1946-51; ptnr. Boxell, Bebout, Torbet & Potter, Toledo, 1951-69; mayor City of Toledo, 1961-67; asst. atty. gen. State of Ohio, 1968-69; judge 6th Dist. Ct. Appeals, 1969-82; judge U.S. Dist. Ct., Toledo, 1982—, sr. judge, 1992—; presenter in field. Sr. editor U. Mich. Law Rev., 1946. Pres. Ohio Mcpl. League, 1965; past assoc. pub. mem. Toledo Labor Mgmt. Commn.; past pres., bd. dirs. Commn. on Rels. with Toledo (Spain); past bd. dirs. Cummings Sch. Toledo Opera Assn., Conlon Ctr.; past trustee Epworth United Meth. Ch.; hon. chmn. Toledo Festival Arts, 1980. Capt. F.A., U.S. Army, 1942-46. Decorated Bronze Star; recipient Leadership award Toledo Bldg. Congress, 1965, Merit award Toledo Bd. Realtors, 1967, Resolution of Recognition award Ohio Ho. of Reps., 1982, award for outstanding rsch. or svc. in law or govt. Ohio State Bar Found., 1995. Fellow Am. Bar Found., Am. Judicature Soc., 6th Jud. Cir. Dist. Judges Assn., Fed. Judges Assn.; mem. ABA, Ohio Bar Assn. (Outstanding Rsch. award 1995), Toledo Bar Assn. (exec. com. 1962-64, award 1992), Lucas County Bar Assn., Toledo Area C. of C. (v.p. 1973-74), U. Toledo Alumni Assn. (past pres.), Toledo Zool. Soc. (past bd. dirs.), Old Newsboys Club, Toledo Club, Kiwanis (past pres.), Phi Kappa Phi. Home: 2418 Middlesex Dr Toledo OH 43606-3114 Office: US Dist Ct 210 US Courthouse 1716 Spielbusch Ave Toledo OH 43624-1347

POTTER, KARL HARRINGTON, philosophy educator; b. Oakland, Calif., Aug. 19, 1927; s. George Reuben and Mabel (Harrington) P.; m. Antonia Fleak, June 26, 1957; children: David Fleak, Julie Ann. Grad., Taft Sch., 1945; AB, U. Calif. at Berkeley, 1950; MA, Harvard U., 1952, PhD, 1955. Instr. philosophy Carleton Coll., 1955-56; mem. faculty U. Minn., 1956-71, prof. philosophy, 1965-70, chmn. dept., 1964-67, dir., 1967-70; prof. philosophy and South Asian studies U. Wash., Seattle, 1971—, chmn. South Asia program, 1972-86, chmn. dept. philosophy, 1986-91. Author: The Padarthatattvanirupanam of Raghunatha Siromani, 1957, Presuppositions of India's Philosophies, 1963, Ency. of Indian Philosophies, 1970, 77, 81, 94, Guide to Indian Philosophy, 1988. With USNR, 1945-46. Fulbright fellow, India, 1952-53, 59-60, 81. Am. Inst. Indian Studies fellow, India, 1963-64, 95. Mem. Assn. Asian Studies (bd. dirs., mem. South Asia regional coun. 1971-74, chmn. coun. 1972-74), Am. Philos. Assn. Univ. Profs., Am. Oriental Soc., Soc. Asian and Comparative Philosophy (pres. 1968-70). Home: 19548 47th Ave NE Seattle WA 98155-1720 Office: U Washington Dept Philosophy Seattle WA 98105

POTTER, LILLIAN FLORENCE, business executive secretary; b. Montreal, Que., Can., Oct. 19, 1912; came to U.S., 1934; naturalized citizen.; d. Thomas Joseph and Lily Rose (Robertson) Quirk; m. Theodore Edward Potter, July 20, 1932 (dec. Apr. 1980); children: Peter Edward, Stephen Thomas. Grad. high sch., Montreal, 1929, grad., 1931. Sr. sec. S.D. Warren div. Scott Paper Co., Westbrook, Maine, 1955-69, editor indsl. publ. S.D. Warren div., 1969-72; editor Nat. Antiques Rev. mag., Portland, Maine, 1972-77; exec. sec. Humboldt Portland Litho div. Humboldt Nat. Graphics, Inc., Fortuna, Calif., 1977—; free lance writer Guy Gannett Pub. Co., Portland, 1960-64. Author: (children's book) Once Upon an Autumn, 1984 (state 1st pl. award, nat. 3d pl. award), (antiques and collectibles) A Re-Introduction to Silver Overlay on Glass and Ceramics, 1992; co-author: (textbook, tchrs. manual) Foundations of Patient Care, 1981; asst. editor, N.E. dist. The Secretary mag., Profl. Secs. Internat., 1960-62; editor Maine Chpt. Bull., 1963-64. Recipient George Washington Honors medal Freedoms Found., Valley Forge, Pa., 1964, Sec. of Yr. award Portland chpt. Profl. Secs. Internat., 1967, Outstanding Svc. award State of Maine Sesquicentennial, 1970, Outstanding Svc. award Island Pond (Vt.) Hist. Soc. 1978. Mem. Maine Media Women (pres. 1970-71, Woman of Yr. 1973, Communicator of Achievement plaque and prize 1991), Maine Writers and Pubs. Alliance, Woman's Lit. Union, Portland Lyric Theater, Island Pond Hist. Soc., Jones Mus. Glass and Ceramics, Westbrook Woman's Club, OES (past matron, past pres.). Republican. Episcopalian. Avocations: reading, researching, antiques, swimming, gardening. Home: 80 Payson St Portland ME 04102-2851

POTTER, RALPH BENAJAH, JR., theology and social ethics educator; b. Los Angeles, May 19, 1931; s. Ralph Benajah and Vivian Irene MacNabb (Borden) P.; m. Jean Ishbel MacCormick, Aug. 15, 1953; children: Anne Elizabeth, Ralph Andrew, James David, Margaret Jean; m. Christine Iva Mitchell, Aug. 25, 1985 (div. 1995); children: Charles Benajah Mitchell Potter, Christopher Ralph Mitchell Potter. B.A., Occidental Coll., 1952; postgrad., Pacific Sch. Religion, 1952-53; B.D., McCormick Theol. Sem., 1955; Th.D. (Presbyn. Grad. fellow 1958-63, Rockefeller fellow 1961-62, Kent fellow 1963-64), Harvard, 1965. Ordained to ministry Presbyn. Ch., 1955; dir., pastor Clay County Presbyn. Larger Parish, Manchester, Ky., 1955-58; sec. social edn. Bd. Christian Edn., United Presbyn. Ch. in U.S.A., Phila., 1963-65; asst. prof. social ethics Harvard Div. Sch.; mem. Center for Population Studies, Harvard U, Cambridge, Mass., 1965-69; prof. social ethics Harvard Divinity Sch., 1969—; mem., prof., Ctr. for Population Studies, Harvard U., 1969-89; theologian-in-residence Am. Ch. in Paris, 1975; sr. rsch. scholar Kennedy Inst. for Bio-ethics Georgetown U., 1974; assoc. Lowell House, Harvard U.; founding fellow Hastings Ctr. Author: War and Moral Discourse, 1969; contbr. chpts. to The Religious Situation, 1968, 1968, Religion and the Public Order, 1968, Toward a Discipline of Social Ethics, 1972, The Population Crisis and Moral Responsibility, 1973, Community in America, 1988, also scholarly articles. Mem. Soc. Christian Ethics, Soc. for Values in Higher Edn., Société Européene de Culture, Am. Acad. Religion, Tocqueville Soc. Home: 7 Swan St Arlington MA 02174-6507 Office: 45 Francis Ave Cambridge MA 02138-1911

POTTER, ROBERT DANIEL, federal judge; b. Wilmington, N.C., Apr. 4, 1923; s. Elisha Lindsey and Emma Louise (McLean) P.; m. Mary Catherine Neilson, Feb. 13, 1954; children: Robert Daniel, Mary Louise, Catherine Ann. AB in Chemistry, Duke U., 1947, LLB, 1950; LLD (hon.), Sacred Heart Coll., Belmont, N.C., 1982. Bar: N.C. 1951. Pvt. practice law Charlotte, N.C., 1951-81; chief judge U.S. Dist. Ct. (we. dist.) N.C., 1981-90, dist. judge, 1990—, now sr. judge. Commr. Mecklenburg County, Charlotte, 1966-68. Served to 2d lt. U.S. Army, 1944-47, ETO. Mem. N.C. Bar Assn. Republican. Roman Catholic. Club: Charlotte City. Office: US Courthouse 250 Federal Bldg 401 W Trade St Charlotte NC 28202

POTTER, ROBERT JOSEPH, technical and business executive; b. N.Y.C., Oct. 29, 1932; s Mack and Ida (Bernstein) P.; married; children: Diane Gail, Suzanne Lee, David Craig. BS cum laude, Lafayette Coll., 1954; MA in Physics, U. Rochester, 1957, PhD in Optics, 1960. Cons. ANPA Research Inst., AEC Brookhaven Nat. Lab., RCA Labs., U.S. Naval Research Labs., 1952-60; mgr. optical physics and optical pattern recognition IBM Thomas J. Watson Research Center, Yorktown Heights, N.Y., 1960-65; assoc. dir. Applied Research Lab., Xerox Corp., Rochester, N.Y., 1965-67; v.p. advanced engring. Xerox Corp., 1967-68, v.p. devel. and engring., 1968-69; v.p., gen. mgr. Spl. Products and Systems div. Spl. Products and Sys. divsn. Xerox Corp., Stamford, Conn. and Pasadena, Calif., 1969-71; v.p. info. tech. group Xerox Corp., Rochester, 1971-73; v.p. info. tech. group Xerox Corp., Dallas, 1973-75, pres. Office Sys. divsn., 1975-78; sr. v.p., chief tech. officer Internat. Harvester Co., Chgo., 1978-82; with R.J. Potter & Co., 1983-84; group v.p. integrated office sys. No. Telecom Inc., Richardson, Tex., 1985-87; pres. and CEO Datapoint Corp., San Antonio, 1987-89; pres., CEO R.J. Potter Co., Dallas, 1990—; dir. Molex Inc. Contbr. articles to profl. jours. Trustee Ill. Inst. Tech. Recipient IBM Outstanding Tech. Contbn. award, 1964, Disting. Achievement award Soc. Mfg. Engrs., 1981; Kroner scholar Lafayette Coll., 1954; Disting. Rochester scholar U. Rochester, 1995. Fellow Optical Soc. Am., Am. Phys. Soc.; mem. Phi Beta Kappa, Sigma Xi. Office: R J Potter Co 5215 N O Connor Blvd Ste 975 Irving TX 75039-3713

POTTER, TREVOR ALEXANDER MCCLURG, lawyer; b. Chgo., Oct. 24, 1955; s. Charles Steele and Barbara (McClurg) P. AB, Harvard Coll., 1978; JD, U. Va., 1982. Bar: Ill. 1983, D.C. 1988. Counsel office of legal policy U.S. Dept. Justice, Washington, 1982-84; asst. gen. counsel FCC, Washington, 1984-85; atty. Wiley, Rein & Fielding, Washington, 1985-91; commr. Fed. Election Commn., Washington, 1991—, vice chmn., 1993, chmn., 1994-95; ptnr. Wiley, Rein & Fielding, Washington, 1996—. Republican. Episcopalian. Mem. ABA (chmn. com. on election law, adminstrv. law sect. 1993—). Office: Fed Election Commn 999 E St NW Fl 9 Washington DC 20463-0001

POTTER, WILLIAM BARTLETT, business executive; b. Washington, Jan. 4, 1938; s. George Holland and Virginia (Bartlett) P.; m. Simone Robert, June 6, 1964; children: Eva Simone, William Bartlett. A.B., Princeton U., 1960; M.B.A., Emory U., 1962. With Merc.-Safe Deposit & Trust Co., Balt., 1962—; asst. sec., asst. treas. Merc.-Safe Deposit & Trust Co., 1964-66, asst. v.p., 1966-68, v.p., 1968-69, sr. v.p., 1969-76, exec. v.p., 1976; exec. v.p. Preston Trucking Co., 1976-77, pres., 1977-86; chmn., pres. Preston Trucking, 1986-92; Preston Corp., 1986-93, chmn., 1994—; bd. dirs. Trinidad Nat. Bank. Mem. Md. Club. Home: PO Box 614 Trinidad CO 81082-0614

POTTER, WILLIAM GRAY, JR., library director; b. Duluth, Minn., Feb. 18, 1950; s. William Gray and Kathryn Martha (Scheuer) P.; m. Marsha Ann Munie, Sept. 23, 1982. BA, So. Ill. U., 1973; MLS, U. Ill., 1975, MA, 1975, PhD, 1984. Libr. U. Wis.-Whitewater, 1975-78; asst. dir. gen. svcs. U. Ill.-Urbana, 1978-85; assoc. dean librs. for tech. svcs., automation and systems Ariz. State U., Tempe, 1985-89; dir. librs. U. Ga., Athens, 1989—. Editor: Serials Automation, 1980, Libr. Trends, 1981, Info. Tech. and Librs., 1984-89; mem. editl. bd. Multi-Media Rev., 1989-92, OCLC Micro., 1990—, Libr. Hi-Tech., 1992—, Coll. and Rsch. Libr., 1996—. Contbr. articles to profl. jours. Bd. dirs. Richard B. Russell Found., 1989—, sec., 1990—; mem. adv. com. Ga. Libr. Svcs. and Constrn. Act; bd. trustees OCLC, 1994—; mem. svc. to the citizen com. Ga. Info. Tech. Policy Coun., 1996—. Mem. ALA, Libr. and Info. Tech. Assn. (pres. 1987-88), OCLC Users Coun. (del. 1990-94, pres. 1991-92), IBM (info. steering com. 1994-95, higher edn. adv. coun. 1995—), Beta Phi Mu. Home: 6 Dearing Pl 420 Waddell St Athens GA 30605-1070 Office: Univ of Georgia Libraries Athens GA 30602

POTTER, WILLIAM JAMES, investment banker; b. Toronto, Aug. 11, 1948; s. William Wakely and Ruby Loretta (Skidmore) P.; m. Linda Lee, Nov. 25, 1972; children: Lisa Michelle, Meredith Lee, Andrew David. AB, Colgate U., 1970; MBA, Harvard U., 1974. With White Weld & Co., Inc., N.Y.C., 1974-75, Toronto Dominion Bank, Toronto (Can.) and N.Y., 1975-78; group mgr. Toronto Dominion Bank, Toronto, 1979-82; 1st v.p. Barclays Bank PLC, N.Y.C., 1982-84; mng. dir. Prudential-Bache Securities, Inc., N.Y.C., 1984-89; pres. Ridgewood Capital Funding Inc., N.Y.C., 1989—; advisor Ladenberg Thalman Internat., 1990-92, Laidlaw Holdings, Inc., 1992-93; bd. dirs. 1st Australia Fund Inc., Md., 1st Australia Prime Income Fund Inc., Md., 1st Australia Prime Income Co. Ltd., New Zealand, Impulsora del Fondo Mex., Mexico City, Alexandria Bancorp, Can., Battery Techs. Inc., Can., 1st Commonwealth Fund, Md., Compuflex Inc., Del. Author: Finance for the Minerals Industry, 1985. Bd. dirs. Glen Ridge (N.J.) Community Fund, 1985—; fin. mem. Glen Ridge Congl. Ch., 1985—; trustee Glen Ridge Ednl. Found., 1994—. Mem. Nat. Fgn. Trade Coun. (bd. dirs., chmn. fin. com.), Harvard Club, Williams Club (N.Y.C.), Nat. Club (Toronto), Glen Ridge Country Club (N.J.), Buck Hill Country Club (Pa.), Internat. Platform Assn. (Washington). Congregationalist. Avocations: golf, tennis. Office: Ridgewood Group Internat Inc 156 W 56th St New York NY 10019-3800

POTTIE, ROSWELL FRANCIS, science and technology consultant; b. St. Peter's, N.S., Can., Oct. 28, 1933; s. John Henry and Margaret Mary (Landry) P.; m. Huguette Lacoste, Aug. 18, 1989; children: Michael F., Gregory J., Lisa M., David S. BS in Chemistry summa cum laude, St. Francis Xavier Univ., 1954; PhD in Chemistry, Notre Dame U., 1958. Postdoctoral fellow Notre Dame (Ind.) U., 1957-58, E.I. Du Pont de Nemours, Inc., Wilmington, Del., 1960-64; postdoctoral fellow NRC Can., Ottawa, 1958-60, research officer, 1964-74, asst. to sr. v.p., 1976-80; Atlantic regional dir. NRC Can., Halifax, N.S., 1980-83; v.p. regional labs. NRC Can., Ottawa, 1983-84, v.p. physical scis. and engring., 1984-86, sr. v.p. labs., 1986-87, exec. v.p., 1987-91; pvt. cons., 1991—; program officer Ministry of State for Sci. and Tech. (secondment), Ottawa, 1974-75; program analyst Treasury Bd. Can. (secondment), Ottawa, 1975-76; bd. govs. Ctr. for Cold Regions Resources Engring., St. John's; mem. N.B. (Can.) Research and Productivity Council, Fredericton, 1981—. Contbr. articles to profl. jours. Coach, exec. baseball, swimming and soccer clubs, Gloucester, Ont., 1970-76; pres. Gloucester Swim Club, 1973-75; exec. North Gloucester Recreation Assn., 1971-74. Recipient Gov. Gen.'s medal, St. Francis Xavier U., 1954. Mem. Can. Research Mgmt. Assn., St. Francis Xavier Alumni Assn. (Ottawa pres. 1970-73), Sigma Xi. Roman Catholic. Avocations: swimming, badminton, carpentry, ancient history. Home: 28 Bellefontaine Ct, Lawrencetown, NS Canada B2Z 1L3

POTTORFF, JO ANN, state legislator; b. Wichita, Kans., Mar. 7, 1936; d. John Edward McCluggage and Helen Elizabeth (Alexander) Ryan; m. Gary Nial Pottorff; children: Michael Lee, Gregory Nial. BA, Kansas State U., 1957; MA, St. Louis U., 1969. Elem. tchr. Pub. Sch., Keats and St. George, 1957-59; cons., elem. specialist Mid Continent Regional Edn. Lab., Kansas City, Mo., 1971-73; cons. Poindexter Assocs., Wichita, 1975; campaign mgr. Garner Shriver Congl. Camp, Wichita, 1976; interim dir. Wichita Area Rape Ctr., 1977; conf. coord. Biomedical Synergistics Inst., Wichita, 1977-79; real estate sales asst. Chester Kappelman Group, Wichita, 1979—; state rep. State of Kans., Topeka, 1985—. Mem. sch. bd. Wichita Pub. Schs., 1977-85; bd. dirs. Edn. Consol. and Improvement Act Adv. com., Kans. Found. for the Handicapped; mem. Children and Youth Adv. com. (bd. dirs.); active Leadership Kans.; chairperson women's network Nat. Conf., State Legislators; mem. Wichita Children's Home Bd. Recipient Disting. Svc. award Kans. Assn. Sch. Bds., 1983, Outstanding Svc. to Sch. Children of Nation award Coun. Urban Bds., 1984, awards Gov.'s Conf. for Prevention of Child Abuse and Neglect, Kans. Assn. Reading. Mem. Leadership Am. Alumnae (bd. dirs., sec.), Found. for Agr. in Classroom (bd. dirs.), Jr. League, Vet. Aux. (pres.), Bd. Nat. State Art Agys., Rotary, Ky. Assn. Rehab. Facilities (Ann. award), Nat. Order Women in Legislature (past bd. dirs.), Rotary, Chi Omega (pres.). Avocations: politics, traveling. Office: Chester Kappelman Group PO Box 8036 Wichita KS 67208-0036

POTTRUCK, DAVID STEVEN, brokerage house executive; b. 1948. BA, U. Pa., 1970, MBA, 1972. Now pres., CEO U.S. Govt., 1972-74; with Arthur Young & Co., 1974-76, sr. cons.; with Citibank N.Am., 1976-81, v.p.; with Shearson/Am. Express, 1981-84, sr. v.p. consumer mktg. and advt.; with Charles Schwab & Co., San Francisco, 1984—; exec. v.p. mktg., br. adminstr. Charles Schwab and Co., Inc.; pres., CEO The Charles Corp., Charles Schwab & Co.; pres., COO The Charles Schwab Corp. Office: Charles Schwab & Co Inc 101 Montgomery St San Francisco CA 94104-4122

POTTS, ANNIE, actress; b. Nashville, Oct. 28, 1952. Student, Calif. Inst. of Arts; BFA, Stephens Coll. Appeared in films including Corvette Summer, 1978, King of the Gypsies, 1978, Heartaches, 1982, Crime of Passion, 1984, Ghostbusters, 1984, Stick, 1985, Pretty in Pink, 1986, Jumpin' Jack Flash, 1986, Pass the Ammo, 1988, Who's Harry Crumb, 1989, Ghostbusters II, 1989, Texasville, 1990, Breaking the Rules, 1992, Toy Story (voice only) 1995; plays include Richard III, Charley's Aunt, Cymbeline; TV appearances include Black Market Baby, 1977, Flatbed Annie and Sweetie Pie: Lady Truckers, 1979, Cowboy, 1983, Why Me?, 1984, Ladies in Waiting; TV series include Goodtime Girls, 1980, Designing Women, 1986-1993, Love and War, 1993-95 (Emmy nomination, Lead Actress - Comedy Series, 1994), Dangerous Minds, 1996. Spokesperson Women for the Arthritis Found.; mem. aux. bd. MADD. *

POTTS, BARBARA JOYCE, historical society executive; b. L.A., Feb. 18, 1932; d. Theodore Thomas and Helen Mae (Kelley) Elledge; m. Donald A. Potts, Dec. 27, 1953; children: Tedd, Douglas, Dwight, Laura. AA, Graceland Coll., 1951; grad., Radiol. Tech. Sch., 1953; grad. program for sr. execs. in state and local govt., Harvard U., 1989. Radiol. technician Independence (Mo.) Sanitarium and Hosp., 1953, 58-59, Mercy Hosp., Balt., 1954-55; city coun. mem.-at-large City of Independence, 1978-82, mayor, 1982-90; exec. dir. Jackson County Hist. Soc., 1991—; chmn. Mid-Am. Regional Coun., Kansas City, Mo., 1984-85; bd. dirs. Mo. Mcpl. League, Jefferson City, 1982-90, v.p., 1986-87, pres., 1987, 88; chmn. Mo. Commn. on Local Govt. Cooperation, 1985-90. Author: Independence, 1985. Mem. Mo. Gov.'s Conf. Edn., 1976, Independence Charter Rev. Bd., 1977; bd. dirs. Hope House Shelter Abused Women, Independence, 1982—, Vis. Nurses Assn., 1990-93, Mid-Continent Coun. U.S. Girl Scouts, 1991-95; pres. Child Placement Svcs., Independence, 1972-89, Greater Kansas City region NCCJ, 1990—; trustee Independence Regional Health Ctr., 1982-90, 94—, Park Coll., 1989—, chmn. bd. trustees, 1995—; mem. Nat. Women's Polit. Caucus, 1978—; mem. adv. bd. Greater Mo. Focus on Leadership, mem. steering com., 1989—; bd. mem. Independence Cmty. Found., 1990—; bd. mem. Harry S. Truman Libr. Inst., 1995—. Recipient George Lehr Meml. award for community svc., 1989, Woman of Achievement award Mid-Continent coun. Girl Scouts U.S.A., 1983, 75th Anniversary Women of Achievement award Mid-Continent coun. Girl Scouts, 1987, Jane Adams award Hope House, 1984, Community Leadership award Comprehensive Mental Health Svcs., Inc., 1984, 90, Graceland Coll. Alumni Disting. Svc. award 1991, Disting. Citizen award Independence C. of C., 1993, Outstanding Community Svc. award Jackson County Inter-Agy. Coun., 1994; named Friend of Edn. Indpendence NEA, 1990. Mem. LWV (Community Svc. award 1990), Am. Inst. Pub. Svc. (mem. bd. nominators), Nat. Trust for Hist. Preservation. Mem. Reorganized LDS Ch. Home: 18508 E 30th Ter S Independence MO 64057-1904

POTTS, CHARLES AARON, management executive, writer; b. Idaho Falls, Idaho, Aug. 28, 1943; s. Verl S. and Sarah (Gray) P.; m. Judith Samimi, 1977 (div. 1986); 1 child, Emily Karen; m. Ann Weatherill, June 19, 1988; 1 child, Natalie Larise. BA in English, Idaho State U., 1965. Lic. real estate broker, Wash. Owner Palouse Mgmt., Inc., Walla Walla, Wash.; founder, dir. Litmus Inc., 1967-77; founding editor COSMEP, Berkeley, Calif., 1968; host poetry radio program Oasis, NPR-KUER, Salt Lake City, 1976-77; N.W. rep. Chinese Computer Communications, Inc., Lansing, Mich., 1988. Author: Little Lord Shiva, 1969, Rocky Mountain Man, 1978, A Rite to the Body, 1989, The Dictatorship of the Environment, 1991, Loading Las Vegas, 1991, How the South Finally Won the Civil War, 1994, others. Rep. to exec. com. 5th Congl. Dist., Wash. State Dem. Party, 1993-95. Recipient First Place Novel award Manuscript's Internat., 1991, Disting. Profl. Achievement award Idaho State U., 1994. Mem. Italian Heritage Assn. (ice cream chair 1990, award 1993), Walla Walla Area C. of C., Downtown W2 Found., Blue Mountain Arts Alliance, Fukuoka Internat. Forum, Chinese Lang. Computer Soc., Soc. Neurolinguistic Programming (master practitioner), Toastmasters. Avocations: tennis, raspberries. Office: Palouse Mgmt 34 S Colville St Walla Walla WA 99362-1920

POTTS, DAVID MALCOLM, population specialist, administrator; b. Sunderland, Durham, Eng., Jan. 8, 1935; came to U.S., 1978; s. Ronald Windle and Kathleen Annie (Cole) P.; m. Carolina Mervla Deys (div. 1979); children: Oliver, Sarah, Henry; m. Marcia Jaffe (dec. 1993); m. Martha Madison Campbell, Mar. 1995. M.A., St. Catherine's Coll., Cambridge, Eng., 1960; M.B., B.Chir., Univ. Coll. Hosp., London, 1962; Ph.D., Sidney Sussex Coll., Cambridge U., 1965. Intern North Middlesex Hosp., London, 1962-64; fellow Sidney Sussex Coll., Cambridge, 1964-67; med. dir. Internat. Planned Parenthood Fedn., London, 1968-78; pres. Family Health Internat., Research Triangle Park, N.C., 1978-91; Bixby prof. of Fam. Planning and Population U of Calif., Berkeley, Calif., 1991—; dir. Population Services Internat., Washington, Alan Guttmacher Inst., N.Y.C.; Tracey Maund lectr. Women's Hosp., Melbourne, Australia, 1989. Author: Abortion, 1977, Society and Fertility, 1979, Textbook of Contraceptive Practice, 1984, Queen Victoria's Gene, 1995; mem. editl. bd. Jour. Biosocial Sci. Recipient Hugh Moore award Population Crisis Com., 1972. Fellow Zool. Soc. Eng.; mem. Internat. Union for Sci. Study of Population. Avocations: history; writing. Home: 3416 Chris Ln San Mateo CA 94403-3937

POTTS, DOUGLAS GORDON, neuroradiologist; b. New Zealand, Jan. 27, 1927; came to U.S., 1960, naturalized, 1966; s. Leslie Andrew and Vera (Morgan) P.; m. Ann Jean Frank, June 16, 1962; children: David Andrew, Kenneth Morgan, Alison Jean. B.Sc., Canterbury Univ. Coll., Christchurch, New Zealand, 1946; M.B., Ch.B., U. Otago, Dunedin, New Zealand, 1951; M.D., U. New Zealand, 1960. Intern Auckland (New Zealand) Hosp., 1952-53, resident radiology, 1954-57; resident Central Middlesex Hosp., London, Eng., 1957-58; sr. registrar Atkinson Morley's Hosp., London, Eng., 1958-59, Nat. Hosp., London, Eng., 1959-60; radiologist Presbyn. Hosp., N.Y.C., 1960-67, N.Y. Hosp., 1967-85; prof. radiology Cornell U. Med. Coll., 1970-85; prof., chmn. dept. radiology U. Toronto, Ont., Can., 1985-91; ret., 1992. Author: (with Pool) Aneurysms and Arteriovenous Anomalies of the Brain, 1965; editor: (with T.H. Newton) Radiology of the Skull and Brain, Vol. 1, 1971, Vol. 2, 1974, Vol. 3, 1977, Vol. 4, 1978, Vol. 5, 1981, Modern Neuroradiology, Vols. 1 and 2, 1983. Mem. Am. Soc. Neuroradiology (pres. 1970-71).

POTTS, ERWIN REA, newspaper executive; b. Pineville, N.C., Apr. 20, 1932; s. Jennings Bryan and Edith Maxine (Matthews) P.; m. Silvia Antuna Montalbo, Feb. 18, 1961; children: Matthew Kingsley, Jeffrey Manuel, Bryan Erwin (dec.). Student, Mars Hill (N.C.) Jr. Coll., 1950-52; A.B. in Journalism, U. N.C., 1954. Reporter, editor Knight Newspapers, Miami, Fla., 1958-70; city editor Miami Herald, 1967-70; v.p., gen. mgr. Tallahassee Democrat, 1970-73, Charlotte (N.C.) Observer, News, 1973-75; pres. McClatchy Newspapers (Sacramento Bee, Fresno Bee, Modesto Bee, Anchorage Daily News, Tri-City Herald, Tacoma News Tribune, Rock Hill Herald, Beaufort Gazette, Hilton Head Island Packet, 10 other newspapers), Sacramento, Calif., Wash., S.C., 1975—; chief exec. officer McClatchy Newspapers (Sacramento Bee, Fresno Bee, Modesto Bee, Anchorage Daily News, Tri-City Herald, Tacoma News Tribune, 13 other newspapers), Sacramento, Calif., Wash., S.C., 1989—. Bd. dirs. Nespaper Advt. Bur.; bd. visitors U. N.C. Sch. Journalism, Stanford U. Knight fellowships. With USMC, 1955-58. Mem. Calif. Newspaper Pubs. Assn., Am. Newspaper Assn. (govt. affairs com.), API (regional adv. bd.). Office: Mc Clatchy Newspapers PO Box 15779 2100 Q St Sacramento CA 95852 also: The Modesto Bee PO Box 3928 1325 H St Modesto CA 95354-2427

POTTS, GERALD NEAL, manufacturing company executive; b. Franklin, N.C., Apr. 10, 1933; s. Joseph Thomas and Virgie (Bryant) P.; m. Ann Eliza Underwood, Dec. 21, 1956 (div. 1991); children: Catherine, Thomas, Alice. B.S., U. N.C., 1954; grad., Advanced Mgmt. Program, Harvard, 1973. With Vulcan Mold & Iron Co., Chgo., 1957-59; sales engr. Vulcan Mold & Iron Co., 1959-62; gen. sales mgr. Vulcan Mold & Iron Co., Latrobe, Pa., 1963-65; v.p. sales Vulcan Mold & Iron Co., 1965-68; v.p. Vulcan, Inc., Latrobe, 1968-72; exec. v.p. Vulcan, Inc., 1972-73, pres., 1973-85, chief exec. officer, 1977-85, chmn., 1981-85; group exec. Teledyne Inc., 1985-92; pres. Woodings Verona Tool Works Inc., 1993—; Active Young Pres.'s Orgn., 1973-83. Bd. dirs. Latrobe Area Hosp., 1967—, chmn., 1985-88; trustee Greater Latrobe Community Chest, 1970-87, pres., 1978-79; adv. bd. U. Pitts. at Greensburg, 1974-80; trustee Seton Hill Coll., Greensburg, 1978-80. Served with AUS, 1954-56. Mem. Laurel Valley Golf Club, Rolling Rock Club, Duquesne Club (Pa.), Masons (32 deg.), Shriners, Chi Phi. Office: PO Box 126 Verona PA 15147-0126

POTTS, JOHN THOMAS, JR., physician, educator; b. Phila., Jan. 19, 1932; married; 3 children. B.A., LaSalle Coll, Phila., 1953; M.D., U. Pa., Phila., 1957. From intern to asst. resident in medicine Mass. Gen. Hosp., Boston, 1957-59; resident Nat. Heart Inst., 1959-60, research fellow in medicine, 1960-63, sr. research staff, 1963-66, head sect. polypeptide hormones, 1966-68; chief endocrine unit Mass. Gen. Hosp., Boston, 1968-81, chief gen med. svc., 1981—; from asst. to assoc. prof. medicine Harvard U. Med. Sch., Boston, 1968-75, prof., 1975-81, Jackson prof. clin. medicine, 1981—; chief endocrine unit Mass. Gen. Hosp., Boston, 1968-81, chief gen. med., 1981—. Recipient Ernest Oppenheimer award, Andre Lichwitz prize Endocrine Soc., 1968, Fred Conrad Koch award Endocrine Soc., 1991, William F. Neumann award Am. Soc. Bone and Mineral Rsch. Fellow AAA; mem. Am. Soc. Biol. Chemistry, Endocrine Soc. (pres. 1987), Assn. Am. Physicians, Am. Fedn. Clin. Research, Am. Soc. Clin. Investigation, Inst. Medicine. Office: Mass Gen Hosp Med Svcs Fruit St Boston MA 02114-2620*

POTTS, KEVIN T., emeritus chemistry educator; b. Sydney, Australia, Oct. 26, 1928; married; children: Mary Ellen, Jeannette, Karen, Susan. B.Sc., U. Sydney, 1950, M.Sc., 1951; D. of Philosophy in Organic Chemistry, Oxford U., Eng., 1954, D.Sc., 1973. Demonstrator chemistry U. Sydney, 1950, teaching fellow, 1951; research asst. organic chemistry Oxford U., 1951-54; scientist Med. Research Council of Eng., 1954-56; research asst. organic chemistry Harvard, 1956-58; lectr. Adelaide, 1958-61; asso. prof. chemistry U. Louisville, 1961-65; assoc. prof. Rensslaer Poly. Inst., 1965-66; prof. chemistry Rensselaer Poly. Inst., 1966-94; prof. emeritus Rensselaer Poly Inst., 1994—; chmn. dept. Rensselaer Poly. Inst., 1973-80. Contbr. articles in field organic chemistry to sci. jours. Grantee Nat. Cancer Inst., Nat. Heart Inst., Dept. Energy, NSF, Am. Chem. Soc.-Petroleum Rsch. Fund. Mem. AAAS, Am. Chem. Soc., Brit. Chem. Soc., Royal Soc. Chemistry. Home: 102 Pelican Cove Sneads Ferry NC 28460-9520 Office: Rennselaer Poly Inst Dept Chemistry 110 Eighth Troy NY 12180

POTTS, RAMSAY DOUGLAS, lawyer, aviator; b. Memphis, Oct. 24, 1916; s. Ramsay Douglas and Ann Clifton (VanDyke) P.; m. Veronica Hamilton Raynor, Dec. 22, 1945 (dec. May 1993); children: Ramsay Douglas, David Hamilton, Lesley Ann, Lindsay Veronica. B.S., U. N.C., 1941; LL.B., Harvard U., 1948. Bar: Tenn. 1948, D.C. 1954, U.S. Supreme Ct. 1957. Commd. 2d lt. USAAF, 1941, advanced through grades to maj. gen. Res., 1961; various combat and operational assignments (8th Air Force and Air Force Res.), 1942-60; chmn. Air Force Res. Policy Com., 1967-68; practice of law Washington, 1955—; spl. asst. to chmn. Nat. Security Resources Bd., 1951; pres. Ind. Mil. Air Transport Assn., 1952-55; ptnr. Shaw, Pittman, Potts & Trowbridge, 1956-86; sr. counsel Shaw, Pittman, Potts & Trowbridge, Washington, 1986—. Publisher: Air Power History, 1989-93; contbr. articles to profl. jours. Mem. State Council Higher Edn. for Va., 1968-71; Trustee Air Force Hist. Found., pres., 1971-75; pres. Washington Area Tennis Patrons Found., 1984-87; vice-chmn. Physicians for Peace, 1989—. Decorated D.S.C., other combat decorations. Mem. ABA, D.C. Bar Assn., Met. Club (Washington), Harvard Club (N.Y.), Army Navy Country Club (Arlington, Va.), Internat. Lawn Tennis Club (U.S., Gt. Brit., India), Phi Beta Kappa. Home: 2818 27th St N Arlington VA 22207-4921 Office: Shaw Pittman Potts & Trowbridge 2300 N St NW Washington DC 20037-1122

POTTS, ROBERT LESLIE, academic administrator; b. Huntsville, Ala., Jan. 30, 1944; s. Frank Vines and Helen Ruth (Butler) P.; m. Irene Elisabeth Johansson, Aug. 22, 1965; children: Julie Anna, Robert Leslie. Student Newbold Coll., Eng., 1963-64; BA, So. Coll., 1966; JD, U. Ala., 1969; LLM, Harvard U., 1971. Law clk. to chief judge U.S. Dist. Ct. (no. dist.) Ala., 1969-70; researcher Herrick, Smith, Donald, Farley & Ketchum, Boston, 1970-71; lectr. Boston U., 1971, U. Ala., 1973-75, 88; ptnr. Potts & Young , Florence, Ala., 1971-84; gen. counsel U. Ala. System, 1984-89, pres. U. North Ala., 1990—; active Nat. Adv. Com. on Instnl. Quality and Integrity, 1994—; bd. dirs. Bank Ind., Florence, 1975-85; adv. com. Rules Civil Procedure, Ala. Supreme Ct., 1973-88; mem. Ala. Bd. Bar Examiners, 1973-79, chmn., 1983-86; trustee Nat. Conf. Bar Examiners, 1986—, chmn., 1994-95, Ala. State U., 1976-79, Oakwood Coll., 1978-81; pres. Ala. Higher Edn. Loan Corp., 1988-93. Mem. ABA, Ala. Bar Assn. (pres. young lawyers sect. 1979-80). Contbr. numerous articles to profl. jours., edn. and schs. Office: U North Ala University Station Florence AL 35632

POTTS, STEPHEN DEADERICK, lawyer; b. Memphis, Nov. 20, 1930; s. Ramsay Douglas and Anne (Van Dyke) P.; m. Irene Potter, Mar. 14, 1953; children: Lori Potts-Dupre, Stephen Deaderick Jr., Stacy Potts Krogh. AB, Vanderbilt U., 1952, LLB, 1954. Bar: Tenn. 1954, D.C. 1961. Assoc. Farris, Evans & Evans, Nashville, 1957-61; ptnr. Shaw, Pittman, Potts & Trowbridge, Washington, 1961-90; dir. U.S. Office Gov. Ethics, Washington, 1990—; mem. Pres.'s Coun. on Integrity and Efficiency; mem. Adminstrv. Conf. of U.S. Past pres. Washington Tennis Patrons Found., 1970-72, Wood Acres Sch. PTA, 1972. 1st lt. U.S. Army, 1954-57. Mem. ABA, U.S. Supreme Ct. Bar Assn., D.C. Bar Assn., Tenn. Bar Assn., Chevy Chase Club (bd. govs. 1982-86), Met. Club, U.S. Tennis Assn. (bd. dirs., won 5 nat., 1 internat. father/son championships, twice ranked 1st in U.S.). Methodist. Office: Of of Government Ethics 1201 New York Ave NW Washington DC 20005-3917

POTTS, THOMAS H., mortgage finance company executive; b. 1949. BA, Princeton U., 1971; MBA, Stanford U., 1976. With Weyerhaeuser Co., Tacoma, 1976-79, Weyerhaeuser Real Estate, Tacoma, 1979-81; exec. v.p., CFO Am. Southwest Fin. Corp., Tucson, 1981-83; treas., v.p. Ryland Group, Columbia, Md., 1984-87; pres., CEO Resource Mortgage Capital, Columbia, Md., 1987—. Office: Resource Mortgage Capital 4880 Cox Rd Glen Allen VA 23060

POTUZNIK, CHARLES LADDY, lawyer; b. Chgo., Feb. 11, 1947; s. Charles William and Laverne Frances (Zdenek) P.; m. Mary Margaret Quady, Jan. 2, 1988; children: Kylie Brommell, Kathryn Mary. BA with high honors, U. Ill., 1969; JD cum laude, Harvard U., 1973. Bar: Minn. 1973. Assoc. Dorsey & Whitney LLP, Mpls., 1973-78, ptnr., 1979—. Mem. Minn. State Bar Assn. (chmn. state securities law subcom., 1987—), Hennepin County Bar Assn., Minn. Securities Adv. Com., Phi Beta Kappa. Mem. Evang. Free Ch. Avocations: hunting, fishing, camping, canoeing, foreign travel. Office: Dorsey & Whitney Pillsbury Ctr S 220 S 6th St Minneapolis MN 55402-4502

POTVIN, ALFRED RAOUL, engineering executive; b. Worcester, Mass., Feb. 5, 1942; s. Alfred Armand and Jacqueline (Morin) P.; m. Janet Holm, Mar. 20, 1965. BEE, Worcester Poly. Inst., 1964; MEE, Stanford U., 1965, Engr. in EE, 1967; MS in Bioengring., U. Mich., 1970, M.S. in Psychology, 1970, PhD in Bioengring., 1971. Registered profl. engr., Tex. Asst. prof. elec. engring. U. Tex., Arlington, 1966-68, assoc. prof. biomed. engring. and elec. engring., 1971-76, prof., 1976-84; chmn. biomed. engring. U. Tex., 1972-84; dir. med. instrumentation systems research div. Eli Lilly & Co., Indpls., 1984-90, dir. tech. assessment and project mgmt., 1990-92; dir. engring., med. devices and diagnostics divsn., 1992-93; prof. elec. engring. Purdue Sch. Engring. and Tech., Ind. U.-Purdue U., Indpls., 1993—; dean Ind. U.-Purdue U., Indpls., 1993—; faculty fellow, life scientist, cons. NASA, Houston, 1972-76, NASA and Moffett Field, 1974-76; clin. prof. biophysics U. Tex. Health Sci. Ctr., Dallas, 1967-84; mem. phys. med. device panel FDA, Washington, 1978-84; mem. adv. bd., reviewer Biomed. Engring. NSF, Washington, 1983-89, 92—; founding dir. Ctr. Advanced Rehab. Engring., 1983-84, mem. adv. bd., 1984-88; mem. adv. bd. Engring. Rsch. Ctrs. NSF, Washington, 1988-92, Biomed. Engr. Worcester Polytech. Inst., Mass., 1987—, Coll. Engrs. Duke U., Durham, N.C., 1987-94, U. Calif., Berkeley, 1989-92, Coll. Engrs. U. Denver, 1990-93, Sch. Engr. and Tech. Ind. U.-Purdue U., Indpls, 1992-93, med. engring. Jet Propulsion Lab., Pasadena, Calif., 1989; chmn. NIH Resource Ctr. Case Western Res. U., Cleve., 1988—; bd. advisors Sch. of Health and Rehab. Sci., U. Pitts., 1993—; mem. adv. com. NIH, 1993. Author: (with W.W. Tourtellotte) Quantitative Examination of Neurologic Functions, 1985; editl. bd. IEEE Spectrum, 1987-90, 92-95, Biomed. Sci. and Tech., 1990-93; co-editor spl. issue on biosensors IEEE Trans. on Biomed. Engring., 1986, spl. issue on status and future directions in biomed. engring. Medicine and Biol. Mag., 1989; mem. editl. bd. Biomed. Sci. and Tech., 1990-92. Mem. Masthead Property Owners Assn., Indpls., 1984—, Manasota Key Property Owners Assn., Englewood, Fla., 1985—. Recipient Life Scientist award NASA, 1974; spl. fellow NIH, 1968. Fellow IEEE (pres. Engring. in Medicine and Biology Soc. 1983, re-elected 1984, gen. chmn. annual conf. 1982, chmn. health care engring. com. 1986, mem. editorial bd. spectrum 1987-89, 92-94, founding mem. steering com. symposium on computer based med. systems 1988-94, Centennial award 1984, co-editor spl. issue Medicine and Biology, 1989), Am. Inst. Med. and Biol. Engring. (bd. dirs. 1991-94, v.p. pub. awareness 1993-94, elected founding fellow 1992, co-pres. world congress on med. biological engring. in Chgo in the yr. 2000, 1993—), Houston Soc. Engrs. in Medicine and Biology (Career Achievement award 1993), Assn. Advancement of Med. Instrumentation; mem. Am. Soc. Engring. Edn. (chmn. biomed. engring. div. 1979-80), Biomed. Engring. Soc. (sr. mem. 1972-88, chmn. edn. and pub. affairs com. 1979-83), Alliance Engrs. in Medicine and Biology (v.p. nat. affairs 1987-89, pres. 1989-92), Assn. Advancement of Med. Instrumentation, Ind. Elec. Mfg. Assn. (bd. dirs. 1993—). Avocations: boating, travel, gourmet dining, skiing.

POTVIN, FELIX, professional hockey player; b. Anjou, Que., Canada, July 23, 1971. Goalie Chicoutimi, QMJHL, 1988-91, St. John's, AHL, 1991-92, Toronto Maple Leafs, 1991—. Recipient Goaltender of the Year Award, Can. Hockey League, 1990-91, Hap Emms Mem. Trophy, 1990-91, Jacques Plante Trophy, 1990-91, Shell Cup, 1990-91, Guy Lafleur Trophy, 1990-91, Baz Bastien Trophy, 1991-92, Dudley Garrett Mem. Trophy, 1991-92. All-Star first team goalie, QMJHL, 1990-91, All-Star first team goalie, AHL, 1991-92, All-Rookie Team, NHL, 1992-93. Office: Toronto Maple Leafs, 60 Carlton St, Toronto, ON Canada M5B 1L1*

POTVIN, PIERRE, physiologist, educator; b. Quebec City, Que., Can., Jan. 5, 1932; s. Rosario and Eva (Montreuil) P.; m. Louise Dube, Aug. 31, 1963; children: Aline, Bernard. BA, Laval U., 1950, MD, 1955; PhD, U. Toronto, 1962. Asst. prof. Faculty of Medicine Laval U., Quebec City, 1956-63, assoc. prof., 1963-68, prof., 1968—, vice dean exec., 1977-86, dean, 1986-94; v.p. Internat. Conf. of Deans of French-Speaking Faculties of Medicine, 1992—; hon. prof. Norman Bethune U. Med. Scis., Changchun, China, 1992. Assoc. editor Modern Medicine Can., 1958-61, Laval Med., 1962-70. Decorated comdr. Ordre Nat. des Palmes académiques (France), officer Ordre Nat. du Lion (Senegal). Fellow Royal Coll. Physicians and Surgeons Can.; mem. Can. Soc. Physiology. Roman Catholic. Avocation: painting. Home: 1915 Bourbonniere, Sillery, PQ Canada G1S 1N3 Office: Laval U Faculty of Medicine, Dept Physiology, Quebec, PQ Canada G1K 7P4

POTVIN, RAYMOND HERVE, sociology educator, author; b. Southbridge, Mass., Oct. 28, 1924; s. Cleophas R. and Eva (Beauvais) P. S.T.B., U. Montreal, 1948; Ph.D., Catholic U. Am., 1958; DHL (hon.), Assumption Coll., 1993. Ordained priest Roman Cath. Ch., 1948; asst. pastor Springfield, Mass., 1948-53; mem. faculty Cath. U., 1958—, prof. sociology, 1967—, chmn. dept., 1968-71, 77-83, asst. acad. v.p. for grad. programs, 1985-88; dir. Inst. Social and Behavioral Research, 1972-74; sr. researcher Boys Town Center, 1974-88; Trustee Population Reference Bur., 1981-87, Center for Applied Research in the Apostolate, 1981-85; Fellow Population Council, 1966-67. Author: (with Charles Westoff) College Women and Fertility Values, 1967, (with Antanas Suziedelis) Seminarians of the Sixties, 1970, Vocational Challenge and Seminary Response, 1971, (with D. Hoge and H. Nelson) Religion and American Youth, 1976, (with Hart Nelsen and Joseph Shields) The Religion of Children, 1977, Seminarians of the Eighties, 1986, (with P. Mucada) Seminary Outcomes: Perseverance and Withdrawal, 1990. Fellow Am. Sociol. Assn., Population Assn.; mem. Soc. Sci. Study of Religion. Office: Cath Univ Dept Sociology Washington DC 20064

POUGH, FREDERICK HARVEY, mineralogist; b. Bklyn., June 26, 1906; s. Francis H. and Alice H. (Beckler) P.; m. Eleanor C. Hodge, Oct. 14, 1938 (dec. May 1966); children: Frederick Harvey, Barbara Hodge. SB, Harvard, 1928, PhD, 1935; MS, Washington U., 1932; student, Ruperto Carola, Heidelberg, Germany, 1932-33. Asst. curator mineralogy Am. Mus. Natural History, N.Y.C., 1935-40; acting curator Am. Mus. Natural History, 1941, curator, 1942-44, curator phys. geology and mineralogy, 1942-52, cons. mineralogist, 1953-64, 66—; gem cons. Jewelers Circular-Keystone, 1940-85; dir. Santa Barbara Mus. Natural History, 1965-66; pres. Mineralogy, Inc., 1978—. Author: Jewelers Dictionary, 1945, 50, 76, 96, All About Volcanoes and Earthquakes, 1953, Hindi translation, 1958, Persian translation, 1959, Bengali translation, 1959, Italian translation, 1960, Arabic translation, 1962, Portuguese translation, 1964, Our Earth, 1961, The Story of Gems and Semi-Precious Stones, 1967, Guide des Roches et Mineraux, 1969, 79, First Guide to Rocks and Minerals, 1991; contbg. editor: Lipidary jour, 1984—. Recipient Bronze medal Royal Geol. Soc., Belgium, 1948, Derby medal Brazilian Geol. Survey, Hanneman award for outstanding contbns. in lit. of mineralogy and gemology, 1988, Mineral. award Carnegie Mus. Nat. History, Pitts., 1989, Lifetime Achievement award Accredited Gemologist Assn., 1993; named Mineralogist of Yr., Am. Fedn. Mineral Soc., 1966. Fellow Mineral Soc. Am., Geol. Soc. Am.; mem. Mineral Soc. Gt. Britain., Gemmological Assn. All Japan (Am. rep. 1985—). Clubs: Harvard (N.Y.C.); Explorers. Address: PO Box 7004 Reno NV 89510-7004

POUL, FRANKLIN, lawyer; b. Phila., Nov. 6, 1924; s. Boris and Anna P.; m. Shirley Weissman, June 26, 1949; children—Leslie Poul Melman, Alan M., Laurie. Student, U. Pa., 1942-43, Haverford Coll., 1943-44; LL.B. cum laude, U. Pa., 1946. Bar: Pa. 1949, U.S. Supreme Ct. 1955. Asso. firm Gray, Anderson, Schaffer & Rome, Phila., 1948-56, Wolf, Block, Schorr and Solis-Cohen, Phila., 1956-60; partner Wolf, Block, Schorr and Solis-Cohen, 1960-93. Bd. dirs. ACLU, Phila., 1955-80, pres., 1975-76. Served with AUS, 1943-46. Mem. ABA, Am. Law Inst., Order of Coif. Office: Wolf Block Shorr & Solis-Cohen 12th Fl Packard Bldg SE Corner 15 Chestnut St Philadelphia PA 19122

POULIN, MARIE-PAULE, Canadian government official; b. Sudbury, Ont., Can., June 21, 1945; d. Alphonse-Emile and Lucille (Ménard) Charette; m. Bernard A. Poulin, May 21, 1977; children: Elaine, Valérie. BA, Laurentian U., Sudbury, 1966; MSW, U. Montréal, Que., Can., 1969; PhD (hon.), Laurentian U., Sudbury, 1995. Lectr. U. Montreal, 1969-70, Coll. of Gen. and Profl. Instrn., Hull, Que., 1972-73; rschr. Ctr. Social Svcs., Hull, 1972-73; interviewer, rschr. French Radio and TV, Ottawa, Ont., 1973-74; prodr. Sta. CBOF-CBC, Ottawa, 1974-78; founder and dir. svcs. in N.E. and N.W. Ont. Sta. CBON (French Network-CBC), Sudbury, 1978-83; exec. dir. regional programming CBC, Ottawa, 1983-84, assoc. v.p. regional broadcasting, 1984-88, sec. gen., 1988-90, v.p. human resources, 1990-92; dep. sec. for comm. and consultation The Privy Coun. Govt. of Can., Ottawa, 1992-93; chmn. Can. Artists and Prodrs. Profl. Rels. Tribunal, Ottawa, 1993—; senator Can. Govt., Ottawa; mem. Senate Standing com. Internal Economy, Budgets and Adminstrn., Nat. Fin., Transport and Comm.; bd. dirs. Cité Collégiale, Ottawa, 1988-91. Commr. for French lang. svcs. Province of Ont., 1986-89; regent U. Sudbury, 1981-83; bd. dirs. Laurentian Hosp., Sudbury, 1980-88, Cambrian Coll.Found., Sudbury, 1983-88; v.p. Art Ctr., Ottawa, 1988-90; pres. Regroupement gens d'affaires, Ottawa, 1991-92. Recipient medal for contbn. to Can. Culture, Coun. of French-Am. Life, 1987, Prix Marcel-Blouin for best morning program in Can., 1983, Profl. Woman of Yr. award Réseau des femmes d'affaires professionnelles, 1990; named Chevalier Ordre de la Pléiade, 1995. Mem. Can.-U.S. Inter-Parliamentary Group, Can.-Japan Inter-Parliamentary Group, Can.-Europe Parliamentary Assn., Can.-France Inter-Parliamentary Assn., Can.-Israel Friendship Group, Can.-Korea Friendship Group, Can.-Italy Friendship Guide, Assn. Grads. of U. Montréal, Can. Circle (exec.). Avocations: running, reading, swimming. Home: 100 Pretoria Ave, Ottawa, ON Canada K1S 1W9 Office: Senate Can, Ottawa, ON Canada K1A 0A4

POULIN, THOMAS EDWARD, marine engineer, state legislator, retail business owner; b. Waterville, Maine, Apr. 23, 1956; s. Donald Richard and Beatrice Delores (Berard) P.; m. Kim E. Marston, July 3, 1981; children: Elizabeth, Brittany, Chanelle. BS in Marine Engring., Maine Maritime Acad., 1978; cert. in tchg., U. Maine, Farmington, 1985. Various marine engring. positions Keystone, Sealand, Maritime Overseas Corp., and U.S. Lines, 1978—; math. tchr. Messalonshee H.S., Oakland, Maine, 1986-90; mem. Maine Ho. of Reps., Oakland and Sidney, 1990—. Mem. budget and adv. coms. Town of Oakland, 1988—, mem. recycling com., 1990—. Roman Catholic. Home: R4 Box 1060 Oakland ME 04963-9410

POULIOT, ASSUNTA GALLUCCI, retired business school owner and director; b. West Warwick, R.I., Aug. 14, 1937; d. Michael and Angelina (DeCesare) Gallucci; m. Joseph F. Pouliot Jr., July 4, 1961; children: Brenda, Mark, Jill, Michele. BS, U. R.I., 1959, MS, 1971. Bus. tchr. Cranston High Sch., R.I., 1959-61; bus. dept. chmn. Chariho Regional High Sch., Wood River Junction, R.I., 1961-73; instr. U. R.I., Kingston, 1973-78; founder, dir. Ocean State Bus. Inst., Wakefield, R.I., 1977-95; fin. aid cons., 1995—; dir. Fleet Nat. Bank, 1985-91; bd. mgrs. Bank of New Eng., 1984-85; commr. Accrediting Coun. Ind. Colls. and Schs., 1995—; speaker in field. Pres. St. Francis Women's Club, Wakefield, 1975; sec. St. Francis Parish Coun., Wakefield, 1980; mem. Econ. Devel. Commn., Wakefield, 1981-85; mem. South County Hosp. Corp., Wakefield, 1978—; fin. dir. Bus and Profl. Women's Club, Wakefield, 1982-84; chmn. Ladies Golf Charity, 1985-91; mem. Computer Info. Systems Com., Chariho Regional Career and Tech. Ctr.; Mem. Galilee Beach Club Assn., R.I. Bus. Edn. Assn. (newsletter editor 1979-81), New Eng. Bus. Coll. Assn. (sec. 1984-86, pres. 1985-87), R.I. Assn. Career and Tech. Schs. (treas., bd. dirs. 1979—), Eastern Bus. Edn. Assn. (conf. leader), Nat. Bus. Edn. Assn. (conf. leader), Career Coll. Assn. (conv. speaker, pub. rels. com., govt. rels. com., membership com., key mem., nominating com., evaluator), Assn. Colls. and Schs. (commr. commn. on postsecondary schs. accreditation 1994—, ednl. cons. 1995—), R.I. Women's Golf Assn., Am. Cancer Soc., U. R.I. Alumi Assn. (Excellence Bus. award 1992), Phi Kappa Phi, Delta Pi Epsilon (pres., newsletter editor). Roman Catholic. Club: Point Judith Country (past ladies golf chmn.). Avocations: golf, gardening. Home: 137 Kenyon Ave Wakefield RI 02879-4242 Office: Ocean State Bus Inst Mariner Sq 140 Point Judith Rd Boxes 1 & 2 Narragansett RI 02882

POULOS, GARY PETER, school system administrator. Dir. Union High Sch. Dist., San Mateo, Calif. Recipient Blue Ribbon Sch. award U.S. Dept. Edn., 1990-91. Office: Union High Sch Dist 605 N Delaware St San Mateo CA 94401-1731

POULOS, MICHAEL JAMES, insurance company executive; b. Glens Falls, N.Y., Feb. 13, 1931; s. James A. and Mary Poulos; m. Mary Kay Leslie; children: Denise, Peter. BA, Colgate U., 1953; MBA, NYU, 1963. CLU, 1970. With sales and mgmt. U.S. Life Ins. Co., N.Y.C., 1958-70, sec., treas. dir., 1968, v.p adminstrn., 1969, mem. exec. com., 1970; with Calif.-Western States Life Ins. Co., Sacramento, 1970-79, pres., chief exec. officer, 1975-79, dir., 1975; with Am. Gen. Corp., Houston, 1979-93, sr. v.p. div. head life ins., 1979-81, pres., 1981-91; mem. exec. com., dir. Am. Gen. Corp., 1981-93, vice chmn., 1991-93; chmn., CEO, pres. Western Nat. Corp., Houston. Mem. Sam Houston Area coun. Boy Scouts Am. Mem. Am. Soc. CLU's, Nat. Assn. Life Underwriters, Houston Assn. Life Underwriters, Am. Mgmt. Assn., Heritage Club, The Houstonian Club. Greek Orthodox. Office: Western National Corp 5555 San Felipe Ste 900 Houston TX 77056*

POULOS-WOOLLEY, PAIGE M., public relations executive; b. Woodland, Calif., Apr. 26, 1958; d. Paul William Jr. and Frances Marie (Gibson) Poulos; m. John Stuart Woolley, Jr., Feb. 3, 1990. Student, U. Calif., Davis, 1977-80. Mgr. pub. rels. Somerset Wine Co., N.Y.C. and San Martin, Calif., 1982-88; dir. comm. The Beverage Source, San Francisco, 1988-89, Rutherford (Calif.) Hill Winery, 1989-90; pres. Paige Poulos Comm., Berkeley, Calif., 1990—; founder, chmn. WINECOM, 1992—. Pub. rels. editor: Practical Winery & Vineyards, 1994—; wine editor Focus Mag. Mem. Pub. Rels. Soc. Am. (bd. dirs. 1993—, sec. 1994, pres. East Bay chpt. 1994-96, editor newsletter food and beverage sect. 1993-95, chmn. food and beverage sect.), Women in Comm., Acad. Wine Comm. (program chair 1994), Internat. Assn. Bus. Communicators. Republican. Episcopalian. Avocations: horseback riding, diving, skiing, gardening. Office: Paige Poulos Comm PO Box 8087 Berkeley CA 94707-8087

POULSON, RICHARD JASPER METCALFE, lawyer; b. Elizabeth City, N.C., Sept. 4, 1938; s. Richard Jasper and Dorothy (Morse) P.; m. Anne Keenan, Dec. 21, 1963 (div. 1976); m. Anne Dare Wrenn, Sept. 25, 1993. BA, U. Va., 1960; JD, Am. U., 1968; ML in Taxation, Georgetown U., 1970. Bar: Va. 1968, D.C. 1969, U.S. Supreme Ct. 1976. V.p. Am. Security & Trust Co., Washington, 1968-70; assoc. Hogan & Hartson, Washington, 1970-73, ptnr., 1973-94; sr. ptnr. Hogan & Hartson, London, 1990-93; chmn. Rapidan Capital Ptnrs., 1994—; CEO, sr. mng. dir. The Appian Group, Washington, 1995—; adj. prof. Georgetown U. Law Ctr., 1971-78; lectr. Law and Fgn. Svc. Schs. Georgetown U.; internat. advisor in field; active Euro-Arab Conciliation and Arbitration System. Trustee, bd. mgrs., U. Va., Charlottesville, 1992—, v.p., 1994-95, pres., 1995—; dir., chmn. exec. com. Mary & Daniel Loughran Found., Washington, 1976—; chmn., dir. Montpelier Steeplechase Found., Orange, Va., 1991—; chmn., trustee U.S. Rugby Football Found., Boston, 1988—. 1st lt. USAR, 1961-63. Mem. Law Society of England and Wales, Metro. Club, Farmington Country Club, Norfolk Yacht Club, Keswick Country Club. Republican. Episcopalian. Avocations: horseback riding, hunting, steeplechase racing, thoroughbred breeding. Home: Hare Forest Farm Orange VA 22960 Office: The Appian Group 9th Fl 1455 Pennsylvania Ave NW Washington DC 20004

POULSON, ROBERT DEAN, lawyer; b. Valparaiso, Ind., June 10, 1927; s. Frank Ferlin and Esther Marie P.; m. Betty Lou Caroline Mercer, Aug. 19, 1950 (dec.); children: Richard D., Thomas C., John R. LL.B., Drake U., 1953, J.D., 1974. Bar: Iowa 1953, Ill. 1954, Colo. 1957. Staff atty. Texaco, Chgo. and Denver, 1953-59; divisional atty. Superior Oil Co., Denver, 1959-64; of counsel Poulson, Odell & Peterson, Denver, 1995—. Mem. Bow Mar City Council, Colo., 1968-72. Served with USN, 1945-47. Mem. Denver, Arapahoe County (Colo.), Colo., Am. bar assns., Rocky Mountain Mineral Law Found. (pres. 1975-76, trustee 1965—), Rocky Mountain Oil and Gas Assn. (chmn. gen. legal com. 1963-66, trustee 1963—), Ind. Petroleum Assn. Am. (dir.), Phi Alpha Delta. Republican. Methodist. Clubs: Univ. (Denver); Masons. Home: 5455 Lakeshore Dr Littleton CO 80123-1542 Office: 1775 Sherman St Ste 1400 Denver CO 80203-4316

POULTER, CHARLES DALE, chemist, educator, consultant; b. Monroe, La., Aug. 29, 1942; s. Erwin and Mary Helen Poulter; m. Susan Raetzsch, Aug. 24, 1964; children: Mary Christa, Gregory Thomas. BS, La. State U., Baton Rouge, 1964; PhD, U. Calif., Berkeley, 1967. NIH postdoctoral fellow UCLA, 1967-68; asst. prof. chemistry U. Utah, Salt Lake City, 1969-75, assoc. prof., 1975-78, prof., 1978-94, John A. Widtsoe prof. chemistry, 1993-95, chair dept. chemistry, 1995—; cons. Amoco Rsch. Ctr., Naperville, Ill., 1985-90, Merck Sharp & Dohme, Rahway, N.J., 1986-90, Bristol-Myers Squibb, Princeton, N.J., 1989-93, Zeneca Ag Products, Richmond, Calif., 1993-95. Fellow AAAS; mem. Am. Chem. Soc. (organic exec. com. 1983-86, biol. divsn. councillor 1993-97, Ernest Guenther award 1991, Utah award 1992). Office: U Utah Dept Chemistry Salt Lake City UT 84112-1102

POULTON, BRUCE ROBERT, former university chancellor; b. Yonkers, N.Y., Mar. 7, 1927; s. Alfred Vincent and Ella Marie (Scanlon) P.; m. Elizabeth Charlotte Jerothe, Aug. 26, 1950; children: Randall Lee, Jeffrey Jon, Cynthia Sue, Peter Gregory. B.S. with honors, Rutgers U., 1950, M.S., 1952, Ph.D., 1956; LL.D., U. N.H. Research instr., then asst. prof. Rutgers U., 1952-56; assoc. prof., then prof., chmn. dept. animal and vet. sci. U. Maine, 1958-66, dir. Bangor Campus, 1967-68, dean, dir. Coll. Life Scis. and Agr., 1968-71, v.p. research and pub. service, 1971-75; chancellor Univ. System N.H., 1975-82, also trustee; chancellor N.C. State U., Raleigh, 1982-89; vis. prof. Mich. State U., 1966-67; mem. regional adv. com. Farm and Home Adminstrn.; mem. exec. com., council on research policy and grad. edn. Nat. Assn. State Univs. and Land Grant Colls.; also mem. senate; mem. Gov.'s Econ. Advisory Council, N.H.; mem. selection com. Kellogg Found.; Lectureship in Agr.; chmn. Rhodes scholarship com. for, N.H.; mem. policy devel. com. New Eng. Innovation Group; adv. com. U.S. Command and Gen. Staff Coll. Author articles in field. Bd. dirs. Research Triangle Inst., Microelectronic Ctr., Triangle Univs. Ctr. Advanced Studies, Aubrey Brooks Found. Served with AUS, 1944-46. Am. Council Edn. fellow acad. adminstrn., 1966-67. Mem. Am. Inst. Nutrition, Brit. Nutrition Soc., Fedn. Am. Soc. Exptl. Biology, Am. Soc. Exptl. Biology, Am. Soc. Animal Sci., Am. Dairy Sci. Assn. (past pres. Eastern div.), AAAS, Sigma Xi, Alpha Zeta. Office: NC State U Office of Chancellor Raleigh NC 27695

POULTON, CHARLES EDGAR, natural resources consultant; b. Oakley, Idaho, Aug. 2, 1917; s. Richard and Narrie Jane (Queen) P.; m. Marcile Belle McCoy, Sept. 29, 1939; children: Richard C., Robert J., Mary Jane Poulton Morris, Betty Jean Poulton Strong. B.S. with high honors, U. Idaho, 1939, M.S., 1948; postgrad., Mont. State Coll., 1946-47; Ph.D., Wash. State U., 1955; postdoctoral, U. Calif. at Berkeley, 1967-68. Adminstr., researcher U.S. Forest Service, Western states, 1937-46; dist. forest ranger U.S. Forest Service, 1941-46; cons. forest ecology U.S. Forest Service, Ala., Fla., 1958-59; asst. prof. range mgmt. Mont. State Coll., Bozeman, 1946-47; instr. range mgmt. U. Idaho, Moscow, 1947-49; prof., dir. range mgmt. program Oreg. State U., Corvallis, 1949-70; prof. range ecology Oreg. State U., 1970-73; dir. Environ. Remote Sensing Applications Lab., 1972-73; dir. range and resource ecology div. Earth Satellite Corp., Berkeley, Calif., 1974-75; sr. officer Rangeland Resources and Pasture, Food and Agr. Orgn. UN, Rome, Italy, 1976-77, 81; Cons., Benton County, Oreg.; (in land use planning), 1972-73, NASA, 1967-71; tng. officer, remote sensing of natural resources NASA-Ames Research Center, 1978-81; cons. natural resource mgmt., bus. devel., 1978—; developed new MS program in interdisciplinary natural resources devel. Asian Inst. of Tech., Bangkok, Thailand, 1986-87, coord. of program, 1987, project work in developing countries. Assoc. editor: Range Mgmt. Jour. Forestry, 1956-62; mem. editorial bd. Ecology, 1965-67; contbr. chpts. to books, articles to profl. jours. Served with USNR, 1945-46. Recipient merit certificate for outstanding service to grassland agr. Am. Grassland Council, 1963. Fellow Soc. Range Mgmt. (charter, pres. Pacific N.W. sect. 1962, Outstanding Achievement award 1986); Mem. (nat. dir. 1965-68, com. on accreditation 1980-83, chmn. com. on internat. affairs 1983), Soc. Am. Foresters (chmn. range mgmt. div. 1955), Nat. Acad. Sci. (panels 1969, 73-74), Sigma Xi, Phi Eta Sigma, Xi Sigma Pi. Mem. Christian Ch. Home: PO Box 2081 Gresham OR 97030-0601

POUNCEY, PETER RICHARD, academic administrarot, classics educator; b. Tsingtao, Shantung, China, Oct. 1, 1937; came to U.S., 1964; s. Cecil Alan and Eugenie Marde (Lintilhac) P.; m. Bethanne McNally, June 25, 1966; 1 son, Christian; m. Susan Rieger, Mar. 21, 1973; 1 dau., Margaret; m. Katherine Dalsimer, June 9, 1990. Lic. Phil., Heythrop Coll., Eng., 1960; B.A., Oxford U., Eng., 1964, M.A., 1967; Ph.D., Columbia U., 1969; AM (hon.), Amherst Coll., 1985; LLD (hon.), Williams Coll., 1985; LHD (hon.), Doshisha U., 1987; LLD (hon.), Wesleyan U., Mass., 1989; LHD (hon.), Trinity Coll., 1990. Instr. classics Fordham U., Bronx, N.Y., 1964-67; asst. prof. Columbia U., N.Y.C., 1969-71, dean Columbia Coll., 1972-76, assoc. prof., 1977-83, prof. classics, 1983-84; pres. Amherst (Mass.) Coll., Mass., 1984-94; pres. emeritus Amherst (Mass.) Coll., 1994—, prof. classics, 1994—; cons. classical lit. Columbia Ency., 1970-73; trustee Columbia Univ. Press, 1972-75. Author: The Necessities of War: A Study of Thucydides' Pessimism, 1980 (Lionel Trilling award 1981). Trustee Brit.-Am. Edn. Found., N.Y.C., 1971-75. Recipient Great Tchr. award Soc. Columbia Grads., 1983. Mem. Am. Philol. Assn., Phi Beta Kappa.

POUND, E. JEANNE, school psychologist, consultant; b. N.Y.C., Oct. 19, 1949; adopted d. W. James and Thelma (Rendall) P.; div.; 1 child, Courtney Jason Pound. BA in English cum laude, U. Mass., 1971; MS in Social Work, U. Wis., 1973; EdS in Sch. Psychology, U. Ga., 1977. Cert. sch. psychologist, Ga., Mass.; cert. sch. social worker, N.Y. Psychiat. social worker White Mountain Community Mental Health Svcs., Littleton, N.H., 1974; sch. social worker Lake Placid (N.Y.) Ctrl. Schs., 1974-75; sch. psychologist Wilbraham (Mass.) Pub. Schs., 1977-80, Stoneham (Mass). Pub. Schs., 1980-81, Richmond County (Ga.) Pub. Schs., 1981-83, Griffin (Ga.) Regional Ednl. Svc. Agy., 1984-87, Atlanta Pub. Schs., 1987—; evaluator of innovative program grants Ga. State Dept. Edn., Atlanta, 1987—; supr. sch. psychology interns Ga. State U., Atlanta, 1994—; mem. Ga. Adv. Panel Spl. Edn., 1995—. Author: (chpt.) Children's Needs-Psychological Perspectives ("Children and Prematurity"), 1987. Mem. APA, Nat. Assn. Sch. Psychologists (cert.), Ga. Assn. Sch. Psychologists (regional rep. 1991-93, chmn. GASP/NASP conv. com. 1995-96), Humane Soc. U.S., World Wildlife Fedn., Kappa Delta Pi, Phi Kappa Phi, Phi Delta Kappa. Avocations: snow skiing, water skiing, weight lifting, aerobic exercise, gardening. Home: 150 Bryson Ln Fayetteville GA 30215-5478 Office: Atlanta Pub Schs Office Youth Svcs 978 North Ave NE Atlanta GA 30306-4456

POUND, RICHARD WILLIAM DUNCAN, lawyer, accountant; b. St. Catharines, Ont., Can., Mar. 22, 1942; s. William Thomas and Jessie Edith Duncan (Thom) P.; m. Julie Houghton Keith, Nov. 4, 1977. B.Commerce, McGill U., Montreal, 1962, B.C.L., 1967; B.A., Sir George Williams U. (now Concordia U.), Montreal, 1963; PhD (hon.), U.S. Sports Acad., 1989. Bar: called to Que. bar 1968, Ont. bar, 1980; chartered accountant, 1964.

Auditor Riddell, Stead, Graham & Hutchinson, Montreal, 1963-65; law clk., then atty. firm Laing, Weldon, Courtois, Clarkson, Parsons & Tétrault, Montreal, 1965-71; mem. firm Stikeman, Elliott, Montreal, Toronto, Ottawa, Calgary, Vancouver, London, N.Y.C., Hong Kong, Taipei, Budepest, Paris, Washington, 1972—; lectr. taxation McGill U. Faculty Law; lectr. Que. Real Estate Assn.; mem. Ct. of Arbitration of Sport, Lausanne, 1991—; officer Order of Can., officer Order nat. du Quebec, Queen's Coun. Author: Five Rings Over Korea: 1994; editor-in-chief: Doing Business in Canada, Canada Tax Cases, Stikeman Income Tax Act (annotated); editl. bd. Can. Tax Svc.; editor Pound's Tax Case Notes, Legal Notes, CGA mag. Pres. Canadian Olympic Assn., 1977-82, sec., 1968-76; mem. Internat. Olympic Com., 1978—, exec. bd., 1983-87, 92—, v.p., 1987-91; bd. govs. McGill U., 1986—, chmn., 1994—; trustee Martlet Found.; former trustee Stanstead Wesleyan Coll.; chmn. McGill U. Athletic Bd.; chmn. McGill U. Fund Coun. Named to Canadian Swimming Hall of Fame, 1969, Sports Fedn. Can. Hall of Fame, 1976. Mem. Can. Bar Assn., Can. Tax Found., Internat. Fiscal Assn., Internat. Assn. Practicing Lawyers, Can. Squash Racquets Assn., Royal Life Savs. Soc., Grads. Soc. McGill U. (former pres.). Clubs: Montreal Amateur Athletic Assn. (pres. 1987-88), Badminton and Squash (Montreal); Hillside Tennis, Jesters, Mt. Bruno Country. Home: 87 Arlington Ave, Westmount, PQ Canada H3Y 2W5 Office: Ste 3900, 1155 Rene Levesque Blvd W, Montreal, PQ Canada H3B 3V2

POUND, ROBERT VIVIAN, physics educator; b. Ridgeway, Ont., Can., May 16, 1919; came to U.S., 1923, naturalized, 1932; s. Vivian Ellsworth and Gertrude C. (Prout) P.; m. Betty Yde Andersen, June 20, 1941; 1 son, John Andrew. BA, U. Buffalo, 1941; AM (hon.), Harvard Coll., 1950; DSc (hon.), SUNY, Buffalo, 1994. Rsch. physicist Submarine Signal Co., 1941-42; staff mem. Radiation Lab. MIT, Cambridge, 1942-46; Soc. Fellows jr. fellow Harvard U., Cambridge, 1945-48; asst. prof. physics Harvard Coll., Cambridge, 1948-50, assoc. prof., 1950-56, prof., 1956-68; chmn. dept. physics, 1968-72, Mallinckrodt prof. physics, 1968-89, emeritus, 1989—; dir. Physics Lab. Havard U., Cambridge, 1975-83; Fulbright rsch. scholar Oxford (Eng.) U., 1951, vis. rsch. fellow Merton Coll., 1980; Fulbright lectr., Paris, 1958; vis. prof. Coll. de France, 1973; vis. fellow Joint Inst. Lab. Astrophysics, U. Colo., 1979-80; Zernike vis. prof. U. Groningen, The Netherlands, 1982; vis. sr. scientist Brookhaven Nat. Lab., 1986-87; vis. prof. U. Fla., 1987; W.G. Brickwedde lectr. Johns Hopkins U., Balt., 1992; Julian Mack lectr. U. Wis., 1992. Author, editor: Microwave Mixers, 1948; Contbr. articles to profl. jours. Trustee Associated Univs., Inc., 1976—. Recipient B.J. Thompson Meml. award Inst. Radio Engrs., 1948, Eddington medal Royal Astron. Soc., 1965, Nat. Medal Sci., NSF 1990; John Simon Guggenheim fellow,1957-58, 72-73. Fellow AAAS, Am. Phys. Soc., Am. Acad. Arts and Scis.; mem. NAS, French Phys. Soc. (mem coun. 1958-61), Acad. Scis. (France, fgn. assoc.), Phi Beta Kappa, Sigma Xi.

POUNDS, BILLY DEAN, law educator; b. Belmont, Miss., Jan. 23, 1930; s. Seth and Warnie (Wroten) P.; m. Genie Smith, June 22, 1952; children: Nancy Angela Pounds Via, Mary Dean Stone. AA, NE C.C., 1950; BS, Miss. State U., 1952, MS, 1953, EdD, 1968. Tchr. Wheeler (Miss.) High Sch., 1952-53; instr. NE Community Coll., Booneville, Miss., 1953-57; paralegal prof. Miss. U. for Women, Columbus, 1959—, dir. paralegal program, 1983—. Author: A Determination and Appraisal Content of Introduction to Political Science, 1968, History of Republic Party in Mississippi, 1964; co-author: Teaching About Communism, 1977. Pres. Lowndes County (Miss.) Kidney Found., 1970, Lowndes County Cancer Soc., 1972. Capt. USAF, 1957-59. Fellow Miss. State U., 1953; named Faculty Mem. of Yr., Miss. Legis., 1988. Mem. Phi Kappa Phi, Gamma Beta Phi, Kappa Delta Epsilon, Phi Delta Kappa, Phi Alpha Theta, Pi Gamma Mu, Pi Tau Chi. Office: Miss U for Women Columbus MS 39701

POUNDS, GERALD AUTRY, aerospace engineer; b. Boaz, Ala., Mar. 21, 1940; s. C.B. and Pauline (DeBord) P.; m. Linda Lee Lindsey, July 29, 1967; children: Kristina Marie, Alissa Michelle. B in Aerospace Engring., Auburn U., 1963, MS in Aerospace Engring., 1965. With Lockheed Martin Aero. Sys., Marietta, Ga., 1960—, engr. staff test and evaluation; lectr. U. Tenn. Space Inst., Tullahoma, 1988-95. Contbr. articles to Jour. Aircraft. Vestry, from jr. warden to sr. warden Christ Episcopal Ch., Kennasaw, Ga., 1974-82; mid. adult retreat coord. Mt. Paran Ch. of God, Atlanta, 1986-91. NSF scholar, 1963-64. Fellow AIAA (assoc.; dep. dir. for test, tech. activities com., 1991—, chmn. Atlanta sect.); mem. Supersonic Tunnel Assn. (co. rep.), Subsonic Aerodynamic Testing Assn. (co. rep.). Home: 562 Stillwaters Dr Marietta GA 30064 Office: Lockheed Martin Aero Sys D/73-66 Z-0605 Marietta GA 30063

POUNDS, WILLIAM FRANK, management educator; b. Fayette County, Pa., Apr. 9, 1928; s. Joseph Frank and Helen (Fry) P.; m. Helen Anne Means, Mar. 6, 1954; children: Thomas Mcclure, Julia Elizabeth. B.S. in Chem. Engring., Carnegie Inst. Tech., 1950, M.S. in Math. Econs., 1959, Ph.D. in Indsl. Adminstrn., 1964. Indsl. engr. Eastman Kodak Co., 1950-51, 55-57; cons. Pitts. Plate Glass Co., 1958-59, asst. to gen. mgr. Forbes finishes div., 1960-61; mem. faculty Sloan Sch. Mgmt., MIT, 1961—, prof. mgmt., 1966—, dean, 1966-80; cons. to industry, 1958—, sr. adv. Rockefeller Family and Assocs., 1981-91; bd. dirs. EG&G, Inc., Putnam Funds, Sun Co., Inc., Idexx Labs., Inc., Mgmt. Scis. for Health, Inc., Perseptive Biosystems, Inc. Trustee Boston Mus. Fine Arts; overseer WGBH Found. Served as aviator lt. (j.g.) USNR, 1951-55. Fellow Am. Acad. Arts and Scis. Home: 83 Cambridge Pky #W1205 Cambridge MA 02142-1241 Office: MIT 50 Memorial Dr Cambridge MA 02142-1347

POUPART-LAFARGE, OLIVIER MARIE, financial executive; b. Angers, France, Oct. 26, 1942; s. Henri M. and Edith M. (LaFarge) Poupart; m. Benedicte M. Gentin, Feb. 12, 1965; children: Arnaud, Bertrand, Henri, Domitille, Astrid. MBA, Hautes Etudes Commerciales, Paris, 1964; BA, U. Paris, 1965. Fin. analyst Credit Lyonnais, London, 1967-68; fin. exec. Roussel Uclaf, Paris, 1968-74; fin. mgr. Bouygues, Paris, 1974-84, CFO, 1984—. Lt. French Air Force, 1964-65. Decorated chevalier Ordre Nat. du Mérite, Legion of Honor (France). Roman Catholic. Home: 4 Imp Nattier, 78000 Versailles France Office: Bouygues, 1 Ave Eugene Freyssinet, 78061 Saint Quentin France

POURCIAU, LESTER JOHN, librarian; b. Baton Rouge, La., Sept. 6, 1936; s. Lester John and Pearlie M. (Hogan) P.; m. Rebecca Anne Thomas, 1975; 1 son, Lester John III. B.A., La. State U., 1962, M.S., 1964; Ph.D. (Higher Edn. Act fellow), Ind. U., 1975. Asst. reference librarian U. S.C., Columbia, 1963-64; reference librarian Florence County Pub. Library, Florence, S.C., 1964-65; reference services coordinator U. Fla., Gainesville, 1966-67; dir. libraries Memphis State U., 1970—, assoc. v.p. for acad. affairs, dir. libraries, 1987—; chmn. coun. of head librarians State Univ. and C.C. System Tenn., 1980, 87; acad. assoc. Atlantic Coun. of U.S., Memphis State U.; fgn. expert, vis. lectr. Beijing U. of Posts & Telecomms., Beijing Normal U., Peking U., Renmen U., Qinghua U., Chingqing Inst. Posts & Telecomms., Guizhou Normal U., Republic of China, 1993; fgn. expert/vis. lectr. Beijing U. Posts and Telecom, 1993, Beijing Normal U., 1993, Peking U., 1993, RenMen U., 1993, Tsinghua U., 1993, Chongqing Inst. Posts and Telecom., 1993, Guizhou Normal U., 1993; fgn. expert, vis. lectr. Nanjing U. Posts and Telecom., Anhui Normal U., Beijing U. Posts and Telecom., 1994, Nanjing U. Posts & Telecomms., Anhui Normal U., Republic of China, 1994. Contbr. articles to profl. jours. Served with USAF, 1955-59. Recipient Adminstrv. Staff award Memphis State U., 1981, Commendation Boy Scouts Am., 1985, Commendation Tenn. Sec. State, 1989, Honor award Tenn. Libr. Assn., 1990; ; named Outstanding Alumnus, La. State U., 1988; named Libr. of Yr., Memphis Libr. Coun., 1989. Mem. Am. Southeastern, Tenn. Libr. Assn., Am. Soc. for Info. Sci., Nat. Assn. Watch and Clock Collectors (chpt. pres. 1983, sec.-treas. 1988, 89), Antique Automobile Am., Mid-Am. Old Time Automobile Assn., Memphis Old Time Car (sec. 1981, pres. 1982, 89), Delta Phi Alpha, Omicron Delta Kappa (Order of Omega), Phi Kappa Phi. Office: Memphis State U U Libr Memphis TN 38152

POUR-EL, MARIAN BOYKAN, mathematician, educator; b. N.Y.C.; d. Joseph and Mattie (Caspe) Boykan; m. Akiva Pour-El; 1 dau., Ina. A.B., Hunter Coll.; A.M., Harvard U., 1951, Ph.D., 1958. Asst. prof. math. Pa. State U., 1958-62, assoc. prof., 1962-64; mem. faculty U. Minn., Mpls., 1964—; prof. math. U. Minn., 1968—; mem. Inst. Advanced Study, Princeton, N.J., 1962-64; mem. coun. Conf. Bd. Math. Scis., 1977-82, trustee, 1978-81, mem. nominating com., 1980-82, chmn., 1981-82; lectr. internat. congresses in logic and computer sci., Eng., 1971, Hungary, 1967, Czechoslovakia, 1973, Germany, 1983, Japan, 1985, 88, China, 1987; lectr. Polish Acad. Sci., 1974; lecture series throughout Fed. Republic of Germany, 1980, 87, 89, 91, Japan, 1985, 87, 90, 93, China, 1987, Sweden, 1983, 94, Finland, 1991, Estonia, 1991, Moscow, 1992, Amsterdam, 1992; mem. Fulbright Com. on Maths., 1986-89. Author: (with I. Richards) Computability in Analysis and Physics, 1989; author numerous articles on mathematical logic (theoretical computer sci.) and applications to mathematical and physical theory. Named to Hunter Coll. Hall of Fame, 1975; NAS grantee, 1966. Fellow AAAS, Japan Soc. for Promotion of Sci.; mem. Am. Math. Soc. (coun. 1980-88, numerous coms., lectr. nat. meeting 1976, also spl. sessions 1971, 78, 82, 84, chmn. spl. sessions on recursion theory 1975, 84), Assn. Symbolic Logic, Math. Assn. Am. (nat. panel vis. lectrs. 1977—, lectr. nat. meetings 1982, 89), Phi Beta Kappa, Sigma Xi, Pi Mu Epsilon, Sigma Pi Sigma. Achievements include research in mathematical logic (theoretical computer science) and in computability and noncomputability in physical theory—wave, heat, potential equations, eigenvalues, eigenvectors. Office: U Minn Sch Math Vincent Hall Minneapolis MN 55455-0488 *In order to practice our careers our family has evolved a pattern of life at variance with the norm. For more than twenty years we have lived apart most of the time. Our strong emotional and personal ties were intensified by this absence of continuous physical nearness. It is my belief that one can succeed personally, socially and professionally without having to accept the constraints of an existing social order.*

POUSSAINT, ALVIN FRANCIS, psychiatrist, educator; b. N.Y.C., May 15, 1934; s. Christopher Thomas V. and Harriet (Johnston) P. BA, Columbia U., 1956; MD, Cornell U., 1960; MS, UCLA, 1964. Intern UCLA Ctr. for Health Sci., 1960-61, resident in psychiatry Neuropsychiat. Inst., 1961-64, chief resident, 1964-65; So. field dir. Med. Com. Human Rights, Jackson, Miss., 1965-66; asst. prof. psychiatry Tufts U. Med. Sch., 1966-69; assoc. prof. psychiatry, assoc. dean students Harvard Med. Sch., 1969-75, 78—, prof. psychiatry, 1993—, dean students, 1975-78; cons. HEW, 1969-73; chmn. select com. on Edn. of Black Youth. Author numerous articles in field. Nat. treas. Black Acad. Arts and Letters, 1969-70, Med. Com. Human Rights, 1966—. Recipient Michael Schwerner award, 1968, Am. Black Achievement award in Bus. and the Professions Johnson Pub. Co., Inc., 1986, John Jay award for Disting. Profl. Achievement Columbia Coll., N.Y., 1987, Medgar Evers Medal of Honor Beverly Hills/Hollywood chpt. NAACP, Hollywood, Calif., 1988, and numerous hon. degrees. Fellow AAAS, Am. Orthopsychiatric Assn., Am. Psychiat. Assn. (mem. com. on Black Psychiatrists 1970-75); mem. Nat. Med. Assn., Am. Acad. of Child Psychiatry, Children's Longwood. Office: Judge Baker Ctr 295 Longwood Ave Boston MA 02115-5794

POUSSAINT, RENEE FRANCINE, journalist; b. N.Y.C., Aug. 12, 1944; d. Christopher Wallace and Bobbie (Vance) P.; m. Henry J. Richardson III, Sept. 10, 1977. B.A., Sarah Lawrence Coll., 1966; M.A., UCLA, 1971; postgrad., Yale Law Sch., 1966-67, Ind. U., 1971-72; student, Sorbonne, Paris, 1964-65; hon. doctorate, Mt. Vernon Coll., Washington, 1985; cert., Columbia U. Journalism Sch., Michele Clark Fellowship Program for Minority Journalists, 1972. Program dir. AIESEC, N.Y.C., 1968-69; editor African Arts Mag., Los Angeles, 1969-71; reporter WBBM-TV, Chgo., 1974-76, CBS Network News, Chgo., Washington, 1976-78; became anchorperson WJLA-TV, Washington, 1978; now correspondent PrimeTime Live, ABC News, New York; dancer Jean Leon Destine Troupe, N.Y.C., 1966; translator U. Calif. Press, Los Angeles, 1970; tutor Operation Rescue, Washington, 1981—. Hon. dir. Nat. Kidney Found., Washington, 1981—; citizen advisor YWCA, Nat. Capitol Area, 1983—; co-chmn. Nat. Capital Area Lung Assn., 1982; membership chmn. Arthritis Found., 1981-82. Recipient Reporting award Ill. Mental Health Assn., 1976; recipient Reporting award Nat. Assn. Media Women, 1977, Broadcasting Excellence award AAUW, 1979, Emmy awards, 1979, 80, 81, 82, Broadcast award NAACP, 1980, Whitney Young Meml. award Washington Urban League, 1983. Mem. AFTRA, NAACP (life), Capitol Press Club. Office: PrimeTime Live 147 Columbus Ave Fl 3 New York NY 10023-5900

POUSSART, DENIS JEAN-MARIE, electrical engineering educator, consultant; b. St. Denis D'Oleron, France, Oct. 3, 1940; arrived in Can., 1952; s. Jean and Anne (Gerardin) P.; m. Nicole Dorion, Dec. 19, 1964; children: Caroline, Brigitte, Pascale. BS, Laval U., Que., Can., 1963; MS, MIT, 1965, PhD, 1968. Registered profl. engr., Que. Prof. elec. & computer engring. Laval U., Quebec, Can., 1968—, chmn. dept. elec. engring., 1988-91; coord. Inst. for Robotics and Intelligent Systems, Can., 1990—; v.p. R & D Centre de Recherche Informatique de, Montreal, Can., 1991—; mem. Sci. & Engring. Rsch. Coun., Can., 1986-88; bd. dirs. Centre de Recherche Industrielle du Que., 1985-89; mem. engring. grant com. Fonds Formation Chercheurs, 1989-91, mem. ctr. grant com., 1993-95. Assoc. editor Indsl. Meteorology, 1988, Can. Jour. Elec. and Computer Engring., 1988; contbr. numerous papers to profl. jours. Mem. IEEE, Can. Acad. Engring., Internat. Soc. Optical Engring., Sigma Xi. Office: Laval U, Dept Elec & Computer Engring, Quebec, PQ Canada G1K 7P4

POUTSMA, MARVIN L., chemical research administrator; b. Grand Rapids, Mich., Aug. 7, 1937; m. Yolanda Arco, July 20, 1968; children: John C., Julie A. BS, Calvin Coll., 1958; PhD, U. Ill., 1962. Staff scientist corp. rsch. Union Carbide, Tarrytown, N.Y., 1961-65, group leader corp. rsch., 1965-68, sr. scientist corp. rsch., 1968-73, sr. group leader corp. rsch., 1972-78; group leader chemistry divsn. Oak Ridge (Tenn.) Nat. Lab., 1978-80, sect. head chemistry divsn., 1980-83, dir. chemistry divsn., 1984-93, dir. chem. & analytical scis. divsn., 1994—. Contbr. chpts. to books and articles to profl. jours. Fellow AAAS; mem. Am. Chem. Soc. Office: Oak Ridge Nat Lab PO Box 2008 Oak Ridge TN 37831-6129

POVICH, DAVID, lawyer; b. Washington, June 8, 1935; s. Shirley Lewis and Ethyl (Friedman) P.; m. Constance Enid Tobriner, June 14, 1959; children: Douglas, Johanna, Judith, Andrew. B.A., Yale U., 1958; LL.B., Columbia U., 1962. Bar: D.C. 1962. Law clk. to assoc. judge D.C. Ct. Appeals, Washington, 1962-63; ptnr. Williams & Connolly, Washington, 1963—, mem. exec. com., 1986-87; speaker Georgetown U. Criminal Practice Inst., Harvard Law Sch. Trial Advocacy Workshop. Bd. dirs., officer Lisner Home for Aged. Mem. D.C. Bar Assn., ABA, Bar Assn. D.C., Barristers (exec. com. 1992-93). Office: Williams & Connolly 725 12th St NW Washington DC 20005-3901

POVICH, LYNN, journalist, magazine editor; b. Washington, June 4, 1943; d. Shirley and Ethyl (Friedman) P.; m. Stephen B. Shepard, Sept. 16, 1979; children: Sarah, Ned. AB, Vassar Coll., 1965. Rechr., reporter, writer, editor Newsweek Mag., N.Y.C., 1965-91; editor-in-chief Working Woman Mag., N.Y.C., 1991—. Recipient Matrix award N.Y. Women in Comms., 1976; named to Acad. of Women Achievers YWCA, 1993. Office: Working Woman 230 Park Ave Fl 7 New York NY 10169-0799

POVICH, (MAURICE) MAURY RICHARD, broadcast journalist, talk show host, television producer; b. Washington, Jan. 17, 1939; s. Shirley and Ethel Povich; m. Constance "Connie" Y. Chung, Dec. 2, 1984; children from previous marriage, Susan, Amy. BA, U. Pa., 1962. Reporter WWDC Radio, Washington, 1962-66; gen. assignment and sports report Sta. WTTG-TV, Washington, 1966; co-anchor Panorama, Washington, 1967-70, host, 1973-76, host and anchor, 1983-86; host People and Povich Sta. WTTG, Washington, 1970-72; news anchor Sta. WMAQ-TV, Chgo., 1977, Sta. KNXT-TV, L.A., 1977-78; anchor Sta. KGO-TV, San Francisco, 1978-79, Sta. KYW-TV, Phila., 1980-83, Sta. WTTG-TV, Washington, 1983-86; host A Current Affair, 1986-90; host, anchor WTTG-TV News, 1983-86; host Maury Povich Show, 1991—; guest on Carol Leiffer show, 1989, Donahue show with Connie Chung, 1989, John MacLaughlin show, 1989, Dick Cavett show, 1989, others; guest speaker Am. Agrl. Editors Assn. Communication Clinic, 1989, ASTA Conf., N.Y.C., 1990, Assn. Broadcast Exec. of Tex., 1990; speaker on tabloid TV, the media and Israel, advertiser blacklists; host Forbes 400, CBS-TV Special, 1992. Author: Current Affairs: A Life on the Edge, 1991. Office: The Maury Povich Show 221 W 26th St New York NY 10001-6703

POVICH, SHIRLEY LEWIS, columnist, former sports editor; b. Bar Harbor, Maine, July 15, 1905; s. Nathan and Rosa (Orlovich) P.; m. Ethyl Friedman, Feb. 21, 1932; children: David, Maurice R., Lynn. Student, Georgetown U., 1922-24. Reporter Washington Post, 1923-25, sports editor, 1926-33, columnist, 1933-45; war corr. Washington Post, PTO, 1945; columnist Washington Post, 1946—; adj. prof. communications Am. U., 1975—. Author: The Washington Senators, 1954, All These Mornings, 1969; also articles in mags. Recipient citation for outstanding svc. as war correspondent, 1945, Grantland Rice award for sportswriting Nat. Headliners Club, 1964, Red Smith award, 1983, award for outstanding career accomplishment in journalism Nat. Press Club, 1995, Lifetime Achievement award Nat. Press. Club, 1995; elected to Baseball Hall of Fame, Cooperstown Writers Divsn., 1976. Mem. Baseball Writers Assn. Am. (pres. 1955). Home: 2801 New Mexico Ave NW Washington DC 20007-3921 Office: Washington Post 1515 L St NW Washington DC 20005-1601

POVISH, KENNETH JOSEPH, retired bishop; b. Alpena, Mich., Apr. 19, 1924; s. Joseph Francis and Elizabeth (Jachcik) P. A.B., Sacred Heart Sem., Detroit, 1946; M.A., Cath. U. Am., 1950; postgrad., No. Mich. U., 1961, 63. Ordained priest Roman Catholic Ch., 1950; asst. pastorships, 1950-56; pastor in Port Sanilac Mich., 1956-57, Munger, Mich., 1957-60, Bay City, Mich., 1966-70; dean St. Paul Sem., Saginaw, Mich., 1960-66; vice rector St. Paul Sem., 1962-66; bishop of Crookston Minn., 1970-75; bishop of Lansing Mich., 1975-95; bd. consulators Diocese of Saginaw, 1966-70; instr. Latin and U.S. history St. Paul Sem., 1960-66. Weekly columnist Saginaw and Lansing diocesan newspapers. Bd. dirs. Cath. Charities Diocese Saginaw, 1969-70. Mem. Mich. Hist. Soc., Bay County Hist. Soc., Lions Club, KC (pres. Mich. Cath. Conf. 1985-95), Kiwanis.

POWDERLY, WILLIAM H., III, lawyer; b. Pitts., Feb. 23, 1930. BS, Georgetown U., 1953; LLB, U. Pitts., 1956. Bar: Pa. 1956. Ptnr. Jones, Day, Reavis & Pogue, Pitts. Office: Jones Day Reavis & Pogue 1 Mellon Bank Ctr 500 Grant St Pittsburgh PA 15219-2502*

POWE, DIANE, nurse anesthetist, educator; b. Elmhurst, N.Y., July 30, 1951; d. Ernest and Dorothy (Bryant) P. BS, Hunter Coll., 1973; MA, Teachers Coll., 1976; postgrad., Va. Tech. U. reg. nurse anesthetist. Commdr. USN, 1976-94; staff nurse anesthetist Kings County Hosp. Ctr., Bklyn., 1984-87, Lewis-Gale Clinic, Salem, Va., 1988—. Mem. Roanoke Symphony Orch. Soc., 1988. Recipient Nat. Defense Svc. medal USN, 1991. Mem. Am. Assn. Nurse Anesthetists, Nat. Employment and Training Assn., Phi Theta Kappa, Omicron Tau Theta. Avocation: traveling.

POWE, RALPH ELWARD, university administrator; b. Tylertown, Miss., July 27, 1944; s. Roy Elward and Virginia Alyne (Bradley) P.; m. Sharon Eve Sandifer, May 20, 1962; children: Deborah Lynn, Ryan Elward, Melanie Colleen. BS in Mech. Engring., Miss. State U., 1967, MS in Mech. Engring., 1968; PhD in Mech. Engring., Mont. State U., 1970. Student trainee NASA, 1962-65; research asst., lab. instr. Miss. State U., 1968, instr. dept. mech. engring., 1968; research asst., teaching asst. Mont. State U., Bozeman, 1968-70, asst. prof. dept. mech. engring., 1970-74; assoc. prof. Miss. State U., 1974-78, prof., 1979-80, assoc. dean engring., dir. engring. and indsl. research sta., 1979-80, assoc. v.p. research, 1980-86, v.p., 1986—; chmn. bd. dirs. Coalition of Experimental Program to Stimulate Competitive Rsch. States, 1994-96; bd. dirs. Gulf Univs. Rsch. Consortium, Tenn.-Tombigbee Project Area Coun.; rep. rsch. coun. Nat. Assn. State Univs. and Land Grant Colls., So. Growth Policies Bd., Miss. Mineral Resources Inst., Sci. and Tech. Coun. States. Disting. Engring. fellow Coll. Engring.; active Miss. Univ. Res. Authority, Coun. on Rsch. Policy, So. Growth Policies Bd.; rep. Miss. Mineral Resources Inst.; gov. rep. Sci. and Tech. Coun. of States; cons. energy conservation programs, coal fired power plants, torsional vibrations, accident analysis; dir. Miss. Energy Rsch. Ctr., 1979-81, Ctr. for Environ. Studies, 1980—; univ. rep. on lignite task force, rep. on bd. dirs. Miss.-Ala. Sea Grant Consortium, chmn. of Council Oak Ridge Associated Univs., rep. to Tenn.-Tombigbee project area coun.; chmn. Miss. Rsch. Consortium; mem. S.E. Univs. Rsch. Assn. Named Outstanding Egr., Engring. Socs. Contbr. articles to profl. jours. Mem. Miss. Econ. Coun., univ. coord. United Way, 1983, 85; tchr. adult Sunday Sch. class 1st Bapt. Ch. Recipient Ralph E. Teeter award Soc. Automotive Engrs., Commdr.'s award Pub. Svc. U.S. Dept. Army, 1995; named Outstanding Engr. in No. Miss. Joint Engr. Soc., Pub. Svc. Commdr.'s award U.S. Army. Fellow ASME; mem. Nat. Assn. State Universities and Land Grant Colls., Starkville Cmty. Theatre Wing. Edn., Wind Energy Soc. Am., Miss. Acad. Scis., Miss. Engring. Soc., Toastmasters, Starkville Quarterback Club, Rotary, Starkville C. of C. (bd. dirs.), Blue Key, Sigma Xi (Miss. State U. research award), Tau Beta Pi, Kappa Mu Epsilon, Pi Tau Sigma, Phi Kappa Phi, Omicron Delta Kappa. Baptist. Lodge: Rotary. Avocations: hunting, fishing, gardening. Home: 110 Pinewood Rd Starkville MS 39759-4128 Office: Miss State U PO Box 6343 Mississippi State MS 39762-6343

POWELL, ALAN, mechanical engineer, scientist; b. Buxton, Derbyshire, Eng., Feb. 17, 1928; came to U.S., 1956; s. Frank and Gwendolen Marie (Walker) P.; m. June Sinclair, Mar. 28, 1956. Student, Buxton Coll., 1939-45; diploma in aeros., Loughborough Coll., 1948; B.Sc. in Engring. with 1st class honors, London U., 1949; honours diploma 1st class, Loughborough Coll., 1949; D.Tech. (hon.), Loughborough U. Tech., 1980; Ph.D., U. Southampton, 1953. Chartered aero. engr., mech. engr. Engr. Percival Aircraft Co., Luton, Eng., 1949-51; research asst. U. Southampton, Eng., 1951-53; lectr. U. Southampton, 1953-56; research fellow Calif. Inst. Tech., Pasadena, 1956-57; engr. Douglas Aircraft Co., 1956; assoc. prof. UCLA, 1957-62, prof. engring., 1962-65, head Aerosonics lab., 1957-65; assoc. tech. dir., head acoustics and vibration lab. David Taylor Model Basin, Dept. Navy, Washington, 1965-66; tech. dir. David Taylor Model Basin, Dept. Navy, 1966-67, David Taylor Naval Ship Research & Devel. Center, Bethesda, Md., 1967-85; mem. Undersea Warfare Research & Devel. Council, 1966-76, chmn., 1971-72; mem. council on Fed. Labs., 1972-85; prof. mech. engring. U. Houston, 1985—, chmn., 1985-87; mem. com. on hearing bioacoustics and biomechs. NAS-NRC, 1961-85, advisor, 1985-95, exec. coun., 1963-65, chmn., 1965-66, mem. naval studies bd. 1990-95; mem. various coms. Naval Studies Bd. and Marine Bd., 1990—; advisor Chinese U. Devel. Project, 1989-91; cons. Douglas Aircraft Co., various aerospace and acoustics cos., 1956-65; mem. adv. coun. Internat. Towing Tank Conf., 1981-85; advisor U.S.-Japan Program Natural Resources, 1987—, mem., 1979-86; gen. chmn. 3d advanced vehicles conf. AIAA and Soc. Naval Architects and Marine Engrs., 1976; chmn. internat. conf. ComputerAided Design, Manufacture and Ops. in Marine and Offshore Industries, 1987-88; cons. Sci. Applications Internat., Inc., 1987-90; governing bd. Am. Inst. of Physics, 1995—. Contbr. articles to profl. jours. Recipient Navy Meritorious Civilian Service award, 1970; Brit. Empire scholar, 1945; named Meritorious Exec. Pres. of U.S., 1982; Capt. Robert Dexter Conrad gold medal for sci. achievement Sec. Navy, 1984. Fellow Royal Aero. Soc. London (Baden-Powell prize 1948, Wilbur Wright prize 1953), Acoustical Soc. Am. (biennial award 1962, assoc. editor Jour. 1962-67, chmn. edn. com. 1964-66, exec. coun. 1966-69, chmn. medals and awards com. 1978-81, v.p. elect 1981-82, v.p. 1982-83, pres. elect 1989-90, pres. 1990-91, past pres. 1991-92, Silver medal in engring. acoustics 1992, designated Nat. Spkr. in Engring. Acoustics 1994—), Inst. Mech. Engrs., Inst. Acoustics (U.K.); mem. AIAA (assoc. fellow, Aeroacoustics award 1980), ASME (Rayleigh lectr. 1988, Per Brüel Gold medal 1991), Inst. Noise Control Engrs. (initial mem., dir. 1974-77, Disting. lectr. 1975, 83, v.p. 1981-84, bd. cert. 1993), Acoustics, Speech and Signal Processing Soc. (exec. com. 1969-72, awards com. 1971-73, bylaws com. chmn. 1973-75), Am. Soc. Naval Engrs. (life), Am. Acad. Mechanics, Tau Beta Pi (hon. life). Office: U Houston Dept Mech Engring Houston TX 77204-4792

POWELL, ALLEN ROYAL, bishop; b. Beaumont, Tex., June 9, 1922; s. Millard and Annie (Surrey) P.; m. Mary Louise Barclay, Dec. 9, 1940; children: Allen R. Jr., Gloria P. Russell, Raymond L., Gwendolyn P. Robinson. Student, Bishop Coll., 1949-51. Pastor Ch. of Living God, Lukin, Tex., 1946-49, Dallas, 1949-51, Kansas City, Kans., 1951-62; dist. overseer Ch. of Living God, Tenn., 1960-66, bishop, 1966-74; bishop Ch. of Living God, Miss., 1974—; pastor Ch. of Living God, Chgo., 1961—, revivalist, counselor, nat. youth instr., exec. bd., Cin., 1966—. Chaplain U.S. Army, 1944-46. Named hon. bishop Five Chs. of Monrovia, 1992. Avocations: printing, singing. Home: 8557 S Wabash Ave Chicago IL 60619-5617 Office: Ch of Living God 14 E 45th St Chicago IL 60653-3111

POWELL, ANICE CARPENTER, librarian; b. Moorhead, Miss., Dec. 2, 1928; d. Horace Aubrey and Celeste (Brian) Carpenter; student Sunflower Jr.

Coll., 1945-47, Miss. State Coll. Women, 1947-48; B.S., Delta State Coll., 1961, M.L.S., 1974; m. Robert Wainwright Powell, July 19, 1948 (dec. 1979); children: Penelope Elizabeth, Deborah Alma. Librarian, Sunflower (Miss.) Pub. Library, 1958-61; tchr. English, Isola (Miss.) High Sch., 1961-62; dir. Sunflower County Library, Indianola, Miss., 1962—; mem. adv. coun. State Instl. Library Services, 1967-71; mem. adv. bd. library services and constrn. act com. Miss. Library Commn., 1978-80, mem. pub. library task force, 1986—; mem. Pub. Library Standards Com., 1988—; mem. state adv. coun. adult edn., 1988-92; mem. steering com. NASA community involvement program Miss. Delta Community Coll., 1990, adult edn. adv. com.; mem. Dist. Workforce Coun., 1994—, Mid Delta Enpowerment Zone Alliance, 1995—; commn. mem. Mid-Delta Empowerment Zone Alliance. Mem. AAUW, NOW, ALA (speaker senate subcom. on illiteracy 1989, honoree ALA 50th Anniversary 1996), Miss. Library Assn. (exec. dir. Nat. Library Week 1975, steering com. 1976, chmn. Right to Read com. 1976, co-chmn., 1987, chmn. legis. com. 1979, chmn. intellectual freedom com. 1975, 80, mem. legis. com. 1973-86, 96, chmn. membership com. 1982, pres. 1984, chmn. nominating com. 1986, chmn. election com. 1989, mem. registration com. 1991—, mem. membership com., mem. nominating com. 1994, mem. publicity com. 1996, mem. fiscal mgmt. com. 1996, mem. awards com. 1996, Peggy May award 1981), Sunflower County Hist. Soc. (pres. 1983-87), Delta Coun. Methodist. Home: PO Box 310 Sunflower MS 38778-0310 Office: Sunflower County Libr 201 Cypress Dr Indianola MS 38751-2415

POWELL, ANNE ELIZABETH, editor; b. Cheverly, Md., Nov. 11, 1951; d. Arthur Gorman and Barbara Anne (MacAran) P.; m. John Alan Ebeling Jr., 1972 (div. 1983). BS, U. Md., 1972. Reporter Fayetteville (N.C.) Times, 1973-75; home editor Columbus (Ga.) Ledger-Enquirer, 1976; assoc. editor Builder mag., Washington, 1977-78; architecture editor House Beautiful's Spl. Publs., N.Y.C., 1979-81; editor Traditional Home mag., Des Moines, 1982-87, Mid-Atlantic Country mag., Alexandria, Va., 1987-89; editor in chief publs. Nat. Trust for Hist. Preservation, Washington, 1989-95; editor-in-chief Landscape Architecture Mag., Washington, 1995—. Author: The New England Colonial, 1988. Mem. Nat. Press Club, Am. Soc. Mag. Editors. Home: 707 S Royal St Alexandria VA 22314-4309 Office: Am Soc Landscape Arch 4401 Connecticut Ave NW Washington DC 20008

POWELL, BARRY BRUCE, classicist; b. Sacramento, Apr. 30, 1942; s. Barrett Robert and Anita Louise (Burns) P.; m. Patricia Ann Cox; children: Elena Melissa, Adam Vincent. BA in Classics, U. Calif., Berkeley, 1963, PhD, 1971; MA, Harvard U., 1965. Asst. prof. Northern Ariz. U., Flagstaff, 1970-73; asst. prof. to prof. U. Wis., Madison, 1973—, chmn. dept. classics, 1985-92, chmn. program integrated liberal studies. Author: Composition by Theme in the Odyssey, 1973, Homer and the Origin of the Greek Alphabet, 1991, Classical Myth, 1995; contbr. articles to profl. jours. Woodrow Wilson fellow, 1965. Mem. Am. Philol. Assn., Am. Sch. Classical Studies at Athens (mng. com), Archeol. Inst. of Am., Classical Assn. of Midwest and South, Am. Academy in Rome, Phi Beta Kappa (former pres. Madison chpt.). Home: 1210 Sweetbriar Rd Madison WI 53705-2228 Office: Univ Wis Dept Classics Madison WI 53707

POWELL, BOLLING RAINES, JR., lawyer, educator; b. Florala, Ala., Aug. 10, 1910; s. Bolling Raines and Marie (Arnold) P.; m. Mary Vilette Spaulding, Dec. 10, 1949; children: Bolling Raines, James Spaulding. B.A., Birmingham-So. Coll., 1930; M.A., LL.B., J.D., U. Va., 1934. Asst. prof. law U. Va., 1938-39; partner Paul V. McNutt, Washington and N.Y.C., 1947-50, Powell, Dorsey and Blum, Washington, 1950-62, Powell, Horkan and Powell, Washington, 1962-75; prof. Wythe Sch. Law, Coll. William and Mary, 1969-80; sole practice Gloucester, Va., 1975—; spl. trial counsel to bd. govs. FRS, 1956-62; bd. advisors Ct. Practice Inst., 1973-78. Editor-in-chief: Va. Law Rev., 1934. Chmn. Gloucester United Taxpayers, 1978—; dir. Boy Scouts Am. Fund Raising Campaign, Gloucester County, 1965. Served to lt. col. AUS, 1942-46. Decorated Legion of Merit. Mem. Va. State Bar (bd. govs. adminstrv. law sect.), Ala. Bar Assn., D.C. Bar Assn., ABA, Raven Soc. U. Va., Phi Beta Kappa, Omicron Delta Kappa. Episcopalian. Clubs: Metropolitan (Washington); Farmington Country (Charlottesville, Va.). Home: Warner Hall Plantation Gloucester VA 23061 Office: PO Box 800 Gloucester VA 23061-0800

POWELL, BOONE, JR., hospital administrator; b. Knoxville, Tenn., Feb. 9, 1937; married. BA, Baylor U., 1959; MA, U. Calif., 1960. Adm. intern Marin Gen. Hosp., Greenbrae, Calif., 1959; adm. resident Baptist Meml. Hosp., Memphis, 1960-61; asst. adminstr. Hendrick Med. Ctr., Abilene, Tex., 1961-69, assoc. adminstr., 1969-70, adminstr., 1970-73, pres., 1973-80; pres. Baylor Health Care System, Dallas, 1980—. Contbr. articles to profl. jours. Mem. Am. Coll. Healthcare Execs., Tex. Hosp. Assn. (chair community svc., trustee). Office: Baylor Health Care System 3500 Gaston Ave Dallas TX 75246-2045

POWELL, BURNELE VENABLE, law educator; b. Kansas City, Kans., Mar. 5, 1947; s. Lorenzo Roland and Teola (Sykes) P.; m. Brenda Joyce Venable, June 30, 1973; children: Bradley Venable, Berkeley Venable. BA, U. Mo., Kansas City, 1970; JD, U. Wis., 1973; LLM, Harvard U., 1979. Bar: Wis. 1973, Mass. 1977. Assoc. regional counsel HUD, Boston, 1973-77; grad. law teaching fellow Harvard U. Law Sch., Cambridge, Mass., 1977-79; asst. prof. U. N.C. Sch. Law, Chapel Hill, 1979-84, assoc. prof., 1984-88, prof., 1988—, assoc. dean, 1990-93; Dean UM KC Sch. Law, Kansas; vis. assoc. prof. law U. Oreg. Sch. Law, Eugene, 1987; vis. prof. law Washington U., St. Louis, summer 1990; cons. Adminstrv. Conf. U.S., Washington, 1983-86; arbitrator Nat. Future Adminstrn., Chgo., 1990. Bd. dirs. Consumers Union, 1993—, Planned Parenthood of Orange and Durham Counties, 1992—. Mem. ABA (coms. 1987—, chmn. standing com. on profl. discipline 1991—, N.C. ethics com. 1990-92), AAUP (chpt. pres. 1990-91), ALI, Am. Bar Found., Assn. Am. Law Schs. (coms. 1981—). Democrat. Unitarian. Home: 2003 S Hawick Ct Chapel Hill NC 27516-7739*

POWELL, CAROL ANN, accountant; b. Bklyn., Dec. 5, 1954; d. William Preston and Adelaide Hertha (Sohl) Batty; m. Michael Robert Powell, Jan. 17, 1976; children: Michael David, David Jason. AAS, Delhi Agrl. and Tech. Coll., 1974; BS, Syracuse U., 1975. CPA, N.Y. Sr. acct. Hall & Yann, CPAs, Fayetteville, N.Y., 1975-78; pvt. practice acct. Cold Spring, N.Y., 1979—; adj. tchr. acctg. Onondaga C.C., Syracuse, N.Y., 1977, Dutchess C.C., Poughkeepsie, N.Y., 1982. Den leader Philipstown Pack 137 Boy Scouts Am., Cold Spring, N.Y., 1987-96; treas. Philipstown Little League, Cold Spring, 1990—, Philipstown Babe Ruth League, Cold Spring, 1994. Mem. AICPA, N.Y. State Soc. CPAs. Methodist. Avocations: piano, quilting. Home: PO Box 312 Cold Spring NY 10516-0312 Office: 159 Main St Cold Spring NY 10516-2818

POWELL, CAROL SUE, pediatric special education educator, nursing consultant; b. Phoenix, Nov. 15, 1944; d. Leonard Newson and Rebecca Jane (Housh) Stephens; m. Howard Powell Jr., Aug. 26, 1967; children: Jim, Howard III, Nicole. LPN, Champaign (Ill.) Sch. Practical Nursing, 1965; BA, Ea. Ill. U., 1975, MS in Edn., 1979; ADN, Lincolnland C.C., 1986. RN, Ill.; lic. EMT; cert. elem. and secondary edn. tchr., Ill.; qualified mental retardation profl., Ill. Nurse Pattie A. Clay Infirmary, Richmond, Ky., 1966-68, Clark County Hosp., Winchester, Ky., 1968-69, Mattoon (Ill.) Hosp., 1970-77; substitute tchr. Mattoon, Charleston, Findlay, Arcola Schs., 1978-79; spl. edn. and kindergarten tchr. Buda (Ill.) Sch. Dist., 1979-81; staff nurse St. John's Hosp., Springfield, Ill., 1981-87; health svc. supr. Assn. for Retarded Citizens, Springfield, 1987-88; staff nurse St. Vincent's Hosp., Taylorville, Ill., 1988-89; spl. edn. tchr., asst. dir. edn., mental retardation profl. Luth. Social Svcs., Beardstown, Ill., 1989—. Nurse Shrine Clinics, Springfield, 1989-96, nurse, EMT first aid meets Boy Scouts Am., Springfield, 1988-96. Methodist. Home: 834 Evergreen Dr Chatham IL 62629-1118 Office: St Luke Health Care Ctr RR3 Box 446 Beardstown IL 62618

POWELL, CHRISTOPHER ROBERT, systems programmer, computer scientist; b. Summit, N.J., Feb. 2, 1963; s. Robin Powell and Nancy Mae (Spurling) Gould; m. Bonnie Jean Manning, June 10, 1989. BS in Math. and Computer Sci., Clarkson U., 1984; postgrad. in Computer Sci., Syracuse U., 1988; postgrad. in Philosophy, SUNY, Binghamton, 1990. Sr. assoc. program IBM Corp., Endicott, N.Y., 1984-90; sr. systems analyst/programmer Supercomputer Systems, Inc., Eau Claire, Wis., 1990-93; prin. systems programmer Network Systems Corp./Channel Networking Strategic Bus. Unit, Brooklyn Park, Minn., 1993—. Appt. City of Spring Lake Park Energy Commn., 1995; vice chmn. Energy Commn., 1996. Mem. Assn. for Computing Machienry, Nat. Systems Programmers Assn., NSC Leadership Forum, Alpha Phi Omega (torchbearer 1987-95), Pi Mu Epsilon, Pi Delta Epsilon. Democrat. Achievements include assisting in Network Systems registration for ISO 9000; core team leader CPU rsch. and implementation. Home: 8220 6th St NE Spring Lake Park MN 55432

POWELL, CLINTON COBB, radiologist, physician, former university administrator; b. Hartford, Conn., Mar. 9, 1918; s. Harry Havey and Nita Florence (Nass) P.; m. Frances Arlene Collins, Apr. 2, 1944; children: Pamela Powell Kellogg, Brenda Joyce, Donna Sue Powell Mason. B.S., Mass. Inst. Tech., 1940; M.D., Boston U., 1944; student, U. Chgo., 1947-48. Diplomate: Am. Bd. Radiology, Nat. Bd. Med. Examiners. Intern U.S. Marine Hosp., Boston, 1944-45; commd. asst. surgeon USPHS, 1946, med. dir., 1956; staff mem. indsl. hygiene research lab. NIH, 1946-47, radiation safety officer, 1948-51; resident radiology USPHS Hosp., Balt., 1951-52; fellow radiology U. Pa. Hosp., 1952-54; staff physician radiation therapy, clin. center NIH, 1954-55; grants analyst, research grants and fellowship br. Nat. Cancer Inst., 1955-56; chief radiol. health med. program, div. spl. health services USPHS, 1956-58; exec. sec. radio and surgery study sect., div. research grants NIH, 1958-59, asst. chief research grants rev. br., div. research grants, 1959-60, dep. chief div., 1960-61; asst. dir. Nat. Inst. Allergy and Infectious Diseases, 1961-62; dir. Nat. Inst. Gen. Med. Scis., NIH, 1962-64; asso. coordinator med. and health scis. U. Calif., 1964-66, coordinator, 1966-71, spl. asst. to pres. for health affairs, 1971-79, spl. asst. emeritus, 1979—; Mem. Internat. Commn. Radiol. Protection, 1965-68; mem. com. Nat. Com. Radiation Protection, 1956-68, exec. com., 1957-67, ad hoc subcom. wide-spread radioactive contamination, 1958-60, subcom. 1, 1960—; mem. radiol. physics fellowship bd. AEC, 1958-63; com. radiation effects Am. Thoracic Soc., 1957—; com. use radioisotopes in hosps. Am. Hosp. Assn., 1953—; subcom. radiol. health Assn. State and Territorial Health Officers, 1956-58. Contbr. numerous articles profl. jours. Served with USNR, 1945-46. Fellow AAAS; mem. Am. Coll. Radiology (commn. radiol. units, standards and protection 1957—, chmn. com. radiation exposure of women), AMA, Am. Pub. Health Assn. (program area com. radiol. health 1959), Radiol. Soc. N.Am., Radiation Research Soc., Health Physics Soc., Assn. for Acad. Health Centers (dir. 1969-70).

POWELL, COLIN LUTHER, retired military officer, author; b. N.Y.C., Apr. 5, 1937; s. Luther and Maud Ariel (McKoy) P.; m. Alma V. Johnson, Aug. 25, 1962; children: Michael, Linda, Annemarie. B.S., CUNY, 1958; M.B.A., George Washington U., 1971. Commd. 2d lt. U.S. Army, 1958; advanced through grades to gen., 1989; comdr. 2d Brigade, 101st Airborne Div., 1976-77; exec. asst. to sec. Dept. Energy, 1979; sr. mil. asst. to sec. Dept. Def., 1979-81; asst. div. comdr. 4th Inf. Div. Dept. Def., Ft. Carson, Colo., 1981-83; mil. asst. to Sec. of Def. Dept. Def., Washington, 1983-86; assigned to U.S. V Corps, Europe, 1986-87; dep. asst. to the pres. for nat. security affairs The White House, Washington, 1987; asst. to Pres. for nat. security affairs Washington, 1987-89; comdr.-in-chief Forces Command, Ft. McPherson, Ga., 1989-94; chmn. Joint Chiefs of Staff The Pentagon, Washington, 1989-93; ret., 1994. Author: My American Journey, 1995. Decorated Legion of Merit, Bronze Star, Air medal, Purple Heart; The White House fellow, 1972-73; recipient Medal of Freedom (2); named hon. knight comdr. Most Honorable Order of the Bath Queen Elizabeth II, 1993. Mem. Assn. U.S. Army. Episcopalian. Office: 909 N Washington St Ste 767 Alexandria VA 22314-1555

POWELL, DEBORAH ELIZABETH, pathologist; b. Lynn, Mass., 1939. MD, Tufts U., 1965. Diplomate Am. Bd. Pathology. Intern Georgetown Med. Ctr., Washington, 1965-66; resident in pathology NIH, Bethesda, Md., 1966-69; with A.B. Chandler Med. Ctr., Lexington, Ky.; prof. U. Ky. Mem. Am. Assn. Pathologists, Internat. Assn. Pathologists, ASC. Office: Acad Faculty 800 Rose St Lexington KY 40536-0001

POWELL, DON WATSON, medical educator, physician, physiology researcher; b. Gadsden, Ala., Aug. 29, 1938; s. Gordon C. and Ruth (Bennett) P.; m. Frances N. Rourke; children: Mary Paige, Drew Watson, Shawne Margaret. BS with honors, Auburn U., 1960; MD with highest honors, Med. Coll. Ala., Birmingham, 1963. Diplomate Am. Bd. Internal Medicine, Am. Bd. Gastroenterology. Intern, resident P.B. Brigham Hosp., Boston, 1963-65; resident Yale U. Sch. Med., New Haven, 1968-69, spl. NIH fellow in physiology, 1969-71; asst. prof. medicine U. N.C., Chapel Hill, 1971-74, assoc. prof., 1974-78, prof., 1978-91; chief divsn. digestive diseases U. N.C., 1977-91, dir. Ctr. Gastrointestinal Biol. Diseases, 1985-91, assoc. chmn. clin. affairs dept. medicine, 1989-91; Edward Randall and Edward Randall, Jr. Disting. Chmn., prof. dept. internal medicine, prof. dept. physiology and biophysics Med. br. U. Tex., Galveston, 1991—; cons. WHO, Geneva, 1980-82, Burroughs-Wellcome, Inc., Research Triangle Park, N.C., 1981-82, Hoffman-LaRoche, Inc., Nutley, N.J., 1982—; mem. merit rev. bd. VA, 1977-80; mem. gen. medicine A-2 study sect. NIH, 1985-89, mem. Nat. Inst. Diabetes Digestive and Kidney Diseases Adv. Coun., 1994—; coun., bd. rep. adv. com. to dir.NIH, 1996—. Assoc. editor: Textbook of Gastroenterology, Atlas of Gastroenterology; mem. editl. bd. Am. Jour. Physiology, Gastrointestinal and Liver Physiology, 1979—, Am. Jour. Med. Sci., 1984-92, Regulatory Peptide Letter, 1990—, Annals of Internal Medicine, 1993-96; contbr. over 100 articles to profl. jours. Capt. U.S. Army Med. Corps, 1965-68. Recipient Rsch. Career Devel. award NIH, 1973-78, Merit award, 1987, Outstanding Physician of Yr. award Gulf Coast chpt. Crohn's Colitis Found. Am., 1994. Fellow ACP (mem. med. knowledge self-assessment program VII gastroenterology com. 1983-85); mem. Am. Physiol. Soc., Am. Gastroenterol. Assn. (v.p. 1991-92, pres. 1993-94), Gastroenterology Rsch. Group (chmn. 1988-89), So. Soc. Clin. Investigation, Federated Socs. Gastroenterology and Hepatology (chmn. 1996—), Assn. Am. Physicians, Assn. Prof. Medicine, Am. Clin. and Climatol. Assn. Avocation: singing. Office: U Tex Med Br 4.108 John Sealy Annex 301 University Blvd Galveston TX 77555-0567

POWELL, DOUGLAS ROBERT, psychology educator; b. Kalamazoo, Sept. 19, 1948; s. Robert Noel and Vonda Lucile (Warner) P.; m. Barbara Jane Lewellen, Aug. 21, 1971; children: Rachel Mae, Philip Douglas. BA, Western Mich. U., 1970, MA, 1971; PhD, Northwestern U., 1974. Rsch. assoc., dir. program devel. Merrill-Palmer Inst., Detroit, 1974-80; assoc. prof. human devel. Wayne State U., Detroit, 1980-84; prof., head child devel. & family studies Purdue U., West Lafayette, Ind., 1984—; cons. Bush Found., St. Paul, 1982—; mem. tech. resource Nat. Edn. Coals Panel, Washington, 1991—; mem. nat. adv. com. U. Chgo. Family Support Project, 1995. Bd. dirs. Tippecanoe County Child Care, Inc., Lafayette, Ind., 1986-88; mem. policy coun. Head Start, Lafayette, 1985-87; mem. standing com. Meth. Children's Village, Detroit, 1981-83. Rsch. grantee Lilly Endowment, Ford Found., Bush Found., Kellogg Found., 1978—; recipient Hoosier Educator of Yr. award Ind. Assn. Edn. Young Children, Indpls., 1990, Mary L. Matthews Outstanding Tchr. award, 1991. Mem. Am. Psychol. Assn., Am. Edn. Rsch. Assn. (chair child devel. group 1992-94), Nat. Assn. Edn. Young Childrem (editor 1985-95), Nat. Coun. Family Rels. Episcopalian. Avocations: music, theatre, gardening. Office: Purdue U CDFS Dept West Lafayette IN 47907

POWELL, DREXEL DWANE, JR., editorial cartoonist; b. Lake Village, Ark., Nov. 7, 1944; s. Drexel Dwane and Minnie Louise (Ruth) P.; m. Janice Sue Lovell, Apr. 10, 1971. B.S. in Agri-Bus, U. Ark. at Monticello, 1970. Cartoonist Sentinel Record, Hot Springs, Ark., 1970-72, San Antonio Light, 1973-74; editorial cartoonist Cin. Enquirer, 1974-75, News and Observer, Raleigh, N.C., 1975—; syndicated L.A. Times Syndicate, 1979—; lectr. in field. Author: Is That All You Do?, 1979, Surely SOMEONE Can Still Sing Bass!, 1981, The Reagan Chronicles, 1987, One Hundred Per Cent Pure Old Jess, 1993; freelance artist; designer book jackets. Served with N.G., 1967-68. Recipient Overseas Press Club citation, 1978, Headliners Club award, 1978; named Disting. Alumnus U. Ark. at Monticello, 1979. Mem. Assn. Am. Editorial Cartoonists. Office: 215 S Mcdowell St Raleigh NC 27601-1331

POWELL, DURWOOD ROYCE, lawyer; b. Raleigh, N.C., Nov. 21, 1951; s. Albert Royce and Ruby Rader (Lowery) P.; m. Leej Ida Copperfield, Mar. 1, 1980. BS, U. N.C., 1974, JD, 1979; LLM in Taxation, Emory U., 1985. Bar: N.C. 1979, U.S. Dist. Ct. (ea., mid. and we. dists.) N.C. 1981, U.S. Tax Ct. 1981, U.S. Ct. Appeals (4th cir.) 1984, U.S. Ct. Claims 1984, U.S. Supreme Ct. 1984, D.C. 1988, U.S. Ct. Appeals (D.C. cir.) 1988, N.Y. 1989. Mgmt. analyst GAO, Norfolk, Va., 1974-76; mem. tax staff Arthur Andersen & Co., Washington, 1979-80; assoc. Biggs, Meadows, Etheridge & Johnson, Rocky Mount, N.C., 1980-82, Biggs Law Firm, Rocky Mount, 1982-83; ptnr. Maupin, Taylor, Ellis & Adams, Raleigh, N.C., 1985—, also bd. dirs.; adj. prof. corp. taxation Grad. Sch. Bus., U. N.C.-Chapel Hill, 1989-92; faculty Duke U. Tax and Estate Planning Conf., 1991; mem. negotiation project Harvard U., Cambridge, Mass., 1992. Contbr. articles to profl. publs. Mem. tax reform com. Duke U., Washington, 1988. Mem. ABA (tax, corp., banking and securities sects.), N.C. Bar Assn. (tax and corp. sects.), Phi Beta Kappa, Phi Eta Sigma. Home: 4917 Rembert Dr Raleigh NC 27612-6239 Office: Maupin Taylor Ellis & Adams 3200 Beech Leaf Ct Raleigh NC 27604-1063

POWELL, EARL ALEXANDER, III, art museum director; b. Spartanburg, S.C., Oct. 24, 1943; s. Earl Alexander and Elizabeth (Duckworth) P.; m. Nancy Landry Powell, July 17, 1971; children—Cortney, Channing, Sumner. AB with honors, William Coll., 1966; AM, Harvard U., 1970, PhD, 1974. Teaching fellow in fine arts Harvard U., 1970-74; curator, Michener Collection U. Tex., Austin, 1974-76, asst. prof. art history, 1974-76; mus. curator, sr. staff asst. to asst. dir. and chief curator Nat. Gallery Art, Washington, 1976-78, exec. curator, 1979-80; dir. Los Angeles County Mus. Art, 1980-92, Nat. Gallery Art, Washington, 1992—; career advisor Harvard U.; mem. fine arts adv. panel Fed. Res. Bank, Commn. Pres. of White House, Pres.' Commn. on Arts and Humanities, Coun. Arts and Humanities, Fed. Coun. Arts and Humanities, Nat. Portrait Gallery Commn., Scholarly Adv. Coun. Author: American Art at Harvard, 1973, Selections from the James Michener Collection, 1975, Abstract Expressionists and Imagists: A Retrospective View, 1976, Milton Avery, 1976, The James A. Michener Collection: Twentieth Century American Painting, catalogue raisonne, 1978, Thomas Cole monograph, 1990. Trustee Pitzer Coll.; mem. vis. com. Williams Coll. Mus. Art. Served with U.S. Navy, 1966-69, comdr. Res., 1976-80. Decorated chevalier Order Arts and Letters, 1985; grand ofcl. Order of the Infante D. Henrique medal, 1995; recipient King Olav medal, 1978, Bicentennial medal Williams Coll., 1995; Harvard U. travelling fellow, 1973-74. Mem. Walpole Soc., Am. Assn. Mus. (co-chmn. commn. on mus. for a new century), Am. Assn. Mus. Dirs., Am. Fedn. Arts (trustee), White House Hist. Assn. (trustee), Nat. Trust Hist. Preservation, Thomas Jefferson Meml. Found.

POWELL, EARL W., chemicals executive; b. 1939. Ptnr. Peat, Marwick, Mitchell & Co., CPAs, Miami, 1965-85; chmn., chief exec. officer Atlantis Plastics, Inc., Miami, 1984—; also pres. Atlantis Plastics, Inc. *

POWELL, EDMUND WILLIAM, lawyer; b. St. Paul, Dec. 23, 1922; s. George L. and Mary (Sexton) P.; m. Ellen M. Williams, May 7, 1949; children—Susan Marie, Sarah Ann, Daniel. Student, St. Thomas Coll., St. Paul, 1941-43, U. Minn., 1943, 46; LL.B., Marquette U., 1948. Bar: Wis. bar 1948. Pvt. practice Milw., 1948—; pres. firm Borgelt, Powell, Peterson & Frauen and predecessors, 1948-90. Served with USNR, 1943-45; to capt. USMCR, 1945-46, 52-53. Fellow Am. Coll. Trial Lawyers; mem. State Bar Wis. (sec. 1964-65, bd. govs. 1961-63, 65-67, sec., dir. ins. sect. 1962-69), Marquette Law Alumni Assn. (pres., dir. 1957-60). Club: Town (Milw.). Home: 4611 N Lake Dr Milwaukee WI 53211-1255 Office: 735 N Water St Milwaukee WI 53202-4100

POWELL, EDWARD LEE, broadcasting company executive; b. Columbus, Ohio, July 3, 1958; s. Louis Andrew and Margaret Letitia (Steen) P.; m. Denise Noel Harlow, July 11, 1981; children: Edward Lee II, Sarah Elizabeth. BS in Bus. Mgmt. and Mktg., Franklin U., 1988. Freelance square dance caller, rec. artist Reynoldsburg, Ohio, 1976—; columnist Columbus Dispatch Newspaper, 1976-79; disc jockey, salesperson Sta. WWWJ, Johnstown, Ohio, 1978-79; disc jockey, ops. dir. Sta. WLGN-AM-FM, Logan, Ohio, 1980-81; disc jockey Sta. WMNI, Columbus, 1980-89, creative dir., disc jockey, 1987-89; disc jockey Sta. WMGG-FM, Columbus, 1986-87; sales assoc. Tom Yontz and Assocs., Eagle Realty, Westerville, Ohio, 1987—; gen. mgr. Radio Sound Network, Columbus, Ohio, 1989-90; prin. Group X, Reynoldsburg, Ohio, 1990—, Radio Cafe Hour/Cafe Prodns. Inc., Branson, Mo., 1993-95; Cons. mktg. and advt. programs, 1984-95, Central Ohio Corp. of Dance Clubs, Columbus, 1982—, direct mail; spokeman, guest on TV; bd. dirs. Y.E.S. (wheelchair) Dancers, Inc., 1986-89, nat. and state square dance conventions, 1976—. Creative dir. advt. campaigns: Levi's, Cavalier; producer, talent advt. campaign Suzuki Motorcycles, 1981 (award of excellence), (record) Phoenix on Her Mind, 1978; author, pub.: So You Want to Be a Caller, 1979; songwriter BMI. Active Ctrl. Ohio Muscular Dystrophy Assn., 1990-92; co-host, organizer Muscular Dystrophy Local Telethon, Beulah Park, Grove City, 1987-89, Reynoldsburg, 1977-80; asst. scoutmaster Boy Scouts Am., 1975-80; hon. dep. sheriff Franklin County, 1988-92. Recipient Eagle Scout award, 1971; Ohio State Life Ins. scholar, 1987, Farmer's Ins. Group scholar, 1986, Honda of Am. Found. scholar, 1986; named one of nation's Top 10 Square Dance Callers, 1979. Mem. Franklin U. Alumni Assn., Columbus Bd. Realtors, Ohio Bd. Realtors, Nat. Bd. Realtors, Cen. Ohio Sq. Dancers, Reynoldsburg Promenaders, Muscular Dystrophy Assn.-Cen. Ohio (past bd. dirs.) Franklin U. Top Execs. Club. Avocations: songwriting, entertainment and consumer marketing, recording and production, square dancing. Home: PO Box 40 Reynoldsburg OH 43068-0040 Office: Group X Inc Radiowriters PO Box 65 Reynoldsburg OH 43068-0065 also: Tom Yontz & Assocs/Eagle Realty 180 Allview Rd Westerville OH 43081-2909

POWELL, ERIC KARLTON, lawyer, researcher; b. Parkersburg, W.Va., July 23, 1958; s. James Milton and Sarah Elizabeth (Gates) P. BA in History, W.Va. U., 1980, BSBA, 1981; JD, Western State U., Fullerton, Calif., 1987. Bar: Ga. 1992, W.Va. 1993, U.S. Dist. Ct. (we. dist.) W.Va. 1993. Reference libr. Western State U., 1984; tchr. acctg. Rosary H.S., Fullerton, 1984-85; law clk. Zonni, Ginnochio Taylor, Santa Ana, Calif., 1986-93; temp. law sch. Gibson, Dunn & Crutcher, Irvine, Calif., 1993; pvt. practice, Parkersburg, 1993—. Asst. scoutmaster Boy Scouts Am., Parkersburg, 1981-83. Mem. ABA, ATLA, W.Va. Trial Lawyers Assn., Nat. Eagle Scout Assn., Elks, Delta Theta Phi. Republican. Presbyterian. Avocations: hiking, reading, canoeing, chess, astronomy. Home: 2002 20th St Parkersburg WV 26101-4125 Office: 500 Green St Parkersburg WV 26101-5131

POWELL, GEORGE EVERETT, JR., motor freight company executive; b. Kansas City, Mo., June 12, 1926; s. George Everett and Hilda (Brown) P.; m. Mary Catherine Kuehn, Aug. 26, 1947; children: George Everett III, Nicholas K., Richardson K., Peter E. Student, Northwestern U. With Riss & Co., Inc., Kansas City, Mo., 1947-52, treas., 1950-52; with Yellow Freight System, Inc., Kansas City, Mo., 1952—, pres., 1957-68, chmn. bd., 1968—; pres. Yellow Freight Systems, Inc. of Del., Overland Park, Kans., 1987-88; dir. 1st Nat. Charter Corp., Butler Mfg. Co. Trustee, mem. exec. com. Mid-West Research Inst., Kansas City, Mo., from 1961, chmn. bd. trustees, from 1968; bd. govs. Kansas City Art Inst., from 1964, chmn. bd. trustees, 1973-75. Served with USNR, 1944-46. Mem. Kansas City C. of C. (bd. dirs. 1964-68). Office: Yellow Corp 10777 Barkley St Overland Park KS 66211-1161

POWELL, GEORGE EVERETT, III, trucking company executive; b. Kansas City, Mo., Oct. 18, 1948; s. George Everett Jr. and Mary Catherine (Kuehn) P.; m. Wendy Jarman, July 29, 1972; children: Jessica Jarman, Ashley Sinclair. BSBA, Ind. U., 1970. From planning analyst trainee to pres., chief exec. officer Yellow Freight System Inc. of Del. (now Yellow Corp.), Overland Park, Kans., 1971—; also chmn. bd. dirs. Yellow Freight System, Inc., Overland Park, Kans.; pres., CEO Yellow Freight System, Inc. of Del. Trustee Midwest Rsch. Inst.; mem. Powell Family Found., Kansas City Pub. TV. Mem. Young Pres.'s Orgn. Home: 5801 Ward Pky Kansas City MO 64113-1155 Office: Yellow Corp 10777 Barkley PO Box 7563 Overland Park KS 66211*

POWELL, HAROLD FRYBURG, food products executive; b. Corry, Pa., Oct. 18, 1932; s. Harold K. and Freda (Fryburg) P.; m. Jacqueline Williams, May 14, 1955; children: Jeffery, Stephen. BS in Econs., U. Pa., 1954; postgrad., Western Res. U. Securities analyst Cen. Nat. Bank, Cleve., 1955-61; asst. treas. Carling Brewing Co., Cleve., 1961-63; div. contr. Carling Brewing Co., St. Louis, 1963-67; mgr. corp. planning Philip Morris Inc., N.Y.C.,

1967-69, asst. to corp. pres., 1969-71; v.p. Benson & Hedges (Can.) Ltd., Toronto, Ont., Can., 1971-74; v.p. fin. Standard Brands Ltd., Montreal, Que., Can., 1974-76, Internat. Standard Brands Inc., N.Y.C., 1976-77; v.p., treas. Standard Brands Inc., N.Y.C., 1977-79, v.p., corp. comptr., 1979-80, sr. v.p., chief fin. officer, 1980-81; pres., chief exec. officer Nabisco Brands Ltd., Toronto, 1982-83; exec. v.p., chief fin. officer Nabisco Brands Inc., N.Y.C., 1984; exec. v.p. Internat. Nabisco Brands Inc., N.Y.C., 1985, pres., 1986-94; exec. v.p., CFO Nabisco Inc., 1994—. Home: 1062 Smith Ridge Rd New Canaan CT 06840-2330

POWELL, HARVARD WENDELL, former air force officer, business executive; b. Duluth, Minn., Feb. 1, 1915; s. Edgar S. and Leona (Bush) P.; m. Audrey Barker, June 18, 1941; children: Mark Horton, Anne Bush. B.S., U. Minn., 1950, J.D., 1951; grad., Indsl. Coll. Armed Forces, 1956. Commd. 2d lt. USAAF, 1940; advanced through grades to brig. gen. USAF, 1959; command pilot, comdr. China, 1943-45; dir. procurement and prodn. USAF, 1958; vice comdr. Air Force Space Systems Div., 1960, ret., 1963; v.p. mgmt. planning and service N.Am. Rockwell, 1963-70; pres., chief exec. officer A.J. Industries, Inc., Los Angeles, 1970—; also dir.; pres. A.J. Land Co., Juneau Hydroelectric, Inc.; dir. Devel. Services, Inc., Sargent Engring. Co., Roberts-Gordon Appliance Ltd., Calif. Bankers Trust Corp.; Mem. Gov. Calif. Commn. Ednl. Reform; dir. small bus. and econ. utilization policy Office Sec. Def., 1971-77; internat. bus. cons., 1977—. Decorated D.F.C., Air medal with 2 oak leaf clusters, Legion of merit with oak leaf cluster. Mem. State Bar Minn., Air Force Assn.

POWELL, JAMES BOBBITT, biomedical laboratories executive, pathologist; b. Burlington, N.C., Aug. 28, 1938; s. Thomas Edward and Sophia (Sharpe) P.; m. Pamela Oughton, Sept. 12, 1969 (div. Sept. 1979); 1 child, Daphne Oughton; m. Anne Ellington, Oct. 20, 1984; children: James Bobbitt (dec.), John Banks, James Rosser, Helen Bobbitt. BA, Va. Mil. Inst., 1960; MD, Duke U., 1964. Diplomate Am. Bd. Pathology. Intern, Duke U. Med. Ctr., Durham, N.C., 1964-65; resident Cornell Med. Ctr., N.Y.C., 1965-67, Englewood Hosp., N.J., 1967-69; founder Biomed. Labs., Burlington, 1969—; pres. Roche Biomed. Labs., 1982-95, pres., CEO Lab. Corp. Am. Holdings, 1995—, Warren Land Co.; bd. dirs. FirstSouth Bank, Burlington, N.C. Trust Co. Contbr. articles to sci. publs. Trustee Elon Coll. (N.C.), 1981—, N.C. Sch. Sci. and Math.; mem. bd. visitors Duke U. Med. Ctr.; chmn. Alamance Found.; interim bd. edn. Alamance-Burlington, N.C. Served as maj. M.C., U.S. Army, 1969-72. Fellow Am. Soc. Clin. Pathologists, Coll. Am. Pathologists; mem. Alamance Country Club. Republican. Methodist. Avocations: tennis, U.S. military history. Home: 2307 York Rd Burlington NC 27215-3360 Office: LabCorp 358 S Main St Burlington NC 27215-5837

POWELL, JAMES HENRY, lawyer; b. N.Y.C., May 1, 1928; s. Milton Jerome and Doris (Unterberg) P.; m. Connie Lu Egger, Oct. 5, 1958; children: David E., Andrew J., Jeffrey K. AB, Harvard U., 1949; LLB, Yale U., 1952. Bar: N.Y. 1952. Assoc. McLaughlin and Stern, N.Y.C., 1955-69; atty. ABC, N.Y.C., 1969-72; assoc. Fried Frank Harris Shriver & Jacobson, N.Y.C., 1972-76; assoc. Patterson Belknap Webb & Tyler, N.Y.C., 1976-80, ptnr., 1980-95. Mem. exec. com. Lexington Dem. Club, 1961-63. With U.S. Army, 1953-55. Mem. Assn. of Bar of City of N.Y., City Athletic Club N.Y.C. (mem. bd. govs. 1973-81), Phi Beta Kappa. Office: 1133 Ave of the Americas New York NY 10036

POWELL, JAMES MATTHEW, history educator; b. Cin., June 9, 1930; s. Matthew James and Mary Loretta (Weaver) P.; m. Judith Catherine Davidorf, May 29, 1954 (dec. 1992); children: James, Michael, Mark, Mary Helen, Miriam, John. B.A., Xavier U., Cin., 1953, M.A., 1955; postgrad., U. Cin., 1955-57; Ph.D., Ind. U., 1960. Instr. Kent State U., Ohio, 1959-61; asst. prof. U. Ill., Urbana, 1961-65; asst. prof. Syracuse U., N.Y., 1965-67, assoc. prof., 1967-72, prof. history, 1972—, dir. Ranke Cataloging Project, 1977—; disting. vis. prof. medieval history Rutgers U., New Brunswick, 1996—. Author: Medieval Monarchy and Trade, 1962, Civilization of the West, 1967, Anatomy of a Crusade, 1213-1221, 1986, 2d edit., 1990, Albertanus of Brescia: The Pursuit of Happiness in the Early Thirteenth Century, 1992; translator: Liber Augustalis, 1971; editor: Innocent III: Vicar of Christ or Lord of the World, 1963, revised and enlarged 2d edit., 1994, Medieval Studies, 1976, 2d edit., 1992; (with George G. Iggers) Leopold von Ranke and the Shaping of the Historical Discipline, 1989, Muslims Under Latin Rule, 1100-1300, 1990; contbr. articles to profl. jours. Grentee NEH, 1977-84, 84, Inst. for Advanced Study, Princeton, N.J., 1989-90, Progetto Radici, Brescia, Italy, 1994-95; Fritz Thyssen Stiftung, 1986, 89; recipient John Gilmary Shea prize Am. Cath. Hist. Assn., 1987,. Mem. Am. Hist. Assn., Am. Cath. Hist. Assn., Medieval Acad. Am., Soc. for Italian Hist. Studies (coun. 1976-79, v.p. 1991-92, pres. 1993-95), Midwest Medieval Conf. (pres. 1965-66), Soc. for Study of the Crusades and the Latin East (sec. 1989-95). Democrat. Roman Catholic. Home: 114 Doll Pky Syracuse NY 13214-1428 Office: Syracuse U Maxwell School Syracuse NY 13244 *The good, the beautiful, the true - these are the words of an unchanging quest. They are our noblest.*

POWELL, JOSEPH HERBERT, hospital administrator; b. Etowah, Tenn., Oct. 5, 1926; s. Newton Carter and Savannah (Smith) P.; m. Ann Marie Lockeman, Mar. 10, 1956; children: Charlotte Marie, Margaret Annabelle, Susan Lea. BS, U. Tenn., 1950; MHA, U. Minn., 1955; LHD (hon.), Union U., Jackson, Tenn., 1986. Cert. hosp. adminstr., Tenn. Adminstrv. resident Bapt. Meml. Hosp., Memphis, 1954-55, adminstrv. asst., 1955-58, asst. adminstr., 1958-72, v.p., 1972-75, exec. v.p., 1975-80, pres., chief exec. officer, 1980-92; pres., chief exec. officer Bapt. Meml. Healthcare System, Memphis, 1981—; pres. emeritus Bapt. Meml. Healthcare System, Memphis, TN; bd. dirs., vice chmn. Blue Cross-Blue Shield, Memphis; trustee Nat. Com. for Quality Healthcare, Washington, 1985—; mem. Hosp. Rsch. and Devel. Inst. bd. dirs. 1985-91, Pensacola, Fla. Bd. dirs. Nations Bank, Memphis, 1986—, NCCJ, Memphis, 1988—; bd. dirs., vice chmn. Future Memphis, 1991—; mem. devel. coun. U. Tenn., 1989-92. 1st lt. U.S. Army, 1945-46, 51-53. Recipient Silver Hope award Multiple Sclerosis Soc., Memphis, 1989, L.M. Graves award Outstanding Achievement Community Health, 1992. Fellow Am. Coll. Healthcare Execs. (Regent 1978-84, Regents Disting. Svc. award 1987); mem. Am. Hosp. Assn. (bd. trustees 1984-88), Internat. Hosp. Fedn., Tenn. Hosp. Assn. (chmn. 1975-76, Disting. Svc. award 1981), Memphis C. of C. (bd. dirs., vice chmn. 1989—), Crescent Club, Econ. Club, Rotary, Omicron Delta Kappa. Home: 4656 Peppertree Ln Memphis TN 38117-3905 Office: Bapt Meml Health Care Found 899 Madison Ave Memphis TN 38146*

POWELL, JOSEPH LESTER (JODY POWELL), public relations executive; b. Vienna, Ga., Sept. 30, 1943; s. Joseph Lester and June Marie (Williamson) P.; m. Nan Sue Jared, Apr. 23, 1966; 1 child, Emily Claire. Student, U.S. Air Force Acad., 1961-64; BA in Polit. Sci., Ga. State U., 1966; post grad., Emory U., 1967-70. Press sec. Gov. Jimmy Carter, Atlanta, 1971-74, 75-76, Pres. Jimmy Carter, Washington, 1977-81; columnist Los Angeles Times Syndicate, 1982-87; news analyst ABC News, Washington, 1982-87; prof. Boston Coll., 1985-86; chmn., CEO Powell Adams & Rinehart, Washington, 1987-91, Powell Tate, Washington, 1991—. Author: The Other Side of the Story, 1984. Baptist. Avocations: golf, tennis, hunting, fishing, Civil War history. Office: Powell Tate 700 13th St NW Fl 10 Washington DC 20005-3960

POWELL, KENNETH EDWARD, investment banker; b. Danville, Va., Oct. 5, 1952; s. Terry Edward and C. Anne (Wooten) P.; m. Cicely Grandin Moorman, Jan. 3, 1976; children: Tanner, Priscilla. Student, Hampden-Sydney Coll., 1971-73; BA in Polit. Sci., U. Colo., 1975; JD, U. Richmond, 1978; LLM in Taxation, Coll. of William and Mary, 1982. Bar: Va. 1978, U.S. Dist. Ct. (ea. dist.) Va. 1979, U.S. Tax Ct. 1980. Ptnr. Maloney, Yeatts & Barr, Richmond, Va., 1978-87; ptnr., owner Hazel & Thomas, P.C., Richmond, 1987-94, mem. bus./tax team, internat. bus. team; v.p. Legg Mason, Richmond, Va., 1994—. Vice chmn. Sci. Mus. Va., Richmond, 1984-91; chmn. Va. Police Found., Inc., 1987; bd. dirs. State Edn. Assistance Authority, 1991—; mem. adv. bd. Va. Opera, 1991—; candidate U.S. Congress, Va., 1986. Recipient Disting. Svc. award Fraternal Order of Police, 1986; named Outstanding Young Man of the Yr., Jaycees, 1981, Outstanding Young Alumni, U. Colo., 1982. Mem. ABA, Va. Bar Assn. (chmn. profl. responsibility com. 1989-92, chmn. com. on legal edn. and admission to the Bar 1991—), Richmond Bar Assn., Richmond C. of C. (bd. dirs. 1988), Va. Econ. Developers Assn. (gen. counsel), Va. Econ. Bridge Initiative. Episcopal. Office: Legg Mason Wood Walker Inc Riverfront Plz East Tower 951 E Byrd St Ste 810 Richmond VA 23219-4039

POWELL, LARRY R., chemicals executive. Pres., CEO DSM Copolymer, Inc., Baton Rouge, La. Office: DSM Copolymer Inc PO Box 2591 Baton Rouge LA 70821-2591*

POWELL, LARRY RANDALL, columnist; b. Texarkana, Tex., Nov. 7, 1948; s. John Calvin and Pearl Mae (Thatcher) P.; m. Martha Jon Muse, Dec. 15, 1991; children: Bret Allen, Bart Randall (twins). AA in Journalism (hon.), Texarkana Community Coll., 1991. Reporter, editor Texarkana Gazette, 1965-68, reporter, asst. mng. editor, 1969-71; sportswriter Shreveport (La.) Times, 1968-69; feature writer Tyler (Tex.) Morning Telegraph, 1969; reporter, editor Fort Worth Press, 1971-75; editor Grand Prairie (Tex.) Daily News, 1975-76; copy editor, page layout editor, nat. editor Dallas Morning News, 1976—, features editor, columnist, 1976—; adj. prof. U. Tex., Arlington, 1982-83. Bd. dirs. Great Pretenders Theatre, Carrollton, Tex., 1981-83, Theatre of the Hill, Cedar Hill, Tex., 1987-88. Recipient 1st pl. headline writing Tex. Gridiron Club, 1974, 1st pl. page one design Tex. UPI Editors Assn., 1980, 3rd pl. spot news reporting, 1975, 2nd pl. page layout, 1975, 2nd pl. page layout Tex. AP Mng. Editors, 1972. Home: 1011 Tarryall Dr Dallas TX 75224-4920 Office: The Dallas Morning News Communications Ctr PO Box 655237 Dallas TX 75265-5237

POWELL, LARSON MERRILL, investment advisory service executive; b. Pittsfield, Mass., Mar. 8, 1932; s. Harry LeRoy and Elsie Madeline (Larson) P.; m. Anne C. Millett, Dec. 8, 1956 (div. Oct. 1993); children: Larson Merrill, Anne Coleman, Miles Sloan. AB Harvard U., 1954; student Columbia U. Law Sch., 1957-59. News editor, reporter Boston Daily Globe, 1954, 56-57; security analyst Moody's Investors Service, N.Y.C., 1959-62, regional mgr., 1964-67, v.p., 1967-68; pres. instl. investment mgmt. div. Anchor Corp., Elizabeth, N.J., 1968-70; pres. Res. Rsch., Ltd., N.Y.C., 1971—, Powell Publs. Corp., N.Y.C., 1980-88. Bd. mgrs. W.Side br. YMCA of Greater N.Y., 1970-79, mem.-at-large citywide bd., 1976-79; chmn. men's com. Am. Mus. Natural History, 1970-72; mem. Boro of Manhattan Cmty. Planning Bd. 7, 1966-69; bd. dirs. Children's Home of Portland, 1986-92, Sweetser Children's Svcs., 1988—, Episcopal Camp and Conf. Center, 1978-80; pres. Wiscasset, Waterville & Farmington Railway Mus., 1994—. With AUS, 1954-56. Fellow Fin. Analysts Fedn.; mem. Internat. Soc. Fin. Analysts, N.Y. Soc. Security Analysts. Episcopalian. Club: Cumberland (Portland, Maine). Editor, pub. Powell Monetary Analyst, 1971—, Powell Gold Industry Guide and Internat. Mining Anlayst, 1976—, Powell Alert, 1980-88. Home: 836 Washington Ave Portland ME 04103-2740 Office: PO Box 4135 Portland ME 04101-0335

POWELL, LESLIE CHARLES, JR., obstetrics and gynecology educator; b. Beaumont, Tex., Dec. 13, 1927; s. Leslie Charles and Tillie Bee (Wallace) P.; m. Jeanne LeBarron Gaston, July 30, 1983; children: Jeffrey Johns, Randall Gardner, Daniel Charles, Gerard Paul. B.S., So. Meth. U., 1948; M.D., Johns Hopkins U., 1952. Diplomate: Am. Bd. Ob-Gyn. Intern, then resident U. Tex., Galveston, 1952-55, instr. ob-gyn, 1957-59, asst. prof., 1959-63, assoc. prof., 1963-68, prof., 1968—; cons. Richmond State Sch., 1969—; vis. prof. ob-gyn. Moi U., Eldoret, Kenya, 199-94; vis. prof. ob-gyn. Womens Hosp., Tudyu Hoa, Vietnam, 1996. Editorial cons.: Tex. Reports Biology and Medicine, 1975, Psychosomatics, 1977, Tex. Medicine, 1978-88; contbr. articles to profl. jours. Pres. Am. Cancer Soc., Galveston County, 1972-73; dir. S.W. conf. Unitarian Ch. Served with M.C., AUS, 1955-57. Recipient Hannah award Tex. Assn. Ob-Gyn, 1955; research grantee HEW, 1969-71; Fulbright scholar Burma, 1975. Mem. Alpha Tau Omega, Phi Beta Pi. Republican. Home: 1906 Back Bay Dr Galveston TX 77551-1211 Office: 800 Ave B U Tex Med Sch Galveston TX 77550

POWELL, LEWIS FRANKLIN, JR., retired United States supreme court justice; b. Suffolk, Va., Sept. 19, 1907; s. Lewis Franklin and Mary Lewis (Gwathmey) P.; m. Josephine M. Rucker, May 2, 1936; children: Josephine Powell Smith, Ann Pendleton Powell Carmody, Mary Lewis Gwathmey Powell Sumner, Lewis Franklin, III. B.S., Washington and Lee U., 1929, LL.B., 1931, LL.D., 1960; LL.M., Harvard, 1932. Bar: Va. 1931, U.S. Supreme Ct. 1937. Practiced law in Richmond, 1932-71; mem. firm Hunton, Williams, Gay, Powell and Gibson, 1937-71; assoc. justice U.S. Supreme Ct., 1972-87; chmn. emeritus Colonial Williamsburg Found.; mem. Nat. Commn. on Law Enforcement and Adminstrn. Justice, 1965-67, Blue Ribbon Def. Panel to study Def. Dept., 1969-70. Served to col. USAAF, 1942-46, 32 months overseas. Decorated Legion of Merit, Bronze Star; Croix de Guerre with palms (France); Trustee emeritus Washington and Lee U.; hon. bencher Lincoln's Inn. Fellow Am. Bar Found. (pres. 1969-71), Am. Coll. Trial Lawyers (pres. 1969-70); mem. ABA (gov., pres. 1964-65), Va. Bar Assn., Richmond Bar Assn. (pres. 1947-48), Bar Assn. City N.Y., Nat. Legal Aid and Defender Assn. (v.p. 1964-65), Am. Law Inst., Soc. Cin., Sons Colonial Wars, Commonwealth Club (Richmond), Phi Beta Kappa, Phi Delta Phi, Omicron Delta Kappa, Phi Kappa Sigma. Presbyterian. Office: care US Supreme Ct 1 First St NE Washington DC 20543

POWELL, LEWIS FRANKLIN, III, lawyer; b. Richmond, Va., Sept. 14, 1952; s. Lewis F. Jr. and Josephine (Rucker) P.; m. Lisa T. LaFata; children: Emily, Hannah. BA, Washington & Lee U., 1974; JD, U. Va., 1978. Bar: Va. 1978, U.S. Dist. Ct. (ea. and we. dists.) Va. 1979, U.S. Ct. Appeals (4th cir.) 1979, U.S. Ct. Appeals (2d cir.) 1983, U.S. Ct. Appeals (11th cir.) 1992, U.S. Supreme Ct. 1985. Law clk. to judge U.S. Dist. Ct. (ea. dist.), Richmond, 1978-79; from assoc. to ptnr. Hunton & Williams, Richmond, 1979—; pres. young lawyers conf. Va. State Bar, 1986-87. Bd. dirs. William Byrd Cmty. Ho., Richmond, 1982-87, Boys Club of Richmond, 1984-90, Maymont Found., Richmond, 1987-92, St. Christopher's Sch., Richmond, 1989—. Mem. Richmond Bar Assn. (chmn. improvement justice com. 1982-83), 4th Cir. Jud. Conf., Am. Law Inst. Avocations: skiing, mountaineering, backpacking, fishing, duck hunting. Office: Hunton & Williams Riverfront Plz East Tower 951 E Byrd St Richmond VA 23219-4040

POWELL, MEL, composer; b. N.Y.C., Feb. 12, 1923. Studied piano from age 4; studied composition with Ernst Toch, L.A., 1946-48; with Paul Hindemith, Yale U., from 1948, MusB, 1952. Mem., chmn. faculty composition Yale U., 1957-69; mem. staff, head faculty composition, formerly dean Calif. Inst. Arts, Valencia, provost, 1972-76, now Inst. fellow, Roy E. Disney chair in mus. composition. Albums include Six Recent Works, 1982-88, The Return of Mel Powell, 1989; composer: Duplicates: A Concerto for Two Pianos and Orchestra (premier L.A. Philharm. 1990, Pulitzer prize for music 1990), Modules for chamber orch. (recorded L.A. Philharm. 1991), Woodwind Quintet (recorded 1991), Setting for Two Pianos (recorded 1992), Settings for Small Orch., 1992 (commissioned by chamber orchs. of St. Paul, L.A., N.J.), Settings for Guitar (recorded 1993), numerous other compositions; subject of profile in New Yorker mag. Recipient Creative Arts medal Brandeis U., 1989; Pulitzer Prize for music, 1990; Guggenheim fellow; Nat. Inst. Arts and Letters grantee. Mem. Arnold Schoenburg Inst. (hon. life). Office: Calif Arts Inst Dept Composition 24700 Mcbean Pky Santa Clarita CA 91355-2340*

POWELL, MIKE, olympic athlete, track and field; b. Phila., Pa., 1964. Grad., UCLA. Olympic track and field participant Seoul, South Korea, 1988; set world record for long jump at World Track and Field Championships. Tokyo, 1991; Olympic track and field participant Barcelona, Spain, 1992. Recipient Long Jump Silver medal Olympics, Seoul, South Korea, 1988, Long Jump Silver medal Olympics, Barcelona, 1992. Office: Footlocker Track Club 233 Broadway Lbby 4 New York NY 10279-0097*

POWELL, NANCY EGAN, elementary education educator; b. Galesburg, Ill., Nov. 5, 1944; d. Robert Matthew and Eva (Fullerton) Egan; m. Dennis Lynn Powell, May 26, 1973; children: Matthew, Susan. BE, Washburn U., 1968; postgrad., Emporia State U., 1973-78, Ottawa U., 1979-85, Avilia U., 1985-89, Portland State U., 1987-88. Cert. K-8, Kans. Tchr. grade 2, permanent substitute tchr. Kansas City Dist. 500, Kans., 1968-69; kindergarten tchr. Kansas City (Kans.) Dist. 500, 1969-91, collaborative kindergarten tchr., 1991—; instr. Math Learning Ctr., Portland State U., 1989—; tchr.'s adv. bd. Kans. Children's Mus., Kansas City, 1988—; presenter S.W. Regional Conf. Kans. Assn. Tchrs. Math., 1989, 90, 92, mem. Kindergarten Curriculum Guide Com., 1988, Math Curriculum Guide Com., 1990, U.S. Russian Joint Conf. Math. Edn., Moscow, 1993, Scope Sequence Writing Team, 1993, Kansas City Math Cadre; mem. Hartcourt Brace Math Tchrs. Adv. Bd., 1995. Mem. Harcourt Brace Math. Tchrs. Adv. Bd., 1995. Troop leader, trainer Santa Fe Trail coun. Girl Scouts U.S., 1982—; troop leader Mid Am. coun. Boy Scouts Am., 1983-90. Grantee Kansas City, Kans. Profl. Devel. Coun. Spl. Edn. Dept., 1990, N.E. Kans. Elem. Sch. Math. Dissemination Project, 1993, 94. Mem. NEA, Internat. Reading Assn., Assn. Childhood Edn. Internat., Nat. Coun. PTA, Nat. Assn. Tchrs. Math., Nat. Assn. Edn. Young Children, Profl. Devel. Coun. Kansas City, Alpha Delta Kappa (v.p. 1986-88, pres. 1988-90, state courtesy chmn. 1992-94). Republican. Methodist. Avocations: art, travel, cooking, reading. Home: 7924 Armstrong Ave Kansas City KS 66112-2547 also: Kansas City Pub Schs Libr Bldg 625 Minnesota Ave Kansas City KS 66101-2805

POWELL, NORBORNE BERKELEY, urologist; b. Montgomery, Ala., July 24, 1914; s. Floyd Berkeley and Eloise (Sadler) P.; m. Elizabeth Mary Balas, Dec. 18, 1939; children—Norborne Berkeley, Barbara Key. M.D., Baylor U., 1938. Diplomate: Am. Bd. Urology. Intern Duke Hosp., Durham, N.C., 1938-39, Charity Hosp., New Orleans, 1939-40; resident Tulane Service, Charity Hosp., 1940-42; practice medicine, specializing in urology Houston, 1942-90; mem. staff Ben Taub Gen. Hosp., Twelve Oaks Hosp., Houston; chief staff Twelve Oaks Hosp., 1974; mem. cons. staff Meth. Hosp., St. Luke's Episc. Hosp.; clin. prof. urology Baylor Coll. Medicine, 1964-90; ret., 1990; Trustee Baylor Med. Found., 1945-55; pres. Twelve Oaks Med. Found., 1976-90. Contbr. articles to profl. jours. Recipient continuing med. edn. award AMA, 1980. Fellow A.C.S., Internat. Coll. Surgeons; mem. Mexican Urol. Assn. (corr.), Am. Urol. Assn. (Sci. Exhbn. 1st prize 1951, continuing med. edn. award 1980), Houston Urol. Soc. (pres. 1955), Can. Urol. Assn. Home: 23 Cedar Cliff Rd Asheville NC 28803-2905

POWELL, REBECCA GAETH, education educator; b. Westlake, Ohio, Oct. 23, 1949; d. John Paul and Ione Roxanne (Poad) Gaeth; m. Jerry Wayne Powell, June 14, 1991; children: Justin Matthew (dec.), Ryan Michael. B Music Edn., Coll. of Wooster (Ohio), 1971; MEd, U. N.C., 1976; D in Edn., U. Ky., 1989. Cert. curriculum and instrn. Elem. tchr. Rittman (Ohio) Elem., 1971-72; presch. tchr. YWCA, Durham, N.C., 1974-76; spl. reading tchr. Claxton Elem. Sch., Asheville, N.C., 1977; instr. and dir. reading, cert. program Mars Hill (N.C.) Coll., 1977-80; health educator Hot Springs (N.C.) Health Program, 1984-85; asst. prof. Ky. State U., Frankfort, 1989-93; assoc. prof. Georgetown (Ky.) Coll., 1993—; Ky. primary sch. rschr. U. Ky. Inst. on Ednl. Reform, Lexington, 1993—; ednl. cons. Jessamine County Schs., Nicholasville, Ky., 1992-93; tchr. educator, trainer, participant pilot project Ky. Tchr. Internship Program, Frankfort, 1990—; chmn. Alliance for Multicultural Edn., Ky., 1993-95; coord. Ctrl. Ky. Whole Lang. Network, 1991-93; mem. Ky. Multicultural Edn. Task Force, 1995—. Editor: (monograph series) Alliance for Multicultural Education, 1994-95; contbr. articles to profl. jours. Dissertation Year fellow U. Ky., Lexington, 1988-89. Mem. Nat. Assn. Multicultural Edn., Nat. Coun. Tchrs. English, Nat. Conf. Rsch. in English, Am. Ednl. Studies Assn., Ky. Coun. Tchrs. English, Alliance for Multicultural Edn. Avocations: crochet, golf. Office: Georgetown Coll 400 E College St Georgetown KY 40324-1696

POWELL, RICHARD C., physicist, educator, researcher; b. Lincoln, Nebr., Dec. 20, 1939; s. William Charles and Allis (Conger) P.; m. Gwendolyn Cline Powell, June 24, 1962; children: Douglas W., David M. BS in Engring., U.S. Naval Acad., 1962; MS in Physics, Arizona State U., 1964, PhD in Physics, 1967. Staff scientist Air Force Cambridge Rsch. Labs., Bedford, Mass., 1964-68, Sandia Nat. Lab., Albuquerque, 1968-71; prof. Okla. State U., 1971-92; prof. dir. optical sci. ctr. U. Ariz., Tucson, 1992—; reviewer numerous physics jours. and funding agys.; cons. laser rsch. with several indsl. and govt. agys. Editor-in-chief Jour. Optical Materials, 1992&; patents include Holographic Gratings in Rare Earth Doped Glasses, with Okla. State U., 1988; contbr. numerous articles to profl. jours. Recipient over 40 grants for rsch. support, 1971—. Fellow Am. Phys. Soc. (co-chmn. Internat. Laser Sci. Conf. 1985, chmn. 1986, vice chmn. Topical Group on Laser Sci., 1986, chmn. 1987, APS rep. Joint Coun. on Quantum Electronics, 1986-90), Optical Soc. Am. (mem. bd. dirs. 1993—, mem. program com. OSA Photoacoustic Spectroscopy Mtg., 1979, mem. nom. com. 1982, organizer Laser Tech. Group Session 1985, com. mem. Meggers award, 1986, 89, 90, chmn. program com. CLEO, 1988, mem. book pub. com., 1992—, mem. awards com., 1994—, mem. organizing com. Adv. Solid State Laser Conf., 1992—, OSA rep. Internat. Coun. on Optics, 1994—; mem. IEEE (mem. solid state lasers adv. com., 1987—, program com. mem. Nonlinear Optical Materials Mtg., 1994), Sigma Xi (hon. lectr. 1983-84). Episcopalian. Avocations: skiing, fishing, softball, jogging, hiking. Office: U Ariz Optical Scis Ctr Tucson AZ 85721

POWELL, RICHARD GORDON, retired lawyer; b. Rochester, N.Y., Jan. 7, 1918. B.S., Harvard U., 1938; LL.B., Columbia U., 1941. Bar: N.Y. 1941, U.S. Supreme Ct. 1955. Assoc. Sullivan & Cromwell, N.Y.C., 1941-52; ptnr. Sullivan & Cromwell, 1952-85. Former mem. bd. mgrs. Englewood (N.J.) Community Chest; trustee, elder 1st Presbyterian Ch. Mem. ABA, Assn. Bar City of N.Y., Am. Law Inst. Home: 200 E 65th St # 33N New York NY 10021-6603

POWELL, RICHARD PITTS, writer; b. Phila., Nov. 28, 1908; s. Richard Percival and Lida Catherine (Pitts) P.; m. Marian Carleton Roberts, Sept. 6, 1932 (dec. Nov. 1979); children: Stephen Barnes, Dorothy Louise; m. Margaret M. Cooper, 1980. Grad., Episcopal Acad., 1926; A.B., Princeton, 1930. Reporter Phila. Evening Ledger, 1930-40; with N.W. Ayer & Son, Phila., 1940-58; mem. pub. relations dept. N.W. Ayer & Son, 1940-42, charge info. services, 1949-58, v.p., 1951-58. Author: mystery books Don't Catch Me, 1943, All Over but the Shooting, 1944, Lay That Pistol Down, 1945, Shoot If You Must, 1946, And Hope to Die, 1947, Shark River, 1950, Shell Game, 1950, A Shot in the Dark, 1952, Say It with Bullets, 1953, False Colors, 1955; novels The Philadelphian, 1957, Pioneer, Go Home, 1959, The Soldier, 1960, I Take This Land, 1963, Daily and Sunday, 1965, Don Quixote, U.S.A, 1966, Tickets to the Devil, 1968, Whom the Gods Would Destroy, 1970, Florida: A Picture Tour, 1972; novel under pen name Jeremy Kirk The Build-Up Boys, 1951; Contbr. short stories, articles, serials to mags. Served as lt. col. AUS, 1942-46; chief news censor 1945, S.W. Pacific Theatre. Home: 1201 Carlene Ave Fort Myers FL 33901-8715

POWELL, ROBERT, insurance company executive; b. 1941. With Equitable Life Ins. Co., N.Y.C., 1963-68; sr. v.p. Johnson & Higgins Inc., N.Y.C., 1968-88, pres. A Foster Higgins & Co. Inc. subs., from 1988, chmn. bd., also bd. dirs. Office: A Foster Higgins & Co Inc 125 Broad St New York NY 10004-2400*

POWELL, ROBERT BARROWS, architectural firm executive; b. Rochester, N.Y., Jan. 29, 1938. BArch, U. Mich., 1960; postgrad., U. Pa., 1960. Registered arch. Arch. Glen Paulsen & Assocs., Bloomfield Hills, 1961-63, Albert Kahn Assocs., Detroit, 1963-66; joined Jickling Lyman Powell Assocs., Inc., Birmingham, Mich., 1966—, prin., 1972—, pres., 1987—; mem. faculty Lawrence Tech. U., 1971—. Prin. works include Woodfield Mall, Bentley Hist. Libr., Taubman Libr., Gerald R. Ford Presdl. Libr., High Tech. Ctr., UAW-GM Human Resources Ctr., First Nat. Bldg., U. Mich. Med. Rcsh. Complex, many others. Treas. exec. com. Bentley Hist. Libr.; active Friends of Terra Cotta. Mem. ALA, AIA (Detroit chpt., Mich. chpt.), Nat. Trust Hist. Preservation, Mich. Archival Assn. Office: Jickling Lyman Powell Assoc 2900 W Maple Rd Ste 210 Troy MI 48084-7050

POWELL, ROBERT ELLIS, mathematics educator, college dean; b. Lansing, Mich., Mar. 16, 1936; s. James Ellis and Mary Frances (Deming) P.; children: Carl Robert, Glenn Arthur, Charles Addison; m. Lisbeth Nilsen, Nov. 21, 1992. B.A., Mich. State U., 1958, M.A., 1959; Ph.D., Lehigh U., 1966. Instr. math. Lehigh U., 1964-66; asst. prof. math. U. Kans., Lawrence, 1966-69; vis. asst. research prof. U. Ky., Lexington, 1967-68; vis. asst. prof. math. Ind. U., Bloomington, summer 1969; assoc. prof. math. Kent State U., Ohio, 1969-74, prof. math., 1974-95; dean grad. coll. Kent State U., 1980-92; prof. math., dean grad. sch., dir. rsch. U. Scranton, Pa., 1995—; bd. dirs. Kent State U. Found., 1981-91, Coun. Grad. Schs., 1990-91; mem. Ohio Bd. Regents' Adv. Com. on Grad. Study, 1980-92, chmn., 1983-84. Co-author: Summability Theory, 1973, rev. edit., 1988, Intuitive Calculus, 1973; contbr. numerous articles to profl. jours. NSF summer grantee, 1964, 65, Fulbright award, 1988. Mem. Math. Assn. Am., Midwest Assn. Grad. Schs. (vice chair 1989-90, chair 1990-91, past chair 1991-92). Home: 3003 Quail Hollow Dr Clarks Summit PA 18411 Office: U Scranton Grad Sch Scranton PA 18510

POWELL, SANDRA THERESA, timber company executive; b. Orofino, Idaho, Jan. 9, 1944; s. Harold L. and Margaret E. (Thompson) P. B.S. in Bus./Acctg., U. Idaho, 1966. CPA, Idaho. Acct., Weyerhaeuser Co., Tacoma, Wash., 1966-67; with Potlatch Corp., 1967—, asst. sec., San Francisco, 1981, sec., asst. treas., 1981-89, treas. 1989-92; v.p. fin. svcs., 1993—, sec., 1993-95. Mem. AICPA, Idaho State Bd. Accountancy, Idaho Soc. CPAs. Office: Potlatch Corp PO Box 193591 San Francisco CA 94119-3591

POWELL, SARA JORDAN, musician, religious worker; b. Waller, Tex., Oct. 6, 1938; d. Samuel Arthur and Mable Ruth (Ponder) Jordan; m. John Atkins Powell, June 24, 1967; 1 child, Marc Benet. B.A., Tex. So. U., 1960; M.R.E., U. St. Thomas, Houston, 1979. Tchr., Chgo. Bd. Edn., 1961-68, Houston Ind. Sch. Dist., 1968-73; youth dir. Gospel Music Workshop Am., Detroit, 1972-76; dir. talent and fine arts Ch. of God in Christ, Memphis, 1974—, dir., cons. ch. hist. mus. and fine arts center, 1980—; mem. nat. reference com. One Nation Under God, Virginia Beach, Va., 1979—; regional sponsor Yr. of the Bible, Washington, 1983; soloist Savoy Record Co., 1972-79; counselor Mike Barber Prison Ministries, 1987—. Bd. dirs. talent coordinator Charles Harrison Mason Edn. Found., 1975—; bd. dirs. James Oglethorpe Patterson Fine Arts Scholarships, 1974—; music and talent dir. Juneteenth U.S.A., 1985—; acad. advisor Oral Roberts U., 1991-92. Recipient 1st Pl. award Record Album, Savoy Record Co., 1972. Best Female Vocalist, Gospel Music Workshop Am., 1973, 74, 75, Gold record, 1978; letter of appeciation Cook County Dept. Corrections, Chgo., 1978; Silver Plate award Assembly of God Ch., Calcutta, India, 1978; letter of appreciation for White House performance, Washington, 1979. Mem. Houston PTA, Houston Peoples Workshop (dir. 1981—), Women in Leadership (adv. bd. 1985—).

POWELL, SHARON LEE, social welfare organization administrator; b. Portland, Oreg., July 25, 1940; d. James Edward Carson and Betty Jane (Singleton) Powell. BS, Oreg. State U., 1962; MEd, Seattle U., 1971. Dir. outdoor edn. Mapleton (Oreg.) Pub. Schs., 1962-63; field dir. Totem Girl Scout Council, Seattle, 1963-68, asst. dir. field services, 1968-70, dir. field services, 1970-72; dir. pub. rels. and program Girl Scout Council of Tropical Fla., Miami, 1972-74; exec. dir. Homestead Girl Scout Council, Lincoln, Nebr., 1974-78, Moingona Girl Scout Coun., Des Moines, 1978—. Pres. agy. dirs. assn. United Way Cen. Iowa, Des Moines, 1987-88, mem. priorities com., 1986-90, chairperson agy. rels., 1994—, chairperson agy. issues, 1989-90; mem. priority goals task group United Way Found., Des Moines, 1985-92; capt. Drake U. Basketball Ticket Drive, Des Moines, 1983-87; sec. Urbandale Citizens Scholarship Found., 1989-93; mem. ad hoc long-range planning com. Urbandale Schs., 1989, mem. budget rev. task group, mem. year-round sch. task group, 1992-93; mem. gender equity task force State of Iowa, 1993—. Mem. AAUW (mem. gender equity task group), Assn. Girl Scouts Execs. (chair nat. conv. 1985-90, nat. bd. dirs. 1985-87, nat. nominating com. 1982-84, nat. treas. 1987-90, nat. pres. 1991—), IRbandale C. of C. (bd. dirs., chair edn. com.), Animal Rescue League of Iowa (bd. dirs. 1992—, shelter chair 1992—), Des Moines Obedience Tng. Club (pres. 1987-89), Des. Moines Golden Retriever Club (bd. dirs., pres. 1992-94), Rotary, Altrusa (treas. Des Moines chpt. 1983-85, cmty. svc. chair 1986-87), Des Moines Kennel Club. Avocations: sailing, dog showing, obedience and conformation. Office: Moingona Girl Scout Coun 10715 Hickman Rd Des Moines IA 50322-3733

POWELL, STEPHANIE, visual effects director, supervisor; b. Dayton, Ohio, Sept. 27, 1946; d. Harley Franklin and Evelyn Luella Pence. Pres., CEO Video Assist Systems, Inc., North Hollywood, Calif., 1979—, Out of the Blue Visual Effects, 1989. Cons.: (motion pictures) Jurassic Park, 1993, Flintstones, 1994, Waterworld, 1995, Get Shorty, 1995; visual effects supr.: Blown Away, 1994, My Brother's Keeper, 1994, Powder, 1995, various commls.; co-visual effects supr. Quantum Leap (TV); developer using 3/4-inch videotape for broadcast; co-developer color videotape for motion picture work. Mem. Acad. TV Arts and Scis., Acad. Magical Arts and Scis. Avocations: horse showing, photography, computer graphics. Office: Video Assist Systems Inc 11030 Weddington St North Hollywood CA 91601-3212

POWELL, THOMAS EDWARD, III, biological supply company executive, physician; b. Elon College, N.C., Aug. 1, 1936; s. Thomas Edward, Jr., and Sophia Maude (Sharpe) P.; m. Betty Durham Yeager, June 19, 1965; children: Frances Powell Barnes, Thomas Edward IV, Caroline Powell Rogers. AB in Biology, Va. Mil. Inst., 1957; MD, Duke U., 1961; MA, Harvard U., 1966. Surgeon USPHS, 1966-68; co-founder Biomed. Reference Labs., Inc., Burlington, N.C., 1969, exec. v.p., 1969-75, chmn. exec. com., 1979-82, also dir.; exec. v.p. Carolina Biol. Supply Co., Burlington, N.C., 1968-80, chmn., 1977-80, 94—, pres., 1980-94; pres. Wolfe Sales Corp., Burlington, 1980-84, Waubun Labs. Inc., Schriever, La., 1980—, Bobbitt Labs., Inc., Burlington, 1983-94; bd. mgrs. Wachovia Bank and Trust Co. N.A., Burlington. Contbr. articles to profl. jours. Bd. dirs. United Way Alamance County, Burlington, 1968—; bd. dirs. Elon Coll., N.C., 1968—, sec., 1975—; bd. dirs. Am. Cancer Soc., Burlington, 1971-81; bd. dirs. Burlington Day Sch., 1973—, pres., 1974-78, 80-84; bd. dirs. N.C. Citizens for Bus. and Industry, Raleigh, 1983-87, Nat. Found. for Study of Religion and Econs., Greensboro, 1984-88, Blue Ridge Sch., Dyke, Va., 1985-90. Served to capt. USAR, 1957-66. Recipient Citizens Service award Elon Coll. Alumni Assn., 1980. Mem. Assn. Biology Lab. Edn., N.C. Acad. Sci., Alamance-Caswell Med. Soc., N.C. Med. Soc., Assn. Venture Founders, Newcomen Soc. Democrat. Mem. United Ch. of Christ. Clubs: Alamance Country (Burlington); Capital City (Raleigh, N.C.); Congl. Country (Washington); N.C. Country (Pinehurst); Hope Valley Country (Durham, N.C.); Greensboro City.

POWELL, THOMAS ERVIN, accountant, consultant; b. Trion, Ga., Mar. 19, 1947; s. Ervin and Myrice (Wike) P.; m. Lana Lois Lang, June 20, 1976; children: Thomas Christopher, Alissa Lynne, Ashley Beth. BS, U. Ctrl. Fla., 1974, MS, 1977; postgrad. studies, U. Fla., 1979. CPA, Fla.; cert. internal auditor. Pub. acct. Peat, Marwick, Mitchell & Co., Orlando, Fla., 1974-75, Arthur Andersen & Co., Orlando, 1975-77; instr. acctg. U. Ctrl. Fla., Orlando, 1977-81; dir. Inst. Internal Auditors, Altamonte Springs, Fla., 1981-95; pvt. practice Windermere, Fla., 1995—; mem. accreditation com. Am. Assembly Collegiate Schs. Bus., 1992-93. Author: Examination Writer's Guide, 1981, rev. edit., 1995; mem. editl. bd. Issues in Acctg. Edn. Jour., 1995—. Vice chmn. audit bd. City of Orlando, 1990-95. With USAF, 1967-71. Mem. AICPA, Am. Acctg. Assn. (profl. exam. com. 1986-89, 93—, v.p. profl. practices 1994—, audit edn. conf. com. 1990-93), Internat. Platform Assn., Inst. Internal Auditors, Fla. Soc. CPAs (edn. com. 1990-93, legis. com. 1991), Nat. Assn. Corp. Dirs., Beta Alpha Psi (adv. coun. 1993—, Alumnus of Yr. U. Ctrl. Fla. 1992), Beta Gamma Sigma. Republican. Baptist. Avocations: guitar, skiing, photography. Home: 1938 Maple Leaf Dr Windermere FL 34786 Office: Thomas E Powell CPA PO Box 766 Gotha FL 34734

POWELL, TREVOR JOHN DAVID, archivist; b. Hamilton, Ont., Can., Feb. 3, 1948; s. David Albert and Morvydd Ann May (Williams) P.; m. Marian Jean McKillop, May 1, 1976. BA, U. Sask., Regina, 1971; MA, U. Regina, Sask., Can., 1980. Staff archivist Sask. Archives Bd., Regina, Sask., 1973-80, dir., 1980-86, acting provincial archivist, 1986-87, provincial archivist, 1988—. Co-author: Living Faith: A Pictorial History of Diocese of Qu'Appelle; author: From Tent to Cathedral: A History of St. Paul's Cathedral, Regina. Archivist Diocese of Qu'Appelle, Regina, Sask., 1971—, registrar, 1979—; archivist, eccles. Province of Rupert's Land, Winnipeg, Man., 1988—; mem. adv. coun. Sask. Order of Merit, 1988-95, Sask Honours, 1995—; mem. selection com. Sask Vol. medal, 1995; chair selection com. Can. 125 medal, 1992. Mem. Soc. Am. Archivists, Can. Hist. Assn., Commonwealth Archivists Assn., Sask. Coun. Archives (sec.-treas. 1987-88, 90-92, pres. 1994—, Can. Coun. Archives rep. 1994—), Assn. Can. Archivists (bd. dirs. 1979-81), Inst. Pub. Adminstrn. Can. Anglican. Avocations: gardening, walking, reading, music, bird watching. Home: 241 Orchard Cres, Regina, SK Canada S4S 5B9 Office: Sask Archives Bd, 3303 Hillsdale St-Univ of Regina, Regina, SK Canada S4S 0A2

POWELL, VIRGINIA W., lawyer; b. Spartanburg, S.C., Feb. 9, 1948. BA, Queens Coll., U. S.C, 1970; JD, U. N.D., 1974. Bar: N.D. 1974, Calif. 1974, Va. 1975, D.C. 1982. Ptnr. Hunton & Williams, Richmond, Va.; adj. instr. trial advocacy Coll. William and Mary, 1982-90, 92—. Mem. Order of Coif, Phi Beta Kappa. Office: Hunton & Williams Riverfront Plz East Tower 951 E Byrd St Richmond VA 23219-4040*

POWELL, WALTER HECHT, labor arbitrator; b. N.Y.C., Apr. 13, 1915; s. Arthur Lee and Stella (Hecht) P.; m. Dorothy Meyer, Mar. 15, 1945; children: Lawrence L., Alan W., Lesley A., Steven H. BS, NYU, 1938, JD, 1940; MA, U. Pa., 1948. Bar: N.Y. 1940, Pa. 1956. Asst. prof. Temple U., Phila., 1946-51, v.p. for pers. resources, 1973-78; asst. dir. pers. Am. Safety Razor, Kingsbury, Ind., 1951-53; v.p., dir. ops. Internat. Resistance Co., Phila., 1953-69, v.p., dir. indsl. rels., 1956-69; sr. v.p. 1st Pa. Banking & Trust Co., Phila., 1969-73; v.p. human resources Temple U., 1973-77; ind. labor arbitrator Phila., 1978—; mem. panel Am. Arbitration Assn., Fed. Mediation and Conciliation Svc., Pa., N.J. labor rels. bds.; lectr. U. Pitts., Temple U., U. Richmond, Vanderbilt U., Am. U., others.; bd. dirs. Auerbach Corp., Phila. Contbr. book chpts., articles to profl. jours. Commr. Phila. Commn. on Human Rels., 1969—; bd. dirs. Opportunities Industralization Ctr. Capt. AUS, 1942-46. Recipient award Phila. C. of C., 1968. Mem. Am. Mgmt. Assn. (adv. coun. 1963—), Indsl. Rels. Assn., Indsl. Rels. Rsch. Assn. (pres. local chpt. 1966), Nat. Acad. Arbitrators. Home and Office: 2401 Pennsylvania Ave Ste 9 A 7 Philadelphia PA 19130-3010

POWELL, WATSON (SCOT) W., III, insurance company executive; b. 1947. Grad., Simpson Coll., 1969. With Am. Rep. Ins. Co., Des Moines, 1969—, vice-chmn., chief exec. officer. Office: Am Rep Ins co 601 6th Ave Des Moines IA 50309*

POWELL, WATSON W., JR., insurance executive; b. 1917. Chmn. bd. dirs. Am. Rep. Ins. Co., Des Moines, Iowa. Office: Am Rep Ins Co 601 6th Ave Des Moines IA 50309-1605*

POWELL, WILLIAM ARNOLD, JR., retired banker; b. Verbena, Ala., July 7, 1929; s. William Arnold and Sarah Frances (Baxter) P.; m. Barbara Ann O'Donnell, June 16, 1956; children: William Arnold III, Barbara Calhoun, Susan Thomas, Patricia Crain. BSBA, U. Ala., 1953; grad., La. State U. Sch. Banking of South, 1966. With Am. South Bank, N.A., Birmingham, Ala., 1953—, asst. v.p., 1966, v.p., 1967, v.p., br. supr., 1968-72, sr. v.p., br. supr., 1972-73, exec. v.p., 1973-79, pres., 1979-83, vice chmn. bd., 1983-93, also bd. dirs.; pres. AmSouth Bancorp., 1979—; bd. dirs. AmSouth Bank Fla., AmSouth Bancorp. Bd. dirs. Salvation Army, United Way Found.; trustee Ala. Hist. Soc., Ala. Ind. Colls.; bd. visitors U. Ala.; past pres. United Way, campaign chmn., 1987; mem. pres.'s coun. U. Ala., Birmingham; bd. dirs., sec.-treas. Warrior-Tombigbee Devel. Assn., Birmingham Mus. Art, Brookwood Med. Ctr.-AMI, Big Bros./Big Sisters of Greater Birmingham. Lt. AUS, 1954-56. Mem. Birmingham Area C. of C. (bd. dirs.), The Club, Mountain Brook, Birmingham Country Club, Green Valley Country Club (Birmingham), Rotary Internat. Home: 2114 Hickory Ridge Cir Birmingham AL 35243-2925

POWER, DENNIS MICHAEL, museum director; b. Pasadena, Calif., Feb. 18, 1941; s. John Dennis and Ruth Augusta (Mott) P.; m. Kristine Moneva Fisher, Feb. 14, 1965 (div. Aug. 1984); children: Michael Lawrence, Matthew David; m. Leslie Gabrielle Baldwin, July 6, 1985; 1 stepchild, Katherine G. Petrosky. BA, Occidental Coll., 1962, MA, 1964; PhD, U. Kans., 1967. Asst. curator ornithology Royal Ont. Mus., Toronto, Can., assoc. curator, 1971-72; asst. prof. zoology U. Toronto, 1967-72; exec. dir. Santa Barbara (Calif.) Mus. Natural History, 1972-94, Oakland Mus. of Calif., 1994—; biol. rschr.; cons. ecology. Editor: The California Islands: Proceedings of a Multidisciplinary Symposium, 1980, Current Ornithology, vol. 6, 1989, vol. 7, 1990, vol. 8, 1991, vol. 9, 1992, vol. 10, 1993, vol. 11, 1993, vol. 12, 1995; contbr. articles to sci. jours. Bd. dirs. Univ. Club Santa Barbara, 1989-92, v.p., 1991-92; bd. dirs. Santa Barbara Chamber Orch., 1990-94, v.p., 1991-94; mem. adv. coun. Santa Cruz Island Found., 1989—; mem. discipline adv. com. for museology Coun. for Internat. Exch. of Scholars, 1991-95. NSF fellow U. Kans., 1967; NRC grantee, 1968-72, 74-78. Fellow Am. Ornithologists Union (life, sec. 1981-83, v.p. 1988-89), Am. Assn. Mus. (mem. coun. 1980-83), Calif. Acad. Scis.; mem. AAAS, Cooper Ornithol. Soc. (bd. dirs. 1976-79, pres. 1978-81, hon. mem. 1993), Calif. Assn. Mus. (bd. dirs. 1990-91, chmn. 1987-89), Western Mus. Conf. (bd. dirs. 1977-83, pres. 1981-83), Am. Soc. Naturalists, Assn. Sci. Mus. Dirs., Ecol. Soc., Am. Soc. Study of Evolution, Soc. Systematic Zoology, Bohemian Club, Sigma Xi. Office: Oakland Mus of California 1000 Oak St Oakland CA 94607-4820

POWER, EDWARD FRANCIS, newspaper editor; b. Norfolk, Va., Oct. 18, 1953; s. Edward Vincent and Elinor (Kuester) P.; m. Marguerite Ulmer, July 25, 1980; children: Edward Graham, Nicholas Conrad. BA, U. Va., 1976, MA, 1978; postgrad., Columbia U., 1979-80. Staff writer The Virginian Pilot/The Ledger-Star, Norfolk, 1983-85, The Phila. Inquirer, 1985-89; from coord. metro editor to dep. mng. editor The Virginian Pilot/The Ledger-Star, 1989—; guest lectr. U. Va., Old Dominion U., Tidewater C.C. Vice-chmn., trustee Virginia Beach Ctr. for the Arts; bd. dirs. World Affairs Coun. Greater Hampton Roads; fundraiser Hampton Roads Com. for Prevention of Child Abuse, 1990-96; chmn. United Way Keel Club, 1991-92, 92-93. Mem. Va. Press Assn. (numerous awards). Avocations: surfing, skiing, sailing, running. Office: Va Pilot/Landmark Comms 150 W Brambleton Ave Norfolk VA 23510

POWER, FRANCIS WILLIAM, newspaper publisher; b. Webster, S.D., Aug. 12, 1925; s. Frank B. and Esther C. (Fowler) P.; m. Margaret Jean Atkinson, Mar. 24, 1951; children: Patricia Ann, John Michael, Kerry Jean. B.B.A., U. N.Mex., 1948. Display advt. sales rep. The Register, Santa Ana, Calif., 1948-51; advt. mgr. Valley Morning Star, Harlingen, Tex., 1951-62; gen. mgr. Pampa (Tex.) Daily News, 1962-69; bus. mgr. Brownsville (Tex.) Herald, 1969-75; pub. The Lima (Ohio) News, 1975-91; v.p. Freedom Comm., Inc., until 1991; ret., 1991. Served with USNR, 1943-46. Roman Catholic. Clubs: Shawnee Country, Rotary, Elks. Office: Freedom Comm Inc 17666 Fitch Irvine CA 92714-6022

POWER, JOHN BRUCE, lawyer; b. Glendale, Calif., Nov. 11, 1936; m. Ann Power, June 17, 1961 (div. 1980); children: Grant, Mark, Boyd. AB magna cum laude, Occidental Coll., 1958; JD, NYU, 1961; postdoctoral, Columbia U., 1972. Bar: Calif. 1962. Assoc. O'Melveny & Myers, Los Angeles, 1961-70, ptnr., 1970—; resident ptnr. O'Melveny & Myers, Paris, 1973-75; mem. Social Svcs. Commn. City of L.A., 1993, pres., 1993; pres. circle, exec. com. Occidental Coll., 1979-82, 91-94, vice chair, 1992-93, chair, 1993-94. Contbr. articles to jours. Dir. Met. L.A. YMCA, 1988—; mem. bd. mgrs. Stuart Ketchum Downtown YMCA, 1985-92, pres., 1989-90; mem. Los Angeles County Rep. Ctrl. Com., 1962-63; trustee Occidental Coll., 1992—. Root Tilden scholar. Mem. ABA (vice chmn. internat. fin. subcom. 1984-91, comml. fin. svcs. com., com. 3d party legal opinions, bus. law sect.), Am. Bar Found. (life), Calif. Bar Assn. (chmn. partnerships and unincorporated assns. com. 1982-83, chmn. uniform commn. code com. 1984-85, exec. com. 1987-91, treas. bus. law sect. 1988-89, vice chmn. 1989-90, chmn. 1990-91, chmn. coun. sect. chairs 1992-93, liaison to state bar commn. on future of legal profession and state bar), L.A. County Bar Assn. (exec. com. comml. law and bankruptcy sect. 1970-73, 86-89), Internat. Bar Assn., Fin. Lawyers Conf. (bd. govs., pres. 1984-85), Exec. Svc. Corps (sec. 1985—, trustee 1994—), Occidental Coll. Alumni Assn. (pres. 1967-68, pres. circle, exec. com. 1979-82, 91-94, vice chair 1992-93, chair 1993-94), Phi Beta Kappa. Office: O'Melveny & Myers 400 S Hope St Los Angeles CA 90071-2801

POWER, JOSEPH EDWARD, lawyer; b. Peoria, Ill., Dec. 2, 1938; s. Joseph Edward and Margaret Elizabeth (Birkett) P.; m. Camille June Repass, Aug. 1, 1964; children—Joseph Edward, David William, James Repass. Student, Knox Coll., Galesburg, Ill., 1956-58; B.A., U. Iowa, 1960, J.D., 1964. Bar: Iowa 1964. Law clk. to judge U.S. Dist. Ct., 1964-65; mem. Bradshaw, Fowler, Proctor & Fairgrave, P.C., Des Moines, 1965—. Bd. dirs. Moingona coun. Girl Scouts U.S.A., 1968-77, pres., 1971-74; mem. Des Moines CSC, 1971-73; bd. dirs. Des Moines United Way, 1976-82, v.p., 1979-81; trustee Am. Inst. Bus., 1987—, chmn., 1992—; bd. dirs. Iowa Law Sch. Found., 1992—, Plymouth Ch. Found., 1991—, Hawley Found., 1994—; bd. dirs. Iowa Natural Heritage Found., 1995—; mem. Des Moines Civil War Roundtable. Fellow Am. Coll. Trust and Estate Counsel (state chair 1994—), Am. Coll. Real Estate Lawyers; mem. ABA, Iowa Bar Assn. (chmn. probate, property and trust law com. 1983-87), Polk County Bar Assn., Des Moines Estate Planners Forum (pres. 1982-83). Republican. Mem. United Ch. of Christ. Clubs: Des Moines, Rotary. Home: 4244 Foster Dr Des Moines IA 50312-2542 Office: Bradshaw Fowler Proctor & Fairgrave 801 Grand Ave Ste 3700 Des Moines IA 50309-2727

POWER, JULES, television producer; b. Hammond, Ind., Oct. 19, 1921; m. Dorothy Kutchinsky; children—Robert, Robin. Grad. with honors (Hardy scholar in speech and communications), Northwestern U., 1944. chmn. Power-Rector Prodns., Inc.; pres. Jules Power Prodns. Sr. producer AM America, ABC-TV; former producer TV show Watch Mr. Wizard, NBC-TV; exec. producer TV show ABC-TV News and Pub. Affairs; creator, exec. producer TV prodn. Discovery, 1962-71; TV spl. How Life Begins, 1968, The Unseen World, 1970; producer ABC-TV series AM America, 1975; exec. producer TV series Over Easy, Pub. Broadcasting System, 1976-83; sr. program cons. Pub. Broadcasting System, 1987—; producer The Scheme of Things, Disney TV Channel, 1983, ednl. films for ABC-McGraw-Hill, Bits, Bytes and Buzzwords, PBS, 1983, State of the Lang., PBS, 1983; exec producer Take Charge, Pub. Broadcasting System; exec. produer for Mary Martin; author: How Life Begins. Pub. info. advisor Buck Ctr. for Aging Rsch. Served with USAAF, World War II. Emmy award, 11 Emmy nominations; Peabody award (2); Thomas Alva Edison award (3); Ohio State award (6); Am. Film Festival 1st place award (2), Internat. Film and TV Festival award (4); Hammond (Ind.) Ann. Achievement award, 1985. Mem. NATAS (past nat. vice-chmn., past pres. N.Y. chpt.), Writers Guild Am. East, Phi Beta Kappa. Home: 78 Red Hill Cir Belvedere Tiburon CA 94920-1773

POWER, MARK, journalist, photographer, educator; b. Washington, Mar. 6, 1937; s. Francis C. and Mary H. P.; m. Virginia North; children: Nancy, John, Rachel, Shelagh. Student, Bowdoin Coll., 1957, student Art Ctr. Coll. Design, 1960-61. Asst. prof. art Corcoran Sch. Art, Washington, 1971-83, assoc. prof. art, 1983—, prof. art, 1989—; art critic Washington Post, 1974-76, 85-87; lectr. in field. Curatorial work exhbns. include Icon Gallery, 1969-71, Corcoran Gallery Art, Dupont Ctr., Washington, 1972-75, 1985; exhibitor (photographs) one-man shows, Dartmouth Coll., 1967, Corcoran Gallery Art, Washington, 1970, 74, 79, Jefferson Pl. Gallery, Washington, 1974, Columbia (Mo.) Gallery, 1974, Diane Brown Gallery, Washington, 1977, Kathleen Ewing Gallery, Washington, 1978, 85,, 92, 95, Contrast Gallery, London, 1981, Galerie Chambre de la Claire, Paris, 1983, "Un/Common Ground" exhbn. Va. Mus. Fine Art, Richmond, 1996; numerous group shows, permanent collections, Libr. Congress, Smithsonian Instn., Iowa Mus. Art, New Orleans Mus. Art, Balt. Mus. Art, Bibliotheque Nationale, Nat. Mus. Am. Art; contbr. over 100 articles on art, film and photography to newspapers and mags. including Washington Post, Washington Star, After-image, Photographies, Art in America, Museum Art, Fotographies Views, San Francisco Camera, Times Lit. Supplement; contbg. editor Photo Rev., Washington Rev. Grantee Va. Mus. of Fine Art, 1995. Mem. Soc. Photog. Educators. Home: 20705 Sycolin Rd Leesburg VA 22075-8918 Office: Corcoran Sch Art 500 17th St NW Washington DC 20006-4804

POWER, MARY SUSAN, political science educator; b. Hazleton, Pa., July 5, 1935; d. Younger L. and Cleo (Boock) P.; 1 dau., Catherine Laverne. B.A., Wells Coll., 1957; postgrad., Exeter U. (Eng.), 1955-56, Yale U., 1958-59; M.A., Stanford U., 1959-60; Ph.D., U. Ill., 1959-61. Asst. prof. Susquehanna U. (Pa.), 1961-64; assoc. prof. U. Ark., Fayetteville, 1965-68; assoc. prof. polit. sci. Ark. State U., State University, 1968-79; prof. Ark. State U., 1979—. Author: Before the Convention, Religion and the Founding Fathers, 1984, Jacques Maritsen and the Quest for a New Commonwealth, 1992; contbr. articles to profl. jours. Mem. State com. Ark. Rep. Com., 1968—, sec., 1978-80; alt. del. Rep. Nat. Conv., 1972, 76, 88; mem. Fed. Edn. Commn. of States, 1982-84, Craighead County Election Commn., 1986—; chmn. Craighead County GOP, 1986-88, vice chmn., 1990—; N.E. regional chmn., 1988—; chmn. Craighead County Sheffield for Gov., 1990; mem. exec. com. Ark. Rep. party, 1990—, N.E. regional chair, 1988-93; N.E. chair Arkansans for Progress, 1990—. Relm Found. fellow, 1960, NSF-Am. Polit. Sci. Assn. fellow, 1963, Nat. Def. Seminar, Nat. War Coll. fellow, 1973, NEH fellow, 1978, Pres.'s fellow Ark. State U., 1988-89. Mem. AAUP (pres. 1983—, state sec. 1978-80), Ark. Polit. Sci. Assn. (bd. dirs., v.p. 1992-93, pres. 1993—), Am. Polit. Sci. Assn., So. Polit. Sci. Assn., Phi Sigma Alpha, Phi Gamma Mu, Phi Kappa Phi (pres. 1991). Republican. Roman Catholic. Office: Ark State U Dept Polit Sci State University AR 72467

POWER, RICHARD D., manufacturing executive; b. 1949. MBA, Boston Coll., 1970. Acct. Price Waterhouse, Boston, 1970-79; with Tyco Labs. Inc., Exeter, N.H., 1979—; officer Mueller Holdings Corp., Exeter, 1988—, now v.p., CFO. Office: Mueller Holdings Corp Ltd 1 Tyco Park Exeter NH 03833*

POWER, THOMAS MICHAEL, economist, educator; b. Milw., May 12, 1940; s. Paul C. and Edith (Thomas) P.; m. Pamela Shore, June 13, 1977; children: Donovan, Kate. BA, Lehigh U., 1962; MA, Princeton U., 1965, PhD, 1971. Instr. Lehigh U., Bethlehem, Pa., 1966-67, Princeton (N.J.) U., 1967-68; from asst. to assoc. prof. U. Mont., Missoula, 1968-78, prof. econ., chmn., 1978—. Author: Economic Value of Quality of Life, 1980, The Economic Pursuit of Quality, 1987, Lost Landscapes and Failed Economies: The Search for an Economic Value of Place, 1996, Environmental Protection and Local Economic Well-Being: The Economic Pursuit of Quality, 1996. Chmn. bd. dirs. Sussex Sch. Bd., Missoula, 1984-93. Woodrow Wilson Nat. fellow, 1963. Mem. Phi Beta Kappa. Avocations: mountaineering, long distance running, skiing. Office: U of Montana Dept Of Econs Missoula MT 59812

POWERS, BRUCE RAYMOND, author, English language educator, consultant; b. Bklyn., Dec. 10, 1927; s. George Osborne and Gertrude Joan (Bangs) P.; m. Dolores Anne Dawson, July 25, 1969; children: Christopher, Patricia. Student U. Conn., 1947-49; AB, Brown U., 1951, MA, (tuition scholar 61-62), 1965; postgrad. U. Pa., 1961. Announcer/engr. Sta. WNLC, New London, Conn., 1946-47; tng. officer CIA, Dept. Def., 1951-55; TV sales/svc. rep. NBC, 1955; TV news writer and reporter Movietone News, United Press Assns., Inc., 1955-56; asst. to pres. Gotham-Vladimir Advt., Inc., 1956-57; asst. account exec. D'Arcy Advt. Co., 1957-58; asst. campaign dir. Cmty. Counselling Svcs., Inc., 1958-59; fund-raising campaign dir. Tamblyn & Brown, Inc., 1959-60; instr. Brown U., Providence, 1963-65, Ryerson Poly. Inst., Toronto, 1966, Nazareth Coll., Rochester, N.Y., 1966-67; asst. prof. English and communication studies Niagara U., Lewiston, N.Y., 1967-86, assoc. prof., 1986-92, prof. emeritus, 1992, chmn. permanent curriculum com. English dept., 1970-71, dir. Film Repertory Center, 1971-92, dir. communication studies program, 1973-87; producer-mgn. dir. Exptl. Film retrospective, N.Y. State Coun. of the Arts, Buffalo, 1972; panelist-judge Artists Com. 2d World Festival of Animated Films, Zagreb, Yugoslavia, 1974; lectr., vis. artist ARTPARK, Lewiston, N.Y., 1975; project dir. Bicentennial Symposium, N.Y. State Am. Revolution Bicentennial Commn., Buffalo, N.Y., 1975-76; research assoc. Center Culture and Tech., U. Toronto, 1977-81; keynote speaker Dupont de Nemours & Co. Health and Safety Conf., Buffalo, 1990. Co-author (with Marshall McLuhan): The Global Village, Oxford, 1989; editor The Film and Study Guide, 1973-74. Served with USNR, 1945-46, PTO. Recipient Carpenter prize in elocution, Brown U., 1951. Mem. MLA, Broadcast Edn. Assn., Soc. Cinema Studies, Am. Soc. Journalism Sch. Adminstrs., Assn. for Edn. in Journalism and Mass Communication, Internat. Exptl. Film Soc. (founding pres. 1971-73), Western N.Y. Audio-Visual Assn., N.Y. Coll. English Assn., Phi Beta Kappa. Roman Catholic. Home: 915 Sun Valley St North Tonawanda NY 14120-1952 Office: 105 Main St Niagara Falls NY 14303-1112 *All creativity is a search for the survival of the Spirit. It always asks the question - "if I am to die why is my life important?".*

POWERS, CLAUDIA MCKENNA, state government official; b. Key West, Fla., May 28, 1950; d. James Edward and Claudia (Antrim) McKenna; m. Richard Garland Powers, Dec. 27, 1971; children: Gregory, Theodore, Matthew, Thurston. BA in Edn., U. Hawaii, 1972; MA, Columbia U., 1975. Cert. tchr., N.Y. Rep. Greenwich (Conn.) Rep. Town Meeting, 1979-93, sec. bldg. com., 1982-84, sec. legis. com., 1986-88, 90-93; mem. Conn. Ho. of Reps., 1993—, ranking mem. govt. adminstrn. and elections com., 1995—. Mem. editorial bd. Greenwich Mag., 1995—. Campaign chmn. Greenwich Rep. Town Com., 1984, 85, chmn., 1986-90; sec. Rep. Round Table, Greenwich, 1988-90; bd. govs. Riverside Assn., Greenwich, 1987-91, sec., 1991-92; class mother Riverside Sch., Greenwich, 1984-90; mem. altar guild Christ Ch., Greenwich, 1990—; adminstrv. coord. Greenwich Teen Ctr., 1990-91; alt. del. Rep. Nat. Conv., New Orleans, 1984—; v.p. LWV of Greenwich, 1990-91. Episcopalian. Home and Office: 15 Hendrie Ave Riverside CT 06878-1808

POWERS, DAVID RICHARD, educational administrator; b. Cambridge Springs, Pa., Apr. 5, 1939; s. William Herman and Elouise Fancheon (Fink) P.; m. Mary Julia Ferguson, June 11, 1960. Student, Pa. State U., 1957-60; BA, U. Pitts., 1963, MA, 1965, PhD, 1971. Dir. CAS advising ctr. U. Pitts., 1966-68, asst. dean faculty, 1968-70, asst. to chancellor, 1970-76, assoc. provost, 1976-78, vice provost, 1978-79; v.p. for acad. affairs George Mason U., Fairfax, Va., 1979-82; vice chancellor for acad. affairs W.Va. Bd. Regents, Charleston, 1982-88; exec. dir. Minn. Higher Edn. Coord. Bd., St. Paul, 1989-94, Nebr. Coord. Commn. Post-secondary Edn., Lincoln, 1994—. Prin. author: Making Participatory Management Work, 1983, Higher Education in Partnership with Industry, 1988; contbr. articles to Ednl. Record, Adult Learning, Forum for Applied Rsch. on Pub. Policy. Grantee USOE Faculty Seminar, Taiwan, 1967, ARC Ctr. for Edn. & Rsch. with Industry Appalachian Regional Commn., 1983, Republic of China Sino-Am. Seminar, 1985; recipient Award for Acad. Quality W.Va. Coun. Faculty, 1986. Mem. Am. Assn. for Higher Edn., Am. Soc. for Pub. Adminstrn., State Higher Edn. Exec. Officers, Civil Air Patrol, Pi Sigma Alpha. Avocation: flying. Home: 1928 High St Lincoln NE 68502-4825 Office: Nebr Coord Comm Post secondary Edn PO Box 95005 Lincoln NE 68509-5005

POWERS, DENNIS ALPHA, biology educator; b. Detroit, May 4, 1938; S. Virginia (Ward) P.; m. 1963 (div. 1993); children: Kathy M., Wendy R., Julie A. BA, Ottawa U., 1963; PhD, U. Kans., 1970. AEC postdoctoral fellow Argonne (Ill.) Nat. Lab.; NSF postdoctoral fellow Marine Biol. Lab., Woods Hole, Mass., 1971-72, SUNY, Stony Brook, 1971-72; asst. prof. biology Johns Hopkins U., Balt., 1973-79, assoc. prof., 1979-82, prof. biology, McCollum-Pratt prof., 1982-89, dir. McCollum-Pratt Inst., chmn. dept. biology, 1983-88; acting dir. Chesapeake Bay Inst., Shady Side, Md., 1984-87; Harold A. Miller prof. biol. sci., dir. Hopkins Marine Sta. Stanford (Calif.) U., 1988—; prin. rsch. scientist Ctr. Marine Biotech., U. Md., Balt., 1986-89; bd. advisors Nat. Aqaurium, Balt. Mem. editorial bd. Sci., Molecular Biology and Evolution, Molecular Phylogenetics and Evolution, Physiol. Zoology, Zool. Studies, Molecular Marine Biology and Biotech.; mem. editorial adv. bd. Advances in Marine Biotech.; contbr. more than 200 articles to profl. jours. Trustee Monterey Bay Aquarium; bd. dirs. Monterey Bay Aquarium Rsch. Inst. With USMC, 1957-59, USMCR, 1959-63. Grantee NSF, NIH, NOAA, others, 1970—; numerous honors and awards. Fellow AAAS; mem. Am. Soc. Biochem. and Molecular Biologists, Am. Soc. of Limnology and Oceanography, Am. Chem. Soc., Am. Soc. Molecular Marine Biology and Biotechnology (pres. editor-in-chief jour.), Soc. Study Evolution, Genetics Soc., Am. Soc. Zoologists, Biophys. Soc., N.Y. Acad. Sci., The Protein Soc., Am. Soc. Biol. Chemists, Sigma Xi. Office: Stanford U Hopkins Marine Sta Pacific Grove CA 93950

POWERS, DORIS HURT, retired engineering company executive; b. Indpls., Jan. 17, 1927; d. James Wallace Hurt Sr. and Mildred (Johnson) Devine; m. Patrick W. Powers, Nov. 12, 1950 (dec. 1989); children: Robert W. Powers, Jaye P., Laura S. Powers. Student, So. Meth. U., 1944-45; BS in Engring., Purdue U., 1949; postgrad., U. Tex., W. Tex., 1952-53, Ecole Normale Du Musique, Paris, 1965-68; grad., Harford County Leadership Acad., 1991. Flight instr. Red Leg Flying Club, El Paso, Lawton, Okla., 1951-57; check pilot Civil Air Patrol, El Paso, Lawton, Okla., 1952-57; ground instr. Civil Air Patrol, Washington, Tex., Okla, 1957-61; exec. v.p. T&E Internat., Inc., Bel Air, Md., 1979-88, pres., 1989-91; exec. v.p. T.E.I.S., Inc., Bel Air, 1979-88, pres., 1989-91; pres. Shielding Technologies, Inc., Bel Air, 1987-95; retired, 1995. Mem. Northeastern Md. Tech. Coun., 1991—; bd. dirs. Leadership Acad., 1991-94. Recipient Svc. award U.S. Army, 1978, Cert. of Appreciation U.S. Army Test and Evaluation Command, 1988, Woman of Distinction award Soroptomist Club, 1996; selected as Old Master Purdue U., 1996. Mem. CAP (lt. maj. 1951-58), Soc. of Women Engrs. (sr., v.p. 1977, treas. 1979, sec. rep. 1986-88, mentor 1986—, speaker 1978—, selected to Coll. of Fellows 1993), Engring. Soc. Balt. (speaker 1980—), 99's (pres. 1951-53), Am. Soc. Indsl. Security, Am. Def. Preparedness Assn., Hartford County Econ. Devel. Coun., Assn. of U.S. Army, Northeastern Md. Tech. Coun. Avocations: ice dancing, music. Home: 11 Glen Gate Ct Bel Air MD 21014

POWERS, DUDLEY, musician; b. Moorhead, Minn., June 25, 1911; s. James Harold and Mary Phoebe (Brainard) P.; m. Dorothy Louise Dasch, May 14, 1935; children: Jean Powers Todd, Eileen Powers Buchanan, Arthur, Anita Powers Palant. Student, Juilliard Mus. Found., 1926-30; MusB, Northwestern U., 1942, MusM, 1945. Cellist Little Symphony of Chgo., 1930-33; cellist Chgo. Symphony, 1933-43, solo cellist, 1943-53; prof. cello Northwestern U., 1931-80; vis. prof. cello U. South Fla., Tampa, 1980-86. Mem. Mischakoff String Quartet, 1935-38, Chgo. Symphony Quartet, 1940-53, Sheridan String Quartet, 1960-72; condr. Youth Symphony Greater Chgo., 1958-80, Eckstein String Quartet, 1972-80; cello recitalist. Home: 5450 B Riverfront Dr Bradenton FL 34208

POWERS, EDWARD ALTON, minister, educator; b. Jamestown, N.Y., Oct. 26, 1927; s. Leslie Edgar and Mabelle Florence (Alton) P.; children: Randall Edward, Christopher Alan, Ann Lynn. BA, Coll. of Wooster, 1948; MDiv, Yale U., 1952; EdD, Columbia U., 1973. Ordained to ministry Congregational Ch., 1951; pastor Hamden, Conn., 1949-53, Pleasant Hill, Ohio, 1953-56; sec. dept. youth work Congl. Christian Ch. Bd. Home Missions, 1956-60; gen. sec. div. Christian edn., bd. home missions Congl. and Christian Chs., 1960-61; div. Christian edn., bd. homeland ministries United Ch. of Christ, 1962-73; gen. sec., div. evangelism, edn., ch. extension United Ch. Bd. Homeland Ministries, 1973-79; mem. faculty Inst. Mgmt. Competency, Am. Mgmt. Assn., N.Y.C., 1980-87; sr. lectr. Grad. Sch. Mgmt. New Sch. for Social Research, 1981—; mem. program bd. div. edn. and ministry Nat. Council Chs., 1963-80; mem. edn. working group World Council Chs.; chmn. Peace Priority Team, United Ch. of Christ, 1970-75, adminstr., editor sexuality study, 1977; ptnr. Cane Powers Cons., and Powers, Wayno & Assocs. Author: Journey Into Faith, 1964, Signs of Shalom, 1973, (with Rey O'Day) Theatre of the Spirit, 1980, In Essentials Unity, 1982, Youth in the Global Village, 1982; also articles. Home: 7 Gramercy Park W Apt 5B New York NY 10003-1759 Office: Graybar Bldg 420 Lexington Ave Rm 300 New York NY 10170-0399

POWERS, EDWARD LATELL, accountant; b. Birmingham, Ala., Jan. 21, 1919; s. Jesse Franklin and Clara (Kircus) P.; m. Frances Gail Watters, Aug. 2, 1939; children: Karen Sue Powers Hoss, Linda Gail Powers Nix. Student, Wayne State U., 1944-45, U. Ala., 1952-53. C.P.A., Ala., N.Y., La., N.C. Accountant So. Cotton Oil Co., Birmingham, 1937-42; examiner pub. accounts Ala. Dept. Examiners Pub. Accounts, 1942; chief accountant Refuge Cotton Oil Co., Columbus, Miss., 1942-43; chief warrant officer, auditor Detroit Ordnance Dist., 1943-46; pub. accountant Screven, Turner & Co., Birmingham, 1946-48, Scarborough, Thomas & Co., Birmingham, 1948-49; sr. ptnr. Blankenship & Powers, Birmingham, 1950-51, Scarborough & Powers, Birmingham, 1951-56; mng. ptnr. Birmingham office, Haskins & Sells (now Deloitte & Touche), 1956-79; Mem., former chmn. Ala. Bd. Pub. Accountancy. Contbr. articles profl. jours. Mem. Mayor's Fact Finding Com., Birmingham, 1964-65; former trustee Bapt. Med.Ctrs.; treas. Lenox Owners Assn. Recipient Army Commendation award Detroit Ordnance Dist., 1945. Mem. AICPA, Ala. Soc. CPAs (past pres.), Soc. States Conf. CPAs (past mem. exec. com.), N.Y. Soc. of CPAs, Beta Alpha Psi. Baptist (deacon). Clubs: Downtown, The Club. Home: 905 Linkside Way Birmingham AL 35242-6430 Office: 3800 Colonnade Pky Birmingham AL 35243-2351

POWERS, EDWIN MALVIN, consulting engineer; b. Denver, July 20, 1915; s. Emmett and Bertha Malvina (Guido) P.; m. Dorothy Lavane Debler, Jan. 18, 1941; children: Dennis M., Kenneth E., James M., Steven R. BS in Chem. Engring., U. Denver, 1939, MS, 1940. Registered profl. engr., N.J., Colo., Fall Out Analysts Engr., U.S. Fed. Emergency Mgmt. Agency, 1975-87. Prodn. supr. Nat. Aniline Div., Buffalo, 1940-45; engr., project supr. Merck & Co., Rahway, N.J., 1945-67, chief project coordinator, 1967-72, purchasing engr., 1972-82; ret., 1982; cons. engr., Conifer, Colo., 1982—. Capt. Air Raid Wardens, River dist., Buffalo, 1942-45. Mem., del. Conifer Home Owners Assns. Protect Our Single Homes, 1984-86, Regional Environ. Assn. Concerned Home Owners, 1985-86, task force area devel. Hwy. 285/ Conifer Area County Planning Bd. Community, 1986-88. Mem. NSPE, Am. Chem. Soc. (emeritus), Am. Inst. Chem. Engrs. (emeritus, treas. N.J. 1960, exec. com. 1961-63), Nat. Soc. Profl. Engrs. Home and Office: 26106 Amy Cir Conifer CO 80433-6102

POWERS, ELIZABETH WHITMEL, lawyer; b. Charleston, S.C., Dec. 16, 1949; d. Francis Persse and Janes Coleman Cotten (Wham) P.; m. John Campbell Henry, June 11, 1994. AB, Mt. Holyoke Coll., 1971; JD, U. S.C., 1978. Bar: S.C. 1978, N.Y. 1979. Law clk. to justice S.C. Cir. Ct., Columbia; assoc. Reid & Priest, N.Y.C., 1978-86, ptnr., 1986—. Exec. editor S.C. Law Rev., Columbia, 1977-78. Bd. dirs. The Seamen's Ch. Inst., 1996—; vol. N.Y. Jr. League, N.Y.C., 1983—. Mem. ABA, S.C. Bar Assn., Nat. Soc. Colonial Dames of Am. (parliamentarian 1994—), Nat. Soc. Colonial Dames in State of N.Y. (pres. 1992-95), Church Club (v.p. 1992-94). Avocations: bridge, tennis. Office: Reid & Priest 40 W 57th St New York NY 10019-4001

POWERS, ESTHER SAFIR, organization design consultant; b. Tel Aviv, Sept. 1, 1948; arrived in Can., 1953, came to U.S., 1977; d. Nisan and Batia (Epstein) Safir; children: Jared Barnet, Elliott Robert. MusB, McGill U., Montreal, Que., Can., 1969; MusM, Ga. State U., 1982, PhD, 1985. Music tchr. North York Bd. Edn., Toronto, Ont., 1969-77; pres. Ested Mgmt., 1975-77, Mescon Group, Atlanta, 1985-95; cons. PeopleTech, 1995—. Contbr. articles to profl. jours., chpt. to book. Pres. bd. dirs. Montessori Sch., Atlanta, 1978; vol. Nat. Coun. Jewish Women, Atlanta, 1990; mem. Ga. Exec. Womens Network; bd. dirs. Coun. Battered Women, 1994—. Mem. Nat. Assn. Sch. Karate, Nat. Soc. for Performance and Instrn. (pres. Atlanta chpt. 1984-85, conf. mgr. 1983-84, internat. v.p. 1988-90, internat. pres. 1991-92, presdl. citation 1988, presdl. award 1989, leadership award 1990). Avocations: karate, music, bicycling, skiing, reading. Office: PeopleTech 1040 Crown Pointe Pky # 570 Atlanta GA 30338-4777

POWERS, EVELYN MAE, education educator; b. Norfolk, Va., Aug. 4, 1946; d. Albert Earl and Dorothy Mae (Weller) P.; m. Curtis Grubb Fitzhugh, June 21, 1969 (div. 1981). BA in Spanish, James Madison U., 1968; MEd, U. Va., 1976, PhD in Social Founds. of Edn., 1985. Spanish teacher pub. high schs., Va., 1969-77; grad. instr. U. Va., Charlottesville, 1977-85; adj. faculty Va. Commonwealth U., Richmond, 1985-88; asst. prof. edn. Lycoming Coll., Williamsport, Pa., 1988-91; asst. prof. social founds. of edn. E. Carolina U., Greenville, N.C., 1991—. Mem. Am. Ednl. Studies Assn., N.C. Founds. of Edn. Profs., So. Atlantic Philosophy of Edn. Soc. (yearbook editor 1994—, archivist 1993-95, Phi Delta Kappa. Home: 307 Joseph St Greenville NC 27858-9242

POWERS, GAY FRANCES, geriatrics nurse; b. Bastrop, Tex., June 9, 1952; d. James Wallace and Patsy Jean (Mach) Greene; m. Rayburn Burnett Powers Jr., Feb. 5, 1983. BS in Nursing, Tex. Womans U., 1976. RN, Tex.; cert. gerontol. nurse. Staff nurse med.-surg. Park Plz. Hosp., Houston, 1976-78, Doctors Meml. Hosp., Tyler, Tex., 1978-80; dir. nursing Pine Village Nursing Home, Tyler, 1980-82, The Clairmont, Tyler, 1987-93; corp. nurse Am. Health Svcs., Tyler, 1993-94; case mgr. Summit Care Corp., Tyler, 1995—. Mem. Tex. Health Care Assn. (nurse coun. 1994), Tex. Nurses Assn. Office: Colonial Manor The Clairmont Tyler TX 75701

POWERS, HARRIS PAT, broadcasting executive; b. Junction City, Kans., Oct. 29, 1934; s. Horace Pierce and Margaret (Harris) P.; m. Jerry Biles, Sept. 23, 1976; children: Rebecca, Randal, Mark, Shawn, Shannon, John. BA, Kans. State U., 1956. From salesman to mgr. Sta. KJCK, Junction City, 1957-73; mgr. Sta. KOYY, Eldorado, Kans., 1974-76; pres., CEO Sta. KTPK-FM, Topeka, 1976—; pres., chief exec. officer Stas. KINA and KQNS, Salina, Kans., 1979-87—; mem. bd. pub. adv. coun. Sta. KTWU, Topeka, 1979-87; pres., CEO Twenty First Century Broadcasting, Inc., Topeka, 1994—; bd. dirs. State Savs. & Loan Assn., Topeka; ptnr. Reichs Fgn. Cars and Parts, Topeka and Junction City. Mem. exec. com. Jayhawk Area coun. Boy Scouts Am., 1979-82; bd. dirs. Topeka Big Bros./ Big Sisters, local chpt. ARC, Downtown Topeka, Inc.; past chmn. Downtown Topeka, Inc.; mem. Radio-TV-Film Curriculum adv. coun. Kans. U., adv. bd. Channel 11 Pub. TV; bd. dirs. Topeka Community Found., Pub. Schs. Found. Recipient numerous C. of C. and Jaycee awards, Disting. Svc. award Topeka Sales and Mktg. Execs., 1983, Grover Cobb award Kans. U., Silver award Profl. Advt. Club. Mem. Nat. Assn. Broadcasters, Internat. Broadcasters Soc., Mid-Am. Broadcasters (past chmn.), Kans. Assn. Broadcasters (past pres., Disting. Svc. award 1993), Kans. Assn. Commerce and Industry, (pres., bd. dirs. 1980-83), Sales and Mktg. Execs. Internat. (past pres. Topeka chpt.), Greater Topeka C. of C. (past vice chmn. devel. com., past v.p. pub. rels.), Kans. C. of C. (bd. dirs.), Topeka Town Club, Elks, Kiwanis (life mem. found.). Republican. Home: 2120 SW Brooklyn Ave Topeka KS 66611-1612 Office: 3003 SW Van Buren St Topeka KS 66611-2224

POWERS, HENRY MARTIN, JR., oil company executive; b. Bath, Maine, July 18, 1932; s. Henry Martin and Eva (Saunders) P.; m. Hepzibah Hinchey Reed, June 20, 1959; children—Henry Martin III, Carlton Reed. B.S., Maine Maritime Acad., 1954. Marine engr. Am. Export Lines, N.Y.C., 1954-58; staff engr. Bull & Roberts Inc., N.Y.C., 1958-59; gen. sales mgr. Williams Bros., Inc., Portland, Maine, 1959-61; v.p. C.H. Sprague & Son Co., Boston, 1961-72; pres. C.H. Sprague & Son Co., 1972—, chmn. bd., 1987—, also bd. dirs.; chmn. Pease Devel. Authority, 1990-93; bd. dirs. Shanley Corp., Strawbery Banke Inc., First N.H. Banks, Seaward Constrn. Co. Vice pres. Seacoast United Fund, 1967-69; chmn. fuels, energy com. New England Council, 1974-75; pres. Portsmouth Council, 1966-67; bd. visitors Maine Maritime Acad. Served to lt. USNR, 1956-58. Mem. Navy League, Mechanic Fire Soc., Algonquin Club (Boston), Cumberland Club (Portland), Masons. Home: 68 River Rd Box 261 Stratham NH 03885 Office: C H Sprague & Son Co 1 Parade Mall Portsmouth NH 03801-3749

POWERS, HUGH WILLIAM, newspaper executive; b. Slaton, Tex., Dec. 20, 1926; s. James Jerome and Myrtle (Black) P.; m. Constance Margaret Cornwall, Aug. 30, 1952; children: Nan Margaret, Sarah Ann. Student, W.Va. U., 1943-47. Mng. editor AGC News Svc., Houston, 1949-56; city editor Houston Press, 1956-64; asst. city editor Houston Chronicle, 1964-65, bus. editor, 1965-67, feature editor, 1967-73, assoc. editor, 1973-95; dir. Taping for the Blind, 1995—. Mem. Press Club of Houston (pres., dir. 1968-72), Ducks Unltd. (dir. Houston chpt. 1989—, chmn. 1995, Tex. State trustee Nat. Del., 1996—), Phi Kappa Psi. Home: 10818 Hillcroft St Houston TX 77096-6031

POWERS, JAMES, record and tape company executive; married. With Handleman Co., Troy, Mich., 1956—, sr. v.p. sales, 1976-86, exec. v.p., 1987—. Served with AUS, 1952-54. Office: Handleman Co 500 Kirts Blvd Troy MI 48084-5225*

POWERS, JAMES FARL, author; b. Jacksonville, Ill., July 8, 1917; s. James Ansbury and Zella (Routzong) P.; m. Elizabeth Alice Wahl, Apr. 22, 1946; children: Katherine, Mary, James, Hugh, Jane. Student, Northwestern U., 1938-40. Instr. writing courses St. John's U., Collegeville, Minn., 1947, 75-93, Marquette U., 1949-51, U. Mich., 1956-57; writer-in-residence Smith Coll., 1965-66. Author: Prince of Darkness and Other Stories, 1947, (short stories) The Presence of Grace, 1956, Morte d'Urban (Nat. Book award 1963, Thormod Monsen award Soc. Midland Authors 1963), 1962, Look How the Fish Live, 1975, (novel) Wheat that Springeth Green, 1988. Decorated Chevalier de l'Ordre des Arts et des Lettres (France); Guggenheim fellow, 1948, Rockefeller fellow, 1954, 57, 67; grantee Am. Acad. of Arts and Letters, 1948. Mem. Am. Acad. of Arts and Letters. Office: care Alfred Knopf Inc 201 E 50th St New York NY 10022-7703

POWERS, JOE L., publishing executive; b. 1945. With TVA, Knoxville, 1966-69; with Thomas Nelson Inc., Nashville, 1969—, v.p., sec. Office: Thomas Nelson Inc Nelson Pl At Elm Hl Pike Nashville TN 37214

POWERS, JOHN H., school system administrator. Supt. Oyster River Sch. Dist., Durham, N.H. Recipient Nat. Superintendent of the Yr. awd., New Hampshire, Am. Assn. of School Administrators, 1992. Office: Oyster River Sch Dist Sau 5 36 Coe Dr Durham NH 03824

POWERS, JOHN Y., federal judge; b. Lake Orion, Mich., Aug. 1, 1929; s. Henry Stephen and Bertha Mae (Youngerman) P.; m. Barbara Mathilda Levero, Aug. 25, 1958; children: Joshua A., Lucas A., John Matthew, Samuel David. Student, Union U., 1947-48; BA, Vanderbilt U., 1951, LLB, 1953. Bar: Tenn. 1954. Enlisted man U.S. Army, Ft. Holabird, Md., 1954; 1st Lt. Judge Adv. Gen. Corps, Charlottesville, Va., 1955-57; with Claims Divsn. Office of the Judge Advocate General, Ft. Holabird, Md., 1955-57; with Adminstrv. divsn. U.S. Dept. Justice, 1957-58; claims rep. State Farm Ins. Co., Miami, Fla., 1958-59; atty. Spears, Moore, Rebman & Wms, Chattanooga, Tenn., 1959-70; ptnr. Hargraves, Curtis & Powers, Chattanooga, Tenn., 1970-74, Noone, Stringer & Powers, Chattanooga, Tenn., 1974-78, Reingold, Powers & Schulman, Chattanooga, Tenn., 1978-84; U.S. magistrate judge ea. dist. Tenn. U.S. Dist. Ct., Chattanooga, Tenn., 1984—. Mem. Tenn. Bar. Assn., Chatanooga Bar Assn. Office: US District Court US Courthouse 900 Georgia Ave Rm 102 Chattanooga TN 37402-2222

POWERS, MARTHA MARY, nursing consultant, education specialist; b. Medford, Mass., Jan. 8, 1940; d. John Francis and Mary (Denning) P. BS, Boston Coll., 1962; MS in Nursing, Boston U., 1978, EdD in Health Edn., 1985. Mem. faculty Boston Coll. Sch. Nursing; asst. prof. nursing Regis Coll., Weston, Mass.; nursing cons., edn. specialist NIH, Bethesda, Md.; cons. health care NATO, Belgium; coord. curriculum Somerville (Mass.) Hosp. Sch. Nursing; researcher medications, cardiac rehab., interaction analysis and leadership. Author: Health Promotion in Home Nursing: A Teaching Manual, 1986; contbr. articles to profl. jours. Chair nominating com. ARC Boston and Massachusetts Bay, past chmn. nursing and health, specialist home nursing, bd. dirs.; vol. Mass. Assn. Blind. Mem. AAUP, ANA, AACN, Mass. Nurses Assn., Nat. League Nursing, Mass. and R.I. League Nursing , N.Y. Acad. Sci., Assn. Nurse Researchers, Phi Lambda Theta.

POWERS, MICHAEL KEVIN, architectural and engineering executive; b. Boston, Feb. 3, 1948; s. Albert Thomas and Claire Marie (Sullivan) P.; m. Patricia Marie Collins, July 10, 1971; children: Kristin Michelle, Jennifer Anne. BSCE, Northeastern U., 1971. Registered profl. engr. N.Y., Vt., Minn., Maine, Mass., N.H., Ky., D.C., Pa., R.I., Pa. Staff engr. Edwards and Kelcey, Boston, 1967-70; project mgr. DeLeuw Cather & Co., Boston, 1971-80; exec. v.p., dir. engring., dir. advanced tech. group Symmes Maini & McKee Assocs., Inc., Cambridge, Mass., 1980—; guest spkr. Tradeline Forum on Bus. and Tech., Boston, 1986-88, Microcontamination Conf. and Expn., Santa Clara, Calif., 1987, Clean Rooms Conf., Balt., 1995, Santa Clara, 1995, Clean Rooms East, Boston, 1996; lectr. facility design MIT, 1989, 92, 93, Wentworth Inst., 1993, 94, Pa. State U., 1995. Contbr. articles to profl. jours. Mem. ASCE, NSPE, Inst. Environ. Scis. (sr.), Internat. Soc. Pharm. Engrs., Parenteral Drug Assn., Mt. River East Condominium Assn. (past trustee). Roman Catholic. Avocations: Alpine skiing, tennis, golf, music. Office: Symmes Maini & McKee Assocs Inc 1000 Massachusetts Ave Cambridge MA 02138-5304

POWERS, PAUL J., manufacturing company executive; b. Boston, Feb. 5, 1935; s. Joseph W. and Mary T. Powers; m. Barbara Ross, June 3, 1961; children: Briana, Gregory, Jeffrey. BA in Econs., Merrimack Coll., 1956; MBA, George Washington U., 1962. Various mfg. and fin. positions with Chrysler Corp., Detroit and overseas, 1963-69; v.p., gen. mgr. Am. Standard, Dearborn, Mich., 1970-78; pres. Abex-Dennison, Columbus, Ohio, 1978-82; group v.p. Comml. Intertech Corp., Youngstown, Ohio, 1982-84, pres., chief ops. officer, 1984-87, chmn., pres., CEO, 1987—; bd. dirs. Acme-Cleve. Corp., Ohio Edison Co., Twin Disc, Inc., Global Marine Inc. Bd. dirs. Youngstown Symphony, 1984-88. Lt. USNR, 1957-63. Mem. NAM (bd. dirs. 1986-93, 95—), Nat. Fluid Power Assn. (bd. dirs. 1984-87), Mfrs. Alliance (bd. dirs. 1995—), Youngstown Area C. of C. (bd. dirs. 1990—). Office: Comml Intertech Corp 1775 Logan Ave # 239 Youngstown OH 44505-2622

POWERS, RAMON SIDNEY, historical society administrator, historian; b. Gove County, Kans., Sept. 24, 1939; s. Sanford and Gladys Fern (Williams) P.; m. Eva Redin, Apr. 11, 1963; children: Elisabeth, Christina. AB, Ft. Hays (Kans.) State U., 1961, MA, 1963; PhD, U. Kans., 1971. Instr. western civilization U. Kans., Lawrence, 1963-67; asst. prof. history U. Mo., Kansas City, 1967-71; instr. Haskell Indian Jr. Coll., Lawrence, 1971-73; rsch. asst. Kans. Legis. Rsch. Dept., Topeka, 1973-77, rsch. analyst, 1977-78, prin. analyst, 1978-88; asst. exec. dir. Kansas State Hist. Soc., Topeka, 1988, exec. dir., 1988—. Contbr. articles to various jours. Chair Eisenhower Centennial Adv. Com., Topeka, 1988-90, Kans. Antiquities Commn., 1988—, State Records Bd., 1988—, Sante Fe Hist. Trail Adv. Coun.; mem. bd. review Kans. Hist. Sites, 1988—; mem. State Hist. Records Adv. Bd., 1988—, Gov.'s Commn. on Travel and Tourism, 1988—, Kans. Bus. Hall of Fame, 1988-96; mem. bd. dirs. Nat. Conf. of State Historic Preservation Officers, 1991—. Recipient regional award Col. Dames Am., 1965, Disting. Alumni award Ft. Hays State U. and Hays Rotary Club, 1978; travel grantee N.J. Hist. Commn., 1971, summer grantee NEH, 1973. Mem. SAR (Thomas Jefferson chpt.), Am. Assn. State and Local History, Kans. Corral of the Westerns, Kans. History Tchrs. Assn., Western History Assn., Travel Industry Assn. (bd. dirs. 1991-93), Greater Topeka C. of C., Topeka Heritage League, Sat. Night Literary Club. Office: Kans History Ctr 6425 SW 6th Ave Topeka KS 66615-1004

POWERS, RICHARD AUGUSTINE, III, judge; b. Phila., Sept. 22, 1932; s. Richard Augustine and Evelyn Lenore (Clark) P.; m. Helen Regina Penza, Aug. 30, 1958; children: Mary, Helen, Joan, Grace, Patricia, Theodore, Robert. B.S. in Econs., LaSalle Coll., 1958; J.D., Temple U., 1962. Bar: U.S. Dist. Ct. (ea. dist.) Pa. 1962; U.S. Supreme Ct., 1993. Assoc., Leo Francis Doyle, Phila., 1962; law clk. to judges U.S. Dist. Ct. (ea. dist.) Pa., 1962-71; U.S. Magistrate judge U.S. Dist. Ct. (ea. dist.) Pa., Phila., 1971—; chief U.S. Magistrate judge, 1994—. lectr. in law Fed. Jud. Center, Washington; lectr. in civil litigation Main Line Paralegal Inst. Contbr. articles to profl. jours. Served with USAR, 1957-63. Recipient award Temple Law Alumni, 1979, LaSalle Law Alumni, 1979. Mem. Nat. Council Fed. Magistrates Judges, Phila. Bar Assn., Pa. Hist. Soc., Genealogical Soc. Pa., Brehon Law Soc., Phila. Museum Art, Smithsonian Contributory Assn., Pa. Hort. Soc., SAR. Roman Catholic. Office: US District Court 2716 US Courthouse Ind Mall W 601 Market St Philadelphia PA 19106-1510

POWERS, RICHARD F., III, finance company executive; b. Boston, Feb. 2, 1946; s. Richard Francis Jr. and Mary Frances (Sullivan) P.; m. Colleen Teresa Cullen, Apr. 8, 1980; 1 child, Alicia Quilty. BS, Boston Coll., 1967; MBA, Columbia Sch. Bus., 1972. Asst. v.p., v.p., 1st v.p., sr. v.p., exec. v.p., dir. Dean Witter, 1972—. Lt. USN, 1967-72. Office: Dean Witter Reynolds Inc Two World Trade Center 66th Fl New York NY 10048

POWERS, STEFANIE (STEFANIE FEDERKIEWICZ), actress; b. Hollywood, Calif., Nov. 2, 1945; m. Patrick de la Chenais, April 1, 1993. Film appearances include Among the Thorns, Experiment in Terror, 1962, McClintock, 1963, Fanatic, 1964, Warning Shot, 1967, Herbie Rides Again, 1973, Escape to Athena, 1979, Invisible Stranger, 1984, Mother's Day, 1984; TV movie appearances include Five Desperate Women, 1971, Sweet Sweet Rachel, 1971, Paper Man, 1971, Ellery Queen: Don't Look Behind You, 1971, Hardcase, 1972, Sky Heist, 1975, Return to Earth, 1976, Washington: Behind Closed Doors, 1977, Nowhere to Run, 1978, A Death in Canaan, 1978, Family Secrets, 1984, Mistral's Daughter, 1984, Hollywood Wives, 1985, Deceptions, 1985, At Mother's Request, 1987, (co-producer) Beryl Markham: A Shadow on the Sun, 1988, She Was Marked for Murder, 1988, Love and Betrayal, 1989, When Will I Be Loved?, 1990, The Burden of Proof, 1992, Survive The Night, 1993, Hart to Hart: Old Friends Never Die, 1994; TV series The Girl from U.N.C.L.E., 1966, The Feather and the Father Gang, 1977, Hart to Hart, 1979-84. Office: care Internat Creative Mgmt 8942 Wilshire Blvd Beverly Hills CA 90211-1934*

POWERS, THOMAS MOORE, author; b. N.Y.C., Dec. 12, 1940; s. Joshua Bryant and Susan (Moore) P.; m. Candace Molloy, Aug. 21, 1965; children: Amanda, Susan, Cassandra. B.A., Yale U., 1964. Reporter Rome (Italy) Daily American, 1965-67, U.P.I., N.Y.C., 1967-70; freelance writer, 1970—; contbg. editor The Atlantic mag., L.A. Times Opinion; editor, founding ptnr. Steerforth Press, So. Royalton, Vt., 1993—. Author: Diana: The Making of a Terrorist, 1971, The War at Home, 1973, The Man Who Kept the Secrets: Richard Helms and the CIA, 1979, Thinking About the Next War, 1982, Total War: What It Is, How It Got That Way, 1988, Heisenberg's War: The Secret History of the German Bomb, 1993. Recipient Pulitzer prize for nat. reporting, 1971. Mem. PEN Am. Center, Council on Fgn. Relations. Office: care Susan P Urstadt PO Box 1676 New Canaan CT 06840-1676

POWERS, WILLIAM FRANCIS, automobile manufacturing company executive; b. Phila., Dec. 11, 1940; s. Francis Simpson and Kathryn Emily (Thoroughgood) P.; m. Linda Nell Shelton, Sept.7, 1963; children—Stephen, Leigh. B.S. in Aerospace Engring., U. Fla., 1963; M.S., U. Tex., 1966, Ph.D., 1968. Aerospace engr. NASA Marshall Space Flight Ctr., Huntsville, Ala., 1960-65; faculty mem. U. Mich., Ann Arbor, 1968-79, prof. aerospace engring., 1976-79; research mgr. Ford Motor Co., Dearborn, Mich., 1980-86, rsch. dir., 1986-87, dir. computer ops. N.Am., 1987-89, program mgr., 1989-91, exec dir. rsch., 1991-94, exec. dir IS and rsch., 1994—; cons. NASA Johnson Space Ctr., Houston, 1971-79, other cos., 1968-79. Contbr. articles to profl. jours. Editor: Astrodynamics, 1975, Jour. Astron. Scis., 1977-80. USSR research exchange scientist U.S. Nat. Acad. Scis., 1976. Fellow AIAA (assoc.), IEEE; mem. ASME, NAE, Soc. Automotive Engrs., Am. Automatic Control Council (v.p. 1986-87, pres. 1988-89), Royal Swedish Acad. Engring. Scis. (fgn.). Home: 2032 Greenview Dr Ann Arbor MI 48103-6110 Office: Ford Motor Company Ford Research Laboratory PO Box 1603 Rm 3153/srl Dearborn MI 48121-1603

POWLEDGE, FRED ARLIUS, freelance writer; b. N.C., Feb. 23, 1935; s. Arlius Raymond and Pauline (Stearns) P.; m. Tabitha Morrison, Dec. 21, 1957; 1 child, Pauline Stearns. AB in English, U. N.C., 1957. Writer, editor AP, New Haven, 1958-60; reporter Atlanta Jour., 1960-63, N.Y. Times, N.Y.C., 1963-66; freelance journalist, 1966—; lectr. New Sch., N.Y.C., 1967-69, 80-82; narrator, co-producer, writer WNET-TV/13, N.Y.C., 1972. Author: Black Power/White Resistance: Notes on the New Civil War, 1967, To Change a Child: A Report on the Institute for Developmental Studies, 1967, Model City: A Test of American Liberalism: One Town's Efforts to Rebuild Itself, 1970, Mud Show: A Circus Season, 1976, Born on the Circus, 1976, The Backpacker's Budget Food Book, 1977, Journeys Through the South, 1979, So You're Adopted: A Book About the Experience of Being Adopted, 1982, Water: The Nature, Uses and Future of Our Most Precious and Abused Resource, 1982, A Forgiving Wind: On Becoming a Sailor, 1983, Fat of the Land, 1984, The New Adoption Maze: And How to Get Through It, 1985, You'll Survive, 1986, Free at Last? The Civil Rights Movement and the People Who Made It, 1991, We Shall Overcome: The Heroes of the Civil Rights Movement, 1993, Working River, 1995. Mem. Bd. Library Trustees, St. Mary's County, Md. With USAR, 1957. Russell Sage fellow Russell Sage Found., 1966-67; travel and study grantee Ford Found., 1971, 93-94. Mem. Nat. Writer's Union.

POWLEN, DAVID MICHAEL, lawyer; b. Logansport, Ind., May 28, 1953; s. Daniel Thomas and Bertha Frances (Cappa) P.; m. Karen Lamb Gentleman, Aug. 5, 1978 (div. Jan. 1984); 1 child, Brooks Ryan. AB, Harvard U., 1975, JD, 1978. Bar: Ind. 1978, U.S. Dist. Ct. (so. dist.) Ind. 1978, U.S. Ct. Appeals (7th cir.) 1985. Assoc. Barnes & Thornburg, Indpls., 1978-84, ptnr., 1985—, chmn. creditors rights dept. Contbr. articles to profl. jours. Mem. ABA (bus. bankruptcy com., secured creditors and chpt. 11 subcom., comml. fin. svcs. com., creditors rights subcom.), Seventh Cir. Bar Assn., Ind. Bar Assn. (chmn. bankruptcy and creditors rights sect. 1990-91), Indpls. Bar Assn. (chmn. edn. com. 1984, chmn. ct. liaison com. 1985, bankruptcy and comml. law sect.), Am. Bankruptcy Inst. (regional programs and seminars subcom.), Comml. Law League Am. (bankruptcy and insolvency sect.), Harvard Club, Indpls. Sailing Club. Republican. Home: 1450 Preston Tr Carmel IN 46032-8971 Office: Barnes & Thornburg 11 S Meridian St Ste 1313 Indianapolis IN 46204-3506

POWLES, PETER B., lawyer; b. Kenya, Feb. 19, 1936. BA, Cambridge U., Eng., 1957, MA, 1962, LLB, 1958. Bar: Eng. 1958, Victoria, Australia 1962, New South Wales, Australia 1963, Ill. 1966, St. Lucia, Windward and Leeward Islands 1966. Ptnr. Baker & McKenzie, Chgo. Office: Baker & McKenzie 1 Prudential Plz 130 E Randolph St Chicago IL 60601*

POWLISON, HOWARD WHITFIELD, religious organization administrator; b. Torracari, Charcas, Bolivia, Oct. 12, 1919; came to U.S., 1932; s. Kenneth Whitfield and Pansy Arvada (Fitch) P.; m. Doris Ruth Waggoner, Sept. 5, 1942; children: Kenneth, Gordon, Douglas, Robert, Cynthia, Steven, Kathleen, Warren, Roland, John, Timothy, Dale, Donald. BA in Biblical Edn., Columbia Bible Coll., 1942; cert., Buffalo Bible Coll., 1943. Ordained minister Bapt. Ch., 1942. Pastor Springbrook (N.Y.) Cmty. Ch., 1942-49, 1st Bapt. Ch., Marilla, N.Y., 1947-52, New Testament Bapt. Ch., Alden, N.Y., 1952-62; precision grinder Consol. Electrodynamics, East Pasadena, Calif., 1962-66; gen. dynamics optical polisher stainless steel mirrors Red Eye Missiles, 1966-68; dir. Christian teens Christian Rsch., Portland, Oreg., 1969-72; assoc. pastor Country Ch., Colton, Oreg., 1973-75; elder, treas. Bethel Ch. - East Portland, 1975-77; sec./treas. Christian Rsch., Inc., Portland, 1977—; chaplain Am. Family Enterprises, 1995—; asst. prin. Bethel Christian Acad., Portland, 1975-77; pastor Canby (Oreg.) Cmty. Ch., 1979-88; mgr., sec. Mineral Rsch. Corp., Portland, 1993-94. Bd. dirs. Love in Action, Portland, 1991-93; mem. com. Concerned Citizens, Portland, 1988; precinct worker Rep., Portland, 1989; foster care vol. Children Svcs., Molalla, Oreg., and Portland, 1975-80. Avocations: crossword puzzles, chess, computers, reading. Office: Berg Christian Enterprises 4525 SE 63rd Ave Portland OR 97206-4617

POWNALL, MALCOLM WILMOR, mathematics educator; b. Coatesville, Pa., Jan. 6, 1933; s. Malcolm and Elizabeth (Moore) P.; m. Gertrude Decker, June 3, 1961; children: Joseph, Elizabeth, Kathryn, Thomas. A.B., Princeton U., 1954; M.A., U. Pa., 1958, Ph.D., 1960. Instr. to prof. math. Colgate U., Hamilton, N.Y., 1959—. Author: Prelude to the Calculus, 1967, Functions and Graphs, 1983, Real Analysis, A First Course with Foundations, 1994. Mem. Math. Assn. Am. (exec. dir. com. on undergrad. program 1966-68, chmn. com. on vis. lectrs. and cons. 1969-83). Democrat. Mem. Soc. of Friends. Office: Colgate Univ Dept Math 13 Oak Dr Hamilton NY 13346-1338

POWSNER, EDWARD RAPHAEL, physician; b. N.Y.C., Mar. 17, 1926; m. Rhoda Lee Moscovitz, June 8, 1950; children: Seth, Rachel, Ethan, David. SB in Elec. Engring., MIT, 1948, SM in Biology, 1949; MD, Yale U., 1953; MS in Internal Medicine, Wayne State U., 1957; MHSA, U. Mich. Diplomate Am. Bd. Nuclear Medicine, Am. Bd. Pathology in clin. pathology and anatomic pathology, Am. Bd. Internal Medicine; lic. physician, Mich., Calif., N.Y. Intern Wayne County Gen. Hosp., Eloise, Mich., 1953-54, resident internal medicine, 1954-55; resident internal medicine Detroit Receiving Hosp., 1955-56; fellow in hematology Wayne State U. and Detroit Receiving Hosp., 1957-58; clin. investigator VA Hosp., Allen Park, Mich., 1958-61, chief nuclear medicine svc., 1961-78; dir. clin. labs. Mich. State U., East Lansing, 1978-81; staff pathologist Ingham Med. Ctr., Lansing, Mich., 1978-81; dir. nuclear medicine St. John Hosp., Detroit, 1982-95; rsch. asst. biology MIT, 1948-49, 50; asst. instr. medicine Wayne State U. Coll. Medicine, 1954-56, instr., 1959-61; assoc. prof. pathology Wayne State U. Sch. Medicine, 1961-68, assoc. medicine, 1961, prof. pathology, 1966-78; prof. pathology Mich. State U., 1978-81, assoc. chairperson, 1980-81, clin. prof., 1981-82; chief clin. labs. Detroit Gen. Hosp., 1969-73; chief lab. svcs. Health Care Inst., Wayne State U., 1976-78; mem. adv. coun. Nuclear Medicine Tech. Cert. Bd., 1990-91. Bd. editors Am. Jour. Clin. Pathology, 1963-76, 83-88; author 1 textbook, 10 chpts., 48 peer reviewed papers, 19 abstracts and other publs. With U.S. Army, 1944-47. Mem. AMA (sect. coun. on pathology), Am. Soc. Clin. Pathologists (rep. 1987-89, 93—, govt. rels. com. 1993—, mem. coun. nuclear medicine 1978-82, chmn. 1982-84), Am. Coll. Nuclear Physicians, Am. Soc. Nuclear Cardiology, Coll. Am. Pathologists, Detroit Acad. Medicine, Mich. Soc. Pathologists, Mich. State Med. Soc., Soc. Nuclear Medicine, Washtenaw County Med. Soc., Sigma Xi, Tau Beta Pi. Office: Eastside Nuclear Medicine 18530 Mack Ave Ste 134 Grosse Pointe MI 48236 also: St John Hosp & Med Ctr 22101 Moross Rd Detroit MI 48236

POYNER, JAMES MARION, retired lawyer; b. Raleigh, N.C., Sept. 18, 1914; s. James Marion and Mary (Smedes) P.; m. Florence I Chan, Feb. 24, 1945; children: Susan Poyner Moore, Chan Poyner Pike, Margaret Poyner Galbraith, Edythe Poyner Lumdsen, James Marion III. B.S. in Chem. Engring, N.C. State U., 1935, M.S., 1937; J.D., Duke U., 1940. Bar: N.C. 1940. Pvt. practice Raleigh, 1946-51; ptnr. Poyner, Geraghty, Hartsfield & Townsend, Raleigh, 1951-86; of counsel Poyner & Spruill, Raleigh, 1986-95, ret., 1995; co-founder Cameron-Brown Co. (now 1st Union Mortgage Co.); life dir. 1st Union Corp., 1st Union Nat. Bank; chmn. bd. dirs. Eastern Standard Ins. Co., George Smedes Poyner Founds. Inc. Orch. leader, trombonist, arranger, Jimmy Poyner and His Orch., 1933-38. Mem. N.C. Senate, 1955-59; Past chmn. bd. trustees St. Mary's Coll.; past chmn. bd. World Golf Hall of Fame; past chmn. trustees N.C. Symphony Soc. Served with Chem. Warfare Service, AUS, 1942-46. Decorated Legion of Merit. Mem. ABA, N.C. Bar Assn. (pres. 1967-68, dir. 1963-67), Am. Judicature Soc. (dir. 1973-77), Raleigh C. of C. (past pres.), Phi Kappa Phi. Episcopalian. Home: 710 Smedes Pl Raleigh NC 27605-1141 Office: 3600 Glenwood Ave Raleigh NC 27612-4945

POYNOR, ROBERT ALLEN, JR., guidance counselor; b. Franklin, Tenn., Aug. 2, 1939; s. Robert Allen and Agnes Elizabeth (Gillespie) P.; divorced; 1 child, Melissa Dawn Hay. BA, Belmont Coll., Nashville, 1967; MEd, Middle Tenn. State U., 1972, EdS, 1975; postgrad., Tenn. State U. Cert. elem. tchr., elem. guidance counselor, elem. prin.-advanced, Tenn. Teller, mgmt. trainee Third Nat. Bank, Nashville, 1962-67; employment rep. S.S. Bd. of the S.B.C., Nashville, 1967-68; tchr. Sumner County Bd. Edn., Gallatin, Tenn., 1968-69; asst. sec.-treas., br. mgr. Security Fed. Savs. and Loan Assn., Nashville, 1969-71; tchr. Sumner County Bd. Edn., Gallatin, 1971-79, 83-85, prin., 1979-83, guidance counselor, 1985—; mem. textbook adoption com. Sumner County bd. Edn., 1968-69, gifted com., 1980-82. Charter sec. 100 Oaks Sertoma Club, Nashville, 1970; treas. Am. Savs. and Loan Inst., Nashville, 1970. With U.S. Army, 1957-59, France. Mem. ASCD, Tenn. ASCD, Tenn. Assn. Counselor Devel., Mid. Tenn. Assn. for Counselor Devel., United Teaching Profession, Sumner County Elem. Prins. (past pres. 1982-83), Sumner County Edn. Assn. (past pres. 1978-79), Phi Delta Kappa. Baptist. Avocations: jogging, reading, yard work, spectator sports, art. Home: 288 Indian Lake Rd Hendersonville TN 37075-4344

POYNTER, JAMES MORRISON, travel educator, travel company executive; b. Kansas City, Mo., July 27, 1939; s. Lewis Alderson and Patricia Connely (Dunn) P.; m. Sorore; children: Lewis, Robert, Michael. BA, George Washington U., 1969, MA, 1975. Cert. travel counselor (honorary). Adminstrv. dir. Inst. Cert. Travel Agents, Arlington, Va., 1967-72; ednl. cons. Saudi Arabian Airlines, Jeddah, 1972-77; specialist employment and tng. Leon County Dept. Human Resources, Tallahassee, 1977-79; pres., CEO Fla. Profl. and Econ. Devel. Corp., Tallahassee, 1979-81; mgr., co-owner The Travel Ctr., Tallahassee, 1979-82, Adventures in Travel, Tallahassee, 1979-82; assoc. prof. travel adminstrn. Met. State Coll. Denver, 1982—; pres. Travel Analysis, Denver, 1988—. Author: Foreign Independent Tours, 1989, Corporate Travel Management, 1990, Travel Agency Accounting Procedures, 1991, Tour Design Marketing and Management, 1992, Travel and Tourism Books in Print, 1992, How to Research and Write A Thesis in Hospitality and Tourism, 1993, Multicultural, Multinational Adjustment and Readjustment, 1995 (with others) Travel Industry Business Management, 1986; compiler editor: Proceedings of the Colloquim on Corporate Travel Curricula Development, 1994, Travel and Tourism Books in Print, 1994, 95. With U.S. Army, 1957-60. Mem. Am. Soc. Travel Agts., Internat. Assn. of Tour Mgrs., Assn. Corp. Travel Execs. (edn. cons. 1988-89, bd govs. 1993-95, v.p. edn. 1994-95, Edn. award 1992, Educator of Yr. award 1993), Soc. Travel and Tourism Educators (bd. dirs. 1989-91, 93-95), Profl. Guides Assn. Am., Rocky Mountain Bus. Travel Assn. (bd. dirs. 1986-87), Rocky Mountain Profl. Guides Assn. (bd. dirs. 1989-90, v.p. 1989-90), Colo. Author's League (treas. 1992). Mem. Am. Soc. Travel Agts., Assn. Corp. Travel Execs. (edn. cons. 1988-89, bd. govs. 1993-95, v.p. edn. 1994-95, Edn. award 1992, Educator of Yr. award 1993), Soc. Travel and Tourism Educators (bd. dirs. 1989-91, 93—), Profl. Guides Assn. Am., Rocky Mountain Bus. Travel Assn. (bd. dirs. 1986-87), Rocky Mountain Profl. Guides Assn. (bd. dirs. 1989-90, v.p. 1989-90), Colo. Author's League (treas. 1992). Republican. Presbyterian.

POYTHRESS, DAVID BRYAN, state commissioner, lawyer; b. Macon, Ga., Oct. 24, 1943; s. John M. and Dorothy (Bayne) P. BA, Emory U., 1964, JD, 1967. Bar: Supreme Ct. Ga. 1967, U.S. Supreme Ct. 1971. Asst. atty. gen. Dept. Law, State of Ga., Atlanta, 1971-72; dep. commr. Ga. Dept. Revenue, Atlanta, 1972-76; commr. Ga. Dept. Med. Assistance, Atlanta, 1976-79; sec. of state State of Ga., Atlanta, 1979-83; ptnr. Kutak Rock & Huie, Atlanta, 1983-84; pvt. practice Atlanta, 1984-86; exec. dir. Ga. Health Network, Atlanta, 1986-89; atty. Chilivis & Grindler, Atlanta, 1989-92; commr. Ga. Dept. Labor, Atlanta, 1992—. With USAF, 1967-71. Mem. State Bar Ga. Democrat. Methodist. Office: Labor Dept 148 Internat Blvd NE Atlanta GA 30303*

POYTHRESS, MARGARET LYNN, occupational health nurse; b. Macon, Ga., Mar. 25, 1941; d. Elwin Mathew and Dorothy Angelle (Davis) P. Diploma, Macon Hosp. Sch. Nursing, 1962; BSN, Med. Coll. Ga., 1980. RN Ga. Staff nurse surg. Emory U. Hosp., Atlanta, 1962-64, charge nurse open heart, 1964-66; staff nurse surg. Macon (Ga.) Hosp., 1966-71, Project Hope/SS Hope, Natal, Brazil, 1972; supr. surgery Med. Ctr. Ctrl. Ga., Macon, 1973-93, asst. mgr. surgery, 1991-93, occupational health nurse, 1993—; mem. infection control com. Med. Ctr. Macon, 1985-88, mem. quality assurance com., 1988-90, mem. nursing practice com., 1985-88, mgmt. com., 1975-93. Mem. AORN, Am. Soc. Ophthalomology RNs, Soc. Head & Neck Nurses, Assn. Hosp. Employee Health Profls., Assn. Profls. Infection Control & Epidemiology. Avocations: collecting art, antiques, old ships, painting. Home: 3385 Matheson Dr Macon GA 31204-3337

POZDRO, JOHN WALTER, music educator, composer; b. Chgo., Aug. 14, 1923; s. John and Rose Anna (Mossman) P.; m. Shirley Allison Winans, June 12, 1954; children—John Winans, Nancy Allison. B.M. in Music, Northwestern U.-Evanston, Ill., 1948, M.M. in Music, 1949; Ph.D. in Music, Eastman Sch. Music, 1958. Instr. Iowa State Tchrs. Coll., Cedar Falls, 1949-50; instr. to assoc. prof. U. Kans., Lawrence, 1950-64, prof. music, 1964—; dir. theory and composition U. Kans., 1961—; teaching fellow Eastman Sch. Music, Rochester, NY, 1956-57; chmn. symposium com. U. Kans., Lawrence, 1958-69. Representative works include Third Symphony, 1960, Piano Sonata No. 4, 1976, Malooley & Fear Monster, 1977, Impressions, Winds, Piano, 1984, Tryptich for Carillon, the Spirit of Mt. Oread, 1989. Winds of Autumn, 1995. Served with U.S. Army, 1943-46. Recipient U. Calif. Berkeley medal for Disting. Svc., 1993; grantee Ford Found., 1960, Nat. Endowment Arts, 1976; nominated for Pulitzer prize in Music, 1960. Mem. ASCAP (award 1965-96), Pi Kappa Lambda. Presbyterian. Avocations: golf; photography, reading. Home: 4700 Muirfield Dr Lawrence KS 66047-1820

POZEN, WALTER, lawyer; b. East Orange, N.J., Oct. 17, 1933; s. Irving Joseph and Berte (Protter) P.; m. Elizabeth Klupt, June 19, 1955 (div. 1967); children: Agatha Elizabeth, Jonathan Walter, Thorn Lord; m. Joan Kennan, Apr. 24, 1971 (div. Apr. 1988). B.A., U. Chgo., 1952, grad. student, 1952-53; J.D., 1956. Bar: Md. 1963. With Strasser, Spiegelberg, Fried & Frank, Washington and N.Y.C., 1956-58; mem. campaign staff Harrison A. Williams for U.S. Senator, 1958; legis. counsel Home Rule Com., Inc., Washington, 1959-60; counsel, assoc. dir. Fgn. Policy Clearing House, Washington, 1960-61; asst. to sec. interior, 1961-67; ptnr. Stroock & Stroock & Lavan, N.Y.C., 1967—, in charge Washington office; ofcl. rep. U.S. del. GATT Ministerial Meeting, Geneva, 1963; mem. Gov.'s Commn. on Historic Preservation, Md.; mem. D.C. Bd. Elections and Ethics.; del. Democratic Nat. Conv., 1964, counsel credentials com., 1968; counsel compliance rev. com. Dem. Nat. Com.; vis. prof. Irving B. Harris Sch. Pub. Policy Studies U. Chgo., 1993—. Author: (with Dr. J.H. Cerf) Strategy for the Sixties, 1960; also articles, book reviews. Bd. dirs. Nat. Symphony Orch.; mem. vis. com. Harris Sch. Pub. Policy Studies, U. Chgo. Mem. D.C. Bar Assn., Md. Bar Assn., Harmonie Club, Fed. City Club. Home: 3806 Klingle Pl NW Washington DC 20016-5433 also: PO Box 121 West Halifax VT 05358-0121 Office: Stroock & Stroock & Lavan 1150 17th St NW Ste 600 Washington DC 20036-4603

POZNANSKI, ANDREW KAROL, pediatric radiologist; b. Czestochowa, Poland, Oct. 11, 1931; came to U.S., 1957, naturalized, 1964; s. Edmund Maurycy and Hanna Maria (Ceranka) P.; children: Diana Jean, Suzanne Christine. B.Sc., McGill U., 1952, M.D.C.M., 1956. Diplomate: Am. Bd. Radiology, Royal Coll. Physicians and Surgeons Can. Intern Montreal (Que., Can.) Hosp., 1956-57; resident Henry Ford Hosp., Detroit, 1957-60; staff radiologist Henry Ford Hosp., 1960-68, U. Mich. Med. Center, Ann Arbor, 1968-79; co.-dir. pediatric radiology C.S. Mott Children's Hosp., Ann Arbor, 1971-79; radiologist-in-chief Children's Meml. Hosp., Chgo., 1979—; prof. radiology U. Mich., 1971-79, Northwestern U. Med. Sch., 1979—; bd. dirs. Nat. Coun. on Radiation Protection, 1983-90; mem. Internat. Commn. on Radiologic Protection, 1981-89; mem. adv. panel on radiologic devices FDA, 1975-77, chmn., 1976-77; trustee Am. Bd. Radiology, 1993—. Author: The Hand in Radiologic Diagnosis, 1974, 2d edit., 1983, Practical Approaches to Pediatric Radiology, 1976; bd. editors: Skeletal Radiology, 1975-95, Radiographics, 1980-84, Pediatric Radiology, 1986-91. Fellow Am. Coll. Radiology; mem. AMA, Am. Roentgen Ray Soc. (pres. 1993-94), Soc. Pediatric Radiology (pres. 1980-81), Radiol. Soc. N.Am., Assn. Univ. Radiologists, John Caffey Soc., Am. Assn. Phys. Anthropologists, Internat. Skeletal Soc. (founder, pres. 1992-94), Can. Assn. Radiologists (hon.), Polish Radiol. Soc. (hon.), Teratology Soc., Alpha Omega Alpha. Home: 2400 N Lakeview Ave Chicago IL 60614-2747 Office: Childrens Meml Hosp 2300 N Childrens Plz Chicago IL 60614-3318

POZNANSKY, MARK JOAB, research institute administrator, educator; b. Montreal, Que., Can., Apr. 25, 1946; s. Eric and Ruth Poznansky; m. Esther Goldberg, Dec. 18, 1981; children: Shoshana, Mirit. BSc in Physiology, McGill U., Montreal, 1967, PhD in Physiology, 1970. Postdoctoral fellow Biophys. Lab., Harvard Med. Sch., Boston, 1970-72, instr., 1972-74, lectr., 1974-76; assoc. prof. dept. physiology U. Alta., Edmonton, Can., 1976-81, prof. lipid and lipoprotein rsch. group, 1982-93; pres., sci. dir. Robarts Rsch. Inst., London, Ont., Can., 1993—; prof. dept. biochemistry U. Western Ont. Faculty Medicine, London, 1993—; in charge rsch. dept. physiology Coll. de France, Paris, 1973-74; rsch. on superoxide dismutase, oxygen free radicals and control of post-reperfusion injury, relating biotech. univ. rsch. to pvt. sector. Home: 80 Sherwood Ave, London, ON Canada N6A 2E2 Office: John P Robarts Rsch Inst, 100 Perth Dr PO Box 5015, London, ON Canada N6A 5K8

POZZATTI, RUDY OTTO, artist; b. Telluride, Colo., Jan. 14, 1925; s. Innocente and Mary L. (Mimiolla) P.; m. Dorothy I. Pozzatti, May 20, 1946; children—Valri Marie, Rudy Otto, Gina Maria, Mia Ines, Illica Lara. B.F.A., U. Colo., 1948, M.F.A., 1950, D.H.L., 1973. Mem. faculty dept. art U. Nebr., Lincoln, 1950-52, 53-56; mem. faculty dept. art Ind. U., Bloomington, 1956-91, prof. fine arts, 1964-91, disting. prof., 1975-91; ret., 1991; dir. Echo Press, Bloomington, 1979—; artist-in-residence Roswell Mus. and Art Ctr.; bd. dirs. Echo Press, Bloomington, Ind. One-man exhbns. include Cleve. Mus. Art, 1955, Whitney Mus. Am. Arts, N.Y.C., 1961, Tyler Sch. Art, Rome, 1969, Sheldon Meml. Art Gallery U. Nebr., 1969, Mitchell Mus. Art, Mt. Vernon, Ill., 4 other sites, 1992-93; represented in permanent collections, Mus. Modern Art, N.Y.C., Libr. Congress, Washington, Art Inst. Chgo., Cleve. Mus. Art. Served with AUS, 1943-46. Recipient George Norlin silver medal U. Colo., 1974; Fulbright grantee, 1952-53, 63-64, grantee U.S. Dept. State, USSR, 1961, Yugoslavia, 1965, Brazil, 1974, Hungary, 1986; Guggenheim fellow, 1963-64; Fellow Ford Found., 1963, grantee, Japan, 1981. Mem. Soc. Am. Graphic Artists, Am. Color Print Soc., Coll. Art Assn. (bd. dirs.), Artists Equity Assn. Roman Catholic. Office: Echo Press 1901 E 10th St Bloomington IN 47408-3972

P'POOL, GERALD W., manufacturing executive; b. Princeton, Ky., Mar. 1, 1933; s. Herbert Claude and Laura Lucille (Adams) P'P.; m. Peggy Simons (div. Sept. 1960); m. Jo Mercer; children: Deborah, Elisha, Jill. Student, Murray (Ky.) State U., 1951-52. Sales rep. Thomas Industries, Inc., Ky., Tenn., N.C. and Fla., 1956-62; mgr. div. Thomas Industries, Inc., Atlanta, 1964-71; mgr. merchandising Thomas Industries, Inc., Louisville, 1971-72, mgr. nat. sales, 1972-78; pres. Paint Applicators div. Thomas Industries, Inc., Johnson City, Tenn., 1978-81; v.p., group mgr., paint applicator, tool and fastener Benjamin Comml. & Indsl. Lighting Mfg., Johnson City, Tenn., 1981-83; sr. v.p. mktg. Thomas Industries, Inc., Louisville, 1983-84, exec. v.p., 1984-87, exec. v.p., mgr. light group, 1987-88. With USN, 1953-54. Avocations: hunting, fishing. Home: 317 S Jefferson St Princeton KY 42445-2111 Office: Thomas Industries Inc PO Box 35120 Louisville KY 40232-5120

PRABHAKAR, ARATI, federal administration research director, electrical engineer; b. New Delhi, Feb. 2, 1959; came to U.S., 1962; d. Jagdish Chandra and Raj (Madan) P. BSEE, Tex. Tech U., 1979; MSEE, Calif. Inst. Tech., 1980, PhD in Applied Physics, 1984; DEng (hon.), Rensselaer Poly. Inst., 1995. Congl. fellow Office Tech. Assessment U.S. Congress, Washington, 1984-86; program mgr. electronic sci. divsn. DARPA, Arlington, Va., 1986-90, dir. defense sci. office, 1990-91, dir. microelectronics tech. office, 1991-93; dir. Nat. Inst. Standards & Tech., Gaithersburg, Md., 1993—. Contbr. articles to profl. jours. Rsch. fellow Calif. Inst. Tech., 1979-84, grad. rsch. program for women Bell Labs., 1979, 80; named Disting. Engr. of 1994, Tex. Tech. U.; elected to Tex. Tech. Elec. Engring. Acad., 1994; recipient Disting. Alumni award Calif. Inst. Tech., 1995. Mem. IEEE, Eta Kappa Nu, Tau Beta Pi. Office: Nat Inst Stds & Tech US Dept of Commerce Rte 270 Bldg 101 Rm A1134 Gaithersburg MD 20899

PRABHUDESAI, MUKUND M., pathology educator, laboratory director, researcher, administrator; b. Lolyem, Goa, India, Mar. 17, 1942; came to U.S., 1967; s. Madhav R. and Kusum M. Prabhudesai; m. Sarita Mukund Usha, Feb. 1, 1972; 1 child, Nitin M. MB, BS (MD), G.S. Med., Bombay, 1967, postgrad., 1973-75. Diplomate Am. Bd. Pathology. Asst. pathologist Fordham Hosp., Bronx, N.Y., 1973-74, assoc. pathologist, 1974-76; assoc. dir. clin. pathology Lincoln Med., Bronx, 1976, dep. dir. pathology, 1977-79; chief pathology and lab. medicine svc., coord. R&D VA Med. Ctr., Danville, Ill., 1979—, dir. electron microscopy lab., 1987—; senator U. Ill. Chgo.; co-investigator U. Ill. Coll. Medicine, Urbana/Champaign, clin. assoc. prof. pathology and medicine Rsch., Rehab., Nutrition, Alcohol, 1982—. Contbr. articles to Am. Jour. Clin. Nutrition, Jour. AMA, Am. Jour. Clin. Pathology. Member Gifted Student Adv. Bd., Danville, 1984-86; v.p. Am. Cancer Soc. Vermilion County chpt., 1982, pres., 1986-88. VA rsch. grantee, 1980-82, 82-85, 83. Fellow Coll. Am. Pathology (inspector 1981—, Ill. state del. to C.A.P. Ho. Dels. 1992—, mem. reference com. 1993); mem. AAAS, Am. Coll. Physician Execs., Ill. State Soc. Pathologists (bd. dirs. 1990—, chmn. membership com. 1990—). Achievements include development of cancer of bladder following portocarval shunting; research in adverse effects of alcohol on lung structure and metabolism; on effects of soy and bran on cholesterol, endocrine response to soy protein, in induction and reversibility of atherosclerosis in trout, effects of ethanol on Vitamin A, lymphatics in atherosclerosis, iron in atherosclerosis, development of dermofluorometer for detection of P.V.D. Office: VA Med Ctr Pathology and Lab Med Svcs 1900 E Main St Danville IL 61832-5100

PRADA, GLORIA INES, mathematics and Spanish language educator; b. San Vicente de Chucuri, Colombia, Dec. 2, 1954; came to U.S., 1985; d. Roberto Gomez and Maria Celina (Serrano) Duran; m. Luis Eduardo Prada, June 19, 1975; children: Luis Ricardo, Nicholas. BS in Math., U. Indsl., Santander, Colombia, 1978. Tchr. h.s. math. Santander Sch. Dist., Bucaramanga, 1973-84; tchr. mid. sch. math., mentor tchr. Hayward (Calif.) Unified Sch. Dist., 1989—; pres. Bilingual Adv. Com., Hayward, 1986-89; mem. Gate Task Force, Hayward, 1990-93, Spanish for Educators Alameda County Office Edn., 1995—. Author: Prada's Spanish Course, 1992, Family Math, 1992, Stations on Probabilities, 1994, (math. replacement unit) Success, 1994. Office: Hayward Unified Sch Dist Winton Intermediate Sch 119 Winton Ave Hayward CA 94544-1413

PRADO, EDWARD CHARLES, federal judge; b. San Antonio, June 7, 1947; s. Edward L. and Bertha (Cadena) P.; m. Maria Anita Jung, Nov. 10, 1973; 1 child, Edward C. AA, San Antonio Coll., 1967; BA, U. Tex., 1969, JD, 1972. Bar: Tex. 1972. Asst. dist. atty. Bexar County Dist. Atty.'s Office, San Antonio, 1972-76; asst. pub. defender U.S. Pub. Defender's Office, San Antonio, 1976-80; judge U.S. Dist. Ct. Tex., San Antonio, 1980; U.S. atty. Dept. Justice, San Antonio, 1980-85; judge U.S. Dist. Ct. (we. dist.) Tex., 1984—. Served to capt. U.S. Army. Named Outstanding Young Lawyer of Bexar County, 1980. Mem. ABA, Tex. Bar Assn., San Antonio Bar Assn., San Antonio Young Lawyers Assn., Fed. Bar Assn. Republican. Roman Catholic. Office: US Courthouse 655 E Durango Blvd San Antonio TX 78206-1102*

PRADO, GERALD M., investment banker; b. Langeloth, Pa., Jan. 19, 1946; s. Caesar S. and Anita A. P.; m. Judith A. Pompe, May 20, 1967; children—Dennis, Eric, Lynn, Christopher. B.A., Washington and Jefferson Coll., 1963-67; M.B.A., U. Pitts., 1983. Sr. acct. Haskins and Sells, Pitts., 1967-72; auditor G.C. Murphy Co., McKeesport, Pa., 1972-76, asst. controller, 1976-78, treas., 1979-80, asst. v.p., treas., 1980-82, v.p., treas., 1982-85; v.p., treas. Russell, Rea & Zappala, Pitts., 1986-87, sr. v.p., 1987-90; pres. Westinghouse Mcht. Banking, Inc., Pitts., 1990-94; prin., co-mgr. Main St. Capital Holdings L.L.C., Pitts., 1994—. Mem. Pa. Inst. CPAs, AICPA, Washington and Jefferson Alumni Assn., Fin. Execs. Inst. Roman Catholic. Home: 205 Overlook Dr McMurray PA 15317-2657 Office: Main St Capital Holdings LLC 600 Grant St Fl 42 Pittsburgh PA 15219

PRADOS, JOHN WILLIAM, educational administrator; b. Spring Hill, Tenn., Oct. 12, 1929; s. Gustave Olivier and Elizabeth (Branham) P.; m. Ruth Lynn Baird, Sept. 2, 1951; children: Elizabeth Prados Bowman, Laura Lynn, Anne Prados Lynch. B.S. in Chem. Engring, U. Miss., 1951; M.S., U. Tenn., 1954, Ph.D., 1957. Registered profl. engr., Tenn. Asst. prof. U. Tenn., Knoxville, 1956-59, asso. prof., 1959-64, prof. chem. engring., 1964—, Univ. prof., 1989—, asso. dean engring., 1969-71, dean admissions and records, 1971-73, acting chancellor Knoxville campus, 1973, acting chancellor Martin campus, 1979; v.p. acad. affairs statewide U. Tenn. System, 1973-81, v.p. acad. affairs and rsch., 1981-88, v.p. emeritus, 1989—, head chem. engring. dept., 1990-93; cons. nuclear divsn. Union Carbide Corp., Oak Ridge, 1957-84, Martin Marietta Energy Sys., Inc., 1984-86; sr. edn. assoc. NSF, Arlington, Va., 1994—. Served with USAF, 1951-53. Recipient Outstanding Tchr. award U. Tenn., 1967, 92. Fellow Am. Inst. Chem. Engrs. (mem. coun. 1975-77, Knoxville-Oak Ridge Chem. Engr. of Yr. 1977, treas. 1996—), Am. Inst. Chemists; mem. Am. Chem. Soc., Am. Soc. Engring. Edn., Engring. Accreditation Commn. Accreditation Bd. Engring. and Tech., Inc (vice chmn. 1981-84, chmn. 1984-85, bd. dirs. 1988—, sec. 1989-90, pres. 1991-92, L.E. Grinter award 1993), So. Assn. Colls. and Schs. (commn. on colls. 1986-92, exec. coun. 1986-89, bd. trustees 1995—), Sigma Xi (dir. at large, chmn. com. 1976—, pres. 1983-84, treas. 1990—), Torch Club, Tau Beta Pi (exec. coun. 1986-90), Alpha Tau Omega. Roman Catholic. Home: 7021 Stagecoach Trl Knoxville TN 37909-1112 Office: U Tenn Dept Chem Engring Knoxville TN 37996-2200

PRADY, NORMAN, journalist, advertising executive, writer, marketing consultant; b. Detroit, Sept. 19, 1933; s. Calvin and Mildred Prady; m. Susan Frank, July 5, 1959 (div. Nov. 1991); children: William Scott, Anne Elizabeth Prady Sheehan. Student, Wayne State U., 1951-53, Fordham U., 1952. Reporter, feature writer Detroit Times, 1955-60; writer various advt. agys. Detroit, 1960-65, creative dir. various advt. agys., 1965-80; exec. v.p., creative dir., prin. Stone, August & Co., Birmingham, Mich., 1980-84; pres. The Norman Prady Co., Farmington Hills, 1985—; editor, pub. The Riverside Journal, Farmington Hills, 1995—. Contbr. features various newspapers. Bd. dirs. ARC, Detroit, 1983—, exec. com., 1987—, vice-chmn. pub. affairs com., 1986—, fin. devel. com., 1987—.

PRAETORIUS, WILLIAM ALBERT, SR., artist, former advertising and real estate executive; b. Forty-Fort, Pa., Oct. 7, 1924; s. George Albert and Elizabeth (Madden) P.; m. Theresa M. Barnes, June 25, 1949; children: Kathleen Ann, William Albert, Gregg Douglas. Student, Biaritz (France) Am. U., 1945-46, N.Y. U., 1947-48. With L.W. Frohlich Intercon Internat., Inc., 1946-72, sr. v.p., dir. ops., 1969-71, chmn. operating com., 1972; sr. v.p., dir. ops. Deltakos div. J. Walter Thompson Co., N.Y.C., 1972-73; sr. v.p. adminstrn. J.W.T. Affiliated Cos., 1973-75; pres. Healthmark Communications, Inc., N.Y.C., 1975-77; dir. Clause Comml. div. Donald J. Clause, Southampton, N.Y., 1977-78; dir. comml. div. Meadow Real Estate, 1978-86; artist, 1987—. Author, pub.: Concepts in Leadership, 1982; contbr. column to East End Bus. Rev, articles to profl. jours; exhbns. of paintings include East Hampton Town Hall, Edwin Winfield Gallery, Sag Harbor. Served with AUS, 1943-46. Mem. Barns Landing Assn. Democrat. Catholic. Home and Studio: 30 Captains Walk East Hampton NY 11937-3169

PRAGER, ALICE HEINECKE, music company executive; b. N.Y.C., Aug. 2, 1930; d. Paul and Ruth (Collin) Heinecke; m. George L. Drescher, 1963. BA, Russell Sage Coll., 1951; postgrad., NYU, 1952-55. V.p. SESAC Inc., N.Y.C., 1956-73, pres., 1973-78, pres., chmn. bd., 1978-92; chmn. bd. Personal Touch Music, Personal Touch, Inc. Mem. Internat. Radio and TV Soc., Am. Women in Radio and TV, Am. Inst. of Mgmt., Advt. Women of N.Y., Nat. Acad. Recording Arts and Scis., Broadcast Pioneers, Country Music Assn. (bd. dirs., 1986), Gospel Music Assn., Vets. Bedside Network (bd. dirs.). Office: The Personal Touch Inc 68-34 Fleet St Forest Hills NY 11375-5051

PRAGER, DAVID, retired state supreme court chief justice; b. Ft. Scott, Kans., Oct. 30, 1918; s. Walter and Helen (Kishler) P.; m. Dorothy Schroeter, Sept. 8, 1945; children: Diane, David III. AB, U. Kans., 1939, JD, 1942. Bar: Kans. 1942. Practiced in Topeka, 1946-59; dist. judge Shawnee County (Kans.) Dist. Ct., 1959-71; assoc. justice Kans. Supreme Ct., Topeka, 1971-87, chief justice, 1987-88; ret., 1988; lectr. Washburn Law Sch., 1948-68. Served to lt. USNR, 1942-46, ETO, PTO. Mem. Kans. Dist. Judges Assn. (past pres.), Order of Coif, Phi Beta Kappa, Phi Delta Theta, Lions Lodge, Arab Shrine Lodge.

PRAGER, ELLIOT DAVID, surgeon, educator; b. N.Y.C., Sept. 10, 1941; s. Benjamin and Sadye Zelda (Newman) P.; m. Phyllis Damon Warner, July 1, 1967; children: Rebecca, Sarah, Katherine. AB, Dartmouth Coll., 1962; MD, Harvard U., 1966. Diplomate Am. Bd. Surgery, Am. Bd. Colon and Rectal Surgery. Surg. resident Roosevelt Hosp., N.Y.C., 1966-71; colonrectal fellow Lahey Clinic, Boston, 1971-72; staff surgeon Sansum Clinic, Santa Barbara, Calif., 1974—; dir. colorectal fellowship Sansum Clinic, Santa Barbara, 1982—, chief of surgery, 1986-94; dir. surg. edn. Cottage Hosp., Santa Barbara, 1994—; mem., vice chair Residency Rev. Com., 1992—. Author: (with others) Operative Colorectal Surgery, 1994, Current Therapy in Colon and Rectal Surgery, 1990; contbr. articles to profl. jours. Lt. comdr. USN, 1972-74. Fellow Am. Coll. Surgeons (adv. coun. 1992—), Am. Soc. of Colon and Rectal Surgeons (v.p. 1992, sec. of program dirs., 1990—). Achievements include 5 patents for colostomy control devices. Office: Sansum Clinic 317 W Pueblo Santa Barbara CA 93102

PRAGER, STEPHEN, chemistry educator; b. Darmstadt, Germany, July 20, 1928; came to U.S., 1941, naturalized, 1950; s. William and Gertrude Ann (Heyer) P.; m. Julianne Heller, June 7, 1948. B.Sc., Brown, 1947; Ph.D., Cornell, 1951. Mem. faculty U. Minn., Mpls., 1952—, assoc. prof. chemistry, 1956-62, prof., 1962-90, prof. emeritus, 1990—; Cons. Union Carbide Corp., Oak Ridge, 1954-74. Asso. editor: Jour. Phys. Chemistry, 1970-79. Fulbright scholar and Guggenheim fellow, 1958, 59; Fulbright lectr. and Guggenheim fellow, 1966-67. Mem. Am. Chem. Soc., Am. Phys. Soc. Home: 3320 Dunlap St N Saint Paul MN 55112-3709 Office: Chemistry Dept U Minn Minneapolis MN 55455

PRAGER, SUSAN WESTERBERG, dean, law educator; b. Sacramento, Dec. 14, 1942; d. Percy Foster Westerberg and Aileen M. (McKinley) P.; m. James Martin Prager, Dec. 14, 1973; children: McKinley Ann, Case Mahone. AB, Stanford U., 1964, MA, 1967; JD, UCLA, 1971. Bar: N.C. 1971, Calif. 1972. Atty. Powe, Porter & Alphin, Durham, N.C., 1971-72; acting prof. law UCLA, 1972-77, prof. Sch. Law, 1977—, Arjay and Frances Fearing Miller prof. of law, 1992—, assoc. dean Sch. Law, 1979-82, dean, 1982—; bd. dirs. Pacific Mut. Life Ins. Co., Newport Beach, Calif. Editor-in-chief, UCLA Law Rev., 1970-71. Trustee Stanford U., 1976-80, 87—. Mem. ABA (council of sect. on legal edn. and admissions to the bar 1983-85), Assn. Am. Law Schs. (pres. 1986), Order of Coif. Office: UCLA Sch Law Box 951476 Los Angeles CA 90095-1476

PRAIRIE, CELIA ESTHER FREDA, biochemistry educator; b. Buenos Aires, Sept. 30, 1940; came to U.S., 1963; d. Rafael Emilio A. and Celia Esther (Seijo) Freda; m. James Roland Prairie, Sept. 19, 1970; children: James Roger, Caryn Elizabeth. BS, U. Buenos Aires, 1961, MS, 1963; PhD, U. Pa., 1967. Fellow Nat. Rsch. Inst., Buenos Aires, 1961-63; rsch. assoc. dept. therapeutic rsch. U. Pa., Phila., 1967-70; postdoctoral rsch. assoc. Lab. Molecular Embryology, Arco Felice, Naples, Italy, 1970; lectr. biology and chemistry depts. Holy Family Coll., Phila., 1974-75, asst. prof. biology dept., 1975-80, assoc. prof., 1980-85, prof. biochemistry, 1985—, chmn. dept. natural scis. and math., 1986-88, acting chmn. biology dept., 1982-86; sr. teaching staff assoc. Marine Biol. Lab., Woods Hole, Mass., 1968-69. Contbr. articles to profl. jours. Bd. dirs. Lower Bucks County Community Ctr., 1970—. Fellow USPHS, 1963-65, U. Pa., 1965-66, Am. Coun. Edn. and Fund for the Improvement of Post Sec. Edn., 1983-84. Mem. AAAS, Nat. Sci. Tchrs. Assn., Am. Inst. Biol. Scis., N.Y. Acad. Scis., Sigma Xi, World Federalist Assn. Democrat. Mem. Religious Soc. of Friends. Avocations: aerobics, yoga, swimming. Home: 31 Fullturn Rd Levittown PA 19056-1924 Office: Holy Family Coll Frankford and Grant Ave Philadelphia PA 19114-2094

PRAISNER, JAN A., electronics executive; b. 1951. MBA, So. Meth. U. CPA. With Price Waterhouse, Digital Equipment Corp.; v.p., contr. Monolithic Memories, Inc.; worldwide mfg. contr. Advanced Micro Devices, Sunnyvale, Calif., 1987-88; v.p. mktg. Aspect Telecomm. Corp., San Jose, Calif., 1988—. *

PRAKAPAS, EUGENE JOSEPH, art gallery director; b. Lowell, Mass., July 29, 1932; s. Joseph S. Prakapas and Viola Schensnol; m. Dorothy A. Seitner, Dec. 1, 1971. BA, Yale U., 1953; MA, Oxford U., Balliol, 1959. Vice-pres., editor-in-chief Trident Press and Pocket Books div. Simon & Schuster, Inc., N.Y.C., 1960-70; co-dir. Carus Gallery, N.Y.C., 1973-75; dir. Prakapas Gallery, N.Y.C., 1976—; vis. curator San Francisco Mus. Modern Art, 1986. Author: Bauhaus Photography, 1985. Lt. (s.g.) USNR, 1953-57. Fulbright fellow, 1957-59; Yale U. scholar, 1949-53. Mem. Art Dealers Assn. Am., Assn. Internat. Photography Art Dealers.

PRAKASH, SATYA, biology educator; b. Pilkhuwa, U.P., India, July 8, 1938; came to U.S., 1962; s. Suraj Bali and Atar Kali; m. Louise Burlant; children: Ulka, Ravi, Anita, Sarita. PhD, Washington U., St. Louis, 1966. Asst. prof. biology U. Rochester, N.Y., 1969-74, assoc. prof., 1974-80, prof., 1980-93; prof. U. Tex. Med. Branch, Galveston, 1993—. NIH grantee, 1972—. Mem. Genetics Soc. Am., Am. Soc. Biochemistry and Molecular Biology. Hindu. Office: U Tex Med Branch Sealy Ctr Molecular Sci Galveston TX 77555

PRAMER, DAVID, microbiologist, educator, research administrator; b. Mt. Vernon, N.Y., Mar. 25, 1923; s. Coleman and Ethel (Toback) P.; m. Rhoda Lifschutz, Sept. 6, 1950; children—Andrew, Stacey. Student, St. John's U., 1940, Tex. A&M Coll., 1941; B.S. cum laude, Rutgers U., 1948, Ph.D., 1952. Vis. investigator Butterwick Research Labs., Welwyn, Eng., 1952-54; from asst. to assoc. prof. microbiology Rutgers U., New Brunswick, N.J., 1954-60; prof. Rutgers U., 1960-67, disting. prof., 1967—, dir. biological scis., 1969-73, dir. univ. research, 1973-75, assoc. v.p. research, 1973-80; dir. Waksman Inst. Microbiology, 1980-88, assoc. v.p. corp. liaison, 1988-93; exec. asst. and disting. prof. emeritus, exec. asst. Rutgers U., New Brunswick, N.J., 1993—; cons. various fed. agys., 1965—; dir. New Brunswick Sci. Co., Edison, R&D Coun. of N.J., Nanodyne, Inc., New Brunswick, Organica, Inc., Great Neck, N.Y.; served on numerous chmn., com. and adv. posts. Author: Life in the Soil, 1964, Experimental Soil Microbiology, 1965, The Microbes, 1971, Engineered Organisms in the Environment, 1985; also over 250 articles in profl. jours.; regional editor World Jour. Soil and Biology and Biochemistry; mem. editl. bd. Soil Sci., BioSci., Applied Microbiology and Biotech. Bd. dirs. Library, Highland Park, N.J., 1966-75, chmn., 1976-78; committeeman Democratic Party, Highland Park, 1958-66. Served to cpl. USAF, 1943-46. Fulbright-Hays Sr. Research fellow, 1969. Fellow Am. Acad. Microbiology; mem. Am. Soc. Microbiology, Internat. Commn. Microbial Ecology (chmn.), Internat. Cell Rsch. Orgn., Phi Beta Kappa, Alpha Zeta, Sigma Xi. Jewish. Avocations: jogging, travel. Home: 208 Hampshire Ct Piscataway NJ 08854-6218 Office: Rutgers Univ Office Rsch & Sponsored Programs Adminstrv Svc Bldg Annex II Piscataway NJ 08855-1179

PRANCKUN, JOHN, manufacturing executive; b. 1947. Grad., Marquette U., 1969. V.p. fin. and adminstrn. Kimble Glass Inc., Vineland, N.J., 1972—; now pres. Kimble Glass Inc., Vineland, NJ. With U.S. Army, 1969-72. Office: Kimble Glass Inc 1022 Spruce Vineland NJ 08360*

PRANGE, ARTHUR JERGEN, JR., psychiatrist, neurobiologist, educator; b. Grand Rapids, Mich., Sept. 19, 1926; s. Arthur Jergen and Martha Frances (Elliott) P.; m. Sarah Elizabeth Bowen, Feb. 4, 1950; children—Christine Anne, Martha Louise, Laura Beth, David Elliott. B.S., U. Mich., 1947, M.D., 1950. Intern Wayne County Gen. Hosp., Eloise, Mich., 1950-51; resident in psychiatry U. N.C., Chapel Hill, 1954-57; instr. U. N.C., 1957-60, asst. prof., 1960-64, asso. prof., 1964-68, prof. psychiatry, 1968-83, Boshamer prof. psychiatry, 1983—, acting chmn. dept. psychiatry, 1983-85, dir. NIMH Clin. Rsch. Ctr., 1979—; vis. scientist Med. Rsch. Coun. Unit, Epson, Surrey, Eng., 1968-69; chmn. clin. projects rsch. rev. com. HEW, NIMH, 1975-76, chmn. bd. sci. counselors, 1986-87; mem. psychopharmacologic drugs adv. com. HEW, FDA, 1979-82. Editor: The Thyroid Axis, Drugs and Behavior, 74; Contbr. articles to med. jours. Recipient NIMH Career Devel. award 1961-69, Career Scientist award, 1969-95, Gold Medal award Soc. of Biol. Psychiatry, 1992. Fellow Am. Psychiat. Assn. (life, Rsch. in Psychiatry award 1996), Am. Coll. Neuropsychopharmacology (life, pres. 1987, Hoch award 1995); mem. Internat. Soc. Psychoneuroendocrinology (founding mem.), N.C. Neuropsychiat. Assn., Collegium Internationale Neuropsychopharmacologicum, Royal Coll. Psychiatrists (London). Home: 218-6 Conner Dr Chapel Hill NC 27514-7070 Office: Univ NC Sch Medicine Dept Psychiatry Chapel Hill NC 27599-7160

PRANGE, HILMAR WALTER, neurology educator; b. Reichenbach/Eule, Silesia, Germany, Aug. 4, 1944; s. Georg Friedrich Reinhold and Gertrud Wilhelmine (Mueller) P.; m. Carin Juliane Schroeter, Mar. 14, 1970; children: Klaus Richard, Juliane. MD, U. Rostock, Germany, 1969, lic. specialist neurology and psychiatry, 1974; Habilitation, Georg-August U., Goettingen, Germany, 1982. Medical diplomate. Med. resident Regional Hosp., Stralsund, Germany, 1969-71; med. asst. then psychiatrist Univ. Hosp., Rostock, 1971-75; asst. med. dir. Ev. Johannes Hosp., Bielefeld, Germany, 1975-76; head neurologic out-patient clinic Univ. Hosp., Goettingen, Germany, 1976-78, asst. med. dir. dept. neurology, 1979-87, dir. neurological intensive care unit, 1987—. Author: Neurosyphilis, 1987, Infectious Diseases of the Central Nervous System, 1995; editor: CNS Barriers and Modern CSF Diagnostics, 1993; contbr. articles to profl. jours. Grantee Deutsche Forschungsgemeinschaft, German MS Soc. Mem. European Neurological Soc., German Med. Assn. (mem. commn. drug security), European Fedn. Neurological Socs. (sec. scientist panel of infectiology). Lutheran. Avocations: cultural history, sports, jogging, swimming, squash.

PRANGE, ROY LEONARD, JR., lawyer; b. Chgo., Sept. 12, 1945; s. Roy Leonard and Marjorie Rose (Kauppi) P.; m. Carol Lynn Poels, June 5, 1971; children: David, Ellen, Susan. BA, U. Iowa, 1967; MA, Ohio State U., 1968; JD, U. Wis.-Madison, 1975. Bar: Wis. 1975, U.S. Dist. Ct. (we. and ea. dists.) Wis. 1975, U.S. Ct. Appeals (7th cir.) 1978, U.S. Supreme Ct. 1978. Assoc. Ross & Stevens, Svc. Corp., Madison, Wis., 1975-79; ptnr. Ross & Stevens, Svc. Corp., 1979-90, Quarles & Brady, Madison, 1990—; lectr. bankruptcy, debtor-creditor rights, U. Wis., Madison, 1982—. Contbr. Wis. Lawyer's Desk Reference Manual, 1987, Comml. Litigation in Wis. Practice Handbook, 1995. 1st lt. U.S. Army, 1969-72. Fellow Am. Coll. Bankruptcy; mem. ABA, Wis. State Bar (dir. bankruptcy, insolvency, creditors rights sect. 1985-91, chair 1990-92, mem. continuing legal edn. com. 1990—), Am. Bankruptcy Inst., Dickens Fellowship (v.p. 1980-84). Avocations: running, soccer, karate, golf. Office: Quarles & Brady PO Box 2113 1 S Pinckney St Madison WI 53703

PRANSES, ANTHONY LOUIS, retired electric company executive, organization executive; b. Claracq, France, May 3, 1920; s. Anthony Kasimer and Georgette (Pilon) F.; m. Margaret Louise Hamill, July 24, 1943; children—Anthony Randolph, Terry Jay, Renee Louise. Student, Sorbonne, Paris, France, 1937-39; B.S. in Metall. Engring, Carnegie Inst. Tech., 1942, grad. student, 1946-48. With Westinghouse Electric Corp., 1945-86; mgr. mfg. planning Westinghouse Electric Corp., Lima, Ohio, 1954-57; plant mgr. Westinghouse Electric Corp., Lima, 1958-59, mgr. mfg. services, 1959-72; mgr. mfg. Westinghouse Electric Corp., 1972-80, cons., 1980-86. Joined Am. Youth Hostels, 1935, founder Pitts. council, 1947, pres. council, 1947-50, mem. nat. bd. dirs., 1954-72, Midwest regional v.p., 1957-59, nat. pres., 1959-62, pres. Lima council, 1962-75, 87-91, chmn. nat. bd. dirs., 1963-67. Served to capt., C.E. AUS, 1942-45. Home: Rural Route 2 6005 Poling Rd Lima OH 45807-9452

PRAS, ROBERT THOMAS, hotel executive; b. Newark, Dec. 14, 1941; s. Leon Lewis and Helen (McCully) P.; m. Constance Wilson, Nov. 30, 1968; children: Andrew, Douglas, Allison. BS, Delaware Valley Coll., 1965. Sanitarian Phila. Dept. Pub. Health, 1965-66; dir. quality assurance Acme Markets, Phila., 1966-68; merchandiser Alpha Beta Acme Markets, LaHabra, Calif., 1968-72; dir. Wakefern Food Corp., Elizabeth, N.J., 1972-79; exec. v.p. Marriott Internat., Washington, 1979—. Mayor Hillsborough (N.J.) Twp., 1979, mem. twp. coun., 1976-77; trustee Delaware Valley Coll., 1995. Mem. Am. Mgmt. Assn., Nat. Restaurant Assn., Mid-Atlantic Consortium of Colls. and Univs. (mem. steering com.). Office: Marriott Internat 10400 Fernwood Rd Bethesda MD 20817-1109

PRASAD, ANANDA SHIVA, medical educator; b. Buxar, Bihar, India, Jan. 1, 1928; came to U.S., 1952, naturalized, 1968; s. Radha Krishna and Mahesha (Kaur) Lall; m. Aryabala Ray, Jan. 6, 1952; children: Rita, Sheila, Ashok, Audrey. BSc, Patna (India) Sci. Coll., 1946, MB, BChir, 1951; PhD, U. Minn., 1957. Intern Patna Med. Coll. Hosp., 1951-52; resident St. Paul's Hosp., Dallas, 1952-53, U. Minn., 1953-56, VA Hosp., Mpls., 1956; instr. dept. medicine Univ. Hosp., U. Minn., Mpls., 1957-58; vis. assoc. prof. medicine Shiraz Med. Faculty, Nemazee Hosp., Shiraz, Iran, 1960; asst. prof. medicine and nutrition Vanderbilt U., 1961-63; mem. faculty, dir. div. hematology dept. medicine Wayne State U., Detroit, 1963-84; assoc. prof. Wayne State U., 1964-68, prof., 1968—, dir. research dept. medicine, 1984—; mem. staff Harper-Grace Hosp., VA Hosp., Allen Park, Mich.; mem. trace elements subcom. Food and Nutrition Bd., NRC-Nat. Acad. Scis., 1965-68; chmn. trace elements com. Internat. Union Nutritional Scis.; mem. Am. Bd. Nutrition; pres. Am. Coll. Nutrition, 1991-93. Author: Zinc Metabolism, 1966, Trace Elements in Human Health and Disease, 1976, Trace Elements and Iron in Human Metabolism, 1978, Zinc in Human Nutrition, 1979, Biochemistry of Zinc, 1993; editor: Clinical, Biochemical and Nutritional Aspects of Trace Elements, 1982, Am. Jour. Hematology, Jour. Trace Elements in Exptl. Medicine; editor: Zinc Metabolism, Current Aspects in Health and Disease, 1977; co-editor: Clinical Applications of Recent Advances in Zinc Metabolism, 1982, Zinc Deficiency in Human Subjects, 1983, Essential and Toxic Trace Elements in Human Health and Disease, 1988, Essential and Toxic Trace Elements in Human Health and Disease: An Update, 1993; mem. editorial bd. Jour. Micro Nutrient Analysis, Jour. Am. Coll. Nutrition; contbr. articles to profl. jours., also reviewer. Trustee Detroit Internat. Inst., Detroit Gen. Hosp. Research Corp., 1969-72. Recipient Rsch. Recognition award Wayne State U., 1964, award Am. Coll. Nutrition, 1976, Disting. Faculty Fellowship award Wayne State U., 1986, Acad. Scholars, Wayne State U., 1992, Medal of Honor, City of Lyon, France, 1989; Pfizer scholar, 1955-56. Master Am. Coll. Nutrition; fellow ACP (recipient Mich. Laureate award), AAAS, Am. Inst. Nutrition, Internat. Soc. Hematology; mem. AMA (Goldberger award 1975), Internat. Soc. Trace Element Rsch. in Humans (pres. 1986-92, chmn. steering com. 1985-86, Raulin award 1989), Am. Soc. Clin. Nutrition (awards com. 1969-70), Am. Fedn. Clin. Rsch. (pres. Mich. 1969-70), Am. Inst. Nutrition (trace elements panel), Am. Physiol. Soc., Am. Soc. Clin. Investigation, Am. Soc. Hematology, Assn. Am. Physicians, Ctrl. Soc. Clin. Rsch., Soc. Exptl. Biology and Medicine (Councillor Mich. 1967-71), Wayne County Med. Soc., Internat. Soc. Internal Medicine, Am. Soc. Clin. Nutrition (Robert H. Herman award 1984), Nutrition Soc. India (Gopalan oration award 1988), Cosmos Club (Washington), Sigma Xi. Home: 4710 Cove Rd Orchard Lake MI 48323-3604 Office: Univ Health Ctr 5-C 4201 Saint Antoine St Detroit MI 48201-2153

PRASHER, GREGORY GEORGE, lawyer; b. Akron, Ohio, Oct. 4, 1948; s. George and Pauline Grace (Markham) P.; m. Patricia Jolyn Siepel, Aug. 22, 1970 (div. Aug. 1993); children: Angela Katheryn, Michael Gregory. BA, Ohio State U., 1969; JD, Duke U., 1972. Bar: U.S. Dist. Ct. (we. and ea. dists.) Mich. 1972, U.S. Ct. Appeals (6th cir.) 1974, U.S. Supreme Ct. 1980. Assoc. Warner, Norcross & Judd, Grand Rapids, Mich., 1972-76; shareholder Clary, Nantz & Wood, Grand Rapids, 1976-84; shareholder, officer Schenk, Boncher & Prasher, Grand Rapids, 1984—; legal counsel Wetlands Found. of West Mich., Grand Rapids, 1985—. Bd. dirs., officer Grand Rapids Summerfest, 1987-94; bd. dirs. Grand Rapids Ballet, 1990-93; precinct del. Rep. Party, Kent County, Mich., 1985-86, Mich. State del., 1986. Mem. Elks. Roman Catholic. Avocations: golf, carpentry, cycling. Office: Schenk Boncher & Prasher 333 Bridge NW # 1220 Grand Rapids MI 49504

PRASIL, LINDA ANN, lawyer, writer; b. Chgo., July 27, 1947; d. Joseph J. and Helen Marie (Palucki) P.; m. John T. Rank, July 25, 1970; 1 child, Sean Patrick Prasil Rank. BA in Interdisciplinary Studies, Am. U., Washington, 1974, JD, 1977; MALS, Mundelein Coll., Chgo., 1992. Bar: Ill. 1977. Ind. contractor Baker & McKenzie, Chgo., 1977-78; atty. Pretzel, Stouffer, Nolan & Rooney, Chgo., 1978-79; sole practitioner Lincolnshire, Ill., 1979—; atty. Leonard M. Ring, Chgo., 1982; grader Ill. State Bar Examiners, Chgo., 1978-90; organizer Kennedy for Pres., Chgo., 1979-80, NOW-ERA Ill., Chgo., 1980, Ill. Polit. Action Com., Chgo., 1981. Legal advisor Holy Cross Talk of Town, Deerfield, Ill., 1992-96; tchr. Holy Cross Drug Awareness Program, Deerfield, 1993-94; religious tchr. Holy Cross, Deerfield, 1983-86. Mem. Ill. State Bar Assn., Internat. Alliance of Holistic Lawyers. Avocations: painting, reading, art projects. Office: 35 Keswick Ct Lincolnshire IL 60069-3425

PRATER-FIPPS, EUNICE KAY, educational administrator; b. Cleve., Aug. 22, 1949; d. Jesse and Bertha (McCollum) Prater; m. Theodis Fipps, Apr. 13, 1990. BS, Kent State U., 1974; MEd, Cleve. State U., 1978. Cert. tchr., secondary prin., Ohio. Tchr. bus. edn. Cleve. Pub. Schs., 1974-80, adminstrv. intern, 1980-83, asst. prin., 1983—. Mem. ASCD, Ohio Assn. Secondary Sch. Adminstrs., Cleve. Coun. Adminstrs. and Suprs. Avocations: travel, reading, outdoor activities. Home: 565 Cynthia Ct Richmond Heights OH 44143 Office: Cleve Pub Schs 3817 MLK Blvd Cleveland OH 44105

PRATHER, DENZIL LEWIS, petroleum engineer; b. Elizabeth, W.Va., Mar. 18, 1921; s. Elias Hugh and Mary Deborah (Lewis) P.; m. Madeline Shimer, May 13, 1945; children: Denzil Jr., Kathy Taylor, Linda Holtgrewe, Mary Smith, Anne Scarbro, David. Student, Potomac State U., 1941-42; BS in Petroleum Engring., Marietta Coll., 1945. Registered profl. engr., W.Va. Supt. Weva Oil Co., Elizabeth, 1945-50; pvt. practice as cons. Midland, Tex., 1950-57; div. mgr. Southwestern Devel. Co., Parkersburg, W.Va., 1957-70; ptnr. Loper and Prather, Parkersburg, 1970-80; pres. Adena Petroleum, Inc., Parkersburg, 1980—. Pres. PTA, Belpre, Ohio, 1961-63; active Congl. Ch., Belpre, 1957-90. 1st lt. USAF, 1942-45. Mem. Soc. Petroleum Engrs. (sr. mem.), Appalachian Geol. Soc., Ohio Acad. Sci., Ohio Acad. History. Democrat. Congregationalist. Home: 814 Boulevard Dr Belpre OH 45714-1208 Office: Adena Petroleum Inc PO Box 250 Mineral Wells WV 26150-0250

PRATHER, GERALD LUTHER, management consultant, retired air force officer, judge; b. LaGrange, Ga., Apr. 7, 1935; s. Luther Pate and Hazel Belle (McCullough) P.; m. Carolyn Pearson, Nov. 22, 1956; children—Dean Allen, Bryan Pate, Jeri Lynn, Angela. B.S.E.E., Auburn U., 1966; M.S. in Mgmt., Air Force Inst. Tech., 1972; postgrad. advanced mgmt., U. Houston, 1978; grad., SQ Officer Sch., Maxwell AFB, 1963, ICAF, Washington, 1974. Enlisted USAF, 1954-56, commd. 2d lt., 1956, advanced through grades to maj. gen., 1981, various assignments as pilot, 1956-68, served in Vietnam, 1967-68; commdr. 1963d Comm. Squadron USAF, Chanute AFB, Ill., 1968-69; comdr. 1918th Comm. Squadron USAF, Scott AFB, Ill., 1969-70; dep. dir. comm.-electronics for 15th Air Force USAF, March AFB, Calif., 1970-72; chief comm. ops div. hdqrs. USAF, Washington, 1972-75; comdr. strategic comm. div. USAF, Offutt AFB, Nebr., 1975-77; comdr. European

Comm. Div. USAF, Ramstein AFB, W. Ger., 1977-80; dir. Command Control, Comm. & Computer Systems, Hdqrs. U.S. Readiness Command USAF, MacDill AFB, Fla., 1980-81; asst. chief of staff of Info. Systems Hdqrs. USAF, Washington, 1981-84; comdr. Air Force Comm. Command USAF, Scott AFB, Ill., 1984-86; ret. USAF, 1986; pvt. practice mgmt. cons. Del Rio, Tex., 1986—; Justice of the Peace Val Verde County, Tex.; lectr. in field; also air traffic controller, parachutist. speech writer Team America 1983 (Freedom Found. nat. award 1984). Scout master Boy Scouts Am., Sacramento, 1963, chmn. com., Sacramento, 1964, cub master, Auburn, Ala., 1965; sponsor Explorer Troop, Boy Scouts Am., Scott AFB, Ill., 1969; alumni Boy Scouts Am., 1984-85; chmn. Amistad Dist. Boy Scouts Am., 1988, chmn. Eagle Scout advancement 1994-96; chmn. Val Verde County United Way campaign, 1989, pres., bd.dirs., 1990. Decorated DSM with oak leaf cluster, Legion of Merit with one oak leaf cluster, DFC, Bronze Star with V device, Air medal with two oak leaf clusters, Republic of Vietnam Gallantry Cross with Palm; recipient Gen. Edwin W. Rawlings award Air Force Inst. Tech., 1972, Comdt.'s award, 1972, also numerous other decorations and awards. Mem. VFW (life), Armed Forces Comm.-Electronics Assn. (assoc. dir. 1984—, internat. v.p. 1982-84, chmn. ethics com. 1982-83, mem. com. 1981-82, Meritorious Gold medal 1976, 83), Air Traffic Control Assn., Soc. Am. Mil. Engrs., Justice of the Peace and Constables Assn., Soc. Logistics Engrs., Telephone Pioneers of Am., Air Force Assn., Air Force Sgts. Assn. (hon.), Non-Commd. Officers Assn. (hon.)m Vietnam Vets. of Am., Ret. Officers Assn., Del Rio C. of C. (bd. dirs. 1990-91, 95-96, v.p. 1991-92, 95-96), Order of Daedalians, Am. Legion, Lions, Civitan, Del Rio Club (v.p. 1989-90). Avocations: gardening, racquetball, sketching, automotive mechanics, private pilot.

PRATHER, LENORE LOVING, state supreme court presiding justice; b. West Point, Miss., Sept. 17, 1931; d. Byron Herald and Hattie Hearn (Morris) Loving; m. Robert Brooks Prather, May 30, 1957; children: Pamela, Valerie Jo, Malinda Wayne. B.S., Miss. State Coll. Women, 1953; JD, U. Miss., 1955. Bar: Miss. 1955. Practice with B. H. Loving, West Point, 1955-60, sole practice, 1960-62, 65-71, assoc. practice, 1962-65; mcpl. judge City of West Point, 1965-71; chancery ct. judge 14th dist. State of Miss., Columbus, 1971-82; supreme ct. justice State of Miss., Jackson, 1982-92; presiding justice State of Miss., 1993—; v.p. Conf. Local Bar Assn., 1956-58; sec. Clay County Bar Assn., 1956-71. 1st woman in Miss. to become chancery judge, 1971, and supreme ct. justice, 1982. Mem. ABA, Miss. State Bar Assn., Miss. Conf. Judges, DAR, Rotary, Pilot Club, Jr. Aux. Columbus Club. Episcopalian. Office: Miss Supreme Ct PO Box 117 Jackson MS 39205-0117 also: PO Box 903 Columbus MS 39703-0903

PRATS, MICHAEL, petroleum engineer, educator; b. Tampa, Fla., Dec. 18, 1925; s. Miguel and Maria (Carbó) P.; m. Mary Blanche Flaherty, Apr. 7, 1951; children: Delicia Anne, Barbara Eileen, Teresa Kaye, Steven Michael. BS in Physics, U. Tex., 1949, MA in Physics, 1951. With Shell Devel. Co., Houston, 1950—, cons. research engr., then sr. research assoc., 1972-89; pres. Michael Prats & Assocs., Houston, 1989—; adj. prof. dept. petroleum engring. U. Tex., Austin, 1991—; participant scientist exchange Royal/Dutch Shell Lab., Amsterdam, The Netherlands, 1954, 55, Shell Internat. Petroleum, The Hague, The Netherlands, 1981, Maraven, S.A., Caracas, Venezuela, 1981-83. Author: Thermal Recovery, 1982, Spanish transl., 1987; contbr. articles to profl. jours.; 21 patents in field. Served to staff sgt. USAAF, 1944-46, PTO. Recipient Diploma of Honor Pi Epsilon Tau, 1986, Disting. Svc. award Rep. Honduras, 1989, Thermal Recovery Disting. Achievement award SPE Thermal Ops. Symposium, 1991, KAPITSA medal Acad. Natural Scis. (Moscow), 1995; named to Internat. Hall of Fame, 1989. Mem. AIME (hon.), NAE, Soc. Petroleum Engrs. (hon., bd. dirs. 1976-79, sr. tech. editor 1987-90, Enhanced Oil Recovery Pioneer 1986, Uren award 1974, Disting. Mem. award 1983, Anthony F. Lucas Gold medal 1993), Soc. Venezolana de Ingenieros de Petroleo, Can. Inst. Mining, Asociacion De Ingenieros Petroleros De Mexico, Mex. Nat. Acad. Engring. (corr.), Acad. Engring. Armenia (fgn. mem.), Russian Acad. Nat. Scis., Pi Epsilon Tau (hon.). Avocation: travel. Address: 2834 Bellefontaine St Houston TX 77025-1610

PRATT, ALBERT, financial consultant, trustee; b. Newton, Mass., May 23, 1911; s. Frederick Sanford and Ella Winifred (Nickerson) P.; m. Alice Mathea Lee, May 24, 1940 (dec. 1976); children: Alice Mathea, Cornelia S., Nina L., Frederick H., Kate Nickerson Pratt Lapping; m. Fanny Gray Little Morgan, Jan. 2, 1977. Grad., Country Day Sch., Newton, 1929; A.B., Harvard, 1933, J.D., 1936. Bar: Mass. bar 1936. With firm Goodwin, Procter & Hoar, Boston, 1936-40; with Paine, Webber, Jackson & Curtis, Inc., Boston, 1946-80; vice chmn. Paine, Webber, Jackson & Curtis, Inc., 1970-76, cons., 1976-80, gen. partner, 1950-54, 57-70, ltd. partner, 1954-57; adv. dir. Blyth, Eastman Paine Webber Inc., Boston, 1980-83; dir., chmn. investment com. Paine Webber Properties, Inc., 1980-84, pres., 1984, cons., 1985—; ptnr. F.S. Pratt & Son, 1946-87; asst. sec. navy, 1954-57; bd. govs. N.Y. Stock Exchange, 1963-66. Pres. United Fund Boston, 1962-64. Served to comdr. USNR, 1940-45. Mem. Investment Bankers Assn. (chmn. N.E. group 1952-53, gov. 1957-60, 64-67, chmn. securities act com. 1959-63, pres. 1965-66), Assn. Harvard Alumni (dir. 1964-70), Boston C. of C. (dir. 1958-61), Assn. Harvard Clubs (pres. 1962-63), Harvard Alumni Assn. (dir. 1958-63), Cruising Club Am., N.Y. Yacht Club, Wianno Club (Osterville, Mass.). Home: Key Largo Anglers Club 50 Clubhouse Rd Key Largo FL 33037-3600 Office: care PaineWebber Properties 265 Franklin St Fl 16 Boston MA 02110-3113

PRATT, BRIAN, construction executive; b. 1952. Graduate, Calif. State Poly. U., 1974. With ARB, Inc., Paramount, Calif., 1974—, ARB Fabricated Syss., Inc. affiliate, Bakersfield, Calif., 1988-92; pres. ARB, Inc., Paramount, 1992—. Office: 14404 Paramount Blvd Paramount CA 90723

PRATT, DAN EDWIN, chemistry educator; b. High Point, N.C., Feb. 7, 1924; s. C. Daniel and Carol Druscilla (Wyatt) P.; m. Mana Clariece Peacock, Aug. 29, 1959; 1 child, Mana Lisa. BS, U. Ga., 1950, MS, 1951; PhD (nuclear sci. fellow 1960), Fla. State U., 1962; postgrad. in food sci., U. Mass. Asst. prof. chemistry U. Ga., 1955-61; assoc. prof., research scientist food sci. and nutrition U. Wis., Madison, 1964-69; research scientist, assoc. prof. Purdue U., West Lafayette, Ind., 1969-76, prof. chemistry, 1976-92, prof. emeritus, 1992—; cons. in lipid chemistry, 1992—; vis. prof. food law Emory U., 1954; vis. rsch. scientist Natick R & D Command, 1980; vis. lectr. U. Viscosa, Brazil, 1982, Harvard U., 1980; vis. scientist Am. Oil Chemists, Cannes, France, 1985; vis. rsch. scientist in lipid chemistry FDA, Washington, 1987, lectr., 1988; cons. to food industry, Taiwan, 1981, Nat. Poultry Industry, Lipid Chemistry, 1990; rsch. scientist Am. Oil Chemists, 1992; rsch. com., rep. Inst. Food Technologists, 1986-89. Contbr. numerous articles profl. jours. Del. Internat. Congress Food Scientists, Tokyo, 1978. With USMCR, 1942-45. Recipient Disting. Scientist Research award Ind. Inst. Food Sci., 1982. Fellow Am. Inst. Chemists, Inst. Food Technologists; mem. Nat. Inst. Food Scientists, Am. Acad. Scis., N.Y. Acad. Scis., Sigma Xi, Phi Kappa Phi, Pi Mu Epsilon, Phi Tau Sigma (exec. sec. 1969), Gamma Sigma Delta. Club: Lafayette Toastmasters (pres. 1975). Home: 12734 Hunters Chase St San Antonio TX 78230-1930 Office: Purdue U Dept Foods And Nutriti West Lafayette IN 47906

PRATT, DANA JOSEPH, publishing consultant; b. Cambridge, Mass., Dec. 9, 1926; s. Carroll Cornelius and Marjory (Bates) P.; m. Therese Louis, July 14, 1957; children—Joseph Caldwell, Michael Louis, Benjamin Lyon. B.Naval Sci., Tufts U., 1946, B.A., 1948. Mgmt. trainee N.J. Bell Telephone Co., Newark, 1948-50; sales asst. Princeton U. Press, N.J., 1950-53; sales mgr. U. Ill. Press, Urbana, 1953-55; field cons. Franklin Book Programs, N.Y.C., 1955-59; staff assoc. Am. Book Pubs. Council, N.Y.C., 1959-62; exec. sec. Assn. Am. Univ. Presses, N.Y.C., 1962-66; asst. dir. Yale U. Press, New Haven, 1966-78; dir. pub. Library of Congress, Washington, 1978-93. Contbr. articles to profl. jours. Served as ensign USNR, comdg. officer PC 566, 1946-47. Mem. Washington Book Pubs. (pres. 1984-85), Soc. for Scholarly Pub. (bd. dirs. 1982-86), Washington Map Soc., Washington Rare Book Group. Home and Office: 7514 Old Chester Rd Bethesda MD 20817-6163

PRATT, DAVID TERRY, mechanical engineering educator, combustion researcher; b. Shelley, Idaho, Sept. 14, 1934; s. Eugene Francis and Bernice (Montague) P.; m. Marilyn Jean Thackston, Dec. 22, 1956; children: Douglas Montague, Elizabeth Joann, Brian Stephens. B.Sc. M.E., U. Wash., 1956; M.Sc., U. Calif., Berkeley, 1962, Ph.D., 1968. Asst. prof. marine engring. U.S. Naval Acad., Annapolis, Md., 1961-64; prof. mech. engring., asst. dean Wash. State U., Pullman, 1968-76; prof. mech. engring. U. Utah, Salt Lake City, 1976-78; prof., chmn. mech. engring. and applied mechanics U. Mich., Ann Arbor, 1978-81; prof., chmn. mech. engring. U. Wash., Seattle, 1981-86, prof. mech. engring., 1987—; research dir. supercomputing Aerojet Propulsion Research Inst., Sacramento, 1986-87. Author (with W.H. Heiser) Hypersonic Airbreathing Propulsion, 1994; editor (with L.D. Smoot) Combustion and Gasification of Pulverized Coal, 1976; contbr. articles to profl. jours. Served to 1st lt. USMC, 1956-60. NSF sci. faculty fellow, 1965-66; Fulbright-Hays sr. research fellow Imperial Coll., 1974-75; David Pierpont Gardner faculty fellow U. Utah, 1976. Mem. ASME, AIAA, Combustion Inst., Am. Soc. Engring. Edn. Lutheran. Office: U Washington Dept Mech Engring Box 352600 Seattle WA 98195

PRATT, DIANE ADELE, elementary education educator; b. Battle Creek, Mich., Oct. 24, 1951; d. John Robert and Kathleen Adele (Cooper) Dickert; m. Stephen Howard Pratt, Apr. 29, 1972; children: Eric Stephen, Elizabeth Adele. BS, Western Mich. U., 1972. Cert. elem. tchr., Ohio, Iowa, Mich. Elem. tchr. Berea (Ohio) Cmty. Schs., 1973-76; ednl. cons. Kolbe Products, Inc., Phoenix and Scottsdale, Ariz., 1982-84; tchr. Lemon Tree Nursery Sch., Battle Creek, 1985-88; instr. Jr. Great Books, 1984-87; elem. tchr. Ft. Dodge (Iowa) Cmty. Schs., 1976-78, 90, substitute tchr., 1988-90, middle sch. tchr., 1990—, team leader, 1994—; exec. sec. Born Free Safari Club, Dodgen Industries, Humboldt, Iowa, 1988; advt. exec. Ft. Dodge Today mag., 1989-92; ednl. tutor, Battle Creek, Ft. Dodge, 1986-96; mem. adv. bd. Inst. for Instrn. Svcs., Battle Creek, 1984-88; dir., instr. Battle Creek Presch. Enrichment Program, 1984; chmn. Ft. Dodge Supr.'s Cmty. Com. to Study K-8 Curriculum, 1988-89, facilitator K-3 human growth and devel. curriculum, 1989-92; mem. standing com. early childhood needs assessment com. Ft. Dodge Comty. Schs., 1989-95; mem. adv. bd., instr. Kids on Kampus Iowa Cen. C.C., Ft. Dodge, 1990-95; speaker State Conv. Childbirth Educators, Lansing, Mich., 1982; trustee Ft. Dodge Comty. Sch. Found. Bd., 1992—, mem. talented and gifted selection com. Ft. Dodge Comty. Schs., 1993—; mem. pub. rels. com. Ft. Dodge Comty Sch. Dist., 1992-94, mem. ednl. outcomes standing com., 1993-94. Author, editor various newsletters. Mem., past chmn. bd. Christian edn. 1st Bapt. Ch., Ft. Dodge, 1978-79, 89—, music com., 1992-94, dir. children's choirs, 1988-90, mem. bell choir, 1990-91, ch. sch. supt. 1993—; membership chmn. Battle Creek Parents, 1981-83; neighborhood coord. mothers' march March of Dimes, Battle Creek, 1981-83; troop leader Lakota coun. Girl Scouts U.S., 1988-90; pres. La Mora Park PTA, 1985-87, Phillips Mid Sch. PTA, Ft. Dodge, 1990-91; bd. dirs. Main Stage Players, jr. theater, Ft. Dodge, 1990-91; sec., pres. Jr. Women's Club, Ft. Dodge, 1977-80; mem. kickoff com. United Way, 1991; membership co-chair Ft. Dodge Athletic Booster Club, 1994—. Recipient Mem. of Yr. award La Mora Park PTA, 1987. Mem. NEA, AAUW (sec., pres. Battle Creek br. 1986-88), PEO (N.J. chpt., Ft. Dodge chpt. 1990—), Iowa Edn. Assn., Ft. Dodge Edn. Assn., Iowa Assn. Middle Level Educators, Iowa Coun. Tchrs. English. Avocations: educational research, cross-country skiing, tennis. Home: 1851 9th Ave N Fort Dodge IA 50501

PRATT, DONALD GEORGE, physician; b. Higgins, Tex., Oct. 19, 1946; s. George Horace and Esta Vici (Barker) P. BS in Biomed. Sci., West Tex. State U., 1970; MD, U. Tex., Galveston, 1974. Diplomate Am. Bd. Family Practice, Am. Bd. Radiology (Radiation Oncology). Intern Scott & White Meml. Hosp., Temple, Tex., 1974-75, resident in gen. surgery and pathology, 1975-77, physician, 1979-83; resident in family practice McLennan County Med. Edn. and Rsch. Found., Waco, Tex., 1977-79; physician Family Practice Assocs., El Paso, Tex., 1983; owner, pvt. contractor Minor Emergency Ctrs., Amarillo, Tex., 1983-85; resident in radiation therapy U. Tex., Galveston, 1985-88; ptnr. Cons. in Radiation Oncology, P.A., Amarillo, 1988—, pres., 1994—; dir. dept. radiation oncology Harrington Cancer Ctr., Amarillo, 1994—; pres. Cons. in Radiation Oncology, 1994—; pres. staff Harrington Cancer Ctr., 1995—; prin. investigator Radiation Oncology Group, 1988-95; pres. of staff Harrington Cancer Ctr., 1995—, also bd. dirs. Mem. AMA, Am. Soc. Therapeutic Radiology and Oncology, Am. Acad. Family Physicians, Tex. Med. Assn., Potter/Randall County Med. Soc., Tex. Radiol. Soc. Home: 3623 Tripp Ave Amarillo TX 79121-1809 Office: Cons Radiation Oncology PA 1600 Coulter Dr Ste 402 Amarillo TX 79106-1719

PRATT, DONALD HENRY, manufacturing company executive; b. Hays, Kans., Dec. 2, 1937; s. Donald Edwin and Ida Marjorie (Dreiling) P.; m. George-Ann Hinkle, June 7, 1960; children—Jacqueline, Donald. B.S.I.E., Wichita State U., 1960; M.B.A., Harvard U., 1965. With Butler Mfg. Co., Galesburg, Ill, 1965-67; with Butler Mfg. Co., Kansas City, MO, 1967—; sr. v.p., gen. mgr. bldgs. div. Butler Mfg. Co., 1978-80, exec. v.p., gen. mgr. bldgs. div., 1980-82, exec. v.p., pres. bldgs. div., 1982-86, pres., 1986—; bd. dirs. Union Nat. Bank, Wichita, Kans., Commerce Bank, Kansas City. Trustee Midwest Research Inst.; bd. dirs. Kansas City Art Inst., Mo. Served to capt. USAF, 1960-63. Mem. Metal Bldg. Mfrs. Assn. (chmn. 1983), Am. Royal of Kansas City (bd. dirs.). Republican. Roman Catholic. Avocation: tennis. Home: 433 Ward Pky Kansas City MO 64112-2102 Office: Butler Mfg Co PO Box 419-917 Kansas City MO 64141*

PRATT, EDMUND TAYLOR, JR., pharmaceutical company executive; b. Savannah, Ga., Feb. 22, 1927; s. Edmund T. and Rose (Miller) P.; m. Jeanette Louise Carneale, Feb. 10, 1951; children: Randolf Ryland, Keith Taylor. BSEE magna cum laude, Duke U., 1947; MBA, U. Pa., 1949; hon. degrees, L.I. U., Marymount Manhattan Coll., Poly. U. of N.Y., St. Francis Coll. With IBM Corp., 1949-52, 54-57, asst. to exec. v.p., 1956-57; with IBM World Trade Corp., 1958-62, contr., 1958-62; asst. sec. fin. mgmt. Dept. Army, 1962-64; contr. Pfizer, Inc., N.Y.C., 1964-67, v.p. ops. internat. subs., 1967-69, chmn. bd., pres. internat. subs., 1969-71, exec. v.p., 1970-71, pres., 1971-72, chmn., chief exec. officer, 1972-91, chmn., 1972-92, chmn. emeritus, 1992—, also bd. dirs.; bd. dirs. Chase Manhattan Corp., Internat. Paper Co., GM, Minerals Techs., Inc., Hughes Electronics; trustee Logistics Mgmt. Inst. Lt. (j.g.) USNR, 1952-54. Mem. Bus. Coun., Bus. Roundtable (past chmn., mem. policy com.), Phi Beta Kappa.

PRATT, GEORGE CHENEY, law educator, retired federal judge; b. Corning, N.Y., May 22, 1928; s. George Wollage and Muriel (Cheney) P.; m. Carol June Hoffman, Aug. 16, 1952; children: George W., Lise M., Marcia Pratt Burke, William T. BA, Yale U., 1950, JD, 1953. Bar: N.Y. 1953, U.S. Supreme Ct. 1964, U.S. Ct. Appeals 1974. Law clk. to Charles W. Froessel (Judge of N.Y. Ct. Appeals), 1953-55; assoc. then ptnr. Sprague & Stern, Mineola, N.Y., 1956-60; ptnr. Andromidas, Pratt & Pitcher, Mineola, 1960-65, Pratt, Caemmerer & Cleary, Mineola, 1965-75; partner Farrell, Fritz, Pratt, Caemmerer & Cleary, 1975-76; judge U.S. Dist. Ct. (Eastern Dist. of N.Y.), 1976-82, U.S. Circuit Ct. Appeals for 2d circuit (Uniondale), N.Y., 1982-93; sr. circ. judge U.S. Cir. of Appeals for 2d Cir., N.Y., 1993-95; prof. Touro Law Sch., Huntington, N.Y., 1993—; counsel Parnon & Pratt L.L.P., N.Y.C., 1995—. Mem. ABA, N.Y. State Bar Assn., Nassau County Bar Assn. Mem. United Ch. of Christ. Office: Touro Law Ctr 300 Nassau Rd Huntington NY 11743-4346

PRATT, JACK E., SR., hotel executive; b. 1927. Commd. USAF, 1942, advanced through grades, resigned, 1951; ptnr. Wes-Tex Vending Co., 1951—; founder, ptnr. Dairy Queen, Mineral Wells, Tex., 1954-64, Bonanza Steakhouse Restaurants, Tex., 1964-68; chmn., CEO Pratt Hotel Corp., Dallas, 1968—. Office: Pratt Hotel Corp 13455 Noel Rd Ste 2200 Dallas TX 75240*

PRATT, JOHN SHERMAN, lawyer; b. Bloomsburgh, Pa., Feb. 7, 1952; s. B.D. and Frances Marie (Quinn) P.; m. Teresa Gayle Plemmons, June 14, 1975; children: Andrew, Caroline, Alexander. BS, Clemson U., 1974; JD, Harvard U., 1977. Bar: Ga. 1977, U.S. Dist. Ct. (no. dist.) Ga. 1977, U.S. Patent and Trademark Office 1979, U.S. Ct. Appeals (5th and 11th cirs.) 1981, U.S. Ct. Appeals (fed. cir.) 1985. Bd. dirs. Wesley Woods Geriatric Hosp. at Emory U., Atlanta, 1991, Ga. Biomed. Partnership, Atlanta, 1991-94. Mem. Am. Intellectual Property Law Assn., Licensing Execs. Soc. Avocation: woodworking. Office: Kilpatrick & Cody 1100 Peachtree St NE Ste 2800 Atlanta GA 30309-4528

PRATT, JOHN WINSOR, statistics educator; b. Boston, Sept. 11, 1931; s. Frederic Wolsey and Theresa (Winsor) P.; m. Joy A. Wilmunen, Nov. 15, 1958; children: Maria Theresa Winsor, Samuel Frederick Wolsey. AB, Princeton U., 1952; PhD, Stanford U., 1956; MA (hon.), Harvard U., 1966. Rsch. assoc. U. Chgo., 1955-57; mem. faculty Harvard U., Cambridge, Mass., 1957—, prof. bus. adminstrn., 1966—; dir. Social Sci. Rsch. Coun., 1971-76; vis. rsch. prof. Kyoto U., Japan, 1972-73; vis. lectr. Keio U. Bus. Sch., Japan, 1982; Yamaichi vis. prof. fin. Tokyo U., 1989-90; chmn. study group on environment. monitoring NRC, 1975-77, chmn. panel on decennial census methodology NRC, 1983-87, mem. com. nat. stats., 1982-88. Co-author: Introduction to Statistical Decision Theory, 1965, rev. edit., 1995, Social Experimentation: A Method for Planning and Evaluating Social Intervention, 1974, Concepts of Nonparametric Theory, 1981; editor: Statistical and Mathematical Aspects of Pollution Problems, 1974; co-editor: Principals and Agents: The Structure of Business, 1985. Trustee Middlesex Sch., Concord, Mass., 1964-67. Guggenheim fellow, 1971. Fellow AAAS (chmn. sect. U. 1977), Am. Statis. Assn. (editor jour. 1965-69, chmn. bus. and econs. sect. 1983), Inst. Math. Stats., Econometric Soc., Am. Acad. arts and Scis.; mem. Internat. Statis. Inst., Bernoulli Soc. Math. Stats. and Probability, Math. Assn. Am. Home: 2 Gray Gdns E Cambridge MA 02138-1402 Office: Harvard Bus Sch Boston MA 02163

PRATT, JOSEPH HYDE, JR., surgeon; b. Chapel Hill, N.C., Mar. 9, 1911; s. Joseph Hyde and Mary (Bayley) P.; m. Hazel Housman, Dec. 11, 1934; children: Judith Housman, Lisa Mary, Joseph Hyde. AB, U. N.C., 1933; MD, Harvrad U., 1937; MS, U. Minn., 1947. Diplomate Am. Bd. Surgery, Am. Bd. Ob-gyn. Intern Boston City Hosp., 1938-39; fellow surgery Mayo Found., Rochester, Minn., 1940-43; mem. staff Mayo Clinic, Rochester, 1943—, head sect. in surgery, 1945-77, sr. gynecol. surgeon, 1958—; prof. clin. surgery Mayo Grad. Sch. Medicine U. Minn., 1963—; prof. surgery Mayo Med. Sch., 1973—. Contbr. articles to med. jours. Mem. ACS (bd. govs. 1966-71, bd. regents 1971-80), AMA, ACOG, Ctrl. Assn. Ob-Gyn., Minn. Ob-Gyn. Soc., Western Surg. Assn., soc. Vaginal Surgeons (pres. 1979-80), Soc. Pelvic Surgeons (pres. 1968), So. Surg. Assn., Ob-Gyn. Travel Club (pres. 1993—), Sigma Xi, Nu Sigma Nu. Republican. Episcopalian. Home: 1159 Plummer Cir SW Rochester MN 55902-2035 Office: 200 1st St SW Rochester MN 55905-0001

PRATT, KATHERINE MERRICK, environmental consulting company executive; b. Alexandria, Egypt, July 4, 1951; d. Theodore and Bettie (Curland) R.; m. Harry Kenneth Todd (div.); 1 child, Kirsten Todd-Pratt. BBA in Mgmt. Systems, U. Iowa, 1980; postgrad., U. Tex., 1985-87. Program data mgr. Rockwell Internat., Dallas, 1981-85; support coord. GTE Govt. Systems, Taunton, Mass., 1987-89, support engr., 1989-93; pres. Enviro-Logistics Inc., Jamestown, R.I., 1993—. Mem. Soc. Logistics Engrs. (officer, mem. standing com. environ. applications, bd. dirs. New Eng. dist., dir. New Eng. dist., nat. chpt. newsletter judge), U.S. Pony Club (Ctrl. New Eng. championship chairwoman). Avocations: sailing, reading, equitation.

PRATT, LAWRENCE ARTHUR, thoracic surgeon, foreign service officer; b. Paris, Ill., Dec. 20, 1907; s. Luther F. and Katherine (Kaufman) P.; m. Mai Thi NgocSuong, May 7, 1974; children: Elizabeth, Lawrie Porter, D. Jane. B.S., Wayne State U., Detroit, 1930, M.B., M.A., M.D., 1934, M.Ed., 1960; LL.B., Woodrow Wilson Coll. Law, Atlanta, 1943. Diplomate: Am. Bd. Surgery, Am. Bd. Thoracic Surgeons. Intern Grace Hosp., 1934-35; practice thoracic surgery Detroit, 1935-41, 46-63; attending thoracic surgeon Grace, Detroit Meml. hosps.; courtesy staff St. John's Hosp.; cons. thoracic surgeon Holy Cross, Highland Park Gen. hosps., Detroit; U.S. fgn. svc. officer, 1963—; vis. prof. medicine U. Saigon, Vietnam, 1963-75; med. dir. Urban Health Clinic of Orange County, Calif., 1981—; exec. v.p. Am. Fedn. Med. Ctrs., Inc., 1953-54; chief med. dental edn. divsn. AID/PH, Vietnam; cons. Vietnam Min. Edn., 1974-75; assoc. dean Minh Duc. Med. Sch., Saigon, 1974-75; cons. HEW, 1975-77; spl. asst. HEW (Divsn. Medicine Bur. Health Manpower), 1976; cons., mem. White House Task Force Internat. Health Policy, 1977; mem. World Bank Task Force Internat. Health Policy and Manpower, 1977, U.S. Pub. Health Assn.; leader design team Health Care Program, Mauritania, West Africa, 1978; physician in charge Refugee Transit Camps, Malaysia, 1980; med. dir. Urban Health Clinic, Orange County, Calif., 1981-84, Spl. Disease Specialist 1981—; cons. physician overseas ops. World Cons., Irvine, Calif., 1984-85; cons. to min. health, Rabat, Morocco, 1986; sr. cons. World Care Inc., 1988—; mem. Nat. Coun. for Internat. Health, 1988—; chmn. bd. dirs. Boarne Seven Seas Devel. Corp., 1993—. Author: Total Development for Survival, 1986. bd. dirs. Sun Yet Middle Sch., Zhongshan, Quandong Province, People's Republic of China, 1986—; chmn. bd. 100 For 1 Systems Corp., 1986—. Lt. col., M.C. AUS, 1941-46. Active U.S-Mexican Border Health Assn., 1986—. Recipient Unit citation; medal of Culture and Edn.; medal of Merit Vietnam). Fellow ACS (life), Am. Coll. Chest Physicians; mem. AMA, Mich. Med. Soc., Wayne County Med. Soc., Internat. Bronchoesophagol. Assn. (founder), Am. Bronchoesophagol. Assn., 4th Aux. Surg. Group Assn. (pres. 1955-56), Wayne State U. Med. Alumni Assn. (pres. 1956-57), Ga. Bar Assn., Am. Bd. of Surgery (diplomat), Am. Bd. of Thoracic Surgery (diplomat). Clubs: Essex Cricket (Eng.); Lambs (N.Y.C.); Scarab (Detroit), Detroit Skating (Detroit); Grosse Pointe Yacht, Grosse Pointe Hunt, Am. Radio Relay League, El Cajon (Calif.) Radio. Home: 2302 Lowell Ln Santa Ana CA 92706-1932

PRATT, LEIGHTON CALVIN, state legislator; b. Hartford, Conn., Apr. 23, 1923; s. Calvin and Jessie (White) P.; m. Sally Burgess, Oct. 21, 1961; children: Randall Leighton, Bruce Charles. BS, U. Vt., 1951; MS, U. R.I., 1953. Plant pathologist Vt. Dept. Agr., Montpelier, 1952-62; tchr. sci. Cabot (Vt.) H.S. and J. H.S., 1962-65; tchr. biology, asst. prin. Newport (Vt.) H.S., 1965-67; tchr. biology North Country Union H.S., Newport, 1967-79; Coos agrl. ext. agt. U. N.H., Durham, 1969-88, prof. emeritus ext. edn., 1988—; mem. N.H. Ho. of Reps., Concord, 1991—. Named hon. state farmer Future Farmers Am., 1986. Mem. Rotary (dir. exch. to Brazil dist. 1986, pres. Lancaster, N.H.), Epsilon Sigma Phi. Republican. Congregationalist. Avocations: travel, gardening. Home: 63 Water St Lancaster NH 03584-1804

PRATT, MICHAEL THEODORE, book publishing company executive, marketing, sales and publishing specialist; b. Troy, Ohio, May 30, 1943; s. James Alden and Dorothy (Kennedy) P.; m. Helen Diane Biddle, Oct. 24, 1964 (div. Sept. 1983); children: Nicole Christine, Jason Alan. Student, Muskingum Coll., New Concord, Ohio, 1961-62, Ashland Coll., Ohio, 1962-63, Temple U., 1963-64, Wharton Sch. (U. Pa.), 1964. Corp. sr. v.p. Random House, Inc., N.Y.C., 1969-90; pres., chief exec. officer Corinthian Internat., Inc., Spring Valley, N.Y., 1990, also bd. dirs.; sr. v.p. St. Martin's Press, N.Y.C., 1991—; bd. dirs. Shambhala Pubs., Inc., J. Alden Pratt, Inc. Mem. Am. Mgmt. Assn. Democrat. Presbyterian. Club: University (Larchmont, N.Y.). Home: 50 Judges Hollow Rd Fairfield CT 06430-1643 Office: St Martin's Press 175 5th Ave New York NY 10010-7703

PRATT, MURRAY LESTER, information systems specialist; b. Mt. Holly, N.J., Mar. 11, 1956; s. John N. and Mildred E. P.; m. Sharon Louise Busby, Aug. 13, 1988; children: Kevin Harrison, Brian Gavel. BS in Indsl. Engring., Northwestern U., 1976; MS in Computer Sci., Ill. Inst. Tech., Chgo., 1983. Systems analyst Gen. Foods USA, Chgo., 1981-84, systems specialist, 1984-87, computer integrated mfg. mgr., 1987-91; KF logistics systems mgr. Kraft Foods, Northfield, Ill., 1991—. Presbyterian. Avocations: current affairs, tennis, volleyball, hiking. Home: 1241 Swainwood Dr Glenview IL 60025-2839 Office: Kraft Foods Dept NF168 Three Lakes Dr Northfield IL 60093-2753

PRATT, PAUL BERNARD, financial services executive; b. Johnson City, Tenn., Aug. 7, 1946; s. Paul Bernard Pratt and Lois Kathern (Arnold) Thomas; m. Diann Marguerite Scroggins, Apr. 2, 1971 (dec.); 1 child, Jennifer Elaine White; m. Patricia Lea Kell Alleman, June 21, 1992 (dec.). BA, Chapman Coll., 1975; MBA, Webster U., 1993; postgrad., Western State U., 1994—. Commd. 2d lt. USMC, 1966, advanced through grades to lt. col., 1983, svc. in RVN, 1969, 70, regimental air officer 2nd Marines, 1977-80, ops. officer MAWTS-1, 1980-83, ops. officer marine corps air sta. Iwakuni SA, 1984-87; asst. dean command and staff coll. USMC, Quantico, Va., 1987-90; dir. morale, welfare and recreation MCAS USMC, El Toro, Calif., 1991-93; ret. USMC, 1993; pres. Success Seminars, Irvine, Calif., 1993—; v.p. ERIC Equities Inc., Santa Ana, Calif., 1993—. Precinct inspector Orange County (Calif.) Voting Commn., 1994; pres. Cath. Parish Coun., Japan, 1986. Recipient Meritorious Svc. medal Pres. of the U.S., 1990, 93. Mem.

Internat. Assn. of Fin. Planners. Avocations: running, biking, chess, reading. Office: ERIC Equities Inc 2021 E 4th St Santa Ana CA 92705-3912

PRATT, PHILIP CHASE, pathologist, educator; b. Livermore Falls, Maine, Oct. 19, 1920; s. Harold Sewell and Cora Johnson (Chase) P.; m. Helen Clarke Deitz, Feb. 4, 1945; children: William Clarke (dec.), Charles Chase (dec.). A.B., Bowdoin Coll., 1941; M.D., Johns Hopkins U., 1944. Diplomate: Am. Bd. Pathology. Intern in pathology Johns Hopkins Hosp., 1944-45, asst. resident in pathology, 1945-46; pathologist Saranac Lab., Saranac Lake, N.Y., 1946-52; asst. dir. Saranac Lab., 1952-55; instr. Ohio State U., 1955-57, asst. prof. pathology, 1957-62, assoc. prof., 1962-66; assoc. prof. Duke U. Med. Ctr., 1966-71, prof., 1971-90, prof. emeritus, 1991—. Author: (with V.L. Roggli and S.D. Greenberg) Pathology of Asbestos Related Diseases, 1993; contbr. numerous articles to profl. publs. Fellow Am. Coll. Chest Physicians, Coll. Am. Pathologists; mem. AAAS, Am. Thoracic Soc., Am. Soc. Exptl. Pathology, Am. Assn. Pathologists and Bacteriologists, Internat. Acad. Pathology, Royal Soc. Health. Unitarian. Office: PO Box 3712 Davison Bldg Durham NC 27710 *The innovative idea is the essential commodity of the academic life. Origins of such ideas are varied but for me usually begin with realization that an existing concept does not adequately explain observed phenomena. When direct reasoning does not produce a new, better concept, the problem is put aside. Weeks later a return to the question often promptly reveals a logical new solution which has arisen without conscious effort. Of course, this must then be subjected to investigation to be either confirmed or refuted.*

PRATT, RICHARD HOUGHTON, physics educator; b. N.Y.C., May 5, 1934; s. Karl Chapman and Gertrude (Gennis) P.; m. Elizabeth Ann Glass, Nov. 1, 1958; children—Jonathan Peter, Kathryn Eileen, Mary Caroline, Paul Chapman. A.B., U. Chgo., 1952, S.M., 1955, Ph.D., 1959. Rsch. assoc. Stanford U., 1959-61, asst. prof., 1961-64; assoc. prof. physics U. Pitts., 1964-69, prof., 1969—, acad. dean semester at sea, fall 1984, adminstrv. dean, spring 1990; program dir. theoretical physics NSF, Washington, 1987-89; cons. Lawrence Livermore Nat. Lab.; prin. investigator Dept. Energy, NSF. Fellow Am. Phys. Soc. (chmn. com. internat. sci. affairs 1993), AAAS; mem. Sierra Club (chmn. Pa. chpt. 1976-80, v.p. Appalachian region 1982-84), Internat. Radiation Physics Soc. (sec. 1985—), Phi Beta Kappa, Sigma Xi. Achievements include research in atomic theory, including photoelectric effect, bremsstrahlung, x-ray scattering; applications to atomic processes in plasmas. Home: 1131 Shady Ave Pittsburgh PA 15232-2809

PRATT, RICHARDSON, JR., retired college president; b. N.Y.C., Mar. 25, 1923; s. Richardson and Laura C. (Parsons) P.; m. Mary Esterbrook Offutt, Aug. 12, 1944; children: Laura Pratt Gregg, Thomas R., David. O. A.B., Williams Coll., 1946, LL.D. (hon.), 1978; M.B.A., Harvard U., 1948; LL.D. (hon.), St Joseph, 1984. Econ. analyst, sec. com. on human relations Exxon Co., 1948-52, dist. mktg. mgr., 1953-63, mktg. planning and evaluation, 1964-71; chmn. Charles Pratt & Co., Inc., 1971—; pres. Pratt Inst., Bklyn., 1972-90; bd. dirs. Dime Savs. Bank N.Y., Bklyn. Union Gas Co.; mayor Village of Lloyd Harbor (N.Y.), 1983—. Trustee Near East Found., Fedn. Protestant Welfare Agys.; mem. governing bd. Bklyn. Bot. Gardens, treas., 1996; chmn. bd. dirs. Greenwood Cemetary. With USNR, 1943-46. Presbyterian. Home: 30 Dock Hollow Rd Cold Spring Harbor NY 11724-1002 Office: Charles Pratt & Co Inc 355 Lexington Ave New York NY 10017-6603

PRATT, ROBERT CRANFORD, political scientist, educator; b. Montreal, Que., Can., Oct. 8, 1926; s. Robert Goodwin and Henrietta (Freeman) P.; m. Renate Hecht, July 15, 1956; children—Gerhard, Marcus, Anna. BA, McGill U., Montreal, 1947; postgrad., Inst. Etudes Politique, Paris, 1948; M. Phil. (Rhodes scholar), Oxford U., Eng., 1952. Lectr. McGill U., 1952-54, 56-58, Makerere U., Uganda, 1954-56; research officer Oxford Inst. Commonwealth Studies, 1958-60; prin. Univ. Coll., Dar-es-Salaam, Tanzania, 1961-65; chmn. internat. studies program U. Toronto, Ont., Can., 1966-71; prof. polit. sci. U. Toronto, 1966—; spl. asst. to pres., Tanzania, 1965, 69; research fellow Internat. Devel. Research Centre, 1978; commonwealth vis. prof. U. London, 1979-80; dir. Research Project on Western Middle Powers and Global Poverty, 1985-89; vis. fellow Devel. Ctr. Orgn. for Econ. Cooperation and Devel., Paris, 1986-87. Author: (with Anthony Low) Buganda and British Overrule, 1960, The Critical Phase in Tanzania, Nyerere and the Emergence of a Socialist Strategy, 1976, Towards Socialism in Tanzania, 1979, (with Robert Matthews) Human Rights in Canadian Foreign Policy, 1988, Internationalism Under Strain: The North-South Policies of Canada, The Netherlands, Norway and Sweden, 1989; (with Roger Hutchinson) Christian Faith and Economic Justice: A Canadian Perspective, 1989); Middle Power Internationalism: The North-South Dimension, 1990, Canadian International Development Assistance Policies: An Appraisal, 1994. Recipient Killam award Can. Council, 1968. Fellow Royal Soc. Can.; mem. Can. Polit. Sci. Assn., Can. African Studies Assn. (past pres.), Can. Assn. for Study of Internat. Devel. (exec. coun.), Ecumenical Forum Can. (past chmn.). Mem. New Democratic Party. Mem. United Ch. Canada. Home: 205 Cottingham St, Toronto, ON Canada M4V 1C4 Office: U Toronto, Dept Polit Sci, Toronto, ON Canada M5S 1A1

PRATT, ROBERT WINDSOR, lawyer; b. Findlay, Ohio, Mar. 6, 1950; s. John Windsor and Isabelle (Vance) P.; m. Catherine Camak Baker, Sept. 3, 1977; children: Andrew Windsor, David Camak, James Robert. AB, Wittenberg U., Springfield, Ohio, 1972; JD, Yale U., 1975. Bar: Ill. 1975, U.S. Dist. Ct. (no. dist.) Ill. 1976, U.S. Ct. Appeals (fed. cir.) 1984, U.S. Dist. Ct. (we. dist.) Mich. 1995. Assoc. Keck, Mahin & Cate, Chgo., 1975-81, ptnr., 1981—. Bd. dirs. Chgo. region ARC, 1985—, vice chmn., 1988-92, chmn., 1992—, bd. dirs. Mid-Am. chpt., 1992—. Mem. ABA, Chgo. Bar Assn., Yale Club (Chgo.). Office: Keck Mahin & Cate 77 W Wacker Dr Ste 4900 Chicago IL 60601-1629

PRATT, ROSALIE REBOLLO, harpist, educator; b. N.Y.C., Dec. 4, 1933; d. Antonio Ernesto and Eleanor Gertrude (Gibney) Rebollo; Mus.B., Manhattanville Coll., 1954; Mus.M., Pius XII Inst. Fine Arts, Florence, Italy, 1955; Ed.D., Columbia U., 1976; m. George H. Mortimer, Esquire, Apr. 22, 1987; children: Francesca Christina Rebollo-Sborgi, Alessandra Maria Pratt Jones. Prin. harpist N.J. Symphony Orch., 1963-65; soloist Mozart Haydn Festival, Avery Fisher Hall, N.Y.C., 1968; tchr. music public schs., Bloomfield and Montclair, N.J., 1962-73; mem. faculty Montclair State Coll., 1973-79; prof. Brigham Young U., Provo, Utah, 1984—, coord. grad. studies dept. music, 1985-87.; biofeedback and neurofeedback rsch. specialist, 1993—. U.S. chair 1st internat. arts medicine leadership conf., Tokyo Med. Coll., 1993. Co-author: Elementary Music for All Learners, 1980; editor Internat. Jour. Arts Medicine, 1991—, (proceedings) 2d, 3d, 4th Internat. Symposia Music Edn. for Handicapped; contbr. articles to Am. Harp Jour., Music Educators Jour., others. Fulbright grantee, 1979; Myron Taylor scholar, 1954. Mem. Am. Harp Soc. (Outstanding Service award 1973), AAUP (co-chmn. legis. rels. com. N.J. 1978-79), Internat. Soc. Music Edn. (chair commn. music in spl. edn., music therapy, and medicine 1985—), Internat. Soc. Music in Medicine (v.p. 1993—), Internat. Assn. of Music for the Handicapped (co-founder, exec. dir., jour. editor), Coll. Music Soc., Music Educators Nat. Conf., Brigham Young U. Grad. Coun., Phi Kappa Phi, Sigma Alpha Iota. Office: Brigham Young U Harris Fine Arts Ctr Provo UT 84602 *Personal philosophy: I believe in offering my students what I have learned from the educational heroes in my life, the teachers whose example is the reason I prepare my classes carefully and thoughtfully. What I am and what I cherish most in life is also the result of a grandmother and father, neither of whose formal education went beyond the third grade, but whose wisdom was timeless.*

PRATT, SHARON L., secondary and elementary education educator; b. Terrell, Tex., Dec. 5, 1946; d. Cecil and Bobbie Lou (Hodge) Brown; m. John E. Pratt, Aug. 31, 1968; 1 child, Randolph W. BS in Edn., U. North Tex., 1969, MS, 1980; ESL cert., East Tex. U., 1987. Cert. elem., English tchr., reading specialist, ESL tchr., Tex. Tchr. Mesquite (Tex.) Ind. Sch. Dist.; elem. tchr. sci. U.S. Govt., Manama, Bahrain; secondary tchr. McDonald Mid. Sch., Mesquite; tchr. ESL and reading improvement North Mesquite High Sch., 1991-92, 96—; adj. faculty devel. reading Cedar Valley C.C., Lancaster, Tex., 1992-95; secondary tchr. Robert T. Hill Mid. Sch. Dallas Ind. Sch. Dist., 1995—; tchr. ESL and adult edn. classes Dallas Ind. Sch. Dist.; instr. ESL class Eastfield Community Coll., Mesquite. Mem. TESOL, Internat. Reading Assn., Tex. State Reading Assn. Home: 1001 Villa Siete Mesquite TX 75181-1237 Office: North Mesquite High Sch 18201 LBJ Fwy Mesquite TX 75150

PRATT, SUSAN G., architect; b. Kansas City, Mo., Sept. 24, 1951; d. John Bohman and Alice Marguerite (Harris) Grow; m. W. Scott Pratt; children: David, Alice; stepchildren: David, Laura. BArch, Kans. State U., 1973. Registered architect, Mich., Wis. Project arch. Skidmore Owings & Merrill, Chgo., 1973-78, 83-85; project arch. Murphy/Jahn, Inc., Chgo., 1978-82, 86—, now v.p.; sr. project arch. Froelich & Marik, L.A., 1982-83, Marshall & Brown, Kansas City, 1985-86. Prin. works include New World Ctr., Hong Kong, Group Repertory Theatre, North Hollywood, Calif., Bi State Indsl. Park, Kansas City, Mo., State of Ill. Ctr., Chgo., John Deere Harvester Works Office Facility, Moline, Ill., Two Liberty Pl., Phila., Livingston Pla., Bklyn., North Loop Block 37, Chgo., 1st and Broadway, L.A., Kudamm 119, Berlin, Cologne/Bonn Airport, Cologne, Jeddah Airport, Saudi Arabia, Sony European Hdqs., Berlin, Munich Airport Ctr., 21st Century Tower, Shanghai, China. Mem. AIA (corp. mem.). Office: Murphy/Jahn 35 E Wacker Dr Chicago IL 60601

PRATT, VAUGHAN RONALD, computer engineering educator; b. Melbourne, Australia, Apr. 12, 1944; s. Ronald Victor and Marjorie (Mirams) P.; m. Margot Frances Koster, Feb. 2, 1969; children: Jennifer Katherine, Jacqueline Andrea. BSc with honors, Sydney U., Australia, 1967, MSc, 1970; PhD, Stanford U., 1972. From asst. to assoc. prof. MIT, Cambridge, 1972-82; head of research Sun Microsystems Inc., Mountain View, Calif., 1983-85; prof. Stanford (Calif.) U., 1981—; pres. Triangle Concepts Inc., Palo Alto, Calif., 1988—. Author: Shellsort and Sorting Networks, 1979. Mem. IEEE, Am. Math. Soc., Assn. for Computing Machinery, Assn. for Symbolic Logic. Office: Stanford U Dept Computer Sci Stanford CA 94305-9045

PRATT, WILLIAM CROUCH, JR., English language educator, writer; b. Shawnee, Okla., Oct. 5, 1927; s. William Crouch and Irene (Johnston) P.; m. Anne Cullen Rich, Oct. 2, 1954; children: Catherine Cullen, William Stuart, Randall Johnston. B.A., U. Okla., 1949; M.A., Vanderbilt U., 1951, Ph.D., 1957. Rotary Internat. fellow U. Glasgow, Scotland, 1951-52; instr. English Vanderbilt U., 1955-57, Miami U., Oxford, Ohio, 1957-59; asst. prof. Miami U., 1959-64, assoc. prof., dir. Freshman English, 1964-68, prof., 1964-90; Fulbright-Hays lectr. Am. lit., prof. Am. lit. Univ. Coll., Dublin, Eire, 1975-76; resident scholar Miami U. European Ctr., Luxembourg, fall 1976; lectr. Yeats Internat. Summer Sch., Sligo, Eire, 1979, 81, 82, 83; writer-in-residence Tyrone Guthrie Ctr., County Monaghan, Ireland, summer 1992, 96. Author: The Imagist Poem, 1963, The Fugitive Poets, 1965, rev. edit., 1991, The College Writer, 1969, College Days at Old Miami, 1984, The Influence of French Symbolism on Modern American Poetry, 1985, Miami Poets, 1988, Homage to Imagism, 1992, The Big Ballad Jamboree, 1996, Singing the Chaos: Madness and Wisdom in Modern Poetry, 1996; contbr. essays, translations, poems, revs. to lit. jours., books. Served to lt. USNR, 1953-55. Mem. MLA, Nat. Coun. Tchrs. English (Ohio awards chmn. 1967-69), Coll. Conf. on Composition, Communication, Internat. Contemporary Lit. and Theatre Soc. (program chmn. 1983, 88), Soc. Study So. Lit. (sec. Ezra Pound Internat. Conf. 1993-97), Phi Beta Kappa, Sigma Alpha Epsilon, Omicron Delta Kappa. Republican. Home: 212 Oakhill Dr Oxford OH 45056-2710 *True happiness is to live in the understanding of what we love, the pursuit of what we believe in.*

PRATTE, LISE, lawyer, corporate secretary; b. Laval, Que., Can., May 16, 1950. LLB, Laval U., 1976; MBA, Montreal U., Que., Can., 1988. Bar: Que. Asst. sec. Malouf Inquiry Commn. on 21st Olympiad, 1977-79, Des Manoirs Sch. Bd., Terrebonne, Que., 1979-82; legal counsel for various corps., mgmt. cons., 1981-82; corp. sec., legal counsel Can. Arsenals Ltd., Le Gardeur, Que., 1982-85; asst. sec., legal counsel Imasco Ltd., Montreal, 1985-88; corp. sec. Bombardier Inc., Montreal, 1988—. Bd. dirs. La Fondation de L'Universite Laval. Mem. Can. Bar Assn., Que. Bar Assn., Inst. Chartered Secs. and Adminstrs., Can. Shareholders Svcs. Assn. (bd. dirs.), Am. Soc. Corp. Secs., Order of Chartered Adminstrs. Avocation: management. Office: Bombardier Inc/29th FL, 800 René-Lévesque Blvd W, Montreal, PQ Canada H3B 1Y8

PRATTE, LOUIS, judge; b. Quebec City, Que., Can., Nov. 29, 1926; s. Garon and Georgine (Rivard) P.; m. Charlotte Tremblay, July 2, 1953; children—Marie, Francois. Grad. Faculte de droit et des scis economiques, Laval U.; diplome d'etudes superieures en droit prive, U. Paris. Bar: Que. 1950. Mem. trial div. Fed. Ct. Can., 1971-73; judge Fed. Ct. Appeal, Ottawa, Ont., 1973—. Office: Fed Ct Appeal, Kent & Wellington Sts, Ottawa, ON Canada K1A OH9

PRATTE, ROBERT JOHN, lawyer; b. Victoria, B.C., Can., Feb. 14, 1948; s. Arthur Louis Jr. and Marie Bertha (Latremouille) P.; children from previous marriage: Merie Elise, Jessica Louise, Allison Adele; m. Erica Catherine Street, Oct. 20, 1984; 1 child, Chelsea Nicole. BA, Northwestern U., 1970; JD, Tulane U., 1976. Bar: Minn. 1976. Ptnr. Best & Flanagan, Mpls., 1976-84; ptnr. Briggs & Morgan, Mpls., 1985—, head mortgage banking group. Editor: Mortgage Lending in Minnesota—A Desktop Reference Guide, 1990. Ex-officio mem. Wilderness Inquiry, Minn.; pres. Twin Cities Northwestern U. Alumni Assn., 1978; active Westminster Presbyn. Ch., Mpls. Fellow Am. Coll. Mortgage Attys.; mem. ABA (real estate financing com. real property sect.), Minn. Bar Assn. (banking com.), Hennepin County Bar Assn., Mortgage Bankers Assn. Minn. (chmn. legal issues com. 1989-94), Calhoun Beach Club (exec. mem.), Minnetonka Country Club. Home: 19080 Carsonwood Ave Deephaven MN 55391 Office: Briggs & Morgan 2400 IDS Ctr 80 S 8th St Minneapolis MN 55402-2100 *Undertake with enthusiasm and pursue to completion the tasks that others are unwilling or unable to do. Never be satisfied with mediocrity. Surround yourself with those who are smarter than you and have the patience and judgement to let them succeed. Success can be measured by the hours you spend with your children-reading, fishing etc.*

PRATTER, GENE E. K., lawyer; b. Chgo., Feb. 25, 1949; d. Eugene Anthony and Laurel Marilyn (Dauer) Kreyche; m. Robert Lawrence Pratter, Oct. 21, 1978; children: Virginia Paige, Matthew Robert. BA, Stanford U., 1971; JD, U. Pa., 1975. Bar: Pa. 1975, U.S. Dist. Ct. (ea. dist.) Pa. 1975, U.S. Ct. Appeals (3d cir.) 1981. Assoc. Duane, Morris & Heckscher, Phila., 1975-83, ptnr., 1983—; judge pro tem Phila. Ct. Common Pleas, 1994—. Bd. overseers U. Pa. Law Sch., Phila., 1994—, lectr. Ctr. on Professionalism. Fund-raiser U. Pa. Law Sch. Contbr. articles to profl. jours. Mem. ABA (litigation sect. com. on ethics and professionalism 1995—), Def. Research Inst., Pa. Bar Assn., Phila. Bar Assn., Stanford U. Alumni Club (fund raiser, officer 1976-83). Republican. Roman Catholic. Office: Duane Morris & Heckscher Ste 4200 One Liberty Pl Philadelphia PA 19103

PRAUSNITZ, JOHN MICHAEL, chemical engineer, educator; b. Berlin, Jan. 7, 1928; came to U.S., 1937, naturalized, 1944; s. Paul Georg and Susi Prausnitz; m. Susan Prausnitz, June 10, 1956; children: Stephanie, Mark Robert. B Chem. Engring., Cornell U., 1950; MS, U. Rochester, 1951; Ph.D., Princeton, 1955; Dr. Ing., U. L'Aquila, 1983, Tech. U. Berlin, 1989; DSc, Princeton U., 1995. Mem. faculty U. Calif., Berkeley, 1955—, prof. chem. engring., 1963—; cons. to cryogenic, polymer, petroleum and petrochem. industries. Author: (with others) Computer Calculations for Multicomponent Vapor-Liquid Equilibria, 1967, (with P.L. Chueh) Computer Calculations for High-Pressure Vapor-Liquid Equilibria, 1968, Molecular Thermodynamics of Fluid-Phase Equilibria, 1969, 2d edit., 1986, (with others) Regular and Related Solutions, 1970, Properties of Gases and Liquids, 3d edit., 1977, 4th edit., 1987, Computer Calculations for Multicomponent Vapor-Liquid and Liquid-Liquid Equilibria, 1980; contbr. to profl. jours. Recipient Alexander von Humboldt Sr. Scientist award, 1976, Carl von Linde Gold Meml. medal German Inst. for Cryogenics, 1987, Solvay prize Solvay Found. for Chem. Scis., 1990, Corcoran award Am. Soc. for Engring. Edn., 1991, D.L. Katz award Gas Processors Assn., 1992, award in petroleum chem. Am. Chem. Soc., 1995; named W.K. Lewis lectr. MIT, 1993; Guggenheim fellow, 1962, 73, fellow Inst. Advanced Study, Berlin, 1985; Miller rsch. prof., 1966, 78; Christensen fellow St. Catherine's Coll. Oxford U., 1994, Erskine fellow U. Canterbury Christchurch, New Zealand, 1996. Mem. AIChE (Colburn award 1962, Walker award 1967, Inst. Lectr. award 1994), Am. Chem. Soc. (E.V. Murphree award 1979, Petroleum Chemistry Rsch. award 1995), NAE, NAS, Am. Acad. Arts and Scis. Office: U Calif 308 Gilman Hall Berkeley CA 94720

PRAVEL, BERNARR ROE, lawyer; b. Feb. 10, 1924. BSChemE, Rice U., 1947; JD, George Washington U., 1951. Bar: D.C. 1951, Tex. 1951, U.S. Supreme Ct. 1951. Ptnr. Pravel, Hewitt, Kimball and Krieger, Houston, 1970—. Patent editor George Washington U. Law Rev., 1950. Precinct chmn. Houston Rep. Com., 1972-74. Served to lt. (j.g.) USNR. Fellow Am. Bar Found., Tex. Bar Found.; mem. ABA (chair intellectual property sect. 1991-92), Tex. Bar Assn. (chmn. patent, trademark sect. 1968-69, bd. dirs. 1976-79, Outstanding Contbn. 1982), Nat. Coun. Patent Law (chmn. 1970-71), Am. Intellectual Property Law Assn. (pres. 1983-84), Houston Intellectual Property Law Assn. (pres. 1983-84, Outstanding Svc. award 1986), Order of Coif, Kiwanis, Tau Beta Pi. Home: 10806 Oak Hollow St Houston TX 77024-3017 Office: Pravel Hewitt Kimball and Krieger 1177 West Loop S Fl 10 Houston TX 77027

PRAW, ALBERT Z., lawyer; b. L.A., Apr. 9, 1948. AB, U. Calif., Berkeley, 1969; JD, UCLA, 1972. Bar: Calif. 1972, U.S. Dist. Ct. (ctrl. dist.) Calif. 1972. Ptnr. Hayutin, Rubinroit, Praw & Kupeitzky, 1979-87, Sidley & Austin, 1987-89, 92-94; sr. v.p., gen. counsel Kaufman and Broad Home Corp., 1989-92; sr. v.p. real estate Kaufman & Broad Home Corp., L.A., 1994—. Mem. ABA (mem. corp., banking and bus. law sects., real property, probate and trust law sects., mem. REA rev. subcom. on real property fin. 1982-83), State Bar Calif. (sr. v.p. and gen. counsel), L.A. County Bar Assn. (mem. bus. and corp., real property sects.), Beverly Hills Bar Assn. Office: Kaufman & Broad Home Corp 12th Fl 10990 Wilshire Blvd Fl 7 Los Angeles CA 90024*

PRAWAT, RICHARD S., education educator; b. Paw Paw, Mich., Dec. 2, 1943; s. Edwin H. and Jessie M. (Reagan) P.; m. Dorothy M. Gallagher; children: Nicole M., Theodore R., Andrew M. BA, Mich. State U., 1966, PhD, 1972. Instr. and rsch. assoc. Macalester Coll., St. Paul, Minn., 1970-72; asst. and assoc. prof. Okla. State Univ., Stillwater, 1972-78; assoc. dir., sr. rsch. assoc. Mich. State U., E. Lansing, 1982-86, assoc. dir., 1985-87, chair person (counseling, educational psychology, spl. edn.), 1991—; presenter numerous ednl. confs. and seminars. Contbr. more than 100 articles to profl. jours. Grantee: Rsch. Found. Okla. State U., 1973, 1976, 77, NIH, 1974, 75, Nat. Inst. Edn. 1980, 82, 84, 86, Ford Found., 1986, U.S. Dept. Edn., 1986, 90, NSF, 1990. Home: 167 Newman Williamston MI 48895 Office: Mich State Univ 449 Erickson East Lansing MI 48824

PRAY, DONALD GEORGE, retired aerospace engineer; b. Troy, N.Y., Jan. 19, 1928; s. George Emerson and Jansje Cornelia (Ouwejan) P.; m. Betty Ann Williams, Oct. 1, 1950; children: Jennifer Loie, Jonathan Cornelius, Judy Karen, Jeffrey Donald. BA in Physics, Tex. Christian U., 1955; MS in Mech. Engring., So. Meth. U., 1979. Sr. structures engr. Gen. Dynamics Corp., Ft. Worth, 1955-62, 67-84; engring. specialist LTV Astronautics Corp., Dallas, 1962-65, sr. engring. specialist, 1989-91; aero. group engr. space div. Chrysler Corp., New Orleans, 1965-67; V-22 group engr. Bell Helicopter Textron, Ft. Worth, 1984-89; E-3 structural integrity program mgr. Tinker AFB, 1991-95; prin. Donald G. Pray, Cons., Ft. Worth, 1959-61. Contbr. articles to tech. publs. Chmn. bd. trustees Cope Cemetery Assn., Johnson County, Tex., 1987—; corps comdr., v.p. bd. dirs. Masqueraders Drum and Bugle Corps, New Orleans, 1965-67; scoutmaster, cubmaster, explorer advisor, dist. com. chmn. Longhorn coun. Boy Scouts Am., Ft. Worth, 1967-75. Recipient Grand Championship Mardi Gras award, 1966. Mem. ASME, NSPE, NRA, SAR, Acoustical Soc. Am., Soc. Mayflower Descendants Tex. (sec. 1983-85, 88-91, gov. 1991-93, dep. gov. gen. 1993—, mem. gen. soc. edn. com. 1990—, chmn. Dallas colony scholarship com. 1988—, gov. Dallas/Ft. Worth colony 1995—), Ft. Worth Rifle and Pistol Club (marksman 1980), Train Collectors Assn., Ft. Worth Geneal. Soc. (bd. dirs. 1993-94), Masons, Scottish Rite, Shriners, Sigma Pi Sigma, Pi Mu Epsilon. Baptist. Achievements include analytical engineering contributions to numerous aircraft and spacecraft programs including B-36, B-58, NX-2, Robot, Dynasoar, Scout, Apollo, F/FB-111, F-16, V-22 Osprey, C-17, E-3 AWACS. Home and Office: 3628 Wedgway Dr Fort Worth TX 76133-2135 Home: Lazy Acres Farm 5750 Lazy Bend Rd Brock TX 76066 *Learn what talents you have been blessed with; then exercise them for the betterment of humanity.*

PRAY, LLOYD CHARLES, geologist, educator; b. Chgo., June 25, 1919; s. Allan Theron and Helen (Palmer) P.; m. Carrel Myers, Sept. 14, 1946; children: Lawrence Myers, John Allan, Kenneth Palmer, Douglas Carrel. B.A., Carleton Coll., 1941; M.S., Calif. Inst. Tech., 1943, Ph.D. (NRC fellow 1946-49), 1952. Geologist Magnolia Petroleum Co., summer 1942, U.S. Geol. Survey, 1943-44; hydrographic officer USN, 1944-46; Geologist U.S. Geol. Survey, 1946-56 part time; instr. to assoc. prof. geology Calif. Inst. Tech., 1949-56; sr. research geologist Denver Research Ctr., Marathon Oil Co., 1956-62, research assoc., 1962-68; prof. geology U. Wis., Madison, 1968-88; emeritus prof. geology, 1989—; short course vis. prof. U. Tex., 1964, U. Colo., 1967, U. Miami, 1971, U. Alta., 1969, Colo. Sch. Mines, 1985; vis. scientist Imperial Coll. Sci. and Tech., London, 1977, U. Calif. Santa Cruz, 1987, Nat. Park Svc. Geology panel, 1993. Author articles sedimentary carbonates, the Permian Reef complex, stratigraphy and structural geology So. N.M. and W. Tex., porosity of carbonate facies, Calif. rare earth mineral deposits. Pres. Colo. Diabetes Assn., 1963-67, v.p., 1968; mem. adv. panel earth scis. NSF, 1973-76. Served as hydrographic officer USNR, 1944-46. Named Layman of Year Am. Diabetes Assn., 1968; recipient Disting. Teaching award U. Wis. Madison, 1988; Disting. Achievement citation Carleton Coll., 1991. Fellow Geol. Soc. Am. (rsch. grants com. 1965-67, com. on nominations 1973, com.Penrose medal 1979-81); mem. Am. Assn. Petroleum Geologists (rsch. com. 1958-61, lectr. continuing edn. program 1966-69, Matson trophy 1967, continuing edn. com. 1978-80, disting. lectr. 1986-87, 87-88), Soc. Sedimentary Geologists (hon. life mem. Permian Basin sect., hon. mem. internat. soc., sec.-treas. 1961-63, v.p. 1966-67, pres. 1969-70), Am. Geol. Inst. (edn. com. 1966-68, ho. bd. dels. 1970-72), Phi Beta Kappa. Office: Univ Wis Dept Geology Madison WI 53706

PRAY, MERLE EVELYN, nurse psychotherapist, educator; b. Washington, Vt., Apr. 19, 1931; d. Clifton Clough and Dorothy (Wadleigh) P. Diploma in nursing, N.H. Sch. Nursing, Concord, 1952; BSN, Loyola U., Chgo., 1977; MS, U. Ill., Chgo., 1983. RN, Ill.; cert. in addictions nursing Nat. Nurses Soc. on Addictions; cert. clin. specialist in adult psychiat. and mental health nursing ANA. Community placement coord. Ill. Dept. Mental Health and Devel. Disability, Chgo., 1977, mental health adminstr., planning area coord., 1978-81; head nurse VA West Side Med. Ctr., Chgo., 1984, clin. specialist, 1985—; adj. clin. instr. psychiat. nursing U. Ill., 1986—. Mem. ANA, Nat. Nurses Soc. on Addictions, Am. Psychiat. Nurses Assn., Ill. Nurses Assn. Home: 175 E Delaware Pl Chicago IL 60611-1756 Office: VA West Side Med Ctr 820 S Damen Ave Chicago IL 60612-3728

PRAY, RALPH MARBLE, III, lawyer; b. San Diego, June 7, 1938; s. Ralph Marble Jr. and Doris (Thomson) P.; m. Karen L. Pray (div. May 1988); children: Matthew Thomson, Kristen Leigh; m. Sandra Anne Shaw, June 7, 1988. BS, U. Redlands, 1960; JD, U. Calif., San Francisco, 1967. Bar: Calif. 1967, U.S. Dist. Ct. (so. dist.) Calif. 1968, U.S. Supreme Ct. 1972, U.S. Dist. Ct. (ea. dist.) Calif. 1985, U.S. Dist. Ct. (ctrl. dist.) Calif. 1989, U.S. Dist. Ct. (no. dist.) Calif. 1992. Assoc. Gray, Cary, Ware & Friedenrich and predecessor, San Diego, 1967-73, ptnr., 1973—; mem. mgmt. com. Gray, Cary, Ames & Frye, San Diego, 1975-80; arbiter Superior Ct., San Diego, 1984—. Lt. USN, 1960-64. Mem. ABA, SAR, NRA, Calif. Bar Assn., Am. Arbitration Soc. (arbiter), San Diego Zool. Soc., Ducks Unltd., Thurston Soc., Rotary Club of Coronado, Calif., Order of Coif. Republican. Episcopalian. Home: 535 C Ave Coronado CA 92118-1824 Office: Gray Cary Ware & Friedenrich 1700 1st Interstate Plz 401 B St San Diego CA 92101-4223

PREBLE, LAURENCE GEORGE, lawyer; b. Denver, Apr. 24, 1939; s. George Enos and Ruth (Jewett) P.; m. Deborah Joan Horton, Aug. 24, 1963; children—Robin Lee, Randall Laurence. B in Petroleum Refining Engring., Colo. Sch. Mines, 1961; J.D. cum laude, Loyola U., Los Angeles, 1968. Bar: Calif. 1969, N.Y. 1987, U.S. Dist. Ct. (cen. dist.) Calif. 1969, D.C. 1983. Assoc. firm O'Melveny & Myers, Los Angeles, 1968-76; ptnr. O'Melveny & Myers, 1976—; adj. prof. law Southwestern U., 1970-75, Loyola U. of L.A.

Sch. Law, 1984-92, Fordham U. Sch. Law, 1992—, Calif. Continuing Edn. of the Bar; lectr., author Practicing Law Inst. Trustee Harvey Mudd Coll., 1991-94, Citizens Bidget Commn. N.Y.C., 1994—. Mem. Los Angeles County Bar Assn. (chmn. real property sect. 1979-80), Calif. Bar Assn. (mem. exec. com. real property sect.), ABA, Am. Coll. Real Estate Lawyers (bd. govs. 1986—), Anglo-Am. Real Property Inst., La Canada-Flintridge C. of C. (pres. 1974-75), Loyola Law Sch. Alumni Assn. (pres. 1978). Office: O'Melveny & Myers 153 E 53rd St Fl 54 New York NY 10022-4611

PRECHT, WILLIAM FREDERICK, environmental specialist; b. N.Y.C., Dec. 26, 1956; s. Frederick C. and Ursula I. (Sennholt) P.; m. Joni Ferden, July 27, 1991; children: Lindsey Leona, Chandler Ilsa. BA in Geology, Marine Sci., SUNY, 1978; MS in Earth Sci., Adelphi U., 1981; MA in Marine Geology and Geophysics, U. Miami, 1994; postgrad. in ocean scis., Nova U. Cert. petroleum geologist; registered petroleum geologist, Pa. Staff geologist Phillips Petroleum Co., Denver, 1981-84; sr. staff geologist Champlin Petroleum Co., Denver, 1984-86; prin. rsch. scientist Reef Resources & Assocs., Billings, Mont., 1986-87; sr. rsch. scientist Reef Resources & Assocs., Miami, Fla., 1987-93; sr. environ. specialist Consulting Engring. & Sci., Miami, 1993-94; environ. dir. Consul-Tech. Engring., Inc., Miami, 1994—; adj. faculty marine scis. Northeastern U., 1987—. Contbr. over 65 articles and abstracts to profl. jours; invited lectr., speaker to over 50 univs. and profl. assns. Pres. Miami Geol. Soc. 1990-91. Recipient fellowship U. Miami, Texaco, 1987-88. Mem. Internat. Soc. for Reef Studies, Soc. for Sedimentary Geology (chmn. carbonate rsch. group 1992-94, Presentation Sci. Excellence award 1985), Am. Assn. Petroleum Geologists (adv. bd. treatise on petroleum geology 1987—, coord. vis. geologists com. 1987—, soc. del. 1990-93), Am. Inst. Profl. Geologists (cert. profl. geologist). Democrat. Achievements include: deciphered the history of reef growth and sea level rise in Belize; investigated the effects of deforestation and runoff on lagoonal reefs in southern Belize; monitors the long term health of Carribean Coral Reefs; designed and implemented large, successful wetland mitigation projects throughout south Fla. Avocations: fly fishing, baseball, ice hockey, skiing, cycling. Home: 7310 Ponciana Ct Miami Lakes FL 33014 Office: Consul-Tech Engring Inc 10570 NW 27th St # 101 Miami FL 33172

PRECOPIO, FRANK MARIO, chemical company executive; b. Providence, Mar. 12, 1925; s. Domenic and Antonetta (Altomari) P.; m. Rita Marie Carr, Apr. 28, 1956; children—Thomas J., Frank J., Michael J. B.Sc. in Chemistry summa cum laude, Brown U., 1948; Ph.D., Yale U., 1952. Research assoc. Gen. Electric Research Ctr., Schenectady, 1951-55; mgr. research and devel. Gen. Electric Co., Erie, Pa., 1955-61; dir. research and devel. wire and cable dept. Gen. Electric Co., Bridgeport, Conn., 1961-66; v.p. tech. Amchem Products, Ambler, Pa., 1966-83; exec. v.p. Henkel Corp., Ambler, 1983-89; ret., 1989. Patentee in field of organic chemistry and high temperature polymers. Trustee Alfred and Mary Douty Found., Phila., 1972-91, William Jeanes Meml. Library, Whitemarsh, Pa., 1968-74. Served to lt. (j.g.) USNR, 1943-46. Recipient Mordica award Wire Assn. Internat., 1983. Fellow Am. Inst. Chemists; mem. Am. Chem. Soc. (chmn. Erie sect. 1958), Sigma Xi. Republican. Roman Catholic. Avocations: antique pewter collecting; antique furniture refinishing; sailing; gardening. *

PRECOURT, GEORGE AUGUSTINE, government official; b. Hartford, Conn., July 26, 1934; s. Charles A. and Antoinette (Gauthier) P.; m. Alma E. Hall, Aug. 28, 1954; children: Debra Ann, Carol Anne, David Charles, Kenneth George. Student, LaSalle U., 1952-55. Prodn. and inventory mgr. Beacon Machine Co., E. Hartford, Conn., 1960-65; purchasing/prodn. control mgr. Redington Counters, Windsor, Conn., 1965-73; gen. mgr. Able Coil & Electronics, Kensington, Conn., 1973-74; chief industries Conn. Svcs. for the Blind, Wethersfield, 1974—, commr., exec. dir., 1989—; regional dir. Nat. Industry for the Blind, Wayne, N.J., 1983—; chmn. New Eng. Conf. Vending Facility Dirs., 1982—; v.p. sales Bernstein Leibstone Assocs., Inc., N.Y.C.; exec. v.p. Tech. Mktg., Inc., Plantation, Fla. Inventor in field; contbr. articles to profl. jours. Vice chmn. E. Hartford Pub. Bldg. Commn., 1971—; chmn. Dem. Town Com. Dist. 6, E. Hartford, 1970-74; del. Dem. State Conv., 1960. With U.S. Army, 1950-52. Named Lion of the Yr., 1972; Spl. Citation, U.S. Pres., 1974. Mem. Am. Assn. Workers for the Blind, Prodn. and Inventory Control Soc., C. of C., Career Edn. Placement Assn. (bd. dir.), Lions, Franco War Vets. Episcopalian. Home: 29 Laurel Ter Manchester CT 06040-6833 Office: State Svcs for the Blind Office of Exec Dir 170 Ridge Rd Wethersfield CT 06109-1044

PREDDY, RAYMOND RANDALL, newspaper publisher; b. Texarkana, Ark., Feb. 1, 1940; s. Raymond Watson and Dorothy Belle (Long) P.; m. Sarah Elizabeth Mitchell, Nov. 20, 1965; children: Lewis, Tiffany. B.S., Northwestern U., 1961, M.S. in Journalism, 1962. Copy editor Louisville Courier-Jour., 1965-69; with Dayton (Ohio) Daily News, 1969-74, asst. city editor, 1971, met. editor, 1971-74; systems mgr. Dayton Newspapers, Inc., 1974-76; bus. mgr. Waco (Tex.) Tribune-Herald, 1976-77, asst. pub., 1977-78; pub. Waco Tribune-Herald, 1978—. Pres. Waco United Way, 1986, Waco Found., 1984-86, Waco Symphony Assn., 1985-86. Served with USN, 1962-65; capt. Res. (ret.). Named Tex. Newspaper Leader of 1994; recipient Pat Taggart award from Tex. Daily Newspaper Assn. Presbyterian. Club: Rotary. Office: Waco-Tribune-Herald 900 Franklin Ave Waco TX 76701-1906

PREDESCU, VIOREL N., electrical engineer; b. Craiova, Dolj, Romania, Sept. 14, 1950; came to U.S., 1986; naturalized, 1993; s. Nicolae I. and Constanta (Ciobanescu) P.; m. Rodica G. Apostoleanu, Sept. 14, 1974; 1 child, Dan Paul. MSEE, Poly. Inst., Bucharest, Romania, 1974. Registered profl. engr., Calif., Nev. Elec. engr. Romania, 1974-86; helper electrician CESSOP Electric Constrn., Tustin, Calif., 1986; elec. designer, drafter Sierra Pacific Tech. Svcs., Inc., Laguna Hills, Calif., 1986; asst. engr. Boyle Engring. Corp., Newport Beach, Calif., 1986-88; project engr. Hallis Engring., Inc., L.A., 1988-89; profl. engr. Elec. Bldg. Systems, Inc., North Hollywood, Calif., 1989-91; mgr. of elec. dept. William J. Yang Assocs., Inc., Burbank, Calif., 1991—. Mem. NSPE, IEEE, N.Y. Acad. Scis. Republican. Christian Orthodox. Achievements include electrical design for large variety of projects: commercial Shanghai: World Trade/Plaza Center, Far East International Building, Dong Hai Plaza Complex, So. Calif. Gas Co. Hdqrs., Torrance, Calif., industrial pump stations, water and wastewater plants, industrial buildings, medium voltage 5-35kv distribution systems, uninterruptible power systems for large computer centers, caltrans, MTA tank farms and large maintenance buildings, Calif. State U. Long Beach Sports Arena (The Pyramid), NASA facilities: JPL, Goldstone Space Center & Edwards, military facilities. Home: 12426 Lemay St North Hollywood CA 91606-1312

PREECE, NORMA, executive secretary; b. Kaysville, Utah, May 19, 1922; d. Walter and Wilma (Witt) Buhler; m. Joseph Franklin Preece, July 26, 1946 (dec. 1991); children: Terry Joe, Shannette Preece Keeler. Grad. high sch., Kaysville, 1940. Telephone operator Mountain States Telephone & Telegraph Co., Kaysville, 1940-43; clk. Civil Svc., Ogden, Utah, 1943-50; newspaper corr. Davis County Clipper, North Davis County, Utah, 1954-85; pub. communication dir. Latter-day Saints Ch., Kaysville, 1988-89; exec. sec. Kaysville Area C. of C., Kaysville, 1985-90; stake missionary Latter-Day Saints Ch., Kaysville, 1991—. Publicity chmn. Boy Scouts Am., Kaysville, 1965-69, Am. Cancer Dr., Davis County, 1967, Kaysville Civic Assn., 1960-80; mem. Utah Press Women Assn., Salt Lake City, 1973-75; active publicity Utah Congress PTA, Salt Lake City, 1977—; judge FFA, Davis County, 1968; campaign com. mem. Rep. Party, Davis County, 1990; ordinance worker LDS Temple, Ogden, Utah, 1992-94, Bountiful, Utah, 1995—; co-chmn. Kaysville City Centennial, 1950. Recipient award for outstanding contbn. Davis High Sch., Kaysville, 1979, Total Citizen award Utah C. of C., 1988, Disting. Svc. award Kaysville Arts Coun., 1981; Outstanding Svc. award Kaysville Jaycees, 1972, Disting. Svc. award, 1985, Cmty. Unsung Hero award City of Kaysville, 1994; named Citizen of Yr., City of Kaysville, 1985. Mem. Lit. Club (Athena chpt., sec. 1984, 87, v.p. 1989, pres. 1990), Fine Arts Club (pres. 1964, sec. 1994). Mem. LDS Ch. Avocations: writing, research, reading, golf, needlework. Home: 347 E 200 N Kaysville UT 84037-2039 Office: Kaysville Area C of C 44 E 100 N Kaysville UT 84037-1910

PREECE, WARREN EVERSLEIGH, editor; b. Norwalk, Conn., Apr. 17, 1921; s. Everett Lowe and Ethel (Miles) P.; m. Deborah Weeks, July 12, 1947; children: Scott Everett, Mark William, Thayer Evelyn. BA cum laude, Dartmouth Coll., 1943; MA, Columbia U., 1947. Instr. English, U. Chgo., 1947-49; reporter Norwalk Hour, 1949-50, writer, copy editor, 1952-56; campaign aide, publicity dir. to U.S. Senator Dodd, 1956-57; exec. sec. bd. editors Ency. Brit., 1957-64, editor, 1964-65, editor-in-chief, 1965-68, gen. editor, 1968-70, editor, 1970-75, vice chmn. bd. editors, 1974-79, bd. editors, 1979—; cons. Center Study Democratic Instns.; Ninth ann. C.N. Williamson lectr. Peabody Coll., Nashville. Author: (with others) The Technological Order, 1962; editor: Encyclopaedia Britannica College Preparatory Series, 1964; bd. editorial advisors Internat. Ency., Tokyo, 1974-88. Bd. dirs., sec. Conn. chpt. ARC, 1955-57; pres. Mass. Protestant Social Svcs. Inc., 1977-78; bd. dirs. Protestant Youth Homes, Baldwinville, Mass., 1976-78; mem. Standing Commn. on Peace with Justice, Episcopal Ch., 1989-94. Served with arty. U.S. Army, 1943-46, 50-52. Mem. Phi Beta Kappa Assos., Phi Beta Kappa, Sigma Nu. Democrat. Episcopalian.

PREEG, ERNEST HENRY, strategic and international studies center executive; b. Englewood, N.J., July 5, 1934; s. Ernest W. and Claudia T. Preeg; m. Florence L. Tate, May 12, 1962; 1 child, Terri E. BS in Marine Transp., N.Y. State Maritime Coll., 1956; MA in Econs., New Sch. for Social Rsch., 1961, PhD, 1964. Officer Mcht. Marine, Am. Export Lines, 1956-61; lectr. econs. Bklyn. Coll., 1962-63; fgn. svc. officer Dept. State, Washington, 1963-88; amb. to Haiti, 1981-83; now William M. Scholl chair internat. bus. Ctr. for Strategic and Internat. Studies, Washington. Author: Traders and Diplomats, 1969, Economic Blocs and U.S. Foreign Policy, 1974, the Evolution of a Revolution, 1981, Haiti and the CBI, 1984, The American Challenge in World Trade, 1988, The Tied Aid and Credit Issue, 1989, Neither Fish Nor Foul: U.S. Economic Aid to the Philippines, 1991, Cuba and the New Caribbean Economic Order, 1993, Trade Policy Ahead, 1995, Traders in a Brave New World, 1995, The Haitan Dilemma, 1996. Coun. Fgn. Rels. fellow, 1967-68. Mem. Am. Fgn. Svc. Assn. Office: CSIS 1800 K St NW Washington DC 20006-2202

PREEG, WILLIAM EDWARD, oil company executive; b. N.Y.C., Oct. 16, 1942; s. Ernest Winfield and Claudia Teresa (Casper) P. BE in Marine Engring., SUNY, 1964; MS in Nuclear Sci. and Engring., Columbia U., 1967, PhD in Nuclear Sci. and Engring., 1970. Project engr. U.S. AEC, N.Y.C., 1964-67; physics specialist Aerojet Nuclear Systems Co., Sacramento, Calif., 1970-71; group leader Los Alamos (N.Mex.) Sci. Lab., 1971-80; dir. fluid-mechanics-nuclear dept. Schlumberger-Doll Rsch., Ridgefield, Conn., 1980-85, v.p., dir. rsch., 1990-94; mgr. nuclear dept. Schlumberger Well Svcs., Houston, 1985-87, v.p. engring., 1987-90; v.p., dir. rsch. Schlumberger Austin Rsch., Austin, 1994—; instr. mech. engring. CCNY, N.Y.C., 1968-70; cons. AEC, Gamma Process Co., Los Alamos Sci. Lab., Lawrence Livermore Lab. Mem. Am. Nuclear Soc., Am. Phys. Soc., Am. Inst. Physics (adv. com on corp. assocs.), Soc. Profl. Well Log Analysts, Soc. Petroleum Engrs. Home: 203 Hurst Creek Rd Austin TX 78734-4223 Office: Schlumberger Austin Rsch 8311 North RR 620 Austin TX 78726

PREER, JEAN LYON, associate dean, information science educator; b. Rochester, N.Y., June 25, 1944; d. Henry Gould and Helen Corinne (McTarnaghan) Lyon; m. James Randolph Preer, June 24, 1967; children: Genevieve, Stephen. BA in History with honors, Swarthmore Coll., 1966; MLS, U. Calif., Berkeley, 1967; JD with highest honors, George Washington U., 1974, PhD, 1980. Bar: D.C. 1975. With Henry E. Huntington Libr., San Marino, Calif., 1967-69; Woodrow Wilson Found. teaching intrn Fed. City Coll., Washington, 1969-70; cons. Inst. for Svcs. to Edn., Silver Spring, Md., 1981-82; vol. edn. divsn. Nat. Archives, Washington, 1981-89; adj. prof. U. D.C., 1984-85; adj. prof. Cath. U. Am., Washington, 1985-87, asst. prof. sch. libr. and info. sci., 1987-92, assoc. prof., 1993—, assoc. dean., 1991-93, 94—, acting dean, 1993-94; adj. assoc. prof. George Washington U., 1985-87. Contbr. articles to profl. jours. Mem. governing bd. Nat. Cathedral Sch., Washington, 1987-91. Fellow Nat. Acad. Edn., 1984-85; grantee Nat. Endowment for Humanities. Mem. Order of Coif, Beta Phi Mu. Home: 2900 Rittenhouse St NW Washington DC 20015-1524 Office: Cath U Am Sch Libr and Info Sci Washington DC 20064

PREER, JOHN RANDOLPH, JR., biology educator; b. Ocala, Fla., Apr. 4, 1918; s. John Randolph Sr. and Ruth (Williams) P.; m. Louise Bertha Brandau; children: James Randolph, Robert William. BS with highest honors, U. Fla., 1939; PhD, Ind. U., 1947. From asst. prof. to assoc. prof. to prof. depts. zoology and biology U. Pa., Phila., 1947-67, chmn. grad. group depts. zoology and biology, 1958-67, admissions officer grad. sch. arts and scis., 1960-61; prof. depts. zoology and biology Ind. U., Bloomington, 1968-77, chmn. dept. biology, 1977-79, disting. prof. depts. zoology and biology, 1977—, disting. prof. emeritus, 1988—. Contbr. 85 articles to profl. jours. and chpts. to books. Served to 1st lt. USAF, 1942-45, ETO. NSF sr. postdoctoral fellow, 1967-68, Guggenheim fellow 1976-77. Mem. AAAS, Nat. Acad. Scis. (elected 1976), Am. Inst. Biol. Scis., Am. Soc. Cell Biology, Am. Soc. Protozoology (pres. 1986-87), Phi Beta Kappa. Democrat. Methodist. Home: 1414 E Maxwell Ln Bloomington IN 47401-5143 Office: Ind Univ care Dept of Biology Bloomington IN 47405

PRÉGENT, GILLES, federal agency administrator, lawyer; b. Lachute, Que., Can., Nov. 19, 1933; s. Aime and Alma (Therrien) P.; m. Claudette Joanisse, Sept. 4, 1957; children: Jacques, Christiane, Thierry. BA, U. Ottawa, Ont., Can., 1954, MA in Polit. Sci., 1956, LLD, 1959. Bar: Que. Legal advisor Que. Mktg. Bd., Montreal, Can., 1959-62; commr. Que. Mktg. Bd., Montreal, 1967-72, vice chmn., 1973-83, chmn., 1984-94; prof. U. Ottawa, 1963-67; chmn. Can. Dairy Commn., Ottawa, 1994—; prof. faculty law Laval U., Quebec City, Can., 1965-75, prof. faculty econs., 1976-77; legal advisor Internat. Assn. Milk Control Agys., Can., USA, 1970-94. Contbr. articles to profl. jours. Mem. coun. Montreal Symphony Orch., 1966-74. Recipient Gov.-Gen. Excellence medal Govt. of Can., 1959. Mem. Internat. Dairy Assn. Roman Catholic. Avocations: skiing, music, travelling, astronomy. Home: 7120 Lisieux St, Saint Leonard, PQ Canada H1S 2G2 Office: Canadian Dairy Commn, 1525 Carling Ave, Ottawa, ON Canada K1A 0Z2

PREGERSON, HARRY, federal judge; b. L.A., Oct. 13, 1923; s. Abraham and Bessie (Rubin) P.; m. Bernardine Seyma Chapkis, June 28, 1947; children: Dean Douglas, Kathryn Ann. B.A., UCLA, 1947; LL.B., U. Calif.-Berkeley, 1950. Bar: Calif. 1951. Pvt. practice Los Angeles, 1951-52; Assoc. Morris D. Coppersmith, 1952; ptnr. Pregerson & Costley, Van Nuys, 1953-65; judge Los Angeles Mcpl. Ct., 1965-66, Los Angeles Superior Ct., 1966-67, U.S. Dist. Ct. Central Dist. Calif., 1967-79, U.S. Ct. Appeals for 9th Circuit, Los Angeles, 1979—; faculty mem., seminar for newly appointed distr. Judges Fed. Jud. Center, Washington, 1970-72; mem. faculty Am. Soc. Pub. Adminstrn., Inst. for Ct. Mgmt., Denver, 1973—; panelist Fed. Bar Assn., L.A. chpt., 1989, Calif. Continuing Edn. of Bar, 9th Ann. Fed. Practice Inst., San Francisco, 1986, Internat. Acad. Trial Lawyers, L.A., 1983; lect. seminars for newly-appointed Fed. judges, 1970-71. Author over 450 published legal opinions. Mem. Community Rels. Com., Jewish Fedn. Coun., 1984—, Temple Judea, Encino, 1955—; bd. dirs. Marine Corps Res. Toys for Tots Program, 1965—, Greater Los Angeles Partnership for the Homeless, 1988—; bd. trustees Devil Pups Inc., 1988—; adv. bd. Internat. Orphans Inc., 1966—, Jewish Big Brothers Assn., 1970—, Salvation Army, Los Angeles Met. area, 1988—; worked with U.S. Govt. Gen. Svcs. to establish the Bell Shelter for the homeless, the Child Day Care Ctr., the Food Partnership and Westwood Transitional Village, 1988. 1st lt. USMCR, 1944-46. Decorated Purple Heart, Medal of Valor Apache Tribe, 1989; recipient Promotion of Justice Civic award, City of San Fernando, 1965, award San Fernando Valley Jewish Fedn. Coun., 1966, Profl. Achievement award Los Angeles Athletic Club, 1980, Profl. Achievement award UCLA Alumni Assn., 1985, Louis D. Brandeis award Am. Friends of Hebrew U., 1987, award of merit Inner City Law Ctr., 1987, Appreciation award Navajo Nation and USMC for Toys for Tots program, 1987, Humanitarian award Los Angeles Fed. Exec. Bd., 1987-88, Grateful Acknowledgement award Bet Tzedek Legal Svcs., 1988, Commendation award Bd. Suprs. Los Angeles County, 1988, Others award Salvation Army, 1988, numerous others. Mem. ABA (vice-chmn., com. on fed. rules of criminal procedure and evidence sect. of criminal 1972—, panelist Advocacy Inst., Phoenix, 1988), L.A. County Bar Assn., San Fernando Valley Bar Assn. (program chmn. 1964-65), State Bar Calif., Marines Corps Res. Officers Assn. (pres. San Fernando Valley 1966—), DAV (Birmingham chpt.), Am. Legion (Van Nuys Post),. Office: US Ct Appeals 9th Cir 21800 Oxnard St Ste 1140 Woodland Hills CA 91367-3657*

PREHEIM, VERN QUINCY, religious organization administrator, minister; b. Hurley, S.D., June 27, 1935; s. Jacob Roy and Selma (Miller) P.; m. Marion Kathryn Keeney, Aug. 28, 1958; children: Jay, Janette, Beth, Brian, Lorie. AA, Freeman Jr. Coll., 1956; BA, Bethel Coll., 1957; BD, Mennonite Bibl. Sem., 1960. Algeria program dir. Mennonite Cen. Com. Mennonite Ch., Algiers, 1960-62; Peace sec. Gen. Conf. Mennonite Ch., Newton, Kans., 1962-65, gen. sec., 1980—, dir. Africa and Middle East, 1965-75, Asia dir., 1975-80; mission bd. sec. Gen. Conf. Mennonite Ch., 1968-72, chmn. gen. bd. dirs., 1974-80. Home: 1112 Lorna Ln Newton KS 67114-1643 Office: Gen Conf Mennonite Ch 722 N Main St Newton KS 67114-1819 *To maintain a sense of direction with a vibrant hope in an uncertain world is imperative for the religious community. Our challenge is also to help others find direction and maintain hope.*

PREHLE, TRICIA A., accountant; b. Queens, N.Y., Oct. 17, 1970; d. William G. and Dolores (Cameron) P. BBA in Acctg., CUNY, Baruch Coll., 1992. CPA, N.Y.; cert. mgmt. acct. Fin. analyst Gruntal & Co., Inc., N.Y.C., 1992—. Mgr. Community Tax Aid, Inc., N.Y.C., 1992—. Mem. Inst. Cert. Mgmt. Accts., Sigma Alpha (Delta chpt.). Home: 60-48 69th Ave Flushing NY 11385-5140 Office: Gruntal & Co Inc 14 Wall St New York NY 10005-2101

PREISER, WOLFGANG FRIEDRICH ERNST, architect, educator, consultant, researcher; b. Freiburg, Germany, June 26, 1941; came to U.S., 1967; s. Gerhard Friedrich and Ursula Helene (von Huelsen) P.; m. Cecilia M. Fenoglio, Feb. 16, 1985; children: Johanna, Timothy, Andreas, Nicholas. Student, Vienna Tech. U., 1963; diploma in Engring., Architecture, U. Karlsruhe, 1967; M.Arch., Va. Poly. Inst. and State U., 1969; Ph.D. in Man-Environ. Relations, Pa. State U., 1973. Architect Germany, Austria, Eng., 1960-66; prof. architecture Va. Poly. Inst. and State U., Pa. State U., U. Ill., U. N.Mex., U. Cin., 1970—; research architect constrn. engring. research lab. U.S. Army, 1973-76; co-dir. Inst. Environ. Edn., U. N.Mex., 1976-86; dir. Ctr. for R & D, U. N.Mex., Albuquerque, 1986-90; dir. research Archtl. Research Cons. Inc., 1976—; lectr. ednl., profl. and civic groups worldwide; v.p. faculty club U. N.Mex., 1976-78; pres. Internat. Club, Va. Poly. Inst. and State U., 1968-69. Editor, author 10 books on programming, post-occupancy evaluation and design rsch.; contbr. over 75 articles in field to profl. jours. Trustee Cin. Chamber Orch., 1992—, v.p., 1995—. Recipient Faculty Devel. award for rsch. U. Cin., 1992, Faculty Achievement award, 1995, Pogue/Wheeler Traveling award, 1993, Dean's Spl. award, 1994, Finland's Inst. Tech. award, 1966, awards Am. Iron and Steel Inst., 1968, Progressive Arch. Ann., 1985, 89, undergrad. teaching award U. Ill., 1976, hon. mention 1st Kyoto award Internat. Coun. of Soc. for Indsl. Design, 1979; Fulbright fellow, 1967, 87, Ford Found. fellow, 1968, Nat. Endowment for Arts fellow, 1979, 82. Mem. Soc. Human Ecology (pres. 1980-86), Environ. Design Research Assn. (vice chmn. 1974-76, sec. 1973-74), Nat. Acad. Scis. (chmn. com. on programming and post-occupancy evaluation, bldg. research bd., 1985-86), Phi Kappa Phi. Research in field. Office: U Cin Coll DAAP Sch Architecture Cincinnati OH 45221-0016

PREISKEL, BARBARA SCOTT, lawyer, association executive; b. Washington, July 6, 1924; d. James and B. Beatrix Scott; m. Robert H. Preiskel, Oct. 28, 1950; children: John S., Richard A. BA, Wellesley Coll., 1945; LLB, Yale U., 1947. Bar: D.C. 1948, N.Y. 1948, U.S. Supreme Ct. 1960. Law clk. U.S. Dist. Ct., Boston, 1948-49; assoc. Poletti, Diamond, Roosevelt, Freidin & Mackay, N.Y.C., 1949-50; assoc. Dwight, Royall, Harris, Hoegel & Caskey, N.Y.C., 1950-54, legal cons., 1954-59; cons. Ford Found. Fund for the Republic, N.Y.C., 1954; dep. atty. Motion Picture Assn. Am., Inc., N.Y.C., 1959-71, v.p., legis. counsel, 1971-77, sr. v.p., gen. atty., 1977-83; pvt. practice N.Y.C., 1983—; bd. dirs. GE, Fairfield, Conn., Mass. Mut. Life Ins. Co., Springfield, Textron, Inc., Providence, Am. Stores Co., Salt Lake City, The Washington (D.C.) Post Co. Mem. Pres.'s Commn. on Obscenity and Pornography, 1968-70, Am. Arbitration Assn., 1971-87, N.Y.C. Bd. Ethics, 1976-89, Inst. Civil Justice, 1984-86, Citizens Com. for Children, N.Y.C., 1966-72, 85-91, Child Adoptive Svc. of State Charities Aid Assn., N.Y.C., 1961-68, Hillcrest Ctr. for Children, N.Y.C., 1958-61, Fedn. Protestant Welfare Agys., N.Y.C., 1959-61, 64-92, N.Y. Philharm. Soc., 1971-94, Am. Women's Econ. Devel. Corp., 1981-93, Med. Edn. for South African Blacks, Inc., Washington, 1985-89; bd. dirs. Wiltwyck Sch., N.Y.C., 1968-78, chmn. bd. dirs., 1950; successor trustee Yale Corp., New Haven, 1977-89; trustee Ford Found., N.Y.C., 1982-94, Am. Mus. of Moving Image, 1986—, Wellesley Coll., 1988—; mem. distbn. com. N.Y. Cmty. Trust, Inc., N.Y.C. 1978—, chmn. dist. com. N.Y. Cmty. Trust, 1990-95; chmn. coun. Advisors Hunter Coll. Sch. Social Work, 1985-89; mem. Dumpson chair com., Fordham U., N.Y.C., 1981-89; bd. dirs. Tougaloo Coll. Econ. Devel. Corp., 1991—. Recipient Meritorious award Nat. Assn. Theatre Owners, 1970, 72, Alumni Achievement award Wellesley Coll., 1975, Tribute to Women in Internat. Industry award YWCA, 1984, Elizabeth Cutter Morrow award, 1985, Outstanding Contbrs. award Am. Women's Econ. Devel., 1985, Dirs. Choice award Nat. Women's Econ. Alliance Found., 1989, Keystone award Fedn. Protestant Welfare Agys., 1991, Civic award Citizen's Union of City of N.Y., 1995. Mem. ABA, Assn. of Bar of City of N.Y. (mem. exec. com. 1972-76), ACLU (bd. dirs.), Century Assn., Cosmopolitan Club, Yale Club, Wellesley Club. Episcopalian. Office: 60 East 42nd St New York NY 10165-3125

PREISLER, HARVEY D., medical facility administrator, medical educator; b. N.Y., Feb. 5, 1941; s. Leonard and Estelle Preisler; m. Angela Preisler; children: Sarah, Mark, Vanessa; m. Arza Raza; 1 child, Sheharzad. BA, Bklyn. Coll., 1961; MD, U. Rochester, 1965. Assoc. prof. medicine SUNY, Buffalo, 1974-88; assoc. chief dept. med. oncology Roswell Park Meml. Inst., Buffalo, 1975-82, chief leukemia svcs., 1982-86, acting chief BMT, 1985-87, chief dept. hematology and oncology, 1986-88; head, sec. cell biology and myeloproliferative Buffalo, 1979-82; founder, chmn. Leukemia Intergroup, 1980-89; dir., prof. medicine, chief divsn. hematology Charles M. Barrett C.C., 1989-91; prof. medicine divsn. hematology U. Cin. Med. Ctr., 1989-92; dir. Rush Cancer Inst., chief hematology/oncology, prof. Rush-Presbyn.-St. Luke's Med. Ctr., Chgo., 1992—; founder, chmn. Buffalo Coop. Group of Cmty. Hematologists for Tex. Myeloid Diseases, 1977-84, Leukemia Intergroup, 1980-89; chmn. teaching session on acute leukemia Am. Soc. Hematology, 1982-84, co-chmn. session XVIII leukemia and myeloid disorders, 1985. Contbr. articles to profl. jours. Mem. med. adv. bd. Lincoln Park Zoo, Chgo., 1994. Grantee NIH, 1988-89, 89-90, 90-91, 92—. Mem. Internat. Soc. Experimental Hematology, Am. Cancer Soc., Am. Assn. Cancer Rsch., Am. Soc. Clin. Oncology, Cell Kinetics Soc., Soc. Internal Medicine. Office: Rush Cancer Inst 1725 W Harrison Ste 809 Chicago IL 60612

PREISS, JACK, biochemistry educator; b. Bklyn., June 2, 1932; s. Erool and Gilda (Friedman) P.; m. Judith Weil Rosen, June 10, 1959; children: Jennifer Ellen, Jeremy Oscar, Jessica Michelle. BS in Chemistry, CCNY, 1953; PhD in Biochemistry, Duke U., 1957. Scientist NIH, Bethesda, 1960-62; asst. prof. dept. biochemistry, biophysics U. Calif., Davis, 1962-65, assoc. prof., 1965-68, prof., 1968-85, chair dept. biochemistry, 1971-74, 77-81; prof. dept. biochemistry Mich. State U., East Lansing, 1985—, chair dept., 1985-89; mem. editorial bd. Jour. Bacteriology, 1969-74, Arch. Biochem. Biophysics, 1969—; mem. editorial bd. Plant Physiology, 1969-74, 77-80, assoc. editor, 1980-92, editor, 1993-95; editor Jour. Biol. Chemistry, 1971-76, 78-83, 94—. Recipient Camille and Henry Dreyfus Disting. scholar award Calif. State U., 1983, Alexander von Humboldt Stiftung Sr. U.S. Scientist award, 1984, Alsberg-Schoch Meml. Lectr. award Am. Assn. Cereal Chemists, 1990, Nat. Sci. Coun. lectr. Republic of China, 1988, award of merit Japanese Soc. Starch Sci., 1992; Guggenheim Meml. fellow, 1969-70, Japan Soc. for Promotion of Sci. fellow, 1992-93; grantee NIH, 1963—, NSF, 1978-89, Dept. of Energy, 1993—, USDA, 1988—. Mem. AAAS, Am. Chem. Soc. (Charles Pfizer award in enzyme chemistry 1971), Biochem. Soc., Am. Soc. Biol. Chemists and Molecular Biology, Am. Soc. Microbiologists, Am. Soc. Plant Physiologists, Soc. for Complex Carbohydrates, Protein Soc. Office: Mich State Univ Dept Of Biochemistry East Lansing MI 48824

PREISS, PATRICIA ELLEN, musician, educator; b. N.Y.C., May 19, 1950; d. Fredric H. and Madeline (Robbins) P.; m. Eric A. Lerner, Nov. 1970 (div. 1975); m. William H. Harris, Aug. 13, 1995. BA, Harvard U., 1973; MFA, Calif. Inst. Arts, 1987. Performer, bassist Carla Bley Band, Willow, N.Y., 1977-78; instr. piano, composition The Hall Sch., Pittsfield, Mass., 1983-84; instr. music Santa Monica (Calif.) C.C., 1989; tchr. piano

The Hackley Sch., Tarrytown, N.Y., 1991; tchr. piano and composition Fraioli Sch. of Music, Greenwich, Conn., 1991—; accompanist SUNY, Purchase, N.Y., 1991-95; pvt. piano tchr., N.Y., Conn., Mass., 1980—; pianist Greenwich Hyatt Hotel, 1995—. Author: Musical Materials, 1987; composer, performer Jamaica's Album, 1984; composer Complete Enlightenment, 1986. Performance grantee Cambridge (Mass.) Arts Coun., 1977, Artists grantee No. Berkshire Coun. on Arts, 1983. Home: 18 Thomas St Cos Cob CT 06807-2146

PREISTER, DONALD GEORGE, greeting card manufacturer, state senator; b. Columbus, Nebr., Dec. 23, 1946; s. Maurice J. Preister and Leona T. (Dusel) Chereck. BS in Edn., U. Nebr., 1977. Unit dir. Boys' Clubs of Omaha, 1973-83; dep. city clk. City of Omaha, 1984-85; tchr. The Great Peace March, U.S., 1986; founder, owner Joy Creations, Co., Omaha, 1988—; instr. Metro C.C., Omaha, 1979-80. Author: (sect.) Drug Abuse Prevention, 1977. Troop leader Boy Scouts Am., Omaha, 1973-83. Served with U.S. Army, 1966-68, Vietnam. Decorated Bronze Star. Mem. Vets. for Peace, Nebr. Sustainable Agr. Soc., Optimist. Democrat. Roman Catholic. Avocations: gardening, running, horses. Home: 3937 W St Omaha NE 68107-3152 Office: State Capitol Dist # 5 Lincoln NE 68509

PRELL, MICHAEL JACK, economist; b. Ft. Worth, Nov. 2, 1944; s. Martin and Ruth Dorothy (Sosin) P.; m. Terri Lynne Hume, Nov. 30, 1969; 1 child, Marisa Hume. AB, U. Calif., Berkeley, 1966, MA, 1967, PhD, 1971. Fin. economist Fed. Res. Bank, Kansas City, Mo., 1970-73; with div. rsch. and stats. Bd. Govs. of Fed. Res. System, Washington, 1973—; economist capital mkts. sect., 1973-74, banking sect., 1974-75; sr. economist govt. fin. sect., 1975-77; chief capital mkts. sect., 1977-78; assoc. dir. div. rsch. and stats., 1978-83, dep. dir., 1983-87, dir., 1987—; assoc. economist Fed. Open Market Com., 1981-87, economist, 1987—; U.S. del. OECD Com. on Fin. Mkts., Paris, 1982—; bd. dirs. Securities Investor Protection Corp., Washington. Mem. Conf. Bus. Economists. Office: Fed Res Bd Rsch & Stats Div 20th St & C St NW Washington DC 20551

PREM, F. HERBERT, JR., lawyer; b. N.Y.C., Jan. 14, 1932; s. F. Herbert and Sybil Gertrude (Nichols) P.; m. Patricia Ryan, Nov. 18, 1978; children from previous marriage: Julia Nichols, F. Herbert III. AB, Yale U., 1953; JD, Harvard U., 1959. Bar: N.Y. 1960. Assoc. Whitman & Ransom, N.Y.C., 1959-66, ptnr., 1967-93, co-chmn. exec. com., 1988-92, chmn., 1993; chmn. Whitman Breed Abbott & Morgan, N.Y.C., 1993—; bd. dirs. Fuji Photo Film U.S.A., Inc., Fuji Med. Sys. U.S.A., Inc., Noritake Co., Inc., Seiko Instruments U.S.A., Inc., Cmty. Action for Legal Svc. Inc., 1967-70, treas.; bd. dirs. Legal Aid Soc. N.Y.C., 1969-73. Bd. dirs. Bagaduce Music Lending Libr., Inc., 1988-95, pres., 1989-93. Lt. (j.g.) USNR, 1953-56. Mem. ABA, Assn. of Bar of City of N.Y. (sec. 1967-69), N.Y. State Bar Assn., Am. Law Inst., Am. Soc. Internat. Law, Univ. Club, Yale Club. Episcopalian. Office: Whitman Breed Abbott & Morgan 200 Park Ave New York NY 10166-0005

PREM, KONALD ARTHUR, physician, educator; b. St. Cloud, Minn., Nov. 6, 1920; s. Joseph E. and Theresa M. (Willing) P.; m. Phyllis Edelbrock, June 14, 1947; children: Mary Kristen, Stephanie, Timothy. B.S., U. Minn., 1947; M.B., 1950, M.D., 1951. Diplomate: Am. Bd. Ob-Gyn (with spl. competence in gynecologic oncology). Intern Mpls. gen. Hosp., 1950-51; fellow dept. obstetrics and gynecology U. Minn., Mpls., 1951-54; instr. U. Minn., 1955-58, asst. prof., 1958-60, assoc. prof., 1960-69, prof., 1969-93; prof. emeritus, 1993—; dir. div. gynecologic oncology U. Minn., 1969-83, head dept. obstetrics and gynecology, 1976-84; prof. dept. surgery, 1993—. Served to capt. USAR, 1941-46; brig. gen. M.C. USAR (Ret.). Decorated Legion of Merit. Mem. Am. Coll. Ob-Gyn, Am. Gynec. and Obstet. Soc., Central Assn. Ob-Gyn, Hennepin County Med. Soc., Soc. Pelvic Surgeons, Minn. Ob-Gyn Soc., Soc. Gynecologic Oncologists, Internat. Soc. Gynecologic Pathologists, Soc. Gynecologic Surgery, Minn. Acad. Medicine, Am. Radium Soc., Mpls. Surg. Soc., Soc. Med. Cons. to Armed Forces, Am. Assn. Pro-Life Ob-Gyn. Roman Catholic. Home: 15660-16 Place N Plymouth MN 55447-2497 Office: PO Box 395 Mayo Bldg 420 Delaware St SE Minneapolis MN 55455-0374

PREMACK, DAVID, psychologist; b. Aberdeen, S.D., Oct. 26, 1925; s. Leonard B. and Sonja (Liese) P.; m. Ann M. James, Oct. 26, 1951; children: Ben, Lisa, Timothy. BA, U. Minn., 1949, PhD, 1955. Rsch. assoc. Yerkes Labs. Primate Biology, Orange Park, Fla., 1955; rsch. assoc., asst. prof. psychology U. Mo., Columbia, 1956-58; assoc. prof. U. Mo., 1959-62, prof., 1963-64; prof. U. Calif., Santa Barbara, 1965-75; vis. prof. Harvard U., 1970-71; prof. U. Pa., 1975—; artist-in-residence Yaddo, Saratoga Springs, N.Y., 1955; fellow Van Leer Jerusalem Inst., 1980, Inst. for Advanced Study, Berlin, 1985-86; vis. scientist Japan Soc. for Promotion Sci., 1980; univ. rsch. lectr. U. Calif., Santa Barbara, 1973; mem. sci. gov. bd. Fyssen Found., Paris, 1989—; assoc. neurosci. rsch. program, La. Jolla, Calif., 1991—. Author: Intelligence in Ape and Man, 1976, (with Ann James Premack) The Mind of an Ape, 1983, Gavagai! Or the Future History of the Animal Language Controversy, 1986 (with Dan Sperber and Ann James Premack) Causal Cognition: A Multidisciplinary Debate, 1995; mem. editorial bd. Jour. Exptl. Psychology: Animal Processes, 1976—, Cognition, 1977—, Brain and Behavior Sci., 1978—, Jour. Cognitive Neurosci. Served with U.S. Army, 1943-46. Ford Found. teaching intern, 1954; USPHS postdoctoral fellow, 1956-59; Social Sci. Research Council fellow, summer 1963; Center for Advanced Study in Behavioral Scis. fellow, 1972-73; Guggenheim fellow, 1979-80; grantee NSF, 1961—, USPHS, 1960-80; recipient Kenneth Craik Research award St. John's Coll.-Cambridge U., 1987, Internat. sci. prize Fyssen Found., Paris, 1987. Fellow AAAS; mem. Soc. Exptl. Psychologists. Office: 3815 Walnut St Philadelphia PA 19104-3604 also: CREA, Ecole Polytechnique, 1 rue Descartes, 75005 Paris France

PREMO, PAUL MARK, oil company executive; b. Syracuse, N.Y., Nov. 20, 1942; s. Matthias George and Kathryn (Whitbread) P.; m. Mary Catherine Hennessy, June 19, 1965; children—Deborah, Mark. B.S. in Chem. Engring., Manhattan Coll., Riverdale, N.Y., 1964; S.M. in Chem. Engring., MIT, 1965. Chem. engr. Chevron Research, Richmond, Calif., 1965-69; fin. analyst Chevron Corp., San Francisco, 1969-72, coordinator, mgr. supply and distbn., 1972-79; mgr. petroleum regulations Chevron USA, San Francisco, 1979-81, sec.-treas., 1981-85, mgr. property tax adminstrn., 1985-86, mgr. natural gas regulatory affairs, 1986-92; exec. cons. Resource Mgmt. Internat., San Rafael, Calif., 1992-95; v.p. Foster Assoc., Inc., San Francisco, 1996—; dir. Ky. Agrl. Energy Corp., Franklin. Trustee Calif. Tax Found., 1985—. Mem. Calif. State C. of C. (tax com.), Western Oil and Gas Assn., Am. Petroleum Inst. (property tax com.), Natural Gas Supply Assn., Inst. Property Taxation, Calif. Taxpayers Assn. (bd. dirs. 1985—), MIT Alumni Assn., Commonwealth (San Francisco), Sigma Xi, Tau Beta Pi. Avocations: sailing, personal computing, woodworking. Home: 310 Hazel Ave Mill Valley CA 94941-5054 Office: Foster Assocs Inc 120 Montgomery St San Francisco CA 94104

PREMPREE, THONGBLIEW, oncology radiologist; b. Thailand, Feb. 1, 1935; s. Korn and Kam (T.) P.; m. Amporn Lohsuwand, Apr. 27, 1963. Pre-Med., Chulalongkorn U., Thailand, 1954; MD, Siriraj U. of Med. Sci., Thailand, 1958; PhD in Radiobiology, John Hopkins U., 1968. Diplomate Am. Bd. Radiology; Fellow in Am. Coll. Radiology. Instr. Dept. Radiology John Hopkins U., Balt., 1968-69; asst. prof. John Hopkins U. Dept. Radiol. Scis., Balt., 1969; staff mem. Dept. of Radiology Ramathibodi Hosp. Mahidol U., Bankok, Thailand, 1969-70; dir. radiobiology Dept. Therapeutic Radiology Tuft New England Med. Ctr., Boston, 1970; asst. prof. sch. of medicine John Hopkins U., Balt., 1971-74; assoc. prof. dept. radiology U. Md. Hosp., Balt., 1974, acting dir., assoc. prof., 1977-79, prof., chief, div. radiation oncology, 1979-83; prof., chmn. dept. radiation oncology U. Hosp., Jacksonville, Fla., 1983—. Contbr. over 100 articles to scientific jours. Recipient PhD Fellowship awards John Hopkins U., 1963-68. Mem. Am. Soc. Therapeutic Radiobiologists, Am. Coll. Radiology, AAAS, AMA, Radiation Research Soc., Fedn. Am. Scientists, Radiol. Soc. N. Am., The John Hopkins Med. & Surgical Assn. Achievements include research in the field of molecular genetics and cancer research. Home: 104 Lamplighter Island Ct Ponte Vedra Beach FL 32082-1940 Office: U Fla 655 W 8th St Jacksonville FL 32209-6511

PRENDERGAST, JOHN THOMAS, editor, writer; b. Phila., Feb. 13, 1958; s. John and Margaret (Walsh) P.; m. Carole Robin Bernstein, May 5, 1990. BA, U. Pa., Phila., 1980; MA, John Hopkins U., Balt., 1988. Asst. editor Wharton Mag., Phila., 1982; staff writer U. Pa., Phila., 1982-84; mng. editor Wharton Annual, Phila., 1984; editor Pa. Outlook, Phila., 1984-85; devel. writer Thomas Jefferson U., Phila., 1985-87; assoc. dir. devel. INFORM, Inc., N.Y.C., 1988; mng. editor Civil Engring., N.Y.C., 1989—. Author: (novel) Jump, 1995 (1st Novel award Mid-List Press, 1994). Democrat. Avocations: reading, travel, films. Home: 118 Union St # 12C Brooklyn NY 11231 Office: Civil Engring 345 E 47th St New York NY 10017

PRENDERGAST, ROBERT ANTHONY, pathologist educator; b. Bklyn., Nov. 6, 1931. BA, Columbia U., 1953; MD, Boston U., 1957. Intern Bellevue Hosp., 1957-58; resident Boston City Hosp., 1958-59, Meml. Sloan-Kettering Hosp., 1959-61; vis. physician Rockefeller U., 1963-65, asst. prof., 1965-70; Assoc. prof. opthamology and pathology, sch. medicine Johns Hopkins U., 1970—; prof. Rsch. Prevent Blindness, Inc., 1971—. Mem. Am. Assn. Immunology, Am. Soc. Exp. Pathology, Transplantation Soc., Reticuloendothelial Soc. Achievements include research in delayed hypersensitivity and cellular immunology, ontogeny of the immune response, transplantation immunology, viral immunopathology, immunopathology of ocular inflammatory diseases. Office: Johns Hopkins Univ Wilmer Inst Opthalmic Immunology Lab Baltimore MD 21287-9142

PRENDERGAST, THOMAS FRANCIS, railroad executive; b. Chgo., June 6, 1952; s. Francis V. and Julia M. Prendergast; m. Christine L. Prendergast, Oct. 1, 1994; 1 child, Kelly. BS in Socio-Technol. Sys., U. Ill., Chgo., 1974. Sr. transit planner Chgo. Transit Authority, 1975-77, sys. safety engr., 1977-79; transit safety sys. specialist Fed. Transit Adminstrn., Washington, 1979-82; dir. sys. safety N.Y.C. Transit, 1982-84, asst. v.p. sys. safety, 1984-87, gen. mgr. S.I. divsn., 1987-89, chief elec. officer, 1989-90, sr. v.p. subways, 1990-94; pres. L.I. R.R., Jamaica, 1994—. Office: LIRR Jamaica Station Jamaica NY 11435

PRENG, DAVID EDWARD, management consultant; b. Chgo., Sept. 30, 1946; s. Edward M. and Frances (Maras) P.; m. JoAnne Ferzoco, Dec. 6, 1969; children: Mark, Laura, Stephen, Michael. BS, Marquette U., 1969; MBA, DePaul U., 1973. Supr. Shell Oil Co., Houston and Chgo., 1969-73; controller Litton Office Products, Houston, 1973-74; v.p. Addington & Assocs., Houston, 1974-76; exec. v.p. Mantech S.W., Inc., Houston, 1976-77; sr. asso. Energy div. Korn/Ferry Internat., Houston, 1977-78; v.p. Kors Marlar & Assocs., 1978-80; pres. Preng & Assocs., 1980-85; pres. Preng Zant & Assocs., 1985-87, Preng & Assoc., 1987—; bd. dirs. Citizens Nat. Bank of Tex., Brit. Am. Bus. Assn. Mem. Sugar Creek Country Club (pres.). Home: 607 Chevy Chase Cir Sugar Land TX 77478-3601

PRENSKY, ARTHUR LAWRENCE, pediatric neurologist, educator; b. N.Y.C., Aug. 31, 1930; s. Herman and Pearl (Newman) P.; m. Sheila Carr, Nov. 13, 1969. A.B., Cornell U., 1951; M.D., N.Y. U., 1955. Diplomate: Am. Bd. Psychiatry and Neurology. Intern Barnes Hosp., St. Louis, 1955-56; resident and research fellow in neurology Harvard U., Mass. Gen. Hosp., Boston, 1959-66; instr. neurology Harvard Med. Sch., 1966-67; mem. faculty Washington U. Sch. Medicine, St. Louis, 1967—; prof. pediatrics and neurology Washington U. Sch. Medicine, to 1975, Allen P. and Josephine B. Green prof. pediatric neurology, 1975—; pediatrician St. Louis Children's Hosp.; neurologist Barnes and Allied Hosps., Jewish Hosp., St. Louis. Author: (with others) Nutrition and the Developing Nervous System, 1975; editor: (with others) Neurological Pathophysiology, 2d edit, 1978, Advances in Neurology, 1976; mem. editorial bd. Pediatric Neurology, 1984-90, Jour. Child Neurology, 1985—. Served with USAF, 1957-59. Fellow Am. Acad. Neurology; mem. Am. Neurol. Assn., Am. Soc. Neurochemistry (mem. council 1973-77), Central Soc. Neurol. Research (pres. 1977-78), Child Neurology Soc. (pres. 1979-80), Am. Pediatric Soc., Internat. Child Neurology Assn., Japanese Soc. Child Neurology, Profs. Child Neurology (pres. 1984-86). Home: 15 Monarch Hill Ct Chesterfield MO 63005-4004 Office: 400 S Kingshighway Blvd Saint Louis MO 63110-1014

PRENTICE, ANN ETHELYND, academic adminstrator; b. Grafton, Vt., July 19, 1933; d. Homer Orville and Helen (Cooke) Hurlbut; divorced; children: David, Melody, Holly, Wayne. AB, U. Rochester, 1954; MLS, SUNY, Albany, 1964; DLS, Columbia U., 1972; LittD (hon.), Keuka Coll., 1979. Lectr. sch. info. sci. and policy SUNY, Albany, 1971-72, asst. prof., 1972-78; prof., dir. grad. sch. library and info. sci. U. Tenn., Knoxville, 1978-88; assoc. v.p. info. resources U. South Fla., Tampa, 1988-93; dean Coll. of Libr. and Info. Svcs. U. Md., 1993—. Author: Strategies for Survival, Library Financial Management Today, 1979, The Library Trustee, 1973, Public Library Finance, 1977, Financial Planning for Libraries, 1983, 2d edit., 1996, Professional Ethics for Librarians, 1985; editor Pub. Literary Quar., 1978-81; co-editor: Info. Sci. in its Disciplinary Context, 1990; assoc. editor Library and Info. Sci. Ann., 1987-90. Cons. long-range planning and pers. Knox County Libr. System, 1980, 85-86, Richland County S.C. Libr. System, 1981, Upper Hudson Libr. Fedn., N.Y., State Libr. Ohio, 1986; trustee Hyde Park (N.Y.) Free Libr., treas., 1973-75, pres., 1976; trustee Mid-Hudson Libr. System, Poughkeepsie, N.Y., 1975-78; trustee adv. bd. Hillsborough County Libr., 1991-93. Recipient Disting. Alumni award SUNY, Albany, 1987, Columbia U., 1991. Mem. ALA, Am. Soc. Info. Sci. (exec. bd. 1986-89, conf. chmn. 1989, pres. 1992-93, chmn. info. policy com. 1994-96), Assn. for Libr. and Info. Sci. Edn. (pres. 1986). Office: Univ Md Coll Libr and Info Svcs 4105 Hornbake Bldg College Park MD 20742

PRENTICE, EUGENE MILES, III, lawyer; b. Glen Ridge, N.J., Aug. 27, 1942; s. Eugene Miles and Anna Margaret (Kiernan) P.; m. Katharine Kirby Culbertson, Sept. 18, 1976; children: Eugene Miles IV, Jessie Kirby, John Francis. BA, Washington and Jefferson Coll., Pa., 1964; JD, U. Mich., 1967. Bar: N.Y. 1973, U.S. Dist. Ct. (so. dist.) N.Y. 1973, U.S. Dist. Ct. (ea. dist.) N.Y. 1974, U.S. Ct. Appeals (2d cir.) 1974, N.Y. Supreme Ct. 1973. With Morgan Guaranty Trust, N.Y.C., 1967-68, 71-73; assoc. White & Case, N.Y.C., 1973-78; assoc. Windels, Marx et al, N.Y.C., 1978-80, ptnr., 1980-84; ptnr. Brown & Wood, N.Y.C., 1984-93, Piper & Marbury, N.Y.C., 1993—; pres. Midland (Tex.) Sports, Inc., 1990—; bd. dirs. Nat. Life Ins. Co., Montpelier, Vt., Tex. League Profl. Baseball, 1990—. Trustee Vt. Law Sch., 1984—, Washington and Jefferson Coll., Pa., 1985—, Nat. Assn. Profl. Baseball Leagues, 1992—, vice chmn. of bd., 1995—, St. Hilda's and St. Hugh's Sch., N.Y.C., 1993—, pres. of bd., 1995—. Capt. U.S. Army, 1968-70. Mem. ABA, Assn. of Bar of City of N.Y., Links Club, Union League Club, N.Y. Athletic Club, Spring Lake Bath & Tennis Club, Lake Mansfield Trout Club (Vt.). Republican. Home: 34 W 95th St New York NY 10025-6701 Office: Bryan Cave LLP 245 Park Ave New York NY 10167

PRENTICE, JAMES STUART, energy company executive, chemical engineer; b. Louisville, Feb. 4, 1944; s. John Edward and Helen (Staples) P.; m. Mary Joan Kelly, July 24, 1965; children: Holly Michelle, Craig Edward, Brian Andrew. B in Chem. Engring., U. Louisville, 1966; MS, Northwestern U., 1967. Research engr. Esso Research and Engring. Co., Baytown, Tex., 1967-71; engr., supr. ops., mkt. mgr. to plant mgr. No. Petrochem. Co., Morris and Des Plaines, Ill., 1971-82; v.p. mfg. No. Petrochem. Co., Omaha, 1982-85; sr. v.p. corp. planning HNG/Internorth, Omaha, 1985-86; sr. v.p. adminstrn. and human resources Enron Corp., Houston, 1986-87; exec. v.p. Enron Liquid Fuels, Houston, 1987-89; sr. v.p. Enron Gas Pipeline Group, Houston, 1989-93; sr. v.p., chief tech. officer Enron Ops. Corp., Houston, 1993-95, sr. v.p. human resources, 1995-96; pres. Enron Clean Fuels Co., 1996—. Patentee in field. Bd. dirs. St. Joseph Hosp. Found. Mem. AIChE, Lakeside Country Club, Petroleum Club of Houston. Roman Catholic. Avocations: tennis, golf. Office: Enron Corp EB4576 PO Box 1188 Houston TX 77251-1188

PRENTICE, NORMAN MACDONALD, clinical psychologist; b. Yonkers, N.Y., Feb. 25, 1925; s. Lester M. and Islay (Macdonald) P.; m. Marilyn E. Shepherd, Dec. 24, 1953 (dec. July 14, 1979); children: Wendy Elizabeth, Lisa Shepherd; m. Joyce Marie Broyles, June 25, 1987. A.B. in Psychology, Princeton U., 1949; M.A. in Clin. Psychology, Harvard U., 1952, Ph.D., 1956. Diplomate Am. Bd. Profl. Psychology. Research fellow child psychiat. unit Mass. Gen. Hosp., Boston, 1953-55; NIMH fellow Judge Baker Guidance Center, Boston, 1955-57; chief adolescent sect. psychologist Children's Hosp., Boston, 1957-58; staff psychologist to coordinator of training Judge Baker Guidance Center, 1958-65; asso. prof. psychology U. Tex., Austin, 1965-68; prof. psychology and ednl. psychology U. Tex., 1968—, dir. clin. psychology tng. program, 1974-76; cons. VA, 1966-80. Contbr. articles to profl. jours. Bd. dirs. Austin Community Nursery Sch., 1966-69, Austin Child Guidance and Evaluation Ctr., 1981-84; trustee Austin-Travis County Mental Retardation Ctr., 1971-73, Art Inst. Boston, 1968-90. With AUS, 1943-45. Decorated Purple Heart. Fellow APA, Am. Psychol. Soc., Am. Orthopsychiat. Assn. (v.p. 1979-80), Soc. for Personality Assessment; mem. Phi Beta Kappa. Office: U Tex Dept Psychology Austin TX 78712-1157

PRENTICE, TIM, sculptor, architect; b. N.Y.C., Nov. 5, 1930; s. T. Merrill and Theodora (Machado) P.; m. Marie Truesdale Bissell, Aug. 23, 1960; children: Nora L., Phoebe A. B.A., Yale U., 1953, M.Arch., 1960. Gen. partner Prentice & Chan, Ohlhausen, Architects and predecessor, N.Y.C., 1966-74; adj. prof. archtl. design Columbia U., 1974-80. One-man shows include Inst. Architecture and Urban Studies, N.Y.C., 1975, Paul Mellon Arts Ctr., Wallingford, Conn., 1983, Aldrich Mus., Ridgefield, Conn., 1989, Bruce Mus., Greenwich, Conn., 1989, Maxwell Davidson Gallery, N.Y.C., 1990, 94, Mattatuck Mus., Waterbury, Conn., 1990, Neville Sargent Gallery, Chgo., 1991, Maxwell Davidson Gallery, N.Y.C., 1992; group shows, New Britain Mus. Am. Art, 1978, Carlson Art Gallery U. Bridgeport, 1978, Indpls. Mus. Art, 1978, Conn. Painting, Drawing and Sculpture Today, 1977, Parsons-Dreyfuss Gallery, N.Y.C., 1980, Allan Stone Gallery, N.Y.C., 1984, Am. Acad. and Inst. Arts and Letters, N.Y.C., 1991, Soma Gallery, San Diego, 1993, Chgo. Cultural Ctr., 1993; kinetic sculpture represented in permanent collections Am. Express Co., N.Y.C., AT&T Long Lines, Bedminster, N.Y., Henry St. Settlement, N.Y.C.; major commns. include CBS Bldg., N.Y.C., 1979, Conn. Natural Gas Co., Hartford, 1980, Mobil Oil, Fairfax, Va., 1982, Tex. Commerce Bank, Houston, 1982, INA CIGNA Corp., Wilmington, Del., 1983, Bank Am. Plaza, N.Y.C., 1984, United Va. Bank, Richmond, 1984, Bradley Internat. Airport, Windsor Locks, Conn., 1987, Hollister Inc., Libertyville, Ill., 1988, Mattatuck Mus., Waterbury, Conn., 1989, Summit Office Bldg., Raleigh, N.C., 1989, Sioux City (Iowa) Pub. Libr., 1990, Tempozan Market Place, Osaka, Japan, 1990, Irving (Tex.) Arts Ctr., 1991, Fed. Res. Bank of N.Y., East Rutherford, N.J., 1992, Math. Lib. Univ. Colo., Boulder, 1992, World Population Coun., N.Y.C., 1993, Peak Galleria, Hong Kong, 1993, Civic Ctr. Torroti, Japan, 1993, Hewlett Packard, Andover, Mass., Nat. Inventors Hall of Fame, 1995, Los Cerritos (Calif.) Ctr., 1995. Served to lt. (j.g.) USNR, 1954-58. Dept. State cultural exchange grantee, 1963-64. Fellow AIA (pres. N.Y. chpt. 1973-74); mem. Nat. Council Archtl. Registration Bds., Mcpl. Arts Soc. N.Y. (pres. 1974-76). Club: Century Assn. Studio: 129 Lake Rd West Cornwall CT 06796-1402

PRENTISS, C.J., state legislator. BA in Edn., Cleve. State U., 1969, MEd, 1975; cert., Kent State U., 1976; grad. Weatherhead Sch. Mgmt., Case Western Res. U., 1978. Mem. Ohio Ho. of Reps., Columbus, 1991—; chair edn. policy Ohio legislative Black Caucus and Black elected Democrats of Cleve., vice-chair edn. com. Nat. Conf. State Legislatures; past vice-chair HouseEdn. com., ways and means, ins.; mem. State Bd. Edn., 1984-90, chair lit. and youth-at-risk com., legis. stds. com., past chair joint select com. on infant health and family support. Past Vice-chair Black Leadership Cleve. Alumni; past mem. gov.'s com. Socially Disadvantaged Black Males. Office: 77 S High St Columbus OH 43266

PRENTISS, PAUL E., lawyer; b. Milford, Mass., June 8, 1943. AB, Middlebury Coll., 1965; JD, Duke U., 1971. Bar: Wis. 1971. Mem. Michael Best & Friedrich, Milw. Mem. editorial bd. Duke Law Jour., 1970-71. Mem. ABA. Office: Michael Best & Friedrich 100 E Wisconsin Ave Milwaukee WI 53202-4108

PRENTKE, RICHARD OTTESEN, lawyer; b. Cleve., Sept. 8, 1945; s. Herbert E. and Melva B. (Horbury) P.; m. Susan Ottesen, June 9, 1974; children: Catherine, Elizabeth. BSE, Princeton U., 1967; JD, Harvard U., 1974. Assoc. Perkins Coie, Seattle, 1974-80, ptnr., 1981—, chief fin. officer, 1989—. Author: School Construction Law Deskbook, 1989; contbr. articles to profl. jours. Pres., trustee Seattle County Day Sch., 1990—. With USN, 1967-70. Fellow Leadership Tomorrow, Seattle, 1985-86. Mem. ABA, Wash. State Bar Assn. (jud. screening com. 1985-91, chmn. 1987-91), Seattle-King County Bar Assn. (chmn. jud. task force 1990-93), Am. Arbitration Assn. (arbitrator 1988—), Princeton U. Rowing Assn. (pres. 1993—, trustee 1976—), Rainier Club, Princeton Club Wash. (trustee 1986—, pres. 1990-92), Seattle Tennis Club. Avocations: art, carpentry, travel, rowing, sports. Office: Perkins Coie 1201 3rd Ave Fl 40 Seattle WA 98101-3000

PREONAS, GEORGE ELIAS, lawyer; b. Dayton, Ohio, Oct. 5, 1943; s. Louis D. and Mary (Drakos) P.; m. Aileen Strike, June 1, 1944; children—Annemarie, Michael, Stephen. B.A., Stanford U., 1965; J.D., U. Mich., 1968. Bar: Ill. 1968, Nev. 1969, Calif. 1974. Ptnr., Seyfarth, Shaw, Fairweather & Geraldson, Los Angeles, 1968—. Mem. Los Angeles County Bar Assn., Calif. Bar Assn., ABA, Ill. Bar Assn., Nev. Bar Assn. Office: Seyfarth Shaw Fairweather 2029 Century Park E Ste 3300 Los Angeles CA 90067-3019

PREOVOLOS, PENELOPE ATHENE, lawyer; b. San Francisco, Sept. 16, 1955; d. James Peter and Lorraine Lucille (Tiscornia) P.; m. Richard Gonzalo Katerndahl, Mar. 24, 1984. AB, U. Calif., Berkeley, 1976; JD, Harvard U., 1979. Bar: Calif. 1979, U.S. Dist. Ct. (no. dist.) Calif. 1979, U.S. Ct. Appeals (9th cir.) 1979. Law clk. to Hon. Charles M. Merrill U.S. Ct. Appeals (9th cir.), San Francisco, 1979-80; assoc. Morrison & Foerster, San Francisco, 1980-85; ptnr. Morrison & Foerster, San Franciso, 1985—; mng. ptnr. San Francisco office Morrison & Foerster, San Francisco, 1995-96. Contbr. articles to profl. jours. Bd. dirs. San Francisco Neighborhood Legal Assistance Found., 1990—. Mem. ABA (antitrust sect.), State Bar of Calif. (sec. antitrust and trade regulation law sect. 1993-94, chair 1994-95). Democrat. Roman Catholic. Avocations: riding (dressage), classical music. Home: 225 Evergreen Dr Kentfield CA 94904-2707 Office: Morrison & Foerster 345 California St San Francisco CA 94104-2635

PRESANT, SANFORD CALVIN, lawyer, educator, author, lecturer; b. Buffalo, Nov. 15, 1952; s. Allen Norman and Reeta (Coplon) P.; m. Ilene Beth Shendell, Dec. 2, 1984; 1 child, Jarrett Matthew. BA, Cornell U., 1973; JD cum laude, SUNY-Buffalo, 1976; LLM in Taxation, Georgetown U., 1981. Bar: N.Y. 1977, D.C. 1977, U.S. Ct. Claims 1978, U.S. Tax Ct. 1977, U.S. Supreme Ct. 1982, Calif. 1992. Staff atty. SEC options task force, Washington, 1976-78; assoc. Barrett Smith Schapiro, N.Y.C., 1978-80, Trubin Sillcocks, N.Y.C., 1980-81; ptnr. Carro, Spanbock, Fass, Geller, Kaster, N.Y.C., 1981-86, Finley, Kumble, Wagner, Heine, Underberg, Manley, Myerson & Casey, N.Y.C., 1987; Kaye, Scholer, Fierman, Hays & Handler, N.Y.C., 1988-95; Battle Bowler LLP, L.A., 1995—; adj. assoc. prof. real estate NYU, 1983—; frequent lectr. in tax law; regular TV appearances on Nightly Business Report, Pub. Broadcasting System, 1986—; co-chmn. NYU Conf. Fed. Taxation of Real Estate Transactions, 1987, 88. Author: (with others) Tax Aspects of Real Investments, 1987, Understanding Estate Partnership Tax Allocations, 1987, Realty Joint Ventures, 1980-86, Tax Sheltered Investments Handbook-Special Update on Tax Reform Act of 1984, Real Estate Syndication Handbook, 1985, Real Estate Syndication Tax Handbook, 1986, The Tax Reform Act of 1986, 1986, The Final Partnership Nonrecourse Debt Allocation Regulations, 1987, Taxation of Real Estate Investments, 1987, Understanding Partnership Tax Allocations, 1987, Tax Aspects of Environmental (Superfund) Settlements, 1994, The Final Regulations Under Section 704(c), 1995, The Proposed Publicly Traded Partnership Regulations, 1995. Kripke Securities law fellow NYU, 1976. Mem. ABA (nat. chmn. audit subcom. of tax sect. partnership com. 1984-86, partnership tax allocation subcom. chmn. 1986-90, nat. chmn. partnership com. 1992-94, chmn. task force publicly traded partnerships 1995—), N.Y. State Bar Assn. (tax sect. partnership com. 1980—), Assn. of Bar of City of N.Y. Republican. Jewish. Office: Battle Fowler 1999 Ave of the Stars Ste 2700 Los Angeles CA 90067

PRESBY, J. THOMAS, financial advisor; b. Newark, Feb. 15, 1940; s. George and Shirley (Kandel) P.; m. Elaine Merle Smith, Aug. 19, 1961; children: Philip, Terry, Mona. BSEE, Rutgers U., 1961; MS in Indsl. Adminstrn., Carnegie-Mellon U., 1963. CPA, Ohio, N.Y. Ptnr. Touche & Ross, N.Y.C., 1972-76; regional ptnr. Touche Ross Internat., Paris, 1976-79, nat. dir. client svcs., 1979-81, exec. dir., 1981-82, ptnr.-in-charge fin. svcs. ctr., 1982-90, mng. ptnr. Ea. Europe, Brussels, 1990-94, chief exec. officer

Europe, Paris, 1991-95; COO Deloitte Touche Tohmatsu Internat., N.Y.C., 1995—. Mem. bus. adv. council Grad. Sch. Indsl. Adminstrn., Carnegie-Mellon U., Pitts., 1984—; trustee Rutgers U., New Brunswick, N.J., 1985-90, Coll. Ins., N.Y.C., 1986-89. Mem. AICPA, Ohio Soc. CPAs, N.Y. Soc. CPAs, Harmonie Club, N.Y. Athletic Club, Tennis Club of Paris. Avocations: antique autos; racquetball; squash. Home: 6 HOlton Ln Essex Fells NJ 07021 Office: Deloitte Touche 1633 Broadway New York NY 10019

PRESCHLACK, JOHN EDWARD, management consultant; b. N.Y.C., May 30, 1933; s. William and Anna M. (Hrubesch) P.; m. Lynn A. Stanley, Dec. 29, 1962; children: John Edward Jr., James S., David C. B.S.E.E., M.I.T., 1954; M.B.A., Harvard U., 1958. Ptnr. McKinsey & Co., Inc., N.Y.C., London, Dusseldorf, W. Ger., 1958-73; pres. ITEK Graphic Products Co., Lexington, Mass., 1973-77; pres., CEO Gen. Binding Corp., Northbrook, Ill., 1977-83, Roberts & Porter, Inc., Des Plaines, Ill., 1984-86; ptnr., sr. dir. Spencer Stuart, Chgo., 1987—; bd. dirs. Blyth Industries, Greenwich, Conn., 1989—. Trustee Chgo. Hort. Soc., 1979—; chmn. Lake Forest (Ill.) Planning Commn., 1982-88; alderman City of Lake Forest, 1989—; mem. devel. com. MIT, 1986-92. With USAF, 1954-56. Decorated Air Force Commendation medal; recipient Corp. Leadership award M.I.T., 1978. Mem. Onwentsia Club, Chgo. Club, Harvard Club of N.Y.C. Republican. Roman Catholic. Avocations: tennis, skiing, travel. Office: Spencer Stuart 401 N Michigan Ave Chicago IL 60611-4212 *Focus on what's right, not who's right; be honest and candid in dealing with others; don't get hung up on who gets credit for what you've done; select and reward outstanding people.*

PRESCOTT, BARBARA LODWICH, educational administrator; b. Chgo., Aug. 15, 1951; d. Edward and Eugenia Lodwich; m. Warren Paul Prescott, Dec. 2, 1979; 1 child, Warren Paul Jr. BA, U. Ill., Chgo., 1973, MEd, 1981; MA, U. Wis., 1978; postgrad., Stanford U., 1983-87. Cert. tchr., learning handicapped specialist, cmty. coll. instr., Calif. Grad. rschr. U. Ill., Chgo., 1979-81; learning handicapped specialist St. Paulus Luth. Sch., San Francisco, 1981-83; grad. rsch. asst. Sch. Edn. Stanford (Calif.) U., 1983-87, writing cons. for law students, 1985-86; learning handicapped specialist/lead therapist Gilroy Clinic Speech-Hearing-Learning Ctr., Crippled Children's Soc., Santa Clara, Calif., 1988-89; ednl. dir. Adolescent Intensive Resdl. Svc. Calif. Pacific Med. Ctr., San Francisco, 1989—; instr. evening San Jose City Coll., 1988-92. Contbr. articles to profl. jours.; author: Proceedings of Internat. Congress of Linguistics, 1987; editor: Proceedings - Forum for Research on Language Issues, 1986; author videotape: Making a Difference in Language and Learning, 1989. Recipient Frederick Bork Teaching Trainee award San Francisco State U., 1983; Ill. State scholar, 1973. Mem. Calif. Assn. Pvt. Specialized Edn. and Svcs., Phi Delta Kappa (v.p. 1984-86), Pi Lambda Theta (sec. 1982-83), Phi Kappa Phi, Alpha Lambda Theta. Home: 1055 Manet Dr Apt 86 Sunnyvale CA 94087-2819

PRESCOTT, DAVID MARSHALL, biology educator; b. Clearwater, Fla., Aug. 3, 1926; s. Clifford Raymond and Lillian (Moore) P.; m. Gayle Edna Demery; children: Lavonne, Jason, Ryan. BA, Wesleyan U., 1950; PhD, U. Calif., Berkeley, 1954. Asst. prof. UCLA Med. Sch., 1955-59; biologist Oak Ridge (Tenn.) Nat. Lab., 1959-63; prof. U. Colo. Sch. Medicine, Denver, 1963-66; prof. molecular, cell and devel. biology U. Colo., Boulder, 1966—, Disting. prof., 1980—; pres. Am. Soc. Cell Biology, 1966. Author: Cell Reproduction, 1976, Cancer: The Misguided Cell, 1986, Cells, 1988; also numerous rsch. reports; editor: Methods in Cell Biology, 15 vols., 1963-78. Adv. com. March of Dimes, 1979-90. Recipient von Humboldt prize Fed. Republic Germany, 1979; grantee NIH, 1985-95, Nat. Found. Cancer Rsch., 1985-89, NSF, 1990-91, 95—; John Simon Guggenheim Meml. Found. fellow, 1990-91. Fellow Am. Acad. Arts and Scis.; mem. NAS, Soc. Protozoologists (pres. 1995—). Avocation: numismatics. Home: 285 Brook Pl Boulder CO 80302-8031 Office: Univ Colo Dept Biology Boulder CO 80309

PRESCOTT, JOHN HERNAGE, aquarium executive; b. Corona, Calif., Mar. 16, 1935; s. Arthur James and Henrietta (Hernage) P.; m. Sandra Baker, Sept. 26, 1985; children by previous marriage—Craig C., Blane R. B.A., UCLA, 1957; postgrad., U. So. Calif., Los Angeles, 1958-60; cert. advanced mgmt. program, Harvard U. Curator Marineland of the Pacific, Palos Verdes, Calif., 1957-70, v.p., 1966-70, gen. mgr., 1970-72; exec. dir., v.p. New Eng. Aquarium, Boston, 1972-95; dir. emeritus, 1995—; corporator Woods Hole (Mass.) Oceanographic Inst., 1976-90; chmn. mem. com. sci. advisers Marine Mammal Commn., Washington, 1977-80; dir. Mus. Inst. Teaching Sci. Boston, 1984-92; chmn. Humpback Whale Recovery Team NOAA, Washington, 1987-93; mem. U.S. del. Internat. Whaling Commn., 1989-94. Author: Aquarium Fishes of the World, 1976. Editor: Georges Bank: Past, Present, Future, 1981, Right Whales: Past and Present Status, 1986. Bd. dirs. Boston Mcpl. Rsch. Bur., 1981-95, Boston Am. Heart Assn., 1983-86, NOAA, Washington, 1987-92; mem. Marine Fisheries Adv. Com., 1991-93, Artery Bus. Com., 1993-95. Recipient commendation for efforts to conserve whales U.S. Ho. of Reps., 1971, Ann. Sci. award for Conservation, Am. Cetacean Soc., 1969. Fellow Am. Assn. Zool. Parks and Aquariums (bd. dirs. 1985-95); mem. AAAS, Soc. Marine Mammalogy, Am. Assn. Mus., Sea Edn. Assn. (trustee 1986-92), Explorers Club (chmn. New Eng. sect. 1981-85). Office: New Eng Aquarium Corp Central Wharf Boston MA 02110-3399

PRESCOTT, JOHN MACK, biochemist, retired university administrator; b. San Marcos, Tex., Jan. 22, 1921; s. John Mack and Maude (Raborn) P.; m. Kathryn Ann Kelly, June 8, 1946; children: Stephen Michael, Donald Wyatt. B.S. in Chemistry, S.W. Tex. State Coll., 1941; M.S. in Biochemistry and Nutrition, Tex. A&M U., 1949; Ph.D. in Biochemistry, U. Wis., 1952. Lab. asst. Dow Chem. Co., Freeport, Tex., 1942-43; faculty Tex. A&M U., College Station, 1946-49, 52-85, prof. biochemistry, 1959-85, dean Coll. Sci., 1970-77, v.p. for acad. affairs, 1977-81, dir. Inst. Occupational and Environ. Medicine, 1981-87, prof. med. biochemistry, 1981-85, prof. emeritus, 1985—, spl. asst. to dep. chancellor for biotech. devel., 1987-88; research asst. U. Wis.-Madison, 1949-51, U. Tex., Austin, 1951-52; vis. prof. Harvard Med. Sch., 1982. Contbr. articles profl. jours. Mem. Tex. Bd. Examiners in Basic Scis., 1974-79, mem. Tex. State Bd. Edn., 1984-88. Served to lt. USAAF, 1943-46; lt. col. USAF Res., 1946-68. Mem. Am. Soc. for Biochemistry and Molecular Biology, Soc. for Exptl. Biology and Medicine, Sigma Xi, Phi Lambda Upsilon. Home: 31 Forest Dr College Station TX 77840-2337

PRESCOTT, PETER SHERWIN, writer; b. N.Y.C., July 15, 1935; s. Orville and Lilias (Ward-Smith) P.; m. Anne Courthope Kirsopp Lake, June 22, 1957; children: David Sherwin, Antonia Courthope. A.B. magna cum laude, Harvard, 1957. Editor E.P. Dutton Co., N.Y.C., 1958-67; lit. editor, syndicated columnist Women's Wear Daily, N.Y.C., 1964-68; mem. faculty Pubs. Sch. for Writers, N.Y.C., 1965-66; lit. editor, columnist Look mag., 1968-71; book critic Newsweek mag., N.Y.C., 1971-91; sr. writer Newsweek mag., 1978-91; lectr. U.S. State Dept., 1978; adj. prof. Grad. Sch. Journalism, Columbia U., 1979-86. Author: A World of Our Own: Notes on Life and Learning in a Boys' Preparatory School, 1970, Soundings: Encounters with Contemporary Books, 1972, A Darkening Green: Notes from the Silent Generation, 1974, The Child Savers: Juvenile Justice Observed, 1981, Never in Doubt: Critical Essays on American Books, 1972-85, 1986, The Norton Book of American Short Stories, 1988. Mem. Dem. town Com., New Canaan, 1969-72; constable Town of New Canaan, 1969-73; bd. dirs. Authors Guild Found., 1970-95, pres., 1971-93; exec. bd. Authors League Fund, 1st v.p., 1994—. With USAR, 1958-64. Recipient George Polk award criticism, 1978, 1st prize Robert F. Kennedy Book Awards, 1981; fellow Guggenheim Found., 1977, NEH, 1993. Mem. PEN Am. Center (exec. bd. 1974-76), Authors League Am. (exec. bd. 1974-76), Assn. Literary Scholars and Critics, Authors Guild (exec. bd. 1971-91), Nat. Book Critics Circle (exec. bd. 1973-75, 92-93), Century Assn., Harvard Club (N.Y.C.), Phi Beta Kappa. Home and Office: 81 Benedict Hill Rd New Canaan CT 06840-2904

PRESCOTT, RICHARD PAUL, JR., computer company consultant; b. Bloomington, Ill., Apr. 20, 1939; s. Richard Paul Sr. and Kathern Grace (Rhodus) P.; m. Winifred Luce Rockefeller, June 15, 1962 (dec. 1966); children: Paul Luce and Peter Grace (dec.). Bus., Ill. Wesleyan U., 1960; MBA, U. Chgo., 1963; PhD, London Sch. Econ., 1966; lic. real estate sales, Ill. State U., 1992. Systems analyst Honeywell EDP, Chgo., 1963-67; info. specialist IBM, White Plains, N.Y., 1967-68; sr. project dir. United Artists, N.Y.C., 1969-70; info. mgr. Blue Cross Assn., Chgo., 1971-72; software cons. Bloomington, Ill., 1973-92, Referral Co. of McLean County, 1992; founding mem., owner Software Info. Svc. Bd., 1993; cons. Gen. Acct. Office, Washington, Sec. of State, Washington, Econ. Devel. Peru, Lima, 1990—. Author: SSA and Blue Cross Instruction Manual, 1970, (software) Easy Tran-sort, 1971, Operating System, 1974. Mem. Rep. Nat. Com., Pres.'s Conf. Econ. Advisors, 1990—. Comdr. USN, 1963—. Decorated Navy Cross, Silver Star, Purple Heart. Mem. DAV, Chgo. Econ. Coun., Am. Legion, Smithsonian Inst., Chgo. Art Inst., Bloomington Symphony, Libr. of Congress Assocs. (charter mem.), Mensa, Theta Chi (chpt. pres.). Methodist. Avocations: sailing, collecting U.S. stamps, reading, computers. Home and Office: 1128 N Colton Ave Bloomington IL 61701-1922

PRESCOTT, WILLIAM BRUCE, minister; b. Denver, Dec. 30, 1951; s. William Rex and Betena Naomi (Fletcher) P.; m. D. Kylene Winters, Nov. 24, 1973; children: William Doyle, Candice Joy. BS in Corrections, U. Albuquerque, 1973; MDiv, Southwestern Bapt. Sem., 1978, PhD, 1986. Ordained minister in Bapt. Ch., 1976. Youth minister Sandia Bapt. Ch., Albuquerque, 1974-75; pastor Clairette (Tex.) Bapt. Ch., 1976-79; instr. philosophy and religion Tarrant County Jr. Coll. NW Campus, Ft. Worth, 1984-86; pastor Easthaven Bapt. Ch., Houston, 1987—; adj. prof. Southwestern Bapt. Theol. Sem., HBU Extension, Houston, 1987-90; police chaplain Houston Police Dept., 1987—; trustee S.E. Area Ministries, Houston, 1988—; exec. bd. Union Bapt. Assn., 1987—, Bapt. Gen. Conv. Tex., 1993—; adv. bd. Tex. Baptists Committed, 1990—; coord. coun. Coop. Bapt. Fellowship, 1994—, Tex. steering com., 1994—. Book reviewer to Southwestern Jour. Theology; contbr. articles to profl. jours. Served on BGCT Bapt. Distinctives Com., 1994—, BGCT Exec. Bd. Nominatin Com., 1996—, CBF Theol. Edn. Ministry Group, 1994-95, CBF Bapt. Principles Ministry Group, 1995—, chmn. CBF Bapt. Distinctives Partnership Team, 1995—; trustee San Andres U., San Andres Island, San Andres Found. Named one of Outstanding Young Men of Am., Jaycees, 1984. Mem. Am. Acad. Religion, Nat. Assn. Bapt. Profs. of Religion, Ams. United Separation Ch. & State, So. Bapt. Alliance, Baptists Committed. Democrat. Home: 2203 Bisontine St Friendswood TX 77546-2391 Office: Easthaven Bapt Ch 9321 Edgebrook St Houston TX 77075-1249

PRESECAN, NICHOLAS LEE, civil, environmental engineer, consultant; b. Indpls., Sept. 4, 1940; s. Nicholas Eli and Dorothy Lee (Moore) P.; m. Joan Westin, Nov. 11, 1940; children: Julie Marie, Mary Lee, Anne Westin. BSCE, Purdue U., 1963; MS in Engring., U. Calif., Berkeley, 1967. Cert. profl. engr., 31 states. Project engr. San Bernardino County (Calif.) Flood Control, 1963, Engring. Sci. Inc., Arcadia, Calif., 1968-70; office mgr. Engring. Sci. Inc., Cleve., 1970-72, v.p., chief engr., 1972-81; v.p. internat. divsn. Engring. Sci. Inc., Arcadia, 1981-84, group v.p., 1984-87; sr. v.p. Engring. Sci. Inc., Pasadena, Calif., 1987—; mem. industry adv. bd. Sch. Engring. and Tech. Calif. State U., L.A., 1986—. Contbr. articles to profl. jours. Commr. Archtl. Commn., Claremont, Calif., 1980-86; councilman Claremont City Coun., 1986-94; mayor City of Claremont, 1989-92; mem. Pasadena Tournament of Roses Assn., 1980—, L.A. 2000 Environ. Com., 1987-88. With USMC, 1963-67. Recipient Disting. Engring. Achievement award Inst. for Advancement of Engring., 1993. Fellow ASCE (mem. internat. adv. com. 1987-90); mem. NSPE, Am. Acad. Environ. Engrs., Am. Water Works Assn. (life), Water Environ. Fedn., Soc. Am. Value Engrs., Rotary. Republican. Avocations: skiing, hiking, fishing, boating, writing. Home: 727 E Alamosa Dr Claremont CA 91711-2008 Office: Parsons Engring Sci Inc 100 W Walnut St Pasadena CA 91124-0001

PRESKA, LORETTA A., federal judge; b. 1949. BA, Coll. St. Rose, 1970; JD, Fordham U., 1973; LLM, NYU, 1978. Assoc. Cahill, Gordon & Reindel, N.Y.C., 1973-82; ptnr. Herzog, Calamari & Gleason, N.Y.C., 1982-92; fed. judge U.S. Dist. Ct. (so. dist.) N.Y., N.Y.C., 1992—. Mem. ABA, N.Y. State Bar Assn., N.Y. County Lawyers Assn., Assn. Bar City N.Y., Fed. Bar Coun., Fordham Law Alumni Assn. (v.p.). Office: US Courthouse Rm 1320 500 Pearl St New York NY 10007

PRESKA, MARGARET LOUISE ROBINSON, education educator, district service professional; b. Parma, N.Y., Jan. 23, 1938; d. Ralph Craven and Ellen Elvira (Niemi) Robinson; m. Daniel C. Preska, Jan. 24, 1959; children: Robert, William, Ellen Preska Steck. B.S. summa cum laude, SUNY, 1957; M.A., Pa. State U., 1961; Ph.D., Claremont Grad. Sch., 1969; postgrad., Manchester Coll., Oxford U., 1973. Instr. LaVerne (Calif.) Coll., 1968-75, asst. prof., asso. prof., acad. dean, 1972-75; instr. Starr King Sch. for Ministry, Berkeley, Calif., summer, 1975; v.p. acad. affairs, equal opportunity officer Mankato (Minn.) State U., 1975-79, pres., 1979-92; project dir. Kaliningrad (Russia) Mil. Re-Tng., 1992—; Disting. svc. prof. Minn. State U., Winona, 1993—, pres. Inst. for Effective Tchg., 1993—; bd. dirs. No. States Power Co., Norwest Corp., Mankato, Minn. Pres. Pomona Valley chpt. UN Assn., 1968-69, Unitarian Soc. Pomona Valley, 1968-69, PTA Lincoln Elem. Sch., Pomona, 1973-74, Campfire Boys and Girls, 1986-88; mem. Pomona City Charter Revision Commn., 1972; chmn. The Fielding Inst., Santa Barbara, 1983-86; bd. dirs. Elderhostel Internat., 1983-87, Minn. Agrl. Interpretive Ctr. (Farmam.), 1983-92, Am. Assn. State Colls. and Univs., Moscow on the Mississippi - Minn. Meets the Soviet Union; nat. pres. Campfire, Inc., 1985-87; chmn. Gov.'s Coun. on Youth, Minn., 1983-86, Minn. Edn. Forum, 1984; mem. Gov.'s Commn. on Econ. Future of Minn., 1985—, NCAA Pres. Commn., 1986-92, NCAA Cost Cutting Commn., Minn. Brainpower Compact, 1985; commr. Great Lakes Govs.' Econ. Devel. Coun., 1986, Minn Gov.'s Commn. on Forestry. Carnegie Found. grantee Am. Coun. Edn. Deans Inst., 1974; recipient Outstanding Alumni award Pa. State, Outstanding Alumni award Claremont Grad. Sch., YWCA Leader award 1982, Exch. Club Book of Golden Deeds award, 1987; named one of top 100 alumni, SUNY, 1985, Hall of Heritage award, 1988, Wohelo Camp Fire award, 1989. Mem. AAUW (pres. Mankato 1990-92), LWV, Women's Econ. Roundtable, St. Paul/Mpls. Com. on Fgn. Rels., Am. Coun. on Edn., Am. Assn. Univ. Adminstrs., Zonta, Rotary, Benedicts Dance Club. Unitarian. Home: 476 W Broadway St Winona MN 55987-5218 Office: Minn State Univ Inst for Effective Teaching 1125 W Wabasha St Winona MN 55987-2452

PRESLAR, LEN BROUGHTON, JR., hospital administrator; b. Concord, N.C., Aug. 13, 1947; s. Len B. and Billie M. (James) P.; m. Joyce W. Whittington, July 11, 1971; children: Bradley E., Whitney A., Andrew C. BA, Wake Forest U., 1971; MBA, U. N.C., Greensboro, 1980. Admissions clk. N.C. Bapt. Hosp., Winston-Salem, 1969-71, systems analyst, 1971-72, budget mgr., 1973, contr., 1973-75, v.p. fin. mgmt., 1975-88, pres., chief exec. officer, 1988—; bd. dirs. Planters Nat. Bank, Winston-Salem, Amos Cottage, Inc. Co-chmn. cabinet United Way, Winston-Salem, 1989—; bd. dirs. N.C. chpt. ARC, 1989—; deacon local Bapt. ch. Fellow Hosp. Fin. Mgmt. Assn. Republican. Baptist. Avocations: gardening, racketball. Office: NC Bapt Hosp Medical Center Blvd Winston Salem NC 27157*

PRESLEY, BRIAN, investment company executive; b. Evansville, Ind., Dec. 28, 1941; s. Harry and Ruth P.; B.S. in Bus. Adminstrn., U. Evansville, 1963; M.B.A. Mich. State U., 1964; diploma Wharton Sch., U. Pa., 1995, m. Mary Nell Minyard, Aug. 17, 1972; children—Debra, Cynthia, David, Jeffrey, Clark, Gregory, Steven. Market research analyst Stanley Works, New Britain, Conn., 1964-68; tax shelter coordinator F.I. Dupont, Memphis, 1968-73; v.p. Bullington Schas, Memphis, 1973-75; pres., mng. gen. ptnr. Presley Assocs., Memphis, 1965-93; pres., CFO CSG, Inc., Memphis, 1975—; gen. ptnr. various real estate and oil and gas partnerships, 1974-1986; pres. Cooper St. Group Securities, Inc., 1983-86 ; div. mgr. Advantage Capital Corp. (divsn. SunAmerica, Inc.), 1986-89, reg. v.p., 1989, CEO 1990-94, mng. dir., mkt. strategist, 1995; pres. Presley Adv. Inc., pub. Presley Adv. Letter; instr. fin. div. continuing edn. Memphis U. Bd. dirs. Apt. Council Tenn., 1980-86, sec.-treas., 1982-83; pres. Memphis Apt. Council, 1983; mem., U. Evansville Nat. Alumni Bd., 1988-91. Producer 2 daily radio stock market commentary shows, 1988; fin. commentator Sta. WEVU-TV (ABC), Ft. Myers/Naples, 1988-89. Mem. Internat. Assn. Fin. Planners (mem. broker dealer adv. coun., 1993—), Admirals Club (life), Naples Sailing and Yacht Club, Pi Sigma Epsilon, Beta Gamma Sigma, Tau Kappa Epsilon Alumni Assn. (pres. Memphis area 1979-80). Presbyterian. Host syndicated radio show for sr. citizens, 1979-81. Home: 425 17th Ave S Naples FL 33940-7404 Office: 1600 S Federal Hwy Pompano Beach FL 33062

PRESLEY, JOHN WOODROW, academic administrator; b. Jonesboro, Ark., Mar. 24, 1948; s. Marvin Woodrow and Willa Louise (Taylor) P.; m. Katherine Bailey Harrison, Oct. 17, 1978. BSE, Ark. State U., 1970; MA, So. Ill. U., 1972, PhD, 1975; BS in Edn., 1970; postgrad., Johns Hopkins U., 1976, U. Tex., 1980. Asst. prof. Augusta (Ga.) Coll., 1974-77, assoc. prof., 1978-84, prof., 1984-89, chmn. Freshman English, 1974-76, chmn. developmental studies, 1976-78, asst. v.p. for acad. affairs, 1988-89; assoc. dean faculty Lafayette Coll., Easton, Pa., 1989-90, acting provost, dean faculty, 1990-91, assoc. provost, dean faculty, 1991-92; dean Coll. of Arts, Scis. and Letters U. Mich., Dearborn, 1992—; presenter in field. Author: The Robert Graves Letters and Manuscripts at Southern Illinois University, 1976, (with W.M. Dodd) Breakthrough: From Reading to Writing, 1981, To Be Exact: A Handbook for Revision, 1982, (with M.G. Kramer) The Prentice-Hall Workbook for Writers, 1983, 4th edit. (with M.G. Kramer and D. Rigg), 1985, 5th, 1988, 6th, 1990, How Like A Life, 1987, (with N. Prinsky) The World of Work, 1987, (with A.I. Philbin) Technical Communications: Method, Application, Management, 1989; contbg. author: The Prentice-Hall Handbook for Writers, 9th edit., 1985, Sparking Connections: Spoken and Written Communications, 1985, Speech Exercises for Basic Writers and Others, 1987; contbr. articles to profl. jours. NDEA fellow, 1972. Mem. Phi Kappa Phi. Home: 7782 Horse Mill Grosse Ile MI 48138 Office: Univ Mich Dearborn 4901 Evergreen Rd Dearborn MI 48128

PRESLEY, PRISCILLA, actress; b. Bklyn., May 24, 1945; m. Elvis Presley, 1967 (div. 1973). Studies with Milton Katselas; student, Steven Peck Theatre Art Sch., Chuck Norris Karate Sch. Prin. Bis and Beau; co-executor Graceland, Memphis. Appearances include (films) The Naked Gun, 1988, The Adventures of Ford Fairlaine, 1990, The Naked Gun 2 1/2, 1991, The Naked Gun 33 1/3, 1994, (TV series) Those Amazing Animals, 1980-81, Dallas, 1983-88, (TV movie) Love Is Forever, 1983; prodr. (TV movie) Elvis and Me, 1988. Office: William Morris 151 El Camino Dr Beverly Hills CA 90212*

PRESLEY, ROBERT BUEL, state senator; b. Tahlequah, Okla., Dec. 4, 1924; s. Doyle and Annie (Townsend) P.; grad. FBI Nat. Acad., Washington, 1962; student Riverside City Coll., 1960; A.A., UCLA, m. Ahni Ratliff, Aug. 20, 1944; children—Donna Thurber, Marilyn Raphael, Robert Buel. Various positions Riverside County Sheriff's Dept. (Calif.), 1950-62, undersheriff, 1962-74; mem. Calif. Senate, 36th Dist., 1974—; lectr. ethics. Served with U.S. Army, 1943-46. Decorated Bronze Star. Mem. FBI Nat. Acad. Assn. (pres. Calif. chpt. 1974). Baptist. Clubs: Lions, Elks, Am. Legion, V.F.W., Moose, Riverside County Democratic Century (pres. 1972-73). Home: 5508 Grassy Trail Dr Riverside CA 92504-1251 Office: Office of State Senate 5114 State Capital Sacramento CA 95814

PRESS, AIDA KABATZNICK, former editor, writer; b. Boston, Nov. 18, 1926; m. Newton Press, June 5, 1947; children: David, Dina Press Weber, Benjamin Presskreischer. BA, Radcliffe Coll., 1948. Reporter Waltham (Mass.) News-Tribune, 1960-63; freelance writer, 1960-63; editl. cons. Mass. Dept. Mental Health, Boston, 1966-72; Waltham/Watertown reporter Boston Herald Traveler, 1963-70; dir. news and publs. Harvard Grad. Sch. Design, Cambridge, Mass., 1972-78; publs. editor Radcliffe Coll., Cambridge, 1978-81, dir., editor of publs., 1981-83, editor Radcliffe Quar., 1971-93, dir. pub. info., 1983-93; cons. editor Regis Coll. Alumnae Mag., Weston, Mass., 1994. Editor emerita Radcliffe Quar., 1993—; contbr. articles to newspapers and mags. Recipient Publs. Distinction award Am. Alumni Coun., 1974, Top 5 coll. Mag., Coun. for Advancement and Support of Edn., 1984, Top 10 Univ Mags., 1991, Gold medal Coll. Mags., 1991, Alumnae Achievement award Radcliffe Coll., 1994. Avocations: hiking, playing recorder.

PRESS, CHARLES, retired political science educator; b. St. Louis, Sept. 12, 1922; s. Otto Ernst and Laura (Irion) P.; m. Nancy Miller, June 10, 1950; children: Edward Paul, William David, Thomas Leigh, Laura Mary. Student, Elmhurst (Ill.) Coll.; B of Journalism, U. Mo., 1948; M.A., U. Minn., 1951, Ph.D., 1953. Faculty N.D. Agrl. Coll., 1954-56; dir. Grand Rapids Area Study, 1956-57; with Bur. Govt., U. Wis., 1957-58; faculty Mich. State U., East Lansing, 1958-91; prof. polit. sci. Mich. State U., 1964-91; emeritus, 1991—; chmn. dept. Mich. State U., 1966-73; cons. Mich. Constl. Conv., 1962-63; supr. Ingham County, 1966-72; tchr. summers, London; tchr. U. N.S.W., Sydney, Mich. State U. Author: Main Street Politics, 1962, (with Charles Adrian) The American Government Process, 1965, Governing Urban America, 1968, 5th edit., 1977, American Politics Reappraised, 1974, (with Kenneth VerBurg) States and Community Governments in a Federal System, 1979, 3d edit., 1991, American Policy Studies, 1981, The Political Cartoon, 1982, (with others) Michigan Political Atlas 1984, (with Kenneth VerBurg) American Politicians and Journalists, 1988, (with Kenneth VerBurg) (weekly newspaper column) The Pros and Cons of Politics. Sec. Ingham County Bd. Health, 1983-93; chmn., mem. East Lansing Bd. Rev., 1966-86; bd. dirs. Urban League, 1971-73; mem. East Lansing Housing and Urban Devel. Commn., 1988-93. Served with AUS, 1943-45. Recipient Disting. Prof. award Mich. State U., 1980, Alumni Merit award Elmhurst (Ill.) Coll., 1995. Mem. Am. Polit. Sci. Assn., Midwest Polit. Sci. Assn. (pres. 1974-75), So. Polit. Sci. Assn., Mich. Conf. Polit. Scientists (pres. 1972-73), Nat. Municipal League. Home: 987 Lantern Hill Dr East Lansing MI 48823-2831 Office: Mich State U 315 S Kedzie Hall East Lansing MI 48824-1032

PRESS, EDWARD, consulting physician; b. N.Y.C., May 4, 1913; s. Louis and Anna (Karpas) P.; m. Ruth Scheffer, July 8, 1951; children: Stephen, Phyllis. B.A., Ohio U., 1934; M.D., NYU, 1937; M.P.H., Harvard U., 1947. Diplomate: Am. Bd. Pediatrics, Am. Bd. Preventive Medicine. Intern Beth Israel Hosp., N.Y.C., 1938-40; resident Lincoln Hosp., Bronx, N.Y., 1940; psychiatric resident E.P. Bradley Home, East Providence, R.I., 1940-41; asst. dir. maternal and child health div. W.Va. Health Dept., 1941-42; pediatric cons. Mich. Health Dept., 1946; regional med. dir. U.S. Children's Bur., Chgo., 1947-50; asso. dir. div. services crippled children U. Ill., 1950-55; field dir. Am. Public Health Assn., N.Y.C., 1955-59; dir. Dept. Public Health, Evanston, Ill., 1959-64; med. asst. to dir. Ill. Dept. Public Health, 1964-67; state health officer (Oreg. Health Div.), Portland, 1967-79; public health cons., 1979—; emeritus sec.-treas. Press Internat. Sales Corp., 1978—; asst. prof. preventive medicine U. Ill., 1950-55; asst. prof. pediatrics Northwestern U., 1964-67; clin. prof. pub. health, preventive medicine and pediatrics Med. Sch., Oreg. Health Scis. U., 1967-79, emeritus clin. prof., 1979—; vice chmn. Tech. Adv. Group for Fire Safe Cigarette Act of 1990-93. Mem. editorial adv. com. The Nation's Health, 1989-91; contbr. articles to profl. jours. Organizer Poison Control Ctr., Chgo., 1953; trustee Underwriters' Labs., Inc., 1969-79. Served to maj. USAAF, 1942-46. Recipient Clifford G. Grulee award Am. Acad. Pediatrics, 1961; recognition award Am. Assn. Poison Control Centers, 1975. Mem. AMA, Am. Pub. Health Assn. (founder and pres. Conf. Emeritus Mems. 1986-89, Excellence in Health Admintrn. award 1992), Nat. Soc. Prevention of Blindness, Am. Assn. Public Health Physicians (pres. 1971-72, Bronze medal 1979), Conf. State and Provincial Health Authorities N.Am. (pres. 1971-72), Assn. State and Territorial Health Officers (mem. exec. com. 1972-75, Arthur G. McCormack award 1978), Am. Assn. Sr. Physicians (pres. 1984-86), Oreg. Pub. Health Assn. (Leadership award 1986), Oreg. Med. Assn. (presdl. citation 1980), Portland City Club, Multnomah Athletic Club, Rotary. Home: 2211 SW 1st Ave Apt 905 Portland OR 97201-5013

PRESS, FRANK, geophysicist, educator; b. Bklyn., Dec. 4, 1924; s. Solomon and Dora (Steinholz) P.; m. Billie Kallick, June 9, 1946; children: William Henry, Paula Evelyn. BS, CCNY, 1944, LLD (hon.), 1972; MA, Columbia U., 1946, PhD, 1949; DSc (hon.), 28 univs. Rsch. assoc. Columbia U., 1946-49, instr. geology, 1949-51, asst. prof. geology, 1951-52, assoc. prof., 1952-55; prof. geophysics Calif. Inst. Tech., 1955-65, dir. seismol. lab., 1957-65; prof. geophysics, chmn. dept. earth and planetary scis. MIT, 1965-77; sci. advisor to pres., dir. Office Sci. and Tech. Policy, Washington, 1977-80; inst. prof. MIT, 1981; pres. Nat. Acad. Scis., 1981-93; Cecil & Ida Green sr. fellow Carnegie Inst. of Washington, Washington, DC, 1993—; mem. Pres.'s Sci. Adv. Com., 1961-64; mem. Com. on Anticipated Advances in Sci. and Tech., 1974-76; mem. Nat. Sci. Bd., 1970-76; mem. lunar and planetary missions bd. NASA; participant bilateral scis. agreement with Peoples Republic of China and USSR; mem. U.S. delegation to Nuclear Test Ban Negotiations, Geneva and Moscow. Author: (with M. Ewing, W.S. Jardetzky) Propagation of Elastic Waves in Layered Media, 1957, (with R.

Siever) Earth, 1986, Understanding Earth, 1994; also over 160 publs.; co-editor: (with R. Siever) Physics and Chemistry of the Earth, 1957—. Decorated Cross of Merit (Germany; Legion of Honor (France); recipient Columbia medal for excellence, 1960, Pub. Svc. award U.S. Dept. Interior, 1972, Gold medal Royal Astron. Soc., 1972, Pub. Svc. medal NASA, 1973, Japan prize Sci. and Tech. Found. Japan, 1993, Pupin medal Columbia U., 1993, Nat. Medal Sci., Pres. of U.S., 1994, Philip Hauge Abelson prize AAAS, 1995; Sherman Fairchild Disting. scholar Calif. Inst. Tech., 1994, Disting. scholar Columbia U., 1995. Mem. NAS, Am. Acad. Arts and Scis., Geol. Soc. Am. (councilor), Am. Geophys. Union (pres. 1973), Soc. Exploration Geophysicists, Seismol. Soc. Am. (pres. 1963), Am. Philos. Soc., French Acad. Scis., Royal Soc. (U.K.), Acad. Scis. of USSR (fgn. mem.), Engring. Acad. Japan (fgn. assoc.). Office: Carnegie Inst Washington 5241 Broad Branch Rd NW Washington DC 20015-1305

PRESS, JEFFERY BRUCE, chemist; b. Rochester, N.Y., May 24, 1947; s. James Herbert and Mildred (Hau) P.; m. Linda Helen Seghers, Dec. 20, 1976; children: Samantha, Michael. BS, Bucknell U., 1969; PhD, Ohio State U., 1973; postgrad., Harvard U., 1973-75. Rsch. chemist Lederle Labs., Pearl River, N.Y., 1975-77, sr. rsch. chemist, 1977-81, group leader, 1981-83; rsch. mgr. Ortho Pharm. Corp., Raritan, N.J., 1983-89; asst. dir. R.W. Johnson Pharm. Rsch. Inst., Spring House, Pa., 1990-94; v.p., dir. rsch. Emisphere Tech. Inc., Hawthorne, N.Y., 1994-95; v.p. R&D Galenica Pharms., Inc., Frederick, Md., 1996—; treas., sec. Organic Reactions, 1995—. Editor: Organic Reactions, 1983—, Chemtracts Organic 1988—, Current Opinion Therapeutic Patents, 1989—, Analgesia, 1993—; patentee in field; contbr. numerous articles to profl. jours. NIH fellow, 1974. Mem. AAAS, Am. Chem. Soc., N.Y. Acad. Scis., Internat. Soc. Heterocyclic Chemistry, Internat. Pure and Applied Chemistry, Drug Info. Assn., Mid-Atlantic Pharmacology Soc., Drug Info. Assn., Sedgewood Club, Tuxedo Club, Phi Beta Kappa, Sigma Xi, Alpha Chi Sigma. Episcopalian. Avocations: golf, building golf clubs, model railroads. Office: 30 W Patrick St Ste 310 Frederick MD 21701

PRESS, MICHAEL S., lawyer; b. N.Y.C., Oct. 30, 1948; s. Irving E. and Florence C. (Mandel) P.; m. Priscilla E. Campo, Oct. 4, 1980; children: Michael S. Press Jr., Priscilla Dorothy. AB, Dartmouth Coll., 1971; JD cum laude, U. Miami, 1974. Bar: N.Y. 1975, U.S. Dist Ct. (so. dist.) N.Y. 1975, (we dist.) N.Y. 1983, (ea. dist.) N.Y. 1987, U.S. Dist. Ct. (ea. dist.) Mich. 1986, U.S. Ct. Appeals (1st cir.) N.Y. 1987, (2nd cir.) N.Y. 1980, (federal cir.) N.Y. 1988, U.S. Tax Ct. 1993, U.S. Supreme Ct. 1985. Assoc. Whitman & Ransom, N.Y.C., 1974-84, ptnr., 1984-93; sole practitioner, 1994—. Mem. bd. editors U. Miami Law Rev., 1973-74. Capt. USAF, 1971-83. Recipient Am. Jurisprudence award U. Miami, 1972, 73. Mem. Piping Rock Club, Hyannisport Club, Beaver Dam Winter Sports Club, Assn. Bar City N.Y., Fed. Bar Coun., Phi Kappa Phi. Republican. Roman Catholic. Home: 36 Harbor Rd Oyster Bay NY 11771-1702 Office: 540 Madison Ave New York NY 10022-3213

PRESS, MICHELLE, editor; b. Memphis, Nov. 22, 1940; d. Sam and Rana (Cohen) Appelbaum; m. Robert Press, June 18, 1960 (div. 1965). B.A., New Sch. for Social Research, 1967. Tchr. U.S. Peace Corps, Malawi, Africa, 1962-64; copy editor Japan Quar., Tokyo, 1967-71; asst. editor Am. Scientist, New Haven, 1971-78, mng. editor, 1978-80, editor, 1981-90; mng. editor Scientific American, N.Y.C., 1981-90, Sci. Am., N.Y.C. Office: Scientific American 415 Madison Ave New York NY 10017

PRESS, WILLIAM HENRY, astrophysicist, computer scientist; b. N.Y.C., N.Y., May 23, 1948; s. Frank and Billie (Kallick) P.; m. Margaret Ann Lauritsen, 1969 (div. 1982); 1 dau., Sara Linda; m. Jeffrey Foden Howell, Apr. 19, 1991; 1 son, James Howell. A.B., Harvard Coll., 1969; M.S., Calif. Inst. Tech., 1971, Ph.D., 1972. Asst. prof. theoretical physics Calif. Inst. Tech., 1973-74; asst. prof. physics Princeton (N.J.) U., 1974-76; prof. astronomy and physics Harvard U., Cambridge, Mass., 1976—; chmn. dept. astronomy Harvard U., 1982-85; mem. numerous adv. coms. and panels NSF, NASA, NAS, NRC; vis. mem. Inst. Advanced Study, 1983—; mem. Def. Sci. Bd., 1985-89, sci. adv. com. Packard Found., 1988—, program com. Sloan Found., 1985-91; chmn. adv. bd. NSF Inst. Theoretical Physics, 1986-87; cons. MITRE Corp., 1977—; trustee Inst. Def. Analysis, 1988—; chief naval ops. Exec. Panel, 1994—. Author: Numerical Recipes, 1986; contbr. articles to profl. jours. Sloan Found. research fellow, 1974-78. Fellow Am. Acad. Arts and Scis., Am. Phys. Soc.; mem. NAS, Am. Astron. Soc. (Helen B. Warner prize 1981), Internat. Astron. Union, Internat. Soc. Relativity and Gravitation, Assn. for Computing Machinery. Office: Harvard U 60 Garden St Cambridge MA 02138-1516

PRESSER, BETH MICHELLE, recreational facility executive, gaming educator; b. Las Vegas, Nev., Mar. 31, 1964; d. Robert and Concetta Ann (Fasso) P. Student, Edison C.C., Ft. Myers, Fla., 1982-84; grad., Casino Career Inst., Atlantic City, N.J., 1987-92. State Cert. in Blackjack, Roulette, Craps, Baccarat, Mini-Baccarat, Pai Gow Poker., N.J., 1992. Cashier, dealer, pit mgr. Carnival Cruises, Miami, Fla., 1984-87; rep. Trump Plaza Casino, Atlantic City, N.J., 1988; dealer Ceasars Casino, Atlantic City, N.J., 1988-93; floor supr. Hollywood Casino, Aurora, Ill., 1993-94; games mgr., tng. ctr. adminstr., instr. Sheraton Casino, Robinsonville, Miss., 1994-95; dealer Horseshoe Casino-Hotel, Robinsonville, Miss., 1995—. Mem. Greenpeace. Democrat. Jewish. Avocation: reading, traveling, swimming. Home: 3170 Edenshire Ln Horn Lake MS 38637

PRESSER, HARRIET BETTY, sociology educator; b. Bklyn., Aug. 29, 1936; d. Phillip Rubinoff and Rose (Gudowitz) Jabish; m. Neil Nathan Presser, Dec. 16, 1956 (div.); 1 child, Sheryl Lynn. BA, George Washington U., 1959; MA, U. N.C., 1962; PhD, U. Calif., Berkeley, 1969. Statistician Bur. Census, Washington, 1959; research assoc. Inst. Life Ins., N.Y.C., 1962-64; lectr. demography U. Sussex, Brighton, England, 1967-68; staff assoc. Population Council, N.Y.C., 1968-69; asst. prof. sociomed. scis. Columbia U., N.Y.C., 1969-73, assoc. prof. sociomed. scis., 1973-76; prof. sociology U. Md., College Park, 1976—, dir. Ctr. on Population, Gender, and Social Inequality,, 1988—, disting. faculty rsch. fellow, 1993-94; fellow in residence Netherlands Inst. for Advanced Study in Humanities & Social Sci., Wassenaar, The Netherlands, 1994-95; fellow Ctr. for Advanced Study in the Behavioral Scis., Stanford, Calif., 1986-87, 91-92; bd. dirs. Population Reference Bur., 1993—; cons. Nat. Inst. for Child Health and Human Devel., 1975—. Editl. bd. Time and Soc., 1991-95, Special Forces, 1984-87, Signs, 19975-85; assoc. editor Jour. Health and Social Behavior, 1975-78. Nat. Inst. for Child Health and Devel. grantee, 1972-78, 83-88, Population Coun. grantee, 1976-79, NSF grantee, 1982-83, 90-94, Rockefeller Found. grantee, 1983-85, 88-94, William and Flora Hewlett Found. grantee, 1989—, Andrew W. Mellon Found. grantee, 1994-95, W. T. Grant Found., 1996—. Mem. Population Assn. Am. (bd. dirs. 1972-75, 2nd v.p. 1983, 1st v.p. 1985, pres.-elect 1988, pres. 1989), Am. Pub. Health Assn. (council mem. population sect. 1976-79), Am. Sociological Assn. (coun. mem. at large 1990-93, chmn., coun. mem. population sect. 1978-83), Sociological Research Assn. (elected). Office: U Md Dept Sociology College Park MD 20742

PRESSER, STANLEY, sociology educator; b. Bklyn., Feb. 18, 1950; s. Sidney and Sydonia (Cohen) P. AB, Brown U., 1971; PhD, U. Mich. 1977. Research investigator Survey Research Ctr. U. Mich., Ann Arbor, 1977-78, head of field office, 1981-83; research assoc. Inst. Research Social Sci.; U. N.C., 1978-81; dir. Detroit Area Study U. Mich., 1983-85; assoc. dir. sociology program NSF, 1985-87, dir., 1987-88; vis. prof. sociology U. Md., College Park, 1988-89, prof. of sociology, dir. Survey Rsch. Ctr., 1989—, dir.joint U Md. and U. Mich. program in Survey Methodology, 1992—; bd. overseers Nat. Opinion Rsch. Ctr. Gen. Social Survey, 1984-85, 93—; spl. cons. Nat. Econ. Research Assocs., 1986-89; cons. U.S. Dept. Justice, Dept. of Commerce, Gen. Acctg. Office, Equal Employment Opportunity Commn., State of Alaska Atty. Gen. Co-author: Questions and Answers in Attitude Surveys, 1981, Survey Questions: Handcrafting the Standardized Questionnaire, 1986; editor Pub. Opinion Quar., 1993—; co-editor: Sourcebook of Harris National Surveys, 1981, Survey Rsch. Methods, 1989. Mem. editl. bd. Pub. Opinion Quar., 1983-87 , Sociol. Methods and Research, 1980-83, Social Psychology Quar., 1979-82. Contbr. articles to profl. jours. and books. Fellow Am. Statis. Assn.; mem. Am. Assn. for Pub. Opinion Rsch. (pres. 1993-94). Office: U of Md Survey Rsch Ctr 1103 Art-Sociology Bldg College Park MD 20742

PRESSER, STEPHEN BRUCE, lawyer, educator; b. Chattanooga, Aug. 10, 1946; s. Sidney and Estelle (Shapiro) P.; m. Carole Smith, June 18, 1968 (div. 1987); children: David Carter, Elisabeth Catherine; m. ArLynn Leiber, Dec. 13, 1987; children: Joseph Leiber, Eastman Leiber. A.B., Harvard U., 1968, J.D., 1971. Bar: Mass. 1971, D.C. 1972. Law clk. to Judge Malcolm Richard Wilkey U.S. Ct. Appeals (D.C. cir.), 1971-72; assoc. Wilmer, Cutler & Pickering, Washington, 1972-74; asst. prof. law Rutgers U., Camden, N.J., 1974-76; vis. assoc. prof. U. Va., 1976-77; prof. Northwestern U., Chgo., 1977—, class 1940 rsch. prof., 1992-93, Raoul Berger prof. legal history, 1992—, assoc. dean acad. affairs Sch. Law, 1982-85. Author: (with Jamil S. Zainaldin) Law and Jurisprudence in American History, 1980, 3d edit., 1995, Studies in the History of the United States Courts of the Third Circuit, 1983, The Original Misunderstanding: The English, The Americans and the Dialetic of Federalist Jurisprudence, 1991, Piercing the Corporate Veil, 1991, revised ann., (with Ralph Ferrara and Meridith Brown) Takeovers: A Strategist's Manual, 2d edit., 1993, Recapturing the Constitution, 1994; assoc. articles editor Guide to American Law, 1985. Mem. acad. adv. bd. Washington Legal Found. Recipient summer stipend NEH, 1975; Fulbright Sr. scholar Univ. Coll., London Sch. Econs. and Polit. Sci., 1983-84, Inst. Advanced Legal Studies, 1996; Adams fellow Inst. U.S. Studies, London, 1996. Mem. Am. Soc. Legal History (bd. dirs. 1979-82), Am. Law Inst., Univ. Club Chgo., Legal Club Chgo. Home: 1015 Cherry St Winnetka IL 60093-2112 Office: Northwestern U Law Sch 357 E Chicago Ave Chicago IL 60611-3008

PRESSLER, LARRY, senator; b. Humboldt, S.D., Mar. 29, 1942; s. Antone Lewis and Loretta Geneive (Claussen) P.; m. Harriet Dent, 1982. B.A., U. S.D., 1964; diploma (Rhodes scholar), Oxford U., Eng., 1965; M.A., Kennedy Sch. Govt., Harvard U., 1971; J.D., Harvard U., 1971. Mem. 94th-95th Congresses from 1st S.D. Dist.; mem. U.S. Senate from S.D., 1979—; U.S. del. Inter-Parliamentary Union for 97th Congress; mem. bd. visitors all mil. svc. academies; now chmn. Commerce Com. U.S. Senate; U.S. Senate com. chmn. commerce, sci. and transp. subcoms.; chmn. comm., aviation, ocieans and fisheries, sci., tech. and space; fin. com. mem.; small bus. com. mem.; mem. spl. com. on aging; congl. del. to UN Gen. Assembly, 1986, 92; mem. U.S. Commn. on Improving the Effectiveness of UN, 1993. Author: U.S. Senators from the Prairie, 1982, Star Wars: The SDI Debates in Congress, 1986. All-Am. del. 4-H agrl. fair, Cairo, 1961, U.S. Rep. (appointed by Vice Pres.) to UN Fall Gen. Assembly, 1986. Served to 1st lt. AUS, 1966-68, Vietnam. Recipient Nat. 4-H Citizenship award, 1962, Report to the Pres. 4-H award, 1962. Mem. Am. Assn. Rhodes Scholars, VFW, ABA Phi Beta Kappa. Office: US Senate 243 Russell Senate Bldg Washington DC 20510

PRESSLEY, FRED G., JR., lawyer; b. N.Y.C., June 19, 1953; s. Fred G. Sr. and Frances (Sanders) P.; m. Cynthia Denise Hill, Sept. 5, 1981. BA cum laude, Union Coll., 1975; JD, Northwestern U., 1978. Bar: Ohio 1978, U.S. Dist. Ct. (so. dist.) Ohio 1979, U.S. Dist. Ct. (no. dist.) Ohio 1985, U.S. Dist. Ct. (ea. dist.) Wis. 1980, U.S. Ct. Appeals (6th cir.). Assoc. Porter, Wright, Morris & Arthur, Columbus, Ohio, 1978-85, ptnr., 1985—. Bd. dirs. Columbus Area Leadership Program, 1981-84, Franklin County Bd. Mental Retardation and Devel. Disabilities, Columbus, 1989—, Union Coll., Schenectady, N.Y., 1992—. Recipient Civic Achievement award Ohio Ho. of Reps., 1988. Mem. ABA. Avocations: jogging, golf, basketball, military history. Office: Porter Wright Morris & Arthur 41 S High St Columbus OH 43215-6101

PRESSLY, THOMAS JAMES, history educator; b. Troy, Tenn., Jan. 18, 1919; s. James Wallace and Martha Belle (Bittick) P.; m. Lillian Cameron, Apr. 30, 1943; children—Thomas James II, Stephanie (Mrs. Kaoruhiko Suzuki). AB, Harvard U., 1940, AM, 1941, PhD, 1950; LLD (hon.), Whitman Coll., 1981. Instr. history Princeton U., 1946-49; asst. prof. U. Wash., 1949-54, assoc. prof., 1954-60, prof., 1960-87, prof. emeritus, 1987—; vis. assoc. prof. Princeton U., 1953-54, Johns Hopkins U., 1969-70. Author: Americans Interpret Their Civil War, 1954; editor: (with W. H. Scofield) Farm Real Estate Values in the United States, 1965, (with others) American Political Behavior, 1974, Diary of George Templeton Strong (abridged), 1988, (with Glenn M. Linden) Voices From the House Divided, 1995. Served with AUS, 1941-45. Ford Found. Faculty fellow, 1951-52; Center for Advanced Study in Behavioral Scis. fellow, 1955-56. Mem. Am. Hist. Assn., So. Hist. Assn. (editorial bd. Jour. So. History 1973-77), Orgn. Am. Historians. Home: 4545 E Laurel Dr NE Seattle WA 98105-3838 Office: U Wash Dept History Seattle WA 98195

PRESSMAN, EDWARD R., motion picture producer; b. N.Y.C.. Grad., Stanford U.; student, London Sch. Econs. Co-founder Pressman-Williams Enterprises. Producer Out of It, 1969, The Revolutionary, 1970, Dealing: or the Berkeley to Boston Forty Brick Lost Bag Blues, 1972, Sisters, 1973, Plenty, 1985, Good Morning Babylon, 1986, Wall Street, 1987, Cherry 2000, 1988, Talk Radio, 1988, Blue Steel, 1989, Reversal of Fortune, 1990; exec. producer Badlands, 1973, Paradise Alley, 1978, Heartbeat, 1979, Half Moon Street, 1986, True Stories, 1986, Masters of the Universe, 1987, Walker, 1987, Paris By Night, 1988, Martians Go Home, 1990, To Sleep With Anger, 1990, Waiting for the Light, 1990; dir., producer Despair, 1978, The Hand, 1981, Das Boot, 1981, Conan the Barbarian, 1982, The Pirates of Penzance, 1982, Crimewave, 1985. Office: Edward R Pressman Film Corp 445 N Bedford Dr Penthouse Beverly Hills CA 90210

PRESSMAN, GLENN SPENCER, lawyer; b. Phila., May 25, 1952; s. Albert and Elaine (Coffae) P.; m. Laura Feldman, Sept. 5, 1982; children: Alexandra, Daniel. BS, Pa. State U., 1974; JD with honors, Drake U., 1981. Bar: Colo. 1981, U.S. Dist. Ct. Colo. 1981, U.S. Ct. Appeals (10th cir.) 1981. Ptnr. Melat Pressman Ezell & Higbie, Colorado Springs, Colo., 1981—. Recipient Order of the Coif, 1981. Democrat. Jewish. Avocations: skiing, mountain climbing. Office: Melat Pressman Ezell Higbie 711 S Tejon Colorado Springs CO 80903

PRESSMAN, MICHAEL, film director; b. N.Y.C., July 1, 1950. Ed., Calif. Inst. Arts. Dir.: (films) The Great Texas Dynamite Chase, 1976, The Bad News Bears in Breaking Training, 1977, Boulevard Nights, 1979, Those Lips, Those Eyes, 1980, Some Kind of Hero, 1982, Doctor Detroit, 1983, Teenage Mutant Ninja Turtles II: The Secret of the Oozie, 1991, To Gillian On Her 37th Birthday, 1996; (TV films) Like Mom, Like Me, 1978, The Imposter, 1984, And the Children Shall Lead, 1985, Private Sessions, 1985, Final Jeopardy, 1985, The Christmas Gift, 1986, Haunted By Her Past, 1987, To Heal A Nation, 1988, Shootdown, 1988, Incident at Dark River, 1989, Man Against The Mob: The Chinatown Murders, 1989, Joshua's Heart, 1990, Quicksand: No Escape, 1992, Miracle Child, 1993; co-exec. prod.: (TV series) Picket Fences, 1992— (Emmy award Outstanding Drama Series, 1993); producer, dir.: (pilot) Chicago Hope, 1993. Mem. Dirs. Guild Am. Office: William Morris Agency 151 El Camino Beverly Hills CA 90212

PRESSMAN, ROBERT, retail executive; b. 1954; s. Fred Pressman. MBA, Boston Univ. With Barney's Inc., 1975—. Office: 106 Seventh Ave New York NY 10012

PRESSMAN, THANE ANDREW, consumer products executive; b. San Diego, June 6, 1945; s. Harold Andrew and Audre Ethelyn (Negus) P.; m. Caroline Hannah Hood Snyder, Nov. 23, 1966; children: Sean, Steven. BS, Springfield (Mass.) Coll., 1967; MS, Syracuse U., 1969. Various to brand mgr. Procter & Gamble Co., Cin., 1968-76, assoc. mgr. advt., 1976-79; v.p. Lamalie Assocs., Inc. Chgo., 1979-81; dir. new products Alberto Culver Co., Melrose Park, Ill., 1981-84; group staff, v.p. Sara Lee Corp., Northbrook, Ill., 1984-85; pres., COO Kitchens of Sara Lee Can., Bramalee, Ont., 1986-88; exec. v.p. Sara Lee Bakery Co., Bramalee and Deerfield, Ill., 1988-90; pres., CEO Crestar Food Products, Inc. (affiliate of H.J. Heinz Co.), Eugene, Oreg., 1991-92, Crestar Food Products Inc. & Crestar Food Products Can. Ltd., Nashville and Mississauga, Ont., Can., 1992-93; pres. Labatt Ont. Breweries, Etobicoke, 1993-95; pres., CEO Labatt U.S.A. LLC., Darien, Conn., 1995—; guest lectr. U. Mich. Grad. Sch. Bus., Ann Arbor, 1977-79; bd. dirs. Brewers Retail Inc., Toronto; bd. dirs. Brewers of Ont., 1994-95, chmn., 1995. Bd. dirs. Am. Field Svc. U.S.A., N.Y.C., 1986-91, trustee AFS Intercultural Programs, N.Y.C., 1988-93; trustee Springfield Coll., 1988—; campaign co-chmn. United Way Cin., Chgo., Bramalea, Deerfield, 19876-94. Mem. Assn. Governing Bds. Univs. and Colls., David Allen Reed Soc., Grocery Product Mfrs. Can., Internat. Dairy Deli Assn., Dixie Curling Club, Eugene Country Club, Richland Country Club, Mississaugua Country Club.

PRESSON, ELLIS WYNN, health services executive; b. Electra, Tex., Mar. 28, 1940; s. Ellis Wilbur and Juanita M. (Morgan) P.; B.B.A., U. Tex., 1963; M.H.A., Washington U., St. Louis, 1965; m. Andrea L., July 5, 1969; children—Eric, Garett, Amber. Adminstrv. asst. Methodist Hosp. of Dallas, 1964-66; asst. adminstr. Dallas County Hosp., 1966-70; pres. Swedish Am. Hosp., Rockford, Ill., 1970-77, Research Med. Center, Kansas City, Mo., 1977-80, Research Health Services, Kansas City, 1980-91, Health Midwest, 1991—. Pres., Comprehensive Mental Health and Retardation, 1972-74; treas. bd. Rockford Med. Edn. Found., 1972-75; preceptor for adminstrn. extern U. Wis., 1975-76; search com. Rockford Sch. Medicine, U. Ill., 1975-76; regional com. mem. Hosp. Adminstrv. Surveillance Program, 1973-76; bd. dirs. Ill. Hosp. and Health Service, 1972-77, Midwest Bioethics Ctr., pres. 1988-89; mem. Health Planning NW Ill., 1973-77; licensing bd. mem. Ill. State Ambulatory Surgery Treatment Center, 1974-76. Mem. Am. Hosp. Assn. (chmn. healthcare systems bd. 1989—), Mo. Hosp. Assn. (chmn. bd., del. to Am. Hosp. Assn., mem. labor relations com., regional policy bd. 1988-90), Kansas City Area Hosp. Assn. (chmn. fin. council, dir.). Clubs: Rotary, Indian Hills Country. Home: 15613 Overbrook Rd Shawnee Mission KS 66224-9603 Office: 2304 E Meyer Blvd Kansas City MO 64132-4104

PRESSON, GINA, journalist, news and documentary production company executive; b. Nuremberg, Germany, Sept. 1, 1959; parents Am. citizens; d. Gerald Vann Presson and Gail Anne (Carter) Presson Nichols; m. William Michael Hammesfahr, Apr. 25, 1987. BA cum laude, Duke U., 1981. Intern reporter, field producer Sta. WTVD-TV, Durham, N.C., 1979-81; assoc. producer, producer, writer, fill-in reporter Sta. KXAS-TV, Dallas/Ft. Worth, 1981-84; reporter, anchor Sta. KFDX-TV, Wichita Falls, Tex., 1984-85; reporter, producer Sta. WTVR-TV, Richmond, Va., 1985-86; reporter Sta. WWBT-TV, Richmond, 1986-88; owner, reporter, producer Presson Perspectives, Clearwater, Fla., 1988—; prodr. Tampa (Fla.) Com. of 100, 1989, Poynter Inst. for Media Studies, 1990—, Leadership Am. and A Presdl. Classroom for Young Ams., 1993; reporter, prodr. Sta. WEDU-TV, Tampa, 1988—, Sta. WTSP-TV, 1992, Sta. WUSF-Radio, 1993. Prodr. program Everyday Heroes, PBS, 1994. Mem. Pinellas Healthy Start Coalition (appointee); publicist First Presbyn. Ch. Svc. Com., St. Petersburg, Fla., 1990—, Habitat for Humanity, Richmond, 1987-88, Children's Miracle Network, Richmond, 1986-88. Recipient Gold medallion Broadcast Promotion and Mktg. Execs., 1982, 10th Dist. Addy award (5 states), Ft. Worth Ad Club, 1982, 83, Tops award Dallas Ad Club, 1982, Best Spot award Tex. Assn. Broadcasters, 1982, 83, Tops award Dallas Ad Club, 1982, Best Spot award Tex. Assn. Broadcasters, 1983, 4th Pl. award in News Spl., Internat. N.Y. Fest., 1992, 94, Gabriel award, 1993, Fla. AP award, 1993, 3rd Pl. Green Eyeshade award (5 states), 1994. Mem. Soc. Profl. Journalists (dept. regional dir. 1990—, pres. Tampa chpt. 1989-90, fund raiser 1988-89, award 1993, dep. chair nat. profl. devel. com.), Duke U. Alumni Assn., Leadership Am., Alpha Delta Pi. Avocations: sailing, windsurfing, photography, reading, cooking. Office: Presson Perspectives 600 Druid Rd E Clearwater FL 34616-3912

PRESTAGE, JAMES JORDAN, university chancellor; b. Deweyville, Tex., Apr. 29, 1926; s. James J. and Mona (Wilkins) P.; m. Jewel Limar, Aug. 12, 1953; children—Terri, James Grady, Eric, Karen, Jay. B.S. cum laude, So. U., Baton Rouge, 1950; M.S., U. Iowa, 1955, Ph.D., 1959. Instr. biology Prairie View Coll., Tex., 1955-56; asst. prof. So. U., Baton Rouge, 1959, assoc. prof. biology, 1959-61, prof. biology, 1961—, dir. computer sci. ctr., 1968-71, 72-73, dean acad. affairs, v.p. acad. affairs, 1973-81, exec. v.p., 1981-82, chancellor, 1982-85, univ. disting. prof., 1985—; univ. disting. prof. biology Dillard U., New Orleans, 1987—; chair divsn. natural scis. Dillard U., 1990—; asst. dir. La. Coordinating Council for Higher Edn., Baton Rouge, 1971-72; mem. commn. on scholars Ill. Bd. Higher Edn., 1975-82; mem. com. on off-campus instrn. La. Bd. Regents, 1975—; mem. La. Data Processing Council, Baton Rouge, 1979-82; vis. prof. biology Dillard U., New Orleans; trustee Am. Coll. Testing Program, 1983—. Mem. exec. bd. Istrouma council Boy Scouts Am.; vice chmn. bd. trustees Greater Mt. Carmel Baptist Ch., Baton Rouge; bd. dirs. Capital Area United Way, Baton Rouge. Served with USN, 1944-46, 50-52; ETO, Korea. Named Most Outstanding Faculty Mem., So. U., 1966-67; Nat. Med. Fellowships fellow U. Iowa, Iowa City, 1956-59; NIH grantee, 1960-65. Mem. Conf. Acad. Deans So. States, NAACP, Sigma Xi, Alpha Chi, Alpha Phi Alpha (chpt. pres.), Sigma Pi Phi. Democrat. Avocations: fishing; reading; gardening. Home: 2145 77th Ave Baton Rouge LA 70807-5508 Office: PO Box 9222 So Br PO Baton Rouge LA 70813

PRESTAGE, JEWEL LIMAR, political science educator; b. Hutton, La., Aug. 12, 1931; d. Brudis L. and Sallie Bell (Johnson) Limar; m. James J. Prestage, Aug. 12, 1953; children—Terri, James, Eric, Karen, Jay. B.A., So. U., Baton Rouge, 1951; M.A., U. Iowa, 1952, Ph.D., 1954; LHD (hon.), U. D.C., 1994. Assoc. prof. polit. sci. Prairie View (Tex.) Coll., 1954-55, 56; assoc. prof. polit. sci. So. U., 1956-57, 58-62, prof., 1962—, chairperson dept., 1965-83, dean pub. policy and urban affairs, 1983-89; Honors prof. polit. sci. Banneker Honors Coll., Prairie View U., 1989—, dean, 1990—; chmn. La. adv. com. to U.S. Commn. on Civil Rights, 1975-85; mem., chmn. nat. adv. coun. on women's ednl. programs U.S. Dept. Edn., 1980-82; vis. prof. U. Iowa, 1987-88. Author: (with M. Githens) A Portrait of Marginality: Political Behavior of the American Woman, 1976; contbr. articles to profl. jours. Rockefeller fellow, 1951-52; NSF fellow, 1964; Ford Found. postdoctoral fellow, 1969-70. Mem. Am. Polit. Sci. Assn. (v.p. 1974-75), So. Polit. Sci. Assn. (pres. 1975-76), Nat. Conf. Black Polit. Scientists (pres. 1976-77), Nat. Assn. African Am. Honors Programs (pres. 1993-94), Am. Soc. for Pub. Adminstrn. (pres. La. chpt. 1988-89, mem. nat. exec. coun. 1989-90), Links Inc., Alpha Kappa Alpha. Home: 2145 77th Ave Baton Rouge LA 70807-5508 Office: So Univ PO Box 125 Prairie View TX 77446-0125 *Commitments which guide my life are: (1) maximum development of personal potential through pursuit of excellence in all endeavors; (2) fair play, respect, compassion and quest of community in relations with fellow human beings; (3) utilization of personal talents in the interest of removing impediments to the good life "for all persons"; (4) pursuit of truth as the pervasive concern in academia; and (5) transmission of the above as priority goals to all with whom I have contact.*

PRESTBO, JOHN ANDREW, newspaper editor, journalist, author; b. Northwood, N.D., Sept. 26, 1941; s. Oscar Bernt and Jeanne (Schol) P.; m. Darlene Parrish, Aug. 14, 1965; children: Bradford Jonathan, Laura Christine. B.S., Northwestern U., 1963, M.S., 1964. Reporter, writer Wall Street Jour., Chgo., 1964-74; staff editor, Page 1 Wall Street Jour., N.Y.C., 1974-75, commodities editor, 1975-77; bur. chief Wall Street Jour., Cleve., 1977-81; markets editor Wall Street Jour., N.Y.C., 1984—, editor Dow Jones World Stock Index, 1993—; v.p. editorial Dow Jones Radio 2, Inc., Princeton, N.J., 1981-83. Author: Sleuthing, 1976; co-author: (with Frederick C. Klein) News and the Market, 1974, (with Douglas R. Sease) Barron's Guide to Making Investment Decisions, 1994; editor: This Abundant Land, 1975, Dow Jones Commodities Handbook, 1976-79, The Dow Jones Guide to the World Stock Market, 1994. Served with USAFR, 1966-73. Recipient Econ. Reporting award Ind. Natural Gas Assn., U. Mo., 1967; recipient Achievement-bur. writing award G.M. Loeb, 1968. Home: 14 Charleston Dr Skillman NJ 08558-1801 Office: Wall Street Jour 200 Liberty St New York NY 10281-1003

PRESTERA, LAURETTA ANNE, newspaper executive; b. Newark, Dec. 15, 1947; d. George Anthony and Carmela (Sallustro) P. BA in Communications, Bridgewater State Coll., 1976; MBA in Mgmt., Fairleigh Dickinson U., 1981. Advt. sales rep. The N.Y. Times, N.Y.C., 1980-81, circulation sales rep., 1981-82, asst. mgr. circulation, 1982-83; home delivery mgr. The N.Y. Times, Torrance, Calif., 1983-84; S.W. mgr. The N.Y. Times, Dallas, 1984-85; west coast mgr. The N.Y. Times, Torrance, 1985-87; nat. sales dir. The N.Y. Times, N.Y., 1987-92; home delivery dir. The N.Y. Times, N.Y.C., 1992-93, group dir. distbn., 1992-95; v.p. circulation, 1995—; treas. The N.Y. Times Distbn. Corp., N.Y. and Calif., 1984-89. Recipient Pub. award The N.Y. Time, 1984. Mem. People for Ethical Treatment of Animals, San Francisco SPCA, L.A. SPCA, Am. Newspaper Pubs. Assn. Roman Catholic. Avocations: animal rights, golf, tennis.

PRESTIA, MICHAEL ANTHONY, accounting executive; b. S.I., N.Y., Oct. 6, 1931; s. Anthony and Antoinette (Folino) P.; m. Nancy Ferrandino, July 4, 1959 (div. May 1970); 1 child, Anthony; m. Janet Swanson, July 22, 1987. BA, NYU, 1953, MBA, 1956. CPA, N.Y. Sr. accountant Gluckman & Schacht, CPAs, N.Y.C., 1953-60; chief financial officer Franklin Broadcasting Co., N.Y.C., 1960-63; chief accountant asst. to bus. officer, sec. Cooper Union for Advancement Sci. and Art, N.Y.C., 1963-66; bus. officer Inst. Pub. Adminstrn., N.Y.C., 1966-71, controller, 1971-78, treas., 1978-84; cons. taxation and tax planning, 1959—. Served with AUS, 1953-55. Mem. AICPA, N.Y. State Soc. CPAs. Home: 53-06 Francis Lewis Blvd Flushing NY 11364-1633 Office: 445 5th Ave New York NY 10016-0126

PRESTON, ANDREW JOSEPH, pharmacist, drug company executive; b. Bklyn., Apr. 19, 1922; s. Charles A. and Josephine (Rizzutto) Pumo; BSc, St. John U., 1943; m. Martha Jeanne Happ, Oct. 10, 1953; children: Andrew Joseph Jr., Charles Richard, Carolyn Louise, Frank Arthur, Joanne Marie, Barbara Jeanne. Cert. bus. intermediary. Mgr. Press Club, Bklyn. Nat. League Baseball Club, 1941-42; purchasing agt. Drug and Pharm. div. Intrassind, Inc., 1947; chief pharmacist Hendershot Pharmacy, Newton, N.J., 1949; agt. Bur. of Narcotics, U.S. Treasury Dept., 1948-49; owner Preston Drug & Surg. Co., Boonton, N.J., 1949-86; CEO Preston Pharmaceutics, Inc., Butler, N.J., 1970-80, Preston Bus. Cons., Inc., Kinnelon, N.J., 1987—; commr. N.J. State Bd. Pharmacy, 1970-72, pres., 1973; organizer State of N.J. Drug Abuse Speakers Program, 1970-76; chmn. Morris County Drug Abuse Coun., 1969-70; lectr. drug abuse and narcotic addiction various community orgns., 1968-78; mem. adv. bd. Nat. Community Bank, Boonton, N.J., 1973. Chmn. bldg. fund com. Riverside Hosp., Boonton, 1963; mem. Morris County (N.J.) Rep. Fin. Com., 1972; pres. Ronald Reagan N.J. Re-Election Adv. Bd., 1984; mem. exec. com. Gov. Tom Kean Annual Ball, 1985-86; chmn. Pharmacists of N.J. for election of Pres. Ford, 1976, Pharmacists for Gov. Tom Kean, 1981-84, N.J. Pharmacists for Reagan/Bush '84; mem. exec. com. Morris County Overall Econ. Devel. Com., 1976-82; chmn. Pharmacists for Fenwick, 1982; v.p. Kinnelon Rep. Club, 1980, Rep. Com., Kinnelon, 1990; adv. com. to Congressman Dean Gallo on Pres. Clinton's Health Security Plan, 1994. Served to lt. (j.g.), USNR, 1943-46. Recipient Bowl Hygeia award Robbins Co., 1969, E.R. Squibb President's award, 1968, N.J. Pharm. Square Club award, 1969. Mem. Am. Pharm. Assn., N.J. Pharm. Assn. (mem. econs. com. 1960-65, pres. 1967-68, Oscar Singer Meml. award 1987, William H. McNeil award 1994), Nat. Assn. of Retail Druggists, Internat. Narcotic Enforcement Officers Assn., N.J. Narcotic Enforcement Officers Assn., Nat. Assn. Realtors, N.J. Assn. Realtors, Morris County Bd. Realtors, Internat. Bus. Brokers Assn. (cert. bus. intermediary), Inst. Bus. Appraisers, Pharmacists Guild Am. (pres. N.Y. div. 1946-47), Pharmacists Guild of N.J., N.J. Public Health Assn., Morris County Pharm. Assn., Morris-Sussex Pharmacists Soc., Am. Legion, St. John's Alumni Assn. Roman Catholic. Clubs: Elks, K.C., Smoke Rise. Contbr. editorials to profl. jours. Home and Office: 568A Pepperidge Tree Ln Kinnelon NJ 07405-2213

PRESTON, COLLEEN ANN, lawyer; b. Monterey, Calif., Oct. 11, 1955; d. Howard Houston and Catherine (Reid) Harrison; m. Raymond C. Preston Jr., June 12, 1982. BA, U. Fla., 1975, JD, 1978; LLM, Georgetown U., 1985. Bar: Fla. 1979, U.S. Ct. Claims 1979, U.S. Ct. Appeals (fed. cir.) 1979. Assoc. Akerman, Senterfitt & Eidson, Orlando, Fla., 1978-79; atty. advisor, office of gen. counsel Sec. USAF, 1979-83; counsel com. on armed svcs. U.S. Ho. Reps., Washington, 1983-89, gen. counsel, 1990-93; spl. asst. to Sec. Def. for legal matters Dept. Def., Washington, 1993, dep. under sec. of def. for acquisition reform, 1993—. Capt. USAF, 1979-83. Avocations: golf, tennis, cross country and downhill skiing, water skiing. Office: 3610 Defense Pentagon Washington DC 20301-3610

PRESTON, DAVID MICHAEL, lawyer; b. Detroit, Apr. 15, 1930; s. David Harold and Ruth (MacDonald) P.; m. Judith Ann Hillner, Aug. 19, 1961; children: Matthew MacDonald, Sarah Elizabeth Parker, Melissa Ann. B.A., U. Mich., 1952, J.D., 1955. Bar: Mich. 1955. Ptnr. firm Long, Preston, Kinnaird & Avant, Detroit and Bloomfield Hills, Mich., 1965-87; ptnr. Barnett, Knight, Preston, Falvay, Drolet & Freeman, Bloomfield Hills, 1987-89, Drolet, Freeman, Preston & Cotton, Bloomfield Hills, 1990-96, Denison Maxwell, Bloomfield Hills, Mich., 1996—. Pres. Tim-Ro-Nan-Go Center for Emotionally Disturbed Children, Birmingham, 1972-74; trustee Oakland Community Coll., 1969-70, 83-84. Mem. Am., Mich., Oakland County bar assns., Beta Theta Pi, Phi Delta Phi. Club: Birmingham Athletic (pres. 1977-78). Home: 577 Westwood Dr Birmingham MI 48009-1129 Office: 33 Bloomfield Hills Pky Ste 100 Bloomfield Hills MI 48304-2945

PRESTON, FAITH, college president; b. Boston, Sept. 14, 1921; d. Howard Knowlton and Edith Smith (Wilson) P.; m. Winthrop Wadleigh, Dec. 19, 1970. B.A., Boston U., 1944; M.A., 1945; Ed.D., Columbia U. Tchrs. Coll., 1964. Tchr. Georgetown (Mass.) High Sch., 1945-47; tchr. Stoneham (Mass.) High Sch., 1947-50, Endicott Jr. Coll., Beverly, Mass., 1950-53; dir. research P.R. Jr. Coll., 1953-55; dean adminstrn., 1955-63, v.p., 1963-65; pres. White Pines Coll., 1965-91, pres. emerita, 1991—, also life trustee. Author: David and the Handcar, 1950, Jose's Miracle, 1955, The Silver Box, 1979, A Gift of Love, 1994. Mem. bd. incorporators Cath. Med. Ctr., Manchester, N.H., 1978-89; bd. dirs. Caregivers; pres. bd. dirs. N.H. Assn. for Blind; trustee funds Chester Congl. Bapt. Ch., deacon, 1988—. Kellogg fellow, 1964. Mem. Am. Assn. Jr. Colls., Phi Lambda Theta, Kappa Delta Pi, Delta Kappa Gamma. Republican. Clubs: Univ. Women's (London); The College (Boston); Fortnightly. Home: PO Box 25 Chester NH 03036-0025 Office: White Pines Coll Office of the Pres 40 Chester St Chester NH 03036-4305 *I am a teacher, and I yearn to impart a few non-textbook lessons. Two are simply said: care, endure.*

PRESTON, FRANCES W., performing rights organization executive; children: Kirk, David, Donald. Hon. degree, Lincoln (Ill.) Coll.; degree (hon.), Berklee Coll. Musicawd. With BMI (Broadcast Music Inc.), Nashville, 1958—, v.p., 1964-85; sr. v.p. performing rights BMI, N.Y.C., 1985, exec. v.p., chief exec. officer, 1986, pres., chief exec. officer, 1986—, also bd. dirs. Mem. Film, Entertainment and Music Commn. Adv. Council State of Tenn., Leadership Nashville, John Work Meml. Found.; trustee Country Music Found., Inc.; mem. Commn. on White House Record Library, Carter adminstrn., Pres.'s Panama Canal Study Com., Carter adminstrn.; bd. dirs. Rock & Roll Hall of Fame; mem. adminstrv. council Confedn. of Internat. Socs. of Authors and Composers; v.p. Nat. Music Council; bd. dirs. Peabody Awards; hon. trustee Nat. Acad. Popular Music. Recipient achievement award Women's Equity Action League, spl. citation award NATAS, Golden Baton award Young Musicians Found.; named one of Am.'s 50 Most Powerful Women Ladies' Home Jour.; named to Country Music Hall of Fame. Mem. Country Music Assn. (life mem. bd. dirs., past chmn., past pres., Irving Waugh Award of Excellence), Nashville Symphony Assn. (past sec., bd. dirs.), NARAS (pres.'s adv. bd., past bd. dirs. Nashville chpt.), Nashville Songwriters Assn. (life mem.), Gospel Music Assn. (life mem. bd., past chmn., past pres.), Am. Women in Radio and TV (past bd. dirs.). Presbyterian. Lodge: Rotary (1st woman mem. Nashville club), Friars Club (Friars Found. Applause award). Office: Broadcast Music Inc 320 W 57th St New York NY 10019*

PRESTON, FREDERICK WILLARD, surgeon; b. Chgo., June 27, 1912; s. Frederick Augustus and Margaret (Atwater) P.; m. Gertrude Eldred Bradford, June 23, 1942 (div. 1961); children: Frederick Willard Jr., David E. (dec. 1994), William B.; m. Barbara Gay Hess, July 30, 1961. BA, Yale U., 1935; MD, Northwestern U., 1940, MS, 1942; MS, U. Minn., 1947. Intern Presbyn. Hosp., Chgo., 1940-41; fellow surgery Mayo Clinic, Rochester, Minn., 1941-42, 46-48; pvt. practice surgery Chgo., 1968-75; mem. surg. faculty Northwestern U. Med. Sch., 1949-75, prof. surgery, 1960-75; assoc. attending surgeon Northwestern Meml. Hosp., 1950-75; attending surgeon Skokie Valley Community Hosp., 1964-75, Henrotin Hosp., 1950-75; chief surg. svc. VA Rsch. Hosp., Chgo., 1953-68; mem. Supreme Acad. Coun. Ofcl. U. Congo, Lubumbashi, 1965-71; chmn. dept. surgery Santa Barbara Gen. Hosp., 1975-78; dir. surg. edn. Santa Barbara Cottage Hosp., 1975-83; rsch. physiologist U. Calif., Santa Barbara, 1976-84. Author, editor: Basic Surgical Physiology, Loose-Leaf Practice of Surgery, Manual of Ambulatory Surgery; cons. editor Internat. Surg. Digest, 1969-70, contbr. numerous articles to profl. jours. Bd. dirs. Schweppe Found., Love Med. Rsch., English Speaking Union, Chgo. chpt., 1960-65; gov. mem., mem. planning com. Shedd Aquarium, 1968-75. 1st lt. to maj. M.C., AUS, 1942-46. Fellow ACS (chpt. pres. 1965-66); mem. AMA, AAAS, Chgo. Surg. Soc. (sec. 1961-64, pres. 1968-69), Chgo. Acad. Scis. (sec. 1963-67), Am. Assn. Cancer Research (pres. Chgo. sec. 1963-64), Am. Geriatrics Soc., Am. Fedn. Clin. Research, Am. Surg. Assn., Central Surg. Assn., Western Surg. Assn. (coun.), Pacific Coast Surg. Assn., Pan Pacific Surg. Assn., Société Internationale de Chirurgie, Soc. Surgery Alimentary Tract, Santa Barbara Club, La Cumbre Golf and Country Club, Chgo. Literary Club, Univ. Club (Chgo.), Sigma Xi. Republican. Episcopalian. Home: 755 Via Airosa Santa Barbara CA 93110-2302

PRESTON, JAMES E., cosmetics company executive; b. 1933. BS, Northwestern U., 1955. With Avon Products, Inc., N.Y.C., 1964—, from mgmt. trainee to dir. sales promotions, 1964-70, dir. personnel, 1970-71, v.p. corp. personnel, 1971-72, from group v.p. mktg. to sr. v.p. field ops. worldwide, 1972-77, exec. v.p., 1977-81, exec. corp. v.p., pres., 1981-88, pres., chief operating officer, 1988-89, chief exec. officer, 1988—, chmn. bd. dirs., 1989—; bd. dirs. ARA Svcs., Woolworth Corp. Mem. Reader's Digest Assn. (bd. dirs. 1994). Office: Avon Products Inc 9 W 57th St New York NY 10019*

PRESTON, JAMES YOUNG, lawyer; b. Atlanta, Sept. 21, 1937; s. James William and Mary Lou (Young) P.; m. Elizabeth Buxton Gregory, June 13, 1959; children: Elizabeth P. Carr, Mary Lane P. Lennon, James Brenton Preston. BA in English, U. N.C., 1958, JD with high honors, 1961. Bar: N.C. 1961. Assoc. to ptnr. Parker, Poe, Adams & Bernstein L.L.P. and predecessors, Charlotte, N.C., 1961—. Pres. Charlotte Area Fund, 1968, Arts & Sci. Coun.--Charlotte/Mecklenburg, Inc., 1986-87, chair nat. conf., Charlotte, 1996—, Wilderness Leadership Initiative, 1994—. Mem. ABA (ho. dels. 1988-92, 95—), N.C. State Bar (pres. 1987-88), Am. Law Inst., Nat. Assn. Bar Presidents (exec. coun. 1989-92), Phi Beta Kappa, Phi Eta Sigma. Democrat. Episcopalian. Avocations: travel, tennis, profl. and civic activities. Office: Parker Poe Adams Bernstein 201 S College St 2500 Charlotte Plz Charlotte NC 28244

PRESTON, JOHN THOMAS, engineering executive; b. Fullerton, Calif., Mar. 18, 1950; s. Seaton Tinsley and Aline Marie (Debbaut) P.; m. Gail Ellen Sandberg. BS, U. Wis., 1972; MBA, Northwestern U., 1976. Mng. dir. Polyscience Corp., Niles, Ill., 1971-77; assoc. dir. MIT, Cambridge, Mass., 1977-82; pres. Visual Comm. Network, Cambridge, Mass., 1982-86; dir. MIT, Cambridge, Mass., 1986-96; pres., CEO Quantum Energy Techs. Inc.; dir. Molten Metal Tech., Waltham, Mass., 1989—, Energy Biosystems, The Woodlands, Tex., 1990—, MIT Enterprise Forum, Cambridge, 1993—, Mass. Tech. Collaborative, 1995—, Clean Harbors, Med. Foods Inc., Univ. Corp. Radiology, 1996—. Named Chevalier dans l'Order National du Mérite Pres. Rep. of France, 1993. Office: Quantum Energy Techs Inc 238 Main St Ste 201 Cambridge MA 02142

PRESTON, KENDALL, JR., electro-optical engineer; b. Boston, Oct. 22, 1927; s. Kendall and Dorothy Fletcher (Allen) P.; m. Sarah Malcolm Stewart, Aug. 23, 1952; 1 child, Louise. B.A. cum laude, Harvard U., 1950, M.S., 1952. Mem. tech. staff Bell Tel. Labs., Murray Hill, N.J., 1952-60; sr. staff scientist Perkin-Elmer Corp., Norwalk, Conn., 1961-74; prof. elec. engring. and bioengring. Carnegie-Mellon U., Pitts., 1974—; prof. radiation engring. Grad. Sch. Pub. Health, U. Pitts., 1977-91; chief engr. Kensal Cons., 1980-92; pres. Pathology Imaging Corp., 1986—, Kensal Corp., 1993—; chmn. Internat. Optical Computing Conf., Zurich, Switzerland, 1974, conf. automatic cytology Engring. Found., N.Y.C., 1971-72, conf. Coherent Radiation Systems, 1973, conf. Comparative Productivity of Non-invasive Techniques for Med. Diagnosis, 1976; U.S. chmn. U.S.-Japan Seminar on Digital Processing of Biomed. Images, Pasadena, Calif., 1975, Japan-U.S. Workshop Parallel Processing, Tokyo, 1979; faculty NATO Advanced Study Inst. on Digital Image Processing and Analysis, Bonas, France, 1976; mem. faculty Internat. Sch. Med. Scis., Erice, Italy, 1988; mem. Tech. Audit Bd., Inc., N.Y.C., 1976—. Author: Coherent Optical Computers, 1972, Kogeretnye Optiches; in Russian, 1974; editor: (with Dr. Onoe) Digital Processing of Biomedical Images, 1976, (with Drs. Ayers, Johnson and Taylor) Medical Imaging Techniques: A Comparison, 1979, (with Drs. Onoe and Rosenfeld) Real-Time Medical Image Processing, 1980, Real-Time/Parallel Computing, 1981; (with Dr. Duff) Modern Cellular Automata, 1984; editor: (with Drs. Duff, Levialdi, Uhr) Multicomputers and Image Processing, 1982, Evaluation of Multicomputers for Image Processing, 1986; assoc. editor: Pattern Recognition; editorial adviser: Biocharacterist, Analytical and Quantitative Cytology, Photonics Spectra; mem. editorial com.: Pattern Analysis and Machine Intelligence; contbr. articles to profl. jours.; patentee in field. Chmn. Ecclesia, YMCA, Summit, N.J., 1958-60; chmn. health svcs. industry com. Automation Rsch. Council, Am. Automatic Control Council, N.J., 1973-76; mem. NSF Fact Finding Team on Egyptian Scientific Instrumentation, 1974-75. With arty. AUS, 1946-47. Recipient silver medal U. Tokyo, Henry Warder Carey prize, Albert Rose award in Elec. Imaging. Fellow IEEE (life, chmn. Conn. PTGEC 1966-67) ; mem. AAAS, Biol. Engring. Soc. Gt. Britain, Biomed. Engring. Soc. (charter), Harvard Engrs. and Scientists (pres. students 1952), N.Y. Acad. Sci., Cum Laude Soc. Clubs: D.U, Hasty Pudding Inst. 1770, Harvard Club of Western Pa. (Pitts.); Country (Brookline, Mass.); Lake (Dublin, N.H.); Hillsboro (Pompano Beach, Fla.); Lawn (New Haven); Capitol Hill (Washington); Athletic (Scottsdale, Ariz.), Harvard-Yale-Princeton (Pitts.). Office: Kensal Corp 5055 E Broadway Blvd Ste C 206 Tucson AZ 85711-3641 also: Carnegie Mellon U Dept Elec & Computer Engring Schenley Park Pittsburgh PA 15213

PRESTON, LOYCE ELAINE, retired social work educator; b. Texarkana, Ark., Feb. 25, 1929; d. Harvey Martin and Florence (Whitlock) P.; student Texarkana Jr. Coll., 1946-47; B.S., Henderson State Tchrs. Coll., 1950; certificate in social work La. State U., 1952; M.S.W., Columbia U., 1956. Tchr. pub. schs., Dierks, Ark., 1950-51; child welfare worker Ark. Dept. Public Welfare, Clark and Hot Spring counties, 1951-56, child welfare cons., 1956-58; casework dir. Ruth Sch. Girls, Burien, Wash., 1958-60; asst. prof. spl. edn. La. Poly. Inst., Ruston, 1960-63; asst. prof. Northwestern State Coll., Shreveport, La., 1963-73; asst. prof. La. State U., Shreveport, 1973-79; ret., 1979. Chpt. sec. La. Assn. Mental Health, 1965-67, Gov's. adv. council, 1967-70; mem. Mayor's Com. for Community Improvement, 1972-76. Mem. AAUW (dir. Shreveport br. 1963-69), Acad. Cert. Social Workers, Nat. Assn. Social Workers (del. 1964-65, pres. North La. chpt., state-wide com. 1968-69), La Conf. Social Welfare, La. Fedn. Council Exceptional Children (pres. 1970-71), La. Tchrs. Assn. Home: 9609 Hillsboro Dr Shreveport LA 71118-4804

PRESTON, MALCOLM, artist, art critic; b. N.J., May 25, 1919; s. Frank and Anniece (Landau) P.; m. Mary Alice Bales, Nov. 27, 1942; children: Jennifer, Amanda. BS, U. Wis., 1940; MA, Columbia U., 1945, PhD, 1951; student, New Sch. Social Rsch., N.Y.C., 1940-42. Display artist and designer, free lance artist, 1939-41; fellow, asst. instr. painting New Sch. Social Research, 1940-41; high sch. tchr., 1944-49; art supr. Manhasset pub. schs., 1945; part-time instr. Adelphi Coll., 1947; chmn. dept. fine arts Hofstra Coll., 1949-74, prof. fine arts, 1954-74, chmn. div. humanities, 1959-74, coordinator arts, 1961-74; dir. Inst. Arts, 1962-74; art critic Newsday, 1968-86, Boston Herald Traveler, 1970-72. Contbr. articles to newspapers and mags.; radio, television shows Met. area; developed and carried out television series Ford Found. grant, Nat. Ednl. Radio and Television Center, Arts Around Us, Am. Art Today, 1956; one-man shows include Ward Eggleston Gallery, N.Y.C., 1950-51, 54, 56, A.C.A. Gallery, 1959, S.A.G., 1962, Palm Beach, 1968, St. Mary's Coll., 1978, Benson Gallery, 1979, The Gallery, Truro, Mass., 1980, 81, 82, Customs House Gallery, 1984, Country Art Gallery, 1986, Wenniger Gallery, 1988, Elaine Benson Gallery, 1991, Galerie Mourlot, Boston, 1992; group shows include New Art Gallery, 1948-49, Ward Eggleston Gallery, 1949-50, also, L.I. Artists Exhibit, Nat. Water Color Exhibit, San Diego, Am. Artists Assn. Gallery, 1951, Roosevelt Field Art Center, 1957, Art U.S.A., 1958, Hansa Gallery Group Show, 1958, Shore Studio Gallery, Provincetown, 1957-58, Kendall Art Gallery, Wellfleet, Mass., 1974, 75, 76, 77, 78, Roko Gallery, 1978, Himelfarb Gallery, 1978, Linden Gallery, 1981-82, Tower Gallery, 1983, Customs House Gallery, 1983, 84, 85, Grand Central Art Gallery, 1984, 85; work represented in permanent collections: Queens's Mus., Guild Hall Mus., Portland Mus., Cape Cod Mus. Fine Arts, Hofstra U., Living Arts Found., Winning Images, Columbus, Ohio, Country Art Gallery, Locust Valley, N.Y. Served as 2d lt. F.A. AUS, World War II. Lowe Found. research grantee, 1950; Ford Found. grantee, 1958; recipient Emily Lowe award, 1949, 50, 52, 54, 56; 1st prize oil Utica, N.Y.; Shell Research award, 1963. Home: PO Box 182 Truro MA 02666-0182 Office: care Galerie Mourlot 14 Newbury St Boston MA 02116-3201

PRESTON, MARK I., investment company executive; b. Schenectady, May 16, 1938; s. Samuel P. and Fay (Zelig) P.; children: Meredith, Laurence. BSBA, Syracuse U., 1959. Gen. mgr. AD-Allure Industries Inc., N.Y.C., 1962-64; pres. Marlin Mfg. Corp., 1965-68; acct. exec. Walston, Inc., 1969-72; v.p. DuPont, Walston, Inc., N.Y.C. and Washington, 1973, Legg Mason Wood Walker, Inc., Balt., 1974-81, sr. v.p. mktg., 1981-85, sr. v.p., dir. of sales, 1986-90, sr. v.p., dir. investor svcs., 1991—. Pres. Balt. County Gen. Hosp. Found., 1983-84; v.p. Safety First Club Md., 1982-90; trustee Balt. County Gen. Hosp., 1983-88; pres. parent bd. Balt. County Gen. Hosp., 1988-90; bd. dirs. blood svcs. bd. ARC, Md. Mem. Int. Assn. Fin. Planners (cert.). Club: Bond (Balt.) (pres. 1984). Home: 2365 Boston St Baltimore MD 21224-3656 Office: Legg Mason Wood Walker Inc 111 S Calvert St Baltimore MD 21202-6174

PRESTON, RICHARD ARTHUR, historian; b. Middlesbrough, England, Oct. 4, 1910; s. Frank and Florence Rachel (Carter) P.; m. Marjorie Fishwick, Sept. 2, 1939; children—David Frank, Carol Jane, Peter Eric. B.A., Leeds U., 1931, M.A., 1932, Dip.Ed., 1933; Ph.D., Yale U., 1936; LL.D., Royal Mil. Coll. Can., 1977. Mem. faculty U. Toronto, 1936-38, U. Coll. South Wales, 1938-45, U. Toronto, 1945-48; mem. faculty Royal Mil. Coll. Can., Kingston, 1948-65; prof. history Royal Mil. Coll. Can., to 1965, Duke U., Durham, N.C., 1965-80; prof. emeritus Duke U., 1980—, dir. Can. studies, 1973-79. Author: Gorges of Plymouth Fort, 1953, Men in Arms, 1956-91, Royal Fort Frontenac, 1958, Kingston Before the War of 1812, 1958, Canada in World Affairs, 1959-61, 1965, Canada and Imperial Defense, 1967, Canada's R.M.C, 1969, For Friends at Home, 1974, Defence of the Undefended Border, 1977, Perspectives in the History of Military Education and Professionalism, 1980, the Squat Pyramid: Canadian Studies in the U.S, 1980, To Serve Canada, 1991. Served with RAF, 1940-45. Commonwealth Fund fellow, 1933-36; Can. Coun. fellow, 1963-64; Social Sci. Rsch. Coun. fellow, 1963-64; Guggenheim fellow, 1972-73; recipient Achievement award City Kingston, 1959, Can. Confedn. medal, 1967, Queen's Jubilee medal, 1975, Donner medal, 1977, No. Telecom. Internat. Can. Studies award and Gold medal, 1983, Kingston Hist. Soc. Centennial award, 1994. Mem. Can. Hist. Assn. (pres. 1961-62), Assn. Can. Studies U.S. (founding pres. 1971-72), Am. Mil. Inst. Home: 25 Old Oak Ct Durham NC 27705-5644

PRESTON, RICHARD MCKIM, lawyer; b. Balt., June 2, 1947; s. Wilbur Day Jr. and May Virginia (Honemann) P.; m. Trisa Jean Thompson, Apr. 28, 1961. BA, Washington & Lee U., 1969, JD cum laude, 1976; MA cum laude, Fairleigh Dickinson U., 1973. Assoc. vomBaur, Coburn, Simmons & Turtle, Washington, 1976-79; assoc. Seyfarth, Shaw, Fairweather & Geraldson, Washington, 1979-82, ptnr., 1982—; mng. ptnr. Constrn. Group, 1987—. Contbr. articles to profl. publs., chpt. to book. Bd. dirs. Jubilee Support Found., Washington, 1989—; mem. Washington & Lee Law Coun., Lexington, Va., 1986-93. Mem. Univ. Club D.C., River Bend Golf and Country Club, Sankaty Head Golf Club. Office: Seyfarth Shaw Fairweather 815 Connecticut Ave NW Washington DC 20006-4004

PRESTON, ROBERT BRUCE, retired lawyer; b. Cleve., Feb. 24, 1926; s. Robert Bruce and Erma May (Hunter) P.; m. Agnes Ellen Stanley, Jan. 29, 1949; children—Robert B., Patricia Ellen Preston Kiefer, Judith Helen Preston Yanover. A.B., Western Res. U., 1950, J.D., 1952. Bar: U.S. Dist. Ct. (no. dist.) Ohio 1953, U.S. Ct. Appeals (6th cir.) 1959, U.S. Supreme Ct. 1964. Assoc. Arter & Hadden, Cleve., 1952-63, ptnr., 1964-93; ret., 1994; dir. Service Stampings Inc., Willoughby, Ohio. Vice pres. Citizens League Cleve., 1965; chmn. Charter Rev. Com., Cleveland Heights, Ohio, 1972; mem. Zoning Bd. Appeals, Cleveland Heights, 1974-76. Mem. Ohio Bar Assn., Greater Cleve. Bar Assn., City Club. Republican. Presbyterian. Avocations: tennis, fishing, travel. Home: 117 Manor Brook Dr South Russell OH 44022-4163 Office: Arter & Hadden 1100 Huntington Bldg Cleveland OH 44115

PRESTON, SAMUEL HULSE, demographer; b. Morrisville, Pa., Dec. 2, 1943; s. Samuel H. and Dora (Berrell) P.; m. Winnifred de Witt, June 19, 1965; children: Samuel, Andrew, Benjamin, Leah. BA in Econs., Amherst Coll., 1965; PhD in Econs., Princeton U., 1968. Asst. prof. demography U. Calif., Berkeley, 1968-72; dir. Ctr. for Demography U. Wash., Seattle, 1972-77; chief, population structure sect. UN, N.Y.C., 1977-79; dir. Population Studies Ctr. U. Pa., Phila., 1979-88. Author: Mortality Patterns in National Populations, 1976, Patterns of Urban and Rural Population Growth, 1980, (with M. Haines) Fatal Years, 1991. Fellow AAAS, Am. Acad. Arts and Scis, Am. Statis. Assn.; mem. NAS, Inst. Medicine, Am. Philos. Soc., Population Assn. Am. (pres. 1984, Irene B. Tauber award for Excellence in Demographic Research 1983), Internat. Union for Sci. Study of Population (council 1981-88). Democrat. Methodist. Home: 234 Walnut Ave Wayne PA 19087-3445 Office: Univ Pa Population Studies Ctr Philadelphia PA 19104

PRESTON, SEYMOUR STOTLER, III, manufacturing company executive; b. Media, Pa., Sept. 11, 1933; s. Seymour Stotler and Mary Alicia (Harper) P.; m. Jean Ellen Holman, Sept. 8, 1956; children: Courtney J., Katherine E., Alicia D., Shelley S. BA, Williams Coll., 1956; MBA, Harvard Coll., 1958. With Pennwalt Corp., Phila., 1961-89; exec. v.p. in charge of chems. and equipment ops., worldwide Pennwalt Corp., 1975-77, pres., COO, 1977-89; pres., CEO Elf Atochem N.Am., Inc. (formerly Atochem N.Am.), Phila., 1990-93; chmn. AAC Engineered Sys. Inc., 1994—; bd. dirs. CoreStates Bank, NA, Scott Specialty Gases, Inc., ADCO Techs., Inc., Albermarle Corp. Trustee Shipley Sch., Bryn Mawr, Pa., 1976-88, Phila. Orch. Assn., 1992-95; trustee Acad. Natural Scis., 1980-95, chmn., 1995—; bd. mgrs. Franklin Inst., Phila., 1980-92; bd. dirs. Lawrenceville (N.J.) Sch., 1982—. 1st lt. USAF, 1958-61. Mem. Soc. for Chem. Industry, Greater Phila. C. of C. (bd. dirs. 1979-94), Radnor Hunt Club (Malvern, Pa.).

PRESTON, THOMAS RONALD, English language educator, researcher; b. Oct. 31, 1936; s. Thomas and Marie Katherine (Nettlow) P.; m. Mary Ruth Atkinson, June 4, 1960; children: Lorel, Mary, Thomas. BA, U. Detroit, 1958; MA, Rice U., 1960, PhD, 1962. Asst. prof. English Duquesne U., Pitts., 1962-63; Asst. prof. English U. Fla., Gainseville, 1963-67; assoc. prof., chmn. dept. Loyola U., New Orleans, 1967-69; prof., chmn. dept. U. Tenn., Chattanooga, 1969-73, U. Wyo., Laramie, 1973-82; prof., dean arts and scis. U. North Tex., Denton, 1982-92; prof. English, 1992—; chmn. Wyo. Council for Humanities, Laramie, 1976-77. Author: Not in Timon's Manner, 1975; editor U. Ga. edit. of Smollett's Humphry Clinker, 1990; contbr. articles on 18th century lit. to profl. jours. Recipient John W. Gardner award Rice U., 1962; George Duke Humphrey award U. Wyo., 1982; NEH grantee, 1979; Am. Council of Learned Socs. grantee, 1980. Mem. South Ctrl. MLA, Am. Soc. for 18th Century Studies, Coll. English Assn., South Ctrl. Soc. for 18th Century Studies (pres. 1986-87). Democrat. Anglican. Home: 11722 S Central Ln Winona TX 75792-6704 Office: U North Tex English Dept Denton TX 76203

PRESTON, WILLIAM HUBBARD, consultant to specialty businesses; b. Bklyn., July 24, 1920; s. Russell Jackson and Mary Louise (Yetman) P.; m. Marcia Whitney Emery, Dec. 18, 1943; children: William Hubbard, Craig Ryder. B.S.M.E. cum laude, Poly. Inst. N.Y., 1942. Asst. supt. Ball & Roller div. SKF Industries, Phila., 1946-51; cons. Booz, Allen & Hamilton, N.Y.C., 1951-53; gen. sales mgr. Joy Mfg. Co., Pitts., 1953-59; exec. v.p. Chase Brass/Kennecott, Waterbury, Conn., 1959-62; pres. Indsl. Group Joy Mfg. Co., Michigan City, Ind., 1962-67, Davis-Standard div., Pawcatuck, Conn., 1967-83; v.p. Crompton & Knowles Corp., N.Y.C., 1967-83; prin. Hubbard Assocs., Hopkinton, Mass., 1983—; bd. dirs. Lefebvre Ltd., Montreal. Served to lt. (j.g.) USNR, 1943-46. Unitarian. Home: 152 Hayden Rowe St Hopkinton MA 01748-2512

PRESTOWITZ, CLYDE VINCENT, economist, research administrator; b. Wilmington, Del., Sept. 6, 1941; s. Clyde Vincent and Lillian (Lang) P.; m. Carol Ann Jay, Mar. 29, 1964; children: Anne, Clyde, Brian. B.A., Swarthmore Coll., 1963; M.A., U. Hawaii, 1965; M.B.A., U. Pa., 1980.

Mgr. market devel. Scott Paper Co., Phila., 1968-72; dir. planning Europe Scott Paper Co., Brussels, 1972-76; v.p. Japan Egon Zehnder Internat., Tokyo, 1976-78; dir. mktg. Am. Can Co., Greenwich, Conn., 1978-79; pres. Prestowitz Assocs., New Canaan, Conn., 1979-81; dep. asst. sec. internat. econ. policy U.S. Dept. Commerce, Washington, 1981-82, acting asst. sec. internat. econ. policy, 1982-83, counselor to sec., 1983-86; Wilson fellow, 1986-87; sr. assoc. Carnegie Endowment for Internat. Peace, Washington, 1987-89; pres. Econ. Strategy Inst., Washington, 1989—; vice-chmn. Pacific Basin Econ. Coun., 1989—. Republican. Presbyterian. Home: 10420 Masters Ter Potomac MD 20854-3862 Office: Econ Strategy Inst 1401 H St NW Ste 750 Washington DC 20005

PRETO-RODAS, RICHARD ANTHONY, foreign language educator; b. N.Y.C., May 30, 1936; s. Manuel and Beatrice Alina (Carvalho) Preto-R. B.A., Fairfield U., 1958; M.A. in Philosophy, Boston Coll., 1960; M.A. in Spanish, U. Mich., 1962, Ph.D. in Romance Langs. (fellow Rackham Sch. Grad. Studies 1965), 1966. Instr. U. Mich., 1964-66; asst. prof. U. Fla., 1966-70; assoc. prof. U. Ill., Urbana-Champaign, 1970-74; prof. U. Ill., 1974-81, chmn. Spanish, Italian, 1978-81; dir. lang. U. South Fla., Tampa, 1981-89, prof. lang., 1989—; cons. MLA; Fulbright vis. prof. comparative lit. Université Stendhal, Grenoble, France, 1994-95. Author: Negritude as A Theme in the Poetry of the Portuguese-Speaking World, 1971, Dialogue and Courtly Lore in Renaissance Portugal, 1971; co-author: Cronicas Brasileiras: A Portuguese Reader, 1980, rev. 1994 as Cronicas Brasileiras, Nova Fase, 40 Historinhas of C.D. de Andrade, 1983; co-editor, contbr: Empire in Transition: The Portuguese World in the Time of Camoes, 1985; contbg. editor: Handbook of Latin American Studies, 1983—; contbg. reviewer World Lit. Today, 1986—. NDEA fellow, 1965. Mem. MLA, Am. Council on Teaching Fgn. Langs., Am. Assn. Tchrs. of Spanish and Portuguese, Phi Beta Kappa. Democrat. Home: 4483 Vieux Carre Cir Tampa FL 33613-3057 Office: CPR-107 U South Fla Tampa FL 33620

PRETTI, BRADFORD JOSEPH, lay worker, insurance company executive; b. Glenwood Springs, Colo., Oct. 11, 1930; s. Joseph John and Ethel Elizabeth (Roe) P.; m. Nancy Ann Clayton, Mar. 30. 1951 (div. 1971); children: Kristi Pretti Micander, Terice Pretti Brownson, Bradford Joseph, Holli; m. Sarah Jane Rupp, Aug. 8, 1974. BA, U. Colo., 1952. Pres. Pub. Adv. Ins. Com., Chaves County, N.Mex., 1965-72; sr. warden St. Thomas á Beckett Ch., Roswell, N.Mex., 1978-79, St. Andrew's Ch., Roswell, N.Mex., 1991-92; mem. Progam Coun. Diocese of Rio Grande, Albuquerque, 1991-92, mem. Venture in Mission Commn., 1980-84, pres. Standing Commn., 1981-85, chmn. Bishop Search Commn., 1987, dep. to Gen. Conv., 1985-88; Cathedral chpt., 1988-91; pres. Roswell Ins. & Surety Agy., RBS Ins., 1974—; instr. Ea. N.Mex. U., Roswell, 1970—. Contbr. articles to jours. in field. Pres. Assurance Home Found., Roswell, 1984—; campaign chmn. United Way of Chaves County, Roswell, 1982, v.p., 1984; bd. dirs. Roswell Hospice Inc., 1984; trustee Roswell Mus. and Art Ctr., 1985, pres. bd. trustees, 1990-92; pres. bd. Roswell Mus. and Art Ctr. Found., 1995; bd. dirs. Sunny Acres, Inc.; chmn. Ea. N.Mex. Med. Ctr. Adv. Coun., 1995. Mem. N.Mex. Ind. Ins. Agts. Assn. (Outstanding Svc. award 1964), Roswell C. of C. (treas. 1984, pres. elect 1985, pres. 1986, Pres.'s Club citation 1983), Mus. Trustees Assn., Am. Contract Bridge League (pres. #382 sect. 1965-68), C Club (Boulder, Colo.). Republican. Episcopalian. Avocation: duplicate bridge. Home: 317 Sherrill Ln Apt 14 Roswell NM 88201-5828 Office: RBS Ins PO Box 280 Roswell NM 88202-0280 *Without a deep, abiding faith our lives are essentially meaningless.*

PRETTYMAN, ELIJAH BARRETT, JR., lawyer; b. Washington, June 1, 1925; s. Elijah Barrett and Lucy Courtney (Hill) P.; children by previous marriage: Elijah Barrett III, Jill Savage Lukoschek. Grad., St. Albans Sch., Washington, 1943; BA, Yale U., 1949; LLB, U. Va., 1953. Bar: D.C. 1954, U.S. Supreme Ct. 1957. Pvt. practice Washington, 1955—; law clk. to Justices Jackson, Frankfurter and Harlan (U.S. Supreme Ct.), 1953-55; assoc. firm Hogan & Hartson, Washington, 1955-63; partner Hogan & Hartson, 1964—; spl. asst. to Atty. Gen. U.S., 1963, White House, 1963-64; also Pres.'s rep. to Interagy. Com. on Transport Mergers; spl. cons. subcom. to investigate problems connected with refugees and escapees U.S. Senate Judiciary Com., Vietnam, 1967-68; outside cons. to subcom. on oversight and investigations, Ho. of Reps. com. on internal and fgn. commerce, 1978; spl. cons. for ABSCAM investigation to Com. on Standards of Ofcl. Conduct, U.S. Ho. of Reps., 1980-81; trustee emeritus, past mem. exec com. Am. U., Washington; past trustee, mem. exec. com. Washington Journalism Ctr.; past bd. dirs. Nat. Council on Crime and Delinquency; mem. adv. com. Media Law Reporter. Author: Death and the Supreme Court, 1961; Editor: (with William E. Jackson) The Supreme Court in the American System of Government (Justice Robert H. Jackson), 1955; contbr. articles to profl. jours. Past corp. mem. Salvation Army; mem. adv. com. Procedures of Jud. Coun., D.C.; mem. adv. bd. Inst. Comm. Law Studies, Cath. U.; bd. govs. St. Albans Sch., 1957-63, 65-72, chmn., 1965-67; past mem. nat. adv. com. Nat. Inst. for Citizen Edn. in Law; mem., bd. dirs., past pres. PEN/Faulkner Found.; v.p., chmn. program com., exec. com. Supreme Ct. Hist. Soc.; mem. internat. adv. bd. Toshiba Corp. With AUS, 1943-45. Fellow ABA; mem. Am. Coll. Trial Lawyers, Jud. Conf. D.C. Cir., D.C. Bar Found. (pres. 1983-84), Met. Washington Bd. Trade, D.C. Bar (1st pres. 1972-73, bd. govs. 1973-74), Am. Judicature Soc. (past v.p., exec. com.), Am. Acad. Appellate Lawyers (past pres.), Lawyers Club (pres.), Vinson Club, Alfalfa Club, Barrister Club, Met. Club, Chevy Chase Club. Methodist (past dir. ch.). Office: Hogan and Hartson Columbia Sq 555 13th St NW Washington DC 20004-1109 Home: 3100 Connecticut Ave NW Washington DC 20008-5148

PRETZINGER, DONALD LEONARD, retired insurance executive; b. Los Angeles, Sept. 17, 1923; s. Leonard K. and Beatrice K. (Haupt) P.; m. Beverly Helen Winnard, Aug. 30, 1946; children: Christine, Kathryn, Kerry. BS with honors, Oreg. State U., 1948; MS, U. So. Calif., 1949. CLU, chartered fin. cons. Secondary tchr. sci. Fillmore (Calif.) High Sch., 1949-50, Los Angeles City Schs., 1950-51; spl. agt. FBI, Washington, 1951-56; sales supr. Farmers Group Inc., Los Angeles, 1956-60, asst. mgr. sales, 1960-63, mgr. sales, 1963-65, regional mgr., 1966-69, v.p. profl. liability, 1978-84; pres., bd. dirs. Farmers Ins. Co. Oreg., 1984-89; ret.; v.p., gen. mgr. Farmers New World Life, Mercer Island, Wash., 1969-78. Pres. Northridge (Calif.) Townhome and Homeowners Assn., 1981-82; bd. dirs. St. Martin in the Fields Episc. Ch., Canoga Park, Calif., 1982-84. Lt. (j.g.) USN, 1942-46, PTO. Mem. Oreg. Ins. Mgrs. (bd. dirs. 1984-88), Oreg. Life and Health Guaranty Assn. (chmn., bd. dirs. 1984-89), Oreg. Ins. Guaranty Assn. (treas., bd. dirs. 1984-89), Oreg. Ins. Coun. (bd. dirs. 1984-89), Masons. Republican. Avocations: tennis, golf, travel. Home: 78585 Autumn Ln Palm Desert CA 92211-1418

PREUS, DAVID WALTER, bishop, minister; b. Madison, Wis., May 28, 1922; s. Ove Jacob Hjort and Magdalene (Forde) P.; m. Ann Madsen, June 26, 1951; children: Martha, David, Stephen, Louise, Laura. BA, Luther Coll., Decorah, Iowa, 1943, DD (hon.), 1969; postgrad., U. Minn., 1946-47; BTh, Luther Sem., St. Paul, 1950; postgrad., Union Sem., 1951, Edinburgh U., 1951-52; LLD (hon.), Wagner Coll., 1973, Gettysburg Coll., 1976; DD (hon.), Pacific Luth. Coll., 1974, St. Olaf Coll., 1974, Dana Coll., 1979, Tex. Luth. Coll., 1994; LHD (hon.), Macalester Coll., 1976. Ordained to ministry Luth. Ch., 1950; asst. pastor First Luth. Ch., Brookings, S.D., 1950-51; pastor Trinity Luth. Ch., Vermillion, S.D., 1952-57; campus pastor U. Minn., Mpls., 1957-58; pastor Univ. Luth. Ch. of Hope, Mpls., 1958-73; v.p. Am. Luth. Ch., 1968-73, pres., presiding bishop, 1973-87; exec. dir. Global Mission Inst. Luther Northwestern Theol. Sem., St. Paul; Disting. vis. prof. Luther-Northwestern Sem., St. Paul, 1988-94; Luccock vis. pastor Yale Div. Sch., 1969; chmn. bd. youth activity Am. Luth. Ch., 1960-68; mem. exec. com. Luth. Council U.S.A.; v.p. Luth. World Fedn., 1977-90; mem. cen. com. World Council Chs., 1973-75, 80-90; Luth. del. White House Conf. on Equal Opportunity. Chmn. Greater Mpls. Fair Housing Com., Mpls. Council Chs., 1960-64; Mem. Mpls. Planning Commn., 1965-67; mem. Mpls. Sch. Bd., 1965-74, chmn., 1967-69; mem. Mpls. Bd. Estimate and Taxation, 1968-73, Mpls. Urban Coalition; sr. public adv. U.S. del. Madrid Conf. of Conf. on Security and Cooperation in Europe, 1980-81; bd. dirs. Mpls. Inst. Art, Walker Art Center, Hennepin County United Fund, Ams. for Childrens Relief, Luth. Student Found., Research Council of Gt. City Schs., Urban League, NAACP; bd. regents Augsburg Coll., Mpls. Served with Signal Corps AUS, 1943-46, PTO. Decorated comdr.'s cross Royal Norwegian Order St. Olav, Order of St. George 1st deg. Orthodox Ch. of Georgia (USSR), 1989; recipient Regents medal Augustana Coll., Sioux Falls, S.D., 1973, Torch of Liberty award Anti-Defamation League, 1973, St. Thomas Aquinas award St. Thomas U. Office: 2481 Como Ave Saint Paul MN 55108-1445

PREUSS, ROGER E(MIL), artist; b. Waterville, Minn., Jan. 29, 1922; s. Emil W. and Edna (Rosenau) P.; m. MarDee Ann Germundson, Dec. 31, 1954 (dec. Mar. 1981). Student, Mankato Comml. Coll., Mpls. Sch. Art. instr. seminar Mpls. Coll. Art and Design, Mpls. Inst. Arts Speakers Bur.; former judge ann. Goodyear Nat. Conservation Awards Program. Painter of nature art; one-man shows include: St. Paul Fine Art Galleries, 1959, Albert Lea Art Center, 1963, Hist. Soc. Mont., Helena, 1964, Bicentennial exhbn., Le Sueur County Hist. Soc. Mus., Elysian, Minn., 1976, Merrill's Gallery of Fine Art, Taos, N.Mex., 1980; exhbns. include: Midwest Wildlife Conf. Exhbn., Kerr's Beverly Hills, Calif., 1947, Laguna Art Mus., Calif., 1947, Joslyn Meml. Mus., Omaha, 1948, Hollywood Fine Arts Center, 1948, Minn. Centennial, 1949, Federated Chaparral Authors, 1951, Nat. Wildlife Art, 1951, 52, N.Am. Wildlife Art, 1952, Ducks Unltd. Waterfowl exhibit, 1953, 54, St. Paul Winter Carnival, 1954, St. Paul Gallery Art Mart, 1954, Salmagundi Club, 1968, Harris Fine Arts Center, Provo, Utah, 1969, Galerie Internationale, N.Y.C., 1972, Holy Land Conservation Fund, N.Y.C., 1976, Faribault Art Ctr., 1981, Wildlife Artists of the World Exhbn., Bend, Oreg., 1984, U. Art Mus., U. Minn., Mpls., 1990, Rochester Art Ctr., 1991, Minn. Hist. Soc.-Hill House, 1992, Bemidji Art Ctr., 1992, Jack London Ctr., Dawson City, Yukon Territory, Can., 1992, Weyerhaeuser Meml. Mus., Little Falls, Minn., 1995, Minn. Valley Nat. Wildlife Refuge Ctr., Bloomington, 1995, Sagebrush Artists Exhbn., Klamath Falls, Oreg., 1995; represented in permanent collections: Demarest Meml. Mus., Hackensack, N.J., Smithsonian Instn., N.Y. Jour. Commerce, Mont. Hist. Soc., Inland Bird Banding Assn., Minn. Capitol Bldg., Mont. State U., Wildlife Am. Collection, LeSueur Hist. Soc., Voyageurs Nat. Park Interpretive Ctr., Krause-Hartig VFW Post, Mpls., Nat. Wildlife Fedn. Collection, Minn. Ceremonial House, U.S. Wildlife Svc. Fed. Bldg., Fort Snelling, Minn., Crater Lake Nat. Park Visitors Ctr., VA Hosp., Mpls., Luxton Collection, Banff, Alta., Can., Internat. Inst. Arts, Geneva, Mont. Capitol Bldg., People of Century-Goldblatt Collection, Lyons, Ill., Harlem Savings Collection, N.Y.C., Weisman Art Mus., Mpls., Minn. Vets. Home, Mpls., Blauvelt Art Mus., Oradell, N.J., Roger Preuss Art Collection, Augustana Ctr. for Western Studies, Sioux Falls, S.D., Minn. Mus. Am. Art, St. Paul, U. Minn. Art Mus., C.M. Russell Mus., Great Falls, Mont., others, numerous galleries and pvt. collections; designer: Fed. Duck Stamp, U.S. Dept. Interior, 1949, Commemorative Centennial Pheasant Stamp, 1981, Gold Waterfowl medallion Franklin Mint, 1983, Gold Stamp medallion Wildlife Mint, 1983, 40th Anniversary Commemorative Fed. Duck Stamp etching, 1989; panelist: Sportsman's Roundtable, Sta. WTCN-TV, Mpls. (emeritus), from 1953; author: Is Wildlife Art Recognized Fine Art?, 1986; contbr.: Christmas Echos, 1955, Wing Shooting, Trap & Skeet, 1955, Along the Trout Stream, 1979; contbr. Art Impressions mag., Can., Wildlife Art, U.S.; also illustrations and articles in Nat. Wildlife and over 300 essays on North American animals, others.; assoc. editor: Out-of-Doors mag.; compiler and artist: Outdoor Horizons, 1957, Twilight over the Wilderness, 1972, 60 limited edition prints Wildlife of America, from 1970; contbr. paintings and text Minnesota Today; creator paintings and text Preuss Wildlife Calendar; inventor: paintings and text Wildlife Am. Calendar; featured artist Art West, 1980-84, Wildlife Art; featured in films Your BFA- Care and Maintenance, Black Ducks Along the Border. Del. Nat. Wildlife Conf.; bd. dirs. emeritus Voyageurs Nat. Park Assn., Deep-Portage Conservation Found., 1977—; bd. dirs. Wetlands for Wildlife U.S.A.; active Wildlife Am.; co-organizer, v.p., bd. dirs. Minn. Conservation Fedn., 1952-54; mem. U.S. Hospitalized Vets. Venison Program, 1957—; trustee Liberty Bell Edn. Found.; Waseca Arts Coun.; founder, dir. Roger Preuss Conseation Preserve for Study of Nature, 1990—. With USNR, World War II. Recipient Stamp Design award U.S. Fish and Wildlife Svc., 1994, Minn. Outdoor award, 1956, Patron of Conservation award, 1956, award for contbns. conservation Minn. Statehood Centennial Commn., 1958, 1st award Am. Indsl. Devel. Coun., citation of merit VFW, award of merit Mil. Order Cootie, 1963, merit award Minn. Waterfowl Assn., 1976, silver medal Nat. SAR, 1978, Svcs. to Arts and Environ. award Faribault Art Ctr., 1981, Ptnrs. for Wildlife award U.S. Fish and Wildlife Svc., 1994; named Wildlife Conservationist of the Yr., Sears Fund.-Nat. Wildlife Fedn. program, 1966, Am. Bicentennial Wildlife Artist, Am. Heritage Assn., 1976; hon. mem. Ont. Chippewa Nation of Can., 1957; named Knight of Mark Twain for contbns. to Am. art Mark Twain Soc., 1978; named to Water, Woods and Wildlife Hall of Fame, named Dean of Wildfowl Artists, 1981, Hon. Ky. Col.; recipient hon. degree U.S. Vets. Venison program, 1980, Western Am. award significant contbns. to preservation arts and history No. Prairie Plains, Augustana Coll. Ctr. for Western Studies, Sioux Falls, S.D., 1992, Pub. Svc. award for outstanding contbns. to Am. conservation and environ. U.S. Dept. Interior, 1996; named creator first signed, numbered photolithographic print pub. in N.Am., 1959; documented Colorado Springs Fine Arts Ctr., 1993, colleague of Frederick R. Weisman Mus., Mpls., 1994; grantee NEH, 1995. Fellow Internat. Inst. Arts (life), Soc. Animal Artists (emeritus), N.Am. Mycol. Assn., Nat. Wildlife Fedn. (nat. wildlife week chmn. Minn.), Minn. Ducks Unltd. (bd. dirs. emeritus), Minn. Artists Assn. (v.p., bd. dirs. 1953-59), Soc. Artists and Art Dirs., Outdoor Writers Am. (emeritus), Soc. Artists and Art Dirs. (emeritus), Am. Artists Profl. League (emeritus), Mpls. Soc. Fine Arts, Wildlife Soc., Minn. Mycol. Soc. (pres. emeritus, hon. life mem.), Le Sueur County Hist. Soc. (hon. life mem.), Minn. Conservation Fedn. (hon. life), Wildlife Artists World (charter mem., internat. v.p. 1986—, chmn. fine arts bd.), Internat. Platform Assn. (emeritus), Great Lakes Outdoor Writers (emeritus), The Prairie Chicken Soc. (patron), The Sharp-tailed Grouse Soc. (patron), Mission Oceanic Arctic, 1992, Beaverbrook Club (hon. life), Minn. Press Club (emeritus), Explorers Club (N.Y.C., emeritus). Office: care Wildlife Am PO Box 580004-a Minneapolis MN 55458-0004 Studio: 2224 Grand Ave Minneapolis MN 55405-3412 *With a modicum of natural skills in painting and writing, my basic goal throughout all my work has been to help people appreciate and understand nature. If I as a naturalist am a small voice for our world's waters, woods, and wildlife, if I have influenced many children and adults to become more environment conscious, if my art brings to others a measure of joy, then my best aspirations for my creations have been fulfilled.*

PREUSS, RONALD STEPHEN, lawyer, educator; b. Flint, Mich., Dec. 1, 1935; s. Edward Joseph and Harriette Beckwith (Pease) P.; 1 child, William Stephen. AB, U. Mo., 1958, MA, 1963; JD, St. Louis U., 1973; postdoctoral, Worcester Coll., Oxford, Eng., 1979, U. Calif., Berkeley, 1979, U. Paris, 1984. Bar: Mo. 1973, U.S. Dist. Ct. (ea. and we. dists.) Mo. 1973, U.S. Tax Ct. 1979. From instr. to assoc. prof. English St. Louis Jr. Coll. Dist., 1965—; ptnr. Anderson & Preuss, Clayton, Mo., 1973—. Author: Laudamus Te, 1962, The St. Louis Gourmet. 1979, 86, English Elegies, 1983, Melville: A Psychic Biography, 1984, Theater I, 1987, Letting Go, 1988; editor St. Louis Gourmet Newsletter, 1981-88; co-editor Criterion mag. 1961-62; columnist Capital Courier newspaper 1962-64. Mem. Eisenhower Commn., 1995. Mem. Mo. Bar Assn., Phi Alpha Delta (John L. Sullivan chpt. vice justice 1971-72, justice 1972-73), Eisenhower Commn. Home: 32 Conway Cove Dr Chesterfield MO 63017-2069 Office: Anderson & Preuss 230 S Bemiston Ave Ste 410 Saint Louis MO 63105-1907

PREUSSER, JOSEPH WILLIAM, academic administrator; b. Petersburg, Nebr., June 18, 1941; s. Louis Henry and Elizabeth Sophia (Oberbrocking) P.; m. Therese Marie Mahoney, Aug. 12, 1967; children: Scott, Michelle, Denise. BA in Social Scis., Wayne State Coll., 1965; MA in Geography, U. Nebr., Omaha, 1971; PhD in Adminstrn., U. Nebr., 1978. Coord. social studies Lewis Cen. Community Sch. Dist., Council bluffs, Iowa, 1967-71; chmn. social sci. div., instr. Platte Jr. Coll., Columbus, Nebr., 1972-73; dean instrn./Platte campus Cen. Community Coll., Columbus, 1973-82, v.p. ednl. planning community edn., pres. Platte campus, 1982-84; pres. Cen. Community Coll., Grand Island, Nebr., 1984—; bd. dirs. devel. Nebr. Tech. Community Coll., 1973-75, sec. , dean instrn., 1974-76, chmn. coun. pres's., 1990-91,; mem. Archdiocese Omaha Bd. Edn., 1980-84; chmn. bd. St. Bonaventure Bd. Edn., 1976-80; pub. speaker in field. Contbr. articles to profl. jours. Bd. dirs. Cen. Nebr. Goodwill Industries, Grand Island, 1987—, treas., 1990-91; chmn. sustaining membership enrollment campaign Overland Trails Boy Scouts Am., 1990; worker YMCA Fund Dr., Columbus, 1980; active Columbus City Planning Commn., 1979-84, chmn., 1981-82. With U.S. Army, 1959-61. Named one Outstanding Young Men of Am., 1976; recipient Pres. award NTCCA, 1986, Nat. Leadership award U. Tex., 1988-89. Mem. Am. Assn. Cmty. and Jr. Colls., Am. Voct. Assn., Nebr. Vocat. Assn. (Outstanding Svc. award 1986), Am. Assn. Ret. People, Nat. Coun. Instructional Officers, Nat. Coun. Instructional Adminstrs., Am. Assn. for Women in Cmty. Colls. (Pres. of Yr. 1996), Saddle Club, Rotary, KC, Greater Columbus Area C. of C., Phi Delta Kappa. Democrat. Roman Catholic. Avocations: golfing, gardening, woodworking.

PREVIN, ANDRE, composer, conductor; b. Berlin, Apr. 6, 1930; came to U.S., 1938, naturalized, 1943; s. Jack and Charlotte (Epstein) P.; m. Mia Farrow, Sept. 10, 1970 (div. 1979); children: Matthew and Sascha (twins), Fletcher, Lark, Daisy; m. Heather Hales, Jan. 1982; 1 child, Lukas. Student, Berlin Conservatory, Paris Conservatory; privately with, Pierre Monteux, Mario Castelnuovo-Tedesco. Mem. faculty Guildhall Sch., London, Curtis Inst., Phila., Berkshire Music Ctr. Rec. artist classical music for RCA, EMI, Phillips, Telarc, Deutsche Gramophone, 1946—; composer chamber music Cello Concerto, Guitar Concerto, piano music, serenades for violin, brass quintet, song cycle on poems by Philip Larkin Every Good Boy Deserves Favour, Principals, Reflections, Piano Concerto, Triolet for Brass Ensemble, Haydn variations for piano solo, 4 lyrics of Toni Morrison for soprano, Cello Sonata, Violin Sonata, Trio for Piano Oboe and Bassoon, Billy the Kid (Songs for Soprano and Piano), Songs of Remembrance (soprano and piano), Sallie Chisum (soprano and orch.), Tango Song and Dance (violin and piano), film scores, 1950-59; condr.-in-chief Houston Symphony, 1967-69; prin. condr. London Symphony Orch., 1968-79, Royal Philharm. Orch., Eng., 1985-91; music dir. L.A. Philharm., 1985-89; condr. laureate London Symphony Orch., 1992—; guest condr. maj. symphony orchs. and festivals in U.S. and Europe including: festivals in Salzburg, Edinburgh, Flanders, Vienna, Osaka, Prague, Berlin, Bergen; music dir. South Bank Music Festival, London, 1972-74, Pitts. Symphony, 1976-84, L.A. Philharmonic, 1984-89; author: Music Face to Face, 1971, Orchestra, 1979, No Minor Chords, 1992. Served with AUS, 1950-51. Knighted (KBE), Her Majesty Queen Elizabeth II, 1996; recipient awards Nat. Grammophone Soc., Acad. Motion Picture Arts and Scis. Mem. Acad. Motion Picture Arts and Scis., Dramatists Guild, Brit. Composers Guild, Nat. Composers and Condrs. League, Degrees Curtis Inst., Royal Acad., Guild Hall Sch./Duquesne U. Home: 6 Sherwood Ln Bedford Hills NY 10507-2200 Address: care Columbia Artists 165 W 57th St New York NY 10019-2201 also: Barbican Centre, Silk St, London England EC2Y8DS

PREVITE, RICHARD, computer company executive; b. Boston, 1935. BS, San Jose State U., 1956, MA. Contr. Sierra Elec. Corp., Menlo Park, Calif., 1961-69; with Advanced Micro Devices, Inc., Sunnyvale, Calif., 1969—, sr. v.p., treas., chief adminstrv. officer, pres., COO, bd. dirs.; bd. dirs. Robinson Nugent, Inc. Office: Advanced Micro Devices Inc PO Box 3453 Sunnyvale CA 94088-3453*

PREVOR, RUTH CLAIRE, psychologist; b. N.Y.C., June 20, 1944; d. Gustav and Greta (Dreifuss) Strauss; m. Sydney Joseph P., July 4, 1963; children: Joy, Grant, Jed. BA, U. P.R., 1966; PhD, Caribbean Ctr. of Postgrad. Studies, San Juan, 1988. Cert. forensic psychologist, critical incident stress debriefing. Asst. dean Caribbean Ctr. of Postgrad. Studies, 1986-87; dir. prenatal edn. Ashford Meml. Hosp., San Juan, 1987; pvt. practice San Juan, 1984—; advisor, field faculty Vt. Coll., Norwich U., 1990-91; trustee Caribbean Ctr. for Advanced Studies, San Juan, Miami, Fla., 1990—. Bd. dirs. Jewish Community Ctr., Miramar, P.R., 1986—, bd. dirs. pre-sch., 1990—; pres. Home and Sch./St. John's Prep., San Juan, 1980-81, P.R. chpt. Hadassah Sch., 1972-74; presdl. adv. com., 1990-92. Mem. Am. Psychol. Assn., Assn. of Psychology of P.R. (hon. award 1984), Caribbean Counselors Assn., Caribe Hilton Club, Nat. Assn. Children with Learning Disabilities, Nat. Register Health Svc. Providers in Psychology. Jewish. Office: Ashford Med Ctr San Juan PR 00907

PREVOST, EDWARD JAMES, paint manufacturing executive; b. Baie Comeau, Que., Can., May 26, 1941; s. Omer and Jeanne (Ouellet) P.; m. Anna Marie Murphy, June 20, 1964; children: Marc, Louise, Eric, Luc. BA in History with honors, Loyola Coll., Montreal, Que., 1962; MBA, U. Western Ont., London, 1964. Cert. Advt. Agy. Practitioner. Account exec. J. Walter Thompson Co. Ltd., Montreal, 1964-66; successively account exec., account supr., group mgr. and v.p. Cockfield Brown & Co. Ltd., Montreal, 1966-69; gen. mgr. CJRP Radio, Quebec City, 1969-71; exec. v.p., chief operating officer Mut. Broadcasting Ltd., 1971-72, pres., chief operating officer, 1973; exec. v.p. Civitas Corp. Ltd., Montreal, 1973-74, pres., chief exec. officer, 1974-82, also chmn. bd. operating cos., 1974-82; pres., chief exec. officer La Brasserie O'Keefe Limitée, Montreal, 1983-89; sr. v.p. Carling O'Keefe Breweries of Can. Ltd., 1983-89; pres., chief exec. officer, dir. SICO Inc., Longueuil, Can., 1989-91; pres., CEO Para Inc., Brampton, Can., 1991—; bd. dirs. BBM Bur. Broadcasting Measurement, 1971-78; mem. Montreal Bd. Trade; treas., vice chmn.-elect Can. Paint & Coatings Assn., 1994—. Gov. Can. Advt. Found., 1982; chmn. Telefilm Can., 1983-86; chmn. Montreal Heart Inst. Rsch. Fund, 1979-81, exec. com. 1981-86. Mem. bd. dirs. L'Assn. des Brasseurs du Que. (chmn. 1984-86), Province Que., Can., C. of C., Can. Assn. Broadcasters (dir. 1975, vice Chmn. radio 1976-77, chmn. 1978-79, past chmn., mem. exec. com. 1980-81), Inter-Am. Assn. Broadcasters Uruguay (sec., past treas.), Young Pres. Orgn. (chmn. Que. chpt. 1987), Assn. des MBA du Que. (chmn. 1985-86). Clubs: St.-Denis (Montreal), Western Bus. Sch. (Montreal) (founding pres. 1972), Royal Montreal Golf. Office: Para Inc, 11 Kenview Blvd, Brampton, ON Canada L6T 5G5

PREVOZNIK, STEPHEN JOSEPH, anesthesiologist, retired; b. McAdoo, Pa., June 21, 1929; s. John George and Mary Margaret (Ficek) P.; m. Rita Agnes Kellett, Aug. 20, 1955; children—Mary Therese, Stephen Joseph, John Cyril, Michael Edward, Margaret Anne, Rita Marie, Thomas William, Jean Marie. R.N., St. Joseph Hosp. Sch. Nursing, Phila., 1951; B.S., U. Notre Dame, 1955; M.D., U. Pa., 1959. Intern Fitzgerald Mercy Hosp., Darby, Pa., 1959-60; resident in anesthesia U. Pa., Phila., 1960-62; practice medicine specializing in anesthesiology Phila., 1962—; mem. staff U. Pa. Hosp.; prof. anesthesia U. Pa., 1977-94, dir. clin. activities, 1971-89; ret., 1994; Chmn. Residency Rev. Com. for Anesthesiology, 1991—. Contbr. to textbooks on anesthesiology. Mem. AMA, Am. Soc. Anesthesiologists, Pa. Soc. Anesthesiologists, Phila. Soc. Anesthesiologists (pres. 1975-77), Internat. Anesthesia Rsch. Soc., U. Anesthetists (exec. coun. 1977-79, sec. 1981-84, dir. anesthesiology pain mgmt. program 1992-94). Home: 204 N Concord Ave Havertown PA 19083-5021 *No one does everything by himself; someone is always there to provide a helping hand. As one progresses and matures, he finds many opportunities to repay what he has received. Without this repayment, the chain is broken and that life is without meaning.*

PREWITT, CHARLES THOMPSON, geochemist; b. Lexington, Ky., Mar. 3, 1933; s. John Burton and Margaret (Thompson) P.; m. Gretchen B. Hansen, Jan. 31, 1958; children: Daniel Hansen. SB, MIT, 1955, SM, 1960, PhD, 1962. Research scientist E.I. DuPont De Nemours & Co. Inc., Wilmington, Del., 1962-69; assoc. prof. SUNY, Stony Brook, 1969-71, prof., 1971-86, chmn. dept. earth and space scis., 1977-80; dir. Geophys. Lab., Carnegie Inst. of Washington, 1986—; sec.-treas. U.S. Nat. Com. for Crystallography, Washington, 1983-85; gen. chmn. 14th Meeting of Internat. Mineral. Assn., Stanford, Calif., 1986; chmn. NRC/Nat. Acad. Scis. com. on physics and chemistry of earth materials, 1985-87; mem. bd. govs. Consortium for Advanced Radiation Svcs. Editor: (jour.) Physics and Chemistry of Minerals, 1976-85; contbr. over 140 articles to profl. jours. Capt. USAR, 1956-65. NATO sr. postdoctoral fellowship, 1975, Churchill overseas fellowship, 1975, Japan Soc. for Promotion of Sci. fellowship, 1983; named Disting. Vis. Prof. Chemistry, Ariz. State U., 1983. Fellow Mineral. Soc. Am. (pres. 1983-84); mem. Geol. Soc. Am., Am. Crystallographic Assn., Materials Research Soc., Mineral. Soc. Gt. Britain and Ireland. Home: 2728 Unicorn Ln NW Washington DC 20015-2234 Office: Carnegie Inst Geophys Lab 5251 Broad Branch Rd NW Washington DC 20015-1305

PREWITT, KENNETH, political science educator, foundation executive; b. Alton, Ill., Mar. 16, 1936; s. Carl Kenneth and Louise (Carpenter) P.; children: Jennifer Ann, Geoffrey Douglas. BA, So. Meth. U., 1958; MA, Washington U., St. Louis, 1959; PhD, Stanford U., 1963. Prof. polit. sci. U. Chgo., 1964-80, chmn. dept. polit. sci., 1975-76; dir. Nat. Opinion Research Center, 1976-79; pres. Social Sci. Research Council, N.Y.C., 1979-85, 95—; sr. v.p. Rockefeller Found., N.Y.C., 1985-95; vis. scholar U. Nairobi, Kenya, 1968-71; adj. prof. polit sci. Columbia U., 1980-83; teaching and rsch. Stanford U., 1964-68; cons. Rockefeller Found., Zaire, 1972, Thailand, 1973; chmn. governing bd. Energy Found.; bd. dirs. Washington U., So. Meth. U.,

Ctr. Advanced Study Behavioral Scis. Author: Political Socialization, 1969, Ruling Elites, 1973, Labryrinths of Democracy, 1973, Introduction to American Government, 1983, 6th edit., 1991. Guggenheim fellow, 1983; fellow Center Advanced Study in Behavioral Scis., 1983. Fellow AAAS, Am. Acad. Arts and Scis. (v.p.); mem. Am. Polit. Sci. Assn. (v.p.), Coun. on Fgn. Rels. Office: Social Sci Rsch Coun 810 7th Ave New York NY 10019

PREWOZNIK, JEROME FRANK, lawyer; b. Detroit, July 15, 1934; s. Frank Joseph and Loretta Ann (Parzych) P.; m. Marilyn Ruth Johnson, 1970; 1 child, Frank Joseph II. AB cum laude, U. Detroit, 1955; JD with distinction, U. Mich., 1958. Bar: Calif. 1959. Pvt. practice, Calif., 1960-91. Served in U.S. Army, 1958-60. Mem. ABA (bus. law sect., law and acctg. com., chmn. auditing standards subcom. 1981-86), State Bar Calif., Order of Coif. Republican. Home and Office: 431 Georgina Ave Santa Monica CA 90402-1909

PREY, BARBARA ERNST, artist; b. Jamaica, N.Y., Apr. 17, 1957; d. Herbert Henry and Margaret (Joubert) Ernst; m. Jeffrey Drew Prey, Jan. 11, 1986; children: Austin William Ernst Prey, Emily Elizabeth Prey. BA with honors, Williams Coll., 1979; MDiv, Harvard U., 1986. Sales staff Tiffany and Co., N.Y.C., summer 1977; summer intern Met. Mus. Art, N.Y.C., summer 1979; personal asst. Prince Albrecht Castell, Castell, Germany, 1980-81; with modern painting dept. Sotheby's Auction House, N.Y.C., 1981-82; sales asst. Marlborough Gallery, N.Y.C., 1982; teaching asst. Boston Coll., 1984, Harvard U., Cambridge, Mass., 1984-85; vis. lectr. Tainan (Taiwan) Coll. and Sem., 1986-87; artist Prosperity, Pa., 1987—; art juror Washington and Jefferson Coll., Washington, Pa., 1990; presenter in field. Illustrator: (book) Boys Harbor Cookbook, 1988, A Dream Became You, (4 book series) A City Grows Up, 1991, (cover) Am. Artist Mag., summer 1994; exhibited paintings in group shows including Mus. of Fine Arts, Nassau County, N.Y., 1988, Nat. Arts Club N.Y.C., 1988, Gallery One, Rockland, Maine, 1992, Williams Coll., Williamstown, Mass., 1993, Johnstown (Pa.) Art Mus., 1993, Blair Art Mus., Hollidaysburg, Pa., 1993, Phila. Mus. of Art Gallery, 1995; exhibited in one-woman shows including Harvard-Yale-Princeton Club, Pitts., 1991; represented in many pvt. collections including Pres. and Mrs. George Bush Farnsworth Mus. Art. Class agt. Williams Coll., Williamstown, Mass., 1981-91; bd. mem. Citizens Libr., Washington, 1992-93; active Bethel Presbyn. Ch. Recipient Fulbright scholarship Fulbright Assn., Germany, 1979-80, grant Roothbert Fund, Chataugua, N.Y., 1982-84, Ch. History award Gordan-Conwell Sem., S. Hamilton, Mass., 1984, Henry Luce Found. grant Henry Luce Found., Taiwan, 1986-87. Mem. Pitts. Watercolor Soc. (Jean Thoburn award 1994), Nat. Mus. Women in the Arts. Republican. Avocations: tennis, skiing, bird watching, reading, cross county skiing.

PREYER, ROBERT OTTO, English literature educator; b. Greensboro, N.C., Nov. 11, 1922; s. William Yost and Mary Norris (Richardson) P.; m. Renee Haenel, June 14, 1947; children: Jill, Sally, Elizabeth; m. Kathryn Conway Turner, July 19, 1966. Grad., Choate Sch., 1939; student, Davidson Coll., 1939-40; AB, Princeton U., 1945; MA, Columbia U., 1948, PhD, 1954. Instr. Smith Coll., 1948-54; asst. prof. Brandeis U., Waltham, Mass., 1954-55, prof., chmn. dept. English and Am. lit., 1963-66, chmn. faculty senate, 1976-80, dir. univ. studies program, 1979—, prof. emeritus, 1988—; vis. lectr. Amherst Coll., 1952; vis. prof. Freiburg U., Germany, 1956-57; guest prof. Heidelberg U., Germany, 1973-74; bd. dirs. Peidmont Fin. Corp., Richardson Corp., Boston, Blacksides Inc., Boston, Adirondack Conservancy, Earl Warren Legal Tng. Program Inc., N.Y.C.; mem. adv. bd. Eyes on the Prize, TV series, 1985. Author: Bentham, Coleridge and The Science of History, 1958; adv. editor: Victorian Studies, 1961—; editor: Victorian Literature; contbr. essays to profl. jours. Chmn. Mass Civil Liberties Fund, 1987-90; mem. bd. overseers humanities Tufts U., 1989-94; mem. adv. coun. dept. English, Princeton U., 1991—; bd. dirs. Mus. Afro-Am. History, Boston. Ensign USNR, 1940-43, PTO. Mem. MLA, ACLU (bd. dirs.), Legal Def. Found. (nat. bd. dirs. 1990—), Cottage Club, St. Botolph Club, Princeton Club, Keene Valley Country Club. Democrat. Home: 6 Maple Ave Cambridge MA 02139-1116

PREZIO, JOSEPH ANTHONY, nuclear medicine physician; b. Troy, N.Y., Dec. 30, 1933. MD, Georgetown U., 1959. Intern Mercy Hosp., Buffalo, N.Y., 1959-60; resident D.C. Gen. Hosp., Washington, 1960-61, Georgetown Hosp., Washington, 1961-62; fellow endocrinology Georgetown Hosp., 1962-64; resident Mercy Hosp.; chmn. dept. nuclear medicine SUNY, Buffalo. Mem. AMA, Am. Coll. Nuclear Physicians, Endocrine Soc., Soc. Nuclear Medicine. Office: PO Box 273 Chautauqua NY 14722-0273 also: SUNY Sch Medicine Dept Nuclear Medicine 105 Parker Hall 3435 Main St Buffalo NY 14214-3001

PREZZANO, WILBUR JOHN, photographic products company executive; b. Chappaqua, N.Y., Dec. 18, 1940; s. Wilbur J. and Adelaide J. Prezzano; m. Sheila Neary, Aug. 29, 1964; children: Timothy J., David N., E. Peter. B.S. in Econs., U. Pa., 1962, M.B.A. in Indsl. Mgmt., 1964. Statistician Eastman Kodak Co., Rochester, N.Y., 1965-66, mem. treas.'s staff, 1966-67, fin. analyst, 1967-68, fin. analyst bus. systems markets div., 1968-69, coordinator sales analysis and fin. info. systems, 1969-71, supr. fin. planning analysis, 1971-73, supt. acctg. analysis, 1973, staff asst. to gen. mgr. Customer Equipment Services Div., 1973-76, mgr. field ops., 1976-78, dir. copy products, mgr. field ops., 1978-79, dir. bus. mktg. planning mktg. div., 1979-80, asst. gen. mgr., 1980, v.p., 1980-82, gen. mgr. U.S. mktg. div., 1982-83, group v.p., gen. mgr. mktg., mgr. internat. photog. ops., 1983-84, gen. mgr. photog. products, 1985-90, gen. mgr. internat., 1990-91, pres. health, 1991-94, exec. v.p., chmn. and pres. Kodak greater China region, 1994—, also bd. dirs.; bd. dirs. First Fed. Savs. & Loan Assn., Rochester. Mem. Genesee Valley Club (Rochester). Office: Eastman Kodak Co 343 State St Rochester NY 14650-0237

PRIAULX, A(LLAN), publishing executive; b. Eugene, Oreg., May 13, 1940; s. Arthur W. and Kathleen Dealtry (Bean) P.; m. Jacqueline Markham, Jan. 10, 1976; children—Sharmon, Elizabeth. Student, Dartmouth Coll., 1958-60, U. Southampton, Eng., 1960, New Sch. for Social Research, 1961-62. Corr. UPI, Buffalo, 1962-63; mgr. bur. UPI, Concord, N.H., 1963-65, Honolulu, 1965-66; news mgr. UPI, Paris, 1966-68; dir. spl. projects McLendon Corp., Dallas, 1968-70; v.p. Register & Tribune Syndicate, N.Y.C., 1970-76; exec. editor King Features Syndicate, N.Y.C., 1976-79, editor, 1979-81, v.p. gen. mgr., 1981-86; v.p. editorial dir. C.N.R. Ptnrs., 1986-87; pres. Resource Media Inc., 1988—; exec. v.p., pub. The Am. Banker Thomson Corp., 1990-92; chmn., chief exec. Resource Media Inc., 1992—; mng. dir. Markham/Novell Comm. Author: (with S.J. Ungar) The Almost Revolution, 1969. V.p., chmn. pub. relations com. United Cerebral Palsy Assns.; mem. exec. vol. core Victim Services Agys. N.Y.C.; bd. dirs. Greyhound Friends Inc. Mem. Overseas Press Club Am., Advt. Club N.Y., Yale Club N.Y., Dartmouth Club N.Y. Episcopalian.

PRIBBLE, EASTON, artist; b. Falmouth, Ky., July 31, 1917; s. Thaddeus Sewell and Louise Ella (Parker) P. Student, U. Cin., 1941. Ind. tchr. N.Y.C., 1950-57; instr. painting and history of art Munson-Williams-Proctor Inst., Utica, N.Y., 1957—; instr. history of art Utica Coll., Syracuse U., 1960-74. One-man exhbns. include Pinacotheca Gallery, N.Y.C., 1947, 48, Alan Gallery, N.Y.C., 1953, 55, 59, Hamilton Coll., Clinton, N.Y., 1975, Munson-Williams-Proctor Inst. Mus. Art, 1957, 76, 82, Kirkland Art Ctr., Clinton, N.Y., 1988, Rome (N.Y.) Art Ctr., 1990; represented in permanent collections Whitney Mus. Am. Art, Hirschorn Mus. and Sulpture Garden, Smithsonian Instn., Parrish Mus., Southampton, N.Y., Munson-Williams-Proctor Inst. Mus. Art., Fallingwater (Frank Lloyd Wright House), Mill Run, Pa., Hudson River Mus., Yonkers, N.Y., Everson Mus., Syracuse, N.Y., Emerson Gallery, Hamilton Coll., The Farnsworth Mus. Art, Rockland, Maine. Fellow Yaddo, Saratoga Springs, N.Y., 1954, 55, 68. Mem. Artists Equity. Home: 24 Rose Pl Utica NY 13502-5614 Office: Munson-Williams-Proctor Inst 310 Genesee St Utica NY 13502-4764

PRIBLE, LARRY R., insurance company executive; b. 1946. With IBM, Indpls., 1967-79; with Indpls. Life Ins., 1980—, now pres., CEO. Office: Indianapolis Life Ins Co 2960 N Meridian St Indianapolis IN 46208*

PRIBRAM, KARL HARRY, psychology educator, brain researcher; b. Feb. 25, 1919. BS, U. Chgo., 1938, MD, 1941; PhD in Psychology (hon.), U. Montreal, Can., 1992. Diplomate Am. Bd. Neurol. Surgery, Am. Bd. Med. Psychotherapists. Lectr. Yale U., New Haven, 1951-58; dir. psychology Inst. of Living, Hartford, Conn., 1951-58; fellow Ctr. for Advanced Studies in Behavioral Sci., Stanford (Calif.) U., 1958-59, assoc. prof., 1959-62, rsch. career prof., 1962-89, prof. emeritus, 1989—; eminent scholar Radford (Va.) U., 1989—; adjunct prof. U. Tenn., 1993—; vis. scholar, hon. lectr. MIT, 1954, Clark U., 1956, Harvard, 1956, Haverford Coll., 1961, U. So. Calif., 1961, U. Leningrad, 1962, U. Moscow, 1962, Beloit Coll., 1966-67, U. Alberta, Can., 1968, Ctr. for Study Dem. Insts., 1967-75, U. Coll., London, 1972, U. Chgo., 1973, Menninger Sch. Psychiatry, 1973-76, Ohio State U., 1975, Inst. for Higher Studies; vis. lectr. Grass Found., 1977; Phillips lectr., Haverford Coll., 1979; Lashley lectr., Queens Coll., 1979; Pres.' Club lectr., Oakland U., 1980; J.E. Wallace Wallin lectr., Augustana Coll., 1981; Hubert Humphrey lectr, Macalester Coll., 1981; John M. Dorseh lectr. in Psychol. Physiology, Wayne State U., 1983; lectr. Internat. Mgmt. Inst., Geneva, Switzerland, 1987, Texas A&M U., 1987, Inst. Med. Psychol., Naples, 1988; disting. lectr. Second Annual Symposium of the Mind, Arlington, Tex., 1988; hon. lectr. Sirius Seminaries, Paris, 1988, Bielfeld, Germany, 1990; and numerous others. Author: Brain and Behavior, vol. 1-4, 1969, What Makes Man Human, 1971, Languages of the Brain: Experimental Paradoxes and Principles in Neuropsychology, 1971; The Neurosciences: Third Study Program, 1971, Brain and Perception: Holonomy and Structure in Figural Processing, 1991, Rethinging Neural Networks: Quantum Fields and Biological Data, 1993, Origins: Brain and Self Organization, 1994, Soale in Conscious Experience: Is the Brain Too Important to be Left to Specialists to Study?, 1995; editor, mem. consulting bd. Neuropsychologia, Jour. Math. Biology, Internat. Jour. Neurosci., Behavioral and Brain Scis., Jour. Mental Imagery, Jour. Human Movement Studies, Jour. Social and Biol. Structures, ReVision, STSM Quarterly, Indian Jour. Psychophysiology, Interim Jour. Psychology, Internat. Jour. Psychophysiology, Cognition and Brain Theory; contbr. over 170 articles to profl. jours. Recipient Lifetime Rsch. Career award in neurosci. NIH, 1962-89, Humanitarian award INTA, 1980, Realia honor Inst. Advanced Philosophic Rsch., 1986, 93, Outstanding Contbns. award Am. Bd. Med. Psychotherapists, Neural Network Leadership award Internat. Neural Network, 1996. Fellow Am. Acad. Arts and Scis., N.Y. Acad. Scis. (hon. life); mem. AAUP, AMA, AAAS, APA (pres. div. physiol. and comparative psychology 1967-68, pres. div. theoretical and philos. psychology 1979-80), Internat. Neuropsychol. Soc. (founding pres. 1967-69), Internat. Assn. Study of Pain, Soc. Exptl. Psychologists, Am. Psychol. Soc., Am. Psychopathological Assn. (Paul Hoch award 1975), Am. Acad. Psychoanalysis, Soc. Biol. psychiatry (Manfred Sakel award 1976), Soc. Clin. and Exptl. Hypnosis (Henry Guze award 1991), Soc. Neurosci., Profs. For World Peace (pres. 1982-85), Sigma Xi. Home: 102 Dogwood Ln Radford VA 24141-3917 Office: Radford Univ Ctr Brain Rsch Box 6977 Radford VA 24142

PRICE, ARTHUR D., food products executive; b. 1944. With Mid Valley Products, Inc., Taylors, S.C., 1964-76, pres.; with Global Trading, Inc., Greenville, S.C., 1976—, pres. Office: Global Trading Inc 14 Creekside Park Ct Greenville SC 29615*

PRICE, B. BYRON, museum director. Dir. Panhandle-Plains Hist. Mus., Canyon, Tex., until 1987; exec. dir. Nat. Cowboy Hall of Fame and Western Heritage Ctr., Oklahoma City, 1987—. Office: Nat Cowboy Hall Fame & Western Heritage Ctr 1700 NE 63rd St Oklahoma City OK 73111-7906

PRICE, BETTY JEANNE, choirchime soloist, writer; b. Long Beach, Calif., June 12, 1942; d. Grant E. and Miriam A. (Francis) Sickles; m. Harvey H. price, Aug. 6, 1975; 1 child, Thomas Neil Gering. Degree in Acctg., Northland Pioneer Coll., Show Low, Ariz., 1977. Missionary to youth Open Bible Standard Missions, Trinidad, 1958-59; typographer Joel H. Weldon & Assocs., Scottsdale, Ariz., 1980-89; exec. chief acct. Pubs. Devel. Corp., San Diego, 1994-95; coord. music and worship College Ave. Bapt. Ch., San Diego, 1994-95; ChoirChime soloist, 1986—; pres., owner Customized Funding Svcs., San Diego, 1996—; founder ubterbat, cibs, bys, Customized Funding Svcs., 1996—. Author: 101 Ways to Fix Broccoli, 1994; ABC's of Abundant Living, 1995; (with others) God's Vitamin C for the Spirit, 1995. Mem. Christian Writers Guild, Nat. Assn. Factoring Specialists, Nat. Entrepreneurs Assn. Avocations: provide musical programs for nursing homes, hospitals, churches, civic groups. Home: PO Box 151115 San Diego CA 92175-1115

PRICE, CHARLES EUGENE, lawyer, legal educator; b. Apalachicola, Fla., Mar. 13, 1926; s. Charles Patrick and Lela Frances (Joseph) P.; m. Lennie F. Bryant, Apr. 25, 1947; 1 child, Charles Eugene Jr. (dec.). B.A. Johnson C. Smith Coll., 1946; A.M. Howard U., 1952; LL.B. Am. Law Sch., 1952; postgrad Johns Hopkins U., 1951-52, Boston U., 1956; J.D. John Marshall U., 1967; C.S., Harvard U., 1980. Bar: Ga. 1968, U.S. Dist. Ct. (no. dist.) Ga. 1978. Sole practice, Atlanta, 1967—; prof. John Marshall Law Sch., Atlanta, 1973-76; dean academics Butler Coll., Tyler, Tex., 1950-53, Fla. Meml. Coll., St. Augustine, 1953-55; Ga. staff NAACP, 1955-60; assoc. prof. Morris Brown Coll., Atlanta, 1960—. Author: The Garvey Movement, 1950. Contbr. articles to profl. jours. Presdl. elector Ga. Electoral Coll., 1972; treas. anti-poverty program, Equal Opportunity Authority, Dekalb County, Ga., 1965-70; bd. dirs. Atlanta SBA, 1966-82. Recipient Leadership award Dekalb NAACP, 1962; Leadership award Ga. NAACP, 1964. Mem. Atlanta Gate City, Ga. State Bar Assn., ABA, Smith Alumni Assn., Alpha Phi Alpha, Alpha Kappa Mu. Presbyterian (elder). Club: Harvard (Cambridge, Mass.). Home: 1480 Austin Rd SW Atlanta GA 30331-2204

PRICE, CHARLES H., II, former ambassador; b. Kansas City, Mo., Apr. 1, 1931; s. Charles Harry and Virginia (Ogden) P.; m. Carol Ann Swanson, Jan. 10, 1969; children: Caroline Lee, Melissa Marie, Charles H., C. B., Pickette. Student, U. Mo., 1951-53; LLD (hon.), Westminster Coll., 1984; LLD (honoris causa), U. Mo., 1988; LHD, Baker U., 1991; DSc (hon.), U. Buckingham, Eng., 1993. Chmn. bd., dir. Price Candy Co., Kansas City, 1969-81, Am. Bancorp., Kansas City, 1973-81; chmn., chief exec. officer Am. Bank & Trust Co., Kansas City, 1973-81; Am. ambassador to Belgium Brussels, 1981-83; Am. ambassador to U.K. London, 1983-89; chmn. bd. Americanc, Inc., St. Joseph, Mo., 1989-92, pres., CEO, 1990-92; chmn. bd. Mercantile Bank Kansas City, Mo., 1992-96, bd. dirs., 1996—; bd. dirs. US Industries, Inc., Hanson PLC, London, N.Y. Times Co., Texaco, Inc., 360 Degree Comm., Inc., Kansas City, Mercantile Bancorp, Inc. Bd. dirs. St. Luke's Hosp., Kansas City, 1970-81, hon. dir., 1989—, advisor Heart Inst. com.; bd. dirs. Midwest Rsch. Inst., Kansas City, chmn., 1990-93. Hon. fellow Regent's Coll., London, 1986; recipient William Booth award Salvation Army, 1985, World Citizen of Yr. award Mayor of Kansas City, 1985, Trustee Citation award Midwest Rsch. Inst., 1987, Disting. Svc. award Internat. Rels. Coun., 1989, Mankind award Cystic Fibrosis Found., 1990, Gold Good Citizenship award SAR, 1991, Chancellor's medal U. Mo. Kansas City, 1992. Mem. Brook Club, Cypress Point Club, Eldorado Country Club, Castle Pines Country Club, Kansas City Country Club, River Club, Swinley Forest Golf Club, White's Club. Republican. Episcopalian. Office: 1 W Armour Blvd Ste 300 Kansas City MO 64111-2087

PRICE, CHARLES T., lawyer; b. Lansing, Mich., Feb. 11, 1944. BA, Ohio Wesleyan U., 1966; JD, Harvard U., 1969. Bar: Ohio 1969, U.S. Dist. Ct. (no. dist.) Ohio 1974, U.S. Ct. Appeals (6th cir) 1981, U.S. Supreme Ct. 1982, Ill. 1989. Ptnr. Baker & Hostetler, Cleve.; pres., pub. Chgo. Sun-Times, 1987-88; exec. v.p. Sun-Times Co., 1989-92. Office: Baker & Hostetler 3200 Nat City Ctr 1900 E 9th St Cleveland OH 44114-3401

PRICE, CINDA LU, psychotherapist; b. Cleve., Jan. 1, 1962; d. William Albert and Betty Lee (Curzon) Benes; m. Benjamin Mark Price, Mar. 7, 1987; children: Jesse Lee, Kaylee Kristine. BS, Kent State U., 1984; MEd, Sam Houston State U., 1989, postgrad., 1992. Lic. profl. counselor, marriage and family therapist, chem. dependency counselor. Supr. Belmont Habilitation Ctr., Barnsville, Ohio, 1984-85; tchr. Klein (Tex.) Ind. Sch. Dist., 1985-87, Conroe (Tex.) Ind. Sch. Dist., 1987-89; psychotherapist Alliance for Healing and Recovery, Houston, 1989-92, Advanced Psychiat. Svcs., Conroe, 1992—; cons. Forest Springs Hosp., Houston, 1990—, Charter Hosp. of Kingwood, Tex., 1993—, Gulf Pines Hosp., Houston, 1993—; owner Advanced Psychiat. Svcs., Conroe, 1992—. Developer First Time Offenders Program, Conroe, 1993, dir., developer intensive outpatient programs for chem. dependency, 1994. Recipient Alumnae Assn. Leadership award Kent State U., 1984. Mem. Tex. Assn. for Counseling and Devel., Am. Assn. Counseling and Devel., Am. Assn. Play Therapy, Am. Assn. Clin. Hypnosis, Internat. Assn. Addiction and Offender Counselors, Tex. Counseling Assn., Kappa Delta Pi, Delta Zeta (v.p. 1982-83, pres. 1983-84). Methodist. Avocations: swimming, horseback riding, water and snow skiing, para-sailing. Office: Advanced Psychiatric Svcs 1712 N Frazier St Ste 213 Conroe TX 77301-1380

PRICE, CLIFFORD WARREN, retired metallurgist, researcher; b. Denver, Apr. 22, 1935; s. Warren Wilson and Vivian Fredricka (Cady) P.; m. Carole Joyce Waterman, June 14, 1969; children: Carla Beth, Krista Lynn Kilton. MetE, Colo. Sch. Mines, 1957; MS, Ohio State U., 1970, PhD, 1975. Design engr. Sundstrand Aviation-Denver, 1957-60; materials specialist Denver Rsch. Inst., 1960-63; sr. metallurgist Rocky Flats div. Dow Chem. Co., Golden, Colo., 1963-66; staff metallurgist Battelle Columbus (Ohio) Labs., 1966-75; sr. scientist Owens-Corning Fiberglas, Granville, Ohio, 1975-80; metallurgist Lawrence Livermore (Calif.) Nat. Lab., 1980-93; retired, 1993. Contbr. articles to profl. jours. Battelle Columbus Labs. fellow, 1974-75. Mem. Metall. Soc. AIME, Microscopy Soc. Am. (treas. Denver 1961-62), Am. Soc. for Metals. Achievements include research on electron, scanning probe and optical microscopy, secondary ion mass spectroscopy, deformation, fracture and recrystallization mechanisms in metals, recrystallization kinetics.

PRICE, DALIAS ADOLPH, geography educator; b. Newtonville, Ind., June 28, 1913; s. Fred J. and Rose (Gillam) P.; m. Lillian O. Alexander, May 14, 1943; children—David, Curtis, Kent, Roger. B.A., U. Ill., 1937, M.A., 1938; Ph.D., U. Wis., 1954. Instr. geography U. Ill., 1938-40; acting head dept. S.W. Mo. State Coll., Springfield, 1940-45; asst. U. Wis., 1945-47; assoc. prof. geography So. Ill. U., 1947-58; prof. geography, head dept. Eastern Ill. U., 1958—. Author articles in field. Mem. Wabash Valley Interstate Commn., 1965—; Bd. suprs. Coles County, Ill., 1967, chmn., 1971-72; Bd. dirs. Charleston Community Hosp., 1966—, Inst. Urban and Regional Affairs, 1967—. Recipient Distng. Svc. award Nat. Weather Svc., 1988, 90.; hon. fellow U. Wis., 1953. Mem. AAUP (sec.-treas. Ill. conf. 1958-62), Ill. Geog. Soc. (sec. 1950, chmn. 1951,62, distinguished geographer award 1976), Charleston C. of C. (bd. dirs. 1961-64), Assn. Am. Geographers, Gamma Theta Upsilon. Democrat. Unitarian. Club: Rotarian (pres. Charleston 1965). Home: 517 W Coolidge Ave Charleston IL 61920-3860

PRICE, DANIEL MARTIN, lawyer; b. St. Louis, Aug. 23, 1955; s. Albert and Edith S. (Werner) P.; m. Kim Ellen Heebner, July 15, 1984; children: Emma Rachel, Joseph Armin, Joshua Simon. BA, Haverford Coll., 1977; diploma in law, Cambridge U., 1979; JD, Harvard U., 1981. Bar: D.C. 1981, Pa. 1987. Assoc. Drinker, Biddle & Reath, Phila., 1981-82, 86-89; dep. gen. counsel Office of U.S. Trade Rep., Washington, 1989-92; ptnr. Powell, Goldstein, Frazer & Murphy, Washington, 1992—; atty., adviser Dept. State, Washington, 1982-84; dep. agt. U.S. Iran-U.S. Claims Tribunal, Hague, The Netherlands, 1984-86; lectr. Haverford Coll., 1982. Articles editor Harvard Law Rev., 1980-81; contbr. Am. Jour. Internat. Law, Internat. Lawyer, Internat. Fin. Law Rev., Internat. Banking and Fin. Law. Am. Keasbey scholar Cambridge U., 1977-78. Mem. ABA (co-chmn. trade com. on N.Am. Free Trade Agreement), Internat. Bus. Forum (legal adv. bd. 1987-89), Coun. on Fgn. Rels., Am. Arbitration Assn. (panel arbitrators 1988), Internat. C. of C. (arbitrator 1994-95), European-Am. C. of C. (trade and investment com.), Orgn. for Internat. Investment (counsel), Phi Beta Kappa. Office: 1001 Pennsylvania Ave NW Washington DC 20004-2505

PRICE, DEBBIE MITCHELL, journalist, newspaper editor; b. Littlefield, Tex., June 3, 1959; d. Horace A. and Diane (Hall) Mitchell; m. Larry C. Price, May 2, 1981. BFA, So. Meth. U., 1980. Reporter Ft. Worth Star-Telegram, 1980-83, 91, Phila. Daily News, 1983-87, Washington Post, 1988-91; columnist Ft. Worth Star-Telegram, 1991-93, exec. editor, 1993—, v.p., 1994—; free-lance writer, Phila., 1987-88. Recipient 1st place Gen. Column Writing award Tex. AP Mng. Editors, 1991, 1st place Mng. Writing award Women's Sports Journalism, 1989, 1st place award Chesapeake Bay AP Mng. Editors, 1990. Mem. Am. Soc. Newspaper Editors, Soc. Profl. Journalists (Ft. Worth chpt.). Office: Ft Worth Star-Telegram Inc PO Box 1870 400 W 7th St Fort Worth TX 76102

PRICE, DENNIS LEE, industrial engineer, educator; b. Taber, Alberta, Can., Oct. 24, 1930; s. Walter and Wilma Harlan (Nance) P.; m. Barbara Ann Shelton; children: Denice Lynn Price Thomas, Philip Walter. BA, Bob Jones U., 1952; BD, MA, Am. Bapt. Sem. of the West, Berkeley, Calif., 1955; MA, Calif. State U., Long Beach, 1967; PhD in Indsl. Engring., Tex. A&M U., 1974. Cert. product safety mgr., hazard control mgr., human factors profl. Clergyman Am. Bapt. Conv., Calif., 1953-66; mem. tech. staff autonetics div. Rockwell Internat., Anaheim, Calif., 1966-69; sr. engr. Martin Marietta Aerospace, Orlando, Fla., 1969-72; rsch. assoc. Tex. A&M U., College Station, 1972-74; teaching asst. Calif. State U., Long Beach, 1963-66; asst. prof. dept. indsl. engring. and operations rsch. Va. Poly. Inst. and State U., Blacksburg, 1974-78, assoc. prof. dept. indsl. and systems engring., 1979-83, prof., 1984-95, prof. emeritus, 1996—, dir. safety projects office, 1975, coord. Human Factors Engring. Ctr., 1986-95; cons., expert witness in safety engring. and human factors, 1978—; mem. U.S. Nuclear Waste Tech. Rev. Bd., 1989-95; mem. U.S. tech. adv. group Internat. Stds. Tech. Com. 159 Ergonomics, 1987-94; chmn. com. on transp. of hazardous materials NRC, 1981-87; chmn. group 3 coun. emerging issues subcom. Transp. Rsch. Bd., 1987-89; chmn. task force on pipeline safety NAS, 1986. Mem. editorial bd. Human Factors, Santa Monica, Calif., 1989-95; author: (with K.B. Johns, J.W. Bain) Transportation of Hazardous Materials, 1983; contbr. chpts. to books, articles to profl. jours.; reviewer in field. Recipient Disting. Svc. award Nat. Rsch. Coun. NAS, 1987, 89, Outstanding Svc. commendation Transp. Rsch. Bd. NAS, 1981; grantee NIOSH, Va. Dept. Transp. and Safety, 1977-82, 86-87, IBM, 1981-84, USN Office of Naval Rsch., 1978-80, USN Naval Systems Weapons Command, 1978-79. Mem. Inst. Indsl. Engrs. (sr.), Am. Soc. Safety Engrs. (profl.), Human Factors Soc. (rep. to rev. panel Guideline for the Preparation of Material Safety Data Sheets), Systems Safety Soc. (Educator of Yr. 1993), Alpha Pi Mu. Avocation: flying. Home: 1011 Evergreen Way Blacksburg VA 24060-5366 Office: Va Poly Inst and State U Dept Indsl and Systems Engring 302 Whittemore Blacksburg VA 24061

PRICE, DONALD, retail executive; b. 1933. Grad., U. Calif., Berkeley, 1956. With Batten, Barton, Durstne & Osborne, Inc., 1958-65; product mgr. mktg. divsn. Block Drug Co. Inc., 1965-67; dir. mktg. CPC Internat., Best Food Divsn., 1967-76; v.p. sales and mktg. mfg. group Great Atlantic and Pacific Tea Co., 1976-78; pres. Groves-Kelco, 1978-79; exec. v.p. WaWa Inc., WaWa, Pa., 1979—. With U.S. Army, 1956-58. Office: WaWa Inc 260 W Baltimore Pike Elwyn PA 19063*

PRICE, DONALD ALBERT, veterinarian, consultant; b. Bridgeport, Ohio, Dec. 25, 1919; s. Arthur David and Louise Ann (Knellinger) P.; m. June Loree Fleming, July 17, 1946; children—Karen Price Privett, Benita Price Esposito, Donna. Grad., Elliott Sch. Bus., 1938; D.V.M., Ohio State U., 1950. Lic. veterinarian, Ohio, Ill., Tex. Adminstrv. asst. Wheeling Steel Corp., W.Va., 1938-41; counselor psychol. dept. Ohio State U., Columbus, 1946-48, lab. asst. vet. parasitology dept., 1948-50; mem. research faculty Tex. A&M U., Sonora, 1950-55; ptnr. San Angelo Vet. Hosp., Tex., 1955-58; assoc. editor AVMA, Chgo., 1958-59, editor in chief, 1959-72, exec. v.p., 1972-85; cons., adj. prof. Tex. A&M U., College Station, 1985—. Served to capt. USAAF, 1941-46. Recipient Disting. Alumnus award Coll. Vet. Medicine, Ohio State U., 1966. Fellow Am. Med. Writers Assn.; mem. AVMA (Service Commendation award 1984, Appreciation award, 1984, chief exec. officer 1972-85), Ill. Vet. Med. Assn. (hon. life), Mich. Vet. Med. Assn. (hon. life), Tex. Vet. Med. Assn. (disting. life), Am. Equine Practitioners Assn. (hon.), Am. Assn. Sheep and Goat Practioners (hon.), Am. Animal Hosp. Assn. (hon.; Merit award 1983), Bexar County Vet. Med. Assn. (hon.), Phi Eta Sigma, Phi Zeta, Alpha Psi. Republican. Presbyterian. Lodge: Masons. Avocations: woodworking; ranching. Home and Office: Rte 1, Box 174-A Hunt TX 78024

PRICE, DONALD RAY, university official, agricultural engineer; b. Rockville, Ind., July 20, 1939; s. Ernest M. and Violet Noreen (Measel) P.; m. Joyce Ann Gerald, Sept. 14, 1963; children—John Allen, Karen Sue, Kimberly Ann, Daniel Lee. B.S. in Agrl. Engring., Purdue U., 1961, Ph.D. in Agrl. Engring., 1971; M.S. in Agrl. Engring., Cornell U., 1963. Registered profl. engr., Fla. From asst. prof. to prof. Cornell U., Ithaca, N.Y.,

1962-80, dir. energy programs, 1975-77, 78-80; program mgr. Dept Energy, Washington, 1977-78, cons.; assoc. dean research U. Fla., Gainesville, 1980-83; dean Grad. Sch., U. Fla., Gainesville, 1983-84; v.p. research U. Fla., Gainesville, 1984—; pres. U. Fla. Research Found., Inc.; chmn. bd. dirs. Progress Research, Inc.; cons. to Pres. Carter, Washington, 1978; bd. dirs. Nat. Food and Engring. Council, Columbia, Mo., 1978-85, S.E. Healthcare Found., Gainesville, Fla., 1985. Contbr. numerous articles on engring. to profl. jours.; patentee mech. device. Mem. Ithaca Sch. Bd., N.Y., 1979-80; deacon Ch. of Christ, Gainesville, Fla., 1983—. Recipient citation Pres. Carter, 1979, Disting. Alumnus award Purdue U., 1990. Fellow Am. Soc. Agrl. Engrs. (dir. 1990, paper awards 1963, 77, 78, Young Engr. of Yr. award 1980); mem. Soc. Research Adminstrs., Nat. Assn. Univ. Research Adminstrs., S.E. Univ. Research Assn., Research Univs. Network. Democrat. Lodge: Rotary. Avocations: tennis, jogging, woodworking. Home: 22415 SW 15th Ave Newberry FL 32669-3205 Office: U Fla 223 Grinter Hall Gainesville FL 32611-2037

PRICE, DOUGLAS ARMSTRONG, chiropractor; b. Pitts., Feb. 17, 1950; s. Walter Coachman and Janet (Armstrong) P.; m. Ann Georgette Martino, Jan. 31, 1989; 4 children. BA, Brown U., 1972; D Chiropractic, Life Chiropractic Coll., Atlanta, 1983. Diplomate Am. Bd. Chiropractic Examiners; cert. rehab. doctor; life extension physician; independent medical examiner, Fla. Owner, CEO Athletic Attic-Westshore, Tampa, Fla., 1976-80, Applied Biomech. and Musculoskeletal Rehab., Tampa, 1989—, All Am. Chiropractic Clinic; pvt. practice Tampa, 1984-94, Manalapan, Fla., 1994—; dir. Myofascial Therapy Found. Producer therapeutic exercise video for cervical and lumbar rehab.; contbr. articles to profl. jours. Magnetic Resonance Imaging fellow; named to Brown U. Athletic Hall of Fame; Southeastern Masters Champion Shotput, Discus, 1990-91. Fellow Am. Coll. Sports Medicine, Chiropractic Rehab. Assn., Am. Gerontology Assn.; mem. APHA, Am. Chiropractic Assn., Fla. Chiropractic Assn., Hillsborough County Chiropractic Soc. (bd. dirs. 1990-93, pres. 1992-93), Palm Beach Chiropractic Soc. Democrat. Roman Catholic. Achievements include research in Russian stimulation applications in low back rehabilitation. Avocations: weightlifting, reading, coaching weight events in track and field. Home: 731 N Atlantic Dr Lantana FL 33462-1911 Office: 204 S Ocean Blvd Mawalapan FL 33462-3312

PRICE, EDGAR HILLEARY, JR., business consultant; b. Jacksonville, Fla., Jan. 1, 1918; s. Edgar Hilleary and Mary Williams (Phillips) P.; m. Elise Ingram, June 24, 1947; 1 son, Jerald Steven. Student, U. Fla., 1937-38. Mgr. comml. flower farm, 1945-49, Fla. Gladiolus Growers Assn., 1949-55; exec. v.p. Tropicana Products, Inc., Bradenton, Fla., 1955-73, dir. div. govt. and industry regulations, to 1979; dir.; exec. v.p. Indsl. Glass Co., Inc., Bradenton, 1963-73; pres., chmn. bd. Price Co., Inc., Bradenton, cons., 1973—; dir. emeritus F.P.L. Group, Inc.; past chmn. Fla. Citrus Commn., Fla. Gov.'s Freeze Damage Survey Team, Spl. Commn. for Study Abolition Death Penalty; bd. dirs. Fla. Power and Light Co., Fla. Fair Assn., Fla. Citrus Expn., Fla. Fruit and Vegetable Assn.; past chmn. Joint Citrus Legis. Com.; past mem. Fla. Plant Bd., Fla. Bd. Control, Fla. Legis. Coun.; exec. com. Growers and Shippers League Fla., Fla. Agrl. Council, Spl. Health Agrl. Research and Edn.; past pres., chmn. bd. Fla. Hort. Soc. Past chmn., commr. census 12th Jud. Circuit; mem. Gov. Fla. Com. Rehab. Handicapped, Fla. Commn. on Ethics, 1976-77, Presdl. Inaugural Fin. com., 1977, Ea. 5th Circuit U.S. Jud. Nominating Commn., 1977—, Fla. Senate from 36th Dist., 1958-66; past chmn. Manatee County Bd. Sch. Dist. Trustees, Local Housing Authority Bradenton, Bradenton Sub. Std. Housing Bd., Bradenton Charter Adv. Com.; del. Dem. Nat. Conv., 1960, dist. del., 1964; past trustee, mem. exec. com. Stetson U.; former trustee New Coll., Aurora Found. Served to 1st lt. USAAF, 1941-45. Named Boss of Yr., Nat. Secs. Assn., 1959, Man of Yr. for Fla. agr. Progressive Farmer mag., 1919; recipient merit award Am. Flag Assn., 1962, Gamma Sigma Delta, 1965, leadership award Fla. Agrl. Ext. Svc., 1963, Outstanding Senator award Fla. Radio Broadcasters, 1965, Allen Morris award s most valuable mem. Fla. Legislature, 1965, Most Valuable Mem. award Fla. Senate, St. Petersburg Times, 1965, Brotherhood awardSarasota chpt. NCCJ, 1966, Disting. Citizen award Manatee County, 1970, Disting. Alumnus award U. Fla., 1972, Svc. to Mankind award Sertoma Internat., 1976, Goodwill Disting. Citizen award, 1979, Crystal Shield award Salvation Army, 1996; inducted into Fla. Agrl. Hall of Fame, 1992, Tampa Bay Bus. Hall of Fame, 1992. Mem. Fla. C. of C. (bd. dirs. emeritus and past chmn.), Manatee C. of C. (past pres.), Fla. Hort. Soc. (past pres., chmn. bd.), Fla. Flower Assn., ARC Clara Barton Soc., Blue Key (hon.), Omicron Delta Kappa (hon.), Kiwanis (pres. 1955), Sigma Alpha Epsilon. Home: 3009 Riverview Blvd W Bradenton FL 34205-3420 Office: PO Box 9270 Bradenton FL 34206-9270 *The turning point in my life came at the age of 32 when I accepted Jesus Christ as my personal Lord and Saviour. I believe every person should live his life up to the fullest extent of his God-given talents and ability. I think we have a responsibility to "pay our dues" for the privilege of living in a free land by being actively involved in our government.*

PRICE, EDWARD DEAN, federal judge; b. Sanger, Calif., Feb. 12, 1919; s. Earl Trousdale and Daisy Shaw (Biggs) P.; m. Katherine S. Merritt, July 18, 1943; children: Katherine Price O'Brien, Edward M., Jane E. B.A., U. Calif., Berkeley, 1947, LL.B., 1949. Bar: Calif. 1949. Assoc. Cleary & Zeff, Modesto, Calif., 1949-51; assoc. Zeff & Halley, Modesto, Calif., 1951-54; ptnr. Zeff, Halley & Price, Modesto, Calif., 1954-63, Zeff & Price, Modesto, Calif., 1963-65, Price & Martin, Modesto, Calif., 1965-69, Price, Martin & Crabtree, Modesto, Calif., 1969-79; judge U.S. Dist. Ct., Fresno, Calif., 1980-90, sr. judge, 1990—; mem. adv. bd. governing com. Continuing Edn. of Bar, San Francisco, 1963-71, governing bd. Calif. State Bar, 1973-76; v.p. Jud. Council, Calif., 1978-79. Contbr. articles to profl. jours. Served with U.S. Army, 1943-46. Mem. ABA, Am. Coll. Trial Lawyers, Am. Bd. Trial Advocates. Democrat. Methodist. Home: 1012 Wellesley Ave Modesto CA 95350-5042 Office: US Dist Ct 5554 US Courthouse 1130 O St Fresno CA 93721

PRICE, FRANCES KIE, hospital administrator; b. Franklin, Ky., Jan. 30, 1950; d. Atha and Dorothy Louise (Poole) Kie; m. James Lewis Price, Feb. 29, 1981; children: Shelley, Tina, Jeremy, James. Ctrl. svc. tech. North Crest Med. Ctr., Springfield, Tenn., 1986-88; surg. technologist Jesse Holman Jones Hosp., Springfield, Tenn., 1988-90, ctrl. svc. mgr., 1990—, recall and chem. inventory mgr., 1993—. Tng. Agy. mgr. Am. Heart Assn., 1993—. Recipient cert. Excellence ARC, 1993; named Parent of Yr. So. Ky. Head Start, 1987. Mem. NAFE, Internat. Assn. Healthcare Ctrl. Svc. Materials Mgmt., Am. Soc. Healthcare Ctrl. Svc. Personnel (Sterile Bowl 1992, advanced mem. award, 1995), Internat. Registry Environ. Engrs. and Profls. (environ. compliance mgr. 1994), Assn. Surg. Technologists, Tenn. Soc. Healthcare Ctrl. Svc. Personnel, Midstate Soc. Healthcare Ctrl. Svc. Personnel, Women's Writers Guild. Office: North Crest Med Ctr 1 N Crest Dr Springfield TN 37172-2941

PRICE, FRANK, motion picture and television company executive; b. Decatur, Ill., May 17, 1930; s. William F. and Winifred A. (Moran) P.; m. Katherine Huggins, May 15, 1965; children: Stephen, David, Roy, Frank. Student, Mich. State U., 1949-51. Writer, story editor CBS-TV, N.Y.C., 1951-53, Columbia Pictures, Hollywood, Calif., 1953-57, NBC-TV, Hollywood, Calif., 1957-58; producer, writer ZIV-TV, Hollywood, Calif., 1958; producer, writer Universal Television, Universal City, Calif., 1959-64, v.p., 1964-71, sr. v.p., 1971-73, exec. v.p. in charge of production, 1973-74, pres., 1974-78; v.p., dir. MCA, Inc., 1976-78; pres. Columbia Pictures Prodn., 1978-79; chmn., chief exec. officer Columbia Pictures, 1979-84, also bd. dirs.; chmn. MCA Motion Picture Group, 1984-86; chmn., chief exec. officer Price Entertainment Inc., 1987-90; chmn. Columbia Pictures, 1990-91; also bd. dirs. Sony Pictures Entertainment; chmn., chief exec. officer Price Entertainment, 1991—; bd. dirs. Savoy Pictures. With USN, 1948-49. Mem. Writers Guild Am., West. Office: Price Entertainment Inc 2425 Olympic Blvd Santa Monica CA 90404-4030

PRICE, GAYL BAADER, residential construction company administrator; b. Gothenburg, Sweden, Mar. 1, 1949; came to U.S., 1951; d. Harold Edgar Anderson and Jeanette Helen (Hallberg) Akeson; m. Daniel J. Baader, Nov. 27, 1971 (div. Sept. 1980); m. Leigh C. Price, Feb. 28, 1983; foster children: Heidi, Heather. BA in Fgn. Lang., U. Ill., 1971. Asst. buyer The Denver, 1971-73, buyer, 1973-75; escrow sec. Transam. Title, Evergreen, Colo., 1975-76, escrow officer, 1976-78, sr. escrow officer, 1978-79, br. mgr., 1979-84; sr. account mgr. Transam. Title, Denver, 1984-87, sales mgr., 1987-91, v.p., 1989-94; cmty. mgr. Village Homes of Colo., Littleton, Colo., 1994—. Vol. Safehouse for Battered Women, Denver, 1986—, Spl. Olympics, 1986—, Adult Learning Source, 1993—, Kids Cure for Cancer, 1994—. Mem. Home Builders Assn. Met. Denver (bd. dirs. 1989—, exec. com. 1991, assoc. mem. coun. 1988-93, co-chair 1990, chair 1991, Arthur Gaeth Assoc. of Yr. 1989), Sales and Mktg. Coun. Met. Denver (bd. 1986-92, 95—, mame chair 1989, chair 1990, Most Profl. award 1989, Sales Master award 1995, Silver Mame award 1996), Douglas County Econ. Devel., Zonta Club Denver II (pres. 1990, Zontian of Yr. 1988), Colo. Assn. Homebuilders (Assoc. of Yr. 1992). Avocations: cooking, volunteer work, travel. Home: 1975 Linda Ln Evergreen CO 80439 Office: Village Homes 6 W Dry Creek Cir Ste 200 Littleton CO 80120-8031

PRICE, GRIFFITH BALEY, mathematician, educator; b. Brookhaven, Miss., Mar. 14, 1905; s. Walter Edwin and Lucy (Baley) P.; m. Cora Lee Beers, June 18, 1940; children: Cora Lee, Griffith Baley, Lucy Jean, Edwina Clare, Sallie Diane and Doris Joanne (twins). BA, Miss. Coll., 1925; MA, Harvard U., 1928, PhD, 1932; LLD (hon.), Miss. Coll., 1962. Instr. math. Union Coll., Schenectady, N.Y., 1932-33, U. Rochester, N.Y., 1933-36, Brown U., Providence, 1936-37; asst. prof., assoc. prof., then prof. math. U. Kans., Lawrence, 1937-75, prof. emeritus, 1975—, chmn. dept. math., 1951-70; exec. sec. Conf. Bd. Math. Scis., Washington, 1960-62. Author: Linear Equations and Matrices (with others), 1966, Sets, Functions, and Probability (with others), 1968, History of Department of Mathematics of University of Kansas, 1976, Multivariable Analysis, 1984, An Introduction to Multicomplex Spaces and Functions, 1991; contbr. articles to rsch. jours. Civil. ops. analyst USAAF, 1943-45, Eng. Mem. AAAS, Am. Math. Soc. (editor 1950-57), Math. Assn. Am. (pres. 1957-58, award Disting. Svc. 1970), N.Y. Acad. Scis., Cosmos Club, Sigma Xi. Achievements include pioneering development of operations research.

PRICE, GRIFFITH BALEY, JR., lawyer; b. Lawrence, Kans., Aug. 15, 1942; s. Griffith Baley and Cora Lee (Beers) P.; m. Maria Helena Martin, June 29, 1968; children: Andrew Griffith, Alexandra Helena. AB (cum laude), Harvard U., 1964; LLB, NYU, 1967. Bar: N.Y. 1967, U.S. Ct. Appeals (6th cir.) 1975, U.S. Ct. Appeals (2nd cir.) 1978, U.S. Ct. Appeals (3d, 5th and 11th cirs.) 1981, U.S. Ct. Appeals (fed. cir.) 1984, D.C. 1991. Assoc. Dewey, Ballantine, Bushby, Palmer & Wood, N.Y.C., 1967-75; ptnr. Milgrim Thomajan & Lee, N.Y.C., 1976-86; of counsel, ptnr. Finnegan, Henderson, Farabow, Garrett & Dunner, Washington, 1987—; adj. prof., lectr. George Washington U. Law Ctr., Washington, 1989-93; frequent lectr. ABA, Practicing Law Inst., Law & Bus., 1982—. Author: (with others, treatise) Milgrim on Trade Secrets, 1986; contbr. articles to publs. Root-Tilden scholar NYU Law Sch., 1964-67. Mem. ABA (intellectual property sect., com. chmn.), Internat. Trademark Assn. (bd. dirs., com. chmn.), Am. Intellectual Property Law Assn. (com. chmn.), Licensing Execs. Soc., N.Y. Athletic Club, Harvard Club (Washington). Presbyterian. Office: Finnegan Henderson Farabow Garrett & Dunner 1300 I St NW Ste 700 Washington DC 20005-3315

PRICE, HARRISON ALAN, business research company executive; b. Oregon City, Oreg., May 17, 1921; s. Harry I. and Isabel (Esson) P.; m. Anne Shaw, Apr. 29, 1944; children: Bret, David, Dana, Holly. B.S., Calif. Inst. Tech., 1942; M.B.A., Stanford U., 1951. Mgr. econ. research Stanford Research Inst., Los Angeles, 1951-55; gen. mgr. Def. Plant div. Harvey Aluminum, Torrance, Calif., 1955-58; founder, pres. Econ. Research Assocs., West Los Angeles, Calif., 1958-73; sr. v.p., mem. Planning Research Corp., Washington, 1973-76, sr. v.p., 1976-78; pres. Harrison Price Co., Los Angeles, 1978—; bd. dirs. LaserStrom, Denver. Trustee Calif. Inst. of Arts. Served with infantry U.S. Army, 1944-46. Club: California. Home: 2141 W Paseo Del Mar San Pedro CA 90732-4556

PRICE, HARRY STEELE, JR., construction materials company executive; b. East Jordan, Mich., Oct. 11, 1910; s. Harry S. and Grace B. (Beers) P.; m. Janet Smith, Apr. 7, 1934; children: Pamela, Harry Steele III, Marlay B. B.S., U. Mich., 1932. Office and field office on heavy constrn. Price Bros. Co., 1932-36, designer, constrn. and operation of gravel plant, 1936-38, in charge concrete sewer and culvert pipe operations, sand and gravel operations, gen. sec., 1938-45, v.p. in charge of pressure pipe div., 1945-67, exec. v.p., 1953-67, chmn., pres., 1967-73, chmn, 1973-80, vice chmn., 1980—. Past commr. Montgomery County Park Dist.; past pres. Dayton Art Inst. Mem. NSPE, ASCE (life), Am. Concrete Pipe Assn. (past pres.), Am. Water Works Assn. (life, past trustee), Buz-Fuz Club, Moraine Country Club, 40 Club, Dayton Racquet Club, St. Andrews Club (Delray Beach, Fla.), Wesquetonsino Golf Club (Harbor Springs, Mich.). Clubs: Dayton City, Buz-Fuz, Moraine Country, 49 Club, Dayton Raquet; St. Andrews (Delray Beach, Fla.); Wequetonsino Golf Club (Harbor Springs, Mich.). Home: 333 Oakwood Ave Apt 2B Dayton OH 45409-2214 Office: 367 W 2nd St Dayton OH 45402-1432

PRICE, JAMES GORDON, physician; b. Brush, Colo., June 20, 1926; s. John Hoover and Rachel Laurette (Dodds) P.; m. Janet Alice McSween, June 19, 1949; children: James Gordon II, Richard Christian, Mary Laurette, Janet Lynn. B.A., U. Colo., 1948, M.D., 1951. Diplomate: Charter diplomate Am. Bd. Family Practice (dir., pres. 1979). Intern Denver Gen. Hosp., 1951-52; practice medicine specializing in family medicine Brush, 1952-78; prof. family practice U. Kans. Med. Ctr., 1978-93; chmn. dept. U. Kans. Med. Center, 1982-90, exec. dean, 1990-93, prof. emeritus in family practice, 1993—; mem. Inst. Medicine, Nat. Acad. Scis., 1973—; med. editor Gen. Learning Corp., 1973-92. Editorial bd.: Med. World News, 1969-79; editor: Am. Acad. Family Physician Home Study Self Assessment Program, 1978-83; contbr.: (column) Your Family Physician, 1973-90. Trustee Family Health Found. Am., 1970-82. Served with USNR, 1943-46. Charter fellow Am. Acad. Family Physicians (pres. 1973); mem. Phi Beta Kappa, Alpha Omega Alpha. Home: 12205 Mohawk Rd Shawnee Mission KS 66209-2137

PRICE, JAMES MELFORD, physician; b. Onalaska, Wis., Apr. 3, 1921; s. Carl Robert and Hazel (Halderson) P.; m. Ethelyn Doreen Lee, Oct. 23, 1943 (div.); children: Alta Lee, Jean Marie, Veda Michele; m. Charlotte E. Schwenk, Sept. 27, 1986; children: Shirley S. Bunn, Cindy S. Davis, Irene S. McCumber. BS in Agr., U. Wis., 1943, MS in Biochemistry, 1944, PhD in Physiology, 1949, MD, 1951. Diplomate Am. Bd. Clin. Nutrition. Intern Cin. Gen. Hosp., 1951-52; mem. faculty U. Wis. Med. Sch., 1952—, prof. clin. oncology, 1959—, Am. Cancer Soc.-Charles S. Hayden Found. prof. surgery in cancer research, 1957—; on leave as dir. exptl. therapy Abbott Labs., 1967—, v.p. exptl. therapy, 1968, v.p. corp. research and exptl. therapy, 1971—, v.p. corp. sci. devel., 1976-78; v.p. med. affairs Norwich-Eaton Pharms., 1978—, v.p. internat. R&D, 1980-82; pres. RADAC Group, Inc., 1982-90, Biogest Products, Inc., 1984-88; mem. metabolism study sect. NIH 1959-62, pathology B study sect., 1964-68;.sci. adv. com. PMA Found.; chmn. research adv. com. Ill. Dept. Mental Health; sci. com. Nat. Bladder Cancer program; mem. Drug Research Bd. Nat. Acad. Scis./NRC. Bd. dirs. Grandview Coll., Des Moines, 1977-78. Served with USNR, 1944-45. Fellow Am. Coll. Nutrition, Royal Soc. Medicine London; mem. Am. Soc. Pharmacology and Exptl. Therapeutics, Am. Assn. Cancer Research, Am. Cancer Soc. (com. etiology 1957-61), Pharm. Mfrs. Assn. (chmn. research and devel. sect. 1974-75), Am. Soc. Biol. Chemists, Am. Inst. Nutrition, Am. Soc. Clin. Nutrition, Research Dirs. Assn. Chgo., Soc. Exptl. Biology and Medicine, Soc. Toxicology. Spl. research trytophan metabolism, metabolism vitamin B complex, chem. carcinogenesis; research and devel. pharm., diagnostic and consumer products; licensing and bus. devel. Avocation: pvt. pilot. Home: PO Box 211 Edmeston NY 13335-0211

PRICE, JEANNINE ALLEENICA, clinical psychologist, computer consultant; b. Cleve., Oct. 29, 1949; d. Q. Q. and Lisa Denise (Wilson) Ewing; m. T. R. Price, Sept. 2, 1976. BS, Western Res. U., 1969; MS, Vanderbilt U., 1974; MBA, Stanford U., 1985. Cert. alcoholism counselor, Calif. Health Service coordinator Am. Profile, Nashville, 1970-72; exec. dir. Awareness Concept, San Jose, Calif., 1977-80, counselor, 1989—, exec. dir., 1989-90, v.p. Image Makers (formerly Awareness Concepts), 1994—; mgr. employee assistance program Nat. Semiconductor, Santa Clara, Calif., 1980-81; mgmt. cons. employee assistant programs. Mem. Gov.'s Adv. Council Child Devel. Programs. Mem. Am. Bus. Women's Assn., NAFE, AAUW, Coalition Labor Women, Calif. Assn. Alcohol counselors, Almaca. Author: Smile a Little, Cry a Lot, Gifts of Love, Reflection in the Mirror, The Light at the Top of the Mountain, The Dreamer, The Girl I Never Knew, An Act of Love, Walk Toward the Light.

PRICE, JOE (ALLEN), artist, former educator; b. Ferriday, La., Feb. 6, 1935; s. Edward Neill and Margaret (Hester) P. BS, Northwestern U., 1957; postgrad., Art Ctr. Coll., L.A., 1967-68; MA, Stanford U., 1970. Free-lance actor, artist N.Y.C., 1957-60; freelance illustrator, actor, L.A., 1960-68; free-lance comml. artist, San Carlos, Calif., 1968-69; package designer Container Corp. Am., Santa Clara, Calif., 1969; prof. studio art and filmmaking, chmn. dept. art Coll. San Mateo, Calif., 1970-94. One-man shows include Richard Sumner Gallery, Palo Alto, Calif., 1975, San Mateo County Cultural Ctr., 1976, 82, Tahir Galleries, New Orleans, 1977, 82, Kerwin Galleries, Burlingame, Calif., 1977, Edits. Gallery, Melbourne, Australia, 1977, Ankrum Gallery, Los Angeles, 1978, 84, Edits. Ltd. West Gallery, San Francisco, 1981, Miriam Perlman Gallery, Chgo., 1982, San Mateo County Arts Council Gallery, 1982, Candy Stick Gallery, Ferndale, Calif., 1984, Assoc. Am. Artists, N.Y.C. and Phila., 1984, Gallery 30, Burlingame, 1991, San Mateo, 1984, Triton Mus. Art, Santa Clara, Calif., 1986, Huntsville (Ala.) Mus. Art, 1987, Gallery 30, San Mateo, 1988-91, Concept Art Gallery, Pitts., 1991, Eleonore Austerer Gallery, San Francisco, 1995; exhibited in groups shows at Berkeley Art Ctr., Calif., 1976, Burlingame Civic Art Gallery, 1976, Syntex Gallery, Palo Alto, Calif., 1977, Gump's Gallery, San Francisco, 1976, 77, Nat. Gallery of Australia, 1978, Sonoma County Gallery, 1979, Gov. Dummer Acad. Art, Byfield, Mass., 1979, Miss. Mus. Art, 1982, C.A.A. Galleries, Chautauqua, N.Y., 1982, Huntsville Mus. Art, 1983, Tahir Gallery, New Orleans, 1983, Hunterdon Art Ctr., N.J., 1984, Editions Galleries, Melbourne, Australia, 1988, Van Stratten Gallery, Chgo., 1988, 6th Internat. Exhbn., Carnegie-Mellon U., Pa., 1988, Forum Gallery, Jamestown, N.Y., 1988, 5th Internat. Biennale Petite Format de Papier, Belgium, 1989, 4th Internat. Biennial Print Exhibit, Taipei Fine Arts Mus., People's Republic China, 1990, Interprint, Lviv '90, USSR, 1990, New Orleans Mus. Art, 1990, Internat. Print Triennale, Cracow, Poland, 1991, 15th Ann. Nat. Invitational Drawing Exhbn. Emporia State U., Kans., 1991, Haggar U. Gallery, U. Dallas, 1991, Directions in Bay Area Printmaking: Three Decades Palo Alto Cultural Ctr., 1992, Am. Prints: Last Half 20th Century, Jane Haslem Gallery, Washington, 1992, Wenniger Graphics, Boston, 1993, Eleonore Austerer Gallery, San Francisco, 1994, Triton Mus. Art, Santa Clara, 1994, Mobile Mus. Art, 1995, Huntsville (Ala.) Mus. Art, 1995; represented in permanent collections San Francisco Mus. Modern Art, Achenbach Found. Graphic Arts, San Francisco, Phila. Mus. Art, New Orleans Mus. Art, Portland Mus. Art, Maine, The Libr. of Congress, Washington. Huntsville Mus. Art, Midwest Mus. Am. Art, Ind., Cracow Nat. Mus., Poland, Cabo Frio Mus., Brazil, Nat. Mus. Am. Art, Smithsonian Inst., Washington. Recipient Kempshall Clark award Peoria Art Guild, 1981, Paul Lindsay Sample Meml. award 25th Chautauqua Nat. Exhbn. of Am. Art, 1982, 1st Ann. Creative Achievement award Calif. State Legislature/Arts Coun. San Mateo County, 1989. Mem. Am. Color Print Soc., Audubon Artists (Louis Lozowick Meml. award 1978, Silver medal of honor award 1991), Boston Printmakers (Ture Bengtz Meml. award 1987), Calif. Soc. Printmakers (mem. council 1979-81), Los Angeles Printmaking Soc., Phila. Print Club (Lessing J. Rosenwald prize 1979), Arts Council of San Mateo Count, Theta Chi. Democrat. Studio and Office: PO Box 3305 Sonora CA 95370-3305 *Personal philosophy: In being an artist, I do not wish to be just a "recorder" of my time, what I see, what I think. To me, the joy of art is in expressing the love of being an artist, for in loving without shame, without fear, and without doubt one transcends to the moment and speaks with integrity. For the rest of my life I wish to reflect on what life is, and to have the courage to create that which touches not only men's eyes, but their hearts and spirits. I seek the profound truth of what it is to be human and the universal truth of what is means to be creative in expressing the love of being.*

PRICE, JOHN ALEY, lawyer; b. Maryville, Mo., Oct. 7, 1947; s. Donald Leroy and Julia Catherine (Aley) P.; m. Deborah Diadra Gunter, Aug. 12, 1995; children: Theodore John, Joseph Andrew. BS, N.W. Mo. State U., 1969; JD, U. Kans., 1972. Bar: Kans. 1972, U.S. Dist. Ct. Kans. 1972, U.S. Ct. Appeals (10th cir.) 1972, Tex. 1984, U.S. Ct. Appeals (5th cir.) 1984, U.S. Supreme Ct., 1987; cert. civil trial law Tex. Bd. Legal Specialization, 1989—. Law clk. U.S. Dist. Ct. Kans., Wichita, 1972-74; assoc., then ptnr. firm Weeks, Thomas and Lysaught, Kansas City, Kans., 1974-82; ptnr. Winstead, Sechrest & Minick, Dallas, 1982-96, litigation sect. coord., 1990-92, intellectual property sect. litigation coord., 1993-95; gen. counsel Travelhost, Inc., Dallas, 1996—; spl. prosecutor Leavenworth County Dist. Atty., 1970-71, Sedgwick County Dist. Atty., Wichita, Kans., 1971-72. Author: Our Boundless Self (A Call to Awake), 1992, A Gathering of Light: Eternal Wisdom for a Time of Transformation, 1993; editor (mag.) Academic Analyst, 1968-69; assoc. editor U. Kans. Law Rev., 1971-72, Dallas Bus. Jour.; author legal publs. Co-dir. Douglas County Legal Aid Soc., Lawrence, Kans., 1971-72; co-pres. Northwood Hills PTA, Dallas, 1984, Westwoood Jr. H.S. PTA, 1989-90; founder New Frontiers Found., 1993; co-founder Wings of Spirit Found., 1994, dir., v.p., 1994—. Mem. ABA, Kans. Bar Assn. (mem. task force for penal reform; Pres.'s Outstanding Svc. award 1981), Tex. Bar Assn., Pro Bono Coll., State Bar Tex., 1992—, World Bus. Acad., Inst. Noetic Scis., UN Assn. (humans rights com. Dallas chpt. 1991-93, bd. dirs. 1991-93), Campaign for the Earth (chpt. coord. Global Report 1991-92, coord. govt. and politics area 1991-92), Blue Key, Order of Coif, Phi Delta Phi, Sigma Tau Gamma (v.p. 1968-69). Mem. Unity Ch. Office: Travelhost Inc 10701 Stemmons Freeway Dallas TX 75220 *Individually, each person creates his or her reality every moment of existence. Collectively, we hold within ourselves a boundless capacity to co-create a world filled with love, compassion and abundance for all sentient beings. The key to a new order of the ages lies within our own hearts, minds and souls.*

PRICE, JOHN RANDOLPH, writer; b. Alice, Tex., Feb. 12, 1932; s. John Randolph and Eva Mae (Boney) P.; m. Janis Bryant Price, June 20, 1953; children: Susan Lynn, Leslie Anne. BS, U. Houston, 1957. Dir. advt. Gates Radio Corp., Quincy, Ill., 1957-62; v.p. Sander Rodkin, Ltd., Chgo., 1962-64; exec. v.p. Stewart, Price, Tomlin, Inc., Chgo., 1964-67; v.p. Goodwin, Dannenbaum, Littman & Wingfield, Inc., Houston, 1967-70; pres. O'Neill, Price, Anderson, Fouchard, Inc., Houston, 1970-74, John Price & Co., Houston, 1974-79, Arnan, Inc., Austin, 1979-81; chmn. bd. The Quartus Found. Inc., Boerne, Tex., 1981—; adv. bd. Global Family, Inc., Palo Alto, Calif., 1990—; Santi Found., Yucalpa, Calif., 1990—, Unity and Diversity World Coun., Inc., L.A., 1992—. Author: The Superbeings, 1981, The Manifestation Process, 1983, The Planetary Commission, 1984, Practical Spirituality, 1985, With Wings as Eagles, 1987, The Abundance Book, 1987, Prayer, Principles & Power, 1987, A Spiritual Philosophy for the New World, 1990, Empowerment, 1992, The Angels Within Us, 1993, Angel Energy, 1995. Chmn. Red Cross Drive, Quincy, Ill., 1960; cons. All Am. City campaign, Quincy, 1962. Staff sgt. USAF, 1952-56. Recipient Joseph S. Cullinan award U. Houston, 1956, Grand Prix Best Consumer Mag. Advt. award, 1970. Mem. Internat. New Though Alliance (Humanitarian award 1992, Joseph Muphy award 1994). Achievements include organizer of first annual World Peace day on December 31, 1986. Office: The Quartus Found Inc PO Box 1768 Boerne TX 78006

PRICE, JOHN ROY, JR., financial executive; b. N.Y.C., Dec. 20, 1938; s. John Roy and Pauline Bernice (Milnes) P.; m. Victoria Scott Pohle, Dec. 19, 1970 (div. 1982); 1 child, Matthew Roy; m. Marion Cobb Hardie, Oct. 1, 1988 (div. 1996). B.A., Grinnell Coll., 1960, Queens Coll., Oxford (Eng.) U., 1962; M.A., Queens Coll., Oxford (Eng.) U., 1965; J.D., Harvard U., 1965. Assoc. Casey, Lane & Mittendorf, N.Y.C., 1965-67; v.p. Bedford-Stuyvesant D & S Corp., N.Y.C., 1967-68; spl. asst. to Pres. U.S., Washington, 1969-71; assoc. Donaldson, Lufkin & Jenrette, N.Y.C., 1971-72; v.p. Mfrs. Hanover Trust, N.Y.C., 1972-75; v.p. Mfrs. Hanover Corp., N.Y.C., 1975-80, sr. v.p. non-bank subs., 1980-83, sr. v.p., sec., 1983-87; mng. dir. Mfrs. Hanover Trust Co., 1987-88, Mfrs. Hanover Securities Corp., 1988-92; mng. dir. govt. affairs Chem. Bank, 1992-96, Chase Manhattan, 1996—; bd. dirs. Am. Trust for Oxford, 1990-94, chmn. Cmty. Devel., Inc., Prin. Fin. Group (formerly Bankers Life Co.), Transcell Techs. Corp., Bankers Assn. for Fgn. Trade, 1990—, pres., 1994—, Nat. Fgn. Trade Coun., 1991—; pres. Am. for Oxford, 1987—; chmn. local devel. corp. Bklyn. Acad. Music, 1980-82. Nat. chmn. Ripon Soc., 1967-68; trustee Grinnell Coll., 1970—; bd. dirs. New Communities Corp., 1976-77; mem. exec. panel Chief of Naval Ops., 1972-79. Rhodes scholar. Mem. Council Fgn. Relations, Phi Beta Kappa. Club: Harvard (N.Y.C.). Home: 3144 Granite Rd Woodstock MD 21163-1004

PRICE, JOSEPH HUBBARD, lawyer; b. Montgomery, Ala., Jan. 31, 1939; s. Aaron Joseph and Minnie Jule (Reynolds) P.; m. Cynthia Winant Ramsey, Sept. 14, 1963 (div. 1980); children—Victoria Reynolds, Ramsey Winant; m. Courtney McFadden, Apr. 26, 1980. A.B., U. Ala., 1961; LL.B., Harvard U., 1964; postgrad. London Sch. Econs., 1964-65. Bar: Ala. 1964, D.C. 1968. Law clerk to justice Hugo L. Black, U.S. Supreme Ct., Washington, 1967-68; assoc. Leva, Hawes, Symington, Martin & Oppenheimer, Washington, 1968-71; v.p. Overseas Pvt. Investment Corp., Washington, 1971-73; ptnr. Leva, Hawes, et. al., Washington, 1973-83, Gibson, Dunn & Crutcher, Washington, 1983—. Mem. CARE Com. Washington; mem. adv. com. Hugo Black Meml. Library, Ashland, Ala. Served to capt. U.S. Army, 1966-67; Vietnam. Decorated Bronze Star; Frank Knox Meml. fellow London Sch. Econs., 1964-65. Mem. ABA, Am. Soc. Internat. Law, Supreme Ct. Hist. Soc., Phi Beta Kappa. Clubs: Metropolitan. Home: 3104 Cathedral Ave NW Washington DC 20008-3419 Office: Gibson Dunn & Crutcher 1050 Connecticut Ave NW Washington DC 20036-5303

PRICE, JOSEPH LEVERING, neuroscientist, educator; b. Mobile, Ala., Oct. 17, 1942; s. Benjamin Joseph and Virginia (Levering) P.; m. Elisabeth Uttenthal, June 23, 1967; children: Anna Elise, Virginia Sigrid, Paul Joseph. BA in Chemistry, U. of the South, 1963; BA in Physiology, U. Oxford, Eng., 1966, PhD in Anatomy, 1969. Instr. Washington U. Sch. Medicine, St. Louis, 1969-71, asst. prof., 1971-76, assoc. prof., 1976-83, prof., 1983—. Mem. editorial bd. Jour. of Comparative Neurology, 1983—; contbr. articles to profl. jours. Jr. warden Christ Ch. Cathedral, St. Louis, 1985-87. Rhodes scholar Oxford U., 1963-66; USPHS predoctoral fellow, 1966-68; recipient C.J. Herrick award Am. Assn. Anatomoists, 1973, Javits Neurosci. Investigator award NIH, 1987. Mem. Soc. for Neurosci., Assn. for Chemoreception Scis., Phi Beta Kappa. Democrat. Episcopalian. Office: Washington U Sch Medicine Dept Anatomy and Neurobiology Saint Louis MO 63110

PRICE, JOSEPH MICHAEL, lawyer; b. St. Paul, Dec. 2, 1947; s. Leon and Rose (Kaufman) P.; m. Louise Rebecca Braunstein, Dec. 19, 1971; children—Lisa, Laurie, Julie. B.A., U. Minn., 1969, J.D., 1972. Bar: Minn. 1972, U.S. Dist. Ct. Minn. 1974. Ptnr., Faegre & Benson, Mpls., 1972—. Mem. Minn. Bar Assn., Hennepin County Bar Assn. Home: 4407 Country Club Rd Minneapolis MN 55424-1148 Office: Faegre & Benson 2200 Norwest Ctr 90 S 7th St Minneapolis MN 55402-3903

PRICE, KAREN OVERSTREET, pharmacist, medical editor; b. South Boston, Va., Oct. 28, 1964; d. Alvin Keith and Catherine Coggin (Marshall) Overstreet; m. David McRoy Price, June 18, 1988. BS in Pharmacy, U. N.C., 1987; MS in Drug Info., L.I. U., 1990. Cert. editor life scis. Bd. Editors in Life Scis. Pharmacist Eckerd, Burlington, N.C., 1988; Lasdon Rsch. fellow Internat. Drug Info. Ctr., Bklyn., 1988-90; drug info. analyst Am. Soc. Hosp. Pharmacists, Bethesda, Md., 1990-91; med. editor Adverceutics, Inc., Laurel, Md., 1991-93; dir. Meniscus Ednl. Inst., Phila., 1993—. Co-author: Athletic Drug Reference, 1991; co-author, co-editor: (computer program) Athletic Drug Reference, 1992; editorial rev. bd. P&T, 1993—; editorial bd. Drugdex Info. Sys., 1994—. Recipient Upjohn award for excellence in rsch. Upjohn Pharms., 1990. Mem. Am. Pharm. Assn. (reviewer 1991—), Am. Med. Writers Assn. (manuscript editor 1991-93, news editor 1994—), Am. Soc. Hosp. Pharmacists, Drug Info. Assn., Rho Chi Honor Soc. Office: Meniscus Ednl Inst 105 N 22nd St Ste 210 Philadelphia PA 19103-1302

PRICE, KATHLEEN MCCORMICK, book editor, writer; b. Topeka, Kans., Dec. 25, 1932; d. Raymond Chesley and Kathleen (Shoffner) McCormick; m. William Faulkner Black, Aug. 25, 1956 (div. 1961); 1 child, Kathleen Serena; m. William Hillard Price, Aug. 13, 1976. BA, U. Colo., Denver, 1971. Book reviewer Denver Post, 1971-78; book editor San Diego Mag., 1978-92; cons. editor St. John's Cathedral, Denver, 1985-95. Author: There's a Dactyl Under My Foot, 1986, The Lady and the Unicorn, 1994. Dir. Colo. Episcopal Vestment Guild. Mem. PEN, Denver Women's Press Club, Denver County Club, La Garita Club, Phi Beta Kappa. Episcopalian. Home: 27 Crestmoor Dr Denver CO 80220-5853

PRICE, LARRY C., photojournalist; b. Corpus Christi, Tex., Feb. 23, 1954; s. David Vernon and Martha C. (Tucker) P.; m. Debbie Mitchell, May 2, 1981. B.J., U. Tex., 1977. Mem. staff U. Tex. Daily Texan, Austin, 1976-77, El Paso Times, Tex., 1977-79, Ft. Worth Star-Telegram, Tex., 1979-83; asst. mng. editor Ft. Worth Star-Telegram, Tex., 1991-93; assoc. editor Ft. Worth Star-Telegram, 1993—; photojournalist Phila. Inquirer, 1983-90, dir. photography, 1987-88, photographer Washington Bur., 1988-90; freelance photographer Washington, 1990-91; vis. prof. U. Tex., Austin, 1983. Contbg. photographer: A Day in the Life of America, 1986, A Day in the Life of Spain, 1987, A Day in the Life of the Soviet Union, 1987, A Day in the Life of California, 1988, A Day in the Life of China, 1989, The Jews in America, 1989, The Power to Heal, 1989, A Day in the Life of Hollywood, 1992, The African Americans, 1993, A Day in the Life of Thailand, 1994, A Day in the Life of Israel, 1994, Jerusalem 3000, 1994. Recipient Pulitzer Prize in spot news photography Columbia U., N.Y.C., 1981, Pulitzer Prize in feature photography, 1985, Best Photographic Reporting From Abroad award Overseas Press Club, 1985, World Press Photo awards, 1987. Mem. Nat. Press Photographer's Assn. Methodist. Home: 2021 Windsor Pl Fort Worth TX 76110-1759

PRICE, LEONTYNE, concert and opera singer, soprano; b. Laurel, Miss., Feb. 10, 1927; d. James A. and Kate (Baker) P.; m. William Warfield, Aug. 31, 1952 (div. 1973). BA, Central State Coll., Wilberforce, Ohio, 1949, DMus, 1968; student, Juilliard Sch. Music, 1949-52; pupil, Florence Page Kimball; LHD, Dartmouth Coll., 1962, Fordham U., 1969, Yale U., 1979; MusD, Howard U., 1962; Dr. Humanities, Rust Coll., 1968. Profl. opera debut in 4 Saints in 3 Acts, 1952; appeared as Bess in Porgy and Bess, Vienna, Berlin, Paris, London, under auspices U.S. State Dept., also N.Y.C. and U.S. tour, 1952-54; recitalist, soloist with symphonies, U.S., Can., Australia, Europe, 1954—; appeared concerts in India, 1956, 64; soloist, Hollywood Bowl, 1955-59, 66, Berlin Festival, 1960; role as Mme. Lidoine in Dialogues des Carmelites, San Francisco Opera, 1957; opera singer, NBC-TV, 1955-58, 60, 62, 64, San Francisco Opera Co., 1957-59, 60-61, 63, 65, 67, 68, 71, as Aida at La Scala, Milan, 1957, Vienna Staatsoper, 1958, 59-60, 61, Berlin Opera, 1964, Rome Opera, 1966, Paris Opera, 1968, recital, Brussels Internat. Fair, auspices State Dept., 1958, Verona Opera Arena, 1958-59, recitals in Yugoslavia for, State Dept., 1958; rec. artist, RCA-Victor, 1958—, appeared Covent Garden, London, 1958-59, 70, Chgo. Lyric Theatre, 1959, 60, 65, Oakland (Calif.) Symphony, 1980, soloist, Salzburg Festival, 1959-63, Tetro alla Scala, Milano, 1960-61, 63, 67, appeared Met. Opera, N.Y.C., 1961-62, 64, 66, 75, 76; since resident mem., until 1985; soloist, Salzburg Festival, 1950, 60, debut, Teatre Dell'Opera, Rome, 1967, Teatro Colon, Buenos Aires, Argentina, 1969, Hamburg Opera, 1970; recordings include A Christmas Offering with Karajani, God Bless America with Charles Gerhardt, Arias from Don Giovanni, Turandot, Aida, Emani, Messa di Requiem, Trovatore, Live at Ordway, The Prima Donna Collection, A Program of Song with D. Garvey, Right as the Rain with André Previn. Hon. bd. dirs. Campfire Girls; hon. vice-chmn. U.S. com. UNESCO; co-chmn. Rust Coll. Upward Thrust Campaign; trustee Internat. House. Decorated Order at Merit Italy; recipient Merit award for role of Tosca in NBC-TV Opera, Mademoiselle mag., 1955, 20 Grammy awards for classical vocal recs. Nat. Acad. Rec. Arts and Scis., citation YWCA, 1961, Spirit of Achievement award Albert Einstein Coll. Medicine, 1962, Presdl. medal of freedom, 1964, Springarn medal NAACP, 1965, Schwann Catalog award, 1968, Nat. Medal of Arts, 1985, Essence award, 1991, others; named Musician of Year, Mus. Am. mag., 1961. Fellow Am. Acad. Arts and Sci.; mem. AFTRA, Am. Guild Mus. Artists, Actors Equity Assn., Sigma Alpha Iota, Delta Sigma Theta. Office: Columbia Artists Mgmt Inc Walter Divsn 165 W 57th St New York NY 10019-2201 also: 1133 Broadway New York NY 10010-7903*

PRICE, LUCILE BRICKNER BROWN, retired civic worker; b. Decorah, Iowa, May 31, 1902; d. Sidney Eugene and Cora (Drake) Brickner; B.S., Iowa State U., 1925; M.A., Northwestern U., 1940; m. Maynard Wilson Brown, July 2, 1928 (dec. Apr. 1937); m. 2d, Charles Edward Price, Jan. 14, 1961 (dec. Dec. 1983). Asst. dean women Kans. State U., Manhattan, 1925-28; mem. bd. student personnel adminstrn. Northwestern U., 1937-41; personnel research Sears Roebuck & Co., Chgo., 1941-42, overseas club dir. ARC, Eng., Africa, Italy, 1942-45; dir. Child Edn. Found., N.Y.C., 1946-56. Participant 1st and 2d Iowa Humanists Summer Symposiums, 1974, 75. Del. Mid Century White House Conf. on Children and Youth, 1950; mem. com. on program and research of Children's Internat. summer villages, 1952-53; mem. bd. N.E. Iowa Mental Health Ctr., 1959-62, pres. bd., 1960-61; mem. Iowa State Extension Adv. Com., 1973-75; project chmn. Decorah Hist. Dist. (listed Nat. Register Historic Places); trustee Porter House Mus., Decorah, 1966-78, emerita bd. dirs., 1982—; participant N. Cen. Regional Workshop Am. Assn. State and Local History, Mpls., 1975, Midwest Workshop Hist. Preservation and Conservation, Iowa State U., 1976, 77; mem. Winneshiek County (Iowa) Civil Service Commn., 1978-87; rep. Class of 1940 Northwestern U. Sch. Edn. and Social Policy, 1986-88. Recipient Alumni Merit award Iowa State U., 1975, Cert. of Appreciation Iowa State U. Extension, 1988. Mem. Am. Coll. Personnel Assn., (life), ARC Overseas Assn. (life, nat. bd.), AAUW (life, mem. bd. Decorah, Named Gift award 1977), Nat. Assn. Mental Health (del. nat. conf. 1958), Norwegian-Am. Mus. (life, Vesterheim fellow), Internat. Platform Assn., Winneshiek County Hist. Soc. (life, cert. of appreciation 1984), DAR, Luther Coll. Heritage Club (life, pres.'s coun. 1993), Pi Lambda Theta, Chi Omega. Designer, builder house for retirement living. Avocation: remembering WWII. Home: 508 W Broadway St Decorah IA 52101-1704

PRICE, MARILYNN MATLOCK, elementary school educator; b. Spokane, Wash., Aug. 20, 1916; d. Jesse William and Mary Frances (Harlow) Matlock; m. Robert Edgar Price, July 17, 1938 (dec. May, 1979); children: Robert Dale, Charlotte Lee Price Wirfs, Carla Jean Price Perkins. Grad., Oreg. Normal Sch., 1936; BS, Oerg. Coll. Edn., 1971. Cert. tchr. Tchr. Tub Springs Sch., Oreg., 1937-38; tchr. grades 1-4 Peedee (Oreg.) Sch., 1942-43; phys. edn. tchr. Dallas (Oreg.) Jr. High Sch., 1943-45, 49-52; tchr. 5th grade Florence (Oreg.) Elem. Sch., 1953-56; tchr. 6th grade Bay City (Oreg.) Elem. Sch., 1958-60, East Sch., Tillamook, Oreg., 1962-82, 1982. Mem. AAUW, Tillamook Hist. Soc., Oreg., DAR (regent Tillamook chpt. 1989-93), Ret. Tchrs. Assn. (sec. 1982-91), Delta Kappa Gamma (pres. Alpha Gamma chpt. 1985-89). Avocations: knitting, crochet, reading, walking. Office: Delta Kappa Gamma Alpha Gamma Chpt Tillamook OR 97141

PRICE, MARION WOODROW, journalist; b. Elizabeth City, N.C., Oct. 13, 1914; s. James Asa and Meddie (Divers) P.; m. Mary Dudley Pittman, Aug. 31, 1940; children—Wiley, Dudley, Mary, Catherine. Student, Wake Forest Coll., 1933-34. Reporter Daily Advance, Elizabeth City, 1935-39, Raleigh (N.C.) Times, 1939-41; mng. editor Kannapolis (N.C.) Ind., 1941-42; reporter AP, Raleigh, 1942-43, News and Observer, Raleigh, 1946-57; mng. editor News and Observer, 1957-72; outdoor editor, 1949-76. Mem. Kerr Reservoir Devel. Commn., 1950-52, Cape Hatteras Seashore Commn., 1949-50, N.C. Wildlife Resources Commn., 1977-89; chmn. N.C. Outer Banks Park Commn., 1962-63, N.C. Seashore Commn., 1963-69, N.C. State Ports Authority, 1969-73. Served with USAAF, 1943-45. Mem. AP Mng. Editors Assn., Outdoor Writers Am. Baptist. Home: Old Ferry Dock Rd Old Ferry Dock Rd PO Box 65 Gloucester NC 28528

PRICE, (WILLIAM) MARK, professional basketball player; b. Bartlesville, Okla., Feb. 15, 1964. Student, Ga. Tech. With Dallas Mavericks, 1986; guard Cleve. Cavaliers, 1986—. Winner NBA Long Distance Shootout, 1993, 94; named to NBA All-Star team, 1989, 92, 93, 94, NBA First Team, 1993, Dream Team II, 1994. Holder career record for highest free-throw percentages during regular and playoff seasons.

PRICE, MARK MICHAEL, building development consultant; b. Cleve., Jan. 20, 1920; s. Mark Michael and Sarah Ann (Moran) P.; ed. U. Detroit, 1940, Cleve. Coll., 1946; m. Ellen Elizabeth Hafford, June 3, 1948; children—Marilyn Michelle, Pamela Susan. Founder Desk Tops Inc., Cleve., 1950, Vistron Door Corp., Cleve., 1962; pres., chief exec. officer Bldg. Devel. Counsel Inc., Washington; founder Desk Tops Inc., Vistron Door Corp. Mem. Cleve. Mayor's Bus. Men's Civic Com., 1977-78. Mem. Soc. Mktg. Profls. Democrat. Roman Catholic. Clubs: Army-Navy, Nat. Press, Capital Hill (Washington), University, Capitol. Office: Bldg Devel Counsel Inc 1225 Connecticut Ave NW Ste 300 Washington DC 20036-2604

PRICE, MICHAEL HOWARD, journalist, critic, composer, cartoonist; b. Amarillo, Tex., Sept. 14, 1947; s. John Andrew and Thelma Adeline (Wilson) P.; m. Christina Renteria, Aug. 31, 1980. BA in Journalism, West Tex. State U., 1970. Edn. writer Amarillo Globe-News, 1968-74, fin. editor, 1974-76, city editor, 1976-77; adminstr. Amarillo Coll., 1977-80; bur. chief Ft. Worth Star-Telegram, 1980-83, features editor, 1983-85, film critic, 1985—; cons. journalism West Tex. State U., Canyon, 1977-90, Tex. Tech U., Lubbock, 1982-85; dirs. The Harvey Group comic-book profls. awards, 1990—. Author: (CD-ROMs) A Century of Fantastic Cinema, 1995, Silver Screen Sensations, 1996, (albums) Cognitive Dissonance, 1994, The Last Temptation of Price, 1995, R. Crumb--The Musical, 1995, Swingmasters Revue, 1995, Claus & Effect, 1996, (books) Forgotten Horrors, 1986, Human Monsters in the Movies, 1994, Krime Duzzin't Pay, 1995, The Guitar in Jazz, 1996, Stitches, 1996, Frights Genuine & Fancied, 1996, (novels) The Prowler, 1989, Carnival of Souls, 1991, Holiday for Screams, 1992. Creative dir. Tex. Gridiron Show, Fort Worth, 1984-85, 92-93. Mem. Soc. Profl. Journalists (bd. dirs. 1992-94), Tex. Tornados Blues Hall of Fame, Soc. Film Critics. Office: Ft Worth Star Telegram Inc 400 W 7th St Fl 3 Fort Worth TX 76102-4701 *In a career of communication, the conventional wisdom of "writing about what you know" no longer applies. Try "writing about what you want to know," and your progress from that point will astonish you.*

PRICE, NICK, professional golfer; b. Durban, South Africa, Jan. 28, 1957; m. Sue Price; children: Gregory, Robyn Frances. Winner PGA Championship, 1992, 1994, British Open, 1994, 3rd PGA Tour Money Leader, 1992, PGA Tour Money Leader, 1993, 10 USPGA Tour Victories, 26 World Wide Victories; recipient Vardon Trophy, 1993; named Player of Yr., 1993. Holds PGA Tournament record for lowest score (269), 1994. Address: care PGA Tour 100 Avenue of the Champions Palm Beach Gardens FL 33410-9601*

PRICE, PAUL BUFORD, physicist, educator; b. Memphis, Nov. 8, 1932; s. Paul Buford and Eva (Dupuy) P.; m. JoAnn Margaret Baum, June 28, 1958; children—Paul Buford III, Heather Alynn, Pamela Margaret, Alison Gaynor. BS summa cum laude, Davidson Coll., 1954, DSc, 1973; MS, U. Va., 1956, PhD, 1958. Fulbright scholar U. (Eng.) Bristol, 1958-59; NSF postdoctoral fellow Cambridge (Eng.) U., 1959-60; physicist R&D Ctr. GE, Schenectady, 1960-69; vis. prof. Tata Inst. Fundamental Rsch., Bombay, India, 1965-66; adj. prof. physics Rensselaer Poly. Inst., 1967-68; prof. physics U. Calif., Berkeley, 1969—, chmn. dept. physics, 1987-91, McAdams prof. physics, 1990-92, dean phys. scis., 1992—, dir. Space Scis. Lab., 1979-85; bd. dirs. Terradex Corp., Walnut Creek, Calif.; vis. com. Bartol Rsch. Inst., 1991-94; adv. bd. Indian Inst. Astrophysics, Bangalore, 1993—; cons. to lunar sample analysis planning team NASA; space sci. bd. Nat. Acad. Scis.; vis. prof. U. Rome, 1983, 92; sci. assoc. Ctr. d'Etude Rsch. Nuclear, 1984; Miller rsch. prof. U. Calif., Berkeley, 1972-73; researcher in space and astrophycs, nuclear physics. Author: (with others) Nuclear Tracks in Solids; Contbr. (with others) articles to profl. jours. Recipient Disting. Svc. award Am. Nuclear Soc., 1964, Indsl. Rsch. awards, 1964, 65, E.O. Lawrence Meml. award AEC, 1971, medal for exceptional sci. achievement NASA, 1973; John Simon Guggenheim fellow, 1976-77. Fellow Am. Phys. Soc., Am. Geophys. Union; mem. Nat. Acad. Scis. (chmn. geophysics sect. 1981-84, sec. class phys.-math. scis. 1985-88, chmn. 1988-91).

PRICE, REYNOLDS, novelist, poet, playwright, essayist, educator; b. Macon, N.C., Feb. 1, 1933; s. William Solomon and Elizabeth (Rodwell) P. AB summa cum laude (Angier Duke scholar), Duke, 1955; BLitt (Rhodes scholar), Merton Coll., Oxford U., Eng., 1958; LittD, St. Andrews Presbyn. Coll., 1978, Wake Forest U., 1979, Washington and Lee U., 1991; Davidson Coll., 1992; LittD, Elon Coll., 1996. Mem. faculty English Duke U., 1958—; asst. prof., 1961-68, assoc. prof., 1968-72, prof., 1972-77, James B. Duke prof., 1977—, acting chmn., 1983; writer in residence U. N.C., Chapel Hill, 1965, U. Kans., 1967, 69, 80, U.N.C., Greensboro, 1971; Glasgow prof. Washington and Lee U., 1971; faculty Salzburg Seminar, 1977. Author: A Long and Happy Life, 1962, The Names and Faces of Heroes, 1963, A Generous Man, 1966, Love and Work, 1968, Permanent Errors, 1970, Things Themselves, 1972, The Surface of Earth, 1975, Early Dark, 1977, A Palpable God, 1978, The Source of Light, 1981, Vital Provisions, 1982, Private Contentment, 1984, Kate Vaiden, 1986, The Laws of Ice, 1986, A Common Room, 1987, Good Hearts, 1988, Clear Pictures, 1989, The Tongues of Angels, 1990, The Use of Fire, 1990, New Music, 1990, The Foreseeable Future, 1991, Conversations with Reynolds Price, 1991, Blue Calhoun, 1992, Full Moon, 1993, The Collected Stories, 1993, A Whole New Life, 1994, The Promise of Rest, 1995, Three Gospels, 1996. Recipient William Faulkner Found. award notable 1st novel, 1962, Sir Walter Raleigh award, 1962, 76, 81, 84, 86, award Nat. Assn. Ind. Schs., 1964, Roanoke-Chowan Poetry award, 1982; Guggenheim fellow, 1964-65; fellow Nat. Endowment for Arts, 1967-68, lit. adv. panel, 1973-76, chmn., 1976; recipient Nat. Inst. Arts and Letters award, 1971, Bellamann Found. award, 1972, Lillian Smith award, 1976, N.C. award, 1977, Nat. Book Critics Circle award, 1986, Elmer H. Bobst award, 1988, R. Hunt Parker award N.C. Lit. and Hist. Soc., 1991. Mem. Am. Acad. Arts and Letters, Phi Beta Kappa, Phi Delta Theta. Home: PO Box 99014 Durham NC 27708-9014 Office: care Harriet Wasserman Lit Agy Inc 137 E 36th St New York NY 10016-3528

PRICE, RICHARD, anthropologist, author; b. N.Y.C., Nov. 30, 1941; s. George Price and Gertrude (Swee) Jaffe; m. Sally Hamlin, 1963; children: Niko, Leah. AB in History and Lit. magna cum laude, Harvard U., 1963, PhD in Social Anthropology, 1970. From lectr. to assoc. prof. anthropology Yale U., New Haven, 1969-74; prof. anthropology Johns Hopkins U., Balt., 1974-87, chmn. dept., 1974-77, 79-85; Marta Sutton Weeks sr. fellow Stanford Humanities Ctr. Stanford (Calif.) U., 1989-90; fellow Shelby Cullom Davis Ctr. for Hist. Studies, Princeton U., 1992; Rockefeller fellow in humanities U. Fla., 1994; vis. prof. U. Paris, 1985-87, U. Minn., Mpls., 1987-88; George I. Miller vis. scholar U. Ill., 1994; Dittman prof. Am. Studies, anthropology and history Coll. William and Mary, 1994—. Author: Maroon Societies, 1973, Saramaka Social Structure, 1975, The Guiana Maroons, 1976, Afro-American Arts of the Suriname Rain Forest, 1980, First-Time: the Historical Vision of an Afro-American People, 1983, To Slay the Hydra, 1983, Stedman's Narrative of a Five Years Expedition, 1988, Alabi's World, 1990, Two Evenings in Saramaka, 1991, The Birth of African-American Culture, 1992, Stedman's Surinam, 1992, Equatoria, 1992, On the Mall, 1994, Enigma Variations, 1995; editor: GK Hall & Co., Boston, 1980—. Recipient Elsie Clews Parsons prize Am. Folklore Soc., 1984, Albert J. Beveridge award Am. Hist. Assn., 1991, Gordon K. Lewis Mem. award for disting. Caribbean scholarship, 1992, J.I. Staley prize, 1993; NEH grantee, NSF grantee, Fulbright grantee; John Simon Guggenheim Meml. fellow. Fellow Am. Anthrop. Assn., Royal Anthrop. Inst. Gt. Britain and Ireland, Royal Dutch Inst. Anthropology; mem. Am. Ethnological Soc., Phi Beta Kappa. Home: Anse Chaudière, 97217 Anses d'Arlet Martinique Office: Coll William & Mary Dept Anthropology Williamsburg VA 23187

PRICE, ROBERT, lawyer, media executive, investment banker; b. N.Y.C., Aug. 27, 1932; s. Solomon and Frances (Berger) P.; m. Margery Beth Wiener, Dec. 18, 1955; children: Eileen Marcia, Steven. AB, NYU, 1953; LLD, Columbia U., 1958. Bar: N.Y. 1958, U.S. Dist. Ct. 1958, U.S. Ct. Appeals 1958, U.S. Supreme Ct 1958, ICC 1958, FCC 1958, IRS 1958. With R.H. Macy & Co., Inc., 1955-58; practiced in N.Y.C., 1958—; law clk. to judge U.S. Dist. Ct. (so. dist.) N.Y., 1958-59; asst. U.S. atty. So. Dist. N.Y., 1959-60; ptnr. Kupferman & Price, 1960-65; chmn. bd. pres. Atlantic States Ind. Inc., 1963-66; dep. mayor N.Y.C., 1965-66; exec. v.p., dir. Dreyfus Corp., N.Y.C., 1966-69; v.p., investment officer Dreyfus Fund, until 1969; chmn., pres., dir. Price Capital Corp., N.Y.C., 1969-72; gen. ptnr., spl. counsel Lazard, Freres & Co., 1972-82; pres. N.Y. Law Jour., Nat. Law Jour.; pres., treas., dir. Price Communications Corp., 1979—; pres., dir. PriCellular Corp., 1988—, TLM Corp., 1989—; adv. com. Bankers Trust Co. N.Y.; dir. Holly Sugar Corp., Lane Bryant, Inc., Graphic Scanning Corp.; chmn. N.Y.C. Port Authority Negotiating Com. for World Trade Ctr., 1965-66; spl. counsel N.Y. State Joint Legis. Com. on Ct. Reorgn.; asst. counsel N.Y. State Joint Legis. Com. on N.Y. Banking Laws; trustee CUNY, 1996—; rep. of N.Y. State Senate on the Mcpl. Assistance Corp. of N.Y.C., 1996—. Author articles. Chmn. govt. and civil svc. divsn. United Jewish Appeal Greater N.Y., 1966; co-chmn. met. N.Y. blood drive ARC, 1966; campaign mgr. John V. Lindsay, Campaigns for Congressman, N.Y.C., 1958, 64, for Nelson A. Rockefeller Oreg. Rep. presdl. primary campaign, 1964, Lindsay campaign for mayor, N.Y.C., 1965; del. N.Y. Rep. State Conv., 1962, 64, 66; del. Rep. Nat. Conv., 1988, 96; lectr. Rep. Nat. Com., 1966; bd. dirs. Am. Friends Hebrew U.; past trustee Columbia U. Sch. Pharm. Scis. With U.S. Army, 1953-55. Recipient Yeshiva U. Heritage award, Pub. Svc. award Queens Catholic War Vets. Mem. ABA, FCC Bar Assn., Assn. Bar City N.Y., N.Y. State Dist. Attys. Assn., Coun. Fgn. Rels., Columbia Law Sch. Alumni Assn. (dir.), Scribes, Tau Kappa Alpha. Home: 25 E 86th St New York NY 10028-0553 Office: Price Communications Corp 45 Rockefeller Plz New York NY 10111-0201

PRICE, ROBERT, electronics consultant; b. West Chester, Pa., July 7, 1929; s. Llewellyn Robert and Elise Maclay (Mirkil) P.; m. Jennifer Ann Livingstone Martin, Apr. 19, 1958; children: Stephen Livingstone, Colin Llewellyn, Edmund Hazleton. A.B., Princeton U., 1950; Sc.D. (Indsl. fellow 1950-52), M.I.T., 1953. Engr. Philco Corp., Phila., 1950; mem. staff Lincoln Lab., M.I.T., 1951-65; mgr. Sperry Research Center, Sperry Corp., Sudbury, Mass., 1965-77; staff cons. communication scis. Sperry Research Center, Sperry Corp., 1977-83; chief scientist M/A-COM Govt. Systems Div., Burlington, Mass., 1983-87, cons., 1987-88; cons. scientist Research div. Raytheon Co., Lexington, Mass., 1988-93; pvt. practice cons. Lexington, Mass., 1993—; vis. lectr. U. Calif., Berkeley, 1962-63; adv. council dept. elec. engring. and computer sci. Princeton U., 1971-77; chmn. Mil. Communication Conf. Bd., 1985. Contbr. sci. and hist. articles on spread spectrum techs.; patentee in spread spectrum communications and magnetic recording. Recipient Edwin Howard Armstrong achievement award IEEE Communications Soc., 1981; Fulbright fellow in radio astronomy Australia, 1953-54. Fellow IEEE (gov. info. theory group 1967-70, 77-79); mem. Internat. Union Radio Sci., Nat. Acad. Engring., Franklin Inst., Phi Beta Kappa, Sigma Xi.

PRICE, ROBERT E., manufacturing company executive; b. 1942. BA, Pomona Coll., 1964. V.p. Fed-Mart Corp., 1964-75; pres., chief exec. officer Price Corp., San Diego, 1976-89; pres., chmn. bd., chief exec. officer Price Enterprises, San Diego, 1989-91, chmn. bd., chief exec. officer, 1991—, also bd. dirs. Office: Price Enterprises 4649 Morena Blvd San Diego CA 92117-3650*

PRICE, ROBERT EBEN, judge; b. Waco, Tex., Jan. 13, 1931; s. Robert Eben and Mary Hamilton (Barnett) P.; m. Ann Hodges, June 4, 1954; children—Eben, Mary, Ann, Emily. B.A., So. Methodist U., 1952, J.D., 1954, LL.M., 1972; postgrad., Air War Coll., 1976. Bar: Tex. 1954, U.S. Supreme Ct., U.S. Ct. Mil. Appeals, U.S. Ct. Claims, U.S. Dist. Ct. (no. dist.) Tex. 1954. Mem. firm Taylor, Mizell, Price, Corrigan & Smith, Dallas, 1956-86; judge Dallas County Probate Ct. No. 2, 1986—; lectr. continuing legal edn. program U. Houston Law Found., 1993—; lectr. law So. Meth. U. Law Sch., 1973—, faculty paralegal cert. program Sch. Continuing Edn., 1987—; lectr. practice skills program State Bar Tex., 1974—. Editor-in-chief: Southwestern Law Jour., 1953-54. Trustee and sec. St. Michael and All Angels Found.; bd. dirs. Downtown Ministry, Diocese of Dallas Episcopal; chmn. legis. and legal awareness subcom., vice chmn. Tex. Gov.'s Com. on Employment of Handicapped, 1978-82. Served as legal officer USAF, 1954-56; col. JAGC Res. ret. Fellow Am. Coll. Trust and Estate Counsel (state membership com., fiduciary litigation com.); mem. ABA (nat. conf. spl. ct. judges com. on probate and surrogates cts. 1992—), Nat. Coll. Probate Judges, Coll. of State Bar Tex., Dallas Bar Assn., State Bar Tex. (lectr. profl. devel. program 1988—), Tex. Coll. Probate Judges (mem. faculty), Phi Alpha Delta, Phi Eta Sigma, Phi Delta Theta. Episcopalian. Home: 4300 Arcady Ave Dallas TX 75205-3704 Office: Probate Ct 2 211 Records Bldg 509 Main St Dallas TX 75202-3504

PRICE, ROBERT EDMUNDS, civil engineer; b. Lyndhurst, N.J., Jan. 8, 1926; s. William Evans and Charlotte Ann (Dyson) P.; B.S. in Civil Engring., Dartmouth Coll., 1946; M.S., Princeton U. 1947; m. Margaret Akerman Menard, June 28, 1947; children—Robert Edmunds, Alexander Menard. Mgr., P&S Standard Vacuum Oil Co., N.Y., London and Sumatra, 1947-55; project engr. Metcalf & Eddy, Cons. Engrs., Boston, 1956-59; structural engr. Lummis Co., Cons. Engrs., Newark, 1960-61; mgr. engring. materials Interpace Corp., Wharton, N.J., 1961-78; pres. Openaka Corp., Denville, N.J., 1979—; cons. cement and concrete design and constrn. Mem. Denville Bd. Health, 1963-66, chmn., 1966; mem. Denville Bd. Adjustment, 1966-69. Served with USNR, 1943-46. Registered profl. engr., N.J., Md. Fellow Am.

Concrete Inst. (dir. 1981-84); mem. ASTM (chmn. subcom. spl. cements 1976-84, hon. mem. com. C-1), Nat. Assn. Corrosion Engrs. Episcopalian. Home: Lake Openaka Denville NJ 07834 Office: Openaka Corp 565 Openaki Rd Denville NJ 07834-9642

PRICE, ROBERT IRA, coast guard officer; b. N.Y.C., Sept. 22, 1921; s. Alfred and Mary Edna (Schweitzer) P.; m. Virginia Louise Miller, June 20, 1946; children: Andrea Jean, Keven Virginia. B.B.A., CCNY, 1942; B.S., U.S. Coast Guard Acad., 1945; postgrad., M.I.T., 1950-53. Registered profl. engr., D.C. Commd. ensign U.S. Coast Guard, 1945, advanced through grades to vice adm., 1978; asst. chief Mcht. Marine Tech. Div., Washington, 1965-67; chief planning staff Office Mcht. Marine Safety, 1967-71; capt. Port of Phila., 1971-73; chief Office Marine Environ. Washington, 1974-76; comdr. 11th Coast Guard Dist. Long Beach, Calif., 1976-78; comdr. Atlantic Area and 3d Coast Guard Dist. N.Y.C., 1978-81; ret., 1981; sr. v.p. J.J. Henry Co. (marine engrs.), N.Y.C., 1981-86; maritime cons., 1986—; prin. U.S. negotiator to tech. programs Intergovtl. Maritime Consultative Orgn., UN, 1962-71. Contbg. author: Ship Design and Construction, 1980; Contbr. articles to profl. jours. Decorated D.S.M. with gold star, Legion of Merit with gold star, Meritorious Service medal with gold star, Coast Guard Commendation medal. Fellow Royal Instn. Naval Architects, Soc. Naval Architects (Land medalist 1982); mem. Sigma Xi. Clubs: Propeller, Army Navy, N.Y. Yacht.

PRICE, ROBERT STANLEY, lawyer; b. Phila., Jan. 21, 1937; s. Benjamin and Estelle B. (Muchnick) P.; m. Emilie W. Kirschbaum, June 27, 1965; children: Louise W., Marianna R. BA, Kenyon Coll., 1958; LLB, Yale U., 1961. Bar: Pa. 1963, U.S. Dist. Ct. (ea. dist.) Pa. 1963, U.S. Ct. Appeals (3d cir.) 1963, N.Y. 1993. Assoc. Dechert, Price & Rhoads, Phila., 1961-63; asst. tax atty. Smith Kline & French, Phila., 1963-67; tax atty. Pa. Central Transp. Co., Phila., 1967-70; tax counsel IU Internat., Phila., 1970-72; ptnr. Townsend, Elliott & Munson, Phila., 1972-76; ptnr. Pepper, Hamilton & Scheetz, Phila., 1977-86; ptnr. Saul, Ewing, Remick & Saul, 1986-93, spl. cons. 1994—. Served with U.S. Army, 1961-62. Mem. Phila. Bar Assn., Pa. Bar, ABA (tax exempt fin. com.), Alpha Delta Phi Internat. (pres. 1975-78). Club: Racquet of Phila. (v.p. 1987-88). Author ABCs of Industrial Development Bonds, 1981, 5th edit., 1990; contbr. articles to legal jours. Home: 1034 W Upsal St Philadelphia PA 19119-3715 Office: Saul Ewing Remick & Saul 3800 Centre Sq W Philadelphia PA 19102

PRICE, SANDRA HOFFMAN, secondary school educator; b. Emden, Ill., July 24, 1935; d. William Frederick and Grace May (Randolph) Hoffman; m. Arthur Elliott Price, Jr., Dec. 27, 1957; 1 child, Anne Marie Price Powell. BS in Math. Tchg., U. Ill., 1957, MA in Math., 1962. Tchr. Ill. Pub. Schs., 1957-69, Libertyville (Ill.) Pub. Sch. Dist. #70, 1970—; adj. staff Coll. Lake County, Grayslake, Ill., 1972-81, Nat.-Louis U., Evanston, Ill., 1996; interdisciplinary team leader Highland Sch., Libertyville, 1979—. Contbr. articles to profl. jours. Pres. Litchfield (Ill.) Women's Club, 1964, Libertyville (Ill.) Edn. Assn., 1979. Univ. scholar-bronze tablet U. Ill., Urbana, 1957; Acad. Yr. fellow NSF, 1961. Mem. Nat. Coun. Tchrs. Math., Phi Beta Kappa, Phi Kappa Phi. Methodist. Office: Libertyville Pub Schs Dist 70 310 W Rockland Rd Libertyville IL 60048-2739

PRICE, THEODORA HADZISTELIOU, individual and family therapist; b. Athens, Greece, Oct. 1, 1938; came to U.S. 1967; d. Ioannis and Evangelia (Emmanuel) Hadzisteliou; m. David C. Long Price, Dec. 26, 1966 (div. 1989); children: Morgan N., Alkes D.L. BA in History/Archaeology, U. Athens, 1961; DPhil, U. Oxford, Eng., 1966; MA in Clin. Social Work, U. Chgo., 1988; Diploma in Piano Teaching, Nat. Conservatory, Athens, 1958. Lic. clin. social worker. Mus. asst. and resident tutor U. Sydney, Australia, 1966-67; instr. anthropology Adelphi U., N.Y.C., 1967-68; archaeologist Hebrew Union Coll., Gezer, Israel, 1968; asst. prof. classical archaeology/art U. Chgo., 1968-70; jr. rsch. fellow Harvard Ctr. Hellenic Studies, Washington, 1970-71; clin. social worker Harbor Light Ctr., Salvation Army, Chgo., 1988-89; therapist Inst. Motivational Devel., Lombard, Ill., 1989-90; caseworker Jewish Family & Community Svc., Chgo., 1989-90; staff therapist Family Svc. Ctrs. of South Cook County, Chicago Heights, 1990-91; pvt. practice child, adolescent, family therapy Bolingbrook, Ill., 1991—; dir. counseling svcs., clin. supr., psychotherapist The Family Link, Inc., Chgo., 1993; therapist children, adolescents and families dept. foster care Catholic Charities, Chgo., 1993-94; individual and family therapist South Ctrl. Cmty. Svcs. Individual-Family Counseling Svcs., Chgo., 1994—; staff therapist Cen. Bapt. Family Svcs., Chgo., 1991, Gracell Rehab., Chgo., 1991-92; casework supr., counselor Epilepsy Found. Greater Chgo., 1992-93; lectr. in field; bd. mem., counselor Naperville Sch. for Gifted and Talented, 1982-84. Author: (monograph) Kourotrophos, Cults and Representations of the Greek Nursing Deities, 1978; contbr. articles to profl. jours. Meyerstein Traveling awardee, Oxford, Eng., 1963, 64; Sophocies venizelos scholar, 1962-65; nominated Internat. Woman of Yr. for 1995-96 Internat. Biog. Ctr., 20th Century Achievement award, 1996. Mem. NASW, Nat. Acad. Clin. Social Workers, Ill. Clin. Social Workers. Avocations: yoga, piano playing. Home and Office: 10 Pebble Ct Bolingbrook IL 60440-1557 *Nobody stands alone, for each of us partakes and contributes to universal energy and creation. Every thought or action has progressively timeless impact. Therefore, working in helping people is influencing the flow of creation.*

PRICE, THOMAS BENJAMIN, former textile company executive; b. W. Jefferson, N.C., Aug. 23, 1920; s. Avery Asper and Jenny L. (Goss) P.; m. Judith Ostberg, Jan. 28, 1950; children: Jonathan R., Gregory W., Timothy C. B.S. in Textile Engring., N.C. State U., 1941. With J.P. Stevens & Co., Inc., 1941-83, corp. v.p., 1964-68, pres. Domestics and Allied Products div., 1971-74, corporate group v.p., 1974-83, also dir., mem. exec. com., chmn.'s office. Served to lt. comdr. USNR, World War II, Korean Conflict. Mem. Am. Arbitration Council, Sigma Tau Sigma, Phi Psi. Clubs: Pine Valley (Clementon, N.J.); Royal Poincianna (Naples, Fla.); Lake Sunapee Golf, Lake Sunapee Yacht (New London, N.H.), U.S. Srs. Golf Assn. Home: 530 Turtle Hatch Rd Naples FL 33940-8541 also: PO Box 1245 New London NH 03257-1245

PRICE, THOMAS EMILE, investment company executive; b. Cin., Nov. 4, 1921; s. Edwin Charles and Lillian Elizabeth (Werk) P.; BBA, U. Tex., 1943; postgrad. Harvard U., 1944; m. Lois Margaret Gahr Matthews, Dec. 21, 1970 (dec. Nov. 26, 1988); 1 child by previous marriage, Dorothy Elizabeth Wood Price; stepchildren: Bruce Albert, Mark Frederic, Scott Herbert, Eric William Matthews. Co-founder Price Y Cia, Inc., Cin., 1946—, sec., 1946-75, treas., 1946—, pres., 1975—, also dir.; co-founder Price Paper Products Corp. (merger Price Y Cia, Inc.), Cin., 1956, treas., 1956-75, pres., 1975-90, sec., 1956-75, also dir.; mem. Cin. Regional Export Expansion Com., 1961-63; dir. Cen. Acceptance Corp., 1954-55; founding mem. and dir. Cin. Royals Basketball Club Co., 1959-73. Referee Tri-State Tennis Championships, 1963-68, Western Tennis Championships, 1969-70, Nat. Father-Son Clay Court Championships, 1974—, Tennis Grand Masters Championships, 1975-77, 80; vol. coach Walnut Hills High Sch. Boys Team, Cin., 1970-81; chmn. and coach Greater Cin. Jr. Davis Cup, 1968-78; co-founder Tennis Patrons of Cin., Inc., 1951, trustee, 1951-79, pres., 1958-63, 68; co-founder Greater Cin. Tennis Assn., 1979. Participant in fund raising drives Cin. Boys Amateur Baseball Fund; chmn. Greater Cin. YMCA World Svc. Fund Drive, 1962-64; trustee Cin. World Affairs Inst., 1957-60, gen. chmn., 1959. 1st lt. USAAF, 1943-46; ETO. Elected to Western Hills High Sch. Sport Hall of Honor; named hon. Almaden Grand Master, 1980. Cin. Met. Tennis Tournament renamed Thomas E. Price Cin. Met. Tennis Torunament, 1991. Mem. Cin. World Trade Club (pres. 1959), U.S. Trotting Assn., Cin. Hist. Soc., U.S. Lawn Tennis Assn. (trustee 1959-60, 62-64, chmn. Jr. Davis Cup com. 1960-62, founder of Col. James H. Bishop award 1962), Ohio Valley Tennis Assn. (trustee 1948—, Gillespie award 1957, Dredge award 1973, pres. 1952-53, Tom Price award named in his honor at Jr. Davis Cup 1988), Western Tennis Assn. (trustee 1951—, mem. championships adv. com. 1969-78, pres. 1959-60, Hall of Fame, 1994, Melvin R. Bergman Disting. Svc. award 1979), Greater Cin. Tennis Assn. (named after and recipient of Tom Price award 1989), Assn. Tennis Profls. (nat. championship adv. 1979—), Cin. Country CLub, Univ. Club, Cin. Tennis Club (hon. life, pres. 1957-58, adv. com. 1959—, Founders and Guardians award 1983), Indoor Tennis CLub, Ea. Hills Indoor Tennis Club, Cin. Rotary, Phi Gamma Delta. Republican. Presbyterian. Nationally ranked boys 15, 1936, jr. tennis player, 1939. History columnist Tennis Talk Greater Cin., 1978-80. Home: 3249 Epworth Ave Cincinnati OH 45211-7037 Office: Dixie Terminal Buildin Ste 216 Cincinnati OH 45202 *Personal philosophy: Follow the Ten Commandments and the Golden Rule.*

PRICE, THOMAS FREDERICK, theatre educator; b. Salt Lake City, June 19, 1937; s. Thomas William P. and Caryl Susan Brown; children: Devin, Jennifer. BA in Drama, Pomona Coll., 1960; MA in Theatre, San Francisco State U., 1962; PhD in Drama, Stanford U., 1968. Asst. prof. English U. of the Pacific, Stockton, Calif., 1968-70; asst. prof. drama U.S. Internat. U., Sch. Performing Arts, San Diego, 1970-74; archivist, curator The Philibrick Theatre Libr., Los Altos Hills, Calif., 1975-85; prof. English Tianjin (China) Normal U., 1985-87; adj. prof. theatre So. Oreg. State Coll., Ashland, 1991-92; assoc. prof. English Tanmkang U., Taipei, Taiwan, 1993—; ednl. broadcaster KPFA-FM, L.A., 1960-62, KSRO-FM, Ashland, Oreg., 1990-92. Author: Edward Gordon Craig and the Theatre of the Imagination, 1985, Dramatic Structure and Meaning, 1992; contbr. articles to profl. jours. Mem. Calif. Scholarship Fedn. (hon. life), Assn. for Theatre in Higher Edn.

PRICE, THOMAS RANSONE, neurologist, educator; b. Hampton, Va., July 31, 1934; s. William Spencer and Virginia (Ransone) P.; m. Nancy Worrell Franklin, June 28, 1958; children: Franklin Ransone, Catherine Blair. BA in Psychology, U. Va., 1956, MD, 1960. Diplomate Am. Bd. Psychiatry and Neurology. Chief resident in neurology U. Va. Hosp., Charlottesville, 1965-66; instr. U. Va. Hosp., 1966-67, U. Md. Sch. Medicine, Balt., 1967-68; asst. prof. U. Md. Sch. Medicine, 1969-72, assoc. prof., 1972-78, prof., 1978—. Editor: Cerebro Vascular Diseases, 1979; contbr. articles to profl. jours. Mem. Gov.'s Task Force on Alzheimers Disease, Md., 1984-88; bd. dirs. Nat. Stroke Assn., 1990—; bd. dirs., treas. Cerebral Cavernous Malformation Found., 1993—. Fellow Am. Neurological Assn., Am. Acad. Neurology (chmn. bylaws com. 1978-79, 83-85), Am. Heart Assn. (chmn. stroke sub-com. 1986-87); mem. Md. Neurologic Soc. (pres. 1979-80). Office: U Md Hosp 22 S Greene St Baltimore MD 21201-1544

PRICE, TOM, journalist; b. Pitts., May 26, 1946; s. H. Samuel and Anna Mae (Nicholson) P.; m. Susan Crites; 1 child, Julianna Margaret. BS Journalism, Ohio U., 1968. Reporter/editor Athens (Ohio) Messenger, 1968-73; freelance writer, 1973-75; Wash. corrs. Dayton Daily News/Cox Newspapers, Washington, 1982-96; urban affairs/politics writer Dayton Journal Herald, 1975-82; freelance writer, 1996—. Co-author: (with Susan Crites Price) The Working Parents Help Book: Practical Advice for Dealing with the Day-to-Day Challenges of Kids and Careers, 1994 (Parent's Choice award, Scholastic Book Club selection), Working Parents Lifeline, Working Solutions Column. Presbyterian. Avocations: photography, hiking, travel, reading.

PRICE, TREVOR ROBERT PRYCE, psychiatrist, educator; b. Concord, N.H., Nov. 29, 1943; s. Trevor Alaric and Beatrice (Dinsmore) Pryce; m. Margaret Ann Bowring, June 8, 1991; children: Meghan Jennifer, Sara Brittany; children by previous marriage: Trevor Breton, Elizabeth Anne. BA, Yale U., 1965; MD, Columbia U., 1969. Diplomate Am. Bd. Psychiatry and Neurology (examiner 1985—), Am. Bd. Internal Medicine, Nat. Bd. Med. Examiners. Intern in medicine Med. Ctr. U. Calif., San Francisco, 1969-70; resident in internal medicine Med. Ctr. of U. Calif., San Francisco, 1972-74; resident in psychiatry Dartmouth Med. Sch., Hanover, N.H., 1974-77, asst. prof., assoc. prof. psychiatry and medicine, 1977-85; assoc. prof., prof. psychiatry U. Pa. Sch. Medicine, Phila., 1985-88; dir. psychiat. in-patient svcs. Hosp. of U. Pa., 1985-88; prof. psychiatry Med. Coll. Pa. and Hahnemann U., Pitts., 1989-90, prof. psychiatry and medicine, 1991—; tenured prof. psychiatry Med. Coll. Pa., 1993; chmn. dept. psychiatry Med. Coll. Pa. and Hahnemann U., Allegheny Campus, Pitts., 1989-95, chmn. dept. physhiatry, 1995—; sr. assoc. dean Med. Coll. Pa. and Hahnemann U., Pitts., 1993-95; pres. Allegheny Neuropsychiat. Inst. Med. Coll. Pa., Pitts., 1992-94; exec. dir. Allegheny Neuropsychiat. Inst., Pitts., 1994—; chmn. Dept. Psychiatry Med. Coll. of Pa., Hahnemann U., 1995—; bd. dirs. Coll. Health Consortium, Inc., Phila., Highland Dr. Rsch. and Edn. Found., Yale Club Pitts., Pitts. Psychoanalytic Found.; mem. blue ribbon bd. Alzheimer's Disease Alliance, Western Pa., 1989—. Mem. editl. bd. Convulsive Therapy, 1984-94, Jour. Neuropsychiatry and Clin. Neurosci., 1992—, Alleghany Gen. Hosp. Jour. Neurosci., 1992—, Seminars in Neuropsychiatry, 1995—; editl. reviewer 12 psychiat. and med. jours., 1978—; contbr. chpts. to books and articles in profl. jours. Mem. N.H. Commn. on Laws Effecting Mental Health, 1974-75; bd. dirs. Advanced Studies Program, Friends of St. Paul's Sch., Concord, N.H., 1983-87. Recipient William C. Menninger award Ctrl. Neuropsychiat. Assn., 1977, Faculty Teaching award dept. psychiatry Dartmouth Med. Sch., 1984, Pres. award for Exceptional Achievement AHERF, 1994, numerous grants. Fellow Am. Psychiat. Assn.; mem. Pa. Psychiat. Assn., Am. Coll. Psychiatrists, Am. Assn. Chairmen of Depts. Psychiatry, Soc. Biol. Psychiatry, Am. Neuropsychiat. Assn. (bd. dirs., exec. dir. 1995), Assn. for Acad. Psychiatry, Am. Assn. Dirs. Psychiat. Residency Tng., Assn. Acad. Psychiatry, Assn. Convulsive Therapy, Assn. Medicine and Psychiatry, Yale Club Pitts., H-Y-P Club Pitts. Avocations: fly fishing, tennis, reading, piano. Office: Med Coll Pa and Hahnemann Univ Dept Psychiatry 320 E North Ave Pittsburgh PA 15212-4772 also: Broad and Vine Sts M/S 403 Philadelphia PA 19102-1192 also: Eastern Pa Psychiat Inst Rm 166 3200 Henry Ave Philadelphia PA 19129 *Life at its best is being continually challenged and fully engaged, yet not self-absorbed.*

PRICE, WESTCOTT WILKIN, III, health care company executive; b. Glendale, Calif., May 6, 1939; s. Westcott Wilkin Jr. and Edna Johnson P.; m. Hillary Clark Haney, Apr. 12, 1941; children: Christopher, Gretchen, Wendy. BS in Bus., U. Colo., 1961; MBA, U. So. Calif., 1967. V.p., COO Calif. Med. Ctrs., L.A., 1970-73; pres., CEO Wm. Flaggs Inc., Commerce, Calif., 1973-80; pres., vice chmn. FHP Inc., Fountain Valley, Calif., 1981—. Bd. dirs. FHP Found., Long Beach, Calif., 1985—; bd. govs. U. So. Calif. Sch. Pub. Adminstrn., Los Angeles, 1987—. Served to lt. (j.g.) USN, 1961-63. Republican. Episcopalian. Club: Calif. (Los Angeles). Office: FHP Internat Corp 9900 Talbert Ave Fountain Valley CA 92708*

PRICE, WILLIAM JAMES, organization executive; b. Alexandria, Ohio, Dec. 3, 1918; s. Lewis J. and Mary (Wright) P.; m. Betty Kistler, Aug. 22, 1943; children—Mary Barbara, Sarah Margaret, Lewis Charles. A.B., Denison U., 1940, Sc.D., 1969; M.S., Rensselaer Poly. Inst., 1941, Ph.D., 1948; DSc (hon.), Denison U., 1969. Research physicist Bendix Aviation Corp., 1942-45, Battelle Meml. Inst., Columbus, Ohio, 1948-50; head dept. physics Air Force Inst. Tech., Dayton, Ohio, 1950-57; chief modern physics br. Aero. Research Lab., Dayton, 1957-59; chief scientist Aero. Research Lab., 1959-63; exec. dir. Air Force Office Sci. Research, 1963-74; mgmt. cons., 1974-78; coordinator World Peacemakers, 1978—; instr. Rensselaer Poly. Inst., 1948; prof. Air Force Inst. Tech., Dayton, Ohio, 1950-57; An organizer Yokefellowship in Nation's Capital, 1964; fed. exec. fellow The Brookings Instn., 1967-68; chmn. Congl. Commn. Govt. Procurement Study Group Research and Devel., 1970-71. Author: Nuclear Radiation Detection, rev. edit, 1964; Co-author: National Security and Christian Faith, 1982, Building Christian Community Pursuing Peace with Justice, 1983, (handbook) World Peacemaker Groups, 1979; Author: also numerous articles. Mem. The Ch. of the Saviour, 1972—; Bd. dirs. Yokefellows Internat., 1967-71, Washington Lift, Inc., 1971-76, World Peacemaker, 1978—. Recipient Alumni citation Denison U., 1965, Outstanding Unit award citation Office Aerospace Research, 1965, Outstanding Unit award citation Air Force Inst. Tech., 1964. Mem. Am. Phys. Soc., A.A.A.S., Phi Beta Kappa, Sigma Xi, Tau Beta Pi (hon.). Home: 11427 Scottsbury Ter Germantown MD 20876-6010

PRICE, WILLIAM JAMES, IV, investment banker; b. Balt., Oct. 6, 1924; s. William James 3d and Frances (Robbins) P.; m. Marjorie Beard, Dec. 6, 1952; children: Marjorie, Jonathan Robbins, William James V, Juliet Robbins. B.S., Yale U., 1949. Propr. Price & Co., 1949-52; with Alex. Brown & Sons, Balt., 1952—, gen. partner, 1959—, mng. dir., 1984-89; bd. dirs. Alex Brown Cash Res. Fund, chmn., 1981—; bd. dirs. Flag Investors Tel. Income Fund, Emerging Growth Fund, Boca Rsch., Inc. Trustee Washington Coll., St. Paul's Sch. Served with inf. AUS, 1943-46, ETO. Decorated Bronze Star, Purple Heart with oak leaf cluster, Combat Infantry badge. Mem. Nat. Assn. Securities Dealers (bd. govs. 1964-66, vice chmn. 1966). Home: 6885 N Ocean Blvd Ocean Ridge FL 33435-3342 Office: Alex Brown & Sons Inc 222 Lakeview Ave West Palm Beach FL 33401-6145

PRICE, WILLIAM RAY, JR., state supreme court judge; b. Fairfield, Iowa, Jan. 30, 1952; s. William Ray and Evelyn Jean (Darnell) P.; m. Susan Marie Trainor, Jan. 4, 1975; children: Emily Margret, William Joseph Dodds. BA with high distinction, U. Iowa, 1974; student, Yale U., 1974-75; JD cum laude, Washington and Lee U., 1978. Bar: Mo. 1978, U.S. Dist. Ct. (we. dist.) Mo. 1978, U.S. Ct. Claims 1978, U.S. Ct. Appeals (8th cir.) 1985. Assoc. Lathrop & Norquist, Kansas City, Mo., 1978-84, ptnr., 1984-92, chmn. bus. litigation sect., 1987-88, 90-92, mem. exec. com., 1989-92; judge Supreme Ct. Mo., Jefferson City, 1992—; mem. G.L.V. Zumwalt monitoring com. U.S. Dist. Ct. (we. dist.) Mo., Kansas City. Pres. Kansas City Bd. Police Commrs.; mem. Together Ctr. & Family Devel. Ctr., Kansas City; chmn. merit selection com. U.S. marshal Western Dist. of Mo., Kansas City; bd. dirs. Truman Med. Ctr., Kansas City. Rockefeller fellow, 1974-75; Burks scholar Washington & Lee U., 1976. Mem. Christian Ch. Office: Supreme Ct Mo PO Box 150 Jefferson City MO 65102-0150

PRICE, WAYNE FRANCIS, counseling administrator; b. Bogue, Kans., Feb. 11, 1935; s. William C. and Lena I. (Hecke) P.; m. Alice M. Fitzpatrick, July 25, 1964; children: Wayne F. Jr., Elizabeth Anne. AB, Ft. Hays State U., 1957; MEd, U. N.D., 1963; postgrad., Wayne State U. Nat. cert. counselor; nat. cert. career counselor; nat. cert. sch. counselor; lic. prof. counselor Mich. Counselor Lamphere High Sch., 1963-64, 69-75; asst. prin. Page Jr. High, Madison Heights, Mich., 1964-68; prin. Page Jr. High, Madison Heights, 1968-69; adj. counselor Oakland Community Coll., Bloomfield Hills, Mich., 1969—; dir. guidance Lamphere Schs., Madison Heights, Mich., 1975—. Contbr. articles to prof. jours. Mem. ACA, Am. Vocat. Assn., Nat. Assn. Collegiate Registrars and Admission Officers, Assn. for Counselor Edn. and Supervision, Am. Coll. Pers. Assn., Am. Fedn. Tchrs., Am. Sch. Coun. Assn., Assn. for Adult Devel. and Aging, Assn. for Assessment in Counseling, Lamphere Fedn. Tchrs., Mich. Assn. for Adult Devel. and Aging, Mich. Assn. Coll. Admission Counselors, Mich. Counseling Assn., Mich. Assn. for Counselor Edn. and Supervision, Mich. Assn. for Measurement and Evaluation in Guidance (pres.), Mich. Assn. Specialists in Group Work, Mich. Career Devel. Assn. (treas. 1994—), Mich. Coll. Pers. Assn., Mich. Sch. Counselors Assn., Mich. Assn. for Humanistic Edn. and Develop., Mich. Assn. for Multi-Cultural Develop., Nat. Assn. Coll. Admission Counselors, Nat. Career Devel. Assn., Oakland Assn. for Counseling and Devel. (former pres.), Phi Delta Kappa. Office: 610 W 13 Mile Rd Madison Heights MI 48071-1858

PRICER, WILBUR DAVID, electrical engineer; b. Des Moines, July 22, 1935; s. Wilbur Ray and Mary Elizabeth (Berner) P.; m. Nancy Loizeaux, Oct. 10, 1964; children: Douglas, Amy, Timothy, Edward. AB in Physics, Middlebury Coll., 1959; BSEE, MIT, 1959, MSEE, 1959. Engr. IBM Corp., Poughkeepsie, 1959-70, sr. engr., East Fishkill, N.Y., 1970-83, sr. mem. tech. staff, Essex Junction, Vt., 1983—; adj. prof. elec. engring. U. Vt., 1984-90; pres. Solid State Circuits Council, 1980-81; mem. editorial bd. Spectrum Mag., 1990-92. Editor Jour. of Solid State Circuits, 1983-86. Patentee in field. Fellow, IEEE; mem. Internat. Solid State Circuits Conf. (program chmn. 1976, chmn. 1988—), program Evaluator Accreditation Bd. for Engring. and Tech., 1990-95, Sigma Xi. Methodist. Home: RR 1 Box 1689 Charlotte VT 05445-9746 Office: IBM Dept N37 Bldg 863-2 Essex Junction VT 05452

PRICHARD, EDGAR ALLEN, lawyer; b. Brockton, Mont., Mar. 6, 1920; s. Clifford B. and Helen (Ouwersloat) P.; m. Nancy M. McCandlish, Apr. 7, 1945; children: Helen Montague (Mrs. Thomas C. Foster), Robert Walton, Thomas Morgan. Student, U. Tulsa, 1937-39, U. Okla., 1940-41; LL.B., U. Va., 1948. Bar: Va. 1947. Ptnr. Boothe, Prichard & Dudley, Fairfax, Va., 1948-87, McGuire, Woods, Battle & Boothe, Fairfax, 1987—; bd. dirs. George Mason Bank Shares, George Mason Bank; bd. editors Va. Law Rev., 1947-48. Mem. gen. bd. Nat. Coun. Chs., 1966-72; councilman City of Fairfax, 1953-64, mayor, 1964-68; chmn. Fairfax Dem. Com., 1962-64, 69-72; mem. Va. Bd. Elections, 1970-75; mem. Lynch Found., pres., 1981-82; trustee Trinity Episcopal Sch. Ministry, 1977—, chmn., 1985-95; bd. visitors George Mason U., 1982-91, rector, 1988-91; chmn. Fairfax Parking Authority, 1991-95; mem. bd. Fairfax Econ. Devel. Authority; mem. George Mason U. Found., pres., 1971-72. Fellow ABA, Va. Bar Assn.; mem. Fairfax Bar Assn. (pres. 1964), Va. State Bar (v.p. 1969), Am. Law Inst., Diosesan Missionary Soc. Va. (pres. 1986-88), Urban Land Inst., 4th Cir. Jud. Conf., Order of Coif, Raven Soc., Fairfax Racquet Club, Inc. (chmn.), Fairfax Country Club, Spl. Forces Club (London), Lambda Alpha, Lambda Chi Alpha. Episcopalian (lay reader, warden). Home: 3820 Chain Bridge Rd Fairfax VA 22030-3904 Office: McGuire Woods Battle & Boothe 8280 Greensboro Dr Mc Lean VA 22102-3807

PRICHARD, JOHN ROBERT STOBO, academic administrator, law educator; b. London, Jan. 17, 1949; arrived in Can., 1951; s. John Stobo and Joan Suzanne (Webber) P.; m. Ann Elizabeth Wilson, Dec. 19, 1975; children: Wilson, Kenneth, John. Honors Econs. student, Swarthmore Coll., 1967-70; MBA, U. Chgo., 1971; LLB, U. Toronto, Ont., Can., 1975; LLM, Yale U., 1976. Asst. prof. faculty of law U. Toronto, 1976-81, assoc. prof., 1981-88, prof., 1988—, assoc. Ctr. for Indsl. Rels., 1979—, dean faculty of law, 1984-1990, pres. univ., 1990—; vis. assoc. prof. Yale U. Law Sch., New Haven, Conn., 1982-83; vis. prof. Harvard U. Law Sch., Cambridge, Mass., 1983-84; mem. Ont. Law Reform Commn., Toronto, 1986-1990; chmn. Fed., Provincial and Territorial Review of Liability and Compensation on Health Care, Ottawa, Ont., 1987-90. Co-author: Canadian Business Corporations, 1977, Canadian Competition Policy, 1979, Choice of Governing Instrument, 1982; co-author, editor: Public Ownership: The Calculus of Instrument Choice, 1983. Mem. Law Soc. Upper Can. Avocation: children, fishing. Office: U Toronto, 27 King's College Cir, Toronto, ON Canada M5S 1A1

PRICHARD, PETER S., newspaper editor; b. Auburn, Calif., Dec. 18, 1944; s. Jarvis B. and Floris C. (Smith) P.; m. Ann O'Donnell, Nov. 13, 1971; children: Oliver W., Lindsay M. AB, Dartmouth Coll., 1966. Wire editor Greenwich (Conn.) Time, 1970-72; reporter Democrat and Chronicle, Rochester, N.Y., 1972-75; assoc. news dir. WOKR TV, Rochester, N.Y., 1975-76; reporter Times Union, Rochester, 1976-78; asst. to chmn. communications Gannett Co. Inc., Rochester, 1980-82, dir. communications, Office of Chief Exec., 1980-82; columns editor USA Today, Washington, 1982-83, dep. assoc. editorial dir., 1983-84, assoc. editorial dir., 1984-86, mng. editor spl. projects, 1986-87, sr. editor, 1988, editor, sr. v.p., news, 1988—; sr. v.p. News Gannett Co. Inc., Washington, 1988—, chief news exec., 1990—. Author: The Making of McPaper: The Inside Story of USA Today, 1987 (Frank Luther Moh Rsch. award Kappa Tau Alpha 1987). Vice chmn., bd. trustees Washington Journalism Ctr., 1989—. With U.S. Army, 1967-69, Vietnam. Decorated Bronze Star. Mem. Nat. Press Club, Am. Soc. Newspaper Editors (Reston, Va.) (various coms. 1985—). Office: USA Today 1000 Wilson Blvd Arlington VA 22209-3901

PRICKETT, DAVID CLINTON, physician; b. Fairmont, W.Va., Nov. 26, 1918; s. Clinton Evert and Mary Anna (Gottschalk) P.; m. Mary Ellen Holt, June 29, 1940; children: David C., Rebecca Ellen, William Radcliffe, Mary Anne, James Thomas, Sara Elizabeth; m. Pamela S. Blackstone, Nov. 17, 1991. AB, W.Va. U., 1944; MD, U. Louisville, 1946; MPH, U. Pitts., 1955. Lab. asst., instr. in chemistry, W.Va. U., 1943; intern, Louisville Gen. Hosp., 1947; surg. resident St. Joseph's Hosp., Parkersburg, W.Va., 1948-49; gen. practice, 1949-50, 55-61; physician USAF, N.Mex., 1961-62, U.S. Army, Calif., 1963-64, San Luis Obispo County Hosp., 1965-66, So. Calif. Edison Co., 1981-84; assoc. physician indsl. and gen. practice Los Angeles County, Calif., 1967—; med. dir. S. Gate plant GM, 1969-71; physician staff City of L.A., 1971-76; relief med. practice Applachia summer seasons, 1977, 1986, 1988-95. Med. Officer USPHS, Navajo Indian Reservation, Tohatchi (N.Mex.) Health Ctr., 1953-55, surgeon, res. officer, 1957-59; pres. W.Va. Pub. Health Assn., 1951-52, health officer, 1951-53, sec. indsl. and pub. health sect. W.Va. Med. Assn., 1956. Author: The Newer Epidemiology, 1962, rev., 1990, Public Health, A Science Resolvable by Mathematics, 1965. Served to 2d lt. AUS, 1943-46. Dr. Thomas Parran fellow U. Pitts. Sch. Pub. Health, 1955; named to Hon. Order Ky. Cols. Mem. Am. Occupational Med. Assn., Western Occupational Med. Assn., Am. Med. Assn., Calif. Med. Assn., L.A. County Med. Assn., Am. Acad. Family Physicians, Phi Chi. Address: PO Box 4032 Whittier CA 90607-4032

PRICKETT, GORDON ODIN, mining, mineral and energy engineer; b. Morris, Minn., Nov. 26, 1935; s. Glenn Irvin and Edna Margaret (Erickson)

P.; m. Jean Carolyn Strobush, Oct. 8, 1958; children: Karen Joan Keating, Laura Jean, Glenn Thomas. B Mining Engring., U. Minn., 1958, MS in Mineral Engring. and Econs., 1965. Registered profl. engr., Mo., Ill. U.S. Steel fellow U. Minn., Mpls., 1963-65; rsch. mineral engr. Internat. Minerals & Chem. Corp., Skokie, Ill., 1965-68; mgmt. sci. cons. Computer Mgmt. Cons., Northfield, Ill., 1968-71; mgr. tech. systems Duval Corp., Tucson, Ariz., 1971-77; dir. mgmt. info. systems Arch Mineral Corp., St. Louis, 1977-78; supr. mine planning projects Peabody Coal Co., St. Louis, 1978-82; mgr. elec. tech. transfer, nuclear plant simulator, rsch. Union Electric Co., St. Louis, 1983-95; tech. network advisor GordMett, Ltd., Aitkin, Minn., 1995—; presenter papers at industry confs. Contbr. articles to profl. jours. Co-founder, chmn. Lake Forest-Lake Bluff (Ill.) Com. for Equal Opportunity, 1968-71; com. Confluence St. Louis, 1987-95; bd. dirs., officer ch. bds., polit. twp. orgn. Lake Forest, Tucson, St. Louis, Aitkin, Minn., 1968—. Lt. USN, 1958-63, naval aviator, Cuba; to comdr. USNR, 1963-79. Mem. AIME (chair program com. 1958—), Assn. Quality and Participation (chair programs 1986-90), Norwegian Soc. St. Louis, LWV (charter mem. Brainerd Lakes uint, 1996—), Engrs. Club St. Louis (chair affiliated socs. and pub. affairs. 1987-88, 93-95). Avocations: running, photography, canoeing, Norwegian Singing Club, skiing. Home and Office: Nord Lake HC 5 Box 16 CC Aitkin MN 56431

PRIDE, CHARLEY, singer; b. Sledge, Miss., Mar. 18, 1939; m. Rozene Pride, Dec. 28, 1956; children—Kraig, Dion, Angela. Grad. high sch. Formerly with constrn. cos., refining plants; profl. baseball player with Detroit, Memphis Red Sox, Birmingham Black Barons (all Negro Am. League), Los Angeles Angels (Am. League). Appeared with WSM Grand Ole Opry, Nashville, 1967, Lawrence Welk Show, ABC-TV; appeared on Joey Bishop Show, ABC-TV; appeared with Ralph Emery Show, WSM-TV, Nashville; appeared with Syndicated Bill Anderson, Bobby Lord and Wilburn Brothers, Hee Haw, Tom Jones Show, Flip Wilson Show, Johnny Cash Show, numerous other TV shows; recorded for RCA; albums include: Country Charley Pride, Charley Pride Sings Heart Songs, Charley, Happiness, She's Just Sunday, Happiness of Having You, Charley Pride IN Person, Christmas in My Hometown, Did You Think to Pray, Roll on Mississippi, There's a Little Bit of Hank in Me, You're My Jamaica, Best of Charley Pride, The Best There Is, Greatest Hits, Night Games, Power of Love, Country Feelin, Songs of Love, A Sunshiny Day, Charley Pride Live, 1994; recorded songs Kiss an Angel Good Mornin', Snakes Crawl at Night, Let the Chips Fall, Day You Stopped Loving Me, Does My Ring Hurt Your Finger, Let Me Help You Work It Out, Is Anyone Goin' to San Antone, Afraid of Losing You Again, Let Me Live, One of These Days, Whole Lotta Love; (Named Most Promising Male Artist, Country Song Roundup 1967, Male Vocalist of Year, Country Music Assn. 1971, 72, Entertainer of Yr. in Country Music 1971, winner Grammy awards for best scored rec. 1971, for best country vocal 1972, Trendsetter award Billboard 1970, Top Male Vocalist award Cashbox, Photoplay Gold Medal award 1976). Served with U.S. Army, 1956-58. Address: care Chardon Inc 3198 Royal Ln Ste 204 Dallas TX 75229-3798

PRIDE, DOUGLAS SPENCER, minister; b. Latrobe, Pa., Jan. 13, 1959; s. Spencer MacVeagh and Kathleen (Tidd) P.; m. Elizabeth Armstrong, June 5, 1982; children: Kathryn Elizabeth and Jennifer Suzanne (twins), Pamela Campbell. BA, Westminster Coll., 1980; MDiv, Pitts. Theol. Sem., 1983, DMin, 1993. Ordained to ministry Presbyn. Ch., 1983. Asst. pastor Shadyside Presbyn. Ch., Pitts., 1983-85, assoc. pastor, 1985-91; pastor The Presbyn. Ch. of Clearfield, Clearfield, Pa., 1992—; chaplain palliative care program West Pa. Hosp., 1983-86, Clearfield Hospice, 1996; bd. dirs. Krislund Camp and Conf. Ctr., chmn., 1995. Bd. dirs. Theol. Sem., 1983-86; mem. alumni coun. Westminster Coll., New Wilmington, Pa., 1986-90, pres., 1989-90; bd. dirs. Bethesda Ctr., Pitts.; 1st v.p. Spina Bifida Assn., Pitts., 1987-89, pres., 1989-93, bd. dirs., 1984—, sec. bd., 1985-87. Mem. Huntingdon Presbytery, Clearfield Curwensville Country Club. Republican. Avocations: tennis, racquetball, reading. Home: 2538 Meadow Rd Clearfield PA 16830-1140

PRIDEAUX, GARY DEAN, linguistics educator; b. Muskogee, Okla., Apr. 21, 1939; arrived in Can., 1966; s. Ivor Dean and Lorene Gertrude (Molohan) P.; m. Pamela Joyce Asquith, Oct. 7, 1989. BA in Physics, Rice U., 1961; PhD in Linguistics, U. Tex., 1966. Asst. prof. linguistics U. Alta., Edmonton, Can., 1966-71, assoc. prof., 1971-78, prof., 1978—; Fulbright lectr. Tottori U., Shimane U., Japan, 1967-68. Author: Psycholinguistics: The Experimental Study of Language, 1985; co-author: Strategies and Structures, 1986; mem. editorial com. Can. Jour. Linguistics, 1983-86; contbr. articles to profl. jours. Grantee Social Scis. and Humanities Rsch. Coun. Can., 1978, 80-82, 90-92, 93-96. Mem. Can. Linguistics Assn. (exec. com. 1972-79), Linguistic Soc. Am., Western Conf. on Linguistics (pres. 1981-82), Linguistic Assn. of Can. and the U.S. Avocations: swimming, sailing. Office: U Alta, Dept Linguistics, Edmonton, AB Canada T6G 2E7

PRIDHAM, THOMAS GRENVILLE, retired research microbiologist; b. Chgo., Oct. 10, 1920; s. Grenville and Gladys Etheral (Sloss) P.; m. Phyllis Sue Hokamp, July 1, 1943 (dec.); children: Pamela Sue, Thomas Foster, Grenville Thomas, Rolf Thomas, Montgomery Thomas; m. Edna Lee Boudreaux, Mar. 6, 1995. BS in Chemistry, U. Ill., 1943, PhD in Bacteriology, 1949. Instr. bacteriology U. Ill., Champaign-Urbana, 1947; rsch. microbiologist No. Regional Rsch. Lab., USDA, Peoria, Ill., 1948-51, 53-65, U.S. Indsl. Chems., Balt., 1951-52; supr. tech. ops. Acme Vitamins, Inc., Joliet, Ill., 1952-53; sr. rsch. biologist U.S. Borax Rsch. Corp., Anaheim, Calif., 1965-67; supervisory rsch. microbiologist No. Regional Rsch. Ctr. USDA, Peoria, 1967-81, head agrl. rsch. culture collection No. Regional Rsch. Lab., 1967-81; ret., 1981; cons. Mycogen Corp., San Diego, 1985-87; U.S. sr. scientist Fed. Republic Germany, Darmstadt, 1977. Contbg. author: Actinomycetales: The Boundary Microorganisms, 1974, Bergey's Manual of Determinative Bacteriology, 1974, Synopsis and Classification of Living Organisms, 1982; mem. editorial bd. Jour. Antibiotics, 1969-81; contbr. articles to Jour. Bacteriology, Applied Microbiology, Phytopathology, Actinomycetes, Mycologia, Devel. Indsl. Microbiology, Jour. Antibiotics, Internat. Bull. Bacteriological Nomenclature Taxonomy, Antibiotics Ann., Antimicrobial Agts., Chemotherapy, also others. With USNR, 1943-45, with Rsch. Res., 1945-54, lt. ret. Fulbright scholar, Italy, 1952; grantee Soc. Am. Bacteriologists, 1957. Fellow Am. Acad. Microbiology (ASM state network 1991—); mem. Am. Soc. Microbiology (com. mem., workshop presenter), Soc. Indsl. Microbiology, Mycol. Soc. Am., U.S. Fedn. Culture Collections (v.p. 1981). Episcopalian. Achievements include patents in fermentative production of riboflavin and of antibiotics; research in microbial culture collection technology and management, systematics of streptomycetes, industrial microbiology, and air pollution. Home: 38 Mayo Branch Brandy Keg Prestonsburg KY 41653

PRIDMORE, CHARLES FRANKLIN, JR., mechanical engineer; b. Washington, June 23, 1949; s. Charles F. Pridmore Sr. and Frances Ray (Couch) Soule; m. Mary Ann Meehan, Sept. 22, 1973; children: Colleen Marie, Scott Andrew. AA, Prince Georges C.C., 1987; BS Tech. Mgmt. cum laude, U. Md., 1990. Draftsman Shull Elec. Co., Brentwood, Md., 1972-74; sr. design draftsman Baxter Travenol, Silver Springs, Md., 1975-80; lead elec. designer Niro Atomizer, Columbia, Md., 1980-81; sr. mech. designer Rixon, Silver Spring, 1981-88; assoc. mech. engr. Rixon-Case Comm., Silver Spring, Md., 1981-88; mech. engr. Telecom. Techniques Corp., Germantown, Md., 1988—, sr. mech. engr., 1988-95; consulting engr. various bio-med. devices, Washington, 1988-90; product engr., lab. mgr. Telecom. Techniques Corp., centest product line, Germantown, 1992-95. Little league coach South Bowie (Md.) Boys/Girls Clubs, 1990, county baseball coach, 1991-94. Mem. Soc. Mfg. Engrs. (sr.), Soc. Plastics Engrs., Mason (32 degree, past master Harmony lodge # 17 FAAM Washington), Alpha Sigma Lambda, Phi Kappa Phi. Republican. Southern Baptist. Avocations: hunting, fishing, training labrador retrievers, gardening, travel. Home: 4106 New Haven Dr Bowie MD 20716-1062 Office: Telecom Techniques Corp 20400 Observation Dr Germantown MD 20876-4092

PRIDMORE, ROY DAVIS, government official; b. Gaffney, S.C., May 18, 1925; s. Davis Bailey and Ethel (Hughes) P.; m. Doris Hedy Glatzl, July 16, 1960; children: Lisa Ann, David Michael. Cert., Columbus U., Washington, 1949, Am. Inst., Washington, 1953, U.S. Dept. Agr. Grad. Sch., Washington, 1957. Pers. asst. Dept. Army, Fort Myer, Va., 1955-58; staff asst. D.C. Hwy. Dept., Washington, 1962-67; adminstrv. asst. Dept. Transp., Washington, 1958-62, adminstrv. officer, 1967-94, ret., 1994. Vice pres. Springboard Swim Club, Springfield, Va., 1984-85. Served with U.S. Army, 1946-47; mem. Res. (ret.). Decorated Legion of Merit. Democrat. Roman Catholic. Avocation: swimming.

PRIEM, RICHARD GREGORY, writer, information systems executive, entertainment company executive; b. Munich, Sept. 18, 1949; came to U.S., 1953; s. Richard Stanley and Elizabeth Teresa (Thompson) P.; m. Janice Lynne Holland, July 27, 1976; children: Michael John, Matthew Warren (dec.), Kathryn Elizabeth. BS in Radio-TV-Film, U. Tex., 1970; grad. with Distinction, U.S. Mil. Police Sch., 1973, 77; MEd in Ednl. Tech., U. Ga., 1979; postgrad., Coll. William and Mary, 1981-82. Cert. fraud examiner. Radio personality, sales exec. KOKE, Inc., Austin, Tex., 1968-73; commd. 2d lt. U.S. Army, 1973, numerous positions including asst. prof. dept. behavioral scis. and leadership U.S. Mil. Acad., staff officer anti terrorism and inspector gen., 1973-94; exec. v.p. It's Your Party, Herndon, Va., 1992—; dep. divsn. mgr. Sci. Applications Internat. Corp., McLean, Va., 1994-95, McLean, 1995—; cons. Dallas Cowboys Football Club, 1981; scouting coord. Army Football, 1983-85. Contbr. articles to profl. jours. Mem. Assn. Cert. Fraud Examiners, Internat. Soc. for Performance Improvement, Am. Soc. Indsl. Security Internat., Phi Kappa Phi, Kappa Delta Pi, Alpha Epsilon Rho. Home: 15386 Twin Creek Ct Centreville VA 20220-3742 Office: Sci Application Internat Corp 1710 Goodridge Dr Mc Lean VA 22102-3701

PRIESAND, SALLY JANE, rabbi; b. Cleve., June 27, 1946; d. Irving Theodore and Rosetta Elizabeth (Welch) P. B.A. in English, U. Cin., 1968; B.Hebrew Letters, Hebrew Union Coll.-Jewish Inst. Religion, 1971, M.A. in Hebrew Letters, 1972; D.H.L. (hon.), Fla. Internat. U., 1973. Ordained rabbi, 1972. Student rabbi Sinai Temple, Champaign, Ill., 1968, Congregation B'nai Israel, Hattiesburg, Miss., 1969-70, Congregation Shalom, Milw., 1970, Temple Beth Israel, Jackson, Mich., 1970-71; rabbinic intern Isaac M. Wise Temple, Cin., 1971-72; asst. rabbi Stephen Wise Free Synagogue, N.Y.C., 1972-77; assoc. rabbi Stephen Wise Free Synagogue, 1977-79; rabbi Temple Beth El, Elizabeth, N.J., 1979-81, Monmouth Reform Temple, Tinton Falls, N.J., 1981—; chaplain Lenox Hill Hosp., N.Y.C., 1979-81. Author: Judaism and the New Woman, 1975. Mem. commn. on synagogue rels. Fedn. Jewish Philanthropies N.Y., 1972-79, mem. com. on aged commn. synagogue rels., 1972-75; mem. task force on equality of women in Judaism pub. affairs com. N.Y. Fedn. Reform Synagogues, 1972-75; mem. com. on resolutions Ctrl. Conf. Am. Rabbis, 1975-77, com. on cults, 1976-78, admissions com., 1983-89; chmn. Task Force on Women in Rabbinate, 1977-83, chmn. 1977-79, mem. exec. bd., 1977-79, com. on resolutions, 1989-92, chmn. com. conv. program, 1993-96; mem. joint commn. on Jewish edn. Ctrl. Conf. Am. Rabbis-Union Am. Hebrew Congregations, 1974-77; mem. task force on Jewish singles Commn. Synagogue Rels., 1975-77; mem. N.Y. Bd. Rabbis, 1975—, Shore Area Bd. Rabbis, 1981—; mem. interim steering com. Clergy and Laity Concerned, 1979-81; bd. dirs. NCCJ, N.Y.C., 1980-82, Jewish Fedn. Greater Monmouth County, trustee, 1988—; trustee Planned Parenthood of Monmouth County, 1982-90; chair religious affairs com. Brookdale Ctr. for Holocaust Studies, 1983-88; v.p. Interfaith Neighbors, 1988—; mem. UAHC-CCAR Joint Commn. on Unaffiliated, 1992—; bd. govs. Hebrew Union Coll.-Jewish Inst. Religion, 1993—; trustee Union Am. Hebrew Congregations, 1994—. Cited by B'nai Brith Women, 1971; named Woman of Yr. Temple Israel, Columbus, Ohio, 1972, Woman of Yr. Ladies Aux. N.Y. chpt. Jewish War Vets., 1973, Woman for All Seasons N.L.I. region Women's Am. ORT, 1973, Extraordinary Women of Achievement NCCJ, 1978, Woman of Achievement Monmouth County Adv. Commn. on Status Women, 1988; recipient Quality of Life award Dist. One chpt. B'nai B'rith Women, 1973, Medallion Judaic Heritage Soc., 1978, Eleanor Roosevelt Humanities award Women's div. State of Israel Bonds, 1980, Rabbinical award Coun. Jewish Fedn., 1988, Woman of Leadership award Monmouth Coun. Girl Scouts U.S., 1991, The Woman Who Dares award Nat. Coun. Jewish Women, 1993. Mem. Hadassah (life), Ctrl. Conf. Am. Rabbis, NOW, Am. Jewish Congress, Am. Jewish Com., Assn. Reform Zionists Am., Jewish Women Internat. (life), Jewish Peace Fellowship, Women's Rabbinic Network, Nat. Breast Cancer Coalition. Home: 10 Wedgewood Cir Eatontown NJ 07724-1203 Office: 332 Hance Ave Tinton Falls NJ 07724-2730

PRIESMAN, ELINOR LEE SOLL, family dynamics administrator, mediator, educator; b. Mpls., Jan. 19, 1938; d. Arthur and Harriet Lucille (Premack) Soll; m. Ira Morton Priesman, Mar. 30, 1958; children: Phillip Sherman, Artyce-Joy Erin. PhD, Union Inst., 1993. Cert. mediator, Va.; cert. family life educator. Nursery sch. tchr. Jewish Comty. Ctr., Santa Monica, Calif., 1958-59; head tchr. Altrusa Day Nursery, Battle Creek, Mich., 1959-60; prin. Arlington/Fairfax Jewish Ctr., Arlington, Va., 1966-67; tchr. grades 1-10 Congregation Olam Tikvah, Fairfax, Va., 1970-75; dir. Creative Play Nursery Sch., Fairfax, Va., 1970-71; tchr. high sch. Temple Sinai, Washington, Va., 1976-78; prin. Congregation Olam Tikvah, Fairfax, Va., 1975-76; asst. to pres.-emeritus Coun. for Advancement and Support of Edn., McLean, Va., 1987-90; cons. to univ. Union for Experimenting Colls. and Univs., McLean, Va., 1988-90; dir. family dynamics inst. Fairfax; mem. doctoral com. Union Inst., Cin., 1991-92, 92—; faculty mentor Ea. U., Albuquerque, 1993—. Author: The Empowered Parent, 1993, A New Perspective on Parenting, 1994 (Spanish, Korean translations 1996), A New Perspective on Parenting for Attorneys and Mediators, 1995; editor: Empowered Parenting newsletter, 1991-92. Pres. No. Va. Artistic Skating Club, Manassas, 1983-85; chair edn. com. Olam Tikvah Synagogue, Fairfax. Recipient Pres.'s award Olam Tikvah Synagogue, 1976. Mem. N.Am. Soc. Adlerian Psychology, Nat. Coun. on Family Rels., Children's Rights Coun., Acad. Family Mediators, No. Va. Mediation Svc. (mediator), Hadassah (life, Alexandria chpt. pres. 1966-67, Esther award 1965). Jewish. Office: Family Dynamics Inst 9302 Swinburne Ct Fairfax VA 22031-3027

PRIEST, GEORGE L., law educator; b. 1947. BA, Yale U., 1969; JD, U. Chgo., 1973. Assoc. prof. U. Puget Sound, Tacoma, 1973-75; law and econ. fellow U. Chgo., 1975-77; prof. U. Buffalo, 1977-80, UCLA, 1980-81, Yale U., New Haven, 1981—; dir. program in civil liability; John M. Olin prof. law and econs., 1986—. Mem. Pres.' Com. on Privatization, 1987-88. Office: PO Box 208215 New Haven CT 06520-8215

PRIEST, HARTWELL WYSE, artist; b. Brantford, Ont., Can., Jan. 1, 1901; d. John Frank Henry and Rachel Thayer (Gavet) Wyse; m. A.J. Gustin Priest, Aug. 4, 1927; children: Paul Lambert, Marianna Thayer. BA, Smith Coll. Former tchr. graphic art Va. Art Inst., Charlottesville; former lectr. on prints and lithography; juror art exhbn. Unitarian Ch., 1993. One-woman shows include Argent Gallery, N.Y.C., 1955, 58, 60, 73, 77, 81, Va., 1969, 71, Nantucket, Mass., 1956, Ft. Lauderdale, Fla. Art Ctr., 1956; Pen & Brush, N.Y.C., 1973, 91, invitational retrospective exhbn. McGuffey Art Ctr., Charlottesville, Va., 1984, Va., N.Y., 1984, 88; work represented in permanent collections Library of Congress Washington, Norton Gallery, Palm Beach, Fla., Soc. Am. Graphic Artists, Hunterdon County Art Ctr., Longwood Coll., Smith Coll., Va. Mus., Richmond, Carnegie Mellon U. and numerous others; solo exhbn. of prints McGuffey Art Ctr., Charlottesville, Va., 1988, 90, 93, Woodstock Artist Gallery, 1990, Soc. Am. Graphic Artists, 1988-89, 92, Bombay, 1989, U. Va. Hosp., 1989, Bergen Mus. Art and Sci., 1991; represented in group shows McGuffey Gallery, 1988, 94, Gallery Show, Richmond, Va., 1988, Nat. Assn. Women Artists, Florence, Italy, 1972, N.Y.C., 1989, 96, ann. show Ojibway Hotel Club, Pointe au Baril, Georgian Bay, Ont., Can., 1991, Soc. Am. Graphic Srts, N.Y.C., 1989, 92, Woodstock, N.Y. Art Assoc., 1990, McGuffey Art Ctr., Charlottesville, Va., 1990, 94, Pen and Brush ann. Graphic Show, N.Y.C., 1991 (award for etching Spring, Ada Rosario Cecere Meml. award), Bergen Mus., N.J., 1991, Ojibway Club, Ont., Can., 1991; Pen and Brush Christmas exhbn., 1994-95, Showing of a Video, Harrisonburg, Va.; represented in traveling group shows Nat. Assn. Women Artists, Puerto Rico, 1987, India, 1989, N.Y.C., 1994; pvt. collection U. Va. Hosp., Charlottesville, 1989; subject of TV documentary Hartwell Priest: Printmaker, 1995. Recipient awards for lithograph Field Flowers, Longwood Coll., 1965, Nat. Assn. Woman Artists, 1965, lithograph West Wind, A Buell award, 1961, print Streets of Silence, T. Giorgi Meml. award, 1973, lithograph Blue Lichen, Pen & Brush, 1984, award for collage, 1985; 1st award for graphics Blue Ridge Art Show, 1985, Gene A. Walker award for print Glacial Rocks, 1986, award for print Blue Ridge Show, 1987, Philip Isenburg award for graphic PreCambrian Rock Pattern, 1988, Ada R. Cecere Meml. award Pen and Brush, 1991, Art award Piedmont Coun. Arts, 1993. Mem. Nat. Assn. Women Artists (Travelling Printmaking Exhbn. 1987-89), Pen and Brush, Soc. Am. Graphic Artists, Washington Print Club, 2d St. Gallery, Charlottesville, McGuffey Art Ctr. Avocations: walking, singing in choir, gardenening, playing Bach and Mozart, playing recorder and piano. Home: 41 Old Farm Rd Charlottesville VA 22903-4725

PRIEST, MELVILLE STANTON, retired consulting hydraulic engineer; b. Cassville, Mo., Oct. 16, 1912; s. William Tolliver and Mildred Alice (Messer) P.; m. Vivian Willingham, Mar. 22, 1941 (dec.); m. Virginia Young, Dec. 16, 1983. BS, U. Mo., 1935; MS, U. Colo., 1943; PhD, U. Mich., 1954. Registered profl. engr., Ala., La., Miss. Jr. engr. U.S. Engrs. Office, 1937-39; from jr. to asst. engr. Bur. Reclamation, 1939-41; from instr. to assoc. prof. civil engring. Cornell U., 1941-55; prof. hydraulics Auburn (Ala.) U., 1955-58, prof. civil engring., head dept., 1958-65; dir. Water Resources Research Inst., Miss. State U., 1965-77; UN adviser on hydraulics, Egypt, 1956, 57, 60; Mem. Ala. Bd. Registration Profl. Engrs., 1962-65. Contbr. articles to profl. jours. Fellow ASCE (pres. Ala. 1962, exec. com., pipeline div. 1971-74), Am. Water Resources Assn. (dir. 1973-75), Sigma Xi, Tau Beta Pi, Chi Epsilon, Pi Mu Epsilon. Address: PO Box 541 Starkville MS 39760

PRIEST, RUTH EMILY, music minister, choir director, composer arranger; b. Detroit, Nov. 7, 1933; d. William and Gertrude Hilda (Stockley) P. Student, Keyboard Studios, Detroit, 1949-52, Wayne State U., Detroit, 1953, 57, Ea. Pentecostal Bible Coll., Peterborough, Ont., Can., 1954-55, Art Ctr. Music Sch., Detroit Inst. Mus. Arts, 1953-54. Legal sec., 1951-90; organist, pianist, vocalist Berea Tabernacle, Detroit, 1943-61; organist Bethany Presbyn. Ch., Ft. Lauderdale, Fla., 1961-67, 69-72; choir dir., organist Bethany Drive-in Ch., Ft. Lauderdale, Fla.; organist First Bapt. Ch., Pompano Beach, Fla., 1967-68, St. Ambrose Episcopal Ch., Ft. Lauderdale, 1969-72; music dir., organist Grace Brethren Ch., Ft. Lauderdale, 1972-75; organist Boca Raton (Fla.) Community Ch., Bibletown, 1975-85; min. music, organist Warrendale Community Ch., Dearborn, Mich., 1985—; ptnr. Miracle Music Enterprises; concert and ch. organist/pianist; organist numerous weddings, city-wide rallies of Detroit and Miami Youth for Christ, Christ for Labor and Mgmt., Holiness Youth Crusade, numerous other civic and religious events; featured weekly as piano soloist and accompanist on Crusade for Christ Telecast, Detroit, 1950-60, CBC-TV, Windsor, Ont., Can.; staff organist Enquire Hotel, Galt Ocean Mile, Ft. Lauderdale, Fla., 1962-67; tchr. piano adult edn. evening sch. program Southfield (Mich.) Pub. Sch. System, 1991—. Ongoing educator in pvt. piano, organ, music theory; Recording artist: Ruth Priest at the Organ, Love Notes from the Heart, Christmas with Ruth. Mem. Am. Guild Organists (past mem. exec. bd. Detroit chpt.). Office: Miracle Music Enterprises PO Box 554 Southfield MI 48037-0554 *I agree with Martin Luther that music is one of God's greatest gifts to mankind. At a very early age my natural response to life was, and still is, an outflow of love to God through the musical gifts with which He has blessed me.*

PRIEST, SHARON DEVLIN, state official; b. Montreal, Quebec, Can.; m. Bill Priest; 1 child, Adam. Tax preparer, instr. H & R Block, Little Rock, 1976-78; account exec. Greater Little Rock C. of C.; owner, founder Devlin Co.; mem. Little Rock Bd. Dirs., 1986—; vice mayor Little Rock, 1989-91, mayor, 1991-93; Sec. of State State of Arkansas, 1994—; bd. dirs. Invesco Inc., New Futures. Bd. dirs., past pres. Metroplan (Environ. Svc. award 1982), YMCA, Southwest Hosp.; mem. Advt. and Promotion commn., Ark. Internat. Visitors Coun., Pulaski Are Transp. Svc. Policy Com., St. Theresa's Parish Coun., Exec. com. for Ark. Mcpl. League, Nat. League of Cities Trans. and Communications Steering Com. and Policy Com., adv. bd. M.M. Cohn., Little Rock City Beautiful Commn., 1980-86; former bd. dirs. Downtown Partnership, Southwest YMCA, 1984, 86, sec.; former mem. Community Housing Resource Bd., 1984-86, Pub. Facilities Bd. Southwest Hosp., 1985-86, Southwest Merchants' Assn., 1985—, 2d v.p., 1985; chmn. Little Rock Arts and Humanities Promotion Commn.; led petition dr. for appropriation for Fourche Creek Plan 7A. Mem. Leadership Inst. Alumni Assn. (4 Bernard de la Harpe awards). Office: Office of Secretary of State State Capitol Bldg 256 Little Rock AR 72201*

PRIEST, TROY ALFRED-WILEY, lawyer; b. Balt., Oct. 5, 1968; s. Roy Otis and Sudie Mae (Payton) P.; m. Françoise Borja Santos, Aug. 10, 1991; 1 child, Gabrielle Borja. BA, Brown U., 1990; JD, Northeastern U., 1993. Bar: Md. 1993, D.C. 1994, U.S. Dist. Ct. Md. 1994, U.S. Dist. Ct. D.C. 1995. Law clk. Hon. Annice M. Wagner chief judge D.C. Ct. of Appeals, Washington, 1993-94; assoc. Houston & Howard, Washington, 1994—; dist. counselor Omega Psi Phi Fraternity, Inc., New Eng., Providence, R.I., 1991-93. Mem. ABA, ATLA, Nat. Bar Assn., Md. Bar Assn., Bar Assn. D.C., Defense Rsch. Inst. Democrat. Baptist. Home: 3504 Aston Manor Ct Apt 301 Silver Spring MD 20904 Office: Houston & Howard 2021 L St NW Ste 304 Washington DC 20036

PRIESTLEY, G. T. ERIC, manufacturing company executive; b. Belfast, Northern Ireland, May 7, 1942; came to U.S., 1990; s. Thomas John McKee P.; m. Carol Elizabeth Gingles Nelson, June 8, 1966; children: Peter, Gaye, Simon. BS, Queens U., 1963; postgrad., Harvard Bus. Sch., 1989. Sales trainee Burroughs Machines Ltd., 1963-64; dealer, sales devel. Regent Oil Co., 1964-66; ops. mgr. RMC (Ulster) Ltd., 1967-70; distbn. mgr. Bass Charrington, Ireland, 1970-71; dir., gen. mgr. Farrans Ltd., 1971-80; dir., CEO Redland plc/British Fuels/Cawoods, 1980-88; dir. Bowater plc, London, 1988-90; pres., CEO Rexam Inc., Charlotte, N.C., 1990—; bd. dirs. REXAM Inc., Bowater, plc., MiTek Inc., St. Louis, Interprint Ltd., Sao Paulo; mem. S.E. regional bd. Wachovia Bank. Bd. advisors U. N.C., Charlotte. Mem. Nat. Assn. Mfrs. (bd. dirs.), Am. Mgmt. Assn. (gen. mgmt. coun.), Moortown Golf Club, Aloha Golf Club, Royal Ulster Yacht Culb, Quail Hollow Golf and Country Club. Home: 9114 Winged Bourne Charlotte NC 28210-5946 Office: Rexam Inc 4201 Congress St Ste 340 Charlotte NC 28209-4621

PRIESTLEY, JASON, actor; b. Vancouver, B.C., Can.. Actor: (TV series) Sister Kate, 1989-90, Beverly Hills 90210, 1990—; (films) Calendar Girl, 1993, Tombstone, 1993, Cold-Blooded, 1995; producer TV series Beverly Hills 90210, 1995-96. Office: c/o Wolf Kasteler 1033 Gayley Ave Ste 208 Los Angeles CA 90024-3417*

PRIEVE, E. ARTHUR, arts administration educator. BBA in Adminstrn. and Art History, U. of Wis., 1959, MBA in Mgmt. and Orgn. Behavior, 1961; DBA in Mgmt. and Psych., George Washington U., Washington, 1965. Asst. dean adminstrv. affairs Sch. Bus. U. Wis., Madison, 1966-69, prof. mgmt. Grad. Sch. Bus., 1969—, dir. exec. MBA program, 1993—; dir. Ctr. For Arts Adminstrn., Madison, 1969—; curriculum cons. for arts adminstrn.; cons. visual, performing and arts svc. orgns.; workshops and presentations on planning, bd. dirs. Mem. Assn. of Arts Adminstrn. Educators (chmn. U.S., Can.). Office: U Wis Ctr Arts Adminstrn 4171 Grainger Hall 975 University Ave Madison WI 53706-1324

PRIGMORE, CHARLES SAMUEL, social work educator; b. Lodge, Tenn., Mar. 21, 1919; s. Charles H. and Mary Lou (Raulston) P.; m. Shirley Melaine Buuck, June 7, 1947; 1 child, Philip Brand. A.B., U. Chattanooga, 1939; M.S., U. Wis., 1947, Ph.D., 1961; extension grad., Air War Coll., 1967, Indsl. Coll. Armed Forces, 1972. Social caseworker Children's Svc. Soc., Milw., 1947-48; social worker Wis. Sch. Boys, Waukesha, 1948-51; supr. tng. Wis. Bur. Probation and Parole, Madison, 1951-56; supt. Tenn. Vocat. Tng. Sch. for Boys, Nashville, 1956-59; assoc. prof. La. State U., 1959-64; ednl. cons. Coun. Social Work Edn., N.Y., 1962-64; exec. dir. Joint Commn. Correctional Manpower and Tng., Washington, 1964-67; prof. Sch. Social Work, U. Ala., 1967-84, prof. emeritus, 1984—, chmn. com. on Korean relationships; Fulbright lectr., Iran, 1972-73; vis. lectr. U. Sydney, 1976; cons. Iranian Ministry Health and Welfare, 1976-78; frequent lectr., workshop leader. Author: Textbook on Social Problems, 1971, Social Work in Iran Since the White Revolution, 1976, Social Welfare Policy Analysis and Formulation, 1979, 2d edit., 1986; editor 2 books; contbr. articles to profl. jours. Adv. Com. for Former Prisoners of War VA, 1981-83; chmn. Prisoner of War Bd., State of Ala., 1984-89; state comdr. Am. Ex-Prisoners of War, Ala., 1985-86, nat. legis. officer, 1985—, nat. dir., 1989-92, nat. sr. vice comdr., 1993—, nat comdr., 1994-95; gov.'s liaison U.S. Holocaust Meml. Coun., 1983-89; mem. Ala. Bd. Vets. Affairs, 1986-89, Ala. Bicentennial Commn. on Constn., 1987-90; bd. dirs. Community Svcs. Programs of W. Ala., 1985-89, others in past. Served to 2d lt. USAAF, 1940-45, prisoner of war, Germany, 1944-45; lt. col. Res., ret. Decorated Air medal with oak leaf cluster; recipient Conservation award Woodmen of the World, 1971; Fulbright rsch. fellow Norway, 1979-80. Fellow Am. Sociol. Assn., Royal Soc. Health; mem. Acad. Cert. Social Workers, Nat. Coun. Crime and Delinquency, Tuscaloosa Country Club, Capitol Hill Club, Alpha Kappa Delta, Beta Beta Beta. Home: 923 Overlook Rd N Tuscaloosa AL 35406-2122 Office: PO Box 870314 Tuscaloosa AL 35487-0314 *The following principles seem most related to my success: 1) From childhood I was encouraged to formulate specific vocational goals and work toward them; 2) support of friends and relatives is secondary, though important; more significant is one's own effort and planning. 3) Objectives and plans usually can be achieved only through persistence and determination. Usually one is forced to sacrifice a measure of peer fellowship and conviviality. 4) Belief in oneself and one's own potentialities makes for a self-fulfilling prophecy.*

PRIGMORE, KATHRYN BRADFORD TYLER, architecture educator, architect; b. St. Albans, N.Y., Nov. 21, 1956; d. Richard Jerome and Shirley Virginia (Neizer) Tyler; m. James Craig Prigmore, June 20, 1986 (div. June 1992); children: Crystal Andrea, Amber Sheriesse. BS in Bldg. Sci., Rensselaer Poly. Inst., 1977, BArch, 1978; MS in Engring., Cath. U. Am., 1981. Registered architect, Va., NCARB. Intern architect VVKR Inc., Alexandria, Va., 1979-82; architect Robert A. Hawthorne, Architects, PC, Washington, 1982; project mgr. Robert Traynham Coles, Architect, PC, Washington, 1982-84; assoc. Segreti Tepper Architects, P.C., Washington, 1984-92; assoc. prof. dept. architecture Howard U., Washington, 1991—, assoc. dean Sch. Architecture and Planning, 1992—; mem. Va. Bd. for Architects, Profl. Engrs., Landscape Architects and Land Surveyors, Nat. Coun. Archtl. Registration Bds., Archtl. Registration Exam and Grading Com.; mem. alumni adv. coun. Sch. Architecture Rensselaer Poly. Inst., 1993—; guest spkr. in field. Contbr. articles to profl. jours. Mem. adv. coun. No. Va. Urban League, 1980-81. Named to Outstanding Young Women in Am., 1983. Mem. AIA (pub. rels. com. Washington chpt. 1983—), AAUW, Nat. Orgn. Minority Archs., Black Women in Architecture and Related Professions (faculty advisor Howard U. chpt. 1992—). Episcopalian. Avocations: writing, gardening. Home: 8911 Union Farm Rd Alexandria VA 22309-3936 Office: Howard U Sch Architecture/Planning 2366 6th St NW Washington DC 20059

PRIGOGINE, VICOMTE ILYA, physics educator; b. Moscow, Russia, Jan. 25, 1917; s. Roman and Julie (Wichmann) P.; m. Marina Prokopowicz, Feb. 25, 1961; children: Yves, Pascal. PhD, Free U. Brussels, 1941; hon. degree, U. Newcastle, Eng., 1966, U. Poitiers, France, 1966, U. Chgo., 1969, U. Bordeaux, France, 1972, U. de Liège, Belgium, 1977, U. Uppsala, Sweden, 1977, U de Droit, D'Economie et des Scis., d'Aix-Marseille, France, 1979, U. Georgetown, 1980, U. Cracovie, Poland, 1981, U. Rio de Janeiro, 1981, Stevens Inst. Tech., Hoboken, 1981, Heriot-Watt U., Scotland, 1985, Universidad Nacional de Educacion a Distancia, Madrid, 1985, U. Francois Rabelais de Tours, 1986, U. Peking, People's Republic of China, 1986, U. Buenos Aires, 1989, U. Cagliari, Sardinia, Italy, 1990, U. Sienne, Italy, 1990; DS (hon.), Gustavus Adolphus Coll., 1990; Membre d'Honneur, l'Academie Nationale d'Argenti, 1990, l'Academie des Sciences Nature, Iles de Republique Federale de Russie, 1991; Pres. d'Honneur, l'Acad. Nat. des Scis. de Republique de San Marino, 1991; Membre d'Honneur, l'Academie Chilienne des Scis., 1991, de l'Université de Nice-Sophia-Antipolis, Nice, France, 1991, de l'Univ. Philippines System, Quezon City, 1991, del'Université de Santiago, Chile, del'Université de Tucumán, Argentine, 1991; Docteur Honoris Causa, Université Lomonosov de Moscow, Russie, 1993, L'Univ. de A L.I. Cuza IASI, Iasi, Romania, 1994, U. de San Luis, Argentina, 1994, Institut Nat. Polytechnique, Lorraine, France, 1994, SUNY, Binghamton, 1995, Vrije U. Brussel, Brussels, Belgium, 1995, Internat. Assn. U. Pres., Seoul, 1995, Institut Royal des Elites, Brussels, 1995, U. Valladolid, Espagne, 1995, U. de Valladolid, Spain, 1995; Laurea ad honorem in philosophy, U. degli Studi Inst. Filosofia, Urbino, Italy, 1996. Prof. U. Brussels, 1947—; dir. Internat. Insts. Physics and Chemistry, Solvay, Belgium, 1959—; prof. physics and chem. engring. U. Tex., Austin, 1967—; dir. Ilya Prigogine Ctr. for Studies in Statis. Mechanics, Thermodynamics and Complex Systems, U. Tex., Austin, 1967—; hon. prof. U. Nankin, People's Republic of China, 1986, Banaras Hindu U., Varasani, India, 1988; Ashbel Smith regental prof. U. Tex., Austin, 1984—; Dir.'s Disting. visitor Inst. for Advanced Study, Princeton (N.J.) U., 1993; counseiller spl. Commn. des Corruluhaute Européennes, 1993; internat. advisor de l'Internat. Inst. Advanced Studies, Kyoto, 1994. Author: (with R. Defay) Traite de Thermodynamique, conformement aux methodes de Gibbs et de De Donder, 1944, 50, Etude Thermodynamique des Phenomenes Irreversibles, 1947, Introduction to Thermodynamics of Irreversible Processes, 1954, 62, 67, translation: Russian, Serbo-Croatian, French, Italian, & Spanish, (with A. Bellemans, V. Mathot) The Molecular Theory of Solutions, 1957, Statistical Mechanics of Irreversible Processes, 1954, 2d edit. 1962, 3d edit. 1967, (with others) Non Equilibrium Thermodynamics, Variational Techniques and Stability, 1966, (with R. Ilerman) Kinetic Theory of Vehicular Traffic, 1971, (with R. Glansdorff) Thermodynamic Theory of Structure, Stability and Fluctuations, 1971, (with G. Nicolis) Self-Organization in Nonequilibrium Systems, 1977, From Being to Becoming-Time and Complexity in Physical Sciences, 1980, French, German, Japanese, Russian, Chinese, Italian, Romanian, & Portuguese edits., (with I. Stengers) Order Out of Chaos, 1983, La Nouvelle Alliance, Les Métamorphoses de la Science, 1979, German, English, Italian, Spanish, Serbo-Croatian, Romanian, Swedish, Dutch, Russian, Japanese, Chinese, Portuguese, Bulgarian, Greek, Korean, & Polish edits., (with G. Nicolis) Die Erforschung des Komplexen, 1987, Exploring Complexity, 1989, Chinese, Russian, Italian, French, Spanish edits., (with I. Stengers) Entre le temps et l'Eternité, 1988, Dutch edit. 1989, Italian edit. 1989, Spanish edit. 1990, Portuguese edit. 1993, Le leggi del Caos, 1993, Das Paradox der Zeit, 1993, (with I. Stengers) Les Lois du Chaos, 1994, Die Gesetze des Chaos, 1995, La Fin des Certitudes, 1996; mem. editl. bd. Ukrainian Phys. Jour., 1990. Mem. sci. adv. bd. Internat. Acad. for Biomed. Drug Rsch., 1990. Fellow RGK Found. Centennial, U. Tex. 1989-90; decorated comdr. Légion d'Honneur, 1989, France, comdr. de l'Ordre de Leopold, 1968, Médaille de la resistance comdr. de l'Ordre Leopold II, 1961, Grande Croix de l'Ordre de Leopold II, 1977, Médaille Civique de Premiere Classe, 1972, comdr. de l'Ordre National du Mérite, France, 1977, comdr. de l'Ordre des Arts et des Lettres, France, 1984; recipient Prix Franqui, 1955, Prix Solvay, 1965, Nobel prize in chemistry, 1977, Honda Prize, 1983, Rumford gold medal Royal Soc. London, 1976, Karcher medal Am. Crystallographic Assn., 1978, Descartes medal U. Paris, 1979, Prix Umberto Biancamano, 1987, award recipient Gravity Rsch. Found., 1988, Artificial Intelligence Sci. Achievement award Internat. Found. for Artificial Intelligence, 1990, Prix Summa de l'Universite Laval, Can., 1993, Medaille Piotr Kapitza decernee par l'Academie des Scis. Naturelles de Russie, 1996—, Medaille de l'Ecole Normale Superieure, Paris, 1995, Medaille d'honneur de l'Inst. Phys. Chemistry-Polish Acad. Scis., 1996—, others. Fellow NAS India (hon.); mem. Royal Acad. Belgium (pres.), Am. Acad. Sci. (medal 1975), Royal Soc. Scis. Uppsala (Sweden), NAS U.S.A. (fgn. assoc.), Soc. Royale des Scis. Liège Belgium (corr.), Acad. Gottingen Germany, Deutscher Acad. der Naturforscher Leopoldina (Cothenius medal 1970), Osterreichische Acad. der Wissenschaften (corr.), Academie Nationale des Sciences, des Letters et des Arts de Modene (Italy, hon.), Commn. Mondiale de la Culture et du Devel. de l'UNESCO (hon.), Chem. Soc. Poland (hon.), Internat. Soc. Gen. Systems Rsch. (pres.-elect 1988), Royal Soc. Chemistry Belgium (hon.), N.Y. Acad. Sci., Internat. Acad. Philosophy Sci., World Acad. Arts and Scis., World Inst. Sci., others. Address: 67 Ave Fond Roy, 1180 Brussels Belgium Office: Inst Internat Physics & Chem, Campus Plaine ULB CP231, Bld du Triomphe 1050 Brussels Belgium Office: U Tex Ilya Prigogine Ctr Studies Statis Mechanics Austin TX 78712

PRIMEAUX, HENRY, III, automotive executive, author, speaker; b. New Orleans, Nov. 16, 1941; s. Henry Jr. and Ethel (Ritter) P.; m. Jane Cathrine Velcich, July 23, 1960; children: Joann Primeaux Longa, Lisa, Henry Joseph. Student, La. State U., New Orleans, 1959-63. Compt. Jimco, New Orleans, 1965-66; owner, mgr. Picone Seafood, New Orleans, 1966-67; v.p. NADW Inc., Metairie, La., 1967-78, Am. Warranty Corp., L.A., 1978-80; pres. F&I Warranty Corp., Arlington, Tex., 1980-87; exec. v.p. F&I Mgmt. Corp., Arlington, 1980-87; pres., chief exec. officer Primco Corp., Arlington, 1987-91; pres. Crown Autoworld Automobile Dealership, Tulsa; cons., corr. Wards Auto Dealer, Deetroit, 1987—, weekly TV program Automotive Satellite TV Network; cons. Nissan Motor Co., L.A., 1988-89, Convergent div. Unisys, Hunt Valley, Md., 1988-90; cons. Mercedes-Benz N.Am.; cons. Automatic Data Processing. Writer Auto Age mag.; author: F&I Handbook. Mem. Rep. Task Force, Rep. Senatorial Inner Circle; bd. dirs. Okla. Spl. Olympics, John Starks Found., Tulsa Ballet, Jr. Achievement, YCMA, Boy Scouts U.S., Children's Med. Ctr.; mem. athletic com. Tulsa Pub. Schs.; mem. nat. adv. bd. GM Sch. to Work Initiative. With USN, 1959-61. Mem. Am. Internat. Automobile Dealers Assn., Assn. of F&I Profls. (bd. dirs. 1990—, pres. 1994), Nat. Auto Dealers Assn. (pres. Tulsa chpt. 1994, Time Quality Dealer of Yr. 1994). Roman Catholic. Home: 10504 S Hudson Pl Tulsa OK 74137-7056 Office: Crown AutoWorld 4444 S Sheridan Rd Tulsa OK 74145-1122

PRIMES, ROBERT, cinematographer. Works include: (films) Dr. Heckyl and Mr. Hype, 1980, The Call Me Bruce?, 1982, Crime Wave, 1985, A Great Wall, 1986, 16 Days of Glory, 1986, Bird On a Wire, 1990, The Hard Way, 1991, Aspen Extreme, 1992; (TV movie) My Antonia, 1995 (Emmy award for outstanding individual achievement in cinematography for a mini-series or spl., 1995). Office: c/o Smith Gosnell Nicholson & Assocs PO Box 1166 Pacific Palisades CA 90272*

PRIMIS, LANCE ROY, newspaper executive; b. Bklyn., June 16, 1946; s. David and Sybil (Schiller) P.; m. Ellen Linda Wildman, June 16, 1946; children: Blair S., Ashley K. BA in English, U. Wis., 1968. Sales rep. Scott Paper Co., N.Y.C., 1968-69; with N.Y. Times, 1969—, retail advt. rep., 1969-72, asst. class advt. mgr., 1972-76, retail advt. mgr., 1976-79, dir. advt. promotion and rsch., 1979, advt. dir., 1979-80, v.p. advt., 1981-82, sr. v.p. advt., from 1982, former v.p., gen. mgr., pres., gen. mgr., 1989-92, pres., CEO, 1992—. Mem. Internat. Newspaper Advt. Execs. (chmn. nat. advertiser rels. com.), Am. Assn. Advt. Agys., Nat. Sales Assn., Proprietary Assn., Cosmetic Toiletry Fragrance Assn., Internat. Newspaper Promotion Assn., N.J. Advt. Club. Office: NY Times Co 229 W 43rd St New York NY 10036-3913*

PRIMM, EARL RUSSELL, III, publishing executive; b. Rhinelander, Wis., Oct. 24, 1958; s. Earl Russell and Betty Joan (Dennis) P. AB in Classics (hon.), Loyola U. Chgo., 1980; MA in Libr. Sci., U. Chgo., 1990. Asst. to edn. dir. J.G. Ferguson Pub. Co., Chgo., 1981-84; prodn. mgr. Joint Commn. on Accreditation of Hosps., Chgo., 1984-85; sr. editor J.G. Ferguson Pub. Co., Chgo., 1985-87; asst. editor U. Chgo. Press., 1987-88; editorial dir. J.G. Ferguson Pub. Co., Chgo., 1988-89; project mgr. Children's Press, Chgo., 1989-92; exec. editor Franklin Watts, Inc., Chgo., N.Y.C., 1992-95; editorial dir. Grolier Children's Pub., Danbury, Conn., 1995—; mem. adv. bd. U. Chgo. Pub. Program, 1990—; judge Lambda Lit. awards, Washington, 1994—. Editorial chief: Career Discovery Encyclopedia, 1990; editor: Civil Rights Movement in America, 2nd edit., 1991, Extraordinary Hispanic Americans, 1991. Mem. crisis counselor Nat. Runaway Switchboard, Chgo., 1985-88; Horizon's hotline counselor, Chgo., 1987-88; bd. dirs. Gerber/Hart Libr. and Archives, Chgo., 1992-94. Named Honors Sr. of Yr., Loyola U. Chgo., 1980; recipient Mertz Latin Scholarship key Loyola U. Chgo., 1980. Mem. Pub. Triangle, Chgo. Book Clinic, Am. Libr. Assn. Democrat. Home: 156 Heatherwood Dr Brookfield CT 06804 Office: Grolier Inc Sherman Twp Danbury CT 06816

PRIMM, JAMES PHILLIP RAY, electro-mechanical engineer; b. Albuquerque, Sept. 5, 1969; s. Ray and Virginia Lou (Schaffer) P. BS in Electro-Mech. Engring. cum laude, Ark. Tech. U., Russellville, 1992. Engring. coop Ark. Nuclear One, Russellville, 1991-94; project engr. Price Sys., Inc., Hot Springs, Ark., 1994—. Guitarist year-long world tour Up With People, 1992-93; rec. two albums as guitarist for contemporary Christian band Emergency Broadcast. Mem. Sigma Phi Epsilon. Home: 501 Plum Hollow Blvd PO Box 7341 Hot Springs National Park AR 71913

PRIMO, JOAN ERWINA, retail and real estate consulting business owner; b. Detroit, Aug. 28, 1959; d. Joseph Carmen and Marie Ann (Nash) P. BA, Wellesley Coll., 1981; MBA, Harvard U., 1985. Acct. exec. Michigan Bell, Detroit, 1981-82, AT&T Info. Sys., Southfield, Mich., 1983; planning analyst Gen. Motors, Detroit, 1984; v.p. Howard L. Green & Assocs., Troy, Mich., 1985-89; prin., founder The Strategic Edge, Inc., Southfield, 1989—. Contbr. articles to profl. jours. Founders soc. mem. Detroit Inst. Arts, 1989—. Mem. Internat. Coun. Shopping Ctrs. (faculty, seminar leader 1987—), Wellesley Club Southeastern Mich. (pres. 1994—), Harvard Bus. Sch. Club Detroit (bd. dirs. 1994—, v.p. 1995—), Ivy Club Detroit (bd. dirs. 1994—, sec. 1995—). Republican. Roman Catholic. Avocations: antiques, travel, theatre, gourmet cooking. Home: 1185 Stonecrest Dr Bloomfield Hills MI 48302-2841 Office: The Strategic Edge 24333 Southfield Rd Ste 211 Southfield MI 48075-2849

PRIMOSCH, JAMES THOMAS, music educator, composer, musician; b. Cleve., Oct. 29, 1956; s. Edward Joseph and Rose Marie (Potochar) P.; m. Mary Marguerite Murphy, April 5, 1986. BA in Composition magna cum laude, Cleve. State U., 1978; MA in Composition, U. Pa., 1980; DMA in Composition awarded with distinction, Columbia U., 1988; studied piano privately with Lambert Orkis, Phila., 1978-80; studied composition with John Harbison, Tanglewood, 1984. Asst. prof. music U. Penn., 1988-94, assoc. prof. music, 1994—; grad. assistantships Columbia-Princeton Electronic Music Ctr., 1982-84, 86-87, preceptorship Columbia U., 1984-85; residency Va. Ctr. Creative Arts, 1985, MacDowell Colony, 1988, Bellagio Conf. Ctr., 1992; regional vis. artist Am. Acad. in Rome, 1994; composer in residence Marlboro Music Festival, 1994. Composer of more than 30 compositions and 19 published works; compositions performed by L.A. Philharm., St. Paul Chamber Orch., Cleve. Chamber Symphony, N.Y. New Music Ensemble; compositions performed at Carnegie Hall, Dorothy Chandler Pavilion, Town Hall, Weill (Carnegie) Recital Hall, and many others; reviewer High Performance Rev. Mag., 1987—. Recipient 3rd prize, People's prize Internat. Gaudeamus Competition, The Netherlands, 1977, Helen L. Weiss prize U. Pa., 1979, David Halstead prize U. Penn., 1980, 3rd prize Shreveport Symphony Composer's Competition, 1980-81, John H. Bearns prize, 1981, 1st. prize Holtkamp Organ Composition Contest, 1982, Eda and Boris Rappoport prize Columbia U., 1984, Tanglewood prize in Composition Berkshire Music Ctr., 1984, Cleve. Arts prize, 1992; recipient Mader Meml. Fund Recognition award, 1980, BMI Student Composers award, 1982; New Music Consort Composition Contest winner, 1987, League of Composers ISCM winner, 1988; Fine Arts scholar Cleve. State U., 1974-78, scholar Cleve. Fortnightly Music Club, 1976-78, Arthur Loesser Meml. scholar, 1977-78, Yale Composer's Workshop at Norfolk, 1981, Columbia U. scholar, 1981-82, Charles Ives scholar Am. Acad. Inst. Arts & Letters, 1985; U. fellow U. Penn., 1978-79, Composers Conf. Johnson Vt., 1979, 80, CBS Found. fellow U. Penn., 1979-80, Margaret Lee Crofts fellow Berkshire Music Ctr. Tanglewood, 1984, Guggenheim fellow, 1985, NEA, 1991-92, Goddard Lieberson fellow Am. Acad. Arts and Letters, 1993; ASCAP Found. Young Composers grant, 1984, 82, Meet The Composer grant 1980, 82, 85, 87, 89, 90, 94, Am. Music Ctr. Copying Assistance grant, 1985, 90, Penn. Coun. On The Arts, 1990, Presser Found. grant U. Penn. Mem. BMI, Pi Kappa Lambda. Roman Catholic. Avocation: reading.

PRIMPS, WILLIAM GUTHRIE, lawyer; b. Ossining, N.Y., Sept. 8, 1949; s. Richard Byrd and Mary Elizabeth (Guthrie) P.; m. Sophia Elizabeth Beutel, Aug. 25, 1973; children: Emily Ann, Elizabeth Armstrong, William Andrew. BA, Yale U., 1971; JD, Harvard U., 1974. Bar: N.Y., 1975. Assoc. LeBoeuf, Lamb, Leiby & MacRae, N.Y.C., 1974-82; ptnr. LeBoeuf, Lamb, Greene & MacRae, N.Y.C., 1983—; counsel to Bd. Zoning Appeals, Bronxville, 1988-89, chmn., 1989-91; bd. dirs. Nat. Integrity Life Ins. Co. Mem. class coun. Yale U., New Haven, 1986-91; trustee Village of Bronxville, 1991—, dep. mayor, 1995—; deacon Reformed Ch. Bronxville, 1989-94. Mem. ABA, N.Y. State Bar Assn., Assn. Yale Alumni (class rep. 1986-91), Yale Club, Bronxville Field Club. Republican. Home: 71 Summit Ave Bronxville NY 10708-1815 Office: LeBoeuf Lamb Greene & MacRae 125 W 55th St New York NY 10019-5369

PRINA, L(OUIS) EDGAR, journalist; b. West New York, N.J., Oct. 7, 1917; s. Louis Edgar and Marion (Duggan) P.; m. Frances Lee Lorick, Feb. 14, 1947; 1 dau., Lee Lorick II. A.B., Syracuse U., 1938, M.A., 1940. Copy editor, asst. night city editor N.Y. Sun, N.Y.C., 1946-48; Washington corr. N.Y. Sun, 1948-50; nat. affairs writer Washington Star, 1950-66; mil. affairs writer/editor Copley News Svc., Washington, 1966-77; bur. chief Copley News Svc., 1977-84, sr. corr., 1984-87; editor Navy mag., Washington, 1961-68; columnist Sea Power mag., 1968—. Author: The Political Virgin, 1958, Flew to South Pole for Overnight Visit, 1966. Served with USN, 1941-46, 51-53; capt. Res. (ret.). Recipient honorable mentionHeywood Broun award, 1956, Disting. Public Svc. award USN, 1965, Alfred Thayer Mahan award Navy League U.S., 1987, Copley Ring of Truth award, 1971, 74-76, 79, 80-81; nominated for Pulitzer Prize (twice). Mem. U.S. Naval Inst., Nat. Press Club (chmn. bd. govs.), White House Corrs. Assn., Explorers Club, Soc. Profl. Journalists (pres. Washington chpt.), Kappa Sigma, Phi Kappa Phi. Roman Catholic. Clubs: Gridiron, Chevy Chase, Met. of Washington. Home: 4813 Quebec St NW Washington DC 20016-3228 Office: National Press Bldg PO Box 2042 Washington DC 20045

PRINCE (PRINCE ROGERS NELSON), musician, actor; b. Mpls., June 7, 1958; s. John L. and Mattie D. (Shaw) Nelson; m. 1996. Singer, songwriter, actor. Albums include For You, 1978, Dirty Mind, 1979, Controversy, 1981, 1999, 1983, film star and soundtrack Purple Rain, 1984, Around the World in a Day, 1985 (Best Soul/Rhythm and Blues Album of the Yr., Downbeat readers poll, 1985), Parade, 1986, Sign O' the Times, 1987, Lovesexy, 1988, Batman: Motion Picture Soundtrack, 1989 (Soundtrack of Yr. award Playboy mag. readers' poll, Best Pop/Rock album Downbeat mag. readers' poll), (with the New Power Generation) Diamonds and Pearls, 1991, (symbol as title), 1992, Come, 1994; films include Purple Rain, 1984 (Acad. award for best original score 1985), film star and soundtrack Under the Cherry Moon, 1986, film star and soundtrack Sign O' the Times, 1987; film appearance and soundtrack Graffiti Bridge, 1990; formerly mem. group Prince and the Revolution (Best Soul/Rhythm and Blues Group of Yr. Downbeat mag. readers poll 1985). Recipient 3 Grammy awards, 1985, Am. Music Achievement award for infuence on look and sound of the 80's; named Rhythm and Blues Musician of Yr. Down Beat mag. readers' poll, 1984, 1992.

PRINCE, ALAN THEODORE, former government official, engineering consultant; b. Toronto, Can., Feb. 15, 1915; s. Theodore and Sarah Helena (McMillan) P.; m. Virginia C. Lea, May 30, 1942; children: Linda Lea Prince Anderson, Mary Catherine Prince Kaschub. BA, U. Toronto, 1937, MA, 1938; PhD, U. Chgo., 1941. Registered profl. engr., Ont. With div. chemistry Nat. Research Council Can., Ottawa, 1940-43, Can. Refractories Ltd., Kilmar, Que., 1943-45; lectr. geology U. Man., 1945-46; with Canadian Dept. Mines and Tech. Surveys, 1946-67, dir. water research br., 1965-67; dir. inland waters br. Dept. Environment, 1967-73; asst. dep. minister planning and evaluation Dept. Energy, Mines and Resources, 1973-75; pres. Atomic Energy Control Bd., Ottawa, 1975-79; cons. Fellow Chem. Inst. Can., Mineral. Soc. Am.; mem. Canadian Inst. Mining and Metallurgy, Assn. Profl. Engrs. Ont. Home: 5445 Riverside Dr, PO Box 106, Manotick, ON Canada K4M 1A2

PRINCE, ANDREW STEVEN, lawyer, former government official; b. Bklyn., Oct. 9, 1943; s. Milton S. and Beatrice M. (Ratkin) P.; m. Rochelle Moskowitz, July 4, 1973; children: Brett, Kenneth. B.S., U.S. Naval Acad., 1965; M.B.A., Harvard U., 1974, J.D., 1974. Bar: N.Y. 1975, U.S. Supreme Ct. 1980. Assoc. firm Shearman & Sterling, N.Y.C., 1974-81; dep. asst. sec. Navy Dept., Washington, 1981-86; exec. v.p. fin., gen. counsel Urquhart and Co., Inc., McLean, Va., 1986-94; pres. BretKen Enterprises, McLean, Va., 1994—; sec. Potash Import & Chem. Corp., N.Y.C., 1979-81; mem. panel of arbitrators Am. Arbitration Assn., N.Y.C., 1979—. Bd. dirs. Harvard Coop. Soc., Cambridge, Mass., 1972-74; bd. dirs. USO, Washington, 1982—, N.Y.C., 1979-81. Served with USN, 1965-70; capt. Res. Mem. Harvard Bus. Sch. Club (exec. v.p.), Mil Order World Wars (judge adv.), Naval Acad. Alumni Assn.

PRINCE, ANGIE BENNETT, psychotherapist; b. Athens, Ga., Sept. 21, 1952; d. Charles Curtis and Margaret Adeline (Hanson) Bennett; m. Thomas Chafer Prince, III, Apr. 7, 1979; children: Rollin Thomas, Nathan Chafer, Merry Katherine. BA, U. Ga., 1975; MEd, Ga. State U., 1978; grad., Psychol. Studies Inst., 1978. Lic. psychol. examiner, counselor, Tenn.; reg. lobbyist, Tenn. V.p. Russell, Montgomery and Assocs., Knoxville and Nashville, Tenn.; counselor, pvt. practice Knoxville Counseling Ctr.; pres. Prince & Assocs., Knoxville. Mem. Knox County Rep. Exec. Com., precinct del.; mem. Jr. League Knoxville; com. mem. Leaderhip Knoxville, 1994; mem. Cedar Springs Presbyn. Ch., leader marriage preparation sem., group leader for survivors of sexual abuse; vol. Cedar Bluffs Schs. Mem. ACA, Am. Mental Health Counselor Assn., N.Am. Assn. Masters in Psychology (charter), Tenn. Assn. Psychol. Examiners (pres. 1994, 95), Knoxville Assn. Psychol. Examiners (past treas.), Christian Assn. Psychologists, Akima Club (assoc.).

PRINCE, CARL E., historian, educator; b. Newark, Dec. 8, 1934; s. Phillip G. and Anne (Silver) P.; children: Elizabeth, Jonathan. B.A. with honors, Rutgers U., 1956, M.A., 1958, Ph.D. in History, 1963. Instr. history Fairleigh Dickinson U., 1960-63; asst. prof. history Seton Hall U., 1963-66, assoc. prof., 1966-68; assoc. prof. N.Y. U., 1968-74, prof., 1974—, chmn. dept. history, 1978-86. Author books: including New Jersey's Jeffersonian Republican, 1789-1817, 1967, The Federalists and the Origins of the U.S. Civil Service, 1977, The Papers of William Livingston, 5 vols., 1979-88, The U.S. Customs Svc., 1989, Brooklyn's Dodgers: The Bums, The Borough and The Best of Baseball, 1996. Mem. exec. bd. N.J. Catholic Hist. Records Commn.; mem. N.J. Hist. Records Commn.; mem. exec. bd. United Negro Coll. Fund Archives.; Chmn. West Orange (N.J.) Citizens Against the Vietnam War, 1965-70; county coord. Essex County (N.J.) Citizens for McCarthy, 1968. Younger scholar fellow NEH, 1968-69; Fulbright scholar, Israel, 1972-73. Fellow N.J. Hist. Soc.; mem. Soc. for Historians of Early Am. Republic (exec. bd. 1980-86, pres. 1983-84), Inst. Early Am. History and Culture (asso.), Columbia U. Seminar in Early Am. History (asso.). Jewish. Office: NYU Dept History 19 University Pl New York NY 10003-4501

PRINCE, CATHY LONG, neuro-orthopedic nurse administrator; b. McCaysville, Ga., Oct. 6, 1956; d. Joseph H. and Charlene E. (Aaron) Long; m. James Darryl Prince, Aug. 19, 1983; 1 child, Christy Renae McDaniel-Short. Diploma, Dalton Vocat. Sch. Health Occupations, 1979; ASN, North Ga. Coll., 1987. RN, Ga. Nursing asst. Fannin Regional Hosp., Blue Ridge, Ga.; EMT, Gilmer County Emergency Med. System, Ellijay, Ga.; EMT Pickens County Emergency Med. System, Jasper, Ga.; advanced clin. nurse NE Ga. Med. Ctr., Gainesville; DON Mountainside Nursing Home, Jasper, Ga. Mem. Nat. Assn. Orhopaedic Nurses, Ga. Info. Control Network. Home: PO Box 26 East Ellijay GA 30539-0026

PRINCE, CHARLES O., III, lawyer; b. 1950. BA, U. So. Calif., 1971, MA, JD, 1975. Bar: Pa. 1975, Md. 1979, Minn. 1982. Formerly gen. counsel Commercial Credit Co.; now sr. v.p., gen. counsel, sec. Traveler's Group, N.Y.C. Office: Traveler's Group 388 Greenick St New York NY 10013*

PRINCE, FRANCES ANNE KIELY, civic worker; b. Toledo, Dec. 20, 1923; d. John Thomas and Frances (Pusteoska) Kiely; m. Richard Edward Prince, Jr., Aug. 27, 1951; children: Anne, Richard III (dec.). Student U. Louisville, 1947-49; AB, Berea Coll., 1951; postgrad., Kent Sch. Social Work, 1951, Creighton U., 1969; MPA, U. Nebr., Omaha, 1978. Instr. flower arranging Western Wyo. Jr. Coll., 1965, 66; editor Nebr. Garden News, 1979-81, 83-90, emeritus, 1990. Author poems. Chmn. Lone Troop coun. Girl Scouts U.S.A., 1954-57, trainer leaders, 1954-68, mem. state camping com., 1959-61, bd. dirs. Wyo. state coun., 1966-69; chmn. Cmty. Improvement, Green River, Wyo., 1959, 63-65, Wyo. Fedn. Women's Clubs State Libr. Svcs., 1966-69; mem. Wyo. State Adv. Bd. on Libr. Inter-Co-op., 1965-69, state libr. bd., 1965-69, Nat. sub com. Commn. on the Bicentennial of the U.S. Constitution, 1986-91; bd. dirs. Sweetwater County Libr. System, 1962-69, pres. bd., 1967-68; adv. coun. Sch. Dist. 66, 1970-79; bd. dirs. Opera Angels, 1971, fund raising chmn., 1971-72, v.p., 1974-80; bd. dirs. Morning Musicale, 1971-82; bazaar com. Children's Hosp., 1970-75; docent Joslyn Art Mus., 1970—; mem. Nebr. Forestry Adv. Bd., 1976—; citizens adv. bd. Met. Area Planning Agy., 1979—; mem. Nebr. Tree-Planting Commn., 1980—; bd. dirs. U.S. Constn. Bicentennial Commn. Nebr., 1986-92, Omaha Commn. on the Bicentennial, 1987-92, Nat. commn. on Bicentennial of U.S. Constitution, 1986-92; bd. dirs. United Ch. Christ, Intermountain, 1963-69, mem. exec. com., 1966-69; bd. dirs. United Ch. Christ, 1985-92. Recipient Libr. Svc. award Sweetwater County Library, 1968; Girl Scout Svcs. award, 1967; Conservation award U.S. Forest Service, 1981; Plant Two Trees award, 1981; Nat. Arbor Day award, 1982; Pres.

award Nat. coun. of State Garden Clubs, 1986, 87, 89, Joyce Kilmer award Nat. Arbor Day Found., 1990; awards U.S. Constn. Bicentennial Commn. Nebr., 1987, 91, Omaha Commn. on the Bicentennial, 1987, Nat. Bicentennial Leadership award Coun. for Advancement of Citizenship, 1989, Nat. Conservation medal DAR, 1991, George Washington silver award Nat. commn. on Bicentennial of U.S. Constitution, 1992, Mighty Oak award Garden Clubs of Nebr., 1992. Mem. AAUW (Vol. of Yr. Omaha br. 1989), New Neighbors League (dir. 1969-71), Ikebana Internat., Symphony Guild, Assistance League Omaha, Omaha Playhouse Guild, ALA, Nebr. Libr. Assn., Omaha Coun. Garden Clubs (1st v.p. 1972, pres. 1973-75, state bd. dirs. 1979—, mem. nat. council bd. dirs. 1979—, pres. award 1988, 89, 90), Internat. Platform Assn., Nat. Trust for Hist. Preservation, Nebr. Flower Show Judges Coun. (chmn. 1995—), Nat. Coun. State Garden Clubs (chmn. arboriculture 1985-90, 93—, chmn. nature conservancy 1991-93), Nebr. Fedn. Garden Clubs (pres. 1978-81), Garden Club (dir. 1970-72, pres. 1972-75). Home: 8909 Broadmoor Dr Omaha NE 68114-4248

PRINCE, GARNETT B., JR., business executive; b. Chattanooga, Feb. 1, 1949; w. Garnett B. and Anna Mae (Elrod) P.; m. Deborah Roemer, Jan. 19, 1971 (div.); m. Charlotte V. McCauley, July 23, 1983; children: Shelly McCauley, Becky, Brandon. Student radio and TV broadcasting, Coastal Carolina Community Coll., Jacksonville, N.C., 1971; student, No. Va. Community Coll., Sterling, 1979-80. Dep. ct. clerk Criminal Ct., Chattanooga, 1971-73; dist. field rep. VA, Chattanooga, 1973-76; leadership tng. cons. Nat. Vocat.-Indsl. Clubs Am., Leesburg, Va., 1976-78, dir. tng. and govt. relations, 1978-84; spl. asst. to sec. U.S. Dept. Labor, Washington, 1984-85; dep. asst. sec. for vets. employment and tng. U.S. Dept. Labor, 1985-88; dep. dir. Nat. Drug Policy Bd., Office of Pres., Washington, 1988-89; regional mgr. state govt. affairs Parke-Davis div. Warner-Lambert Co., Atlanta, 1989—; dir. fed. health care policy Warner-Lambert Co., Washington, 1991—, dir. govt. devel., 1995—. Co-author: The Meetings Kit, 1985. Trustee U.S. Internat. Youth Yr. Com., Washington, 1985. Served with USMC, 1967-71. Mem. Mil. Order Purple Heart, DAV, VFW, Am. Legion. Republican. Lodge: Masons. Avocations: golf; bowling; swimming. Home and Office: 17 Uvilla Est Shenandoah Junction WV 25442-9538

PRINCE, GERALD JOSEPH, Romance languages educator; b. Alexandria, Egypt, Nov. 7, 1942; came to U.S., 1959, naturalized, 1964; s. Tully Rudolph and Marguerite (Bigio) P.; m. Ellen Friedman, June 25, 1967. B.A., Bklyn. Coll., 1963; M.A., U. Fla., 1963; Ph.D., Brown U., 1968. Instr. French lang. U. Pa., Phila., 1967-68, asst. prof., 1968-73, assoc. prof., 1973-81, prof. Romance langs., 1981—, chmn. comparative lit. program, 1984-87; co-dir. Ctr. Cultural Studies, 1987—. Author: Métaphysique et Technique dans l'Oeuvre Romanesque de Sartre, 1968, A Grammar of Stories, 1973, Narratology: The Form and Function of Narrative, 1982, A Dictionary of Narratology, 1987, Narrative as Theme, 1992. Contbr. articles and revs. to scholarly jours. Recipient award of honor, Bklyn. Coll., 1978, Lindback award for excellence in teaching U. Pa., 1974. Mem. MLA, N.E. MLA (officer 1983-86), Am. Comparative Lit. Assn. (adv. bd. 1983-87), Phi Beta Kappa, Phi Kappa Phi, Pi Delta Phi. Office: Ctr Cultural Studies Univ Pa 521 Williams Hall Philadelphia PA 19104

PRINCE, GREGORY SMITH, JR., academic administrator; b. Washington, May 7, 1939; s. Gregory Smith and Margaret (Minor) P.; m. Toni Layton Brewer; children: Tara Wyndom, Gregory S. III. BA, Yale U., 1961, M in Philosophy, 1969, PhD, 1973; cert. in teaching English as a Second Language, Georgetown U., 1961; DHL (hon.), Amherst Coll., 1991, LLD (hon.), 1991. Instr. New Asia Coll., Kowloon, Hong Kong, 1961-62, Chinese U., Kowloon, 1962-63, Yale China Assn., Kowloon, 1961-63, Woodberry Forest (Va.) Sch., 1963-65; dean summer programs Dartmouth Coll., Hanover, N.H., 1970-72, asst. dean faculty, 1972-78, assoc. dean faculty, 1978-89; pres. Hampshire Coll., Amherst, Mass., 1989—; mem. coun. on race and ethnic justice ABA; bd. dirs. Mass Ventures. Producer: (film) A Way of Learning, 1988. Trustee Montshire Mus. Sci., Hanover, 1973-89, Washington Campus, 1978—; trustee, chmn. Univ. Press New England, Hanover, 1983-84; trustee, pres. Yale-China Assn., New Haven, 1969-84; bd. dirs., pres. Five Colls., Inc., Amherst, 1989—; bd. dirs. Mass. Internat. Festival for Arts, 1994—; chmn. bd. dirs. Assn. Ind. Colls. and Univs. Mass., 1994-95; mem. commn. on accreditation Am. Coun. Edn. Coe fellow Stanford U., 1965, Woodrow Wilson fellow Yale U., 1966, NDEA fellow, 1967-70. Mem. Internat. Assn. of Chiefs Police Found. (bd. dirs. 1991-95). Democrat. Episcopalian. Home: 15 Middle St Amherst MA 01002-3009 Office: Hampshire Coll 893 West St Amherst MA 01002-3372

PRINCE, HAROLD, theatrical producer; b. N.Y.C., Jan. 30, 1928; s. Milton A. and Blanche (Stern) P.; m. Judith Chaplin, Oct. 26, 1962; children: Charles, Daisy. AB, U. Pa., 1948, DFA (hon.), 1971; LittD, Emerson Coll., 1971. chmn. Performing Arts Libr., N.Y.C. Co-producer Pajama Game, 1954-56 (Antoinette Perry award), Damn Yankees, 1955-57 (Antoinette Perry award), New Girl in Town, 1957-58, West Side Story, 1957-59, Fiorello, 1959-61 (Antoinette Perry award, Pulitzer prize), Tenderloin, 1960-61, A Call on Kuprin, 1961, They Might Be Giants, London, 1961, Side by Side by Sondheim, 1976; producer Take Her, She's Mine, 1961-62, A Funny Thing Happened on the Way to the Forum, 1962-64 (Antoinette Perry award), Fiddler on the Roof, 1964-72 (Antoinette Perry award), Poor Bitos, 1964, Flora the Red Menace, 1965; dir., producer: She Loves Me, 1963-64 (London 1964), Superman, 1966, Cabaret, 1966-69 (Antoinette Perry award 1968), Zorba, 1968-69, Company, 1970-72 (Antoinette Perry award 1972), A Little Night Music, 1973-74 (Antoinette Perry award 1975), Pacific Overtures, 1976; co-dir., producer Follies, 1971-72, Faust; co-producer, dir. Candide, 1974-75, Merrily We Roll Along, 1981, A Doll's Life, 1982; dir. A Family Affair, 1962, Baker Street, 1965, Great God Brown, 1972-73, The Visit, 1973-74, Love for Love, 1974-75, Ashmedai, 1976, On The Twentieth Century, 1978, Evita (London, 1978, Broadway, 1979, L.A., 1980, Australia, 1980, Chgo., 1980, Detroit, 1982), Sweeney Todd, The Demon Barber of Fleet Street, Broadway, 1979, London, 1980, Silverlake, 1980, Willie Stark, 1981, Candide, 1982, Madama Butterfly, 1982, Turandot, 1983, Play Memory, 1984, End of the World, 1984, Diamonds, 1984, Grind, 1985, Cabaret Revival, 1987, Roza, 1987, Phantom of the Opera, London, 1986, N.Y.C., (Antoinette Perry award) 1988, La Fanciula del West, Don Giovanni, N.Y. City Opera, 1989, Faust, Met. Opera, 1990; adapter, dir. Grandchild of Kings, 1992, Kiss of the Spider Woman, the Musical, 1992 (London), 1993 Broadway, Show Boat, 1993 (Toronto), 1994 (Broadway, Antoinette Perry award, 1995); co-producer films The Pajama Game, 1957, Damn Yankees, 1958; dir. films Something for Everyone, 1970, A Little Night Music, 1978. Mem. coun. Nat. Endowment Arts; pres. League N.Y. Theatres, 1964-66; chmn. Performing Arts Libr., N.Y.C. Recipient 20 Antoinette Perry (Tony) Meml. awards, Critics Circle awards, Pulitzer prize, 1961, Best Mus. awards London Evening Std., Kennedy Ctr. Honors, 1994. Office: 10 Rockefeller Plz New York NY 10020-1903

PRINCE, JERRY LADD, engineering educator; b. Manchester, Conn., Aug. 10, 1957; s. Ralph Peery and Lela (Ladd) P.; m. Carol Ann Morello, June 12, 1982; children: Emily, Benjamin, Mark, David. SM, MIT, 1982, PhD, 1988. Rsch. asst. MIT, Cambridge, 1979-82; engr. Brigham and Women's Hosp., Boston, 1982-83; teaching asst. MIT, Cambridge, 1983-84, rsch. asst., 1984-88; mem. tech. staff The Analytical Scis. Corp., Reading, Mass., 1988; asst. prof. Johns Hopkins U., Balt., 1989-94, assoc. prof. elec. and computer engrng., 1994—. Contbr. articles to profl. jours. Mem. IEEE (assoc. editor Transactions on Image Processing 1992-95), Sigma Xi. Office: Johns Hopkins Univ 3400 N Charles St Baltimore MD 21218-2608

PRINCE, JOHN LUTHER, III, engineering educator; b. Austin, Tex., Nov. 13, 1941; s. John Luther and Glynda (Chollett) P.; m. Martha Ann Hight, Mar. 4, 1960; children: Cynthia Kay, John Luther IV, Alan Douglas, David William. BSEE, So. Meth. U., 1965; MEE, N.C. State U., 1968, PhD, 1969. Research engr. RTI, Res. Tri. Park, N.C., 1968-70; mem. tech. staff Tex. Instruments, Dallas, 1970-75; from assoc. prof. to prof. Clemson (S.C.) U., 1975-80; dir. R.A. Intermedics, Inc., Freeport, Tex., 1980-83; prof. U. Ariz., Tucson, 1983—; acting dir. packaging scis. Semiconductor Rsch. Corp., 1991-92; cons. numerous semi-conductor and electronics cos., 1983—; dir. Electronic Packaging Lab., 1984-91, Ctr. for Electronic Packaging Rsch., 1991—, SEMATECH Ctr. of Excellence for Contamination and Defect Control, 1988-90. Contbr. articles to profl. jours. Named Ariz. Innovator of the Yr., 1992; NSF fellow, 1965-68. Fellow IEEE; mem. Am. Philatelic Soc. Lutheran. Avocations: stamp collecting, classic cars, motorcycles. Home: 7542 N San Lorenzo Dr Tucson AZ 85704-3141 Office: U Ariz Tucson AZ 85721

PRINCE, JULIUS S. (BUD), retired foreign service reserve officer; b. Yonkers, N.Y., July 21, 1911; s. Julius and Clara B. (Rich) P.; m. Eleanora Molloy, July 6, 1943; children: Thomas Marc, Tod Ainslee (dec.), Richard M. Johnson. B.A., Yale U., 1932; M.D., Columbia U., 1938, M.P.H., 1948; Dr.P.H., Harvard, 1957. Intern Sinai Hosp., Balt., 1939-40; asst. resident medicine N.Y. U. div. Goldwater Meml. Hosp., 1941-42; dist. state health officer N.Y. State Dept. Health, Jamestown, 1948-58; chief pub. health div. USAID, Ethiopia, 1958-67; prin. investigator demonstration and evaluation project AID, Ethiopia, 1959-67; chief Africa div. Population and Humanitarian Affairs, Population Office, AID, Washington, 1967-73; dir. Africa Regional Population Office, Accra, Ghana, 1973-74; chief health, population and nutrition projects AID, Ghana, 1974-76; cons. internat. health APHA, 1977-78, Pacific Cons., Inc., 1978-82, RONCO Inc., 1982; pub. health specialist/sr. health advisor One Am., Inc., 1982-87; sr. pub. health and nutrition specialist Internat. Sci. and Tech. Inst. Inc., 1985-94; cons. on internat. health, 1985—; report on sustainability of AID supported health, population and nutrition programs, Ghana, 1963-85, Ctr. Devel. Info. and Evaluation AID, 1988, Annotated History of AID-Supported Health and Nutrition Rsch.: From Outset to Present, Introduction and Background, AID Office Health, 1991, Compendium of Abstracts, 1985-92, rsch. by historically black colls. and univs. under AID Univ. Ctr./Rsch. and Univ. Devel. Linkages, 1985-92. Contbr. chpt. to book. Served from lt. to maj. M.C. Royal Canadian Army, 1942-46. Recipient Letter of Commendation, Adj. Gen. Can. Army, 1946, Superior honor award AID, 1968, Letter of Commendation, 1977. Fellow APHA, Soc. Applied Anthropology, Washington Acad. Scis., Royal Soc. Health; mem. AMA, N.Y. State Pub. Health Assn. (pres. 1957), Pan Am. Med. Assn., Am. Assn. World Health (emeritus mem. bd. dirs.), Internat. Soc. Hypertension in Blacks, Population Assn. Am., Soc. Internat. Devel., Nat. Coun. Internat. Health (award 1992), World Med. Assn., Soc. Prospective Medicine, Am. Heart Asns., Can. Soc. Internat. Health. Home and Office: 7103 Pinehurst Pky Chevy Chase MD 20815-3144

PRINCE, KENNETH STEPHEN, lawyer; b. Newton, Mass., Jan. 28, 1950; s. Samuel and Edna L. Prince; m. Patricia Denning, Jan. 15, 1977 (dec. Nov. 1985); 1 child, Kenneth Stephen Jr.; m. Jane M. McCabe, Sept. 5, 1987; 1 child, Allison Pamela. BA, U. Pa., 1972; JD, Boston Coll., 1975. Bar: N.Y. 1976, Mass. 1975, U.S. Dist. Ct. (so. and ea. dists.) N.Y. 1978. Assoc. Shearman & Sterling, N.Y.C., 1975-83, ptnr., 1984—; antitrust group practice leader Shearman & Sterling, 1992—. Mem. N.Y. Law Inst. (exec. com. 1984—), Order of Coif.

PRINCE, LARRY L., automotive parts and supplies company executive; b. 1937. With Genuine Parts Co., Atlanta, 1958—, v.p., then group v.p., 1977-83, exec. v.p., 1983-86, pres., chief oper. officer, 1986-90, chief exec. officer, 1989—, chmn. bd. dirs., 1990—, also bd. dirs. Office: Genuine Parts Co 2999 Circle 75 Pky NW Atlanta GA 30339-3050*

PRINCE, LEAH FANCHON, art educator and research institute administrator; b. Hartford, Conn., Aug. 12, 1939; d. Meyer and Annie (Forman) Berman; m. Herbert N. Prince, Jan. 30, 1955; children: Daniel L., Richard N., Robert G. Student, U. Conn., 1957-59, Rutgers U., Newark, 1962; BFA, Fairleigh Dickinson U., 1970; postgrad., Caldwell Coll. for Women, 1973-75, Parsons Sch. of Design, N.Y.C., 1978. Cert. tchr. art, N.J. Tchr. art Caldwell-West Caldwell (N.J.) Pub. Schs., 1970-75; pres. Britannia Imports Ltd., Fairfield, N.J., 1979-89; tchr. religious studies Bohrer-Kaufman Hebrew Acad., Randolph, N.J., 1981-82; co-founder and corp. sec. Gibraltar Biol. Labs., Inc., Fairfield, 1970—; dir., co-founder Gibraltar Inst. for Rsch. and Tng., Fairfield, 1984—; cons. Internat. Antiques and Fine Arts Industries, U.K., 1979-89; cons. in art exhibitry Passaic County Coll., Paterson, N.J., 1989-93; art curator Fairleigh Dickinson U., Rutherford, N.J., 1972-74; curator history of design Bloomfield (N.J.) Coll., 1990-91; lectr. nat. meeting Am. Soc. Microbiology, New Orleans, 1989; spkr. in field. Exhibited in group shows at Bloomfield (N.J.) Coll., 1990, Caldwell Women's Club, N.J., 1991, State Fedn. Women's Clubs Ann. Show, 1992 (1st pl. award 1992), Newark Art Mus., 1992, West (N.J.) Essex Art Assn., 1990, Somerset (N.J.) Art Assn. Ann. Juried Show, 1994, Mortimer Gallery, Gladstone, N.J., 1994, Tewksbury His. Soc. (1st pl. award 1994); one-woman shows include Passaic County Coll., N.J., 1990, Caldwell Coll., N.J., 1990. Chair ann. juried art awards Arts Coun. of Essex Bd. Trustees, Montclair, N.J., 1984-90; chair fundraising Arts Coun. Essex County, N.J., 1989. Recipine 1st place award N.J. Tewksbury Hist. Soc., 1994. Mem. AAUW, Somerset Art Assn., Nat. Mus. of Women in the Arts, Barnegat Light Yacht Club. Republican. Avocations: boating, tennis, the Arts. Home: 5 Standish Dr Morristown NJ 07960-3224

PRINCE, MILTON S., investment company executive; b. Bklyn., Jan. 20, 1912; s. Abraham and Frances (Raps) P.; m. Beatrice Ratzkin, Jan. 18, 1942; children: Andrew, Thomas. BS, Carnegie Inst. Tech., 1935; LLB, St. Johns U., Bklyn., 1938, JSD, 1939. Bar: N.Y. 1940, U.S. Dist. Ct. (ea. and so. dists.) N.Y. 1950, U.S. Ct. Mil. Appeals, U.S. Supreme Ct. 1954. Sole practice, Bklyn., 1940-41; mng. ptnr., gen. counsel Prince & Prince, Bklyn., 1946—. Trustee U.S. Naval Acad. Found., Annapolis, Md., 1964—; dir., excom. USO, N.Y.C., 1965—; nat. council mem., Bklyn. council officer, dir. Boy Scouts Am., Irving, Tex. and Bklyn., 1972—; state advisor U.S. Congl. Adv. Bd., 1982-88. Served with USN, 1941-45, to capt. USNR, to rear admiral N.Y. State Naval Militia, 1955—. Recipient USN Disting. Pub. Svc. award, 1972, Shofar award Boy Scouts Am., 1984, Bklyn. citation, 1990; decorated various medals Dept. Def. Mem. Navy League U.S. (nat. dir., officer 1962—), U.S. Naval Inst. (silver), ABA, Mil. Order World Wars (dir., past comdr. 1966-67, Meritorious Achievement award 1964), Naval Order U.S. (ex. com. 1960-88), Salmagundi Club (N.Y.C.), Coasters Harbor Yacht Club (Newport, R.I.), Mcpl. Club, Bklyn. Club, Army-Navy Club (Washington), Rotary. Avocations: sailing, golf, travel, pub. service.

PRINCE, MORTON BRONENBERG, physicist; b. Phila., Apr. 1, 1924; s. David H. and Jennie (Bronenberg) P.; m. Blanche E. Stern, June 15, 1947; 1 child, Judith Ann. A.B., Temple U., 1947; Ph.D., MIT, 1951. Mem. tech. staff Bell Telephone Labs., Inc., Murray Hill, N.J., 1951-56; v.p., gen. mgr. Hoffman Electronics Corp., El Monte, Calif., 1956-61; with electro optical systems div. Xerox, Pasadena, Calif., 1961-69; pres. SSR Instruments Co., Santa Monica, Calif., 1970-74; v.p., gen. mgr. Meret Inc., Santa Monica, 1974-75; with U.S. Dept. Energy, Washington, 1975-93. Contbr. chpts. to books, articles to profl. jours. Served with U.S. Army, 1943-46. Recipient Marconi premium Inst. Radio Engrs., Gt. Britain, 1959, Becquerel prize European Commn., 1994. Fellow IEEE; mem. Am. Phys. Soc., Internat. Solar Energy Soc. Club: Cosmos. Home: 7301 Coventry Ave Apt 601 Elkins Park PA 19027-2953

PRINCE, ROBB LINCOLN, manufacturing company executive; b. Duluth, Minn., June 30, 1941; s. Milton H. and Katherine (Lincoln) P.; m. Jacqueline H. Marik, June 19, 1965; children: Daniel, Deborah. BA in Econs., Carleton Coll., 1963; MBA in Mktg., U. Pa., 1965. With mktg. planning United Airlines, Chgo., 1965-72; dir. planning Jostens Inc., Mpls., 1973-74, treas., 1975-79, v.p., treas., 1979-95, ret., 1995; dir. FORTIS Mut. Funds, Analysts Internat. Corp. With USN, 1966-69. Mem. Wharton Alumni Club (bd. dirs.). Office: 5108 Duggan Plz Edina MN 55439-1453

PRINCE, THOMAS E., bank executive; b. 1947. With Security Pacific Corp., L.A., 1968-92; exec. v.p., CFO, treas. Downey Savs Loan Assn., Newport Beach, Calif., 1992—. Office: Downey Savs Loan Assn 3501 Jamboree Rd Newport Beach CA 92660*

PRINCE, THOMAS RICHARD, accountant, educator; b. New Albany, Miss., Dec. 7, 1934; s. James Thompson and Callie Florence (Howell) P.; m. Eleanor Carol Polkoff, July 14, 1962; children: Thomas Andrew, John Michael, Adrienne Carol. B.S., Miss. State U., 1956, M.S., 1957; Ph.D. in Accountancy, U. Ill., 1962. C.P.A., Ill. Instr. U. Ill., 1960-62; mem. faculty Northwestern U., 1962—, prof. acctg. and info. systems, 1969—, chmn. dept. accounting and info. systems Grad. Sch. Mgmt., 1968-75, prof. health svcs. mgmt., 1980—; cons. in field; dir. Applied Research Systems, Inc. Author: Extension of the Boundaries of Accounting Theory, 1962, Information Systems for Management Planning and Control, 3d edit, 1975, Financial Reporting and Cost Control for Health Care Entities, 1992. Served to 1st lt. AUS, 1957-60. Mem. Am. Accounting Assn., Am. Inst. C.P.A.s, Am. Econ. Assn., Inst. Mgmt. Scis., Fin. Execs. Inst., AAAS, Ill. Soc. C.P.A.s, Nat. Assn. Accts., Alpha Tau Omega, Phi Kappa Phi, Omicron Delta Kappa, Delta Sigma Pi, Beta Alpha Psi. Congregationalist. Home: 303 Richmond Rd Kenilworth IL 60043-1138 Office: Northwestern U Leverone Hall Evanston IL 60208

PRINCE, WILLIAM J., church officer; m. Evelyn Imel; 1 child. 4th pres. Mt. Vernon Nazarene Coll., 1980-89; pres. So. Nazarene U., 1989; bd. gen. supts. Ch. of the Nazarene, Indpls., 1989—; former supt. Pitts. dist.; pres. European Nazarene Bible Coll., 1970-76; pastor Lone Pine, Reseda and Ventura, Calif., Mpls., and Dayton; min. teaching and preaching missions in Haiti, Guatemala, South Africa, Zambia, Zimbabwe, Swaziland, Kenya; leader preacher missions in Hawaii; participant European Congress on Evangelism, Amsterdam, The Netherlands; speaker to students, Shanghai, 1989; speaker commencement Luzon Nazarene Theol. Sem. Office: Church of Nazarene 6401 Paseo Blvd Kansas City MO 64131-1213

PRINCE, WILLIAM TALIAFERRO, federal judge; b. Norfolk, Va., Oct. 3, 1929; s. James Edward and Helen Marie (Taliaferro) P.; m. Anne Carroll Hannegan, Apr. 12, 1958; children: Sarah Carroll Prince Pishko, Emily Taliaferro, William Taliaferro, John Hannegan, Anne Martineau, Robert Harrison. Student, Coll. William and Mary, Norfolk, 1947-48, 49-50; AB, Williamsburg, 1955, BCL, 1957, MLT, 1959. Bar: Va. 1957. Lectr. acctg. Coll. William and Mary, 1955-57; lectr. law Marshall-Wythe Sch. Law, 1957-59; assoc. Williams, Kelly & Greer, Norfolk, 1959-63, ptnr., 1963-90; U.S. magistrate judge Eastern Dist. of Va., Norfolk, 1990—; pres. Am. Inn of Ct. XXVII, 1987-89. Bd. editors: The Virginia Lawyer, A Basic Practice Handbook, 1966. Bd. dirs. Madonna Home, Inc., 1978-93, Soc. Alumni of Coll. William and Mary, 1985-88. Fellow Am. Coll. Trial Lawyers, Am. Bar Found., Va. Law found. (bd. dirs. 1976-90); mem. ABA (ho. of dels. 1984-90), Am. Judicature Soc. (bd. dirs. 1984-88), Va. State Bar (coun. 1973-77, exec. com. 1975-80, pres. 1978-79). Roman Catholic. Home: 1227 Graydon Ave Norfolk VA 23507-1006 Office: Walter E Hoffman US Courthouse 600 Granby St Ste 181 Norfolk VA 23510-1915

PRINCIPAL, VICTORIA, actress; b. Fukuoka, Japan, Jan. 3, 1950; d. Victor and Ree (Veal) P.; m. Harry Glassman, 1985. Attended, Miami-Dade Community Coll.; studied acting with Max Croft, Al Sacks and Estelle Harman, Jean Scott, Royal Acad. Dramatic Arts. Worked as model, including TV commls.; appearences include (film) The Life and Times of Judge Roy Bean, 1972, The Naked Ape, 1973, Earthquake, 1974, I Will I Will For Now, 1976, Vigilante Force, 1976; (TV movies) Last Hours Before Morning, 1975, Fantasy Island, 1977, The Night They Stole Miss Beautiful, 1977, Pleasure Palace, 1980, Not Just Another Affair, 1982, Mistress, 1987, The Burden of Proof, 1990, Just Life, 1992, Beyond Obsession, 1994; exec. prodr., actress Naked Lie, 1989, Blind Witness, 1989, Sparks: The Price of Passion, 1990, Don't Touch My Daughter, 1991, Seduction: Three Tales from the Inner Sanctum, 1993, River of Rage: The Taking of Maggie Keene, 1993; exec. prodr. Midnight's Child, 1992; (TV series) Dallas, 1978-87; (theatre) Love Letters, 1990; author: The Body Principal, 1983, The Beauty Principal, 1984, The Diet Principal, 1987. Office: ICM 8942 Wilshire Blvd Beverly Hills CA 90211*

PRINCZ, JUDITH, publishing executive. BA, Wheaton Coll., 1974. Retail circulation asst. Family Media, 1975-76; asst. mgr. direct mail Redbook, 1977; subscription mgr. Women Sports, 1977; circulation mgr. Sport mag., 1978-79; circulation dir. Weight Watcher's, 1979-83; assoc. pub. Am. Baby mag., N.Y.C., 1983-89, v.p., pub., 1989—; v.p., group pub. Cahners Childcare Group, 1992—. Office: American Baby/Healthy Kids 249 W 17th St New York NY 10011*

PRINDIVILLE, ROBERT ANDREW, investment executive; b. Chgo., Aug. 18, 1935; s. James A. and Mary (Greening) P.; m. Kathleen Hardie, Aug. 8, 1959; children: Eleanor, Victoria, Christopher, Charles, Anne, Mary Alice, Genevieve. BS, Marquette U., 1958. With Pimco Advisors L.P., Stamford, Conn., 1958—; pres. Pimco Advisors Funds; bd. dirs. Chgo. Bd. Option Exchange, 1978-82. Mem. City Midday Club, Baltusrol Golf Club. Office: PIMCO Advisors LP 2187 Atlantic St Stamford CT 06902

PRINDLE, WILLIAM ROSCOE, consultant, retired glass company executive; b. San Francisco, Dec. 19, 1926; s. Vivian Arthur and Harriette Alnora (Nickerson) P.; m. June Laverne Anderson, June 20, 1947; children—Carol Susan, William Alastair. B.S., U. Calif., Berkeley, 1948, M.S., 1950; Sc.D., M.I.T., 1955. Asst. tech. dir. Hazel-Atlas Glass Co., 1954-56; mgr. research Hazel-Atlas Glass div. Continental Can Co., Wheeling, W.Va., 1956-58, gen. mgr. research and devel., 1959-62; mgr. materials research Am. Optical Co., Southbridge, Mass., 1962-65; v.p. research Southbridge and Framingham, Mass., 1971-76; dir. research Ferro Corp., Cleve., 1966-67, v.p. research, 1967-71; exec. dir. Nat. Materials Adv. Bd., NRC-NAS, Washington, 1976-80; dir. adminstrv. and tech. svcs. R & D div. Corning Glass Works, N.Y., 1980-85, dir. materials rsch., 1985-87; assoc. dir. R & D, Engring. div. Corning Glass Works (now Corning, Inc.), N.Y., 1987-90; div. v.p., assoc. dir. tech. group Corning Inc., N.Y., 1990-92; ret.; pres. XII Internat. Glass Congress, 1980, Internat. Commn. on Glass, 1985-88. Served with U.S. Navy, 1944-46. Named Outstanding Ceramist of New Eng., New Eng. sect. Am. Ceramic Soc., 1974, Toledo Glass and Ceramic award NW Ohio sect., 1986, Albert Victor Bleininger Meml. award Pitts. sect., 1989; Friedberg Meml. lecture Nat. Inst. Ceramic Engrs., 1990. Fellow Am. Ceramic Soc. (disting. life, pres. 1980-81), Soc. Glass Tech., Am. Soc. for Metals Internat.; mem. NAE, AAAS, Cosmos Club (Washington), Sigma Xi, Phi Gamma Delta. Home and Office: 1556 Crestline Dr Santa Barbara CA 93105-4611

PRINE, JOHN, singer, songwriter; b. Maywood, Ill., Oct. 10, 1946. Pres. Oh Boy Records, Nashville. Began performing original compositions, 1969; songs include Paradise, Sam. Stone, Hello in There, Dear Abby; albums include Bruised Orange, Common Sense, Diamonds in the Rough, John Prine, Pink Cadillac, Prime Prine, Storm Windows, Sweet Revenge, Aimless Love, German Afternoons, 1986, John Prine Live, 1988, The Missing Years, 1991 (Grammy award for best contemporary folk rec.), Great Days: The John Pride Anthology, 1993, Lost Dogs & Mixed Blessings, 1995. Served with U.S. Army. Address: Oh Boy Records 33 Music Sq W Ste 102-a Nashville TN 37203-3226

PRINEAS, RONALD JAMES, epidemiologist, educator; b. Junee, New South Wales, Australia, Sept. 19, 1937; came to U.S., 1973; s. Peter John and Nancy (MacDonald) P.; m. Julienne Swynny, Apr. 21, 1961; children: Matthew Leigh, Anna Mary, John Paul, Miranda Jane. MBBS, U. Sydney, Australia, 1960; PhD, U. London, 1969. Med. house officer Prince Henry Hosp., Sydney, 1961; sr. med. house officer Royal Perth Hosp., Australia, 1962; registrar in medicine Royal Glasgow Infirmary, Scotland, 1963-64; research fellow London Sch. Hygiene and Tropical Medicine, 1964-67, lectr., 1967-68; asst. in medicine U. Melbourne, Australia, 1968-72; prof. epidemiology U. Minn., Mpls., 1973-88, prof. medicine, 1974-88; prof., chair epidemiology and pub. health U Miami, Fla., 1988—; cons. WHO, Geneva, 1976—, Nat. Heart Lung and Blood Inst., 1976—; prin. investigator Nat. Health Lung and Blood Inst., 1973—. Author books, including; Blood Pressure Sounds; Their Measurement and Meaning, 1978; The Minnesota Code Manual of Electrocardiographic Findings, 1982; also numerous articles. Recipient numerous cardiovascular disease research grants and contracts. Mem. Fla. affiliate Am. Heart Assn., Mpls., 1973—, chmn. adv. groups, 1975—. Fellow Royal Coll. Physicians Edinburgh, Am. Coll. Cardiology, Am. Pub. Health Assn., Soc. Epidemiologic Research, Am. Heart Assn. Council on Epidemiology, Internat. Soc. Hypertension, Council on Human Biology, Internat. Soc. Cardiology, Soc. Controlled Clin. Trials, Am. Coll. Epidemiology, Am. Soc. Epidemiology, Internat. Soc. Human Biology; mem. Royal Coll. Physicians London. Avocations: reading; raising a family. Office: U Miami Sch Medicine Dept Epidemiology & Pub Health PO Box 669R Miami FL 33101-0116

PRINGLE, BARBARA CARROLL, state legislator; b. N.Y.C., Apr. 4, 1939; d. Nicholas Robert and Anna Joan (Woloshinovich) Terlesky; m. Richard D. Pringle, Nov. 28, 1959; children: Christopher, Rhonda. Student, Cuyahoga C.C. With Dun & Bradstreet, 1957-60; precinct committeewoman City of Cleve., 1976-77; elected mem. Cleve. City Coun., 1977-81;

mem. Ohio Ho. of Reps., Columbus, 1982—; 20th dist. state ctrl. commet-teewoman, 1982-92; mem. family svcs. com., ranking mem. children and youth subcom., pub. utilities com.; mem. Ohio Children's Trust Fund, Supreme Ct. Domesticc Violence Task Force. Vol. Cleve. Lupus Steering Com., various community orgns.; charter mem. Statue of Liberty Ellis Island Found. Recipient cert. of appreciation Cleve. Mcpl. Ct., 1977, Exch. Club Bklyn., 1978, Cmty. Recreation Appreciation award City of Cleve., 1978, Key to City of Cleve., 1979, Cleve. Area Soapbox Derby cert., 1976, 77, 81, cert. of appreciation Ward 9 Youth League, 1979-82, No. Ohio Patrolman's Benevolent Assn. award, 1983, Cuyahoga County Firefighters award, 1983, Outstanding Pub. Servant award for Outstanding Svc. to Hispanic Cmty., 1985, Nat. Sr. Citizen Hall of Fame award, 1987, cert. of appreciation Cleve. Coun. Unemployed Workers, 1987, Ohio Farmers Union award, 1990, award of appreciation United Labor Agy., 1993, Susan B. Anthony award, 1995. Mem. Nat. Order Women Legislators, Fedn. Dem. Women of Ohio, Nat. Alliance Czech Catholics, St. Michael Ch. Altar and Rosary Soc., Ward 15 Dem. Club, Polish Falcons. Democrat. Home: 708 Timothy Ln Cleveland OH 44109-3733

PRINGLE, EDWARD E., legal educator, former state supreme court chief justice; b. Chgo., Apr. 12, 1914; s. Abraham J. and Lena (Oher) P.; m. Pauline Judd, Aug. 17, 1941; children: Bruce, Eric. LL.B., U. Colo., 1936, LL.D., 1976; LL.D., U. Denver, 1979. Bar: Colo. Practiced in Denver, 1936-42, 47-57; with fed. govt. service Washington, 1943-47; dist. judge Colo. Dist. Ct., Denver, 1957-61; justice Supreme Ct. Colo., Denver, 1961-79; chief justice Supreme Ct. Colo., 1970-78; dir. research and writing program U. Denver Coll. Law, 1979-90, prof. emeritus, 1990—. Contbr. articles to profl. jours. Bd. dirs. Am. Med. Center, Denver; mem. Nat. Commn. for Establishment of Nat. Inst. Justice. Served with USAAF, 1942. Recipient William Lee Knous award U. Colo. Law Sch., 1975. Mem. Am., Colo., Denver bar assns., Conf. Chief Justices (chmn. 1973-74), Am. Judicature Soc. (Herbert Lincoln Harley award 1973, chmn. bd. 1974-76), Nat. Center State Cts. (pres. 1977-79). Jewish. Club: Masons (33 deg.). Office: U Denver Coll Law 1900 Olive St Denver CO 80220-1857

PRINGLE, LAURENCE PATRICK, writer; b. Rochester, N.Y., Nov. 26, 1935; s. Laurence Erin and Marleah Elizabeth (Rosehill) P.; m. Judith Malanowicz, June 23, 1962 (div. 1970); children: Heidi Elizabeth Jeffrey Laurence, Sean Edmund; m. Susan Deborah Klein, Mar. 13, 1983; children: Jesse Erin, Rebecca Anne. BS in Wildlife Biology, Cornell U., 1958; MS in Wildlife Biology, U. Mass., 1961. Tchr. sci. Lima (N.Y.) Cen. Sch., 1961-62; editor Nature and Sci. mag. Am. Mus. Natural History, N.Y.C., 1963-70; free-lance writer, 1970—; writer-in-residence Kean College, Union, N.J., 1985-86. Author: (children's books) Dinosaurs and Their World, 1968, The Only Earth We Have, 1969, From Field to Forest, 1970, In a Beaver Valley, 1970, One Earth, Many People, 1971, Ecology: Science of Survival, 1971, Cockroaches: Here, There, Everywhere, 1971, From Pond to Prairie, 1972, This Is a River, 1972, Pests and People: The Search for Sensible Pest Control, 1972, Estuaries: Where Rivers Meet the Sea, 1973, Into the Woods: Exploring the Forest Ecosystem, 1973, Follow a Fisher, 1973, Twist, Wiggle and Squirm: A Book about Earthworms, 1973, Recycling Resources, 1974, Energy: Power for People, 1975, City and Suburb: Exploring an Ecosystem, 1975, Chains, Webs and Pyramids: The Flow of Energy in Nature, 1975, Water Plants, 1975, The Minnow Family: Chubs, Dace, Minnows and Shiners, 1987, Listen to the Crows, 1976, Our Hungry Earth: The World Food Crisis, 1976, Death is Natural, 1977, The Hidden World: Life under a Rock, 1977, The Controversial Coyote: Predation, Politics and Ecology, 1977, The Gentle Desert: Exploring an Ecosystem, 1977, Animals and Their Niches: How Species Share Resources, 1977, The Economic Growth Debate: Are There Limits to Growth?, 1978, Dinosaurs and People: Fossils, Facts and Fantasies, 1978, Wild Foods, 1978, Nuclear Power: From Physics to Politics, 1979, Natural Fire: Its Ecology in Forests, 1979, Lives at Stake: The Science and Politics of Environmental Health, 1980, What Shall We Do with the Land?: Choices for America, 1981, Frost Hollows and Other Microclimates, 1981, Vampire Bats, 1982, Water: The Next Great Resource Battle, 1982, Radiation: Waves and Particles/Benefits and Risks, 1983, Wolfman: Exploring the World of Wolves, 1983, Feral: Tame Animals Gone Wild, 1983, The Earth Is Flat—and Other Great Mistakes, 1983, Being a Plant, 1983, Nuclear War: From Hiroshima to Nuclear Winter, 1985, Animals at Play, 1985, Here Come the Killer Bees, 1986, Throwing Things Away: From Middens to Resource Recovery, 1986, Restoring Our Earth, 1987, Home: How Animals Find Comfort and Safety, 1987, Rain of Troubles: The Science and Politics of Acid Rain, 1988, Living in a Risky World, 1989, Nuclear Energy: Troubled Past, Uncertain Future, 1989, Bearman: Exploring the World of Black Bears, 1989, The Animal Rights Controversy, 1989, Saving Our Wildlife, 1990, Global Warming: Assessing the Greenhouse Threat, 1990, The Golden Book of Insects and Spiders, 1990, Killer Bees (rev. edit.) 1991, Batman: Exploring the World of Bats, 1991, Living Treasure: Saving Earth's Threatened Biodiversity, 1991, Antarctica: The Last Unspoiled Continent, 1992, The Golden Book of Volcanoes, Earthquakes, and Powerful Storms, 1992, Chemical and Biological Weapons: The Cruelest Weapons, 1993, Oil Spills: Damage, Recovery, and Prevention, 1993, Jackal Woman: Exploring the World of Jackals, 1993, Scorpion Man: Exploring the World of Scorpions, 1994, Dinosaurs! Strange and Wonderful, 1995, Vanishing Ozone: Protecting Earth from Ultraviolet Radiation, 1995, Coral Reefs: Earth's Undersea Treasures, 1995, Dolphin Man: Exploring the World of Dolphins, 1995, Fire in the Forest: A Cycle of Growth and Renewal, 1995, Taking Care of the Earth: Kids in Action, 1996, Smoking : A Risky Business, 1996; (fiction) Jesse Builds a Road, 1989, Octopus Hug, 1993; (adult books) Wild River, 1972, Rivers and Lakes, 1985. Recipient Spl. Conservation award Nat. Wildlife Fedn., 1978, Eva L. Gordon award Am. Nature Study Soc 1983. Mem. the Authors Guild. Home and Office: PO Box 252 West Nyack NY 10994-0252

PRINGLE, LEWIS GORDON, marketing professional, educator; b. Lansing, Mich., Feb. 13, 1941; s. Gordon Henry and Lucile Roxana (Drake) P.; children: Lewis Gordon Jr., William Davis, Thomas Benjamin. B.A., Harvard U., 1963; M.S., M.I.T., 1965, Ph.D., 1969. Vice pres., dir. mktg. sci. BBDO, Inc., N.Y.C., 1968-73, exec. v.p., dir. rsch. svcs., corp. dir., 1978-91; exec. v.p. BBDO Worldwide, 1986-91; chmn., CEO BBDO Europe, 1986-91, LG Pringle and Assocs., 1992-95; Joseph C. Seibert prof. of mktg. Farmer Sch. Bus. Adminstrn., Miami U., Oxford, Ohio, 1995—; asst. prof. mktg. Carnegie-Mellon U., 1973-74. Author numerous articles in field. Active local Boy Scouts Am. Ford Found. fellow, 1967. Fellow Royal Statis. Soc.; mem. Market Rsch. Coun., Am. Psychol. Assn., European Soc. Mktg. and Opinion Rsch., Am. Mktg. Assn., Inst. Ops. Rsch. and Mgmt. Sci. Home: 71 Hunting Ridge Rd Greenwich CT 06831-3122 Office: Farmer Sch Bus Adminstrn Miami Univ Oxford OH 45056

PRINGLE, ORAN ALLAN, mechanical and aerospace engineering educator; b. Lawrence, Kan., Sept. 14, 1923; s. Oran Allan and Mae (McClell) P.; m. Billie Hansen, June 25, 1947; children—Allan, Billie, James, Rebecca. B.S. in Mech. Engring, U. Kan., 1947; M.S., U. Wis., 1948, Ph.D., 1967. Registered profl. engr., Mo. Mech. engr. Black and Veatch (cons. engrs.), Kansas City, Mo., 1947-48; engr. Boeing Airplane Co., Wichita, 1952—; prof. U. Mo., Columbia, 1948—. Co-author: Engineering Metallurgy, 1957; contbr. articles to profl. lit. Bd. dirs. United Cerebral Palsy Boone County, Mo. Served with AUS, 1943-45. Ford Found. grantee. Mem. Am. Soc. M.E. (chmn. fastening and joining com., design engring. div.), Sigma Xi. Home: 1820 University Ave Columbia MO 65201-6004 Office: Dept Mech and Aerospace Engring U Mo Columbia MO 65201

PRINGLE, ROBERT MAXWELL, diplomat; b. N.Y.C., Nov. 12, 1936; s. Henry Fowles and Helena Huntington (Smith) P.; m. Barbara Ann Cade, Sept. 26, 1964; children: James Maxwell, Anne Elizabeth. BA, Harvard U., 1958; PhD, Cornell U., 1967. Dir. econ. policy staff Bur. African Affairs Dept. State, 1981-83; dep. chief mission Ouagadougou, Burkina Faso, 1983-85, Port Moresby, Papua New Guinea, 1985-87; ambassador to Mali, 1987-90; dir. cen. African affairs U.S. Dept. State, 1990-93; dir. ecology and terrestrial conservation U.S. Dept. of State, 1993-95; dir. sr. seminar U.S. Dept. State, 1995—. Author: Rajahs and Rebels: The Ibans of Sarawak under Brooke Rule, 1970, Indonesia and the Philippines: American Interests in Island Southeast Asia, 1980. Mem. Assn. Asian Studies, African Studies Assn. Avocations: photography, gardening, scuba diving. Home: 216 Wolfe St Alexandria VA 22314

PRINS, DAVID, speech pathologist, educator; b. Herkimer, N.Y., Oct. 4, 1930; s. Tunis W. and Harriet Z. (Baker) P.; m. Gloria B. Fleming, June 4, 1955; children: Leslie, Steven, Douglas, Michael. BA, Central Coll. Iowa, 1952; MA, U. Mich., 1957, PhD, 1961. Tchr. Denison (Iowa) H.S., 1954-55; instr. U. Mich., 1960-63, asst. prof., 1963-66, assoc. prof., 1966-69; asst. dir. U. Mich. Speech and Hearing Camp, 1960-64, dir., 1964-69; dir. program in speech and hearing scis. U. Wash., 1974-75, assoc. prof., 1969-72, prof., 1973-92, chmn. dept. speech and hearing scis., 1975-79, assoc. dean Coll. Arts & Scis., 1979-88, prof. emeritus, 1992—; vis. prof. U. Va. Contbr. articles in field of stuttering and articulation disorders to profl. jours. Served with U.S. Army, 1952-54. Mem. AAAS, Am. Speech and Hearing Assn., Wash. Speech and Hearing Assn., Mich. Speech and Hearing Assn. (past pres.), Phi Beta Kappa, Phi Kappa Phi. Office: U Wash Dept Speech And Scis Seattle WA 98105-6246

PRINS, ROBERT JACK, college administrator; b. Grand Rapids, Mich., Oct. 12, 1932; s. Jacob and Marie (Vanden Brink) P.; m. Ruth Ellen John, Oct. 10, 1950; children: Linda, Douglas, Debra, Nancy, Eric, Sarah. BA, Hope Coll., 1954; DBA, Coll. Emporia, 1974. With Mich. Bell Telephone Co., Detroit area, 1954-66; dir. devel. Bethesda Hosp., Denver, 1966-68; v.p. planning and devel. Park Coll., Parkville, Mo., 1969-70; chief adminstrv. officer Coll. of Emporia, Kans., 1970-75; dir. fin. and devel. The Abbey Sch., Canon City, Colo., 1975-79; dir. devel. Kirksville Coll. Osteo. Medicine, Mo., 1979-84; v.p. devel. McKendree Coll., Lebanon, Ill., 1984-86; pres. Iowa Weslyan Coll., Mt. Pleasant, 1986—; bd. dirs. Iowa Coll. Found., Iowa Commn. on Nat. and Cmty. Svc.; mem. adv. bd. Iowa Commn. on Status of Women, Iowa Assn. Ind. Colls. and Univs.; mem. edn. adv. com. Potomak Internat., Taipei, Taiwan. Mem. Nat. Assn. Ind. Colls. and Univs., Coun. for Advancement and Support of Edn., Mt. Pleasant C. of C. *Education may be the key to opportunity but only solid performance on the job insures success.*

PRINZ, RICHARD ALLEN, surgeon. MD, Loyola U., Chgo., 1972. Diplomate Am. Bd. Surgery. Intern Barnes Hosp., St. Louis, 1972-73, resident in surgery, 1973-74; resident in surgery Loyola U., Chgo., 1974-77, attending surgeon, 1980-93; staff Rush Presbyn.-St. Luke's Med. Ctr., Chgo., 1993—; prof., chmn. Rush U., Chgo., 1993—. Mem. Alpha Omega Alpha. Office: Rush Presbyn/St Luke Med Ct 810 Professional Bldg 1725 W Harrison St Chicago IL 60612*

PRIOR, GARY L., lawyer; b. Niagara Falls, N.Y., June 26, 1943; s. Harold D. and Adeline Thelma (Lee) P.; m. Nancy O'Shaughnessy, Aug. 12, 1975; children: Joseph Lee, Julia Elizabeth. BS, Tulane U., 1965; JD, U. Chgo., 1968. Bar: Ill. 1968, U.S. Dist. Ct. (no. dist.) Ill. 1968, U.S. Ct. Appeals (7th cir.) 1973, U.S. Ct. Appeals (3rd cir.) 1974, U.S. Trial Bar 1983, U.S. Supreme Ct. 1989, U.S. Dist. Ct. (we. dist.) Wis. 1992, U.S. Dist. Ct. (ea. dist.) Wis. 1993. Assoc. Rooks, Pitts & Poust, Chgo., 1968-71; assoc. McDermott, Will & Emery, Chgo., 1971-74, ptnr., 1974—, dir. trial dept. tng., 1980-85, mem. securities approval com., 1986—, mem. nominating com., chmn., 1988-89, partnership com., 1989-92, mem mgmt. com., 1991-93. Mem. Chgo. Bar Assn., Phi Delta Phi. Avocations: farming, sports, family. Home: 623 W Briar Pl Chicago IL 60657-4520 Office: McDermott Will & Emery 227 W Monroe St Chicago IL 60606-5016*

PRIOR, RONALD L., nutritionist; b. McCook, Nebr., Mar. 9, 1945. BS, U. Nebr., 1967; PhD in Nutrition, Cornell U., 1971. NIH postdoctoral trainee N.Y. State Vet. Coll. Cornell U., 1971-73; rsch. chemist, asst. prof. meat animal rsch. ctr., Clay ctr., USDA U. Nebr., 1973-83; pres. Sunshine Audio, Inc., 1983-87; gen. ptnr. R&M Enterprises, 1983-87; sci. program officer, nutritionist USDA human nutrition rsch. ctr. aging Tufts U., 1987—; lectr. animal nutrition lab. Cornell U., 1968, 69, U. Nebr., 1978-81; chmn. ruminant nutrition workshop U.S. Meat Animal Rsch. Ctr., 1977, 2d ann. ruminant nutrition conf. Fedn. Am. Soc. Exptl. Biology & Medicine, 1981; coop scientist spl. fgn. currency rsch. programs U. Alexandria, Egypt and Warsaw Agr. U., Poland. Contbr. over 90 articles to profl. jours. Mem. AAAS, Am. Soc. Animal Sci. (chmn. ruminant nutrition session 1973), Am. Inst. Nutrition, Sigma Xi. Office: USDA Human Nutrition Rsch Ctr Tufts U 711 Washington St Rm 919 Boston MA 02111-1524

PRIOR, WILLIAM ALLEN, electronics company executive; b. Benton Harbor, Mich., Jan. 14, 1927; s. Allen Ames and Madeline Isabel (Taylor) P.; m. Nancy Norton Sayles, July 7, 1951 (div. Oct. 1971); children: Stephanie Sayles, Alexandra Taylor, Robert Eames, Eleanor Norton; m. Carol Luise Becker-Ehmck, Oct. 30, 1971; children: Michael Becker-Ehmck, Jeffrey Renner. AB in Physics, Harvard Coll., 1950, MBA, 1954. Salesman IBM, Mineola, L.I., N.Y., 1950-52; sales engr. Lincoln Electric Co., Cleve., 1954-57; ptnr. Hammond Kennedy & Co., N.Y.C., 1957-66; v.p. The Singer Co., N.Y.C., 1967-68; pres. Tansitor Electronics, Bennington, Vt., 1969-71, Aerotron Inc., Raleigh, N.C., 1971-82; v.p. J. Lee Peeler & Co., Durham, N.C., 1986-89; pres. Accudyne, Inc., Raleigh, 1990—; dir. Carroll's Foods, Warsaw, N.C.; chmn. Royal Blue Capital, Inc., Raleigh. Cpl. USAAF, 1945-46, Germany. Mem. IEEE, North Ridge Country Club (Raleigh), Raleigh Racquet Club, 50 Group, Harvard Club of N.Y.C. Republican. Avocations: tennis, skiing, computer programming. Home: 329 Meeting House Cir Raleigh NC 27615-3133 Office: Accudyne Inc 5800 Mchines Pl Raleigh NC 27604-1839

PRIORE, ROGER L., biostatistics educator, consultant; b. Buffalo, Apr. 21, 1938; s. Anthony J. and Linda M. (DeMarchi) P.; m. Carol A. Cooper, Sept. 3, 1960; children—Howard W., Susan L., John D. B.A., SUNY-Buffalo, 1960, M.S., 1962; Sc.D., Johns Hopkins U., 1965. Jr. cancer research scientist Roswell Park Meml. Inst., Buffalo, 1960-65, sr. cancer research scientist, 1965-67, assoc. cancer research scientist, 1967-69, prin. cancer research scientist, 1974-79, dir. computer sci., 1979-83, dir. dept. biomath., 1983-91, dir. mgmt. info. systems, 1988-91; asst. rsch. prof. SUNY, Buffalo, 1966-68, assoc. rsch. prof., 1968-69, rsch. prof., dir. grad. studies in biometry, 1980-91; rsch. prof. Niagara U., 1968-91; cons. in stats. and computing, 1991—; clin. prof. dept. social and preventive medicine SUNY, Buffalo, 1991—; pres. Compustat Assocs., Inc., Buffalo, 1993—; clin. prof. dept. statistics SUNY, Buffalo, 1995—; cons. Am. Joint Com. on Cancer, 1980-88. Contbr. articles to profl. jours. Mem. Am. Statis. Assn., Soc. for Epidemiol. Rsch., Sigma Xi. Office: 342 Dan Troy Dr Buffalo NY 14221-3514

PRIORY, RICHARD BALDWIN, electric utility executive; b. Lakehurst, N.J., May 15, 1946; s. Joseph Albert Jr. and Betty (Baldwin) P.; m. Joan Ellen Rourke, May 30, 1968; children: Jennifer Joan, Richard Baldwin Jr. BS in Civil Engring. magna cum laude, W.Va. Inst. Tech., 1969; MS in Engring., Princeton U., 1973; grad. utility exec. program, U. Mich., 1982; grad. advanced mgmt. program, Harvard U., 1991. Registered profl. engr., N.C., S.C. Design engr., project engr. Union Carbide Corp., 1969-72; asst. prof. structural engring. U. N.C., Charlotte, 1973-76; design engr. Duke Power Co., Charlotte, N.C., 1976-78, prin. engr., 1978-81, mgr. project mgmt. divsn., 1981-84, v.p. design engring., 1984-88, sr. v.p. generation and info. svcs., 1988-91, exec. v.p. Power Generation Group, 1991-94, pres., COO, 1994—; mem. Duke Power Co.; bd. dirs.; mem. Duke Fluor Daniel Mgmt. Com.; mem. power generation com. Assn. of Edison Illuminating Cos. Bd. visitors U. N.C., Charlotte; bd. dirs. N.C. State U. Engring. Found.; bd. trustees N.C. chpt. Nature Conservancy; mem., past chmn. bd. dirs. Charlotte-Mecklenburg Edn. Found.; pres., bd. trustees Discovery Place, Inc., 1992-93; past mem. Charlotte-Mecklenburg Pub. Broadcasting Found.; vice chmn. campaign drive United Way Ctrl. Carolinas, Inc., 1990; mem. adv. coun. N.C. Alliance for Competitive Technologies. Mem. ASCE, Nat. Acad. Engring, Charlotte Engrs. Club. Avocation: golf. Office: Duke Power Co 422 S Church St Charlotte NC 28242-0001

PRIP, JANET, metalsmith; b. Hornell, N.Y., June 17, 1950; d. John Axel and Karen E. (Jensen) P.; m. Roger A. Birn, Oct. 7, 1978; 1 child, Alexander P. Birn. BFA, R.I. Sch. Design, 1974. Ptnr., designer Trillium Fine Gold and Silver Jewelry, Providence, 1974-78, P's & Q's Costume Jewelry, Providence, 1978-81; freelance designer Providence, 1981-86; freelance artist Cranston, R.I., 1986—. One-woman show include Craft and Folk Art Mus., L.A., 1990, R.I. Sch. Design Mus., Providence, 1991, 94, Boston Mus. Fine Arts, 1992, Art Gallery Western Australia, 1992, Joanne Rapp Gallery, Scottsdale, Ariz., 1993, Am. Craft Mus., N.Y.C ., 1993, others. Recipient Merit award Guild Am. Crafts Awards, 1987; fellow Nat. Endowment Arts , 1986. Avocations: gardening, travel. Home: 163 Arnold Ave Cranston RI 02905

PRISBREY, REX PRINCE, retired insurance agent, underwriter, consultant; b. Washington, Utah, Mar. 18, 1922; s. Hyrum William and Susan (Prince) P.; m. Pinka Julieta Lucero, Nov. 16, 1943; children: Karol Sue Prisbey Lewallen, Pamela Blanche Prisbrey Ebert, Michael Rex. BA in Acctg., Denver U., 1949. CLU. Ptnr. Allen Stamm & Assocs., home builders, Farmington, N.Mex., 1949-52; acct. Linder Burke & Stevenson, Santa Fe, N.Mex., 1949-52; agt. State Farm Ins. Cos., Farmington, 1952-56; mgr. State Farm Ins. Cos., Phoenix, 1956-60; contractor, agt. State Farm Ins. Cos., Scottsdale, Ariz., 1960—; v.p., treas. Original Curio Store Inc., Santa Fe. Pres. Farmington Jr. C. of C., 1952; v.p. N.Mex. Jr. C. of C., 1953. 1st lt. USAAF, 1941-46, CBI. Decorated DFC, Air medal with oak leaf cluster; recipient Disting. Life Underwriter award Cen. Ariz. Mgrs. Assn., 1979. Mem. Am. Soc. CLU's, Scottsdale Assn. Life Underwriters (pres. 1980-81), Airplane Owners and Pilots Assn., Hump Pilots Assn. (life, speaker at meml. of Hump Flyers, Kunming, China 1993), Pinewood Country Club (bd. dirs., treas., v.p. 1985—), Civitans (pres. Scottsdale 1962-63). Avocations: flying, golf, photography. Home: 4011 N 65th St Scottsdale AZ 85251-4235

PRITCHARD, CLAUDIUS HORNBY, JR., retired university president; b. Charleston, W.Va., June 28, 1927; s. Claudius Hornby and Katherine (Ellison) P.; m. Marjorie Walker Pullen, Aug. 9, 1952; children: Virginia Aiken, Katherine Winston, Olivia Reynolds, Claudius V. BA, Hampden-Sydney Coll., 1950; MA, Longwood Coll., 1965; PhD, Fla. State U., 1971. Comml. loan teller Am. Nat. Bank and Trust Co., Danville, Va., 1950-53; asst. cashier Planters Bank & Trust Co., Farmville, Va., 1953-55; asst. to pres. Hampden-Sydney (Va.) Coll., 1955-57, bus. mgr. and treas., 1957-67, v.p. devel., 1967-71; sr. budget analyst-edn. State of Fla., Tallahassee, 1971-72; pres. Sullins Coll., Bristol, Va., 1972-76; v.p. adminstrn. Maryville U., St. Louis, 1976-77, pres., 1977-92, pres. emeritus, 1992—; adv. dir. Commerce Bank of St. Louis, 1982-92. Author: Col. D. Wyatt Aiken (1828-1887) South Carolina's Militant Agrarian, 1970; contbr. articles to profl. jours. Bd. dirs. West St. Louis County YMCA, Chesterfield, Mo., 1985-92; bd. visitors Charleston So. Univ., 1993—. Served with USNR, 1945-46. Fla. State U. fellow, 1969-70, Arthur Vining Davis fellow Am. Council on Edn., 1974. Mem. AAUP, Am. Assn. Higher Edn., So. Hist. Assn., S.C. Hist. Soc., Mo. Colls. Fund (bd. dirs., chmn. 1987-88), Ind. Colls. and Univs. Mo., Chesterfield C. of C. (pres. 1987, named Chesterfield Citizen of Yr. 1986), Rotary. Republican. Presbyterian.

PRITCHARD, CONSTANCE JENKINS, human resources specialist, trainer, consultant; b. Washington, May 6, 1950; d. William Morton and Marguerite Kathleen (Marshall) Jenkins; m. Paul Ralph Pritchard, June 30, 1973; children: Laura, Leslie. BA in English and History, Hiram (Ohio) Coll., 1972; MA in Linguistics, U. S.C., 1978, EdD in Student Pers. Svcs., 1991. Tchr. Sterling High Sch., Somerdale, N.J., 1972-76; instr. U. S.C., Aiken, 1982-93; dir. advisement ctr., 1984-89, asst. dean for career planning, placement and orientation, 1989-93; trainer, cons. Pritchard Group, North Augusta, S.C., 1989—; adminstr. Grace United Meth. Ch., North Augusta, S.C., 1993—. Scout leader Girl Scouts Am., S.C., 1987-89; trainer Leadership Aiken County, 1991—; bd. dirs. United Way of Aiken County, 1993—, Aiken County ARC, 1994—. Recipient citation for excellence in career programming Am. Assn. Career Edn., 1992; named Woman of Achievement, Miss. S.C. Pageant, 1993. Mem. Nat. Comty. Leadership Assn., Coll. Placement Coun. (Excellence award 1992, Award for Excellence in Rsch. 1992), Nat. Assn. Acad. Adminstrs. (newsletter editor 1987-89), Student Affairs Profl. Orgn., Cen. Savannah River Area Human Resource Assn. (sec. 1992-93), North Augusta Rotary (Rotarian of Yr. 1990-91), North Augusta C. of C. (bd. dirs. 1995—). Avocations: sailing, reading, family. Office: The Pritchard Group PO Box 6756 North Augusta SC 29861

PRITCHARD, DALTON HAROLD, retired electronics research engineer; b. Crystal Springs, Miss., Sept. 1, 1921; s. Cecil Harold and Marvie Prudence (Lofton) P.; m. Caroline Ann Hnatuk, Apr. 27, 1947; 1 child, Mary Ann Pritchard Poole. B.S.E.E., Miss. State U., 1943; postgrad., Harvard, MIT Radar Sch., 1943-44. Mem. tech. staff RCA Labs., Riverhead, N.Y., 1946-50; mem. tech. staff RCA Labs., Princeton, N.J., 1950-75, fellow tech. staff, 1975-87; session chmn., mem. program com. Internat. Conf. on Consumer Electronics, Chgo., 1980-85. Contbr. articles to profl. jours.; patentee in field. mem. N.J. Gov.'s Sci. Adv. Council, Princeton, 1981-85. Served to capt. U.S. Army Signal Corps. Decorated Bronze Star; recipient Eduard Rhein prize Edward Rhein Found., Berlin, Fed. Republic of Germany, 1980; Disting. Engring. fellow Miss. State U., 1991. Fellow IEEE (Vladimir Zworykin award 1977, David Sarnoff award 1981), Soc. Info. Display, Nat. Assn. Engrs., Nat. Acad. Engring., Sigma Xi, Tau Beta Pi, Kappa Mu Epsilon. Republican. Baptist. Avocations: amatuer radio; tennis. Home: 3 Bent Tree Ln Hilton Head Island SC 29926-1906

PRITCHARD, DAVID J., oil company executive; b. 1948. BA, Cambridge (Eng.) U., 1969, MA, 1969. With BP Pipelines (Alaska) Inc., Anchorage, 1969-93; pres., CEO Alyeska Pipeline Svc. Co., Anchorage, 1993—. Office: Alyeska Pipeline Svc Co 1835 S Bragaw St Anchorage AK 99512-0001*

PRITCHARD, DONALD WILLIAM, oceanographer; b. Santa Ana, Calif., Oct. 20, 1922; s. Charles Lorenzo and Madeleine (Sievers) P.; m. Thelma Lydia Amling, Apr. 25, 1943; children—Marian Lydia, Jo Anne, Suzanne Louise, Donald William, Albert Charles. B.A., UCLA, 1942; M.S. Scripps Instn. Oceanography, La Jolla, 1948, Ph.D., 1951; D.Sc. (hon.), Coll. William and Mary, 1985. Research asst. Scripps Instn. Oceanography, 1946-47; oceanographer USN Electronics Lab., 1947-49; assoc. dir. Chesapeake Bay Inst., Johns Hopkins, Balt., 1949-51; dir. Chesapeake Bay Inst., Johns Hopkins, 1951-74, chief scientist, 1974-79, prof., 1958-79, chmn. dept. oceanography, 1951-68; assoc. dir. for research, prof. Marine Scis. Rsch. Ctr., SUNY at Stony Brook, 1979-86, acting dir., dean, 1986-87, assoc. dean, 1987-88, prof. emeritus, 1988—; cons. C.E., U.S. Army, USPHS, AEC, Internat. AEA, NSF, Adv. Panel Earth Scis.; mem. adv. bd. to Sec. Natural Resources, State of Md. Bd. editors Jour. Marine Rsch., 1953-70, Bull. Bingham Oceanographic Collection, 1960-70, Geophys. Monograph Bd., Am. Geophys. Union, 1959-70, Johns Hopkins Oceanographic Studies, 1962-78; contbr. articles to profl. jours. Served from 2d lt. to capt. USAAF, 1943-46. Recipient Mathias Sci. medal The Chespeake Rsch. Consortium, 1990. Fellow Am. Geophys. Union (past pres. oceanography sect.); mem. AAAS, Nat. Acad. Engring., Nat. Acad. Engring., Am. Soc. Limnology and Oceanography (past v.p.), Am. Meteorol. Soc., Sigma Xi (past chpt. pres.). Office: SUNY Marine Scis Rsch Ctr Stony Brook NY 11794

PRITCHARD, HUW OWEN, chemist, educator; b. Bangor, Wales, July 23, 1928; s. Owen and Lilian Venetia (McMurray) P.; m. Margaret Ramsden, Nov. 3, 1956; children—Karen, David. B.Sc., U. Manchester, 1948, M.Sc., 1949, Ph.D., 1951, D.Sc., 1964. Asst. lectr. chemistry Manchester (Eng.) U., 1951-54, lectr., 1954-65; prof. chemistry York U., Ont., Can., 1965—. Contbr. articles to profl. jours. Fellow Royal Soc. Can. Office: Chemistry Dept York Univ, Downsview, ON Canada M3J 1P3

PRITCHARD, JAMES BENNETT, archaeologist, educator, author; b. Louisville, Oct. 4, 1909; s. John Hayden and Mary (Bennett) P.; m. Anne Elizabeth Cassedy, June 30, 1937; children: Sarah Anne (Mrs. Robert F. Hayman), Mary Bennett (Mrs. Clifton Mitchell). AB, Asbury Coll., 1930; BD, Drew U., 1935; PhD, U. Pa., 1942, LHD (hon.), 1991; STD, Phila. Div. Sch., 1961; DD, Ch. Div. Sch. of Pacific, 1962; LHD (hon.), Swarthmore Coll., 1977; DD (hon.), U. Uppsala, Sweden, 1977. Prof. O.T. lit. Crozer Theol. Sem., 1942-54; ann. prof. Am. Sch. Oriental Research, Jerusalem, 1950-51; archeol. dir. expdn. to Jericho, Jordan, 1951; vis. prof. Am. Sch. Oriental Research, 1956-57, 61-62; dir. expdns. to el-Jib, Jordan, 1956-62; to Tell es-Sa'idiyeh, Jordan, 1964-67, Am. Sch. Oriental Research, Sarafand, Lebanon, 1969, 70, 71, 72, 74; prof. O.T. lit. Ch. Div. Sch. Pacific, 1954-62; curator Bib. archeology Univ. Mus., 1962-78, assoc. dir., 1967-76, dir., 1976-77; prof. religious thought U. Pa., 1962-78; Winslow lectr. Gen. Theol. Sem., 1960; Fulbright-Hays vis. prof. archaeology Am. U. Beirut, 1966-67; mem. Inst. Advanced Study, Princeton, N.J., 1978; Sec., Am. Schs. Oriental Research, 1963-71. Author: Palestinian Figurines, 1943, Ancient Near Eastern Texts, 1950, 55, 69, The Ancient Near East in Pictures, 1954, 69, Archaeology and the Old Testament, 1958, The Excavation at Herodian

Jericho, 1958, The Ancient Near East, 1958, vol. 2, 1975, Hebrew Inscriptions from Gibeon, 1959, The Water System at Gibeon, 1961, Gibeon, Where the Sun Stood Still, 1962, Bronze Age Cemetery at Gibeon, 1963, Winery, Defenses and Soundings at Gibeon, 1964, Sarepta, 1975, Recovering Sarepta, A Phoenician City, 1978, The Cemetery at Tell es-Sa'idiyeh, 1980, Excavations on the Tell, 1964-66, 1985, The Times Atlas of the Bible, 1987, The Times Concise Atlas of the Bible, 1991, Sarepta IV, 1988, The Harper Concise Atlas of the Bible, 1991; assoc. editor: Jour. Am. Oriental Soc, 1948-52; editor, 1952-54. Trustee Am. U. Beirut, 1970-79. Decorated Order of Istiqlal, 1st Class Jordan, 1964. Mem. Am. Philos. Soc. (Benjamin Franklin medal 1990), Am. Oriental Soc., Archeol. Inst. Am. (pres. 1973, 74, Disting. Archeol. Achievement award 1983). Clubs: Franklin Inn, Penn. Home: 108 Tunbridge Rd Haverford PA 19041-1038 Office: Univ Mus 33rd And Spruce St Philadelphia PA 19104

PRITCHARD, JOEL, state lieutenant governor; b. Seattle, May 5, 1925; children: Peggy, Frank, Anne, Jeanie. Student, Marietta Coll.; PhD (Hon.), Seattle U. Pres. Griffin Envelope Co., Seattle; mem. Wash. Ho. of Reps., Olympia, 1958-66, Wash. State Senate, 1966-70, U.S. Ho. of Reps., Washington, 1972-84; dir. govt. rels. Bogle & Gates, 1985-88; lt. gov. State of Wash., Olympia, 1989—; mem. Merchant Marine and Fisheries Com. U.S. Ho. of Reps., subcom. on Asia and the Pacific Fgn. Rels. Com., Panama Canal Consultative Commn., 1987-88; U.S. del. to UN Gen. Assembly, 1983. With U.S. Army, PTO, WWII. Office: Lt Gov's Office PO Box 40482 304 Legislative Bldg Olympia WA 98504-0482

PRITCHARD, KATHLEEN JO, not-for-profit association administrator; b. Milw., Feb. 6, 1951; d. Owen J. and Madelon (Coogan) P.; m. William A. Durkin Jr., Oct. 22, 1982; children: Elizabeth Durkin, Christine Durkin, W. Ryan Durkin. BA in Anthropology, U. Wis., Oshkosh, 1973; MA in Pub. Adminstrn., U. Wis., 1980; PhD in Polit. Sci., U. Wis., Milw., 1986. Rsch. analyst Wis. Coun. on Criminal Justice, Madison, 1974-77; planning analyst Wis. Dept. Health and Social Svcs., Madison, 1977-80; assoc. lectr. U. Wis., Milw., 1980-89; vis. asst. prof. Marquette U., Milw., 1986, 90-91; policy cons. dept. adminstrn. City of Milw., 1992; Outcomes Project dir. United Way of Greater Milw., 1992—; faculty advisor Model OAS, UN advisor, Milw., 1986-91; campus rep. spkr. Wis. Inst. for Study of War, Peace and Global Cooperation, Milw., 1989-90; mem. United Way Am. Task Force on Impact, 1995. Contbr. articles to profl. jours. Recipient Alice Paul Dissertation award Women's Caucus for Polit. Sci., 1984; Grad. Sch. fellow U. Wis., Milw., 1983, fellow Kenyon Coll. Summer Inst., 1983. Mem. Am. Polit. Sci. Assn., Internat. Polit. Sci. Assn., Phi Kappa Phi (chpt. officer 1989).

PRITCHARD, PAUL C(LEMENT), conservation association executive; b. Huntington, W.Va., Aug. 27, 1944; m. Susan Ford; children: Robin Elizabeth, Marcus, Stephen, Christopher. B.A. (scholar), U. Mo., 1966; M.S.P., U. Tenn., 1971; postgrad. in Bus. Mgmt, Harvard U., 1973-74, U. Mich., 1980. Chief natural resources planning Ga. Dept. Natural Resources, Atlanta, 1972-74; Pacific region coordinator NOAA, U.S. Dept Commerce, 1974-75; exec. dir. Appalachian Trial Conf., Inc., Harpers Ferry, W.Va., 1975-77; asst. to sec. U.S. Dept. Interior, Washington, 1977; dep. dir. Heritage Conservation and Recreation Service U.S. Dept. Interior, 1977-80; pres. Nat. Parks and Conservation Assn., Washington, 1980—. Editor: Views of the Green, 1985; contbr. articles to profl. jours. Chmn. Nat. Pk. Trust; League of Conservation Voters. Recipient Spl. Achievement award Dept. Commerce, 1975; Meritorious Achievement award Dept. Interior, 1980; Gulf Conservation award, Schweitzer prize in Humanities. Office: Nat Parks & Conservation Assn 1776 Massachusetts Ave NW 2nd fl Washington DC 20036-1904

PRITCHARD, WILBUR LOUIS, telecommunications engineering executive; b. N.Y.C., May 31, 1923; s. Harmon and Jessie H. (Roth) P.; m. Kathleen H. Moss, Apr. 24, 1949; children: Hugh, Sarah, Ruth. BSEE, CCNY, 1943, ScD (hon.), 1993; postgrad., MIT, 1948-52. Registered profl. engr., Mass., Md. Microwave engr., mgr. Wayland Lab. Raytheon Co., Waltham, Mass., 1946-60; dir. engring. Europe Raytheon Co., Rome, 1960-62; group dir. satellite communication systems Aerospace Corp., El Segundo, Calif., 1962-67; v.p., dir. Comsat Labs., Clarksburg, Md., 1967-73; pres. Fairchild Space & Electronics Co., Germantown, Md., 1973-74, Satellite Systems Engring., Bethesda, Md., 1974-87, SSE Telecom, Inc., Bethesda, 1987-89, Direct Broadcast Satellite Corp., Bethesda, 1982-86, W.L. Pritchard & Co., Inc., Bethesda, 1989—; chmn. panel on broadcast satellites Nat. Acad. Scis., Falmouth, Mass., 1967; mem. space applications bd. Nat. Acad. Engring., Colo., 1968; mem. space applications adv. com. NASA, Washington, 1984, space and earth scis. adv. com., 1984-88, Nat. Acad. Engring. com. on Voice of Am., 1986-89. Author: (with others) China Space Report, 1980, Satellite Communication Systems Engineering, 1986, 2d edit., 1993; contbr. numerous articles to profl. jours.; holder 12 patents. Recipient Systems Command award USAF, 1967, Lloyd V. Berkner Space Utilization award Am. Astronautical Soc., 1983. Fellow IEEE, AIAA (Aerospace Comm. award 1972), Brit. Interplanetary Soc.; mem. Nat. Acad. Engring., Soc. Satellite Profls., Am. Astronautics Soc. (sr.), Internat. Acad. Astronautics, Club Cosmos (Washington). Home: 9201 Laurel Oak Dr Bethesda MD 20817-1937 Office: WL Pritchard & Co Inc 7315 Wisconsin Ave Ste 520E Bethesda MD 20814-3209

PRITCHARD, WILLIAM ROY, former university system administrator; b. Portage, Wis., Nov. 15, 1924; s. William Roy and Lillian Edith (Roberts) P.; m. Deanna Elaine Pritchard; children: Rosan June, William Roy, Caryl Jean, Alyn Evan, Cynthia Bedeau. Student, U. Wis., 1942-43; D.V.M., Kans. State U., 1946, D.Sc. (hon.), 1970; D.Sc. (hon.), Tufts U., 1988; Ph. D., U. Minn., 1953; J.D., Ind. U., 1957; D.Sc. (hon.), Purdue U., 1977. Asst. prof. U. Wis., 1946-49; asso. prof. U. Minn., 1949-53; prof. Purdue U., 1953-57; prof., head vet. sci. U. Fla., 1957-61; asso. dir. Vet. Med. Research Inst., Ia. State U., 1961-62; prof. U. Calif.-Davis, 1962—, dean Sch. Vet Medicine,, 1962-82; asso. dir. Agrl. Expt. Sta., 1962-72; coordinator internat. agrl. programs U. Calif. system, 1977-81; vis. fellow Woodrow Wilson Sch. Pub and Internat. Affairs, Princeton, 1968-69; John Thomson lectr. U. Queensland, 1966; co-dir. nat. veterinary edn. program Duke U., 1987-92; spl. research hemmorrhagic diseases animals. Cons. Dept. Agr., Def. Dept., USPHS, VA, Calif. Dept. Health, FDA, 1962—; bd. cons. agr. Rockefeller Found., 1962-66; nat. med. cons. surgeon gen. USAF, 1962-64; mem. FAO/WHO Expert Panel Vet. Edn., President's Sci. Advisory Com. Panel World Food Supply, 1966-67, President's Sci. Advisory Com. Panel Biology and Med. Sci., 1969-70, Joint Research Com. Bd. Internat. Food and Agr. AID, 1977-81. Served with U.S. Army, 1942-44. Recipient Gov. Fla. award, 1961, Disting. Svc. award Kans. State U., 1963, Outstanding Achievement award U. Minn., 1976, Disting. Pub. Svc. award U. Calif.-Davis, 1991, Gold Headed Cane award Am. Soc. Vet. Epidemiology, 1992. Mem. AAAS, APHA, Am. Vet. Med. Assn. (Internat. Vet. Congress award 1988), Nat. Acad. of Practice in Vet. Medicine (elected 1986), Am. Soc. Vet. Epidemiologists, Conf. of Pub. Health Vets. (hon. life), U.S. Animal Health Assn., Nat. Assn. State Univs. and Land-Grant Colls. (internat. affairs com. 1965-70), Order of Coif, Sigma Xi, Phi Zeta, Gamma Alpha. Home: 2409 Madrid Ct Davis CA 95616-0141

PRITCHARD SCHOCH, TERESA NOREEN, lawyer, law librarian, executive; b. Brackley, Eng., Apr. 2, 1953; came to U.S., Dec. 1953; d. Boston Forrest and Noreen PHyliss (Taylor) P.; m. Claude M. Schoch, 1992. BA magna cum laude, Oakland U., 1974; MLS, Wayne State U., 1976, JD cum laude, 1981. Bar: Fla. 1985, Mich. 1981. Law librarian Honigman Miller Schwartz & Cohn, Detroit, 1979-81; assoc. Honigman, Miller, Schwartz & Cohn, Detroit, 1981-83, Rumberger, Kirk et al, Orlando, Fla., 1984-85; dir. rsch. svcs. Gunster, Yoakley, Criser & Stewart, West Palm Beach, Fla., 1985-91; pres. Pritchard Info., Inc., Palm Beach Gardens, Fla., 1991-92; v.p. Digital Directory Assistance, Bethesda, Md., 1993—. Columnist Online, Database; contbr. articles to profl. jours. Online Authorship award, 1994. Mem. Fla. Bar Assn., Mich. Bar Assn. (judicial and profl. ethics com. 1982-84), Am. Assn. Law Libraries (cert.). Protestant. Avocations: aerobics, gourmet cooking. Office: Digital Directory Assistance 6931 Arlington Rd Ste 405 Bethesda MD 20814-5231

PRITCHETT, ROBERT MARVIN, JR., religious organization administrator; b. Centreville, Md., Oct. 15, 1946; s. Robert Marvin Sr. and Bertha (Rozier) P.; m. Christine Emma Jones, June 25, 1966; children: Kaynette Linesha, Dana Marvea. BS, U. Md., 1985; postgrad., Howard U., 1985-87; MA in Religion, Liberty U., 1990. Ordained African Meth. Episcopal Ch.-2d Episcopal Dist., 1979. Pastor Wrights AME Ch., Elkton, Md., 1977-80, St. James AME Ch., Havre De Grace, Md., 1980-85, Adams Chapel AME Ch., Balt., 1985-88; pastor, administr. Faith Unity Fellowship, Millington, Md., 1988—; instr. African M.E. Ch., Balt., 1978-82, Parks and Recreation, Queen Anne's County, Md., 1989-91; dir., instr. Fellowship Biblical & Theol. Inst., Millington, 1993—. Author: (manuals) Christian Education, Retooling for the 21st Century, 1986, Discipline, 1992; editor: Faith Unity Fellowship Ministry Manual, 1992. Mem. Grasonville (Md.) Cmty. Ctr., 1980; advisor, founder Black Bros. for Change, Grasonville, Md., 1988; bd. mem. Commn. Drug & Alcohol, Centreville, 1993. Recipient Cert. of Recognition, U.S. Army, Aberdeen, Md., 1983, Cert. of Recognition, NAACP, Grasonville, 1991. Avocations: fishing, walking, bowling, reading, traveling. Home: 1 Charles Wood Ct Baltimore MD 21207 Office: Fellowship Biblical and Theol Inst 31850 Millington Rd Millington MD 21651

PRITCHETT, SAMUEL TRAVIS, finance and insurance educator, researcher; b. Emporia, Va., Dec. 18, 1938; s. Harvey Eugene and Mary (Brown) P.; m. Bertha Yates, Feb. 20, 1960; children: John Travis, Meri Katherine. BSBA, Va. Poly. Inst. and State U., 1960, MSBA, 1967; DBA, Ind. U., 1969. CLU, ChFC, CPCU. Claim rep. Equitable Life Assurance Soc., Richmond, Va., 1960-64, asst. div. claim mgr., 1964-65; asst. prof. bus. adminstrn. U. Richmond, 1969-70; asst. prof. ins. Va. Commonwealth U., Richmond, 1970-72, assoc. prof. ins., 1972-73; assoc. prof. fin. and ins. U. S.C., Columbia, 1973-76, prof. fin. and ins., 1976—, J.H. Fellers prof., 1981-83, W.F. Hipp prof. ins., 1983—; acad. dir. MBA program Ind. U., Bloomington, 1993-95, vis. prof. ins., 1995-96; chmn. Risk theory Soc., Columbus, Ohio, 1987-88; acad. dir. internat. exec. devel. program Bamerindus Seguros, Curtiba, Brazil, 1995. Author: Risk Management and Insurance, 7th edit., 1996, Stock Life Insurance Company Profitability, 1986, Individual Annuities as a Source of Retirement Income, 2d edit., 1982, An Economic Analysis of Workers' Compensation in South Carolina, 1994; assoc. editor Jour. Risk and Ins., 1982-86, editor, 1987-91; assoc. editor Fin. Svcs. Rev., 1989-95; asst. editor Jour. Am. Soc. CLU and ChFC, 1993—; mem. acad. rev. bd. Jour. Fin. Planning, 1990-91; mem. editl. bd. Jour. Bus. Rsch., 1976-83, Am. Jour. Small Bus., 1975-79; contbr. articles to profl. jours. Active S.C. Joint Ins. Study Com., 1981-86, 89-95. Mem. Am. Risk and Ins. Assn. (pres. 1980-81), Acad. Fin. Svcs. (pres. 1987-88), So. Risk and Ins. Assn. (pres. 1977-78), Fin. Mgmt. Assn., Profl. Ins. Agts. Found. (named Ins. Educator of Yr. 1989), Beta Gamma Sigma (pres. chpt. 1980-81), Gamma Iota Sigma (nat. trustee 1976-92). Home: 7740 Castleton Ln Columbia SC 29223-2508 Office: U SC Coll Bus Columbia SC 29208 *Apply to others religious values such as honesty, humility, respect, and service. Cultivate a strong work ethic and select admirable mentors.*

PRITCHETT, THOMAS RONALD, retired metal and chemical company executive; b. Colorado City, Tex., Sept. 2, 1925; s. John Thomas and Meddie Omeira (Terry) P.; m. Mary Margaret Hallenbeck, Dec. 23, 1948; children: Rhonda Jean, Thomas Rand, Rebecca Ann. BS in Chemistry and ChemE., U. Tex., 1948, MS, 1949, PhD, 1951. Registered profl. engr. Calif. Rsch. chemist Def. Rsch. Lab., Austin, Tex., 1948-51, Monsanto Chem. Co., Dayton, Ohio, 1951-52; sect. head, rsch. investigator, asst. dir., tech. mgr. Kaiser Aluminum & Chem. Corp., Pleasanton, Calif., 1952-68, v.p., dir. rsch., 1968-89; cons. Alamo, Calif., 1989—. Contbr. articles to profl. jours. Mem. adv. bd. Sch. Engring. U. Calif.-Berkeley. Served with U.S. Army, 1944-46. Fellow Am. Soc. Metals; mem. AIME, Aluminum Assn. (chmn. tech. com. and acad. com.), Nat. Assn. Corrosion Engrs., Am. Chem. Soc., Electrochem. Soc., Materials Properties Council (bd. dirs.), Sigma Xi, Phi Lambda Upsilon. Home and Office: 1430 Laurenita Way Alamo CA 94507-1133

PRITCHETT, SIR VICTOR SAWDON, author; b. Ipswich, Eng., Dec. 16, 1900; s. Sawdon and Beatrice (Martin) P.; m. Dorothy Roberts, Oct. 2, 1936; children: Josephine, Oliver. Ed., Alleyn's Sch., Dulwich; D.Litt. (hon.), Leeds U., 1973, Columbia U., 1978, U. Sussex, 1980, Harvard U., 1985. Free-lance journalist France, Ireland, Spain and U.S., 1921-28; lit. critic New Statesman, London, 1928-78; dir. New Statesman, 1951-78; Christian Gauss lectr. Princeton U., 1953; Beckman prof. U. Calif., Berkeley, 1960; writer-in-residence Smith Coll., 1966-71; Zisskind prof. Brandeis U., Waltham, Mass., 1969; vis. prof. Sch. Fine Arts, Columbia U., 1972; Clark lectr. Cambridge (Eng.) U., 1969, Vanderbilt U., 1981. Author: Marching Spain, 1928, Clare Drummer, 1929, The Spanish Virgin, 1930, Elopement into Exile, 1932, Nothing Like Leather, 1935, You Make Your Own Life, 1938, It May Never Happen, 1945, The Living Novel, 1949, Mr. Beluncle, 1951, The Spanish Temper, 1954, Books in General, 1962, In My Good Books, 1953, The Working Novelist, 1965, When My Girl Comes Home, 1961, Dead Man Leading, 1949, The Key to My Heart, 1963, London Perceived, 1962, The Offensive Traveller, 1964, New York Proclaimed, 1965, (with Elizabeth Bowen and Graham Greene) Why Do I Write?, 1948, Dublin: A Portrait, 1967, A Cab at the Door, 1967, Blind Love, 1970, Meredith's English Comedy, 1970, Midnight Oil, 1971, Balzac, 1973, The Camberwell Beauty, 1974, The Gentle Barbarian: Turgenev: Selected Stories, 1978, The Myth Makers, 1979, On the Edge of the Cliff, 1980, The Tale Bearers (essays), 1980, Collected Stories, 1981, More Collected Stories, 1983, The Turn of the Year, 1984, The Oxford Book of Short Stories, 1981, Man of Letters (essays), 1986, Chekhov, 1987, A Careless Widow, 1989, At Home and Abroad, 1989, Lasting Impressions (essays), 1990, Complete Short Stories, 1990, Complete Essays, 1992; contbr. stories to leading mags. Decorated comdr. Order Brit. Empire, 1968, created knight, 1975, Companion of Honor, 1993; recipient Royal Soc. Lit. award, 1969, 87, W.H. Smith award, 1990, Elmer Holmes Bobst award NYU, 1991, Golden Pen award Internat. PEN, 1993. Mem. Soc. Authors (pres. 1978). Clubs: Savile (London), Beefsteak (London). Address: 12 Regents Park Terr, London NW1, England

PRITIKIN, DAVID T., lawyer; b. Freeport, Ill., May 2, 1949. BA summa cum laude, Cornell U., 1971; JD magna cum laude, Harvard U., 1974. Bar: Ill. 1974, U.S. Ct. Appeals (9th cir.) 1975, U.S. Ct. Appeals (7th cir.) 1976, U.S. Supreme Ct. 1977, U.S. Ct. Appeals (fed. cir.) 1993. Ptnr. Sidley & Austin, Chgo.

PRITIKIN, JAMES B., lawyer, employee benefits consultant; b. Chgo., Feb. 18, 1939; s. Stan and Anne (Schwartz) P.; m. Barbara Cheryl Demovsky, Apr. 20, 1968 (dec. 1988); children: Gregory, David, Randi; m. Mary Szatkowski, July 7, 1990; 1 child, Peyton. BS, U. Ill., 1961; JD, DePaul U., 1965. Bar: Ill. 1965, U.S. Dist. Ct. (no. dist.) Ill. 1965, U.S. Supreme Ct. 1985; cert. matrimonial arbitrator. Pvt. practice, Chgo., 1965-68, 1984—; ptnr. Sudak, Grubman, Pritikin, Rosenthal & Feldman, Chgo., 1969-80, Pritikin & Sohn, Chgo., 1980-84; pres. Prepaid Benefits Plans Inc., Chgo., 1978—; exec. dir. The Ctr. for Divorce Mediation Ltd. Fellow Internat. Acad. Matrimonial Lawyers, Am. Acad. Matrimonial Lawyers; mem. ABA, Ill. Bar Assn., Chgo. Bar Assn. (cir. ct. Cook County liaison com.), Chgo. Pub. Schs. Alumni Assn. (v.p. 1984—). Office: 221 N La Salle St Chicago IL 60601-1206

PRITIKIN, ROLAND I., opthalmologic surgeon, writer, lecturer; b. Chgo., Jan. 9, 1906; s. Edward and Bluma (Saval) P.; m. Jeanne DuPre Moore, May 25, 1940 (dec. May 1988); children: Gloria Anne, Karin (Mrs. Craig Howard Heiser). B.S., Loyola U., 1928, M.D., 1930; diploma, U.S. Army Command and Gen. Staff Coll., 1964. Diplomate: Am. Bd. Ophthalmology. Eye department Loyola U. School Medicine, 1933-35; resident Ill. Eye and Ear Infirmary, 1936-38, staff, 1939-48; vis. eye surgeon, Shikarpur, Sind, Pakistan, under Sir Henry Holland, 1939, 57, 60, 63, 66, 71, vis. eye surgeon Ethiopia, 1972; cons. Rockford industries, 1946—; pvt. practice ophthalmology Rockford, 1946—; pres. staff Winnebago County (Ill.) Hosp., 1950; lecture, research tour, Western Europe, Near and Middle East, 1951, vis. eye surgeon, Pakistan, 1960; cons. in ophthalmology HHS; hearing officer Social Security Adminstrn.; vis. eye clinics Vienna, Zurich, Paris, 1934. Author: Essentials of Ophthalmology, 1950, 3d edit., 1975, World War Three Is Inevitable, 1976; contbr. Ency. Americana supplements, 1946-80, reg. vols., 1955-72, articles on ophthalmology various med. jours., also sects. on spectacles and contact lenses to Acad. Am. Ency. Med. Res. Officers; chmn. meeting on computers in ophthalmology Internat. Symposium on Bio-Engring. in Ophthalmology, Haifa, Israel, 1975, Ctr. For Global Security, 1978—; life mem. Weizmann Inst., Sci. Served as col. M.C. AUS, 1941-45; brig. gen. Ill. N.G., ret. Recipient 1st award World Medical Assn., 1964; Quetta Mission Hosp. medal, 1964; Physician's Recognition award AMA, 1972, 75, 77, 83, 86, 89, 92, Cert. award VFW, 1986, Cert. award Chapel of the Four Chaplains, 1980, Super Sr. award Winnebago County Coun. on Aging, 1991, Cert. Appreciation for 25 yrs. vol. cons. ophthalmology U.S. Army Health Svcs. Command; named Commodore State of W.Va., 1980, Ky. Col., 1982; decorated Army Commendation medal, 1965, Order St. John of Jerusalem by Queen Elizabeth II, 1970; promoted to Comdr. by Queen Elizabeth II, 1993. Fellow Indsl. Med. Assn., Am. Med. Writers Assn., Soc. Mil. Ophthalmologists (bd. govs., 1st life), AMA, A.C.S., Internat. Coll. Surgeons, AAAS, Am. Geriatrics Soc., Royal Soc. Health, Am. Coll. Nuclear Medicine (distinguished mem., founding mem.), Instituto Barraquer, Barcelona; assoc. Royal Soc. Medicine London; mem. Internat. Assn. Secs. Ophthalmol. and Otolaryngol. Socs. (editor ophthalmology 1973-80), Ill., Winnebago County med. socs., Am. Nuclear Soc., Am. Acad. Ophthalmology and Otolaryngology, Chgo. Ophthal. Soc., Assn. Mil. Surgeons U.S., Rock River Valley Ophthalmology Assn. (sec. 1978—), World Med. Assn., Pan-Am. Assn. Ophthalmology, Am. Assn. History of Medicine, Assn. Am. Phys. and Surg., Internat. Assn. Prevention of Blindness, Joseph Waring Meml. Library Assn. History of Medicine, Soc. Med. Cons. to Armed Forces, N.Y. Acad. Scis., Contact Lens Soc. of Ophthalmologists, Nat. Soc. Prevention Blindness, Henry Holland Hosps. Alumni Assn. and Fund (pres.), Internat. Assn. Against Trachoma, Assn. Research Ophthalmology, Soc. Nuclear Medicine, Pan Am. Soc. Ophthalmic Microsurgery (charter), Ophthalmol. Soc. Canary Islands (hon.), Internat. Soc. History Medicine (hon.), Am. Coll. Eye Surgeons (life mem.), C. of C., 33d Div. War Vets. Assn. (surgeon 1975-85), Am. Legion, Res. Officers Assn. U.S., Internat. Agy. Prevention Blindness, Ophthalmol. Soc. Pakistan (life), others. Club: Univ. (Rockford). Inventor surg. and diagnostic equipment for the eye. Home: Independence Village 3655 N Alpine Rd Apt B-302 Rockford IL 61114-7324 Office: Talcott Bldg Rockford IL 61101

PRITSKER, A. ALAN B., engineering executive, educator; b. Phila., Feb. 5, 1933; s. Robert and Gertrude (Liebowitz) P.; m. Anne Gruner, 1956; children: Caryl DuBrock, Pamela Poteet, Kenneth, Jeffrey. B.S.E.E., Columbia U., 1955, M.S. in Indsl. Engring., 1956; Ph.D., Ohio State U., 1961; DSc (hon.), Ariz. State U., 1992. Registered profl. engr., Tex., Ariz. Engr. Battelle Inst., 1956-62; Prof. engring. Ariz. State U., Tempe, 1962-69; prof. engring. Va. Poly. Inst., Blacksburg, 1969-70; prof. engring. Purdue U., West Lafayette, Ind., 1970-81, adj. prof. engring., 1981—; pres. Pritsker Corp., West Lafayette, 1973-86, 91—, chmn., 1973—; cons. Rand Corp., Gen. Electric Co., Gen. Motors Corp., Bethlehem Steel Co. Author: Simulation With Gasp IV, 1974, Modeling and Analysis Using Q-Gert Networks, 1979, Management Decision Making, 1984, Introduction to Simulation and SLAM II, 1986, TESS: The Extended Simulation Support System, 1987, SLAM II Network Models for Decision Support, 1989, Papers, Experiences, Perspectives, 1990. Recipient Gilbreth Indsl. Engring. award Am. Inst. Indsl. Engrs., 1991. Fellow Inst. Indsl. Engrs. (Rsch. and Innovation award 1978, Gilbreth award 1991); mem. NAE, Inst. Mgmt. Scis. (coll. on simulation, Disting. Svc. award 1991), Ops. Rsch. Am. Office: Pritsker Corp PO Box 2413 West Lafayette IN 47906-0413

PRITZ, MICHAEL BURTON, neurological surgeon; b. New Brunswick, N.J., Oct. 8, 1947; s. John Ernest and Helen Violet (Rockoff) P.; m. Edmay Marie Gregorcy, Feb. 18, 1973; children: Edmond Louis, Benjamin David. BS, U. Ill., 1969; PhD, Case Western Res. U., 1973, MD, 1975. Diplomate Am. Bd. Neurol. Surgery. Asst. prof. neurol. surgery U. Calif. Irvine Med. Ctr., Orange, 1981-85, assoc. prof., 1985-93; prof., 1993, U. Calif. Irvine Med. Ctr., Orange, 1993—; prof. sect. neurol. surgery Ind. U. Sch. Medicine, Indpls., 1993—, prof. neurol. surgery, 1993—. Contbr. articles to profl. jours. Recipient Herbert S. Steuer award Case Western Res. U., Cleve., 1975; NSF fellow, 1968; Edmund J. James scholar U. Ill., Champaign, 1968-69. Mem. Soc. Neurosci., Am. Assn. Anatomists, Am. Assn. Neurol. Surgeons, Congress Neurol. Surgeons, Soc. Neurol. Surgeons of Orange County (pres. 1985-86, sec.-treas. 1984-85).

PRITZKER, JAY, travel company executive , lawyer; b. Chgo., Aug. 26, 1922; married; children: Tom, John, Dan, Gigi. BS, Northwestern U., 1941, JD, 1947. Bar: Ill. 1947. Ptnr. Pritzker and Pritzker, Chgo., 1947—, Chgo. Mill and Lumber Co., 1948—, Mich.-Calif. Lumber Co., 1951—; chmn., CEO, bd. dirs. Amarillo Gear Co., 1965—; chmn., sec., CEO Marmon Group Inc., 1967—, chmn., sec., chmn. bd. dirs., 1972—; chmn. bd. dirs., CEO Hyatt Corp.; chmn. bd. dirs. Hyatt Corp., Hyatt Internat., Marmon Holdings, Inc.; dir. Berisford plc, Royal Caribbean Cruises Ltd., others. Life trustee Univ. Chgo.; chmn. internat adv. bd. Columbia Univ. Sch. Internat. and Pub. Affairs. Lt. USN, 1942-46. Office: Pritzker and Pritzker 200 W Madison St Ste 3800 Chicago IL 60606-3414*

PRITZKER, LEON, statistician, consultant; b. N.Y.C., June 26, 1922; s. Harry and Sophie (Greene) P.; m. Mary Anne Watts; children: William Earl, David Ronald, Paul Mark, Carol Ann, Phillip Joseph. BS, CCNY, 1942; MA, U. Pa., 1947. Statistician U.S. Bur. of Census, Washington, 1947-61, chief response rsch. br., 1961-67; dir. mktg. info. svcs. Anheuser-Busch Cos., St. Louis, 1967-73, dir. mgmt. systems, 1973-84; exec. v.p., staff ops. Campbell Taggart, Inc., Dallas, 1985-90; cons., 1990—; vis. faculty Case Inst. Tech., Cleve., 1954-55; cons. Cen. Statis. Bur., Govt. Israel, Jerusalem, 1961, Inst. Stats., Govt. Turkey, Ankara, 1967. Contbr. articles to profl. jours. With U.S. Army, 1943-46. Fellow Am. Statis. Assn.; mem. Ops. Rsch. Soc., Internat. Assn. Survey Statisticians.

PRITZKER, NICHOLAS J., diversified services corporation executive. Formerly exec. v.p. devel. Hyatt Corp., Chgo.; pres. Hyatt Devel. Corp., Chgo. Office: Hyatt Devel Corp 200 W Madison St Chicago IL 60606-3414*

PRITZKER, ROBERT ALAN, manufacturing company executive; b. Chgo., June 30, 1926; s. Abram Nicholas and Fanny (Doppelt) P.; m. Mayari Sargent; children: James, Linda, Karen, Matthew , Liesel. B.S. in Indsl. Engring., Ill. Inst. Tech., Chgo., 1946; postgrad. in bus. adminstrn., U. Ill. Engaged in mfg., 1946—; chief exec. officer, pres., dir. Marmon Corp., Chgo., Marmon Indsl. Corp., Chgo.; pres., dir. The Colson Group, Inc., Marmon Holdings, Inc., Marmon Industries, Inc., Chgo.; bd. dirs. Hyatt Corp., Chgo., Dalfort Corp., Union Tank Car Co.; vis. prof. Oxford U.; chmn. Nat. Assn. Mfrs. Chmn. bd. Pritzker Found., Chgo.; trustee, chmn. Ill. Inst. Tech., Chgo. Symphony Orch.; immediate past chmn. Field Mus. of Natural History; bd. dirs. Rush-Presbyn.-St. Luke's Med. Ctr. Mem. NAE, Nat. Assn. Mfrs. (former chmn.). Office: Marmon Group Inc 225 W Washington St Chicago IL 60606-3418

PRITZKER, THOMAS JAY, lawyer, business executive; b. Chgo., June 6, 1950; s. Jay Arthur and Marian (Friend) P.; m. Margot Lyn Barrow-Sicree, Sept. 4, 1977; children—Jason, Benjamin, David. B.A.,, Claremont Men's Coll, 1971; M.B.A., U. Chgo., 1972, J.D., 1976. Assoc. Katten, Muchin, Zavis, Pearl and Galler, Chgo., 1976-77; exec. v.p. Hyatt Corp., Chgo., 1977-80, pres., 1980—; chmn. exec. com. Hyatt Hotels Corp., 1980—; ptnr. Pritzker & Pritzker, Chgo., 1976—; pres. Rosemont Shipping, Chgo., 1980—; chmn. of the bd. Health Care Compare Corp., Chgo. Trustee Art Inst. Chgo. 1988—, U. Chgo.; chmn. Indo-U.S. Subcommn. Mem. ABA, Ill. Bar Assn., Chgo. Bar Assn. Clubs: Standard (Chgo.); Lake Shore Country (Glencoe, Ill.). Office: Hyatt Corp 200 W Madison St Chicago IL 60606

PRIVETERA, LORA MARIE, lawyer; b. Toms River, N.J., July 6, 1967; d. Joseph Alfred and Gloria Estelle (Perez) P. BA, Georgian Ct. Coll., 1989; JD, Temple U., 1992. Bar: N.J. 1992, Pa. 1992. Visitation counsellor Ocean County Superior Ct., Toms River, N.J., 1992-93; lawyer Tanner & Tanner, Barnegat, N.J., 1993-95. Mem. ABA. Republican. Roman Catholic. Office: 703 Millcrek Rd Ste F-2 Manahawkin NJ 08050

PRIVETT, HOWARD J., lawyer; b. Monahans, Tex., Aug. 27, 1929. Student, Pepperdine U., 1946-50; LLB summa cum laude, U. Calif., San Francisco, 1957. Bar: Calif. 1958. Ptnr. Baker & Hostetler, L.A.; ret., 1995. Editor-in-chief Hastings Law Jour., 1956-57. Fellow Am. Coll. Trial Lawyers, Chancery Club.

PRIVO, ALEXANDER, finance educator, department chairman; m. Elena Privo. BS, Touro Coll., N.Y.C., 1982; M Profl. Studies, New Sch. for Social

Rsch., N.Y.C., 1985; MS in Edn., CUNY, 1988; PhD in Adminstrn. and Mgmt., Walden U., 1991. Cert. govt. fin. mgr.; cert. secondary tchr. math., ESL, social studies, bus., acctg., Russian, N.y. Dir. acctg. and fin. reporting Assoc. Retail Stores Inc., N.Y.C., 1982-85; tchr. acctg. N.Y.C. Bd. Edn., 1985—; prof., dept. bus. and econs. Touro Coll., 1987—; dean CUNY, 1987-90; chmn. dept. bus. econs. Touro Coll., 1991—; coord. mentoring program CUNY and N.Y.C. Bd. edn., 1985-92; cons. and prof. Russian (former Soviet Union); exec. training program MBA Baruch Coll., CUNY, 1990—; coord. cooperative edn. program NYC BD. Edn./CUNY, 1992—. Curriculum devel. grantee. Mem. ASCD, Am. Acctg. Assn., Assn. Govt. Accts., Nat. Bus. Edn. Assn., Internat. Bus. Edn. Assn., Met. Bus. Edn. Assn., N.Y. Educators (doctorate), Am. Mgmt. Assn., Kappa Delta Pi. Home: 43-33 46th St Apt F15 Sunnyside NY 11104-2036

PRIVOTT, W. J., agricultural products company executive; b. 1938. BS in Chem. Engring., N.C. State U., 1961, PhD, 1964. With Monsanto Co., St. Louis, 1964-91, pres., 1991-94; CEO, pres. Novus Internat. Inc., St. Louis, 1994—. Office: Novus Internat Inc 530 Maryville Centre Dr Saint Louis MO 63141*

PRIZER, CHARLES JOHN, chemical company executive; b. Lake Forest, Ill., Apr. 24, 1924; s. Charles Sumner and Josephine Mary (Jansz) P.; m. Dorothy Gore, June 15, 1944; children: John, Sharon Lee, Mark Sumner, Linda Ann. B.S., U. Ill., 1944; M.S., Drexel U., 1956. With Eastman Kodak Co., 1944-46, Edwal Labs., 1946-51; with Rohm & Haas Co., Phila., 1951-85; v.p., dir. N.Am. region Rohm & Haas Co., 1978-83, group v.p. corp. ops., 1983-85; exec. v.p. Clean Sites, Inc., Alexandria, Va., 1986; prin. Mill Creek Co., 1987-93, Prizer & Wilkinson, 1988-93, Dotsu Enterprises, Inc., 1991-93, CJP Enterprises, Inc., 1992—. Mem. Am. Inst. Chem. Engrs., Am. Chem. Soc. Office: 4325 Gulf Of Mexico Dr Unit 307 Longboat Key FL 34228-2418

PRIZIO, BETTY J., property manager, civic worker; b. L.A., Jan. 23, 1928; d. Harry W. and Irene L. (Connell) Campbell; divorced; children: David P., John W., Robert H., James R. AA in Social Sci., L.A. City Coll., 1949. Owner, mgr. indsl. bldgs. and condominiums indsl. bldgs. and condominiums,, Tustin, Calif., 1976—; owner Baskets and Bows by Jean, Tustin, 1994—; ind. mktg. exec., Melaleuca. Bd. dirs. Founders Chpt. Aux., Providence Speech and Hearing Ctr., 1986-88, aux. pres., 1986-89; vol. Western Med. Ctr. Aux., 1985-89, chmn. gift shop com., 1987-88, 2d v.p., 1992, jr. vol. adv., mem. bd. dirs. fund raising group, mem. scholarship com., mem. Focus on Women com. 1990—; mem. adv. coun. Chapman U., Orange, Calif., 1986-87, bd. mem. Pres. Assocs., 1985-86; bd. dirs. Chapman Music Assocs., 1986—, Tustin Hist. Soc., 1988—, Santa Ana YWCA, 1976-77; mem. adv. coun. Orange County chpt. Freedoms Found. at Valley Forge, 1985—; mem. Orange County chpt. Charter 100, 1985-87; active United Meth. Ch.; others. Mem. Tustin Hist. Soc. (bd. dirs. 1988-90). Republican. Avocations: gardening, arts and crafts, travel, photography. Home: 17342 Village Dr Tustin CA 92680-2546

PRIZZI, JACK ANTHONY, investment banking executive; b. Rochester, N.Y., July 5, 1935; s. Samuel Anthony and Mary Ann (Emanuele) P.; B.S. in Chemistry, Va. Mil. Inst., 1956; M.S. in Phys. Chemistry, U. Va., 1961, M.B.A., 1963; m. Geraldine A. Bias, Feb. 16, 1957 (div. 1971); children—Lynne Marie, Michael Vincent, Karen Annette. Chem. engr. E.I. duPont DeNemours & Co., Inc., Niagara Falls, N.Y., 1956-57; engr. Project Mercury, NASA, 1959; mgr. planning and devel. PPG Industries, Pitts., 1963-68; gen. mgr. Process Components Inc., Norfolk, Va., 1968-70; ptnr. Alan Patricof Assocs., N.Y.C., 1970-74, Beacon Ptnrs., N.Y.C., 1974-76, 77-79, Stuart Bros., N.Y.C., 1976-77; v.p. Walter E. Heller & Co., exec. v.p. Heller Capital Services Inc., N.Y.C., 1979-84; sr. v.p. DnC Am. Banking Corp., N.Y.C., 1984-86; mng. dir. DnC Capital Corp., 1986-89; pres., CEO Jack A. Prizzi & Co., 1989—; spl. ltd. ptnr. Harvest Ptnrs., 1993—; bd. dirs. Tex. Meridian Resources Corp.; instr. advanced grades N.Y. Power Squadron. Vol. Urban Cons. Group. Served to capt. U.S. Army, 1957-59. Grantee Office Naval Research, 1960, Calif. Research Corp., 1960-61. Mem. Assn. for Corp. Growth, Am. Chem. Soc., Raven Soc., N.Y. Athletic Club. Home: 21 W 58th St Apt 12E New York NY 10019-1634 Office: Harvest Ptnrs 767 3rd Ave New York NY 10017-2023

PRO, PHILIP MARTIN, judge; b. Richmond, Calif., Dec. 12, 1946; s. Leo Martin and Mildred Louise (Beck) P.; m. Dori Sue Hallas, Nov. 13, 1982; 1 child, Brenda Kay. BA, San Francisco State U., 1968; JD Golden Gate U., 1972. Bar: Calif. 1972, Nev. 1973, U.S. Ct. Appeals (9th cir.) 1973, U.S. Dist. Ct. Nev. 1973, U.S. Supreme Ct. 1976. Pub. defender, Las Vegas, 1973-75; asst. U.S. atty., Dist. Nev., Las Vegas, 1975-78; ptnr. Semenza, Murphy & Pro, Reno, 1978-79; dep. atty. gen. State of Nev., Carson City, 1979-80; U.S. magistrate U.S. Dist. Ct. Nev., Las Vegas, 1980-87; U.S. dist. judge, 1987—; instr. Atty. Gen.'s Advocacy Inst., Nat. Inst. Trial Advocacy, 1992; chmn. com. adminstrn. of magistrate judge system Jud. Conf. U.S., 1993—. Bd. dirs. NCCJ, Las Vegas, 1982—, mem. program com. and issues in justice com. Mem. ABA, Fed. Judges Assn. (bd. dirs. 1992—), Nev. State Bar Assn., Calif. State Bar Assn., Nev. Judges Assn. (instr.), Assn. Trial Lawyers Am., Nev. Am. Inn Ct. (pres. 1989—), Ninth Cir. Jury (instructions com.), Nat. Conf. U.S. Magistrates (sec.), Nev. Am. Inn of Ct. (pres. 1989-91). Republican. Episcopalian. Office: US Dist Ct 341 Fed Bldg 300 Las Vegas Bldv S Las Vegas NV 89101

PROBASCO, CALVIN HENRY CHARLES, clergyman, college administrator; b. Petaluma, Calif., Apr. 5, 1926; s. Calvin Warren and Ruth Charlene (Winans) P.; m. Nixie June Farnsworth, Feb. 14, 1947; children—Calvin, Carol, David, Ruth. B.A. cum laude, Biola Bible Coll., La Mirada, Calif., 1953; D.D. (hon.), Talbot Theol. Sem., La Mirada, 1983. Ordained to ministry, 1950. Pastor Sharon Baptist Ch., El Monte, Calif., 1951-58, Carmichael Bible Ch., Calif., 1958—; pres. Sacramento Bible Inst., Carmichael, 1968—. Mem. Ind. Fundamental Chs. Am. (rec. sec. 1978-81, pres. 1981-84, 1st v.p. 1987-88), Delta Epsilon Chi. Republican. Office: Carmichael Bible Ch 7100 Fair Oaks Blvd Carmichael CA 95608-6452

PROBERT, WALTER, lawyer, educator; b. Portland, Oreg., Jan. 13, 1925; s. Raymond and Mildred Marie (Pyburn) P.; m. Barbara Louise Stevenson, Mar. 22, 1952; children: Richard Walter, James Stevenson. Student, Alfred U., 1944; B.S., U. Oreg., 1948, J.D., 1951; J.S.D. (Grad. fellow), Yale U., 1957. Bar: Oreg. 1951. Practiced in Portland, 1951-52; asst. prof. Western Res. U., 1953-57, asso. prof., 1957-59; prof. U. Fla., Gainesville, 1959—; endowed prof. U. Fla., 1985—; vis. prof. Northwestern U., 1960-61, U. Tex., summer 1970, U. Wash., 1972-73; vis. research prof. U. Denver, 1966-67; lectr. Balliol Coll., Oxford U., 1968; dir. law and social sci. program NSF, 1973-74. Author: Law, Language, and Communication, 1972; faculty editor Western Res. U. Law Rev., 1953-59; contbr. articles to profl. jours. Served with AUS, 1943-47. Recipient grants for law-communication research. Mem. ATLA, Assn. Am. Law Schs. (mem. panel advocates), Oreg. Bar Assn., Internat. Assn. Philosophy of Law and Social Philosophy, Law and Soc. Assn., Am. Psychology-Law Soc., Am. Soc. Polit. and Legal Philosophy, Phi Beta Kappa, Order of Coif, Order of St. Ives, Delta Theta Phi. Home: 1522 SW 35th Pl Gainesville FL 32608-3530

PROBST, LAWRENCE F., III, computer company executive. BS, U. Del., 1972. Dist. sales mgr. Johnson & Johnson, 1972-80; nat. accounts mgr. The Clorox Co., 1980-82, Mediagenic (formerly Activision Inc.), 1982-84; chmn., CEO Electronic Arts, San Mateo, Calif., 1984—. Office: Electronic Arts 1450 Fashion Island Blvd San Mateo CA 94404-2063

PROBSTEIN, RONALD FILMORE, mechanical engineering educator; b. N.Y.C., Mar. 11, 1928; s. Sidney and Sally (Rosenstein) P.; m. Irene Weindling, July 30, 1950; 1 child, Sidney. B.M.E., NYU, 1948; M.S.E., Princeton U., 1950, A.M., 1951, Ph.D., 1952; A.M. (hon.), Brown U., 1957. Research asst. physics N.Y. U., 1946-48, instr. engring. mechanics, 1947-48; research asst. dept. aero. engring. Princeton U., 1948-52, research assoc., 1952-53, asst. prof., 1953-54; asst. prof. divs. engring., applied math. Brown U., 1954-55, assoc. prof., 1955-59, prof., 1959-62; prof. mech. engring. M.I.T., 1962-89, Ford prof. engring., 1989—; Disting. prof. engring. U. Utah, 1973; sr. partner Water Purification Assos., Cambridge, 1974-82; chmn. bd. Water Gen. Corp., Cambridge, 1982-83; sr. corp. tech. advisor Foster-Miller, Inc., 1983—; commr. commn. on engring. and tech. systems NRC, 1980-83; sci. advisor to bd. Corrpro Cos., 1993—. Author: Hypersonic Flow Theory, 1959, Hypersonic Flow, Inviscid Flows, 1966, Water in Synthetic Fuel Production, 1978, Synthetic Fuels, 1982, Physicochemical Hydrodynamics, 1989, 2d edit., 1994; editor: Introduction to Hypersonic Flow, 1961, Physics of Shock Waves, 1966, Jour. PhysicoChem. Hydrodynamics, 1987-89; contbr. articles to profl. jours.; patentee in field. Guggenheim fellow, 1960-61. Fellow Am. Acad. Arts and Scis. (councilor 1975-79), Am. Phys. Soc., ASME (Freeman award 1971), AIAA, AAAS; mem. NAE, Internat. Acad. Astronautics, Am. Inst. Chem. Engrs. Home: 5 Seaver St Brookline MA 02146-5714 Office: 77 Massachusetts Ave Cambridge MA 02139-4301

PROBUS, MICHAEL MAURICE, JR., lawyer; b. Louisville, Jan. 26, 1963; s. Michael Maurice and Jerilyn Ann (Burks) P.; m. Luz Marie Probus, May 22, 1985; children: Michael Julian, Lauren Michael. BA, U. Dallas, 1985; JD, U. Tex., 1988. Bar: Tex. 1988, U.S. Dist. Ct. (we. dist.) Tex. 1990, U.S. Ct. Appeals (5th cir.) 1993. Jud. law clk. to chief judge U.S. Dist. Ct. Tex., Houston, 1988-90; assoc. Law Offices of Michael A. Wash, Austin, Tex., 1990—. Pro bono atty. Vol. Legal Svcs., Austin, 1994—; active TTLA Advocates, Austin, 1994—. Mem. ABA, Tex. Trial Lawyers Assn., Travis County Bar Assn. (mem. CLE com. 1993—). Democrat. Roman Catholic. Office: Law Offices Michael A Wash 600 Congress Ave # 3200 Austin TX 78701

PROCHNOW, DOUGLAS LEE, lawyer; b. Omaha, Jan. 9, 1952; s. Albert Delmer and Betty Jean (Wood) P. BA with high distinction, U. Nebr., 1974; JD, Northwestern U., 1977. Bar: Ill. 1977, U.S. Dist. Ct. (no. dist.) Ill. 1977, U.S. Ct. Appeals (7th cir.) 1989. Assoc. Wildman, Harrold, Allen & Dixon, Chgo., 1977-84, ptnr., 1985—. Spl. asst. corp. counsel City of Chgo., 1986-87. Mem. ABA, Ill. Bar Assn., Chgo. Bar Assn., Assn. Trial Lawyers Am. (assoc.), Ill. Trial Lawyers Assn., Soc. Trial Lawyers, Def. Rsch. Inst., Phi Beta Kappa, Phi Eta Sigma. Home: 1230 N State Pky Apt 6D Chicago IL 60610-2261 Office: Wildman Harrold Allen & Dixon 225 W Wacker Dr Chicago IL 60606-1224

PROCHNOW, HERBERT VICTOR, former government official, banker, author; b. Wilton, Wis., May 19, 1897; s. Adolph and Alvina (Liefke) P.; m. Laura Virginia Stinson, June 12, 1928 (dec. Aug. 1977); 1 child, Herbert Victor. BA, U. Wis., 1921, MA, 1922, LLD, 1956; PhD, Northwestern U., 1947, Northwestern U., 1963; LLD (hon.), LittD, Millikin U., 1952; LLD, Ripon Coll., Wis., 1950, Lake Forest Coll., 1964, Monmouth Coll., 1965, U. N.D., 1966; DHL, Thiel Coll., 1965. Prin. Kendall (Wis.) High Sch.; asst. prof. bus. adminstrn. Ind. U.; advt. mgr. Union Trust Co., Chgo.; officer First Nat. Bank of Chgo., pres., 1962-68, dir., 1960-68, hon. dir., 1968-73; former dir. Carter H. Golembe Assocs., Inc., 1972-76; dir. Banco di Roma, Chgo., 1973-87; columnist Chgo. Tribune, 1968-70; sec. fed. adv. coun. Fed. Res. System, 1945-94; apptd. spl. asst. to sec. of state, 1955, dep. under sec. of state for econ. affairs, 1955-56; alt. gov. for U.S. Internat. Bank and Internat. Monetary Fund, 1955-56; pres. Internat. Monetary Conf., 1968, now cons., hon mem. Co-author: The Next Century Is America's, 1938, Practical Bank Credit, 1963, (with Herbert V. Prochnow, Jr.) A Dictionary of Wit, Wisdom and Satire, 1962, The Public Speaker's Treasure Chest, 1976, rev. edit., 1986, The Successful Toastmaster, 1966, A Treasury of Humorous Quotations, 1969, The Changing World of Banking, 1973, The Toastmaster's Treasure Chest, 1979, rev. edit., 1988, A Treasure Chest of Quotations for All Occasions, 1983; author: Great Stories from Great Lives (an anthology), 1944, Meditations on the Ten Commandments, 1946, The Toastmaster's Handbook, 1949, Term Loans and Theories of Bank Liquidity, 1949, Successful Speakers Handbook, 1951, 1001 Ways to Improve Your Conversations and Speeches, 1952, Meditations on the Beatitudes, 1952, The Speaker's Treasury of Stories for All Occasions, 1953, The Speaker's Handbook of Epigrams and Witticisms, 1955, Speakers Treasury for Sunday School Teachers, 1955, A Treasury of Stories, Illustrations, Epigrams and Quotations for Ministers and Teachers, 1956, The New Guide for Toastmasters, 1956, Meditations on The Lord's Prayer, 1957, The New Speaker's Treasury of Wit and Wisdom, 1958, A Family Treasury of Inspiration and Faith, 1958, The Complete Toastmaster, 1960, Speaker's Book of Illustrations, 1960, 1000 Tips and Quips for Speakers and Toastmasters, 1962, 1400 Ideas for Speakers and Toastmasters, 1964, Tree of Life, 1972, Speaker's Source Book, 1972, A Speaker's Treasury for Educators, Convocation Speakers, 1973, 1,000 Quips, Stories, and Illustrations for All Occasions, 1973, Toastmaster's Quips and Stories and How to Use Them, 1982; editor: American Financial Institutions, 1951, Determining the Business Outlook, 1954, The Federal Reserve System, 1960, World Economic Problems and Policies, 1965, The Five Year Outlook for Interest Rates, 1968, The One-Bank Holding Company, 1969, The Eurodollar, 1970, The Five Year Outlook for Interest Rates in the U.S. and Abroad, 1972, Dilemmas Facing the Nation, 1979, Bank Credit, 1981, Speaker's and Toastmaster's Handbook, 1990, 5100 Quotations for Speakers and Writers, 1992. Mem. O.S.S., 1942-45, U.S. delegation GATT, Geneva, 1956; del. Colombo Conf., Singapore, 1955, OECD, Paris, 1956; former lectr. Loyola U., Ind. U., Northwestern U.; bd. dir. grad. sch. of banking U. of Wis., 1945-81; trustee, cons. McCormick Theol. Sem.; hon. trustee Chgo. Sunday Evening Club. With AEF, 1918-19. Decorated Order of Vasa (Sweden), comdr. Cross Order of Merit (Fed. Republic of Germany).; recipient Bus. Statesmanship award Harvard U. Bus. Sch. Assn. Chgo., 1965, Ayres Leadership award Stonier Grad. Sch. Banking, Rutgers U., 1966, Silver Plaque NCCJ, 1967. Mem. Chgo. Coun. on Fgn. Rels. (pres. 1966-67), Am. Econ. Assn., Chgo. Assn. Commerce and Industry (pres. 1964-65), Rotary, Beta Gamma Sigma (nat. honoree). Clubs: Comml., Glen View; Univ., Chgo., Union League (Chgo.), Bankers (past pres.). Home: 2950 Harrison St Evanston IL 60201-1249 Office: 1 First National Plz Chicago IL 60670

PROCHNOW, HERBERT VICTOR, JR., lawyer; b. Evanston, Ill., May 26, 1931; s. Herbert V. and Laura (Stinson) P.; m. Lucia Boyden, Aug. 6, 1966; children: Thomas Herbert, Laura. A.B., Harvard U., 1953, J.D., 1956; A.M., U. Chgo., 1958. Bar: Ill. 1957, U.S. Dist. Ct. (no. dist.) Ill. 1961. With 1st Nat. Bank Chgo., 1958-91, atty., 1961-70, sr. atty., 1971-73, counsel, 1973-91, adminstrv. asst. to chmn. bd., 1978-81; pvt. practice, 1991—. Author: (with Herbert V. Prochnow) A Treasury of Humorous Quotations, 1969, The Changing World of Banking, 1974, The Public Speaker's Treasure Chest, 1986, The Toastmaster's Treasure Chest, 1988; also articles in legal publs. Mem. ABA, Ill. Bar Assn., Chgo. Bar Assn. (chmn. com. internat. law 1970-71), Am. Soc. Internat. Law, Phi Beta Kappa. Clubs: Harvard (N.Y.C.); Chicago (Chgo.), Legal (Chgo.), Law (Chgo.), Onwentsia, Economic (Chgo.), University (Chgo.). Home: 949 Woodbine Pl Lake Forest IL 60045-2275 Office: 155 N Michigan Ave Chicago IL 60601-7511

PROCHNOW, JAMES R., lawyer; b. Hutchinson, Minn., Sept. 22, 1943. BA, Hamline U., 1965; JD, William Mitchell Law Sch., 1969. Bar: Minn. 1969, U.S. Supreme Ct. 1973, Colo. 1975. Staff civil divsn. Dept. Justice, Washington, 1973-74; legal counsel to Pres. The White House, Washington, 1974; ptnr. Baker & Hostetler, Denver, Patton Boggs, 1995—. Editor in chief William Mitchell Opinion, 1968-69; antitrust notes editor The Barrister, 1978-81. Mem. ABA, Denver Bar Assn., Colo. Bar Assn., Assn. Trial Lawyers Am., Colo. Trial Lawyers Assn. Office: Patton Boggs 1660 Lincoln St Ste 1975 Denver CO 80264*

PROCKOP, DARWIN JOHNSON, biochemist, physician; b. Palmerton, Pa., Aug. 31, 1929; s. John and Sophie (Gurski) P.; m. Elinor Sacks, Apr. 15, 1961; children: Susan Elizabeth, David John. AB, Haverford Coll., 1951; MA, Oxford U., 1953; MD, U. Pa., 1956; PhD, George Washington U., 1962; DSc (hon.), U. Oulu, 1983, U. So. Fla., 1993. Investigator NIH, 1957-61; assoc., asst. prof., asso. prof., prof. medicine and biochemistry U. Pa., Phila., 1961-72; prof., chmn. dept. biochemistry U. Medicine and Dentistry of N.J. (Rutgers Med. Sch.), Piscataway, N.J., 1972-86; prof., chmn. dept. biochemistry and molecular biology Jefferson Med. Coll., Phila., 1986-96; prof., dir. Ctr. for Gene Therapy, Med. Coll. Pa./Hahnemann U., Phila., 1996—; dir. Jefferson Inst. Molecular Medicine, 1986-96. Contbr. articles to profl. jours.; research on collagen. Served with USPHS, 1958-61. Fulbright fellow Oxford U., 1951-53; NIH, grantee, 1961—; recipient Disting. Alumnus award George Wash. U., 1991, U. Pa., 1994. Mem. NAS, Inst. Medicine, Acad. Finland, Soc. Biol. Chemists, Am. Soc. Clin. Investigation, Am. Assn. Physicians, Phi Beta Kappa, Alpha Omega Alpha. Home: 291 Locust St Philadelphia PA 19106-3913

PROCTER, JOHN ERNEST, former publishing company executive; b. Gainesboro, Tenn., July 23, 1918; s. Leon and Mary (Poteet) P.; m. Jane Sprott, May 23, 1941; children: Mary Carol, Valere Kay. Student, Vanderbilt U., 1940-41, U. Miami (also extension div.), 1943-44, U. Tenn., 1946-50; LL.D. (hon.), Ohio No. U., 1971; D.L. (hon.), Ky. Wesleyan Coll., 1981. With Methodist Pub. House, Nashville, 1945-83; v.p., pub. Methodist Pub. House, 1964-70, pres., pub., 1970-83; dir. 3d Nat. Bank, Nashville. Bd. dirs. Tenn Council on Econ. Edn. Served to capt. USAAF and USAF, 1944-45, 50-52. Decorated Certificate of Valor; Air medal with 7 oak leaf clusters; D.F.C. Mem. Adminstrv. Mgmt. Soc. (past pres. Nashville, area. sec.-treas. 1967-68, Merit Key award 1961, Diamond Merit award 1967), Nashville C. of C. (past mem. bd. govs.), Assn. Am. Pubs. (past dir.). Clubs: Golf Club of Tenn., Belle Meade Golf & Country. *The modest success I have achieved is the result of an intense commitment to intellectual honesty, sensitivity to the needs of my associates, the setting of challenging and realistic goals, striving for efficiency by doing things right and being effective by doing the right things, always with faith in myself and my associates.*

PROCTOR, BARBARA GARDNER, advertising agency executive, writer; b. Asheville, N.C.; d. William and Bernice (Baxter) Gardner; B.A. Talladega Coll., 1954; m. Carl L. Proctor, July 20, 1961 (div. Nov. 1963); 1 son, Morgan Eugene. Music critic, contbg. editor Down Beat Mag., Chgo., from 1958; internat. dir. Vee Jay Records, Chgo., 1961-64; copy supr. Post-Keyes-Gardner Advt., Inc., 1965-68, Gene Taylor Assos., 1968-69, North Advt. Agy., 1969-70; contbr. to gen. periodicals, from 1952; founder Proctor & Gardner Advt., Chgo., 1970—, now pres., chief exec. officer. Mem. Chgo. Urban League, Chgo. Econ. Devel. Corp. Bd. dirs. People United to Save Humanity, Better Bus. Bur. Cons. pub. relations and promotion, record industry. Recipient Armstrong Creative Writing award, 1954; awards Chgo. Fedn. Advt. Clubs, N.Y. Art Dirs. Club. Woman's Day; Frederick Douglas Humanitarian award, 1975; named Chgo. Advt. Woman of Year, 1974. Mem. Chgo. Media Women, Nat. Assn. Radio Arts and Sci., Women's Advt. Club, Cosmopolitan C. of C. (dir.), Female Execs. Assn., Internat. Platform Assn., Smithsonian Instn. Assos. Author TV documentary Blues for a Gardenia, 1963. Office: Proctor & Gardner Advt Inc 111 E Wacker Dr Ste 321 Chicago IL 60601-4208*

PROCTOR, CONRAD ARNOLD, physician; b. Ann Arbor, Mich., July 14, 1934; s. Bruce and Luena Marie (Crawford) P.; m. Phyllis Darlene Anderson, June 23, 1956; children: Sharon Darlene Proctor Heimbach, Barbara Jan Brown, David Conrad, Todd Bruce. MD, U. Mich., 1959, MS, 1964. Cert. Am. Bd. Otolaryngology. Intern St. Joseph Mercy Hosp., Ann Arbor, 1959-60; jr. clin. instr. Univ. Hosp., Ann Arbor, 1961-63, sr. clin. instr., 1963-65; chief dept. otolaryngology Munson Army Hosp., Ft. Leavenworth, Kans., 1965-67; mem. attending staff William Beaumont Hosp., Royal Oak, Mich., 1967—; instr. Am. Acad. Otolaryngology, Washington, 1968-82, guest examiner, Chgo., 1978-79; Midwest dir. Macrocellular Cellular Phone Sys., 1990—. Author: Current Therapy in Otolaryngology, 1984-85; (booklet) Dietary Treatment of Meniere's Syndrome, 1983, Hyperinsulinemia and Tinnitus, 1988; (manual) Hereditary Sensorineural Hearing Loss, 1978, Etiology, Treatment of Fluid Retention in Meniere's Syndrome, 1992; (med. jour.) Abnormal Insulin Levels and Vertigo, 1981. Dir. Christian edn. Bloomfield Hills (Mich.) Bapt. Ch., 1969-72, fin. chmn., 1975-78, Sunday sch. tchr., 1967—. Served to capt. U.S. Army, 1965-67. Recipient 1st pl. award for med. rsch. Students Am. Med. Assn., 1959, Merit award Am. Acad. Otolaryngology, 1978; holder 4 world records Internat. Game Fish Assn. Mem. AMA, Mich. State Med. Assn., Oakland County Med. Assn., Am. Bd. Otolaryngology, ACS, Triological Soc., Otosclerosis Study Group, Internat. Game Fish Assn., Phi Eta Sigma, Phi Kappa Phi, Phi Beta Kappa. Republican. Clubs: Panangling Ltd. (Chgo.); Victors and Presidents (Ann Arbor). Avocations: baseball, football, tennis, Arctic exploration, fishing. Home: 1645 Kirkway Ln Bloomfield Hills MI 48302-1360 Office: 3535 W 13 Mile Rd Royal Oak MI 48073-6700

PROCTOR, DONALD FREDERICK, otolaryngology educator, physician; b. Red Bank, N.J., Apr. 19, 1913; s. Frederick R. and Gertrude (Chauncey) P.; m. Janice Carson, June 10, 1937; children: Douglas, Nan. A.B., Johns Hopkins, 1933, M.D., 1937. Diplomate: Am. Bd. Otolaryngology. With otol. lab. Johns Hopkins Hosp., 1937-38, mem. otolaryn. house staff, 1938-40; resident otolaryngology Balt. City Hosps., 1940-41; pvt. practice otolaryngology Balt., 1941-56; asso. prof. otolaryngology Med. Sch., Johns Hopkins, 1946-51, 58-73, prof. anesthesiology, 1951-55, 77-84, asst. prof. physiology, laryngology and otolaryngology, 1955-58, 77-84, prof. laryngology and otology, 1973-84, prof. environ. health sci., 1965-84, prof. emeritus, 1984—, chief bronchoscopic clinic, 1962-66, chief research program air hygiene, dept. environmental medicine, 1955—; with dept. physiology U. Rochester, 1946-47; fellow anesthesiology U. Pa., 1951-52. Author: Anesthesia and Otolaryngology, 1957, Tonsils and Adenoids in Childhood, 1960, Nose Paranasal Sinuses and Ears in Childhood, 1962, Breathing, Speech, and Song, 1980; editor: Respiratory Defense Mechanisms, 1977, The Nose, Upper Airway Physiology and Atmospheric Environment, 1982, A History of Breathing Physiology, 1995; author articles, book chpts. deafness, respiration, air hygiene, air polllution, mucous membrane. Fellow A.C.S., Am. Acad. Otolaryngology; mem. Am. Bronchoesophagol. Assn., Am. Indsl. Hygiene Assn., Air Pollution Control Assn., Am. Physiol. Soc., Phi Beta Pi, Sigma Xi. Club: 14 West Hamilton Street (Balt.). Home: 4300 N Charles St Apt 9-f Baltimore MD 21218-1066

PROCTOR, EDWARD GEORGE, lawyer; b. Chgo., July 16, 1929; s. Harold Proctor and Catherine Elliott; m. Kathleen Friend, Apr. 4, 1959; children: Brian, Diana, Edward, Laurel, Abigail, John. BS, Loyola U., Chgo., 1951; JD, Loyola U., 1953. Bar: Ill. 1953. From assoc. to ptnr. Kirkland & Ellis, Chgo., 1953-78; ptnr. Reuben & Proctor, Chgo., 1978-87, Isham, Lincoln, Beale (merger with Reuben & Proctor), Chgo., 1987-88, Hinshaw & Culbertson, Chgo., 1988—; adj. prof. Loyola U. Sch. of Law; trustee Loyola U.; chmn. bus. dept. Hinshaw & Culbertson. Co-chmn. Com. to Elect Mary Ann McMorrow to Ill. Supreme Ct., 1991-92; mem. Legal Assistance Found. Friends Com. Chgo.; former tchr. CCD classes St. Barnabas Ch., Chgo.; former fundraiser Mt. Carmel H.S., Morgan Park Acad., St. Ignatius Coll. Prep. Recipient Medal of Excellence Loyola U. Sch. Law, 1989, plaque of Appreciation Cath. Charities, 2 plaques of Appreciation Loyola Alumni Assn. Fellow ABA (life); mem. Ill. Bar Assn., Chgo. Bar Assn. (comml. fin. and transactions coms.), Bankruptcy Inst., Loyola Law Alumni Assn. (past pres.), Olympia Fields Country Club (past pres.), Lambda Alpha Internat. Roman Catholic. Avocation: golf. Office: Hinshaw & Culbertson 222 N La Salle St Chicago IL 60601-1003

PROCTOR, JESSE HARRIS, JR., political science educator; b. Durham, N.C., Sept. 3, 1924; s. Jesse Harris and Rosa Belle (Rogers) P.; m. Ella Jane Callahan, Mar. 27, 1948; children: Edward Sidney, Thomas Christopher, Kenneth Stuart. A.B., Duke U., 1948; M.A., Fletcher Sch. Law and Diplomacy, 1949; Ph.D., Harvard U., 1955. Instr., asst. prof. polit. sci. MIT, 1949-56; asst. prof., assoc. prof. polit. sci. Am. U. in Cairo, 1956-58, prof., 1991-92; asst. prof., then assoc. prof. and prof. polit. sci. Duke U., 1958-70; Charles A. Dana prof. polit. sci. Davidson (N.C.) Coll., 1970-91, prof. emeritus, 1991—, chmn. dept. polit. sci., 1972-89; vis. assoc. prof. polit. sci. U. Coll., Nairobi, Kenya, 1964-65; vis. prof. polit. sci., U. Dar es Salaam, Tanzania, 1969-70; Fulbright lectr. St. Stephen's Coll., Delhi U., India, 1982-83. Editor: Islam and International Relations, 1965; contbg. author: Federalism in the Commonwealth, 1963, The Aftermath of Sovereignty, 1973, Prospects for Constitutional Democracy, 1976; Contbr. articles to profl. jours. Served with USAAF, 1943-46. Mem. Phi Beta Kappa, Pi Sigma Alpha, Omicron Delta Kappa. Home: PO Box 567 Davidson NC 28036-0567

PROCTOR, JOHN FRANKLIN, lawyer; b. Scottsboro, Ala., May 6, 1931; s. James Moody and Lucy (May) P.; m. Anne Esco, Dec. 3, 1988; children from previous marriage: James Moody, Laura. B.S., U. Ala., 1953, LL.B., 1957. Bar: Ala. bar 1957. Asst. atty. gen., 1957-59; pvt. practice Scottsboro, 1959-90; judge Jackson County Ct., 1959-63; pvt. practice, 1963-66, 68—; judge 9th Jud. Circuit, 1966-68; fed. adminstrv. law judge, 1990—. Served with U.S. Army, 1953-55. Mem. Ala. Bar Assn. (commr. 1979-90), Rotary, Sigma Chi, Phi Alpha Delta. Methodist. Home: 3110 Olde Town Ln Chattanooga TN 37415 Office: Office Hearings and Appeals 300 Uplain Bldg Chattanooga TN 37411

PROCTOR, JOHN P., lawyer; b. Kewaunee, Wis., 1942. BA, Princeton U., 1964; LLB, U. Pa., 1967. Bar: D.C. 1968, U.S. Ct. Mil. Appeals 1970, U.S. Ct. Appeals (D.C. cir.) 1975, N.Y. 1984. Ptnr. Winston & Strawn, Washington. Mem. ABA (vice chmn. air quality com., nat. resources law sect. 1984—), Fed. Bar Assn. Office: Winston & Strawn 1400 L St NW Washington DC 20005-3509*

PROCTOR, KENNETH DONALD, lawyer; b. Balt., Apr. 28, 1944; s. Kenneth Chauncey and Sarah Elizabeth (Kent) P.; m. Judith Danner Harris, Aug. 2, 1969; children—Kenneth Scott, Kent Harris, Janet Cameron. B.S., Lehigh U., 1966; J.D., U. Md., 1969. Bar: Md. 1969, U.S. Dist. Ct. Md. 1970, U.S. Ct. Appeals (4th cir.) 1980, U.S. Supreme Ct. 1974. Law clk. to presiding judge Md. Ct. Appeals, 1969-70; assoc. Miles & Stockbridge, Balt., 1970-73, 74-76, ptnr., Balt., 1976-81, Towson, Md., 1981—; asst. atty. gen. Md., Balt., 1973-74; Trustee, Gilman Sch., Balt., 1982-85. Mem. ABA, Md. State Bar Assn., Balt. County Bar Assn. Democrat. Episcopalian. Office: Miles & Stockbridge 600 Washington Ave Baltimore MD 21204-3913

PROCTOR, MARK ALAN, real estate executive, television panelist, commentator; b. Daytona Beach, Fla., June 3, 1948; s. John George and Christine (Crosier) P.; m. Carolyn Louise Morgan, July 24, 1982; 1 child, Morgan Alan. AA, Miami-Dade Community Coll., Miami, Fla., 1968; BA, Fla. Internat. U., 1975; postgrad., Fla. State U., 1978. Pub. relations asst. Woody Kepner & Assoc., Inc., Miami, 1968-70; dir. admission World Jai-Alai, Inc., Miami, 1970-75; sales assoc. R.C. Peacock & Co., Miami, 1975-77; systems cons. Fla. Game & Fish Commn., Tallahassee, Fla., 1977-79; communications dir. Fla. Dental Assn., Tampa, Fla., 1980-81; sales mgr. Gen. Devel. Corp., Tampa, 1981-83; broker-salesman Select Properties & Investment Corp., Tampa, 1983-87; pres. Proctor Properties, Brandon, Fla., 1987—; mem. Hillsborough County Indsl. Devel. Authority, Tampa, 1988—, vice chmn. 1991-92, 93-94; mem. Hillsborough County Housing Resource Bd.,1989—, pres., 1991-92, 92-93; mem. policy bd. Tampa Com. of 100, 1988-89; participant Joint Civil Orientation Conf., U.S. Dept. Def.; gov.'s appointee State of Fla. Growth Mgmt. Com., 1993; bd. dirs. Homes for Hillsborough, Inc.; pres. Dist. Six, Inc., 1994—. Editor, contbr. articles to Wildlife Inventory, 1979; contbr. articles to Fla. Dental Jour., 1980-81, Fla. Conservation News, 1986, Tampa Realtor, 1986; regular guest analyst weekly current events TV show Tampa Bay Week, Sta. WEDU-Channel 3, 1993—, Bayside, Sta. WTOG-Channel 44, 1994—. Pres. Hillsborough Assn. Chambers, Tampa, 1988-89, Arts and Crafts Cmty. Edn. Svcs., Inc. Tampa, 1991-92; pres. Rep. Exec.Com., Tampa, 1984; mem. Pres. Roundtable of Greater Brandon, 1989-90, co-chair Highlighting Hillsborough Paint Your Heart Out, 1992, 93-94, Brandon Balloon Festival and Marathon, 1994, alumni assn. Leadership Hillsborough, 1994-95; ch. moderator United Ch. of Christ, 1994. Recipient Comty. Svc. award 1989, Greater Brandon; named outstanding vol. Bay Area Youth Svcs., Tampa, 1984, Up & Comer of Yr., Price Waterhouse-Tampa Bay Bus. Jour., 1988, to Pres. Coun. U. S. Fla. Coll. Bus. Adminstrn., Tampa, 1989. Mem. Greater Tampa Assn. Realtors (pres. 1990, chmn. exec. bd. 1991, Realtor of Yr. 1985, W.H. Copeland award for outstanding comty. svc. 1991, Civic Achievement award 1991), Fla. Assn. Realtors (state dir. 1987-90, chmn. local govt. subcom. 1990, issues mobilization com. 1991, dist. v.p. 1994, Honor Soc. 1988-90), Nat. Assn. Realtors (congl. coord. 1987-89, polit. affairs com. 1991), Women's Coun. Realtors (affiliate), Real Estate Investment Coun., Greater Brandon C. of C. (pres. 1988,. Republican. Avocations: fishing, hunting, politics, travel. Home: 1716 Silverwood Dr Brandon FL 33510-2643 Office: Proctor Properties 409 S Kings Ave Brandon FL 33511-5919

PROCTOR, RICHARD J., geologist, consultant; b. L.A., Aug. 2, 1931; s. George Arthur and Margaret Y. (Goodman) P.; m. Ena McLaren, Feb. 12, 1955; children: Mitchell, Jill, Randall. BA, Calif. State U., L.A., 1954; MA, UCLA, 1958. Engring. geologist, Calif.; cert. profl. geologist Am. Inst. Profl. Geologists. Chief geologist Met. Water Dist., L.A., 1958-80; pres., cons. geologist Richard J. Proctor, Inc., Arcadia, Calif., 1980—; vis. assoc. prof. Calif. Inst. Tech., Pasadena, 1975-78. Co-author: Citizens Guide to Geologic Hazards, 1993; editor: Professional Practice Guidelines, 1985, Engineering Geology Practice in Southern California, 1992. Pres., dir. Arcadia Hist. Soc., 1993-96. Fellow Geol. Soc. Am. (Burwell Meml. award 1972); mem. Assn. Engring. Geologists (pres. 1979), Am. Inst. Profl. Geologists (pres. 1989, Van Couvering Meml. award 1990, hon. mem. 1992), Am. Geol. Inst. (sec.-treas. 1979-83).

PROCTOR, RICHARD OWEN, public health administrator, army officer; b. Austin, Tex., Nov. 18, 1935; s. William Owen and Arlene Gertrude (Holdeman) P.; m. Martha June Whitlock, Nov. 19, 1955; children: Tanya Marie, Sheilia Renee, Michael Lee, Terry Glen, Richard Lowell, Roger Owen. BA, Oklahoma City U., 1957; MS, Baylor U. Coll. Medicine, Houston, 1964, MD, 1964; MPH and TM, Tulane U., 1970; diploma, U.S. Army War Coll., 1983. Diplomate Am. Bd. Pediatrics, Am. Bd. Preventive Medicine. Commd. capt. U.S. Army, 1964, advanced through grades to brig. gen.; instr. Imperial Ethiopian Coll. A&M Arts, Alemaya, 1957-59; dep. comdr. U.S. Army Hosp., Kagnew Station, Ethiopia, 1967-69, U.S. Army Med. Lab., Ft. Sam Houston, Tex., 1973-75; instr. U.S. Army Acad. Health Scis., Ft. Sam Houston, 1975-77; surgeon U.S. Army VII Corps, Moeringen, Fed. Republic Germany, 1978-81; prof., chmn., comdt. of students Uniformed Svcs. U. of Health Scis., Bethesda, Md., 1981-82; comdr. Raymond Bliss Army Community Hosp., Ft. Huachuca, Ariz., 1983-85; surgeon U.S. Army Tng. and Doctrine Command, Ft. Monroe, Va., 1985-88; comdg. gen. William Beaumont Army Med. Ctr., El Paso, Tex., 1988-91; dir. pub. health Region 6 Tex. Dept. Health, Houston, 1991—; cons. WHO/PAHO, Bolivia, 1971; lectr. on medicine, anthropology, theology, history, substance abuse prevention; past adj. or clin. faculty positions Baylor U., Tulane U., U. Tex. Author: (with others) Principles of Pediatrics: Healthcare of the Young, 1978, Current Pediatrics Diagnosis and Treatment, 1978, 80, Primary Pediatric Care, 1987, 2d edit., 1992, Comprehensive Adolescent Health Care, 1992; author multiple articles on viremia with Sabin polio vaccines. Asst. scout master Boy Scouts Am., Bowie, Md., 1971-73; scout committeeman Boy Scouts Am., Moeringen, 1978-81. Decorated D.S.M., Legion of Merit (twice); recipient scholarship Broadhurst Found., Tulsa, 1953-57; rsch. fellow NIH, 1960-61; Tropical Medicine fellow La. State U., 1970. Fellow Am. Acad. Preventive Medicine, Am. Acad. Pediatrics, Royal Soc. Medicine; mem. Assn. Mil. Surgeons of U.S., Nat. Eagle Scout Assn. Methodist. Avocations: ranching, conservation, living history. Home: RR 4 Box 1193 Paris TX 75462-9708 Office: Ste J 5425 Polk Ave Houston TX 77023-1497

PROCTOR, ROBERT SWOPE, retired petroleum company executive; b. Columbus, Ohio, June 15, 1922; s. William Edward and Elsie M. (Swope) P.; m. Mary M. Thornton, Dec. 31, 1945; children: Robert M., Jill, Mary, Ann, Kathleen. MSME, Oreg. State U., 1947. With Standard Oil Co. Calif., Inc., 1947-76; gen. mgr. El Segundo (Calif.) refinery, 1969-71; v.p., dir. Western Operation Inc., San Francisco, 1971-76; v.p. mfg. Chevron U.S.A., San Francisco, 1976-84. Served to 1st lt., C.E. AUS, 1943-45. Mem. Calif. Mfrs. Assn. (dir.). Republican. Home: PO Box 1639 Zephyr Cove NV 89448-1639 *I have been very fortunate in life. I did not set life long goals early in life, rather always tried to develop myself and do the best I could for family, country and community.*

PROCTOR, SAMUEL, history educator; b. Jacksonville, Fla., Mar. 29, 1919; s. Jack and Celia (Schneider) P.; m. Bessie Rubin, Sept. 8, 1948; children: Mark Julian, Alan Lowell. B.A., U. Fla., 1941, M.A., 1942, Ph.D., 1958. Mem. faculty U. Fla., Gainesville, 1946—, prof. history and social scis., 1963-74, disting. service prof. history, 1974—, Julien C. Yonge prof. Fla. history, 1976—, univ. historian, 1953—, dir. oral history program, 1968—; curator History Fla. State Mus.; dir. Doris Duke Southeastern Indian Oral History Program, Ctr. for Study of Fla. History and Humanities. Author: Napoleon Bonaparte Broward, Florida's Fighting Democrat, 1950, Florida Commemorates the Civil War Centennial, 1962, Florida One Hundred Years Ago, 1966, Florida History Preservation Planning, 1971, Gator History: History of the University of Florida, 1986, The University of Florida, 1990, N.B. Broward, 1993; editor, author introduction: Dickison and His Men: Reminiscences of the War in Florida, 1962; series editor: Bicentennial Floridiana Facsimile Series; editor: Eighteenth Century Florida and Its Borderlands, 1975, Eighteenth Century Florida and the Carribean, 1976, Eighteenth Century Florida, Life on the Frontier, 1976, Eighteenth Century Florida and the Revolutionary South, 1977, Eighteenth Century Florida and the Impact of The American Revolution, 1978, Tacachale, Essays on the Indians of Florida and Southeastern Georgia during the Historic Period, Jews of the South; assoc. editor: Fla. Hist. Quar., 1962-64, editor, 1963-93; contbr. articles to profl. jours. Served with U.S. Army, 1943-46. Mem. Fla. Blue Key, Phi Beta Kappa, Tau Epsilon Phi, Pi Kappa Phi, Phi Alpha Theta. Democrat. Jewish. Home: 2235 NW 9th Pl Gainesville FL 32605-5201 Office: Univ Fla Dept History Gainesville FL 32611

PROCTOR, WILLIAM LEE, college president; b. Atlanta, Jan. 27, 1933; s. Samuel Cook and Rose Elizabeth (Nottingham) P.; m. Pamela Evans Duke; children: Samuel Matthews (dec.), Priscilla Nottingham. BS, Fla. State U., 1956, MS, 1964, PhD, 1968. Tchr. Seminole County Pub. Schs., Longwood, Fla., 1956-57, 58-62, Orange County Fla. Pub. Schs., Orlando, Fla., 1957-58; athletic coach Fla. State U., Tallahassee, 1962-65, asst. dean men, 1965-67, grad. fellow, 1967-68; supt. of schs. Rock Hill (S.C.) Sch. Dist. #3, 1968-69; dean of men U. Cen. Fla., Orlando, 1969-71; pres. Flagler Coll., St. Augustine, Fla., 1971—; cons. on higher edn. policy Heritage Found., Washington, 1983—; mem. Commn. on Colls., So. Assn. Colls. and Schs., 1995—; mem. adv. coun. State Postsecondary Rev. Entity, 1994-95. Bd. dirs. Nat. Accrediting Coun. for Agys. Serving the Blind, Flagler Health Svcs., Inc., St. Augustine, 1977-95, Penny Farms Retirement Cmty., pres., 1991—; bd. dirs. Fla. Ind. Coll. Fund, Lakeland, Vickers Landing Retirement Cmty., pres. bd., 1990—; trustee Fla. Sch. for Deaf and Blind, St. Augustine, 1984—. Recipient Disting. Educator award Fla. State U. Coll. Edn., 1989, Phil Carrol award Soc. for Advancement Mgmt., 1990, Disting. Svc. award Fla. Sch. for Deaf and Blind, 1990, Patrick Henry Medallion patriotic achievement Mil. Order of World Wars, 1991, Stetson S Club Achievement award, 1993; named to Fla. State U. Athletic Hall of Fame, 1988. Mem. Am. Assn. Pres. of Ind. Colls., State Hist. Assn., Ind. Colls. and Univs. of Fla. (legis. chmn. 1974-77, vice chmn. 1976-77, chmn. 1978-79), St. Johns County C. of C. (dir.), Rotary (pres. 1978-79, govs. dist. 697 1988-89). Republican. Presbyterian. Avocations: history, jogging, karate. Office: Flagler Coll Office of the Pres PO Box 1027 Saint Augustine FL 32085-1027

PROCYK, JUDSON M., metropolitan archbishop. Ordained priest, 1957. Bishop Byzantine Catholic Metropolitan Diocese of Pitts., 1994-96; Met. Archbishop Byzantine Metropolitan Archdiocese of Pitts., 1996—. Office: 66 Riverview Ave Pittsburgh PA 15214

PROEBSTING, EDWARD LOUIS, JR., retired research horticulturist; b. Woodland, Calif., Mar. 2, 1926; s. Edward Louis and Dorothy (Critzer) P.; m. Patricia Jean Connolly, June 28, 1947; children: William Martin, Patricia Louise, Thomas Alan (dec.). BS, U. Calif., Davis, 1948; PhD, Mich. State U., 1951. Asst. horticulturist Wash. State U., Prosser, 1951-57, assoc. horticulturist, 1957-63, horticulturist, 1963-93, supt. Irrigated Agrl. Rsch. and Ext. Ctr., 1990-93; ret., 1993; vis. prof. Cornell U., Ithaca, N.Y., 1966; vis. scientist Hokkaido U., Sapporo, Japan, 1978, Victoria Dept. Agr., Tatura, Australia, 1986—. Contbr. numerous articles to profl. jours. Scoutmaster Boy Scouts Am., Prosser, 1963-76, dist. chmn., 1976-78. Served to lt. USNR, 1943-46, 52-54. Recipient Silver Beaver award Boy Scouts Am.; fellow Japan Soc. Promotion Sci., Sapporo, 1978, Res. Bank. Australia, 1986. Fellow AAAS, Am. Soc. Hort. Sci. (pres. 1983-84, sci. editor jour. 1993—). Methodist. Avocations: backpacking, native plants. Home: 1929 Miller Ave Prosser WA 99350-1532 Office: Wash State U Irrigated Agrl/Ext Ctr 24106 N Bunn Rd Prosser WA 99350-9678

PROEFROCK, CARL KENNETH, academic medical administrator; b. Curtis, Ill., Mar. 30, 1928; s. Carl Robert and Anna Lorraine (Hagel) P.; m. Margaret Muntz (dec. 1984); children: Philip, Andrew, Elizabeth, Liesl; m. Janelle Dillon, Sept. 8, 1988. BA, Carthage Coll., Kenosha, Wis., 1949; MDiv, Chgo. Luth. Theol. Sem., 1953. Sr. com. orgn. specialist N.Y.C. Housing and Devel. Adminstrn., 1966-68; exec. dir. Model Cities Program, Manchester, n.H., 1968-70, Health Assn. Rochester and Monroe (N.Y.), 1970-73, Mahoning Shenango Area Health Edn. Network, Youngstown, Ohio, 1973-78; spl. asst. to dean Northeastern Ohio Univs. Coll. Medicine, Rootstown, 1978-79; v.p. Med. Coll. Ohio, Toledo, 1979-88, sr. v.p. govtl. affairs, 1988-93; pres. KPA Assocs., Inc., 1993—; v.p. Found. for Applied Rsch., Washington, 1976; chmn. adv. bd. Ohio AHEC, Columbus, 1976; program adminstr. Ohio Statewide Area Health Edn. Ctr., Toledo, 1988-93. Mem. budget allocation com. United Appeal, Youngstown, 1975-78; mem. dist. planning coun. Ohio Dept. Mental Health, Youngstown, 1977-78; chmn. Toledo Area Coun. Tech., 1986. Mem. Nat. Area Health Edn. Ctrs. Assn. (bd. dirs. 1988—), Nat. Assn. Univ. Rsch. Adminstrs., Soc. Rsch. Adminstrs., Internat. Assn. Univ. Rsch. Parks, Soc. Univ. Patent Adminstrs., Nat. Assn. Health Manpower Edn. Systems, Northeastern Ohio Med. Educators Assn. (bd. dirs.), Rotary. Lutheran. Home: 189 Rose Hill Dr Pawleys Island SC 79585 Office: KPA Assocs PO Box 194 Pawleys Island SC 29585

PROFFITT, JOHN RICHARD, investment banking executive; b. Grand Junction, Colo., Sept. 12, 1930; s. Hillus D. and Joy Elaine (Lindsay) P.; m. Claire Boyer Miller, May 8, 1965 (div. 1992); children: Cameron Lindsay, William Boyer. BA in Edn., U. Ky., 1953, MA in Polit. Sci., 1961; postgrad., U. Mich., 1959-65. Asst. dean of men, instr. polit. sci. dept. U. Ky., Lexington, 1957-59; teaching fellow U. Mich., Ann Arbor, 1961-63, 63-65; asst. dir. Nat. Commn. on Accrediting, Washington, 1966-68; dir. accreditation and eligibility staff U.S. Dept. HEW, Washington, 1968-75; dir. div. eligibility and agy. evaluation U.S. HEW, Washington, 1975-80; dir. div. instnl. and state incentive programs U.S. Dept. Edn., Washington, 1980-82; pres. The Clairion Corp., Bethesda, Md., 1982-84, Nat. Asbestos Removal, Inc., Beltsville, Md., 1985-90; pres. Commonwealth Environ. Svcs., Inc., Alexandria, Va., 1987-91, also chmn. bd. dirs.; chmn. Internat. Environ. Engrs., Inc., Alexandria, Va., 1991-92; pres. Canterbury Internat., Vienna, Va., 1992—; cons. Conn. State Commn. Higher Edn., Hartford, 1967, Am. Coun. Edn., Washington, 1970; cons. U.S. Dept. Hew, 1967, 68; mem. study steering com. Am. Vocat. Assn., Washington, 1968; exec. sec. Nat. Adv. Com. on Accreditation and Instnl. Eligibility, Washington, 1968-80; mem. gen. com. Nat. Study Sch. evaluation, Alexandria, 1970-78; mem. task force Edn. Commn. of the States, Denver, 1972; subcom. chmn. Fed. Interagy. Com. on Edn., Washington, 1974-76; lectr., presenter profl. confs. Co-author: Accreditation and Certification in Relation to Allied Health Manpower, 1971; contbg. author: Health Manpower: Adapting in the Seventies, 1971, Accreditation in Teacher Education, 1975, Transferring Experiential Credit, 1979; contbr. articles to profl. and govtl. agy. publs., 1968-79. v.p., bd. dirs. Nat. Accreditation Coun. for Agys. Serving the Blind, N.Y.C., 1985; pres., chmn. bd. dirs. Found. for Advancement of Quality Svcs. for the Blind, Alexandria, 1988. 1st lt. USAF, 1953-55, Japan and Korea. Higher edn. fellow Univ. Mich., 1959. Mem. Club Internat. (Chgo.), Island Club (Hope Sound, Fla.), Thoroughbred Club Am. (Lexington, Ky.), Tower Club (Vienna, Va.), Sigma Nu. Democrat. Episcopalian. Avocations: conservation, animal welfare, travel, antiques, art. Home: 11008 Spring House Ct Potomac MD 20854-1452

PROFFITT, KEVIN, archivist; b. Hamilton, Ohio, Dec. 24, 1956; s. Henry C. and Marjorie O. (Elam) P.; m. Joan Moriarity, May 17, 1986. BA, Miami U., Oxford, Ohio, 1979; MA, Wright State U., 1980. Archivist Am. Jewish Archives, Cin., 1981—. Contbr. articles to profl. jours. Mem. Soc. Am. Archivists, Acad. Cert. Archivists (cert.), Midwest Archives Conf., Soc. Ohio Archivists (pres. 1987-89). Office: Am Jewish Archives 3101 Clifton Ave Cincinnati OH 45220-2404

PROFFITT, WALDO, JR., newspaper editor; b. Plainview, Tex., Oct. 8, 1924; s. Waldo and Susan Ann (Smith) P.; m. Marjorie Baltzegar, Sept. 14, 1946 (div. 1963); children: Ann Herbert, Deborah, Geoffrey Harrison, Laurence Scott; m. Anne Collier Greene, Feb. 6, 1966; 1 child, Robert Waldo. BA cum laude, Harvard U., 1948. Reporter Bangor (Maine) Commercial, 1948-50; assoc. dir. Harvard News Office, Cambridge, Mass., 1952-54; city editor Charlotte (N.C.) News, 1954-58; mng. editor Journal, Lorain, Ohio, 1958-61; editorial dir. Sarasota (Fla.) Herald-Tribune, 1961-84; editor, 1984—. Lt. U.S. Army, 1943-46, ETO, lt. USAF, 1950-52. Mem. Am. Soc. Newspaper Editors, Fla. Soc. Newspaper Editors (pres. 1978). Democrat. Unitarian. Home: 1581 Hillview Dr Sarasota FL 34239-2047 Office: Sarasota Herald-Tribune PO Box 1719 Sarasota FL 34230-1719

PROFICE, ROSENA MAYBERRY, elementary school educator; b. Natchez, Miss., Oct. 8, 1953; d. Alex Jr. and Louise V. (Fuller) Mayberry; m. Willie Lee Profice, Feb. 12, 1977; children: Jamie Martez, Alesha Shermille. BS in History, Jackson State U., 1974, MS in Elem. Edn., 1975, Edn. Splty. in Elem. Edn., 1977. Cert. elem. reading and social studies tchr., Miss. Tchr. reading Ackerman (Miss.) H.S., 1975-76, North Hazlehurst (Miss.) Elem. Sch., 1976-79; tchr. reading and elem. edn. Natchez-Adams Sch. Sys., Natchez, 1979—. Mem. NEA, Miss. Assn. Educators, Concerned Educators of Black Students, Internat. Reading Assn., Nat. Alliance Black Sch. Educators, Natchez Assn. for the Preservation of Afro-Am. Culture (bd. dirs. 1996-97), Linwood Circle Ruritan Club (bd. dirs. 1992-93, sec. 1994-95), Jackson State U. Alumni Assn., Zion Hill #1 Bapt. Ch. Democrat. Baptist. Avocations: reading, travel, shopping. Home: 11 Elbow Ln Natchez MS 39120-5346

PROFT, PAT, screenwriter, film producer; b. Mpls., Apr. 3, 1947; s. Bob and Marguerite Proft; m. Karen Philipp; 1 child, Patrick. Writer: (T.V. series) The Jim Stafford Show, 1975, The Smothers Brothers Show, 1975, When Things Were Rotten, 1975, Cher, 1975-76, Welcome Back Kotter, 1975-79, Van Dyke and Company, 1976 (Emmy award nomination outstanding writing 1976), The Redd Foxx Comedy Hour, 1977-78, The Mary Tyler Moore Comedy Hour, 1979, Detective School, 1979, Police Squad!, 1982, (TV spls.) Bob Hope Special: Bob Hope's Christmas Party, 1975, Cher, 1975, Ringo, 1978, The Roy Clarke Special, 1979, All Commercials: A Steve Martin Special, 1980, Gary Owens All Nonsense News Network, 1982, (TV pilots) Ultra Quiz, 1981, Twilight Theatre II, 1982, High School, U.S.A., 1984, (films) (with Neal Israel) Bachelor Party, 1984, (with Israel and Hugh Wilson) Police Academy, 1984, (with Israel and Peter Torokvei) Real Genius, 1985, (with Jim Abrahams, David Zucker, and Jerry Zucker) The Naked Gun: From the Files of Police Squad!, 1988, (with D. Zucker) Naked Gun 2 1/2: The Smell of Fear, 1991, Brain Donors, 1992, (with D. Zucker and Robert LoCash) Naked Gun 33 1/3: The Final Insult, 1994; writer, exec. prodr.: (films) (with Israel) Moving Violations, 1985, Lucky Stiff, 1989, (with Abrahams) Hot Shots!, 1991, (with Abrahams) Hot Shots! Part Deux, 1993; writer, prodr.: (TV series) Marie, 1980, Buckshot, 1980; tech. advisor: Johnny Dangerously, 1984; appearances include (films) Modern Problems, 1981, Bachelor Party, 1984, (TV series) Madhouse 90, 1972, The Burns and Schreiber Comedy Hour, 1973, Joey & Dad, 1975, Van Dyke and Company, 1976, Detective School, 1979, (TV movies) Fast Friends, 1979, (TV pilots) Twilight Theatre, 1982.

PROFUSEK, ROBERT ALAN, lawyer; b. Cleve., Jan. 14, 1950; s. George John and Geraldine (Hobl) P.; m. Linda Gail Schmidt, May 7, 1972; children: Robert Charles, Kathryn Anne. B.A., Cornell U., 1972; J.D., NYU, 1975. Bar: Ohio 1975, Tex. 1981, N.Y. 1994. Assoc. Jones, Day, Reavis & Pogue, Cleve., 1975-81, Dallas, 1981-82, ptnr., 1982—, N.Y., 1993. bd. dir. Maybelline, Inc. Contbr. articles to profl. jours. Mem. ABA, N.Y. Bar Assn., Assn. Bar City of N.Y., Tex. Bar Assn., Greenwich Country Club. Republican. Episcopalian. Home: 541 North St Greenwich CT 06830-3801 Office: Jones Day Reavis & Pogue 32nd Flr 599 Lexington Ave Fl 32 New York NY 10022-6030

PROGAR, DOROTHY, retired library director; b. Bruceville, Tex., Sept. 14, 1924; d. Florence Scott and George Thomas Watkins; m. Walter L. Progar, Aug. 3, 1946; 1 child, James Scott. Student, Mich. State U.; BA, Baylor U.; postgrad., Tex. Woman's U. With Waco-McLennan County Libr., 1961-92, circulation libr., 1961-65, young adult libr., 1965-67, ref. libr., 1967-69, asst. dir., 1969-72, assoc. dir., 1972-78, dir. librs., 1978-92. Contbr. articles to profl. jours. Mem. Ctrl. Tex. Lit. Coalition; mem. Strecker Mus. Assocs. Bd.; bd. dirs. Heart O'Tex. Fair and Rodeo, LaRue's Learning Ctr.; mem. adv. bd. Salvation Army. Recipient Waco-McLennan County Pathfinder in Pub. Svc. award, 1988, Silver Bridge award Cen. Tex. chpt. Pub. Rels. Soc. Am., 1990; Dorothy Progar Day proclaimed by City of Waco, 1986. Mem. ALA, Tex. Libr. Assn. (exec. bd. 1986-89), Tex. Mcpl. Libr. Dirs. Assn. (pres. 1987-88, Libr. Dir. of Yr. award 1989), Baylor Alumni Assn., Friends of Baylor Fine Arts Bd., Advt. Club Waco (Silver Medal award 1988), Rotary. Baptist. Avocations: reading, sports, people. Home: 1800 Trinity Dr Waco TX 76710-2842

PROIES, MICHAEL CONSTANTINE, apparel company executive; b. Bklyn., Feb. 12, 1947; s. Michael C. and Marcella E. (James) P.; B.S., Fordham U., 1969; m. Rita D. Gentleman, Sept. 30, 1972; children—Michael, Mark, Craig. With Main Hurdman & Cranston, N.Y.C., 1969-72; mgr. acctg. Gulf & Western Mfg. Co., N.Y.C., 1972-75; div. controller Kayser Roth Corp., N.Y.C., 1975-77, asst. corp. controller, 1980-81, corp. controller, 1981, v.p., chief fin. officer, 1981-82; sr. v.p. K.R. Hosiery Co., 1982-86, chmn. exec. co., 1986-87, pres., No-Nonsense Fashions, Inc., 1987—; acting pres. No Nonsense Fashions,Inc., 1986—; C.P.A., N.Y. Mem. Am. Inst. C.P.A.s, N.Y. State Soc. C.P.A.s. Republican. Office: MPC Consulting 4108 O'Brien Pl Greensboro NC 27410*

PROKASY, WILLIAM FREDERICK, academic administrator; b. Cleve., Nov. 27, 1930; s. William Frederick and Margaret Lovinia (Chapman) P.; children: Kathi Lynn, Cheryl Anne. B.A., Baldwin-Wallace Coll., 1952; M.A., Kent State U., 1954; Ph.D., U. Wis., 1957. Grad. asst. Kent State U., 1953-54; W.A.R.F. fellow U. Wis., 1954-55, teaching asst., 1955-57; asst. prof., then asso. prof. Pa. State U., 1957-66; prof. psychology, chmn. dept. U. Utah, 1966-69, Disting. rsch. prof., 1971-72, dean social and behavioral sci., 1968-70; dean U. Utah (Coll. Social and Behavioral Sci.), 1970-79; acting dean U. Utah (Grad. Sch. Social Work), 1979-80; prof. psychology dean Coll. Liberal Arts and Scis., U. Ill., Champaign-Urbana, 1980-88; prof., v.p. for acad. affairs U. Ga., 1988—; cons. in field. Editor: Classical Conditioning, 1965, (with A.H. Black) Classical Conditioning II, 1971, (with D. Raskin) Electrodermal Responding in Psychological Research, 1973, Psychophysiology, 1974-77; editor (with I. Gormezano and R. Thompson) Classical Conditioning III, 1986; assoc. editor Learning and Motivation, 1969-76; cons. editor Jour. Exptl. Psychology, 1968-80. Del. Utah Dem. Conv., 1968-70, 72-74; trustee Utah Planned Parenthood Assn., 1977-80, Utah bd. dirs. ACLU, 1978-80; v.p., bd. dirs. Champaign-Urbana Symphony, 1986-88; bd. advs. Ga. Mus. of Art, 1989—. NSF sr. postdoctoral fellow, 1963-64, recipient Alumni Merit award Baldwin Wallace Coll., 1992. Fellow AAAS, Am. Psychol. Assn. (chmn. bd. sci. affairs 1977-78, coun. of reps. 1980-86, bd. dirs. 1983-86, bd. editl. affairs 1993—); mem. Fedn. Behavioral, Pyschol. and Cognitive Scis. (v.p. 1984-85, pres. 1985-87), coun. of Sci. Soc. Pres.'s (exec. bd. 1987-91, chmn. 1990), Psychonomic Soc., Coun. Rsch. Librs. (bd. dirs. 1990—), NASULGC (exec. com. coun. on acad. affairs 1995—), Am. Assn. Higher Edn., Soc. Psychophysiol. Rsch. (bd. dirs. 1978-84, pres. 1982-83), Utah Psychol. Assn. (exec. bd. 1968-70, pres. 1971-72), Assn. Advancement Psychology (bd. dirs. 1982-83), Sigma Xi (pres. U. Utah chpt. 1972-73), Phi Kappa Phi.

PROKOPIS, EMMANUEL CHARLES, computer company executive; b. Peabody, Mass., July 5, 1942; s. Charles Emmanuel and Stevia (Kassotis) P.; m. Mary Catherine Dudeck, Dec. 6, 1969; children: Peter Matthew, Christina Eve. BBA, U. Mass., 1966. Mgr., pricing, budgeting, acctg. The Mitre Corp., Mass., Va., 1969-74; mgr. contracts liaison Pratt & Whitney Aircraft div., Conn., Fla., 1974-78; mgr. fin. planning, corp. office United Techs. Corp., Hartford, Conn., 1978-81; contr. magnet wire and insulation div. United Techs. Corp., Fort Wayne, Ind., 1981-83; v.p. fin., chief fin. officer The Mostek Corp. (subs.) United Techs. Corp., Carrollton, Tex., 1983-85; sr. v.p. fin. and ops., chief fin. officer The Lotus Devel. Corp., Cambridge, Mass., 1985-87; fin. mgr. mfg. and engring. Digital Equipment Corp., 1987-91, v.p. budgeting, 1991-92; exec. v.p. MAST Industries, 1992, Ziff Comm., 1992-93; v.p. corp. contr. Digital Equipment Corp., 1994—. 1st lt. U.S. Army, 1966-69, Vietnam. Decorated Bronze Star. Greek Orthodox.

PROKOPOFF, STEPHEN STEPHEN, art museum director, educator; b. Chgo., Dec. 24, 1929; s. Stephen George and Jadwiga M. (Borejszo) P.; m. Paula M. Delle Donne, Oct. 26, 1957 (div. 1981); children—Alexander, Ilya; m. Lois A. Craig, June 21, 1982. B.A., U. Calif.-Berkeley, 1951, M.A., 1952; Ph.D., NYU, 1962. Dir. Hathorn Gallery, Skidmore Coll., Saratoga Springs, NY, 1966-67; dir. Inst. Contemporary Art, U. Pa., Phila., 1967-71, Mus. Contemporary Art, Chgo., 1971-78, Inst. Contemporary Art, Boston, 1978-82, Krannert Art Mus., U. Ill., Champaign, 1982-92, Univ. Art Mus., U. Iowa, Iowa City, 1992—. Co-author and co-designer (with Joan Siegfried): 19th Century Architecture of Saratoga Springs, New York, 1972 (named 1 of 50 Best Designed Books of Yr.); co-author (with text by Marcel Franciscono) The Modern Dutch Poster: The First Fifty Years, 1986; contbr. articles to art periodicals. Grantee Fulbright, 1956-57, German Govt., 1958, U.S. State Dept., 1974, Am. Council on Germany, 1980, 82. Mem. Coll. Art Assn., Assn. Art Mus., Assn. Art Mus. Dirs. Avocations: music; reading; study of architecture. Home: 200 Ferson Ave Iowa City IA 52246-3507 Office: U Iowa U Art Mus 150 N Riverside Dr Iowa City IA 52246-3536

PROM, STEPHEN GEORGE, lawyer; b. Jacksonville, Fla., July 8, 1954; s. George W. and Bonnie M. (Porter) P.; divorced; children: Ashley Brooke, Aaron Jacob, Adam Glenn. AA in Polit. Sci. with high honors, Fla. Jr. Coll., 1974; BA in Polit. Sci. with high honors, U. Fla., 1977, JD with honors, 1979. Bar: Fla. 1980, U.S. Dist. Ct. (mid. dist.) Fla. 1980, U.S. Dist. Ct. (no. dist.) Fla. 1981, U.S. Tax Ct. 1982, U.S. Ct. Appeals (11th cir.) 1985, U.S. Supreme Ct. 1985. Assoc. Rogers, Towers, Bailey, Jones & Gay, Jacksonville, 1979-83, Foley & Lardner, Jacksonville, 1983-86; ptnr. Christian & Prom, Jacksonville, 1986-87, Prom, Korn & Zehmer, P.A., Jacksonville, 1987-95, Brant, Moore, Macdonald & Wells, P.A., 1995—. Sr. mgmt. editor U. Fla. Law Rev., 1978-79. Mem. Leadership Jacksonville, 1984, Jacksonville Community Coun. Inc., 1985-86; bd. dirs. Mental Health Resource Ctr., Jacksonville, 1984-87, Mental Health Resource Foun., Jacksonville, 1985-87, Mental Health Found., Inc., 1987-89, mem. community bd., 1989-91; bd. dirs. Youth Crisis Ctr., Jacksonville, 1984-86, Young Profls. Bd. Multiple Sclerosis Soc., 1988-89; bd. dirs. The Team, Inc., 1992—; vol. Jacksonville, Inc., 1993—, Jacksonville Found., Inc., 1993—, Positively Jacksonville!, Inc., 1993—. Mem. ABA (tax, health law sects.), Fla. Bar Assn. (tax, health law bd., bd. govs. young lawyers sect. 1983-87), Jacksonville Bar Assn. (chmn. health law sect.), Jacksonville Beaches Bar Assn., Am. Acad. Hosp. Attys., Am. Hosp. Assn., Nat. Health Lawyers Assn., Fla. Acad. Hosp. Attys. (bd. dirs. 1994—), Epping Forest Yacht Club (bd. govs., sail fleet capt.), Ponte Vedra Club, North Fla. Cruising Club, Phi Beta Kappa, Phi Theta Kappa, Phi Kappa Phi. Republican. Baptist. Avocations: sailing, surfing, weightlifting, tennis, jogging. Office: Brant Moore et al Barnett Ctr Ste 3100 50 N Laura St Jacksonville FL 32201-4548

PROMISEL, NATHAN E., materials scientist, metallurgical engineer; b. Malden, Mass., June 20, 1908; s. Solomon and Lyna (Samwick) P.; m. Evelyn Sarah Davidoff, May, 17, 1931; children: David Mark, Larry Jay. B.S., M.I.T., 1929, M.S., 1930; postgrad., Yale U., 1932-33; D.Engring. (hon.), Mich. Tech. U., 1978. Asst. dir. lab. Internat. Silver Co. Meriden, Conn., 1930-40; chief materials scientist and engr. Navy Dept., Washington, 1940-66; exec. dir. nat. materials adv. bd. Nat. Acad. Scis., Washington, 1966-74; cons. on materials and policy, internationally, Washington, 1974—; mem., chmn. NATO Aerospace Panel, 1959-71; U.S. rep. (materials) OECD, 1967-70; U.S. chmn. U.S./USSR Sci. Exch. Program (materials), 1973-77); hon. guest USSR Acad. Scis.; permanent hon. pres. Internat. Conf. Materials Behavior; mem. Nat. Materials Adv. Bd.; adv. com. Oak Ridge Nat. Lab., Lehigh U., U. Pa., U.S. Navy Dept. Labs., U.S. Congress Office Tech. Assessment. Contbr. 65 articles to profl. publs.; contbr., editor: Advances in Materials Research, 1963, Science and Technology of Refractory Metals, 1964, Science, Technology and Application of Titanium, 1970; other books. Named Nat. Capitol Engr. of Yr. Coun. Engring. and Archtl. Socs., 1974; recipient Outstanding Accomplishment awards Navy Dept., 1955-64, Nat. Materials Advancement award, Fedn. Materials Socs., 1994; annual hon. lectr. Electrochem. Soc., 1970. Fellow AIME (hon. mem., ann. disting. lectr. Metall. Soc. 1984), Soc. Advanced Materials and Process Engring., Am. Soc. Materials Internat. (pres. 1972, hon. mem., Carnegie lectr. 1967, ann. hon. lectr. 1984), Brit. Inst. Materials; mem. NAE, ASTM (hon., ann. disting. lectr. 1964), Fedn. Materials Soc. (pres. 1972-73, 1st Decennial award 1982), Soc. Automotive Engrs. (chmn. aerospace materials divsn. 1959-74), Alpha Sigma Mu (hon.). Inventor in electroplating, 1930-40; metall. devels., 1941-66. Home and Office: Hyatt Classic Residence 8100 Connecticut Ave Apt 1406 Chevy Chase MD 20815-2820 *Ten key words and phrases for a professional career: identified goals, long range vision, can-do attitude, integrity, objectivity, understanding and tolerance, faith and trust, professionalism, dedication and perseverance, sense of humor.*

PROMISLO, DANIEL, lawyer; b. Bryn Mawr, Pa., Nov. 15, 1932; s. Charles and Pearl (Backman) P.; m. Estelle Carasso, June 10, 1961; children: Mark, Jacqueline, Steven. BSBA, Drexel U., 1955; JD magna cum laude, U. Pa., 1966. Bar: Pa. 1966. Pres., owner Hist. Souvenir Co., Phila., 1957—; assoc. Wolf, Block, Schorr & Solis-Cohen, Phila., 1966-70, ptnr., 1977-94, mem. exec. com., 1987-89, of counsel, 1994—; founder, pres. dir. Inst. for Paralegal Tng., Phila., 1970-75, cons., 1975-77. Editor: Corporate Law, 1970, Real Estate Law, 1971, Estates and Trusts, 1971, Civil Litigation, 1972, Employee Benefit Plans, 1973, Criminal Law, 1974; contbr. articles in field to profl. jours. Bd. dirs. Phila. Drama Guild, 1977-95, chmn., 1982-86; bd. dirs. Phila. Israel Econ. Devel. Program, 1983-88, Inst. for Arts in Edn., 1990-93; bd. dirs. WHYY, Inc., 1994—, vice chmn., 1995-96, chmn., 1996—; bd. dirs. Cancer Recovery, Inc., 1995—. Mem. Order of Coif, Blue Key, Phi Kappa Phi. Democrat. Jewish. Avocations: movies, basketball, tennis. Office: Wolf Block Schorr & Solis-Cohen SE Corner 15 Chestnut St Philadelphia PA 19122

PRONOVOST, STEPHEN H., principal; b. Flushing, N.Y., Aug. 16, 1946; s. Wilbert L. and Margaret N. (Harriman) P.; m. Rose Marie Farrinella, May 20, 1972; children: Jason, Evan. BS, Boston U., 1970, MEd, 1975. Dir. edn. and tng. Paul A. Dever State Sch., Taunton, Mass., 1971-76; extended day coord. Assabet Valley Regional Vocat. H.S., Marlboro, Mass., 1976-84; asst. vocat. chmn. Assabet Valley Regional Vocat. H.S., Marlboro, 1984-89, prin., 1989—; sch. stds. task force Dept. of Edn., Mass., 1993-94, statewide assessment adv. com., 1994—; community edn. adv. coun. Bd. of Edn., 1990-93; asst. dir. Competency Based Vocat. Edn., 1982-83; presenter in field. With U.S. Army, 1966-69. Leadership Acad. fellowship Bd. Edn., 1988-89. Mem. Mass. Secondary Sch. Adminstn. Assn. (vice chair curriculum com. 1990—), Mass. Assn. Vocat. Adminstrn., Mass. Assn. Vocat. Edn. Specialists Needs (pres.). Avocation: model railroading. Office: Assabet Valley Regional Vocat HS 215 Fitchburg St Marlborough MA 01752-1219

PRONZINI, BILL JOHN (WILLIAM PRONZINI), author; b. Petaluma, Calif., Apr. 13, 1943; s. Joseph and Helene (Guder) P. Coll. student, 2 years. Author: 50 novels (including under pseudonyms), 4 books of nonfiction, 6 collections of short stories, 1971—; first novel, The Stalker, 1971; editor 80 anthologies; contbr. numerous short stories to publs. Recipient Scroll award, Best First Novel, Mystery Writers Am., 1972, Life Achievement award Pvt. Eye Writers Am., 1987. Democrat. Office: PO Box 2536 Petaluma CA 94953-2536

PROOPS, JAY D., agricultural products executive. Pres. Vigoro Corp., Chgo., Ill., until 1994, v. chmn., 1994—. Office: Vigoro 225 N Michigan Ave Chicago IL 60601-7601*

PROPHET-COMPTON, DEBBIE JO, pilot; b. Springfield, Mo., Apr. 9, 1956; d. Tom Haggard and Dorothy O. (Leach) Prophet; m. James S. Compton, June 21, 1980. BSN manga cum laude, St. Louis U., 1981, JD, MBA with honorsMBA, 1982. Lic. comml. pilot. Nurse burn unit St. John's Hosp., St. Louis, 1981-85; nurse ICU St. Louis U., 1983-85, utilization mgr., 1986; CEO Brittany Group Inc., St. Louis, 1989-90; owner CFS, Inc., St. Louis, 1991—; chairperson, bd. com. Deaconess Found., St. Louis, 1989-92. Mem. DAR, 1987. Named one of Outstanding Young Women ofAm., 1989. Mem. U.S. Pilot Assn., Mo. Pilots Assn., Women's Pilot Assn. (The 99's), Aircra t Owners and Pilots Assn., Exptl. Aircraft Assn., Pilot/Lawyer Bar Assn., Women's Commerce Assn., Internat. Aerobatic Club. Avocations: snorkeling, tennis, golf, flying. Home: 18025 Deercliff Ct Glencoe MO 63038-1519 Office: CFS Inc 580 Beechcraft Ave Chesterfield MO 63005-3601

PROPHETT, ANDREW LEE, political science educator; b. Lynchburg, Va., Mar. 1, 1948; s. Elisha and Evatna (Gilliam) P. BS in History, Hampton U., 1970; MEd in Social Studies, U. Ill., 1972; postgrad., U. Va., 1986-91. Cert. tchr., N.J. and Va. Tchr. U.S. and African history Camden (N.J.) H.S., 1970-85; tchr. social studies Randolph-Henry H.S., Charlotte Court House, Va., 1986—; instr. polit. sci. and African-Am. history Southside Va. C.C., Keysville, 1988—; mem. Campbell County (Va.) Sch. Bd.; trustee, chmn. edn. com. Staunton River Adv. Commn., Randolph, Va., 1994—; summer participant Armonk Inst. Study Tour of Germany, 1995. Mem. Campbell County Dems., Rustburg, Va., 1986—; pres. Campbell County NAACP, Rustburg, 1992—; mem. youth adv. bd. Gethsemane Presbyn. Ch., Drakes Branch, Va., 1994—, deacon, 1995—. Mem. NEA, Va. Edn. Assn., Va. Geog. Soc., Phi Delta Kappa. Democrat. Presbyterian. Home: RR 1 Box 268 Brookneal VA 24528-9631 Office: Randolph-Henry H S PO Box 668 Charlotte Court House VA 23923

PROPST, CATHERINE LAMB, biotechnology company executive; b. Charlotte, N.C., Mar. 10, 1946; d. James Pinckney and Eliza Mayo (Mills) P. BA magna cum laude, Vanderbilt U., 1967; M of Philosophy, Yale U., 1970, PhD, 1973. Head microbiology div. GTE Labs., Waltham, Mass., 1974-77; various mgmt. positions Abbott Labs., North Chgo., Ill., 1977-80; v.p. rsch. and devel. Ayerst Labs., Plainview, N.Y., 1980-83; v.p. rsch. and devel. worldwide Flow Gen. Inc., McLean, Va., 1983-85; pres. and chief exec. officer Affiliated Sci. Inc., Ingleside, Ill., 1985—; vis. prof. genetics U. Ill., Chgo., 1989-90; founder and exec. dir. Ctr. for Biotech., Northwestern U., 1990-95; pres., Ill. Biotechnology Ctr., 1995—; bd. dirs. several cos. Author and editor: Computer-Aided Drug Design, 1989, Nucleic Acid Targeted Drug Design, 1992; contbr. articles to profl. jours. Named to Outstanding Working Women in the U.S., 1982; recipient many sci. and bus. awards. Fellow Soc. Indsl. Microbiology (bd. dirs. 1990-93), Nat. Coun. Biotech Ctrs. (bd. dirs. 1995—); mem. AAAS, Am. Chem. Soc., Nat. Wildlife Fedn., Consortium for Plant Biotech. Rsch. (bd. dirs. 1994—), Phi Beta Kappa, Sigma Xi. Episcopalian. Avocations: horseback riding, skiing, raising German Shephard dogs. Office: Affiliated Sci Inc PO Box 437 Ingleside IL 60041-0437 also: Ill Biotechnology Ctr Chgo Technology Park 2201 W Campbell Park Dr Chicago IL 60612

PROPST, HAROLD DEAN, retired academic administrator; b. Newton, N.C., Feb. 7, 1934; s. Charles Clayton and Sarah Isabel (Hilderbrand) P. B.A., Wake Forest Coll., 1956; M.A., Peabody Coll., 1959, Ph.D., 1964; LL.D., Mercer U., 1985. Tchr. Vandalia Pub. Schs., Ohio, 1959-60; instr. Wake Forest Coll., Winston-Salem, N.C., 1960-61; asst. prof. English, Radford Coll., Va., 1962-64, assoc. prof., 1964-65, prof., 1965-69, chmn. dept. English, 1965-66, 68-69; dean Armstrong State Coll., Savannah, Ga., 1969-76, v.p. for acad. affairs, 1976-79; vice chancellor for acad. devel. Univ. System Ga., Atlanta, 1979-81, exec. vice chancellor, 1981-85, chancellor, 1985-94. Editor: (novel) John Brent, 1970; contbr. articles to profl. jours., monographs, books. Bd. visitors Radford Coll., 1970-74; former pres. bd. Family Counseling Ctr., Savannah; former pres. bd. Family Counseling Ctr., Savannah; former bd. dirs. Savannah Symphony, Savannah Heart Assn., Alliance Theatre, Atlanta; mem. So. Region Edn. Bd., 1985-94. With USN, 1956-58. Fellow Carnegie Found., 1958, Ford Found., 1960; recipient Disting. Alumnus award Wake Forest U., 1986. Mem. Am. Assn. State Colls and Univs. (com. on accreditation 1982-86), Acad. for Ednl. Devel. (study com. on campus govt. 1976-77). Baptist.

PROPST, ROBERT BRUCE, federal judge; b. Onatchee, Ala., July 13, 1931; s. Franklin Glenn and Mildred (Moore) P.; m. Elma Jo Griffin, Dec. 29, 1962; children: Stephen, David, Joanne. B.S., U. Ala., 1953, J.D., 1957. Pvt. practice law Wilson, Propst, Isom, Jackson, Bailey & Bott, 1957-80; Judge U.S. Dist Ct. (no. dist.) Ala., Birmingham, 1980—. Served to 1st lt. U.S. Army, 1953-55. Mem. ABA, Ala. Bar Assn., Birmingham Bar Assn., Calhoun County Bar Assn., Jaycees (pres. 1954-60). Methodist. Club: Exchange (Anniston, Ala.). Avocation: golf. Office: US Dist Ct 581 US Courthouse 1729 5th Ave N Birmingham AL 35203-2000*

PROROK, ROBERT FRANCIS, lawyer; b. Pitts., Feb. 21, 1952; s. Stephen F. and Nellie (Mamula) P.; m. Joanne Marie Dolata, May 26, 1979; children: Matthew, Christine. BA, U. Pitts., 1974, JD, 1977. Bar: Pa. 1977, U.S. Dist. Ct. (we. dist.) Pa. 1977, U.S. Ct. Appeals (3d cir.) 1979, U.S. Supreme Ct. 1985, U.S. Dist. Ct. (ea. dist.) Mich. 1989, U.S. Tax Ct. 1989. Law clk. U.S. Dist. Ct. Western Dist. Pa., Pitts., 1977-80; ptnr. Reed Smith Shaw & McClay, Pitts., 1980—. Mem. Pa. Bar Assn. (continuing edn. com. 1990-91), Pitts. Pers. Assn. (program com. 1991). Republican. Roman Catholic. Avocation: golf. Office: Reed Smith Shaw & McClay Mellon Sq 435 6th Ave Pittsburgh PA 15219-1809*

PROSCINO, STEVEN VINCENT, food products company executive; b. Phila., Nov. 22, 1954; s. Vincent and Marjorie (Gefrorer) P.; m. Anna Moore, May 31, 1986; children: Matthew, Vincent. BS in Math./Physics, Coll. William and Mary, 1977; BSME, Rensselaer Poly. Inst., 1977; MBA, U. Pa., 1983. Registered profl. engr., Pa. Project mgr. Air Products, Allentown, Pa., 1977-81; dir. MIS/engring. Metal Container Corp., St. Louis, 1985-94; exec. v.p. Campbell Taggart Inc., Clayton, Mo., 1994—. Mem. Algonquin Country Club. Avocations: golf, tennis. Office: Campbell Taggart Inc 8400 Maryland Ave Saint Louis MO 63105-3647

PROSKIN, ARNOLD W., state assemblyman, lawyer; b. Albany, N.Y., Apr. 2, 1938; s. Betty (Levin) P.; m. Martha Pollack, June 4, 1960; children: Lisa, Heath, Wendy, Michael. Student, SUNY, Albany, 1961; LLD, Boston Coll., 1964. Bar: N.Y. 1964, U.S. Dist. Ct. (no. dist.) N.Y., U.S. Dist. Ct. (so. dist.) N.Y., U.S. Supreme Ct. 1968. Pvt. practice Albany, N.Y., 1964—; dist. atty. Office of Dist. Atty. Albany County, N.Y., 1969-73; judge Albany County Ct., 1973-76; ptnr. The Proskin Law Firm, Albany, 1976—; mem. N.Y. State Assembly, Albany, 1984-94; mem. judiciary, codes and ethics standing com., guidance standing com., racing and wagering standing com., chmn. steering com. minority conf.; mem. legis. ethics com.; mem. civil practice, property rights, estates and trust, court ops. and constl. amendments subcoms.; past mem. ins., corps., authorities, commns., election law, labor and housing standing coms. Active Temple Ohav Shalom, Gov. Clinton Coun., Boy Scouts Am. Adv. Bd., Jewish War Vets., Adv. Bd. Barn Raisers. With USN, 1956-58. Recipient N.Y. State Vocat. Schs. award, 1971, Histradrut Pub. Svc. Coun. award, 1973; named Outstanding Young Man of Yr., N.Y. State Jaycees, 1972, Man of Yr., Internat. Order of Alhambra, 1975, Mem. of Yr., Independent Order of Odd Fellows, 1985. Mem. ABA, Am. Judicature Soc., N.Y. State Bar Assn., N.Y. State Dist. Attys. Assn., Saratoga County Bar Assn., Albany Bar Assn., Nat. Dist. Attys. Assn., County Judge's Assn. State N.Y., Am. Legion, B'nai B'rith Gideon Lodge, Masons, Shiners, West Albany Athletic Assn., Latham Area C. of C. Office: The Proskin Law Firm 423 Loudon Rd Albany NY 12211-1722

PROSKY, ROBERT JOSEPH, actor; b. Phila., Dec. 13, 1930; s. Joseph and Helen (Kuhn) Porzuczek; m. Ida Mae Hove, June 4, 1960, children—Stefan, John, Andrew. Student, Temple U., Am. Theatre. Appeared at Arena Stage, Washington, 23 years including roles in Death of a Salesman, Twelfth Night, Enemy of the People, Galileo; appeared on Broadway in Moonchildren, View from the Bridge, Glengarry Glen Ross, A Walk in the Woods, 1988 (Tony award nomination 1988, Best Actor award Outer Critics Circle, toured USSR and Lithuania 1989), Camping with Henry and Tim; films include Thief, 1981, Lords of Discipline, 1983, Christine, 1983, The Natural, 1984, Broadcast News, 1987, Outrageous Fortune, 1987, Things Change, 1988, Gremlins II, 1989, Something About Love, 1990, Green Card, 1990, Life in the Food Chain, 1990, Far and Away, 1992, Hoffa, 1992, Life on the High Wire, 1992, Rudy, 1992, Last Action Hero, 1993, Mrs. Doubtfire, 1993, Miracle on 34th Street, 1994, Scarlet Letter, 1995, Dead Man Walking, 1995; TV appearances include role of Sgt. Jablonski in Hill Street Blues, The Murder of Mary Phagan, 1988, Home Fires Burning, 1988, From the Dead of Night, 1989, Heist, 1989, Dangerous Pursuit, 1990, Johnny Ryan, 1990, The Love She Sought, 1990, Double Edge, 1992, Teamster Boss: The Jackie Presser Story, 1992, narrator Lifestories; mem. first Am. co. to tour Soviet Union, 1972. Recipient Tony award nomination for Glengarry Glen Ross, 1985, Joseph Jefferson award nomination, 1985, Drama Desk award, 1985, Helen Hayes award, 1995.

PROSPERI, DAVID PHILIP, public relations executive; b. Chgo., June 20, 1953. BSBA, U. Ill., 1975; MBA in Internat. Bus., George Washington U., 1983. Moving cons. Fed. Safety Moving & Storage, Elmhurst, Ill., 1975-79; press aide 1980 Reagan for Pres. campaign, Los Angeles, 1979-80, Reagan-Bush Campaign, Alexandria, Va., 1980-81; asst. press sec. to the Pres. White House, Washington, 1981-82; mgr. govt. affairs The Superior Oil Co., Washington, 1982-84; press sec. U.S. Dept. Energy, Washington, 1985; asst. to sec. dir. pub. affairs U.S. Dept. Interior, Washington, 1985-88; asst. sec. transp. U.S. Dept. Transp., Washington, 1989-90; sr. v.p. Chgo. Bd. Trade, 1990-95, 1995—; prin. Coun. on Excellence in Govt. Bd. dirs. Corp. Pub. Broadcasting, 1992-93. Republican. Roman Catholic. Avocations: basketball, tennis, spending time with family. Office: Chgo Bd Trade 141 W Jackson Blvd Ste 1740A Chicago IL 60604-3001

PROSPERI, LOUIS ANTHONY, lawyer; b. Altoona, Pa., Jan. 12, 1954; s. Louis Alfred and Ann Francis (DiDimenico) P.; m. Susan Lynn Irwin, Sept. 14, 1985. BS in Bus. Adminstrn. summa cum laude, Georgetown U., 1975; JD cum laude, Harvard U., 1978. Bar: Pa. 1978, U.S. Dist. Ct. (we. dist.) Pa. 1978, U.S. Ct. Appeals (Fed. cir.) 1985, U.S. Ct. Fed. Claims, 1985, U.S. Tax Ct. 1979. From assoc. to ptnr. Reed, Smith, Shaw & McClay, Pitts., 1978-94; pvt. practice Law Office Louis A. Prosperi, Pitts., 1994—. Mem. Allegheny County Bar Assn., Pitts. Tax Club. Republican. Roman Catholic. Club: Longue Vue (Verona, Pa.). Avocations: golf, tennis, paddle tennis, cross-country skiing. Home: 3036 Grasmere Ave Pittsburgh PA 15216-1862 Office: Law Office of Louis A Prosperi Grant Bldg 310 Grant St Ste 3601 Pittsburgh PA 15219-2203

PROSSER, C. LADD, physiology educator, researcher; b. Avon, N.Y., May 12, 1907; s. Clifford James and Izora May (Ladd) P.; m. Hazel Blanchard, Aug. 25, 1934; children—Jane Ellen, Nancy Ladd, Loring Blanchard. A.B., U. Rochester, 1929; Ph.D., Johns Hopkins U., 1932; hon. degree, Clark U., 1975. Asst. prof. physiology Clark U., Worcester, Mass., 1934-39; asst. prof physiology U. Ill., Urbana, 1939-47, assoc. prof. physiology, 1947-52, prof. physiology, 1952-74, prof. emeritus, 1975—; asst. sect. chief Metallurgy Lab. U. Chgo., 1943-46; vis prof. U. Hawaii, U. Wash., U. Mass., Ariz. State U. Author: Adaptational Biology, 1986; author, editor: Comparative Animal Physiology, 1st edit., 1951, 4th edit. 1991; contbr. numerous articles to profl. jours. Guggenheim fellow, 1963-64; Fulbright fellow, 1971-72. Fellow Am. Acad. Arts and Scis.; mem. Nat. Acad. Scis., Soc. Gen. Physiologists (pres. 1958-59), AAAS (v.p. 1960), Am. Soc. Zoologists (pres. 1961), Am. Physiol. Soc. (pres. 1969-70), Bavarian Acad. Sci. Unitarian. Avocations: music; gardening. Home: 101 W Windsor Rd Urbana IL 61801-6663 Office: U Ill 524 Burrill Hall Urbana IL 61801

PROSSER, FRANKLIN PIERCE, computer scientist; b. Atlanta, July 4, 1935; s. Edward Theron and Eunice (McDaniel) P.; m. Brenda Mary Lau, June 16, 1960; children: Edward, Andrea. B.S., Ga. Inst. Tech., 1956, M.S., 1958; Ph.D., Pa. State U., 1961. Prof. computer sci. Ind. U., Bloomington, 1969—; assoc. dir. Wrubel Computing Center, 1969-81, chmn. dept. computer sci., 1971-77, 87-93, spl. asst. for acad. computing, 1979-81; v.p. Logic Design, Inc., 1982-92; cons. Lockheed Theoretical Physics Lab., Palo Alto, Calif., 1967. Mem. AAAS, IEEE. Home: 1200 S Longwood Dr Bloomington IN 47401-6072 Office: Ind U Dept Computer Sci Bloomington IN 47405

PROSSER, JOHN MARTIN, architect, educator, university dean, urban design consultant; b. Wichita, Kans., Dec. 28, 1932; s. Francis Ware and Harriet Corinne (Osborne) P.; m. Judith Adams, Aug. 28, 1954 (dec. 1982); children: Thomas, Anne, Edward; m. Karen Ann Cleary, Dec. 30, 1983; children: Jennifer. B.Arch., U. Kans., 1955; M.Arch., Carnegie Mellon U., 1961. Registered architect, Kans., Colo. Architect, Robinson and Hissem, Wichita, 1954-56, Guirey, Srnka, and Arnold, Phoenix, 1961-62, James Sudler Assocs., Denver, 1962-68; ptnr., architect Nuzum, Prosser and Vetter, Boulder, 1969-73; from asst. prof. to prof. U. Colo., Boulder, Denver, 1968—, acting dean, 1980-84, dean, 1984; dir. environ. design U. Colo., Boulder, 1969-72, dir. urban design, 1972-85; cons. John M. Prosser Assoc., Boulder and Denver, 1974—; vis. prof. urban design Oxford Poly., Eng., 1979; vis. Critic Carnegie Mellon U., U. N.Mex., Colo. Coll.; pres. Denver chpt. AIA, 1983 . Author, narrator PBS TV documentary Cities Are For Kids Too, 1984. Prin. works include (with others) hist. redesign Mus. Western Art, Denver (design honor 1984), Villa Italia, Lakewood, Colo., Denver, Auraria Higher Edn. Ctr., Pueblo C.C. campus plan and new acad. facilities, comprehensive campus plan Denver U., Lamar C.C., Ft. Lewis Coll., Pueblo City Ctr. Urban Design, Westminstrer Golf Course Community, Denver Botanic Gardens 20-Yr. Concept Plan, Colo. Coll. Historic Preservation Plan, Commerce City Golf Course Community. Bd. dirs. Denver Parks and Recreation Bd., 1987-93; chmn. design rev. bd. Univs. Colo., Boulder, Denver and Colorado Springs, 1981—; mem. archtl. control com. Denver Tech. Ctr., 1984—, Meridian Internat. Bus. Ctr., 1984—, DTC West, 1991—, Denver Internat. Bus. Ctr., 1993—; planning cons. Denver Internat. Airport Environs Devel. Projects. Capt. USAF, 1956-59. Co-recipient 2d place nat. award Am. Soc. Interior Designers, 1984, honor award Colo. Soc. Architects, 1984. Mem. Urban Land Inst. Democrat. Club: Denver Country (pres. 1986-87). Avocation: Arlberg Ski. Home: 1620 Monaco Pky Denver CO 80220-1643 Office: U Colo 1200 Larimer St Denver CO 80204-5300

PROSSER, MICHAEL HUBERT, communications educator; b. Indpls., Mar. 29, 1936; s. Marshall Herbert and Clydia Catharine (O'Dea) P.; m. Carol Mary Hogle, Nov. 27, 1958 (div. 1983); children: Michelle Ann Prosser-Evans, Leo Michael, Louis Mark; m. Joan Ann Kirkeby, Dec. 6, 1986. BA, Ball State U., 1958, MA, 1959; PhD, U. Ill., 1964. Tchr. Latin Urbana (Ill.) Jr. High Sch., 1960-63; asst. prof. speech SUNY, Buffalo, 1963-69; assoc. prof. speech Ind. U., Bloomington, 1969-72; prof. rhetoric and comm. U. Va., Charlottesville, 1972—, chair, 1972-77; William A. Kern prof. in comm. Rochester Inst. Tech., 1994—; chair AFS Global Awareness Day, U. Va., 1983-90, Global Awareness Day, 25th Ann. of Intercultural Comm.; confts. Rochester Inst. Tech., 1995; vis. lectr. comm. Queens Coll. CUNY, 1966, 67; vis. assoc. prof. speech Calif. State U., Hayward, 1971; vis. prof. curriculum Meml. U. Newfoundland, St. John's, 1972, St. Paul U. and U. Ottawa (Can.), 1975; cons. intercultural comm. U.S. Info. Agy., Washington, 1977; disting. vis. prof. speech Kent (Ohio) State U., 1978; Fulbright prof. English, U. Swaiziland, Kwalusene, 1990-91, Am. U. of Bulgaria, 1994-95 (declined); fellow New Coll. U. Va., 1992-94; Gannett lectr. Rochester Inst. Tech., 1995, Kern lectr., 1995-96. Author: The Cultural Dialogue, 1978 (translated into Japanese 1982); editor: An Ethic for Survival, 1969, Sow the Wind, Reap the Whirlwind: Heads of State Address the United Nations (2 vols.), 1970, Intercommunication Among Nations and Peoples, 1973; co-editor: Readings in Classical Rhetoric, 1969, Readings in Medieval Rhetoric, 1973. Mem. Haiti commn. Cath. Diocese Richmond, 1989-93; bd. dirs. Rochester Assn. UN, 1995—; chair pro tem Rochester Area Fulbright Chpt., 1995. Recipient Disting. Alumnus award Ball State U., 1978. Mem. Internat. Soc. for Intercultural Edn., Tng. and Rsch. (pres. 1984-86, Citizen of World 1986, Outstanding Sr. Interculturalist 1990), Internat. Comm. Assn. (v.p., Disting. Svc. award 1978), Fulbright Assn., Internat. Speech Comm. Assn., N.Y. State African Studies Assn., Rochester Assn. for UN (bd. dirs.), Am. Field Svc. (pres. intercultural programs 1982-86, Charlottesville), Assn. for Edn. in Journalism and Mass Media. Democrat. Roman Catholic. Avocations: social justice and peace advocacy, youth, travel. Office: Rochester Inst Tech Coll of Liberal Arts 92 Lomb Memorial Dr Rochester NY 14623-5604

PROSSER, MICHAEL JOSEPH, community college staff member; b. Syracuse, N.Y., May 9, 1948; s. Palmer Adelbert and Viola Mary (Clairmont) P. AA, Riverside (Calif.) City Coll., 1971; BA in History, Calif. State Coll., San Bernardino, 1977; MSLS, U. So. Calif., L.A., 1981. Cert. cmty. coll. instr., librarian, Calif. Libr. clk. Riverside C.C., 1968-81, learning resources asst., 1981—. Author: California and the Pacific Plate: A Bibliography, 1979. Tutor, Queen of Angels Ch., Riverside, 1985—, facilitator/patrons, 1985—. With U.S. Army, 1969-71. Mem. ASCD, Calif. Media Libr. Educators Assn., Calif. Libr. Assn. Democrat. Roman Catholic. Home: 6800 Palos Dr Riverside CA 92503-1330 Office: Riverside Cmty Coll 4800 Magnolia Ave Riverside CA 92506-1242

PROTAS, RON, dance company executive. Gen. dir. Martha Graham Ctr. Contemporary Dance, N.Y.C, assoc. artistic dir.; now artistic dir. Martha Graham Dance Co., N.Y.C. Office: Martha Graham Dance Co 316 E 63rd St New York NY 10021-7702*

PROTHRO, JERRY ROBERT, lawyer; b. Midland, Tex., Dec. 22, 1946; s. Jack William Prothro and Nita Marie (Stovall) Milligan; m. Leslie Joan Lepar, Aug. 15, 1970 (div. 1994); children: Laura Kay, Evan Jackson. BA, Southwestern U., 1969; JD, U. Tex. Sch. Law, 1972. Lawyer, capt. U.S. Army, JAGC, 1972-76; assoc. Turpin, Smith & Dyer, Midland, 1976-85; ptnr. Boyd, Sanders, Wade, Cropper & Prothro, Midland, 1985-91; pvt. practice Dallas and Midland, Tex., 1991—; mem. admissions com. M/O div. U.S. Dist. Ct. for Western Dist. Tex., 1987—; speaker in field. Treas., v.p.

Southwestern U. Alumni Bd., Georgetown, Tex., 1980-90, pres.-elect, 1991, pres., 1992-94, trustee, 1992-94; adminstrv. bd. First United Meth. Ch., Midland, 1989—; chmn. Permian Basin AIDS Coalition Bd., 1994; active Midland County Hist. Commn., 1980-85. Named Univ. scholar Southwestern U., 1969; recipient Disting. Svc. medal U.S. Army, 1974. Mem. Midland County Young Lawyers (pres. 1979-80), Midland County Bar Assn., 5th Cir. Bar Assn., Pi Kappa Alpha Social Frat., Blue Key Leadership Frat., Pi Gamma Mu Social Sci. Frat. Methodist. Avocations: antique collecting, camping, men's movement activity. Office: PO Box 93 Midland TX 79702-0093 also: 4107 Hawthorne Ste A Dallas TX 75219

PROTIGAL, STANLEY NATHAN, lawyer; b. Wilmington, Del., June 3, 1950; s. Bernard Protigal. BS in Aircraft Maintenance Engring., Northrop U., 1973; JD, Vt. Law Sch., 1978. Bar: U.S. Patent Office 1977, D.C. 1978. Assoc. Sixbey F. & L., Arlington, Va., 1978-79, atty., 1979-82; patent atty. Allied-Signal Bendix Aerospace, Teterboro, N.J., 1982-88; patent counsel Micron Tech., Inc., Boise, Idaho, 1988-94; pvt. practice Boise, Idaho, 1994-96; of counsel Barnard, Pauly & Bellamy, Seattle, 1996—. Mem. IEEE, MENSA. Avocations: pvt. pilot, bicycling, skiing. Office: Box 58888 Seattle WA 98138-1888

PROTO, PAUL WILLIAM, government consulting company executive; b. New Haven, Mar. 1, 1954; s. Cosmo and Nina (Aceto) P.; m. Carol Lynn Culver, May 3, 1986; children: Melissa, Nicole, Cosmo. AS, Dean Jr. Coll., 1974; BA, U. Redlands, 1976; MA, U. Mich., 1981. Sr. advocate Legal Svcs., Inc., Bridgeport, Conn., 1976-81; govt. benefit cons. Disability Svcs., Inc., Southfield, Mich., 1981-86; pres. Govt. Entitlement Svcs., Southfield, 1986-93, Social Security Cons. Svcs., Tampa, Fla., 1992—; v.p. advocacy and edn. Govt. Benefit Specialists, Tampa, 1993—; cons., lectr. Legal Svcs., Inc., Washington, 1977-79. Author: A Stroll Through the Maze: The Social Security Process, 1993, Navigating Rough Waters. . .Understanding the Relationship Between Workers' Compensation and Federal Benefits, 1994; scriptwriter for videotape Social Security Disability and You, 1992. Bd. dirs. Social Security Task Force, Conn., 1978-81; mem. Mayor's Alliance for People with Disabilities, Tampa, 1993—. Named Employer of Yr., Pontiac (Mich.) Jaycees, 1991. Mem. Worker Compensation Claim Profls. (instr. 1993-94), Nat. Orgn. Social Security Claim Reps. Avocations: taekwando, running, screenwriting. Home: 15864 Sanctuary Dr Tampa FL 33647-1075

PROUGH, RUSSELL ALLEN, biochemistry educator; b. Twin Falls, Idaho, Nov. 5, 1943; s. Elza Leroy and Beulah Elsie (Huddleston) P.; M. Betty Marie Ehlers, Dec. 26, 1965; children: Jennifer Sally, Kimberly Marie. BS in Chemistry, Coll. of Idaho, 1965; PhD in Biochemistry and Biophysics, Oreg. State U., 1969. Postdoctoral fellow VA Hosp., Kansas City, Mo., 1969-72; instr. biochemistry U. Tex. Southwestern Med. Sch., Dallas, 1972-73, asst. prof. biochemistry, 1973-77, assoc. prof. biochemistry, 1977-82, prof. biochemistry, 1982-86; prof., chmn. dept. biochemistry U. Louisville Sch. Med., 1986—; mem. NIH Toxicology Study Sect., 1984-88, State of Nebr. Smoking Disease and Cancer Rsch. Program, 1984-91. Assoc. editor Drug Metabolism and Disposition, 1994—. Recipient Rsch. Career Devel. award USPHS. Mem. Am. Soc. Biochemistry and Molecular Biology, Am. Assn. Cancer Rsch., Am. Soc. Pharmacology and Exptl. Therapeutics, Internat. Soc. for Study of Xenobiotics, Sigma Xi. Lutheran. Office: U of Louisville Dept of Biochemistry Louisville KY 40292

PROUGH, STEPHEN W., savings and loan executive; b. 1945. COO Westcorp, Irvine, Calif., 1983—, bd. dirs. Office: Downey Savs Loan Assn 3501 Jamboree Rd Newport Beach CA 92660-2939*

PROULX, EDNA ANNIE, writer; b. Norwich, Conn., Aug. 22, 1935; d. George Napolean and Lois Nelly (Gill) Proulx; m. James Hamilton Lang, June 22, 1969 (div. 1990); children: Jonathan Edward Lang, Gillis Crowell Lang, Morgan Hamilton Lang. BA cum laude, U. Vt., 1969; MA, Sir George Williams U., Montreal, Can., 1973; DHL (hon.), U. Maine, 1994. Author: Heart Songs and Other Stories, 1988, Postcards, 1992 (PEN/Faulkner award 1993), The Shipping News, 1993 (Nat. Book award for fiction 1993, Chgo. Tribune Heartland award 1993, Irish Times Internat. Fiction award 1993, Pulitzer Prize for fiction 1994); contbr. more than 50 articles to mags. and jours. Kress fellow Harvard U., 1974, fellow Vt. Coun. Arts, 1989, NEA, 1991, Guggenheim Found., 1992; rsch. grantee Inter.-U. Ctr., 1975; resident Ucross Found., 1990-92. Mem. PEN Am. Ctr., Phi Beta Kappa, Phi Alpha Theta. Avocations: canoeing, reading, fishing, carpentry. Office: c/o Scribners Pub Co 866 3rd Ave Fl 7 New York NY 10022-6221

PROUT, CURTIS, physician; b. Swampscott, Mass., Oct. 13, 1915; s. Henry Byrd and Eloise (Willett) P.; m. Daphne Brooks, June 27, 1939 (div. 1985); children: Diana P. Cherot, Daphne P. Cook, Rosamond P. Warren, Phyllis P. Brosius; m. Diane Neal Emmons, Dec. 7, 1985. AB, Harvard U., 1937, MD, 1941. Diplomate Am. Bd. Internal Medicine. Intern Peter Bent Brigham Hosp., Boston, 1942; resident in internal medicine Johns Hopkins Hosp., Balt., 1943; research fellow Mass. Gen. Hosp., Boston, 1943-45; practice medicine specializing in internal medicine, 1945—; asst. dir. Univ. Health Services Harvard U., Cambridge, Mass., 1961-72; dir. prison health project Office of Econ. Opportunity, 1972-74; asst. dean Harvard Med. Sch., Boston, 1980-90, asst. clin. prof., 1975-82; trustee Humane Soc. of Mass., Boston, 1975-87; bd. dirs. Nat. Commn. on Correctional Health Care, 1980—, chmn., 1990; dir., treas. The Med. Found., Boston, 1980—. Chmn. Bd. Health, Dover, Mass., 1960-75. Fellow Am. Coll. Physicians, Mass. Med. Soc.; mem. AMA, Am. Clin. and Climatol. Assn. Clubs: Tavern (Boston) (pres. 1980-82); Manchester Yacht (Mass.). Avocations: sailing, writing. Home: 115 School St Manchester MA 01944-1232 Office: 319 Longwood Ave Boston MA 02115-5710

PROUT, GEORGE RUSSELL, JR., medical educator, urologist; b. Boston, July 23, 1924; s. George Russell and Marion (Snow) P.; m. Loa Katherine Wheatley, Oct. 17, 1950; children: George Russell III, Elizabeth Louise. Student, Union Coll., 1943, DSc (hon.), 1990; MD, Albany Med. Coll., 1947, DSc (hon.), 1988; MA (hon.), Harvard U., 1969. Intern Grasslands Hosp., Valhalla, N.Y., 1947-48; resident N.Y. Hosp., N.Y.C., 1952-56; asst. attending physician Meml. Ctr. for Cancer and Allied Disease, N.Y.C., 1956-57; asst. clinician in surgery James Ewing Hosp., N.Y.C., 1956-57; assoc. prof., chmn. div. urology U. Miami, 1957-60; prof., chmn. div. urology Med. Coll. Va., 1960-69; chief urol. svc. Mass. Gen. Hosp., Boston, 1969-89; prof. surgery Harvard Med. Sch., 1969-89; emeritus prof. surgery Harvard Med. Sch., Boston, 1989—; hon. urologist Mass. Gen. Hosp., Boston, 1993—; chmn. Adjuvants in Surg. Treatment of Bladder Cancer; mem. adv. task force to Nat. Cancer Inst., 1968—, expert cons. divsn. surveillance, 1991—, Finland coop. ATBC study, 1991—; chmn. Nat. Bladder Cancer Group, 1973-86. Editor-in-chief Urologic Oncology, 1994—. With USNR, 1950-52. Fellow ACS, Acad. Medicine Toronto (corr.); mem. AMA, AAUP, Am. Urol. Assn., Can. Urol. Assn., Am. Cancer Soc., Soc. Pelvic Surgeons, Soc. Surg. Oncology, Soc. Univ. Urologists, Dallas. So. Clin. Soc. (hon.), Am. Assn. Genitourinary Surgeons, Soc. Pediatric Urology, Soc. Urol. Oncology, Soc. Internat. Urologists, Soc. Basic Urol. Rsch., Alpha Omega Alpha. Home and Office: 27 W Prospect Bay Dr Grasonville MD 21638-9668 Winter address: 224 Corsair Rd Marathon FL 33050

PROUT, RALPH EUGENE, physician; b. Los Angeles, Feb. 27, 1933; s. Ralph Byron and Fern (Taylor) P.; m. Joanne Morris, Sept. 17, 1980; children: Michael, Michelle. BA, La Sierra Coll., 1953; MD, Loma Linda U., 1957; D of Nutri-Medicine (hon.), John F. Kennedy Coll., 1987. Diplomate: Nat. Bd. Med. Examiners. Intern Los Angeles County Hosp., 1957-58; resident internal medicine White Meml. Hosp., Los Angeles, 1958-60; resident psychiatry Harding Hosp., Worthington, Ohio, 1960-61; practice medicine specializing in internal medicine Napa, Calif., 1961-63; staff internist Calif. Med. Facility, Vacaville, 1963-68, chief med. officer, 1968-84; chief med. cons. Calif. Dept. Corrections, 1977-86, chief med. services, 1983; med. cons. Wellness Cons., Placerville, Calif., 1986—; pres. Addiction Medicine treatment Ctr., Placerville, Calif., 1991-95; instr. Sch. Medicine, Loma Linda U., 1965-66; clin. assoc. U. Calif.-Davis Sch. Medicine, 1978-84; med. cons. Substance Abuse Pine Grove Camp, 1985-90. Treas. Vacaville Republican Assembly, 1972-75; del. Republican Central Com. Solano County, 1975-78; Bd. dirs. Napa-Solano County United Crusade, Vallejo, Calif., 1969-71, v.p., 1970-71; bd. dirs. Project Clinic, Vacaville, 1974-77, Home Health Com. Inter-Community Hosp., Fairfield, 1978-80; pres. MotherLode Citizens for Drug-Free Youth, Amador County, 1985—. Named One of Outstanding Young Men of Am., 1968. Mem. AMA, Internat. Acad. Nutrition and Preventive Medicine, Calif. Soc. Internal Medicine, Am. Soc. Internal Medicine, Am. Assn. Sr. Physicians, Internat. Assn. New Sci., Union Concerned Scis., Mother Lode Citizens for Drug-Free Youth, Native Sons of Golden West, Alpha Omega Alpha. Republican. Home and Office: 24405 Shake Ridge Rd Volcano CA 95689-9728 *When we ask better questions, the answers will follow.*

PROUTY, NORMAN R., investment banker; b. N.Y.C., Feb. 4, 1939; s. Norman R. and Eleanor (Ryan) P.; m. Alden Finch, July 18, 1964 (div. Mar. 1989); children: Brooks Silliman, Nicholas Alden, Honor Howland; m. Allison LoveJoy Simmons, Jan. 27, 1990; 1 child, Annabel Scarlett LoveJoy. BA, Yale U., 1961. V.p., sr. credit officer Citibank, N.Y.C., 1961-81; gen. ptnr. Lazard Frères & Co., N.Y.C., 1981-95; pres. Brook Capital Corp., Greenwich, Conn., 1996—. Trustee Pitzer Coll., Nature Conservancy of N.Y. State, 1992—; bd. overseers The Claremont Colls., 1990. Mem. Anglers' Club, The Brook, Racquet and Tennis Club, Fishers Island Club. Avocations: fishing, shooting, skiing, sailing, tennis. Home: 5 Mountain Wood Dr Greenwich CT 06830 Office: Brook Capital Corp Greenwich CT 06803

PROVENCHER, ROGER ARTHUR, international consultant; b. Manchester, N.H., June 20, 1923; s. Arthur J. and Rose Albina (Briere) P.; m. Josette Marguerite Camus, Jan. 3, 1946 (dec. 1976); children: Frances Provencher-Kambour, Carl; m. Mary Lou Sack, Mar. 17, 1989. BA, U. N.H., 1949; Doctorat D'Universite', U. Paris, 1950. Joined Dept. State, 1950; asst. commr. gen. Expo 67, Montreal, Que., Can., 1965-67; mgmt. analyst Washington, 1968; assigned to Nat. War Coll., 1969-70; 1st sec., counselor Am. embassy, Moscow, 1970-73; counselor for administrv. affairs Am. embassy, Vientiane, Laos, 1973-74, Tehran, Iran, 1974-77; sr. counsellor Internat. Telecommunication Union, Geneva, 1977-82; mng. dir. Pan African Airlines (Nigeria) Ltd., Lagos, 1962-63. V.p. Rollingwood Community Assn. 1st lt. AUS, 1943-46, ETO. Recipient Meritorious Honor award Dept. State, 1958, 62, also Superior Honor award, 1975. Mem. Nat. War Coll. Alumni Assn., Am. Fgn. Service Assn. (dir.), Lambda Pi. Home and Office: PO Box 326 Ladysmith VA 22501-0326 *A public servant must never forget that his responsibility rests on serving the public. The public have contributed their trust and hope in their investments. Their aspirations must be honored even if at times, physical, ideological, conjugal or other personal stresses invite abdication.*

PROVENCHER, YVES, airport executive. Gen. mgr. Montreal (Can.) Internat. Airport. Office: Montreal Internat Airport, 12655 Commerce A-4 7th Fl, Mirabel, PQ Canada J7N 1E1*

PROVENSEN, ALICE ROSE TWITCHELL, artist, author; b. Chgo.; d. Jay Horace and Kathryn (Zelanis) Twitchell; m. Martin Provensen, Apr. 17, 1944; 1 child, Karen Anna. Student, Art Inst. of Chgo., 1930-31, U. Calif., L.A., 1939, Art Student League, N.Y., 1940-41; D.H.L. (hon.), Marist Coll., 1986. With Walter Lanz Studios, Los Angeles, 1942-43; OSS, 1944-45. Exhibited (with Martin Provensen) Balt. Mus., 1954, Am. Inst. Graphic Arts, N.Y., 1959, Botolph Group, Boston, 1964; exhibited one person shows: Henry Feiwel Gallery, N.Y.C., 1991, Children's Mus., Washington, 1991, Moscarelle Mus. Art, Williamsburg, Va., 1991; books represented in Fifty Books of Yr. Selections, Am. Inst. Graphic Arts, 1947, 48, 52 (The Charge of the Light Brigade named Best Illustrated Children's Book of the Yr. N.Y. Times 1964, co-recipient Gold medal Soc. Illustrators 1960); author/illustrator: books including Karen's Opposites, 1963, Karen's Curiosity, 1963, What is a Color?, 1967, (with Martin Provensen) Who's In the Egg, 1970, The Provensen Book of Fairy Tales, 1971, Play on Words, 1972, My Little Hen, 1973, Roses are Red, 1973, Our Animal Friends, 1974, The Year at Maple Hill Farm, 1978, A Horse and a Hound, A Goat and a Gander, 1979, An Owl and Three Pussycats, 1981, Town and Country, 1984, Shaker Lane, 1987, The Buck Stops Here, 1990, Punch in New York, 1991 (Best Books N.Y. Times 1991), My Fellow Americans, 1995; illustrator: (with Martin Provensen) children's books including Mother Goose Book, 1976, Old Mother Hubbard, 1977, A Peaceable Kingdom, 1978, The Golden Serpent, 1980, A Visit to William Blake's Inn, 1981, Birds, Beasts and the Third Thing, 1982, The Glorious Flight, 1984 (Caldecott medal 1984), The Voyage of the Ludgate Hill, 1987; also textbooks.

PROVINE, JOHN C., lawyer; b. Asheville, N.C., May 15, 1938; s. Robert Calhoun and Harriet Josephine (Thoms) P.; m. Martha Ann Monson, Aug. 26, 1966 (div. Jan. 1975); m. Nancy Frances Lunsford, Apr. 17, 1976; children: Robert, Frances, Harriet. AB, Harvard U., 1960; JD, U. Mich., 1966; MBA, NYU, 1972, LLM in Taxation, 1975. Bar: N.Y., Tenn., U.S. Dist. Ct. (so. and ea. dists.) N.Y., U.S. Ct. Appeals (2nd and 6th cirs.), U.S. Dist. Ct. (mid. dist.) Tenn., U.S. Supreme Ct. From assoc. to ptnr. White & Case, N.Y.C., 1966-74, ptnr., 1974-81, 92-94; ptnr. White & Case, Jakarta and Ankara, 1982-91; counsel Dearborn & Ewing, Nashville, Tenn., 1982. Lt. USN, 1960-63. Mem. ABA, N.Y. Bar Assn., Tenn. Bar Assn., Assn. of Bar of City of N.Y. Avocations: bluegrass music, rural activities. Home and Office: 6630 Manley Ln Brentwood TN 37027-3401

PROVINE, LORRAINE, secondary school educator; b. Altus, Okla., Oct. 6, 1944; d. Claud Edward and Emmie Lorraine (Gasper) Allmon; m. Joe A. Provine, Aug. 14, 1966; children: Sharon Kay, John David. BS, U. Okla., 1966; MS, Okla. State U., 1988. Tchr. math. U.S. Grant High Sch., Oklahoma City Schs., 1966-69; tchr. East Jr. High Sch., Ponca City (Okla.) Schs., 1969-70; tchr. Ponca City High Sch., 1978-79, 81—. Mem. NEA, Coun. for Exceptional Children, Internat. Soc. Tchrs. in Edn., Math. Assn. Am., Nat. Coun. Tchrs. Math., Sch. Sci. and Math. Assn., Okla. Edn. Assn., Okla. Coun. Tchrs. Math., Assn. Women in Math., Ponca City Assn. Classroom Tchrs. (treas. 1983-86,91—), Okla. Assn. Mothers Clubs (life, state bd. dirs. 1977-87, pres. 1984-85), Delta Kappa Gamma. Republican. Baptist. Avocations: reading, knitting, sewing. Home: 1915 Meadowbrook St Ponca City OK 74604-3012 Office: Ponca City HS 927 N 5th Ponca City OK 74601

PROVORNY, FREDERICK ALAN, lawyer; b. Bklyn., Sept. 7, 1946; s. Daniel and Anna (Wurm) P.; m. Nancy Ileene Wilkins, Nov. 21, 1971; children: Michelle C., Cheryl A., Lisa T., Robert D. BS summa cum laude, NYU, 1966; JD magna cum laude, Columbia U., 1969. Bar: N.Y. 1970, U.S. Supreme Ct. 1973, D.C. 1975, Mo. 1977, Md. 1987, Calif. 1989; CPA, Md., Mo. Law clk. to Judge Harold R. Medina U.S. Ct. Appeals (2d cir.), N.Y.C., 1969-70; asst. prof. law Syracuse (N.Y.) U., 1970-72; assoc. Debevoise, Plimpton, Lyons & Gates, N.Y.C., 1972-75, Cole & Groner P.C., Washington, 1975-76; with Monsanto Co., St. Louis, 1976-86, asst. co. counsel, 1978-86; pvt. practice Washington, 1986-89; ptnr. Provorny & Jacoby, Washington, 1989-91; counsel Shaw, Pittman, Potts & Trowbridge, Washington, 1991-93; ptnr. Tydings & Rosenberg, Balt., 1993-94; pvt. practice Balt., 1994-95, Washington, 1995—; adj. prof. law, U. Balt. Sch. Law, 1996—; lectr. Bklyn. Law Sch., 1973-74; pres. Sci. and Tech. Assocs., Inc., 1986-91. Contbr. articles to profl. jours. Trustee Christian Woman's Benevolent Assn. Youth Home, 1979-83. Mem. ABA, Am. Law Inst., Am. Arbitration Assn. (panel comml. arbitrators), Philo-Mt. Sinai Lodge 968, Masons, Beta Gamma Sigma. Jewish. Home: 11803 Kemp Mill Rd Silver Spring MD 20902-1511 Office: Ste 650 1920 N St NW Washington DC 20036

PROVOST, DAVID EMILE, financial services executive; b. Detroit, Oct. 28, 1949; s. Emile L. and Terese M. (Disnard) P.; m. Nancy B. McCormick; children: Emilie N., Natalie E. BBA, Northeastern U., BS in Acctg., 1975; MBA, Boston U., 1981. Controller, Lion Precision Corp., Newton, Mass., 1973-76, Life Support Equipment, Woburn, Mass., 1976-80; treas. Nixdorf Computer, Burlington, Mass., 1980-82, pres. Nixdorf Leasing Inc., 1982-88; fin. v.p.-treas. Unitarian Universalist Assn., Boston, 1988—; assoc. prof. Middlesex Coll., Bedford, Mass., 1982-86. Treas., First Parish, Dedham, Mass., 1981-86, Boston Ballet Soc., 1982-85; trustee Soc. Ministerial Relief, Boston, 1988—, Liberal Religious Charitable Soc., Boston, 1988—, Interfaith Ctr. Corp. Responsibility, N.Y.C., 1989—, Devel. Capital Inst., Washington, 1994—. Served with U.S. Army, 1970-72. Democrat. Unitarian-Universalist. Home: 93 Cedar St Lexington MA 02173-6651 Office: Unitarian Universalist Assn of Congregations 25 Beacon St Boston MA 02108-2824

PROVOST, THOMAS TAYLOR, dermatology educator, researcher; b. Pitts., Mar. 21, 1938; s. Charles Thomas and Marcelle K. (Taylor) P.; m. Carol Sara Christie, July 2, 1960; children: Charles T., Christie Lynn, Thomas Wright. AB, U. Pitts., 1958, MD, 1962. Resident in dermatology Dartmouth Med. Ctr., Hanover, N.H., 1966-67, U. Oreg. Med. Ctr., Portland, 1967-68; fellow in immunology SUNY, Buffalo, 1969-72, asst. prof. dermatology, 1972-75, assoc. prof., 1975-78; assoc. prof. Johns Hopkins U. Med. Sch., Balt., 1978-82, prof., dept. chmn., 1982—. Lt. commdr. USPHS, 1962-64. Mem. Soc. Investigative Dermatology, Soc. Clin. Investigation. Avocation: boating. Office: Johns Hopkins U Sch of Medicine 720 Rutland Ave Baltimore MD 21205-2109

PROVUS, BARBARA LEE, executive search consultant; b. Washington, Nov. 20, 1949; d. Severn and Birdell (Eck) P.; m. Frederick W. Wackerle, Mar. 29, 1985. Student, NYU, 1969-70; BA in Sociology, Russell Sage Coll., 1971; MS in Indsl. Rels., Loyola U., Chgo., 1978; postgrad., Smith Coll., 1971. Sec. Booz, Allen & Hamilton, Chgo., 1973-74, mgr. tng., 1974-77, dir. rsch., 1977-79, cons. search, 1979-80; mgr. mgmt. devel. Federated Dept. Stores, Cin., 1980-82; v.p. Lamalie Assocs., Chgo., 1982-86; prin., founder Sweeney, Shepherd, Bueschel, Provus, Harbert & Mummert, Inc., Chgo., 1986-91; founder Shepherd Bueschel & Provus Inc., Chgo., 1992—. Bd. dirs. Anti-Cruelty Soc., Chgo., 1990—, pres., 1996—. Mem. Assn. Exec. Search Cons. (dir. 1989-92), The Chgo. Network (bd. dirs. 1993—), Econ. Club Chgo. Avocations: collecting rubber bands, modern art, baseball. Home: 3750 N Lake Shore Dr Chicago IL 60613-4238 Office: Shepherd Bueschel & Provus Inc 401 N Michigan Ave Ste 3020 Chicago IL 60611

PROWN, JULES DAVID, art historian educator; b. Freehold, N.J., Mar. 14, 1930; s. Max and Matilda (Cassileth) P.; m. Shirley Ann Martin, June 23, 1956; children: Elizabeth Anderson, David Martin, Jonathan, Peter Cassileth, Sarah Peiter. AB, Lafayette Coll., 1951, DFA (hon.), 1979; AM, U. Del., 1956, Harvard U., 1953; PhD, Harvard U., 1961. Dir. Hist. Soc. Old Newbury, Newburyport, Mass., 1957-58, Old Gaol Mus., York, Maine, 1958-59; asst. to dir. Harvard U., Fogg Art Mus., Cambridge, Mass., 1959-61; instr. to Paul Mellon prof. history of art Yale U., New Haven, 1961—, curator Am. art, 1963-68; vis. lectr. Smith Coll., Northampton, Mass., 1966-67; dir. Yale Ctr. for Brit. Art, New Haven, 1968-76; assoc. dir. Nat. Humanities Inst., New Haven, 1977; trustee Whitney Mus., N.Y.C., 1975-94; mem. editorial adv. bd. Am. Art-Smithsonian, Washington, 1986—, On Common Ground, 1993—; mem. vis. com. Harvard U. Art Museums, 1993—. Author: John Singleton Copley, 2 Vols., 1966, American Painting from Its Beginnings to the Armory Show, 1969, The Architecture of the Yale Center for British Art, 1977, (catalogue) American Art from Alumni Collections, 1968. Recipient George Washington Kidd award Lafayette Coll., 1986. Fellow The Athenaeum of Phila. (hon.); mem. Am. Antiquarian Soc., Coll. Art Assn., Am. Studies Assn., Conn. Acad. Arts & Scis., Walpole Soc., Royal Soc. Arts. Office: Yale U History of Art Dept 56 High St New Haven CT 06510-2306

PROXMIRE, WILLIAM, former senator; b. Lake Forest, Ill., Nov. 11, 1915; s. Theodore Stanley and Adele (Flanigan) P.; m. Ellen Hodges. Grad., Hill Sch., 1934; B.A., Yale, 1938; M.B.A., Harvard, 1940, M.P.A. in Pub. Adminstrn, 1948. Assemblyman Wis. Legislature, 1951; nominee gov. Wis., 1952, 54, 56; pres. Artcraft Press, Waterloo, Wis., 1953-57; U.S. senator from Wis., 1957-89; former chmn. Sen. Banking, Housing and Urban Affairs com., Cong. JointEcon. com. Author: Can Small Business Survive?, 1964, st of the Big Time Spenders, 1972, You Can Do It, 1977, The Fleecing of America, 1980, Your Joy Ride to Health, 1993. Democrat.

PRSHA, MARIE ALICE, administrator, educator; b. Pitts., Aug. 19, 1927; d. Joseph Albert and Sabina Elizabeth (Rauch) Yoest; m. William John Prsha, July 14, 1951 (wid. Oct. 1977); children: Jon Michael, Mark Steven, Jeffrey Alan, Jeanne-Marie. Grad., Queen of Angels Coll. Nursing, 1950; BS in Health Sci., Chapman U., 1984, MS in Health Adminstrn., 1989. RN, PHN, Calif. Clin. nurse, charge/ob-gyn. Queen of Angels Clinic, L.A., 1950-52; staff nurse Huntington Meml. Hosp., Pasadena, Calif., 1993-94, St. Luke Hosp., Pasadena, 1955-56, La Vina Resp. Disease, Altadena, Calif., 1966; nurse nutritionist, high risk counselor ARC, San Diego, Calif., 1980-91; asst. dir. WIC svcs. ARC, San Diego, 1991-93; nutrition edn. coord. dept. health svcs. County of San Diego WIC Program, 1993—; mem. adv. bd. Southeast Asian Devel. Disabilities Prevention Program, San Diego, 1993—. Nurse educator Univ. Calif., San Diego, 1989-90. Recipient scholarship Immaculate Heart Coll., L.A., 1949; traineeship USPHS, San Diego, 1969. Mem. NLN, Am. Pub. Health Assn., Queen of Angels Alumni Assn., Chapman Univ. Alumni Assn. Republican. Roman Catholic. Avocations: reading, poetry, music, personal fitness, aviation. Home: 4872 Dixie Dr San Diego CA 92109-2430 Office: County of San Diego Dept Health Svcs 1700 Pacific Hwy San Diego CA 92101-2417

PRUCHA, JOHN JAMES, geologist, educator; b. River Falls, Wis., Sept. 22, 1924; s. Edward Joseph and Katharine (Schladweiler) P.; m. Mary Elizabeth Helfrich, June 12, 1948; children—David, Stephen, Katharine, Carol, Mark, Barbara, Margaret, Christopher, Anne, Andrew. Student, Wis. State U., River Falls, 1941-43; Ph.B., U. Wis., 1945, Ph.M., 1946; M.A., Princeton, 1948, Ph.D., 1950. Asst. prof. geology Rutgers U., 1948-51; sr. geologist N.Y. State Geol. Survey, 1951-56; rsch. geologist Shell Devel. Co., 1956-63; prof. geology Syracuse U., 1963-90, prof. emeritus, 1990—, chmn. dept., 1963-70, 88-89, dean Coll. Arts and Scis., 1970-72, vice chancellor acad. affairs, 1972-85; pres. Syracuse U. Press, 1973-85, bd. dirs., 1985-90. Author: Basement Tectonics of Rocky Mountains, 1965, Structural Behavior of Salt, 1967, Stratigraphy and Structure of Southeastern New York, 1959, Fracture Patterns, 1979, Zones of Structural Weakness, 1992, (with Norman A. Foss) Kinnickinnic Years, 1993. Trustee Le Moyne Coll., 1971-78; bd. dirs. Cultural Resources Coun., Syracuse, 1974—, pres., 1978-80; bd. dirs. Everson Mus. Art, Syracuse, 1977-83, v.p., 1980-81; mem. regents vis. com. N.Y. State Mus., 1993—. Recipient John Mason Clarke medal N.Y. State Geol. Survey, 1990. Fellow AAAS, Geol. Soc. Am.; mem. Am. Assn. Petroleum Geologists, Am. Geophys. Union. Home: 112 Ardsley Dr Syracuse NY 13214-2110 Office: Syracuse Univ 204 Heroy Geology Lab Syracuse NY 13244-1070

PRUDE, ELAINE S., principal. Prin. John S. Bradfield Elem. Sch., Dallas. Recipient Elem. Sch. Recognition award U.S. Dept. Edn., 1989-90. Office: John S Bradfield Elem Sch 4300 Southern Ave Dallas TX 75205-2663

PRUDEN, ANN LORETTE, chemical engineer, researcher; b. Norfolk, Va., Sept. 3, 1948; d. James Otis and Elora Maie (Bagwell) P.; m. Alan Todd Royer, Aug. 13, 1983; children: James Sebastian Royer, Annabelle Grace Royer. BS in Chemistry, Maryville (Tenn.) Coll., 1970; MA in Chem. Engring., Princeton (N.J.) U., 1978; PhD, 1981. Chemist Mobil Rsch. and Devel. Corp., Princeton, N.J., 1970-73, rsch. chemist, 1973-76, rsch. engr., 1980-86, sr. rsch. engr., 1986-92, supr., 1992—; mem. Quality Director's Network, Indsl. Rsch. Inst., Washington, 1992—. Contbg. author: Photocatalytic Purification and Treatment of Water and Air, 1993; contbr. articles to profl. jours. Fellow Mobil R&D Corp., Princeton, N.J., 1976-79. Mem. ASTM, AIChE, Am. Chemical Soc. Achievements include research in heterogeneous catalysis, organizational effectiveness. Avocations: gardening, textile handwork, singing. Office: Mobil Chemical Co Rte 27 and Vineyard Rd PO Box 3029 Edison NJ 08818-3029

PRUDEN, JAMES WESLEY, newspaper editor, columnist; b. Jackson, Miss., Dec. 18, 1935; s. James Wesley and Anne (Wilder) P.; m. Ann Fontaine Rice, Oct. 15, 1960 (div. 1961). Student, U. Ark.-Little Rock, Little Rock, 1954-55. Sportswriter Ark. Gazette, Little Rock, 1953, asst. state editor, 1954-56; reporter The Comml. Appeal, Memphis, 1956-63; fgn. corr. The Nat. Observer, Washington, 1963-77; free-lance journalist, 1977-82; chief polit. corr. The Washington Times, 1982-84, dep. mng. editor, 1984-87, mng. editor, 1987-92, editor-in-chief, 1992—. Author: Vietnam: The War, 1965. Ark. del. to Dem. Nat. Conv., L.A., 1960. With USAF, 1957-58, Ark. Air Nat. Guard, 1954-63. Recipient H.L. Mencken prize Balt. Sun, 1991. Mem. Sigma Delta Chi. So. Bapt. Office: The Washington Times 3600 New York Ave NE Washington DC 20002-1947

PRUD'HOMME, ROBERT KRAFFT, chemical engineering educator; b. Sacramento, Jan. 28, 1948; s. Earle Sutter and Adele E. (Wilkens) P.; m. N. Beth Morton, June 2, 1973; children: Wendy A., Graham C., Jodie B. BSChemE, Stanford U., 1969; Grad. Spl. Studies, Harvard U., 1973; PhD ChemE, U. Wis., 1978. Asst. prof. chem. engring. Princeton (N.J.) U.,

1978-84, assoc. prof., 1984-91, prof., 1991—; rsch. engr. AT&T Bell Labs., Murray Hill, N.J., 1984-85; bd. dirs. Rheometrics Inc., Piscataway, N.J.; McCabe lectr. Dept. Chem. Engring. N.C. State U. Contbr. articles to profl. jours. Deacon Cornerstone Ch., Hopewell, N.J., 1989-92. Capt. U.S. Army, 1969-73. Decorated Bronze Star, Army Commendation Medal; recipient Presdl. Young Investigator award NSF. Mem. Am. Chem. Soc., Am. Inst. Chem. Engrs. (bd. dirs. material sci. and engring. div. 1982-93), U.S. Soc. Rheology (exec. com. 1989-91), Soc. Petroleum Engrs. Achievements include research in areas of polymer fluid mechanics, polymer characterization and transport phenomena. Office: Princeton U Dept Chem Engring Princeton NJ 08544

PRUETT, JAMES WORRELL, librarian, musicologist; b. Mt. Airy, N.C., Dec. 23, 1932; s. Samuel Richard and Gladys Dorne (Worrell) P.; m. Lilian Maria-Irene Pibernik, July 20, 1957; children—Mark, Ellen. B.A., U. N.C., Chapel Hill, 1955, M.A., 1957, Ph.D., 1962. Mem. faculty U. N.C., Chapel Hill., 1961-87; prof. music U. N.C., 1974-87, music librarian, 1961-76, chmn. dept. music, 1976-86; chief music div. Library of Congress, Washington, 1987-94; vis. prof. U. Toronto, 1976; cons. in music, 1995—. Editor: Studies in the History, Style and Bibliography of Music in Memory of Glen Haydon, 1969; author: Research Guide to Musicology, 1985. Contbr. profl. jours., encys. Newberry Library fellow, summer 1966. Mem. Internat. Musicol. Soc., Am. Musicol. Soc. (chpt. chmn. 1964-66, mem. coun. 1974-77), Music Libr. Assn. (pres. 1973-75, editor jour. 1974-77), Internat. Assn. Music Libraries, Cosmos Club (Washington). Home: 343 Wesley Dr Chapel Hill NC 27516-1520

PRUETT, JEANNE, singer, songwriter; m. Jack Pruett (div. 1982); children: Jack, Jael; m. Eddie Fulton. owner J Bar E Ranch, Franklin, Tenn. Debut on, Grand Ole Opry, 1964, regular appearances, 1974—; recs. include Hold on to My Unchanging Love, 1971, Satin Sheets, 1973, I'm Your Woman, Honey on His Hands, You Don't Need to Move a Mountain, Just Like Your Daddy, I'm Living a Lie, 1977, Back to Back, 1979, Temporarily Yours, 1980, It's Too Late, 1980; songwriter for recs. include, Marty Robbins. Office: Grand Ole Opry 2800 Opryland Dr Nashville TN 37214-1200

PRUETT, KYLE DEAN, psychiatrist, writer, educator; b. Raton, N.Mex., Aug. 27, 1943; s. Ozie Douthitt Pruett and Velma Lorraine Smith; children: Elizabeth Storr, Emily Farrar. BA in History, Yale U., 1965; D of Medicine, Tufts U., 1969. Intern Mt. Auburn Hosp.-Harvard U., 1969-70; resident in psychiat. medicine Tufts-New England Med. Ctr., Boston, 1970-72; child psychiatry fellow Child Study Ctr., Yale U., New Haven, 1972-74, asst. clin. prof. psychiatry, 1975-79, assoc. clin. prof., 1979-87, clin. prof., 1987—; dir. child devel. unit Yale U., 1982—; attending physician dept. child psychiatry Yale-New Haven Hosp., 1972—; cons. psychiatrist Guilford (Conn.) Pub. Schs., 1977—; vis. scholar Sch. Medicine, U. Vt., 1987, Sch. Medicine, U. N.Mex., 1988; mem. editorial bd. Med. Problems of Performing Artists jour., 1983—, Good Housekeeping mag., 1987—; bd. dirs. Zero to Three: Nat. Ctr. for Clin. Infant Programs, Washington; cons. CBS News, Lifetime. Author: The Nurturing Father, 1988 (Am. Health Book award 1988); contbr. numerous articles to profl. jours.; host biweekly TV series Your Chid 6 to 12 with Dr. Kule Pruett Lifetime TV, 1993-94. Mem. med. adv. bd. Scholastic, Inc., 1988—, Yale U. Program for Humanities in Medicine, 1989—, World Assn. for Infant Mental Health, 1979—, CBS-TV Family Time, 1989—, Wellesley Child Study Ctr.; prin. tenor Conn. Chancel Opera Co., New Haven, 1983—. Vis. fellow Anna Freud Clinic, London, 1975; recipient Mayoral Citation, City of Indpls., 1987. Mem. Am. Acad. Child and Adolescent Psychiatry, Am. Psychiat. Assn., Soc. for Rsch. in Family Therapy, Physicians for Social Responsibility, Nat. Assn. Physician Broadcasters (CBS news cons. 1989—), Zero to Three (Nat. Ctr. for Clin. Infant Programs pres.-elect 1995—), Yale U. Glee Club Alumni Assn. (pres. 1985-89). Avocations: rowing, sailing, skiing, vocal chamber music, running. Home: 10 Fernwood Dr Guilford CT 06437-2349 Office: Yale Child Study Ctr 333 Cedar St New Haven CT 06510-3206

PRUGH, GEORGE SHIPLEY, lawyer; b. Norfolk, Va., June 1, 1920; s. George Shipley and Florence (Hamilton) P.; m. Katherine Buchanan, Sept. 27, 1942; children: Stephanie Dean, Virginia Patton. A.B., U. Calif., Berkeley, 1941; J.D., U. Calif., San Francisco, 1948; postgrad., Army War Coll., 1961-62; M.A., George Washington U., 1963. Bar: Calif. 1949, U.S. Supreme Ct. 1954. Legal advisor U.S. Mil. Assistance Command, Vietnam, 1964-66; legal adviser U.S. European Command, Stuttgart, Ger., 1966-69; Judge Adv., U.S. Army Europe, Heidelberg, Ger., 1969-71; Judge Adv. Gen. Washington, 1971-75; ret., 1975; prof. law Hastings Coll. Law, U. Calif., San Francisco, 1975-82. Author: (with others) Law at War, 1975; (play) Solferino; contbr. articles to profl. jours. Mem. Sec. Def. Task Force on Racial Discrimination in Adminstrn. Mil. Justice, 1973; mem. U.S. del. Diplomatic Conf. on Law of War, Geneva, 1974, 75. 2d lt. U.S. Army; maj. gen. JAGC, 1971. Decorated D.S.M. with oak leaf cluster, Legion of Merit with oak leaf cluster. Mem. ABA, Am. Judicature Soc., Internat. Soc. Mil. Law and Law of War (hon. pres.), Civil Affairs Assn. (hon. dir.), Selden Soc., Calif. Bar, Order of Coif, Bohemian Club, Army and Navy Club (Washington), Phi Delta Phi. Episcopalian.

PRUGOVECKI, EDUARD, mathematical physicist, educator, author; b. Craiova, Romania, Mar. 19, 1937; emigrated to Can., 1965; s. Slavoljub and Helena (Piatkowsky) P.; m. Margaret Rachelle Loveys, July 19, 1973. Dipl. Phys., U. Zagreb, Croatia, 1959; Ph.D., Princeton U., 1964. Rsch. asst. Inst. Ruder Boskovic, Zagreb, 1959-61; rsch. asst. Princeton (N.J.) U., 1961-64, research assoc., 1964-65; postdoctoral fellow Inst. Theoret. Physics, Edmonton, Alta., Can., 1965-67; lectr. U. Alta., Edmonton, 1966-67; asst. prof. math. physics U. Toronto, 1967-69, assoc. prof., 1969-75, prof., 1975—; vis. prof. Centre National de Recherche Scientifique, Marseille, France, 1974. Author: monographs Quantum Mechanics in Hilbert Space 1971, 2d rev. edit., 1981, Stochastic Quantum Mechanics and Quantum Spacetime, 1984, 2d rev. edit., 1986, Quantum Geometry, 1992, Principles of Quantum General Relativity, 1995; contbr. articles to profl. jours. Grantee NRC Can., 1971-79; grantee Nat. Sci. and Engring. Research Council, 1980—. Mem. Sci. for Peace. Office: U Toronto, 100 Saint George St, Toronto, ON Canada M5S 1A1

PRUIS, JOHN J., business executive; b. Borculo, Mich., Dec. 13, 1923; s. Ties J. and Trientje (Koop) P.; m. Angeline Rosemary Zull, Sept. 14, 1944; children: David Lofton, Daniel J., Dirk Thomas. B.S., Western Mich. U., 1947; M.A., Northwestern U., 1949, Ph.D., 1951; Litt.D. (hon.), Yeungnam U., Taegu, Korea, Ind. State U.; LL.D. (hon.), Ball State U., U. So. Ind. Tchr. pub. schs. Mich., 1942-43; supervising tchr. Campus Sch., Western Mich. U., 1947-48; instr. speech U. No Ia., 1951-52; from asst. prof. to assoc. prof. speech So. Ill. U., 1952-55; mem. faculty Western Mich. U., 1955-68, sec. bd. trustees, 1964-68, v.p. adminstrn., 1966-68; pres. Ball State U., 1968-78; v.p. corp. rels. Ball Corp., 1978-88; Cons., examiner North Central Assn., 1959-78; also bd. dirs. N. Central Assn. V.p. Country dr. chmn. Kalamazoo Cmty. Chest, 1964; bd. dirs. Kalamazoo chpt. Am. Cancer Soc., 1963-68, Del. County United Way, Muncie Symphony Assn., Ball Meml. Hosp., Big Bros./Big Sisters, Ind. Legal Found.; trustee U. So. Ind., 1985-90; exec. v.p. George and Frances Ball Found. With USNR, 1943-46; capt. Res., ret. Mem. Am. Assn. Higher Edn., Speech Communication Assn., Muncie C. of C., Blue Key, Rotary, Phi Delta Kappa, Omicron Delta Kappa, Beta Gamma Sigma. Presbyterian.

PRUITT, ALICE FAY, mathematician, engineer; b. Montgomery, Ala., Dec. 17, 1943; d. Virgil Edwin and Ocie Victoria (Mobley) Maye; m. Mickey Don Pruitt, Nov. 5, 1967; children: Derrell Gene, Christine Marie. BS in Math., U. Ala., Huntsville, 1977; postgrad. in engring., Calif. State U., Northridge, 1978-79. Instr. math. Antelope Valley Coll., Quartz Hill, Calif., 1977-78; space shuttle engr. Rockwell Internat., Palmdale, Calif., 1979-81; programmer, analyst Sci. Support Svcs. Combat Devel. and Experimentation Ctr., Ft. Hunter-Liggett, Calif., 1982-85; sr. engring. specialist Loral Vought Systems Corp., Dallas, 1985-92; mgr. new concepts devel. army tactical sys. and tech. Nichols Rsch. Corp., Huntsville, Ala., 1992—. Mem. DeSoto (Tex.) Coun. Cultural Arts, 1987-89. Mem. AAUW (sch. bd. rep. 1982, legal advocacy fund chairperson 1989-91), Toastmasters Internat., Phi Kappa Phi. Republican. Methodist. Avocations: dancing, gourmet cooking. Office: Nichols Rsch Corp PO Box 40002 4040 S Memorial Pkwy Huntsville AL 35815-1502

PRUITT, ANNE LORING, academic administrator, education educator; b. Bainbridge, Ga., Sept. 19, 1929; d. Loring Alphonzo and Anne Lee (Ward) Smith; m. Harold G. Logan; children: Leslie; stepchildren: Dianne, Pamela, Sharon, Ralph Pruitt, Jr., Harold, Minda, Andrew Logan. BS, Howard U., Washington, 1949; MA, Tchrs. Coll. Columbia U., N.Y.C., 1950, EdD, 1964; HumD hon., Ctrl. State U., Wilberforce, Ohio, 1982. Counsel for women Howard U., 1950-52; tchr., dir. guidance Hutto H.S., Bainbridge, 1952-55; dean students Albany State Coll., Ga., 1955-59, Fisk U., Nashville, 1959-61; prof. edn. Case Western Res. U., Cleve., 1963-79; prof. ednl. policy and leadership Ohio State U., Columbus, 1979-95, prof. emeritus, 1995—, assoc. dean Grad. Sch., 1979-84, assoc. provost, 1984-86, dir. Ctr. for Tchg. Excellence, 1986-94; dean in residence Coun. Grad. Schs., Washington, 1994—; cons. So. Regional Edn. Bd., Atlanta, 1967-78, So. edn. Found., Atlanta, 1978-87. Author: New Students and Coordinated Counseling, 1973, Black Employees in Traditionally White Institutions in the Adams States 1975-77, 1981, In Pursuit of Equality in Higher Education, 1987; co-author: (with Paul Isaac) Student Services for the Changing Graduate Student Population, 1995. Mem. bd. trustees Urban League, Cleve., 1965-71, Ctrl. State U., 1973-82, Case Western Res. U., 1987—, Columbus Area Leadership Program, 1988-91; bd. dirs. ARC, Cleve., 1978-79, Am. West Airlines Found., 1992-95; mem. adv. com. USCG Acad., New London, Conn., 1980-83; Ohio State U. rep. to AAUW, 1989-94; univ. co-chairperson United Way, 1990-91; trustee Marburn Acad., 1991-95; mem. Columbus 1992 Edn. Com., 1988-92; mem. edn. subcom. Columbus Found., 1991-94; mem. exec. com. Renaissance League, 1992-94. Recipient Outstanding Alumnus award Howard U. Alumni Assn., 1975; Am. Council on Edn. fellow, 1977; named one of Am.'s Top 100 Black Bus. and Profl. Women Dollars & Sense Mag., 1986; recipient Disting. Affirmative Action award Ohio State U., 1988; named Sr. Scholar Am. Coll. Personnel Assn., 1989, Woman of Achievement award YMCA, 1993. Mem. NSF (mem. com. on equal opportunities in sci. and engring. 1989-95), Am. Coll. Pers. Assn. (pres. 1976-77), Coun. Grad. Schs. in U.S. (chairperson com. on minority grad. edn. 1980-84), Am. Ednl. Rsch. Assn., Ohio Assn. Counselor Edn. (pres. 1966-67), Links Club, Inc., Cosmos Club. Office: Coun Grad Schs 1 Dupont Cir NW Ste 430 Washington DC 20036-1110

PRUITT, BASIL ARTHUR, JR., surgeon, army officer; b. Nyack, N.Y., Aug. 21, 1930; s. Basil Arthur and Myrtle Flo (Knowles) P.; m. Mary Sessions Gibson, Sept. 4, 1954; children: Scott Knowles, Laura Sessions, Jeffrey Hamilton. AB, Harvard U., 1952, postgrad., 1952-53; MD, Tufts U., 1957. Diplomate: Am. Bd. Surgery (bd. dirs. 1982-88); cert. surg. critical care. Intern Boston City Hosp., 1957-58, resident in surgery, 1958-59, 61-62; commd. capt., M.C. U.S. Army, 1959, advanced through grades to col., 1972; resident Brooke Gen. Hosp., Ft. Sam Houston, Tex., 1962-64; chief clin. div. Inst. Surg. Rsch., Ft. Sam Houston, Tex., 1965-67; chief profl. services 12th Evacuation Hosp., Vietnam, 1967-68; comdr., dir. U.S. Army Inst. Surg. Research, Brooke Army Med. Center, Ft. Sam Houston, 1968-95; clin. prof. gen. surgery Med. Sch. U. Tex., San Antonio, 1975—; prof. surgery U. of the Health Scis., Bethesda, Md., 1978—; mem. surgery, anaesthesiology and trauma study sect. NIH, 1978-82; mem. Shriners Burns Adv. Bd., 1992-95; mem. Shriners Rsch. Adv. Bd., 1995—; mem. rev. bd. for surgery, VA, 1990-93. Author med. books; contr. chpts. to textbooks, articles to profl. jours.; assoc. editor: Jour. Trauma, 1975-94, editor, 1995—; mem. edit. bd.: Archives Surgery, 1981-93, Consultations in Surgery, Correspondence Society of Surgeons, Collected Letters, 1978—, Circulatory Shock, 1985-93, Jour. Burn Care and Rehabilitation, 1984-87, Jour. Investigative Surgery, 1987—, Shock Research, 1993—, Current Opinion in Surgical Infections, 1993—. Decorated Bronze Star, Legion of Merit, Disting. Svc. medal. Fellow ACS (gov. 1973-79, pre and postoperative care com. 1969-79, com. on trauma 1974-84, internat. rels. com. 1983-93, chmn. 1987-89), Am. Coll. Critical Care Medicine; mem. Am. Burn Assn. (pres. 1975-76), Internat. Soc. Burn Injuries (nat. rep. 1974-82, co-chmn. disaster planning com. 1982-86, pres.-elect 1990-94, pres. 1994—), Smoke Burn and Fire Assn. (adv. coun.), Am. Trauma Soc. (dir., pres. Tex. divsn. 1974-75, sec. 1986-88, 2d v.p. 1988-90, pres.-elect 1990-92, pres. 1992-94), Soc. Univ. Surgeons, Am. Surg. Assn. (2d v.p. 1980-81), Tex. Surg. Assn., Western Surg. Assn. (dist. rep. 1984-88, pres. 1993-94), So. Surg. Assn., Halsted Soc. (pres. 1985-86), Am. Assn. Surgery Trauma (recorder 1976-80, pres. 1982-83), Surg. Biol. Club III, Soc. Internat. Surgery, Assn. Acad. Surgery, Surg. Infection Soc. (recorder 1980-84, pres. 1985-86), Internat. Surg. Group, North Am. Burn Soc. (pres. 1993-94), Shock Soc. (clin. counselor 1995—). Home: 402 Tidecrest Dr San Antonio TX 78239-2517 Office: Journal of Trauma 7330 San Pedro Ste 336 San Antonio TX 78216

PRUITT, DEAN GARNER, psychologist, educator; b. Phila., Dec. 26, 1930; s. Dudley McConnell and Grace (Garner) P.; m. France Juliard, Dec. 27, 1959; children: Andre Juliard, Paul Dudley, Charles Alexandre. A.B., Oberlin Coll., 1952; M.S., Yale U., 1954, Ph.D., 1957. Postdoctoral fellow U. Mich., 1957-59; research assoc. Northwestern U., 1959-61; asst. prof., assoc. prof. U. Del., 1961-66; assoc. prof., prof., Disting. prof. SUNY-Buffalo, 1966—, dir. Grad. Program in Social Psychology, 1969-73, 76-77, 85-88. Author: Negotiation Behavior, 1981, (with J. Z. Rubin) Social Conflict, 1986, 94; (with P.J. Carnevale) Negotiation in Social Conflict, 1993; editor; (with R.C. Snyder) Theory and Research on the Causes of War, 1969, (with K. Kressel) Mediation Research, 1989. Grantee Office Naval Rsch., 1965, NIMH, 1969, NSF, 1969, 74, 76, 80, 83, 86, 88, 93, Guggenheim Found., 1978-79. Fellow Am. Psychol. Assn., Am. Psychol. Soc., Soc. for Psychol. Study Social Issues; mem. Internat. Assn. for Conflict Mgmt. (pres. 1990-92), Internat. Soc. Polit. Psychology (v.p. 1984-85, Harold D. Lasswell award 1992), Phi Beta Kappa, Sigma Xi. Home: 9006 Friars Rd Bethesda MD 20817-3320 Office: SUNY Buffalo Dept Psychology Buffalo NY 14260

PRUITT, DOROTHY J. GOOCH, home economics educator, educational administrator; b. Granville County, N.C., June 10, 1935; d. Edgar N. and Lorine (Henley) Gooch; m. William Leonard Pruitt, July 22, 1958. BS, East Carolina U., 1956; MEd, U. N.C.-Chapel Hill, 1971; sixth yr. cert. Nova U., 1984, EdD, 1985. Home econs. tcr. Granville County Schs., Oxford, N.C., 1956-69; cons. State Dept. Pub. Instrn., Raleigh, N.C., 1972-82; prin. Granville County Schs., Oxford, N.C., 1982-91, ret. 1991; part time instr. Vance Granville C.C., 1994—; mem. Bd. Edn. Bd. dirs. N.C. Sch. Bd. Assn., Raleigh, 1980-82; chmn. Granville County Bd. Edn., 1979-82; v.p. Jr. Woman's Club, Oxford, 1965-66 (named Club Woman of Yr. 1965). Named Granville County Prin. of Yr., 1987-88, 90-91. Mem. N.C. Assn. Sch. Adminstrs., Am. Sch. Curriculum Devel. Assn., Am. Sch. Curriculum Assn., Am. Ednl. Research Assn., N.C. Future Homakers of Am. (hon.), Alpha Delta Kappa (corr. sec. 1970). Baptist. Home and Office: 106 Country Club Dr Oxford NC 27565

PRUITT, GEORGE ALBERT, academic administrator; b. Canton, Miss., July 9, 1946; s. Joseph Henry and Lillie Irene (Carmichael) P.; 1 child, Shayla Nicole. BS, Ill. State U., 1968, MS, 1970, DHL (hon.), 1994; PhD, Union Grad. Sch., Cin., 1974; D Pub. Svc. (hon.), Bridgewater State Coll., 1990, MA (hon.), 1990; LLD (hon.), Ill. State U., 1994; DHL honoris causa, SUNY Empire State Coll., 1996. Asst. to v.p. for acad. affairs Ill. State U., Normal, 1968-70, dir. high potential students program, 1968-70; dean students Towson State U., 1970-72; v.p., exec. asst. to pres., assoc. prof. urban affairs Morgan State U., 1972-75; v.p., prof. Tenn. State U., 1975-81; exec. v.p. Council for Advancement Experiential Learning, Columbia, Md., 1981-82; pres. Thomas A. Edison State Coll., Trenton, 1982—; bd. mgrs. Trenton Savs. Bank; mem. commn. on ednl. credit and credentials, labor/higher edn. coun. Am. Coun. on Edn.; advisor group XII, Nat. Fellowship program W.K. Kellogg Found., 1990-94, advisor group XV, 1995—; bd. dirs. SEEDCO; bd. trustees Ctr. for Analysis of Pub. Issues, Princeton, N.J., 1993—; mem. nat. adv. com. on instnl. quality and integrity U.S. Dept. Edn., 1994—. Trustee Union Inst., Cin., Mercer Med. Ctr.; bd. dirs. N.J. Assn. Colls. and Univs., N.J. div. Am. Cancer Soc., 1992—. Recipient Resolution of Commendation Bd. Trustees Morgan State U., 1975, Outstanding Svc. to Edn. award Tenn. State U., 1981, Gubernatorial citation Gov. of Tenn., 1981, Good Guy award George Washington coun. Boy Scouts Am., 1991, Humanitarian award NCCJ, 1992; apptd. hon. mem. Gen. Assembly Tenn., 1981, hon. mem. U.S. Congress from 5th Tenn. dist., 1981; named ole of the Most Effective Coll. Pres. in U.S., Exxon Edn. Found. Study, 1986. Mem. Coun. for Advancement Exptl. Learning, Am. Assn. State Colls.and Univs., Coun. for Advancement and Support of Edn., Am. Coun. Edn., Mid. States Assn. Colls. and Schs. (accreditation evaluator commn. on higher edn.), Mercer County C. of C. (trustee). Office: Thomas Edison Coll 101 W State St Trenton NJ 08608-1101

PRUITT, MELINDA DOUTHAT, elementary school special education educator; b. Warner Robins, Ga., Jan. 24, 1958; d. J.P. and Grace Imogene (Elkins) Douthat; m. Jeffrey Hal Pruitt, Aug. 20, 1983. BS in Phys. Edn., U. Tenn., 1980, MS in Deaf Edn., 1982. Cert. tchr., Tenn., career ladder III tchr. Elem. tchr. and Title I tchr. math. Ellijay (Ga.) Elem. Sch., Gilmer County Schs.; tchr. spl. edn. Jonesborough (Tenn.) Mid. Sch., Washington County Schs.; tchr. deaf edn. King Springs Elem. Sch., Johnson City (Tenn.) Schs.; tchr. spl. edn., team leader Mosheim (Tenn.) Elem. Sch., Greene County Schs.; speaker, presenter in field. Cheerleading sponsor coach West Greene H.S.; mem. local PTA; active cmty orgns. and ch. Mem. NEA, Tenn. Edn. Assn., Coun. on Edn. of Deaf (cert.), Greene County Edn. Assn. (negotiating team, pres.), Ruritan Club (Midway Vol. chpt.), Pi Lambda Theta. Home: 190 Lonesome Rd Midway TN 37809-4946

PRUITT, THOMAS P., JR., textiles executive; b. 1922. Grad., N.C. State U., 1948; with Springs Mills, 1948-52. With Springs Mills, Lancaster, S.C., 1945-52; with Carolina Mills, Maiden, N.C., 1952—, v.p., now exec. weaving ops. Office: Carolina Mills Inc 618 Carolina Ave Maiden NC 28650-1100

PRUITT, WILLIAM CHARLES, JR., minister, educator; b. Reed, Okla., May 31, 1926; s. William Charles and Helen Irene (Sanders) P.; m. Ellen Ruth Palmer, Aug. 25, 1953; children: Philip, Suzanne, John. BS, Stephen F. Austin State U., 1956, MEd, 1958; BD, MRE, Bapt. Missionary Assn. Theol. Sem., 1959, DRE, 1963; MLS, East Tex. State U., 1963. Ordained to ministry Bapt. Missionary Assn. Am., 1955. Pastor Mt. Pleasant Bapt. Ch., Bedias, Tex., 1955-60, Calvary Bapt. Ch., Commerce, Tex., 1960-63, Glenfawn Bapt. Ch., Laneville, Tex., 1963-66, New Hope Bapt. Ch., Winkler, Tex., 1966-70, Pleasant Ridge Bapt. Ch., Centerville, Tex., 1970-74, Redland Bapt. Ch., Centerville, 1970-79, Concord (Tex.) Bapt. Ch., 1983—; dir. libr. svc., instr. Bapt. Missionary Assn. Theol. Sem., 1958-67, prof. missions and religious edn., 1967-72; instr. psychology Jacksonville Coll., 1971-76; asst. dir. East Tex. Adult Edn. Coop., 1973-93; supr. Adult Learning Ctr. Rusk State Hosp., 1988-96. Tex. wing chaplain CAP, 1971-77; exec. dir. Armed Forces Chaplaincy Com., Bapt. Missionary Assn. Am., Jacksonville, Tex., 1965-95. Mem. Mil. Chaplains Assn. U.S., Lions. Home: Rte 8 Box 327 Jacksonville TX 75766 Office: PO Box 912 Jacksonville TX 75766-0912

PRUS, VICTOR MARIUS, architect, urbanist; b. Poland, Apr. 19, 1917; s. Marien Raymond and Susanna (Hoffman) P.; m. Maria Fisz, Sept. 22, 1948. Diploma in architecture, Warsaw Tech. U., 1939; Ing.Arch., M.Arch., U. Liverpool, 1946. Sr. exec. officer Festival of Britain, London, 1948-51; prin. Victor Prus (Architect), London, 1948-52, Montreal, Que., Can., 1953-76; prin. Victor Prus & Assos. (Architects and Urbanists), Montreal, 1976—; asst. to Buckminster Fuller Princeton U., 1953; vis. prof. McGill U., 1953, 66, 72, Washington U., St. Louis, 1978. Works include New Internat. Airport, Barbados, Montreal Conv. Ctr., Observatory, Mauna Kea, Hawaii, Grand Théâtre de Québec, Conservatory of Music, Montreal Metro stas., Bonaventure, Langelier, Mt. Royal, Brudenell River Resort, P.E.I., Can., Place Longueuil Comml. Centre, Rockland Shopping Centre, Centaur Theatres, Expo '67 Stadium and James Lyng Sch., Montreal. Served with RAF, 1941-45. Decorated Polish Cross of Valour (2); recipient Massey medal, 1961, Can. Architect award, 1971, 1st prize for Que. Performing Arts Centre, 1964, 1st prize for RCAF Meml., 1969, 1st prize for Montreal Congress Center, 1978. Fellow Royal Archtl. Inst. Can., AIA (hon.); mem. Royal Can. Acad. Arts, Royal Inst. Brit. Architects, Can. Inst. Planners. Home and Office: 108 Senneville Rd, Senneville, PQ Canada H9X 1B9

PRUSINER, STANLEY BEN, neurology and biochemistry educator, researcher; b. Des Moines, May 28, 1942; s. Lawrence Albert and Miriam (Spigel) P.; m. Sandra Lee Turk, Oct. 18, 1970; children: Helen Chloe, Leah Anne. AB cum laude, U. Pa., 1964, MD, 1968; PhD (hon.), Hebrew U., Jerusalem, 1995. Diplomate Am. Bd. Neurology. Intern in medicine U. Calif., San Francisco, 1968-69, resident in neurology, 1972-74, asst. prof. neurology, 1974-80, assoc. prof., 1980-84, prof., 1984—, prof. biochemistry, 1988—, acad. senate faculty rsch. lectr., 1989-90; prof. virology U. Calif., Berkeley, 1984—; mem. neurology rev. com. Nat. Inst. Neurol. Disease and Strokes, NIH, Bethesda, Md., 1982-86, 90-92; mem. sci. adv. bd. French Fedn., L.A., 1985—; mem. sci. rev. com. Alzheimer's Disease Diagnostic Ctr. & Rsch. Grant Program, State of Calif., 1985-89; chmn. sci. adv. bd. Am. Health Assistance Found., Rockville, Md., 1986—. Editor: The Enzymes of Glutamine Metabolism, 1973, Slow Transmissible Diseases of the Nervous System, 2 vols., 1979, Prions--Novel Infectious Pathogens Causing Scrapie and CJD, 1987, Prion Diseases of Humans and Animals, 1992, Molecular and Genetic Basis of Neurologic Disease, 1993, Prions Prions Prions, 1996—; contbr.more than 200 articles to profl. jours. Mem. adv. bd. Family Survival Project for Adults with Chronic Brain Disorders, San Francisco, 1982—, San Francisco chpt. Alzheimer's Disease and Related Disorder Assn., 1985—. Lt. comdr. USPHS, 1969-72. Recipient Leadership and Excellence for Alzheimer's Disease award NIH, 1990—, Potamkin prize for Alzheimer's Disease Rsch., 1991, Presl. award, 1993, Med. Rsch. award Met. Life Found., 1992, Christopher Columbus Discovery award NIH and Med. Soc. Genoa, Italy, 1992, Charles A. Dana award for pioneering achievements in health, 1992, Dickson prize for outstanding contbns. to medicine U. Pitts., 1992, Max Planck Rsch. award Alexander von Humboldt Found. and Max Planck Soc., 1992, Gairdner Found. Internat. award, 1993, Disting. Achievement in Neurosci. Rsch. award Bristol-Myers Squibb, 1994, Albert Lasker award for Basic Med. Rsch., 1994, Caledonian Rsch. Found. prize Royal Soc. Edinburgh, 1995, Paul Ehrlich and Ludwig Darmstaedter award Germany, 1995, Paul Hoch award Am. Psychopathol. Assn., 1995, Wolf prize in medicine, 1996, ICN Virology prize, 1996; Alfred P. Sloan Rsch. fellow U. Calif., 1976-78; Med. Investigator grantee Howard Hughes Med. Inst., 1976-81; grantee for excellence in neurosci. Senator Jacob Javits Ctr., NIH, 1985-90. Mem. NAS (Inst. Medicine, Richard Lounsbery award for extraordinary achievements in biology and medicine 1993), Am. Acad. Arts and Scis., Am. Acad. Neurology (George Cotzias award for outstanding rsch. 1987, Presdl. award 1993), Am. Assn. Physicians, Am. Soc. Microbiology, Am. Soc. Neurochemistry, Internat. Soc. Neurochemistry, Am. Soc. Virology, Am. Neurol. Assn., Am. Soc. Clin. Investigation, Am. Soc. Cellular Biology, Am. Soc. Molecular Biol. Biochemistry, Protein Soc., Concordia Argonaut Club.

PRUSOFF, WILLIAM HERMAN, biochemical pharmacologist, educator; b. N.Y.C., June 25, 1920; s. Samuel and Mary (Metrick) P.; m. Brigitte Auerbach, June 19, 1948 (dec. Apr. 1991); children—Alvin Saul, Laura Ann. B.A., U. Miami, Fla., 1941; M.A., Columbia U., 1947, Ph.D., 1949. Research assoc., instr. pharmacology Western Res. U., 1949-53; mem. faculty Yale Med. Sch., 1953—; prof. pharmacology, 1966-90, prof. emeritus. sr. rsch. scientist, 1990—, acting chmn. dept., 1968; cons. in field, 1965—. Mem. Am. Assn. Cancer Rsch., Am. Chem. Soc., Am. Soc. Biol. Chemists, Am. Soc. Pharmacology and Exptl. Therapeutics, Soc. Chinese Bioscientists in Am., Sigma Xi, Internat. Soc. for Antiviral Rsch. Achievements include rsch. in virology, photochemistry, mechanism drug action, synthesis potential drugs; synthesized Idoxuridine; developed (in collaboration with D.T.S. Lin) Stavudine for therapy of AIDS. Home: De Forest Dr Branford CT 06471 Office: Yale U Sch Medicine New Haven CT 06510

PRUSSING, LAUREL LUNT, state official, economist; b. N.Y.C., Feb. 21, 1941; d. Richard Valentine and Maria (Rinaldi) Lunt; m. John Edward Prussing, May 29, 1965; children: Heidi Elizabeth, Erica Stephanie, Victoria Nicole Johanna. AB, Wellesley Coll., 1962; MA, Boston U., 1964; postgrad., U. Calif., San Diego, 1968-69, U. Ill., 1970-76. Economist Arthur D. Little, Cambridge, Mass., 1963-67, U. Ill., Urbana, 1971-72; mem. county bd. Champaign County, Urbana, 1972-76, county auditor, 1976-92; mem. local audit adv. bd. Office Ill. Compt., Chgo., 1984-92. Contbr. to Illinois Local Government: A Handbook, 1990. Founder Com. for Intelligent Tax Reform, Urbana, 1982—, Com. for Elected County Exec., Urbana, 1986—; state rep. 103d dist. Ill. Gen. Assembly, 1993-95; dem. cand. Ill. 15th dist. U.S. Congress, 1996. Named Best Freshman Legislator Ind. Voters Ill., 1994; recipient Friend of Agriculture award Ill. Farm Bur., 1994; named to Legis. Honor Roll Ill. Environ. Coun., 1994. Mem. LWV, Govt. Fin. Officers Assn., U.S. and Can. (com. on acctg., auditing and fin. reporting 1980-88, Fin. Reporting award 1981-91, Disting. Budget award 1986), Nat. Assn. Local Govt. Auditors (charter), Ill. Assn. County Auditors (pres. 1984-85). Democrat. Home: 2106 Grange Dr Urbana IL 61801-6609

PRUTER, KARL HUGO, bishop; b. Poughkeepsie, N.Y., July 3, 1920; s. William Karl and Katherine (Rehling) P.; m. Nancy Lee Taylor, 1943; children: Hugo Jr., Robert, Karl, Stephen, Maurice, Katherine, Nancy Goodman. B.A., Northeastern U., 1943; M.Div., Lutheran Theol. Sem., Phila., 1945; M.A. in Edn., Roosevelt U., 1963; M.A. in History, Boston U., 1968. Guest lectr. Landerziehungsheim, Stein, West Germany, 1964-65; ordained priest Christ Catholic Ch., 1965; pastor Ch. of the Transfiguration, Boston, 1965-70; bishop Christ Cath. Ch. Author: The Theology of Congregationalism, 1953, The Teachings of the Great Mystics, 1969, A History of the Old Catholic Church, 1973, The People of God, 1975, The Jewish Christians in the United States, 1985. Address: Cathedral Ch Prince of Peace Highlandville MO 65669

PRUYN, WILLIAM J., energy industry executive; b. Boston, Aug. 25, 1922; s. William J. and Ida M. (Langan) P.; m. Mary Anton, May 19, 1945; children: William J., Barbara, Marilyn, Ann Marie, Stephen, Christopher. Student, Bentley Coll., 1939-41, Harvard U., 1944-45, 64; BBA, Northeastern U., 1948. Pub. acct. Meahl, McNamara & Co., 1946-51; with Eastern Gas & Fuel Assocs. (name changed to Eastern Enterprises 1989), Boston, 1951-91, sr. v.p., 1972-76, trustee, 1973—, pres., chief adminstrv. officer, 1976-77, pres., chief exec. officer, 1977-85, chmn. bd., chief exec. officer, 1986-87, chmn. bd., 1987-91; ret., 1991. Bd. dirs. Med. Found., Inc.; trustee Northeastern U., New Eng. Aquarium; mem. pres.'s adv. council Bentley Coll. Served with USNR. Mem. Corinthian Yacht Club. Home: 17 Vassar Rd Marblehead MA 01945-2851

PRUZANSKY, JOSHUA MURDOCK, lawyer; b. N.Y.C., Mar. 16, 1940; s. Louis and Rose (Murdock) P.; m. Susan R. Bernstein, Aug. 31, 1980; 1 child, Dina Gabrielle. BA, Columbia Coll., 1960, JD, 1965. Bar: N.Y., 1965, U.S. Dist. Ct. (ea. and so. dists.) N.Y., 1968, U.S. Supreme Ct., 1980. Ptnr. Scheinberg, DePetris & Pruzansky, Riverhead, N.Y., 1965-85, Greshin, Ziegler & Pruzansky, Smithtown, 1985—; mem. exec. coun. N.Y. State Conf. Bar Leaders, 1984—, chmn., 1988-89; mem. grievance com. Appellate Divsn. 10th Judicial Dist., 1992-96; mem. adv. bd. Ticor Title Guarantee Co., 1992—; mem. L.I. adv. bd. Marine Midland Bank, 1995—. Trustee Evan Frankel Found., 1993—, Suffolk Acad. Law, Suffolk County, N.Y., 1979-89; mem. secondary sch. adv. com. Columbia U.; mem. Suffolk adv. bd. Fund for Modern Cts. Fellow ABA Found., N.Y. State Bar Found. (bd. dirs. 1994—); mem. ABA (probate and real property sect.), N.Y. State Bar Assn. (ho. dels. 1982—, v.p. 1991-92, 95-96, pres. elect 1996—, mem.-at-large exec. com. 1992-95, nominating com. 1986-91, spl. com. women and law 1986-91, task force on adminstrv. adjudication 1986—, task force om small firms 1991—, chair-by-laws com. 1991—, trusts and estates sect.), Suffolk County Bar Assn. (bd. dirs. 1979-89, pres. 1985-86), N.Y. County Lawyers Assn., Nassau County Bar Assn., Suffolk Bar Pac (chmn. 1987-88), Columbia U. Law Alumni Assn Suffolk County (dir. 1989—). Office: Greshin Ziegler & Pruzansky 199 E Main St Smithtown NY 11787-2899

PRUZZO, JUDITH JOSEPHINE, office manager; b. Oklahoma City, July 11, 1945; d. Joseph Michael and Mary Amelia (Reinhart) Engel; m. Neil Alan Pruzzo, Aug. 20, 1966 (dec. Sept. 1991); children: Maria Pruzzo Richards, Eric Alan, Brian Samuel, Lisa Michelle. BS in Pharmacy, Southwestern Okla. U., 1968. Registered pharmacist, Mo., Okla., Tex.; cert. by Coun. Homeopathy. Nurse's aide Valley View Hosp., Ada, Okla., 1963-64; pharmacy technician Gibson Pharmacy, Ada, Okla., 1966; pharmacist Trinity Luth. Hosp., Kansas City, Mo., 1968-69, Rsch. Hosp., Kansas City, Mo., 1969-73, East Town Osteo. Hosp., Dallas, 1973; office mgr., profl. homeopath Neil A. Pruzzo, DO, P.A., Richardson, Tex., 1975-91; profl. homeopath, nutritional counselor Pruzzo Clinic, Inc., Richardson, 1992—; lectr., presenter homeopathy and weight loss. Mem. Dallas Symphony Assn., 1992—, Stradivarious patron, 1994—. Women's Bowling Assn. scholar, 1963; named Ada Dist. Dairy Princess, Okla. Dairy Princess Contest, 1965. Mem. Internat. Found. Homeopathy, Nat. Ctr. Homeopathy, Am. Pharm. Assn., Homeopathic Assn., Naturopathic Physicians (assoc.), Southwestern State U. Alumni Assn. (life), Kappa Epsilon (life, v.p. 1967-68). Avocations: classical music, aerobic walking, reading, competitive ballroom dancing, travel. Home: 4303 Shadow Glen Dr Dallas TX 75287-6828 Address: 8345 Walnut Hill Dallas TX 75231

PRYCE, DEBORAH D., congresswoman; b. Warren, Ohio, July 29, 1951. BA cum laude, Ohio State U., 1973; JD with honors, Capital U., 1976. Bar: Ohio 1976. Former asst. city prosecutor, asst. city atty., first asst. city prosecutor Columbus, Ohio; former judge Franklin County Mcpl. Ct., Columbus; mem. 103rd Congress from 15th Ohio dist., Washington, D.C., 1993—; mem. coms. rules. Republican. Presbyterian. Avocations: skiing, traveling.

PRYCE, EDWARD LYONS, landscape architect; b. Lake Charles, La., May 26, 1914; s. George Samuel and Dora (Cook) P.; m. Woodia Bernice Smith, Nov. 2, 1940; children—Marilyn C., Joellen G. B.S., Tuskegee Inst., 1937; B.L.A., Ohio State U., 1948; M.S. in Landscape Architecture, U. Calif., Berkeley, 1953. Head dept. ornamental horticulture Tuskegee Inst., 1948-55, supt. of bldgs. and grounds, 1955-69, prof. dept. architecture, 1969-77; pvt. practice landscape architecture Tuskegee, Ala., 1948—; chmn. Ala. State Bd. Examiners for Landscape Architects, 1981—. Mem. Tuskegee City Planning Commn., 1970-76; mem. Tuskegee Model Cities Commn., 1968-72, Ala. State Outdoor Recreation Planning Bd., 1978—. Recipient Alumni Merit award Tuskegee Inst., 1977, Disting. Alumnus award Ohio State U., 1980. Fellow Am. Soc. Landscape Architects. Baptist. Office: PO Box 246 1901 Montgomery Rd Tuskegee AL 36087

PRYCE, JONATHAN, actor; b. North Wales, June 1, 1947. Appearences include (stage) Liverpool Everyman, 1972, Nottinguam Playhouse-Comedians, Comedians, 1977 (Tony award, Theatre World award), Hamlet (Olivier award), Macbeth, Julius Caesar, The Caretaker, 1981, Accidental Death of an Anarchist, 1984, Miss Saigon, 1991 (Tony award), Oliver, 1995; (films) Voyage of the Damned, 1976, Breaking Glass, 1980, Loophole, 1981, Praying Mantis, 1982, The Plowman's Lunch, 1983, Something Wicked This Way Comes, 1983, Brazil, 1985, The Doctor and the Devils, 1985, Haunted Honeymoon, 1986, Jumpin Jack Flash, 1986, Hotel London, 1987, Man On Fire, 1987, The Adventures of Baron Munchausen, 1988, Consuming Passions, 1988, The Rachel Papers, 1989, Glengarry Glen Ross, 1992, The Age of Innocence, 1993, Carrington, 1995 (Best Actor award Cannes Film Festival 1995); (TV movie) Barbarians at the Gate, HBO, 1993 (Emmy nomination, Supporting Actor - Miniseries or Special, 1993). Office: Duva Flack and Assocs Elin Flack 200 W 57th St Ste 1407 New York NY 10019

PRYCE, WILLIAM THORNTON, ambassador; b. San Diego, July 19, 1932; s. Roland Fremont and Katharine (Hartmann) P.; m. Joan MacClurg, Mar. 22, 1958; children: Kathy Ellen, Jeffrey Fremont, Scott Fisher. BA, Wesleyan U., 1953; MA, Tufts U., 1954. Joined Fgn. Svc., Dept. State, 1958; spl. asst. to under sec. of state for econ. affairs, asst. sec. for Latin Am. affairs Washington, 1964-65; polit. officer Am. ambassies in Moscow, Panama, Guatemala, 1966-74; dir. Soviet ednl. and cultural programs Dept. State, Washington, 1974-76; exec. asst. to amb.-at-large Ellsworth Bunker Washington, 1977-78; polit. counselor Am. Embassy, Mexico City, 1978-81; dep. chief of mission Am. Embassy, La Paz, Bolivia, 1981-82, Panama City, Panama, 1982-86; alt. U.S. rep. Orgn. Am. States, Washington, 1986-89; spl. asst. to pres. for nat. security affairs NSC, Washington, 1989-92; U.S. amb. to Honduras, 1993—. Lt. USN, 1955-58. Recipient Meritorious Honor award Dept. State, 1986, Superior Honor award, 1989, Sr. Performance award 1982-87, 89, 90, 92. Mem. Am. Fgn. Svc. Assn., City Tavern Club. Episcopalian. Home and Office: Am Embassy US Embassy APO AA 34022

PRYE, ELLEN ROSS, graphic designer; b. Waynesboro, Va., Mar. 12, 1947; d. John Dewey and Betty Lou (Hardman) Ross; m. Warren Douglas Drumheller, June 7, 1969 (div. 1987); children: Amy Heather Drumheller, Warren Daniel Drumheller; m. John Paul Prye, July 24, 1993. BS, James Madison U., 1990. Cert. tchr. art K-12, Va/. Graphic artist The News-Virginian, Waynesboro, 1990-92, advt. prodn./composing mgr., 1992-94; graphic designer The Humphries Press, Inc., Waynesboro, Va., 1994—. Recipient Distinction award Shenandoah Valley Art Ctr., 1989, 1st Design of Newsletter Printing Industries of Va., 1995. Mem. Va. Press Assn. (Merit certs. 1991, 93). Presbyterian. Avocations: ceramics, watercolor, horseback riding. Home: 1830 S Talbott Pl Waynesboro VA 22980-2252 Office: The Humphries Press Inc 1400 Hopeman Pkwy Waynesboro VA 22980

PRYOR, CHARLES WINGFIELD, JR., nuclear technology company executive; b. Lynchburg, Va., Dec. 31, 1944; s. Charles Winfield and Elizabeth (Baldock) P.; m. Mary Jane Meacham, Apr. 19, 1990; children: Chip, Blake Newton, Laurie, Reed Newton. BSCE with honors, Va. Inst. Tech. and State U., 1966, MS in Structural Engring., 1968, PhD in Structural Engring., 1970; postgrad., Northeastern U., 1980. Registered profl. engr., Va. Instr. engring. mechanics Va. Poly. Inst. and State U., Blacksburg, 1969-70; sr. engr. McDonnell Douglas Aerospace Co., 1970-72; various positions nuclear power generation div. Babcock & Wilcox Co., 1972-83; v.p., gen. mgr. nuclear power div., 1983-89, v.p., 1989-91; pres., CEO, B&W Nuclear Svc. Co.; chmn. bd. B&W Fuel Co., 1989-91; pres., CEO B&W Nuclear Techs., Inc., Lynchburg, Va., 1991—; now mngr. Pryor Inc.; numerous presentations in field; bd. dirs., mem. internat. adv. com. Nuclear Energy Inst., Washington; chmn. bd. Centra Health, Inc.; mem. com. of 100 engring. adv. bd. Va. Poly. Inst. and State U. Contbr. numerous articles to tech., profl. and managerial jours. Chmn. bd. Employee Assistance Ctrl. Va., Ctrl. Va. Ptnrs. in Edn.; bd. dirs. Va. Ctr. for Innovative Tech., Ctrl. Va. C.C. Found., Ctrl. Va. YMCA, NCCJ; trustee Lynchburg Coll.; mem. Blue Ridge Econ. Devel. Coun., Coun. for Va. Urban Renewal; past div. dir. United Way Ctrl. Va. Decorated chevalier Ordre Nat. du Merite (France); named Va. Outstanding Industrialist, State of Va., 1993. Mem. Am. Nuclear Soc., Greater Lynchburg C. of C. (past pres.), Sigma XXi, Tau Beta Pi, Phi Kappa Phi, Chi Epsilon. Episcopalian. Home: RR 4 Box 195C Lynchburg VA 24503-9726 Office: Pryor Inc PO Box 10-935 Lynchburg VA 24506-0935*

PRYOR, DAVID HAMPTON, senator; b. Camden, Ark., Aug. 29, 1934; s. Edgar and Susan (Newton) P.; m. Barbara Lunsford, Nov. 27, 1957; children—David, Mark, Scott. B.A. in Polit. Sci, U. Ark., 1957, LL.B., 1961. Bar: Ark. 1964. Practiced in Camden; mem. firm Pryor and Barnes; founder, pub. Ouachita Citizen newspaper, Camden, 1957-60; mem. Ark. Ho. of Reps., 1961-65, 89th-92d Congresses from 4th Ark. dist.; gov. of Ark., 1974-79, senator from Ark., 1979-96; ranking min. mem. Select Com. On Aging, Nutrition and Forestry Subcom. on Prodn. and Price Competitiveness, Fin. Subcom. on Long Term Growth, Debt. and Deficit Reduction; mem. Govt. Affairs, Sen. Dem. Conf. Com., Sen. Dem. Steering and Coord. Com., Dem. Senatorial Campign Com. Office: US Senate 267 Russell Senate Bldg Washington DC 20510*

PRYOR, DIXIE DARLENE, elementary education educator; b. Anderson, Ind., May 22, 1938; d. Thurman Earle and Alice D. (Watson) Rinker; m. Charles Lee Pryor, Mar. 13, 1958; children: Charles A., Deborah Lee Pryor Evans, Laurinda Ann Pryor Owen. BS, Ball State U., 1967, MEd, 1974. Tchr. Anderson (Ind.) Pub. Schs., 1967-72, Wawasee Cmty. Sch. Corp., Syracuse, Ind., 1972—; bd. dirs. Internat. Palace Sports-Scholarship, North Webster, Ind. Bd. dirs. North Webster Day Care. Named Outstanding Mem. Tippkee Reading Coun., 1995, Outstanding Educator Honor Srs., 1995; recipient Ind. State Reading Assn., 1995. Mem. Ind. State Reading Assn.(pres. 1994-95, Outstanding Mem. award 1996), Kiwanis (com. chair North Webster 1988—, sec. 1996-97). Republican. Methodist. Avocations: travel, reading. Home: 4630 E Armstrong Rd Leesburg IN 46538-9588

PRYOR, HAROLD S., retired college president; b. Overton County, Tenn., Oct. 3, 1920; s. Hubert S. and Ethel (Stockton) P.; m. LaRue Vaughn, June 26, 1946. B.S., Austin Peay State U., 1946; M.A., George Peabody Coll., 1947; Ed.D., U. Tenn., 1951. Instr. George Peabody Coll., Vanderbilt U., 1946-47, E. Tenn. State U., 1947-49, U. Tenn., Knoxville, 1949-51; head dept. edn. Austin Peay State U., 1952, dir. tchr. edn., 1954-68; pres. Columbia (Tenn.) State Community Coll., from 1968, now pres. emeritus; dir. First Farmers and Merchants Nat. Bank, Columbia, 1970—, First Farmers and Mchts. Corp., 1982—; Columbia State Found., 1971—. Contbr. articles to profl. jours. With U.S. Army, 1943-46. Grantee Dept. Labor; Grantee HEW. Mem. NEA, Tenn. Coll. Assn. (past pres.), Tenn. Edn. Assn., Am. Assn. Higher Edn., Comparative Edn. Soc., Graymere Country Club, Kiwanis, Kappa Delta Pi, Phi Delta Kappa. Democrat. Presbyterian.

PRYOR, RICHARD, actor, writer; b. Peoria, Ill., Dec. 1, 1940; s. Leroy and Gertrude (Thomas) P.; children: Elizabeth Ann, Richard, Rain, Renee. G-rad. high sch. Appeared on: Ed Sullivan, Merv Griffin and Johnny Carson television shows in 1960s; appeared in motion pictures The Busy Body, 1967, The Green Berets, 1968, Wild In The Streets, 1968, The Phynx, 1970, Dynamite Chicken, 1970, Lady Sings the Blues, 1972, Hit, 1973, Wattstax, 1973, The Mack, 1973, Some Call It Loving, 1973, Uptown Saturday Night, 1974, Adios Amigos, 1976, The Bingo Long Travelling All-Stars and Motor Kings, 1976, Car Wash, 1976, Silver Streak, 1976, Greased Lightning, 1977, Which Way is Up?, 1977, Blue Collar, 1978, California Suite, 1978, The Wiz, 1978, Richard Pryor Live in Concert, 1979, The Muppet Movie, 1979, Wholly Moses, 1980, In God We Trust, 1980, Stir Crazy, 1980, Bustin' Loose, 1981, Some Kind of Hero, 1982, The Toy, 1982, Superman III, 1983, Richard Pryor Here and Now, 1983, Brewster's Millions, 1985, Critical Condition, 1987, Moving, 1988, See No Evil, Hear No Evil, 1989, Harlem Nights, 1989, Another You, 1991; writer, producer, dir. Jo Jo Dancer Your Life Is Calling, 1986; writer scripts for Flip Wilson; co-writer TV spls. for Lily Tomlin, 1973 (Emmy award); movie script Blazing Saddles, 1973 (Am. Writers Guild award, Am. Acad. Humor award), Lily, 1974 (Am. Acad. Humor award); recorded That Nigger's Crazy, 1974 (Grammy award, certified Gold and Platinum album), Bicentennial Nigger, 1976 (Grammy award); star Richard Pryor Show, NBC-TV, 1977; owner Richard Pryor Enterprises, Inc., Los Angeles, 1975—. Served with U.S. Army, 1958-60. Mem. Nat. Acad. Rec. Arts and Scis., Writers Guild Am.

PRYOR, RICHARD WALTER, telecommunications executive, retired air force officer; b. Poplar Bluff, Mo., Nov. 6, 1932; s. Walter V. and Mary (Clifford) P.; m. Barbara LeCompte, Feb. 19, 1955; children: Richard, Susan Davis, Robert, William. B in Gen. Studies, U. Nebr., Omaha, 1972; MA, Webster Coll., St. Louis, 1975; grad., U. No. Colo., 1975. Commd. 2d lt. USAF, 1953, advanced through grades to maj. gen., 1982, ret., 1982, instr. Acad., DVMT engr. space and missile systems, chief of staff Communication Services; mgr. worldwide def. communication system Def. Communications Agy., 1980-81; pres. ITT World Communications, N.Y.C., 1982-84, ITT Indsl. Transmission Co., N.Y.C.; sr. v.p. engring. ops. ITT Communication Services GP; pres., gen. mgr. ITT Christian Rovsing-Copenhagen DK, 1984-86; chmn. Christian-Rovsing Inc., Tulsa; exec. v.p. Electronic Data Systems (EDS) Comm. Corp., Dallas, 1986-89; pres., COO IMM Corp.-Interdigital AMEX, Phila., 1989-92; chmn., CEO. officer Ultranav Corp, Dallas; chmn. Prism Video, Dallas; CEO Trans-Tech Holdings Corp., Dallas. Contbr. articles to tech. publs. Assoc. dir. Boy Soucts Am., N.Y.C., 1983. Recipient Cert. of Appreciation Okla. Mental Health Assn., 1979, Kansas City Lions Club, 1974. Mem. Armed Forces Communications and Electronics Assn. (pres. N.Y.C. 1983, nat. dir.), Air Force Assn., Oklahoma City Soc. Profl. Engrs., Phi Alpha Theta. Republican. Roman Catholic. Clubs: Bolling AFB Officers; Canoe Brook Country (Short Hills, N.J.); Army-Navy (Washington). Home: 7802 Mason Dells Dr Dallas TX 75230-6035 Office: Provident Towers 5001 Spring Valley 2d Fl Dallas TX 75244

PRYOR, WILLIAM AUSTIN, chemistry educator; b. St. Louis, Mar. 10, 1929; s. Saul Arnold and Adeline (Franzel) P. Ph.B., U. Chgo., 1948, B.S., 1951; Ph.D., U. Calif. at Berkeley, 1954. Chemist Calif. Research Corp., Richmond, 1954-60; lectr. U. Calif. at Berkeley, 1956-60; asst. prof. Purdue U., Lafayette, Ind., 1960-63; assoc. prof. La. State U., Baton Rouge, 1963-67; prof. La. State U., 1967-72, Thomas and David Boyd prof. chemistry and biochemistry, 1972—; mem. depts. chemistry and biochemistry Inst. Environ. Studies, La. State U. Med. Ctr., New Orleans; mem. Pennington Biomed. Rsch. Ctr., Baton Rouge; dir. Biodynamics Inst. La. State U., 1985—; vis. prof. Washington U., St. Louis, 1968, UCLA, 1970, U. Calif., Berkeley, 1971, Duke U., 1978, U. Calif., Davis, 1978, U. Calif., San Deigo, 1978, U. Calif., Davis, 1994, Harvard U., 1995, Tufts U., 1995; cons. to chem. co., 1963—. Author: Free Radicals, 1966, (with Melvin Calvin) Organic Chemistry of Life; Free Radicals in Biology, Vols. 1-6, 1976-84, Organic Free Radicals, 1978, Frontiers in Free Radical Chemistry, 1980, Methods in Enzymology, 1984, 90, 94, (with A. T. Diplock, L. J. Macklin, L. Packer) Vitamin E: Biochemistry and Health Implications, 1989, (with J. N. Diana) Tobacco Smoking and Nutrition: Influence of Tobacco-Associated Health Risks, 1993. Grantee AEC, 1960-64, NIH, 1964—, NSF, 1964—, Air Force Office Sci. Rsch., 1964-68, Dow Chem. Co., 1964—, Du Pont, U.S. Army, 1965-69, Exxon Rsch. and Devel. Co., 1966—, Owens-Corning Fiberglass, 1983—; Disting. Faculty fellow La. State U. Found., 1969, NIH Spl. Postdoctoral fellow, 1970-71, John Simon Guggenheim fellow, 1970-71; recipient Merit award NIH, 1986-96, Harold Harper Meml. award Am. Coun. for Advancement of Medicine, 1987. Fellow Am. Inst. Chemists, AAAS; mem. Am. Chem. Soc. (S.W. sect. award 1975, Petroleum Chemistry award 1980, Southern Chemist award 1983, Charles E. Coates award 1989), Chem. Soc. London (VERIS award for nutrition rsch.), Faraday Soc., Gerontol. Soc., Radiation Rsch. Soc., Am. Aging Assn., Pan-Am. Med. Assn. (hon. life), Soc. for Free Radical Search (founding mem., internat. coun.), Oxygen Soc. (founding mem., pres.-elect 1995-96, pres. 1997-98). Patentee in field. Home: 3631 S Lakeshore Dr Baton Rouge LA 70808-3631 Office: La State U Biodynamics Inst 711 Choppin Baton Rouge LA 70803-1800

PRYOR, WILLIAM DANIEL LEE, humanities educator; b. Lakeland, Fla., Oct. 29, 1926; s. Dahl and Lottie Mae (Merchant) P. AB, Fla. So. Coll., 1949; MA, Fla. State U., 1950, PhD, 1959; postgrad. U. N.C., 1952-53. Pvt. art study with Florence Wilde; pvt. voice study with Colin O'More and Anna Kaskas; pvt. piano study with Waldemar Hille and audited piano master classes of Ernst von Dohnányi. Asst. prof. English, dir. drama Bridgewater Coll., 1950-52; vis. instr. English Fla. So. Coll., MacDill Army Air Base, summer 1951; grad. teaching fellow humanities Fla. State U., 1953-55, 57-58; instr. English, U. Houston, University Park, 1955-59, asst. prof., 1959-62, assoc. prof., 1962-71, prof., 1971—; assoc. editor Forum, 1967, editor, 1967-82; vis. instr. English, Tex. So. U., 1961-63; vis. instr. humanities, govt. U. Tex. Dental Br., Houston, 1962-63; lectr. The Women's Inst., Houston, 1967-72; lectr. humanities series Jewish Community Center, 1972-73; originator, moderator weekly television and radio program The Arts in Houston on Stas. KUHT-TV and KUHF-FM, 1956-57, 58-63. Contbg. author: National Poetry Anthology, 1952, Panorama das Literaturas das Americas, vol. 2, 1958-60; contbr. articles to scholarly jours.; dir. Murder in the Cathedral (T.S. Elliot), U. Houston, 1965; performed in opera as Sir Edgar in Der Junge Lord (Henze), Houston Grand Opera Assn., 1967; played the title role in Aella (Chatterton), Am. premiere, U. Houston, 1970. Bd. dirs. Houston Shakespeare Soc., 1964-67; bd. dirs., program annotator Houston Chamber Orch. Soc., 1964-76; narrator Houston Symphony Orch., Houston Summer Symphony Orch., Houston Chamber Orch., U. Houston Symphony Orch., St. Stephen's Music Festival Symphony Orch., New Harmony, Ind.; narrator world premier of The Bells (Jerry McCathern), 1969, U. Houston Symphony Orch., 1969, Am. premier Symphony No. Seven, Antartica (Vaughn-Williams), Houston Symphony Orch., 1967, L'Histoire du Soldat (Stravinski), U. Houston Symphony Orch., 1957, Am. premier Babar the Elephant (Poulenc-Francais), Houston Chamber Orch., 1967, Le Roi David (Honegger), 1979, Voice of God in opera Noye's Fludde (Britten), St. Stephen's Music Festival, 1981; bd. dirs., program annotator Music Guild, Houston, 1960-67, v.p., 1963-67, adv. bd. 1967-70; bd. dirs. Contemporary Music Soc., Houston, 1958-63; mem.-at-large bd. dirs. Houston Grand Opera Guild, 1966-67; mem. repertory com. Houston Grand Opera Assn. 1967-70; bd. dirs. Houston Grand Opera, 1970-75, adv. bd., 1978-79; mem. cultural adv. com. Jewish Community Center, 1960-66; bd. dirs. Houston Friends Pub. Library, 1962-67, 73-75, 1st v.p., 1963-67; adv. mem. cultural affairs com. Houston C. of C., 1972-75; adv. bd. dirs. The Wilhelm Schole, 1980—, Buffalo Bayou Support Com., 1985-87. Recipient Master Teaching award Coll. Humanities and Fine Arts U. Houston, 1980, Favorite Prof. award Bapt. Student Union, U. of Houston, 1991. Mem. MLA, Coll. English Assn., L'Alliance Francaise, English-Speaking Union, Alumni Assn. Fla. So. Coll., Fla. State U., Am. Assn. U. Profs., South Cen. Modern Lang. Assn., Conf. Editors Learned Jours., Coll. Conf. Tchrs. English, Nat. Council Tchrs. of English, Am. Studies Assn., Phi Beta (patron), Phi Mu Alpha Sinfonia, Alpha Psi Omega, Pi Kappa Alpha, Sigma Tau Delta (cited as an Outstanding Prof. of English U. Houston chpt. 1990), Tau Kappa Alpha, Phi Kappa Phi, Caledonian Club (London). Episcopalian. Avocations: tennis, racquetball, swimming, traveling. Home: 2625 Arbuckle St Houston TX 77005-3929 Office: 3801 Cullen Blvd Houston TX 77004

PRYSTOWSKY, HARRY, physician, educator; b. Charleston, S.C., May 18, 1925; s. Moses Manning and Raye (Karesh) P.; m. Rhalda Betsy Bressler, Mar. 8, 1951; children: Michael Wayne, Ray Ellen, Jay Bressler. BS, The Citadel, 1944, DSc (hon.), 1974; MD, Med. Coll. S.C., 1948, LHD (hon.), 1975; DSc (hon.), U. Fla., 1988. Diplomate: Am. Bd. Obstetrics and Gynecology (dir., asso. examiner). Intern Johns Hopkins Hosp. and Med. Sch., 1948-49, resident, 1950-51, 53-55, instr., 1955-56, asst. prof., 1956-58; research fellow U. Cin. Sch. Medicine, 1949; research fellow physiology Yale Med. Sch., 1955-56; prof., chmn. obstetrics and gynecology U. Fla. Coll. Medicine, 1958-73; provost Milton S. Hershey Med. Center, Pa. State U., 1973-84, sr. v.p. health affairs, 1984-86; dean Coll. Medicine, 1973-86; sr. v.p. emeritus health affairs, dean emeritus Pa. State U., 1986—; bd. dirs. STV Group Inc. Contbr. articles to med. jours. Capt., M.C. U.S. Army, 1951-53. Named 1 of 10 Outstanding Young Men Am. U.S. Jaycees; recipient Alumni Centennial award Med. U. S.C. Mem. Soc. Gynecol. Investigation, Am. Assn. Obstetricians and Gynecologists, Am. Gynecol. Soc., Assn. Profs. Gynecology and Obstetrics (pres.), U. Fla. Alumni Assn. (hon.), Pa. State U. Honorary Alumnus award, Alpha Omega Alpha. Home: 8877 Collins Ave Apt 208 Surfside FL 33154-3519

PRZELOMSKI, ANASTASIA NEMENYI, retired newspaper editor; b. Cleve., Dec. 11, 1918; d. Ernest Nicholas and Anna (Ress) Nemenyi; m. Edward Adrian Przelomski, July 4, 1946 (dec. July 1995). A.B., Youngstown State U., 1939; M.Ed., U. Pitts., 1942. Tchr. Youngstown Pub. Sch., Ohio, 1939-42; reporter Vindicator, Youngstown, 1942-57, asst. city editor, 1957-73, city editor, 1973-76, mng. editor, 1976-88, ret., 1988. Named Woman of Yr., Youngstown Bus. and Profl. Women's Club, 1977, bus. category Woman of Yr., YWCA, 1986; recipient Community Service award Youngstown Fedn. Women's Clubs, 1981, Woman of Yr. award YWCA, 1983; named to Ohio Woman's Hall of Fame, 1986. Mem. AP Mng. Editors Assn., UPI Ohio Editors Assn. (bd. dirs. 1984-88), Ohio Assn. AP, Ohio Soc. Newspaper Editors, Youngstown State U. Alumni Assn. (trustee 1978-83), Catholic Collegiate Assn., Phi Kappa Phi. Republican. Roman Catholic. Avocations: travel; golf. Home: 4000 Logan Gate Rd Youngstown OH 44505-1773

PRZEMIENIECKI, JANUSZ STANISLAW, engineering executive, former government senior executive and college dean; b. Lipno, Poland, Jan. 30, 1927; came to U.S., 1961, naturalized, 1967; s. Leon and Maria (Sarnacka) P.; m. Stefania (Fiona) Rudnicka, July 17, 1954; children: Anita, Christopher. B.S., U. London, 1949, Ph.D., 1958; diploma in Aeros., Imperial Coll. Sci. and Tech., 1953; D.Sc. in Engring., U. London, 1988. Registered profl. engr., Ohio. Head structural research and devel. sect. Bristol Aircraft Ltd., Eng., 1954-61; assoc. prof. Sch. Engring., Air Force Inst. Tech., Wright-Patterson AFB, Ohio, 1961-64; prof. mechanics Sch. Engring., Air Force Inst. Tech., 1964-66, asst. dean, assoc. dean research, 1966-69, dean, 1969-89, Inst. sr. dean, 1970-95; pres. Astra Technologies, Inc., Fla., 1996—; cons. in field. Author: Theory of Matrix Structural Analysis, 1968, Mathematical Methods in Defense Analyses, 1990, Defense Analyses Software, 1991; assoc. editor: Jour. Aircraft, 1970-71; editl. bd.: Internat. Jour. Numerical Methods in Engring., 1969-75; editor: Mechanics of Structural Systems (textbook series) 1973-89; editor: Critical Technologies for Nat. Defense, 1991, Acquisition of Defense Systems, 1993; contbr. articles to profl. jours. Chmn. bd. trustees The Air Force Inst. Tech. Found., Ohio, 1987-88, trustee, 1993-95; trustee Engring. and Sci. Found. of Dayton, 1984-95. Decorated Polish Underground Army Cross, Warsaw Uprising Cross, Armed Forces medal; recipient USAF superior performance award, 1965, exceptional civilian svc. decoration, 1978, Presdl. rank of Meritorious Exec., 1981, Disting. Exec., 1982, Outstanding Engr. award Dayton Engring. and Sci. Found., 1986, Outstanding Civilian Svc. medal, 1995, Comdrs. Cross of the Polonia Restituta Order, Pres. of Poland, 1995. Fellow Royal Aeros. Soc. (Usborne Meml. prize 1959), AIAA (editor-in-chief ednl. series 1981—, Pendray medal 1992), City and Guilds of London Inst.; mem. Am. Soc. Engring. Edn., NSPE, Ohio Acad. Sci., Polish Inst. Arts and Scis., Tau Beta Pi. Home: 510 Pennyroyal Pl Venice FL 34293-7233

PRZYBYLOWICZ, EDWIN PAUL, chemical company executive, research director; b. Detroit, June 29, 1933; s. Ignacy and Antonette Olga (Krezalek) P.; m. Roberta Richardson, June 5, 1954; children: Christine, Margaret, Paul, Sue, Anne, Thomas, Catherine, James, Elizabeth, Sara, Edward. BS in Chemistry, U. Mich., 1953; PhD in Analytical Chemistry, MIT, 1956. Research chemist, lab. head. Eastman Kodak Co., Rochester, N.Y., 1956-68, asst. div. head, 1969-74, tech. asst. to dir. of research labs., 1974-75, dir.

photographic program devel., 1975-77, asst. dir. research labs., 1977-81, program mgr. copy products, 1981-83, asst. dir. research labs., 1983-85, dir. research, 1985-91; acad. assignment Nat. Bur. Standards, Washington and MIT, Cambridge, 1968-69; mem. U.S.-Polish Joint Commn. for Cooperation in Sci. and Tech., Nat. Rsch. Coun. Adv. Panel on Cen. Europe, numerous coms. in field; seminar speaker MIT Sloan Sch.; workshop facilitatator Insl. Rsch. Inst.; bd. dirs. Cytologics, more. Co-Author: Activation Analysis with Neutron Generators, 1973, Chem. Analysis, A Series of Monographs on Analytical Chemistry and Its Applications, 1973; patentee in field. Pres. Webster Bd. (N.Y.) Edn., 1965-72; bd. dirs. St. Paul's Ch. Bd., Webster, 1980-85. Eastman Kodak fellow MIT, 1955; recipient Moses Gomberg Prize in Chemistry U. Mich., 1953. Mem. Am. Chem. Soc., Nat. Acad. Engring., Indsl. Rsch. Inst., AAAS. Republican. Roman Catholic. Avocations: tennis, sailing, cross-country skiing, woodworking, geneology. Home: 1219 Crown Point Dr Webster NY 14580-9532 Office: Rochester Inst Tech Ctr for Imaging Science 54 Lomb Memorial Dr Rochester NY 14623

PRZYBYLSKI, SANDRA MARIE, speech pathologist; b. Berwyn, Ill.; d. Raymond and Julie Marie (Vocelka) Hammers; m. James Przybylski; children: Eric, Sara. BS, U. Iowa, 1968; MA, U. Ill., 1971. Cert. clin. speech pathologist; speech/lang., educable mentally retarded education, learning disabilites and elem. tchr., life, Mo. Speech, lang. pathologist LaPlata (Mo.) Sch. Dist., 1974-87, Maysville (Mo.) Sch. Dist., 1990-92, Bucklin (Mo.) Sch. Dist., 1992—. Named one of Outstanding Young Women of Am., 1980, to Disting. Svc. Registry-Speech and Hearing, 1990. Mem. Am. Speech, Lang., Hearing Assn., Autism Soc. Am., Mo. Edn. Assn., Mo. Speech Language Hearing Assn.

PSALTIS, HELEN, medical and surgical nurse; b. Rockford, Ill., Nov. 27, 1931; d. Harry and Martha (Triantafelakis) P. Diploma, St. Margaret Hosp., Hammond, Ind., 1953; BSN, DePaul U., 1961; MS in Health Edn., Purdue U., 1971; MSN, Purdue U., Calumet, Ind., 1988. RN, Ind., cert. sch. nurse, Ind. Sch. nurse Pub. Sch. City of E. Chgo., Ind.; asst. supr., staff nurse, instr. St. Catherine Hosp., East. Chgo., Ind.; instr., head nurse, staff nurse St Margaret Hosp., Hammond. Mem. ANA, Nat. League for Nursing, Sigma Theta Tau. Home: 4303 Ivy St East Chicago IN 46312-3026

PSALTIS, JOHN COSTAS, manufacturing company executive; b. Drama, Greece, Jan. 5, 1940; came to U.S., 1955; naturalized, 1961; s. Costas Dimitriou and Kay Psaltis; m. Dorothy May Coons, Sept. 18, 1961; children: Costas John, Kay Joanne. BSBA, Loyola U., Chgo., 1971; diploma corp. fin. mgmt, Harvard U., 1979, postgrad. internat. sr. mgrs. program, 1981. With Molex Inc., mfrs. electronic connectors, Lisle, Ill., 1973—; contr. internat. ops. Molex Inc., 1973-78, mem. corp. mgmt. com., 1978-91; mem. corp. exec. com., 1991—; treas. Molex Inc., 1978-79, v.p., treas., 1982-87, corp. v.p., treas., CFO, 1994—, pres. for Americas, 1982-87, treas., bd. dirs. Molex Internat. Inc., 1979—; sec.-treas., dir. Molex Far East Svcs. Ltd.; sec-treas. Molex Electronics Ltd.; sec., dir. Molex Electronics Ltd. U.K., Molex Euorpean Svcs. Ltd.; bd. dirs. Molex Japan, Molex Singapore Pte. Ltd., Molex Italia Spa, Molex Korea Co. Ltd., Molex Malaysia Ltd.; auditor Touche Ross & Co., 1971-72, sr. auditor, 1972-73. Mem. adv. com. Inst. for Internat. Mktg., Ill. Benedictine Coll. With USAR, 1958-66. Mem. Fin. Execs. Inst., Am. Mgmt. Assn. (fin. coun., briefing adv. bd.), Leading CFO's, Strategic Planning Inst., Pers. Inventory Mgmt. Sys. (coun. on value for 90's), Chicagoland C. of C. (bd. dirs. 1989—, exec. com., v.p. world trade div. 1994, past chmn. fin. and audit com.). Office: 2222 Wellington Ave Lisle IL 60532-3820

PSATHAS, GEORGE, sociologist, educator; b. New Haven, Feb. 22, 1929; s. Milton Emanuel and Melpa (Joannides) P.; m. Irma M. Amatruda, Feb. 5, 1951; children: Christine Ann, David George, Anthony Paul. BA, Yale U., 1950; MA, U. Mich., 1951; PhD, Yale U., 1956; diploma, N.E. Sch. Photography, 1979. Instr. to asst. prof. Ind. U., Bloomington, 1955-63; lectr. Harvard U., Cambridge, Mass., 1961-62; assoc. prof. Washington U., St. Louis, 1963-68, rsch. assoc. Social Sci. Inst., 1963-68; program dir. community mental health tng. program NIMH/Washington U., 1966-68; prof. sociology Boston U., 1968—, acting chair, 1968-69; assoc. chair Boston U., Mass., 1969-70, 76-78, chair, 1984-85; dir. Ctr. for Applied Social Sci. Boston U., 1970-73, co-dir. post-doctoral rsch. tng. program in sociology and mental health Nat. Inst. Mental Health, 1976-79; co-dir. Sociology and Health Svcs. Rsch. Tng. Program NCHSR and Boston (Mass.) U., 1970-78; vis. lectr. MRC Med. Sociology-U. Aberdeen, Scotland, 1974, U. Colo., 1963, U. London, 1973; vis. prof. Panteios Sch. Polit. Sci., Athens, 1982, Internat. U. Japan, Yamato-Machi, 1988, Doshisha U., Kyoto, Japan, 1989; Brit. Acad. vis. prof. U. Manchester, Eng., 1996; guest prof. Inst. for Human Scis., Vienna, 1996; chair Mass. Interdisciplinary Discourse Analysis seminar, 1989-95; cons. NSF, 1978, 79, 89, 94, 95, Rsch. Coun. Can., 1983-84, Social Sci. Rsch. Coun. Eng., 1981-82; active Ctr. Advanced Rsch. in Phenomenology, 1980—; presenter 70 presentations at profl. and scholarly socs. Editor: Phenomenological Sociology, 1973, Everyday Language, 1979, Interaction Competence, 1990, Situated Order, 1994; editor-in-chief: Human Studies, Boston, 1978—; assoc. editor Social Problems, 1958-61, Visual Sociology, 1993—; author: Student Nurse in Diploma School of Nursing, 1968, Phenomenology & Sociology, 1989, Conversation Analysis, 1994; cons. editor Temple Univ. Press, Kluwer Academic Pubs., Qualitative Sociology; author 11 book chpts.; contbr. numerous articles to profl. jours. Cons. Human Rels. Lab., Boston, Bethel, St. Louis, 1967, 69, Sch. for the Blind, Kallithea, Athens, Greece, 1982; tng. dirs. com. Nat. Ctr. for Health Svcs. Rsch., Washington, 1971-73; bd. dirs. Carroll Ctr. for the Blind, Newton, Mass., 1974-79. Named Post-Doctoral fellow NIMH Dept. Social Rels., Harvard U., Cambridge, 1961-62; recipient Sci. Faculty Devel. award NSF, 1978-79, Fulbright grant Fulbright Commn., Greece and Turkey, 1982. Mem. AAUP (sec. 1977-79, v.p. Boston U. chpt. 1979-80), Am. Sociol. Assn., Ea. Sociol. Assn., Internat. Visual Sociology Assn., Internat. Inst. for Ethnomethodology (chair 1990—), Soc. for Phenomenology & Existential Philosophy, Soc. for Phenomenology and Human Scis. (co-chair 1981-85, exec. com. 1993—), Soc. Study Social Problems (treas., bus. mgr. 1959-61). Home: 150 Mt Vernon St Newtonville MA 02160 Office: Sociology Dept Boston Univ Boston MA 02215

PSOMIADES, HARRY JOHN, political science educator; b. Boston, Sept. 8, 1928; s. John and Koula (Yalmanides) P.; m. Dorothy Smith, Aug. 18, 1962 (dec. Aug. 27, 1984); children—Kathy Alexis, Christine Anne. B.A., Boston U., 1953; M.Internat. Affairs, Columbia U., 1955; cert., Middle East Inst., 1956, Ph.D. (Ford Found. fellow), 1962; Litt.D. (hon.), Holy Cross/Hellenic Coll., 1985. Lectr. govt. Columbia U., 1959-65, asst. dean Grad. Sch. Internat. Affairs, 1959-65, dir. Carnegie Endowment Fellowships in Diplomacy, 1959-71; assoc. prof. polit. sci. Queens Coll., City U. N.Y., 1965-69, prof., 1970—, chmn. dept. polit. sci., 1967-71, dep. exec. officer Ph.D. program in polit. sci., 1975-76, program dir. seminar on the modern Greek state, 1976—; dir. Center Byzantine and Modern Greek Studies, 1976—; cons. faculty U.S. Army Command and Gen. Staff Coll., 1968-86; U.S. Dept. State Fgn. Service Inst., 1968-71; mem. screening com. Fgn. Area Fellowships Program for Asia and Middle East Joint Com., Social Sci. Research Council and Am. Council Learned Socs., 1967-69. Author: Greece and Turkey: Mutual Economic Interests, 1964, (with Thomas Spelios) A Pictorial History of the Greeks, 1967, The Eastern Question: The Last Phase, 1968, (with T.A. Couloumbis) Foreign Interference in Greek Politics: An Historical Perspective, 1976, (with A. Scourby) The Greek American Community in Transition, 1982, (with R.S. Orfanos) Education and Greek Americans: Process and Prospects, 1987, (with S. Thomadakes) Greece, The New Europe and the Changing International Order, 1993; editor: Jour. Modern Hellenism, 1984—; contbr. articles to profl. jours. Served with U.S. Army, 1946-50; to col. USAR, 1950-83. Hon. fellow Soc. Macedonian Studies, Thessaloniki, Greece, 1970—. Fellow Middle East Studies Assn. N.Am.; mem. Am. Polit. Sci. Assn., Middle East Inst., Modern Greek Studies Assn. (mem. exec. com. 1972-76), Phi Beta Kappa. Greek Orthodox. Home: 440 Riverside Dr New York NY 10027-6828 Office: Dept Polit Sci Queens Coll Flushing NY 11367

PSUTY, NORBERT PHILLIP, marine sciences educator; b. Hamtramck, Mich., June 13, 1937; s. Phillip and Jessie (Proszykowski) P.; m. Sylvia Helen Zurinsky, June 13, 1959; children: Eric Anthony, Scott Patrick, Ross Phillip. BS, Wayne State U., 1959; MS, Miami U., Oxford, Ohio, 1960; PhD, La. State U., 1966. Rsch. assoc. Coastal Studies Inst., La. State U., Baton Rouge, 1962-64; instr. dept. geography and dept. geology U. Miami, Coral Gables, Fla., 1964-65; asst. prof. geography U. Wis., Madison, 1965-69; assoc. prof. geography and geol. scis. Rutgers U., New Brunswick, N.J., 1969-73, prof., 1973—, chmn. dept. marine and coastal scis., 1991—, dir. Marine Scis. Ctr., 1972-76, dir. Ctr. for Coastal and Environ. Studies, 1976-90; assoc. dir. Inst. Marine and Coastal Scis., New Brunswick, N.J., 1990—; mem. sci. com. Thalassas, Vigo, Spain, 1985—. Co-author: Living with the New Jersey Shore, 1986, Coastal Dunes, 1990; mem. editorial bd Coastal Mgmt., 1981—, Jour. Coastal Rsch., 1987—; contbr. numerous articles to scholarly jours., chpts. to books, monographs. Mem. Water Policy Bd., East Brunswick, N.J., 1981-83, N.J. Shoreline Adv. Bd., Trenton, 1984-86; chmn. N.J. Gov.'s Sea Level Rise Com., Trenton, 1987-90; mem. N.J. State Beach Erosion Commn., 1994—; referee U.S. Volleyball Assn. Recipient Disting. Pub. Svc. award Pres. of Rutgers U. 1988; numerous grants including NSF, Nat. Park Svc., EPA, Office Naval Rsch., Nat. Sea Grant Program, NOAA, 1961—. Mem. AAAS, Assn. Am. Geographers (Honors award 1993), Coastal Soc. (pres. 1980-82), Internat. Geog. Union (vice chair commn. on coastal environ. 1988-92, chmn. commn. on coastal systems, 1992-96, editor newsletter 1984-96), N.J. Acad. Sci. (pres. 1982). Avocations: gardening, reading. Office: Rutgers U Inst Marine & Coastal Scis Cook Campus New Brunswick NJ 08903

PTAK, FRANK S., manufacturing executive; b. Chgo., Apr. 23, 1943; s. Frank J. and Stella R. (Los) P.; m. Karen M. Novoselsky, May 2, 1971; children: Jeffrey B., Jacquelyn F., Russell E. BS, De Paul U., 1965. CPA, Ill. Sr. auditor Arthur Young & Co., Chgo., 1965-69; sr. rsch. cons. Kemper Fin. Svcs., Chgo., 1969-71; asst. sec., mgr. acquisitions Sara Lee Corp., Chgo., 1971-73, asst. treas., 1973-74, asst. to chmn., 1974, v.p. planning, 1974-75; bus. devel. mgr. ITW Conex, Des Plaines, Ill., 1975-77; mktg. mgr. ITW Shakeproof, Elgin, Ill., 1977-78, group pres., 1977-78; group pres. ITW Metal Components Cos., Glenview, Ill., 1978-91; exec. v.p. Global Automotive Components ITW Corp., Glenview, 1991—. Patentee in field. Mem. AICPA, Assn. Corp. Growth, ITW Patent Soc. Jewish. Home: 849 Edgewood Ct Highland Park IL 60035-3714 Office: ITW Corp 3600 W Lake Ave Glenview IL 60025-1215

PTAK, JOHN ANTHONY, talent agent; b. San Diego, Sept. 23, 1942; s. John and Doris Elizabeth P.; m. Margaret Elizabeth Black, May 21, 1981; 1 child, Hillary Elizabeth. BA, UCLA, 1967. Theatre mgr., booker Walter Reade Orgn., Beverly Hills, Calif., 1967-69; adminstrv. exec. Am. Film Inst., Beverly Hills, 1968-70; talent agent Internat. Famous Agy. (now ICM), L.A., 1971-75, William Morris Agy., Beverly Hills, 1976-91, Creative Artists Agy., Beverly Hills, 1991—; cons. Nat. Endowment for Arts, Washington, 1980—; co-chmn. Am. Film Inst. Ctr. for Film & Video Preservation, L.A., 1991—; mem. Nat. Film Preservation Bd., Washington, 1992—. Avocations: tennis, travel. Office: Creative Artists Agy 9830 Wilshire Blvd Beverly Hills CA 90212-1804

PTASHNE, MARK STEVEN, biochemistry educator; b. Chgo., June 5, 1940; s. Fred and Mildred P. BA, Reed Coll., 1961; PhD, Harvard U., 1968. Lectr. biochemistry Harvard U., Cambridge, Mass., 1968-71, prof., 1971—, chmn. dept. biochemistry and molecular biology, 1980-83, Herchel Smith prof. of molecular biology, 1993—; Feodor Lynen lectr. U. Miami, Fla., 1988. Author: A Genetic Switch, 1986; contbr. numerous articles to sci. jours. Recipient Eli Lilly award, 1975, prix. Chalres-Leopold Mayer Acad. des Scis., Inst. de France, 1977, Louisa Gross Horwitz prize Bd. Trustees Columbia U., 1985, Gairdner Found. Internat. award, 1985; co-recipient Ledle award Harvard U., 1986, GM Sloan prize, 1990. Fellow N.Y. Acad. Sci., Am. Acad. Sci.; mem. NAS, Fedn. Am. Scis. (bd. sponsors 1981). Avocations: opera, classical music. Office: Harvard U Dept Molecular & Cellular Biology 7 Divinity Ave Cambridge MA 02138

PTASZEK, EDWARD GERALD, JR., lawyer; b. Cleve., Sept. 29, 1950; s. Edward Gerald and Roseanne (Venetta) P. BS in Fin., Bowling Green U., 1972; JD, Case Western Res. U., 1978. Bar: Ohio 1978, U.S. Dist. Ct. (no. dist.) Ohio, U.S. Tax Ct. Assoc. Baker & Hostetler, Cleve., 1978-85, ptnr., 1985—. Mem. ABA, Cleve. Bar Assn., Columbus Bar Assn., Lakewood Club, Club at Social Ctr. Office: Baker & Hostetler 3200 National City Ctr 1900 E 9th St Cleveland OH 44114-3401*

PTASZKOWSKI, STANLEY EDWARD, JR., civil, structural engineer; b. N.Y.C., June 11, 1943; s. Stanley Edward and Elsie Helena (Heihs) P. AAS, Acad. Aeronautics, Flushing, N.Y., 1967; BS in Civil Engring., U. Mo., 1975. Registered profl. engr., Tex., profl. sanitarian, Tex. Engr. Brown & Root, Inc., Houston, Tex., 1975-79; sr. engr. Marathon Marine Engring. Co., Houston, 1979-84, Gen. Dynamics, Ft. Worth, 1984-91, Bridgefarmer & Assocs., Dallas, 1991-93; prin. Pasko Consultants, Arlington, Tex., 1993—; sr. site constrn. engr. Raytheon Svc. Co., Ft. Worth, 1994—. Mem. AIAA (sr.), Nat. Soc. Profl. Engrs., Tex. Soc. Profl. Engrs., Soc. Profl. Bldg. Designers (cons.). Lutheran. Avocations: lic. pvt. pilot, golf, racquet ball. Home: 2002 Park Hill Dr Arlington TX 76012

PUCCIO, JOHN, hospital administrator; b. 1946. With Peat, Marwick, Mitchell & Co., N.Y.C., 1970-76; v.p. fin. Bklyn. Hosp. Ctr., 1976—. Office: Bklyn Hosp Ctr 121 Dekalb Ave Brooklyn NY 11201-5425*

PUCEL, ROBERT ALBIN, electronics research engineer; b. Ely, Minn., Dec. 27, 1926; s. Joseph and Theresa (Francel) P.; m. Catherine Ann Silva, June 30, 1952; children: Robert W., James J., Valerie A., Marc R., David J. BS, MIT, 1951, MS, 1951, DSc, 1955. With rsch. div. Research div. Raytheon Co., Lexington, Mass., 1955-93; staff mem. microwave tube group Research div. Raytheon Co., 1951-55, solid state physics group, 1955-65, project mgr. microwave semicondr. group, 1965-70, cons. to microwave semicondr. group, 1970-74, cons. scientist semicondr. group, 1974-93; pres. RCP Cons., Needham, Mass., 1994—; lectr. on monolithic microwave integrated circuits. Editor: Monolithic Microwave Integrated Circuits, 1985; contbg. author: Advances in Electronics and Electron Physics, vol. 38, 1975, Gallium Arsenide Technology, 1985. Served with USNR, 1945-46. Recipient Excellence in Technology award Raytheon, 1988. Fellow IEEE (life); mem. Microwave Theory and Techniques Soc. (editorial rev. bd., nat. lectr. 1980-81, Microwave prize 1976, Microwave Career award 1990), Nat. Acad. Engring., Electron Devices Soc. Inventor low-distortion FET; co-inventor Spacistor, Overlay FET. Office: RCP Cons 427 South St Needham MA 02192-2761

PUCHTA, CHARLES GEORGE, lawyer; b. Cin., Feb. 19, 1918; s. Charles George and Kate (Carlisle) P.; m. Jean Geary, Dec. 12, 1959; children: Polly Carlisle Puchta Wells, Charles George, Jr. AB, U. Cin., 1940, LLD, 1943. Bar: Ohio 1943, Ky. 1964, U.S. Dist. Ct. (so. dist.) Ohio 1944, U.S. Ct. Appeals (6th cir.) 1960. Assoc. Frost & Jacobs, Cin., 1943-53, ptnr., 1953-83, chmn. exec. com., 1978-83, sr. ptnr., 1983—. Pres. Cin. C. of C., 1978, C. of C. Found., 1978; pres. Cin. Nature Ctr., 1979-81, chmn., 1981-84; trustee U. Cin. Endowment Fund, 1979—; trustee U. Cin. Found., 1978-85, emeritus, 1989—, Greater Cin. Ctr. for Econ. Edn., 1981-93, Cin. Mus. Natural History, 1988-90, Jewish Hosp., 1992-95; chmn. Bus. Mobilized for Xavier campaign, 1976; chmn. exec. com. Hebrew Union Coll. Assoc. Ann. Tribute Dinner, 1988-89; former trustee, sec. Cin. Country Day Sch.; former mem., pres., bd. dirs. Bradley U. Parents Assn.; mem. adv. bd. Juvenile Diabetes Found., 1982—. Mem. ABA, Ohio Bar Assn., Ky. Bar Assn., Cin. Bar Assn., Cin. Country Club, Queen City Club, Comml. Club (sec. 1983-85), Commonwealth Club (v.p. 1985-86), Queen City Optimists Club (past pres.). Republican. Methodist. Home: 2444 Madison Rd Apt 1402 Cincinnati OH 45208-1277 Office: Frost & Jacobs 2500 PNC Ctr 201 E 5th St Cincinnati OH 45202-4117

PUCIE, CHARLES R., JR., public affairs executive; b. Asheville, N.C., Oct. 8, 1943. BSFS in Internat. Affairs, Georgetown U., 1965. Fin. analyst Chase Manhattan Bank, 1969-70; account exec. Doremus, 1970-73, v.p., 1973-80; sr. v.p., regional mgr. Doremus, Washington, 1980-85; sr. v.p., group dir., internat. counseling Hill and Knowlton, 1986-90, exec. v.p., 1991; mng. dir., sr. prin. Capitoline Internat. Group, Washington, 1991—; chmn., CEO C.I.H. Ltd., 1992—; CEO Capitoline/MS&L, G.P., 1995—. Capt. aviator U.S. Army, 1966-69, Vietnam. Office: Capitoline/MS&L GP 1615 NW 1150 # L Washington DC 20036

PUCK, THEODORE THOMAS, geneticist, biophysicist, educator; b. Chgo., Sept. 24, 1916; s. Joseph and Bessie (Shapiro) Puckowitz; m. Mary Hill, Apr. 17, 1946; children: Stirling, Jennifer, Laurel. B.S., U. Chgo., 1937, Ph.D., 1940. Mem. commn. airborne infections Office Surgeon Gen., Army Epidemiol. Bd., 1944-46; asst. prof. depts. medicine and biochemistry U. Chgo., 1945-47; sr. fellow Am. Cancer Soc., Calif. Inst. Tech., Pasadena, 1947-48; prof. biophysics U. Colo. Med. Sch., 1948—, chmn. dept., 1948-67, disting. prof., 1986—; dir. Eleanor Roosevelt Inst. Cancer Research, 1962-95; Disting. research prof. Am. Cancer Soc., 1966—; nat. lectr. Sigma Xi, 1975-76. Author: The Mammalian Cell as a Microorganism: Genetic and Biochemical Studies in Vitro, 1972. Mem. Commn. on Physicians for the Future. Recipient Albert Lasker award, 1958, Borden award med. rsch., 1959, Louisa Gross Horwitz prize, 1973, Gordon Wilson medal Am. Clin. and Climatol. Assn., 1977, award Environ. Mutagen Soc., 1981, E.B. Wilson medal Am. Soc. Cell Biology, 1984, Bonfils-Stanton award in sci., 1984, U. Colo. Disting. Prof. award, 1987, Henry M. Porter medal, 1992; named to The Colo. 100, Historic Denver, 1992; Heritage Found. scholar, 1983; Phi Beta Kappa scholar, 1985. Fellow Am. Acad. Arts and Scis.; mem. Am. Chem. Soc., Soc. Exptl. Biology and Medicine, AAAS (Phi Beta Kappa award and lectr. 1983), Am. Assn. Immunologists, Radiation Research Soc., Biophys. Soc., Genetics Soc. Am., Nat. Acad. Sci., Tissue Culture Assn. (Hon. award 1987), Paideia Group, Santa Fe Inst. Sci. Bd., Phi Beta Kappa, Sigma Xi. Achievements include pioneering contributions to establishment of somatic cell approaches to mammalian cell genetics, to the identification and classification of the human chromosomes; measurement of mutation in mammalian cells; demonstration of the reverse transformation reaction and the genome exposure defect in cancer; development of quantitative approaches to mammalian cell radiobiology. Office: Eleanor Roosevelt Inst Cancer Rsch 1899 Gaylord St Denver CO 80206-1210 *Our age is threatened by distorted emphasis on power, material wealth, and competitiveness, and by an explosive increase in population which exceeds our traditional regulative capacities. But it also holds promise for new and profound understanding of ourselves - of our basic human biological intellectual and emotional needs. There is room for hope.*

PUCKET, SUSAN, newspaper editor. Exec. food editor features desk Atlanta Jour. and Constn. Office: Atlanta Jour and Constn 72 Marietta St NW Atlanta GA 30303-2804

PUCKETT, ALLEN WEARE, health care information systems executive; b. Pasadena, Calif., Mar. 17, 1942; s. Allen Emerson Puckett and Betty Jane (Howlett) Ward; m. Joan Adrienne Roth, Apr. 10, 1965 (div. 1980); children: Glenn A., Tod A.; m. Laura Treadgold, July 10, 1992. BS, U. Calif., Berkeley, 1963; JD, Harvard U., 1966. Bar: Calif. 1966. Prin. McKinsey & Co., San Francisco, 1966-78; pres. Atman Corp., San Francisco, 1979-83; v.p. VWR Sci., San Francisco, 1980-83, Univar Corp., Seattle, 1984-85; sr. v.p. fin. VWR Corp., Seattle, 1986-90, Momentum Distbn. Inc., Seattle, 1990; v.p. cen. ops. Eldec Corp., Lynnwood, 1990-92; pres., CEO Phycom Corp., 1993—. Recipient Nathan Burkan prize ASCAP, 1966. Mem. Wash. Athletic Club. Democrat. Avocations: skiing, scuba diving, music. Home: 1624 38th Ave E Seattle WA 98112-3134 Office: Phycom Corp 3380-146th Pl SE Bellevue WA 98007

PUCKETT, C. LIN, plastic surgeon, educator; b. Burlington, N.C., Oct. 19, 1940; s. Harry W. and Lula C. Puckett; m. Florence Elizabeth Loy, June 18, 1961 (div. 1976); children: Loy C., Lisa A., Leslie A.; m. Patricia Louise Wells, June 17, 1984 (div. 1994); 1 child, Henry James; m. Theresa G. Teel, Nov. 24, 1995. MD, Bowman Gray Sch. Medicine, 1966. Assoc. in surgery Duke U. Med. Ctr., Durham, N.C., 1971-73; assoc. prof., head div. plastic surgery U. Mo. Med. Ctr., Columbia, 1976-81; prof., head attending plastic surgeon U. Mo. Med. Ctr., Truman VA Hosp., Columbia, 1982—. Contbr. numerous articles to profl. jours. Fellow ACS (gov. 1992); mem. AMA, Am. Assn. Hand Surgery (bd. dirs. 1982-84, chmn. nominating com. 1985, v.p. 1987, pres.-elect 1988, pres. 1988—), Am. Assn. Plastic Surgeons (trustee 1995), Am. Cleft Palate Assn., Am. Soc. Plastic and Reconstructive Surgeons Inc. (bd. dirs. 1985—, asst. sec. 1988, trustee 1990, chmn. bd. trustees 1992, parlamentarian 1993, historian 1994, sec. 1995), Am. Bd. Plastic Surgery (cert., bd. dirs. 1988-94, chmn. 1993-94), Am. Soc. Surgery of the Hand, Am. Trauma Soc., Internat. Microsurg. Soc., Mo. Chpt. ACS, Plastic Surgery Rsch. Coun., So. Med. Assn., Assn. Acad. Chmn. Plastic Surgery (bd. dirs. 1985—, pres. 1987-88), Sigma Xi, Alpha Omega Alpha. Republican. Avocation: breeding Quarter horses, angus cattle. Home: RR 1 Box 146 Ashland MO 65010-9801 Office: U Mo Med Ctr Dept Plastic Surgery 1 Hospital Dr # M349 Columbia MO 65201-5276

PUCKETT, ELIZABETH ANN, law librarian, law educator; b. Evansville, Ind., Nov. 10, 1943; d. Buell Charles and Lula Ruth (Gray) P.; m. Joel E. Hendricks, June 1, 1964 (div. June 1973); 1 child, Andrew Charles; m. Thomas A. Wilson, July 19, 1985. BS in Edn., Eastern Ill. U., 1964; JD, U. Ill., 1977, MS in L.S., 1977. Bar: Kans. 1978, Ill. 1979. Acquisitions/reader services librarian U. Kans. Law Library, Lawrence, 1978-79; asst. reader services librarian So. Ill. U. Law Library, Carbondale, 1979-81, reader services librarian, 1981-83; assoc. dir. Northwestern U. Law Library, Chgo., 1983-86, co-acting dir., 1986-87; dir./assoc. prof. South Tex. Coll. Law Library, Houston, 1987-89; dir./prof. South Tex. Coll. Law Libr., Houston, 1990-94, U. Ga. Law Libr., Athens, 1994—. Co-author: Evaluation of System-Provided Library Services to State Correctional Centers in Illinois, 1983; co-editor Uniform Commercial Code: Confidential Drafts, 1993. Mem. ABA, Am. Assn. Law Librs. (mem. exec. bd. 1993-96). Avocations: reading, antiques. Office: U Georgia Law Libr Athens GA 30602-6018

PUCKETT, HOYLE BROOKS, agricultural engineer, research scientist, consultant; b. Jesup, Ga., Oct. 15, 1925; s. Lawrence Parham and Martha Elizabeth (Mizell) P.; m. Faye Eloise Bowden, June 22, 1945; children: Carol P. Keeley, Hoyle B. Jr., Kristina P. Berbaum. BS in Agrl. Engring., U. Ga., 1948; MS in Agrl. Engring., Mich. State U., 1949; student, Ga. Inst. Tech., 1964-65. reg. profl. engr. Ill. Rsch. engr. GS 7-9 USDA/ARS, Oxford, N.C., 1949-55; res. engr. GS 11-13 USDA/ARS, Urbana, Ill., 1955-68, res. ldr. GS 14-15, 1968-85; ret., 1985; engring. cons. pvt. practice, Champaign, Ill., 1985—. Fellow Am. Soc. Agrl. Engrs.; mem. Exchange Club of Urbana. Home: 407 W University Ave Apt 104 Champaign IL 61820-3944

PUCKETT, KIRBY, professional baseball player; b. Chgo., Mar. 14, 1961; s. Catherine Puckett; m. Tonya Hudson; children: Catherine, Kirby, Jr. Student, Bradley U., Ill., Triton Coll., Ill. Baseball player Minnesota Twins, Mpls., 1982—. Author: I Love This Game!, 1993, Be The Best You Can Be, 1993. Founder, benefactor Kirby Puckett Eight-Ball Invitational to benefit Children's Heart Fund, United Way. Recipient All-Star Most Valuable Player award, 1993, Gold Glove award, 1986-89, 1991-92, Silver Slugger award, 1986-89, 92, 94, All-Star team, 1986-94; named to Sporting News All-Star Team, 1986-89, 92, 94, Am. League All-Star Team, 1986-89, Am. League Batting Champion, 1989, Minn. Twins Most Valuable Player 1985, 86, 88, 89, 92; named Calif. League Player of the Yr., 1983, Most Valuable Player, Am. League Championship Series, 1991, Best Hitter and Most Exciting Player, Baseball America, 1992; inducted Triton Coll. Hall of Fame, 1993. Mem. Alexis de Tocqueville Soc. Achievements include: led Major League in hits 1988-92, highest batting average among active batters 1988-92, seasons with 200 or more hits: 1986-89, 92. Office: Minnesota Twins Hubert H Humphrey Metrodome 501 Chicago Ave Minneapolis MN 55415-1517*

PUCKETT, RICHARD EDWARD, artist, consultant, retired recreation executive; b. Klamath Falls, Oreg., Sept. 9, 1932; s. Vernon Elijah and Leona Belle (Clevenger) P.; m. Velma Faye Hamrick, Apr. 14, 1957 (dec. 1985); children: Katherine Michelle Briggs, Deborah Alison Bolinger, Susan Lin Rowland, Gregory Richard. Student So. Oreg. Coll. Edn., 1951-56, Lake Forest Coll., 1957-58; Hartnell Jr. Coll., 1960-70; B.A., U. San Francisco, 1978. Asst. arts and crafts dir., Fort Leonard Wood, Mo., 1956-57; arts and crafts dir., asst. spl. services officer, mus. dir., Fort Sheridan, Ill., 1957-59; arts and crafts dir., Fort Irwin, Calif., 1959-60, Fort Ord, Calif., 1960-86; dir. arts and crafts br. Art Gallery, Arts and Crafts Center Materials Sales Store, 1960; opening dir. Presidio of Monterey Army Mus., 1968; dir. Model Army Arts and Crafts Program. Recipient First Place, Dept. Army and U.S. Army Forces Command awards for programming and publicity, 1979-81, 83-85, 1st and 3d place sculpture awards Monterey County Fair Fine Arts Exhibit, 1979, Comdrs. medal for civilian svcs., 1986, numerous other awards,

Golden Acad. award, Internat. Man of Yr. award, 1991-92. Mem. Am. Craftsman Assn. (former), Glass Arts Soc., Monterey Peninsula Art Assn., Salinas Fine Arts Assn., Rogue Valley Art Assn., Am. Park and Recreation Soc. One-man shows: Seaside City Hall, 1975, Fort Ord Arts and Crafts Center Gallery, 1967, 73, 79, 81, 84, 86, Presidio of Monterey Art Gallery, 1979, Rogue Valley Art Assn.; Glass on Holiday, Gatlinburg, Tenn., 1981, 82; exhibitions in Mo., Ill., and pvt. collections; designed and opened first Ft. Sheridan Army Mus., Presidio of Monterey Mus. Home: 110 Ashland Ave Medford OR 97504-7523 also: 1152 Jean Ave Salinas CA 93905

PUCKETT, ROBERT HUGH, political scientist, educator; b. Kansas City, Mo., July 16, 1935; s. John William and Marjorie (Shirlaw) P.; m. Barbara Ann Chandley, Dec. 23, 1964; 1 child, Sarah Anne. BA, De Pauw U., 1957; MA, U. Chgo., 1958, PhD, 1961. Asst. prof. polit. sci. Mary Washington Coll., Fredericksburg, Va., 1961-63; vis. scholar, postdoctoral fellow social sci. rsch. coun. MIT, Cambridge, 1963-64; asst. prof. govt. and fgn. affairs U. Va., Charlottesville, 1964-66; asst. prof. social sci. Mich. State U., East Lansing, 1966-68; prof. polit. sci. Ind. State U., Terre Haute, 1968—; cons. in field.; cons. Rand Corp., 1962, U.S. Army, 1985-89, U.S. Dept. Edn., 1987-88, USN, 1990-95; del. Ind. Gov.'s Conf. on Librs. and Info. Svcs., 1990. Author: America Faces the World: Isolationist Ideology in American Foreign Policy, 1972, (with Oscar H. Rechtschaffer) Reflections on Space, 1964, The United States and Northeast Asia, 1993; contbr. articles to polit. sci. jours. Bd. dirs. So. Ind. Health Sys. Agy., 1978-81; adv. com. U.S. Army Command and Gen. Staff Coll., 1985-89; mem. Pres.'s Commn. on White House Fellowships, 1990-93; bd. advisors to pres. Naval War Coll., 1990-95. Mem. DePauw U. Alumni Assn. (pres. chpt. 1973-74), Am. Polit. Sci. Assn., Indpls. Com. Fgn. Rels., Midwest Polit. Sci. Assn., Internat. Studies Assn., Ind. Consortium for Security Studies, Ind. Acad. Social Scis., Ind. Polit. Sci. Assn. (v.p. 1977-79), Coun. Fgn. Rels., Ind. Coun. on World Affairs, Inter-Univ. Seminar on Armed Forces and Soc., Japan-Am. Soc. Ind., Nat. Strategy Forum, Econ. Club Indpls., Columbia Club, MVP Club (Terre Haute), Phi Beta Kappa, Sigma Iota Rho, Phi Eta Sigma, Pi Sigma Alpha, Pi Kappa Alpha, Alpha Phi Omega. Mem. DePauw U. Alumni Assn. (pres. chpt. 1973-74), Am. Polit. Sci. Assn., Indpls. Com. Fgn. Rels., Midwest Polit. Sci. Assn., Internat. Studies Assn., Ind. Consortium for Security Studies, Ind. Acad. Social Scis., Ind. Polit. Sci. Assn. (v.p. 1977-79), Coun. Fgn. Rels., Ind. Coun. on World Affairs, Inter-Univ. Seminar on Armed Forces and Soc., Japan-Am. Soc. Ind., Nat. Strategy Forum, Econ. Club Indpls., Columbia Club (Indpls.), MVP Club (Terre Haute), Phi Bata Kappa, Sigma Iota Rho, Phi Eta Sigma, Pi Sigma Alpha, Pi Kappa Alpha, Alpha Phi Omega. Home: 122 Marigold Dr Terre Haute IN 47803-1538 Office: Dept Polit Sci Ind State U Terre Haute IN 47809

PUCKETTE, STEPHEN ELLIOTT, mathematics educator, mathematician; b. Ridgewood, N.J., Oct. 18, 1927; s. Charles McDonald and Elizabeth Argyle (Gettys) P.; m. Upshur Smith, June 22, 1957; children: Robert B. E., Miller S., Emily E., Charles McD., Charlotte Elliott. BS, U. of the South, 1949; MS, Yale U., 1950, MA, 1951, PhD, 1957. Asst. prof. math. U. of the South, Sewanee, Tenn., 1956-64; vis. asst. prof. math. U. Ga., Athens, 1962-63; assoc. prof. math. U. Ky., Lexington, 1966-69; dean of arts and scis., prof. U. of the South, Sewanee, Tenn., 1969-79; prof. associé U. Nationale, Cote d'Ivoire, Côté d'Ivoire, Ivory Coast, 1979-80; prof. math. U. of the South, Sewanee, Tenn., 1980-93, prof. emeritus, 1993—; vis. prof. U. N.C., Chapel Hill, 1986-87; vis. lectr. Math. Assn. Am., Washington DC, 1967-77. NSF faculty fellow, Yale U., 1964-65; Fulbright scholar (France), 1952-53; Fulbright lectr. (Ivory Coast), 1979-80. Mem. Am. Math. Soc., Societé Mathématique de France, Deutsche Mathematiker-Vereinigung, London Math. Soc. Democrat. Episcopalian. Home: Morgan's Steep Sewanee TN 37375 Office: Univ of the South Math Dept Sewanee TN 37375

PUCKO, DIANE BOWLES, public relations executive; b. Wyndotte, Mich., Aug. 15, 1940; d. Mervin Arthur and Bernice Letitia (Shelly) Bowles; m. Raymond J. Pucko, May 22, 1965; children: Todd Anthony, Gregory Bowles. BA in Sociology, Bucknell U., Lewisburg, Pa., 1962. Accredited in pub. rels. Asst. to pub. rels. dir. Edward C. Michener Assocs., Inc., Harrisburg, Pa., 1962-65; advt./pub. rels. coord. Superior Switchboard & Devices, Canton, Ohio, 1965-66; editorial dir. women's svc. Hutchins Advt. Co., Inc., Rochester, N.Y., 1966-71; pres. Editorial Communications, Rochester and Elyria, Ohio, 1971-77; mgr. advt. and sales promotion Tappan Air Conditioning, Elyria, 1977-80; mgr. pub. affairs Kaiser Permanente Med. Care Program, Cleve., 1980-85; corp. dir. pub. affairs Keystone Health Plans, Inc., Camp Hill, Pa., 1985-86; v.p., dir. client planning Young-Liggett-Stashower, Cleve., 1986; v.p., dir. pub. rels. Marcus Pub. Rels., Cleve., 1987-91; sr. v.p. Proconsul, Cleve., 1991-95, also bd. dirs.; sr. ptnr. pub. rels. Poppe Tyson, Cleve., 1995—; mgr., role model Women in Mgmt. Field Placement program, Cleve. State U., 1983—; prof. advisor, pub. rels. adv. bd. Pub. Rels. Student Soc. Am., Kent State U., 1988—. Bd. trustees, mem. exec. com., chmn. pub. rels. adv. com. Ronald MacDonald House of Cleve., 1993—; bd. dirs., chmn. pub. rels. com. Assn. Retarded Citizens, Cleve., 1987-91. Recipient Woman Profl. Excellence award YMCA, 1984, MacEachern award Acad. Hosp. Pub. Rels., 1985, Bell Ringer award Cmty. Rels. Report, 1985, Bronze Quill Excellence award Internat. Assn. Bus. Communicators, 1992, 93, Cleve. Comms. award Women in Comms. Internat., 1993, 95, Tower award Bus./Profl. Advt. Assn., 1993, 95, Creativity in Pub. Rels. award, 1994, Silver Screen award U.S. Internat. Film & Video Festival, 1995. Fellow Pub. Rels. Soc. Am. (bd. dirs. 1983-85, 86-94, officer 1991-95, mem. counselors acad. 1986—, Silver Anvil award 1985, Mktg./Consumer Rels. award East Ctrl. dist. 1992, 95, Lighthouse award 1995); mem. Press Club Cleve. (bd. dirs. 1989—, v.p. 1990—), Cleve. Advt. Club, Women's City Club Cleve. Republican. Methodist. Avocation: soccer. Home: 656 University Ave Elyria OH 44035-7239 Office: Erieview Tower 1301 E 9th St Cleveland OH 44114

PUDDINGTON, IRA EDWIN, chemist; b. Clifton, N.B., Can., Jan. 8, 1911; s. Charles Edwin and Elizabeth (Currie) P.; m. Hazel Jean Duncan, Aug. 27, 1936; 1 child, James Donald. B.S., Mt. Allison U., Sackville, N.B., Can., 1933, D.Sc. (hon.), 1967; M.S., McGill U., Montreal, Que., Can., 1936, Ph.D., 1938; D.Sc. (hon.), Carleton U., Ottawa, Ont., Can., 1975, Meml. U., St. John's, Nfld., Can., 1977. Chemist Nat. Research Council Can., Ottawa, 1938-52, dir. div. chemistry, 1952-75. Contbr. numerous articles to profl. jours.; patentee (over 50) in field. Fellow Am. Inst. Chemists (Pioneer award 1984), Royal Soc. Can., Chem. Inst. Can. (pres. 1967-68, Montreal medal 1971); mem. Am. Chem. Soc., Can. Soc. Chem. Engring. (R.S. Jane award 1975). Mem. United Ch. of Can. Avocations: sailing; gardening. Home: 2324 Alta Vista Dr, Ottawa, ON Canada K1H 7M7 Office: Nat Research Council Can, Div Chemistry, Ottawa, ON Canada K1A 0R9

PUDER, JANICE, special education educator; b. Phila., Apr. 6, 1950; d. Allen Thrasher and Dorothy Ruth (Mathis) P.; foster child: Corienna Gallagher. AA, Pasadena (Calif.) City Coll., 1970; BA, U. Calif., Chico, 1973; postgrad., U. Calif./Chico and San Jose,, U. Pacific, 1973-74, 82; MA, Santa Clara U., 1995. Cert. elem./secondary edn. tchr., Calif. Tchr. New Covenant Christian High Sch., Palo Alto, Calif., 1977-81; spl. edn. tchr. Sunnyvale (Calif.) Christian Jr. and Sr. High, 1981-82; adapted phys. edn. and cons. to spl. edn. local plan area 3 Santa Clara County Office Edn., 1983-92, adapted phys. edn. specialist, 1992—. Vol. Christian Counseling. Mem. PEO. Avocations: Bible study, reading, sports, advocate for foster daughter. Home: 174 N Buena Vista Ave San Jose CA 95126-2823

PUDNEY, GARY LAURENCE, television executive; b. Mpls., July 20, 1934; s. Lawrence D. and Agnes (Hansen) P. BA, UCLA, 1956. V.p. ABC, Inc., N.Y.C., 1968—; v.p., sr. exec. in charge of spls. and talent ABC Entertainment, 1979-89; pres. The Gary L. Pudney Co., Beverly Hills, Calif., 1988—; chief oper. officer Paradigm Entertainment, Beverly Hills, 1989-92; xec. producer World Music Awards, ABC-TV, 1993, World's Greatest Magic, NBC-TV, 1994—, Grand Illusions, 1994, Caesar's World Entertainment, 1994-95, Lance Burton and Houdini, NBC-TV, 1995, Champions of Magic, ABC-TV, 1996, Hidden Secrets of Magic, NBC-TV, 1996, 30th Anniversary, Ceasars Palace-ABC. Exec. producer for United Cerebral Palsy Aspen and Lake Tahoe Pro-Celebrity Tennis Festivals, 4 yrs., AIDS Project L.A. Dinner, 1985, The 25th Anniversary of the L.A. Music Ctr. Bd. dirs. nat. Cerebral Palsy Found., Ctr. Theatre Group Ahmanson Theatre, L.A., Ctr. Theatre Group of L.A. Music Ctr.; mem. bd. La Quinta Arts Found., 1991—. Recipient Helena T. Deveraux Meml. award, 1985, Humanitarian award Nat. Jewish Ctr. for Immunology and Respiratory Medicine, 1986, Gift of Love award Nat. Ctr. Hyperactive Children, 1988, Winner award Excellence The L.A. Film Adv. Bd. Mem. Hollywood Radio and TV Soc. (bd. dirs.), Acad. TV Arts and Scis. (exec. com.), Met. Mus. Art, Mus. Modern Art. Democrat. Lutheran.

PUENTE, TITO ANTHONY, orchestra leader, composer, arranger; b. N.Y.C., Apr. 20, 1923; s. Ernest Anthony and Ercilia (Ortiz) P.; m. Margaret Asencio, Oct. 19, 1963; children: Ronald, Audrey, Tito Anthony. Student, Julliard Conservatory Music, N.Y. Sch. Music, Schillinger System; MusD (hon.), SUNY, Albany, 1987. Orch. leader appearing in numerous night clubs and ballrooms, throughout U.S., 1949—; appeared in Woody Allen's Radio Days, John Candy's Armed & Dangerous, 1986-87; recorded 96 albums; appeared in concert Red Sea Jazz Festival, Israel, all major jazz festivals, including Montreaux, Monterey, Munich, North Sea, others, Tribute in P.R., 1986, Los Angeles Ford Theatre Tribute, 1987; composer Para Los Rumberos, 1960, Oye Como Va, 1962, numerous other works recorded with Dizzy Gillespie, Lionel Hampton, George Shearing, Woody Herman, other major jazz artists; sold out performance Radio City Music Hall & Apollo Theatre, 1986; appeared Madison Square Garden, N.Y.C., 1986, Los Angeles Amphitheatre, 1986, on Bill Cosby Show, 1987, Regis Philbin, Bill Boggs shows, 1987; guest artist with Bklyn. Philharmonic Symphony Orch., N.Y. and Phila., 1987. Founder T. Puente Scholarship fund, 1980. Served with USN, 1942-45. Recipient Bronze medallion City of N.Y., 1969, Key to City Los Angeles, 1976, Key to City of Chgo., 1985, Key to City of Miami, 1986; named Musician of Month on several occasions by Downbeat, Metronome, Playboy and trade mags., 1950's; named King of Latin Music, La Prensa newspaper, 1955; his band named Best Latin Am. Orch. New York Daily News, 1977; recipient 6 Grammy nominations, Grammy award, 1978, 83, 85, 90; N.Y. Music award, 1986. Office: Thomas Cassidy Inc 366 Horseshoe Dr Basalt CO 81621

PUERNER, JOHN, newspaper publishing executive. V.p., dir. mktg. and devel. Chgo. Tribune; now pres., pub. The Orlando Sentinel, Fla., 1993—. Office: The Orlando Sentinel 633 N Orange Ave Orlando FL 32801-1349

PUFFER, RICHARD JUDSON, retired college chancellor; b. Chgo., Aug. 20, 1931; s. Noble Judson and Lillian Katherine (Olson) P.; m. Alison Foster Cope, June 28, 1952; children—Lynn, Mark, Andrew. Ph.B., Ill. Wesleyan U., 1953; M.S. in Edn, Ill. State U., 1962; PhD (Roy Clark Meml. scholar), Northwestern U., 1967. Asst. plant supt. J.A. Olson Co., Winona, Miss., 1957-59; tchr. Leroy Community Unit Dist. (Ill.), 1959-60; tchr., prin. Community Unit, Dist. 7, Lexington, Ill., 1960-62; asst. county supt. schs. Cook County, Ill., 1962-65; dean arts and scis. Kirkwood Community Coll., Cedar Rapids, Iowa, 1967-69; v.p. Black Hawk Coll., Moline, Ill., 1969-77; pres. Black Hawk Coll., 1977-82, chancellor, 1982-87; pres. The Ark Computer Ctr., 1989-92; dir. W. Ctrl. Ill. Ednl. TV Corp., Springfield, Ill., 1977-87; cons. examiner North Central Assn., 1978-87; bd. mem. Unitarian Universalist Dist. of Mich., 1995—. Editor: Cook County Ednl. Digest, 1962-65. Bd. dirs. Cedar Rapids Symphony, 1967-69, United Way of Rock Island and Scott Counties, Ill., 1978-80; sec., treas. Ill. Ednl. Retirement Cts., 1987-91; vice-chmn. Illini Hosp. Bd., 1988-93, chmn., 1993-95; bd. dirs. Illowa coun. Boy Scouts Am., 1979-83, v.p., 1981-83. With USNR, 1953-57. Mem. Rotary (pres. 1975-76, East Moline, Ill.), Green Medallion, Blue Key, Phi Delta Kappa, Pi Gamma Mu. Home and Office: 6191 Grace Ave Ludington MI 49431

PUGH, EDISON NEVILLE, metallurgist; b. Glamorgan, Wales, May 5, 1935; naturalized U.S. citizen; BSc, U. Wales, 1956, PhD in Metallurgy, 1959. Sci. officer def. stds. labs. NSW br. Australian Dept. Supply, 1959-63; scientist rsch. inst. advanced studies Martin Marietta Corp., Md., 1963-65, staff scientist, 1965-66, sr. rsch. scientist, 1966-69; assoc. prof. engring. and applied sci. George Washington U., 1969-70; assoc. prof. metallurgy and mining engring. U. Ill., Urbana, 1970-73, prof., 1973-80; mem. staff Nat. Inst. Stds. & Tech., 1980-85, chief metallurgy divsn., 1985—. Fellow Am. Soc. Metals Internat., Nat. Assn. Corrosion Engrs. (Willis Rodney Whitney award 1984). Office: Nat Inst of Stds Tech Materials Sci Engring Lab Materials Bldg Rm B268 Gaithersburg MD 20899

PUGH, EMERSON WILLIAM, electrical engineer; b. Pasadena, Calif., May 1, 1929; s. Emerson Martindale and Ruth Hazel (Edgin) P.; m. Elizabeth Burnam Russell; children: William Russell, Sarah Elizabeth, David Emerson. BS in Physics, Carnegie Mellon U., 1951, PhD in Physics, 1956. Asst. prof. physics Carnegie Mellon U., Pitts., 1956-57; with IBM, 1957-93, rsch. staff mem. rsch. div., Poughkeepsie, N.Y., 1957-61, engring. mgr. components div., 1962-65, group dir. data processing group, Harrison, N.Y., 1965-66, dir. tech. planning rsch. div., Yorktown Heights, N.Y., 1966-68, asst. to v.p. IBM Corp., Armonk, N.Y., 1968-71, rsch. mgr. rsch. div., Yorktown Heights, 1971-85, mgr. tech. history, 1985-93; vis. scientist IBM Lab., Zurich, Switzerland, 1961-62; mem. United Engring. Trustees Bd., N.Y.C., 1986-92; mem. Engring. Soc. Libr. Bd., N.Y.C., 1986-89; trustee Chalres Babbage Found., 1990—. Author: Principles of Electricity and Magnetism, 1960, Memories That Shaped an Industry, 1984, IBM's Early Computers, 1986, IBM's 360 and Early 370 Systems, 1991, Building IBM, 1995; also articles; 10 patents. Fellow IEEE (v.p. 1986-87, pres. 1989, chmn. friends com. Ctr. for History Elec. Engring. 1991-94, dir. found. bd. 1996—), AAAS, Am. Phys. Soc. Home: 40 Brandon Dr Mount Kisco NY 10549-3720 Office: IBM T J Watson Rsch Ctr PO Box 218 Yorktown Heights NY 10598-0218

PUGH, GEORGE WILLARD, law educator; b. Napoleonville, La., Aug. 17, 1925; s. William Whitmell and Evelyn (Foley) P.; m. Jean Earle Hemphill, Sept. 6, 1952; children: William Whitmell III, George Willard, David Nicholls, James Hemphill. B.A., La. State U., 1947, J.D., 1950; J.S.D., Yale U., 1952; Dr. h.c., U. Aix-Marseille III, France, 1984. Bar: La. 1950. Instr. La. State U. Law Sch., 1950, mem. faculty, 1952-94, prof. law, 1959-94, Julius B. Nachman prof. law, 1984-94; prof. law emeritus, 1994—; faculty summer session abroad U. Thessaloniki Greece summer 1974, Aix-en-Provence, France, 1985; mem. faculty summer program U. San Diego, Paris, 1977; part-time rsch. cons. La. State Law Inst., 1953-54; 1st jud. adminstr. Jud. Coun. Supreme Ct. La., 1954-56; vis. prof. U. Tex., summer 1961; vis. Doherty prof. law U. Va., 1966-67; mem. faculty orientation program in Am. law Assn. Am. Law Schs., 1968, law teaching clinic, summer 1969; vis. prof. U. Aix-Marseille III, France, 1983, fall 1987, U. Catholique de Louvain, Belgium, fall 1987; cons. La. State U.S. Vietnam Legal Adminstrn. Project, 1969. Author: Louisiana Evidence Law, 1974, supplement, 1978; co-author: Cases and Materials on the Adminstration of Criminal Justice, 2d edit., 1969, Handbook on Louisiana Evidence Law, 1989, 8th edit., 1996; coord., reporter Code of Evidence for La. Bd. dirs. Legal Aid Soc. Baton Rouge, 1965-89, chmn., 1963-64; adv. bd. St. Alban's Episcopal Student Ctr., La. State U., 1965-68, 70-72. Served with AUS, World War II. Fellow Comparative Study Adminstrn. Justice, 1962-65. Mem. Am., La., Baton Rouge bar assns., Order of Coif, Omicron Delta Kappa, Lambda Chi Alpha. Democrat. Episcopalian. Home: 167 Sunset Blvd Baton Rouge LA 70808-5073

PUGH, JOYE JEFFRIES, educational administrator; b. Ocilla, Ga., Jan. 23, 1957; d. Claude Bert and Stella Elizabeth (Paulk) Jeffries; m. Melville Eugene Pugh, Sept. 21, 1985. AS in Pre-law, S. Ga. Coll., 1978; BS in Edn., Valdosta State Coll., 1980, MEd in Psychology, Guidance and Counseling, 1981; EdD in Adminstrn., Nova U., Ft. Lauderdale, Fla., 1992. Cert. tchr., adminstr., supr., Ga. Personnel adminstr. TRW, Inc., Douglas, Ga., 1981-83; recreation dir. Ocilla (Ga.), Irwin Recreation Dept., 1983-84; exec. dir. Sunny Dale Tng. Ctr., Inc., Ocilla, 1984—; pres. and registered agt. Irwin County Resources, Inc., Ocilla, 1988—, Camelot Ct., Inc., 1994—. Contbr. articles on handicapped achievements to newspapers, mags. (Ga. Spl. Olympics News Media award, 1987, Assn. for Retarded Citizens News Media award, 1988). Adv. bd. Area 12 Spl. Olympics, Douglas, Ga., 1984-88; pres. Irwin County Spl. Olympics, 1984—, mem. adv. task force Spl. Olympics Internat. for 6-7 yr. olds, 1995—, elected to Ga. Spl. Olympics bd. dirs., 1995-98, serve on the comm. and mktg. com. for Ga. Spl. Olympics, 1995-96; exec. dir., fund raising chmn. Irwin Assn. for Retarded Citizens, Ocilla, 1984—; arts and crafts chmn. Ga. Sweet Tater Trot 5k/1 Mile Rd. Races, 1993—; bd. dirs., com. mem., mktg. com. Ga. Spl. Olympics, 1995—; founder, chmn. Joseph Mascolo Celebrity Events, 1985—. Recipient Spirit of Spl. Olympics award Ga. Spl. Olymics, Atlanta, 1986, Cmty. Svc. award Ga. Assn. for Retarded Citizens, Atlanta, 1987, Govs.' Vol. award Ga. Vol. Awards, Atlanta, 1988, Presdl. Sports award AAU, Indpls., 1988, Humanitarian award Sunny Dale Tng. Ctr., Inc., Ocilla, 1988, Golden Poet award New Am. Poetry Anthology, 1988, Outstanding Coach-Athlete Choice award Sunny Dale Spl. Olympics, Ocilla, 1992, Dist. Coach award, 1993, Outstanding Unified Sports Ptnr. of Yr. award, 1995. Mem. DAR, Mut. Unidentified Flying Object Network (Ga. state sect. dir., asst. state dir.), Ga. State Assn. for Retarded Citizens, Ctrs. Dirs. Ga., Ocilla Rotary Club (program dir. 1995—, bd. dirs. 1995—, sec. 1996—), Sunny Dale Unified Track Club (founder 1991—), Sunny Dale Unified Track Club (founder 1991—), Sunny Dale Ensemble (founder), Ocilla/Irwin County C. of C. Baptist. Avocations: playing musical instruments, jet skiing, weight lifting, dancing, singing. Home: 201 Lakeside Cir Douglas GA 31533-9656 Office: Sunny Dale Tng Ctr Inc Mascolo Dr Box 512 Ocilla GA 31774-9801

PUGH, KEITH E., JR., lawyer; b. L.A., Mar. 17, 1937; s. Keith Emerson and Serena (Reynolds) P.; m. Kathleen Perry, Aug. 28, 1958 (div. Mar. 1973); children—Linda, Lisa, Scott; m. Pamela Carolyn Winberry, May 20, 1973; children—Alexander, Caroline. Student, Principia Coll., 1955-58; J.D., U. So. Calif., 1962. Bar: Calif. 1962, D.C. 1969, U.S. Supreme Ct. 1976, U.S. Ct. Internat. Trade 1983, U.S. Ct. Appeals (fed. cir.) 1994. Dep. atty. gen. antitrust sect. Office Calif. Atty. Gen., San Francisco, 1962-65; assoc. Broad, Busterud & Khourie, San Francisco, 1965-66, Office Joseph Alioto, San Francisco, 1966-68, Howrey & Simon, Washington, 1968-69; ptnr. Howrey & Simon, 1970—, also mem. mgmt. com., 1980—. Mem. ABA, Fed. Cir. Bar Assn., State Bar Calif., D.C. Bar Assn., Annapolis Yacht Club, Capitol City Club, Phi Delta Phi. Avocation: boating. Home: 3939 Fordham Rd NW Washington DC 20016-1937 Office: Howrey & Simon 1299 Pennsylvania Ave NW Washington DC 20004-2400

PUGH, LAWRENCE R., apparel executive; b. Jan. 22, 1933; m. Jean Pugh; 2 children. Grad., Colby Coll., 1956. Div. sales mgr. Borden Inc., 1958-66; product mgr., gen. mktg. mgr. Hamilton Beach Co., 1966-70; dir. mktg. Ampex Corp., 1970-72; group pres. Beatrice Foods Co., 1972-80; pres. V.F. Corp., Wyomissing, Pa., 1980-83, chmn., chief exec. officer, 1983-96; chmn. bd. V.F. Corp., Wyomissing, 1996—. Office: VF Corp 1047 N Park Rd Reading PA 19610

PUGH, MARION STIRLING, archaeologist, author; b. Middletown, N.Y., May 12, 1911; d. Louis and Lena May (Randall) Illig; m. Matthew Williams Sirling, Dec. 11, 1933 (dec. 1975); children: Matthew Williams, Jr. (dec.), Ariana Stirling Withers; m. John Ramsey Pugh, Aug. 7, 1977 (dec. Mar. 1994). BS, Rider Coll., 1930; postgrad. George Washington U., 1931-33. Office sec. Bur. Am. Ethnology, Smithsonian Instn., Washington, 1931-33; archaeologist with Matthew W. Stirling, Fla., 1934-38, Smithsonian Instn.-Nat. Geog. Soc. archeol. expdn. Mex., 1939-46, Panama, 1948-53, Ecuador, 1957, Costa Rica, 1962. Author: (with Matthew Stirling) Tarqui, an Early Site in Manabi, Ecuador, 1962, El Limon, an Early Tomb Site in Cocle Province, Panama, 1963, Archaeological Notes on Almirante Bay, Bocas del Toro, Panama, 1963, The Archeology of Taboga, Uraba and Taboguilla Islands, Panama, 1963; contbr. articles to Nat. Geog. mag. and Ames. mag. Trustee The Textile Mus., Washington, 1968—, pres. 1984-87. Co-recipient Franklyn L. Burr award Nat. Geog. Soc., 1941, Disting. Svc. medal Peruvian Embassy, 1985. Fellow Am. Anthrop. Assn., Gen. Div. Anthropology; mem. Am. Ethnol. Soc., Soc. Latin Am. Anthropology, Washington Anthrop. Soc., Washington Acad. Sci., Soc. Woman Geographers (pres. 1960-63, 69-72, mem. exec. council 1954-74, Gold medal 1975). Avocations: swimming, textiles. Home: 20351 Airmont Rd Round Hill VA 22141

PUGH, RICHARD CRAWFORD, lawyer; b. Phila., Apr. 28, 1929; s. William and Myrtle P.; m. Nanette Bannen, Feb. 27, 1954; children: Richard Crawford, Andrew Lembert, Catherine Elizabeth. AB summa cum laude, Dartmouth Coll., 1951; BA in Jurisprudence, Oxford (Eng.) U., 1953; LLB, Columbia U., 1958. Bar: N.Y. 1958. Assoc. firm Cleary, Gottlieb, Steen & Hamilton, N.Y.C., 1958-61; ptnr. Cleary, Gottlieb, Steen & Hamilton, 1969-89, counsel, 1989—; disting. prof. law U. San Diego, 1989—; mem. faculty Law Sch. Columbia U., 1961-89, prof., 1964-69, adj. prof., 1969-89; lectr. Columbia-Amsterdam-Leyden (Netherlands) summer program Am. law, 1963, 79; dep. asst. atty. gen. tax div. U.S. Dept. Justice, 1966-68; Cons. fiscal and fin. br. UN Secretariat, 1962, 64. Editor: Columbia Law Rev., 1957-58; editor: (with W. Friedmann) Legal Aspects of Foreign Investment, 1959, (with others) International Law, 1993, Taxation of International Transactions, 1996, Taxation of Business Enterprises, 1995. Served with USNR, 1954-56. Rhodes scholar, 1953. Mem. ABA, Am. Law Inst., Am. Coll. Tax Counsel, Am. Soc. Internat. Law, Internat. Fiscal Assn. (pres. U.S. br. 1978-79). Home: 7335 Encelia Dr La Jolla CA 92037-5729 Office: Univ San Diego Sch Law Alcala Park San Diego CA 92110-2429

PUGH, ROBERT GAHAGAN, lawyer; b. Shreveport, La., Aug. 25, 1924; m. Jo Ann Powell; children: Robert G. Jr., Jean Anne Pugh Cottingham, Lamar Powell. BS, Centenary Coll., Shreveport; LLB, La. State U. Bar: La. 1949. Former tchr. St. John's High Sch., Shreveport; former prof. law and medicine La. State U. Med. Ctr., Shreveport. Author: Juvenile Laws of Louisiana, Their History and Developmment. La. commr. Nat. Conf. Commrs. on Uniform State Laws; bd. regents State of La., mem. Judiciary Commn.; coun. mem. Lat. State Law Inst.; del. La. Constl. Conv., 1973; chmn. La. Indigent Defender Bd. Navigator USAAF, World War II; intelligence and security officer USAF, Korea. Recipient Disting. Atty. award La. Bar Found., 1990; named to Hall of Fame La. State U. Law Ctr. Fellow at large Am. Bar Found; mem. ABA (La. ho. of dels., chmn. standing com. on membership 1977-84, mem. sect. on real property, probate and trust law, sect. taxation), Bar Assn. for 5th Fed. Cir. (pres. 1985-87), La. Bar Assn. (pres. 1975-76), Shreveport Bar Assn. (pres. 1971-72), Fed. Bar Assn., Can. Bar Assn., La. Bar Found., Nat. Conf. Bar Pres. (pres. 1981-82), Am. Judicature Soc., Am. Law Inst., Bartolus Soc., La. State U. Law Sch. Alumni Assn. (pres. 1977), The Shreveport Club, East Ridge Country Club (past pres.), Order of Coif (hon.). Roman Catholic. Office: Commercial National Tower 333 Texas St Ste 2100 Shreveport LA 71101-5303

PUGH, RODERICK WELLINGTON, psychologist, educator; b. Richmond, Ky., June 1, 1919; s. George Wilmer and Lena Bernetta (White) P.; m. Harriet Elizabeth Rogers, Aug. 29, 1953 (div. 1955). B.A., Fisk U., 1940; M.A., Ohio State U., 1941; Ph.D., U. Chgo., 1949. Diplomate: Am. Bd. Profl. Psychology. Instr. Albany (Ga.) State Coll., 1941-43; psychology trainee VA, Chgo., 1947-49; lectr. Roosevelt U., Chgo., 1951-54; staff clin. psychologist VA Hosp., Hines, Ill., 1950-54, asst. chief psychologist for psychotherapy, 1954-58, chief clin. psychology sect., 1958-60, supervising psychologist, coord. psychol. internship tng., 1960-66; pvt. practice clin. psychology Chgo., 1958—; assoc. prof. psychology Loyola U., Chgo., 1966-73, prof., 1973-88, emeritus prof. psychology, 1989—; Cons. St. Mary of the Lake Sem., Niles, Ill., 1965-66, Ill. Div. Vocational Rehab., 1965-82, Center for Inner City Studies, Northeastern State U., Chgo., 1966-67, VA Psychology Tng. Program, 1966—, Am. Psychol. Assn. and Nat. Inst. Mental Health Vis. Psychologists Program, 1966-89; juvenile problems research rev. com. NIMH, 1970-74; cons. Center for Minority Group Mental Health Programs, 1975-77, cons. psychology edn. br., 1978-82; lectr. U. Ibadan, Nigeria, 1978; Mem. profl. adv. com. Div. Mental Health, City of Chgo., 1979-82; mem. adv. com. U.S. Army Command and Gen. Staff Coll., 1981-83. Author: Psychology and the Black Experience, 1972; Contbr.: chpt. in Black Psychology, 1972; Cons. editor: Contemporary Psychology, 1975-79; contbr. articles to profl. jours. Sec. bd. trustees Fisk U., 1968-78. Served to 2d lt. AUS, 1943-46, ETO. Vis. scholar Fisk U., 1966, vis. prof. in psychology, 1994. Fellow Am. Psychol. Soc., Am. Psychol. Assn. (nat. adv. panel to Civilian Health and Med. Program of Uniformed Services 1980-83, joint coun. on profl. edn. in psychology 1988-90); mem. Midwestern Psychol. Assn., Ill. Psychol. Assn. (chmn. legis. com. 1961, council mem. 1960-62, Disting. Psychologist award 1988), Soc. for Psychol. Study Social Issues, Assn. Behavior Analysis, AAUP, Sigma Xi, Alpha Phi Alpha, Psi Chi. Home: 5201 S Cornell Ave Chicago IL 60615-4207 Office: 30 N Michigan Ave Chicago IL 60602-3400 also: Loyola U 6525 N Sheridan Rd Chicago IL 60626-5311

PUGH, STEPHEN HENRY, JR., lawyer; b. Chgo., Oct. 17, 1942; s. Stephen Henry Pugh Sr. and Mardella (James) Barran; m. Joyce Pugh, Dec. 26, 1968; children: Preston L. Leslie. AB in Classics/Philosophy, Loyola U., Chgo., 1968, JD, 1973. Summer clk. U.S. Atty. for No. Dist., Chgo., 1972; law clk. Hon. James B. Parsons, Chgo., 1973-74; spl. trial atty. U.S. Dept.

Justice, Chgo., 1974-77; assoc. Chapman & Cutler, Chgo., 1978-83, ptnr., 1983-91; ptnr., shareholder Pugh, Jones & Johnson, P.C., Chgo., 1991—. Bd. mem. Emergency Fund for Needy People, Chgo.; mem. Character and Fitness Commn., Chgo., Atty. Registration and Disciplinary Commn., Chgo. Sgt. USAF, 1970. Named Bd. Mem. of Yr., Parkway Cmty. House/Hull Assn., 1986; recipient cert. appreciation ISBA Practicing Lawyers Bus. Fair, 1988, Testimonial of Appreciation, Loyola U. Sch. Law, 1994. Mem. ABA, Nat. Bar Assn., Ill. State Bar Assn., Cook County Bar Assn., Chgo. Bar Assn., Monroe Club, Hyde Park Athletic Club. Avocations: golf, tennis. Office: Pugh Jones & Johnson PC 180 N LaSalle St #2910 Chicago IL 60601

PUGH, THOMAS DOERING, architecture educator; b. Jacksonville, Fla., May 27, 1948; s. William Edward Jr. and Lina Lillian (Doering) P.; m. Virginia Margaret McRae, June 14, 1972; children: Rachel McRae, Jordan Faith, Nathan Calder. B Design, U. Fla., 1971, MA Arch., 1974. Asst. prof. architecture U. Ark., Fayetteville, 1976-78; pres. Thomas D. Pugh Constrn. Co., Inc., Fayetteville, Ark., 1978-87; assoc. prof. Fla. A&M U. Sch. Architecture, Tallahassee, 1987—; interim dir. Inst. Bldg. Scis. Fla. Agrl. and Mech. U., Tallahassee, 1991-93, dir., 1993—; vis. rsch. fellow Tech. U. Eindhoven, The Netherlands, 1993-94; chmn. radon adv. bd. Fla. State U. Sys., 1988—; mem. Fla. Coordinating Coun. on Radon Protection; jurof Progressive Architecutre-AIA Nat. Archtl. Rsch. Awards, 1995. Bd. dir. Tallahassee Habitat for Humanity, 1987-92; crew leader Habitat for Humanity Internat., Americus, Ga., 1988, 90. Recipient Bronze medal Fla. Assn. AIA, Gainesville, 1975; Named Vol. of Yr. Tallahassee Dem. and Vol. Tallahassee, Inc., 1991. Mem. AIA, ASCE (sec. spl. task com. radon mitigation 1990-91), Assn. Collegiate Schs. Architecture (coun. on archtl. rsch. 1994). Democrat. Lutheran. Avocations: sailing, woodworking. Office: Fla A&M Univ Sch Architecture 1936 S Martin Luther King Tallahassee FL 32307-4200

PUGH, THOMAS WILFRED, lawyer; b. St. Paul, Minn., Aug. 3, 1949; s. Thomas Leslie and Joann Marie (Tauer) P.; m. Susan Elizabeth Beattie, Sept. 12, 1971; children: Aimee Elizabeth, Douglas Thomas. AB cum laude, Dartmouth Coll., 1971; JD cum laude, U. Minn., 1976. Assoc. Thuet & Lynch, South St. Paul, 1976-79; ptnr. Thuet, Lynch & Pugh, South St. Paul, 1980-85; atty., pres. Thuet, Pugh & Rogosheske, Ltd., South St. Paul, 1986—; mem. Minn. Ho. of Reps., St. Paul, 1989—; mem. Supreme Ct. Task Force Conciliation Ct., St. Paul, 1992, Dakota County Tech. Coll. Adv. Bd., 1991—. Bd. dirs. Wakota Arena, South St. Paul, 1984-87; pres. Luther Meml. Ch., South St. Paul, 1983-84. Daniel Webster scholar Dartmouth Coll., 1970, Rufus Choate scholar, 1971. Mem. Minn. State Bar Assn., 1st Dist. Bar Assn., Ducks Unltd., Pheasants Forever, South St. Paul C. of C. (local issues chair 1982, Dedicated Svc. award 1983), South St. Paul Jaycees (pres. 1978-79, Key award 1979), Lions. Lutheran. Avocations: tennis, golf, hunting, fishing, reading. Office: Thuet Pugh & Rogosheske 833 Southview Blvd South Saint Paul MN 55075-2237

PUGLIESE, MARIA ALESSANDRA, psychiatrist; b. Phila., Sept. 16, 1948; d. Peter Francis and Ida Agnes (Rosa) P.; m. J. Paul Hieble, Sept. 14, 1985; children: Helen Elisa Hieble, Jesse Paul Hieble. BS, Chestnut Hill Coll., 1970; MD, U. Pa., 1974. Diplomate Am. Bd. Psychiatry and Neurology; with added qualifications in addiction psychiatry. Intern in pediatrics Children's Hosp. of Phila., 1974-75; resident in psychiatry Inst. Pa. Hosp., Phila., 1975-78, attending psychiatrist, 1978—; attending psychiatrist Malvern (Pa.) Inst., 1982—. Office: 111 N 49th St Philadelphia PA 19139-2718

PUGLIESE, ROBERT FRANCIS, lawyer, business executive; b. West Pittston, Pa., Jan. 15, 1933. BS, U. Scranton, 1954; LLB, Georgetown U., 1957, LLM, 1959; grad. advanced mgmt. program Harvard U., 1976. Bar: D.C. 1957, U.S. Dist. Ct. 1957, U.S. Ct. Claims 1958, U.S. Tax Ct. 1957, U.S. Ct. Appeals 1957. Assoc. Hedrick & Lane, Washington, 1957-60; tax counsel Westinghouse Electric Corp., Pitts., 1961-70, gen. tax counsel, 1970-75, v.p., gen. tax counsel, 1975-76, v.p., gen. counsel, sec., 1976-86, sr. v.p., 1987, exec. v.p., 1988-92; spl. counsel Eckert, Seamans, Cherin & Mellott, Pitts., 1993—. Mem. exec. com. U. Scranton; bd. dirs. St. Clair Meml. Hosp. Mem. Assn. Gen. Counsel. Office: Eckert Seamans Cherin & Mellott 600 Grant St Ste 42 Pittsburgh PA 15219-2703

PUGLIESE, ROBERT J., lawyer; b. Charles City, Iowa, July 7, 1953. BA, Drake U., 1974; JD, U. Ill., 1978. Bar: Ill. 1978, U.S. Dist. Ct. (no. dist.) Ill. 1978. Ptnr. Lord, Bissell & Brook, Chgo. Mem. ABA. Office: Lord Bissell & Brook Harris Bank Bldg 115 S La Salle St # 3400 Chicago IL 60603-3801*

PUGMIRE, ROBERT, wholesale distribution executive. V.p. Nat. Clothing Co., Inc., Kirkland, Wash.; asst. gen. mgr. & asst. v.p., now gen. mgr. & v.p. Price Cosko, Issaquah, WA, 1988—. Office: Price Cosko 999 Lake Dr Issaquah WA 98207*

PUGSLEY, FRANK BURRUSS, lawyer; b. Kansas City, Mo., Apr. 3, 1920; s. Charles Silvey and Emma (Burruss) P.; m. Aline East, May 7, 1943; children—John, Susan Pugsley Patterson, Nancy Pugsley Young. B.S. in Mech. Engring, U. Tex., Austin, 1942; J.D., DePaul U., Chgo., 1950. Bar: Ill. 1950, Tex. 1953, U.S. Supreme Ct. 1960. Engr. Gen. Electric Co., Schenectady, 1946-50; patent atty. Gen. Electric Co., 1950-52; assoc. Baker & Botts, Houston, 1952-60; ptnr. Baker & Botts, 1960-84, sr. ptnr., 1974-84; lectr. Southwestern Legal Found., Practising Law Inst., Bur. Nat. Affairs Conf. Contbr. articles to legal jours. Trustee West Univ. Methodist Ch., Houston, 1959-65; bd. dirs. St. Stephens Episcopal Day Sch., 1960-62; adminstrv. bd. St. Luke's United Meth. Ch., 1981-83. Served to lt. USNR, 1942-46. Fellow Tex. Bar Found.; mem. ABA (chmn. intellectual property law sec. 1980-81), Am. Intellectual Property Law Assn. (pres. 1966-67), Tex. Bar Assn. (chmn. intellectual property law sect. 1960-61), Houston Bar Assn., Petroleum Club, Frisch Auf! Valley Country Club, Friars. Home: 3602 Nottingham St Houston TX 77005-2221 Office: 3000 One Shell Plz Houston TX 77002

PUGSLEY, JOHN EAST, financial executive, accountant; b. Schenectady, N.Y., Dec. 28, 1946; s. Frank Burruss and Aline (East) P.; m. Kathleen Ellen Partain, Aug. 24, 1974; children: Frank East, Paul Burruss. BSEE, U. Houston, 1971, MS in Acctg., 1977. CPA, profl. engr. Power cons. Houston Lighting & Power, 1971-77; CPA Deloitte & Touche, Houston, 1977-83; v.p. fin. Capital Excavation Co., Austin, Tex., 1983-94. Commr. Western Hills Youth Football, Austin, 1991-93. Mem. FEI, Tex. Soc. CPAs. Office: Capital Excavation Co PO Box 1301 Austin TX 78767-1301

PUHALA, JAMES JOSEPH, lawyer; b. Pitts., Sept. 5, 1942; s. Leo Andrew and Agnes (Ruglovsky) P.; m. Linda Sue Lash, Oct. 1, 1977; children: Stephen, Susan, Matthew. BBA, U. Dayton, 1964; MBA, U. Pitts., 1965; JD, Duquesne U., 1974. Bar: Pa. 1974, U.S. Dist. Ct. (we. dist.) Pa. 1974. Mgr. internat. taxes Dravo Corp., Pitts., 1974-79, sr. counsel, 1979-86, group gen. counsel, 1986-87, v.p., gen. counsel, sec., 1987—. Decorated D.F.C., Bronze Star. Mem. Am. Corp. Counsel Assn., Allegheny County Bar Assn., Mobile Bar Assn. (assoc.). Home: 1061 Lindendale Dr Pittsburgh PA 15243 Office: Dravo Corp 3600 One Oliver Plaza Pittsburgh PA 15222-2682

PULASKI, CHARLES ALEXANDER, JR., lawyer; b. Flushing, N.Y., Oct. 22, 1941; s. Charles Alexander and Mary Ann (Spencer) P.; m. Linda Shannon Holden, Aug. 16, 1965; 1 child, Alison. BA in Econs., Yale U., 1964, LLB, 1967. Bar: Conn. 1968, U.S. Dist. Ct. Conn. 1968, U.S. Ct. Appeals (2d cir.) 1968, Iowa 1974, U.S. Dist. Ct. (no. and so. dists.) Iowa 1975, U.S. Ct. Appeals (8th cir.) 1975, Ariz. 1986, U.S. Dist. Ct. Ariz. 1986, U.S. Supreme Ct. 1970. Prof. law U. Iowa, 1975-80, Ariz. State U., Tempe, 1980-88; assoc. Snell & Wilmer, Phoenix, 1986-87; ptnr. Snell & Wilmer, 1988—. Author: Criminal Procedure Case Book, 1982, also numerous articles in law revs. Recipient Kalven award, Law and Soc. Assn., 1987. Mem. ABA, Ariz. Bar Assn., Am. Coll. Tax Counsel. Office: Snell & Wilmer 1 Arizona Ctr Phoenix AZ 85004

PULASKI, LORI JAYE, career officer; b. Madison, Wis., June 22, 1962; d. Stanley Harold and Phyllis Mabel (Billock) P.; m. Joseph Kawika Kim, Sept. 14, 1986 (div. Aug. 1991). BS, USAF Acad., 1984; MA in Aero. Sci., Imbry Riddle Aero. U., 1995. Commd. 2d lt. USAF, 1984, advanced through grades to capt., 1988; evaluator/instr. pilot USAF, Carswell AFB, Tex., 1986-92; flight safety officer USAF, Edwards AFB, Calif., 1992-94, evaluator/instr. pilot, 1994—; command flight safety officer Hqrs. Aircombat Command USAF, Langley AFB, Va., 1995. Avocations: flying, skiing, scuba diving, bicycling. Home: 106 Derosa Dr Hampton VA 23666

PULEO, FRANK CHARLES, lawyer; b. Montclair, N.J., Nov. 25, 1945; s. Frank and Kathren (Despenzerie) P.; m. Alice Kathren Leek, June 1, 1968; children—Frank C., Richard James. B.S.E., Princeton U., 1967; J.D., N.Y.U., 1970. Bar: N.Y., 1971. Ptnr., Milbank, Tweed, Hadley & McCloy, N.Y.C., 1970—. Mem. ABA (mem. com. on fed. regulation securities), N.Y. State Bar Assn. Office: Milbank Tweed Hadley & McCloy 1 Chase Manhattan Plz New York NY 10005-1401

PULGRAM, ERNST, linguist, philologist, Romance and classical linguistics educator, writer; b. Vienna, Austria, Sept. 18, 1915; came to U.S. 1939, naturalized 1943; s. Sigmund and Gisela (Bauer) P.; m. Frances McSparran, Nov. 29, 1985. Dr. Phil. in Romance and Classical Philology, U. Vienna, 1947, Dr. phil. honoris causa, 1990; PhD in Comparative Linguistics, Harvard U., 1946. Asst. prof. Union Coll., Schenectady, N.Y., 1946; asst. prof. U. Mich., Ann Arbor, 1948-51, assoc. prof., 1951-56, prof., 1956—, H. Keniston disting. prof. romance and classical linguistics, 1979-86, prof. emeritus, 1986—; vis. prof. U. Florence, Italy, 1956-57, U. Cologne, Germany, 1970, U. Heidelberg, Germany, 1972, U. Regensburg, Germany, 1975, U. Vienna, 1977, Internat. Christian U., Tokyo, 1982, U. Innsbruck, Austria, 1983, U. Munich, Germany, 1987; lectr. numerous univs., internat. linguistic congresses; cons. Sch. Langs. and Linguistics, Georgetown U., Washington. Author: Theory of Names, 1951, The Tongues of Italy, 1958, Introduction to Spectrography of Speech, 1959, Syllable, Word, Nexus, Cursus, 1970, Latin-Romance Phonology, Prosodics and Metrics, 1975, Italic, Latin, Italian: 600 B.C.-A.D. 1250, 1978, Practicing Linguist, Essays 1950-1985 (2 vols.), 1986; editor: Studies Presented to Joshua Whatmough, 1957, Romanitas: Studies in Romance Linguistics, 1984; contbr. articles to profl. jours.; author revs.; mem. editorial bd. Current Issues in Linguistic Theory (Amsterdam), Mich. Germanic Studies, Jour. Linguistics and Philology, Mediterranean Language Rev. Served to pvt. inf. U.S. Army, 1942-44; PTO. fellow Am. Council of Learned Socs., 1951-52, 59-60, Guggenheim Found., 1954-55, 62-63; recipient Henry Russell award U. Mich., 1951, Festschrift, Amsterdam, 1980. Mem. Linguistic Soc. Am. (exec. com., com. on appointment of hon. mems., program com.), Internat. Linguistic Assn., Internat. Phonetics Assn., Linguistic Assn. Can. and the U.S. (founding mem., pres. 1978-79). Avocations: collecting drawings and watercolors; hiking; swimming. Home: 1050 Wall St Ann Arbor MI 48105-1974

PULGRAM, WILLIAM LEOPOLD, architect, space designer; b. Vienna, Austria, Jan. 1, 1921; came to U.S., 1940; s. Sigmund and Gisela (Bauer) P.; married, Jan. 12, 1952; children: Deirdre, Laurence, Anthony, Christopher. BS, Ga. Inst. Tech., 1949, BArch, 1950; postgrad., Ecole des Beaux Arts, Fontainebleau, France, 1951. Archtl. designer various firms, Atlanta, 1951-58; assoc., chief interior design FABR&P, Atlanta, 1958-63; exec. v.p., gen. mgr. associated Space Design Inc., Atlanta, 1963-70, pres., chief exec. officer, 1971-85, chmn., chief exec. officer, 1985-86, chmn. emeritus, 1986-88; architect, cons. Atlanta, 1988—; cons. UN, 1986; com. mem. NAS, 1980-84; lectr. at colls., univs., U.S. and abroad. Author: Designing the Automated Office, 1984, Japanese transl., 1985; contbr. articles to jours. in field. Mem., lectr. High Mus. Art, Atlanta, 1970—. With U.S. Army, 1943-46. Named to Hall of Fame, Interior Design mag., 1986. Fellow AIA (chmn. interiors 1978-84, archt. res. coun. AIA Found. 1983-85); mem. Architects, Designers and Planners for Social Responsibility (nat. bd. dirs. 1989—), Am. Soc. Interior Designers, Atlanta C. of C., Atlanta City Club, Lake Lanier Sailing Club. Mem. Unitarian Universalist Ch. Home and Office: W L Pulgram FAIA Cons 4317 E Conway Dr NW Atlanta GA 30327-3528

PULHAMUS, MARLENE LOUISE, elementary school educator; b. Paterson, N.J., Sept. 11, 1937; d. David Weeder and Elfrieda (Ehler) Wemmell; m. Aaron R. Pulhamus, Aug. 20, 1960; children: Steven, Thomas, Nancy. Student, Trenton State U., 1957; BS, William Paterson U., 1959; postgrad., Rutgers U., 1992. Cert. elem. tchr., N.J. Kindergarten tchr. Wayne (N.J.) Bd. Edn., 1959-63; kindergarten tchr. Paterson Bd. Edn., 1974-75, 2d grade tchr., 1975-81; basic skills instr. Paterson Pub. Schs., 1981—, tchr. accelerated program 1st grade, 1992—; trainer for insvc. groups of learning ctrs. and math. with manipulatives for local pub. schs., trainer for local pub. schs. Contbr. Lessons 4Mat in Action, 3d edit. Pres. Friends of Eisenhower Libr., Totowa, N.J., 1975-77; coord. ch. sch. Preakness Reformed Ch., Wayne, 1990—. Recipient Gov.'s award for tchg. excellence State of N.J. Commn. Edn., 1991, 4Mation program award, 1994. Mem. ASCD, NEA, AAUW, Nat. Coun. Tchrs. Math., Nat. Assn. for Edn. Young Children, N.J. Edn. Assn., Passaic County Edn. Assn., Paterson Edn. Assn. (mem. exec. bd., 1985-89, legis. chmn. 1986-89). Home: 47 Easedale Rd Wayne NJ 07470-2486 Office: Paterson Pub. Sch # 3 448 Main St Paterson NJ 07501-2818

PULIAFITO, CARMEN ANTHONY, ophthalmologist, laser researcher; b. Buffalo, Jan. 5, 1951; s. Dominic F. and Marie A. (Nigro) P.; m. Janet H. Pine, May 19, 1979. AB cum laude, Harvard Coll., 1973, MD magna cum laude, 1978; postgrad., U. Pa. Diplomate Am. Bd. Ophthalmology. Intern Faulkner Hosp., Tufts U. Sch. Medicine, 1978-79; resident Mass. Eye and Ear Infirmary, Boston, 1979-82, retina fellow, 1982-83; instr. Harvard Med. Sch., Boston, 1983-85, asst. prof., 1985-89, assoc. prof., 1989-91; dir. divsn. continuing edn. dept. ophthalmology Harvard Med. Sch., 1989-91; vis. scientist MIT Regional Laser Ctr., Cambridge, 1982—, asst. prof. health scis. and tech. program, 1987-89, assoc. prof., 1989-91; mem. staff Mass. Eye and Ear Infirmary, Boston, 1983; dir. Morse Laser Ctr., Mass. Eye and Ear Infirmary, 1986-91, dir. New Eng. Eye Ctr., 1991—; prof., chmn. dept. ophthalmology Tufts U. Sch. Medicine, 1991—; adj. prof. biomed. engring. Tufts U., 1991—; chmn. med. bd. New Eng. Med. Ctr. Hosps., 1994—, ophthalmologist in chief, 1991—; assoc. examiner Am. Bd. Ophthalmology, 1990—. Author: (with D. Albert) Foundations of Ophthalmic Pathology, 1979, (with R. Steinert) Principles and Practice of Ophthalmic YAG Laser Surgery, 1984, Lasers in Surgery and Medicine: Principles and Practice, 1996, (with M.R. Hee, J.S. Schuman and J.G. Fujimoto) Optical Coherence Tomography of Ocular Diseases, 1996, (with E. Reichel) Atlas of Indocyanine Green Angiography, 1996; editor-in-chief Lasers in Surgery and Medicine, 1987-95, Ophthalmic Surgery and Lasers, 1995—; contbr. about 100 articles to profl. jours. Pres. Am. Soc. for Laser Medicine and Surgery, 1994-95; v.p. Mass. Soc. Eye Physicians and Surgeons, 1994-96; assoc. examiner Am. Bd. Ophthalmology, 1990—; retina trustee Assn. Rsch. in Vision and Ophthalmology, 1995—. Recipient Richard and Hinda Rosenthal award in visual scis., 1994, Man of Vision award Boston Aid to the Blind, 1993, Leon Goldman award Biomed. Optics Soc., 1993, I Migliori award Pirandello Lyceum of Mass., 1994. Fellow Am. Acad. Ophthalmology, Am. Soc. for Laser Medicine and Surgery (pres. 1994-95); mem. Mass. Soc. Eye Physicians and Surgeons (v.p. 1994-96). Roman Catholic. Home: 69 Pigeon Hill Rd Weston MA 02193-1641 Office: New Eng Eye Ctr 750 Washington St Boston MA 02111-1533

PULIDO, MIGUEL LAZARO, marketing professional; b. Havana, Cuba, Dec. 17, 1934; s. Jose Fabriciano and Maria Dolores (Perez) P.; m. Janie Ham, Nov. 28, 1980; 1 child, Michael James. AE, Sugar Techs., Havana U., 1956; MS, La. State U., 1961, PhD, 1965; completed Exec. Program, U. Va., 1986. Agrl. engr. Agrl. and Indsl. Bank Cuba, Havana, 1956-58, mgr. agrl. and eastern devel. div., 1958-59; agrl. engr. Productora Superfosfatos, Havana, 1959-60; asst. mgr. Tech. Svcs. div. Velsicol Chem. Co., Chgo., 1965-67; v.p. internat. mktg. Buckman Labs., Memphis, 1985—. Editor Jour. Fitopatologia, 1969-74; contbr. articles to profl. jours. Fellow Pan Am. U., 1960-62. Mem. AAAS, Am. Phytopathol. Soc., Weed Sci. Soc., Plant Growth Regulator Soc., Biol. Soc., Internat. Sugarcane Techs. Soc., Tech. Assn. Pulp and Paper Industry. Republican. Office: Buckman Labs Internat Inc 1256 N Mclean Blvd Memphis TN 38108-1241

PULITZER, EMILY S RAUH (MRS. JOSEPH PULITZER, JR.), art consultant; b. Cin., July 23, 1933; d. Frederick and Harriet (Frank) Rauh. AB, Bryn Mawr Coll., 1955; student, Ecole du Louvre, Paris, France, 1955-56; MA, Harvard U., 1963. Mem. staff Cin. Art Mus., 1956-57; asst. curator drawings Fogg Art Mus., Harvard, 1957-64, asst. to dir., 1962-63; curator City Art Mus., St. Louis, 1964-73; mem. painting and sculpture com. Mus. Modern Art, 1975—; chmn. visual arts com. Mo. Arts Council, 1976-81; co-chmn. fellows Fogg Art Mus., 1978—; mem. bd. Inst. Mus. Services, 1979-84; commr. St. Louis Art Mus., 1981-88, vice chmn., 1988; chair collections com. Harvard U. Arts Museums, 1992—; bd. dirs. Pulitzer Pub. Co. Bd. dirs. Forum, St. Louis, 1980—, pres., 1990-94; bd. dirs. Mark Rothko Found., 1976-88, Grand Ctr., 1993-95, St. Louis Symphony Orch., 1994—; bd. dirs. arts in transit com. Bi-State Devel. Agy., vice-chmn., 1987—; mem. Leadership St. Louis, 1990-91; mem. overseers com. to visit Harvard Art Mus., 1990—; trustee Mus. Modern Art, 1994—. Mem. Am. Fedn. Arts (dir. 1976-89), St. Louis Mercantile Libr. Assn. (bd. dirs. 1987-93), Women's Forum of Mo. Home: 4903 Pershing Ave Saint Louis MO 63108-1201

PULITZER, MICHAEL EDGAR, publishing executive; b. St. Louis, Feb. 23, 1930; s. Joseph and Elizabeth (Edgar) P.; m. Cecille Stell Eisenbeis, Apr. 28, 1970; children: Michael Edgar, Elizabeth E. Voges, Robert S., Frederick D., Catherine D. Culver, Christina H. Eisenbeis, Mark C. Eisenbeis, William H. Eisenbeis. Grad., St. Mark's Sch., Southborough, Mass., 1947; AB, Harvard U., 1951, LLB, 1954. Bar: Mass. 1954. Assoc. Warner, Stackpole, Stetson & Bradlee, Boston, 1954-56; reporter Louisville Courier Jour., 1956-60; reporter, news editor, asst. mng. editor St. Louis Post-Dispatch, 1960-71, assoc. editor, 1978-79; pub. Ariz. Daily Star, Tucson, 1971—; pres. chief operating officer Pulitzer Pub. Co. (and subs.), 1979-84, vice chmn., 1984-86, pres., chmn., 1986—, also bd. dirs., chief exec. officer, 1988—. Trustee St. Louis U., 1989—. Clubs: St. Louis Country; Mountain Oyster (Tucson). Office: Pulitzer Pub Co 900 N Tucker Blvd Saint Louis MO 63101-1069

PULITZER, ROSLYN K., social worker, psychotherapist; b. Bronx, N.Y., Apr. 25, 1930; d. George and Laura Eleanor (Holtz) P. BS in Human Devel. and Life Cycle, SUNY, N.Y.C., 1983; MSW, Fordham U., 1987; postgrad., Masterson Inst., N.Y.C., 1991. cert. in psychoanalytic psychotherapy of the personality disorders, Masterson Inst., N.Y.C.; lic. clin. social worker, N.Y. Clinic dir. Resources Counseling and Psychotherapy Ctr., N.Y.C., 1985-89; social worker, clin. supr. methadone maintenance treatment program Beth Israel Med. Ctr., N.Y.C., 1989—; cons. therapist, clin. supr. Identity House, N.Y.C., 1980—, exec. dir., 1985, clin. dir., 1993-94. Mem. regional adv. coun. N.Y. State Div. Human Rights, N.Y.C., 1975-76; mem. Community Bd. 6, N.Y.C., 1978-81; founder, legis. chmn. N.Y. State Women's Polit. Caucus, 1978-80. Mem. NASW, Acad. Cert. Social Workers, Soc. Masterson Inst., N.Y. Milton Erickson Soc. for Psychotherapy and Hypnosis (cert.). Avocations: photography, snorkeling. Home: 110 Bank St Apt 5F New York NY 10014-2171

PULLEN, EDWIN WESLEY, anatomist, university dean; b. Flushing, N.Y., June 2, 1923; s. Edwin Leeson and Henrietta Esther (Treharne) P.; m. Ruthann Chambers, Sept. 7, 1946; children—Wayne, Jeffrey, Susan, Kimberly. A.B. (Pres.'s scholar), Colgate U., 1943; M.S., U. Mass., 1948; Ph.D. (DuPont fellow), U. Va., 1953. Instr. anatomy U. Va., 1951-53, asst. prof., 1953-57, assoc. prof., 1957-73, prof., 1973-91; assoc. dean U. Va. (Sch. Medicine), 1974-91, ret., 1991—. Served with USNR, 1943-46. Mem. Am. Assn. Anatomists, AAAS, Sigma Xi. Home: 2700 Magnolia Dr Charlottesville VA 22901-2019

PULLEN, KEATS A., JR., electronics engineer; b. Onawa, Iowa, Nov. 12, 1916; s. Keats A. and Mabel Jeannette (Faus) P.; m. Phyllis Kouwenhoven, Jan. 6, 1945; children: Peter K., Paul V., Keats A. 3d, Andrew W., Victoria F. B.S. in Physics, Calif. Inst. Tech., 1939; Dr.Engring., Johns Hopkins U. Registered profl. engr., Md. Electronic research engr. Ballistic Research Labs., Aberdeen Proving Ground, Md., 1946-78; electronic engr. Army Material Systems Analysis Activity, Aberdeen Proving Ground, 1978-90; cons. engr., 1990—. Author 9 books; Contbr. articles to profl. jours. Recipient Marconi Meml. award Vet. Wireless Operator's Assn., 1982. Fellow IEEE (officer Balt. sect. 1962-66); mem. Am. Def. Preparedness Assn., Assn. U.S. Army, Armed Forces Communications and Electronics Assn. (ex-pres. Aberdeen chpt.), Am. Assn. of Concerned Engrs. (bd. dirs.), Sigma Xi. Episcopalian. Home: 2807 Jerusalem Rd Kingsville MD 21087-1050

PULLEN, NANCY ELLEN, marketing consultant; b. Tucson, Aug. 22, 1949; d. John Paul Pullen and Ellen Lyle (Jorgenson) Pullen Foules; m. David Lynn Preuss; Aug. 22, 1981; children: Donald, Elizabeth. BSBA, Stephen F. Austin State U., 1971; MSBA, U. Denver, 1973. Brand asst. to brand mgr. Procter & Gamble, Cin., 1973-81; mktg. mgr. Heublein Wine Divsn., San Francisco, 1981-82; account dir. Foote, Cone & Belding, S.A., Barcelona, Spain, 1981-85; sr. account dir. Addison Design Cons., San Francisco, 1985-88; exec. v.p. and prin. PSL Mktg. Resources, San Francisco, 1988—; speaker in field. Bd. dirs. Calif./Nev. United Meth. Found., San Francisco, 1993—. Mem. Roundtable for Women in Foodsvcs., Am. Mktg. Assn., San Francisco C. of C. Avocations: lay minister, cub scout leader, reading. Home: 677 Spruce St Berkeley CA 94707-1745 Office: PSL Mktg Resources Inc 10 Lombard St # 400 San Francisco CA 94111-1109

PULLEN, PENNY LYNNE, non-profit administrator, former state legislator; b. Buffalo, Mar. 2, 1947; d. John William and Alice Nettie (McConkey) P.; BA in Speech, U. Ill., 1969. TV technician Office Instructional Resources, U. Ill., 1966-68; community newspaper reporter Des Plaines (Ill.) Pub. Co., 1967-72; legislative asst. to Ill. legislators, 1968-77; mem. Ill. Ho. of Reps., 1977-93, chmn. ho. exec. com., 1981-82, minority whip, 1983-87, asst. minority leader, 1987-93; pres., founder Life Advocacy Resource Project, 1992—; exec. dir. Ill. Family Inst., 1993-94; dir. Legal Svcs. Corp., 1989-93; mem. Pres.'s Commn. on AIDS Epidemic, 1987-88; mem. Ill. Goodwill Del. to Republic of China, 1987. Del. Atlantic Alliance Young Polit. Leaders, Brussels, 1977, Rep. Nat. Conv, 1984; mem. Republican Nat. Com., 1984-88; summit conf. observer as mem. adhoc Women for SDI, Geneva, 1985; former mem. Maine Twp. Mental Health Assn.; active Nat. Coun. Ednl. Rsch., 1983-88. Recipient George Washington Honor medal Freedoms Found., 1978, Dwight Eisenhower Freedom medal Chgo. Captive Nations Com., 1977, Outstanding Legislator awards Ill. Press Assn., Ill. Podiatry Soc., Ill. Coroners Assn., Ill. County Clks. Assn., Ill. Hosp. Assn., Ill. Health Care Assn.; named Ill. Young Republican, 1968, Outstanding Young Person, Park Ridge Jaycees, 1981, One of 10 Outstanding Young Persons, Ill. Jaycees, 1981. Mem. Am. Legis. Exchange Council (dir. 1977-91, exec. com. 1978-83, 2d vice chmn. 1980-83), DAR. Lodge: Kiwanis.

PULLEN, RICHARD OWEN, lawyer, communications company executive; b. New Orleans, Nov. 6, 1944; s. Roscoe LeRoy and Gwendolen Sophia Ellen (Williams) P.; m. Frances G. Eisenstein, Jan. 24, 1976 (div. 1986). B.A. in Econs., Whitman Coll., 1967; J.D., Duke U., 1972. Bar: D.C. 1973. Fin. mgmt. trainee Gen. Electric Co., Lynn, Mass., 1967-69; sr. atty. domestic facilities div. Common Carrier Bur., FCC, Washington, 1972-79, atty. advisor Office of Opinions and Rev., 1979-81; chmn. definitions and terminology of joint industry, govt. com. for preparation of U.S. Proposals 1977 Broadcasting Satellite World Adminstrv. Radio Conf.; v.p. Washington office Contemporary Comm. Corp., New Rochelle, N.Y., 1981-91; v.p., gen. counsel Comm. Innovations Corp., New Rochelle, 1991—. With USCGR, 1967-75. Mem. ABA, Fed. Comm. Bar Assn., Fed. Bar Assn., Internat. Platform Assn. Republican. Unitarian.

PULLEYBLANK, EDWIN GEORGE, history educator emeritus, linguist; b. Calgary, Alta., Can., Aug. 7, 1922; s. W. George E. and Ruth Elizabeth (Willoughby) P.; m. Winona Ruth Relyea, July 17, 1945 (dec. Jan. 1978); children: David Edwin, Barbara Jill, Marcia Ruth. B.A., U. Alta., 1942; Ph.D., U. London, 1951. Research officer Nat. Research Council, Ottawa, 1943-46; lectr. Sch. Oriental and African studies U. London, 1948-53; prof. Chinese U. Cambridge, 1953-66; prof. Asian studies U. B.C., 1966-87, prof. emeritus, 1988—, head dept., 1968-75; editorial adviser Ency. Brit. Author: The Background of the Rebellion of An Lu-shan, 1955, Middle Chinese, 1984, Lexicon of Reconstructed Pronunciation in Early Middle Chinese, Late Middle Chinese and Early Mandarin, 1991, Outline of Classical Chinese Grammar; editor: (with W.G. Beasley) Historians of China and Japan, 1961; contbr. articles to profl. jours. Fellow Royal Soc. Can.; mem. Royal Asiatic Soc. (coun. 1956-59), Philol. Soc. London (coun. 1961-66), Assn. Asian Studies (dir. 1969-73), Can. Liguistic Assn., Can. Soc. Asian Studies (pres. 1971-74), Am. Oriental Soc. (pres. 1990-91), Internat. Assn. of Chinse

Linguistics (pres. 1995-96). Office: U BC, Dept Asian Studies, Vancouver, BC Canada V6T 1Z1

PULLEYN, S(AMUEL) ROBERT, publishing company executive; b. Milford, Pa., Nov. 18, 1946; s. Samuel Robert and Jeanne (Phillips) P.; m. Kathryn Susan Mathews, June 20, 1971 (div. 1986); 1 child, Micah Marion. B.A., Lake Forest Coll., 1969; postgrad., U. N.Mex., 1971. Dir. New Directions Ctr., Albuquerque, 1971-72; pres. Mediaworks Film Co., Albuquerque, 1972-74; pub. Fiberarts, Albuquerque, 1974-79; pres., pub. Lark Communications Corp., Asheville, N.C., 1979-85, Nine Press, Inc., Asheville, 1985-90, Altamont Press, Asheville, 1988—; adj. instr. U. N.C., Asheville, 1985; lectr. in fields of pub., art and textiles; coord. Small Mags. Pubs. Group, 1983-88. Author: Everlasting Floral Gifts, 1989, Wreaths 'Round the Year, 1990; editor: Fiberarts Design Book, 1980, Fiberarts Design Book II, 1983, The Basketmaker's Art, 1985, The Wreath Book, 1988, Fiberarts Design Book IV, 1990; mem. editorial bd. The Arts Jour., 1985-88; contbr. articles to profl. jours. Bd. dirs. Children's Grammar Sch., Asheville, 1980-84, Beaucatcher Prodns., 1987-90, The Preservation Soc., 1989-92, Planned Parenthood, 1994—. Democrat. Home: Scotton Hills Craine Rd Marshall NC 28753 Office: Altamont Press Inc 50 College St Asheville NC 28801-2818

PULLIAM, EUGENE SMITH, newspaper publisher; b. Atchison, Kans., Sept. 7, 1914; s. Eugene Collins and Myrta (Smith) P.; m. Jane Bleecker, May 29, 1943; children: Myrta, Russell, Deborah. A.B., DePauw U., 1935, LL.D., 1973. Reporter, UP, Chgo., Detroit, Buffalo, 1935-36; news editor Radio Sta. WIRE, Indpls., 1937-41; city editor Indpls. Star, 1947-48; mng. editor Indpls. News, 1948-62; asst. publisher Indpls. Star and News, 1962-76; pres. Phoenix Newspapers, 1979—; exec. v.p. Central Newspapers, Indpls., 1979—. Mem. Am. Soc. Newspaper Editors, Am. Newspaper Pubs. Assn. Found. (past pres.), Soc. Profl. Journalists, Delta Kappa Epsilon. Club: Crooked Stick Golf. Office: Indpls Star Indpls Newspapers Inc 307 N Pennsylvania St Indianapolis IN 46204-1811 also: Phoenix Newspapers Inc 120 E Van Buren St Phoenix AZ 85004-2227

PULLIAM, FREDERICK CAMERON, educational administrator; b. Mesa, Ariz., Jan. 5, 1936; s. Fredrick Posy and Nathana Laura (Cameron) P.; AA., Hannibal LaGrange Coll., 1955; AB, Grand Canyon Coll., 1958; M.Ed., U. Mo., Columbia, 1966, Ed.S., 1976, EdD, 1981; m. Deborah Jean Botts, June 1, 1979; 1 child, Sarah Elizabeth; children by previous marriage: Cameron Dale, Joy Renee. tchr., Centerview (Mo.) Public Schs., 1958-59; ordained to ministry So. Baptist Conv., 1955; minister Bethel Bapt. Ch., Kansas City, Mo., 1959-61; adminstr. Fiti'uta, Manu'a sch., Am. Samoa, 1966-69; cons. in fin. Mo. State Tchrs. Assn., Columbia, 1969-79; supt. schs. Midway Heights C-VII, Columbia, 1979-83; dir. elem. edn. Brentwood Pub. Schs. (Mo.), 1983-90; founder, coordinator Mo. Computer-Using Educators Conf., 1982-84; contbg. writer St. Louis Computing News, 1984—; adj. asst. prof. ednl. studies U. Mo., St. Louis, 1986-90; assoc. prof. edn. Mo. So. State Coll., 1990—, dir. clinical and field experiences in tchr. edu., Mo. So. Stae Coll., 1994—; adj. assoc. prof. grad. studies Southwest Baptist Univ., 1991-95; cons. sch. fin., curriculum improvement. Mem. Columbia Am. Revolution Bicentennial Commn. Inst. Devel. Ednl. Activity fellow, 1969, 78-84. Mem. Am. Assn. of Colls. for Tchr. Edn., Assn. Childhood Edn. Internat. Nat. Assn. Supervision and Curriculum Devel. (bd. dirs. 1984-90),Mo. Gov's. Transition Team (edn. adv. com. 1992-93), Phi Delta Kappa (chpt. pres.). Contbr. articles to profl. jours. Home: 2140 Kayla Ln Mount Vernon MO 65712-1243 Office: Mo So State Coll 224 Taylor Hall Joplin MO 64801-1595

PULLIAM, RUSSELL BLEECKER, editor, elder; b. Indpls., Sept. 20, 1949; s. Eugene S. and Jane B. Pulliam; m. Ruth Eichling, Nov. 26, 1977; children: Christine, Daniel, John, Sarah, David, Anna. BA, Williams Coll., 1971. Reporter, editor AP, N.Y.C. and Albany, N.Y., 1971-76; editorial writer, columnist Indpls. News, 1978-92, editor, 1992—; deacon Second Reformed Presbyn. Ch., Indpls., 1983-89, elder, 1989—; mem., bd. dirs. Cen. Ind. Radio Reading Inc. Contbr. articles to religious jours. Bd. dirs. Community Outreach Ctr., Noble Ctrs. Marion County Assn. for the Mentally Retarded, Indpls., 1984—; participant Stanley K. Lacey Leadership Series, 1980—; mem. adv. bd. Youth as Resources. Recipient Casper award Community Svc. Coun., 1980, 81, 82, 86; 1st place editorial writing Hoosier State Press Assn., 1979, 80, 3d place editorial writing UPI, 1983, 2d and 3d place, 1986; named Sagamore of the Wabash Gov. of Ind., 1980. Mem. Prison Fellowship, Ind. Assn. for Home Educators, Indpls. C. of C., Soc. Profl. Journalists (treas. Ind. chpt. 1982—, found. bd. 1991—, 2d place editorials and columns 1984, 85, hon. mention editorials 1988, 3d place columns 1989), Nat. Conf. Editorial Writers. Home: 1025 W 52nd St Indianapolis IN 46208-2463 Office: Indpls News 307 N Pennsylvania St Indianapolis IN 46204-1811

PULLING, RONALD WILSON, SR., aviation systems planner, civil engineer, consultant; b. L.A., Oct. 30, 1919; s. Albert Elmer and Mary (Porter) P.; m. Florence Dorothy Rooke, June 24, 1945 (dec.); children: Mary Anna, Ronald Jr. (dec.), William. BSCE, U. Calif., Berkeley, 1940; PFPA, Princeton U., 1963-64; PhD (hon.), Sierra Madre City Coll., 1981. Registered profl. engr., Calif., Fla., Hawaii, Md., Va. Civil engr. CAA, Honolulu, 1943-51; chief facility materials div. CAA, Oklahoma City, 1951-63; chief airport planning div. FAA, Washington, 1964-66, dep. dir. Office of Policy, 1966-68, dep. assoc. adminstr. for plans, 1968-73; sr. v.p. William L. Pereira Assoc., Washington, 1973-74; staff cons. TAMS Cons. Inc., Washington, 1975—; pres. Ronald W. Pulling Assoc., Alexandria, 1976—; v.p. United Global Airlines, Sierra Madre, Calif., 1984—. Author: (with others) Airport Economic Planning, 1971, Airport Planning, 1972; contbr. articles to profl. jours.; corr. Sierra Madre News, 1988-94. Recipient Meritorious Svc. award FAA, 1971, Disting. Career Svc. award, 1973. Fellow ASCE (James Laurie prize 1981); mem. NAE (elected), Transp. Rsch. Bd. (Disting. Svc. award 1984), Am. Planning Assn., Am. Inst. Cert. Planners (cert.), Springfield (Va.) Golf Club, Nat. Aviation Club. Episcopalian. Avocations: golf, creative writing, travel. Home: 4809 Polk Ave Alexandria VA 22304-2257 Office: R W Pulling Assoc PO Box 9526 Alexandria VA 22304-0526

PULLING, THOMAS LEFFINGWELL, investment advisor; b. N.Y.C., May 1, 1939; s. T.J. Edward and Lucy (Leffingwell) P.; m. Lisa Canby, Sept. 14, 1962 (div. 1968); children: Elizabeth, Edward L.; m. Sheila Sonne, Mar. 12, 1970 (div. 1980);children: Victoria, Diana, Christopher; m. Eileen Kingsbury-Smith, Dec. 21, 1989. BA cum laude, Princeton U., 1961. Asst. treas. J.P. Morgan & Co. Inc., N.Y.C., 1962-68; v.p. N.Y. Securities Co., N.Y.C., 1968-71, L.M. Rosenthal & Co., N.Y.C., 1971-76; mng. dir. Smith Barney (formerly Shearson Lehman Hutton), N.Y.C., 1977—; CEO Smith Barney Investment ADvisors, 1985—. Bd. dirs. Henry Luce Found., 1988—, Woodlawn Cemetery, 1980—; trustee South St. Seaport Mus., Long Island U., 1994—. with USMC, 1962-67. Mem. Century Assn., Pilgrims of the U.S. (N.Y.C.), Piping Rock Club (Locust Valley, N.Y.), Surf Club (Miami, Fla.), Univ. Club (N.Y.C.). Republican. Episcopalian. Home: 34 Yellow Cote Rd Oyster Bay NY 11771-4111 Office: Smith Barney 388 Greenwich St New York NY 10013-2375

PULLMAN, BILL, actor; b. Hornell, N.Y., 1953; m. Tamara Pullman, 3 children. Attended, SUNY, Oneonta; MFA, U. Mass., Amherst. theatre instr. Mont. State U., Bozeman. Actor: (theatre) The Rover, 1981, Ah, Wilderness!, 1983, The Old Flag, 1983, Dramathon '84, 1984, Curse of the Starving Class, 1985, All My Sons, 1986, Barabbas, 1986, Nanawatai, 1986, Demon Wine, 1988, Control Freaks, 1993, (films) Ruthless People, 1986, Spaceballs, 1987, The Serpent and the Rainbow, 1988, Rocket Gibraltar, 1988, The Accidental Tourist, 1989, Cold Feet, 1989, Brain Dead, 1989, Sibling Rivalry, 1990, Going Under, 1991, Bright Angel, 1991, Newsies, 1992, A League of Their Own, 1992, Singles, 1992, Sommersby, 1993, Sleepless in Seattle, 1993, Malice, 1993, Mr. Jones, 1993, The Favor, 1994, Wyatt Earp, 1994, While You Were Sleeping, 1995, Casper, 1995, (TV movies) Home Fires Burning, 1989, Crazy in Love, 1992, The Last Seduction, 1994. Office: UTA 9560 Wilshire Blvd 5th Fl Beverly Hills CA 90212

PULLMAN, MAYNARD EDWARD, biochemist; b. Chgo., Oct. 26, 1927; s. Harry and Gertrude (Atlas) P.; m. E. Phyllis Light, Sept. 12, 1948; children: H. Cydney, B. Valerie, Jacky Leigh. B.S., U. Ill., 1948, M.S., 1950; Ph.D. (NIH fellow), Johns Hopkins U., 1953. Fellow in pediatrics Johns Hopkins Hosp., 1953-54; asst. Pub. Health Rsch. Inst., City N.Y., 1954-56; assoc. Pub. Health Rsch. Inst., 1956-61, assoc. mem., 1961-65, mem., 1965-89, chief, 1973-87, assoc. dir., 1983-89; sr. rsch. scientist Coll. Physicians and Surgeons Columbia U., 1989-92; vis. prof. biochemistry U. São Paulo (Brazil) Sch. Medicine, 1963-64; research assoc. prof. biochemistry Sch. Medicine NYU, 1966-76, research prof., 1976-90; biochemistry study section mem. NIH, 1969-73. Editorial bd.: Jour. Biol. Chemistry, 1967-71, 78-80. NIH grantee, 1956-85; Shubert Found. grantee, 1972-74. Fellow N.Y. Acad. Scis.; mem. AAAS, Am. Soc. Biol. Chemistry and Molecular Biology, Brit. Biochem. Soc., Am. Chem. Soc. Home and Office: 338 Archer St Freeport NY 11520-4233

PULOS, ARTHUR JON, industrial design executive; b. Vandergrift, Pa., Feb. 3, 1917; s. John and Argyro (Tsakalos) Palukakos; m. Elizabeth Jane McQueen, Jan. 28, 1944; children—Cristofer, Maria, Demetra. B.F.A., Carnegie Inst. Tech., 1939; M.F.A., U. Oreg., 1943. Teaching asst. design and crafts U. Oreg. at Eugene, 1939-41; assoc. prof. design U. Ill., 1946-55; prof., chmn. dept. design Syracuse (N.Y.) U., 1955-82, prof. emeritus, 1982—; pres. Pulos Design Assos., Syracuse, 1958-87; Mem. planning council Expo 67, Montreal, Can., Fed. Design Assembly, 1974, Am. Design Bicentennial, 1974-75; mem. policy panel for architecture, planning and design Nat. Endowment for Arts, 1978—; cons. Colonial Williamsburg; lectr. in, USSR, Romania, Pakistan, Japan Ministry of Internat. Trade and Industry, others for UNESCO, USIA. Author: Careers in Industrial Design, 1978, Contact-Selling Design Services, 1975, American Design Ethic, 1983, The American Design Adventure, 1988; contbr. articles in design and design edn. to profl. jours. Bd. dirs. Everson Mus. Art, Syracuse, 1983—; mem. Budapest Cultural Forum, 1985. Served to 1st lt. USAF, 1944-46. Ford Found. fellow; Nat Endowment Arts fellow, 1984; Graham Found. grantee, 1987; recipient Chancellor's citation Syracuse U., 1982; Bronze Apple award, N.Y.C., 1983, Worldesign award, N.Y.C., 1988, Misha Black Meml. medal for design edn. Royal Soc. Arts, London, 1993. Fellow Indsl. Design Soc. Am. (pres. 1973-74; Disting. Educator award 1988), Internat. Council Socs. Indsl. Design (pres. 1980-81, senator 1982—, keynote speaker ICSID Congress in Japan 1989), Am. Steel Inst. (juror, cons.), Design Inst. Australia (hon.), Mexican Acad. Design (hon.) Japan Design Fedn. Internat. Competition (chmn. Jury, Osaka 1983), Alpha Rho Chi, Alpha Zi Alpha. Unitarian. Home: 3 The Orch Fayetteville NY 13066

PULSE, DAVID LUTHER, electrical engineer; b. Kansas City, Mo., Mar. 5, 1964; s. Joe Hyder and Diana Lillian (Woods) P. BSEE, U. Mo., 1986. Registered profl. engr., Mo., Kans., Okla., Ark. Project engr. City of Liberty, Mo., 1986; lab. instr. U. Mo., Columbia, 1986; distbn. engr. Empire Dist. Electric Co., Joplin, 1987-93; pres. EJL Electronics Engring., Joplin, 1991—; sr. distbn. engr. Empire Dist. Electric Co., Joplin, 1993-95, sr. system planning engr., 1995—; power quality adv. com. Kans. Electric Utilities Rsch., Topeka, 1993—, KRD 246 harmtracer rev. com., 1990, host engr.-power quality assessment, Wichita, 1991—; host engr. DPQ rsch. project Electric Power Rsch. Inst., Palo Alto, Calif., 1989—; utility power quality cons. WSU Power Quality Rsch. Lab., Wichita, Kans., 1989—. Author: Grounding-A Comprehensive Approach, 1990, Wiring for Sensitive Electronic Loads, 1992; contbr. articles to profl. jours. Advisor, judge Mo. Jr. Acad. of Sci., Kirksville, Mo., 1983—; hunter edn. instr. Mo. Dept. of Conservation, Jefferson City, 1989—. Mem. IEEE (sr.), Mo. Soc. Profl. Engrs. (chair com. 1987—), Mo. Acad. Sci., Mo. Jaycees (Outstanding Local Officer 1994), Jasper County Jaycees (past pres., chmn. bd. 1988—), Tau Beta Pi, Eta Kappa Nu, Kappa Alpha. Achievements include development of Dransoft 5.0-Power Quality Analysis Software Package, Empire Dist.'s Power Quality Program; rsch. in grounding techniques for electric power quality. Office: Empire Dist Electric Co 602 Joplin St Joplin MO 64802

PULSIFER, EDGAR DARLING, leasing service and sales executive; b. Natick, Mass., Jan. 11, 1934; s. Howard George and Elvie Marion (Morris) P.; m. Alice Minarik, Feb. 16, 1957 (div. Oct. 1979); children: Mark Edgar, Audrey Carol, Lee Howard; m. Barbara Ann Chuhak, Apr. 19, 1980. BSEE, MIT, 1955. With sales and service dept. Beckman Instruments, Fullerton, Calif., 1956-59; regional sales mgr. Hewlett Packard, Palo Alto, Calif., 1959-72, Gen. Automation, Anaheim, Calif., 1973-74; exec. v.p. Systems Mktg., Elk Grove Vlg., Ill., 1975-79; pres. Consol. Funding, Mt. Prospect, Ill., 1979—. Served as 1st lt. U.S. Army, 1956. Mem. MENSA, Coast Guard Auxiliary. Republican. Episcopalian. Clubs: North Shore Country (Glenview, Ill.), Itasca (Ill.) Country. Avocations: coins, stamps, curling, scuba diving, golf. Home: 370 Dulles Rd Des Plaines IL 60016-2755 Office: Consol Funding Corp P O Box 801 Mount Prospect IL 60056-0801

PUMPER, ROBERT WILLIAM, microbiologist; b. Clinton, Iowa, Sept. 12, 1921; s. William R. and Kathrine M. (Anderson) P.; m. Ruth J. Larkin, June 24, 1951; 1 son, Mark. B.A., U. Iowa, 1951, M.S., 1953, Ph.D., 1955. Diplomate: Am. Soc. Microbiology. Asst. prof. Hahnemann Med. Coll., Phila., 1955-57; prof. microbiology U. Ill. Med. Sch., Chgo., 1957—, Raymond B. Allen Med. lectr., 1970, 74, 76, 87. Co-author: Essentials of Medical Virology; contbr. articles to profl. jours. Served with USAAF, 1942-46. Recipient Chancellors' award U. Ill., Bombeck award for excellence in med. edn., 1992. Mem. Tissue Culture Assn., Sigma Xi, Phi Rho Sigma. Lutheran. Home: 18417 Argyle Ave Homewood IL 60430-3007 Office: U Ill Med Sch Dept Microbiology 808 S Wood St Chicago IL 60612-7300

PUMPHREY, JANET KAY, editor; b. Balt., June 18, 1946; d. John Henry and Elsie May (Keefer) P. AA in Secondary Edn., Anne Arundel C.C., Arnold, Md., 1967, AA in Bus. and Pub. Adminstrn., 1976. Office mgr. Anne Arundel C.C., 1964—; mng. editor Am. Polygraph Assn., Severna Park, Md., 1973—; archives dir. Am. Polygraph Assn., Severna Park, 1973—; owner JKP Publ. Svcs., 1990—; dir. Am. Polygraph Assn. Reference Svc., 1995—. Editor: (with Albert D. Snyder) Ten Years of Polygraph, 1984, (with Norman Ansley) Justice and the Polygraph, 1985, 2d edit., 1996, A House Full of Love, 1990, Mama, There's A Mouse in My House, 1996. Mem. Rep. Nat. Sustaining Com. Mem. NAFE, Am. Polygraph Assn. (hon.), Md. Polygraph Assn. (affiliate), Anne Arundel County Hist. Soc., Alumni Assn. Anne Arundel Community Coll. Republican. Methodist. Avocations: travel, poetry, gardening, mystery writer. Home: 3 Kimberly Ct Severna Park MD 21146-3703 Office: JKP Pub Svcs PO Box 1535 Severna Park MD 21146-8535

PUMPIAN, BETTY ANN G., advertising executive; b. Balt., Sept. 19, 1935; d. Emanuel Henry and Carlyn Rose (Freudenthal) Goldstone; m. Paul H. Pumpian, June 24, 1956. BS in Mktg., U. Balt., 1956. Network coord., asst. buyer Parkson Advt., N.Y.C., 1957-61; traffic mgr. Sta. KORK, Las Vegas, Nev., 1961; project coord., bookkeeper Art Dept., L.A., 1961-62; network and planning coord. Ogilvy & Mather, L.A., 1962-75, asst. media dir., 1975-78, assoc. media dir., 1978-80, v.p., dir. nat. broadcast and programming, 1980-89; nat./regional broadcast adminstr. Bozell, Inc., L.A., 1989-90; v.p., sr. network negotiator Western Internat. Media, L.A., 1991—; lectr. Adweek Seminars, L.A., 1989-91. Chmn. 1st Coun. Dist. Horsemen's Adv. Com., L.A., 1978-81; chmn. L.A. Equine Adv. Com., 1978-83; pres. Cal-Western Appaloosa Inc., 1981-82, bd. dirs; mem. horse drugging adv. com. Calif. Dept. Food and Agr., Sacramento, 1987—. Recipient Commendation award L.A. City Coun., 1983, Achievement cert. YWCA, L.A., 1976. Mem. Appaloosa Horse Club (dir., chmn. planning and rev. 1987-88, 93-94, chmn. rules 1988-92, chmn. mktg. 1992—, chmn. youth 1992-93, v.p. 1994-95). Republican. Avocation: breeding and racing Appaloosa horses. Office: Western Internat Media 8544 W Sunset Blvd West Hollywood CA 90069-2310

PUNCH, JERRY LEROY, audiology educator, researcher; b. Newton, N.C., Mar. 3, 1943; s. Coyle L. and Nancy (Sigmon) P.; m. Susan Jeannette Milner, Oct. 13, 1976; children: Wendy, Keith, Corey, Janelle. BA in Psychology, Wake Forest U., 1965; MS in Audiology and Speech Pathology, Vanderbilt U., 1967; PhD in Audiology, Northwestern U., 1972. Audiology trainee VA, Winston-Salem, N.C., 1965; clin. audiologist, supr. Bill Wilkerson Hearing and Speech Ctr., 1967-68; asst. prof. audiology U. Miss., 1971-73, Memphis State U., 1973-75; rsch. assoc. Biocomms. Lab. U. Md., 1975-80; project dir. Am. Speech-Lang.-Hearing Assn., 1980-81, dir. rsch. divsn., 1980-84; assoc. prof., chief audiology sect., dept. otolaryngology Ind. U. Sch. Medicine, 1984-87; sr. rsch. audiologist Audio-Diagnostics divsn. Nicolet Instrument Corp., 1987-89; prof., chair dept. audiology and speech scis. Mich. State U., East Lansing, 1990—; cons. Dept. VA, Mich. Dept. Social Svcs. Editl. cons. Jour. Speech and Hearing Rsch., Ear and Hearing, Am. Jour. Audiology, Jour. Acoustical Soc. Am.; contbr. numerous articles to profl. jours. Fellow Am. Acad. Audiology; mem. Am.-Speech-Lang.-Hearing Assn. (cert. of clin. competence in audiology), Mich. Speech-Lang.-Hearing Assn., Am. Auditory Soc. Avocations: golf, photography. Office: Mich State U Dept Audiology/Speech Scis East Lansing MI 48824

PUOTINEN, ARTHUR EDWIN, college president, clergyman; b. Crystal Falls, Mich., Sept. 7, 1941; s. Kaleva Weikko and Ines Pauline (Maki) P.; m. Judith Cathleen Kapoun, Aug. 8, 1964; children: Anne, Marjetta, Sara. AA, Suomi Coll., 1961; BA, Augustana Coll., Rock Island, Ill., 1963; MDiv, Luth. Sch. Theology, Chgo., 1967; MA, U. Chgo., 1969, PhD, 1973; MBA, Wake Forest U., 1984. Pastor Trinity Luth. Ch., Chgo., 1968-70; asst. prof. religion Cen. Mich. U., Mt. Pleasant, 1971-74; dean faculty Suomi Coll., Hancock, Mich., 1974-78; v.p. acad. affairs Lenoir-Rhyne Coll., Hickory, N.C., 1978-83; assoc. dean acad. affairs Roanoke Coll., Salem, Va., 1983-84; exec. dir. Luth. Ednl. Conf. of N.Am., Washington, 1984-88; pres. Grand View Coll., Des Moines, 1988—; dir. Iowa Luth. Hosp., Des Moines, 1989—; pastor S.E. Iowa Synod, Evang.-Luth. Ch. Am. Author: Finnish Radicals..., 1979; contbr. articles to books and jours. Grantee NEH, U.S. Dept. Edn. Mem. Des Moines Club, Pioneer Club, Rotary. Democrat. Avocations: jogging, reading, travel. Home: 528 Valley West Ct West Des Moines IA 50265-4047 Office: Grand View Coll 1200 Grandview Ave Des Moines IA 50316-1529

PURAVS, JOHN ANDRIS, journalist; b. Ruckersdorf, Germany, Feb. 23, 1945; s. Janis Alfreds and Alma Otilija (Grundulis) P.; m. Trudi Ann Tiedeman, July 2, 1966 (div. Feb. 1982). BA, U. Mich., 1966. Reporter Saginaw (Mich.) News, 1966-78, suburban editor, 1978-79, editorial editor, 1979—, chmn. editorial bd., 1981—; commentator Sta. WUCM-TV, Univ. Ctr., Mich. Contbr. articles to profl. jours. Mem. adv. bd. Saginaw State Valley State U. Coll. Edn., 1991—. 1st lt. U.S. Army, 1967-69, Vietnam. Medill fellow Northwestern U., 1970; Regents-Alumni scholar U. Mich., 1962-66, Chgo. House Coun., 1963-64; numerous journalism awards. Mem. Soc. Profl. Journalists, Am. Coun. on Germany (fellow 1980, Haus Rissen fellow 1982, del. German-Am. Biennial Conf. 1989), Saginaw Valley Press Club (pres. 1976), Nat. Conf. Editl. Writers (group chmn. 1991), Latvian Club Saginaw. Avocations: sports, history, geo-politics. Home: 3925 Cabaret Trl W Apt 4 Saginaw MI 48603-2205 Office: Saginaw News 203 S Washington Ave Saginaw MI 48607-1244

PURCELL, ANN RUSHING, state legislator, office manager medical business; b. Reidsville, Ga., May 12, 1945; d. William Robert and Katie (Dasher) Rushing; m. Dent Wiley Purcell, May 26, 1966; children: Edwin Wiley, Mieke Ann, Mikki Marie. BS in Edn., Ga. So. Coll., 1966. Cert. secondary tchr. Tchr. math. Evans (Ga.) High Sch., 1966-68; tchr. math., earth and sci. Beaumont Jr. High Sch., Lexington, Ky., 1969-70; substitute tchr. Tallahassee, Fla., 1970's; agt. Noblin Realty, Tallahassee, 1970's; office mgr. Radiation Therapy Assocs., PC, Savannah, Ga., 1979—; state legislator Ho. of Reps. Ga. Gen. Assembly, Atlanta, 1991—. Author: Purcells of South Georgia and Other Related Families, 1976. Bd. dirs. Med. Assn. Ga. Polit. Action Com., Atlanta, 1988-89, Girl Scout Coun. Savannah, 1991—, Ga. So. U. Found., 1992—; mem. adv. com. Effingham County Extension Svc., 1992—; fin. chmn. State YMCA, 1991—; bd. adv. Claxton Youth Detnetion Ctr. Recipient Friend of Medicine award Med. Assn. Ga., 1991, 93, 94, Guardian of Small Bus. award Nat. Fedn. Ind. Bus., 1992, 94, Commendation cert. Ga. Emergency Mgmt. Agy., 1995. Mem. Aux. to the Med. Assn. Ga. (pres. 1985), Aux. to the Ga. Med. Soc. (pres. 1981-82), Ga. Salzburger Soc., Effingham County Pub. Officials Assn., Rotary Internat. Democrat. Methodist. Avocations: painting, genealogy, fishing. Home: 410 Willowpeg Way Rincon GA 31326-9111 Office: State Capitol SW Ste 401 Atlanta GA 30334-1600

PURCELL, ARTHUR HENRY, environmental engineering educator, consultant; b. Evanston, Ill., Aug. 11, 1944; s. Edward and Ethel (Lohman) P.; m. Deborah Ross Purcell, Feb. 2, 1973; 1 child:Christina Jean Ethel. B.S., Cornell U., 1966; M.S., Northwestern U., 1971, Ph.D., 1972. Environmentalist U.S. Army Environ. Office, 1971; assoc. dir. office of sci. and govt. AAAS, 1973-74; co-founder, dir. Resource Policy Inst., Washington, 1975—; assoc. professorial lectr. dept. civil, mech. and environ. engring. George Washington U., 1975-89; professorial lectr. Ctr. for Tech. and Adminstrn., Am. U., 1980-81; cons. engr., 1974—; staff prin. Pres.'s Commn. on Accident at Three Mile Island, 1979; chmn. D.C. Adv. Neighborhood Commn., 1981-84, 86—; spl. cons. Econ. Commn. for Europe, 1982—; lectr. USIA, Europe, 1982, 90; vis. scientist Hazardous Substances Control Rsch. Ctr. UCLA, 1989; assoc. prof., lectr. environ. mgmt. U. Soc. Calif., West Coast U.; chmn. First Internat. Conf. on Waste Minimization and Clean Tech., Geneva, 1989; keynote lectr. Envirotech '90, Vienna, Austria, 1990, EC/Finnish Rsch. Inst. series on setting priorities in environ. mgmt., Finland, 1992, Italy, 1993; sr. environ. engr. Jacobs Engring. Group, 1991; chmn. Pollution Prevention Tech. Conf., L.A., 1994; mem. environ. mgmt. faculty West Coast U., 1994—. Contbr. publs. and lects. on resource policy, materials research and sci. and tech. policy to popular and profl. jours.; author: The Waste Watchers, 1980; contbg. travel writer Washington Post and others; editorial bd. Resources Policy. Chmn. Scientist and Engrs. for Carter, 1976-77; mem. Jimmy Carter Sci. Policy Task Force, 1976, Pres.'s Commn. on Scholars, 1978—; sr. adviser sci. Mondale-Ferraro campaign, 1984; mem. Environmentalists for Pete Wilson, 1990. Recipient Environ. Program award Friends of UNEP, 1988; German Marshall Fund Travel award scholar, 1980, 82. Mem. World Coun. for Biosphere, Sigma Xi. Democrat. Office: 1745 Selby Ave No 11 Los Angeles CA 90024-5774 *We are all environmentalists. We have to be. So we are all part of the solution to solving the world's ecological dilemmas. Let's get on with the job.*

PURCELL, BRADFORD MOORE, publishing company executive; b. Garden City, N.Y., Oct. 1, 1929; s. William Lawrence and Margaret (Moore) P.; m. Louise Rauth, July 10, 1954; children: Margaret, Philip, Mark, Louisa, Christopher. B.A., Williams Coll., 1951; M.B.A., Columbia U., 1957. Sr. v.p. devel. McGraw Hill, Inc., 1976-79, sr. v.p., 1979-81, group v.p. tng. systems, 1981-83, sr. v.p. mktg., 1983-85; pres. W.H. Smith Pubs Inc., N.Y.C., 1985-91; Rsch. Books Inc., 1992. Served to 1st lt. USAF, 1951-53. Home: RR 3 21-31 Croton Lake Rd Katonah NY 10536 Office: Rsch Books Inc 38 Academy St # 1507 Madison CT 06443-2611

PURCELL, DALE, college administrator, consultant; b. Baxley, Ga., Oct. 20, 1919; s. John Groce and Agnes (Moody) P.; m. Edna Jean Rowell, Aug. 2, 1944; children: David Scott, Steven Dale, Pamela Jean; m. Mary Louise Gerlinger, Aug. 26, 1962; adopted children: Amelia Allerton, Jon Allerton. B.A., U. Redlands, 1948, M.A., 1949; postgrad., Northwestern U., 1951-52; LL.D., Lindenwood Colls., 1974. Topographer U.S. E.D., 1939; U.S. counter-intelligence agt., 1940-42; assoc. prof. Ottawa U., 1953-54, asst. to pres., 1954-58; gen. sec. Earlham Coll., 1958-61; dir. devel. U. So. Fla., 1961-63; pres. MITAC, Inc., Beverly Hills, Calif., 1961-72; exec. dir. Cancer Research Center, Columbia, Mo., 1963-65; pres. Dale Purcell Assocs., 1972-92, Westminster Coll., Fulton, Mo., 1973-76; a founding dir. Am. Sports Medicine Inst., Birmingham, Ala., 1987-92; chmn. Corp. Health Solutions, Arlington, Tex., 1988—; cons. Hughston Sports Medicine Found., Columbus, Ga., Berry Coll., Mt. Berry, Ga., Hope Coll., Holland, Mich., William Woods Coll., Fulton, Mo., Eureka (Ill.) Coll., Brescia Coll., Owensboro, Ky., Cranbrook Insts., Bloomfield Hills, Mich., Penrose Hosp., Colorado Springs, Colo., Northwestern Coll., Orange City, Iowa, Centro Medico Docente, Caracas, Venezuela, Wayland Acad., Beaver Dam, Wis., Cen. Coll., Pella, Iowa, U. Stirling, Scotland, U. Ottawa, Ont., Can., Washington & Lee U., Lexington, Va., Taylor U., Upland, Ind., Menninger Found., Topeka, Kans., Ill. Wesleyan U., Bloomington, Cox Med. Ctr., Springfield, Mo., Nat. Council Family Rels. Mpls., Albert Schweitzer Ctr., Great Barrington, Mass., Stephens Coll., Columbia, Mo., Hist. Savannah Found., Ga. Served to capt. USMCR, 1942-46, 52-53. Recipient Disting. Achievement award Berry Coll., 1974, medal Pres. of China, 1945, medal Pres. of Korea, 1953. Mem. Pi Kappa Delta (Alpha chpt.). Presbyterian (elder 1964—). Clubs: HousaTonics (pres.) (Salisbury, Conn.), St. Louis (Clayton), Univ. (St. Louis and N.Y.C.), Litchfield County. Home: Woodlands 120 Belden St Falls Village CT 06031-1112

PURCELL, EDWARD MILLS, physics educator; b. Taylorville, Ill., Aug. 30, 1912; s. Edward A. and Mary Elizabeth (Mills) P.; m. Beth C. Busser,

Jan. 22, 1937; children: Dennis W., Frank B. B.S. in Elec. Engring, Purdue U., 1933, D. Engring. (hon.), 1953; Internat. Exchange student, Technische Hochschule, Karlsruhe, Germany, 1933-34; A.M., Harvard U., 1935, Ph.D., 1938. Instr. physics Harvard U., 1938-40, asso. prof., 1946-49, prof. physics, 1949-58, Donner prof. sci., 1958-60, Gerhard Gade Univ. prof., 1960-80, emeritus, 1980—; sr. fellow Soc. of Fellows, 1949-71; group leader Radiation Lab., MIT, 1941-45. Contbg. author: Radiation Lab. series, 1949, Berkeley Physics Course, 1965; contbr. sci. papers on nuclear magnetism, radio astronomy, astrophysics, biophysics. Mem. Pres.'s Sci. Advisory Com., 1957-60, 62-65. Co-winner Nobel prize in Physics, 1952; recipient Oersted medal Am. Assn. Physics Tchrs., 1968, Nat. Medal of Sci., 1980, Harvard medal, 1986. Mem. NAS, Am. Philos. Soc., Am. Phys. Soc., Am. Acad. Arts and Scis., Royal Soc. (fgn. mem.). Office: Harvard U Lyman Lab Cambridge MA 02138

PURCELL, GEORGE RICHARD, artist, postal employee; b. Clayton, N.Y., May 4, 1921; s. George Thomas and Katherine Eileen (Eagan) P.; m. Mary Sutter, Apr. 3, 1961. BS, Niagara U., 1947; postgrad., Syracuse U., 1952-53, 55-56. With Eagan Real Estate, Syracuse, 1948-49; claims interviewer N.Y. State Div. Unemployment Ins., 1949-50, 52; with U.S. Postal Service, Syracuse, 1957—, cert. classifier of mails, 1975-77, with registry dept., 1977—; tutor philosophy, 1971—. Exhibited in Central N.Y. Art Open, 1981, Drake Gallery, Fayetteville, N.Y., 1982, Assoc. Artists Gallery, Syracuse, 1983, 91, Fayetteville Art Festival, 1984, Recreation Generation Art Exhibit, 1982—, DeWitt (N.Y.) Libr., 1986—, N.Y. State Fair, 1990, Art Telauc WCNY-TV, Syracuse, N.Y., 1990—, Cazenovia Coll. Art Auction, 1994. Founder, pres. Syracuse chpt. Cath. Med. Mission Bd., 1973-76, rep., 1976—; del. Predsl. Trust, 1992; senator of high chamber Internat. Parliament for Safety and Peace, also dep. of assembly; active Cath. Near-East Welfare Assn., Book Mission Program, New Mems. Art Show Manlius Libr., 1991, Rep. Nat. Com., Heritage Found, Washington. Decorated Legion de L'Aigle de mer, Order of Holy Cross of Jerusalem, Order Knight Templars of Jerusalem, knight Order of Holy Grail, knight Lofsensischen Ursinius Orden, baron Royal Order of Bohemian Crown. Served with U.S. Army, 1943-46. N.Y. State War Service scholar, 1955. Fellow Australian Inst. Co-ordinated Rsch. (life); mem. Am. Biog. Inst. (life assoc., rsch. bd. advisors nat. div.), Internat. Soc. Neoplatonic Studies, World Jewish Congress, Soc. Ancient Greek Philosophy, Inst. des Hautes Etudes, Alliance Universelle pour La Paix (hon. prof.), Osterrichische Albert Sweitzer Gesselshaft, Lofsensischen Ursinius Orden (knight), Internat. Parliament for Safety and Peace (senator high chamber dept. mem. assembly), German Order of the Holy Grail (knight), Heritage Found., Acad. Maison Des Internationale Intellectuels, Australian Inst. of Co-Ordinated Rsch. (life fellow), Contemporary Personalities. Roman Catholic.

PURCELL, JAMES FRANCIS, consultant, former utility executive; b. Miles City, Mont., May 13, 1920; s. Robert E. and Mary A. (Hickey) P.; m. Dorothy Marie Abel, Nov. 4, 1944; children—Angela, Ann, Alicia, Anita, Alanna, James Francis, Andrea, Adria, Michael, Gregory, Amara. A.B. magna cum laude, U. Notre Dame, 1942; MBA, Harvard U., 1943. With McGraw-Hill Pub. Co., N.Y.C., 1946-48; dir. public relations Am. Maize Products Co., N.Y.C., 1948-51; public relations cons. Selvage & Lee, Chgo., 1951-53; with No. Ind. Public Service Co., Hammond, 1953—, v.p. public relations, 1961-75, sr. v.p., 1975-84, bd. dirs., chmn. environ. and consumer affairs com.; owner, pres. James F. Purcell and Assocs., 1984—. Chmn. bd. govs. Our Lady of Mercy Hosp., Dyer, Ind., 1979-83; past chmn. Hammond Community Chest drive; past mem. nat. president's council St. Mary's (Ind.) Coll.; bd. dirs. Catholic Charities, 1965-85; chmn. bd. dirs. Bishop Noll Found., 1988-90. Served to lt. USNR, 1943-46. Named Man of Year Notre Dame U., 1967. Mem. Pub. Rels. Soc. Am. (past pres. Hoosier chpt.), N.W. Ind. Assn. Commerce and Industry (v.p., dir. 1979-83), Newcomen Soc. N. Am., Briar Ridge Country Club (Schererville), Serra Club (past pres. Calumet region), Notre Dame Club, Harvard U. Bus. Sch. Club of Chgo. Office: 2842 45th Ave Highland IN 46322

PURCELL, JAMES LAWRENCE, lawyer; b. Wilkes-Barre, Pa., July 29, 1929; s. Joseph Ligouri and Mary Theresa (Walter) P.; m. Mary Louise Gallagher, Nov. 22, 1956 (dec. 1968); children: Joseph, Joan, James Lawrence, Catherine; m. Regina M. Bligh, May 31, 1971; 1 son, Daniel. Student, King's Coll., 1947-49; LL.B., St. John's U., 1952; LL.M., NYU, 1955. Bar: N.Y. 1953, U.S. Ct. Appeals (2d cir.) 1953, U.S. Tax Ct. 1954, U.S. Supreme Ct. 1956, U.S. Dist. Ct. (so. and ea. dists.) N.Y. 1957, D.C. 1970. Assoc. Dewey, Ballantine, Bushby, Palmer & Wood (and predecessor firms), N.Y.C., 1952-55, Crisona Bros., N.Y.C., 1955-58, Paul, Weiss, Rifkind, Wharton & Garrison, N.Y.C., 1958-64; ptnr. Paul, Weiss, Rifkind, Wharton & Garrison, 1964—; mem. bd. advs. Nat. Ctr. for Paralegal Tng., N.Y.C., 1978—. Bd. dirs. King's Coll., Wilkes-Barre, Pa., 1977—. Fellow Am. Bar Found.; mem. ABA, Assn. Bar City N.Y., Nassau County Bar Assn. Roman Catholic. Office: Paul Weiss Rifkind Wharton Garrison 1285 Avenue of Americas New York NY 10019-6064

PURCELL, JAMES NELSON, JR., international organization administrator; b. Nashville, July 16, 1938; s. James Nelson and Mary Helen P.; m. Walda Jean Primm, July 16, 1961; children: Deirdre Ann, Carole Elizabeth. B.A. in Polit. Sci., Furman U., 1961; M.P.A. (Maxwell Grad. Sch. fellow), Syracuse U., 1962. Mgmt. intern U.S. AEC, N.Y.C., Washington, Oak Ridge, 1962; budget analyst U.S. AEC, Oak Ridge, Washington, 1962-66; mgmt. analyst AID, State Dept., Washington, 1966-68; budget preparation specialist Office Mgmt. and Budget/Exec. Office of the Pres., 1968-69, dept. chief budget preparation, 1969-72; sr. budget examiner Internat. Ednl. Exch. program Office of Pres., 1972-74; chief Justice-Treasury br. Office Mgmt. and Budget/Exec. Office of the Pres., 1974-76; chief resources programming and mgmt. div. Bur. Ednl. and Cultural Affairs, Dept. State, Washington, 1976-77; exec. dir. Bur. Adminstrn., Dept. State, Washington, 1978-79; dep. asst. sec. Bur. Refugee Programs, Dept. State, Washington, 1979-82, dir., 1982-87; dir. gen. Internat. Orgn. for Migration, Geneva, 1988—. Mem. Am. Soc. Pub. Adminstrn. Home: 6 Chateau-Banquet, CH-1202 Geneva Switzerland Office: IOM/Case postale 71, 17 Rt des Morillons, 1211 Geneva Switzerland

PURCELL, JOHN R., holding company executive. Sr. v.p. fin. Gannett Co. Inc., 1968-77; exec. v.p. CBS, 1977-81; chmn. bd., CEO SFN Cos., Inc., 1982-86; pres. DM Holdings, Stamford, Conn., 1991—. Office: DM Holdings Inc 70 Seaview Ave Stamford CT 06902-6040*

PURCELL, KENNETH, psychology educator, university dean; b. N.Y.C., Oct. 21, 1928; s. Herman and Ann (Bulkin) P.; m. Claire Dickson Kepler, Dec. 17, 1949 (div. Dec. 1986); children: Kathleen Ann, Andrew Kepler; m. Marjorie Bayes, Jan. 17, 1987. B.A., Ph.D., U. Nebr. Asst. prof. U. Ky., 1956-58; dir. behavior sci. div. Children's Asthma Research Inst.; asst. prof. U. Colo. Med. Center, 1958-68; prof., dir. clin. tng. psychology U. Mass., 1968-69, chmn. dept. psychology, 1969-70; prof. psychology, chmn. dept. U. Denver, 1970—, dean Coll. Arts and Scis., 1976-84, prof. psychology, 1984—. Author papers in field. Served to 2d lt. AUS, 1953-56. Fellow Am. Psychol. Assn., Soc. Research Child Devel., AAAS, Colo. Psychol. Assn. (dir. 1962-64). Home: 3759 E Noble Rd Littleton CO 80122-2042 Office: Univ Denver Coll Arts And Scis Denver CO 80208

PURCELL, LEE, actress; b. N.C., June 15, 1953; m. Gary A. Lowe; 1 child, Gary; 1 stepchild. Student, Royal Acad. Dramatic Art; studies with Margot Lister, Milton Katselas, Jeff Corey, Robert F. Lyons. Appeared in (films) Adam at 6 A.M., 1970, The Toy Factory, 1971, Dirty Little Billy, 1972, Kid Blue, 1973, Mr. Majestyk, 1974, Almost Summer, 1978, Stir Crazy, 1980, Valley Girl, Eddie Macon's Run, 1983, Laura's Dream, 1986, (TV) Highjack, 1973, Stranger in Our House, 1978, Kenny Rogers as the Gambler, 1980, Killing at Hell's Gate, 1981, Magnum P.I., Murder, She Wrote, 1985, My Wicked Wicked Ways: The Legend of Errol Flynn, 1986, Secret Sins of the Father, 1994 (Emmy nomination, Supporting Actress - Special, 1994), (stage) Richard III, A Streetcar Named Desire, The Taming of the Shrew, A Midsummer Night's Dream. Recipient Bronze Halo Career Achievement award So. Calif. Motion Picture Council, 1985. Mem. Actors' Equity Assn., Screen Actors Guild, AFTRA, Acad. Motion Picture Arts and Scis., Acad. TV Arts And Scis. Avocations: writing, collecting antiques and music boxes. Office: Artists Agency 1000 Santa Monica Blvd Ste 305 Los Angeles CA 90067*

PURCELL, MARY LOUISE GERLINGER, educator; b. Thief River Falls, Minn., July 17, 1923; d. Charles and Lajla (Dale) Gerlinger; student Yankton Coll., 1941-45, Yale Div. Sch., 1949-50, NYU, summer 1949; MA (alumni fellow), Tchrs. Coll. Columbia, 1959, EdD, 1963; m. Walter A. Kuyawski, June 9, 1950 (dec. July 1954); children: Amelia Allerton, Jon Allerton; m. 2d, Dale Purcell, Aug. 26, 1962. Teen-age program dir., YWCA, New Haven, 1945-52; dir. program in family rels., asst. prof. sociology and psychology Earlham Coll., Richmond, Ind., 1959-62, conf. coord. undergrad. edn. for women, 1962; chmn. div. home and community Stephens Coll., Columbia, Mo., 1962-73, chmn. family and community studies, 1962-78, dir. Learning Unltd., continuing edn. for women, 1974-78, developer course The Contemporary Am. Woman, 1962, cons., 1962; prof., Auburn (Ala.) U., 1978-88, prof. emerita, 1988—, head dept. family and child devel., 1978-84, spl. asst. to v.p. acad. affairs, 1985-86. chmn. search com. for v.p. acad. affairs, 1984; vis. prof. Ind. U. Summer Sch., 1970. Cons. student personnel svcs., Trenton (N.J.) State Coll., 1958-59, 61. Recipient Alumni Achievement award Yankton Coll., 1975. Mem. AAUW, Am. Home Econs. Assn. (bd. dirs. 1967-69, chair 1st subject matter unit 1969, family relations and child devel. sect. 1986-89), Groves Conf. on Family, Nat. Council Family Relations (dir., chmn.-elect affiliated councils, 1981-82, chmn., 1982-84, nat. program chmn. 1977, chmn. film awards com., chmn. spl. emphases sect., bd. dirs., Ernest G. Osborne award for excellence in teaching 1979), Delta Kappa Gamma. Presbyterian. Contbr. articles to coll. bulls., jours. Home: 120 Belden St Falls Village CT 06031-1112

PURCELL, PATRICK B., motion picture company executive; b. Dublin, Ireland, Mar. 16, 1943; s. James P. and Rita (Donohoe) P.; m. Simone Gros-Long, Feb. 1, 1968; children: Alexander J., Christopher P., Benjamin J. Student, Staffordshire Coll. Commerce, 1964-66; M.B.A., Fordham U., 1973. CPA, Calif. Various positions in pub. and pvt. acctg. Eng. and U.S., 1960-70; with Paramount Pictures Corp., N.Y.C., Los Angeles, 1970—, v.p. fin., 1980—83, exec. v.p. fin. and adminstrn., 1983-89, exec. v.p., chief fin. and adminstrv. officer, 1989—. Fellow Chartered Assn. Cert. Accts.; mem. AICPA, Calif. Soc. CPAs, Fin. Execs. Inst., Inst. Taxation. Roman Catholic. Club: Jonathan. Home: 1449 Capri Dr Pacific Palisades CA 90272-2706 Office: Paramount Pictures 5555 Melrose Ave Hollywood CA 90038

PURCELL, PATRICK JOSEPH, newspaper publisher; b. N.Y.C., Nov. 9, 1947; s. Patrick Joseph and Sarah (Muller) P.; m. Maureen T. Shuart, Aug. 8, 1970; children: Kathleen, Erin, Patrick, Kerry. B.B.A., St. John's U., 1969; M.B.A., Hofstra U., 1977. Various supr. positions N.Y. Daily News, N.Y.C., 1969-80; assoc. pub. Village Voice, N.Y.C., 1980-82; v.p. advt. N.Y. Post, N.Y.C., 1982-83; v.p. sales and mktg. Skyband Inc., N.Y.C., 1983; pres., pub. Boston Herald, 1984—, owner, 1994—; pub. The N.Y. Post, 1986-88; exec. v.p. News Am./Newspapers, 1986-90, pres., 1990-93, CEO, 1993-94; East Coast pres. Am. Ireland Fund, 1996—; bd. dirs. Bay Bank, MetroWest Sub. Regional Bd., The Genesis Fund. Bd. dirs. NCCJ, Boston, 1984-86, Boy Scouts Am., Boston, 1984-85, Cath. Charitable Bur., Boston, 1984-86, John F. Kennedy Found.; mem. Greater Boston Assn. Retarded Citizens, 1984-86; chmn. Boston Against Drugs, 1988—; mem. White House Conf. for a Drug Free Am., 1987—. Mem. Boston Better Bus. Bur., Am. Newspaper Pub. Assn., New Eng. Newspaper Assn., Boston C. of C. (bd. dirs. 1984-86), Downtown Crossing Assn. (bd. dirs.). Roman Catholic. Clubs: Publicity, Ad (Boston). Avocations: jogging; skiing. Office: Boston Herald 1 Herald St Boston MA 02118-2200

PURCELL, PHILIP JAMES, financial services company executive; b. Salt Lake City, Sept. 5, 1943; m. Anne Marie Mc Namara, Apr. 2, 1964. B.B.A., U. Notre Dame, 1964; M.Sc. in Econs., London Sch. Econs. and Polit. Sci., U. London, 1966; M.B.A., U. Chgo., 1967. Mng. dir., cons. McKinsey & Co., Inc., Chgo., 1967-78; v.p. planning and adminstrn. Sears, Roebuck and Co., Chgo., 1978-82; from pres., CEO, to chmn., CEO Dean Witter Discover & Co., N.Y.C., 1982—; also bd. dirs. Dean Witter InterCapital Inc., N.Y.C.; bd. dirs. Dean Witter Realty Inc., Dean Witter Reynolds, Inc., N.Y. Stock Exchange, SPS Payment Systems Inc., Transaction Svcs. Inc.; mem. coun. Grad. Sch. Bus., Univ. Chgo.; chmn. Discover Card Svcs. Inc.; chmn., CEO Novus Credit Svcs. Inc. Bd. trustees U. Notre Dame Bus. Sch., Ind. Served with USNR. Roman Catholic. Clubs: Economic of Chgo., The Chgo. Office: Dean Witter/Discover 2 World Trade Ctr New York NY 10048

PURCELL, RICHARD FICK, lawyer, food companies advisor and counsel; b. Washington, Apr. 19, 1924; s. Richard J. and Clara A. (Fick) P.; m. Judith Wyckoff, Nov. 28, 1964; children: Richard Wyckoff, Edward Thomas, Carolyn Elizabeth P. Reichenbach. BA, George Washington U., 1948; MA, Columbia U., 1949; cert., U. Fribourg (Switzerland), 1949; LLB, Harvard U., 1952; grad., Command and Gen. Staff Coll., Ft. Leavenworth, Kans., 1970, Indsl. Coll. Armed Forces, 1971. Bar: D.C. 1953, Mass. 1953, Minn. 1953, N.Y. 1954, U.S. Ct. Appeals (D.C. and 2d cirs.) 1954, U.S. Dist. Ct. D.C. 1954, U.S. Dist. Ct. (so. and ea. dists.) N.Y. 1954, U.S. Ct. Mil. Appeals 1954, U.S. Supreme Ct. 1963. Assoc. Shearman & Sterling, N.Y.C., 1954-74; v.p., dep. gen. counsel 1st Nat. City Bank (now Citibank N.A.), N.Y.C., 1974-75; sr. v.p., gen. counsel The Connell Co. and related cos., Westfield, N.J., 1975-93; food co. cons. and counsel, 1993—; bd. dirs. Combined Life Ins. Co., N.Y. Author: Government Administration of Wage Incentives in Wartime, 1949, Church and State in Colonial Connecticut, 1953; contbr. to Cath. Ency., legal and banking jours.; law editor (Banking Law Jour.), 1965-67; mem. adv. bd. Letter of Credit Update, 1987—. Lt. col. F.A., U.S. Army, 1943-46, 52-53, PTO, ETO. Mem. ABA (task force on study and revision of UCC Article 5), D.C. Bar Assn., Minn. Territorial Pioneers, Mil. Order of World Wars, Army and Navy Club (Washington), Harvard Club (N.Y.C.). Republican. Roman Catholic. Office: PO Box 257 Oldwick NJ 08858-0257

PURCELL, ROBERT HARRY, virologist; b. Keokuk, Iowa, Dec. 19, 1935; s. Edward Harold and Elsie Thelma (Melzl) P.; m. Carol Joan Moody, June 11, 1961; children: David Edward, John Leslie. BA in Chemistry, Okla. State U., 1957; MS Biochemistry, Baylor U., 1960; MD, Duke U., 1962. Intern in pediatrics Duke U. Hosp., Durham, N.C., 1962-63; officer USPHS, 1963, advanced through grades to med. dir. (O-6), 1974; with Epidemic Intelligence Svc., Communicable Disease Ctr. Atlanta; assigned to vaccine br. Nat. Inst. Allergy and Infectious Diseases, Bethesda, Md., 1963-65; sr. surgeon Lab. Infectious Diseases, NIH, Bethesda, Md., 1965-69, med. officer, 1969-72, med. dir., 1972-74, head hepatitis viruses sect., 1974—; organizer, invited participant, speaker numerous nat. and internat. symposia, confs., workshops, meetings; temporary advisor WHO, 1967—; expert cons. in hepatitis U.S.—China, U.S.—Taiwan, U.S.—Japan, U.S.—Russia, U.S.—India, U.S.—Pakistan Bilateral Sci. Agreements; lectr. various virology classes. Mem. editl. bd. and/or reviewer Am. Jour. Epidemiology, Gastroenterology, Hepatology, Infection and Immunity, Jour. Clin. Microbiology, Jour. Infectious Diseases, Jour. Med. Virology, Jour. Nat. Cancer Inst., Nature, Sci.; contbr. over 500 articles to profl. jours., chpts. to books; numerous patents in field. Decorated D.S.M.; recipient Superior Svc. award USPHS, 1972, Meritorious Svc. medal USPHS, 1974, Gorgas medal, 1977, Disting. Alumni award Duke U. Sch. Medicine, 1978, Eppinger prize 5th Internat. FALK Symposium on Virus and Liver, Switzerland, 1979, Medal of City of Turin, Italy, 1983, Gold medal Can. Liver Found., 1984, Inventor's Incentive award U.S. Commerce Dept., 1984; fellowships Baylor U., 1959-60, Duke U., 1960-62. Fellow Washington Acad. Scis.; mem. Am. Epidemiology Soc., Am. Soc. Microbiology, Am. Soc. Virology, Am. Acad. Microbiology, AAAS, Soc. Epidemiol. Rsch., Infectious Diseases Soc. Am. (Squibb award 1980), N.Y. Acad. Scis., Am. Soc. Clin. Investigation, Assn. Am. Physicians, Am. Coll. Epidemiology, Am. Assn. Study of Liver Diseases, Internat. Assn. Study and Prevention Virus Associated Cancers, Internat. Assn. Biol. Standardization, Internat. Assn. Study Liver, Soc. Exptl. Biology and Medicine (Disting. Scientist award 1986), Nat. Acad. Scis. Office: NIH Lab Infectious Diseases NIH Bldg 7 Rm 202 7 Center Dr MSC 0740 Bethesda MD 20892-0740

PURCELL, STEVEN RICHARD, international management consultant, engineer, economist. B of Mech. and Indsl. Engring., NYU Coll. Engring., 1950; MS in Indsl. Engring., Columbia U., 1951; EdM, Harvard U., 1968. Registered profl. engr., Can. Lectr. engring. NYU Coll. Engring., N.Y.C., 1948-50; gen. mgr. Dapol Plastics Co., Inc., Boston, 1956-58; gen. div. mgr. Am. Cyanamid Co., Sanford, Maine, 1958-61; sr. prin., mgmt. cons. investment banking Purcell & Assocs., N.Y.C., 1961-66; prof., chmn. Bristol Coll., Fall River, Mass., 1966-68; assoc. dean grad. faculty adminstrv. studies York U., Toronto, Ont., Can., 1969-71; chief economist Dept. Manpower and Immigration, Ottawa, Ont., Can., 1970-71; cons. Treasury Bd., Ottawa, 1971-72; dir. urban and internat. environ. policy Ministry of State for Urban Affairs Internat. Activities, Ottawa, 1973-74; mem. com. on challenges of modern soc. NATO, Ottawa, 1973-74; mem. sci., econ. policy com. OECD UN, Ottawa, 1973-74; prof. Grad. Sch. Bus. Adminstrn. and Econs. Algonquin Coll., Ottawa, 1974-76; advisor, cons. House of Commons, 1976-77; sr. prin. Purcell & Assocs., Internat. Mgmt. Cons., Washington, 1977-80, chmn., CEO, 1981—; chmn., CEO Phoenix Internat. Capital Associates, Washington, 1981—; exec. dir. nat. coastal zone mgmt. adv. com. NOAA U.S. Dept. Commerce, Washington, 1980-81; profl. lectr. Northeastern U. Grad. Sch. Bus. Adminstrn., Boston, 1953-56, U. Toronto, 1968-69, George Washington U. Grad. Sch. Bus. Adminstrn., Washington, 1979; vis. prof. Rensselaer Poly. Inst. Advanced Mgmt. Program, 1967, U. Ottawa Grad. Sch. Bus. Adminstrn., 1971-74; lectr. Council for Internat. Progress in Mgmt., N.Y.C., 1960, Royal Bank Can. Mgmt. Assn., Toronto, Ont., 1970; corp. appointment cons. Harvard U., Cambridge, Mass., 1967-68; cons. Govt. Venezuela, 1967-68, Can. Inst. Bankers, Toronto, 1969-70; internat. sr. adviser NASA, 1985-86, mem. nat. adv. bd. Ctr. for Nat. Policy; dir. Rental Resource Corp., 1986-89. Contbr. articles on indsl. orgn., sci. policy and fin. to profl. jours. Lt. AC, USNR, 1943-46. Mem. UN Assn., Soc. for Advancement of Mgmt. (pres. 1949-50, leadership award 1950), Tau Beta Pi, Alpha Pi Mu (v.p. 1949-50), Columbia Univ. Club (Washington, trustee 1982-84, chmn., sr. trustee 1984-85), Harvard Univ. Club. Office: 12904 Mayflower Ln Bowie MD 20720-3368

PURCELL, STUART MCLEOD, III, financial planner; b. Santa Monica, Calif., Feb. 16, 1944; s. Stuart McLeod Jr. and Carol (Howe) P. AA, Santa Monica City Coll., 1964; BS, Calif. State U., Northridge, 1967; grad., CPA Advanced Personal Fin. Planning Curriculum, San Francisco, 1985. CPA, Calif.; CFP. Sr. acct. Pannell Kerr Forster, San Francisco, 1970-73; fin. cons. Purcell Fin. Services, San Francisco, 1973-74, San Rafael, Calif., 1980-81; controller Decimus Corp., San Francisco, 1974-76, Grubb & Ellis Co., Oakland, Calif., 1976-78, Marwais Steel Co., Richmond, Calif., 1979-80; owner, fin. counselor Purcell Wealth Mgmt., San Rafael, 1981—; guest lectr. Golden Gate U., San Francisco, 1985—; leader ednl. workshops, Larkspur, Calif., 1984; speaker Commonwealth Club Calif., 1989, 91. Contbr. articles to newspapers and profl. jours. Treas. Salvation Army, San Rafael-San Anselmo-Fairfax, Calif., 1987—; chmn. fin. planners div. United Way Marin County, Calif., 1984; mem. fundraising com. Marin County March of Dimes, 1987—, Marin County Arthritis Found., 1988—; mem. Marin Estate Planning Council. Served to lt. (j.g.) USNR, 1968-76. Named Eagle Scout, 1959, Best Fin. Advisor Marin County Independent-Jour. newspaper, 1987, Top Producer Unimarc, 1986; recipient Outstanding Achievement award United Way, 1984; named to The Registry of Fin. Planning Practitioners, 1987. Mem. AICPA, Calif. Soc. CPAs, Nat. Speakers Assn., Internat. Assn. for Fin. Planners (exec. dir. North Bay chpt., San Francisco 1984), Internat. Soc. Pre-Retired Planners, Soc. CPA-Fin. Planners (dist. membership chmn. San Francisco 1986), Registry Fin. Planning Practitioners, Sigma Alpha Epsilon. Presbyterian. Avocations: travel, auto racing, skiing, gardening. Home: 45 Vineyard Dr San Rafael CA 94901-1228 Office: Purcell Wealth Mgmt 1811 Grand Ave Ste B San Rafael CA 94901-1925

PURCELL, WILLIAM PAXSON, III, state legislator; b. Phila., Oct. 25, 1953; s. William Paxson Jr. and Mary (Hamilton) P.; m. Deborah Lee Miller, Aug. 9, 1986; 1 child, Jesse Miller. AB, Hamilton Coll., 1976; JD, Vanderbilt U., 1979. Bar: Tenn. 1979, U.S. Ct. Appeals (6th cir.) 1985, U.S. Supreme Ct. 1986. Staff atty. West Tenn. Legal Svcs., Nashville, 1979-81; asst. pub. defender Metro Pub. Defender, Nashville, Tenn., 1981-84, sr. asst. pub. defender, 1984-85; assoc. Lionel R. Barrett, P.C., Nashville, 1985-86; ptnr. Farmer, Berry & Purcell, Nashville, 1986-90; mem. Tenn. Ho. of Reps., Nashville, 1986-96, also majority leader, 1990-96; chmn. select com. on children and youth Tenn. Ho. of Reps., 1989-96; exec. dir. Vanderbilt Legal Aid Soc., 1978-79; chmn. NCSL Assembly of State Issues, 1995; chmn. policy makers' program adv. bd. Danforth Found. Mem. exec. com. 6th dist. Dems., Nashville, 1986-88, Dem. Nat. Com., 1994-96; chmn. human svcs. com. Nat. Conf. State Legislatures, Washington, 1993; com. chmn. Dem. Legis. Campaign, 1994-96. Toll fellow Coun. State Govts., 1988; named Legislator of Yr. Tenn. Conservation League, Dist. Attys. Gen. Conf. Mem. ABA, Tenn. Bar Assn., Tenn. Pediatric Soc., Nashville Bar Assn., Dem. Legis. Leaders Assn. (chmn. 1994—). Methodist. Home: PO Box 60331 Nashville TN 37206-0331 Office: 18 A Legislative Plz Nashville TN 37243

PURCIFULL, DAN ELWOOD, plant virologist, educator; b. Woodland, Calif., July 1, 1935; s. Ernest Lee and Virginia (Margaroli) P.; m. Marcia Ann Weatherby, Sept. 7, 1966; children: Scott, Douglas. B.S., U. Calif., Davis, 1957, M.S., 1959, Ph.D., 1964. Asst. prof. plant pathology U. Fla., Gainesville, 1964-69, assoc. prof. U. Fla., 1969-75, prof., 1975—; dept. grad. coord., 1988-91; mem. plant virus subcom. Internat. Com. for Taxonomy of Viruses, 1973-75, mem. potyvirus study group, 1987-93; mem. plant virology adv. com. Am. Type Culture Collection, 1993—; mem. Internat. Legume Virus Working Group. Assoc. editor Phytopathology, 1971-73, Plant Disease, 1987-89; contbr. articles to profl. jours. Mem. Morningside Nature Center Commn., City of Gainesville, 1978-81, treas., 1981. Served with U.S. Army, 1957. Fellow AAAS, Am. Phytopathol Soc. (Lee Hutchins award 1981, Ruth Allen award 1992); mem. Fla. State Hort. Soc., N.Y. Acad. Sci., Am. Soc. Virology, Sigma Xi. Home: 3106 NW 1st Ave Gainesville FL 32607-2504

PURCIFULL, ROBERT OTIS, insurance company executive; b. Grinnell, Iowa, July 1, 1932; s. Chauncey O. and Mildred E. (Clendenen) P.; m. Mary G. White, Sept. 12, 1953; children: Jane, Robert Otis, Patricia, Elizabeth. B.A., Grinnell Coll., 1954. C.L.U. With Occidental Life Ins. Co., Calif., 1960-78; 1st. v.p. charge agys. Occidental Life Ins. Co., Los Angeles, 1968-71; exec. v.p. sales Occidental Life Ins. Co., 1971-76; pres., chief exec. officer Transmerica Ins. Mgmt., Inc., Los Angeles, 1972-78, Countrywide Life Ins. Co., Los Angeles, 1973-76; dir. Countrywide Life Ins. Co., 1973-78; chmn. bd., pres. Plaza Ins. Sales Inc., San Francisco; pres. Canadian div. Occidental Life Ins. Co., 1977-78; pres., chief exec. officer Occidental Life of Can., 1977-78; pres., chief operating officer, dir. Penn Mut. Life Ins. Co., Phila., 1979-80; sr. v.p. life divsn. Am. Gen. Corp., 1981-82; pres. Lincoln Am. Life Ins. Co., Am. Gen. Life Ins. Co. Del., Am. Gen. Life Ins. Co. Tex., Am. Amicable Life Ins. Co., Pioneer Am., 1982-84; vice chmn. Pioneer Security Life Ins. Co., 1982-84; pres., CEO Gulf Life Ins. Co., Interstate Fire Co., Jacksonville, Fla., 1984-88, also dir.; pres. Am. Gen. Group Ins. Co. Fla., 1986-89; vice chmn. Gulf Life Ins. Co., 1988-91; chmn., CEO ROP & Assocs. Past pres. Vols. of Am., L.A.; councilman City of Upper Arlington, Ohio, 1962-66; trustee Life Underwriters Tng. Coun., Washington, 1975-78; campaign chmn. Jacksonville United Way, 1988, 89, chmn., 1989-90; pres. Jacksonville Univ. Coun., 1992, 93; pres. Jacksonville Symphony Orch., 1993-94; chmn. bus. adv. coun. U. North Fla.; bd. dirs. Acordia Benefits Fla. Mem. Life Ins. Mktg. and Rsch. Assn. (bd. dirs. 1982-85), Rancho Las Palmas Club, San Jose Club, River Club. Home: 12940 Riverplace Ct Jacksonville FL 32223-1773

PURCUPILE, JOHN STEPHEN, lawyer; b. Ventura, Calif., Nov. 8, 1954; s. John Charles and Sylvia Marie (Pilgrim) P.; m. Anna Marie Leone, June 20, 1981; children: John Justin, Jessica Marie. BA, Case Western Reserve U., 1980; JD, Duquesne U., 1983. Bar: Pa. 1983, U.S. Dist. Ct. (we. dist.) Pa. 1983, U.S. Supreme Ct. 1987. Lawyer Stone & Stone, Pitts., 1983-85; law clk. Ct. of Common Pleas Hon. Livingstone M. Johnson, Pitts., 1985-88; lawyer Egler, Garrett & Egler, Pitts., 1988—. Home: 335 Kennedy Rd Prospect PA 16052 Office: Egler Garrett & Egler 428 Forbes Ave Pittsburgh PA 15219-1603

PURDES, ALICE MARIE, adult education educator; b. St. Louis, Jan. 8, 1931; d. Joseph Louis and Angeline Cecilia (Mozier) P. AA, Belleville Area Coll., 1951; BS, Ill. State U., Normal, 1953, MS, 1954; cert., Sorbonne U., Paris, 1964; PhD, Fla. State U., Tallahassee, 1976. Cert. in music edn., elem. edn., secondary edn., adult edn. Teaching/grad. asst. Ill. State U., 1953-54; music supr. Princeton (Ill.) Pub. Schs., 1954-55; music dir. Venice (Ill.) Pub. Schs., 1955-72, secondary vocal music dir., 1955-72; coord. literacy program Venice-Lincoln Tech. Ctr., 1983-86, chair lang. arts dept., 1983—; tchr. in space candidate, 1985. Mem. St. Louis chpt. World Affairs Coun., UN

Assn., Nat. Mus. of Women in the Arts, Humane Soc. of Am.; charter mem. St. Louis Sci. Ctr., Harry S. Truman Inst.; contbr. Old Six Mile Mus., 1981, Midland Repertory Players, Alton, Ill., 1991; chair Cystic Fibrosis Spring Bike-A-Thon, Madison, Ill., 1981, Granite City, Ill., 1985. Recipient gold medal Nat Senior Olympics, 1989, Senior World Games, 1992, several scholarships. Mem. AAUW, Music Educators Nat. Conf., Ill. Music Educators Assn., Am. Choral Dirs. Assn., Fla. State Alumni Assn., Ill. Adult and Continuing Educators Assn., Am. Fedn. Tchrs. (pres. 1957-58), Western Cath. Union, Croation Fraternal Union, Nat. Space Soc., Travelers Abroad (pres. 1966-68, 89—), Internat. Platform Assn., Archaeol. Inst. Am., Friends St. Louis Art Mus., St. Louis Numis. Assn. Madison Rotary Club (internat. amb., Humanitarian award 1975), Slavic and East European Friends (life), Lovejoy Libr. Friends, Ill. State U. Alumnia Assn. Roman Catholic. Avocations: bowling, travel. Home: PO Box 274 Madison IL 62060-0274 Office: Venice-Lincoln Tech Ctr S 4th St Venice IL 62090-1063

PURDOM, PAUL WALTON, JR., computer scientist; b. Atlanta, Apr. 5, 1940; s. Paul Walton and Bettie (Miller) P.; m. Donna Armstrong; children—Barbara, Linda, Paul. B.S., Calif. Inst. Tech., 1961, M.S., 1962, Ph.D., 1966. Asst. prof. computer sci. U. Wis.-Madison, 1965-70, asst. prof., 1971-82; mem. tech. staff Bell Telephone Labs., Naperville, Ill., 1970-71; assoc. prof., chmn. computer sci. dept. Ind. U., Bloomington, 1977-82, prof. computer sci., 1982—; grant researcher FAW, Ulm, Germany. Author: (with Cynthia Brown) The Analysis of Algorithms; assoc. editor: Computer Surveys; contbr. articles to profl. jours. NSF grantee, 1979, 81, 83, 92, 94. Mem. AAAS, Soc. for Indsl. and Applied Math., Assn. Computing Machinery, Sigma Xi. Democrat. Methodist. Home: 2212 S Belhaven Ct Bloomington IN 47401-6803 Office: Ind U Dept Computer Science 215 Lindley Hall Bloomington IN 47405-4101

PURDOM, THOMAS JAMES, lawyer; b. Seymour, Tex., Apr. 7, 1937; s. Thomas Exer and Juanita Florida (Kuykendall) P.; m. Betty Marie Shoemaker, May 31, 1969; 1 son, James Robert. Student, U. Syracuse, 1956-57, U. Md., 1958-59; BA, Tex. Tech. Coll., 1962; JD, Georgetown U., 1966. Bar: Tex. 1966, U.S. Supreme Ct. 1978, U.S. Ct. Appeals (5th cir.) 1983. Ptnr. Griffith & Purdom, Lubbock, Tex., 1966-67; asst. dist. atty. 72d Jud. Dist., Lubbock, 1967-68; county atty. Lubbock County, Tex., 1968-72; pres. Purdom Law Offices, P.C. and predecessor firms, Lubbock, Tex., 1972—; mem. com. for Vol. 5 pattern jury charges, 1988-94. Author: West's Texas Forms Vols. 16, 17, 18, 1984-94; (with others) Family Law, Texas Practice and Procedure,, 1981. Served with USAF, 1956-60. Fellow Tex. Bar Found.; mem ABA, Lubbock County Bar Assn. (bd. dirs. 1970), State Bar Assn. Tex. (sec. family law sect. 1974-75, chmn. family law sect. 1975-77, mem. examining commn. for family law specialization), Am. Acad. Matrimonial Lawyers (cert. family law, Tex. bd. legal specialization), Tex. Assn. Def. Counsel, Delta Theta Phi. Democrat. Baptist. Home: 3619 55th St Lubbock TX 79413-4713 Office: Purdom Law Offices PC 1801 Avenue Q Lubbock TX 79401-4826

PURDY, ALAN HARRIS, biomedical engineer; b. Mt. Clemens, Mich., Dec. 13, 1923; s. Harry Martin and Elinor (Harris) P.; m. Anna Elizabeth Sohn, Aug. 16, 1968 (dec.); children: Catherine, Charles, Susan, Harry. BSME, U. Miami, 1954; MS in Physiology, UCLA, 1967; PhD in Engring., U. Mo., 1970. Cert. clin. engr., Washington. Project engr. in acoustics Arvin Industries, Columbus, Ind., 1954-56, AC Spark Plug Co., Flint, Mich., 1956-60; asst. prof. engring. Calif. Poly. U., Pomona, 1960-62; assoc. dir. biomed. engring. U. Mo., Columbia, 1967-71; dep. assoc. dir. Nat. Inst. for Occupational Safety and Health, Rockville, Md., 1971-81; scientist, biomed. engr. Nat. Inst. for Occupational Safety and Health, Cin., 1983-86; asst. dir. Fla. Inst. Oceanography, St. Petersburg, 1981-83; pres. Alpha Beta R & D Corp., Cape Coral, Fla., 1986—; cons. Smithy Muffler Corp., L.A., 1961-62, Statham Instruments, L.A., 1966; cons. faculty, Tex. Tech. U., Lubbock, 1972-73; lectr. U. Cin., 1980. Patentee in diving, acoustical and occupational safety fields. Pilot CG Aux., Ft. Myers, Fla., 1989—; mem. Dem. Exec. Com., Lee County, 1989—. With USAF, 1942-43. Nat. Heart Inst. spl. fellow, 1963-67; Fulbright scholar, Yugoslavia, 1984. Mem. Acoustical Soc. Am., Biomed. Engring. Soc., Am. Inst. Physics, Internat. Oceanopgraphic Found., Exptl. Aircraft Assn., Aircraft Owners and Pilots Assn., DAV. Democrat. Home and Office: 5228 SW 5th Pl Cape Coral FL 33914-6504

PURDY, ALAN MACGREGOR, financial executive; b. Iowa City, Iowa, Apr. 23, 1940; s. Rob Roy MacGregor and Frances Norrine (Edwards) P.; m. Sarah Lane Robins, June 13, 1964; children—William Wallace, John Alan, Tammi Ann. A.B., Duke U., 1962; M.B.A., Wharton Sch. Fin. and Commerce, U. Pa., 1968. Bus. analyst Gen. Mills, Inc., Mpls., 1968-71; sr. fin. analyst Dayton Hudson Corp., Mpls., 1972-73, mgr. capital expenditure analysis, 1973, dir. corp. analysis, 1973-75, dir. planning and analysis, 1975-77; v.p., treas. Fleming Cos., Inc., Oklahoma City, 1977-81; v.p. fin., chief fin. officer John A. Brown Co. subs. Dayton Hudson Corp., Oklahoma City, 1981-83; sr. v.p., chief fin. officer B. Dalton Co. subs. Dayton Hudson Corp., Mpls., 1983-86, Robinson's of Fla. subs. May Co., St. Petersburg, 1986-87, Miller's Outpost (subs. Amcena Corp.), Ontario, Calif., 1988-92, Builders Emporium subs. Collins and Aikman Group, Irvine, Calif., 1993; Remedy Temp, San Juan Capistrano, Calif., 1994—. Served with USN, 1962-66. Home: 2190 Hillview Dr Laguna Beach CA 92651-2626 Office: Remedy Temp 32122 Camino Capistrano San Juan Capistrano CA 92675-3717

PURDY, CHARLES ROBERT, corporate executive; b. St. Louis, Oct. 2, 1937; s. Wilbur Charles and Myrtle (Baker) P.; m. Carolyn Joan Leppa, Aug. 29, 1959; children—Maureen Carol, Kelly Ann, Jeffrey Scott, Mark Edward. B.S.C., DePaul U., 1959. Jr. accountant Price Waterhouse & Co., Chgo., 1958-61, sr. accountant, 1961-62; asst. controller Scot Lad Foods, Inc., Chgo., 1962-64, adminstrv. v.p., 1964-66, exec. v.p., dir., 1966-69, pres., dir., 1969-71; vice-chmn., chief exec. officer, dir. Scot Lad Foods, Inc., Lansing, Ill., 1977-78; prin. Purdy Enterprises, Chgo., 1971-77, 78—; chmn. Computrition Inc, Chatsworth, Calif., 1989—. Recipient DePaul U. Alumni Assn. Achievement award, 1971-72. Mem. Delta Sigma Pi, Beta Gamma Sigma, Beta Alpha Psi. Club: Olympia Fields (Ill.) Country. Office: 20300 Western Ave Olympia Fields IL 60461

PURDY, DAVID LAWRENCE, biotechnical company executive; b. N.Y.C., Sept. 18, 1928; s. Earl and Mabel (Roberts) P.; m. Margaret Helen Rye, July 7, 1951; children: Susan Lee, John F. (dec.), Ross David (dec.), Thomas Griffith. BSME, Cornell U., 1951; degree in advanced & creative engring., GE, 1955, degree in profl. bus. mgmt., 1956. Devel. engr. GE, Valley Forge, Pa., 1953-64; mgr. energy conversion divsn. Nuclear Materials and Equipment Corp. (acquired by ARCO), Apollo, Pa., 1964-69, Atlantic Richfield Corp., Apollo, 1969-72; founder, pres., chmn. Biocontrol Tech., Inc., Indiana, 1972—; chmn., treas. Diasense, Inc., Indiana, 1989—. Contbr. over 22 articles to profl. jours. 1st lt. USAF, 1961-63. Fellow ASME (life); mem. AAAS, Am. Diabetes Assn. Achievements include patents for generator of electrical energy by radioisotope thermoelectric conversion, for radioisotope powered cardiac pacemaker, for radioisotope powered artificial heart, for thermoelectric apparatus for high thermoelectric efficiency by cascading materials, for method of metals joining and articles produced by such method - brazing copper to tungsten, for thermoelectric apparatus for high thermoelectric efficiency by cascading materials, for generator of electrical energy by radioisotope thermoelectric conversion, for rate responsive pacemaker, for artificial pancreas, for noninvasive glucose sensor. Office: Biocontrol Tech Inc 300 Indian Springs Rd Indiana PA 15701-9704

PURDY, JAMES, writer; b. 1923. Ed., Spain. Editor, other positions Cuba, Mexico. Author: Don't Call Me by My Right Name, 1956; 63, Dream Palace, 1956, 1980, Color of Darkness, 1957, Malcolm, 1959, 1980, paperback, 1987, The Nephew, 1960, , 1980, paperback, 1987, (play) Children is All, 1962, Cabot Wright Begins, 1964, Eustace Chisholm and The Works, 1967, An Oyster is A Wealthy Beast, 1967, Mr. Evening, 1968, Jeremy's Version, 1970, On the Rebound, 1970, (poems) The Running Sun, 1971, Collected Poems, 1990, (novel) I am Elijah Thrush, 1971; Sunshine is an Only Child, 1973, Sleepers in Moon Crowned Valleys, The House of the Solitary Maggot, 1974, (selected stories) Color of Darkness, Children is All, The Candles of Your Eyes, 1991, (fairy tale) Kitty Blue, 1993 (Eng. edit. The Netherlands); (novel) In a Shallow Grave, 1976; (plays and stories) A Day After the Fair, 1977; (recordings) Eventide, 63; Dream Palace, 1968, 1980; (novel) Narrow Rooms, 1978; (poetry) I Will Arrest the Bird that has No Light, 1978, Lessons and Complaints, 1978; Sleep Tight, 1978, Proud Flesh, 4 short plays, 1980; (novel) Mourners Below, 1981, The Berry-Picker, 1981, Scrap of Paper, 1981, Dawn, 1985, (novel) On Glory's Course, 1983, (poems) Don't Let the Snow Fall, 1985, Are You in the Winter Tree?, 1987, (novel) In the Hollow of His Hand, 1986, (collected stories) The Candles of your Eyes, 1987, Garments the Living Wear, 1989, (fiction) Reaching Rose, 1994, (play) Ruthanna Elder, 1989; subject of book: James Purdy (Stephen D. Adams), 1976, Collected Poems, 1990, (plays) In The Night of Time and Four Other Plays, 1992, A Day After the Fair, 1993, (novel) Out With The Stars, 1992, In the Night of Time and Four Other Plays, 1992, (plays) Foment, 1994, Brice, 1994, Where Quentin Goes, 1994; intro. to Weymouth Sands (by John Cowper Pwys); contbr. article to Life Mag., 1965. Recipient Morton Dauwen Zabel Fiction award Am. Acad. Arts and Letters, 1993, Oscar Williams and Gene Durwood award for poetry and art, 1995; subject of The Not-Right House, Essays on the Books of James Purdy (Bettina Schwarzschild), 1969-70. Address: 236 Henry St Brooklyn NY 11201-4280

PURDY, KEVIN M., estate planner; b. Escondido, Calif., Jan. 26, 1952; s. Kenneth C. and Helen M. (Moore) P.; m. Janice M. Cook, May 12, 1982. BA in Philosophy, Psychology, U. Redlands, 1974. CFP. Pres. Timeline Pub., San Diego, Calif., 1980-90; estate planner CIGNA Fin. Advisors, San Diego, Calif., 1990—; pub. speaker. Author: A Brief History of the Earth and Mankind, 1986, A Brief History of Mankind, 1987. Fundraiser San Diego Hist. Soc., 1993-94. Avocations: photography, music, travel, investment analysis. Office: CIGNA Fin Advisers 4275 Executive Sq Ste 400 La Jolla CA 92037-1476

PURDY, WILLIAM CROSSLEY, chemist, educator; b. Bklyn., Sept. 14, 1930; s. John Earl and Virginia (Clark) P.; m. Myrna Mae Moman, June 17, 1953; children—Robert Bruce (dec.), Richard Scott, Lisa Patrice, Diana Lori. B.A., Amherst Coll., 1951; Ph.D., MIT, 1955. Instr. U. Conn., Storrs, 1955-58; faculty U. Md., College Park, 1958-76, prof. chemistry, 1964-76, head div. analytical chemistry, 1968-76; prof. chemistry McGill U., 1976-86, assoc. in medicine, 1976—, Sir William Macdonald prof. chemistry, 1986—, assoc. vice prin. (acad.), 1986-91; vis. prof. Institut für Ernährungswissenschaft, Justus Liebig-Universität, Giessen, Germany, 1965-66; nat. lectr. Am. Assn. Clin. Chemistry, 1971; Fisher Sci. Lecture award Chem. Inst. Can., 1982; cons. Surg. Gen., U.S. Army, 1959-75; sci. adviser Balt. dist. FDA. Author: Electro-analytical Methods in Biochemistry, 1965, also numerous articles; mem. bd. editors Clin. Chemistry, 1971-80, Anal. Letters, 1979-95, Anal. Chim. Acta, 1979-84, Clin. Biochemistry, 1983-91, Pure and Applied Chemistry, 1983-91; adv. bd. editors Analytical Chemistry, 1971-73. Bd. govs. Trafalgar Sch. Girls, Montreal, 1980-90, chmn., 1983-87; bd. trustees Trafalgar-Ross Found., Montreal, 1983-90, chmn., 1983-87. Fellow Nat. Acad. Clin. Biochemistry, Royal Soc. Chemistry (London), Chem. Inst. Can., Can. Acad. Clin. Biochemistry; mem. Am. Chem. Soc., Am. Assn. Clin. Chemistry (Outstanding Contbns. to Clin. Chemistry award 1984), Can. Soc. Clin. Chemists (Outstanding Contbr. through Rsch award, 1990), Sigma Xi. Achievements include research in application of modern analytical methods to biochem. and clin. systems, separation sci., electroanalytical chemistry. Home: 1321 Sherbrooke St W C-40, Montreal, PQ Canada H3G 1J4 Office: McGill U, 801 Sherbrooke St W, Montreal, PQ Canada H3A 2K6

PURI, MADAN LAL, mathematics educator; b. Sialkot, Feb. 20, 1929; came to U.S., 1957, naturalized, 1973; s. Ganesh Das and S. V. P.; m. Uma Kapur, Aug. 24, 1962; 3 children. B.A., Punjab U., India, 1948, M.A., 1950, D.Sc., 1975; Ph.D., U. Calif. at Berkeley, 1962. Head dept. math. D.A.V. Coll., Punjab U., 1955-57; instr. U. Colo., 1957-58; teaching asst., research asst., jr. research statistician U. Calif. at Berkeley, 1958-62; asst. prof., asso. prof. math. Courant Inst., N.Y. U., 1962-68; vis. asso. prof. U. N.C., summers 1966-67; prof. math. Ind. U., Bloomington, 1968—; guest prof. stats. U. Gottingen, West Germany, 1972, Alexander von Humboldt guest prof., 1974-75; guest prof. U. Dortmund, West Germany, 1972, Technische Hochschule Aachen, West Germany, 1973, U. Goteborg, Chalmers U. Tech., both Sweden, 1974; vis. prof. U. Auckland, N.Z., 1977, U. Calif., Irvine, 1978, U. Wash., Seattle, 1978-79, U. Bern (Switzerland), 1982, Va. Poly. Inst., 1988; disting. visitor London Sch. Econs. and Polit. Sci., 1991; vis. prof. U. Göttingen, Germany, 1991, June-July 1992; rsch. fellow Katholieke U., Nijmegen, The Netherlands, 1992; vis. prof. U. Des Scis. et Tech. de Lille, France, 1994, U. Basel, Switzerland, 1995—. Coauthor: Non Parametric Methods in Multivariate Analysis, 1971, Non Parametric Methods in General Linear Models, 1985. Editor Statochastic Process and Related Topics, 1975, Statistical Inference and Related Topics, 1975, Non Parametric Techniques in Statistical Inference, 1970; co-editor: Nonparametric Statistical Inference, Vols. I and II, 1982, New Perspectives in Theoretical and Applied Statistics, 1987, Mathematical Statistics and Probability Theory, Vol. A, 1987, Statistical Sciences and Data Analysis, 1993, Recent Advances in Statistics and Probability, 1994. Recipient Sr. U.S. Scientist award, Humboldt Preis, 1974-75, 83. Fellow Royal Statis. Soc., Inst. Math. Statistics, Am. Statis. Assn.; mem. Math. Assn. Am., Internat. Statis. Inst., Bernoulli Soc. Math. Stats. and Probability. Office: Ind U Dept Math Rawles Hall Bloomington IN 47405

PURIS, MARTIN FORD, advertising agency executive; b. Chgo., Feb. 22, 1939; s. Martin and Virginia Lee (Farmer) P.; m. Mary M. Herrmann; children: Kimberly Mayo, Jason Patterson. Student, DePauw U., 1961. With Campbell-Ewald Co., N.Y.C., 1962-64, Young & Rubicam, Inc., N.Y.C., 1964-66; v.p. Carl Ally, Inc., N.Y.C., 1966-74; pres., CEO Ammirati & Puris, Inc., N.Y.C., 1974-94; chmn., ceo, chief creative officer Ammirati, Puris, Lintas, N.Y.C., 1995—; chmn. bd. The Upward Fund, Inc., N.Y.C.; media advisor Pres. George Bush. Vice-chmn., trustee Mystic Seaport Mus. Recipient awards Art Dir. Club, Copy Club, N.Y.C., Cannes Film Festival. Mem. Am. Assn. Advt. Agys. (gov.), N.Y. Yacht Club, Nantucket Yacht Club, Am. Yacht Club, Union Club. Republican. Roman Catholic. Avocations: sailing, tennis, riding, hunting. Office: Ammirati Puris Lintas 1 Dag Hammarskjold Plz New York NY 10017*

PURL, O. THOMAS, retired electronics company executive; b. East St. Louis, Ill., June 5, 1924; s. Ruthford Keith and Muriel Agnes (Thompson) P.; m. Martha Elaine Smalley, Feb. 21, 1948; children—Thomas Keith, Jeanne Marie Purl Elder. B.S., U. Ill., 1948, U. Ill., 1951; M.S., U. Ill., 1952, Ph.D., 1955. Head high-power traveling wave tube sect., mem. tech. staff Hughes Research Lab., Culver City, Calif., 1955-58; sect. head, dept. mgr., group v.p., v.p. shareholder relations and planning coordination Watkins-Johnson Co., Palo Alto, Calif., 1958-86. Contbr. articles to profl. jours. Chmn. career guidance com. Santa Clara Valley Joint Engring. Council, 1971-73; bd. dirs. Jr. Achievement of Santa Clara County, 1975-79. Served to 1st lt. USAAF, 1943-46. Fellow IEEE (chmn. Santa Clara Valley subsect. 1972); mem. Sigma Xi, Eta Kappa Nu, Phi Kappa Phi, Sigma Tau. Club: Commonwealth of Calif. Patentee in field. Home: 466 La Mesa Portola Valley CA 94028

PURNELL, CHARLES GILES, lawyer; b. Dallas, Aug. 16, 1921; s. Charles Stewart and Ginevra (Locke) P.; m. Jane Carter; children: Mimi, Sarah Elizabeth, Charles H., John W. Student Rice Inst., 1938-39; BA, U. Tex., 1941; student Harvard Bus. Sch., 1942; LLB, Yale U., 1947. Bar: Tex. 1948. Ptnr. Locke, Purnell, Boren, Laney & Neely, Dallas, 1947-89, Locke, Purnell, Rain & Harrell, 1989-90, of counsel, 1990—; exec. asst. to Gov. of Tex., Austin, 1973-75. Bd. dirs. Trinity River Authority of Tex., 1975-81; vice chmn. Tex. Energy Adv. Council, 1974. Served to lt. U.S. Navy, 1942-45; PTO. Mem. ABA, Tex. Bar Assn., Tex. Bar Found. Episcopalian. Clubs: Yale, Dallas Country, Dallas Petroleum, La Jolla (Calif.) Beach and Tennis. Home: # 1 Saint Laurent Place Dallas TX 75225 Office: Locke Purnell Rain Harrell 2200 Ross Ave Ste 2200 Dallas TX 75201-6766

PURNELL, FLORIE ELIZABETH, trainer; b. Winston-Salem, N.C., Mar. 29, 1955; d. Bernard Owen and Mary Elizabeth (Thompkins) Taylor; m. Rodney James Roundtree, Mar. 9, 1973 (div. Apr. 1978); 1 child, Rodney James; m. Fason Anderson, May 28, 1988; children: Rachel, Jasmin. AAS in Bus. Adminstrn., Forsyth Tech. Coll., Winston-Salem, 1981; BS in Bus. Adminstrn., High Point Coll., Winston-Salem, 1985; MS in Human Resource Counseling, N.C. A&T State U., Greensboro, 1992. Supr. Piedmont Airlines, Winston-Salem, 1974-88; counselor Tokyo English Life Line, Tokyo, 1990-91; trainer Oak Assocs., Tokyo, 1991-92; program dir. Am. C. of C., Tokyo, 1993-94; adult edn. coord. Internat. Sch. Kuala Lumpur, Malaysia, 1995—; aerobics instr. Pres. Girl Talk, Tokyo, 1991-92. Mem. Am. Counseling Assn. Democrat. Baptist. Avocation: reading. Home: Apt 8 191 Condominium, 191 Jalan Ampang, 50450 Kuala Lumpur Malaysia

PURNELL, MAURICE EUGENE, JR., lawyer; b. Dallas, Feb. 17, 1940; s. Maurice Eugene Sr. and Marjorie (Maillot) P.; m. Diane Blake, Aug. 19, 1966; children: Maurice Eugene III, Blake Maillot. BA, Washington and Lee U., 1961; MBA, U. Pa., 1963; LLB, So. Meth. U., 1966. Bar: Tex. 1966. Ptnr. Locke, Purnell, Boren, Laney & Neely, Dallas, 1966-87; shareholder Locke Purnell Rain Harrell P.C., Dallas, 1987—; bd. dirs. Leggett & Platt, Inc. Bd. dirs. Dallas Summer Musicals. Mem. ABA, Tex. Bar Assn., Dallas Bar Assn. Am. Judicature Soc., Dallas C. of C. Clubs: Brook Hollow Golf, Koon Kreek Klub (Dallas). Home: 4409 Versailles Ave Dallas TX 75205-3012 Office: Locke Purnell Rain Harrell PC 2200 Ross Ave Ste 2200 Dallas TX 75201-6766

PURNELL, RONALD JERRY, special education educator; b. Crisfield, Md., July 7, 1957; s. Marvin Jerry and Shirley Virginia (Parks) P.; m. Minnie Kathleen Tyler, July 21, 1979; children: Ronald Jerry II, Melissa Ruth. BS in Elem. Edn., Salisbury State U., 1981; Assocs. Provisional Cert., U. Md., 1986, M in Spl. Edn., 1992. Cert. elem. edn. grades K-8, spl. edn. grades K-12. Media specialist asst. Somerset County Schs., Princess Anne, Md., 1979-80; tchr. grades 2 and 3 Deal Island (Md.) Sch., 1980-81; tchr. spl. edn. Sarah M. Peyton Sch., Marion, Md., 1991-92, Crisfield (Md.) H.S., 1982—; varsity soccer coach Crisfield (Md.) H.S., 1981—, jr. varsity basketball coach, 1982—, baseball coach, 1984, jr. varsity baseball coach, 1992—. Chmn. Mike Sterlin 10K, Crisfield, 1988—; pres. Crisfield (Md.) Youth Soccer Club, 1991—, Crisfield (Md.) Youth Basketball Club, 1994—; mgr. Crisfield (Md.) Little League, 1992, 93. Named Coach of Yr. 2nd team Bayside Athletic Conf., 1991, Mgr. of Yr., Crisfield (Md.) Little League, 1993. Mem. Coun. for Exceptional Children. Baptist. Avocations: running, boating, collecting Indian artifacts, playing basketball. Home: 26546 Asbury Ave Crisfield MD 21817-2216

PURPURA, DOMINICK P., neuroscientist, university dean; b. N.Y.C., Apr. 2, 1927; m. Florence Williams, 1948; children—Craig, Kent, Keith, Allyson. A.B., Columbia U., 1949; M.D., Harvard U., 1953. Intern Presbyn Hosp., N.Y.C., 1953-54; asst. resident in neurology Neurol. Inst., N.Y.C., 1954-55; Prof., chmn. dept. anatomy Albert Einstein Coll. Medicine, Yeshiva U., N.Y.C., 1967-74, sci. dir. Kennedy Ctr., 1969-72, dir. Kennedy Ctr., 1972-82, prof., chmn. dept. neurosci., 1974-82, dean, 1984—; dean Stanford U., Calif., 1982-84; mem. neurophysiol. panel Internat. Brain Rsch. Orgn., pres. 1987—; v.p. med. affairs UNESCO, 1961—; chmn. internat. congress com. Internat. Brain Rsch. Orgn./World Found. Neuroscientists, 1983—. Mem. editorial bd. Brain Rsch., 1965—, editor-in-chief, 1975—; editor-in-chief Brain Rsch. Revs., 1975—, Developmental Brain Rsch., 1981—, Molecular Brain Rsch., 1985—, Cognitive Brain Rsch., 1991—. Served with USAAF, 1945-47. Fellow N.Y. Acad. Scis.; mem. Inst. Medicine of Nat. Acad. Scis., Nat. Acad. Scis., Am. Acad. Neurology, Am. Assn. Anatomists, Am. Assn. Neurol. Surgeons, Am. Epilepsy Soc., Am. Physiol. Soc., Assn. Research in Nervous and Mental Disease, Soc. Neurosci., Sigma Xi. Office: Yeshiva U Albert Einstein Coll Medicine 1300 Morris Park Ave Bronx NY 10461-1926

PURPURA, PETER JOSEPH, museum curator, exhibition designer; b. Bklyn., Nov. 29, 1939; s. Salvatore and Vincenza (Scozzari) P. B in Indsl. Design, Pratt Inst., 1962. Package designer Walter Dorwin Teague Assocs., N.Y.C., 1961-65; exhibit designer Will Burtin, Inc., N.Y.C., 1965-69; sr. exhibits designer Corning Glass Works, N.Y., 1969-71; assoc. exhibits dir. Met. Mus. Art, N.Y.C., 1971-72; exhibits dir. Mus. Sci., Boston, 1972-74; curator, dir. Explorers Hall, Nat. Geographic Soc., Washington, 1974-82; pres. Purpura & Kisner Inc., N.Y.C., 1983—; vis. design instr. Cornell U., 1971; lectr. Parsons Sch. Design, 1988, Phila. U. for Arts, 1992, 93, 94, 95. Recipient Gold medal award Internat. Film and TV Festival of N.Y., 1973, Edison award for excellence GE, 1985. Mem. Indsl. Designers Soc. Am. (v.p. Mid Atlantic chpt. 1978); Am. Assn. Museums. Office: Purpura & Kisner 142 E Court St Doylestown PA 18901-4338

PURSE, CHARLES ROE, real estate investment company executive; b. Redhill, Surrey, Eng., May 19, 1960; came to U.S., 1960.; s. James Nathanial II and Rolande Marie-Louise (Redon) P.; m. Carole Lynn Sadler, July 5, 1986; children: Hayley Elizabeth, Cameron James. BA, Dartmouth Coll., 1982; MBA, Northwestern U., 1985. Account officer Northern Trust Bank, Chgo., 1982-85; asst. v.p. Citicorp Real Estate, Inc., Chgo., 1985-88; v.p. Citibank, Ltd., Sydney, Australia, 1988-91, Citibank Realty Investment Advisors, N.Y.C., 1991-94; sr. v.p. The Yarmouth Group, N.Y.C., 1994—. V.p., bd. dirs. Perrot Meml. Libr., Old Greenwich, Conn., 1993. Mem. Nat. Assn. Comml. Real Estate Investment Fiduciaries, Pension Real Estate Assn., The Country Club (Cleve.), Cromer Golf Club (Sydney, Australia), The Hillsboro Club (Hillsboro Beach, Fla.). Republican. Avocations: golf, photography, skiing, tennis. Office: The Yarmouth Group Inc 10 E 50th St New York NY 10022-6831

PURSELL, CARROLL WIRTH, history educator; b. Visalia, Calif., Sept. 4, 1932; s. Carroll Wirth and Ruth Irene (Crowell) P.; m. Joan Young, Jan. 28, 1956 (dec. 1985); children: Rebecca Elizabeth, Matthew Carroll; m. Angela Woollacott, Dec. 20, 1986. B.A., U. Calif., Berkeley, 1956, Ph.D., 1962; M.A., U. Del., 1958. Asst. prof. history Case Inst. Tech., Cleve., 1963-65; asst. prof. U. Calif., Santa Barbara, 1965-69; asso. prof. U. Calif., 1969-76, prof., 1976-88; Adeline Barry Davee Disting. prof. history Case Western Res. U., Cleve., 1988—; Mellon prof. Lehigh U., Bethlehem, Pa., 1974-76; vis. research scholar Smithsonian Instn., 1970. Author: Early Stationary Steam Engines in America, 1969, Military Industrial Complex, 1972, From Conservation to Ecology, 1973, White Heat, 1994, The Machine in America, 1995. Fellow AAAS; mem. Soc. History of Tech. (pres. 1990-92, Leonardo da Vinci medal 1991), History of Sci. Soc., Orgn. Am. Historians, Am. Hist. Assn., Phi Beta Kappa. Democrat. Office: Case Western Res U Dept History Cleveland OH 44106

PURSEY, DEREK LINDSAY, physics educator; b. Glasgow, Scotland, Oct. 22, 1927; came to U.S., 1964; s. Henry Edwin and Margaret Martin (Lindsay) P.; m. Barbara Ann Parker, Aug. 4, 1962; 1 child, John. BS, U. Glasgow, 1948, PhD, 1952. Asst. lectr. theoretical physics King's Coll., London, 1951-54; lectr. math. physics U. Edinburgh, Scotland, 1954-59; vis. lectr. UCLA, 1959-60; mem. sch. math. Inst. for Advanced Studies Princeton U., 1960-61; lectr. in theoretical physics U. Glasgow, Scotland, 1961-64; vis. prof. Iowa State U., Ames, 1964-65, prof. physics, 1965-93, emeritus prof. physics, 1993—. Contbr. articles to profl. jours. Fellow Royal Soc. Edinburgh, Am. Phys. Soc.; mem. Am. Assn. Advancement Sci., Sigma Xi. Democrat. Presbyterian. Avocations: church-related activities; photography; music; reading; wilderness camping.

PURSLEY, CAROL COX, psychologist; b. Chattanooga, Dec. 7, 1951; d. George Edwin and M. Sue (Clarke) Cox; m. James V. Pursley; 1 child, Drew Vinson; stepchildren: Nancy, John. BS, U. Tenn., 1973, MS, 1975; PhD, U. Ky., 1983. Registered rehab. supplier, Ga.; cert. rehab. counselor; lic. psychologist, Ky., Ga.; lic. profl. counselor, Ga. Dir. rehab. Goodwill Industries, Knoxville, Tenn., 1975-77; rsch. and evaluation asst. region IV rehab. continuing edn. U. Tenn., Knoxville, 1977; crisis intervention cons., job placement counselor KACRC, Knoxville, 1977-78; instr., cons. region IV rehab. continuing edn. program U. Tenn., Knoxville, 1978-79; teaching/rsch. asst. U. Ky., Lexington, 1979-80; rehab. specialist Internat. Rehab. Assocs., Louisville, 1980; psychologist and assoc. clin. staff Ea. State Hosp., Lexington, 1981-84; rehab. cons. Southeastern Transitions, Atlanta, 1985-86; pvt. practice rehab. cons. Marietta, Ga., 1986—; rehab. counselor U.S. Dept. of Labor OWCP Program, 1987—; pvt. practice psychotherapy and testing Marietta and Atlanta, 1994—; allied health profl. Ridgeview Inst., 1994-95, clin. psychology staff mem., 1995—; assessments/group therapy, allied health profl. for Rehab. Evaluation and Comprehensive Treatment Program Kennestone Hosp. at Windy Hill, Marietta, 1988-92; clin. assoc. Am. Bd. Med. Psychotherapists, 1986—; strategy meeting cons. Sony Music Entertainment, N.Y.; cons. ADA; expert witness Ga. Composite Bd. Profl. Counselors, Social Workers and Marriage and Family Therapists, 1991—; cons. to Gov.'s Rehab. Adv. Com., 1990. Chairperson-elect Vol. State Rehab. Counseling Assn., Knoxville, 1976; mem. Mayor's Adv. Com. for Handicapped, Knoxville, 1974-76. Facility Improvement grantee s.e. region Rehab. Svcs. Adminstrn., 1975-77, Facility Establishment grantee United

Cerebral Palsy, 1977. Mem. APA, Am. Coll. Forensic Examiners, Ga. Psychol. Assn., Ky. Psychol. Assn., Nat. Assn. Rehab. Providers in Pvt. Sector (rsch. and tng. com. 1988-94), Pvt. Rehab. Suppliers of Ga. (chairperson ethics com. 1989-91, named person of distinction state PRSG chpt. newsletter 1990, ethics com. 1986-92), Phi Kappa Phi. Avocations: photography, video filming, boating, interior decorating/design. Office: 2520 E Piedmont Rd Ste F Marietta GA 30062-1700

PURSLEY, MICHAEL BADER, electrical engineering educator, communications systems research and consulting; b. Winchester, Ind., Aug. 10, 1945; s. Bader E. and Evelyn L. (Bennett) P.; m. Lou Ann Hinchman, July 6, 1968; 1 child, Jessica Ann. B.S., Purdue U., 1967, M.S., 1968; Ph.D., U. So. Calif., 1974. Mem. tech. staff Hughes Aircraft Co., Los Angeles, 1967; engr. Northrop Co., Hawthorne, Calif., 1968; staff engr. Hughes Aircraft Co., Los Angeles, 1968-74; acting asst. prof. UCLA, 1974; asst. prof., then assoc. prof. elec. engring. U. Ill., Urbana, 1974-80, prof., 1980-93; Holcombe prof. elec. and computer engring. Clemson (S.C.) U., 1992—; assoc. Ctr. Advanced Study, 1980-81; vis. prof. UCLA, 1985; cons. U.S. Army, Huntsville, Ala., 1977, Ft. Monmouth, N.J., 1983-86, 91; cons. ITT, Ft. Wayne, Ind., 1979—; pres. SIGCOM, Inc., 1986-90; prin. scientist Techno-Scis. Inc., 1990—. Contbr. chpts. to books. Fellow IEEE (pres. info. theory group 1983, Centennial medal 1984); mem. Inst. Math. Stats. Office: Clemson U 102 Riggs Hall Box 340915 Clemson SC 29634-0915

PURSWELL, BEVERLY JEAN, veterinary medicine educator, theriogenologist; b. Atlanta; d. Henry D. and Frances (Martin) P.; m. C.M. Wall, Jan. 1, 1990. DVM, U. Ga., 1977, MS, 1981, PhD, 1985. Equine vet., 1977-79; theriogenology resident Medical Microbiology, 1979-85; assoc. prof. vet. medicine Va. Poly. Inst. and State U., Blacksburg, 1985—. Mem. AVMA, Soc. for Theriogenology (bd. dirs. 1989—, sec.-treas., v.p. 1992-93, pres. 1993-94), Va. Vet. Med. Assn. (bd. dirs. 1990-96, v.p. 1996-97). Avocations: dressage, livestock breeding. Office: Va Poly Inst and State U Coll Vet Medicine Duck Pond Rd Blacksburg VA 24061

PURTELL, LAWRENCE ROBERT, lawyer; b. Quincy, Mass., May 2, 1947; s. Lawrence Joseph and Louise Maria (Loria) P.; m. Cheryl Lynn Tymon, Aug. 3, 1968; children: Lisa Ann, Susan Elizabeth. AB, Villanova U., 1969; JD, Columbia U., 1972. Bar: N.Y. 1973, N.J. 1978, Conn. 1988. Assoc. White & Case, N.Y.C., 1972-73; judge advocate USMC, Washington, 1973-76; assoc. White & Case, N.Y.C., 1977-79; corp. counsel Great Atlantic & Pacific Tea Co., Montvale, N.J., 1979-81; asst. gen. counsel United Techs. Corp., Hartford, Conn., 1981-84, assoc. gen. counsel, 1984-92, sec., gen. counsel, 1989-92; v.p., gen. counsel and sec. Carrier Corp., 1992-93; sr. v.p., gen. counsel and corp. sec. Mc Dermott Internat., New Orleans, La., 1993-96; sr. v.p., gen. counsel Koch Industries, Wichita, Kans., 1996—. Capt. USMC, 1973-76. Roman Catholic. Avocations: running. Home: 8911 Summerfield Wichita KS 67206 Office: Koch Industries Inc PO Box 2256 Wichita KS 67201

PURTLE, JOHN INGRAM, lawyer, former state supreme court justice; b. Enola, Ark., Sept. 7, 1923; s. John Wesley and Edna Gertrude (Ingram) P.; m. Marian Ruth White, Dec. 31, 1951; children: Jeffrey, Lisa K. Student, U. Central Ark., 1946-47; LLB, U. Ark., Fayetteville, 1950. Bar: Ark. 1950, U.S. Dist. Ct. (ea. dist.) Ark. 1950. Pvt. practice Conway, Ark., 1950-53, Little Rock, 1953-78; mem. Ark. State Legislature, 1951-52, 69-70; assoc. justice Ark. Supreme Ct., 1979-90; ret. N000, Little Rock, Ark., 1990; pvt. practice Little Rock, Ark., 1990—. Tchr., deacon Baptist Ch. Served with U.S. Army, 1940-45. Mem. ABA, Ark. Bar Assn., Am. Judicature Soc., Ark. Jud. Council. Democrat. Office: 300 S Spring St Ste 620 Little Rock AR 72201-2422

PURVES, ALAN CARROLL, English language educator, education educator; b. Phila., Dec. 14, 1931; s. Edmund Randolph and Mary Carroll (Spencer) P.; m. Anita Woodruff Parker, June 18, 1960 (dec. 1975); children: William Carroll, Theodore Rehn; m. Anne Hathaway Nesbitt, July 14, 1976. A.B., Harvard U., 1953; M.A., Columbia U., 1956, Ph.D., 1960. Lectr. Hofstra Coll., 1956-58; instr. Columbia U., 1958-61; asst. prof. English Barnard Coll., N.Y.C., 1961-65; examiner in humanities Ednl. Testing Service, 1965-68; assoc. prof. English U. Ill., Urbana, 1968-70, prof., 1970-73, dir. curriculum lab., 1973-86; dir. U. Ill. (Curriculum Lab.), 1976-86; prof. edn. and humanities SUNY, Albany, 1986-96, prof. emeritus, 1996—, dir. Ctr. for Writing and Literacy, 1987—; staff assoc. Ctrl. Midwest Regional Ednl. Lab., St. Ann, Mo., 1968-70; cons. Coll. Entrance Exam. Bd., 1987-90, Grad. Record Exam. Bd., 1988-91, N.Y. State Found. for Sci. and Tech., N.Y. State Edn. Dept. Acad. Sys. Inc., MLA; pres. The Scribes, Inc. Editl. Svcs. Author: The Essays of Theodore Spencer, 1968, The Elements of Writing about a Literary Work, 1968, Testing in Literature, 1971, How Porcupines Make Love, 1972, Literature and the Reader, 1972, Responding, 1973, Literature Education in Ten Countries, 1973, Educational Policy and International Assessment, 1975, Common Sense and Testing in English, 1975, Evaluation in English, 1976, Achievement in Reading and Literature: New Zealand in International Perspective, 1979, Evaluation of Learning in Literature, 1980, Achievement in Reading and Literature: The U.S. in International Perspective, 1981, The Implementation of Language and International Schools, 1981, An International Perspective on the Evaluation of Written Composition, 1982, Experiencing Children's Literature, 1984, How to Write Well in College, 1984, Contrastive Rhetoric, 1988, Cultural Literacy and General Education, 1988, International Study of Writing Achievement, 1988, The Scribal Society, 1989, International Research And Educational Reform, 1989, How Porcupines Make Love II, 1990, The Idea of Difficulty in Literature, 1991, Literate Systems and Individual Lives, 1991, Tapestry: A Multicultural Anthology, 1992, International Study of Writing Achievement 2, 1992, Encyclopaedia of English Studies and Language Arts, 2 vols., 1994, Creating the Writing Portfolio, 1995, How Porcupines Make Love III, 1995, Creating the Literature Portfolio, 1996; editor: Research in the Teaching of English, 1971-77, IMEN Rev., 1986-92. Pres. Wonalancet (N.H.) Corp., 1967-69, 75-77; mem. vestry Episcopalian ch., 1970-73, 77-79, 88-91, 92-94, warden 1994—). With AUS, 1953-55. Fellow Internat. Assn. Evaluation Edn. Achievement Internat., 1971, Coolidge Colloquium, 1994; recipient Fulbright Hayes award, 1977, 86, Leppert award, 1980, noted lectr. award U. B.C., 1991, disting. rsch. award NCRE, 1994. Mem. MLA, Nat. Coun. Tchrs. English (trustee rsch. found. 1969-72, 83-86, mem. com. rsch. 1968-77, 82-85, v.p. 1977-78, pres. 1979-80), Newcomen Soc. (hon.), N.Y. State Coun., Nat. Conf. Rsch. English, Internat. Assn. for Evaluation of Ednl. Achievement (chmn. 1986-90), Farm Bur. (edn. com. 1991—), Wonalancet Outdoor Club (pres. 1965-69), Appalachian Mountain Club, Harvard Club. Home: 468 Pinewoods Rd Melrose NY 12121-9747

PURVES, WILLIAM KIRKWOOD, biologist, educator; b. Sacramento, Calif., Oct. 28, 1934; s. William Kirkwood and Dorothy (Brandenburger) P.; m. Jean McCauley, June 9, 1959; 1 son, David William. B.S., Calif. Inst. Tech., 1956; M.S., Yale U., 1957, Ph.D., 1959. NSF postdoctoral fellow U. Tubingen, Fed. Republic Germany, 1959-60; Nat. Cancer Inst. postdoctoral fellow UCLA, 1960-61; asst. prof. botany U. Calif., Santa Barbara, 1961-65; assoc. prof. biochemistry U. Calif., 1965-70, prof. biology, 1970-73, chmn. dept. biol. scis., 1972-73; prof. biology, head biol. sci. group U. Conn., Storrs, 1973-77; Stuart Mudd prof. biology Harvey Mudd Coll., Claremont, Calif., 1977-95, prof. emeritus, 1996—, chmn. dept. biol., 1985-95; chmn. dept. computer sci. Harvey Mudd Coll., 1985-90; adj. prof. plant physiology U. Calif., Riverside, 1979-85; vis. fellow computer sci. Yale U., 1983-84; vis. scholar Northwestern U., 1991. Author: Life, the Science of Biology, 1983, 4th edit., 1995. NSF sr. postdoctoral fellow U. London, 1967; NSF sr. postdoctoral fellow Harvard U., 1968; NSF rsch. grantee, 1962-83. Fellow AAAS; mem. Am. Soc. Plant Physiologists, Sigma Xi. Home: 2817 N Mountain Ave Claremont CA 91711-1550 Office: Harvey Mudd Coll 301 E 12th St Claremont CA 91711-5901

PURVIS, GEORGE FRANK, JR., life insurance company executive; b. Rayville, La., Nov. 22, 1914; s. George Frank and Ann Mamie (Womble) P.; m. Virginia Winston Wendt, May 16, 1942; children: Virginia Reese (Mrs. William H. Freshwater), Winston Wendt, George Frank III. AA, Kemper Mil. Sch., 1932; LLB, La. State U., 1935. Bar: La. bar 1935. Sole practice Rayville, 1935-37; atty. Office Sec. State State of La., Baton Rouge, 1937-41; also dep. ins. commr. State of La., 1945-49; atty. La. Ins. Dept., also spl. asst. to atty. gen., 1937-41; with Pan-Am. Life Ins. Co., New Orleans, 1949—, exec. v.p., 1962-64, pres., chief exec. officer, 1964—, chmn. bd., 1969—, also bd. dirs.; pres., bd. dirs. Compania de Seguros Panamericana, S.Am.; pres. Pan-Am. de Colombia Compania de Seguros de Vida, S.A.; chmn., bd. govs. Internat. Ins. Seminars, Inc., 1984—; mem. Industry Sector Adv. Com. for Trade Policy Matters, 1986; lectr. ins. law Tulane U., New Orleans, 1949-56; bd. dirs. 1st Nat. Bank Commerce in New ORleans, Republic Airlines, Inc., 1st Commerce Corp., So. Airlines-Republic Airlines, Pan Am de Mex. Cos. de Seguros Sobre la Vida, S.A., 1964-88; dir. Northwest Airlines, 1986-87. Compiler, author: Louisiana Insurance Code, 1948; contbr. articles to profl. jours. Chmn. big donors com. New Orleans Christmas Seal Campaign, 1961, gen. campaign chmn., 1962, chmn. profl. group VIII, 1963; vice chmn. New Orleans United Fund campaign, 1965, gen. chmn., 1967; pres. Tb Assn. Greater New Orleans, 1967, La. State U. Found., 1967, YMCA, New Orleans, 1968—, Internat. House, 1977, Met. Area Com., 1979; geog. chmn. U.S. Savs. Bond Campaign, Greater New Orleans, 1971; mem. Bd. City Park Commrs., 1965-79, mem. bd. commrs. Port of New Orleans, 1979—, pres. bd. commrs., 1982; chmn. S.S. Huebner Found. Ins. Edn., 1977—, Bus. Task Force on Edn., Inc., 1980—; mem. adv. bd. Bapt. Hosp., 1985—, Salvation Army, 1986—; bd. dirs. Family Svc. Soc. New Orleans, Council for a Better La., New Orleans Philharm. Symphony Soc., Summer Pop Concerts, Bur. Govt. Rsch. New Orleans; mem. Govs. Cost Control Commn., 1981-89; trustee Greater New Orleans Found., 1987—, chmn. bd. trustees La. Ind. Coll. Fund Inc., 1987-88, mem. 1987—. Served with USNR, 1941-45. Decorated Order of Vasco Nunez de Balboa (Panama); named Alumnus of Yr., La. State U., 1975, role model Young Leadership Coun., 1993; recipient award Inst. for Human Understanding, 1975, Weiss Meml. award, 1976, Vol. Activist award, 1978, award of excellence Greater New Orleans Fedn. Chs., 1983, Disting. Svc. award Navy League, 1983, Humanitarian award Nat. Jewish Hosp./Nat. Asthma Ctr., 1984, internat. ins. award Internat. Ins. Adv. Coun., 1986, 1st ann. award for outstanding efforts in promoting trade with L.Am., Rotary Club, 1987, Hall of Fame award La. State U., 1987, Man of Yr. award Fedn. Ins. and Corp. Counsel, 1988, Integritas Vitae award Loyola U. of South, 1991, Bus. Hall of Fame award Jr. Achievement, 1993, cert. of appreciation La. Air N.G., 1995; selected role model Young Bus. Leadership Coun., 1993. Mem. ABA, La. Bar Assn., La. Law Inst., Am. Judicature Soc., Assn. Life Ins. Counsel, Am. Life Conv. (past chmn. legal sect., exec. com., v.p. La., chmn. 1972), Health Ins. Assn. Am. (dir., chmn. 1970), Ins. Econs. Soc. Am. (chmn. 1980-81), La. Assn. Legal Res. Life Ins. Cos. (pres. 1963-68), New Orleans Assn. Life Underwriters (award for Loyal and Unselfish Service to the Ins. Industry 1987), Internat. Trade Adminstrn. (industry sector and functional adv. coms. for trade policy matters), C. of C. Greater New Orleans Area (dir., pres. 1970), Phi Delta Phi, Omicron Delta Kappa, Delta Kappa Epsilon. Episcopalian. Home: 5501 Dayna Ct New Orleans LA 70124-1042

PURVIS, HOYT HUGHES, political scientist, academic administrator, educator; b. Jonesboro, Ark., Nov. 7, 1939; s. Hoyt Somervell and Jane (Hughes) P.; children: Pamela R., Camille C. BJ, U. Tex., 1961, MJ, 1963; postgrad., U. Nancy, France, 1962-63, Vanderbilt U., Nashville, 1963-64. Researcher/writer So. Edn. Reporting Svc., Nashville, 1963-64; reporter Houston Chronicle, 1964-65; press sec., spl. asst. Sen. J.W. Fulbright, Washington, 1967-74; dir. pubs. and lectr. LBJ Sch. Pub. Affairs, U. Tex., Austin, 1974-76; fgn./def. advisor and dep. staff dir. Sen. Majority Leader and Sen. Dem. Policy Com., Washington, 1977-80; sr. rsch. fellow LBJ Sch. Pub. Affairs, U. Tex., 1980-82; dir. and prof. Fulbright Inst. Internat. Rels., U. Ark., Fayetteville, 1982—. Author: Interdependence, 1992; co-author: Legistling Foreign Policy, 1984, Seoul & Washington, 1993; editor: The Presidency and the Press, 1976, The Press: Free and Responsible?, 1982; coeditor: Old Myths and New Realities in U.S.-Soviet Relations, 1990. Mem. adv. coun. Sci. Info. Liaison Office, Ark. Gen. Assembly, Little Rock, 1984—; chmn. Fayetteville City Cable Bd., 1991-93; apptd. J. Wm. Fulbright Fgn. Scholarship Bd., 1994—, vice chair, 1995, chmn., 1996. Rotary fellow, 1962-63, others; recipient Fulbright Coll. Master Tchr. award, Disting. Faculty Achievement award U. Ark. Alumni Assn. Mem. Internat. Studies Assn. (regional v.p. 1984-86), Am. Polit. Sci. Assn., Assn. for Edn. in Journalism and Mass Communication, Phi Beta Delta, Delta Phi Alpha. Methodist. Home: PO Box 1872 Fayetteville AR 72702-1872 Office: Fulbright Inst Internat Rels 722 W Maple St Fayetteville AR 72701-3229

PURVIS, JOHN ANDERSON, lawyer; b. Greeley, Colo., Aug. 31, 1942; s. Virgil J. and Emma Lou (Anderson) P.; m. Charlotte Johnson, Apr. 3, 1976; 1 child, Whitney; children by previous marriage: Jennifer, Matt. B.A. cum laude, Harvard U., 1965; J.D., U. Colo., 1968. Bar: Colo. 1968, U.S. Dist. Ct. Colo. 1968, U.S. Ct. Appeals (10th cir.) 1978, U.S. Ct. Claims, 1980. Dep. dist. atty. Boulder, Colo., 1968-69; asst. dir. and dir. legal aid U. Colo. Sch. Law, 1969; assoc. Williams, Taussig & Trine, Boulder, 1969; head Boulder office Colo. Pub. Defender System, 1970-72; assoc. and ptnr. Hutchinson, Black, Hill, Buchanan & Cook, Boulder, 1972-85; ptnr. Purvis, Gray, Schuetze and Gordon, 1985—; acting Colo. State Pub. Defender, 1978; adj. prof. law U. Colo., 1981, 84-88, 94, others; lectr. in field. Chmn., Colo. Pub. Defender Commn., 1979-89; mem. nominating commn. Colo. Supreme Ct., 1984-90; mem. com. on conduct U.S. Dist. Ct., 1993—; chmn. Boulder County Criminal Justice Com., 1975-81, Boulder County Manpower Coun., 1977-78. Recipient Ames award Harvard U., 1964; Outstanding Young Lawyer award Colo. Bar Assn., 1978. Mem. Internat. Soc. Barristers, Am. Coll. of Trial Lawyers, Colo. Bar Assn. (chair litigation sect. 1994-95), Boulder County Bar Assn., Colo. Trial Lawyers Assn., Am. Trial Lawyers Assn., Trial Lawyers for Pub. Justice. Democrat. Address: 1050 Walnut St Ste 501 Boulder CO 80302-5144

PURVIS, RICHARD GEORGE, former superintendent of schools; b. Milw., Oct. 31, 1945; s. Robert E. and Violet (Roberts) P.; m. Janis Ann Borden, Jan. 27, 1966; children: Kelly Lyn, Cassie Ann. BS, Ea. N.Mex. U., 1967, MS, 1970; postgrad., Tex. Tech U., 1992—. Tchr. Jefferson County Schs., Arvada, Colo., 1967-68; tchr. Clovis (N.Mex.) Mcpl. Schs., 1968-71, asst. prin., 1971-72, jr. high prin., 1972-80, high sch. prin., 1980-85, supt., 1985-92; v.p. Ea. N.Mex. Research & Study Council, Portales, 1988—. Bd. dirs. Project Uplift, Albuquerque, 1983—. Named Adminstr. of Yr. N.Mex. Music Educators Assn., 1991, Nat. Superintendent of the Yr. awd., N.Mex., Am. Assn. of School Administrators, 1992. Mem. N.Mex. Supts. Assn. (bd. dirs. 1987—, pres. 1990, Supt. of Yr. 1992), Am. Assn. Sch. Adminstrs., N.Mex. Sch. Adminstrs., Assn. Supervision and Curriculum Devel., Rotary. Republican. Christian Ch. Avocations: hunting, fishing, travel.

PURYEAR, JAMES BURTON, college administrator; b. Jackson, Miss., Sept. 2, 1938; s. Harry Henton and Doris (Smith) P.; m. Joan Copeland, June 13, 1965; children: John James, Jeffrey Burton, Joel Harry. BS, Miss. State U., 1960, MEd, 1961; PhD, Fla. State U., 1969. Lic. profl. counselor, Ga. Assoc. dir. YMCA, Starkville, Miss., 1962-64, dir., 1964-65; dir. fin. aid Fla. State U., Tallahassee, 1967-69; asst. dir. student affairs Med. Coll. of Ga., Augusta, 1969-70, dir. student affairs, 1970-86, v.p. student affairs, 1986—. Adv. bd. mem. Ga. Fed. Bank, Augusta, 1978-85; chmn. bd. First Bapt. Ch., Augusta, 1978-80; pres. Learning Disabilities Assn., Augusta, 1987, PTA, 1994; bd. dirs. Augusta Tng. Shop for Handicapped, 1994—; exec. bd. mem. Boy Scouts Am. Yearbook Dedication MCG Student Yearbook, 1975; scholar Med. Coll. Ga., 1988; recipient Svc. to Mankind award Sertoma, 1988. Mem. Nat. Assn. Student Pers. (S.E. regional bd. 1985), Am. Coll. Pers. Assn., So. Assn. Coll. Student Affairs, Rotary (pres. 1978, Paul Harris fellow 1985). Baptist. Avocations: golf, photography, scouting. Office: Student Affairs Med Coll Ga Augusta GA 30912

PURYEAR, JOAN COPELAND, English language educator; b. Columbus, Miss., May 10, 1944; d. John Thomas and Mamie (Cunningham) Copeland.; m. James Burton Puryear, June 13, 1965; children: John James, Jeffrey Burton, Joel Harry. BA summa cum laude, Miss. State U., Starkville, 1965; MA, Fla. State U., 1969; EdD, U. Ga., 1987. Cert. tchr., Ga. English instr. Fla. State U., Tallahassee, 1965-69, Augusta (Ga.) Coll., 1987-88; head English dept. Augusta Tech. Inst., 1989-93; chairperson gen. edn. and devel. studies, 1993—, mem. dean's coun., mgmt. team and grant proposal team, 1994—; chmn. State Exec. Bd. English, Ga.,1 990-92, East Ctrl. Consortium English, Ga., 1990-92; mem. Augusta Tech. Inst. Tech. Com., 1990—; chmn. Capital Funds Raising Family Campaign, Augusta Tech. Inst., vice chmn. Capital Fund Raising Cmty. Campaign; mem. and co-chmn.-elect Continuous Improvement Coun., 1996—, Augusta Tech. Inst.; facilitator Total Quality Mgmt. Tech. Tng.; mem. steeringt com. Continuous Improvement Coun.; chmn. editing com. Augusta Tech. Inst. Self Study, 1992-93, chmn. long range planning goals and objectives com., 1994. Mem. Cmtys. in Schs., 1996—; trustee Augusta Tech. Inst. Found. Bd., 1996—; co-pres. Davidson Fine Arts Sch. PTA; pres. Med. Coll. Spouse's Club, Augusta, 1972; dir. Women's Mission Orgn., First Bapt. Ch., Augusta, 1982, dir. Youth Sunday Sch., 1992, chmn. 175th Anniversary, 1992, deacon, 1996—. Mem. Modern Lang. Assn., Nat. Coun. Tchrs., Am. Vocat. Assn., Ga. Vocat. Assn., So. Assn. Colls. (accreditation team 1994), Phi Theta Kappa (adv. 1992—). Baptist. Avocations: flower arranging, home decorating, reading. Office: Augusta Tech Inst 3116 Deans Bridge Rd Augusta GA 30906-3375

PUSATERI, JAMES ANTHONY, judge; b. Kansas City, Mo., May 20, 1938; s. James A. and Madeline (LaSalle) P.; m. Jacqueline D. Ashburne, Sept. 1, 1962; children—James A., Mark C., Danielle L. B.A., U. Kans., 1960, LL.B., 1963. Bar: Kans. 1963, U.S. Dist. Ct. Kans. 1963, U.S. Ct. Appeals (10th cir.) 1964. Assoc. Payne, Jones, Chartered, Olathe, Kans., 1963-65; assoc. James Cashin, Prairie Village, Kans., 1965-69; asst. U.S. atty. Dept. Justice, Kansas City, Kans., 1969-76; judge U.S. Bankruptcy Ct. Dist. Kans., Topeka, 1976—. Mem. Prairie Village City Council, 1967-69. Mem. Kans. Bar Assn., Topeka Bar Assn., Nat. Conf. Bankruptcy Judges, Am. Bankruptcy Inst. Office: US Dist Ct 444 SE Quincy St Topeka KS 66683

PUSATERI, LAWRENCE XAVIER, lawyer; b. Oak Park, Ill., May 25, 1931; s. Lawrence E. and Josephine (Romano) P.; m. Eve M. Graf, July 9, 1956; children: Joanne, Lawrence F., Paul L., Mary Ann, Eva. JD summa cum laude, DePaul U., 1953. Bar: Ill. 1953. Asst. state's atty. Cook County, 1957-59; ptnr. Newton, Wilhelm, Pusateri & Naborowski, Chgo., 1959-77; justice Ill. appellate ct., Chgo., 1977-78; ptnr. Peterson, Ross, Schloerb & Seidel, Chgo., 1978-91, Peterson & Ross, 1991—; pres. Conf. Consumer Fin. Law, 1984-92, chmn. gov. com., 1993—; mem. Ill. Supreme Ct. Com. on Pattern Jury Instrns., 1981—; mem. U.S. Senate Jud. Nominations Commn. State Ill., 1993, 95; exec. dir. State of Ill. Jud. Inquiry Bd., 1995—; mem. Merit Selection Panel for U.S. Magistrate; lectr. law DePaul U., Chgo., 1962, Columbia U., N.Y.C., 1965, Marquette U., Milw., 1962-82, Northwestern U. Law Sch., Def. Counsel Inst., 1969-70; apptd. by U.S. Senator Paul Simon to Merit Screening Com. Fed. Judges, U.S. Atty. and U.S. Marshal, 1993, others; mem. task force indigent appellate def. Cook County Jud. Adv. counsel, 1992—; mem. Ill. Gen. Assembly, 1964-68. Contbr. articles to profl. jours. Chmn. Ill. Crime Investigating Commn. 1967-68, chmn. Ill. Parole and Pardon Bd., 1969-70; bd. dirs. Ill. Law Enforcement Commn., 1970-72; chmn. Com. on Correctional Facilities and Services; exec. v.p. and gen. counsel Ill. Fin. Svcs. Assn., 1980-95; chmn. law forum Am. Fin. Svcs. Assn., 1975-76; mem. spl. commn. on adminstrn. of justice in Cook County, Ill. (Greylord Com.) 1984-90, bd. dirs. Chgo. Crime Commn., 1986-91; mem. Ill. Supreme Ct. Spl. Commn. on the Adminstrn. of Justice, Ill. Supreme Ct. Appointment, 1991. Served to capt. JAGC, AUS, 1955-58. Named One of Ten Outstanding Young Men in Chgo., Chgo. Jr. Assn. Commerce and Industry, 1960, 65; recipient Outstanding Legislator award Ill. Gen. Assembly, 1966. Mem. ABA (com. consumer fin. svcs. 1975—, ho. dels. 1981-90, judicial adminstrn. divsn. 1980—, mem. exec. com. lawyer's conf. 1994—, mem. bench and bar rels. com. 1994—, mem. adv. com. to Ill. State Del., Jud. Adminstrn. Divsn. in Recognition of Leadership in Improvement of Adminstrn. of Justice award 1993), Ill. State Bar Assn. (pres. 1975-76, com. on fed. jud. and related appointments; Abraham Lincoln Legal Writing award 1959, mem. adv. com., state del., 1994—, bd. dirs.), Chgo. Bar Assn. (bd. mgrs. 1965-66), Fred B. Snite Found (sec., counsel 1976-85), Gertrude and Walter Swanson Found., Mid-Am. Club Chgo. Republican. Roman Catholic.

PUSCH, WILLIAM GERARD, lawyer; b. La Porte, Ind., Jan. 29, 1935; s. William C. and Margaret (Elshout) P.; m. Mikellanne Peet, June 1, 1963; children: Jeffrey, Gregory, Anne. BA with honors, U. Mich., 1957; JD, Stanford U., 1960. Bar: Wash. 1961, U.S. Dist. Ct. (we. dist.) Wash. 1961. Ptnr. Davis Wright Tremaine (and predecessor firms), Seattle, 1961—. Editor: Wash. Partnership Law, 1981-84; bd. editors: Stanford Law Rev., 1959-60. Mem. ABA, Wash. State Bar Assn. (chair partnership law com., 1988—, exec. com. bus. law sect.), Seattle-King County Bar Assn., Order of Coif. Avocations: gardening, fishing, golf. Home: 8434 W Mercer Way Mercer Island WA 98040-5633 Office: Davis Wright Tremaine 2600 Century Sq 1501 4th Ave Seattle WA 98101-1662

PUSCHECK, HERBERT CHARLES, social sciences educator; b. Marshfield, Wis., July 14, 1936; s. Herbert and Ella (Sanger) P.; m. Elizabeth E., Oct. 17, 1959; children: Elizabeth E. and Lisa Marie. BS in Gen. Engring., U.S. Mil. Acad., 1958; MS in Elec. Engring., Purdue U., 1964, PhD in Ops. Rsch., 1969. Officer U.S. Army, various cites, 1958-78; dir. spl. studies Office of Sec. Def., Washington, 1974-78, dep. asst. sec. def., 1987-94; prof. Nat. Def. U., Washington, 1979; assoc. dir. Selective Svc. System Hdqrs., Washington, 1980-82; asst. chief staff Army Materiel Command, Alexandria, Va., 1983-86; army chair Def. Systems Mgmt. Coll., Ft. Belvoir, Va., 1986-87; prof. pub. and internat. affairs George Mason Univ., Fairfax, 1994—; pres. H & BI (investments), Alexandria, 1985—. Contbr. articles to profl. jours. Co-chmn. Mt. Vernon Coun., Fairfax, Va., 1977-79. Recipient Meritorious Achievment award Pres., 1989. Mem. Mil. Ops. Rsch. Soc. (v.p. 1972-74, sponsor 1988-94). Avocations: sailing, hiking, fly fishing. Home: 8106 W Boulevard Dr Alexandria VA 22308-1711

PUSCHEL, PHILIP P., textiles executive; m. Roberta J. Green. AB, Hamilton Coll., 1960; MBA, Stanford U., 1962. V.p. F Schumacher & Co., N.Y.C., 1971, pres., CEO, 1981, chmn. bd., CEO officer, 1989—. With USN, 1962-65. Office: F Schumacher & Co 79 Madison Ave New York NY 10016-7802

PUSCHETT, JULES B., medical educator, neprhrologist, researcher; b. Hazelton, Pa., Mar. 13, 1934; m. Diane Puschett; children: Mitchell, Lynne. BA magna cum laude, Lehigh U., 1955; MD, U. Pa., 1959. Intern Jackson Meml. Hosp., Miami, 1959-60; resident, fellow endrocrinology and metabolism Univ. Hosp., Balt., 1963-66; postdoctoral fellow in medicine NIH Inst. Arthritis and Metabolic Disease, Bethesda, Md., 1966-68; fellow, renal-electrolyte sect. U. Pa. Sch. Medicine, Phila., 1966-68; rsch. assoc. VA Hosp., Phila., 1968-70, staff to chief renal-electrolyte sect. dept. medicine, 1968-73, clin. investigator, 1970-73; head renal-electrolyte divsn. Allegheny Gen. Hosp., Pitts., 1973-78; dir. renal-electrolyte divsn. fellowship tng. program U. Pitts. Sch. Medicine, 1976-78; chief renal-electrolyte divsn. dept. medicine U. Ark. for Med. Scis., Little Rock, 1979-80, U. Pitts. Sch. Medicine, 1980-90; interim chief sect. nephrology dept. medicine Tulane U. Sch. Medicine, New Orleans, 1990-92; chmn. dept. medicine Tulane U. Sch. Medicine, New Orleans, 1990—; instr. medicine U. Pa. Sch. Medicine 1967-79, assoc. in medicine 1969-70, asst. prof. medicine 1970-73; clin. assoc. prof. medicine U. Pitts. Med. Sch. 1973-78; prof. medicine U. Ark. Med. Scis. 1979-80; prof. medicine U. Pitts. Sch. Medicine 1980-90; prof. medicine Tulane U. Sch. Medicine 1990—. Editor: The Diuretic Manual, 1984, Diuretics: chemistry, Pharmacology and Clinical Applications, 1984, Disorders of Fluid and Electrolyte Balance: diagnosis and Management, 1985, Diuretics II: Chemistry, Pharmacology and Clinical Applications, 1986, Diuretics III, 1989, Diuretics IV, 1993; contbr. over 170 articles to profl. jours.; spkr. and presenter in field; editl. bd. Am. Jour. Med. Scis., Am. Jour. Nephrology (sect. editor Physiology for the Nephrologist), Cardiovasc. Risk Factors, Internat. Jour. Artificial Organs, Southern Med. Jour. Chmn. 1st Ann. Kidney Ball, Nat. Kidney Found. of Western Pa., 1988, chmn. 2d Ann. Kidney Ball, 1989. With USN 1960-63. Coxe Meml. schlar, Lehigh U., 1951; named Outstanding Tchr. Yr., Owl Club, Tulane U., 1991, 94. Fellow ACP; mem. AMA, AAAS, Am. Fedn. Clin. Rsch., Am. Soc. Artificial Internal Orgnas. Am. Soc. Nephrology (chmn. audit com. 1992), Nat. Kidney Found. (pub. policy com. 1989, vol. svc. award 1990), Internat. Soc. Nephrology, Am. Heart Assn. Coun. on the Kidney in Cardiovasc. Disease (chmn. subcom. on scientific confs. 1991-92, exec. com. 1991-95, long-range planning com. 1992—), Am. Heart Assn. Coun. for High Blood Pressure Rsch., Am. Physiol. Soc., Fedn. Am. Socs. for Exptl. Biology, Am. Geriat. Soc., Ctrl. Soc. for Clin. Rsch., Soc. for Exptl. Biology and Medicine, Am. Soc. Clin. Pharmacology and Therapeutics, Am. Coll. Clin. Pharmacology, Endocrine Soc., Am. Soc. Renal Biochemistry and Metabolism, Am. Soc. Hypertension (Outstanding Tchr. Yr. 1986), Internat. Soc. Nutrition and Metabolism in Renal Disease, Am. Soc. Bone and Mineral Rsch., European Dialysis and Transplant Assn., Nat. Kidney Found. of Western Pa. (med. adv. com. 1981, chmn. 1981-83, Gift of Life award 1991), Nat. Kidney Found. of La. (mem.-at-large, trustee 1992), So. Med. Assn., So. Soc. Clin. Investigation (councilor 1992-94, sec.-treas. 1994-95), La. State Med. Soc., Orleans Parish Med. Soc. (membership com. 1993, long-range planning com.

1993), La. Soc. Internal Medicine, S.E. Clin. Club, Midwestern Salt and Water Club, Phi Beta Kappa, Alpha Epsilon Delta. Office: Tulane Univ Sch Medicine Dept Medicine SL 12 1430 Tulane Ave New Orleans LA 70112-2699

PUSEY, WILLIAM ANDERSON, lawyer; b. Richmond, Va., Mar. 17, 1936; s. Paul H. and Vernelle (Barnes) P.; m. Patricia Powell, Sept. 3, 1960; children: Patricia Brent, William A. Jr., Margaret Glen. AB, Princeton U., 1958; JD, U. Va., 1962. Bar: Calif. 1963, Va. 1964, D.C. 1987. Assoc. McCutchen, Brown, et al, San Francisco, 1962-63; dep. dist. atty. Alameda County, Oakland, Calif., 1963-64; assoc., ptnr. Hunton & Williams, Washington, D.C., Fairfax and Richmond, Va., 1964—; trustee Ea. Mineral Law Found., Morgantown, W.Va., 1985—, pres., 1987-88. Chmn. bd. dirs. Presbyn. Sch. Christian Edn., Richmond, 1984-85. Mem. Order of Coif, Phi Beta Kappa, Omicron Delta Kappa. Home: 3910 N Glebe Rd Arlington VA 22207-4221 Office: Hunton & Williams 2000 Pennsylvania Ave NW Washington DC 20006-1812

PUSEY, WILLIAM WEBB, III, retired dean, foreign language educator; b. Wilmington, Del., Nov. 16, 1910; s. William Webb, II and Edith White (Lobdell) P.; m. Mary Hope Smith, June 18, 1940 (dec. Sept. 1990); children: Mary Faith Pankin, Diana P. Pickral. BS., Haverford Coll., 1932; A.M., Harvard U., 1933; Ph.D., Columbia U., 1939; Litt.D. (hon.), Washington and Lee U., 1983. Exchange scholar Bonn, Germany, 1934-35; asst. in German Columbia U., 1935-37, instr. German and humanities, 1937-39; assoc. prof., head German dept. Washington and Lee U., 1939-47, prof., head German dept., 1947-76, prof. German on Thomas Ball Found., 1956-60, S. Blount Mason, Jr. prof. German, 1974-81, dean coll., 1960-71, acting pres., 1967, dean emeritus, S. Blount Mason, Jr. prof. emeritus, 1981—. Author: Louis Sebastien Mercier in Germany, 1939, The Interrupted Dream, 1976, Elusive Aspirations, 1983; editor: (with A.G. Steer and B.Q. Morgan) Readings in Military German, 1943; contbr. articles and revs. to profl. jours. Served as lt. (j.g.), lt., lt. comdr. USNR, 1942-45, Washington, London, Berlin. Recipient Am. Council Learned Socs. faculty study fellowship, 1952-53. Mem. Phi Beta Kappa. Address: 18 Buck Island Rd Palmyra VA 22963-2054

PUSHINSKY, JON, lawyer; b. N.Y.C., May 30, 1954; s. Paul and Harriet (Rosenberg) P.; m. M. Jean Clickner, July 31, 1982; children: Matthew Clickner-Pushinsky, Jeremy Clickner-Pushinsky. BA, U. Pa., 1976, MA, 1976; JD, U. Pitts., 1979. Bar: Pa. 1979, U.S. Dist. Ct. (we. dist.) Pa. 1979, U.S. Ct. Appeals (3rd cir.) 1980, U.S. Supreme Ct. 1988. Staff counsel W.Va. Legal Svcs. Plan, Wheeling, 1979-80; pvt. practice Pitts., 1980—. Dem. candidate Superior Ct. Pa., 1993, 95; solicitor Cmty. Human Svcs. Corp., Pitts., 1992—; consulting lawyer ARC-Allegheny, Pitts., 1981—. Recipient Civil Libertarian award ACLU of Pa., 1994, Cmty. Citation of Merit Allegheny County Mental Health/Mental Retardation Bd., 1992, Cert. Appreciation Pitts. Commn. on Human Rels., 1992. Mem. Pa. Trial Lawyers Assn., Allegheny County Bar Assn. (appellate practice com., civil rights com.). Democrat. Avocations: reading, hiking, movies. Office: 429 4th Ave Pittsburgh PA 15219-1503

PUSHKAREV, BORIS S., research foundation director, writer; b. Prague, Czechoslovakia, Oct. 22, 1929; came to U.S., 1949, naturalized, 1954; s. Sergei G. and Julie T. (Popov) P.; B.Arch., Yale U., 1954, M.C.P., 1957; m. Iraida Vandellos Legky, Oct. 20, 1973; Instr. city planning Yale U., New Haven, 1957-61; chief planner Regional Plan Assn., N.Y.C., 1961-69, v.p. research, 1969-89, sr. v.p., 1989-90; adj. assoc. prof. N.Y.U., 1967-79; chmn. Russian Research Found. for Study of Alternatives to Soviet Policy, 1981—. Bd. dirs. Russian Solidarists; lectr. New Humanitarian U., Moscow, 1993—. Recipient Nat. Book award (with C. Tunnard), 1964. Mem. Am. Assn. for Advancement of Slavic Studies, editorial bd. POSSEV. Russian Orthodox. Author: (with Christopher Tunnard) Man-Made America, 1963; (with Jeffrey Zupan) Urban Space for Pedestrians, 1975, Public Transportation and Land Use Policy, 1977; Urban Rail in America, 1982, Russia and the Experience of the West, 1995; contbr. articles to profl. jours. Home: 300 Winston Dr Cliffside Park NJ 07010-3236

PUSKAR, MILAN, pharmaceuticals executive; b. 1935. Grad., Youngstown State U., 1961. V.p. Mylan Pharm. Inc., 1961-72; divsn. v.p. ICN Pharms., Inc., 1972-75; pres. Mylan Lab. Inc., 1976—. Office: Mylan Labs Inc 1030 Century Bldg Pittsburgh PA 15222*

PUSTILNIK, DAVID DANIEL, lawyer; b. N.Y.C., Mar. 10, 1931; s. Philip and Belle (Gerberholtz) P.; m. Helen Jean Todd, Aug. 15, 1959; children: Palma Elyse, Leslie Royce, Bradley Todd. BS, NYU, 1952, JD, 1958, LLM, 1959; postgrad., Air War Coll., 1976. Bar: N.Y. 1959, U.S. Supreme Ct. 1962, Conn. 1964. Legis. tax atty. legis. and regulations div. Office Chief Counsel, IRS, Washington, 1959-63; atty. Travelers Ins. Co., Hartford, Conn., 1963-68; assoc. counsel Travelers Ins. Co., Hartford, 1968-73, counsel, 1973-75, assoc. gen. counsel, 1975-87, dep. gen. counsel, 1987-93; mem. adv. coun. Hartford Inst. on Ins. Taxation, 1978-93, vice chmn., 1991-92, chmn., 1992-93. Grad. editor NYU Tax Law Rev., 1958-59. Trustee Hartford Coll. for Women, 1985-91; life sponsor Am. Tax Policy Inst. Served to col. USAFR. Kenneson fellow NYU, 1958-59. Fellow Am. Coll. Tax Counsel; mem. ABA (chmn. ins. cos. com. 1976-78), Am. Coun. Life Ins. (chmn. co. tax com. 1982-84), Am. Ins. Assn. (chmn. tax com. 1979-81), Assn. Life Ins. Counsel (chmn. tax sect. 1991-93), Twentieth Century Club, Sea Pines Country Club. Democrat. Jewish.

PUSTILNIK, SEYMOUR W., mathematics educator, education educator; b. N.Y.C., Apr. 3, 1927; s. Morris and Susan Pustilnik; m. Phyllis Lampert, Apr. 8, 1962; children: Michael, Susan. BA in Math., U. Mich., 1948; MA in Math., Bowling Green State U., 1950. Grad. asst. math. Bowling Green (Ohio) State U., 1948-49; assoc. prof. math. CUNY, 1956-86; asst. prof. math. edn. NYU, N.Y.C., 1988-90; dir. SWP Co., Brooklyn, N.Y. Author, editor (pamphlet) Rehabilitation and Redevelopment: A Plan to Rehabilitate the Homeless Men on the Cooper Square Site through Urban Renewal, 1961. Mem. Cmty. Sch. Bd., Dist. 13, Bklyn., 1973-77; chmn. Com. for Coop. of Parents, Tchrs., and Prin., Bklyn., 1973-77, Com. for Kindergarten through 6th Grade P.S. 8, Bklyn., 1972-76. Mem. Am. Math. Soc. (presenter), Nat. Coun. Tchrs. Math., Math. Assn. Am. (presenter), Soc. Lit. and Sci. (presenter), Soc. Utopian Studies (presenter), Learning Styles Network, N.Y. State Math. Assn. of 2-Yr. Colls., Melus, Soc. for Study of Multi-Ethnic Lit. (presenter). Avocations: literary criticism, theater, educational games. Home: 140 Cadman Plz W Brooklyn NY 11201-1852

PUSTOVAR, THOMAS M., manufacturing executive, heavy; b. 1957. V.p. Wheelbrator Engineered Sys., Saint Paul, Minn. Office: Wheelbrator Engineered Systems 55 Schumann Blvd Naperville IL 60563*

PUTH, JOHN WELLS, consulting company executive; b. Orange, N.J., Mar. 14, 1929; s. Leonard G. and Elizabeth R. (Wells) P.; m. Betsey Leeds Tait, Mar.1, 1952; children: David Wells, Jonathan Craig, Alison Leeds. BS cum laude, Lehigh U., 1952. Dir. mktg. Purolator Products, Rahway, N.J., 1955-61; pres., chief exec. officer Bridgeport (Conn.) Hardware Mfg. Co. subs. Purolator, 1962-65; group v.p. H.K. Porter Co., Pitts., 1965-72; pres., CEO Disston Inc., Pitts., 1972-75, Vapor Corp., Niles, Ill., 1975-83; chmn., pres., CEO Clevite Industries Inc., Glenview, Ill., 1983-89; pres. JW Puth Assocs., Skokie, Ill., 1989—; bd. dirs. L.B. Foster, Pitts., A.M. Castle & Co., Franklin Park, Ill., Lindberg Corp., Chgo., V.J. Growers Inc., Apopka, Fla., Sys. Software Assocs., Chgo., Pierce Mfg., Appleton, Wis., TNT Freightways, Inc., Rosemont, Ill., George W. Schmidt Inc., Niles, Ill., MSP Commn., Lansing, Mich., Golder, Thomas Cressy & Funds, Chgo., Brockway Std., Atlanta, Am. Acads., Cary, Ill., Allied Products Corp., Chgo. Chmn. bd. trustees Hadley Sch. for Blind, Winnetka, Ill., 1982-84; trustee Lehigh U., Kenilworth Union Ch.; bd. dirs. Iaccoca Inst. With U.S. Army, 1946-47, PTO. Mem. Chgo. Club, Econ. Club, Comml. Club, Indian Hill Country Club, Old Elm Club, Loblolly Pines Club. Republican. Presbyterian. Home: 180 De Windt Rd Winnetka IL 60093-3744

PUTKA, ANDREW CHARLES, lawyer; b. Cleve., Nov. 14, 1926; s. Andrew George and Lillian M. (Koryta) P. Student, John Carroll U., 1944, U.S. Naval Acad., 1945-46; A.B., Adelbert Coll., Western Res. U., 1949; J.D., Western Res. U., 1952. Bar: Ohio 1952. Practice law Cleve.; instr. govt. Notre Dame Coll.; v.p. Koryta Bros. Coal Co., Cleve., 1952-56; supt. div. bldg. and loan assns. Ohio Dept. Commerce, 1959-63; pres., chmn. bd., chief exec. officer Am. Nat. Bank, Parma, Ohio, 1963-69; dir. fin. City of Cleve., 1971-74; dir. port control, 1974-78; dir. Cleve. Hopkins Internat. Airport, 1974-78. Mem. Ohio Ho. of Reps., 1953-56, Ohio Senate, 1957-58; dep. auditor, acting sec. Cuyahoga County Bd. Revision, 1970-71; mem. exec. com. Cuyahoga County Democratic Com., 1973-81, Assn. Ind. Colls. and Univs. Ohio, 1983-89; bd. govs. Sch. Law, Western Res. U., 1953-56; mem. exec. com. World Service Student Fund, 1950-52; U.S. rep. Internat. Pax Romana Congress, Amsterdam, 1950, Toronto, 1952; mem. lay advisory bd. Notre Dame Coll., 1968-90, trustee, 1990-93, hon. trustee, 1993—; mem. adv. bd. St. Andrew's Abbey, 1976-88 ; trustee Case-Western Res. U., Newman Found. No. Ohio, 1980-93, hon. trustee, 1993—; 1st v.p. First Cath. Slovak Union of U.S., 1977-80; pres. USO Council of Cuyahoga County, 1980-83. Voted an outstanding legislator Ohio Press Corrs., 1953; named to All-Star Legislative team Ohio Newspaper Corrs., 1955; named one of Fabulous Clevelanders Cleve. Plain Dealer, John Henry Newman honor Soc. Mem. Cuyahoga County, Cleve. Bar Assn., Nat. Assn. State Savs. and Loan Suprs. (past. nat. pres.), U.S. Savs. and Loan League (mem. legis com, 1960-63), Am. Legion, Ohio Mcpl. League (bd. trustees 1973), Parma C. of C. (bd. dirs., treas. 1965-67), Newman Fedn. (past nat. pres.), NCCJ, Catholic Lawyers Guild (treas.), Am. Ohio Bankers Assn., Am. Inst. Banking, Adelbert Alumni Assn. (exec. com.), Cathedral Latin Alumni Assn. (trustee 1952—), Internat. Order of Alhambra (internat. parliamentarian 1971—, past grand comdr., supreme advocate 1973), Amvets, KC, Pi Kappa Alpha, Delta Theta Phi (past. pres. Cleve. alumni senate, master inspector 1975). Home: 28 Pond Dr Cleveland OH 44116-1062

PUTMAN, DALE CORNELIUS, management consultant, lawyer; b. Ponca, Nebr., Apr. 29, 1927; s. Merle H. and Catherine V. (Sheahan) P.; m. Alice Anselmi, Sept. 8, 1951; children: Mark, Lee, Neil, Bruce, Kirk, Nancy, Wendy. B.S., U. Nebr., 1949, LL.B., 1951. Bar: Nebr. 1951, Iowa 1951, Mo. 1977. Mgr. Interstate Assn. Credit Mgmt., Sioux City, Iowa, 1951-52; sec., legal counsel Metz Baking Co., Sioux City, 1953-66; v.p. Metz Baking Co., 1966-69, exec. v.p., 1969-72, pres., 1972-76; chief operating officer Interstate Brands Corp., Kansas City, Mo., 1976-77; pres., dir. Interstate Brands Corp., 1977-80, pres., chief exec. officer, 1980-84; chmn., chief exec. officer, pres., dir. Interstate Bakeries (formerly DPF, Inc.), 1980-84; pvt. practice mgmt. cons., 1984—. Served with U.S. Army, 1945-46. Knight, Order of the Holy Sepulchre of Jerusalem. Republican. Roman Catholic. Home: 8405 Reinhardt Ln Shawnee Mission KS 66206-1316

PUTMAN, ROBERT DEAN, golf course architect; b. Wallace, Idaho, Dec. 18, 1924; m. Sally Harmon, 1945; 3 children. Grad., Fresno State Coll. Art dir. Sta. KJEO-TV, Fresno, Calif. Prin. works include Arvin Mcpl. Golf Course, Wasco, Calif., Madera (Calif.) Mcpl. Golf Course, Rancho Canada Golf Course, Carmel Valley, Calif., La Manga Golf Couse, Costa Blanca, Spain, Monterey (Calif.) Country Club Shore Course, San Joaquin Country Club, Fresno, Visalia (Calif.) Mcpl. Golf Course, River Island Golf Course, Poterville, Calif., Kings River Country Club, Kingsburg, Calif. Office: Robert Dean Putman GCA 5644 N Briarwood Ave Fresno CA 93711-2501

PUTNAM, BONNIE COLLEEN, elementary education educator; b. Unionville, Mo., July 29, 1936; d. Randall Lee and Edith Nora (Colton) Pickering; m. Robert Lyle Putnam, Aug. 16, 1953; 1 child, Michael Lee. BA in Edn. cum laude, Wichita State U., 1966; MA in Edn., N.E. Mo. State U., 1971. Cert. elem. edn. Classroom tchr. Liberal (Kans.) Schs., 1966-68, Putnam County R-3 Schs., Unionville, 1968-70, Albia (Iowa) Cmty. Schs., 1970—; mem. state adv. bd. So. Prairie Area Edn. Agy., Ottumwa, Iowa, 1972-74; instr. Performance Learning Sys., Nevada, Calif., 1983-92. Sec., trustee Albia (Iowa) Pub. Libr., 1975—; co-chair Albia (Iowa) Schs. Fun Walk/Run. Named Woman of Yr., Beta Sigma Phi Sorority, Albia, 1992. Mem. NEA, Internat. Reading Assn., Iowa State Reading Assn., Rathbun Area Reading Coun. (past pres.), Iowa State Edn. Assn. (presenter Mobile Insvc. Tng. Lab. 1977-83), Albia Cmty. Edn. Assn. (treas., Tchr. of Yr. 1974), Delta Kappa Gamma (sec. 1980—), Golden Key Honor Soc. Avocations: gardening, traveling, reading. Home: RR 3 Box 237 Albia IA 52531-9803 Office: Albia Cmty Schs 120 Benton Ave E Albia IA 52531-2035

PUTNAM, FRANK WILLIAM, biochemistry and immunology educator; b. New Britain, Conn., Aug. 3, 1917; s. Frank and Henrietta (Holzmann) P.; m. Dorothy Alice Linder, Nov. 18, 1942; children—Frank William, Beverly Susan. B.A., Wesleyan U., Middletown, Conn., 1939, M.A., 1940; Ph.D., U. Minn., 1942; M.A. (hon.), Cambridge (Eng.) U., 1973. Instr., research asso. Duke U. Med. Sch., 1942-46; biochemist CWS, Camp Detrick, Md., 1946; asst. prof. U. Chgo., then assoc. prof. biochemistry, 1947-55; Lasdon research fellow Cambridge U., 1952-53; prof. biochemistry, head dept. U. Fla., 1955-65; prof. biology, dir. div. biol. scis. Ind. U., Bloomington, 1965-69; prof. molecular biology and zoology Ind. U., 1972-74, disting. prof. molecular biology and biochemistry, 1974-88, prof. emeritus, 1989—; bd. visitors Duke U. Med. Center, 1970-75; chmn. com. nomenclature of human immunoglobulins Internat. Union Immunol. Socs., 1971-76; chmn. basic sci. rev. bd. VA, 1972-76; chmn. cancer cause and prevention adv. com. Nat. Cancer Inst., 1974-75; sci. adv. com. Papanicolaou Cancer Research Inst., 1976-82; research rev. com. ARC, 1973-77; sci. com. Brussels Colloquium on Protides of Biol. Fluids, 1970-90; chmn. virus cancer program adv. com. Nat. Cancer Inst., 1975-77; sr. med. adv. group VA, 1976-80; council div. biol. scis. and Pritzker Med. Sch., U. Chgo., 1977-87; chmn. Assembly Life Scis. Nat. Acad. Scis., 1977-81; mem. U.S. Nat. Com. Biochemistry, 1973-79; pres. sci. adv. com. G.E.R.M.I., Lyon, France, 1981-87. Co-author, editor: The Plasma Proteins, vol. 1, Isolation, Characterization and Function, 1960, vol. 2, Biosynthesis, Metabolism, Alterations in Disease, 1960, The Plasma Proteins, 2d edit., Structure, Function, and Genetic Control, Vol. 1, 1975, Vol. 2, 1975, Vol. 3, 1977, Vol. 4, 1984, Vol. 5, 1987; mem. editorial bd. Archives of Biochemistry and Biophysics, 1954-59, Science, 1968-82, Immunochemistry, 1972-75, Biomed. News, 1969-73, Fedn. Proc, 1958-63; Author numerous research papers. Trustee Argonne Univs. Assn., 1981-82; bd. govs. U. Chgo. Argonne Nat. Lab., 1983-89, chmn. Sci. and tech. com., 1983-87; bd. dirs. Radiation Research Found., 1981-87. Markle scholar med. scis., 1950-56; Guggenheim fellow, 1970; fellow Churchill Coll., Cambridge U., 1973—; recipient Distinguished award teaching and research Wesleyan U., 1964, Distinguished Service award in medicine U. Chgo., 1968; Outstanding Achievement award U. Minn., 1974. Fellow AAAS, N.Y. Acad. Scis.; mem. Nat. Acad. Scis., Am. Acad. Arts and Scis. (Midwest council 1975-84), Pan-Am. Assn. Biomed. Scis. (sec.-gen. 1975-78), Japan Electrophoresis Soc. (hon.), Am. Inst. Biol. Scis. (life), Am. Soc. Biol. Chemists (sec. 1958-63), Soc. Exptl. Biology and Medicine, Am. Assn. Immunologists, Am. Chem. Soc. (chmn. div. biol. chemistry 1966-67), Soc. Peruana de Patologia (hon.), Fedn. Socs. Exptl. Biology (chmn. secs. com. 1958-63), Phi Beta Kappa, Sigma Xi, Phi Lambda Upsilon, Delta Sigma Rho. Club: Cosmos. Address: 5025 E Heritage Woods Rd Bloomington IN 47401-9314

PUTNAM, FREDERICK WARREN, JR., bishop; b. Red Wing, Minn., June 17, 1917; s. Frederick W. and Margaret (Bunting) P.; m. Helen Kathryn Prouse, Sept. 24, 1942; children: James Douglas, John Frederick, Andrew Warren. B.A., U. Minn., 1939; M.Div., Seabury-Western Theol. Sem., 1942, D.D., 1963; postgrad., State U. Iowa, 1946-47. Ordained to ministry Episcopal Ch. as deacon, priest, 1942. Pastor in Windom and Worthington, Minn., 1942-43, Iowa City, 1943-47, Evanston, Ill., 1947-59, Wichita, Kans., 1960-63; Episcopalian chaplain State U. Iowa, 1943-47; suffragan bishop Episcopal Diocese, Okla., 1963-79; bishop Episc. Ch. in, Navajoland, 1979-83; assisting bishop Diocese of Minn., 1983-89; acting rector St. George's, Pearl Harbor, Hawaii, 1984-85, St. Clement's, Honolulu, 1986, St. John's, Kula, Maui, Hawaii, 1988, St. Elizabeth's, Honolulu, 1990; interim rector St. Stephen's Episcopal Ch., Edina, Minn., 1991-92, Trinity Episcopal Ch., Pocatello, Idaho, 1994; vis. bishop Diocese of N.J., 1995; bd. dirs. Kiyosoto Ednl. Experiment Program, 1954-91, v.p., 1989-91; cons. Oklahoma City Community Relation Commn., 1966-70; Pres. Okla. Conf. Religion and Race, 1963-67; v.p. Greater Oklahoma City Council Chs., 1966-67; nat. chaplain Brotherhood of St. Andrew, 1967-79, mem. brotherhood legion, 1972—; priest assoc. Order Holy Cross, 1942—; exec. com. Conf. Diocesan Execs., 1969-76, pres., 1972-74; mem. Okla. Commn. United Ministries in Higher Edn., 1970-79, pres., 1973-75; mem. nat. com. on Indian work Episc. Ch., 1977-80; chaplain Okla. Assn. Alcoholism and Alcohol Abuse, 1974-78; hon. life mem. Oklahoma City and County Criminal Justice Council, 1978—; Bechtel lectr. U. Denver, 1966. Editor: (pub.) Sharers Mag., 1957-63; contbr. articles to profl. publs. Founder, pres. Oklahoma City Met. Alliance for Safer City, 1971-78; Trustee Seabury-Western Theol. Sem., 1959-65, Episcopal Theol. Sem. Southwest, 1966-69, St. Simeon's Episcopal Home, 1963-79, St. Crispins Episcopal Conf. Center, 1963-79, Casady Sch., 1963-79, Holland Hall Sch., 1963-79, Episcopal Soc. Cultural and Racial Unity, 1967-70; trustee Neighborhood Services Orgn., treas., 1969; founder, 1st pres. Friends of Wichita Pub. Library, 1962; bd. dirs. Minn. Photographic Exbn.; chmn. Mpls.-St. Paul Internat. Photographic Exhbn., 1987, 89; State Bd. Minn. Common Cause, 1989—, state chmn., 1993—. Recipient Disting. Service award Evanston Jr. C. of C., 1952; Merit award Photog. Soc. Am. Fellow Coll. Preachers; mem. ACLU, Assoc. Parishes (pres. 1960-64), Mpls. Soc. Fine Arts (mem. photo coun.), Photog. Soc. Am., Am. Com. for KEEP (v.p. 1961-70, 90), Walker Art Ctr., Sierra Club, Met. Sr. Fedn., Audubon Club, Am. Assn. Ret. Persons, Minn. Hort. Soc., Hist. Soc. Episcopal Ch., Archaeol. Conservancy, Ancient Bibl. Manuscripts Ctr., Claremont, Calif., World Future Soc., Photographic Soc. Am. (assoc. 1989—, mem. v.p., 1995—), Twin Cities Assn. Camera Clubs (v.p. 1987), U. Minn. Alumni Assn., Minn. Hist. Soc., St. Paul Camera Club, N.Am. Rights Fund., People for the Am. Way, Episcopal Peace Fellowship, Amnesty Internat., Greenpeace, Liturgical Conf., Living Ch. Found., Worldwatch Inst., Clan Douglas Soc., Crossroads Camera Club, Phi Kappa Psi. Clubs: Normandale Tennis and Swim. Home: 5229 Meadow Rdg Edina MN 55439-1412

PUTNAM, GEORGE W., JR., army officer; b. Ft. Fairfield, Maine, May 5, 1920; s. George W. and Rae B. (Merrithew) P.; m. Elaine Anderson (dec. 1973); m. Claudine Mahin (div. 1995); m. Helen Guerin, 1995; children: James M., J. Glenn; stepchildren: Philip Mahin, Leslie Mahin. Served as enlisted man U.S. Army, 1941-42, commd. 2d lt., 1942, advanced through grades to maj. gen., 1970; comdg. gen. (1st Cavalry Div.), Vietnam, 1970-71; dir. Mil. Personnel Mgmt., Hdqrs. Dept. Army, Washington, 1971-75; comdg. gen. U.S. Army So. European Task Force, Vicenza, Italy, 1975-77, U.S. Army Phys. Disability Agy., Washington, 1977-81; ret. U.S. Army, 1981; dir. Army Coun. Rev. Bds., 1977-81; pres. Nat. Capital Retiree Coun., 1982-85. Internat. judge 5th and 6th World Helicopter Championships, 1986, 89, 94, chief judge 7th World Championship, 1992; U.S. mem. Internat. Helicopter com. Fedn. Aeronautique Internationale, 1988-91, 93—; bd. dirs. Army Aviation Mus. Found., 1987—, pres., 1993—. Inducted Army Aviation Hall of Fame, 1980. Mem. Nat. Aero. Assn. (sr. v.p. 1991-95, v.p. Fedn. Aero. Internat. affairs 1995—), Army Aviation Assn. Am. (sr. v.p., pres. 1983-87, pres. scholarship found. 1991-93), Helicopter Club Am. (pres. 1988-90). Home: 4106 N Richmond St Arlington VA 22207

PUTNAM, HUGH DYER, environmental scientist, educator, consultant; b. Carrington, N.D., Feb. 12, 1928; s. Hugh Rodney and Blanche Putnam; m. Natalie Joy Knott, Dec. 23, 1950; children: Mark, Lynn, Charles. BA in Microbiology, U. Minn., 1953, MS in Microbiology, 1956, PhD in Pub. Health Biology/Environ. Health, 1963. Rsch. asst. U. Minn., 1952-54, teaching asst., 1954-55, instr., 1956-59, rsch. fellow, 1959-63; asst. prof. sanitary sci., asst. rsch. prof. U. Fla., Gainesville, 1963-66, assoc. prof. environ. sci., 1966-70, prof. environ. engring. studies, 1970-74, adj. prof. environ. engring. scis., 1974-85; founder, v.p. environ. scis. divsn. Environ. Sci. and Engring., Inc., Gainesville, 1965-74; v.p., prin. scientist Water and Air Rsch., Inc., Gainesville, 1974-94; vis. prof. U. Minn., 1974-75; mem. ad hoc com. on environ. rsch. and toxicology NAS; mem. environ. biology review panel EPA; vice chmn. sect. 1000 15th Edit. Standard Methods for Water and Wastewater, chmn. sect. 1000 16th and 17th Edits.; coord. water and wastewater biol. examination sect. 17th Edit. Standard Methods; mem. site selection bd. U.S. Army Med. Rsch. abd Devel. Command Effect of Munition Wastes on Aqatic Life; mem. site vis. team for evaluation NERQ Corvalis Ecol. programs Inst. Ecology, Madisin, Wis.; guest lectr. NASA, U. Minn, Duluth, USAF Acad.; cons. EPA, TVA, Muscle Shoals, Ala., Met. Waste Control Commn., St. Paul, Dept. Water and Power, L.A. Contbr. over 75 profl. reports and publs. to sci. jours. Mem. tech. awareness com. City of Tampa Water Reuse Com. Master sgt. U.S. Army, 1946-48, 50-52. Recipient Best Paper award TAPPI Environ. Conf. Planning Com., 1993. Mem. Am. Soc. Limnology and Oceanography, Water Environment Fedn., Internat. Soc. Theoretical and Applied Limnology, Sigma Xi. Office: Water & Air Rsch Inc 6821 SW Archer Rd Gainesville FL 32608-4720

PUTNAM, J. STEPHEN, financial executive; m. Pamela Schirmer; 3 children. BA, Bowdoin Coll., 1965. Pres. Robert Thomas Securities, Inc., St. Petersburg, Fla.; sr. v.p. Raymond James & Assocs., Inc.; bd. dirs., exec. v.p. Raymond James Fin., Inc.; treas. Meerschaert Mut. Fund; v.p., bd. dirs. F.L. Putnam Securities. Bd. dirs., former chmn. bd. St. Joseph's Coll., North Windham, Maine; bd. dirs., chmn. Citizens Scholarship Found. Am., Inc.; pres. Palm Harbor (Fla.) Cmty. Svc. Agy. Decorated Bronze Star, Army Commendation medal. Mem. NASD (by-laws and spl. com. to investigate investment adv. regulation), Fla. Securities Dealers Assn. (bd. dirs.), Youth Soccer Assn. Office: Rober Thomas Securities Inc 880 Carillon Pky Saint Petersburg FL 33716-1102

PUTNAM, LINDA LEE, communication educator, researcher; b. Frederick, Okla., Aug. 10, 1945; d. Allard Warren and Etta Wanona (Tucker) Loutherback; m. Thomas Milton Putnam III, Mar. 28, 1970; 1 child, Ashley Ann. BA, Hardin-Simmons U., 1967; MA, U. Wis., 1968; PhD, U. Minn., 1977. Instr. U. Mass., Amherst, 1968-69; instr., chair dept. speech-theatre Normandale Community Coll., Bloomington, Minn., 1969-77; prof. communication Purdue U., West Lafayette, Ind., 1977-93; dept. head Tex. A & M Univ., 1993—; vis. scholar Stanford U., U. Calif.-Berkeley, San Francisco, 1984, Harvard U.-Harvard Negotiation Project, 1992. Editor: Communication and Organization, 1983(Best Publ. award 1985), Handbook of Organizational Communication, 1987 (Best Publ. award 1988), Communication and Negotiation, 1992. Del. Dem. State Conv., Mpls., 1972-74; treas. local dist. Dem. Farm Labor Party, Mpls., 1973-74, co-chairperson, 1974-75; block chair Am. Can. Soc. Fund Raiser, West Lafayette, 1986-87. Recipient AMOCO Teaching award Purdue U., 1986, Andersch award Ohio U., 1991, Disting. Alumni award Hardin-Simmons U., 1991, Charles H. Woolbert Rsch. award Speech Comm. Assn., 1993. Fellow Internat. Comm. Assn. (chair 1986-88, orgn. com. divsn. 1995); mem. Acad. Mgmt. (chair power negotiation, conflict mgmt. com. 1989-91), Speech Comm. Assn. (mem. at large 1984-87), Ctrl. States Speech Assn. (sec. comm. theory com. 1978-79, Scholar Showcase award 1989), Internat. Assn. for Conflict Mgmt. (bd. dirs. 1990-92, pres. 1994). Avocation: cooking. *In an age when change is inevitable, we often fear and try to avoid the unknown. In our drive for security, we forget that one of our richest blessings is change—the change that preserves diversity and the balance of power.*

PUTNAM, MICHAEL COURTNEY JENKINS, classics educator; b. Springfield, Mass., Sept. 20, 1933; s. Roger Lowell and Caroline (Jenkins) P. AB, Harvard U., 1954, AM, 1956, PhD, 1959; LLD (hon.), Lawrence U., 1985. Instr. classics Smith Coll., Northampton, Mass., 1959-60; faculty classics Brown U., Providence, 1960—; prof. Brown U., 1967—, chmn., 1968, 70-72, 77-78, prof. comparative lit., 1980—, MacMillan prof. of classics, 1985—; acting dir. Ctr. for Hellenic Studies, Harvard U., 1961-62, sr. fellow, 1971-86; Townsend prof. classics Cornell U., 1985; Mellon prof.-in-charge Am. Acad. in Rome, 1989-91; scholar in residence Am. Acad. in Rome, 1969-70, mem. classical jury, 1982-83, trustee, 1991—; assoc. univ. seminar on classical civilization Columbia U., N.Y.C., 1972—; mem. cath. Commn. on Intellectual and Cultural Affairs, 1969—; mem. adv. coun. dept. classics Princeton U., 1981-87, chmn., 1983-87; cons. Am. Coun. Learned Socs., 1987—; mem. Inst. for Advanced Study, 1987-88; vis. scholar Phi Beta Kappa, 1994-95. Author: The Poetry of the Aeneid, 1965, Virgil's Pastoral Art, 1970, Tibullus: A Commentary, 1973, Virgil's Poem of the Earth, 1979, Essays on Latin Lyric, Elegy and Epic, 1982, Artifices of Eternity: Horace's Fourth Book of Odes, 1986, Virgil's Aeneid: Interpretation and Influence, 1995; contbr. articles to profl. jours. Sole trustee Lowell Obs., Flagstaff, Ariz., 1967-87, bd. advisors, 1987—; trustee Bay Chamber Concerts, Camden, Maine, 1972-88, incorporator, 1988-94; mem. bd. cons. Portsmouth Abbey Sch., 1985-89; hon. sec. Keats-Shelley Meml. Assn., Rome, 1989-91. Rome Prize fellow Am. Acad. in Rome, 1963-64; Guggenheim Meml. fellow, 1966-67; sr. fellow NEH, 1973-74, cons. 1974-78, 87—; Am. Council Learned Soc. fellow, 1983-84. Fellow Am. Acad. Arts and Scis.; mem. Am. Philol. Assn. (bd. dirs. 1972-75, mem. com. on award of merit 1975-78, chmn. 1977-78, 1st v.p. 1981, pres. 1982, del. Am. Coun. Learned Socs. 1984-87, Charles J. Goodwin award of merit 1971), Archaeol. Inst. Am., Classical Assn. New Eng., Medieval Acad. Am., Vergilian Soc. Am. (trustee

1969-73, v.p. 1974-76), Accademia Nazionale Virgiliana, Acad. Lit. Studies, Art Club. Office: Brown U Dept Classics Providence RI 02912

PUTNAM, PAUL ADIN, retired government agency official; b. Springfield, Vt., July 12, 1930; s. Horace Adin and Beatrice Nellie (Baldwin) P.; m. Elsie Mae (Ramseyer) June 12, 1956; children: Pamela Ann, Penelope Jayne, Adin Tyler II, Paula Anna. B.S., U. Vt., 1952; M.S., Wash. State U., 1954; Ph.D., Cornell U., 1957. Research animal scientist Agrl. Research Service, USDA, Beltsville, Md., 1957-66, investigation leader beef cattle nutrition, 1966-68, chief beef cattle research br., 1968-72; asst. dir. Beltsville Agrl. Research Ctr., 1972-80, dir., 1980-84; dir. cen. plains area Ames, Iowa, 1984-87; assoc. dir. mid. south area Stoneville, Miss., 1987-88, dir. mid south area, 1988-94. Contbr. articles to profl. jours. Recipient Kidder medal U. Vt.; Outstanding Performance awards USDA, also cert. merit; Danforth fellow; Borden fellow; Purina Research fellow. Fellow AAAS (rep. sect. O), Am. Soc. Animal Sci. (pres., North Atlantic sect., chmn. various coms., N.E. sect. Disting. Service award); mem. Am. Dairy Sci. Assn., Orgn. Profl. Employees USDA (pres. Beltsville chpt.), Council for Agrl. Sci. and Tech. Home: 36 Putnam Rd Springfield VT 05156-9115

PUTNAM, PETER BROCK, author, lecturer; b. Georgia, June 11, 1920; s. Brock and Margaret (Faber) P.; m. Durinda Dobbins, Aug. 12, 1944; children: Brock II, Barbara Durinda, John Gerry. Grad., Hill Sch., 1938; B.A., Princeton, 1942, Ph.D., 1950. Lectr. history Princeton, 1950-55; v.p. Unitarian Universalist Assn., 1965-67; cons. recording for the blind and dyslexic, 1988—. Author: Keep Your Head Up, Mr. Putnam, 1952, Seven Britons in Imperial Russia, 1952, Cast off the Darkness, 1957, Triumph of the Seeing Eye, 1962, Peter, the Revolutionary Tsar, 1973, Love in the Lead, 1979; Translator: (Marc Bloch): Apologie Pour l'Histoire, 1953. Pres. Chapin Sch., 1961-63; exec. com. Princeton Alumni Coun., 1972-76; bd. dirs. Recording for Blind, 1955—, pres., 1976-80; bd. dirs. Mass. Assn. Blind, 1967-71, Star Island Corp.; pres. Unitarian Ch., 1954-57; bd. dirs. Lucerna Fund, 1976—; trustee Seeing Eye, 1981-90; trustee Continental Assn. Funeral and Meml. Socs., 1983-89; pres. Meml. Soc. Fund, 1983-87, Talking Books for Hosps., 1983-87. Mem. Author's League, Princeton Meml. Assn. (bd. dirs. 1956—, pres. 1988—). Clubs: Cottage, Princeton Triangle (trustee 1962-87), Nassau Club. Home: 48 Roper Rd Princeton NJ 08540-4070 *The fear of uncertainty is the principal fear from which all others flow. It is always necessary to act on insufficient evidence. The acceptance of uncertainty is a major step on the road to maturity. A sense of humor is indispensable.*

PUTNAM, RICHARD JOHNSON, federal judge; b. Abbeville, La., Sept. 27, 1913; s. Robert Emmett and Mathilde (Young) P.; m. Dorethea Gooch, Jan. 27, 1940; children: Richard Johnson, Claude Robert, Mary Stacy, Cynthia Anne. BS cum laude, Springhill Coll., Mobile, 1934; LLB, Loyola U., New Orleans, 1937. Bar: La. 1937. Pvt. practice law Abbeville, 1937-54; dist. atty. 15th Jud. Dist., La., 1948-54; judge 15th Jud. Dist. Ct., La., 1954-61; dist. judge U.S. Dist. Ct. (we. dist.) La., La., 1961-75; sr. U.S. dist. judge, 1975—; temporary judge U.S. Ct. Appeals for 5th cir., 1983; rep. fed. cts. Coun. La. Law Inst., 1976-89, sr. mem. inst. coun., 1989—; liaison judge for we. dist. 5th Cir. Archives - Hist. Com. , 1980; chmn. sr. judges adv. bd. Fed. Judges Assn., 1983—. Served from ensign to lt. USNR, 1942-45. Recipient Student Coun. Key Loyola U., 1937. Mem. Dist. Judges Assn., ABA, La. Bar Assn., Fifth Cir. Dist. Judges Assn., Am. Legion, VFW, St. Thomas Moore Soc. (Svc. award 1937), Delta Theta Phi. Lodge: KC. Office: US Dist Ct 249 Fed Bldg 705 Jefferson St Lafayette LA 70501*

PUTNAM, ROBERT E., writer, editor; b. Mt. Sterling, Ill., Sept. 13, 1933; s. John Harold and Florence Pauline (Curran) P.; m. Linda J. Wiant, Aug. 30, 1960; children: Justine, Robbie, Dylan. B.A., U. Ill., 1959; M.A., Roosevelt U., 1969. Asso. engr. Western Electric Co., Chgo., 1960-62; with Am. Tech. Pubs., Inc., Chgo., 1964—; editor-in-chief Am. Tech. Pubs., Inc., 1973—, v.p. editorial, 1980-82. Author: Fundamentals of Carpentry, 1967, Concrete Block Construction, 3d edit, 1973, Bricklaying Skill and Practice, 3d edit, 1974, Architectural and Building Trades Dictionary, 3d edit, 1974, Fundamentals of Carpentry: Tools, Materials and Practices, 5th edit, 1977, Basic Blueprint Reading: Residential, 1980, Builder's Comprehensive Dictionary, 1984, 89, Construction Blueprint Reading, 1985, Building Trades Blueprint Reading, 1985; Welding Print Reading, 1986, Motorcycle Operation and Service, 1986, Masonry, 1988. Served with U.S. Army, 1953-55. Mem. Am. Welding Soc., Am. Soc. Tng. and Devel., Am. Soc. for Quality Control, Nat. Soc. Performance and Instrn. (Chgo. chpt.). Home: 256 Lester Rd Park Forest IL 60466-2039

PUTNAM, RUTH ANNA, philosopher, educator; b. Berlin, Germany, Sept. 20, 1927; d. Martin and Marie (Kohn) Hall; m. Hilary W. Putnam, Aug. 11, 1962; children: Samuel, Joshua, Polly Maxima. BS in Chemistry, UCLA, 1954, PhD in Philosophy, 1962. Instr. Philosophy UCLA, 1957-59; acting asst. prof. U. Oreg., 1959-62; from lectr. to prof. Wellesley (Mass.) Coll., 1963—, chair dept. Philosophy, 1979-82, 91-93; dir. summer seminar NEH, 1986, 89; mem. extramural grad. fellowships Wellesley Coll., faculty benefits com., com. budget, academic review bd., taskforce on affirmative action, bd. of admissions; presenter in field. Contbr. chpts. to books, articles to profl. jours., encyclopedias. Mem. Am. Philos. Assn. (program com. ea. divsn. 1977). Jewish. Office: Wellesley Coll 106 Central St Wellesley MA 02181-8209

PUTNAM, WILLIAM LOWELL, science association administrator; b. Springfield, Mass., Oct. 25, 1924; s. Roger Lowell and Caroline Piatt (Jenkins) P.; m. Joan Fitzgerald, Sept. 29, 1951 (dec. April 1993); children: Katherine Elizabeth, W. Lowell. Grad., Harvard Coll., 1945. With Springfield C. of C., 1950-52; founder, chmn. Springfield TV Corp., 1952-84; with Carroll Travel Bur., 1984—; vice chmn. Assn. Maximum Svc. Telecasters, 1975-84; sec.-treas. NBC Affiliates, 1980-83. Sole trustee Lowell Obs., Flagstaff, Ariz.; chmn. Springfield Pk. Commn., 1991-95. 1st lt. U.S. Army, 1943-45. Decorated Silver Star, Bronze Star, Purple Heart. Mem. Assn. Canadian Mountain Guides (hon.), Alpine Club Can. (hon.), Appalachian Mountain Club (hon.), Am. Alpine Club (pres. 1974-76, treas. 1977-91, hon.), Am. Mountain Guides Assn. (dir.), Internat. Union Alpine Clubs (Am. del., v.p.). Avocation: alpinism. Office: Lowell Obs Flagstaff AZ 86001

PUTNEY, JOHN ALDEN, JR., insurance company executive; b. Bklyn., Mar. 5, 1939; s. John Alden and Anne Marie (Davenport) P.; m. Theresa Rose DeFrisco, Feb. 9, 1964; children: Angela, Alexander. B.S. cum laude in Math, St. John's U., 1960. Systems engr. IBM, N.Y.C., 1961-64; mktg. rep. IBM, 1964-66; cons. Topas Computer Corp., N.Y.C., 1966-67; dir., v.p., sec. Topas Computer Corp., 1967-70; with Tchrs. Ins. and Annuity Assn., N.Y.C., 1971—, v.p., 1977-79, sr. v.p., 1979-80, exec. v.p., 1980—, office and info. systems area mgr., 1979-87, mgr. ops. support area, 1987-95, mgr. pension and annuity svc. area, 1995—. Served with USMC, 1960. Home: 9 Concord Ave Larchmont NY 10538-3105 Office: Tchrs Ins & Annuity Assn 730 3rd Ave New York NY 10017-3206

PUTNEY, MARK WILLIAM, lawyer, utility executive; b. Marshalltown, Iowa, Jan. 25, 1929; s. Lawrence Charles and Geneva (Eldridge) P.; m. Ray Ann Bartnek, May 25, 1962; children: Andi Bartnek, William Bradford, Blake Reinhart. BA, U. Iowa, 1951, JD, 1957. Bar: Iowa 1957, U.S. Supreme Ct. 1960. Ptnr. Bradshaw, Fowler, Proctor & Fairgrave, Des Moines, 1961-72, of counsel, 1992-94; chmn., CEO. Bradford & Blake Ltd., Des Moines, 1992—; pres., chmn., chief exec. officer Iowa Resources, Inc.,, 1984-90; chmn., chief exec. officer Iowa Power & Light Co., 1984-90, Iowa Gas Co.,, 1984-85, Midwest Resources Inc., 1990-92. Civilian aide to Sec. Army for Iowa, 1975-77; bd. dirs. Greater Des Moines YMCA, 1976-86, Boys' Home Iowa, 1982-86, Hoover Presdle. Libr. Assn., 1983—, U. Iowa Found., 1984—, Edison Electric Inst., 1986-89; bd. dirs. Greater Des Moines Com., 1984—, pres. 1988; bd. dirs. Assoc. Edison Illuminating Cos., 1988-93, pres., 1991-92; chmn. Iowa Com. Employer Support of Guard and Res., 1979-86; bd. dirs. Des Moines Devel. Corp., 1984-92, chmn., 1989-90. With USAF, 1951-53. Mem. Iowa Utility Assn. (chmn. 1989, dir.), Des Moines Club (pres. 1977), Desert Forest Golf Club (Carefree, Ariz.), Masons, Shriners, Delta Chi, Phi Delta Phi. Republican. Episcopalian. Home: 600 Stevens Port Dr Dakota Dunes SD 57049-5188 Office: # 101 600 Stevens Point Dr Dakota Dunes SD 57049

PUTNEY, PAUL WILLIAM, lawyer; b. Phila., Feb. 6, 1940; s. R. Emerson and Dorothea (Schulz) P.; m. Joan E. High, June 9, 1961; children: Joanna E., Andrew E. AB, Princeton U., 1962; JD, Harvard U., 1965. BarP Pa. 1965, U.S. Dist. Ct. (ea. dist.) Pa. 1966, U.S. Supreme Ct. 1977, N.Y. 1988. Assoc. Dechert Price & Rhoads, Phila., 1965-73, ptnr., 1973-74, 77-87; mng. ptnr. Dechert Price & Rhoads, N.Y.C., 1987-94; chmn. trust and estates dept., 1994—; dep. chief broadcast bur. FCC, Washington, 1974-77; chmn. Phila. Presbytery Homes, Inc., 1987-93. Mem. ABA (past chair com. fin. planning for bus. owners, task force on legal fin. planning of real property, trust and probate sect.). Office: Dechert Price & Rhoads 4000 Bell Atlantic Tower 1717 Arch St Philadelphia PA 19103-2713

PUTTER, IRVING, French language educator; b. N.Y.C., Dec. 3, 1917; s. Joseph and Anna (Schrank) P.; children—Paul Stephen, Candace Anne Putter. B.A., CCNY, 1938; M.A., State U. Iowa, 1941; Ph.D., Yale U., 1949. Mem. faculty U. Calif.-Berkeley, 1947-88; prof. French U. Calif. at Berkeley, 1961-88, chmn. dept., 1968-71, humanities research fellow, 1971-72, 78-79, 84-85. Author: Leconte de Lisle and His Contemporaries, 1951, The Pessimism of Leconte de Lisle: Sources and Evolution, 1954, The Pessimism of Leconte de Lisle: The Work and The Time, 1961, La Dernière Illusion de Leconte de Lisle: Lettres Inédites a Emilie Leforestier, 1968; also numerous articles.; editor, translator: Chateaubriand: Atala, René, 1952. Guggenheim fellow, 1955-56; Fulbright fellow, 1955-56. Home: 115 St James Dr Piedmont CA 94611-3603

PUTTERMAN, FLORENCE GRACE, artist, printmaker; b. N.Y.C., Apr. 14, 1927; d. Nathan and Jean (Feldman) Hirsch; m. Saul Putterman, Dec. 19, 1947. BS, NYU, 1947; MFA, Pa. State U., 1973. Founder, pres. Arts Unlimited, Selinsgrove, Pa., 1969—; curator Milton Shoe Collection, 1970—; artist in residence Title III Program Cultural Enrichment in Schs. Program, 1969-70; instr. Lycoming Coll., Williamsport, Pa., 1972-74, Susquehanna U., Selinsgrove, PA, 1984—. Exhibited one-woman shows, Everson Mus., Syracuse, N.Y., 1976, Hagerstown, Md., 1978, Stuhr Mus., Grand Island, N.B., 1979, Muhlenburg Ctr. for the Arts, Pa., 1985, Harmon Gallery, Fla., 1985, The State Mus. of Pa., 1985-86, Segal Gallery, N.Y., 1986, Canton Inst. Fine Arts, Ohio, 1986, Fla. Biennial Polk Mus., Lakeland, Fla., 1987, 89, Artists Choose Artists, Tampa Mus., 1987, Auburn Works on Paper, 1987, Ala., Ruth Volid Gallery, Chgo., 1989, Polk Mus. Art, Lakeland, Fla., 1989, Lowe Gallery, Atlanta, 1990, Mickelson Gallery, Washington, 1990, Palmer Mus., Pa. State U., 1990, Payne Gallery, Moravian Coll., 1991, Everhart Mus., Scranton, Pa., 1991, Lowe Gallery, L.A., 1992, Center Gallery, Bucknell U., Pa., 1993, Lore Degenstein Gallery, Susquehanna U., Selinsgrove, Pa., 1993, Lowe Gallery, Atlanta, 1993, Down Roll Gallery, Sarasota, Fla., Gallery 10, Washington, Donn Roll Contemporary, Sarasota, Fla., 1996; group shows include Libr. Congress, Soc. Am. Graphic Artists, Ball State Drawing Ann., Muncie, Ind., Arts Club N.Y., Colorprint, U.S.A., Smithsonian Traveling Exhbn., Boston Printmakers, N.C. Print & Drawing, Chautauqua Nat., U. Dallas Nat. Print Invitational, Segal Gallery, Rutgers Drawing, Polk Mus., Tampa Mus., Sichaun Fine Art Inst., Mickelson Gallery, Harmon Gallery, Mus. Art U. Ariz., 1988, U. Del., Newark, 1988 Mid Am. Biennial, Owensboro Mus. Art, VCCA Exhbn. Mcpl. Gallery, Regensburg, Federal Republic of Germany, 1989, Erie (Pa.) Art Mus., 1990, 1990 twenty year survey Palmer Mus., Pa. State U., Univ. Park, Payne Gallery Moravian Coll., Bethlehem, Pa., 1991, Everhart Mus., Scranton, Pa., 1991, U. Del. Biennial, Phila. Watercolor Soc., Noyes Mus., N.J., 1992, Erie (Pa.) Mus., 1991, Mus. Fine Arts, Hanoi, 1991, Spanish Embassy, Madrid, 1992, Anita Shapolsky Gallery, N.Y., 1990, American Women's Artists, Foster Harman Gallery Sarasota, Fla., 1993, Humphrey Gallery, N.Y., 1992, Anita Shapolsky Gallery, N.Y., 1993, Fla. Printmakers, Miami, 1993, Fla. Artists Ringling Mus., 1994, Walter Wickiser Gallery, N.Y., 1995. Recipient award Silvermine Guild Conn. Appalachian Corridors, Arena, 1976, Gold medal of honor Audubon Artists ann. competition, Whitehead award Boston Printmakers, 1985, Shellenberg award Artists Equity, 1985, award N.C. Print & Drawing, 1985, award Chautauqua Nat., 1985, Johnson & Johnson award 3rd Ann. Nat. Printmaking Coun. of N.J., 1985, Purchase award N.J. State Mus., 1987, Disting. Alumni award Pa. State U. Sch. Arts & Architecture, 1988, Ethel Klassen Meml. award Fla. Artists Group, 1992, Earl Horter award Phila. Watercolor Club, 1992, award of excellence, 1995, Stella Drabkin Meml. award Colorprint Soc.; Va. Ctr. for the Creative Arts fellow, 1983-84; Nat. Endowment Arts grantee. Mem. Soc. Am. Graphic Artists (v.p.), Nat. Assn. of Women Artists (Nat. Medal of Honor, Elizabeth Blake award). Home: 220 Morningside Dr Sarasota FL 34236-1113 *I examine the world through painting. I consider the act of art a spiritual experience. My work is informed by nature and visually recalled and then made permanent on paper or canvas. Maintaining a feeling of being in harmony with the world allows for periods of quiet meditation and creativity.*

PUTTERMAN, LOUIS G., economics educator; b. N.Y.C., Apr. 27, 1952; s. Milton and Eileen L. (Goldstein) P.; (div.); 1 child, Laura Lee; m. Vivian Tseng, Apr. 5, 1981; children: Serena Rose, Mark Isaac. BA summa cum laude, Columbia U., 1976; MA in Internat. Relations, Yale U., 1978, PhD in Econs., 1980; MA (hon.), Brown U., 1983. From asst. prof. to prof. econs. Brown U., R.I., 1980—; rsch. assoc., Ctr. for East Asian Rsch. Harvard U., Cambridge, Mass., 1987-93. Author: Peasants, Collectives and Choice, 1986, Division of Labor and Welfare, 1990, Continuity and Change in China's Rural Development: Collective and Reform Eras in Perspective, 1993; co-author: Economics of Cooperation and the Labor-Managed Economy, 1987; editor: The Economic Nature of the Firm, 1986, 2d edit., 1996, State and Market in Development: Synergy or Rivalry, 1992; mem. editl. bd. Modern China, 1990—, Comparative Economic Studies, 1991-93, Annals of Public and Cooperative Economics, 1992—, Jour. Comparative Econs., 1989-91; assoc. editor Pacific Econ. Rev., 1996—. Recipient Sloan Rsch. fellowship, Alfred P. Sloan Found., 1983, Fellowship in Chinese Studies, Wang Inst., 1986. Mem. Am. Economic Assn., Assn. for Comparative Economic Studies, Phi Beta Kappa. Office: Brown U Dept Econs 64 Waterman St Providence RI 02912-9029

PUTTERMAN, WILLIAM ZEV, foundation executive, television producer; b. Bronx, N.Y., Nov. 6, 1928; s. David Joseph and Amy Belle (Racoosin) P.; m. Anita Ruth Woien, Mar. 3, 1964 (div. 1971); children: Rachel Amy, Naomi Leah; m. Mary Elizabeth Kudlacik, Nov. 18, 1984. Student Colgate U., 1946-47; BA with honors in Philosophy, Syracuse U., 1949. Stage mgr. on Broadway, 1958; dir. Off-Broadway, 1960-61; with with Synanon found., 1962-64; prodr. Sta. KGO-TV, ABC, San Francisco, 1964-66; exec. prodr. Sta. KTTV, Metromedia, 1967-68; program cons. Sta. KABC-TV, ABC, L.A., 1969; dir. program devel. Metromedia TV, Inc., L.A., 1969-70; dir. nat. programs Sta. KQED, PBS, San Francisco, 1970-79; dir. comm. Werner Erhard and Assocs., San Francisco, 1980-83; v.p. program devel. Furia/Oringer Prodns., Inc., Sherman Oaks, Calif., 1984-86; supervising prodr. The Landsburg Co., L.A., 1986-88; pres. Zev Putterman Prodns., Tucson, 1989—; exec. dir. Amity Found., Tucson, 1991—; prodr. Alan Landsburg Prodns., L.A., 1972; vis. lectr. Calif. State U., Northridge, 1966; instr. U. Calif. Ext., Berkeley, 1972; lectr. Berkeley Film Inst., 1977, 79; mem. Norman Corwin student documentary program adv. bd. U. So. Calif., 1989—; U.S. del. Internat. Pub. TV Screening Conf., Milan, 1978. Prodr. On Location, Am. Broadcasting System, 1972, The Boarding House, PBS, 1975, Leukemia Soc.'s Televent '90, Nat. Leukemia Broadcast Coun., L.A., 1990; supervising prodr. Photoplay, 1986, 87; exec. prodr. Internat. Animation Festival, 1976, World Press, 1975-77, Music from Aspen/MoreMusic from Aspen spls., 1977, People vs. Inez Garcia, 1977, Turnabout, 1978, Transport of Delight, 1978, Black Filmmakers Hall of Fame spls., 1977, 78, Inside the Cuckoo's Nest, 1978; numerous others. Bd. dirs. Found. for Mideast Comm., 1985—, The Holiday Project, 1983-88, Am. Jewish Congress, 1985—, Marin Cmty. Workshop, 1977-78; mem. adv. coun. New Israel Fund, 1986—; bd. dirs. Chabad of No. Calif., 1975-84, chmn., 1984. Recipient Golden Eagle award for Vasectomy, Coun. for Internat. Non-Theatrical Events, 1973, for Private Lives of Americans, 1974, The Place for No Story, 1975, 13 Emmy awards, DuPont-Columbia award for "1985", 1970. Mem. NATAS, Nat. Assn. TV Program Execs., Nat. Assn. Fund Raising Execs., Internat. Documentary Assn., Theta Beta Phi. Democrat. Jewish. Avocations: arab-Jewish reconciliation, drug addict rehabilitation. Office: Amity Inc PO Box 32200 Tucson AZ 85751

PUTTERS, SARAH L., pediatrics nurse; b. Clarks, Nebr., July 24, 1931; d. Hilmer E. and Emma Ellen (Hannigan) Wallin; m. William Charles Putters, Jan. 3, 1954; children: Charles, Patricia, Pamela. BSN, U. Kans., Kansas City, 1973; MSN, PNP, U. Mo., Kansas City, 1975. Cert. PNP ANA; Nat. Assn. Pediatric Nurse Assocs. and Practitioners. Pediatric nurse practitioner U. Miss., Jackson, 1976-77; asst. prof. nursing U. West Fla., Pensacola, 1978-80; project coord. N.W. Fla. Dist. I Child Protection Team, 1981-90; pvt. practice as PNP Milton, Fla., 1990—; health cons. Headstart Westinghouse Health Systems, Atlanta, 1976-79; faculty advisor student nurse assn. Univ. N.W. Fla., 1978-80; mem. task force Dist. I N.W. Fla. Child Abuse Prevention Project, 1983—; cons. in field. Active Escambia Co. Pub. Health Trust, Pensacola, 1979-82, Gov.'s Constituency Children, Pensacola, 1985-90; bd. dirs. Hospice N.W. Fla., Pensacola, 1981-84, Favor Ho. Spouse Abuse Ctr., Pensacola, 1982-85, Guardian Ad Litum Dist. I, 1983-91. Grantee in field. Mem. Advanced Registered Nurse Practitioner (chair dist. I group 1993-94), Fla. Nurses Assn. (2d v.p. dist. I 1980-81, 1st v.p. 1982-83, pres. 1984-86, bd. dirs. 1987—, Fla. Nurse of Yr. 1986). Democrat. Episcopalian. Avocations: golfing, swimming, gardening, reading. Office: Health Svcs & Consultation Inc 9950 N Palafox St Pensacola FL 32534-1227

PUTTNAM, SIR DAVID TERENCE, film producer; b. London, Feb. 25, 1941; s. Leonard Arthur and Marie Beatrix P.; m. Patricia Mary Jones, 1961; two children. LLD (hon.) Bristol (Eng.) U., 1983; DLitt (hon.) Leicester U., 1986, Leeds U., 1992, U. Bradford, 1993. Knighted, 1995. With advt. firms, 1958-66; photographer's agt., 1966-68; film producer, 1968—. Chmn., Columbia Pictures, 1986-88. Producer films including That'll Be the Day, 1971, Mahler, 1973, Bugsy Malone, 1975, The Duellists (Spl. Jury prize Cannes 1977), 1977, Midnight Express, 1977 (2 Acad. awards), Chariots of Fire (4 Acad. awards and 3 BAFTA awards including Best Film award 1981, 4 Oscars including Best Picture), Local Hero, 1982, The Killing Fields, 1984 (3 Am. Acad. awards, 8 Brit. Acad. awards, BAFTA award for Best Picture), Cal, 1984, The Mission, 1986 (Palme d'Or 1986, Acad. award), Memphis Belle, 1990, Meeting Venus, 1991, Being Human, 1992, War of the Buttons, 1993, The Burning Season, 1994 (Golden Globe award best film for TV), Le Confessional, 1995. Chmn. Nat. Film and TV Sch., ITEL;pres. Atelier du Cinema European; vis. prof. films Bristol U.; dir. Anglia TV. Claridge's Hotel, Chrysalis Group, Survival Anglia; trustee Nat. Energy Found.; hon. fellow The Chartered Soc. Designers; hon. fellow Manchester Polytechnic. Decorated Officier dans l'Ordre des Arts et des Lettres, 1986; comdr. of the Most Excellent Order of the Brit. Empire, 1982, Kt., 1995; recipient Michael Balcon award for Outstanding Contbn. Brit. Film Industry, BAFTA, 1982. Fellow Royal Soc. Arts, Royal Photographic Soc., Royal Geog. Soc. Address: 13/15 Queen's Gate Pl Mews, London SW7 5BG, England

PUTZEL, CONSTANCE KELLNER, lawyer; b. Balt., Sept. 5, 1922; d. William Stummer and Corinne (Strauss) Kellner; m. William L. Putzel, Aug. 28, 1945; 1 son, Arthur William. A.B., Goucher Coll., 1942; LL.B., U. Md., 1945, J.D., 1969. Bar: Md. 1945. Social worker Balt. Dept. Pub. Welfare, 1945-46; atty. New Amsterdam Casualty Co., Balt., 1947; staff atty. Legal Aid Bur., Balt., 1947-49; mem. Putzel & Putzel, P.A., Balt., 1950-89; sole practitioner Balt., 1989—; instr. U. Balt. Sch. Law, 1975-77, Goucher Coll., 1976-77; chmn. character com. Ct. Appeals for 3d Cir., 1976—. Author: Divorce Organization System, 1984, 3d edit., 1993, Representing the Older Client in Divorce, 1992. Mem. Md. Com. on Status of Women, 1972-76; mem. Com. to Implement ERA, 1973-76; Pres. U. Md. Law Alumni Assn., 1978; bd. dirs. Legal Aid Bur., 1951-52, 71-73. Fellow Am. Acad. Matrimonial Lawyers, Internat. Acad. Matrimonial Lawyers; mem. ABA, Md. Bar Assn. (bd. govs. 1972-73, chmn. family law sect. 1978-79). Home: 8207 Spring Bottom Way Baltimore MD 21208-1859 Office: 29 W Susquehanna Ave Baltimore MD 21204-5201

PUTZEL, MICHAEL, journalist, consultant; b. Washington, Sept. 16, 1942; s. Max and Nell (Converse) P.; m. Ann Blackman, Feb. 23, 1974; children: Leila Elizabeth, Christof Blackman. BA, UNC in Polit. Sci., 1967. Reporter Charleston (W.Va.) Gazette, 1963-66; newsman AP, Raleigh, N.C., 1967-68, N.Y.C., 1968-69; war corr. AP, Vietnam, 1969-72; reporter AP, Washington, 1972-79; asst. metro editor Washington Post, Washington, 1979; White House corr. AP, Washington, 1979-84; chief White House corr. AP, 1984-87; chief of bur. AP, Moscow, 1987-90; diplomatic corr. AP, Washington, 1990-91; Washington bureau chief Boston Globe, 1991-92; White House corr. Boston Globe, Washington, 1993-94; columnist "Plugged In", 1994-95; founder, CEO Trysail, Inc., Washington, 1996—. With USAR, 1964-65. Recipient AP Mgn. Editors citation, 1975, 81, Merriman Smith Meml. award White House Corr. Assn., 1986. Home: 4938 Quebec St NW Washington DC 20016-3231 Office: Trysail Inc 1155 Connecticut Ave NW Ste 300 Washington DC 20036

PUTZELL, EDWIN JOSEPH, JR., lawyer, mayor; b. Birmingham, Ala., Sept. 29, 1913; s. Edwin Joseph and Celeste (Joseph) P.; children: Cynthia Putzell Reidy, Edwin Joseph III; m. Dorothy Corcoran Waters, Aug. 5, 1967. AB, Tulane U., 1935; LLB, Harvard U., 1938. Bar: N.Y. 1939, Mo. 1947, U.S. Supreme Ct. 1945. Atty. Donovan, Leisure, Newton & Lumbard, N.Y.C. and Washington, 1937-42; asst. dir., exec. officer Office of Strategic Svcs., 1942-45; asst. treas. Monsanto Co., St. Louis, 1945-46, asst. sec., atty., 1946-51, sec., 1951-77, dir. law dept., 1953-68, v.p., gen. counsel, 1963-77; ptnr. Coburn, Croft, Shepherd, Herzog & Putzell, St. Louis, 1977-79; of counsel Coburn, Croft & Putzell, St. Louis, 1979—; mayor City of Naples, Fla., 1986-90. Dir. St. Louis Symphony Soc., 1955-69; pres. The Conservancy, Inc., 1981-85, chmn. bd. dirs., 1984-85; vice chmn. St. Louis County Bd. Police Commrs., 1964-72, Big Cypress Basin Bd., South Fla. Water Mgmt. Dist., 1985-86; pres. Social Planning Coun., St. Louis, 1954-57; chmn. Naples Airport Authority, 1979-83, 94—; vice chmn. Westminster Coll., 1976-79; chmn. Sta. KETC-TV, St. Louis, 1977-79; trustee St. Luke's Hosp., 1973-79; bd. dirs. Hospice of Naples, Cmty. Found. Collier County, The Moorings, Inc., Collier/Naplescape, Inc. Mem. ABA, Mo. Bar Assn., St. Louis Bar Assn., Am. Soc. Corp. Secs. (pres. 1968-69), Assn. Gen. Counsel, Bogey Club, Noonday Club, Port Royal Club, Hole in the Wall Golf Club, Naples Yacht Club, Phi Beta Kappa, Delta Sigma Phi. Episcopalian. Home: 1285 Gulf Shore Blvd N Naples FL 33940-4911

PUYAU, FRANCIS ALBERT, physician, radiology educator; b. New Orleans, Dec. 1, 1928; s. Frank Albert and Rose Sue (Jones) P.; m. Geraldine Sally diBenedetto, June 6, 1951; children: Michael, Stephen, Jeanne Marie, Julie, Melissa. B.S., Notre Dame U., 1948; M.D., La. State U., 1952. Diplomate Am. Bd. Pediatrics, Am. Bd. Pediatric Cardiology, Am. Bd. Radiology. Intern Charity Hosp., New Orleans, 1952-53; resident in pediatrics Charity Hosp., 1955-57; instr. pediatrics La. State U. Sch. Medicine, New Orleans, 1957-59; asst. prof. La. State U. Sch. Medicine, 1959-61, clin. asso. prof., 1968-71, prof. radiology and pediatrics, 1971-74, acting head dept. radiology, 1971-72, head dept., 1972-74; asst. prof. pediatrics Vanderbilt U., 1961-68; fellow dept. diagnostic radiology Charity Hosp., New Orleans, 1968-70; prof. radiology and pediat. Tulane U. Sch. Medicine, New Orleans, 1974—, prof. medicine, 1974-95; acting chmn. dept. pediatrics Tulane U. Sch. Medicine, 1976-78; cons. St. Tammany Hosps., Covington, La., 1968-81; dir. cardiac catherization lab. dept. cardiology Charity Hosp., New Orleans, 1970-85; staff radiologist Our Lady of the Lake Regional Med. Ctr., Baton Rouge, 1986-93; mem. staff Hotel Dieu, New Orleans, 1973-80; head x-ray dept. Children's Hosp. of New Orleans, 1976-82. Contbr. articles to med. jours. Served with USPHS, 1953-55. Fellow Am. Coll. Cardiology, Am. Coll. Radiology; mem. East Baton Rouge Med. Soc., So. Soc. Pediatric Research, Am. Coll. Radiology, La. Radiology Soc., New Orleans Radiology Soc. (pres. 1985), New Orleans Pediatric Soc., Soc. Chmn. Acad. Radiology Depts., Radiol. Soc. N.Am., Am. Roentgen Ray Soc., Assn. Univ. Radiologists, Southern Yacht Club (New Orleans), City Club New Orleans, Alpha Omega Alpha. Roman Catholic. Home: 458 Shady Lake Pky Baton Rouge LA 70810-4322 Office: Tulane U Med Ctr Dept Radiology 1415 Tulane Ave New Orleans LA 70112-2605

PUZO, MARIO, author; b. N.Y.C., Oct. 15, 1920; s. Antonio and Maria (Le Conti) P.; m. Erika Lina Broske, 1946; children: Anthony, Joey, Dorothy, Virginia, Eugene. Student, New Sch. for Social Research, Columbia U. Lit. reviewer various mags.; former civil service employee; former editor Male Mag. Author: The Dark Arena, 1955, The Fortunate Pilgrim, 1964, The Runaway Summer of Davie Shaw, 1966, The Godfather, 1969, The Godfather Papers and Other Confessions, 1972, Inside Las Vegas, 1977, Fools Die, 1978, The Sicilian, 1984, The Fourth K, 1991; screenwriter: (with Francis Ford Coppola) The Godfather, 1972 (Academy award best adapted screenplay 1972, Screen award Writers Guild Am. West 1972, Golden Globe award best screenplay 1973), (with Coppola) The Godfather,

Part II, 1974 (Academy award best adapted screeplay 1974, Screen award Writers Guild Am. West 1974), (with George Fox) Earthquake, 1974, (with Robert Benton, David Newman, and Leslie Newman) Superman, 1978, (with D. Newman and L. Newman) Superman II, 1981, (with Coppola and William Kennedy) The Cotton Club, 1984, (with Coppola) The Godfather, Part III, 1990 (Golden Globe award best screenplay 1990), (with John Briley and Cary Bates) Christopher Columbus: The Discovery, 1992. Office: Greenberg Glusker Fields Claman & Machtinger 1900 Avenue Of The Stars Los Angeles CA 90067-4301

PYATT, EVERETT ARNO, government official; b. Kansas City, Mo., July 22, 1939; s. Arno Doyne and Myrl Elizabeth (Osborn) P.; m. Susan Evelyn Kristal, Sept. 28, 1968; children: Jennifer, Laura, Jeffrey. B.E., B.S., Yale U., 1962; M.B.A., U. Pa., 1977. Staff engr. office dir. def. research and devel. Office Sec. Def., Dept. Def., Washington, 1962-72; dir. acquisition planning Office Asst. Sec. Def. for Program Analysis and Evaluation, 1972-75; dir. logistics resources Office Asst. Sec. Def. for Installations and Logistics, 1975-77; prin. dep. asst. sec. for logistics Dept. Navy, Washington, 1977-79, prin. dep. asst. sec. for shipbldg. and logistics, 1981-84; asst. sec. for shipbldg. and logistics Dept. Navy, 1984-89; exec. advisor Coopers & Lybrand, 1989—; pres. EV Ventures; dep. chief fin. officer Dept. Energy, 1979-81; dir. Dept. Energy (Office of Alcohol Fuels), 1980. Recipient Disting. Civilian Svc. medal USN, 1980-81, 87, Superior Civilian Svc. medal, 1981, Outstanding Svc. medal Dept. Energy, 1981, Pres.'s award of meritorious excellence, 1983, Disting. Civilian Pub. Svc. award Dept. Def., 1989; Office of Sec. Def. fellow, 1975-77. Mem. IEEE. Club: Yale. Home: 4560 25th Rd N Arlington VA 22207-4147 Office: Coopers & Lybrand 1530 Wilson Blvd Arlington VA 22209-2447

PYATT, KEDAR DAVIS, JR., research and development company executive; b. Wadesboro, N.C., May 20, 1933; s. Kedar D. and Frances (Hales) P.; m. Mary Mackenzie, June 2, 1956; children: Geoffrey, Kira, David, Rebecca. BS in Physics, Duke U., 1955; PhD in Physics, Yale U., 1960. With Gen. Atomic, San Diego, 1959-67; sr. v.p., chief tech. officer, rechr., mem. bd. dirs. S-Cubed divsn. Maxwell Labs., Inc., San Diego, 1967—. Recipient Exceptional Pub. Svc. medal Dept. Def., 1985. Office: S-Cubed Divsn Maxwell Labs 3398 Carmel Mountain Rd San Diego CA 92121

PYATT, LEO ANTHONY, real estate broker; b. Key Port, N.J., Oct. 20, 1925; s. Ralph James and Anna Regina (Kussmaul) P.; m. Geraldine Genevive Gibb, May 31, 1947; children: Steven Lee, Rebecca Lynn. Student, Franklin U., 1947-49. Salesperson Standard Oil Co., Columbus, Ohio, 1947-49, Borden Dairy Co., Columbus, 1950-57, Frito-Lay, Inc., Columbus, 1958-74; sec., treas. Snack Time, Inc., Columbus, 1974-75; agt. N. NE Realty Co., Columbus, 1976-86; owner-broker Pyatt's Rose Realty Co., Columbus, 1986—. Presiding judge County Rep. Party, Franklin County, 1991; mem. Citizens for an Alternative Tax System. With USN, 1943-46, PTO. Decorated Air medal, Philippine Liberation award. Republican. Roman Catholic. Avocations: writing, travel, hiking, reading. Home: 4400 Wanda Lane Rd Columbus OH 43224-1026 Office: Pyatts Rose Realty Co 4400 Wanda Lane Rd Columbus OH 43224-1026

PYE, GORDON BRUCE, economist; b. Oak Park, Ill., Oct. 30, 1933; s. Harold Charles and Florence Martha P. B.S. in Chem. Engring, M.I.T., 1955, Ph.D. in Econs, 1963. Asst. prof. bus. adminstrn. U. Calif., Berkeley, 1963-66; assoc. prof. U. Calif., 1966-69, prof., 1969-72; econ. cons. Standard Oil Co. Calif. (name changed to Chevron Corp.), San Francisco, 1972-74; v.p., sr. economist Irving Trust Co., N.Y.C., 1974-78, sr. v.p., mgr. econ. research and planning div., 1978-89; prin. Gordon B. Pye Assocs., N.Y.C., 1990—. Assoc. editor: Fin. Analysts Jour, 1972-89. Mem. Forecasters Club N.Y. (pres. 1980-81). Home: 230 E 50th St New York NY 10022-7702

PYE, LENWOOD DAVID, materials science educator, researcher, consultant; b. Little Falls, N.Y., May 16, 1937; s. Lenwood George and Elizabeth Marie Pye; m. Constance Lee Lanphere, Sept. 6, 1958; children: DeAnn, Lorie, Lisa, Brien. BS, Alfred U., 1959, PhD, 1968. Rsch. engr. PPG Industries, Pitts., 1959-60; rsch. scientist Bausch & Lomb, Rochester, N.Y., 1960-61, 62-64; prof. glass sci. N.Y. State Coll. Ceramics, N.Y. State Coll. Ceramics, Alfred U., 1968-96, dean, 1996—, dir. Inst. Glass Sci. and Engring., 1984-96, dir. Industry-Univ. Ctr. Glass Rsch., 1986-96; dean, prof. Alfred U., 1996—; past mem. steering com. The Internat. Commn. on Glass; bd. dirs. Alfred Tech. Resources, Inc., Schott Glass Technologies; dir. Paul Vicker Gardner Glass Ctr. 1st lt. U.S. Army, 1960-62. Recipient Dominick Labino lectr. award 1995. Mem. Am. Ceramics Soc., Optical Soc. Am., U.K. Soc. Glass Tech., Can. Ceramic Soc., German Soc. Glass Technology (hon.), Acad. Ceramic Sci. Office: Alfred U NY State Coll Ceramics Office of the Dean New York NY 14802

PYE, LUCIAN WILMOT, political science educator; b. Shansi, China, Oct. 21, 1921; s. Watts Orson and Gertrude (Chaney) P.; m. Mary Toombs Waddill, Dec. 24, 1944; children: Evelyn, L. Christopher, Virginia. B.A., Carleton Coll., 1943; M.A., Yale U., 1949, Ph.D., 1951. Instr., then asst. prof. polit. sci. Washington U., St. Louis, 1949-52; research assoc. Yale U., 1951-52, Princeton, 1952-56; vis. lectr. Columbia U., 1956; mem. faculty Mass. Inst. Tech., 1956-92, prof. polit. sci., 1960-92, Ford prof., 1972-92, chmn. sect., 1961-63; sr. staff mem. Mass. Inst. Tech. (Center Internat. Studies), 1956—; vis. assoc. prof. Yale U., 1959-61; vis. prof. George Washington U., 1993, Ballial Coll., Oxford U., 1994, Fletcher Sch., Tufts U., 1994; chmn. com. comparative politics Social Sci. Rsch. Coun., 1963-73; mem. adv. com. adminstr. AID, 1961-68; Dept. State, 1962-68, MSC, 1968—; trustee Asia Found., 1963—; gov. East-West Ctr., Honolulu, 1976-80; bd. dirs., v.p. Nat. Com. U.S.-China Rels. Author: Guerrilla Communism in Malaya, 1956, Politics, Personality and Nation Building, 1961, Aspects of Political Developments, 1966, Southeast Asia's Political Systems, 1967, The Spirit of Chinese Politics, 1968, Warlord Politics, 1971, China: An Introduction, 1972, Mao Tse-tung: The Man in The Leader, 1976, Dynamics of Chinese Politics, 1982, Asian Power and Politics, 1985; co-author: The Politics of the Developing Areas, 1960, The Emerging Nations, 1961; Editor: Communications and Political Development, 1963, Political Culture and Political Development, 1965, Political Science and Area Studies, 1975. Served as 1st lt. USMCR, 1945-46. Fellow Center Advanced Study Behavioral Scis., 1963. Fellow Am. Acad. Arts and Scis., Am. Philos. Soc.; mem. Assn. Asian Studies (dir.), Am. Polit. Sci. Assn. (dir., pres. 1989), Council Fgn. Relations (dir.), Asia Soc. (dir.), Pilgrim Soc., Phi Beta Kappa. Unitarian. Club: Cosmos. Home: 72 Fletcher Rd Belmont MA 02178-2017 Office: Mass Inst Tech Dept Polit Sci Cambridge MA 02139

PYFFER, LINDA J., nursing administrator, consultant; b. Phila., Dec. 11, 1946; d. William George and Irma Gertude (Leister) Heuser; m. Harry Pyffer, June 26, 1965; children: Annette Marie, Harry Vincent. Diploma, Northeastern Hosp. Sch. Nursing, 1983. RN, Pa.; cert. quality mgmt. RN, staff nurse isolation unit Parkview Hosp., Phila., 1983-85; RN, asst. DON Cheltham York Rd. Nursing Home, Phila., 1985-88; RN, staff nurse Northeastern Hosp., Phila., 1988-89; RN utilization rev. Attleboro Nurse/Rehab. Ctr., Langhorne, Pa., 1989-90; RN, asst. DON utilization rev. Chapel Manor Nursing Home, Phila., 1990; asst. DON, medicare coord. utilization rev. coord. Germantown Home, Phila., 1990-91; mem. utilization rev. team Dept. of Welfare, Norristown, Pa., 1991-92; RN, asst. DON Twp. Manor Nursing Home, Elkins Park, Pa., 1992-93; assessment and medicare coord. quality assurance and infection control Golden Slipper Uptown Home, Phila., 1993—; mem. utilization rev. in long term care Chapel Manor Nursing & Rehab. Ctr., Phila., 1990. Named Pa. Charge Nurse of Yr., Pa. Nursing Assn., 1986. Mem. Nat. Assn. DON, Assn. Profls. Infection Control, Wissmoming Yacht Club (sec. to commadore 1990—). Democrat. Roman Catholic. Avocations: reading, painting, boating, writing. Home: 2146 Dixon Ave Croydon PA 19021-5106

PYKE, JOHN SECREST, JR., lawyer, polymers company executive; b. Lakewood, Ohio, July 11, 1938; s. John S. and Elma B. Pyke; student Haverford Coll., 1956-58; BA, Columbia Coll., 1960, postgrad. Columbia Sch. Grad. Faculties, 1960-61; JD, Columbia Law Sch., 1964; m. Judith A., Dec. 26, 1970; 1 child, John Secrest, III. Bar: N.Y. 1965. Assoc. firm Townsend & Lewis (now Thacher, Proffit & Wood), N.Y.C., 1964-68; atty. M.A. Hanna Co., Cleve., 1968—, sec., 1973—, v.p., gen. counsel, 1979—. Trustee, Western Res. Acad., Hudson, Ohio, 1976—. Mem. ABA, Assn. Bar City N.Y., Am. Soc. Corp. Secs., Am. Corp. Counsel Assn., Union Club, Clifton Club, Cleve. Yachting Club. Author: Landmark Preservation, 1969, 2d edit., 1972. Office: MA Hanna Co 200 Public Sq Ste 36-5000 Cleveland OH 44114-2304

PYKE, RONALD, mathematics educator; b. Hamilton, Ont., Can., Nov. 24, 1931; s. Harold and Grace Carter (Digby) P.; m. Gladys Mary Davey, Dec. 19, 1953; children: Darlene, Brian, Ronald, Gordon. BA (hon.), McMaster U., 1953; MS, U. Wash., 1955, PhD, 1956. Asst. prof. Stanford U., Calif., 1956-58; asst. prof. Columbia U., N.Y.C., 1958-60; prof. math. U. Wash., Seattle, 1960—; vis. prof. U. Cambridge, Eng., 1964-65, Imperial Coll., London, 1970-71, Colo. State U., Ft. Collins, 1979, Technion, Israel, 1988, 90, 92; pres. Inst. Math. Stats., 1986-87; mem. bd. math. scis. NRC/NAS, 1984-88, chmn. com. applications and theoretical stats., 1985-88. Editor Ann. Prob., 1972-75; contbr. articles to profl. jours. NSF grantee, 1961-91. Fellow Internat. Statis. Inst. (v.p. 1989-91), Am. Statis. Assn., Inst. Math. Stats. (pres. 1986-87); mem. Am. Math. Soc., Statis. Soc. of Can. Office: U Wasington Dept Math Box 354350 Seattle WA 98195-4350

PYKE, THOMAS NICHOLAS, JR., government science and engineering administrator; b. Washington, July 16, 1942; s. Thomas Nicholas and Pauline Marie (Pingitore) P.; m. Carol June Renville, June 22, 1968; children—Christopher Renville, Alexander Nicholas. BS, Carnegie Inst. Tech., 1964; MS in Engring., U. Pa., 1965. Electronic engr. Nat. Bur. Standards, Gaithersburg, Md., 1964-69, chief computer networking sect., 1969-75, chief computer systems engring. div., 1975-79, dir. ctr. for computer systems engring., 1979-81, dir. ctr. programming sci. and tech., 1981-86; asst. adminstr. for satellite and info. services NOAA, Washington, 1986-92, dir. high performance computing and comm., 1992—; dir. The Globe Program The White House, Washington, 1994—; organizer profl. computer confs., 1970-86; mem. Presdl. Adv. Com. on Networking Structure and Function, 1980, Interagy. com. on Info. Resources Mgmt., 1983-84, bd. dirs., 1984-87, vice chmn. 1986-87 (Exec. Excellence award 1991), chmn. Interagy. Working Group on Data Mgmt. for Global Change, 1987-93; speaker in field. Editorial bd. Computer Networks Jour., 1976-86; contbr. articles to profl. jours. Bd. dirs. Glebe Commons Assn., Arlington, Va., 1976-79, v.p., 1977-79; chmn. Student Congress, Carnegie Inst. Tech., 1963-64; mem. Task Force on Computers in Schs., Arlington, 1982-85; pres. PTA, Arlington, 1983-84. Recipient silver medal Dept. Commerce, 1973, gold medal, 1995; award for exemplary achievement in pub. adminstrn. William A. Jump Found., 1975, 76, Presdl. Rank award of Meritorious Exec., 1988; Westinghouse scholar Carnegie Inst. Tech., 1960-64; Ford Found. fellow U. Pa., 1964-66. Fellow Washington Acad. Scis. (Engring. Sci. award 1974); mem. Am. Fedn. Info. Processing Socs. (bd. dirs. 1974-76), IEEE (sr. mem.), Computer Soc. of IEEE (bd. govs. 1971-73, 75-77, vice chmn. tech. com. on personal computing 1982-86, chmn. 1986-87), AAAS, Assn. Computing Machinery, Sigma Xi, Eta Kappa Nu, Omicron Delta Kappa, Pi Kappa Alpha (chpt. v.p. 1963-64). Episcopalian. Office: The Globe Program 744 Jackson Pl NW Washington DC 20503-0003

PYLE, DONALD ALAN, music educator, tenor; b. Ridgewood, N.J., Jan. 12, 1933; s. Aime A. and Muriel Ann (Barbour) P.; m. Barbara Jean Sly, July 6, 1961 (dec.); m. 2d, Virginia R. Tinker, June 4, 1968. Student Juilliard Sch. Music, 1956-59; B.A. in Vocal Performance, U. So. Fla., 1969; Mus. M., Mus. D., Fla. State U., 1972. Mem. company South Shore Music Circus, Cohassett, Mass., 1958-59; tenor soloist John Harms Chorus, St. Michael's Episcopal Ch., Juilliard Opera Theatre, N.Y.C., Temple Bethel, Englewood, N.J., St. Leo Coll., Dade City, Fla., 1956-61; teaching asst. Fla. State U., Tallahassee, 1969-71, adj. faculty, 1971-72; instr. U. Mo.-Columbia, 1972-76, acting dean, Swinney Conservatory Music, Central Meth. Coll., Fayette, Mo., 1976-77, dean, prof. voice, 1977-90; asst. dean. Sch. Fine Arts, U. Conn., 1990-93, assoc. dean, 1994—; tenor soloist numerous U.S. colls. and univs.; tenor soloist world premiers Songs from the Ark, The Labyrinth, Of Mice and Men; performances include: Strauss's Ariadne Auf Naxos, Bacchus, Verdi Requiem, Otello, Rigoletto, Duke, Bizet's Carmen, Don Jose, Handel's Acis & Galatea, Massanet's Le Cid, Flotow's Martha, Lionel, Purcell's Dido & Aeneas, Puccini's Turandot, Calaf, Rossini's Stabat Mater, Bach's St. Matthew's Passion, Mendelsohn's The Elijah and Les Troyens (under Sir Thomas Beecham); recordings for Koch Recordings Internat., RCA. Served to sgt. USMC, 1951-54. U. So. Fla. scholar, 1966. Mem. Nat. Assn. Tchrs. Singing, Nat. Assn. Schs. Music, Blue Key, Gold Key, Phi Delta Kappa, Omicron Delta Kappa, Phi Mu Alpha, Pi Kappa Lambda, Phi Kappa Phi. Roman Catholic.

PYLE, JERRY, automotive executive. Pres. Gulf States Toyota, Houston, 1981—. Office: Gulf States Toyota PO Box 40306 7701 Wilshire Pl Houston TX 77240-0306*

PYLE, KENNETH BIRGER, historian, educator; b. Bellefonte, Pa., Apr. 20, 1936; s. Hugh Gillespie and Beatrice Ingeborg (Petterson) P.; m. Anne Hamilton Henszey, Dec. 22, 1960; children: William Henszey, Anne Hamilton. AB magna cum laude, Harvard U., 1958; PhD, Johns Hopkins U., 1965. Asst. prof. U. Wash., 1965-69, assoc. prof., 1969-75, prof. history and Asian studies, 1975—, dir. Henry M. Jackson Sch. Internat. Studies, 1978-88; pres. Nat. Bur. Asian Rsch., 1988—; vice chmn. Japan-U.S. Friendship Commn., 1989-92, chmn., 1992-95; co-chmn. Joint Com. on U.S.-Japan Cultural and Ednl. Coop., 1992-95; vis. lectr. history Stanford U., 1964-65; vis. assoc. prof. history Yale U., 1969-70. Author: The New Generation in Meiji, Japan, 1969, The Making of Modern Japan, 1978, rev. edit., 1996; editor: The Trade Crisis: How Will Japan Respond?, 1987, The Japanese Question: Power and Purpose in a New Era, 1992, rev. edit., 1996; founding editor Jour. Japanese Studies, 1974-86, chmn. editl. bd., 1987-89, assoc. editor, 1989—. Bd. dirs. Maure and Mike Mansfield Found., 1979-88; bd. govs. Henry M. Jackson Found., 1983—; adv. bd. Japan Found., 1989—, Japan-Am. Student Conf., 1991—. Ford Found. fellow, 1961-64; Fulbright-Hays fellow, 1970-71; Social Sci. Research Council-Am. Council Learned Socs. fellow, 1970-73, 77, 83-84. Mem. Assn. Asian Studies, Am. Hist. Assn., Coun. Fgn. Rels. Presbyterian. Home: 8416 Midland Rd Medina WA 98039 Office: Henry M Jackson Sch Internat Studies U Wash Seattle WA 98195

PYLE, LUTHER ARNOLD, lawyer; b. Pontotoc County, Miss., Dec. 5, 1912; s. Thomas Luther and Lillie Dean (Reynolds) P.; m. Elizabeth McWillie Browne, Aug. 9, 1941; children—William A., Robert Bradford, Ben Cameron. LL.B., Cumberland U., 1936, J.D., 1960. Bar: Miss. 1936, D.C. 1974, U.S. Dist. Ct. (no. dist.) Miss. 1936, U.S. Dist. Ct. (so. dist.) Miss. 1946, U.S. Ct. Apls. (5th cir.) 1946, U.S. Ct. Appeals (11th cir.) 1981, U.S. Supreme Ct. 1959. Sole practice, New Albany, Miss., 1936-42; pros. atty. Union County, Miss., 1940-42; assoc. Cameron & Wills, Jackson, Miss., 1946-52; chancellor 5th chancery ct. dist. Miss., 1952-58; ptnr. Watkins, Pyle, Ludlam, Winter & Stennis, Jackson, 1958-80; ptnr. Barnett, Alagia & Pyle, Jackson, 1981-83; of counsel Pyle, Dreher, Mills & Dye, 1993—; participant World Law Conf., Manila, 1977, Madrid, 1979; bd. dirs. Miss. Bar Commn., 1959-63. Mem. exec. bd. Andrew Jackson council Boy Scouts Am., 1946; bd. govs. Jackson Little Theatre, 1964-67; pres. Jackson Jr. C. of C., 1949; chmn. downtown div. United Givers, Mental Health Assn. Served to lt. col. JAG Corps, U.S. Army, 1942-46. Recipient Silver Beaver award Boy Scouts Am. Fellow Miss. Bar Found.; mem. Fed. Bar Assn., ABA (chmn. continuing legal edn. 1958-74), Am. Judicature Soc. (dir.), Hinds County Bar Assn., Miss. Bar Assn. (chmn. jud. adminstrn. com. 1966-70), U.S. Supreme Ct. Hist. Soc., U.S. C. of C., Jackson C. of C. (dir. 1960-63), Miss. Dept. Res. Officers Assn. (pres. 1950), Am. Legion (past comdr.). Episcopalian. Clubs: University (dir. 1972-92), Jackson Country, Annandale Golf. Contbr. articles to profl. jours. Home: 1803 E Northside Dr Jackson MS 39211-6029 Office: Pyle Dreher Mills & Dye 775 Woodlands Pky # 100 Ridgeland MS 39157-5212

PYLE, ROBERT MILNER, JR., financial services company executive; b. Orange, N.J., Oct. 24, 1938; s. Robert M. and Dorothy (Collings) P.; m. C. Page Neville, May 31, 1969; children: Cynthia Neville, Laura Collings. BA, Williams Coll., 1960; JD, U. Va., 1963. Bar: N.Y. 1964. Assoc. Mudge Rose Guthrie & Alexander, N.Y.C., 1963-68; with Studebaker-Worthington, Inc., N.Y.C., 1968-77; sec. Studebaker-Worthington, Inc., 1972-76, assoc. gen. counsel, 1974-77; with Singer Co., N.Y.C., 1977-79; corp. counsel, asst. to sec. Singer Co., 1977-78, sr. corp. counsel, asst to sec., 1979; v.p., counsel Am. Soc. Corp. Secs., Inc., N.Y.C., 1979-89, v.p., sec., counsel, 1989-91; v.p., sr. asst. sec. Am. Express Co., N.Y.C., 1991—; Career counseling rep. for Williams Coll., 1977—. Trustee Pingry Sch., Martinsville, N.J., 1972-74; trustee Arts Coun. Suburban Essex Inc., 1979-84, chmn. bd., 1981-84; bd. govs. Colonial Dances, Ltd., N.Y.C., 1970-74; bd. dirs. Millburn-Short Hills Hist. Soc., 1985-90, v.p., 1985-87; trustee Suburban Cmty. Music Ctr., 1985-87. Mem. ABA, Assn. Bar City N.Y., Am. Soc. Corp. Secs. (hon.), Pingry Sch. Alumni Assn. (pres. 1972-74, bd. dirs. 1966-78, cert. of merit 1968), Pilgrims U.S., Met. Squash Racquets Assn. (past treas.), Racquet and Tennis Club, Bay Head Yacht Club (N.J.), Short Hills Club, Sigma Phi, Delta Theta Phi, Pi Delta Epsilon. Republican. Episcopalian. Office: Am Express Tower World Fin Ctr New York NY 10285-5003

PYLE, ROBERT NOBLE, public relations executive; b. Wilmington, Del., Oct. 23, 1926; s. Joseph Lybr and LaVerne Ruth (Noble) P.; m. Claire Thoron; children: Robert Noble Jr., Mark C., Nicholas A., Sarah L. B.A., Dickinson Coll., 1948; postgrad., Wharton Sch., U. Pa., 1949, U. Minn. Pres. Robert N. Pyle, Inc., Wilmington, 1949-52; adminstrv. asst. to U.S. Congress, Washington, 1952-63; bus. and polit. cons. and lobbyist Robert N. Pyle & Assoc., Washington, 1970—; pres. Ind. Bakers Assn., 1981—; sec./treas. Bulgarian Am. Bus. Ctr. Contbr. numerous articles to profl. jours.; reporter covering Nurnburg Trials, Paris Peace Conf. for, Stars & Stripes, Europe, 1946. Part-time field man Rep. Nat. Congl. Com., 1959-74; Selective Service Bd.; Served with U.S. Army, 1945-46, ETO. Mem. City Tavern Club, Nat. Press Club, Kenwood Golf & Country Club. Presbyterian. Home: 2613 Dumbarton St NW Washington DC 20007-3103 Office: 1223 Potomac St NW Washington DC 20007-3212

PYLE, THOMAS ALTON, instructional television and motion picture executive; b. Phoenix, Sept. 8, 1933; s. Thomas Virgil and Evelyn B. (Redden) P.; m. Victoria K. Bileck, Apr. 21, 1957; children: Pamela V., Brett T. BA, Ariz. State U., 1956. Freelance unit mgr. theatrical motion picture industry, N.Y.C. and L.A., 1956-60; v.p. sales Depicto Films Corp., N.Y.C., 1960-65; prodr. John Sutherland Prodns., N.Y.C. and L.A., 1965-67; v.p. mktg. Audio Prodns. Ednl. Svcs., N.Y.C., 1967-71; exec. v.p. Data Plex Systems, N.Y.C., 1971-74; divsn. pres., exec. prodr. Sterling Inst. Video Prodns., Washington, 1974-80; pres. Applied Video Concepts, Inc., Washington, 1980-83; pres., CEO Nat. Sci. Ctr. Found., Burke, Va., 1983-85; CEO Network for Instrnl. TV, Inc., Reston, Va., 1987—; active in new bus. and project fundraising; bd. dirs. Cmty. Ednl. Svcs., Balt., So. Fla. Instrnl. TV, Delaware Valley (Del.) Ednl. Telecomms. Network, Inc., Instrnl. Opportunities/St. Louis, Inc.; cons. Wireless Cable Industry, 1993—. Writer, dir., producer film on Pres. John F. Kennedy, 1962; producer film biography on Pres. Lyndon B. Johnson, 1964. V.p. Dexter Park Assn., Spring Valley, N.Y., 1968-74, Solaridge Cluster Assn., Reston, Va., 1990. Recipient numerous awards from nat. and internat. film and video festivals, also 2 Commendation awards White House, 2 Acad. award nominations. Mem. AAAS, Internat. Platform Assn., N.Y. Acad. of Scis. Republican. Methodist. Avocation: photography. Office: Network Instructional TV 11490 Commerce Park Dr Ste 110 Reston VA 22091-1532

PYLE, WILLIAM CARMODY, human resource management educator, researcher; b. Indpls., Nov. 28, 1939; s. William Branham and Florence Evelyn (Carmody) P.; m. Barbara Bostian, Aug. 1978 (div. 1982); stepchildren: Lori Weaver, Jeffrey Bostian, Kyle Bostian; 1 foster child, Ramin Sobhian. BBA, U. Notre Dame, 1961; MBA, Butler U., 1962; PhD, U. Mich., 1971. Rsch. fellow U. Mich., Ann Arbor, 1967-69, rsch. assoc., 1969-72, dir. human resource acctg. program, 1972-74; assoc. prof. indsl. rels., dir. human resource rsch. program U. Minn., Mpls., 1974-78; dir. Human Resource Rsch. Ctr., U. Mass., Amherst, 1978-86; prof. mgmt. Eckerd Coll., St. Petersburg, Fla., 1986-90, Holder prof. mgmt. and internat. bus., 1990—, founding dir., chmn., 1986—; cons. to over 100 Fortune 500 firms, 1970—. Contbr. articles to profl. jours. 1st lt. USAF, 1962-65. Recipient award for outstanding contbn. to field of human resource mgmt. Am. Soc. for Pers. Adminstrn., 1971. Mem. Bahai Faith. Achievements include director of research project to implement first human resource accounting system. Avocations: classical music, reading. Home: 6600 Sunset Way Unit 520-B St Petersburg Beach FL 33706 Office: Eckerd Coll Human Resource Inst 4200 54th Ave S Saint Petersburg FL 33711

PYLES, RODNEY ALLEN, archivist, county official; b. Morgantown, W.Va., June 21, 1945; s. Melford John and Luci L. (Scarcella) P.; m. Carol Louise Wrobleski, May 20, 1972; 1 child, Janessa Louise. B.A., M.A. (Benedum scholar 1966-67, grad. research asst. 1967-68, grad. teaching fellow 1968-69), W.Va. U., 1967, 69. Instr. polit. sci. Alderson-Broaddus Coll., Philippi, W.Va., 1969-71; asst. curator W.Va. U. Library, 1971-77; dir. archives and history div. W.Va. Dept. Culture and History, 1977-85; dep. chief Assessor's Office Monongalia County, 1985-88; assessor Monongalia County, 1989—. Mng. editor: W.Va. History quar, 1977-85. Mem. Morgantown (W.Va.) Dem. exec. com., 1966-69, Monongalia County (W.Va.) Dem. exec. com., 1972-74; mem. Morgantown Libr. Bd., 1988-91; pres. Morgantown Hist. Landmarks Commn., 1986—. Mem. Soc. Am. Archivists, Mid-Atlantic Regional Archives Conf., W.Va. Hist. Soc. (exec. sec. 1977-90), W.Va. Libr. Assn., Am. Assn. State and Local History (state awards chmn. 1980-85, state membership com. 1981-87), Monongalia Hist. Soc. (pres. 1986-88), W.Va. Polit. Sci. Assn. (treas. 1991—), W.Va. Assessors' Assn. (pres. 1992-93), KC (pres. bowling league 1995-96). Roman Catholic. Home: 536 Harvard St Morgantown WV 26505-2157 Office: County Court House Rm 215 Morgantown WV 26505

PYLIPOW, STANLEY ROSS, retired manufacturing company executive; b. Coudersport, Pa., Apr. 4, 1936; s. Stanley Edward and Helen L. (Haskins) P.; m. Phyllis Beverly Moore, Dec. 1, 1956; children—David, James, Vicky, Kenneth, Sandra. B.B.A. in Acctg. cum laude, St. Bonaventure U., 1957. Various fin. positions Chicopee Mfg., New Brunswick, N.J., 1957-65; various positions to v.p., gen. mgr. Domestic Coatings div. Mobil Chem. Co., N.Y.C., 1965-73; asst. corp. controller Monsanto Co., St. Louis, 1974-76; controller, dir. planning Monsanto Comml. Products, St. Louis, 1976-79; sr. v.p., chief fin. officer Fisher Controls Internat., Inc., St. Louis, 1979-92; ret., 1992; adv. bd. RBA Group; bd. dirs. Ligyori Publs.; mem. Acctg. Edn. Change Commn., 1985-89. Treas., City of Town and Country, Mo., 1980-84; bd. dirs. Ecumenical Housing Prodn. Corp., St. Louis, 1980-90; sr. warden St. Peter's Episcopal Ch., St. Louis, 1984-87. Served to 1st lt., U.S. Army, 1958. Named Exec. of Yr., Profl. Secs. Internat., 1982. Mem. Inst. Mgmt. Accts. (chmn. com. chpt. ops. 1984-86, rsch. com. 1986-87, v.p. 1983-84, exec. com. 1988-90, pres. 1990-91, chmn. 1991-92), Fin. Execs. Inst., Inst. Mgmt. Cons., Bellerive Country Club. Republican. Avocations: golf, fitness, spectator sports. Home: 244 Carlyle Lake Dr Saint Louis MO 63141-7544

PYM, BRUCE MICHAEL, lawyer; b. Alameda, Calif., Sept. 29, 1942; s. Leonard A. and Willamay (Strandberg) P. B.B.A., U. Wash., 1964, J.D., 1967. Bar: Wash. 1967, U.S. Dist. Ct. (we. dist.) Wash. 1968, U.S. Ct. Appeals (9th cir.) 1968, U.S. Tax Ct. 1969, U.S. Supreme Ct. 1971. Law clk. Wash. State Supreme Ct., Olympia, 1967-68; assoc. Graham & Dunn, Seattle, 1968-73, shareholder, 1973-92; ptnr. Heller, Ehrman, White & McAuliffe, Seattle, 1992—; mng. ptnr. Northwest Offices, 1994—. Bd. dirs. United Way of King County, 1986-92, chmn., 1990. Mem. ABA, Wash. State Bar Assn., Seattle-King County Bar Assn. (pres. 1984-85). Office: Heller Ehrman White & McAuliffe 701 5th Ave Ste 6100 Seattle WA 98104-7016

PYNCHON, THOMAS RUGGLES, JR., author; b. Glen Cove, N.Y., May 8, 1937; s. Thomas R. Pynchon. BA, Cornell U., 1958. Former editorial writer Boeing Aircraft Co., Seattle. Author: V, 1963 (William Faulkner novel award 1963), The Crying of Lot 49, 1966 (Rosenthal Found. award Nat. Inst. Arts and Letters 1967), Gravity's Rainbow, 1973 (Nat. Book award 1974), Slow Learner, 1984, Vineland, 1989; contbr. short stories to publs. including N.Y. Times Mag., N.Y. Times Book Rev., Cornell Writer, Saturday Evening Post, Kenyon Rev. Served with USNR. Recipient Howells medal Nat. Inst. and Am. Acad. Arts and Letters, 1975. Office: Little Brown & Co 34 Beacon St Boston MA 02108-1415

PYNE, EBEN WRIGHT, banker; b. N.Y.C., June 14, 1917; s. Grafton H. and Leta Constance (Wright) P.; grad. Groton Sch., 1935; AB, Princeton, 1939; m. Hilda Holloway, Dec. 16, 1941; children: Constance Howland Pyne Ranges (dec.), Lillian Stokes (Mrs. Lillian Pyne-Corbin), Mary Alison (Mrs. M. Alison McNaughton). Clerk 1st Nat. City Trust Co. (formerly City Bank

Farmers Trust Co., 1939, v.p., asst. to pres., 1952-56, exec. v.p., 1956, pres., dir., 1957-61; asst. cashier Nat. City Bank of N.Y., 1946-50, asst. v.p., 1950-52, v.p., 1952-53, sr. v.p., 1960-82; vice chmn., bd. dirs. The Home Group Inc.; bd. dirs. U.S. Life Ins. Co. City of N.Y., Home Ins. Co., U.S. Internat. Reins., Inc., Gen. Devel. Corp., Slattery Group, Inc. , L.I. Lighting Co. Mem. N.Y. State Met. Transp. Authority, 1965-75; commr. N.Y.C. Transit Authority, Triborough Bridge and Tunnel Authority, Manhattan and Bronx Surface Transit Authority, Stewart Airport, S.I. Rapid Transit Operating Authority, all 1965-75; adv. bd. Nassau County council Boy Scouts Am.; bd. dirs. Winthrop U. Hosp.; trustee Juilliard Sch., St. Luke's Hosp. ; mem. exec. com. Pres.'s Pvt. Sector on Cost Control. Served as maj. AUS, 1940-46. Decorated Bronze Star. Mem. Pilgrims of U.S. (exec. com.), Bklyn. Inst. Arts and Scis. (trustee), N.Y. Zool. Soc. (trustee). Clubs: Piping Rock (Locust Valley, L.I.); Bond, Racquet and Tennis, River (N.Y.C.); Ivy (Princeton, N.J.). Home: 134 Willets Rd Box 195 Old Westbury NY 11568

PYNE, FREDERICK WALLACE, genealogist, clergyman, retired civil engineer, retired mathematics educator; b. El Paso, Tex., Aug. 19, 1926; s. Frederick Cruger and Helen Louise (Wallace) P.; m. Jo Ann Rammes, July 18, 1952; children: Stephen VanRensselaer, Anne Wallace, Elizabeth Glover, Mary Clinton. BS in Civil Engring., Tri-State U., 1951; MS in Engring., Johns Hopkins U., 1966. Profl. engr., Md., Pa. Del., N.Y.; registered land surveyor; registered sanitarian; ordained priest Episcopal Ch., 1993; certified genealogist. Mcpl. engr., 1951-54; hwy. engr., pub. health engr., chief engr. State of Md., Balt., 1954-81; civil engr., biomedical engr. Dept. Def., Frederick, Md., 1981-88; adj. prof. math. Frederick C.C., 1988-94; priest Episcopal Ch. Author: The John Pyne Family in America, 1992. County surveyor Carroll County, Md., 1966-74; scout commr. Boy Scouts Am., Carroll and Frederick Counties, 1956—. Lt. inf. U.S. Army, 1944-51. Named Disting. Commr. Boy Scouts Am., 1993. Fellow ASCE; mem. Am. Acad. Environ. Engrs. (diplomate), Md. Soc. Surveyors (bd. dirs. 1972-78); life mem. SAR (Md. state registrar 1994—), Descs. Signers Declaration Independence (pres.-gen. 1975-78), Soc. Colonial Wars, Mayflower Soc. Republican. Avocations: history, languages, stamp collecting. Home: 7997 Windsail Ct Frederick MD 21701-9304

PYSCH, RICHARD LAWRENCE, principal; b. New Kensington, Pa., Apr. 27, 1950; s. Michael and Mary Louise (Klauscher) P.; m. Carolyn Vargo, Oct. 14, 1978; children: Matthew, Benjamin. BA, U. Pitts., 1972, MEd, 1977, PhD, 1987; MA, Carnegie-Mellon U., 1974. Tchr. The Village Acad., Bethel Park, Pa., 1975-78; program dir. The Bradley Ctr., Dorseyville, Pa., 1978; tchr. Fox Chapel Area Sch. Dist., Pitts., 1979-87; asst. high sch. prin. Pine-Richland Sch. Dist., Pitts., 1987-88, elem. curriculum coord., prin., 1988—. Contbr. articles to profl. jours. Mem. Juvenile Diabetes Found., Pitts., Hampton Athletic Assn., Pitts., Am. Cancer Soc., Pitts. Gateways grantee Pa. Dept. Edn., 1994. Mem. ASCD, Nat. Elem. Sch. Prins. Assn., Pa. Assn. Elem. Prins., Phi Delta Kappa. Avocations: exercising, civil war enthusiast. Home: 3342 Oaknoll Rd Gibsonia PA 15044-8483 Office: Hance Elem Sch 5518 Molnar Dr Gibsonia PA 15044-9308

PYTELL, ROBERT HENRY, lawyer, former judge; b. Detroit, Sept. 27, 1926; s. Henry Carl and Helen (Zielinski) P.; m. Laurie Mazur, June 2, 1956; children: Mary Beth, Mark Henry, Robert Michael. JD, U. Detroit, 1951. Bar: Mich. 1952. Prin. R.H. Pytell & Assocs., P.C., Detroit, 1952—; asst. U.S. atty. Ea. Dist. Mich., 1962-65; judge Mcpl. Ct., Grosse Pointe Farms, Mich., 1967-85. With USNR, 1945-46. Mem. Nat. Acad. Elder Law Attys., Am. Coll. Trust and Estate Coun., Comml. Law League Am., Crescent Sail Yacht Club (Grosse Pointe), Delta Theta Phi. Roman Catholic. Office: 18580 Mack Ave Grosse Pointe MI 48236-3251

PYTTE, AGNAR, academic administrator; b. Kongsberg, Norway, Dec. 23, 1932; came to U.S., 1949, naturalized, 1965; s. Ole and Edith (Christiansen) P.; m. Anah Currie Loeb, June 18, 1955; children: Anders H., Anthony M., Alyson C. A.B., Princeton U., 1953; A.M., Harvard U., 1954, Ph.D., 1958. Mem. faculty Dartmouth Coll., 1958-87, prof. physics, 1967-87, chmn. dept. physics and astronomy, 1971-75, assoc. dean faculty, 1975-78, dean grad. studies, 1975-78, provost, 1982-87; pres. Case Western Res. U., Cleve., 1987—; researcher in plasma physics; mem. Project Matterhorn, Princeton, 1959-60, U. Brussels, 1966-67, Princeton U., 1978-79; bd. dirs. Goodyear Tire & Rubber Co.; A.O. Smith Corp. Bd. dirs. Sherman Fairchild Found. Inc., 1987—, Cleve. United Way; bd. trustees Univs. Rsch. Assn., Ohio Aerospace Inst., Cleve. Inst. Music, Cleve. Orch. Mem. Am. Phys. Soc., Ohio Sci. and Tech. Coun., Cleve. Roundtable, Cleve. Tech. Leadership Coun., Phi Beta Kappa, Sigma Xi. Office: Case Western Res U Office of Pres Cleveland OH 44106

QADRI, YASMEEN, educational administrator, consultant; b. Hyderabad, India, June 12, 1955; came to U.S., 1979; d. Ghulam and Bilquees Mahmood; m. Najeeb Qadri, Oct. 8, 1978; children: Kamran, Farhan, Sumayya. BA, St. Francis Coll., Hyderabad, 1976; MA in Psychology, Osmania U., Hyderabad, 1978; MA in Social Sci., U. Ctrl. Fla., Orlando, 1991, EdD in Curriculum and Instrn., 1994. Tchr. Indian Embassy Sch. and Minaret-e-Jeddah, Jeddah, Saudi Arabia, 1981-84; asst. adminstr. Muslim Acad. Ctrl. Fla., Orlando, 1991-93, adminstr., 1993—, prin., 1994—; profl. interaction Trinity Prep. Sch., Orlando, 1993—. Cons. NCCJ, Orlando, 1992—. Recipient Cert. of Appreciation, Orange County Pub. Schs., 1992, Islamic Coun. Calif., 1993. Mem. ASCD, Muslim Women's Assn., Kappa Delta Pi. Muslim. Avocations: counseling, multicultural education, cooking, tourism. Office: Muslim Acad Ctrl Fla 1005 N Goldenrod Rd Orlando FL 32807-8326

QASIM, SYED REAZUL, civil engineering educator, researcher; b. Allahabad, India, Dec. 1, 1938; came to U.S., 1960; s. Syed Zamir and Fakhira (Begum) Q.; m. Mujtaba Rizvi, Dec. 17, 1966; children: Zeba Saira, Saba Bano. BCE, Aligarh (India) Muslim U., 1957; MCE, W.Va. U., 1962, PhD in Environ. Engring., 1965. Registered profl. engr., Tex., Ohio. Sr. lectr. Allahabad Agrl. Inst., 1958-59; asst. dist. engr. Allahabad Mcpl. Corp., 1959-60; pool officer Indian Agrl. Rsch. Inst., New Delhi, 1965-66; design civil engr. Alden E. Stilson and Assocs., Columbus, Ohio, 1966-68; sr. civil engr. Battelle Meml. Inst., Columbus, 1968-70; assoc. prof. Poly. Inst. Bklyn., 1970-73; assoc. prof. U. Tex., Arlington, 1973-78, prof. civil engring., 1978—; cons. Chiang, Patel & Yerby, Inc., Dallas, 1981—, Gutierrez, Smouse, Wilmut & Assocs., Dallas, 1984—, Kuwait Inst. for Sci. Rsch., 1992, Hong Kong Rsch. Coun., 1994—; TOKTEN (Transfer of Knowledge through Expatriate Nats.) cons. to UN Devel. Program, 1992. Author: Wastewater Treatment Plants: Planning, Design and Operation, 1994, Sanitary Landfill Leachate: Generation, Control and Treatment, 1994; contbr. articles to profl. jours. Recipient Halliburton award U. Tex. Arlington Coll. Engring., 1988-89, Disting. Rsch. award U. Tex. Arlington, 1990-91; Fulbright scholar India, 1986. Mem. ASCE, NSPE (chmn. awards com. 1969-70), Water Environ. Fedn., Am. Water Works Assn., Tech. Transfer Soc., Sigma Xi, Chi Epsilon, Tau Beta Pi. Home: 907 Leslie Dr Arlington TX 76012-4109 Office: U Tex at Arlington Dept Civil Engring Box 19308 Arlington TX 76019

QIAN, JIN, law librarian; b. Shanghai, China; came to the U.S., 1987; s. Bingchun and Shiyi Qian. BA, Shanghai Tchrs. U., ; 1981; MA, Fordham U., 1988; MLS, St. John's U., 1990. Libr. trainee N.Y. Pub. Libr., N.Y.C., 1988; reference asst. N.Y. Hist. Soc., N.Y.C., 1989-90; asst. libr. Wilson, Elser et al., N.Y.C., 1990-92, head libr., 1992—. Presdl. scholar Fordham U., 1987. Mem. Law Libr. Assn. Greater N.Y., Am. Assn. Law Librs., Spl. Librs. Assn., ALA. Home: 36-34 Crescent St Long Island City NY 11106-3922 Office: Wilson Elser & Moskowitz 150 E 42nd St New York NY 10017-5612

QIAO, LIANG, pathologist; b. Tanghe, China, Oct. 20, 1962; s. Wancheng and Wenfang (Zhao) Q.; m. Wei Liu, July 14, 1986; 1 child, George Z. MD, Sun Yat-sen U. of Med. Sci., Guangzhou Guangdong, China, 1983, MS in Pathology, 1988. Resident physician Henan Med. U., Zhengzhou, China, 1983-85; fellow in pathology Sun Yat-sen U. of Med. Sci., Guangzhou, China, 1985-88; attending physician Henan Med. U., Zhengzhou, China, 1988-90; vis. scholar SUNY at Stony Brook, 1990-91; rsch. assoc. Meml. Sloan-Kettering Cancer Ctr., N.Y.C., 1991-92; physician, rsch. assoc. N.Y. Med. Coll., Valhalla, N.Y., 1992-93, Cornell Med. Coll., N.Y.C., 1993—. Apptd. editor Chinese Jour. of Gastroenterology and Hepatology, 1994—; contbr. rsch. articles to Leukemia Rsch., Urological Rsch. and other profl. jours. Mem. Am. Assn. for Cancer Rsch., Internat. Soc. Analytical Cytology, Histochem. Soc. Achievements include rsch. in Suramin affects proliferation of prostate cancer; rsch. on proliferation antigen expression on leukemia and status of prostate cancer; rsch. on HLA expression on thyroid carcinoma. Office: Cornell U Med Coll 1300 York Ave # F231 New York NY 10021-4805

QUAAL, WARD LOUIS, broadcast executive; b. Ishpeming, Mich., Apr. 7, 1919; s. Sigfred Emil and Alma Charlotte (Larson) Q.; m. Dorothy J. Graham, Mar. 9, 1944; children: Graham Ward, Jennifer Anne. A.B., U. Mich., 1941; LL.D. (hon.), Mundelein Coll., 1962, No. Mich. U., 1967; D.Pub. Service, Elmhurst Coll., 1967; D.H.L. (hon.), Lincoln Coll., 1968, DePaul U., 1974. Announcer-writer Sta. WBEO (now sta. WDMJ), Marquette, Mich., 1936-37; announcer, writer, producer Sta. WJR, Detroit, 1937-41; spl. events announcer-producer WGN, Chgo., 1941-42, asst. to gen. mgr., 1945-49; exec. dir. Clear Channel Broadcasting Service, Washington, 1949-52, pres., chief exec. officer, 1964-74; v.p., asst. gen. mgr. Crosley Broadcasting Corp., Cin., 1952-56; v.p., gen. mgr., mem. bd. WGN Inc., Chgo., 1956; exec. v.p., then pres. WGN Continental Broadcasting Co. (now Tribune Broadcasting Co.), 1960-75; pres. Ward L. Quaal Co., 1975—; dir. Tribune Co., 1961-75; dir., mem. exec. com. U.S. Satellite Broadcasting Co., 1982—; bd. dirs. Christine Valmy Inc., Nat. Press Found., chmn. exec. com., dir. WLW Radio Inc., Cin., 1975-81; co-founder, dir. Universal Resources Inc., 1961-86; mem. FCC Adv. Com. on Advanced TV Sys., 1988-96. Author: (with others) Broadcast Management, 1968, rev. edit., 1996; co-prodr. (Broadway play) Teddy and Alice, 1988. Mem., Hoover Commn. Exec. Br. Task Force, 1949-59; mem. U.S.-Japan Cultural Exchange Commn., 1960-70; mem. Pres.'s Council Phys. Fitness and Sports, 1983-93; bd. dirs. Farm Found., 1963-73; bd. trustees Hollywood (Calif.) Mus., 1964-78, MacCormac Jr. Coll., Chgo., 1974-80; chmn. exec. com. Council for TV Devel., 1969-72; mem. bus. adv. coun. Chgo. Urban League, 1964-74; bd. dirs. Broadcasters Found., Internat. Radio and TV Found., Sears Roebuck Found., 1970-73; trustee Mundelein Coll., 1962-72, Hillsdale Coll., 1966-72. Served as lt. USNR, 1942-45. Recipient Disting. Bd. Gov.'s award Nat. Acad. TV Arts and Scis., 1966, 87, Freedoms Found. award, Valley Forge, 1966, 68, 70, Disting. Alumnus award U. Mich., 1967, Loyola U. Key, 1970, Advt. Man of Yr. Gold medallion, Chgo. Advt. Club, 1968, Disting. Svc. award Nat. Assn. Broadcasters, 1973, Ill. Broadcaster of Yr. award, 1973, Press Vet. of Yr. award, 1973, Comm.award of distinction Brandeis U., 1973, Founder & Leadership award Broadcast Pioneers Libr., 1991; first recipient Sterling Medal, Barren Found., 1985, Lifetime Achievement award in broadcasting Ill. Broadcasters Assn., 1989; 1st person named to Better Bus. Bur. Hall of Fame, Council of Better Bus. Burs. Inc., 1975; named Radio Man of Yr. Am. Coll. Radio, Arts, Crafts & Scis., 1961, Laureate in Order of Lincoln, Lincoln Acad. Ill., 1965, Communicator of Yr., Jewish United Fund, 1969, Advt. Club Man of Yr., 1973; named to Broadcasting mag. Hall Fame, 1991, Delta Tau Delta Disting. Svc. Chpt., 1970. Mem. NATAS (bd. govs. 1966-76, Silver Circle award 1993), Nat. Press Found. (bd. dirs. 1991—), Nat. Assn. Broadcasters (bd. dirs. 1952-56), Fed. Comm. Bar Assn., Broadcast Music Inc. (bd. dirs. 1953-70), Assn. Maximum Svc. Telecasters Inc. (bd. dirs. 1952-72), Broadcast Pioneers (pres., bd. dirs. 1962-73), Broadcast Pioneers Libr. (pres. 1981-84), Broadcast Pioneers Ednl. Fund Inc., Am. Advt. Fedn. (ethics com.), Delta Tau Delta (Alumni Achievement award 1990, disting. svc. chpt.), The George Town Club (Washington), Mid-Am. Club, Exmoor Country Club (Chgo.). Office: Ward L Quaal Co 401 N Michigan Ave Ste 3140 Chicago IL 60611-4207

QUACKENBUSH, CATHY ELIZABETH, secondary school educator; b. Carthage, N.Y., Sept. 20, 1949; d. James Adrian and Miriam June (Fickes) Seaman; m. Roger E. Quackenbush, March 31, 1973; 1 child, Thomas Bradford. AAS, SUNY, Morrisville, 1969; BS, SUNY, Albany, 1971, MS, 1976; attended, U. Ga., 1978, Cornell U., 1984, U. Calif., 1986, SUNY, Albany, 1986-87. Cert. tchr., N.Y. Tchr., 7th grade sci. Bethlehem Ctrl. Middle Sch., Delmar, N.Y., 1971-92; tchr., biology Bethlehem Ctrl. High Sch., Delmar, N.Y., 1992—; bd. dirs. Bethlehem Opportunities Unlimited-Corp. for Substance Abuse Prevention, Delmar, 1983-91, 95; organizer and co-adv. Bethlehem Ctrl. Leadership Club, 1985-89; chair Middle Sch. Final Assessment Com., 1990-91, Middle Sch. Restructuring Com., 1991-92; organizer and leader Student Ednl. Tours to Kenya, East Africa, 1985, 89, 91, 94; rater and question writer for N.Y. State Regents Competency Exam in Sci., N.Y. State Edn. Dept., Albany, 1990-92. Sunday sch. tchr. Bethany Reformed Ch., 1988-92. N.Y. State Environ. Coun. and N.Y. State Outdoor Edn. Assn. grantee N.Y. State Outdoor Edn. Inst., 1979, NSF grantee DNA Inst. for Middle Sch. Tchrs., 1990, Human Genetics and Bioethics grantee Greenwall Found., 1993, Molecular Biology for Tchrs. grantee Howard Hughes Med. Inst., 1993, co-inst., 1994, 95. Mem. Delta Kappa Gamma Soc. (sec. 1987-90, 2d v.p. 1990-92). Avocations: traveling, sailing. Home: 25 Robinhood Rd Albany NY 12203-5133 Office: Bethlehem Ctrl High Sch 700 Delaware Ave Delmar NY 12054-2436

QUACKENBUSH, JUSTIN LOWE, federal judge; b. Spokane, Wash., Oct. 3, 1929; s. Carl Clifford and Marian Huldah (Lowe) Q.; m. Marie McAtee; children: Karl Justin, Kathleen Marie, Robert Craig. BA, U. Idaho, 1951; LLB, Gonzaga U., Spokane, 1957. Bar: Wash. 1957. Dep. pros. atty. Spokane County, 1957-59; ptnr. Quackenbush, Dean, Bailey & Henderson, Spokane, 1959-80; dist. judge U.S. Dist. Ct. (ea. dist.) Wash., Spokane, 1980—, now sr. judge; part-time instr. Gonzaga U. Law Sch., 1960-67. Chmn. Spokane County Planning Commn., 1969-73. Served with USN, 1951-54. Mem. ABA, Wash. Bar Assn., Spokane County Bar Assn. (trustee 1976-78), Internat. Footprint Assn. (nat. pres. 1967), Spokane C. of C. (trustee, exec. com. 1978-79). Episcopalian. Club: Spokane Country. Lodge: Shriners. Office: US Dist Ct PO Box 1432 Spokane WA 99210-1432

QUACKENBUSH, MARGERY CLOUSER, psychoanalyst, administrator; b. Reading, Pa., Apr. 30, 1938; d. Carl Brumbach and Katherine Elvina (Althouse) Clouser; m. Robert Mead Quackenbush, July 3, 1971; 1 child, Piet Robert. BA, Pratt Inst., 1960; MA, Calif. Grad. Inst., 1982. Cert. in psychoanalysis Ctr. for Modern Psychoanalytic Studies. Instr. Pratt Inst., Bklyn., 1978-79, Fash. Inst. of Tech., N.Y.C., 1980-81; counselor Wiltwyck, Bronx Ctr., 1981-82; adminstr. Nat. Assn. for Advancement of Psychoanalysis, N.Y.C., 1982—; pvt. practice in psychoanalysis N.Y.C., 1980—. Mem. Lenox Hill Dem. Club, N.Y.C., 1993-95; spkr. various community groups, 1991-95. Recipient Maison Blanche award, 1959, Miriam Berkman Spotnitz award, 1992. Mem. Nat. Assn. for Advancement of Psychoanalysis, Nat. Soc. DAR, Alumni Assn. of the Ctr. for Modern Psych. Studies (sec. 1992-94, Alumni Assn. program dir., v.p. 1995-96). Democrat. Avocations: reading, writing, golf, horseback riding. Home: 460 E 79th St #14E New York NY 10021 Office: Nat Assn Advancement Psychoanalysis 80 8th Ave #1501 New York NY 10011

QUACKENBUSH, ROBERT DEAN, management consultant; b. Lansing, Mich., Oct. 12, 1947; s. Gerald G. and Margaret Lee (McLean) Q.; m. Donna Jean Cleary, Aug. 4, 1976; children: Dana McLean, Grant Robert. BA, Elmhurst Coll., 1969; postgrad., John Marshall Law Sch., 1969, 71. Mgmt. cons. Nineveh, Pa., 1982—; instr. Washington and Jefferson Coll., 1982-85. Author: Lake Lauzon, 1991. With U.S. Army, 1970-71, Vietnam. Mem. Anawana Club. Avocations: fishing, snorkeling, travel. Home and Office: PO Box 14 Nineveh PA 15353-0014

QUACKENBUSH, ROBERT MEAD, artist, author, psychoanalyst; b. Hollywood, Calif., July 23, 1929; s. Roy Maynard and Virginia (Arbogast) Q.; m. Margery Clouser, July 3, 1971; 1 child: Piet Robert. Bachelor Profl. Arts, Art Ctr. Coll. of Design, Pasadena, Calif., 1956; grad., Ctr. Modern Psychoanalytic Studies, N.Y.C., 1991; MSW, Fordham U., 1994. Art dir. Scandinavian Airlines System, N.Y.C. and Stockholm, 1956-61; pvt. practice N.Y.C., 1961—; psychoanalyst New Hope Guild Ctrs. for Emotionally Disturbed Children, Bklyn., 1994—; educator Robert Quackenbush Studios, N.Y.C.; lectr. U.S., Europe, Middle East and South Am.; TV performer Ednl. TV; mem. faculty N.J. Ctr. for Modern Psychoanalysis. Author/artist over 160 books for young readers including Old MacDonald Had A Farm, 1972, Clementine, 1974, There'll Be a Hot Time in the Old Town Tonight, 1974, Pop! Goes the Weasel and Yankee Doodle, 1976, The Holiday Song Book, 1977, Along Came the Model T! How Henry Ford Put the World on Wheels, 1978, Who Threw That Pie?, The Birth of Comedy Movie, 1979, Henry's Awful Mistake, 1980, Piet Potter's First Case, 1980, The Boy Who Waited for Santa Claus, 1981, Detective Mole Mystery Series (winner Edgar Allen Poe Spl. award 1982), Henry's Important Date, 1981, No Mouse for Me, 1981, Here a Plant, There a Plant, Everywhere a Plant, Plant! The Story of Luther Burbank, 1982, Henry Babysits, 1983, I Don't Want to Go, I Don't Know How to Act, 1983, Taxi to Intrigue, 1984, Who Said There's No Man on the Moon? The Story of Jules Verne, 1985, Who Let Muddy Boots into the House? The Story of Andrew Jackson, 1986, Mouse Feathers, 1988, Danger in Tibet, 1989, Robert Quackenbush's Treasury of Humor, 1990, Benjamin Franklin and His Friends, 1991, Evil Under the Sean, 1992, James Madison & Dolly Madison and Their Times, 1993, Arthur Ashe and His Match with History, 1994, Clara Barton and Her Victory Over Fear, 1994; prodr.: TV series Dear Mr. Quackenbush and The Great American Storybook for Educational Television; films include American Songfest, 1978. With U.S. Army 1951-53. Recipient 2 Citations for outstanding Troop Info. & Edn. instrn. from commdg. gen. 31st Inf. Divsn. 1953, 3 time winner Am. Flag Inst. award for outstanding contbn. to field of children's lit., 1976, 77, 81, Edgar Allen Poe Spl. award, 1982. Mem. Mystery Writers of Am., Authors' Guild, Authors' League of Am., Holland Soc. of N.Y., Nat. Assn. for Advancement of Psychoanalysis (trustee, v.p. pub. rels., founder Gradiva awards), Soc. Modern Psychoanalysts (cert.). Avocations: travel, antique restoration. Home: 460 E 79th St Apt 14E New York NY 10021-1445 Office: Robert Quackenbush Studios 223 E 78th St New York NY 10021-1222 *Humor became a key to survival in my family when I was growing up during the depression and World War II. Thus humor became the keynote of all the books I wrote - I want young readers to know that as long as we keep our sense of humor, our spirits cannot be crushed.*

QUACKENBUSH, ROGER E., retired secondary school educator; b. Cooperstown, N.Y., Jan. 22, 1940; s. Eugene W. and Marion I. (Clark) Q.; m. Cathy E. Quackenbush, Mar. 31, 1973; children: Michele, Stacey, Thomas. BS, SUNY, Albany, 1961, MS, 1966; PhD, Columbia Pacific U., San Rafael, Calif., 1984; postgrad., numerous univs. Cert. permanent biology and gen. sci. tchr., N.Y. Tchr. gen. sci. and math Troy (N.Y.) Pub. Sch. System, 1961-64; tchr. earth sci. and biology Schuylerville (N.Y.) Cen. H.S., 1964-66; tchr. biology Bethlehem Cen. H.S., Delmar, N.Y., 1966-95; cons. advanced placement biology Niskayuna (N.Y.) H.S., 1995-96; mentor student tchrs., 1968-90; instr. Tchr. Expectation Student Achievement program, 1985-91; lectr. on marine mammals SUNY, Albany, 1986; instr. DNA Sci. and Tech. for high sch. students SUNY, Albany, 1996; lectr. on whales; workshop leader on use microcomputers in classroom; mem. Mid States Commn. on Evaluation Local High Schs.; past mem. adv. bd. Upstate N.Y. Jr. Sci. and Humanities Symposium; test writer Regents biology exams. N.Y. State Dept. Edn.; presenter/cons. N.Y. State Edn. Dept. alt. assessment writer's workshop, 1994; leader, naturalist for whale watch trips and Kenya safaris; workshop presenter for DNA-molecular biology lab. techniques; workshop presenter on the use of the Tex. Instruments calculator and the Calculator Based Lab. sys. in the sci. classroom; mem. Select Seminar on Evaluating Tchrs., 1985; mem. Wells Conf. Regents Biology Syllabus Revision, 1991. Editor/writer of alternative assessments for N.Y. State Edn. Dept., 1993-94; contbr. numerous articles to profl. jours.; author: Swahili Phrasebook, 1993. Hon. admisssions liaison officer USAF Acad., 1988. Recipient Excellence in Tchg. award, 1989, letter of commendation U. Chgo., 1978, MIT, 1985, U.S. Army, 1989, Tufts U., 1990, 94, Tchr. of Yr. award, Tufts U., 1985, Golub Tchr.-Scholar award SUNY, 1991, 96; Chpt. II grantee N.Y. State Dept. Edn., 1987, NSF grantee, 1965, 67, 68, 72, 87, 90, Future Directions, 1990, Greenwall Found., 1993, hon. mention Tandy Tech. Scholar award, 1994, Tandy Tech. Scholar prize for excellence in sci. tchg., 1995, Outstanding Tchr award U. Chgo., 1995; named Hon. Grad. Marshal, 1991, 94, hon. N.Y. State Biology Mentor, 1995. Mem. NEA, Nat. Assn. Biology Tchrs., BALSA, Soc. Marine Mammalogy, Am. Cetacean Soc., Cetacean Soc. Internat., Sci. Tchrs. Assn. N.Y. State (past sect. dir., past state bd. dirs.), NEA of N.Y., Phi Delta Kappa. Home: 25 Robinhood Rd Albany NY 12203-5133

QUADE, QUENTIN LON, political science educator; b. Ft. Dodge, Ia., Jan. 28, 1933; s. Louis Anton and Vera (Chrisman) Q.; m. Phyllis F. Fleskes, Jan. 2, 1954; children: Zachary, Christopher, Matthew, Stephanie, Leslie. B.S., Creighton U., 1957; M.A., Notre Dame U., 1958, Ph.D., 1965. Instr. polit. sci. St. Louis U., 1959-61; faculty polit. sci. Marquette U., Milw., 1961—, prof., 1968—, Raynor prof. polit. sci., 1991—, dean Grad. Sch., 1968, assoc. acad. v.p., grad. dean, 1970-72, acad. v.p., 1972-74, exec. v.p., 1974-90; dir. Ctr. for Parental Freedom in Edn., 1992—. Author: U.S. and Wars of National Liberation, 1966, (with T.J. Bennett) American Politics: Responsible and Efffective?, 1969, Pope and Revolution, 1982, Paths to Parental Freedom and School Choice, 1995, Financing Education: The Struggle Between Governmental Monopoly and Parental Freedom, 1996. Served with USAF, 1950-53. Roman Catholic. Home: 7326 Maple Ter Milwaukee WI 53213-3153 Office: 615 N 11th St Milwaukee WI 53233-2305 *Love the truth. Know the good. Do it.*

QUADE, VICTORIA CATHERINE, editor, writer; b. Chgo., Aug. 15, 1953; d. Victor and Virginia (Uryasz) Q.; m. Charles J. White III, Feb. 15, 1986; children: Michael, David, Catherine. BS in Journalism, No. Ill. U., 1974. Staff reporter news divsn. The News-Tribune, LaSalle, Ill., 1975-77; staff writer news divsn. The News-Sun, Waukegan, Ill., 1977-81; staff writer ABA Jour., Chgo., 1981-85; mng. editor ABA Press, Chgo., 1985-90, editor, 1990—, sr. editor, 1994—. Author: Rain and Other Poems, 1976, Laughing Eyes, 1979, Two Under the Covers, 1981; co-author: (plays) (with Maripat Donovan) Late Nite Catechism: Saints, Sisters & Ejaculation, 1993, Room for Advancement, 1994; editor Human Rights mag.; contbr. to numerous anthologies and publs. Recipient numerous awards from Soc. Nat. Assn. Publs., AP, UPI. Mem. Am. Soc. Bus. Press Editors (award), Chgo. Newspaper Guild (award), Am. Soc. Assn. Execs. (Gold Circle award 1989, 90). Avocations: traveling, photography. Office: ABA 750 N Lake Shore Dr Chicago IL 60611-4403

QUADRACCI, HARRY V., printing company executive, lawyer; b. 1936. JD, Columbia U., 1959. Assoc. N.Y.C., Milw., 1961-71; corp. counsel W.A. Krueger Co., Brookfield, Wis., 1961-71; pres. Quad Graphics, Inc., Pewaukee, Wis., 1971—. Office: Quad Graphics Inc W224 N3322 Duplainville Rd Pewaukee WI 53072-4137*

QUADT, RAYMOND ADOLPH, metallurgist, cement company executive; b. Perth Amboy, N.J., Apr. 16, 1916; s. Adolph and Florence (MacCracken) Q.; 1 child, Brian. B.S., Rutgers U., 1939; M.A., Columbia U., 1943; M.S., Stevens Inst. Tech., 1948. Tchr. high sch. Plainfield, N.J., 1939-42; research metallurgist Am. Smelting & Refining Co., Barber, N.J., 1942-48; dir. aluminum devel. Am. Smelting & Refining Co., 1948-50; v.p. Hunter Douglas Corp., Riverside, Calif., 1950-57; v.p. research and devel. Bridgeport Brass Co., 1958-60, v.p. spl. metals, 1962-63; v.p. Nat. Distillers and Chem. Corp., N.Y.C., 1963—; chmn. bd. Loud Co., Pomona, Calif., 1963—; pres., gen. mgr. Reactive Metals Inc., 1960-62; v.p., gen. mgr. Pascoe Steel Corp., Pomona, 1965-73; pres. Phoenix Cement Co., 1973-80, cons., 1980-83; chmn. bd. Trendex, Inc., Phoenix, 1983-87, Mesco, Phoenix, 1983-88; vice chmn. Sunstate Bancshares Inc., Casa Grande, Ariz., 1982; bd. dirs. Republic Nat. Bank, Phoenix, 1982—; chmn. Express Delivery, Phoenix, 1991-94, Mariah Internat., Inc., Phoenix, 1992-93; v.p., sec. Ariz. Custom Motorcoaches, Mesa, Ariz., 1995—. Mem. Am. Soc. Metals, Pomona C. of C. (pres. 1970), Phi Beta Kappa. Home and Office: 6454 S Willow Dr Tempe AZ 85283-3968

QUAID, DENNIS, actor; b. Houston, Apr. 9, 1954; s. William Rudy and Juanita B. Q.; m. Meg Ryan, 1991; 1 child, Jack Henry. Student, U. Houston, 1972-75. Appearances include (film) Crazy Mama, 1975, I Never Promised You A Rosegarden, 1977, Sept. 30, 1955, 1978, Our Winning Season, 1978, The Seniors, 1978, Breaking Away, 1979, G.O.R.P., 1980, The Long Riders, 1980, Caveman, 1981, All Night Long, 1981, The Night the Lights Went Out in Georgia, 1981, Tough Enough, 1983, Jaws 3-D, 1983, The Right Stuff, 1983, Dreamscape, 1984, Enemy Mine, 1986, Innerspace, 1987, The BigEasy, 1987, Suspect, 1987, D.O.A., 1988, Everybody's All-American, 1988, Great Balls of Fire, 1989, Postcards from the Edge, 1990, Come See the Paradise, 1990, Undercover Blues, 1993, Wilder Napalm, 1993, Flesh and Bone, 1993, Wyatt Earp, 1994; (theatre) The Last of the Knucklemen, 1983, True West, 1984, (TV movies) Are You In the House Alone?, 1978, Amateur Night at the Dixie Bar and Grill, 1979, Bill, 1981, Johnny Belinda, 1982, Bill: On His Own, 1983, Wyatt Earp, 1994, Something to Talk About, 1995, Dragonheart, 1996. *An artist must take chances in* *performing his craft. If he is to succeed he must be willing to fall flat on his face.**

QUAID, RANDY, actor; b. Houston, Oct. 1, 1950; s. William R. and Juanita B. Quaid; m. Ella Marie Jolly, May 11, 1980 (div.); 1 child. Student, Houston Baptist Coll., 1969-70, U. Houston, 1970-71. Film appearances include Targets, 1968, The Last Picture Show, 1971, What's Up Doc, 1972, Lolly Madonna XXX, 1972, The Last Detail, 1973 (Acad. award, Golden Globe nominations for best supporting actor), Paper Moon, 1973, Apprenticeship of Duddy Kravitz, 1974, Breakout, 1974, Missouri Breaks, 1975, Bound for Glory, 1976, The Choirboys, 1977, Three Warriors, 1978, Midnight Express, 1979, Foxes, 1980, Long Riders, 1980, Heart Beeps, 1981, National Lampoon's Vacation, 1983, The Wild Life, 1984, The Slugger's Wife, 1985, Fool for Love, 1986, The Wraith, 1986, Caddyshack II, 1988, Moving, 1988, Parents, 1989, Out Cold, 1989, Blood Hounds of Broadway, 1989, National Lampoon's Christmas Vacation, 1989, Quick Change, 1990, Martians Go Home, 1990, Days of Thunder, 1990, Quick Change, 1990, Texasville, 1990, Freaked, 1993, The Paper, 1994, Bye Bye, Love, 1995; appeared in TV films Getting Away From It All, 1972, The Great Niagara, 1974, The Last Ride of the Dalton Gang, 1979, To Race the Wind, 1980, Guayana Tragedy: The Story of Jim Jones, 1980, Of Mice and Men, 1981, Inside the Third Reich, 1982, Cowboy, 1983, A Street Car Named Desire, 1984, LBJ: The Early Years, 1986, Dead Solid Perfect, 1988, Evil in Clear River, 1988, Murder in the Heartland, 1993, Frankenstein, 1993, Next Door, 1994; TV series Saturday Night Live, 1985-87, Davis Rules, 1991-92; off-Broadway play True West, 1983. Mem. Acad. Motion Picture Arts and Scis. *

QUAIFE, MARJORIE CLIFT, nursing educator; b. Syracuse, N.Y., Aug. 21. Diploma in Nursing with honors, Auburn Meml. Hosp; BS, Columbia U., 1962, MA, 1978. Cert. orthopaedic nurse; cert. in nursing continuing edn. and staff devel.; BLS instr. Staff instr. Columbia Presbyn. Hosp., N.Y.C.; content expert for computer assisted instrn. program-ctrl. venous catheters. Contbr. articles to numerous profl. publs. Mem. ANA, N.Y. State Nurses Assn., Nat. Assn. Orthopaedic Nurses, Nat. Assn. Nursing Staff Devel., Nat. Assn. Vascular Access Networks, Intravenous Nurses Soc., Sigma Theta Tau.

QUAIL, BEVERLY J., lawyer; b. Glendale, Calif., June 19, 1949; d. John Henry and Dorothy Marie (Sanblom) Q.; m. Timothy D. Roble; children: Benjamin W., Elizabeth L. BA magna cum laude, U. So. Calif., 1971; JD, U. Denver, 1974. Bar: Colo. 1974. Dir. Dufford & Brown, P.C., Denver, 1975—; broker Colo. Assn. Realtors, 1982—; lectr. continuing legal edn. Colo.; v.p., bd. mem. Girls Club Denver, 1984-87; bd. dirs. Swedish Hosp. Found., Legal Aid of Colo. Found., Central City Opera House Assn. Mem. ABA (chmn. real property litigation and dispute resolution com., coun. real property, probate & trust sect. 1990-95, co-chair membership com. 1993-95, sec. 95—), Am. Coll. Real Estate Lawyers (bd. govs. 1990-95, treas. 95—), Colo. Real Estate Council, Cen. City Opera House Assn., Phi Beta Kappa. Clubs: Univ. (coms.), Castle Pines Golf, Cherry Hills Country (Denver). Author Colo. Real Estate Forms-Practice, Real Property Practice & Litigation; editor newsletter The Colo. Lawyer, 1983-87; contbr. articles to profl. jours. Office: Ballard Spahr Andrews & Ingussel 1225 17th St Ste 2300 Denver CO 80202-5523

QUAIN, MITCHELL I., investment executive; b. N.Y.C., Nov. 15, 1951; m. Cherie Quain; children: Sam, Rhonda, Jacob, Samuel, Michelle. BSEE, U. Pa., 1973; MBA, Harvard U., 1975. CFA. Mng. dir., head equity capital markets Schroder Wertheim & Co., N.Y.C., 1975—; bd. dirs. Allied Products Corp., Mech. Dynamics, Inc., Strategic Distbn., Inc. Mem. bd. overseers Sch. Engring. & Applied Scis., U. Pa.; trustee St. Lukes Acad. Office: Schroder Wertheim and Co 787 7th Ave New York NY 10019-6018

QUAINTANCE, ROBERT FORSYTH, JR., lawyer; b. Evanston, Ill., Apr. 22, 1950. BA, Amherst Coll., 1972; JD, NYU, 1977. Bar: Vt., 1977, N.Y. 1980. Clk. Vt. Supreme Ct., 1977-78; instr. NYU Sch. Law, 1978-80; assoc. Debevoise & Plimpton, N.Y.C., 1980-87; ptnr. Debevoise & Plimpton, 1987—; lectr. in field. Contbr. articles to profl. jours. Mem. Assn. of Bar of City of N.Y. Office: Debevoise & Plimpton 875 3rd Ave New York NY 10022-6225*

QUAINTON, ANTHONY CECIL EDEN, diplomat; b. Seattle, Apr. 4, 1934; s. Cecil Eden and Marjorie Josephine (Oates) Q.; m. Susan Long, Aug. 7, 1958; children: Katherine, Eden, Elizabeth. B.A., Princeton U., 1955; B.Litt., Oxford (Eng.) U., 1958. Research fellow St. Antony's Coll., Oxford, 1958-59; with Fgn. Service, State Dept., 1959—; vice consul Sydney, Australia, 1960-62; Urdu lang. trainee, 1962-63; 2d sec., econ. officer Am. embassy, Karachi, Pakistan, 1963-64, Rawalpindi, Pakistan, 1964-66; 2d sec., polit. officer Am. embassy, New Delhi, 1966-69; sr. polit. officer for India Dept. State, Washington, 1969-72; 1st sec. Am. embassy, Paris, 1972-73; counselor, dep. chief mission Am. embassy, Kathmandu, Nepal, 1973-76; ambassador to Central African Empire, Bangui, 1976-78, Nicaragua, Managua, 1982-84, Kuwait, 1984-87; dir. Office for Combatting Terrorism, Dept. State, Washington, 1978-81; dep. insp. gen. Dept. State, 1987-89; ambassador Peru, 1989-92; asst. sec. of state for diplomatic security Dept. State, Washington, 1992-95, dir. gen. fgn. svc., 1995—. English Speaking Union fellow, 1951-52; Marshall scholar, 1955-58; recipient Rivkin award, 1972, Herter award, 1984. Mem. Am. Fgn. Svc. Assn., Lions Internat., Met. Club, Phi Beta Kappa. Home: 3424 Porter St NW Washington DC 20016-3126 Office: Dept State M/DGP Rm 6218 2201 C St NW Washington DC 20520-0001

QUALE, ANDREW CHRISTOPHER, JR., lawyer; b. Boston, July 7, 1942; s. Andrew Christopher and Luella (Meland) Q.; m. Sally Sterling Ellis, Oct. 15, 1977; children: Andrew, Addison. BA magna cum laude, Harvard U., 1963, LLB cum laude, 1966; postgrad., Cambridge (Eng.) U., 1966-67. Bar: Mass. 1967, N.Y. 1971. Fellow Internat. Legal Ctr., Bogota, Colombia, 1967-68; cons. Republic of Colombia, Bogota, 1968-69; assoc. Cleary, Gottlieb, Steen and Hamilton, N.Y.C., 1969-75; ptnr. Coudert Brothers, N.Y.C., 1975-82, Sidley and Austin, N.Y.C., 1982—; bd. dirs. Den Danske Corp.; adj. prof. Sch. of Law U. Va., Charlottesville, 1976-88; cons. privatizations World Bank, UN, Harvard Inst. Internat. Devel., 1982—. Contbr. to profl. publs. Pres. Bronxville (N.Y.) Sch. Bd., 1991-93; founder bd. dirs. Bronxville Sch. Found., 1991-95. Mem. ABA, Assn. Bar City N.Y., N.Y. State Bar Assn., N.Y.C. Bar Assn. (chmn. Inter-Am. affairs com. 1982-85), Bronxville Field Club, Norfolk (Conn.) Country Club, Doolittle Club (Norfolk). Office: Sidley & Austin 875 3d Ave New York NY 10022

QUALE, JOHN CARTER, lawyer; b. Boston, Aug. 16, 1946; s. Andrew C. and Luella (Meland) Q.; m. Diane Zipursky, Jan. 19, 1992; children: Virginia Ann, Jane Harris, John Andrew. AB cum laude, Harvard Coll., 1968, JD cum laude, 1971. Bar: Mass. 1971, D.C. 1972. Assoc. Kirkland & Ellis, Washington, 1971-78, ptnr., 1978-83; ptnr. Wiley, Rein & Fielding, Washington, 1983—; Speaker mass media trade groups. Contbr. articles to profl. jours. Trustee Fed. Comm. Bar Assn. Found., 1992-93. Mem. ABA, Fed. Comm. Bar Assn. (treas. 1982-83, exec. com. 1993—), Barristers, Met. Club. Office: Wiley Rein & Fielding 1776 K St NW Washington DC 20006-2304

QUALLEY, CHARLES ALBERT, fine arts educator; b. Creston, Iowa, Mar. 19, 1930; s. Albert Olaf and Cleora (Dietrick) Q.; m. Betty Jean Griffith, Nov. 26, 1954; children: Janet Lynn, John Stuart. B.F.A., Drake U., 1952; M.A., U. Iowa, 1956, M.F.A., 1958; Ed.D., Ill. State U., 1967. Art tchr. Des Moines Pub. Schs., 1952,, 54-55; critic art tchr. U. Iowa, 1955-57; prof. fine arts U. Colo., Boulder, 1958-90, prof. emeritus, 1990—; chmn. dept. fine arts U. Colo., 1968-71, assoc. chmn., 1981-82; vis. prof. Inst. for Shipboard Edn., semester at sea, 1979, Ill. State U., 1985. Author: Safety in the Art Room, 1986; contbg. editor Sch. Arts, 1978-85, mem. editorial adv. bd., 1985-87; author column Safetypoint, 1981-85. Served with AUS, 1952-54, Korea. Mem. Nat. Art Edn. Assn. (v.p. 1980-82, pres. 1987-89, dir. conv. svcs. 1990—, fellow 1990—, Art Educator of Yr. 1993), Nat. Art Edn. Found. (trustee 1987—, chair bd. trustees 1996—), Colo. Art Edn. Assn. (editor 1965-67, 75, pres. 1976-78), Delta Phi Delta, Omicron Delta Kappa, Pi Kappa Delta. Home: 409 Fillmore Ct Louisville CO 80027-2273

QUALLS, JUNE CAROL, elementary education educator; b. Ft. Worth, June 22, 1954; d. Earl Clayton and Viola Maurine (McFaul) Irvin; m. Richard Eugene Qualls, Apr. 20, 1984. BS, Tarleton State Coll., 1976; MEd, East Tex. State U., 1979, cert. in spl. edn., 1992, cert. in edml. diagnostics, 1993. Cert. elem. tchr., Tex. Tchr. kindergarten Elisha M. Pease Elem. Sch., Dallas, 1979-80, 87-91, Mt. Auburn Elem. Sch., Dallas, 1983-84; tchr. jr. high sch. Maypearl (Tex.) Ind. Sch. Dist., 1980-83; edn. specialist Alaska Headstart-Rural Cap, Anchorage, 1984-85; multi-level tchr. Tom Thumb Montessori Sch., Anchorage, 1985-87; tchr. 2d grade John Neely Bryan Elem. Sch., Dallas, 1991-92; tchr. kindergarten, chairperson kindergarten John Q. Adams Elem. Sch., Dallas, 1993-94, mentor tchr., 1993-94; tchr. spl. edn. resource/content mastery, 1995-96; mentor tchr. Elisha M. Pease Elem. Sch., 1989-90; math. coord. Maypearl Jr. H.S., 1980-83. Contbg. writer curriculum materials for gifted edn. Mem. Internat. Reading Assn., ASCD, Alliance Dallas Educator, Tex. State Reading Assn., Ellis County Reading Assn., Parent-Tchr. Orgn., Nat. Parks and Conservation Assn., Greenpeace. Avocations: scuba diving, camping, archaelogical interests. Office: Dallas Ind Sch Dist JQ Adams Elem Sch 8329 Lake June Rd Dallas TX 75217-2169

QUALLS, ROBERT L., manufacturing executive, banker, former state official, educator; b. Burnsville, Miss., Nov. 6, 1933; s. Wes E. and Letha (Parker) Q.; m. Carolyn Morgan, Feb. 10, 1979; 1 dau., Stephanie Elizabeth. BS, Miss. State U., 1954, MS, 1958; PhD, La. State U., 1962; LLD, Whitworth Coll., 1974; DBA (hon.), U. of the Ozarks, 1984. Prof., chmn. div. econs. and bus. Belhaven Coll., Jackson, Miss., 1962-66; asst. to pres. Belhaven Coll., 1965-66; asst. prof. finance Miss. State U., State College, 1967-69, adj. prof., 1969-73; sr. v.p., chmn. venture com. Bank of Miss., Tupelo, 1969-73; v.p. Wesleyan Coll., Macon, Ga., 1974; pres. U. of the Ozarks, Clarksville, Ark., 1974-79; mem. cabinet Bill Clinton Gov. of Ark., 1979-80; exec. v.p. Boatmen's Bank of Ark., Little Rock, 1980-85; chmn., CEO, dir. Boatmen's, Harrison, Ark., 1985-86; pres., dir. First Bank Fin. Services, Inc., 1980-85, Advt. Assocs., Inc., 1980-85; pres., chief oper. officer Baldor Electric Co., Ft. Smith, Ark., 1986—, CEO, 1992; mktg. cons. Ill. Central Industries, Chgo., 1964; mem. faculty, thesis examiner Stonier Grad. Sch. Banking, Rutgers U., 1973-86; mem. faculty Miss. Sch. Banking, U. Miss., 1973-78; course coordinator Sch. Banking of the South, La. State U., 1978-88, Banking Sch., Duke U., 1977; lectr. Southwestern Sch. Banking, So. Meth. U., 1983; adj. prof. bus. adminstrn. U. Central Ark., 1985-86. Author: Entrepreneurial Wit and Wisdom, 1986; co-author: Strategic Planning for Colleges and Universities: A Systems Approach to Planning and Resource Allocation, 1979; mem. editorial adv. bd.: Bank Mktg. Mag., 1984-86. Chmn. cmty. svc. and continuing edn. com. Tupelo Cmty. Devel. Found., 1972-73; mem. Miss. 4-H adv. coun., 1969; active Boys Scouts Am.; mem. Lee County Dem. Exec. Com., 1973-74; trustee Wal-Mart Found., 1975-79, Oklahoma City U., 1990-95; trustee, mem. exec. com. U. Ozarks, 1982-88; mem. Pres.'s Roundtable U. Ctrl. Ark., 1982-87; mem. exec. com. Coll. Bus. Adv. Bd., U. Ark., Little Rock, 1980-85; bd. dirs. U. Ark. Med. Sch. Found., 1991—, Ark. Inst., 1991-94, Associated Industries Ark., treas., 1993-94,v.p., 1994-95. Lt. AUS, 1954-56. Found. for Econ. Edn. fellow, 1964; Ford Found. faculty research fellow Vanderbilt U., 1963-64; recipient Pillar of Progress award Johnson County, 1977. Mem. Am. Bankers Assn. (mktg. planning and rsch. com. 1972-73), Ark. Coun. Ind. Colls. and Univs. (chmn. 1978-79), Johnson County C. of C. (pres. 1977), Fort Smith C. of C. (dir. 1995—), Blue Key, Omicron Delta Kappa, Delta Sigma Pi, Sigma Phi Epsilon (citation 1977), Masons (32 deg.), Clarksville Rotary (pres. 1979). Presbyterian. Office: Baldor Electric Co 5711 S 7th St Fort Smith AR 72901-8394

QUALLS, ROXANNE, mayor of Cincinnati. Former exec. dir. Women Helping Women; former dir. No. Ky. Rape Crisis Ctr.; former dir. Cin. office Ohio Citizen Action; councilwoman City of Cin., 1991-93, mayor, 1993—; former chairperson Cin. City Council's Intergovtl. Affairs and Environment Com.; former vice chairperson Community Devel., Housing and Zoning Com.; 2d v.p. OKI Regional Coun. Govts.; mem. Gov.'s Commn. on Storage and Use of Toxic and Hazardous Materials, Solid Waste Adv. Com. of State of Ohio, Gov.'s Waste Minimization Task Force; former chair bd. commrs. Cin. Met. Housing Authority; bd. dirs. Shuttlesworth Housing Found. Hon. chair Friends of Women's Studies; mem. Jr. League Adv. Coun. Recipient Woman of Distinction award Girl Scouts U.S., 1992, Woman of Distinction award Soroptimists, 1993, Outstanding Achievement award Cin. Woman's Polit. Caucus, 1993. Office: City Hall 801 Plum St Ste 150 Cincinnati OH 45202-5704*

QUALSET, CALVIN O., agronomy educator; b. Newman Grove, Nebr., Apr. 24, 1937; s. Herman Qualset and Adeline (Hanson) Vakoc; m. Kathleen Boehler; children: Douglas, Cheryl, Gary. BS, U. Nebr., 1958; MS, U. Calif., Davis, 1960, PhD, 1964. Asst. prof. U. Tenn., Knoxville, 1964-67; from asst. prof. to assoc. prof. U. Calif., Davis, 1967, prof., 1973-94, prof. emeritus, 1994—, chmn. dept. agronomy and range sci., 1975-81, 91-94, assoc. dean coll. agrl. and environ. sci., 1981-86; dir. Genetic Resources Conservation Program, Davis, 1985—; sci, liaison officer U.S. Agy. Internat. Devel., Washington, 1985-93, mem. rsch. adv. com., 1989-92; mem. nat. plant genetic resources bd. USDA, Washington, 1982-88. Contbr. over 180 articles to profl. jours. Fulbright fellow, Australia, 1976, Yugoslavia, 1984. Fellow AAAS (chmn. agr. sect. 1992), Am. Soc. Agronomy (pres. 1994), Soc. Conservation Biology, Soc. Econ. Botany; mem. Genetic Soc. Am., Crop Sci. Soc. Am. (pres. 1989). Achievements include development of 10 cultivars of wheat, oat triticale. Office: Genetic Res Conserv Prog Univ of Calif Davis CA 95616

QUALTER, TERENCE HALL, retired political science educator; b. Eltham, New Zealand, Apr. 15, 1925; emigrated to Can., 1957; s. Michael Frederick and Mary (Hall) Q.; m. Shirley Anne Card, May 19, 1951; children: Karen Anne, Matthew John, Paul Michael, Adam James. B.A., U. New Zealand, 1951; Ph.D., U. London-London Sch. Econs., 1956. Newscaster New Zealand Broadcasting Service, Wellington, 1948-51; various positions London, 1951-57; lectr. United Coll., Winnipeg, Man., Can., 1957-58; spl. lectr. U. Sask., Can., 1958-60; lectr. polit. sci. U. Waterloo, Ont., Can., 1960-61; asst. prof. polit. sci. U. Waterloo, 1961-64, assoc. prof., 1964-67, prof. polit. sci., 1967—, chmn. dept. polit. sci., 1965-67, 70-73. Author: Propaganda and Psychological Warfare, 1962, The Election Process in Canada, 1970, Graham Wallas and the Great Society, 1980, Opinion Control in the Democracies, 1985, Conflicting Political Ideas in Liberal Democracies, 1986, Advertising and Democracy in the Mass Age, 1991. Served with Royal New Zealand Air Force, 1944-47. Grantee Can. Council, NRC Can., Social Sci. and Humanities Research Council Can. Home: 249 Stonybrook Dr, Kitchener, ON Canada

QUANDT, RICHARD EMERIC, economics educator; b. Budapest, Hungary, June 1, 1930; came to U.S., 1949, naturalized, 1954; s. Richard F. and Elisabeth (Toth) Q.; m. Jean H. Briggs, Aug. 6, 1955; 1 son, Stephen. BA, Princeton U., 1952; MA, Harvard U., 1955, PhD, 1957; Dr. Econs. (hon.), Budapest U. Econs. Scis., 1991, Kossuth Lajos U., Hungary, 1994, Gödöllö Agrl. U., 1995. Mem. faculty Princeton U., 1956—, prof. econs., 1964-95, prof. emeritus, sr. rsch. economist, 1995—, Hughes-Rogers prof. econs., 1976-95; prof. emeritus, 1995—; chmn. dept. Princeton U., 1968-71, 85-88; dir. Fin. Rsch. Ctr., 1982—; rsch. prof. Ford Found., 1967-68; prof. emeritus, sr. rsch. economist Princeton U., 1995—; cons. Alderson Assocs., 1959-61; sr. cons. Mathematica, Inc., 1961-67; cons. Internat. Air Transport Assn., 1974-75, N.Y. Stock Exch., 1976-77, N.Y. State Dept. Edn., 1978; adviser Am.-Hungarian Found., 1977-78; editorial advisor Holt, Rinehart & Winston, 1968-72; fin. adviser Inst. for Rsch. in History, 1986; sr. advisor Andrew W. Mellon Found., 1989—; mem. adv. coun. Budapest U. Econ. Scis., 1992-93; vis. prof. Birkbeck Coll., 1981, U. Leicester, 1989-92; mem. Census Adv. Com., 1983-86; mem. adv. com. Coll. Fin. and Acctg., Budapest, 1993-94. Author: (with J. M. Henderson) Microeconomic Theory: A Mathematical Approach, 1958, 2d edit., 1971, 3d edit., 1980, (with W.L. Thorp) The New Inflation, 1959, (with B.G. Malkiel) Strategies and Rational Decisions in the Securities Option Market, 1969; editor: The Demand for Travel: Theory and Measurement, 1970; (with S.M. Goldfeld) Nonlinear Methods in Econometrics, 1972, Studies in Nonlinear Estimation, 1976; (with P. Asch) Racetrack Betting: The Professor's Guide to Strategies, 1986, (with M. Peston) Prices, Competition and Equilibrium, 1986, The Econometrics of Disequilibrium, 1988, (with H.S. Rosen) The Conflict Between Equilibrium and Disequilibrium Theories, 1988; also numerous articles; editorial bd.: Applied Econs., Econs. of Planning, Rev. Econ. and Stats., 1980-91; assoc. editor: Econometrica, 1976-80, Jour. Am. Statis. Assn, 1974-80, Bell Jour. Econs., Jour. of Comparative Econs., 1988-91, Empirica, 1988-93. Trustee Corvina Found., 1992—. Recipient merit citation Jagiellonian U., Poland, 1991, gold medal Eötvös Lóránd U., Budapest, 1991; Guggenheim fellow, 1958-59; McCosh fellow, 1964; NSF sr. postdoctoral fellow, 1971-72. Fellow Am. Statis. Assn., Econometric Soc. (mem. coun. 1985-88), Am. Acad. Arts and Scis.; mem. Am. Econ. Assn., Math. Programming Soc., Am. Philos. Soc., Hungarian Librs. Assn. (hon.). Home: 162 Springdale Rd Princeton NJ 08540-4948 Office: Princeton U Fin Rsch Ctr Dept Econs Princeton NJ 08544

QUANDT, WILLIAM BAUER, political scientist; b. Los Angeles, Nov. 23, 1941; s. William Carl and Dorothy Elaine (Bauer) Q.; m. Anna Spitzer, June 21, 1964 (div. 1980); m. Helena Cobban, Apr. 21, 1984; 1 child, Lorna. B.A., Stanford U., 1963; Ph.D., MIT, 1968. Researcher Rand Corp., Santa Monica, Calif., 1968-72; staff mem. Nat. Security Council, Washington, 1972-74, sr. staff mem., 1977-79; assoc. prof. U. Pa., Phila., 1974-76; sr. fellow Brookings Instn., Washington, 1979-94; prof. govt. and fgn. affairs U. Va., Charlottesville, 1994—; sr. assoc., Cambridge Energy Research Assocs., Mass., 1983—. Author: Revolution and Political Leadership: Algeria, 1954-68, The Politics of Palestinian Nationalism, 1973, Decade of Decisions, 1977, Saudi Arabia in the 1980's, 1981, Camp David: Peacemaking and Politics, 1986, The United States and Egypt, 1990, Peace Process, 1993. Social Scis. Research Council fellow, 1966; Council Fgn. Relations fellow, 1972; NDEA fellow, 1963. Mem. Council Fgn. Relations, Middle East Inst., Middle East Studies Assn. (pres. 1987-88). Avocations: tennis; travel; photography. Home: 2318 44th St NW Washington DC 20007-1101 Office: U Va Dept Govt and Fgn Affairs Cabell Hall 255 Charlottesville VA 22901

QUANT, HAROLD EDWARD, financial services company executive, rancher; b. Aug. 21, 1948; s. Harold Atwell and Dorothy Ann Quant; m. Michelle Bumpers, June 27, 1982; children: Andrew, Angela, Emily. BSBA, San Jose State U., 1976. Account exec. Dun & Bradstreet, San Jose, Calif., 1970-81; pres. Telecredit Collection Svcs., Inc., L.A., 1981-85; v.p. FCA, Arlington, Tex., 1986-90; pres., CEO Creditwatch, Inc., Arlington, 1990—, chmn. bd. dirs. Sgt. USMC, 1965-70, Vietnam. Decorated Bronze Star, Purple Heart. Mem. Century II Club. Republican. Mem. Worldwide Ch. of God. Avocation: horses. Office: Creditwatch Inc 2201 N Collins St Ste 300 Arlington TX 76011-2655

QUARCOO, MARILYNNE SMITH, school system administrator; b. Boston, Dec. 11, 1950; d. Ernest Harold and Doris Mae (Jemmotte) S.; m. Gideon Kwame Quarcoo, Mar. 26, 1978; 1 child, Esinam Dede. BA in Elem. Edn., Boston Coll., 1972, M Edn. Edn. Psych., 1974. Reading tchr. K-8 Brookline (Mass.) Pub. Sch., 1974-75, multicultural tchr., 1975-77, tchr. second grade, 1977-87; METCO dir. K-12 Wellesley (Mass.) Pub. Sch., 1987-90; elem. prin. Cabot Sch. Newton (Mass.) Pub. Schs., 1990—; staff devel. cons. Brookline, 1978-80; curriculum developer Wellesley Pub. Schs., 1990; facilitator Wheelock Coll., Boston, 1992; presenter AERA convention, 1994. Mem. NAACP; trustee Agassiz Village Campe, Waltham, Mass., 1991-94. Recipient award for racial, ethnic and religious harmony, Newton, Mass., 1994, Marion V. Thomas award. Mem. ASCD, AERA, Nat. Alliance Black Sch. Educators, Brookline Sch. Found. Avocations: travel, reading. Office: Cabot Sch 229 Cabot St Newton MA 02160-2018

QUARLES, CARROLL ADAIR, JR., physicist, educator; b. Abilene, Tex., Nov. 24, 1938; s. Carroll Adair and Marguerite Marie (Vollmers) Q.; m. Sonja Gale Bandy, May 14, 1971; children: Jennifer Anne, John Patrick. BA, Tex. Christian U., 1960; PhD, Princeton U., 1964. Rsch. physicist Brookhaven Nat. Lab., Upton, N.Y., 1964-67; mem. faculty Tex. Christian U., Ft.Worth, 1967—; assoc. prof. physics Tex. Christian U., Ft. Worth, 1970-76; prof. Tex. Christian U., Ft.Worth, 1976—; W.A. Moncrief Jr. prof. physics Tex. Christian U., 1986—; chmn. dept. physics Tex. Christian U., Ft. Worth, 1978-84, 96—; assoc. dean Coll. Arts and Scis. Tex. Christian U., Ft.Worth, 1974-78. Contbr. articles to profl. jours. Mem. AAAS, Am. Phys. Soc. (sec.-treas. Tex. sect. 1993—), Am. Assn. Physics Tchrs. (pres. Tex. sect. 1984), Sigma Xi, Phi Beta Kappa (pres. Delta of Tex. chpt. 1982-84), Alpha Chi, Pi Mu Epsilon. Roman Catholic. Office: Tex Christian U Dept Physics Fort Worth TX 76129

QUARLES, JAMES CLIV, law educator; b. Charlottesville, Va., Mar. 18, 1921; s. James Cliv and Lucy (Sinclair) Q.; m. Prudence White, Sept. 1, 1944 (dec.); children: Rebecca Wayne (Mrs. Douglas S. McLeod), James Peyton, Christopher Sinclair.; m. Audrey Clark Keeter, June 10, 1983. B.A., U. Va., 1942, LL.B., 1945. Bar: Va. 1944, Ga. 1955. Law clk. U.S. circuit judge, 1945-47; instr. law Walter F. George Sch. Law, Mercer U., 1947-48, asst. prof., 1948-49, assoc. prof., 1949-52, prof., 1952-69, acting dean, 1950-51, 56-58, dean, 1958-69; prof. law U. Fla., Gainesville, 1969—; Exec. dir. Fla. Law Revision Commn., 1969-71; chmn. research group Ga. Criminal Law Study Com., 1961-66; Mem. Gainesville Human Relations Adv. Bd., 1972-85, chmn., 1975-77, 81-83; bd. dirs. Macon Legal Aid Soc., 1956-60; mediator State Atty.'s Citizen Dispute Resolution Program, 1983—. Editor: Cases and Materials on Florida Constitutional Law, 1977; contbr. articles to legal publs. Mem. ABA; Ga. Bar Assn.; Macon Bar Assn.; Mem. Am. Law Inst., State U. System Law Faculty Assn. (pres. 1975—), Order Coif, Raven Soc., Pi Delta Epsilon. Democrat. Presbyn. Home: 9519 NW 27th Pl Gainesville FL 32606-5179

QUARLES, JAMES LINWOOD, III, lawyer; b. Huntington, W.Va., Oct. 12, 1946; s. James Linwood Jr. and Beatrice (Hardwick) Q.; m. Sharon Taft, Dec. 20, 1969; children: Jessica, Matthew. BS cum laude, Denison U., 1968; JD cum laude, Harvard U., 1972. Bar: Mass. 1974, U.S. Dist. Ct. Mass. 1975, U.S. Ct. Appeals (D.C. cir.) 1975, U.S. Ct. Appeals (6th cir.) 1979, U.S. Supreme Ct. 1980, D.C. 1981, U.S. Ct. Appeals (2d cir.) 1981, U.S. Ct. Appeals (1st and 4th cirs.) 1983, Md. 1985. Law clk. to presiding justice U.S. Dist. Ct. Md., Balt., 1972-73; with Watergate Spl. Pros. Force, Washington, 1973-75; from assoc. to sr. ptnr. Hale and Dorr, Boston and Washington, 1975—. Mem. Am. Law Inst. Democrat. Office: Hale & Dorr 1455 Pennsylvania Ave NW Washington DC 20004-1008

QUARTARARO, PHIL, recording industry executive. Pres., CEO, CHB Virgin Records Am. Inc. Office: Virgin Records Am Inc 338 N Foothill Rd Beverly Hills CA 90210-3608*

QUARTON, WILLIAM BARLOW, broadcasting company executive; b. Algona, Iowa, Mar. 27, 1903; s. William B. and Ella B. (Reaser) Q.; m. Elnora Bierkamp, Aug. 24, 1935; 1 dau., Diane (Mrs. Waldo F. Geiger). Student, U. Iowa, 1921-22, George Washington U., 1923-25. Joined radio sta. KWCR, Cedar Rapids, Iowa, 1931; comml. mgr. radio sta. WMT, 1936, gen. mgr., 1943; exec. v.p. Am. Broadcasting Stas., Inc., 1959-68, chmn., 1968-70; chmn. bd. KWMT Inc., Ft. Dodge, Iowa, 1968-88, Cable Communications Iowa, Inc., 1971-83; pres. WMT-TV, Inc., 1959-68; chmn. adv. bd. CBS-TV Affiliates, 1960; Mem. bd. Iowa Ednl. Broadcasting Network, 1967-77; bd. govs. Pub. Broadcasting Service, 1973-78. Trustee Coe Coll., 1946-78; trustee, mem. exec. com. Herbert Hoover Presdl. Library; bd. regents State Iowa, 1965-71. Mem. Cedar Rapids C. of C. (pres. 1944), Nat. Assn. Broadcasters (chmn. TV bd. 1962-63, chmn. joint bd. 1963-64). Clubs: Ft. Lauderdale Country (Fla.), Coral Ridge Yacht (Ft. Lauderdale); Cedar Rapids Country. Lodge: Rotary. Home: 134 Kyrie SE Cedar Rapids IA 52403-1712 Office: 1810 I E Tower Cedar Rapids IA 52401

QUATE, CALVIN FORREST, engineering educator; b. Baker, Nev., Dec. 7, 1923; s. Graham Shepard and Margie (Lake) Q.; m. Dorothy Marshall, June 28, 1945 (div. 1985); children: Robin, Claudia, Holly, Rhodalee; m. Arnice Streit, Jan., 1987. B.S. in Elec. Engring, U. Utah, 1944; Ph.D., Stanford U., 1950. Mem. tech. staff Bell Telephone Labs., Murray Hill, N.J., 1949-58; dir. research Sandia Corp., Albuquerque, 1959-60, v.p. research, 1960-61; prof. dept. applied physics and elec. engring. Stanford (Calif.) U., 1961—, chmn. applied physics, 1969-72, 78-81, Leland T. Edwards prof. engring., 1986—; assoc. dean Sch. Humanities and Scis., 1972-74, 82-83; sr. rsch. fellow Xerox Rsch. Ctr., Palo Alto, Calif., 1984-94. Served as lt. (j.g.) USNR, 1944-46. Recipient Rank prize for Opto-electronics, 1982, Pres.'s Nat. medal of Sci. 1992. Fellow IEEE (medal of honor 1988), Am. Acad. Arts and Scis., Acoustical Soc.; mem. NAE, NAS, Am. Phys. Soc., Royal

Microscop. Soc. (hon.), Royal Soc. (fgn. mem.), Sigma Xi, Tau Beta Pi. Office: Stanford University Dept Applied Physics Stanford CA 94305-4090

QUAY, THOMAS EMERY, lawyer; b. Cleve., Apr. 3, 1934; s. Harold Emery and Esther Ann (Thomas) Q.; divorced; children: Martha Wyndham, Glynis Cobb, Eliza Emery; m. Winnifred B. Cutler, May 13, 1989. A.B. in Humanities magna cum laude (Univ. scholar), Princeton U., 1956; LL.B. (Univ. scholar), U. Pa., 1963. Bar: Pa. 1964. Assoc. Pepper, Hamilton & Scheetz, Phila., 1963-65; with William H. Rorer, Inc., Ft. Washington, Pa., 1965—; sec., counsel William H. Rorer, Inc., 1974-79, v.p., gen. counsel, sec., 1979-88; v.p. legal planning and adminstrn. Rorer Group, 1988-90; counsel Reed Smith Shaw and McClay, Phila., 1991-93; pvt. practice, Bala Cynwyd, Pa., 1993—; v.p., gen. counsel Athena Inst., Haverford, Pa., 1995—. Bd. dirs. Main Line YMCA, Ardmore, Pa., 1971-73, chmn. bd., 1972-73; editor 10th Reunion Book Princeton Class of 1956, 1966, 25th Reunion Book, 1981—, class sec., 1966-71, class v.p., 1971-81, pres., 1981-86. Lt. (j.g.) USNR, 1957-60. Recipient Svc. Commendation Main Line YMCA, 1973. Mem. ABA, Pa. Bar Assn., Phila. Bar Assn., Pharm. Mfrs. Assn. (chmn. law sect. 1983), Pa. Biotech. Assn. (chmn. legis. com., mem. exec. com. 1991-93), Phila. Drug Exch. (chmn. legis. com. 1975-78), Cannon Club of Princeton U., Sharswood Law Club of U. Pa., Princeton Club of Phila. Democrat. Presbyterian. Home: 30 Coopertown Rd Haverford PA 19041-1013 Office: 9 Union Ave Ste 202 Bala Cynwyd PA 19004-3323

QUAYLE, J(AMES) DANFORTH, former vice president United States, entrepreneur; b. Indpls., Feb. 4, 1947; s. James C. and Corinne (Pulliam) Q.; m. Marilyn Tucker, Nov. 18, 1972; children: Tucker Danforth, Benjamin Eugene, Mary Corinne. BS in Polit. Sci., DePauw U., Greencastle, Ind., 1969; JD, Ind. U., 1974. Bar: Ind. 1974. Ct. reporter, pressman Huntington (Ind.) Herald-Press, 1965-69, assoc. pub., gen. mgr., 1974-76; mem. consumer protection div. Office Atty. Gen., State of Ind., 1970-71; adminstrv. asst. to gov. State of Ind., 1971-73; dir. Ind. Inheritance Tax Div., 1973-74; mem. 95th-96th Congresses from 4th Dist. Ind.; U.S. Senator from Ind., 1981-89, V.P. of U.S., 1989-93; author, speaker, columnist, corp. bds. $D, $D; tchr. bus. law Huntington Coll., 1975, author, speaker, columnist, corp. bds. Author: Standing Firm, 1994. Capt. Ind. Army N.G., 1970-76. Mem. Huntington Bar Assn., Hoosier State Press Assn., Huntington C. of C. Club: Rotary. Office: 11711 N Pennsylvania St 100 Carmel IN 46032

QUAYLE, MARILYN TUCKER, lawyer, wife of former vice president of United States; b. 1949; d. Warren and Mary Alice Tucker; m. J. Danforth Quayle, Nov. 18, 1972; children: Tucker, Benjamin, Corinne. BA in Polit. Sci., Purdue U., 1971; JD, Ind. U., 1974. Pvt. practice atty. Huntington, Ind., 1974-77; ptnr. Krieg, DeVault, Alexander & Capehart, Indpls., 1993—. Author: (with Nancy T. Northcott) Embrace the Serpent, 1992, The Campaign, 1996. Office: Krieg DeVault Alexander & Capehart 1 Indiana Sq Ste 2800 Indianapolis IN 46204-2017

QUAYTMAN, HARVEY, painter; b. Far Rockaway, N.Y., 1937. Student, Syracuse U., 1955-57; BFA, Tufts U., 1959, Sch. of Mus. of Fine Arts, Boston, 1959; grad. cert., Tufts U., 1959. One-man shows include AIA Gallery, London, 1962, Ward-Nasse Gallery, Boston, 1964, Royal Marks Gallery, N.Y., 1966, Contemporary Arts Mus., Houston, 1967, 73, Paula Cooper Art Gallery, 1969, 71, Onnasch Galerie, Cologne, Germany, 1971, Galerie Ostergren, Malmo, Sweden, 1973, Henri 2, Washington, 1973, Cunningham Ward Gallery, 1974, David McKee Gallery, N.Y., 1975, 77, 78, 80, 82, 84, 86, 87, 91, 93, 94, 96, Nina Nielsen Gallery, Boston, 1976, 78, 80, 83, 86, 89, 93, 94, Galerie Arnesen, Copenhagen, Galerie Nordenhake, Stockholm, 1982, 86, 87, 90, Galerie Engstrom, Stockholm, 1982, Storrer Gallery, Zurich, 1983, Galleria Katarina, Helsinki, Finland, 1984, Dolan/Maxwell Gallery, Phila., 1987, Hoffman/Borman Gallery, L.A., 1988, Persons & Lindell Gallery, Helsinki, 1990, Gilbert Brownstone Gallery, Paris, 1990, Tony Oliver Gallery, Melbourne, Australia, 1990, Art Gallery New South Wales, Sydney, Australia, 1991, Haines Gallery, San Francisco, 1994, 95, Room NYC, 1995, Henie-Onstad Art Ctr., Oslo, 1996, Riis Gallery, Oslo, 1996, Art Soc., Trondheim, Norway, 1996; group exhbns. include Paula Cooper Gallery, 1968, 69, 70, 71, 73, The Jewish Mus., N.Y.C., 1969, Akron Art Inst., 1969, Art Inst. Chgo., 1972, Poindexter Gallery, N.Y.C., 1973, Phyllis Kind Gallery, N.Y.C., 1973, Power Gallery Contemporary Art, Sydney, 1973, Balt. Mus. Art, 1974, Albright-Knox Art Gallery, Buffalo, 1974, Inst. Contemporary Art, Boston, 1974, High Mus. Art, Atlanta, 1974, 76, PSI, Queens, N.Y., 1977, Mus. Modern Art, N.Y.C., 1978, 87-88, Nina Nielsen Gallery, Boston, 1979, 84, 90, Gallerie Schlegl, Zurich, 1979, Grand Palais, Paris, 1980, Axiom Gallery, Melbourne, 1981, Israel Mus., Jerusalem, 1982, Weatherspoon Art Gallery, Greensboro, N.C., 1982, Jersey City Mus., 1983, Galerie Norballe, Copenhagen, 1983, Harvard U., 1983, Hokkaido (Japan) Mus. Modern Art, 1984, Galerie Grafiart, Turku, Finland, 1984, Hill Gallery, Birmingham, Mich., 1985, 94, Jay Gorney Modern Art, N.Y.C., 1985, Pamela Auchincloss Gallery, Santa Barbara, Calif., 1986, Asher/Faure Gallery, L.A., 1987, Corcoran Bienvale, Washington, 1987, Ateneum, Helsinki, Finland, 1987, Dart Gallery, Chgo., 1988, Germans Van Eck Gallery, N.Y.C., 1989, Ljubjana Bienale 18, Yugoslavia, 1989, Tony Oliver Gallery, 1992, Rose Art Mus., Waltham, Mass., Ark. Art Ctr., Little Rock, Galerie Denis Cade, N.Y., 1994, Tel Aviv Mus. Art, 1994, Henie-Onstaad Ctr., Oslo, 1994, The Painting Ctr., N.Y., 1994, Bill Maynes Contemporary Art, N.Y., 1994, Haines Gallery, San Freacisco, 1994, Stephen Wirtz Gallery, 1995; public collections include Mus. Modern Art, N.Y.C., Tate Gallery, London, Whitney Mus. Am. Art, N.Y.C., Corcoran Gallery Art, Washington, Mus. Fine Arts, Boston, Henie-Onstad Mus., Oslo, Israel Mus., Jerusalem, Kuntsthalle Malmo, Sweden, Mus. Contemporary Art, Helsinki, Allen Meml. Art Mus., Oberlin, Ohio, Del. Art Mus., Wilmington, Denver Mus. Art, Fogg Art Mus., Cambridge, Mass., High Art Mus., Atlanta, Houston Mus. Fine Arts, Lannan Mus., L.A., The Lousiana Mus., Humlebaeck, Denmark, Newberger Mus., Purchase, N.Y., Nat. Gallery Art, Canberra, Australia, Nat. Gallery Art, Wellington, New Zealand, Pasadena (Calif.) Art Mus., Pori Mus., Finland, Rose Art Mus., Waltham, Mass., Tel Aviv Mus., Va. Mus. Fine Arts, Richmond, Worcester (Mass.) Mus. Art., Henie-Onstad Art Ctr., Oslo, Queensland Art Gallery, Australia, Cleve. Ctr. for Contemporary Art, The Phillips Collection, Washington.., Bill Maynes Contemporary Art, N.Y., Haines Gallery, San Francisco, Stephen Wirtz Gallery, Phillips Collection, Washington D.C. Grantee: CAPS, 1972, 75, Elizabeth Found. for the Arts, 1994; Guggenheim fellow, 1979, 85, Artist's fellow NEA, 1983. Mem. NAD. Avocation: early 20th century model airplane building. Home: 231 Bowery New York NY 10002-1237

QUEBE, JERRY LEE, architect; b. Indpls., Nov. 7, 1942; s. Charlie Christopher and Katheryn Rosella (Hankins) Q.; m. Julie Ann Gordon (div.); 1 child, Dana Ann; m. Lisbeth Jane Gray, Mar. 16, 1986. BArch, Iowa State U., 1965. Registered architect, Ill., Calif. Mem. staff Hansen Lind Meyer, Iowa City, 1965-70, assoc., 1970-74, prin., 1975-77; prin., v.p. Hansen Lind Meyer, Chgo., 1977-86; prin., exec. v.p. VVKR, Inc., Alexandria, Va., 1986-88; prin., exec. v.p. Perkins & Will, Chgo., 1988-93, prin., mem. office of chief exec., 1994-96, also bd. dirs.; chmn. Cedar Rapids/Iowa City Architects Council, 1974. Author: Drafting Practices Manual, 1978; contbr. articles to profl. jours. Pres. bd. dirs. Mental Health Assn. of Greater Chgo., 1990-95. Fellow AIA; mem. Am. Hosp. Assn., Chgo. Health Exec. Forum, Forum for Health Care Planning (bd. dirs. 1992—). Avocations: photography, scuba diving, sports car racing, reading. Home: 1908 N Sedgwick St Chicago IL 60614-5410 Office: Perkins & Will 1908 N Sedgwick Chicago IL 60614-5410

QUEBEDEAUX, BRUNO, horticulture educator; b. Arnandville, La., June 8, 1941; s. Bruno Sr. and Iola (Guidry) Q.; m. Maureen Fahey, Aug. 13, 1966; children: Mark E., Annette M., Michael J., Adele M. BS, La. State U., 1962, MS, 1963; PhD, Cornell U., 1968. Horticulturist Tex. A&M U., College Station, 1963-65; rsch. scientist E.I. du Pont de Nemours & Co., Wilmington, Del., 1968-80; team leader/COP U.S. AID Contract, Mauritania, 1980-83; chmn. dept. horticulture U. Md., College Park, 1983-90, prof., 1983—; sci. advisor USDA Plant Genome Rsch. Program, Washington, 1989-96. Assoc. editor Crop Sci. Soc. Am., Madison, Wis., 1979-82; editor: Horticulture and Human Health, 1988; author: (publ.) Oxygen: New Factor Controlling Reproductive Growth, 1973. Bd. dirs. League of Internat. Food Edn., Washington, 1987-90; sch. bd. chmn. Internat. Sch. Nauakchott, Mauritania, 1980-82; asst. scout master Boy Scouts Am., Wilmington, 1978-80; bd. dirs. Chapelcroft Civic Assn., Wilmington, 1978-80, v.p., 1975-77. Recipient Merit award USDA/ARS Nat. Resources, 1989. Fellow Am. Soc. Hort. Sci. (v.p. internat. merit 1988-89, L. Ware award 1962); mem. Am. Soc. Plant Physiology (pres. 1989-90, pres. Washington sect. 1990-91), Am. Soc. Agronomy (assoc. editor 1979-82), N.Y. Acad. Sci., Alpha Zeta. Achievements include patents for Method of Increasing Sugar Content in Crops, for Carbomoyl Phosphonate as Plant Growth Regulators, for Ureidotriazoles as Cytokinins and Yield Increasing Agents for Crop Plants, for Ureidotriazoles as Cytokinins and Plant Antisenescence Agents, for Selected Amidoxy Compounds as Flower Preservatives; research on oxygen regulation of plant growth. Home: 2417 Laurelwood Ter Silver Spring MD 20905-6419 Office: Dept Hort Lanscape Arch U Md College Park MD 20742-5611

QUEEN, EVANGELINE PALMER, private school educator, administrator, psychologist; b. S.C., May 15, 1905; d. Laurence Palmer and Daisy Dene (Nix) White; m. Edward Jerome Queen, Feb. 26, 1942; 1 child, Evangeline Marie. AB, Howard U., 1928; MA, Columbia U., 1933; PhD, NYU, 1951. Tchr. elem., jr. and sr. high D.C. Pub. Schs., Washington, 1927-39, rsch. asst. and asst. to chief examiner, 1939-49, asst. prin., 1949-64; founder, owner, dir., tchr. Avalon Montessori Sch., Washington, 1962—; assoc. prof. psychology D.C. Tchrs. Coll., Washington, 1972-75; tutor The Kingsbury Ctr., Washington, 1991—. Mem. St. Anthony Ch., Washington, 1952—, parish coun. rep. Mem. APA (life), AARP, N.Am. Montessori Tchrs. Assn., D.C. Psychol. Assn. (charter, life), Assn. Montessori Internat., Am. Montessori Soc. (life), Nat. Assn. Secondary Sch. Prins., D.C. Assn. Secondary Sch. Prins., Montessori Tchrs. Assn., Washington Montessori Inst. Tchr. Network, Nat. Ret. Tchrs. Assn. (Golden Age mem.), Delta Pi Epsilon (charter), St. Aiden Sch. (charter). Democrat. Roman Catholic. Avocations: music, genealogical research, travel, gardening, china painting. Home: 1424 Girard St NE Washington DC 20017-2940 Office: Avalon Montessori Sch 2814 Franklin St NE Washington DC 20018-1435

QUEEN, EVELYN E. CRAWFORD, judge, law educator; b. Albany, N.Y., Apr. 6, 1945; d. Iris (Jackson) Crawford; m. Charles A. Queen, Mar. 6, 1971; children: Angelia, George. BS, Howard U., 1968, JD, 1975. Bar: N.Y. 1976, D.C. 1977, U.S. Ct. Appeals (D.C. cir.) 1977, U.S. Dist. Ct. (D.C. dist.) 1978, U.S. Supreme Ct. 1980. Park ranger Nat. Park Svc., Washington, 1968-69; pers. specialist NIH, Bethesda, Md., 1969-75; staff atty. Met. Life Ins. Co., N.Y.C., 1975-76; atty. advisor Maritime Adminstrn.-U.S., Washington, 1976-78; att. U.S. atty.-D.C. Justice Dept., Washington, 1978-81; hearing commr. D.C. Superior Ct., Washington, 1981-86, judge, 1986—; adj. law prof. Howard U., 1988, D.C. Sch. Law, 1993, 94. Recipient spl. achievement awards HEW, 1975, certs. of appreciation and placques Dept. Justice, 1981, Trefoil award Hudson Valley coun. Girl Scouts U.S.A., 1988. Mem. ABA, Nat. Bar Assn., Nat. Assn. Women Judges, Washington Bar Assn. Office: DC Superior Ct 500 Indiana Ave NW Washington DC 20001-2131

QUEENAN, JAMES F., JR., judge; m. Helen E. Wood; 5 children. BA cum laude, Boston Coll., 1953, JD magna cum laude, 1958. Bar: Mass. 1958, U.S. Supreme Ct. 1966, U.S. Tax Ct. 1968, U.S. Dist. Ct. Mass. 1959. Law clk. Mass. Supreme Judicial Ct., Boston, 1958-59; ptnr. Bowditch & Dewey, Worcester, Mass.; judge U.S. Bankruptcy Ct. Dist. Mass., Worcester, 1986—; adj. prof. bankruptcy law Suffolk U. Law Sch.; former mem. spl. com. on legal edn. Mass. Supreme Jud. Ct., Mass. Jud. Conduct Commn. Co-editor, co-author: Chapter 11 Theory and Practice, 6 vols.; former assoc.editor The Am. Bankruptcy Law Jour.; former editor-in-chief Mass. Law Rev.; contbr. articles to profl. jours. Chmn.task force Worcester Area C. of C., pres. Friends of the Worcester Public Libr. Mem. Mass. Bar Assn. (bd. of delegates, sec., chmn. bus. bankruptcy com.). Office: US Bankruptcy Ct 595 Main St Worcester MA 01608

QUEENAN, JOSEPH MARTIN, JR., writer, magazine editor; b. Phila., Nov. 3, 1950; s. Joseph M. and Agnes Catherine (McNulty) Q.; m. Francesca Jane Spinner, Jan. 7, 1977; children: Bridget Noelle, Gordon Pasha. B.A., St. Joseph's U., 1972. Editor in chief Uncle Sam Mag., N.Y.C., 1981-82; mng. editor Moneysworth, Am. Bus., N.Y.C., 1982-83; editor in chief Am. Bus., Moneysworth, Better Living, N.Y.C., 1983-86; staffwriter Barron's, 1987-89; sr. editor Forbes Mag., N.Y.C., 1989; freelance writer, 1989—. Author: Imperial Caddy, 1992, If You're Talking to Me Your Career Must Be in Trouble, 1994, The Unkindest Cut, 1996. Democrat. Roman Catholic.

QUEENEY, JACK, public relations executive. Ptnr. Fin. Rels. Bd., Chgo. Office: Fin Rels Bd John Hancock Ctr 875 N Michigan Ave Chicago IL 60611*

QUEHL, GARY HOWARD, association executive, consultant; b. Green Bay, Wis., Mar. 25, 1938; s. Howard and Virginia Babcock (Dunning) Q.; children: Scott Boyer, Catherine Mary. BA, Carroll Coll., 1960; MS, Ind. U., 1962, EdD, 1965; LHD (hon.), Buena Vista Coll., 1977, Davis and Elkins Coll., 1979; EdD (hon.), Columbia Coll., S.C., 1987. Asst. dean students Wis. State U., 1962; asst. dean coll. Wittenberg U., 1965-76; v.p., dean coll. Lindenwood Colls., St. Charles, Mo., 1967-70; exec. dir. Coll. Center of the Finger Lakes, Corning, N.Y., 1970-74; pres. Council of Ind. Colls., Washington, 1974-86, Council for Advancement and Support of Edn., Washington, 1986-90, Quehl Assocs., Quehl Group, Lafayette, Calif., 1990—; cons. in field, 1990—. Editor, author books in field. Mem. secretariat Nat. Center for Higher Edn.; bd. dirs. Carroll Coll., Muskingum Coll., Elmira Coll., Nat. Assn. Ind. Colls. and Univs., ind. sector, Cornell Coll. Mem. Am. Council Edn., Am. Conf. Acad. Deans, Nat. Panel for Women in Higher Edn., North Central Assn. Acad. Deans (past pres.). Mem. United Ch. Christ.

QUELER, EVE, conductor; b. N.Y.C.. Student, Mannes Coll. Music, CCNY. Music dir. Opera Orchestra of N.Y. Music staff N.Y.C. Opera, 1958-70; assoc. condr. Ft. Wayne (Ind.) Philharm., 1970-71; founder, music dir. Opera Orch., N.Y., 1968; condr. Lake George Opera Festival, Glen Falls, N.Y., 1971-72, Oberlin (Ohio) Music Festival, 1972, Romantic Festival, Indpls., 1972, Mostly Mozart Festival, Lincoln Center, 1972, New Philharmonia, London, 1974, Teatro Liceu, Barcelona, 1974, 77, San Antonio Symphony, 1975; guest condr. Paris Radio Orch., 1972, P.R. Symphony Orch., 1975, 77, Mich. Chamber Orch., 1975, Phila. Orch., 1976, Montreal Symphony, 1977, Cleve. Orch., 1977 (Recipient Martha Baird Rockefeller Fund for Music award 1968, named Musician of Month Mus. Am. Mag. 1972), N.Y.C. Opera, 1978, Opera Las Palmas, 1978, Opera de Nice, 1979, Nat. Theatre of Prague, 1980, Opera Caracas, Venezuela, 1981, San Diego Opera, 1984, Australian Opera, Sydney, 1985, Kirov Opera, St. Petersburg, Russia, 1993, Hamburg Opera, Germany, 1994, Pretoria, South Africa, 1995, Hamilton, Ont., 1995; recording CBS Masterworks, 1974, 76, Hungaroton Records, 1982-85. Office: c/o Alix Barthelmes Manager Opera Orchestra NY 239 W 72nd St #2R New York NY 10023-2734

QUELLE, FREDERICK WILLIAM, JR., physicist; b. Chgo., Sept. 4, 1934; s. Fred William and Viola Mildred (Miller) Q.; m. Claudia Jean Suba, June 18, 1961 (div. 1979); children: Frederick William, Geoffrey William. B.S., Ill. Inst. Tech., 1955; M.A., Harvard U., 1957, Ph.D., 1964. Staff mem. Lincoln Labs., Lexington, Mass., 1955-61; mem. solid state and molecular theory group M.I.T., Cambridge, 1958-63; physicist Office Naval Research, Boston, 1961—; pres. Tech. Engring. Devel. Co., Cohasset, Mass., 1978—; head ONR laser team, 1968-78, SHAD Space Navigation Team, 1979—; Navy mem. Adv. Group on Electronic Devices, 1975-80; mem. Exploratory Research and Devel. Com., 1980-89. Contbr. articles in field to profl. jours. Gen. Communication Co. fellow Harvard U., 1955. Mem. Am. Phys. Soc., Sigma Xi, Sigma Pi Sigma. Patentee in field. Home: 120 Nichols Rd Cohasset MA 02025-1146 Office: 495 Summer St Boston MA 02210-2109 *The name of the game is to cover as much unplowed ground and tread on as much snow where no man has ever walked as one can in his lifetime.*

QUELLER, FRED, lawyer; b. N.Y.C., July 10, 1932; s. Victor and Helen (Cenzer) Q.; m. Stephanie Tarler, Aug. 29, 1965; children: Jessica, Danielle. BA, CCNY, 1954; JD, NYU, 1956. Bar: N.Y. 1956, U.S. Dist. Ct. (so. and ea. dists.) N.Y. 1958, U.S. Supreme Ct. 1960, U.S. Ct. Appeals (2d cir.) 1967, Fla. 1980; cert. diplomate civil trial advocacy Nat. Bd. Trial Advocacy, cert. adv. Am. Bd. Trial Advs. Sole practice, N.Y.C., 1956-70; ptnr. Queller & Fisher, N.Y.C., 1970—, now sr. prtnr.; lectr. N.Y. County Lawyers Assn., Practicing Law Inst., Med. Soc. State of N.Y., N.Y. Women's Bar Assn., Victims for Victims, Council of N.Y. Law Assocs., Bklyn. Coll. Inst. for Retired Profls. and Execs., Nassau Acad. Law, Mt. Sinai Med. Ctr., 1975-91, App. Divsn. of the Supreme Ct. State of N.Y. 2d Judicial Dept., Violent Crimes Compensation bd. of N.J.; The Coll. of Ins., Transamerica Ins. Co., Park Slope Sr. Ctr., Touro Coll. Jacob D. Fuchsberg Sch. of Law; panelist Med. Malpractice Panel of Supreme Ct. State of N.Y., County of N.Y. 1973-91; arbitrator Compulsory Arbitration Service of State of N.Y., 1st Jud. Dept., 1975-91; co-chmn. jud. screening com. of lawyers' com., 1979; adminstrv. sec. ad hoc com. for Preservation of an Elected Judiciary, 1977-80; counsel com. for elected judiciary, 1981-84; mem. coordinating council on lawyer competence of Conf. of Chief Justices, 1983-84. Contbr. articles to profl. jours. Chmn. Big Apple Pothole and Sidewalk Protection Corp., 1982-83, pres. 1984-87. Mem. Am. Soc. Legal and Indsl. Medicine, Assn. Bar City of N.Y., Bronx Bar Assn., Am. Bd. Trial Advs. (lectr., pres. N.Y. chpt. 1988-90, vice-chmn. N.Y. Am. Bd. Trial Advs. Key Person Com. 1995), N.Y. State Bar Assn. (com. on automobile liability 1981-93, com. on products liability ins. 1986-93, torts reparation com. 1983-93), ABA (trial techniques com. 1984), Fla. Bar Assn., Met. Women's Bar Assn. (bd. dirs. 1975-83, lectr. 1975-87, treas. 1978-80, v.p. 1980-81), N.Y. Criminal and Civil Cts. Bar Assn., Bklyn. and Manhattan Trial Counsel Assn., N.Y. County Lawyers Assn., Bklyn. Bar Assn., Judiciary/Trial Lawyers Joint Com. of O.C.A., Trial Lawyers for Pub. Justice, N.Y. State Trial Lawyers Inst. (dean 1988-95), N.Y. State Trial Lawyers Assn. (bd. dirs. 1970—, 86-93, lectr. 1975—, v.p. 1980-83, pres. 1984-86, chmn. products liability com. 1980-81, chmn. brief bank com. 1982-84, chmn. expert bank com. 1982-84, nominating com. 1986-95, Pres.'s award 1986, Disting. Service award 1986), Assn. Trial Lawyers of City N.Y. (bd. dirs. 1975—), Assn. Trial Lawyers Am., Nat. Judicature Soc., Nat. Coalition Victims Attys. and Cons., Nat. Adv. Coun., Nat. Com. for Furtherance Jewish Edn. (bd. dirs. 1980-95, Man of Yr. 1984), Inst. Jewish Humanities (bd. dirs. 1985—, Humanitarian award 1988), Jewish Trial Lawyer's Guild (gov. 1977—), Lawyers Polit. Action Com. (trustee 1984-86), NYU Law Rev. Alumni Assn, Assoc. editor NYU Law Rev., 1955-56. Office: Queller & Fisher 110 Wall St New York NY 10005-3801

QUELLMALZ, HENRY, printing company executive; b. Balt., May 18, 1915; s. Frederick and Edith Margaret (Shaw) Q.; m. Marion Agar Lynch, Aug. 2, 1940; children: Lynn Quellmalz Johnson, Susan Quellmalz Mastan, Jane Quellmalz Carey. . BA with high honors, Princeton U., 1937. Pres. Princeton Advt. Agy., 1936-37; dir. pers. Macy's Men's Store, 1938-40; asst. mgr. Fowlers Dept. Store, Glens Falls, N.Y., 1940-41; pers. dir. U.S. Army Post Exchs., Ft. Meade, Md., 1941-44; with Boyd Printing Co., Albany, N.Y., 1944—, pres., 1952-84, chmn. bd., 1984—; v.p. Q Corp. U.S.; agt. for WHO publs., 1965—. Campaign chmn. ARC, Albany, 1956, 57; bd. govs. Doane Stuart Sch., Albany, 1977-79, treas. bd., 1977-78; vice chmn. Family Svc. Assn. Am. Salute to Families, 1979—, Nat. UN Day com., 1980-82; mem. adv. bd. Ind. Coll. Fund of N.Y., 1971-91, corp. trustees, 1992—; bd. dirs. Am. Assn. World Health, 1977-82, Combined Health Appeal of Capitol Dist., Inc., 1984, Camelot Home for Boys, 1975; trustee St. Peter's Hosp. Found., Albany, 1982—, asst. sec., 1987-89, chmn. bd. dirs., 1989-91. With AUS, 1943. Recipient Pres.'s award Am. Assn. Mental Deficiency, 1976; 25 Yrs. Svc. award N.Y. State Bar Assn., 1983, 34 Yrs. Svc. Award Am. Sociol. Assn., 1985. Mem. Albany Area C. of C., Printing Industry Am. Assn. East Ctrl. N.Y. (pres. 1958), Ft. Orange Club, Hudson Mohawk Assn. of Colls. and Univs. (Spl. award for svcs. 1995). Democrat. Episcopalian. Home: 1 Park Hill Dr Apt 6 Albany NY 12204-2142 Office: 49 Sheridan Ave Albany NY 12210-2735

QUELLO, JAMES HENRY, government official; b. Laurium, Mich., Apr. 21, 1914; s. Bartholomew and Mary Katherine (Cochis) Q.; m. Mary Elizabeth Butler, Sept. 14, 1937; children: James Michael, Richard Butler. BA, Mich. State U., 1935, D of Humanities (hon.), 1977; D of Pub. Svc. (hon.), No. Mich. U., 1975. V.p., sta. mgr. Goodwill Stas., Inc., Detroit, 1947-72; v.p. Capital Cities Communications Corp., 1968; commr. FCC, Washington, 1974—; communications cons., Detroit, 1972-74; commr. FCC, Washington, 1974—; commr. Detroit Housing and Urban Renewal Commn., 1951-72. Contbr. articles to mags., newspapers. Bd. dirs. Greater Detroit Hosp. Assn.; trustee Mich. Vet. Trust Fund; mem. Gov.'s Spl. Commn. on Urban Problems, Mich., Gov.'s Spl. Study Com. on Legis. Compensation, Mayor's Com. on Human Relations; bd. dirs. Am. Negro Emancipation Centennial; mem. exec. bd. Boy Scouts Am.; TV-radio chmn. United Found. Lt. col. AUS, 1940-45. Decorated Bronze Star with oak leaf cluster, Croix de Guerre (France); recipient Internat. Pres.'s award Nat. Assn. TV Program Execs., 1985, Silver Satellite award Am. Women in Radio and TV, 1988, 93, Sol Taishoff award Washington Area Broadcasters Assn., 1989, 93, Pub. Svc. award Fed. Comm. Bar Assn., 1993, Disting. Svc. award Media Inst., 1993, Golden Eagle Amb. award Pa. Assn. Broadcasters, 1993, Disting. Alumni award Mich. State U., Club Dir. award Detroit Adcraft Club, 1993, L.I. Coalition for Fair Broadcasting award, 1993, Nat. Disting. Svc. award Nat. Assn. Pub. TV, 1993, Obie award Ohio Ednl. TV Stas., 1993, Gold Eagle Leadership award Wireless Cable Assn. Internat., 1993, Pres. award Alaska Broadcasting Assn., 1994, Chmn. award Nat. Religious Broadcasters, 1994, Ga. Broadcasters award Broadcasters of Am., 1994, 1st Amendment award Radio & TV News Dirs. Found., 1994. Mem. Nat. Assn. Broadcaster (mem. gov. liaison com. 1964-72, Keystone award 1990, Disting. Svc. award 1994, Honor award for protecting the technical integrity of radio and TV 1994, Broadcasting Cable Hall of Fame, 1995), Mich. Assn. Broadcasters (pres. 1958, legis. chmn. 1959-72, dir., Outstanding Mich. Citizen 1989, Pioneer award 1994), Greater Detroit Bd. Commerce, Adcraft (Detroit), Detroit Athletic, Army and Navy Country Club, Nat. Press Club (Washington), Sigma Alpha Epsilon. Clubs: Adcraft (Detroit); Detroit Athletic, Army and Navy Country; Nat. Press (Washington). Office: FCC 1919 M St NW Washington DC 20036-3505

QUENCER, ROBERT MOORE, neuroradiologist, researcher; b. Jersey City, Nov. 14, 1937; s. Arthur Bauer and Isabell (Moore) Q.; m. Christine F. Thomas, Sept. 16, 1972; children: Kevin, Keith. BS, Cornell U., 1959, MS, 1963; MD, SUNY, Syracuse, 1967. Diplomate Am. Bd. Radiology, Nat. Bd. Med. Examiners; cert. of added qualifications in neuroradiology. Intern Jackson Meml. Hosp., Miami, Fla., 1967-68; resident in radiology Columbia U., N.Y.C., 1968-71, fellow in neuroradiology, 1971-72; asst. prof. Downstate Med. Ctr., Bklyn., 1972-76; assoc. prof. U. Miami, 1976-79, prof., 1979-92, chmn., prof., 1992—, chief sect. neuroradiology, 1976-86, dir. divsn. magnetic resonance imaging, 1986-92; vis. prof. U. Tenn. Coll. Medicine, Memphis, 1982, Downstate Med. Ctr. Coll. Medicine, Bklyn., 1992, U. Vt. Coll. Medicine, Burlington, 1983, N.Y. Med. Coll., Valhalla, 1984, U. Va. Sch. Medicine, Charlottesville, 1984, U. Ky. Sch. Medicine, Lexington, 1985, Yale U. Sch. Medicine, New Haven, 1986, Columbia U. Sch. Medicine, N.Y.C., 1986, The Mayo Clinic & Found., Rochester, Minn., 1987, Med. Coll. Va., Richmond, 1988, U. Pa. Sch. Medicine, Phila., 1988, Harvard U. Sch. Medicine/Mass. Gen. Hosp., Boston, 1989, U. Conn., Farmington, 1990, Kumamoto, Japan, 1993, U. Man., Can., 1992; Phaler lectr. Phila. Roentgen Soc., 1995; dir. programs in dept. radiology U. Miami Sch. Medicine, 1984, 86, Med. Coll. Wis., Tucson, 1990, 92, Kauai, Hawaii, 1991, Whistler, B.C., 1990; guest lectr. at ASEAN Congress of Radiology, Malaysia, 1992, Royal Australia Radiology Soc., Brisbane, 1993; adv. cons. NIH, 1987, 90; sci. merit reviewer V.A., 1987; presenter, lectr. in field. Author: Neurosonography, 1988; dep. editor Am. Jour. Neuroradiology, 1984—; assoc. editor for neuroimaging Yearbook of Neurology and Neurosurgery, 1991—; book reviewer Am. Jour. Neuroradiology, 1984—, Paraplegia, 1989—, Radiographics, 1991—, Pediatrics, 1993—; mem. editorial bd. Jour. Clin. Neuro-Ophthalmology, 1980—; contbr. articles to profl. jours. Pres. Am. Soc. Neuroradiology, 1994-95; prin. investigator NIH Grant on imaging/pathology of spinal cord injury. Lt. (j.g.) USN, 1959-61. Fellow Am. Coll. Radiology, Am. Soc. Neuroradiology (pres. 1994-95, program com. 1985-89, 92, editl. com. 1984—, publs. com. 1984—); mem. AMA, Radiol. Soc. N.Am. (program subcom. on neuroradiology 1990-94), Southeastern Neuroradiol. Soc. (founder, pres. 1980-81, examiner for bd. certification in radiology and neuroradiology), Dade County Med. Assn., Soc. Chmn. Acad. Radiology Depts., Fla. Radiol. Soc. (magnetic resonance com. 1991-92), Alpha Omega Alpha. Avocations: golf, travel. Office: U Miami 1150 NW 14th St Miami FL 33136-2106

QUENEAU, PAUL ETIENNE, metallurgical engineer, educator; b. Phila., Mar. 20, 1911; s. Augustin L. and Jean (Blaisdell) Q.; m. Joan Osgood Hodges, May 20, 1939; children: Paul Blaisdell, Josephine Downs (Mrs. George Stanley Patrick). BA, Columbia U., 1931, BSc, 1932, M of Engring.,

1933; postgrad., Cambridge (Eng.) U., 1934; DSc, Delft (Netherlands) U. Tech., 1971. With INCO, 1934-69; dir. rsch. Internat. Nickel Co., 1940-41, 46-48, v.p., 1958-69, tech. asst. to pres., 1960-66, asst. to chmn., 1967-69; vis. scientist Delft U. Tech., 1970-71; prof. engring. Dartmouth Coll., 1971-87, prof. emeritus, 1987—; cons. engr., 1972—; vis. prof. U. Minn., 1974-75, U. Utah, 1987-91; geographer Perry River Arctic Expdn., 1949; chmn. arctic rsch. adv. com. USN, 1957; gov. Arctic Inst. N.Am., 1957-62; mem. engring. coun. Columbia U., 1965-70; mem. vis. com. MIT, Cambridge, 1967-70; mem. extractive metallurgy and mineral processing panels NAS; pres. Q-S Oxygen Processes Inc., 1974-79, also bd. dirs. Author: (with Hanson) Geography, Birds and Mammals of the Perry River Region, 1956; Cobalt and the Nickeliferous Limonites, 1971; editor: Extractive Metallurgy of Copper, Nickel and Cobalt, 1961; (with Anderson) Pyrometallurgical Processes in Nonferrous Metallurgy, 1965; The Winning of Nickel, 1967; contbr. articles to profl. jours.; patentee 34 U.S. patents including processes and apparatus employed in the pyrometallurgy, hydrometallurgy and vapometallurgy of nickel, copper, cobalt, lead, zinc and iron, extractive metallurgy oxygen tech. including INCO oxygen flash smelting, oxygen top-blown rotary converter, lateritic ore matte smelting, nickel high pressure carbonyl and iron ore recovery processes; co-inventor Lurgi QSL direct lead-making, QSOP direct coppermaking and nickelmaking reactors, Lurgi direct steelmaking reactors, and Dravo oxygen sprinkle copper smelting furnaces. Bd. dirs. Engring. Found., 1966-76, chmn. bd. dirs., 1973-75. With U.S. Army, WWII, ETO; col. C.E., USAR ret. Decorated Bronze Star, ETO medal with 5 battlestars, Commendation medal; Evans fellow Cambridge U., 1934; recipient Egleston medal Columbia U., 1965, Fletcher award Dartmouth Coll., 1991. Fellow Metall. Soc. of AIME (dir. 1964, 68-71, pres. 1969, Extractive Metallurgy Lecture award 1977, Paul E. Queneau Internat. Symposium on Extractive Metallurgy of Copper, Nickel and Cobalt 1993); mem. AIME (Douglas Gold medal 1968, v.p. 1970, dir. 1968-71, Henry Krumb lectr. 1984, keynote lectr. ann. meeting 1990), NAE, NSPE, Can. Inst. Mining and Metallurgy, Inst. Mining and Metallurgy U.K. (overseas mem. council 1970-80, Gold medal 1980), Sigma Xi, Tau Beta Pi. Office: Dartmouth Coll Thayer Sch Engring Hanover NH 03755

QUENNELL, NICHOLAS, landscape architect, educator; b. London, Sept. 30, 1935; s. Cecil William and Beatrice Irene Quennell; m. Grace Tankersley, Apr. 30, 1983. AA, Archtl. Assn., London, 1957; MLA, Harvard U., 1969. Registered architect, N.Y., Pa., N.J., Conn., U.K.; registered landscape architect, N.Y., N.J., Conn., Mass., N.C. Architect London County Coun., 1959-61, Jose Luis Sert, Cambridge, Mass., 1961-62, Lawrence Halprin & Assocs., San Francisco, 1962-65, Vollmer Assocs., N.Y.C., 1965-68; prin. Nicholas Quennell Assocs., N.Y.C., 1968-79, Quennell Rothschild Assocs., N.Y.C., 1979—; v.p. The Mcpl. Art Soc. (dir. 1978-85), N.Y.C., 1985-92, dir. The Archtl. League, N.Y.C., 1984-89. Bd. dirs. nat. Assn. for Olmsted Pks., Washington, 1988-90, chmn., 1990-93; mem. Art Commn. of City of N.Y., 1992—, pres., 1993—. Fellow Am. Soc. of Landscape Architects; mem. Century Assn. Office: Quennell Rothschild Assocs 118 W 22nd St New York NY 10011-2416

QUENON, ROBERT HAGERTY, retired mining consultant and holding company executive; b. Clarksburg, W.Va., Aug. 2, 1928; s. Ernest Leonard and Josephine (Hagerty) Q.; m. Jean Bowling, Aug. 8, 1953; children: Evan, Ann, Richard. B.S. in Mining Engring., W.Va. U., 1951; LL.B., George Washington U., 1964; PhD (hon.), U. Mo., 1979, Blackburn Coll., 1983, W.Va. U., 1988. Mine supt. Consol. Coal Co., Fairmont, W.Va., 1956-61; mgr. deep mines Pittston Co., Dante, Va., 1964-66; gen. mgr. Riverton Coal Co., Crown Hill, W.Va., 1966-67; mgr. ops. coal and shale oil dept. Exxon Co., Houston, 1967; pres. Monterey Coal Co., Houston, 1969-76; sr. v.p. Carter Oil Co., Houston, 1976-77; exec. v.p. Peabody Coal Co., St. Louis, 1977-78; pres., chief exec. officer Peabody Coal Co., 1978-83; pres., chief exec. officer Peabody Holding Co., Inc., St. Louis, 1983-90, chmn., 1990-91; bd. dirs. Newmont Gold Co., Denver, Union Electric Co., St. Louis, Laclede Steel Co., St. Louis; bd. dirs., chmn. Fed. Res. Bank St. Louis, 1993-95, dep. chmn., 1990-92; mem. coal industry adv. bd. Internat. Energy Agy., 1980—, bd. chmn., 1984-90; chmn. Bituminous Coal Operator's Assn., 1980-83, 89-91. Trustee Blackburn Coll., Carlinville, Ill., 1975-83, St. Louis U., 1981-91; pres. St. Louis Art Mus., 1985-88. Served with AUS, 1946-47. Recipient Eavenson award Soc. Mining, Metallurgy, and Exploration, 1994. Mem. Am. Mining Congress (vice-chmn. 1980-91), Nat. Coal Assn. (chmn. bd. 1978-80), U.S. C. of C. (dir. 1982-88). Office: PO Box 11328 Saint Louis MO 63105-0128

QUENTEL, ALBERT DREW, lawyer; b. Miami, Fla., Nov. 27, 1934; s. Charles Edward Jr. and Alberta Amelia (Drew) Q.; m. Paula Staelin Hagar, Feb. 9, 1957; children: Albert D. Jr., Stephen C., Marshall Lee, Paul G., Peter E., Michael J. BA, U. Fla., 1956, JD with honors, 1959. Bar: Fla. 1959. Assoc. Mershon, Sawyer, Johnston, Dunwody & Cole, Miami, 1959-64, ptnr., 1965-71; princ. Greenberg, Traurig, Hoffman, Lipoff, Rosen & Quentel, P.A., Miami, 1971—. Editor-in-chief U. Fla. Law Rev., 1959; contbg. author: Florida Real Property Practice, 1965, Real Estate Partnerships Selected Problems and Solutions, 1991, Commercial Real Estate Finance, 1993. Mem. Gov.'s Growth Mgmt. Adv. Com., Tallahassee, 1985-87; bd. dirs. Nat. Parkinson Found., Miami, 1980—, v.p., 1985—. Mem. NRA (life 1989—), Am. Coll. Real Estate Lawyers, Urban Land Inst., Fla. Bar Assn. (chmn. pub. rels. com. 1970-72, chmn. editorial com. jour. 1972-73), Lions (pres. Key Biscayne, Fla. club 1973), Miami Club (pres. 1991-92), Bath Club, Blue Key, Beta Theta Pi (pres. local chpt. 1954-55), Phi Eta Sigma, Phi Kappa Phi. Republican. Congregationalist. Avocations: reading, shooting, photography. Home: 3410 Poinciana Ave Miami FL 33133-6525 Office: Greenberg Traurig Hoffman Lipoff Rosen & Quentel PA 1221 Brickell Ave Miami FL 33131-3200

QUERSHEY, SAFI U., computer company executive; b. 1951. BS in Engring., U. Tex., 1975. Test specialist A M Internat., 1975-77; engr. Computer Automation Corp., Irvine, Calif., 1977-78, Telefile Computer Corp., Irvine, 1978-79; chmn bd. AST Research%, 1979—. Office: AST Research Inc 16215 Alton Pkwy Irvine CA 92718*

QUERY, JOY MARVES NEALE, medical sociology educator; b. Worcestershire, Eng.; came to U.S., 1952; d. Samuel and Dorree (Oakley) Neale; children: Jonathan, Margo, Evan. A.B., Drake U., 1954, M.A., 1955; postgrad., U. Syracuse, 1955-56; Ph.D., U. Ky., 1960. Tchr. secondary schs. Staffordshire, Eng., 1947-52; dep. prin. Smethwich Hall Girls' Sch., Staffordshire, 1948-52; instr. U. Ky., 1956-57, asst. prof., 1960; assoc. prof. sociology Transylvania Coll., Lexington, Ky., 1961-66; assoc. prof. N.D. State U., Fargo, 1966-68; prof. sociology and psychology N.D. State U., 1969-75, also chmn. sociology and psychology depts., 1969-70, chmn. sociology and anthropology dept., 1968-73; prof. div. psychiatry behavioral sci., dept. neurosci. U. N.D. Sch. Medicine, Fargo, 1975-89, prof. emeritus, 1989—; on sabbatical leave Yale U., 1974-75; coord. AIDS Edn. State Program NIMH, 1989-93. Mem. bd. adv. editors Sociological Inquiry jour., 1987-93; contbr. articles and papers to profl. jours. Field dir. Girl Scouts U.S.A., 1953-55; mem. Lexington Civil Rights Commn., 1960-66; bd. dirs. Fargo-Moorhead Family Service Agy., 1967-70; mem. Mayor's Coordinating Council for Youth, Fargo-Moorhead, 1976—; pres. Hospice of Red River Valley, 1986-87 (Svc. award 1987). Named Profl. Woman of Yr. Fargo-Moorhead YWCA, 1981, Disting. Lectr. of Yr., N.D. State U., 1991, Outstanding Educator U. N.D. Sch. Medicine Class of 1992; recipient Burlington No. award, 1987, Alumni award U. Ky., 1988, Disting. Svc. award Gt. Plains Sociol. Assn., 1988; Joy M. Query scholarship at N.D. State U., U. Md. Coll. Medicine created in her honor, 1987. Fellow Internat. Assn. Social Psychiatry; mem. AAUP, Am. Sociol. Asns., N.D. Mental Health Assn. (pres. Red River Valley chpt., Heritage award 1987), midwest Sociol. Soc. (dir. 1970-73, 75-78, mem. standards, tng. and employment com. 1988-89), Alpha Kappa Delta. Unitarian. Home: 1202 Oak St Fargo ND 58102-2707 Office: U ND Sch Medicine 1919 Elm St Fargo ND 58102-2416

QUESENBERRY, KENNETH HAYS, agronomy educator; b. Springfield, Tenn., Feb. 28, 1947; s. James William and Cora Geneva (Moore) Q.; m. Joyce Ann Kaze, July 28, 1947; children: James Kenneth, Kendra Joyce. BS, Western Ky. U., 1969; PhD U. Ky., 1975. D. F. Jones predoctoral fellow U. Ky., Lexington, 1972-75; asst. prof. U. Fla., Gainesville, 1975-80, assoc. prof. agronomy, 1980-86, prof. agronomy, 1986—; Contbr. articles to profl. jours. Chair So. Pasture and Forage Crop Improvement Conf., 1991. Served with U.S. Army, 1969-71, Vietnam. Named Prof. of Yr., Coll. Agr., U. Fla., 1976. Fellow Am. Soc. Agronomy; mem. Crop Sci. Soc. Am. (chair divsn. C-8 1993-94) . Democrat. Avocations: sports, antique furniture refinishing. Achievements include rsch. in germplasm enhancement of forages with release of four cultivars of tropical grasses and two clovers and genetic transformation of clovers. Office: Univ Fla PO Box 110500 Gainesville FL 32611-0500

QUESNEL, GREGORY L., transportation company executive; b. Woodburn, Oreg., May 24, 1948. BA in Finance, U. Oregon; MA in Bus. Adminstrn., U. Portland; grad. Exec. Program in Bus. Adminstrn., Columbia U. Dir. fin. acctg. Consolidated Freightways, Portland, 1975-78, dir. mgmt. and cost acctg., 1978-86; fin. officer CF MotorFreight, Consolidated Freightways, Portland, 1986-89; v.p. acctg. Emery Worldwide, Consolidated Freightways, Scranton, Pa., 1989-91; exec. v.p., CFO Consolidated Freightways, Inc., Palo Alto, Calif., 1991—. Mem. Fin. Exec. Inst., Chief Fin. Execs. (conf. bds. coun., conf. bds. coun. of fin. execs.).

QUEST, JAMES HOWARD, advertising executive; b. Johnstown, Pa., June 21, 1934; s. Norris R.D.O. and Edna Jane (Nichols) Q.; m. Sarah Jo Ames, June 11, 1960 (dec. 1973); m. Leslie Reiman; children: Daniel, Anna, Benjamin. BS in Hotel Adminstrn., Cornell U., 1956. Brand mgr. Procter & Gamble, Cin., 1956-60; v.p. SSC&B Advt., N.Y.C., 1961-64; group product dir. Pfizer Consumer Products, N.Y.C., 1964-67; v.p. Am. Home Products, N.Y.C., 1967-71, RS&L Advt., N.Y.C., 1971-75; sr. v.p., mem. bd. dirs. The Marschalk Co., Advt., N.Y.C., 1975-80; chmn., chief exec. officer Posey & Quest Advt., Greenwich, Conn., 1980-90; exec. v.p. TBWA Advt., N.Y.C., 1990-95; CEO Quest Assoc. LTD., Stamford, Conn., 1995—; speaker AAAA, N.Y.C., 1985-87, Assn. Nat. Advertisers, 1987-89; guest lectr. Cornell Sch. Hotel Adminstrn., 1985. Author: (with others) Developing New Products, 1980, Executive Chess, 1987. Bd. dirs., exec. com. Children of Alcoholics Found., N.Y.C., 1987—; mem. Cornell U. Coun.; v.p. Cornell Class of 1956. With U.S. Army, 1956-58. Mem. Cornell Soc. Hotelmen, Cornell Club (N.Y.C.), Friars Club N.Y., Woodway Country Club, Darien, Conn. Avocations: tennis, golf., travel, writing. Home: 14 Alfred Ln Stamford CT 06902-1238 Office: Quest Assocs Ltd PO Box 3005 Stamford CT 06905-0005

QUESTEL, MAE, actress; b. Bronx, N.Y., Sept. 13, 1908; d. Simon and Frieda (Glauberman) Q.; m. Leo Balkin, Dec. 22, 1930 (dec.); children: Robert (dec.), Richard; m. Jack E. Shelby, Nov. 19, 1970. Student in drama, J.G. Geiger, N.Y.C., 1916-24; scholar, Theatre Guild, N.Y.C., 1923, Columbia U., 1949, Theatre Wing, 1951. Appeared in vaudeville at, Palace Theatre, 1930, on RKO theater circuit, 1931-38; radio shows include Betty Boops Frolics, NBC, 1932; cartoon voices Betty Boop, 1931—, Olive Oyl, 1933—, Mr. Bugs Goes to Town, 1934, Little Audrey, 1946; TV cartoon Winky Dink and You, 1956-60, Popeye (as Olive Oyl), 1981; stage appearances include Dr. Social, 1948, A Majority of One, 1959-61, Come Blow Your Horn, 1963, Enter Laughing, 1963, Bajour, 1964, The Warm Peninsula, 1966, Walk Like A Lion, 1969, Barrel Full of Pennies, 1970, Where Have You Been, Billy Boy, 1969, Betty Boop—60 Yrs., N.Y.C., 1990, Betty Boop (Olive Oyl), U. Nebr., Lincoln, 1990; appeared: films A Majority of One, 1961, It's Only Money, 1962, Funny Girl, 1967, Move, 1969, Zelig, 1983, Hot Resorts, 1984, Who Framed Roger Rabbit?, 1988, New York Stories: A Trilogy, 1988-89, Christmas Vacation, 1989; TV spokeswoman for Scott Paper Co. as Aunt Bluebell films, 1971-78; other commls. include Playtex, 1970-72, Romilar, 1970-72, Folger's Coffee, 1970-72, Speidel Watch Bands, 1980, S.O.S, 1981, Parker Bros. video game Popeye, 1983-84; soap opera Somerset, 1976-77, All My Children, 1983; other TV appearances include Good Morning America, 1980, Good Day Show, 1980, Picture Pages, 1981, Entertainment Tonight, Joan Rivers and Her Friends; also numerous recs. including Good Ship Lollipop; (Troupers award for outstanding contbn. to entertainment 1979, Annie award Internat. Animated Film Soc. 1979). Named Living Legend NYU Sch. Social Work, 1979. Mem. Screen Actors Guild, AFTRA, Actors Equity Assn., Nat. Acad. TV Arts and Scis. (award 1978), Hadassah. Clubs: Troupers (award 1963), Variety. Mae Questel Day named by City of Indpls., 1968. Home: 27 E 65th St Apt 7C New York NY 10021-6556 *My mother was a singer and a mimic - took me to the theater when I was about 3 yrs. old - performed in school and for many charities - always wanted to entertain - at seventeen won a "Betty Boop" contest. I have never turned down anything - performed on radio, tv, soap, theater and movies - always acted - because I just love show business.*

QUESTER, GEORGE HERMAN, political science educator; b. Bklyn., July 14, 1936; s. Jacob George and Elizabeth (Mattern) Q.; m. Aline Marie Olson, June 20, 1964; children: Theodore, Amanda. A.B., Columbia U., 1958; M.A., Harvard U., 1964, Ph.D., 1965. Instr., then asst. prof. govt. Harvard U., 1965-70; assoc. prof. govt. Cornell U., 1970-73, prof., 1973-82; prof. polit. sci. U. Md., College Park, 1982—; vis. prof. U.S. Naval Acad., Annapolis, Md., 1991-93. Author: Deterrence Before Hiroshima, 1966, Nuclear Diplomacy, 1970, The Politics of Nuclear Proliferation, 1973, The Continuing Problem of International Relations, 1974, Offense and Defense in the International System, 1977, American Foreign Policy: The Lost Consensus, 1982, The Future of Nuclear Deterrence, 1986, The International Politics of Television, 1990. Served with USAF, 1958-61. Fellow Center Advanced Study Behavioral Scis., 1974-75. Mem. Council Fgn. Relations, Inst. Strategic Studies, Am. Polit. Sci. Assn. Home: 5124 37th St N Arlington VA 22207-1862 Office: Univ Md Lefrak # 2181 College Park MD 20742

QUESTROM, ALLEN I., retail executive; b. Newton, Mass., Apr. 13, 1941; s. Irving Allen and Natalie (Chadbourne) Q.; m. Carol Brummer, Sept. 9, 1967. BS, Boston U., 1964. From exec. trainee to div. mdse. mgr. Abraham & Straus, Bklyn., 1965-73; v.p., gen. mdse. mgr. home store Bullock's, L.A., 1973-74, sr. v.p., gen. mdse. mgr. all stores, 1974-77; exec. v.p. Bullock's div. Federated Dept. Stores, L.A., 1977-78; pres. Rich's div. Federated Dept. Stores, Atlanta, 1978-80, chmn. bd., chief exec. officer, 1980-84, chmn. bd., chief exec. officer Bullock's/Bullocks Wilshire div., 1984-88; corp. exec. v.p. Federated Dept. Stores, Cin., 1987-88, vice-chmn., 1988; pres., chief exec. officer Neiman Marcus Group Inc., Dallas, 1988-90; chmn., chief exec. officer Federated Dept. Stores Inc., Cin., 1990—; also chmn., chief exec. officer Allied Stores Corp., Cin., 1990—. Avocations: skiing; golf; travel. *

QUETGLAS, MOLL JUAN, plastic and maxillofacial surgeon; b. Cuidadela, Menorca, Spain, Feb. 11, 1922; s. Honesto Quetglas Montserrat and Catalina Moll Coll; m. Conception Marimon Alvarez; children: Juan, Alfonso, Carlos. Degree, U. Barcelona, Spain, 1945; MD, U. Madrid, 1970. Diplomate Bd. Plastic Surgery, Bd. Maxillofacial Surgery and Plastic and Reconstructive Surgery, Bd. Gen. Surgery and Traumatology. Gen. practice medicine Mahon, Spain, 1945-52; resident in gen. surgery Madrid, 1953-55; head surg. svc. Mil. Hosp., Larache, Morocco, 1955-59, Tenerife, Canary Island, 1960-61; head surg. svc. Social Security, Madrid, 1962-84; head plastic surgery svc. Ctrl. Mils. Hosp., Madrid, 1962-87; prof. U. Madrid, 1978-87; dir. hosps. Social Security, 1968-71; mem. exec. com. I.S.A.P.S., 1975-76; prof. anatomy Med. Sch., Salamanca (Spain) U., 1972; asst. plastic surgery svc. Walter Reed Hosp., Washington, 1969. Author: Brief Handbook of Plastic and Aesthetic Surgery of the Face, 1971; co-author: Treatise of Medical Rehabilitation, 1967, 2d edit., 1970, Iberoamerican Text of Plastic Surgery, 1986, 2d edit., 1994, Art of Aesthetic Plastic Surgery, 1989, Ualoracion de las Secuelas Traumaticas en el Aparato Locomotor, 1995, Rehabilitacion Media-Editorial Masson, 1996; dir., founder Spanish Jour. Plastic Surgery, 1968-76; hon. dir. Jour. Plastic Jour., 1983; editor: Facial Traumatology, 1983; dir. Jour. Ibero-L.Am. Jour. Plastic Surgery, 1975—; contbr. over 100 articles to med. jours. Col. M.C., Spanish Army, 1987. Recipient Ex-Combatiente, Donador de Sangre, Cruz de San Hermenegildo, Placa de San Hermenegildo, Cruz del Merito Militar, Spanish Army Min., medal Complutense U. Madrid. Mem. Internat. Confedn. Plastic Surgery, Spanish Soc. Plastic Surgery (mem. exec. com. 1969-71, pres. 1972-74), Plastic Surgery Soc. Ecuador (hon.), Plastic Surgery Soc. Argentina (hon.), Plastic Surgery Soc. Chile (hon.), Spanish Soc. Traumatology, Assn. Mil. Plastic Surgeons, Assn. Mil. Surgeons, Acad. Surgery Madrid, N.Y. Acad. Scis., Helenic Soc. Plastic Reconstructive Surgery.

QUIAT, GERALD MARVIN, lawyer; b. Denver, Jan. 9, 1924; s. Ira L. and Esther (Greenblatt) Q.; m. Roberta M. Nicholson, Sept. 26, 1962; children: James M., Audrey R., Melinda A., Daniel P., Ilana L., Leonard E. AA, U. Calif., Berkeley, 1942; AB, LLB, U. Denver, 1948, changed to JD, 1970. Bar: Colo. 1948, Fed. Ct. 1948, U.S. Dist. Ct. Colo. 1948, U.S. Ct. Appeals (10th cir.) 1948, U.S. Surpeme Ct. 1970. Dep. dist. atty. County of Denver, Colo., 1949-52; partner firm Quiat, Seeman & Quiat, Denver, 1952-67, Quiat & Quiat (later changed to Quiat, Bucholtz & Bull, P.C.), 1968; pres. Quiat, Bucholtz & Bull & Laff, P.C. (and predecessors), Denver, 1968-85; pvt. practice Denver, 1985—; bd. dirs., chmn. audit com. Guaranty Bank & Trust Co., Denver; past bd. dirs. and chmn. bd. ROMED, RMD, Inc. Past trustee Holding Co., Rose Med. Ctr., Denver, pres., chmn. bd. dirs., 1976-79; mem. Colo. Civil Rights Com., 1963-71, chmn., 1966-67, 69-70, hearing officer, 1963-71; bd. dirs. Am. Cancer Rsch. Ctr., Denver, chmn. bd., 1991-93; chmn. bd. Am. Med. Ctr., 1993-95; mem. nat. civil rights com., hon. mem. nat. exec. com., hon. nat. commr. Anti-Defamation League, B'nai B'rith, mem. exec. com., chmn. bd. Mountain States region, 19809-82. With inf. U.S. Army, 1942-45. Decorated Bronze Star. Mem. ABA, Colo. Bar Assn., Colo. Trial Lawyers Assn. (pres. 1970-71), Am. Legion (comdr. Leyden-Chiles-Wickersham post 1 1955-56, past judge adv. Colo. dept.), Rotary (chmn. constn. and bylaws com. Denver club). Home: 8130 Lt Wm Clark Rd Parker CO 80134 Office: Penthouse Suite 1720 S Bellaire St Denver CO 80222-4304

QUICK, ALBERT THOMAS, law educator, university dean; b. BattleCreek, Mich., June 28, 1939; s. Robert and Vera Quick; m. Brenda Jones; children: Lori, Traci, Becki, Breton, Regan, Leigh. BA, U. Ariz., 1962; MA, Cen. Mich. U., 1964; JD, Wayne State U., 1967; LLM, Tulane U., 1974. Bar: Mich. 1968, Ky. 1987. Asst. prosecutor Calhoun County, Marshall, Mich., 1968-69; assoc. Hatch & Hatch, Marshall, 1969-70; asst. prof. U. Maine, Augusta, 1970-73; prof. law U. Louisville, 1974-87, spl. asst. to univ. provost, 1983-87; dean, prof. law Ohio No. U., Ada, 1987-95; prof. law, dean U. Toledo, Ohio, 1995—. Co-author: Update Federal Rules of Criminal Procedure; contbr. articles to profl. jours. Recipient Medallion of Justice Nat. Bar Assn., 1995. Mem. ABA, Assn. Am. Law Schs. (criminal justice sect.), Ky. State Bar Assn., Mich. State Bar Assn., Willis Soc., Ohio State Bar Assn., Toledo Bar Assn., Rotary, Phi Kappa Phi. Episcopalian. Avocations: racquetball, tennis, art, reading. Office: Univ Toledo Coll Law 2801 W Bancroft St Toledo OH 43606-3328

QUICK, EDWARD RAYMOND, museum director, educator; b. L.A., Mar. 22, 1943; s. Donald Russell Quick and Gertrude Ruth (Albin) Thornbrough; m. Ruth Ann Lessig; children: Jeannette Lee, Russell Raymond. BA, U. Calif., Santa Barbara, 1970, MA, 1977. Adminstr. supr. Civil Service, Santa Ana, Calif., 1971-75; sr. computer operator Santa Barbara Rsch. Ctr., 1975-77; asst. collections curator Santa Barbara Mus. Art, 1977-78; registrar Montgomery (Ala.) Mus. Fine Arts, 1978-80; head dept. registration and preparation Joslyn Art Mus., Omaha, 1980-85; dir. Sheldon Swope Art Mus., Terre Haute, Ind., 1985-95, Berman Mus., Anniston, Ala., 1995—; advisor Ind. Arts Commn., Indpls., 1986-91; mem. Arts in Pub. Places Commn., Terre Haute, 1986-93; bd. dirs. Arts Iliana, Terre Haute, 1986-91; pres. Friends Vigo County Pub. Libr., 1988-95, treas., 1990-93. Author: Code of Practice for Couriering Museum Objects, 1985, Gilbert Brown Wilson and Herman Melville's "Moby Dick", 1993; co-author: Registrars in Record, 1987, The American West, 1996. Bd. dirs. Vol. Action Ctr., Terre Haute, 1987-90, Terre Haute Community Relief Effort for Environ. and Civic Spirit, 1989. With USAF, 1961-65, Air N.G., 1979—. Mem. Am. Assn. Mus., Assn. Ind. Mus., Am. Assn. for State and Local History, Internat. Coun. Mus., Rotary Internat., Alpha Gamma Sigma. Republican. Avocation: working on nat. and internat. couriering of art objects. Office: Berman Mus 840 Museum Dr PO Box 2245 Anniston AL 36202-6261

QUICK, LESLIE CHARLES, III, brokerage house executive; b. Bklyn., Mar. 15, 1953; s. Leslie C. Jr. and Regina A. (Clarkson) Q.; m. Eileen Manning, July 7, 1979; children: L. Christopher, Ryan F., Kelsey M., Maura G. BBA in Fin., St. Bonaventure U., 1975; postgrad., Stanford U., 1987. Prin., pres. Quick & Reilly Group, N.Y.C., 1975—. Trustee St. Bonaventure U., N.Y., 1985—; bd. dirs. Mt. Iraneus-Franciscan Mountain Retreat, St. Bonaventure, N.Y., 1981—, Ireland/U.S. Coun. for Commerce and Industry, Inc., 1991—, St. Vincents Hosp., N.Y.C., 1992—. Mem. Securities Industry Assn. (bd. dirs. 1993), Nat. Assn. Securities Dealers (com. dist. 10 1989-91), Nat. Acad. Design (bd. advisors 1992—), Downtown Athletic Club, Plainfield Country Club (Edison, N.J.). Roman Catholic. Avocations: golf, family activities. Office: Quick & Reilly Group Inc 26 Broadway New York NY 10004-1703*

QUICK, NORMAN, bishop. Bishop of R.I. Ch. of God in Christ, Bklyn.

QUICK, THOMAS CLARKSON, brokerage house executive; b. Westbury, N.Y., Feb. 26, 1955; s. Leslie Charles and Regina (Clarkson) Q. BS in Bus., Fairfield U., 1977. Br. mgr. Quick & Reilly Inc., Palm Beach, Fla., 1977-81; dir., v.p. The Quick & Reilly Group, Palm Beach, 1981—; v.p. Quick & Reilly Inc., Palm Beach, 1981-86; pres. Quick & Reilly Inc., N.Y.C., 1986—, also bd. dirs.; trustee Security Industry Found. for Econ. Edn., Securities Industry Inst. Trustee Nat. Corp. Theater Fund; mem. investment adv. bd. and endowment com. St. Jude Children's Rsch. Hosp., Memphis, 1986—; chmn. com. Wall Street Friends of St. Jude Children's Rsch. Hosp., 1979—, mem. endowment com. Mem. The Investment Assn. N.Y., N.Y. Stock Exch., Securities and Industry Assn. (econ. edn. com.), Am. Assn. of Sovereign Mil., Order of Malta, Young Pres.'s Orgn., Univ. Club, Friendly Sons of St. Patrick, Apawamis Country Club (Rye, N.Y.), The Beach Club (Palm Beach, Fla.). Home: 30 Sutton Pl New York NY 10022 Office: Quick & Reilly Inc 26 Broadway New York NY 10004-1703

QUICK, WILLIAM THOMAS, author, consultant; b. Muncie, Ind., May 30, 1946; s. Clifford Willett and Della May (Ellis) Q. Student, Ind. U., 1964-66. Pres. Iceberg Prodns., San Francisco, 1986—. Author: Dreams of Flesh and Sand, 1988, Dreams of Gods and Men, 1989, Yesterday's Pawn, 1989, Systems, 1989, Singularities, 1990; (as Quentin Thomas) Chains of Light, 1992; (as Margaret Allan) The Mammoth Stone, 1993, Keeper of the Stone, 1994, The Last Mammoth, 1995; (as W.T. Quick) Star Control: Interbellum, 1996. Mem. Sci. Fiction and Fantasy Writers Am., The Authors Guild. Home and Office: 1558 Leavenworth St San Francisco CA 94109-3220

QUIE, PAUL GERHARDT, physician, educator; b. Dennison, Minn., Feb. 3, 1925; s. Albert Knute and Nettie Marie (Jacobson) Q.; m. Elizabeth Holmes, Aug. 10, 1951; children: Katie, Bill, Paul, David. B.A., St. Olaf Coll., 1949; M.D., Yale U., 1953; PhD (hon.), U. Lund, 1993. Diplomate Am. Bd. Pediatrics, Nat. Bd. Med. Examiners (mem.). Intern Hennepin County Hosp., 1953-54; pediatric resident U. Minn. Hosps., 1957-59; mem. faculty U. Minn. Med. Sch., 1959—, prof. pediatrics, 1968—, prof. microbiology, 1974—; assoc. dean of students, 1992—; Am. Legion meml. heart research prof. U. Minn. Med. Sch., 1974-91, Regents prof., 1991, interim dir. Ctr. for Biomed. Ethics, 1985-86; attending physician Hennepin County Hosp., 1959-91; cons. U. Minn. Nursery Sch., 1959-91; chief of staff U. Minn. Hosp., 1979-84; vis. physician Radcliffe Infirmary, Oxford, Eng., 1971-72; mem. Adv. Allergy and Infectious Disease Coun., 1976-80; mem. pediat. com. NRC, 1978; mem. bd. sci. counselors Gamble Inst., 1985-90; vis. prof. U. Bergen, 1991; hon. prof. U. Hong Kong Med. Sch., 1995; vis. prof. pediat. Chubu Hosp., Nagasaki, Japan, 1996. Mem. editorial bd. Pediatrics, 1970-76, Rev. Infectious Diseases, 1989-92. Served with USNR, 1954-57; med. officer. Recipient E. Mead-Johnson award Am. Acad. Pediatrics, 1971; Guggenheim fellow, 1971-72; John and Mary R. Markle scholar, 1960-65; Alexander Von Humbolt fellow, 1986. Mem. Inst. Medicine of NAS, N.W. Pediatrics Soc., Minn. Med. Found. (pres. 1986-88), Am. Fedn. Clin. Rsch., Am. Soc. Microbiology, Infectious Diseases Soc. Am. (coun. 1977-82, pres. 1985, Bristol award 1994), Soc. Pediatric Rsch., Am. Pediatric Soc. (coun. 1976-83, pres. 1987-88), Am. Soc. Clin. Investigation, Minn. Acad. Pediatrics, Am. Acad. Pediatrics, Assn. Am. Physicians, Minn. Acad. Medicine (pres. 1993-94). Research in function of human leukocytes. Home: 2154 Commonwealth Ave Saint Paul MN 55108-1717 Office: U Minn Hosp PO Box 483 Minneapolis MN 55440-0483

QUIGG, JEAN, principal. Prin. Frostwood Elem. Sch., Houston. Recipient Elem. Sch. Recognition award U.S. Dept. Edn., 1989-90. Office: Frostwood Elem Sch 12214 Memorial Dr Houston TX 77024-6207

QUIGLEY, AUSTIN EDMUND, literature and language educator; b. Newcastle-upon-Tyne, Eng., Dec. 31, 1942; came to U.S., 1969; s. Edmund and Marguerita Mary (Crilley) Q.; m. Patricia Doreen Denison, June 1, 1979. BA with honors, U. Nottingham, Eng., 1967; MA, U. Birmingham, Eng., 1969; PhD, U. Calif., Santa Cruz, 1971. Asst. prof. U. Mass., 1971-73; from asst. prof. to prof. U. Va., 1973-90, chmn. dept. English, 1986-90; H. Gordon Garbedian prof. English and comparative lit. Columbia U., N.Y.C., 1990—, chmn. PhD program theatre Hammerstein Ctr. Theatre Studies, 1990—; dean Columbia Coll., 1995—; chmn. Lionel Trilling Seminars, 1993—; vis. prof. U. Konstanz, Germany, 1981, U. Geneva, 1982, U. Nottingham, Eng., 1983-84; lectr. at univs., convs. and theatres. Author: The Pinter Problem, 1975, The Modern Stage and Other Worlds, 1985; contbr. many articles on modern lit., drama, lit. theory to profl. jours.; mem. edit. bd. New Lit. History, Va., 1974—, Modern Drama, Toronto, 1978—, The Pinter Rev., Tampa, Fla., 1987—, Theater/Theory/Text Performance, Ann Arbor, Mich., 1988—. Danforth fellow U. Calif., 1970-71, fellow NEH, London, 1977-78. Mem. MLA (exec. com. drama div. 1987-92), Linguistics Assn. Gt. Britain, Samuel Beckett Soc., Harold Pinter Soc., Am. Soc. Theatre Rsch., Shakespeare Assn. Am., Phi Beta Kappa, Omicron Delta Kappa. Avocations: tennis, squash, soccer, hiking. Office: Columbia Univ Dept English 208 Hamilton Hall New York NY 10027

QUIGLEY, JACK ALLEN, service company executive; b. Bloomington, Ill., Apr. 11, 1914; s. Thomas M. and Margaret (Brown) Q.; m. Eleanor T. Steen, Nov. 17, 1946 (dec. 1996); children: J. Timothy, J. William, Margaret N., Richard A. B.S., Northwestern U., 1935. With Means Services, Inc., 1935—, personnel dir., 1935-37, div. mgr., 1937-41, gen. mgr., 1946-48, v.p., dir., 1948-50, pres., dir., 1950-72, chmn. bd., chief exec. officer, 1972-96; cons., 1981—; Co-chmn. First and Second Internat. Linen Supply Congresses, 1959, 62; founder, chmn. Chgo. Pres.'s Orgn., 1966-68, Young Pres.'s Orgn., 1951-62. Served with USAF, World War II. Mem. Linen Supply Assn. Am. (pres. 1955-57, founder chmn. rsch. group 1957-60), Chief Execs. Forum, Royal Poinciana Golf Club (Naples, Fla.). Home: 114 Moorings Park Dr Apt A-812 Naples FL 33942-2112 *Died, March 26, 1996.*

QUIGLEY, JEROME HAROLD, management consultant; b. Green Bay, Wis., Apr. 19, 1925; s. Harold D. and Mabel (Hansen) Q.; BS, St. Norbert Coll., 1951; m. Lorraine A. Rocheleau, May 3, 1947; children: Kathy, Ross, Michael, Daniel, Mary Beth, Andrew, Maureen. Personnel adminstr. Gen. Motors Corp., 1959-64; dir. indsl. rels. Raytheon Co., Santa Barbara, Calif., 1964-67; dir. personnel U. Calif., Santa Barbara, 1967-72; corp. dir. indsl. rels. Gen. Rsch. Corp., 1972-73; dir. indsl. rels. ISS Sperry Univac, 1973-75; corp. dir. indsl. rels. Four-Phase Systems, Inc., Cupertino, Calif., 1975; sr. v.p. human resources UNC, Annapolis, Md., 1975-86; pres. Profl. Guidance Assocs. Inc., 1986—. Aviator with U.S. Navy, 1943-47. Mem. Am. Electronics Assn., Assn. Former Intelligence Officers, Machinery and Allied Products Inst., Assn. Naval Aviation, Tailhook Assn., Navy Aviation Mus. Found., Navy League, Soc. for Human Resource Mgmt., Scottsdale Radisson Racquet Club. Republican. Roman Catholic. Office: Profl Guidance Assocs Inc 7789 E Joshua Tree Ln Scottsdale AZ 85250-7962

QUIGLEY, JOHN BERNARD, law educator; b. St. Louis, Oct. 1, 1940; s. John Bernard and Ruth Rosina (Schieber) Q. BA, Harvard U., 1962, MA, LLB, 1966. Bar: Ohio 1973, Mass. 1967, U.S. Dist. Ct. (so. dist.) Ohio 1976, U.S. Ct. Appeals (6th cir.) 1986, U.S. Supreme Ct. 1989. Research assoc. Harvard U. Law Sch., Cambridge, Mass., 1967-69; prof. law Ohio State U., Columbus, 1969—. Author: Basic Laws on the Structure of the Soviet State, 1969, The Soviet Foreign Trade Monopoly, 1974, Palestine and Israel: A Challenge to Justice, 1990, The Ruses for War: American Interventionism since World War II, 1992. Mem. Nat. Lawyers Guild (v.p. 1977-79), Am. Soc. Internat. Law, AAUP. Avocations: tennis, speed skating, violin. Office: Ohio State U Coll of Law Coll of Law 55 W 12th Ave Columbus OH 43210-1338

QUIGLEY, JOHN MICHAEL, economist, educator; b. N.Y.C., Feb. 12, 1942. B.S. with distinction, U.S. Air Force Acad., 1964; M.Sc. with honors, U. Stockholm, Sweden, 1965; A.M., Harvard U., 1971, Ph.D., 1972. Commd. 2d lt. USAF, 1964, advanced through grades to capt., 1968; asst. prof. econs. Yale U., 1972-74, assoc. prof., 1974-81; prof. pub. policy U. Calif., Berkeley, 1979—, prof. econs., 1981—, chmn. dept. econs., 1992—; vis. prof. econs. and stats. U. Gothenberg, 1978; cons. numerous govt. agys. and pvt. firms; econometrician Hdqrs. U.S. Air Force, Pentagon, 1965-68; research assoc. Nat. Bur. Econ. Research, N.Y.C., 1968-78; mem. com. on nat. urban policy Nat. Acad. Sci., 1985—. Author, editor, contbr. articles to profl. jours.; editor in chief Reg. Sci. and Urban Econs., 1987—; mem. editorial bd. Land Econs., 1974-81, Jour. Urban Econs., 1978—, Coun. on Pub. Policy and Mgmt., 1979—, AREUEA Jour., 1985—, Property Tax Jour., 1990—, Jour. Housing Econs., 1990—. Fulbright scholar, 1964-65; fellow NSF, 1968-69, Woodrow Wilson, 1968-71, Harvard IBM, 1969-71, NDEA, 1969-71, Thord-Gray Am. Scandinavian Found. 1971-72, Social Sci. Research Council, 1971-72. Mem. Am. Econ. Assn., Econometric Soc., Regional Sci. Assn. (bd. dirs. 1986—), Nat. Tax Assn., Assn. for Pub. Policy and Mgmt. (bd. dirs. 1986-89, v.p. 1987-89), AREUEA (bd. dirs. 1987—, v.p. 1995—). Home: 875 Hilldale Ave Berkeley CA 94708-1319 Office: U Calif 2607 Hearst Ave Berkeley CA 94709-1005

QUIGLEY, LEONARD VINCENT, lawyer; b. Kansas City, Mo., June 21, 1933; s. Joseph Vincent and Rosemary (Cannon) Q.; m. Lynn Mathis Pfohl, May 23, 1964; children: Leonard Matthew, Cannon Louise, Daniel Pfohl, Megan Mathis. A.B., Coll. Holy Cross, 1953; LL.B. magna cum laude, Harvard U., 1959; LL.M. in Internat. Law, NYU, 1962. Bar: N.Y. 1960. Assoc. Cravath, Swaine & Moore, N.Y.C., 1959-67; ptnr. Paul, Weiss, Rifkind, Wharton & Garrison, N.Y.C., 1968; gen. counsel Archaeol. Inst. Am., Boston. Served to lt. USN, 1953-56. Mem. ABA, Can. Bar Assn., N.Y. State Bar, Coun. Fgn. Rels., Assn. Bar City N.Y., Harvard Club (N.Y.C.), West Side Tennis Club (Forest Hills, N.Y.).

QUIGLEY, MARTIN SCHOFIELD, publishing company executive, educator; b. Chgo., Nov. 24, 1917; s. Martin Joseph and Gertrude Margaret (Schofield) Q.; m. Katherine J. Dunphy, July 2, 1946; children: Martin, Elin, William, Kevin, Karen, Patricia, John, Mary Katherine, Peter. AB magna cum laude, Georgetown U., 1939; MA, Columbia U., 1973, EdD, 1975. Reporter Motion Picture Herald, N.Y.C. and Hollywood, Calif., 1939-41; with overseas br. OWI, 1942; secret war work U.S. Govt., 1943-45; various editorial and mgmt. posts Quigley Pub. Co., Inc., N.Y.C., 1946—; pres. Quigley Pub. Co., Inc., 1964—; staff, dept. higher and adult edn. Tchrs. Coll., 1974-75; prof. higher edn. grad. courses Baruch Coll. CUNY, 1977-89; prof. higher edn. grad. courses Tchrs. Coll. Columbia U., 1979-80, 90; prof. higher edn. grad. courses Seton Hall U., 1981-82; pres. QWS, Inc., 1975-80; ednl. cons.; cons. supt. schs. N.Y. Archdiocese, 1962-70. Author: Great Gaels, 1944, Roman Notes, 1946, Magic Shadows--the story of the origin of motion pictures, 1948, Government Relations of Five Universities in Washington, D.C., 1975, Peace Without Hiroshima-Secret Action at the Vatican in Spring of 1945, 1991, First Century of Film, 1995; co-author: Catholic Action in Practice, 1962, Films in America, 1969; editor: New Screen Techniques, 1953. Pres. N.Y. Christian Family Movement, 1960-62, mem. nat. exec. com., 1960-65; founder, chmn. N.Y. Ind. Schs. Opportunity Project, 1965-77; pres. Found. Internat. Coop., 1960-65; bd. dirs. Will Rogers Inst., Motion Picture Pioneers; treas. Religious Edn. Assn. U.S. and Can., 1975-81, chmn., 1981-84; trustee Village of Larchmont, N.Y., 1977-79, mayor, 1980-84; mem. Laymen's Nat. Bible Assn., 1981—; trustee Am. Bible Soc., 1984—; bd. dirs. William J. Donovan Meml. Found., 1994—. Roman Catholic. Club: Larchmont Yacht. Home: 8 Pheasant Run Larchmont NY 10538-3423 Office: 159 W 53rd St New York NY 10019-6050

QUIGLEY, PHILIP J., telecommunications industry executive; b. 1943. With Advanced Mobile Phone Svc. Inc., 1982-84, v.p., gen. mgr., Pacific region; with Pac Tel Mobile Access, 1984-86, pres., chief exec. officer; with Pac Tel Personal Communications, 1986-87, pres., chief exec. officer; exec. v.p., chief oper. officer Pac Tel Corp., 1987; with Pacific Bell, San Francisco, 1987—; now chmn., pres., chief exec. officer Pacific Bell Group, Pacific Telesis, San Francisco. Office: Pacific Bell 140 New Montgomery St San Francisco CA 94105-3705*

QUIGLEY, ROBERT LAWRENCE, cardiothoracic surgeon, educator; b. Halifax, N.S., Can., Dec. 16, 1957; came to U.S., 1988; s. John Howden and Gloria Lorraine (Monseur) Q.; m. Debra Kristine Crumb, Sept. 4, 1993. BS, Dalhousie U., Halifax, 1978; MD, U. Toronto, Ont., Can., 1982; DPhil, Oxford (Eng.) U., 1988. Diplomate Am. Bd. Surgery, Am. Bd. Critical Care, Am. Bd. Thoracic Surgery. Intern U. Toronto, 1982-83, resident in surgery, 1983-85; rsch. fellow Oxford U., 1985-88; resident in Surgery Duke U. Med. Ctr., Durham, N.C., 1988-90, fellow in cardiothoracic surgery, 1990-92; asst. prof. surgery Northwestern U.-Evanston (Ill.) Hosp., 1992-95, dir. Surg. Rsch. Lab., 1994-95; assoc. cardiothoracic surgery Guthrie Clinic, Sayre, Pa., 1995—. Recipient rsch. award Med. Rsch. Coun. Can., 1986-88, Golden Apple award med. students Duke U. Med. Ctr., 1990; faculty fellow ACS, 1994-96. Fellow Am. Coll. Surgeons, Am. Coll. Chest Physicians; mem. Soc. Critical Care Medicine, Alpha Omega Alpha. Avocations: running, sailing, water and snow skiing, swimming. Home: 316 Drive C Strathmont Pk Elmira NY 14905 Office: Guthrie Clinic Dept Surgery Guthrie Sq Sayre PA 18840

QUIGLEY, THOMAS J., lawyer; b. Mt. Carmel, Pa., July 22, 1923; s. James S. and Helen C. (Laughlin) Q.; m. Joan R. Reifke, Aug. 11, 1956; children: Thomas J., Jr., Joan E., James S. AB, Bucknell U., 1947; LLB, Yale U., 1950. Bar: Ohio, U.S. Dist. Ct. Ohio, U.S. Ct. Appeals (6th and D.C. cirs.). With Squire, Sanders & Dempsey, 1950—, adminstr. labor dept., 1971-80, mng. ptnr., Washington, 1980-85; nat. vice chmn., 1985-86; nat. chmn., 1986-90. Immediate past pres., dir. exec. com. Nat. Symphony Orch., nat. trustee Musical Arts Assn. Cleve. 1st lt. USAAF, 1942-45. Decorated D.F.C., Air medal with oak leaf cluster, Belgium's Order of the Crown. Mem. ABA, Ohio Bar Assn., D.C. Bar Assn., Cleve. Bar Assn., Belgian-Am. C. of C. (bd. dirs.), Yale Law Sch. Alumni. Assn. (bd. dirs.), Case-Western Res. Univ. Law Sch. (vis. com.). Roman Catholic. Clubs: Yale (N.Y.C.), Edgartown Yacht (Mass.), Chevy Chase, Metropolitan (Wash.). Office: Squire Sanders & Dempsey PO Box 407 1201 Pennsylvania Ave NW Washington DC 20004 also: Soc Ctr Bldg Cleveland OH 44114

QUILICO, LOUIS, baritone; b. Montreal, Que., Can., Jan. 14, 1925; s. Louis and Jeanne (Gravel) Q.; m. Lina Pezzolongo, Oct. 30, 1949 (dec. Sept. 1991); children: Donna Maria, Gino; m. Christina Petrowska, Nov. 30, 1993; children: Alexander, Dominique. Studied, Conservatoire de la Province de Que., Ont., Can., Mannes Coll. Music, N.Y.C., Conservatoir de Santa Cecilia, Rome. Prof. U. Toronto, Ont., Acad. Vocal Art, Phila. Operatic debut in La Traviata, N.Y.C. Opera, 1956; performed with major opera cos. including Royal Opera, Covent Garden, Staatsoper, Opera Nat. de Belgique, L'Opera de Quebec, Canadian Opera Co., Bolshoi Opera, Opera Co. of Phila., San Francisco Opera, Seattle Opera, San Diego Opera, Opera Soc. of Washington (D.C.), many others; created numerous roles; resident mem., Met. Opera, (Winner Nos Futurs Étoi Les, Montreal 1953, Met. Opera Audition of the Air 1955). Named Esquire Montreal Expo, 1967; decorated companion Order of Can. Roman Catholic. Office: care Robert Lombardo Assocs One Harkness Plaza 61 W 62nd St Ste 6F New York NY 10023-7201 also: Ann Summers Int, Box 188 Station A, Toronto, ON Canada M5W 1B2

QUILL, LEONARD WALTER, banker; b. Wilmington, Del., Dec. 11, 1931; s. Timothy Joseph and Katherine (McCann) Q.; m. Martina Mary Quinn, July 12, 1958; children—Martina, Teresa, Katherine, Timothy, Leonard, James. B.S., U. Del., M.B.A. With Wilmington Trust Co., Wilmington, Del., 1957—, now mgr. comml. banking dept., sr. v.p., treas.; chmn. of bd., ceo, 1996—; dir. Wilmington Econ. Devel. Corp. Bd. dirs. United Way Del., 1983—. Served to sgt. USAF, 1951-53. Mem. Del. Bankers Assn. (bd. dirs. 1985—), Roman Catholic. Home: 1104 Arundel Dr Wilmington DE 19808-2135 Office: Wilmington Trust Co 1100 N Market St Wilmington DE 19810-1246*

QUILLEN, CECIL DYER, JR., lawyer, consultant; b. Kingsport, Tenn., Jan. 21, 1937; s. Cecil D. and Mary Louise (Carter) Q.; m. Vicey Ann Childress, Apr. 1, 1961; children: Cecil D., Ann C. BS, Va. Poly. Inst., 1958; LLB, U. Va., 1962. Bar: Va. 1962, N.Y. 1963, Tenn. 1974. Atty. patent dept. Eastman Kodak Co., Rochester, N.Y., 1962-65, atty. patent sect. Tenn. Eastman Co. (div. Eastman Kodak), Kingsport, Tenn., 1965-69, mgr., 1969-72, mgr. licensing, 1972-74, sec. and asst. chief counsel, 1974-76, dir. patent litigation Eastman Kodak, 1976-82, dir. antitrust litigation Eastman Kodak, 1978-82, v.p. and chief counsel Tenn. Eastman, 1983-85, v.p., and assoc. gen. counsel Eastman Kodak, 1986, sr. v.p., gen. counsel, dir., 1986-92; sr. adv., Putnam, Hayes & Bartlett, Inc., Washington, 1992—. Mem. ABA, Va. State Bar, Am. Intellectual Property Law Assn., Va. Poly. Inst. Com. of 100, Assn. of Gen. Counsel.

QUILLEN, JAMES HENRY (JIMMY QUILLEN), congressman; b. Wayland, Va., Jan. 11, 1916; s. John A. and Hannah (Chapman) Q.; m. Cecile Cox, Aug. 9, 1952. Ed. high sch.; LL.D. (hon.), Milligan Coll., Tenn., 1978. With Kingsport Press, 1934-35, Kingsport Times, 1935-36; founder newspaper Kingsport Mirror (semi-weekly), 1936, pub., 1936-39; founder Johnson City (Tenn.) Times, 1939, pub., 1939-44; pub. Johnson City (Tenn.) Times (converted to daily), 1940; Mem. Tenn. Ho. of Reps., 1954-62, minority leader, 1959-60, mem. legislative council, 1957, 59, 61, mem. rules com., subcom. legis. process, Rep. chmn. emeritus; mem. U.S. Congress from Tenn., 1963—. Served to lt. USNR, 1942-46. Mem. Am. Legion, VFW, C. of C. Republican. Methodist. Clubs: Lions, Ridgefields Country (Kingsport); Capitol Hill (Washington). Office: US Ho Reps 102 Cannon Ho Office Bldg Washington DC 20515*

QUILLEN, MARY ANN, university administrator, consultant; b. Md., Dec. 10, 1947; 1 child, Jessica. BS, Del. State U., 1977; Cert. Spl. Edn., Pa. State U., 1981; MS, U. Pa., 1991. Adminstrv. asst. Manor Jr. Coll., Jenkintown, Pa., 1977-79; spl. edn. tchr. Wordsworth Acad., Ft. Washington, Pa., 1979-82; tchr. specialist Rens, Inc., Langhorne, Pa., 1982-83; area rep. Pa. State U., King of Prussia, 1983-85; dir. continuing edn. Ea. Montgomery County AVTS, Willow Grove, Pa., 1985-93; mgr. Drexel U., Phila., 1993—; con. in field. Vice chair Montgomery County Commn. on Women and Families, Norristown, Pa., 1992—; coord. Domestic Violence Forum for Montgomery County, Norristown, 1994—. Mem. ASTD, AAUW, Pa. Assn. for Adult and Continuing Edn., U. Pa. Alumni Assn. (dir. comm. com. 1993—). Avocations: gourmet cooking, gardening, reading. Home: 1000 Valley Forge Cir #1103 King Of Prussia PA 19406

QUILLEN, WILLIAM TATEM, judge, lawyer, educator; b. Camden, N.J., Jan. 15, 1935; s. Robert James and Gladys Collings (Tatem) Q.; m. Marcia Everhart Stirling, June 27, 1959; children: Carol Everhart, Tracey Tatem. B.A., Williams Coll., 1956; LL.B., Harvard U., 1959; LL.M., U. Va., 1982. Bar: Del. 1959. Assoc. Richards, Layton & Finger, Wilmington, Del., 1963-64; adminstrv. asst. to Gov. of Del., 1965; assoc. judge Superior Ct. of Del., 1966-73; chancellor State of Del., 1973-76; sr. v.p. Wilmington Trust Co., 1976-78; justice Supreme Ct. of Del., 1978-83; ptnr. Potter Anderson & Corroon, Wilmington, 1983-86; gen. counsel, v.p. Howard Hughes Med. Inst., 1986-91; sec. of state State of Del., Dover, 1993-94; assoc. judge Superior Ct. Del., Wilmington, 1994—; mem. adj. faculty Widener U. Sch. Law, Wilmington, 1976-83, 85-86, 95—, disting. vis. prof. law, 1992-94. Trustee Widener U., 1979-91; Democratic candidate for gov. Del., 1984. Served with JAGC, USAF, 1959-62. Mem. Am. Bar Assn., Del. State Bar Assn., Phi Beta Kappa. Democrat. Presbyterian. Club: Wilmington.

QUILLIAN, WARREN WILSON, II, pediatrician, educator; b. Miami, Fla., Jan. 21, 1936; s. Warren Wilson and Rosabel (Brown) Q.; m. Sallie Ruth Creel, July 26, 1958; children: Rutledge, Ruth, Warren C., Frances. MD, Emory U., 1961. Diplomate Am. Bd. Pediat. (examiner 1966—, bd. dirs. 1974-80, 1992—, treas. 1978, v.p. 1979, pres. 1980). Intern in pediatrics Vanderbilt U., Nashville, 1961-62; resident Children's Hosp. Med. Ctr., Harvard U., Boston, 1962-63; chief resident Grady Meml. Hosp., Emory U., Atlanta, 1963-64; pvt. practice, Coral Gables, Fla., 1966; instr., asst. clin. prof., assoc. clin. prof., now clin. prof. pediat. U. Miami Med. Sch., 1966—; active staff, bd. dirs. Miami Children's Hosp.; active staff Jackson Meml. Hosp.; chief pediat. Doctors' Hosp.; mem. courtesy staff Mercy Hosp., Bapt. Hosp., South Miami Hosp., Cedars of Lebanon Hosp.; chmn. health adv. com. Dade County Schs.; bd. dirs., v.p. Am. Bd. Pediat. Found., 1991—; mem. adv. bd. McGlannon Sch.; cons. Fla. Div. Med. Svcs.; bd. dirs. Bank Coral Gables. Contbr. articles to med. jours. Hon. bd. dirs. Soc. for Abused Children of Children's Home Soc., Miami, 1980-84; mem. Coral Gables Code Enforcement Bd., 1986-88; team-sch. physician Coral Gables Sr. H.G., 1980-88; bd. dirs. Dade County March of Dimes, Miami, 1968-72; bd. advisors Dade County Assn. Retarded Children, 1968-76; trustee Emory U., 1991—; mem. coun. ministries, youth coord., mem. fin. com., Sunday sch. tchr. United Meth. Ch. Coral Gables, 1966—; mem. parrish rels. com.; mem. bd. advisors The Growing Place. Capt. M.C., U.S. Army, 1964-66. Recipient citation of merit Emory U., 1980, alumni commendation Miami Children's Hosp., 1983, Teaching award U. Miami Sch. Medicine, 1995. Fellow Am. Acad. Pediat.; mem. AMA, Fla. Med. Assn. (sch. health com.), Fla. Pediatric Soc. (past chmn. sch. health com.), So. Med. Assn., Dade County Med. Assn. (sch. health com., continuing edn. com.), Empirical Soc. (past pres.), So. Soc. for Pediatric Rsch., So. Perinatal Soc., Greater Miami Pediatric Soc. (past pres., chmn. legis. and sch. health com.), Miami Med. Forum (past pres., Maxwell Cup 1985), Alpha Omega Alpha, Omicron Delta Kappa, Alpha Epsilon Upsilon, Phi Delta Theta. Democrat. Avocations: fishing, golf. Office: 305 Granello Ave Coral Gables FL 33146-1806

QUILLIAN, WILLIAM FLETCHER, JR., retired banker, former college president; b. Nashville, Apr. 13, 1913; s. William Fletcher and Nonie (Acree) Q.; m. Margaret Hannah Weigle, June 15, 1940; children—William Fletcher III, Anne Acree, Katherine, Robert. A.B., Emory U., 1935, Litt.D. (hon.), 1959; B.D., Yale, 1938, Ph.D., 1943; postgrad., U. Edinburgh, 1938-39, U. Basel, 1939; Day fellow from, Yale, 1938-39; Rosenwald fellow, 1940-41; LL.D., Ohio Wesleyan U., 1952, Hampden-Sydney Coll., 1978, Randolph-Macon Coll., 1967; D.H.L., Randolph-Macon Woman's Coll., 1978. Ordained to ministry Meth. Ch., 1942. Student asst. Stamford (Conn.) Presbyn Ch., 1936-38; del. Gen. Com. of World Student Christian Fedn., Bievres, France, 1938; discussion leader World Conf. Christian Youth, Amsterdam, Holland, 1939; pastor Clarendon (Vt.) Community Ch., summer 1940; asst. prof. philosophy Gettysburg Coll., 1941-43, prof., 1943-45; prof. philosophy Ohio Wesleyan U., 1945-52; pres. Randolph Macon Woman's Coll., 1952-78; pres. emeritus Randolph Macon Woman's Coll., 1978—; sr. v.p. Central Fidelity Bank, 1978-88; exec. dir. Greater Lynchburg (Va.) Community Trust, 1988—; v.p., bd. dirs. Pride of Virginia Meats, Inc.; tchr. Garrett Biblical Inst., summer 1951. Author: The Moral Theory of Evolutionary Naturalism, 1945, Evolution and Moral Theory in America, Evolutionary Thought in America, 1950; Contbr. articles to philos. and religious jours. Pres. bd. dirs. United Way Cen. Va., campaign chmn., 1987; bd. dirs. Alpha Tau Omega Found., Lynchburg Gen. Hosp.; hon. life trustee Va. Found. Ind. Colls., pres., 1958-61. Mem. Assn. Va. Colls. (past pres.), So. U. Conf. (pres. 1967-68), So. Assn. Colls. for Women (pres. 1956), Nat. Assn. United Methodist Colls. and Univs. (pres. 1973), Am. Philos. Assn., Soc. for Values in Higher Edn. (mem. central com. 1945-48, chmn. 1947-48), Nat. Assn. Bibl. Instrs., AAUP, Greater Lynchburg C. of C. (dir. pres. 1979-80), Phi Beta Kappa., Omicron Delta Kappa, Alpha Tau Omega (dir. found.). Home: 1407 Club Dr Lynchburg VA 24503-2503 Office: Central Fidelity Bank Lynchburg VA 24505

QUILLIGAN, EDWARD JAMES, obstetrician, gynecologist, educator; b. Cleve., June 18, 1925; s. James Joseph and Maude Elvira (Ryan) Q.; m. Betty Jane Cleaton, Dec. 14, 1946; children—Bruce, Jay, Carol, Christopher, Linda, Ted. B.A., Ohio State U., 1951, M.D., 1951; M.A. (hon.), Yale, 1967. Intern Ohio State U. Hosp., 1951-52, resident, 1952-54; resident Western Res. U. Hosps., 1954-56; asst. prof. obstetrics and gynecology Western Res. U., 1957-63, prof., 1963-65; prof. obstetrics and gynecology UCLA, 1965-66; prof., chmn. dept. Ob-Gyn Yale U., 1966-69; prof., chmn. dept. Ob-Gyn U. So. Calif., 1969-78, assoc. v.p. med. affairs, 1978-79; prof. Ob-Gyn. U. Calif., Irvine, 1980-83, vice chancellor health affairs, dean Sch. Medicine, 1987-89; prof., chmn. ob.-gyn. dept. U. Wis., 1983-85; prof., chmn. Ob-Gyn Davis Med. Ctr. U. Calif., Sacramento, 1985-87; vice chancellor Health Scis., dean Coll. Med. U. Calif., Irvine, 1987-89, prof. ob-gyn, 1987-94, prof. emeritus ob-gyn., 1994; exec. dir. med. edn. Long Beach (Calif.) Meml. Health Svcs., 1995—. Contbr. articles to med. jours.; co-editor-in-chief: Am. Jour. Obstetrics and Gynecology. Served to 2d lt. AUS, 1944-46. Recipient Centennial award Ohio State U., 1970. Mem. Soc. Gynecologic Investigation, Am. Gynecol. Soc., Am. Coll. Obstetrics and Gynecology, Sigma Xi. Home: 24 Urey Ct Irvine CA 92715-4045 Office: UC Irvine Med Ctr Dept Ob-Gyn Bldg 40 101 The City Dr S Orange CA 92668-3201

QUIMBY, FRED WILLIAM, pathology educator, veterinarian; b. Providence, Sept. 19, 1945; s. Edward Harold and Isabel (Barber) Q.; m. Cynthia Claire Connelly, Aug. 21, 1965; children—Kelly Ann, Cynthia Jane. V.M.D., U. Pa., 1970, Ph.D., 1974. Diplomate Am. Coll. Lab. Animal Medicine. Hematology fellow New Eng. Med. Ctr., Boston, 1974-75, instr. pathology, 1975-76, asst. prof., 1976-79; assoc. prof. pathology Cornell Med. Coll., N.Y.C., 1979-92, prof. pathology, 1993—; assoc. prof. N.Y. State Vet. Coll., Ithaca, 1979-93, prof. pathology, 1993—; dir. lab. animal medicine Tufts-New Eng. Med. Ctr., Boston, 1975-79; dir. Ctr. Rsch. Animal Resources, Cornell U., Ithaca, 1979—. Editor: Clinical Chemistry of Laboratory Animals, 1988, Animal Welfare, 1992, Lab. Animal Sci., 1992-93, consulting editor, 1993—; chmn. editorial bd. ILAr News, 1988-91; contbr. 100 sci. papers and abstracts. Greenfield Trust scholar, 1966-70; N.H. Rural Rehab. Corp. scholar, 1966-70; U. Pa. scholar, 1969-70; recipient Charles River prize Am. Vet. Med. Assn., 1995. Mem. Am. Assn. Lab. Animal Sci. (pres. Northeast br. 1978-79; B. Trum award 1979), World Vet. Assn. (sec. exec. com. animal welfare 1990—). Episcopalian. Home: 115 Terrace View Dr Ithaca NY 14850-6256 Office: NYSCVM Cornell U 221 Vrt Ithaca NY 14853

QUIMBY, GEORGE IRVING, anthropologist, former museum director; b. Grand Rapids, Mich., May 4, 1913; s. George Irving and Ethelwyn (Sweet) Q.; m. Helen M. Ziehm, Oct. 13, 1940; children: Sedna H., G. Edward, John E., Robert W. B.A., U. Mich., 1936, M.A., 1937, grad. fellow, 1937-38; postgrad., U. Chgo., 1938-39; LHD (hon.), Grand Valley State U., Mich., 1992. State supr. Fed. Archaeol. Project in La., 1939-41; dir. Muskegon (Mich.) Mus., 1941-42; asst. curator N.Am. archaeology and ethnology Field Mus. Natural History, 1942-43, curator exhibits, anthropology, 1943-54, curator N.Am. archeology and ethnology, 1954-65, research assoc. in N. Am. archaeology and ethnology, 1965—; curator anthropology Thomas Burke Meml. Wash. State Mus.; prof. anthropology U. Wash., 1965-83, emeritus prof., 1983—, mus. dir., 1968-83, emeritus dir., 1983—; lectr. U. Chgo., 1947-65, Northwestern U., 1949-53; Fulbright vis. prof., U. Oslo, Norway, 1952; archaeol. expdns. and field work, Mich., 1935, 37, 42, 56-63, Wis., 1936, Hudson's Bay, 1939, La., 1940-41, N.Mex., 1947, Lake Superior, 1956-61. Author: Aleutian Islanders, 1944, (with J. A. Ford) The Tchefuncte Culture, an Early Occupation of the Lower Mississippi Valley, 1945, (with P. S. Martin, D. Collier) Indians Before Columbus, 1947, Indian Life in the Upper Great Lakes, 1960, Indian Culture and European Trade Goods, 1966, A Thing of Sherds and Patches: The Autobiography of George Irving Quimby, American Antiquity, vol. 58, 1, 1993; prodr. documentary film (with Bill Holm) In the Land of the War Canoes, 1973, Edward S. Curtis in the Land of the War Canoes: A Pioneer Cinematographer in the Pacific Northwest, 1980; Contbr. articles to profl. jours. Honored by festschrift U. Mich. Mus. Anthropology, 1983. Fellow AAAS, Am. Anthrop. Assn.; mem. Soc. Am. Archaeology (pres. 1958, 50th Anniversary award 1983, Disting. Svc. award 1989), Am. Soc. Ethnohistory, Wis. Archeol. Soc., Soc. Historical Archeology (council 1971-74, 75-78, J.C. Harrington medal 1986), Assn. Sci. Mus. Dirs. (pres. 1973-74), Arctic Inst. N.Am., Am. Assn. Museums (council 1971-74), Sigma Xi, Phi Sigma, Chi Gamma Phi, Zeta Psi. Home: 6001 52nd Ave NE Seattle WA 98115-7711 Office: U Washington Thomas Burke Meml Wash State Mus Seattle WA 98195

QUIMBY, ROBERT SHERMAN, retired humanities educator; b. St. Albans, Vt., Feb. 20, 1916; s. Christopher Sherman and Lura Mae (Wills) Q.; m. Shirley Lenore Lay, Oct. 19, 1957. B.S. in Edn. U. Vt., 1937, M.A., 1938; Ph.D., Columbia U., 1952; postgrad., Am. Sch. Classical Studies, Athens, Greece, 1958. Teaching asst. in history U. Vt., Burlington, 1938-39, 41-42; instr. history U. Vt., 1942-44, Cornell U., Ithaca, N.Y., 1944-45; instr. history of civilization Mich. State U., East Lansing, 1945-52; asst. prof. humanities Mich. State U., 1952-59, assoc. prof., 1959-68, prof., 1968-81, prof. emeritus of humanities, 1981—; Mem. Mich. Commn. of United Ministries in Higher Edn., 1970-87, sec., 1975-77. Author: The Background of Napoleonic Warfare; contbr. articles to profl. jours. and encys. George Ellis fellow Columbia U., 1939-41. Mem. Am. Inst. Archaeology, Mich. Hist. Soc., Am. Mil. Inst., U.S. Naval Inst., Rwy. and Locomotive Hist. Soc. Republican. Episcopalian. Club: University. Address: 145 Columbia Ave Apt 207 Holland MI 49423-2983 Address (winter): 3400 S Ironwood Dr Lot 379 Apache Junction AZ 85220-7114

QUIN, LOUIS DUBOSE, chemist, educator; b. Charleston, S.C., Mar. 5, 1928; s. Louis DuBose and Olga vonOven (Jatho) Q.; children: Gordon, Howard, Carol. B.S., The Citadel, 1947; M.A., U. N.C., 1949, Ph.D., 1952. Research chemist Am. Cyanamid Co., Stamford, Conn., 1949-50; research project leader FMC Corp., South Charleston, W.Va., 1952-54, 56; mem. faculty dept. chemistry Duke U., Durham, N.C., 1956-86; prof. Duke U., 1967-81, James B. Duke prof. chemistry, 1981-86, chmn. dept., 1970-76; prof. chemistry U. Mass., Amherst, 1986—, head dept., 1986-94; Mem. Durham Human Relations Commn., 1978-81. Author: Heterocyclic Chemistry of Phosphorus, 1981; contbr. articles to profl. jours. Served to 1st lt. U.S. Army, 1954-56. Fellow AAAS; mem. Am. Chem. Soc., Chem. Soc. (London). Office: U Mass Dept Of Chemistry Amherst MA 01003

QUINBY, WILLIAM ALBERT, lawyer, mediator, arbitrator; b. Oakland, Calif., May 28, 1941; s. George W. and Marge (Diaz) Q.; m. Marion Bach, Nov. 27, 1964; 1 child, Michelle Kathleen. BA, Harvard U., 1963; JD, U. Calif., San Francisco, 1967. Bar: Calif. 1967. V.p., dir., shareholder Crosby, Heafey, Roach & May, Oakland, Calif., 1967—; bd. dirs. Haws Drinking Faucet Co., Berkeley, Calif.; mem. faculty Hastings Coll. Advocacy, San Francisco, 1980; co-moderator Counsel Connect's Calif. ADR Discussion Group; lectr. currents devels. in banking arbitration and mediation; mem. fellowship rev. com. HEW; mem. panel disting. neutrals Ctr. for Pub. Resources, Inc.; mem. mediation panel Nat. Assn. Securities Dealers. Author: Six Reasons--Besides Time and Money--to Mediate Rather Than Litigate, Why Health Care Parties Should Mediate Rather Than Litigate, Starting an ADR Practice Group in a Law Firm, Mediation Process Can Amicably Solve Business Disputes and Not a Gold Rush (But Silver, Maybe), ADR Practice in a Large Law Firm Produces No Overnight Bonanzas. Bd. dirs. Big Bros. East Bay, Oakland, 1983-87, Easter Seals Soc. East Bay, 1973, Oakland East Bay Symphony; chmn. bd. dirs. Bay Area Tumor Inst. Scholar Harvard U., 1962-63. Mem. ABA, ATLA, Calif. Bar Assn., Alameda County Bar Assn., Calif. Bus. Trial Lawyers Assn., Am. Arbitration Assn. (large, complex case panel, comml. mediation and arbitration panels), Oakland C. of C. (bd. dirs., exec. com.), Alameda County Barristers Club (bd. dirs., pres. 1972), Harvard Club, San Francisco Calimari Club, Lakeview Club, Bohemian Club. Republican. Avocations: running, skiing, tennis, travel, gardening. Office: Crosby Heafey Roach & May 1999 Harrison St Oakland CA 94612-3517

QUINE, WILLARD VAN ORMAN, philosophy educator; b. Akron, Ohio, June 25, 1908; s. Cloyd Robert and Hattie Ellis (Van Orman) Q.; m. Naomi Ann Clayton, Sept. 19, 1930; children: Elizabeth Roberts, Norma; m. Marjorie Boynton, Sept. 2, 1948; children: Douglas Boynton, Margaret McGovern. AB in Math. summa cum laude, Oberlin Coll., 1930, LittD (hon.), 1955; AM in Philosophy, Harvard U., 1931, PhD, 1932, LLD (hon.), 1979; MA, Oxford U., 1953, LittD (hon.), 1970; LittD (hon.), Ohio State U., 1957; hon. doctorate, U. Lille, France, 1965, Uppsala U., Sweden, 1980, U. Berne, Switzerland, 1982, U. Granada, Spain, 1986; LittD (hon.), Akron U., 1965, Washington U., St. Louis, 1966, Temple U., 1970, Cambridge (Eng.) U., 1978, Syracuse U., 1981; LHD (hon.), U. Chgo., 1967, Ripon Coll., 1983, Adelphi U., 1989. Instr., tutor philosophy Harvard U., Cambridge, Mass., 1936-41, assoc. prof., 1941-48, prof., 1948—, Edgar Pierce prof. philosophy, 1955-78, chmn. dept. philosophy, 1952-53; vis. prof. U. Sao Paulo, Brazil, 1942, Rockefeller U., 1968, Coll. de France, 1969; George Eastman vis. prof. Oxford U., 1953-54, U. Tokyo, 1959; mem. Inst. Advanced Study, Princeton U., 1956-57; Gavin David Young lectr. in philosophy U. Adelaide, Australia, 1959; Paul Carus lectr. Am. Philos. Assn., 1971; Hagerstrom lectr. U. Uppsala, Sweden, 1973; Ferrater Mora lectr., Gerona, Spain, 1990. Author: A System of Logistic, 1934, Mathematical Logic, 1940, Elementary Logic, 1941, O Sentido da Nova Logica, 1944, Methods of Logic, 1950, From a Logical Point of View, 1953, Word and Object, 1960, Set Theory and Its Logic, 1963, The Ways of Paradox, 1966, Selected Logic Papers, 1966, Ontological Relativity, 1969, Philosophy of Logic, 1970, (with J.S. Ullian) The Web of Belief, 1970, The Roots of Reference, 1974, Theories and things, 1981, The Time of My Life, 1985, Quiddities, 1987, La Scienza e i Dati di Senso, 1987, Pursuit of Truth, 1989, The Logic of Sequences, 1990, From Stimulus to Science, 1995; co-author: Philosophical Essays for A.N. Whitehead, 1936; Philosophy of A.N. Whitehead, 1941; Philosophy of Rudolf Carnap, 1963; Words and Objections, 1969, Aspectos de la Filosofia de W.V. Quine, 1975, Philosophy of W.V. Quine, 1986, Symposio Quine, 1988, Perspectives on Quine, 1989; also articles. Served to lt. comdr. USNR, 1942-46. Recipient Nicholas Murray Butler Gold medal Columbia U., 1970, Frantisek Polacky gold medal, Czech Republic, 1991, Charles U. silver medal, Prague, 1993, Rolf Schock prize in philosophy, Sweden, 1993; Harvard U. Soc. Fellows jr. fellow, 1933-36, sr. fellow, 1948-78; univ. scholar Harvard U.; James Walker fellow Harvard U.; Sheldon traveling fellow, Europe, 1932-33; Rockefeller fellow, Bellagio, 1975; fellow Ctr. Advanced Study Behavioral Scis., 1958-59, Ctr. Advanced Studies, Wesleyan U., 1965; Sir Henry Savile fellow Merton Coll., Oxford, 1973-74. Fellow Am. Philos. Soc., Brit. Acad. (corr.); mem. Am. Philos. Assn. (pres. East div. 1957), Assn. Symbolic Logic (pres. 1953-56), Am. Acad. Arts and Scis., Nat. Acad. Scis., Institut de France (corr.), Norwegian Acad., Institut Internat. de Philosophie, Instituto Brasileiro de Filosofia (corr.), Academie Internationale de la Philosophie de Sci., Phi Beta Kappa. Office: Harvard U Dept Philosophy Emerson Hall Cambridge MA 02138

QUINLAN, GUY CHRISTIAN, lawyer; b. Cambridge, Mass., Oct. 28, 1939; s. Guy Thomas and Yvonne (Carver) Q.; m. Mary-Ella Holst, Apr. 18, 1987. AB, Harvard Coll., 1960, JD, Harvard U., 1963. Bar: N.Y. 1964, U.S. Dist. Ct. (so. and ea. dists.) N.Y. 1965, U.S. Ct. Appeals (2d cir.) 1967, U.S. Supreme Ct. 1969, U.S. Ct. Appeals (8th cir.) 1973, (10th cir.) 1977, (4th cir.) 1993, (11th cir.) 1995, U.S. Tax Ct. 1977. Assoc. Rogers & Wells, N.Y.C., 1963-70, ptnr., 1970-90, of counsel, 1991—. Past pres. Unitarian Universalist Svc. Com., Yorkville Common Pantry; past pres. Unitarian Universalist Dist. of Met. N.Y.; mem. adv. council on ministerial studies Harvard U. Div. Sch. Mem. ABA, N.Y. State Bar Assn., Fed. Bar Coun., Am. Judicature Soc., Am. Assn. Internat. Commn. Jurists, Lawyers Alliance for World Security. Democrat. Club: Harvard (N.Y.C.). Office: Rogers & Wells 200 Park Ave New York NY 10166-0153

QUINLAN, J(OSEPH) MICHAEL, lawyer; b. Rockville Centre, N.Y., Nov. 2, 1941; s. Joseph Charles Quinlan and Harriet Veronica (Gorman) Greene; m. Agnes Mary Quinlan, May 5, 1973; children: Kara Ann, Kristen Mary. BS. in Social Sci., Fairfield U., 1963; JD, Fordham U., 1966; LLM, George Washington U., 1970. Bar: N.Y. 1966, D.C. 1967, Va. 1993, U.S. Ct. Mil. Appeals 1967, U.S. Supreme Ct. 1970. Exec. asst. to warden U.S. Penitentiary, Leavenworth, Kans., 1973-74; of counsel N.E. region U.S. Bur. Prisons, Phila., 1974-75, exec. asst. to dir., Washington, 1975-78; supt. Fed. Prison Camp, Eglin AFB, Fla., 1978-80; warden Fed. Correctional Inst., Otisville, N.Y., 1980-85; dep. asst. dir. U.S. Bur. Prisons, Washington, 1985-86, dep. dir., 1986-87; dir. U.S. Bur. Prisons, 1987-92; dir. strategic planning, Corrections Corp. Am., 1993—, pres. Correctional Training Network, 1995—; dir., bd. dirs. United Kingdom Detention Svcs., London. 1st vice chmn. bd. dirs. Horton Meml. Hosp., Middletown, N.Y., 1982-85; criminal justice cons. Lt. Col. USAFR, 1966-93. Recipient SES Presdl. Disting. Rank award, 1988, SES Presdl. Meritorious Rank award, 1991, Exceptional Leadership award U.S. Atty. Gen., 1991, Nat. Pub. Svc. award Nat. Acad. Pub. Adminstrn./Am. Soc. Pub. Adminstrn., 1992, John Marshall award Dept. Justice, 1993. Fellow Nat. Acad. Pub. Adminstrn.; mem. ABA (corrections and sentencing com. 1985—, Am. Correctional Assn. (mem. legis. com.), Nat. Com. Comm. Corrections, N.Y. Bar Assn., D.C. Bar Assn., Va. Bar Assn. Roman Catholic. Avocations: reading, family activities.

QUINLAN, KATHLEEN, actress; b. Pasadena, Calif., Nov. 19, 1954. Actress: (theatre) Taken in Marriage, 1979 (Theatre World award 1979), Accent on Youth, 1983, Les Liaisons Dangereuses, 1988, (feature films) One is a Lonely Number, 1972, American Graffiti, 1973, Lifeguard, 1976, Airport '77, 1977, I Never Promised You a Rose Garden, 1977, The Promise, 1979, The Runner Stumbles, 1979, Sunday Lovers, 1981, Hanky Panky, 1982, Independence Day, 1982, Twilight Zone: The Movie, 1983, The Last Winter, 1983, Warning Sign, 1985, Wild Thing, 1987, Sunset, 1988, Clara's Heart, 1988, The Doors, 1991, Trial by Jury, 1994, Apollo 13, 1995 (Acad. award nominee for best actress 1996); (TV movies) Can Ellen Be Saved?, 1974, Lucas Tanner, 1974, Where Have All the People Gone?, 1974, The Missing Are Deadly, 1975, The Turning Point of Jim Malloy, 1975, The Abduction of Saint Anne, 1975, Little Ladies of the Night, 1977, She's in the Army Now, 1981, When She Says No, 1984, Blackout, 1985, Children of the Night, 1985, Dreams Lost, Dreams Found, 1987, Trapped, 1989, The Operation, 1990, Strays, 1991, An American Story, 1992, Stolen Babies, 1993, Last Light, 1993, Perfect Alibi, 1994. Mem. Actors' Equity Assn., Screen Actors Guild. *

QUINLAN, MARY LOU, advertising executive. Pres. N.W. Ayer, N.Y.C. Office: NW Ayer 825 8th Ave New York NY 10019*

QUINLAN, MICHAEL ROBERT, fast food franchise company executive; b. Chgo., Dec. 9, 1944; s. Robert Joseph and Kathryn (Koerner) Q.; m. Marilyn DeLashmutt, Apr. 23, 1966; children: Kevin, Michael. BS, Loyola U., Chgo., 1967, MBA, 1970. With McDonald's Corp., Oak Brook, Ill., 1966—, v.p., 1974-76, sr. v.p., 1976-78, exec. v.p., 1978-79, chief ops. officer, 1979-80, pres. McDonald's U.S.A., 1980-82, pres., 1982-89, chief oper. officer, 1982-87, chief exec. officer, 1987—, chmn., 1989—, also bd. dirs. Republican. Roman Catholic. Clubs: Butterfield Country, Oakbrook Handball-Racquetball. Office: McDonald's Corp 1 Kroc Dr Oak Brook IL 60521-2275*

QUINLAN, WILLIAM JOSEPH, JR., lawyer; b. Chgo., Nov. 4, 1939; s. William Joseph and Catherine E. (Bowman) Q.; m. Susan L. Collins, June 16, 1962; children—Kathleen, Michael, Julie, Jennifer. A.B. cum laude, Loyola, U., Chgo., 1961, J.D. cum laude, 1966. Bar: Ill. 1966, U.S. Dist. Ct. (no. dist.) Ill. 1966, U.S. Tax Ct. 1968, U.S. Ct. Appeals (7th cir.) 1972. Assoc. Wilson & McIlvaine, Chgo., 1966-73; ptnr. McDermott, Will & Emery, Chgo., 1973-78, sr. ptnr., 1978—; dir. Wickman Machine Tools, Elk Grove Village, Ill., 1978-81, Eiger Machinery, Inc., Bensenville, Ill., 1981—. Contbr. articles to profl. publs. Mem. St. Athanasius Bd. Edn., Evanston, Ill., 1976, pres., 1978. Mem. ABA (com. on fed. regulation of securities), Chgo. Bar Assn. (chmn. subcom. on securities law), Ill. Bar Assn., Blue Key, Phi Alpha Delta. Roman Catholic. Clubs: Union League, Wilmette Harbor Assn. Office: McDermott Will & Emery 227 W Monroe St Chicago IL 60606-5016

QUINN, AIDAN, actor; b. Chgo., Mar. 8, 1959. Actor: (films) Reckless, 1984, Desperately Seeking Susan, 1985, The Mission, 1986, Stakeout, 1987, Crusoe, 1989, The Handmaid's Tale, 1990, The Lemon Sisters, 1990, Avalon, 1990, At Play in the Fields of the Lord, 1991, The Playboys, 1992, Benny & Joon, 1993, Blink, 1994, Legends of the Fall, 1994, Mary Shelley's Frankenstein, 1994, The Stars Fell on Henrietta, 1994, Haunted, 1994; (plays) The Man in 605, Fool for Love, 1983, Hamlet, 1984, A Lie of the Mind, 1985, A Streetcar Named Desire, 1988 (Theatre World award 1988), Scheherazade, The Irish Hebrew Lesson, (TV) An Early Frost, 1985 (Emmy award nominee 1985), Perfect Witness, 1989, Lies of the Twins, 1991, A Private Matter, 1992. Office: Creative Artists Agy 9830 Wilshire Blvd Beverly Hills CA 90212-1804*

QUINN, ANDREW PETER, JR., lawyer, insurance executive; b. Providence, Oct. 22, 1923; s. Andrew Peter and Margaret (Canning) Q.; m. Sara G. Bullard, May 30, 1952; 1 child, Emily H. AB, Brown U., 1945; LLB, Yale U., 1950. Bar: R.I. 1949, Mass. 1960, U.S. Tax Ct. 1960, U.S. Supreme Ct. 1986. Pvt. practice Providence, 1950-59, Springfield, Mass., 1959-88; ptnr. Letts & Quinn, 1950-59; with Mass. Mut. Life Ins. Co., 1959-88, exec. v.p., gen. counsel, 1971-88; of counsel Day, Berry & Howard, Hartford, Conn. and Boston, 1988—; pres., trustee MML Series Investment Fund, 1971-88; bd. dirs. Sargasso Mut. Ins. Co., Ltd., 1986-95, pres., 1986-89, chmn. bd. dirs., 1989-93. Trustee, MacDuffie Sch., 1974-87, chmn. bd., 1978-85; trustee Baystate Med., Springfield, 1977-80. Lt. (j.g.) USNR, 1944-46. Mem. ABA (co-chmn. nat. conf. lawyers and life ins. cos. 1973), Assn. Life Ins. Counsel (pres. 1983-84), Am. Coun. Life Ins. (chmn. legal sect. 1971), Life Ins. Assn. Mass. (chmn. exec. com. 1975-77), Brown U. Alumni Assn. (bd. dirs. 1969-72), N.Y. Yacht club, Longmeadow Country Club, Dunes Club, Hillsboro Club, Conn. Valley Brown U. (past pres.). Home: 306 Ellington Rd Longmeadow MA 01106-1559 Office: Day Berry & Howard City Pl Hartford CT 06103-3499

QUINN, ANTHONY RUDOLPH OAXACA, actor, writer, artist; b. Chihuahua, Mexico, Apr. 21, 1915; naturalized, 1947; s. Frank and Nellie (Oaxaca) Q.; m. Katherine de Mille, Oct. 2, 1937 (div.); children: Christina, Kathleen, Duncan, Valentina; m. Iolanda Addolori, Jan. 1966; children: Francesco, Daniele, Lorenzo. Student pub. schs. Actor in plays including Clean Beds, 1936, Gentleman from Athens, 1947, Street Car Named Desire, Let Me Hear the Melody, Beckett, 1961, Tchin-Tchin, 1963, Zorba, 1983-86; has appeared in over 200 motion pictures including Guadalcanal Diary, 1943, Buffalo Bill, 1944, Irish Eyes are Smiling, 1944, China Sky, 1945, Back to Bataan, 1945, Where Do We Go From Here?, 1945, Tycoon, 1947, The Brave Bulls, 1951, Mask of the Avenger, 1951, World in his Arm, 1952, Against all Flags, 1952, Viva Zapata (Acad. award 1952), Ride Vaquero, 1953, City Beneath the Sea, 1953, Seminole, 1953, Blowing Wild, 1953, East of Sumatra, 1953, Long Wait, 1954, Magnificent Matador, 1955, Ulysses, 1955, Naked Street, 1955, Seven Cities of Gold, 1955, Lust for Life, (Acad. award best supporting actor 1956), La Strada, 1954, Man from Del Rio, 1956, Wild the Wind, 1957, Attila the Hun, 1958, The Wild Party, 1956, The Ride Back, 1957, The Hunchback of Notre Dame, 1957, The River's Edge, 1957, Hot Spell, 1958, Heller with a Gun, Savage Innocents, 1959, The Black Orchid, 1958, Last Train From Gun Hill, 1958, Warlock, 1959, Heller in Pink Tights, 1960, Portrait in Black, 1960, Guns of Navarrone, 1961, Becket, 1961, Barabbas, 1962, Lawrence of Arabia, 1962, Requiem for a Heavyweight, 1963, The Visit, 1963, Behold a Pale Horse, 1964, Zorba the Greek, 1964, High Wind in Jamaica, 1965, Guns for San Sebastian, 1968, The Shoes of the Fisherman, 1968, The Secret of Santa Vittoria, 1969, A Dream of Kings, 1969, Flap, 1970, A Walk in Spring Rain, 1970, R.P.M., 1970, The City, 1971, Jesus of Nazareth, 1971, Across 110th Street, 1972, Arruza, Deaf Smith and Johnny Ears, 1973, The Don Is Dead, 1973, Mohammed Messenger of God, 1977, Caravans, 1978, The Children of Sanchez, 1978, The Greek Tycoon, 1978, The Inheritance, 1978, The Passage, 1979, Lion of the Desert, 1981, High Roll, 1981, Valentina, 1984, The Salamander, 1984, Treasure Island, 1986, Stradivarius, 1987, Revenge, 1990, Ghosts Can't Do It, 1990, A Star for Two, 1990, Jungle Fever, 1990, Only the Lonely, 1991, Mobsters, 1991, The Last Action Hero, 1993, Somebody to Love, 1994, A Walk in the Clouds, 1995, Project Mankind, 1996; appeared in TV prodns. of The Life of Christ, Onassis: The Richest Man in the World, 1988, Old Man and the Sea, 1990, This Can't Be Love, 1994; script writer: Metro-Goldwyn-Mayer prodn. The Farm; author: The Original Sin, 1972, Self-Portrait, 1995; artist 13 major exhbns. oil paintings, sculptures and serigraphs, Hawaii, 1982, 87, San Francisco, 1983, N.Y.C., 1984, 89, San Antonio, 1984, Houston, 1984, Washington, 1985, Beverly Hills, Calif., 1986, Mexico City, 1990, Paris, 1990, Zurich, Switzerland, 1990, Vienna, Austria, 1991, Buenos Aires, 1992, Las Vegas, 1993. Office: 60 E End Ave # 32-C New York NY 10028*

QUINN, ART JAY, veterinarian; b. Bennington, Kans., Aug. 2, 1936; s. Arthur Jess and Edith Mae (Reigle) Q. BS, Kans. State U., 1959, DVM, 1961. Diplomate Am. Coll. Vet. Ophthalmologists. Pvt. practice Albuquerque, 1961-75; field rep. Am. Animal Hosp. Assn., Denver, 1968-69; prof. Coll. Vet. Medicine, Okla. State U., Stillwater, 1975-95; prof. emeritus Coll. Vet. Medicine, Okla. State U., 1995—. Contbr. articles to profl. jours. Capt. U.S. Army, 1962-64. Recipient Kans. Vet. Med. Assn. Small Animal Proficiency award, 1961, Upjohn award, 1961, AAHA Western Region Practitioner award, 1993; Sarkey Found. grantee, 1981. Mem. AVMA, Am. Animal Hosp. Assn., Am. Coll. Vet. Ophthalmologists, Am. Assn. Vet. Clinicians, North Cen. Okla. Vet. Med. Assn. Democrat. Home: 1528 S Shalamar Dr Stillwater OK 74074-1648 Office: Okla State U Coll Vet Medicine Stillwater OK 74078

QUINN, BETTY NYE, former classics educator; b. Buffalo, Mar. 22, 1921; d. Fritz Arthur and Alma (Svenson) Hedberg; A.B., Mt. Holyoke Coll., 1941; A.M., Bryn Mawr Coll., 1942, Ph.D., 1944; m. John F. Quinn, Sept. 21, 1950. Analyst, U.S. Army, 1944-46, CIA, 1947; instr., asst. prof. Vassar Coll., Poughkeepsie, N.Y., 1948-59, dir. pub. relations, 1952-59, assoc. prof., 1959-68; prof. classics Mt. Holyoke Coll., South Hadley, Mass., 1968-91, prof. emeritus, 1991—. Am. Acad. Rome fellow, 1942-43; Am. Philos. Soc. grantee, 1952. Mem. Am. Philos. Assn., Mediaeval Acad. Am., Classics Assn. New Eng. (pres. 1970-71) Vergilian Soc. Am. Republican. Lutheran. Home: 27 W Parkview Dr South Hadley MA 01075-2164

QUINN, CHARLES NICHOLAS, journalist; b. Utica, N.Y., July 28, 1930; s. Charles Dunaway and Elsa (Zarth) Q.; children—Diana David, Ben, Jane. B.A., Cornell U., 1951; M.S., Columbia U. Sch. Journalism, 1954. Reporter Providence Jour., 1954-56, N.Y. Herald Tribune, 1956-62; corr. NBC News, N.Y.C., 1962-66, Washington, 1966-71, Rome, 1971-74; mng. editor, chief corr. NBC Radio News, Washington, 1978-80; corr. Ind. Network News, Washington, 1980-81; electronic media rep. Am. Petroleum Inst., Washington, 1981-91. Reported on hunger in U.S. on: Huntley-Brinkley Report, (co-recipient Emmy 1969). Served with arty. U.S. Army, 1951-53. Mem. Nat. Press Club (bd. govs. 1990-91).

QUINN, CHARLES NORMAN, lawyer; b. Abington, Pa., Nov. 5, 1943; s. Charles Ransom and Lela Josephine (Cooper) Q.; m. Mary Bernadette Bradley, Oct. 4, 1975 (div. Oct. 1976); m. Vicki Lou Erickson Heinze, Nov. 11, 1978; stepchildren: Scott L., Kymbra Lynn. BSME, Purdue U., 1965; ME, Pa. State U., 1970; JD, Villanova (Pa.) U., 1973. Bar: U.S. Dist. Ct. (ea. dist) Pa. 1974, U.S. Ct. Appeals (fed. cir.) 1984. Systems engr. GE Co., King of Prussia, Pa., 1965-70; atty. Paul and Paul, Phila., 1973-75, Penwalt Corp., Phila., 1976-80, A.R. Miller, P.C., Phila., 1981-85; ptnr. Miller & Quinn, Phila., 1986-91; atty., of counsel Dann Dorfman Herrell & Skill, Phila., 1992—. Contbr. articles to profl. jours. Mem. ABA, Phila. Patent Law Assn. (treas. 1980-83, gov. 1987-89), Phila. Intellectual Property Law Assn., Am. Intellectual Property Law Assn., Phila. Bar Assn. Avocations: golf, classical music, personal computers. Home: 617 Marydell Dr West Chester PA 19380-6328 Office: Dann Dorfman Herrell & Skillman 1601 Market St Ste 720 Philadelphia PA 19103-2337

QUINN, DAVID W., building company executive; b. 1942. BA, Midwestern U. Ptnr. Arthur Andersen, Dallas, 1967-84; COO Alpert Cos., 1984-87; exec. v.p. Centex Corp., Dallas, 1987—, also bd. dirs. Office: Centex Corp 3333 Lee Pky Dallas TX 75219-5111*

QUINN, DENNIS B., English language and literature educator; b. Bklyn., Oct. 3, 1928; s. Herbert John and Thelma Leona (Warren) Q.; m. Eva M. Jensen, Aug. 13, 1952; children—Timothy, Monica, Alison. Student, Creighton U., 1948-50; B.A. in English, U. Wis., 1951, M.A. in English, 1952, Ph.D. in English, 1958. Instr. English U. Kans., Lawrence, 1956-60, asst. prof. English, 1960-64, assoc. prof. English, 1964-68, prof. English, 1968—, dir. Pearson Coll., 1968-75, dir. integrated humanities program, 1971-79. Contbr. articles on Medieval and Renaissance literature and children's literature to profl. jours. Served with U.S. Army, 1946-48; Japan. Recipient student Fulbright award, Leiden, The Netherlands, 1955-56, research Fulbright award, Salamanca, Spain, 1962-63; H. Bernard Fink Outstanding Tchr. award U. Kans., 1965, H.O.P.E. Teaching award, 1969; NEH grantee, 1971. Roman Catholic. Avocations: gardening, travel. Home: 1102 W 25th St Lawrence KS 66046-4441 Office: Univ Kansas Dept English Lawrence KS 66045

QUINN, ELIZABETH R., elementary education educator; b. Covina, Calif., Oct. 7, 1951; d. John Howard and Rosemary (Branine) Roberts; m. D. Whitney Quinn, July 18, 1980. BA, Ariz. State U., 1973; Marriage, Family and Child Counseling, Azuza Pacific U., 1980; BS, Calif. State U., Fullerton, 1993. Tchr. Saddleback Valley Unified Sch. Dist., Mission Viejo, Calif., 1976—, mentor tchr., 1992—; Cert. life standard elem. credential K-8, Calif. Named Tchr. of Yr. Kiwanis, Mission Viejo, 1992. Mem. Calif. Tchrs. Assn., Saddleback Valley Educators. Avocations: reading, gourmet cooking, weight lifting.

QUINN, EUGENE FREDERICK, government official, clergyman; b. Oil City, Pa., Sept. 16, 1935; s. Frederick Anthony and Wilma (Scott) Q.; m. Charlotte Alison Smith, Aug. 25, 1965; children: Christopher Edward Vermilye, Alison Moore. AB, Allegheny Coll., 1957; MA in African studies, UCLA, 1966, MA in History, 1969, PhD in History, 1970; diploma in theol. studies, Va. Theol. Sem., 1974. Ordained to ministry Episcopal Ch. U.S.A., 1975. Info. officer Am. Embassy, Rabat, Morocco, 1958-59; cultural affairs officer Am. Embassy, Port-au-Prince, Haiti, 1959-61; country pub. affairs officer Ouagadougou, Upper Volta, 1961-63; field rep. Joint U.S. Affairs Office, Saigon, Vietnam, 1964-66; country pub. affairs officer Am. embassy, Yaounde, Cameroun, 1966-68; counselor embassy for press and cultural affairs Am. embassy, Prague, Czechoslovakia, 1975-78; apptd. career mem. Sr. Fgn. Service with class of counselor, 1981, minister-counselor, 1986; dir. fgn. service personnel Voice of Am., Washington, 1981-83; dep. asst. sec. pub. affairs Dept. Transp., 1983-85; dir. Office Pub. Affairs Voice of Am., 1985-86; internat. coord. for Bicentennial U.S. Constn., dir.'s office U.S. Info. Agy., 1986-91; cons. internat. affairs, 1992—; dir. rule of law programs, conf. on security and cooperation in Europe, Office of Dem. Instns. and Human Rights, Warsaw, 1993-95. Author: Federalist Papers' Reader, 1992, To Heal the Earth, 1994; editor: Diplomacy for the Seventies, 1969; editorial bd. Fgn. Service Jour., 1972-75, Dept. State Open Forum Jour., 1982-83; contbr. articles to profl. jours., chpts. to books. Trustee N.J. Ednl. Consortium, 1970-72; coord. USIA Yorktown Bicentennial Activities, 1981; assisting clergyman St. Columbia Ch., Washington, 1973-75, 78-81, Nat. Cathedral, Washington, 1981-82, 95, Grace Ch., Silver Spring, Md., 1981-82, Epiphany Ch., Washington, 1983, 86-92; chaplain Anglo-Am. Diplomatic Cmty., Prague, 1975-78, Warsaw, 1993-95; vicar St. James Ch., Bowie, Md., 1983-84; rector Christ Ch., Accokeek, Md., 1985, St. John's Ch., Pomonkey, Md.; assisting clergyman All Saints Ch., Chevy Chase, Md., 1981-82, 86-90; interim pastor Ch. of Holy Communion, Washington, 1992-93; chair environ. com. Episcopal Diocese of Washington Peace Commn., 1991-92; mem. Environ. Stewardship Team, Episcopal Ch., 1992-95. Recipient Meritorious Honor award USIA, 1964, 66, 85; Merit medal Republic of Vietnam, 1965, medal of honor, 1966. Club: Cosmos (Washington). Home and Office: 5702 Kirkside Dr Chevy Chase MD 20815-7116

QUINN, FRANCIS A., bishop; b. L.A., Sept. 11, 1921. Ed., St. Joseph's Coll., Mountain View, Calif., St. Patrick's Sem., Menlo Park, Calif., Cath. U., Washington, U. Calif., Berkeley. Ordained priest Roman Cath. Ch., 1946; ordained titular bishop of Numana and aux. bishop of San Francisco, 1978; bishop Diocese of Sacramento, 1979-94, bishop emeritus, 1994—. Office: 2110 Broadway Sacramento CA 95818-2518

QUINN, FRANCIS XAVIER, arbitrator and mediator, author, lecturer; b. Dunmore, Pa., June 9, 1932; s. Frank T. and Alice B. (Maher) Q.; m. Marlene Stoker Quinn; children: Kimberly, Catherine, Cameron, Lindsay, Megan. AB, Fordham U., 1956, MA, 1958; STB, Woodstock Coll., 1964; MSIR, Loyola U., Chgo., 1966; PhD in Indsl. Rels., Calif. Western U., 1966. Assoc. dir. St. Joseph's Coll. Inst. Indsl. Rels., Phila., 1966-68; Manpower fellow Temple U., 1969-74, asst. to dean Sch. Bus. Adminstrn., 1972-78; arbitrator Fed. Mediation and Conciliation Svc., Nat. Mediation Bd., Am. Arbitration Assn., Nat. Assn. Railroad Referees, Dem. Nat. Steering Com.; ; apptd. to Rail Emergency Bd., 1975, to Fgn. Service Grievance Bd., 1976, 78, 80—; chmn. Hall of Fame com. Internat. Police Assn., 1990—, Tulsa City-County Mayor's Task Force to Combat Homelessness, 1991-92; mem. exec. bd. Tulsa Met. Ministries, 1990-92, Labor-Religion Coun. Okla., 1990—. Named Tchr. of Yr., Freedom Found., 1959; recipient Human Rels. award City of Phila., others. Mem. Nat. Acad. Arbitrators (chair SW Region 1995—), Indsl. Rels. Rsch. Assn., Assn. for Social Econs., Soc. for Dispute Resolution, Am. Arbitration Assn. (arbitrator), Internat. Soc. Labor Law and Social Security, Internat. Ombudsman Inst. Democrat. Author: The Ethical Aftermath of Automation, Ethics and Advertising, Population Ethics, The Evolving Role of Women in the World of Work, Developing Community Responsibility. Editor: The Ethical Aftermath Series; contbr. articles to profl. jours. Home: 230 Hazel Blvd Tulsa OK 74114-3926

QUINN, JACK, congressman, English language educator, sports coach; b. South Buffalo, N.Y., 1951; s. Jack Sr. and Norma Ide Q.; m. Mary Beth McAndrews, 1974; children: Jack III, Kara. BA, Siena Coll.; MA in Edn., SUNY, Buffalo. English language tchr. Orchard Park (N.Y.) Schs.; town councilman Town of Hamburg, N.Y.; also town supv. Town of Hamburg; mem. 103d-104th Congresses from 30th N.Y. Dist., 1993—; mem. transp. and infrastructure com., mem. vet. affairs com., mem. congl. reform task force, mem. joint econ. com. Recipient Humanitarian award Erie County for the Disabled, Pub. Svc. award Niagara Frontier Parks and Recreation Soc., Disting. Grad. award Nat. Cath. Elem. Schs. Assn., Bronze Good Citizen medal SAR, New Horizons award Drug Edn. of Internat. Assn. of Lions Club, Red, White and Blue award Am. Legion of N.Y., Honor medal Hilbert

Coll., Fin. Reporting award Govt. Fin. Officer's Assn., Disting. Career Svc. award Siena Coll., 1995. Mem. Hamburg C. of C., Greater Buffalo C. of C., Buffalo KC, Hamburg Kiwanis Club. Republican. Roman Catholic. Office: US Ho Reps 331 Cannon HOB Washington DC 20515-3230*

QUINN, JACK J., professional hockey team executive; b. Boston; s. John Quinn; m. Connie Quinn; children: Beth, Kay, Connie, John. Exec. v.p. St. Louis Blues, 1983-86, pres., 1986-95, chrm., ceo, 1995—. Office: St Louis Blues Kiel Ctr 1401 Clark Saint Louis MO 63103*

QUINN, JAMES W., lawyer; b. Bronxville, N.Y., Oct. 1, 1945; s. James Joseph Quinn and Marie Joan (Blossy) Tisi; m. Kathleen Manning, Kellianne, Christopher, Tierney, Kerrin. AB cum laude, U. Notre Dame, 1967; JD, Fordham U., 1971. Bar: N.Y. 1972, U.S. Dist. Ct. (so. and ea. dists.) N.Y. 1973, U.S. Ct. Appeals (2nd cir.) 1976, U.S. Supreme Ct. 1984, U.S. Ct. Appeals (3rd, 7th and 9th cirs.) 1985, U.S. Ct. Appeals (8th cir.) 1991. Assoc. Weil, Gotshal & Manges, N.Y.C., 1971-77, 78-79, ptnr., 1979—; ptnr. Fleisher & Quinn, N.Y.C., 1977-78; adj. assoc. prof. law Fordham U., N.Y.C., 1985-87. Editor Fordham U. Law Rev., 1969-71; contbr. articles to legal jours. Mem. ABA (litigation sect., co-chmn. subcom. alternate means of dispute resolution of com. corp. counsel, program chmn. trial practice com., sports and entertainment forum), Assn. of Bar of City of N.Y. (com. of state jurisdiction, com. on entertainment sports, com. on anti-trust regulation, chmn. sports law com.). Home: 1 Maple Way Armonk NY 10504-2602

QUINN, JANE BRYANT, journalist, writer; b. Niagara Falls, N.Y., Feb. 5, 1939; d. Frank Leonard and Ada (Laurie) Bryant; m. David Conrad Quinn, June 10, 1967; children—Matthew Alexander, Justin Bryant. B.A. magna cum laude, Middlebury Coll., 1960. Assoc. editor Insiders Newsletter, N.Y.C., 1962-65, co-editor, 1966-67; sr. editor Cowles Book Co., N.Y.C., 1968; editor-in-chief Bus. Week Letter, N.Y.C., 1969-73, gen. mgr., 1973-74; syndicated financial columnist Washington Post Writers Group, 1974—; contbr. fin. column to Women's Day mag., 1974-95; contbr. fin. column Good Housekeeping, 1995—; contbr. NBC News and Info. Service, 1976-77; bus. corr. WCBS-TV, N.Y.C., 1979, CBS-TV News, 1980-87, ABC-TV Home Show, 1991-93; contbg. editor Newsweek mag., 1978—. Author: Everyone's Money Book, 1979, 2d edit., 1980, Making the Most of Your Money, 1991, A Hole in the Market, 1994. Mem. Phi Beta Kappa. Office: Newsweek Inc 251 W 57th St New York NY 10019-1802

QUINN, JANITA SUE, city secretary; b. Breckenridge, Tex., Apr. 14, 1950; d. Doyle Dean and Peggy Joyce (Melton) Allen; m. John Lloyd Rippy, June 27, 1969 (div. Mar. 1976); children: Johna DeAnn, Jason Allen; m. Ervel Royce Quinn, Jan. 31, 1987; stepchildren: Amy Talitha, Jason Ervel. Student, Odessa (Tex.) Jr. Coll., 1968-70, U. Tex. of Permian Basin, Odessa, 1978-79, 85-86. New accts. clk. State Nat. Bank, Odessa, Tex., 1975-76; accts. receivable clk. Woolley Tool Corp., Odessa, Tex., 1976-78; data entry operator M-Bank, Odessa, Tex., 1978-79; asst. county treas. Ector County, Odessa, Tex., 1979-83, county treas., 1983-88; office mgr., co-owner Nat. Filter Svc., Inc., San Antonio, 1988-91; temporary employment Kelly Temporary Svcs., Abilene, Tex., 1991; sec. Pride Refining, Inc., Abilene, Tex., 1991-93; city sec. City of Eastland, Tex., 1993—. Mem., treas., bd. dirs. Family Outreach Svc. Taylor County; vol. tchr. Parenting for Parents and Adolescents; recorder, del. West Tex. Corridor II Com., Eastland and Dallas, 1993; county del. Taylor County dem. Party, Abilene, 1992; state del. Tex. Dem. Party, Dallas, 1991; pres., charter mem. Bluebonnet chpt. City Secs. Region 6 Group, 1994-96. Named Outstanding Mcpl. Clk., Bluebonnet Chpt. Mcpl. Clks./Sec., 1994. Mem. Tex. Mcpl. Clks. Assn., County Treas. Alumni Assn. (recorder 1991-93), Rotary Internat. Democrat. Ch. of Christ. Avocations: teaching parenting classes, knitting, golfing, gen. craft painting. Office: City of Eastland 416 S Seaman St Eastland TX 76448-2750

QUINN, JARUS WILLIAM, physicist, former association executive; b. West Grove, Pa., Aug. 25, 1930; s. William G. and Ellen C. (DuRoss) Q.; m. Margaret M. McNerney, June 27, 1953; children: J. Kevin, Megan, Jennifer, Colin, Kristin. BS, St. Joseph's Coll., 1952; postgrad., Johns Hopkins U., 1952-55; PhD, Cath. U. Am., 1964. Rsch. assoc. physics Johns Hopkins U., 1954-55; staff scientist Rsch. Inst. Advanced Study, 1956-57; rsch. assoc. physics Cath. U. Am., 1958-60, instr., 1961-64, asst. prof., 1965-69; exec. dir. Optical Soc. Am., Washington, 1969-93; governing bd. Am. Inst. Physics, 1973-94; pres. Stellar Focus, Sunnyvale, Calif., 1994-95. Bd. govs. Am. Assn. Engrng. Socs., 1990-93. Fellow Optical Soc. Am. (Distinguished Service Award, 1993), mem. Am. Phys. Soc., Am. Soc. Assn. Execs., Coun. Engrng. and Sci. Soc. Execs. Home: 357 Fearrington Post Pittsboro NC 27312-8517

QUINN, JOHN ALBERT, chemical engineering educator; b. Springfield, Ill., Sept. 3, 1932; s. Edward Joseph and Marie (Von De Bur) Q.; m. Frances Wilkie Daly, June 22, 1957; children: Sarah D., Rebecca V., John E. B-SChemE, U. Ill., 1954; PhDChemE, Princeton U., 1959. Mem. faculty chem. engrng. U. Ill., Urbana, 1958-70; prof. U. Pa., Phila., 1971—, Robert D. Bent prof., 1978—, chmn. dept. chem. engrng., 1980-85; vis. prof. Imperial Coll. U. London, 1965-66; vis. scientist MIT, 1980; vis. prof. U. Rome/La Sapienza, 1992; mem. sci. adv. bds. Sepracor, Inc., Marlborough, Mass., 1984—, Whitaker Found., Mechanicsburg, Pa., 1987—; Mason lectr. Stanford U., 1981; Katz lectr. U. Mich., 1985; Reilly lectr. U. Notre Dame, 1987. Contbr. articles to profl. publs.; editl. advisor Jour. Membrane Sci., 1975—, Indsl. and Chem. Engrng. Rsch., 1987-88, Revs. in Chem. Engrng., 1980—; pioneer rschr. on mass transfer and interfacial phenomena. Sr. postdoctoral fellow NSF, 1965-66; Sherman Fairchild scholar Calif. Inst. Tech., 1985. Fellow AAAS, Am. Inst. Med. and Biol. Engrng.; mem. NAE, AIChE (Allan P. Colburn award 1966, Alpha Chi Sigma award 1978), Am. Acad. Arts and Scis., Am. Chem. Soc., Internat. Soc. Oxygen Transport to Tissue, Sigma X, Phi Lambda Upsilon, Tau Beta Pi. Home: 275 E Wynnewood Rd Merion Station PA 19066-1627 Office: Univ Pa Towne Bldg 220 S 33rd St Philadelphia PA 19104-6315

QUINN, JOHN COLLINS, publishing executive, newspaper editor; b. Providence, Oct. 24, 1925; s. John A. and Kathryn H. (Collins) Q.; m. Lois R. Richardson, June 20, 1953; children: John Collins, Lo-anne, Richard B., Christopher A. A.B., Providence Coll., 1945; M.S., Columbia U. Sch. Journalism, 1946. Successively copy boy, reporter, asst. city editor, Washington corr., asst. mng. editor, day mng. editor Providence Jour.-Bull., 1943-66; with Gannett Co. Inc., Rochester, N.Y., 1966-90; exec. editor Rochester Democrat & Chronicle, Times-Union, 1966-71; gen. mgr. Gannett News Service, 1967-80, pres., 1980-88, v.p. parent co., 1971-75, sr. v.p. news and info., 1975-80, sr. v.p., chief news exec. parent co., editor USA TODAY, 1983-89; exec. v.p. Gannett Co., Arlington, Va., 1983-90; trustee Gannett Found., Arlington, 1988-91; trustee, dep. chmn. Freedom Forum, Arlington, 1991—. Named to R.I. Hall of Fame, 1975, Editor of Yr. Nat. Press Found., 1986; recipient William Allen White citation, 1987, Women in Communications Headliner award, 1986; Paul Miller/Okla. State U. medallion, 1988. Mem. AP Mng. Editors (past dir., nat. pres. 1973-74), Am. Soc. Newspaper Editors (dir., chmn. editorial bd., chmn. conv. program, nat. pres. 1982-83). Roman Catholic. Home: 365 S Atlantic Ave Cocoa Beach FL 32931-2719 Office: Freedom Forum 1101 Wilson Blvd Arlington VA 22209-2248

QUINN, JOHN E., lawyer; b. Pitts., Oct. 28, 1950. BA, Duquesne U., 1972, JD, 1976. Bar: Pa. 1976, U.S. Dist. Ct. (we. dist.) Pa. 1976, U.S. Ct. Appeals (3d cir.) 1981. Ptnr. Evans, Portnoy & Quinn, Pitts. Mem. ABA, Pa. Bar Assn., Allegheny County Bar Assn. (vice chmn., chmn. lawyer referal com. 1983-87), Pa. Trial Lawyers Assn. (bd. govs. 1989-91), Assn. Trial Lawyers Am. Office: Evans Portnoy & Quinn One Oxford Ctr 36th fl Pittsburgh PA 15219*

QUINN, JOHN R., archbishop; b. Riverside, Calif., Mar. 28, 1929; s. Ralph J. and Elizabeth (Carroll) Q. Student, St. Francis Sem., Immaculate Heart Sem., San Diego, 1947-48; Ph.B., Gregorian U., Rome, 1950, Licentiate in Sacred Theology, 1954, S.T.L., 1954. Ordained priest Roman Cath. Ch., 1953, as bishop, 1967. Assoc. pastor St. George Ch., Ontario, Calif., 1954-55; prof. theology Immaculate Heart Sem., San Diego, 1955-62, vice rector, 1960-62; pres. St. Francis Coll. Sem., El Cajon, Calif., 1962-64; rector Immaculate Heart Sem., 1964-68; aux. bishop, vicar gen. San Diego, 1967-72; bishop Oklahoma City, 1972-73, archbishop, 1973-77; archbishop San Francisco, 1977-95; archbishop emeritus; provost U. San Diego, 1968-72; pastor St. Therese Parish, San Diego, 1969; apptd. consultor to Sacred Congregation for the Clergy in Rome, 1971; pres. Nat. Conf. Cath. Bishops, 1977-80, chmn. Com. of Liturgy; chmn. com. on Family Life U.S. Cath. Conf.; chmn. Bishops' Com. on Pastoral Rsch. and Practices, Bishops' Com. on Doctrine; mem. Bishops' Com. on Sems., Pontifical Commn., Seattle, 1987-88, Bishops' Com. for Pro-Life Activies, 1989—; apptd. pontifical del. for religious in U.S., 1983; pres. Calif. Cath. Conf., 1985; mem. Synod of Bishops, Rome, 1994; chmn. Nat. Conf. Cath. Bishops Com. on Doctrine, 1994—. Trustee U. San Diego, 1991-93. Mem. Cath. Theol. Soc. Am., Canon Law Soc. Am., Am. Cath. Hist. Soc. Address: 445 Church St San Francisco CA 94114-1720*

QUINN, MICHAEL DESMOND, diversified financial services executive; b. Balt., Sept. 4, 1936; s. Michael Joseph and Gladys (Baldwin) Q.; m. Mary Annette McHenry, Apr. 11, 1961; children: Cailin A., Maureen K., Patricia B., Marianne P. BA, U. Md., 1970. With Weaver Bros., Inc. of Md., Balt., 1960—, investment v.p., corporate dir. interim loan dept., 1978-86; chmn. bd. Wye Mortgage Co., L.P., 1977—, Christiana Capital Group, Inc.; chmn., chief exec. officer Alliance Recovery Group, Inc., 1990—, Estate Trust Co., Inc.; faculty evening coll. Johns Hopkins U., Essex Community Coll., 1967—. Mem. gov.'s task force Md. Housing Ins. Fund; mem. Md. Health Claims Arbitration Panel; bd. visitors U. Md.; dist. adv. coun. U.S. Small Bus. Adminstrn. With USN, 1956-58. Mem. Md. Mortgage Bankers Assn. (pres. bd. govs.), Real Estate Bd. Greater Balt. (bd. dirs.), Home Builders Assn. Md., Md. Bankers Assn., Balt. Econ. Soc., N.Am. Soc. Corp. Planning, Greater Balt. Com., Ancient Order Hibernians, Balt Jr. Assn. Commerce (Richard Troja Meml. award 1967, Outstanding Young Man of Balt. 1969), Balt. County C. of C. (bd. dirs.). Home: 8207 Robin Hood Ct Baltimore MD 21204-1900 Office: 7400 York Rd Ste 300 Baltimore MD 21204-7502

QUINN, PAT (JOHN BRIAN PATRICK QUINN), professional sports team manager; b. Hamilton, Ont., Can., Jan. 29, 1943; s. John Ernest and Jean (Ireland) Q.; m. Sandra Georgia Baker, May 1, 1963; children: Valerie, Kathleen. BA in Econs., York U., 1972; JD, Del. Law Sch., 1987. Player Toronto Maple Leafs, Ont., 1968-70, Vancouver Canucks, B.C., Can., 1970-72, Atlanta Flames, 1972-77; coach Phila. Flyers, 1977-82, L.A. Kings, 1984-86; head coach Team Canada, 1986; pres., gen. mgr. Vancouver Canucks, 1987—, head coach, 1990—; player rep. NHL, Atlanta, 1973-77, bd. govs., 1987—. Named Def. Man of Yr., Vancouver Canucks, 1971, Coach of Yr. NHL, 1979-80, Coach of Yr., Sporting News, 1980, 92, Coach of the Yr. Hockey News, 1980, 92, Coach of the Yr. Acad. Awards of Sports, named to the Longest Unbeaten Record in Profl. Sports of 35 Games, 1979-80, named to the Best Record in the History of the Canucks Franchise, 1991-92; recipient Jake Milford award, 1994, Jack Diamond award, 1994. Roman Catholic. Avocations: sports, reading. Office: Vancouver Canucks, Nat Hockey League, 800 Griffiths Way, Vancouver, BC Canada V6B 6G1

QUINN, PAT MALOY, engineering company executive; b. Clay Ctr., Kans., May 28, 1932; s. Lawrence Maloy and Lois Shouse (Benjimen) Q.; m. Virginia Lois White, June 1, 1957; children: Michael Maloy, Jennifer Quinn Williams, Patrick Maloy, Amy Anne. BA in Literature, Kans. State U., 1951, BS in Civil Engrng., 1960. Civil engr. Schaub Baton Assn., Manhattan, Kans., 1957-66; civil engr. Louis Berger Internat., East Orange, N.J., 1966—, v.p., 1976-84; chief structural engr. Louis Berger Internat., Thailand, 1966-68; chief engr. Louis Berger Internat., Indonesia, 1968-72; project mgr. Louis Berger Internat., Peru, 1973, The Philippines, 1974; v.p. Louis Berger Internat., Iran, 1974-76; group v.p. Louis Berger Internat., Washington, 1984—. 1st lt. U.S. Army, 1954-57, Germany. Mem. ASCE, ASME, NSPE. Office: Louis Berger Internat Ste 900 1819 H St NE Washington DC 20000

QUINN, PATRICK, tranportation executive. Pres., co-chmn. U.S Xpress Enterprises, Inc., Chattanooga, Tenn., 1985—. Office: US Xpress Enterprises Inc 2931 S Market St Chattanooga TN 37410

QUINN, PATRICK MICHAEL, wholesale food executive; b. Grand Rapids, Mich., Mar. 5, 1934; s. Robert George and Albertine Frances (Kolzinski) Q.; m. Rita Lee Ronán, Aug 6, 1955; children: Suzanne, Brian, Karen, Timothy, Catherine, Patricia. BSBA, Aquinas Coll., 1958. Sales mgr. Nabisco, Inc., Grand Rapids, 1958-73; exec. v.p. D&W Food Ctrs., Grand Rapids, 1973-85; pres., chief exec. officer Spartan Stores, Inc., Grand Rapids, 1985—; bd. dirs. Aquinas Coll., Grand Rapids; adv. bd. N. Am. Wholesale Grocers Assn., Falls Church, Va. Chmn. United Way Appeal, Grand Rapids, 1988. With U.S. Army, 1953-55. Mem. Nat. Grocers Assn. (vice chmn., bd. dirs. 1983—, chmn. 1989). Roman Catholic. Avocations: reading, hunting, fishing, golf. Office: Spartan Stores Inc 850 76th St SW Grand Rapids MI 49518*

QUINN, PHILIP LAWRENCE, philosophy educator; b. Long Branch, N.J., June 22, 1940; s. Joseph Lawrence and Gertrude (Brown) Q. AB, Georgetown U., 1962; MS, U. Del., 1967; MA, U. Pitts., 1968, PhD, 1970; MA (hon.), Brown U., 1972. Asst. prof. philosophy Brown U., Providence, R.I., 1969-72, assoc. prof. philosophy, 1972-78, prof. philosophy, 1978-85, William Herbert Perry Faunce prof. philosophy, 1982-85; John A. O'Brien prof. philosophy U. Notre Dame, South Bend, Ind., 1985—. Author: (book) Divine Command and Moral Requirements, 1978; editor Faith and Philosophy, 1990-95; contbr. articles to profl. jours. Fulbright fellow, 1962-63; Danforth fellow, 1967-69. Mem. Am Philos. Assn. (sec., treas. ea. divsn. 1982-85, chmn. career opportunities com. 1985-90, exec. com. ctrl. divsn. 1987-90, v.p. ctrl. divsn. 1993-94, pres. 1994-95, chair ctrl. divsn. nominating com. 1995-96, acting chair Nat. Bd. of Officers 1995-96, chair 1996-99), Philosophy of Sci. Assn. (nominating com. 1984-86), Soc. Christian Philosophers (exec. com. 1981-84), N.Y. Acad. Scis. Roman Catholic. Avocations: reading, swimming, film, theatre. Home: 1645 W Turtle Creek Dr South Bend IN 46637-5660 Office: Univ Notre Dame Dept Philosophy Notre Dame IN 46556

QUINN, ROBERT, diversified financial service company. Gen. mgr. Automatic Data Processing, Inc., Chgo. Office: Automatic Data Processing 209 W Jackson Chicago IL 60606

QUINN, ROBERT HENRY, surgeon, medical school administrator; b. Omaha, July 3, 1919; s. Henry Thomas and Esther Mary (Hecklin) Q.; m. Ruth Elizabeth Binder, Aug. 1, 1942; children: Karen, Terrence, Thomas, Lisa. B.S., Creighton U., 1941, M.D., 1943. Intern St. Joseph's Hosp., Denver, 1943; resident in ob-gyn Northwestern U., 1946-47, Luth. Deaconess Hosp., Chgo., 1948; gen. practice medicine Sioux Falls, S.D., 1946-54; surgery fellow Ochsner Clinic, New Orleans, 1954-58; practice medicine specializing in surgery Sioux Falls, S.D., 1958-75; asso. dean U. S.D. Sch. Medicine, Sioux Falls, 1974-81; prof., chmn. div. surgery U. S.D. Sch. Medicine, 1977-82, v.p., dean, 1982-87, acting chmn. dept. surgery, 1982-89, prof. surgery emeritus, 1989—; chief staff McKennan Hosp., Sioux Falls, 1966; assoc. dean West River Campus, 1987-89; mem. adv. bd. clin. fellowship Bush Found., 1983-88. Bd. dirs. Karl Mundt Found., 1970—, McCrossan Boys Ranch, 1985—, Rapid City Regional Eye Inst. Found., 1987. Served with M.C., USNR, 1943-46. Recipient Disting. Service award U. S.D., 1978, Alumni Merit award Sch. Medicine Creighton U., 1985. Mem. AMA (mem. council on continuing physician edn. 1978-81, cert. of appreciation ho. of dels. 1971-75), ACS, Assn. Surg. Chmn., Ochsner Surg. Soc., S.D. State Med. Assn. (pres. 1969-70), Alpha Omega Alpha. Republican. Roman Catholic. Club: Rotary. Home: 110 Fairway Dr Spearfish SD 57783-3109 Office: 3526 5th St Ste 200 Rapid City SD 57701

QUINN, THOMAS JOSEPH, lawyer; b. Worcester, Mass., May 26, 1954; s. John Peter and Winifred Agnes (McDonough) Q.; children: Meghan, Conor, Alexander. BA summa cum laude, St. Francis Coll., Biddeford, Maine, 1975; JD, U. Notre Dame, 1978. Bar: Maine 1978, Mass. 1979, U.S. Dist. Ct. Maine 1978, U.S. Ct. Appeals (1st cir.) 1991. Rsch. asst. to prof. Alan Dershowitz Harvard Law Sch., Cambridge, Mass., 1977; law clk. to Hon. Charles A. Pomeroy Supreme Jud. Ct. of Maine, Portland, 1978-79; assoc., ptnr. Douglas, Whiting, Quinn & Denham, Portland, 1979-93; ptnr. Beals & Quinn, Portland, 1993—; instr. U. So. Maine, Portland, 1982-86. Author: (screenplay) Choice of Law, 1992; notes editor, author Jour. of Legislation, 1978-79; contbg. author Maine Lawyers Rev. Mem. City of Portland Historic Preservation Com., 1993-95. Mem. Am. Bd. Trial Advocates, Maine Bar Assn., Cumberland County Bar Assn., Maine Trial Lawyers Assn. Avocations: painting, travel, writing. Home: 415 Brighton Ave Portland ME 04102-2326 Office: Beals & Quinn 77 Middle St Portland ME 04101-4214

QUINN, TIMOTHY CHARLES, JR., lawyer; b. Caro, Mich., Mar. 3, 1936; s. Timothy Charles and Jessie (Brown) Q.; m. Linda Ricci, June 21, 1958; children: Gina M., Samantha E., Timothy Charles III. BA, U. Mich., 1960; JD, Columbia U., 1963. Bar: N.Y. 1963, U.S. Dist. Ct. (so. and ea. dists.) N.Y. 1965, U.S. Ct. Appeals (2d cir.) 1967. Assoc. Clark, Carr & Ellis, N.Y.C., 1963-69, Casey, Tyre, Wallace & Bannerman, N.Y.C., 1969-71, Arsham & Keenan, N.Y.C., 1971; assoc. Conboy, Hewitt, O'Brien & Boradman, N.Y.C., 1972-74, ptnr., 1975-83, mem. exec. com., 1981-83; ptnr. Quinn, Cohen, Shields & Bock, N.Y.C., 1983-88, Quinn & Suhr, White Plains, N.Y., 1988-95, Quinn, Marantis & Rosenberg, White Plains, N.Y., 1995—; arbitrator N.Y.C. Civil Ct., 1982-88 , Am. Arbitration Assn., N.Y.C., 1966—, 9th Jud. Dist., 1988—. Mem. ABA, N.Y. State Bar Assn., Westchester County Bar Assn., Assn. of Bar of City of N.Y., N.Y. State Trial Lawyers Assn., Nat. Assn. R.R. Trial Counsel, Conf. Freight Loss and Damage Counsel, N.Y. Law Inst., Def. Rsch. Inst., Westchester Country Club. Avocation: golf. Home: 34 Pinehurst Dr Purchase NY 10577-1307 Office: Quinn Marantis & Rosenberg 3 Barker Ave White Plains NY 10601

QUINN, TOM, communications executive; b. L.A., Mar. 14, 1944; s. Joseph Martin and Grace (Cooper) Q.; m. Amy Lynn Friedman, Nov. 24, 1982; children—Douglas, Lori, Shelby. BS, Northwestern U., 1965. Reporter, newswriter ABC Radio, Chgo. and L.A., 1965; reporter, prodr. Sta. KXTV, Sacramento, 1966; day editor City News Svc., L.A., 1966-68, chmn., 1980-85; pres. Americom Broadcasting, Inc., L.A., 1985—; pres. Radio News West, L.A., 1968-70; campaign mgr. Jerry Brown for Sec. State, L.A., 1970; dep. sec. state Calif., Sacramento, 1971-74; campaign mgr. Brown for Gov., L.A., 1974; sec. Calif. Dept. Environ. Affairs, Sacramento, 1975-79; pres. Sta. KFSO Radio, Fresno, 1985—; pres. K-HITS Radio, Reno, Nev.; dir. Parallel Comms. Co. Chmn. Tom Bradley Mayoral Campaign, 1985. Recipient Headliner of Yr. award Greater L.A. Press Club, 1978; Environ. Protection award Calif. Trial Lawyers Assn., 1979. Democrat. Office: 6255 W Sunset Blvd Bldg 1901 Los Angeles CA 90028-7420

QUINN, WILLIAM FRANCIS, lawyer; b. Rochester, N.Y., July 13, 1919; s. Charles Alvin and Elizabeth (Dorrity) Q.; m. Nancy Ellen Witbeck, July 11, 1942; children: William Francis, Stephen Desford, Timothy Charles, Christopher Thomas, Ann Cecily, Mary Kaiulani, Gregory Anthony. B.S. summa cum laude, St. Louis U., 1940; LL.B. cum laude, Harvard U., 1947. Bar: Hawaii 1948. Ptnr. Robertson, Castle & Anthony, Honolulu, 1947-57; gov. Ter. of Hawaii, 1957-59, state Hawaii, 1959-62; partner Quinn & Moore, Honolulu, 1962-64; exec. v.p. Dole Co., Honolulu., 1964-65; pres. Dole Co., 1965-72; ptnr. Jenks, Kidwell, Goodsill & Anderson, Honolulu, 1972-73, Goodsill Anderson & Quinn, 1973-82, Goodsill Anderson Quinn & Stifel, 1982-91; mem. sr. adv. bd. 9th Cir. Jud. Coun. Served with USNR, 1942-46. Decorated knight of Holy Sepulchre Order. Republican. Roman Catholic. Clubs: Waialae Country, Pacific (Honolulu). Home: 1365 Laukahi St Honolulu HI 96821-1407 Office: Alii Place 1099 Alakea St Ste 1800 Honolulu HI 96813-4500

QUINN, WILLIAM WILSON, army officer, manufacturing executive; b. Crisfield, Md., Nov. 1, 1907; s. William Samuel and Alice (Wilson) Q.; m. Bette Williams, Dec. 16, 1939; children: Sally, Donna, William Wilson. Student, St. John's Coll., Annapolis, Md., 1927-29; B.S., U.S. Mil. Acad., 1933; postgrad., Inf. Sch., Ft. Benning, Ga., 1938-39, Command and Staff Sch., Ft. Leavenworth, Kans., 1941, Nat. War Coll., Washington, 1948-49. Commd. 2d lt. inf. U.S. Army, 1933, advanced through grades to lt. gen., 1961; co. comdr. inf., 1933-36; provost marshal city of Manila, 1937-38; assigned G-2 IV Corps, 1943-44, G-2 7th Army Invasion S. France, 1944-45; dir. Strategic Service Unit, 1946-47, G-2 X Corps, Inchon Landing, Inchon Landing, Korea, 1950; comdg. officer 7th Inf. Div. 17th Inf. Regt., Korea, 1951; office Chief of Staff U.S. Army, 1952; asst. divsn. comdr. 47th Inf. Div., 1953; chief Army sect. Joint U.S. Mil. Adv. Group to Greece, 1953-55; asst. divsn. comdr. 9th Inf. Div., Germany, 1955-56; comdg. gen. Ft. Carson, Colo., 1956; comdg. gen. 4th Inf. Div. Ft. Lewis, Washington, 1957; chief pub. info. Dept. Army, 1960-61; dep. dir. Def. Intelligence Agy., 1961-64; comdg. gen. 7th U.S. Army Germany, 1964-66; ret., 1966; v.p. Martin Marietta Corp., Washington, 1966-72; pres. Quinn Assos., Washington, 1972—. Author articles. Vice chmn. Goldwater Edn. Found. Decorated D.S.M. with cluster, Silver Star, Legion of Merit with cluster, Air medal with clusters, Purple Heart, Bronze star with V device, Officer, Legion of Honor, France; recipient Presdl. Unit citation, Korea, Das. Grosse Verdienstkreuz mit Stern, Germany. Mem. SAR, Army Navy Club, Chevy Chase Club, Bohemian Club of San Francisco, Kappa Alpha. Episcopalian. Address: 9787 Unionville Rd Easton MD 21601-5223

QUINN, YVONNE SUSAN, lawyer; b. Spring Valley, Ill., May 13, 1951; d. Robert Leslie and Shirley Eilene (Morse) Q.; m. Ronald S. Rolfe, Sept. 1, 1979. BA, U. Ill., 1973; JD, U. Mich., 1976, MA in Econs., 1977. Bar: N.Y. 1978, U.S. Dist. Ct. (ea. and so. dists.) N.Y. 1978, U.S. Ct. Appeals (3d, 5th, 9th, 10th and D.C. cirs.) 1982, U.S. Ct. Appeals (2d cir.) 1992, U.S. Ct. Appeals (4th cir.) 1994, U.S. Supreme Ct. 1982. Assoc. Cravath, Swaine & Moore, N.Y.C., 1977-80; assoc. Sullivan & Cromwell, N.Y.C., 1980-84, ptnr., 1984—. Mem. ABA, Assn. of Bar of City of N.Y., India House Club. Office: Sullivan & Cromwell 125 Broad St New York NY 10004-2400

QUINNAN, GERALD VINCENT, JR., medical educator; b. Boston, Sept. 7, 1947; s. Gerald Vincent and Mary (Lally) Q.; children: Kevin, Kylie, Kathleen, John, Gerald; m. Leigh A. Sawyer. AB in Chemistry, Coll. Holy Cross, 1969; MD cum laude, St. Louis U., 1973. Diplomate Am. Bd. Internal Medicine. Intern, resident, fellow Boston U. Med. Ctr., 1973-77; med. officer Bur. Biologics, USPHS, Bethesda, Md., 1977; advanced through grades to asst. surgeon gen. USPHS, 1992; dir. herpes virus br., dep. dir. div. virology Bur. Biologics, Bethesda, 1980-81; dir. div. virology Ctr. for Drugs and Biologics, Bethesda, 1981-88; dep. dir. Ctr. Biologics Evaluation and Rsch., Bethesda, 1988-93, acting dir., 1990-92; prof. uniformed svcs. U. Health Scis., Bethesda, 1993—. Contbr. chpts. to books, numerous articles to profl. jours.; editl. bd./reviewer several jours. Fellow Infectious Diseases Soc. Am.; mem. AAAS, Am. Soc. for Microbiology, Am. Soc. for Clin. Investigation, Sigma Xi, Alpha Omega Alpha. Roman Catholic. Office: Uniformed Svcs U Hlth Scis Div Tropical PH 4301 Jones Bridge Rd Bethesda MD 20814

QUINNELL, BRUCE ANDREW, retail book chain executive; b. Washington, Jan. 6, 1949; s. Robert Kay and Marion Louise (Moseley) Q.; m. Aug. 31, 1972 (div. June 1986); children: Paul David, Andrea Carolyn; m. Marcia Melodie Mundie. BS in Acctg., Va. Poly. Inst. and State U., 1971, MA in Acctg., 1972. CPA, Ohio, Mo., Tex., Tenn. Sr. auditor Ernst & Whinney, Columbus, Ohio, 1972-75; treas., chief fin. officer Midway Ford Truck Ctr., Kansas City, Mo., 1975-82; sr. v.p., chief fin. officer Rsch. Health Svcs., Kansas City, 1982-85; sr. v.p. VHA Enterprises Inc., Irving, Tex., 1985-87; v.p., treas., chief fin. officer Dollar Gen. Corp., Nashville, 1987-92; exec. v.p. Pace Membership Warehouse, Englewood, Colo., 1992-93; exec. v.p., COO Walden Book Co., Stamford, Conn., 1993, pres., 1994—. Bd. dirs. Advs. Tenn. State U. Coll. Bus., Nashville, 1991-92, Jr. Achievement Mid. Tenn., 1992. Mem. Fin. Execs. Inst., Am. Inst. CPA'S, Nat. Investor Rels. Inst. Republican. Lutheran. Avocations: racquetball, golf, scuba diving. Office: Waldenbooks 100 Phoenix Dr PO Box 996 Ann Arbor MI 48106-9700

QUINN-JUDGE, PAUL MALACHY, journalist; b. London, Feb. 2, 1949; came to U.S., 1977; s. Charles and Marion Judge; m. Sophia Whitney Sears, May 1, 1971; children: Emma, Katharine. MA, Trinity Coll., Cambridge U., Eng., 1971. Saigon rep. Am. Friends' Svc. Com., Saigon, S. Vietnam, 1973-75; S.E. Asia rep. Am. Friends' Svc. Com., Singapore, 1976-80; freelance corr. Christian Sci. Monitor, Bangkok, 1992-94; Moscow corr. Christian Sci. Monitor, Moscow, Russia, 1986-89, The Boston Globe, Moscow, Russia, 1989-92; nat. security corr. The Boston Globe, Washington, 1992—; freelance corr. Far Eastern Econ. Rev., Bangkok, 1980-86; diplomatic corres. The Boston Globe, 1994—; cons. BBC-The Second Russian Revolution (TV series), London, 1990-91. Avocations: running, wine. Home: 3401 Pauline

Dr Chevy Chase MD 20815-3917 Office: The Boston Globe Washington Bur 1130 Connecticut Ave NW Washington DC 20036-3904

QUINN-KERINS, CATHERINE, psychologist; b. Neptune, N.J., Mar. 12, 1951; d. James R. and Jane (Forman) Quinn; m. Daniel Kerins, Jan. 14, 1978; children: Katie, Amanda, Benjamin. BA magna cum laude, Fairleigh Dickinson U., 1973; postgrad., Hahneman Med. Coll., 1974-75; MEd, U. Del., 1975; PhD, U. Pa., 1983. Lic. psychologist, Pa. Treatment coord., psychologist St. Gabriel's Hall, Audubon, Pa., 1975-86; clin. psychologist InterPsych Assocs., King of Prussia, Pa., 1985-87; full-time ind. practice Audubon, 1987—; mem. allied health staff Phoenixville (Pa.) Hosp., 1990—; mem. part-time faculty dept. psychology Neuman Coll., Aston, Pa., 1977. V.p. Montessori Children's House of Valley Forge, Wayne, Pa., 1985-87. Mem. APA, Am. Assn. Anxiety Disorders, Obsessive Compulsive Found., Phi Omega Epsilon, Phi Zeta Kappa, Psi Chi. Avocations: spending time with her children, walking on the beach, artwork, reading. Home: 2018 Blackbird Cir Norristown PA 19403-1845 Office: 2605 Egypt Rd Norristown PA 19403-2317

QUINSLER, WILLIAM THOMSON, retired investment advisor; b. Watertown, Mass., June 21, 1924; s. Phillips Brooks and Eleanor (Macurdy) Q.; m. Barbara Jean Faust, June 15, 1957; children: William Thomson, Jr., Harry Faust, Catharine Marten Quinsler Örn. B.S. in Elec. Engring., U. Ariz., 1950. Registered profl. engr., Ariz. Engr. Ariz. Pub. Service Co., Phoenix, 1950-53; staff cons. treasury dept. Ariz. Pub. Service Co., 1953, supr. treasury dept., 1954, mgr. fin. services, 1955-62, asst. treas., 1962-69, sec., asst. treas., 1969-83; founding dir. Utility Svcs. Ins. Co. Ltd., Hamilton, Bermuda, 1970-84; pres., chief oper. officer Utility Svcs. Ins. Co. Ltd., 1982-84; trustee Tax-Free Trust of Ariz., 1986—, chmn. audit com., 1992—. Mem. adv. bd. Apache Nat. Forest Service; mem. Phoenix Symphony Assn. Served with USAAF, 1943-46. Mem. IEEE, NSPE, Ariz. Soc. Profl. Engrs., Am., Pacific Coast gas assns., Am. Soc. Corp. Secs., Pacific Coast Electric Assn., C. of C., Ariz. Cattle Growers Assn., Greenlee County Cattle Growers Assn., Phoenix Soc. Fin. Analysts (past pres. and dir.). Home and Office: 5428 E Calle Del Medio Phoenix AZ 85018-4530

QUINSON, BRUNO ANDRE, publishing executive; b. Norwich, Conn., Jan. 1, 1938; s. Louis Jean and Suzanne Marie (Richard) Q.; m. Mary Ann Goodman, May 3, 1980; children by previous marriage: Timothy Bruno, Marc Albert (dec.), Christopher Louis; stepchildren: J. Geoffrey Taylor, Luke J. Taylor, Adam J. Taylor, Joshua P. Taylor. BA, Williams Coll., 1958; postgrad., NYU, 1960-61. Product mgr. Simon & Schuster, N.Y.C., 1960-65; pub., gen. mgr. Golden Press (div. Western Pub. Co., Inc.), 1965-70; pres. Larousse & Co., Inc., N.Y.C., 1970-82, also bd. dirs.; pres. trade and reference div. Macmillan Pub. Co., N.Y.C., 1982-88; pres., chief exec. officer Henry Holt & Co. Inc., N.Y.C., 1988-96; bd. dirs. Henry Holt & Co., Inc., N.Y.C.; bd. dirs. Fitzhenry & Whiteside, The Voyager Co., Nat. Book Found., chmn., 1993-96; treas. Columbia Univ. Press, 1994—; mem. exec. bd. MacMillan Ltd., 1995-96; chmn. bd. dirs. Motovun Group Assn., 1996—. Bd. dirs. Rye (N.Y.) Art Ctr., treas., 1973-74; bd. dirs. Northside Ctr. for Child Devel., 1981-89, chmn., 1987-89, mem. adv. bd., 1990—; bd. dirs. 1115 Fifth Ave. Corp., 1983-94, 96—; bd. dirs. Lycee Francais de New York, 1994—. Mem. Am. Assn. Pubs. (bd. dirs. 1991-95), Century Assn., Manhattan Theater Club (bd. dirs. 1991—), Norfolk Country Club, The River Club. Office: Henry Holt & Co Inc 115 W 18th St New York NY 10011-4113

QUINT, ARNOLD HARRIS, lawyer; b. Boston, Jan. 3, 1942; s. Milton and Esther (Kirshen) Q.; m. Susan Arenson, July 23, 1967; children: Edward, Michael. AB, Haverford (Pa.) Coll., 1963; LLB, Yale U., 1966. Bar: D.C. 1967. Supervisory atty. Fed. Power Commn., Washington, 1967-70; assoc. Hunton & Williams, Washington, 1970-74, ptnr., 1974—. Mem. ABA, Fed. Energy Bar Assn. (com. chmn. 1979-83, bd. dirs. 1989-92). Office: Hunton & Williams 2000 Pennsylvania Ave NW PO Box 19230 Washington DC 20036

QUINT, BERT, journalist; b. N.Y.C., Sept. 22, 1930; s. George and Sadye (Slonim) Q.; m. Diane Frances Schwab, Apr. 10, 1975; children: Lara Gabrielle, Amy Frances. BS, NYU, 1952. Reporter Worcester (Mass.) Telegram, 1953-54, AP, 1953-54, N.Y. Herald Tribune, 1956-58; mag. editor, free lance corr. N.Y. Herald Tribune, Wall Street Jour., CBS News, others, Mexico City, 1958-65; corr. CBS News, 1965-93; adj. prof. broadcast journalism U. Colo., Boulder, 1993—; journalist/anchor/writer TV & home-video documentaries,pres. Quint Colo. Inc., 1994—. Writer, anchor TV & Video Documentaries, 1996; contbr. articles to profl. jours. Recipient Radio Reporting award Overseas Press Club, 1971. Mem. Soc. Profl. Journalists, Fgn. Corr. Assn. Mex. (pres.). Home and Office: 539 Bari Ct Boulder CO 80303-4312

QUINT, IRA, retail executive; b. N.Y.C., May 29, 1930; s. Theodore Isaac and Rebecca (Ginandes) Q.; m. Carol Ann Goldsmith (div. Feb. 1984); children: Susan Amy, Stephanie Ann. B.S., NYU, 1951; M.B.A., Harvard U., 1954. Group nat. mdse. mgr. Sears Roebuck & Co., Chgo., 1954-78; pres. Colonial Corp. Am., N.Y.C., 1978-79; pres., CEO Venture Stores, St. Louis, 1979-81; exec. v.p. Montgomery Ward, Chgo., 1981-85; pres. Lane Bryant Stores, N.Y.C., 1985-90; pres., chief exec. officer Conston Corp., Phila., 1990-92; pres. Quint Consultancy, N.Y.C., 1992—. Club: Harvard (N.Y.C.). Home: 130 E 67th St New York NY 10021-6136 Office: 130 E 67th St New York NY 10021-6136

QUINTANA, JOSE BOOTH, health care executive; b. Coral Gables, Fla., July 13, 1946; s. Jose Luis and Carmen Elaine (Booth) Q.; m. Mary Jo Gregg, Sept. 7, 1968; children: Stephanie Elizabeth, Meredith Caroline. BSBA, U. Fla., 1968; MHA, Duke U., 1974; PhD, U. Ala., 1984. Commd. 2d lt. USAF, 1969, advanced through grades to lt. col., 1985, resigned, 1989; dir. pers. and adminstrv. svcs. USAF Regional Hosp., March AFB, Calif., 1969-71, adminstrv. asst. hosp. svcs., 1971-72; adminstr. USAF Hosp., Ubon Royal Thai Air Base, Thailand, 1974, Kunsan Air Base, South Korea, 1974-75; dir. pers. and adminstrv. svcs. USAF Regional Hosp., Maxwell AFB, Ala., 1975, dir. patent info., 1975-76, dir. med. resource mgmt., 1976-78; chief med. readiness ops. divsn. Office of Surgeon, USAF in Europe, Ramstein AFB, West Germany, 1978-81; strategic planner, health affairs and plans divsn. Office Air Force Surgeon Gen., Bolling AFB, Washington, 1984-86, sr. health rsch. analyst, directorate med. plans and resources, 1986-89; health svcs. rsch. and devel. coord., rsch. svc. VA Med. Ctr., Birmingham, Ala., 1989—, exec. asst. to dir. (quality), 1991—; asst. prof. dept. health svcs. adminstrn. U. Ala., Birmingham, 1989—; lectr. in field. Contbr. articles to profl. jours. Fellow ACHE; mem. Am. Soc. Quality Control (mem. edn. com. 1993), Ala. Hosp. Assn. (mem. quality innovation com. 1992—), Assn. Health Svcs. Rsch., Assn. Univ. Programs in Health Adminstrn., Acad. Mgmt., Phi Kappa Phi, Beta Gamma Sigma. Republican. Southern Baptist. Avocations: computers, bridge, bible study. Office: U Ala Dept Health Svcs Adminstrn 1675 University Blvd # 512 Webb Birmingham AL 35233

QUINTANA, MARGARET ANN, financial analyst, banker; b. Marianna, Fla., June 21, 1952; d. John Amos and Ella-Margaret Estright (Callin) Dickenson; m. Enrique Quintana Jr., Aug. 25, 1973. AA with honors, Fla. Jr. Coll., Jacksonville, 1982, AS in Banking with honors, 1983; BBA in Acctg. cum laude, U. North Fla., 1985, MBA, 1986. CPA, Fla. Internal auditor Atlantic Nat. Bank, Jacksonville, Fla., 1985; auditor Coopers & Lybrand, Jacksonville, 1986-88; asst. contr. Fla. Physicians Ins. Co., Jacksonville, 1988-92; sr. auditor, tax acct. Grenadier, Appleby, Collins & Co., Jacksonville, 1992-93; fin. analyst Am. Nat. Bank, Jacksonville, 1993—. Mem. acctg. del. to Soviet Union, People to People Amb. Program, 1991; cashier chmn. Jacksonville Jazz Festival, 1992—; mem. adminstrv. coun. Spring Glen United Meth. Ch., Jacksonville, 1992—, chmn. worship com., 1992-93, chmn. children's ministry, 1993—. Recipient 5-Yr. Recognition cert. Am. Express Internat. Banking Corp., 1979, Outstanding Svc. award Alpha Sigma Pi, 1985. Mem. AICPA, Inst. Mgmt. Accts., Inst. Internal Auditors, Fla. Inst. CPAs (Grad. Study scholar 1985), U. North Fla. Alumni Assn. (v.p. 1989-90, Recognition award 1989), Jacksonville Rose Soc. (v.p., treas. 1991-94), Phi Theta Kappa (sec., pres. 1982-84, Recognition award 1983, 84, Most Disting. Alumni Mem. 1984, Honors Inst. scholar 1984, Hall of Honor 1984), Phi Kappa Phi. Avocations: dancing, travelling, collecting jewelry, Egyptology, growing and arranging roses. Home: 5224 Hoof Print Dr N Jacksonville FL 32257-3369 Office: Am Nat Bank 1551 Atlantic Blvd Jacksonville FL 32207-3345

QUINTERO, JOSE, theatrical director; b. Panama City, Panama, Oct. 15, 1924; s. Carlos Rivira and Consuelo (Palmerola) de Q. Student, Goodman Theater, Chgo., 1934-35, U. So. Calif. and L.A. City Coll., 1948. Producer, dir. Circle in the Square Theatre, N.Y.C., 1951-63; instr. Fla. State U., U. Houston. Producer, dir.: (plays) Desire Under the Elms, Cradle Song, La Ronde, The Iceman Cometh, The Girl on the Via Flaminia, Summer and Smoke, The King and the Duke, Burning Bright, Yerma, Dark of the Moon, The Balcony, Our Town, Plays for Bleecker Street, (Broadway plays) A Moon for the Misbegotten (Tony award), The Innkeepers, Portrait of a Lady, Gabrielle, In the Summer House, The Girl on the Via Flaminia, The Skin of Our Teeth, Long Days Journey into Night, A Touch of the Poet, Look We've Come Through, Great Day in the Morning, Strange Interlude, Diamond Orchid, Anna Christie, Faith Healer, Clothes for a Summer Hotel, Welded, 1981, Cat On A Hot Tin Roof, 1984, Long Days Journey Into Night, 1987, Private Lives, 1990, Our Town, 1993, others, (film) The Roman Spring of Mrs. Stone, 1961, (TV movies) Hughie, Medea, Our Town; dir. Eugene O'Neill play for Nat. Pub. Radio, 1988/93. Decorated Cabellero de la Order de Vasco Nunez de Balboa; recipient spl. citation La Asamblea Nacional de Panama, Drama Desk award, Tony award, Page One award, Disting. Artist award, 1985, L.A. Drama Circle award, O'Neill Gold Medal award, 1988, South Ea. Theatre Conf. award for life achievement; named to Theatre Hall of Fame. Mem. Dirs. Guild Am., Soc. Stage Dirs. and Choreographers, Am. Fellows of Theatre. Address: The Lantz Office 888 7th Ave Ste 2500 New York NY 10106

QUINTERO, RONALD GARY, management consultant; b. Detroit, Jan. 5, 1954; s. John Urdiales and Jean Lorraine (Morton) Q.; m. Barbara Kay McDaniel, June 15, 1985; children: Jean Marie, Alexandra Lisa. AB, Lafayette Coll., 1975; MS, NYU, 1976, APC, 1978. CPA, CFA, CFP, cert. mgmt. acct., cert. fraud examiner, cert. insolvency and reorgn. acct., cert. turnaround profl. Sr. mgr. Peat, Marwick, Mitchell & Co., N.Y.C., 1975-85; workout cons. Zolfo, Cooper & Co., N.Y.C., 1985-87; assoc. Bear, Stearns & Co., Inc., N.Y.C., 1987-88; prin. R. G. Quintero & Co., N.Y.C., 1988—; mng. dir. Chartered Capital Advisers, Inc., N.Y.C., 1988—; adj. prof. New Sch. for Social Rsch., N.Y.C., 1983-85; adj. prof. N.Y. Inst. Fin., N.Y.C., 1988—; instr. Ctr. for Profl. Edn., Berwyn, Pa., 1991—. Author: (book and cassette) Mergers and Acquisitions, 1990; contbg. author several books; contbr. articles to profl. jours.; creator: Quintero Index of Bankrupt Stocks. Mem. AICPAs, Am. Bankruptcy Inst., N.Y. Soc. CPAs (chmn. com. 1990-91, Max Block Disting. Article award 1990, Outstanding Discussion Leader 1991), Turnaround Mgmt. Assn. (bd. dirs., exec. com.). Avocations: squash, softball, running, computers, reading. Office: R G Quintero & Co 145 4th Ave New York NY 10003-4906

QUINTIERE, GARY G., lawyer; b. Passaic, N.J., Nov. 26, 1944; s. Benjamin and Sadie (Riotto) Q.; m. Judy Rosenthal, Aug. 16, 1966; children: Karen, Geoffrey. AB in Govt., Lafayette Coll., 1966; JD, George Washington U., 1969. Law clk. to Judge Philip Nichols, Jr. U.S. Ct. Appeals (Fed. cir.), Washington, 1969-70; from assoc. to ptnr. Miller & Chevalier, Washington, 1970-85; ptnr. Morgan, Lewis & Bockius, Washington, 1985—. Mem. ABA, D.C. Bar Assn., Va. Bar Assn. Avocations: tennis, skiing, golf. Home: 14 Mercy Ct Potomac MD 20854-4540 Office: Morgan Lewis & Bockius 1800 M St NW Washington DC 20036-5802

QUINTON, PAUL MARQUIS, physiology educator, researcher; b. Houston, Tex., Sept. 17, 1944; s. Curtis Lincoln and Mercedes Genale (Danley) Q.; m. Liesbet Joris, Dec. 31, 1992; 1 child, Marquis. BA, U. Tex., 1967; PhD, Rice U., 1971. Asst. prof. physiology and medicine UCLA Med. Sch., 1975-79; asst. prof. biomed. scis. U. Calif., Riverside, 1979-81, assoc. prof., 1981-84, prof., 1984—; assoc. prof. physiology UCLA, 1981-91. Assoc. ed. Am. Journal Physiology: Cell Biology (Bethesda), assoc. ed. Experimental Physiology (Cambridge). Recipient Rsch. Career Devel. award NIH, 1978, Paul di Sant'Agnese Disting. Sci. Achievement award Nat. Cystic Fibrosis Found., 1991, Joseph Levy Meml. award Internat. Cystic Fibrosis (Mucovisidosis) Assn., 1994. Office: U Calif Biomed Scis 2263 Weber Hall W Riverside CA 92521

QUIRICO, FRANCIS JOSEPH, retired state supreme court justice; b. Pittsfield, Mass., Feb. 18, 1911; s. Luigi and Lucia (Giovanetti) Q. LL.B., Northeastern U., 1932, LL.D., 1970; J.D. (hon.), Suffolk U., 1971; LL.D. (hon.), Am. Internat. U., 1974, New Eng. Sch. Law, 1975, Western New Eng. Coll., Springfield, Mass., 1981, North Adams (Mass.) State Coll., 1981. Bar: Mass. 1932, U.S. Ct. Appeals (1st cir.), U.S. Supreme Ct. 1939. Pvt. practice law Pittsfield, 1932-56, city solicitor, 1948-52; justice Superior Ct. Mass., 1956-69, Supreme Jud. Ct. Mass., 1969-81; recalled to active service with Superior Ct., 1981-86, Appeals Ct., 1986-87. Served with USAAF, 1942-46. Mem. Berkshire County Bar Assn., Am. Law Inst., Am. Legion. Roman Catholic.

QUIRK, FRANK JOSEPH, management consulting company executive; b. N.Y.C., Feb. 27, 1941; s. Frank J. and Madeline B. Quirk; BA, Cornell U., 1962, MBA, 1964; m. Betty Josephine Mauldin, Jan. 7, 1967; children: Laura Josephine, Katherine Elizabeth. Assoc., Booz, Allen & Hamilton, Inc., Chgo. and Washington, 1967-72; exec. v.p. Macro Internat., Inc., Silver Spring, Md., 1972-79, pres., CEO, 1980—. Bd. dirs. Profl. Svcs. Coun. Served to capt. U.S. Army, 1964-66. Club: Belle Haven Country. Home: 2110 Foresthill Rd Alexandria VA 22307-1128 Office: Macro Internat Inc 11785 Beltsville Dr Beltsville MD 20705-3121

QUIRK, JOHN JAMES, investment company executive; b. N.Y.C., July 10, 1943; s. Francis J. and Madeline A. (Meizinger) Q.; m. Kathryn Anne O'Brien, Mar. 21, 1963; children: John James, Ashlin Carter, Merritt Andrew. B.A., Georgetown U., 1965; M.B.A., U. Va., 1967. Asst. treas., mgr. corp. fin. dept. W.R. Grace & Co., N.Y.C., 1967-74; asst. v.p., asst. treas. City Investing Co., N.Y.C., 1974-77; v.p., treas. City Investing Co., 1978-81, sr. v.p., treas., 1982-85; chmn. bd. Quirk Carson Peppet Inc., 1985—; dir. Global Union Bank, N.Y.C., Entertainment Completions Inc., Haywood & Co. Clubs: Racquet and Tennis; Wee Burn (Conn.). Home: 445 Hollow Tree Ridge Rd Darien CT 06820-3030 Office: 126 E 56th St New York NY 10022

QUIRK, KENNETH PAUL, accountant; b. Lake Charles, La., Aug. 29, 1953; s. Charles Patrick and Helen (Lejeune) Q.; m. Teresa Ann Tucker, Mar. 26, 1982 (div. Mar. 1988); 1 child, Heather Marie. BS in Acctg., McNeese State U., 1978; postgrad. MBA on-line, U. Phoenix, 1995—. CPA, La. Staff acct. Quirk, Cargile, Hicks & Reddin, Lake Charles, 1979-80, Browning-Ferris Industries, Lake Charles, 1980-81, La. Savs. Assn., Lake Charles, 1981-90, Calcasieu Marine Nat. Bank, Lake Charles, 1990—. Author fin. acctg. software sys. Mem. Young Men's Bus. Club, Lake Charles, 1986-90, Girl Scouts U.S., Lake Charles, 1989-90. Mem. AICPA, Soc. La. CPAs, Assn. for Computing Machinery. Republican. Episcopalian. Avocations: jazz drumming, geneaology.

QUIRK, PETER RICHARD, engineering company executive; b. New Orleans, Dec. 28, 1936; s. Andrew John and Elise (Richard) Q.; m. Marilyn Ann Montalban, Aug. 16, 1958; children: Karen, Cheryl, Brian, Kathleen, Aimee, Elizabeth. BS, La. State U., 1959. Registered profl. engr., La. Sr. staff engr. Continental Oil Co., Ponca City, Okla., 1959-64; pres. Walk, Haydel & Assocs. Inc., New Orleans, 1964—, now pres. and CEO; mem. Bur. Govtl. Rsch., Natural Gas Assn. of New Orleans, 1991—. Active World Trade Ctr., 1972—; bd. dirs. Closer Walk Ministries, 1984—, Covenant Ho. New Orleans, 1989—, Met. Area Com., 1989—, La. State U. Found., 1989—, Phi Kappa Theta Nat. Found., 1990—, Cath. Found., 1993—; bd. dirs. United Way of Greater New Orleans, 1996, chmn. gen. campaign, 1991, co-chair Day of Caring, 1995; bd. dirs. U. New Orleans Higher Edn. Coun., 1992—; mem. adv. bd. U. New Orleans Ctr. for Energy Resources Mgmt., 1992—; chair exec. com. Archbishop's Cmty. Appeal, 1993—; chair Cystic Fibrosis Found. Ann. Walk, 1993. 2d lt. C.E., AUS, 1960. Recipient A.E. Wilder Jr. award Cons. Engr. Coun. L.A., 1989, Vol. Activist award, 1993, Man of Achievement award Phi Kappa Theta Nat. Found., 1991, Order St. Louis award. Mem. Instrument Soc. Am., NSPE, Constrn. Mgmt. Assn. Am. (bd. dirs. 1987-90), La. Engring. Soc., Am. Cons. Engrs. Council (trustee polit. action com. 1984-90, fellow 1988), Cons. Engrs. Council La. (pres. 1982-83), New Orleans and River Region C. of C., La. Chem. Industry Alliance, Greater New Orleans Bus. Roundtable, Paper Industry Mgmt. Assn., Phi Kappa Theta. Republican. Roman Catholic. Clubs: Serra (New Orleans pres. 1986, 94-95), Engineers (New Orleans pres. 1984-85). Home: 1201 Beverly Gardens Dr Metairie LA 70002-1903 Office: Walk Haydel & Assocs Inc 600 Carondelet St New Orleans LA 70130

QUIRKE, LILLIAN MARY, retired art educator; b. West Haven, Conn., Oct. 1, 1928; d. Mortimer Francis and Ellen Louise (Bird) Q. BS, BA, So. Conn. U., 1950; MA, Long Beach State U., 1953; EdD, Columbia U., 1963. Cert. elem. and art tchr., Conn., Calif. Tchr. Long Beach (Calif.) Pub. Schs., 1950-54; jr. high art tchr. Army Dependents Sch., Frankfurt, Germany, 1954-55; art tchr. Navy Dependents Sch., Naples, Italy, 1955-56; art instr. So. Conn. U., New Haven, 1956-64, Foothill C.C., Los Altos, Calif., 1964-67; from art instr. to prof. DeAnza C.C., Cupertino, Calif., 1967-88; adj. prof. Queens (N.Y.) Coll., 1990-91. Author: The Rug Book, 1979; contbr. articles to profl. jours.; mem. editl. bd. Art Edn. mag., 1985-87. Active Dem. and Rep. Ctrl. Coms., San Jose, Calif., 1968-71; mem. arts rev. com. Cupertino Pub. Libr., 1977-81. Title IV grantee, 1967, grantee State of Calif., 1968, NDEA grantee U.S. Office Edn., 1966. Mem. Nat. Art Edn. Assn. (life, sec. Pacific chpt. 1954—, founder higher edn. sect. 1973), Calif. Art Edn. Assn. (rsch. chair 1969-72), Artists and Tech. (bd. dirs. 1984-88). Avocations: quilting, boating, cooking, computer graphics. Home: 5916 Rio Royalle Rd Saint Augustine FL 32084-7304

QUIST, GORDON JAY, federal judge; b. Grand Rapids, Mich., Nov. 12, 1937; s. George J. and Ida F. (Hoekstra) Q.; m. Jane Capito, Mar. 10, 1962; children: Scot D., George J., Susan E., Martha J., Peter K. BA, Mich. State U., 1959; JD with honors, George Washington U., 1962. Bar: D.C. 1962, Ill. 1964, U.S. Dist. Ct. (no. dist.) Ill. 1964, U.S. Supreme Ct. 1965, Mich. 1967, U.S. Dist. Ct. (we. dist.) Mich. 1967, U.S. Ct. Appeals (6th cir.) 1967. Assoc. Hollabaugh & Jacobs, Washington, 1962-64, Sonnenschein, Carlin, Nath & Rosenthal, Chgo., 1964-66; assoc. Miller, Johnson, Snell & Cummiskey, Grand Rapids, 1967-72, ptnr., 1972-92, mng. ptnr., 1986-92; judge U.S. Dist. Ct. (we. dist.) Mich., Grand Rapids, 1992—. Bd. dirs. Wedgewood Acres-Ch. Youth Home, 1968-74, Mary Free Bed Hosp., 1979-88, Christian Ref. Publs., 1968-78, 82-88, Opera Grand Rapids, 1986-92, Mary Free Bed Brace Shop, 1988-92, Better Bus. Bur., 1972-80, Calvin Theol. Sem., 1992-93; bd. dirs. Indian Trails Camp, 1970-78, 82-88, pres., 1978, 88. Mem. Am. Indicature Soc., Mich. State Bar Assn., Univ. Club Grand Rapids, Order of Coif. Avocations: reading, travel. Office: 482 Ford Fed Courthouse 110 Michigan St NW Grand Rapids MI 49503-2313

QUITTMEYER, CHARLES LOREAUX, business educator; b. Peekskill, N.Y., Dec. 23, 1917; s. Ernest Martin and Edith Grace (Loreaux) Q.; m. Maureen J. Rankin, June 2, 1956; children: Peter Charles, David Rankin, Andrew Robert, Jane Loreaux. A.B., Coll. William and Mary, 1940; M.B.A., Harvard U., 1947, Ph.D. (fellow), Columbia U., 1955. Bus. and govt. positions, 1941-42, 47-48; asst. prof. bus. adminstrn. Coll. William and Mary, Williamsburg, Va., 1948-54, prof., head dept., 1962-68, founding dean Sch. Bus. Adminstrn., 1968-83, Floyd Dewey Gottwald prof. bus. adminstrn., 1982-88, Floyd Dewey Gottwald prof. bus. adminstrn. emeritus, 1988—; lectr., asst. prof. mktg. U. Buffalo, 1954-57; rsch. assoc., assoc. prof. commerce U. Va., 1957-61; sr. scientist Tech. Ops., Inc., 1961-62; dir., adv. bd. First & Mchts. Nat. Bank, Peninsula, 1972-83; dir., treas., exec. com. Williamsburg Landing, Inc., 1983-89. Contbr. to Ency. Brit., also papers in field. Mem. bd. suprs. James City County, 1969-71, chmn., 1971; mem. Peninsula Airport Commn., 1971-81, sec., 1973-81; lifetime mem. Sch. Bus. Adminstrn. Bd. Sponsors, Inc. Coll. of William and Mary. Served to capt., F.A. and M.I. AUS, 1942-46. Recipient William and Mary Alumni medallion, 1976. Mem. Acad. Mgmt., Am. Econ. Assn., So. Bus. Adminstrn. Assn. (pres. 1976-77), Soc. of Alumni Coll. William and Mary (dir. 1984-90), Phi Beta Kappa, Beta Gamma Sigma. Episcopalian. Club: Harvard of Virginia. Home: 210 Kingswood Dr Williamsburg VA 23185-3223

QURAISHI, MOHAMMED SAYEED, health scientist, administrator; b. Jodhpur, India, June 23, 1924; came to U.S., 1946, naturalized, 1973; s. Mohammed Latif and Akhtar Jahan Q.; m. Akhtar Imtiaz, Nov. 12, 1953; children: Rana, Naveed, Sabah. B.Sc., St. John's Coll., 1942; M.Sc., Aligarh Muslim U., 1944; Ph.D., U. Mass., 1948. Sr. mem. UN, WHO Team to Bangladesh, 1949-51; entomologist Malaria Inst. Pakistan, 1951-55; sr. rsch. officer Pakistan Council Sci. and Indsl. Rsch., 1955-60; sr. sci. officer Pakistan AEC, 1960-64; assoc. prof. entomology U. Man., 1964-66; assoc. prof. entomology N.D. State U., Fargo, 1966-70, prof., 1970-74; chief scientist biology N.Y. State Sci. Svc., Albany, 1974-75; entomologist, toxicologist, chief pest control and consultation sect. NIH, Bethesda, Md., 1976-84; health scientist adminstr., exec. sec. microbiology and infectious disease rsch. com. Nat. Inst. Allergy and Infectious Diseases, Bethesda, Md., 1984-88, sci. rev. adminstr. spl. revs., 1988—; sr. scientist Cen. Treaty Orgn., Inst. Nuclear Sci., Tehran, Iran, 1960-64; program mgr. interdepartmental contract Project THEMIS, Dept. Def., 1968-74; vis. scientist Harvard Sch. of Pub. Health, 1995. Author: Biochemical Insect Control: Its Impact on Economy, Environment and Natural Selection, 1977; mem. editorial bd. Jour. Environ. Toxicology and Chemistry, 1981-84; author numerous sci. papers. Chmn. NIH Asian-Am. Cultural Assn., 1980-81. Recipient Sustained High Quality Performance award, 1980, Merit Pay Performance awards, 1984, 86, 87, Recognition and Appreciation of Spl. Achievement award NIH, 1988, Spl. Recognition award for Svcs. to NIH, Asian Am. Cultural Com., 1989, Appreciation in Recognition of Outstanding Support for Combined Fed. Campaign, 1991. Mem. Am. Chem. Soc., Soc. Environ. Toxicology and Chemistry (mem. publs. com. in charge spl. publs. 1982-84), Sigma Xi, Phi Kappa Phi. Home: 19813 Cochrane Way Gaithersburg MD 20879-1637 Office: NIH Rm 4C22 Solar Bldg 6003 Executive Blvd Bethesda MD 20892

QURAISHI, NISAR ALI, internist; b. Rawalpindi, Punjab, Pakistan, May 15, 1946; came to U.S., 1970; s. Jehan Dad and Sahib Jan (Qureshi) Q.; m. Shahida Parveen, June 25, 1970; children—Abid, Zahid. M.B., B.S. Dacca (Pakistan) Med. Coll., 1969. Diplomate Am. Bd. Internal Medicine. House surgeon Dacca Med. Coll., 1969, sr. house physician, 1969-70; intern Beekman Downtown Hosp., N.Y.C., 1970-71, resident, 1971-74; assoc. attending N.Y. Infirmary-Beekman Downtown Hosp., N.Y.C., 1982—; physician in charge exercise EKG, Mobil Oil Corp., N.Y.C., 1977-86. Mem. N.Y. County Med. Soc., N.Y. State Med. Soc., AMA, ACP, Am. Soc. Internal Medicine. Office: 303 Greenwich St New York NY 10013 Office: 1 Chopin Ct Jersey City NJ 07302-3240

QUREISHI, A. SALAM, computer software and services company executive; b. Aligarh, India, July 1, 1936; s. M.A. Jabbar and Saira (Sattar) Q.; m. Naheed Fatima; children: Lubna, Leila. BS in Physics and Math., Aligarth U., India, 1954; MS in Stats., Patna U., India, 1957. Mgr. applications IBM Corp., Palo Alto, Calif., 1961-67; founder, pres., chmn. bd. Optimum Sys., Inc., Palo Alto, Calif., 1967-71; chmn. bd. Sysorex Internat., Inc., Mountain View, Calif., 1972—. Republican. Home: 925 Mountain Home Rd Redwood City CA 94062 Office: Sysorex Internat Inc 225 E Middlefield Rd Mountain View CA 94043-3909

QURESHEY, SAFI U., electronics manufacturing company executive; b. Karachi, Pakistan, Feb. 15, 1951; s. Razi and Ishrat (Temuri) Q.; m. Anita Sue Savory, Sept. 19, 1976; children: Uns, Zeshan, Anisa. BS in Physics, U. Karachi, 1971; BSEE, U. Tex., 1975. Test specialist Documentor div. A.M. Internat., Santa Ana, Calif., 1975-77; test engr. Computer Automation, Irvine, Calif., 1977-78; design engr. Telefile Computer Products, Irvine, 1978-80; founder, pres. AST Research, Inc., Irvine, 1980—; CEO AST Research Inc., 1988—. Mem. So. Calif. Tech. Execs. Network (bd. dirs.). Islamic. Avocations: bicycling, golf. Office: AST Rsch Inc 16215 Alton Pky Irvine CA 92718*

QURESHI, NILOFER, biochemist; b. Karachi, Pakistan, July 31, 1947; came to U.S., 1970; d. Ahmed Hussain A. and Ayesha Kazi; m. Asaf A. Qureshi, Nov. 26, 1970; 1 child, Arif A. BS, St. Joseph's Coll., Karachi, Pakistan, 1967; MS, Karachi U., 1969; PhD in Physiol. Chemistry, U. Wis., 1975. Sr. exec. ops. rsch. Sui Gas Transmission Co., Karachi, 1975-76; rsch. assoc. VA Hosp. and U. Wis., Madison, 1976-77, project assoc., 1977-81; rsch. biochemist VA Hosp., Madison, 1981—; adj. assoc. prof. dept. bacteriology U. Wis., 1993—. Contbr. over 85 articles to profl. jours. NIH grantee. Mem. Am. Soc. Biochemistry and Molecular Biology (congl. liaison com.), Internat. Endotoxin Soc. (charter mem.), Am. Soc. Microbiology, Am. Chem. Soc. Avocations: reading, interior decoration. Home: 8251 Raymond Rd Madison WI 53719-5045 Office: VA Hosp 2500 Overlook Ter Madison WI 53705-2254

QUTUB, CAROL HOTELLING, elementary education educator; b. Portland, Oreg., Jan. 8, 1939; d. Cecil Claire and Mina Alice (Jarrett) Hotelling; m. Ibrahim Qutub, Mar. 1961 (div.); children: Robert, Noelle Schoos, Bilal. BA in Math., U. Oreg., 1960, postgrad., 1992, PhD; MA in Edn., Portland State U., 1968. Math. tchr. Grant Union Sch. Dist., Sacramento, Calif., 1960-61; statistician Aeorojet Gen., Sacramento, 1961-67; tchr. Clackamas, Oreg., 1967-93; elem. tchr. math. and computer Portland Pub. Schs., 1967-93, chmn. math. text book com., 1979-80. Contbr. articles to profl. jours. Mem. NEA (rep.), Nat. Coun. Tchrs. Math., Am. Ednl. Rsch. Assn., Internat. Soc. for Tech. in Edn., Phi Lambda Theta. Avocations: piano playing, skiing, boating, traveling. Home: 4610 SW 37th Ave Portland OR 97221-3910 Office: Portland Pub Schs 7452 SW 52nd Ave Portland OR 97219-1315

QUTUB, MUSA YACUB, hydrogeologist, educator, consultant; b. Jerusalem, June 2, 1940; came to U.S., 1960; s. Yacub and Sarah Qutub; married; children: Hanhia, Jennan, Sarmad, Muntaser, Aya, Saif, Tahsneen. B.A. in Geology, Simpson Coll., Indianola, Iowa, 1964; M.S. in Hydrogeology, Colo. State U., 1966; Ph.D in Water Resources, Iowa State U. Sci. and Tech., 1969. Instr. earth sci. Iowa State U., Ames, 1966-69; from asst. prof. to prof. Northeastern Ill., Chgo., 1969-80, prof. geography and environ. studies, 1980—; cons. hydrogeology, Des Plaines, Ill., 1970—; sr. adviser Saudi Arabian Ministry Planning, Riyadh, 1977-78; leader U.S. environ. sci. del. to People's Republic of China, 1984; pres., founder Islamic Info. Ctr. Am. Author: Secondarty Environmental Science Methods, 1973; contbr. numerous articles to profl. jours.; editor Environ. Resource, Directory Environ. Educators and Cons. World. NSF grantee, 1970-71, 71-72, 72-73, 75, 76, Hew grantee, 1974, grantee Ill. Dept. Edn., 1970. Mem. AAAS, NSF (cons.), Am. Waterworks Assn., Am. Men and Women Sci., Nat. Assn. Geology Tchrs. (pres. central sect. 1974), Environ. Sci. Inst. (edn. com.), Internat. Assn. Advancement of Earth and Environ Sci. (pres. 1975—, founder), Ill. Earth Sci. Edn. (pres. 1971-73, founder), Phi Delta Kappa. Muslim. Avocations: tennis, track, cross country, soccer.

RAAB, G. KIRK, biotechnology company executive; b. N.Y.C., Sept. 27, 1935; s. George Rufus and Ann Maria (Wood) R.; m. Mollie Elizabeth Painter, Dec. 6, 1986; children; Julia Woodson, Dean Kirk; children from previous marriage: Kristina Elizabeth, Alyson Ann, Michael George. B.A. with honors, Colgate U., 1959. With Pfizer Inc., 1959-65; gen. mgr. A.H. Robins Co., Mex., 1965-68; v.p. Latin Am. Beecham Group Ltd., 1968-75; v.p. Latin Am., then exec. v.p. internat. Abbott Labs., North Chicago, Ill., 1975-79, corp. group v.p., 1980-81, pres., COO, dir., 1981-85; pres., COO Genentech Inc., San Francisco, 1985—, pres., CEO, 1985-95; chmn., bd. dirs. various biotech. cos. Trustee Colgate U. San Francisco Symphony, KQED; bd. dirs. Found. Nat. Sci. and Tech. medals, Oclassen Pharms. Inc., Shaman Pharms. Inc.

RAAB, HARRY FREDERICK, JR., physicist; b. Johnstown, Pa., May 9, 1926; s. Harry Frederick and Marjorie Eleanor (Stiff) R.; m. Phebe Ann Duerr, June 16, 1951; children: Constance Diane, Harry Frederick, Cynthia Ann Raab Morgenthaler. Student Navy Electronics Tech. Sch., 1944-45; SB and SM E.E., MIT, 1951; postgrad. Oak Ridge Sch. Reactor Tech., 1954-55. Reactor control engr. Bettis Atomic Power Lab. Westinghouse Electric Corp., West Mifflin, 1951-54, mgr. surface ship physics, 1955-62, mgr. light water breeder reactor physics, 1962-72; chief physicist Navy Nuc. Propulsion Directorate, Washington, 1972-95; retired 1995. Patentee light water breeder reactor. Active Laymen's Missionary League, Episc. Diocese of Pitts., 1957-72; lay eucharistic min. and lector Episc. Ch. of the Good Shepherd, Burke, Va., 1972—, Sunday Sch. tchr., 1957-72, dir. liturgy, 1987—, stewardship chmn., 1979-82, 84, 92-93, chmn. presch. bd., 1994—, healing ministry, 1989—, sr. warden, 1983, 85; mem. stewardship com. Diocese of Va., 1983—, chmn. stewardship, 1995—; chaplain for mentally retarded No. Va. Tng. Ctr., 1983—; bd. dirs. Phoenix Cmty. Svcs., 1995—; lay chaplain Fairfax Hosp., 1995—. With USNR, 1944-46, PTO. Fellow Am. Nuc. Soc.; mem. Internat. Platform Assn., Sigma Xi, Tau Beta Pi, Eta Kappa Nu. Republican. Lodge: Masons. Home: 8202 Ector Ct Annandale VA 22003-1342 *Always treat others with respect. Strive for excellence. Always act with honestyand integrity. Remember Henry Ford's observation: "If you say that you can, or if you say you cannot, you are right."*

RAAB, HERBERT NORMAN, retail executive; b. N.Y.C., Nov. 7, 1925; s. Jacob and Pauline (Neuwirth) R.; m. Blanche Muriel Levin, Jan. 27, 1952 (dec. Mar. 1981); children: Nancy Renée, James Harris; m. Carmen Sandra Fernandez, Aug. 17, 1986. AB, Harvard U., 1947; postgrad., Harvard U. Bus. Sch., 1947-48, Seton Hall U. Law Sch., 1972-75. V.p. Bamberger Div. R.H. Macy Inc., N.Y.C., 1968-75, v.p., 1975-78; pres. and chief exec. officer W&J Sloane, N.Y.C., 1978-80; pvt. practice cons. N.Y.C., 1980-84; sr. v.p. Wayside Furniture Co., Milford, Conn., 1984-90; adj. prof. U. Bridgeport (Conn.), 1986-91. Jewish.

RAAB, IRA JERRY, lawyer; b. N.Y.C., June 20, 1935; s. Benjamin and Fannie (Kirschner) R.; divorced; children: Michael, Shelley; m. Katie Rachel McKeever, June 30, 1979 (div. 1991); children: Julie, Jennifer, Joseph. BBA, CCNY, 1955; JD, Bklyn. Law Sch., 1957; MPA, NYU, 1959, postgrad., 1961; MS in Pub. Adminstrn., L.I. U., 1961; MBA, Adelphi U., 1990. Bar: N.Y. 1958, U.S. Dist. Ct. (so. and ea. dists.) N.Y. 1960, U.S. Supreme Ct. 1967, U.S. Tax Ct. 1976, U.S. Ct. Appeals (2d cir.) 1977. Pvt. practice Woodmere, N.Y., 1958—; agt. Westchester County Soc. Prevention of Cruelty to Children, White Plains, N.Y., 1958; counsel Dept. Correction City of N.Y., 1959, trial commr. Dept. Correction, 1976, asst. corp. counsel Tort divsn., 1963-70; staff counsel SBA, N.Y.C., 1961-63; counsel Investigation Com. on Willowbrook State Sch., Boro Hall, S.I., N.Y., 1970; gen. counsel Richmond County Soc. Prevention of Cruelty to Children, Boro Hall, 1970-81; pro bono counsel N.Y.C. Patrolmen's Benevolent Assn., 1974-81; rep. to UN Internat. Criminal Ct., 1977-78; arbitrator Small Claims Ct., Day Cts., N.Y.C., 1970—, L.I. Better Bus. Bur., 1976-93, Nassau County Dist. Ct., 1978-93; hearing officer Nassau and Suffolk County Supreme Ct., 1982—; spl. master N.Y. County Supreme Ct., 1977—; judge N.Y.C. Parking Violations Bur., 1991-93; small claims arbitrator N.Y.C. Civil Ct. and Nassau County Dist. Ct., 1970—, U.S. Dist. (ea. dist.) N.Y., 1986—; lectr. cmty. and ednl. orgns; instr. paralegal course Lawrence Sch. Dist., N.Y., 1982-84. Chmn. Businessmen's Luncheon Club, Wall St. Synagogue, 1968-79; sec. Cmty. Mediation Ctr., Suffolk County, 1978-80, exec. v.p., 1980-81; vice chmn. Woodmere Inc., Com., 1980-81; mem. adv. bd. Nassau Expressway Com., 1979-80; bd. dirs. Woodmere Mchts. Assn., 1979-80, v.p., 1979-83, chmn., 1984-93; candidate for dist. ct. judge Nassau County, 1987, 88, 89, 91, 93, 94; candidate for supreme ct. justice Nassau and Suffolk Counties, 1995. Recipient Consumer Protection award FTC, 1974, 76, 79, Recognition award Pres. Ronald Reagan, 1986, Man of Yr. award L.I. Coun. of Chambers, 1987. Mem. ABA (chmn. cts. and cmty. com. 1988-93, exec. com. jud. adminstrn. divsn. lawyers conf. 1989-95), Am. Judges Assn. (nat. treas. 1978-82, 82-83, 89-96, chmn. civil ct. ops. com. 1975-76, chmn. ednl. film com. 1974-77, editl. bd. Ct. Rev. mag. 1975-79, 82-86, chmn. spkrs. bur. com. 1976-77, chmn. legis. com. 1983-95, historian 1988—, William H. Burnett award 1983), Am. Judges Found. (pres. 1977-79, chmn. bd. trustees 1979-83, treas. 1974-75, 76-77, trustee 1983—), Assn. Arbitrators of Civil Ct. City of N.Y. (past pres.), N.Y. State Bar Assn. (sec. dist., city town and villages cts. com.), Nassau County Bar Assn. (criminal cts. com., matrimonial and family ct. com., ct. com., ethics com.), Profl. Group Legal Svc. Assn. (past pres.), Internat. Assn. Jewish Lawyers and Jurists (com. to draft Internat. Bill of Rights to Privacy 1982, coun. 1981—, bd. govs. 1984-95), Am. Arbitration Assn. (arbitrator 1975-94, adv. bd. cmty. dispute ctr. 1979-81), K.P. (past chancellor comdr.). Democrat. Home and Office: 375 Westwood Rd Woodmere NY 11598-1624

RAAB, LAWRENCE EDWARD, English educator; b. Pittsfield, Mass., May 8, 1946; s. Edward Louis and Marjorie (Young) R.; m. Judith Ann Michaels, Dec. 29, 1968; 1 child, Jennifer Caroline. BA, Middlebury Coll., 1968; MA, Syracuse U., 1972. Lectr. Am. U., Washington, 1970-71; jr. fellow U. Mich. Soc. Fellows, Ann Arbor, 1973-76; prof. English Williams Coll., Williamstown, Mass., 1976—. Author: (poems) Mysteries of the Horizon, 1972, The Collector of Cold Weather, 1976, Other Children, 1987, What We Don't Know About Each Other, 1993 (National Book award nominee, 1993). Creative Writing fellow Nat. Endowment Arts, 1972, 84; recipient Bess Hokin prize Poetry mag., 1983; residencies at Yaddo, 1979-80, 82, 84, 86-90, 94, MacDowell Colony, 1993, 95. Office: Williams Coll English Dept Williamstown MA 01267

RAAB, SELWYN, journalist; b. N.Y.C., June 26, 1934; s. William and Berdie (Glantz) R.; m. Helene Lurie, Dec. 25, 1963; 1 dau., Marian. B.A., Coll. City N.Y., 1956. Reporter N.Y. World-Telegram and Sun, N.Y.C., 1960-66; producer, news editor NBC-TV News, N.Y.C., 1966-71; exec. producer WNET-News, N.Y.C., 1971-74; reporter New York Times, 1974—. Author: Justice in the Back Room, 1967; co-author: Mob Laywer, 1994. Recipient award for best mag. consumer protection article U. Mo. Sch. Journalism, 1969, Deadline awards for excellence in television reporting Sigma Delta Chi, 1971, 73, 1st prize for excellence in television reporting N.Y. State A.P., 1973, Best Television Reporting award N.Y. Press Club, 1973, Heywood Broun Meml. award, 1974, Page One award Newspaper Guild of New York, 1975, Best Feature Story award N.Y. Press Club, 1984, N.Y.C. Patrolmen's Benevolent Assn. award, 1985. Office: NY Times 229 W 43rd St New York NY 10036-3913

RAAB, SHELDON, lawyer, Bklyn. Nov. 30, 1937; s. Morris and Eva (Shereshevsky) R.; m. Judith Deutsch, Dec. 15, 1963; children: Michael Kenneth, Elisabeth Louise, Andrew John. AB, Columbia U., 1958; LLB cum laude, Harvard U., 1961. Bar: N.Y. 1961, U.S. Ct. Appeals (2d cir.) 1963, U.S. Dist. Ct. (so. and ea. dists.) 1967. Dep. asst. atty. gen. State of N.Y., 1961-63, asst. atty gen., 1963-64; assoc. Fried, Frank, Harris, Shriver & Jacobson and predecessor firm, N.Y.C., 1964-69, ptnr., 1970-81, inc. ptnr., 1981—. Mem. exec. com. lawyers' div. United Jewish Appeal, 1982—. Mem. ABA, Am. Law Inst., N.Y. State Bar Assn. (trial lawyers sect. 1968—), Assn. of Bar of City of N.Y. (adminstrv. law com. 1968-71, spl. com. electric power and environment 1971-73, chmn. energy com. 1974-79, fed. cts. com. 1981-84, state superior cts. juris. com. 1985-88). Democrat. Office: Fried Frank Harris Shriver & Jacobson 1 New York Plz New York NY 10004

RAABE, WILLIAM ALAN, tax author and educator; b. Milw., Dec. 14, 1953; s. William Arthur and Shirley (Semmann) R.; m. Mary Jane Swiggum, Aug. 7, 1976 (div. July 1984); m. Nancy Elizabeth Miller, Mar. 1989; children: Margaret Elisabeth, Martin William. BS, Carroll Coll., 1975; MAS, U. Ill., 1976, PhD, 1979. Wis. Disting. prof. U. Wis., Milw., 1979—; tax edn. cons. Price Waterhouse, N.Y.C., 1990—; vis. assoc. prof. Ariz. State U., Tempe, 1985; vis. faculty Ernst. & Young, N.Y.C., 1990—, Calif. CPA Found., 1986, AICPA, 1984—; developer Estate Tax Planner, McGraw Hill Software, N.Y.C., 1980-88; expert witness, 1985—. Author West's Federal Taxation, 1985—, West's Federal Tax Research, 1986—, Income Shifting After Tax Reform, 1987, Multistate Corporate Tax Guide, 1985—; contbr. articles to profl. jours. Bd. dirs., pres. Luth. High Sch. Assn. Milw., 1991—, Bethesda Luth. Home, Watertown, Wis., 1989-91, Concord Chamber Orch., Milw., 1983-88; mem. Econ. Devel. Com., Wauwatosa, Wis., 1986-89; faculty athletic rep. to NCAA from U. Wis. Milw., 1990-96; mem. Milw. Symphony Chorus, Master Singers of Milw. Fellow Am. Acctg. Assn., Nat. Ctr. for Tax Edn. and Rsch.; mem. U. Wis. Milw. Tax Assn. (bd. dirs. 1981—), Wis. Inst. CPAs (Educator of Yr. 1987). Office: Univ Wis UWM Tax Assn PO Box 742 Milwaukee WI 53201-0742

RAAD, VIRGINIA, pianist, lecturer; b. Salem, W.Va., Aug. 13, 1925; d. Joseph M. and Martha (Joseph) R. BA in Art History, Wellesley Coll., 1947; spl. student, New Eng. Conservatory Music, 1947-48; diplôme, Ecole Normale de Musique, Paris, 1950; Doctorate with honors (French Govt. grantee 1950-52, 54-55), U. Paris, 1955; student, Alfred Cortot, Jeanne Blancard, Berthe Bert, Jacques Chailley. Artist in residence Salem (W.Va.) Coll., 1957-70; ind. concert pianist, 1960—; musician in residence N.C. Arts Council, at community colls., 1971-72; adjudicator Nat. Guild Piano Tchrs., Nat. Fedn. Music Clubs; panelist, grant reviewer NEH, 1978-84, 92—; mem. com. Nat. Endowment Arts, 1978; Am. rep. Debussy Centennial Colloque, Paris, 1962. Perfomances, concerts, lectrs. master classes at Carleton Coll., U. Fla., Viterbo Coll., Portland State U., Notre Dame U., Mt. Mary Coll., Mundelein Coll., Trinity Coll., Washington, Phillips Gallery, Washington, Norton Gallery, Rollins Coll., Marietta Coll., Huntington (W.Va.) Galleries, W.Va. U., Coll. William and Mary, Channel 13 (Sta. WQED), Pitts., Channel 24 (WNPB, Morgantown, W.Va., Lincoln (Pa.) U., U. Pitts., U. Mich., Dearborn, Fordham U., Piano Tchrs. Congress of N.Y.C., So. Conn. State U., Wellesley Coll., Middlebury Coll., Ladycliff Coll., numerous other colls. and univs.; contbg. author: Debussy et l'Evolution de la Musique au XX Siècle, 1965; author: The Piano Sononity of Claude Debussy, 1994; recording artist: EDUCO, 1995—; contbr. articles to profl. jours. Active Amnesty Internat. Urgent Action Network; alumna regional representative Wellesley Coll. Named Outstanding W.Va. Woman Educator Delta Kappa Gamma, 1965; included in Schlesinger Library on History of Women in Am. Radcliffe Coll., 1967; grantee Govt. France, Am. Coun. Learned Socs. Mem. Soc. Française de Musicologie, Am. Musicol. Soc. (regional officer 1960-65), Am. Soc. for Aesthetics (grant reviewer), Internat. Musicol. Soc., Music Tchrs. Nat. Assn. (adjudicator, musicology program chair 1983-87), W.Va. Music Tchrs. Assn., Coll. Music Soc., Alpha Delta Kappa (hon.). Republican. Roman Catholic. Avocations: hiking, gardening, birding. Address: 60 Terrace Ave Salem WV 26426-1116 *Whether on the concert stage or in the classroom, I am a teacher with the desire to enlarge each person's vision in the arts.*

RAAFLAUB, KURT A., classics educator; b. Buea, Cameroon, Feb. 15, 1941; s. Fritz and Heidi (Ninck) R.; m. Deborah Dickmann Boedeker, July 14, 1978. MA, U. Basel, Switzerland, 1967, PhD, 1970. Asst. prof. ancient history Free U. Berlin, Fed. Republic Germany, 1972-78; asst. prof. ancient history Brown U., Providence, 1978-80, assoc. prof. classics and history, 1980-83, prof., 1983—, John Rowe Workman Disting. prof. classics and humanistic tradition, 1989-92, chmn. dept. classics, 1984-89; co-dir. Ctr. for Hellenic Studies, Washington, 1992—. Author: Dignitatis Contentio, 1974, Die Entdeckung der Freiheit, 1985; co-author: Studien zum Attischen Seebund, 1984, Aspects of Athenian Democracy, 1990; editor or co-editor: Social Struggles in Archaic Rome, 1986, Between Republic and Empire: Interpretations of Augustus and His Principate, 1990, Athens and Rome, Florence and Venice: City-States in Classical Antiquit6y and Medieval Italy, 1991, Anfänge politischen Denkens in der Antike: Die nahöstlichen Kulturen und die Griechen, 1993, Studies in the Ancient Greek Polis, 1995, Democracy 2500: Questions and Challenges, 1996, Studies in the Ancient Greek Polis, Vol. 2, 1996; contbr. articles to profl. jours. Mem. Historisches Kolleg Munich, 1989-90. Am. Coun. Learned Socs. fellow, 1983-84, Ctr. for Hellenic Studies fellow, 1976-77, NEH fellow, 1989. Mem. Philol. Assn., Assn. Ancient Historians, Am. Inst. Archaeology. Avocation: music. Home and Office: Ctr Hellenic Studies 3100 Whitehaven St NW Washington DC 20008-3614

RAASH, KATHLEEN FORECKI, artist; b. Milw., Sept. 12, 1950; d. Harry and Marion Matilda (Schwabe) Forecki; m. Gary John Raash, June 13, 1987. BS, U. Wis., Eau Claire, 1972; MFA, U. Wis., Milw., 1978. One-, two- and three-person shows include Sight 225 Gallery, Milw., 1979, 81, Nicolet Coll., Phinelander, Wis., 1981, Messing Gallery, St. Louis, 1982, Arts Consortium, Cin., 1982, Ctr. Gallery, Madiwon, Wis., 1982, Otteson Theatre Gallery, Waukesha, Wis., 1982, Foster Gallery, Eau Claire, 1984, Duluth (Minn.) Art Inst., 1984, West Bend (Wis.) Gallery of Fine Arts, 1987, U. Wis.-Waukesha Fine Arts Gallery, 1988, Marion Art Gallery, Milw., 1990, Layton Honor Gallery, Milw., 1991, West Bend Art Mus., 1995, Gwenda Jay Gallery, Chgo., 1995, Wis. Acad., Madison, 1996; exhibited in group shows at River Edge Galleries, Wis., 1990, 91, 94, 95, Peltz Gallery, Milw., 1990, 91, 92, 93, 94, 95, Minnetonka Ctr. Arts, Wazata, Minn., 1996; represented in permanent collections United Bank and trust of Madison, Fine Arts Gallery U. Wis., Miller Brewing Co., Independence Bank Waukesha, U. Wis. Home and Studio: W 1630 Bear Trail Rd Gleason WI 54435

RABAGO, KARL ROGER, lawyer; b. Landstuhl, Germany, Nov. 5, 1957; (parents Am. citizens); s. Rogerio I. and Christa J. (Ubelhor) R.; m. Pamela Houston, June 9, 1979; children: Timothy K., Troy R., Kara R. BBA in Bus. Mgmt., Tex. A&M U., 1977; JD with honors, U. Tex., 1984; LLM in Mil. Law, U.S. Army JAG Sch., Charlottesville, Va., 1988; LLM in Environ. Law, Pace U., 1990. Bar: Tex. 1984, U.S. Ct. Mil. Appeals 1985. Commd. 2d lt. U.S. Army, 1977, advanced through grades to maj., 1989; officer 2d Squadron, 9th Armored Cav., 24th Inf. Div., Ft. Stewart, Ga., 1978-81; trial counsel 5th Inf. Div., Ft. Polk, La., 1984-86, def. counsel, 1986-87; asst. prof. law U.S. Mil. Acad., West Point, N.Y., 1988-90; resigned, 1990; assoc. prof. U. Houston Law Ctr., 1990-92; commr. Pub. Utility Commn. Tex., Austin, 1992-94; dept. asst. sec. U.S. Dept. Energy, Washington, 1995-96; energy program mgr. Environ. Def. Fund, Austin, 1996—. Democrat. Roman Catholic. Office: Environ Def Fund 44 East Ave Ste 304 Austin TX 78701

RABASSA, GREGORY, Romance languages educator, translator; b. Yonkers, N.Y., Mar. 9, 1922; married 1966. A.B., Dartmouth Coll., 1945, Litt.D. hon., 1982; M.A., Columbia U., 1947, Ph.D. in Portuguese, 1954. Instr. Spanish Columbia U., 1947-52, assoc., 1952-58, asst. prof., 1958-63, assoc. prof. Spanish and Portuguese, 1963-68; prof. Romance langs. Queens Coll., CUNY Grad. Sch., Flushing, N.Y., 1968-86; Disting. prof. Queens Coll., CUNY Grad. Sch., 1986—; assoc. editor Odyssey Rev., 1961-64. Contbr. articles to profl. jours. Staff sgt. OSS, 1942-45. Decorated Croce al Merito di Guerra (Italy), Order of San Carlos (Colombia); recipient Nat. Book award for transl., 1967, transl. prize PEN Am. Ctr., 1977, Gode award Am. Transl. Assn., 1980, PEN transl. medal, 1982, arts award N.Y. Gov., 1985, transl. prize Wheatland Found., 1988, lit. award Am. Acad. and Inst. Arts and Letters, 1989, presdl. medal Dartmouth Coll., 1991, Ivan Sandrof award The Nat. Book Critics Cir., 1993, Lit. Lion award N.Y. Pub. Libr., 1993, Mellon Humanities award Loyola U., Chgo., 1995, Gabriela Mistral prize, Chile, 1996; Fulbright-Hays fellow, 1965-66, NEH fellow, 1979-80. Mem. Renaissance Soc. Am., MLA, Am. Assn. Tchrs. Spanish and Portuguese, Latin Am. Studies Assn., Am. Lit. Translators Assn., Hispanic Soc. Am., PEN Club, Phi Beta Kappa. Office: Dept of Romance Lang CUNY Queens College Flushing NY 11367

RABB, BRUCE, lawyer; b. Cambridge, Mass., Oct. 4, 1941; s. Maxwell M. and Ruth (Cryden) R.; m. Harriet Rachel Schaffer, Jan. 4, 1970; children: Alexander Charles, Katherine Anne. AB, Harvard U., 1962; Cert. d'Etudes Politiques, Institut d'Etudes Politiques, Paris, 1963; LLB, Columbia U., 1966. Bar: N.Y. 1966. Law clk. to judge U.S. Ct. Appeals (5th cir.), 1966-67; assoc. Stroock & Stroock & Lavan, N.Y.C., 1967-68, 71-75, ptnr., 1976-91; ptnr. Kramer, Levin, Naftalis & Frankel, N.Y.C., 1991—; staff asst. to Pres. U.S., 1969-70; vice-chmn. Lawyers Com. Human Rights, 1977-95; bd. dirs. Chiquita Italia, SPA; supr. bd. dirs. Agora-Gazeta, sp.zo.o., 1993—; pub. mem. Adminstrv. Conf. U.S., 1982-86, 89-92, spl. counsel, 1986-88. Bd. dirs. Citizens Union of N.Y., 1981-87, 88-94, 95—; bd. dirs. Am. Friends of Alliance Israelite Universelle, 1987—, Human Rights Watch, 1987—; mem. Human Rights Watch/Ams., 1982—, Human Rights Watch/Helsinki, 1985—, Fund for Free Expression, 1987—, Human Rights Watch/Middle East, 1989—, vice chmn., 1990—; mem. internat. adv. com. Internat. Parliamentary Group for Human Rights in the Soviet Union, 1984-88, Prin. of the Coun. for Excellence in Govt., 1990—; sec. Lehrman Inst., 1978-88. Mem. ABA (adv. panel Internat. Human Rights Trial Observer project), Am. Law Inst., Assn. of Bar of City of N.Y. (fed. legis., internat. law chair 1992-95, internat. human rights, civil rights, legal edn. and admission to bar, internat. trade coms., coun. on fgn. rels.), Harvard Club N.Y.C., Met. Club of Washington. Office: Kramer Levin et al 919 3rd Ave New York NY 10022

RABB, GEORGE BERNARD, zoologist; b. Charleston, S.C., Jan. 2, 1930; s. Joseph and Teresa C. (Redmond) R.; m. Mary Sughrue, June 10, 1953. BS, Coll. Charleston, 1951, LHD (hon.), 1995; MA, U. Mich., 1952, PhD, 1957. Teaching fellow zoology U. Mich., 1954-56; curator, coord. rsch. Chgo. Zool. Park, Brookfield., Ill., 1956-64; assoc. dir. rsch. and edn. Chgo. Zool. Park, 1964-75, dep. dir., 1969-75, dir., 1976—; rsch. assoc. Field Mus. Natural History, 1965—; lectr. dept. biology U. Chgo., 1965-89; mem. Com. on Evolution Biology, 1969—; pres. Chgo. Zool. Soc., 1976—; mem. steering com. Species Survival Commn., Internat. Union Conservation of Nature, 1983—, vice chmn. for N.Am., 1986-88, dep. chmn., 1987-89, chmn., 1989—; chmn. policy adv. group Internat. Species Info. System, 1974-89, chmn. bd., 1989-92; mem. bd. dirs. Ill. State Mus., 1994—. Fellow AAAS; mem. Am. Soc. Ichthyologists and Herpetologists (pres. 1978), Herpetologists League, Soc. Systematic Zoology, Soc. Mammalogists, Soc. Study Evolution, Ecol. Soc. Am., Soc. Conservation Biology (council mem. 1986), Am. Soc. Zoologists, Soc. Study Animal Behavior, Am. Assn. Museums, Am. Soc. Naturalists, Am. Assn. Zool. Parks and Aquariums (dir. 1979-80), Internat. Union Dirs. Zool. Gardens, Am. Com. Internat. Conservation (chmn. 1987—), Chgo. Coun. Fgn. Relations (Chgo. com.), Sigma Xi. Club: Economic (Chgo.), Tavern. Office: Brookfield Zoo 3300 Golf Rd Brookfield IL 60513-1060

RABB, HARRIET SCHAFFER, lawyer, educator; b. Houston, Sept. 12, 1941; d. Samuel S. and Helen G. Schaffer; m. Bruce Rabb, Jan. 4, 1970; children: Alexander, Katherine. BA in Govt., Barnard Coll., 1963; JD, Columbia U., 1966. Bar: N.Y. 1966, U.S. Supreme Ct. 1969, D.C. 1970. Instr. seminar on constl. litigation Rutgers Law Sch., 1966-67; staff atty. Center for Constl. Rights, 1966-69; spl. counsel to commr. consumer affairs N.Y.C. Dept. Consumer Affairs, 1969-70; sr. staff atty. Stern Community Law Firm, Washington, 1970-71; asst. dean urban affairs Law Sch., Columbia U., N.Y.C., 1971-84, prof. law, dir. clin. edn., 1984—; George M. Jaffen prof. law and social responsibility Law Sch., Columbia U., 1991—, vice dean, 1992—; gen. counsel Dept. Health and Human Svcs., Washington, 1993—; mem. faculty employment and tng. policy Harvard Summer Inst., Cambridge, Mass., 1975-79. Author: (with Agid, Cooper and Rubin) Fair Employment Litigation Manual, 1975, (with Cooper and Rubin) Fair Employment Litigation, 1975. Bd. dirs. Ford Found., 1977-89, N.Y. Civil Liberties Union, 1972-83, Lawyers Com. for Civil Rights Under Law, 1978-86, Legal Def. Fund NAACP, 1978-93, Mex. Am. Legal Def. and Edn. Fund, 1986-90, Legal Aid Soc., 1990-93; mem. exec. com. Human Rights Watch, 1991-93; trustee Trinity Episcopal Sch. Corp., 1991-93. Office: Dept Health and Human Svcs 200 Independence Ave SW Rm 722A Washington DC 20201-0004

RABB, MAXWELL M., lawyer, former ambassador; b. Boston, Sept. 28, 1910; s. Solomon and Rose (Kostick) R.; m. Ruth Criedenberg, Nov. 2, 1939; children: Bruce, Sheila Rabb Weidenfeld, Emily Rabb Livingston, Priscilla Rabb Ayres. AB, Harvard U., 1932, LLB, 1935; LLD (hon.), Wilberforce U., 1957; DHL (hon.), Mt. St. Mary's Coll., 1983; LLB (hon.), Pepperdine U., 1985, St. Thomas U., 1986; DHL (hon.), Hebrew Union Coll., 1990. Bar: Mass. 1935, N.Y. 1958. Mem. firm Rabb & Rabb, Boston, 1935-37; adminstrv. asst. to U.S. Senator H.C. Lodge Jr., Mass., 1937-43; adminstrv. asst. U.S. Senator Sinclair Weeks, Mass., 1944; legal and legis. cons. Sec. Navy Forestal, 1946; practice law Boston, 1946-51; cons. U.S. Senate Rules Com., 1952; presdl. asst. to Pres. Eisenhower, sec. to Cabinet, 1953-59; partner Stroock & Stroock & Lavan, N.Y.C., 1959-81, of counsel, 1989-91; of counsel Kramer, Levin, Natalis, Nessen, Kamin & Frankel, N.Y.C., 1991—; amb. to Italy, 1981-89; bd. dirs. Sterling Nat. Bank, MIC Industries, Data Software Sys. Inc., Alusit Internat. Corp., Liberty Cable Co., Inc. Exec. asst. campaign mgr. Eisenhower presdl. campaign, 1951-52; del. Republican Nat. Conv., 1952, 56, 76, 80; mem. exec. com. U.S. Commn. for UNESCO, 1959-60; chmn. U.S. del. UNESCO conf., Paris, 1958; mem. Coun. on Fgn. Rels., 1978—; pres. Congregation Emanu-El, N.Y.C., 1973-81; mem. bd. advisors John F. Kennedy Sch. Govt., Harvard U.; trustee Cardinals Cooke and O'Connor Inner City Scholarship Fund, The Lighthouse, 1995—, N.Y. Med. Coll., Eisenhower Inst., Annenberg Inst., John Cabot U., Italy, George Marshall Meml. Found.; mem. bd. mgrs. Seamen's Ch. Inst.; mem. presdl. adv. panel on South Asian Relief assistance, 1971; mem. panel conciliators World Bank Internat. Ctr. for Settlement of Investment Disputes, 1967-73, U.S. rep., 1974-77; mem. Presdl. Commn. on Income Maintenance Programs, 1968-69; hon. chmn. bd. Am. Friends of Alliance Israelite Universelle; vice chmn. United Cerebral Palsy, Inc., Nat. Com. on Am. Fgn. Policy, Coun. for U.S. and Italy; mem. adv. bd. Auburn U. Served as lt. amphibious corps USNR, 1944-46. Decorated Commendation Ribbon, commendatore Order of Merit, 1958, Grand Cross ofOrder of Merit (Italy), 1982; Grand Cross of Order of Malta, 1989. Mem. ABA, Am. Law Inst., Amb.'s Club of Reps. Abroad (hon. chmn.), Harvard Club (N.Y.C.), Harmonie Club (N.Y.C.), Army and Navy Club (Washington), Met. Club (Washington). Home: 480 Park Ave New York NY 10022-1613 also: Wilson Hill Rd Colrain MA 01340 Office: Kramer Levin Natalis et al 919 3rd Ave New York NY 10022

RABB, THEODORE K., historian, educator; b. Teplice-Sanov, Czechoslovakia, Mar. 5, 1937; came to U.S., 1956, naturalized, 1978; s. Oskar Kwasnik and Rose (Oliner) Rabinowicz; m. Tamar Miriam Janowsky, June 7, 1959; children: Susannah Rabb Bailin, Jonathan Richard, Jeremy David. B.A., Queen's Coll. Oxford U., Eng., 1958; M.A., Queen's Coll. Oxford U., 1962, Princeton U., 1960; Ph.D., Princeton U., 1961. Instr. Stanford U., 1961-62; instr. Northwestern U., 1962-63; asst. prof. Harvard U., 1963-67; mem. faculty Princeton U., 1967—, prof. history, 1976—; vis. assoc. prof. Johns Hopkins U., 1969, SUNY-Binghamton, 1973-74; visitor Inst. Advanced Studies, Princeton, 1973, 82; mem. nat. bd. cons. NEH, Nat. Coun. History Edn. (chair); N.J. Com. for Humanities (chair); chief historian Renaissance Television Series; bd. dirs. Humanities West; cons. in field. Author: The Thirty Years War, 2d edit, 1972, Enterprise and Empire, 1967, The Struggle for Stability in Early Modern Europe, 1975, The Origins of Modern Nations, 1981, Renaissance Lives: Portraits of an Age, 1993, Origins of the Modern West, 1993; co-author: The Western Experience, 6th edit., 1994, Peoples and Nations, 1982; editor: Jour. Interdisciplinary History, 1970—; co-editor: Action and Conviction in Early Modern Europe, 1969, The Family in History, 1973, Marriage and Fertility, 1981, Industrialization and Urbanization, 1981, Climate and History, 1981, The New History, 1982, Hunger and History, 1985, Population and Economy, 1986, Art and History, 1988, La Fame nella storia, 1991, Origin and Prevention of Major Wars, 1988. Bd. govs. Hebrew U. Fellow and/or grantee Folger Shakespeare Library, Am. Philos. Soc., Social Sci. Research Council, Am. Council Learned Socs., Guggenheim Found., NEH. Mem. Am. Hist. Assn. (chmn. com. quantitative rsch. history, chmn. nominating com.), Social Sci. History Assn. (exec. com., treas.), Am. Assn. Advancement Humanities (dir., sec.-treas.), Nat. Coun. History Stds., C.C. Humanities Assn. (steering com.), Royal Hist. Soc., Internat. Commn. History Parliamentary and Rep. Instns., Renaissance Soc. Am., Hakluyt Soc., Nat. Coun. History Edn. (chair), Historians Early Modern Europe, Conf. Brit. Studies. Office: Princeton University History Dept Princeton NJ 08544

RABBITT, EDWARD THOMAS, singer, songwriter; b. Bklyn., Nov. 27, 1941; m. Janine Girardi; children: Demelza Anne, Timmy (dec.), Thomas Edward. Nightclub and concert singer, 1962—; founder Hare Trigger band, composer more than 300 songs, including Kentucky Rain, 1970, Pure Love, 1974, Drivin' My Life Away, 1980, I Love a Rainy Night; recs. of own compositions include: Two Dollars in the Jukebox, Forgive and Forget, Rocky Mountain Music, Drinkin' My Baby Off My Mind; recorded albums: Horizon, 1981 (2 Gold Album awards.), Best of Eddie Rabbitt, Step by Step, 1981, Rabbitt Trax, 1985, The Best Year of My Life, 1985, I Wanna Dance with You, 1987, Greatest Country Hits, 1991. Office: Moress Nanas Shea Entertainment 1209 16th Ave S Nashville TN 37212-2901

RABE, DAVID WILLIAM, playwright; b. Dubuque, Iowa, Mar. 10, 1940; s. William and Ruth (McCormick) R.; m. Elizabeth Pan, 1969 (div.); 1 child; m. Jill Clayburgh, Mar. 1979. BA in English, Loras Coll., 1962; MA, Villanova U., 1968. Feature writer Register, New Haven, 1969-70; asst. prof. Villanova U., 1970-72. Author: (plays) The Basic Training of Pavlo Hummel, 1971 (Obie award disting. playwriting 1971, Drama Desk award 1971, Drama Guild award 1971), Sticks and Bones, 1971 (Elizabeth Hull-Kate Warriner award Dramatists Guild 1971, Variety Poll award 1971, Outer Critics' Circle award 1972, Tony award best play 1972, N.Y. Drama Critics' Circle citation 1972), The Orphan, 1973, In the Boom Boom Room, 1974, Burning, 1974, Streamers, 1976 (N.Y. Drama Critics' Circle award best Am. play 1976), Goose and Tomtom, 1976, Hurlyburly, 1985, Those the River Keeps, 1990, Crossing Guard, 1994, (screenplays) I'm Dancing as Fast as I Can, 1982, Streamers, 1983, Casualties of War, 1989, State of Grace, 1990, The Firm, 1993, (novel) Recital of the Dog, 1992. With U.S. Army, 1965-67. Recipient AP award, 1970, Am. Acad. Arts and Letters award, 1974, Nat. Inst. and Am. Acad. award, 1976; Rockefeller Found. grantee, 1969; Guggenheim fellow, 1976.

RABE, ELIZABETH ROZINA, hair stylist, horse breeder; b. Granby, Quebec, Canada, Sept. 28, 1953; d. John J. and Christina Maria (De Vaal) Gluck; m. Oct. 21, 1972 (div. 1981); children: Diana Marie Claire, Michelle Diane. Diploma in hairstyling, Art Inst. Film hairstylist Internat. Alliance Theatrical, Stage Employees and Moving Pictures Machine Operators Local 706, L.A., 1977-94. Recipient Design Patent hock support horse brace U.S. Design Patent Office, Washington, 1994. Home: 522 W Stocker St Apt 1 Glendale CA 91202-2299

RABE, LAURA MAE, mathematician, educator; b. Cin., May 28, 1945; d. Howard Lawrence and Alberta Catherine (Held) R. BS, U. Cin., 1967, MS, 1972, supr. cert., 1982. Tchr. Colerain H.S., Cin., 1967—, chairperson math. dept., 1980—; presenter grant writing workshop Miami U., Oxford, Ohio, 1994; pressenter in field. Named Hixon Tchr. of Yr., 1996; grantee GTE, 1994-95, NSF, 1980, Dartmouth Univ., 1995, 96. Mem. NEA, Nat. Coun. Tchrs. Math., Ohio Coun. Tchrs. Math., Greater Cin. Coun. Tchrs. Math. Roman Catholic. Avocations: travel, camping, water skiing, snow skiing, photography. Office: Colerain HS 8801 Cheviot Rd Cincinnati OH 45251-5907

RABEL, ED, news correspondent. BA in Political Sci., Morris Harvey Coll., 1963; LHD (Hon.), U. Charleston, 1985. Dir., anchor CBS Affiliate-WCHS-TV, 1962-66; chief so. correspondent CBS, 1967-70; war correspondent CBS, Saigon, 1970-71; middle east correspondent CBS, Tel Aviv, 1971-73; roving correspondent CBS, Atlanta, Ga., 1973-81; nat. correspondent CBS Evening News, N.Y., 1981-85; sr. correspondent NBC Nightly News, Wash., 1985-88; chief Latin Am. correspondent NBC Nightly News, Miami, 1988-89; sr. correspondent NBC Nightly News, Wash., 1989-93; Pentagon correspondent NBC Evening News, Wash., 1993—; trustee bd. dirs. U. Charleston. Recipient News and Documentary Emmy award, CBS Evening News, 1981, CBS Reports, 1981, George Polk award, 1982, three time Emmy nominee, CBS Sunday Morning, Communication award Nat. Easter Seal Soc., 1990. Home: 507 Scenic Way Great Falls VA 22066-3011 Office: NBC News Washington Bur 4001 Nebraska Ave NW Washington DC 20016-2733

RABELO, LUIS CARLOS, engineering educator, consultant; b. David, Chiriqui, Panama, Feb. 6, 1960; came to U.S., 1985; s. Luis Carlos and Consuelo (Mendizabal) R. BSEE, BS in Mech. Engring., Tech. U., Panama, 1983; MSEE, Fla. Inst. Tech., 1987; MS in Engring. Mgmt., U. Mo., 1988, PhD in Engring. Mgmt., 1990. Ops. engr. Aeroperlas Airlines subs. Contadora Corp., Panama City, 1982-83; ops. analyst Contadora Corp., Panama City, 1983-84, ops. mgr., 1984-85; grad. rsch. asst. engring. mgmt. dept. U. Mo., Rolla, 1988-90, grad. teaching asst. engring. mgmt. dept., 1989-90, rsch. engr. engring. mgmt. dept. Ctr. for Tech. Transfer, 1990-91; asst. prof. dept. indsl. and sys. engring. Ohio U., Athens, 1991—; cons. Metalurgia Panama, Panama City, 1982-83, Talema Electronics Inc., Rolla, 1988, S&S Contract Furniture, Inc., Marquand, Mo., 1989, Ohio Tech. Transfer Orgn., Athens, 1993, AMP, Inc., 1992, guest rschr. Automated Mfg. Rsch. Facility Nat. Inst. Standards and Tech., Gaithersburg, Md., 1992-95; lectr. in field. Contbr. articles to profl. jours., chpts. to books. Postdoctoral fellow U. Mo., 1990-91; grantee Ohio Rsch. Challenge Program, 1992-93, 94-95, U.S. NSF, 1994, Nat. Inst. Standards and Tech., 1992, 93, 95—; recipient Disting. Alumni award Tech. U. Panama, 1995. Mem. IEEE, Am. Soc. Engring. Edn., Internat. Neural Networks Soc., Soc. Mfg. Engrs., Inst. Indsl. Engrs., Inst. Ops. Rsch. and Mgmt. Scis., Sigma Xi. Roman Catholic. Avocations: soccer, swimming, chess. Home: PO Box 945 Athens OH 45701 Office: Ohio U Dept Indsl & Mfg Sys Engring Athens OH 45701

RABEN, NINA, molecular biologist, biochemist; b. Moscow, Russia, Jan. 13, 1945; came to the U.S., 1987; d. Anatoly S. and Liza M. (Vinogradsky) R.; m. Mark Belenky, Sept. 23, 1966; 1 child, Masha Belenky. MD, 1st Moscow (Russia) Med. Inst., 1967; PhD in Biochemistry, USSR Acad. Med. Sci., Moscow, 1973. Rschr. USSR Surgery Ctr., Moscow, 1968-73, sr. investigator, 1973-79; vis. assoc. Nat. Inst. of Diabetes, Digestive and Kidney Diseases, Bethesda, Md., 1987-90; vis. scientist Nat. Inst. of Arthritis and Musculoskeletal Diseases, Bethesda, 1990-94; rsch. chemist NIAMS, NIH, Bethesda, 1994—; translator of English lang. books and articles Moscow Pub., Houses Mags., 1968—. Contbr. articles to profl. jours.; patentee in field. Mem. AAAS. Jewish. Home: 5455 Grove Ridge Way Rockville MD 20852 Office: NIAMS NIH 9000 Rockville Pike Bethesda MD 20892

RABENSTEIN, DALLAS LEROY, chemistry educator; b. Portland, Oreg., June 13, 1942; 8. Melvin Leroy and Rose Marie (Nelson) R.; m. Gloria Carolyn Duncan, Aug. 30, 1964; children: Mark, Lisa. BS, U. Wash., 1964; PhD, U. Wis., 1968. Lectr. U. Wis., Madison, 1967-68; research chemist Chevron Research Co., Richmond, Calif., 1968-69; from asst. prof. to prof. chemistry U. Alta., Edmonton, Can., 1969-85; prof. U. Calif., Riverside, 1985—, chmn. chemistry dept., 1989-92, dean Coll. Natural and Agrl. Scis., 1993-94; vis. prof. U. Oxford, 1976-77; McElvain lectr. U. Wis., 1981; Dow lectr. U. B.C., 1988; Eli Lilly lectr., Ind. U., 1993. Contbr. articles to profl. jours. NIH grantee. Fellow AAAS, Chem. Inst. Can. (Fisher Sci. Lecture award 1984); mem. Am. Chem. Soc. Avocations: reading, gardening, music. Home: 5162 Palisade Cir Riverside CA 92506-1521 Office: U Calif Dept Chemistry Riverside CA 92521

RABER, MARVIN, consultant, retired utility company executive; b. Bklyn., Aug. 3, 1937; s. Robert Abraham and Claire (Miller) R.; m. Miriam Lewin, Dec. 18, 1960; children: Steven, Suzanne Beth. BChemE, Poly. Inst. Bklyn., 1958; MChemE, NYU, 1963. Registered profl. engr., N.Y., Md. Engr. Nuclear Devel. Corp. Am./United Nuclear Corp., White Plains, N.Y., 1958-66; section chief, v.p. subs. Hittman Corp. (Hittman Nuclear & Devel. Corp.), Columbia, Md., 1966-70; sect. mgr. Combustion Engring., Inc., Windsor, Conn., 1970-78; v.p. strategic planning Gen. Pub. Utilities Corp., Parsippany, N.J., 1978-95; ret., 1995; founder Raber Cons., Randolph, N.J., 1995—. Co-patentee subcooled liquid inlet fog cooled nuclear reactor, 1965, reactor power reduction system and method, 1978. Mem. Am. Mgmt. Assn., The Planning Forum, Am. Nuclear Soc., NSPE. Jewish. Avocation: boating. Home: 5 Bayberry Ln Randolph NJ 07869-3801

RABEY, T. W., JR., financial company executive. BA, Calif. State, 1976. With E.F. Hutton Co. Inc., Bakerfield, Calif., 1977-79; asst. treas. Contel Group, Atlanta, 1987-91; v.p. GTE Fin. Corp., Stamford, Conn., 1991—. Office: GTE Finance Corp 1 Stamford Forum Stamford CT 06901-3516*

RABIDEAU, MARGARET CATHERINE, media center director; b. Chgo., Nov. 24, 1930; d. Nicholas and Mary Agnes (Burke) Oberle; m. Gerald Thomas Rabideau, Nov. 27, 1954; children: Mary, Margaret, Michelle, Gregory, Marsha, Grant. BA cum laude, U. Toledo, 1952, MA in Ednl. Media Tech., 1978. Cert. tchr. K-12 media tech., supr. ednl. media, tchr. English and journalism. Asst. dir. pub. rels. U. Toledo, 1952-55; publicity writer United Way, Toledo, 1974-75; tchr. Toledo Pub. Schs., 1975-80, libr., media specialist, 1980-90; dir. media svcs. Sylvania (Ohio) Schs., 1990—; task force to evaluate coll. programs Ohio Dept. Edn., 1987; on-site evaluation team, Hiram Coll., Ohio, 1991; north ctrl. evaluation team Northwestern Ohio, 1985—. Citizen task force Toledo/Lucas County Libr., Ohio, 1991, mem. friends of the libr., 1990—; task force Sta. WGTE-TV PBS Sta., Toledo, 1993; instr. U. Toledo, 1990; A-Site media svcs. Maumee Valley Computer Assn., 1994. Mem. ALA, U. Toledo Alumni Assn., Ohio Ednl. Libr. Media Assn. (N.W. dir. 1993—, vocat. dir. 1985-89, Libr. Media Specialist of Yr. 1993), Am. Ednl. Comm. and Tech., Maumee Valley Computer Assn. (task force), Phi Delta Kappa (Outstanding Newsletter Nat. award 1990, pres. Toledo chpt.). Avocations: running, travelling, cross stitching. Home: 1038 Olson St Toledo OH 43612-2828 Office: Sylvania Schs 6850 Monroe St Sylvania OH 43560-1922

RABIDEAU, PETER WAYNE, university dean, chemistry educator; b. Johnstown, Pa., Mar. 4, 1940; s. Peter Nelson and Monica (Smalley) R.; m. Therese Charlene Newquist, Sept. 1, 1962 (div.); children—Steven, Michael, Christine, Susan; m. Jennifer Lee Mooney, Nov. 15, 1986; children: Mark, Leah. B.S., Loyola U., Chgo., 1964; M.S., Case Inst. Tech., Cleve., 1967; Ph.D., Case Western Res U, Cleve., 1968. Postdoctoral asst. U. Chgo., 1968-69, instr., 1969-70; asst. prof. Ind. U.-Purdue U., Indpls., 1970-73, assoc. prof., 1973-76, prof., 1976-90, chmn. dept. chemistry, 1985-90; dean Coll. Basic Scis. La. State U., Baton Rouge, 1990—; program officer NSF, 1988-89. Contbr. numerous articles to profl. jours. Recipient research award Purdue Sch. Sci. at Indpls., 1982. Mem. AAAS, Am. Chem. Soc. (chmn. Ind. sect. 1974, councilor 1981-90). Home: 15160 Old Oak Ave Baton Rouge LA 70810-5546 Office: La State U Office of the Dean 338 Choppin Baton Rouge LA 70803

RABIL, ALBERT, JR., humanities educator; b. Rocky Mount, N.C., May 8, 1934; s. Albert and Sophie Mae (Safy) R.; m. Janet Spain, Aug. 29, 1956; children—Albert, III, J. Alison. B.A., Duke U., 1957; M.Div., Union Theol. Sem., 1960; Ph.D., Columbia U., 1964. Instr. religion Trinity Coll., Hartford, Conn., 1964-65, asst. prof., 1965-68; asst. prof. hist. theology Chgo. Theol. Sem., 1969-71; assoc. prof. SUNY-Old Westbury, 1971-74, prof., 1974-77, disting. teaching prof. humanities, 1977—; program dir. NEH Summer Inst., 1992, 94, 95, 96. Author: Merleau-Ponty, 1967 (Ansley award 1964), Erasmus and the New Testament, 1972, Laura Cereta, 1981, (with others) Her Immaculate Hand, 1983, Erasmus' Paraphrases of Romans and Galatians, 1983, Erasmus' Annotations on Romans, 1994; editor: Renaissance Humanism (3 vols.), 1988; editor, translator: Knowledge, Goodness, and Power, 1991, Henricus Cornelius Agrippa Declamation on the Nobility and Preeminence of the Female Sex, 1996; co-editor Renaissance Quarterly, 1992—; series co-editor The Other Voice in Early Modern Europe, 1993—; editorial bd. Soundings: An Interdisciplinary Jour., 1992-94. Travelling fellow Union Theol. Sem., 1960, Soc. for Values in Higher Edn., 1961; grantee. Fulbright Found., 1961, NEH, 1974, 81, 94. Mem. Erasmus Rotterdam Soc. (mem. editorial bd. 1980—), Soc. for Values in Higher Edn. (bd. dirs. 1981-90, 94—), Renaissance Soc. Am. (bd. dirs. 1991—). Democrat. Home: 324 Post Ave Apt 9H Westbury NY 11590-2249 Office: SUNY PO Box 210 Old Westbury NY 11568-0210

RABIL, MITCHELL JOSEPH, lawyer; b. Smithfield, N.C., Sept. 19, 1931; s. Albert G. and Eva (Nassif) R.; BS, Wake Forest Coll., 1953; LLB, Georgetown U., 1961; m. Antoinette M. Olivry, Nov. 25, 1956 (div. Oct. 1986); children: Elizabeth, Nathalie, Marcus, Gregory; m. Dolores E. Bleam, Jan. 21, 1989; children: Susan Starr Vermes, Scott Starr. Bar: N.C. 1961, N.J. 1967, D.C. 1980, Pa. 1981, U.S. Tax Ct. 1962, U.S. Supreme Ct. 1979. Supervisory acct. GAO, Washington, 1956-60; fin. analyst, staff acct. SEC, Washington, 1960-62; tax atty. Office Chief Counsel, IRS, Phila. and N.Y.C., 1962-66; assoc. Archer, Greiner, Hunter & Read, Camden, N.J., 1966-71; ptnr. Myers, Matteo, Rabil, Norcross & Landgraf, Cherry Hill, N.J., 1971-89, Montgomery, McCracken, Walker and Rhoads, Cherry Hill, 1989-95, Mitchell J. Rabil & Assocs., P.A., 1995—. Mcpl. chmn. Riverton (N.J.) Rep. Com., 1976-83; chmn. area 2 Burlington County Rep. Com., 1976-82; bd. dirs. Archway Programs, West Jersey Chamber Music Soc., 1990-91, Zurbrugg Meml. Hosp., 1991-93. Served with AUS, 1953-55. C.P.A., N.J., N.C. Mem. Am. Bar Assn., AICPA, N.J. Bar Assn., Phila. Bar Assn., N.J. Soc. CPAs, Am. Assoc. Atty. CPAs (bd. mem., sec., Del. Valley, Greater Phila. chpt. pres.), Cherry Hill C. of C. (bd. dirs. 1990-94), World Affairs Council Phila., Union League (Phila.), Riverton Country Club, Rotary Club (Cherry Hill, N.J. past pres. 1980-81, past dir.). Roman Catholic. Home: 107 Wayside Ct Delran NJ 08075-2000 Office: Mitchell J Rabil & Assoc 1010 Kings Hwy S Bldg 1-D Cherry Hill NJ 08034-2431

RABIN, BRUCE STUART, immunologist, physician, educator; b. Buffalo, Jan. 25, 1941; s. Eli and Dorothy R.; children: Andrew L., Alison J. B.A., Case Western Res. U., 1962; M.D., SUNY, Buffalo, 1969, Ph.D. (NIH predoctoral fellow, 1967), 1969. Diplomate Am. Bd. Med. Lab. Immunology. Asst. prof. pathology SUNY and Ctr. for Immunology, Buffalo, 1970-72; asst. prof. pathology Sch. Medicine, U. Pitts., 1972-76, assoc. prof. pathology, 1976-86, prof. pathology, 1986—, prof. psychiatry, 1987—, dir. Brain, Behavior and Immunity Ctr., 1989—; dir. div. clin. immunopathology Univ. Health Ctr. of Pitts., 1972—, med. dir. clin. lab. svcs., 1985—; interim chmn. dept. pathology, U. Pitts. Sch. Medicine, 1990-91; mem. merit rev. bd. for immunology VA Central Office, 1980-83; mem. study sect. NIMH, 1988-91. Assoc. editor Clin. Immunology Newsletter, 1980, Brain Behavior and Immunity, Clin. Immunology and Immunopathology; contbr. sci. papers in field to profl. publs. NIH research grantee, 1973—. Mem. AAAS, Pitts. Pathology Soc., Am. Assn. Pathologists, Acad. Clin. Lab. Physicians and Scientists, Am. Acad. Allergy, Am. Assn. Immunologists, Am. Assn. Clin. Histocompatibility Testing, Am. Soc. Clin. Pathologists (clin. immunopathology coun. 1978-84, editor Clin. Immunology Check Sample Program), Am. Acad. Microbiology (com. on postdoctoral edn. 1980), Assn. Med. Lab. Immunologists (pres. 1988), Psychoneuroimmunology Rsch. Soc. (pres. 1995). Home: 318 Schenley Rd Pittsburgh PA 15217-1173 Office: Presbyn-U Hosp Clin Immunopathology DeSoto & O'Hara Sts Pittsburgh PA 15213-2582

RABIN, HERBERT, physics educator, university official; b. Milw., Nov. 14, 1928; 2 children. B.S., U. Wis., 1950; M.S., U. Ill., 1951; Ph.D. in Physics, U. Md., 1959. Physicist elec. div. U.S. Naval Research Lab., 1952-54, physicist solid state physics div., 1954-62, head radiation effects sect. optical materials br., 1962-67, head quantum optics sect., applied optics br., 1967-68, head quantum optics br., 1968-71, asso. dir. research for space sci. and tech., 1971-77, asso. dir. research for space and communication sci. and tech., 1977-79; dep. asst. sec. of Navy for research, applied and space tech. Office of Navy Secretariat, Washington, 1979-83; dir. engring. research ctr., prof. elec. engring., assoc. dean Coll. Engring., U. Md., College Park, 1983—; vis. scientist Technisch Hochschule, Stuttgart, Germany, 1960-61; mem. staff physics dept. George Washington U., 1955-73; cons. Sch. Engring. of Sao Carlos, U. Sao Paulo, Brazil, 1964, 70. Contbr. articles to tech. jours.; patentee in field. Recipient Meritorious Civilian Svc. award USN, 1969, Disting. Civilian Svc. award, 1976, 93; Disting. Civilian Svc. award Dept. Def., 1979, cert. of commendation NASA, 1986, Centennial medal U. Md. Coll. Engring., 1994. Fellow Am. Phys. Soc., AAAS, Optical Soc. Am., AIAA; mem. IEEE (sr. mem.), Brazilian Acad. Scis. (corr.). Home: 7109 Radnor Rd Bethesda MD 20817-6332 Office: U Md Engring Rsch Ctr College Park MD 20742

RABIN, JACK, lawyer; b. Bklyn., Aug. 19, 1930; s. Leo and Bertha R.; m. Roberta Edith Libson, Oct. 25, 1953; children: Keith Warren, Michael Jay, Adam Douglas. Student Bklyn. Coll., 1948-50; LLB, Bklyn. Law Sch., 1953. Bar: N.Y. 1953, U.S. Ct. Mil. Appeals 1955, U.S. Dist. Ct. (so. and ea. dists.) N.Y. 1957, U.S. Tax Ct. 1960, U.S. Ct. Claims 1964, U.S. Supreme Ct. 1964, U.S. Ct. Appeals (2d cir.) 1968. Ptnr. Hoffberg, Rabin & Engler and predecessor firms, N.Y.C., 1968-82, Javits, Hinckley, Rabin & Engler, N.Y.C., 1982-84, Phillips, Nizer, Benjamin, Krim & Ballon, N.Y.C., 1984—; arbitrator gen. comml. and constrn. panel Am. Arbitration Assn., 1968—; instr. Real Estate Inst., NYU, 1976-78; ct. apptd. mediator U.S. Dist. Ct. (so. dist.), N.Y., 1994—. Assoc. editor Bklyn Law Rev., 1952, editor-in-chief, 1953, also author law rev. note. Served to 1st lt. JAGC, U.S. Army, 1953-57, col. Res. Mem. N.Y. State Bar Assn., Res. Officers Assn. U.S. (pres. Rockland County chpt. 1967-68), B'nai B'rith (pres. New City, N.Y. 1965-66). Jewish. Home: 10 W 66th St New York NY 10023-6206 Office: Phillips Nizer Benjamin Krim & Ballon 666 5th Ave New York NY 10103-0084

RABIN, KENNETH HARDY, public relations executive; b. Rochester, N.Y., Apr. 6, 1943; s. Martin and Ruby (Hardy) R.; m. Renee Efland, June 2, 1967; children: Max, Glennie. BA cum laude, Cornell U., 1965; MAT, Yale U., 1966; MA, U. N.C., 1968; PhD, Vanderbilt U., 1974. Accredited pub. relations practitioner. Fgn. svc. info. officer U.S Info. Agy., Uganda, Nigeria, 1967-70; news dir. U. Tenn., Chattanooga, 1970-72; communications specialist Meharry Med. Coll., Nashville, 1972-73; asst. editor Peabody Jour. of Edn. Vanderbilt U., Nashville, 1973-74; assoc. prof. pub. relations Am. Univ., Washington, 1974-80; dir. U.S. pub. affairs Squibb Corp., Princeton, N.J., 1980-83; exec. v.p., dir. health care commn. Hill and Knowlton, Washington, 1984-92; mng. dir. Interscience Comm. Ltd., Washington, 1992—. Co-editor: Regulating Change, 1990, Informing the People, 1981; mem. editorial bd. Pub. Rels. Rev., 1978—. Bd. dirs. Am. Soc. Hypertension, 1993—; mem. bus. adv. bd. Nat. Downs Syndrome Soc., N.Y.C., 1985—. Mem. Am. Med. Writers Assn. (assoc.), Nat. Assn. Sci. Writers (assoc.), Pub. Relations Soc. Am. (Silver Anvil award, 1986). Democrat. Jewish. Avocations: reading, tennis, video. Home: 3918 Ingomar St NW Washington DC 20015-1916 Office: Interscience Comm Ltd 1615 L St NW # 1150 Washington DC 20036-5610

RABIN, PAUL, insurance company executive; b. 1938. With U.S Gov., 1960-70; treas. Va. Surety Co. Inc., Chgo., 1970—. Office: Virginia Surety Co Inc 123 N Wacker Dr Ste 26 Chicago IL 60606-1700*

RABIN, STANLEY ARTHUR, metal products manufacturer; b. N.Y.C., 1938. B.A., B.S. in Metall. Engring., Columbia U., 1958; M.B.A., U. Santa Clara, 1969. With Comml. Metals Co., Inc., Dallas, 1970—, pres., 1978—, now also chief exec. officer, mem. exec. com., dir. Office: Comml Metals Co Inc PO Box 1046 7800 N Stemmons Fwy Dallas TX 75247-4217*

RABINER, LAWRENCE RICHARD, electrical engineer; b. Bklyn., Sept. 28, 1943; s. Nathan Marcus and Gloria Hannah (Bodinger) R.; m. Suzanne Login, June 23, 1968; children—Sheri Lynn, Wendi Beth, Joni Elizabeth. B.S., MIT, 1964, M.S., 1964, Ph.D., 1967. Mem. tech. staff AT&T Bell Labs., Murray Hill, N.J., 1967-70, supr. human machine voice communications group, 1971-85, head speech rsch. dept., 1985-90, dir. info. principles rsch. lab., 1990-95, v.p. user experience rsch. divsn., 1995-96; v.p. Speech and Image Processing Svcs., 1995—. Author: Theory and Application of Digital Signal Processing, 1975, Digital Speech Processing, 1979, Multirate Digital Signal Processing, 1983, Fundamentals of Speech Recognition, 1993. Bd. dirs. Summit Jewish Community Ctr., N.J., 1985-90. Fellow NAE, NAS, IEEE (pres. ASSP Soc. 1974-75, Piori award 1980), Soc. award 1980, Centennial award 1984), Acoustical Soc. Am. (Biennial award 1974, v.p. 1994-95). Republican. Jewish. Avocations: stamp collecting, bridge, racquetball. Home: 58 Sherbrook Dr Berkeley Heights NJ 07922-2346

RABINER, SUSAN, editor; b. Bklyn., May 5, 1948; d. Nathan M. and Gloria (Bodinger) R.; m. Alfred G. Fortunato, Mar. 27, 1974; children: Anna, Matthew. B.A. cum laude, Goucher Coll., 1969. Asst. editor Random House, N.Y.C., 1969-72; editor Oxford U. Press, N.Y.C., 1973-79, sr. editor, 1980-86; sr. editor St. Martin's Press, N.Y.C., 1986-87, Pantheon Books, N.Y.C., 1987-90, Basic Books, Inc., N.Y.C., 1990—; editl. dir., 1995—; vis. lectr. Yale U., New Haven, 1983, 84. Home: 1009 Brent Dr Wantagh NY 11793-1043 Office: Basic Books Inc 10 E 53rd St New York NY 10022-5244

RABINOVICH, RAQUEL, painter, sculptor; b. Buenos Aires, Argentina, Mar. 30, 1929, came to U.S., 1967, naturalized, 1973; d. Enrique Rabinovich and Julia Dinitz; m. Jose Luis Reissig, Feb. 14, 1956 (div. 1981); children—Celia Karen, Pedro Dario, Nora Vivian. Student U. Córdoba, Argentina, 1950-53, Sorbonne, Paris, 1957, U. Edinburgh, Scotland, 1958-59; lectr. Whitney Mus., 1983-86, Marymount Manhattan Coll., 1984-90. Exhbns. include Hecksher Mus., Huntington, N.Y., 1974, Susan Caldwell Gallery, N.Y.C., 1975, CUNY Grad. Ctr., 1978, The Jewish Mus. Sculpture Ct., N.Y.C., 1979, Ctr. Inter-Am. Rels., 1983, Bronx Mus. Arts, N.Y.C., 1986, Fordham U. Lincoln Ctr., N.Y.C., 1985, Ams. Soc., 1990, Erik Stark Gallery, 1991, Montgomery Ctr., 1992, Trans-Hudson Gallery, 1993, Noyes Mus., 1994, Nelson Atkins Mus. Art, 1995, Intar Gallery, N.Y.C., 1996, others; represented in collections World Bank Fine Art Collection, Washington, Univ. Art Mus., Austin, Cin. Art Mus., Walker Art Ctr., others. NEA fellow, 1991-92; grantee N.Y. State Coun. Arts, 1995—. Avocations: travel, music. Home and Studio: 141 Lamoree Rd Rhinebeck NY 12572-3013

RABINOVICH, SERGIO, physician, educator; b. Lima, Peru, Apr. 8, 1928; m. Nelly; children—Gina, Sergio, Norca, Egla. M.D., San Fernando Med. Sch., U. San Marcos, Lima, Peru, 1953. Intern San Fernando Med. Sch., U. San Marcos, Lima, 1947-54; resident in medicine Grasslands Hosp., Valhalla, N.Y., 1954-57, Henry Ford Hosp., Detroit; prof., head dept. internal medicine U. Arequipa Med. Sch., 1960-61; asst. prof. dept. internal medicine U. Iowa, Iowa City, 1963-65; asst. prof. U. Iowa, 1965-69; attending physician and cons. VA Hosp., Iowa City, 1965-73; assoc. prof. U. Iowa, 1969-73; prof., chief dept. medicine div. infectious disease So. Ill. U. Sch. Medicine, Springfield, 1973—; prof., chmn. dept. medicine So. Ill. U. Sch. Medicine, 1974-88, pres. Faculty Coun., 1992-93. Author: (with I.M. Smith, S.T. Donta) Antibiotics and Infection, 1974. Fellow ACP, Infectious Disease Soc. Am.; mem. AMA, Am. Soc. Microbiology, N.Y. Acad. Sci., Am. Fedn. Clin. Research, AAAS, Am. Thoracic Soc., Ill. Thoracic Soc. (pres. 1978-79), Central Soc. Clin. Research, Sigma Xi. Office: So Ill U Sch Medicine 800 N Rutledge St Springfield IL 62702-4911

RABINOVITCH, BENTON SEYMOUR, chemist, educator emeritus; b. Montreal, Que., Can., Feb. 19, 1919; came to U.S., 1946; s. Samuel and

Rachel (Schachter) R.; m. Marilyn Werby, Sept. 18, 1949; children—Peter Samuel, Ruth Anne, Judith Nancy, Frank Benjamin; m. Flora Reitman, 1980. BSc, McGill U., 1939, PhD, 1942; DSc (hon.), Technion Inst., Haifa, 1991. Postdoctoral fellow Harvard, 1946-48; mem. faculty U. Wash., Seattle, 1948—, prof. chemistry, 1957—, prof. chemistry emeritus, 1985—; Cons. and/or mem. sci. adv. panels, cons. NSF, Nat. Acad. Scis.-NRC; adv. com. phys. chemistry Nat. Bur. Standards. Former editor: Ann. Rev. Phys. Chemistry; mem. editorial bd.: Internat. Jour. Chem. Kinetics, Rev. of Chem. Intermediates, Jour. Phys. Chemistry, J. Am. Chem. Soc. (assoc. editor). Served to capt. Canadian Army, 1942-46, ETO. Nat. Research Council Can. fellow, 1940-42; Royal Soc. Can. Research fellow, 1946-47; Milton Research fellow Harvard, 1948; Guggenheim fellow, 1961; vis. fellow Trinity Coll., Oxford, 1971; Recipient Sigma Xi award for original research, Debye award in phys. chemistry, 1984, Polanyi medal Royal Soc. Chemistry. Fellow Am. Phys. Soc., Am. Acad. Arts and Scis., Royal Soc. London; mem. Am. Chem. Soc. (past chmn. Puget Sound sect., past chmn. phys. chemistry div., editor jour.), Faraday Soc. Spl. research Unimolecular gas phase reaction. Home: 12530 42nd Ave NE Seattle WA 98125-4621

RABINOVITZ, JASON, film and television consultant; b. Boston, Aug. 17, 1921; s. Morris J. and Martha (Leavitt) R.; m. Frieda Pearlson, July 18, 1948; children: Abby, Judith, Daniel, Jonathan. B.A. magna cum laude, Harvard U., 1943, M.B.A. with distinction, 1948. With Chase Nat. Bank, N.Y.C., 1948-49; asst. to sec.-treas. United Paramount Theatres, Inc., N.Y.C., 1949-53; dir. Microwave Assocs., Burlington, Mass., 1952-54; asst. controller ABC, N.Y.C., 1953-56; adminstrv. v.p. ABC-TV Network, N.Y.C., 1956-57; with Metro-Goldwyn-Mayer, Inc., N.Y.C., 1957-69; treas., CFO Metro-Goldwyn-Mayer, Inc., 1963, financial v.p., 1967-69; dir., exec. v.p., gen. mgr. Ency. Brit. Ednl. Corp., Chgo., 1971-73; sr. v.p., gen. mgr. Am. Film Theatre, N.Y.C., 1974-75; v.p., asst. to pres. Metro-Goldwyn-Mayer, Inc., Culver City, Calif., 1976-79; v.p. fin. Metro-Goldwyn-Mayer, Inc., 1979-83; sr. v.p. fin. and corp. adminstrn. MGM/UA Entertainment Co., 1983-84; cons. motion picture and TV, 1984—; dir. Pacific Rim Entertainment, 1993-95. Served to capt., parachutist AUS, 1942-46. Decorated Bronze Star. Mem. Phi Beta Kappa, Phi Eta Sigma. Home: 1675 Stone Canyon Rd Los Angeles CA 90077-1912

RABINOVITZ, JOEL, lawyer, educator; b. 1939. A.B., Cornell U., 1960; LL.B., Harvard U., 1963. Bar: N.Y. 1963, Calif. 1981. Asst. prof. U. Fla., Gainesville, 1966-68; vis. assoc. prof. UCLA, 1968-69, acting prof., 1969-72, prof., 1972-79; ptnr. with Irell & Manella, L.A., 1981—; vis. prof., NYU, 1976; dep. Internat. Tax Counsel, Dept. Treasury, 1980-81. Office: Irell & Manella 1800 Avenue Of The Stars Los Angeles CA 90067-4211

RABINOW, JACOB, electrical engineer, consultant; b. Kharkov, Russia, Jan. 8, 1910; came to U.S., 1921, naturalized, 1930; s. Aaron and Helen (Fleisher) Rabinovich; m. Gladys Lieder, Sept. 26, 1943; children: Jean Ellen, Clare Lynn. B.S. in Elec. Engring, Coll. City N.Y., 1933, E.E., 1934; D.H.L. (hon.), Towson State U., 1983. Radio serviceman N.Y.C., 1934-38; mech. engr. Nat. Bur. Standards, Washington, 1938-54; pres. Rabinow Engring. Co., Washington, 1954-64; v.p. Control Data Corp., Washington, 1964-72; research engr. Nat. Bur. Standards, 1972-89; cons. Inst. Standards and Tech., Gaithersburg, Md., 1989—; Regent's lectr. U. Calif.-Berkeley, 1972; lectr., cons. in field. Author. Recipient Pres.'s Certificate of Merit, 1948; certificate appreciation War Dept., 1949; Exceptional Service award Dept. Commerce, 1949; Edward Longstreth medal Franklin Inst., 1959; Jefferson medal N.J. Patent Law Assn., 1973; named Scientist of Yr. Indsl. R&D mag., 1980. Fellow IEEE (Harry Diamond award 1977), AAAS; mem. Nat. Acad. Engring., Philos. Soc. Washington, Audio Engring. Soc., Sigma Xi. Club: Cosmos (Washington). Patentee in field. Home: 6920 Selkirk Dr Bethesda MD 20817-4750 Office: Inst Standards and Tech Gaithersburg MD 20899 *I believe that inventions enrich both the material wealth and the cultural life of a nation and the world. Being a product of original thought, they are an art form and should be supported as such.*

RABINOWITCH, DAVID GEORGE, sculptor; b. Toronto, Ont., Can., Mar. 6, 1943; came to U.S., 1972; s. Joseph and Ruthe (Calverley) R.; m. Sheila Martin, June 1966 (div. 1981); m. Catrina Neiman, Mar. 14, 1983. BS, U. Western Ont., London, 1966. Instr. sculpture Yale U., New Haven, 1974-75; prof. sculpture Staatliche Kunstakademie Düsseldorf, Germany, 1984—; sculptor in residence Atelier Calder, Saché, France, 1994. Sculptures include Box Troughs, 1963, Fluid Sheet Pieces, 1964, Gravitational Vehicles, 1965, Tubers and Wood Constructions, 1966-67, Phantoms, 1967, Sectioned Mass Constructions, 1968, Metrical Constructions, 1973—, Tyndale Constructions, 1974—, Construction of Vision Drawings, 1969—, Ottonian Drawings, 1977—, Collinasca Cycle (Woodcuts), 1991-92. Recipient CAPS award N.Y. State Coun., 1974, Lynch-Staunton award of distinction Can. Coun., Ottawa, Ont., 1977; J.S. Guggenheim Meml. Found. fellow, N.Y.C., 1975, Nat. Endowment Arts fellow, Washington, 1986-87. Mem. Royal Can. Acad. Arts and Scis. Avocations: music. Studio: 49 E 1st St New York NY 10003-9324

RABINOWITZ, HOWARD K., physician, educator; b. Pitts., Sept. 25, 1946; s. Mac and Anne (Morgan) R.; m. Carol A. Gelles, Feb. 4, 1968; children: Elyse, Daniel J. Student, Rutgers Coll., 1964-67; MD, U. Pitts., 1971. Diplomate Am. Bd. Family Practice, Am. Bd. Pediatrics. From instr. to assoc. prof. Dept. Family Medicine Jefferson Med. Coll., Phila., 1976-90, vice chmn., 1990-95; prof., 1990—; bd. dirs. Am. Bd. Family Practice, Lexington, Ky., pres., 1992-93. Contbr. articles to profl. jours. With USPHS, 1972-74. RWJ Health Policy fellow, 1993-94. Fellow Phila. Coll. Physicians; mem. AMA, Soc. Tchrs. Family Medicine, Am. Acad. Family Physicians. Office: Jefferson Medical College Dept Family Medicine 1015 Walnut St Ste 401 Philadelphia PA 19107-5005

RABINOWITZ, JACK GRANT, radiologist, educator; b. Monticello, N.Y., July 9, 1927; s. Abraham and Bessie (Sussman) R.; m. Rica Gedalia Arnon, Oct. 19, 1972; children—Antoine, Anne, Pierre, Yaron, Tal. B.A., UCLA, 1949; M.D., U. Berne, Switzerland, 1955. Diplomate: Am. Bd. Radiology. Intern Kings County Hosp., Bklyn., 1955-56; resident Kings County Hosp., 1956-59; instr. radiology Downstate Med. Center, Bklyn., 1960-61; asst. prof. radiology Downstate Med. Center, 1967-70, prof. radiology, 1970-73; asst. radiologist Mt. Sinai Sch. Medicine, N.Y.C., 1962-65; asst. prof. radiology Mt. Sinai Sch. Medicine, 1965-66, asso. prof. radiology, 1966-67, prof., chmn. dept. radiology, 1978-95, prof., 1995—; asso. attending radiologist Mt. Sinai Hosp., N.Y.C., 1965-67, dir. radiology, 1978—; radiologist-in-chief Bklyn.-Cumberland Med. Center, Bklyn., 1967-70; dir. diagnostic radiology Kings County Hosp. Center, Bklyn., 1970-73; prof., chmn. dept. diagnostic radiology U. Tenn., Memphis, 1973-78; cons. in radiology VA Hosp., Bronx, N.Y. Author: Pediatric Radiology, 1978, Radiology for the Primary and Emergency Care of Physicians, 1981. Fellow Am. Coll. Radiology; mem. Radiol. Soc. N. Am., Am. Roentgen Ray Soc., Assn. Univ. Radiologists, AMA, Soc. Chmn. Acad. Radiology Depts., Tenn. Radiol. Soc., Tenn. Med. Soc., Memphis and Shelby County Med. Soc., Memphis Roentgen Soc. Office: Mt Sinai Hosp 1 Gustave L Levy Pl New York NY 10029-6504

RABINOWITZ, JAY ANDREW, state supreme court justice; b. Phila., Feb. 25, 1927; s. Milton and Rose (Rittenberg) R.; m. Anne Marie Nesbit, June 14, 1957; children: Judith, Mara, Max, Sara. B.A., Syracuse U., 1949; LL.B., Harvard, 1952. Bar: N.Y. 1952, Alaska 1958. Pvt. practice law N.Y.C., 1952-57; law clk. to presiding judge U.S. Dist. Ct., Fairbanks, Alaska, 1957-58; asst. U.S. atty. Fairbanks, 1958-59; dep. atty. gen., chief civil div. State of Alaska, 1959-60; judge Superior Ct. Alaska, 1960-65; justice Alaska Supreme Ct., 1965—; chief justice Alaska Supreme Ct., Juneau, 1972-75, 78-81, 84-87, 90-92. Served with AUS, 1945-46. Mem. ABA (chmn. task force jud. evaluation), N.Y. Bar Assn., Alaska Bar Assn. (commr. on uniform laws 1971—). Office: Alaska Supreme Ct 303 K St Anchorage AK 99501-2013*

RABINOWITZ, LEONARD, apparel executive. Grad., NYU, 1968. With Good Fellow, Inc., N.Y.C., 1968-72; dir. sales Baggs, Inc., L.A., 1972-74; v.p. Fashion Makers, L.A., 1974-75; chmn. bd. dirs. Calif. Fashion Ind. (Carol Little), L.A., 1975—. Office: Carol Little 3434 So Grand Ave Los Angeles CA 90007*

RABINOWITZ, MARK ALLAN, lawyer; b. Chgo., Feb. 9, 1954; s. Marvin Harold and Pauline Betty (Robins) R.; m. Linda Kay Beauseigneur, Feb. 7, 1982. BA summa cum laude, U. Ill., 1975; JD, Harvard U., 1978. Bar: Ill. 1978, U.S. Dist. Ct. (no. dist.) Ill. 1978, U.S. Ct. Appeals (7th cir.) 1979. Ptnr. Levy & Erens, Chgo., 1978-85, McDermott, Will & Emery, Chgo., 1985-93, Rudnick & Wolfe, Chgo., 1993—. Mem. Phi Beta Kappa. Avocations: history, polit. theory, philosophy. *

RABINOWITZ, MAYER ELYA, librarian, educator; b. N.Y.C., Jan. 31, 1939; s. Simcha Rabinowitz and Dvora (Resnikoff) Masovetsky; m. Renah Lee Levine, June 16, 1965; children: Adi, Dalya, Ayelet. BA, B in Hebrew Lit., Yeshiva U., 1960, MA, 1961; M in Hebrew Lit., Jewish Theol. Sem., 1965, PhD, 1974. Ordained rabbi, 1967. Instr. Jewish Theol. Sem., N.Y.C., 1970-74, asst. prof., 1974-76, dean students Tchrs. Inst., 1974-76, assoc. prof., 1976—, assoc. dean grad sch., 1976-79, dean grad. sch., 1979-88, libr., 1988—; mem. com. on Jewish law and standards Rabbinical Assembly, N.Y.C., 1978—; chair Joint Bet Din Conservative Movement, N.Y.C., 1990—. Author: Sefer Hamordekhai Gittin, 1990; contbr. articles to profl. jours. Mem. Assn. Jewish Studies, Assn. Jewish Librs. Office: Jewish Theol Sem 3080 Broadway New York NY 10027-4650

RABINOWITZ, MAYNARD, publishing executive; b. 1942. BA, Columbia U., 1963; LLB, Harvard U., 1966. Pvt. practice N.Y.C., 1966-75; ptnr. Townsend, Rabinowitz, Pantaleoni & Valente P.C., N.Y.C., 1975—; with Enquirer/Star Group Inc., 1990—; v.p.- sec. Enquirer/Star Inc., Lake Worth, Fla., 1989—; now v. chmn. fin. adm. and legal affairs American Media inc; vice chmn. bd. dirs. Am. Media, Inc., Lake Worth, Am. Media Ops., Inc., Lake Worth. Office: American Media Inc 600 S East Coast Ave Lake Worth FL 33464-0001*

RABINOWITZ, SAMUEL NATHAN, lawyer; b. Hazleton, Pa., Sept. 16, 1932; s. Morris M. and Bodia (Janowitz) R.; m. Barbara G. Cohen, Mar. 27, 1955; children—Fredric E., Mark I., Joshua A. BA, Pa. State U., 1955; JD, Temple U., 1959. Bar: D.C. 1959, Pa. 1960. Agt. IRS, Phila., 1956-60; sole practice Phila., 1960-61; ptnr. Blank, Rome, Comisky & McCauley, Phila., 1961—; mem. trust com. Continental Bank, Phila., 1983-91; faculty Temple U. Sch. Law. Contbr. articles to profl. jours. Active Phila. Friends Boys Town Jerusalem; bd. dirs. Jerusalem Soc. Boys Town, Phila. Friends of Ben Gurion U. the Negev, Jewish Nat. Fund Coun., Phila.; bd. dirs., pres. Jewish Cmty. Ctrs. Greater Phila.; past chmn. Albert Einstein Soc. Albert Einstein Med. Ctr., past trustee; trustee Jewish Fedn. Phila. (officer Fedn. Endowments Corp.). Fellow Am. Coll. Trust and Estate Counsel; mem. ABA, Pa. Bar Assn., Phila. Bar Assn. (chmn. probate and trust sect. 1985-86), Green Valley Country Club, Elkview Country Club, Vesper Club, Locust Club, Pyramid Club, Golden Slipper, B'nai B'rith, Maccabi/USA Sports for Israel (exec. com., counsel). Home: 1161 Norsam Rd Gladwyne PA 19035-1419 Office: Blank Rome Comisky et al 1200 Four Penn Ctr Plz Philadelphia PA 19103

RABINOWITZ, STANLEY SAMUEL, rabbi; b. Duluth, Minn., June 8, 1917; S. Jacob Mier and Rose (Zeichik) R.; m. Anita Bryna Lifson, June 24, 1945; children: Nathaniel Herz, Sharon Deborah, Judith Leah. B.A., State U. Iowa, 1939; M.A., Yale U., 1950; M. Hebrew Lit., Jewish Theol. Sem., 1944, Doctor Hebrew Lit., 1971. Ordained rabbi, 1943; dir. United Synagogue, N.Y.C., 1943-46; rabbi B'nai Jacob Synagogue, New Haven, Conn., 1946-53, Adath Jeshurun Synagogue, Mpls., 1953-60; rabbi Adas Israel Synagogue, Washington, 1960-86, rabbi emeritus, 1986—; v.p. Rabbinical Assembly, N.Y.C., 1974-76, pres., 1976-78; vice chmn. B'nai B'rith Youth Commn., 1965-76; pres. Mercaz, 1977-83. Club: Cosmos (Washington). Home: 3115 Normanstone Ter NW Washington DC 20008-2732 Office: Adas Israel Synagogue 2850 Quebec St NW Washington DC 20008-5200

RABINS, MICHAEL JEROME, mechanical engineer, educator; b. N.Y.C., Feb. 24, 1932; s. Herman and Ida (Olinsky) R; m. Joan Rose, Apr. 6, 1956; children: Andrew, Evan, Alexandra. BS, MIT, 1953; MS, Carnegie Inst. Tech., 1954; PhD, U. Wis., 1959. Lic. engr., Calif., Tex. Asst. prof. U. Wis., Madison, 1959-60; asst. prof. NYU, N.Y.C., 1960-64, assoc. prof., 1964-70; prof. Polytechnic Inst. N.Y., Bklyn., 1970-75; dir. Office Univ. Rsch., U.S. Dept. Transp., Washington, 1975-77; chmn. mech. engring. dept. Wayne State U., Detroit, 1977-85, assoc. dean, 1985-87; prof. mech. engring., head dept. Tex. A&M U., College Station, 1987-89; TEES rsch. prof., 1989-91; dir. engring. ethics & professionalism program Tex. A&M U., College Station, 1992—. Author: Controls and Dynamics Systems Response, 1970, Introducing Systems and Controls, 1974, Engineering Ethics: Concepts and Cases, 1995. Chmn. Detroit 3 Ctr. Transp. Com., 1977-87. Recipient Superior Svc. award Dept. Transp., Washington, 1976, Cert. of Merit, Mayor of Detroit, 1980. Fellow ASME (exec. com., chmn., editor jour., v.p. 1985-87, bd. govs. 1989-90, com. on program rev. 1992-96, Disting. Svc. award 1974); mem. Am. Soc. Engring. Edn. (projects bd. 1987-90), Am. Automatic Control Coun. (pres. 1984-86, Edn. award 1991). Avocations: reading, Chinese cooking, stained glass, classical music. Office: Tex A&M U Mech Engring Dept College Station TX 77843

RABJOHN, NORMAN, chemistry educator emeritus; b. Rochester, N.Y., May 1, 1915; s. Alfred Augustus and Elizabeth Mary (Hooper) R.; m. Dora I. Taylor, Sept. 9, 1943; 1 son, James Norman. B.S., U. Rochester, 1937; M.S., U. Ill., 1939, Ph.D., 1942. Instr. chemistry U. Ill., Champaign-Urbana, 1942-44; research Goodyear Tire, Akron, Ohio, 1944-48; from assoc. prof. to prof. chemistry U. Mo., Columbia, 1948-83; prof. emeritus, 1983—. Mem. editorial bd.: Organic Syntheses, 1960—; assoc. editor: Chem. Revs., 1965-67. Fellow AAAS; mem. Am. Chem. Soc. (chmn. council com. publs. 1970-71), Phi Beta Kappa, Sigma Xi, Phi Lambda Upsilon, Alpha Chi Sigma. Home: 100 E Ridgeley Rd Columbia MO 65203-3530

RABKIN, MITCHELL THORNTON, physician, hospital administrator, educator; b. Boston, Nov. 27, 1930; s. Morris Aaron and Esther (Quint) R.; m. Adrienne M. Najarian, June 24, 1956; children: Julia Margaret, David Gregory. A.B. magna cum laude, Harvard U., 1951, M.D. cum laude, 1955; D.Sc. (hon.), Brandeis U., 1983; D.Pharm. (hon.), Mass. Coll. Pharmacy, 1983; D.Sc. (hon.), Curry Coll., 1989, Northeastern U., 1994; D in Hum. Let. (hon.), Salem (Mass.) State Coll., 1995. Intern Mass. Gen. Hosp., Boston, 1955-56; resident in internal medicine Mass. Gen. Hosp., 1956-57, 59-60, chief resident, 1962, mem. staff, 1963-72, bd. consultation, 1972-80, hon. physician, 1981—; clin. fellow NIH, Bethesda, Md., 1957-59; gen. dir. Beth Israel Hosp., Boston, 1966-80; pres. Beth Israel Hosp., 1980—; asst. prof. medicine Harvard U., 1969-70, assoc. prof., 1971-83, prof., 1983—; mem. Health Care Adv. Coun. U.S. Gen. Acctg. Office, 1991—. Served with USPHS, 1957-59. Fellow ACP, AAAS; mem. Am. Fedn. Clin. Rsch., Mass. Med. Soc., Soc. Med. Adminstrs., Assn. Am. Med. Colls. (past chmn. coun. teaching hosps., chmn. elect. 1995-96), Conf. Boston Teaching Hosps. (past chmn., Inst. Medicine, NAS, Century Assn. (N.Y.C.), Harvard Club of Boston. Jewish. Office: Beth Israel Hosp 330 Brookline Ave Boston MA 02215-5400

RABÓ, JULE ANTHONY, chemical research administrator, consultant; b. Budapest, Hungary; came to U.S., 1957; m. Sheelagh Ennis; children: Benedict, Sebastian. BSChemE, Poly. U., Budapest, 1946, DSc in Chemistry, 1949, D honoris causa, 1986. From asst. prof. to assoc. prof. Poly U., Budapest, 1946-54; assoc. dir. Hydrocarbon Rsch. Inst., Budapest, 1951-56; rsch. assoc. Union Carbide Corp., Buffalo, 1957-60; rsch. mgr. Union Carbide Corp., Tarrytown, N.Y., 1960-72, corp. fellow, 1969-82, sr. corp. rsch. fellow, 1982—; sr. corp. rsch. fellow UOP, Tarrytown, 1988—; cons. in chemistry and catalysis, Armonk, N.Y.; former mem. adv. bd. Ctr. for Advanced Materials, Lawrence-Berkeley Lab.; mem. adv. bd. dept. chemistry Lehigh U. Author: Zeolite Chemisty and Catalysts; former mem. editorial bd. Jour. Catalysis, Applied Catalysis; contbr. articles to profl. jours.; patentee in field. Recipient Kossuth award Govt. of Hungary, 1953, Excellence in Catalysis award N.Y. Catalysis Soc., 1982, Humboldt award, Fed. Republic of Germany, 1990. Mem. Am. Chem. Soc. (E.V. Murphree award 1988), Am. Catalysis Soc. (Eugene J. Houdry award 1989), Hungarian Acad. Sci. (Varga medal 1991), Am. Inst. Chemists (Chem. Pioneer award 1993).

RABOLT, JOHN FRANCIS, optics scientist; b. N.Y.C., May 14, 1949; married, 1990; 2 children. BS, SUNY, Oneonta, 1970; PhD in Physics, Ill. U., Carbondale, 1974. Nat. Rsch. Coun., NAS assoc. Nat. Bur. Standards, 1976-77; scientist polymers rsch. staff rsch. lab IBM Corp., San Jose, Calif., 1978-96; co-dir. NSF Ctr. on polymer interfaces and macromolecular assemblies Stanford U.-IBM-U. Calif. Davis rsch. partnership, 1994-96; prof. and chair materials sci. U. Del., Newark, 1996. Recipient Coblentz award, 1985, Williams-Wright award, 1990, Ellis R. Lippincott award Optical Soc. Am., 1993. Achievements include research in the use of Fourier transform (FT) infared and FT and Conventional Raman spectroscopy to investigate crystal and molecular structure of long chain molecules and polymers, integrated optical techniques in conjunction with Raman Spectoscopy to investigate submicron polymer films and polymer surfaces, FTIR studies of self assembled and Langmoir-Blodgett films on metals and dielectrics, and co-development of FT Raman spectroscopy. Office: Spencer Lab Univ Delaware Newark DE 19716

RABON, WILLIAM JAMES, JR., architect; b. Marion, S.C., Feb. 7, 1931; s. William James and Beatrice (Baker) R; m. Martha Ann Hibbitts, Mar. 7, 1987. BS in Arch., Clemson (S.C.) Coll., 1951; BArch, N.C. State Coll., 1955; MArch, MIT, 1956. Registered architect, Calif., Ky., N.C., Ohio, Pa., Ga. Designer archtl. firms in N.Y.C. and Birmingham, Mich., 1958-61; designer, assoc. John Carl Warnecke and Assocs., San Francisco, 1961-63, 64-66, Keyes, Lethbridge and Condon, Washington, 1966-68; prin. archtl. ptnr. A.M. Kinney Assocs. and William J. Rabon, Cin., 1968-85; v.p., dir. archtl. design A.M. Kinney, Inc., Cin., 1977-85; v.p., dir. programming svcs. Design Art Corp., 1977-85; sr. architect. John Portman & Assocs., Atlanta, 1985-88; dir. architectural design Robert and Co., Atlanta, 1988-89; studio dir., design prin. Carlson Assocs., Atlanta, 1990-93; prin. Rosser Internat., 1993—; lectr. U. Calif., Berkeley, 1963-65; asst. prof. archtl. design Cath. U. Am., 1967-68. Prin. works include Kaiser Tech. Ctr., Pleasanton, Calif. (Rsch. Devel. Lab. of Yr. award), 1970, Clermont Nat. Bank, Milford, Ohio, 1971, Pavilion bldg. Children's Hosp. Med. Ctr., Cin. (Cin. AIA design award), 1973, EG&G, Hydrospace, Inc., Rockville, Md. (Potomac Valley AIA design award), 1970, Mead Johnson Park, Evansville, Ind. (Rsch. Devel. Lab. of Yr. merit award), 1973, Hamilton County Vocat. Sch., Cin., 1972, hdqrs. lab. EPA, Cin., 1975, Arapahoe Chem. Co. Rsch. Ctr., Boulder, Colo. (Rsch. Devel. Lab. of Yr. award 1976, Concrete Reinforced Steel Inst. Nat. Design award, Regional AIA Design award), 1976, corp. hdqrs. Ohio River Co., Cin., 1977, Children's Hosp. Therapy Ctr., Cin. (Cin. AIA design award 1978, award of merit Am. Wood Council 1981), VA Hosp. addition, Cin. (Cin. ASHRAE Design award 1980), NALCO Chem. Co. Rsch. Ctr., Naperville, Ill. (Ohio and Cin. AIA design awards 1980, 81), 1980, Proctor & Gamble-Winton Hill Tunnel, Cin. (Ohio AIA design award), 1978, Toyota Regional Ctr., Blue Ash, Ohio (Ohio AIA and Ohio Masonry Council combined design award 1981), planning cons. Nat. Bur. Standards, Republic of China, 1982, East and West fleet hdqrs. and Data Ctr. Librs. of Royal Saudi Arabian Navy, 1985, corp. hdqrs. The Drackett Co., Cin., 1983, corp. hdqrs. Brown & Williamson, Louisville, 1984, Inst. Paper Sci. and Tech., Atlanta, 1989, 93, Animal Sci. Complex, Athens, Ga., 1996. 1st lt. AUS, 1951-53, Korea. Decorated Silver Star, Bronze Star with V device, Bronze Star, Purple Heart with bronze cluster; MIT Grad. Sch. scholar, 1956; Fulbright scholar, Italy, 1957-58. Mem. AIA, Nat. Council Archtl. Registration Bds.

RABOSKY, JOSEPH GEORGE, engineering consulting company executive; b. Sewickley, Pa., May 20, 1944; s. Mary Helen (Mayer) Rabosky; m. Suzanne Lazzelle, Aug. 23, 1969. BS, Pa. State U., 1966; MS in Engring., W.Va. U., 1969, MSCE, 1973; PhD, U. Pitts., 1984. Registered profl. engr., Pa., Tenn., W.Va., Mo., Ohio. Project engr. Chester Engrs., Coraopolis, Pa., 1969-70, mgr., 1989-92; project mgr. Calgon Corp., Pitts., 1970-73, sect. leader, 1979-85, mktg. mgr., 1985-86; sr. environ. specialist Mobay Chem. Corp., Pitts., 1975-79; project engr. Morris Knowles, Inc., Pitts., 1973-74; project mgr. Penn Environ. Cons., 1974-75; engring. mgr. Baker/TSA, Inc., Pitts., 1986-89; pres. AquaTerra, Inc., Moon Twp., Pa., 1992-95, Rabosky & Assocs., Moon Township, Pa., 1995—; adj. prof. U. Pitts., 1985-88, Pa. State U.-Beaver, McKeesport and New Kensington campuses, 1985—. Bd. dirs. Moon Twp. Mcpl. Authority, 1980-89. Mem. ASCE, Am. Acad. Engrs. (diplomate, waste water), Water Environ. Fedn., Pa. Water Environ. Assn. (chmn. rsch. com. 1984-89, 91-92, mem. program com. 1984-89, mem. long planning com. 1993-95, 2d v.p. 1994-95, 1st v.p. 1995-96, pres. 1996—), Western Pa. Water Pollution Control Assn. (officer, pres. 1992-93), Internat. Water Conf. (mem. exec. bd. 1989-94, gen. chmn. 1992-93). Home: 104 Wynview Dr Moon Township PA 15108-1033 Home: 104 Wynview Dr Moon Township PA 15108-1033

RABSON, ALAN SAUL, physician, educator; b. N.Y.C., July 1, 1926; s. Abraham and Florence (Shulman) R.; m. Ruth L. Kirschstein, June 11, 1950; 1 son, Arnold B. BA, U. Rochester, 1948; MD, SUNY, Bklyn., 1950. Intern Mass. Meml. Hosp., Boston, 1951-52; resident in pathology NYU Hosp., 1952-54, USPHS Hosp., New Orleans, 1954-55; pathologist Nat. Cancer Inst., Bethesda, Md., 1955—; prof. pathology Georgetown U. Med. Sch., 1974—, Uniformed Services U. Health Scis., 1978—, George Washington U., 1978—. Contbr. articles to med. jours. Mem. Am. Assn. Pathologists, Phi Beta Kappa, Sigma Xi, Alpha Omega Alpha. Address: NIH-National Cancer Institute Bldg 31-Cancer Biology 9000 Rockville Pike Bethesda MD 20892-0001

RABSON, ROBERT, plant physiologist, retired science administrator; b. Bklyn., Mar. 4, 1926; s. Samuel and Rose (Strauss) R.; m. Eileen K. Rabson, Aug. 27, 1950; children: Michael, Barbra, Laurel. BS, Cornell U., 1951, PhD, 1956. Rsch. assoc. biolog. div. Oak Ridge (Tenn.) Nat. Lab., 1956-58; asst. prof. U. Houston, 1958-62, assoc. prof., 1962-63; biochemist civ. biology and medicine AEC, Washington, 1963-67, asst. br. chief, 1967-73; first officer plant breeding and genetics sect. FAO/IAEA, Vienna, Austria, 1973-76; mem. divsn. biomed. and environ. sci. Energy Rsch. & Devel. Dept. Energy, 1976-79; dir. div. energy bioscis. Dept. Energy, Washington, 1979-95; mem. adv. bd. Rsch. Sch. Biol. Sci. Australian Nat. U., 1991-95. Mem. plant scis. adv. bd. McKnight Found., Mpls., 1981-92. With U.S. Army, 1944-46, PTO, ETO. Fellow AAAS; mem. Am. Soc. Plant Physiologists (chmn. publ. com. 1984-86, treas. 1988-91, Adolph Gude award 1986).

RABSTEJNEK, GEORGE JOHN, management consultant; b. Queens, N.Y., June 14, 1932; s. George John and Rose Anna (Krasa) R.; m. Patsy Kidd, July 17, 1964; 1 child, Marley Ann. B in Indsl. Engring., Ga. Inst. Tech., 1954; postgrad., U. Conn. Sch. Law, 1960, NYU Sch. Bus., 1965-69; advanced mgmt. program, Harvard U., 1975. Supr. purchasing Westinghouse Electric, Bridgeport, Conn., 1957-61; project mgr. systems div. IBM Corp., Poughkeepsie, N.Y., 1961-65; dir. material mgmt. svcs. divsn. Harbridge House, Inc., Boston, 1965-69, v.p., group head, 1969-75, exec. v.p., 1975-76, pres., 1976-83, CEO, 1983-92, chmn., 1983-93, ret., 1993; chmn. bd. dirs. R.P.W., Inc., Bluelight, Inc. Contbr. articles to profl. jours. Vice chmn. World Affairs Coun. Boston, 1988, pres., 1984-87; trustee Internat. Coord. Coun., Boston, 1984—; trustee Mass. Eye and Ear Infirmary, Boston, 1984—, vice chmn. bd. dirs.; mem. Draper Labs. Corp., 1994; mem. adv. bd. Town of Cohasset, Mass., 1975; chmn. nat. adv. bd. Ga. Inst. Tech., 1991-92; mem. exec. adv. bd. Ivan Allen Coll.; mem. bd. visitors Northeastern U.; bd. dirs. Ctr. for Tech. Commercialization. Comdr. USNR, 1958-75. Recipient Disting. Alumni award Sch. Indsl. and Sys. Engring., Ga. Inst. Tech., named to Acad. Disting. Engring. Alumni. Mem. Am. Inst. Indsl. Engrs., Nat. Security Indsl. Assn. (v.p. 1987—), Nat. Def. Transp. Assn. (Def. Transp. award 1980), Assn. Naval Aviators, Navy League, Reynolds Soc. (chmn.), Nat. Security Industry Assn. (trustee 1990-93), Harvard Club, Algonquin Club (Boston), Cohasset Golf Club (Mass.), Cohasset Yacht Club, Cohasset Tennis and Squash Club, Mill Reef Club, Antigua, B.W.I., Comml. Club, F St. Club (Washington), Phi Kappa Sigma. Republican. Unitarian. Home: 181 Border St Cohasset MA 02025-2043

RABUN, JOHN BREWTON, JR., criminal justice agency administrator; b. Augusta, Ga. Nov. 16, 1946; s. John Brewton and Alsie Imor (Bateman) R.; m. Anna Betsy Park, Dec. 27, 1967; children: Kerry Kristin, John Candler. B.A., Mercer U., 1967; postgrad. So. Bapt. Theol. Sem., 1967-70; M.S. in Social Work, U. Louisville, 1971. Cert. social worker, Ky., D.C. Exec. dir. Ky. Civil Liberties Union, Louisville, 1971-72; dir. Community Residential Treatment Services, Louisville, 1973-78; program mgr. Field Services, Louisville, 1978-80; program mgr. Exploited and Missing Child Unit, Louisville, 1980-84; v.p., chief oper. officer Nat. Ctr. for Missing & Exploited Children, Washington, 1984—; mem. Alderman's Task Force on Social Svcs., Louisville, 1982, Mayor's City Youth Commn., Louisville, 1983-84; trainer and/or cons. to numerous agys. in U.S., U.K., Can., Mex. Contbr. articles to criminal justice and healthcare publs. and books. Recipient Key to City of Louisville, 1983, Disting. Alumnus award U. Louisville, 1985, Russell L. Colling lit. award Internat. Assn. for Healthcare Security and Safety, 1991, Russell Colling Lit. award Internat. Assn. for Healthcare Security and Safety, 1991; named hon. chief of police, City of Louisville, 1982. Mem. ACLU, Nat. Assn. Social Workers, Nat. Sheriff's Assn., Nat. Coun. Juvenile and Family Ct. Judges, Internat. Juvenile Officers Assn., Acad. Cert. Social Workers, Internat. Assn. Chiefs of Police. Baptist (deacon). Avocations: photography, hunting, fishing, Internet. Home: 13519 Oak Ivy Ln Fairfax VA 22033-1230 Office: Nat Ctr for Missing and Exploited Children 2101 Wilson Blvd Ste 550 Arlington VA 22201-3062

RABUNSKI, ALAN E., lawyer; b. N.Y.C., Jan. 18, 1948; s. Leo and Noima (Alperovich) R.; m. Jean Scheinberg, Oct. 31, 1976; children: Jonathan Sandler, Benjamin Jacob. BA, CUNY, 1971; JD with honors, John Marshall Law Sch., 1975; LLM in Taxation, NYU, 1978. Bar: N.Y. 1975, Ill. 1975, U.S. Tax Ct. 1981. Law clk. Hon. Allan Stouder Ill. Appellate Ct., Kankakee, 1975-76; pvt. practice law N.Y.C., 1976-94; ptnr. Rabunski & Katz, LLP, N.Y.C., 1994—; lectr. NYU Sch. of Continuing Edn., N.Y.C., 1985-89; lectr. in field. Coach Little League, Larchmont, N.Y., 1988-91; mem. Bd. Assessment Rev., Larchmont, 1992-94; arbitrator Civil Ct. of City of N.Y. Mem. ABA, N.Y. State Bar Assn. (trusts and estates law sect. com. taxation, tax sect. com. on estates, trusts, practice and procedure). Home: 72 Pinebrook Dr Larchmont NY 10538 Office: Rabunski & Katz LLP 230 Park Ave New York NY 10169

RABURN, RANDALL K., school system administrator. Supt. Edmond (Okla.) Pub. Schs. Recipient Nat. Superintendent of the Yr. awd., Oklahoma, Am. Assn. of School Administrators, 1993. Office: Edmond Pub Schs 1216 S Rankin St Edmond OK 73034-4769

RABUSKA, MICHÈLE JOANNE, financial analyst; b. Waterbury, Conn., Dec. 6, 1963; d. Peter Constantine and Joan Elfreida (Bergstrom) R. BA in Govt., Wesleyan U., 1995; postgrad., Trinity Coll., Hartford, Conn., 1995—. With bus. office St. Francis Hosp. and Med. Ctr., Hartford, Conn., 1990-93; customer rels. specialist St. Francis Hosp. and Med. Ctr., Hartford, 1993-96; fin. analyst VSM & Co., P.C., Farmington, Conn., 1996—; adminstrv. support, personal computer trainer, cons. The 1000 Corp., Hartford, 1993-94; cons. St. Francis Hosp. Profl. Svcs., 1995. Election pollwatcher Hartford Courant newspaper, 1992—; mem. Pub. Concern Found., Washington, 1993-94, Amnesty Internat., 1989—. Grantee State of Conn., 1993, 94; scholar Wesleyan U., 1993, 94, Etherington scholar Wesleyan U., 1993, 94. Mem. St. Francis Hosp. Women's Aux., We Adopt Greyhounds, Phi Theta Kappa, Alpha Zeta Psi. Republican. Russian Orthodox. Avocations: glass etching and jewelry making, print-making, inline skating. Home: 47-C Congress St Hartford CT 06114-1025 Office: VSM & Co., P.C. 231 Farmington Ave Farmington CT 06032-1922

RABUZZI, DANIEL D., medical educator; b. Pitts., June 19, 1935; s. Daniel Ralph and Victoria (Bruni) R.; m. Kathryn Allen, June 11, 1958; children: Daniel, Matthew, Douglas. AB, Harvard Coll., 1957; MD, U. Pa., 1961. Diplomate Am. Bd. Otolaryngology. Instr. otolaryngology U. Md., Balt., 1967-68; asst. prof. SUNY, Syracuse, 1968-71, assoc. prof., 1971-77, prof., 1977-81, clin. prof. otolaryngology, 1984—; prof., chmn. N.Y. Med. Coll. and N.Y. Eye & Ear Infirmary, N.Y.C., 1981-84; pres. St. Joseph's Hops. Med. Staff, Syracuse, 1990-92. Contbr. 54 articles to profl. jours. and chpts. to books. Capt. U.S. Army, 1966-68. Fellow ACS; mem. Am. Soc. Head and Neck Surgery, Am. Acad. Otoloaryngology, Am. Cancer Soc. (pres. County unit 1978-80), Onondaga County Med. Soc. (pres. 1987-88). Avocations: Roman archeology, European travel, golfing, historical readings. Office: Ctrl NY Ear Nose & Throat Cons 1100 E Geneseee Syracuse NY 13210

RABY, WILLIAM LOUIS, author; b. Chgo., July 16, 1927; s. Gustave E. and Helen (Burgess) R.; m. Norma Claire Schreiner, Sept. 8, 1956; children: Burgess, Marianne, Marlene. BSBA, Northwestern U., 1949; MBA, U. Ariz., 1961, PhD, 1971. Ptnr. VAR CPA Firms, 1950-76, Touche Ross & Co., N.Y.C., 1977-87; pres. Ariz. State Bd. Accountancy, 1993-94; mem. Ariz. State Bd. Tax Appeals, 1994—; prof. acctg. emeritus Ariz. State U., 1994—; columnist Tax Notes mag., Arlington, Va., 1990—. Author: The Income Tax and Business Decisions, 1964, Building and Maintaining a Successful Tax Practice, 1964, The Reluctant Taxpayer, 1970, Tax Practice Management, 1974, Introduction to Federal Taxation, annually, 1980-91, Tax Practice Management: Client Servicing, 1986; editor: Raby Report on Tax Practice, 1986—, PPC Guide To Successful Tax Practice, 1991; mem. editorial adv. bd. Taxation for Accountants, The Tax Adviser; contbr. articles to profl. jours. Mem. AICPA (chmn. fed. tax divsn. 1980-83, v.p. 1983-84, coun. 1983-90), Tax Ct. Bar. Presbyterian (elder, chmn. adv. coun. on ch. and soc. 1979-81). Office: PO Box 26846 Tempe AZ 85285-6846

RACE, GEORGE JUSTICE, pathology educator; b. Everman, Tex., Mar. 2, 1926; s. Claude Ernest and Lila Eunice (Bunch) R.; m. Annette Isabelle Rinker, Dec. 21, 1946; children: George William Daryl, Jonathan Clark, Mark Christopher, Jennifer Anne (dec.), Elizabeth Margaret Rinker. M.D., U. Tex., Southwestern Med. Sch., 1947; M.S. in Pub. Health, U. N.C., 1953; Ph.D. in Ultrastructural Anatomy and Microbiology, Baylor U., 1969. Intern Duke Hosp., 1947-48, asst. resident pathology, 1951-53; intern Boston City Hosp., 1948-49; asst. pathologist Peter Bent Brigham Hosp., Boston, 1953-54; pathologist St. Anthony's Hosp., St. Petersburg, Fla., 1954-55; staff pathologist Children's Med. Center, Dallas, 1955-59; dir. labs. Baylor U. Med. Center, Dallas, 1959-86; chief dept. pathology Baylor U. Med. Center, 1959-86, vice chmn. exec. com. med. bd., 1970-72; cons. pathologist VA Hosp., Dallas, 1955-71; adj. prof. anthropology and biology So. Meth. U., Dallas, 1969; instr. pathology Duke, 1951-53, Harvard Med. Sch., 1953-54; asst. prof. pathology U. Tex. Southwestern Med. Sch., 1955-58, clin. assoc. prof., 1958-64, clin. prof., 1964-72, prof., 1973-94, prof. emeritus, 1994—, dir. Cancer Center, 1973-76, assoc. dean for continuing edn., 1973-94, emeritus assoc. dean, 1994—; pathologist-in-chief Baylor U. Med. Ctr., 1959-86, prof. biomed. studies Baylor Grad. sch., 1989-94; chmn. Baylor Rsch. Found., 1986-89; prof. microbiology Baylor Coll. Dentistry, 1962-68, prof. pathology, 1964-68, prof., chmn. dept. pathology 1969-73, dean A. Webb Roberts Continuing Edn., 1973-94; spl. advisor on human and animal diseases to gov. State of Tex., 1979-83. Editor: Laboratory Medicine (4 vols.), 1973, 10th edit., 1983; Contbr. articles to profl. jours., chpts. to textbooks. Pres., Tex. div. Am. Cancer Soc., 1970; chmn. Gov.'s Task Force on Higher Edn., 1981. Served with AUS, 1944-46; flight surgeon USAF, 1948-51, Korea. Decorated Air medal. Fellow Coll. Am. Pathologists, Am. Soc. Clin. Pathologists, AAAS; mem. AMA (chmn. multiple discipline research forum 1969), Am. Assn. Pathologists, Internat. Acad. Pathology, Am. Assn. Med. Colls., Explorer's Club (dir., v.p. 1993—), Sigma Xi. Home: 3429 Beverly Dr Dallas TX 75205-2928

RACE, JOHN STEPHEN, electronics manufacturing and technology executive; b. Evansville, Ind., Sept. 19, 1942; s. John Edward and Mary Rosetta (Doran) R.; m. Lisa Kame; children: Kimberly Anne, John Kevin, Erin Nichole. BS in Physics, Ind. U., 1964. Adminstr. quality improvement RCA, Bloomington, Ind., 1964-70, mgr. quality control, 1971-72; mgr. prodn. engring. and quality assurance RCA, Juanez, Mexico, 1972-74, mgr. mfg. and prodn. engring., 1975-76; mgr. mfg. technology RCA, Indpls., 1976-80; pres. Hirata Corp. of Am., Indpls., 1980—, also bd. dirs. Contbr. articles to profl. jours. Appointed to Ind. dist. export council, Indpls., 1982—, vice chmn. 1988—; subcom. chair Peace Games, Indpls., 1977—. Mem. Soc. Mfg. Engrs., Machine Vision Assn., Robotics Inst. Am., Midwest Bdminton Assn., U.S. Badminton Assn. (dir.), Sigma Pi Sigma. Home: 5122 Jensen Rd Martinsville IN 46151-8401 Office: Hirata Corp of Am 3901 Industrial Blvd Indianapolis IN 46254-2509*

RACHELEFSKY, GARY S., medical educator; b. N.Y.C., 1942. Intern Bellevue Hosp. Ctr., N.Y.C., 1967-68; resident in pediatrics Johns Hopkins Hosp., 1968-70, Ctr. Disease Control, 1970-72; fellow UCLA Med. Ctr., 1972-74; clin. prof., assoc. dir. A/I Tng. Program UCLA. Mem. Am. Acad. Allergy, Asthma and Immunology (bd. dirs., pres.-elect). Office: 11620 Wilshire Blvd Ste 200 Los Angeles CA 90025-1767

RACHIE, CYRUS, lawyer; b. Willmar, Minn., Sept. 5, 1908; s. Elias and Amanda (Lien) R.; m. Helen Evelyn Duncanson, Nov. 25, 1936; children: John Burton Rachie, Janice Carolyn MacKinnon, Elisabeth Dorthea Becker. Student, U. Minn., 1927-28; JD, George Washington U., 1932, William Mitchell Coll. Law, 1934. Bar: Minn. 1934, U.S. Supreme Ct. Atty. Minn. Hwy. Dept., 1934-43; spl. asst. atty. gen. Minn., 1946-50; counsel Luth. Brotherhood (fraternal life ins. co.), 1950-61; pvt. practice law Mpls., 1961-62; v.p., counsel Gamble-Skogmo, Inc., Mpls., 1962-64; v.p., gen. counsel Aid Assn. Lutherans, Appleton, Wis., 1964-70; sr. v.p., gen. counsel Aid Assn. Lutherans, 1970-73; with Rachie & Rachie, 1973-83; pvt. practice, 1983—. Councillor Nat. Luth. Coun., 1959-66, sec., 1962-64, mem. exec. com., 1965-66; United Luth. Ch. in Am. del. to 4th Assembly Luth. World Fedn., Helsinki, 1963; past pres. Luth. Welfare Soc. Minn.; past chmn. Mpls. Mayor's Coun. on Human Rels.; chmn. finance United Fund drive, 1967-68; past mem. bd. dirs. Mpls. YMCA; trustee emeritus William Mitchell Coll. Law Augsburg Coll. With USNR, 1943-46. Recipient Disting. Alumnus award William Mitchell Coll. Law, 1987. Mem. ABA Minn. Bar Assn., Am. Legion, Minn. Fraternal Congress (past pres.). Lutheran. Club: Rotarian. Home: 7500 York Ave S Apt 101 Minneapolis MN 55435-4736 *I always try to keep in mind that the Christian Cross consists of both vertical and horizontal lines. The vertical is the longest line and represents a direct line from all of us on the bottom to God on the top and we must commune with Him. The horizontal represents an encompassing line that takes in all of mankind. If my life activities do not include the implementation of both lines of the cross, I will not have a balanced and Christian life.*

RACHLEFF, OWEN SPENCER (OWEN SPENCER RACKLEFF), actor, author; b. N.Y.C., July 16, 1934; s. Harold Kirman and Theresa (Friedman) R. BFA, Columbia, 1956; MA, London U., 1959. Editor Harry N. Abrams, Inc., Am. Heritage Co.; asst. prof. humanities N.Y. U., 1962-74. Profl. actor (theater prodns.) Catsplay, 1978, The Lesson, 1978, Arms and the Man, 1980, Escoffier: King of Chefs, 1981-92, A New Way to Pay Old Debts, Enter Laughing, 1984, The Imaginary Invalid, 1985, The Jew of Malta, 1987, Sunday Promenade, 1989, Variations Without Fugue, 1992, Impropriety, 1995; (films) The Dain Curse, 1977, Question of Honor, 1981, Murder of Mary Phagan, 1988; (TV shows) The Bloodhound Gang, Ryan's Hope, All My Children; author: Rembrandt's Life of Christ, 1968, Young Israel, 1969, Great Bible Stories and Master Paintings, 1970, The Occult Conceit, 1971, Sky Diamonds, 1973, Secrets of Superstitions, 1976, Exploring the Bible, 1981, The Occult in Art, 1990; (plays) Javelin, 1966, Uncle Money, 1980, Escoffier: King of Chefs, 1982, Tosca '43, 1984, The Fabulous La Fontaine, 1990; (novels) Eric's Image, 1982, Enigma, 1988. MacDowell Colony fellow, 1970. Mem. Actors Equity Assn., Screen Actors Guild, AFTRA, Dramatists Guild. Home and Office: 135 E 71st St New York NY 10021-4258 *It's a lucky man who has a goal and is not sidetracked. Personally, I was fooled into looking for comfort and security while in my twenties. As a result, a dream I'd cherished of a life in the theatre grew dim; dim, but not extinguished. At age 42 I opted for myself and pursued the dream.*

RACHLIN, HARVEY BRANT, author, music company executive; b. Phila., June 23, 1951; s. Philip and Mazie (Drucker) R.; m. Marla Sivak Goldwert, June 28, 1987; 1 child, Glenn. BA in Biology, Hofstra U., Hempstead, N.Y., 1973. With music pub. cos., 1973—; owner Western Hemisphere Music Co., Ellipsis Music Mgmt. Co., Manhasset Hills, N.Y., 1975—, pres. 1982—; faculty Five Towns Coll., Seaford, N.Y., 1978-84. Author: The Songwriter's Handbook, 1977 (N.Y. Pub. Libr. Book for Teen Age 1979-82); The Encyclopedia of the Music Business, 1981 (Outstanding Reference Source, Libr. Jour., 1981, ASCAP-Deems Taylor award 1982); Love Grams, 1983; The Money Encyclopedia, 1984 (Outstanding Fin. Reference Book, Libr. Jour., 1984, Ency. Britannica Home Libr. selection); The Kennedys: A Chronological History 1823—, 1986; The Songwriter's and Musician's Guide to Making Great Demos, 1988 (N.Y. Pub. Libr. Book for Teen Age 1989); The Making of a Cop, 1991, The Songwriter's Workshop, 1991, The TV and Movie Business: An Encyclopedia of Careers, Technologies, and Practices, 1991, The Making of a Detective, 1995, Lucy's Bones, Sacred Stones, and Einstein's Brain, 1996; free-lance music journalist; contbr. Law and Order Mag., 1992—, Songwriter's Market 1979, 80, 87, 92; guest on The Dinah Shore Show, 1978, The Sally Jessy Raphael Show, 1993; compositions performed L.I. Mandolin and Guitar Orch., 1988. Recipient Outstanding Reference Book Yr. Am. Libr. Assn., 1981, Outstanding Reference Book Yr. Libr. Jour., 1984. Mem. ASCAP, Am. Guild Authors and Composers, L.I. Songwriters Workshop (bd. dirs.). Home: 878 Warner Rd Valley Stream NY 11580-1526

RACHLIN, LAUREN DAVID, lawyer; b. Buffalo, Feb. 6, 1929; s. Harry A. and Thelma (Goldberg) R.; m. Jean K. Rachlin, June 27, 1954; children: Laura Gail, Ellen Joan, James N. BS, U. Buffalo, 1948; JD, Harvard U., 1951. Bar: N.Y. 1952, U.S. Dist. Ct. (no. and we. dists.) N.Y. 1952, U.S. Supreme Ct. 1958, U.S. Ct. Appeals (2nd cir.) 1967, U.S. Tax Ct. 1952, U.S. Ct. Internat. Trade 1978. Ptnr. Rachlin & Rachlin, Buffalo, 1952-81; sr. ptnr. Kavinoky & Cook, Buffalo, 1981—; lectr. in inernat. law and trade; U.S. appointee to Bi-nat. Dispute Settlement Panel created under U.S.-Can. Free Trade Agreement, 1989-93; U.S. appointee N. Am. Free Trade Agreement Bi-Nat. Dispute Settlement Panel, 1994-96; arbitrator internat. C. of C. Am. Arbitration Assn. U.S. del. to UN Human Rights Commn., 1970; cons. to temporary commn. N.Y. State Constl. Conv.; mem. Erie County Charter Rev. Commn.; mem.-at-large U.S. Nat. Commn. for UNESCO, 1972-76, chmn. human rights task force; mem. industry functional adv. com. Customs for Trade Policy Matters of U.S. Dept. Commerce, Office U.S. Trade Rep., 1987—. Mem. ABA (fgn. investment in U.S. real estate com., internat. bus. law com., subcom. on trade import), N.Y. State Bar Assn. (founding chmn. internat. sect. 1987-89, chmn. internat. divsn. 1989-94), World Arbitration Inst. (adv. bd., bd. dirs.), Am. Assn. Exporters & Importers (various coms.), Internat. Law Assn., Am. Soc. Internat. Law, Internat. Bar Assn., U.S. Inst. Human Rights (adv. coun.), Customs and Internat. Trade Bar Assn., Erie County Bar Assn., Union Internationale des Advocats. Office: Kavinoky & Cook 120 Delaware Ave Buffalo NY 14202-2704

RACHLIN, STEPHEN LEONARD, psychiatrist; b. N.Y.C., Mar. 6, 1939; s. Murray and Sophie (Rodnitsky) R.; m. Florence Einsidler, Nov. 22, 1962; children: Michael Ira, Robert Alan. BA, NYU, 1959; MD, Albert Einstein Coll. Medicine, 1963. Diplomate Nat. Bd. Med. Examiners, Am. Bd. Forensic Psychiatry, Am. Bd. Psychiatry and Neurology with added qualifications in forensic psychiatry. Internship UCLA, 1963-64; resident, chief resident in psychiatry Mt. Sinai Hosp., N.Y., 1964-67; staff psychiatrist Bronx Psychiat. Ctr., Bronx, N.Y., 1969-72; asst. chief svc. Bronx Psychiat. Ctr., 1970-72, chief svc., 1972-74; dep. dir. Meyer-Manhattan Psychiat. Ctr., N.Y.C., 1974-76; acting dir. Meyer-Manhattan Psychiat. Ctr., 1976-77; dep. dir. Manhattan Psychiat. Ctr., N.Y.C., 1977; clin. dir. dept. psychiatry & psychology Nassau County Med. Ctr., E. Meadow, N.Y., 1978-80; assoc. chmn. dept. psychiatry & psychology Nassau County Med. Ctr., 1979-80, chmn. dept. psychiatry & psychology, 1980-94; assoc. prof. clin. psychiatry sch. medicine SUNY, Stony Brook, 1978-87, prof. clin. psychiatry, 1987-94; spl. prof. law Hofstra U., Hempstead, N.Y., 1983-95. Editor in chief Psychiat. Quar., 1990—; assoc. editor Bull. of the Am. Acad. os Psychiatry and the Law, 1989—; contbr. articles to profl. jours. Lt. comdr. USNR, 1967-69. Mem. Am. Psychiat. Assn. (chmn. com. adminstrv. psychiatry 1987-92, mem. assembly 1991-94, mem. com. confidentiality 1993—), N.Y. State Psychiat. Assn. (chmn. com. on pub. psychiatry 1986-94), Am. Assn. Psychiat. Adminstrs. (pres. 1989-90), Am. Acad. Psychiatry and Law (pres. tri-state chpt. 1988-90), Am. Assn. Gen. Hosp. Psychiatrists (pres. 1993-94), Am. Bd. Forensic Psychiatry (dir. 1990-94, treas. 1992-93), Am. Hosp. Assn. (gov. coun. sect. psychiat. and substance abuse 1991-92), Hosp. Assn. N.Y. State (chmn. mental health 1992, 93). Office: PO Box 117-h Scarsdale NY 10583

RACHOFSKY, DAVID J., lawyer; b. Oceanside, N.Y., Nov. 17, 1936; s. Lester M. and Marjorie A.; m. Faith Allen; children: Robert, Patricia, Edward. BSEE, MIT, 1958; JD, Temple U., 1968. Bar: Pa., U.S. Dist. Ct. (ea. dist.) Pa., U.S. Tax Ct., U.S. Ct. Fed. Claims, Pa. Supreme Ct. 1968. Ptnr. Dechert Price & Rhoads, Phila., 1968—; lectr. law Temple U. Law Sch., 1976—. Contbr. articles to profl. jours. With USAF, 1969-72. Mem. ABA, Phila. Bar Assn., Internat. Fiscal Assn. (chmn. mid-Atlantic region 198587, mem. coun. 1986-92, v.p., sec. 1992-96, exec. v.p. 1996—), Internat. Bus. Forum (tax sect. coun.). Office: Dechert Price & Rhoads 1717 Arch St Philadelphia PA 19103-2713

RACHOW, LOUIS A(UGUST), librarian; b. Shickley, Nebr., Jan. 21, 1927; s. John Louis and Mable (Dondlinger) R. B.S., York Coll., 1948; M.S. in L.S., Columbia U., 1959. Librarian York Coll., Nebr., 1949-54; instr. library asst. Queens Coll., N.Y.C., 1956-57; serials acquisition asst. Columbia U. Law Library, N.Y.C., 1957-58; asst. librarian Univ. Club, N.Y.C., 1958-62; librarian Hampden-Booth Theatre Library at the Players, N.Y.C., 1962-86, curator, 1986-88; library dir. Internat. Theatre Inst. U.S., N.Y.C., 1989—; cons. theatre sect. U. Calif., San Diego, new campuses program, 1964, Music Ctr. Operating Archives, Los Angeles, 1985; mem. library adv. bd. Eugene O'Neill Meml. Theatre Center, 1966—. Editor, compiler: Guide to Performing Arts, 1968; assoc. editor Am. Notes and Queries, 1971-74, asst. editor, 1967-71; mem. editorial adv. bd. Nat. Dir. for Performing Arts and Civic Ctrs.; editor Performing Arts series Gale Info. Guide, 1976-83, Theatre and Performing Arts Collections, 1981; contbr. articles and revs. to profl. jours. Mem. adv. bd. Am. Theatre Co., OKC Theatre Prodns. Served with AUS, 1954-56. Mem. Theatre Libr. Assn. (rec. sec. 1966-67, pres. 1967-72, 81-83, v.p. 1976-80, editor Broadside 1973-81), ALA, Spl. Librs. Assn. (sec.-treas. mus. group N.Y.C. chpt. 1964-66), N.Y. Libr. Club (pres. 1979-80), Am. Theatre Assn., New Drama Forum Assn. (pres. 1983-86), Am. Soc. Theatre Rsch., N.Y. Tech. Svcs. Librs., Archons of Colophon (convener 1982-83), Episcopal Actors Guild Am. (bd. dirs. 1976—), Broadway Theatre Inst. Outer Critics Cir., Players Club. Home: 528 W 114th St New York NY 10025-7841 Office: Internat Theatre Inst/US 47 Great Jones St New York NY 10012

RACHWALSKI, FRANK JOSEPH, JR., financial executive; b. Chgo., Mar. 26, 1945; s. Frank Joseph and Julia Alice (Cwikowski) R.; children: Mark, Karla, Brian. B.B.A., Loyola U., Chgo., 1967, M.B.A., 1969. Chartered fin. analyst. Systems analyst N. Am. Life/U.S. Life, Chgo., 1963-73; portfolio mgr. Kemper Fin., Chgo., 1973—; sr. v.p. Zurich Kemper Investments, Inc., Chgo., 1979—; v.p. Kemper Investors Life Ins. Co., Chgo., and subs. cos., Cash Equivalent Fund Inc., Chgo. Mem. Investment Analyst Soc. Chgo. Roman Catholic. Club: River Forest Country Club. Avocations: tennis, exercise, golf. Home: 380 S Kenilworth Ave Elmhurst IL 60126-3927 Office: Kemper Fin Services Inc 120 S La Salle St Fl 21 Chicago IL 60603-3402

RACICOT, MARC F., governor; b. Thompson Falls, Mont., July 24, 1948; s. William E. and Patricia E. (Bentley) R.; m. Theresa J. Barber, July 25, 1970; children: Ann, Timothy, Mary Catherine, Theresa, Joseph. BA, Carroll Coll., Helena, Mont., 1970; JD, U. Mont., 1973; postgrad., U. Va., 1973, Cornell U., 1977. Bar: Mont. 1973. With U.S. Army, 1973-76; advanced through grades to capt., 1973; legal assistance officer U.S. Army, Ft. Lewis, Wash., 1973; chief trial counsel U.S. Army, Kaiserslautern, Fed. Republic of Germany, 1975-76; resigned, 1976; dep. county atty. Missoula (Mont.) County, 1976-77; bur. chief County Prosecutor Svcs. Bur., Helena, Mont., 1977-89; asst. atty. gen. State of Mont., Helena, 1977-89; spl. prosecutor for the Atty. Gen.'s Office State of Mont., atty. gen., 1989-93, gov., 1993—. Founder Missoula Drug Treatment Program, 1977; active United Way, Helena; bd. visitors U. Mont. Sch. Law. Inducted into Basketball Hall of Fame Carroll Coll., 1982. Mem. Mont. Bar Assn., Carroll Coll. Century Club. Republican. Roman Catholic. Office: State Capitol RM 204 Helena MT 59620*

RACINE, RENE, academic administrator, astronomer; b. Quebec City, Can., Oct. 16, 1939; married; two children. BA, Laval U., 1958, BSc, 1963; MA, U. Toronto, 1965, PhD, 1967. Carnegie fellow Hale Obs., Calif., 1967-69; from asst. prof. to assoc. prof. astronomy U. Toronto, 1969-76; prof. U. Montreal, 1976—; dir. Can.-France-Haw Tel Corp., 1980-84, Observatory Astron., Mont Megantic, 1976-80, 84-90. Mem. Am. Astron. Soc., Can. Astron. Soc. (pres. 1974-76). Achievements include research in galactic structure, galaxies, open and globular clusters, optical instrumentation/telescopes. Office: U Montreal, 4734 PO Box 6128 Sta Ctr Ville, Montreal, PQ Canada H3C 3J7

RACITI, CHERIE, artist; b. Chgo., June 17, 1942; d. Russell J. and Jacque (Crimmins) R. Student, Memphis Coll. Art, 1963-65; B.A. in Art, San Francisco State U., 1968; M.F.A., Mills Coll., 1979. Assoc. prof. art San Francisco State U., 1984-89, prof., 1989—; lectr. Calif. State U., Hayward, 1974, San Francisco Art Inst., 1978; mem. artist com. San Francisco Art Inst., 1974-85, sec., 1980-81. One woman show U. Calif., Berkeley, 1972, Nicholas Wilder Gallery, Los Angeles, 1975, San Francisco Art Inst., 1977, Marianne Deson Gallery, Chgo., 1980, Site 375, San Francisco, 1989, Reese Bullen Gallery, Humboldt State U., Arcata, Calif., 1990; group shows include Whitney Mus. Art, 1975, San Francisco Sci. Fiction, The Clocktower, N.Y.C., Otis-Parsons Gallery, Los Angeles, 1984-85, San Francisco Art Inst., 1985, Artists Space, N.Y.C., 1988, Angles Gallery, Santa Monica, 1987, Terrain Gallery, San Francisco, 1992, Ctr. for the Arts, San Francisco, 1993. Bd. dirs. New Langton Arts, 1988-92. Eureka fellow Fleishhacker Found., San Francisco; recipient Adaline Kent award San Francisco Art Inst., 1976, Djerassi resident, 1994, Tyrone Guthrie Ctr. resident, Ireland, 1995. Office: San Francisco State U Art Dept 1600 Holloway Ave San Francisco CA 94132-1722

RACKLEFF, OWEN SPENCER See RACHLEFF, OWEN SPENCER

RACKOW, JULIAN PAUL, lawyer; b. Phila., Dec. 16, 1941; s. Lawrence Lionel and Blanche (Wachman) R.; m. Paulette Schorr, June 23, 1963; children: Jeffrey A., Andrea B. AB, Cornell U., 1963; JD, Harvard U., 1966. Bar: Pa. 1966, U.S. Dist. Ct. (ea. dist.) Pa. 1966. Assoc. atty. Goodis, Greenfield, Narin & Mann, Phila., 1966-69; ptnr., co-chmn. dept. real estate Blank, Rome, Comisky & McCauley, Phila., 1970—. Sec., mem. exec. com., bd. dirs. Ctrl. Phila. Devel. Corp., 1990—, pres. 1996-97. Mem. Pa. Bar Assn., Phila. Bar Assn., Harvard Law Sch. Assn. Phila. (v.p., exec. com. 1991—). Avocations: tennis, travel, piano. Office: Blank Rome Comisky & McCauley 4 Penn Center Plz Fl 1200 Philadelphia PA 19103-2512

RACLIN, ERNESTINE MORRIS, banker; b. South Bend, Ind., Oct. 25, 1927; d. Ernest M. and Ella L. Morris; m. O.C. Carmichael, Jr., Sept. 28, 1946; children: Carmen Carmichael Murphy, O.C., III, Ernestine Carmichael Nickle, Stanley Clark; m. Robert L. Raclin, July 22, 1977. Student, St. Mary's Coll., South Bend, 1947; LL.D. (hon.), U. Notre Dame, 1978, Ind. State U., 1981; L.H.D. (hon.), Converse Coll., 1974; D (hon.), Vincennes U., 1987, U. So. Ind., 1988; D in Tech. (hon.), Purdue U., 1992. Chmn. 1st Source Corp., 1976, South Bend, Ind.; Chmn. 1st Source Bank; former bd. dirs. First Chgo. Corp., First Nat. Bank Chgo.; bd. dirs. No. Ind. Pub. Service Co. Trustee U. Notre Dame, 1973—; bd. govs. United Way Am., 1973-80; adv. bd. Ind. U. South Bend; bd. dirs. Mich. Public Broadcasting, United Way of Ind.; bd. dirs., former chmn. Project Future, Ind. Acad. Bd. Regents; mem. nat. fin. com. George Bush for Pres., steering com., co-chair Ind. fin. com. Bush/Quayle, 1992. Recipient E.M. Morris Meml. award Ind. Acad., Community Service award St. Mary's Coll., Ivy Tech's Excellence in Edn. award, Edmund F. Ball award Ind. Pub. Broadcasting Soc., Castaldi award United Way Ind., Top Vol. award United Way Ind., 1987, Helping Hands award Hospice of St. Joseph County. Mem. St. Joseph County C. of C. South Bend (dir. 1977— , chmn.-elect 1986, Woman of Yr. award 1970, Disting. Bus. Leader award, 1993), Ind. State C. of C. (mem. edn. task force). Republican. Presbyterian. Clubs: Summit (South Bend); Ocean (Delray Beach, Fla.); Signal Point (Niles, Mich.), Audubon (Naples, Fla.), Collier's Res. Country (Naples). Office: 1st Source Corp PO Box 1602 South Bend IN 46634-1602

RACZKIEWICZ, PAUL EDWARD, hospital administrator; b. Lockport, N.Y., June 17, 1944; s. Edward Paul and Helen (Lentivech) R.; m. Rosemary Raczkiewicz, Jan. 16, 1973; children: Ann, Edward, Ellen. AA, Niagara County C.C., 1965; BS, SUNY, Brockport, 1968; Master in Hosp. and Health Care Adminstrn., St. Louis U., 1973. Dir. profl. svcs. Alton (Ill.) Meml. Hosp., 1973; v.p., corp. officer St. Elizabeth Hosp., Granite City, Ill., 1973-86; exec. v.p. St. Elizabeth Med. Ctr., Granite City, 1986—; pres., chief exec. officer St. Elizabeth Captive Med. Ins. Co.; v.p. Providence Mgmt. and Mktg. Svcs., Provide Med. Equipment Supply Co.; pres.-elect HAMSTL, Hosp. Industry Data Inst., bd. dirs. HIDI Ill. State rep. for HAMSTL; mem. adv. com., adv. bd. regional incinerator project Shared Resource Enterprises (HAMSTL). Past pres. bd. Tri-Cities Area United Way; mem. quality measurement tech. com. St. Louis Bus. Coalition. With U.S. Army, 1969-71. Fellow Am. Coll. Healthcare Execs.; Ill. Hosp. Assn. (past pres. region 4, cost containment coun., coun. institutional regulation), Assn. Ind. Hosps., Southwestern Ill. Indsl. Assn. (govt. affairs com.). Office: St Elizabeth Medical Ct 2100 Madison Ave Granite City IL 62040-4701

RADANDT, FRIEDHELM K., college president; b. Gross-Jestin, Germany, Oct. 23, 1932; came to U.S., 1960; married; 3 children. Diploma in Theology, Bapt. Theol. Sem., Germany, 1957; AM, U. Chgo., 1961, PhD in German, 1967. Instr. German Lake Forest Coll., 1961-64, assoc. prof., 1970-77, acting dean faculty, 1973-74, dean faculty, 1974-77; from instr. to asst. prof. U. Chgo., 1964-70; prof. humanities, v.p. acad. affairs Northwestern Coll., Iowa, from 1977, pres., 1979-85; pres. King's Coll., Briarcliff Manor, N.Y., 1985—. Author: Transitional Time in Keller's Zuricher Novellen, 1974, From Baroque to Storm and Stress, 1720-1775, 1977. Office: The King's Coll Office of Pres Briarcliff Manor NY 10510-9985

RADANOVICH, GEORGE P., congressman. BS in Agr. Bus. Mgmt., Calif. State Polytechnic U. Radanovich Wine, Mariposa, Calif., 1982—; County supr.; chair County Planning Commn.; mem. U.S. Ho. of Reps., 104th Congress, Washington, 1995—; mem. Budget Com., Resources Com., subcoms. Water & Power Resources, Nat. Parks, Forests & Lands. U.S. Ho. of Reps., 104th Congress, also mem. Resources Com. Task Force dealing with Endangered Species Act. Mem. Calif. Agrl. Leadership Program Class XXI, Rotary (Paul Harris Fellowship). Office: US House Reps 313 Cannon Washington DC 20515*

RADCLIFF, WILLIAM FRANKLIN, lawyer; b. Fredericksburg, Ind., May 21, 1922; s. Samuel Pearl and Hester Susan (Sherwood) R.; m. Elizabeth Louise Doeller Haines, May 15, 1982; children—Forrest Lee, Stephanie Anne; foster children—Cheryl Lynn, Sandra Lee, Richard Alan, Lezlie Laverne; stepchildren—Mark David, Laura Louise, Pamela Lynn, Veronica Leigh. B.A., Yale U., 1948; J.D., Ind. U., 1951. Bar: Ind. 1951. With DeFur, Voran, Hanley, Radcliff & Reed and predecessors, Muncie, Ind., 1951—, ptnr., 1954—; dir., mem. exec. com. Am. Nat. Bank and Trust Co., Muncie . Pres. Delaware County Mental Health Assn., 1962-63; founding mem. Ind. Mental Health Meml. Found., 1962, sec., 1962-84; bd. dirs. Delaware County Cancer Soc.; trustee Acad. Community Leadership. Served with AUS, 1940-46, PTO. Mem. ABA, Ind. Bar Assn., Muncie Bar Assn., Muncie-Delaware County C. of C. (pres. 1972-73). Clubs: Muncie Tennis and Country (bd. dirs., sec.), Muncie, Delaware Country (pres. 1972-73), Exchange (pres. 1962) (Muncie). Lodge: Masons. Home: 1809 N Winthrop Rd Muncie IN 47304-2532 Office: 201 E Jackson St Muncie IN 47305-2832 *Be yourself. Do not try to be someone else. Use your God given talents to the best of your ability and be content with the success that such effort brings.*

RADCLIFFE, GEORGE GROVE, retired life insurance company executive; b. Balt., Nov. 12, 1924; s. George G. and Elsie (Winter) R.; m. Bettie Howell, Feb. 10, 1951 (div.); 1 child, Cynthia; m. Kathleen Moore Smith, 1991. B.A., Johns Hopkins U., 1947; grad. Advanced Mgmt. Program., Harvard U. Grad. Sch. Bus. Adminstrn., 1962. With Balt. Life Ins. Co., 1947-89, v.p. treas., 1963-69, exec. v.p., 1969-72, pres., 1972-89, chief exec. officer, 1974-89, chmn. bd., 1980-89, pres., 1981-86, ret., 1989; dir., 1989—, EA Engring. Sci. and Tech., Inc. Chmn. bd. trustees Johns Hopkins U., 1984-90, trustee, 1975-93, trustee emeritus, 1993—. Mem. Johns Hopkins Club, Delta Upsilon. Methodist. Clubs: Maryland (Balt.), Tred Avon Yacht Club. Home and Office: PO Box 166 Oxford MD 21654-0166

RADCLIFFE, REDONIA WHEELER (DONNIE RADCLIFFE), journalist, author; b. Republican City, Nebr.; d. Donnel F. and Lois (Woolman) Wheeler; m. Robert C. Radcliffe, 1957; 1 son, M. Donnel Nunes. B.A., San Jose (Calif.) State U., 1951. Reporter, women's editor, county editor The Salinas Californian, 1951-59; free-lance writer Europe, 1959-66; reporter Washington Star, 1967-72; reporter, columnist Washington Post, 1972-95. Author: Simply Barbara Bush: A Portrait of America's Candid First Lady, 1989, Hillary Rodham Clinton: A First Lady for Our Time, 1993; contbr.: The Fall of a President, 1974, Guide to Washington, 1989. Address: 2795 Spout Ln Lusby MD 20657-2989

RADDING, ANDREW, lawyer; b. N.Y.C., Nov. 30, 1944; m. Bonnie A. Levinson, Oct. 7, 1972; children: Judith Lynne, Joshua David. BBA, CCNY-Baruch Sch., 1965; JD, Boston U., 1968. Bar: N.Y. 1968, Md. 1977, D.C. 1977, U.S. Supreme Ct. Grad. fellow Northwestern U. Sch. Law, 1968-69; asst. csl. U.S. Ho. of Reps. Select Com. on Crime, 1969-72; asst. U.S. atty. for Dist. Md., 1972-77; ptnr. Francomano, Radding & Mannes, Balt., 1977-80, Burke, Gerber, Wilen, Francomano & Radding, Balt., 1980-85, Blades & Rosenfeld P.A., Balt., 1985—; mem. adj. faculty clin. practice skills, criminal law, fed. criminal practice U. Balt. Sch. Law, 1980—; mem. trial experience com. U.S. Dist. ct., 1986-88; apptd. by gov. State Adminstrv. Bd. of Election Laws, 1995-96. Bd. dirs. Copper Hill Condominium, 1979-82, pres., 1981-82; subcom. Md. Republican Conv., 1981; sen. C.M. Mathias Jud. Selection com., 1986, chmn. U.S. Dist. Ct. Bicentennial Program, 1989-90. Mem. ABA, Md. Bar Assn., Balt. City Bar Assn. (jud. selection com. 1990-92, 94—), Fed. Bar Assn. (Balt. chpt. pres. 1986-87), Balt. City Bar Assn. (jud. selection com. 1990-92, 94—, chmn. 1996—, ethics com. 1991-92), U.S. Atty. Alumni Assn. Md. (pres. 1978—), Md. Inst. Continuing Profl. Edn. for Lawyers (bd. govs. 1987-92, inquiry panel atty. grievance com. 1991—), Am. Arbitration Assn. (arbitrator), U.S. Arbitration and Mediation (mediator). Republican. Jewish. Avocations: playing tennis, baseball. Office: Blades & Rosenfeld PA 20 S Charles St Baltimore MD 21201-3220

RADEBOLDT-DALY, KAREN ELAINE, medical nurse; b. Bklyn., Mar. 3, 1944; d. Harry Phillip and Lillian Florence (Renton) McAnaney; m. Richard William Radeboldt, Aug. 19, 1968 (dec. Aug. 1985); children: Karyn, Kellianne, Kimberly, Kristi-Jo, Richard; m. William J. Daly, Sr., Jan. 22, 1995. Lic. practical nurse, Wyckoff Heights Sch. Nursing, Bklyn., 1968; RN, Orange County C.C., Middletown, N.Y., 1990. LPN, N.Y., RN, N.Y.; cert. med.-surg. nurse, N.Y. Nurses aide, lic. practical nurse Wyckoff Heights Hosp., Bklyn., 1967-90; staff nurse, med.-surg. nurse Westchester Med. Ctr., Valhalla, N.Y., 1990—. Mem. Am. Jour. Nursing. Adventist. Avocations: reading, sewing, bowling, walking, motorcycle riding. Home: RD 1 Box 417 Daly Rd Middletown NY 10940 Office: Westchester Med Ctr Valhalla NY

RADECKI, TADEUSZ, computer and information science educator, researcher; b. Borawe, Poland, Jan. 15, 1950; came to U.S., 1984; s. Stanislaw and Helena (Sutnik) R. M.Sc. in Elec. Engring. Cybernetics, Tech. U. Wroclaw, 1973, Ph.D. in Computer Sci., 1978. Researcher, lectr. Tech. U. Wroclaw, 1973-78, asst. prof., 1978-80; vis. research fellow U. Sheffield, Eng., 1980-81; sr. vis. research fellow U. London, 1982-83; vis. assoc. prof. La. State U., Baton Rouge, 1984-85; vis. assoc. prof. U. Nebr., Lincoln, 1985-87, assoc. prof. computer sci., 1987—; vis. research fellow research and devel. dept. Brit. Library, 1979; sr. vis. research fellow Sci. and Engring. Research Council, Gt. Britain, 1981; vis. scientist U. Regina, Can., 1985; invited lectr. U.K., U.S., Can., Fed. Republic Germany, and Belgium. Contbr. articles to profl. jours.; Mem. editorial bd. Info. Processing & Mgmt. jour., 1984—, guest editor spl. issue, 1988; mem. editorial bd. Info. Tech. jour., 1981-85. Mem. Assn. for Computing Machinery, Am. Assn. Artificial Intelligence, Com. on Informetrics/Fédération Internationale de Documentation, EURO Working Group on Fuzzy Sets, Brit. Computer Soc. Info. Retrieval Specialist Group, Tau Beta Pi. Office: U Nebr Dept Computer Sci Engr Lincoln NE 68588

RADEKA, VELJKO, electronics engineer; b. Zagreb, Yugoslavia, Nov. 21, 1930; came to U.S., 1962; s. Milan and Neda Radeka; m. Jelena Horvat, May 17, 1958; children: Dejan, Dina. Diploma Engr., U. Zagreb, 1955, D. Engring. Scis., 1961. Scientist Inst. Ruder Boskovic, Zagreb, 1955-62, 64-66; scientist Brookhaven Nat. Lab., Upton, N.Y., 1962-64, 66-72; sr. scientist, head instrumentation div. Brookhaven Nat. Lab., 1972—. Contbr. in field. Fellow IEEE: mem Am. Phys. Soc., Nuclear and Plasma Physics Soc., Bellport Bay Yacht Club. Home: 29 Academy Ln Bellport NY 11713-2742 Office: Brookhaven Nat Lab Upton NY 11973

RADELL, NICHOLAS JOHN, management consultant; b. South Range, Mich., Sept. 2, 1930; s. Nicholas and Anna (Pekkala) R.; m. Jennifer L. Beemer, May 19, 1989; childrenfrom previous marriage: Susan Diane, Sally Anne, Nicholas Steven; stepchildren: Andrew Justin Beemer, Shana Kristen Beemer. B.S., U. Mich., 1952, M.B.A., 1956. C.P.A., Mich. registered profl. engr., Mich. Application engr. Square D Co., Detroit, 1954-55; mem. firm Touche, Ross, Bailey & Smart (C.P.A.'s), Detroit, 1956-61; with Cresap, McCormick & Paget Inc., Chgo., 1961-83, ptnr., 1967-69, v.p., dir., 1969-82, region mgr., 1971-82; v.p., dir. Cresap, a Towers Perrin Co., 1983-90; chmn. Towers Perrin Australia, 1989-90; v.p. Mercer Mgmt. Consulting, Chgo., 1991-95. Contbg. author: Handbook of Process Planning and Estimating, 1962, Scientific Inventory Management, 1963, Introduction to Manufacturing Management, 1969, Managing Radical Change, 1995. Bd. dirs. Chgo. Conv. and Tourism Bur., 1983, U. Mich. Alumni Assn., 1989. 1st lt. USAF, 1952-54. Fellow Inst. Prodn. Engrs. U.K. (hon.); mem. Soc. Mfg. Engrs. (bd. dirs., nat. v.p. 1971, pres. 1973), Am. Assn. Engring. Socs. (chmn. 1984), Inst. Indsl. Engrs., Chgo. Club, Mid-Day Club, Met. Club, Phi Gamma Delta. Presbyterian. Home: 1230 Sunset Rd Winnetka IL 60093-3628

RADEMACHER, RICHARD JOSEPH, librarian; b. Kaukauna, Wis., Aug. 20, 1937; s. Joseph Benjamin and Anna (Wyuts) R.; m. Mary Jane Liethen, Feb. 12, 1966; children: Alicia Mary, Ann Marie, Amy Rose. A.B., Ripon Coll., 1959; M.S., Library Sch. U. Wis., 1961. Dir. Kaukauna Public Library, 1964-66, Eau Claire (Wis.) Public Library, 1966-69; librarian Salt Lake City Public Library, 1969-76; dir. Wichita (Kans.) Public Library, 1976—. Bd. dirs. Salt Lake Art Center, Reading Room for the Blind.; mem. Kans. Com. for the Humanities, 1977-82; mem. exec. bd. Wichita Girl Scouts, 1977—. Served with AUS, 1962-64. Mem. ALA; Mem. Mountain Plains Library Assn. (sect. chmn.); mem. Kans. Library Assn. (pres. 1982-83); Mem. Wichita Library Assn. Office: Wichita Pub Libr 223 S Main St Wichita KS 67202-3715

RADEMAKER, STEPHEN GEOFFREY, lawyer; b. Balt., July 18, 1959; s. Thomas Joseph and Ruth Virginia (Wentz) R.; m. Danielle Pletka; 1 child, Andrew. BA with Highest Distinction, U. Va., 1981, JD, 1984, MA in Fgn. Affairs, 1985. Bar: Va. 1984, D.C. 1985. Assoc. Covington & Burling, Washington, 1984-86; law clk. to Hon. James L. Buckley U.S. Ct. Appeals (D.C. cir.), Washington, 1986; counsel to vice chmn. U.S. Internat. Trade Commn., Washington, 1986-87; spl. asst. to asst. sec. for Inter-Am. affairs Dept. State, Washington, 1987-89; assoc. counsel to Pres. of U.S. and dep. legal advisor to NSC, Washington, 1989-92; gen. counsel Peace Corps, Washington, 1992-93; Rep. chief counsel Com. Fgn. Affairs U.S. Ho. of Reps., Washington, 1993-95, chief counsel Com. Internat. Rels., 1995—. Recipient Raven award U. Va.,1984; S. Philip Heiner scholar U. Va., 1983. Mem. Va. Bar Assn., D.C. Bar Assn., Coun. Fgn. Rels., Phi Beta Kappa, Omicron Delta Kappa. Republican. Lutheran. Avocations: skiing, cycling, scuba diving. Office: US House Reps 2170 Rayburn St Com Internat Rels Washington DC 20515

RADEN, LOUIS, tape and label corporation executive; b. Detroit, June 17, 1929; s. Harry M. and Joan (Morris) R.; m. Mary K. Knowlton, June 18, 1949; children: Louis III, Pamela (Mrs. T.W. Rea III), Jacqueline. BA, Trinity Coll., 1951; postgrad. NYU, 1952. With Time, Inc., 1951-52; with Quaker Chem. Corp., 1952-63, sales mgr., 1957-63; exec. v.p. Gen. Tape & Supply, Inc., Detroit, 1963-68, pres., chmn. bd., 1969—; pres. Mich. Gun Clubs, 1973-77. Fifth reunion chmn. Trinity Coll., 1956, pres. Mich. alumni, 1965-72, sec. Class of 1951, 81-86, pres. 1986-91, The McCook Fellow Soc.; trustee, v.p. Mich. Diocese Episcopal Ch., 1980-82, mem. urban evaluation com., 1975-78, chmn. urban evaluation com., 1978, chmn. urban affairs com., 1977-79; vice chmn., bd. dirs. Robert H. Whitaker Sch. Theology, 1983-85; vice chmn. Mich. Diocese Econ. Justice Commn., 1989—, bd. dirs. Poverty and Social Reform Inst., 1992—; founding sponsor World Golf Hall of Fame; mem. Founders Soc. Detroit Inst. Arts; trustee Mich. Housing Trust Fund, 1993—. Recipient Person of Yr. award Mich. Diocese Econ. Justice Commn., 1994; inductee Hall of Fame Robert H. Whitaker Sch. Theology, 1996. Mem. NRA (life), Nat. Skeet Shooting Assn. (life, nat. dir. 1977-79, 5 Man Team World Champion award 1977, pres. coun.), Mich. Skeet Assn. (all state team 1975-80, inductee Hall of Fame 1994), Greater Detroit Bd. Commerce, Automotive Industry Action Group, Mich. C. of C., U.S. C. of C., Greater Hartford Jaycees (exec. v.p. 1955-57, Key Man award 1957), Theta Xi (life, Disting. Service award 1957, alumni pres. 1952-57, regional dir. 1954-57). Republican. Clubs: Detroit Golf, Detroit Gun (bd. dirs., 1996—), Katke-Cousins Golf, Midland Country, Black Hawk Indians, Pinehurst Country; Oakland U. Pres.'s, Round Table, Detroit Sportsmen's Congress. Home: 1133 Ivyglen Cir Bloomfield Hills MI 48304-1236 Office: Gen Tape & Supply Inc 7451 W 8 Mile Rd Detroit MI 48221-1262

RADER, CHARLES GEORGE, chemical company executive; b. Niagara Falls, N.Y., Apr. 9, 1946; s. Carl Franklin and Eileen (Adler) R.; m. Sheila Ann Dunlop, Oct. 30, 1971; children: Carla Beth, Kevin Alexander. B-SChemE, Rensselaer Polytech. Inst., 1968; MS, U. Rochester, 1970; PhD, SUNY, Buffalo, 1974. Sr. research engr. Occidental Chem. Corp., Grand Island, N.Y., 1974-77, group leader, 1977-78; tech. mgr. Occidental Chem. Corp., Niagara Falls, N.Y., 1978-81; tech. dir. Occidental Chem. Corp., Grand Island, 1981-84, dir. tech., 1984—; now v.p., tech. & develop.; v.p. D.S. Ventures, Dallas, 1987—; bd. dirs. TreaTek, Grand Island. Patentee in field; contbr. articles to profl. jours. Industrial adv. bd. dept. chem. enring. SUNY, Buffalo. Mem. Am. Inst. Chem. Engrs., Am. Chem. Soc. (Jacob F. Schoellkopf Medal, 1995), Electrochem. Soc., Regional Tech. Strategy Com., Niagara Frontier Assn. Research and Devel. Dirs., Tau Beta Pi, Phi Lambda Upsilon, Sigma Xi, Delta Tau Delta. Office: Occidental Chem Corp Tech Ctr 2801 Long Rd Grand Island NY 14072-1244*

RADER, DIANE CECILE, lawyer; b. San Francisco, Sept. 8, 1949; d. Dale A. and Genevieve A. (Couture) R. BA, Portland State U., 1987; JD, Lewis and Clark Coll., 1990. Bar: Oreg. 1990, Idaho 1992, U.S. Dist. Ct. Idaho, U.S. Dist. Ct. Oreg. Founder, cons. D.C. Rader & Assocs., Portland, 1972-88; real estate broker Rader Realty, Portland, 1982—; pvt. practice law Boise, 1992—; with Rader and Rader, Ontario, Oreg., 1990—; bd. dirs. Criminal Justice Adv. Bd., Malheur County, Oreg. Asst. mng. editor: Internat. Legal Perspectives, 1989-90. Polit. cons. and fundraiser various parties and campaigns, Oreg., 1972-88; fundraiser, cons. charitable orgns., Oreg., 1972—, others. Mem. ABA, ATLA, Nat. Assn. Criminal Def. Lawyers, Oreg. Trial Lawyers Assn., Oreg. Criminal Def. Lawyers Assn., Oreg. State Bar (pub. svc. and info. com. 1994-97, chmn. pub. rels. subcom. 1994—), Phi Alpha Delta. Avocations: piano, writing, arts, outdoor sports, travel. Office: Rader & Rader 381 W Idaho Ontario OR 97914

RADER, DOTSON CARLYLE, author, journalist; b. Minn., July 25, 1941; s. Paul Carlyle and Lois (Schacht) R. Student, Columbia, 1962-68. Editor Defiance: A Radical Rev. (Warner Communications, Inc.), 1969-71; contbg. editor Evergreen Rev., 1969-73, Esquire, N.Y.C., 1973-77, N.Y. mag., 1977-80; cons. Nat. Com. for Lit. Arts at Lincoln Center, N.Y.C., 1980—; Mem. sponsoring bd. New Politics, 1972—; host Free Time Show, WNET-TV, N.Y.C., 1972-73. Author: I Ain't Marchin' Anymore!, 1969, Government Inspected Meat and Other Fun Summer Things, 1971, Blood Dues, 1973, Tennessee: Cry of the Heart; An Intimate Memoir of Tennessee Williams, 1985; screenplay The Bronze Lily, 1974, The Dream's on Me: A Love Story, 1976, Miracle, 1978; novel Beau Monde, 1981; play (with Mike Miller) Shattered Glass, 1990; contbg. editor Parade Mag., 1984—. Mem. Student Peace Union, 1961-63, Students for a Democratic Soc., 1964-69, War Resisters League, 1970—; pres. Humanitas, Columbia, 1963-67; vice chmn. Peoples Coalition for Peace and Justice, 1972. Named hon. ambassador State of W. Va., 1982; recipient award for nat. journalism Odyssey Inst., 1982, Spl. Olympics award for nat. journalism Joseph P. Kennedy Found., 1985. Mem. PEN, Overseas Press Club, The Dramatists Guild.

RADER, LOUIS T., corporation executive, educator; b. Frank, Can., Aug. 24, 1911; came to U.S., 1934, naturalized, 1940; s. Italo and Louise (Bonamico) R.; m. Constance Wayland, Sept. 10, 1938; children—Louis Albert, John Newton. B.S., U. B.C., 1933; Ph.D. in Elec. Engring, Calif. Inst. Tech., 1938. Engr. Gen. Electric Co., 1937-45; prof., head dept. elec. engring. Ill. Inst. Tech., 1945-47; with Gen. Electric Co., 1947-59, gen. mgr. splty. control div., 1951-59; v.p., dir. ITT, N.Y.C., 1959-61; group v.p. U.S. Commercial, 1961—; pres. Univac div. Sperry Rand Corp., N.Y.C., 1962-64; v.p., gen. mgr. Indsl. Process Control div. Gen. Electric Co., N.Y.C., 1964-69; prof. elec. engring. U. Va., 1969-82, prof. emeritus, 1982—, prof., Grad. Sch. Bus., 1969-82; vis. com. div. engring. and applied sci. Calif. Inst. Tech., 1968-75. Recipient Alumni distinguished service award Calif. Inst. Tech., 1966; Va. Engring. Found. award, 1982. Fellow IEEE; mem. Am. Soc. Engring. Edn., Nat. Acad. Engring., Sigma Xi, Tau Beta Pi, Beta Gamma Sigma, Eta Kappa Nu, Omicron Delta Kappa. Home: PO Box 1721 Waynesboro VA 22980 Office: U Va Darden Grad Sch Bus PO Box 6550 Charlottesville VA 22906-6550

RADER, PATRICK NEIL, accountant; b. Oak Ridge, Tenn., May 16, 1952; s. Daniel Hurley Jr. and Mary Lou (Arms) R.; m. Deborah Lynn Bryant, Dec. 20, 1975 (div. May 1978); 1 child, Andrew Neil; m. Caroline Elizabeth Snow, Dec. 30, 1983; children: Laura Ashley, Mary Beth, Patrick Samuel. BSBA with high honors, U. Tenn., 1974, MBA, 1986. CPA, Tenn.; CFP. Fin. officer Union Carbide Corp., Oak Ridge, 1975-79, fin. mgr., 1979-84; capital acctg. mgr. Martin Marietta Corp., Oak Ridge, 1984-86, materials mgr., 1986-90, bus. mgr., 1990—; tech. advisor software devel. Co-author: (user's manual) Subcontract Guidelines, 1986. Mem. AICPA, Inst. CFP. Baptist. Avocations: boating, antique collecting.

RADER, PAUL ALEXANDER, minister, administrator; b. N.Y.C., Mar. 4, 1934; s. Lyell M. and Gladys Mina (Damon) R.; m. Kay Fuller, May 29, 1956; children: Edith Jeanne, James Paul, Jennifer Kay. BA, Asbury Coll., Wilmore, Ky., 1956; BD, Asbury Theol. Sem., 1959; LLD (hon.), Asbury Coll., Wilmore, Ky., 1984; ThM, So. Bapt. Theol. Sem., Louisville, 1961; D Missiology, Fuller Theol. Sem., 1973. Ordained to ministry Salvation Army, 1961. Tng. prin. The Salvation Army, Seoul, 1973-74, edn. sec., 1974-77, chief sec., 1979-83; tng. prin. The Salvation Army, Suffern, N.Y., 1983-86; divisional comdr. for Ea. Pa. and Del. The Salvation Army, Phila., 1986-88; chief sec. ea. ter. The Salvation Army, N.Y.C., 1988; territorial comdr. U.S.A. western ter. The Salvation Army, Rancho Palos Verdes, Calif., 1989—; adj. prof. Seoul Theol. Sem., 1980-82; trustee Asian Ctr. for Theol. Studies and Mission, 1980-83, Asbury Coll., 1988—; pres. The Salvation Army Calif. Corp., Rancho Palos Verdes, 1989—. Recipient Alumnus A award Asbury Coll., 1982, Disting. Alumni award Asbury Theol. Sem., 1989; Paul Harris fellow Rotary Internat., 1989. Mem. Am. Soc. Missiology, Internat. Assn. Mission Studies. Office: The Salvation Army 639 Sabrina Way Vista CA 92084-6264

RADER, PAUL MACFARLAND, healthcare administrator; b. Mpls., Feb. 12, 1939; s. Paul Carlyle and Lois Pauline (Schacht) R.; m. Linda Emmy Frances Tschaepe, Dec. 19, 1981; 1 child, James E. Bayles. BA, U. Minn., 1973, MHA, 1975; cert., Am. Grad. Sch. Instl. Mgmt., Phoenix, 1985; PhD, Knightsbridge U., Copenhagen, 1993. Dir. mktg. Reality, Inc., Alexandria, Va., 1962-71; assoc. dir. U. Minn. Hosps., Mpls., 1973-76; sr. cons. James Hamilton Assocs., Mpls., 1976-79; v.p. Roseville (Calif.) Community Hosp., 1979-81; exec. v.p. Whittaker Saudi Arabia, Ltd., Khamis Mushayt, Saudi Arabia, 1981-83; ops. dir. Commonwealth Health Ctr. Project, Saipan, Mariana Islands, 1983-85; exec. dir. Chinese Hosp., San Francisco, 1986-89; chief exec. officer Woodland Pk. Hosp., Portland, Oreg., 1989-91; sr. v.p. Healthcare Enterprise Internat., Washington, 1991-95; pres. Internat. Healthcare Devel. Group Ltd., Warsaw, Poland, 1995—; exec. cons. World Bank/USAID, Washington, 1985. Mem. Chinese Am. Citizens' Alliance, San Francisco, 1986-90, Rep. Inner Circle, Washington, 1985, Chinatown Social Agcy. Consortium, San Francisco, 1986-89. Recipient Merit awd. Trust Territory/Pacific, Saipan, Mariana Islands, 1984. Fellow Am. Coll. Healthcare Execs.; mem. Am. Hosp. Assn., Am. Heart Assn., Soc. for Healthcare Planning, Healthcare Execs. of N. Calif., West Bay Hosp. Conf. (trustee 1987-88), Oreg. Assn. Hosps. Avocations: travel, reading, writing. Home: 1 Canyon Dr Alexandria VA 22305 Office: Internat Healthcare Devel Group Ltd, ul Kaniowska 110, 01-529 Warsaw Poland

RADER, RALPH TERRANCE, lawyer; b. Clarksburg, W.Va., Dec. 5, 1947; s. Ralph Coolidge and Jeanne (Cover) R.; m. Rebecca Jo Vorderman, Mar. 22, 1969; children: Melissa Michelle, Allison Suzanne. BSME, Va. Poly. Inst., 1970; JD, Am. U., Washington, 1974. Bar: Va. 1975, U.S. Ct. Customs and Patent Appeals 1977, U.S. Dist. Ct. (ea. dist.) Mich. 1978, Mich. 1979, U.S. Ct. Appeals (6th cir.) 1979, U.S. Dist. Ct. (we. dist.) Mich. 1981, U.S. Ct. Appeals (fed. cir.) 1983. Supervisory patent examiner U.S. Patent Office, Washington, 1970-77; patent atty., ptnr. Cullen, Sloman, Cantor, Grauer, Scott & Rutherford, Detroit, 1977-88; ptnr., Dykema, Gossett, 1989-96; ptnr. Rader, Fishman & Grauer, 1996—. Contbr. articles to profl. jours. Mem. adminstrv. bd. First United Methodist Ch., Birmingham, Mich., 1980—. With U.S. Army, 1970-76. Recipient Superior Performance award U.S. Patent Office, Washington, 1971-77. Mem. Am. Patent Law Assn., ABA, Mich. Patent Law Assn., Mich. Bar. (mem. governing council patent trademark and copyright law sect. 1981-84), Engring. Soc. Detroit, Masons, Tau Beta Pi, Pi Tau Sigma, Phi Kappa Phi. Methodist. Home: 4713 Riverchase Dr Troy MI 48098-4186 Office: Rader Fishman & Grauer 1533 N Woodward Ave Ste 140 Bloomfield Hills MI 48304-2820

RADER, RANDALL RAY, federal judge; b. 1949. BA magna cum laude, 1974; JD with honors, George Washington U., 1978. Bar: D.C., U.S. Ct. Appeals (fed. cir.) 1990, U.S. Claims Ct., U.S. Supreme Ct. Legis. asst. to Congresswoman Virginia Smith U.S. Ho. of Reps., 1975-78; mem. staff Ways and Means Com. U.S. Ho. Reps., 1978-81; chief counsel subcom. on Constn. U.S. Senate Judiciary Com., chief counsel, staff dir. subcom. on patents, copyrights and trademarks, 1981-87; counsel to Senator Orrin Hatch, 1981-87; judge U.S. Ct. Claims, Washington, 1988-90, U.S. Ct. Appeals (fed. cir.), Washington, 1990—; lectr. patent law U. Va. Sch. Law, trial advocacy George Washington U. Nat. Law Ctr. Contbr. articles to prof. jours.; co-editor: Criminal Justice Reform, 1983. Mem. Fed. Bar Assn. Office: US Ct Appeals Fed Cir 717 Madison Pl NW Ste 913 Washington DC 20439-0001

RADER, ROBERT MICHAEL, lawyer; b. Camden, N.J., Sept. 9, 1946; s. Raymond Cornelius and Martha Lou (Freas) R.; m. Eileen Charnesky, June 5, 1976; children: Brennan Matthew, Ashley Marie. BA cum laude, Lafayette Coll., 1968; JD, Cornell U., 1971. Bar: N.J. 1972, D.C. 1977. Law sec. to chief judge U.S. Dist. Ct. N.J., Newark, 1971-73; trial atty. U.S. Justice Dept., Washington, 1973-78; assoc. Conner & Wetterhahn P.C., Washington, 1978-79, ptnr., 1980—. Contbr. articles to profl. jours. Ward chmn. Falls Church Rep. com., Va., 1980-86. Mem. Phi Beta Kappa. Roman Catholic. Club: River Bend Country (Great Falls, Va.). Home: 812 Hickory Vale Ln Great Falls VA 22066-2810 Office: Winston & Strawn 1400 L St NW Washington DC 20005-3509*

RADER, TINA LOUISE, pathology technologist; b. Allentown, Pa., Apr. 9, 1959; d. Marlin Robert and Gioconda Maria (Alpago) R. BS in Med. Tech., Bloomsburg U., 1981; M Health Sci., Quinnipiac Coll., 1987. Med. technologist Lehigh Valley Hosp. Ctr., Allentown, Pa., 1981-84, Brigham & Womens Hosp., Boston, 1984-85; pathologists' asst. Dartmouth-Hitchcock Med. Ctr., Lebanon, N.H., 1987-89, New Eng. Med. Ctr., Boston, 1989-91, R.I. Hosp., Providence, 1991-94, Fox Chase Cancer Ctr., Phila., 1994—. Fellow Am. Assn. Pathologists' Assts. (edn. com. chairperson 1990—). Avocations: horseback riding, needlework, reading. Office: Fox Chase Cancer Ctr Dept Pathology 7701 Burholme Ave Philadelphia PA 19111-2412

RADEST, HOWARD BERNARD, clergyman, educator; b. N.Y.C., June 29, 1928; s. Louis and Gussie (Permison) R.; m. Rita Stollman, Dec. 22, 1951; children: Robert, Michael. A.B., Columbia U., 1949, Ph.D., 1971; M.A. (Hillman fellow 1950), New Sch. Social Research, 1951. Dir. youth activities N.Y. Soc. Ethical Culture, 1955-56; leader Ethical Culture Soc. Bergen County, Teaneck, N.J., 1956-64, Ethical Culture Movement, 1956—; mem. Coun. Ethical Leaders, 1958—; exec. dir. Am. Ethical Union, N.Y.C., 1964-70; asso. prof. philosophy Ramapo Coll., N.J., 1971-73; prof. Ramapo Coll., 1973-79; dir. Ethical Culture Schs., 1979-91; adj. prof. philosophy U. S.C., Beaufort, 1991—; co-chmn., sec. gen. Internat. Humanist and Ethical Union, 1970-86, bd. trustees, 1986—; assoc. Am. Civilization Seminar Columbia U., chmn. moral edn. seminar, 1983-91; adv. bd. NBC, 1988-94; dir. Camp Elliott, Jeffersonville, N.Y., 1963, 64; dean Humanist Inst., 1982-92; dean emeritus; cons. state based programs NEH, Beaufort Meml. Hosp., 1994—, Hilton Head Hosp., 1994—; mem. assessment com. Vols. in Medicine, 1994—. Author: Understanding Ethical Religion, 1958, On Life and Meaning, 1963, Toward Common Ground, 1969, To Seek a Humane World, 1971, Can We Teach Ethics, 1989, The Devil and Secular Humanism, 1990, Community Service Encounter with Strangers, 1992, Humanism with a Human Face, 1996; also articles; editor: Ramapo Papers, 1976-79, International Humanism; edtl. bd. Religious Humanism, Free Inquiry, The

Humanist. Mem. bd. Encampment for Citizenship, 1963-71, Mental Health Assn. Bergen County, Bergen Co. Mental Health Bd., 1964-67, Assn. Moral Edn., 1986-94; mem. bd. past treas., v.p. N.J. Welfare Conf., 1958-64; mem. bd., past pres. Health and Welfare Coun. Bergen County, 1956-64; bd. mgrs. Bergen Pines County Hosp., 1966-70; Bergen County (N.J.) Mem. Democratic Com., 1970-71. Served with AUS, 1953-55. Mem. AAUP (treas. N.J. coun. 1973-74), Com. Sane Nuclear Policy (sponsor N.J.), Am. Assn. UN, Am. Philos. Assn., Soc. Advancement Am. Philosophy, N.Am. Com. Humanism (trustee 1985—), S.C. Philos. Assn., Grad. Faculties Alumni Columbia U. (trustee 1989-91), Network Progressive Educators (steering com. 1988-91), Phi Beta Kappa. Home: 108 Devil's Elbow Ln Hilton Head Island SC 29926

RADEWAGEN, FRED, publisher, organization executive; b. Louisville, Mar. 20, 1944; s. Hobart Fred and Mildred Lillian (Carlsen) R.; m. Amata Catherine Coleman, Dec. 4, 1971; children—Erika Catherine, Mark Peter, Kirsten Alexandra. B.A., Northwestern U., 1966; M.S., Georgetown U., 1968. Rsch. asst. Republican Nat. Com., Washington, 1967-68; dir. mgmt. services Republican Presdl. Campaign and Inaugural Com., Washington, 1968-69; liaison officer Trust Terr. Washington, 1969-71; staff coordinator for territorial affairs Dept. Interior, Washington, 1971-75; assoc. dir. govtl. and polit. participation programs C. of C. U.S., 1975-76, dir., 1976-79; dir. resource devel. Rep. Govs. Assn., Washington, 1979-81; dir. state and fed. relations Rep. Govs. Assn., 1981-82; Washington rep. Gov. of Am. Samoa, 1982-85, 89-93; pub. Washington Pacific Report, 1982—; dir. Pacific Islands Washington office, 1984—; rep. Cook Islands, Washington, 1986-89; pres. Washington and Pacific Assocs., 1975-84; staff exec. Bus. Alliance for Congl. Action, 1974-77; lectr. Insts. for Orgn. Mgmt., 1977-79; exec. dir. Nat. Chamber Alliance for Politics, 1977-79; mem. U.S. del. UN Trusteeship Coun., 1972, advisor U.S. del. to Com. of Twenty-Four, 1982-83; mem. Am. Samoa dels. to South Pacific Conf., 1982-83, 89, 91, Post-Forum Dialogue, 1991, UN Conf. on Environment and Devel., 1992; del. Am. Coun. Young Polit. Leaders, 1982-83, mem. coun., 1984—; exec. dir. U.S.- New Zealand Coun., 1995. Mem. Alexandria Rep. City Com., 1979-80; del. Va. Rep. State Conv., 1981, 89, 93, 94; participant Rep. Nat. Convs., 1968, 80, 84, 88, 92; past mem. Christian edn. com. Westminster Presbyn. Ch. Mem. Northwestern U. Alumni Assn. (past Washington bd. govs.), Washington Roundtable for Asian/Pacific Press, Nat. Capital Interfrat. Forum (past pres.), Nat. Eagle Scout Assn. (life), Mensa, Delta Tau Delta (past pres. Washington alumni). Clubs: Ill. State Soc. (past v.p.), Capitol Hill (life), Circumnavigators. Home: 103 E Luray Ave Alexandria VA 22301-2027 also: 1245 N Taft Ave Berkeley IL 60163-1043 also: 1019 3rd St Rehoboth Beach DE 19971-1503 Office: PO Box 26142 Alexandria VA 22313-6142

RADFORD, LINDA ROBERTSON, psychologist; b. Winnipeg, Man., Can., Nov. 6, 1944; came to U.S., 1954; d. William and Edith Aileen (Wheatley) Robertson; 1 child, Drew Richard; m. Richard D. Polley, Sept. 21, 1991. BA, Seattle Pacific U., 1970; MEd, U. Wash., 1972, PhD, 1980. Lic. psychologist, Fla.; cert. clin. hypnotherapist. Dir. support svcs. Highline-West Seattle Mental Health Clinic, 1973-75; rsch. asst. in human affairs Battelle, Seattle, 1976-80, rsch. scientist, 1982-87; sr. cons. Martin Simmonds Assoc., Seattle, 1980-82; pres., owner R.R. Assocs., Seattle and Miami, 1982—; pres. PGI Inc., Miami and London, 1989—; pvt. clin. psychologist Bay Harbor Island, Fla., 1991—, West Palm Beach, Fla., 1991—; chmn., chief exec. officer Swiver Corp., North Miami, Fla., 1994—; chair Swiver Corp., 1994—; vis. sr. assoc. Joint Ctr. for Environ. and Urban Problems, North Miami, Fla., 1986-88; cons. Health Ministry Govt. Thailand, Bangkok, 1989—. Contbr. articles to profl. jours. Community Mental Health Ctr fellow, Seattle, 1972-73. Mem. Am. Psychol. Assn., Am. Soc. Clin. Hypnosis, N.Y. Acad. of Sci. Avocations: tennis, music, snorkeling, racquetball, fishing. Home: 9264 Bay Dr Surfside FL 33154-3026 Office: 1160 Kane Concourse Ste 401 Bal Harbour FL 33154-2020 also Office: Ste 680 1645 Palm Beach Lakes Blvd West Palm Beach FL 33409

RADICE, ANNE-IMELDA, museum director; b. Buffalo, Feb. 29, 1948; d. Lawrence and Anne (Marino) R. AB, Wheaton Coll., 1969; MA, Villa SchiFanoia, Florence, Italy, 1971; PhD, U. N.C., 1976; MBA, Am. U., 1984. Asst. curator Nat. Gallery of Art, Washington, 1972-76; archtl. historian U.S. Capitol, Washington, 1976-80, curator Office of Architect, 1980-85; dir. Nat. Mus. Women in the Arts, 1985-89; chief div. of creative arts USIA, 1989-91; sr. dep. chmn. Nat. Endowment for Arts, Washington, 1991-92; acting chmn., 1992-93; exec. v.p. Gray & Co. II, Miami, Fla., 1993; prodr. World Affairs TV Prodn., 1994; assoc. producer Think Tank, 1994; chief spl. projects, confidential adviser Courtney Sale Ross, 1994-96; v.p., COO ICL Internat., 1996—; cons. in pub. rels. and TV, 1994—. Contbr. articles to profl. jours.

RADICE, SHIRLEY ROSALIND, education educator; b. Newark, June 2, 1935; d. Gerald Alexander and Pauline Deborah (Baitz) Deitz; m. Richard Charles Radice, Dec. 17, 1955; children: Carol, Richard Neil. BA, Kean Coll., Union, N.J., 1960, MA, 1963; EdD, Rutgers U., 1985. Tchr. Edison (N.J.) Bd. Edn., 1960-64, 70—, trainer, 1990—; instr. grad. sch. edn. Rutgers U., 1992—; mem. grant com. N.J. Dept. Higher Edn., 1988-90; lectr. Rutgers U., 1989—, instr. in edn., 1992—; staff devel. specialist Edison, 1994—; ednl. cons. in field; presenter Rutgers U. Ann. Reading Conf., 1996. Contbr. articles to profl. jours. Recipient N.J. Gov.'s Recognition award for outstanding contbn. to edn., 1991; grantee Ford Found., 1966, State of N.J., 1973, NSF/Smithsonian Inst., 1995. Mem. AAUP, ASCD, Nat. Assn. Sci. Tchrs., N.J. Sci. Tchrs. Assn., Nat. Assn. Math. Tchrs., Nat. Tchrs. Assn. (del. 1980-87), N.J. Tchrs. Assn., Edison Tchrs. Assn. (co-chmn. legis. com. 1975-76), Kappa Delta Phi. Avocations: gardening, piano.

RADIGAN, FRANK XAVIER, pharmaceutical company executive; b. Paterson, N.J., Apr. 13, 1933; s. John Joseph and Susan Clair (Brett) R.; m. Julia Lou Smith, Aug. 27, 1960 (div. Nov. 1988); children: Francis Gregory, Patricia Louise, Brett Frasier; m. Carol E. Berkley, June 26, 1992; children: Dana, Trici. AB in Sociology, Seton Hall U., 1955; MBA Mktg., U. Hartford, 1968. Asst. mgr. Beneficial Fin. Co., Newark, 1955-57; hosp. rep. Becton-Dickinson Co., Rutherford, N.J., 1957-58; dist. mgr. Merck Sharp & Dohme, West Point, Pa., 1958—. Chmn. St. John the Baptist Social Justice, New Freedom, Pa., 1981-85; mem. Passaic County Dem. Com., 1985-86. Capt. USAR, 1956. Mem. Am. Mktg. Assn., Md. Pharmacists Assn. (chmn. indsl. rels. com.), W.Va. Pharm. Soc., Balt. Pharm. Assn. (hon. pres. 1989), Hopewell Fish and Game Assn., Bon Air Country Club, Elk, Lion (pres. Glen Rock 1975-76, 86-88). Roman Catholic. Avocation: horsebreeding. Home and Office: 2440 Bradenbaugh Rd White Hall MD 21161-9661

RADIGAN, JOSEPH RICHARD, human resources executive; b. N.Y.C., Apr. 9, 1939; s. Joseph Anthony and Mae Cecilia (Holden) R.; m. Margaret Mary Krug, Apr. 23, 1962; children—Kateri, Laureen, Kenneth. BA, Fordham Coll., 1961; MA, Fordham U., 1962; grad. advanced mgmt. program, Harvard U., 1982; grad., Air War Coll., 1982, Navy War Coll., 1989. Mgr. employee relations Gen. Electric Co., N.Y.C., 1965-79; cons. orgn. planning Gen. Electric Co., Fairfield, Conn., 1981-83; dir. orgn. and mgmt. Kennecott Co., Stamford, Conn., 1979-81; sr. v.p. human resources Donaldson, Lufkin & Jenrette Inc., N.Y.C., 1983-86, The Equitable, N.Y.C., 1986-90; sr. v.p., gen. mgr. Manchester Co., N.Y.C., 1991-92; pres. Cove Communications, 1991-92; sr. v.p. human resource Blue Cross/Blue Shield Ga., 1993—. Mem. Cardinal's Com. of Laity. 1st lt. U.S. Army, 1962-65, col. USAR. Mem. Wall Street Pers. Mgrs. Assn. (sec. 1984-85), Knights of Malta. Republican. Roman Catholic. Home: 6 Cardinal Ln Westport CT 06880-1714

RADIN, ALEX, former association executive, consultant; b. Chattanooga, June 14, 1921; s. Joseph and Mollie (Pernat) R.; m. Sara Leah Gordon, Sept. 6, 1943 (dec. Nov. 20, 1964); children—Jay Jacob, William Gordon m. Carol Nita Schuman, Sept. 21, 1979. B.A., U. Chattanooga, 1948. Reporter Chattanooga Times, Chattanooga, 1938-42; adminstrv. asst. Office of Price Adminstrn., Washington, 1942-43; adminstrv. analyst Dept. of State, Washington, 1945-48; asst. to gen. mgr. Am. Pub. Power Assn., Washington, 1948-51, exec. dir., 1951-86; pres. Radin & Assocs. Inc., 1986—; cons. U.S. Senate Com. on Interior and Insular Affairs, Washington, 1959; mem. exec. com. Am. Nuclear Energy Coun., Washington, 1973-88; v.p. Consumer Fedn. Am., Washington, 1978-86; mem. So. States Energy Bd.'s Adv. Com. on TVA, 1986-87; chmn. Monitored Retrievable Storage Rev. Commn., 1988-89; rep., sec. U.S. Dept. Energy, Independent Mgmt. and Fin. Rev. of Yucca Mt. (Nev.) Project, 1994-95; mem. adv. bd. Ford Found. Energy Policy Project, 1973-74. Columnist, Pub. Power Mag.; contbr. articles to newspapers and mags. Mem. adv. bd. Dance Theatre of Harlem, N.Y.C., 1985—. Recipient Leland Olds award Western States Water and Power Consumers Conf., 1970, Philip Hart Disting. Consumer Svc. award Consumer Fedn. Am., 1985, Alex Radin Disting. Svc. award Am. Pub. Power Assn., 1986. Democrat. Jewish. Club: Nat. Press. Avocations: photography; music; art; hiking. Home: 2510 Virginia Ave NW Apt 610N Washington DC 20037-1904 Office: Radin & Assocs Inc 1200 New Hampshire Ave NW Washington DC 20036-6802

RADIN, NORMAN SAMUEL, retired biochemistry educator; b. N.Y.C., July 20, 1920; s. Joseph and Bertha (Sherson) R.; m. Norma Levinson, Dec. 23, 1947; children: Lon, Laurie. B.A., Columbia U., 1941, Ph.D., 1949. Asst. research chemist Nat. Def. Research Com., Carnegie Inst. Tech., 1942-45; research chemist Biochem. Inst., U. Tex., Austin, 1950-52; prin. scientist Hines Hosp., VA, Maywood, Ill., 1952-54, VA Research Hosp., Chgo., 1954-57; mem. faculty dept. biochemistry Northwestern U. Med. Sch., Chgo., 1952-60; assoc. prof. Northwestern U. Med. Sch., 1957-60; research scientist Mental Health Research Inst., U. Mich., 1960-91, prof. biol. chemistry, 1973-84, prof. neurochemistry, 1984-91; prof. emeritus in neurochemistry, 1992—. Editor book in field. NIH fellow, 1946-48; AEC fellow, 1949-50. Mem. Am. Soc. Biol. Chemists, Am. Soc. Neurochemistry, Internat. Soc. Neurochemistry. *In reviewing how best I might help humanity, I came to the conclusion that the greatest human need is higher intelligence. This feature is the characteristic which reflects the major product of the evolutionary process. Evolution has brought man to a point so high that he can destroy civilization, but not high enough to realize the foolishness of so many efforts. The best hope for higher intelligence seems to me to lie in neurochemical research. This analysis led me to devote my life to neurochemistry.*

RADKE, BEVERLY IDA, elementary education educator; b. Sutherland, Iowa, May 17, 1945; d. Henry John and Eleonora Ella (Koehlmoos) Jalas; m. Lee Allen Radke, Aug. 12, 1971. BA, Buena Vista Coll., 1967. Cert. elem. edn. tchr. Kindergarten tchr. Cherokee (Iowa) Schs., 1967—. Mem. NEA, Iowa State Edn. Assn., Cherokee Edn. Assn. (pres., sec. 1988-90), Alpha Delta Kappa (chaplain). Lutheran. Avocations: playing piano and organ, fishing, gardening. Home: 5353 120th St Holstein IA 51025 Office: Cherokee Schs 515 W Cedar PO Box 801 Cherokee IA 51012

RADKE, JAN RODGER, pulmonologist, hospital program administrator; b. Detroit, Nov. 16, 1942; s. Edward V. and Dorothy M. Radke; m. Judith Hogan, June 20, 1987; children: Jennifer, John, Colin, Cameron. BS, Mich. State U., 1965; MD, U. Wis., 1969. Diplomate Am. Bd. Internal Medicine, Am. Bd. Pulmonary. Intern Henry Food Hosp., 1969-70, resident internal medicine, 1970-71, resident, 1974-75, chief med. resident internal medicine, 1975-76, fellow pulmonary/critical care, 1977-78; v.p. satellite program Henry Ford Health Systems, Detroit, 1989; assoc. v.p. ambulatory program, assoc. prof. medicine Loyola U. Med. Ctr., Maywood, Ill., 1990-93, v.p. health care svcs., 1993-96; pres., CEO Univ. Care Plus, 1996—; exec. dir. MSRDP and ambulatory care U. Tex. Med. Sch. and Hermann Hosp., Houston, 1996—. Lt. comdr. USNR, 1971-73. Fellow ACP, Am. Coll. Chest Physicians; mem. Am. Thoracic Soc., Am. Coll. Physician Execs. Avocation: bird watching. Office: U Tex-Houston Med Sch 6431 Fannin Houston TX 77030

RADKE, RODNEY OWEN, agricultural research executive, consultant, research biologist; b. Ripon, Wis., Feb. 5, 1942; s. Edward Ludwig and Vera Ione (Phillips) R.; m. Jean Marie Rutsch, Sept. 1, 1963; children: Cheryl Lynn, Lisa Diane, Daniel E. BS, U. Wis., 1963, MS, 1965, PhD, 1967. Cert. environ. insp. Rsch. sci. Monsanto Agrl. Co., St. Louis, 1969-75, sr. research group leader, 1975-79, research mgr. 1979-81, mgr. research, 1981-93; pvt. practice cons., 1993—. Contbr. articles to profl. jours. Served to capt. U.S. Army, 1967-69. Mem. Weed Sci. Soc. North Ctrl. Weed Sci. Soc. Lutheran. Club: First Capitol Soccer (coach 1981-92) (St. Charles). Avocations: power boating; soccer; gardening; woodshop. Home and Office: 1119 Grand Prix Dr Saint Charles MO 63303-6313

RADLER, FRANKLIN DAVID, publishing holding company executive; b. Montreal, Que., Can., June 3, 1942; m. Rona Lassner, Mar. 26, 1972; children: Melanie, Melissa. MBA, Queen's U., Can., 1967. Pres., chief oper. officer, dir. Hollinger Inc., Toronto; exec. v.p. Argus Corp. Ltd., Toronto; chmn. Am. Pub. Co., Jerusalem Post Ltd., Palestine Post Ltd. Office: Hollinger Inc, 1827 W 5th Ave, Vancouver, BC Canada V6J 1P5 also: Hollinger Inc, 10 Toronto St, Toronto, ON Canada M5C 2B7*

RADLEY, VIRGINIA LOUISE, humanities educator; b. Marion, N.Y., Aug. 12, 1927; d. Howard James and Lula (Ferris) R. B.A., Russell Sage Coll., 1949, L.H.D., 1981; M.A., U. Rochester, 1952; M.S., Syracuse U., 1957, Ph.D., 1958. Instr. English Chatham (Va.) Hall, 1952-55; asst. dean students, asst. prof. English Goucher Coll., 1957-59; dean freshmen, asst. prof. English Russell Sage Coll., 1959-60, assoc. dean, assoc. prof. English, 1960-61, prof. chmn. dept., 1961-69; dean coll., prof. English Nazareth Coll., Rochester, N.Y., 1969-73; provost for undergrad. edn., central adminstrn. SUNY, Albany, 1973-74; exec. v.p., provost Coll. Arts and Scis., SUNY, Oswego, 1974-76; acting pres. Coll. Arts and Scis., SUNY, 1976-78; pres. SUNY, Oswego, 1978-88; prof. English and Humanities SUNY, 1988-93; scholar-in-residence Russell Sage Coll., 1993—; vis. prof. Syracuse U., summer 1957-59, Nazareth Coll., summer 1965; cons. N.Y. State Dept. Edn.; chmn. commn. on women Am. Coun. on Edn., 1978-81, sr. assoc. Office of Women, 1990—; trustee Marymount Manhattan Coll., 1988-90; mem. commn. on higher edn. Middle States Assn., 1979-86; disting vis. prof. Russell Sage Coll., 1994-95. Author: Samuel Taylor Coleridge, 1966, Elizabeth Barrett Browning, 1972, also articles. Mem. MLA (chmn. regional sect. Romanticism 1969), English Inst., Pi Lambda Theta. Republican. Home: 75 Plank Rd Poestenkill NY 12140-1706

RADLOFF, ROBERT ALBERT, real estate executive; b. Chgo., Mar. 30, 1947; s. Henry O. and Virginia G. (Grothus) R.; m. Ann Macy Beha, June 21, 1975; children: Macy, Allison. BS in Fin., Boston U., 1969. V.p. Kuras & Co., Inc., Boston, 1971-76; sr. v.p. Boston Co. Real Estate Counsel, Inc., 1976-81, pres., 1981-89, chmn., 1989-91; real estate investments counselor Boston, 1991—; bd. dirs. Boston Pvt. Bank and Trust Co. Bd. dirs. First Night, Boston, 1990, Mass. Cultural Coun., 1992, Friends of Vieilles Maison Francais, 1992; trustee Isabella Stewart Gardner Mus., 1995; overseer Children's Hosp., WGBH Ednl. Found. Mem. Am. Soc. Real Estate Counselors (cert.), Somerset Club. Avocations: art, tennis, travel. Office: 33 Kingston St Boston MA 02111-2208

RADLOFF, WILLIAM HAMILTON, editor, writer; b. Milw., Mar. 5, 1914; s. Alfred Carl and Florence (Hamilton) R.; m. Mary Ellen Borgman, Nov. 10, 1940; children: Thomas M., Susan M. BA, Ripon Coll., 1936. Reporter, writer Milw. Sentinel, 1937-42; reporter, writer Milw. Jour., 1946-49, asst. city editor, 1949-60, asst. feature editor, 1960-61, feature editor, 1961-69; asst. story editor 20th Century Fox Film Corp., L.A., 1969-72; freelance writer, poet L.A., 1972—. Author, editor numerous news and feature articles. Lt. U.S. Army, Counter Intelligence, 1942-46, PTO. Recipient Letter of Commendation, Japanese Occupation. Home: 313 S Anita Ave Los Angeles CA 90049-3805

RADMER, MICHAEL JOHN, lawyer, educator; b. Wisconsin Rapids, Wis., Apr. 28, 1945; s. Donald Richard and Thelma Loretta (Donahue) R.; children from previous marriage: Christina Nicole, Ryan Michael; m. Laurie J. Anshus, Dec. 22, 1983; 1 child, Michael John. B.S., Northwestern U., Evanston, Ill., 1967; J.D., Harvard U., 1970. Bar: Minn. 1970. Assoc. Dorsey & Whitney, Mpls., 1970-75, ptnr., 1976—; lectr. law Hamline U. Law Sch., St. Paul, 1981-84; gen. counsel, rep., sec. 150 federally registered investment cos., Mpls. and St. Paul, 1977—. Contbr. articles to legal jours. Active legal work Hennepin County Legal Advice Clinic, Mpls., 1971—. Mem. ABA, Minn. Bar Assn., Hennepin County Bar Assn. Club: Mpls. Athletic. Home: 4329 E Lake Harriet Pky Minneapolis MN 55409-1725 Office: Dorsey & Whitney Pillsbury Ctr S 220 S 6th St Minneapolis MN 55402-4502 *A key to a successful and happy life is achieving a balance. Intellectual, academic and vocational goals are important, but their pursuit should be balanced with ample time spent with family and friends, travel and enjoying reading, music, art and sports. Don't be afraid to try something new; realize that education should be a lifelong pursuit. Much frustration can be avoided by realizing that life is full of trade-offs. You can't experience the joy of raising children and have the complete freedom of the child-free. Finally, while you should strive for perfection, be content with less. We are only human, and live in an imperfect, yet wonderful, world.*

RADNAY, PAUL ANDREW, physician; b. Szolnok, Hungary, Aug. 6, 1913; came to U.S., 1949, naturalized, 1954; s. Ferenc and Ida (Varsa) R.; m. Eva Balazs, Aug. 6, 1939. MD, U. Szeged, 1937. Diplomate Hungarian Bd. Surgery, Hungarian Bd. Dentistry, Am. Bd. Anesthesiology. Intern Univ. Clinics, Budapest and Szeged, Hungary, 1936-37; chief head and neck surgery outpatient dept. Orszagos Tarsadalom Biztosito Intezet, Budapest, 1945-49; asst. prof. Polyclinic Hosp., Budapest, 1945-49; resident in anesthesiology Queens Gen. Hosp., Jamaica, N.Y., 1953-54; dir. anesthesia sect. cardio-thoracic surgery Montefiore Hosp., Med. Ctr., Bronx, N.Y., 1970-79; cons. Montefiore Hosp., Med. Ctr., Bronx, 1979-83, emeritus attending anesthesiologist, 1983-95; prof. anesthesiology Albert Einstein Coll. Medicine, Bronx, 1981-83, prof. emeritus, 1983-95; prof. respiratory therapy program Manattee Community Coll., Bradenton, Fla. Editor: Anesthetic Considerations for Pediatric Cardiac Surgery, 1980, 2 English, 1 Spanish edits.; contbr. articles to profl. lit. Pres. Am.-Hungarian Med. Assn., 1966-67; vice chmn. bd. dirs. Am.-Hungarian Found., 1974-90; bd. dirs. Sarasota Opera Assn. Capt. M.C., Hungarian Army, intrmittantly, 1934-45. Decorated Cross Knighthood Order St. Martin, Austria; decorated Cross St. John of Jerusalem, Knights of Malta; recipient Disting. Svc. award Am. Hungarian Found., 1978, Incentive N.Y. County Med. Soc., 1983; recipient Goldzieher award Am.-Hungarian Med. Assn., 1976, also Disting. Svc. award. Fellow Am. Coll. Anesthesiologists, N.Y. Acad. Medicine, N.Y. Cardiological Soc., Internat. Coll. Surgeons; mem. Am. Soc. Anesthesiologists, N.Y. State Soc. Anesthesiologists, N.Y. County Med. Soc., N.Y. State Med. Soc., Soc. Cardiovascular Anesthesiologists, Hungarian Soc. Anesthesialogists and Intensive Therapists (hon.). Home: Sarasota Fla. *A good physician has humility. He must give the patient consideration first as a human being, and secondly as a patient who requires treatment. One must never see the sick only as a source of financial reward. In academic life one should be a clinician, a teacher and a researcher. The contribution which appears to be insignificant may one day become the base of a major discovery. Deceased.*

RADNER, ROY, economist, educator, researcher; b. Chgo., June 29, 1927; s. Samuel and Ella (Kulansky) R.; m. Virginia L. Honoski, July 26, 1949 (dec. Apr. 1976); children: Hilary A., Erica H. (dec.), Amy E., Ephraim L.; m. Charlotte Virginia Kuh, Jan. 22, 1978. PhB with honors, U. Chgo, 1945, BS in Math., 1950, MS in Math., 1951, PhD in Math. Stats., 1956. Rsch. asst. Cowles Commn. for Rsch. in Econs. U. Chgo., 1951, rsch. assoc., 1951-54, asst. prof., 1954-55; mem. Cowles Found. for Rsch. in Econs. Yale U., New Haven, 1955-57, asst. prof. econs., 1955-57; assoc. prof. econs. and stats. U. Calif., Berkeley, 1957-61, prof. econs. and stats., 1961-79, chmn. dept. econs., 1966-69; Taussig prof. econs. Harvard U., Cambridge, Mass., 1977-78, vis. prof. Kennedy Sch. Govt., 1978-79; mem. tech. staff AT&T Bell Labs, Murray Hill, N.J., 1979-84, disting. mem. tech. staff, 1985-95; rsch. prof. econs. NYU, N.Y.C., 1983-95, prof. econs. and info. sys., 1995—; mem. com. on fundamental rsch. relevant to edn. NRC-NAS, 1976-77, mem. commn. on human resources, 1976-79; mem. assembly of behavioral and social scis. NRC, 1979-82, mem. com. on risk and decision making, 1980-81, mem. working group on basic rsch. in behavioral and social scis., 1985-86; mem. panel on contingent valuation methology NOAA, U.S. Dept. Commerce, 1992-93; mem. steering com. Enjeux et Procedures de Decentralization Commisariat du Plan, Paris, 1992—; active Com. on Prevention of Nuclear War, also various other profl. coms., bds., panels. Author: (books, monographs) Notes on Theory of Economic Planning, 1963, (with D. Jorgenson and J.J. McCall) Optimal Replacement Policy, 1967, (with J. Marshack) Economic Theory of Teams, 1972, (with L.S. Miller) Demand and Supply in U.S. Higher Education, 1975, (with C.V. Kuh) Mathematicians in Academia, 1980; also articles on econ. theory, orgn. theory, econs. of edn.; co-editor: Decision and Organization, 1972, Education as an Industry, 1976, Information, Incentives and Economic Mechanisms, 1987, Perspectives on Deterrence, 1989, Bargaining with Incomplete Information, 1992; assoc. editor Mgmt. Sci., 1959-70, Econometrica, 1961-68, Jour. Econ. Theory, 1968—, Am. Econ. Rev., 1970-82, Games and Econ. Behavior, Econ. Theory, Econ. Design, Rev. Acctg. Studies. 2d lt. U.S. Army, 1945-48, PTO. William Cook scholar U. Chgo., 1944-45; fellow Ctr. Advanced Study in Behavioral Scis., Stanford, Calif., 1955-56, Guggenheim Found. fellow, 1961-62, 65-66, overseas fellow Churchill Coll., Cambridge U., Eng., 1969-70, 89. Fellow AAAS (disting. fellow), Econometric Soc. (v.p. 1970-72, pres. 1972-73), Am. Acad. Arts and Scis., Am. Econ. Assn. (disting. fellow); mem. NAS (chair econ. sect. 1994—), Inst. Math. Stats. Avocations: music, backpacking, cross-country skiing. Home: 3203 Davenport St Washington DC 20008 Office: Stern Sch Business NYU MEC 9-68 44 W 4th St New York NY 10012-1126

RADNER, SIDNEY HOLLIS, retired rug company executive; b. Holyoke, Mass., Dec. 8, 1919; s. William I. Radner; m. Helen Jane Cohen, Dec. 12, 1946; children: William Marc, Richard Scott. Student, Yale U., 1941. Ret. pres. Am. Rug Co., Holyoke; lectr., cons., investigator on crooked gambling, U.S. Armed Forces, FBI, Govt. of Can., state and mcpl. police squads; dir. Houdini Magical Hall of Fame, Niagara Falls, Ont., Can.; dir., organizer Annual Ofcl. Houdini Seance. Author: Radner on Poker, Radner on Dice, Radner on Roulette and Casino Games, How to Detect Card Sharks; contbr. articles to profl. jours.; appeared in First TVseries Turn of A Card, 1953, BBC Omnibus: Houdini, 1971, CNN, 1993, 94, Tonight Show, 1956, Today Show, Merv Griffin Show, CNBC, PBS, CBC, In Search Of..., First TV series exposing crooked gambling techniques, 1956; cons. to Houdini TV spl. A&E. Past pres. Holyoke C. of C.; co-founder Volleyball Hall of Fame; past bd. dirs. Greater Springfield (Mass.) Better Bus. Bur.; hon. curator, dir. Houdini Hist. Ctr., Appleton, Wis. Served with criminal investigation divsn. U S. Army, 1942-46. Mem. Soc. Am. Magicians (occult investigation com.), Internat. Brotherhood Magicians, Magic Circle London (mem. Inner Magic Circle), Magicians Guild (charter), Magic Collector's Assn. (charter, Honor award 1992), Am. Platform Assn., Houdini Club Wis. (hon.), Nat. Assn. Bunco Investigators, China-Burma-India Vets. Assn. (life), Rotary, Masons, Shriners. Jewish. Home: 1050 Northampton St Holyoke MA 01040-1321 Office: 1594 Dwight St Holyoke MA 01040-2356

RADNOFSKY, BARBARA A., lawyer, mediator/arbitrator; b. Broomall, Pa., July 8, 1956; m. Daniel Edward Supkis Jr.; children: Danielle Esther, Max David, Michaela Sarah. BA magna cum laude, U. Houston, 1976; JD with honors, U. Tex., 1979. Bar: Tex. Assoc. Vinson & Elkins, L.L.P., Houston, 1979-87, ptnr., 1987—; mem. faculty intensive trial advocacy programs U. Tex. Sch. Law, Internat. Acad. Trial Lawyers; spkr. in field; mediator/arbitrator in field; mem. Disting. Panel of Neutrals of Ctr. for Pub. Resources. Contbr. articles to profl. jours. Albert Jones scholar U. Tex. Sch. Law; named Outstanding Young Lawyer Houston, Houston Young Lawyers Assn., 1988-89. Mem. ABA (chmn. Nat. Trial Competition 1983), Tex. Young Lawyers Assn. (Outstanding Young Lawyer Tex. 1988-89), Nat. Health Lawyers Assn. Avocations: sailing, ballet, modern dance, basketball. Office: Vinson & Elkins 3300 First City Tower 1001 Fannin St Houston TX 77002

RADNOR, ALAN T., lawyer; b. Cleve., Mar. 10, 1946; s. Robert Clark and Rose (Chester) R.; m. Carol Sue Hirsch, June 22, 1969; children: Melanie, Joshua, Joanna. B.A., Kenyon Coll., 1967; M.S. in Anatomy, Ohio State U., 1969, J.D., 1972. Bar: Ohio 1972. Ptnr., Vorys, Sater, Seymour & Pease, Columbus, Ohio, 1972—; adj. prof. law Ohio State U., Columbus, 1979—. Contbr. articles to profl. jours. Bd. dirs., trustee Congregation Tifereth Israel, Columbus, 1975—, 1st v.p., 1983-85, pres., 1985-87; trustee Columbus Mus. Art, 1995. Named Boss of Yr., Columbus Assn. Legal Secs., 1983. Mem. ABA, Ohio State Bar Assn., Columbus Bar Assn. (chmn. dr.-lawyer com. 1979-80), Columbus Def. Assn. (pres. 1980-81), Def. Research Inst., Internat. Assn. Def. Counsel, Ohio Hosp. Assn. Democrat. Jewish. Avocations: reading; sculpture. Home: 400 S Columbia Ave Columbus OH 43209-1629 Office: Vorys Sater Seymour & Pease 52 E Gay St PO Box 1008 Columbus OH 43216-1008

RADOCK, MICHAEL, foundation executive; b. Belle Vernon, Pa., July 17, 1917; s. Nicholas M. and Pauline (Radich) R.; m. Helen Adelaide Hower, Sept. 2, 1944; children: Robert Hower, William Michael. AB magna cum laude, Westminster Coll., New Wilmington, Pa., 1942, LittD (hon.), 1965; MS in Journalism, Northwestern U., 1946; postgrad., Case Western Res. U., 1950-52. Reporter Fayette City (Pa.) Jour., 1937-39; corr. for Pa. newspapers, 1937-39; reporter, sports editor Charleroi (Pa.) Daily Mail, 1942; dir. news bur., asst. prof. journalism Westminster Coll., 1942-45; dir. pub. relations, prof. journalism Kent (Ohio) State U., 1945-53; with corp. pub. relations Ford Motor Co., Dearborn, Mich., 1953-61; established Inst. for Pub. Rels. Kent (Ohio) State U., 1947; v.p. univ. relations, prof. journalism U. Mich., Ann Arbor, 1961-81; sr. v.p. devel. and univ. relations, prof. journalism U. So. Calif., Los Angeles, 1981-82; v.p. resource devel. Aspen Inst. Humanistic Studies, N.Y.C., 1982-83; advisor to pres. C.S. Mott Found., Flint, Mich., 1983-90, cons., 1990—; mem. faculty Harvard U. Inst. in Ednl. Mgmt., 1972, 73, Williamsburg Devel. Inst., 1979-81; vis. prof. journalism U. Wyo., Laramie, 1952, U. Kent, Canterbury, Eng., 1989; trustee Westminster Coll., 1972-82; mem. adv. bd. Pub. Rels. News; cons. NSF, 1972-73; mem. adv. bd. Chronicle of Non-Profit Enterprise, 1990—. Contbr. Handbook of Institutional Advancement, 1977, (books) Lesly's Public Relations Handbook, 1978, Public Relations Career Directory, 1987, 88, 89, 93, 95, Lesly's Handbook of Public Relations and Communications, 1990. Mem. Fulbright Bd. Fgn. Scholarships, Washington, 1972-74; mem. exec. bd. U. Mich., 1979-81, mem. bd. in control of intracollegiate athletics, 1961-81; trustee Glacier Hills Retirement Ctr., Ann Arbor, 1988-93, Ann Arbor Area Cmty. Found., 1989-92, Mich. Hist. Ctr. Found., 1990—; chmn. White House Sci. and Tech. Adv. Com. on Black Colls., Washington, 1986-88. Recipient Disting. Service award Kent State U., 1965, Frank Ashmore award for disting. service to edn. Am. Coll. Pub. Relations Assn., 1968-69; Disting. Service award for leadership in institutional advancement for minority colls. and univs., 1980. Fellow Pub. Rels. Soc. Am. (accredited); mem. Inst. for Pub. Rels. Rsch. and Edn. (bd. trustees 1980-84), Soc. of Profl. Journalists, Nat. Soc. Fund Raising Execs., Higher Edn. Roundtable. Republican. Presbyterian. Home: 851 Green Hills Dr Ann Arbor MI 48105-2719

RADOFF, LEONARD IRVING, librarian, consultant; b. Houston, Jan. 9, 1927; s. Morris Aaron and Jenny (Goldberg) R.; m. Lisel Ruth Ephraim, July 25, 1953; 1 child, Lesley Radoff Rappaport. B.A., Rice U., Houston, 1949; M.L.S., U. Tex., Austin, 1965. Cert. secondary sch. tchr., Tex. Tchr. math Aldine Ind. Sch. Dist., Houston, 1959-61, sch. librarian, 1961-63; head pub. services Abilene Pub. Library, Tex., 1964-65; library dir. Pasadena Pub. Library, Tex., 1966-70; chief br. services Houston Pub. Library, 1971-92, ret., 1992; library bldg. cons. Houston, 1975—. Treas. Literacy Vol. Am., Houston, 1984-85; mem. Northside Interests, Houston, 1982-85. Served with USN, 1945-46. Hoenthal scholar, 1948. Mem. Tex. Library Assn., ALA, Freedom to Read Found., Houston Great Books Council (leader trainer 1953-59, pres. 1967-69). Avocations: tutoring; listening to music; stamp collecting. Home: 4013 Gano St Houston TX 77009-4119

RADOJCSICS, ANNE PARSONS, librarian; b. Mansfield, Ohio, Mar. 23, 1929; d. Richard Walbridge Parsons and Iva Pearl (Ruth) Kemp; m. Joseph Michael Radojcsics, July 8, 1950; children: Kurt Joseph, Jo Anne Radojcsics Kent. Diploma, Bethel Woman's Coll., Hopkinsville, Ky., 1949; BS, Miss. State U., 1972, MEd, 1974. Cert. secondary tchr., Miss. Chemist Humphries Borg-Warner Co., Mansfield, 1950-53; asst. reference libr. Mansfield Pub. Libr., 1953-59; libr. media specialist Verona (Miss.) Sch., 1970-92, supr. Verona computer lab., 1985-92; libr. media specialist Pierce St. Elem. Sch., Miss., 1992-95; ret., 1995; libr. Saints Libr., Miss., 1995—; supr. libr. Guntown (Miss.) Sch., 1988-90, Shannon (Miss.) Sch., 1988-92; chmn. assessment project Miss. Libr.-Miss. Dept. Edn., Jackson, 1986-92; coord. region I Miss. Conf. on Libr. and Info. Svc., 1990; mem. Miss. Edn. TV Adv. Coun., 1985—; cons. content instrnl. prodn.-libr. rsch. skills Miss. Ednl. Tv., 1995. Author: Clay Tablets to Media Centers: Library Development from Ancient to Modern Times, 1975; (tchr. guide) Media Mania, 1996 Mississippi Educational TV. Bd. dirs., past pres. SAFE, Inc., Tupelo, Miss., 1978-92, bd. dirs. emeritus, 1992—; mem. Lee County Adult Lit. Task Force, Tupelo, 1987-90; schs. chmn. Target Tupelo, 1981-85. Recipient Ed Ransdell Instructional TV award, 1991. Mem. AECT, DSMS, AAUW (pres. Tupelo chpt. 1977-81, 1993—, Miss. divsn. 1984-86)), Miss. Profl. Educators, Mississippians for Ednl. Broadcasting, Miss. Ednl. Computer Assn., Miss. Libr. Assn. (project chmn. com. on. sch. librs. 1989, awards chmn. 1987-88, ednl. comml. and tech. roundtable chair 1993), Miss. Profl. Educators Tupelo/Lee County (treas. 1993-95, pres. 1995—), Apple Computer User Group (co-organizer). Democrat. Episcopalian. Avocations: aerobics, reading, church music and liturgy, quilt making. Home: Carr Vista 105 Michael St Tupelo MS 38801-8608

RADOJEVIC, DANILO, ballet dancer; b. Sydney, Australia, Sept. 8, 1957. Mem. corps de ballet Austrialian Ballet Co., soloist, from 1977; soloist Am. Ballet Theatre, N.Y.C., 1978-81; prin. dancer Am. Ballet Theatre, 1981-1993; prin. guest artist with Basel Ballet, 1988, Royal Ballet of Flanders, 1988; mem. ballet faculty Univ. of California, Irvine, 1994—. Created role of Head Fakir, La Bayadere, also leading male role in Grand Pas Romantique; created ballet Sirens, Univ. of California, Irvine. Gold medalist Internat. Ballet Competition Moscow, 1977. Office: Univ of Calif Irvine Dance Dept HTC 101 Irvine CA 92717

RADOMSKI, JACK LONDON, toxicology consultant; b. Milw., Dec. 10, 1920; s. Joseph Elwood and Evelyn (Hansen) R.; BS, U. Wis., 1942; PhD, George Washington U., 1950; m. Margery Dodge, 1947 (dec. 1970); m. Teresa Pascual, Feb. 19, 1971; children—Mark, Linda, Eric, Janet, Mayte. Chemist, Gen. Aniline & Film Corp., Binghamton, N.Y. 1942-44; pharmacologist FDA, Washington, 1944-52, acting chief acute toxicity br., 1952-53; prof. pharmacology U. Miami, Coral Gables, Fla., 1953-82; pres. Covington Tech. Services, Andalusia, Ala., 1982-88; pvt. practice cons. in toxicology, Hudson, Fla., 1988—; cons. WHO, IARC, GAO, EPA, HEW, NIOSH. Contbr. articles to profl. jours. Recipient Spl. award Commr. FDA, 1952; diplomate in gen. toxicology Acad. Toxicol. Scis., 1982. Mem. Am. Soc. Pharmacology and Exptl. Therapeutics, Soc. Toxicology, Am. Assn. Cancer Research, N.Y. Acad. Scis., Am. Bd. Forensic Examiners. Home and Office: 6432 Driftwood Dr Port Richey FL 34667-1018 *The single most important thing in life is to make a continuous, intensive effort to comprehend things as they really are, as distinct from as we wish them to be. Failure to perceive the world and everything in it accurately and objectively, admittedly a difficult and frequently fearful task, causes untold misery and misfortune to individuals, organizations and nations. Success in all endeavors is in direct proportion to the degree we achieve this goal.*

RADUAZO, ANTHONY F., lawyer; b. Portsmouth, N.H., Oct. 16, 1945; s. Anthony and Geraldine (Huntress) R.; m. Elizabeth A. Raduazo; children: Ann M., Phillip A. BA in Liberal Arts, Ctrl. Mich. U., 1967; JD, Detroit Coll., 1974. Bar: Mich. 1974, U.S. Dist. Ct. (ea. dist.) Mich. 1978, U.S. Dist. Ct. (we. dist.) Mich. 1983, U.S. Ct. Appeals (6th cir.) 1983. Tchr., coach Plymouth (N.H.) Pub. Schs., 1967-68, Raymond (N.H.) Pub. Schs., 1968-69; sales staff Addison Wesley Pub. Co., Menlo Park, Calif., 1969-70; mktg. supr. Addison Wesley Pub. Co., Menlo Park, 1970-71; asst. prosecuting atty. Washtenaw County Mich., Ann Arbor, 1974-78; asst. city atty. City of Jackson, Mich., 1979-81, city atty., 1981—. Treas. Jackson (Mich.) County Rep. Com., 1987-88, 91-93, vice chair, 1989-91. Mem. Mich. Assn. Mcpl. Attys. (pres. 1993-95), Mich. Pub. Risk and Ins. Mgmt. Assn. (pres. 1985-86), Mich. Mcpl. League Legal Def. Fund (chair 1993-95). Office: City Attys Office 161 W Michigan Ave Jackson MI 49201

RADUEGE, HARRY DALE, JR., career military officer; b. Columbus, Ohio, Jan. 9, 1947; s. Harry Dale and Ruth Pauline (Roederer) R.; m. Julee Lydia Hux, Oct. 17, 1970; children: Chad Dale, Rian Elise, Ashley Jean. BS in Edn., Capital U., 1970; MS in Bus. Mgmt., Troy State U., 1976; MS in Telecommunications, U. So. Miss., 1978. Commd. 2d lt. USAF, 1970, advanced through grades to col., 1991; exec. officer tactical communications area USAF, Langley AFB, Va., 1978-80; comdr. communications detachment USAF, Pirinclik, Turkey, 1980-81; chief readiness div. hdqrs. communications command USAF, Scott AFB, Ill., 1981-84; chief C3 engring. div. hdqrs. space command USAF, Colorado Springs, Colo., 1984-88; chief strategic info. warning systems staff of Chmn. Joint Chiefs of Staff, Washington, 1989-90, chief satellite communications div., 1990-91, exec. asst. to dir. command control, communications and computer systems staff, 1991-92; asst. deputy chief staff comm. computer systems Hdqs. Air Combat Command, Langley AFB, Va., 1992—. Asst. scoutmaster Boy Scouts Am., USAF Acad., Colo., 1985-86, scoutmaster, 1987-88; youth group leader Burke (Va.) Community Ch., 1990—. Named one of Outstanding Young Men Am., 1979. Mem. Armed Forces Communications-Electronics Assn. (bd. dirs. 1986-87, v.p. programs 1987-88, profl. achievement award, meritorious svc. award 1985, medal of merit 1988), AIAA (sr. mem. tech. com. 1991—). Home: 2105 McClelland Ave Tampa FL 33621 Office: Hdqs Air Combat Command/SC Langley Afb Hampton VA 23665

RADWICK, MELISSA JANE, elementary counselor; b. Memphis, Nov. 26, 1954; d. Nelson Arthur and Mary Jane (Loss) Haas; m. Douglas Martin, Oct. 23, 1976; children: Nathan, Eric. BA in Elem. Edn., Mich. State U., 1975; MA in Health Edn., U. Mich., 1981; counseling endorsement, Ctrl. Mich. U. 6th grade tchr. North Branch (Mich.) Schs., 1976-93, elem. counselor, 1993—; student asst. coord. North Br. Schs., 1991-93, Ruth Fox. Mid. Sch., 1996, coord. parent class, 1991—, chmn. cmty. teen, 1993—; county schs. rep. Continuum Care Com., Lapeer, Mich., 1992-93. Grantee Genesee Intermediate Dist., 1991, 93—. Mem. AAUW, PEO. Republican. Lutheran. Avocations: coaching soccer and baseball, reading, traveling, cross-country skiing. Home: 8635 Gera Rd Birch Run MI 48415-9717

RADY, ERNEST S., thrift and loan association executive; b. 1938. Chmn. bd. Western Thrift & Loan, Orange, Calif., 1973—; chmn. bd., CEO Westcorp, Irvine, Calif., 1975—. Office: Westcorp 23 Pasteur Irvine CA 92718-3816*

RADZINOWICZ, MARY ANN, language educator; b. Champaign, Ill., Apr. 18, 1925; d. Arthur Seymour and Ann (Stacy) Nevins; m. Leon Radzinowicz, June 16, 1958 (div. 1978); children: Ann Stacy Radzinowicz Prior, William Francis Henry. BA, Radcliffe Coll., 1945; MA, Columbia U., 1947, PhD, 1953; MA (hon.), U. Cambridge, Eng., 1960. Prof. Vassar Coll., Poughkeepsie, N.Y., 1947-50, 52-59, Girton Coll., Cambridge, Eng., 1960-80, U. Cambridge, 1973-80, Cornell U., Ithaca, N.Y., 1980-90; Jacob Gould Schurman prof. English emeritus Cornell U., Ithaca, 1990—; mem. adv. bd. 2d, 3d, 4th Internat. Milton Symposia, 1985—. Author: Toward Samson Agonistes, 1978 (Hanford prize 1979), Milton's Epics and Psalms, 1989; editor American Colonial Prose, 1984, Paradise Lost, Book VIII, 1974; mem. editorial bd. Milton Quarterly, 1981—, Christianity and Literature, 1989—. Mem. MLA, Renaissance Soc. Am., Milton Soc. Am. (honored scholar 1987), John Donne Soc. Home: Ballyconry House, Ballyvaughan County Clare Ireland Office: Cornell U Dept English Lit Ithaca NY 14850

RAE, BARBARA JOYCE, former employee placement company executive; b. Prince George, B.C., Can., May 17, 1930; d. Alfred and Lottie Kathleen (Davis) Holmwood; m. George Suart, Feb. 14, 1984; children: Jamie, Glenn, John. MBA, Simon Fraser U., Burnaby, B.C., 1975. Chmn., CEO Adia Can., Ltd., Vancouver, B.C., 1953-95; also bd. dirs.; bd. dirs. Can. Imperial Bank Commerce, Grosvenor Internat. Ltd., B.C. Telephone Co., B.C. Telecom, Noranda, Inc., Xerox Can. Ltd.; dir. Can. Inst. Adv. Rsch., 1995—, B.C. Womens Hosp. & Health Ctr. Found., 1994—, KTCS Pub. Broadcasting; bd. govs. Multiple Sclerosis Soc., 1995—. Chancellor Simon Fraser U., 1987-93; mem. Jud. Appts. Com., B.C., 1988-90; commr. Triennial Commn. on Judges Salaries and Benefits; mem. adv. coun. Imagine Campaign, 1988; mem. Primier's Econ. Adv. Coun., B.C., 1987-91; mem. Price Minister's Com. on Sci. and Tech., B.C., 1989-94; gen. chmn. United Way Lower Mainland, 1987, Salvation Army Red Shield Vancouver Campaign, 1986; bd. dirs. Vancouver Bd. Trade, 1972-76; nat. co-chmn. Can. Coun. Christians and Jews. Decorated Order of Can., Order of B.C.; recipient Outstanding Alumnae award Simon Fraser U., 1985, Disting. Alumni Svc. award, 1995, Bus. Women of Yr. award Vancouver YWCA, 1986, West Vancouver Achievers award, 1987, B.C. Entrepreneur of Yr. award, 1987, Nat. Vol. award, 1990, Can. Woman Entrepreneur B.C. award, 1992. Home: 2206 Folkestone Way #3, West Vancouver, BC Canada V7S 2X7

RAE, JOHN JOSEPH, lawyer; b. Battle Creek, Mich., Sept. 11, 1935; s. James Gordon and Mary Kathryn (McGrail) R.; m. Patricia Ann Rae, Dec. 30, 1961; children: Elizabeth, Susan, Mary. BS in Social Sci. cum laude, John Carroll U., Cleve., 1957; JD, DePaul U., Chgo., 1961. Bar: Ill. 1961, Mich. 1965. Assoc. McDermott, Will & Emery, Chgo., 1961-65; pvt. practice Battle Creek, Mich., 1965-75; pros. atty. Calhoun County, Marshall, Mich., 1975-76; city atty. City of Midland, Mich., 1977—; mem. State Bar Ethics Com., Lansing, Mich., 1994. Editor Calhoun County Bar Assn. Newsletter; contbr. articles to profl. jours. Vice-chairperson bd. trustees Mid-Mich. Dispute Resolution Ctr., Saginaw, 1994. Capt. U.S. Army, 1959-69. Mem. ABA, Nat. Inst. Mcpl. Law Officers, Am. Trial Lawyers Assn., State Bar Mich. (profl. and jud. ethics com.), Midland County Bar Assn. Roman Catholic. Avocations: reading, music. Office: City of Midland 333 W Ellsworth St Midland MI 48640-5134

RAE, MATTHEW SANDERSON, JR., lawyer; b. Pitts., Sept. 12, 1922; s. Matthew Sanderson and Olive (Waite) R.; m. Janet Hettman, May 2, 1953; children: Mary-Anna, Margaret Rae Mallory, Janet S. Rae Dupree. AB, Duke, 1946, LLB, 1947; postgrad., Stanford U., 1951. Bar: Md. 1948, Calif. 1951. Asst. to dean Duke Sch. Law, Durham, N.C., 1947-48; assoc. Karl F. Steinmann, Balt., 1948-49, Guthrie, Darling & Shattuck, L.A., 1953-54; nat. field rep. Phi Alpha Delta Law Frat., L.A., 1949-51; research atty. Calif. Supreme Ct., San Francisco, 1951-52; ptnr. Darling, Hall & Rae (and predecessor firms), L.A., 1955—; mem. Calif. Commn. Uniform State Laws, 1985—, chmn., 1993-94; chmn. drafting com. for revision Uniform Prin. and Income Act of Nat. Conf., 1991—. Vice pres. L.A. County Rep. Assembly, 1959-64; mem. L.A. County Rep. Ctrl. Com., 1960-64, 77-90, exec. com., 1977-90; vice chmn. 17th Congl. Dist., 1960-62, 28th Congl. Dist., 1962-64; chmn. 46th Assy. Dist., 1962-64, 27th Senatorial Dist., 1977-85, 29th Senatorial Dist., 1985-90; mem. Calif. Rep. State Ctrl. Com., 1966—, exec. com., 1966-67; pres. Calif. Rep. League, 1966-67; trustee Rep. Assocs., 1979-94, pres., 1983-85, chmn. bd. dirs., 1985-87. 2d lt. USAAF, WWII. Fellow Am. Coll. Trust and Estate Counsel; academician Internat. Acad. Estate and Trust Law (exec. coun. 1974-78); mem. ABA, L.A. County Bar Assn. (chmn. probate and trust law com. 1964-66, chmn. legis. com. 1980-86, chmn. program com. 1981-82, chmn. membership retention com. 1982-83, truste 1983-85, dir. Bar Found., 1987-93, Arthur K. Marshall award probate and trust law sect. 1984, Shattuck-Price Meml. award 1990), South Bay Bar Assn., State Bar of Calif. (chmn. state bar jour. com. 1970-71, probate com. 1974-75; exec. com. estate planning trust and probate law sect. 1977-83, chmn. legis. com. 1977-89; co-chmn. 1991-92; probate law cons. group Calif. Bd. Legal Specialization 1977-88; chmn. conf. dels. 1987-90), Lawyers Club L.A., (bd. govs. 1981-87, 1st v.p. 1982-83), Am. Legion (commdr. Allied post 1969-70), Legion Lex (bd. dirs. 1964—, pres. 1969-71), Air Force Assn., Aircraft Owners and Pilots Assn., Town Hall (gov. 1970-78, pres. 1975), World Affairs Coun., Internat. Platform Assn., Breakfast Club (law, pres. 1989-90), Commonwealth Club, Chancery Club (v.p. 1995—), Rotary, Phi Beta Kappa (councilor Alpha Assn. 1983—, v.p. 1984-86, 94—), Omicron Delta Kappa, Phi Alpha Delta (supreme justice 1972-74, elected to Disting. Svc. chpt. 1978), Sigma Nu. Presbyterian. Home: 600 John St Manhattan Beach CA 90266-5837 Office: Darling Hall & Rae 777 S Figueroa St Fl 37 Los Angeles CA 90017-5800

RAE, ROBERT KEITH, lawyer, former Canadian premier of Ontario; b. Ottawa, Ont., Can., Aug. 2, 1948; s. Saul Forbes and Lois Esther (George) R.; m. Arlene Perly, Feb. 23, 1980; children: Judith Florence, Lisa Ruth, Eleanor Grace. BA, U. Toronto, Ont., 1969, LLB, 1977; BPhil, Oxford U., 1971. Bar: Ont. 1980. M.P. from Broadview-Greenwood dist. Ho. of Commons, 1978-82, fin. spokeman New Dem. Party, 1979-82; mem. for York South, provincial legislature Ont., 1982-96, leader official opposition, 1987-90; premier Province of Ont., Toronto, 1990-95; spl. lectr. in indsl. rels. U. Toronto, 1976-77. Contbr. articles on law and politics to profl. jours. Mem. com. on univ. govt. U. Toronto, 1968-69; community worker London, Eng., 1973-74; extensive legal aid and community worker, Toronto, 1974—; asst. to Can. gen. counsel United Steelworkers Am., 1975-77; vice chmn. Can.-U.S. Interparliamentary Group, 1979-82. Rhodes scholar Balliol Coll., Oxford, 1969. Avocations: tennis, golf, skiing, fishing, music.

RAEBER, JOHN ARTHUR, architect, construction specifier consultant; b. St. Louis, Nov. 24, 1947; s. Arthur William and Marie (Laux) R.; m. Sandi Hartupee, Aug. 16, 1969. AA, Jefferson Coll., 1968; AB, Washington U., 1970, MArch, 1973. Registered architect, Calif., Mo.; cert. constrn. specifier; cert. Nat. Coun. Arch. Specification writer Hellmuth, Obata & Kassabaum, St. Louis, 1973-78, constrn. administr., 1978-79; mgr. of specifications Gensler & Assocs., San Francisco, 1979-82; ind. constrn. specifier San Francisco, 1982—; adj. prof. architecture Calif. Coll. Arts and Crafts, San Francisco, 1986—; access code advisor Constrn. Industry & Owners, 1982—; spkr., instr. seminars orgns., univs., 1982—; mem. Calif. State Bldg. Standards Commn. Accessibility Adv. Panel, Sacramento, 1981, Calif. Subcom. Rights of Disabled Adv. Panel, Sacramento, 1993. Author: CAL/ABL: Interpretative Manual to California's Access Barriers Laws, 1982; co-author: (with Peter S. Hopf) Access for the Handicapped, 1984; columnist Constrn. Specifier Mag., 1988-95. Vol. Calif. Office Emergency Svcs. Safety Assessment, Sacramento, 1991—. Fellow AIA (San Francisco chpt. codes com., Calif. coun. codes and standards com., nat. masterspec rev. com. 1982-84, nat. codes com. corr.), Contrns. Specifications Inst. (cert., columnist newsletter San Francisco chpt. 1984—, Ben John Small award for Outstanding Stature as practicing specifications writer 1994, pres. St. Louis chpt. 1978-79, pres. San Francisco chpt. 1993-94, tech. com., edn. com., publs. com., Specifications Proficiency award San Francisco chpt. 1989, Tech. Commendation award 1987); mem. Specifications Cons. in Ind. Practice (nat. pres. 1990-92, nat. sec./treas. 1988-90), Am. Soc. Testing and Materials, Internat. Conf. Bldg. Officials, Phi Theta Kappa. Avocations: history, anthropology, sci. fiction. Home and Office: 519 Teresita Blvd San Francisco CA 94127-1830

RAEBURN, ANDREW HARVEY, performing arts association executive, record producer; b. London, July 22, 1933; arrived in U.S., 1964, Can., 1993; s. Walter Augustus Leopold and Dora Adelaide Harvey (Williams) R. BA in History, King's Coll., Cambridge U., Eng., 1958; MA, King's Coll., Camridge U., Eng., 1962. Mus. dir. Argo Record Co., London, 1959-64; asst. to music dir., program editor Boston Symphony Orch., 1964-73; dir. artists and repertory New World Records, N.Y.C., 1975-79; artistic adminstr. Detroit Symphony Orch., 1979-82; exec. dir. Van Cliburn Found. Inc., Ft. Worth, 1982-85; performing arts cons., 1985-93; exec. v.p. The Peter Pan Children's Fund, 1990-91; exec. dir. Esther Honens Internat. Piano Competition Found., 1993-95, pres., 1995—; cons. music; radio and TV commentator; mem. faculty Boston U., 1966-67; condr. New World String Orch., 1978. Author record liner notes, Argo, RCA, Time-Life records, 1960-79, program notes, Boston Symphony Orch., 1968-73. Served with Royal Arty. Brit. Army, 1952-55. Home: Apt 406, 929 18th Ave SW, Calgary AB, AB Canada T2T 0H2 Office: 116 8th Ave SE 3rd Fl, Calgary, AB Canada T2G OK6

RAEBURN, JOHN HAY, English language educator; b. Indpls., July 18, 1941; s. Gordon Maurice and Katherine (Calwell) R.; m. Gillian Kimble, Aug. 18, 1963 (div. July 1979); children—Daniel Kennedy, Nicholas Kimble; m. Kathleen Kamerick, July 5, 1986. A.B. with honors, Ind. U., 1963; A.M., U. Pa., 1964, Ph.D., 1969. Asst. prof. U. Mich., Ann Arbor, 1967-74; vis. lectr. U. Iowa, Iowa City, 1974-75, assoc. prof., 1976-83, prof. English, 1983—; chmn. Am. Studies dept., 1983-85, 94—; chmn. English dept. U. Iowa, Iowa City, 1985-91; assoc. prof. U. Louisville, 1975-76. Author: Fame Became of Him: Hemingway as Public Writer, 1984; editor: (with others) Frank Capra: The Man and His Films, 1975. Mem. Am. Studies Assn. Democrat. Home: 321 Hutchinson Ave Iowa City IA 52246-2407 Office: U Iowa Dept Am Studies Dept English 202 Jefferson Building Iowa City IA 52242-1418

RAEDER, MYRNA SHARON, lawyer, educator; b. N.Y.C., Feb. 4, 1947; d. Samuel and Estelle (Auslander) R.; m. Terry Oliver Kelly, July 13, 1975; children: Thomas Oliver, Michael Lawrence. BA, Hunter Coll., 1968; JD, NYU, 1971; LLM, Georgetown U., 1975. Bar: N.Y. 1972, D.C. 1972, Calif. 1972. Spl. asst. U.S. atty. U.S. Atty.'s Office, Washington, 1972-73; asst. prof. U. San Francisco Sch. Law, 1973-75; assoc. O'Melveny & Myers, L.A., 1975-79; assoc. prof. Southwestern U. Sch. Law, L.A., 1979-82, prof., 1983—, Irwin R. Buchalter prof. law, 1990; mem. faculty Nat. Judicial Coll., 1993—; advisor drafting com. to revise uniform rules of evidence Nat. Conf. Commrs. on Uniform State Laws, 1996. Prettyman fellow Georgetown Law Ctr., Washington, 1971-73. Author: Federal Pretrial Practice, 2d edit., 1995, ALI, 1989. Fellow Am. Bar Found.; mem. ABA (chmn. com. on fed. rules and criminal procedure criminal justice sect. 1987-93, vice-chair pubs. criminal justice sect. 1994—, trial evidence com. litigation sect. 1980—, adv. to nat. conf. commrs. uniform state laws drafting com. uniform rules of evidence 1996), Assn. Am. Law Schs. (chair elect evidence sects. 1996, com. on sects. 1984-87, chairperson women in legal edn. sect. 1982), Nat. Assn. Women Lawyers (bd. dirs. 1991—, pres.-elect 1993, pres. 1994—), Women Lawyers Assn. L.A. (bd. dirs., coord. mothers support group 1987—), Order of Coif, Phi Beta Kappa. Office: Southwestern U Sch Law 675 S Westmoreland Ave Los Angeles CA 90005-3905

RAEL, HENRY SYLVESTER, retired health administrator; b. Pueblo, Colo., Oct. 2, 1928; s. Daniel and Grace (Abyeta) R.; m. Helen Warner Loring Brace, June 30, 1956 (dec. Aug. 1980); children: Henry Sylvester, Loring Victoria. AB, U. So. Colo., 1955; BA in Bus Adminstrn., U. Denver, 1957, MBA, 1958. Sr. boys counselor Denver Juvenile Hall, 1955-58; adminstrv. asst. to pres. Stanley Aviation Corp., Denver, 1958-61; Titan III budget and fin. control supr. Martin Marietta Corp., Denver, 1961-65; mgmt. adv. services officer U. Colo. Med. Center, Denver, 1965-72; v.p. fin., treas. Loretto Heights Coll., Denver, 1972-73; dir. fin. and adminstrn. Colo. Found. for Med. Care, 1973-86, Tri-County Health Dept., Denver, 1986-96; instr. fin. mgmt., mem. fin. com. Am. Assn. Profl. Standards Rev. Orgn., 1980-85; speaker systems devel., design assns., univs., 1967-71. Mem. budget lay adv. com. Park Hill Elem. Sch., Denver, 1967-68, chmn., 1968-69; vol. worker Boy and Girl Scouts, 1967-73; bd. dirs. Community Arts Symphony, 1981-83, 85-87; controller St. John's Episcopal Cathedral, 1982-83; charter mem. Pueblo (Colo.) Coll. Young Democrats, 1954-55; block worker Republican party, Denver, 1965-68, precinct committeeman, 1978-84 ; trustee Van Nattan Scholarship Fund, 1974-96; bd. dirs. Vis. Nurse Assn., 1977-84, treas., 1982-84. Served with USAF, 1947-53; res. 1954-61. Recipient Disting. Service award Denver Astron. Soc., 1968, Citation Chamberlin Obs., 1985; Stanley Aviation masters scholar, 1957; Ballard scholar, 1956. Mem. Assn. Systems Mgmt. (pres. 1971-72), Hosp. Systems Mgmt. Soc., Budget Execs Inst. (v.p. chpt. 1964-65, sec. 1963-64), Colo. Pub. Employees Retirement Assn. (bd. dirs. 1993), Denver Astron. Soc. (pres. 1965-66, bd. dirs. 1982-94), Am. Assn. Founds. for Med. Care (fin. com. 1981-82), Nat. Astronomers Assn. (exec. bd. 1965—). Epsilon Xi, Delta Psi Omega. Episcopalian. Home: 4600 E Kentucky Ave A-511 Denver CO 80222-2641

RAEMER, HAROLD ROY, electrical engineering educator; b. Chgo., Apr. 26, 1924; s. Leo and Fannie (Marx) R.; m. Paulyne Barkin, Dec. 21, 1947; children: Daniel, Liane, Diane. B.S., Northwestern U., 1948, M.S., 1949, Ph.D., 1959. Teaching asst. Northwestern U., 1950-52; physicist Bendix Research Labs., Detroit, 1952-55; staff engr. Cook Research Labs., Chgo., 1955-60; sr. engring. specialist Sylvania Applied Research Lab., Waltham, Mass., 1960-63; assoc. prof. elec. engring. Northeastern U., Boston, 1963-65, prof., 1965—, chmn. dept., 1976-77, acting chmn., 1982-84, Snell prof. engring., 1986-93; prof. emeritus, 1994—; vis. lectr. Harvard U., 1962, hon. research assoc., 1972-73; vis. scientist MIT, 1984-85; cons. in field. Author: Statistical Communication: Theory and Applications, 1969, Radar Systems Principles, 1996; contbr. articles to profl. jours. Served with USAAF, 1943-46. Mem. IEEE (sr.), AAAS, Am. Soc. for Engring. Edn., Sigma Xi, Pi Mu Epsilon, Eta Kappa Nu, Tau Beta Pi. Home: 1200 Noanett Needham MA 02194-2442 Office: Dept Elec and Computer Engring Northeastern U Boston MA 02115

RAETZ, CHRISTIAN R. H., biochemistry educator; b. Berlin, Germany, Nov. 17, 1946. B.S. in Chemistry, Yale U., 1967; M.D., Harvard U., 1973, Ph.D., %. House officer Peter Bent Brigham Hosp., Boston, 1973-74; research assoc. Nat. Inst. Gen. Med. Scis., USPHS, Bethesda, Md., 1974-76; asst. prof. biochemistry U. Wis.-Madison, 1976-79, assoc. prof., 1979-82, prof., dir. Ctr. for Membrane Biosynthesis Research, 1982—; mem. biochemistry study sect. NIH. Contbr. numerous articles to profl. jours. Mem. editorial bd. Jour. Biol. Chemistry. Recipient James Tolbert Shipley Research prize Harvard U. Med. Sch., 1973, Harry and Evelyn Steenbock

Career Advancement award, 1976, Research Career Devel. award NIH, 1978-83, Dreyfus Tchr.-Scholar award, 1979; H. I. Romnes Faculty fellow U. Wis., 1984; NIH grantee. Mem. Am. Soc. Biol. Chemists, Japanese Soc. Promotion Sci., Phi Beta Kappa, Alpha Omega Alpha. Office: U Wis-Madison Dept Biochemistry 420 Henry Mall Madison WI 53706-1502

RAEUCHLE, JOHN STEVEN, computer analyst; b. Washington, Sept. 21, 1955; s. Richard Frank and Ruth Darlene (Fulton) R. BS, Tex. Christian, 1978. Programmer Tex. Christian U., Fort Worth, 1976-78, Warrex Computer Systems, Fort Worth, 1978-79; systems programmer Tandy Data Processing, Fort Worth, 1979-84; sr. programmer, analyst Commodity News Svcs., Leawood, Kans., 1984-86, Logica Data Architects, St. Louis, 1986-89; computer analyst Credit Systems, Inc., St. Louis, 1989-95; software engr. Master Card Internat., St. Louis, 1995—. Mem. St. Louis Ambassadors, 1989—; active Boy Scouts Am., 1964—. Recipient awrd of merit Boy Scouts Am., Commrs. Key, 1982. Mem. St. Louis Jaycees Found. (treas. 1990-94, sec. 1994-96, pres. 1996—), Mo. Jaycees (state officer 1989-94), Kansas City Jaycees (bd. dirs. 1985-87), Kansas City Jaycees Found., St. Louis Jr. C. of C. (pres. 1988-89). Democrat. Methodist. Avocations: camping, bowling, hiking. Home: 52 Country Creek Dr Saint Peters MO 63376-3041 Office: Master Card Internat 12115 Lackland Rd Saint Louis MO 63146

RAFAEL, RUTH KELSON, archivist, librarian, consultant; b. Wilmington, N.C., Oct. 28, 1929; d. Benjamin and Jeanette (Spicer) Kelson; m. Richard Vernon Rafael, Aug. 26, 1951; children: Barbara Martinez Yates, Brenda Elaine. BA, San Francisco State U., 1953, MA, 1954; MLS, U. Calif.-Berkeley, 1968. Cert. archivist, 1989. Tchr. San Francisco Unified Sch. Dist., 1956-57; libr. Congregation Beth Sholom, San Francisco, 1965-83; archivist Western Jewish History Ctr. of Judah L. Magnes Mus., Berkeley, Calif., 1968, head archivist, libr., curator of exhibits, 1969-94; cons. NEH, Washington, NHPRC, Congregation Sherith Israel, San Francisco, Mount Zion Hosp., San Francisco, Benjamin Swig archives project, San Francisco, Koret Found., Camp Swig, Saratoga, Calif.; project dir. Ethnicity in Calif. Agriculture, 1989, San Francisco Jews of European Origin, 1880-1940, an oral history project, 1976; curator exhibits Western U.S. Jewry. Author: Continuum, San Francisco Jews of Eastern European Origin, 1880-1940, 1976, rev. edit., 1977; (with Davies and Woogmaster) poetry book Relatively Speaking, 1981; Western Jewish History Center: Archival and Oral History Collections, Judah L. Magnes Meml. Mus., 1987; contbg. editor Western States Jewish History, 1979—. Mem. exec. bd. Bay Area Library Info. Network, 1986-88. Bur. Jewish Edn. scholar, San Francisco, 1983; NEH grantee, 1985. Mem. Calif. Libr. Assn., Soc. Am. Archivists, Soc. Calif. Archivists, No. Calif. Assn. Jewish Librs. (pres. 1975-76), Jewish Arts Coun. of the Bay (bd. dirs. 1981-83)

RAFAJKO, ROBERT RICHARD, medical research company executive; b. Chgo., Sept. 3, 1931; s. Edward Michael and Mildred Eleanor (Simo) R.; m. Mary Ann Filipi, June 24, 1954 (div. 1979); children: Rorie Rae, Ronald Raymond, Robin Rene, Rod Richard, Rebecca Rae.; m. Anne Thorne Sloan, Jan. 26, 1982; 1 son, Andrew Sloan. BA, Coe Coll., 1953; MS, U. Iowa, 1958, PhD, 1960. Research assoc. Merck Sharp and Dohme, West Point, Pa., 1960-61; research scientist Microbiol. Assos., Bethesda, Md., 1961-66; v.p., gen. mgr. Med. Research Cons., Rockville, Md., 1966-69; v.p. research and devel. N. Am. Biols., Rockville, 1969-74; pres. Biofluids, Inc., Rockville, 1974—; pres. Tysan Serum, Inc., Rockville, 1974—, Kytaron Inc, Rockville, 1987—; breeder thoroughbred horses, 1980—. Contbr. 23 articles to profl. jours. Chmn. PVAAU Swimming Program, Washington, Md. and Va., 1973-76; bd. dirs. Montgomery County Swim League, Montgomery County, Md., 1968-76. Served with USAF, 1954-55. Mem. AAAS, N.Y. Acad. Scis., Am. Soc. Microbiology, Tissue Culture Assn., Am. Horse Council, Horsemans Benevolent and Protective Assn. Republican. Presbyterian. Avocations: scuba diving, photography, collecting stamps, travel. Home: 12053 Wetherfield Ln Potomac MD 20854 Office: Biofluids Inc 1146 Taft St Rockville MD 20850-1310

RAFEEDIE, EDWARD, federal judge; b. Orange, N.J., Jan. 6, 1929; s. Fred and Nabeeha (Hishmeh) R.; m. Ruth Alice Horton, Oct. 8, 1961; children: Fredrick Alexander, Jennifer Ann. BS in Law, U. So. Calif., 1957, JD, 1959; LLD (hon.), Pepperdine U., 1978. Bar: Calif. 1960. Pvt. practice law Santa Monica, Calif., 1960-69; mcpl. ct. judge Santa Monica Jud. Dist., Santa Monica, 1969-71; judge Superior Ct. State of Calif., Los Angeles, 1971-82; dist. judge U.S. Dist. Court for (cen. dist.) Calif., Los Angeles, 1982—. Trustee Santa Monica Hosp. Med. Ctr., 1979—; With U.S. Army, 1950-52, Korea. Office: US Dist Ct 312 N Spring St Los Angeles CA 90012-4701

RAFELSON, BOB, film director; b. N.Y.C., 1933. Dir.: (films) Head, 1968, Five Easy Pieces, 1970 (Acad. awad nomination for best picture), The King of Marvin Gardens, 1972, Stay Hungry, 1976, The Postman Always Rings Twice, 1981, Black Widow, 1987, Mountains of the Moon, 1990, Man Trouble, 1992, (short film) Wet, 1993, Armed Response, 1994, (rock video - Lionel Richie) All Night Long, 1983; author: (TV series) Play of the Week; creator (TV series) The Monkees; dir. (series) The Painted Word. Recipient N.Y. Film Critics award for Five Easy Pieces, 1970.

RAFELSON, MAX EMANUEL, JR., biochemist, medical school administrator; b. Detroit, June 17, 1921; s. Max Emanuel and Lillian (Kay) R.; m. Trudy Diane Hellem, Mar. 31, 1973; children—Mark Thomas, Anne Elizabeth. B.S., U. Mich., 1943; Ph.D., U. So. Cal., 1951. Postdoctoral rsch. fellow U. Stockholm, Sweden, 1951-52; asst. prof. biol. chemistry U. Ill. Coll. Medicine, Chgo., 1953-55, assoc. prof., 1955-60, prof., 1961-70; assoc. dean biol. and behavioral scis. Rush Med. Coll., Rush-Presbyn.-St. Luke's Med. Center, 1970-71, v.p. info. scis., 1971-77, v.p., 1972—; prof. biochemistry Rush Med. Coll., 1972-90, prof. and chmn. emeritus, 1990—; John W. and Helen H. Watzek meml. chmn. biochemistry Presbyn.-St. Lukes Hosp., Chgo., 1961-70; vis. prof. U. Paris, France, 1960, 77-78, U. Ulm, Fed. Republic Germany, 1986; assoc. mem. commn. influenza Dept. Def., 1961—. Author: Basic Biochemistry, 1965, 68, 71, 80, Conuse Biochemistry, 1995; contbr. articles on biochemistry, blood platelets, viruses, protein structure, endothelial cells and metabolism to profl. publs. Served with USNR, 1943-46. Mem. Am. Soc. Biol. Chemists, Biochem. Soc. (London), Am. Chem. Soc., AAAS, Nat. Acad. Clin. Biochemistry, Société de Chemie Biologique, Sigma Xi. Home: 2246 N Seminary Ave Chicago IL 60614-3507 Office: Rush-Presbyn-St Luke's Med Ctr 1653 W Congress Pky Chicago IL 60612-3833

RAFF, JOSEPH ALLEN, publishing and travel executive, author; b. N.Y.C., Sept. 28, 1933; s. Bertram and Billie (Martin) R.; m. Judy Ann Oberfelder, Aug. 5, 1959. B.A., U. N.C., 1955, postgrad., 1956-57; postgrad., Harvard, Ind. U., Ohio U. Wire editor A.P., Charlotte, N.C., 1958; staff writer Burlington (N.C.) Times News, then Raleigh (N.C.) Times, Sports Illus., N.Y.C., 1958-61; editor Rome Daily Am., 1961; pres. Temple Fielding Enterprises, Mallorca, Spain; cons. internat. pub. relations, internat. tour packaging. Author: Fielding's Europe, Fielding's Economy Europe, Fielding's Britain; host (film) Shopping London; contbr. numerous articles to mags., newspapers. Decorated chevalier Ordre de Couteaux (France). Mem. Soc. Am. Travel Writers. Clubs: Overseas Press, Nautico de Puerto de Pollensa. Home and Office: PO Box 50, Mallorca Spain

RAFFAY, STEPHEN JOSEPH, manufacturing company executive; b. McAdoo, Pa., Oct. 25, 1927; s. Stephen John and Stephanie (Severa) R.; m. Audree Eugenia Kuehne, Sept. 12, 1953; children: Andrea, Stephen, Leslie. B.A., Columbia, 1950, M.S., 1951. C.P.A., N.Y. Sr. accountant Arthur Andersen & Co., N.Y.C., 1951-56; asst. controller Emhart Corp., Farmington, Conn., 1956-61, asst. treas., 1961-63, treas., 1963-67, v.p. internat., 1967-72, v.p., group pres., 1972-79, exec. v.p., 1979-84, vice chmn., chief adminstrv. officer, 1984-87, dir., 1980-87; sr. v.p. Dexter Corp., Windsor Locks, Conn., 1987-90; bd. dirs. Reflexite Corp., Fresnel Optics, Inc., Schaar Inds., Inc., United Plumbing Tech., Inc., Trust Co. Conn., Rossi Enterprises, Inc. Bd. dirs. Hartford Symphony Soc. With AUS, 1946-47. Mem. AICPA, Conn. Soc. CPAs. Office: 93 Westmont St West Hartford CT 06117-2929

RAFFEL, JEFFREY ALLEN, urban affairs educator; b. Bklyn., June 19, 1945; s. George A. and Renee (Lane) R.; m. Joanne Ruth Traum, Aug. 27, 1966; children: Allison, Lori, Kenneth. AB, U. Rochester, 1966; PhD, MIT, 1972. Asst. prof. U. Del., Newark, 1971-76, assoc. prof., 1976-82, dir. M Pub. Adminstrn. program, 1980-86, prof., 1982—, chair pub. mgmt. faculty, 1994—; acting assoc. dean Coll. Urban Affairs and Pub. Policy U. Del., 1989; chair pub. mgmt. faculty U. Del., Newark, 1994—; pub. svc. fellow, spl. asst. to gov. for intergovtl. rels. State of Del., 1979-80; chair urban edn. policy group Nat. Assn. State Univs. and Land Grant Colls., 1987-93; mem. state supt.'s adv. com. on tchr. recruitment, Del., 1988-91. Author: Politics of School Desegregation, 1980; co-author: Systematic Analysis of University Libraries, 1969, Selling Cities: Attracting Homebuyers Through Schools and Housing Programs, 1995; mem. editl. bd. Pub. Productivity Rev., N.Y.C., 1984—; contbr. articles to urban affairs publs. Treas. Nottingham Swim Club, Inc., Newark, 1985-88; co-chair Gov.'s Task Force on Enhancing Ednl. Dollar, 1986-87; chair long-range planning com. and membership com. Delmarva coun. Boy Scouts Am., 1988-89; mem. Gov.'s Sch. Reform Partnership, Del, 1990—. Recipient cert. of recognition, NCCJ Greater Wilmington, 1980, numerous profl. and civic awards. Mem. ACLU (Del. chpt. sec. 1992—), Del. Assn. Pub. Adminstrn. (pres. 1981-82), Am. Soc. Pub. Adminstrn., Am. Edn. Rsch. Assn. Avocations: golf, reading. Home: 4 High Pond Dr Newark DE 19711-2597 Office: U Del Coll Urban Affairs Pub Policy Newark DE 19716

RAFFEL, LEROY B., real estate development company executive; b. Zanesville, Ohio, Mar. 13, 1927; s. Jacob E. and Anne M. (Oliker) R.; m. Shirley Balbot, Sept. 11, 1949; children: Kenneth, Janet, James, Nancy. B.S., U. Pa., 1949. Pres. Raffel Bros., Inc., Youngstown, Ohio, 1949-78; ret., 1978; pres. York Mahoning Co., Youngstown, 1950-64, Arby's, Inc., Youngstown, 1964-70; chmn. bd. Arby's, Inc., 1971-79; ret., 1979; pres. Brom Equity Devel., Inc., Miami, Fla., 1979—. Served with USNR, 1945-46. Home: 2141 NE 190th Ter N Miami Bch FL 33179-4352 Office: Brom Equity Devel Inc # 207 1380 NE Miami Garden Dr Miami FL 33179-4843

RAFFEL, LOUIS B., trade association administrator; b. Chgo.; s. Martin G. and Donnette (Rogers) R.; m. Trudi Weiner; children: Lawrence, Sharon, Mark. B.S., U. Ill. Account exec. Glassner & Assos., Chgo., 1957-60, Buchen Pub. Rels., Chgo., 1960-62; asst. pub. rels. dir. Am. Meat Inst., Chgo., 1962-68; pub. rels. dir. Nat. Dairy Council, Chgo., 1968-70, Armour & Co., Chgo., 1970-72; v.p. for pub. rels. and advt. Greyhound Corp., Phoenix, 1972-76; pres. Am. Egg Bd., Chgo., 1976—. Served with U.S. Army, 1955-57. Mem. Am. Soc. Assn. Execs. (cert.), Pub. Rels. Soc. Am. (pres. Phoenix chpt. , Silver Anvil), Chgo. Soc. Assn. Execs. (bd. dirs.), Publicity Club Chgo. (pres., Pub-Clubber award). Home: 1724 Seton Rd Northbrook IL 60062-1341 Office: AEB 1460 Renaissance Dr Park Ridge IL 60068-1331

RAFFERTY, JAMES GERARD, lawyer; b. Boston, July 9, 1951; s. James John and Helen Christine (Kennedy) R.; m. Rhonda Beth Friedman, May 17, 1981; children: Jessica Faith, Evan Louis Quinn. BA, Brown U., 1974; MA, Princeton U., 1980; JD, Georgetown U., 1984. Bar: Md. 1985, D.C. 1985, U.S. Tax Ct. 1988, U.S. Ct. Appeals (4th cir.) 1989, U.S. Ct. Appeals (3d cir.) 1992. Assoc. Piper & Marbury, Washington, 1984-91, Pepper, Hamilton & Scheetz, Washington, 1991-92; founding ptnr. Harkins Cunningham, Washington, 1992—. Contbr. articles to legal jours. Mem. ABA (chmn. com. on affiliated and related corps. tax sect. 1994-95). Roman Catholic. Avocation: golf. Office: Harkins & Cunningham 1300 19th St NW Ste 600 Washington DC 20036

RAFFERTY, JAMES PATRICK, violinist, violin educator; b. Toledo, Ohio, June 1, 1947; s. James A. and Eileene L. (Davis) R.; m. Barbara Elizabeth Janiec, Aug. 17, 1985; children: Erin Colleen, Sean Patrick. MusB in Performance, Bowling Green State U., 1970. Violinist St. Louis Symphony Orch., 1971-72, Cleve. Orch., 1972-74, Cin. Symphony Orch., 1974-78; concertmaster Cin. Symphony Chamber Orch., 1976-78; assoc. concertmaster Dallas Symphony Orch., 1978-86; acting concertmaster Seattle Symphony Orch., 1980, 81, San Diego Symphony Orch., 1981; assoc. concertmaster Dallas Chamber Orch., 1981-86; concertmaster Dallas Bach Orch., 1981-86, Milw. Symphony Orch., 1986-91; assoc. prof. violin U. Ala., Tuscaloosa, 1991—; instr. violin Wis. Conservatory Music, Milw., 1986-91; sr. lectr. U. Wis., Milw., 1987, 89-91. Soloist Milw. Symphony Orch., Dallas Bach Orch., Dallas Fine Arts Orch., Dallas Symphony Orch., Brevard Music Ctr. Orch., Cin. Symphony Orch., St. Louis Symphony Orch., others; music festivals include Interlochen Music Camp, 1965, Brevard Music Ctr., 1967, 69, 81, 93—, Berkshire Music Festival, 1968, Grant Teton Music Festival, 1979-80, Southern Music Festival, 1992, Brevard Music Festival, 1993—; performed with New Marlboro Chamber Players, Am. Chamber Trio, Grand Teton Music Festival, Brevard Music Ctr., Fine Arts Chamber Players, Walden Chamber Player, Paganini Trio, Stradivari Trio, 1971—, Cadek Trio, 1991—. Mem. Music Tchrs. Nat. Assn., Am. String Tchrs. Assn., Music Educators Nat. Conf. Office: U Ala Sch Music PO Box 870366 Tuscaloosa AL 35487-0366

RAFFERTY, NANCY SCHWARZ, anatomy educator; b. Jamaica, N.Y., June 11, 1930; d. Franklin and Louise (Barry) Schwarz; m. Keen Alexander Rafferty, Aug. 7, 1953; children: Burns Arthur, Katherine Louisa. B.S., Queens Coll., 1952; M.S., U. Ill., 1953, Ph.D., 1958. Instr. anatomy Johns Hopkins U., 1963-66, asst. prof., 1966-70; asst. prof. anatomy Northwestern U., Chgo., 1970-72; assoc. prof. Northwestern U., 1972-76, prof., 1976-94, prof. emeritus, 1994—; corp. mem., gen. libr. reader Marine Biol. Lab., Woods Hole, Mass. Contbr. articles on cell biology of the crystalline lens to profl. jours. USPHS fellow, 1958-63; USPHS grantee. Mem. Assn. Research in Vision and Ophthalmology, Internat. Soc. for Eye Research, Am. Assn. Anatomists, AAAS, Am. Soc. Cell Biology, Visual Scis. (study sect. of NIH), Sigma Xi, Phi Sigma. Home: 59 Harbor Hill Rd Woods Hole MA 02543-1219 Office: Marine Biol Lab Woods Hole MA 02543

RAFFERTY, WILLIAM BERNARD, lawyer; b. Balt., May 15, 1912; s. John Patrick and Dorothy Amalye (Hartje) R.; m. Elizabeth Catherine Henkel, Dec. 26, 1938; children: Patricia Carol Buchan, Susan Elizabeth Magri, Dorothy Lee Schultz. AB with honors, U. Md., 1934, LLB with honors, 1936. Bar: Md. 1936, U.S. Supreme Ct. 1942. Ptnr. Miles & Stockbridge (and predecessor firms), Balt., 1936-41, ptnr., 1941-92, of counsel, 1992-94, ret., 1994; bd. dirs. Fidelity Fed. Savs. and Loan Assn., Henkel-Harris Co. Inc., Rolling Road Realty Co., Balt., 1975—; lectr. pub. utility law U. Balt. Law Sch., 1951-56. Pres., Roland Park Civic League, 1954-57. Fellow Md. Bar Found.; mem. Wednesday Law Club (pres. 1953), Merchants. Democrat. Presbyterian. Home: 9 Midvale Rd Baltimore MD 21210-2113 Office: Miles & Stockbridge 10 Light St Baltimore MD 21202-1435

RAFFI (RAFFI CAVOUKIAN), folksinger, children's entertainer; b. Cairo, July 8, 1948. Attended, U. Toronto. Recordings include: Singable Songs for the Very Young, 1976, More SIngable Songs for the Very Young, 1977, Love Light, 1977, The Corner Grocery Store, 1979, Baby Beluga, 1980, Rise and Sun, 1982, Raffi's Christmas Album, 1983, One Light One Sun, 1985, Everything Grows, 1987, Raffi in Concert with the Rise and Shine Band, 1989, Evergreen, Everblue: An Ecology Album for the '90's, 1990; Broadway appearances: A Family Concert, 1993, Bananaphone, 1994; videos: A Young Children's Concert with Raffi, 1985, Raffi and the Rise and Shine Band, 1988; author: Down By the Bay, 1988, Shake My Sillies Out, 1988, Baby Beluga, 1990, (with Debi Pike) Like Me and You, 1994. Recipient Order of Can., 1983, Parents' Choice award Parents' Choice Mag.,. Office: Troubadour Records Ltd, 1075 Cambie St, Vancouver, BC Canada M2M 3W3

RAFFIN, THOMAS A., physician; b. San Francisco, Jan. 25, 1947; s. Bennett L. and Carolyn M. Raffin; m. Michele Raffin, June 19, 1987; children: Elizabeth S., Ross Daniel, Jake Bennett, Nicholas Ethan. AB in Biol. Sci., Stanford Med. Sch., 1968, MD, 1973. Diplomate Am. Bd. Pulmonary Medicine, Am. Bd. Internal Medicine (also in Critical Care Medicine). Intern Peter Bent Brigham Hosp., 1973-75; fellow in respiratory medicine sch. medicine Stanford U., Stanford, Calif., 1975-78, med. fiberoptic bronchoscopy service dir. med. ctr., 1978—, acting asst. prof. sch. medicine, 1978-80, assoc. dir. med. ctr. intensive care units, med. dir. dept. respiratory therapy hosp., 1978—, assoc. prof. medicine sch. medicine, 1986-95, acting chief div. respiratory medicine, 1988—; chief div. pulmonary and critical care Stanford U., 1990—, prof. medicine sch. of medicine, 1995—; co-dir. Stanford U. Ctr. for Biomed. Ethics, 1989—; chmn. ethics com. Stanford U. Med. Ctr., 1987—. Author: Intensive Care: Facing the Critical Choices, 1988; contbr. articles to profl. jours. V.p. lung cancer com., No. Calif. Oncology Group, 1983-85; com. mem. NIH Workshop, 1984. Recipient Henry J. Kaiser Found. award, 1981, 84, 88, Arthur L. Bloomfield award, 1981. Fellow ACP (rep. coun. subsplty. socs. 1986), Am. Coll. Chest Physicians (program com. mem. 1985—); mem. AAAS, Am. Fedn. for Clin. Rsch., Am. Thoracic Soc., Santa Clara County Lung Assn. and Med. Soc., Calif. Med. Assn. (chmn. sect. chest diseases 1984-85), Soc. for Critical Care Medicine, Calif. Thoracic Soc. Jewish. Avocations: painting, gardening. Home: 13468 Three Forks Ln Los Altos CA 94022-2404 Office: Stanford U Med Ctr Dept Medicine Div Pul & Crit Care Med # H3151 Stanford CA 94305

RAFII, SHAHIN, medicine educator; b. Tehran, Iran, May 16, 1960; came to U.S., 1977; s. Daniel and Touran Rafii. BA cum laude in Chemistry, Cornell U., 1982; MD, Albert Einstein Coll. Medicine, 1986. Diplomate Am. Bd. Internal Medicine, Am. Bd. Oncology, Am. Bd. Hematology. Intern in internal medicine N.Y. Hosp., N.Y.C., 1986-87, resident, 1987-89; fellow in hematology and oncology N.Y. Hosp.-Cornell U. Med. Coll., 1989-92, chief fellow, 1991, instr. medicine, 1992-94, asst. prof., 1994—, cons. in hematology and oncology, 1992—. Contbr. articles to med. jours.; designer elec. circuit. Recipient Jack Friedman young investigator award N.Y. Hosp.-Cornell U. Med. Coll., 1993, trainee's award Soc. for Study Blood, 1993, scholar award Am. Soc. Hematology, 1994, clin. investigator award NIH, 1994, Tolly Vinik award, 1994; fellow NSF, 1981, rsch. fellow N.Y. Heart Assn., 1990-92. Mem. Phi Beta Kappa, Alpha Omega Alpha. Avocations: karate, swimming, weightlifting. Office: NY Hosp-Cornell U Med Ctr 525 E 70th St Rm C-606 New York NY 10021-4872

RAFKIN, ALAN, television and film director; b. N.Y.C., July 23, 1928; s. Victor and Til (Bernstein) R.; children—Dru, Leigh Ann. B.S., Syracuse U., 1950. guest lectr. Bowling Green State U., 1975. Actor Robert Q. Lewis TV Show, 1955, daytime shows, CBS-TV; dir. Verdict is Yours, 1960, Mary Tyler Moore Show, 1970-71, Sanford and Son, 1972, Bob Newhart Show, 1972-73, Rhoda, 1973, Let's Switch, 1975, MASH, 1976-77, Love, American Style, 1970-71, Laverne & Shirley, 1977-83; TV movie: One Day at a Time: Barbara's Crisis, 1981-82; films include Ski Party, 1965, The Ghost and Mr. Chicken, 1966, The Ride to Hangman's Tree, 1967, Nobody's Perfect, 1968, The Shakiest Gun in the West, 1968, Angel in my Pocket, 1969, How to Frame a Figg, 1971. Served with U.S. Army, 1950-52. Democrat. Jewish.

RAFSHOON, GERALD MONROE, communications executive; b. N.Y.C., Jan. 11, 1934; s. Jack and Helen (Goodman) R.; m. Eden White Donohue, Mar. 3, 1978; children by previous marriage: Susan, Patricia, Janet, Scott. B.J., U. Tex., 1955. Copywriter Rich's Dept. Store, Atlanta, 1959; Southeastern advt. and publicity mgr. 20th Century Fox Film Corp., Atlanta, 1959-62; nat. advt. mgr. 20th Century Fox, N.Y.C., 1962-63; pres. Gerald Rafshoon Advt., Inc., Atlanta, 1963-77; chmn. bd. Gerald Rafshoon Advt., Inc., 1977-78; asst. to pres. U.S. for communications White House Washington, 1978-79; media and communications dir. Carter Presdl. Campaign, 1976, Carter Re-election Campaign, 1980; pres. Rafshoon Communications, Washington, 1980-88, Rafshoon Prodns., Washington, 1981-88, Consol. Prodns., Inc., Washington, 1988-91; vice-chmn. Consol. Entertainment, Inc., L.A., 1988-91; pres. Gerald Rafshoon Prodn., 1991—; guest scholar Brookings Instn., Washington, 1991—. Exec. prodr. TV spl. and movies including: The Atlanta Child Murders (CBS-TV), 1985, Circle of Violence (CBS-TV), 1986, The Nightmare Years (TNT), 1989, Bob Hope 75th Birthday Spl. (NBC-TV), 1977, Iran (TNT), 1990, Abraham (TNT), 1993, Jacob (TNT), 1994, Joseph (TNT), 1995 (Emmy for Best Miniseries NATAS 1995), Moses (TNT), 1995, Samson and Delilah, 1996; ind. film prodn., 1991—. Trustee Kennedy Center for Performing Arts. Served to lt. USN, 1955-58. Office: 1775 Massachusetts Ave NW Washington DC 20036-2188

RAGAINS, CHARLES C., public relations executive; b. Owensboro, Ky., July 24, 1943. BA in Sociology, Mich. State U., 1965, MA in Journalism, 1967. Pub. rels. rep. Burroughs, 1969-72, mgr. pub. rels. internat. group, 1972-74, mgr. corp. publs. and employee comm., 1974-82; dir. advt. and mktg. comm. Burroughs Corp., Detroit, 1982-88; v.p. Anthony M. Franco, Inc., Detroit, 1987-89, sr. v.p., 1989-91, exec. v.p., COO, 1991-92; pres., owner, 1992—. Mem. NIRI (sec. Detroit chpt. 1978-79). Office: Anthony M Franco Inc 400 Renaissance Ctr Ste 600 Detroit MI 48243-1509*

RAGAN, CHARLES RANSOM, lawyer; b. N.Y.C., Aug. 13, 1947; s. Charles Alexander Jr. and Josephine Forbes (Parker) R.; m. Barbara Thiel McMahon, Aug. 30, 1969; children: Alexandra Watson, Madeline McCue. AB, Princeton U., 1969; JD, Fordham U., 1974. Bar: N.Y. 1975, U.S. Ct. Appeals (3d cir.) 1975, Calif. 1976, U.S. Ct. Appeals (9th cir.) 1976, U.S. Dist. Ct. (no. dist.) Calif. 1976, U.S. Supreme Ct. 1981, U.S. Dist. Ct. (so. dist.) N.Y. 1982, U.S. Ct. Appeals (2d cir.) 1984. Law clk. to Hon. R.J. Aldisert U.S. Ct. Appeals (3rd cir.), 1974-76; assoc. Pillsbury, Madison & Sutro, San Francisco, 1976-81, ptnr., 1982—; mem. exec. com. 9th Cir. Judicial Conf., 1987-91; mem. Civil Justice Reform Act Adv. Group, No. Dist. Calif., 1995—. Contbr. articles to profl. jours. Mem. Inst. Transnational Arbitration (bd. dirs., advisor), San Francisco Bar Assn. (chair feds. cts. 1982-89), Chartered Inst. Arbitrators (assoc.). Avocations: biking, ballet, spectator sports. Office: Pillsbury Madison & Sutro 225 Bush St San Francisco CA 94104-4207

RAGAN, DAVID, publishing company executive; b. Jackson, Tenn., Aug. 26, 1925; s. Amos and Esther Lee (Tacker) R.; m. Violet Claire Sills, Dec. 27, 1948; children—David Nathaniel, Sarah Sills, Jennifer Leigh. B.A. in English, Union U., Jackson, 1947; M. Theatre Arts, Calif. Sch. Theatre, 1950. Radio writer Grand Central Sta., 1950; syndicated columnist Hollywood South Side, 1951; mng. editor Tele-Views mag., 1952; free-lance writer, 1952-57, 74-77, 82—; editor TV and Movie Screen Sterling Group, Inc., N.Y.C., 1957-61; mng. editor Motion Picture mag. Fawcett Pub. Co., N.Y.C., 1961-64; editor TV Radio Mirror, Macfadden-Bartell Pub. Co., N.Y.C., 1964-71; pub., editorial dir. Movie Digest, Words and Music, Planet mags. Nat. Periodical Publs. (Warner Communications), N.Y.C., 1971-74; editorial dir. Photoplay, Motion Picture, TV Mirror mags.; Macfadden Women's Group, N.Y.C., 1977-79; entertainment editor Globe Nat. Weekly, N.Y.C., 1979-82. Author: Who's Who in Hollywood 1900-1976, 1977, Movie Stars of the '30s, 1985, Movie Stars of the '40s, 1985, Mel Gibson: An Intimate Biography, 1985, Who's Who in Hollywood: The Largest Cast of Film Personalities Ever Assembled, rev., 1992; co-author: Richard Pryor: This Cat's Got Nine Lives, 1982; contbr. articles to profl. jours. Served with U.S. Army, 1952-54. Mem. Screen Actors Guild, TV Acad., Alpha Tau Omega, Tau Kappa Alpha. Republican. Presbyterian. Home: 1230 Park Ave New York NY 10128-1724

RAGAN, JAMES THOMAS, communications executive; b. San Diego, Mar. 15, 1929; m. Susan Held, Nov. 9, 1957; children: James, Maria, Carey, Andrew. BA, Oxford U., Eng., 1951, MA, 1955. With Gen. Electric Co., 1954-69; pres., chief operating officer Athena Communications Corp. subs. Gulf & Western Industries, Inc., N.Y.C., 1969-74; v.p. broadcast services Western Union Telegraph Co., 1974-76, v.p. satellite services, 1976-82, pres. Western Union personal communications corp., v.p. communication systems group, 1982-85; pres. Associated Info. Services Corp., 1985-86, Bunting, Inc., 1985-86; ptnr. Pierce Kennedy Hearth, 1988-91; CEO Nat. Lang. Assocs. Lanarea Pub., Guilford, Conn., 1990—. Patentee recreational sports equipment. Pres. Wilton (Conn.) Pop Warner Football League, 1972-73. Served with USMCR, 1952-54, maj. (ret.). Mem. Sachem's Head Assn. (v.p., treas.), Sachem's Head Yacht Club (Guilford, Conn.), Madison (Conn.) Winter Club (pres.). Clubs: Racquet and Tennis (N.Y.C.); Sachem's Head Yacht (Guilford, Conn.); Madison Winter (pres.). Home: 630 Colonial Rd Guilford CT 06437-3139 Office: Nat Lang Assocs PO Box 442 Guilford CT 06437-0442

RAGATZ, THOMAS GEORGE, lawyer; b. Madison, Wis., Feb. 18, 1934; s. Wilmer Leroy and Rosanna (Kindschi) R.; m. Karen Christensen, Dec. 19, 1965; children—Thomas Rolf, William Leslie, Erik Douglas. BBA, U. Wis.-Madison, 1957, LLB, 1961. Bar: Wis. 1961, U.S. Dist. Ct. (ea. and we. dists.) Wis. 1961, U.S. Tax Ct. 1963, U.S. Ct. Appeals (7th cir.) 1965, U.S. Supreme Ct. 1968; CPA, Wis. Staff acct. Peat, Marwick, Mitchell & Co., Mpls., 1958; instr. Sch. Bus., U. Wis.-Madison, 1958-60, formerly lectr. in acctg. and law Law Sch. U. Wis.; law clk. Wis. Supreme Ct. , 1961-62; assoc. Boardman Suhr Curry & Field, Madison, 1962-64, ptnr., 1965-78; ptnr.

Foley & Lardner, Madison, 1978—, mgr. ptnr., 1984-93; dir. Sub-Zero Freezer Co., Inc., Wis. Tales & Trails, Inc., Acme Equipment Corp., Mortenson, Matzell & Meldrem, Inc., Norman Bassett Found.; dir., past pres. Wis. Amateur Sports Corp.; lectr. seminars on tax subjects. Editor in chief Wis. Law Rev., 1960-61; chmn. Nat. Conf. Law Revs., 1960-61; author: The Ragatz History, 1989; contbr. articles to profl. jours. Formerly dir. United Way, Meth. Hosp. Found.; mem. U. Wis. Found., United Way of Dane County; chmn. site selection com. U. Wis. Hosp.; bd. regents U. Wis., panel provision of legal svcs.; former moderator 1st Congl. Ch.; past pres. First Congl. Ch. Found.; bd. dirs. Met. YMCA, Madison, 1983-90, YMCA Found.; pres. Bus. & Edn. Partnership, 1983-89, also bd. dirs. Fellow Am. Bar Found.; mem. ABA, Seventh Cir. Bar Assn., Wis. Bar Found., State Bar Wis. (sec. 1969-70, bd. govs. 1971-75, chmn. fin. com. 1975-80, chmn. tax sect., chmn. spl. com. on econs., chmn. svcs. for lawyers com.), Dane County Bar Assn. (pres. 1978-79, chmn. jud. qualification com., sec.), Am. Judicature Soc., Wis. Inst. CPAs, Madison Club (pres. 1980-81), Order of Coif, Bascom Hill Soc., Beta Gamma Sigma, Sigma Chi, Order of Constantine. Republican. Home: 3334 Lake Mendota Dr Madison WI 53705-1469 Office: Foley & Lardner 150 E Gilman St PO Box 1497 Madison WI 53701-1497 also: Foley & Lardner 1st Wisconsin Ctr 777 E Wisconsin Ave Milwaukee WI 53202-5302

RAGENT, BORIS, physicist; b. Cleve., Mar. 2, 1924; s. Samuel and Bertha (Lev) R.; m. Dorothy Kohn, Sept. 11, 1949; children—David Stefan, Lawrence Stanton, Jesse Ron. Student, Ohio State U., 1941-44; B.S.E.E., Marquette U., 1944; Ph.D. in Physics, U. Calif., Berkeley, 1953. Registered profl. engr., Calif. Engr. Victoreen Instrument Co., Cleve., 1946-48; engr., physicist Radiation Lab., U. Calif., Berkeley, 1948-53; physicist Livermore, 1953-56, Broadview Research Corp., Burlingame, Calif., 1956-59, Vidya div. Itek Corp., Palo Alto, Calif., 1959-66, Ames Research Ctr., NASA, Moffett Field, Calif., 1966-87, San Jose (Calif.) State U. Found., 1987—; lectr. Stanford U., U. Calif. Extension. Served in USNR, 1944-46. Mem. AAAS, Am. Phys. Soc., Optical Soc. Am., Am. Geophys. Union, Sigma Xi. Office: Ames Research Ctr NASA Mail Stop 245-1 Moffett Field CA 94035

RAGGI, REENA, federal judge; b. Jersey City, May 11, 1951. BA, Wellesley Coll., 1973; JD, Harvard U., 1976. Bar: N.Y. 1977. U.S. atty. Dept. Justice, Bklyn., 1986; ptnr. Windels, Marx, Davies & Ives, N.Y.C., 1987; judge U.S. Dist. Ct. (ea. dist.) N.Y., Bklyn., 1987—. Office: US Courthouse 225 Cadman Plz E Brooklyn NY 11201-1818

RAGGIO, KENNETH GAYLORD, lawyer, mediator; b. Dallas, Oct. 18, 1949; s. Grier H. and Louise (Ballerstedt) R.; m. Patricia Thornbury, June 28, 1980; children: Jeffrey, Michael. BA, U. Tex., Austin, 1971, JD, 1974. BarL Tex. 1974, U.S. Dist Ct. (no. dist.) Tex. 1974. Pvt. practice Austin, 1974-76; shareholder Raggio & Raggio, Inc., Dallas, 1977—; speaker, lectr. in field of tracing and characterization of property, and applying tech. to clients cases. Contbr. to profl. publs. Recipient Cici Simon Meml. award Children's Rights Coun., 1993. Mem. ABA (chair family law sect. 1991-92, spl. com. on project 2000, 1991-95), Tex. Bar Found., Am. Acad. Matrimonial Lawyers, Internat. Acad. Matrimonial Lawyers, Tex. Acad. Family Law Specialists, State Bar Tex., Dallas Bar Assn. (chair family law sect. 1980-81). Office: Raggio & Raggio Inc 3316 Oak Grove Ave Dallas TX 75204-2365

RAGGIO, LOUISE BALLERSTEDT, lawyer; b. Austin, Tex., June 15, 1919; d. Louis F. and Hilma (Lindgren) Ballerstedt; m. Grier H. Raggio, Apr. 19, 1941; children: Grier, Thomas, Kenneth. B.A., U. Tex., 1939; student, Am. U. Washington, 1939-40; J.D., So. Methodist U., 1952. Bar: Tex. 1952, U.S. Dist. Ct. (no. dist.) Tex. 1958. Intern Nat. Inst. Pub. Affairs, Washington, 1939-40; asst. dist. atty. Dallas County, Tex., 1954-56; shareholder Raggio and Raggio, 1956—. Sec. Gov.'s Commn. on Status of Women, 1970-71; trustee Tex. Bar Found., 1982-86, chmn., 1984-85, chmn. fellows, 1993—, Dallas Women's Found., 1993—, Nat. Conf. Bar Founds., 1986-92. Recipient Zonta award, Bus. and Profl. Women's Club award, So. Meth. U. Alumni award, Woman of Yr. award Tex. Fedn. Bus. and Profl. Women's Clubs, 1985, award Internat. Women's Forum, 1990, Disting. Law Alumni award So. Meth. U., 1992; Disting. Trial Lawyer award, 1993, Outstanding Trial Lawyer award Dallas Bar Assn., 1993, Pacemaker award Nat. Bus. Women Owners Assn., 1994, Thomas Jefferson award ACLU, 1994, Courage award Women Journalists North Tex., 1995; inducted into Tex. Women's Hall of Fame, 1985. Fellow Am. Bar Found.; mem. ABA (chmn. family sect. 1975-76, Best Woman Lawyer award 1995), LWV (pres. Austin 1945-46), State Bar Tex. (chmn. family law sect. 1965-67, dir. 1979-82, citation for law reform 1967, Pres.'s award 1987, Sarah T. Hughes award 1993), Dallas Bar Found. (pres. fellow com. 1991), Am. Acad. Matrimonial Lawyers (gov. 1973-81, trustee found. 1992—), Bus. and Profl. Women's Club (pres. Town North 1958-59), Phi Beta Kappa (pres. Dallas chpt. 1970-71, 90-92). Unitarian. Home: 3561 Colgate Ave Dallas TX 75225-5010 Office: Raggio and Raggio 3316 Oak Grove Ave Dallas TX 75204-2365 *All things are possible in our expanding universe if we can tune in to the infinite power available to all of us. Our ancestors concentrated on the problems—let us be a part of the solutions so desperately needed in our complex and troubled world.*

RAGGIO, WILLIAM JOHN, state senator, lawyer; b. Reno, Oct. 30, 1926; s. William John and Clara M. (Cardelli) R.; student La. Poly. Inst., 1944-45, U. Okla., 1945-46; BA, U. Nev., 1948; JD, U. Cal. at Hastings, 1951; m. Dorothy Brigman, August 15, 1948; children: Leslie Ann, Tracy Lynn, Mark William. Bar: Nev. 1951, U.S. Supreme Ct. 1959. Atty., Reno and Las Vegas; asst. dist. atty. Washoe County, Nev., 1952-58, dist. atty., 1958-71; ptnr. firm Wiener, Goldwater, Galatz & Raggio, Ltd., 1971-72, Raggio, Walker & Wooster Reno and Las Vegas, 1974-78, Raggio, Wooster & Lindell, 1978-92, sr. ptnr. Vargas & Bartlett, 1992—; mem. Nev. Senate, 1973—, minority floor leader, 1977-81, 82-87, 91, majority flr. leader, 1987—; mem. legis. commn., vice chmn. criminal law and adminstrn. com. Council State Govts., 1972-75; bd. dirs. Am. Savs. & Loan Assn.; v.p., dir. Sahara Resorts, Casino Properties, Inc., Sahara Las Vegas, Inc. Adv. bd. Salvation Army, Reno; mem. Nev. Am. Revolutionary Bicentennial Commn., 1975-81; mem. Republican State Cen. Com. Bd. dirs. YMCA, Reno chpt. NCCJ, Salvation Army; nat. chmn. Am. Legislative Exchange Council, dir. Sierra Health Svcs.; trustee Nat. Dist. Attys. Found. (vice chmn. 1962-65); trustee Community Action Program Washoe County. Republican candidate for U.S. Senate, 1970. Served with USNR, 1944-46; to 2d lt. USMCR, 1946-47. Named Young Man of Yr., Reno-Sparks Jr. C. of C., 1959; recipient Disting. Nevadan award, 1968, Fellows award The Salvation Army, Torch of Liberty award The Anti-Defamation League, SIR award Assoc. Gen. Contractors, 1995. Fellow Am. Bd. Criminal Lawyers (v.p. 1978—); mem. ABA (state chmn. jr. bar conf. 1957-60, ho. dels.) Am. Judicature Soc., Navy League, Air Force Assn., Nat. (nat. pres. 1967-68; named Outstanding Prosecutor 1965), Nev. State (sec. 1959, pres. 1960-63) Dist. Attys. Assn., NCCJ (Brotherhood award 1965), Nev. Peace Officers Assn., Internat. Assn. Chiefs Police, Am. Legion, Elks, Lion Club, Prospectors Club, Alpha Tau Omega, Phi Alpha Delta. Republican. Roman Catholic. Home: PO Box 281 Reno NV 89504-0281

RAGHAVAN, RAMASWAMY SRINIVASA RAJU, astrophysics and nuclear physics researcher; b. Tanjore, India, Mar. 31, 1937; came to U.S., 1962; m. Pramila Raghavan, 1967. MA, U. Madras, India, 1957, MSc, 1958; PhD in Physics, Purdue U., 1965. Rsch. asst. Tata Inst. Fundamental Rsch., Bombay, India, 1959-62, Purdue U., Lafayette, Ind., 1962-65; fellow Bartol Rsch. Found., Swarthmore, Pa., 1965-66; vis. prof. U. Bonn, Germany, 1966-67; rsch. scientist Tech. U. Munich, Munich, 1967-72; mem. staff Bell Labs., Murray Hill, N.J., 1972-89; disting. mem. staff physics AT&T Bell Labs., Murray Hill, N.J., 1989—; assoc. grad. faculty Rutgers U., 1974-87; co-spokesman for solar neutrino physics and astrophysics Borexino Internat. Collaboration, Italy, 1988—. Editl. bd. Hyperfine Interactions Jour., 1983-92. Fellow Am. Phys. Soc. Achievements include original research in frontier topics in nuclear physics, elementary particle physics, astrophysics, solid state physics and microelectronics applications; invented several methods for neutrino astronomy of the sun. Avocations: crossword puzzles, history. Office: Bell Labs 1E432 600 Mountain Ave New Providence NJ 07974

RAGHU, RENGACHARI, medicine, nutrition, biotechnology and chemistry consultant, agriculture consultant; b. Amur, Tamilnadu, India, Mar. 22, 1943; came to U.S., 1975; s. Rengachari Veeraraghavachari and Sakunthala Krishnaswamy Rengachari; m. Kamala Rengan, Dec. 1, 1972; children: Anand, Adithya. HMB, Hanemann Homeopathic Inst., Bangalore, India, 1963; MS, Annamalai U., Chidambaram, India, 1965; MBA, S.P. Mandalia's Inst., Bombay, 1973; PhD, Bhaba Atomic Rsch. Ctr., Bombay, 1974. Asst. mgr. Amoor (India) Estates, 1962-65; mgr. Sakunthala Chemists, Tiruvarur, India, 1962-65; sr. rsch. fellow TB Ctr, Madras, India, 1965-68; sr. sci. officer Bhaba Atomic Rsch. Ctr., Bombay, 1968-75; dir. rsch. divsn. ob-gyn. Meharry Med. Coll., Nashville, 1975-85; chief clin. chemistry Apollo Hosps., Madras, 1985-89; rsch. cons. Vanderbilt U., Nashville, 1988-89; chmn. clin. biochemistry Nat. Chiropractic Coll., Lombard, Ill., 1989-90; pres. Internat. High Tech. Transfer, Nashville, 1990—. Contbr. over 50 articles to sci. publs.; inventor no-share syringe. Bd. dirs. March of Dimes, Nashville, 1979-83, Juvenile Diabetes Fedn., Nashville, 1983-85, Jr. C. of C., Nashville, 1981-83; mem. bd. trustees Hindu Cultural Ctr., Nashville, 1983-90; mem. commerce adv. com. State of Tenn., Nashville, 1980-84; intern Mr. Bob Clement, U.S. House of Reps., U.S. Congress, Washington, 1994; mem. nat. steering com. Davidson County, Nashville, State of Tenn. Clinton/Gore '96 Campaign. March of Dimes fellow, N.Y., 1975-78; rsch. grantee Nat. Cancer Inst., Washington, 1981-86. Fellow Indian Phytopathology Soc. (life); mem. Am. Clin. Chemists, Soc. Biol. Chemists, Soc. Exptl. Biol. Medicine, Soc. Pharmacology, Soc. Preventive Medicine. Democrat. Home: 822 Kendall Dr Nashville TN 37209-4512 Office: Internat High Tech Transfer 822 Kendall Dr Nashville TN 37209-4512

RAGINSKY, NINA, artist; b. Montreal, Apr. 14, 1941; d. Bernard Boris and Helen Theresa R.; 1 child, Sofia Katrina. BA, Rutgers U., 1962; studied painting with, Roy Lichtenstein; studied sculpture with, George Segal; studied Art History with Allan Kaprow, Rutgers U. Freelance photographer Nat. Film Bd., Ottawa, Ont., Can., 1963-81; instr. metaphysics Emily Car Coll. Art, Vancouver, B.C., Can., 1973-81; painter Salt Spring Island, B.C., 1989—; sr. artist, jury Can. Coun.; selected Can. rep. in Sweden for Sweden Now Mag., 1979; tchr., lectr. in field, 1973—. One woman shows include Vancouver Art Gallery, Victoria Art Gallery, Edmonton Art Gallery, Art Gallery Ont., San Francisco Mus. Art, Acadia U., Nancy Hoffman Gallery, N.Y.C., Meml. U. Newfoundland Art Gallery; exhibited in group shows at Rutgers U., 1962, Montreal Mus. Fine Arts, 1963, Nat. Film Bd., Ottawa, 1964, 65, 67, 70, 71, 76, 77, Internat. Salon Photography, Bordeaux, France, 1968, Nat. Gallery Ottawa, 1968, Eastman House Rochester, N.Y., 1969, Vancouver Art Gallery, 1973, 80, Mural for Conf. Ctr. Ottawa, 1973, Field Mus., Chgo., 1976, Edmonton Art Gallery, 1978, 79, Walter Philips Gallery, 1979, Glenbow Mus. Gallery, 1979, Harbour Front Community Gallery, 1980, Hamilton Art Gallery, 1980, Musée Maisil de St. Lambert, 1981, Mendel Art Gallery, 1981, Dunlop Art Gallery, Regina, Can., 1981; represented in permanent collections Nat. Film Bd. Stills divsn., Ottawa, Ont., Banff (Alta.) Sch. Fine Arts, Nat Gallery Ottawa, Can., George Eastman House, Wadsworth Atheneum, Edmonton Art Gallery, various pvt. collections. Bd. dirs. Island Watch, Salt Spring Island, B.C., 1993; founder, coord. Salt Spring Island Ecosys. Stewardship Project, 1993; founder, coord. Salt Spring Island Waterbird Watch Collective, 1994—. Mem. Royal Can. Acad. Arts, Order Can. (officer 1985). Avocations: gardening, birding, subject of numerous publs. Home and Office: 272 Beddis Rd, Salt Spring Island, BC Canada V8K 2J1

RAGLAND, ALWINE MULHEARN, judge; b. Monroe, La., July 28, 1913; m. LeRoy Smith, 1947 (dec.); children—LeRoy, Caroline Smith Christman; m. 2d., L. Percy Ragland (dec.). A.A., Principia Coll., St. Louis; J.D., Tulane U., 1935. Bar: La. 1935. Sole practice, Tallulah, La., 1935-74; mem. firm Mulhearn & Smith, 1972-74; judge 6th Jud. Dist. Ct., Lake Prvidence, La., 1974-90; atty. for inheritance tax collector Madison Parish, La., 1968-74; former city atty., Delta, La.; temporary judge La. Ct. Appeals (2d cir.), 1976; atty., Tallulah, La., 1991. Charter bd. dirs. Silver Waters council Girl Scouts U.S.A.; past pres. Band Boosters Assn. Tallulah High Sch., Tallulah High Sch. PTA; past dist. dir., past bd. dirs, lay reader 1st Ch. Christ Scientist, Vicksburg, Miss.; past bd. dirs. Delta Christian Sch. Mem. ABA, La. Bar Assn., 6th Jud. Bar Assn., La. Def. Counsel Assn. (jud. assoc. mem.), Am. Judges Assn., La. Judges Assn., Am. Judicature Soc., La. Council Juvenile and Family Ct. Judges (past pres.), Nat. Council Juvenile Ct. Judges, So. Juvenile Ct. Judges, Assn. Trial Lawyers Am., La. Trial Lawyers Assn., Family Conciliation Cts. and Services, Nat. Juvenile Ct. Service Assn., La. Conf. Social Welfare, Practicing Law Inst., Nat. Assn. Women Judges, La. Assn. Def. Counsel. Home and Office: 206 Monroe St Tallulah LA 71282-5226

RAGLAND, CARROLL ANN, law educator; b. New Orleans, Nov. 28, 1946; d. Herbert Eugene Watson and Mary May (LeCompte) Leathers; children: Robert A. Sinex, Jr., Stacie Bateman, Joy Montgomery. JD, San Francisco Law Sch., 1980. Bar: Calif. 1980. Pvt. practice Santa Rosa, Calif., 1980-85; child custody mediator Sonoma County Superior Ct., Santa Rosa, 1985-86; chief dep. county counsel Butte County Counsel, Oroville, Calif., 1986-87; chief dep. dist. atty. Butte County Dist. Atty., Oroville, 1987-94; referee Shasta County Superior Ct., Redding, Calif., 1995-96; commr. Shasta County Superior Ct., Redding, 1996—; dean faculty, law prof. Calif. No. Sch. of Law, Chico, 1987—; instr. Shasta Coll., 1996—. Commr. Yuba County Juvenile Justice and Delinquency Prevention Commn., Marysville, Calif., 1993-94. Fellow Lawyers in Mensa. Avocations: scuba diving, reading, crossword puzzles. Office: Shasta County Superior Ct 1431 Market St Redding CA 96001

RAGLAND, INES COLOM, principal; b. Washington, Mar. 12, 1947; d. Jose Luis Sr. and Frances Yerby (Pannill) Colom; m. Banjamin Michael Ragland, Dec. 17, 1977 (div. May 1991); children: Michelle Elizabeth, Rachael Christine. BA in Secondary Edn., Longwood Coll., 1969, MS in Secondary Adminstrn., 1992. Clk. Va. State Water Control Bd., Richmond, 1969; tchr. Spanish Richmond City Pub. Schs., 1969-74; planning supr. Va. State Water Control Bd., 1974-78; asst. prin., tchr., prin. Grove Ave. Bapt. Christian Sch., Richmond, 1978-83; guidance tchr., asst. prin. Victory Christian Acad., Richmond, 1990—; cons. in field. Mission participant, El Salvador, 1992. Mem. ASCD. Avocations: civil war research, church. Office: Victory Christian Acad 8491 Chamberlayne Rd Richmond VA 23227-1550

RAGLAND, JACK WHITNEY, artist; b. El Monte, Calif., Feb. 25, 1938; s. Jack Rider and Dorsey (Whitney) R.; m. Marilee J. Weaver, July 31, 1969; children—Roxanne, Natasha. B.A., Ariz. State U., 1960, M.A., 1964; postgrad., UCLA, 1961-64. Grad. asst. tchr. Ariz. State U., 1960-61; grad. teaching asst. UCLA, 1961-64; head art dept. Simpson Coll., Indianola, Iowa, 1964-76; demonstrator Nat. Art Materials Trade Assn., Denver, 1993, Pasadena Conv. Ctr., 1994. One-man shows include Kleine Gallery, Vienna, Austria, Billy Son Gallery, Coralville, Iowa, Tamarack Gallery, Stillwater, Minn., Percival Galleries, Des Moines, Simpson Coll., Internat. Art Svc., Pan Pacific Hotel, San Diego, Lakes Art Center, Okaboji, Iowa, Greenstone Ct. Collection, Fallbrook, Calif., Santa Barbara (Calif.) Art Co.; exhibited in group shows, Lyn Kottler Gallery, N.Y.C., Phoenix Art Mus., Tucson Festival Art, Talisman Gallery, Bartlesville, Okla., Exhibiting Artists Fedn., Poultney, Vt., Des Moines Art Center, Danskin Gallery, Palm Desert, Calif., Joslyn Mus. Art, Omaha, Lagerquist Gallery, Atlanta, Glez-Harkins Gallery, Palm Desert, Calif., Cabrillo Art Ctr., Point Loma, Calif., San Diego, NAMTA Art Show, San Francisco, 1995, Eagle Gallery, La Jolla, Calif., Tirage Gallery, Alta Dena, Calif., Polson Gallery, Pasadena, Show Case Houses, Pasadena, Rancho Santa Fe, Calif., 1995; represented in permanent collections, Albertina Museum, Vienna, Kunsthaus, Basel, Switzerland, Bibliothèque National, Paris, Los Angeles County Mus., Simpson Coll., Phoenix Art Mus., Ariz. State collection, Graphische Bundes Versuchsanstalt, Vienna, Austria, also pvt. collections, works include stained glass windows, Meth. Ch., Perry, Iowa.; works reproduced Applause mag, 1971, New Woman mag, 1974, Artists of Cen. and No. Calif., Vol. II, San Diego Better Homes and Gardens Lifestyles mag., 1995, San Diego Decorating mag., 1995, Pasadena Showcase House Design Mag., 1995. Recipient grand purchase prize Ariz. Ann. Art Show, 1961, 1st prize in prints Iowa State Fair, 1974, 1st prize So. Calif. Expn., Del Mar; featured in Am. Artist mag. Oct. 1993. Home: 5490 Rainbow Heights Rd Fallbrook CA 92028-9619 *To capture the spiritual essence of a subject through form and color is the goal of my art.*

RAGLE, GEORGE ANN, accountant; b. Detroit, Dec. 21, 1946; d. Joseph Theodore and Josephine Theresa (Mastrogiovanni) Gibson; m. James Albert, Sept. 3, 1976; children: Gina Ann, Jeffrey Allen. Assoc. Bus., Oakland C.C., Farmington Hills, Mich., 1974; B Accountancy, Walsh Coll., Troy, Mich., 1975; MBA, Ctrl. Mich. U., 1981. Cert. sch. bus. adminstr., Mich. Tax analyst Burroughs Corp., Detroit, 1976, Robillard & Joyce, St. Clair Shores, Mich., 1977-78; acctg. mgr. Baker Driveaway, Bloomfield Hills, Mich., 1978-79; staff acct. Macomb County Contr., Mt. Clemens, Mich., 1979-80; sr. acct. Macomb Intermediate Sch. Dist., Mt. Clemens, 1980-86; dir. bus. Mt. Clemens Community Schs., 1986-88, Pinconning (Mich.) Area Sch., 1988-90; dir. bus. and pers. St. Clair Intermediate Sch. Dist., Port Huron, Mich., 1990—. Bd. officer, treas. Fraser (Mich.) Pub. Schs. Bd. Edn., 1984-88; mem. Anchor Bay Schs. Bd. Edn., New Baltimore, Mich., 1991-95, treas., 1991-92, 94-95. Mem. Assn. Sch. Bus. Ofcls., Mich. Sch. Bus. Ofcls., Mich. Assn. Sch. Pers. Adminstrs., Macomb/St. Clair Sch. Bus. Ofcls. Avocation: gourmet cooking. Home: 52134 Charleston Ln New Baltimore MI 48047-1191 Office: St Clair Intermediate Sch Dist 499 Range Rd Port Huron MI 48061

RAGLE, JOHN LINN, chemistry educator; b. Colorado Springs, Colo., Feb. 4, 1933; s. Richard Charles and Jane Addams (Hulbert) R.; m. Roberta Ann Litzerman, July 26, 1990. BS, U. Calif., Berkeley, 1954; PhD, Wash. State U., 1957. Asst. prof. U. Mass., Amherst, 1957-60, assoc. prof., 1964-67, prof., 1968-75, 1976—; rsch. assoc. Cornell U., Ithaca, N.Y., 1960-62; scientist Northrop Space Labs., Hawthorne, Calif., 1962-64; vis. assoc. prof. U. B.C., Vancouver, Can., 1967-68; vis. prof. Technische Hochschule, Darmstadt, Fed. Republic Germany, 1975-76. Contbr. articles to profl. jours. Recipient Sr. U.S. Scientist award von Humboldt Stiftung, 1975. Mem. Am. Phys. Soc., Am. Chem. Soc. Republican. Avocations: music, computers, amateur radio, hiking, gardening. Office: U Mass Dept Chemistry Amherst MA 01003

RAGNO, NANCY NICKELL, educational writer; b. Phila., Sept. 2, 1938; d. Paul Eugene and Sara Jane (Mensch) Nickell; m. Joseph Diego Ragno, Aug. 25, 1961; 1 child, Michelle Angela. BA, Lebanon Valley Coll., 1960; MA, NYU, 1968. Cert. tchr., N.J. Tchr. N.J. pub. schs., 1961-68; project editor Prentice-Hall, Inc., Englewood Cliffs, N.J., 1968-70, Harcourt Brace Jovanovich, N.Y.C., 1970-72; sr. editor Silver Burdett Co., Morristown, N.J., 1972-76; editor, writer Houghton Mifflin Co., Boston, 1976-77; sr. editor J.B. Lippincott Co., Phila., 1977-79; sr. author Silver Burdett Ginn, Morristown, 1984—. Author: (textbook series) Silver Burdett English, 1984, World of Language, 1992, (sound filmstrip) The City and the Modern Writer, 1970, Buying on the Installment Plan, 1974. Bassoonist Harrisburg (Pa.) Symphony Orch., 1959, Plainfield (N.J.) Symphony Orch., 1976, Somerset (N.J.) County Orch., 1989, Princeton (N.J.) Community Orch., 1992. Mem. ASCD, Nat. Coun. Tchrs. English, Internat. Reading Assn., Am. Soc. Journalists and Authors, Textbook Authors Assn., Authors Guild, U.S. Power Squadron. Democrat. Mem. Ch. of Christ. Avocations: music, writing, boating. Home: 38 Tortoise Ln Tequesta FL 33469

RAGO, ANN D'AMICO, public relations professional, educator; b. Pitts., Aug. 24, 1957; d. Jack and Florence (Zappa) D'Amico; m. John Thomas Rago, Aug. 31, 1984; children: Annie J., Emily J. BA, Duquesne U., Pitts., 1979, MA, 1987. From communications assoc. to dir. pub. relations Duquesne U., 1979-89, coord. univ. relations, 1989-93, exec. dir. pub. affairs, 1993—, adj. prof. comm. Editor University Record, 1989 (silver medal). Bd. dirs. Support Pitts., 1989-91; sch. dir. Carylnton Sch. Bd., Pitts., 1989-93, pres. sch. bd., 1990. Recipient Gold award for publs./external prospectus 9th Ann. Admissions Advt. Awards, 1994, Gold award for Total Pub. Rels. Campaign, 10th Ann. Admissions Advt. Awards, 1995, Gold award for Total Pub. Rels. Campaign, 11th Ann. Admissions Awards, 1996, 1st Place award in Category 35, Internal Pub. Rels. Campaign, Pitts. chpt. Women in Comm., Inc., 1996. Mem. Pub. Rels. Soc. Am. (1st place award 1993), Internat. Assn. Bus. Communicators (award of excellence 1991, award of honor 1993, award of merit 1994), Am. Mgmt. Assn., Press Club Western Pa., Sigma Delta Chi. Office: Duquesne U 405 Adminstrn Bldg Pittsburgh PA 15282

RAGON, ROBERT RONALD, clergyman; b. Flintstone, Ga., Sept. 10, 1939; s. Robert Emmett and Frances Cora (Stoner) R.; m. Judith Ann Ward, Apr. 27, 1962; children: Ronald Russell, Regina Renee. BS, U. Chattanooga, 1962; BDiv, MDiv, Columbia Theol. Sem., Decatur, Ga., 1967. Ordained to ministry Presbyn. Ch., 1967. Pastor Trion (Ga.) Presbyn. Ch., 1967-72; dir., pastor Chattooga County Presbyn. Ministries, Trion, 1971-72; pastor Brainerd Presbyn. Ch., Chattanooga, 1972—; moderator Knoxville Presbytery, 1979-80; founder An Order of Slaves of Christ, Chattanooga, 1970; stated clk. Presbytery of S.E., 1990-93. Author: Covenant Agreement: O.S.C., 1970, The Journey, 1990. Trustee King Coll., Bristol, Tenn., 1983-86. Mem. Masons (Ga. chaplain 1980), KT (sec. 1991), Shriners, Kiwanis (bd. dirs. Chattanooga 1986-90). Republican. Avocation: investments. Home: 4229 Happy Valley Rd Flintstone GA 30725-2222 Office: Brainerd Presbyterian Church 7 N Tuxedo Ave Chattanooga TN 37411-3728

RAGONE, DAVID VINCENT, former university president; b. N.Y.C., May 16, 1930; s. Armando Frederick and Mary (Napier) R.; m. Katherine H. Spaulding, Dec. 18, 1954; children: Christine M., Peter V. S.B., MIT, 1951, S.M., 1952, Sc.D., 1953. Asst. prof. chem. and metall. engring. U. Mich., Ann Arbor, 1953-57, assoc. prof., 1957-61, prof., 1961-62; asst. dir. John J. Hopkins Lab for Pure and Applied Sci., also chmn. metallurgy dept. Gen. Atomic div. Gen Dynamics, La Jolla, 1962-67; Alcoa prof. metallurgy Carnegie-Mellon U., Pitts., 1967-69; assoc. dean Carnegie-Mellon U. (Sch. Urban and Pub. Affairs), 1969-70; dean Thayer Sch. of Engring., Dartmouth Coll., 1970-72, Coll. Engring., U. Mich., 1972-80; pres. Case Western Res. U., Cleve., 1980-87; vis. prof., dept. materials sci. and engring. MIT, Cambridge, 1987-88, sr. lectr. dept. materials sci. and engring., 1988—; gen. ptnr. Ampersand Spity. Materials Ventures, 1988-92; ptnr. Ampersand Specialty Materials Ventures, 1992—; trustee Mitre Corp.; bd. dirs. Cabot Corp., Augat Inc., Sifco Inc. Mem. Nat. Sci. Bd., 1978-84; mem. tech adv. bd. U.S. Dept. Commerce, 1967-75; chmn. adv. com. advanced auto power systems Council on Environ. Quality, 1971-75; Trustee Henry Luce Found. Named Outstanding Young Engr., Engring. Soc. Detroit, 1957. Mem. Univ. Club (N.Y.C.), Longwood Cricket Club (Boston), Sigma Xi, Tau Beta Pi. Office: MIT Dept Materials Sci Eng Rm 8-301 Cambridge MA 02139

RAGSDALE, CARL VANDYKE, motion picture producer; b. Illmo, Mo., May 16, 1925; s. Vandyke and Iona Lee (Bledsoe) R.; m. Diane E. Ringrose, Sept. 18, 1976; children: John Sheldon, Susan Lee. Student, Wash. U., 1942-43; BA, Denison U., 1950. Commd. ensign USN, 1945, advanced through grades to capt., 1972; ops. officer on staff comdr. in-chief Pacific, 1945; officer-in-charge Western Pacific Fleet Camera Party, 1946-47; capt. Res., 1954-85; photo officer USS Eldorado, Korea, 1950-52; dir.-prodr. USN Photo Ctr., 1952-53; comdg. officer Naval Res. Combat Camera Group—Atlantic, 1972-74; comdg. officer Naval Res. Office Info., N.Y.C., 1975-76, Houston, 1977-83; v.p. Depicto Films Inc., N.Y.C., 1954-62; pres. Carl Ragsdale Assocs. Inc., Houston and N.Y.C., 1962—. Producer films including A Year Towards Tomorrow, 1966, While I Run This Race, 1967. Vice chmn. USS San Jacinto Com., 1987; chmn. USS Houston (CA30) Found., 1991—. Decorated Navy Commendation medal with Gold star, Navy Meritorious Svc. medal; recipient Oscar award Acad. Motion Picture Arts and Scis., 1966, nomination, 1967, Silver Anvil award Pub. Rels. Soc. Am., 1983, Meritorious Pub. Svc. award, U.S. Navy, 1995. Mem. Dirs. Guild Am., Naval Res. Assn., Naval Order of U.S. (founder Tex. commandery), Am. Legion, DAV, Naval Aviation Commandery, Navy League, Inst. Diving, Underwater Photog. Soc., Soc. Motion Picture and TV Engrs., Houston C. of C., Mil. Affairs Com., N.Y. Athletic Club, Riverbend Country Club, Masons, Shriners. Republican.

RAGSDALE, GEORGE ROBINSON, lawyer; b. Raleigh, N.C., Mar. 26, 1936; s. George Young and Susan (Jolly) R.; m. Adora Prevost, Oct. 20, 1962; children: John Robinson, George Young II, Adora P. AB, U. N.C., 1958, LLB, 1961. Asst. to chief counsel U.S. Senate Subcom. on Constnl. Rights, Washington, 1961-62; law ptnr. Bailey & Ragsdale, Raleigh, 1962-65; legal counsel to Dan K. Moore, Gov. of N.C., Raleigh, 1965-68; judge Superior Ct. of N.C., Raleigh, 1968-70; ptnr. Moore, Ragsdale, Liggett, Ray & Foley, Raleigh, 1970-86, LeBoeuf, Lamb, Leiby & MacRae, Raleigh, 1987-93, Ragsdale, Liggett & Foley, 1994—; lectr. N.C. Assn. Def. Counsel.

Trustee U. N.C., Chapel Hill, 1979-87, vice-chmn. bd. trustees, 1983-84, chmn., 1984-85; trustee U. N.C. Endowment, 1980—, chmn., 1984-85; bd. dirs. U. N.C. Instnl. Devel. Found., Inc., 1985—, U. N.C.-Chapel Hill Found.; bd. visitors U. N.C., The Ednl. Found., Inc. Mem. ABA, N.C. Bar Assn., Wake County Bar Assn., Assn. Bar of City of N.Y., Def. Rsch. Inst., Raleigh C. of C., Kiwanis, Sphinx Club of Raleigh, Terpsichorean Club, Raleigh Execs. Club, Carolina Country Club, Laurel Ridge Country Club. Episcopalian. Office: Ragsdale Liggett & Foley 2840 Plaza Pl PO Box 31507 Raleigh NC 27622

RAGSDALE, KEITH ELLEN, nurse, educator, administrator; b. Austin, Tex., Dec. 27, 1949; d. Kenneth B. and Janet (Dittlinger) R. AAS, Del Mar Coll., 1971; BS, Purdue U., 1973; MS, U. Colo., 1974; EdD, Nova Southeastern U., 1994. Asst. prof. rsch. and mgmt. U. So. Miss., Hattiesburg, 1974-75; asst. prof. community health Tex. Christian U., Ft. Worth, 1975-78; assoc. prof., acting asst. dean U. N.D., Grand Forks, 1978-79; chair divsn. nursing and allied health Austin C.C., 1982-95, dir. acad. support, 1995—. Contbr. articles to profl. publs. Mem. Nat. League for Nursing (v.p. Tex. chpt.), World Future Soc., Tex. Assn. ADN's (chmn. legis. com.), Tex. Deans and Dirs., Tex. Jr. Coll. Tchrs. Assn., Sigma Theta Tau. Home: Rte 1 1300 Cardinal Dr Paige TX 78659-9742 Office: Austin CC 1020 Grove Blvd Austin TX 78741-3337

RAGSDALE, RICHARD ELLIOT, healthcare management executive; b. St. Louis, Dec. 20, 1943; s. Billie Oscar and Isabelle (Roques) R.; m. Anne Elizabeth Ward, Aug. 20, 1968; children: Richard, Kevin, Bethany. B.B.A., Ohio U., 1965; M. in Internat. Commerce, Am. Grad. Sch. Internat. Mgmt., 1968. Asst. treas. Chase Manhattan Bank, N.Y.C., 1968-73; v.p., treas. Hosp. Affiliates Internat., Nashville, 1973-80; v.p., treas., chief fin. officer INA Health Care Group, Dallas, 1980-81; sr. v.p., chief fin. officer, dir. Republic Health Corp., Dallas, 1981-83, sr. exec. v.p., dir., 1983-85; chmn. Community Health Systems Inc., Brentwood, Tenn., 1985—, Great No. Health Mgmt., Ltd., London, 1986-89, Pro Med Co., Inc., Ft. Worth, 1994—; bd. dirs. RehabCare Group, Inc., St. Louis; chmn. ProMed Co., Inc. Ft. Worth, Tex. Coach Spring Valley Athletic Assn., Dallas, 1985; trustee Watkins Inst., 1988-94; trustee Benton Hall Sch., 1988—, chair, 1991—; trustee Maryville Coll., 1990—, chair, 1992—. Recipient Thunderbird Disting Alumni award Entrepreneurship, 1990, Jonas Meyer Disting. Alumni award, 1993. Mem. Fedn. Am. Hosps. (legis. commn. 1984-95). Republican. Avocations: SCUBA diving, drag racing. Office: Community Health Systems Inc 155 Franklin Rd Ste 400 Brentwood TN 37027-4646

RAHAL, ROBERT W., automotive company executive; b. Medina, Ohio, Jan. 10, 1953; s. Michael G. and Barbara (Woodward) R.; m. Deborah Ann Kuhl, Nov. 16, 1980; children: Michaela, Jarrad, Graham. BA in History, Denison U., Granville, Ohio, 1975. Profl. race car driver, 1982—; owner Bobby Rahal, Inc., Dublin, Ohio, 1988—. Hon. chmn. Easter Seals, Cen. Ohio, Columbus, 1985—; chmn. Children's Hosp., Columbus, 1988—; trustee Columbus Zoo, 1986—. Winner numerous car races including the Indianapolis 500, 1986; named CART champion, 1986, 87, 92. Avocations: golf, antiques, antique cars, reading. Office: Bobby Rahal Inc PO Box 39 Hilliard OH 43026-0039*

RAHALL, NICK JOE, II (NICK RAHALL), congressman; b. Beckley, W.Va., May 20, 1949; s. Joe and Alice Rahall; children: Rebecca Ashley, Nick Joe III, Suzanne Nicole. AB, Duke U., 1971. Staff asst. U.S. Senator Robert C. Byrd, 1971-74; sales rep. Sta. WWNR, Beckley, 1974; pres. Mountaineer Travel Co., Beckley, 1975-77, W.Va. Broadcasting, 1980—; mem. 95th-104th Congresses from 4th (now 3rd) W.Va. dist., Washington, 1977—; mem. transp. and infrastructure com. with subcom. on r.r.'s and surface transp., mem. resources com. with subcom. on energy and mineral resources and nat. parks, forests and lands; bd. dirs. Rahall Comm. Corp. Del. Dem. Nat. Conv., 1972, 74, 78, 80, 84, 88, 92; W.Va. chmn. March of Dimes, 1979. Named Young Man of Year, Beckley Jaycees, 1972; Outstanding Young Man in W.Va., W.Va. Jaycees, 1977; recipient Achievement award Logan Cripple Children Soc., 1978; Citizenship award K.C., 1978, Disting. Svc. award Am. Fedn. Govt. Employees W.Va., 1984, Young Dem. of Yr. Dem. Nat. Conv., 1980, Outfitter of Yr. Profl. Outfitters, 1987, Seneca award Sierra Club 1988, River Conservation award Am. River 1988; named Coal Man of Yr. Coal Industry News, 1979. Mem. NAACP, NRA, Elks, Moose, Masons (33d degree) Shriners. Presbyterian. Office: US Ho of Reps 2269 Rayburn HOB Washington DC 20515-4803

RAHE, MARIBETH SEMBACH, bank executive; b. Evanston, Ill., Oct. 3, 1948; d. Daniel F. and Boysie (Beebe) Sembach; m. Martin E. Rahe, May 31, 1975. BA, Bowling Green State U., 1970; postgrad., Ohio State U., 1970-72; MA in Internat. Mgmt., Am. Grad. Sch. Internat. Mgmt., 1974. Internat. banking officer Harris Bank, Chgo., 1974-77; asst. v.p. Harris Bank, London, 1977-80; v.p. Morgan Guaranty Trust Co., London, 1980-83, N.Y.C., 1983-84; sr. rep. Sparebanken Oslo Akershus, N.Y.C., 1984-85; v.p. Morgan Guaranty Trust Co., N.Y.C., 1985-87, J.P. Morgan Investment Mgmt., N.Y.C., 1987-88; sr. v.p. Harris Bank, Chgo., 1988-91, dept. exec., 1991-94, sr. exec. v.p., 1994-95, vice chmn. bd., 1995—; bd. dirs. Harris Bankcorp., Trustmark Ins. Co. Bd. dirs. Children's Meml. Hosp., Rush Presbyn. Hosp., U. Chgo.; trustee Ill. Inst. Tech. Recipient Outstanding Alumni award Am. Grad. Sch., 1991. Mem. Am. Bankers Assn. (vice chmn. 1991-92, chmn. 1992-93, exec. com. pvt. banking, banking advisor 1993—), Com. of 200, Econ. Club, Chgo. Women's Network, Chgo. Club. Republican. Lutheran. Office: Harris Trust & Savs Bank 111 W Monroe St Chicago IL 60603-4003

RAHE, RICHARD HENRY, psychiatrist, educator; b. Seattle, May 28, 1936; s. Henry Joseph and Delora Lee (Laube) R.; m. Laurie Ann Davies, Nov. 24, 1960 (div. Dec. 1990); children: Richard Bradley, Annika Lee. Student, Princeton U., 1954-57; MD, U. Wash., 1961. Diplomate Am. Bd. Psychiatry and Neurology. Chief resident in psychiatry U. Wash. Sch. Medicine, Seattle, 1965; rsch. psychiatrist USN, San Diego, 1965-75; commdg. officer Naval Health Rsch. Ctr., San Diego, 1976-80; exec. officer Long Beach (Calif.) Naval Hosp., 1980-82; commdg. officer Guam Naval Hosp., Agana, 1982-84; prof. psychiatry U.S. Univ. Health Scis. Mil. Med. Sch., Bethesda, Md., 1984-86, U. Nev. Sch. Medicine, Reno, 1986—; dir. Mil. Stress Studies Ctr., Bethesda, 1984-86, Nev. Stress Ctr., Reno, 1986—. Contbr. numerous articles to sci. jours., chpts. to books; photographer prints and video. Med. dir. Nev. Mental Health Inst., Sparks, 1991-94. Capt. USN, 1965-86. Recipient Humanitarian award Vietnamese Refugee Com., 1974, Dept. of State award for treatment of Am. hostages held in Iran, 1981. Fellow Am. Psychiat. Assn.; mem. Am. Psychosomatic Soc. (past pres.), World Psychiat. Assn. (past. pres. mil. sect.). Avocations: hiking, skiing, swimming. Home: 638 Saint Lawrence Ave Reno NV 89509-1440 Office: VA Med Ctr Code 151-C 1000 Locust St Reno NV 89520-0102

RAHEEL, MASTURA, textile scientist, educator; b. Lahore, Pakistan, Mar. 1, 1938; d. Sultan Mohamad and Firdous Dean; M.S., Punjab U., 1959, Okla. State U., 1962; Ph.D., U. Minn., 1971; m. Akbar Javed Raheel, Jan. 25, 1959; children: Seemal, Salman. Asst. prof., head dept. textiles and clothing Home Econs. Coll., Lahore, Pakistan, 1960-77; lectr. textiles and clothing U. Minn., 1977-78; vis. prof. Ind. U., Bloomington, 1978; asst. prof. textile sci. U. Ill., Urbana, 1978-84, assoc. prof., 1984-91, chmn. div. textiles, apparel and interior design, 1987-89, prof., 1991—. Recipient Gold medal, 1960; Ford. Found. fellow, 1960-62, 68-71, rsch. grantee, 1979—. Mem. Internat. Textile and Apparel Assn., Am. Chem. Soc., Am. Assn. Textile Chemists and Colorists, Am. Home Econs. Assn. (Mfr. Fiber Rsch. award 1989), Coll. International de L'enseignement Textile, Omicron Nu, Sigma Xi. Contbr. rsch. articles to profl. and tech. jours. Home: 2611 Willoughby Rd Champaign IL 61821-7567 Office: U Ill 239 Bevier Hall Urbana IL 61801

RAHHAL, DONALD K., obstetrician, gynecologist; b. Clinton, Okla., 1942. MD, U. Okla. Coll. Medicine, 1971. Diplomate Am. Bd. Ob.-Gyn. (bd. dirs.). Resident Indiana U. Hosp., Indpls., 1971-74; obstetrician-gynecologist Mercy Health Ctr., Okla. City, 1981—, Deaconess Hosp., Okla. City, 1981—; clin. prof. U. Okla. Coll. Medicine, Okla. City, 1981—. Mem. ACOG, AMA, Am. Bd. Med. Specialties (del.), Coll. Acad. Obstetricians, Gynecologists. Office: 4200 Memorial Dr Ste 410 Oklahoma City OK 73120-9349*

RAHILL, MARGARET FISH, retired museum curator; b. Milw., Feb. 21, 1919; d. Joseph Benedict and Margaret (Scherdan) Schmidt; m. William James Fish, Nov. 14, 1941 (dec. 1945); 1 child, Mary Fish Arcuri; m. Frank M. Rahill, Mar. 14, 1951 (dec. Oct. 1986); children: Marguerite, Laura Rahill Maramba. BA, U. Wis., 1958; student, Mt. Mary Coll., 1958. With pub. rels. Blackland Army Air Base, Waco, Tex., 1942-43; reporter, art critic Milw. Sentinel, 1945-62; with pub. rels. dept. Milw. Art Mus., 1962-63, Layton Sch. Art, Milw., 1965-68, Bel Canto Chorus, Milw., 1965-68; curator in charge Charles Allis Art Mus., Milw., 1968-91; prin. Book Bay, Milw., 1962-72; vis. instr. journalism Marquette U., Milw., 1972-73; mem. organizing com. Florentine Opera Club, 1962, with pub. rels. dept. 1962-65, Bel Canto Chorus, 1966-68; mem. organizing com. Wis. Chamber Orch., Milw., 1975-76; v.p. art, councillor-at-large Wis. Acad. Sci. Arts and Letters, Madison, 1981-85; juror numerous art competitions, Wis., 1962-91. Contbr. articles to profl. jours. Active City of Milw. Art Commn., 1982-90, pres., 1984-85. Recipient Gridirm award Milw. Press Club, 1955, 57, 59, 60, Community Svc. award Milw. Art Commn., 1976, Ann. Bookfellows award Milw. Pub. Libr., 1977, Devel. award Milw. County Hist. Soc., 1982, Promotion of Hispanic Culture award Centro de la Communidad Unida, 1988. Mem. Wis. Painters and Sculptors (hon.), Wis. Crafts Coun. (hon.). Roman Catholic. Avocations: Oriental art studies, child care, reading. Home: 4801 Connecticut Ave NW Apt 302 Washington DC 20008-2203

RAHL, LESLIE LYNN, risk advisor, entrepreneur; b. N.Y.C., May 16, 1950; d. Myron and Esther (Botwin) Horwitz; m. Jeffrey Mark Lynn, Dec. 20, 1969 (div. 1981); m. J. Andrew Rahl Jr., Apr. 30, 1989; 1 child, Kevin; stepchildren: Kaitlin, Stephen. SB, MIT, 1971, MBA, 1972. V.p. swaps and derivatives Citibank, N.Y.C., 1972-91; pres. Leslie Rahl Assocs., N.Y.C., 1991-94; co-prin. Capital Market Risk Advisors, N.Y.C., 1994—; presenter in field. Contbr. articles to profl. jours. Recipient On the Rise award Fortune. Mem. Internat. Assn. Fin. Engrs. (bd. dirs. 1993—), Madison Beach Club. Avocation: wine tasting. Office: Capital Market Risk Advisors 565 Fifth Ave New York NY 10017

RAHM, BARBARA JANE, counselor; b. Waukegan, Ill., Nov. 16, 1941; d. Alton Romeo and Jane Romaine (Gregory) Kaste; m. Kenneth J. Schultz, Aug. 24, 1963 (div. Dec. 1990); children: Annemarie Katharine, Kristin Elise, Carleen Janette. B of Edn., U. Wis., 1963; MA in Guidance, Northeastern U., 1991. Cert. counselor. Audio-visual dir., libr. Sch. Dist. 155, Crystal Lake, Ill., 1984-88; counselor, case mgr. Family Svc. Assn., Elgin, Ill., 1991-93; sch. counselor Simmons Mid. Sch., Aurora, Ill., 1993—. Mem. ACA. Home: 1085 Hecker Dr Elgin IL 60120-4604

RAHM, DAVID ALAN, lawyer; b. Passaic, N.J., Apr. 18, 1941; s. Hans Emil and Alicia Katherine (Onuf) R.; m. Susan Eileen Berkman, Nov. 23, 1972; children: Katherine Berkman, William David. AB, Princeton U., 1962; JD, Yale U., 1965. Bar: N.Y. 1966, D.C. 1986. Assoc. Paul, Weiss, Rifkind & Wharton, N.Y.C., 1965-66, 1968-69; asst. counsel N.Y. State Urban Devel. Corp., N.Y.C., 1969-72, assoc. counsel, 1972-75; counsel real estate div. Internat. Paper Co., N.Y.C., 1975-80; ptnr. Stroock & Stroock & Lavan, N.Y.C., 1980-83, sr. ptnr., 1984—; mem. legis. com. Real Estate Bd. N.Y., 1988-92; lectr. Old Dominion Coll., Norfolk, Va., 1967-68, NYU, 1986—; mem. editl. bd. Comml. Leasing Law and Strategy, 1988-95; mem. N.Y.C. bd. advisors Commonwealth Land Title Ins. Co., 1996—. Contbr. articles to profl. jours. Fund raiser corp. com. N.Y. Philharm., N.Y.C., 1980-84; trustee Manhattan Sch. Music, 1989—, treas., 1991-94, chmn., 1994—; mem. N.Y.C. bd. advs. Commonwealth Land Title Ins. Co., 1996—. Mem. ABA (comml. leasing com. 1987-88, 94—, pub./pvt. devel. com. 1989—, real property sect.), Assn. of Bar of City of N.Y. (housing and urban devel. com. 1977-80, 81-84, real property com. 1989-92), Princeton Club. Democrat. Presbyterian. Avocations: music, reading, travel. Office: Stroock Stroock & Lavan 7 Hanover Sq New York NY 10004-2616

RAHM, SUSAN BERKMAN, lawyer; b. Pitts., June 25, 1943; d. Allen Hugh and Selma (Wiener) Berkman; m. David Alan Rahm, Nov. 23, 1972; children: Katherine, William. BA with honors, Wellesley Coll., 1965; postgrad., Harvard U., 1966-68; JD, NYU, 1973. Bar: N.Y. 1974, D.C. 1988. Assoc. Marshall, Bratter, Greene, Allison & Tucker, N.Y.C., 1973-81, ptnr., 1981-82; ptnr. Kaye, Scholer, Fierman, Hays & Handler, N.Y.C., 1982—, chair real estate dept., 1993—; N.Y. adv. bd., Chgo. Title Ins. Co., 1995. Editor: New York Real Property Service, 1987. Bd. dirs. Girls Inc., 1989-93; mem. aux. bd. Mt. Sinai Hosp., N.Y.C., 1976-78. Recipient cert. of outstanding svc. D.C. Redevel. Land Agy., 1969, She Knows Where She's Going award Girls' Clubs of Am., 1987. Mem. ABA, Assn. of Bar of City of N.Y., N.Y. Bar Assn. (real property law com., co-chmn. real-estate devel. . 1987-91), Am. Coll. Real Estate Lawwyers, Comml. Real Estate Women N.Y. (bd. dirs. 1988-94), v.p. 1988-91, pres. 1991-93). Office: Kaye Scholer Fierman Hays & Handler 425 Park Ave New York NY 10022-3506

RAHMAN, MUHAMMAD ABDUR, mechanical engineer; b. Sylhet, Assam, India, Mar. 1, 1930; came to U.S., 1950; s. Haji Sajjad Ali Khan and Momotaj Khanom. BSME, U. Toledo, 1953, MSME, 1968; PhD in Engring., Calif. Coast U., 1985. Registered prof. engr., Calif. Mech. design engr. various cons. firms, L.A., 1955-61; aerospace engr. Douglas Aircraft Co., Santa Monica, Calif., 1962-63, N.Am. Aviation, Inc., L.A., 1963-64, NASA Manned Spacecraft Ctr., Houston, 1964-70; safety engr. U.S. Dept. Labor, OSHA, Washington, 1975-86; invention researcher Arlington, Va., 1987—; Contbr. articles to profl. jours. Mem. N.Y. Acad. Scis. Democrat. Islam. Achievements include patent for solar energy collector, supersonic MHD generator system; copyrights for hypothesis on unified field theory and creation of the universe, on the mechanism of superconductivity, a note of caution of superconductivity in reference to permeability and permitivity, concentration on suggesting methods to build superconductors and biomedical engineering instrumentation for cancer in particular, others. Home and Office: 1805 Crystal Dr # 1013-s Arlington VA 22202-4402

RAHMAN, RAFIQ UR, oncologist, educator; b. Mirali, Pakistan, Mar. 3, 1957; came to U.S., 1985; s. Rakhman and Bibi (Sana) Gul; m. Shamim Ara Bangash; children: Maryam, Hassan, Haider. BS, MB, U. Peshawar, Pakistan, 1980. Bd. cert. internal medicine, med. oncology; lic. physician Pa., Ala., Ky. House officer in internal medicine Khyber Teaching Hosp.-U. Peshawar, Pakistan, 1980-81, house officer in gen. surgery, 1981, jr. registrar med. ICU, 1983-84; jr. registrar internal medicine Khyber Teaching Hosp., 1981-82; sr. registrar internal medicine Khyber Teaching Hosp.-Lady Reading Hosp. & Postgrad. Inst., Peshawar, 1984-85; Audrey Meyer Mars fellow in med. oncology Roswell Park Cancer Inst., Buffalo, 1985-86; resident in internal medicine SUNY-Buffalo Gen. Hosp.-Erie County Med. Ctr.-VA Med. Ctr., 1986-88; chief resident in internal medicine SUNY-Buffalo-Erie County Med. Ctr., 1988; fellow in hematology and med. oncology SUNY-Buffalo-Roswell Park Cancer Inst., 1989-90; hematologist, med. oncologist Daniel Boone Clinic and Harlan A.R.H., 1991-92; clin. asst. prof. medicine U. Ky., 1991—; attending physician, hematology/med. oncologist Hardin Meml. Hosp., Elizabethtown, 1993—, chief medicine, 1996; tchr. med. students Med. Sch., SUNY; participant CALGB protocol studies Roswell Park Cancer Inst., investigator. Editor English sect. Cenna mag. Cenna; contbr. articles to profl. jours. Mem. Pakistan Med. & Dental Coun., Ky. Med. Assn., Harlan County Med. Soc., Hardin-LaRue County Med. Soc. Avocations: traveling, aeromodeling, swimming, studying political science and history. Home: 400 Briarwood Cir Elizabethtown KY 42701-8913 Office: 1107 Woodland Dr Ste 105 Elizabethtown KY 42701-2749

RAHMAN, YUEH-ERH, biologist; b. Kwangtung, China, June 10, 1928; came to U.S., 1960; d. Khon and Kwei-Phan (Chan) Li; m. Aneesur Rahman, Nov. 3, 1956; 1 dau., Aneesa. B.S., U. Paris, 1950; M.D. magna cum laude, U. Louvain, Belgium, 1956. Clin. and postdoctoral research fellow Louvain U., 1956-60; mem. staff Argonne (Ill.) Nat. Lab., 1960-72, biologist, 1972-81, sr. biologist, 1981-85; prof. pharmaceutics Coll. Pharmacy, U. Minn., Mpls., 1985—, dir. grad. studies, pharmaceutics, 1989-92, head dept. pharmaceutics, 1991—; vis. scientist State U. Utrecht, Netherlands, 1968-69; adj. prof. No. Ill. U., DeKalb, 1971-85; cons. NIH.; Mem. com. of rev. group, div. research grants NIH, 1979-83. Author. Recipient IR-100 award, 1976; grantee Nat. Cancer Inst., Nat. Inst. Arthritis, Metabolic and Digestive Diseases. Fellow Am. Assn. Pharm. Scientists; mem. AAAS, Am. Soc. Cell Biology, N.Y. Acad. Scis., Radiation Rsch. Soc., Assn. for Women in Sci. (1st pres. Chgo. area chpt. 1978-79). Unitarian. Patentee in field. Home: 902 Dartmouth Pl SE Minneapolis MN 55414-3158 Office: Coll Pharmacy U Minn Minneapolis MN 55455

RAHN, ALVIN ALBERT, former banker; b. St. Paul, Apr. 8, 1925; s. Albert and Manda (Lau) R.; m. Helen Lyngen, June 10, 1950; children: Jennifer, Karen, Paul. B.B.A., U. Minn., 1949; postgrad., Stonier Sch. Banking, 1968. C.P.A., Minn. With income tax div. Minn. Dept. Taxation, 1949-61, asst. dir., 1957-61; with 1st Bank System Inc., Mpls., 1961-85; treas. 1st Bank System Inc., 1969-85, chief fin. officer, 1973-74, sr. v.p., 1974-85. Served with USNR, 1943-46. Mem. Am. Inst. C.P.A.s, Minn. Soc. C.P.A.s, Fin. Execs. Inst. Home: 5601 Dewey Hill Rd Minneapolis MN 55439-1919

RAHN, RICHARD WILLIAM, economist, business executive; b. Rochester, N.Y., Jan. 9, 1942; s. William Fred and Evelyn Janet (Chapman) R.; children: Margie Lynn, Richard William Jr.; m. Anneli Heinonen. BA, U. South Fla., 1963; MBA, Fla. State U., 1964; PhD, Columbia U., 1972; LLD (hon.), Pepperdine U., 1993. Instr. Fla. State U., Tallahassee, 1964-66; mem. grad. faculty dept. mgmt. Poly. Inst. N.Y., 1964-72, assoc. prof., 1973, adminstrv. officer, 1970-72; head dept., 1972-73; mng. dir. Ripon Soc., Cambridge, Mass., Washington, 1973-74; pres. Richard W. Rahn & Assocs. (Managerial Economists), Washington, 1974-76; econ. cons. N.Y. Merc. Exch., 1974-80; exec. dir., 1976-80; bd. dirs. Am. Coun. for Capital Formation, Washington, 1976—; v.p., chief economist C. of C. of U.S., 1980-91; exec. v.p. Nat. Chamber Found., 1985-91; adj. prof. George Mason U., Fairfax, Va., 1974-80; adj. scholar Hudson Inst., CATO Inst.; commentator on nat. radio and TV; bd. dirs. IRET. Editor-in-chief Jour. Econ. Growth, 1986-91; contbr. articles to profl. jours., newspapers and mags. Mem. N.Y. County Republican Com., 1973, Nat. Social Security Adv. Council, 1982-83. Mem. Nat. Assn. Bus. Econs. (pres. Washington chpt. 1980), Adj. Scholar Discovery Inst. (pres. 1992—, CEO Novecon Mgmt. and Novecon Ltd.), Bus. Leadership Coun. (chmn. bd. 1995—), Mont Pelerin Soc., Pvt. Sector Coun. (bd. advisors). Republican. Club: Internat. Home: 8917 Potomac Forest Dr Great Falls VA 22066-4111 Office: 1020 16th St NW Ste 200 Washington DC 20036-5702

RAHR, STEWART, health medical products executive; b. 1946. BA, N.Y. Univ., 1968. CEO Kinray, pres., 1978, sole stockholder, 1984. Office: 152-35 Tenth Ave Whitestone NY 11357

RAIBLE, PETER SPILMAN, minister; b. Peterborough, N.H., Nov. 22, 1929; s. Robert Jules and Mildred (Galt) R.; m. Dee Dee Rainbow, June 18, 1950 (div. 1968); children: Stephen M., Robin S., Robert R., Deborah R.; m. Marcia McClellan Barton, June 5, 1987. PhB, U. Chgo., 1949; BA, U. Calif., Berkeley, 1952; MDiv, Starr King Sch. Ministry, 1953, D in Sacred Theology (hon.), 1974. Ordained to ministry Unitarian Ch. Asst. minister First Unitarian Ch., Providence, 1953-55; minister Unitarian Ch., Lincoln, Nebr., 1955-61, Univ. Unitarian Ch., Seattle, 1961—; bd. pres. Starr King Sch., Berkeley, 1967-68; mem. exec. com. Coun. Chs., Seattle, 1982-88; adj. prof. Meadville Lombard, 1987-88, N.W. Theol. Union, 1989, Seattle U., 1995. Author: How to Case a Church, 1982, Manual for Ordination Installation Services, 1994; book editor: Jour. Liberal Ministry, 1965-71; editor UU Polity Manual, 1992. Bd. dirs. Coun. Planning Affiliates, Seattle, 1969-73, Wash. State chpt. ACLU, Seattle, 1963-67; chmn. ministerial adv. com. Planned Parenthood Ctr., Seattle, 1963-68; pres. UN Assn., Lincoln, 1959-61; pres. Unitarian Universalist Ptnr. Ch. Coun., 1995—. Cpl. USAF, 1948-49. Merrill fellow Harvard U., Cambridge, Mass., 1972. Mem. Unitarian Universalist Ministers Assn. (pres. 1973-75), Pacific N.W. Dist. Unitarian Universalist Assn. (exec. 1962-64, pres. 1985-87, mem. commn. on appraisal 1977-81), Unitarian Universalist Ptnr. Ch. Coun. (pres. 1995—). Office: U Unitarian Ch 6556 35th Ave NE Seattle WA 98115-7332

RAICHLE, ELAINE LUCAS, retired art educator; b. Fremont, Nebr., Dec. 14, 1915; d. Arthur Wilson and Lily Kathryn (Christensen) Lucas; m. Donald Roderick Raichle, Dec. 15, 1942; children; Douglas, Donald, Alan, Lynne. BA, Midland Coll., 1939; MA, Columbia U., 1949, EdD, 1955. Cert. fine arts tchr., Nebr. Elem. tchr. Cedar Bluffs (Nebr.) Sch., 1937-35, Garden City (Nebr.) Sch., 1935-36; primary tchr. Fremont Pub. Schs., 1936-39, supr. art, 1939-42; art tchr. Irvington (N.J.) High Sch., 1951-53; supr. art edn. Irvington Pub. Schs., 1953-87; mem. bd. trustees Classroom Renaissance N.J. Dept. Edn., Trenton, 1968-72; founder, trustee N.J. Sch. Arts, Trenton, 1980—; advisor art dept. Kean. Coll. N.J., Union, 1974—. Co-editor: Art Education Issues, 1989, History of Art Educators of New Jersey, 1990, The Year of Crafts, 1994, Art: A Cultural Connection, 1995, Art History: Our Heritage, 1996; contbr. numerous articles to profl. jours. Founder, pres. Irvington Symphony Orch., 1968-87, Irvington Cultural Com., 1968-87; co-founder Arts Adminstrs., N.J., 1968; designer Teen Arts N.J., 1970. Lt. (j.g.) USN, 1942-44. Named Citizen of Yr. Irvington C. of C., 1988; recipient Art awards Gov. N.J., 1989, 91. Fellow N.J. Art Edn. Assn. (disting.); mem. Nat. Art Edn. Assn. (N.J. Art Educator of Yr. 1990, Art Adminstr. eastern divsn. 1991), N.J. Congress Parents and Tchrs. (arts chmn. 1966-74, life), Art Educators N.J. (chmn. speakers com. 1988-95, Disting. Art Educator award 1990), Getty Confs. Art Edn., N.J. Coun. on Edn. (founder), Ret. Art Educators N.J., Nat. Ret. Art Educators (treas. 1988-96), Arts Alliance in Edn., Hands and Minds Inst. Avocations: theater, gardening, bridge, travel. Home: 43 Meadow Lakes 08 Hightstown NJ 08520-3348

RAICHLE, MARCUS EDWARD, radiology, neurology educator; b. Hoquiam, Wash., Mar. 15, 1937; m. Mary Elizabeth Rupert, 1964; children: Marcus Edward, Timothy Stephen, Sarah Elizabeth, Katherine Ann. BS, U. Wash., 1960, MD, 1964. Diplomate Am. Bd. Psychiatry and Neurology. Intern Balt. City Hosps., 1964-65, resident, 1965-66; asst. neurologist N.Y. Hosp. Cornell Med. Ctr., N.Y.C., 1966-68, neurologist, chief resident, 1968-69; clin. instr. dept. medicine divsn. neurosci. U. Tex. Med. Sch., San Antonio, 1969-70; rsch. instr. Washington U. Sch. Med., St. Louis, 1971-72, from asst. prof. neurology to assoc. prof. neurology, 1972-78, from asst. prof. radiology (radiation scis.) to assoc. prof. radiology Edward Mallinckrodt Inst. Radiology, 1972-79, from asst. prof. to assoc. prof. biomedical engring., 1974-79, prof. neurology, 1978—, prof. radiology Edward Mallinckrodt Inst. Radiology, 1979—, prof. biomedical engring., 1979—; instr. dept. neurology Cornell U. Med. Coll., N.Y.C., 1968-69; asst. neurologist Barnes Hosp., St. Louis, 1971-75, assoc. neurologist, 1975-78, neurologist, 1978—; cons. neurologist St. Louis Children's Hosp., 1975—; neurologist Jewish Hosp., St. Louis, 1984—, St. Louis Regional Hosp., 1985—; mem. neurology study sect. A NIH, 1975-79; mem. com. cerebrovascular diseases Nat. Inst. Neurol. Diseases and Stroke, long range planning effort, 1978, basic sci. task force, 1979, mem ad hoc adv. panel, Nat. Inst. Neurol. Diseases and Stroke, 1983, chmn. PET grants spl. rev. com., 1983, chmn. brain imaging ctrs. spl. rev. com., 1985; mem. adv. bd. McDonnell-Pew Program cognitive neuroscience, 1989; other coms. Editorial bds. Stroke, 1974-82, Neurology, 1976-82, Annals of Neurology, 1979-86, Journal Cerebral Blood Flow and Metabolism, 1983-86, dep. chief editor, 1981-83, Brain, 1985-90, Human Neurobiology, 1985-87, Brain Research, 1985-90, Synapse, 1987-90, Journal Neuroscience, 1989—, Journal Cognitive Neuroscience, 1989—, Cerebral Cortex, 1990—, Journal Nuclear Medicine, 1990—, Biological Psychiatry, 1993—, Learning and Memory, 1993—; over 120 pub. papers; contbr. over 75 book chpts., revs. Major USAF, 1969-71. Recipient numerous awards, lectrs., fellows; sr. McDonnell fellow McDonnell Ctr. Studies Higher Brain Function, Washington U., St. Louis, 1982—. Mem. AAAS, Am. Heart Assn. (stroke coun. 1974—, cardiovascular D rsch. study com. 1975-78, Academia Rodinensis Pro Remediatione (acting), Am. Acad. Neurology, Am. Neurological Assn. (councillor 1986-88, nom. com. 1990-91), Am. Physiological Soc., Assn. Rsch. Nervous and Mental Disease, Birmingham Med. Rsch. Expeditionary Soc., Explorers Club (N.Y.), Internat. Soc. Cerebral Blood Flow and Metabolism (sec. 1985-89, pres. elect 1989-91, pres. 1991-93), Inst. Medicine/NAS, Internat. Double Reed Soc., Soc. Neuroscience (pub. rels. com. 1988—), St. Louis Soc. Neurological Scis., Soc. Nuclear Medicine.

RAICHLEN, FREDRIC, civil engineering educator, consultant; b. Balt., Oct. 12, 1932; s. Samuel Israel and Ethel Lee (Fribush) R.; m. Judith Kurschner, May 29, 1968; children: Robert, David. B of Engring., Johns Hopkins U., 1953; MSc, MIT, 1955, DSc, 1962. Registered profl. engr., Calif., N.J. Asst. prof., assoc. prof. civil engring. Calif. Inst. Tech., Pasadena, 1962-72, prof. civil engring., 1972—; fellow, asst. prof. civil engring. MIT, 1962; consulting engr., Pasadena, 1962—. 1st lt. USAF, 1956-59. Fellow ASCE (recipient John C. Moffatt and Frank E. Nichol Harbor and Coastal Engring. award 1994); mem. NAE, Internat. Assn. Hydraulic Rschrs., Sigma Xi. Home: 2157 Homet Rd San Marino CA 91108 Office:

Calif Inst Tech Dept Civil Engineering 1201 E California Blvd Pasadena CA 91125-0001

RAIDER, LOUIS, physician, radiologist; b. Chattanooga, Sept. 7, 1913; s. Leaha Reevin; m. Emma Silberstein, Oct. 19, 1940; children: Lynne Dianne, David Bernard, Paula Raider Olichney. BS, Bklyn. Coll., 1935; MD, Dalhousie U., 1941. Diplomate, cert. Am. Bd. Radiology. Intern Met. Hosp., N.Y.C., 1940-41, resident in radiology, 1941-42; resident in radiation therapy Bellevue Hosp., N.Y.C., 1942-43; fellow in cancer therapy NIH, N.Y.C., 1943-44; chief of radiology Vets. Hosp., New Orleans, 1947-50; radiologist, chief radiology Providence Hosp., Mobile, Ala., 1950-76; clin. prof. Med. Sch. U. South Ala., Mobile, 1987—. Contbr. articles to profl. jours. Maj. AUS, 1944-47. Fellow Am. Coll. Radiology, Am. Coll. Chest Physicians; mem. Radiol. Soc. N.Am., Am. Roentgen Ray Soc., AMA, Ala. Acad. Radiology (pres. 1970-71, Silver medal 1989), So. Med. Assn. (chmn. sect. radiology 1973-74), Soc. Thoracic Radiology, So. Radiol. Conf., Am. Soc. Emergency Radiology. Democrat. Jewish. Home: 1801 S Indian Creek Dr Mobile AL 36607-2309 Office: Hosp U South Ala 2451 Fillingim St Mobile AL 36617-2238

RAIKEN, ESTHER CAGEN, librarian; b. Cleve., Dec. 22, 1907; d. Charles and Ida (Kaufman) Hirsch; m. Samuel Lawrence Cagen, June 18, 1934 (dec. Jan. 1982); children: Lenore, Barbara (dec.), Robert; m. Oscar Harris Raiken, Sept. 18, 1988. BS, Western Res. U., 1962, MLS, 1963. Head children's rm. Lee Br. Libr., Cleveland Heights, Ohio, 1953-57; head Fairfax Sch. libr. Cleveland Heights Sch. Libr. System, 1957-69; instr. children's lit. Case Western Res. U., Cleve., 1964-67, Cleve. State U., 1967-69; dir. pilot media ctr. Belvoir Elem. Sch., Cleveland Heights, 1969-74; libr. Convent of Sacred Heart, San Francisco, 1974-76, Congregation Sherith Israel, San Francisco, 1980—. NDEA scholar Kent (Ohio) U., 1964. Mem. Assn. Jewish Librs. (award presenter 1991, Best Book of Yr. award 1991), AAUW, Beta Phi Mu. Democrat. Jewish. Avocations: reading, walking, travel. Home: 1900 Jackson St San Francisco CA 94109-2860

RAIKES, CHARLES FITZGERALD, lawyer; b. Mpls., Oct. 6, 1930; s. Arthur FitzGerald and Margaret (Hawthorne) R.; m. Antonia Raikes, Dec. 20, 1969; children: Jennifer Catherine, Victoria Samantha. B.A., Washington U., 1952; M.A., Harvard U., 1955, LL.B., 1958. Bar: N.Y. State 1959. Assoc. White & Case, N.Y.C., 1958-69; assoc. gen. counsel Dun & Bradstreet, Inc., N.Y.C., 1969-72; v.p., gen. counsel Dun & Bradstreet, Inc., 1972-73; v.p., gen. counsel The Dun & Bradstreet Corp., N.Y.C., 1973-76, sr. v.p., gen. counsel, 1976-94, of counsel, 1994-95; cons. Bd. Govs. Fed. Reserve System, 1958—. Served with U.S. Army, 1952-54. Woodrow Wilson fellow, 1952. Mem. Assn. Bar City of N.Y., Harvard Club, Sky Club, Phi Beta Kappa. Home: 26 Crooked Trl Rowayton CT 06853-1106 Office: Dun & Bradstreet Corp 187 Danbury Rd Wilton CT 06897-4003

RAIKLEN, HAROLD, aerospace engineering consultant; b. Boston, June 7, 1920; s. Michael Isaac and Jennie Zelda (Jaffee) R.; m. Shirley Gesetz, Nov. 24, 1954; children: David R., Margery Claire. B, MIT, 1947, M, 1949. Dir. electronics and electrics Rockwell, El Segundo, Calif.; v.p. program mgr. Saturn II Rockwell, Downey and Seal Beach, Calif., 1965-70; v.p. rsch. and engring. Rockwell, Downey, Calif., 1970-72; v.p. B-1 bomber engring. Rockwell, El Segundo, Calif., 1972-80, v.p. strategic aircraft, 1980-82; amateur anthropologist, Long Beach, Calif., 1982—. Contbr. articles to profl. jours.; co-patentee in anti-skid sys. Co-recipient Collier trophy USAF, 1976, Pub. Svc. award NASA, 1969. Assoc. fellow AIAA (Aircraft Design award 1979); mem. IEEE (life), Old Crows Assn., Pi Tau Sigma, Tau Beta Pi, Phi Kappa Phi. Home and Office: 4300 Cerritos Ave Long Beach CA 90807-2462

RAILTON, WILLIAM SCOTT, lawyer; b. Newark, July 30, 1935; s. William Scott and Carolyn Elizabeth (Guiberson) R.; m. Karen Elizabeth Walsh, Mar. 31, 1979; 1 son, William August; children by previous marriage: William Scott, Anne Greenwood. BSEE, U. Wash., 1962; JD with honors, George Washington U., 1965. Bar: D.C. 1966, Md. 1966, Va. 1993, U.S. Patent Office 1966. Assoc., then ptnr. Kemon, Palmer & Estabrook, Washington, 1966-70; sr. trial atty. Dept. Labor, Washington, 1970-71, asst. counsel for trial litigation, 1971-72; chief counsel U.S. Occupational Safety and Health Rev. Commn., Washington, 1972-77; acting gen. counsel U.S. Occupational Safety and Health Rev. Commn., 1975-77; ptnr. Reed, Smith, Shaw & McClay, Pitts., 1977—; lectr. George Washington U. Law Sch., 1977-79, seminar chmn. Occupational Safety and Health Act, Govt. Inst., 1979—; lectr. Practicing Law Inst., 1976-79. Author: (legal handbooks) The Examination System and the Backlog, 1965, The OSHA General Duty Clause, 1977, The OSHA Health Standards, 1977; OSHA Compliance Handbook, 1992; contbg. author: Occupational Safety and Health Law, 1988, 93. Regional chmn. Montgomery County (Md.) Republican party, 1968-70; pres. Montgomery Sq. Citizens Assn., 1970-71; bd. dirs., pres. Foxvale Farms Homeowners Assn., 1979-82; pres. Orchards on the Potomac Homeowners Assn., 1990-92; dir. Great Falls Hist. Soc., 1991-94; scoutmaster Troop 55 Boy Scouts Am., 1993—. With USMC, 1953-58. Recipient Meritorious Achievement medal Dept. Labor, 1972, Outstanding Service award OSHA Rev. Commn., 1977. Mem. ABA (mgmt. co-chmn. occupational safety and health law com. 1995—), Md. Bar Assn., Va. Bar Assn., Bar Assn. D.C. (vice chmn. young lawyers sect. 1971), Order of Coif, Sigma Phi Epsilon, Phi Delta Phi. Home: 10102 Walker Lake Dr Great Falls VA 22066-3502 also: East Tower 1301 K St NW #1100 Washington DC 20005 *Lawsuits are won by pre-trial preparation. A litigator should be candid with his clients and honest in his dealings with associates, opponents and the courts; an attorney should also volunteer his service to the community of which he is a part.*

RAIMI, BURTON LOUIS, lawyer; b. Detroit, May 5, 1938; s. Irving and Rae (Abel) R.; m. Judith Morse, Mar. 31, 1963 (div. Mar. 1985); children: Diane L., and Matthew D. BA, Brandeis U., 1960; JD with honors, U. Mich., 1963; LLM, George Washington U., 1964. Bar: Mich. 1963, D.C. 1964, Fla. 1991; U.S. Ct. Appeals (4th, 7th, 8th, 9th, 10th and D.C. cirs.). Atty. NLRB, Washington, 1964-69; assoc. Morgan, Lewis & Bockius, Washington, 1969-71; dep. gen. counsel FDIC, Washington, 1971-78; ptnr. Rosenman and Colin, Washington, 1978-86, Dechert Price & Rhoads, Washington, 1986-93; shareholder McCaffrey & Raimi, P.A., Naples and Sarasota, Fla., 1994—; speaker various insts. Mem. ABA (chmn. bank receiverships subcom. of banking com.), D.C. Bar Assn. (past chmn. banking law com., com. on interests on lawyers trust accounts), Fla. Bar. Avocations: sailing, racketball, tennis, travel. Home: 4452 Staghorn Ln Sarasota FL 34238-5626 Office: McCaffrey & Raimi PA 1800 2d St Ste 753 Sarasota FL 34237-6091

RAIMI, SAMUEL M., film director; b. Royal Oak, Mich., Oct. 23, 1959; s. Leonard Ronald and Celia Barbara (Abrams) R. Student in humanities study, Mich. State U., East Lansing, 1977-79. V.p. Renaissance Pictures, Ferndale, Mich., 1979—. Writer, dir. (films) Evil Dead, 1981, Crimewave, 1985 (Best Dir. award 1986), Evil Dead II, 1986, Darkman, 1990, Army of Darkness: Evil Dead 3, 1993; co-writer: (screenplay) The Hudsucker Proxy, 1994; prodr. Hard Target, 1993, Timecop, 1994; dir. (film) The Quick and the Dead, 1995; appeared in films Spies Like Us, 1985, Thou Shall Not Kill...Except, 1987, Maniac Cop, 1988, Miller's Crossing, 1990, Innocent Blood, 1992, Intruder, 1994, Terminal Force, 1995; appeared on TV Journey to the Center of the Earth, 1993, Body Bags, 1993, The Stand, 1994; prodr., writer Mantis, 1993; exec. prodr. syndicated TV series The Legendary Journeys of Hercules, 1994-96, Xena: Warrior Princess, 1995-96, (series) American Gothic, 1995-96. Recipient Best Horror Film, Knokke'heist Film Festival Belgium, 1982, Best Horror Film and Best Spl. Effects, Sitges Film Festival, Spain, 1982, 1st Prize of the Critics, 1st Prize of the Pub., Paris Festival Sci. Fiction, Fantasy and Horror, 1983, Best Horror Film of Yr., Fangoria Mag., 1983. Mem. Mich. State U. Soc. for Creative Film Making (founder, pres. 1978, 79), Calif. Rare Fruit Growers. Office: ICM 8942 Wilshire Blvd Beverly Hills CA 90211-1934

RAIMO, BERNARD, JR. (BERNIE RAIMO), lawyer; b. Kansas City, Mo., May 29, 1944; m. Sharon Marie Brady, Aug. 23, 1974; children: Sara Elizabeth, Peter Bernard. BA, U. Notre Dame, 1965; MA, U. Md., 1967; JD with honors, George Washington U., 1972. Bar: D.C. Staff asst. to Sen. Stuart Symington Mo., 1968-72; asst. corp. counsel Washington, 1972-76; legis. analyst Am. Petroleum Inst., 1976-78; counsel Permanent Select Com. Intelligence U.S. Ho. Reps., Washington, 1978-91, chief counsel Ho. Com. Standards of Official Conduct, 1991-95; minority counsel Ho. Com. Standards of Official Conduct, 1995—. Office: Ho Com Standards of Official Conduct HT 2 The Capitol Washington DC 20515-6328

RAIMONDI, ALBERT ANTHONY, mechanical engineer; b. Plymouth, Mass., Mar. 29, 1925; s. William and Amelia (Taddia) R. B.S., Tufts U., 1945; M.S., U. Pitts., 1963, Ph.D. in Mech. Engring, 1968. Rsch. engr. Westinghouse Rsch. Labs., Pitts., 1945-68; mgr. lubrication mechanics Westinghouse Rsch. Labs., 1968-85, mgr. tribology and exptl. mechanics, 1978-90, cons. engr. mechanics and tribology dept., 1990—. Contbr.: Am. Soc. Lubrication Engr. Handbook, 1968, 84; editor: jours. Am. Soc. Lubrication Engrs, 1971-76; assoc. editor: Trans. Am. Soc. Lubrication Engrs., 1960-71; Contbr. articles to profl. jours. Fellow Soc. for Tribologists and Lubrication Engrs. (Hunt award 1959, nat. award 1968, Westinghouse Maj. Innovation award 1990). Home: 125 8th St Turtle Creek PA 15145-1805 Office: Westinghouse Sci & Tech Ctr 1310 Beulah Rd Pittsburgh PA 15235-5068

RAIMONDI, RUGGERO, opera singer; b. Bologna, Italy, Oct. 3, 1941; m. Isabel Maier, 1987. Studies with, Teresa Pediconi, Rome, Armando Piervenanzi. Debut as opera singer in La Boheme, Spoleto, Italy, 1964; opera singer in major houses, Europe and U.S.; Met. debut in Ernani, N.Y.C., 1970; favorite roles include Don Giovanni, Philip II, Boris and Don Quichotte; recorded Verdi Requiem, Vespri Siciliani, La Boheme, Aida, Attila, Don Carlos, Macbeth, Simon Boccanegra, Don Giovanni, Boris Godunov, Tosca, Turandot, Barbiere di Siviglia, Mosè, Nozze di Figaro, Italiana in Algieri, Cenerentola; appeared in films Don Giovanni (Joseph Losey), 1978, Six Characters in Search of a Singer (Maurice Bejart), 1983, Carmen (Francesco Rosi), 1986, others; in opera prodn., 1986—. Decorated Officier des Arts et Lettres, Chevalier de l'Ordre de Malte, Ufficiale della Repubblica Italiana. Office: 140 bis, rue Lecourbe, F-75015 Paris France

RAINBOLT, JOHN VERNON, II, lawyer; b. Cordell, Okla., May 24, 1939; s. John Vernon (Mike) and Mary Alice (Power) R.; m. Janice Glaub, Oct. 2, 1976; children—John Vernon, III, Sara McLain, Charles Joseph. B.A., Okla. U., 1961, LL.B., 1964; postgrad. George Washington U. 1971-73. Bar: Okla. 1964, D.C. 1971, U.S. Supreme Ct. 1971. Legis. counsel, adminstrv. asst. U.S. Rep. Graham Purcell, Washington, 1967-72; counsel agr. com. U.S. Ho. of Reps., Washington, 1972-74, chief counsel, 1975; commr. Commodity Futures Trading Commn., Washington, 1975-78; sole practice, Washington, 1978—; ptnr. Miles & Stockbridge, Washington, 1982-86; advisor agr. policy Tokyo Roundtable White House, 1978-81; mem. Adminstrn. Conf., U.S., 1976-79; mem. CFTC Adv. Com. on Regulatory Coord. Author and draftsman Commodity Futures Trading Commn. Act, 1974; contbr. articles to legal jours. Served to 1st lt. Inf., U.S. Army, 1964-67. Vice chmn. Commodity Futures Trading Commn., 1975-78. Mem. ABA (chmn. subcom. on fgn. markets and traders 1982-85), U.S. Futures Industry Assn. (assoc., internat. com., Japan chpt.). Clubs: Commodity of Washington. Office: 655 15th St NW Ste 300 Washington DC 20005-5701

RAINER, JOHN DAVID, psychiatrist, educator; b. N.Y.C., July 13, 1921; s. Louis W. and Daisy (Harris) Rosen; m. Barbara Antin, Dec. 23, 1944; children: Jeff, Peter. AB, Columbia Coll., N.Y.C., 1941; MA, Columbia U., 1944, MD, 1951; DLitt (hon.), Gallaudet U., 1968. Rotating intern Mt. Sinai Hosp., N.Y.C., 1951-52; resident psychiatry N.Y. State Psychiat. Inst., N.Y.C., 1952-55; rsch. assoc. in psychiatry Columbia U., N.Y.C., 1956-59; asst. clin. prof. psychiatry Columbia U., 1959-67; chief psychiat. rsch. (genetics) N.Y. State Psychiat. Inst., N.Y.C., 1965-91; assoc. clin. prof. psychiatry Columbia U., N.Y.C., 1967-70; assoc. prof. clin. psychiatry Columbia U., 1970-72, prof. clin. psychiatry, 1972—; tng. and supervising analyst Columbia Psychoanalytic Ctr., N.Y.C., 1972—; attending psychiatrist Presbyterian Hosp., N.Y.C., 1972—. Editorial bd. mem. Am. Annals of the Deaf, Neuropsychobiology, Jour. Preventive Psychiatry; contbr. over 150 articles to profl. jours. Pres. Lake Isle Civic Assn., Eastchester, N.Y., 1989-91. With U.S. Army, 1945-46. Recipient Samuelson award N.Y. League for Hard of Hearing, 1974. Fellow Am. Psychiat. Assn. (life), Am. Psychoanalytic Assn. (life), Am. Coll. Psychoanalysts; mem. Am. Soc. Human Genetics, Am. Psychopathol. Assn. (life), Eastern Psychiat. Rsch. Assn. (pres. 1971-73), Westchester Psychoanalytic Soc. (pres. 1975-76), Phi Beta Kappa, Alpha Omega Alpha. Achievements include establishment of first psychiatric program for deaf people. Home: 9 Innisfree Pl Eastchester NY 10707-1207 Office: NY State Psychiat Inst 722 W 168th St New York NY 10032-2603

RAINER, REX KELLY, civil engineer, educator; b. Montgomery, Ala., July 17, 1924; s. Kelly Kenyon and Pearl (Jones) R.; m. Betty Ann Page, Aug. 28, 1945; children: Rex Kelly, John Kenyon. B.S., Auburn (Ala.) U., 1944, M.S., 1946; Ph.D., Okla. State U., 1967. Asst. engr. L. & N. R.R. Co., Cin., 1944-45; design engr. Polglaze & Basenberg, Birmingham, Ala., 1945-51; pres., chmn. Rainer Co., Inc., Orlando, Fla., 1951-62; prof. civil engring. Auburn U., 1962-67, head civil engring. dept., 1967; exec. v.p., 1980; hwy. dir. State of Ala., 1979-80, fin. dir., 1981-82; spl. asst. to gov. of Ala., 1981-82; dir. Office for Advancement Devel. Industry U. Ala., Birmingham, 1982-86; pres., cons. engr. Rex K. Rainer, Inc., 1982—; cons. to ins. cos., constrn. engring. firms; mem. Ala. Bd. Registration Profl. Engrs. and Land Surveyors, 1977-89. Contbr. articles to profl. jours. Mem. Municipal Planning Bd., 1963-65, Indsl. Park Devel. Bd., 1969-71, So. Regional Edn. Bd., 1982-86. Served with AUS, 1943. Fellow ASCE (sec., treas. 1970, pres. Ala. chpt. 1976-77, chmn. Constrn. Rsch. Coun., chmn. hwy. div. publs. com.; Civil Govt. award 1981); mem. Assn. Gen. Contractors Am. (bd. dirs. 1955), Am. Soc. for Engring. Edn. (chmn. constrn. engring. com.), Am. Pub. Works Assn., Phi Kappa Phi, Tau Beta Pi, Chi Epsilon. Home: 901 Ogletree Rd Auburn AL 36830-7207

RAINER, WILLIAM GERALD, cardiac surgeon; b. Gordo, Ala., Nov. 13, 1927; s. Jamie Flournoy and Lula (Davis) R.; m. Lois Sayre, Oct. 7, 1950; children: Vickie, Bill, Julia, Leslie. Student, Emory U., Atlanta, Ga., 1943-44, U. Ala., 1944-45; MD, U. Tenn., Memphis, 1948; MS in Surgery, U. Colo., Denver, 1958. Diplomate Am. Bd. Surgery, Am. Bd. Thoracic Surgery. Intern Wesley Hosp., Chgo., 1949; gen. practice medicine Blue Island, Ill., 1950-52; resident Denver VA Hosp., 1954-59; practice medicine specializing in cardiac surgery Denver, 1960—; bd. dirs. St. Joseph Hosp. Found., Denver. Contbr. articles to profl. jours. Lt. U.S. Army, 1952-54. Decorated Bronze Star; recipient Disting. Alumnus award U. Tenn. Health Sci. Ctr., 1992. Mem. Soc. Thoracic Surgeons (sec. 1980-85, pres. 1989), Colo. Med. Soc. (pres. 1984-85), Denver Med. Soc. (pres. 1984), Am. Coll. Chest Physicians (pres. 1984), Am. Bd. Thoracic Surgeons (bd. dirs. 1982-88), Am. Surg. Assn., Am. Assn. Thoracic Surgery, Societé Internationale de Chirugie, Denver Athletic Club. Avocations: photography, traveling. Office: 2005 Franklin St Ste 700 Denver CO 80205-5408

RAINES, CHARLOTTE AUSTINE BUTLER, artist, poet; b. Sullivan, Ill., July 1, 1922; d. Donald Malone and Charlotte (Wimp) Butler; m. Irving Isaack Raines, Sept. 26, 1941; children: Robin Raines Collison, Kerry Raines Lydon. BA in Studio Arts magna cum laude, U. Md., 1966. One-woman show at Castle Theatre, 1988, C.T.V. Awards Hall, Md., 1993; exhbd. in numerous group shows including Corcoran Gallery, 1980, Md.'s Best Exhbn., 1986, Md. State House, 1990, four-artist video documentary, 1992, U. Md. Univ.-Coll. Gallery, 1996; represented in various pvt. collections; selected works in U.S. Dept. State Arts in Embassies Program; contbr. poems to lit. publs. Mem. Artists Equity Assn., Writers' Ctr., Phi Kappa Phi. Avocations: piano, jogging, gardening. Studio: 4103 Longfellow St Hyattsville MD 20781-1748

RAINES, FRANKLIN DELANO, investment banker; b. Seattle, Jan. 14, 1949; s. Delno Thomas and Ida Mae (Fortson R.; m. Wendy Farrow, Sept. 11, 1982; children: Laura Farrow, Andrea Landon. BA magna cum laude, Harvard U., 1971, JD cum laude, 1976; postgrad., Oxford U., 1971-73. Assoc. dir. Seattle Model Cities Program, 1972-73; assoc. Preston, Thorgrimson, Ellis, Holman & Fletcher, Seattle, 1976-77; asst. dir. White House Domestic Policy Staff, Washington, 1977-78; assoc. dir. U.S. Office of Mgmt. and Budget, Washington, 1978-79; v.p. Lazard, Freres & Co., N.Y.C., 1979-82, sr. v.p., 1983-84, gen. ptnr., 1985-90; ltd. ptnr., 1990-91; vice chmn. Fed. Nat. Mortgage Assn., Washington, 1991—. Mem. bd. overseers Harvard U.; trustee U. Puget Sound, German Marshall Fund of U.S., French-Am. Found., Am. Mus. Natural History, Mitre Corp.; mem. Nat. Adv. Coun. Edn. Disadvantaged Children, N.Y.C. Commn. on Early Childhood Edn., White House Confs. on Children and Youth, N.Y. Gov.'s Task Force on Poverty and Welfare Reform, Commn. on Behavioral and Social Scis.; bd. dirs. Ctr. Law and Social Policy, Am. Inst. Rsch., Washington, Black Student Fund, Washington, Nat. Inst. Dispute Resolution. Rhodes scholar, 1971. Mem. AAAS, Coun. Fgn. Rels., Nat. Acad. Social Ins., Washington State Bar Assn., D.C. Bar Assn. Avocations: running, tennis. Office: Fed Nat Mortgage Assn 3900 Wisconsin Ave NW Washington DC 20016-2806

RAINES, HOWELL HIRAM, newspaper editor, journalist; b. Birmingham, Ala., Feb. 5, 1943; s. W.S. and Bertha Estelle (Walker) R.; m. Laure Susan Woodley, Mar. 22, 1969 (div.); children: Ben Hayes, Jeffrey Howell. BA, Birmingham So. Coll., 1964; MA, U. Ala., 1973. Reporter Birmingham Post-Herald, 1964-65, Sta. WBRC-TV, Birmingham, 1965-67, Tuscaloosa (Ala.) News, 1968-69, Birmingham News, 1970-71; polit. editor Atlanta Constitution, 1971-74, St. Petersburg (Fla.) Times, 1976-78; Atlanta bur. chief N.Y. Times, 1978-80, White Ho. corr., 1980-82, nat. polit. corr., 1982-84, dep. Washington editor, 1985-86, London bur. chief, 1987-88, Washington editor, 1988-92; editl. page editor N.Y. Times, N.Y.C., 1993—. Author: Whiskey Man, 1977, My Soul is Rested, 1977, Fly Fishing Through the Midlife Crisis, 1993. With U.S. Army N.G., 1965-71. Recipient Pulitzer Prize for feature writing, 1992. Office: NY Times 229 W 43rd St New York NY 10036-3913

RAINES, JEFF, biomedical scientist, medical research director; b. N.Y.C., Sept. 5, 1943; s. Otis J. and Mildred C. (Wetzler) R.; B.S. in Mech. Engring., Clemson U., 1965; M. in Mech. Engring., U. Fla., 1967; MD Harvard U., 1968; Ph.D. in Biomed. Engring. (NIH fellow), M.I.T., 1972; children: Gretchen Christena, Victoria Jean. Mem. staff M.I.T., Cambridge, 1968-70; biophysicist dept. surgery Mass. Gen. Hosp., Boston, 1972-77, dir. Vascular Lab., 1972-77; instr. surgery Harvard Med. Sch., Boston, 1973-77; preceptor Harvard/M.I.T. Sch. Health Scis., 1976-77; research dir., dir. Vascular Lab., Miami (Fla.) Heart Inst., Miami Beach, 1977-88; adj. prof. bioengring. U. Miami, Coral Gables, 1977—; prof. surgery U. Miami (Fla.) Sch. Medicine, 1977—, prin. investigator series NIH programs and pharm. firms, 1977—; Harvard Travelling fellow lectr. in Europe, 1975. Recipient Apollo Achievement award NASA, 1969. Fellow Am. Coll. Cardiology, Am. Coll. of Radiology, Am. Assn. of Physicists in Medicine; mem. Biomed. Engring. Soc., Instrument Soc. Am., Am. Heart Assn., Internat. Cardiovascular Soc., Cardiovascular System Dynamics Soc. (founding mem.; editor 1976—, pres. 1980-82), New Eng. Cardiovascular Soc., AAAS, ASME, Kiwanis, Sigma Xi, Tau Beta Pi. Republican. Presbyterian. Clubs: La Gorce Country, Harvard, M.I.T. Contbr. numerous articles on biomechanics, cardiovascular diagnosis, dynamics and instrumentation to sri. jours.; patentee med. devices; developer math. models of arterial hemodynamics and clin. use of autotransfusion. Home: 770 Claughton Island Dr Miami FL 33131 Office: U Miami Sch Medicine R-669 PO Box 16069 Miami FL 33101-6069

RAINES, TIMOTHY, professional baseball player; b. Sanford, Fla., Sept. 16, 1959; m. Virginia Raines; children: Tim Jr., André Darrell. Baseball player Montreal Expos, 1977-90, Chgo. White Sox, 1990-95, N.Y. Yankees, 1996—; mem. Nat. League All-Star Team, 1981-87. Recipient Silver Slugger award 1986, Sporting News Gold Shoe award, 1984; named Minor League Player of the Yr. The Sporting News, 1980, Nat. League Batting Champion, 1986; named to Sporting News Nat. League Rookie of Yr., 1981, Sporting News All-Star Team, 1983, 86, Nat. League Stolen Base Leader, 1981-84, N.L. All-Star Game, 1981-87 (named MVP 1987). Office: N.Y. Yankees E 161st St and River Ave Bronx NY 10451*

RAINESS, ALAN EDWARD, psychiatrist; b. N.Y.C., Sept. 24, 1935; s. George W. and Ida Rainess; m. Alice Maree Haber, June 5, 1968; children: Alice Jeanne Rainess Kules, James Alan (dec.). AB, Columbia Coll., 1957; MD, U. Paris, 1965. Diplomate Am. Bd. Psychiatry and Neurology. Intern Meadowbrook Hosp., East Meadow, L.I., 1965-66; resident in psychiatry N.Y. VA Hosp., N.Y.C., 1966-67; teaching fellow in psychiatry Harvard Med. Sch., Boston, 1967; chief resident in psychiatry Boston City Hosp., 1967; resident in psychiatry Walter Reed Med. Ctr., Washington, 1970-72; clin. dir. St. Elizabeth's Hosp., Washington, 1973-76; asst. chief psychiatry Andrews AFB Hosp., Camp Springs, Md., 1976-80, chief neurology, 1989-91; resident in neurology Wilford Hall USAF Med. Ctr., San Antonio, 1980-83; chief medicine and neuropsychiatry Air Univ. Hosp., Maxwell AFB, Ala., 1983-89, chief neurology, 1991-94; psychiatrist Manhattan Psychiat. Ctr., N.Y.C., 1994—; asst. clin. prof. psychiatry Georgetown U. Med. Sch., Washington, 1974-79; assoc. prof. neurology and psychiatry Uniformed Svcs. U. Health Scis., Bethesda, Md., 1989-94. Maj. U.S. Army, 1968-73, col. USAF, 1976-94. Fellow Am. Psychiat. Assn.; mem. Am. Soc. Psychoanalytic Physicians (pres. N.Y. chpg. 1996), Masons. Home: 345 E 93rd St Apt 22H New York NY 10128-5522 Office: Manhattan Psychiat Ctr New York NY 10035

RAINEY, ARTHUR H., lawyer; b. Harrisburg, Pa., Oct. 8, 1943; s. David Cotter and Helen Hambleton (Hull) R.; m. Nancy Jeanne Bowen, July 29, 1967; 1 child, Douglas H. AB cum laude, Dartmouth Coll., 1965; JD cum laude, U. Pa., 1968. Bar: Pa. 1968, U.S. Supreme Ct. 1972, U.S. Ct. Appeals (3d cir.) 1973, U.S. Dist. Ct. (ea. dist.) Pa. 1973, U.S. Dist Ct. (mid. dist.) Pa. 1988. Assoc. Dechert, Price & Rhoads, Phila., 1968, 73-79, ptnr., 1979—. Lt. JAGC, USNR, 1968-72. Office: Dechert Price & Rhoads 4000 Bell Atlantic Tower 1717 Arch St Philadelphia PA 19103-2713

RAINEY, CLAUDE GLADWIN, retired health care executive; b. Enloe, Tex., Apr. 21, 1923; s. Claude C. and Pauline (Whitlock) R.; m. Peggy Ballard, July 27, 1947; children—Kathy Suzanne, David Claude, Mark Jeffery, Joel Allen, Peggy Jan, Susan Elise. Student pub. health and adminstrv. medicine, Columbia U., 1961-62. Med. adminstrv., officer dept. medicine and surgery VA, Temple, Tex., 1946-51; med. adminstrv., officer dept. medicine and surgery VA, Muskogee, Okla., 1951-56; med. adminstr. Fite Clinic, Lakeland Med. Ctr., Muskogee, Okla., 1956-59; hosp. adminstr. M.-K.-T. R.R. Employees Hosp. Assn., Denison, Tex., 1959-62, also sec., treas. trustee; hosp. adminstr., cons. Denison Hosp. Authority, Meml. Hosp., 1962-66; adminstr. Seton Hosp., Austin, Tex., 1966-74; exec. v.p. Fort Worth Osteo. Hosp., 1974-83; pres. Health Care of Tex., Inc., Fort Worth, 1983-88, ret. Pres. North Grayson County chpt. Am. Cancer Soc., 1960-66, bd. dirs., Tex., 1961—. Served with USNR, 1942-46. Fellow Am. Coll. Hosp. Adminstrs., Am. Coll. Osteo. Hosp. Adminstrs. (award of merit 1984); mem. Am. Hosp. Assn., Tex. Hosp. Assn., Am. Osteo. Hosp. Assn. (Disting. Service award 1985).

RAINEY, GORDON FRYER, JR., lawyer; b. Oklahoma City, Apr. 26, 1940; s. Gordon F. and Esther (Bliss) R.; m. Selina Norman, Aug. 3, 1968; children—Kate, Melissa, Gordon III. B.A. in English, U. Va., 1962, LL.B., 1967. Bar: Okla. 1967, Va. 1968. Assoc. Rainey, Flynn, Wallace, Ross & Cooper, Oklahoma City, 1967-68; assoc. Hunton & Williams, Richmond, Va., 1968-75, ptnr., 1975—; chmn. of exec. com. Hunton & Williams, dir. Crestar Fin. Corp., Crestar Bank, Weidmuller North Am., Inc., Health Corp. of Va., Meml. Regional Med. Ctr., Inc.; bd. mgrs. U. Va. Alumni Assn.; trustee Ch. Schs. Diocese Va.; campaign chmn. United Way of Greater Richmond, 1982, trustee, 1981-84; bd. dirs., past pres. Sheltering Arms Hosp., 1984; trustee Sheltering Arms Found.; chmn. Gov.'s Econ. Devel. Adv. Coun. Dist. 12; mem. Gov.'s Blue Ribbon Strike Force Commn. on Govtl. Reform; past mem. bd. govs. St. Catherine's Sch.; chmn. bd. dirs. Leadership Met. Richmond; mem. Mayor's Emergency Shelter Task Force, 1981; pres., bd. dirs. Met. Bus. Found. Served to 1st lt. U.S. Army, 1962-64, Korea. Recipient Communication and Leadership award Toastmasters Internat., 1983. Mem. ABA (sect. on bus. law, banking law com., mem. com. on devel. in investment services), Richmond Metro C. of C. (bd. dirs., past chmn.). Republican. Episcopalian. Clubs: Forum (Richmond, Va.). Office: Hunton & Williams Riverfront Plz East Tower 951 E Byrd St Richmond VA 23219-4040

RAINEY, JEAN OSGOOD, public relations executive; b. Lansing, Mich., Apr. 5, 1925; d. Earle Victor and Blanche Mae (Eberly) Osgood; m. John Larimer Rainey, Nov. 29, 1957 (dec. Oct. 1991); children: Cynthia, John Larimer, Ruth. Grad., Lansing Bus. U., 1942. Pub. rels. dir. Nat. Assn. Food Chains, Washington, 1954-59; v.p. pub. rels. Manchester Orgns., Washington, 1959-61; ptnr. Rainey, McEnroe & Manning, Washington, 1962-73; v.p. Manning, Selvage & Lee, Washington, 1973-79, pres. Washington div., 1979-84, sr. counsellor, 1985—; owner Jean Rainey Assocs., Washington, 1986-87; sr. v.p. Daniel J. Edelman Inc., 1987-96; owner Sean Raney Assocs., Washington. Author: How to Shop for Food, 1972. Pres. Hyde Home and Sch. Assn., Washington, 1969-71; co-chmn. Nat. Com. for Reelection of the Pres., 1972. Mem. Pub. Rels. Soc. Am. (accredited), Am. Women in Radio and TV (pres. Washington chpt. 1962-63, mem. nat. bd. 1963-65), Am. News Women's Club (pres. 1973-75). Republican. Episcopalian. Clubs: City Tavern, International. Home: Apt 250B 4000 Cathedral Ave NW Washington DC 20016-5249 Office: PO Box 251 Main Lobby W 4000 Cathedral Ave NW Washington DC 20016-5249

RAINEY, JOHN DAVID, federal judge; b. Freeport, Tex., Feb. 10, 1945; s. Frank Anson and Jewel Lorene (Hortman) R.; m. Judy Davis, Aug. 17, 1968; children, John David Jr., Jacob Matthew, Craig Thomas. BBA, So. Meth. U., 1967, JD, 1972. Bar: Tex. 1972, U.S. Dist. Ct. (no. dist.) Tex. 1974, U.S. Tax Ct. 1974, U.S. Ct. Appeals (5th cir.) 1981, U.S. Supreme Ct. 1981, U.S. Dist. Ct. (so. dist.) Tex. 1986. Assoc. Taylor, Mizell, Price, Corrigan & Smith, Dallas, 1973-79; ptnr. Gilbert, Gilbert & Rainey, Angleton, Tex., 1979-82, Rainey & LeBoeuf, Angleton, 1982-86; judge 149th Dist. Ct., Brazoria County, Tex., 1987-90, U.S. Dist. Ct. (so. dist.) Tex., 1990—; bd. dirs. Angleton Bank of Commerce. Mem. City of Angleton Planning and Zoning Commn., 1981-84; mem. Angleton Charter Rev. Commn., 1984, chmn. 1982. Served with U.S. Army, 1969-70. Mem. ABA, State Bar Tex., Brazoria County Bar Assn. (pres. 1983-84). Republican. Methodist. Lodge: Lions (pres. Angleton 1986-87). Avocations: hunting, fishing, woodworking. Office: US Dist Ct 515 Rusk St Ste 8613 Houston TX 77002-2603*

RAINEY, JOHN MARK, administrator; b. Laurel, Miss., Mar. 16, 1947; s. Eleanor I. Rainey; children: Trisha, Kelly, Christopher, Heather, Melissa. BFA, U. So. Miss., 1972; M of Ednl. Adminstrn., Ctrl. Mich. U., 1976; postgrad., Western Mich. U., 1994—. Instr. vocat. media, broadcasting, asst. prin. Sch. Dist. of the City of Saginaw, Mich., 1976-77, specialist, media and publ. svcs., 1977-79; prin., coord. of media and printing svcs. Salina elem. Sch. Dist. of the City of Saginaw, 1979-80, coord. media and publ. svcs., 1980-84, supr. Saginaw pub. schs. media ctr., 1984-92; dir. regional ednl. media ctr. and instrn. ctr. Kalamazoo Valley Intermediate Sch. Dist., 1992—; adj. prof. Ctrl. Mich. U., Mt. Pleasant, 1989—, Western Mich. U., Kalamazoo, 1992—; bd. dirs. TeleCity USA, Kalamazoo, 1994—, Community Cable Access, Kalamazoo, 1994—. Author: (manual) Critical Viewing Skills/Television, Copyright Manual for Educators, HyperCard for the Teacher, Macintosh Basics-Your Recipe for the Macintosh computer. Bd. dirs. Pub. Awareness Com. Saginaw Community Found., 1990-92; commr. Saginaw City Human Rels. Commn., 1990-92. With USAF, 1965-69. Recipient Outstanding Secondary Educator of Am. award, 1974. Mem. AAUW, ASCD, Nat. Staff Devel. Coun., Assn. for Ednl. Comm. and Tech. (pres. 1992-93, Richard B. Lewis Meml. award 1991), Action for Children's TV, Phi Delta Kappa (Leadership award 1991). Office: Kalamazoo Valley Intermed Sch Dist 1819 E Milham Rd Kalamazoo MI 49002

RAINEY, WILLIAM E., medical educator. BS in Biology, U. North Tex., 1980, MS in Biology, 1981; PhD in Cell Biology, U. Tex. SW Med. Ctr., 1985. Asst. prof. ob-gyn. U. Tex. Southwestern Med. Ctr.; vis. scientist Flinders Med. Ctr., Adelaide, Australia, 1995. Grantee NIH, Am. Heart Assn.; Given Inst. Pathobiology fellow, 1984, Noble Found. fellow, 1984-85, Fogarty Internat. fellow, 1987-88. Mem. Fedn. Am. Socs. for Exptl. Biology, Endocrine Soc., Soc. Gynecol. Investigation, Am. Fertility Soc. Office: U Tex SW Med Ctr Dept Ob-Gyn 5323 Harry Hines Blvd Dallas TX 75235-9032

RAINEY, WILLIAM JOEL, lawyer; b. Flint, Mich., Oct. 11, 1946; s. Ralph Jefferson and Elsie Matilda (Erickson) R.; m. Cynthia Hetsko, June 15, 1968; children: Joel Michael, Allison Elizabeth. A.B., Harvard U., 1968; J.D., U. Mich., 1971. Bar: N.Y. 1973, Wash. 1977, Ariz. 1987, Mass. 1992, U.S. Dist. Ct. (so. and ea. dists.) N.Y. 1973, U.S. Ct. Appeals (2nd cir.) N.Y. 1973, U.S. Dist. Ct. (we. dist.) Wash. 1977, U.S. Supreme Ct. 1976, U.S. Ct. Appeals (9th cir.) Wash. 1978, U.S. Dist. Ct. Ariz. 1987, U.S. Dist. Ct. Mass. 1992, U.S. Ct. Appeals (1st cir.) Mass. 1992. Assoc. atty. Curtis, Mallet-Prevost, Colt & Mosle, N.Y.C., 1971-76; atty., asst. corp. sec. Weyerhaeuser Co., Tacoma, Wash., 1976-85; v.p., corp. sec., gen. counsel Southwest Forest Industries Inc., Phoenix, 1985-87; sr. v.p., corp. sec., gen. counsel Valley Nat. Corp. and Valley Nat. Bank, Phoenix, 1987-91; v.p., gen. counsel Cabot Corp., Boston, 1991-93; exec. v.p., gen. coun., corp. sec. Fourth Fin. Corp., Wichita, Kans., 1994-96; sr. v.p., gen. counsel, corp. sec. Payless Shoe Source, Inc., Topeka, 1996—. Editor U. Mich. Jour. Law Reform, 1970-71. Bd. dirs. 1st Ave. Svc. Ctr., Seattle, 1977-85, Mcpl. League Seattle and King County, 1982-84, Phoenix Symphony Orch. Assn., 1988-91, Salvation Army, 1988-91, Big Bros./Big Sisters, 1994-96; chmn. Bellevue (Wash.) Planning Commn., 1984. Maj. USAR, 1970-91. Mem. ABA (chmn. task force 1984-91), Wash. State Bar Assn., State Bar of Ariz., Boston Bar Assn., Assn. Bank Holding Cos. (steering com. 1989-91, chmn. lawyers com. 1990-91), Harvard Club of Phoenix (bd. dirs. 1989-91). Avocations: backpacking, running, fishing. Home: 901 Deer Run Dr Lawrence KS 66049 Office: Payless Shoe Source Inc PO Box 1189 Topeka KS 66601-1189

RAINIER, ROBERT PAUL, publisher; b. Adrian, Mich., Oct. 19, 1940; s. Paul Leslie and Mildred Sofia (Magdefrau) R.; m. Dorothy Krauss, May 28, 1966; children: Michele Carole, Kenneth Charles. BA, Northwestern U., 1962, MA, 1964. Various positions with mktg. and sales dept. Times Mirror/McGraw Hill Book Co., N.Y.C., 1964-70, sponsoring editor coll. div., 1970-74, editor in chief humanities, 1974-79; pub. engring. coll. dept. Holt-Rinehart and Winston, N.Y.C., 1979-80, editor in chief, sci. and engring., 1980-81, pub. humanities, 1981-83, v.p., editor in chief, 1983-84; v.p., editor in chief CBS Coll. Pub., N.Y.C., 1984-86; dir. publs. AICPA, N.Y.C., 1986—. Vestryman St. Johns Episcopal Ch., Larchmont, N.Y., 1987-90, fundraiser, 1988-89. Staff sgt. N.Y. N.G., 1964-70. Mem. The Dessoff Choirs (treas. 1993—), Soc. Nat. Assn. Publs. (bd. dirs. 1988—, pres. 1992-93). Democrat. Episcopalian. Avocations: music, sports. Home: 21 Summit Ave Larchmont NY 10538-2913

RAINIS, EUGENE CHARLES, brokerage house executive; b. N.Y.C., Sept. 24, 1940; s. Charles William and Louise Theresa (Nold) R.; m. Jane Margaret Micucci, Nov. 28, 1964; children—Ellen, David, Mark. B.S., Fordham U., 1962; M.B.A., U. Pa., 1964. Security analyst trainee Merrill, Lynch Pierce Fenner & Smith, N.Y.C., 1963-65; ptnr. Brown Bros. Harriman & Co., N.Y.C., 1965—, also bd. dirs.; chmn. bd. dirs. Jefferson Ins. Co. N.Y., Monticello Ins. Co. Trustee St. Vincents Hosp., N.Y.C., Fordham U., N.Y.C., Cath. Health Care Network. Mem. Inst. Chartered Fin. Analysts, Down Town Assn. (N.Y.C.), Knights of Malta, Harbour Ridge Golf Club (Palm City, Fla.). Republican. Roman Catholic. Avocations: fishing; trap and skeet shooting. Office: Brown Bros Harriman & Co 59 Wall St New York NY 10005-2818

RAINS, HARRY HANO, lawyer, arbitrator, mediator; b. N.Y.C., Jan. 27, 1909; s. Jackson and Rose (Heller) R.; m. Muriel, May 17, 1942; 1 child, Peggy Jane Rains Goodman. LL.B., St. Lawrence U., 1932; M.P.A., NYU, 1947, LL.M. in Labor Law, 1954. Bar: N.Y. 1933, U.S. Supreme Ct. 1965, U.S. Dist. Ct. (so. and ea. dists.) N.Y. 1947. Referee N.Y. State Dept. Labor, 1936-38, unemployment ins. mgr., 1939-42; sole practice Mineola, N.Y., 1933-42; sr. ptnr. firm Rains & Pogrebin, N.Y.C., 1947-81, of counsel, cons., 1982—; labor arbitrator, mediator, lectr.; prof. labor law CCNY, 1935-37, 46-47; prof. labor law Hofstra U., 1947-54, Harry H. Rains Disting. prof. arbitration and alternative dispute settlement law, 1982—; mem. faculty L.I. U., 1953; dir. Sealectro Corp., John Hassall Co., Inc. Contbr. articles to profl. jours. Mem. Fed. Mediation and Conciliation Service, 1948—; mem. N.Y. State Pub. Employment Relations Bd. Panel Mediators and Fact Finders, 1968—. Served to capt. QMC, AUS, 1942-46. Mem. ABA, Fed. Bar Coun., N.Y. State Bar Assn., Nassau County Bar Assn., Nat. Acad. Arbitrators, Indsl. Rels. Rsch. Assn., Am. Arbitration Assn. (panel labor arbitrators), L.I. C. of C. (bd. dirs.), Univ. Club (Garden City, N.Y.). Home: 14871 David Dr Fort Myers FL 33908-1638 Office: Rains Bldg 210 Old Country Rd Mineola NY 11501

RAINS, MERRITT NEAL, lawyer; b. Burlington, Iowa, July 26, 1943; s. Merritt and Lucille (Lepper) R.; m. Jean Baldwin, July 26, 1980 (div. 1995); children: Robert Baldwin, Kathleen Kellogg. B.A. in Polit. Sci. with honors, U. Iowa, 1965; J.D., Northwestern U., 1968. Bar: Ohio 1968. Assoc. Arter & Hadden, Cleve., 1968-76, ptnr., 1976—, mem. exec. com., 1981—, mem. mgmt. com., 1987-90, mng. ptnr., 1990-92; master bencher Inns of Ct., 1990—; lectr. on profl. topics, including alternative dispute resolution, distbn. law, litigation practice and procedure, and antitrust. Contbr. articles to profl. jours. Former trustee Legal Aid Soc. Cleve.; trustee Cleve. Play House, mem. adv. coun., 1988—; trustee Citizens League Greater Cleve., 1975-76, recipient cert. merit 1975), Def. Rsch. Inst., Internat. Assn. Def. Counsel, Ohio Assn. Civil Trial Attys., Union Club, Cleve. Skating Club, Cleve. Playhouse Club, City Club, Print Club, Rowfant Club, Phi Beta Kappa, Omicron Delta Kappa, Phi Delta Phi. Home: 12546 Cedar Rd Cleveland Heights OH 44106 Office: Arter & Hadden 1100 Huntington Bldg Cleveland OH 44115

Cleve. Art Assn. With U.S. Army, 1968-70. Fellow Am. Bar Found.; mem. ABA, Ohio Bar Assn., Bar Assn. Greater Cleve. (chmn. young lawyers sect.

RAINS, MURIEL BARNES, retired educator, real estate agent; b. Atlanta, Feb. 6, 1916; d. George Washington and Nancy Blodgett (Enos) Barnes; m. David Dean Rains (dec.); children: Rose Muriel, David Dean II. BS, Wilberforce (Ohio) U., 1937; MA, Tex. So. U., 1955; postgrad., Temple U., 1956-81. Cert. tchr., N.J., Tex., Del., Pa.; cert. news reporter, Ohio. News reporter Ohio State News, Columbus, 1937-40; tchr. Houston Pub. Schs., 1950-56, Camden (N.J.) Pub. Schs., 1956-63, various schs., Wilmington, Del., 1963-78; various schs., Claymont, Del., 1978-81; real estate agt., Phila., 1980—; former mem. city profl. growth com. Wilmington Pub. Schs., 1963-67; instr. in physics Brandywine Coll., Wilmington; co-author WOMP (Wilmington Occupational Project). Poetry author; contbr. articles to profl. jours. Active Houston Interracial Commn., 1950-56, State Reception Com., Houston, 1949. Mem. AAUW, Am. Assn. Math. Tchrs., Nat. Hist. Soc., Germantown Civic League (rec. sec., 1986-91), Alpha Kappa Alpha (life). Episcopalian. Avocations: tutoring, interior decorating, scene and portrait painting, swimming, poetry. Home and Office: 6909 Boyer St Philadelphia PA 19119-1908

RAINSFORD, BETTIS C., textile company executive. Exec. v.p., chief fin. officer Delta Woodside Industries Inc., Greenville, S.C. Office: Delta Woodside Industries Inc 108 1/2 Courthouse Sq Box 388 Edgefield SC 29824*

RAINWATER, R. STEVEN, systems engineer; b. Tyler, Tex., Dec. 13, 1962; s. Clois Miles and Nancy Jane Rainwater; m. Susan C. Chance, May 11, 1991. AA, Northlake Coll., Irving, Tex., 1981-83; student, U. Tex., 1983-88. Programmer Profl. Info. Libr., Dallas, Tex., 1984-89; systems engr. Kimball Computer Video Tech., Irving, Tex., 1989-91; pres. Network Cybernetics Corp., Irving, 1992—; cons. Chaparal Steel Inc., Midlothian, Tex., 1988-89; sys. operator The Interocitor BBS, Irving, 1990—. Author computer software. Mem. Soc. Motion Picture and TV Engrs. Avocation: artificial intelligence rsch. Home: 2821 Vassar Dr Irving TX 75062-4575 Office: Network Cybernetics Corp Ste 202 4201 Wingren Rd Irving TX 75062-2763

RAISBECK, GORDON, systems engineer; b. N.Y.C., May 4, 1925; s. Milton Joseph and Marcelle (Ellinger) R.; m. Barbara Wiener, Dec. 22, 1948; children: Michael Norbert, Lucy Margaret, Alison Jane, Timothy Gordon, James Gregory. Rhodes scholar, Oxford (Eng.) U., 1947-48; B.A., Stanford U., 1944; Ph.D., MIT, 1949. Registered profl. engr., Mass., Maine. Instr. M.I.T., Cambridge, 1948-49; mem. tech. staff Bell Telephone Labs., Inc., Murray Hill, N.J., 1949-61; dir. transmission line research Bell Telephone Labs., Inc., 1954-61; mem. profl. staff research and devel. Advanced Research Projects Agy., Washington, 1959-60; mem. profl. staff Arthur D. Little, Inc., Cambridge, 1961-86; dir. systems engring. Arthur D. Little, Inc., 1966-70, dir. phys. systems research, 1970-75, v.p. systems engring., 1973-86, part-time 1982-86; cons. mgmt. of technol. innovation, 1982—; instr. Drew U., Stanford U., MIT. Contbr. articles to profl. jours.; author: Information Theory: An Introduction for Engineers and Scientists, 1964. Served to lt. (j.g.) USNR, 1944-46, ATO, PTO. Rhodes scholar, 1947. Fellow IEEE, Acoustical Soc. Am.; mem. Oceanic Engring. Soc. IEEE (sec. 1988-92), Engring. Mgmt. Soc. IEEE, N.Y. Acad. Scis., New Coll. Soc., Math. Assn. Am., Oxford Soc., Maine Soc. Profl. Engrs., NSPE, Inst. Ops. Rsch. and the Mgmt. Scis., Assn. Am. Rhodes Scholars, Amateur Chamber Music Players, Chamber Music Am., Sigma Xi. Democrat. Episcopalian. Patentee in field (22). Home and Office: 40 Deering St Portland ME 04101-2212 also: RR #1 Barrington Blanche Rd, Cape Negro, NS Canada B0W 1E0

RAISBECK, JAMES DAVID, engineering company executive; b. Milw., Sept. 29, 1936; m. Sherry Raisbeck; children: Jennifer Lee; stepchildren: Eric Valpey, Laura Valpey. BS in Aerodynamics, Purdue U., 1961. Rsch. aerodynamist Boeing Comml. Airplane Co., Seattle, 1961-66; new airplane and rsch. outplant mgr. Boeing Airplane Co., Wright-Patterson AFB, Ohio, 1966-68; program mgr. comml. STOL airplane programs Boeing Co., 1968-69; pres., CEO Robertson Aircraft Corp., Seattle, 1969-73; v.p, tech. Am. Jet Industries, Van Nuys, Calif., 1973-74; CEO Raisbeck Group, San Antonio and Seattle, 1974-80, Raisbeck Engring., Inc., Seattle, 1980—. Named Disting. Engring. Alumnus 1979, Purdue U. Fellow AIAA (assoc.); mem. Soc. Automotive Engrs., NBAA, Purdue U. Alumni Assn., Tau Beta Phi, Phi Eta Sigma, Sigma Gamma Tau. Achievements include numerous patents in aircraft design. Office: Raisbeck Engring Inc 4411 S Ryan Way Seattle WA 98178-2083

RAISER, MARY M., chief of protocol; b. Buffalo, Aug. 5, 1942; d. Robert and Eleanor (Verduin) Millonzi; m. Charles Victor Raiser II, Sept. 7, 1963 (dec. July 1992); 1 child, Mary van Schuyler. Student, Smith Coll., 1960-63; BS in Edn., U. Va., 1964; MA, SUNY, Buffalo, 1978; postgrad., George Washington U., 1990—. Tchr. grade 5 Pub. Sch. #56, 1965-66; tchr. grades 5-8 Emwood Franklin Sch., Buffalo, 1973-75; regional dir. western N.Y. office Sen. Daniel P. Moynihan, Buffalo, 1977-79; spl. asst. Sen. Daniel P. Moynihan, Washington, 1979-81; chief of protocol to U.S. Pres., v.p., sec. of state Dept. State and White House, Washington, 1993—. Founder Smith Coll. Club Scholarship; pres. Del. Assn., 1971; chair Quality of Life Task Force, Com. Alternative Forms of Govt., Buffalo, 1976; chair vols. D.C. chpt. ARC, 1985-86, bd. dirs., 1986-90, chair comm. com., 1986-90, mem. mgmt. com. D.C. chpt.; bd. dirs. Cmty. Mus. Sch., Buffalo, 1967-70, Jr. Group, Albright-Knox Gallery, Buffalo, 1967-70, Sasha Bruce House, Washington, 1981-83, Higher Achievement Program, Washington, 1989-90, Ellington Fund of Duke Ellington Sch. for the Arts D.C. Pub. Performing Arts H.S., 1989-92, Nat. Symphony Orch., 1992—; participant, fundraiser local and statewide elections Buffalo, 1970-92; fundraiser Dem. Nat. Com., Congressmen Matsui, LaFalce, Dicks, Nowak, Sens. Gore, Robb, others, 1970-92; mem. fin. com. Moynihan for Sen., 1981-82; mem. arrangements com. Dem. Nat. Conv., 1984, mem. site selection com., 1987-88; mem. Albert Gore Jr. Presdl. Fin. Com., 1987-88; chair devel. com., bd. dirs. Women's Campaign Fund, 1988-90, Dem. chair, 1990-93; founder women's coun. Dem. Senatorial Campaign Com., 1992—. Episcopalian. Office: Office of Protocol Dept State 2201 C St NW Rm 1232 Washington DC 20520-0001

RAISH, DAVID LANGDON, lawyer; b. Cleve., Mar. 12, 1947; s. John E. Raish and Roslyn V. (Skeels) Pettibone; m. Roslyn Anne Dinnick, Sept. 12, 1969; children: David Jr., Anne, Julia. BA, Yale U., 1969; JD, Harvard U., 1973. Bar: Mass. 1975, D.C. 1981. Law clk. to hon. James R. Browning U.S. Ct. Appeals-9th Cir., San Francisco, 1973-74; assoc. Ropes & Gray, Boston, 1974-82, ptnr., 1982—; mem. Com. on U.S. Activities of Foreigners and Tax Treaties, ABA Tax sect. 1981—, chair, 1991-93. Author: Cafeteria Plans, 1985, Cash or Deferred Arrangements, 1986, Compensation and Benefits for Key Employees of Tax-Exempt Organizations, 1995; editor Tax Highlights Boston Bar Assn., 1985-93. Tenor Tanglewood Festival Chorus. Office: Ropes & Gray One International Pl Boston MA 02110

RAISIAN, JOHN, university institute director, economist; b. Conneaut, Ohio, July 30, 1949; s. Ernest James and Ruby Lee (Owens) R.; m. Joyce Ann Klak, Aug. 17, 1984; children: Alison Kathleen, Sarah Elizabeth. BA, Ohio U., 1971; PhD, UCLA, 1978. Rsch. assoc. Human Resources Rsch. Ctr., U. So. Calif., L.A., 1972-73; cons. Rand Corp., Santa Monica, Calif., 1974-75, 76; vis. asst. prof. econs. U. Wash., Seattle, 1975-76; asst. prof. econs. U. Houston, 1976-80; sr. economist Office Rsch. and Evaluation, U.S. Bur. Labor Stats., Washington, 1980-81; spl. asst. for econ. policy Office Asst. Sc. for Policy, U.S. Dept. Labor, Washington, 1981-83, dir. rsch. and tech. support, 1981-84; pres. Unicon Rsch. Corp., L.A., 1984-86; sr. fellow Hoover Instn., Stanford, Calif., 1986—, assoc. dir., dep. dir., 1986-90, dir., 1990—; exec. dir. Presdl. Task Force on Food Assistance, Washington, 1983-84. Mem. editorial bd. Jour. Labor Rsch., 1983—; contbr. articles to profl. jours. Advisor Nat. Coun. on Handicapped, Washington, 1985-86, Nat. Commn. on Employment Policy, Washington, 1987-88; chmn. minimum wage bd. Calif. Indsl. Welfare Commn., 1987; mem. nat. adv.com. Student Fin. Assistance, Washington, 1987-89; corp. mem. Blue Shield Calif. Recipient Best Publ. of Yr. award Econ. Inquiry, Western Econ. Assn., 1979, Disting. Teaching award U. Houston Coll. Social Scis., 1980, Disting. Svc. award U.S. Dept. Labor, 1983; predoctoral fellow Rand Corp., 1976. Mem. Am. Econs. Assn., Western Econ. Assn. (chmn. nominating com. 1992), Commonwealth Club of Calif., World Affairs Coun., Mont Pelerin Soc., Coun. on Fgn. Rels., Nat. Assn. Scholars, Phi Beta Kappa. Republican. Avocations: wine collecting, sports enthusiast. Office: Stanford U Hoover Hoover Inst War-Revolution Stanford CA 94305-6010

RAISIG, PAUL JONES, JR., lawyer; b. Jamestown, N.Y., June 21, 1932; s. Paul Jones and Marian Elizabeth (Christian) R.; m. Carolyn Virginia Sides, June 12, 1955; children: Dawn Virginia, Paul Christian, Anne Sibley. B.G.E., U. Nebr., 1961; M.B.A., U. Ala., 1965; JD, Campbell U., 1989. Bar: N.C., 1989, D.C. 1991, U.S. Supreme Ct. 1992. Commd. 2d lt. U.S. Army, 1953, advanced through grades to col., 1973, ret., 1977, served in Vietnam, 1963, btn. comdr., Vietnam, 1968; dep. dir. U.S. Army Reorganization, 1973; v.p. Armed Forces Relief and Benefit Assn., Washington, 1977-79; sr. cons. Dept. Def., Washington, 1979-80; exec. dir. Am. Fedn. Info. Processing Socs., Arlington, Va., 1980-84; v.p., dir. Designs, Ltd., Alexandria, Va., 1985-86; ptnr. Barrington, Herndon & Raisig, P.A., Fayetteville, N.C., 1989-92; adj. prof. bus. law and bus. mgmt. Campbell U., 1992-96; cons. in field. Decorated Legion of Merit (4), Bronze Star medal (2), Air medal (7), Purple Heart (2), Meritorious Service medal, Army Commendation medal with V Device (3). Mem. U.S. Council for World Communications, Beta Gamma Sigma. Club: University. Home and Office: Buffalo Lake 7612 Mallard Dr Sanford NC 27330-8444 *As we go about climbing the mountains in our lives, we must always remember to take the high road - for that is the only way to truly reach the top.*

RAISLER, KENNETH MARK, lawyer; b. New Rochelle, N.Y., May 15, 1951; s. Herbert A. and Norma (Glaubach) R.; m. Sara Ann Kelsey, June 11, 1978; children: Caroline Elisabeth, Katharine Kelsey, David Mark. BSBA, Yale Coll., 1973; JD, NYU, 1976. Bar: N.Y. 1977, D.C. 1977, U.S. Dist. Ct. (so. dist.) N.Y. 1977, U.S. Dist. Ct. D.C. 1977, U.S. Ct. Appeals (2d cir.) 1977, U.S. Ct. Appeals (D.C. cir.) 1977, U.S. Ct. Appeals (7th cir.) 1982, U.S. Ct. Appeals (10th cir.) 1983, U.S. Supreme Ct. 1985. Law clk. U.S. Dist. Ct. (so. dist.) N.Y., N.Y.C., 1976-77; asst. U.S. atty., Washington, 1977-82; dep. gen. counsel Commodity Futures Trading Commn., Washington, 1982-83, gen. counsel, 1983-87; ptnr. Rogers & Wells, N.Y.C., 1987-92, Sullivan & Cromwell, N.Y.C., 1992—. Mem. Assn. of Bar of City of N.Y. (chair futures regulation com. 1988-91). Office: Sullivan & Cromwell 125 Broad St New York NY 10004-2400

RAISZ, LAWRENCE GIDEON, medical educator, consultant; b. N.Y.C., Nov. 13, 1925; s. Erwin Joseph and Marie Georgette (Patai) R.; s. Helen Martin, June 5, 1948; children: Stephen, Matthew, Jonathan, Katherine, Nicholas. Student, Harvard U., 1943, MD, 1947; DOdontology (hon.), U. Umea, Sweden, 1990. Diplomate Am. Bd. Internal Medicine, Nat. Bd. Med. Examiners. Intern Harvard Med. Svc., Boston City Hosp., 1947-48; resident in medicine Cushing VA Hosp., 1950, Boston VA Hosp., 1952-54; asst. and instr. in physiology NYU-Bellevue Med. Ctr., 1948-50; asst. and instr. in medicine sch. medicine Boston U., 1953-56; chief renal sect. Boston VA Hosp., 1954-56; asst. chief radioisotope svc. Syracuse VA Hosp., 1956-57; asst. prof. medicine Coll. Medicine SUNY, Syracuse, 1956-61; assoc. prof. pharmacology and medicine Sch. Medicine U. Rochester, 1961-66, assoc. prof. medicine Sch. Medicine, 1966-68, prof. pharmacology, toxicology, and medicine Sch. Medicine, 1966-74, chief div. of clin. pharmacology Sch. Medicine, 1961-74; prof. medicine, head div. of endocrinology and metabolism Sch. Medicine U. Conn., Farmington, 1974—; program dir. Gen. Clin. Rsch. Ctr. U. Conn Health Ctr., Farmington, 1993—; sr. assoc. physician Strong Meml. Hosp., Rochester, 1961-68, physician, 1968-74; acting chmn. dept. pharmacology Sch. Medicine, U. Rochester, 1962-63, vis. prof. pharmacology, toxicology and medicine Sch. Medicine and Dentistry, 1974-76; vis. assoc. prof. pharmacology Sch. Medicine Stanford U., 1966; vis. prof. Coll. Medicine U. Lagos, Nigeria, 1973; mem. gen. B study sect. NIH, 1986-88; mem. subspecialty bd. on endocrinology and metabolism Am. Bd. Internal Medicine, 1990—; mem. U.S.-Japan Malnutrition Panel, 1985-91; clin. investigator Syracuse VA Hosp., 1957-60; William N. Creasy Vis. Prof. Clin. Pharmacology Med. Sch. Dartmouth Coll., 1977; chmn. Gordon Conf. on Bones and Teeth, 1980; Edwin B. Astwood lectr. Endocrine Soc., 1983. Mem. numerous editorial bds.; contbr. more than 300 articles to profl. jours. With USNR, 1943-45; capt. AUS, 1950-52. Spl. Rsch. fellow Nat. Inst. Arthritis and Metabolic Disease, Strangeways Rsch. Lab., 1960-61, Nat. Inst. Dental Rsch. NIH, 1971-72; Burroughs-Wellcome scholar in Clin. Pharmacology, 1963-68; recipient Prix Andre Lichtwitz, 1980, Class of 1947 Disting. Prof. award Med. Sch. U. Wis., 1988. Mem. AAAS, Am. Fedn. for Clin. Rsch., Am. Soc. for Clin. Investigation, Am. Soc. for Pharmacology and Exptl. Therapeutics, Endocrine Soc., Assn. Am. Physicians, Conn. Endocrine Soc. (pres. 1976), Am. Soc. for Bone and Mineral Rsch. (pres. 1980-81, William F. Neuman award 1986), Conn. Acad. Sci. and Engring., Sigma Xi. Avocations: travel, skiing, wind surfing. Home: 118 Waterville Rd Farmington CT 06032-1624 Office: U Conn Health Ctr 263 Farmington Ave Farmington CT 06030-1850

RAITT, BONNIE LYNN, blues singer, guitarist; b. Burbank, Calif., Nov. 8, 1949. Student, Radcliffe Coll. Performer blues clubs, East Coast; concert tours in Britain, 1976, 77; albums include Bonnie Raitt, 1971, Give It Up, 1972, Takin' My Time, 1973, Streetlights, 1974, Home Plate, 1975, Sweet Forgiveness, 1977, The Glow, 1979, Green Light, 1982, Nine Lives, 1986, Nick of Time, 1989 (Grammys 1990, Rock-Best Vocal Performance, Female, Pop-Best Vocal Performance, Female, Album of Yr.), I'm in the Mood (with John Lee Hooker) (Grammy 1990, Blues-Best Traditional Record), The Bonnie Raitt Collection, 1990, Luck of the Draw, 1991 (Grammy 1992, Rock-Best Vocal Performance, Female, Grammy for Best Duet with Delbert McClinton), Longing In Their Hearts, 1994 (Grammy award Best Pop Album), Road Tested, 1996; songs include Something to Talk About (Grammy 1992, Best Pop Vocal Performance, Female), Good Man, Good Woman (with Delbert McClinton) (Grammy 1992, Rock-Best Vocal by a Duo or Group). Recipient numerous Grammy nominations, four Grammy awards 1990, three Grammy awards 1992. Office: PO Box 626 Los Angeles CA 90078*

RAJAB, MOHAMMAD HASAN, biostatistician, educator; b. Oct. 8, 1955; married; 2 children. BS in Agrl. Scis., Damascus (Syria) U., 1976; MS in Quantitative Genetics, Tex. A&M U., 1983, MS in Stats., 1987, PhD in Quantitative Genetics, 1987. Instr. Coll. Agr., Damascus (Syria) U., 1976-80, asst. prof. quanititative genetics, 1987-90; tchg. asst. dept. stats. Coll. Sci., Tex. A&M U., College Station, 1986-87; vis. asst. prof. Tex. A&M U., College Station, 1990; rsch. sci. dept. stats. Coll. Sci., Tex. A&M U., College Station, 1990-93, asst. prof. dept. psychiatry-behavioral scis. Coll. Medicine, 1993—; vis. asst. prof. Inst. für Tierenranhrung, U. Bonn, Bermany, 1990; co-investigator Coordinating Ctr. Partial Hospitalization of High-Rise Suicidal Youth Study, NIH, 1990-94, statistician ctrl. vein occlusion study, 1994—; epidemiologist biostats. dept. Scott and White Hosp., Temple, Tex., 1993—; presenter in field. Contbr. articles to profl. jours. Acad. scholar USAID, 1980; recipient Govt. award Damascus U., 1976. Mem. Am. Statis. Assn., Soc. Clin. Trials, Biometrics Soc., Sigma Xi. Office: Texas A&M U Health Sci Ctr Coll Med Temple Campus 600 S 25th St Temple TX 76504-5371 also: Scott and White Biostats Dept 2401 S 31st St Temple TX 76508-0001

RAJAN, FRED E. N., clergy member, church administrator. Exec. dir. Commn. for Multicultural Ministries of the Evangelical Lutheran Church in America, Chicago, Ill. Office: Evangelical Lutheran Church Am 8765 W Higgins Rd Chicago IL 60631-4101

RAJANI, PREM RAJARAM, transportation company financial executive; b. Bombay, Nov. 9, 1949; came to U.S., 1973; s. Rajaram N. and Devibai Rajani; m. Rekha Rohera, Apr. 21, 1977; children: Anand, Harshada. B Tech., Indian Inst. Tech., Bombay, 1973; MBA in Acctg. and Fin., Columbia U., 1975. Sr. ops. auditor Pfizer, Inc., N.Y.C., 1975-78; sr. projects fin. analyst Sea-Land Industries subs. RJR, Edison, N.J., 1978-80, fin. mgr. joint ventures, 1980-81, mgr. corp. planning and analysis, 1981-84; mgr. corp. fin. Sea-Land Corp., Edison, 1984-87; asst. treas.-internat. Sea-Land Svc. Inc. subs. CSX Corp., Edison, 1987-88, asst. treas.-domestic, 1988, staff v.p., treas., 1988-94, staff v.p. fin. and planning Americas, 1994—. Mem. Nat. Assn. Corp. Treas., Soc. Internat. Treas. Office: Sea-Land Svc Inc 6000 Carnegie Blvd Charlotte NC 28209

RAJAONARIVELO, PIERROT J., diplomat; b. Madagascar, June 17, 1945; m. Honorine Renee Razafindralamb; 3 children. MA in Law and Polit. Sci., U. Madagascar, 1973; postgrad. in mgmt. tng., Columbia U., 1974-75; grad. degree in Mgmt., U. Paris, 1980. Comml. attaché Mission of Madagascar to UN, N.Y.C., 1973-77; with econ. and comml. sect. Embassy of Madagascar, Paris, 1978-80; dir. mktg. Société industrielle et commerciale, 1981-83; dir. internal trade Govt. Madagascar, 1983-84, dir. gen. fgn. trade, 1984-88; dir. gen. commerce, ministry commerce Govt. Madagascar, Antananarivo, 1988-89; amb. to U.S. Govt. Madagascar, Washington, 1989—; chmn. bd. govs. Société malgache de Commerce et de distributien, 1983-89; mem. bd. govs. BFV Bank, 1986-89, chmn., 1989. Mem. African Group Ambs. in Washington (chmn. econ. com. 1994—). Office: Embassy of Madagascar 2374 Massachusetts Ave NW Washington DC 20008-2801

RAJESHWAR, KRISHNAN, chemist, educator; b. Trivandrum, India, Apr. 15, 1949; m. Rohini Chidambaram, 1977; children: Reena, Rebecca. BSc, U. Col, India, 1969; postgrad., Indian Inst. Technol. Sci., 1971, PhD in Chemistry, 1974. From asst. to assoc. prof. chemistry U. Tex., Arlington, 1983-89, prof. chemistry, 1989—; rsch. chemist Prods Formulation Group Foseco Internat., India, 1974-75, rsch. fellow in chemistry St. Francis, Xavier U., Can., 1975-76; rsch. fellow Colo. State U., 1976-78, vis. asst. prof., 1978-79, sr. rsch. assoc., 1979-83; cons. U. Wyo Rsch. Corp. & Forensic Labs., Edwards Aerospace Inc., Tex. Mem. Am. Chem. Soc. (Wilford T. Doherty award 1994), Electrochem. Soc. Achievements include research in charge storage and transport mechanisms in a variety of metals, semiconductors and polymers, environmental electrochemistry and photoelectrochemistry. Office: U Texas Dept Chemistry & Biochemistry PO Box 19065 Arlington TX 76019

RAJOTTE, RAY V., biomedical engineer, researcher; b. Wainwright, Alta., Can., Dec. 5, 1942; s. Sam and Bernadette (Tremblay) R.; m. Gloria A. Yackimetz, Aug. 20, 1966; children: Brian, Michael, Monique. RT, No. Alta. Inst. Tech., 1965; BSc in Elec. Engring., U. Alta., 1971, MSc in Elec. Engring., 1973, PhD in Biomed. Engring., 1975. Postdoctoral fellow U. Alta. Dept. Medicine, Edmonton, 1975-76, Oak Ridge (Tenn.) Nat. Lab., 1976-77, Washington U., St. Louis, 1977, UCLA, 1977; rsch. assoc. dept. medicine U. Alta., Edmonton, 1977-79, asst. prof. dept. medicine, 1979-82, asst. prof. dept. medicine & surgery, 1983-84, assoc. prof., 1984-88, prof., 1988—; dir. Islet Cel Transplant Lab. U. Alta., 1982—, Divsn. Exptl. Surgery U. Alta., 1988—; assoc. dir. Surg.-Med. Rsch. Inst. U. Alta., 1984-87, dir., 1987—; co-dir. Juvenile Diabetes Fund Diabetes Interdisciplinary Rsch. Program U. Alta., 1992—. Co-editor: The Immunology of Diabetes Mellitus, 1986; mem. adv. bd. Diabetologia jour., 1993—; author over 350 publs. in field; contbr. 18 chpts. to books. Mem. Cell Transplantation Soc. (founding mem., councillor 1991—), Internat. Pancreas and Islet Transplant Assn. (founding mem., treas. 1991—), Can. Transplantation Soc. (Western councillor 1987—), European Assn. for Study of Diabetes, Assn. Profl. Engrs., Geologists & Geophysicists Alta., Soc. Cryobiology, Am. Diabetes Assn., Can. Soc. Clin. Investigation, N.Y. Acad. Sci., Transplantation Soc., Can. Diabetes Assn., Acad. Surg. Rsch., Internat. Diabetes Fedn. Achievements include patent for glucose sensor. Office: U Alta, Surgical-Med Rsch Inst, Edmonton, AB Canada T6G 2N8

RAJSIC, ROBERT, secondary school educator. Tchr. River Forest High Sch., Hobart, Ind. Named Outstanding High Sch. Tchr. Inland Steel Ryerson Found., 1992. Office: River Forest High Sch Indiana St Huber Blvd Hobart IN 46342

RAJSKI, PEGGY, film director, film producer; b. Stevens Point, Wis.. Attended, U. Wis. Films include: (prodn. mgr.): Lianna, 1982, Almost You, 1984; (prodr., prodn. mgr.) The Brother From Another Planet, 1984, Matewan, 1987, Eight Men Out, 1988; (prodr.) The Grifters, 1990, Little Man Tate, 1991 (also 2nd. unit dir.), Used People, 1992; (prodr. video) Bruce Springsteen's Glory Days; (dir.) Trevor, 1994 (Acad. award for Best Live Action Short Film). Office: 140 Riverside Dr Ste 5E New York NY 10024-2605*

RAJUR, SHARANABASAVA BASAPPA, chemistry educator, researcher; b. Benakanhal, India, June 1, 1956; came to U.S., 1987; s. Basappa and Basamma Rajur; m. Krupa Sharanabasava Mensinkal, June 30, 1990; 1 child, Vinaya S. PhD, Karanatak U., Dharwad, India, 1987. Rsch. asst. Karnatak U., 1984-85; lectr. organic chemistry Kittle Coll., Dharwad, 1985-86; asst. prof. Coll. of Pharmacy, Dharwad, 1986-87; rsch. assoc. U. Tex. Southwestern Med. Ctr., Dallas, 1987-90, Boston Coll., 1990-93; rsch. scientist Millipore Corp., Bedford, Mass., 1993-94; profl. researcher, group leader Boston Coll., 1994-95; sr. rsch. fellow Mass. Gen. Hosp., Boston, 1995—. Reviewer Jour. Pharm. Scis., 1990-93; contbr. articles to profl. jours. Recipient grant Dept. Mental Health Clinics, 1988-89. Mem. AAAS, Am. Chem. Soc., Indian Chem. Soc. Hindu. Achievements include patent for developing FMOC protected peptide nucleic acid (PNA) derivatives. Avocations: tennis, swimming, skiing. Home: 36 Westgate Rd Chestnut Hill MA 02167 Office: Mass Gen Hosp Harvard Med Sch Surg Rsch 149 13th St Boston MA 02129

RAKEL, ROBERT EDWIN, physician, educator; b. Cin., July 13, 1932; s. Edwin J. and Elsie (Machino) R.; m. Peggy Klare; children: Barbara, Cindy, Linda, David. BS in Zoology, U. Cin., 1954, MD, 1958. Diplomate: Charter diplomate Am. Bd. Family Practice (v.p., dir.). Intern St. Mary's Hosp., Cin., 1958-59; resident in internal medicine USPHS Hosp., Seattle, 1959-61; resident in gen. practice Monterey County Hosp., Salinas, Calif., 1961-62; practice medicine Newport Beach, Calif., 1962-69; chmn. family practice program U. Calif., Irvine, 1969-71; prof., head dept. family practice U. Iowa, 1971-85; assoc. dean acad. and clin. affairs, Richard M. Kleberg, Sr. prof., chmn. dept. family medicine Baylor Coll. Medicine, Houston, 1985—; dir. family practice residency program Hoag Meml. Hosp., Newport Beach, 1969-71; med. staff Mercy Hosp., Iowa City, 1971-85; chief family practice service St. Luke's Episc. Hosp., The Meth. Hosp., Houston, 1985—; trustee The Hospice of Tex. Med. Ctr., 1986—, Inst. of Religion Tex. Author: Selected References in Family Medicine, 1973, (with H.F. Conn & T.W. Johnson) Family Practice, 1973, (with H.F. Conn.) Textbook of Family Practice, 1978, editor 3d edit., 1984, 5th edit., 1995, Principles of Family Medicine, 1977; author foreword Neurology for the Everyday Practice of Medicine, R.G. Feldman, 1984; contbr. Dictionary of Am. Med. Biography Vols. I and II, 1984; editor: Conn's Current Therapy, 1984—, Yearbook of Family Practice, 1977-90, (series) Procedures for Your Practice Patient Care, Vol. 18, Essentials of Family Practice, 1992, Saunders Manual Med. Practice, 1996; mem. 13 editorial bds. med. jours.; contbr. articles to med. jours.; contbr. Encyclopedia Britannica, 1995. Served with USPHS, 1959-61. Recipient Mead-Johnson Scholar award in Gen. Practice, 1971. Fellow Am. Acad. Family Physicians (pres. Orange County chpt. Calif. 1969, commn. on edn. 1970-76, Thomas W. Johnson award 1973); mem. AMA (sect. on med. schs. 1985—, gov. council of sect. 1986-88), Tex. Med. Assn., Am. Bd. Family Practice (bd. dirs. 1973-79, v.p. 1977-79, chmn. exam. com. 1974-79, recert. com. 1973-79, others), Am. Bd. Med. Spltys. (com. splty. evaluation 1978-81), Nat. Bd. Med. Examiners (bd. dirs. 1975-79), Soc. Tchrs. Family Medicine (dir. 1971-79, sec. 1971-73), Council Acad. Socs., Assn. Am. Med. Colls., History of Medicine Soc. (founder, chmn. U. Iowa 1978-85, founder, chmn. Baylor Coll. Medicine 1986—), Am. Osler Soc. (bd. dirs. 1989—, pres. 1994), Cosmos Club. Home: 2420 Underwood St Houston TX 77030-3506 Office: Baylor Coll Medicine 1 Baylor Plz Houston TX 77030-3411

RAKES, GANAS KAYE, finance and banking educator; b. Floyd, Va., May 2, 1938; s. Samuel D. and Ocie J. (Peters) R.; m. Mary Ann Simmons, Oct. 1, 1961; 1 child, Sabrina Darrow. BS, Va. Tech., 1960, MS, 1964; D of Bus. Adminstrn., Washington U., St. Louis, 1971. Assoc. prof. commerce U. Va., Charlottesville, 1968-80; O'Bleness prof. fin. and banking Ohio U., Athens, 1980—; chmn. fin. dept. Coll. of Bus. Adminstrn., 1983—; bd. dirs. Caldwell Savs. and Loan Co.; pres. bd. dirs. Enterprise Devel. Corp. Contbr. articles to profl. jours. Served to 1st lt. U.S. Army, 1961-63. Mem. Fin. Mgmt. Assn., Midwestern Bus. Adminstrs. Assn., Eastern Fin. Assn., Rotary, Reynolds Nat. Club. Republican. Episcopalian. Avocation: sailing. Office: Ohio U Dept of Fin Athens OH 45701

RAKESTRAW, WARREN VINCENT, lawyer; b. Dayton, Ohio, July 6, 1940; s. David Warren and Lou Ann (Hobbs) R.; m. Susan M. Rich, 1993. B.S., Ohio U., 1963; J.D., Capital U., 1968. Bar: Ohio bar 1968. Asst. atty. gen. State of Ohio, Columbus, 1968; legis. dir. to U.S. Senator William B. Saxbe, Washington, 1969-74; asst. atty. gen. U.S. Dept. Justice, Washington, 1974-75; counsel to ambassador New Delhi, India, 1975-77; partner firm Chester Hoffman & Willcox, Columbus, 1977-86; sole practice Columbus, 1986—. Mem. ABA (Ohio, Fla., D.C. chpts.), Sigma Chi, The Athletic Club of Columbus. Home: 8403 Beeswing Ct Muirfield Village Dublin OH 43017 Office: 4930 Reed Rd Columbus OH 43220-3144

RAKIC, PASKO, neuroscientist, educator; b. Ruma, Yugoslavia, May 15, 1933; came to U.S., 1969; m. Patricia Goldman, 1969. MD, U. Belgrade, Yugoslavia, 1959, ScD in Neuroembryology, 1969. With inst. path. physiology Med. Sch. U. Belgrade, 1959-61, resident in neurosurgery, 1961-62; NIH research fellow neuropathology Harvard Med. Sch., Boston, 1962-66; asst. prof. Inst. Biol. Rsch., Belgrade, 1967-68; from asst. prof. to assoc. prof. neuropathology and neuroscience Harvard Med. Sch., 1969-77; prof. neurosci. Yale Med. Sch., New Haven, 1977-78, Dorys McConnell Duberg prof. neurosci., 1978—, also chmn. neurobiology sect. Author of 200 sci. papers and gen. books on brain orgn. and devel. Mem. NAS, Am. Acad. Arts and Sci., Soc. Neurosci. (pres. 1996—). Office: Yale U Sch Medicine Sect Neurobiology 333 Cedar St New Haven CT 06510-3206

RAKITA, LOUIS, cardiologist, educator; b. Montreal, Que., Can., July 2, 1922; came to U.S., 1951, naturalized, 1962; s. S. and Rose (Weinman) R.; m. G. Blanche Michlin, Dec. 4, 1945; 1 son, Robert M. B.A., Sir George Williams Coll., Montreal, 1942; M.D., C.M., McGill U., 1949. Diplomate: Am. Bd. Internal Medicine. Intern Montreal Gen. Hosp., 1949-50; resident in medicine Jewish Gen. Hosp., Montreal, 1950-51; fellow in medicine Alton Ochsner Med. Found., New Orleans, 1951-52; chief resident in medicine Cleve. City Hosp., 1952-53, Am. Heart Assn. fellow, 1954-55; Am. Heart Assn. fellow Inst. for Med. Research, Cedars of Lebanon Hosp., Los Angeles, 1953-54; practice medicine specializing in internal medicine and cardiology Cleve., 1954—; instr. medicine Western Res. U., Cleve., 1954-55; sr. instr. Western Res. U., 1955-57, asst. prof., 1957-61, asso. prof., 1961-71; asst. vis. physician Cleve. City Hosp., 1954-57, vis. physician, 1957—; advanced fellow Cleve. Met. Gen. Hosp., 1959-61, dir. cardiology, 1966-87, immediate past dir., div. cardiology, 1987—; asso. div. of research in med. edn. Case Western Res. U., Cleve., 1969-75; prof. medicine Case Western Res. U., 1971-93, prof. emeritus medicine, 1993; chmn. Phase IIA Cardiovascular com. Case Western Res. U., 1965-70, Faculty Senate Subcom. for Devel. and Evaluation of Ednl. Methods, 1969, chmn. Univ. Com. on Ednl. Planning, 1971-73, Faculty Coun. Sch. Medicine, 1979-80, Faculty Coun. Steering Com. Sch. Medicine, 1979-80, mem. bd. trustees Com. on Univ. Plans, 1971-73, Faculty Senate, Exec. Coun.; cons. in cardiology Luth. Med. Ctr., Cleve., 1970—, Crile VA Hosp., Cleve., 1969—; vis. cardiologist Sunny Acres Hosp., Cleve., 1973—; cardiologist rep. of del. to USSR, 1973. Author: (with M. Broder) Cardiac Arrhythmias, 1970, (with M. Kaplan) Immunological Diseases, 1972; Contbr. (with M. Kaplan) articles on cardiovascular diseases to profl. pubs. Served with RCAF, 1942-45. Recipient Research Career Devel. award USPHS, 1962-69. Fellow ACP (Laureate award Ohio chpt. 1992), Am. Coll. Cardiology, Royal Coll. Physicians and Surgeons Can. (cert.), Am. Heart Assn. (mem. exec. com. N.E. Ohio chpt. 1972—, trustee 1969—, pres. N.E. Ohio chpt. 1972-74, coun. on clin. cardiology 1972—, chmn. various coms., v.p. North Ctrl. Region 1985-86, bd. dirs. 1985-86, hon. life trustee Northeast Ohio affiliate, vice chmn. task force on product licensing feasibility 1987—, Award of Merit 1987, Gold Heart award 1989); mem. AAUP, Am. Fedn. Clin. Rsch., Ctrl. Soc. Clin. Rsch., Soc. Exptl. Biology and Medicine, Cleve. Med. Libr. Assn. (trustee 1972—), Nat. Bd. Med. Examiners, The Press of Case Western Res. U. (adv. com. 1970), Nat. Heart and Lung Inst., Nat. Insts. Health (left ventricular assist device clin. trial program divsn. extramural affairs, data rev. bd. 1981—, adv. com. med. devices applications program 1971-75), Sigma Xi. Home: 24151 S Woodland Rd Cleveland OH 44122-3315 Office: 2500 Metrohealth Dr Cleveland OH 44109-1900

RAKOFF, JED SAUL, federal judge, author; b. Phila., Aug. 1, 1943; s. Abraham Edward and Doris Tobiah (Michell) R.; m. Ann Rosenberg, Aug. 4, 1974; children: Jena Lynn, Elana Beth, Keira Jan. BA, Swarthmore Coll., 1964; MPhil, Balliol Coll., Oxford U., Eng., 1966; JD, Harvard U., 1969. Bar: N.Y. 1971, D.C. 1983, U.S. Supreme Ct. 1986. Law clk. U.S. Ct. Appeals (3rd cir.), Phila., 1969-70; assoc. Debevoise, Plimpton, Lyons & Gates, N.Y.C., 1970-73; asst. U.S. atty. So. Dist. N.Y., N.Y.C., 1973-80, chief bus. and securities fraud prosecutions U.S. Atty.'s Office, 1978-80; ptnr. Mudge Rose Guthrie Alexander & Ferdon, N.Y.C., 1980-90, Fried Frank Harris Shriver & Jacobson, N.Y.C., 1990-96; judge U.S. Dist. Ct. (so. dist.) N.Y., 1966—; lectr. in law Columbia Law Sch., 1988—. Author: (with S. Arkin et al) Business Crime, 6 vols., 1982, Criminal Defense Techniques, 6 vols., 1982, (with H. Goldstein) RICO: Civil and Criminal Law and Strategy, 1989, (with L. Blumkin and R. Sauber) Corporate Sentencing Guidelines: Compliance and Mitigation, 1993; editor-in-chief Bus. Crimes Bull., 1994-95; columnist N.Y. Law Jour., 1985-95; contbr. numerous articles to law revs. Mem. exec. bd. N.Y. chpt. Am. Jewish Com., 1971-95. Fellow Am. Coll. Trial Lawyers (chmn. N.Y. State 1993-94), Am. Bd. Criminal Lawyers; mem. ABA, N.Y. State Bar Assn., Assn. of Bar of City of N.Y. (chmn. criminal law com. 1986-89), Fed. Bar Coun., N.Y. Coun. Def. Lawyers (dir. 1990-94). Democrat. Jewish. Office: U.S. Courthouse 500 Pearl St New York NY 10007

RAKOFF, VIVIAN MORRIS, psychiatrist, writer; b. Capetown, South Africa, Apr. 28, 1928; s. David Wilfred and Bertha Lillian (Woolf) R.; m. Gina Shochat, Nov. 27, 1959; children: Simon, Ruth, David. B.A., U. Capetown, 1947, M.A. with 1st class honors, 1949; M.B.B.S., U. London, 1957; diploma psychiat. medicine, McGill U., 1963. Intern St. Charles Hosp., London, 1957, Victoria Hosp., Capetown, 1958; resident Groote Schuur Hosp., Capetown, 1959-61, Jewish Gen. Hosp., Montreal, 1961-62, Verdun Protestant Hosp., Montreal, 1961-62; staff psychiatrist Jewish Gen. Hosp., Montreal, 1963-66, dir. research psychiatry, 1967-68; dir. postgrad. edn. dept. psychiatry U. Toronto, Ont, Can, 1968-75; prof. psychiat. edn. U. Toronto, Ont., Can., 1975-80, prof., chmn. dept. psychiatry, 1980-90; prof. emeritus U. Toronto, 1990—; head dept. psychiatry Sunnybrook Hosp., Toronto, 1978-80; dir., psychiatrist-in-chief Clarke Inst. Psychiatry, Toronto, 1980-90. Author: plays Nonquasi, 1967; Mandelstam's Witness, 1975; editor: Psychiatric Diagnosis, 1977, A Method of Psychiatry, 1979. Fellow Royal Coll. Physicians and Surgeons, Am. Psychiat. Assn., Am. Coll. Psychiatrists; mem. Sigma Xi. Jewish. Office: Clarke Inst Psychiatry, 250 College St, Toronto, ON Canada M5T 1R8

RAKOLTA, JOHN, construction company executive; b. 1923. Student, U. Detroit. With Walbridge Aldinger Co., Livonia, Mich., 1945—, sec., treas., 1955-70, pres., treas., 1970-78, pres., 1978-80, now chmn. bd. dirs., 1980—. Office: Walbridge Aldinger Co 613 Abbott St Detroit MI 48226-2522*

RAKOWICZ-SZULCZYNSKA, EVA MARIA, molecular oncologist; b. Poznan, Poland, Nov. 22, 1951; came to U.S., 1984; d. Tadeusz and Wieslawa Maria (Hankiewicz) Rakowicz; divorced; 1 child, Adriana Maria. MS in Biochemistry, A. Mickiewicz U., Poznan, 1974; PhD in Biochemistry, Acad. Medicine, Poznan, 1977, DMS in Human Genetics & Molecular Biol., 1981. Asst. prof. Inst. Human Genetics, Poznan, 1978-82, assoc. dir., 1982-86, assoc. prof., 1982-89; assoc. scientist, lab. head Wistar Inst., Phila., 1984-90, rsch. asst. prof., 1991-92; assoc. prof. epp. U. Nebr. Med. Ctr., Omaha, 1992—, assoc. prof. Eppley Inst., 1993—, assoc. prof. biochemistry, 1995—; mem. Eppley Cancer Ctr., Omaha, 1995—. Author: Nuclear Localization of Growth Factors and of Monoclonal Antibodies, 1993; contbr. articles to Am. Jour. Pathology, Carcinogenesis, others. Grantee Nebr. Dept. Health, 1993—, Elson U. Pardee Found., 1993-94, Olson Ctr. for Women's Health, 1993—. Grantee Nebr. Dept. of Health, 1993—, Elas U. Pardee Found., 1993-94, Olson Ctr. for Women's Health, 1993—. Mem. AAAS, Am. Assn. Cancer Rsch., N.Y. Acad. Scis. Roman Catholic. Achievements include patents for Methods for Detecting Growth Factor Receptor Expression, Methods for Screening Monoclonal Antibodies for Therapeutic Use; patent pending for diagnosis and therapy of breast and gynecological cancer. Office: U Nebr Med Ctr Dept Ob/Gyn 600 S 42d St Omaha NE 68198-3255

RALEIGH, CECIL BARING, geophysicist; b. Little Rock, Aug. 11, 1934; s. Cecil Baring and Lucile Nell (Stewart) R.; m. Diane Lauster, July 17, 1982; children: Alison, Marianne, Lawrence, David. B.A., Pomona (Calif.) Coll., 1956; M.A., Claremont (Calif.) Grad. Sch., 1958; Ph.D., UCLA, 1963. Fellow Research Sch. Phys. Sci., Australian Nat. U., Canberra, 1963-66; geophysicist U.S. Geol. Survey, Menlo Park, Calif., 1966-80; program mgr. for earthquake prediction research program U.S. Geol. Survey, 1980-81; dir. Lamont-Doherty Geol. Obs. and prof. geol. scis. Columbia U., Palisades, N.Y., 1981-89; dean Sch. Ocean and Earth Sci. and Tech. U. Hawaii, Honolulu, 1989—; chmn. bd. dirs. DOSECC, Inc., 1985-88; CEO Ctr. for a Sustainable Future, Inc., 1996—; mem. Gov.'s Task Force on Sci. Tech., 1996—; mem. NAS/NRC Ocean Studies Bd.; chmn. NAS/NRC Yucca Mountain Panel; bd. dirs. JOI, Inc., High Tech. Devel. Corp. Author papers control earthquakes, rheology of the mantle, mechanics of faulting, crystal plasticity. Recipient Interdisciplinary award U.S. Nat. Com. Rock Mechanics, 1969, 74; Meritorious Service award Dept. Interior, 1974; Barrows Dist. Alumnus award Pomona Coll. Fellow Am. Geophys. Union, Geol. Soc. Am. Democrat. Inventor formation fracturing method. Office: U Hawaii Sch Ocean Earth Sci & Tech Honolulu HI 96822

RALES, MITCHELL P., automotive parts company executive; b. 1956; married. Pres. Danaher Corp., Washington, 1984—, also bd. dirs.; with Equity Group Holdings, Washington, 1979—. Office: Danaher Corp 1250 24th St NW Washington DC 20037-1124

RALES, STEVEN M., automotive parts company executive; b. Pitts., Mar. 31, 1951; married. BA, DePauw U., 1973; JD, America U., 1978. With Equity Group Holdings, Washington, 1979—; chmn. bd., chief exec. officer Danaher Corp., Washington, 1984—, now chmn. bd. Office: Danaher Corp 1250 24th St NW Washington DC 20037-1124*

RALIS, PARASKEVY, art educator, artist; b. N.Y.C., Sept. 16, 1951; d. Harry and Katerina (Koumi) R. AA, Miami-Dade Community Coll., 1970; BFA, Fla. Internat. U., 1973; MS, Nova U., 1977. Tchr. Miami (Fla.) Park Elem. Sch., 1973-80; instr. visual arts, photography Am. Sr. High Sch., 1980-81; tchr. Holmes Elem. Sch., 1981-84, Horace Mann Jr. High Sch., 1983-85; instr. magnet program visual arts, photography R.R. Moton South Ctr. for the Expressive Arts, 1984—, head dept. fine arts spl. area, 1986-89, 93-94, magnet lead tchr., 1992-93; magnet dept. head R.R. Moton South Ctr. for the Expressive Arts, Miami, 1993-94; chairperson grant writing com. R.R. Moton Expressive Arts Ctr., 1990; mem. SBM Sch. Cadre, 1993-94, R.R. Moton's Sch. Based Mgmt. Cadre, 1994-95. Prin. works include Twenty-First M. Allen Hortt Meml. Exhbn., Contemporary Reflections of the 19th Century, 1979, Media Plus, 1980, Inception, 1981, Artspace, 1982, Class Impressions, 1983, Southern Exposure, 1986; exhibited in group shows at Met. Mus. Art and Art Ctr., Coral Gables, Fla., 1986, Broward Community Coll. Fine Arts Gallery, 1985, Mus. Art, Ft. Lauderdale, 1979, 84, North Miami Mus. and Art Ctr., 1983, Fla. Internat. U., 1980, Nat. Exhibit Am. Art, Chautauqua, N.Y., 1985, Images I Miami Dade Community Coll., 1988, Omni Internat. Mall Artworks Gallery, 1990, 91, 92, The Ctr. for Visual Comms., 1993, Sheldon Lurie Art Against AIDS Auction IV, Biltmore Hotel, Coral Gables, Fla., 1994, Rex Art Tchrs. Exhibit, 1996; inventor first art game in U.S. History, 1978; Photog. of James Brown, 1981. Mem. Dade County Art Tchrs. Assn. (bd. dirs., publicity chmn., Pres.'s award 1984), Fla. Art Educators Assn. (presenter 1994), United Tchrs. of Dade (liaison to Dade Art Educators Assn. 1981-94, 95—, arts advocacy chair 1995-96), Art Edn. Assn. (chair photography com. conv. 1990). Greek Orthodox. Home: 798 NE 71st St Miami FL 33138-5718 Office: RR Moton S Ctr for Excellence Expressive Arts Ctr 18050 Homestead Ave Miami FL 33157-5529

RALL, DAVID PLATT, pharmacologist, environmentalist; b. Aurora, Ill., Aug. 3, 1926; s. Edward Everett and Nell (Platt) R.; children: Jonathan D., Catharyn E.; m. Mary Gloria Monteiro, Apr. 22, 1989. BS, North Ctrl. Coll., Naperville, Ill., 1946; MS, Northwestern U., 1948, MD, PhD, 1951. Intern Bellevue Hosp., N.Y.C., 1952-53; officer USPHS, 1953-90, asst. surgeon gen., 1971-90; sr. investigator Lab. Chem. Pharmacology, Nat. Cancer Inst., NIH, Bethesda, Md., 1953-55, Clin. Pharmacology and Exptl. Therapeutics Service, 1956-58, head service, 1958-63; chief Clin. Pharmacology and Exptl. Therapeutics Service (Lab. Chem. Pharmacology), 1963-69; assoc. sci. dir. for exptl. therapeutics Nat. Cancer Inst., 1966-71; dir. Nat. Inst. Environ. Health Scis., 1971-90, dir. Nat. Toxicology Program, 1978-90; adj. prof. pharmacology U. N.C., Chapel Hill, 1972-90, Foreign Secretary NAS Inst. Medicine, 1994—. Trustee Environ. Def. Fund, 1991—; treas. Ramazzini Soc., 1992—. Fellow AAAS; mem. Am. Assn. Cancer Rsch., Am. Soc. Clin. Investigation, Am. Soc. Pharmacology and Exptl. Therapeutics, Inst. Medicine, Soc. Toxicology. Home and Office: 5302 Reno Rd NW Washington DC 20015-1908

RALL, JOSEPH EDWARD, physician; b. Naperville, Ill., Feb. 3, 1920; s. Edward Everett and Nell (Platt) R.; m. Caroline Domm, Sept. 28, 1944 (dec. Apr. 1976); children: Priscilla, Edward Christian. B.A., North Central Coll., 1940, D.Sc. (hon.), 1966; M.S., Northwestern U., 1944, M.D., 1945; Ph.D., U. Minn., 1952; Dr. honoris causa, Faculty of Medicine, Free U. Brussels, Belgium, 1975; M.D. (hon.), U. Naples, 1985. Assoc. mem. Sloan Kettering Inst., N.Y.C., 1950-55; chief clin. endocrinology br. Nat. Inst. Arthritis, Metabolism and Digestive Diseases, NIH, 1955-62; dir. intramural research Nat. Inst. Arthritis, Diabetes, Digestive and Kidney Diseases, 1962-83; dep. dir. intramural research NIH, 1983-91; sr. investigator Nat. Inst. Diabetes and Digestive and Kidney Diseases, NIH, 1991; scientist emeritus NIH, 1995; mem. NRC, 1960-65. Author numerous articles, chpts. in books on thyroid gland and radiation. Chmn. Coun. of Scientists for Internat. Human Frontier Sci. Program, 1989-93. Served to capt. M.C. AUS, 1946-48. Recipient Van Meter prize Am. Goiter Assn., 1950, Fleming award, 1959, Outstanding Achievement award Mayo Clinic and U. Minn., 1964; Disting. Service award Am. Thyroid Assn., 1967; Disting. Service award HEW, 1968, Disting. Exec. rank, sr. exec. service, 1980, R.H. Williams Disting. Leadership award in endocrinology, 1983, Disting. Achievement award N.Y. Hosp., Cornell Med. Ctr., 1987; named Outstanding Alumnus N. Central Coll., 1966. Mem. NAS, AAAS, Am. Acad. Arts and Scis., Am. Soc. Clin. Investigation, Am. Phys. Soc., Endocrine Soc., Assn. Am. Physicians, Societe de Biologie (France), Royal Acad. Medicine (Brussels). Home: 3947 Baltimore St Kensington MD 20895-3913 Office: NIH Bldg 10 Rm 8N307 Bethesda MD 20892

RALL, LLOYD LOUIS, civil engineer; b. Galesville, Wis., Dec. 7, 1916; s. Louis A. and Anna (Kienzle) R.; m. Mary Moller, July 12, 1952; children: Lauris, David, Christopher, Jonathan. BCE, U. Wis., 1940. Commd. 2d lt. U.S. Army, 1940, advanced through grades to col., 1972, engr. forward area strategic air force, 1944-45, ret., 1977; chief construct divsn. Far East forces U.S. Army, Tokyo, 1945-47; engr., mem. mil. survey mission U.S. Army, Turkey, 1947; with office joint chiefs of staff U.S. Army, Washington, 1947-49, exec. officer R&D office chief engrs., 1949-51; asst. dist. engr. U.S. Army, Seattle, 1952-54; dept. engr. Comm. Zone U.S. Army, France, 1954-56; commanding officer 540th combat engr. group U.S. Army, 1956-57, prof. mil. sci. and tactics Mo. Sch. Mines and Metallurgy, 1957-60; dep. dir. topography office chief engrs. U.S. Army, Washington, 1960-64; dir. geographic intelligence and mapping U.S. Army, Ft. Belvoir, Va., 1964-66, dep. asst. dir. defense intelligence mapping, 1966-69, asst. dir. defense intelligence agy. mapping and charting, 1969-72; dir. Washington ops. Itek Optical Systems, Washington, 1977-91; mem. nat. tech. adv. com. Antarctica Mapping, 1960-64. Decorated Legion of Merit with oak leaf cluster, Bronze star. Home: 301 Cloverway Dr Alexandria VA 22314-4817

RALLI, CONSTANTINE PANDIA, lawyer; b. Bronxville, N.Y., Apr. 6, 1948; s. Pandia C. and Mary (Motter) R.; m. Alison Rhoads, Aug. 11, 1973; children: Pandia C., Christopher A. BA, Middlebury Coll., 1970; JD,

Fordham U., 1973; LLM in Taxation, NYU, 1986. Bar: N.Y. 1974, U.S. Ct. Appeals (2d cir.) 1974, U.S. Dist. Ct. (so. and ea. dists.) N.Y. 1975, U.S. Dist. Ct. Conn. 1987, U.S. Tax Ct. 1977, Fla. 1985, Conn. 1985. Assoc. Davis Polk & Wardwell, N.Y.C., 1973-81; ptnr. Hall, McNicol, Hamilton & Clark, N.Y.C., 1981-88, LeBoeuf, Lamb, Greene & MacRae, N.Y.C., 1988—; sec., bd. dirs. Fairfield-Maxwell Ltd., Campo Tankers SA, N.Y.C., 1987-95. Bd. dris. Samaritan Counseling Ctr., Rye, N.Y., 1987-90, Rye Free Reading Room, 1990-93, Rye Presbyn. Ch., 1986-89. Mem. Union Club, Am. Yacht Club, Ekwanok Country Club (Manchester, Vt.). Republican. Presbyterian. Home: 11 Rockridge Rd Rye NY 10580-4130 Office: LeBoeuf Lamb Green & MacRae 125 W 55th St New York NY 10022-3502 also: 6 Landmark Sq Stamford CT 06901-2501

RALLIS, JOHN, manufacturing holding company executive; b. 1937. Grad., Brown U. Active Foamex L.P. and Predecessor Co., Marcus Hook, Pa., 1952—; pres/CEO Foamex Internat. Co., Marcus Hook, Pa. Office: Foamex Internat Inc 1000 Columbia Ave Linwood PA 19061*

RALLS, KATHERINE, zoologist; b. Oakland, Calif., Mar. 21, 1939; d. Alvin Wallingsford and Ruth (McQueen) Smith; m. Kenneth M. Ralls, June 1958 (div. Sept. 1968); children: Robin, Tamsen, Kristin. AB, Stanford U., 1960; MA, Radcliffe Coll., 1962; PhD, Harvard U., 1965. Guest investigator Rockefeller U., N.Y.C., 1968-70, adj. asst. prof. biology, 1970-76; asst. prof. Sarah Lawrence Coll., Bronxville, N.Y., 1970-73; rsch. zoologist Inst. Rsch. in Animal Behavior, N.Y. Zool. Soc., 1970-73; zoologist Nat. Zool. Park, Smithsonian Instn., 1976—; mem. psychobiology adv. panel NSF, 1982-83; mem. sea otter recovery team U.S. Fish and Wildlife Svc., 1989—, mem. Calif. condor recovery team, 1990—. Mem. editorial bd. Signs, 1975-78; contbr. articles to profl. jours. Radcliffe Inst. fellow, 1973-74, Smithsonian Instn. fellow, 1973-76. Fellow AAAS, Animal Behavior Soc.; mem. Am. Soc. Mammalogists (bd. dirs. 1984-87, 2d v.p. 1990-91, 92), Internat. Union Conservation of Nature and Natural Resources (captive breeding specialist group 1979—,otter specialist group 1989—), Am. Assn. Zool. Pks. and Aquaria (species survival plan subcom. 1981-88), Soc. Marine Mammalogy (editorial bd., book rev. editor Marine Mammal Sci. 1983-89), Soc. Conservation Biology (bd. govs. 1985-90), Animal Behavior Soc., Assn. Women in Sci., Wildlife Soc. Achievements include research in relationship between mammalian social behavior and other aspects of mammalian biology, conservation biology, genetic problems of small populations, and threatened and endangered mammals. Office: Nat Zoo Smithsonian Instn Washington DC 20008

RALPH, DAVID CLINTON, communications educator; b. Muskogee, Okla., Jan. 12, 1922; s. Earl Clinton and Rea Jane (Potter) R.; m. Kathryn Juanita Wicklund, Nov. 29, 1947; children: David Randall, Steven Wicklund. AA, Muskogee Jr. Coll., 1941; BS in Theatre, Northwestern U., 1947, MA in Theatre, 1948, PhD in Speech, 1953. Lectr. Ind. U., Hammond, 1947-48; instr. speech U. Mo., Columbia, 1948-53; tchr. debate-forensics summer program for high sch. students Northwestern U., Evanston, Ill., 1949-51; asst. prof. speech Mich. State U., East Lansing, 1953-57, assoc. prof., 1957-64, prof. speech and theatre, 1964-68, prof. communication, 1968—, dir. communication undergrad. program, 1968-88; cons. on pub. speaking, 1948—. Co-author: Group Discussion, 1954, 2d edit., 1956, Principles of Speaking, 1962, 3d edit., 1975; contbr. articles to profl. jours., chpts. to books. Coach Jr. League Boys' Baseball, Lansing, Mich., 1958-74; mem. civilian aux. to Lansing Fire Dept., 1987—. Lt. USNR, 1942-46, PTO, ETO. Named Hon. State Farmer, Future Farmers Am., 1965; recipient Community Svc. award Mich. State U. Sr. Class Coun., 1979, Outstanding Faculty award, 1987, 91; Teaching Excellence award State of Mich., 1990. Mem. AAUP, Speech Communication Assn., Internat. Communication Assn., Cen. States Communication Assn., Golden Key (hon., faculty advisor), Omicron Delta Kappa. Democrat. Methodist. Avocation: model trains and fire engines. Office: Mich State U Dept Communication East Lansing MI 48824

RALPH, ROGER PAUL, arbitrator; b. Hammond, Ind., May 19, 1953; s. Bobby Gene Ralph and Nora Gwynn (Cornell) Baldwin; m. LaDonna Susan McDonald, July 15, 1972; children: Jarrod Keith, Rebecca Ann, Elizabeth Susan. BS in History, U. So. Ind., 1984; JD, Ind. U., 1987. Bar: Ind. 1987. Mill worker Ozark-Mahoning Co., Rosiclare, Ill., 1977-78; constrn. laborer Laborer's Internat. Union North Am. Local No. 561, Evansville, Ill., 1978-86; labor atty. Fillenworth Dennerline Groth & Towe, Indpls., 1987-88; litigation atty. Ricos & Price, Indpls., 1989-92; pvt. practice labor arbitrator Indpls., 1989—; chmn. Ind. Edn. Employment Rels. Bd., Indpls., 1992—. Democrat. Avocation: bluegrass music. Home: 808 Serenity Way Greenwood IN 46142 Office: Ind Edn Employment Rels Bd 100 North Senate Ave300 Indianapolis IN 46204-2820*

RALPH, THOMAS A., lawyer; b. Phila., Feb. 17, 1941; s. Thomas L. and Ruth A. R.; m. Margaret Walton; children: Weatherly H., William W., Elizabeth F. BA, Dartmouth Coll., 1963; LLB, U. Pa., 1968. Bar: Pa. 1968. Mng. ptnr. Dechert Price & Rhoads, Brussels, Belgium, 1978-80; ptnr. Dechert Price & Rhoads, Phila., 1976—. Trustee Shipley Sch., 1989—; bd. dirs. World Affairs Coun. Phila., 1991—. 1st lt. USAR, 1963-65. Office: Dechert Price & Rhoads 4000 Bell Atlantic Tower 1717 Arch St Philadelphia PA 19103-2793*

RALPH, WILLIAM J., lawyer; b. Springfield, Ill., June 30, 1953. BS summa cum laude, Ohio State U., 1974; JD, Columbia U., 1978. Bar: Ill. 1978, U.S. Dist. Ct. (no. dist.) Ill. 1978. Ptnr. Winston & Strawn, Chgo. Office: Winston & Strawn 35 W Wacker Dr Chicago IL 60601-1614*

RALSTON, ANTHONY, computer scientist, mathematician, educator; b. N.Y.C., Dec. 24, 1930; s. Alfred Joseph and Ruth (Bien) R.; m. Jayne Madeleine Rosenthal, Feb. 14, 1958; children: Jonathan, Geoffrey, Steven, Elizabeth. BS, MIT, 1952, PhD, 1956. Mem. tech. staff Bell Tel. Labs., 1956-59; lectr. U. Leeds, 1959-60; mgr. tech. computing Am. Cyanamid Co., 1960-61; assoc. prof. math. Stevens Inst. Tech., 1961-64, prof., 1964-65; dir. computer services SUNY, Buffalo, 1965-70, prof., 1965-95; chmn. dept. computer sci. SUNY, 1967-80; prof. emeritus SUNY, Buffalo, 1995—; bd. examiners Grad. Record Exam in Computer Sci., 1976-82; mem. computer sci. and tech. bd. NRC, 1976-79, math. sci. edn. bd., 1985-89; acad. visitor Imperial Coll., London, 1995—. Author: A First Course in Numerical Analysis, 1965, 2d edit., 1978, Introduction to Programming and Computer Science, 1971, Discrete Algorithmic Mathematics, 1991; editor: Ency. of Computer Science, 1976, 2d edit., 1982, 3d edit., 1992, ABACUS, 1983-88; co-editor: Mathematical Methods for Digital Computers, Vol. 1, 1960, Vol. 2, 1967, Vol. 3, 1977, The Influence of Computers and Informatics in Mathematics and Its Teaching, 1993. 2d lt. U.S. Army, 1957. Fellow AAAS, Royal Soc. of Arts, Assn. Computing Machinery (pres. 1972-74, mem. coun. 1968-76, Disting. Svc. award 1982); mem. Math. Assn. Am. (bd. govs. 1984-87), Am. Fedn. Info. Processing Soc. (pres. 1975-76), Com. Concerned Scientists (bd. dirs.). Home: Flat 4, 58 Prince Consort Rd, 00000000 London SW7 2BA, England

RALSTON, GILBERT ALEXANDER, writer, educator; b. L.A., Jan. 5, 1912; s. Alexander Gilbert and Jeanette (Johnston) R.; grad. Pasadena Coll., 1929-32; grad. Am. Acad. Dramatic Arts, 1935; B.C.A., Sierra Nev. Coll., 1972; D in Psychology, Fielding Inst., 1983, PhD in Health Sci., 1987, Columbia Pacific U., 1986; m. Mary K. Hart, Dec. 20, 1938; children—Michael, David. Actor, stage mgr. theatre prodns. N.Y.C., 1931-35; writer, dir. radio shows NBC, N.Y.C., 1936-38; prodn. supr. Compton Advt., Inc., N.Y.C., West Coast, 1939-42; organizer, mgr. radio dept. Proctor & Gamble, Cin., 1943-47, exec. producer inc. TV div., 1947-50; free lance producer TV films, 1950-55; exec. producer in charge TV drama CBS, 1955, dir. network programs originating in N.Y.C., 1956; producer High Adventure documentaries with Lowell Thomas, 1957; chmn. sch. communication arts Tahoe (Cal.) Paradise Coll., 1968; dean sch. communicative arts Sierra Nevada Coll., Incline Village, Nev., 1960-73, pres., 1973-83, pres. emeritus, 1983—; pres. Ralston Sch. Communicative Arts, Genoa, Nev., 1971—, Ralston Sch. Massage; v.p. Rule of Three Prodns., Los Angeles, 1973—; lectr. Fordham U., City Coll. City U. N.Y., Loyola U. of Los Angeles, St. Mary's Coll. of Calif. Mem. Authors Guild, ASCAP, Western Writers Am., Writers Guild Am., Am. Massage and Therapy Assn. Author: Ben, 1972; (with Richard Newhafer) The Frightful Sin of Cisco Newman, 1972; Dakota Warpath, 1973; Dakota: Red Revenge, 1973; Dakota Cat Trap, 1974; Dakota Murder's Money, 1974; Dakota: Chain Reaction, The Deadly Art, 1975, The Third Circle, 1976, The Tao of Touch, 1983, Gods Fist, 1989, Hamelin House, 1989, Hunter Fentress, 1990, Fattura Della Morte, 1990, others. Author screenplays: No Strings Attached, 1962; A Gallery of Six, 1963; A Feast of Jackals, 1963; Cockatrice, 1965; Kona Coast, 1967; Night of the Locust, 1969; Ben, 1971, Third Circle, 1975, Sure, 1975. Author screen adaptations: Willard (by Stephen Gilbert), 1970; Bluebonnet (by Boris Sobelman and Jack H. Robinson), 1971; Dakota Red, 1987. Author scripts for TV under sometime pseudonym Gil Alexander: High Adventure, Naked City, Route 66, Follow the Sun, Bus Stop, The Untouchables, Alcoa Theatre, Ben Casey, Richard Boone Show, 12 O'Clock High, The Name of the Game, Daktari, Laredo, Combat, Big Valley, Gunsmoke, Amos Burke, Slattery's People, Alfred Hitchcock, Star Trek, It Takes a Thief, O'Hara, Cannon, numerous others. Address: PO Box 490 Sullivans Island SC 29482-0490

RALSTON, HENRY JAMES, III, neurobiologist, anatomist, educator; b. Berkeley, Calif., Mar. 12, 1935; s. Henry James and Sue Harris (Mahnke) R.; m. Diane Cornelia Daly, Oct. 29, 1960; children: Rachel Anne, Amy Sue. BA, U. Calif., Berkeley, 1956, MD, 1959. Intern Mt. Sinai Hosp., N.Y.C., 1959-60; resident in medicine U. Calif., San Francisco, 1960-61, prof., 1973—, chmn. dept. anatomy, 1973—, chair acad. senate, 1986-88; spl. postdoctoral fellow Univ. Coll., London, 1963-65, Univ. lectr., 1981; asst. prof. anatomy Stanford (Calif.) U., 1965-69; assoc. prof. U. Wis., Madison, 1969-73; cons. NIH; mem. com. for future of anat. scis., Macy Found., 1977-80; vis. prof. French Med. Rsch. Inst.-INSERM, Paris, 1981-82; chair step I U.S. Med. Lic. Examination Com. Nat. Bd. Med. Examiners, 1992-96. With M.C. U.S. Army, 1961-63. Recipient Henry J. Kaiser award for excellence in tchg., 1978, Jacob Javits Neurosci. Investigator award NIH, 1988-95; USPHS grantee, 1966—. Mem. AAAS, Soc. Neurosci., Soc. Study Pain, Am. Pain Soc., Am. Assn. Anatomists (pres. 1987-88, chair publs. com. 1989-91), Anat. Assn. Gt. Britain, Phi Beta Kappa, Anat. Assn. Gt. Britain, Phi Beta Kappa. Research in field of organization of mammalian nervous system studied by electron microscopy, mechanisms subserving pain in animals and humans. Office: U Calif Dept Anatomy PO Box 0452 San Francisco CA 94143

RALSTON, JOANNE SMOOT, public relations counseling firm executive; b. Phoenix, May 13, 1939; d. A. Glen and Virginia (Lee) Smoot; m. W. Hamilton Weigelt, Aug. 15, 1991. B.A. in Journalism, Ariz. State U., 1960. Reporter, The Ariz. Republic, Phoenix, 1960-62; co-owner, pub. relations dir. The Patton Agy., Phoenix, 1962-71; founder, pres., owner Joanne Ralston & Assocs., Inc., Phoenix, 1971-87, 92—; pres. Nelson Ralston Robb Comm., Phoenix, 1987-91; pres. Joanne Ralston & Assoc., Inc., Scottsdale, Ariz., 1992—. Contbr. articles to profl. jours. Bd. dirs. Ariz. Parklands Found., 1984-86, Gov.'s Council on Health, Phys. Fitness and Sports, 1984-86; task force mem. Water and Natural Resources Council, Phoenix, 1984-86; mem. Ariz. Republican Caucus, 1984—, others. Recipient Lulu' awards (36) Los Angeles Advt. Women, 1964—, Gold Quill (2) Internat. Assn. Bus. Communicators, Excellence awards Fin. World mag., 1982-93, others; named to Walter Cronkite Sch. Journalism Hall of Fame, Coll. Pub. Programs Ariz. State U., 1987; name one of 25 Most Influential Arizonians, Phoenix Mag., 1991. Mem. Pub. Relations Soc. Am. (counselor sect.), Internat. Assn. Bus. Communicators, Phoenix Press Club (pres. bd.), Investor Rels. Inst., Phoenix Met. C. of C. (bd. dirs. 1977-84, 85-91), Phoenix Country Club. Republican. Avocations: horses, skiing.

RAM, CHITTA VENKATA, physician; b. Machilipatnam, India, Oct. 24, 1948; s. Chitta M. Row and Chitta (Cheruvu) Sarojini; m. Ashalata Ram, Feb. 17, 1979; children: Gita, Radha. B.Sci, Marathwada U., Aurangabad, India, 1966; MD, Osmania U., Hyderabad, India, 1972. Diplomate Am. Bd. Internal Medicine. Resident in internal medicine Brown U., R.I. Hosp., Providence, 1974-76; fellow in hypertension Hosp. U. Pa., Phila., 1976-77; faculty assoc. U. Tex. Southwestern Med. Ctr., Dallas, 1977-78, asst. prof., 1978-83, assoc. prof., 1983-89; prof., 1989—; dir. hypertension clinic Parkland Meml. Hosp., Dallas, hypertension unit St. Paul Med. Ctr., Dallas; pres. med. staff St. Paul Med. Ctr., 1996—. Contbr. numerous articles to profl. jours. and chpts. to textbooks; editl. cons., reviewer numerous nat. and internat. jours. and pubs. Pres. Tex. IndoAm. Physician Soc., Dallas, 1988; trustee Dallas/Ft. Worth Hindu Temple Soc., Dallas, 1988. Named Outstanding Tchr. St. Paul Med. Ctr., 1982; recipient Mother of India award, 1992. Fellow ACP, Am. Coll. Cardiology, Am. Coll. Chest Physicians (regent), Am. Coll. Clin. Pharmacology; mem. Am. Assn. Physicians from India (pres.-elect 1994-95, pres. 1995-96), Tex. Indo-Am. Physicians Soc. also: St Paul Med Ctr # 600 5939 Harry Hines Blvd Ste 600 Dallas TX 75235-6243

RAM, TRACY SCHAEFER, ballet company manager; b. San Francisco, June 4, 1960; d. Donald Worth and Leslie Lorraine Wells Schaefer; m. Michael Francis Ram, May 29, 1987. BA in Polit. Sci. and Mass Communications, U. Calif., Berkeley, 1982. Legal asst. Morrison & Foerster, San Francisco, 1982-84; asst. to gen. mgr. San Francisco Ballet, 1984-86, mgr. co., 1986-96. Democrat. Home: 761 Noe St San Francisco CA 94114-2941 Office: San Francisco Ballet 455 Franklin St San Francisco CA 94102-4438

RAMACHANDRAN, VENKATANARAYANA DEEKSHIT, electrical engineering educator; b. Mysore, India, May 3, 1934; s. K.C. Venkatanarayana Deekshit and Subbamma Deekshit R.; m. Kamala Visweswaraiya, June 12, 1960; 1 child, Ravi P. BS, U. Mysore, 1953; B in Engring., Indian Inst. Sci., Bangalore, 1956, M in Electronics, 1958, PhD, 1965. Registered profl. engr. Sr. research asst. Indian Inst. Sci., 1958-59, lectr., 1959-66; asst. prof. N.S. Tech. Coll., Halifax, Can., 1966-69; prof. elec. engring. Concordia U. (formerly Sir George Williams Univ.), Halifax, Can., 1971—; acting chmn. dept. elec. and computer engring. Montreal, various times; grad. program dir. dept., 1969-84; adj. prof. U. Windsor, Ont., Can., 1983—, Ecole Tech. Superieure U. Quebec, Montreal, 1989—; mem. program com. Internat. Symposium on Operator Theory of Networks and Systems, 1975; vice chmn. Internat. Symposium on Circuits and Systems IEEE, Montreal, 1984, mem. tech. program com., 1987; internat. coordinator Internat. Conf. on Computers, Systems and Signal Processing, Indian Inst. Sci., 1984. Author papers in profl. jours., 120 papers presented to confs., others. Named to Order of Engrs. of Que.; recipient Merit award Concordia Council on Student Life, 1981-82. Fellow Inst. Electronics and Telecomms. India (edit. bd. jour. 1986), Inst. Engrs. India, Inst. Elec. Engrs. Eng., Engring. Inst. Can. (sec. Montreal chpt. 1979-80, centennial bd. 1983-84), IEEE; mem. Circuits and Systems chpt. IEEE (chmn. Montreal sect. 1978-84), Can. Soc. Elec. Engrs. (editor jour. 1983-85, editor bull. 1981-83), Am. Soc. Engring. Edn. (chmn. awards com. St. Lawrence chpt. 1987-88, Western Elec. Fund award 1983, Myril B. Reed Best Rsch. Paper award 1984, Outstanding Svc. 1993). Office: Concordia Univ, Faculty of Engring, 1455 de Maisonneuve Blvd W, Montreal, PQ Canada H3G 1M8

RAMAKRISHNAN, VENKATASWAMY, civil engineer, educator; b. Coimbatore, India, Feb. 27, 1929; came to U.S., 1969, naturalized, 1981; s. Venkataswamy and Kondammal (Krishnaswamy) R.; m. Vijayalakshmi Unnava, Nov. 7, 1962; children: Aravind, Anand. B.Engring., U. Madras, 1952, D.S.S., 1953; D.I.C. in Hydropower and Concrete Tech, Imperial Coll., London, 1957; Ph.D., Univ. Coll., U. London, 1960. From lectr. to prof. civil engring., head dept. P.S.G. Coll. Tech., U. Madras, 1952-69; vis. prof. S.D. Sch. Mines and Tech., Rapid City, 1969-70, prof. civil engring., 1970—, dir. concrete tech. research, 1970-71, head grad. div. structural mechanic and concrete tech., 1971—; program coordinator materials engring. and sci. Ph.D. program S.D. Sch. Mines and Tech., —, 1985-86; disting. prof. S.D. Sch. Mines and Tech., Rapid City, 1996—. Author: Ultimate Strength Design for Structural Concrete, 1969; also over 200 articles. Recipient Outstanding Prof. award S.D. Sch. Mines and Tech., 1980, 1st Rsch. award, 1994; Colombo Plan fellow, 1955-60. Mem. Internat. Assn. Bridge and Structural Engring., ASCE (vice chmn. constrn. div. publs. com. 1974), Am. Concrete Inst. (chmn. subcom. gen. considerations for founds., chmn. com. 214 on evaluation of strength test results, sec.-treas. Dakota chpt. 1974-79, v.p. 1980, pres. 1981), Instn. Hwy. Engrs., Transp. Rsch. Bd. (chmn. com. on admixtures and curing, chmn. com. on mech. properties concrete), Am. Soc. Engring. Edn., NSPE, Internat. Coun. Gap-Graded Concrete Rsch. and Application, Sigma Xi. Address: 1809 Sheridan Lake Rd Rapid City SD 57702-4219 *To me, success is a coin with hard work on one side and perseverance with devotion on the other. No matter what—head or tails—the message is the same: keep on working. Goals in my life were pursuit of truth and beauty. The structures I have created, and my writings based on research have given me greater satisfaction than any wealth, position, or power.*

RAMALEY, JUDITH AITKEN, academic administrator, endocrinologist; b. Vincennes, Ind., Jan. 11, 1941; d. Robert Henry and Mary Krebs (McCullough) Aitken; m. Robert Folk Ramaley, Mar. 1966 (div. 1976); children: Alan Aitken, Andrew Folk. BA, Swarthmore Coll., 1963; PhD, UCLA, 1966; postgrad., Ind. U., 1967-69. Rsch. assoc., lectr. Ind. U., Bloomington, 1967-68, asst. prof. dept. anatomy and physiology, 1969-72; asst. prof. dept. physiology and biophysics U. Nebr. Med. Ctr., Omaha, 1972-74, assoc. prof., 1974-78, prof., 1978-82, assoc. dean for rsch. and devel., 1979-81; asst. v.p. for acad. affairs U. Nebr., Lincoln, 1980-82; prof. biol. scis. SUNY, Albany, N.Y., 1982-87, v.p. for acad. affairs, 1982-85, acting pres., 1984, exec. v.p. for acad. affairs, 1985-87; exec. vice chancellor U. Kans., Lawrence, 1987-90; pres. Portland (Oreg.) State U., 1990—; bd. dirs. Bank of Am.; mem. endocrinology study sect. NIH, 1981-84; cons.-evaluator North Cen. Accreditation, 1978-82, 89-90; mem. regulatory panel NSF, 1979-82; mem. Ill. Commn. Scholars, 1980—. Co-author: Progesterone Function: Molecular and Biochemical Aspects, 1972; Essentials of Histology, 8th edit., 1979; editor: Covert Discrimination, Women in the Sciences, 1978; contbr. articles to profl. jours. Bd. dirs. Family Svc. of Omaha, 1979-82, Albany Symphony Orch., 1984-87, mem. exec. com., 1986-87, Urban League Albany, 1984-87, 2d v.p., mem. exec. com., 1986-87, Upper Hudson Planned Parenthood, 1984-87, Capital Repertory Co., 1986-89, Assn. Portland Progress, 1990—, City Club of Portland, 1991-92, Metro Family Svcs., 1993—, Campbell Inst. for Children, Portland Met. Sports Authority, 1994; bd. dirs. NCAA Pres. Commn., 1991, chair divsn. II sub-com., 1994, mem. joint policy bd., 1994; chmn. bd. dirs. Albany Water Fin. Authority, 1987; mem. exec. com. United Way Douglas County, 1989-90; mem. adv. bd. Emily Taylor Women's Resource Ctr., U. Kans., 1988-90; mem. Silicon Prarie Tech. Assn., 1989-90, Portland Opera Bd., 1991-92, Portland Leaders Roundtable, 1991—; mem. bd. devel. com. United Way of Columbia-Williamette, 1991—; active Oreg. Women's Forum, 1991—, Portland Met. Sports Authority; progress bd. Portland-Multinomah County, 1993—. NSF grantee, 1969-71, 71-77, 75-82, 77-80, 80-83. Fellow AAAS; mem. Nat. Assn. State Univs. and Land Grant Colls. (exec. com., mem. senate 1986-88, vice chair commn. urban agenda 1992—), Assn. Am. Colls. and Univs. (bd. dirs. 1995—), Endocrine Soc. (chmn. edn. com. 1980-85), Soc. Study Reprodn. (treas. 1983-85), Soc. for Neuroscis., Am. Physiol. Soc., Am. Coun. on Edn. (chmn. commn. on women in higher edn. 1987-88), Assn. Portland Progress (bd. dirs.), Portland C. of C. (bd. dirs. 1995), Western Assn. of Schs. and Colls. (commr. 1994). Office: Portland State U Office of the President PO Box 751 Portland OR 97207-0751

RAMAMURTHY, SUBRAMANIAN, management consultant; b. Coimbatore, Madras, India, Nov. 25, 1948. B Tech., Indian Inst. Tech., Madras/Tamilnadu, 1970; MS in Engring., U. Madras, 1972; PhD, Cornell U., 1977. Registered profl. engr., N.J., Mich. Asst. prof. U. Ill., 1977-79; stress analyst ConRail, Phila., 1979-81; engr. Stone & Webster Engring. Corp., Cherry Hill, N.J., 1981-87; staff engring. group leader Stone & Webster Engring. Corp., 1982, structural engr., 1982; lead engr. Stone & Webster Engring. Corp., Monroe, Mich., 1985; sr. structural engr. Stone & Webster Engring. Corp., 1986; pres. Optimum Mgmt. Inc., Canton, Mich., 1987, also bd. dirs.; mem. adv. coun. Southeastern Mich. Coun. Govts.; mem. bus. adv. coun. Macomb Math. and Sci. Tech. Ctr.; projects advisor Lincoln Arc Welding Found., Cleve.; bus. columnist News-Herald. Bus. columnist News-Herald; contbr. numerous articles to profl. jours. Profit bus. cons. Jr. Achievement, 1993. Recipient Global Guru award Leadership Detroit XII. Mem. ASCE (treas. Cherry Hill chpt. 1983-85, vice chmn. com. on electronic computation 1983-86, chmn. engring. mgmt. 1988), ASME, Leadership Detroit XII (Global Guru 1991), Greater Detroit C. of C. (coun. small enterprises Detroit chpt. 1990-92, communication adv. com. 1990—), So. Wayne C. of C. (econ. devel. com.). Achievements include institution of locomotive underframe buckling specifications and fatigue failure predictions of freight car bolsters. Office: Optimum Mgmt Inc 127 S Main St Plymouth MI 48170-1680

RAMANARAYANAN, MADHAVA PRABHU, science administrator, researcher, educator; b. Varapuzha, Kerala, India, Feb. 5, 1945; came to U.S., 1972; s. Srinivasa Madhava and Priyothama (Shenoy) Prabhu; m. Leelavati Murthy, Sept. 2, 1972; children: Malini, Ananth. BS, American Coll., Madurai, India, 1964, MS, 1966; PhD, Indian Inst. Sci., Bangalore, India, 1972. Post-doctoral research worker dept. biochemistry Coll. Physicians and Surgeons of Columbia U., N.Y.C., 1972-75; staff assoc. Inst. Cancer Research, Columbia U., N.Y.C., 1975-81; dir. research & devel. Diagnostic Reagent Tech., Teaneck, N.J., 1981-85; v.p. research & devel. Visual Diagnostics, Inc., Teaneck, 1985-88; pres. Windsor Park Labs., Inc., Teaneck, 1988—; lectr., instr. postgrad. courses Am. Acad. Otolaryngic Allergy. Contbr. sci. articles to profl. jours. Fellow Am. Inst. Chemists, Nat. Acad. Clin. Biochemistry; mem. N.Y. Acad. Scis., Am. Chem. Soc., Internat. Union Pure and Applied Chemistry, Am. Assn. for Clin. Chemistry.

RAMANATHAN, KAVASSERI VAIDIANATHA, accounting educator, researcher, consultant; b. Trichur, Kerala, India, Nov. 26, 1932; came to U.S., 1966; s. Kavasseri Viswanatha and Saraswathy (Apathira) Vaidianathan; m. Rajalakshmi Ramanathan, Apr. 22, 1959; 1 dau., Saraswathy. B.Com., Calcutta U., India, 1954; M.B.A., Northwestern U., 1962, Ph.D., 1970. Systems mgr. Philips India Ltd., Calcutta, 1955-59; prof. acctg. Indian Inst. Mgmt., Ahmedabad, 1963-66; assoc. prof. acctg. U. Wash., Seattle, 1969-79, prof. acctg., 1979—, chmn. exec. M.B.A. program, 1982-86; dir. Russian programs, 1992—; vis. scientist Battelle Meml. Inst., Seattle, 1974-77; vis. prof. Harvard U., Cambridge, Mass., 1979-80; vis. fellow Australian Nat. U., Canberra, 1983, Monash U., Australia, 1983; vis. prof. NYU, N.Y.C., 1986-87, U. Auckland, 1992. Author: Management Control in Nonprofit Organizations, 1982; editor: Accounting for Managerial Decision Making, 1974, Readings in Management Control in Nonprofit Organizations, 1982. Adviser Sandeepany West, Piercy, Calif., 1981-82; bd. dirs. Arsha Vidya Pitam, Los Gatos, Calif., 1982—; pres. Ragamala, Seattle; founder, chmn. Hindu Temple & Community Ctr. Pacific N.W., Seattle, 1988—. Fulbright scholar Calcutta, 1960-63. Fellow Indian Inst. of Cost and Works Accts.; mem. Am. Acctg. Assn. , Fin. Execs. Inst., Inst. of Mgmt. Accts. Home: 19311 63rd Ave NE Seattle WA 98155-3331 Office: Univ Wash Dj 10 Dept Acctg # 10 Seattle WA 98195

RAMANI, RAJA VENKAT, mining engineering educator; b. Madras, India, Aug. 4, 1938; came to U.S., 1966; s. Natesa and Meenakshi (Srinivasan) Rajaraman; m. Geetha V. Chalam, July 9, 1972; children: Deepak, Gautam. BSc. with honors, Indian Sch. Mines, Dhanbad, Bihar, 1962; MS, Pa. State U., 1968, PhD, 1970. Registered profl. engr., Pa., 1971; lic. first class mine mgr., 1965. Mining engr., mgr. Andrew Yule & Co., Asansol, West Bengal, India, 1962-66; grad. asst. Pa. State U., University Park, 1966-70, asst. prof., 1970-74, assoc. prof., 1974-78, prof. mining engring., 1978—, chmn. mineral engring. mgmt. sect., 1974—, head dept. mineral engring., 1987—; chmn. com. post-disaster survival/rescue NAS, Washington, 1979-81; cons. UN, UN Devel. Program, Dept. Econ. and Social Devel., N.Y.C., 1983-96; cons./expert panels U.S. Dept. Labor, 1979, 92, 96, HHS, 1977, 92, U.S. Dept. State, 1986, 87, U.S. Dept. Interior, 1995, Dept. Environ. Resources, Commonwealth of Pa., 1990, 92; co-dir. Generic Mineral Tech. Ctr. on Respirable Dust, U.S. Bur. Mines, 1983—, Nat. Mines/Land Reclamation Ctr., 1988—, Std. Oil Ctr. of Excellence on Longwall Tech., 1983-89. Sect. editor, author: Computer Methods for the Eighties, 1979, SME Mining Engineering Handbook, 1992; editor State-of-the-Art in Longwall-Shortwall Mining, 1981, Proceedings: 19th Internat. APCOM Symposium, 1986, 2d and 3d Respirable Dust Symposia, 1988, 91, Longwall Thick Seam Mining, 1988. Computers in Mineral Industry, 1994. Recipient Disting. Alumni award Indian Sch. Mines, Dhanbad, 1978, Ednl. Excellence award Pitts. Coal Mining Inst., 1986, Environ. Conservation award AIME, N.Y.C., 1990, Howard N. Eavenson award SME/AIME, N.Y.C., 1991, Percy H. Nicholls award AIME/ASME Joint Soc., 1994, Robert Stefanko Best Paper award SME/AIME, 1993, Coal Divsn. Disting. Svc. award SME/AIME, 1993; Fulbright scholar to Soviet Union Coun. Internat. Exch. of Scholars, Washington, , 1989-90; Henry Krumb lectr. AIME, 1994. Mem. Internat. Coun. for Application of Computers in the Mineral Industry (chmn. 1984-87, Disting. Achievement award 1989), Soc. Mining, Metall. and Exploration (Disting. Mem. 1989, pres. 1995), Mine Ventillation Soc. South Africa, Inst. for Ops. Rsch. and Mgmt. Scis. Achievements include research in health, safety, environmental and productivity aspects in underground and surface mining engineering. Home: 285 Oakley Dr State College PA 16803-1349 Office: Dept Mineral Engring Pa State U University Park PA 16802

RAMANUJA, TERALANDUR KRISHNASWAMY, structural engineer; b. Mysore, Mysore, India, June 23, 1941; came to U.S., 1967, naturalized, 1979; s. Teralandur R. and Padmammal Krishnaswamy; m. Jayalakshmi Ramanuja, Jan. 18, 1971; children: Srinivasan, Rekha. BSCE, U. Mysore, 1962; MS in Structural Engring., U. Notre Dame, 1969. Registered profl. engr., Ill., Mich., Ind., N.Y. Sub-divisional officer Mil. Engring. Svcs., Bangalore, India, 1962-67; structural engr. Clyde E. Williams and Assocs., South Bend, Ind., 1969-73; head structural engring. dept. Ayres, Lewis, Norris & May, Cons. Engrs., Ann Arbor, Mich., 1973-76; sr. project mgr. Johnson & Anderson Cons. Engrs., Pontiac, Mich., 1976-78; supr. Bechtel Power Corp., Ann Arbor, 1978-85; supr. Shoreham Nuclear Power Sta. Lilco, N.Y.C., 1985-89; supervising engr. Clinton (Ill.) Power Sta. Ill. Power Co., 1989—. Fellow ASCE; mem. Am. Concrete Inst.; mem. Chi Epsilon. Achievements include structural and foundation design of facilities for fossil and nuclear power plants, water/waste treatment plants, petrochemical plants, pulp and paper mills and for heavy equipment/machinery for these plants; seismic and dynamic analysis of structures, systems and components in nuclear power plants. Home: 2006 Hidden Lake Rd Bloomington IL 61704-7283 Office: Ill Power Co Clinton Power Sta PO Box 678 Clinton IL 61727-0678

RAMAPRASAD, SUBBARAYA, medical educator; b. Mysore, India, May 20, 1954; came to the U.S., 1980; s. Puttaniah and Sharadamma Subbaraya; m. Padma Ramaprasad, Sept. 28, 1987; 1 child, Sanjay. PhD, Indian Inst. Sci., 1979. Instr. U. Ark. Med. Scis., Little Rock, 1989-91, asst. prof., 1991-94, assoc. prof., 1995—. Contbr. articles to profl. jours. Grantee NIMH, 1994, Ark. Sci. Tech. Authority, 1991. Mem. Internat. Soc. Magnetic Resonance Medicine, N.Y. Acad. Sci., Sigma Xi. Hindu. Avocation: photography. Home: 5 Sams Cove Little Rock AR 72212 Office: U Ark Med Sci Dept Radiol 4301 W Markham St Little Rock AR 72205

RAMAT, CHARLES S., apparel executive. Chrm. bd., pres., ceo, asst. sec. Aris Industries Inc, N.Y.C. Office: Aris Industries Inc 475 5th Ave New York NY 10017-5704*

RAMATY, REUVEN ROBERT, physicist, researcher; b. Timisoara, Rumania, Feb. 25, 1937; came to U.S., 1963; s. Nikolas and Elizabeth (Markowitz) Reiter; m. Vera Marie Klein, Aug. 8, 1961; children: Daphne, Deborah. BSc, Tel-Aviv (Israel) U., Israel, 1961; PhD, UCLA, 1966. Rsch. assoc. UCLA, 1966-67; rsch. assoc. NASA/Goddard Space Flight Ctr., Greenbelt, Md., 1967-69, astrophysicist, 1969-80, head Theory Office, 1980-93, sr. scientist, 1993—; adj. prof. U. Md., College Park, 1983—; orgnizer several internat. confs. Contbr. over 200 articles and papers to sci. jours. Fellow Am. Phys. Soc. (chmn. div. cosmic physics 1977-78, councilor div. astrophysics 1985-89); mem. Am. Astron. Soc. (chmn. div. high energy astrophysics 1984-85), Internat. Astron. Union. Achievements include research in the origin of the elements, the origin of cosmic rays and high energy processes in solar flames. Avocations: linguistics, foreign languages, history, geography. Office: Goddard Space Flight Ctr Greenbelt MD 20771

RAMBERG, WALTER DODD, architect; b. Charlotte, N.C., Feb. 17, 1932; s. Walter Gustav Charles and Julia Elisabeth (Lineberger) R.; m. Lucinda Jenifer Ballard, Nov. 25, 1961 (dec. 1989); children: Lucinda E.G., Jenny S.F., Julia E.L.; m. Frances Seska Peck, Sept. 14, 1996. B.A., Yale U., 1953, M.Arch., 1956. Fulbright fellow Kyoto (Japan) U., 1956-58; apprentice architect Paul Rudolph, New Haven, 1958-61; project designer Meyer & Ayers, Balt., 1961-63; partner Howe & Ramberg, Washington, 1963-65; prin. Walter Dodd Ramberg (Architect), Washington, 1965—; prof. architecture Cath. U. Am., 1977—; mem. design adv. panel Balt. Dept. Housing and Community, 1973—; mem. bd. architecture rev. Baltimore County, 1986-89. Designer: N.W. Balt. High Sch, 1963 (P.A. Excellence in Design award); architect: Bridge for Washington Cathedral, 1965 (Excellence in Design award Washington Bd. Trade, AIA), Kidder Guest House, 1965 (1st Honor award Balt. AIA), Azrael House, 1969 (Honor award Balt. AIA), Cutts House, 1973 (Honor award Balt. AIA), Woody House, 1975 (Merit award Balt. AIA), Lineberger Meml. Library, 1976 (Merit award Nat. AIA, ALA); contbr. articles to profl. publs. Served to lt. USCGR, 1958-59. Mem. AIA (corp.), AAUP, Soc. Archtl. Historians. Episcopalian. Club: Met. (Washington). Home: 1651 Belfast Rd Sparks MD 21152-9788 Office: 1830 T St NW Washington DC 20009-7138

RAMBO, A. TERRY, anthropologist, research program director; b. San Francisco, Apr. 3, 1940; s. Arthur Ira Rambo and Dorothy V. (Miller) Schlee; m. Dawn Jean Bowman, Jan. 24, 1971 (dec. July 1987); children: Charmaine Malia, Claire Norani. AB in Anthropology with distinction, U. Mich., 1963; MA in Anthropology, Am. U., 1969; PhD in Anthropology, U. Hawaii, 1972. Rsch. scientist Human Scis. Rsch., Inc., McLean, Va., 1964-69; acting asst. prof. anthropology U. Hawaii, 1971-72; asst. prof. anthropology Wash. State U., 1972-73; vis. prof. social sci. Grad. Sch. Politics and Econs., Dalat U., Saigon, Vietnam, 1973-75; lectr. dept. anthropology and sociology U. Malaya, 1975-80; sr. fellow, coord. program on renewable resources mgmt. East-West Ctr. Environ. and Policy Inst., Honolulu, 1980-92; dir. program on environ., coord. Indochina initiative East-West Ctr., Honolulu, 1992—; bd. dirs. S.E. Asian Univs. Agroecosystem Network; cons. in field. Author: Primitive Polluters, 1985, Comparison of Peasant Social Systems of Northern and Southern Vietnam, 1973; co-editor: An Introduction to Human Ecology Research on Agricultural Systems in Southeast Asia, 1984, Cultural Values and Human Ecology in Southeast Asia, 1985, Ethnic Diversity and the Control of Natural Resources in Southeast Asia, 1988, Agroecosystems of the Midlands of Northern Vietnam: A Report on a Preliminary Human Ecology Field Study of Three Districts in Vinh Phu Province, 1990, Profiles in Cultural Evolution, 1991, The Challenges of Vietnam's Reconstruction, 1992, Too Many People, Too Little Land: The Human Ecology of a Wet Rice-Growing Village in the Red River Delta of Vietnam, 1993, The Challenges of Highland Development in Vietnam, 1995, Red Books, Green Hills: The Impact of Economic Reform on Restoration Ecology in the Midlands of Northern Vietnam, 1996; also reports, papers, monographs, procs. in field; contbr. articles to profl. publs., chpts. to books. Grantee Asia Soc./SEADAG, 1969-70, U. Malaya, 1976-79, Ford Found., 1978-79, 84, 85-87, 87-89, 91-93, 95—, U. Hawaii-East-West Ctr., 1981-82, 84-85, Rockefeller Bros. Fund, 1988-89, 90-92, 94-95, MacArthur Found., 1990-91, 91-93, 93—, Luce Found., 1995-96; Nat. Def. Fgn. Lang. fellow, 1970-71, Ford Found. S.E. Asia rsch. fellow, 1972, 73-74, 75-76. Avocations: gardening, backpacking, reading. Office: East-West Ctr Program on Environment 1777 East-West Rd Honolulu HI 96848

RAMBO, DAVID L., religious organization administrator. Pres. The christian and Missionary Alliance, Nyack, N.Y., 1988—. Office: Christian and Missionary Alliance PO Box 35000 Colorado Springs CO 80935-3500

RAMBO, SYLVIA H., federal judge; b. Royersford, Pa., Apr. 17, 1936; d. Granville A. and Hilda E. (Leonhardt) R.; m. George F. Douglas, Jr., Aug. 1, 1970. BA, Dickinson Coll., 1958; JD, Dickinson Sch Law, 1962; LLD (hon.), Wilson Coll., 1980, Dickinson Sch. Law, 1993, Dickinson Coll., 1994. Bar: Pa. 1962. Atty. trust dept. Bank of Del., Wilmington, 1962-63; pvt. practice Carlisle, 1963-76; public defender, then chief public defender Cumberland County, Pa., 1974-76; judge Ct. Common Pleas, Cumberland County, 1976-78, U.S. Dist. Ct. (mid. dist.) Pa., Harrisburg, 1979-92; chief judge Pa. & Md., 1992—; asst. prof., adj. prof. law Dickinson Sch. Law, 1974-76. Mem. Nat. Assn. Women Judges, Phi Alpha Delta. Democrat. Presbyterian. Office: US Dist Ct Federal Bldg PO Box 868 Harrisburg PA 17108-0868

RAMBO, WAYNE HERBERT, English language and education educator; b. Camden, N.J., Aug. 1, 1947; s. Herbert Jordan and Gladys Marie (Savage) R.; m. Alice Carolyn Huber, Nov. 3, 1944; children: Theodore Yung-Kyo, Faith Yung Gin. BA, Clearwater Christian Coll., 1969; MA, Glassboro State Coll., 1976; EdD, Temple U., 1982. Cert. sch. adminstr., Pa. Elem. prin. Phila. Assn. Christian Schs., 1969-72, dir. pub. rels., 1972-75; teaching asst. Temple U., Phila., 1975-79; rsch. grants analyst Inst. Exptl. Psychiatry, Phila., 1979—; prof. English, acad. skills Camden County Coll., Blackwood, N.J., 1986—; prof. humanities, social sci., biometrics Med. Coll. Hahnemann U., Phila., 1990—; adj. prof. comm. Rowan State Coll., Glassboro, N.J., 1990—, Gloucester County Coll., Sewell, N.J., 1995—; adj. prof. speech and English, Salem (N.J.) Coll., 1991—; cons. Ednl. Testing Svc., Princeton, N.J., 1989—, N.J. Dept. Higher Edn., Trenton, 1991, N.J. Divsn. Vocat. Edn., Trenton, 1981-82; adj. prof. composition and lit. Hahnemann U., Phila., 1994—. Author: Developing Critical Thinking Skills Through Reading and Writing: Expanding Bloom's Taxonomy to Differentiate Between Consumptive and Productive Cognitive Behavior, 1982, Gunning Rambo Readability Writability, 1994; contbg. author: Paragraphy and Essays, 1993; author symposium in field. 1st pres. Marie J. Carrol Found., Merchantville, N.J., 1984; bd. dirs. Merchantville Bd. Edn., 1979—, pres., 1989-92. Avocations: restoration of historical homes, building trades, travel. Home: 37 Rogers Ave Merchantville NJ 08109-2528 Office: Inst for Exptl Psychiatry 111 N 49th St Philadelphia PA 19139-2718

RAMER, BRUCE M., lawyer; b. Teaneck, N.J., Aug. 2, 1933; s. Sidney and Anne S. (Strassman) R.; children: Gregg B., Marc K., Neal I. BA, Princeton U., 1955; LLB, Harvard U., 1958. Bar: Calif. 1963, N.J. 1958. Assoc., Morrison, Lloyd & Griggs, Hackensack, N.J., 1959-60; ptnr. Gang, Tyre, Ramer & Brown, Inc., L.A., 1963—; bd. dirs. Silver King Comms., Inc. Exec. dir. Entertainment Law Inst., Law Ctr. of U. So. Calif.; bd. of councilors Law Ctr. U. So. Calif.; past pres. L.A. chpt.; chmn., bd. govs., bd. govs. Am. Jewish Com. (nat. v.p. 1982-88, pres. L.A. chpt. 1980-83, chair Western region 1984-86, community svc. award, 1987); chmn. Pacific Rim Inst.; trustee Loyola Marymount U., Los Angeles Children's Mus., 1986-89; vice chair United Way, 1991-93, corp. bd. dirs., 1981-93, chair coun. pres. 1989-90, mem. cmty. issues coun., 1989-90, chair discretionary fund distbn. com., 1987-89; bd. dirs., chair Geffen Playhouse UCLA, bd. dirs. L.A. Urban League, 1987-93, Jewish Fedn. Coun. of Greater L.A. (mem. Cmty. Rels. com.), Jewish TV Network, Sta. KCET-TV; mem., bd. dirs. Rebuild L.A.; vice chmn., bd. govs. Calif. Cmty. Found.; recipient Ann. Brotherhood award Nat. Conf. of Christians and Jews, 1990; mem. Fellows of Am. Bar Found. Pvt. U.S. Army, 1958-59, 2d lt., 1961-62. Mem. ABA, L.A. County Bar Assn., Calif. Bar Assn., Beverly Hills Bar Assn. (Exec. Dirs. award 1988, Entertainment Lawyer of Yr. award 1996), L.A. Copyright Soc. (pres. 1974-75), Calif. Copyright Conf. (pres. 1973-74), Princeton Club (pres. 1975-78). Office: Gang Tyre Ramer & Brown Inc 132 S Rodeo Dr Beverly Hills CA 90212

RAMER, HAL REED, academic administrator; b. Kenton, Tenn., June 8, 1923; s. Clude Orion and Dixie Clayton (Carroll) R. BS, George Peabody Coll., 1947; MSW, U. Tenn., 1952; PhD, Ohio State U., 1963. Asst. dean men Ohio State U., Columbus, 1953-58, dir. internat. house, 1958-60, staff asst. to pres., 1960-62; asst. commr. State Dept. Edn., Nashville, 1963-70; founding pres. Vol. State C.C., Gallatin, Tenn., 1970—; bd. dirs. Sumner Regional Health Sys., Inc. Mem. adv. bd. First Union Bank Mid. Tenn., Hendersonville, Tenn., com. March of Dimes, Gallatin; trustee Nashville United Way, 1970s; bd. govs. Aquinas Coll., Nashville, 1967—; bd. dirs. Y.M.C.A.; former chmn. Tenn. Fulbright-Hays Sch. Commn. With USAAF, 1943-45; col. Tenn. Def. Force. Recipient Distinctive Svc. award Devel. Coun. Peabody Coll., Nashville, 1960s, Distinguished Svc. award Tenn. Dept. Edn., 1970, Outstanding Leader award Vanderbilt U. chpt. Phi Delta Kappa, 1987, Gov.'s Svc. award State of Tenn., 1993, Sertoma Club Svc. to Mankind award, 1995-96, Disting. Alumnus award Peabody Coll., 1996; named Rotarian of the Yr., 1979; Paul Harris fellow Rotary Internat., 1981. Mem. Am. Legion, Coun. Pres. C.Cs. (chmn. state Tenn. 1988-89), Tenn. Coll. Assn. (pres. 1985-86), Nat. Alumni Assn. Peabody Coll. (pres. 1970-71, bd. trustees), Tenn. Acad. Sci., Tenn. and Sumner Co. Hist. Socs. (bd. dirs.), English Speaking Union Internat. (Nashville chpt.), So. Assn. Colls. and Schs., Univ. Club Nashville, Gallatin and Hendersonville C. of C., Torch Club Internat., Alpha Tau Omega, Kappa Phi Kappa, Alpha Phi Omega, Phi Delta Kappa. Methodist. Avocations: antiques, antique cars, photography. Home: 148 Kenner Ave Nashville TN 37205-2219 Office: Vol State CC Office of Pres Nashville Pike Gallatin TN 37066

RAMER, JAMES LEROY, civil engineer; b. Marshalltown, Iowa, Dec. 7, 1935; s. LeRoy Frederick and Irene (Wengert) R.; m. Jacqueline L. Orr, Dec. 15, 1957; children: Sarah T., Robert H., Eric A., Susan L. Student U. Iowa, 1953-57; MCE, Washington U., St. Louis, 1976, MA in Polit. Sci., 1978; postgrad. U. Mo., Columbia, 1984—. Registered profl. engr., land surveyor. Civil and constrn. engr. U.S. Army C.E., Tulsa, 1960-63; civil and relocations engr. U.S. State Dept., Del Rio, Tex., 1964; project engr. H. B. Zachry Co., San Antonio, 1965-66; civil and constrn. engr. U.S. Army C.E., St. Louis, 1967-76, tech. advisor for planning and nat. hydropower coordinator, 1976-78, project mgr. for EPA constrn. grants, Milw., 1978-80; chief architecture and engring. HUD, Indpls., 1980-81; civil design and pavements engr. Whiteman AFB, Mo., 1982-86, project mgr. maintenance, 1993—; soil and pavements engr. Hdqtrs. Mil. Airlift Command, Scott AFB, Ill., 1986-88; project manager AF-1 maintenance hangar; cattle and grain farmer, 1982—; pvt. practice civil-mech. engr., constrn. mgmt., estimating, cost analysis, cash flow, project scheduling, expert witness, Fortuna, Mo., 1988—, chief construction inspector divsn. Design and Construction, State of Mo., 1992-93; adj. faculty civil engring. Washington U., 1968-78, U. Wis., Milw., 1978-80. Ga. Mil. Coll., Whiteman AFB., Longview Coll., Kansas City; adj. research engr. U. Mo., Columbia, 1985-86. Author tech. writing operation and maintenance manuals, fin. reports and environ. control plans, tech. & indsl. models; holder 25 U.S. patents in diverse art, 8 copyrights. Achievements include developer solar waterstill, deep shaft hydropower concept. Mem. ASCE, NSPE, AAUP, Soc. Am. Mil. Engrs. Lutheran. Club: Optimists Internat. Home: RR 1 Box 50-aa Fortuna MO 65034-9720

RAMER, LAWRENCE JEROME, corporation executive; b. Bayonne, N.J., July 29, 1928; s. Sidney and Anne (Strassman) R.; m. Ina Lee Brown, June 30, 1957; children: Stephanie Beryl, Susan Meredith, Douglas Strassman. B.A. in Econs, Lafayette Coll., 1950; M.B.A., Harvard U., 1957; LLD (hon.), Lafayette Coll., 1992. Sales rep., then v.p. United Sheet Metal Co., Bayonne, 1953-55; with Am. Cement Corp., 1957-64; v.p. mktg. div. Riverside Cement Co., 1960-62, v.p. mktg. parent co., 1962-64; vice chmn. bd., chief exec. officer Clavier Corp., N.Y.C., 1965-66; exec. v.p., vice chmn. bd. Pacific Western Industries, Los Angeles, 1966-70; pres., chief exec. officer Nat. Portland Cement Co. Fla., 1975-89; chmn. bd. Sutro Partners, Inc., Los Angeles, 1977-89, Somerset Mgmt. Group, 1975-92, Luminall Paints Inc., Los Angeles, 1972-95; chmn. bd., chief exec. officer Bruning Paint Co., Balt., 1979—, Pacific Coast Cement Co., Los Angeles, 1979-90; pres., chief exec. officer Ramer Equities, Inc., 1990—; chmn. Lawrence J. Ramer Family Found., 1986—; bd. dirs. Project Orbis, N.Y.C., The Music Ctr., L.A., Music Ctr. Operating Co., L.A., Canyon Ranch, Tucson, Music Ctr. Found., L.A.; chmn. bd. dirs. Ctr. Theatre Group-Taper Ahmanson Theatres, L.A. Chmn. bd. trustees Lafayette Coll., Easton, Pa.; trustee, chmn. bd. trustees Calif. Inst. Arts, Valencia, Calif.; bd. dirs. Non-Traditional Casting Project, N.Y.; nat. bd. govs. Am. Jewish Com., N.Y. Office: Ramer Equities Inc Ste 1090 1999 Avenue Of The Stars Los Angeles CA 90067-6034

RAMER, WINNIFRED ROBISON, school nurse; b. Duluth, Minn., Jan. 25, 1933; d. Thomas Jefferson and Mable Jeanette (Thorstad) Robison; m. Louis William Ramer, July 30, 1954; children: Jan Carol, Leigh Ellen, Linda Jeanette, Anna Lynn. Diploma, St. Luke's Sch. Nursing, 1954; BS in Health Arts, Coll. of St. Francis, Joliet, Ill., 1980. RN, Minn., Ind. Staff nurse St. Luke's Hosp., Duluth, 1954; pediatric nurse Davis Clinic, Marion, Ind., 1955-57; surg. charge nurse Ball Meml. Hosp., Muncie, Ind., 1957-59; mem. I.V. team Cmty. Hosp., Indpls., 1960-64; pvt. duty nurse Hancock County Meml. Hosp., Greenfield, Ind., 1965-74; sch. nurse, health coord. Warren Ctrl. H.S., Indpls., 1974—; staff nurse detox unit Fairbanks Hosp., Indpls., 1991—; camp nurse MW Lodge, Three Lakes, Wis., summers, 1971-88. Mem. AIDS adv. bd., curriculum rev. bd., OSHA stds. policy originator Met. Sch. Dist. Warren Twp., Indpls. Mem. Nat. Assn. Sch. Nursing (dist. rep. 1987-89). Presbyterian. Avocations: sewing, riding, breeding show horses. Home: 7908 Bellwood Dr Indianapolis IN 46226-6307 Office: Warren Ctrl HS 9500 E 16th St Indianapolis IN 46229-2008

RAMETTE, RICHARD WALES, chemistry educator; b. Hartford, Conn., Oct. 9, 1927; s. Joel Edward and Grace Margaret (Wales) R.; m. Lenora Kathryn Kelleher, Aug., 21, 1949; children: Cheryl Lee, James Edward, John Richard, David Joel, William Michael. BA, Wesleyan U., Middletown, Conn., 1950; PhD, U. Minn., 1954. Prof. chemistry Carleton Coll., Northfield, Minn., 1954-90, Laurence M. Gould prof. chemistry, 1971-90, prof. emeritus, 1990—; sci. advisor FDA, Mpls., 1969-80. Author: Chemical Equilibrium and Analysis, 1981. Asst. scoutmaster Boy Scouts Am., Northfield, 1968-73; calligraphy instr. Northfield Arts Guild, 1974-80. Served with USN, 1946-48. Recipient Chemistry Teaching award Mfg. Chemists, 1966, Analytical Chemistry Teaching award Am. Chem. Soc., 1991, Disting. Alumnus award Wesleyan U., 1995. Home: 805 Highland Ave Northfield MN 55057-1327

RAMEY, CARL ROBERT, lawyer; b. Binghamton, N.Y., Feb. 15, 1941; s. Clinton W. and Hester May (Wisdom) R.; m. Maryan Sitzenkopf, Aug. 11, 1962 (div. Sept. 1987); children: Mark Alan, Christian David; m. Karen Reichard, Nov. 28, 1987. AB, Marietta Coll., 1962; MA, Mich. State U., 1964; JD, George Washington U., 1967. Bar: D.C. 1968, U.S. Dist. Ct. D.C. 1968, U.S. Ct. Appeals (2d, 3d, 4th, 5th, 7th and 9th cirs.), U.S. Supreme Ct. 1972. Assoc. McKenna, Wilkinson & Kittner, Washington, 1967-71, ptnr., 1971-86; ptnr. Wiley, Rein & Fielding, Washington, 1986—. Contbr. articles to profl. jours., chpt. to Copyright Law Symposium, 1969; editorial staff George Washington Law Rev., 1965-67. Recipient First Prize award Nat. Nathan Burkan Meml. Writing Competition, ASCAP, 1969. Mem. ABA, Fed. Communications Bar Assn. (treas. 1977-78), D.C. Bar Assn. Republican. Episcopalian. Avocations: skiing, tennis, boating, biking. Office: Wiley Rein & Fielding 1776 K St NW Washington DC 20006-2304

RAMEY, CECIL EDWARD, JR., lawyer; b. Shreveport, La., Nov. 9, 1923; s. Cecil Edward and Blanche (Gwin) R.; m. Betty Loper, June 15, 1945; children—Martha L., L. Christine, Stephen E. BS summa cum laude, Centenary Coll., 1943; LLB, Yale U., 1949; postgrad., Tulane U., 1950-51. Bar: Wis. 1949, La. 1951. Assoc. Miller, Mack & Fairchild, Milw., 1949-50; mem. faculty Tulane U., 1950-54; assoc. Hargrove, Guyton, Van Hook and Hargrove, Shreveport, 1954-56, ptnr., 1956-63; ptnr. Hargrove, Guyton, Van Hook and Ramey, Shreveport, 1963-73; ptnr. Hargrove, Guyton, Ramey and Barlow, Shreveport, 1973-89, of counsel, 1989-94; of counsel Barlow and Hardtner, L.C., Shreveport, 1994—; adj. prof. Centenary Coll., 1992—. Former chmn. Citizens Capital Improvements com. City of Shreveport; former mem. governing bd. Shreveport YMCA; former chmn. bd. trustees Broadmoor Meth. Ch., Shreveport, chmn. bd. stewards; former bd. dirs., former chmn. Shreveport-Bossier Found.; former trustee Centenary Coll. With AC, U.S. Army, 1943-46. Named Shreveport's Outstanding Young Man of Yr., 1956, Mr. Shreveport, 1968; recipient Clyde E. Fant Meml. award community service United Way, 1979. Fellow Am. Coll. Trust and Estate Counsel; mem. ABA, La. Bar Assn., Shreveport Bar Assn., La. Law Inst., Shreveport C. of C. (pres. 1974), Centenary Coll. Alumni Assn. (past pres.), Shreveport Club, Order of Coif, Phi Delta Phi, Kappa Sigma. Club: Shreveport. Home: PO Box 873-C RR 1 Box 873 C Karnack TX 75661-9801 Office: Barlow and Hardtner LC 401 Edwards St Shreveport LA 71101-3289

RAMEY, DENNY L., bar association executive director; b. Portsmouth, Ohio, Feb. 22, 1947; s. Howard Leroy and Norma Wylodine (Richards) R.; m. Jeannine Gayle Dunmyer, Sept. 24, 1971 (div. Nov. 1991); children: Elizabeth Michelle, Brian Michael. BBA, Ohio U., 1970; MBA, Capital U., 1976. Cert. assn. exec. Adminstrv. mgr. Transit Warehouse div. Elston Richards Storage Co., Columbus, Ohio, 1970-73; mgr. continuing profl. edn. Ohio Soc. CPA's, Columbus, 1973-79; exec. dir. Engrs. Found. of Ohio, Columbus, 1979-80; asst. exec. Ohio State Bar Assn., Columbus, 1980-86, exec. dir., sec., treas., 1986—; treas., exec. com., bd. dirs. Ohio Bar Liability Ins. Co., Columbus, 1986—; treas. Ohio State Bar Found., 1986—; treas. Ohio Legal Ctr. Ins., Columbus, 1988-91; sec. Ohio Printing Co., Ltd., 1991; v.p. Osbanet, Inc., 1993—. Mem. Nat. Assn. Bar Execs. (chmn. various coms.), Am. Soc. Assn. Execs., Ohio Soc. Assn. Execs., Heritage Golf Club, The Player's Club. Methodist. Avocations: tennis, golf, sports, music, wine appreciation. Office: Ohio State Bar Assn 1700 Lake Shore Dr PO Box 16562 Columbus OH 43216-6562

RAMEY, PETER M., holding company executive. Sec. Lou Fusz Motor Co., Inc., Saint Louis, 1987—; now comptroller Lou Fusz Motor Inc., St. Louis. Office: Lou Fusz Motor Co Inc 925 N Lindbergh Blvd Saint Louis MO 63141-5901*

RAMEY, SAMUEL EDWARD, bass soloist; b. Colby, Kans., Mar. 28, 1942; s. Robert Guy and Grace Irene (Mallory) R.; m. Carrie Tanate, Jan. 10, 1970. Student, Kans. State U., 1960-62; B.Mus., Wichita State U., 1968. Debut in Carmen, N.Y.C. Opera, 1973, leading bass, 1973—, European debut, Glyndebourne Festival, 1976, debut, Hamburg Staatsoper, 1978, Paris Opera, 1979, Houston Grand Opera, 1975, San Francisco Opera, 1978, Chgo. Lyric Opera, 1979, Festival International Aix-en-Provence, 1979, 80, Teatro della Scala, 1981, Vienna Staatsoper, 1981, in Rinaldo, Met. Opera, 1984; recording artist opera and oratorio, Philips, Angel, RCA, Deutsche Grammophone, London, CBS Records. Named Kansan of the Year Native Sons and Daughters of Kansas, 1994. Office: Columbia Artists Mgmt Inc Arbib Div 165 W 57th St New York NY 10019-2201

RAMIREZ, ANTHONY BENJAMIN, lawyer; b. Frizell, Kans., Jan. 17, 1937; s. Jesus Ruiz and Francisca (Lopez) R.; m. Jeanette Marilyn Lee, Sept. 19, 1964; children: Christopher Benjamin, Andrew Anthony. BA, St. Benedict's Coll., Atchison, Kans., 1959; JD, St. Louis U., 1967. Bar: Mo. 1967, U.S. Dist. Ct. (ea. dist.) Mo. 1968. Legal staff probate divsn. St. Louis City Cir. Ct., 1967-72; atty. various law offices St. Louis, 1972-81; ptnr. Coleman, Ross, Goetz, Robert & Ramirez, 1981-86; pvt. practice, 1986—; legal advisor Mexican Consulate in St. Louis, 1979—; adj. prof. law Webster U., St. Louis, 1988-93. Editor (newsletter) DeNuevo, 1978-80; co-host Latin Rhythms radio program KDHX FM, 1992-93. Bd. dirs. Confluence St. Louis, 1990-96, ARC, Bi-State chpt. St. Louis, 1990-94; mem. Coro Fellows Program, 1994-95; facilitator Hispanic Leaders Group Greater St. Louis, 1985-93, sec., 1993-95, chmn., 1995—; Mo. del. White House Conf. on Small Bus., 1986; mem. SBA St. Louis Dist. Adv. Coun., 1985-93; mem. Fordyce Two Leadership Summit, 1990; commr. Mo. Commn. on Human Rights, 1983-87; charter mem. Gov.'s Coun. on Hispanic Affairs, 1980. Staff sgt. U.S. Army, 1959-60, 61-64. Named Mo. Minority Advocate of Yr. U.S. SBA, St. Louis, 1984; recipient Pres. award Hispanic C. of C., St. Louis, 1986, St. Louis Cmty. award of merit KPLR-TV, St. Louis, 1989. Mem. ABA, Nat. Assn. Criminal Def. Attys., Mo. Bar Assn., Bar Assn. Metro St. Louis, Law Alumni Assn. St. Louis U. Sch. Law (v.p. 1984-88), Hispanic C. of C. Met. St. Louis (co-founder, pres. 1982-85, chmn. bd. 1983-88). Republican. Roman Catholic. Office: 1221 Locust St Ste 503 Saint Louis MO 63103-2364

RAMIREZ, CARLOS DAVID, publisher; b. San Juan, P.R., Aug. 19, 1946; s. Carlos David and Maria (Melendez) R.; children: Christine, David. AAS, CCNY, 1969, BBA, 1972; PhD, Pace U., 1995. Asst. controller TRW, London Am. Mktg. Corp. (Midland Bank), Meridien Mktg. Corp.; dep. dir. fin. svcs. ITM Group, N.Y.C., 1980; controller El Diario-La Prensa, N.Y.C., 1981—; pres., pubr. El Diario-La Prensa, 1984—; exec. v.p. Latin Comm. Group Inc.; mem. bd. dirs. and sec. Latin Comm. Arcup, Inc. Mem. Gov. Cuomo's Task Force for the Elderly, Commn. Operation Welcome Home, N.Y.C.; bd. dirs. N.Y.C. Partnership, Inst. for Ednl. Leadership, El Museo del Barrio; trustee Pace U., Partnership for a Drug-Free Am.; adv. bd. Nat. P.R. Forum, Inst. for P.R. Policy. Mem. N.Y. Press Club, Am. Newspapers Pubs. Assn., , Nat. Assn. Hispanic Journalists, Nat. Assn. Hispanic Pubs., N.Y. C. of C. (bd. dirs.), Nat. Advt. Bur., Nat. Hispanic Coalition. Roman Catholic. Office: El Diario La Presna 143 Varick St New York NY 10013-1106

RAMIREZ, MANUEL ARISTIDES (MANNY RAMIREZ), professional baseball player; b. Santo Domingo, Dominican Republic, May 30, 1972. Grad. high sch., N.Y.C. Outfielder Cleve. Indians, 1993—. Mem. Cleve. Indians Am. League Champions, 1995. Office: Cleveland Indians 2401 Ontario St Cleveland OH 44115*

RAMIREZ, MARIA FIORINI, economist, investment advisor; b. Naples, Italy, Jan. 1, 1948; came to U.S., 1961; d. Fernando and Clelia Ambrosio Fiorini; m. George M. Ramirez, 1973. BBA, Pace U., 1972, postgrad., 1974-76. Analyst Meinhardt-CIT Comml. Fin., N.Y.C., 1967-68; credit analyst Am. Express Internat. Bank, N.Y.C., 1968-72; credit mgr. Banca Nazionale del Lavoro, N.Y.C., 1972-73; credit mgr., asst. v.p. Merrill Lynch G.S.I.,

1973-74, economist, 1974—, v.p., sr. money market economist Merrill Lynch Econs. Inc., 1981-84; sr. v.p., sr. money market economist Becker Paribas Inc., N.Y.C., 1984; corp. first v.p., money market economist Drexel Burnham Lambert Inc., N.Y.C., 1984-86, mng. dir., chief money market economist, 1986—; pres. Maria Ramirez Capital Cons. Inc. (subs. Hancock Freedom), N.Y.C., 1990—; pres. and CEO Maria Fiorini Ramirez, Inc., 1992—; bd. dirs. various orgns. Roman Catholic. Home: PO Box 992 Belcher Ln Far Hills NJ 07931 Office: 1 World Fin Ctr 200 Liberty St Fl 4 New York NY 10281-1003

RAMIREZ, MARIO EFRAIN, physician; b. Roma, Tex., Apr. 3, 1926; s. Efren M. and Carmen (Hinojosa) R.; m. Sarah B. Aycock, Nov. 25, 1949; children: Mario, Patricia Ann, Norman Michael, Jaime Eduardo, Roberto Luis. Student, U. Tex., 1942-45; MD, U. Tenn., 1948. Diplomate Am. Bd. Family Physicians. Intern Shreveport (La.) Charity Hosp., 1949; resident; practice medicine specializing in family practice Shreveport (La.) Charity Hosp., Roma; pvt. family practice Roma, 1950-75, Rio Grande City, Tex., 1975-93; owner, adminstr. Ramirez Meml. Hosp., Roma, 1958-75; assoc. med. dir. South Tex. Blue Cross Blue Shield Tex., McAllen, 1993-95. County judge Starr County, Rio Grande City, 1969-78; chmn. South Tex. Devel. Coun., 1975-76, Tri-County Cmty. Action Coun., 1971-78; mem. coordinated bd. Tex. Colls. and Univs., 1979-85; mem. devel. bd. U. Tex., 1986—; presdl. appointee bd. regents Uniformed Svcs. U. Tex. Health Scis., 1985-92; mem. bd. regents U. Tex. Sys., 1989-95, vice chmn. bd., 1991-92. Recipient Spl. citation Surgeon Gen., 1967, Disting. Alumnus award U. Tex., 1975, 78, Achievement award Lab World, 1978, Presdl. citation U. Tex., 1979, Outstanding Alumnus award U. Tenn., 1991; named Family Dr. of Yr., Good Housekeeping mag. and Am. Acad. Family Physicians, 1978, Border Texan of the Yr., 1995; honoree Founder's Day for contbns. to higher edn. U. Tex. Pan Am., 1989. Fellow Am. Acad. Family Physicians; mem. AMA (vice chmn. com. health care of poor 1971-75, Benjamin Rush Bicentennial award 1976, Council of Med. Services 1985-94), Tex. Med. Assn. (chmn. com. health care of poor 1971, Disting. Service award 1972, pres. 1979-80), Tex. Acad. Family Physicians (v.p. 1973, pres. 1975, Distinguished Service award 1967, Outstanding Leadership award 1975-76, v.p. Valley chpt. 1960-61, pres. 1961-62), Hidalgo-Starr Counties Med. Soc. (pres. 1964). Clubs: Lions, K.C, Rotary, Alhambra. Address: 212 W Pine Ridge Ln Mcallen TX 78503-3129

RAMIREZ, MARTIN RUBEN, educator, administrator, consultant; b. San Luis Potosi, Mex., Aug. 17, 1962; s. Victorio Niño and Concepcion (Zuñiga) R.; m. Maureen Therese McDermott, July 27, 1991. BS in Civil Engring., Northwestern U., 1984, MS, 1986, PhD in Theoretical and Applied Mechanics, 1991. Asst. to v.p. engring. Perkins & Will, Chgo.; cons. engr. Alfred Benesch & Co., Chgo., 1985-86; asst. prof. mech. engring. Johns Hopkins U., Balt., 1990-94; cons., dir. curriculum and learning assessment IMSA, Aurora, Ill., 1996—; cons. Wiss-Jenney Elsther, Northbrook, Ill., 1985-86, Mitsubishi Heavy Industries, Hunt Valley, Md., 1994; founder, dir. program on engring. edn. Johns Hopkins U., 1993. Reviewer for several jours. Me. adv. coun. Baltimore County Schs., 1994. Recipient Young Investigators award NSF, 1993; Lilly fellow, 1992; NSF grad. fellow, 1985. Mem. ASCD, ASCE (assoc.), ASME, Am. Soc. Engring. Edn. (chair Frontiers in Edn. Conf. 1993), U.S. Assn. for Computational Mechanics, IEEE Computer Soc., Am. Acad. Mechanics. Avocation: bicycling. Office: IMSA 1500 W Sullivan Rd Aurora IL 60506

RAMIREZ, MICHAEL P., editorial cartoonist; b. Tokyo; s. Ireneo Edward and Fumiko Maria R. Syndicated cartoonist Copley News Svc., 1986—; cartoonist The Comml. Appeal, Memphis, 1990—. Recipient Pulitzer Prize for editorial cartooning, 1994. Office: The Commercial Appeal 495 Union Ave Memphis TN 38103

RAMIREZ, RICARDO, bishop; b. Bay City, Tex., Sept. 12, 1936; s. Natividad and Maria (Espinosa) R. B.A., U. St. Thomas, Houston, 1959; M.A., U. Detroit, 1968; Diploma in Pastoral Studies, East Asian Pastoral Inst., Manila, 1973-74. Ordained priest Roman Catholic Ch., 1966; missionary Basilian Fathers, Mex., 1968-76; exec. v.p. Mexican Am. Cultural Ctr., San Antonio, 1976-81; aux. bishop Archdiocese of San Antonio, 1981-82; bishop Diocese of Las Cruces, N.M., 1982—; cons. U.S. Bishop's Com. on Liturgy, from 1981; advisor U.S. Bishop's Com. on Hispanic Affairs, from 1981. Author: Fiesta, Worship and Family, 1981. Mem. N.Am. Acad. on Liturgy, Hispanic Liturgical Inst., Padres Asociada Derechos Religiosos Educativos y Sociales. Lodges: K.C; Holy Order Knights of Holy Sepulcher. Office: Diocese of Las Cruces 1280 Med Park Dr Las Cruces NM 88005-3239*

RAMIREZ, TINA, artistic director; b. Caracas, Venezuela; d. Gloria Maria Cestero and Jose Ramirez Gaonita. Studied dance with Lola Bravo, Alexandra Danilova, Anna Sokolow. Toured with Federico Rey Dance Co.; founder, artistic dir. Ballet Hispanico, N.Y.C., 1970—; panelist NEA, N.Y. Sate Coun. on Arts; mem. advisory panel N.Y.C. Dept. Cultural Affairs; bd. dirs. Dance Theater Workshop. Appearances include (Broadway) Kismet, Lute Song, (TV) Man of La Mancha. Recipient Arts and Culture Honor award Mayor of N.Y.C., 1983, Ethnic New Yorker award N.Y.C., 1986, Gov.'s Arts award N.Y. State Gov. Mario Cuomo, 1987; honoree Nat. Puerto Rican Forum, Hispanic Inst. for Performing Arts. Office: Ballet Hispanico 167 W 89th St New York NY 10024-1901*

RAMIREZ-RIVERA, JOSE, physician; b. Mayaguez, P.R., June 26, 1929; S. Jesus Ramirez and Nieves Rivera; m. Leila Suner, May 14, 1971; children: Federico, Steven, Sally, Juliette, Natasha, Leila. B.A., Johns Hopkins U., 1949; M.D., Yale U., 1953. Diplomate Am. Bd. Internal Medicine. Intern U. Md. Hosp., 1953-54; resident in medicine Univ. Hosp., Balt., 1954-55, fellow in hematology, 1958-59, resident, 1959; staff physician VA Hosp., Balt., 1960-67; assoc. chief of staff VA Hosp., 1962-68; asst. in medicine Johns Hopkins U., 1960-67, instr. in medicine, 1967-68; asst. prof. medicine U. Md., 1961-68; assoc. prof. Duke U., Durham, N.C., 1968-70; dir. med. edn. and clin. investigation Western Region P.R., 1970-80; chief medicine Mayaguez (P.R.) Med. Ctr., 1971-82; prof. medicine U. P.R., San Juan, 1974—, dir. univ. med. svcs. Med. Sci. Campus, 1982-86; dir. Rincon Rural Health Project, 1975-82, assoc. chief staff for edn. VA Med. Ctr., San Juan, 1990-92. Contbr. articles to med. jours. Bd. dirs. Soc. Edn. Suroeste. With USPHS, 1955-57. Fellow ACP (pres. P.R. chpt. 1986-88), Royal Soc. Medicine (London), Coll. Chest Physicians; mem. Am. Fedn. Clin. Rsch., P.R. Lung Assn. (bd. dirs. 1975-80), Soc. Autores Puertorriguenos, PEN Club, Alliance Francaise of P.R. (v.p. 1995-96, pres. 1996—). Roman Catholic. Office: Dept Vets Affairs Med Ctr One Veterans Pla San Juan PR 00927-5800

RAMIS, HAROLD ALLEN, film director, screenwriter, actor; b. Chgo., Nov. 21, 1944; s. Nathan and Ruth (Cokee) R.; m. Erica Mann; children: Violet, Julian, Daniel. B.A., Washington U., St. Louis, 1966; ArtsD (hon.), Washington U., 1993. Assoc. editor Playboy mag., 1968-70; actor, writer Second City, Chgo., 1970-73, Nat. Lampoon Radio Hour, Lampoon Show, 1974-75; actor, head writer SCTV, 1977-78; producer, head writer Rodney Dangerfield Show, ABC-TV, 1982. Screenwriter (with Douglas Kenny and Chris Miller) National Lampoon's Animal House, 1978, (with Janice Allen, Len Blum and Dan Goldberg) Meatballs, 1979, (with Douglas Kenny, Brian Doyle-Murray) Caddyshack, 1980, (with Len Blum and Dan Goldberg) Stripes, 1981, (with Dan Aykroyd) Ghostbusters, 1984, (with Brian Doyle-Murray) Club Paradise, 1986; co-screenwriter (with Peter Torokvei) Armed and Dangerous, 1986; writer (with Dan Akroyd) Ghostbusters II, 1989; dir. feature films: Caddyshack, 1980, National Lampoon's Vacation, 1983, Club Paradise, 1986; exec. producer, co-screenwriter (with Rodney Dangerfield) Back to School, 1986; film appearances include: Stripes, 1981, Ghostbusters, 1984, Baby Boom, 1987, Stealing Home, 1988, Ghostbusters II, 1989; dir., exec. producer, co-writer Groundhog Day, 1993; dir., co-prodr. Stuart Saves His Family, 1995. Mem. AFTRA, Screen Actors Guild, Writers Guild Am., Dirs. Guild Am. Office: CAA 9830 Wilshire Blvd Beverly Hills CA 90212-1804 also: Ocean Pictures Inc 10202 Washington Blvd Culver City CA 90232-3119

RAMLER, SIEGFRIED, school administrator, educator; b. Vienna, Austria, Oct. 30, 1924; s. Lazar and Eugenia Ramler; m. Piilani Andrietta Ahuna, Jan. 27, 1948; children: David K., Dita L., Laurence K., Malia R. Diplôme supérieur, U. Paris, 1958; MA, U. Hawaii, 1961. Interpreter Internat. Mil. Tribunal, Nuremberg, Germany, 1945-46, chief interpreting br., 1946-49; chair fgn. lang. dept. Punahou Sch., Honolulu, 1951-71, dir. instnl. svcs., 1971-91, dir. Wo Internat. Ctr., 1990-95; exec. dir. Found. for Study in Hawaii and Abroad, Honolulu, 1969-90; vis. fellow East-West Ctr., 1995—. Contbr. articles to profl. publs. Sec., bd. dirs. crown Prince Akihito Scholarship Found., 1989—. Decorated medal Freedom Found., 1958, Order of the Palmes Académiques, French Govt., 1964, Order of the Sacred Treasure, Japanese Govt., 1992, Ordre National du Mérite, French Govt., 1993. Mem. ASCD, Internat./Global Edn. Com. (chair nat. adv. com. 1987-93), Japan-Am. Soc. Hawaii (pres. 1986-87, program chmn. 1975-94, Alliance Française of Hawaii (pres. 1961, bd. dirs. 1992—). Avocations: running, travel, swimming. Home: 921 Maunawili Cir Kailua HI 96734-4620 Office: East West Ctr 1777 East West Rd Honolulu HI 96848

RAMM, DOUGLAS ROBERT, psychologist; b. New Haven, Dec. 11, 1949; s. Robert Frederick and Gladys (Torgrimson) R. B.A., Ithaca Coll., 1972; M.A., Duquesne U., 1974; Ph.D., 1979; m. Barbara Stephens, Aug. 10, 1974; children—Jennifer, Jessica. Staff psychologist Westmoreland Hosp, Greensburg, Pa., 1976-79; chief clin. psychologist, dir. child and adolescent psychiat. services Westmoreland Hosp., Greensburg, 1979-82; pvt. practice, Greensburg, 1980—; pres. Ctr. for Sci. Study of Values and Morality, 1995—; cons. U. Pitts., Pa. Bur. Vocat. Rehab., Westmoreland County Ct. of Common Pleas. Mem. Am. Psychol. Assn., Am. Philos. Assn., Pa. Psychol. Assn., Soc. Personality Assessment, Nat. Acad. Neuropsychologists, Am. Bd. Med. Psychotherapists, N.Y. Acad. Scis., Nat. Register Health Svc. Providers in Psychology, Am. Coll. Forensics Examiners. Methodist. Home: 225 Humphrey Rd Greensburg PA 15601-4571 Office: 1717 Penn Ave Ste 327 Pittsburgh PA 15221

RAMMING, MICHAEL ALEXANDER, school system administrator; b. St. Louis, Feb. 4, 1940; s. William Alexander and Emily Louise (Reingruber) R.; m. Susan Ray Oliver, July 9, 1962; children: Michael Murray, Todd Alexander. BS, Centenary Coll., 1963; MA, Washington U., St. Louis, 1968. Cert. adminstr. secondary schs., Mo. Teacher and coach Ladue Sch. Dist., St. Louis, 1963-88, adminstr., 1988—. Vol. Sr. Olympics, St. Louis, 1992, 93. Mem. Nat. Assn. Secondary Sch. Prins., Mo. Assn. Secondary Sch. Prins., Nat. Interscholastic Athletic Adminstrs. Assn., Mo. Interscholastic Athletic Adminstrs. Assn. (25 Yr. Svc. award). Avocations: tennis, walking, travel. Home: 13309 Kings Glen Dr Saint Louis MO 63131-1022 Office: Ladue Horton Watkins High Sch 1201 S Warson Rd Saint Louis MO 63124-1266 *As I look back I feel that participation in sports as a player, coach, and fan provided me with a wealth of leadership, community building, daring, sharing, and the ability to accept success and failure.*

RAMO, ROBERTA COOPER, lawyer; b. Denver, Aug. 8, 1942; d. David D. and Martha L. (Rosenblum) Cooper; m. Barry W. Ramo, June 17, 1964. BA magna cum laude, U. Colo., 1964, LHD (hon.), 1995; JD, U. Chgo., 1967; LLD (hon.) U. Mo., 1995, U. Denver, 1995. Bar: N.Mex., 1967, Tex. 1971. With N.C. Fund, Durham, N.C., 1967-68; nat. teaching fellow Shaw U., Raleigh, N.C., 1968-70; mem. Sawtelle, Goode, Davidson & Troilo, San Antonio, 1970-72, Rodey, Dickason, Sloan, Akin & Robb, Albuquerque, 1972-74; sole practice law, Albuquerque, 1974-77; dir., shareholder Poole, Kelly & Ramo, Albuquerque, 1977-93; shareholder Modrall, Sperling, Roehl, Harris & Sisk, 1993—; bd. dirs. United N.Mex. Bank of Albuquerque, 1983-88; lectr. in field. Bd. dirs., past pres. N.Mex. Symphony Orch., 1977-86; bd. dirs. Albuquerque Cmty. Found., N.Mex. First, 1987-90, Coll. of Law Practice Mgmt.; trustee Manzano Day Sch., 1975-77; bd. regents U. N.Mex., 1989-94, pres. 1991-93, chmn. presdl. search com. 1990; mem. vis. com. U. Chgo. Law Sch., 1987-90; mem. adv. bd. N.Mex. Performing ARts Ctr. 1987-90, others. Recipient Disting. Pub. Svc. award Gov. of N.Mex., 1993. Fellow Am. Bar Found.; mem. Albuquerque Bar Assn. (bd. dirs., pres. 1980-81), N.Mex. Bar Assn. (chmn. bus., banking and corp. sect. 1979-80, Outstanding Contbn. award 1981, 84), ABA (pres. 1995, bd. govs. 1994—, vice chmn. 1981-82, chmn. law practice sect. 1984, ALI/ABA com., chmn. select com. of the ho. 1991, mem. coun. law practice mgmt. sect. 1974—, chmn. coun. of sect. officers 1984-86, chmn. legal tech. adv. commn. 1984-88, chmn. coord. coun. on legal tech. 1989-94, chmn. ABA celebration of bicentennial of constitution at ann. meeting 1986-87, past mem. tax sect. com. on employee benefits, past mem. tax sect. com. on profl. svc. corps., others), Am. Bar Retirement Assn. (bd. dirs. 1990-94), Am. Judicature Soc. (bd. dirs. 1988-91), Greater Albuquerque C. of C. (bd. dirs. exec. com. 1987-91). Co-author: New Mexico Estate Administration System, 1980; contbr. articles to profl. jours. and chpts. to books; editor: How to Create a System for the Law Office, 1975; contbg. editor: Tex. Probate Sys., 1974. Address: Modrall Sperling Roehl Harris & Sisk PO Box 2168 Albuquerque NM 87103-2168

RAMO, SIMON, engineering executive; b. Salt Lake City, May 7, 1913; s. Benjamin and Clara (Trestman) R.; m. Virginia Smith, July 25, 1937; children: James Brian, Alan Martin. BS, U. Utah, 1933, DSc (hon.), 1961; PhD, Calif. Inst. Tech., 1936; DEng (hon.), Case Western Res. U., 1960, U. Mich., 1966, Poly. Inst. N.Y., 1971; DSc (hon.), Union Coll., 1963, Worcester Polytechnic Inst., 1968, U. Akron, 1969, Cleve. State U., 1976; LLD (hon.), Carnegie-Mellon U., 1970, U. So. Calif., 1972, Gonzaga U., 1983, Occidental Coll., 1984, Claremont U., 1985. With Gen. Electric Co., 1936-46; v.p. ops. Hughes Aircraft Co., 1946-53; with Ramo-Wooldridge Corp., 1953-58, Ramo-Wooldridge Corp., 1954-58; dir. TRW Inc., 1954-85, exec. v.p., 1958-61, vice chmn. bd., 1961-78, chmn. exec. com., 1969-78, cons., 1978—; pres. The Bunker-Ramo Corp., 1964-66; chmn. bd. TRW-Fujitsu Co., 1980-83; bd. dirs. Arco Power Techs.; vis. prof. mgmt. sci. Calif. Inst. Tech., 1978—; Regents lectr. UCLA, 1981-82, U. Calif. at Santa Cruz, 1978-79; chmn. Center for Study Am. Experience, U. So. Calif., 1978-80; Faculty fellow John F. Kennedy Sch. Govt., Harvard U., 1980-84; mem. White House Energy Research and Devel. Adv. Council, 1973-75; mem. adv. com. on sci. and fgn. affairs U.S. State Dept., 1973-75; chmn. Pres.'s Com. on Sci. and Tech., 1976-77; mem. adv. council to Sec. Commerce, 1976-77, Gen. Atomics Corp., 1988—, Aurora Capital Ptnrs., 1991—, Chartwell Investments, 1992—; co-chmn. Transition Task Force on Sci. and Tech. for Pres.-elect Reagan; mem. roster consultants to adminstr. ERDA, 1976-77; bd. advisors for sci. and tech. Republic of China, 1981-84; chmn. bd. Aetna, Jacobs & Ramo Venture Capital, 1987-90, Allenwood Ventures Inc., 1987—. Author: The Business of Science, 1988, other sci., engring. and mgmt. books. Bd. dirs. L.A. World Affairs Coun. 1973-85, Mus. Ctr. Found., L.A., L.A. Philharm. Assn., 1981-84; life trustee Calif. Inst. Tech., Nat. Symphony Orch. Assn., 1973-83; trustee emeritus Calif. State Univs.; bd. visitors UCLA Sch. Medicine, 1980—; bd. dirs. W.M. Keck Found., 1983—; bd. govs. Performing Arts Coun. Mus. Ctr. L.A., pres., 1976-77. Recipient award IAS, 1956; award Am. Inst. Elec. Engrs., 1959; award Arnold Air Soc., 1960; Am. Acad. Achievement award, 1964; award Am. Iron and Steel Inst., 1968; Disting. Svc. medal Armed Forces Communication and Electronics Assn., 1970; medal of achievement WEMA, 1970; awards U. So. Calif., 1971, 79; Kayan medal Columbia U., 1972; award Am. Cons. Engrs. Coun., 1974; medal Franklin Inst., 1978; award Harvard Bus. Sch. Assn., 1979; award Nat. Medal Sci., 1979; Disting. Alumnus award U. Utah, 1981; UCLA medal, 1982; Presdl. Medal of Freedom, 1983; named to Bus. Hall of Fame, 1984; recipient Aesculapian award UCLA, 1984, Durand medal AAIA, 1984, John Fritz medal, 1986, Henry Townley Heald award Ill. Inst. Tech., 1988, Nat. Engring. award Am. Assn. Engring. Socs., 1988, Franklin-Jefferson medal, 1988, Howard Hughes Meml. award, 1989. Fellow IEEE (Electronic Achievement award 1953, Golden Omega award 1975, Founders medal 1980, Centennial medal 1984), Am. Acad. Arts and Scis., Am. Acad. Polit. Sci.; mem. N.Y. Acad. Scis., Nat. Acad. Engring. (founder, coun. mem. Bueche award), Nat. Acad. Scis., Am. Phys. Soc., Am. Philos. Soc., Inst. Advancement Engring., Coun. Fgn. Rels., Pacific Coun. Internat. Policy, Internat. Acad. Astronautics, Eta Kappa Nu (eminent mem. award 1966), Theta Tau (Hall of Fame laureate). Office: 9200 W Sunset Blvd Ste 801 Los Angeles CA 90069-3603

RAMO, VIRGINIA M. SMITH, civic worker; b. Yonkers, N.Y.; d. Abraham Harold and Freda (Kasnetz) Smith; B.S. in Edn., U. So. Calif., DHL (hon.), 1978; m. Simon Ramo; children—James Brian, Alan Martin. Nat. co-chmn. ann. giving U. So. Calif., 1968-70, vice chmn., trustee, 1971—, co-chmn. bd. councilors Sch. Performing Arts, 1975-76, co-chmn. bd. councillors Schs. Med. and Engring.; vice-chmn. bd. overseers Hebrew Union Coll., 1972-75; bd. dirs. The Muses of Calif. Mus. Sci. and industry, UCLA Affiliates, Estelle Doheny Eye Found., U. So. Calif. Sch. Medicine; adv. council Los Angeles County Heart Assn., chmn. com. to endow Chair in cardiology at U. So. Calif.; vice-chmn., bd. dirs. Friends of Library U. So. Calif.; bd. dirs., nat. pres. Achievement Rewards for Coll. Scientists Found., 1975-77; bd. dirs. Les Dames Los Angeles, Community TV So. Calif.; bd. dirs., v.p. Founders Los Angeles Music Center; v.p. Los Angeles Music Center Opera Assn.; v.p. corp. bd. United Way; v.p. Blue Ribbon-400 Performing Arts Council; chmn. com. to endow chair in gerontology U. So. Calif.; vice chmn. campaign Doheny Eye Inst., 1986. Recipient Service award Friends of Libraries, 1974, Nat. Community Service award Alpha Epsilon Phi, 1975, Disting. Service award Am. Heart Assn. 1978, Service award U. So. Calif., Spl. award U. So. Calif. Music Alumni Assn., 1979, Life Achievement award Mannequins of Los Angeles Assistance League, 1979, Woman of Yr. award PanHellenic Assn., 1981, Disting. Service award U. So. Calif. Sch. Medicine, 1981, U. So. Calif. Town and Gown Recognition award, 1986, Asa V. Call Achievement award U. So. Calif., 1986, Phi Kappa Phi scholarship award U. So. Calif., 1986, Vision award Luminaires of Doheny Eye Inst., 1994. Mem. UCLA Med. Aux., U. So. Calif. Pres.'s Circle, Commerce Assos. U. So. Calif., Cedars of Lebanon Hosp. Women's Guild (dir. 1967-68), Blue Key, Skull and Dagger.

RAMOS, ALBERT A., electrical engineer; b. L.A., Feb. 28, 1927; s. Jesus D. and Carmen F. (Fontes) R.; B.S. in Elec. Engring., U. So. Calif., 1950, M.S. in Systems Mgmt., 1972; Ph.D., U.S. Internat. U., 1975; m. Joan C. Pailing, Sept. 23, 1950; children—Albert A., Richard R., James J., Katherine. With guided missile test group Hughes Aircraft Co., 1950-60; with TRW DSG, 1960-91, sr. staff engr. Norton AFB, San Bernardino, Calif., 1969-91, ret., 1991. Served with USNR, 1945-46. Registered profl. engr., Calif. Mem. IEEE, NSPE, Air Force Assn., Mexican-Am. Engring. Soc., Mexican-Am. Profl. Mgmt. Assn. (mem. administering commn. dept. community svcs.), Sigma Phi Delta, Eta Kappa Nu, Tau Beta Pi. Home: 8937 Napoli Dr Las Vegas NV 89117-1182

RAMOS, ELEANOR LACSON, internist; b. Quezon City, The Philippines, Mar. 26, 1956; d. Pol and Evelyn (Manahan) Ramos. BS, Tufts U., 1977; MD, Tufts Med. Sch., Boston, 1981. Diplomate Am. Bd. Internal Medicine, Am. Bd. Nephrology. Resident in internal medicine N.E. Med. Ctr., Boston, 1981-84; fellow in nephrology Brigham & Women's Hosp., Boston, 1984-88, med. dir. renal transplant svc., 1988-90; med. dir. renal transplant svc. U. Fla., Gainesville, 1990-94; assoc. dir. immunology clin. rsch. Bristol-Myers Squibb Pharm. Rsch. Inst., Wallingford, Conn., 1994—; asst. clin. prof. medicine Yale U., 1995—. Mem. Am. Soc. Transplant Physicans (chairperson patient care and edn. com. 1994-95, Young Investigator award 1988), Am. Soc. Nephrology, Internat. Soc. Nephrology, Alpha Omega Alpha. Office: Bristol-Myers Squibb Immunology Clin Rsch 5 Research Pky PO Box 5100 Wallingford CT 06492-7660

RAMOS, LUZ MARIA, elementary education educator; b. Santurce, Puerto Rico; arrived in U.S., 1989; d. Gerardo and Maria Luz (Moczó) López; m. Angel Manuel Ramos, Oct. 28, 1961; children: Joan Marie, Angel Manuel Jr. (dec.). Student, U. Ctrl. Fla., 1992; BA in Natural Sci., U. Puerto Rico, 1965. Cert. elem. educator, Fla. Asst. trust officer Banco Popular de Puerto Rico, 1956-73; prof. banking inst. Inst. de Banca, Puerto Rico, 1984-89; dir. banking dept. Inst. de Banca, 1988; tchr. Spring Lake Elem., Ocoee, Fla., 1992—. Vol. svc. Orange County Pub. Schs., 1989-90; mem. dept. edn. evaluation banking program Voc. Sch. Miguel Such., San Juan, 1987. Recipient Outstanding Professor award Inst. de Banca, 1989. Mem. Orange County Classroom Tchrs. Assn. Roman Catholic. Avocations: reading, gardening, computer, museums, public libraries. Home: 5166 Wood Ridge Ct Orlando FL 32818 Office: Spring Lake Elem 115 Spring Lake Cir Ocoee FL 34761-1686

RAMOS, MELVIN JOHN, artist, educator; b. Sacramento, July 24, 1935; s. Clifton John and Agnes (Enos) R.; m. Lolita Alice Helmers, Aug. 14, 1955; children: Bradley, Scot, Rochelle. B.A., Calif. State U.-Sacramento, 1957, M.A., 1958. Tchr. Elk Grove High Sch., (Calif.), 1957-60, Mira Loma High Sch., Sacramento, 1960-66; prof. art Calif. State U.-Hayward, 1966—. Exhibited one man shows, Louis Meisel Gallery, N.Y.C., 1974, 76, 81, 85, 89, Mus. Haus Lange, 1975, Oakland Mus., 1977, Rose Art Mus., 1980, group shows, Whitney Mus., N.Y.C., 1969, 78, 83, Bklyn Mus., 1970, Mus. Modern Art, N.Y.C., 1970; Ludwig Mus. Cologne, 1992, Mus. of Cont. Art La., 1993; represented in permanent collections, San Francisco Mus. Modern Art, Oakland Mus., Indpls. Mus., Mus. Modern Art, N.Y.C., Crystler Mus., Va., Smithsonian Instn., Washington, Guggenheim Mus., N.Y.C., Nat. Gallery, Washington, Kunsthaus, Darmstadt, W.Ger., Whitney Mus. Am. Art; author: Mel Ramos: Watercolors, 1979. Democrat. Roman Catholic. Home: 5941 Ocean View Dr Oakland CA 94618-1842 Office: 25800 Hillary St Hayward CA 94542

RAMOS, ROSE MARY, elementary education educator; b. San Antonio, Aug. 8, 1942; d. Henry Barbosa and Bertha Alice (Cuellar) Gonzalez; m. Jesus Ramos Jr., Sept. 11, 1965; children: Rebecca Anne, Veronica Anne. BS in Elem. Edn., Our Lady of Lake U., San Antonio, 1965; MA in Edn., U. Houston, 1992. Cert. elem. educator, kindergarten, reading specialist, bilingual and ESL. Tchr. San Antonio Ind. Sch. Dist., 1965-89, Ft. Bend County (Tex.) Ind. Sch. Dist., 1989—. Mem. Nat. Space Soc., Tex. State Reading Assn., Tex. Educators of Speakers of Other Langs., Greater Houston Area Reading Assn., San Antonio Conservation Soc., Internat. Reading. Assn. Democrat. Roman Catholic. Avocations: reading, life sciences, writing, researching instructional ideas for Spanish bilingual students transitioning into English. Home: 3614 Belle Grove Ln Sugar Land TX 77479-2257

RAMOS MOREAU, IRIS VIOLETA, English educator; b. Santurce, Puerto Rico, Dec. 24, 1948; d. Jose A. and Violeta (Moreau) Ramos; m. Orlando R. Gonzalez Hernandez, June 27, 1970; children: Michelle Marie, Suzanne Elaine, Rebecca Christine. BA in English, U. Puerto Rico, 1970, MA, 1983, postgrad., 1994—. Cert. English tchr., Puerto Rico. English tchr. Tomas C. Ongay Vocat. High Sch., Bayamon, Puerto Rico, 1970-85; asst. prof. bus. English dept. coll. bus. adminstrn. U. Puerto Rico, Rio Piedras, 1985—; English prof. Bayamon Regional Coll., 1984, Interam. U., 1985; curriculum cons. Humacao (P.R.) C.C.; mem. curriculum adv. com. coll. bus. adminstrn. U. P.R., 1988-92, mem. adv. com., 1991-94; mem. pers. com. bus. English dept. U. P.R. Rio Piedras Campus, 1992-94. Mem. adv. bd. ANG Family Program, Isla Verde, Puerto Rico, 1985—, PTA, Guaynabo, Puerto Rico, 1988—, Tintillo's Residents, Guaynabo, 1992—; judge competitions Puerto Rico Forensics, 1994. Mem. Assn. Bus. Communication of Ams. (mem.-at-large, founder, sec. bd. dirs. 1992—, mem. adv. bd. 1992—), ASCD, Puerto Rico TESOL, U.S.A. TESOL, Assn. for Bus. Communication, Nat. Bus. Edn. Assn., Alpha Delta Kappa. Roman Catholic. Avocations: jogging, aerobics, cooking, decorating. Home: D-4 9th St Ext Victor Braegger Guaynabo PR 00966 Office: U Puerto Rico San Juan PR 00931

RAMSAY, DONALD ALLAN, physical chemist; b. London, July 11, 1922; s. Norman and Thirza Elizabeth (Beckley) R.; m. Nancy Brayshaw, June 8, 1946; children: Shirley Margaret, Wendy Kathleen, Catharine Jean, Linda Mary. BA, Cambridge (Eng.) U., 1943, MA, 1947, PhD, 1947, ScD, 1976; D honoris causa, U. Reims, France, 1969; Filosofie hedersdoktor, U. Stockholm, Sweden, 1982. With divs. chemistry Nat. Research Council Can., Ottawa, Ont., 1947-49; with divs. physics Nat. Research Council Can., 1949-75; with Herzberg Inst. Astrophysics, 1975-87, sr. research officer, 1961-68, prin. research officer, 1968-87; vis. prof. U. Minn., 1964, U. Orsay, 1966, U. Stockholm, 1967, 71, 74, U. Calif., Irvine, 1970, U. Sao Paulo, 1972, 78, U. Bologna, 1973, U. Western Australia, 1976, Australian Nat. U., 1976, Tex. Christian U., 1988, U. Wuppertal, Germany, 1988, U. Canterbury, Christchurch, New Zealand, 1991, U. Ulm, Germany, 1992, 96; guest worker Steacie Inst. Molecular Scis. Editor: (with J. Hinze) Selected Works of Robert S. Mulliken, 1975; contbr. numerous articles on molecular spectra and molecular structure to profl. jours. Recipient commemorative medal for 125th anniversary Confederation Can., 1992, Alexander von Humboldt Rsch. award, 1993-95; decorated Queen Elizabeth Silver Jubilee medal. Fellow Royal Soc. London, Royal Soc. Can. (hon. treas. 1976-79, 88-91, Centennial medal 1982), Am. Phys. Soc., Chem. Inst. Can. (Chem. Inst. Can. medal 1992). Mem. United Ch. of Canada (organist 1954—). Club: Leander (Henley-on-Thames, Eng.). Home: 1578 Drake Ave, Ottawa, ON Canada K1G 0L8 Office: Nat Research Council, 100 Sussex Dr, Ottawa, ON Canada K1A 0R6

RAMSAY, GUSTAVUS REMAK, actor; b. Balt., Feb. 2, 1937; s. John Breckinridge and Caroline V. (Remak) R. BA, Princeton U., 1958. Appeared in plays Hang Down Your Head and Die, 1964, Half A Sixpence, 1965, Lovely Ladies, Kind Gentlemen, Sheep on the Runway, 1970, On the Town, 1971, The Real Inspector Hound, After Magritte, 1972, Jumpers, 1974, Private Lives, 1975, Landscape of the Body, Dirty Linen, 1977, The Rear Column, 1978, All's Well That Ends Well, 1978, Every Good Boy Deserved Favor, 1980, Save Grand Central, 1980, The Winslow Boy, 1980-81, The Dining Room, 1982, as St. John Quartermaine in Quartermaine's Terms, 1983— (Obie award), Woman in Mind, 1988, The Devil's Disciple, 1988, Love Letters, 1989, Prin, 1990, Nick & Nora, 1991, St. Joan, 1993, The Moliere Comedies, 1995, The Heiress, 1995; appeared in movies Tiger Makes Out, The Stepford Wives, The Great Gatsby, The Front, Class, Simon, The House on Carroll Street, Mr. and Mrs. Bridge, Shadows and Fog, King of the Hill; TV movies The Dining Room, Heartbreak House, Kennedy, Liberty, Concealed Enemies, Dream House, Mellon, Lincoln and Seward, 1992, Dead Ahead: The Exxon Valdez Disaster, Truman. With U.S. Army, 1959-62. Democrat. Presbyterian. Home: 115 Central Park W New York NY 10023-4153

RAMSAY, JOHN BARADA, research chemist, educator; b. Phoenix, Dec. 28, 1929; s. John A. and Helen G. Ramsay; m. Barbara Ann Hilsenhoff, Apr. 18, 1953; children: Bryan J., Kathleen L., Carol A., David A. BS in Chemistry, Tex. Western U., 1950; PhD in Analytical Chemistry, U. Wis., 1954. Mem. staff Los Alamos Nat. Lab., 1954-70, 73-95; assoc. prof. Coll. Petroleum and Minerals, Dhahran, Saudi Arabia, 1970-73; cons. U.S. Navy, USAF, 1980—; adj. prof. U. N.Mex., Los Alamos, 1980-85. Author sci. articles. Recipient award of excellence U.S. Dept. Energy, 1984, 92. Mem. N.Mex. Acad. Sci. (pres. 1988), Am. Inst. Archeol. (chpt. pres. 1979, 96), Nat. Ski Patrol (appt. 7651), Westerners Internat. (chpt. pres. 1988-90), Sigma Xi. Democrat. Home: 6 Erie Ln Los Alamos NM 87544-3810

RAMSAY, KARIN KINSEY, publisher, educator; b. Brownwood, Tex., Aug. 10, 1930; d. Kirby Luther and Ina Rebecca (Wood) Kinsey; m. Jack Cummins Ramsay Jr., Aug. 31, 1951; children: Annetta Jean, Robin Andrew. BA, Trinity U., 1951. Cert. assoc. ch. edn., 1980. Youth coord. Covenant Presbyn. Ch., Carrollton, Tex., 1961-76; dir. ch. edn. Northminster Presbyn. Ch., Dallas, 1976-80, Univ. Presbyn. Ch., Chapel Hill, N.C., 1987-90, Oak Grove Presbyn. Ch., Bloomington, Minn., 1990-93; coord. ecum. ministry Flood Relief for Iowa, Des Moines, 1993; program coord. 1st Presbyn. Ch., Green Bay, Wis., 1994-95; publicity & tour dir. Hist. Resources Press, Green Bay, 1994—; mem. Presbytery Candidates Com., Dallas, 1977-82, Presbytery Exams. Com. Dallas, 1979-81; clk. coun. New Hope Presbytery, Rocky Mount, N.C., 1989-90; creator, dir. Thee Holy Fools and This Is Me retreats. Author: Ramsay's Resources, 1983—; contbr. articles to jours. in field. Design cons. Brookhaven Hosp. Chapel, Dallas, 1977-78; elder Presbyn. Ch. U.S.A., 1982—; coord. Lifeline Emergency Response, Dallas, 1982-84. Mem. Internat. Platform Assn., Assn. Presbyn. Ch. Educators. *Yesterday taught me the lessons which made today possible. Today is the challenging link between yesterday and tomorrow. Tomorrow is an opportunity built on the foundation of today. Today is special.*

RAMSAY, LOUIS LAFAYETTE, JR., lawyer, banker; b. Fordyce, Ark., Oct. 11, 1918; s. Louis Lafayette and Carmile (Jones) R.; m. Joy Bond, Oct. 3, 1945; children—Joy Blankenship, Richard Louis. JD, U. Ark., 1947; LLD (hon.), U. Ark., Fayetteville, 1988, U. Ark., Pine Bluff, 1992. Bar: Ark. 1947, U.S. Dist. Ct. Ark. 1947, U.S. Ct. Appeals (8th cir.) 1948, U.S. Supreme Ct. 1952. Sr. counsel Ramsay, Bridgforth, Harrelson & Starling and predecessor firm Ramsay, Cox, Lile, Bridgforth, Gilbert, Harrelson & Starling, Pine Bluff, Ark., 1948—; pres. Simmons First Nat. Bank, Pine Bluff, Ark., 1970-78; chmn. bd., chief exec. officer Simmons First Nat. Bank, 1978-83; chmn. bd. dirs. Blue Cross-Blue Shield of Ark., Usable Life Ins. Co.; chmn. exec. com. Simmons First Nat. Corp., Pine Bluff. Mem. bd. Econ. Devel. of Jefferson County; mem. ofcl. bd. First United Meth. Ch. With USAF, 1942-45, maj. Res., 1945-49. Recipient Disting. Alumnus award U. Ark., 1982, Outstanding Lawyer award Ark. Bar Assn./Ark. Bar Found., 1966, 87. Mem. ABA (mem. spl. com. on presdl. inability and vice presdl. vacancy 1966), Ark. Bar Assn. (pres. 1963-64), Ark. Bar Found. (pres. 1960-61, Joint Bar Assn.,-Bar Found. Outstanding Lawyer award 1966, Lawyer Citizen award 1987), Ark. Bankers Assn. (pres. 1980-81), Pine Bluff C. of C. (pres. 1968), Rotary (pres. Pine Bluff 1954-55). Methodist. Lodge: Rotary (Pine Bluff) (pres. 1956-57). Office: Ramsay Bridgforth Harrelson & Starling PO Box 8509 Pine Bluff AR 71611-8509

RAMSAY, WILLIAM C., ambassador; b. Pontiac, Mich., Sept. 13, 1943; m. Lorna E. Ramsay. BS, Mich. State U., 1965, MBA, 1968; MA, Stanford U., 1983. Asst. comml. attache Kinshasa, Zaire, 1971-73; comml. attache Abidjan, Cote d'Ivoire, 1973-75; econ. trainer Fgn. Svc. Inst. U.S. Dept. State, Washington, 1975; econ/comml. officer Off Fuels and Energy, Bur. Econ. and Bus. Affairs, 1976-79; res. officer U.S. Mission to Com. of European Cmtys., Brussels, 1979-82; from dep. chief to dir. Off Energy Producing Country Affairs Bur. Econ. and Bus. Affairs, 1986-88; sr. seminar Fgn. Svc. Inst., 1988-89; U.S. Amb. to People's Republic of Congo, 1993—. With USAR. Office: US Amb Brazzaville Republic of Congo US Dept of State Rm 3529 Washington DC 20521-2090

RAMSAY, WILLIAM CHARLES, writer; b. N.Y.C., Nov. 6, 1930; s. Claude Barnett and Myrtle Marie (Scott) R.; m. Charlotte Appleton Kidder, June 10, 1988 (dec. Sept. 1995); children from previous marriages: Alice, John, Carol Ramsay Scott, David. BA in English Lit., U. Colo., 1952; MA in Physics, UCLA, 1957, PhD in Physics, 1962. NFS postdoctoral fellow U. Calif., San Diego, 1962-64; asst. prof. U. Calif., Santa Barbara, 1964-67; tech. mgr. Systems Assocs., Inc., Long Beach, Calif., 1967-72; sr. environ. economist U.S. AEC, Bethesda, Md., 1972-75; tech. adviser U.S. Nuclear Regulatory Agy., Washington, 1975-76; sr. fellow Resources for the Future, Washington, 1976-83, Ctr. for Strategic and Internat. Studies, Washington, 1983-85; sr. staff officer NAS, Washington, 1985-86; freelance writer, editor, publ. Washington, 1986—; cons. Vols. in Tech. Assistance, Arlington, Va., 1987-90, Internat. Resources Group, Washington, 1991; treas., bd. dirs. Jordan Conservation and Rsch. Ctr., Inc. Author: Unpaid Costs of Electrical Energy, 1979, Bioenergy and Economic Development, 1985; co-author: Managing the Environment, 1972, Energy in America's Future, 1979; editor, pub. Fiction-Online (electronic lit. jour.). Buenos Aires Convention fellow, 1952, NSF fellow, 1962; NATO scholar, 1960, 62. Mem. Am. Phys. Soc., Am. Astron. Soc., Internat. Assn. Energy Economists, Washington Ind. Writers, Writers' Ctr. (bd. dirs.). Avocations: piano, musical composition. Home and Office: 2930 Foxhall Rd NW Washington DC 20016-3429

RAMSBY, MARK DELIVAN, lighting designer and consultant; b. Portland, Oreg., Nov. 20, 1947; s. Marshall Delivan and Verna Pansy (Culver) R.; divorced; children: Aaron Delivan, Venessa Mercedes. Student, Portland (Oreg.) State U., 1966-67. With C.E.D., Portland, 1970-75; minority ptnr. The Light Source, Portland, 1975-78, pres., 1978-87; prin. Illume Lighting Design, Portland, 1987-90; ptnr. Ramsby, Dupuy & Seats, Inc., Portland, 1990-91; dir. lighting design PAE Cons. Engrs., Inc., Portland, 1991—; pvt. practice cons. Portland, 1979—. Recipient Top 100 Outstanding Achievement award Metalux Lighting, 1981-85, 100% award, 1985, Edwin F. Guth award of merit, 1990, Edison award of excellence, 1990, Edwin F. Guth award of excellence, 1993, 94, Paul Waterbury award of Merit, 1995. Mem. Illuminating Engring. Soc. Am. (sec.-treas. Oreg. sect. 1978-79, Oreg. Section and Regional and Internat. awards 1989, 90, 93, 94, Lighting Design awards), Internat. Assn. Lighting Designers. Republican. Lutheran. Avocations: lighting design, historical restoration, flyfishing, downhill skiing. Office: PAE Cons Engrs 808 SW 3rd Ave Ste 300 Portland OR 97204-2426

RAMSDEN, NORMA LA VONNE HUBER, nurse; b. Lewiston, Idaho, Aug. 1, 1921; d. Lawrence Henry and Gertrude Melissa (Ryder) Huber; m. John Burton Wormell, Nov. 18, 1942 (div. 1950); m. Everett Glenn Ramsden, Dec. 25, 1957; 1 child, Valerie Ann Ramsden Brooks. Diploma in nursing, St. Joseph's Hosp., Lewiston, 1952. Psychiatric nurse Oreg. State Hosp., Salem, 1952-57; clin. instr. Idaho State Hosp., Orofino, Idaho, 1957-58; night nurse ICU Tri State Hosp., Clarkston, Wash., 1969-94; adv. bd. Rogers Counseling Ctr., Clarkston, 1969—; ret., 1994. Leader Camp Fire Girls Am., 1958-61, 69-71; Episcopalian vestry, 1992-94, fellowship chmn., 1994—; vol. Interlink, 1994—. Recipient Woman Achievement award Altrusa Club, 1985. Mem. Am. Nurses Assn., Anatone Grange, Pollyette (pres., sec., treas.). Avocations: hiking, sewing, oil painting, gardening. Home: 817 Highland Ave Clarkston WA 99403

RAMSEY, BILL (WILLIAM MCCREERY), singer, actor, composer-lyricist, television executive; b. Cin., Apr. 17, 1931; s. William McCreery II and Olivia (James) R.; m. Erica Moeckli, Dec. 14, 1962 (div. Feb. 1982); 1 son, Joachim.; m. Petra Bock, Aug. 3, 1983. Student, Yale U., 1949-51, Goethe U., Frankfurt/Main, Germany, 1955, 57, U. Cin., 1956-57. guest prof. vocal jazz and presentation in pop and jazz program Hamburg U. Music and Drama, Hamburg, 1983-86. Partime profl. singer, 1949; appeared on Horace Heidt show, Hollywood, Calif., 1951, Eddie Fisher tour, Europe, 1953, Raymond Burr tour, Europe and North Africa, 1954, series jazz concerts, Germany and Am., 1953-55; 1st American to appear at German Jazz Festival, 1955, 1st American jazz vocalist after war to tour Yugoslavia, 1955, 1st TV portrait, Frankfurt/Main, 1955, 1st films in Baden-Baden, Munich, Hamburg, 1955; full-time profl. jazz and pop vocalist, 1957—, numerous recs.; actor numerous films, TV shows; songwriting, disc jockey work with Radio Luxembourg, Europawelle Saar, Radio Salzburg; 1st American jazz singer to tour Poland after war, also appearances Polish Jazz Festival, 1957, 67, Czek Jazz Festival, 1966; 1st pop record hit German version of Purple People Eater, 1958; program dir. Televico AG, Zurich/Gockhausen, Swiss TV and Film Prodn. Co., 1968-72, rec. artist for Polydor, Electrolia, Columbia, Cornet, Warner Bros., Stockfish, Ariola, Dino, Bear Family; in addition to singing, TV moderator on all three German Programs as well as in Austria since 1970. With USAF, 1951-55. Recipient top positions in various jazz polls. Mem. German Authors and Composers Soc. Address: Elbchaussee 118, D-22763 Hamburg Germany

RAMSEY, CHARLES EUGENE, sociologist, educator; b. Paragon, Ind., Apr. 24, 1923; s. Sarcefield Dodson and Stella (Goss) R.; m. Alberta Mae Jordan, July 19, 1943; children—James D., Charles W., Jane E., Suzanne. B.S., Ind. State Tchrs. Coll., 1947; M.S., U. Wis., 1950, Ph.D., 1952. Faculty U. Wis., 1951-52, U. Minn., 1952-54, Cornell U., 1954-62, Colo. State U., 1962-65; prof. sociology U. Minn., Mpls., 1965-77; chmn. dept. sociology U. Tex., Arlington, 1977-83; vis. prof. Inter-Am. Instn. Agrl. Sci., Costa Rica, 1961, Exptl. Sta., U. P.R., 1961-62; research cons. to various univs., agys. Author: (with Lowry Nelson and Cooley Verner) Community Structure and Change, 1960, (with David Gottlieb) The American Adolescent, 1965, Understanding the Deprived Child, S.R.A. 1967, Problems of Youth, 1967, (with D.J. McCarty) The School Managers: Power and Conflict in American Public Education, 1971, (with William A. Stacey) Social Statistics, 1992; also articles. Mem. Am. Sociol. Assn., Rural Sociol. Soc., Sigma Xi. Developed and tested theory of variations in community power structure, types of sch. bds., and roles of sch. supt., developed method of comparative measurement of level of living for different countries. Home: 1102 De Pauw Dr Arlington TX 76012-5339 Office: U Tex Dept Sociology Arlington TX

RAMSEY, DAVID SELMER, retired hospital executive; b. Mpls., Feb. 19, 1931; s. Selmer A. and Esther D. (Dahl) R.; m. Elinor Corfield, Aug. 15, 1953; children—Scott, Stewart, Thomas. B.S., U. Mich., 1953, M.S. in Microbiology, 1954, M.H.A., 1962. Research asst. Detroit Inst. Cancer Research, 1954-60; asst. adminstr. Harper Hosp., Detroit, 1962-68; assoc. adminstr. Harper Hosp., 1968-72; exec. v.p. Iowa Meth. Med. Ctr., Des Moines, 1972-83; pres. Iowa Meth. Med. Ctr., 1983-93, Iowa Health Sys., 1993-95. Avocations: golf; tennis; photography. Home: 25213 Quail Haven Dr Rio Verde AZ 85263

RAMSEY, DOUGLAS KENNETH, television anchor, journalist; b. Norman, Okla., June 15, 1951; s. Edwin P. and Madeline (Willoquet) R.; m. Ann Polya, Dec. 30, 1977 (div. 1985). BA in Polit. Sci., UCLA, 1970; MA in European Studies, Coll. Europe, Bruges, 1971; MA in Internat. Affairs, Johns Hopkins U., 1972. Freelance corr. Washington Post, Brussels, 1973-74; writer The Economist, London, 1975; corr. The Economist, Tokyo, 1976-79, NBC News, N.Y.C., 1985-87; bus. editor Newsweek, N.Y.C., 1979-82; exec. prodr. Bus. Times on ESPN, N.Y.C., 1982-85; mng. editor. Fin. News Network, N.Y.C., 1987-91; anchor CNBC, Ft. Lee, N.J., 1991-95; pres. Global Media Assocs., 1995—. Author: (non-fiction) The Corporate Warriors; contbr. columns to N.Y. Times, L.A. Times, Fin. Times. Mem. Authors Guild. Office: Sta KUSI-TV 4575 Viewridge Ave San Diego CA 92123

RAMSEY, FORREST G., computer company executive. BS, U.S. Naval Acad., 1952; MBA, U. Colo., Boulder, 1965. Chmn. Am. Sys. Corp., Chantilly, Va., 1976—. with USN, 1952-57. Office: Am Systems Corp 14200 Park Meadow Dr Chantilly VA 22021-2219*

RAMSEY, FORREST GLADSTONE, JR., engineering company executive; b. Wichita, Kans., Oct. 25, 1930; s. Forrest Gladstone and Anastasia Ruth (Linot) R.; m. Gwendolyn Moreton, June 22, 1953 (div. Jan. 1982); children: Deborah Jenkins, Rebecca Johnson, Susan Klopp, Diane Hayes, Forrest G. III, Mark, Kenneth; m. Carmen Bergen, Apr. 30, 1988. BS in Engring., U.S. Naval Acad., 1952; postgrad., Wichita State U., 1957-58, U. Colo., 1958-64. Commd. ensign USN, 1952, res., 1957; planner, engr. Boeing Corp., Wichita, Kans., 1957-58; engr., logistician Martin-Marietta, Denver, 1959-65; div. dir. Computer Scis., Washington, 1965-73; program dir. Systems Cons., Washington, 1973-76; CEO Am. Sys. Corp., Washington, 1976-92, chmn., bd. dirs., 1992—. Mem. Profl. Svcs. Coun. (vice chmn. 1990), Naval Submarine League (bd. dirs. 1982-90). Roman Catholic. Home: 8 Hidden Vly Palmyra VA 22963-9500

RAMSEY, FRANK ALLEN, veterinarian, retired army officer; b. Rocksprings, Tex., May 1, 1929; s. Reynolds Allen and June (Burdette) R.; m. Lucette C. Reboul, Jan. 1958; children: Randal R., Ramsay A.; m. 2d, Mary Lou Cain, June 1991. D.V.M., Tex. A & M U., 1954; grad., U.S. Army Command and Gen. Staff Coll., 1965, U.S. Army War Coll., 1972. Commd. 1st. lt. U.S. Army Vet. Corps, 1955, advanced through grades to brig. gen., 1980; chief vet. service Ft. Leonard Wood, Mo., 1958-61; acad. vet. U.S. Mil. Acad., West Point, N.Y., 1962-64; vet. staff officer U.S. Army Combat Devel. Command Med. Service, Ft. Sam Houston, Tex., 1965-67; asst. chief profl. programming and planning br. Office Surgeon Gen., Washington, 1967-68, chief profl. programming and planning br., 1968-71, chief food inspection policy office, 1972-73, sr. vet. staff officer, 1973-77; asst. chief of staff Vet. Service, 7th Med. Command, Army Europe and 7th Army, Heidelberg, W. Ger., 1977-80; asst. for vet. services to surgeon gen. and chief U.S. Army Vet. Corps, Hdqrs. Dept. Army, Washington, 1980-85; ret., 1985. Decorated Army Commendation medal, Legion of Merit with oak leaf cluster, D.S.M. Mem. AVMA, Assn. Fed. Veterinarians, Assn. Mil. Surgeons U.S., Assn. Equine Practitioners, Am. Assn. Food Hygiene Veterinarians, Conf. Pub. Health Veterinarians, Tex. Vet. Med. Assn. Presbyterian. Lodge: Masons (32 degree). Home: 8 El Norte Cir Uvalde TX 78801-4021

RAMSEY, GEORGE BERNARD, financial planning consultant; b. Phila., Nov. 22, 1931; m. Josephine Marie Martinelli, Sept. 22, 1960; children: G. Christopher, J. Timothy. AS, Valley Forge Mil. Acad., 1950; BA, U. Pa., 1954. With IDS Fin. Svcs. Inc. (now Am. Express Fin. Advisors, Inc.), 1963—; tng. mgr. IDS Fin. Svcs. Inc., 1964-66, divsn. v.p., 1969-87; pers. and bus. fin. planner Am. Express Fin. Advisors, Inc., Sea Isle City, N.J., 1987—. Contbr. numerous articles to profl. publs. Mem. Nat. Assn. Securities Dealers, Internat. Assn. for Fin. Planning, Sea Isle C. of C., Cape May County C. of C., South Jersey C. of C., Valley Forge Mil. Acad. Alumni Assn., Sea Isle City Civic Clubs, Sigma Phi Epsilon. Avocations: fishing, golf, boating, continued career advancement courses, music. Home: 52d St and Atlantic Ocean Sea Isle City NJ 08243 Office: Am Express Fin Advisors 3514 Landis Ave Ste 4 Sea Isle City NJ 08243-2178 also: 275 Forest Hills Blvd Naples FL 33962

RAMSEY, HENRY, JR., university official, lawyer, retired judge; b. Florence, S.C., Jan. 22, 1934; s. Henry Ramsey and Mary Ann Brunson; reared by Charles Arthur and and Nellie Tillman; m. Evelyn Yvonne Lewis, June 11, 1961 (div. Sept. 1967); children: Charles, Githaiga, Robert, Ismail; m. Eleanor Mason Ramsey, Sept. 7, 1969; children: Yetunde, Abeni. Student, Howard U.; BA, U. Calif., Riverside, 1960; LLB, U. Calif., 1963; student Inst. Edn. Mgmt., Harvard U., 1992; LLD, William Mitchell Coll. Law, 1996. Bar: Calif., 1964, U.S. Supreme Ct., 1967. Dep. dist. atty. Contra Costa County, Calif., 1964-65; pvt. practice Ramsey & Rosenthal, Richmond, Calif., 1965-71; prof. law U. Calif., Berkeley, 1971-80; judge Superior Court County of Alameda State Calif., Oakland, 1980-90; dean Sch. Law, Howard U., Washington, 1990—, v.p. for legal affairs, acting gen. counsel, 1994-95; vis. prof. law U. Tex., Austin, 1977, U. Colo., Boulder, 1977-78, Am. Indian Law Ctr., U. N.Mex., 1980; mem., pres. Coun. Legal Edn., Opportunity, Washington, 1987-93; chair Law Sch. Admission Coun.-Bar Passage Rate Study Group, 1990-93; mem. Fellows of Am. Bar Found. Adv. Rsch. Com., 1995—; panelist Washington, D.C. region Ctr. for Pub. Resources, Institute for Dispute Resolution. Mem. City Coun. Berkeley, 1973-77, Criminal Justice Planning Bd., County of Alameda, 1973-76; trustee City of Berkeley Libr., 1973-74, Fibreboard Asbestos Compensation Trust, 1994—; bd. dirs. Redevel. Agy., Berkeley, 1971-73. With USAF, 1951-55. Recipient Jefferson Jurist award Calif. Assoc. Black Lawyers, 1986, Disting. Alumnus award U. Calif., 1987, Disting. Svc. award Wiley Manuel Law Found., 1987. Mem. ABA (mem. sect. legal edn. and admissions to bar 1982—, chair 1991-92, mem. standards rev. com. 1992-95), Nat. bar Assn., Nat. Ctr. State Cts. (mem. commn. trial ct. performance stds. 1987-95, Dist. Svc. award 1990), Am. Law Inst., Am. Judicature Soc., Calif. Judges Assn., Cosmos Club, Fed. City Club, Alpha Phi Alpha. Democrat. Avocations: cooking, reading, gardening, travel. Office: Howard U Sch of Law 2900 Van Ness St NW Washington DC 20008-1106

RAMSEY, IRA CLAYTON, retired pipeline company executive; b. Quitman, Ga., May 13, 1931; s. James Redding and Ruth Frances (Treadaway) R.; m. Marianne Vinzant, Dec. 23, 1962; children: Clayton Hamilton, Robin Leigh. BBA, U. Ga., Atlanta, 1954; LLB, Atlanta Law Sch., 1950; postgrad., U. Tex., 1968, U. Pitts., 1973. With Plantation Pipe Line Co., Atlanta, 1948—, asst. sec., 1967-70, treas., contr., 1970-90, v.p. fin., 1990-96. Trustee Ga. Found. for Ind. Colls. With U.S. Army, 1954-56. Mem. Fin. Execs. Inst. Baptist. Home: 780 Wesley Oak Rd NW Atlanta GA 30328-4738

RAMSEY, JACKSON EUGENE, management educator; b. Cin., Dec. 20, 1938; s. Leonard Pershing and Edna Willa (Blakeman) R.; m. Inez Mae Linn, Apr. 22, 1961; children: John Earl, James Leonard. BS in Metall. Engring., U. Cin., 1961; MBA, SUNY-Buffalo, 1969, PhD, 1975. Registered profl. engr., Va., Ohio. Welding engr. Gen. Electric Co., Cin., 1961-62, Westinghouse-Bettis Lab., Pitts., 1962-66; prodn. control mgr. Columbus-McKinnon Corp., Buffalo, 1966-71; asst. prof. mgmt. SUNY, Buffalo, 1971-73; prof. mgmt. James Madison U., Harrisonburg, Va., 1973—, provost; cons. in field. Chmn. Harrisonburg Reps., 1978-86, vice chmn., 1974-78; vice chmn. 6th Dist. Rep. Com., 1984-94. Served with USMCR, 1956-62. Named Outstanding Young Scholar, Xerox Corp., 1976. Mem. Acad. of Mgmt., Am. Inst. for Decision Scis., Inst. of Mgmt. Sci., Am. Soc. for Metals, Nat. Soc. Profl. Engrs. Republican. Baptist. Author: R D Strategic Decision Criteria, 1986; Handbook for Professional Managers, 1985; Budgeting Basics, 1985; Library Planning and Budgeting, 1986. Contbr. articles to profl. jours. Home: 282 Franklin St Harrisonburg VA 22801-4019 Office: James Madison U Coll Intergrated Sci & Tech Harrisonburg VA 22807

RAMSEY, JAROLD WILLIAM, English language educator, author; b. Bend, Oreg., Sept. 1, 1937; s. Augustus S. and Wilma E. (Mendenhall) R.; m. Dorothy Ann Quinn, Aug. 16, 1959; children: Kate, Sophia, John. B.A. with honors, U. Oreg., 1959; Ph. D., U. Wash., 1966. Acting instr. U. Wash., Seattle, 1963-65; asst. prof. English U. Rochester, (N.Y.), 1965-70, assoc. prof., 1970-81; prof. U. Rochester, (N.Y.), 1981—, dir. undergrad. rsch., 1990—; vis. prof. English U. Victoria, B.C., Can., 1974, 75-76; dir. NEH summer seminars on Indian lit., 1985, 88. Author: The Space Between Us, 1970, Love in an Earthquake, 1973 (Lillian Fairchild award 1973), Dermographia, 1982, Reading the Fire, 1983, Hand-shadows, 1989, (play) Coyote Goes Upriver, premier 1985, (cantata) (with Samuel Adler) The Lodge of Shadows, premiere 1988; editor: Coyote Was Going There, 1977, Nehalem Tillamook Tales, 1990, The Stories We Tell: Oregon Folk Literature (with Suzi Jones), 1994. Recipient Don Walker award Western Am. Lit., 1979, Borestone Mount Found. Best Poems award, 1972, 75, 76; Helen Bullis prize, 1984, Poetry prize Quar. Rev., 1989; Alumni Achievement award U. Oreg. Alumni Assn, 1990; Nat. Endowment Arts writing grantee, 1974, 76; Ingram Merrill Found. writing grantee, 1976. Mem. MLA (chair com. on lits. and langs. of Am. 1991-92), Assn. Study Am. Indian Lit. (pres. 1981), Am. Folklore Soc., Phi Beta Kappa. Democrat. Home: 519 Wellington Ave Rochester NY 14619-1828 Office: U Rochester English Dept Rochester NY 14619

RAMSEY, JERRY VIRGIL, educator, financial planner, radio broadcaster; b. Tacoma, July 24, 1940; s. Virgil Emory and Winifred Victoria (Carothers) R.; m. Elaine Sigrid Perdue, June 24, 1967; 1 child, Jason Perdue. BA in Elem. Edn., U. Puget Sound, 1967; MEd in Tchr. Tng. and Curriculum Devel., U. Wash., 1971; PhD in Econ. Geography, Columbia Pacific U., 1995. Tchr. Tacoma Pub. Schs., 1967-95; fin. planner Primerica Corp., Tacoma, 1986-90, Gig Harbor Fin. Svcs., 1986—, Waddell & Reed, Inc., Tacoma, 1990-93; N.Am. Mgmt., 1993—; real estate investor, CEO Ramsey Properties, Gig Harbor, Wash., 1970—; radio broadcaster KGHP, KJUN/ The Country Club Network, KMAS, 1990—; lectr. Pacific Luth. U., Tacoma, 1972-86. Precinct committeeman Pierce County Rep. Com., Tacoma, 1968-78, 95—; mem. steering com. Peninsula Neighborhood Assn., Gig Harbor, Wash., 1991-92. With USAF, 1959-62. Recipient Golden Acorn award PTA, 1975, Meritorious Teaching award Nat. Coun. Geog. Edn., 1978, achievement award Rep. Nat. Com., 1985; grantee U.S. Office Edn., 1971. Mem. NEA (life), Knife and Fork Club (pres. 1983), Kiwanis (pres. Tacoma 1976), Phi Delta Kappa. Methodist. Avocation: real estate investing, management and education. Office: Ramsey Properties Gig Harbor Fin Svcs PO Box 1311 Gig Harbor WA 98335-3311

RAMSEY, JOHN ARTHUR, lawyer; b. San Diego, Apr. 1, 1942; s. Wilbert Lewis and Lillian (Anderson) R.; m. Nikki Ann Ramsey, Feb. 9, 1943; children: John William, Bret Anderson, Heather Nichole. AB, San Diego State U., 1965; JD, Calif. Western Sch. Law, 1969. Bar: Colo. 1969, Tex. 1978. Assoc., Henry, Cockrell, Quinn & Creighton, 1969-72; atty. Texaco Inc., 1972-80, asst. to pres. Texaco U.S.A., 1980-81, asst. to div. v.p., Houston, 1981-82, div. atty., Denver, 1982-88; ptnr. Holland & Hart, 1989—. Bd. dirs. Selective Service, Englewood, Colo., 1972-76; chmn. council Bethany Lutheran Ch., Englewood, 1976. Mem. ABA (vice chmn. oil, natural gas exploration and prodn. com. sect. natural resource law 1983-88, chmn. 1989—, coun. sect. natural resources, energy and environ. law 1993). Republican. Editor-in-chief: Calif. Western Law Rev., 1969. Office: Holland & Hart 555 17th St Ste 2900 Denver CO 80202-3929

RAMSEY, JOHN HANSBERRY, executive search firm executive, investment banker; b. Scranton, Pa., May 4, 1941; s. Robert Martin and Elizabeth Mary (Durrick) R.; children: Mark Joseph, Craig Andrew, Alison Dianne. B.S., Tufts U., 1963; M.B.A. with distinction, Harvard U., 1968. Commd. 2d lt. USAF, 1963, advanced through grades to maj., 1971, resigned, 1972; sr. v.p., treas., chief fin. officer Union Commerce Corp./ Bank, Cleve., 1972-81; sr. v.p. devel. Am. Savs. and Loan Assn. of Fla., 1982-84; co-founder, pres. Mark Stanley & Co., Miami, Fla., 1983—; co-founder EMA Ptnrs. Internat., 1988—; treas., dir. Union Commerce Leasing Corp., 1974-75; treas. Union Capital Mgmt. Corp., 1974-75. Participant Leadership Cleve., 1980-81; co-fin. chmn. Cuyahoga County George Bush for Pres. Campaign, 1980; trustee mem. Beacon Council. Decorated Bronze Star, AF Commendation Medal. Mem. Fin. Execs. Inst., Greater Miami C. of C., Venture Coun. Forum, Harvard Club N.Y., Harvard Bus. Sch. So. Fla. Republican. Office: Mark Stanley & Co PO Box 149071 Coral Gables FL 33114-9071

RAMSEY, LISTON BRYAN, state legislator; b. Marshall, N.C., Feb. 26, 1919; s. John Morgan and Della Lee (Bryan) R.; m. Florence McDevitt; 1 childm Martha Louise Ramsey Geouge. Student, Mar Hill Coll., 1936-38. Mem. N.C. Ho. of Reps., Raleigh, 1961—, speaker of House, 1981-88; exec. com. So. Legis. Conf., 1981-88; chmn. 11th congl. dist. Dem. Exec. Com., 1972, 74, 76, 80; del. Dem. Nat. Conv., 1968; mem. Govtl. Ops. Commn., 1973-76, 95-96; co-chmn., 1981-88; co-chmn. Legis. Svcs. Commn., 1971, 73-74, 75-76, 81-88, Legis. Rsch. Commn., 1975-76, 81-88, Joint Com. on Separation Powers, 1982; mem. Adv. Budget Commn., 1973-80, 91—, Blue Ribbon Study Commn. on Transp., 1979-80. County chmn. Dem. Exec.

Com., 1958-60, 62; bd. alderman Town of Marshall, 1949-61. Served as sgt. U.S. Army, 1944-46. Recipient Roy A. Taylor Service award, 1978, N.C. Pub. Service award, 1985, Friend Edn. award N.C. Assn. Edn., 1985; Liston B. Ramsey Regional Activity Ctr., Western Carolina U. dedicated and named after him, 1986. Mem. Am. Legion, VFW, N.C. AFL-CIO (hon.). Baptist. Lodges: Elks, Masons. Office: NC Ho of Reps State Legislative Bldg Raleigh NC 27601-1096

RAMSEY, LLOYD BRINKLEY, retired savings and loan executive, retired army officer; b. Somerset, Ky., May 29, 1918; s. William Harold and Mary Ella (Barnett) R.; m. Glenda Burton, Feb. 22, 1941; children: Lloyd Ann (Mrs. Kyle D. Wallace), Larry Burton, Judi Carol (Mrs. David E. Derr). A.B., U. Ky., 1940; postgrad., Yale U., 1946, Command and Gen. Staff Coll., Ft. Leavenworth, Kans., 1949-50, U.S. Army War Coll., Carlisle Barracks, Pa., 1953-54, Harvard, 1961. Commd. 2d lt. U.S. Army, 1940, advanced through grades to maj. gen., 1968; bn. comdr. 7th Inf., 3d Inf. Div., 1944-45; instr. Inf. Sch., Ft. Benning, Ga., 1946-49; assigned Office G-2 Dept. Army Gen. Staff, 1950-53; sec. joint staff UN Far East Command, 1954-57; comdg. officer 1st Inf. Brigade, 1957-58; with Office Chief Legis. Liaison, Dept. Army Gen. Staff, 1960-63, Office Asst. Chief Staff Force Devel., 1963-64; dep. chief information, 1966-67; div. comdr. Am. 23d Div., Vietnam, 1969-70; provost marshall gen. Army, Washington, 1970-74; ret. Army, 1974; chmn. bd. McLean Savs. & Loan Assn., Va., 1974-88. Decorated D.S.M. with oak leaf cluster, Silver Star medal with two oak leaf clusters, Legion of Merit with oak leaf cluster, D.F.C., Bronze Star medal with three oak leaf clusters, Air medal with 16 oak leaf clusters, Army Commendation medal with oak leaf cluster, Purple Heart with four oak leaf clusters, Combat Inf. badge; mem. Order Brit. Empire; Croix de Guerre France; Vietnamese Nat. Order; Vietnamese Armed Forces Honor medal; Vietnamese Gallantry Cross with palm. Mem. Sigma Chi, Omicron Delta Kappa. Baptist. Home: 6451 Dryden Dr Mc Lean VA 22101-4625 *Accept a man for what he is, not for what you want him to be.*

RAMSEY, MARJORIE ELIZABETH, early childhood education educator; b. Kimball, Minn., May 25, 1921; d. William Emil and Emma Edith (Ryti) Leppa; children: Rebecca, Cynthia. B.S., St. Cloud State Coll., 1955, M.S., 1957; Ed.D. (Ford Found. fellow), George Peabody Coll., 1961. Tchr., prin., vis. lectr. Minn., 1940-57; asst. prof. St. Cloud State Coll., Minn., 1957-59; supr. edn. Montgomery County, Md., 1961-64; research assoc. George Peabody Coll., Nashville, 1964-68; supr. Vanderbilt U., Nashville, 1964-69; assoc. prof. early childhood edn. Kent (Ohio) State U., 1969-73, prof., 1973-79, dean student pers. Coll. Edn., 1973-79; head div. edn., dir. tchr. edn. Ga. Southwestern Coll., Americus, 1979-89, Ga. Adv. Coun. Edn., 1983-89. Author: Music: A Way of Life for the Young Child, 1978, 4th edit., 1991, Kindergarten: Programs and Practices, 1980; contbr. articles to profl. jours. Mem. AAUW, Edn. Internat. (publs. com. 1980-86), Mid-South Writers Assn. Home: 242 S Reese St Memphis TN 38111-4517

RAMSEY, MARL, school system administrator. Supt. Osseo Area Schs. # 279, Maple Grove, Minn. State finalist Nat. Supt. of Yr., 1993. Office: Osseo Area Schs # 279 11200 93rd Ave N Osseo MN 55369-3669

RAMSEY, NORMAN F., physicist, educator; b. Washington, Aug. 27, 1915; s. Norman F. and Minna (Bauer) R.; m. Elinor Jameson, June 3, 1940 (dec. Dec. 1983); children: Margaret, Patricia, Janet, Winifred; m. Ellie Welch, May 11, 1985. AB, Columbia U., 1935; BA, Cambridge (Eng.) U., 1937, MA, 1941, DSc, 1954; PhD, Columbia U., 1940; MA (hon.), Harvard U., 1947; DSc (hon.), Case Western Res. U., 1968, Middlebury Coll., 1969, Oxford (Eng.) U., 1973; DCL (hon.), Oxford (Eng.) U., 1990; DSc (hon.), Rockefeller U., 1986, U. Chgo., 1989, U. Sussex, 1990, U. Houston, 1991, Carleton Coll., 1991, Lake Forest Coll., 1992, U. Mich., 1993, Phila. Coll. Pharmacy & Sci., 1995. Kellett fellow Columbia U., 1935-37, Tyndall fellow, 1938-39; Carnegie fellow Carnegie Inst. Washington, 1939-40; assoc. U. Ill., 1940-42; asst. prof. Columbia U., 1942-46; assoc. MIT Radiation Lab., 1940-43; cons. Nat. Def. Research Com., 1940-45; expert cons. sec. of war, 1942-45; group leader, asso. div. head Los Alamos Lab., 1943-45; assoc. prof. Columbia U., 1945-47; head physics dept. Brookhaven Nat. Lab. of AEC, 1946-47; assoc. prof. physics Harvard U., 1947-50, prof. physics, 1950-66, Higgins prof. physics, 1966—; sr. fellow Harvard Soc. of Fellows, 1970—; Eastman prof. Oxford U., 1973-74; Luce prof. cosmology Mt. Holyoke Coll., 1982-83; prof. U. Va., 1983-84; dir. Harvard Nuclear Lab., 1948-50, 52-53, Varlan Assos., 1963-66; mem. Air Forces Sci. Adv. Com., 1947-54; sci. adviser NATO, 1958-59; mem. Dept. Def. Panel Atomic Energy; exec. com. Cambridge Electron Accelerator and gen. adv. com. AEC. Author: Nuclear Moments and Statistics, 1953, Nuclear Two Body Problems, 1953, Molecular Beams, 1956, 85, Quick Calculus, 1965; contbr.: articles Phys. Rev.; other sci. jours. on nuclear physics, molecular beam experiments, radar, nuclear magnetic moments, radiofrequency spectroscopy, masers, nucleon scattering. Trustee Asso. Univs., Inc., Brookhaven Nat. Lab., Carnegie Endowment Internat. Peace, 1962-85, Rockefeller U., 1977-90; pres. Univs. Research Assocs., Inc., 1966-72, 73-81, pres. emeritus, 1981—. Recipient Presdl. Order of Merit for radar devel. work, 1947, E.O. Lawrence and AEC, 1960, Columbia award for excellence in sci., 1980, medal of honor IEEE, 1983, Rabi prize, 1985, Monte Ferst award, 185, Compton medal, 1985, Rumford premium, 1985, Oersted medal, 1988, Nat. medal of Sci., 1988, Nobel prize for Physics, 1989, Pupin medal Columbia Engrng. Sch. Alumni Assn., 1992, Sci. for Peace prize, 1992, Einstein medal, 1993, Vannevar Bush award, 1995, Alexander Hamilton award, 1995; Guggenheim fellow Oxford U., 1954-55. Fellow Am. Acad. Sci., Am. Phys. Soc. (coun. 1956-60, pres. 1978-79, Davisson-Germer prize 1974); mem. NAS, French Acad. Sci., Am. Philos. Assn., AAAS (chmn. physics sect. 1977), Am. Inst. Physics (chmn. bd. govs. 1980-87), Phi Beta Kappa (senator 1979-88, v.p. 1982-85, pres. 1985-88), Sigma Xi. Home: 24 Monmouth Ct Brookline MA 02146-5634 Office: Harvard U Lyman Physics Lab Cambridge MA 02138

RAMSEY, PAUL GLENN, internist; b. Pitts., 1949. MD, Harvard U., 1975. Diplomate Am. Bd. Internal Medicine. Intern Cambridge Hosp., 1975-76; resident in medicine Mass. Gen. Hosp., Boston, 1976-78; resident in medicine U. Wash., Seattle, 1980-81, fellow infectious diseases, 1978-80, prof., 1991—, chmn. dept. medicine, 1992—; physician-in-chief U. Wash. Med. Ctr., 1992—. Mem. ACP, AFCR, AAP, ADA, APM, SGIM. Office: U Wash Hosp RG-20 Dept Medicine Seattle WA 98165

RAMSEY, PETER CHRISTIE, bank executive; b. N.Y.C., Oct. 1, 1942; s. Norman Carnegie and Rosalie Amelia (Christie) R.; m. Maryalice Ives, Nov. 15, 1969. BA, Brown U., 1964. Mgmt. trainee Irving Trust Co., N.Y.C., 1965-67; account exec. Hayden Stone, N.Y.C., 1967-72; regional sales mgr. Autex, Inc., Chgo., 1972-78; v.p. Chem. Bank, N.Y.C., 1978—. Mem. coun. of chairs YMCA Greater N.Y., N.Y.C., 1987-90; chmn. bd. mgrs. McBurney YMCA, N.Y.C., 1980-92. Mem. Brown U. Club. Home: 345 E 80th St New York NY 10021-0644

RAMSEY, ROBERT LEE, judge, lawyer; b. Glen. Allen, Va., Jan. 9, 1929; s. Hubert Smith and Louise Estelle (Ennis) R.; m. Dorothea Catherine Cherubini, Mar. 28, 1958 (div. 1972); children: Craig John, Matthew Lee, Scott Garrett; m. Lynn Marie Giubbini, July 15, 1978. BA, Hofstra U., 1954; LLB, Union U., 1957, JD, 1968; MPA, SUNY-Albany, 1966; LLM, So. Meth. U., 1969. Bar: N.Y. 1958, Tex. 1970, Calif. 1990. Assoc. Kouray & Kouray, Schenectady, 1957-60; spl. agt. FBI, U.S. Dept. Justice, Washington, 1960-64; asst. atty. gen. State of N.Y., Albany, 1964-65; ptnr. Kalteux & Ramsey, Schenectady, 1965-68; chief asst. dist. atty. Schenectady County, N.Y., 1965-68; asst. gen. counsel Internat. Air Transport Assn., Montreal, Que., Can., 1969-70; sr. atty. Air Transport Assn. Am., Washington, 1970; sole practice Dallas, 1970-76; adminstrv. law judge U.S. Dept. Labor, San Francisco, 1976-77; adminstrv. law judge U.S. Dept. Labor, Washington, 1977-81, chmn., chief adminstrv. appeals judge Benefits Rev. Bd., 1981-88; adminstrv. law judge U.S. Dept. Labor, San Francisco, 1988-89; ptnr. Mullen & Filippi, San Francisco, 1989-91; adminstrv. law Judge Calif. Pub. Utilities Commn., San Francisco, 1991; mem. adj. faculty So. Meth. U. Sch. Law, 1970-75;. Served with USMC, 1946-48, 50-52. Mem. ABA, State Bar Tex., State Bar Calif., Fed. Adminstrv. Law Judges Conf. Republican. Presbyterian. Home: 4725 Fairway Dr Rohnert Park CA 94928-1304 Office: Calif Pub Utilities Commn 505 Van Ness Ave San Francisco CA 94102-3214

RAMSEY, SANDRA LYNN, psychotherapist; b. Camp LeJeune, N.C., Feb. 7, 1951; d. Robert A. and Lola J. (Hann) R.; m. Edward G. Schmidt, July 9, 1988; children: Seth, Sarah, Anna, Rachel. Student, U. Calif., Long Beach, 1969-70, Orange Coast Coll., Costa Mesa, Calif., 1971-72; BA in Psychology with distinction, U. Nebr., 1987, MA in Counseling Psychology, 1989. Vol. coord., client adv. Rape/Spouse Abuse Crisis Ctr., Lincoln, 1989-90; mental health therapist Health Am., HMO, Lincoln, 1991-94; pvt. practice, Lincoln, 1994—; adj. faculty S.E. Cmty. Coll; contract therapist Lincoln Pediatric Group, 1990-91, Family Svc. Assn., Lincoln, 1990-91, Cmty. Preservation Assocs., Lincoln, 1991-94. Mem. Nebr. Domestic Violence Sexual Assault Coalition; vol. ARC Disaster Mental Health Svcs. Portenier scholar U. Nebr., 1986-87. Mem. APA (assoc., divsn. 50 addictions), Am. Assn. Sex Educators, Counselors, and Therapists, Assn. Pvt. Practice Therapists, Nebr. Assn. for Counseling and Devel., Am. Mental Health Counselors Assn., Sex Info. and Edn. Coun. of the U.S., Golden Key, Psi Chi. Avocations: gardening, reading, travel.

RAMSEY, STEPHEN DOUGLAS, lawyer, environmental manager; b. Oklahoma City, Okla., May 10, 1947; s. Oliver F. and Gladys O'Neil (Smith) R.; m. Abigail Havens, June 11, 1977 (div. 1983); 1 child, Andrew Havens; m. Ann Jones, Nov. 4, 1990. AB, Princeton U., 1969; JD, U. Tex., 1978. Assoc. Coffee, Goldston & Bradshaw, Austin, Tex., 1972-77; atty. U.S. Dept. Justice, Washington, 1978-79, asst. chief pollution control sect., land and nat. resourses div., 1979-80, chief environ. enforcement sect., 1980-85; ptnr. Sidley & Austin, 1985-90; v.p. corp. environ. programs GE, 1990—. Author: Superfund Handbook, 1985. Mem. com. to nominate alumni trustees Princeton U., (N.J.), 1977-80; pub. weigher Travis County, Austin, Tex., 1972-74; bd. dirs. Clean Sites, Inc., 1991—, Environ. Law Inst., 1993—, Inst. For Sustainable Cmty, 1995—, Keystone Ctr., 1995—. Recipient Atty. Gen. Disting. Svc. award Dept. Justice, 1983. Mem. ABA (nat. resources and adminstrv. law sects., chmn. environ. values subcom.), Tex. Bar Assn., D.C. Bar Assn. Democrat. Baptist.

RAMSEY, WILLIAM DALE, JR., petroleum company executive; b. Indpls., Apr. 14, 1936; s. William Dale and Laura Jane (Stout) R.; m. Mary Alice Ihnet, Aug. 9, 1969; children: Robin, Scott, Kimberly, Jennifer. AB in Econs., Bowdoin Coll., 1958. With Shell Oil Co., 1958-95, salesman, Albany, N.Y., 1960, merchandising rep., Milton, N.Y., 1961-63, real estate and mktg. investments rep., Jacksonville, Fla., 1963-65, dist. sales supr., St. Paul, 1965-67, employee relations rep., Chgo., 1967-69, spl. assignment mktg. sfaff-adminstrn., N.Y.C., recruitment mgr., Chgo., 1970-72, sales mgr., Chgo., 1973-75, sales mgr., Detroit, 1975-79, dist. mgr. N.J. and Pa., Newark, 1979-84, Mid-Atlantic dist. mgr. (Md., D.C., Va.) 1984-87, econ. advisor head office, Houston, 1987-89; mgr. mktg. concepts head office, Houston, 1989-94, mgr. tech. head office, Houston, 1994-95, prin. Ramsey Cons., 1995—; dir. N.Am. Fin. Services, 1971-72; lectr., speaker on energy, radio, TV, appearances, 1972—; guest lectr. on bus. five univs., 1967-72; v.p., dir. Malibu East Corp., 1973-74; prin. Robotics Rsch. Consortium, 1991—; mem. Am. Right of Way Assn., 1963-65. James Bowdoin scholar Bowdoin Coll., 1958. Active Chgo. Urban League, 1971-75; mem. program com., bus. adv. council Nat. Rep. Congl. Com., 1981-87, rep. nat. com., 1994—; mem. Gov.'s Council on Tourism and Commerce, Minn., 1965-67; mem. Founders Soc., Detroit Inst. Arts, 1978-80; bd. dirs. N.J. Symphony Orch. Corp., 1981-85. Capt. U.S. Army, 1958-60. Mem. Internat. Svc. Robot Assn., N.J. Petroleum Council (exec. com. 1979-84 vice chmn. 1982-84), Midwest Coll. Placement Assn., Md. Petroleum Council (exec. com. 1984-87). Presbyterian. Clubs: Ponte Vedra (Fla.); Bowdoin Alumni (Houston); Morris County (N.J.) Golf; Kingwood (Tex.) Country, Houston Soc. Club; Bethesda (Md.) Country. Author: Corp. Recruitment and Employee Relations Organizational Effectiveness Study, 1969; Inventor 6 patents pending.

RAMSEY, WILLIAM EDWARD, retired naval officer, space systems executive; b. San Diego, Sept. 7, 1931; s. Paul Hubert and Isabelle (Turton) R.; m. Peggy Scott Booth, Oct. 23, 1954; children—Timothy Scott, William Blake, Christopher Booth. B.S., U.S. Naval Acad., 1953. Commd. ensign U.S. Navy, 1953, advanced through grades to vice adm., 1985; comdg. officer USS Pensacola, Little Creek, Va., 1972-73; instr. Naval War Coll., Newport, R.I., 1973-75; comdg. officer in USS Dwight D. Eisenhower, Norfolk, Va., 1975-79; comdr. Carrier Group One, Coronado, Calif., 1979-81; dir. Navy space systems div. Dept. Navy, Washington, 1981-85; dept. comdr.-in-chief U.S. Space Command, Peterson AFB, Colo., 1985-89; ret. U.S. Space Command, 1989; v.p., dir. space systems div. CTA, Inc., Rockville, Md., 1989—, also dir. corp. bus. devel. Decorated Bronze star, Air medal (11), Navy Commendation medal (3), Legion of Merit (2), Def. Disting. Svc. medal. Fellow Assn. Naval Aviation (trustee), Daedelian Soc., Soc. Exptl. Test Pilots; mem. Am. Inst. Aeros. and Astronautics, Tailhook Soc., Nat. Sec. Indsl. Assn., Armed Forces Commmunications and Elect. Assn. Episcopalian. Club: Nat. Space (bd. govs. 1983—). Avocations: golf; tennis. Home: 615 Bayshore Dr Pensacola FL 32507 Office: CTA Inc Space Systems Dv Rockville MD 20852

RAMSEY, WILLIAM RAY, professional society administrator; b. Minerva, Ohio, Aug. 25, 1926; s. Carl Andrew and Alwilda Pauline (Foss) R.; m. Betty Jane Hawkins, Dec. 2, 1950 (dec. Dec. 1975); children: Thomas, Kevin (dec.), Mary Joanne, Robert, Matthew; m. Linda Rae Foss, May 14, 1977. B.S., Mt. Union Coll., 1948; postgrad., Kent State U., 1948; M.H.A., Washington U., St. Louis, 1950; postgrad. in health systems mgmt, Harvard Bus. Sch., 1974. Exec. sec. King County Med. Soc., Seattle, 1953-61; field rep. AMA, Chgo., 1961-64; asst. dir. div. field service AMA, 1964-68; exec. dir. Am. Soc. Internal Medicine, San Francisco, 1968-78; exec. v.p. Am. Soc. Internal Medicine, Washington, 1978-85; ret., 1985. Served with USAAF, 1944; with USAF, 1950-53. Mem. Am. Assn. Med. Soc. Execs. (dir. 1978-81). Home: 16055 Volz Rd Moores Hill IN 47032

RAMSEYER, J. MARK, law educator; b. 1954. BA, Goshen Coll., 1976; AM, Mich. U., 1978; JD, Harvard U., 1982. Bar: Ill. 1983. Law clk. to Hon. S. Breyer U.S. Ct. Appeals (1st cir.), Boston, 1982-83; assoc. Sidley & Austin, Chgo., 1983-85; acting prof. UCLA, 1986-89, prof., 1989-92; prof. U. Chgo. Law Sch., 1992—. Office: U Chgo Law Sch 111 E 60th St Chicago IL 60637

RAMSIER, PAUL, composer, psychotherapist; b. Louisville, Ky., Sept. 23, 1927; s. Paul and Lucie (Herrmann) R. PhD., N.Y.U., 1972; MSW, SUNY, Stony Brook, 1976. Composer N.Y.C., 1950—, psychotherapist in pvt. practice, 1977—; adj. prof. music N.Y.U., 1970—. Composer numerous musical compositions including Divertimento Concertante on a Theme of Couperin, 1965, Road to Hamelin, 1978, Eusebius Revisited, 1980, Silent Movie, 1985, Zoo of Dreams, 1994, Stargazer, 1995. Huntington Hartford fellow, 1960, MacDowell fellow, 1963, Yaddo fellow, 1970; NEA grantee, 1975; recipient Disting. Alumnus award U. Louisville, 1983, Composer award Internat. Soc. Bassists, 1995. Mem. ASCAP. Home and Office: 210 Riverside Dr New York NY 10025-6802

RAMSTAD, JIM, congressman, lawyer; b. Jamestown, N.D., May 6, 1946; s. Marvin Joseph and Della Mae (Fode) R. BA, U. Minn., 1968; JD with honors, George Washington U., 1973. Bar: N.D. 1973, D.C. 1973, U.S. Supreme Ct. 1976, Minn., 1979. Adminstrv. asst. to speaker Minn. Ho. Reps., 1969; spl. asst. to Congressman Tom Kleppe, 1970; pvt. practice law, Jamestown, 1973, Washington, 1974-1978, Mpls., 1978-90; mem. Minn. Senate, 1981-90, asst. minority leader, 1983-87; mem. 102nd-103rd Congresses from 3rd Minn. dist., 1990—; adj. prof. Am. U., Washington, 1975-78. Bd. dirs. Children's Heart Fund, Lake Country Food Bank. Served as 1st lt. U.S. Army Res., 1968-74. Mem. Minn. Bar Assn., D.C. Bar Assn., N.D. Bar Assn., Hennepin County Bar Assn., U. Minn. Alumni Assn. (nat. dir.), Am. Legion, Wayzata C. of C., TwinWest C. of C., U. Minn. Alumni Club (past pres. Washington), Lions, Phi Beta Kappa, Phi Delta Theta. Republican. Office: 103 Cannon House Office Bldg Washington DC 20515

RAMUS, JOSEPH S., marine biologist; b. Grosse Pointe Farms, Mich., May 7, 1940; married; three children. AB, U. Calif., Berkeley, 1963, PhD in Botany, 1968. From asst. prof. to assoc. prof. biology Yale U., New Haven, 1968-78; from assoc. prof. to prof., acting dir. marine lab. Duke U., Beaufort, 1978-90; dir. marine lab. Duke U., Beaufort, N.C., 1990—. Mem. AAUP, Am. Soc. Limnology & Oceanology, Phycol. Soc. Am., Am. Geophys. Union. Office: Duke U Marine Lab Marine Lab 135 Duke Marine Lab Rd Beaufort NC 28516 Office: Duke U Marine Lab Piver's Island Beaufort NC 28516

RAN, SHULAMIT, composer; b. Tel Aviv, Oct. 21, 1949; came to U.S., 1963; m. Abraham Lotan, 1986. Studied composition with, Paul Ben-Haim, Norman Dello, Joio, Ralph Shapey; student, Mannes Coll. Music, N.Y.C., 1963-67. With dept. music U. Chgo., 1973—, William H. Colvin prof. music; composer-in-residence Chgo. Symphony Orch., 1990—, Lyric Opera of Chgo., 1994—. Compositions include 10 Children's Scenes, 1967, Structures,l 968, 7 Japanese Love Poems, 1968, Hatzvi Israel Eulogy, 1969, O the Chimneys, 1969, Concert Piece for piano and orch., 1970, 3 Fantasy Pieces for Cello and Piano, 1972, Ensembles for 17, 1975, Double Vision, 1976, Hyperbolae for Piano, 1976, For an Actor: Monologue for Clarinet, 1978, Apprehensions, 1979, Private Game, 1979, Fantasy-Variations for Cello, 1980, A Prayer, 1982, Verticals for piano, 1982, String Quartet No. 1, 1984, (for woodwind quintet) Concerto da Camera I, 1985, Amichai Songs, 1985, Amichai Songs, 1985, Concerto for Orchestra, 1986, (for clarinet, string quartet and piano) Concerto da Camera II, 1987, East Wind, 1987, String Quartet No. 2, 1988-89, Symphony, 1989-90, Mirage, 1990, Inscriptions for solo violin, 1991, Chicago Skyline for brass and percussion, 1991, Legends for Orch., 1992-93, Invocation, 1994, Yearning for violin and string orch.; commd. pieces include for Am. Composers Orch., Phila. Orch., Chgo. Symphony, Chamber Soc. of Lincoln Ctr., Mendelssohn String quartet, Da Capo Chamber Players, Sta. WFMT; composer and soloist for 1st performances Capriccio, 1963, Symphonic Poem, 1967, Concert Piece, 1971. Recipient Acad. Inst. Arts and Letters award, 1989, Pulitzer prize for music, 1991, Friedheim award for orchestral music Kennedy Ctr., 1992; Guggenheim fellow, 1977, 90. Office: U Chgo Dept Music 1010 E 59th St Chicago IL 60637-1404

RANBERG, CHUCK, television writer, producer. Writer (TV series) Kate and Allie, 1986-88, Working it Out, 1991, Baby Talk, 1991-92; co-prodr. (TV series) Frasier, 1992 (Emmy award for Outstanding Comedy Series 1995). Office: c/o Writers Guild Am 8955 Beverly Rd West Hollywood CA 90069*

RANCE, QUENTIN E., interior designer; b. St. Albans, Eng., Mar. 22, 1935; came to U.S., 1981; s. Herbert Leonard and Irene Ann (Haynes) R.; m. India Adams, May 17, 1974. Grad., Eastbourne (Eng.) Sch. Art, 1960. Soft furnishings buyer Dickeson & French Ltd., Eastbourne, 1960-61, outside sales mgr., 1961-62; design dir. Laszlo Hoenig, Ltd., London, 1962-73; mng. dir. Quentin Rance Interiors Ltd., London, 1973-81; pres. Quentin Rance Enterprises, Inc., Encino, Calif., 1981—. Works featured in Designers West, 1983, Design House Rev., 1983, Profiles mag., 1987, Nat. Assn. Mirror Mfrs. Jour., 1988, Designer Specifier, 1990. Mem. Founders for Diabetic Research/City of Hope. Served with RAF, 1953-55. Recipient Hon. Mention award Nat. Assn. Mirror Mfrs., 1987, 1st Pl. Nat. Pub. Svc. award, Designer Specifier, 1990. Fellow Chartered Soc. Designers (Eng.); mem. Am. Soc. Interior Designers (profl., chpt. bd. dirs. 1983-87, 89-91, chmn. Avanti 1983-85, admissions chmn. 1985—, Presdl. citations 1984, 87, 91, 95), Knights of Vine. Avocations: bicycling, antiques, fine wines, philately, theatre. Home and Office: 18005 Rancho St Encino CA 91316-4214 *Personal philosophy: Good design is always there to be seen, there to be appreciated, and there for expanding one's own boundaries of creativity.*

RANCK, EDNA RUNNELS, academic administrator, researcher; b. Waterville, Maine, Aug. 24, 1935; d. Everett Elias and Edna May (King) Runnels; m. James Gilmour Ranck, June 30, 1971 (dec. May 1979); children: Matthew, Christopher, Joshua Duggan; m. Martin Fleischer, Apr. 19, 1982; stepchildren: Christina, Laura Ranck. BA cum laude, Fla. State U., Tallahassee, 1957; MDiv magna cum laude, Drew U. Theol. Sch., Madison, N.J., 1971, MEd in Edn. Adminstrn., 1978; EdD in Curriculum and Teaching, Columbia U. Tchrs. Coll., N.Y.C., 1986. Dir. Collinsville Child Care Ctr., Morristown, N.J., 1971-78; exec. dir. Children's Svcs. Morris County, Morristown, N.J., 1980-84; co-mgr. N.J. Child Care Clearinghouse, Trenton; coord. N.J. Child Care Adv. Coun., Trenton, 1987-92; dir. N.J. Office Child Care Devel., Trenton, 1992; child care coord. N.J. Dept. Human Svcs., Trenton, 1992—; mem. adj. faculty Kean Coll. N.J., Union, 1983; dir. Sprout House Preschool, Chatham, N.J., 1984-87; mem. Morris County Human Svcs. Adv. Coun., Morristown, N.J., 1986-87. Author: Dodge Foundation Project, 1984; Young Children, 1987; contbr. articles to profl. jours. Mem. exec. bd. Drew U. Alumni Assn. Theol. Sch., 1986-92; mem. Drew U. Alumni Study Commn., 1993, Non-Govt. Orgn. rep. to UN Internat. Fedn. Educative Cmtys., 1992—. Recipient Volpe Commitment in Child Care award, N.J. Child Care Assn., 1991. Mem. Child Care Action Campaign Panel, Acad. Child and Youth Care Workers, Phi Beta Kappa, Pi Sigma Alpha. republican. United Methodist. Avocations: writing, travel, swimming, clothing design. Home: 15 Rosedale Ave Madison NJ 07940-2148 Office: NJ Dept Human Svcs 222 S Warren St CN700 Trenton NJ 08625-0700

RANCOURT, JAMES DANIEL, optical engineer. BA in Physics, Bowdoin Coll., 1963; MS in Physics, Carnegie Tech., 1965; PhD in Optical Scis., U. Ariz., 1974. Engr. Itek Corp., Lexington, Mass., 1965-69; rsch. assoc. U. Ariz., Tucson, 1969-74; engr. OCLI, Santa Rosa, Calif., 1970—. Author: Optical Thin Films Users Handbook, 1987; patentee in field. Fellow Optical Soc. Am. Achievements include 13 patents. Office: OCLI 2789 Northpoint Pky Santa Rosa CA 95407-7350

RAND, ALBERT, computer systems company executive; b. 1927. BS, MIT, 1950. With Gen. Electric Co., Lynn, Mass., 1956-60; assoc. Dynamics Rsch. Corp., Wilmington, Mass., 1960—, now CEO; now pres. Andover, MA. Office: Dynamics Research Corp 60 Frontage Rd Andover MA 01887*

RAND, CALVIN GORDON, arts and education producer and consultant; b. Buffalo, May 15, 1929; s. George Franklin and Isabel (Williams) R.; m. Patricia Clemens Andrew, Aug. 18, 1951; children—Robin, Melissa, Jennifer, Lucinda, Elizabeth. B.A., Princeton U., 1951; M.A., Columbia U., 1954; Dr of Letters (hon.), York U., Can., 1984. Head history dept. Riverdale Sch., N.Y.C., 1955-60; lectr. philosophy SUNY-Buffalo, 1961-68, acting dir. cultural affairs, 1968-71; founder, pres. The Niagara Inst., Niagara-on-the-Lake, Can., 1971-79; pres. Am. Acad. in Rome, N.Y.C., 1980-84; ind. producer, theatre and film cons., N.Y.C., 1985-90; founding chmn., dir. Shaw Festival Theatre, Niagara-on-the-Lake, 1964-78,. bd. govs., 1979; trustee Playwrights Horizons Theatre, N.Y.C., 1982-92; bd. dirs. Niagara Inst.; pres. Arts in Edn. Inst.; mem. N.Y. State Coun. on Arts, 1978-82, Arts Coun. Western N.Y., 1987-93; chmn. World Ency. Contemporary Theater; chmn. arts coun. SUNY, Buffalo, 1987—, adj. prof. theater, 1988—. Contbr. articles to profl. jours. Bd. dirs. Burchfield Art Ctr., Buffalo, 1991—, Irish Classical Theater, 1993—; trustee Albright-Knox Gallery, Buffalo, 1976-80, 84-88, 90-94. Recipient spl. citation Ont. Arts Coun., 1976, Fellowship Fund award Niagara Inst., 1980, Centennial Arts award Nichols Sch., 1992; named Man of Yr., Coun. World Affairs, 1976, Buffalo Courier Express, 1976, Arts Patron of Yr., Western N.Y. Arts Coun. and C. of C., 1989; Vanier Coll. fellow York U. Mem. Players Club, Princeton Club, Saturn Club. Home and office: 930 Fifth Ave New York NY 10021-2651

RAND, DUNCAN D., librarian; b. Biggar, Sask., Can., Oct. 28, 1940; s. Dawson Ellis and Elizabeth Edna (Gabie) R.; m. Nancy Jean Daugherty, Sept. 7, 1963; children: Jacqueline Nancy, Duncan Dawson, Thomas Nelson, John David, Jennifer Nancy. B.A., U. Sask., 1963; B.L.S., McGill U., 1964. Young adult librarian Regina Pub. Library, Sask., 1964-65; coordinator library services Regina Separate Sch. Bd., 1965-68; asst. chief librarian Regina Pub. Library, 1968-71; dep. dir. London Pub. Library and Art Mus., 1971-73, acting dir., 1973-74; chief librarian Lethbridge Pub. Library, Alta., 1974—; dir. So. Alta. Art Gallery. Editor: Sask. Geneal. Soc. Bull, 1968-71. Vice pres. Alta. council Boy Scouts. Mem. Libr. Assn. Alta (dir., pres. 1986-87), Can. Libr. Assn. (dir.), Can. Assn. Pub. Librs. (chair 1976-77), Sask. Geneal. Soc. (pres.), Assn. Profl. Librs. of Lethbridge (chmn. 1982-84), Samaritans (bd. dirs. 1993—), Allied Arts Coun. (bd. dirs. 1993—), Rotary, Ipaloh (archivist, sec. 1980-94). Office: 810 5th Ave S, Lethbridge, AB Canada T1J 4C4

RAND, HARRY ISRAEL, lawyer; b. N.Y.C., July 27, 1912; s. Samuel and Rose (Hirth) R.; m. Anna Tulman, Oct. 22, 1938; children: Steven, Deborah, Naomi. BS, CCNY, 1932; JD, NYU, 1936. Bar: N.Y. 1936, U.S. Supreme Ct. 1943, D.C. 1947, U.S. Dist. Cts. (so. and ea. dists.) N.Y. 1959, 60, U.S.

Ct. Appeals (2d cir.) 1966. Atty. U.S. Pub. Works Adminstrn., 1938-39, U.S. Dept. Interior, 1939-43, U.S. Dept. Justice, 1943-48; pvt. practice Washington, 1948-58; mem. Weisman, Celler, Allan, Spett & Sheinberg, N.Y.C., 1959-67, Botein, Hays & Sklar, N.Y.C., 1967-89; counsel Herrick, Feinstein, N.Y.C., 1990—. Mem. Assn. of Bar of City of N.Y., Am. Law Inst. Home: 66 Hillandale Rd Westport CT 06880-5319 also: 320 W 86th St New York NY 10024-3139 Office: Herrick Feinstein LLP Two Park Ave New York NY 10016

RAND, HARRY ZVI, art historian, poet; b. N.Y.C., Jan. 10, 1947; m. Jennifer Rand; 1 child, Leah Zoë. BA, CCNY, 1969; AM, Harvard U., 1971, PhD, 1974. Contbg. editor Arts mag., N.Y.C., 1975-91, 1975—; assoc. curator Nat. Mus. Am. Art, Washington, 1977-79, curator, 1979-93, chmn. dept., 1978-84, sr. curator, 1993—; adv. bd. mem. Awards in Visual Arts, Winston-Salem, N.C., 1982-92, Austrian Internat. Art Inst., 1989—; arts advisor Virlane Found., New Orleans, 1980—; cons. NAS, 1983, Cosanti Found., 1989—, Exodus Found., 1992—, World Bank, 1994—. Co-author: The Genius of American Painting, 1973; author: Seymour Lipton, 1979, Arshile Gorky, 1981, 91, Recent Trends in Collecting, 1982, The Beginning of Things, 1983, Martha Jackson Meml. Collection, 1985, Der Maler Hundertwasser, 1986, Manet's Contemplation at the Gare Saint-Lazare, 1987, paperback edit. 1991, Paul Manship, 1989, Julian Stanczak, 1990, Hundertwasser, 1991, 92, Jochen Seidel, 1992, Color, 1993; hon. editor Leonardo mag., 1983—; patentee in field. Bd. dirs. Soc. to Prevent Trade in Stolen Art, 1995. N.Y. State Regents scholar, 1965-68; travelling fellow Harvard U., 1973, Andrew W. Mellon Found. fellow, 1976-77; Rockefeller Found. devel. grantee, 1982-83, Rsch. Opportunities grantee Smithsonian Instn., 1985, 86, 87, 88, 89, 90, 91, 92, 94, 95, Spl. Scholarly Studies grantee, 1987—, Ednl. Outreach grantee, 1995. Fellow Explorers Club; mem. World Art Coun. (steering com. Geneva 1992—). Home: 5511 Greystone St Chevy Chase MD 20815-5556 Office: Nat Mus Am Art MRC 210 8th and G Sts NW Washington DC 20560

RAND, JOELLA MAE, nursing educator, counselor; b. Akron, Ohio, July 9, 1932; d. Harry S. and Elizabeth May (Miller) Halberg; m. Martin Rand; children: Craig, Debbi Stark. BSN, U. Akron, 1961, MEd in Guidance, 1968; PhD in Higher Edn. Adminstrn., Syracuse U., 1981. Staff nurse Akron Gen. Hosp., 1953-54; staff-head nurse-instr. Summit County Receiving, Cuyahoga Falls, Ohio, 1954-56; head nurse psychiat. unit Akron Gen. Hosp., 1956-57; instr. psychiatric nursing Summit County Receiving, Cuyahoga Falls, 1957-61; head nurse, in-service instr. Willard (N.Y.) State Hosp., 1961-62; asst. prof. Alfred (N.Y.) U., 1962-76, assoc. prof., assoc. dean, 1976-78, acting dean, 1978-79, dean, 1979-90, dean coll. profl. studies, 1990-91, prof. counseling, 1991—; cons. N.Y. State Regents Program for Non-Collegiate Sponsored Instrn., 1984; cons. collegiate programs N.Y. State Dept. Edn., 1985, Elmira Coll., 1991, U. Rochester, 1992-93; accreditation visitor Nat. League for Nursing, 1984-92; ednl. cons. Willard Psychiat. Hosp., 1992-93; mem. profl. practice exam. subcom. Regents Coll., 1990-95. Recipient Teaching Excellence award Alfred U., 1977, Mary E. Gladwin Outstanding Alumni award Akron U. Coll. Nursing, 1983, Alfred Alumni Friends award, 1989, Grand Marshall commencement Alfred U., 1993. Mem. N.Y. State Coun. of Deans (treas. 1984-88), Genesee Regional Consortium (v.p.), Western N.Y. League Nursing (bd. dirs. 1991-93), Genesee Valley Edn. Com. (chair 1984-86), Sigma Theta Tau (treas. Alfred chpt. 1984-85). Avocations: boating, fishing, public speaking in areas of family and child abuse. Office: Alfred U 343 Myers Hall Alfred NY 14802

RAND, KATHY SUE, public relations executive; b. Miami Beach, Fla., Feb. 24, 1945; d. William R. and Rose (Lasser) R.; m. Peter C. Ritsos, Feb. 19, 1982. BA, Mich. State U., 1965; M in Mgmt., Northwestern U., 1980. Asst. editor Lyons & Carnahan, Chgo., 1967-68; mng. editor Cahners Pub. Co., Chgo., 1968-71; pub. rels. writer Super Market Inst., Chgo., 1972-73; account supr. Pub. Communications Inc., Chgo., 1973-77; divisional mgr. pub. rels. Quaker Oats Co., Chgo., 1977-82; exec. v.p., dep. gen. mgr. Golin/Harris Communications, Chgo., 1982-90; exec. v.p. Lesnik Pub. Rels., Northbrook, Ill., 1990-91; mng. dir. Manning, Selvage & Lee, Chgo., 1991—. Dir. midwest region NOW, 1972-74; mem. Kellogg Alumni Adv. Bd.; bd. dirs. Jr. Achievement of Chgo. Mem. Pub. Rels. Soc. Am. (Silver Anvil award 1986, 87), Pub. Club Chgo. (Golden Trumpet awards 1982-87, 90, 94, 95), Northwestern Club Chgo., Kellogg Alumni Club, Beta Gamma Sigma. Home: 400 Riverwoods Rd Lake Forest IL 60045-2547

RAND, LAWRENCE ANTHONY, investor and financial relations executive; b. Bklyn., Nov. 19, 1942; s. Gerald M. and Elaine Shirley (Borenstein); m. Madelon L., July 4, 1942; children: Allan, Joshua, Emily. AB with honors, Brown U., 1964; MA, NYU, 1965, postgrad., 1966-67. Lectr. NYU, 1967, CUNY, 1968; analyst CIA, Langley, Va., 1967-68; account supr. Ruder & Finn Inc., N.Y.C., 1968-71; co-founder, sr. v.p. Kekst & Co, N.Y.C., 1971—, also bd. dirs.; chmn., bd. dirs. ALS Assn., L.A., 1987-92. Chmn. ethics com. Village of Rye Brook, N.Y. Mem. City Athletic Club, Brown U. Club, Bailiwick Club (Greenwich, Conn.). Office: Kekst & Co 437 Madison Ave New York NY 10022-7001

RAND, LEON, academic administrator; b. Boston, Oct. 8, 1930; s. Max B. and Ricka (Muscanto) Rakisky; m. Marian L. Newton, Aug. 29, 1959; children: Debra Ruth, Paul Martin, Marta Leah. B.S., Northeastern U., 1953; M.A., U. Tex., 1956, Ph.D., 1958. Postdoctoral fellow Purdue U., 1958-59; asst. prof. to prof. U. Detroit, 1959-68; prof., chmn. dept. chemistry Youngstown (Ohio) State U., 1968-74, dean grad. studies and research, 1974-81, acting acad. v.p., 1980; vice chancellor acad. affairs Pembroke (N.C.) State U., 1981-85; chancellor Ind. U.-S.E., New Albany, 1986-96; bd. dirs. INB Banking Co., Jeffersonville, Ind, Jewish Hosp., Louisville, Ky., 1991—. Bd. dirs., mem. exec. com. Louisville (Ind.) Area chpt. ARC; bd. dirs. Floyd Meml. Hosp., New Albany, 1987-90. Mem. Am. Chem. Soc., Am. Inst. Chemists, Metroversity (bd. dirs.), Sigma Xi, Phi Kappa Phi. Home: 3119 Brazil Lake Pky Georgetown IN 47122-8605 Office: Office of Chancellor Ind U SE New Albany IN 47150

RAND, PAUL, graphic designer, educator; b. N.Y.C., Aug. 15, 1914. Student, Pratt Inst., 1929-32, Art Students League, 1934; DFA (hon.), Phila. Coll. Art, Parson Sch. Design, U. Hartford Sch. Visual Arts, Kutztown U.; MA, Yale U.; postgrad., Pratt Inst., 1996. Art dir. Esquire/Apparel Arts; creative dir. William H. Weintraub Advt. Agy., N.Y.; prof. graphic design Sch. Art Yale U., New Haven, 1956-91, prof. emeritus; cons. IBM, 1956-92, Cummins Engine Co., 1962—, Westinghouse Electric, 1960-81, numerous others; tchr. Yale Summer Sch. Program, Brissago, Switzerland. Author: Thoughts on Design, 1946, Design and the Play Instinct, 1965, The Trademarks of Paul Rand, 1960, A Paul Rand Miscellany, 1984, Paul Rand: A Designer's Art, 1985, Design, Form and Chaos, 1993, From Lascaux to Brooklyn, 1996; contbr. numerous articles to profl. publs.; represented in permanent collections various museums, U.S., Europe and Japan. Pres.'s fellow RISD; recipient Florence prize for Visual Comm., City of Florence, 1987. Home: 87 Good Hill Rd Weston CT 06883

RAND, PETER ANDERS, architect; b. Hibbing, Minn., Jan. 8, 1944; s. Sidney Anders and Dorothy Alice (Holm) R.; m. Nancy Ann Straus, Oct. 21, 1967; children—Amy, Dorothy. B.A., St. Olaf Coll., 1966; cert. Oslo Internat. Summer Sch., Norway, 1964; student U. Minn. Sch. Architecture, 1969-72. Registered architect, Minn. Designer, architect, dir. pub. relations Setter, Leach & Lindstrom, Inc., Mpls., 1972-78; dir. bus. devel. and head Eden Prairie Office, Archtl. Design Group, Inc., Minn., 1979-80; dir. mktg. and publs. Minn. Soc. AIA, 1981-82, exec. dir., 1982-85, exec. v.p./CEO, 1986—; pub. Architecture Minn. mag.; cons., archtl. designer. Bd. dirs. Project for Pride in Living, 1979-88, chmn. 1980-86; trustee Bethlehem Luth. Ch., 1980-86, chmn. bd. trustees, 1985, chmn. com. on worship, 1993-96, mem. ch. coun., 1993-96; mem. Minn. Ch. Ctr. Commn., 1981-89, chmn., 1985-88; sec. Council of Component Execs. of AIA, 1987, 92; bd. dirs. Minn. Council of Chs. 1985-89, sec. 1989, Mpls. Council of Chs., 1985-88, Arts Midwest, 1987-96, treas. 1989, v.p. 1990-91, chmn., 1992-93; bd. dirs. Nordic Ctr., 1989—, Preservation Alliance of Minn., 1995—. Served with U.S. Army, 1966-69. Fellow AIA (jour. honor award 1981, Nat. Svc. award 1993); mem. MSAADA Architects & Engrs. (bd. dirs. 1994—), Minn. Soc. AIA, Nat. Trust Hist. Preservation, Torske Klubben. Home: 1728 Humboldt Ave S Minneapolis MN 55403-2809 Office: 275 Market St Ste 54 Minneapolis MN 55405-1627

RAND, PETER W., medical research administrator, cardiologist; b. Boston, Oct. 16, 1929; m. 1953. AB, Harvard U., 1951, MD, 1955. Intern Maine Med. Ctr., Portland, 1955-56, resident internal medicine, 1956-57, 59-60, dir. rsch. dept., 1965-89, chmn. pre-med., 1974—; asst. clin. prof. medicine Coll. Medicine U. Vt., 1972-80; adj. prof. applied immunology U. So. Maine, 1988—. Fellow cardiology Maine Med. Ctr., 1960-61, USPHS, 1961-63; grantee NIH, 1963. Mem. Am. Fedn. Clin. Rsch., Am. Physiol. Soc., Am. Heart Assn., Soc. Rheology, Microcirculation Soc. Office: ME Med Ctr Rsch Inst 22 Bramhall St Portland ME 04102*

RAND, PHILLIP GORDON, chemist; b. Meredith, N.H., Nov. 5, 1934; s. Roger Orville and Mary Isabel (Gordon) R.; m. Lela Joyce Magouirk, Aug. 14, 1955; children: Bruce Edward, Brenda Lea, Steven Alan. B.A., John Brown U., 1956; M.S., U. Wyo., 1958; Ph.D., Purdue U., 1963. With Miles Labs., Elkhart, Ind., 1963-89; prin. rsch. scientist Miles Labs., 1978-83, sr. devel. scientist, 1983-89; sales rep. Crain Industries, 1990-92; quality control technician Ross Labs., 1992-94; sr. scientist Environ. Test Systems, 1994—. Mem. Am. Chem. Soc. Republican. Methodist. Clubs: Toastmasters, Gideons. Patentee in field. Home: 1320 W Lexington Ave Elkhart IN 46514-2048

RAND, ROBERT WHEELER, neurosurgeon, educator; b. L.A., Jan. 28, 1923; s. Carl W. and Catherine (Humphrey) R.; m. Helen L. Pierce, Dec. 17, 1949; children: Carl W., Richard P. Student, Harvard U., 1940-42, UCLA, 1942-44; MD, U. So. Calif., 1947; MS, U. Mich., 1951, PhD in Anatomy, 1952; JD, U. West L.A., 1974. Intern, resident in neurosurgery U. Mich., Ann Arbor, 1947-52; from instr. to prof. neurol. surgery UCLA, 1953-89; expert witness malpractice cases Superior Ct. Author: Spinal Cord Tumors in Childhood, 1960, Microneurosurgery, 3d edit., 1985; contbr. articles to profl. jours.; inventor neuropledgets, thermomagnetic surgery coil system, microballoon for aneurysm occlusion, Malcolm-Rand graphite cranial frame, cobalt scalpel. Lt. comdr. USNR, 1943-46, 54-56. Recipient Profl. award UCLA, 1973. Fellow ACS; mem. AMA, Calif. Med. Assn., L.A. County Med. Assn., Am. Surg. Assn., Internat. Coll. Surgeons, Assn. Neurol. Surgeons, Soc. Neurol. Surgeons, Western Neurosurg. Soc., L.A. Country Club. Office: John Wayne Inst St John's Hosp 1328 22nd St Santa Monica CA 90404-2032

RAND, SIDNEY ANDERS, retired college administrator; b. Eldred, Minn., May 9, 1916; s. Charles William and Ida Alice (Pedersen) R.; m. Dorothy Alice Holm, Sept. 1, 1942 (dec. Jan. 1974); children: Peter Anders, Mary Alice; m. Lois Schiager Ekeren, Nov. 23, 1974. BA, Concordia Coll., Moorhead, Minn., 1938, DD (hon.), 1956; degree in theology, Luther Sem., St. Paul, 1943; LHD (hon.), Colo. Coll., 1976; LLD (hon.), Carleton Coll., 1980, St. Olaf Coll., 1980, Coll. of St. Scholastica, 1985; DTh (hon.), St. John's U., 1980; LHD (hon.), Augustana Coll., 1988. Faculty Concordia Coll., Moorhead, Minn., 1945-51; pres. Waldorf Coll., Forest City, Iowa, 1951-56; exec. dir. coll. edn. Am. Luth. Ch., Mpls., 1956-63; pres. St. Olaf Coll., Northfield, Minn., 1963-80; U.S. ambassador to Norway, Oslo, 1980-81; higher edn. cons. Mpls., 1981—; pres. Augustana Coll., Sioux Falls, S.D., 1986-87, 92-93, Suomi Coll., Hancock, Mich., 1990-91; sr. cons. Minn. Pvt. Coll. Council, St. Paul, 1981-87. Pastor Nashwauk (Minn.) Luth. Ch., 1943-45; pres. Fund for Theol. Edn., Princeton, N.J., 1984-87; mem. Gov.'s Tax Commn., Minn., 1984-85; chmn. Minn. Citizens for Ct. Reform, 1984-87. Decorated Comdr. Norwegian Order of Merit, 1986; named Knight 1st Class Order of St. Olaf Kingdom of Norway, 1974; recipient Wittenberg award, 1996. Mem. AIA (hon.), Phi Beta Kappa, Torske Klubben Club. Home: 19 S 1st St Apt 907B Minneapolis MN 55401-1839

RAND, WILLIAM, lawyer, former state justice; b. N.Y.C., Oct. 11, 1926; s. William and Barbara (Burr) R.; married; children: Alicia, Carley Coudert, William Coudert, Paula Burr. AB, Harvard U., 1948; LLB, Columbia U., 1951. Bar: N.Y. 1951, U.S. Dist. Ct. N.Y. 1951, U.S. Supreme Ct., 1958, U.S. Ct. Appeals (2d cir.) 1961, U.S. Ct. Appeals (4th cir.) 1985. Asst. dist. atty. New York County, 1954-59; asst. counsel to gov. of State of N.Y., 1959-60; assoc. Coudert Bros., N.Y.C., 1961-62, ptnr., 1963—; justice N.Y. County Supreme Ct., 1962; justice Village of Cove Neck, Oyster Bay, N.Y., 1974—. Mem. exec. com. New York County Reps., 1968-72. Served with USN, 1944-46, PTO. Clubs: Piping Rock (Locust Valley, N.Y.); Seawanhaka Corinthian Yacht (Oyster Bay); Racquet and Tennis (N.Y.C.). Home: 73 Cove Neck Rd Oyster Bay NY 11771-1821 Office: Coudert Bros 1114 Avenue Of The Americas New York NY 10036-7703

RANDA, RUDOLPH THOMAS, judge; b. Milw., July 25, 1940; s. Rudolph Frank and Clara Paula (Kojis) R.; m. Melinda Nancy Matera, Jan. 15, 1977; children—Rudolph Daniel, Daniel Anthony. B.S., U. Wis.-Milw., 1963; J.D., U. Wis.-Madison, 1966. Bar: Wis. 1966, U.S. Dist. Ct. (ea. and we. dists.) Wis., 1966, U.S. Ct. Appeals (7th cir.) 1973, U.S. Supreme Ct. 1973. Sole practice, Milw., 1966-67; prin. city atty. Office Milw. City Atty., 1970-75; judge Milw. Mcpl. Ct., 1975-79, Milwaukee County Circuit Ct., 1979-81, 1982-92, Appellate Ct., Madison, Wis., 1981-82; federal judge U.S. Dist. Ct. (ea. dist.) Wis., 1992—; chmn. Wis. Impact, Milw., 1980—; lectr. Marquette U. Law Sch., Milw., 1980—. Served to capt. U.S. Army, 1967-69, Vietnam. Decorated Bronze Star medal. Mem. Milw. Bar Assn., Wis. Bar Assn., Trial Judges Wis., Am. Legion (adjutant Milw. 1980), Thomas More Lawyers Soc. (former pres. Milw.), Milw. Hist. Soc., Phi Alpha Theta. Roman Catholic. Office: US Courthouse 517 E Wisconsin Ave Rm 247 Milwaukee WI 53202-4504

RANDALL, CAROLYN MAYO, chemical company executive; b. Atlanta, June 11, 1939; d. Frank and Winifred (Layton) Mayo; m. James Allen Hall, Dec. 28, 1960 (dec. 1973); children: James Allen Hall Jr., Christopher Mayo Hall, Charlotte Ann Hall O'Neal. BA, U. Ga., 1959. Ptnr. Mayo Chem. Co., Marietta, Ga., 1989—. Bd. dirs. Mayo Edn. Found; active Alliance Theater Atlanta, Salvation Army Aux., Voters Guild Met. Atlanta, Friendship Force Atlanta, Kennestone Hosp. Cancer Group, Am. Cancer Soc. Mem. Cobb County Gem & Mineral Soc. (trustee), S.E. Fedn. Mineralogical Soc. (historian), Atlanta Preservation Soc., Nat. Trust Historic Preservation, Ga. Trust Hist. Preservation, Nat. Meml. Day Assn., Better Films Assn. Met. Atlanta (bd. dirs.), Ret. Officers Assn. (ladies aux. bd. dirs.), Ga. Mineral Soc., Native Atlantians Club, 100 Club (pres.), The Frogg Club, Terrell Mill Estates Women's Club (bd. dirs.), Dobbins AFB OFficers Wives Club (bd. dirs.), Alpha Chi Omega, Atlanta Steinway Soc. (bd. dirs.), French-Am. Ch. of C., Raban Gap Nacoochee Guild, Freedoms Found. of Valley Forge, Atlanta Butterfly Club, Make A Wish Found., The Etowah Found., The Civil War Trust. Republican. Episcopal. Avocations: mineral and gem collecting, bridge. Home: 3244 Beechwood Dr Marietta GA 30067-5420

RANDALL, CHANDLER CORYDON, church rector; b. Ann Arbor, Mich., Jan. 22, 1935; s. Frederick Stewart and Madeline Leta (Snow) R.; m. Marian Archias Montgomery, July 2, 1960; children: Sarah Archais, Elizabeth Leggett, Rebekah Stewart. AB in History, U. Mich., 1957; S.T.B. in Theology, Berkeley Divinity at Yale U., 1960; PhD in Hebraic Studies, Hebrew Union Coll., 1969; D.D. (honoris causa), Berkeley Divinity at Yale U., 1985. Rector St. Paul's Episcopal Ch., Richmond, Ind., 1967-71; rector Trinity Episcopal Ch., Ft. Wayne, Ind., 1971-88, St. Peter's Episcopal Ch., Del Mar, Calif., 1988—; bd. dirs. Living Ch. Found., Milw.; bibl. theologian Episcopal Ch. Stewardship, N.Y.C., 1985; alumni coun. Berkeley Divinity at Yale, New Haven, Conn., 1981-87; bishop's cabinet Diocese of No. Ind., South Bend, 1983-87. Author: Satire in the Bible, 1969, An Approach to Biblical Satire, 1990; contbr. articles to profl. jours. Founder Canterbury Sch., Ft. Wayne, 1977; commr. Ind. Jud. Qualifications Commn., Indpls., 1981-87; pres. Ft. Wayne Plan Commn., 1977; bd. dirs. Ft. Wayne Park Found., 1983-88; platform com. Ind. Republican Party, Indpls., 1974. Recipient Disting. Svc. medal U. Mich., 1981, Scheuer scholar Hebrew Union Coll., 1963-66, Liberty Bell award Ft. Wayne Bar Assn., 1988; named Sagamore of the Wabash, Gov. Ind., 1987. Mem. Am. Schs. Oriental Research, Yale U. Alumni Club (pres. 1982-88), Quest Club (pres.), Rotary Club, Chi Psi (nat. chaplain 1982). Republican. Avocations: college recruiting, genealogy. Office: St Peters Episcopal Church PO Box 336 Del Mar CA 92014-0336

RANDALL, CLAIRE, church executive; b. Dallas, Oct. 15, 1919; d. Arthur Godfrey and Annie Laura (Fulton) R. A.A., Schreiner Coll., 1948; BA, Scarritt Coll., 1950; DD (hon.), Berkeley Sem., Yale U., 1974; LHD (hon.), Austin Coll., 1982; LLD, Notre Dame U., 1984. Assoc. missionary edn. Bd. World Missions Presbyterian Ch., U.S., Nashville, 1949-57; dir. art Gen. Council Presbyterian Ch., U.S., Atlanta, 1957-61; dir. Christian World Mission, program dir., assoc. dir. Ch. Women United, N.Y.C., 1962-73; gen. sec. Nat. Council Ch. of Christ in U.S.A., N.Y.C., 1974-84; nat. pres. Ch. Women United, 1988-92; ret., 1992—. Mem. Nat. Commn. on Internat. Women's Yr., 1975-77, Martin Luther King Jr. Fed. Holiday Commn., 1985. Recipient Woman of Yr. in Religion award Heritage Soc., 1977; Empire State Woman of Yr. in Religion award State of N.Y., 1984; medal Order of St. Vladimir, Russian Orthodox Ch., 1984. Democrat. Episcopalian. Avocations: golf, swimming; painting; reading; music. Home: 13427 W Countryside Dr Sun City West AZ 85375-4711

RANDALL, CLIFFORD WENDELL, civil engineer; b. Somerset, Ky., May 1, 1936; s. William Lesbert and Geneva (James) R.; m. Phyllis Amis, Aug. 15, 1959; children: Andrew Amis, William Otis. B.S. in Civil Engring., U. Ky., 1959, M.S. in San. Engring., 1963; Ph.D. (AEC trainee 1963-65), U. Tex., 1966. Asst. prof. civil engring. U. Tex., Arlington, 1965-68; mem. faculty Va. Poly. Inst. and State U., 1968—, prof. civil engring., 1972—, Charles Lunsford prof., 1981—; vis. prof. U. Cape Town, South Africa, 1983; chmn. environ. engring. and scis. program Va. Poly. Inst. and State U., 1979—; lectr. Shanghai Archtl. and Mcpl. Engring. Inst., Wuhan Tech. U., 1987; dir. Occoquan Watershed Monitoring Program, 1971—; mem. U.S. nat. com. Internat. Water Quality, 1976-88, chair 1986-88, mem. 1992 Biennial Conf. Com., chair conf. arrangements, Washington; tng. grant cons. EPA, 1970-71; cons. to industry, 1969—; WHO cons. to Nat. Environ. Engring. Rsch. Inst. India, 1983-84; gov. appointee sci. and tech. adv. com. EPA Chesapeake Bay Restoration Project, 1984—, chmn. 1993—. Author tech. papers in field; co-author: Biological Process Design for Wastewater Treatment, 1980, Stormwater Management in Urbanizing Areas, 1983, Design and Retrofit of Wastewater Treatment Plants for Biological Nutrient Removal, 1992. Troop com. chmn. local Boy Scouts Am., 1978-82, chmn. dist. Camporee com., 1977; camp pres. Gideons Internat., 1976-78, 80, 95—, state cabinet mem., 1985-88; vice moderator Highlands Bapt. Assn., 1980-81, moderator, 1982-83; mem. bd. deacons Blacksburg Bapt. Ch., 1971-74, 79-82, chmn., 1974. Lt. U.S. Coast and Godetic Survey, 1959-62. Ford Found. fellow, 1964-65; recipient citation Engring. News-Record, 1988, Disting. Svc. award U.S. nat. com. Internat. Assn. Water Quality, 1989, Salute to Excellence Gov. of Md., 1994, Pub. Svc. award Va. Tech., 1996; named Conservationist of Yr. Chesapeake Bay Found., 1986. Mem. ASCE (chmn. water resources mgmt. com. 1977, environ. engring. rsch. coun. 1989-90, svc. award 1978, 80, meritorious tech. paper award 1969), Am. Water Works Assn. (cert. recognition for acad. excellence 1980, 89), Water Environ. Fedn. (bd. dirs. 1981-84, cert. of merit for full scale rsch. 1982, Bedell award 1983, svc. award 1984), Internat. Assn. Water Quality (Mem. gov. bd. 1986-88, USA rep. on sci. and tech. com. 1994—, mem. nutrient removal specialist group mgmt. com. 1990—, chmn. 1994—), Va. Water Pollution Control Assn. (v.p. 1974-75, pres. 1975-76), Assn. Environ. Engring. Profs. (sec.-treas. 1979-80, bd. dirs. 1978-80, 93—, v.p. 1994-95, pres. 1995-96). Home: 1302 Crestview Dr Blacksburg VA 24060-5609 Office: Va Poly Inst & State U Dept Civil Engring 330 Norris Hall Blacksburg VA 24061

RANDALL, DAVID JOHN, physiologist, zoologist, educator; b. London, Sept. 15, 1938. BSc, U. Southampton, 1960, PhD, 1963, FRSC, 1981. From asst. to assoc. prof. U. B.C., 1963-73, prof. zoology, 1973—, assoc. dean grad. studies, 1990—; vis. lectr. Bristol U., 1968-69; vis. sci. Marine Labs U. Tex., 1970, Zool. Sta., Naples, Italy, 1973; NATO vis. sci. Acadia U., 1975, Marine Lab U. Tex., 1977; chief sci. Alpha Helix Amazon Expedition, 1976; mem. adv. bd. J. Comp Physiology, 1977-92, J. Exp. Biol., 1981-84; chmn. animal biol. com. Nat. Res. Coun., Can., 1974; vis. prof. U. Nairobi, 1988, George Washington U., 1988-89; concurrent prof. Nanjing U., China, 1993—; external examiner U. Singapore, 1990-91. Assoc. editor: Marine Behavior Physiology. Recipient Award of Excellence Am. Fisheries Soc., 1994. Fellow Royal Soc. Can.; mem. Can. Soc. Zoologists (Fry medal 1993), Soc. Exp. Biologists. Office: U BC, Dept Zoology 6270 Unv Blvd, Vancouver, BC Canada V6T 1Z4

RANDALL, ELIZABETH ELLEN, press clippings company executive; b. Maple Hill, Kans., Mar. 21, 1915; d. Edwin and Ann (Scott) Sage; m. George Albert Randall, May 29, 1941; children: Cheryl Ann, Rebecca Lynn. Student, Kans. State U., 1932-34. Tchr. elem. sch Maple Hill, Kans., 1932-34, Dover, Kans., 1934-46; reader Luce Press Clippings, Topeka, 1959-63, supr., 1964, office mgr., 1964—. Tchr. Jr. High Ch. Sch., 1949-61; mem. pastoral com. Dover Federated Ch., 1991—. Mem. Dover 4-H Club (leader 1960-62), Dover Rebekah Lodge, Eastern Star, Am. Leg. Aux., Disabled Am. Vets. Aux., 14th Armored Divsn. Aux. Democrat. Avocations: collecting antiques, plates and dolls, needlework. Home: 5731 SW 22nd Ter Topeka KS 66614-1831 Office: Luce Press Clippings 912 S Kansas Ave Topeka KS 66612-1211

RANDALL, FRANCIS BALLARD, historian, educator, writer; b. N.Y.C., Dec. 17, 1931; s. John Herman, Jr. and Mercedes (Moritz) R.; m. Laura Regina Rosenbaum, June 11, 1957; children: David R., Ariane R. B.A., Amherst Coll., 1952; M.A., Columbia, 1954, Ph.D., 1960. Instr. history Amherst Coll., 1956-59; instr., asst. prof. history Columbia, 1959-61, vis. prof., 1967-68; mem. humanities faculty Sarah Lawrence Coll., Bronxville, N.Y., 1961—, chmn., 1985-89; trustee Sarah Lawrence Coll., 1971-76. Author: (with others) Essays in Russian and Soviet History, 1963, Stalin's Russia, an Historical Reconsideration, 1965, N.G. Chernyshevskii, 1967, Vissarion Belinskii, 1987. Freedom rider civil disobedience to racism, 1961, war draft resistance arrests, 1967, 70. Fulbright fellow for study in India, 1965; Wye fellow, 1986. Mem. Am. Hist. Assn., Am. Assn. for Advancement Slavic Studies, Am. Assn. U. Profs. (chpt. chmn. 1966-69), Phi Beta Kappa, Sigma Xi. Home: 425 Riverside Dr # 10I New York NY 10025-7730 Office: Humanities Dept Sarah Lawrence Coll Bronxville NY 10708

RANDALL, GENE, news correspondent, anchor; b. Port Chester, N.Y., Jan. 10, 1942; m. Susan Biggs; children: Christopher, Gina, Dominic. BA in English, Georgetown U., 1964. Anchor, corr. Sta. WLWT, Cin., 1966-71; anchor Sta. WTVC, Chattanooga, 1972-74; corr., anchor Sta. KTVI, St. Louis, 1974-76, Sta. WMAQ-TV, Chgo., 1976-80; bur. chief/corr. NBC, Moscow, 1980-83; nat. corr. CNN, Washington, 1983—. Recipient Emmy awards for Best TV Talk Show, 1975, Best Spot News Story, 1976, U.S. Operation in Somalia, 1993, DuPont award, 1993. Office: CNN Bldg Wash Bureau 820 1st St NE Washington DC 20002-4243

RANDALL, GERALD J., insurance company executive; b. Sparta, Wis., Mar. 6, 1931; s. Jean Oliver and Mabel E. (Olson) R.; m. Beverly J. Gehrig, Apr. 23, 1955; children: Robin Jean, Scott Gerald, Susan Kay. BBA, U. Wis., 1954, JD, 1957. Bar: Wis., U.S. Supreme Ct.; CLU, ChFC. With Conn. Mutual Life Ins. Co., Hartford, 1957-61, asst. counsel advanced sales, 1961-69, asst. v.p. advanced sales, 1969-70, 2d v.p. advanced sales, 1970-73, v.p. pension divsn., 1973-80, sr. v.p., 1980-81; pres. Diversified Ins. Svcs. Am., Inc. subs. Conn. Mutual Life Ins. Co., 1981-84; pres. Conn. Mutual Fin. Svcs., Inc. subs. Conn. Mutual Life Ins. Co., 1984-88, sr. v.p. advanced sales SBU, 1988-94; broker Mass. Mutual Life Ins. Co., 1995—; instr. CLU dip. courses U. Conn., 1965-72; founder, charter mem., pres. Estate & Bus. Planning Coun. Hartford, 1969-70; mem. exec. program Dartmouth Coll., 1973, Columbia U., 1988; chmn. pension com. Am. Coun. Life Ins., 1976. Contbr. articles to profl. jours. Mem. Jaycees, 1960-65; bd. dirs. Hartford Better Bus. Bureau, 1981-84, greater Hartford YMCA, 1989—. 1st Lt. U.S. Army, 1955-56. Recipient CLU Inst. scholarship, 1971. Mem. ABA, Wis. Bar Assn., Hartford Life Underwriters Assn., Estate & Bus. Planning Coun. Hartford, Life Ins. Mgmt. Rsch. Assn. (chmn. advanced sales com. 1978-79), Gen. Agents and Mgrs. Assn., Assn. Advanced Life Underwriting, Hartford Club. Republican. Congregationalist. Avocations: antique cars, travel, jogging, antique watch collecting. Home: 178 Tall Timbers Rd Glastonbury CT 06033-3351 Office: Mass Mut Life Ins Co 178 Tall Timbers Rd Glastonbury CT 06033-3351

RANDALL, JAMES R., manufacturing company executive; b. 1924; married. BS in Chem. Engring., U. Wis., 1948. Tech. dir. Cargill Inc., 1948-68; v.p. prodn. and engring. Archer-Daniels-Midland Co., Decatur, Ill., 1968-69, exec. v.p., 1969-75, pres., 1975—, also dir. Served with AUS, 1943-46. Office: Archer-Daniels-Midland Co 4666 E Faries Pky Decatur IL 62526-5666*

RANDALL, LILIAN MARIA CHARLOTTE, museum curator; b. Berlin, Feb. 1, 1931; came to U.S., 1938; d. Frederick Henry and Elizabeth Agnes (Ziegler) Cramer; m. Richard Harding Randall, Apr. 11, 1953; children: Christopher, Julia, Katharine. BA cum laude, Mount Holyoke Coll., 1950; MA, Radcliffe Coll., 1951, PhD, 1955; LHD (hon.), Towson State U., 1993. Asst. dir. Md. State Arts Coun., 1972-73; curator manuscripts and rare books Walters Art Gallery, Balt., 1974-85, rsch. curator manuscripts, 1985-95; rsch. cons., 1995—; vis. lectr. dept. art history Johns Hopkins U., 1964-68; hon. vis. lectr. U. Mich., Ann Arbor; lectr. in field. Author: Images in the Margins of Gothic Manuscripts, 1966, Gatherings in Honor of Dorothy Miner, 1974, The Diary of George A. Lucas: An American Art Agent in Paris, 1909-1957, 1979, Illuminated Manuscripts: Masterpieces in Miniature, 1984, Medieval and Renaissance Manuscripts in the Walters Art Gallery, Vol. I, France, 875-1420, 1989, Vol. II, France, 1420-1540, 1992; contbr. numerous articles to profl. jours. Mem. Williston Libr. com., 1988-89; reviewer, panelist NEH, 1980—. Grantee AAUW, 1953-54, ACLS, 1960, 65, Bunting Inst., 1961-63, Ford Found., 1967-69, Am. Philosophical Soc., 1971, NEA, 1975, Samuel H. Kress Found., 1979, 81-84, NEH, 1977-84, 89—; grantee publ. subsidy Md. State Arts Coun., 1972, Mcpl. Art Soc. Balt., 1972, Andrew W. Mellon Found., 1988, Getty Grant program, 1990-92, NEA Mus. program, 1992-93. Fellow Medieval Acad. Am. (libr. preservation com., various coms. 1985-87, 90-93); mem. Internat. Ctr. Medieval Art (bd. dirs. 1978-82, 96—), Coll. Art Assn. (Arthur Kingsley Porter prize 1957), Balt. Bibliophiles (bd. dirs. 1966-80, pres. 1980-83), Pyramid Atlantic (bd. dirs. 1985-88), Phi Beta Kappa, Grolier Club. Home: 301 Kendall Rd Baltimore MD 21210-2562

RANDALL, LINDA LEA, biochemist, educator; b. Montclair, N.J., Aug. 7, 1946; d. Lowell Neal and Helen (Watts) R.; m. Gerald Lee Hazelbauer, Aug. 29, 1970. BS, Colo. State U., 1968; PhD, U. Wis., 1971. Postdoctoral fellow Inst. Pasteur, Paris, 1971-73; asst. prof. Uppsala (Sweden) U., 1975-81; assoc. prof. Washington State U., Pullman, 1981-83, prof. biochemistry, 1983—; guest scientist Wallenberg Lab., Uppsala U., 1973-75; study section NIH, 1984-88. Editorial bd. Jour. of Bacteriology, 1982—; co-editor: Virus Receptors Part I, 1980; contbr. articles to profl. jours. Recipient Eli Lilly Award in Microbiology and Immunology, Am. Soc. Microbiology, Am. Assn. Immunologists, Am. Soc. Exptl. Pathology, 1984, Faculty Excellence Award in Rsch., Washington State U., 1988, Disting. Faculty Address, 1990, Parke-Davis award, 1995. Fellow Am. Acad. Microbiology; mem. AAAS, Am. Microbiol. Soc., Am. Soc. Biol. Chemists, Protein Soc. Avocation: dancing. Office: Washington State U. Biochemistry/Biophysic Dept Pullman WA 99164-4660

RANDALL, MALCOM, health care administrator; b. East St. Louis, Ill., Aug. 9, 1916; s. John Leeper and Merle Dorothy Randall; m. Christine Sheppard, Nov. 10, 1972. A.B., McKendree Coll., 1939; M.H.A., St. Louis U., 1955. Chief br. office VA, St. Louis, 1946-49, asst. area dir. area office, 1949-53; spl. asst. to dir. VA Hosp., St. Louis, 1953-56; hosp. adminstr. VA Hosp., Spokane, Wash., 1956-57, Chgo., 1957-58, Indpls., 1958-60, Wood, Wis., 1960-64; hosp. dir. VA Hosp., Miles City, Mont., 1964-66; med. ctr. dir. and med. dist. dir. VA, Gainesville, Fla., 1966—; regional rep. VA, Gainesville, 1991—; prof. health and hosp. adminstrn. U. Fla., Gainesville, 1966—; pres. N. Cen. Fla. Health Planning Council; mem. Fla. State Health Planning Council; chmn. Gov.'s Commn. on Alzheimer's Disease; mem. Alachua County Emergency Med. Svcs. Coun.; bd. dirs. emeritus 1st Union Nat. Bank Fla., Regional Med. Programs; mem. editorial bd. Jour. Am. Coll. Health Care Execs.; cons. on health care Univ. Clin. Ctr., Ljubljana, Slovenia, 1982—, Ministry of Health, Hungary and Med. U. Debrecen, 1989—. Contbr. numerous articles to profl. jours. Bd. dirs. Civitan Regional Blood Ctr., Gainesville, 1970. Served to capt. USN, 1942-46. Recipient Presdl. Rank award Pres. U.S., 1983, Meritorious Svc. award U. Fla., 1984, Exceptional Svc. award, 1985, Exec. Performance award, 1986, all VA; named Citizen of Yr., Gainesville, 1977. Fellow Am. Coll. Health Care Execs. (council regents, VA liaison); mem. Inst. Medicine, Nat. Acad. Sci., Assn. Am. Med. Colls. (bd. dirs., council tchg. hosps.), Am. Health Planning Assn. (bd. dirs.), Am. Hosp. Assn. (governing council met. and fed. hosp. sect.). Club: Heritage. Lodge: Rotary. Home: 1617 NW 19th Cir Gainesville FL 32605-4092 Office: VA Med Ctr Archer Rd Gainesville FL 32608 *A core set of values should be the base for all of your activities, both professional and personal.*

RANDALL, PRISCILLA RICHMOND, travel executive; b. Arlington, Mass., Mar. 19, 1926; d. Harold Bours and Florence (Hoefler) Richmond; m. Raymond Victor Randall, Mar. 2, 1946; children: Raymond Richmond, Priscilla Randall Middleton, Susan Randall Geery. Student, Wellesley Coll., 1943-44; Assoc., Garland Coll., 1946; student, Winona State U., 1977-81. Pub. relations dir. Rochester Meth. Hosp., Rochester, Minn., 1960-69; dir. pub relations Sheraton Rochester, 1969-71; pres. Med. Charters, Rochester, 1970-75, Ideas Unltd., Rochester, 1969-77; chief exec. officer Randall Travel, Rochester, 1977-89; pres. Randall Travel Delray, Delray Beach, Fla., 1989—; pres. Bar Harbour Apts. Inc., Delray Beach, 1989. Editor, Inside Story, 1960-69, Rochester Meth. Hosp. News, 1960-69; producer Priscilla's World, 1972-75. Pres. Rochester Meth. Hosp. Aux., 1957-59, Downtown Bus. Assn., Rochester, 1985. Recipient Woman of Achievement Bus. YWCA, Rochester, 1983, Golden Door Knob, Bus. and Prfl. Women, Rochester, 1979. Mem. Inst. Cert. Travel Agts. (life), Assn. Retail Travel Agts. (life, nat. bd. 1988-90, sec. to bd. 1988-90, sec.-treas. Arlington, Va. nat. bd. 1990), Am. Soc. Travel Agts., Pacific Area Travel Agts., Minn. Exec. Women in Travel, Cruise Line Internat. Assn. (master cruise counselor), Women's Golf Com. Little Club (Gulfstream, Fla.) (sec.), Hibiscus Garden Club (Delray Beach, Fla.) (sec.). Avocation: travel writing. Home: 86 Macfarlane Dr Apt 2C Delray Beach FL 33483-6901 Office: Randall Travel Delray Inc 1118 E Atlantic Ave Delray Beach FL 33483-6936

RANDALL, RICHARD RAINIER, geographer; b. Toledo, July 21, 1925; s. Robert Henry and Maree (Gard) R.; m. Patricia Lee Spencer, June 9, 1962; children: Allison Maree, Susan Rebecca, Richard Rainier Jr. BA, George Washington U., 1949, MA, 1950; PhD, Clark U., 1955; postgrad., Graz U., Austria. Geog. analyst U.S. Govt., Washington, 1955-61; Washington rep. Rand McNally & Co., Washington, 1961-72; owner Randall Assocs., Washington, 1972-73; exec. sec. U.S. Bd. Geog. Names, Washington, 1973-93; geographer Def. Mapping Agy., Washington, 1973-93; ret., 1993, cons. on geog. names,, 1993—; convenor UN Working Group on Undersea and Maritime Feature Names, 1975-84; mem., prin. U.S. tech. advisor U.S. and U.K. Conf. on Geog. Names, 1976, 79, 81, 84, 86, 88, 92; dep. head U.S. del. UN Conf. on Geog. Names, 1977, 87, head, 1982, 92; prin. U.S. expert UN Group Experts on Geog. Names, 1975, 77, 79, 82, 84, 86, 87, 89, 92; pres. com. on geog. terminology Pan Am. Inst. Geography and History, 1973-77, pres. working group on geog. names and gazetters, 1981-94. Contbr. articles to profl. jours.; inventor flexible fishhook. V.p. North Cleveland Park Citizens Assn., Washington, 1968. With U.S. Army, 1943-46, ETO. Fulbright scholar, NRC, Austria, 1953-54. Mem. Am. Congress on Surveying and Mapping (dir. cartography divsn. 1973-75, dir. press rels. 1961-72, program dir. cartography divsn. ann. meeting 1967), Am. Geog. Soc., Assn. Am. Geographers (chmn. Mid-Atlantic divsn. 1978, dir. press rels. ann. conf. 1968), Am. Names Soc., Am. Austrian Soc. (v.p. 1955-57), Explorers Club, Cosmos Club. Republican.

RANDALL, ROBERT L(EE), ecological economist; b. Aberdeen, S.D., Dec. 28, 1936; s. Harry Eugene and Juanita Alice (Barstow) R. MS in Phys. Chemistry, U. Chgo., 1960, MBA, 1963. Market devel. chemist E.I. du Pont de Nemours & Co., Inc., Wilmington, Del., 1963-65; chem. economist Battelle Meml. Inst., Columbus, Ohio, 1965-68; mgr. market and econ. rsch. Kennecott Copper Corp., N.Y.C., 1968-74, economist, 1974-79, dir. new bus. venture devel., 1979-81; pres., mng. dir. R.L. Randall Assocs., Inc., 1981—; economist U.S. Internat. Trade Commn., Washington, 1983—; founder, pres., exec. dir. The RainForest ReGeneration Inst., 1986—; indsl. panel policy rev. of effect of regulation on innovation and U.S.-internat. competetion U.S. Dept. Commerce, 1980-81; participant preparatory com. UN Conf. on Environ. and Devel., Rio de Janeiro, 1991; del. observer internat. negotiating com. Framework Conv. on Climate Change, 1991—. Contbr. articles to profl. jours.; contbg. author: Computer Methods for the '80's. Mem. AAAS (organizer ann. meeting Tropical Forest Regeneration Symposium), AIME (econs. coun. sec. mineral econ. subsect.), Am. Econ. Assn., Am. Statis. Assn., Am. Chem. Soc., Soc. Mining Engrs., Chemists Club of N.Y.C., Metall. Soc., N.Y. Acad. Scis., Nat. Econs. Club Washington (sec., reporter), Assn. Environ. and Resource Economists, Internat. Soc. Ecol. Economists, Gay Activist Alliance N.Y.C. (chmn. state, fed. legis. com. 1975); Wanderbirds Hiking Club (hike leader, treas., Washington, Capital Hiking Club (hike leader, Washington); chm. State and Federal Legislature, 1975. Home: 1727 Massachusetts Ave NW Washington DC 20036-2153 Office: US Internat Trade Com 500 E St NW Washington DC 20436-0003

RANDALL, RONALD FISHER, grocery store chain executive; b. Sioux City, Iowa, June 25, 1934; s. F. Dwain and J. Gale (Fisher) R.; m. Lavonne E. Woltoff, Dec. 27, 1961 (dec. May 1966); children—DaLinda, Ronald; m. Charlys Fern Stewart, Mar. 7, 1969. B.S. in Engring., U.S. Naval Acad., 1958. Dir. ops. Randall Stores, Mitchell, S.D., 1958-72, pres., 1972-81, pres., chmn. bd., 1981—; pres. Coca-Cola Bottling Co. of Central S.D. Inc., Mitchell; dir. Comml. Bank, Mitchell, Dakota Mfg. Inc., Mitchell. Clubs: Interlachen Country (Mpls.); Minnehaha Country (Sioux Falls, S.D.). Office: Randall Stores Inc PO Box 1200 Mitchell SD 57301-1019*

RANDALL, TONY (LEONARD ROSENBERG), actor; b. Tulsa, Feb. 26, 1920; m. Florence Gibbs. Student, Northwestern U., Columbia; studies, Neighborhood Playhouse Sch. of Theater, N.Y.C. Founder, artistic dir. Nat. Actors' Theatre, N.Y.C. Appearances include: (theatre) Circle of Chalk, 1941, Candida, 1941, The Corn is Green, 1942, The Barretts of Wimpole St., 1947, Antony and Cleopatra, 1948, Caesar and Cleopatra, 1950, Oh Men, Oh Women, 1954, Inherit the Wind, 1955-56, Oh Captain, 1958, UTBU, 1966, Two Into One, 1988, M. Butterfly, 1989, A Little Hotel on the Side, 1992, Three Men on a Horse, 1993, The Government Inspector, 1994, tour with Jack Klugman The Odd Couple, 1994; (tv) Mr. Peepers, 1952-55, Max Liebman Spectaculars, Tonight Show, 1956, The Odd Couple, 1970-75, also The Tony Randall Show, 1976-77, Love Sydney, 1981-83; (motion pictures) Oh Men, Oh Women, 1957, Will Success Spoil Rock Hunter, 1957, The Mating Game, 1959, Pillow Talk, 1959, Let's Make Love 1960, Lover Come Back, 1962, Bang, Bang, You're Dead, 1966, Huckleberry Finn, 1974, Scavenger Hunt, 1979, Foolin' Around, 1980, The King of Comedy, 1983, My Little Pony, 1986, That's Adequate, It Had to Be You; appeared in TV movies: Kate Bliss and the Ticker Tape Kid, 1978, Sidney Shorr: A Girl's Best Friend, 1981, Off Sides, 1984, The Man in the Brown Suit, 1989, The Odd Couple Returns, 1993; author: (with Michael Mindlin) Which Reminds Me, 1989. Served from pvt. to 1st lt. Signal Corps, AUS, 1942-46. Recipient Emmy award for The Odd Couple 1975. Office: care Nat Actors' Theatre 1560 Broadway Ste 409 New York NY 10036-1525*

RANDALL, WILLIAM B., manufacturing company executive; b. Phila., Jan. 8, 1921; s. Albert and Ann (Fine) R.; m. Geraldine Kempson, Aug. 10, 1943; children: Robert, Erica Lynn, Lisa. Student, Rider Coll., Trenton, N.J., 1940-41. Gen. Sales mgr. Lowres Optical Mfg. Co., Newark, 1946-49; pres., founder Rand Sales Co., N.Y.C., 1949-58; gen. mgr. Sea & Ski Co. div. Botany Industries, Inc., Millbrae, Calif., 1958-61; pres., dir. Botany Industries, Inc., 1961-66, v.p., 1961-65; pres. Renauld of France, Reno, 1967-68; chmn. bd. Renauld Internat., Reading, Pa., 1963-65; pres., chief operating officer Renauld Internat., Ltd., Burlingame and Reno, 1966-67; pres., chmn. bd. Randall Internat., Ltd., 1967-68; sr. exec. v.p. Forty-two Prods. Ltd., 1969-71; pres. Exec. Products Internat. Ltd., 1969-71, New Product Devel. Ctr., Carlsbad, Calif., 1971—; pres. Internat. Concept Ctr. Exec. Products Internat. Ltd., Irvine, 1971—, pres. Sun Research Ctr., 1974—; pres. La Costa Products Internat., 1975-86; mng. dir. merchandising La Costa Hotel and Spa, 1986-88; pres., chief exec. officer Randall Internat., Carlsbad, 1989—; bd. dirs. Bank of La Costa, Garden Botanika. Served to 1st lt., navigator USAAF, 1942-45. Mem. Am. Mgmt. Assn., Nat. Wholesale Druggists Assn., Nat. Assn. Chain Drug Stores, Hon. Order Ky. Cols., Baja Beach and Tennis Club (bd. dirs.). Home: 7150 Arenal Ln Carlsbad CA 92009-6701 *I play to win. I like to win. And I hate good losers.*

RANDALL, WILLIAM SEYMOUR, leasing company executive; b. Champaign, Ill., July 5, 1933; s. Glenn S. and Audrey H. (Honnold) R.; m. Sharon Larsen; children: Steve, Cathy, Mike, Jennifer. B.S., Ind. State U., 1959. Controller Amana Refrigeration Co., Iowa, 1966-70; div. controller Trane Co., Clarksville, Tenn., 1970-74; corporate controller Trane Co., La Crosse, Wis., 1974-79; v.p., chief fin. officer Sta-Rite Industries, Milw., 1979-82; pres., owner Profl. Staff Resources, Inc., Milw., 1982—. Served with AUS, 1953-55. Mem. Financial Execs. Inst. Lodge: Rotary. Home: 13365 Tulane St Brookfield WI 53005-7141 Office: 14430 W Bluemound Rd Ste 103 Milwaukee WI 53226

RANDALL, WILLIAM THEODORE, state official; b. Seattle, July 8, 1931; s. Heaton Henry Randall and Mabel Maud (Johnson) Landstrom; m. Barbara Ann Bouffard; children: Julie Randall Waybright, Linda A. Randall Wiggins, Mary Lee Randall Lane. BA in Far Ea. Studies, U. Wash., 1953, BA in Polit. Sci., 1959, MEd in Edn. Adminstrn., 1966; EdD in Edn. Adminstrn., Ariz. State U., 1969. Agt. Aetna Ins. Co., Seattle, 1957-59; tchr. Shoreline Pub. Schs., Seattle, 1959-61, prin., 1961-66, dir. rsch., 1969-70; asst. supt. Wash. Sch. Dist., Phoenix, 1970-73; supt. Scottsdale (Ariz.) Pub. Schs., 1973-80; pres. William Randall Assocs., Phoenix, 1980-83; supt. Creighton Sch. Dist., Phoenix, 1983-88; commr. edn. State of Colo., Denver, 1988—; cons. Edge Learning Corp., Tempe, Ariz., 1978-82; edn. advisor Gov. of Ariz., 1985; pres.-elect Ariz. Adminstrs., Inc., 1986-88. Author: Stress Management, 1978; co-author: Role of Teacher, 1979, Management Development, 1980. Chmn. Ariz. Child Care Coalition, Phoenix, 1986; bd. dirs. Colo. Childrens Trust, Denver, 1989—; mem. exec. bd. Communities for Drug Free Colo., Denver, 1988. Sgt. U.S. Army, 1955-57. Named Adminstr. of Yr. Shoreline Edn. Assn., Seattle, 1966, Ariz. Supt. of Yr. Ariz. Sch. Adminstrs., Phoenix, 1988. Avocations: hiking, skiing. Office: Colo Dept Edn 201 E Colfax Ave Denver CO 80203-1704*

RANDAZZO, ANTHONY, dancer; b. Ann Arbor, Mich.. Student, Nat. Ballet Can. Mem. Nat. Ballet of Can.; soloist San Francisco Ballet, 1987-88, prin. dancer, 1988—. Performances with San Francisco Ballet include The Sleeping Beauty, Swan Lake, Handel—A Celebration, Ballet d'Isoline, Valses Poeticos, Intimate Voices, La Fille Mal Gardee, The Four Temperaments, Symphony in C, Theme and Variations, Ballo dell Regina, Glinka Pas de Trois, Duo Concertant, Forgotton Land, The Comfort Zone, Dream of Harmony, Nutcracker, In The Middle, Somewhat elevated, Stravinsky Violin Concerto, Terra Firma, Dance House, Sonata, Romeo and Juliet, New Sleep, Rodeo, Connotations, Rodin, La Sylphike, Variations de Ballet, Krazy Kat, Harvest Moon, The Wonder Fantasy; ballets with other cos., including Etudes, Nutcracker, Napoli, Don Juan, Don Quixote, The Merry Widow. Office: 133 W 71st St New York NY 10023-3834 also: San Francisco Ballet 455 Franklin St San Francisco CA 94102-4438

RANDAZZO, GARY WAYNE, newspaper executive; b. Georgetown, Tex., Sept. 23, 1947; s. Frank Birchmans and Edna Earle (Forbis) R.; m. Joyce Sue McNorton, Oct. 7, 1966; children: Gary Wayne Jr., Vanessa Rene, Michael Jason, Daniel Paul. BBA, U. Tex., 1974; MBA, Tex. A&I U., Corpus Christi, 1976. Instr. Del Mar Coll., Corpus Christi, 1974-76; bus. mgr. Corpus Christi Caller-Times, 1976-81; pres., pub. Huntsville (Tex.) Item, 1981-83; pres. Am. Property Data, Houston, 1984-87; gen. mgr. Health Care News, Houston, 1987-89; v.p. sales Houston Chronicle, Houston, 1995—. Mem. Leadership Houston. Mem. Kiwanis. Home: 9610 Oxted Ln Spring TX 77379-6600 Office: Houston Chronicle 801 Texas St Houston TX 77002-2906

RANDEL, RONALD DEAN, physiologist, educator; b. Lewis, Kan., May 22, 1938; s. Emery Howard and Pauline (Mahan) R.; m. Colleen Kay O'Brien, Sept. 4, 1966; 1 child, Lowell Warren. BS in Animal Sci., Washington State U., 1965; PhD in Animal Physiology, Purdue U., 1971. Research fellow Purdue U., West Lafayette, Ind., 1965-71; visiting scientist U.S. Range Livestock Experiment Station, Miles City, Mont., 1971-72; research physiologist USDA, Agrl. Rsch. Svc., Miles City, 1972-74; assoc. prof. Texas A & M U., Overton, Tex., 1974-78, prof., 1978—; cooperating scientist USDA-Office Internat. Coop. and Devel./Taiwan Livestock Rsch. Inst., Ping Tung, 1987—; presenter in field. Mem. editl. bd. Jour. Animal Sci., 1990-93, 95—, Theriogeneology, 1994—; contbr. numerous papers to profl. jours., 2 chpts. to books, also numerous paper presentations, misc. papers, and symposia. Adult leader 4-H, Rusk County Riding Club Overton, 1981-90. With USN, 1958-62. Named Alpha Zeta agrl. hon. Wash. State U., 1964, Phi Kappa Phi scholastic hon. Wash. State U., 1964, Sigma Xi rsch. hon. Purdue U., 1970, Award in Excellence for Rsch. Tex. A&M U., 1987, 90, Svc. award Dept. Animal Sci., 1994; sr. Fulbright rsch. fellow James Cook U. of N. Queensland, Townsville, Australia, 1984; Donald Henry Barron lectr., 1995. Mem. Am. Soc. of Animal Sci., Soc. for the Study of Reproduction, Assn. Latino Americana de Prodn. Animal, Reproductive Performance of Domestic Ruminants (W-112Reg. Proj. Com.; pres. 1986). Protestant. Home: 604 W Patricia Dr Overton TX 75684-1526 Office: Tex A&M U Agrl Rsch & Extension Drawer E Overton TX 75684

RANDELL, JOSEPH DAVID, airline executive; b. Corner Brook, Newfoundland, Can., Feb. 20, 1954; s. Sterling A. and Mercedes O. (Locke) R.; m. Kathryn Janet Oxford, Sept. 3, 1977; children: David, Adam, Leah, Rebecca. B in Indsl. Engring., Tech. U. Nova Scotia, Halifax, 1976; MBA, Meml. U. Newfoundland, St. John's, 1985. Mgr. market devel. Ea. Provincial Airways, Gander, Newfoundland, 1976-77, asst. to v.p. mktg., 1977-78; dir. product planning Ea. Provincial Airways, Halifax, 1978-79; asst. mgr. Locke's Elec. Ltd., Corner Brook, 1979-80; v.p. Atlantis Corp. Ltd., St. John's, 1981-86; trans. cons. Atlantis Cons. Ltd., St. John's, 1980-81; exec. v.p. Air Nova Inc., Halifax, 1986-88, pres., CEO, 1988—; Dir. Air Transp. Assn. Can., Ottawa, 1991, 92. Dir. Bedford (Can.) Econ. Devel. Commn., 1992; mem. Tech. U. of Nova Scotia President's Adv. Program; mem. adv. bd. of the Frank H. Sobey Faculty of Commerce, Saint Mary's U. Sexton Scholar, Tech. U. Nova Scotia, 1976. Mem. Assn. Profl. Engrs. of Nova Scotia, Young President's Orgn. Anglican. Avocations: swimming, downhill and cross country skiing, tennis. Home: 110 Peregrine Crescent, Bedford, NS Canada B4A 3C1 Office: Air Nova, 310 Goudey Dr, Halifax Internat Airport, Enfield, NS Canada B2T 1E4

RANDELL, RICHARD C., mathematics educator; b. Fairfield, Iowa, Aug. 23, 1946; m. Linda Randell; children: John, Alex. BS, U. Iowa, 1968; MS, U. Wis., 1971; PhD, 1973. Asst. prof. U. Mich., Ann Arbor, 1973-79; vis. mem. Inst. Advanced Study, Princeton, N.J., 1976-78; asst., assoc. prof. U. Okla., Norman, 1979-81, U. Iowa, 1981-87; prof., 1987—, dept. chair, 1991-94; mem., governing bd. Iowa Math. Coalition, Cedar Falls, 1990-95. Editor, author: Singularities, 1989; contbr. articles to profl. jours. recipient Rsch. grants U.S. Nat. Sci. Found., 1974-87. Mem. Am. Math. Soc. Office: Dept Math University of Iowa Iowa City IA 52242

RANDELS, ED LEE, lawyer; b. Albuquerque, Nov. 17, 1953; s. James L. and Betty J. (Ridgeway) R.; m. Kathryn J. Eddleman, July 11, 1975; children: Nancy L, Joshua L. BA, Mid-Am. Nazarene Coll., Olathe, Kans., 1975; JD, U. Kans., 1982. Bar: Kans. 1982, U.S. Dist. Ct. Kans. 1982, U.S. Ct. Appeals (10 cir.) 1994. Asst. county atty. Montgomery County, Indpendence, Kans., 1982-85, Miami County, Paola, Kans., 1985-86; asst. city atty. City of Wichita, Kans., 1986-92; asst. county counselor Sedgwick County, Wichita, Kans., 1992—; law day dir. Miami County Bar Assn., Paola, Kans., 1985-86. Contbr. articles to profl. jours. Mem. Kans. Bar Assn., Wichita Bar Assn., Christian Legal Soc. Republican. Nazarene. Office: Sedgwick County Counselor 525 N Main Rm 359 Wichita KS 67203

RANDHAWA, BIKKAR SINGH, psychologist, educator; b. Jullundur, India, June 14, 1933; came to Can., 1961, naturalized, 1966; s. Pritam S. and Sawaran K. (Basakhi) R.; m. Leona Emily Bujnowski, Oct. 8, 1966; children—Jason, Lisa. BA in Math., Panjab U., 1954, BT in Edn., 1955, MA in History, 1959; BEd, U. Alta., Can., 1963; MEd in Measurement and Evaluation, U Toronto, 1967, PhD, 1969. Registered psychologist. Tchr. secondary sch. math. Panjab, 1955-61; asst. headmaster, then headmaster, 1955-61; tchr. high sch. math. and sci. Beaver County, Riley, Alta., 1964-65, Camrose County, Alta., 1961-64; tchr. high sch. math. and sci. Edmonton (Alta.) Public Schs., 1965-67; tutor in math. for social sci. Ont. Inst. Studies in Edn., Toronto, 1968-69; mem. faculty U. Sask., Saskatoon, 1969-76, 77—; prof. ednl. psychology U. Sask., 1977—, asst. dean research and field services, 1982-87; prof., coord. Visual Scholars' Program, U. Iowa, 1976-77; cons. in field. Contbr. articles profl. jours. Fellow Am. Psychol. Assn., Am. Psychol. Soc. (charter), Can. Psychol. Assn.; mem. Am. Ednl. Rsch. Assn., Can. Soc. Study Edn., Sask. Psychol. Assn., Phi Delta Kappa (pres. Saskatoon chpt. 1971, 85). Home: 510 Forsyth Crescent, Saskatoon, SK Canada S7N 4H8 Office: U Sask, 3117 Edn Bldg 28 Campus Dr, Saskatoon, SK Canada S7N OX1

RANDI, JAMES (RANDALL JAMES HAMILTON ZWINGE), magician, writer, educator; b. Toronto, Ont., Can., Aug. 7, 1928; naturalized U.S. citizen, 1987; s. George Randall and Marie Alice (Paradis) Zwinge. Student, Oakwood Collegiate Inst., Toronto, 1940-45; LittD (hon.), U. Indpls., 1995. Internationally known conjuror; regent's lectr. UCLA, 1984; skeptical lectr. on paranormal subjects. Author: The Magic of Uri Geller, 1975 (with Bert Sugar) Houdini, His Life and Art, 1978, Flim-Flam, 1982, Test Your ESP Potential, 1983, The Faith Healers, 1987, The Magic World of the Amazing Randi, 1989, The Mask of Nostradamus, 1990, James Randi: Psychic Investigator, 1991, Conjuring, 1992, An Encyclopedia of Claims, Frauds, and Hoaxes of the Occult and Supernatural, 1995; host TV spls. Recipient Blackstone award Internat. Platform Assn., 1983, 87, Forum award Am. Phys. Soc., 1988, Nat. Consumer Svc. award Nat. Coun. Against Health Fraud, 1988, Gold medal U. Ghent, Belgium, 1989, Humanist Disting. Svc. award Am. Humanist Assn., 1990, medal with golden wreath Hungarian Soc. for Dissemination Sci. Knowledge, 1992; MacArthur Found. fellow, 1986, Spl. fellow Acad. Magical Arts and Scis., 1987. Founding fellow Com. for Sci. Investigation of Claims of the Paranormal (exec. bd. dirs. 1973-91); Soc. Am. Magicians (inducted into Hall of Fame 1988, named Internat. Amb. of Magic 1988). Performed at White House, 1974. Home and Office: 12000 NW 8th St Fort Lauderdale FL 33325-1406 *Irrationalism and the anti-science movement continue to grow, fed by the irresponsible media. Quack medicine, Creation "Science," TV psychics and other pseudoscientific matters are heedlessly and increasingly embraced by the public. This flight into superstition must be checked; that can be done if legislators accept their responsiblity to look into the activities of those who publish wild claims with no foundation in fact. We are facing a crisis.*

RANDINELLI, TRACEY ANNE, magazine editor; b. Morristown, N.J., Apr. 6, 1963; d. Andrew R. and Patricia Ann (Brenner) R. BA in Comm., U. Del., 1985. Copywriter Macy's N.J., Newark, 1985-86; edit. asst. Globe Comms. Corp., N.Y.C., 1986-87; from asst. editor to assoc. editor Scholastic Math and DynaMath Mags. Scholastic, Inc., N.Y.C., 1987-89, editor Scholastic Math Mag., 1989-95; mng. editor Zig Zag Mag. Games Pub. Group, N.Y.C., 1995; sr. editor 321 Contact Mag. Children's Television Workshop, N.Y.C., 1996—. Mem. Soc. Children's Book Writers, Ednl. Press Assn. Am. (Disting. Achievement award feature articles divsn. 1991, 95).

RANDLE, JOHN, professional football player; b. Hearne, Tex., Jan. 12, 1967. Student, Trinity Valley C.C., Tex., Tex. A&I U. Defensive tackle Minn. Vikings, 1990—. Selected to Pro Bowl, 1993, 94; named to The Sporting News NFL All-Pro Team, 1994. Achievements tied AFC record for most sacks, 1994. Office: c/o Minn Vikings 9520 Viking Dr Eden Prairie MN 55344*

RANDLE, ROLINDA CAROL, elementary education educator; b. Fort Worth, Nov. 3, 1959; d. John Arthur and Ann Junette (Jones) Richards; m. Joseph L. Randle, June 12, 1982; children: Joseph Jr., Jennifer Michelle, Ja'Lissa Maurnice. BS in Edn., Tex. Christian U., 1982; postgrad., Tarleton State U. Cert. elem. edn., English, mid-mgmt., Tex. 2d grade tchr. Sunset Valley Elem. Sch., Austin, Tex., 1982-84; 6th grade tchr. Rosemont Middle Sch., Fort Worth, 1985-87; 6th grade tchr., adminstrv. intern Meadowbrook Middle Sch., Fort Worth, 1987—; pres./ceo Triple "J" Enterprises, Ft. Worth, 1996—; mem. site-based decision making team Rosemont Middle Sch., 1985-87, Meadowbrook Middle Sch., 1987-90, mem. leadership team, 1994—, mem. tech. com., 1991—; indsl. tech. trainer Fort Worth Ind. Sch. Dist., 1994—; owner, pres., CEO Triple J Enterprises. Fellow Summer Writing Inst; mem. United Educators Assn., NEA, Jack-n-Jill of Am. Inc., ASCD, Delta Sigma Theta. Methodist. Avocations: reading, computers, family activities. Home: 4733 Leonard St Fort Worth TX 76119-7540

RANDLETT, MARY WILLIS, photographer; b. Seattle, May 5, 1924; d. Cecil Durand and Elizabeth (Bayley) Willis; m. Herbert B. Randlett, Oct. 19, 1950 (div.); children—Robert, Mary Ann, Peter, Susan. B.A., Whitman Coll., Walla Walla, Wash., 1947. Freelance photographer, 1949—; one-person shows include Seattle Sci. Center, 1971, Western Wash. State U., 1971, Seattle Art Mus., 1971, Art Gallery of Greater Victoria, 1972, Alaska State Mus., 1972, State Capitol Mus., 1983, Whatcom Mus. History and Art,

Bellingham, Wash., 1986, Janet Huston Gallery, LaConner, Wash., 1990, Gov.'s Gallery, Office of Gov., Olympia, Wash., 1991, Stonington Gallery, Seattle, 1992, Valley Mus. Art, LaConner, 1992, others; group shows: Am. Soc. Mag. Photographers, 1970, Whatcom Mus., Bellingham, Wash., Henry Gallery, Seattle, 1971, 74, Royal Photog. Soc., 1979, Heard Mus., Phoenix, 1979, Gov.'s Invitational State Capital Mus., Olympia, Wash., 1983, Helmi: Interpretations N.W. Indian Art State Capital Mus., 1984, The Small Show Santa Fe Ctr. for Photography, 1987, Wash. State Capital Mus., 1988, Wash. State Capital Mus., Olympia, 1988, 89, 93, Tacoma (Wash.) Art Mus., 1989, Helen Day Art Ctr., Stowe, Vt., 1989, Valley Mus. Northwest Art, LaConner, 1991, Allen Libr. U. Wash., Seattle, 1991, Wing Luke Asian Mus., Seattle, 1991, Cheney Cowles Mus., Spokane, 1991, Security Pacific Gallery, Seattle, 1992, Benham Gallery, Seattle, 1993, Stonington Gallery, 1993, Rainier Club, Seattle, 1994, Valley Mus. of Northwest Art, La Conner, Wash., 1994, Port Angeles Fine Arts Ctr., Port Angeles, Wash., 1994, Mus. History and Industry, Seattle, 1994, Whatcom Mus., Bellingham, Wash., 1994, others; works represented in permanent collections Met. Mus., Nat. Collection of Fine Arts, Nat. Portrait Gallery, Washington State Library, Manuscript div. U. Wash., Pacific Northwest Bell, Seattle, Swedish Med. Center, Seattle, Whatcom Mus., Bellingham, Henry Gallery, Seattle, Wash. State Capitol Mus., Olympia, Phillips Collection, Washington; works appeared in books: The Master and His Fish (Roderick Haig-Brown), 1982; Theodore Roethke: The Journey to I and Otherwide (Neal Bowers), 1982; Mountain in the Clouds (Bruce Brown), 1982; Masonry in Architecture (Louis Redstone), 1982; Writings and Reflections from the World of Roderick Haig-Brown, 1982; Pike Place Market (Alice Shorett and Murray Morgan), 1982; The Dancing Blanket, (Cheryl Samuel), 1982, Collected Poems of Theodore Roethke, 1982; Spires of Form (Victor Scheffer), 1983; Assault on Mount Helicon (Mary Barnard), 1983; New as a Wave (Eve Triem), 1983; Sketchbook: A Memoir of the '30's and the Northwest School (William Cumming), 1983; Good Intentions (Jane Adams), 1985; Blackbirds of the Americas (Gordon Orians and Tony Angell), 1985; Historic Preservation in Seattle (Larry Kreisman), 1985; Down Town Seattle Walking Tours (Mary Randlett and Carol Tobin), 1986; Seattle, the Seattle Book, 1986; When Orchids were Flowers (Kate Knap Johnson), 1986, Jacob Lawrence, American Painter, (Ellen Wheat), 1986, Manic Power: Robert Lowell and His Circle, (Jeffrey Meyers), 1987, The Isamu Noguchi Garden Museum, (Isamu Noguchi), 1987, Washington's Audacious State Capitol and its Builders, (Norman Johnston), 1988, The Bloedel Reserve: Gardens in the Forest, (Lawrence Kreisman), 1988, Washingtonians: A Biographical Portrait of the State on the Occasion of its Centennial, 1988, Directory of Literary Biography: Canadian Writers 1920-59, 2d series, 1989, Crafts of America, 1989, The Lone Tree Tragedy (Bruce Brown), 1989, Northwest Coast Handbook of North American Indians, 1990, Dancing on the Rim of the World, 1990, Openings, Original Essays by Contemporary Soviet and American Writers (eds. Robert Atwan, Valeri Vinokurov), 1990, George Tsutakawa (Martha Kingsbury), 1990, Contemporary American Poetry (ed. Al Polin Jr.), 1991, Natural History of Puget Sound Country (Arthur Kruckberg), 1991, Bones (Joyce Thompson), 1991, Cebu (Peter Basho), 1991, Catalogue of Historic Preservation Publications, 1992, Art in Seattle's Public Places (James Rupp), 1992, The Olympic Rainforest (Ruth Kirk with Jerry Franklin), 1992, Steelhead Fly Fishing, (Trey Combs), 1992, Illustrated Guidelines for Rehabilitation Historic Buildings, 1993, A History of African American Artists (Bearden and Henderson), 1994, Childrens Literature Review Vol. 1, 1994, Invisible Gardens: The Search for Modernism the American Landscape (Walker and Simo), 1994, Seeing Seattle (Roger Sale), 1994, Reaching Home (Jay and Matson), 1994, Redesigning the American Lawn: A Search for Environmental Harmony (Gordone Geballe, Diana Balmari and F. Herbert Bormann), 1995, Reaching Home: Pacific Salmon, Pacific People (Foves, Jay and Matson), 1995, Carl F. Gould: A Life in Architecture and the Arts (T. William Booth and William H. Wuksib), 1995, others; works also appeared in newspapers and mags. Nat. Endowment for Arts grantee, 1976; recipient Wash. State Gov.'s award for spl. commendation for contbns. in field of photography, 1983, Individual Artist award King County Arts Commn., 1989. Mem. Am. Soc. Mag. Photographers. Home: PO Box 10536 Bainbridge Island WA 98110

RANDOLPH, ALAN DEAN, chemical engineering educator; b. Muskogee, Okla., Mar. 25, 1934; married 1957, 3 children. BSChE, U. Colo., 1956; MSChE, Iowa State U., 1959, PhD in Crystallization, 1962. Asst. tech. Shell Chem. Corp., 1956-58; rsch. proj. engr. Am. Potash & Chem. Corp., Calif., 1962-65; head crystallization sec. Res. Dept., 1965; assoc. prof. chem. engr. U. Fla., 1965-68; prof. Chem. Engring. Dept. U. Ariz., 1968-94; prof. emeritus, 1994—; vis. prof. U. Colo. London, 1981, U. Calif. Berkeley, 1974-75, U. Queenslana, Brisbane, Australia, 1975, U. Coll., London, 1982; cons. Comt. Nuclear Waste Immobilization, 1971-79, Los Alamos Sci. Lab, 1960-87, US Borax, 1978-82. Recipient Marston medal, Iowa State U., 1977. Fellow Am. Inst. Chem. Engrs. Achievements include research on mathematical simulation description and control of particulate systems, especially crystallization processes, theoretical and experimental study of nucleation-growth rate kinetics and residence-time distribution of particulate systems. Home: 2131 N Rainbow Vista Dr Tucson AZ 85712-2910

RANDOLPH, ARTHUR RAYMOND, federal judge, lawyer; b. Riverside, N.J., Nov. 1, 1943; m. Eileen J. O'Connor, May 18, 1984; children from previous marriage: John Trevor, Cynthia Lee. BS, Drexel U., 1966; JD summa cum laude, U. Pa., 1969. Bar: Calif. 1970, D.C. 1973, U.S. Supreme Ct. 1973. Law clk. to hon. judge Henry J. Friendly U.S. Ct. Appeals, 2d Cir., N.Y.C., 1969-70; asst. to solicitor gen. U.S. Dept. Justice, Washington, 1970-73, dep. solicitor gen., 1975-77; ptnr. Sharp, Randolph & Green, Washington, 1977-83, Randolph & Truitt, Washington, 1983-87, Pepper, Hamilton & Scheetz, Washington, 1987-90; judge U.S. Ct. Appeals (D.C. cir.), Washington, 1990—; spl. asst. atty. gen. State of Mont., 1983-90, State of N.Mex., 1985-90, State of Utah, 1986-90; mem. adv. panel Fed. Cts. Study Com., 1989-90; spl. counsel Com. on Stds. of Ofcl. Conduct, U.S. Ho. of Reps., 1979-80; adj. prof. law Georgetown U. Law Ctr., 1974-78; exec. sec. Atty. Gen.'s Com. on Reform of Fed. Jud. System, 1975-77; mem. com. on Fed. Rules of Evidence U.S. Justice Dept., 1972; chmn. Com. on Govtl. Structures, McLean, Va., 1973-74; adj. prof. law sch. George Mason U., 1992; mem. com. codes conduct Jud. Conf. U.S., 1993—, chmn., 1995—. Recipient Spl. Achievement award U.S. Dept. Justice, 1971. Mem. Am. Law Inst., Calif. Bar Assn., D.C. Bar Assn., Order of Coif. Office: US Ct Appeals 3rd Constitution Ave NW Washington DC 20001

RANDOLPH, CARL LOWELL, chemical company executive; b. Pasadena, Calif., May 30, 1922; s. Carl L. and Lulu (McBride) R.; m. Jane Taber, June 25, 1943; children—Margaret, Stephen. B.A., Whittier Coll., 1943; M.S., U. So. Calif., 1947, Ph.D., 1949; LL.D. (hon.), Whittier Coll., 1982; D. Pub. Service (hon.), U. Alaska, 1983. Prin. chemist Aerojet-Gen. Corp., 1949-57; v.p. U.S. Borax Research Corp., Anaheim, Calif., 1957-63; asst. to pres. U.S. Borax & Chem. Corp., Los Angeles, 1963-66; v.p. U.S. Borax & Chem. Corp., 1966-68, exec. v.p., 1968-69, pres., 1969-86, vice chmn., 1983-87. Trustee, chmn. bd. Whittier Coll., emeritus, 1969—; bd. dirs., chmn., Ind. Colls. So. Calif., 1982—. Served from ensign to lt. (j.g.) USNR, 1944-46. Mem. Phi Beta Kappa, Sigma Xi. Home: 1407 Seaview Way Anacortes WA 98221-9794

RANDOLPH, DAVID, conductor; b. N.Y.C., Dec. 21, 1914; s. Morris and Elsie (Goodman) R.; m. Mildred Greenberg, July 18, 1948. BS, CCNY, 1936; MA, Tchrs. Coll., Columbia U., 1941. Music specialist OWI, N.Y.C., 1943-47; adj. prof. music NYU, 1948-85, Mostly Mozart course, 1976-85; lectr. Town Hall, N.Y.C., 1955-60, Columbia U., 1957, Cosmopolitan Club, N.Y.C., 1962-63; pre-concert lectr. N.Y. Philharmonic, Avery Fisher Hall, 1964-86,Cleve. Orch., 1981, Vienna Symphony Orch., 1988; tchr. conducting Dalcroze Sch., 1948-49; music commentator Little Orch. Soc. Concerts and Broadcasts, 1950-62, Met. Opera Intermission Broadcasts; vis. prof. music SUNY-New Paltz, 1970-72, Fordham U., 1972-73; lectr. New Sch. for Social Rsch., 1973—, IBM, N.Y.C., 1978-86, Beethoven Soc., 1977, 83; prof. music Montclair State Coll., Upper Montclair, N.J., 1973-87; guest condr. Rockland County (N.Y.) Ann. Choral Festival, 1972, 73; adviser film Music to Live By, mem. N.J. Arts Council, 1967-70; mem. music com. Gov. N.J.'s Commn. to Study Arts, 1965; honored guest Handel Festival, Halle, Fed. Republic Germany, 1991. Condr. Randolph Singers, 1944-62 (appeared on NBC Today, and Tonight Shows), United Choral Soc., 1961-86, N.J. Ballet Orch., 1977, 83, Masterwork Chamber Orch., 1982, 83, The Philharmonia Orch. in Brahms' Requiem, London, 1988, Barge Concert, N.Y.C., 1987, 89; guest condr., Conn. Symphony Orch., 1961; condr. concert tour Spain with Am. choruses and Radio TV Orch. of Moscow, 1992; music annotator, CBS, N.Y.C., 1947-48; yearly choral seminar leader Mohonk Mountain House, 1986-95; music dir., condr. Masterwork Chorus and Orch., 1955-93, St. Cecilia Chorus and Orch., N.Y.C., 1965—; numerous performances at Carnegie Hall including Brahms' Requiem, Mozart's Requiem, Mozart's C Minor Mass, Beethoven's Missa Solemnis, Bach's Mass in B Minor, St. John Passion, St. Matthew Passion, Christmas Oratorio, Vaughan Williams' A Sea Symphony, Hodie, Verdi's Requiem, Mendelssohn's Elijah, Die erste Walpurgisnacht, Poulenc's Gloria, Dvorak's Requiem, Kodaly's Te Deum, Berlioz' Requiem, Avery Fisher Hall, Lincoln Ctr., N.Y.C. and Kennedy Ctr., Washington (including 168 complete performances of Handel's Messiah); broadcaster: David Randolph Concerts, WNYC and numerous radio stas. of Nat. Assn. Ednl. Broadcasters, 1946-79, Young Audience telecasts, CBS-TV, 1958-59, series of candid rehearsals of Bach's Mass in B minor, PBS, 1965; host: weekly broadcasts Lincoln Ctr. Spotlight, Sta. WQXR, N.Y.C., 1966-67; regular guest critic First Hearing program Sta. WQXR, N.Y.C., and 68 other stas., 1986—; author: This Is Music, 1964, numerous album jacket notes; editor: David Randolph Choral Series; writer, narrator: Instruments of the Orchestra, 1958, 95, Stereo Review's Guide to Understanding Music, 1973; music critic, High Fidelity Mag., 1952-57; composer: A Song for Humanity, 1968, Andante for Strings, Edward; contbg. author: The N.Y. Times Guide to Listening Pleasure, 1968; Recs. for Columbia, Vanguard, Westminster, Concert Hall Soc., Esoteric records; analyzed Mendelssohn's Symphony No. 3 on records for Book of Month Club; The Instruments of the Orchestra on Vanguard CD. Recipient 1st award for edn. by radio Ohio State Inst., 1948, 50, 51, Sylvania TV award, 1959, Disting. Alumni award Columbia U., 1982, cert. of appreciation May of City of N.Y. at Carnegie Hall, 1991; endowed David Randolph Disting. Artist-in-Residence Program at New Sch. in N.Y., 1996. Address: 420 E 86th St Apt 4-c New York NY 10028-6450

RANDOLPH, FRANCIS FITZ, JR., cable television executive; b. N.Y.C., July 13, 1927; s. Francis Fitz and Sarah Tod (Bulkley) R.; m. Catherine Ann Meyers, June 6, 1969. BA, Yale U., 1950; LLB, Columbia U., 1953. Bar: U.S. Ct. Appeals (2d cir.) 1954. Law clk. to presiding judge U.S. Ct. Appeals 2d cir., 1953-54; assoc. Cravath, Swaine & Moore, N.Y.C., 1954-61, ptnr., 1962-81; vice chmn. Cablevisions Systems Corp., Woodbury, N.Y., 1982-94; ret., 1994. Exec. com. NAACP Legal Def. Fund, N.Y., 1968-80; trustee Vassar Coll., 1980-92. With USN, 1946. Mem. N.Y. Bar Assn., Assn. of Bar of City of N.Y., Down Town Assn., Union Club; Silver Spring Country Club (Ridgefield, Conn.). Democrat. Office: Cablevision Systems Corp 1 Media Crossway Dr Woodbury NY 11797-2062

RANDOLPH, JACKSON HAROLD, utility company executive; b. Cin., Nov. 17, 1930; s. Dward Bradley and Cora Belle (Puckett) R.; m. Angelina Losito, June 20, 1958; children: Terri, Patti, Todd, Craig. B.B.A., U. Cin., 1958, M.B.A., 1968. C.P.A., Ohio. Acct. Arthur Andersen & Co., Cin., 1958-59; with Cin. Gas & Electric Co., 1959—, v.p. fin. and corp. affairs, 1981-85, exec. v.p., 1985-86, chmn., pres., chief exec. officer, 1986—, also dir.; chmn., CEO CINergy Corp., 1994—; also pres. Union Light Heat and Power Co., Covington, Ky.; bd. dirs. Cen. Trust Bank, N.A., Cin. Fin. Corp., PNC Corp.; chmn., CEO CINergy Corp., 1994—. V.p., bd. dirs. Gen. Protestant Orphan Home, Cin., 1981-86; treas., bd. dirs. Cin. chpt. ARC, 1975—; mem. adv. com. Catherine Booth Home, 1980—, Dan Beard council Boy Scouts Am., 1985. Served with USN, 1951-55. Mem. Cin. Country Club, Queen City Club, Met. Club, Bankers Club, Delta Sigma Pi, Phi Eta Sigma, Beta Gamma Sigma. Home: 414 Bishopsbridge Dr Cincinnati OH 45255-3900 Office: CINergy Corp 139 E 4th St Cincinnati OH 45202-4003 also: Union Light Heat & Power Co 107 Brent Spence Sq Covington KY 41011-1433*

RANDOLPH, JENNINGS, JR. (JAY RANDOLPH), sportscaster; b. Cumberland, Md., Sept. 19, 1934; s. Jennings and Mary Katherine (Babb) R.; m. Sue Henderson, May 28, 1966; children: Jennings, Brian Robert, Rebecca Sue. B.A., Salem (W.Va.) Coll., 1963. Sports and promotion dir. Sta. WHAR, Clarksburg, W.Va., 1958-61; sportscaster Sta. KLIF, Dallas, 1963-66; Sta. KMOX, St. Louis, 1966-68; with Sta. KSDK-TV, St. Louis, 1968—; sports dir. Sta. KSDK-TV, 1968-88, spl. sports corr., 1988—, also on nationally televised broadcasts for various sports events.; TV announcer Fla. Marlins Baseball Club, Ft. Lauderdale, 1993—; TV announcer St. Louis Cardinals, 1970-87, Cin. Reds., 1988; mem. NBC's broadcast staff for 1988 Olympics, Seoul, Korea and 1992 Summer Games, Barcelona, Spain; host nationally syndicated The Golf Show. Trustee Salem Coll., 1976-89. With U.S. Army, 1954-56. Inducted into Boys and Girls Clubs of Am. Hall of Fame, 1990. Mem. Nat. Assn. Sportscasters, Delta Tau Delta. Amateur golf champion. Office: The Fla Marlins 2267 NW 199th St Opa Locka FL 33056-2600

RANDOLPH, JOE WAYNE, machine manufacturing executive; b. Madisonville, Ky., Aug. 5, 1938; s. Albert Clay and Helen (Brown) R.; m. Mary Ann Rabenau, July 20, 1963; children: Ann E., Charles J. BS, Murray State U., 1962, MS, 1964; MBA, Washington U./Lindenwood Coll., 1978. High sch. tchr. Benton (Ky.) Sch. System, 1962-64, St. Charles (Mo.) Sch. System, 1964-65; mfg. mgr. Sunnen Products Co., St. Louis, 1967—. 1st lt. U.S. Army, 1965. Named Col., Hon. Order of Ky. Cols., 1990. Mem. AAIM Mgmt. Assn. (prodn. exec. round table, leader 1984—), Elks. Avocations: golf, fishing, travel, hunting. Home: 5700 Highway 2 Augusta MO 63332-1419 Office: Sunnen Products Co 7910 Manchester Rd Saint Louis MO 63143-2712

RANDOLPH, JUDSON GRAVES, pediatric surgeon; b. Macon, Ga., July 19, 1927; s. Milton Fitz and Abigail Theresa (Graves) R.; m. Susan Comfort Adams, June 14, 1952; children: Somers, Garrett, Judson, Adam, Comfort. BA, Vanderbilt U., 1950, MD, 1953. Intern in surgery U. Rochester, N.Y., 1953-54; asst. resident in pathology Vanderbilt U., 1954-55; asst. resident, then sr. resident in surgery Mass. Gen. Hosp., Boston, 1956-58; asst. resident in surgery Children's Hosp., Boston, 1955-56, sr. resident, then chief resident, 1958-61, asst. surgeon, 1961-63; teaching fellow to instr. surgery Med. Sch. Harvard U., 1960-63; jr. assoc. in surgery Peter Bent Brigham Hosp., Boston, 1961-63; surgeon-in-chief Children's Hosp., Washington, 1964-91; mem. faculty Med. Sch. George Washington U., 1964-91, prof. surgery and child health, 1968-91; prof. surgery Meharry Med. Coll., 1992—; cons. Nat. Naval Med. Ctr., NIH, Walter Reed Army Med. Ctr.; trustee Children's Hosp. Nat. Med. Ctr., 1972-84, Vanderbilt U., 1980—. Editor: Pediatric Surgery, 3d edit., 2 vols., 1979, 4th edit., 2 vols., 1985, The Injured Child, 1980; mem. editl. bd. Surgery, 1978-92; contbr. numerous articles to med. jours. With USNR, 1945-46, PTO. Mem. ACS (gov. 1969-75), AMA, Am. Acad. Pediats. (chmn. exec. com. surg. sect. 1974-75), Am. Assn. Thoracic Surgery, Am. Pediat. Surg. Assn. (gov. 1980—, pres. 1984), Washington Acad. Surgery (pres. 1989), Soc. U. Surgeons, Am. Surg. Assn., So. Surg. Assn., Am. Bd. Surgery (bd. dirs. 1973-79, diplomate), Alpha Omega Alpha (faculty), Cosmos Club (Washington). Methodist.

RANDOLPH, LILLIAN LARSON, medical association executive; b. Spokane, Wash., May 3, 1932; d. Charles P. and Juanita S. (Parrish) Larson; m. Philip L. Randolph, Nov. 12, 1952; children: Marcus, Andrew. BA, U. Wash., 1954, MA, 1956; PhD, U. Calif., Berkeley, 1966; EdD, N.Mex. State U., 1979. Researcher U. Wash., Seattle, 1954-59; asst. prof. Calif. State U., Hayward, 1964-68, U. Tex., El Paso, 1972-74; dir. S.W. Conservatory of Music, El Paso, 1972-74; adj. prof. Loyola U. and DePaul U., Chgo., 1974-78; asst. prof. DeVry Inst. Tech., Lombard, Ill., 1982-84; mgr. AMA, Chgo., 1985—; cons. Weber Co., Chgo., 1979-85. Author: Fundamentals of Government Organizations, 1971, Third Party Settlement of Disputes, 1973. Mem. AAUP, Phi Beta Kappa. Home: 408 W Wilshire Dr Wilmette IL 60091-3154

RANDOLPH, NANCY ADELE, nutritionist, consultant; b. St. Louis, Sept. 7, 1941; d. Robert Andrew and Mary Jane (Hilliker) R.; m. John Reginald Randolph-Swainson, Sept. 16, 1989. BS, U. Ariz., 1963; MEd, Boston U., 1971; postgrad., Harvard U., 1983. Intern instn. adminstrn. Mills Coll., Oakland, Calif., 1963-64; staff dietitian St. Lukes Hosp., St. Louis, 1964-65; clin. dietitian New England Deaconess Hosp., Boston, 1965-66; dietitian mgr. The Seiler Corp., Waltham, Mass., 1966-67; instr., acting dir. Whidden Hosp. Sch. Nursing, Everett, Mass., 1967-72; instr. nutrition Northeastern U. Coll. Nursing, Boston, 1972; renal/rsch. dietitian Lemuel Shattuck Hosp., Jamaica Plain, Mass., 1979-81; New England regional dietitian coord. Beverly Enterprises, Virginia Beach, Va., 1985-88; state nutritionist, surveyor Mass. Dept. Pub. Health/Health Care Quality, Boston, 1988-89; cons. nutritionist Randolph Assocs., West Palm Beach and Sarasota, Fla., 1990—; cons. dietitian Jewish Rehab Ctr., Swampscott, Mass., 1972-79, Lenox Hill Rehab. Ctr., Lynn, Mass., 1972-79, Jesmond Nursing Home, Nahant, Mass., 1972-88, numerous other health care facilities in New England, 1972-88. Mem. Am. Dietetic Assn. (cert.), Fla. Dietetic Assn., Cons. Nutritionists Practice Group, Cons. Dietitians in Health Care.

RANDOLPH, ROBERT DEWITT, lawyer; b. Sligo, Pa., Mar. 6, 1929; s. DeWitt Lyman and Hazel Irene (McCall) R.; m. Betty Ann McElhattan, May 8, 1953 (dec. Aug. 1979); children: Douglas, Andrew; m. Susan Denise Hopkins, Oct. 15, 1988. BA, Westminster Coll., 1951; LLB, Harvard U., 1957. Bar: Ohio 1958, Pa. 1960, U.S. Supreme Ct. 1981. Assoc. Buckingham, Doolittle & Burroughs, Akron, Ohio, 1957-59, Rose, Houston, Cooper & Schmidt, Pitts., 1959-60, 61-65; fgn. svc. officer U.S. Dept. State, Washington, 1960-61; ptnr. Houston, Cooper, Spear & German, Pitts., 1965-70, Randolph & O'Connor, Pitts., 1970-74, Buchanan Ingersoll P.C., Pitts., 1974-93. Pres. Assn. Retarded Citizens Allegheny, Pitts., 1990-92. With U.S. Army, 1951-54. Mem. Duquesne Club, St. Clair Country Club. Democrat. Presbyterian. Avocations: golf, skiing. Home: 750 Washington Rd Pittsburgh PA 15228

RANDOLPH, ROBERT LEE, economist, educator; b. East St. Louis, Ill., Jan. 2, 1926; s. John Andrew and Willye (Smith) R.; m. Patricia Smith, June 13, 1954 (div. 1986); 1 dau., Heather Elizabeth. A.B., DePauw U., Greencastle, Ind., 1948; M.S., U. Ill., Urbana, 1954, Ph.D., 1958; postdoctoral student, Case Western Res. U., 1960, U. Mich., 1962. From instr. to assoc. prof. econs. Springfield (Mass.) Coll., 1958-65, chmn. dept., 1960-63, dir. eve. and summer schs., 1960-64; dep. exec. dir. Equal Employment Opportunity Commn., Washington, 1967-68; dep. assoc. dir. Job Corps, 1965-67; exec. v.p. Chgo. State U., 1969-73; pres. Westfield (Mass.) Coll., 1973-79; vice-chancellor Mass. State Coll. System, 1979-81; pres. Ala. State U., 1981-83; prof. econs. U. Montevallo, Ala., 1983-86; pres. Randolph Assocs., Birmingham, Ala., Boston, 1983-91, Hyannis, Mass., 1991—; pres. State C.C., East St. Louis, Ill., 1993-95; cons. to industry. Author articles, monographs. Vice pres. Springfield Urban League, 1962-66; Bd. dirs. Wesson Hosp., Springfield, Holyoke (Mass.) Hosp., Sickle-Cell Anemia Found. Served to lt. (j.g.) USNR, 1943-45, 50-51. Decorated Bronze Star; recipient Danforth Found. award, 1943; Republic Steel Found. award, 1961; Vice Pres.'s award excellence pub. service U.S. Govt., 1967; Outstanding Alumni award Lincoln High Sch., E. St. Louis, 1973, Alumni Svc. award U. Ill., 1990, DePauw U., 1991; Navy V-12 scholar, 1943-45; State of Ill. scholar, 1952-56; Bailey fellow, 1957-58, Carnegie fellow, 1962. Mem. Am. Assn. State Colls. and Univs. (chmn. personnel com. 1974-75), Am. Assn. Polit. and Social Scis., Am. Econ. Assn., Phi Delta Kappa, Alpha Phi Omega, Kappa Alpha Psi. Clubs: Quandrangle (Chgo.); Internat. (Washington). Home: 101 John Joseph Rd Harwich MA 02645

RANDOM, IDA, production designer. Art dir.: (films) On Golden Pond, 1981, Partners, 1982, Frances, 1982; prodn. designer: (TV movies) The Kid from Nowhere, 1982, First Flight, 1989, (films) The Big Chill, 1983, Irreconcilable Differences, 1984, Body Double, 1984, Silverado, 1985, About Last Night..., 1986, Throw Momma from the Train, 1987, Who's That Girl?, 1987, Rainman, 1988 (Academy award nomination best art direction 1988), The War of the Roses, 1989, How I Got into College, 1989, Defending Your Life, 1991, Hoffa, 1992, Housesitter, 1992, Wyatt Earp, 1994. Office: care Spyros Skouras Sanford Skouras Gross & Assoc 1015 Gayley Ave Fl 3 Los Angeles CA 90024-3424

RANDS, BERNARD, composer, educator; b. Sheffield, Eng., Mar. 2, 1934. B.Music, U. Wales, 1956, M.Music, 1958; pvt. student composition, 1958-62. Former concert performer Europe, Australia and U.S.; co-founding artistic dir. Contemp Music. Fest, Calif. Inst. Arts; lectr. U. Wales, 1963-67; vis. fellow Princeton U., N.J., 1967-68; mem. faculty music, Granada fellow creative arts York U., 1968-75; composer in residence U. Ill, 1969-70; fellow creative arts Brasenose Coll., Oxford U., Eng., 1972-73; prof. music U. Calif.-San Diego, 1976-85, founder, conductor SONOR; prof. music Boston U., 1985-89, Harvard U., 1989—; composer in residence Phila. Orch., 1989. Compositions include Actions for Six, 1963, Wildtrack 1, 2 & 3, 1969-75, Mésalliance, 1972, AUM, 1974, Madrigali, 1977, déjà, 1979, Obbligato, 1980, Canti Lunatici, 1980/81, Canti del Sole for tenor and orch., 1982/83 (Pulitzer prize 1984), Le Tambourin: Sts. #1 and 2, 1984, Hiraeth for cello and orch., 1987, Ceremonial II, 1988, "...in the receding mist...", 1988, "...among the voices...", 1988, "...body and shadow...", 1989, Bells, 1989, Canti dell' Eclisse for bass and orch., 1991, Canti d'Amor, 1991, "...where the murmurs die...", 1991-92, Symphony, 1994, Canzoni per Orch., 1995. Harkness Internat. fellow Commonwealth Fund N.Y., 1966; grantee Nat. Endowment Arts, 1977; recipient Calif. Arts Council award, 1978, Koussevitzky award, 1984, 94, Barlow award, 1994. Office: Harvard U Dept Music Cambridge MA 02138

RANERE, BARBARA PHYLIS, elementary principal; b. Hammonton, N.J., July 12, 1942; d. John J. and Jeanette E. (Testa) R. BS in Secondary Edn., Seton Hall U., South Orange, N.J. Cert. tchr., N.J. Tchr. grade 6 St. Peter Sch., River Edge, N.J., 1962-63; tchr. grades 7-8 Our Lady Queen of Peace, Maywood, N.J., 1963-74; prin. St. Peter Elem. Sch., Merchantville, N.J., 1974-80; formation directress Villa Walsh Mother House of Religious Tchrs. Filippini, Morristown, N.J., 1980-88; tchr. grade 8 St. Joseph Sch., Hammonton, 1988-90, prin., 1990—; mem. Camden Diocesan Regionalization Bd. Mem. Nat. Cath. Edn. Assn., Nat. Coun. Tchrs. Math., N.J. Prins. and Suprs. Assn. Home: 219 N 3rd St Hammonton NJ 08037-1735 Office: St Joseph Regional Elem Sch 133 N 3rd St Hammonton NJ 08037-1733

RANEY, LEON A., librarian; b. Charleston, Ark., Jan. 14, 1939; s. J.D. Raney and Grace (Dunn) Pugh; m. Mary Lee Wilson, May 17, 1958; children: Joel, Jason. BSE, U. Ctrl. Ark., 1960; MS, La. State U., 1962; PhD, Ind. U., 1972. Libr. Grant Parish Libr., Colfax, La., 1962-64; catalog dept. head Ark. State U. Libr., Jonesboro, 1964-66; acquisitions libr. U. Okla. Libr., Norman, 1966-69; grad. teaching fellow Ind. U., Bloomington, 1969-72; dean librs. S.D. State U., Brookings, 1972—; cons. libr. Botswana Agrl. Coll., Gabrone, 1981, Northwestern Coll., Orange City, Iowa, 1983, U. Wis., River Falls, 1993; mem. exec. bd. S.D. Libr. Network, 1987—. Author libr. bldg. program S.D. State U., 1973; editor Index to S.D. Experiment Station Publications, 1978; contbr. articles to profl. jours. Mem. Pub. Libr. Bd., Brookings, 1985-88; chair adminstv. bd. Brookings United Meth. Ch., 1987; mem. S.D. Pub. Employees Retirement Bd., 1984-87. Grad. scholar La. State U., Baton Rouge, 1961-62; higher edn. fellow Ind. U., Bloomington, 1969-72. Mem. ALA (mem. coun. 1978-84), Mountain Plains Libr. Assn., S.D. Libr. Assn. (pres. 1991-92, Libr. of Yr. 1983, Disting. Svc. award 1995), Brookings Mason (master 1979), Rotary, Elks. Home: 404 12th Ave Brookings SD 57006-2265 Office: SD State U Briggs Libr Box 2115 Brookings SD 57007

RANGAN, CHAKRAVARTHI RAVI, environmental engineer; b. Madras, India, June 9, 1956; came to U.S., 1988; s. Chakravarthi and Tara Rangan; m. Rashmi Mishra, Nov. 8, 1981; 1 child, Artika. BS, Directorate Marine Engring., Calcutta, 1977; MS, U. Del., 1990. Profl. engr., Del. Jr. engr. Seven Seas Transp., Bombay, 1977-80; 1st engr. Garware Shipping Corp., Bombay, 1980-83; chief engr. Tolani Shipping Co., Bombay, 1985-88; from environ. engr. I to environ. engr. IV Del. Dept. Natural Resources & Environ. Control, New Castle, 1990—. Mem. ASTM (subcom. 1993—), Inst. Engrs. India, Inst. Marine Engrs. India, Inst. Engrs. U.K., Nat. Assn. Corrosion Engrs. Avocations: automobile repair, woodworking. Home: 4944 Mermaid Blvd Wilmington DE 19808-1005 Office: Del Dept Natural Resources & Environ Control 715 Grantham Ln New Castle DE 19720-4801

RANGEL, CHARLES BERNARD, congressman; b. Harlem, N.Y., June 11, 1930; s. Ralph and Blanche (Wharton) R.; m. Alma Carter, July 26, 1964; children: Steven, Alicia. BS, NYU, 1957; JD, St. John's U. Sch. Law, 1960; LLD (hon.), Wagner Coll., 1982, Atlanta U., 1983, St. John's U., Mt. Sinai Sch. Medicine, NYU, Howard U., 1988, Hofstra U., 1989. Bar: N.Y. 1960. Asst. U.S. atty. So. Dist. N.Y., 1961-62; mem. N.Y. State Assembly, 1966-70, 92nd-103rd Congresses from 19th (now 15th) N.Y. dist., Washington, D.C., 1971—; mem. Ways and Means Com., subcom. on trade, subcom on human resources; mem. Joint Com. on Taxation. Served with AUS, 1948-52,

Korea. Decorated Bronze Star, Purple Heart (U.S.); Korean presdl. citations. Home: 40 W 135th St New York NY 10037-2504 Office: US Ho of Reps 2354 Rayburn Ho Office Bldg Washington DC 20515

RANGELL, LEO, psychiatrist, psychoanalyst; b. N.Y.C., Oct. 1, 1913; s. Morris and Pauline (Kaiser) R.; m. Anita J. Buchwald, Feb. 22, 1939; children: Judith Ellen, Susan Roberta, Richard Neal, Paul Charles. AB, Columbia, 1933; MD, U. Chgo., 1937. Diplomate Am. Bd. Neurology and Psychiatry, 1943. Intern Bklyn. Jewish Hosp., 1937-39; resident neurology Montefiore Hosp., N.Y.C., 1939; resident psychiatry Grasslands Hosp., Valhalla, N.Y., 1940, N.Y. State Psychiat. Inst. and Hosp., N.Y.C., 1941; pvt. practice neurology and psychiatry N.Y.C., 1942-43; instr. neurology Columbia U. Coll. Physicians and Surgeons, 1942-46; Stroock rsch. fellow neuropsychiatry Montefiore Hosp., 1942-43; psychoanalytic tng. N.Y. Psychoanalytic Inst., later L.A. Psychoanalytic Inst., 1941-49; tng. analyst L.A. Psychoanalytic Inst., 1956—, dir. extension divsn., 1956-57, mem. bd. trustees, 1958—; pvt. practice psychoanalysis and neuropsychiatry Beverly Hills and L.A., 1946—; cons. Reiss-Davis Clinic Child Guidance, L.A., 1953-65; clin. prof. psychiatry Sch. Medicine UCLA, 1953—; clin. prof. psychiatry/psychoanalysis U. Calif., San Francisco, 1976—; fellow Ctr. Advanced Study Behavioral Scis., Stanford, 1962-63, Ctr. Advanced Psychoanalytic Studies, Princeton, N.J., 1962-70, Ctr. Advanced Psychoanalytic Studies, Aspen, Colo., 1970, 86; John B. Turner vis. prof. psychiatry Columbia U. Psychoanalytic Clinic for Tng. and Rsch., N.Y.C., 1971-72. Mem. editl. bd. Israel Annals Psychiatry and Related Disciplines, 1973—, Jour. Phila. Psychoanalytic Assn., Rev. Psychoanalytic Books, 1980—; contbr. numerous articles to profl. jours. Pres. bd. dirs. Westwood Hosp., L.A., 1959-60. Maj. M.C., USAAF, 1943-46. Guggenheim fellow, 1971-72; Recipient Internat. Clin. Essay prize Brit. Inst. Psychoanalysis, 1951, 53, Disting. Alumni award U. Chgo. Sch. Medicine, 1987, Sigourney Hon. award, 1991. Mem. Am. Psychoanalytic Assn. (pres. 1961-62, 66-67, bd. editors 1956-60, 62-66, 76-79, cons. 1979-81, 82-84, Edn. award Phila. chpt. 1978, Jour. award 1981, Hartmann award N.Y. chpt. 1985), L.A. Psychoanalytic Soc. (hon., pres. 1956-57, 64-65), Internat. Psychoanalytic Assn. (v.p. 1967-69, pres. 1969-71, 71-73, hon. v.p. 1994—), Am. Psychiat. Assn., So. Calif. Psychiat. Assn. (hon. mem. 1986), Peurvian Psychoanalytic Soc. (hon. mem. 1987). Home and Office: 456 N Carmelina Ave Los Angeles CA 90049-2704 also: Spindrift Rd Carmel Hglds CA 93923

RANGOS, ALEXANDER W., waste management enironmental services administrator. Student, U. Pitt.; pres., COO, Chambers Devel. Co., 1994—. Vice chmn. USA Waste Service Inc., Pittsburgh, PA, 1994—. Office: USA Waste Service Inc. 10700 Frankstown Rd Pittsburgh PA 15235-3039*

RANGOS, JOHN G., SR., waste management company executive; b. Steubenville, Ohio, July 27, 1929; s. Gust and Anna (Svokas) R.; children: John G. Jr., Alexander William, Jenica Anne. Attended, Houston Bus. Coll., 1949-50; grad., U.S. Signal and Communications Sch., Ft. Gordon, Ga. Formerly gen. agt. Rockwell Mfg. Co., Pitts.; also formed several cos. and pioneered technol. advances in waste transp. and disposal resources recovery and recycling during 1960s; pres., chief exec. officer Chambers Devel. Co., Inc. (merged as USA Waste service Inc.), Pitts., 1971—; now bd. mem. Innovations include converting powerplant boiler ash into a useful product for cinder block material and anti-skid material for hwys.; contbd. to invention of techniques for recycling bituminous by-products, disposing of sewage sludge; co-developer of techniques for disposing liquid indsl. waste; developer of a resource recovery system which converts waste-generated methane into energy. Fundraising chmn. UNICEF; contbr. Children's Hosp., Pitts., United Cerebral Palsy, Muscular Dystrophy, Leukemia Soc.; bd. trustees Lukemia Soc. Am.; bd. dirs. The Pitts. Opera, Carnegie Mellon U., Duquesne U., Allegheny Conf., The Carnegie, Carnegie Sci. Ctr., U. Pitts., Boy Scouts Am., Children's Hosp., Presentation of Christ Diocese, Clergy Liturgy Council; nat. del. U.S. Olympic Conf.; active Truman Libr. Found. Served with U.S. Army, 1951-54, Korea. Decorated Nat. Def. medal, U.N. medal, Korean Campaign medal; named Pitts. Man of Yr. in bus. and labor Vector's Community Svc. Orgn., 1990, Man of Yr. in bus. Juvenile Diabetes Found., 1990, Outstanding Philathropist of Yr. Nat. Soc. Fundraising Execs., 1990; recipient Nat. Patriots award Congrl. Medal of Honor Soc., 1991, Ellis Island award Am. Hellenistic Edn. Progressive Assn., 1991, Environ. Recognition award Soc. Preservation Greek Heritage, 1991, Art Rooney award Cath. Youth Assn., 1992, B'Nai B'rith Internat. Corp. Leadership award, 1992, Aristotelian award Am. Hellenistic Edn. Progressinve Assn., 1992, Man of Yr. award Hellenic-Am. C. of C., 1992, Handicapped Svc. award Boy Scouts of Am., 1992, Jr. Achievement award S.W. PA Corp., 1992, Acad. of Achievement award Am. Hellenistic Edn/ Progressive Assn., 1992; elected Archon of Ecumenical Patriarchate Order St. Andrew the Apostle, Greek Orthodox Ch., 1988. Mem. Nat. Dem. Club, Young Dems., Internat. Platform Assn. Clubs: The Allegheny, The Pitts. Press, U. Pitts. Golden Panther, Churchill Valley Country. Lodges: Masons (32nd degree), Shriners (Syria). Avocations: racquetball, golf, tennis, collecting art. Home: 1 Trimont Ln Apt 2200A Pittsburgh PA 15211-1255 Office: USA Waste Service Inc 10700 Frankstown Rd Pittsburgh PA 15235-3039*

RANHEIM, DAVID A., lawyer; b. Tyler, Minn., 1942. BA summa cum laude, Macalester Coll., 1964; JD, NYU, 1967. Ptnr. Dorsey & Whitney, Mpls. Office: Dorsey & Whitney Pillsbury Center So 220 S 6th St Minneapolis MN 55402-4502*

RANIERI, LEWIS S., financial services company executive. Mem. exec. com. Salomon Bros. Inc., N.Y.C., vice-chmn., 1986-89; founder Hyperion Capital (now Hyperion Partners LP), N.Y.C., 1989—; now chmn. Office: Bank United 3200 Southwest Fwy Houston TX 77027-7528 Office: Hyperion Capital Mgmt Inc 520 Madison Ave New York NY 10022-4213*

RANIS, GUSTAV, economist, educator; b. Darmstadt, Germany, Oct. 24, 1929; s. Max and Bettina (Goldschmidt) R.; m. Ray Lee Finkelstein, June 15, 1958; children: Michael Bruce, Alan Jonathan, Bettina Suzanne. BA summa cum laude, Brandeis U., 1952, hon. degree, 1982; MA, Yale U., 1953, PhD, 1956. Asst. adminstr. program and policy AID/Dept. of State, 1965-67; dir. Econ. Growth Ctr. Yale U., New Haven, 1967-75, prof. econs., 1964—, Frank Altschul prof. internat. econs., 1981—; dir. Yale Ctr. Internat. and Area Studies, 1996—; Ford Found. vis. prof. U. De Los Andes, Bogota, Colombia, 1976-77; Ford Found. faculty fellow Colegio de Mex., 1971-72; fellow Inst. for Advanced Study, Berlin, 1993-94; cons. World Bank, AID, Ford Found., ILO, FAO, Inter-Am. Devel. Bank. Author: (with John Fei) Development of the Labor Surplus Economy: Theory and Policy, 1964, (with Fei and Shirley Kuo) Growth with Equity: The Taiwan Case, 1979, (with Keijiro Otsuka and Gary Saxonhouse) Comparative Technology Choice in Development, 1988, (with F. Stewart and E. Angeles-Reyes) Linkages in Developing Economies: A Philippine Study, 1990, (with S.A. Mahmood) Political Economy of Development Policy Change, 1992; editor: Taiwan: From Developing to Mature Economy, 1992, En Route to Modern Economic Growth: Latin America in the 1990s, 1994; co-editor: The State of Development Economics, 1988, Science and Technology: Lessons for Development Policy, 1990. Trustee Brandeis U., 1967-93, chmn. acad. affairs com., 1986-93. Social Sci. Rsch. Coun. fellow, Japan, 1955-56. Mem. Am. Econ. Assn., Coun. Fgn. Rels., Overseas Develop. Coun. (mem. adv. com.). Home: 7 Mulberry Rd Woodbridge CT 06525-1716 Office: Yale U Econ Growth Ctr 27 Hillhouse Ave New Haven CT 06511-3703

RANK, EVERETT GEORGE, government official; b. Fresno, Calif., Dec. 1, 1921; s. Everett George and Evelyn Lydia (Dawson) R.; m. Evelyn Ingeborg Karschen, Apr. 30, 1948; children—Patricia, Judy, Ginny. Student pub. sch., Clovis, Calif. Farmer Fresno, 1946-81; chmn. Fresno County Agrl. Stblzn. and Conservation Service, 1959-69, Calif. Agrl. Stblzn. and Conservation Service, Berkeley, 1969-73; western regional dir. Agrl. Stblzn. and Conservation Service, Dept. Agr., Washington, 1974-76, adminstr., 1981-86. Pres. Clovis Unified Sch. Bd., 1959-72; bd. govs. U. Calif.-Fresno, 1977-81. Served with USN, 1941-45, PTO. Mem. Masons (32 degreer), Shriners. Republican. Baptist. Avocation: golf. Home: 11868 Old Friant Rd Fresno CA 93720-9701

RANK, JOHN THOMAS, lawyer; b. Chgo., Aug. 22, 1947; s. Gerald T. and Estelle M. (Lawler) R.; m. Linda Ann Prasil, July 25, 1970; 1 child, Sean Patrick. BA, U. Notre Dame, 1969; JD, Stanford U., 1972. Bar: Ill. 1972, Calif. 1973, U.S. Ct. Mil. Appeals 1973, U.S. Supreme Ct. 1977, U.S. Dist. Ct. (no. dist.) Ill. 1979. Assoc. Baker & McKenzie, Chgo., 1977-84, ptnr., 1984—. Served as capt. U.S. Army, 1973-77. Mem. ABA, Am. Arbitration Assn. (arbitrator), Calif. Bar Assn., Ill. Bar Assn., Ill. Assn. Hosp. Attys., Chgo. Bar Assn., Chgo. Trial Lawyers Club. Roman Catholic. Avocation: tennis. Office: Baker & McKenzie One Prudential Plz 130 E Randolph St Chicago IL 60601

RANK, LARRY GENE, social welfare association administrator; b. Auburn, Ind., July 14, 1935; s. Lloyd R. Rank and Elizabeth M. (Williamson) Jackson; m. Bette Whitehurst, May 2, 1959; children: Kevin, Karen. Grad., Am. Inst. Banking, 1962, U. Balt., 1969, Grad. Sch. Banking, Brown U., 1975, Nat. Council Savs. Instns., 1985. Asst. treas. Provident Savs. Bank, Balt., 1967-70, v.p., 1975-76, treas., v.p., 1976-79, sr. v.p., treas., 1979-82; exec. v.p. Provident Bank Md., Balt., 1982-85, pres., chief operating officer, 1985-90; dir. Provident Bank Md., 1984-90; mng. dir. Jannotta, Bray & Assocs. Inc., Balt., 1991-92; exec. dir. Big Bros. and Big Sisters Ctrl. Md. Inc., 1993—. Bd. dirs. Children's Cancer Found., Inc., Balt., 1984-90, Balt. chpt. ARC, 1990-92, bd. dirs., 1984—; divsn. chmn. United Way of Ctrl. Md., Balt., 1984-85, group chair, chair pub. sector mktg. com., Mktg. Task Force, bd. dirs., 1991-93; blood chmn. ARC, 1984-87, bd. dirs., first vice chair, 1988-89, Balt. Regional chpt., mem. campaign cabinet, hon. chmn 1988 ARC Humanitarian Award Dinner; chair Gov.'s Vol. Awards Selection com., 1989; chmn. Am. Heart Assn.-Heart Ball, 1989, bd. dirs. Am. Heart Assn., 1989-95, treas. 1992-94; mem. Vol. Coun. on EqualOpportunity; bd. trustees Md. Banking Sch., chmn. bd. trustees; chmn. bd. Neighborhood Housing Svcs., 1990; exec. com. Nat. Jewish Ctr. Immunology and Respiratory Medicine; mem. 1988 Com. for a Capital Affair; bd. dirs. Balt. Goodwill Industries, 1989—, 1st vice chmn., 1992; trustee Northwest Hosp. Ctr., 1988, exec. com., 1989-95, chair capital campaign, 1990—, sec., 1992, 1st v.p. 1992-94, vice-chmn. bd., 1996—. Mem. Nat. Coun. Savs. Instns. (mem. ecn. com. 1984-85), Assn. Corp. Growth (pres. 1985-86), Assn. Balt. Area Grantmakers, Am. Inst. Banking (chmn. sr. exec. commn. 1989), Balt. Mentoring Inst. (bd. dirs.), Md. Hosp. Assn. (mem. PAC com.), Deacon Club, Wake Forest Wildcat Club, Villanova Club, Hunt Valley Golf Club, Camden Club. Lutheran. Avocations: golf, sports, books, travel. Office: 3600 Clipper Mill Rd # 250 Baltimore MD 21211-1934

RANKAITIS, SUSAN, artist; b. Cambridge, Mass., Sept. 10, 1949; d. Alfred Edward and Isabel (Shimkus) Rankaitis; m. Robbert Flick, June 5, 1976. B.F.A. in Painting, U. Ill., 1971; M.F.A. in Visual Arts, U. So. Calif., 1977. Rsch. asst., art dir. Plato Lab., U. Ill., Urbana, 1971-75; art instr. Orange Coast Coll., Costa Mesa, Calif., 1977-83; chair dept. art Chapman Coll., Orange, Calif., 1983-90; Fletcher Jones chair in art Scripps Coll., Claremont, Calif., 1990—; represented by Robert Mann Gallery, N.Y.C.; overview panelist visual arts Nat. Endowment for Arts, 1983, 84. One-woman shows include Los Angeles County Mus. Art, 1983, Internat. Mus. Photography, George Eastman House, 1983, Gallery Min. Tokyo, 1988, Ruth Bloom Gallery, Santa Monica, 1989, 90, 92, 95, Schneider Mus., Portland, Ore., 1990; Ctr. for Creative Photography, 1991, Robert Mann Gallery, N.Y.C., 1994, Mus. Contemporary Photography, Chgo., 1994; represented in permanent collections U. N.Mex. Art, Santa Monica Coll., Ctr. for Creative Photography, Mus. Modern Art, Santa Barbara Mus. Art, Los Angeles County Mus. Art, Mpls. Inst. Arts, San Francisco Mus. Modern Art, Mus. Modern Art, Lodz, Poland, Princeton U. Art Mus., Stanford U. Art Mus., Contemporary Art Mus., Honolulu, others. Active L.A. Ctr. for Photographic Studies, 1988—, mem. adv. bd. trustees. Nat. Endowment for Arts fellow, 1980, 88, U.S./France fellow, 1989, Agnes Bourne fellow in Painting and Photography, Djerassi Found., 1989; recipient Graves award in Humanities, 1985. Mem. Coll. Art Assn., L.A. Contemporary Exhbns. (adv. trustee L.A. Ctr. for Photographic Studies), L.A. County Mus. Art. Studio: Studio 5 1403 S Santa Fe Ave Los Angeles CA 90021-2500

RANKIN, ALFRED MARSHALL, JR., business executive; b. Cleve., Oct. 8, 1941; s. Alfred Marshall and Clara Louise (Taplin) R.; m. Victoire Conley Griffin, June 3, 1967; children: Helen P., Clara T. BA in Econs. magna cum laude, Yale U., 1963, JD, 1966. Mgmt. cons. McKinsey & Co., Inc., Cleve., 1970-73; with Eaton Corp., Cleve., 1974-81, pres. materials handling group, 1981-83, pres. indsl. group, 1984-86, exec. v.p., 1986, vice chmn., chief oper. officer, 1986-89; pres., COO NACCO Industries, Inc., Cleve., 1989-91, pres., CEO, 1991-94, also bd. dirs., chmn., pres., CEO, 1994—, chmn., 1994—; bd. dirs. B.F. Goodrich Co., The Std. Products Co., Vanguard Group. Former pres., trustee Hathaway Brown Sch.; trustee Univ. Hosps. Cleve., Mus. Arts Assn., Univ. Ctr., Inc., Cleve. Mus. Art, Greater Cleve. Growth Assn., John Huntington Art and Poly. Inst., Cleve. Tomorrow, The Cleve. Found. Mem. Ohio Bar Assn. Republican. Clubs: Chagrin Valley Hunt, Union, Tavern, Pepper Pike, Kirtland Country (Cleve.); Rolling Rock (Ligonier, Pa.); Met. (Washington). Home: 5875 Landerbrook Dr Ste 300 Mayfield Heights OH 44124 Office: NACCO Industries Inc 5875 Landerbrook Dr Mayfield Heights OH 44124

RANKIN, CLYDE EVAN, III, lawyer; b. Phila., July 3, 1950; s. Clyde Evan, Jr. and Mary E. (Peluso) R. A.B., Princeton U., 1972; J.D., Columbia U., 1975; postgrad. Hague Acad. Internat. Law, 1975. Bar: N.Y., N.J., D.C., U.S. Supreme Ct. Law clk. to judge U.S. Dist. Ct. So. Dist. N.Y., 1975-77; assoc. Debevoise, Plimpton, Lyons & Gates, N.Y.C., 1977-79; assoc. Coudert Bros., N.Y.C., 1979-83, ptnr., 1984—. Trustee The Rensselaerville (N.Y.) Inst., 1989—. Stone scholar, 1974. Mem. ABA, Assn. of Bar of City of N.Y., N.Y. State Bar Assn., D.C. Bar Assn., N.J. Bar Assn. Roman Catholic. Club: Amateur Comedy (N.Y.C.). Contbr. article to legal jour. Office: Coudert Bros 1114 Avenue Of The Americas New York NY 10036-7703

RANKIN, HAYWOOD FORNEY, diplomat; b. Washington, July 31, 1946; s. Forney Anderson and Jean Smith (Cantrell) R.; m. Sabine Irmgard Schmid, Aug. 5, 1982; children: Johanna, Susanna. AB in Sociology, U. N.C., 1968, JD, 1971; BS in Geology, Oxford U., Eng., 1982. Bar: N.C. 1971. Law clk. to chief justice N.C. Supreme Ct., Raleigh, 1971-72; vice consul Am. Consulate Gen., Tangier, Morocco, 1973-75; consul Am. Consulate Gen., Port Said, Egypt, 1977-79; polit. analyst Bureau Intelligence and Rsch. Dept. State, Washington, 1982-84; polit. officer Am. Embassy, Damascus, Syria, 1984-86; chief polit. sect. Am. Embassy, Baghdad, Iraq, 1986-88; dep. chief mission Am. Embassy, Muscat, Oman, 1989-92, Algiers, Algeria, 1992-94; dep. dir. Office Near East South Asia Bur. Intelligence & Rsch., Washington, 1994—. Recipient Meritorious Honor award, 1986, Superior Honor award, 1992. Democrat. Presbyterian. Avocations: travel, photography. Home: 4948 Ashby St NW Washington DC 20007 Office: Am Embassy Abidjan Dept State Washington DC 20521-2010

RANKIN, HELEN CROSS, cattle rancher, guest ranch executive; b. Mojave, Calif; d. John Whisman and Cleo Rebecca (Tilley) Cross; m. Leroy Rankin, Jan. 4, 1936 (dec. 1954); children—Julia Jane King Sharr, Patricia Helen Denvir, William John. A.B., Calif. State U.-Fresno, 1935. Owner, operator Rankin Cattle Ranch, Caliente, Calif., 1954—; founder, pres. Rankin Ranch, Inc., Guest Ranch, 1965—; mem. sect. 15, U.S. Bur. Land Mgmt.; mem. U.S. Food and Agrl. Leaders Tour China, 1983, Australia and N.Z., 1985; dir. U.S. Bur. Land Mgmt. sect. 15. Pres., Children's Home Soc. Calif., 1945; mem. adv. bd. Camp Ronald McDonald. Recipient award Calif. Hist. Soc., 1983, Kern River Valley Hist. Soc., 1983. Mem. Am. Nat. Cattlemen's Assn., Calif. Cattlemen's Assn., Kern County Cattlemen's Assn., Kern County Cowbelles (pres. 1949, Cattlewoman of Yr. 1988), Calif. Cowbelles, Nat. Cowbelles, Bakersfield Country Club, Bakersfield Raquet Club. Republican. Baptist. Office: Rankin Ranch Caliente CA 93518

RANKIN, JACQUELINE ANNETTE, communications expert, educator; b. Omaha, Nebr., May 19, 1925; d. Arthur C. and Virdie (Gillispie) R. BA, Calif. State U., L.A., 1964, MA, 1966; MS in Mgmt., Calif. State U., Fullerton, 1977; EdD, U. LaVerne, Calif., 1981. Tchr. Rowland High Sch., La Habra, Calif., 1964-66, Lowell High Sch., La Habra, Calif., 1966-69, Pomona (Calif.) High Sch., 1969-75; program asst. Pomona Adult Sch., 1975-82; dir. Child Abuse Prevention Program, 1985-86; instr. Northern Va. Univ.; faculty evening divsn. Mt. San Antonio C.C., 1966-72; asst. prof. speech Ball State U., Muncie, Ind., 1993; instr. No. Va. U., Alexandria, Annendale, Manassas, Woodbridge, 1995—; assoc. faculty dept. comm. and theatre, Ind. U., Purdue U., Indpls., 1993; trainer internat. convs., sales groups, staffs of hosps., others; lectr., cons. in field. Author: Body Language: First Impressions, Body Language in Sales and Negotiations; columnist Jackie's World, Topics Newspapers, Indpls. Mem. ARC, Fairfax Adv. Coun., Fairfax County Dem. Com. Mem. Ph Lambda Theta, Phi Delta Kappa. Home and Office: 7006 Elkton Dr Springfield VA 22152-3330

RANKIN, JAMES WINTON, lawyer; b. Norfolk, Va., Sept. 9, 1943; s. Winton Blair and Edith (Griffin) R.; m. Donna Lee Carpenter, June 25, 1966 (dec.); children—Thomas James, William Joseph, Elizabeth Jeanne; m. JoAnne Katherine Murray, Feb. 11, 1978. A.B. magna cum laude, Oberlin Coll., 1965; J.D. cum laude, U. Chgo., 1968. Bar: Ill. 1968, U.S. Dist. Ct. (no. dist.) Ill. 1969, U.S. Ct. Appeals (7th cir.) 1971, U.S. Ct. Appeals (5th cir.) 1979, U.S. Supreme Ct. 1975, Calif. 1986. Law clk. U.S. Dist. Ct. (no. dist.) Ill., 1968-69; assoc. Kirkland & Ellis, Chgo., 1969-73, ptnr., 1973—. Mem. ABA, Order of Coif, Mid-Am. Club, Univ. Club, Mich. Shores Club, Kenilworth Club, Ephriam Yacht Club. Presbyterian. Home: 633 Kenilworth Ave Kenilworth IL 60043-1070 Office: Kirkland & Ellis 200 E Randolph St Chicago IL 60601-6436

RANKIN, JOANNA MARIE, astronomy educator; b. Denver, Mar. 10, 1942; d. Robert McCurdy and Julia Bernice (Pelsor) R.; life ptnr. Mary Rose Fillmore. BS, So. Meth. U., 1965; MS, Tulane U., 1966; PhD in Astrophysics, U. Iowa, 1970. Asst. prof. astronomy dept. Cornell U., Ithaca, N.Y., 1974-78; acting head computer dept. Arecibo (P.R.) Obs., 1976; sr. rsch. assoc. history dept. Ctr. for Radiophysics and Space Rsch., Cornell U., Ithaca, 1978-80; assoc. prof. physics dept. U. Vt., Burlington, 1980-88, prof. physics and astronomy physics dept., 1988—; organizer Internat. Astron. Union Colloquium 128, Lagow, Poland, 1990; organizer, participant in internat. astron. collaborations with astronomers, India, USSR, Poland, 1985-90; lectr. in field. Contbr. articles to profl. jours. Bd. dirs. Vt. Pro-Choice, 1987-90; activist Women's Internat. League for Peace and Freedom, Burlington, Vt., 1981-86; mem. War Resister's League, N.Y.C., 1982—; supporter Lesbian Herstory Archives, N.Y.C., 1987—; creator, collector polit. poster art show, 1983-85. Recipient NASA traineeship U. Iowa, 1966-70; named Van Allen/Link fellow astron. dept. U. Iowa, 1970, finalist Kellogg Nat. fellow Kellogg Found., 1984, Fulbright fellow, 1994, Indo-U.S. fellow, 1990; rsch. grantee NSF, 1972, 73, 78, 89, 94. Mem. Internat. Astron. Union, Am. Astron. Soc., Fedn. Am. Scientists, Am. Women in Sci., Nat. Women's Studies Assn. Avocations: hiking, camping, sailing. Office: U Vt Physics Dept Burlington VT 05405

RANKIN, M. DOUGLAS, electronics executive; b. 1938. V.p. sales and mkgt. Inmos Corp., Colo. Springs, 1980-86, Signetics Corp., Sunnyvale, Calif., 1983-86; sr. v.p. sales, mktg. Actel Corp., Sunnyvale, Calif., 1986—; now sr. v.p. strategic accounts. Office: Actel Corp 955 E Arques Ave Sunnyvale CA 94086-4521*

RANKIN, MARTHA MILLER COTTINGHAM (MARTY RANKIN), elementary school educator; b. Bennettsville, S.C., Dec. 24, 1927; d. Colin James and Lily Clarkston (Miller) Cottingham; m. Donald McCray Rankin, Aug. 28, 1949; children: Martha Miller (dec.), Donald McCray Jr., Mary Colin. BS, Queens Coll., 1949; MEd, Francis Marion Coll., 1989. Cert. reading tchr., S.C. Spl. edn. tchr. Marlboro County Bd. Edn., Bennettsville, 1956-58, 1st grade tchr., 1958-59, 5th grade tchr., 1959-67, 81-91, 2d grade tchr., 1969-72, art tchr. K-2, 1991—; grade 5 rep., advisor social studies curriculum Marlboro County Bd. Edn., 1989-91, observer assessments of performance in teaching, 1991-95. Commr. Marlboro Coounty Parks and Recreation; bd. dirs. Atlanta Area Presbyn. Homes, 1980-90; pres. Pee Dee Presbytery, 1977-79, Women of Ch. Pee Dee Presbytery, 1977-79; elder 1st Presbyn. Ch., Bennettsville, 1983—; reenactor 2d Regiment S.C. Line C. E., Columbia, 1974-81. Mem. Nat. Art Edn. Assn., S.C. Art Edn. Assn., NEA, S.C. Edn. Assn., Marlboro County Edn. Assn. (sec., treas., legis. rep.), Delta Kappa Gamma (pres., v.p., program chmn., sec. 1968—). Avocations: reading, walking, crafts, painting. Home: 1683 Highway 15-401 E Bennettsville SC 29512-7212

RANKIN, ROBERT, retired educational foundation executive; b. Des Moines, Sept. 14, 1915; s. Wiley Strange and Estelle Blanche (Renne) R.; m. Martha Jean Roberts, Sept. 7, 1940; children: Mary Renne (Mrs. Joseph L. Sturdevant Jr.), Margaret Lloyd, Wiley Robert, William Roberts. B.A., U. Iowa, 1937; B.D., Yale, 1940, M.A., 1942; D.D. (hon.), Lindenwood Coll., St. Charles, Mo., 1964, Northland Coll., Ashland, Wis., 1981; D.H.L. (hon.), U. So. Calif., 1967. Ordained to ministry Methodist Ch., 1944, United Ch. Christ, 1960; minister Sunnyvale, Calif., 1942-44; campus minister, lectr. religion, dir. YMCA Oberlin Coll., 1946-51; chaplain, assoc. prof. religion Claremont Colls., 1951-58; exec. dir. Rockefeller Bros. Theol. Fellowship Program, Princeton, N.J., 1954-55; assoc. dir. Danforth Found., St. Louis, 1958-66; v.p. Danforth Found., 1966-80, dir. programs campus ministry, 1958-80, assoc. program, 1958-75; cons. Fund Theol. Edn., Lilly Endowment, Pres.'s Commn. on Campus Unrest; chmn. St. Louis Met. Conf. Edn. Culturally Disadvantaged, 1962; cons. to bd. dirs. Nat. Inst. for Campus Ministry, 1974-83; mem. St. Louis region selection panel White House fellows, 1975, 77, chmn., 1978; mem. Nat. Commn. Higher Edn., United Meth. Ch., 1975-77; chmn. exec. com. Wingspread Conf., 1969-73. Author, editor: The Recovery of Spirit in Higher Education, 1980; author articles, chpts. in books; edit. adv. bd. Religion and Intellectual Life, 1984—. Trustee Sch. Theology at Claremont, 1955-59, advisor, 1985—, Am. Friends of Wilton Park, 1975, Healing Community St. Louis, 1976-81, Claremont, 1984-90, Nat. Task Force for Disability and the Art, 1978-81, Evangelicals for Social Action; mem. Com. on Disability City of Claremont; resident Pilgrim Place, Claremont, 1981; advisor Pilgrim Festival, 1983—, Pilgrim Aquatic Fitness Ctr., 1993—. Recipient E. Harris Harbison hon. award for gifted teaching, 1970; Fellow Wilton Park Conf., Sussex, Eng.; Fellow Soc. Values Higher Edn. Mem. Nat. Assn. Coll. and Univ. Chaplains, Assn. for Religion and Intellectual Life, Nat. Campus Ministry Assn., Am. Friends Svc. Com., Am. Assn. UN, Am. Acad. Religion, Am. Assn. for Higher Edn., ACLU, NAACP, Sigma Chi, Univ. Claremont Club. Mem. United Ch. of Christ. Home: 737 Alden Rd Claremont CA 91711-4221

RANKIN, ROBERT ARTHUR, journalist; b. Richmond, Va., May 31, 1949; s. Arthur Norton and Martha Louise (Rountree) R.; m. Janis Johnson, May 11, 1979; 1 child, Benjamin John. BA in Polit. Sci., Randolph Macon Coll., 1971; MA in Govt., U. Va., 1974. Reporter Richmond News Leader, Va., 1972-75; reporter Congl. Quar., Washington, 1975-78; editorial writer Miami Herald, Fla., 1980-85, Phila. Inquirer, 1985-87; nat. corr. Washington bur. Knight Ridder Newspapers, 1987—. V.p. Civic Assn. Hollin Hills, Alexandria, Va., 1991-92. Co-recipient Pulitzer prize for editorial writing 1983, Olive Branch award N.Y.U. Ctr. for War, Peace and The News Media, 1990; recipient 1st prize Va. Press Assn., 1974; best editorial award Phila. chpt. Sigma Delta Chi, 1987; Walter Bagehot fellow Columbia U., 1978-79. Mem. White House Corres. Assn., Nat. Press Club. Office: Knight Ridder Newspapers 700 National Press Building Washington DC 20045-1701

RANKIN, THOMPSON L., utilities executive, agricultural executive. With Lykes Bros. Inc., Tampa, Fla., 1961—, chmn., pres.; chmn., CEO Lykes Energy Inc., Tampa; chmn., pres. Lykes Pasco, Inc., Dade City, Fla.; chmn., CEO People's Gas Sys., Tampa, 1993—; chmn., pres. Shore Mgmt. Inc., Tampa. Office: Lykes Bros PO Box 1690 Tampa FL 33601 Office: Lykes Bros 111 E Madison St Tampa FL 33602*

RANKIN, WILLIAM BROWN, II, airport administrator. BS in Aviation Mgmt., Mid. Tenn. State U.; MS in Aviation Mgmt., Embry-Riddle U. Airport mgr. Smith-Reynolds Airport, Winston-Salem, N.C., 1974-85; airport dir. Cedar Rapids (Iowa) Regional Airport, 1985-89; mgr. ops. divsn. Washington Nat. Airport, 1989-94; dir. aviation El Paso (Tex.) Internat. Airport, 1994—. Dir. El Paso Conv. and Tourism Bd.; past dir. Cedar Rapids Conv. and Vis. Bur., Greater Downtown Assn. Cedar Rapids, Auburn U. Scholarship Com. Mem. Am. Assn. Airport Execs. (accredited), S.E. Airport Mgrs. Assn., N.C. Assn. Airports (past dir.). Office: El Paso Internat Airport 6701 Convair Dr El Paso TX 79925

RANKIN, WILLIAM PARKMAN, educator, former publishing company executive; b. Boston, Feb. 6, 1917; s. George William and Bertha W. (Clowe) R.; m. Ruth E. Gerard, Sept. 12, 1942; children: Douglas W., Joan W. BS, Syracuse U., 1941; MBA, NYU, 1949, PhD, 1979. Sales exec. Redbook mag., N.Y.C., 1945-49; sales exec. This Week mag., N.Y.C., 1949-55, adminstrv. exec., 1955-60, v.p., 1957-60, v.p., dir. advt. sales, sales devel. dir.,

1960-63, exec. v.p., 1963-69; gen. exec. newspaper div. Time Inc., N.Y.C., 1969-70; gen. mgr. feature svc. Newsweek, Inc., N.Y.C., 1970-74, fin. and ins. advt. mgr., 1974-81; prof., asst. to the dir. Walter Cronkite Sch. Journalism and Telecommunication, Ariz. State U., Tempe, 1981—; lectr. Syracuse U., NYU, Berkeley Sch. Author: Selling Retail Advertising, 1944; The Technique of Selling Magazine Advertising, 1949; Business Management of Consumer Magazines, 1980, 2 ed. 1984, The Practice of Newspaper Management, 1986. Mem. Dutch Treat Club. Home: 1220 E Krista Way Tempe AZ 85284-1545 also: Bridge Rd Bomoseen VT 05732 Office: Ariz State U Walter Cronkite Sch Journalism/Telecom Tempe AZ 85287-1305

RANNEY, (JOSEPH) AUSTIN, political science educator; b. Cortland, N.Y., Sept. 23, 1920; s. Frank Addison and Florence Edith (Ranney) R.; m. Elizabeth Mackay (div. Oct. 1975); m. Nancy Boland; children: Joseph, Douglas, Gordon, David. BS, Northwestern U., 1941, LLD (hon.), 1995; MA, U. Oreg., 1943; PhD, Yale U., 1948, DSS (hon.), 1985; LLD (hon.), SUNY, 1986, Northwestern U., 1995. Statistician Douglas Aircraft Corp., Chgo., 1942-44; instr. Yale U., New Haven, 1945-47; from instr. to prof. U. Ill., Urbana, 1947-63; prof. U. Wis., Madison, 1963-76; resident scholar Am. Enterprise Inst., Washington, 1976-86; prof. U. Calif., Berkeley, 1986-91, prof. emeritus, 1991—, chmn. dept. polit. sci., 1987-90. Author: The Doctrine of Responsible Party Government, 1954, Governing, 1958, Curing the Mischiefs of Faction, 1975, Channels of Power, 1983. Mem. Presdl.-Congl. Commn. on Polit. Activity Govtl. Employers, Washington, 1967-68, Dem. Nat. Com. Commn. on Party Structure, Washington, 1969-72, Commn. on Presdl. Debates, Washington, 1980-88; chmn. Gov.'s Commn. on Registration and Voting Participation, Madison, Wis., 1964, social sci. rsch. coun. Com. on Govtl. Processes, 1964-71, coun. on social scis. policy Yale U., 1983-88. Recipient Wilbur Lucius Cross medal Yale U. Grad. Sch., 1977; sr. rsch. fellow NSF, 1970, John Simon Guggenheim fellow, 1974, fellow Ctr. for Advanced Study in Behavioral Scis., 1978. Mem. Am. Polit. Sci. Assn. (pres. 1975-76), Am. Acad. Arts and Scis. (v.p. 1981-84). Home: 990 Regal Rd Berkeley CA 94708-1430 Office: Univ Calif Dept Polit Sci Berkeley CA 94720

RANNEY, CARLETON DAVID, plant pathology researcher, administrator; b. Jackson, Minn., Jan. 23, 1928; s. Carleton Oran and Ada Elizabeth (Harriman) R.; m. Mary Kathryn Ransleben, July 16, 1949; children: David Clayton, Mary Elizabeth. AA, Chaffey Jr. Coll., Ontario, Calif., 1952; BS, Tex. A&M U., 1954, MS, 1955, PhD, 1959. Plant pathologist Crops Rsch. Div. Agrl. Rsch. Svc. USDA, College Station, Tex., 1955-58, Stoneville, Miss., 1958-70; investigations leader Crops Rsch. Div. Agrl. Rsch. Svc. USDA, Beltsville, Md., 1970-72; area dir. Ala. No. Miss. area Agrl. Rsch. Svc. USDA, Starkville, Miss., 1973-78; area dir. Delta States area Agrl. Rsch. Svc. USDA, Stoneville, Miss., 1978-84; area dir. Mid-South area Agrl. Rsch. Svc. USDA, Stoneville, 1984-87; asst. dir. Miss. Agrl. and Forestry Exptl. Stas., Stoneville, 1987-94, head Delta br. sta., 1987-94, emeritus plant pathologist, 1994—; adj. prof. agronomy Miss. State U., 1970-94; sr. exec. svc. USDA, Stoneville, Miss., 1984-87; adv. bd. Belt Wide Meetings Nat. Cotton Coun., Memphis, Tenn., 1987-96. Contbr. articles to profl. jours. Sect. advisor SE2 Order of Arrow, Boy Scouts Am., Miss. and West Tenn., 1973-83; pres. Delta Area coun. Boy Scouts Am., Clarksdale, Miss., 1990-911 vice chmn. Leland Habitat for Humanity, 1995—. Recipient Silver Beaver Boy Scouts Am., Stoneville, 1981, Disting. Svc. Order of Arrow, Stoneville, 1983. Mem. Agron. Soc. Am., Nat. Cotton Disease Coun. (sec. 1959-60, chmn. 1961-62), Lions Club (pres. 1995-96), Sigma Xi, Alpha Zeta, Phi Kappa Phi. Methodist. Achievements include development of fungicide control seedling diseases; definition of relationship of microclimate to boll rot of cotton; development of non-mercurial seed treatments. Office: Delta Rsch & Ext Ctr PO Box 197 Stoneville MS 38776-0197

RANNEY, GEORGE A., JR., lawyer; b. Chgo., Apr. 11, 1940. BA magna cum laude, Harvard U., 1962; JD, U. Chgo., 1966. Bar: Ill. 1966. Law clk. to Hon. Carl McGowan U.S. Ct. Appeals, Washington, 1966-67; dep. dir. Bur. Budget, State of Ill., 1969-73; counsel, v.p. Inland Steel Co., 1973-86; ptnr. Mayer, Brown & Platt, Chgo.; mem. Commn. Uniform State Laws, 1969-73; chmn. State Task Force on Future Ill., 1978-80; lectr. U. Chgo., 1975-79. Editor-in-chief U. Chgo. Law Rev., 1966-67. Mem. ABA, Chgo. Bar Assn. Office: Mayer Brown & Platt 190 S La Salle St Ste 3900 Chicago IL 60603-3410*

RANNEY, GEORGE ALFRED, lawyer, former steel company executive; b. Chgo., May 30, 1912; s. George Alfred and Cornelia (Williams) R.; m. Nora Ryerson, June 18, 1938 (dec. Mar. 1987); children: George Alfred, Edward R., David M., Nancy R. (Mrs. David F. Levi). A.B., Yale, 1934, LL.B., 1939. Bar: Ill. 1939. Mem. firm Sidley, Austin, Burgess & Smith, Chgo., 1939-62; v.p., gen. counsel Inland Steel Co., Chgo., 62-68; sr. v.p. Inland Steel Co., 1968-71, vice chmn., 1971-77, also dir. Trustee U. Chgo. Served as 1st lt. AUS, 1942-45. Mem. Am., Ill., Chgo. bar assns. Episcopalian. Home: 17370 W Casey Rd Libertyville IL 60048-9748

RANNEY, HELEN MARGARET, physician, educator; b. Summer Hill, N.Y., Apr. 12, 1920; d. Arthur C. and Alesia (Toolan) R. AB, Barnard Coll., 1941; MD, Columbia U., 1947; ScD, U. S.C., 1979. Diplomate: Am. Bd. Internal Medicine. Intern Presbyn. Hosp., N.Y.C., 1947-48, resident, 1948-50, asst. physician, 1954-60; practice medicine specializing in internal medicine, hematology N.Y.C., 1954-70; instr. Coll. Phys. and Surg. Columbia, N.Y.C., 1954-60; assoc. prof. medicine Albert Einstein Coll. Medicine, N.Y.C., 1960-64, prof. medicine, 1965-70; prof. medicine SUNY, Buffalo, 1970-73; prof. medicine U. Calif., San Diego, 1973-90, chmn. dept. medicine, 1973-86, Disting. physician vet. adminstr., 1986-91; mem. staff Alliance Pharm. Corp., San Diego, 1991—. Master ACP; fellow AAAS; mem. NAS, Inst. Medicine, Am. Soc. for Clin. Investigation, Am. Soc. Hematology, Harvey Soc., Am. Assn. Physicians, Am. Acad. Arts and Scis., Phi Beta Kappa, Sigma Xi, Alpha Omega Alpha. Office: Alliance Pharm Corp 3040 Science Park Rd San Diego CA 92121-1102

RANNEY, MAURICE WILLIAM, chemical company executive; b. Buffalo, Jan. 13, 1934; s. Maurice Lynford and Helen Hart (Birdsall) R.; m. Theresa Ann Berthot, Oct. 24, 1953 (div. 1974); children: William, Linda, Laurel, James, Michael; m. Elisa Ramirez Villegas, Dec. 21, 1974; 1 stepchild, Elisa. BS in Chemistry, Niagara U., 1957, MS in Organic Chemistry, 1959; PhD in Phys. Organic Chemistry, Fordham U., 1967. Group leader, tech. mgr. Union Carbide Corp., Tarrytown, N.Y., 1957-75; gen. mgr. Union Carbide Japan KK, 1976-80; exec. v.p. Showa Union Gosei Co., Ltd., 1976-80; rep. dir. Union Carbide Svcs. Eastern Ltd., 1976-80; dir. Nippon Unicar Co., Ltd., 1976-80, Union Showa KK, 1976-80; pres. Union Carbide Formosa Co., Ltd., Hong Kong, Tokyo, 1980-82; bus. dir. Union Carbide Eastern, Inc., Tokyo, 1982-85; pres., rep. dir. Union Carbide Japan KK, 1986-94; pres. Union Indsl. Gas Corp.; rep. dir. Oriental Union Chem. Corp., 1980-82; mng. dir. Nippon Unicar Co., Ltd., 1982-85; v.p. internat. Union Carbide Chems. and Plastics Co., 1986-94; vice chmn., rep. dir. Nippon Unicar, 1986-95; pres. Nihon Parylene, 1992; lectr. in field. Author: Flame Retardant Textiles, 1970, Power Coatings, 1971, Synthetic Lubricants, 1972, New Curing Techniques, 1976, Fuel Additives, 1976, Durable Press Fabrics, 1976, Silicones, Vols. I, II, 1977, Reinforced Plastics and Elastomers, 1978, Offshore Oil Technology, 1979, Oil Shale and Tar Sands, 1980, Primary Electrochemical Cell Technology, 1981; contbr. articles to profl. jours. Union Carbide fellow, Mellon Inst. Indsl. Rsch., 1958-60. Achievements include numerous patents in field. Home: # 6 Cotton Hall Ln Hilton Head Island SC 29938

RANSIL, BERNARD J(EROME), research physician, methodologist, consultant, educator; b. Pitts., Nov. 15, 1929; s. Raymond Augustine and Louise Mary (Berhalter) R. BS, Duquesne U., 1951; PhD in Phys. Chemistry, Cath. U. Am., 1955; MD, U. Chgo., 1964. NRC-NAS postdoctoral fellow Nat. Bur. Stds., Washington, 1955-56; cons. heat div. thermodynamics sect. Nat. Bur. Standards, Washington, 1956-62; cons. NASA exobiology project, Washington, 1962-68; rsch. assoc. and dir. diatomic molecule project Lab. Molecular Structure and Spectra, physics dept. U. Chgo., 1956-63; intern Harbor Gen. Hosp., UCLA, Torrance, 1964-65, Guggenheim fellow, 1965-66; from rsch. assoc. in medicine to assoc. prof. in medicine Harvard Med. Sch., Boston, 1966—; from rsch. assoc. and clin. fellow to clin. assoc. Harvard II and IV Med. Svcs., 1966-74; core lab. scientist clin. rsch. ctr. Thorndike Meml. Lab Boston City Hosp., Boston, 1966-74; asst. physician Beth Israel Hosp., Boston, 1974-96, sr. physician, 1996—; dir. Core Lab. Clin. Rsch. Ctr., 1974-89, Data Analysis Lab., 1989-94; cons. statistical computing Boston City Hosp., Beth Israel Hosp., 1966—; cons. Prophet project NIH, Bethesda, Md., 1971-88, exec. com., 1986-91, Howard Hughes Med. Inst., Boston, 1979-80, Coop. Cataract Rsch. Group, Boston, 1981-83, Mass. Alzheimer's Disease Rsch. Ctr., Boston, 1992-94; guest lectr. Seton Hall U., 1970—; vis. scientist Rockefeller U., 1985, Scripps Rsch. Found., 1986, Calif. State U., 1986, U. Pitts. Med. Sch., 1987. Author: Abortion, 1969, Background to Abortion, 1979; editor: Life of a Scientist: Autobiography of Robert S. Mulliken, 1989 (videocassettes) Elements of Statistics and Data Analysis, 1985, diatomic molecule studies (computational chemistry), 1960-80; contbr. numerous articles and book revs. in sci. jours., non-sci. periodicals in many fields. Recipient alumni rsch. award Cath. U. Am., 1969, Duquesne U. centennial award, 1978. Mem. numerous profl. socs. Home: 226 Calumet St Boston MA 02120-3303

RANSOHOFF, MARTIN, motion picture producer; b. New Orleans, 1927. Grad., Colgate U., 1949. Founder Filmways, Inc., N.Y.C., 1952, chmn. bd., pres., until 1972; pres. Martin Ransohoff Prodns., Inc., 1972—. Prodns. include Boy's Night Out, 1962, The Americanization of Emily, 1964, Topkapi, 1964, The Loved One, 1965, The Cincinnati Kid, 1965, The Sandpiper, 1965, Ice Station Zebra, 1969, Catch 22, 1970, See No Evil, 1971, Ten Rillington Place, 1971, Save the Tiger, 1972, Fuzz, 1972, The White Dawn, 1974, Nightwing, 1979, Silver Streak, 1976, The Wanderers, 1976, A Change of Seasons, 1980, American Pop, 1981, Hanky Panky, 1982, Class, 1983, Jagged Edge, 1985, Welcome Home, 1989; TV prodns. Mister Ed, The Beverly Hillbillies, Petticoat Junction, The Addams Family.

RANSOM, BILL, author; b. Puyallup, Wash., June 6, 1945; s. Bert and LaVerne (Marcoe) R.; m. Kathy Ann Potocki, June 17, 1967 (div.); 1 child, Hali Kalae. Student, Wash. State U., 1963-65, U. Puget Sound, 1965-67; BA in English and Sociology Edn., U. Wash., 1970; postgrad., U. Nev., 1970-72. Nat. Endowment for Arts and Wash. State Arts Commn. poet-in-residence Tacoma and Port Townsend, Wash., 1972-75; Manpower Tng. Act master poet for Wash. and Colo., 1974; instr. writing So Utah U, Cedar City; dir. Port Townsend Writer's Conf., 1973-77; instr. So. Utah U. Author: Finding True North, 1974 (Nat. Book award and Pulitzer prize nominee 1974), Last Rites, 1978; author: (chapbook) Waving Arms At The Blind, 1975, (novel with Frank Herbert) The Jesus Incident, 1979, (chapbook) The Single Man Looks at Winter, 1983, Last Call, 1984, (novels with Frank Herbert) The Lazarus Effect, 1982, The Ascension Factor, 1988, (novels) Jaguar, 1990, Viravax, 1993, Learning the Ropes, 1995, Burn, 1995; author documentary of Artists-in-Schs. Program, Look: Listen, 1975; freelance journalist, Ctrl. Am., 1982-84; contbr. articles, stories, poems to mags., newspapers. Mem. PEN (selected stories for syndicated fiction project 1983, 85), AAUW, Sci. Fiction and Fantasy Writers Am., Poets & Writers, Inc., Associated Writing Programs. Office: 9160 W 2400 S Cedar City UT 84720

RANSOM, BRIAN CHARLES, artist, educator, musician, composer; b. Portland, Oreg., Sept. 27, 1954; s. James Charles Willis and Margret Marie (Wallace) R.; m. Emily Lucile Phelps, June 21, 1982 (div. Oct. 1987); children: Willis, Stefan, Jacob; m. Amanda Marie Donta, June 3, 1995. Student, U. Puget Sound, 1972-73, R.I. Sch. Design, Providence, 1973-74; BFA in Visual Art, N.Y. State Coll. Ceramics, Alfred, 1978; MA in Ceramics/Anthropology, U. Tulsa, 1984; MFA in Sculpture, Claremont (Calif.) Grad. Sch., 1985. Tchr. U. Tulsa, 1983-84, Pitzer Coll., Claremont, 1984-85, UCLA, Westwood, Calif., 1988-89, Chaffey Coll., Rancho Cucamonga, Calif., 1990-95, Scripps Coll., Claremont, 1991; artist in residence/ceramics Tierra Del Sol, Claremont, 1992-95; asst. prof. ceramics Eckerd Coll., St. Petersburg, Fla., 1995—; condr. various workshops and lectrs. Founder, creator The Ceramic Ensemble, 1986; one-man shows include Maude Kerns Gallery, Eugene, Oreg., 1981, Courtyard Gallery, Portland, Oreg., 1982, Whitebird Gallery, Cannon Beach, Oreg., 1982, U. Tulsa, 984, Claremont Grad. Sch., 1985, New Harmony (Ind.) Gallery of Contemporary Art, 1986, Lawrence Gallery, Portland, 1986, Nexus Gallery, Phila., 1987, Norra Eccles Mus. Art, Logan, Utah, 1987, Cera Cossa Coll., Ridgecrest, Calif., 1989, Couturier Gallery, L.A., 1989, 90, 94, Art Space, Winnipeg, Man., Can., 991, Conejo Valley Art Mus., Thousand Oaks, Calif., 1991, Mendecine Arts Ctr., Calif., 1995; exhibited in group shows at Portland Art Mus., 1973, Devo Gallery, Portland, 1980, Johnson Atilier Art Ctr., Tulsa, 1983, Hansen Howard Gallery, Ashland, Oreg., 1985, Scripps Coll., Claremont, 1986, Reflections Gallery, La Mesa, Calif., 1986, Contemporary Crafts Gallery, Portland, 1987, Oreg. Sch. Arts and Crafts, Portland, 1988, Wita Gardner Gallery, San Diego, 1988, Faith Nightingale Gallery, San Diego, 1990, Irvine (Calif.) Fine Arts Ctr., 1992, Hollywood (Calif.) Bowl Mus., 1992, El Camino Coll., Torrence, Calif., 1994, Wabash Coll., Crawfordsville, Ind., 1994; represented in permanent collections Everson Mus., N.Y. State Coll. Ceramics Alfred U. Mus.,; recs.: Between Two Worlds, 1986, Try to Tell Fish About Water, 1986, The Destroyer, 1987, Echoes, 1989, Tales of the Human Dawn, 1990, Sounding Clay, 1990, At Home with Mother Earth, 1994, Internal Medicine, 1995. Recipient Fulbright/Hayes Congl. fellowship, 1978-79, Oreg. Arts Commn. fellowship, 1982, rsch. fellowship U. Tulsa, 1985, COGS fellowship Claremont Grad. Sch., 1985, fellowship in sculpture Nat. Endowment Arts, 1986, Artist in Residence fellowship Calif. Arts Coun., 1992-95; named Emerging Artist Nat. Ceramic Educators' Conf. Am., 1986. Mem. Coll. Art Assn., Sierra Club. Avocations: bicycling, sailing, hiking, camping. Office: Art Dept Eckerd Coll Saint Petersburg FL 33711

RANSOM, CLIFTON LOUIS, JR., lawyer, real estate investor; b. Houston, May 25, 1935; s. Clifton Louis and Birdelle (Wykoff) R.; m. Dorothy Ellen Peterson, Dec. 25, 1974. BS in Math., Tex. So. U., 1956; BA in Philosophy, St. Joseph's Coll., Rensselaer, Ind., 1964; MA in Bibl. Theology, St. Louis U., 1970; JD, Tex. So. U., 1974; LLM in Taxation, Washington Law Sch., Salt Lake City, 1991. Bar: Tex. 1974, U.S. Dist. Ct. (so. dist.) Tex. 1976, U.S. Ct. Appeals (5h cir.) 1980, U.S. Supreme Ct. 1980, U.S. Tax Ct. 1991; ordained priest Roman Cath. Ch., 1968. Priest Diocese of Galveston-Houston, 1968-74; atty. Tex. Welfare Dept., Houston, 1975-80, Gulf Coast Legal Found., Houston, 1980—. Bd. dirs. Hope Is Victory AIDS Found., Houston, 1993—. Lt. (j.g.) USN, 1957-60. Democrat. Home: 3919 Point Clear Dr Missouri City TX 77459-3710 Office: Gulf Coast Legal Found 1415 Fannin Ste 200 Houston TX 77002

RANSOM, DAVID MICHAEL, diplomat; b. St. Louis, Nov. 23, 1938; s. Clifford Fredic and Inez Natalie (Green) R.; m. Marjorie Ann (Marilley) Ransom; children: Elizabeth Inez, Katherine Hope, Sarah Grace. AB, Princeton U., 1960; MA, Johns Hopkins Sch. of Advanced Internat. Studies, 1962; student, The Nat. War Coll., 1982-83. With U.S. Dept. State, Yemen, Iran, Lebanon, Saudi Arabia, 1965-71; nat. security coun. staff White House U.S. Dept. State, Washington, 1971-73; dep. chief mission-Am. Embassy Sanaa U.S. Dept. State, Yemen Arab Rep., 1975-78; dir., dept. dir. near east divsn. internat. security affairs Office of Sec. of Def., U.S. Dept. of Def., Washington, 1978-82; dep. chief of mission-Am. Embassy Abu Dhabi U.S. Dept. State, United Arab Emirates, 1983-85; dep. chief of mission-Am. Embassy Damascus U.S. Dept. State, Syria, 1985-88; country dir. Arabian Peninsula-Near East bureau U.S. Dept. State, Washington, 1988-90, country dir. Greece, Turkey, Cyprus-European bureau, 1990-93; Am. ambassador to State of Bahrain-Am. Embassy Manama U.S. Dept. State, 1994. 1st lt. inf. USMC, 1962-65. Mem. Met. Club (Washington). Episcopalian. Avocations: scuba diving, canoeing, skiing. Office: Bahrain Am Embassy FPO AE 09834-5100

RANSOM, EVELYN NAILL, language educator, linguist; b. Memphis, Apr. 20, 1938; d. Charles Rhea and Evelyn (Goodlander) Naill Ransom; m. Gunter Heinz Hiller, June 7, 1960 (div. Mar. 1964). AA, Mt. Vernon Jr. Coll., 1958; BA, Newcomb Coll., 1960; MA, N.Mex. Highlands U., 1965; PhD, U. Ill., 1974. Cert. secondary tchr., N.Mex. Instr. Berlitz Sch. Langs., New Orleans, 1961; tchr. MillerWall Elem. Sch., Harvey, L.A., 1961-62; teaching asst. N.Mex. Highlands U., Las Vegas, 1963-64; instr. U. Wyo., Laramie, 1965-66; teaching asst. U. Ill., Urbana, 1966-70; prof. English lang. Ea. Ill. U., Charleston, 1970-93; vis. prof. in linguistics No. Ariz. U., Flagstaff, 1990-91, adj. faculty, 1993-94; adj. faculty Ariz. State U., Tempe, 1995—; referee Pretext: Jour. of Lang. and Lit., Ill., 1981; co-chair roundtable Internat. Congress of Linguistics, 1987; linguistics del. People to People, Moscow, St. Petersburg, Prague, 1993; dissertation reader SUNY, Buffalo, 1982; vis. scholar UCLA, 1977; conductor workshop LSA summer inst. Author: Complementation: Its Meanings and Forms, 1986; contbr. articles to profl. publs. Organizer Prairie Women's Cir., Champaign, 1981-83; mem. Women's Ctr., Yavapai County, Ariz., 1993. Nat. Def. Fgn. Lang. fellow, 1969; grantee Ea. Ill. U., 1982, 87, 88, NSF, 1988. Mem. Linguistic Soc. Am., Linguistic Assn. S.W. Avocations: computer applications for the humanities, chess, motorhoming. Home: # 135 201 E Southern Ave # 135 Apache Junction AZ 85219-3740

RANSOM, JEREMY, ballet dancer; b. St. Catharines, Ont.. Grad., Nat. Ballet Sch. With Nat. Ballet Canada, Toronto, Ont., 1980—, 2d soloist, 1984-85, 1st soloist, 1985-90, prin. dancer, 1990—; performed with Zurich Ballet, Switzerland, 1986-87, Australian Ballet. Created roles in David Allan's Occasion, Capriccio, Etc!; Glen Tetley's Alice; James Kudelka's The Actress, The Miraculous Mandarin; also L'Ile Inconnue, Oiseaux Exotiques. Office: National Ballet of Canada, 157 King St East, Toronto, ON Canada M5C 1G9

RANSOM, MARGARET PALMQUIST, public relations executive; b. Davenport, Iowa, Aug. 13, 1935; d. Herman Philip and Margaret (Burchell) Palmquist; m. David Duane Ransom, July 16, 1960; 1 child, David Burke. BA in Speech and English, Augustana Coll., 1957. Tchr. speech and English Beloit (Wis.) High Sch., 1957-59; tchr. English Lake Forest (Ill.) High Sch., 1959-60, Warren High Sch., Gurnee, Ill., 1960-62, 64-66; asst. to dean Grad. Sch. Bowling Green (Ohio) State U., 1963; freelance writer Coll. Bd. Examinations, 1966; market rsch. analyst Kitchens of Sara Lee, Deerfield, Ill., 1972-74; pub. affairs mgr. Sara Lee Bakery, Deerfield, 1975-89; sr. cons. Ransom Pub. Svc. Cons., Libertyville, Ill., 1990-94; cons. Olsten Staffing Svcs., Chgo., 1994—; judge nat. competitions Pub. Rels. Soc. Am., 1986-89; spkr. on motivation and orgn.; chmn. Ill. Dept. Employment Security's Job Security Employers Com., 1995—. Bd. dirs. Early Childhood Adv. Coun., Northeastern Ill. State U., 1989-91; mem. Main St. Libertyville com., 1990-92; creator Job Market Place '96, Lake County. Recipient Ill. Citizens Svc. medal, 1993. Mem. AAUW, Bus. and Profl. Women Lake County, Mortar Bd. Avocations: computer science, reading, original art. Office: 1037 Mayfair Dr Libertyville IL 60048-3548 *This is the day the Lord has made. Let us rejoice and be glad. Carpe diem!.*

RANSOM, PERRY SYLVESTER, civil engineer; b. Atlanta, July 3, 1929; s. Perry Sylvester and Eva James (Smith) R.; m. Wilma Ruth Cone, June 1, 1951; children: Beverly Kay, Barbara Ann. BSCE, Auburn U., 1958. Registered profl. engr., La., Miss., Ala.; cert. land surveyor, La., Miss. Asst. timekeeper Swift & Co., Montgomery, Ala., 1947-51; trainman Atlantic Coast Line RR, Montgomery, 1951-58; lab. mgr. A.W. Williams Inspection Co., Mobile, Ala., 1958-60; owner, CEO Cons. Engrs., Inc., Biloxi, Miss., 1960—. Mem. Civitan Club, Mobile, 1959, Rotary Internat., Moss Point, Miss., 1965; pres. Gulf Coast chpt. Miss. Engring. Soc., Biloxi, 1965-66, chmn. Pepp sect., Jackson, 1967-68; bd. dirs. Miss. sect. ASCE, Jackson, 1972-74. With U.S. Army, 1951-53. Named Boss of Yr., Miss. Nat. Sec. Assn., 1975-76, for Outstanding Svc., Miss. Engring. Soc., 1966, Outstanding Supporter, Boys Clubs Am., Biloxi, 1991; recipient Cert. of Appreciation, Boys Clubs Am., Biloxi, 1990. Mem. Miss. Cons. Engrs. Coun., Aircraft Owners and Pilots Assn., VFW (Merit/Disting. Svc. 1989), Masons (life). Republican. Baptist. Home: 711 Twin Oaks Dr Ocean Springs MS 39564-4221 Office: Cons Engrs Inc 430 Caillavet St Biloxi MS 39530-2050

RANSOM, RICHARD EDWARD, state supreme court justice; b. Hampton, Iowa, Dec. 9, 1932. BA, U. N.Mex., 1954; LLB, Georgetown U., 1959. Bar: N.Mex. 1959, D.C. 1959. Trial lawyer Albuquerque, 1959-86; justice N.Mex. Supreme Ct., Santa Fe, 1987—; chief justice N. Mex. Supreme Ct., 1992-94, sr. justice, 1994—. 1st lt. USMC, 1954-56. Fellow Am. Coll. Trial Lawyers, Internat. Soc. Barristers, Internat. Acad. Trial Lawyers. Office: N Mex Supreme Ct PO Box 848 237 Don Gaspar Ave Santa Fe NM 87504-0848*

RANSOM, WILLIAM HARRISON, lawyer; b. Flint, Mich., Aug. 15, 1938; s. Earl Jarvis and Aileen (Halpin) R.; m. Marilyn Jean Novotny, Aug. 27, 1960; children: Nancy Aileen Maggard, Andrew William, Elizabeth Hope. BA in Econs., U. Mich., 1960, JD, 1963. Bar: Ohio, 1964. Assoc. Squire, Sanders & Dempsey, Cleve., 1964-74, ptnr., 1974-91, counsel, 1992—. Mem. ABA (tax sect. benefits com.), Ohio Bar Assn., Cleve. Bar Assn. Office: Squire Sanders & Dempsey 3900 Key Tower 127 Public Sq Cleveland OH 44114-1216

RANSOME, ERNEST LESLIE, III, retail company executive; b. Riverton, N.J.; s. Percy A. and Clarice (Frishmuth) R.; m. Nancy Ellis Clark, Aug. 16, 1947 (div. Jan. 1984); children: Leslie Ransome Hudson, Elizabeth Ransome, Jane Ransome Bromley; m. Myradean Alcott, Feb. 12, 1984. AB in Econs., Princeton U., 1947. Ins. exec. Johnson & Higgins, Phila., 1947-48; asst. to dean Princeton (N.J.) U., 1948-50; asst. treas. Giles & Ransome, Bensalem, Pa., 1950-55; v.p. adminstrn. Giles & Ransome, Bensalem, 1955-69, exec. v.p., 1969-82, vice chmn., 1982-88, chmn. bd., 1988—; v.p. Ransome Airlines, Bensalem, Pa., 1966-86; bd. dirs. Mannington Mills, Salem, N.JH., chmn., 1991-92; bd. dirs. Sun Distbrs., Phila. Mem. Zoning Bd. Borough of Riverton, N.J., 1965-69; bd. trustees Riverton Library, 1959-79; campaign chmn. Zurbrugg Hosp., Riverside, N.J., 1971. 2d lt. USMC, 1944-46. Mem. Pine Valley Golf Club (pres. 1977-88, chmn. 1988—), Royal and Ancient Golf Club (St. Andrews, Scotland). Republican. Episcopalian. Avocation: golf.

RANSONS, ELLEN FRANCES, high school administrator; b. Orange, Calif., Oct. 2, 1954; d. Kenneth London and Billie Margaret (Jensen) Keith; m. Silvio Theodore Ransons, Apr. 1, 1978; children: Paul, Keith, Amy. BA, Calif. State U., Fullerton, 1977; MEd, Whittier (Calif.) Coll., 1988. Cert. tchr. English, social sci., Calif., Wash.; adminstrv. cert., Calif., Wash. Tchr. Mission H.S., San Gabriel, Calif., 1977-86, Suzanne Mid. Sch., Walnut, Calif., 1986-95; assoc. prin. academics Eastside Cath. H.S., Bellevue, Wash., 1995—; mentor tchr. Walnut Valley Unified Sch. Dist., 1994-95. Editor student lit. publs.; author newsletter. Mem. SPARK, Walnut, 1992-94. Mem. NEA, ASCD, Assn. Calif. Sch. Adminstrs., Nat. Coun. Tchrs. English, Calif. League of Mid. Schs., Am. Assn. of Sch. Adminstrs. Democrat. Roman Catholic. Avocations: cooking, reading, writing prose and poetry. Home: 18801 215th Way NE Woodinville WA 98072 Office: Eastside Cath High Sch 11650 SE 60th Bellevue WA 98006

RANTA, RICHARD ROBERT, university dean; b. Virginia, Minn., Nov. 18, 1943; s. V. Robert and Bernice (Smith) R.; 1 child, Erick H.; m. Carol Crown. AS, Hibbing (Minn.) Community Coll., 1963; BS, U. Minn., 1965; MA, Cornell U., 1967; PhD, U. Iowa, 1974. Floor dir. Sta. KDAL-TV, Duluth, Minn., 1964-65; asst. prof. U. Va., Charlottesville, 1969-72; asst. prof. U. Memphis, 1972-75, assoc. prof., 1975-91, prof., 1991—, interim dean Univ. Coll., 1975, asst. v.p. academic affairs, 1976-78, dean Coll. Comm. and Fine Arts, 1977—; gen. mgr. High Water Records, Memphis, 1980—; bd. dirs. Concerts Internat., Memphis, pres., 1988-90; TV cons., free-lance producer, 1973—. Assoc. prodr.: (TV program) Nat. Arthritis Telethon, 1985-90; Rec. Acad. graphics and prodn. coord. Grammy Awards TV program, 1983—; author articles in Communication Adminstrn. Bull., 1977—, editl. bd., 1991—, exec. com., 1996—. Chmn., v.p. Tenn. Humanities Coun., Nashville, 1980-82; v.p. Memphis Devel. Found., 1983-86; bd. dirs. Leadership Memphis, 1987-90, 94—, chmn. mktg. com., 1987-90, chmn. selection com., 1994-95; bd. dirs. Life Blood, Memphis, 1984-92; treas. Memphis-Shelby County Film, Tape and Music Commn., 1986—; mem. adv. com. Tenn. Film, Entertainment and Music Commn., Nashville, 1987-93, chmn., 1993-95; chmn. bd. dirs. Crime Stoppers Memphis Assn., 1993-95; chmn. Memphis Arts Festival, 1992-94. Recipient Edn. Operational Models grant Ednl. Testing Svc., 1975, Communication Lab. grant HEW, 1976, Disting. Alumnus award Minn. Cmty. Coll. System, 1984; named to Recording Hall of Fame Selection panel, Nat. Rec. Acad., L.A., 1986—. Mem. NARAS (v.p. 1986-88, 92-93, chmn. edn. com. 1983—, trustee 1982-86, 88-92, 93—, pres. Memphis chpt. 1984-86, bd. govs. 1978—), So. States Comm. Assn. (pres. 1987-88, fin. bd. 1985-87, 93-95, exec. dir. 1995—), Tenn. Speech Comm. Assn. (pres. 1986-87, editor Communicator 1993—), Speech Comm. Assn. (vice chmn., then chmn. exptl. learning com. 1979-83, mem. fin. and adminstrn. coms. 1989-93, chmn. fin. com. 1991-93), So. Arts Fedn. (bd. dirs. 1994—), Internat. Coun. Fine Arts Deans (parliamentarian 1996—), Delta Sailing Assn. Club (sec. 1984—). Avocations: sailing, tennis, photography. Office: U Memphis Coll Communication & Fine Arts Memphis TN 38152

RANTS, CAROLYN JEAN, college official; b. Hastings, Nebr., Oct. 3, 1936; d. John Leon and Christine (Helzer) Halloran; m. Marvin L. Rants, June 1, 1957 (div. July 1984); children: Christopher Charles, Douglas John. Student, Hastings Coll., 1954-56; BS, U. Omaha, 1960; MEd, U. Nebr., 1968; EdD, U. S.D., 1982. Tchr. elem. Ogallala (Nebr.) Community Sch., 1956-58, Omaha Pub. Schs., 1958-60, Hastings Pub. Schs., 1960-64, Grosse Pointe (Mich.) Community Schs., 1964-67; asst. prof., instr. Morningside Coll., Sioux City, Iowa, 1974-82, dean for student devel., 1982-84, v.p. for student affairs, 1984-94, interim v.p. for acad. affairs, 1992-94; v.p. enrollment and student svcs., 1994—. Mem. new agy. com., chmn. fund distbn. and resource deployment com. United Way, Sioux City, 1987-94, co-chair, United Way Day of Caring, 1996; mem. Iowa Civil Rights Commn., 1989—; bd. dirs. Leadership Sioux City, 1988-93, pres., 1992-93; bd. dirs. Siouxland Y, Sioux City, 1985-90, pres., 1988; bd. dirs. Girls, Inc., 1995—, WACO, 1996—; mem. Vision 2020 Cmty. Planning Task Force, 1990-92. Mem. Iowa Women in Ednl. Leadership (pres. Sioux City chpt. 1986), Nat. Assn. Student Pers. Adminstrs.(region IV-E adv. bd.), Nat. Assn. for Women Deans, Adminstrs. and Counselors, Iowa Student Pers. Adminstr. (chmn. profl. devel. Iowa chpt. 1988-89, pres. 1991-92, Disting. Svc. award 1995), AAUW (corp. rep., coll./univ. rep. 1994-96), P.E.O. (pres. Sioux City chpt., Tri-State Women's Bus. Conf. (treas., planning com. Sioux City chpt. 1987-89), Quota Club (com. chmn. Sioux City 1987-89, v.p. 1992-94, pres. 1994-95, Siouxland Woman of Yr. award 1988), Sertoma (officer, bd. govs., regional dir.), Omicron Delta Kappa, Delta Kappa Gamma (state 1st v.p. 1993—, state pres. 1995—). Republican. Methodist. Avocations: handbells, cross-stitching. Home: 2904 S Cedar St # 4 Sioux City IA 51106-4246 Office: Morningside Coll 1501 Morningside Ave Sioux City IA 51106-1717

RANU, HARCHARAN SINGH, biomedical scientist, administrator, orthopaedic biomechanics educator; b. Lyallpur, India; came to U.S., 1976; s. Jodh Singh and Harnam Kaur R. BSc, Leicester Poly., Eng., 1963; MSc, U. Surrey, Guilford, Eng., 1967, Cambridge (Eng.) U., 1972; PhD, Middlesex Hosp. Med. Sch. and Poly. of Cen. London, 1975; diploma, MIT, 1984. Chartered engr., Eng. Med. scientist Nat. Inst. Med. Rsch. of the Med. Rsch. Coun., London, 1967-70; rsch. fellow Middlesex Hosp. Med. Sch. and Poly. of Cen. London, 1971-76; rsch. scientist Plastics Rsch. Assn. of Great Britain, Shawbury, Eng., 1977; asst. prof. Wayne State U., Detroit, 1977-81; prof. biomed. engring./orthopaedic biomechanics biomaterials La. Tech. U., Ruston, 1982—; prof., chmn. dept. biomechanics N.Y. Coll. Osteo. Medicine, Old Westbury, 1989-93; prof., asst. to pres. and dir. doctoral program Life Coll., Marietta, Ga., 1993—; dir. tng. Rehab. Rsch. and Devel. Ctr., 1983-85; mem. La. Tech. U. Libr. Com., 1983-85; chmn. design competition Assn. Biomed. Engrs.; mem. steering com. So. Biomed. Engring. Confs., 1983—; chmn. tech. in health care conf. U. Cambridge, 1985; chmn. Internat. Symposium on Bioengring., Calcutta, India, 1985; dir. orthopaedic biomechanics rsch. labs., staff Nassau County Med. Ctr., Long Island, 1989—; prof., asst. to pres., dir. doctoral program Life Coll., Marietta, Ga., 1993—; mem. biomed. engring. faculty com. La. Tech. U., faculty com., rsch. awards com., grad. studies com., grad. faculty, acad. bd. dirs; vis. scientist Dryburn Hosp., Durham, Eng., 1985-87, cons., 1988—; vis. prof. U. Istanbul, 1982, Lab. de Recherch Orthopediques, Paris, 1985—, Kings Coll. Med. Sch. U. London, 1989—, Indian Inst. Tech., New Delhi, Postgrad Inst. Med. Edn. and Rsch., Chandigarh, India, 1989—, Inst. Biol. Physics USSR Acad. Sci., Moscow, 1990, Polytech. Ctrl. London, 1991—; adj. prof. Coll. Physicians and Surgeons Columbia U., N.Y.C., 1988—, Inst. Biol. Physics USSR Acad. Sci., Moscow, 1990, N.Y. Coll. Podiatric Medicine, 1991—, CUNY, 1992—; cons. Lincoln Gen. Hosp., Ruston, La., 1982-85, La. State U. Med. Ctr., Shreveport, 1982—, St. Luke's and Roosevelt Hosp. Ctr., N.Y., 1988—, Foot Clinics N.Y., 1991—, Vets. Affairs Med. Ctr., N.Y., 1992—, various biomed. rsch. & legal corps., U.S., United Kingdom; mem. media resource svc. Inst. Pub. Info., N.Y., 1989—; med. scientist, cons. NATO, 1982—; presenter, lectr., dir. organizer numerous sci. orgns. and nat. & internat. confs.; external examiner for doctoral candidates All India Inst. Med. Scis., New Delhi, Indian Inst. of Tech., New Delhi, Banaras Hindu U., Varanasi, India, 1994—. Author: Rheological Behavior of Articular Cartiliage Under Tensile Loads, 1967, Effects of Ionizing Radiation on the Mechanical Properties of Skin, 1975, Effects of Fractionated Doses of X-irradiation on the Mechanical Properties of Skin--A Long Term Study, 1980, Effects of Ionizing Radiation on the Structure & Physical Properties of the Skin, 1983, 3-D Model of Vertebra for Spinal Surgery, 1985, Application of Carbon Fibers in Orthopaedic Surgery, 1985, Relation Between Metal Corrision & Electrical Polarization, 1989, The Distribution of Stresses in the Human Lumbar Spine, 1989, Medical Devices & Orthopaedic Implants in the United States, 1989, Spinal Surgery by Modeling, 1989, Multipoint Determination of Pressure-Volume Curves in Human Intervertebral Discs, 1993, Evaluation of Volume-Pressure Relationship in Lumbar Discs Using Model and Experimental Studies, 1994, A Mechanism of Laser Nuclectomy, 1994, Microminiaturization in Laser Surgery in Vivo Intradiscal Pressure Measurements in Lumbar Intervertebral Discs, 1994, An Experimental and Mathematical Simulation of Fracture of Human Bone Due to Jumping, 1994; editor The Lower Extremity, 1993—; guest editor IEEE Engring. in Medicine & Biology, 1991; mem. editorial bd. Med. Instrumentation, 1988—, Jour. Biomed. Instrumentation & Tech., 1988—, Jour. Med. Engring. & Tech., 1989—, Joul, 1990—, Jour. Long-Term Effects Med. Implants, 1991—, Biomed. Sci. & Tech., 1991—; reviewer Jour. Biomechanics, 1981—, Clin. Biomechanics, 1984—, Jour. Biomed. Engring., 1981, Phys. Therapy, 1990—, IEEE Biomed. Transactions, 1991—, Jour. Engring. in Medicine, 1989—; contbr. articles to profl. jours. Faculty advisor India Students Assn. Wayne State U., 1980. Recipient Edwin Tate award U. Surrey, 1968, Third Internat. Olympic Com. World Congress On Sprots Scis. award, Atlanta, 1995; numerous rsch. grants. Fellow ASME (bioengring. com. 1990—, award L.I. chpt. 1991), Biol. Engring. Soc. (London) (President's prize 1984), Instn. Mech. Engrs. (chmn. revv. bd. for corp. memberships, James Clayton awards 1974-76); mem. Am. Soc. Biomechanics (edn. com. 1990—), Orthopaedic Rsch. Soc., Biomed. Engring. Soc., India Assn., India Assn. North La. Sikh. Research includes microfracture simulation of human vertebrae under compressive loading, laserectomy of the human nucleus pulposus and its effect on the intradiscal pressure, pressure-volume relation in human intervertebral discs, in vitro and in vivo intradiscal pressure measurements before and after laserectomy of the human nucleus pulposus, gait analysis of a diabetic foot. Office: Sch of Grad Studies Life Coll Marietta GA 30060

RANUM, OREST ALLEN, historian, educator; b. Lyle, Minn., Feb. 18, 1933; s. Luther George and Nada (Chaffee) R.; m. Patricia McGroder, July 4, 1955; children—Kristin, Marcus. B.A., Macalester Coll., St. Paul, 1955; M.A., U. Minn., 1957, Ph.D., 1961. Asst. prof. U. So. Calif., 1960-61, Columbia U., N.Y.C., 1961-63; assoc. prof. Columbia U., 1963-69; prof. history Johns Hopkins U., Balt., 1969—; mem., chmn. GRE Ednl. Testing Service, Princeton, 1973-78. Author: Richelieu and Councilors, 1963; Paris, Age of Absolutism, 1968; Artisans of Glory, 1981, The Fronde, 1993. Recipient Bronze medal City of Tours, France, 1980. Mem. Am. Hist. Assn., Soc. French Hist. Studies, Inst. de France (corr.), Académie des Sciences Morales et Politiques (Paris; corr. 1989), Société de l'Histoire de France, Collège de France (internat. chair 1994-95). Home: 208 Ridgewood Rd Baltimore MD 21210-2539 Office: History Dept Johns Hopkins U Baltimore MD 21218

RANUS, ROBERT D., food marketing executive; b. 1940. BS in Acctg., U. Buffalo, 1961, MBA, 1962. CPA, N.Y. With Price Waterhouse & Co., 1963-78, Fox Industries, 1978-80; v.p. fin. and adminstrn. Pitts. divsn. Wetterau, Inc., 1980-86; 1st v.p. adminstrn. Roundy's Inc., 1986-87, v.p., CFO, bd. dirs., 1987—. Office: Roundys Inc 23000 Roundy Dr Pewaukee WI 53072-4001*

RANZAHUER, GUILLERMO GONZALEZ, bishop; b. Huatusco, Veracruz, Mex., Mar. 12, 1928; s. Edmundo Ranzahuer Cárcamo and Lucia (Gónzalez) Lecuona. Ordained priest Roman Catholic Ch.; consecrated bishop of Diocese of San Andres Tuxtla. Office: Constitucion Y Morelos, San Andres Tuxtla, Veracruz CP 95700, Mexico

RAO, DABEERU C., epidemiologist; b. Santhabommali, India, Apr. 6, 1946; came to U.S., 1972; s. Ramarao Patnaik and Venkataratnam (Raghupatruni) R.; m. Sarada Patnaik, 1974; children: Ravi, Lakshmi. BS in Stats., Indian Statis. Inst., Calcutta, 1967, MS, 1968, PhD, 1971. Research fellow U. Sheffield, Eng., 1971-72; asst. prof., geneticist U. Hawaii, Honolulu, 1972-78, assoc. prof.-geneticist, 1978-80; assoc. prof., dir. div. biostats. Washington U. Med. Sch., St. Louis, 1980-82, prof. depts. biostats., psychiatry and genetics, 1982—, adj. prof. math., 1982—, dir. div. biostats., 1980—. Author: A Source Book for Linkage in Man, 1979, Methods in Genetic Epidemiology, 1983, Genetic Epidemiology of Coronary Heart Disease, 1984; editor-in-chief Genetic Epidemiology jour., 1984-91; contbr. articles to profl. jours. Grantee NIH, 1978—. Mem. Am. Statis. Assn., Am. Soc. Human Genetics, Internat. Genetic Epidemiology Soc. (pres. 1996), Behavior Genetics Assn., Soc. Epidemiol. Res., Biom. Soc. Office: Box 8067 Div Biostatistics Washington U Sch Medicine 660 S Euclid Ave Saint Louis MO 63110

RAO, DESIRAJU BHAVANARAYANA, meteorologist, oceanographer, educator; b. Visakhapatnam, India, Dec. 8, 1936; came to U.S., 1960, naturalized, 1974; s. Desiraju Sreeramulu and Desiraju Hanumayamma Adavikolanu; m. Padmavati Kavuru; children: Desiraju Pramila, Desiraju Kavitha. B.Sc., Andhra U., Waltair, India, 1956, M.Sc., 1959; M.S., U. Chgo., 1962, Ph.D., 1965. Rsch. scholar Indian Naval Phys. Labs., Cochin, 1959-60; postdoctoral fellow Nat. Center Atmospheric Rsch., Boulder, Colo., 1965-67; rsch. scientist marine scis. br. Can. Dept. Energy, Mines and Resources, Ottawa, Ont., 1967-68; asst. prof. atmospheric sci. Colo. State U., Ft. Collins, 1968-71; assoc. prof. energetics, also Center Gt. Lakes Studies, U. Wis.-Milw., 1971-74, prof., 1974-76; head phys. limnology and meteorology group Gt. Lakes Environ. Rsch. Lab., NOAA, Ann Arbor, Mich., 1975-80; adj. prof. limnology and meteorology U. Mich., Ann Arbor, 1977-80; head oceans and ice br. Lab. for Atmospheric Sci., Goddard Space Flight Ctr., NASA, Greenbelt, Md., 1980-84; chief marine prediction br. Nat. Meteorol. Ctr., NOAA, Washington, 1984-95; chief Ocean Modeling Br., Nat. Ctrs. Environ. Prediction NOAA, Washington, 1995—; adj. prof. meteorology U. Md., College Park, 1981—; cons. in field. Contbr. articles on atmospheric, oceanic and lake dynamics to sci. jours. Fellow Am. Meteorol. Soc. (v.p. Denver chpt. 1969-70); Mem. Am. Soc. Limnology and Oceanography, AAAS, Internat. Water Resources Assn. (charter), Am. Geophys. Union, Internat. Assn. for Gt. Lakes Research, The Oceanography Soc. (charter), Sigma Xi. Home: 13101 Hugo Pl Silver Spring MD 20906-5916 Office: 5200 Auth Rd Room 209 Camp Springs MD 20746

RAO, NANNAPANENI NARAYANA, electrical engineer; b. Kakumanu, Andhra Pradesh, India; m. Sarojini Jonnalagadda, June 10, 1955; children: Vanaja, Durgaprasad, Hariprasad. BSc in Physics, U. Madras, India, 1952; DMIT in Electronics, Madras Inst. Tech., 1955; MSEE, U. Wash., 1960, PhD in Elec. Engring, 1965. Acting instr. elec. engring. U. Wash., 1960-64, acting asst. prof., 1964-65; asst. prof. elec. engring. U. Ill., Urbana, 1965-69; asso. prof. U. Ill., 1969-75, prof., 1975—, assoc. head elec. and computer engring., 1987—; cons. Fakultas Teknik, Univ. Indonesia, Jakarta, 1985-86, 87. Author: Basic Electromagnetics with Applications, 1972, Elements of Engineering Electromagnetics, 4th edit., 1994; contbr. numerous articles to profl. jours. Recipient Engring. award Telugu Assn. N.Am., 1983, Fakultas Teknik award Universitatas Indonesia, 1986. Fellow IEEE (Undergrad. Teaching award 1994); mem. Am. Soc. Engring. Edn. (AT&T Found. award for excellence in instrn. engring. students 1991), Internat. Union Radio Sci. (U.S. Commn. G). Activities include rsch. carried out in the general area of ionospheric propagation. Home: 2509 S Lynn St Urbana IL 61801-6841 Office: U Ill Dept Elec & Computer Engring 1406 W Green St Urbana IL 61801-2918

RAO, POTARAZU KRISHNA, government executive; b. Andhra Pradesh, India, Mar. 26, 1930; s. Satyanarayana and Annapoorna (Mullapudi) P.; m. Rukmani Krutivinti, Aug. 5, 1954; children: Ramanarayan, Sreedhar. BS, Andhra U., 1950, MS, 1952; MS, Fla. State U., 1957; PhD, NYU, 1968. Meteorologist Can. Meteorol. Svc., Montreal, Can., 1960-61; rsch. phys. scientist Nat. Oceanic and Atmospheric Adminstrn./Nat. Environ. Satellite Data and Info. Svc., Washington, 1961-74, chief atmospheric energetics br., acting dir., 1976-80, chief satellite applications lab., 1980-86, dir. office of rsch. and applications, 1986—; program dir., weather modification NSF, Washington, 1971-72; advisor on satellite programs World Meteorological Orgn., Geneva, 1974-76; bd. dirs. Nat. Oceanic and Atmospheric Adminstrn. Climate and Global Change Program, Washington; adv. bd. Coop. Inst. for Rsch. in Atmospheres, Ft. Collins, Colo., 1986—. Editor: Weather Satellites, 1990; contbr. articles to profl. jours. Founder, trustee Sri Siva Vishnu Temple, Lanham, Md. Fellow Am. Meteorol. Soc., Royal Meteorol. Soc. (U.K.), N.Y. Acad. Scis. Hindu. Avocations: tennis, photography. Home: 15824 Buena Vista Dr Rockville MD 20855 Office: NESDIS/NOAA Rsch & Applications NOAA Science Ctr 5200 Auth Rd Washington DC 20233

RAO, SETHURAMIAH LAKSHMINARAYANA, United Nations official; b. Mysore, Karnataka, India, Apr. 28, 1942; came to U.S., 1967; s. Ramakrishniah Sethuramiah and Bhageerathi; m. Sudha Bagur Viswanath, Aug. 1, 1971; children: Rekha, Kumar. MSc, U. Mysore, 1963; MPH, U. N.C., 1968; cert., U. Mich., 1969; PhD, U. Pa., 1971. Asst. prof. Brown U., Providence, 1971-73; UN adviser Govt. of Sri Lanka, Colombo, 1974-77; chief population and devel. UN Population Fund, N.Y.C., 1978-82, chief policy br., 1982-90; country dir. UN Population Fund, Addis Ababa, Ethiopia, 1991-92; dep. dir. info. & extern rels. UN Population Fund, N.Y.C., 1992-95, dir. tech. and evaluation divsn., 1996—; sec. UN Population Fund segment of UN Devel. Program/UN Population Fund exec. bd. Author: Socio-Religious Factors in Fertility, 1973; co-author: Population Problems of Sri Lanka, 1977, Population Program Experience, 1991; contbr. articles to profl. jours. V.p. Mysore Self Reliance Assn., Mangalore, 1963-65, Indo-Am. Forum for Polit. Edn., N.Y., 1989-90; founder, pres. New Eng. Kannada Koota, Providence, 1972-73. Mem. Delta Omega. Avocations: traveling, debate, bridge playing. Home: 143 Nelson Rd Scarsdale NY 10583-5811 Office: UN Population Fund 220 E 42nd St New York NY 10017-5806

RAOS, JOHN G., manufacturing executive. Pres. and COO U.S. Industries, Inc., Iselin, N.J. Office: US Industries Inc 101 Wood Ave S Iselin NJ 08830-2715

RAPAPORT, FELIX THEODOSIUS, surgeon, editor, researcher, educator; b. Munich, Germany, Sept. 27, 1929; s. Max W. and Adelaide (Rathaus) R.; m. Margaret Birsner, Dec. 14, 1969; children: Max, Benjamin, Simon, Michel, Adelaide. AB, NYU, 1951, MD, 1954. Diplomate Am. Bd. Surgery. Intern Mt. Sinai Hosp., N.Y.C., 1955-56; resident, chief resident NYU Surg. Services, 1958-62, USPHS postdoctoral fellow in pathology, 1956; exec. officer Naval Med. Rsch. Unit No. 1, U. Calif., Berkeley, 1956-58; trainee in allergy and infectious diseases NYU, 1958-61; head, transplantation and immunology div. NYU Surg. Svcs., 1965-77; dir. rsch. Inst. Reconstrn. and Plastic Surgery, NYU, 1965-77; assoc. prof. surgery NYU Med. Ctr., 1965-70, prof., 1970-77; prof. surgery, prof. pathology, dir. transplantation svc. SUNY, Stony Brook, 1977-95, disting. prof., 1995—, chmn. dept. surgery, 1989-91; guest investigator Hosp. St. Louis, Paris, 1963-79; Claude Bernard vis. prof. exptl. medicine Coll. de France, Paris, 1985; sr. attendingsurgeon SUNY Hosp., 1980—, surgeon-in-chief, 1989-91; pres. bd. dirs. regional N.Y. Transplant Program, 1972-89; cons. VA Hosp., N.Y.C., 1963-77, Northport, N.Y., 1977—; adv. panel on medicine and dentistry U.S. Office of Naval Res., 1974-78; adv. com. NIAID, 1964-68; merit review bd. immunology V.A. Dept. of Medicine and Surgery, 1974-78. Editor in chief Transplantation Proc., 1968—; assoc. editor Am. Jour. Kidney Diseases, 1981-86, Am. Jour. Craniofacial Genetics and Developmental Biology, 1980-85, Cellular Immunology, 1980—; contbr. over 500 articles to profl. jours.; author, editor 20 books on transplantation. Bd. dirs. United Network for Organ Sharing, 1986-88. Served to lt. comdr. M.C. USNR, 1956-58. Decorated comdr. Order Sci. Merit, chevalier Ordre National du Merite, France, 1970, officer Legion of Honor (France), 1990; recipient Gold medal Societe d'Encouragement au Bien, 1979, Gold medal City of Paris, France, 1980, Commandeur Ordre des Palmes Academiques, France, 1981, Samuel L. Kountz award Howard U., 1989, Lester Hoenig award Nat. Kidney Found., 1990, Sol Berson award NYU, 1990, Disting. Achievement in Med. Scis. award Touro Coll. B. Levine Sch. Health Scis., 1991, USPHS Res. Career Devel. award, NIAID, 1961-62, Career Scientst award Health Rsch. Coun., 1963-72, Maimonides Physician award, new Skwere Institutions, 1995. Mem. ACS, French Acad. Scis., Soc. Univ. Surgeons, N.Y. Surg. Soc., Am. Burn Assn., Am. Surg. Assn., Am. Assn. Immunologists, Soc. Exptl. Biology and Medicine, Harvey Soc., Am. Soc. Transplant Surgeons, Am. Soc. Transplant Physicians, Soc. for Organ Sharing (hon. pres.), Am. Assn. Clin. Histocompatibility Testing, Internat. Soc. Exptl. Hematology, Transplantation Soc. (founding sec., v.p., treas., councillor, historian, pres. 1986-88), Alpha Omega Alpha. Jewish. Current Work: induction of specific tolerance to major transplantable organs in man; research concerned with effects of irradiation and bone marrow transplantation in the production of host unresponsiveness to tissue allografts. Office: SUNY Stony Brook Dept Surgery Health Sc Ctr Stony Brook NY 11794

RAPAPORT, MARK SAMUEL, lawyer; b. N.Y.C., July 31, 1947; s. Joseph and Sadie (Schwartz) R.; m. Jennifer Munnell, Nov. 22, 1971. B.A. cum laude, U. Wis., 1968, J.D. cum laude, 1973. Bar: Wis. 1973, N.Y. 1974, Calif. 1981. Assoc. Dewey, Ballantine, Bushby, Palmer & Wood, N.Y.C., 1973-80; assoc. Hahn and Cazier, Los Angeles, 1980-82, ptnr. 1982—. Mem. donor fin. planning com. Greater Los Angeles affiliate Heart Fund, 1981—; mem. devel. com. The Dance Gallery, 1984—. Mem. State Bar Calif. (vice chmn. trust adminstrn. subcom. 1982—, probate com. 1985—), ABA (investments by fiduciaries com. 1979—), N.Y. State Bar Assn., State Bar of Wis. Note and comment editor Wis. Law Rev., 1972-73. Office: Morgan Lewis & Bockius 801 S Grand Ave Ste 2200 Los Angeles CA 90017-4613*

RAPER, CHARLES ALBERT, retired management consultant; b. Charleston, W.Va., Aug. 18, 1926; s. Kenneth B. and Louise (Williams) R.; m. Margaret Ann Weers, Dec. 26, 1947; children: Kathleen, Josephine, Charles. Student, Okla. State U., 1945; B.S., U. Ill., 1949. Sales mgr. Meyer Furnace Co., Peoria, Ill., 1949-54; v.p. mktg. Master Consol., Inc., Dayton, Ohio, 1954-61; mgmt. cons. McKinsey & Co., Inc., Chgo., 1961-67; v.p. mktg. Gen. Portland Inc., Dallas, 1967-69; pres. Gen. Portland Inc., 1969-75, also dir.; v.p., gen. mgr. Scholl Inc., Chgo., 1975-81; pres. Oxford Group of Sara Lee, 1981-84; mgmt. cons. McKinsey & Co., 1984—. Vice chmn. devel. bd. U. Tex. at Dallas; exec. bd. Circle 10 council Boy Scouts Am. Served with USNR, 1944-46. Mem. Dallas C. of C. (chmn. bd. dirs. 1974—), Sales Execs. Club, Phi Gamma Delta. Methodist. Club: Cherokee Country. Home: 301 Townsend Pl NW Atlanta GA 30327-3035

RAPER, WILLIAM BURKETTE, retired college president; b. nr. Wilson, N.C., Sept. 10, 1927; s. William Cecil and Beulah Maybelle (Davis) R.; m. Rose Mallard, Aug. 19, 1951; children: Olivia, Kristie, Burkette, Elizabeth, Stephen, Laura. AB, Duke U., 1947, MDiv, 1951; MS (Kellogg fellow), Fla. State U., 1962; LLD, Atlantic Christian Coll. (now Barton Coll.), 1960. Ordained to ministry Free Will Baptist Ch., 1946; pastor Hull Rd. Free Will Bapt. Ch., Snow Hill, N.C., 1951-55; pres. Mt. Olive (N.C.) Coll., 1954-95, ret., 1995; dir. Wachovia Bank and Trust Co.; promotional dir. Free Will Bapt. State Conv. N.C., 1953-54; pres. council Ch.-Related Colls. N.C., 1966-67; mem. N.C. Edn. Assistance Authority, 1972-76; sec. Ind. Coll. Fund of N.C., 1976-78; Mem. N.C. Gov.'s Com. on Hwy. Traffic Safety, 1968; regional coordinator U.S. Office Edn. Program with Developing Instns., 1968-70; dir. Edn. Professions Devel. Act Grant for Strengthening Devel. in Pvt. Two-Year Colls., 1970-72; trustee N.C. Coll. Found., 1977-94; adv. com. Ind. Coll. Presidents, U. N.C. Recipient Disting. Service award Mt. Olive Jr. C. of C., 1961; named N.C. Young Man of Year, 1961. Mem. Am. Assn. Community and Jr. Colls. (commn. on legislation 1963-66, cons. 1968-71, chmn. commn. on student personnel 1970-71), N.C. Assn. Ind. Colls. and Univs. (exec. com. 1967-70, 76-77, 83-85), N.C. Assn. Colls. and Univs. (pres. 1969-70), Masons. Democrat. Office: Mt Olive Coll Office of Pres Emeritus Mount Olive NC 28365

RAPER, WILLIAM CRANFORD, lawyer; b. Asheville, N.C., Aug. 17, 1946; s. James Sidney and Kathryn (Cranford) R.; m. Patricia Dotson, Sept. 28, 1974; children: Kimber-leigh, Heather, James. AB, U. N.C., 1968; JD, Vanderbilt U., 1972. Bar: N.C. 1972, U.S. Ct. Appeals (4th cir.) 1972, U.S. Supreme Ct. 1977, U.S. Ct. Appeals (fed. cir.) 1985. Law clk. to Senator Sam Ervin Jr. Washington, 1971; law clk. to presiding justice U.S. Ct. Appeals (4th cir.), Richmond, Va., 1972-73; ptnr. Womble, Carlyle, Sandridge & Rice, Winston-Salem, N.C., 1974—. Mem. ABA, N.C. Bar Assn., N.C. Assn. of Def. Attys. (charter). Office: Womble Carlyle Sandridge & Rice 3300 One First Union Ctr 301 S College St Charlotte NC 28202-6025

RAPHAEL, ALBERT ASH, JR., lawyer; b. N.Y.C., June 4, 1925; s. Albert Ash and Clare (Schindler) R.; m. Dorothy Buck, Oct. 7, 1960; 1 child, Bruce William. A.B., Yale U., 1947; LL.D., Harvard U., 1950. Bar: N.Y. 1950, Vt. 1972. Mem. firm Gallert, Hilborn & Raphael, N.Y.C., 1950-60, Alter, Lefevre, Raphael, Lowry, and Gould, N.Y.C., 1960-78; individual practice Waitsfield, Vt., 1972-86, 95—; ptnr. Raphael and Ware, Waitsfield, 1986-95; Dir. various real estate cos. Mem. bd. zoning appeals, Waitsfield, 1974-83, selectman, 1976-82, chmn. bd. selectmen, 1981-82. Served with F.A., AUS, 1943-46. Mem. Vt. Bar Assn., Assn. of Bar of City of N.Y. Home: PO Box 1149 Waitsfield VT 05673-1149 Office: PO Box 1149 Raphael Rd Waitsfield VT 05673

RAPHAEL, BRETT, artistic director, choreographer; b. New Haven, Conn., Nov. 10, 1954; s. Howard Boone Jacobson and Dana Raphael. Artistic dir. L.I. Ballet, Huntington, 1979-80, Conn. Ballet, Stamford, 1980—; mem. faculty Harkness House, N.Y.C., 1978-79, Alvin Ailey Am. Dance Theatre, N.Y.C., 1990-92, divsn. continuing edn. SUNY, 1984-96. Choreographer 15 original ballets Conn. Ballet, Boston Ballet, Netherlands Dans Theatre, Joffrey II Dancers; restager Nutcracker, Giselle, Coppelia. Named Choreographer of Yr. by Internat. Beaux Arts Soc., N.Y.C., 1979. Office: CT Ballet 20 Acosta St Stamford CT 06902

RAPHAEL, COLEMAN, business school dean; b. N.Y.C., Sept. 16, 1925; s. Morris and Adella (Leav) R.; m. Sylvia Moskowitz, Feb. 28, 1948; children—Hollis, Gordon. B.Civil Engring., CCNY, 1945; M.C.E., Poly. Inst. Bklyn., 1951, Ph.D. in Applied Mechanics, 1965. Registered profl. engr., N.Y., Fla. Structural research engr., test research engr. Republic Aviation Corp., 1945-47; instr. mech. engring. Pratt Inst., Bklyn., 1947-51; from sr. research engr. to mgr. space systems div. Republic Aviation Corp., 1951-65; gen. mgr. space and electronics systems div., then v.p. Fairchild Hiller Corp., Germantown, Md., 1965-70; with Atlantic Rsch. Corp., Alexandria, Va., 1970-86, chmn. bd., 1980-86; chmn. bd. SJI Industries, 1968-70; dean bus. sch. George Mason U., Fairfax, Va., 1986-91; ret., 1991; bd. mem., prin. owner Applied Bus. Systems, Bethesda, Md., 1990—; bd. dirs. ENVIPCO (chmn. 1995), Fairfax, Va., Night Owl Security, Landover, Md., Geico, Chevy Chase, Md.; mem. engring. adv. com. Montgomery Coll., Md., 1968-69, George Washington U., 1977-82; mem. Gov. Va. Task Force Nuclear Power Plants, 1969; chmn. energy com. Gov. Md. Sci. Adv. Coun., 1974-76; bd. visitors U. Pitts., 1980-82. Author textbook, papers, reports in field. Chmn. U.S. Bond drive, Alexandria, 1975-76; chmn. adv. com. Montgomery County Bldg. Codes, 1976-77. Recipient Citizenship award Montgomery County Press Assn., 1967, Disting. Service award Montgomery County C. of C., 1969, Disting. Citizenship award State of Md., 1970. Mem. AIAA (chmn. mgmt. com. 1976), Aircraft Industries Assn., Nat. Space Club, disting Alumus, Poly. Inst. of Bklyn., 1982. Home: 508 Hermleigh Rd Silver Spring MD 20902-1608

RAPHAEL, FREDERIC MICHAEL, author; b. Chgo., Aug. 14, 1931; s. Cedric Michael and Irene (Mauser) R.; m. Sylvia Betty Glatt, Jan. 17, 1955; children: Paul Simon, Sarah Natasha, Stephen Matthew Joshua. M.A. (Major Open scholar), St. John's Coll., Cambridge (Eng.) U., 1954. Author: (novels) Obbligato, 1956, The Earlson Way, 1958, The Limits of Love, 1960, A Wild Surmise, 1961, The Graduate Wife, 1962, The Trouble with England, 1962, Lindmann, 1963, Darling, 1965, Two for the Road, 1966, Orchestra and Beginners, 1967, Like Men Betrayed, 1970, Who Were You With Last Night?, 1971, April, June and November, 1972, Richard's Things, 1973, California Time, 1975, The Glittering Prizes, 1976, Heaven and Earth, 1984, After the War, 1988, A Double Life, 1993, Old Scores, 1995; short stories Sleeps Six, 1979, Oxbridge Blues, 1980, Think of England, 1986, The Hidden I, 1990, The Latin Lover, 1994, Old Scores, 1995; screenplays Nothing But the Best, 1964, Darling, 1965, Two For the Road, 1967, Far From the Madding Crowd, 1967, A Severed Head, 1971, Daisy Miller, 1973, The Glittering Prizes, 1976, Rogue Male, 1976, Something's Wrong, 1978, Oresteia of Aeschylus, 1978, The Best of Friends, 1980, School Play, 1980, Richard's Things, 1981, Oxbridge Blues, 1984, After The War, 1989, The Man in the Brooks Brothers Shirt, 1990, Armed Response, 1995 (cinema and/or TV) Nothing But the Best, 1964 (Best Comedy Screenplay award Writers' Guild of U.K.), Darling, 1965, (U.S. Academy award, Best Original Screenplay Original British Academy and Writers' Guild of U.K.), Two For the Road, 1967 (nom. for Oscar, Best Screenplay Original), Far From the

Maddening Crowd, 1968, A Severed Head, 1971, Daisy Miller, 1973, The Glittering Prizes, 1976 (Writer of the Yr. award Royal TV Soc.), Rogue Male, 1976, The Best of Friends and Sch. Play, 1980, Richard's Things, 1981, Oxbridge Blues, 1984; (criticism) Somerset Maugham and His World, 1977, Byron, 1982, Euripides' Medea, 1995; translator (with Kenneth McLeish) book revs. The Poems of Catullus, 1978, The Oresteia of Aeschylus, 1979, Aeschulus Complete Plays, 1991, Of Gods and Men, 1993; editor: (with Kenneth McLeish) Essays Bookmarks, 1975, Cracks In The Ice (Views & Reviews), 1978, A List of Books, 1981; screenwriter, dir. The Man in the Brooks Brothers Shirt, 1990. Recipient Oscar award for original screen-play Darling, 1966, Ace awards 1987, 92; named Writer of Yr. Royal TV Soc., 1976. Fellow Royal Soc. Lit. Address: Lagardelle, St Laurent-la-Vallée, 24170 Belves France

RAPHAEL, LOUISE ARAKELIAN, mathematician, educator; b. N.Y.C., Oct. 24, 1937; d. Aristakes and Antionette (Sudbeaz) Arakelian; m. Robert Barnett Raphael, June 12, 1966 (div. 1985); children: Therese Denise, Marc Philippe. BS in Math., St. John's U., 1959; MS in Math., Cath. U., Washington, 1962; PhD in Math, Cath. U., 1967. Asst. prof. math. Howard U., Washington, 1966-70, vis. prof., 1981-82, assoc. prof., 1982-86, prof., 1986—; assoc. prof. Clark Coll., Atlanta, 1971-79, prof., 1979-82; vis. assoc. prof. MIT, Cambridge, 1977-78, vis. prof., 1989-90. Contbr. over 35 rsch. articles to profl. jours. Program dir. NSF, Washington, 1986-88; acting adminstrv. officer Conf. Bd. Math. Scis., 1985-86. Grantee NSF, 1975-76, 79-81, 89-91, Army Rsch. Office, 1981-89, Air Force Sci. Rsch., 1981-82, 91-95, Nat. Security Agy., 1994—. Mem. AAAS, Am. Math. Soc. (com. mem.), Math. Assn. Am. (chmn. minorities in math. task force 1988, 1st v.p. 1996—), Soc. Indsl. and Applied Math., Sigma Xi. Democrat. Roman Catholic. Office: Howard U Dept Math Washington DC 20059

RAPHAEL, SALLY JESSY, talk-show host; b. Easton, Pa., Feb. 25, 1943; children: Allison (dec.), Andrea; m. Karl Soderlund; 2 step-daughters, 1 adopted son, also foster children. BFA, Columbia U. Anchored radio program Jr. High Sch. News Sta. WFAS-AM, White Plains, N.Y., 1955; host of cooking program WAPA-TV, San Juan, P.R., 1965-67; radio and television broadcaster Miami and Ft. Lauderdale, Fla., 1969-74; host Sta. WMCA-Radio, N.Y.C., 1976-81; talk show host NBC Talk-net, N.Y.C., 1982-88, ABC Talkradio, N.Y.C., 1988-91; syndicated TV talk-show host N.Y.C., 1983—; part-time owner of a perfume factory, 1964-68; owner of an art gallery, 1964-69; owner, The Wine Press, N.Y.C., 1979-83; ind. producer TV films, 1991;. Author: (with M.J. Boyer) Finding Love, 1984, (with Pam Proctor) Sally: Unconventional Success, 1980; film appearances include: Resident Alien, 1990, The Addams Family, 1991, The Associate, 1996, Meet Wally Sparks, 1996; TV appearances include: Murphy Brown, Dave's World, The Nanny, The Tonight Show, Nightline, Diagnosis Murder, Conspiracy of Silence, Touched By An Angel. Recipient Bronze medal, Internat. Film & Television Festival of NY, 1985; Emmy award as outstanding talk-show host, daytime, 1988, 89. Office: Multimedia Entertainment 515 W 57th St New York NY 10019-2901

RAPHAEL-HOWELL, FRANCES JAYNE, clinical psychologist; b. Alexandria, Va., Apr. 26, 1945; d. Robert Arthur and Isabelle Georgiana (Francis) Raphael; m. Frederick Alfred Howell, June 14, 1977; children: Robert, Carolyn, Cheryl. BS in Psychology, Howard U., 1971; MA in Clin. Psychology, Clark U., 1976, PhD, 1992; pre-doctoral intern, Children's Hosp. Med. Ctr., Boston, 1974-75. Cert. clin. psychologist; play therapist and supr. Assn. for Play Therapy. Spl. edn. tchr. Boston U. Mini Sch., 1975-76; instr. psychopathology U. Mass., Boston, 1976; psychologist Boston U. Med. Ctr., 1976-77; psychologist cons. Head Start, Boston, 1977; psychologist Montgomery County Pub. Schs., 1978; clin. psychologist D.C. Pub. Schs., Washington, 1978-91, supr. psychol. svcs., 1991-93; dir. Title I Pupil Pers. Svcs., Washington, 1993—; instr. urban edn. Grad. Sch. George Washington U., 1995-96; instr. play therapy Trinity U., 1996; presentations at confs. and workshops. Bd. dirs. Washington Humane Soc. Harvard U. fellow, 1974-75. Mem. APA (div. Clin. Psychology), Am. Bd. Forensic Examiners, Assn. for Play Therapy, Inc., D.C. Assn. for Sch. Psychologists. Democrat. Methodist. Home: 3010 W St SE Washington DC 20020-3361 Office: DC Pub Schs Winston Ednl Ctr 31st and Erie Sts SE Washington DC 20020

RAPHAELSON, JOEL, retired advertising agency executive; b. N.Y.C., Sept. 27, 1928; s. Samson and Dorothy (Wegman) R.; m. Mary Kathryn Hartigan, Aug. 20, 1960; children: Matthew, Katherine, Paul. B.A., Harvard U., 1949. Copywriter Macy's, N.Y.C., 1950-51, BBDO, N.Y.C., 1953-58; with Ogilvy & Mather, Inc., N.Y.C., 1958-94, v.p., joint copy chief, 1964-66, dir., 1968-75, mem. exec. com., 1970-75; creative cons. Ogilvy & Mather, Inc., Europe, 1975-76; exec. creative dir. Ogilvy & Mather, Inc., Chgo., 1976-82; sr. v.p. internat. creative svcs. Ogilvy & Mather Worldwide, 1982-92, spl. assignments as editor, writer, speechwriter, cons., 1993-94, ret., 1994; lectr. bus. writing for Am. Assn. Advt. Agys., other bus. orgns.; cons. Ogilvy & Mather Worldwide. Author: (with Kenneth Roman) How To Write Better, 1978, Writing That Works, 1981, rev. expanded edit., 1992; editor: The Unpublished David Ogilvy, 1986, Viewpoint (co. jour.), 1983-94. Cons. Lyric Opera Chgo., Snake River Inst., Jackson Hole, Wyo., Exec. Svc. Corps, Chgo. Home: 20 E Cedar St Chicago IL 60611-1149

RAPHEL, ROBIN, federal official; b. Vancouver, Wash., Sept. 16, 1947; m. Leonard Arthur Ashton; 2 children. BA, U. Wash.; Diploma in Hist. Studies, Cambridge U., Eng.; MA, U. Md. Lectr. history Damavand Coll., Tehran, Iran; analyst CIA; with Fgn. Svc., 1977, Islamabad, Pakistan, 1977-78; with office investment affairs bur. econs. Dept. of State, 1978-80, staff asst. to asst. sec. Near East and South Asian affairs, 1980-81, econ. officer Israel desk, 1981-82, spl. asst. to under sec. polit. affairs, 1982-84; 1st sec. polit. affairs London, 1984-88; polit. counselor Pretoria, South Africa, 1988-91, New Delhi, 1991-93; asst. sec. South Asian affairs Dept. of State, Washington, 1993—. Mem. Am. Econ. Assn., Am. Fgn. Svc. Assn., Phi Beta Kappa. Office: S Asian Affairs 2201 C St NW Washington DC 20520-0001*

RAPIN, ISABELLE, physician; b. Lausanne, Switzerland, Dec. 4, 1927; d. Rene and Mary Coe (Reeves) R.; m. Harold Oaklander, Apr. 5, 1959; children: Anne Louise, Christine, Stephen, Peter. Physician's Diploma. Faculte de Medicine, U. Lausanne, 1952, Doctorate in Medicine, 1955. Diplomate Am. Bd. Psychiatry and Neurology. Intern in pediatrics N.Y. U. Bellevue Med. Center, 1953-54; resident in neurology Neurol. Inst. of N.Y., Columbia-Presbyn. Med. Center, 1954-57, fellow in child neurology, 1957-58; mem. faculty Albert Einstein Coll. Medicine, Bronx, N.Y., 1958—; prof. neurology and pediatrics Albert Einstein Coll. Medicine, 1972—; attending neurologist and child neurologist Einstein Affiliated Hosps., Bronx.; Mem. Nat. Adv. Neurol. and Communicative Disorders and Stroke Coun., NIH, 1984-88. Contbr. chpts. to books, articles to med. jours. Recipient award Conf. Ednl. Adminstrs. Serving the Deaf, 1988. Fellow Am. Acad. Neurology (exec. bd. 1995—); mem. AAAS, Internat. Child Neurology Assn. (sec.-gen. 1979-82, v.p. 1982-86, Frank R. Ford lectr. 1990), Am. Neurol. Assn. (v.p. 1982-83), Child Neurology Soc. (Hower award 1987), Internat. Neuropsychology Soc., N.Y. Acad. Scis., Assn. for Rsch. in Nervous and Mental Diseases (v.p. 1986). Office: Albert Einstein Coll Medicine 1410 Pelham Pky S Bronx NY 10461-1101

RAPKE, JACK, agent. Co-head of motion picture divsn., then co-chmn. Creative Artists Agy., Beverly Hills, Calif. Office: Creative Artists Agy 9830 Wilshire Blvd Beverly Hills CA 90212-1804*

RAPOPORT, ANATOL, peace studies educator, mathematical biologist; b. Lozovaya, Russia, May 22, 1911; emigrated to U.S., 1922, naturalized, 1928; s. Boris and Adel (Rapoport) R.; m. Gwen Goodrich, Jan. 29, 1949; children: Anya, Alexander, Charles Anthony. PhD, U. Chgo., 1941; DHL, U. Western Mich., 1971; LLD, U. Toronto, 1986; DS, Royal Mil. Coll. Can., 1995; Ehrendoktor, U. Bern, Germany, 1995. Faculty dept. math. Ill. Inst. Tech., 1946-47; com. math. biology U. Chgo., 1947-54; fellow Ctr. Advanced Study Behavioral Scis., Stanford, 1954-55; asso. prof. Mental Health Research Inst., prof. math. biology U. Mich., 1955-70; prof. psychology and math. U. Toronto, 1970-80; dir. Inst. for Advanced Studies, Vienna, 1980-83; prof. peace studies U. Toronto, 1984—. Author: Science and the Goals of Man, 1950, Operational Philosophy, 1953, Fights, Games, and Debates, 1960, Strategy and Conscience, 1964, Prisoner's Dilemma, 1965, Two-Person Game Theory, 1966, N Person Game Theory, 1970, The Big Two, 1971, Conflict in Man Made Environment, 1974, Semantics, 1975, The 2 x 2 Game, 1976, Mathematische Methoden in den Sozialwissenschaften, 1980, Mathematical Models in the Social and Behavioral Sciences, 1983, General System Theory, 1986, The Origins of Violence, 1989, Decision Theory and Decision Behavior, 1989, Canada and the World, 1992, Peace: An Idea Whose Time Has Come, 1992, Gewissheiten and Zweifel, 1994; editor General Systems, 1956-77. Served to capt. USAAF, 1942-46. Fellow Am. Acad. Arts and Scis.; mem. Am. Math. Soc., Internat. Soc. Gen. Semantics (pres. 1953-55), Canadian Peace Research and Edn. Assn. (pres. 1972-75), Soc. for Gen. Systems Research (pres. 1965-66), Sci. for Peace (pres. 1984-86). Home: 38 Wychwood Park, Toronto, ON Canada M6G 2V5

RAPOPORT, BERNARD, life insurance company executive; b. San Antonio, July 17, 1917; s. David and Riva (Feldman) R.; m. Audre Jean Newman, Feb. 15, 1942; 1 child, Ronald B. B.A., U. Tex.-Austin, 1939. Chmn. bd., chief exec. officer Am. Income Life Ins. Co., Waco, Tex., 1951—; chmn. bd. regents U. Tex., 1991; apptd. by pres. adv. com. for trade policy and negotiations, 1994—. Mem. Nat. Council on Crime and Delinquency, San Francisco, 1979—, Jerusalem Found., N.Y.C., 1979—, Hebrew Union Coll., Cin., 1980—, Union Am. Hebrew Congregations, 1981—; Nat. Hispanic Ctr. for Advanced Studies and Policy Analysis, Oakland, Calif., 1981—; assoc. mem. U. Cancer Found., Houston, 1976—, Jt. Ctr. Polit. and Econ. Studies, 1987—; appointed mem. Adv. Com. for Trade Policy and Negotiation; chmn. United Negro Coll. Fund, Waco, 1979-80, United Way of Waco, 1982-83; trustee Paul Quinn Coll., Waco, 1963-90, Boy's Club, Waco, 1982—. Fellow City of Jerusalem., 1994. Democrat. Jewish. Club: Brazos. Avocations: tennis; politics; reading. Home: 2332 Wendy Ln Waco TX 76710-2011 Office: Am Income Life Ins Co PO Box 2608 Waco TX 76797

RAPOPORT, BERNARD ROBERT, lawyer; b. N.Y.C., Jan. 18, 1919; s. Max and Rose (Gerard) R.; m. Robyrta Wechter, May 31, 1959; 1 son: Michael. AB, Cornell U., 1939, JD, 1941. Bar: N.Y. 1941, Fed. Ct. (so. dist.) 1946. Assoc. firm Proskauer, Rose, Goetz, Mendelsohn, N.Y.C., 1941-50; gen. counsel M. Lowenstein Corp., N.Y.C., 1950-86, bd. dirs., 1961-86, treas., 1975-86, sec., 1970-86; dir., treas., sec. Leon Lowenstein Found. Served to capt. Signal Corps, U.S. Army, 1942-45. Mem. ABA, Assn. of Bar of City of N.Y. Address: 910 5th Ave New York NY 10021-4155

RAPOPORT, DAVID E., lawyer; b. Chgo., May 27, 1956; s. Morris H. and Ruth (Tecktiel) R.; m. Andrea Gail Albun; children: Alyson Faith, Steven Andrew. BS in Fin., No. Ill. U., 1978; JD with high honors, Ill. Inst. Tech., 1981; cert. in trial work Lawyers Postgrad. Inst., Chgo., 1984; cert. civil trial specialist Nat. Bd. Trial Adv., 1991. Bar: Ill. 1981, Wis. 1995, U.S. Dist. Ct. (no. dist.) Ill. 1981, U.S. Dist. Ct. (trial bar) Ill. 1993, U.S. Dist. Ct. (so. and cent. dists.), U.S. Ct. Appeals (7th cir.) 1981, U.S. Ct. Appeals (4th cir.) 1996. Litigation clk. Steinberg, Polacek & Goodman, Chgo., 1979-81; assoc. Katz, Friedman, Schur and Eagle, Chgo., 1981-90, 1993; ptnr. Katz, Friedman, Schur and Eagle, 1990, Baizer & Rapoport, Chgo., Highland Park, Ill., 1990-96; founding ptnr. Rapoport & Kupets Law Offices, 1996—; instr. legal writing Ill. Inst. Tech.-Kent Coll. Law, Chgo., 1981, guest lectr., 1985—; instr. Ill. Inst. Cont. Legal Edn., 1995—; arbitrator Cir. Ct. Cook County, Ill., Million Dollar Advocates Forum, 1995—; mem. plaintiff's steering com. In Air Disaster at Charlotte Douglas Airport, 1994. Fellow Roscoe Pound Found.; mem. ABA, Am. Trial Lawyers Assn., Assn. Trial Lawyers of Am., Ill. Bar Assn., Ill. Trial Lawyers Assn., Chgo. Bar Assn. (mem. workers compensation com. 1981—, tort litigation com. 1982—), Ill. Inst. for Continuing Legal Edn., Trial Lawyers for Pub. Justice, Trial Lawyers for Civil Justice, Lake County Bar Assn. Contbr. chpt. to book. Office: Rapoport & Kupets Law Offices 77 W Washington St Fl 20 Chicago IL 60602-2801 also: O'Hare Internat Ctr 10275 W Higgins Rd Ste 370 Rosemont IL 60018

RAPOPORT, JUDITH, psychiatrist; b. N.Y.C., July 12, 1933; d. Louis and Minna (Enteen) Livant; m. Stanley Rapoport, June 25, 1961; children: Stuart, Erik. BA, Swarthmore Coll., 1955; MD, Harvard U., 1959. Lic. psychiatrist. Cons., child psychiatrist NIMH/St. Elizabeth's Hosp., Washington, 1969-72; clin. asst. prof. Georgetown U. Med. Sch., Washington, 1972-82, clin. assoc. prof., 1982-85, clin. prof. psychiat., 1985—; med. officer biol. psychiatry br. NIMH, Bethesda, Md., 1976-78, chief, child mental illness unit, biol. psychiat. br., 1979-82, chief, child psychiatry lab. of clin. scis., 1982-84, chief, child psychiatry div. intramural rsch. programs, 1984—; prof. psychiatry George Washington U. Sch. Med., Washington, 1979—; prof. pediatrics Georgetown U., Washington, 1985—; cons. in field. Author: (non-fiction) The Boy Who Couldn't Stop Washing, 1989 (best seller literary guild selection 1989), Childhood Obsessive Compulsive Disorder, 1989. Fellow Am. Psychiat. Assn., Am. Acad. Child Psychiat.; mem. D.C. Psychiat. Assn., Inst. Medicine. Home: 3010 44th Pl NW Washington DC 20016-3557 Office: NIMH Bldg 10 Rm 6N240 Bethesda MD 20892

RAPOPORT, MILES S., state official; m. Sandra Luciano; children: Jeff, Ross. BA in Polit. Sci., NYU, 1971. Exec. dir. Conn. Citizen Action Group, 1979-84; mem. Conn. Ho. of Reps., asst. majority leader, 1987-92, house chmn. govt. adminstrn. and elections com., mem. fin., revenue and bonding com.; sec. of state State of Conn., 1994—. Address: 30 Montclair Dr West Hartford CT 06107-1246 Office: State Capitol # 104 Hartford CT 06106*

RAPOPORT, ROBERT MORTON, medical educator; b. Oakland, Calif., Nov. 20, 1952; married; 2 children. BA in Biological Scis., U. Calif., Santa Barbara, 1974; PhD in Pharmacology, U. Calif., L.A., 1980; postdoc. studies in Pharmacology, U. Va., 1980-81, Stanford U., 1981-83. Rsch. pharmacologist VA Med. Ctr., Palo Alto, Calif., 1983-84, Cin., 1984—; asst. prof. dept. pharmacology and cell biophysics U. Cin., 1984-91, assoc. prof., 1991—; asst. dir. med. pharmacology, 1994; spkr. in field. Reviewer manuscripts. various jours., grants various assns.; contbr. over 100 articles to profl. publs. Grantee U. Calif., 1977, VA, 1983-86, 85-86, 87-90, NIH, 1985-87, 88-93, Am. Heart Assn. S.W. Ohio, 1985-86, 86-87, 88-89, 89-91, 91-92, U. Cin., 1985-86, Am. Heart Assn., 1987-90, 1995—, Veterans Affairs, 1994-95, 95—, Univ. Rsch. Coun., 1994-95, Parke-Davis, 1994, 95; recipient Rsch. Career Devel. award, 1986-91. Office: Dept Pharmacology Univ Cincinnati 231 Bethesda Ave Cincinnati OH 45267*

RAPOPORT, RONALD JON, journalist; b. Detroit, Aug. 14, 1940; s. Daniel B. and Shirley G.; m. Joan Zucker, Sept. 2, 1968; children—Rebecca, Julie. B.A., Stanford U., 1962; M.S., Columbia U., 1963. Reporter Mpls. Star, 1963-65; asso. editor Sport mag., 1965-66; sports reporter AP, N.Y.C., San Francisco, 1966-70, Los Angeles Times, 1970-77; sports columnist Chgo. Sun-Times, 1977-88, Los Angeles Daily News, 1988-95; sports commentatorWeekend Edit. Nat. Pub. Radio, 1986—. Author: (with Chip Oliver) High for the Game, 1971, (with Stan Love) Love in the NBA, 1975, (with Jim McGregor) Called for Travelling, 1979; editor: A Kind of Grace: A Treasury of Sportswriting by Women, 1994. Served with U.S. Army Res., 1963. Address: 5744 Buffalo Van Nuys CA 91401

RAPOPORT, SONYA, artist; b. Boston; d. Louis Aaron and Ida Tina (Axelrod) Goldberg; m. Henry Rapoport; children—Hava Rapoport de Fereres, David, Robert. Student Mass. Coll. Art, 1941-42; B.A., NYU, 1945; M.A., U. Calif.-Berkeley, 1949. One woman shows N.Y.C. Pub. Library, 1979, New Sch. Social Research, N.Y.C., 1981, NYU Grad. Sch. Bus. Adminstrn., 1982, Sarah Lawrence Coll., Bronxville, N.Y., 1984, Kuopio Mus., Finland, 1992; group shows include Union Gallery San Jose State U., Calif., 1979, Ctr. for Visual Arts, Oakland, Calif., 1979, Walker Art Ctr., Mpls., 1981, Nat. Library, Madrid, 1982, SUNY Library, Purchase, 1983, Otis Art Inst. of Parsons Sch. of Design, Los Angeles, 1984, Cleve. Inst. Art, 1984, FISEA93 4th Internat. Symposium on Electronic Art, Mpls.also others; respresented in permanent collections Stedelijk Mus., Amsterdam, Indpls. Mus. Art, Grey Art Gallery, NYU, San Francisco Mus. Modern Art, San Jose State U. Found.-Union Gallery, Crocker Art Mus., Sacramento, Hall of Justice, Hayward, Calif.; book artist Shoe-Field, Chinese Connections, About Me, Objects on My Dresser, (interactive books) Gateway to Your Ka, Your Fate is in Your Feet, Digital Mudra2; producer A Shoe-In, Biorhythm, Coping with Sexual Jealousy, (computer assisted interactive installations) The Animated Soul, Digital Mudra, Transgenic Bagel; contbr. to profl. publs. Home: 6 Hillcrest Ct Berkeley CA 94705-2805

RAPP, CHARLES WARREN, computer scientist, researcher; b. Evanston, Ill., Nov. 30, 1961; s. Daniel Warren and Eunice Marie (Gockel) R. BS in Math. and Computer Sci., U. Ill., Chgo., 1984; MS in Computer Sci., Oreg. State U., 1986. Mem. tech. staff AT&T Bell Labs., Naperville, Ill., 1984-90; cons. BALR Corp., Oak Brook, Ill., 1990-91; sr. devel. engr. Clear Comm., Lincolnshire, Ill., 1991—. Author: (chpt.) Current Trends in SNePS, 1990. Mem. Assn. for Computing Machinery, Am. Assn. Artificial Intelligence. Republican. Lutheran. Office: Clear Comm Corp 100 Tri-State Internat Lincolnshire IL 60069

RAPP, FRED, virologist; b. Fulda, Germany, Mar. 13, 1929; came to U.S., 1936, naturalized, 1945; s. Albert and Rita (Hain) R.; children: Stanley I., Richard J., Kenneth A.; m. Pamela A. Miles, Aug. 28, 1988. BS, Bklyn. Coll., 1951; MS, Albany Med. Coll., Union U., 1956; PhD, U. So. Calif., 1958. Jr. bacteriologist to bacteriologist divsn. labs. and rsch. N.Y. State Dept. Health, 1952-55; from teaching asst. to instr. dept. med. microbiology Sch. Medicine U. So. Calif., 1956-59; cons. supervisory microbiologist Hosp. Spl. Surgery, N.Y.C., 1959-62; also virologist div. pathology Philip D. Wilson Research Found., N.Y.C.; asst. prof. microbiology and immunology Cornell U. Med. Coll., N.Y.C., 1961-62; assoc. prof. Baylor U. Sch. Medicine, Houston, 1962-66, prof., 1966-69; prof., chmn. dept. microbiology and immunology Pa. State U. Coll. Medicine, Hershey, Pa., 1969-90; Evan Pugh prof. microbiology Pa. State U. Coll. Medicine, University Park, 1978-90, prof. emeritus, 1990—, assoc. provost, dean health affairs, 1973-80, sr. mem. grad. faculty, assoc. dean acad. affairs, research and grad. studies, 1987-90, professor emeritus, 1990—; researh career prof. of virology Am. Cancer Soc., 1966-69, prof. virology, 1977-90; dir. Coll. Med. Pa. State U. (Specialized Cancer Research Ctr.), 1973-84; mem. del. on viral oncology, U.S./USSR Joint Com. Health Cooperation; chmn., Gordon Rsch. Conf. in Cancer, 1975; virology Task Force, 1976-79; chmn. Atlantic Coast Tumor Virology Group, Nat. Cancer Insts. Health, 1971-77; mem. council for projection and analysis Am. Cancer Soc., 1976-80; chmn. standards and exam. com. on virology Am. Bd. Med. Microbiology, 1977, 80; chmn. subsect. on virology program com. Am. Assn. Cancer Research, 1978-79; mem. adv. council virology div. Internat. Union Microbiol. Socs., 1978-84; referee Macy Faculty Scholar Award Program, 1979-81; mem. programme com. Fifth Internat. Congress for Virology, Strasbourg, France, 1981; mem. basic cancer rsch. group U.S.-France Agreement for Cooperation in Cancer Research, 1980-84; mem. organizing com. Internat. Workshop on Herpes viruses, Bologna, Italy, 1980-81, NATO Internat. Advanced Study Inst., Corfu Island, Greece, 1981; mem. Herpes viruses Study Group, 1981-84; mem. sci. adv. com. Wilmot Fellowship Program, U. Rochester Med. Ctr., 1981-90 ; mem. scientific rev. com. Hubert H. Humphrey Cancer Research Ctr., Boston U., 1981; mem. fin. com. Am. Soc. Virology, 1982-89, mem. council, 1984-88; mem. adv. com. persistent virus-host interactions research program R.J. Reynolds Scientific Bd./Wistar Inst., 1983-90; mem. med. adv. bd. Herpes Resource Ctr., Am. Social Health Assn., 1983-90; bd. dirs. U.S.-Japan Found. Biomedicine, 1983-90; mem. council Soc. Exptl. Biology and Medicine, 1983-87; mem. scientific adv. com. Internat. Assn. Study and Prevention of Virus-Associated Cancers, 1983-90; mem. Basil O'Connor Starter Research Adv. Com., 1984-90; mem. council for research and clin. investigation awards Am. Cancer Soc., 1984-90; mem. recombinant DNA adv. com. NIH, 1984-87; mem. outstanding investigator grant rev. com. Nat. Cancer Inst., 1984-90; mem. organizing com. Fourth Symposium Sapporo Cancer Seminar, Japan, 1984, Second Internat. Conf. Immunobiology and Prophylaxis of Human Herpes virus Infections, Ft. Lauderdale, Fl., 1984-85, Internat. Congress of Virology, Sendai, Japan, 1984; mem. internat. sci. com. Internat. Meeting on Adv. in Virology, Catania, Italy, 1984-85; mem. adv. bd. Cancer Info., Dissemination and Analysis Ctr. Carcinogenesis and Cancer Biology, 1984-89; mem. internat. programme com. 7th Internat. Congress of Virology, Edmonton, Can., 1985-87; councilor div. DNA viruses Am. Soc. Microbiology, 1985-87; mem. adv. com. rsch. on etiology, diagnosis, natural history, prevention and therapy of multiple sclerosis Nat. Multiple Sclerosis Soc., 1985-89; mem. sci. adv. bd. Tampa Bay Rsch. Inst., 1985-91; mem. sci. adv. coun. Pitts. Ctr. AIDS Rsch. U. Pitts., 1988; mem. recombinant DNAdv. com. Working Group on Transgenic Animals NIH, 1988; mem. adv. com. 15th Internat. Herpes Virus Workshop, Washington, 1989-90. Sect. editor on oncology: Intervirology, 1972-84, assoc. editor, 1978-84, editor-in-chief, 1985-90; adv. bd. Archives Virology, 1976-81; editorial bd. Jour. Immunology, 1966-73, Jour. Virology, 1968-88; assoc. editor Cancer Research, 1972-79; editorial bd. Virology, 1979-83, editor, 1983-90; mem. adv. bd. Ency. Americana, 1992—. Recipient 1st CIBA-Geigy Drew award for biomed. research, 1977, Nat. award for teaching excellence in microbiology, U. Medicine and Dentistry N.J. Med. Sch., 1988; Wellcome vis. professorship in microbiology, 1989-90; Disting. fellow Inst. Advanced Biotech., 1991. Mem. AAAS, AAUP, Am. Acad. Microbiology (fellow, diplomate), Soc. Microbiology (mem. com. med. microbiology and immunology, bd. pub. sci. affairs 1979-88, chmn. DNA viruses div. 1981-82, divsn. councilor DNA viruses), Am. Soc. Virology (chmn. fin. com. 1987-88, emeritus 1991), Am. Assn. Immunologists, The Harvey Soc., Soc. Exptl. Biology and Medicine (emeritus 1993), Am. Assn. Cancer Rsch. (emeritus 1991), Assn. Med. Sch. Microbiology Chmn. (pres. 1980-81), Sigma Xi (Monie A. Ferst award 1990, nat. lectr. 1977-79), Alpha Omega Alpha. Home: 68 Azalea Dr Hershey PA 17033-2602

RAPP, GEORGE ROBERT, JR. (RIP RAPP), geology and archeology educator; b. Toledo, Sept. 19, 1930; s. George Robert and Gladys Mae (Warner) R.; m. Jeannette Messner, June 15, 1956; children: Kathryn, Karen. BA, U. Minn., 1952; PhD, Pa. State U., 1960. Asst. then assoc. prof. S.D. Sch. Mines, Rapid City, 1957-65; assoc. prof. U. Minn., Mpls., 1965-75; prof. geology and archeology U. Minn., Duluth, 1975-95, dean Coll. Letters and Sci., 1975-84, dean Coll. Sci. and Engring., 1984-89, dir. Archeometry Lab., 1975—; Regents' prof. geoarchaeology, 1995—; prof. Ctr. for Ancient Studies, U. Minn., Mpls., 1970-93, prof. interdisciplinary archaeol. studies, 1993—, Regents' prof. geoarchaeology, 1995—; cons. USIA, Westinghouse Corp., Exxon Corp., Ford Found. Author, editor: Excavations at Nichoria, 1978, Troy: Archeological Geology, 1982, Archeological Geology, 1985, Excavations at Tel Michal, 1989, Encyclopedia of Minerals, 1989, Phytolith Systematics, 1992; mem. editorial bd. Jour. Field Archeology, 1976-85, Jour. Archeol. Sci., 1977-79, Geoarcheology Jour., 1984—, Am. Jour. Archeology, 1985-92. NSF postdoctoral fellow, 1963-64, Fulbright-Hayes sr. rsch. fellow, 1972-73. Fellow AAAS (chmn. sect. E, 1987-88, nat. coun. 1992-95), Geol. Soc. Am. (Archeol. Geology award 1983), Mineral. Soc. Am.; mem. Nat. Assn. Geology Tchrs. (pres. 1986-89), Soc. for Archeol. Sci. (pres. 1983-84), Assn. Field Archeology (pres. 1979-81), Archaeol. Inst. Am. (Pomerance medal 1988), Sigma Xi (bd. dirs. 1990—). Avocation: classical music, archaeological excavations in Greece, Turkey, Cyprus, Israel. Office: U Minn-Duluth Archaeometry Lab Duluth MN 55812

RAPP, GERALD DUANE, lawyer, manufacturing company executive; b. Berwyn, Nebr., July 19, 1933; s. Kenneth P. and Mildred (Price) R.; m. Jane Carol Thomas, Aug. 14, 1954; children—Gerald Duane Jr., Gregory T., Amy Frances. B.S., U. Mo., 1955; J.D., U. Mich., 1958. Bar: Ohio bar 1959. Practice in Dayton, 1960—; ptnr. Smith & Schnacke, 1963-70; asst. gen. counsel Mead Corp., Dayton, 1970, v.p. human resources and legal affairs, 1973, v.p., corp. sec., 1975, v.p., gen. counsel, corp. sec., 1976, v.p., gen. counsel, 1979, sr. v.p., gen. counsel, 1981-91, counsel to bd. dirs., 1991-92; of counsel Bieser, Greer & Landis, 1992—; pres. R-J Holding Co., Weber Canyon Ranch, Inc. Sr. editor U. Mich. Law Rev., 1957-58. Past chmn. Oakwood Youth Commn.; past v.p., bd. dirs. Big Bros. Greater Dayton; mem. pres.'s visitors com. U. Mich. Law Sch.; past trustee Urbana Coll.; past pres., trustee Ohio Ctr. Leadership Studies, Robert K. Greenleaf Ctr., Indpls.; past pres. bd. trustees Dayton and Montgomery County Pub. Libr.; past. mem. bd. visitors Law Schs. of Dayton. 1st lt. U.S. Army, 1958-60. Mem. ABA, Ohio Bar Assn., Dayton Bar Assn., Moraine Country Club, Dayton Racquet Club, Dayton Lawyers Club, Met. Club Washington, Phi Kappa Psi, Phi Delta Phi, Beta Gamma Sigma. Presbyterian. Office: Bieser Greer & Landis 400 National City Ctr Dayton OH 45402-1908

RAPP, PETER F., medical facility administrator. BA in Econs., Denison U., 1972; M Mgmt. in Hosp. and Health Adminstrn., Northwestern U., 1974. Asst./assoc. adminstr. for support svcs. Ohio State U. Hosps., Columbus, 1974-81, assoc. adminstr. profl. svcs., 1981-83; assoc. adminstr. profl. svcs. Vanderbilt U. Hosp., Nashville, 1983-84; interim CEO, interim CO Med. Coll. Va. Hosps., 1985-86; CFO, 1984-94; gen. dir. U. Minn. Hosp. and Clinic, Mpls., 1994—. Office: U Minn Hosp and Clinic Box 502 UMHC 420 Delaware St SE Minneapolis MN 55455

RAPP, RICHARD TILDEN, economist, consultant; b. Miami, Fla., Nov. 30, 1944; s. Melville Benjamin and Rachel (Marx) R.; m. Wilma J. Levin, Aug. 20, 1967; children: Ethan, Sandra. BA cum laude, Bklyn. Coll., 1965; MA, U. Pa., 1966, PhD, 1970. Asst. prof. SUNY, Stony Brook, 1970-75, assoc. prof. econ. history, 1976-77; pres., chief exec. officer Nat. Econ. Research Assocs., Inc., White Plains, N.Y., 1977—; cons. on internat. trade and competition econs. Author: Industry and Economic Decline in Seventeenth-Century Venice, 1976, Trade Warfare and the New Protectionism, 1986; co-author: European Economic History, 1975. Nat. adv. bd. Santa Fe Opera, 1989—. Kent fellow Danforth found., 1968-70; Fulbright fellow, 1968-69. Mem. Am. Econ. Assn., Inst. for Advanced Study. Home: 52 Whippoorwill Lake Rd Chappaqua NY 10514-2314 Office: Nat Econ Rsch Assocs Inc 50 Main St White Plains NY 10606-1920

RAPP, ROBERT ANTHONY, metallurgical engineering educator, consultant; b. Lafayette, Ind., Feb. 21, 1934; s. Frank J. and Goldie M. (Royer) R.; m. Heidi B. Sartorius, June 3, 1960; children: Kathleen Rapp Raynaud, Thomas, Stephen, Stephanie Rapp Surface. BSMetE, Purdue U., 1956; MSMetE, Carnegie Inst. Tech., 1959, PhDMetE, 1960; D (hon.), Inst. Polytech., Toulouse, France, 1995. Asst. prof. metall. engring. Ohio State U., Columbus, 1963-66, assoc. prof., 1966-69, prof., 1969—, M.G. Fontana prof., 1988—, Univ. prof., 1989-95; disting. univ. prof. emeritus, 1995—; cons. KB Alloys; vis. prof. Ecole Nat. Superior d'Electrochimie, Grenoble, France, 1972-73, U. Paris-Sud, Orsay, 1985-86, Ecole Nat. Superior de Chimie, Toulouse, France, 1985-86, U. New South Wales, Australia, 1987; Acta/Scripta Metallurgica lectr., 1991; rsch. metallurgist WPAFB, Ohio, 1960-63. Editor: Techniques of Metals Research, vol. IV, 1982, High Temperature Corrosion, 1984; translator Metallic Corrosion (Kaesche), 1986; bd. rev. jour. Oxid. Metals; contbr. numerous articles to profl. jours. Recipient Disting. Engring. Alumnus award Purdue U., 1988, B.F. Goodrich Collegiate Inventor's award, 1991, 92, Ulrick Evans award Brit. Inst. Corrosion, 1992; Guggenheim fellow, 1972; Fulbright scholar Max Planck Inst. Phys. Chemistry, 1959-60. Fellow Am. Soc. Metals Internat. (B. Stoughton award 1968, Howe gold medal 1974), Mining Metals and Materials Soc., Electrochem. Soc. (HTM Divsn. Outstanding Achievement award 1992), Nat. Assn. Corrosion Engrs. (W.R. Whitney award 1986), French Soc. Metals and Materials (hon.), Chevalier des Palmes Acad. Lutheran. Home: 1379 Southport Dr Columbus OH 43235-7649

RAPP, ROBERT NEIL, lawyer; b. Erie, Pa., Sept. 10, 1947; m. Sally K. Meder; 1 child: Jeffrey David. BA, Case Western Res. U., 1969, JD, 1972; MBA, Cleve. State U., 1989. Bar: Ohio 1972, U.S. dist. Ct. (no. dist.) Ohio 1973, U.S. Ct. Appeals (6th crct.) 1981, U.S. Supreme Ct. 1980. Assoc. Metzenbaum, Gaines & Stern, Co., L.P.A., Cleve., 1972-75; ptnr. Calfee, Halter & Griswold, Cleve., 1975—; adj. prof. law Case Western Res. U., 1975-78, 94—, Cleve. Marshall Coll. Law, Cleve. State U., 1976-82; disting. lawyer-in-residence Cornell U. Law Sch., 1993; mem. legal adv. bd. Nat. Assn. Securities Dealers, 1992-96; arbitrator Nat. Futures Assn., Nat. Assn. Securities Dealers, Inc,; ind. arbitrator securities and futures law matters. Contbr. numerous articles to law jours. Mem. ABA (sect. bus. law: mem. com. fed. regulation of securities, subcom. broker-dealer regulation, sect. litigation: mem. com. securities litigation), Am. Arbitration Assn. (securities arbitrator, mem. comml. adv. coun. Cleve. region), Ohio State Bar Assn. (elected mem. coun. dels. 1976-82, corp. law com. 1980—), Cleve. Bar Assn. (chmn. young lawyers sect. 1976-77), assoc. mem. cert. grievance com., sect. securities law: exec. coun. 1980-85, chmn. govt. liaison com. 1980-81). Office: Calfee Halter & Griswold 1400 McDonald Investment Ct Cleveland OH 44114-2688

RAPPA, MICHAEL GEORGE, occupational and environmental medicine physician; b. Milw., Mar. 26, 1960; s. Raymond Anthony and Carol Kathleen (McKenzie) R.; m. Adriana D'Angelo, June 1, 1985; children: Walter, Brian, Erik, Christine. BS, U. West Fla., 1982, MBA, 1984; DO, Southeastern U., Miami, 1988; MPH with honors, Johns Hopkins U., 1992. Diplomate Am. Bd. Preventive Medicine; cert. chemist Am. Chem. Soc. Commd. 2d lt. US Army, 1984, advanced through grades to maj., 1994; intern William Beaumont Army Med. Ctr./Ft. Bliss, El Paso, Tex., 1988-89, occupational health physician, 1989-91; occupational medicine resident U.S. Army Environ. Hygiene Agy., Aberdeen Proving Ground, Md., 1991-93; occupational and environmental medicine cons. U.S. Army Ctr. Health Promotion & Preventive Medicine, Aurora, Colo., 1993-95; assoc. med. dir. occupational and preventive health BroMenn Healthcare, Bloomington, Ill., 1995—. U.S. Army scholar, 1984-88. Mem. APHA, Am. Chemical Soc., Am. Coll. Occupational and Environ. Medicine, Am. Coll. Preventive Medicine, Assn. Mil. Osteo. Physicians and Surgeons, Am. Osteo. Assn., Delta Omega Alpha. Avocations: jogging, hiking, raquetball. Home: 1917 Redbud Ln Bloomington IL 61704 Office: BroMenn Healthcare 807 N Main St Bloomington IL 61701

RAPPACH, NORMA JEANNE, health occupations educator; b. Hastings, Pa., Mar. 7, 1938; d. James Eugene and Katherine Luella (Lear) Fairbanks; m. James Davis Mrus, June 30, 1959 (div. Aug. 1978); children: Timothy James, Susan Marie Mrus Hughes, Joseph Michael; m. Ronald Michael Rappach, Aug. 9, 1979; stepchildren: Kelley Rae, Lynn Rae Rappach Paris. Diploma, Trumbull Meml. Sch. Nursing, 1959; cert. EMT/paramedic, Cuyahoga C.C., 1978; AAS with honors, Kent State U., 1983, vocat. tchr. cert., 1996; BSN magna cum laude, Youngstown State U., 1986. RN, Ohio; cert. diversified health occupations instr., Ohio. Pediatric staff nurse Trumbull Meml. Hosp., Warren, Ohio, 1960-62, part-time pvt. duty nurse, 1969-71; geriatric staff nurse Meadows Manor, Terre Haute, Ind., 1965-66; Vocat. Tchr.; substitute sch. nurse Howland Local Schs., Warren, 1972-78, cert. emergency med. instr. Ohio Dept. Edn., Columbus, 1973-78; substitute indsl. nurse Packard Electric divsn. GM, Warren, 1974-76; sch. nurse Lordstown Local Schs., Warren, 1978-93; diversified health occupations instr. Gordon D. James Career Ctr., Lordstown Schs., Warren, 1993—; part-time nurse obstetrical office, Warren, 1961-73; part-time gen. office nurse, Warren, 1960-72; part-time geriatric nurse Gillette's Nursing, Warren, 1972-74; instr. nurse aid tng. Ohio Bd. Nursing, 1993—. Adviser Teen Inst. for Alcohol Abuse, Warren, 1981; county emergency med. coord. Trumbull County, Warren, 1976-77; pres. Trumbull County Emergency Med. Com., 1976-77; HIV/AIDS coord. Lordstown Local Schs., 1985-93, mem. diversified health adv. bd., 1990—; vol. nurse, 1st aid/CPR/HIV-AIDS instr., ARC, Warren, 1990—; parish nurse Blessed Sacrament Ch., Warren, 1992-94. Named Profl. Woman of Yr., Trumbull County Fair, 1977, Hon. Firewoman, Howland Twp. Fire Dept., 1978, Vocat. Citizenship award Omicron Tau Theta chpt. Kent State U., 1995; nursing scholar Warren Kiwanis Club, 1956. Mem. Am. Fedn. Tchrs., Ohio Vocat. Assn. Avocations: reading, computers, crafts.

RAPPAPORT, CHARLES OWEN, lawyer; b. N.Y.C., May 15, 1950; s. Edward and Edith (Novick) R.; m. Valerie B. Ackerman, Oct. 11, 1987; children: Emily Randle, Sarah Elisabeth. BA, Columbia U., 1970; JD, NYU, 1975. Bar: N.Y. 1976. Assoc. Simpson, Thacher & Bartlett, N.Y.C., 1975-82, ptnr., 1982—. Home: 26 N Moore St Apt 4W New York NY 10013-2461 Office: Simpson Thacher & Bartlett 425 Lexington Ave New York NY 10017-3903

RAPPAPORT, GARY BURTON, defense equipment and computer company executive; b. Mpls., Apr. 27, 1937; s. Max and Beatrice (Berkinsky) R.; m. Susan Heller, Nov. 26, 1961; children: Debra Lynn, Melissa Ellen. B.S., U. Pa., 1959. Asst. to pres. Napco Industries, Inc., Hopkins, Minn., 1959-61, v.p., 1961-65, exec. v.p., 1964-65, pres., 1965-74, chmn. bd., chief exec. officer, 1974-84; chmn. bd., chief exec. officer Venturian Corp., Hopkins, 1984—; dir. La Maur, Inc., Mpls., 1980-87. Chmn. bd. govs. Mt. Sinai Hosp., Mpls., 1979-81. Served with Air N.G., 1960-64. Jewish. Office: 1600 2nd St S Hopkins MN 55343-7485

RAPPAPORT, LAWRENCE, plant physiology and horticulture educator; b. N.Y.C., May 28, 1928; s. Aaron and Elsie R.; m. Norma, Nov. 21, 1953; children: Meryl, Debra Kramer, Craig. BS in Horticulture, U. Idaho, 1950; MS in Horticulture, Mich. State Coll., 1951; PhD in Horticulture, Mich. State U., 1956. Lectr. U. Calif., Davis, 1956-67, jr. olericulturist dept. vegetable crops, 1956-58, asst. olericulturist, 1958-63, assoc. olericulturist, 1963-67, prof., 1968-91, prof. emeritus, 1991—, dir. plant growth lab., 1975-78, chairperson dept. vegetable crops, 1978-84; vis. scientist Calif. Inst. Tech., 1958; co-dir. Horticulture Subproject, Calif./Egypt project, 1978-82. Contbr. articles to profl. jours. 1st pres. Davis Human Rels. Coun., 1964-66; v.p. Jewish Fedn. Sacramento, 1969; pres. Jewish Fellowship, Davis, 1985-89. Sgt. maj. U.S. Army, 1952-53, Korea. Decorated Bronze star; Guggenheim Found. fellow, 1963, Fulbright fellow, 1964, USPHS Spl. fellow, 1970, Am. Soc. Horticulture Sci. fellow, 1987, Sir Frederick McMaster fellow, 1991. Achievements include discovery of evidence for gibberellin-binding protein in plants; evidence for the signal hypothesis operating in plants, positive evidence for phytochrome-mediated gibberellin metabolism and stem growth; isolation of somaclonal variants of celery bearing stable resistance to Fusarium oxysporum f. sp. apii. Home: 637 Elmwood Dr Davis CA 95616-3514 Office: U Calif Dept Vegetable Crops Asmundson Hall Rm 210 Davis CA 95616

RAPPAPORT, MARTIN PAUL, internist, nephrologist, educator; b. Bronx, N.Y., Apr. 25, 1935; s. Joseph and Anne (Kramer) R.; BS, Tulane U., 1957, MD, 1960; m. Bethany Ann Mitchell; children: Karen, Steven. Intern, Charity Hosp. of La., New Orleans, 1960-61, resident in internal medicine, 1961-64; pvt. practice medicine specializing in internal medicine and nephrology, Seabrook, Tex., 1968-72, Webster, Tex., 1972—; mem. courtesy staff Mainland Ctr. Hosp. (formerly Galveston County Meml. Hosp.), Houston, 1968—, Bapt. Meml. System, 1969-72, 88—; mem. staff Clear Lake Regional Med. Ctr., 1972—; cons. staff St. Mary's Hosp., 1973-79; cons. nephrology St. John's Hosp., Nassau Bay, Tex.; fellow in nephrology Northwestern U. Med. Sch., Chgo., 1968; clin. asst. prof. in medicine and nephrology U. Tex., Galveston, 1969—; lectr. emergency med. technician course, 1974-76; adviser on respiratory therapy program Alvin (Tex.) Jr. Coll., 1976-82; cons. nephrology USPHS, 1979-80. Served to capt. M.C., U.S. Army, 1961-67. Diplomate Am. Bd. Internal Medicine, Nat. Bd. Med. Examiners. Fellow ACP, Am. Coll. Chest Physicians; mem. Internat., Am. Socs. Nephrology, So. Med. Assn., Tex. Med. Assn., Tex. Soc. Internal Medicine (bd. govs. 1994—), Am. Soc. Artificial Internal Organs, Tex. Acad. Internal Medicine, Harris County Med. Soc., Am. Geriatrics Soc., Bay Area Heart Assn. (bd. govs. 1969-75), Clear Lake C. of C., Phi Delta Epsilon, Alpha Epsilon Pi, Tulane Alumni Assn. Lodge: Rotary. Home: 1818 Linfield Way Houston TX 77058-2324 Office: PO Box 57609 Webster TX 77598-7609

RAPPAPORT, STUART R., lawyer; b. Detroit, Apr. 13, 1935; s. Reuben and Zella (Golechen) R.; m. Anne M. Plotnick; children: Douglas, Erica Rappaport Witt. BA in History, U. Mich., 1956; JD, Harvard U., 1959. Bar: Calif. 1962. Trial lawyer, chief trials, bur. chief, chief. asst. pub. defender L.A. County Pub. Defender's Office, L.A., 1962-87; cons. on def. of capital cases Santa Clara County Pub. Defender's Office, San Jose, Calif., 1987-95; mem. standing adv. com. on criminal law Judicial Coun. Calif., San Francisco, 1993—; mem. discipline evaluation com. State Bar of Calif. Contbr. articles to profl. jours. Recipient Lifetime Achievement award Calif. Attys. for Criminal Justice. Mem. Calif. Pub. Defenders Assn. (pres. 1982-83, Lifetime Achievement award), L.A. County Pub. Defenders Assn. (pres.). Democrat. Jewish. Office: PO Box 960 Mendocino CA 95460

RAPPAPORT, THEODORE SCOTT, electrical engineering educator; b. Bklyn., Nov. 26, 1960; s. Eugene and Carol Ann (Cooper) R.; m. Brenda Marie Velasquez, May 30, 1981; children: Matthew B., Natalie M., Jennifer L. BSEE, Purdue U., 1982, MSEE, 1984, PhD, 1987. Registered profl. engr., Va. Engring. coop. Magnavox Govt./Ind. Elec. Co., Fort Wayne, Ind., 1980-81; engr. Harris Corp., Melbourne, Fla., 1983, systems engr., 1986; rsch., teaching asst. Purdue U., West Lafayette, Ind., 1982-87; prof. Va. Poly. Inst. and State U., Blacksburg, 1992—; founding dir. Mobile & Portable Radio Rsch. Corp.; cons. Ralph M. Parsons Co., Pansonic, Inc., Ericsson/GE Mobile Comm. Co-author, co-editor 6 books on wireless personal comm. including Wireless Communications, Cellular Raido and Personal Communications; contbr. articles to profl. jours. V.p. Gilbert Linkous Elem. Sch. PTA, Blacksburg, 1990-91; exec. com., asst. den leader Boy Scouts of Am., Blacksburg, 1992. Named Marconi Young scientist IEEE, 1990, one of Young Men of Am., 1988, Pres. Faculty fellow NSF, 1992. Fellow Radio Club Am. (dir.); mem. NSPE, IEEE (sr. mem., developer first wireless textbook and learning program 1995), Am. Radio Relay League, Am. Soc. Engring. Edn. Achievements include patents in Tunable Discone Antenna, computer-based bit error simulation for digital wireless communications, real-time DSP receivers.

RAPPEPORT, IRA J., lawyer; b. Phila., Jan. 13, 1954. BA with honors, Washington U., 1975; JD with honors, Villanova U., 1978. Bar: Calif. 1978. Assoc. Pillstory Madison & Sutro, 1978-83; assoc. Memel, Jacobs, Pietro & Gersh, 1983-85, ptnr., 1985-87; ptnr. McDermott, Will & Emory, L.A., 1987—. Mng. editor Villanova Law Rev., 1977-78. Recipient Scribes award Villanova Sch. Law, 1978. Mem. Am. Acad. Hosp. Attys., L.A. County Bar Assn. (mem. healthcare law sect.), Beverly Hills Bar Assn. (mem. healthcare law sect.), Century City Bar Assn. (mem. healthcare law sect.), Nat. Health Lawyers Assn., Calif. Soc. Healthcare Attys. Office: McDermott Will & Emery 2049 Century Park E Fl 34 Los Angeles CA 90067-3208*

RAPPLEYE, RICHARD KENT, financial executive, consultant, educator; b. Oswego, N.Y., Aug. 10, 1940; s. Robert Edward and Evelyn Margaret (Hammond) R.; m. Karen Tobe Greenberg, Sept. 7, 1963; children: Matthew Walker, Elizabeth Marion. AB, Miami U., Oxford, Ohio, 1962; postgrad. in theology Boston U., 1962-63; MBA, U. Pa., 1964; postgrad. in law DePaul U., 1965-66. CPA, Ill. Auditor DeLoitte Haskins & Sells, Chgo., 1962-67, mgmt. cons., 1967-71; controller, United Dairy Industry Assn., Rosemont, Ill., 1971, dir. fin. and adminstrn., 1971-73, exec. v.p., 1973-74; asst. to exec. v.p. Florists' Transworld Delivery, Southfield, Mich., 1974-75, group dir. fin. and adminstrn., 1975-80; asst. treas. Erb Lumber Co., Birmingham, Mich., 1980, v.p. fin., chief fin. officer, 1981-83; v.p., sec.-treas. C.S. Mott Found., Flint, Mich., 1983—; lectr. U. Mich., Flint, 1987-91; cons. in field; instr. Oakland U., Rochester, Mich., 1981-83; bd. dirs. Mich. Nat. Bank, Treas. Council Mich. Founds, 1986-92. Mem. AICPAs, Mich. Assn. CPAs. Unitarian. Lodge: Masons, Rotary. Home: 503 Arlington St Birmingham MI 48009-1639 Office: CS Mott Found 503 S Saginaw St Flint MI 48502-1807

RAPPOLT, WILLIAM CARL, banker; b. N.Y.C., Oct. 17, 1945; s. William Herbert and Loretta (Risk) R.; m. Pamela Hodgkins, June 7, 1969; children: Gabrille, Sarah, William. BS, Lafayette Coll., 1967; MBA, Columbia U., 1969. Fgn. exch. dealer Brown Bros. Harriman & Co., N.Y.C., 1970-72; v.p., mgr. trading 1st Nat. State Bank of N.J., Newark, 1972-74; v.p. fgn. exch. trading United Calif. Bank, N.Y.C., 1974-76; sr. v.p., mgr. trading Fidelity Bank Phila., 1976-84; exec. v.p., treas. M&T Bank, Buffalo, 1984—; exec. v.p. 1st Empire State Corp.; mem. fgn. exch. com. Fed. Res., N.Y.C., 1976—. Lt. USNR, 1969-71. Mem. Forex USA (pres. 1988—), Delta Upsilon (trustee 1978—). Methodist. Avocation: horseback riding. Office: M&T Bank 1 M & T Plz Buffalo NY 14211-1638

RAPSON, RICHARD L., history educator; b. N.Y.C., Mar. 8, 1937; s. Louis and Grace Lillian (Levenkind) R.; m. Susan Burns, Feb. 22, 1975 (div. June 1981); m. Elaine Catherine Hatfield, June 15, 1982; 1 child, Kim Elizabeth. BA, Amherst Coll., 1958; PhD, Columbia U., 1966. Asst. prof. Amherst (Mass.) Coll., 1960-61, Stanford (Calif.) U., 1961-65; from assoc. prof. to prof. history U. Hawaii, Honolulu, 1965—, founder, dir. New Coll., 1968-73; bd. dirs. Semester at Sea, U. Pittsburgh, 1979—; psychotherapist, Honolulu, 1982—. Author: Indivisualism and Conformity in the American Character, 1967, Britons View America, 1971, The Cult of Youth, 1972, Major Interpretations of the American Past, 1978, Denials of Doubt, 1980, Cultural Pluralism in Hawaii, 1981, American Yearnings, 1989; co-author: (with Elaine Hatfield) Love, Sex and Intimacy: Their Psychology, Biology and History, 1993, Emotional Contagion, 1994, Love and Sex: Cross-Cultural Perspectives, 1995; mem. editl. bd. Univ. Press Am., 1981—. Woodrow Wilson fellow, Wilson Found., Princeton, 1960; Edward Perkins scholar, Columbia U., 1961; Danforth tchr., Danforth Found., St. Louis, 1965; recipient E. Harris Harbison for Gifted Teaching award, Danforth Found., 1973, Outstanding Tchr. award Stanford U. 25th Reunion Class, 1992. Mem. Am. Hist. Assn., Orgn. Am. Hist., Nat. Womens Hist. Project, Phi Beta Kappa, Outrigger Canoe Club, Honolulu Club. Avocations: squash, travel, classical music. Office: U Hawaii Dept History 2530 Dole St Honolulu HI 96822-2303

RARIDEN, KAREN L., television executive; b. Bloomington, Ind., Feb. 15, 1953. BS in Radio/TV and English, Ind. U., 1975, MS in Telecomms., 1977. With WTHI-TV, Terre Haute, Ind., 1978-82; prodr. WANE-TV, Ft. Wayne, Ind., 1983, WRTV-TV, Indpls., 1993-94; prodr., reporter WPTA-TV, Ft. Wayne, 1983-84, mng. editor, 1984-85; asst. news dir. WOTV-TV, Grand Rapids, Mich., 1985-88; assignment mgr. WBNS-TV, Columbus, Ohio, 1988-89; mng. editor WTTV-TV, Indpls., 1990-93; spl. project prodr. WRTV-TV, Indpls., 1993-94, mng. editor, 1994—. Recipient Best News Feature award Ind. divsn. AP, 1982, Best Newscast award UPI, 1984, Best Documentary award Mich. class UPI, 1986, News Sta. of Yr. award Mich. class UPI, 1987, Emmy award for Spl. Coverage Mich. chpt. NATAS, 1987, Best Spor News award SPJ Ind., 1990, Best Newscast award SPJ Ind., 1992, Best In-Depth Series award AP Ind., 1994. Office: WRTV-TV 1330 N Meridian Indianapolis IN 46202-2303

RARIDON, RICHARD JAY, computer specialist; b. Newton, Iowa, Oct. 25, 1931; s. Jack Allison and Letha Helen (Woods) R.; m. Mona Marie Herndon, May 28, 1956; children—Susan Gayle, Ann Chaney. B.A., Grinnell Coll., 1953; M.A., Vanderbilt U., 1955, Ph.D., 1959. Assoc. prof. phys. sci. Memphis State U., 1958-62; research scientist Oak Ridge Nat. Lab., 1962-92; cons. ORNL, fusion energy divsn., 1992—; environ. specialist Coop. Sci. Edn. Center, Oak Ridge, 1971-72. Contbr. articles to profl. jours. Radiol. Physics fellow AEC, 1953-55. Fellow AAAS, Tenn. Acad. Sci. (pres. 1971); mem. Assn. Acads. Sci. (sec.-treas. 1972-76, pres. 1977), Sigma Xi. Home: 111 Columbia Dr Oak Ridge TN 37830 Office: Oak Ridge Nat Lab Oak Ridge TN 37831-8071

RASCH, ELLEN MYRBERG, cell biology educator; b. Chicago Heights, Ill., Jan. 31, 1927; d. Arthur August and Helen Catherine (Stelle) Myrberg; m. Robert W. E. Rasch, June 17, 1950; 1 son, Martin Karl. PhB with honors, U. Chgo., 1945, BS in Biol. Sci., 1947, MS in Botany, 1948, PhD, 1950. Asst. histologist Am. Meat Inst. Found., Chgo., 1950-51; USPHS postdoctoral fellow U. Chgo., 1951-53, rsch. assoc. dept. zoology, 1954-59; rsch. assoc. Marquette U., Milw., 1962-65, assoc. prof. biology, 1965-68, prof. biology, 1968-75, Wehr Disting. prof. biophysics, 1975-78; rsch. prof. biophysics East Tenn. State U., James H. Quillen Coll. Medicine, Johnson City, 1978-94, interim chmn. dept. cellular biophysics, 1986-94, prof. anatomy and cell biology, 1994—. Mem. Wis. Bd. Basic Sci. Examiners, 1971-75, sec. bd., 1973-75. Recipient Post-doctoral fellowship USPHS, 1951-53, Research Career Devel. award, 1967-72; Teaching Excellence and Disting. award Marquette U., 1975; Kreeger-Wolf vis. disting. prof. in biol. sci. Northwestern U., 1979. Mem. Royal Microscopic Soc., Am. Soc. Cell Biology, Am. Soc. Zoologists, Am. Soc. Ichthyologists and Herpetologists, The Histochem. Soc., Phi Beta Kappa, Sigma Xi. Contbr. articles to various publs. Home: 1504 Chickees St Johnson City TN 37604-7103 Office: East Tenn State U Dept Anatomy & Cell Biology PO Box 70, 421 Johnson City TN 37614-0421

RASCHE, ROBERT HAROLD, economics educator; b. New Haven, June 29, 1941; s. Harold A. and Elsa (Bloomquist) R.; m. Dorothy Anita Bensen, Dec. 28, 1963; children: Jeanette Dorothy, Karl Robert. B.A., Yale U., 1963; A.M., U. Mich., 1965, Ph.D., 1966. Asst. prof. U. Pa., Phila., 1966-72; assoc. prof. econs. Mich. State U., East Lansing, 1972-75, prof., 1975—; vis. scholar St. Louis Fed. Res., 1971-72, 76-77, San Francisco Fed. Ses., 1985, Bank of Japan, Tokyo, 1990; vis. scholar Fed. Res. Bank of St. Louis, 1994-96; disting. vis. prof. econs. Ariz. State U., Tempe, 1986; rsch. assoc. Nat. Bur. Econ. Rsch., Cambridge, Mass., 1982-91; mem. Mich. Gov. Coun. Econ. Advisers, 1992—; mem. Shadow Open Market Com., 1973—. Mem. Am. Econs. Assn. Lutheran. Home: 1736 Hitching Post Rd East Lansing MI 48823-2144 Office: Mich State U Dept Econs East Lansing MI 48824-1038

RASCO, CAROL HAMPTON, federal official; b. Columbia, S.C., Jan. 13, 1948; d. Frank Barnes and Mary Ruby (Dallas) Hampton; children: Howard Hampton, Mary-Margaret. Student, Hendrix Coll., 1965-66; BSE, U. Ark., 1969; MS, U. Ctrl. Ark., 1972. Elem. sch. tchr. Springdale and Fayetteville (Ark.) Pub. Schs., 1969-71; counselor Bryant (Ark.) Middle Sch., 1972-73; liaison to human svcs. and health agys. Gov. Bill Clinton, Little Rock, Ark., 1983-85; exec. asst. for govtl. ops. Gov. Bill Clinton, Little Rock, 1985-91, sr. exec. asst., 1991-92; liaison to Nat. Govs. Assn., 1985-92; asst. to President U.S. for domestic policy White House, Washington, 1993—. V.p., pres. Ark. Symphony Orch. Soc. Guild Bd., 1975-78, mem. exec. com., 1976-78; pres. Fullbright Elem. Sch. PTA, 1982-83; child advocate coord. Little Rock Conf. United Meth. Women's Bd., 1979-80; family life coord. Little Rock Conf. United Meth. Ch. Coun. Ministries, 1980-82; active Friends of Ark. Repertory Theatre Bd., 1977-79, First United Meth. Ch., 1973—, chmn. bd. stewards, 1981, chmn.coun. on ministries, 1980, lay leader, 1982, chmn. child devel. ctr. bd., 1982, bd. trustees, 1988-90, Ark. Devel. Disabilities Svcs. Bd., 1979-82; vol. Ark. Coalition for Handicapped, 1974-77, Little Rock Mcpl. Ct. Vols. in Probation, 1975-78, Gov. Task Force on Coordination of Svcs. Sch.-Aged Children, 1979, Little Rock Pub. Sch. Spl. Edn. Adv. Com., 1981-91, Pulaski County Coord. for Bill Clinton for Gov., 1982. Recipient Germaine Menteil Vol. Activist award, 1976, Community Svc. award Channel 4-GOVCP, 1979. Spl. Friend of Children award Ark. Advocates for Children and Families, 1985. Democrat. Avocations: reading, travel, cooking. Office: The White House Office of Domestic Policy 1600 Pennsylvania Ave NW Washington DC 20502*

RASCÓN, ARMANDO, artist; b. Calexico, Calif., Dec. 9, 1956; s. Reynoldo and Maria (Herrera) R. BA in Fine Art, U. Calif., Santa Barbara, 1979. Owner Terrain Gallery, San Francisco, 1988—; mem. artist's com. San Francisco Art Inst., 1988-90; guest faculty dept. art U. Calif., Davis, 1988, Calif. Coll. Arts and Crafts, Oakland, 1991, dept. art practice U. Calif., Berkeley, 1995; co-juror McMilan award, San Francisco Art Inst., 1993; juror New Langton Arts, San Francisco, 1993, Emeryville (Calif.) Celebration of the Arts, 1993, Intersection for the Arts, San Francisco, 1993; juror, panelist Artist Trust Fellowship Grants, Visual Arts, Seattle, 1994; lectr. San Francisco Mus. Modern Art, 1995; presenter various lectrs., panels, workshops, confs. One-person shows include Randolph St. Gallery, Chgo., 1992, Santa Barbara Contemporary Arts Forum, 1992, Intar Gallery, N.Y.C., 1994, Walter/McBean Gallery, San Francisco Art Inst., 1994, L.A. Ctr. Photographic Studies, 1995; exhibited in group shows at Primary Colors Gallery, Sacramento, Calif., 1984, Alternative Mus., N.Y.C., 1984, 89, San Francisco Art Inst., 1987, Matrix Gallery, U. Art Mus., U. Calif., Berkeley, 1989, Walter/McBean Gallery, San Francisco Art Inst., 1991, Robbin Lockett Gallery, Chgo., 1992, U. Art Mus., U. Calif., Santa Barbara, 1992, Centre Contemporain Regional d'Art, Nantes, France, 1993, Mus. Folkwang, Essen, Germany, 19993, Olive Art Ctr., Calif. Coll. Arts and Crafts, Oakland, 1994, San Francisco State U., 1995, Mus. Modern Art, N.Y.C., 1994, Mexican Mus., San Francisco, 1995. Bd. mem. San Francisco Art Commn. Gallery, 1988-91, New Langton Arts, San Francisco, 1988-92; commr. Art Commn. City of San Francisco, 1995. Recipient Hazel S. Lagerson scholarship U. Calif., Santa Barbara, 1975, fellowship grant in painting Nat. Endowment for Arts, Washington, 1987, Adaline Kent award San Francisco Art Inst., 1994, Goldie award in visual art San Francisco Bay Guardian, 1994. Home & Office: 165 Jessie St 2nd Fl San Francisco CA 94105

RASDAL, WILLIAM D., electronics executive; b. 1933. Gen. mgr. TRW, 1960-72, v.p., 1972-80; pres., COO Granger Assoc., Santa Clara, Calif., 1980-85; chb, CEO Symmetricom Inc., San Jose, Calif., 1986—. Office: Symmetricom Inc 85 W Tasman Dr San Jose CA 95134*

RASHAD, AHMAD (BOBBY MOORE), sports broadcaster, former professional football player; b. Portland, Oreg., Nov. 19, 1949; m. Phylicia Allen; 1 child, Condola Phylea. Student, U. Oreg. With St. Louis Cardinals, 1972-73, Buffalo Bills, 1974-76, Seattle Seahawks, 1976, Minn. Vikings, 1976-82; sports broadcaster NBC, N.Y.C., 1982—; played in Pro Bowl (Nat. Football League All-Star Game), 1979. Author: Vikes, Mikes and Something on the Backside, 1988. Named to Nat. Football Conf. All-Star Team Sporting News, 1978, 79. Office: care NBC Sports 30 Rockefeller Plz New York NY 10112

RASHBA, EMMANUEL IOSIF, physicist, educator; b. Kiev, Ukraine, Oct. 30, 1927; came to U.S., 1991; s. Iosif Ovsei and Rosalia (Mirkine) R.; m. Erna Kelman, Aug. 18, 1927; 1 child, Julia. Diploma with Honor, U. Kiev,

Ukraine, 1949; PhD, Ukrainian Acad. Scis., 1956; DSc, Acad. of Sci. of USSR, 1963. Jr. and sr. scientist Inst. of Physics Ukrainian Acad. of Scis., Kiev, Ukraine, 1954-60; head theoretical divsn. Inst. of Semiconductors Ukrainian Acad. of Scis., Kiev, 1960-66; head divsn. of theory of semiconductors, prin. scientist Landau Inst. for Theoretical Physics, Acad. Sci. of Russia, Moscow, 1966—; vis. prof. dept. physics NYU, N.Y.C., 1991-92; vis. rsch. prof. dept. physics U. Utah, Salt Lake City, 1992—. Co-author: Spectroscopy of Molecular Excitons, 1981, English edit. 1985, Collection of Problems in Physics, 1978, 2d edit. 1987, English edit. 1986, Japanese edit. 1989; author, co-author of monographic revs.; assoc. editor Jour. Luminescence, 1985—; editl. bd. Letters to the Jour. of Exptl. and Theoretical Physics, 1967-88. Recipient Lenin prize Govt. of USSR, 1966, A.F. Ioffe prize Acad. of Scis. of the USSR, 1987. Fellow Am. Phys. Soc. Achievements include prediction electro-dipole spin resonance (related term in energy is known as Rashba term), spin beats in magnetotransport oscillations, giant oscillator strengths for impurity excitons (Rashba effect), self-trapping barrier, and coexistence of free and self-trapped states; development of advanced theory of rectification in semiconductor devices, of molecular excitons, of the electron conductivity of polymers, of self-trapping rate, of optical properties of incompressible quantum liquids. Office: U Utah Dept of Physics 201 J Fletcher Bldg Salt Lake City UT 84112

RASHID, KAMAL A., program director, researcher; b. Sulaimania, Kurdistan, Iraq, Sept. 11, 1944; came to U.S., 1972; s. Ahmad Rashid and Habiba M. Muhiedin; m. Afifa B. Sabir, May 23, 1970; children: Niaz K., Neian K., Suzanne K. BS, U. Baghdad, Iraq, 1965; MS, Pa. State U., 1974, PhD, 1978. Lab. instr. U. Baghdad, Iraq, 1966-72; mem. faculty U. Basrah, Iraq, 1978-80, U. Sulaimania, Iraq, 1980-83; sr. rsch. assoc., vis. prof. Pa. State U., University Park, 1983—, rsch. assoc. prof., 1992—; dir. Biotech. Tng. Program program Pa. State U., 1989—, dir. summer symposium molecular biology, 1991—; v.p. Cogenic Inc., State College, Pa., 1989-90; cons., spkr. biotech. tng. program developer. Contbr. articles to profl. jours. Iraqi Ministry Higher Edn. scholar. Mem. Am. Chem. Soc., Environ. Mutagen Soc., Pa. Biotech. Assn. (mem. edn. com.), Rotary. Avocations: travel, swimming, reading. Home: 100 Berwick Dr Boalsburg PA 16827-1611 Office: Pa State U 203 S Frear University Park PA 16807

RASHKIND, PAUL MICHAEL, lawyer; b. Jamaica, N.Y., May 21, 1950; s. Murray and Norma (Dorfman) Weinstein; m. Robin Shane, Dec. 20, 1975; children: Adam Charles, Noah Hamilton, Jennifer Elizabeth. AA, Miami-Dade Jr. Coll., 1970; BBA, U. Miami, Coral Gables Fla., 1972, JD, 1975. Bar: Fla. 1975, D.C. 1981, N.Y. 1981, U.S. Dist. Ct. (so. dist.) Fla. 1975, U.S. Ct. Appeals (5th cir.) 1976, U.S. Supreme Ct. 1978, U.S. Dist. Ct. (mid. dist.) Fla. 1979, U.S. Ct. Appeals (2d and 11th cirs.) 1981, U.S. Ct. Appeals (4th and 6th cirs.) 1986, U.S. Dist. Ct. (no. dist.) Fla. 1987, U.S. Dist. Ct. (no dist.) Calif. 1989; diplomate Nat. Bd. Trial Advocacy-Criminal Law, bd. cert. Criminal Trial Law, Fla. Bar. Asst. state atty. Dade County State Attys. Office, Miami, Fla., 1975-78, chief asst. state atty. in charge of appeals, 1977-78; atty. Sams, Gerstein & Ward, P.A., Miami, 1978-83; ptnr. Bailey, Gerstein, Rashkind & Dresnick, Miami, 1983-92, supr. asst. Fed. Defender Chief of Appeals, Miami, 1992—; spl. master Ct. Appointment, Miami, 1982-83; arbitrator Dade County Jail Inmates Grievance Program, Miami, 1981-92; mem. Fla. Bar Unauthorized Practice of Law Com. C, 11th Jud. Cir., Miami, 1980-84, Fed. Ct. Practice Com., 1992—. Contbr. articles on ethics and criminal law to profl. jours. Pres., bd. dirs. Lindgren Homeowners Assn., Miami, Fla., 1981-86. Fellow Am. Bd. Criminal Lawyers (bd. govs. 1980-86; mem. ABA (ethics com. criminal justice sect. 1979-92, vice chmn. 1985-87, chmn. 1987-89, ethics advisor to chair, 1992—), Fla. Bar Assn. (commn. on Lawyer professionalism 1988-89, criminal law cert. com. 1989-94, standing com. on professionalism 1989-94), N.Y. Bar Assn., D.C. Bar Assn., Dade County Bar Assn., Assn. Trial Lawyers Am., Acad. Fla. Trial Lawyers (chmn. criminal law sect. 1985-86, diplomate 1986—), Nat. Assn. Criminal Def. Lawyers, Soc. Bar and Gavel, Iron Arrow, Hon. Order Ky. Cols., Omicron Delta Kappa, Delta Sigma Rho-Tau Kappa Alpha, Pi Sigma Alpha, Phi Rho Pi, Delta Theta Phi. Democrat. Jewish. Office: Office Fed Defender 301 N Miami Ave Ste 321 Miami FL 33128-7787

RASI, HUMBERTO MARIO, educational administrator, editor, minister; b. Buenos Aires, Argentina, Mar. 23, 1935; came to U.S., 1962, naturalized, 1968; s. Mario and Gertrudis Frida (Heyde) R.; m. Julia Cuchma, Feb. 28, 1957; children—Leroy Mario, Sylvia Beatrice. B.A., Instituto Superior del Profesorado, Buenos Aires, 1960; M.A., San Jose State U., 1966; Ph.D., Stanford U., 1971. Ordained to ministry Seventh-day Adventist Ch., 1980. Mem. faculty Instituto Florida, Buenos Aires, 1957-61; asst. editor Pacific Press Publ. Assn., Mountain View, Calif., 1962-66; asst. prof., assoc. prof. modern langs. Andrews U., 1969-76, prof., dean Sch. Grad. Studies, 1976-78; chief editor internat. publs. Pacific Press Publ. Assn., 1978-83, v.p. editorial devel., 1984-86; assoc. world dir. edn. Gen. Conf. Seventh-day Adventists, Silver Spring, Md., 1987-90, world dir. edn., 1990—; exec. dir. Inst. for Christian Teaching, 1987—. Author: The Life of Jesus, 3 vols., 1984-85; contbg. editor Handbook of L.Am. studies, Libr. of Congress, 1972-82; gen. editor Comentario Biblico Adventista, 7 vols., 1978-90; co-editor: Meeting the Secular Mind, 1985; editor Coll. and Univ. Dialogue, 1989—, editor-in-chief, 1996—; compiler Christ in the Classroom, 16 vols., 1991—; also articles on modern Hispanic lit., current events and religious trends; bd. dirs. Andrews U., Loma Linda U. NEH postdoctoral fellow Johns Hopkins U., 1975-76. Mem. Instituto Internacional de Literatura Iberoamericana. Office: 12501 Old Columbia Pike Silver Spring MD 20904-6601

RASIN, RUDOLPH STEPHEN, corporate executive; b. Newark, July 5, 1930; s. Simon Walter and Anna Rasin; m. Joy Kennedy Peterkin, Apr. 11, 1959; children: Rudolph Stephen, James Stenning, Jennifer Shaw Denniston. B.A., Rutgers Coll., 1953; postgrad., Columbia, 1958-59. Mgr. Miles Labs., Inc., 1959-61; devel. mgr. Gen. Foods Corp., White Plains, N.Y., 1961-62; asst. to pres., chmn. Morton Internat. Inc., Chgo., 1962-72; pres. Rasin Corp., Chgo., 1971—; bd. dirs. Federated Foods Inc. Bd. dirs. Ctr. for Def. Info., 1972—, English Speaking Union, Ct. Theatre. Served with USAF, 1954-56. Mem. Hinsdale Golf Club, Mid Am. Club (Chgo.), Lake Geneva Country Club, Williams Coll. Club (N.Y.C.), Chgo. Club. Republican. Mem. United Ch. of Christ. Home: 328 E 8th St Hinsdale IL 60521-4504 Office: One First Nat Plz Ste 2690 One First Nat. Plz Ste Chicago IL 60603

RASKIN, EDWIN BERNER, real estate executive; b. Savannah, Ga., Mar. 19, 1919; s. Isaac and Hannah (Berner) R.; m. Rebecca Kornman, Nov. 13, 1946; children: Susan, Joan. B.B.A., Tulane U., 1940. Cert., Inst. Real Estate Mgmt. Pres., Superior Shoe Co. and Nat. Shoe Co., Savannah, Ga., 1946-50; pres. A.L. Kornman Co., Nashville, 1947-54; from pres. to sr. chmn. Edwin B. Raskin Co., Nashville, 1954—. Served to capt. USAAF, 1942-46. Mem. Nashville Bd. Realtors, Tenn. Assn. Realtors, Nat. Assn. Real Estate Bds., Inst. Real Estate Mgmt. (past pres. middle Tenn. chpt.). Club: Old Natchez (Nashville). Lodge: Rotary. Home: 419 Ellendale Ave Nashville TN 37205-3401 Office: Edwin B Raskin Co 110 Westwood Pl Brentwood TN 37027-5015

RASKIN, FRED CHARLES, transportation and utility holding company executive; b. N.Y.C., Sept. 11, 1948; s. Harry and Isabel (Wexler) R.; m. Lorraine Mary Sabourin, Apr. 25, 1974; children: Elizabeth Harris, Alexander Eastwood. B.S., Syracuse U., 1970; J.D., NYU, 1973. Bar: R.I. 1973, Mass. 1974; CPA, Ohio. Assoc. counsel Fleet Nat. Bank, Providence, 1973-75, Bank of Boston, 1975-78; asst. gen. counsel Eastern Enterprises, Boston, 1978-79, treas., 1979-81, v.p., treas., 1981-84; sr. v.p. fin. Eastern Assoc. Coal Co., Pitts., 1984-87; exec. v.p. Midland Enterprises, Inc., Cin., 1987-90, pres., 1991—; Dept. of Energy Nat. Coal coun. Mem. Fin. Execs. Inst., Treas.' Home: 9866 Bennington Dr Cincinnati OH 45241-3617 Office: Midland Enterprises Inc 300 Pike St Cincinnati OH 45202-3108

RASKIN, MARCUS GOODMAN, writer, educator; b. Milw., Apr. 30, 1934; s. Benjamin Samuel and Anna (Goodman) R.; m. Barbara Raskin (div.); m. Lynn Randels, May 4, 1985; children: Erika Raskin Littlewood, Jamin Ben, Noah Annin, Eden McArtor. B.A., U. Chgo., 1954, J.D., 1957. Advisor to Congressional Liberal Project Group, 1959-61; mem. spl. staff NSC, 1961-63; advisor Bur. Budget, Washington, 1963; co-founder, co-dir. Inst. Policy Studies, 1963-77, disting. fellow, 1978—; prof. govt. and pub. policy George Washington U., Washington, 1993—; mem. Presdl. Commn. on Edn. Research and Devel., 1963-65, U.S. Disarmament del. 18 Nation Geneva Conf., 1962; cons. Office of Sci. and Tech., 1963-65. Author and co-author: The Limits of Defense, 1962, After Twenty Years, 1965, The Vietnam Reader, 1965, An American Manifesto, 1970, Washington Plans an Aggressive War, 1971, Being and Doing, 1971, Notes on the Old System, 1975, The Problem of the Federal Budget, 1976, The Federal Budget and Social Reconstruction, 1978, The Politics of National Security, 1978, The Common Good, 1986, New Ways of Knowing, 1987, Winning America, 1988, Essays of a Citizen, 1991, Abolishing the War System, 1993, Visions and Revisions, 1995; mem. editorial bd. The Nation, 1979—; editor: Paths for the 21st Century; contbr. articles on public policy, polit. philosophy and edn. to major jours. Bd. dirs. Inst. So. Studies, 1977-87; trustee Antioch Coll., 1965-71; chmn. SANE Edn. Fund. Recipient U. Chgo. Alumni award, 1971; Johns Hopkins Centennial fellow, 1976; citation award for disting. educator Pa. State Legislature, 1980. Office: Inst Policy Studies 1601 Connecticut Ave NW Washington DC 20009-1035 *The first question to open in nature is the secret of humankind. Then we will be in a position to live with each other - ourselves - and make sense of the self-inflicted problems that now beset humanity. We will be able to initiate a social reconstruction in our institutions that better fit with people as liberated and critically thinking human beings. This is the intellectual and political project in which I am engaged.*

RASKIN, MICHAEL A., retail company executive; b. N.J., Feb. 26, 1925; s. Harry and Elizabeth Rose (Furstenberg) R.; m. Mary Bonetta Whalen, June 12, 1948; children: Robin Raskin Crowell, Hillary Raskin Maass, Mary Allison Sullivan. A.B., Pa. State Coll., 1947; M.B.A., Columbia U., 1948. With Abraham & Straus, 1949-65; successively mdse. v.p., dir. stores, sr. v.p. Abercrombie & Fitch, N.Y.C., 1966-68; exec. v.p. Dayton's div. Dayton Hudson Corp.; pres. Jos. Magnin Co., San Francisco, 1978—; chmn., CEO, bd. dirs. Imnar Corp., San Francisco, Info. Please; chmn. exec. com. Acajoe Internat.; bd. dirs. Fortune Almac, Canterbury Cuisine, Cultural Devel. Assocs., HELP Inc., Express Yourself Through Art, Inc., Munsingwear, Inc., B&B Acceptance Corp. Bd. dirs. Amyotrophic Lateral Sclerosis Assn.

RASKIND, LEO JOSEPH, law educator; b. Newark, Nov. 2, 1919; s. Isaac and Fannie (Michelson) R.; m. Mollie Gordon, June 14, 1948; children—Carol Inge, John Richard. A.B., UCLA, 1942; M.A., U. Wash., 1949; Ph.D. (Fulbright fellow), London Sch. Econs., 1952; LL.B., Yale, 1955. Faculty Stanford Law Sch., 1955-56; lectr., research asso. Yale Law Sch., 1956-58; faculty Vanderbilt Law Sch., 1958-64, Ohio State U. Coll. of Law, 1964-70, U. Minn., 1970-90; vis. prof. Bklyn. Law Sch., 1991-95; vis. tchr. NYU, 1964, 83, U. Tex., 1964, U. Utah, 1967, So. Meth. U., 1973, U. N.C., 1978, Lyon III, 1984, Kiel U., 1988; vis. prof. Bklyn. Law Sch., 1991-94, Coll. Law, U. Tenn. Knoxville, 1994, Law Sch., U. Calif., Davis, 1995, Bklyn. Law Sch., 1995. Co-author: Casebook Corporate Taxation, 1978, Casebook Antitrust Law, 1983; mem. adv. bd. BNA jour. Served to capt. AUS, 1942-46. Mem. Am. Law Inst. Office: Bklyn Law Sch 250 Joralemon St Brooklyn NY 11201-3798

RASKY, HARRY, producer, director, writer; b. Toronto, Ont., Can., May 9, 1928; emigrated to U.S., 1955; s. Louis Leib and Pearl (Krazner) R.; m. Ruth Arlene Werkhoven, Mar. 21, 1965; children: Holly Laura, Adam Louis. BA, U. Toronto, 1949, LLD, 1984. Reporter No. Daily News, Kirkland Lake, Ont., 1949; news editor-producer Sta. CHUM, Toronto, 1950, Sta. CKEY, 1951-52; co-founder new documentary dept. CBC, 1952-55; assoc. editor Saturday Night Mag., 1955; producer-dir-writer Columbia Broadcasting Corp., 1955-60, NBC-TV, N.Y.C., 1960-61, ABC-TV, N.Y.C., 1963-69, CBC-TV, Toronto, 1971-78; pres. Harry Rasky Prodns., N.Y.C. and Toronto, 1971—, Maragall Prodns., Toronto, 1978—; guest lectr. film and TV at various univs., colls. Creator: Raskymentary (recipient numerous awards, including Emmy award 1978, 86, San Francisco Film Festival award 1978, Grand prize N.Y. TV-Film Festival 1978, Jerusalem medal 1975); numerous films include Travels Through Life with Leacock, 1976, The Peking Man Mystery, 1978, Arthur Miller on Home Ground, 1979, (TV film) Hall of Kings (Emmy award, 1965); producer, dir., writer: numerous films including Next Year in Jerusalem, 1973, The Wit and World of G. Bernard Shaw, 1974, Tennessee Williams South, 1975, Homage to Chagall-The Colours of Love, 1977 (200 internat. prizes including Oscar nomination, Emmy 1986), Stratasphere, The Mystery of Henry Moore, Karsh: The Searching Eye; play Tiger Tale, 1978, The War Against The Indians, 1992 (Humanities Prize, Great Plains Film Festival, Lincoln, Nebr., Golden Hugo award Chgo. Film Festival), Prophecy, 1994 (Golden Angel award, honored by Smithsonian, Jerusalem Found.); author: memoirs Nobody Swings on Sunday—The Many Lives of Harry Rasky, 1980, Tennessee Williams a Portrait in Laughter and Lamentation, 1986, Karsh: The Searching Eye, 1986, To Mend the World, 1987, Stratas: An affectionate tribute, 1988, Degas co-prodn. Met. Mus. of N.Y., 1988, The Great Teacher, 1989, Robertson Davies-The Magic Season, 1989; 19 hour retrospective of his films on Rasky's Gallery: Poets, Painters, Singers and Saints, CBC, 1988, The War Against the Indians, 1993 (12 Internat. awards, adopted Huron Nation title Keeper of teh Flame. Mem. YMCA; mem. adv. coun. Univ. Coll./U. Toronto. Recipient honors City of Venice, Italy, 1970, Golden Eagle, Grand prize N.Y. Intenat. TV and Film Festival of N.Y., 1977, Cert. of Merit, Acad. Motion Picture Arts and Scis., 1984, Red Ribbon, Am. Assn. Film and Video, N.Y.C., 1988, Blue Ribbon, Am. Film Festival, Emmy award, 1990, Moscow award for cultural contbn. to 20th Century USSR, 1991, Retrospective of Films, 1990, Golden Hugo award Chgo. Film Festival, 1993; named Best Non-Fiction Dir., Dirs. Guild Am., N.Y.C. and L.A., 1988, hon. Mayor N.Y.C., 1977, City of Toronto, 1979; Harry Rasky Day named in his honor, City of Toronto, 1988; Moscow Film Festival honoree, 1991; adopted by Huron Indians, named Keeper of the Spirit, adopted by Ojibway Tribe, named Mountain Eagle. Mem. Writers Guild Am. (best non-fiction dir. 1986), Dirs. Guild Am., Writers Union Can., Am., Acad. TV Arts and Scis., Assn. Can. TV and Radio Artists, Producers Assn. Can., Acad. Motion Picture Arts and Scis., Overseas Press Club, Acad. of Can. TV and Film Can. (lifetime achievement award 1992), PEN (Toronto), Nat. Arts Club. Jewish. Avocations: swimming, lecturing. Home: 15 Gregory Ave, Toronto, ON Canada M4W 2X7 Office: care CBC, Box 500 Terminal A, Toronto, ON Canada M5W 1E6 *I have tried to find the positive forces in life and out of them create works of art of a lasting nature with the idea of improving the lives of others. This, plus the adventure of passing on the tradition of my father and his, is my life.*

RASMUS, JOHN A., magazine executive; b. St. Louis, Mar. 20, 1954; s. Robert Nelson and Annette (Avery) R.; m. Sue A. Alexander; 1 child, Grace Alexander. B.S., Boston U., 1975. Assoc. editor Chgo. Mag., 1975-78, editorial dir., 1978; mng. editor Outside mag., Chgo., 1979-84, editor, 1984-90; exec. editor Outside Business mag., Chgo., 1986-90; columnist Universal Press Syndicate, 1987-90; editor Men's Jour. mag. Wenner Media, Inc., N.Y.C., 1990—; instr. Medill Sch. Journalism, Northwestern U., Evanston, Ill., 1985-86. Mem. Am. Soc. Mag. Editors (Nat. Mag. award 1984, 95). Office: Wenner Media Inc 1290 Avenue Of The Americas New York NY 10104

RASMUSON, BRENT (JACOBSEN), photographer, graphic artist; b. Logan, Utah, Nov. 28, 1950; s. Eleroy West and Fae (Jacobsen) R.; m. Tess Bullen, Sept. 30, 1981; children: John, Mark, Lisa. Grad. auto repair and painting sch., Utah State U. Pre-press supr. Herald Printing Co., Logan, 1969-79; profl. drummer, 1971-75; owner Valley Automotive Specialties, 1971-76; exec. sec. Herald Printing Co., 1979-89; owner Brent Rasmuson Photography, Smithfield, Utah, 1986—, Temple Photographs by Brent Rasmuson, Smithfield, 1996—. Author photo prints of LDS temples: Logan, 1987, 96, Manti, 1989, Jordan River, 1989, 96, Provo, 1990, Mesa, Ariz., 1990, 96, Boise, Idaho, 1990, 96, Salt Lake LDS Temple, 1990, 96, Idaho Falls, 1991, 96, St. George, 1991, 96, Portland, Oreg., 1991, 96, L.A., 1991, 96, Las Vegas, Nev., 1991, Seattle, Wash., 1992, Oakland, Calif., 1993, 96, Ogden, 1996; author photo print: Statue of Angel Moroni, 1994; author photos used to make neckties of LDS temples: Salt Lake, Manti, Logan, L.A., Oakland, Seattle, Las Vegas, Mesa, Portland, St. George, Jordan River, scenic tie Mammoth Hot Springs in Yellowstone Park, 1995; landscape scenic photographs featured in Best of Photography Ann., 1987, 88, 89, also in calendars and book covers. Mem. Internat. Platform Assn., Assoc. Photographers Internat., Internat. Freelance Photographers Orgn. Republican. Mem. LDS Ch. Avocations: landscape design, gardening, audio and video recording and mixing. Home and Office: 40 N 200 E Smithfield UT 84335-1543

RASMUSON, ELMER EDWIN, banker, former mayor; b. Yakutat, Alaska, Feb. 15, 1909; s. Edward Anton and Jenny (Olson) R.; m. Lile Vivian Bernard, Oct. 27, 1939 (dec. 1960); children: Edward Bernard, Lile Muchmore (Mrs. John Gibbons, Jr.), Judy Ann; m. Col. Mary Louise Milligan, Nov. 4, 1961. BS magna cum laude, Harvard U., 1930, AM, 1935; student, U. Grenoble, 1930; LLD, U. Alaska, 1970, Alaska Pacific U., 1993. C.P.A., N.Y., Tex., Alaska. Chief accountant Nat. Investors Corp., N.Y.C., 1933-35; prin. Arthur Andersen & Co., N.Y.C., 1935-43; pres. Nat. Bank of Alaska, 1943-65, chmn. bd., 1966-74, chmn. exec. com., 1975-82, now chmn. emeritus; mayor City of Anchorage, 1964-67, dir., emeritus and cons., 1989; civilian aide from Alaska to sec. army, 1959-67; Swedish consul Alaska, 1955-77; Chmn. Rasmuson Found.; Rep. nominee U.S. Senate from Alaska, 1968; U.S. commr. Internat. N. Pacific Fisheries Commn., 1969-84; mem. Nat. Marine Fisheries Adv. Com., 1974-77, North Pacific Fishery Mgmt. Council, 1976-77, U.S. Arctic Research Commn., 1984-92. Mem. City Coun. Anchorage, 1945, chmn. city planning commn., 1950-53; pres. Alaska coun. Boy Scouts Am., 1953; regent U. Alaska, 1950-69; trustee King's Lake Camp, Inc., 1944—, Alaska Permanent Fund Corp., 1980-82; bd. dirs. Nat. Mus. Natural History Smithsonian Inst. 1994—. Decorated knight first class Order of Vasa, comdr. Sweden; recipient silver Antelope award Boy Scouts Am., Japanese citation Order of the Sacred Treasure, Gold and Silver Star, 1988; outstanding civilian service medal U.S. Army; Alaskan of Year award, 1976. Mem. Pioneers Alaska, Alaska Bankers Assn. (past pres.), Defense Orientation Conf. Assn., NAACP, Alaska Native Brotherhood, Explorers Club, Phi Beta Kappa. Republican. Presbyn. Clubs: Masons, Elks, Anchorage Rotary (past pres.); Harvard (N.Y.C.; Boston); Wash. Athletic (Seattle), Seattle Yacht (Seattle), Rainier (Seattle); Thunderbird Country (Palm Desert, Calif.); Bohemian (San Francisco); Eldorado Country (Indian Wells, Calif.); Boone & Crockett. Home: PO Box 100600 Anchorage AK 99510-0600

RASMUSSEN, ALICE CALL, nursing educator; b. Grand Rapids, Mich., Dec. 16, 1947; d. Amon Burton and Jessie Pearl (Dann) Call; m. Charles P. Rasmussen, Apr. 16, 1972. BSN, Andrews U., 1971; MSN, Med. Coll. Ga., 1977; postgrad., Ferris State U., 1990. Staff nurse Lockwood-MacDonald Hosp., Petoskey, Mich., 1971-72; instr. Lake Michigan Coll., Benton Harbor, Mich., 1973-86; nursing coord. Lake Mich. Coll., Benton Harbor, Mich., 1986—; Mem. Mich. Bd. Nursing. Mem. AAUW, NAFE, Mich. League for Nursing, Mich. Coun. Nursing Edn. Adminstrs., Nat. Ordn. ADN, Mich. Assn. Women in Edn., S.W. Mich. Nurse Educator Network, Sigma Theta Tau. Home: 9088-1 4th St Berrien Springs MI 49103-1600 Office: Lake Mich Coll 2755 E Napier Ave Benton Harbor MI 49022-1881

RASMUSSEN, DAVID GEORGE, lawyer; b. Mpls., Mar. 6, 1943; s. Ivan Raymond and Helen Ann (Wojcichowski) R.; m. Patricia Ann Howell, July 12, 1969; children: Andrea, Christopher, Mary Patricia. BSEE, U. Minn., 1967; JD, Wayne State U., 1972. Bar: Pa. 1972, U.S. Patent Office 1973, D.C. 1982, Mass. 1987. Elec. engr. Univac, Phila., 1967-69; patent atty. Howson & Howson, Phila., 1972-73, Dupont Co., Wilmington, Del., 1973-75, U.S. Dept. Navy, Washington, 1975-79; div. patent counsel Burroughs Corp., Washington, 1979-84; corp. patent counsel Analog Devices Inc., Boston, 1984—. Served as staff sgt. USAF, 1963-69. Mem. ABA, Am. Intellectual Property Assn., Boston Patent Law Assn., Fed. Bar Assn., Am. Corp. Counsels Assn. Democrat. Roman Catholic. Avocation: outdoor sports. Office: Analog Devices Inc 3 Technology Way Norwood MA 02062-2634

RASMUSSEN, DAVID TAB, physical anthropology educator; b. Salt Lake City, June 17, 1958; s. David Irvin and Deon (Robison) R.; m. Asenath Marian Bernhardt, May 23, 1987. BA, Colo. Coll., 1980; PhD, Duke U., 1986. Rsch. assoc. Duke Primate Ctr., Durham, N.C., 1986-87; vis. asst. prof. Rice U., Houston, 1987-88; asst. prof. UCLA, 1988-91; asst. prof. phys. anthropology Washington U., St. Louis, 1991-93, assoc. prof., grad. coord. dept. anthropology, 1993—; rsch. assoc. Los Angeles County Mus., L.A., 1989—, Carnegie Mus., Pitts.; condr. paleontol. fieldwork in Africa and N.Am. Editor: Origin and Evolution of Humans and Humanness, 1993; contbr. numerous articles to sci. jours. Achievements include finding fossils of early primates from 30 to 50 million years old; research on anthropoid origins, on mammal and bird evolution. Avocations: birding, mountain climbing, canoeing. Office: Washington U Dept Anthropology Saint Louis MO 63130-4862

RASMUSSEN, ELLEN L., secondary school educator; b. Clark, S.D., Nov. 25, 1936; d. Lloyd R. and Zella Dollie (Fisk) Acker; m. Donald M. Rasmussen, Aug. 6, 1960; children: LaDonna, Diann, Curtis. BS, S.D. State U., 1963. Cert. secondary edn. tchr., S.D. Educator Strandburg (S.D.) Sch. Dist., 1956-61, Brookings (S.D.) Pub. Sch., 1963, Hurley (S.D.) Sch. Dist., 1963-64, Bridgewater (S.D.) Sch. Dist., 1964-65, Lakeview (Oreg.) High Sch., 1965-66; educator South Lane Sch. Dist. 45J3, Cottage Grove, Oreg., 1966-95, ret., 1995. Mem. NEA, Nat. Coun. Tchrs. Math., Oreg. Coun. Tchrs. Math., Oreg. Edn. Assn., Lane Unified Bargaining Coun. (sec.-treas. 1988-91), Three Rivers Edn. Coun. (treas. 1991-95), South Lane Edn. Assn. (treas. 1982-95). Lutheran. Avocations: travel, sewing, crafts, gardening. Home: 1218 W D St Springfield OR 97477-8111 Office: Lincoln Mid Sch 1565 S 4th St Cottage Grove OR 97424-2955

RASMUSSEN, FRANK MORRIS, lawyer; b. Modesto, Calif., Sept. 21, 1934; s. Elmer Christian and Mary Evelyn (Bonham) R.; m. Carolyn Anne Humbert, Aug. 22, 1959; children—Kathryn Anne, James Russell, Peter Bonham. A.B., Wabash Coll., 1956; LL.B., Harvard U., 1960. Bar: Ohio 1960, U.S. Dist. Ct. (no. dist.) Ohio, U.S. Mil. Ct. Appeals 1962. Assoc. Squire, Sanders & Dempsey and predecessor firms, Cleve., 1960-70, ptnr., 1970—; sec. United Screw & Bolt Co., Cleve.; sec., bd. dirs. Ohio Aerospace Inst., Cleve., A.E. Ehrke & Co., Cleve.; bd. dirs. Nat. Machinery Corp., Tiffin, Ohio, Hartzell Propellor, Inc., Piqua, Ohio, Weatherhead Industries, Inc., Ohio, Health-Mor, Inc., Cleve. Trustee, past pres. Interchurch Coun. of Greater Cleve.; trustee, chmn. Cleve. Coun. on World Affairs, 1970—; trustee, past pres. Greater Cleve. Neighborhood Ctrs. Assn., 1975-90; trustee Wabash Coll. Alumni Assn., 1970-83. Mem. ABA, Ohio Bar Assn., Bar Assn. Greater Cleve. Union. Office: Squire Sanders & Dempsey 4900 Society Ctr 127 Public Sq Cleveland OH 44114-1304*

RASMUSSEN, GAIL MAUREEN, critical care nurse; b. Can., Feb. 22, 1941; d. Thomas Alfred and Bernice Hilda (Sayler) Salisbury; m. Byron Karl Rasmussen, June 28, 1964; children: Stephen, Carla, Wade, Gregory. AS, Riverside City Coll., 1961; BSN, U. Phoenix, 1987; MS in Health Professions Edn., Osteo. Coll. the Pacific, 1991. RN, Calif.; CCRN. Staff nurse Meml. Med. Ctr., Long Beach, Calif., 1961-63, UCLA Med. Ctr., 1963-64; clin. nurse critical care unit Intercomty. Med. Ctr. (name changed to Citrus Valley Health Ptnrs.- Intercomty. Campus), Covina, Calif., 1964-71, 78-95, 96; instr. ACLS, Los Angeles County, 1991—. Mem. AACN.

RASMUSSEN, GUNNAR, engineer; b. Esbjerg, Denmark, Nov. 23, 1925; s. Karl Sigurd and Frederikke Valentine (Gjeruiff) R.; m. Hanna Hertz, June 27, 1973; children: Jan, Lise, Per, Thue. Student, Aarhus Teknikum, Denmark, 1950. Mgr. quality control Brüel and Kjaer, Nerum, Denmark, 1950-54, with devel. div., 1955-69, with product planning div., 1969-74, with innovation div., 1975—; lectr. Danish Tech. U., Copenhagen, 1974-79, Med. Air Force Acad., Jegersborg, Denmark, 1978-79; examiner Danish Engring. Acad., Copenhagen, 1972—, Chalmers Tech. U., Gothenburg, Sweden, 1984-85. Editor: Intensity Measurements, 1989; inventor measurement microphones, accelerometers; contbr. articles to profl. jours. Chairman Audio Engring. Soc. Denmark, Copenhagen, 1976. Recipient Danish Design prize for microphones, 1962, medal for contbn. to intensity techniques SETIM, 1990. Fellow Acoustical Soc. Am., Can. Acoustical Soc., Danish Medico Tech. Soc.; mem. Internat. Union Pure and Applied Physics (vice chmn. internat. commn. on accoustics), Danish Acoustical Soc. (bd. dirs.), Internat. Electronical Commn., Internat. Orgn. for Standarization. Home: Hojbjerggardsvej 15, 2840 Holte Denmark Office: GRAS Sound & Vibration, Skelstedet 10 B, DK-2950 Vedbaek Denmark

RASMUSSEN, HARRY PAUL, horticulture and landscape educator; b. Tremonton, Utah, July 18, 1939; s. Peter Y. and Lorna (Nielsen) R.; m. Mary Jane Dalley, Sept. 4, 1959; children—Randy Paul, Lorianne, Trent Dalley, Rachelle. A.S., Coll. of So. Utah, 1959; B.S., Utah State U., 1961; M.S., Mich. State U., 1962, Ph.D., 1965. Research scientist Conn. Agr. Expt.

Sta., New Haven, 1965-66; researcher, instr. Mich. State U., East Lansing, 1966-81; chmn. dept. horticulture and landscape architecture Wash. State U., Pullman, 1981-88; dir. Utah Agrl. Expt. Sta., Utah State U., 1988—; assoc. v.p. Utah State U., Logan, 1992—. Contbr. articles to profl. jours., chpts. to books. Mem. bd. control YMCA, Lansing, Mich., 1976; mem. council Boy Scouts Am., Lansing, 1980; stake pres. Ch. of Jesus Christ of Latter-day Saints, Lansing, 1973-81. NDEA fellow, 1961-65. Fellow Am. Soc. Horticulture Sci.; mem. AAAS, Scanning Electron Microscopy (chmn. plant sect. 1976-83). Home: 1949 N 950 E Logan UT 84341-1813 Office: Utah State U 235 Agr Sci Bldg Logan UT 84322

RASMUSSEN, HOWARD, medical educator, medical institute executive; b. Harrisburg, Pa., Mar. 1, 1925; s. Frederick and Faith (Elliott) R.; m. Jane Claire Spence, June 10, 1950; children: Gail, Paul, Jane, Craig. AB in Chemistry and Physics, Gettysburg Coll., 1948; MD, Harvard U., 1952; PhD in Biochemistry and Physiology, Rockefeller U., 1959; DSc, Gettysburg Coll., 1964. Asst. prof. physiology Rockefeller U., N.Y.C., 1959-61; assoc. prof. biochemistry U. Wis., Madison, 1961-64; prof. sch. medicine U. Pa., Phila., 1964-75, Benjamin Rush prof. biochemistry, 1964-75, prof. biochemistry and biophysics, 1964-76, chmn. dept. biochemistry, 1964-70, prof. pediatrics, 1975-76; Guggenheim fellow Cambridge U., 1971-72; prof. medicine and cell biology sch. medicine Yale U., New Haven, 1976-93; prof. medicine, surgery, cell biology, anatomy Med. Coll. Ga., Augusta, 1993—; dir. SCOT Urolithiasis Ctr., Sch. Medicine, Yale U., 1977-82, chief divsn. endocrinology, 1980-86, dir. med. scientist tng. program, 1983-91; dir. Inst. for Molecular Medicine and Genetics, Med. Coll. Ga., 1993—; Wellcome vis. prof. U. Va., Richmond, 1988; Klenk lectr. U. Koln, West Germany, 1989; Lily lectr. XI Internat. Conf. Calcium Regulation, Florence, Italy, 1992. Author: Calcium and cAMP as Synarchic Messengers, 1981, The Physiological and Cellular Basis of Metabolic Bone Disease, 1984. Bd. trustees Gettysburg Coll., 1985-93. Staff sgt. U.S. Army, 1942-44. Recipient Cotlove award Acad. Clin. Lab. Physicians and Scientists, 1993, Andre Lichtwitz prize, 1971. Fellow AAAS. Avocations: opera, hiking. Office: Med Coll Ga 1120 15th St CB-2803 Augusta GA 30912

RASMUSSEN, JAMES LAURENCE, federal government administrator; b. Stevens Point, Wis., May 9, 1936; s. Laurence Jay and Gertrude Marie (Larsen) R.; m. Sonja Gandrud, June 14, 1959; children: Eric John, Kristi Bartho. BA in Math., Physics, St. Olaf Coll., 1958; BS in Meteorology, U. Utah, 1959; MS in Atmospheric Sci., Colo. State U., 1963, PhD in Atmospheric Sci., 1968. From asst. to assoc. prof. Colo. State U., Fort Collins, 1968-72; from sci. coord. to dir. US Global Atmospheric Rsch. program Nat. Oceanic and Atmospheric Adminstrn. (North), Rockville, Md., 1972-76; mgr. global weather experiment World Meteorol. Program, Geneva, Switzerland, 1976-79; dir. tech. cooperation World Meteorol. Program, Geneva, 1979-81; dir. climate analysis ctr. Nat. Weather Svc., Camp Springs, Md., 1981-84; dir. office of meteorology Nat. Weather Svc., Silver Spring, Md., 1984-89; dir. world weather watch World Meteorol. Orgn., Geneva, 1989-94; dir. environ. rsch. labs. Nat. Oceanic and Atmospheric Adminstrn., Silver Spring, Md., 1994—. Contbr. articles to profl. jours. 1st lt. USAF, 1958-61. Recipient Gold medal U.S. Dept. Commerce, Washington, 1975, Alumni Achievement award Colo. State U., Fort Collins, 1993. Fellow Am. Meteorol. Soc. (mem. coun., commr.); mem. Am. Geophys. Union. Achievements include the organization and management of very large international research programs: Global Weather experiment, 1979, Global Atmospheric Research program, Atlantic Tropical experiment, 1974 and the World Climate program.Avocations: golf, hiking, skiing. Office: Environ Rsch Labs 1315 East-West Hwy Silver Spring MD 20910

RASMUSSEN, JOHN OSCAR, chemist, scientist; b. St. Petersburg, Fla., Aug. 8, 1926; s. John Oscar and Hazel (Ormsby) R.; m. Louise Brooks, Aug. 27, 1950; children—Nancy, Jane, David, Stephen. B.S., Calif. Inst. Tech., 1948; Ph.D., U. Calif. at Berkeley, 1952; M.A. (hon.), Yale U., 1969. Mem. faculty dept. chemistry U. Calif., Berkeley, 1952-68, 73-91, prof. chemistry, 1971-91, ret., 1991, mem. research staff, 1952-68; sr. rsch. assoc. Lawrence Berkeley Nat. Lab., 1972—; prof. chemistry Yale U. 1969-73; asso. dir. Yale Heavy Ion Accelerator Lab., 1970-73; vis. research prof. Nobel Inst. Physics, Stockholm, 1953; vis. prof. Inst. Nuclear Sci. U. Tokyo, 1974, Fudan U., Shanghai, 1979, hon. prof., 1984. Contbr. articles on radioactivity, nuclear models, heavy ion reactions. Served with USN, 1944-46. Recipient E.O. Lawrence Meml. award AEC, 1967; NSF sr. postdoctoral fellow Niels Bohr Inst., Copenhagen, 1961-62, NORDITA fellow, 1979, Guggenheim Meml. fellow, 1973, Alexander von Humboldt sr. rsch. fellow Tech. U. Munich, 1991. Fellow Am. Phys. Soc., AAAS; mem. Am. Chem. Soc. (Nuclear Applications in Chemistry award 1976), Fedn. Am. Scientists (chmn. 1969). Office: Lawrence Berkeley Lab MS 70A # 3307 Berkeley CA 94720

RASMUSSEN, NEIL WOODLAND, insurance agent; b. Portland, Oreg., Sept. 14, 1926; s. Ernest Roy and Lulu Mildred (Woodland) R.; m. Mary Ann Cannon, Aug. 10, 1957; children: Kirk, Sally, P. Cannon, Eric (dec.). BA, Stanford U., 1949. Registered mut. funds rep. Warehouseman Consol. Supply Co., Portland, Oreg., 1949-50, sales rep., 1955-56; sales rep. Consol. Supply Co., Eugene, Oreg., 1950-52; sales rep. Consol. Supply Co., Salem, Oreg., 1956-64, br. mgr., 1964-82; agt. life and health ins. N.Y. Life Ins. Co., Salem, 1982—. Lt. Cmdr. USN, 1952-55, Res. ret. Recipient Nat. Quality award Nat. Assn. Life Underwriters, 1986-88. Mem. Salem Assn. Life Underwriters, Res. Officers Assn. (bd. dirs. 1988-91, v.p. 1988-91), Rotary (bd. dirs. East Salem 1980-83, sr. active mem. 1990-92, Paul Harris fellow). Republican. Episcopalian. Avocations: golf, fishing, camping. Office: NY Life Ins Co 530 Center St NE Salem OR 97301-3744

RASMUSSEN, RICHARD ROBERT, lawyer; b. Chgo., July 5, 1946; s. Robert Kersten Rasmussen and Marisa Bruna Batistoni; children: Kathryn, William. BS, U. Oreg., 1970, JD, 1973. Bar: Oreg. 1973. Atty. U.S. Bancorp, Portland, Oreg., 1973-83, v.p. law div., 1983-87, mgr. law div., 1983—, sr. v.p., 1987—, mgr. corp. sec. div., 1990—. Mem. editorial bd. Oreg. Bus. Law Digest, 1979-81, Oreg. Debtor/Creditor newsletter, 1980-84; contbr. articles to profl. jours. Chmn. mgmt. com. YMCA of Columbia-Willamette, Portland, 1978-79; bd. dirs. Camp Fire, 1988-89, v.p., 1990-91; bd. dirs. Portland Repertory Theatre, 1994—. Mem. Oreg. State Bar Assn. (chmn. corp. counsel com. 1979-81, debtor/creditor sect. 1982-83; sec. com. on sects. 1982-83), ABA, Multnomah County Bar Assn., Beta Gamma Sigma. Club: Founder's (Portland). Avocations: mountaineering, white-water rafting, tennis, basketball. Office: US Bancorp Law Div 111 SW 5th Ave Portland OR 97204-3604

RASMUSSEN, WAYNE R., law educator, consultant; b. Sioux Falls, S.D., May 8, 1936; s. Ezra Christian and Loretta Mae Belle (Schlafer) R.; m. Carol Joy Longsdorf Prue, June 4, 1960 (div. May 1973); children: Joy, Corbin; m. Mary Dee Fowlkes, May 20, 1973; children: Thomas, Frances, Heather. BA, ThB, St. Paul Bible Coll., 1963; JD, John Marshall Law Sch., Atlanta, 1989. Bar: Ga. 1989, Calif. 1992; CPCU. Claims adjuster Travelers Ins. Co., St. Paul, 1966-70; claims supr. Travelers Ins. Co., Washington, 1970-72; asst. mgr. claims Travelers Ins. Co., Atlanta, 1972-77; asst. v.p. Continental Ins. Co., N.Y.C., 1977-82; mgr. state claims Continental Ins. Co., Charlotte, N.C., 1982-86; pvt. practice, Atlanta, 1989—; prof. law John Marshall Law Sch., 1989—; ins. cons., Atlanta, 1990—. Aux. police officer N.Y. Police Dept., N.Y.C., 1978-82. With USAF, 1954-58. Named Outstanding Prof. of Yr., John Marshall Law Sch., 1992. Mem. Soc. of CPCU (treas. 1980), Soc. of CLU. Avocations: skiing, walking. Office: 5496 E Mountain St Stone Mountain GA 30083-3076

RASMUSSON, GARY HENRY, medicinal chemist; b. Clark, S.D., Aug. 2, 1936; s. Rudolf M. and Alice Ernestine (Henry) R.; m. Nancy Elaine Torkelson, June 7, 1958; children: Randall, Korise, Tamara, Todd. BA, St. Olaf Coll., 1958; PhD, MIT, 1962. Postdoctoral fellow Stanford U., Palo Alto, Calif., 1962-64; sr. chemist Merck, Sharp & Dohme Rsch. Labs., Rahway, N.J., 1964-72, rsch. fellow, 1972-77, sr. rsch. fellow, 1977-85, sr. investigator, 1985-94; v.p. chemistry Biofor, Inc., Waverly, Pa., 1996. Medicinal discovery new type drug 5alpha reductase inhibitors, 1986. Named Inventor of Yr. Intellectual Property Owners, Washington, 1993. Mem. AAAS, Am. Chem. Soc. Lutheran.

RASNAKE, JAMES HAMILTON, JR., portfolio manager; b. Atlanta, Nov. 24, 1935; s. James Hamilton Sr. and Dorothy (Turner) R.; children: Brooke, Robin. BBA, U. Ga., 1961. V.p., cert. fin. mgr. Merrill Lynch, Atlanta, 1961—. Named Outstanding Young Man of Atlanta, Jaycees, 1972. Mem. Ga. Security Dealers Assn. (pres. 1982). Republican. Episcopalian. Home: 252 Pineland Rd NW Atlanta GA 30342-4019 Office: Merrill Lynch 3500 Piedmont Rd NE Ste 600 Atlanta GA 30305-1503

RASOR, DINA LYNN, investigator, journalist; b. Downey, Calif., Mar. 21, 1956; d. Ned Shaurer and Genevieve Mercia (Eads) R.; m. Thomas Taylor Lawson, Oct. 4, 1980. BA in Polit. Sci., U. Calif., Berkeley, 1978. Editorial asst. ABC News, Washington, 1978-79; researcher Pres.'s Commn. on Coal, Washington, 1979; legis. asst. Nat. Taxpayers Union, Washington, 1979-81; founder, dir. Project on Mil. Procurement, Washington, 1981-89; investigative reporter Lawson-Rasor Assocs., El Cerrito, Calif., 1990-92; pres., CEO, investigator Bauman & Rasor Group, El Cerrito, Calif., 1993—. Author: The Pentagon Underground, 1985; editor: More Bucks, Less Bang, 1983; contbr. articles to profl. jours. Recipient Sigma Delta Chi Outstanding Leadership award Soc. Profl. Journalists, 1986; named to register Esquire Mag., 1986, Nat. Jour., 1986. Mem. United Ch. Christ.

RASOR, ROBERT D., lawyer; b. Bloomington, Ind., Aug. 3, 1948. BA, DePaul U., 1970; JD, Northwestern U., 1973. Bar: Ill. 1973, U.S. Dist. Ct. (no. dist.) Ill. 1973. Ptnr. Lord, Bissell & Brook, Chgo. Mem. ABA, Ill. State Bar Assn., Chgo. Bar Assn. Office: Lord Bissell & Brook Harris Bank Bldg 115 S La Salle St # 2600 36 Chicago IL 60603-3801*

RASPORICH, ANTHONY WALTER, university dean; b. Port Arthur, Ont., Can., Jan. 9, 1940; s. Milan and Sophia (Grgurich) R.; m. Beverly Jean Matson. BA, Queen's U., Kingston, Ontario, 1962, MA, 1965; PhD, U. Man., Winnipeg, 1970. Tchr. Kingston Bd. Edn., 1962-63; prof. history U. of Calgary, Alta., 1966—, dean social scis. faculty, 1986-94. Author: For a Better Life, 1982, Oil and Gas in Western Canada 1900-80, 1985; editor: The Making of the Modern West, 1984; co-editor: Canadian Ethnic Studies, 1980-95, Sports in the West, 1990. C.D. Howe postdoctoral fellow, fellow Assn. Univs. Colls. Can., Thunder Bay, Ontario, 1970, Vis. Can. Studies, Sussex, Eng., 1979, Killam Found., Calgary, 1979, Social Scis. Human Rsch. Coun., Ottawa, Can., 1981. Mem. Canada Ethnic Studies Assn., Can. Hist. Assn. Office: U Calgary, Dept History, Calgary, AB Canada T2N 1N4

RASSBACH, HERBERT DAVID, marketing executive; b. Glen Ridge, N.J., Mar. 23, 1944; s. Merrill Augustus and Ruth Bruce (Sims) R.; m. Sherry Miriam Reichel, July 14, 1974. BS, Del. State Coll., 1971; MBA, Drexel U., 1979. Prodn. planning mgr. Standard Brands Chem. Industries, Edison, N.J., 1971-74; order fulfillment mgr. P Q Corp., Valley Forge, Pa., 1974-77, mkt. devel. project mgr., 1977-82; market mgr. Willson Safety Products, Reading, Pa., 1983-85; pres. HDR Group, mktg. and mgmt. cons., Wayne, Pa., 1986—; guest speaker Wharton Sch. U. Pa., 1988, Temple U., Phila., 1989, Wharton Club, 1995. Committeeman Upper Merion Twp., Pa., 1977; Media Comms. bd., Upper Merion Twp., 1989, vice chmn., 1990, 92-96, chmn., 1991. Mem. Drexel U. Alumni Assn. (v.p. Montgomery County chpt. 1988-91), Alpha Kappa Mu, Delta Mu Delta. Democrat. Avocations: golf, tennis, racquetball, travel, American History, arts. Home: 635 Mallard Rd Wayne PA 19087-2346 Office: HDR Group PO Box 904 Valley Forge PA 19482-0904

RASSEL, RICHARD EDWARD, lawyer; b. Toledo, Jan. 10, 1942; s. Richard Edward and Madonna Mary (Tuohy) R.; m. Elizabeth Ann Frederick, Dec. 5, 1967 (wid. June 1977); children: Richard III, Elizabeth; m. Dawn Ann Lynch, Sept. 17, 1983; children: Lauren, Brian. BA, U. Notre Dame, 1964; JD, U. Mich., 1966. Bar: Mich. 1966, U.S. Dist. Ct. (ea. dist.) Mich. 1969, U.S. Ct. Appeals (6th cir.) 1971, U.S. Supreme Ct. 1980. Law clk. to presiding judge Mich. Ct. Appeals, Detroit, 1966; shareholder, chmn. CEO Butzel & Long, Detroit, 1970—; bd. dirs. Lex Mundi Law Firm Alliance, Robertson-Jamieson Corp. Contbr. articles to profl. jours.; lectr. in field. Past pres., bd. dirs. Birmingham Cmty. House; mem. bd. advisors U. Detroit Grad. Sch. Bus.; mem. steering com. Friends of Legal Aid; pres. Rosa Parks Scholarship Found., Detroit, Detroit Police Athletic League, S.E.E.D. Found.; bd. dirs. Met. Affairs Coalition, Mich. Jobs Commn., Detroit Legal News. Fellow Am. Coll. Trial Lawyers, Mich. Bar Found.; mem. ABA (forum com., vice chmn. law and media com. tort and ins. practice sect.), Am. Arbitration Assn., Fed. Bar Assn., State Bar Mich. (past chmn. media and the law com., chmn. TV in the cts. com.), Detroit Bar Assn. (exec. com., U.S dist. cts. com.), Libel Def. Resource Ctr. (vice chmn. def. counsel sect.), Detroit C. of C. (bus. attraction and expansion coun. southeast Mich.), Leadership Detroit Alumni Assn., U.S. Navy League, Detroit Athletic Club, Birmingham Athletic Club, Otsego Club, Village Club. Roman Catholic. Home: 700 Browning Ct Bloomfield Hills MI 48304-3715 Office: Butzel Long 150 W Jefferson Ste 900 Detroit MI 48226-4430

RASSMAN, JOEL H., real estate company executive, accountant; b. N.Y.C., May 16, 1945. BBA, CUNY, 1967. CPA, N.Y. Mng. dir. Ernst & Young, N.Y.C., 1967-73; ptnr. Kenneth Leventhal & Co. (now Ernst & Young), N.Y.C., 1973-84; sr. v.p. Toll Bros., Inc., Huntingdon Valley, Pa., 1984—. Mem. AICPA, N.Y. State Soc. CPA's.

RAST, WALTER, JR., hydrologist, water quality management; b. San Antonio, Jan. 14, 1944; s. Walter and Jane Irene (Tudyk) R.; m. Claudia Leigh Jones, July 16, 1971; children: Margaret Amanda, Elizabeth Miranda. BA in Zoology, U. Tex., Austin, 1970; MS in Molecular Biology, U. Tex., Richardson, 1974, MS in Environ. Sci., 1976, PhD in Environ. Sci., 1978. Limnologist Gt. Lakes Regional Office, Internat. Joint Commn., Windsor, Ont., Can., 1977-79; environ. advisor U.S. Hdqrs. sect. Internat. Joint Commn., Washington, 1979-82; rsch. hydrologist U.S. Geol. Survey, Sacramento, 1982-86, Austin, 1986-92; dep. dir. water programme UNEP, Nairobi, Kenya, 1993—; adj. prof. dept. biology Wayne State U., Detroit, 1978-79; adj. prof. dept. aquatic biology S.W. Tex. State U., San Marcos, 1992—; mem. core editorial group program on man and biosphere UNESCO, 1982-89, chmn. sci. adv. com., 1988—; instr. Austin Community Coll., 1989—; reviewer sci. books and films AAAS, Washington, 1989-92. Co-author: Control of Eutrophication of Lakes and Reservoirs, 1989; co-editor: Phosphorus Management Strategies for Lakes, 1979; mem. editorial bd. Internat. Jour. Devel., 1993—; contbr. articles to sci. jours. Scholar Richardson Environ. Action League, 1976-77. Mem. N.Am. Lake Mgmt. Soc. (co-chmn. scholarship com. 1988—, mem. internat. com. and lake cert. com. 1988—, tech. chmn. 9th internat. symposium 1989), Am. Soc. Limnology and Oceanography, Internat. Soc. Applied and Theoretical Limnology. Roman Catholic. Avocations: jogging, model railroads, piano, reading, amateur politics. *One of the most difficult things for a person to do is undertake necessary and even unpleasant tasks, at the same time others are content to offer excuses as to why they cannot be done. Fortunately, a sufficient number of people display this virtue to make it all worthwhile.*

RASTEGAR, NADER E., real estate developer, businessman; b. Tehran, Iran, May 12, 1953; came to U.S., 1982; s. Morteza and Rabe'eh (Baghai-Kermani) R.; m. Soheila Gharai, Apr. 1979; children: Roya Z., Scheherazade B., Maryam A. BSc, U. Wis., 1976; MBA, Iran Ctr. Mgmt. Studies, 1979. Pres. Shahgard Indsl. Co., Tehran, 1977, Renafa, Inc., Atlanta, 1984—. Contbr. articles to various publs. Active various profl., historical, philatelical and environ. socs. and groups. Lt. Iranian Armed Forces, 1977-78. Avocations: historical research, social welfare, environmental issues, philatelics. Office: Renafa Inc 1603 Lenox Tower N 3400 Peachtree Rd NE Atlanta GA 30326-1107

RASTOGI, ANIL KUMAR, medical device manufacturer executive; b. India, July 13, 1942; came to U.S., 1969, naturalized, 1978; s. R.S. and K.V. Rastogi; m. Anjali Capur, Mar. 18, 1970; children: Priya, Sonya. B.S. with honors, Lucknow U., 1963, M.S., 1964; Ph.D. in Polymer Sci., McGill U., 1969. Mem. staff Owens-Corning Tech. Ctr., Granville, Ohio, 1969-87; lab. supr. Owens-Corning Tech. Ctr., 1975-76; lab. mgr. materials tech. labs Ownes-Corning Tech. Ctr., Granville, Ohio, 1976-79; lab. mgr. product devel. labs. Owens-Corning Tech. Ctr., Granville, Ohio, 1979-80, research dir., 1980-83, dir. corp. diversification portfolio, 1983-87; v.p. Mead Imaging, Miamisburg, Ohio, 1987-89; pres. Mead Cycolor Div., Dayton, Ohio, 1989-92; v.p., gen. mgr.infusion systems div. Pharmacia Deltec, Inc., St. Paul, 1992-93; exec. v.p. Pharmacia Deltec, Inc., 1993-94; COO SIMS Deltec, Inc., St. Paul, 1994-95; pres., COO Sabratek Corp., Niles, Ill., 1995—; mem. adv. bd. Central Ohio Tech. Coll.; lectr., cons. in field. Author of 11 bus. and tech. publs.; patentee in field. Bd. dirs. Licking County Family Services Assn.; bd. dirs. Tech. Alliance of Central Ohio; v.p. local United Way; bd. dirs. and treas. Columbus Bus. Tech. Ctr.; mem. Overview Adv. Com. Strategic Hwy. Research Program. Fellow NRC Can., 1966-69. Mem. AAAS, Am. Mgmt. Assn., Am. Chem. Soc., Soc. Plastics Engrs., Comml. Devel. Assn., Med. Alley (bd. dirs.), Health Ind. Mfrs. Assn., Sigma Xi. Club: Toastmasters (past pres.). Lodge: Rotary. Home: 4445 Foothill Trl Saint Paul MN 55127-6002 Office: Sabratek Corp 5601 W Howard Niles IL 60714

RATAJ, EDWARD WILLIAM, lawyer; b. St. Louis, Oct. 14, 1947; m. Elizabeth Spalding, July 4, 1970; children: Edward, Suzanne, Anne, Thomas, Charles. BS in Acctg., St. Louis U., 1969, JD, 1972. Assoc. Bryan, Cave, McPheeters & McRoberts, St. Louis, 1972-82, ptnr., 1983—. Office: Bryan Cave McPheeters & McRoberts 1 Metropolitan Sq Saint Louis MO 63102-2750

RATAJ, ELIZABETH ANN, artist; b. Flint, Mich., Oct. 3, 1943; d. Lloyd Milton Clem and Mildred (Lamrock) Clem-Taylor; m. David Henry Rataj, Oct. 17, 1970. BA, Bob Jones U., 1966; BFA, U. Iowa, 1987. Educator Oscoda (Mich.) Area Schs., 1966-71, 73-83, Ft. Wayne (Ind.) Pub. Schs., 1971-72, St. Louis Pub. Schs., 1983-85. Represented in permanent collections Mich. Edn. Assn., Lansing, 1978, Munson Williams Proctor Mus., Utica, N.Y., 1989, Jesse Besser Mus., Alpena, Mich., 1993; two-person shows include The Art Ctr., Mount Clemens, Mich., 1996; group shows include Mus. Modern Art Miami, 1995, San Bernardino County Mus., Redlands, Calif., 1995, Austin Pedy State U., Clarksville, Tenn., 1995, The Art Ctr., Mount Clemens, Mich., 1996. Mem. Delta Kappa Gamma (1978-82, 86-87, 76-87), Nat. Mus. of Women in the Arts (charter).

RATAJCZAK, MARIUSZ, hematologist, researcher; b. Szczecin, Poland, Feb. 8, 1955; came to U.S., 1989; s. Zdzislaw and Teresa (Tomczak) R.; m. Janina Obrzud, Dec. 26, 1977; children: Teresa, Eva, Victor. MD, Med. U. Szczecin, 1981; PhD, Polish Acad. Scis., Warsaw, 1986. Assoc. prof. Polish Acad. Scis., 1986-89; sr. rschr. U. Pa., Phila., 1990—; asst. prof., 1995—. Contbg. author: Molecular Biology of Haematopoiesis, 1992, Nucleic Acids and Molecular Biology, 1994; contbr. articles to sci. jours. Fellow Am. Soc. Hematology.

RATCLIFF, CARTER GOODRICH, writer, art critic, poet; b. Seattle, Aug. 20, 1941; s. Francis Kenneth and Marian Elizabeth (Carter) R.; m. Phyllis Derfner, Jan. 28, 1976. BA, U. Chgo., 1963. Dir. poetry workshop St. Mark's Poetry Project, N.Y.C., 1969-70; editorial assoc. Artnews, N.Y.C., 1969-72; advisory editor Art Internat., Lugano, Switzerland, 1970-75; instr. modern and contemporary art and art theory The Sch. of Visual Arts, N.Y.C., 1972-83; instr. modern and contemporary art Phila. Coll. of Art, 1973; instr. art history NYU Sch. of Continuing Edn., 1973-75; contbg. editor Saturday Review, N.Y.C., 1980-82, Art in America, N.Y.C., 1976—; mem. editorial adv. com. Sculpture, Washington, 1992—; via. prof. post-war Am. art SUNY, Purchase, 1983-84; vis. prof. modern and contemporary art and art theory Pratt Inst., Bkyn., 1984-85; vis. prof. art criticism and theory Hunter Coll., CUNY, 1985-86, 95-96. Author: (books, poetry), Fever Coast, 1973, Give Me Tomorrow, 1983; (books) John Singer Sargent, 1982, Andy Warhol, 1983, Robert Longo, 1985, Komar and Melamid, 1989, Gilbert and George: The Singing Sculpture, 1993, Jackson Pollock, 1996; (catlog essays) Joseph Cornell, 1980, Willem de Kooning: The North Atlantic Light, 1983, Sean Scully, 1993, Ellsworth Kelly, 1996; contbr. over 350 articles on art to magazines and catalogs including The Times Literary Supplement, The L.A. Times Book Review, Art in America, Art Internat., Artnews, Architectural Forum; lectr. at many instns. including Met. Mus., N.Y.C., Mus. Modern Art, N.Y.C., Whitney Mus. of Am. Art, Pratt Inst., U. So. Calif., U. Chgo., Detroit Inst. of Art, San Francisco Art Inst. Home and Office: 26 Beaver St New York NY 10004

RATCLIFF, JAMES LEWIS, administrator; b. Indpls., Mar. 3, 1946; s. Perry Albert and Viola Ruth (Hall) R.; m. Carol Rocklin Kay, Dec. 24, 1984 (dec.); m. Barbara Marie Montgomery, Aug. 31, 1995. Student, Raymond Coll.; B of History, Polit. Sci., Utah State U., 1968; MA in History, Wash. State U., 1972, PhD, 1976. Dir. Ctr. for the Study of Higher Edn. Pa. State U., University Pk.; prof., leader higher edn. section Iowa State U., Ames; assoc. prof. Fla. Atlantic U., Boca Raton; asst. prof. Wash. State U., Pullman. U.S. Dept. Edn. grantee. Mem. Am. Assn. Community Jr. Colls., Assn. Study Higher Edn. (bd. dirs.), Coun. Universities Colls. (past pres., bd. dirs.), European Assn. for Inst. Rsch.,Consortium Higher Edn. Rschs., Phi Delta Kappa, Phi Kappa Phi, Phi Alpha Theta.

RATCLIFFE, G(EORGE) JACKSON, JR., business executive, lawyer; b. Charleston, W.Va., Mar. 22, 1936; s. George Jackson and Dorothy (Ward) R.; m. Nancy Lenhardt, Oct. 5, 1963; children: George Jackson III, Dorothy Margaret. AB, Duke U., 1958; JD, U. Va., 1961. Bar: N.Y. 1964, Ohio 1962. Assoc. Taft, Stettinius & Hollister, Cin., 1961-63; lawyer IBM Corp., 1963-65; assoc. Perkins, Daniels & McCormack, N.Y.C., 1965-70, ptnr., 1970; v.p., sec., gen. counsel Helme Products Inc., N.Y.C., 1970, exec. v.p., 1971-74, pres., 1974; v.p., sec., gen. counsel Hubbell Inc., Orange, Conn., 1975-80, sr. v.p. fin. and law, 1980-83, exec. v.p. adminstrn., 1983-87, chmn. bd., 1987—, pres., chief exec. officer, 1987—; bd. dirs. Aquarian Co., Bridgeport, Conn., Olin Corp., Stamford, Conn., Praxair Inc., Danbury, Conn.; mem. listed co. adv. com. N.Y. Stock Exch. Mem. Conn. Bus. and Industry Assn. (bd. dirs.), Nat. Elec. Mfrs. Assn. (bd. govs.), Brooklawn Country Club (Fairfield, Conn.), Aspetuck Fish and Game Club (Bridgeport), Clove Valley Rod and Gun Club (LaGrangeville, N.Y.), Loblolly Pines Club (Hobe Sound, Fla.), Merion Golf Club (Ardmore, Pa.), Blind Brook Country Club (Purchase, N.Y.), Links Club (N.Y.). Home: 278 Sherwood Dr Southport CT 06490-1049 Office: Hubbell Inc PO Box 549 584 Derby Milford Rd Orange CT 06477-4024*

RATH, ALAN T., sculptor; b. Cin., Nov. 25, 1959; s. George and Carolyn R. BSEE, MIT, 1982. One-man exhbns. include San Jose (Calif.) Art Mus., 1990, Dorothy Goldeen Gallery, Santa Monica, Calif., 1990, 92, Walker Art Ctr., Mpls., 1991, Mus. Contemporary Art, Chgo., 1991, Carl Solway Gallery, Cin., 1991, Inst. Contemporary Mus., Honolulu, 1992, Ctr. Fine Art, Miami, Fla., 1992, Galerie Hans Mayer, Dusseldorf, Germany, 1992, Hiroshima (Japan) City Mus. Contemporary Art, 1994, Worcester (Mass.) Art Mus., 1994, John Weber Gallery, N.Y.C., 1994, Haines Gallery, San Francisco, 1995, Contemporary Art Mus., Houston, 1995, Aspen Art Mus., Colo., 1996; group exhbns. include Visiona, Zurich, 1989, Arc Electronics, Linz, Austria, 1989, L.A. Contemporary Exhbns., 1989, Mus. Folkwang, Essen, Germany, 1989, Cite des Arts et des Nouvelles Technologies, Montreal, 1990, Staftmuseum Siegburg, Siegburg, Germany, 1990, San Francisco Mus. Modern Art, 1990, Denver ArtMus., 1991, Whitney Am. Art, N.Y.C., 1991, Alvar Alto Mus., Jyvaskyla, Finland, 1992, Internat. Ctr. Photography, N.Y.C., 1992, Padigilione d'Arte Contemporanea, Ferrara, Italy, 1992, John Weber Gallery, N.Y.C., 1993, Spiral Art Ctr., Tokyo, 1994. Grantee NEA, 1988; Guggenheim fellow, 1994. Office: IKON 830 E 15th St Oakland CA 94606-3631

RATH, BERNARD EMIL, trade association executive; b. Arnstein, Fed. Republic of Germany, Oct. 9, 1949; arrived in Can., 1952; U.S. resident, 1985; s. Rudolph and Elfriede (Kraft) R.; m. Susan Elaine Garner, July 8, 1972; children: Vanessa, Andrew, Lauren. BA in Polit. Sci., McMaster U., Can., 1972, BA in Phys. Edn., 1972; Diploma Edn., U. Western Ont., Can., 1973. Sales rep. Doubleday Pubs., Toronto, Ont., Can., 1973-75; sales mgr. Macmillian Pubs., Toronto, Ont., Can., 1975-77, nat. sales mgr., 1977-79; exec. dir. Can. Booksellers, Toronto, 1979-83, Am. Booksellers Assn., N.Y.C., 1984—; pres. Booksellers Order Service, N.Y.C., 1984—. Pub. Booksellers Publishing, N.Y.C., 1984—; contbr. articles to profl. jours. Am. Soc. Assn. Execs. Home: 33 Chester Ct Cortlandt Mnr NY 10566-6361 Office: Am Booksellers Assn 560 White Plains Rd Tarrytown NY 10591-5112*

RATH, FRANK E., SR., electronics executive; b. 1915. Grad., Carnegie Inst. of Tech., Pitt., 1937. Chief engr. U.S. Steel Corp., Pitts., 1937-49; chmn, CEO Spang & Co., Butler, Pa., 1958—. Office: Spang & Co PO Box 751 Butler PA 16003-0751*

RATH, FRANK E., JR., electronics executive; b. 1946. BS, Carnegie Mellon U., 1968. With Ernst & Ernst CPAs, Pitts., 1968-70; with Spang & Co., Butler, Pa., 1974—, pres., 1977—. Office: Spang & Co PO Box 751 Butler PA 16003-0751*

RATH, GUSTAVE J(OSEPH), industrial engineering educator, psychologist; b. N.Y.C., May 19, 1929; s. Gustave Julian and Margaret Rose (Payor) R.; m. Clouia Poock, Sept. 1, 1953 (div. 1976); 1 child, G. Alexander; m. Karen Sue Braatz Stoyanoff, Oct. 15, 1977. BS, MIT, 1952; MS, Ohio State U., 1955, PhD, 1957. Psychologist IBM, Peekskill, N.Y., 1957-59; mgr. ops. rsch. Admiral Co., Chgo., 1959-60; mgr. behavioral tech. Raytheon Co., Lexington, Mass., 1960-63; prof. indsl. enging. and mgmt. sci. Northwestern U., Evanston, Ill., 1963—; pres. Fundamental Systems, Inc., Evanston, 1967-70, Cassell, Rath & Stoyanoff, Ltd., Evanston, 1979-84; v.p. Resource Profls., Inc., Evanston, 1990—. Author: Punch Card Data Processing, 1966; co-author: Marketing for Congregations, 1992, Benchmarks of Quality in the Church, 1994; author, co-author chpts. in books. Mem. commn. on appraisal Unitarian-Universalist Assn., 1995—. 1st lt. USAF, 1952-54. Danforth fellow, 1983; Sloan Found. grantee, 1970. Fellow AAAS, APA, Am. Psychol. Soc., Sigma Xi, Tau Beta Pi. Achievements include invention of computer-assisted instrn. Office: Northwestern U Dept Indsl Engring 2145 Sheridan Rd Evanston IL 60208-0834

RATH, HOWARD GRANT, JR., lawyer; b. L.A., Sept. 2, 1931; s. Howard Grant and Helen (Cowell) R.; m. Peyton McComb, Sept. 13, 1958 (dec. Apr. 1984); children: Parthenia Peyton, Francis Cowell; m. Dorothy Moser, Aug. 29, 1986. BS, U. Calif., 1953; JD, U. So. Calif., 1958. Bar: Calif. 1959, U.S. Dist. Ct. (cen. dist.) Calif., 1959, U.S. Ct. Claims 1974, U.S. Tax Ct. 1960. Assoc. O'Melveny & Myers, L.A., 1959-66; tax counsel, dir. tax adminstrn., asst. treas. Northrop Corp. L.A., 1966-74; sr. tax ptnr. Macdonald, Halsted & Laybourne, L.A., 1974-86, Hill & Weiss, L.A., 1986-90; ptnr. Lewis, D'Amato, Brisbois & Bisgaard, L.A., 1990—; dir. Rath Packing Co., Waterloo, Iowa, 1966-81. 1st lt. U.S. Army, 1953-55. Mem. ABA, State Bar Calif., L.A. County Bar Assn., Order of Coif, Phi Beta Kappa. Republican. Episcopalian. Club: Valley Hunt (pres. 1981-82). Office: Lewis D'Amato Brisbois & Bisgaard 221 N Figueroa St Ste 1200 Los Angeles CA 90012-2601

RATH, R. JOHN, historian, educator; b. St. Francis, Kans., Dec. 12, 1910; s. John and Barbara (Schauer) R.; m. Isabel Jones, June 26, 1937; children: Laurens John (dec.), Donald (dec.), Isabel Ferguson. A.B., U. Kans., 1932; A.M., U. Calif., Berkeley, 1934; Ph.D., Columbia U., 1941. Instr. history U. Ark., 1936-37, summer vis. prof., 1947; pre-doctoral field fellow Social Sci. Research Council in Austria and Italy, 1937-38; instr. history Coll. Puget Sound, Tacoma, Wash., 1938-39; head dept. history and polit. sci. Lindenwood Coll., St. Charles, Mo., 1939-41; assoc. prof. history Miss. State Coll. for Women, 1941-43; chief bur. documentary evidence UNRRA Bur. Documents and Tracing, U.S. Zone of Ger., 1945-46; asst. prof. history U. Ga., 1946-47; assoc. prof. history, assoc. editor Jour. Central European Affairs, U. Colo., 1947-51, vis. prof., summer 1958; prof. history U. Tex., Austin, 1951-63; prof. history, chmn. dept. history and polit. sci. Rice U., 1963-68, Mary Gibbs Jones prof., 1968-80, prof. emeritus, 1980—; prof. history U. Minn., Mpls., 1980-85; vis. prof. U. Wis., 1955, Duke U., 1963; Guggenheim fellow in Italy, 1956-57. Author: The Fall of the Napoleonic Kingdom of Italy, 1941, The Viennese Revolution 1948, 1957, L'amministrazione austriaca nel Lombardo Veneto, 1814-21, 1959, The Austrian Provisional Regime in Lombardy Venetia, 1969, The Deterioration of Democracy in Austria, 1927-1992, 1996; contbg. author: The Fate of East Central Europe (editor Stephen Kertesz), 1956, East Central Europe and the World (edited S. Kertesz), 1962; also Ency. Americana; founder, editor: Austrian History Newsletter, 1960-63, Austrian History Yearbook, 1965-82; contbr. Die Aufloesung des Habsburgerreiches, 1970, Native Fascism in the Successor States, 1971, Beitraege zur Zietgeschichte, 1976, The Austrian Socialist Experiment, 1985, The Mirror of History, 1988, Austria, 1938-88, 1995. Served in AUS, 1943-45. Recipient 1st class Austrian Cross of Honor in arts and scis., 1963. Mem. Am. Hist. Soc. (com. internat. activities 1960-66, exec. com. modern European history sect. 1963-66), So. Hist. Soc. (chmn. European sect. 1961-62, exec. coun. 1965-68), Soc. Italian Hist. Studies (Sr. Scholar Citation 1984), Conf. Ctrl. European History (nat. exec. bd. 1959-61, chmn. 1970, com. on Austrian history 1957-68, 70-81, exec. sec. 1957-68), Am. Assn. Study of Hungarian History (chmn. 1978), Southwestern Social Sci. Assn. (pres. 1976-77), Austrian Acad. Sci. (corr.), Deputazione di Storia Patria par le Venezie (corr.), Phi Beta Kappa. Home: 5015 35th Ave S Apt 130 Minneapolis MN 55417-1562

RATH, THOMAS DAVID, lawyer, former state attorney general; b. East Orange, N.J., June 1, 1945; s. Harvey and Helen R.; m. Christine Casey, Dec. 18, 1971; children—Erin, Timothy. A.B., Dartmouth Coll., 1967; J.D., Georgetown U., 1971. Bar: N.J. 1971, N.H. 1972, U.S. Supreme Ct. 1978. Law clk. Judge Clarkson Fisher, U.S. Dist. Ct. N.J., 1971-72; atty. criminal div. Office of Atty. Gen., State of N.H., 1972-73; asst. atty. gen. Office of Atty. Gen., 1973-76, dep. atty. gen., 1976-78, atty. gen., 1978-80; ptnr. Orr & Reno, P.A., Concord, 1980-87, Rath & Young, P.A., Concord, 1987-91; founding ptnr. Rath, Young, Pignatelli & Oyer, P.A., Concord, 1991—; polit. analyst WHDH-TV, Boston, WGBH Pub. TV, Boston, WENH, N.H. Pub. TV, WBUR-Boston Radio; chief strategist Alexander for Pres.; vice chmn. of bd. Primary Bank, 1995; pres. Play Ball, N.H., 1994—; commentator, polit. analyst WMUR-TV and Yankee Network. Host State of the State, Yankee Cable Network; co-host Close-Up, WMUR-TV. chmn. campaign Warren B. Rudman for U.S. Senate, 1980, 86; bd. overseers Aquinas House, Dartmouth Coll.; nat. dir. Baker Exploratory Com., 1986-87; sec. bd. trustees Concord Hosp.; treas. N.H. Rep. party, 1981-93; trustee DWC, 1981-87, chmn., 1982-86; mem. Baker Exploratory Com., 1986-87; trustee Concord Hosp., 1980-86; sr. nat. cons. Dole for Pres.; del. Rep. Nat. Conv., 1984, 88, 92, rules com., 1988, 92. Mem. Nat. Assn. Attys. Gen. (vice-chmn. Eastern region, vice chmn. standing com. on energy), N.H. Bar Assn. (Spl. Pres. award 1992). Roman Catholic. Club: Dartmouth Coll. (v.p. Merrimack County). Office: Rath Young and Pignatelli Two Capital Plaza PO Box 1500 Concord NH 03302-1500

RATHBONE, PERRY TOWNSEND, art museum director; b. Germantown, Pa., July 3, 1911; s. Howard Betts and Beatrice (Connely) R.; m. Euretta de Cosson, Feb. 10, 1945; children: Peter Betts, Eliza, Belinda. A.B., Harvard U., 1933, postgrad., 1933-34; Arts D., Washington U., St. Louis, 1958; L.H.D., Northeastern U., 1960, Suffolk U., Williams Coll., 1970; A.F.D., Bates Coll., 1964, Boston Coll., 1970, R.I. Sch. Design, 1982. Co-dir. Harvard Soc. Contemporary Art, 1931-33; ednl. asst. Detroit Inst. Arts, 1934-36; instr. fine arts Wayne U., Detroit; curator Alger House (suburban br. Detroit Inst. Arts) and gen. rsch. asst. to Dir. Valentiner, 1936-39; asst. to Dir. Valentiner (dir. gen. masterpieces of art), N.Y. World's Fair; later dir.); dir. City Art Mus., St. Louis, 1940-55; dir. Mus. Fine Arts, Boston, 1954-72; dir. Mus. Fine Arts, 1955-72, dir. emeritus, cons., 1972—; dir. Christie's USA, 1973-77; sr. v.p., dir. Christie's Internat., 1977-86; cons. to Christie's Internat., 1987—; Pres. St. Louis Art Commn., 1940-55, St. Louis Little Symphony, 1950-55; adviser council Harvard Found. for Advanced Study and Research, 1953-58; mem. vis. com. Fogg Art Mus., Harvard, 1955-66; mem. U.S. nat. commn. Internat. Council of Museums; adviser program for humanities Ford Found., 1957-73; adviser art com. Chase Manhattan Bank, 1958-76; pres. Met. Boston Arts Center, Inc., 1958-61, chmn. bd., 1961-72; mem. Rockefeller Panel on Performing Arts, 1963-64, Skowhegan Sch. Painting and Sculpture, 1965-77; fine arts vis. com. R.I. Sch. Design, 1966-68, trustee, 1969-74; adviser Urasenke Found., Kyoto, Japan, 1974—; vice chmn. Mass. Art Commn.; v.p. Cosmopolitan Art Found., 1974-13 ; mem. Cambridge Arts Council, 1978-79, 79—. Author: Charles Wimar, 1946, Max Beckmann, 1948, Mississippi Panorama, 1950, Westward the Way, 1954, Lee Gatch, 1960, (with Peter Selz) Max Beckmann, 1964, Handbook of the Forsyth Wickes Collection, 1968, Museum of Fine Arts, Boston, Western Art, 1971, Andrew Wyeth (in Japanese), 1974; also numerous articles in mus. bulls. and art jours.; Contbr. to: (with Peter Selz) Great Drawings of All Times, 1962, The Arts and Public Policy in the U.S., chpt. 3, 1984. Mem. bd. overseers Brandeis U., Strawbery Banke, Inc.; trustee Am. Fedn. Arts, 1959-79, New Eng. Conservatory of Music, 1960-80, Boston Arts Festival, Cape Cod Art Assn., Internat. Exhbns. Found., 1965-81, Royal Oak Found., 1974-92, Opera Co. of Boston, 1976-90. Lt. comdr. USNR, 1942-45, PTO. Decorated chevalier Légion d'Honneur; Benjamin Franklin fellow Royal Soc. Art; fellow R.I. Sch. Design, 1981. Mem. Am. Assn. Mus. (v.p. 1960—, coun.), St. Louis Round Table, Mass. Hist. Soc., Colonial Soc. Mass., Assn. Art Mus. Dirs. (pres. 1959-60, 69-70, trustee 1969-72), Am. Acad. Arts and Scis., Royal Art Soc. London, Phi Beta Kappa (hon. Harvard chpt.), Century Club (N.Y.C.), Tavern Club (Boston), Odd Volumes Club (Boston), Harvard Club (Boston). Episcopalian. Home: Univ Green 130 Mount Auburn St Apt 506 Cambridge MA 02138-5779

RATHBUN, JOHN WILBERT, American studies educator; b. Sioux City, Iowa, Oct. 24, 1924; s. Wilbert W. and Paulina Amanda (Baldes) R.; m. Mary Regina Walsh, Aug. 2, 1947 (div. Sept. 19, 1985); children: Mary Walsh, John Philip. Ph.B., Marquette U., Milw., 1951, M.A., 1952; Ph.D., U. Wis., 1956. Mem. faculty Calif. State U., Los Angeles, 1956—; prof. English/Am. studies Calif. State U., 1959—, chmn. dept. Am. studies, 1969-75, prof. emeritus, 1991—. Author: American Literary Criticism, 1800-1860, vol. 1, 1979, (with Harry Hayden Clark) American Literary Criticism, 1860-1905, vol. 2, 1979, Literature and Literary Analysis, 1983; (with Monica Grecu) American Literary Critics and Scholars, 1800-1850, vol. 1, 1987, 1850-1880, vol. 2, 1880-1900, 1988, vol. 3, 1988; contbr. articles to profl. jours. Served with AUS, 1943-46. Recipient Service citation Calif. State U., Los Angeles, 1977, Univ. Meritorious Achievement award, 1986; Fulbright fellow Romania, 1979-81. Mem. Am. Studies Assn. (council 1974), So. Calif. Am. Studies Assn. (pres. 1973), Coll. English Assn. So. Calif. (pres. 1966-67), MLA. Democrat. Office: 5151 State University Dr Los Angeles CA 90032-4221

RATHER, DAN, broadcast journalist; b. Wharton, Tex., Oct. 31, 1931; m. Jean Goebel; children: Dawn Robin, Danjack. B.A. in Journalism, Sam Houston State Coll., Huntsville, Tex., 1953; student, U. Houston, South Tex. Sch. Law. Instr. journalism Sam Houston State Coll., for 1 year; later worked for U.P.I. and Houston Chronicle; with CBS; joined staff of radio Sta. KTRH (CBS affiliate), Houston; staying about 4 years as news writer, reporter, and later, as news dir.; became dir. news and pub. affairs with CBS Houston TV affiliate KHOU-TV, in the late 1950's; became White House corr., 1964; and then transferred to overseas burs., including chief of London bur., 1965-66, then worked in Vietnam, returned to White House position in fall of 1966; appearing nightly on segments of CBS Evening News; became anchorman-corr. for CBS Reports, 1974-75; co-editor 60 Minutes, CBS-TV, 1975-81; anchorman Dan Rather Reporting, CBS Radio Network, 1977—, Midwest desk CBS news coverage of nat. election night returns, 1972-88; mem. CBS news team nat. polit. convs., 1964—; anchorman, mng. editor CBS Evening News with Dan Rather, 1981—; Writer, sportscaster KSAM-TV; co-editor show Who's Who, CBS-TV, 1977; Anchored numerous CBS News spl. programs including: (with Charles Kuralt) co-anchor, The Moon Above, The Earth Below, 1989; as White House corr. accompanied Pres. on numerous travels, including visits to the Mideast, USSR, People's Republic of China. Author: (with Gary Gates) The Palace Guard, 1974, (with Mickey Herskowitz) The Camera Never Blinks, 1977, The Camera Never Blinks Twice: The Further Adventures of a Television Journalist, 1994, (with Peter Wyden) Memoirs, I Remember, 1991. Recipient numerous Emmy awards; honors include dedication of Dan Rather Comm. Bldg., classroom facility Sam Houston State U., Huntsville, Tex. Office: CBS News 524 W 57th St New York NY 10019-2902

RATHER, LUCIA PORCHER JOHNSON, library administrator; b. Durham, N.C., Sept. 12, 1934; d. Cecil Slayton and Lucia Lockwood (Porcher) Johnson; m. John Carson Rather, July 11, 1964; children: Susan Wright, Bruce Carson. Student, Westhampton Coll., 1951-53; A.B. in History, U. N.C., 1955, M.S. in Library Sci., 1957; PhD in History, George Washington U., 1994. Cataloger Library of Congress, Washington, 1957-64; bibliographer Library of Congress, 1964-66, systems analyst, 1966-70; group head MARC Devel. Office, 1970-73, asst. chief, 1973-76, acting chief, 1976-77, dir. for cataloging, 1976-91; Chmn. standing com. on cataloguing Internat. Fedn. Library Assns., 1976-81; sec. Working Group on Content Designators, 1972-77; chmn. Working Group on Corp. Headings, 1978-79, Internat. ISBD Rev. Com., 1981-87. Co-author: the MARC II Format, 1968. Recipient Libr. Congress Disting. Svc. award, 1991, Disting. Alumnus award U. N.C. Sch. Libr. and Info. Sci., 1992. Mem. ALA (Margaret Mann award 1985, Melvil Dewey award 1991), Phi Beta Kappa. Democrat. Presbyterian. Home: 10308 Montgomery Ave Kensington MD 20895-3327

RATHJENS, GEORGE WILLIAM, political scientist, educator; b. Fairbanks, Alaska, June 28, 1925; s. George William and Jennie (Hansen) R.; m. Lucy van Buttingha Wichers, Apr. 5, 1950; children: Jacqueline, Leslie, Peter. B.S., Yale U., 1946; Ph.D., U. Calif., Berkeley, 1951. Instr. chemistry Columbia U., 1950-53; staff weapons systems evaluation group Dept. Def., 1953-58; research fellow Harvard U., 1958-59; staff spl. asst. to Pres. U.S. for sci. and tech., 1959-60; chief scientist Advanced Research Projects Agy., Dept. Def., 1961, dep. dir., 1961-62; dep. asst. dir. U.S. ACDA, 1962-64, spl. asst. to dir., 1964-65; dir. weapons systems evaluation div. Inst. Def. Analyses, 1965-68; prof. dept. polit. sci. MIT, 1968—. Fellow Am. Acad. Arts and Scis.; mem. Coun. for Livable World (bd. dirs.), Fedn. Am. Scientists (councilor), Fedn. Am. Scientists Fund (chmn.), Coun. Fgn. Rels., Inst. Strategic Studies. Office: Mass Inst Tech 77 Massachusetts Ave Cambridge MA 02139-4301

RATHKE, DALE LAWRENCE, community organizer and financial analyst; b. Rangely, Colo., Mar. 16, 1950; s. Edmann Jacob and Cornelia Ruth (Ratliff) R. BA, Yale U., 1971; MA, Princeton U., 1974, ABD, 1977. Dir. internal ops. Assn. of Cmty. Orgns. for Reform Now (ACORN), New Orleans, 1977—; CFO Citizens' Cons. Inc., New Orleans, 1979—; fin. dir. ACORN Housing Corp., New Orleans, 1984—; pres., sec.-treas. Broad St. Corp., New Orleans, 1986—, Elysian Fields Corp., New Orleans, 1986—, Greenwell Springs Corp., New Orleans, 1989—, ACORN Fund, Inc., New Orleans, 1991—, ACORN Beneficial Assn., Inc., New Orleans, 1991—. Pres., sec.-treas. Assn. for Rights of Citizens, New Orleans, 1980—, ACORN Cultural Trust, Inc., 1988—; active Overture to Cultural Season, 1987—, New Orleans Mus. Art, 1990—. Mem. Yale Club of N.Y.C., Princeton Club of N.Y.C. Avocations: 18th century French furniture, English country homes. Office: ACORN 1024 Elysian Fields Ave New Orleans LA 70117-8402

RATHKE, SHEILA WELLS, advertising and public relations executive; b. Columbia, S.C., Aug. 9, 1943; d. Walter John and Betty Marie (McLaughlin) Wells; m. David Bray Rathke, Sept. 1966 (div. Apr. 1977); 1 child, Erinn Michele. BA summa cum laude, U. Pitts., 1976, postgrad., 1976-77. Loan coord. Equibank, Pitts., 1961-65; office mgr. U.S. Steel Corp., Pitts., 1966-70; various account and mgmt. positions Burson-Marsteller, Pitts., 1977-87, exec. v.p., gen. mgr., 1987-94; CEO Can. ops. Burson-Marsteller, Toronto, Montreal, Ottawa, Vancouver, 1994-96; sr. v.p., dir. corp. devel. Young and Rubicam, Inc., N.Y.C., 1996—; bd. dirs. Y & R Group of Cos., Can., 1994-96; instr. Slippery Rock Coll., Pitts., 1984-85; adviser Exec. Report Mag., Pitts., 1986-88. Trustee U. Pitts., 1976-80; mem. alumni bd. dirs., trustee Robert Morris Coll., 1992-95; bd. dirs. Vocat. Rehab. Ctr., 1987-93, Freewheelers, 1989-92, Pitts. Hist. Soc., River City Brass Band. Named Disting. Alumnus, U. Pitts., 1992. Mem. Female Execs. Am., Am. Assn. Advt. Agys. (chair ea. region 1994-95), Pitts. Advt. Club (bd. dirs. 1988-91, pres. 1990), Alpha Sigma Lambda (charter). Avocations: skiing, reading, gardening, traveling, music. Home: 330 E 38th St New York NY 10016 Office: Young and Rubicam Inc 285 Madison Ave New York NY 10017-6486

RATHMAN, WILLIAM ERNEST, lawyer, minister; b. Middletown, Ohio, Jan. 10, 1927; s. Ernest Daniel and Marguerite (Sebald) R.; m. Constance Schedler, Nov. 28, 1958; children: Marchie, William E. Jr. Grad., Phillips Exeter Acad., 1944; BA, Kenyon Coll., 1948; postgrad., Harvard U., 1950, Ohio State U. Coll. of Law, 1951, United Theol. Seminary, Dayton, Ohio, 1975. Bar: Ohio 1952; ordained to ministry Episc. Ch., 1975. Pvt. practice law Middletown, Ohio, 1952-78; sr. ptnr. Rathman, Elliott & Boyd, Middletown, 1979-84, Rathman, Combs, Schaefer, Valen & Kaup, Middletown, 1985-88, Rathman, Combs, Schaefer & Kaup, Middletown, 1989-95; of counsel, 1995—; spl. counsel to County of Butler, 1956-64, City of Middletown, 1965-66, Ohio Atty. Gen., 1967-69; acting judge Middletown Mcpl. Ct., 1969-74. Pres. Middletown Community Found., 1972-76, Middletown Chamber Found., 1977-80, Butler County Park Commn., 1986-90; trustee-at-large Ohio Found. of Ind. Colls., Columbus, 1972-90; trustee, mem. exec. com. Middletown United Way, 1963-90; trustee Middleton Req. Hosp. Found., 1986-90; adv. bd. Middletown campus Miami U., 1984-90. With USN, 1944-46, capt. USAF, 1959, comdr. Am. Legion, 1965. Named Exec. Yr., Middletown chpt. Nat. Secs. Assn., 1969; recipient Outstanding Community Svc. award Middletown post Am. Legion, 1975, Outstanding Svc. award Parstoral Counselling Svc., 1983, Vol. of Yr. award Middletown Area United Way, 1986. Fellow Am. Coll. Trust and Estate Counsel; mem. ABA (estate tax com. 1966-69), Ohio Bar Assn. (coun. dels. 1980-93), Butler County Bar Assn. (pres. 1980), Middletown Bar Assn. (pres. 1967), Fed. Bar Assn. (pres. Cin. chpt. 1975), Ohio State Bar Found. (trustee 1992-96, Ohio Supreme Ct. bd. of commrs. on grievances and discipline 1996—), City Club (Hamilton, Ohio), Jefferson Lodge, Browns Run Country Club, Masons (master 1959-60), Scottish Rite Valley of Cin. (treas. 1986, 33rd degree mason 1988—, chmn. bd. 1990), Bankers Club. Republican. Episcopalian. Home: 501 Thornhill Ln Middletown OH 45042-3750 Office: Rathman Combs Schaefer & Kaup 2 N Main St Middletown OH 45042-1918

RATHMELL, SANDRA LEE, women's health nurse; b. St. Louis, Apr. 3, 1944; d. Charles Chester and Estelle Lucille (Simon) Dunham; m. Thomas S. Rathmell, Sept. 17, 1965 (div. May 1990); children: John Thomas, Tamara Lynn. Diploma, St. Luke's Hosp., 1965. RN, Ariz., Mo., Del. Staff nurse Dover (Del.) AFB Hosp., 1966-68, Luth. Med. Ctr., St. Louis, 1975-82, Maricopa Med. Ctr., Phoenix, 1982-84, Chandler (Ariz.) Regional Hosp., 1984-96; instr. hosp. postpartum classes, St. Louis, Phoenix. Mem. St. Luke's Alumni Assn.

RATHORE, NAEEM GUL, retired United Nations official; b. Lahore, Punjab, Pakistan, Nov. 21, 1931; arrived in country, 1950; s. Jalaluddin and Zohra (Butt) R.; m. Carol Salima, Sept. 19, 1951; 1 child, Amna Elona. BS, Mich. U., 1952; MA in Polit. Sci., Columbia U., 1955, PhD in Internat. Affairs, 1965. Dir. personnel and adminstrn. UNRWA, Beirut, 1975-76; exec. sec. Internat. Civil Svc. Commn. UN, N.Y.C., 1980-81, sec. First Com., 1980-84, asst. dir. Office Under-Sec. Gen./Dept. Polit. Affairs, 1984-87, chief Div. of Palestinian Rights, 1987-89, acting dir. Dept. Polit. Affairs, 1983—, coord. Pakistan Expatriates in UN Systems, 1992—, adviser to the Pakistan amb., and permanent rep. of Pakistan, 1994—; lectr. Pakistan studies NEar and Mid. E. Inst., Columbia U., N.Y., 1954-55; prof., head dept. internat. affairs U. Islamabad, 1974; active numerous coms., panels and task forces with Office of Human Resources Mgmt., UN, field including chmn. N.Y. Gen. Svc. Classification Appeals and Rev. Com., 1986-92; pres. FICSA, 1971-74; chmn. UN staff com., 1971-74; active External Exam. in Polit. Affairs (France, Japan, others). Author: In Defense of of the International Civil Service: Statements and Submission, 1974, United Nations Secretariat: Problems and Prospects, 1974, other publs. in field; contbr. articles to profl. jours. Mem. Fedn. of Nat. Civil Svcs. (pres. 1971-74). Muslim. Avocations: reading, writing newspaper columns, horseback riding, scuba diving, swimming. Home: 1305 Elm St Concord MA 01742-2103

RATHORE, UMA PANDEY, utilities executive; b. Unnao, India, Mar. 5, 1950; came to U.S., 1978; d. O Nath and R Devi Pandey; m. Ram N.S. Rathore, Dec. 18, 1978; children: Dinesh, Rana. BS, Kanpur U., 1967, MS, 1969. Adviser, Consul Gen. of Iceland to India, 1976-85; v.p. Nevaid Cons., 1974-82; with North Jersey Utilities, Mount Freedom, N.J., 1983—, pres.; sr. ptnr. Translantic Cons.; founder Maxim Imports, 1994—; ind. mgmt. cons. Mem. ethics bd. Randolph Twp., N.J., 1986-91, county and state rep. Shongrum Sch. PTA, 1989—, mem. multicultural com., 1993-94; membership chmn. LWV, 1979-81, com. person Dem. dist. 3 Randolph Twp., 1992, 94, mem. ethics com., 1994, mem. com., 1995; mem. drug action com. Randolph Twp., 1994, 95; mem. Dem. task force N.J. Women's Polit. Caucus, 1994; county and state rep. Randolph Intermediate Sch. PTA, 1993-94; legis. chair Morris County Coun. PTA, counselor Region I; mem. Morris Mus., Macculloch Hall, Frelinghuysen Arboretum. Mem. Internat. Platform Assn., Dau. Brit. Empire (supporting mem.). Democrat. Avocations: reading, jogging, hiking, mountaineering. Home and Office: 3 Hickory Pl Randolph NJ 07869-4528

RATHWELL, PETER JOHN, lawyer; b. Windsor, Ont., Can., Aug. 20, 1943; came to U.S., 1947; s. Harold Wilfred and Jean Isabel (Lucas) R.; m. Ann Wickstrom Williams, Sept. 10, 1977; 1 child, James Michael. BA, U. Ariz., 1965, JD, 1968. Bar: Ariz. 1968. Assoc. Boettcher, Crowder & Schoolitz, Scottsdale, Ariz., 1972-73; ptnr. Snell & Wilmer, Phoenix, 1973—; seminar lectr. Nat. Bus. Inst. Inc., 1987-90. Mem. exec. com. Jr. Achievement Ctrl. Ariz., Phoenix, 1980-92; chmn. scholarship fund St. Mary H.S., 1982-91; mem., chmn. Phoenix Parks Bd., 1982-87; trustee Orme Sch., 1991—, chair devel. com., 1995-96; treas. Smith Scholarship Trust U. Ariz. Law Sch., 1985—. Capt. JAGC, USAF, 1969-72. Fellow State Bar Ariz. Found. (founding mem.), Maricopa County Bar Found. (founding mem.); mem. Am. Bankruptcy Inst., Ariz. Bar Assn. (chmn. discipline hearing com. 1987-93, mem. bankruptcy sect.), S.W. Bankruptcy Conf. (bd. advisors 1995—), Maricopa County Bar Assn. (seminar lectr. 1987), Comml. Law League Am., Phoenix Zoo Wildest Club in Town (founding mem. 1972). Republican. Avocations: fishing, raising cattle, riding, stamp collecting. Home: 4523 E Mountain View Rd Phoenix AZ 85028-5213 Office: Snell & Wilmer 1 Arizona Ctr Phoenix AZ 85004

RATKOWSKI, DONALD J., mechanical engineer, consultant; b. Cleve., July 29, 1938; m. Joyce Ellen Kotlarczyk, July 15, 1961; children: Rhonda, Tamyra, Cheryl, Randall. Student, Ariz. State U.; AAS, Alliance Coll., 1959, DSc (hon.), 1986. Sr. project engr. semiconductor products div. Motorola, 1960-70, 75-77; v.p. engring. Danker & Wohlk, 1970-75; founder, pres. Paragon Optical Inc., 1976-90; exec. v.p. Pilkinton Vision Care, 1987-90, cons., 1990-91; pres. DJR Resources Inc., Chandler, Ariz., 1990—; mem. adv. bd. Am. Sec. Coun., 1988-89; mem. steering com. Optometry Coll., Marcinkowski Acad. Medicine, Poland, 1989-91; founder Rigid Gas Permeable Lens Inst., 1985; speaker Nat. Contact Lens Examiners, 1984-91. Contbr. articles to profl. jours.; patentee in field. Sustaining mem. Rep. Nat. Com., 1983-90; mem. U.S. Congl. Adv. Bd., 1990. Recipient Alumnus of Yr. award Alliance Coll., 1985. Mem. Opticians Assn. Am. (assoc. mem. adv. coun. 1987-88), Contact Lens Soc. Am. (bd. dirs. 1986-88, founder scholarship program 1988, hon. chmn. steering com. edn. fund 1989-91), Contact Lens Mfrs. Assn. chmn. external communication com. 1981-90, bd. dirs. 1982-84, Trailblazer award 1987, program chmn. 1989-90, Leonardo DaVinci award 1990), Ariz. Soc. Plastic Engrs. bd. dirs. 1976-78, 83, v.p. 1980-81, pres. 1981-82), Sigma Tau Gamma (Outstanding Alumni award 1985). Home: 31 E Oakwood Hills Dr Chandler AZ 85248-6200 Office: DJR Resources Inc 574 E Alamo Dr Ste 60 Chandler AZ 85225-1225

RATLIFF, CHARLES EDWARD, JR., economics educator; b. Morven, N.C., Oct. 13, 1926; s. Charles Edward and Mary Katherine (Liles) R.; m. Mary Virginia Heilig, Dec. 8, 1945; children: Alice Ann, Katherine Virginia, John Charles. B.S., Davidson Coll., 1947; A.M., Duke U., 1951, Ph.D., 1955; postgrad., U. N.C., Harvard, Columbia. Instr. econs. and bus. Davidson Coll., 1947-48, asst. prof., 1948-49; scholar econs. Duke, 1949-51; mem. faculty Davidson (N.C.) Coll., 1951—, prof., 1960—, chmn. dept. econs., 1966-83, Charles A. Dana prof., 1967-77, William R. Kenan prof., 1977-92, prof. emeritus, 1992—; prof. econs. Forman Christian Coll., Lahore, Pakistan, 1963-66, 69-70; summer vis. prof. U. N.C. at Charlotte, 1958, 60, Appalachian State U., 1962, Punjab U., Pakistan, 1963-64, Kinnaird Coll., Pakistan, 1965, Fin. Svcs. Acad., Pakistan, 1966, NDEA Inst. in Asian History, 1968; lectr. U.S. Cultural Affairs Office, East and West Pakistan, 1969-70. Author: Interstate Apportionment of Business Income for State Income Tax Purposes, 1962, A World Development Fund, 1987, Economics at Davidson: A Sesquicentennial History, 1987; co-author textbooks and monographs; contbg. author: Dictionary of the Social Sciences, Distinguished Teachers on Effective Teaching, 1986, Those Who Teach, 1988, Britain-USA: A Survey in Key Words, 1991; mem. editorial bd. Growth and Change: A Journal of Urban and Regional Policy, 1993—; contbr. articles to profl. jours. Mem. Mayor's Com. Comty. Rels., Davidson, 1973-80, chmn., 1973-78; mem. Mecklenburg County Housing and Devel. Commn., 1975-81; mem. exec. com. Mecklenburg Dem. Com., 1967-69, precinct com., 1967-69, 72-74, 89—, issues com., 1979—, nat. bd. dirs. Rural Advancement Fund Nat. Sharecroppers Fund, Inc., 1978-94, exec. com., 1981-94, treas., 1981-94; mem. Mecklenburg County Comty. and Rural Devel. Exec. Com., 1981—; bd. dirs. Bread for the World, Inc., 1983-84, Pines Retirement Comty., 1990—, Crisis Assistance Ministry, 1992—, Davidson Coll. Devel. Corp., 1992-95, Our Towns Habitat for Humanity, 1996—; bd. advisors Mecklenburg Ministries, 1992—. Ford Found. rsch. grantee, 1960-61, Fulbright-Hays grantee, 1973; rsch. fellow Inter-Univ. Com. Econ. Rsch. on South, 1960-61; recipient Thomas Jefferson award Davidson Coll., 1972, Gold medalist Prof. of Yr. award Coun. Advancement and Support of Edn., 1985, Tchg. Excellence and Campus Leadership award Sear Roebuck Found., 1991, Hunter-Hamilton Love of Tchr. award, 1992. Mem. AAUP, So. Econ. Assn. (exec. com. 1961-63, v.p. 1975-76, N.C. corr. So. Econ. Jour.), Am. Econ. Assn., So. Fin. Assn. (exec. com. 1966-68), Nat. Tax Assn. (chmn. interstate allocation and apportionment of bus. income com. 1972-74), Assn. Asian Studies, Fulbright Alumni Assn., Old Catawba Soc., Phi Beta Kappa, Omicron Delta Kappa (Teaching award 1991). Home: 301 Pinecrest St PO Box 597 Davidson NC 28036-0597

RATLIFF, FLOYD, biophysics educator, scientist; b. La Junta, Colo., May 1, 1919; s. Charles Frederick and Alice (Hubbard) R.; m. Orma Vernon Priddy, June 10, 1942; 1 child, Merry Alice. BA magna cum laude, Colo. Coll., 1947, DSc (hon.), 1975; MS, Brown U., 1949, PhD, 1950; NRC postdoctoral fellow, Johns Hopkins, 1950-51. Instr., then asst. prof. Harvard U., 1951-54; assoc. Rockefeller Inst., 1954-58; mem. faculty Rockefeller U., 1958-89, prof. biophysics and physiol. psychology, 1966-89, prof. emeritus, 1989—, head lab. biophysics, 1974-86; pres. Harry Frank Guggenheim Found., N.Y.C., 1983-89, bd. dirs., 1983—; rsch. assoc. Sch. Am. Rsch., Santa Fe, N.Mex., 1989—; cons. to govt., 1957-89, to John D. and Catherine T. MacArthur Found., 1986. Author: Mach Bands: Quantitative Studies on Neural Networks in the Retina, 1965, Paul Signac and Color in Neo-Impressionism, 1992, also articles; editor: Studies on Excitation and Inhibition in the Retina, 1974; editorial bd.: Jour. Gen. Physiology, 1969-86. Bd. dirs. Esperanza, Santa Fe, 1990-93, pres., 1992-93. Served to 1st lt. AUS, 1941-45, ETO. Decorated Bronze Star; recipient Howard Crosby Warren medal Soc. Exptl. Psychologists, 1966; Edgar D. Tillyer medal Optical Soc. Am., 1976; medal for disting. service Brown U., 1980; Pisart Vision award N.Y. Assn. for Blind, 1983. Fellow AAAS; mem. NAS, Am. Inst. Physics, Am. Psychol. Assn. (disting. sci. contbn. award 1984), Am. Psychol. Soc. (William James fellow 1989), Manhattan Philos. Soc., Internat. Brain Rsch. Orgh., Am. Philos. Soc., China Inst. Am., Oriental Ceramic Soc. (London), Oriental Ceramic Soc. (Hong Kong), 20th Century Chinese Ceramic Soc., Asia Soc., Japan Soc., Phi Beta Kappa, Sigma Xi. Home: 2215 Calle Cacique Santa Fe NM 87505-4944

RATLIFF, GERALD LEE, dean, speech and theatre educator; b. Middletown, Ohio, Oct. 23, 1944; s. Ray and Peggy (Donisi) R. BA magna cum laude, Georgetown (Ky.) Coll., 1967; MA, U. Cin., 1970; PhD, Bowling Green (Ohio) State U., 1975. Area head English theatre Glenville State Coll., 1970-72; prof., chair theatre Montclair State Coll., Upper Montclair, N.J., 1975-92; dean Sch. Fine and Performing Arts Ind.-Purdue U., Ft. Wayne, Ind., 1993-95; dean Coll. Arts and Architecture Mont. State U., Bozeman, Mont., 1995—; feature writer Lexington (Ky.) Herald-News, 1967-68. Author: Beginning Scene Study: Aristophanes to Albee, 1980, Speech and Drama Club Activities, 1982, Oedipus Trilogy, 1984, Combating Stagefright, 1985, Playscript Interpretation and Production, 1985, (Machiavelli's) The Prince, 1986, (with Suzanne Trauth) Introduction to Musical Theatre, 1986, Playing Scenes: A Sourcebook for Performance, 1993, Playing Contemporary Scenes: A Sourcebook for Performance, 1996; contbr. articles and revs. to profl. jours. Exec. coun. mem. Assn. for Commn. Adminstrn., 1995—; bd. dirs. Am. Conf. Acad. Deans. Fulbright scholar, 1989; recipient Nat. Medallion of Honor award Theta Alpha Phi, 1989; Alumni Assn. faculty rsch. grantee, 1980, 83, 86. Mem. Speech Communication Assn. (legis. coun. 1987-88, chair theatre div. 1986-87), Am. Assn. Theatre in Secondary Edn. (nat. bd. dirs. 1986-87), Secondary Sch. Theatre Assn. (nat. bd. dirs. 1983-86), Internat. Arts Assn. (v.p. 1975-76), Eastern Communication Assn. (exec. sec. 1986-89, 1st v.p. elect 1989, exec. com. 1986—, pres. 1991, Disting. Svc. award 1993), Theta Alpha Phi (nat. pres. 1984-87, nat. coun. 1979-82, 84-87). Avocations: writing, softball. Home: 317 S 16th C Bozeman MT 59715 Office: Mont State U Theatre Dept Bozeman MT 59717

RATLIFF, LOUIS JACKSON, JR., mathematics educator; b. Cedar Rapids, Iowa, Sept. 1, 1931; s. Louis Jackson and Ruth Sara (Sidlinger) R. BA, State U. Iowa, 1953, MA, 1958, PhD, 1961. Lectr. Ind. U., Bloomington, 1961-63, U. Calif., Riverside, 1963-64; asst. prof. math. U. Calif., 1964-67, assoc. prof., 1967-69, prof., 1969—. Author: Chain Conjectures in Ring Theory, 1978; assoc. editor Procs. of AMS, 1987-92, Comm. in Algebra, 1990-95; contbr. articles to profl. jours. 1st lt. USAF, 1953-57. NSF fellow, 1960-62, grantee, 1965-69, 71-88; recipient Disting. Teaching award, U. Calif.-Riverside, 1983. Mem. Am. Math. Soc., Phi Beta Kappa. Democrat. Seventh Day Adventist. Home: 3139 Newell Dr Riverside CA 92507-3147 Office: U Calif Dept Math Riverside CA 92521

RATLIFF, WILLIAM DURRAH, JR., lawyer; b. Gainesville, Tex., Nov. 17, 1921; s. William Durrah and Fay (Tippit) R.; m. Barbara Warner, June 20, 1947; children: William Durrah III, Robert Warner, Bryan Prichard, Barbara Louise, Edwin Brent, Dorothy Jeanne. B.B.A., U. Tex., 1943, LL.B., 1948. Bar: Tex. 1948; cert. in estate planning and probate law, Tex. Ptnr. Shannon, Gracey, Ratliff & Miller, 1968-90, of counsel, 1991—; bd. dirs. Aztec Mfg. Co. Bd. dirs. Southwestern Expn. and Livestock Show. Fellow Tex. Bar Found. (sustaining life), Am. Coll. Trust and Estate Counsel. Clubs: River Crest Country, Fort Worth. Home: 5820 El Campo Ave Fort Worth TX 76107-4640 Office: 500 Throckmorton St Ste 1600 Fort Worth TX 76102-3803

RATMANSKY, ALEXEI, dancer; b. St. Petersburg, Russia. Studied with A. Markeyeva, Pyotr Pestov, Moscow Bolshoi Ballet Sch.; grad. choreographer's divsn., Moscow State Inst. Theatrical Arts, 1992. Dancer Kiev Ballet, 1986-88, prin. dancer, 1988-92; soloist Royal Winnipeg (Man., Can.) Ballet, 1992—; guest artist Ballet Nat. du Québec. Dance performances include Tarantella (George Ballanchine), Spectre de la Rose (Michel Fokine), Giselle (Peter Wright), La Sylphide, Cinderella, Square Dance (Ballanchine), Tchaikovsky Pas de Deux (Ballanchine), Lilac Garden (Antony Tudor), La Bayadere Act II (Petipa), Nutcracker (John Neumeier), Romeo and Juliet (Rudi van Dantzig), Don Quixote, Pas de Dix (Ballanchine). Recipient First prize Second Nat. Ballet Competition, Donietsk, Russia, 1987, Vaslav Nijinsky prize First Internat. Diaghilev Ballet Competition, Moscow, 1992, 2nd prize for choreography Serge Lifar Ballet Competition, 1994; named Honored Artist of Ukraine, 1992.

RATNER, ALBERT B., building products company executive, land developer; b. Cleve., 1927. Grad., Mich. State U., 1951. With Forest City Enterprises, Inc., Cleve., 1964—, sec., 1960-68, exec. v.p., from 1968, now pres., chief exec. officer, dir., also co-chmn brd; mem. exec. com., dir. Univ. Circle Devel. Corp.; dir. Am. Greetings Corp. Mem. Internat. Council Shopping Ctrs. Office: Forest City Enterprises Inc 10800 Brookpark Rd Cleveland OH 44130-1119*

RATNER, BUDDY DENNIS, bioengineer, educator; b. Bklyn., Jan. 19, 1947; s. Philip and Ruth Ratner; m. Teri Ruth Stoller, July 7, 1968; 1 child, Daniel Martin. BS in Chemistry, Bklyn. Coll., 1967; PhD in Polymer Chemistry, Polytech. Inst. Bklyn., 1972. Postdoctoral fellow U. Wash., Seattle, 1972-73, from rsch. assoc. to assoc. prof., 1973-86, prof., 1986—; dir. Nat. ESCA and Surface Analysis Ctr., Seattle, 1984-96; dir. U. Washington Engineered Biomaterials NSF Engring. Rsch. Ctr., 1996—. Editor: Surface Characterization of Biomaterials, 1989, Plasmas and Polymers, 1994—; mem. editl. bds. 9 jours. and book series; contbr. more than 270 articles to profl. jours. Recipient faculty achievement/outstanding rsch. award Burlington Resources Found., 1990, Perkin Elmer Phys. Electronics award for excellence in surface sci.; grantee NIH. Fellow AAAS, Am. Inst. Med. Biol. Engring. (founder), Am. Vacuum Soc.; mem. AIChE, Adhesion Soc., Am. Chem. Soc., Internat. Soc. Contact Lens Rsch., Materials Rsch. Soc., Soc. for Biomaterials (pres. 1991, 92, Clemson award 1989, fellow 1994). Achievements include 10 patents in field. Office: U Wash Dept Chem Engring PO Box 351750 Seattle WA 98195

RATNER, DAVID LOUIS, legal educator; b. London, Sept. 2, 1931. AB magna cum laude, Harvard U., 1952, LLB magna cum laude, 1955. Bar: N.Y. 1955. Assoc. Sullivan & Cromwell, N.Y.C., 1955-64; assoc. prof. Cornell Law Sch., Ithaca, N.Y., 1964-68, prof., 1968-82; prof. law U. San Francisco Law Sch., 1982—, dean, 1982-89; exec. asst. to chmn. SEC, Washington, 1966-68; chief counsel Securities Industry Study, Senate Banking Com., Washington, 1971-73; vis. prof. Stanford (Calif.) U., 1974, Ariz. State U., Tempe, 1974, U. San Francisco, 1980, Georgetown U., Washington, 1989-90, U. Calif., Hastings, San Francisco, 1992; mem. Larkspur (Calif.) Planning Commn., 1992—. Fulbright scholar Monash U., Australia, 1981. Author: Securities Regulation: Cases and Materials, 5th edit., 1996, Securities Regulation in a Nutshell, 5th edit., 1996, Institutional Investors: Teaching Materials, 1978. Fellow Royal Soc. Arts (London); mem. Am. Law Inst., Cosmos Club (Washington), Phi Beta Kappa. Home: 84 Polhemus Way Larkspur CA 94939-1928 Office: U San Francisco Law Sch 2130 Fulton St San Francisco CA 94117-1080

RATNER, ELLEN FAITH, radio talk show host, writer; b. Cleve., Aug. 28, 1951; d. Harry Ramer and Anne Spott. BA, Goddard Coll., 1974; EdM, Harvard U., 1978. Coord. women's svcs. Homophile Comty. Health Svc., Boston, 1971-73; co-dir., co-founder Boundaries Therapy Ctr., Acton, Mass., 1973-86; dir. psychiat. day treatment program South Shore Mental Health Ctr., Quincy, Mass., 1974-81; v.p. rsch., devel. and svc., dir. ARC Rsch. Found. Addiction Recovery Corp., Rockville, Mass., 1986-90; health care cons., dir. Found. for Addiction Rsch., 1990-94; pres. Talk Radio News Svc., White House corr. Good Day USA "The Washington Reality Check", Washington, 1991—; pres. Talk Radio News Svc. White House corr. Good Day USA "Washington Day", 1995; tchr. Curry Coll., Milton, Mass., 1979-80; cons. program devel. Addiction Recovery Corp., 1984-86; developer, planner The Art's in Mileau Treatment of Phychiatric Outpatients, Quincy, 1980, New Eng.'s first conf. on Chem. Dependency and AIDS, 1988. Author: The Other Side of the Family: A Book for Recovery from Abuse, Incest and Neglect, 1990; appeared on nat. TV and radio shows including C-SPAN, The Oprah Winfrey Show, CNN, Nat. Empowerment TV, others; mem. adv. bd. The Counselor Mag., 1987-90. Bd. trustees, mem. exec. com., vis. com. presdl. search com. Goddard Col., Plainfield, Vt. 1977-81; bd. trustees Samaritan Coll., L.A., 1988-90; bd. dirs. Nat. Lesbian and Gay Health Found., Washington, 1985-92, pres., exec. com., program com., program chair; v.p. Harry Ratner Human Svcs. Fund, Cleve., 1991—; mem. adv. bd. Women of Washington, Inc., 1992—; bd. dirs. Theater Chamber Players, Kennedy Ctr., Washington, 1988-91, An Uncommon Legacy Found., N.Y.C., 1993—, The Ctr. for Spiritual Enlightment, Falls Church, Va., 1994—. Recipient Comty. Svc. award Lesbian and Gay Counseling Svc., Boston, 1985, The Addams-Brown award Nat. Lesbian and Gay Health Found., 1993. Mem. Nat. Assn. Radio Talk Show Hosts, Mass. Assn. Day treatment Adminstrs. (chair regulations and standards com. 1979-81), Lily Dale Assembly. Democrat. Jewish. Avocation: writing works on spiritualism. Office: Talk Radio News Svc 2514 Mill Rd NW Washington DC 20007-2950

RATNER, GERALD, lawyer; b. Chgo., Dec. 17, 1913; s. Peter I. and Sarah (Soreson) R.; m. Eunice Payton, June 18, 1948. PhB, U. Chgo., 1935, JD cum laude, 1937. Bar: Ill. 1937. Since practiced in Chgo.; sr. ptnr. Gould & Ratner and predecessor firm, 1949—; officer Henry Crown & Co., CC Industries, Inc., Material Svc. Corp., Freeman United Coal Mining Co., Mineral and Land Resources Corp.; lectr., writer on real estate law; mem. vis. com. for Law Sch., U. Chgo. Capt. AUS, 1942-46. Mem. ABA, Ill. Bar Assn., Chgo. Bar Assn., Order of Coif, U. Chgo. Pres. Coun. and Endowment Assn., Phi Beta Kappa. Home: 900 Lake Shore Dr Apt 2902 Chicago IL 60611 Office: 222 N La Salle St Chicago IL 60601-1003

RATNER, HARVEY, health club owner, operator; m. Barbara Ratner; children: Mark, Edward, David, Rachel. Co-founder Northwest Racquet, Swim and Health Clubs, Minn., 1963—; co-owner Minn. Timberwolves (NBA), Mpls., 1989-95; owner, operator Northwest Racquet Club, St. Louis Park, Minn., 1995—. Supporter numerous Mpls.-St. Paul charities including Crisis Nursery Ctr., Groves Learning Ctr., Mpls. Children's Med. Ctr., Intervarsity Christian Fellowship, Mpls. Fedn., also arts orgns. Office: Minn Timberwolves Northwest Racquet Club 5525 Cedar Lake Rd Saint Louis Park MN 55416

RATNER, MARK ALAN, chemistry educator; b. Cleve., Dec. 8, 1942; s. Max and Betty (Wohlvert) R.; m. Nancy Ball, June 19, 1969; children—Stacy, Daniel. A.B., Harvard U., 1964; Ph.D., Northwestern U., 1969; Amanuensis (hon.), Aarhus U., Denmark, 1970; Akad Rat (hon.), Tech. U., Munich, W. Ger., 1971. Asst. prof. NYU, 1971-75; prof. chemistry Northwestern U., Evanston, Ill., 1975—, Dow rsch. prof., 1988-90; cons. U.S. Army, Huntsville, Ala., 1973-75; lectr. IBM, Yorktown Heights, N.Y., 1973; dir. Electrochem. Industries, Israel, 1980—; assoc. dean arts and scis. Northwestern U., Evanston, 1980-84; vis. prof. Rush Presbyn. Sch. Medicine, 1990—. Contbr. numerous articles and manuscripts to profl. jours. Bd. dirs. Hillel Found., Evanston, 1984—. Fellow A.P. Sloan Found., 1973-76, Inst. Advanced Study, Israel, 1979. Fellow AAAS, Am. Phys. Soc.; mem. Am. Chem. Soc., Rumplestiltskin Soc., Sigma Xi. Jewish. Avocations: scientific education; canoeing; conservation. Home: 615 Greenleaf Ave Glencoe IL 60022-1745 Office: Northwestern U Chemistry Dept 2145 Sheridan Rd Evanston IL 60208-0834

RATNOFF, OSCAR DAVIS, physician, educator; b. N.Y.C., Aug. 23, 1916; s. Hyman L. and Ethel (Davis) R.; m. Marian Foreman, Mar. 31, 1945; children: William Davis, Martha. AB, Columbia U., 1936, MD, 1939; LLD, U. Aberdeen, 1981; ScD (hon.), Case Western Res. U., 1996. Intern Johns Hopkins Hosp., Balt., 1939-40; Austin fellow in physiology Harvard Med. Sch., Boston, 1940-41; asst. resident Montefiore Hosp., N.Y.C., 1942; resident Goldwater Meml. Hosp., N.Y.C., 1942-43; asst. in medicine Columbia Coll. Physicians and Surgeons, N.Y.C., 1942-46; fellow in medicine Johns Hopkins, 1946-48, instr. medicine, 1948-50, instr. bacteriology, 1949-50; asst. prof. medicine Western Res. U., Cleve., 1950-56; assoc. prof. Case Western Res. U., 1956-61, prof., 1961—; asst. physician (Univ. Hosp.), Cleve., 1952-56; assoc. physician (Univ. Hosp.), 1956-67, physician, 1967—. Author: Bleeding Syndromes, 1960; mem. editorial bd. Jour. Lab. Clin. Medicine, 1956-62, assoc. editor, 1986-91; editor: Treatment of Hemorrhagic Disorders, 1968, (with C. D. Forbes) Disorders of Hemostasis, 1984, 2d edit., 1991; mem. editorial bd. Circulation, 1961-65, Blood, 1963-69, 78-81, Am. Jour. Physiology, 1966-72, Jour. Applied Physiology, 1966-72, Jour. Lipid Rsch., 1967-69, Jour. Clin. Investigation, 1969-71, Circulation Rsch., 1970-75, Annals Internal Medicine, 1973-76, Perspectives in Biology and Medicine, 1974—, Thrombosis Rsch., 1981-84, Jour. Urology, 1981-88, Internat. Jour. Hematology, 1991—; contbr. articles to med. jours. Career investigator Am. Heart Assn., 1960-86. Served to maj. M.C., 1943-46, Ind. Recipient Henry Moses award Montefiore Hosp., 1949, Disting. Achievement award Modern Medicine, 1967, James F. Mitchell award, 1971, Murray Thelin award Nat. Hemophilia Found., 1971, H.P. Smith award Am. Soc. Clin. Pathology, 1975, Joseph Mather Smith prize Columbia Coll. Physicians and Surgeons, 1976, Disting. Achievemtn in Med. Sci. award U. Hosps. of Cleve, 1992, Saltzman award Mt. Sinai Hosp. of Cleve., 1994; named to Heart Hall of Fame, N.E. Ohio Heart Assn., 1989. Master ACP (John Phillips award 1974); fellow AAAS; mem. NAS (Kovalenko award 1985), AMA, Am. Fedn. Clin. Rsch., Soc. Scholars Johns Hopkins U., Am. Soc. Clin. Investigation, Ctrl. Soc. Clin. Rsch. (Disting. Svc. award 1992), Assn. Am. Physicians (Kober lectr. 1985, Kober medal 1988), Am. Soc. Hematology (Dameshek award 1972), Internat. Soc. Hematology, Internat. Soc. Thrombosis (Grant award 1981, spl. award 1993), Am. Physiol. Soc., Am. Soc. Biol. Chemists. Home: 2916 Sedgewick Rd Cleveland OH 44120-1840 Office: Univ Hosps of Cleve Cleveland OH 44106

RATNY, RUTH LUCILLE, publishing company executive, writer; b. Chgo., Dec. 8, 1937; d. Herman Joseph and Bertha (Levy) R. Student, De Paul U., 1950-54. Creative v.p. Niles Communications Ctrs., Chgo., 1954-64; prin. Ruth L. Ratny Mktg. Communications, Chgo., 1964-69; owner Screen mag., Chgo., 1979—; bd. dirs. Ind. Feature Project/Midwest. Bd. dirs. Chgo. Internat. Film Festival. Named Advt. Women of Yr., 1979, Midwest Advt. Person of Yr., 1979; recipient Recognition award Chgo. Coalition, 1983, Clio awards, 1960-61, Women in Film's Recognition award, 1993. Mem. Women in Film, Women's Advt. Club, Pearl S. Buck Found. Mem. Christian Sci. Ch.

RATTAZZI, SERENA, art museum and association administrator; b. Taranto, Italy, Aug. 20, 1935; came to U.S., 1969; d. Umberto and Ligetta (Maresca) Bardelli; m. Mario Cristiano Rattazzi, Jan. 15, 1962; 1 child, Claudia. BA, Liceo Umberto I, Naples. Italy, 1953; MSW, U. Naples, 1958; postgrad. in legal problems of mus. adminstrn., Am. Legal Inst., ABA, 1985, 86, 87, 89. Pub. rels., publs. asst. Albright-Knox Art Gallery, Buffalo, 1974-76, coord. pub. rels., 1976-82, asst. dir. for adminstrn., 1982-84; asst. dir. for adminstrn. The Bklyn. Mus., 1984-85, vice dir. for adminstrn., 1985-89, assoc. dir., 1989-90; dir. Am. Fedn. Arts, N.Y.C., 1990—; adv. bd. The Pitts. Ctr. for Arts, 1989-92, A.I.R. Gallery, N.Y.C., 1990-93; field reviewer Inst. Mus. Svcs., Washington, 1990; adv. coun. dept. art history and archaeology Columbia Univ., 1992—. Mem. ArtTable Inc. (bd. dirs. 1986-88, pres. 1986-88), Am. Assn. Museums (standing profl. com. on pub. rels. mgmt. 1978-82, bd. 1990—). Avocation: reading. Office: Am Fedn Arts 41 E 65th St New York NY 10021-6508

RATTERMAN, DAVID BURGER, lawyer; b. Louisville, Sept. 8, 1946; s. Joseph A. and Esther M. (Burger) R.; m. Mary Miles Sledd, May 31, 1969; children—Andrew August, Sara Chandler. B.S.M.E., U. Ky., 1968; J.D., U. Louisville, 1975, M.B.A., 1980. Bar: Ky. 1976, U.S. Dist. Ct. (we. dist.) Ky. 1976, U.S. Dist. Ct. (so. dist.) Ga. 1979, U.S. Ct. Claims 1990, U.S. Ct. Appeals (6th cir.) 1986, U.S. Ct. Appeals (5th cir.) 1987, U.S. Ct. Appeals (Fed. cir.) 1991, U.S. Supreme Ct. 1981. Design engr. Square D Co., Lexington, Ky., 1968-70; ptnr. Goldberg & Simpson, Louisville, 1975—; tchr. seminars in constrn. law; legal counsel Ky. Council for the Blind, 1975-85. Contbr. articles to profl. jours. Mem. sch. bd. St. Leonard Sch., 1981-84, pres. 1983-84; counsel County Govt. Handicapped Compliance Commn., 1980-85; bd. dirs. United Crescent Hill Ministries, 1974-81, Clifton Neighborhood Devel. Corp., 1974-81. Served with USN, 1970-73, to comdr. Res. Decorated Naval Commendation medal. Fellow Am. Bar Found. (sustaining life fellow), Am. Inst. Steel Constrn. (sec., gen. counsel 1989—), Am. Coll. Constrn. Lawyers; mem. ABA, Am. Arbitration Assn., Ky. Bar Assn. (ho. of dels. 1986-92, founding chmn. sect. constrn. and pub. contract law), Louisville Bar Assn., Constrn. Specifications Inst., Rotary Club Louisville (bd. dirs. 1991-93). Roman Catholic. Home: Unit 209 2525 George Rogers Clark Pl Louisville KY 40206-2505 Office: Goldberg & Simpson 3000 National City Tower Louisville KY 40202

RATTHAHAO, SISOUPHANH, minister. Dir. Lao Ministry Dist. of the Christian and Missionary Alliance.

RATTI, RONALD ANDREW, economics educator; b. Neath, West Glamorgan, Wales, Oct. 10, 1948; came to U.S., 1970; s. Ronald Rudolph and Janet (Marshall) R. BA, U. Lancaster, 1970; MA, Case Western Res. U., 1972; PhD, So. Meth. U., 1975. Asst. prof. to assoc. prof. U. Mo., Columbia, 1975-85, prof. econs., 1985—, chmn. dept., 1982-89; vis. scholar Fed. Res. Bank Kansas City, Mo., 1978, Fed. Res. Bank St. Louis., 1984-85; acad. visitor London Sch. Econs., 1985. Contbr. articles to profl. jours. Office: U Mo Dept Econs 118 Profl Bldg Columbia MO 65211

RATTLE, SIMON, conductor; b. Liverpool, Eng., 1955. Studied conducting and piano, Royal Acad. Music; PhD (hon.), Birmingham U., 1985. At age 15 occasional percussion player Royal Liverpool Philharm. Orch.; prin. condr., artistic adviser City of Birmingham Symphony Orch., 1980-91, mus. dir., 1990—; prin. guest condr. L.A. Philharm. Orch., 1981-93, princ. guest condr. of the Orch. of the Age of Enlightenment, 1992—, Rotterdam Philharm. Orch., 1981-84; prin. condr. London Choral Soc., 1979-84; assoc. condr. Royal Liverpool Philharm. Orch., 1977-80, BBC Scottish Symphony Orch., 1977-80; artistic dir. South Bank Summer Music, 1981-83; asst. condr. Bournemouth Symphony Orch. and Bournemouth Sinfonietta, 1974-76; debut at Glyndebourne Festival Opera, 1977, appeared regularly since; debuts at English Nat. Opera, 1985, Berlin Philharmonic, 1987, Los Angeles Opera, 1988, Royal Opera House, 1990, Vienna Philharmonic, 1993, Philadelphia Orchestra, 1993. Decorated comdr. Brit. Empire, knight Brit. Empire; chevalier des Arts et Lettres (France); recipient 1st prize John Player Internat. Condrs. Competition, 1974, Edison award, 1987, Gramophone Record of Yr., 1988, Gramophone Opera award, 1989, Internat. Record Critics award, 1990, Grand Prix in Honorem de l'Academie Charles Cros, 1990, Artist of Yr. Gramophone award, 1993, Montblanc de la Culture prize, Paris, 1993. Office: care Harold Holt Ltd, 31 Sinclair Rd, London W14 ONS, England also: Frank Salomon Assoc 201 W 54th St Apt 4C New York NY 10019-5521

RATTNER, JEROME BERNARD, biologist, anatomist, educator; b. Cin., Sept. 12, 1945; m. Eileen; children: John P., Nathalie. BS, Miami U., 1967; MS, U. Tex., 1969; PhD in Biology, Washington U., 1973. Fellow cell biology U. Calif., Irvine, 1973-75, rsch. asst., 1976-81; NATO fellow in biology Nat. Ctr. Sci. Rsch., France, 1975-76; asst. prof. anatomy, molecular biology U. Calgary, Can., 1981-85, assoc. prof. anatomy Dept. Med. Biochemistry, 1985—. Office: U CalgaryDept Med Biochemistry, 3330 Hospital Dr NW, Calgary, AB Canada T2N 4N1*

RATTNER, STEVEN LAWRENCE, investment banker; b. N.Y.C., July 5, 1952; s. George Seymour and Selma Ann (Silberman) R.; m. P. Maureen White, June 22, 1986; children: Rebecca White, Daniel Irvin, David William, James Brennan. AB in Econ. honors, Brown U., 1974. Asst. to James Reston, corr. N.Y. Times, Washington, N.Y.C., London, 1974-82; assoc., v.p. Lehman Bros. Kuhn Loeb, N.Y.C., 1982-84; assoc., v.p., prin., mng. dir., head communications group Morgan Stanley & Co., N.Y.C., 1984-89; mng. dir., head comms. group Lazard Fréres & Co., LLC, N.Y.C., 1989—; dir. Falcon Cable Holding Group, 1993—. Contbr. articles to various publs. including N.Y. Times, Wall St. Jour., L.A. Times, Newsweek. Trustee Brown U., 1987-93, 94—, Met. Mus. Art, 1996—; trustee Ednl. Broadcasting Corp., 1990—, vice chmn., 1994—; dir. N.Y.C. Outward Bound Ctr., 1990—; mem. bd. advisors Russian-Am. Press and Info. Ctr., 1993—. Harvey Baker fellow Brown U. 1974, Poynter fellow Yale, 1979. Mem. Coun. Fgn. Rels., Royal Inst. for Internat. Affairs (assoc.). Home: 998 5th Ave New York NY 10028-0126

RATTNER, WILLIAM EDWARD, lawyer; b. Chgo., Sept. 26, 1936; s. Herbert and Ethel (Weiss) R.; m. Gale Golovan, Nov. 27, 1963; 1 child, David Herbert. BS in Econ., U. Pa., 1958; JD, Harvard U., 1961. Bar: Ill. 1962, U.S. Dist. Ct (no. dist.) Ill. 1962, U.S. Ct. Appeals (7th cir.) 1963, U.S. Tax Ct. 1969, U.S. Dist. Ct. (no. dist.) Tex. 1989. Atty. Peterson, Lowry, Rall, Barber & Ross, Chgo., 1962-67, Schwartz & Freeman, Chgo., 1967-72; ptnr. Levy & Erens, Chgo., 1972-86, Hopkins & Sutter, Chgo., 1986—; adj. prof. Northwestern U. Law Sch. Vice chmn., pres. Chgo. chpt., nat. bd. govs. Am. Jewish Com.; chmn. City of Evanston (Ill.) Bd. Ethics. With U.S. Army, 1961-67. Mem. ABA, Chgo. Bar Assn. (vice chmn. urban affairs com. 1970-72), 7th Cir. Bar Assn., Chgo. Coun. Lawyers, Mid-Day Club. Home: 1046 Michigan Ave Evanston IL 60202-1436 Office: Hopkins & Sutter 3 First National Plz Chicago IL 60602

RATZENBERGER, JOHN DESZO, actor, writer, director; b. Bridgeport, Conn., Apr. 6, 1947; s. Dezso Alexander and Bertha (Grohowski) R.; m. Elizabeth Georgia Stiny, Sept. 9, 1984; children: James John, Nina Katherine. Grad. high sch., Bridgeport, Conn.; Doctorate, Sacred Heart U., 1992. Actor, writer, dir. own theater troupe Sal's Meat Market, 1971-75; touring actor Europe, 1971-81; pres., founder Eco-Pack Industries, Kent, Wash. Appeared in plays Curse of the Starving Class, The Connection; films include The Ritz (film debut), 1974, Yanks, Ragtime, Motel Hell, Superman I, II, A Bridge Too Far, Firefox, The Empire Strikes Back, Protocol, Gandhi, Outland; TV performances include Songs of a Sourdough, The Good Soldier, (series) Cheers, 1982-1993; co-author TV plays: Friends in Space, 1978, Scalped, 1979. Recipient cash award Arts Council of Great Britain. Mem. AFTRA, SAG, Writers Guild Am., Dirs. Guild, Am. Farmland Trust, Brit. Actors Equity Assn., Greenpeace, Wilderness Soc., Nat. Resources Def. Coun., Sierra Club (San Francisco). Avocations: sailing, reading, woodworking.

RATZLAFF, JAMES W., investment company executive. BS, U. Kans., 1958; JD, George Washington U., 1968. Sr. ptnr. Capital Group Ptnrs., L.P., 1991—; pres. bd. dirs. Fundamental Investors, Am. Balanced Fund, AMCAP Fund, Am. Funds Svc. Co., The Growth Fund of Am., The Income Fund of Am.; vice chmn., bd. dirs. Am. Mut. Fund; exec. v.p., bd. dirs. The Investment Co. of Am.; bd. dirs. New Perspective Fund. Office: Capital Rsch & Mgmt Co PO Box 7650 4 Embarcadero Ctr San Francisco CA 94111-4106

RATZLAFF, RUBEN MENNO, religion educator, minister; b. Burrton, Kans., Jan. 8, 1917; s. Henry and Julia (Foth) R.; m. Frances Irene King,

Sept. 7, 1941; children: Keith Lowell, Paul Dennis, Mark Henry, Loren Lee; m. Doris Carr Arneson, Aug. 1, 1992. BA, Johnson Bible Coll., 1940; BD, Butler U., 1955, MA, 1959. Ordained to ministry Chs. of Christ, 1938. Min. Pleasant Hill Christian Ch., Hall, Ind., 1948-50; min. Christian Ch., Clermont, Ind., 1950-55, Kennard, Ind., 1955-59; prof. San Jose (Calif.) Christian Coll., 1959—; ann. vis. lectr. Springdale Coll., Selly Oak Colls., Birmingham, Eng., 1985—; vis. lectr. Zimbabwe Christian Coll., Harare, 1995. Author: Ezra Nehemiah, 1982; contbr. articles to profl. jours. Recipient Hebrew award Hebrew Synagogue, 1950. Mem. Theta Phi. Home: 1567 Willowdale Dr San Jose CA 95118-1346 Also: 72 Wellman Croft, Selly Oak, Birmingham B29 6NS, England Office: San Jose Christian Coll 790 S 12th St San Jose CA 95112-2304 *What amazes me most is that God the Almighty sends His Son to knock at our door, and wait with His hat in His hand while we decide whether to follow Him.*

RATZLAFF, VERNON PAUL, elementary education educator, consultant; b. Mt. Lake, Minn., May 16, 1925; s. Peter Benjamin and Helen (Dick) R.; m. Bonnie Lou Sommers, Dec. 17, 1955; children: Paul, Gwen, Jay, Peter. BA in Elem. Edn., German, Goshen Coll., 1954; MA, U. N.D., 1971; student, U. Minn., 1956-57, U. Oreg., 1965, U. No. Ariz., 1968. Cert. tchr. Elem. tchr. Richfield (Minn.) Pub. Schs., 1954-74; tchr. Tuba City (Ariz.) Pub. Sch., 1975—; resource person to tchrs., Grand Forks, N.C., 1970-72, resource person to upper elem. tchrs. and children, Richfield, 1967-70; adminstr. of Christian Sch. Hopi Mission, Oraibi, Ariz., 1971-75; math tchr. Nortland Pioneer Coll.; established "Look Folks-No Fail" classrooms. Author: Side by Side " Up from the Pit to Become a Shining Star" (Where Students Take Responsibility for Learning), 1990; contbr. articles to numerous jours. Mem. NEA, Ariz. Edn. Assn., Am. Assn. Retired People. Republican. Avocations: cooking, painting, writing, gardening, preaching. Home: 440 Circle View Dr Flagstaff AZ 86001-4812 *Personal philosophy: Tell me, I forget, Show me, I remember, Involve me, I understand.*

RAU, DAVID EDWARD, real estate company executive; b. Lincoln, Nebr., Sept. 27, 1956; s. Leo George and Anne Marie (Pavel) R.; m. Kathy Georgette Wilcox, May 17, 1980; children: Andrew David, Peter Nicholas, Victoria Anne. BBA, U. Ariz., 1978. CPA, Ariz., N.Mex. Sr. Peat Marwick Main, Albuquerque, 1978-82; supervising sr. Peat Marwick Main, Phoenix, 1982-83; asst. treas. Kroy Inc., Scottsdale, Ariz., 1983-85; acct. Zolondek & Blumenthal, Phoenix, 1985; v.p., controller Del Webb Corp., Phoenix, 1985—; bd. dirs. Ariz. Tax Rsch. Assn. Chmn. Phoenix chpt. walk Juvenile Diabetes Found., 1990, pres. 1992, 93, 94; mem. Ariz. Town Hall; advisor Phoenix Sky Harbour Ctr. Tech. Adv. Panel, 1987; treas. Drugs Don's Work in Ariz., 1994—. Mem. Ariz. Soc. CPAs, Albuquerque Jaycees (treas. 1981-82), Nat. Assn. Real Estate Cos. (tax com.), Ariz. C. of C. (bd. dirs.), Beta Alpha Psi. Republican. Roman Catholic. Avocations: skiing, fishing, family. Office: Del E Webb Corp 2231 E Camelback Rd Phoenix AZ 85016-3453

RAU, LEE ARTHUR, lawyer; b. Mpls., July 22, 1940; s. Arthur W. and Selma A. (Lund) R.; m. Janice R. Childress, June 27, 1964; children—Brendan D., Patrick C., Brian T. BSB, U. Minn., 1962; JD, UCLA, 1965. Bar: Calif. 1966, D.C. 1972, Va. 1986, U.S. Dist. Ct. D.C. 1973, U.S. Dist. Ct. (ea. dist.) Va. 1988, U.S. Ct. Mil. Appeals 1966, U.S. Ct. Appeals (D.C. cir.) 1972, U.S. Ct. Appeals (3d cir.) 1975, U.S. Ct. Appeals (6th cir.) 1980, U.S. Ct. Appeals (4th cir.) 1988, U.S. Supreme Ct. 1971. Trial atty. evaluation sect. antitrust div. U.S. Dept. Justice, Washington, 1965-66, appellate sect., 1970-72; assoc. Reed Smith Shaw & McClay, Washington, 1972-74, ptnr., 1975—; former mem. constl. and adminstrv. law adv. com. Nat. Chamber Litigation Ctr. Inc.; sec., bd. dirs. Old Dominion Land Co., Inc. Contbr. articles to profl. jours. Sec. bd. dris. Reston Found., 1982-93; bd. dirs. Reston Interfaith Inc., 1973-89, pres. 1984-88; bd. dirs. Greater Reston Arts Ctr., 1988-96, pres., 1989-91, sec., 1991-95; mem. Washington Dulles Task Force, 1982-91; mem. exec. com. and ops. com. Fairfax-Falls Ch. United Way, mem. regional coun., 1988-92. Capt. JAGC, U.S. Army, 1966-70. Named Restonian of Yr., 1990; decorated Commendation with oak leaf cluster; recipient Best of Reston award. Mem. ABA (antitrust, adminstrv. law, corp. banking and bus., sci. and tech. sects.), D.C. Bar Assn. (past chmn. energy study group), Calif. Bar Assn., U.S. C. of C. (antitrust policy com.). Democrat. Lutheran. Home: 1930 Upper Lakes Dr Reston VA 22091-3620 Office: Reed Smith Shaw & McClay 8251 Greensboro Dr Ste 1100 Mc Lean VA 22102-3809

RAU, RALPH RONALD, retired physicist; b. Tacoma, Sept. 1, 1920; s. Ralph Campbell and Ida (Montgall) R.; m. Maryjane Uhrlaub, June 2, 1944; children: Whitney Leslie, Little Elise. B.S. in Physics, Coll. Puget Sound, 1941; M.S. in Physics, Calif. Inst. Tech., 1943, Ph.D. in Physics, 1948. Asst. prof. physics Princeton U., 1947-56; Fulbright research prof. physics Ecole Polytechnique, Paris, 1954-55; physicist Brookhaven Nat. Lab., Upton, N.Y., 1956-66; chmn. dept. physics Brookhaven Nat. Lab., 1966-70, assoc. dir. for high energy physics, 1970-81; adj. prof. U. Wyo.; vis. prof. MIT, 1984-88; staff scientist Desy Lab., Hamburg, Fed. Republic Germany, 1984-85. Trustee U. Puget Sound, 1978-84. Named Alumnus Cum Laude U. Puget Sound, 1968; recipient Alexander von Humboldt U.S. Sr. Scientist award 1988. Mem. Am. Phys. Soc., N.Y. Acad. Sci. Office: Brookhaven Nat Lab Upton NY 11973

RAU, ROBERT NICHOLAS, pipe distribution executive; b. Phila., Oct. 14, 1927; s. Nicholas A. and Mary A. (McCandless) R.; m. Alice Marie Farrington, May 21, 1949; children: Robert N., Donna-Marie Murphy, Karen Gamble, Patricia A. Pinkston. Student, Drexel U., 1947-48. Clk. to inside sales Hajoca Corp., Phila., Lansdale, Pa., 1951-54; inside sales to v.p. Standard Pipe and Supply, Bala Cynwyd, Pa., 1954-71; pres. BBL Co., Kulpsville, Pa., 1971-94, CEO, 1994—. Contbr. articles to profl. jours. Coach Spl. Olympics, 1982—; active Boy Scouts of Am. With USN, 1945-46, PTO. Named Vol. of Yr., Spl. Olympics, 1991, Knowles-Rubin Steine Award of Excellence, 1996. Mem. ASTM (sec. 1975—), Nat. Assn. Steel Pipe Distbrs. (dir. 1977—, v.p. 1988-89, pres. 1989-92, Pres.' award 1992, award of Excellence 1996). Republican. Roman Catholic. Avocations: cross country skiing, spl. olympics, grandchildren, travel.

RAU, WILLIAM ARTHUR, management consultant; b. Portsmouth, Ohio, May 29, 1939; s. Arthur Henry and Ruth (Carson) R.; m. Carolyn Jackson, Oct. 21, 1972; children: Sarah Ruth, Anne Forest, Katherine Carson, Arthur Henry II. BS in Arts and Scis., Ohio U., 1963, MS in Accountancy, 1967, MBA in Gen. Bus., 1981. Acct. Peat, Marwick, Mitchell & Co., Columbus, 1966-68; v.p. fin., chief fin. officer The Williams Mfg. Co., Portsmouth, 1968-76, Mercy Hosp. Corp., Portsmouth, 1976-87, U.S. Health Corp. So. Ohio, Portsmouth, 1987-94; mgmt. cons., prin. The Waverly Group, Portsmouth, Ohio, 1994—; mem. exec. adv. bd. Coll. Bus., Ohio U., Athens, 1983—. Bd. dirs. YMCA, Portsmouth, 1971-81, Gt. Lakes regional bd. dirs., 1980-81. Fellow Am. Coll. Healthcare Execs.; mem. Fin. Execs. Inst., Inst. Mgmt. Accts., Healthcare Fin. mgmt. Assn. Avocation: golf. Office: The Waverly Group 3309 Sheridan Rd Portsmouth OH 45662

RAUB, DONALD WILMER, minister, author; b. Quakertown, Pa., Dec. 24, 1931; s. Harvey Wilmer and Estella Martha (Bleam) R.; m. Dolores Jean Kern, Oct. 20, 1951; children: Diane, Donald, Deborah, Devlyn. DRE, Evang. Bible Sem., Lake Worth, Fla., 1987. Ordained minister Evang. Ch. Alliance, 1951. Evangelist Evang. Ch. Alliance, Bradley, Ill., 1951-58; pastor Troy (Ohio) Gospel Tabernacle, 1959-60; writer and photographer Quakertown (Pa.) Free Press, 1963-73; pastor East Rockhill Chapel, 1965—; with Merck & Co., West Point, Pa., 1968-94; ret., 1994; advisor Lebanon (Pa.) Gospel Assn., 1992-94; lectr. in field. Author: I, Being of Sound Mind, 1988, 2d edit., 1989, Unusual Experiences and Special Moments, 1990, The Value of Christian Holiness, 1992; inventor fin. game: Independence, 1976; patentee in field; contbr. articles to profl. jours. Bd. dirs. Transylvania Bible Sch., Freeport, Pa., 1957—, North Penn Symphony Orch. Soc., Lansdale, Pa., 1980-90; v.p. Transylvania, Inc., 1994—. Mem. Songwriters of N.Am. (founder). Republican. Avocation: horticulture.

RAUCH, ARTHUR IRVING, management consultant; b. N.Y.C., Sept. 18, 1933; s. David and Miriam (Frankel) R.; m. Roxane M. Spiller, Aug. 19, 1962 (div. 1977); children: David S., Janine B.; m. Lynn R Saidenberg, Oct. 11, 1987. BA magna cum laude Dartmouth Coll., 1954, MS, 1955. Chartered fin. analyst. Security analyst Lionel D. Edie & Co., N.Y.C., 1959-64; group dir. rsch. Eastman Dillon, Union Securities & Co., N.Y.C., 1964-68; v.p., sr. analyst Laird, Inc., N.Y.C., 1968-69, dir. rsch., 1969-71, sr. v.p., 1970-73; ptnr. Oppenheimer & Co., N.Y.C., 1973-77; v.p. corp. devel. Rorer Group Inc., Ft. Washington, Pa., 1977-84; v.p. corp. fin. Arnhold & S. Bleichroeder, Inc., 1984-88; cons. corp. devel. ICN Pharms. Inc., N.Y.C., 1988-89; mem. investment com. Becker Fund, 1969-73; bd. dirs. Sonomed Tech., Inc., 1983—, exec. com. Dartmouth Class of 1954, 1968-79, 94—. Lt. (j.g.) USNR, 1956-59. Rufus Choate scholar Dartmouth Coll. Mem. N.Y. Soc. Security Analysts, Assn. Corp. Growth, Fin. Analysts Fedn. (corp. info. com.), Phi Beta Kappa. Home and Office: 250 E 73rd St Apt 19C New York NY 10021-4314

RAUCH, GEORGE WASHINGTON, lawyer; b. Marion, Ind., July 18, 1919; s. George W. and Emma Asenath (Nolen) R.; m. Audrey M. Cranfield, Feb. 28, 1943 (div.); children: George Washington III, Nancy Lynn, Jane Nolen; m. Dorothy D. Farlow, June 26, 1970. B.S., Ind. U., 1941; LL.B., U. Va., 1947. Bar: Ind. 1948, Ill. 1957, Mass. and Fla. 1972. Practice law Batton, Harker and Rauch (and predecessor firms), Marion, Ind., 1948-57; v.p., gen. counsel The Greyhound Corp., Chgo., 1957-61; mem. firm Hubachek & Kelly Ltd. and predecessor firms, Chgo., 1961-82; pres. Hubachek & Kelly Ltd., 1972-80; of counsel firm Chapman and Cutler, Chgo., 1982-95; gen. counsel Household Finance Corp., 1967-78, dir., 1967-92, mem. fin. com., 1969-92, exec. com., 1972-92; dir. Edwards Engring. Corp., Constrn. Materials Co., Indsl. Air & Hydraulics Co., 1976-90; dir. Burch Co., 1972—, pres., 1975—; dir. 1242 Lake Shore Dr. Corp., 1971-83, pres., 1973-74; mem. Nat. Conf. Commrs. on Uniform Laws, 1955-57. Served as aviator USNR, 1941-45; lt. comdr. Mem. Raven Soc., Sankaty Head Golf Club (Nantucket, Mass.), Casino Club (Nantucket), Beach Club (Palm Beach, Fla.), Masons, Shriners, Phi Delta Phi, Delta Tau Delta. Home: 455 Australian Ave Palm Beach FL 33480-4526 also: 83 Baxter Rd PO Box 149 Siasconset MA 02564-0149

RAUCH, IRMENGARD, linguist, educator; b. Dayton, Ohio, Apr. 17, 1933; d. Konrad and Elsa (Knott) R.; m. Gerald F. Carr, June 12, 1965; children: Christopher, Gregory. Student, Nat. U. Mex., summer 1954; B.S. with honors, U. Dayton, 1955; M.A., Ohio State U., 1957; postgrad. (Fulbright fellow), U. Munich, Fed. Republic Germany, 1957-58; Ph.D., U. Mich., 1962. Instr., German and linguistics U. Wis., Madison, 1962-63, asst. prof., 1963-66; assoc. prof. German U. Pitts., 1966-68; assoc. prof. German and linguistics U. Ill., Urbana, 1968-72, prof., 1972-79; prof. U. Calif., Berkeley, 1979—. Author: The Old High German Diphthongization: A Description of a Phonemic Change, 1967, The Old Saxon Language: Grammar, Epic Narrative, Linguistic Interference, 1992; editor: (with others) Approaches in Linguistic Methodology, 1967, Spanish edit., 1974, Der Heliand, 1974, Linguistic Method: Essays in Honor of Herbert Penzl, 1979, The Signifying Animal: The Grammar of Language and Experience, 1980, Language Change, 1983, The Semiotic Bridge: Trends From California, 1989, On Germanic Linguistics: Issues and Methods, 1992, Insights in Germanic Linguistics I: Methodology in Transition, 1995, Insights in Germanic Linguistics II: Classic and Contemporary, 1996; editor of three series: Berkeley Insights in Linguistics and Semiotics, Berkeley Models of Grammars, Studies in Old Germanic Languages and Literatures; contbr. articles to profl. jours. Named outstanding woman on campus U. Ill. Sta. WILL, 1975; recipient Disting. Alumnus award U. Dayton, 1985; research grantee U. Wis., summer 1966, U. Ill., 1975-79, Eastern Ill. U., 1976, Nat. Endowment Humanities, 1978, U. Calif., Berkeley, 1979—; travel grantee NSF, Linguistics Soc. Am., 1972; Guggenheim fellow, 1982-83; IBM Distributed Acad. Computing Environment, 1986; NEH grantee, 1988. Mem. Linguistics Soc. Am., MLA, Am. Assn. Tchrs. German, Society for Germanic Philogy, Philological Assn. of the West Coast, Phonetics Assn., Semiotic Soc. Am. (pres. 1982-83), Semiotic Circle of Calif. (founder), Internat. Assn. for Semiotic Studies (pres., dir. 5th congress 1994), Alpha Sigma Tau, Delta Phi Alpha. Home: 862 Camden Ct Benicia CA 94510-3633 Office: U Calif Dept German Berkeley CA 94720

RAUCH, JANET MELODIE, elementary school educator; b. Mpls., June 17, 1952; d. James Harlan and Myrna Luverne (Prinsen) R. BA, Wheaton Coll., 1974; MA in Tchg., Rockford Coll., 1980; cert. of advanced study, No. Ill. U., 1985. Cert. elem. tchr., spl. edn. tchr., Ill. Elem. sch. tchr. Christian Life Ctr. Sch., Rockford, Ill., 1974-80; remedial reading tchr. Washington Elem. Sch., Belvidere, Ill., 1980—. Mem. NEA, Ill. Edn. Assn., Belvidere Edn. Assn. (bldg. rep. 1980-82), No. Ill. Reading Coun., Nat. Assn. Christian Schs., Alpha Delta Kappa (sec. 1994—). Avocations: church choral singing, flute, violin, guitar, travel. Home: 1112 Fox Chase Ln Rockford IL 61107-6214

RAUCH, JOHN KEISER, JR., architect; b. Phila., Oct. 23, 1930; s. John Keiser and Marjorie (Gretz) R.; m. Carol Pfaff, Mar. 11, 1953 (div. June 1978); children: John David, Charles Daniel, Kathryn Mari, Peter, Carol Anne; m. Carol A. McConochie, Jan. 10, 1981. Student, Wesleyan U., Middletown, Conn., 1948-51; B.Arch., U. Pa., 1957. Draftsman Cope & Lippincott, Phila., 1957-60; architect Venturi and Short, Phila., 1960-64; partner Venturi and Rauch (Architects and Planners), Phila., 1964-79; partner Venturi, Rauch and Scott Brown, 1980-82, v.p., mng. prin., 1982-87, mgmt. cons., mediator, arbitrator, 1988—; instr. U. Pa. Grad. Sch. Fine Arts, 1969-70, 89; lectr. dept. architecture Princeton (N.J.) U., 1990-94. Trustee Found. for Architecture, 1977-84, mem. adv. com., 1994—; treas. Phila. Rehab., Inc., 1984-94; pres. Reading Terminal Market Pres. Fund, 1988-93, bd. dirs., 1994—; bd. dirs. United Cerebral Palsy Assn., 1988-91. Recipient Good Neighbor award Mellon/PSFS Bank, 1992. Fellow AIA (Firm award 1983, John Harbeson Disting Svc. Phila. Chpt. award 1992); mem. Pa. Soc. Architects. Democrat. Home and Office: 620 Gate House Ln Philadelphia PA 19118-4303

RAUCH, KATHLEEN, computer executive; b. Franklin Square, N.Y., Oct. 30, 1951; d. William C. and Marian (Shull) R.; B.A., U. Rochester, 1973; M.A. in L.S., U. Mich., 1974; postgrad. N.Y. U., 1981-82. Media specialist Sutton (Mass.) Sch., 1974-76; program cons. Advanced Mgmt. Rsch. Internat., N.Y.C., 1976-79; pub. rels. cons., N.Y.C., 1979; pres. N.Y. chpt. NOW, N.Y.C., 1979-80; computer programmer Blue Cross/Blue Shield of Greater N.Y., N.Y.C., 1981-82; computer programmer analyst Fed. Res. Bank of N.Y., 1983-84; systems officer Citibank, N.A., 1984-85; systems analyst Fed. Res. Bank of N.Y., 1986-89; computer and children's libr. East Meadow (N.Y.) Pub. Libr., 1989-91; pres. Panorama Children's Videos, Inc., 1988-93; microcomputer specialist N.C. State U., 1992-93; prin., v.p. The Computer Lab., Inc., 1993—. Mem. ALA, NOW (dir. pub. rels. N.Y.C. chpt. 1978, v.p. programs 1978, chmn. bd. 1981, founding mem., sec. svc. fund NOW, N.Y.C. chpt. 1981), Assn. for Women in Computing (v.p. membership 1984, exec. v.p. 1985, treas. 1986, mem.-at-large 1987, pres. 1988), N.C. Libr. Assn., Triangle Bus. and Profl. Guild. Home and Office: The Computer Lab Inc 8711 Six Forks Rd Ste 160 Raleigh NC 27615-2968

RAUCH, LAWRENCE LEE, aerospace and electrical engineer, educator; b. L.A., May 1, 1919; s. James Lee and Mabel (Thompson) R.; m. Norma Ruth Cable, Dec. 15, 1961; children: Lauren, Maury Rauch. AB, U. So. Calif., 1941; postgrad., Cornell U., 1941; AM, Princeton U., 1948, PhD, 1949. Instr. math. Princeton U., 1943- 49; faculty U. Mich., 1949—, prof. aerospace engring., 1953-79, emeritus, 1979, chmn. instrumentation engring. program, 1952-63, chmn. computer, info. and control engring. program, 1971-76, asso. chmn. dept. elec. and computer engring., 1972-75; chief technologist telecommunication sci. and engring. div. NASA/Calif. Inst. Tech. Jet Propulsion Lab., 1979-85; vis. prof. Ecole Nationale Supérieure de L'Aéronautique et de l'Espace, Toulouse, France, 1970, Calif. Inst. Tech., Pasadena, 1977-85, U. Tokyo, 1978; cons. govt. and industry, 1946—; chmn. telemetering working group, panel test range instrumentation Research and Devel. Bd. Dept. Def., 1952-53; mem. exec. com. (Nat. Telemetering Conf.), 1959-64; Western Hemisphere program chmn. (1st Internat. Telemetering Conf.), London, 1963, program chmn., U.S.A., 1967; supr. air blast telemetering, Bikini, 1946; mem. project non-linear differential equations Office Naval Research, 1947-49; mem. research adv. com. on communications, instrumentation and data processing NASA, 1963-68. Author: Radio Telemetry, 1956; also numerous sci. articles and papers on radio telemetry. Recipient award for outstanding contbn. to WWII Army and Navy, 1947, award for outstanding contbn. to telemetering field Nat. Telemetering Conf., 1960; Donald P. Eckman award for disting. achievement in edn. Instrument Soc. Am., 1966; Pioneer award Internat. Telemetering Conf./USA, 1985. Fellow IEEE (spl. award contbns. radio telemetry 1957, adminstrv. com. profl. group space electronics and telemetry 1958-64), AAAS. Explorers Club: mem. Am. Math. Soc., AIAA, U. Mich. Research Club, Phi Beta Kappa, Sigma Xi, Phi Eta Sigma, Phi Kappa Phi. Achievements include patent in field; development of first electronic time-division multiplex radio telemetering system, of pre-detection recording; radio telemetry of first U.S. jet aircraft, of air blast over pressure for Operation Crossroads at Bikini Atoll; analysis of optimum demodulation of frequency-modulated signals. Address: 759 N Citrus Ave Los Angeles CA 90038-3401

RAUCH, RUDOLPH STEWART, III, periodical editor, arts education executive; b. Bryn Mawr, Pa., July 5, 1943; s. Rudolph Stewart and Frances (Brewster) R.; m. Sheila Prentice, Oct. 31, 1972; children: Edward Prentice, Michael Brewster. BA, Princeton U., 1965. Corr. Time mag., N.Y.C., 1969-70, Bonn, W. Ger., 1970-71, Saigon, Vietnam, 1971-72, Rio De Janeiro, Brazil, 1972-74, Buenos Aires, Argentina, 1974-76, Atlanta, 1976-79; dep. chief of corrs. Time mag., N.Y.C., 1979-80; asst. to chmn. bd. Time Inc., N.Y.C., 1981-84; internat. dir. mag. devel. Time Inc., 1984-85; exec. editor N.Y. N.J. Conn. Real Estate, 1986-87; mng. editor Constitution, 1989-94; mng. dir. Met. Opera Guild, Inc., N.Y.C., 1994—. Edward R. Murrow Press fellow Council on Fgn. Relations, 1980-81. Mem. Coun. Fgn. Rels., Knickerbocker Club, Century Assn. Office: Met Opera Guild 70 Lincoln Ctr Plz New York NY 10023

RAUCHER, HERMAN, novelist, screenwriter; b. Bklyn., Apr. 13, 1928; s. Benjamin Brooks and Sophie (Weinshank) R.; m. Mary Kathryn Martinet, Apr. 20, 1960; children: Jacqueline Leigh, Jennifer Brooke. BS, NYU, 1949. Asst. trade ad mgr. 20th Century Fox Films, N.Y.C. and Los Angeles, 1950-54; copy dir. Walt Disney Studios, N.Y.C., 1954-55; copy supr. Calkins & Holden Advt., N.Y.C., 1955-57; copy dir., v.p., dir. Reach McClinton Advt., N.Y.C., 1957-63; v.p., creative dir. Maxon Advt., N.Y.C., 1963-64; creative supr. Gardner Advt., N.Y.C., 1964-65; v.p. advt., cons. Benton & Bowles Advt., N.Y.C., 1965-67; freelance novelist, screenwriter, 1967—; pres. Bearfilm Prodns., 1971-76. Author: (novels and screenplays) Watermelon Man, 1970, Summer of '42 (nominated Acad. award for best original screenplay 1971, Writers Guild award nomination, Photoplay award), Ode to Billy Joe, 1975, A Glimpse of Tiger, 1972, (novels) Sweet November, 1968, Maynard's House, 1979, (screenplays) The Other Side of Midnight, 1977, Class of 44, 1972, Hieronymus Merkin (Best Original Screenplay award Writers Guild of Great Britain 1969), There Should Have Been Castles, 1978, also various dramas appearing on TV in Alcoa Hour, Studio One, Matinee Theatre, Goodyear Playhouse, (TV mini-series under pseudonym) Master of the Game, 1984, (TV pilot) Remember When, 1974; playwright: Harold, 1962, Two Weeks Somewhere Else, 1967; contbg. editor: Greenwich Time; contbr. to book revs. to N.Y. Times. Served with U.S. Army, 1950-52. Mem. Writers Guild Am., Authors League Am., Am. Film Inst., Dramatists Guild, Acad. of Motion Picture Arts and Scis.

RAUE, JORG EMIL, electrical engineer; b. Stettin, Germany, June 13, 1936; came to U.S., 1952; s. Ludwig and Liselotte (Barth) R.; m. Anke Volkmann, June 29, 1957; children: Monika Kay, Jennifer Faye. BSEE, Milw. Sch. Engring., 1961; MSEE, Marquette U., 1965, PhDEE, 1968. Mem. faculty Milw. Sch. Engring., 1961-68, chmn. dept., 1968-69; research engr. TRW Systems, Redondo Beach, Calif., 1969-76; mgr. dept. TRW Systems, Redondo Beach, 1976-79; sr. research scientist TRW Electronic Systems, Rendondo Beach, Calif., advanced systems mgr., 1980-93; tech. cons. Calif., 1993—; chmn. dept. elec. engring. Calif. Polytech State U., San Luis Opispo, 1979-80; mem. faculty Marquette U., Milw., 1968-69, Loyola U., Los Angeles, 1970-72, U. So. Calif., Los Angeles, 1983—. Contbr. articles to profl. jours. Served with U.S. Army, 1955-58. Recipient Disting. Tchr. award Milw. Sch. Engring., 1968; named Outstanding Alumnus Milw. Sch. Engring., 1985. Fellow IEEE; mem. Microwave Soc. of IEEE (sec. adminstrn. com. 1985—), Sigma Xi. Avocations: tennis, bicycling, flying. Home and Office: 28813 Rothrock Dr Palos Verdes Peninsula CA 90274

RAUENHORST, GERALD, architectural, construction and development executive; b. Mpls., Dec. 8, 1927; s. Henry and Margaret (Keltgen) R.; m. Henrietta Schmoll, Sept. 2, 1950; children: Judith, Mark, Neil, Joseph, Michael, Susan, Amy. BA, U. St. Thomas, 1948, Dr. Laws (hon.), 1971; B.S.C.E., Marquette U., 1951. Instr. in civil engring. Marquette U., 1950-51; engr. Peter Rasmussen & Son, Oshkosh, Wis., 1951-52, Viking Constrn., Mpls., 1952-53; pres., founder. Rauenhorst Corp., Mpls. 1953— (name changed to Opus Corp. chrm. bd., ceo, 1982—); deputy chrm. 1991-93, chmn. bd. dirs. Fed. Res. Bank, Mpls., 94-95, dir., chmn. human resources com. ConAgra, Omaha; bd. dirs. Cornerstone Properties, Inc., N.Y. Chmn. bd. trustees Marquette U., 1985-87. Recipient Disting. Engring. award Marquette U., 1974; named Alumnus of Yr., Marquette U., 1969, Coll. St. Thomas, 1978, Minn. Exec. of Yr., Corp. Report Mag., 1983, Devel. of Yr., NAIOP, 1992, # 1 Developer in Country Nat. Real Estate Investor Mag., 1995; named to Minn. Bus. Hall of Fame, 1980. Mem. ASCE, Am. Soc. Profl. Engrs., World Press Orgn., Minn. Soc. Profl. Engrs., Mpls. Club, Interlachen Club. Roman Catholic. Avocations: fishing, golf, pottery. Office: Opus Corp PO Box 150 Minneapolis MN 55440-0150

RAUH, CARL STEPHEN, lawyer; b. Washington, Dec. 14, 1940; s. Joseph L. and Olie (Westheimer) R. A.B., Columbia U., 1962; LL.B., U. Pa., 1965; LL.M., Georgetown U., 1968. Bar: D.C. 1966, U.S. Supreme Ct. 1969. Asst. U.S. atty. for D.C., 1966-69; atty. Dep. Atty Gen.'s Office Dept. Justice, Washington, 1969-71; 1st asst. atty. gen. U.S. V.I., 1971-73; prin. asst. U.S. atty. for D.C., 1974-79, U.S. atty. for D.C., 1979; ptnr. Dunnells, Duvall, Bennett & Porter, Washington, 1980-90, Skadden, Arps, Slate, Meagher & Flom, Washington, 1990—. Mem. D.C. Jud. Nomination Commn., 1985-90. Recipient Dir.'s award Dept. Justice, 1976; Atty. Gen.'s Disting. Service award, 1980. Fellow Am. Coll. Trial Lawyers; mem. ABA, D.C. Bar Assn., Nat. Assn. Former U.S. Attys., Asst. U.S. Attys. Assn. (Harold J. Sullivan award 1980). Office: 1440 New York Ave NW Washington DC 20005-2111

RAUH, JOHN DAVID, manufacturing company executive; b. Cin., May 28, 1932; s. Carl J. and Grace (Stix) R.; m. Elizabeth Gibbons, June 19, 1954; children: Carol Miller, Daniel Gibbons.; m. Mary Stoner, Dec. 23, 1984; children: Brooks Tomb, Howard Tomb. AB, Harvard U., 1954, MBA, 1956. Gen. mgr. Rauh Shirt Co., Cin., 1959-61, Clopay Corp., Cin., 1961-85; pres. Clopay Corp., 1972-75, chmn., chief exec. officer, 1975-85, also chmn.; adj. faculty mktg. Colby-Sawyer Coll., New London, N.H., 1989—; fellow Kennedy Sch., Harvard, 1989. Pres. Charter Com. Greater Cin., 1969-76; canidate U.S. Senate, N.H., 1990, 92. 1st lt. Finance Corps. AUS, 1956-59. Home: 11 Clearwater Dr # 729 Sunapee NH 03782-2608

RAUH, RICHARD PAUL, architect; b. Covington, Ky., Mar. 27, 1948; s. Robert Paul and Pauline (Farmer) R.; m. Mary Darlene Bailey, Oct. 6, 1975. AB, Columbia U., 1970; BArch, MArch., Harvard U., 1974; DMD, U. Ky., 1980. Registered arch., 30 states; lic. dentist, Ky., Va. Asst. prof. U. Ky. Coll. Arch., Lexington, 1976-80, adj. asst. prof., 1980-81; prin. Carpenter/Rauh, Lexington, 1978-80; prin. Rabun Hatch Portman McWhorter Hatch & Rauh Architects, Atlanta, 1981-85; prin. Richard Rauh & Assocs., Archs., Atlanta, 1984—; cons. Macon (Ga.) Heritage Found., Tampa Preservation Bd., Battle House Found., Mobile, Ala., City of Norwood, Ohio, St. Petersburg (Fla.) Preservation, Inc., City of West Palm Beach, Booker Creek Preservation Inc. Works published in numerous books and mags.; works include: Norfolk Hilton Hotel, Va., 1985, Omni Netherland Plaza Hotel restoration, Cin., 1982-83, Bridgeport Plaza Hilton Hotel, Conn., 1985, Carew Tower Block restoration, Cin., 1983-91, master plan Gaines Ctr. for Humanities U. Ky. Lexington, 1984, La Concha Hotel, Key West, Fla., 1986, Carolina Head Injury Ctr., Durham, N.C., 1987, Albany (Ga.) Holiday Inn Hotel, 1989, Shenandoah Head Injury Ctr., Manassas, Va., 1989, Kenner Toy Products Gen. Offices, Cin., 1990, Cinn. Club, 1991, Tower Pl.-Emery Arcade Restoration, Cinn., 1991, Urban Design Masterplan, Mobile, Ala., 1993; author (with David G. Wright) Design Courses at Schools of Architecture in Western Europe: A Documentary Study, 1975. Pres., Hist. South Hill Assn., Lexington, 1978-80; bd. dirs. Margaret Mitchell House, Inc., 1987-92, pres. 1989, Preservation Action, Washington, 1988—, Atlanta Neighborhood Planning Unit Bd., 1996; mem. Atlanta Planning adv. bd. Sheldon fellow, Harvard U., 1974-75, Appleton fellow, 1974-75; recipient LUMEN excellence award Illuminating Engring. Soc. N.Am., 1985; Harvard Book award Harvard Club Cin., 1965; U.S. Dept. Interior grantee Ky. Heritage Commn., 1978, U.S. Dept. of HUD Urban

Devel. Action grantee, 1988; recipient honor awards Nat. Trust Historic Preservation U.S., 1985, AIA South Atlantic Regional council, 1984, Ga. Assn. AIA, 1984, 88, 89, 94, Ky. Soc. Archs. AIA, 1986, Nat. award Soc. Am. Reg. Archs., 1986, 89, 90, 94, Build Am. award AGC/Motorola, 1992, Greater Cin. Beautiful award City of Cin., 1984, Ohio Hist. Soc., 1987, Fla. Keys Preservation Bd., 1987, City of Miami Beach, 1990, Nat. Hist. Landmark Designation U.S. Dept. Interior, 1995. Mem. Art Deco Soc. Am., Harvard Club of Ga., Harvard Club of Ky., Filson Club (Ky.), Order Ky. Cols. Democrat. Presbyterian. Home: 2986 Howell Mill Rd NW Atlanta GA 30327-1656 Office: Richard Rauh & Assocs 3400 Peachtree Rd NE Atlanta GA 30326-1107

RAUHALA, ANN ELAINE, reporter; b. Sudbury, Ont., Can., Dec. 7, 1954; d. Esko Alexander and Iona Anna (Tormala) R.; m. Lorne Franklin Slotnick, Feb. 27, 1990; 1 child, Sam Aleksander Nathan. BA in Arts, U. Toronto, 1977; B in Applied Arts, Ryerson U., 1979. Copy editor Globe and Mail, Toronto, Ont., 1979-83, asst. fgn. editor, 1983-86, reporter, 1986-89, fgn. editor, 1989-95, columnist, 1993-95; TV reporter Can. Broadcasting Corp., Toronto, 1995—; panelist, organizer Can. Assn. Journalists of Toronto, 1990, Ottawa, Ont., 1992, Winnipeg, Man., 1993. Bd. dirs. YMCA, Toronto, 1989-92, Montrose Child Care, Inc., Toronto, 1992—. Recipient Robertine Berry award Can. Rsch. Inst. for Advancement of Women, Ottawa, 1987. Avocations: film, travel, literature. Office: Can Broadcasting Corp, PO Box 500 Sta A, Toronto, ON Canada M5W 1E6

RAUHUT, HORST WILFRIED, research scientist; b. Duesseldorf, Germany, May 4, 1930; came to U.S., 1964; s. Gustav Adolf and Johanna (Klose) R.; m. Magdalena Winkel, July 16, 1957; children: Birgit, Monika, Michael Winfred. BSc, U. Bonn., Germany, 1954, MSc, 1956; D in Natural Scis., U. Munich, 1958. Lab. supr. Henkel of CIE, Duesseldorf, 1959-64; chemist Harry Diamond Lab., U.S. Army, Washington, 1964-68, Morton Internat., Woodstock, Ill., 1968-71, Acme Resin, Forest Park, Ill., 1971-73; rsch. scientist Dexter Electronic Materials, Olean, N.Y., 1973—; dir., program coord. Plastics Engrs., Chgo., 1971-73; instr. Jamestown C.C., Olean, 1977; author, presenter tech. seminars, 1976-88. Author: Ueber Bicyclische Ketale mit Spiran-Struktur, 1958, Microelectronics Packaging and Processing Engrs. Tutorial on Epoxies, 1994; contbr. articles to sci. jours. Treas. Haskell Cmty., Cuba, N.Y., 1977-94, local historian, 1991. Named Outstanding New Citizen, Citizenship Coun. Met. Chgo., 1970. Mem. Am. Chem. Soc., Soc. Plastics Engrs. (dir. thermoset divsn. 1973-81, chmn. divsn. 1981-82, mem. internat. rels. com. 1973-84, thermoset divsn. award 1978, chmn.'s award 1982, award for significant contbn. to plastics industry 1988). Democrat. Achievements include Belgian, French and German patents for epoxy compositions, U.S. patents for foam sandwich structure, for flammable striker; research in areas of synthetic organic chemistry, adhesives/adhesion, ordnance, epoxy encapsulation compounds, low-stress technology and dielectric analysis. Avocations: photography, hiking, history. Home: 3551 Willow Rd Cuba NY 14727-9425 Office: Dexter Electronic Materials 211 Franklin St Olean NY 14760-1211

RAUL, ALAN CHARLES, lawyer; b. Bronx, N.Y., Sept. 9, 1954; s. Eugene and Eduarda (Müller-Mañas) R.; m. Mary Tinsley, Jan. 30, 1988; children: Caroline Tinsley, William Eduardo Tinsley. AB magna cum laude, Harvard U., 1975, MPA, 1977; JD, Yale U., 1980. Bar: N.Y. 1982, D.C. 1982, U.S. Ct. Appeals (D.C. cir.) 1982, U.S. Dist. Ct. D.C. 1986, U.S. Ct. Internat. Trade 1988, U.S. Claims Ct. 1988, U.S. Ct. Appeals (fed. cir.) 1988, U.S. Supreme Ct. 1988, U.S. Ct. Appeals (9th cir.) 1991, U.S. Ct. Appeals (4th cir.) 1994, U.S. Ct. Appeals (11th cir.) 1996. Law clk. to judge U.S. Ct. Appeals (D.C. cir.), Washington, 1980-81; assoc. Debevoise & Plimpton, N.Y.C., 1981-86; White House assoc. counsel Pres. Reagan, Washington, 1986-88; gen. counsel Office Mgmt. and Budget, Washington, 1988-89, USDA, Washington, 1989-93; prin. Beveridge & Diamond P.C., Washington, 1993—; cons. Reagan-Bush campaign, N.Y.C., 1984; com. mem. Food and Drug Law Inst. Co-chairperson, co-founder Lawyers Have Heart; chmn. bd. USDA Grad. Sch., 1991-93; bd. dirs. Am. Heart Assn., Nations Capital Affiliate, 1993—; treas. Citizens Assn. Georgetown; mem. Nat. Policy Forum's Environ. Policy Coun. Recipient Disting. Achievement award Am. Heart Assn., 1991, Vol. of Yr. award, 1993. Mem. ABA (coun. sect. internat. law and practice 1992—, chmn. com. on nat. security and internat. law 1990-92, standing com. on election law 1995—), Assn. of Bar of City of N.Y. (chmn. subcom. on Cen. Am. issues 1985, mem. com. on inter-Am. affairs 1983), Federalist Soc. (mem. nat. practitioners adv. coun., chair environment and property rights practice group), Coun. on Fgn. Rels. Office: Beveridge & Diamond PC 1350 I St NW Ste 700 Washington DC 20005-3305

RAULERSON, PHOEBE HODGES, school superintendent; b. Cin., Mar. 16, 1939; d. LeRoy Allen and Thelma A. (Stewart) Hodges; m. David Earl Raulerson, Dec. 26, 1959; children: Julie, Lynn, David Earl, Jr., Roy Allen. BA in Edn., U. Fla., 1963, MEd, 1964. Tchr. several schs., Okeechobee, Fla., 1964-79; asst. prin. Okeechobee Jr. H.S., 1979-81, prin., 1983-84; asst. prin. South Elem. Sch., Okeechobee, 1981-82; asst. prin. Okeechobee H.S., 1982-83, prin., 1984-96; sch. supt. for curriculum and instrn., 1996—; mem. Dept. Edn. Commr.'s Task Force on H.S. Preparation, 1993-94, chair Task Force Tchr. Preparation & Certification, 1995-96. Mem. Okeechobee Exchange Club. Recipient Outstanding Citizen award Okeechobee Rotary Club, 1986; week named in her honor, Okeechobee County Commrs., 1990. Mem. Am. Bus. Women's Assn., Fla. Assn. Secondary Sch. Prins. (pres. 1993-94, Fla. Prin. of Yr. award 1990), Fla. Assn. Sch. Adminstrs. (bd. dirs. 1992-95), Okeechobee Cattlewomen's Assn. Democrat. Episcopalian. Home: 3898 NW 144th Dr Okeechobee FL 34972-0930 Office: Okeechobee County Sch Dist 700 SW 2d Ave Okeechobee FL 34974

RAULINAITIS, PRANAS ALGIS, electronics executive; b. Kaunas, Lithuania, May 13, 1927; came to U.S., 1954, naturalized, 1960; s. Pranas Viktoras and Paulina (Gervaite) R.; m. Angele Staugaityte, Oct. 4, 1952; 1 son, Pranas Darius. With Commonwealth Rys. of Australia, Melbourne, 1949-53; asst. to fin. acct. Kitchen & Sons, Pty. Ltd., Melbourne, 1953-54; v.p. Photo div. Interphoto Corp., Los Angeles, 1954-71; sr. v.p., sec. Craig Corp., Los Angeles, 1971-87; pres. PAR Enterprises, Burbank, Calif., 1987—; adviser Ministry Fgn. Affairs Republic of Lithuania, 1992. Former pres. Lithuanian Am. Coun., Inc. of Calif.; bd. dirs. Lithuanian-Am. assns.; founder, treas. Baltic Am. Freedom League; former mem. Am. Soc. Internat. Law. Home and Office: Par Enterprises 1501 W Riverside Dr Burbank CA 91506-3027

RAULLERSON, CALVIN HENRY, political scientist, consultant; b. Utica, N.Y., Dec. 18, 1920; s. Calvin Thomas and Cora (White) R.; m. Olive Lewis, Dec. 1, 1956; children: Kevin Greer, Cheryl Harp, Earl Henry. A.B., Lincoln (Pa.) U., 1943; M.P.A., NYU, 1949; postgrad., Harvard, 1947, Harvard Bus. Sch., 1979. Instr. polit. sci. Lincoln U., 1946, 49; editor, dir. research Christian E. Burckell Assocs., Yonkers, N.Y., 1950-52; asst. to exec. dir. United Negro Coll. Fund, 1952-57, dir. ednl. services, 1957-61; dir. African programs Am. Soc. African Culture, Lagos, Nigeria, 1961-64; exec. dir. Am. Soc. African Culture, N.Y.C., 1964-66; chief Peace Corps, East and So. Africa, 1966-69; dir. Kenya, 1969-71, Africa regional dir., 1971-73; exec. asst. to dean Sch. Medicine, spl. asst. to pres. for internat. programs, spl. cons. research and devel., exec. dir. Internat. Ctr. for Arid and Semi-Arid Lands, Tex. Tech U., 1973-78; asst. prof. health orgn. mgmt., Health Svcs. Ctr. Tex. Tech U., 1973-78; asst. adminstr. Bur. Pvt. Devel. Cooperation, AID, 1978-81; v.p. African Am. Inst., 1981-84; assoc. Keene, Monk Assocs., Middleburg, Va., 1985-86; dir. internat. programs One Am., Inc., 1987-88; pres. internat. group LABAT Anderson, 1988-94; v.p. internat. group Gardner Kamya Inc., Washington, 1994-95; sr. project mgr. Labat-Anderson Inc., Mount Clemens, Va., 1995—; mgmt. cons. Mgmt. Devel. Consortium, Phelps Stokes Fund, 1973-75; Mem. information resources com. group on bus. affairs Assn. Am. Med. Colls.; mem. adv. com. on desertification AAAS, 1976-78; mem. Career Ministers Selection Bd., Dept. State, 1980; U.S. del. U.N. Conf. Desertification Nairobi, 1977; chmn. U.S. del. Com. on Food Aid and Policy, World Food Program, Rome, 1980; research analyst Pres.'s Com. on Fair Employment Practices, 1944; treas. U.S. planning com. 1st World Festival Negro Art, Dakar, 1965-66; del. Internat. Conf. on African History, U. Ibadan (Nigeria), 1962, Internat. Conf. on African Affairs, U. Ghana, 1963. Assoc. editor: Who's Who in the United Nations, 1952; Contbr. to: Negro Yearbook, 1952. Mem. nat. adv. com. Peace Corps, 1986-89; trustee African Wildlife Found., 1992—, chmn. strategic planning com., 1993-95. Rockefeller travel grantee East and Central Africa, 1960; Woodrow Wilson scholar, 1978-79. Clubs: Harvard (Washington). Home: 5823 Bradley Blvd Bethesda MD 20814-1104

RAUM, ARNOLD, federal judge; b. Lynn, Mass., Oct. 27, 1908; s. Isaac and Ida (Ross) R.; m. Muriel Leidner Slaff, Jan. 26, 1944 (div.); m. Violet Gang Kopp, Apr. 26, 1957; stepchildren—Robert E., Elizabeth A., Katherine F. AB summa cum laude, Harvard, 1929, LLB magna cum laude, 1932. Bar: Mass. 1932, U.S. Supreme Ct. 1935, D.C. 1935, bars of various other fed. cts 1935. Sheldon fellow Cambridge U., Eng., 1932; atty. for RFC, 1932-34; spl. asst. to atty. gen. U.S., 1934-50; spl. prosecutor in connection with fed. grand jury investigation of corruption La., 1939; 1st dep. solicitor gen. U.S., also occasional acting, 1939-1950; directed litigation of all Fed. tax cases as well as other types of cases in U.S. Supreme Court, 1939-1950; made arguments in numerous Supreme Ct. cases, including Calif. Tidelands case; judge U.S. Tax Ct., Washington, 1950—; lectr. on taxation Yale Law Sch., 1937-38; mem. faculty Harvard Law Sch., 1947. Editor Harvard Law Rev. 1930-32. Served as lt. comdr. USCGR, World War II. Hon. mem. D.C. Bar Assn., Fed. Bar Assn.; mem. Am. Law Inst., Phi Beta Kappa. Club: Cosmos (Washington). Home: 2622 31st St NW Washington DC 20008-3519 also: 1211 Crandon Blvd Key Biscayne FL 33149 Office: US Tax Ct 400 2nd St NW Washington DC 20217-0001

RAUMA, JOHN GUNNAR, architect, educator; b. Virginia, Minn., Jan. 22, 1926; s. Andrew Nestor and Susan Josephine (Kunnari) R.; m. Wanda Ruth McIntire, July 11, 1950; children—Ann, Peter, Allan, David. B.S., Marquette U., 1947; B.Arch., U. Minn., 1950; M.Arch., MIT, 1952. Registered architect, Minn. Designer Magney Tuler Seiter, Mpls., 1948-50; instr. architecture U. Calif.-Berkeley, 1952-54; v.p. design Thorshon & Cerny, Mpls., 1954-59, The Cerny Assoc., Mpls., 1959-63; prof. U. Minn., Mpls., 1956—; dir. grad. studies in architecture U. Minn., 1985—; pres. Griswold Rauma Egge Olson, Architects, 1963—; advisor Capitol Area Archtl. and Planning Bd., State of Minn., St. Paul, 1982—, Minn. State History Ctr. Design Competition, St. Paul, 1983—. Prin. works include Sch. of Architecture Bldg., U. Minn., Ch. of Risen Savior, Mpls., passenger terminal St. Paul Internat. Airport, auditorium and classroom bldg. U. Minn. Recipient numerous archtl. awards. Fellow AIA (com. on aesthetics 1966, pres. Minn. sect. 1970), Mpls. C. of C. (chmn. devel. com. 1965). Avocations: sailing; watercolor painting. Home: 1067 Antoinette Ave Minneapolis MN 55405-2102 Office: U Minn Dept Arch 89 Church St SE Minneapolis MN 55455

RAUP, DAVID MALCOLM, paleontology educator; b. Boston, Apr. 24, 1933; s. Hugh Miller and Lucy (Gibson) R.; m. Susan Creer Shepard, Aug. 25, 1956; 1 son, Mitchell D.; m. Judith T. Yamamoto, May 30, 1987. B.S., U. Chgo., 1953; M.A., Harvard U., 1955, Ph.D., 1957. Instr. Calif. Inst. Tech., 1956-57; mem. faculty Johns Hopkins U., 1957-65, assoc. prof., 1963-65; mem. faculty U. Rochester, 1965-78, prof. geology, 1966-78, chmn. dept. geol. scis., 1968-71, dir. Center for Evolution and Paleobiology, 1977-78; curator geology, chmn. dept. geology Field Mus. Natural History, Chgo., 1978-80; dean of sci. Field Mus. Natural History, 1980-82; prof. geophys. sci. U. Chgo., 1980-95, chmn. dept., 1982-85, Sewell L. Avery disting. service prof., 1984-95; prof. emeritus, Sewell L. Avery disting. svc. prof. emeritus, 1995—; geologist U.S. Geol. Survey, part-time, 1959-77; vis. prof. U. Tubingen, Germany, 1965, 72. Author: (with S. Stanley) Principles of Paleontology, 1971, 78, The Nemesis Affair, 1986, Extinction: Bad Genes of Bad Luck?, 1991; editor: (with B. Kummel) Handbook of Paleontological Techniques, 1965; contbr. articles to profl. jours. Recipient Best Paper award Jour. Paleontology, 1966; Schuchert award Paleontol. Soc., 1973; grantee Calif. Rsch. Corp., 1955-56, Am. Assn. Petroleum Geologists, 1957, Am. Philos. Soc., 1957, NSF, 1960-66, 75-81, Chem. Soc., 1965-71, NASA, 1983-95. Fellow Geol. Soc. Am.; mem. Nat. Acad. Sci., Paleontol. Soc. (pres. 1976-77), Am. Soc. Naturalists (v.p. 1983), Soc. for Study Evolution, AAAS, Sigma Xi. Home: RR 1 Box 168-y Washington Island WI 54246-9753

RAUSCH, HOWARD, information service executive; b. N.Y.C., June 29, 1928; s. Sol and Helen (Kartiganer) R.; m. Sidra Cohn, Apr. 22, 1979. A.B., Syracuse U., 1950. Reporter Phila. Bull., 1961; copy editor Wall St. Jour., 1961-63, N.Y. Times, 1963-64; editor, fgn. corr. McGraw-Hill, N.Y.C. and Moscow, 1964-68; pres. Advanced Tech. Publs., Inc., Newton, Mass., 1968-80; editor, pub. Laser Focus mag., 1968-80; editor, founder Energy Research, 1975-80; editor Electronic Business, 1980-82; founder, pub. Lightwave Jour., 1983-90; tech. dir. Optical Soc. Am., Washington, 1991-93; pres. Capitol Gains, Info. and Cons. Svcs., Washington, 1993—. Home and Office: 2541 Waterside Dr NW Washington DC 20008-2820

RAUSCHENBERG, BRADFORD LEE, museum research director; b. Atlanta, Sept. 11, 1940. BS in Archaeology and Biology, Ga. State Coll., 1963; MA in History, Wake Forest U., 1995. Archaeologist Ga. Hist. Commn., 1963-64; site supr., asst. Stanley South, State Archaeologist of N.C., 1964-66; antiquarian, asst. Dir. Restoration Old Salem, Inc., Winston-Salem, N.C., 1966-73; asst. to dir. Mus. Early So. Decorative Arts, Winston-Salem, 1973-76, rsch. fellow, 1976-87, dir. rsch., 1987-93; dir. rsch. Mus. Early So. Decorative Arts and Old Salem, Inc., Winston-Salem, 1993—; cons., lectr. in field. Author: British Regional Carving (1600-1640), and Furniture (1600-1800), 1984, Wachovia Historical Society: 1895-1995, 1995. With USCG, 1964-72. Recipient Halifax Resolves award, 1986; grantee NEH, 1972-81, Kaufman Americana Found., 1981-82. Mem. Am. Ceramic Circle (grantee), Orgn. Am. Historians, No. Ceramic Soc., So. Hist. Assn., Friends of Swiss Ceramic Circle, Regioanl Furniture Soc., Furniture History Soc., Soc. Hist. Archaeology, Soc. Post-Medieval Archaeology, Soc. Historians Early Am. Republic. Address: 221 Harmon Ct Winston Salem NC 27106-4613 Office: Mus Early So Decorative Arts PO Box 10310 Winston Salem NC 27108-0310

RAUSCHENBERG, ROBERT, artist; b. Port Arthur, Tex., Oct. 22, 1925; m. Sue Weil, 1950 (div. 1952); 1 child, Christopher. Student, U. Tex., Kansas City Art Inst., Academie Julian, Paris, Black Mountain Coll., N.C., Art Students League, N.Y.C.; LHD (hon.), Grinnell Coll., 1967; DFA (hon.), U. So. Fla., 1976. One man shows include Parsons Gallery, N.Y.C., 1951, Stable Gallery, N.Y.C., 1953, White Chapel Art Gallery, London, 1964, Leo Castelli Gallery, 1972, 73, Galerie Ileana Sonnabend, Paris, 1971, 72, 73, Ace Gallery, Los Angeles, 1973, Vancouver Art Gallery, 1978, Tate Gallery, London, 1981, Phoenix Art Mus., 1982, G.H. Dalsheimer Gallery, Balt., 1983, Castelli Graphics, 1984, others; exhbn. art constructions Rome and Florence Italy, 1953, Leo Castelli Gallery, N.Y.C., 1957—; rep. internat. art festivals, Carnegie Inst. Internat. exhbns., Sao Paulo Biennial, 1959, Exposition Internat. du Surrealisme, Paris, 1959-60, Amsterdam, others; group shows include Mus. Modern Art, 1959, Guggenheim Mus., 1961, 92, N.Y. Collection in Stockholm, 1972, Whitney Mus., N.Y.C., 1972, 73, Garage Show, Rome, 1973, Automme Festival d'Artes, Paris, 1973, Mus. South Tex., Corpus Christi, 1974, N.Y. Cultural Center, 1973, retrospective exhbn., Nat. Collection Fine Arts, Smithsonian Inst., Washington, 1976, Mus. Modern Art, N.Y.C., 1977, Albright Knox Gallery, 1977, San Francisco Mus. Modern Art, 1977, Art Inst. Chgo., 1977, Staatliche Kunsthalle, Berlin, 1980, Kunsthalle, Düsseldorf, 1980, Louisiana Mus., Copenhagen, 1980, Stadelsches Kunstinstitut, Frankfurt, 1981, Städtische Galerie im Lembachhaus, Munich, 1981, Tate Gallery, London, 1981, Galerie Beyeler, Basle, 1984, Juan March, Madrid, 1985, Inst. Contemporary Art, London, 1987, L.A. County Mus. Art, 1987, Galerie Alfred Kren, Cologne, Germany, 1988-89, Tretyakov Gallery, Moscow, 1989, Nat. Art Gallery, Kuala Lampur, Malaysia, 1990; permanent collections include Albright-Knox Art Gallery, Whitney Mus. Am. Art, Wadsworth Atheneum, Tate Gallery, Mus. Modern Art, Neue Galerie Aachen, Fed. Republic Germany, Hirshhorn Mus., Moderna Museet, Stockholm, others; reprodn. photographs by silk screen stenciling technique to allow change in scale; set and costume designer, lighting expert, stage mgr. Merce Cunningham Dance Co., 1964; choreographer: dance Pelican; others; works include electronic sculpture Soundings; paintings Tut-Scape; originator Overseas Culture Interchange traveling exhbn., 1985—. Served with USNR, World War II; neuropsychiat. tech. Calif. Naval Hosps. Recipient 1st prize Internat. Exbn. Prints Gallery Modern Art, Ljubljana, Yugoslavia, 1963, 1st prize Venice Biennale, 1964, 1st prize Corcoran Biennial Contemporary Am. Painters, 1965, Skowhegan Sch. Painting and Sculpture medal, 1982, NAD assoc., 1983, Grammy award, 1984. Mem. Am. Acad. and Inst. Arts and Letters. *

RAUSCHER, ELIZABETH ANN, physics educator, researcher; b. Berkeley, Calif., Mar. 18, 1943; d. Philip Jenkins and Claire Elsa (Soderblom) Webster; m. Warren Carleton Rauscher, Oct. 5, 1962 (div. June 1965); 1 child, Brent Allen; m. William Lloyd Van Bise, Mar. 1, 1995. BS in Chemistry and Physics, U. Calif., Berkeley, 1962, MS in Nuclear Engring., 1964, PhD in Nuclear Sci., 1979. Staff rschr. Lawrence Berkeley Lab. U. Calif., 1963-79; staff rschr. Lawrence Livermore Nat. Lab., Livermore, Calif., 1966-69; prof., instr. U. Calif., 1971-74; instr., rschr. Stanford (Calif.) Linear Accelerator Ctr., 1971-72; rschr. SRI Internat., Menlo Park, Calif., 1974-76; dir. Tecnic Rsch. Labs., San Leandro, Calif., 1979—; v.p. Magtek Labs, Inc., Reno, 1988-94; prof. physics U. Nev., Stanford, 1990—; cons. McDonnell-Douglass, L.A., 1978, 80, Learned Soc. Can., Montreal, 1981, USN, Silver Spring, Md., 1983, NASA, Martin-Marietta, New Orleans, 1988-89; adviser Engring. Inst., Provo, Utah, 1979. Patentee in field. Del. UN, N.Y.C., 1979, mem. UN com., 1989; adviser Congress Office Tech. Assessment, Washington, 1979-81; adviser, cons. City Coun., Reno, 1993. Recipient Outstanding Contbn. award Am. Astron. Soc., 1978, Honor award Rosebridge Grad. Sch., 1988; grantee USN, 1970-74, 82-83, PF Found., 1978, 79, 81; Delta Delta Delta scholar, 1960; Iota Sigma Pi Woman's fellow, 1961. Mem. IEEE, Am. Phys. Soc. (chair), Am. Chem. Soc. (v.p.), Lawrence Berkeley Lab. Fundametal Physics (chair, pres.), Psychology Rsch. Group San Franciso (bd. dirs., pres.). Avocations: poetry, photography, art, skin and scuba diving.

RAUSCHER, TOMLINSON GENE, electronics company executive; b. Oneida, N.Y., May 27, 1946; s. Grant Koster and Rosalind Rebecca (Smith) R.; B.S., Yale U., 1968; M.S., U. N.C., Chapel Hill, 1971; Ph.D., U. Md., 1975; M.B.A., U. Rochester, 1984; children—David Grant, Tasha Candice, April Abigail, Nathan Tomlinson. Computer specialist Naval Research Lab., Washington, 1972-75; mgr. software tech. applications NCR Corp., Cambridge, Ohio, 1975-76; sr. computer architect Amdahl Corp., Sunnyvale, Calif., 1976-77; mgr. software systems GTE Labs., Waltham, Mass., 1977-78; mgr. product devel. and software systems design Xerox Corp., Rochester, N.Y., 1978-95, mgr. sys. products family group, 1995—; vis. asst. prof. Ohio U., 1976; adj. prof. Rochester Inst. Tech., 1991—. Cert. computer programmer, data processor. Winner Masters Pole Vault—Empire State Games Championship, Eastern Region Masters Championship, Can. Nat. Masters Championship, U.S. Nat. Championship, N.Am. Masters Championship; named All-Am. champion. Mem. IEEE (sr.), Assn. Computing Machinery, Greater Rochester Track Club. Author: (with A. Agrawala) Foundations of Microprogramming—Architecture, Software and Applications, 1976, Software Development and Management for Microprocessor-Based Systems, 1987; contbr. articles on time to market, orgn., mgmt., software engring., computer architecture, microprogramming to profl. jours.; patentee computer systems design. Home: 85 Sunset Blvd Pittsford NY 14534-2142 Office: Xerox Corp 300 Main St East Rochester NY 14445-1728 *You can accomplish more with others than by yourself. Delegate decision making responsiblity to those who have the knowledge to make those decisions.*

RAUSEO, VICTOR, television writer and producer. Writer TV series, including Dorothy, 1979, Welcome Back Kotter, 1979, Private Benjamin, 1981-82, Just Our Luck, 1983-84, Alice, 1979-85, Our Time, 1985, Roomies, 1987, I Married Dora, 1988, Hooperman, 1989, Doogie Howser, M.D., 1989-91; exec. prodr. TV series Frasier, 1992— (Emmy award for outstanding comedy series 1995). Office: care ICM 8942 Wilshire Blvd Beverly Hills CA 90211

RAUSHENBUSH, WALTER BRANDEIS, law educator; b. Madison, Wis., June 13, 1928; s. Paul A. and Elizabeth (Brandeis) R.; m. Marylu de Watteville, May 3, 1956; children: Lorraine Elizabeth, Richard Walter, Carla de Watteville, Paul Brandeis. AB magna cum laude in Govt., Harvard U., 1950; JD with high honors, U. Wis., 1953. Bar: Wis. 1953. Ptnr. LaFollette, Sinykin & Doyle, Madison, 1956-58; mem. faculty U. Wis.-Madison, 1958—, prof. law, 1966-95; prof. emeritus, 1995—; vis. prof. law U. San Diego, 1992-9, 96, 97; project dir. real estate transfer study Am. Bar Found., 1967-72; trustee nat. Law Sch. Admission Coun., 1968-70, 72-95, chmn. pre-law com., 1970-74, chmn. svcs. com., 1976-78, pres., 1980-82; legal advisor Madison Citizens Fair Housing, 1961-63, Wis. Citizens Family Planning, 1965-73; mem. real property drafting com. Multistate Bar Exam., 1986—. Author: Wisconsin Construction Lien Law, 1974, (with others) Wisconsin Real Estate Law, 1984, 4th edit., 1994, Brown on Personal Property, 3d edit., 1975, Real Estate Transactions Cases and Materials, 1994. Served with USAF, 1953-56, col. Res. ret. Mem. ABA, State Bar Wis., Dane County Bar Assn., AAUP, Order of Coif, Phi Beta Kappa, Phi Delta Phi (province pres. 1963-75). Presbyterian (elder). Club: Stage Harbor Yacht (Chatham, Mass.). Home: 3942 Plymouth Circle Madison WI 53705 Office: U Wis Law Sch Madison WI 53706-1399

RAUTENBERG, ROBERT FRANK, consulting statistician; b. Milw., Sept. 14, 1943; s. Raymond Clarence and Anne Josephine (Winter) R.; m. Meredith Taylor, June 2, 1965 (div. Feb. 1975); 1 child, Matthew Carl. PhD in Bus. Adminstrn., Pacific Western U., 1983; post doctorate rsch., Sorbonne U., Paris. Pvt. practice acctg. Kansas City, Mo., 1975-76; pres. Seven Diamond Enterprises, San Francisco, 1976-78; chief exec. officer Assurance Systems, San Francisco, 1984—. Author: The Analytical Management Handbook, 1985, Supplement to the Analytical Management Handbook, 1991; contbr. articles to profl. jours. and conf. proceedings. Fellow Royal Statis. Soc.; mem. Internat. Soc. Bayesian Analysis (charter). Episcopalian. Avocations: swimming, skiing, traveling. Home: 711 Leavenworth St San Francisco CA 94109-6084 Office: Assurance Systems PO Box 191333 San Francisco CA 94119-1333 *Personal philosophy: I am always surprised at the willingness of the human spirit to face new challenges.*

RAVAL, DILIP N., pharmaceutical executive; b. 1933. BS in Physics and Chemistry, U. Bombay, India, 1953, MS in Clin. Biochemistry, 1955; PhD in Physics and Chemistry, U. Oregon, 1962. Mgr. Varian Arrowgraph, Calif., 1955-68; dir. U. Calif. Med. Ctr., San Francisco, 1968-70; dir. rsch. Alcon Labs., Inc., Fort Worth, 1970-72, gen. mgr. science and tech., 1972-75, v.p. rsch. and devel., 1975-88, sr. v.p. rsch. and devel., 1988—; now exec. v.p. rsch. and devel. Office: Alcon Laboratories Inc 6201 South Fwy Fort Worth TX 76134-2001*

RAVE, JAMES A., bishop. Bishop of Northwestern Ohio, Evang. Luth. Ch. in Am., Toledo. Office: Evang Luth Ch Am 621 Bright Rd Findlay OH 45840-6987

RAVECHÉ, HAROLD JOSEPH, university administrator, physical chemist; b. N.Y.C., Mar. 18, 1943; s. Harold Edward Raveche and Helen Patricia (DeVincent) Gravino; m. Elizabeth Marie Scott, Jan. 26, 1974; children—John Vincent, Justin Blaise, Bernice Helen, Elizabeth Ann. B.A. in Chemistry, Hofstra U., 1963; Ph.D. in Phys. Chemistry, U. Calif.-San Diego, 1968. NRC postdoctoral assoc. Nat. Bur. Standards, Gaithersburg, Md., 1968-70, research chemist, 1970-78, chief thermophysics div., 1978-85; dean Sch. of Sci., prof. chemistry Rensselaer Poly. Inst., Troy, N.Y., 1985-88; pres. Stevens Inst. Tech., Hoboken, N.J., 1988—; bd. dirs. Nat. West N.J. and Bancorp, Atlantic Energy Inc.; commr. of sci. and tech., N.J. Editor: Perspectives in Statistical Physics, 1980; contbr. articles to profl. jours. Pres. Potomac Highlands Citizens Assn., Md., 1978-80. Recipient Disting. Young Scientist of Yr. award Md. Acad. Scis., 1975, U.S. Sr. Exec. Service award Nat. Bur. Standards, 1983, Equal Employment Opportunity award Nat. Bur. Standards, 1984. Mem. AAAS (commn. on sci. edn. 1972-75), Am. Phys. Soc. (adv. council 1975-78), Soc. for Indsl. and Applied Math. (adv. bd. conf. on large-scale computational problems 1984-88), Am. Chem. Soc., Sigma Xi. Roman Catholic. Avocations: hiking, swimming, skiing, music, theater. Office: Stevens Inst Tech Office of Pres Castle Point On Hudson Hoboken NJ 07030

RAVELLETTE, BARBARA LYNN, account executive; b. Buffalo, N.Y., Mar. 23, 1954; d. Roy Aaron and Ruth Christine (Steffens) Stewart; m. William Edgar Ravellette Jr., Jan. 17, 1985; 1 child, Jacquelyn Christine. BS, Ind. State U., 1974; MS, Butler U., 1981. Elem. tchr. Clark Pleasant Cmty. Sch., Whiteland, Ind., 1976-81; regional reading cons. Ginn Pub. Co. and Laidlaw Bros., Chgo., 1981-86; so. Ind. sales rep. MacMillian Pub., Greenwood, Ind., 1986-89; mgr. electronic transmission Agy. for Instrnl. Tech., Bloomington, Ind., 1989—; negotiator rep. Clark Pleasant Sch.

Coop., Whiteland, 1976-81; nat. presenter Agy. for Instrnl. Tech., 1989—; pres. Quonset Investment Club, Bloomington, 1991-94; tutor in field. Participant Leadership Bloomington, Ind., 1994. Mem. Assn. Ind. Media Educators, Nat. Coun. Tchrs. Math. Avocations: fitness, reading, public speaking, parenting. Office: AIT Box A Bloomington IN 46204

RAVEN, BERTRAM H(ERBERT), psychology educator; b. Youngstown, Ohio, Sept. 26, 1926; s. Morris and Lillian (Greenfeld) R.; m. Celia Cutler, Jan. 21, 1961; children: Michelle G., Jonathan H. BA, Ohio State U., 1948, MA, 1949; PhD, U. Mich., 1953. Research assoc. Research Ctr. for Group Dynamics, Ann Arbor, Mich., 1952-54; lectr. psychology U. Mich., Ann Arbor, 1953-54; vis. prof. U. Nijmegen, U. Utrecht, Netherlands, 1954-55; psychologist RAND Corp., Santa Monica, Calif., 1955-56; prof. UCLA, 1956—, chair dept. psychology, 1983-88; vis. prof. Hebrew U., Jerusalem, 1962-63, U. Wash., Seattle, U. Hawaii, Honolulu, 1968, London Sch. Econs. and Polit. Sci., London, 1969-70; external examiner U. of the W.I., Trinidad and Jamaica, 1980—, rsch. assoc. Psychol. Rsch. Ctr., 1993—; participant Internat. Expert Conf. on Health Psychology, Tilburg, The Netherlands, 1986; cons., expert witness in field, 1979—. co-dir. Tng. Program in Health Psychology, UCLA, 1979-88; cons. World Health Orgn., Manila, 1985-86; cons., expert witness various Calif. cts., 1978—. Author: (with others) People in Groups, 1976, Discovering Psychology, 1977, Social Psychology, 1983, Social Psychology: People in Groups (Chinese edition), 1994; editor: (with others) Contemporary Health Services, 1982, Policy Studies Rev. Ann., 1980; editor: Jour. Social Issues, 1969-74; contbr. articles to profl. jours. Guggenheim fellow, Israel, 1962-63; Fulbright scholar The Netherlands, 1954-55, Israel, 1962-63, Britain, 1969-70; Citation from Los Angeles City Council, 1966, Rsch. on Soc. power by Calif. Sch. of profl. psychology, L.A., 1991; NATO sr. fellow, Italy, 1989. Fellow APA (chair bd. social and ethical responsibility 1978-82), Am. Psychol. Soc., Soc. for Psychol. Study of Social Issues (pres. 1973-74, coun. 1995—); mem. AAAS, Am. Sociol. Assn., Internat. Assn. Applied Psychology, Soc. Exptl. Social Psychology, Assn. Advancement of Psychology (founding, bd. dirs. 1974-81), Internat. Soc. Polit. Psychology (governing coun. 1996—), Interam. Psychol. Soc., Am. Psychology-Law Soc. Avocations: guitar, travel, international studies. Home: 2212 Camden Ave Los Angeles CA 90064-1906 Office: UCLA Dept Psychology Los Angeles CA 90095-1563

RAVEN, CORINNE, principal. Prin. Mother McAuley Liberal Arts High Sch., Chgo. Recipient Blue Ribbon Sch. award U.S. Dept. Edn., 1990-91. Office: Mother McAuley Liberal Arts High Sch 3737 W 99th St Chicago IL 60642-3321

RAVEN, GREGORY KURT, retail executive; b. Elmhurst, Ill., Sept. 14, 1949; s. Eugene Alexander and Eloise Irene (McGhee) R.; m. Margot Clesta Theis, Feb. 2, 1974; children: Scott, Bryan, Ashley, Michael. B.B.A., Bucknell U., 1971. Second v.p. Chase Manhattan Bank, N.Y.C., 1973-76; corp. fin. specialist, dir. corp. fin. Gt. Atlantic and Pacific Tea Co., Inc., Montvale, N.J., 1977-80, asst. treas., 1980-82, treas., asst. chief fin. officer, 1982-87; v.p., treas. Revco Drug Stores, Twinsburg, Ohio, 1987-88, exec. v.p. fin. and chief fin. officer, 1988-95; pres., CEO Hills Stores Co., Canton, Mass., 1996—. Republican. Office: Revco Drug Stores Inc 1925 Enterprise Pky Twinsburg OH 44087-2207

RAVEN, PETER HAMILTON, botanical garden director, botany educator; b. Shanghai, China, June 13, 1936; s. Walter Francis and Isabelle Marion (Breen) R.; children—Alice Catherine, Elizabeth Marie, Francis Clark, Kathryn Amelia. AB with highest honors, U. Calif.-Berkeley, 1957; PhD, UCLA, 1960; DSc (hon.), St. Louis U., 1982, Knox Coll., 1983, So. Ill. U., 1983, Miami U., 1986, U. Goteborg, 1987, Rutgers U., 1988, U. Mass., 1988, Leiden U., The Netherlands, 1990; HHD (hon.), Webster U., 1989; D.Sc. (hon.), Universidad Nacional de La Plata, Argentina, 1991, Westminster Coll., 1992, U. Mo., 1992, Washington U., 1993, U. Conn., 1993; DSc (hon.), U. Cordoba, Argentina, 1993. Taxonomist, curator Rancho Santa Ana Botanic Garden, Claremont, Calif., 1961-62; asst. prof., then assoc. prof. biol. scis. Stanford U., Calif., 1962-71; dir. Mo. Bot. Garden, St. Louis, 1971—; adj. prof. biology St. Louis U., 1973—; Engelmann prof. botany Washington U., St. Louis, 1976—; adj. prof. biology U. Mo., St. Louis, 1976—; sr. rsch. fellow New Zealand Dept. Sci. and Indsl. Rsch., 1969-70; v.p. XIII Internat. Bot. Congress, Sydney, 1981; home sec. Nat. Acad. Scis., 1987—; chmn. report rev. com. NRC, 1989—; mem. pres. com. Adv. on Sci. and Tech., 1994—; hon. vice-chair 27th Internat. Geographical Cong., 1992; hon. v.p. XV Internt. Bot. Cong., Tokyo, 1993; mem. Nat. Sci. Bd., 1990-94; mem. jury Internat. St. Francis Prize for Environment, 1990-93; mem. exec. com. Joint Appeal by Religion and Sci. for Environment, 1991—; mem. external adv. bd. Com. on Peabody Mus., Yale U., 1992-94; mem. coun. World Resources Inst., 1992—; mem. adv. com. Africa Ctr. for Resources and Environment, 1992—, Third World Found. N.Am., 1993; mem. adv. com. to biodiversity com. Chinese Acad. Scis., 1993—; mem. Exec. Com. Round Table, St. Louis, 1993—; mem. hon. fgn. adv. bd. Botanical Garden Orgn. Thailand, 1993—. Author: Native Shrubs of Southern California, 1966, (with P.R. Ehrlich, R.W. Holm) Papers on Evolution, 1969, (with H. Curtis) Biology of Plants, 1971, 4th edit., 1986, (with R.F. Evert and S.E. Eichhorn) 5th edit., 1992, (with B. Berlin and D. Breedlove) Principles of Tzeltal Plant Classification, 1974, (with G.B. Johnson) Biology, 1986, 3d edit., 1992, Understanding Biology, 1988, 3d edit., 1995; editor: (with L.E. Gilbert) Coevolution of Animals and Plants, 1981, (with F.J. Radovsky & S.H. Sohmer) Biogeography of the Tropical Pacific, 1984, (with others) Topics in Plant Population Biology, 1979, (with K. Iwatsuki and W.J. Bock) Modern Aspects of Species, 1986; editor-in-chief Brittonia, 1963-66; mme. editorial bd. Flora Neotropica, 1965-84; editor (with D.E. Osterbrock) Origins and Extinctions, 1988, paperback, 1992, (with R.M. Polhill) Advances in Legume Systematics, 1981 (with L. Berg and G.B. Johnson) Environment, 1995; mem. editorial bd. Evolution, 1963-65, 76-79, Memoirs of N.Y. Botanical Garden, 1966-84, N.Am. Flora, 1966-84, Am. Naturalist, 1967-70, Annual Rev. Ecology and Systematics, 1971-75, Flora of Ecuador, 1974—, Evolutionary Theory, 1975—, Adansonia, 1976—, Jour. Biogeography, 1978—, Science, 1979-82, Proceedings of U.S. Nat. Acad. Scis., 1980-87, World Book, Inc., 1982-86, Diversity, 1985-90, Bothalia, 1985—, Serie Botánica of the Anales del Instituto de Biología UNAM, 1989, Ecol. Applications, 1989-92, others; mem. adv. bd. Applied Botany Abstracts, 1981—, Tropical Plant Sci. Research, 1982—, Darwiniana, 1985—; mem. internat. editl. com. Acta Botánica Mexicana, 1987—; mem. internat. editl. adv. bd. Candollea, 1995—; mem. editl. bd. Botanical Bulletin Academia Sinica, 1988—, Botanical Mag., 1988-92, Chinese Jour. of Botany, 1991—, Edinburgh Jour. of Botany, 1994—; co-chmn. editl. com. Flora of China, 1988—; advisor Plants Today, 1988-89; contbr. over 400 articles to profl. jours. bd. curators U. Mo., 1985-90; commr. Tower Grove Park, St. Louis, 1971—; mem. Arnold Arboretum Vis. Com., 1974-81, chmn. 1976-81; bd. overseers Morris Arboretum, 1977-adv. bd. Nat. Tropical Botanical Garden, 1975—; mem. Smithsonian Council, 1985-90; chmn. St. Louis Area Mus. Collaborative, 1985-91, Commn. for Flora Neotropica, 1985—; mem. Commn. on Mus. for New Century, 1981-84; mem. sci. and engring. panel Com. on Scholarly Communication with People's Republic China, 1981-85; chmn. com. to visit dept. organismic and evolutionary biology Harvard U., 1982-84, mem. 84-85; ednl. adv. bd. John Simon Guggenheim Meml. Found., 1986—; research assoc. botany Bernice P. Bishop Mus., 1985—; hon. trustee Acad. Sci. of St. Louis, 1986—; chmn. Internat. Union for the Conservation of Nature, World Wildlife Fund, 1984-87, hon. chmn. 1987-90; mem. adv. and tech. bd. Fundación de Parques Nacionales and Fundación Neotrópica, Costa Rica, 1988—; mem. Nat. Coun. World Wildlife Fund and Conservation Foun., 1989—, U.S. bd. dirs. 1983-88, bd. dirs. Conservation Found., 1985-88, sci. adv. com. Conservation Internat., 1988—, chmn's. coun., 1989, World Wildlife Fund, 1987-90, Conservation Found., 1989—, Found. Flora Malesianna, 1992—, Sci. Svc., 1993—; hon. scientific adv. com. XVII Pacific Sci. Congress, 1990-91; adv. bd. The Winslow Found., 1993—, The Internat. Sci. Camp The Earth We Share, 1993—; exec. bd. Internat. Sci. Found. for the Former Soviet Union, 1992—; internat. adv. bd. Fifth ICSEB Congress, Hungary, 1994—. Commn. mem. U.S. MAB, 1994-95. Recipient A.P. DeCandolle prize, Geneva, 1970; Disting. Service award Japan Am. Soc. So. Calif., 1977; award of Merit, Bot. Soc. Am., 1977; Achievement medal Garden Club Am., 1978; Willdenow medal Berlin Bot. Garden, 1979; Disting. Service award Am. Inst. Biol. Scis., 1981; Joseph Priestly medal, Dickinson Coll., 1982; Gold Seal medal Nat. Council of State Garden Clubs, 1982; Internat. Environ. Leadership medal UN Environ. Program, 1982; Spl. citiation Doña Doris Yankelewitz de Monge, 1985, Internat. Prize for Biology, Govt. Japan, 1986, Hutchinson medal Chgo. Hort. Soc., 1986, Archie F. Carr medal, 1987, Global 500 Honor Roll UN Environ. Program, 1987, Am. Fuchsia Soc. Achievement Medal, 1987, George Robert White Medal of Honor Mass. Horticultural Soc., 1987, Robert Allerton Medal Nat. Tropical Bot. Garden, 1988, Nat. Conservation Achievement award Nat. Wildlife Fedn., 1989, Delmer S. Fahrney medal Franklin Inst., Phila., 1989, (with E.O. Wilson) Environ. prize Institut de la Vie (Paris), 1990, Order of Golden Ark (officer), The Netherlands, 1990, award for Support of Sci. Coun. Sci. Soc. Pres., 1990, (with Norman Myers) Volvo Environ. prize, 1992, Pres.'s Conservation Achievement Awd., 1993, Nature Conservancyvement award TNC, 1993, Internat. award Internat. Inst. of St. Louis, 1994, Founder's Coun. Centennial Merit award The Field Mus. of Natural History, 1994, Sword of St. Ignatius Loyola award St. Louis U., 1994, Tyler Environ. Achievement prize, 1994, and numerous other botanical awards and honors; Guggenheim fellow, 1969-70; John D. and Catherine T. MacArthur Found. fellow, 1985-90, NSF postdoctoral fellow, Brit. Mus. London, 1960-61. Fellow Am. Acad. Arts and Scis. (com. on membership 1980-82), Linnean Soc. London (fgn. mem.), Calif. Acad. Scis. (CAS Fellow, Fellows' medal 1988), AAAS, Indian Nat. Sci. Acad., Third World Acad. Scis., World Acad. Art & Sci.; mem. NSF (systematic biology panel 1973-76, chmn. adv. com. for biol. behavioral and social scis. 1984-90), NAS (com. on human rights 1984-87, home sec. 1987—), Royal Danish Acad. Scis. and Letters (fgn. hon.), Royal Swedish Acad. Scis. (fgn.), Royal Soc. New Zealand (hon.), NRC (gov. bd. 1983-86, 87-88, chmn. com. on research priorities in tropical biology 1977-79, assembly life scis. 1979-81, com. on selected research problems in humid tropics 1980-82, commn. internat. relations 1981-82), Calif. Bot. Soc. (v.p. 1968-69), Am. Soc. Plant Taxonomists (pres. 1972), Assn. Systematics Collections (pres. 1980-82, Fed. Council Arts and Humanities, Nat. Geographic Soc. (com. on research and explortion 1982—), Internat. Orgn. Plant Biosystematists (v.p. 1989-92, pres. 92-95), Internat. Assn. for Plant Taxonomy (council 1981—), Orgn. Tropical Studies (treas. 1981-84, v.p. devel. 1984-85, pres. 1985-88, past pres. 1988-90, bd. dirs. 1981-91), Am. Soc. Naturalists (pres. 1983), Miller Inst. Basic Research in Sci. (adv. bd. 1983-89), Am. Inst. Biol. Scis. (pres. 1983-84), Mo. Acad. Scis., Geol. Soc. Am., Bot. Soc. Am. (pres. 1975, chmn. com. on sci. exchange with People's Republic China 1978-84), Assn. Tropical Biology (bd. dirs. 1981-85), Am. Assn. Mus. (exec. com. 1980-83), Assn. Sci. Mus. Dirs., Assn. Pacific Systematists, Sociedad Argentina de Botanica (socio honorario), Fundación Miguel Lillo (hon.), Soc. Systematic Zool., Sociedad Botánica de México (life), Assn. pour l'Etude Taxonomique de la Flore d'Afrique Tropicale, Orgn. for Phyto-Taxonomic Investigation of Mediterranean Area (council 1975-89), All-Union Botanical Soc. USSR (hon. fgn. mem.), Accademia Nazionale delle Scienze detta dei XL (fgn.), Am. Philosophical Soc, Russian Acad. Scis. (fgn. mem.), Nat. Acad. Scis. India (fgn. fellow 1990—), Academia de Ciencias Exactas, Físicas y Naturales, Austrian Acad. Scis., Academia Chilena de Ciencias, Academia Nacional de Ciencias, Academy Scis. Ukraine, Chinese Acad. Scis., Nature Conservancy (Pres. Conservation Achievement Awd., 1993), Phi Beta Kappa, Sigma Xi. Office: Mo Bot Garden PO Box 299 Saint Louis MO 63166-0299

RAVEN, ROBERT DUNBAR, lawyer; b. Cadillac, Mich., Sept. 26, 1923; s. Christian and Gladys L. (Dunbar) R.; m. Leslie Kay Erickson, June 21, 1947; children: Marta Ellen, Matt Robert, Brett Lincoln. AB with honors, Mich. State U., 1949; LLB, U. Calif., Berkeley, 1952. Bar: Calif. 1953. Assoc. Morrison & Foerster and predecessor, San Francisco, 1952-56, ptnr., 1956-94, sr. of counsel, 1994—; chmn. Morrison & Foerster (and predecessor), San Francisco, 1974-82; mem. Jud. Coun. of Calif., 1983-87. Bd. dirs. Bay Area USO, 1964-73, pres., 1968-70; mem. San Francisco Mayor's Criminal Justice Coun., 1971-72; co-chmn. San Francisco Lawyer's Com. for Urban Affairs, 1976-78; bd. dirs. Lawyers Com. for Civil Rights Under Law, 1976—. With USAAF, 1942-45. Decorated Air medal with oak leaf cluster. Mem. ABA (pres. 1989, mem. standing com. fed. judiciary 1975-80, chmn. 1978-80, chmn. standing com. on legal aid and indigent defendants 1981-83, chair standing com. dispute resolution 1991-93, chair sect. dispute resolution 1993-94), Am. Arbitration Assn. (bd. dirs. 1988-96), CPR Inst. for Dispute Resolution (exec. com.), Internat. Acad. Trial Lawyers, State Bar Calif. (gov. 1978-81, pres. 1981), Fed. Bar Assn., Bar Assn. San Francisco (pres. 1971), Am. Law Inst., Am. Bar Found., Am. Judicature Soc., Boalt Hall Alumni Assn. (pres. 1972-73), World Trade Club (San Francisco), Order of Coif. Democrat. Home: 1064 Via Alta Lafayette CA 94549-2916 Office: Morrison & Foerster 345 California St Fl 35 San Francisco CA 94104

RAVENAL, EARL CEDRIC, international relations educator, author; b. N.Y.C., Mar. 29, 1931; s. Alan M. and Mildred S. (Sherman) R.; m. Carol Bird Myers, May 26, 1956; children: Cornelia Jane, John Brodhead, Rebecca Eliza. B.A., Harvard U., 1952; postgrad., U. Cambridge, Eng., 1952-53; M.M.P. diploma, Harvard Bus. Sch., 1958; M.A., Johns Hopkins U., 1971; Ph.D., John Hopkins U., 1975. Treas. Elbe File & Binder Co., Inc., Fall River, Mass., 1955-64, pres., 1965-67; dir. Asian div. systems analysis Office Sec. Def., Washington, 1967-69; prof. internat. relations Johns Hopkins U. Sch. Advanced Internat. Studies, Washington, 1973-78, Georgetown U. Sch. Fgn. Service, Washington, 1976—; mem. bd. advisors Ctr. for Def. Info., Washington, 1971—, Inst. for Study of Diplomacy, 1983—. Author: (with others) Peace with China?, 1971, (with James Chace) Atlantis Lost, 1976, Never Again, 1979, Toward World Security, 1978, Strategic Disengagement and World Peace, 1979, NATO's Unremarked Demise, 1979, Defining Def., 1984, NATO: The Tides of Discontent, 1985, Large-Scale Foreign Policy Change, 1989, Designing Defense, 1991; contbg. editor Inquiry Mag., 1976-85, Critical Rev., 1987—; contbr. articles in field to profl. jours. Advisor Democratic Presdl. Campaign, 1972; advisor Jerry Brown Presdl. Campaign, 1976, Libertarian Presdl. Campaign, 1980; shadow def. sec. Libertarian Party, 1993—. Served with JAGC U.S. Army, 1953-55. Henry fellow U. Cambridge, 1952-53; mem. faculty Salzburg Seminar in Am. Studies, 1977; fellow Bellagio Ctr. Rockefeller Found., 1975, Woodrow Wilson Internat. Ctr. for Scholars, 1973, Washington Ctr. for Fgn. Policy Research, 1974, Inst. Policy Studies, 1977-80; sr. fellow Cato Inst., 1985-91. Mem. Council Fgn. Relations, Am. Polit. Sci. Assn., Internat. Inst. Strategic Studies, Fed. Am. Scientists, Internat. Studies Assn. Libertarian. Clubs: Cosmos (Washington); Fed. City (Washington); Harvard (N.Y.C.); Signet (Cambridge, Mass.); Tred Avon Yacht (Oxford, Md.). Home: 4439 Cathedral Ave NW Washington DC 20016-3562

RAVENHILL, PHILIP LEONARD, curator, art historian; b. Bath, U.K., June 2, 1945; s. Leonard and Martha (Wilson) R.; children: Geoffrey, Brendan, Amanda. BA in Philosophy, Nyack Coll., 1968; MA in Anthropology, New Sch. for Social Rsch., 1970, PhD, 1976. Rsch. assoc. Inst. d'Ethno-Sociologie Univ. d'Abidjan, 1972-74, rsch. assoc. Inst. d'Histoire, d'Art et d'Archéologie Africains, 1975-77, attaché de recherche, 1978-79, chargé de recherche, 1979-82; sr. rsch. fellow Internat. African Inst., London, 1982-87; project dir. West African Mus. Project, Abidjan, Ivory Coast, 1982-87; chief curator Nat. Mus. African Art, Smithsonian Inst., Washington, 1987—; cons. on cultural preservation and edn. The Ford Found., West Africa, 1982, 84-87; mem. steering com. Smithsonian Inst. Forum on Material Culture, 1988-91, West African Mus. Project Internat. African Inst., 1987-96; dir. joint Nat. Mus. African Art-Musée National du Mali film team, 1989; co-chair Eighth Triennial Symposium on African Art, 1989; bd. dirs. West African Mus. Programme; N.Am. coord. ICOM Conf., 1991; cons. in field; participant numerous confs. Author: (book) Dreams & Reverie, 1996, The Art of the Personal Object, 1991; author, field coord. video films for exhbns.; contbr. articles to profl. jours. Home: Smithsonian Inst Nat Mus African Art 3817 Calvert St NW Washington DC 20007

RAVENHOLT, REIMERT THOROLF, epidemiologist; b. Milltown, Wis., Mar. 9, 1925; s. Ansgar Benedikt and Kristine Henriette (Petersen) R.; divorced; children: Janna, Mark, Lisa, Dane; m. Betty Butler Howell, Sept. 26, 1981. B.S., U. Minn., 1948, M.B., 1951, M.D., 1952; M.P.H., U. Calif.-Berkeley, 1956. Intern USPHS Hosp., San Francisco, 1951-52; epidemic intelligence service officer USPHS Communicable Disease Ctr., Atlanta, 1952-54; dir. epidemiology and communicable disease div. Seattle-King County Health Dept., 1954-61; epidemiology cons. European area USPHS, Paris, 1961-63; assoc. prof. preventive medicine U. Wash. Med. Sch., Seattle, 1963-66; dir. Office of Population, AID, Washington, 1966-79, World Health Surveys, Ctrs. for Disease Control, 1980-82; asst. dir. epidemiology and research Nat. Inst. Drug Abuse, Rockville, Md., 1982-84; chief epidemiology br. FDA, Rockville, Md., 1984-87; dir. World Health Surveys, Inc., Seattle, 1987-93; pres. Population Health Imperatives, Seattle, 1993—. Contbr. articles to profl. publs. Served with USPHS, 1951-54, 61-63. Recipient Disting Honor award AID, 1973, Hugh Moore Meml. award IPPF and Population Crisis Com., 1974. Fellow Am. Coll. Epidemiology, APHA (Carl Schultz award 1978); mem. Am. Coun. on Sci. and Health (bd. dirs.), N.W. Danish Found. (bd. dirs.), Cosmos Club (Washington). Independent. Home: 3156 E Laurelhurst Dr NE Seattle WA 98105-5333

RAVENTOS, ANTOLIN, radiology educator; b. Wilmette, Ill., June 3, 1925; s. Enrique Antolin and Juanita (Gillespie) R.; m. Anne Patricia Gray, 1976. Student, Northwestern U., 1941-44; S.B., U. Chgo., 1945, M.D., 1947; M.Sc., U. Pa., 1954. From instr. to prof. radiology Sch. Medicine U. Pa., Phila., 1950-70; prof. radiology Sch. Medicine, U. Calif.-Davis, 1970-91, chmn. dept., 1970-77, prof. emeritus, 1991—. Assoc. editor: Cancer, 1964-91. Served with AUS, 1944-46, 52-54. Fellow Am. Coll. Radiology (chancellor 1964-70), Am. Radium Soc. (pres. 1972-73). Home: PO Box 3136 El Macero CA 95618-0736 Office: 44434 Country Club Dr El Macero CA 95618-1043

RAVETCH, IRVING, screenwriter; b. Newark, Nov. 14, 1920; s. I. Shalom and Sylvia (Shapiro) R.; m. Harriet Frank Jr., Nov. 24, 1946. BA, UCLA, 1941. Screenwriter: (films) (with La Cava) Living in a Big Way, 1947, The Outriders, 1950, Vengeance Valley, 1951; (with Harriet Frank, Jr.) The Long, Hot Summer, 1958, The Sound and the Fury, 1959, Home from the Hill, 1959, The Dark at the Top of the Stairs, 1960, House of Cards, 1969, The Cowboys, 1972, Conrak, 1974, The Spikes Gang, 1974, Norma Rae, 1979 (Academy award nomination best adapted screenplay 1979), Murphy's Romance, 1985, Stanley and Iris, 1990; writer, prodr.: (with Frank) Hud, 1963 (Academy award nomination best adapted screenplay 1963, N.Y. Film Critics Circle award best screenplay 1963), Hombre, 1967, The Reivers, 1969; story: (with Frank) Ten Wanted Men, 1955. Recipient N.Y. Film Critics award, 1963, Writers' Guild Am. award, 1988; Oscar nomination for Hud, Acad. Motion Picture Arts and Scis., 1963, Norma Rae, 1979. Office: care William Morris Agy Inc 151 S El Camino Beverly Hills CA 90212

RAVID, KATYA, medical educator; m. Shmuel Ravid; children: Yinon Arie, Noga Leah, Jonathan David. BSc, Technion-Israel Inst. Tech., Haifa, Israel, 1979, PhD, 1985. Postdoctoral fellow dept. biochemistry Brandeis Univ., Waltham, Mass., 1986-88; postdoctoral assoc. dept. biology Mass. Inst. Tech., Cambridge, 1988-91; instr. molecular medicine Harvard Medical Sch., Boston, 1992; asst. prof. biochemistry Boston Univ. Sch. Medicine, Boston, 1993-95, assoc. prof. biochemistry rsch. assoc. prof. medicine, 1993—, investigator Whitaker Cardiovascular Inst., 1993—, scientific dir. Core Transgenci facility, 1993—; peer reviewer Am. Heart Assn. 1995—. Contbr. articles to profl. jours. With Israeli Def. Forces, 1977-79. Recipient numerous rsch. grants. Mem. The Am. Soc. Hematology, Am. Soc. Cell Biology, Am. Soc. Biochemistry and Molecular Biology, Am. Assn. Advancement of Sci. Office: Boston Univ Sch Medicine Dept Biochemistry 80 East Concord St Boston MA 02118

RAVIOLA, ELIO, anatomist, neurobiologist; b. Asti, Italy, June 15, 1932; came to U.S., 1970; s. Giuseppe and Luigina (Carbone) R.; m. Trude Kleinschmidt; 1 child, Giuseppe. M.D. summa cum laude, U. Pavia, Italy, 1957, Ph.D. in Anatomy, 1963. Resident in neurology and psychiatry U. Pavia, asst. prof., 1958-70; asso. prof. anatomy Harvard U. Med. Sch., Boston, 1970-74; prof. human anatomy Harvard U. Med. Sch., 1974-89, Bullard prof. neurobiology, 1989—, prof. ophthalmology, 1989—. Editorial bd.: Jour. Cell Biology, 1978-80; asso. editor: Anat. Record, 1972—. Mem. Am. Acad. Arts and Scis., Am. Soc. Cell Biology, Am. Assn. Anatomists, Soc. of Neurosci. Club: Harvard (Boston). Achievements include research on mechanism of vision. Office: Harvard U Med Sch Dept Neurobiology 220 Longwood Ave Boston MA 02115-5701

RAVIS, HOWARD SHEPARD, conference planner and publishing consultant; b. Waterbury, Conn., Mar. 3, 1934; s. Paul Morton and Ida Ruth (Levin) R.; m. Sophie G. Simons, Nov. 1, 1959; 1 dau., Heidi. B.S. in Journalism, Boston U., 1959. Sports editor Milford (Conn.) Citizen, 1959-60; editor Stratford (Conn.) News, 1960-61; news editor Wallingford (Conn.) Post, 1961-62; editor Needham (Mass.) Chronicle, 1962-66; reunion coordinator Boston U. Alumni Assn., 1966; copy desk man, writer Boston Globe, 1966; news editor Scholastic Tchr. mag., 1966-67; mgmt. and careers editor Electronic Design mag., 1967-68; mng. editor Teacher mag., 1968-74; editor, assoc. pub. Folio: The Magazine for Mag. Mgmt., New Canaan, Conn., 1974-77; v.p. seminar programming, also creative dir. Conf. Mgmt. Corp., Stamford, Conn., 1978-80; speaker; bd. dirs. Ossining (N.Y.) Open Door Med. Assocs., 1973-77; chmn. United Ossining Party, 1973, Ossining Citizens Com. Edn., 1972-73; treas., bd. dirs. Ossining Interfaith Council for Action, 1970-73. Editor: Magazine Publishing Management, 1976, the Handbook of Magazine Publishing, 2d edit., 1983. Rep. Town Meeting, Needham, 1966; mem. nat. alumni coun. Boston U., 1977-91; trustee Ossining Pub. Libr., 1986-96, v.p., 1988-89, pres., 1989-91, 95-96. With AUS, 1956-58. Recipient Jesse H. Neal Editorial Achievement award Am. Bus. Press, 1976; Top News Writing award New Eng. Press Assn., 1962. Mem. Boston U. Alumni Assn. (chmn. Westchester County 1972-83). Democrat. Home: 5 Amawalk Ct Ossining NY 10562-4509

RAVITCH, DIANE SILVERS, historian, educator, author, government official; b. Houston, July 1, 1938; d. Walter Cracker and Ann Celia (Katz) Silvers; m. Richard Ravitch, June 26, 1960 (div. 1986); children: Joseph, Steven (dec.), Michael. BA, Wellesley Coll., 1960; PhD, Columbia U., 1975; LHD (hon.), Williams Coll., 1984, Reed Coll., 1985, Amherst Coll., 1986, SUNY, 1988, Ramapo Coll., 1990, St. Joseph's Coll., N.Y., 1991. Adj. asst. prof. Tchrs. Coll., Columbia U., N.Y.C., 1975-78, assoc. prof., 1978-83, adj. prof., 1983-91; asst. sec. office ednl. rsch. and improvement U.S. Dept. Edn., Washington, 1991-93, counselor to the sec. edn., 1991-93; vis. fellow Brookings Instn., Washington, 1993-94, non-resident sr. fellow, 1994—; sr. rsch. scholar NYU, 1994—; adj. fellow Manhattan Inst., 1996—. Author: The Great School Wars, 1974, The Revisionists Revised, 1977, The Troubled Crusade, 1983, The Schools We Deserve, 1985, National Standards in American Education, A Citizens Guide, 1995, (with others) Educating an Urban People, 1981, The School and the City, 1983, Against Mediocrity, 1984, Challenges to the Humanities, 1985, What Do Our 17 Year Olds Know?, 1987, The American Reader, 1990; co-editor: The Democracy Reader, 1992; editor: Learning from the Past, 1995, Debating the Future of American Education, 1995. Chair Ednl. Excellence Network, 1988-91, 94—; trustee N.Y. Pub. Libr., N.Y.C., 1981-87, hon. life trustee, 1988—; trustee N.Y. Coun. on Humanities, 1996—; bd. dirs. Woodrow Wilson Nat. Fellowship Found., 1987-91, Coun. Basic Edn., 1989-91. Recipient Award for Disting. Svc., N.Y. Acad. Pub. Edn., 1994; Guggenheim fellow, 1977-78; Phi Beta Kappa vis. scholar. Mem. Nat. Acad. Edn., Am. Acad. Arts and Scis., Soc. Am. Historians, N.Y. Hist. Soc. (trustee 1995—). Office: NYU 32 Press Bldg Washington Place New York NY 10003-6644

RAVITZ, LEONARD, JR., physician, scientist, consultant; b. Cuyahoga County, Ohio, Apr. 17; s. Leonard Robert and Esther Evelyn (Skerball) R. BS, Case Western Res. U., 1944; MD, Wayne State U., 1946; MS, Yale U., 1950. Diplomate Am. Bd. Psychiatry and Neurology, 1952. Rsch. asst. EEG to A.J. Derbyshire, PhD Harper Hosp., Detroit, 1943-46; electromagnetic field measurement project dept. asst. sec. Sec. Defense in Charge of Health & Medical E.H. Cushing, 1958; spl. trainee in hypnosis to Milton H. Erickson, MD Wayne County Gen. Hosp., Eloise, Mich., 1945-46, 46-80; rotating intern St. Elizabeth's Hosp., Washington, 1946-47; jr./sr. asst. resident in psychiatry Yale-New Haven Hosp.; asst. in psychiatry and mental hygiene Yale Med. Sch., 1947-48, assoc. in psychiatry and mental hygiene, 1948-49, rsch. fellow to Harold S. Burr, PhD, sect. neuro-anatomy, 1949-50, sr. resident in neuropsychiatry Richard S. Lyman svc., 1950-51; instr. Duke U. Med. Sch., Durham, 1950-51; assoc. to R. Burke Suitt, MD, Pvt. Diagnostic Clinic, Duke Hosp., Durham, 1951-53; assoc. Duke U. Med. Sch., 1951-53; vis. asst. prof. neuropsychiatry and asst. to vis. prof. Richard S. Lyman, MD, Meharry Med. Ctr., Nashville, 1953; asst. dir. profl. edn. in charge tng. U. Wyo. Nursing Sch. affiliates; chief rsch. rehab. bldg. Downey VA Hosp. (now called VA Hosp.), N. Chicago, Ill., 1953-54; assoc. psychiatry Sch. Medicine and Hosp., U. Pa., Phila., 1955-58; electromagnetic field measurement project office dep. asst. sec. def. in charge health & med. E.H. Cushing M.D. Dept. Def., Pentagon, 1958; dir. tng. and rsch. Ea. State Hosp., Williamsburg, Va., 1958-60; pvt. practice neuropsychiatry specializing in hypnosis Norfolk, Va., 1961—; psychiatrist, cons. Divsn. Alcohol Studies and Rehab. Va. Dept. Health (later Va. Dept. Mental Health and Mental Retardation), 1961-81; psychiatrist Greenpoint Clinic, Bklyn., 1983-87, 17th

St. Clinic, N.Y.C., 1987-92, Downstate Mental Hygiene Assocs., Bklyn., 1983—; sec.-treas. Euclid-97th St. Clinic, Inc., Cleve., 1957-63, pres., 1963-69; spl. tng. in epistemology and methodologic foundations of sci. knowledge F.S.C. Northrop, PhD, 1973-92; electrodynamic field rschr. with Harold S. Burr, PhD, sect. neuro-anatomy Yale Med. Sch., 1948-73; cons. hypnosis with Milton H. Erickson, MD, 1945-80; clin. asst. prof. psychiatry SUNY Health Sci. Ctr. Med. Sch., 1983—; pvt. cons., Cleve., 1961-69, Upper Montclair, N.J., 1982—; lectr. sociology Old Dominion U., Norfolk, 1961-62, cons. nutrition rsch. project Old Dominion U. Rsch. Found., 1978-90; spl. med. cons. Frederick Mil. Acad., Portsmouth, Va., 1963-71; cons. Tidewater Epilepsy Found., Chesapeake, Va., 1962-68, USPH Hosp. Alcohol Unit, Norfolk, 1980-81, Nat. Inst. Rehab. Therapy, Butler, N.J., 1982-83; participant 5th Internat. Congress Hypnosis and Psychosomatic Medicine, Gutenburg U., Mainz, Germany, 1970; organizer symposia on hypnosis in psychiatry and medicine, field theory as office practice, history of certain forensic and psychotherapeutic aspects of the study of man, Eastern State Hosp., Coll. William and Mary, James City County Med. Soc., Va. Soc. Clin. Hypnosis, Williamsburg, Va., 1959-60; founding pres. Found. for Study Electrodynamic Theory of Life, 1989—. Asst. editor Jour. Am. Soc. Psychosomatic Dentistry and Medicine, 1980-83; mem. editorial bd. Internat. Jour. Psychosomatics, 1984—; contbr. sects. to books, articles, book revs., abstracts to profl. publs. Sr. v.p. Willoughby Civic League, 1971-75. 1st lt. AUS, 1943-46. Lyman Rsch. Fund grantee, 1950-53. Fellow AAAS, Am. Psychiat. Assn. (life), N.Y. Acad. Scis., Am. Soc. Clin. Hypnosis (charter, cons. cert. program), Royal Soc. Health (London); mem. Va. Soc. Clin. Hypnosis (founding pres. 1959-60), Norfolk Acad. Medicine, Soc. for Investigation of Recurring Events, Va. Med. Soc., Sigma Xi, Nu Sigma Nu. Achievements include discovery of electromagetic field correlates of hypnosis, emotions, psychiatric/medical disorders, aging, and electic phenomena in humans which parallel those of other life forms, earth and atmosphere underwriting beginning short- and long-range predictions, such seemingly disparate phenomena united under a single regulating principle defined in terms of measurable field intensity and polarity. Office: SUNY Health Sci Ctr Med Sch Dept Psychiatry 450 Clarkson Ave Box 1203 Brooklyn NY 11203-2012 also: PO Box 9409 Norfolk VA 23505-0409

RAVITZ, ROBERT ALLAN, advertising agency executive; b. Omaha, May 26, 1938; s. Ben and Frances (Cooper) R.; m. Muriel Strickler, May 12, 1977; 1 dau. by previous marriage, Anne Cooper (dec.); stepchildren: Matthew and Todd Wilson. B.S., Northwestern U., 1960. Trainee/account exec. Edward H. Weiss Advt., Chgo., 1962-65; account exec. Tatham-Laird & Kudner Advt., Chgo., 1965-68; v.p., account supr. Stern, Walters & Simmons Advt., Chgo., 1968-72; sr. v.p., mgmt. rep. McCann-Erickson Inc., Chgo., 1972-77, N.Y.C., 1977-85; exec. v.p. Grey Advt., 1985—; mem. Svcs. Policy Adv. Com. U.S. Trade Rep.; guest lectr. Adv. Edn. Found.; bd. dirs. Meridian Coun.; trustee Naval Inst.; adj. prof. NYU. Rear Adm. USNR, ret. Mem. Naval Res. Assn., Navy League U.S. Jewish. Clubs: Rotan Point (Rowayton, Conn.), Wings (N.Y.C.), Army-Navy (Washington). Home: 15 Westview Ln Norwalk CT 06854-2413 Office: Grey Advt Inc 777 3rd Ave New York NY 10017

RAVIV, SHEILA, public relations executive. Degree, Ind. U., U. Wis. Faculty mem. Sch. Medicine and Health Sci. George Washington U.; dir. rsch. Ministry Social Welfare, Israel; dir. Nat. Vol. Orgns. for Ind. Living for the Aging; asst. dir. Nat. Coun. on the Aging; sr. v.p., dir. of constituency rels. Burson-Marsteller, 1988-91, mem. Am. bd. dirs., 1993, exec. v.p., dir. constituency rels., 1991-94; pres., CEO Burson-Marsteller/Washington, 1994—. Office: Burson-Marsteller 1850 M St NW Washington DC 20036-5803*

RAVNIKAR, VERONIKA A., medical educator; b. Bklyn., Jan. 16, 1950; m. Dr. Leonard Sicilian; 3 children. AB in premedicine magna cum laude, Immaculata (Pa.) Coll., 1971; MD, SUNY Upstate, 1975. Diplomate Am. Bd. Ob-gyn. Resident in ob-gyn Prentice Women's Hosp. of Northwestern Med. Ctr., Chgo., 1975-79; fellow in reproductive endocrinology and infertility Brigham and Women's Hosp.-Harvard Med. Sch., Boston, 1979-81, obstetrician-gynecologist, 1981-89; asst. prof. ob-gyn, and reproductive biology Harvard Med. Sch., 1987-92, part-time lectr., 1992—; prof. U. Mass. Med. Ctr., 1992—, obstetrician-gynecologist, 1993—, dir. divsn. reproductive endocrine and infertility, 1992—; cons. in field. Mem. editl. bd. Women's Health Digest Med., 1994, Prevention Mag., 1994. Recipient rsch. paper award Dist. VI meeting, Milw., 1979, rsch. paper award Boston Obstetrical Soc., 1981; Bristol Myers grantee, NIH grantee; Grace La Gendre fellow Com. of Nat. Bus. and Profl. Women's Club in N.Y., 1973. Fellow Am. Coll. Obstetricians and Gynecologists; mem. Am. Fertility Soc., Soc. Reproductive Endocrinologists, The Endocrine Soc., Assn. Gynecologic Laparoscopists, Am. Heart Assn., North Am. Menopause Soc. (founding mem.), others. Home: 423 Commonwealth Ave Newton MA 02159

RAWDIN, GRANT, lawyer, financial planning company executive; b. N.Y.C., Nov. 17, 1959; s. Eugene and Nona (Neubauer) R.; children: Alexander, Jacob, Jesse. BA, Temple U., 1981, JD, 1987. Bar: Pa. 1987, N.J. 1987; CFP, Colo. Tax acct. Hepburn Willcox Hamilton & Putnam, Phila., 1978-81; mgr. tax acctg. dept. Duane Morris & Heckscher, Phila., 1981-86, dir. personal fin. planning, 1986-87; pres. Wescott Fin. Planning Group Inc. subs. Duane Morris & Heckscher, Phila., 1987—, also bd. dirs.; mem. adj. faculty Coll. for Fin. Planning, Denver, 1987—; lectr. Inst. Tax and Fiduciary Mgmt., 1988—. Bd. dirs. People's Emergency Ctr., Am. Poetry Ctr.; pres. PEC Found. Mem. ABA, Phila. Bar Assn., Internat. Assn. Fin. Planners (chmn.), Inst. CFP (bd. dirs. 1987-93). Home: 7615 Seminole Ave Elkins Park PA 19027 Office: Wescott Fin Planning Group Inc 1 Liberty Pl Philadelphia PA 19103-7396

RAWDON, CHERYL ANN, elementary school educator; b. Dallas, June 13, 1957; d. Billy Wayne and Carol Ann (Murdock) R.; 1 child, Meagan. BS, East Tex. State U., 1979. Cert. kindergarten, elem., jr. high sch. reading and English tchr., Tex. Tchr. reading and spelling Canton (Tex.) Ind. Sch. Dist. Jr. High Sch.; tchr. pre 1st grade Midlothian (Tex.) Ind. Sch. Dist., tchr. kindergarten. Mem. First Bapt. Ch., Midlothian, tchr. Sunday sch., mem. choir, mission friends tchr., Awana leader; active numerous cmty. orgns. Recipient Golden Poet award, 1989, 90. Mem. Canton Tchrs. Assn. (pres.), Tex. State Tchrs. Assn., Canton Classroom Tchrs. Assn.

RAWITCH, ROBERT JOE, journalist, educator; b. L.A., Oct. 11, 1945; s. Sam and Jean (Reifman) R.; m. Cynthia Z. Knee, Oct. 27, 1968; children—Dana Leigh, Jeremy Aaron, Joshua Eric. BA in Journalism, Calif. State U.-Northridge, 1967; MS in Journalism, Northwestern U., 1968. Reporter L.A. Times, 1968-80, asst. met. editor, 1980-82, editor Valley sect., 1982-83, suburban editor, 1983-89, exec. editor Valley and Ventura County edits., 1989-93; dir. editorial ops. Valley and Ventura County edits., 1993-95; lectr. Calif. State U.-Norridge, 1971-83, 95—. Co-author: Adat Ari El, The First Fifty Years, 1988. Chmn. Calif. Freedom of Info. Com., 1978-79; pres. Calif. First Amendment coalition, 1991-93; bd. dirs. Temple Adat Ari El, 1987-92; pres. Calif. Soc. Newspaper Editors, 1995-96. Recipient Greater L.A. Press Club award, 1973, 75, 79, L.A. Jewish Youth of Yr. award United Jewish Fund, 1963, Clarence Darrow Found. award, 1979. Mem. Soc. Profl. Journalists (nat. bd. dirs. 1979-82). Avocation: tennis. Office: L A Times 20000 Prairie St Chatsworth CA 91311-6507

RAWL, ARTHUR JULIAN (LORD OF CURSONS), retail executive, accountant, consultant, author; b. Boston, July 6, 1942; s. Philip and Evelyn (Rosoff) R.; m. Karen Lee Werby, June 4, 1967; 1 child, Kristen Alexandra. BBA, Boston U., 1967, postgrad, 1972-74. CPA, Mass., N.Y., La. Audit mgr. Touche Ross & Co., Boston, 1967-77; audit mgr. Touche Ross & Co., N.Y.C., 1977-79, ptnr., 1979; ptnr. Touche Ross & Co., Newark, 1980-88, N.Y.C., 1988-89; ptnr. Deloite & Touche, N.Y.C., 1989; exec. v.p., chief fin. officer Hanlin Group, Inc., Linden, N.J., 1990-94, United Auto Group, Inc., N.Y.C., 1994—; bd. dirs. BiakalInterPlast (USSR), Kuperwood Enterprises, Hanlin Group, Inc.; mem. adj. faculty Boston U., 1971-75. Contbr. articles to profl. journals, mags. and trade publs. Mem. Newton Upper Falls (Mass.) Hist. Commn., 1977; bd. dirs. Sherburne Scholarship Fund Boston U., 1977-80; mem. Englewood (N.J.) Planning Bd., 1981-83; trustee Englewood Bd. Edn., 1983-85, 89-93, pres., 1991-92; trustee, treas. exec. com. Englewood Econ. Devel. Corp., 1986-89; fin. and compensation com. Dwight Englewood Sch., 1985-90; mem. parent devel. com. Mt. Holyoke Coll., 1991-94. Served to 2d class petty officer USN, 1960-63. Fellow AICPA, Mass. Soc. CPAs, N.Y. Soc. CPAs; mem. Am. Legion, Navy League U.S., N.J. Hist. Soc. (bd. govs., exec. com., nominating com., treas. 1987—), St. George's Soc. N.Y., Univ. Club, Essex Club, Sloane Club (London). Home: 72 Booth Ave Englewood NJ 07631-1907 Office: United Auto Group Inc 375 Park Ave New York NY 10152

RAWLEY, JAMES ALBERT, history educator; b. Terre Haute, Ind., Nov. 9, 1916; s. Frank S. and Annie B. (Vanes) R.; m. Ann F. Keyser, Apr. 7, 1945; children: John Franklin, James Albert. A.B., U. Mich., 1938, A.M., 1939; Ph.D., Columbia U., 1949. Instr., Columbia U., 1946-48; Instr. N.Y. U., 1946-51, Hunter Coll., 1951-53; asso. prof. to prof. Sweet Briar Coll., 1953-64, chmn. history dept., 1953-57, chmn. div. social studies, 1962-64; prof. U. Nebr., 1964-87, prof. emeritus, 1987—, chmn. history dept., 1966-67, 73-82, acting dean univ. libraries, 1984-85, honors MASUA lectr., 1984-85, Carl Happold Disting. prof., 1986-87; resident scholar Rockefeller Study and Conf. Center, Italy, 1977; vis. prof. U. Hanover, 1990; mem. adv. bd. Salmon P. Chase Papers and Abraham Lincoln Prize. Author: Edwin D. Morgan: Merchant in Politics, 1811-1883, 1955, Turning Points of the Civil War, 1966, Race and Politics, 1969, The Politics of Union, 1974, The Transatlantic Slave Trade, 1981, Secession: The Disruption of the American Republic, 1844-1861, 1989, Abraham Lincoln and a Nation Worth Fighting For, 1996; editor: The American Civil War: An English View, 1964; editor: Lincoln and Civil War Politics, 1969; contbr.: Essays in American Historiography, 1960. Served to 1st lt. AUS, 1942-46. Recipient Outstanding Research and Creativity award U. Nebr., 1983, George Howard-Louise Pound Disting. Career award U. Nebr., 1991; NEH fellow Huntington Library, 1979. Fellow Royal Hist. Soc.; mem. Am. Hist. Assn., So. Hist. Assn., Nebr. State Hist. Soc. (past pres.), Orgn. Am. Historians, Soc. Am. Historians, Civil War Round Table Nebr. (charter pres. 1989-90), Lincoln U. Club, Lincoln Country Club, Phi Beta Kappa. Home: 2300 Bretigne Dr Lincoln NE 68512-1910

RAWLINGS, HUNTER RIPLEY, III, university president; b. Norfolk, Va., Dec. 14, 1944; married; 4 children. BA, Haverford Coll., 1966; PhD in Classics, Princeton U., 1970. Asst. prof. U. Colo., Boulder, 1970-75, assoc. prof., 1975-80, prof. classics, 1980-88, v.p. acad. affairs, rsch., dean System Grad. Sch., 1984-88; pres. U. Iowa, 1988-95; pres., prof. classics Cornell U., Ithaca, N.Y., 1995—; chair Iowa Commn. on Fgn. Lang. Studies and Internat. Edn., 1988-91; bd. dirs. Tompkins County Trust Co. Author: The Structure of Thucydides' History, 1981; editor-in-chief: Classical Jour., 1977-83; contbr. articles to jours. Bd. dirs. Norwest Bank Iowa, N.A., 1988-95, Am. Coun. Edn., 1994, Tompkins County Trust Co., 1996—. Jr. fellow Ctr. Hellenic Studies, 1975-76. Fellow Am. Acad. Arts and Scis.; mem. Assn. Am. Univs. (exec. com. 1990-92), Am. Coun. on Edn. (bd. dirs. 1994—), Nat. Fgn. Lang. Ctr. (mem. nat. adv. bd. 1995—). Office: Cornell U Office of Pres Ithaca NY 14853

RAWLINGS, JOHN OREN, statistician, researcher; b. Archer, Nebr., July 26, 1932; s. Cecil Curtis and Mildred Louise (Suck) R.; m. Mary Jane Reichardt, Aug. 17, 1952; children: Gweneth Marie, Bradley John, Kalen Louise. BSc, U. Nebr., 1953, MSc, 1957; PhD, N.C. State U., 1960. Geneticist USDA/Agrl. Rsch. Svc., Raleigh, N.C., 1959-60; asst. statis. N.C. State U., Raleigh, 1960-61, asst. prof., 1961-63, assoc. prof., 1963-68, prof., 1968-94; prof. emeritus, 1994—. Author: Applied Regression Analysis: A Research Tool, 1988; contbr. over 75 articles to profl. jours. Lt. U.S. Army, 1953-55. U. Reading (Eng.) fellow, 1967-68. Fellow Am. Soc. Agronomy, Am. Stats. Assn.; mem. Crop Sci. Soc. Am., Biometrics Soc., Gamma Sigma Delta (Cert. merit 1979), Sigma Xi (Rsch. award 1964), Phi Kappa Phi. Home: 6216 Splitrock Trl Apex NC 27502-9778

RAWLINGS, PAUL C., retired government official; b. Cave City, Ark., June 21, 1928; s. Otha A. and Leona (King) R.; m. Catherine Terral, 1951 (div. 1970); children: William A., Rebecca, Neal; m. Erma Martin, June 20, 1971. Grad., Little Rock Jr. Coll.; LL.B., Ark. Law Sch., 1950. Bar: Ark. 1950. Practiced in Little Rock, 1950, 52-73; adminstrv. law judge Office Hearings and Appeals, Social Security Adminstrn., HEW, Hattiesburg, Miss., 1973-92; ret. adminstrv. law judge sr. status, 1992; partner firm Terral, Rawlings, Matthews & Purtle, until 1973; asst. atty. gen., Ark., 1955-56. Bd. dirs. Ark. Enterprises for Blind, 1964-67. Served with AUS, 1950-52. Mem. Ark. Bar Assn., Law Sci. Acad. Methodist (past chmn. bd. adminstrn., trustee). Club: Lion (past pres.). Home: 3002 Navajo Cir Hattiesburg MS 39402-2446

RAWLINS, BENJAMIN W., JR., bank holding company executive; b. 1938; married. BA, Vanderbilt U., 1961; MBA, Ga. State U., 1969. With Union Planters Nat. Bank, Memphis, 1974—, v.p., 1974-84, pres., chief exec. officer, 1984-86, chmn., pres., 1986—; pres., chief exec. officer Union Planters Corp., Memphis, 1984—, also dir. Office: Union Planters Corp 7130 Goodlet Farms Pkwy Cordova TN 38018*

RAWLINS, STEVEN WAYNE, management consultant; b. Hopkinsville, Ky., Sept. 28, 1956; s. Malcolm Franklin and Frances Ann (Ledford) R.; m. Terri Machelle Rogers, July 21, 1979; children: Brandon Christopher, Jason Todd. AA, U. Ky., 1976; BS, U. Ala., 1983; MBA, Vanderbilt U., 1990. Asst. sec. Liberty Nat. Bank West Ky., Hopkinsville, 1976-82; systems mgr. White Hydraulics, Inc., Lafayette, Ind., 1982-84; acctg. mgr. White Hydraulics, Inc., Hopkinsville, 1984-86, contr., 1986-90, v.p. adminstrn., 1990-94; sr. ptnr. Rawlins Group Internat., Hopkinsville, 1994—. Bd. dirs. Western Ky. State Fair, 1986, Westwood Day Care Ctr., 1987-88. Democrat. Mem. Ch. of Christ. Club: Pennyrile Indsl. Mgmt. (sec.-treas. 1985-86). Avocations: hunting, boating, flying. Home: 120 James Lynn Dr Hopkinsville KY 42240-9001 Office: Rawlins Group Internat 1910 S Virginia St Ste 203 Hopkinsville KY 42240-6009

RAWLINSON, HELEN ANN, librarian; b. Columbia, S.C., Mar. 30, 1948; d. Alfred Harris and Mary Taylor (Moon) R. BA, U. S.C., 1970; MLS, Emory U., 1972. Asst. children's librarian Greenville (S.C.) County Library, 1972-74, br. supr., 1974-76, asst. head extension div., 1976-78; children's room librarian Richland County Pub. Library, Columbia, 1978-81; sr. adult services librarian Richland County Pub. Library, 1981-82, chief adult services, 1982-85, dep. dir., 1985—; mem. adv. com. S.C. Pre-White House Conf. on Libr. and Info. Svcs., chmn. program com.; mem. tech. com. Columbia World Affairs Coun. Mem. ALA, S.E. Libr. Assn., S.C. Libr. Assn. (2d v.p. 1987-89, editl. com. 1993, chmn. pub. libr. sect. 1995), U. S.C. Thomas Cooper Soc. (bd. dirs.). Mem. ALA, S.E. Libr. Assn., S.C. Libr. Assn. (2d v.p. 1987-93, editl. com. 1993, chmn. pub. libr. sect. 1995). Baptist. Home: 1316 Guignard Ave West Columbia SC 29169-6137 Office: Richland County Pub Libr 1431 Assembly St Columbia SC 29201-3101

RAWLINSON, NORA, publishing executive. Editor in chief Pubs. Weekly, N.Y.C. Office: Publishers Weekly 249 W 17th St New York NY 10011-5300*

RAWLS, EUGENIA, actress; b. Macon, Ga.; d. Hubert Fields and Louise (Roberts) R.; m. Donald Ray Seawell, Apr. 5, 1941; children: Brook Ashley, Donald Brockman. Grad., Wesleyan Conservatory, Macon, 1932; student, U. N.C., 1933; L.H.D., U. No. Colo., Greeley, 1978; D.F.A., Wesleyan Coll., Macon, Ga., 1982. Participant 25th Anniversary of Lillian Smith Book Awards, Atlanta, 1993. Author: Tallulah—A Memory, 1979; Broadway appearances include The Children's Hour, 1934, Pride and Prejudice, 1936, The Little Foxes, 1939, 41, Guest in the House, 1942, Rebecca, 1945, The Second Mrs. Tanqueray, 1940, The Shrike, 1952, Private Lives, 1949, The Great Sebastians, 1956, First Love, 1961, The Glass Menagerie, 1964, 67, Our Town, 1967, Tallulah: A Memory; appeared at Lincoln Ctr., 1971, London, 1974, U.S. tour, 1979, Denver Ctr. Performing Arts, 1980, Theatre of Mus., N.Y.C., 1980, Four Arts Soc., Palm Beach, Fla., 1981, Herbst Theater, San Francisco, 1981, Kennedy Ctr. (cable TV), 1981, Nat. Theatre Great Britain, 1984, Queen Elizabeth II, 1984-86; one-woman show Affectionately Yours Fanny Kemble, London, 1974, U.S. tour, 1979, Nat. Portrait Gallery, Washington, 1983, Grolier Club Exhbn., N.Y.C., 1988; appeared in The Enchanted, 1973, Sweet Bird of Youth, 1975, 76, Daughter of the Regiment, 1978, Just the Immediate Family, 1978, Women of the West, U.S. tour, 1979, Am. Mus. in Britain, Bath, Eng., 1981, Kennedy Ctr. and Denver Ctr. Performing Arts, 1980; one-woman show Fanny Kemble, Arts Theatre, London, 1969, Queen's Hall, Edinburgh, 1980, St. Peter's Ch., N.Y.C., 1980, Internat. Theater Festival, Denver, 1982, also Kennedy Center; appeared as Emily, Denver, 1976; with Abbey Theatre, Dublin, Ireland, 1972; one-woman show tour of Europe, 1972; appeared as: Fanny Kemble, Shakespeare World Congress, Washington, 1976; TV appearances, U.S. Steel Hour, Love of Life, Women of the West; (for edn1. TV) Tallulah: A Memory (performed for presdl. inauguration), 1977; Memory of a Large Christmas, Folger Shakespeare Library, 1977; mem., Sarah Caldwell Opera Co., Boston, 1978; rec. talking books for blind; mem. com.: Plays for Living, 1964-67; Rockefeller Found. artist-in-residence, Denver U., 1967, 68, U. Tampa, Fla., 1970, artist-in-residence, U. No. Colo., 1971, 72, 73; artist Annenberg Theatre, Desert Art Mus., Palm Springs, Calif., 1988, 89, "Our Town" Pitts. Pub. Theatre, 1990; author: (poems) A Moment Ago, 1984; participant Edwin Forrest Day Celebrating Shakespeare's 427th Birthday The Actors' Fund of Am.'s Nursing and Retirement Home Lucille Lortel Theatre, 1991; appeared in Our Town, Pitts. Pub. Theater, 1990-91, Three Sisters, 1991—. Mem. Internat. Women's Forum, Vail, Colo., 1989. Recipient Alumna award U. N.C., 1969; Disting. Achievement award Wesleyan Coll., 1969; Gold Chair award Central City (Colo.) Opera House Assn., 1973; (with husband) Frederick H. Koch Drama award U. N.C., 1974; citation Smithsonian Instn., 1977. Address: care Donald Seawell 1050 13th St Denver CO 80204-2157

RAWLS, S(OL) WAITE, III, business executive; b. Norfolk, Va., July 15, 1948; s. Sol Waite Jr. and Ann Arendel (Peace) R.; m. Margaret Louise Thorn, Sept. 26, 1970. BA, Va. Mil. Inst., 1970; MBA, U. Va., 1975, JD, 1975. Mng. dir. Chem. Bank, N.Y.C., 1975-88, with retail banking dept., 1975-77, with comml. lending dept., 1977-79, with securities trading and sales dept., 1980-88; vice chmn. Continental Bank Corp., Chgo., 1988-91; exec. v.p. Fixed Income Chgo. Corp., 1993-95; pres. Ferrell Rawls & Co., Greenwich, Conn., 1995—; bd. dirs. Liberty Brokerage, Inc., N.Y.C.; vice chmn., bd. dirs. Nat. Ctr. for Pub. and Pvt. Initiatives, Inc.; bd. dirs. Nevander Asset Mgmt., Inc.; mem. fin. instruments adv. com. Chgo. Merc. Exch.; vis. prof. Darden Sch., U. Va., 1991-92; mem., former chmn. com. Chgo. Risk Mgmt. Ctr. Bd. dirs. Chgo. Urban League Devel. Corp., Camp Found.; trustee Mus. Sci. and Industry, The Civil War Trust, 1994—, Va. Mil. Inst. Found., 1993—, Darden Found. of the Darden Sch., U. Va., 1991—; chmn. nat. adv. coun. The Seeing Eye, Inc.; mem. Chgo. Com. Mem. Econ. Club Chgo., Chgo. Club, Chgo. Golf Club, Farmington Country Club, Torrington Country Club. Baptist. Avocations: golf, quail hunting, art, antiques.

RAWN, WILLIAM LEETE, III, architect; b. Berkeley, Calif., Aug. 8, 1943; s. William Leete Jr. and Betsy (Blanckenburg) R. BA, Yale U., 1965; JD, Harvard U., 1969; MArch, MIT, 1979. Bar: D.C., 1969. Assoc. Arent, Fox, Kintner, Plotkin & Kahn, Washington, 1969-71; asst. to pres. U. Mass., Boston, 1971-73, asst. chancellor phys. planning, 1973-75; architect Davis Brody & Assocs., N.Y.C., 1979-83, William Rawn Assocs., Boston, 1983—. Designer serigraphs, 1971-79; contbr. articles to profl. jours., newspapers. Mem. Boston Civic Design Com., 1990; trustee 1000 Friends of Mass., Boston, 1990, Bennington Coll., Inst. Contemporary Art, Boston, 1994. Recipient Urban Design citation Progressive Architecture, U. Va./City of Charlottesville Urban Plan, 1995. Fellow AIA (hon., Nat. AIA Award of Excellence, 1993, AIA Award in Urban Design, 1996, Nat. AIA Honor Award in Arch. 1994, 95, Louis Sullivan award 1995); mem. Boston Soc. Architects (20 regional and local AIA design awards 1985-96), D.C. Bar Assn., Yale Club of N.Y.C., Harvard Club (Boston). Office: William Rawn Assocs Archs Inc 101 Tremont St Ste 204 Boston MA 02108-5004

RAWNSLEY, HOWARD MELODY, physician, educator; b. Long Branch, N.J., Nov. 20, 1925; s. Walter A. and Elizabeth (Melody) R.; m. B. Eileen Fiddes, Sept. 5, 1967; children—Virgilia Ingram, Elizabeth Sue. A.B., Haverford Coll., 1949; M.D., U. Pa., 1952. Diplomate Am. Bd. Pathology (trustee 1988—). Intern Hosp. U. Pa., 1952-53, resident, 1953-57; practice medicine, specializing in pathology Phila., 1957-75; mem. Wm. Pepper Lab., U. Pa., 1957-75, asst. dir., 1960-68, dir., 1968-75; assoc. dir. Clin. Research Ctr., 1962-67, acting dir., 1969—70, asst. prof. pathology and medicine, 1960-65, assoc. prof., 1965-69, prof., 1969-75; prof. pathology Dartmouth Hitchcock Med. Ctr., Hanover, N.H., 1975-95, chmn. dept., 1980-87, sr. v.p. med. affairs, 1987-94, emeritus, 1995—; cons. VA Hosp. Served with AUS, 1944-46. Woodward fellow in chemistry, 1953-55. Mem. AMA, ARC (biomed. svcs. com. 1990-92), Pathology Soc. Phila. (pres.), Coll. Am. Pathologists (bd. govs. 1985-93), Am. Soc. Clin. Pathologists. Home: 7 Haskins Rd Hanover NH 03755-2204

RAWSKI, CONRAD H(ENRY), humanities educator, medievalist; b. Vienna, Austria, May 25, 1914; came to U.S., 1939, naturalized, 1944; s. Stanislaus and Johanna (Buberl-Maffei) R.; m. Helen Orr, July 5, 1957; children: Thomas George, Judith Ellen Rawski Kleen. M.A., U. Vienna, 1936, Ph.D., 1937; postgrad., Péter Pázmány Egyetem, Budapest, 1938-39, Harvard U., 1939-40; M.S. in L.S, Western Res. U., 1957. Lectr. in music U. Louisville, 1940; asst. prof., assoc. prof., prof. music Ithaca (N.Y.) Coll., 1940-56; dir. grad. studies, dean Ithaca (N.Y.) Coll. (Sch. Music), 1951-56; head fine arts dept. Cleve. Public Library, 1957-62; assoc. prof., prof. library sci., coordinator Ph.D. program in info. sci. M.A. Baxter Sch. Info. and Libr. Sci., Case Western Res. U., Cleve., 1957-80; prof., sr. research scholar M.A. Baxter Sch. Info. and Libr. Sci., Case Western Res. U., 1980-85, prof. emeritus for life, dean emeritus, 1985; music columnist Boston Evening Transcript, 1939-40, Ithaca Jour., 1943-50; lectr. in musicology, medieval studies, info. sci. Fellow Fund for the Advancement of Edn., Ford Found., 1952-53, Nat. Endowment for Humanities, 1979. Author: Petrarch: Four Dialogues for Scholars, 1967, Toward a Theory of Librarianship, 1973, Petrarch's Latin Prose Works and the Modern Translator, 1977, Introduction to Research in Information Sciane, 1982; translator, editor: Petrarch's Remedies for Fortune Fair and Foul, 5 vols., 1991, Petrarch to Boccaccio: The Griseldis Letters, 1994, Francisci Petrarchae lectoris Adminiculum: Late Antique and Medieval Latin Words in the Works of Petrarch, 1996; contbr. papers on Petrarch's Latin prose works, Petrarch's Latinity, medieval music, info. sci. and theory to profl. jours. and encys. Mem. Renaissance Soc. Am., Medieval Acad. Am., Soc. for Medieval Latin, ALA (nat. Beta Phi Mu award 1979), Am. Musicol. Soc., Wembley Club. Club: Rowfant of Cleve. Address: 17877 Lost Trl Chagrin Falls OH 44023-5835

RAWSKI, EVELYN SAKAKIDA, history educator; b. Honolulu, Feb. 2, 1939; d. Evan T. and Teruko (Watase) Sakakida; m. Thomas G. Rawski, Dec. 16, 1967. B.A., Cornell U., 1961; M.A., Radcliffe Coll., 1962; Ph.D., Harvard U., 1968. Asst. prof. history U. Pitts., 1967-72, assoc. prof., 1973-79, prof. history, 1980—; univ. prof., 1996—. Author: Agricultural Change and the Peasant Economy of South China, 1972, Education and Popular Literacy in Ch'ing China, 1979; co-author: Chinese Society in the Eighteenth Century, 1987; co-editor: Popular Culture in Late Imperial and Modern China, 1988, Harmony and Counterpoint: Chinese Music in Ritual Context, 1996. Am. Coun. Learned Soc. grantee, 1973-74; NEH fellow, 1979-80, Chinese Studies fellow Am. Coun. Learned Soc./Sci. Rsch. Coun., 1989, Guggenheim Meml. Found. fellow, 1990, Woodrow Wilson Internat. Ctr. fellow 1992-93. Mem. Assn. Asian Studies (China-Inner Asia coun., bd. dirs. 1976-79, v.p. 1994-95, pres. 1995-96). Home: 5317 Westminster Pl Pittsburgh PA 15232-2120 Office: U Pitts Dept History Pittsburgh PA 15260

RAWSON, CLAUDE JULIEN, English educator; b. Shanghai, Feb. 8, 1935; came to U.S., 1985; m. Judith Ann Hammond, July 14, 1959; children: Hugh, Tim, Mark, Harriet, Annabel. BA, Oxford (Eng.) U., 1955, MA, BLitt, 1959. English lectr. U. Newcastle, Eng., 1957-65; from lectr. to prof., chmn. dept. U. Warwick, Coventry, Eng., 1965-85, hon. prof., 1986—; George Sherburn prof. English U. Ill., Urbana, 1985-86; George M. Bodman prof. English Yale U., New Haven, Conn., 1986-96, Maynard Mack prof. English, 1996—; vis. prof. U. Pa., Phila., 1973, U. Calif., Berkeley, 1980. Author: Henry Fielding and the Augustan Ideal, 1972, 2d edit., 1991, Gulliver and the Gentle Reader, 1973, 2d edit., 1991, Order from Confusion Sprung, 1985, 2d edit., 1992, Satire and Sentiment 1660-1830, 1994; editor: Modern Lang. Rev. and Yearbook of English Studies, London, 1974-78; gen. editor: Cambridge (Eng.) History of Literary Criticism, 1983—, Unwin Critical Libr., London, 1974—, Blackwell Critical Biographies, 1985—; chmn., gen. editor: Yale Boswell Papers, 1990—. Recipient Cert. of Merit for Disting. Svc. Conf. of Editors of Learned Jours., 1988; Andrew Mellon fellow Clark and Huntington Libr., 1980, 90, Guggenheim fellow, 1991-92, Sr. Faculty fellow Yale U., 1991-92; NEH grantee, 1991. Mem. Modern Humanities Rsch. Assn. (life mem., com. mem. 1974-88), Internat. Soc. 18th Century Studies, Am. Soc. for 18th Century Studies, Brit. Soc. for 18th

Century Studies (pres. 1973-74). Office: Yale U Dept English PO Box 208302 New Haven CT 06520-8302

RAWSON, DAVID P., ambassador; b. Addison, Mich., Sept. 10, 1941; m. Sandra Miller; 2 children. BA, Malone Coll.; MA, PhD, Am. U. Joined Fgn. Svc., 1971; asst. for Zaire, desk officer for Rwanda and Burundi Dept. State, 1971-72; polit. officer Dept. State, Kigali, Rwanda, 1973-75, Bamako, Mali, 1975-78; chief polit. sect. Dakar, Senegal, 1978; spl. asst. for trade and devel. Pearson Fellowship Program Trumbull County Commrs., Warren, Ohio; dep. chief of mission Antananarivo, Madagascar, 1983-85, Mogadishu, Somalia, 1986-88; fellow Woodrow Wilson Sch. Pub. Affairs Princeton U.; dir. Office West African Affairs Dept. State, 1989-90; sr. fellow Ctr. for Study Fgn. Affairs, 1991-92; advisor Coun. on Fgn. Diplomacy's Exec. Exchange Program Mobil South, Inc., 1993; amb. to Rwanda Kigali, 1993—. Recipient 3 Superior Honor awards, 2 Sr. Performance Pay awards, Alumnus of Yr. award Malone Coll. Mem. African Studies Assn., Mande Studies Assn., Lenawee County Farm Bureau, Am. Fgn. Svc. Assn. Office: Am Embassy Kigali Dept State Washington DC 20521-2050

RAWSON, ELEANOR S., publishing company executive; m. Kennett Longley Rawson (dec.); children—Linda, Kennett Longley. V.p., exec. editor David McKay Co.; exec. v.p., editor-in-chief Rawson, Wade Publishers, Inc.; v.p. Scribner Book Cos.; pub. Rawson Assocs. divsn. Macmillan; v.p., chmn. Rawson Assocs. (divsn. Macmillan Pub. Co.); teaching staff Columbia U.; now pub. Rawson Assocs./Simon & Schuster; lectr. NYU, New Sch., N.Y.; organizer, panelist various writers' confs.; mem. exec. coun., nominating chair Am. Assn. Pubs., 1970-74. Former editorial staff writer Am. mag.; free-lance writer radio and mags., newspaper syndicates; fiction editor Collier's mag., Today's Woman. Trustee, past v.p. Museums at Stony Brook. Mem. Assn. Women's Nat. Book Assn., P.E.N., Am. Assn. Museums, Yale Club, Cosmopolitan Club, Old Field Club, Women's Forum, Women In Media, Women in Comms. Office: 1230 Ave of the Americas New York NY 10020-4941

RAWSON, RAYMOND D., dentist; b. Sandy, Utah, Nov. 2, 1940; s. James D. and Mable (Beckstead) R.; m. Linda Downey, July 23, 1959; children: Raymond Blaine, Mark Daniel, Pamela Ann, David James, Kristi Lynn, Kenneth Glenn, Richard Allen. B.S., U. Nev. at Las Vegas, 1964; D.D.S., Loma Linda U., 1968; M.A., U. Nev., 1978; m. Linda Downey, July 23, 1959; children: Raymond Blaine, Mark Daniel, Pamela Ann, David James, Kristi Lynn, Kenneth Glenn, Richard Allen. Diplomate Am. Bd. Forensic Odontology (pres. 1984), Am. Bd. Oral Medicine. Gen. practice dentistry, Las Vegas, 1968—; instr. dental hygiene, dental dir. Clark County Community Coll., 1977—, dep. coroner, chief dental examiner, 1977—; adj. prof. U. Nev., 1977—, adj. assoc. prof. oral diagnosis and forensic dentistry Northwestern U., Chgo., 1985—. Contbr. articles to profl. jours. Active Boy Scouts Am., 1968—; chmn. youth and family health comm. assembly on fed. issues, Nat. Conf. State Legislators, mem. steering comm. Reforming States Group, council of State Govts.; recipient Community Heroes award, Nat. Conf. Christians and Jews, Las Vegas, 1994; pres. Red Rock Stake; bishop Ch. Jesus Christ Latter-day Saints, 1978-84; asst. majority leader Nev. State senator. Fellow Am. Acad. Forensic Scis. (pres., chmn.), ADA (editorial rev. bd. jour.), Federation Dentaire International, Omicron Kappa Upsilon (commr. edn. commn. of the states). Republican. Office: 6375 W Charleston Blvd Las Vegas NV 89102-1139

RAWSON, ROBERT H., JR., lawyer; b. Washington, Oct. 18, 1944. AB, Princeton U., 1966; MA, Oxford U., Eng., 1968; JD, Harvard U., 1971. Bar: Ohio 1971, D.C. 1972. Ptnr. Jones, Day, Reavis & Pogue, Cleve. Rhodes scholar. Mem. Phi Beta Kappa. Office: Jones Day Reavis & Pogue North Point 901 Lakeside Ave E Cleveland OH 44114-1116*

RAWSON, ROBERT ORRIN, physiologist; b. East St. Louis, Apr. 25, 1917; s. Orrin Garfield and Mabel Estelle (Casteel) R.; m. Barbara Ellis, Nov. 19, 1966; children—David Garfield, Mary Ellen, Judith Ann. Student, Ill. State Normal U., 1935-37; B.S. in Psychology, U. Ill., 1940; Ph.D. in Physiology, Loyola U., 1961. Broadcaster radio and TV St. Louis and Chgo., 1941-56; instr. biology U. Ill., Chgo., 1956-58; instr. physiology Yale U. Sch. Medicine, 1961-68, asst. prof., 1968-75, sr. research asso., lectr., 1975-82; asst., then asso. fellow John B. Pierce Found. of Conn., New Haven, 1961-69, fellow, 1969-83, fellow emeritus, 1982. Contbr. articles to profl. jours. Mem. Inland Wetlands Commn., Guilford, Conn., 1980-86; mem. Mcpl. Preservation Bd., Guilford, 1980-86;sec. Madison Planning and Zoning Commn., 1987—. NIH grantee. Mem. Am. Physiol. Soc. Republican. Episcopalian. Home: 273 Legend Hill Rd Madison CT 06443-1864 Office: 290 Congress Ave New Haven CT 06519-1403

RAWSON, WILLIAM ROBERT, lawyer, retired manufacturing company executive; b. Montclair, N.J., Mar. 14, 1925; s. William Howard and Maude Elizabeth (Wheeler) R.; m. Elizabeth S. Crandall, Sept. 30, 1949; children—Shirley, Jean, Elizabeth. A.B., Brown U., 1947; LL.B., N.Y. U., 1950. Bar: N.J. 1950, Ill. 1974. Practice of law Bloomfield, N.J., 1950-52; legal asst. Thomas A. Edison Industries, West Orange, N.J., 1952-57; asst. counsel T.A. Edison div. McGraw-Edison Co., Elgin, Ill., 1957-67; v.p. adminstrn., div. T.A. Edison div. McGraw-Edison Co., 1967-72, asst. gen. counsel, 1972-77, corp. v.p. adminstrn., 1977-80, v.p. law, adminstrn. also corporate sec., 1980-85; corp. counsel L. Kaiser/Estech div. Vigoro Industries, Inc., Savannah, Ga., 1985-89; dir. Chgo. Econ. Devel. Corp. Chmn. Millburn (N.J.) Planning Bd. and Bd. Adjustment, 1962-70, Millburn Red Cross, 1969-70; mem. twp. coun., dep. mayor Twp. of Millburn, 1970-72; v.p. Elgin (Ill.) United Way, 1978-79; bd. dirs. United Way Suburban Chgo., 1981-85; pres. Regional Adult Literacy Partnership, Savannah, 1990-91; pres., bd. dirs. The Landings Homeowners Assn., 1992-94, pres., 1992-93. Lt. (j.g.) USN, 1943-46. Mem. ABA, Ill. State Bar Assn., Am. Arbitration Assn. (arbitrator constrn. industry panel 1985—), Elgin C. of C. (v.p. 1978-79). Republican. Episcopalian. Home: 4 Sandsfield Way Savannah GA 31411-2511

RAY, ANNETTE D., business executive; b. Decatur, Ind., Mar. 24, 1950; d. Gilbert O. and Florence L. Hoffman; m. Richard M. Ray, Nov. 28, 1975; children: Michelle Ann, Ellen Marie, Laura Leigh, David Richard, Ruth Anne. AA, Concordia Jr. Coll., Ann Arbor, Mich., 1970; BS, Concordia Tchrs. Coll., Seward, Nebr., 1972; attended, Ctrl. Fla. C.C., Ocala, 1974. Lic. real estate, Ind.; lic. tchr., Ind., Fla. Elem. tchr. St. John's Luth., Ocala, 1972-74; mgr. apt. complex Victoria Sq. Apts., Ft. Wayne, Ind., 1974-75; substitute tchr. East Allen County Schs., Allen County, Ind., 1976-79, Circut A Luth. Schs., Adams and Allen County, Ind., 1977-81; corp. sec., treas., office mgr. Heritage Wire Die, Monroeville, Ind., 1987—. Co-author, coeditor: 1928-1988 A Rememberance, 1988. Vol. Monroeville C. of C., 1987—, Concerned Area Residents Quality Edn., Allen County, 1990—, Am. Cancer Soc., Allen County, 1991—, chairperson Celebrity Bagger Day, 1995, 96; bd. dirs. Hoagland (Ind.) Hist. Soc., 1985—. Lutheran. Avocations: remodeling old homes, reading, genealogy, gardening, floral arranging. Home: 16901 Berning Rd Hoagland IN 46745-9753 Office: Heritage Wire Die Inc 19819 Monroeville Rd Monroeville IN 46773-9113

RAY, BETTY JEAN G., lawyer; b. New Orleans, June 7, 1943; d. William E. George and Iris U. (Berthold) Grizzell; m. Gerald L. Ray, June 9, 1962; children: Gerald L. Ray, Jr., Brian P. BS Psychology, La. State U., 1976, JD, 1980. Bar: La., 1980; U.S. Dist. Ct. (ea., mid. and we. dists.) La. 1981; U.S. Ct. Appeal (5th cir.) 1981. Jud. law clk. 19th Jud. Dist. Ct., Baton Rouge, 1980-81; atty. Jean G. Ray, Baton Rouge, 1981-83; counsel Gulf Stream, Inc., Baton Rouge, 1982-83; staff atty. La. Dept. Justice, Baton Rouge, 1983-84, asst. atty. gen., 1984-87; staff atty. FDIC, Shreveport, La., 1987-88, mng. atty., 1988-94; spl. dep. receiver Receivership Office, La. Dept. Ins., Baton Rouge, 1994-95; spl. counsel Brook, Pizza & van Loon, L.L.P., Baton Rouge, 1995—. Mem. La. Bar Assn., Baton Rouge Bar Assn., Order of Coif, Phi Beta Kappa, Phi Delta Phi (scholar 1980). Episcopalian. Home: 1143 Oakley Dr Baton Rouge LA 70806 Office: Brook Pizza & van Loon Ste 402 9100 Bluebonnet Centre Blvd Baton Rouge LA 70809

RAY, BRADLEY STEPHEN, petroleum geologist; b. Ada, Okla., Feb. 15, 1957; s. Walter Lloyd and Betty Louise (McCurley) R. BS in Geology, Baylor U., 1980; MS in Geology, U. Tex., 1985. Cert. geologist. Asst. geologist Hunt Oil Co., Dallas, 1978, geologist, 1979-81; ind. oil and gas producer Dallas, 1981—; chmn. adv. bd. Geol. Info. Libr. Dallas, 1988—; bd. dirs. Global Mapping Internat. Trustee Dallas Bapt. U., 1988-94, Criswell Coll., 1990-92; chmn. The Habitats Project, 1993—; co-chmn. Peoples and Habitats Project, 1994—; mem. Peoples Info. Network. Mem. Am. Assn. Petroleum Geologists, Ind. Petroleum Assn. Am., Soc. Ind. Profl. Earth Scientists, Dallas Geol. Soc., Tex. Ind. Producers and Royalty Owners, Okla. Ind. Petroleum Assn., Geol. Soc. Am., Computer Oriented Geol. Soc., Nat. Stripper Well Assn., Energy Club, Oklahoma City Geol. Soc., Colbert-Tracht Club. Republican. Baptist. Home: 4925 Greenville #1348 Dallas TX 75206 Office: 1348 One Energy Sq Dallas TX 75206

RAY, BRUCE DAVID, lawyer; b. Denver, Dec. 19, 1955; s. John Denver Ray and Jane (Guiney) Mitchell; m. Faith Theofanus, Aug. 20, 1978; children: Ellena, Constance, Christian. BA magna cum laude, U. Colo., 1978; JD, Union U., Albany, N.Y., 1981. Bar: Colo. 1981. Spl. environ. counsel URS-Berger, San Bernardino, Calif., 1982-84; asst. regional counsel EPA, Denver, 1984-90; spl. asst. U.S. atty. U.S. Dept. Justice, Denver, 1987-90; environ. counsel Schuller Corp., Denver, 1990—. Asst. editor Natural Resources and Environment, 1989—; contbr. articles to legal jours. First v.p. St. Catherine Greek Orthodox Ch. of S.E. Denver, 1994-95. Recipient bronze medal EPA, 1986, 91, gold medal, 1989, Environ. Excellence award, 1987, Best Article award, 1988, Roasch prize Albany Law Sch., 1981. Mem. ABA (sect. on natural resources, energy and environ. law), Colo. Bar Assn. (environ. law coun. 1987—, chmn. 1995-96), Aurora Bar assn., Environ. Law Inst., Air and Waste Mgmt. Assn., Phi Beta Kappa. Avocation: German language and literature, modern Greek. Office: Schuller Corp 717 17th St Denver CO 80202-3330

RAY, CHARLES AARON, foreign service officer; b. Center, Tex., July 5, 1945; m. Myung Wook Soe, Nov. 3, 1973; children: David Edward, Denise Ellen. BSBA, Benedictine Coll., 1972; MS in Sys. Mgmt., U. So. Calif., 1981. Commd. 2d lt. U.S. Army, 1965, advanced through grades to maj., ret., 1982; consular officer U.S. Consulate Gen., Guangzhou, China, 1983-84; chief consular sect. U.S. Consulate Gen., Shenyang, China, 1985-87; chief adminstrv. sect. U.S. Consulate Gen., Chiangmai, Thailand, 1988-91; spl. asst. to dir. Office Def. Trade Controls, Washington, 1991-93; dep. chief of mission Am. Embassy, Freetown, Sierra Leone, 1993-96; detailed to Nat. War Coll., Washington, 1996—. Editl. cartoonist Spring Lake News, 1975-79; contbr. articles to Asia Mag., 1974-79; editor mag. Psyop Digest, 1976-78; exec. editor Def. Trade News, 1992-93. Mem. Heritage Found., Washington, 1991. Avocations: taekwondo, softball, tennis, painting, poetry. Office: Am Embassy, Walpole & Siaka Stevens St, Freetown Sierra Leone Office: Nat War Coll, Fort Lesley J McNair, Washington $D

RAY, CHARLES KENDALL, retired university dean; b. Boise City, Okla., Mar. 15, 1928; s. Volney Holt and Mamie (Burton) R.; m. Doris Derby, Aug. 26, 1951. B.A., U. Colo., 1951; M.A., Columbia, 1955, Ed.D., 1959. Teaching prin. Bur. Indian Affairs, Savoonga, Alaska, 1951-54; mem. faculty U. Alaska, 1957-93, prof. edn., 1960-93, dean Sch. Edn., 1961-80, dir. summer sessions, 1980-93. Author: A Program of Education for Alaska Natives, 1959, Alaskan Native Secondary School Dropouts, 1961. Mem. N.E.A., Am. Assn. Sch. Adminstrs., Am. Assn. U. Profs., Am. Assn. Colls. Tchr. Edn. (state liaison officer), Phi Delta Kappa. Home: 2000 First Ave #2204 Seattle WA 98121-9999

RAY, CREAD L., JR., retired state supreme court justice; b. Waskom, Tex., Mar. 10, 1931; s. Cread L. and Antonia (Hardesty) R.; m. Janet Watson Keller, Aug. 12, 1977; children: Sue Ann (dec.), Robert E., Glenn L., David B., Marcie Lynn, Anne Marie. B.B.A., Tex. A&M U., 1952; J.D., U. Tex., 1957; L.H.D. (hon.), Wiley Coll., Marshall, Tex., 1980. Bar: Tex. 1957. Practiced in Marshall, 1957-59; judge Harrison County, 1959-61; justice 6th dist. Ct. Civil Appeals, Texarkana, 1970-80, Supreme Ct. Tex., 1980-90; ret. Supreme Ct. Tex., Austin, 1990; prin. C.L Ray, Austin, 1991—. Past pres. Marshall Jaycees, Marshall C. of C.; mem. Tex. Ho. of Reps., 1966-70; active local, regional, nat. Boy Scouts Am.; trustee Wiley Coll. Lt. col. USAF, 1952-54, Korea; ret. Recipient various Boy Scouts awards. Mem. State Bar Tex., N.E. Tex. Bar Assn. (past pres.), VFW, Am. Legion, Rotary, Tex. Aggies. Democrat. Methodist. Home: 604 Beardsley Ln Austin TX 78746 Office: 400 W 15th St Ste 600 Austin TX 78701-1647

RAY, DENNIS JAY, utilities and business educator, researcher; b. Hobbs, N.Mex., Jan. 29, 1950; s. J.W. and Beatrice Doris (Smith) R.; m. Mary Barnard, June 7, 1973; children: Mark Wilson, Kathryn Barnard, William Eric. BSEE, U. N.Mex., 1972; MBA in Finance, U. Wis., 1983, PhD in Bus., 1987. Rsch. analyst Pub. Svcs. Commn. Wis., Madison, 1977-79; rsch. asst. U. Wis., Madison, 1979-82; program mgr. Wis. Pub. Utility Inst., Madison, 1982-87, dir, 1987—; asst. prof. sch. bus. U. Wis., Madison, 1992—; mem. rsch. adv. com. Wis. Ctr. for Demand-Side Rsch., Madison, 1992-95; mem. Power Sys. Engrng. Rsch. Consortium. Contbr. articles to profl. jours. Chmn. pastoral rels. com. First Bapt. Ch., Madison, 1988-89, chmn. budget com., 1993-94; bd. dirs. Capital City United Youth Soccer, Madison, 1990-91, Wayland Found., Madison, 1992—. Mem. IEEE, Am. Econ. Assn., Transp. and Pub. Utilities Group (vice chmn. 1994, chmn. 1995). Avocations: travel, camping, computers, softball. Office: Wis Pub Utility Inst U Wis Madison Sch Bus 975 University Ave Madison WI 53706-1324

RAY, DONALD HENSLEY, biologist; b. Hamilton AFB, Calif., Sept. 23, 1952; s. Cecil C. and Harriet Ellen (Graham) R.; m. Joni Lynn Rogers, June 26, 1976. AA, Okaloosa Walton Jr. Coll., 1972; BS in Biology, U. West Fla., 1974. Range technician Vitro Services, Eglin AFB, Fla., 1972; survey asst. Lowe Engrs., Fort Walton Beach, Fla., 1972; research asst. Hennison, Durham, Richardson Engrs., Pensacola, Fla., 1973-74, U. West Fla., Pensacola, 1974; v.p. Theta Analysis, Inc., Pensacola, 1974-75, pres., 1975; biologist Fla. Dept. Environ. Regulation, Gulf Breeze, Fla., 1976—, biol. scientist supr., 1989—, environ. specialist, 1990, environ. supr., 1992; charter affiliate Jour. Freshwater Invertebrate Biology, Port Washington, Wis., 1982; staff mem. Gov.'s Fla. Rivers Study com., Tallahassee, Fla., 1985; research subcom. Bayou Area Foresight com., Pensacola, 1987—; mem. Fla. Dept. Environ. Regulations Biocriteria Com., Tallahassee, 1991; mem. environ. adv. com. Pensacola Jr. Coll., Milton, Fla., 1991. Contbr. articles to profl. jours. Mem. N.Am. Benthological Soc., Southeastern Pollution Biologists Assn. (exec. com., moderator 1985—), Fla. Benthological Assn., Sigma Xi. Discovered hydroperla phormidia species U.S. Nat. Mus. Natural History at Smithsonian Inst., Washington, 1981. Avocations: sports, natural history. Office: Fla Dept Environ Protection 160 Governmental Ctr Pensacola FL 32501

RAY, DOUGLAS, newspaper editor. Now editor, v.p. Daily Herald/Sunday Herald, Arlington Heights, Ill. Office: Daily Herald/Sunday Herald Paddock Publs PO Box 280 Arlington Heights IL 60006-0280

RAY, EDWARD JOHN, economics educator, administrator; b. Jackson Heights, N.Y., Sept. 10, 1944; s. Thomas Paul and Cecelia Francis (Hiney) R.; m. Virginia Beth Phelps, June 14, 1969; children: Stephanie Elizabeth, Katherine Rebecca, Michael Edward. B.A., Queens Coll., CUNY, 1966; M.A., Stanford U., 1969, Ph.D., 1971. Asst. prof. econs. Ohio State U., Columbus, 1970-74, assoc. prof., 1974-77, prof., 1977—, chmn. dept. econs., 1976-92, assoc. provost acad. affairs Office Acad. Affairs, 1992-93; sr. vice provost, chief info. officer Office Acad. Affairs, 1993—; cons. Dept. Labor, 1974-76, Dept. Commerce, 1977; cons. AID, Office Tech. Assessment, winter 1982. Contbr. numerous articles on econs. to profl. jours. Active Upper Arlington Civic Assn., Columbus, 1983—. Mem. Am. Econs. Assn., Western Econ. Assn., Econ. History Assn., Phi Beta Kappa. Home: 1977 Rosebery Dr Columbus OH 43220-3044 Office: Ohio State U Acad Affairs 203 Bricker Hall 190 N Oval Mall Columbus OH 43210-1321

RAY, FRANK ALLEN, lawyer; b. Lafayette, Ind., Jan. 30, 1949; s. Dale Allen and Merry Ann (Fleming) R.; m. Carol Ann Olmutz, Oct. 1, 1982; children: Erica Fleming, Robert Allen. BA, Ohio State U., 1970, JD, 1973. Bar: Ohio 1973, U.S. Dist. Ct. (so. dist.) Ohio 1975, U.S. Supreme Ct. 1976, U.S. Tax Ct. 1977, U.S. Ct. Appeals (6th cir.) 1977, U.S. Dist Ct. (no. dist.) Ohio 1980, Pa. 1983, U.S. Dist. Ct. (ea. dist.) Mich. 1983, U.S. Ct. Appeals (1st cir.) 1986; cert. civil trial adv. Nat. Bd. Trial Advocacy. Asst. pros. atty. Franklin County, Ohio, 1973-75, chief civil counsel, 1976-78; dir. econ. crime project Nat. Dist. Attys. Assn., Washington, 1975-76; assoc. Brownfield, Kosydar, Bowen, Bally & Sturtz, Columbus, Ohio, 1978, Michael F. Colley Co., L.P.A., Columbus, 1979-83; pres. Frank A. Ray Co., L.P.A., Columbus, 1983-93, Ray & Todaro Co., LPA, Columbus, 1993-94, Ray, Todaro & Alton Co., L.P.A., 1994-96, Columbus, Ray, Todaro, Alton & Kirstein Co., L.P.A., 1996—; mem. seminar faculty Nat. Coll. Dist. Attys., Houston, 1975-77; mem. nat. conf. faculty Fed. Jud. Ctr., Washington, 1976-77; bd. mem. bar examiners Ohio Supreme Ct., 1992-95, Rules Adv. Com., 1995—. Editor: Economic Crime Digest, 1975-76; co-author: Personal Injury Litigation Practice in Ohio, 1988, 91. Mem. fin. com. Franklin County Rep. Orgn., Columbus, 1979-84; trustee Ohio State U. Coll. Humanities Alumni Soc., 1991-93. 1st lt. inf. U.S. Army, 1973. Named to Ten Outstanding Young Citizens of Columbus, Columbus Jaycees, 1976; recipient Nat. award of Distinctive Svc., Nat. Dist. Attys. Assn., 1977. Fellow Internat. Soc. Barristers, Columbus Bar Found., Roscoe Pound Found., Ohio Acad. Trial Lawyers; mem. ABA, Am. Bd. Trial Advocates, Columbus Bar Assn. (com. profl. ethics and grievances 1990-93, chmn. professionalism com. 1994-96, bd. govs. 1996—), Ohio State Bar Assn. (com. negligence law 1990—), Assn. Trial Lawyers Am. (state del. 1990-92), Ohio Acad. Trial Lawyers (trustee 1984-87, sec. 1987-88, pres.-elect 1988-89, pres. 1989-90, legis. coord. 1986-88, Pres.' award 1986), Franklin County Trial Lawyers Assn. (trustee 1982-83, treas. 1984-85, chmn. com. negligence law 1983-87, sec. 1985-86, v.p. 1986-87, pres. 1987-88, Pres's. award 1990), Inns of Ct. (sec. Judge Robert M. Duncan chpt. 1991-93, pres. 1993-94). Presbyterian. Home: 2030 Tremont Rd Columbus OH 43221-4330 Office: 175 S 3rd St Ste 350 Columbus OH 43215-5134

RAY, FRANK DAVID, government agency official; b. Mt. Vernon, Ohio, Dec. 1, 1940; s. John Paul and Lola Mae (Miller) R.; children: Susan M., Frank D. II; BS in Edn., Ohio State U., 1964, JD, 1967. Bar: Ohio 1967, U.S. Dist. Ct. 1969, U.S. Cir. Ct. Appeals (6th cir.) 1970, U.S. Supreme Ct. 1971. Legal aide to atty. gen. Ohio, 1965-66; bailiff probate ct., Franklin County, Ohio, 1966-67, gen. referee, 1967-68; with firm Stouffer, Wait and Ashbrook, Columbus, Ohio, 1967-71; jour. clk. Ohio Ho. of Reps., 1969-71; dist. dir. SBA, 1971—; mem. Ohio Pub. Defender Commn., 1983-91; mem. U.S. Dept. Commerce So. Ohio Dist. Export Council, 1988—; mem. Ohio Export Promotion and Trade Coun., 1992—, Ohio Rural Devel. Coun., 1993—; mem. vocat. edn. adv. com. Columbus Pub. Schs., 1993—; mem. Columbus Mayor's Econ. Devel. Council, 1983-84; mem. Small Bus. and High Tech. adv. com. Ohio Div. Securities, 1983-84; mem. tech. alliance Central Ohio Adv. Bd., 1983-89; mem. Ohio Small Bus. and Entrepreneurship Coun., 1994—. Mem. Upper Arlington (Ohio) Bd. Health, 1970-75; pres. Buckeye Republican Club, 1970, Franklin County Forum, 1970; chmn. Central Ohio chpt. Nat. Found.-March of Dimes, 1974-77; trustee Columbus Acad. Contemporary Art, 1976. Recipient Service award Nat. Found.-March of Dimes, 1974, 75, 76, 77; Am. Jurisprudence award for Excellence, 1967, In Search of Excellence award SBA, 1985; named Ohio Commodore, 1973. Mem. Leadership Columbus (grad. 1976), Delta Upsilon, Alpha Epsilon Delta. Clubs: Ohio Press, Ohio State U. Pres. Home: 4200 Dublin Rd Columbus OH 43221-5005

RAY, GARY J., food products executive. Chmn bd. dirs. Rochelle (Ill.) Foods Inc.; exec. v.p. operations Hormel Foods, Austin, Minn. Office: Hormel Foods 1 Hormel Pl Austin MN 55912*

RAY, GAYLE ELROD, sheriff; b. Murfreesboro, Tenn., Oct. 22, 1945; d. Jesse Smith and Jennie Hare (McElroy) Elrod; m. Roy Norman Ray, Dec. 27, 1970; children: Molly Elizabeth, Austin Elrod. BA, Mid. Tenn. State U., 1967; MA, U. Ark., 1969; MBA, Belmont U., 1989. Instr. English La. State U., Baton Rouge, 1969-72, Tenn. State U., Nashville, 1972-76; program coord. Vanderbilt U., Nashville, 1992-94; sheriff Davidson County, Nashville, 1994—. Pres. LWV, Nashville, 1987-89; mem. Women's Polit. Caucus, Nashville, 1987—; mem. alumni bd. Leadership Nashville, 1993. Recipient Polit. Star award Davidson County Dem. Women, 1993. Avocations: reading, hiking.

RAY, GENE WELLS, industrial executive; b. Murray, Ky., Apr. 23, 1938; s. Terry Lee and Loreen (Lovett) R.; m. Becky Huie, Mar. 5, 1956 (dec. 1976); children: Don Dickerson, Kathy Pratt, Nancy Dickerson. BS in Math., Physics and Chemistry, Murray State U., 1956; MS in Physics, U. Tenn., 1962, PhD in Theoretical Physics, 1965. With tech. staff Aerospace Corp., San Bernardino, Calif., 1965-68; mgr. strategic div. USAF (OA), Washington, 1968-70; scientist, sr. v.p., systems group mgr. Sci. Applications Inc., La Jolla, Calif., 1970-81, also bd. dirs.; pres., chief exec. officer Titan Systems Inc., San Diego, 1981-85, ceo, 1985—; assoc. prof. Carson Newman Coll., Tenn., 1964-65. Inventor mass flow meter. 1st lt. USAR, 1963-68. Republican. Avocations: tennis, wine collecting. Home: PO Box 2464 Rancho Santa Fe CA 92067-2464 Office: Titan Corp 3033 Science Park Rd San Diego CA 92121-1101*

RAY, GEORGE EINAR, lawyer; b. Gloucester, Mass., Apr. 23, 1910; s. Matti and Sandra Sofia (Kujala) R.; m. Mary Lee Osborne, Sept. 7, 1940 (dec.); children: Mary Danforth White, Priscilla Ray Sartwelle, Elizabeth Ray Haenchen, George Einar Jr., Clifford Osborne, Michael Gritton (dec.). AB, Harvard U., 1932, JD, 1935. Bar: Mass. 1935. Practiced in N.Y.C., 1936-38, Boston, 1942-44; lawyer Ray, Trotti, Hemphill, Finfrock & Needham, P.C., Dallas, 1946-94, pvt. practice, Dallas, 1995—; faculty assoc. Columbia Law Sch., 1935-36; atty. U.S. Bd. Tax Appeals, Washington, 1938-41; spl. asst. to atty. gen. U.S., tax div. Dept. Justice, 1941; prin. atty. Office Tax Legis. Counsel, U.S. Treasury Dept., 1941-42; adj. prof. So. Meth. U. Law Sch., N.Y.U. Tax Inst., Practicing Law Inst.; attended Sch. Mil Govt., Columbia, 1944; head dept. internat. law Naval Sch. Mil. Govt., Princeton, 1944-45; chief counsel Office Army-Navy Liquidation Commr., M.T.O., 1945; dep. exec. dir. Office Fgn. Liquidation Commr., State Dept., 1946. Author: Incorporating the Professional Practice, 1972, 3d edit., 1984; also articles in legal publs. Lt. comdr. USNR, World War II. Mem. Am., Tex., Dallas County bar assns., Tex. Bar, Tex. Bar Found., Southwestern Legal Found., Harvard Law Sch. Assn. Tex. (ex-pres.), Dallas Estate Council (pres. 1949-50). Baptist (deacon). Clubs: Northwood, Harvard (pres. 1950-51), Salesmanship, Dallas Knife and Fork (pres. 1967-68). Home: 12615 Breckenridge Dr Dallas TX 75230-2001 Office: 5949 Sherry Ln Dallas TX 75225

RAY, GEORGE WASHINGTON, III, English language educator; b. Binghamton, N.Y., Dec. 4, 1932; s. George Washington and Margaret (Nicholson) R.; m. Elizabeth DuPree Osborn, Dec. 29, 1956; children—Virginia, George, Melissa, Grace Elizabeth. A.B., Wesleyan U., 1954; postgrad., Colgate U., 1957-59; Ph.D., U. Rochester, 1966. Instr. English U. Rochester, N.Y., 1961-62, U. Va., Charlottesville, 1962-64; instr. English Washington and Lee U., Lexington, Va., 1964-66; asst. prof. Washington and Lee U., 1966-69, assoc. prof., 1969-74, prof., 1974—, acting chmn. dept., 1985, 91-92; vis. fellow Univ. Coll., Oxford (Eng.) U., 1980. Editor: Duke of Byron, 1979, The Chi Psi Story, 1995. Bd. dirs. Rockbridge Concert-Theater Series, 1966-83, Lime Kiln Arts Inc., 1983-86, Rockbridge Area Mental Health Assn., 1975-78 . Served as 1st lt. USMC, 1954-57. Recipient various fellowships. Mem. Va. Humanities Conf. Southeastern Renaissance Conf., Renaissance Soc. Am., Chi Psi (nat. Disting. Svc. award 1985, trustee ednl. trust 1989-95, nat. pres. 1995—), Am. Soc. Theatre Rsch. Democrat. Presbyterian (elder 1979-85, 89-91). Home: 13 Sellers Ave Lexington VA 24450-1930 Office: Dept English Washington and Lee U Lexington VA 24450

RAY, GILBERT T., lawyer; b. Mansfield, Ohio, Sept. 18, 1944; s. Robert Lee Ray and Renatha (Goldie) Washington; m. Valerie J. Reynolds, June 14, 1969; children: Tanika, Tarlin. BA, Ashland Coll., 1966; MBA, U. Toledo, 1968; JD, Howard U., 1972. Assoc. O'Melveny & Myers, Los Angeles, 1972-79, ptnr., 1980—. Bd. dirs. Host Marriott Svcs. Corp., L.A. Area C. of C., NAACP Legal Def. Fund, Haynes Found., Conv. and Visitor Bur. Mem. Riviera Club (L.A.), The Calif. Club. Democrat. Office: O'Melveny & Myers 400 S Hope St Los Angeles CA 90071-2801

RAY, H. M., lawyer; b. Rienzi, Miss., Aug. 9, 1924; s. Thomas Henry and Isabelle (Dunlap) R.; m. Merle Burt, Nov. 28, 1953 (dec. Dec. 1993); children: Howard Manfred, Mark Andrew. J.D., U. Miss., 1949. Bar: Miss. 1949. U.S. atty. No. Dist. Miss. Oxford, 1961-81; pvt. practice law Corinth, Miss., 1949-61, Jackson, Miss., 1981-85, 90—; asst. atty. gen. State of Miss., Jackson, 1986-90; mem. Atty. Gen.'s Adv. Com. U.S. Attys., 1973-78, chmn., 1976; vis. lectr. UN, Asia and Far East, UN (Inst. for Prevention Crime and Treatment of Offenders), Tokyo, 1977; pros. atty. Alcorn County,

Miss., 1956-57, 68-61; mem. Miss. Ho. of RReps., 1948-51; mem. Miss. Gov.'s Com. to Study Laws Regarding Use of Deadly Force on Fleeing Felons, 1982-83, Miss. Gov.'s Constl. Study Commn., 1985-86. Co-author: Miss. Workmens' Compensation Act, 1948. Chmn. Corinth-Alcorn County Airport Bd., 1959-61; trustee Alcorn County Public Library, 1959-62. Served with USAAC, 1943-45, ETO; with USAF, 1951-53. Recipient Corinth's Young Man of Yr. award, 1958. Presbyterian (elder). Clubs: Kiwanis (lt. gov. 1955-56, dist. chmn. 1956-57, pres. Corinth 1943-53). Home: 12 Windy Ridge Cv Jackson MS 39211-2904 Office: PO Box 2449 Jackson MS 39225-2449

RAY, HUGH MASSEY, JR., lawyer; b. Vicksburg, Miss., Feb. 1, 1943; s. Hugh Massey and Lollie Landon (Powell) R.; m. Florence Hargrove, Sept. 3, 1966; children—Hugh, Hallie. B.A., Vanderbilt U., 1965, J.D., 1967. Bar: Tex. 1967, U.S. Dist. Ct. (so. dist.) Tex. 1967, U.S. Dist.Ct. (we. dist.) La. 1979, U.S. Dist. Ct. (we. dist.) Tex. 1979, U.S. Dist Ct. (no. dist.) Tex. 1980, U.S. Ct. Appeals (11th cir.) 1982, U.S. Dist. Ct. (no. dist.) Calif. 1989, D.C. 1991, N.Y. 1992. Asst. U.S. atty. So. Dist. Tex., 1967-68; assoc. Andrews & Kurth, Houston, 1968-77, ptnr., 1977—; lectr. Ctrl. and Estern European Law Initiative, Vilnius, Lithuania, 1996. Co-author: Bankruptcy Investing, 1992; editor-in-chief Creditor's Rights in Texas, 1975; contbr. articles to law revs. Mem. ABA (chmn. real property practice com. 1975-77, chmn. continuing legal edn. com. young lawyers divsn. 1976-78, vice chmn. 1979, chmn. oil and gas subcom. bus. bankruptcy com. 1985-89, chmn. executory contracts subcom. 1989-93, chmn. bus. bankruptcy com. 1993—, chair com. on trust indentures and indenture trustees 1995—), Fed. Bar Assn., Houston Bar Assn., Tex. Bar Assn. (chmn. bankruptcy com. 1985-88), Am. Law Inst., Tex. Bd. Legal Specialization (cert.), Houston Country Club, Tex. Club, Houston Club. Episcopalian. Home: 5785 Indian Cir Houston TX 77057-1302 Office: Andrews & Kurth 4200 Tex Commerce Tower Houston TX 77002

RAY, JAMES ALLEN, research consultant; b. Lexington, Ky., Feb. 21, 1931; s. Allen Brice and Elizabeth Logan (Simpson) R.; m. Mary Ruth Johnston, June 8, 1958; children: James Edward, Allen Bruce, John David. BS in Geology, U. N.C., 1958; MS, N.C. State Coll., 1962. Chief petrographic research Master Builders div. Martin Marietta Corp., Cleve., 1959-73, asst. dir. research, 1973-77, dir. research, 1977-78, v.p. research, 1979-80, v.p. creative research, 1980-82; cons., 1982—; pres. James A. Ray Corp. 1986—. Patentee in field. Served with USAF, 1951-55. Recipient Jefferson cup Martin Marietta Corp., 1977. Fellow Am. Inst. Chemists, Inc.; mem. ASTM, Res. Officers Assn. (life), Nat. Rifle Assn. (life), Ret. Officers Assn. (life). Republican. Home: 9891 Stamm Rd PO Box 1072 Mantua OH 44255

RAY, JEANNE CULLINAN, lawyer, insurance company executive; b. N.Y.C., May 5, 1943; d. Thomas Patrick and Agnes Joan (Buckley) C.; m. John Joseph Ray, Jan. 20, 1968 (dec. 1993); children: Christopher Lawrence, Douglas James. Student, Univ. Coll., Dublin, Ireland, 1963; AB, Coll. Mt. St. Vincent, Riverdale, N.Y., 1964; LLB, Fordham U., 1967. Bar: N.Y. 1967. Atty. Mut. Life Ins. Co. N.Y. (MONY), N.Y.C., 1967-68, asst. counsel, 1969-72, assoc. counsel, 1972-73, counsel, 1974-75, asst. gen. counsel, 1976-80, assoc. gen counsel, 1981-83, v.p. pension counsel, 1984-85, v.p. area counsel group and pension ops., 1985-87; v.p. sector counsel group and pension ops., 1988, v.p., chief counsel exec. and corp. affairs, 1988-89; v.p. law, sec. MONY Securities Corp., N.Y.C., 1980-85; v.p. law, sec. MONY Advisers, Inc., N.Y.C., 1980-88; sec. MONYCO, Inc., N.Y.C., 1980-85; v.p., counsel MONY Series Fund, Inc., Balt., 1984-87; v.p., assoc. gen. counsel Tchrs. Ins. and Annuity Assoc. Coll. Ret. Equities Fund (TIAA-CREF), N.Y.C., 1989-91, v.p., chief counsel ins., 1991-93. Contbr. articles to legal jours. Cubmaster, den mother Greater N.Y. coun. Boy Scouts Am., N.Y.C., 1978-84, mem. bd. rev. and scouting com., 1985-93. Mem. ABA (chmn employee benefits com. Tort and Ins. Practice sect. 1981-82, vice-chmn. 1983-93), Assn. Life Ins. Counsel (chmn. policyholders tax com. tax sect. 1982-91, vice chmn. tax sect. 1991-93, chmn. tax sect. 1993-93), Assn. Bar of Cityof N.Y. (chmn. 1992-93), Investment Co. Inst. (pension com. 1993-93). Democrat.Roman Catholic.

RAY, JENNY, artist; b. Ontario, Oreg.; d. Thompson and Othela Jean Towell Carper; m. Gary Wayne Limbaugh, Apr. 14, 1971; children: Cindy Sue, Tina Marie, Kay Jean, Tamara Rae, Cody Wayne. Cosmetologist, Pendleton (Oreg.) Coll. Beauty, 1972; student, Blue Mountain C.C., 1979-80, Ea. Oreg. State Coll., 1991-92. Owner Butter Creek Beauty Salon, Hermiston, Oreg., 1977-80, Pretty Quick Constrn. Co., Hermiston, Oreg., 1978-93, McCord's Corner Art Gallery, Baker City, Oreg., 1986-88, Creations, Inc., Baker City, 1984-85, Western Mountain Art, Inc., Joseph, Oreg., 1982—, Age of Bronze Art Foundry, Joseph, 1992—. Author: Self Esteem Repair in Recovery, 1992; artist oil portraits of famous native Americans, 1985—; one woman shows at McCords Corner Art Gallery, 1986, Klondikes of Baker City, 1987, Baker County Chamber Office, 1988, Sumpter Valley R.R. Baker, 1988. Asst. dir. Ch. of Christ Christian Sch., Hermiston, 1980, Wallowa Valley Players, Joseph, 1990-92; econ. devel. com. Wallowa Valley Arts Coun., Enterprise, Oreg., 1993—; exec. dir. Wallowa Valley Mktg. Assn., Joseph, 1994; chair Jane Jefferson Club, Pendleton, Oreg., 1975; del. Umatilla County Dem. Com., Pendleton, 1976; campaign chair Jimmy Carter Campaign, Umatilla County, 1976; mem. Dakota Sioux Tribe. Recipient Cert. of Merit Pendleton Coll. Beauty, 1980; Western Art Prodns. scholar, 1988. Mem. Lakota Sioux Tribe, Nat. Mus. of the Am. Indian (charter), Nat. Mus. of Women in the Arts, Smithsonian Assocs., Grant County Art Assn., Union County Art Guild, The Cross Roads Art Ctr. Avocations: fishing, hiking, raising and training Egyptian Arabian horses, camping, writing. Home: PO Box 320 Joseph OR 97846-0320 Office: Western Mountain Art Inc 84587 Walker Ln Joseph OR 97846-8228

RAY, JOHN WALKER, otolaryngologist, educator, broadcast commentator; b. Columbus, Ohio, Jan. 12, 1936; s. Kenneth Clark and Hope (Walker) Ray; m. Susanne Gettings, July 15, 1961; children: Nancy Ann, Susan Christy. AB magna cum laude, Marietta Coll., 1956; MD cum laude, Ohio State U., 1960; postgrad. Temple U., 1964, Mt. Sinai Hosp. and Columbia U., 1964, 66, Northwestern U., 1967, 71, U. Ill., 1968, U. Ind., 1969, Tulane U., 1969. Intern, Ohio State U. Hosps., Columbus, 1960-61, clin. rsch. trainee NIH, 1963-65, resident dept. otolaryngology, 1963-65, 1966-67, resident dept. surgery 1965-66, instr. dept. otolaryngology, 1966-67, 70-75, clin. asst. prof., 1975-82, clin. assoc. prof., 1982-92, clin. prof., 1992—; active staff, past chief of staff Bethesda Hosp.; active staff, past chief of staff Good Samaritan Hosp., Zanesville, Ohio, 1967—; courtesy staff Ohio State U. Hosps., Columbus, 1970—, Meml. Hosp., Marietta, Ohio, 1992—; radio-TV health commentator, 1982—. Past pres. Muskingum chpt. Am. Cancer Soc.; trustee Ohio Med. Polit. Action Com.; bd. dirs. Zanesville Art Ctr. Capt. USAF, 1961-63. Recipient Barraquer Meml. award, 1965; named to Order of Ky. Col., 1966, Muskingum County Country Music Hall of Fame. Diplomate Am. Bd. Otolaryngology. Fellow ACS, Am. Soc. Otolaryn. Allergy, Am. Acad. Otolaryngology-Head and Neck Surgery (gov.), Am. Acad. Facial Plastic and Reconstructive Surgery; mem. Nat. Assn. Physician Broadcasters, Muskingum County Acad. Medicine (past pres.), AMA (del. hosp. med. Staff sect.), Ohio Med. Assn. (del.), Columbus Ophthalmol. and Otolaryngol. Soc. (past pres.), Ohio Soc. Otolaryngology (past pres.), Pan-Am. Assn. Otolaryngology and Bronchoesophagology, Pan-Am. Allergy Soc., Am. Acad. Invitro Allergy, Am. Auditory Soc., Am. Soc. Contemporary Medicine and Surgery, Acad. Radio and TV Health Communicators, Fraternal Order Police Assocs., Phi Beta Kappa, Alpha Tau Omega, Alpha Kappa Kappa, Alpha Omega Alpha, Beta Beta Beta. Presbyterian. Contbr. articles to sci., med. jours; collaborator with surg. motion picture: Laryngectomy and Neck Dissection, 1964. Office: 2945 Maple Ave Zanesville OH 43701-1753

RAY, KELLEY, production company technical director. MA in Animation, Photography and Graphic Design, Ill. Inst. Tech. Tech. dir. MetroLight Studios, L.A. Office: MetroLight Studios 5724 W 3rd St Ste 400 Los Angeles CA 90036-3078

RAY, LEO ELDON, fish breeding and marketing company executive; b. Logan County, Okla., Dec. 9, 1937; s. Wilbur Houston and Florence Ivy (Doggett) R.; B.S. in Zoology, U. Okla., 1963; m. Judith Kay Croddy, Aug. 29, 1959; children—Tana Kim, Tod Kent, Kacy Kay. Research asst. U. Okla., 1961-63; tchr. public schs., Dumas, Tex., 1963-64, Grants, N.Mex., 1964-65, Anaheim, Calif., 1965-69; co-owner Fish Breeders, Niland, Calif., 1969-87; owner, pres. Fish Breeders of Idaho, Inc., Buhl, 1971—, Fish Processors, Inc., 1971—. Served with U.S. Army, 1957-60. Mem. Calif. Catfish Farmers Am. (past pres.), Catfish Farmers Am. (past pres., dir.), U.S. Trout Farmers Assn. (past pres., dir.). Address: 4647 River Rd # D Buhl ID 83316-5104

RAY, MICHAEL EDWIN, lawyer; b. Charlotte, N.C., Dec. 13, 1949; s. Daniel Shaw Ray and Jane (Horne) Keziah; m. Janet Langston Jones, July 14, 1973; children: John Daniel, Jennifer Marjory. BA, Furman U., 1972; JD, U. S.C., 1978. Bar: N.C. 1978, S.C. 1978, U.S. Dist. Ct. (ea., mid. and we. dists.) N.C. 1978, U.S. Ct. Appeals (4th cir.) 1981, U.S. Ct. Appeals (Fed. cir.) 1989. Legal adminstr. Wyche Burgess Freeman & Parham, Greenville, S.C., 1973-75; assoc. Womble Carlyle Sandridge & Rice, Winston-Salem, N.C., 1978-85, ptnr., 1985—. Active S.C. Manpower Planning Coun., Columbia, 1971-72. T. B. Clarkson scholar Furman U., 1971-72. Mem. ABA, N.C. Bar Assn., S.C. Bar Assn., Fed. Cir. Bar Assn. (bd. govs. 1994—), Am. Intellectual Property Law Assn., N.C. Assn. Def. Attys., Forsyth County Bar Assn., Furman U. Alumni Assn. (bd. govs. 1995—), Lex Mundi, Ltd. (dir., 1995—). Democrat. Presbyterian. Avocations: sailing, woodworking, guitar. Home: 4269 Stonehenge Ln Winston Salem NC 27106-3535 Office: Womble Carlyle Sandridge & Rice PO Box 84 Winston Salem NC 27102-0084

RAY, NORMAN WILSON, career officer; b. Hillsboro, Ill., June 26, 1942; s. Glen B. and Courtenay (Sandifer) R.; m. Priscilla Songer, Dec. 27, 1964; children: Melinda Caron, Molly Ellen. BS, U.S. Naval Acad., 1964. Commd. ensign USN, 1964, advanced through grades to vice adm., 1992, pilot Patrol Squadron 50, 1965; with Test Pilot Sch., 1969; project test pilot Naval Air Test Ctr. USN, 1970-72; advanced VP systems project officer Naval Air Systems USN, Washington, 1972-75; pilot Patrol Squadron 16 USN, Jacksonville, Fla., 1975-78; comdr. Patrol Squadron 56 USN, 1978-81; air readiness officer ASW Systems Project Office USN, Washington, 1981-82; naval armaments officer, dep. nat. armaments rep. U.S. Mission to NATO, Brussels, 1982-84; air ASW br. head, dep. div. dir. for force level plans and warfare appraisal Dir. Naval Warfare, Washington, 1984-87; exec. asst., naval aide Under Sec. Navy, Washington, 1987-88; comdr. Naval Air Sta., Jacksonville, 1988-89; exec. asst. Sec. Navy, Washington, 1989-90; dir. Office of Program Appraisal USN, 1990-92; dep. chmn. NATO Mil. Com., Brussels, 1992-95; ret., 1995; asst. sec. gen. for def. support NATO, 1995—. Decorated D.S.M., Legion of Merit with 2 gold stars. Mem. Army and Navy Club (Washington and Arlington, Va.). Avocation: golf. Office: NATO Mil Com IMS/DEL PSC 80 Box 300 APO AE 09724

RAY, PAUL DUBOSE, lawyer; b. Barnwell, S.C., July 1, 1966; s. Albert DuBose and Harriet Jane (LaMaster) R. BA, Furman U., 1988; JD, U. S.C., 1991. Bar: S.C. Asst. contracts atty. County of Charleston, S.C., 1992-94; projects officer County of Charleston, 1994; pres. Palmetto Practice Systems, Charleston, 1994—. Mem. Phi Beta Kappa. Office: Palmetto Practice Sys 21 Broad St Charleston SC 29401

RAY, PAUL RICHARD, JR., executive search consultant; b. Columbus, Ga., Nov. 6, 1943; s. Paul Richard and Sarah (Campbell) R.; m. Elizabeth Richards, June 29, 1968; children: Paul Richard III, John Ray, Alice Ray. BSBA, U. Ark., 1966; JD, U. Tex., 1969. Bar: Tex. 1970. Dir. mktg., various mktg. positions tobacco divsn. R.J. Reynolds Tobacco Co., Winston-Salem, N.C., 1969-78; cons. Paul R. Ray & Co., Ft. Worth, 1978, v.p., 1978-79, sr. v.p., 1979-83, exec. v.p., 1983-84, pres., 1984—, COO, 1984-86; CEO Pau R. Ray & Co., Ft. Worth, 1986—. Bd. dirs. Cook-Ft. Worth Children's Med. Ctr., United Way Met. Tarrant County; mem. liberal arts adv. bd. U. Tex.; mem. dean's exec. adv. bd. U. Ark. Mem. ABA, Assn. Exec. Search Cons. (chmn. 1995-97), Tex. Bar Assn., Young Pres.' Orgn., River Crest Country Club, City Club. Office: Paul Ray Berndtson Inc 301 Commerce St Ste 2300 Fort Worth TX 76102-4123

RAY, REBECCA LEA, communication consultant, educator; b. Yokohama, Japan, Nov. 19, 1955; (parents Am. citizens); d. Gerald C. and Beverly (Lindstrom) R. BA in Theatre, Speech and English, U. Fla., 1976; MA in English Lit., Fla. Atlanta U., 1978; cert., Shakespeare Inst., Stratford-upon-Avon, Eng., 1979; PhD in Comm. Arts and Scis., NYU, 1985. Tchr., dir. speech and drama program Palm Beach Gardens (Fla.) High Sch., 1978-81; tchr., co-dir. drama program Southside High Sch., Rockville Centre, N.Y., 1982-86; assoc. prof. Stroudsburg U., East Stroudsburg, Pa., 1986-92; prin. Rebecca Ray & Assocs., Long Valley, N.J., 1986-95; sr. mgmt. devel. specialist Merrill Lynch, Princeton, N.J., 1995—; adj. asst. prof. NYU, 1988—; instr. Oxford (Eng.) U., summer 1992; corp. trainee for Fortune 500 cos. in the areas of presentation skills, interviewing strategies, sexual harassment, and comm. skills; presenter at nat. convs.; chmn. numerous profl. panels. Author: (one-act plays) Reflections on Loss, 1982, Brat, 1991; editor: Bridging Both Worlds: The Communication Consultant in Corporate America, 1993. Mem. ASTD, Speech Comm. Assn., Ea. Comm. Assn., Dramatists Guild-Author's League Am., Phi Delta Kappa, Kappa Delta Sorority. Avocations: travel, writing.

RAY, ROBERT D., health insurance company executive; b. Des Moines, Sept. 26, 1928; s. Clark A. and Mildred (Dolph) R.; m. Billie Lee Hornburger, Dec. 21, 1951; children: Randi Sue, Lu Ann, Vicki Jo. BA in Bus. Admin., Drake U., 1952, JD, 1954. Bar: Iowa 1954. Ptnr. Lawyer, Lawyer & Ray, Des Moines; gov. State of Iowa, 1969-83; pres., chief exec. officer Life Investors Inc. subs. Aegon NV, Cedar Rapids, Iowa, 1983-89; also chmn., bd. dirs. Life Investors Devel. Co. subs. Life Investors Inc., Cedar Rapids; pres., chief exec. officer IASD Health Svcs. Corp. dba in Iowa as Blue Cross & Blue Shield of Iowa and in S.D. as Blue Cross of S.D., Des Moines, 1989—; chmn., pres., bd. dirs. Bankers United Life Assurance Co. subs. Life Investors Devel. Co., Cedar Rapids. Office: Blue Cross and Blue Shield Iowa 636 Grand Ave Des Moines IA 50309-2502*

RAY, ROGER BUCHANAN, retired communications executive, lawyer; b. Tampa, Fla., Aug. 12, 1935; s. Ralph Jackson and Virginia Marie (Stewart) R.; m. Mary Frye Gaillard, Dec. 27, 1957; children: Mary Katherine, Roger Buchanan Jr. BA in Acctg., U. South Fla., 1967; MBA with honors, U. Notre Dame, 1984; JD, Stetson U., 1991. Bar: Fla. 1992. Acct. Gen. Telephone Co. Fla., Tampa, 1959-67; internal audit mgr. GTE Service Co., N.Y.C., 1967-69; budget dir. Gen. Telephone Co. of S.E., Durham, N.C., 1969-74; v.p., controller Gen. Telephone Co. Mich., Muskegon, 1974-78; regional v.p. fin. GTE Service Corp., Westfield, Ind., 1978-82; v.p. fin. Gen. Telephone Co. Wis., 1982-84, Gen. Telephone Co. Ohio, 1982-84, Gen. Telephone Co. Pa., 1982-84, Gen. Telephone Co. Ill., 1982-84; v.p. fin., bd. dirs. Gen. Telephone Co. Mich., 1982-84, Gen. Telephone Co. Ind., 1982-84; v.p. fin., mem. exec. com., bd. dirs. GTE Communications Systems, Phoenix, 1985-87; asst. state's atty. 13th jud. cir. Tampa, Fla. bar, 1992; asst. state atty. 6th Jud. Cir., Pinellas County, Fla., 1992-96; ret., 1996. Lay eucharistic min., vestry mem., sr. warden Ch. of Ascension, Clearwater, Fla. Mem. Fin. Execs. Inst., Clearwater Bar Assn., Notre Dame Alumni Assn., Kappa Alpha. Republican. Episcopalian. Avocations: jogging, golf, reading, church work. Home: 2337 Kings Point Dr Largo FL 34644-1010

RAY, THOMAS KREIDER, clergyman. Bishop No. Mich. region Episcopal Ch., 1982—. Office: Diocese of No Mich 131 E Ridge St Marquette MI 49855-4208

RAY, WAYNE ALLEN, epidemiologist; b. Yakima, Wash., July 2, 1949; s. Allen and Patsy (McKay) R.; m. Janine Elise Thorson, June 11, 1972; children: Lily Amelia, Lea Camille. BS, U. Washington, 1971; MS, Vanderbilt U., 1974, PhD, 1981. Research assoc. Vanderbilt U. Sch. Medicine, Nashville, 1974-75, research instr., 1975-78, research asst. prof., 1979-83, asst. prof., 1984-85, dir. div. pharmacoepidemiology, 1984—, assoc. prof., 1985—. Contbr. articles to profl. jours. Recipient Burroughs Wellcome scholar in Pharmacoepidemiology Am. Coll. Preventive Medicine, 1984. Mem. Am. Statis. Assn., Assn. Computing Machinery, Computer Soc. of IEEE, Soc. Epidemiologic Research, Am. Pub. Health Assn., Phi Beta Kappa. Avocations: gardening. Office: Vanderbilt Univ Sch Medicine Nashville TN 37232

RAY, WILLIAM F., banker; b. Cin., Sept. 17, 1915; s. William F. and Adele (Daller) R.; m. Helen Payne, 1939; children: Katharine Ray Sturgis, Barbara Ray Stevens, Mary Ray Struthers, Margaret Ray Gilbert, Whitney Ray Dawson, William F. III, Susan. A.B., U. Cin., 1935; M.B.A., Harvard, 1937. With Brown Bros. Harriman & Co., 1937—, asst. mgr., 1944-49; mgr. Brown Bros. Harriman & Co., Boston, 1950-67; ptnr. Brown Bros. Harriman & Co., N.Y.C., 1968-94; ptnr. Brown Bros. Harriman & Co., Boston, 1994-95, ltd. ptnr., 1996—; trustee emeritus Altantic Mut. Ins. Co., N.Y.C.; mem. internat. bd. advisors Australia and new Zealand Banking Group, Ltd., 1987-91; bd. dirs. U.S.-New Zealand Bus. Coun., 1990-95. Bd. dirs. Robert Brunner Found., 1957-94, Downtown-Lower Manhattan Assn., Inc., 1978-89; bd. dirs., trustee Am. Friends of the Australian Nat. Gallery. Mem. Bankers Assn. for Fgn. Trade (pres. 1966-67), Harvard Bus. Sch. Assn. (pres. 1963-64, exec. coun.), Robert Morris Assocs. (pres. N.E. 1962-63), Pilgrims U.S., Am. Australian Assn. (patron), U.S.-New Zealand Bus. Coun., S.R. (lfe), Asia Soc. (Ann. award 1988), Skating Club Boston (pres. 1956-58), Brookline (Mass.) Country Club, Union Club N.Y.C., India House N.Y.C., Fishers Island (N.Y.) Club, Mountain Lake Club (Lake Wales, Fla.), Order of Australia (hon., officer), Order of Malta, Somerset Club Boston, Phi Beta Kappa Assocs. (hon. bd. dirs.). Republican. Home: 10 Longwood Dr Westwood MA 02090-1146 Office: Brown Bros Harriman & Co 40 Water St Boston MA 02109-3604

RAY, WILLIAM JACKSON, psychologist; b. Birmingham, Ala., Sept. 3, 1945; s. Norman M. and Mary K. Agnew; m. Judith Mebane, Aug. 22, 1987; children from previous marriage: Adam, Lauren. BA, Eckerd Coll., 1967; MA, Vanderbilt U., 1969, PhD, 1971; Fellow in med. psychology, Langley Porter Neuropsychiat. Inst., U. Calif. Med. Center, San Francisco, 1971-72. Prof., dir. clin. psychology tng. program Pa. State U., 1972—, dir. clin. trng., 1991—. Author: (with R.M. Stern) Biofeedback, 1977, (with others) Evaluation of Clinical Biofeedback, 1979, (with R.M. Stern and C.M. Davis) Psychophysiological Recording, 1980, Methods Toward a Science of Behavior and Experience, 1981, 4th edit., 1992, (with E. Susman & L. Feajous) Emotion, Cognition, Health and Development in Children and Adolescents, 1992, (with L. Michelson) Handbook of Dissociation, 1996; series editor: Plenum Series in Behavioral Psychophysiology and Medicine. Recipient Nat. Media award Am. Psychol. Found., 1976, 78. Mem. AAAS, APA, APS, Soc. Psychophysiol. Rsch. Office: Dept Psychology Pa State U University Park PA 16802

RAY, WILLIAM MELVIN, newsletter publishing executive; b. Dutchmills, Ark., Mar. 13, 1935; s. William Estes and Verda Lou (Robbins) R.; m. Janet Drachman, June 6, 1969; children: Matthew Stephen, Susannah Brett. BA, U. Redlands, 1959. Reporter Sun-Telegram, San Bernardino, Calif., 1959-60; sports editor Times-Delta, Visalia, Calif., 1961-62; reporter Progress-Bull., Pomona, Calif., 1962-63; copy editor, reporter Newsday, Garden City, N.Y., 1963-65; news editor Nat. Petroleum News, McGraw-Hill, N.Y.C., 1966-71; Washington editor/chief editor Energy Newsletters, McGraw-Hill, 1972-80; v.p., gen.mgr. Energy Newsletters, McGraw-Hill, N.Y.C., 1980—; new product champion McGraw-Hill, N.Y.C., 1989-92, chmn. newsletter editl. bd., 1985-88, seminar spkr., 1985—. Author: Newsletter Publishing, 1990, Business Newsletter Promotion, 1991. Office: The McGraw-Hill Companies 1221 Ave of the Americas New York NY 10020

RAYBURN, BILLY J., Church administrator. Dir. of cross cultural ministries Ch. of God. Office: Ch of God PO Box 2430 Cleveland TN 37320-2430

RAYBURN, CAROLE (MARY AIDA) ANN, psychologist, researcher, writer; b. Washington, Feb. 14, 1938; d. Carl Frederick and Mary Helen (Milkie) Miller; m. Ronald Allen Rayburn (dec. Apr. 1970). BA in Psychology, Am. U., 1961; MA in Clin. Psychology, George Washington U., 1965; PhD in Ednl. Psychology, Cath. U. Am., 1969; MDiv in Ministry, Andrews U., 1980. Lic. psychologist, Md., Mich. Psychometrician Columbian Prep. Sch., Washington, 1963; clin. psychologist Spring Grove State Hosp., Catonsville, Md., 1966-68; pvt. practice, 1969, 71—; staff clin. psychologist Instl. Care Svcs. Div. D.C. Children's Ctr., Laurel, Md., 1970-78; psychologist Md. Dept. Vocat. Rehab., 1973-74; psychometrician Montgomery County Pub. Schs., 1981-85; lectr. Strayer Coll., Washington, 1969-70; forensic psychology expert witness, 1973—; guest lectr. Andrews U., Berrien Springs, Mich., 1979, Hood Coll., Frederick, Md., 1986-88; instr. Johns Hopkins U., 1986, 88-89; adj. faculty Profl. Sch. Psychology Studies, San Diego, 1987; adj. asst. prof. Loyola Coll., 1987; cons. Julia Brown Montessori Schs., 1972, 78, 82—, VA Ctr., 1978, 91-93. Editor: (with M.J. Meadow) A Time to Weep and a Time to Sing, 1985; contbg. author: Montessori: Her Method and the Movement (What You Need to Know), 1973, Drugs, Alcohol and Women: A National Forum Source Book, 1975, The Other Side of the Couch: Faith of thge Psychotherapist, 1981, Clinical Handbook of Pastoral Counseling, 1985, An Encyclopedic Dictionary of Pastoral Care and Counseling, 1990, Religion Personality and Mental Health, 1993; author copyrighted inventories Religious Occupationl and Stress Questionnaire, 1986, Religion and Stress Questionnaire, 1986, Organizational Relationships Survey, 1987, Attitudes Toward Children Inventory, 1987, State-Trait Morality Inventory, 1987, Body Awareness and Sexual Intimacy Comfort Scale (Basics), 1993; cons. editor Profl. Psychology, 1980-83; assoc. editor Jour. Pastoral Counseling, 1985-90, guest editor, 1988; contbr. numerous articles to profl. jours. Recipient Svc. award Coun. for Advancement Psychol. Professions and Scis., 1975, cert. D.C. Dept. Human Resources, 1975, 76, cert. recognition D.C. Psychol. Assn., 1976, 1985; AAUW rsch. grantee, 1983. Fellow APA (pres. divsn. psychology of religion 1995-96, psychology of women, clin. psychology, cons. psychology, psychotherapy, state assn. affairs, chair equal opportunity affirmative action divsn. clin. psychology 1980-82, mem. editl. bd. Jour. Child Clin. Psychology 1978-82, pres. clin psychology women's sect. 1984-86, program chair 1991-94, divsn. psychology women chair task force on women and religion 1980-81, divsn. psychology issues in grad. edn. and clin. tng. 1988—, pres. 1995-96), Am. Orthopsychiat. Assn., Md. Psychol. Assn. (editor newsletter 1975-76, chpt. recognition 1978, chair ins. com. 1981-83, pres. 1984-85, exec. adv. com. 1985—), Am. Assn. Applied & Preventive Psychology (sec. 1992-93, chair fellows com. 1992-93); mem. Assn. Practicing Psychologists Montgomery-Prince George's Counties (pres. 1986-88, editor newsletter 1990—), Balt Assn. Cons. Psychologists (pres. D.C. chpt. 1991-92), Psi Chi (hon.). Achievements include research on stress in religious professionals, women and stress, women and religion, pastoral counseling, state-trait morality inventory, leadership, psychotherapy, children. Address: 1200 Morningside Dr Silver Spring MD 20904-3149

RAYBURN, GEORGE MARVIN, business executive, investment executive; b. Cape Girardeau, Mo., Jan. 30, 1920; s. Walter Marvin and Alma Fay (McBride) R.; m. Louise Tinder, Feb. 6, 1990; 1 child from previous marriage, George Marvin. Student, Central Coll., Fayette, Mo., 1937-39; B.S. in Bus. Adminstrn, Washington U., St. Louis, 1941, M.S. in Bus. Adminstrn, 1947. Auditor Internat. Harvester Co., 1941-45; accountant Tallman Co., 1946-47; asst. prof. U. Omaha, 1947-49; assoc. prof. Millikin U., 1949-52; pvt. practice as George M. Rayburn (C.P.A.), 1948-52; regional internal auditor Olin-Mathieson Chem. Corp., 1952-55; comptroller Orchard Paper Co., 1955-56; asst. controller St. L.S.F. Ry., St. Louis, 1956-62; sec., treas. St. L.S.F. Ry., 1963-69, v.p., 1969-72; pres., dir. N.M. & Ariz. Land Co., 1966-81; chmn., dir. G.M. Resources, Inc., 1982—. Author: Standard Costs Applied to Distribution Costs, 1947, Budgets Bewitched or Bewildered, 1960. Served to capt. AUS, 1942-45, 51-52. Mem. AICPA, Am. Accounting Assn., Financial Execs. Inst., Planning Forum Inc., Delta Sigma Pi, Phi Sigma Phi, Phi Kappa Delta. Methodist. Home and Office: 12410 W 82nd Pl Lenexa KS 66215-2738

RAYBURN, TED RYE, newspaper editor; b. Manchester, Tenn., Dec. 16, 1956; s. Ted and Thelma (Taylor) R.; m. Kimberly Ann Pearce, June 4, 1983. BS in Mass Comm., Mid. Tenn. State U., 1986. State corr. Nashville Banner, Murfreesboro, Tenn., 1978-79; reporter, photographer, sports editor Murfreesboro Press, 1978-80; state corr. The Tennessean, Murfreesboro, 1979-80; copy editor Jackson (Tenn.) Sun, 1980-82, asst. copy desk chief, 1982-85; copy editor Tennessean, Nashville, 1985-90, page one editor, 1990—, asst. copy desk chief, 1994—. Avocations: film, literature, jazz music. Office: The Tennessean 1100 Broadway Nashville TN 37203-3116

RAYBURN, WENDELL GILBERT, academic administrator; b. Detroit, May 20, 1929; s. Charles Jefferson and Grace Victoria (Winston) R.; m.

Gloria Ann Myers, Aug. 19; children: Rhonda Renee, Wendell Gilbert; 1 stepson, Mark K. Williams. B.A., Eastern Mich. U., 1951; M.A., U. Mich., 1952; Ed.D., Wayne State U., Detroit, 1972. Tchr., adminstr. Detroit public schs., 1954-68; from asst. dir. to dir. spl. projects U. Detroit, 1968-72, asso. dean acad. support programs, 1972-74; dean Univ. Coll., U. Louisville, 1974-80; pres. Savannah (Ga.) State Coll., 1980-88, Lincoln U., Jefferson City, Mo., 1988—; chair adv. com. Office for Advancement of Pub. Black Colls., 1989—. Trustee Candler Gen. Hosp., 1982-85, Telfair Acad. Arts, 1980-87; bd. dirs. Candler Health Svcs., 1985-88, YMCA Blue Ridge Assembly, 1986-88, Internat. Food and Agrl. Devel. and Econ. Cooperation, 1988-94, Meml. Cmty. Hosp., Jefferson City, 1988-94, United Way Mo., 1989—, Mo. Capital Punishment Resource Ctr., 1990-95, Stephens Coll., Columbia, Mo., 1993—, Capital Regional Med. Ctr., 1994—; campaign chair Jefferson City Area United Way, 1994-95. With AUS, 1952-59. Decorated Commendation medal with pendant; recipient Disting. Alumni award Wayne State U., 1993, Whitney M. Young Jr. award Lincoln Found., 1980, Disting. Citizens award City of Louisville, 1980. Mem. Mo. Bar Assn. (foresight com.), Am. Assn. Higher Edn., Am. Assn. State Colls. and Univs. (bd. dirs. 1988—, chmn. 1992-93), Nat. Assn. State Univs. and Land Grant Colls., Nat. Assn. for Equal Opportunity in Higher Edn., Coun. on Pub. Higher Edn. for Mo. (chmn. 1991-93), Coun. of 1890 Colls. and Univs., Jefferson City C. of C. (bd. dirs. 1988—), Rotary (bd. dirs. Jefferson City 1989—, pres. 1994-95), Kappa Alpha Psi, Sigma Pi Phi. Episcopalian. Office: Lincoln U Office of Pres Jefferson City MO 65101

RAYBURN, WILLIAM FRAZIER, obstetrician, gynecologist, educator; b. Lexington, Ky., Aug. 19, 1950; s. Charles Calvin and Charlotte Elizabeth (Ballard) R.; m. Pamela Rae Gilleland, Nov. 27, 1976; children: Lindsay Ann, Britany Beth, Drake Tanner. BS, Hampden Sydney Coll., 1971; MD, U. Ky., 1975. Diplomate Nat. Bd. Med. Examiners, Am. Bd. Ob.-Gyn. (examiner), Divsn. Maternal-Fetal Medicine. Intern family medicine U. Iowa Hosps. and Clinics, Iowa City, Iowa, 1975-76; resident ob.-gyn. U. Ky. Med. Ctr., Lexington, 1976-79; fellow in maternal-fetal medicine dept. ob.-gyn. Ohio State U. Hosps., Columbus, 1979-81; asst. prof. ob.-gyn. U. Mich. Med. Sch., Ann Arbor, 1981-83, assoc. prof. ob.-gyn., 1983-86; assoc. prof. dept. ob.-gyn. and pharmacology U. Nebr. Coll. of Medicine, Omaha, 1985-88, prof. dept. ob-gyn. and pharmacology, 1988-92; prof. dept. ob-gyn. and pharmacology U. Okla. Coll. Medicine, Oklahoma City, 1992—, John W. Records endowed chair, 1992—; chief of obstetrics U. Okla. Coll. of Medicine, Okla. City, 1992—; dir. maternal fetal medicine dept. ob-gyn U. Mich. Med. Ctr., 1981-85, med. edn.; reviewer for Ob and Gyn., Am. Jour. Ob-Gyn., Jour. Reproductive Medicine, Internat. Jour. Gyn. and Ob., New Eng. Jour. Medicine, Jour. Maternal-Fetal Medicine, Jour. Maternal-Fetal Investigation; U. Nebr. Med. Ctr., 1985-92, U. Okla. Health Sci. Ctr., 1992—, Presbyn. Hosp., Okla. City, 1992—. Author: (books) Obstetrics/Gynecology: Pre Test Self Assessment and Review, 1982; (with others), Every Woman's Pharmacy: A Guide to Safe Drug Use, 1983, Obstetrics for the House Officer, 1984, 2d rev. edition, 1988, Every Woman's Pharmacy, 1984, The Women's Health and Drug Reference, 1993, Oklahoma Notes: Obstetrics and Gynecology, 1994, 2d. rev. edit., 1996, Obstetrics and Gynecology for the House Officer, 1996; editor: (with F.P. Zuspan) Drug Therapy in Obstetrics and Gynecology, 1982, 3d rev. edit., 1992; editor: (jour. issues) Diagnosis and Management of the Malformed Fetus, Jour. Reprod. Medicine, 1982, Operative Obstetrics, Clinics in Perinatology, 1983, Controversies in Fetal Drug Therapy, Clin. Obstetrics and Gynecology, 1991; contbr. 46 chpts. to books, articles to over 150 profl. jours. including Am. Jour. Obstetric Gynecology, Obstetrics Gynecology, Jour. Reproductive Medicine, Am. Jour. Perinatology and many others; also speaker and lectr. at sci. confs. and seminars and author of audio visual ednl. material for universities and in continuing med. edn.; contbr. numerous abstracts at sci. meetings; reviewer for Ob. and Gyn., Am. Jour. Ob.-Gyn., Jour. Reproductive Medicine, Internat. Jour. Gyn. and Ob., New Eng. Jour. Medicine, Jour. Maternal-Fetal Medicine, Jour. Maternal-Fetal Investigation. Dir. maternal and infant care programs U. Nebr. Med. Ctr., Omaha, 1986-92; U.S. Pharmacopeia Conv. field reviewer, 1983—. Recipient Residents' prize paper award Ky. Ob.-Gyn. Soc., 1978, 79, Faculty Teaching award for Excellence, 1993, 94.car. Fellow Am. Coll. Obstetricians and Gynecologists (Ephraim McDowell) prize paper award 2d pl. 1978, 1st pl. 1979, Searle-Donald F. Richardson Prize Paper award 1980, Best Doctors in Am., 1996); mem. Soc. Perinatal Obstetricians, Assn. of Profs. in Gyn.-Ob., Soc. for Gynecol. Investigation, Teratology Soc., N.Y. Acad. Sci., Neurobehavioral Teratology Soc., Okla. State Med. Soc. Achievements include contributions to the knowledge of drug effcts on developing fetus and of principals of induction of labor and to the influence he has had on peers not only through teaching and patient care but through his extensive writing. Office: U Okla Health Sci Ctr PO Box 6901 4 SP Rm 710 Oklahoma City OK 73190

RAYEN, JAMES WILSON, art educator, artist; b. Youngstown, Ohio, Apr. 9, 1935; s. James Wendell and Marjorie (Wilson) R. BA, Yale U., 1957, BFA, 1959, MFA, 1961. Instr. Wellesley (Mass.) Coll., 1961-67, asst. prof., 1967-69, assoc. prof., 1969-76, prof., 1976-80, Elizabeth Christy Kopf prof., 1980—. One-man shows include Durlacher Bros., N.Y.C., 1966, Eleanor Rigelhaupt Gallery, Boston, 1968, Brockton (Mass.) Mus., 1973, Chapel Gallery, West Newton, Mass., 1984, Gallery on the Green, Lexington, Mass., 1990, Rice Polak Gallery, 1995; paintings commd. by New Eng. Med. Ctr., Boston, Mariott Hotel Corp., Cambridge, Mass., Hyatt Hotel Corp., Washington. Trustee Boston Concert Opera, 1984-88, bd. dirs., 1986-90, pres. Boston Concert League, 1988-90; bd. dirs. Boston Acad. Music, 1991—; trustee, bd. dirs. North Bennet St. Sch. Grantee Italian govt., 1959-60, Ford Found., 1969; recipient Mass. Artists Found. award in printmaking, 1989. Democrat. Episcopalian. Avocation: garden design. Home: 108 Fox Hill St Westwood MA 02090-1120 Office: Wellesley Coll 106 Central St Wellesley MA 02181-8209

RAYFIEL, DAVID, screenwriter; b. N.Y.C., Sept. 9, 1923; s. Leo F. and Flora (Marks) R.; m. Lila Paris, 1950 (div. 1953); 1 child, Eliza; m. Maureen Stapleton, 1963 (div. 1969); m. Lynne Schwarzenbek, 1988. AB, Bklyn. Coll., 1947; MFA, Yale U., 1950. Scripts include (with Daniel Taradash) Castle Keep, 1968, (with Roland Kibbee) Valdez Is Coming, 1970, (with Lorenzo Semple, Jr.) Three Days of the Condor, 1975 (Edgar Allan Poe award best screenplay Mystery Writers of Am. 1975), Lipstick, 1976, (with Bertrand Tabernier) Death Watch, 1982, (with Tavernier) Round Midnight, 1986, (with Judith Rascoe) Havana, 1990, The Firm, 1993, (with Marshall Brickman) Intersection, 1994, (with Barbara Benedek) Sabrina, 1995; plays include P.S. 193, 1962, Nathan Weinstein, Mystic, Connecticut, 1966.

RAYFIELD, ALLAN LAVERNE, electronics company executive; b. Mobile, Ala., May 11, 1935; s. Allan Edger and Clara Louise (Dalee) R.; m. Joan Pilgrim Boucher, July 5, 1958; children: Michael Jon, Mark Allan. BSCE, Pa. State U., 1959; MBA, Rensselaer Poly. Inst., 1965; grad. Advanced Mgmt. Program, Harvard U. Bus. Sch., 1976. Various positions medium A.C. motors GE, Schenectady, 1964-72; gen. mgr. armament systems dept. GE, Burlington, Vt., 1972-77; gen. mgr. transp. equipment dept. GE, Erie, Pa., 1977-80; chmn. bd., chief exec. officer Gen. Electric do Brasil, Sao Paulo, 1980; pres. GTE Communications Products Corp., Stamford, Conn., 1980-83, GTE Diversified Products, Stamford, 1983-87; pres. GTE Products and Systems, Stamford, 1987-89, also bd. dirs., sr. v.p. joint venture ops., 1989; with Forstmann-Rayfield, Southport, Conn., 1989-90; chmn. Internat. Telecharge, Inc., Dallas, 1990-91; pres., CEO M/A-Com. Inc., Lowell, Mass., 1991—, also bd. dirs.; corporator Burlington Savs. Bank, 1978-79; bd. dirs. Parker Hannifin Corp., Cleve. Trustee Com. for Econ. Devel., 1985-89, 94—; mem. bd. overseers Rensselaer Poly. Inst.; pres. Greater Burlington Indsl. Devel. Coun., 1975-77; bd. dirs. YMCA, Burlington, 1976-79, Erie, 1978-79; pres. Family Y, Erie, 1975-77. Recipient Clarence E. Davies award Rensselaer Poly. Inst., 1981, Disting. Alumni award Pa. State U., 1988; named Alumni Fellow, Pa. State U., 1985. Mem. Nat. Assn. Mfrs. (bd. dirs. 1988-89, 92—), Nat. Action Coun. for Minorities in Engring. (trustee 1984-89), Peugot Yacht Club, Eastern Yacht Club, Tau Beta Pi, Chi Epsilon. Republican. Methodist. Office: M/A-Com Inc 100 Chelmsford St Lowell MA 01851-2649

RAYFIELD, GORDON ELLIOTT, playwright, political risk consultant; b. Newark, Sept. 1, 1950; s. Bernard George and Rhoda Gertrude (Glucklisch) R.; m. Jean Metzger, July 12, 1981; children—Michael Evan, Jillian Amy. B.A., The American U., 1972; Ph.D., CUNY, 1980. Adj. lectr. Hunter Coll., CUNY, 1977-79, Bklyn Coll., Bklyn., 1977-79; research assoc. Ralph Bunche Inst., UN, N.Y.C., 1978-79; dir. Assn. Polit. Risk Analysts, N.Y.C., 1980-84, 87-90; polit. risk analyst Gen. Motors Corp., N.Y.C., 1979-86; prin. Rayfield Assocs., N.Y.C., 1986—; writing instr. Rutgers U., 1993. Editor newsletter Polit. Risk Rev., 1983-87; columnist World Wide Projects, 1985-87; author: (plays) Fever of Unknown Origin, 1988, Bitter Friends, 1989, Living Proof, 1995, ABC-TV aftersch. spl. It's Only Rock and Roll, 1991 (nominated Writer's Guild award, nominated Daytime Emmy award), PBS dramatic spl. In the Shadow of Love, 1991 (nominated Emmy award), Fox TV Pilot Skin-to-Skin, 1992, HBO life stories: Portrait of a Bulimic (nominated Cable Ace award); episodes of Law and Order, Schoolbreak Spl. Stand Up, 1995 (Writers' Guild award 1996, nominated Emmy award). Mem. Dramatists Guild, Writers Guild of Am. East, Assn. Polit. Risk Analysts (co-founder 1980, pres. 1981-83). Home and Office: 47 Nance Rd West Orange NJ 07052-1630

RAYGOZA, LYNETTE ROSALIND, educational administrator; b. Hanford, Calif., Sept. 16, 1953; d. King and Lupe (Vasquez) R. BA in History, St. Mary's Coll., Moraga, Calif., 1976. Adminstrv. asst. fin. aid office U. Calif., Davis, 1980-83, systems coord. fin. aid office, 1983-87; asst. dir. fin. aid office Santa Clara (Calif.) U., 1987-90, mgr. student systems and registration svcs., 1990—. Precinct capt. Dem. Party, Santa Clara, 1988; precinct worker Vasconcillos Campaign, Santa Clara, 1992; vol. Green Initiative, Palo Alto, 1990, United Farm Workers Inst., 1978. Mem. Nat. Assn. Student Fin. Aid Adminstrs., Western Assn. Student Fin. Aid Adminstrs., Calif. Assn. Student Fin. Aid Adminstrs., Nat. Assn. SIGMA Users, Am. Coun. on Edn., Nat. Idenfication Program. Roman Catholic. Avocations: swimming, baseball, reading, walking. Home: # 279 151 Buckingham Dr Apt 279 Santa Clara CA 95051-6524

RAYLESBERG, ALAN IRA, lawyer; b. N.Y.C., Dec. 6, 1950; s. Daniel David and Sally Doris (Mantell) R.; m. Caren Thea Coven, Nov. 20, 1983; children: Lisa Maris, Jason Todd. BA, NYU, 1972; JD cum laude, Boston U., 1975. Bar: N.Y. 1976, U.S. Dist. Ct. (so. dist.) N.Y. 1976, U.S. Dist. Ct. (ea. dist.) N.Y. 1978, U.S. Tax Ct. 1981, U.S. Ct. Appeals (2d and 5th cirs.) 1982, U.S. Ct. Appeals (1st cir.) 1986. Assoc. Orans, Elsen & Polstein, N.Y.C., 1975-77; assoc. Guggenheimer & Untermyer, N.Y.C., 1977-83, ptnr., 1983-85; ptnr. Rosenman & Colin, N.Y.C., 1985—; adj. instr. N.Y. Law Sch., 1980-83; instr. Nat. Inst. of Trial Advocacy; mem. adv. group comml. divsn. N.Y. State Supreme Ct., mem. mediation panel. Mem. exec. bd. Town Club of New Castle ; bd. dirs. Fund for Modern Cts., 1994—. Mem. ABA, Fed. Bar Coun., Assn. Bar City N.Y., N.Y. County Lawyers Assn. (bd. dirs. 1995—, fed. ct. com. 1988—, co-chmn. appellate ct. com. 1992-93, chair appellate ct. com. 1993—), Securities Industry Assn. (legal and compliance divsn.), N.Y. Coun. Def. Lawyers. Democrat. Jewish. Office: Rosenman & Colin 575 Madison Ave New York NY 10022-2511

RAYMOND, ARTHUR EMMONS, aerospace engineer; b. Boston, Mar. 24, 1899. BS, Harvard U., 1920; MS, MIT, 1921; DSc (hon.), Poly. Inst. Bklyn., 1947. Engr. Douglass Aircraft Co., 1925-34, v.p. engring., 1934-60; cons. Rand Corp., 1960-85; ret., 1985; mem. Nat. Adv. Com. Aero., 1946-56; cons. NASA, 1962-68. Trustee Aerospace Corp., 1960-71, Rsch. Analysis Corp., 1965-71. Recipient Nat. Air and Space Mus. Trophy/Lifetime Achievement award Smithsonian Instn., 1991. Fellow AIAA (hon.); mem. NAS, Nat. Acad. Engring. Achievements include research in aeronautics and astronautics. Home: 65 Oakmont Dr Los Angeles CA 90049-1901

RAYMOND, CYNTHIA DIANE ARMSTRONG, elementary school educator; b. Akron, Ohio, Mar. 4, 1947; d. Robert Cook and Dorothy Kelly (Goodson) Armstrong; m. Neil Vanness Raymond, June 22, 1968; 1 child, Cathryn Alise. BA in Edn., Lynchburg Coll., 1968; MEd in Elem. Edn., Mercer U., 1972. Tchr. Houston County Schs., Warner Robins, Ga., 1968-70, Robins AFB Sch. System, Warner Robins, 1970-72, North Hanover Twp. Schs., McGuire AFB, N.J., 1972-73; remedial reading tchr. Capitol Sch. Dist., Dover, Del., 1977-78; tchr. U.S. Dept. Def. Dependent Schs., Stuttgart, Germany, 1979-82, Dayton (Ohio) Pub. Schs., 1987—; tchr. rep. Alexander M. Patch Elem. Parent-Tchr. Adv. Coun., Stuttgart, 1980-82. Active Girl Scouts U.S. neighborhood bd. RAF Bentwaters, Eng. and Beavercreek, Ohio, 1979-86; chmn. Operation Stork, RAF Bentwaters, 1982-85; developer, chmn. Operation Loveprint, RAF Bentwaters, 1985; troop leader Stuttgart unit Girl Scouts U.S., 1980-82. Mem. AAUW (chpt. pres., chpt. 1st v.p., chpt. sec.), NEA, Anglo-Am. Womens Club, Fedn. German-Am. Womens Club, Officers Wives Club (sch. tour guide Air Force Mus., Dayton, columnist monthly mag. officer), Federated Womens Club, Warner Robins Womens Club, Wright-Patterson AFB Officer Wives Club. Avocations: travel, theater, walking, reading, cross-stitch. Home: 1580 Applewood Dr Beavercreek OH 45434-6900

RAYMOND, DAVID WALKER, lawyer; b. Chelsea, Mass., Aug. 23, 1945; s. John Walker and Jane (Beck) R.; m. Sandra Sue Broadwater, Aug. 12, 1967 (div.); m. Margaret Byrd Payne, May 25, 1974; children: Pamela Payne, Russell Wyatt. BA, Gettysburg Coll., 1967; JD, Temple U., 1970. Bar: Pa. 1970, D.C. 1971, U.S. Supreme Ct. 1974, Ill. 1975, U.S. Dist. Ct. (no. dist.) Ill. 1981. Govtl. affairs atty. Sears, Roebuck and Co., Washington, 1970-74, atty. Sears hdqrs. law dept., Chgo., 1974-80, asst. gen. counsel advt., trademarks and customs, 1981-84, asst. gen. counsel adminstrn., 1984-86, mgr. planning and analysis corp. planning dept., 1986-89, sr. corp. counsel pub. policy corp. law dept., 1989-90; assoc. gen. counsel litigation and adminstrn. law dept. Sears Mdse. Group, 1990-92, dep. gen. counsel, 1992-93, v.p. and gen. counsel, 1993-95, v.p. law, Sears Roebuck and Co., 1996—. Staff Temple Law Quar., 1968-69, editor, 1969-70; mem. bd. trustees No. Ill. U., 1996—. Mem. ABA, Ill. Bar Assn., Chgo. Bar Assn., Phi Alpha Delta. Presbyterian. Office: Sears Roebuck and Co Law Dept 3333 Beverly Rd Hoffman Estates IL 60179

RAYMOND, DENNIS KENNETH, army officer; b. Witherbee, N.Y., Feb. 21, 1947; s. Kenneth Andrew and Theresa Lillian (Barnes) R.; m. Vivian Velsini, Aug. 23, 1969 (div. June 1982); 1 child, Dennis Kenneth Jr. (dec.); m. Sondra Lynne Mayhew, Apr. 24, 1987; 1 child, Aaron Paul. BSEE, Norwich U., 1969; MA in Internat. Rels., Salve Regina Coll., Newport, R.I., 1983; MS in Sys. Mgmt., U. So. Calif., 1986; postgrad., Indsl. Coll. Armed Forces, Ft. McNair, Washington, 1991-92. Indsl. engr. N.Y. State Electric & Gas Co., Binghamton, 1969-70; commd. 2d lt. U.S. Army, 1970, advanced through grades to col., 1993; comdg. officer TUSLOG Detachment 169, Sinop, Turkey, 1977-79; brigade C-E officer air def. arty, then ops. officer 9th Inf. Divsn., Ft. Lewis, Wash., 1979-82; comm. sys. engr. Command Sys. Integration Office, Washington, 1983-86; chief current sys. divsn. Command Sys. Integration Agy., Arlington Hall Station, Va., 1986-89; product mgr. western hemisphere transmission sys. Project Mgmt. Office, Def. Comm. and Army Transmission Sys., Ft. Monmouth, N.J., 1989-91, spl. asst. to program exec. officer, 1992-93; project mgr. satellite comms. Program Exec. Office for Comm. Sys., Ft. Monmouth, 1993—. Recipient Order of Silver Mercury, Signal Corps Regtl. Assn., 1995. Mem. IEEE, Armed Forces Comm. and Electronics Assn. (v.p., bd. dirs. 1994—, pres. Ft. Monmouth chpt. 1994-95), Assn. U.S. Army (bd. dirs. 1995—). Roman Catholic. Avocations: golf, hunting, woodworking, collectibles. Office: PM SATCOM SFAE-C35-SC Bldg 209 Fort Monmouth NJ 07703

RAYMOND, GEORGE MARC, city planner, educator; b. Odessa, Russia, Jan. 1, 1919; came to U.S., 1937, naturalized, 1942; s. Mark J. and Rachelle (Schneiderman) R.; m. Kathleen E. Waid, Oct. 3, 1942 (div. Mar. 1978); 1 dau., Valerie M.; m. Lois Jean Gainsboro, Mar. 26, 1979. BArch, Columbia, 1946. Planning dir. Harrison, Ballard & Allen, Inc., N.Y.C., 1952-54; founder, pres. Raymond, Parish, Pine & Weiner, Inc., 1954-83; pres. George M. Raymond Assocs., 1983—; prof. planning, chmn. dept. city and regional planning Pratt Inst., Bklyn., 1959-75; founder, dir. Pratt Ctr. for Community Improvement, Bklyn., 1963-70; lectr. planning Columbia U., 1955-58; lectr. planning and urban renewal New Sch. Social Rsch., 1967-72; pres. Assn. Collegiate Sch. Planning, 1968-69; chmn. Westchester County Housing Implementation Commn., 1992-93. Editor: Pratt Planning Papers, 1963-73, (with Astrid Monson) Pratt Guide to Housing, Planning and Urban Renewal for New Yorkers, 1965. V.p. Citizens Housing and Planning Coun. N.Y.C., 1967-86, N.Y. Assn. Environ. Profls., 1977-79; pres. Westchester Citizens Housing Coun., 1964-66, Met. Com. on Planning, 1950-51; founder, pres. Friends of Music Concerts, 1954-57, Spoken Arts Soc., 1966-67; bd. dirs. Nat. Housing Conf.; past 1st v.p. Federated Conservationists Westchester County; past dir. Phipps Houses, Wave Hill, Settlement Housing Fund; chmn. Westchester County Housing Opportunity Commn., 1994—; land use adv. com. N.Y. State Legis. Commn. on Rural Resources, 1992—. Mem. Am. Soc. Cons. Planners (pres. 1968-70), Am. Inst. Cert. Planners, Am. Planning Assn. (pres. N.Y. met. chpt. 1983-95). Home: 192 Locust Ln Irvington NY 10533-2315 Office: 560 White Plains Rd Tarrytown NY 10591-5112

RAYMOND, KENNETH NORMAN, chemistry educator, research chemist; b. Astoria, Oreg., Jan. 7, 1942; s. George Norman and Helen May (Dunn) R.; m. Jane Galbraith Shell, June 19, 1965 (div. 1976); children: Mary Katherine, Alan Norman; m. Barbara Gabriele Sternitzke, June 17, 1977; children: Gabriella Petra, Christopher Norman. B.A., Reed Coll., 1964; Ph.D., Northwestern U., 1968. Asst. prof. chemistry U. Calif.-Berkeley, 1968-74, assoc. prof., 1974-78, prof., 1978—; vice chmn. dept. U. Calif. Berkeley, 1982-84, chmn., 1993—; mem. study sect. NIH, 1983; mem. chemistry adv. com. NSF, 1985-87. Editor: Biorganic Chemistry II, 1977; assoc. editor Biology of Metals, 1987-91; editl. bd. Inorganic Chemistry, 1976-86, Accounts Chem. Rsch., 1982-90, Inorganica Chemica Acta f-Block Elements, 1984-90, Jour. Coordination Chemistry, 1981—, Jour. Inorganic and Nuclear Chemistry, 1974-81, Jour. Am. Chem. Soc., 1983-95, Metallobiochemistry, 1992-93, Metals in Biology, 1993—; U.S. editl. advisor Springer-Verlag in Chemistry, 1972-91; contbr. articles to profl. jours.; author more than 260 papers, 8 patents in field. Alfred P. Sloan rsch. fellow, 1971-73; Miller rsch. prof., 1977-78; Guggenheim fellow, 1980-81; recipient E.O. Lawrence award, Dept. Energy, 1984, Humboldt Rsch. award for U.S. Scientists, 1982, Alfred R. Bader award Am. Chem. Soc., 1994. Mem. Am. Chem. Soc. (chair divsn. inorganic chemistry 1996), Am. Crystallographic Soc., Sigma Xi. Democrat. Office: U Calif Berkeley Dept Chemistry Berkeley CA 94720

RAYMOND, LEE R., oil company executive; b. Watertown, S.D., Aug. 13, 1938; m. Charlene Raymond. BSChemE, U. Wis., 1960; PhDChemE, U. Minn., 1963. Various engring. positions Exxon Corp., Tulsa, Houston, N.Y.C. and Caracas, Venezuela, 1963-72; mgr. planning Internat. Co. div. Exxon Corp., N.Y.C., 1972-75; pres. Exxon Nuclear Co. div. Exxon Corp., 1979-81, exec. v.p. Exxon Enterprises Inc. div., 1981-83; sr. v.p., dir. Exxon Corp., N.Y.C., 1984-86, pres., dir., 1987-93, chmn., CEO, 1993—; v.p. Lago Oil, Netherlands Antilles, 1975-76, pres., dir., 1976-79; pres., dir. Esso Inter-Am. Inc., Coral Gables, Fla., 1983-84, sr. v.p., dir., 1984—; bd. dirs. J.P. Morgan & Co., Inc., N.Y.C., Morgan Guaranty Trust Co. of N.Y., N.Y.C.; chmn. Am. Petroleum Inst. Bd. dirs. United Negro Coll. Fund, New Am. Schs. Devel. Corp., 1991—, Project Shelter PRO-AM, 1991—, Dallas Citizens Coun.; trustee Wis. Alumni Rsch. Found., 1987—, Bus. Coun. Internat. Understanding, Inc., 1988—; trustee So. Meth. U.; mem. Tri Lateral Commn., U. Wis. Found.; mem. emergency com. Am. trade; ptnr. emeritus N.Y.C. Partnership; mem. bd. govs. United Way Am.; active Am. Coun. on Germany, Dallas Com. Fgn. Rels., Dallas Wildcat Com., 1993. Mem. Am. Soc. Engring. (nat. adv. coun.), Am. Soc. Royal Bot. Garden (founder), Bus. coun., Bus. Roundtable (policy taxation task force 1993), Nat. Petroleum Coun., Coun. Fgn. Rels., Singapore-U.S. Bus. Coun.

RAYMOND, MAURICE A., management consultant; b. New Bedford, Mass., Jan. 8, 1938; s. J. Donat and Marie Anne (Begin) R.; m. E. Beatty Elliott, Jan. 12, 1963; children: Catherine S., Elizabeth B. BS in Chemistry, Providence Coll., 1958; PhD in Chemistry, U. Fla., Gainesville, 1962; postgrad., U. New Haven, 1968-70. R & D mgr. Olin Corp., New Haven, 1962-74; mktg. mgr. Olin Corp., Stamford, Conn., 1974-75, bus. mgr., 1975-82, venture mgr., 1982-85; corp. dir. R & D Tremco Inc., Div. of B.F. Goodrich Co., Beachwood, Ohio, 1985-89; dir. rsch. Rhone-Poulenc, Inc., Princeton, N.J., 1990-95; cons. pvt. practice, 1994—; lectr. on polymer sci. St. Joseph's Coll., West Hartford, Conn., 1968. Author nine papers published in profl. jours.; patentee in field. Mem. Planning and Zoning Bd., North Branford, Conn., 1976. Recipient Petroleum Rsch. Fund fellowship, 1960. Mem. Am. Chem. Soc., Indsl. Rsch. Inst., Comml. Devel. Assn., Sierra Club, Raritan Yacht Club, Delta Epsilon Sigma. Republican. Roman Catholic. Avocations: sailing, fishing, hiking, travel. Home: 107 Sayre Dr Princeton NJ 08540-5814

RAYMOND, SPENCER HENRY, lawyer; b. Omaha, Jan. 19, 1926; s. Anan and Florence (Hostetler) R.; m. Priscilla Falley, Dec. 28, 1950 (div. Dec. 1973); children: Margaret Raymond Stickel, Anan, Elizabeth Raymond Hybel, Daniel; m. Joan R. Strouse, Jan. 28, 1993. BS, Princeton U., 1950; JD, Harvard U., 1953. Bar: Ill. 1953. Assoc. Jenner & Block, Chgo., 1953-62, ptnr., 1962—. Trustee Rush North Shore Med. Ctr., Skokie, Ill., 1959-90, Glencoe (Ill.) Union Ch., 1976-82. With USN, 1944-46. Mem. ABA, Ill. State Bar Assn. (mem. trusts and estates sect. coun. 1989-93), Chgo. Bar Assn. (chmn. probate com. 1976-77, chmn. real property sect. 1979-80), Am. Acad. Hosp. Attys., Am. Coll. Trust and Estate Counsel, Chgo. Co. of Lawyers, Law Club, Legal Club Chgo., Harvard Law Soc. Ill. (pres. 1985), Sheridan Investment Co. (pres. 1973, 93, Chgo.). Home: 183 Lake St Glencoe IL 60022-2108 Office: Jenner & Block 1 E IBM Plz Chicago IL 60611

RAYMONDA, JAMES EARL, retired banker; b. Piseco, N.Y., Feb. 20, 1933; s. Floyd E. and Bertha (Kramer) R.; m. Marie A. Countryman, Aug. 18, 1956; children—David J., Diane J., Daniel J. B.S. magna cum laude, Syracuse U., 1955. With Fleet Bank (formerly Oneida Nat. Bank & Trust Co. Cen. N.Y.), Utica, 1957—; v.p., comptroller Norstar Bank (formerly Oneida Nat. Bank & Trust Co. Central N.Y.), 1968—, adminstrv. v.p., until 1973, exec. v.p., 1973—, regional pres., 1987-90; chmn. reg. bd. Fleet Bank, 1990-94. Treas. Oneida County chpt. Nat. Found.; pres. Whitestown Jaycees, 1964; adv. com., sec. Whitestown Sr. Ctr., 1965-87; trustee St. Elizabeth Hosp., Utica, N.Y.; gen. chmn. campaign Greater Utica United Way, 1977, pres., 1979-80, 95; mem. Utica Found. bd., Oneida County Hist. Soc. bd. Recipient Len Wilbur award Utica Kiwanis, 1980, Indsl. Man Yr. award, 1981, Humanitarian of Yr. award St. Elizabeth Hosp., 1989, Business Man of Year award Utica Observer Dispatch, 1990. Mem. KC (Utica), Nat. Assn. Accts., C. of C. Greater Utica Area (v.p. adminstrn., Person of Yr. 1991), Rotary (pres. 1985-86, dist. gov. 1993-94). Home: 35 Chateau Dr Whitesboro NY 13492-2528

RAYMUND, STEVEN A., computer company executive; b. 1955. BS, U. Oreg.; Georgetown U. Sch. Fgn. Svc. Pres., CEO, chmn. bd., dir. Tech Data Corp., 1981—. Office: Tech Data Corp 5350 Tech Data Dr Clearwater FL 34620-3122*

RAYNAULD, ANDRE, economist, educator; b. Quebec, Que., Can., Oct. 20, 1927; s. Léopold and Blanche (Gauthier) R.; m. Michelle Nolin, Oct. 15, 1951; children: Francoy, Olivier, Dominique, Isabelle. BA cum laude, U. Montreal, 1948, MA in Indsl. Rels. magna cum laude, 1951; D. in Econs., U. Paris, 1954; D. in Econs. (hon.), U. Ottawa, 1976, U. Sherbrooke, 1976. Mem. faculty U. Montreal, 1954-71, founder, dir. Ctr. Econ. Research and Devel., 1970-72; vis. prof. U. Toronto, 1962-63; chmn. Economic Council Can., Ottawa, 1971-76; mem. Que. Nat. Assembly, Montreal, 1976-80; prof. U. Montreal, 1980-93, prof. emeritus, 1993—; exec. com. Can. Social Sci. Rsch. Coun., 1961-63, 64-65; pres. Inst. Canadien Affaires Publiques, 1961-62; bd. govs. Can. Labour Coll., 1962-66; dir., exec. com. CBC, 1964-67; trustee CBC Pension Fund, 1967-70; pres. Soc. Canadienne de Sci. Economique, 1967-69; mem. Royal Commn. Bilingualism and Biculturalism, 1969-70, Can. Coun. Urban and Regional Rsch., 1971, Quebec Coun. Planning and Devel., 1971; chmn. com. inquiry French-lang. tchr.-tng. Western provinces Dept. Sec. State, 1971; mem. interfutures study group OECD, Paris, 1976-78; mem. bd. Inst. Rsch. Pub. Policy, 1980—; rsch. fellow Devel. Ctr. OECD, Paris, 1986-94; invited prof. College de France, Paris, 1987. Author: Economic Growth in Quebec, 1961, The Canadian Economic System, 1967, La propriete des entreprises au Quebec, 1974, Institutions Economiques Canadiennes, 2d edition, 1977, Le financement des exportations, 1979, Government Assistance to Export Financing, 1984, The External Financing of Tunisia's Imports, OECD, 1988, Financing Exports to Developing Countries, OECD, 1992; co-editor: Economic Integration in Europe and North America, 1992, Can. Jour. Econs., 1965-70. Recipient ann. award des Diplomes de l'U. de Montreal, 1974; apptd. Officer of Order of Can., 1986; fellow Walter Levy Coun. on Fgn. Rels., Boston, 1977. Fellow Royal Soc. Can.; mem. Can. Econs. Assn. (pres. 1983-84), Am. Econs. Assn., Atlantic Econ. Soc. (disting. assoc.). Liberal. Roman Catholic. Home: 4820 Roslyn St, Montreal, PQ Canada H3W 2L2

RAYNER, ROBERT MARTIN, financial executive; b. London, Sept. 21, 1946; s. Henry John and Kathleen Mary (Edwards) R.; m. Mindy S. Miller, May 28, 1979. BSc with honors in Eng., Bristol (Eng.) U., 1968; MBA, London Bus. Sch., 1976. Sr. engr. Halcrow and Ptnrs., London, 1968-74; fin. dir. Pepsico Inc., Purchase, N.Y., 1976-88; pres. constrn. materials group, sr. v.p., CFO ESSROC Corp., Nazareth, Pa., 1988-94, COO, 1994—; bd. dirs. ESSROC Materials Inc., Nazareth, San Juan Cement Co., P.R., Ciment Quebec Inc., St. Basile. Mem. Inst. Civil Engrs. Avocations: running, golf, theatre, music. Office: ESSROC 3251 Bath Pike Nazareth PA 18064

RAYNER, WILLIAM ALEXANDER, retired newspaper editor; b. Winnipeg, Man., Can., Nov. 7, 1929; s. William and Annie Mitchell (McDonald) R.; divorced; 1 child, Robert William. Student Can. schs. Sports editor Trail Times, B.C., 1954-55; sportswriter Victoria (B.C.) Times, 1955-57, Vancouver (B.C.) Herald, 1957; copy editor, reporter Montreal (Que.) Star, 1957-58; asst. sports editor Vancouver Sun, 1958-62, copy editor, then slotman, 1962-74, news editor, 1974-83, systems mgr., 1983-88, ret., 1988; copy editor Toronto Globe & Mail, 1962. Author: Vancouver Sun Style Guide, 1976. Dir. B.C. Newspaper Found. Mem. Vancouver Press Club.

RAYNOLDS, DAVID ROBERT, buffalo breeder, author; b. N.Y., Feb. 15, 1928; s. Robert Frederick and Marguerite Evelyn (Gerdau) R.; m. May (Kean) Raynolds, May 12, 1951; children: Robert, Linda, Martha, Laura, David A.F. AB, Dartmouth Coll., 1949; MA, Wesleyan U., Middletown, Conn., 1955; predoctoral, Johns Hopkins Sch. Advanced Internat. Studies, Washington, 1956; grad., Nat. War Coll., Washington, 1973. Account exec. R.H. Morris Assoc., Newtown, Conn., 1949-50; fgn. svc. officer Dept. of State, Washington, 1956-76; pres. Ranch Rangers, Inc., Lander, Wyo., 1976—; pres. Nat. Buffalo Assn., Ft. Pierre, S.D., 1987-88. Author: Rapid Development in Small Economies (Praeger); contbr. articles to profl. jours. Mem. mgmt. com. Wyo. Heritage Soc.; bd. dirs. Liberty Hall Found., Wyo. Community Found. With U.S. Army, 1950-53. Recipient Meritorious Svc. Award, Dept. of State, Washington, 1966. Mem. The Explorers Club, Fremont County Farm Bur., Fgn. Svc. Assn., Am. Legion, Rotary, Elks. Republican. Episcopalian. Avocation: travel. Office: Table Mountain Group PO Box 1310 Lander WY 82520-1310

RAYNOLDS, HAROLD, JR., retired state education commissioner; b. Chgo., Feb. 7, 1925; s. Harold and Dorothy (Smith) R.; m. Ann Richards Ellis, June 1950 (div. 1968); children—Christopher, Timothy, Madeline, Dorothy, m. Patricia Adele Miller, Jan. 20, 1973. BS, Cornell U., 1948, MA, 1953; postgrad., NYU, 1968-69. Cert. supt. schs., N.Y., Maine, Alaska. Supt. schs. Cape Elizabeth Sch. Dist., Maine, 1969-74; supt. schs. Portland Sch. Dist., Maine, 1974-79; commr. edn. State of Maine, Augusta, 1979-83, State of Alaska, Juneau, 1983-86, Commonwealth of Mass., 1986-91; interim supt. Windsor Ctrl. Supervisory Union Sch. Dist., Woodstock, Vt., 1991-92; vice chair Windsor Ctrl. Supervisory Union Sch. Dist., Woodstock, 1993—; supt. Springfield (Vt.) Sch. Dist., 1994—. Contbr. articles to ednl. jours. Mem. sch. com., Pomfret, Vt., 1993—; vice chair Windsor Ctrl. Supervisory Union Bd., 1993—; mem. Vt. Senate, 1965-66; chmn. Vt. Bd. Edn., Montpelier, 1963-68; trustee U. Maine, Orono, 1979-83; Dem. candidate for U.S. Congress, Vt., 1962. Staff sgt. U.S. Army, 1943-45, ETO. Mem. Am. Assn. Sch. Adminstrs., Chief State Sch. Officers, Phi Delta Kappa. Unitarian-Universalist. Avocations: reading; gardening; cross-country skiing; theater; music.

RAYNOLDS, JOHN F., III, executive search consultant. Chmn. Ward Howell Internat., N.Y.C., 1993—. Office: Ward Howell Internat 99 Park Ave New York NY 10016

RAYNOR, JOHN PATRICK, university administrator; b. Omaha, Oct. 1, 1923; s. Walter V. and Mary Clare (May) R. AB, St. Louis U., 1947, MA, 1948, Licentiate in Philosophy, 1949, Licentiate in Theology, 1956; PhD, U. Chgo., 1959. Ordained priest Roman Cath. Ch., 1954. Joined Soc. of Jesus, 1941; instr. St. Louis U. High Sch., 1948-51, asst. prin., 1951; asst. to dean Coll. Liberal Arts, Marquette U., 1960, asst. to v.p. acad. affairs, 1961-62, v.p. acad. affairs, 1962-65, pres., 1965-90, ret., 1990; now, chancellor Marquette Univ., Milwaukee, Wis.; dir. Kimberly-Clark Corp. Mem. Greater Milw. Com.; Pub. Policy Forum; corp. mem. United Community Services Greater Milw.; hon. bd. dirs. Goethe House; mem. Froedtert Meml. Luth. Hosp. Corp.; hon. com. mem. Endowment Fund Metro Milw. Luth. Campus Ministry; trustee Milw. Heart Research Found., Inc.; bd. dirs. Greater Milw. Edn. Trust, Mus. Sci., Econs. & Tech., Inc. Discovery World. Recipient Disting. Service award Edn. Commn. of States, 1977. Mem. Nat. Cath. Edn. Assn., North Central Assn. (examiner, cons.), Am. Council Edn., Wis. Assn. Ind. Colls. and Univs. (past pres., exec. com.), Wis. Found. Ind. Colls. (past pres.), Assn. Jesuit Colls. and Univs. (past chmn., dir., mem. exec. com.), Internat. Fedn. Cath. Colls. and Univs., Met. Milw. Assn. Commerce, Phi Beta Kappa, Phi Delta Kappa, Alpha Sigma Nu. Office: Marquette U 615 N 11th St Milwaukee WI 53233-2305

RAYNOR, RICHARD BENJAMIN, neurosurgeon, educator; b. N.Y.C., Aug. 16, 1928; s. Murray and Mildred (Pitt) R.; m. Barbara Golob; children: Geoffrey, Michele. BSME, U. Mich., 1950; MD, U. Vt., 1955. Diplomate Am. Bd. Neurol. Surgery. Intern Mt. Sinai, N.Y.C., 1955-56; residency Neurol. Inst. Presbyn. Hosp., N.Y.C., 1956-57, Nat. Hosp., London, 1957; residency neurosurgery Neurol. Inst. Presbyn. Hosp., 1958-62; assoc. in neurosurgery Coll. Physicians and Surgeons Columbia U., N.Y.C., 1965-77; clin. assoc. prof. NYU, N.Y.C., 1977-84, clin. prof., 1984—; pvt. practice neurosurgery, N.Y.C., 1965—. Consulting editor Spine; contbr. more than 40 articles to profl. jours., chpts. to books. Served as capt. U.S. Army, 1962-64. Fellow Am. Coll. Surgeons; mem. Cervical Spine Research Soc. (pres. 1986-87), Am. Assn. Neurol. Surgeons, Congress Neurol. Surgeons. Club: University (N.Y.C.). Avocations: skiing, squash. Office: 112 E 74th St New York NY 10021-3562

RAYNOVICH, GEORGE, JR., lawyer; b. Pitts., Dec. 30, 1931; s. George Sr. and Zora (Mamula) R.; m. Mary Ann Senay, July 11, 1953; children: George III, Andrew. BS, U. Pitts., 1957; JD, Duquesne U., 1961. Bar: Pa. 1962, U.S. Dist. Ct. (we. dist.) Pa. 1962, U.S. Patent and Trademark Office 1962, U.S. Supreme Ct. 1966, U.S. Ct. Appeals (fed. cir.) 1986. Patent agt. Consolidation Coal Co., Library, Pa., 1959-62; ptnr. Stone & Raynovich, Pitts., 1962-75; atty. Wheeling-Pitts. Steel Corp., Pitts., 1975-77, gen. counsel, sec., 1978-85, v.p., 1980-85, bd. dirs., 1983-85; sr. atty. Buchanan Ingersol P.C., Pitts., 1986-88, 89—; ptnr. Price & Raynovich, Pitts., 1988-89. Councilman Borough of Baldwin, Allegheny County, Pa., 1972-75, govt. study commr., 1973. 1st lt. USAF, 1952-56. Mem. ABA, Pa. Bar Assn., Allegheny County Bar Assn., Pitts. Intellectual Property Law Assn., Fed. Cir. Bar Assn., Acad. Trial Lawyers Allegheny County. Democrat. Mem. Serbian Orthodox Ch. Home: 335 Jean Dr Pittsburgh PA 15236 Office: Buchanan & Ingersoll PC One Oxford Ctr 301 Grant St 20th Fl Pittsburgh PA 15219-1410

RAYSON, EDWIN HOPE, lawyer; b. Earlville, Ill., Jan. 13, 1923; s. Edwin H. and Lillian (Astley) R.; m. Evelyn Sherry Kirkland, Oct. 1, 1983; children: Jane Rayson Young, Edwin Hope III, G. Scott. A.B., U. Tenn., 1944, LL.B., 1948. Bar: Tenn. 1948. Pvt. practice Knoxville, 1948—; ptnr. Kramer, Rayson, Leake, Rodgers & Morgan, 1949—; lectr. labor law U. Tenn. Coll. Law, 1951-71. Served to lt. (j.g.) USNR, 1944-46. Mem. Order of Coif, Sigma Chi, Omicron Delta Kappa. Home: 501 River Rd Loudon TN 37774-5555 Office: Plaza Towers Knoxville TN 37901

RAYSON, GLENDON ENNES, internist, preventive medicine specialist, writer; b. Oak Park, Ill., Dec. 2, 1915; s. Ennes Charles and Beatrice Margaret (Rowland) R. AB, U. Rochester, 1939; MD, U. Ill., Chgo., 1948; MPH, Johns Hopkins U., 1965; MA, Northwestern U., 1965. Diplomate Am. Bd. Internal Medicine, Am. Bd. Preventive Medicine. Resident in internal medicine Presbyn.-St. Luke's Hosp., Chgo., 1953-56; physician-in-charge Contagious Disease Hosp., Chgo., 1956-58, asst. med. supt., 1958-64; rsch. assoc. Sch. Hygiene and Pub. Health Johns Hopkins U., Balt., 1966-71; internist Johns Hopkins Hosp., 1971-82, Columbia Free State Health Plan, Balt., 1984-91; pvt. practice Balt., 1984—; with Neurodiagnostics Assocs., 1990—; attending internist emergency rm. South Balt. Gen. Hosp., 1982-84; asst. prof. health sci. U. Ill., Chgo., 1958-64; fellow in gastroenterology and endocrinology Presbyn.-St. Luke's Hosp., 1956-58. Contbr. articles to med. jours., chpt. to book. Vol. physician, Vietnam, 1968, 71, 72, 73; mem. Citizens Amb. Program Delegation to Vietnam, 1993. Capt. M.C., USAF, 1951-53. Fellow Am. Coll. Preventive Medicine, Am Geriatrics Soc.; mem. AMA, Am. Pub. Health Assn. Avocations: writing poetry, short stories, composing songs. Home: 337 Poplar Point Rd Perryville MD 21903-1803 Office: 218 N Charles St Apt 1407 Baltimore MD 21201-4027

RAYWARD, WARDEN BOYD, librarian, educator; b. Inverell, New South Wales, Australia, June 24, 1939; s. Warden and Ellie Rayward. B.A., U. Sydney, 1960; diploma in libr., U. NSW, 1964; M.S. in L.S, U. Ill., 1965; Ph.D., U. Chgo., 1973. Asst. state library NSW, 1961-64, research librarian planning and devel., 1970; lectr. Sch. Librarianship U. NSW, 1971-72, head sch. Info., Libr. and Archive Studies, 1986-92, prof., 1992—, dean Faculty of Profl. Studies, 1993—; asst. prof. U. Western Ont., 1973-74; asst. prof. Grad. Library Sch. U. Chgo., 1975-77, assoc. prof., 1978-80, prof., 1980-86; dean U. Chgo. Grad. Library Sch., 1980-86; cons. NEH, 1976-79, U.S. Dept. Edn., 1981; bd. govs. Charles Stuart U., 1994—; bd. dirs. Internat. House-U. N.S.W., 1992—. Author: The Universe of Information: The Work of Paul Otlet for Documentation and International Organization, 1975 (also transl. Russian and Spanish); editor: The Variety of Librarianship: Essays in Honour of John Wallace Metcalfe, 1976, The Public Library: Circumstances and Prospects, 1978, Library Quar., 1975-79, Library History in Context, 1988, Libraries and Life in a Changing World: the Metcalfe Years 1920-1970, 1993; editor, translator: International Organization and the Dissemination of Knowledge: Selected Papers of Paul Otlet, 1990; editor Confronting the Future, University Libraries in the Next Decade, 1992, Developing a Profession in Librarianship in Australia: Travel Diaries and Other Papers, 1996; mem. internat. editorial adv. bd. World Book of Encyclopedia, 1990—; contbr. articles to profl. jours. Coun. on Library Resources fellow, 1978; vis. fellow U. Coll. London, 1986, 90, Mortenson fellow U. Ill., 1992-93. Mem. ALA, Australian Library and Info. Assn., Bibliog. Soc. Australia and New Zealand, Am. Soc. for Info. Sci. Office: U New South Wales, PO Box 1, Kensington NSW 2033, Australia

RAZOR, BEATRICE RAMIREZ (BETTY RAZOR), enterostomal therapy nurse, educator, consultant; b. Miami, Ariz., Oct. 18, 1931; d. Jorge William and Eleanor (Reyes) Ramirez; m. James Howard Razor, Sept. 5, 1953; children: James Steven, Susan Marie, Jorge William, Edward Thomas. AA, East L.A. City Coll., 1953; RN, L.A. County Sch. Nursing, 1953; cert. enterstomal therapy, U. So. Calif., 1979, 95; BS in Health Scis., Chapman U., 1979. RN, Calif., Alaska. Staff nurse Providence Hosp., Anchorage, 1953-54; svc. coord. Native Svc. Hosp., Anchorage, 1954-56; staff nurse, head nurse to enterstomal therapy nurse coord. Meth. Hosp. of So. Calif., Arcadia, 1973-83; clin. instr. Pasadena (Calif.) City Coll., 1983-93; enterstomal nursing instr. Azusa (Calif.) Pacific U., 1983-93; enterstomal nursing coord. City of Hope Nat. Med. Ctr., Duarte, Calif., 1983-93; enterstomal nursing instr. U. So. Calif., L.A., 1990—; enterstomal nursing cons. Arcadia, 1993—; cons. San Gabriel Valley Ostomy Ctr., Covina, Calif., 1982-94; lectr. Am. Cancer Assn., 1983—, San Gabriel Valley Ostomy Assn., 1979—, Citrus Coll. Sch. Nursing, 1982-85, Pasadena City Coll. Sch. Nursing, 1981-93, Pharmacy Tech. Assn. Conf., 1982-93, Arroyo H.S., 1980, 81, 83, 90, Congress for World Coun. Enterstomal Therapists, Lyon, France, 1992, Symposium on Advanced Wound Care, 1989, 91, City of Hope Planned Giving Program, 1989-93, Oncology Nursing Soc., 1987, 89, also others. Author: Seminars in Oncology Nursing, 1993; also articles. Merit badge cons. San Gabriel Valley coun. Boy Scouts Am., 1965-94; chmn. Byron-Thompson Cmty. Svcs., El Monte, 1983—; mem., chmn. nursing edn. com. Am. Cancer Soc., Pasadena, 1980-90; mem. chronic disease prevention adv. com. State of Calif., Sacramento, 1982-90; sec. El Monte Rep. Women. Recipient Silver Beaver award Boy Scouts Am., 1978, cmty. svc. award City of El Monte, 1983, Svc. award Calif. PTA, Nurse of Yr. award City of Hope, 1992. Mem. Oncology Nursing Soc., World Coun. Enterstomal Therapy (editl. bd. 1990—), United Ostomy Assn. (med. advisor San Gabriel Valley chpt. 1980-95), Wound, Ostomy and Continence Nursing Soc. (pub. rels. coord. Pacific Coast chpt. 1992—, bd. dirs. 1992—, pres. 1988-92), Sigma Theta Tau. Republican. Lutheran. Avocations: backpacking, painting, gardening, clay pottery. Office: Enterstomal Nursing Cons 701 S 1st Ave Arcadia CA 91732

RAZZANO, FRANK CHARLES, lawyer; b. Bklyn., Feb. 25, 1948; s. Pasquale Anthony and Agnes Mary (Borgia) R.; m. Stephanie Anne Lucas, Jan. 10, 1970; children: Joseph, Francis, Catherine. BA, St. Louis U., 1969; JD, Georgetown U., 1972. Bar: N.Y. 1973, U.S. Dist. Ct. (so. dist.) N.Y. 1973, U.S. Dist. Ct. (es. dist.) N.Y. 1973, N.J. 1976, D.C. 1981, Va. 1984, U.S. Dist. Ct. N.J. 1976, U.S. Dist. Ct. Md. 1977, U.S. Dist. Ct. (no. dist.) Calif. 1981, U.S. Dist. Ct. D.C. 1982, U.S. Dist. Ct. (ea. dist.) Va. 1989, U.S. Dist. Ct. (we. dist.) Va. 1990, U.S. Ct. Appeals (2d cir.) 1973, U.S. Ct. Appeals (3d cir.) 1975, U.S. Ct. Appeals (D.C. and 5th cirs.) 1983, U.S. Ct. Appeals (4th cir.) 1984, U.S. Ct. Appeals (6th cir.) 1990, U.S. Supreme Ct. 1976. Assoc. Shea & Gould, N.Y.C., 1972-75; asst. U.S. atty. Dist. of N.J., Newark, 1975-78; asst. chief trial atty. SEC, Washington, 1978-82; ptnr. Shea & Gould, Washington, 1982-94, mng. ptnr., 1991-92; ptnr. Camhy Karlinsky Stein Razzano & Rubin, Washington, 1994—; lectr. in field. Civil law editor Rico Law Reporter; mem. adv. bd. Corp. Confidentiality and Disclosure Letter; hon. adv. com. Jour. Internat. Law and Practice, Detroit Coll. Law; contbr. articles to legal jours. Scoutmaster Vienna coun. Boy Scouts Am., 1984. Recipient spl. achievement award Justice Dept., 1977, spl. commendation, 1978, Outstanding Achievement award Detroit Coll. of Law, 1993. Mem. ABA (chmn. criminal law com., sect. bus. law 1996—), Va. Bar, D.C. Bar (chmn. litigation sect. 1987-89, vice-chmn. coun. sects. 1988-89), Assn. Securities & Exch. Commn. Alumni (pres. 1993-95), Phi Beta Kappa, Eta Sigma Phi. Roman Catholic. Home: 1713 Paisley Blue Ct Vienna VA 22182-2326

RAZZAQUE, MUHAMMAD MAHBUBUR, nuclear engineer; b. Sylhet, Bangladesh, Mar. 23, 1948; came to U.S., 1973; s. Abdur and Aliya R.; m. Sayeeda; 1 child, Saima Anika. BS, U. Wis., 1976, MS, 1977; PhD, U. Tex., 1981. Engr. Va. Power Co., Richmond, 1982-84; prof. nuclear engr. Iowa State U., Ames, 1984-91; nuclear engr. U.S. Nuclear Regulatory Commn., Washington, 1991—; cons. on nuclear safety UN Devel. Program, 1986-87; prin. co-investigator U.S. Dept. Energy, Washington, 1985-89; spkr. Atomic Energy Commn., Dhaka, 1987. Contbr. over 15 articles to profl. jours. Mem. Am. Nuclear Soc. Avocations: reading, walking, outdoor cooking. Office: US Nuclear Regulatory Commn M/S O-8E23 Washington DC 20555-0001

RE, EDWARD DOMENIC, law educator, retired federal judge; b. Santa Marina, Italy, Oct. 14, 1920; s. Anthony and Marina (Maetta) R.; m. Margaret A. Corcoran, June 3, 1950; children: Mary Ann, Anthony John, Marina, Edward, Victor, Margaret, Matthew, Joseph, Mary Elizabeth, Mary Joan, Mary Ellen, Nancy Madeleine. BS cum laude, St. John's U., 1941, LLB summa cum laude, 1943, LLD (hon.), 1968; JSD, NYU, 1950; DPed, Aquila, Italy, 1960; LL.D. (hon.), St. Mary's Coll., Notre Dame, Ind., 1968, Maryville Coll., St. Louis, 1969, N.Y. Law Sch., 1976, Bklyn. Coll., CUNY, 1978, Nova U., 1980, Roger Williams Coll., 1982, Dickinson Sch. Law, Carlisle, Pa., 1983, Seton Hall U., 1984, Stetson U., 1990, William Mitchell Coll. Law, 1992, St. Francis Coll., Bklyn., 1993; L.H.D. (hon.), DePaul U., 1980, Coll. S.I., CUNY, 1981, Pace U., 1985, Am. U. of Rome, 1995; D.C.S. (hon.), U. Verona, Italy, 1987; J.D. (hon.), U. Bologna, Italy, 1988, U. Urbino, Italy, 1994. Bar: N.Y. 1943. Appointed faculty St. John's U., N.Y., 1947, prof. law, 1951-69, adj. prof. law, 1969-80, Disting. prof., from 1980; vis. prof. Georgetown U. Sch. Law, 1962-67; adj. prof. law N.Y. Law Sch., 1972-82, Martin disting. vis. prof., from 1982; spl. hearing officer U.S. Dept. Justice, 1956-61; chmn. Fgn. Claims Settlement Commn. of U.S., 1961-68; asst. sec. ednl. and cultural affairs U.S. Dept. State, 1968-69; judge U.S. Customs Ct. (now U.S. Ct. Internat. Trade), N.Y.C., 1969-91, chief judge, 1977-91, chief judge emeritus, 1991—; mem. Jud. Conf. U.S., 1986-91, adv. com. on appellate rules, 1976-88, com. on internat. jud. rels., 1994—; chmn. adv. com. on experimentation in the law Fed. Jud. Ctr., 1978-81; mem. bd. higher edn. City of N.Y., 1958-69, emeritus, 1969—; Jackson lectr. Nat. Coll. State Trial Judges, U. Nev., 1970. Author: Foreign Confiscations in Anglo-American Law, 1951, (with Lester D. Orfield) Cases and Materials on International Law, rev. edit., 1965, Selected Essays on Equity, 1955, Brief Writing and Oral Argument, 6th edit., 1987, (with Joseph R. Re) 7th edit., 1993, (with Zechariah Chafee Jr.) Cases and Materials on Equity, 1967, Cases and Materials on Equitable Remedies, 1975; (with Joseph R. Re) Law Students' Manual on Legal Writing and Oral Argument, 1991; chpt., freedom in internat. soc. Concept of Freedom (editor Rev. Carl W. Grindel), 1955; Cases and Materials on Remedies, 1982, (with Joseph R. Re) 4th edit., 1996; contbr. articles to legal jours. Served with USAAF, 1943-47; col. JAGC, ret. Decorated Grand Cross Order of Merit Italy; recipient Am. Bill of Rights citation; Morgenstern Found. Interfaith award; USAF commendation medal; Distinguished service award Bklyn. Jr. C. of C., 1956. Mem. ABA (ho. of dels. 1976-78, chmn. sect. internat. and comparative law 1965-67), Am. Fgn. Law Assn. (pres. 1971-73), Am. Law Inst., Fed. Bar Coun. (pres. 1973-74), Am. Soc. Comparative Law (pres. 1969-91), Am. Justinian Soc. Jurists (pres. 1974-76), Internat. Assn. Jurists: Italy-USA (pres. 1991—), Internat. Assn. Judges (prin. rep. to UN 1993—), Scribes Am. Soc. Writers on Legal Subjects (pres. 1978). Office: St Johns U Sch Law Jamaica NY 11439

REA, ANN W., librarian; b. Jefferson City, Mo., Aug. 3, 1944; d. William H. and Ruby (Fogleman) Webb; m. Glen N. Rea, Sept. 28, 1974; children: Sarah, Rebecca. BA, U. Mo., 1966; MLS, U. So. Calif., 1968. Libr. St. Charles (Mo.) County Libr., 1967-71; libr. adult svcs. Paterson (N.J.) Free Pub. Libr., 1971-74; libr. Beal Coll. Libr., Bangor, Maine, 1983—. Mem. Am. Libr. Assn., Maine Libr. Assn. Office: Beal Coll Libr 629 Main St Bangor ME 04401-6848

REA, DAVID K., geology and oceanography educator; b. Pitts., June 2, 1942; m. Donna M. Harshbarger, Feb. 11, 1967; children: Gregory, Margaret. AB, Princeton U., 1964; MS, U. Ariz., 1967; PhD, Oreg. State U., 1974. Prof. geology & oceanography U. Mich., Ann Arbor, 1975—; assoc. dir. NSF Climate Dynamics Program, Washington, 1986-87; interim dir. Ctr. for Great Lakes and Aquatic Scis., 1988-89, chmn. dept. geol. scis., 1995—. Contbr. more than 300 articles, reports to profl. publs. Recipient numerous NSF rsch. grants, 1976—. Office: U Mich Dept Geological Sci Ann Arbor MI 48109-1063

REA, STEPHEN, actor; b. Belfast, Ireland, 1949; m. Dolours Price, 1983; children: Oscar, Danny. Student, Queens Univ., Belfast. Formed (with Brian Friel) Field Day Theatre Co., 1980. Stage appearances include (London) The Shadow of a Gunman, The Cherry Orchard, Miss Julie, High Society; (Royal Court Theatre) Endgame, The Freedom of the City; (Field Day Theatre Co.) Translations, Communication Card, St. Oscar, Boesman and Lena, Hightime and Riot Act, Double Cross, Pentecost, Making History, Three Sisters (dir. only), The Cure at Troy (dir. only); (Broadway) Someone Who'll Watch Over Me, 1992 (Tony award nominee 1993), Uncle Vanya, 1995; films include Angel, 1982, Danny Boy, 1984, Company of Wolves, 1985, The Doctor and the Devils, 1985, Loose Connections, 1988, Life Is Sweet, 1991, The Crying Game, 1992 (Acad. award nominee best actor 1993), Bad Behavior, 1993, Princess Caraboo, 1993, Angie, 1994, Interview with the Vampire, 1994, Ready to Wear (Prêt-à-Porter), 1994, All Men Are Mortal, 1994, Citizen X, 1994, The Devil and the Deep Blue Sea, 1994; TV appearances include Four Days in July, Lost Belongings, Scout, St. Oscar, Not with a Bang, Hedda Gabler. Office: Peters Fraser & Dunlop Ltd, 503 The Chambers Lots Rd, Chelsea Harbor London SW10 OXF, England

REA, WILLIAM, oil industry executive. With Arthur Young, Jacksonville, Fla., 1977-80, Charter Co., Jacksonville, Fla., 1980-83, Haskell Co., Jacksonville, Fla., 1983-88; v.p., cfo TR Trading Inc., Long Beach, Calif., 1989—. Office: TR Trading Inc 1 World Trade Ctr Ste 2550 Long Beach CA 90831-2550*

REA, WILLIAM J., district judge; b. 1950; BA, Loyola U., 1942, LLB, U. Colo., 1949. With U.S. Census Bur., Denver, 1949-50; adjuster Farmers Ins. Group, L.A., 1950; pvt. practice law, L.A., 1950-64, Santa Ana, Calif., 1964-68; judge Superior Ct., L.A., 1968-84; judge U.S. Dist. Ct. (cen. dist.) Calif., L.A., 1984—. Past pres. L.A. chpt. Nat. Exec. Com.; chmn. Constn. and By-Laws Com. With USN, WWII. Mem. L.A. County Bar Assn. (Outstanding Jurist award 1985), So. Calif. Def. Counsel Assn. Disting. Svc. award 1982), Internat. Acad. Trial Lawyers (Trial Judge of Yr. 1982), L.A. Trial Lawyers Assn., Am. Bd. Trial Advs. (nat. pres.). Office: US Dist Ct 312 N Spring St Los Angeles CA 90012-4701*

REACH, REBECCA M., nursing educator, university dean. BSN, No. Ill. U., 1964; MSN in Cmty. Health Nursing, U. Evansville, 1978. RN, Ark. Cmty. health nurse Peoria (Ill.) City and County Health Dept., 1964-65, Jackson County Health Dept., Murphysboro, Ill., 1972-74; staff nurse Proctor Hosp., Peoria, 1965-66; charge nurse Herrin (Ill.) Hosp., 1966-72; DON, Franklin-Williamson Bi-County Health Dept., Johnston City, Ill., 1975-77, Egyptian Health Dept., Eldorado, Ill., 1977-79; coord. allied health related occupations John A. Logan Coll., Carterville, Ill., 1979-81; mem. faculty, chmn. nursing and health scis. dept. U. N.Mex., Gallup, 1981-86; prof. nursing, chmn. dept. Sinclair C.C., Dayton, Ohio, 1986-94; prof. nursing, chmn. dept. U. Ark., Little Rock, 1994—, also dean nursing; presenter in field; nurse specialist accreditation teams Am. Coun. Ind. Colls. and Schs., 1989—; coord. educator exch. visits to Russia, 1990, 92, 94; mem. new program site visit team Ohio Bd. Regents,1991, 93. Former mem. editl. bd. ADvancing Clin. Care (formerly AD Nurse); contbr. articles to nursing jours. Recipient cert. of appreciation Navajo C.C., 1982, excellence in writing award Am. Jour. Nursing and N.Mex. Nurses Assn., 1983, 84, 85; grantee FITNE, 1992. Mem. ANA, Nat. League for Nursing, Nat. Orgn. for Advancement ADN, Ark. Nurses Assn., Nursing Adminstrs. in Nursing Edn. Programs in Ark., Clin. Experience Planning and Coordinating Coun. (chmn.), Ark. for Nursing, Fuld Inst. Tech. in Nursing, Sigma Theta Tau. Office: Sinclair Comm Coll Dept of Nursing 444 W 3rd St Dayton OH 45402-1421

READ, ALLAN ALEXANDER, minister; b. Toronto, Ont., Can., Sept. 19, 1923; s. Alec P. and Lillice (Matthews) R.; m. Mary Beverly Roberts, Sept. 28, 1949; children—John Allan, Elizabeth Anne, Peter Michael, Martha Ruth. B.A., U. Toronto, Can., 1946; Licentiate in Theology, Trinity Coll., Toronto, 1947, D.D., 1972; D.D., Wycliffe Coll., Toronto, 1972; D.S.T. (hon.), Thornloe Coll., Sudbury, Ont., 1982. Ordained diaconate, 1948, priest, 1949, Anglican Ch. of Canada. Rector 7 chs. Diocese Toronto-Anglican Ch., Parish of East and West Mono, Ont., Can., 1947-54; rector Diocese of Toronto-Trinity Anglican Ch., Christ Ch. Vespra, Barrie, Ont., Can., 1954-72; founder Barrie East End Mission, Parish of St. Giles, 1954; chaplain Simcoe County Gaol, 1954-72; Suffragan bishop Diocese of Toronto-Anglican Ch., Toronto, Ont., Can., 1972-81; bishop Diocese of Ont., Kingston, Ont., Can., 1981-92; canon St. James Cathedral, Toronto, 1957-61; mem., chmn. provincial synod rural chmn. com., 1953-63, Diocese of Toronto Exec. Com., 1959-71, Diocesan Com. Prayer and Evang., 1950-70, Ont. Guelph Agr. Coll. Planning Com. on Courses for Clergy in Rural Areas, 1950-54, Anglican Gen. Synod Com. on Ministry in Rural Areas, 1952-65; Diocesan Com. Corrections, 1950-72, Gen. Synod Com. Music and Hymn Book, 1965-71, chmn. and chaplin, Boy Scout Com., Barrie #1, 1954-71, Govt. of Ont. Dept. Lands and Forests adv. com. on reforestation, 1950-54, provincial synod, 1955-91, rural ch. unit gen. synod Anglican Ch. Can., 1959-89; archdeacon of Simcoe, 1961-72, Can. churchmn. bd. trustees; participant World Anglican Congress, Toronto, 1963; mem. Anglican World Wide Lambeth Conf., 1978, 88; dir. Anglican Found., Toronto; priest-in-charge St. Patrick's Cathedral, Trim, Ireland, 1992, Parish of Dunster Diocese of Bath and Wells, Eng., 1993, Parish of St. Ippolyts, Diocese St. Alban's, Eng., 1994, Parish of St. Mary the Virgin Westerham, Diocese of Rochester Eng., 1995, Cathedral of St. John and St. Patrick, Ch. of Ireland, Eire, 1956. Author: Unto The Hills, 1951; Shepherds in Green Pastures, 1953. Patron Grenville Christian Coll., Brockville, Ont., 1981—; mem., hon. pres. Can. Coll. Organists, Simcoe Br., 1954-71; hon. Reeve, Black Creek Pioneer Village, 1981-82; mem. Barrie and Dist. High Sch. Bd., 1961-70; exec. com. Alcohol and Drug Concerns, 1971-83. Recipient Rural Workers Fellowship award Episcopal Ch. U.S., 1952, Citizenship awards Gov. of Ont., 1980, 85, 90; named Citizen of Yr. City of Barrie, 1967. Mem. Rural Workers Fellowship (hon. pres. 1967—), Barrie Ministerial Assn. (sec. 1954-81). Home: 39 Riverside Dr, RR 1, Kingston, ON Canada K7L 4V1

READ, DAVID HAXTON CARSWELL, clergyman; b. Cupar, Fife, Scotland, Jan. 2, 1910; came to U.S., 1956; s. John Alexander and Catherine Haxton (Carswell) R.; m. Dorothy Florence Patricia Gilbert, 1936; 1 son, Rory David Gilbert. Grad., Daniel Stewart's Coll., Edinburgh, 1927; M.A. summa cum laude, U. Edinburgh, 1932, D.D., 1957; student, Montpelier,

Strasbourg, Paris, 1932-33, Marburg, 1934; B.D., New Coll., Edinburgh, Scotland, 1936; D.D., Yale U., 1959, Lafayette Coll., 1965, Hope Coll., 1969; Litt.D., Coll. Wooster, 1966; L.H.D., Trinity U., 1972, Hobart Coll., 1972, Knox Coll., 1979; D.H.L., Japan Internat. Christian U., 1979, Rockford Coll., 1982. Ordained to ministry Ch. Scotland, 1936; min. Colsdtream West, 1936-39; minister Greenbank Ch., Edinburgh, 1939-49; chaplain U. Edinburgh, 1949-55; chaplain to Her Majesty the Queen, Scotland, 1952-56; minister Madison Ave. Presbyn. Ch., 1956-89, minister emeritus, 1989—. Author: The Spirit of Life, 1939, Prisoners' Quest, 1944, The Communication of the Gospel, 1952, The Christian Faith, 1956, I Am Persuaded, 1962, Sons of Anak, 1964, God's Mobile Family, 1966, Whose God is Dead?, 1966, The Pattern of Christ, 1967, Holy Common Sense, 1966, The Presence of Christ, 1968, Christian Ethics, 1968, Virginia Woolf Meets Charlie Brown, 1968, Religion without Wrappings, 1970, Overheard, 1971, Curious Christians, 1972, An Expanding Faith, 1973, Sent from God, 1974, Good News in the Letters of Paul, 1976, Go . . . And Make Disciples, 1978, Unfinished Easter, 1978, The Faith is Still There, 1980, This Grace Given, 1984, Grace Thus Far, 1986, Preaching About the Needs of Real People, 1988, Christmas Tales for All Ages, 1989; translator (from German): The Church to Come, 1939; editor-in-chief The Living Pulpit, 1992; contbr. articles religious jours., periodicals, U.S. and Eng., The Living Pulpit, 1992—. Chaplain Brit. Army, 1939-45. Mem. Century Assn. (N.Y.C.), Pilgrims Club. Prisoner of war, 1940-45. Home: 258 Riverside Dr Apt 9A New York NY 10025-6161

READ, ELEANOR MAY, financial analyst; b. Arcadia, N.Y., July 4, 1940; d. Henry and Lena May (Fagner) Van Koevering; 1 child, Robin Jo. Typist, clk., sec., credit corr. Sarah Coventry, Inc., Newark, N.Y., 1957-61; exec. sec. Mobil Chem. Co., Macedon, N.Y., 1961-68; bus. mgr. Henry's Hardware, Newark, 1968-72; with Xerox Corp., Fremont, Calif., 1973—, internat. clk. analyst, personnel adminstrv. asst., employment coordinator, exec. sec., cycle count analyst., acctg. specialist, tax preparer H&R Block, 1985-92. Mem. Xerox/Diablo Mgmt. Assn., Am. Mgmt. Assn., Profl. Businesswomen's Assn., NAFE. Office: Xerox/AMTX 5450 Campus Dr Canandaigua NY 14425

READ, FRANK THOMPSON, law educator; b. Ogden, Utah, July 16, 1938; s. Frank Archie and Fay Melrose (Thompson) R.; m. Lenet Hadley; 5 children. BS with high honors, Brigham Young U., 1960; JD, Duke U., 1963. Bar: Minn. 1963, Mo. 1966, N.Y. 1968, Okla. 1975. Pvt. practice Mpls., St. Paul, 1963-65; atty. AT&T, Kansas City, Mo., and N.Y.C., 1965-68; asst. prof. law, asst. dean Law Sch., Duke U., 1968-70, assoc. prof., asst. dean, 1970-72, prof., assoc. dean, 1972-73, prof., 1973-74; dean, prof. law U. Tulsa Coll. Law, 1974-79, Ind. U. Sch Law., Indpls., 1979-81, U. Fla. Coll. Law, 1981-88; dean, chief exec. officer Hastings Coll. Law, U. Calif., San Francisco, 1988-93; dep. cons. sect. on legal edn. ABA, Indpls., 1993-95; pres., dean S. Tex. Coll. Law, 1995—; trustee Law Sch. Admission Coun., 1976-88, pres., 1984-85; chmn. Okla. Jud. Coun., 1976-78, pres., 1984-85; vis. prof. U. N.C., So. Meth. U., Brigham Young U. Author: Let Them Be Jugged: The Judicial Integration of the Deep South, 1978, The Oklahoma Evidence Handbook, 1979, Read's Florida Evidence, 2 vols., 1987; contbr. articles to profl. jours. Mem. ABA (sect. legal edn.), Am. Law Inst., Assn. Am. Law Schs., Order of Coif, Phi Kappa Phi. Home: 1303 San Jacinto St Houston TX 46032-5824

READ, FREDERICK WILSON, JR., lawyer, educator; b. Providence, July 30, 1908; s. Frederick Wilson and Araminta Rowena (Briggs) R.; m. Evelyn Elaine Avery, Feb. 21, 1942; children: Frederick Wilson III, Cynthia Avery. Student, Trinity Coll., 1925-26; AB, Columbia U., 1930, LLB, 1932. Bar: N.Y. 1933, Mass. 1939, U.S. Supreme Ct. 1955. Assoc. Hervey, Barber & McKee, N.Y.C., 1932-35, Menken, Ferguson & Idler, N.Y.C., 1937-39; atty. legal dept. Nat. Realty Mgmt. Co., N.Y.C., 1935-37, French Air Commn., N.Y.C., 1939-40; mem. legal and contracts depts. Brit. Purchasing Commn., Brit. Air Commn., N.Y.C. and Washington, 1940-41; atty. Glenn L. Martin Co., Middle River, Md., 1941-42; with Home Life Ins. Co., N.Y.C., 1945-73; atty. Home Life Ins. Co., 1945-47, asst. counsel, 1947-54, counsel, 1954-64, gen. counsel, 1964-71, v.p., gen. counsel, 1971-73; counsel Daiker, D'Elia, Turtletaub & Cantino, Port Washington, N.Y., 1973-77, D'Elia, Turtletaub & Cantino, 1977-80, Capobianco, D'Elia, Turtletaub, Cantino & Aitken (P.C.), 1980-83, D'Elia & Turtletaub, 1983—; prof. Coll. Ins., 1974-84, N.Y. Law Sch., 1974-76; counsel N.Y.C. Life Underwriters Assn., 1974-83, hon. mem., 1984—. Mem. Bd. Edn., Port Washington, 1949-52, 59-66, pres., 1950-52, v.p., 1962-66; trustee McAuley Water St. Mission, 1970-81, trustee emeritus, 1981—; dir. John Philip Sousa Meml. Band Shell, Inc., 1990—; mem. sr. adv. coun. Port Washington Pub. Libr., 1991—. Capt. USNR, 1942-45; mem. Res. (ret.). Recipient Bishops Cross, 1988. Fellow Am. Bar Found. (life); mem. ABA (rep. ho. dels. 1969-77, sr. lawyer div. com. liaison with state and local bar sr. lawyers 1986—), N.Y. State Bar Assn. (assn. ins. program com. 1973-84, vice-chmn. 1974-77, chmn. 1977-84), Nassau County Bar Assn. (chmn. assn. ins. plans com. 1973-83, dir. 1977-80), Assn. of Bar of City of N.Y. (ins. law com. 1946-49, 61-64, mil. justice and mil. affairs com. 1951-68, chmn. 1965-68), Assn. Life Ins. Counsel (sec.-treas. 1960-63, v.p. 1965-66, pres. 1967-68), Judge Advs. Assn. (life), Am. Council Life Ins., Health Ins. Assn. Am., Am. Soc. CLUs, Ins. Soc. of N.Y. (1974-84), Cow Neck Peninsula Hist. Soc. (trustee, 3d v.p.-legal 1974-83, trustee emeritus 1983—), U.S. Naval Inst. (life), Naval Res. Assn. (life), Ret. Officers Assn., Nat. Maritime Hist. Soc., Acad. Political Sci., Alpha Delta Phi. Episcopalian. Clubs: Lions (Port Washington) (bd. dirs. 1980-82, 87—); Masons. Home: 2 Lynn Rd Port Washington NY 11050-4447 Office: 927 Port Washington Blvd Port Washington NY 11050-2910

READ, GREGORY CHARLES, lawyer; b. St. Louis, Jan. 21, 1942; s. Charles Hadley and Margaret Olive (Kumlien) R.; m. Mary Beth Bartulis, Aug. 28, 1965; children: Laura Elizabeth, Andrew Nathan. BA, U. Ill., 1964, JD, 1967. Bar: Ill. 1967, Calif. 1971, U.S. Dist. Ct. (no., ea. and cen. dists.) Calif., U.S. Ct. Claims, U.S. Ct. Appeals (9th cir.), U.S. Ct. Appeals (fed. cir.), U.S. Supreme Ct. Law clk. to Hon. Henry Wise U.S. Dist. Ct. Ill., Danville, 1967; assoc. Sedgwick, Detert, Moran & Arnold, San Francisco, 1971-76, ptnr., 1976—. Contbr. articles to profl. jours. Lt. JAGC, USN, 1968-70. Mem. ABA, Am. Bd. Trial Advocates, Ill. Bar Assn., Calif. Bar Assn., Internat. Assn. Def. Counsel, Def. Rsch. Inst. Home: 66 La Cuesta Orinda CA 94563-2326 Office: Sedgwick Detert Moran & Arnold 1 Embarcadero Ctr Fl 16 San Francisco CA 94111-3607

READ, SISTER JOEL, academic administrator. BS in Edn., Alverno Coll., 1948; MA in History, Fordham U., 1951; hon. degrees, Lakeland Coll., 1972, Wittenburg U., 1976, Marymount Manhattan Coll., 1978, DePaul U., 1985, Northland Coll., 1986, SUNY, 1986. Former prof., dept. chmn. history dept. Alverno Coll., Milw., pres., 1968—; pres. Am. Assn. for Higher Edn., 1976-77; mem. coun. NEH, 1977-83; bd. dirs. Ednl. Testing Svc., 1987-93, Neylan Commn., 1985-90; past pres. Wis. Assn. Ind. Colls. and Univs.; mem. Commn. on Status of Edn. for Women, 1971-76, Am. Assn. Colls., 1971-77; mem. exec. com. Greater Milw. com. GMC Edn. Trust. Mem. exec. bd. Milw. YMCA. First recipient Anne Roe award Harvard U. Grad. Sch. Edn., 1980. Fellow Am. Acad. Arts and Scis.; mem. Found. for Higher Edn. Office: Alverno Coll Office of the President PO Box 343922 Milwaukee WI 53234-3922

READ, JOHN CONYERS, management consultant; b. N.Y.C., May 21, 1947; s. Edward Cameron Kirk and Louise (Geary) R.; m. Alexandra Gould, Mar. 30, 1968; children: Cameron Kirk, Trevor Conyers, Alexandra. AB, Harvard, 1969, MBA, 1971. Ops. rsch. analyst HEW, Washington, 1971-72; exec. asst. to dir. Cost of Living Council, Washington, 1973; chief econ. adviser to Gov. Mass., 1974; exec. asst., counselor to sec. labor Washington, 1975; asst. sec. labor for employment standards, 1976-77; dir. corp. employee rels., pers. Cummins Engine Co., Columbus, Ind., 1977-80, plant mgr., 1980-85; v.p. Midrange Engines, 1986-90; v.p., gen. mgr. engine group Donaldson Co., Inc., Mpls., 1990-92; exec. v.p., 1992-94; cons. nat. productivity and energy policies; chmn. NAM Task Force on Wage and Price Policies, 1978-80. Author Ford Found. monograph on occupational disease and workers' compensation; contbr. articles to newspapers and mags. Trustee Nat. Ctr. Occupl. Readjustment, 1984-87, N.C. Outward Bound Sch., dir., 1995—; chmn. Charleston Pvt. Industry Coun., 1985; mem. plant closing task force U. S. Dept. Labor, 1986, mfg. task force NRC, 1989, critical industries task force Def. Dept., 1989. Mem. Nat. Assn. Mfrs. (bd. dirs., chair employee rels. com. 1993-95). Home: 2697 E Lake Of The Isles Pky Minneapolis MN 55408-1051

READ, MICHAEL OSCAR, editor, consultant; b. Amarillo, Tex., July 11, 1942; s. Harold Eugene and Madeline (Welch) R.; m. Jill Kay Vanderby, July 6, 1963 (div. Apr. 1967); 1 child, Rebecca Anne; m. Fawn Dale Barby, Apr. 10, 1977; 1 child, Nathan Michael. AA in Chemistry, Amarillo Coll., 1962; BA in Journalism, Tex. Tech. U., 1965. News editor Olton (Tex.) Enterprise, 1963-64; reporter, photographer Lubbock (Tex.) Avalanche-Jour., 1964-67, copy editor, 1967-70, city editor, 1970-72; copy editor Houston Post, 1972-74, systems editor, 1974-89, dir. news tech., 1989-95; electronic media content coord. Houston Chronicle, 1995—; bd. dirs. News Media Credit Union, Houston, Meadows (Tex.) Econ. Devel. Corp.; tchr. Let's Compute!, Stafford, Tex., 1985—; cons. Newspaper Pub. Sys., Stafford, 1989—; mem. joint Newspaper Assn. Am.-Internat. Press. Telecomm. Coun. Com. Wire Svc. Standards. Author weekly newspaper column, 1977—. Vol. United Way, Houston, 1973—; bd. dirs. Meadows Community Improvement Assn., 1985-91, Meadows Utility Dist., 1988-93. Eldon Durrett scholar, 1961-65. Mem. Am. MENSA, Am. Philatelic Soc., Am. 1st Day Cov. Soc. (life), U.S. Chess Fedn. (life), Soc. Profl. Journalists (conv. com. 1989-90), Press Club of Houston. Avocations: philately, photography, gardening. Home: 12023 Alston Dr Stafford TX 77477-1505 Office: Houston Chronicle 801 Texas Ave Houston TX 77002

READ, PHILIP LLOYD, computer design and manufacturing executive; b. Flint, Mich., Jan. 9, 1932; s. Harry Samuel and Maude Elizabeth (Jones) R.; m. Ann Elizabeth Goodall, June 23, 1956; children: Thomas, Elizabeth, Jane. AB, Oberlin Coll., 1953; MS in Physics, U. Mich., 1954, PhD in Physics, 1961. Physicist GE, Schenectady, N.Y., 1960-67; mgr. GE, Milw., 1967-70, gen. mgr., 1970-75; corp. v.p., divsn. gen. mgr. Computervision Corp., Bedford, Mass., 1975-81, sr. v.p., COO, 1981-83, sr. v.p., 1983-88, also bd. dirs. Contbr. articles to profl. jours.; patentee in field. Mem. Am. Phys. Soc. Avocations: photography, tennis. Home and Office: 80 Witherell Dr Sudbury MA 01776-1248

READ, PIERS PAUL, author; b. Beaconsfield, Eng., Mar. 7, 1941; s. Herbert Edward and Margaret (Ludwig) R.; m. Emily Albertine Boothby, July 29, 1967; children: Albert Nathaniel, Martha Marianna, William Edward, Beatrice Mary. B.A., St. John's Coll., Cambridge U., 1962, M.A., 1963. Sub-editor Times Lit. Supplement, 1963-64; adj. prof. writing Columbia U., 1980; lit. panel mem. Arts Coun. Gt. Britain, 1974-76; gov. Cardinal Manning Boys Sch., 1985; chmn. Cath. Writers Guild, 1993. Author: (novels) Game in Heaven with Tussy Marx, 1966, The Junkers, 1968 (Sir Geoffrey Faber Meml. prize 1969), Monk Dawson, 1970 (Somerset Maugham award, Hawthornden prize 1970), The Professor's Daughter, 1971, The Upstart, 1973, Polonaise, 1976, A Married Man, 1980, The Villa Golitsyn, 1982, The Free Frenchman, 1986, A Season in the West, 1988 (James Tait Black Meml. prize), On the Third Day, 1990, (non-fiction) Alive: The Story of the Andes Survivors, 1974 (Thomas More medal), The Train Robbers, 1978, Ablaze: The Heros and Victims of Chernobyl, 1993, The Patriot, 1996, (TV plays) Coincidence, The Family Firm, The House of Highbury Hill. Mem. Brit. bd. of Aid to Church in Need, 1988. Ford Found. fellow, 1963-64; Harkness fellow, 1967-68. Fellow Royal Soc. Lit.; mem. Soc. Authors (com. mgmt. 1972-74), Inst. Contemporary Arts (com. mgmt. 1972-74). Roman Catholic. Address: 50 Portland Rd, W11 4LG London England

READ, WILLIAM LAWRENCE, business executive, former naval officer; b. Bklyn., July 8, 1926; s. Reginald A. and Martha (Bedell) R.; m. Martha Miller, Nov. 25, 1950; children: Allison, William Lawrence, John Alexander. BS., U.S. Naval Acad., 1949; M.S., George Washington U., 1970. Commd. ensign U.S. Navy, 1949, advanced through grades to vice adm., 1977; comdr. U.S.S. Van Voorhis, 1961-63, U.S.S. King, 1966-68, Escort Squadron Ten, 1968-69, Cruiser-Destroyer Flotilla Three, 1972-73; sr. aide to SACEUR, 1970-72, mil. asst. to sec. Def., 1963-65, asst. chief Navy Personnel for officer devel. and distbn., 1973-74, dir. Ship Acquisition Div., Office Chief Naval Ops., 1974-77, comdr. Naval Surface Force, U.S. Atlantic Fleet, 1977-79; v.p. constrn. mgmt. Lone Star Industries, Greenwich, Conn., 1979-83; bd. dirs. Olin Corp., Meml. Health Sys. Decorated D.S.M., Legion of Merit, Navy Commendation medal with combat V, Navy Disting. Service Order 2d class (Republic of Vietnam). Mem. Surface Navy Assn. (bd. dirs.). Episcopalian. Home: 8117 Lee Haven Rd Easton MD 21601-7455

READ, WILLIAM MCCLAIN, retired oil company executive; b. Phila., July 30, 1918; s. William Tucker and Grace (McNeal) R.; m. Esther Donahoo, Sept. 15, 1945; children: Deborah Read Yoder, Suzanne Read DiFulvio, William W. B.A., Washington and Lee U., 1940; postgrad., U. Pa., 1941-42. Personal asst. Atlantic Refining Co., Phila., 1943-50, dir. tng., 1950-72; v.p. employee relations Atlantic Richfield Co., Los Angeles, 1972-78, sr. v.p. employee relations, 1978-83; now ret. Author: Now You Are a Supervisor, 1962; contbr. articles to profl. jours. Chmn. Verdugo Hills Hosp., Glendale, Calif., 1980-81, 85-86; dir. Hosp. Coun. So. Calif., L.A., 1982-84, chmn. trustees com., 1983-84; chmn. bd. dirs. Pacific Clinics, 1993. Recipient Algernon Sydney Sullivan award Washington and Lee U., 1940. Mem. Phi Beta Kappa, Omicron Delta Kappa. Home: 4141 Cambridge Rd Flintridge CA 91011

READE, CLAIRE ELIZABETH, lawyer; b. Waltham, Mass., June 2, 1952; d. Kemp Brownell and Suzanne Helen (Dorntge) R.; m. Earl Phillip Steinberg, Nov. 22, 1980; children: Evan Samuel, Emma Miriam. BA, Conn. Wesleyan U., 1973; JD, Harvard U., 1979; MA in Law and Diplomacy, Tufts U., 1979. Bar: Mass. 1980, D.C. 1983. Sheldon fellow Harvard U., Cambridge, Mass. and, Republic of China, 1979-80; assoc. Ropes & Gray, Boston, 1980-82; assoc. Arnold & Porter, Washington, 1982-86, ptnr., 1987—. Exec. editor: International Trade Policy: The Lawyer's Perspective, 1985; contbr. articles to profl. jours. Mem. ABA (co-chair internat. trade com.), D.C. Bar Assn., Fed. Bar Assn., Am. Soc. Internat. Law, Washington Coun. Lawyers, Women in Internat. Trade. Office: Arnold & Porter 555 12th St NW Washington DC 20004-1202

READE, LEWIS POLLOCK, diplomat, engineer; b. N.Y.C., Nov. 1, 1932; s. Herman Ross and Dorothy Stella (Pollock) R.; m. Anne Carol Kulka, July 3, 1953 (div. Feb. 1968); children: Steven Gordon, Nicholas Edward; m. Margaret Ann Kilpatrick, Mar. 30, 1968; 1 child, Jonathan Collins. BS in Mech. Engrin., U. Miami, 1953; postgrad., Hofstra U., 1953-54, U. Balt., 1957-59. Product engr. Sperry Gyroscope, Lake Success, N.Y., 1953-54; project engr. ARMA, Garden City, N.Y., 1954-55; field engr. Westinghouse Electric Corp., Balt. & Rome, 1957-66; v.p. Westinghouse Learning Corp., Washington & Pitts., 1966-70; v.p. corp. planning & devel. Tyco Labs., Waltham, Mass., 1970-71; chmn., chief exec. officer, treas. Kellett Corp., Willow Grove, Pa., 1971-72; exec. v.p. Big Bros./Big Sisters of Am., Phila., 1973-80; mission dir. U.S. Agency Internat. Devel., Kingston, Jamaica, Amman, Jordan, & Jakarta, Indonesia, 1980-92; dir. gen. U.S.-Asia Environ. Ptnrship., Washington, 1992—. Sgt. US Army, 1955-57. Mem. Athenaeum of Phila., Soc. Internat. Devel., Am. Fgn. Svc. Assn., Vesper (Phila.), Soc. Hill (Phila.), Internat. (Washington), Jamaica Club (Kingston), Royal Jordanian Automobile Club, Am. Club (Jakarta, Indonesia). Home: 827 F St NE Washington DC 20002-5321 Office: US-AEP Dept State 321 21st St NE Ste 3208 Washington DC 20002

READER, GEORGE GORDON, physician, educator; b. Bklyn., Feb. 8, 1919; s. Houston Parker and Marion J. (Payne) R.; m. Helen C. Brown, May 23, 1942; children: Jonathan, David, Mark, Peter. BA, Cornell U., 1940, MD, 1943; DSc (hon.), Drew U., 1988. Diplomate Am. Bd. Internal Medicine. Intern N.Y. Hosp., N.Y.C., 1944; resident N.Y. Hosp., 1947-49, attending physician, 1962-92; hon. staff, 1992—; dir. comprehensive care and teaching program N.Y. Hosp., 1952-66, chief med. clinic, 1952-72; practice medicine specializing in internal medicine N.Y.C., 1949-93; chief div. ambulatory and community medicine N.Y. Hosp.-Cornell Med. Center, N.Y.C., 1969-72; prof. medicine Cornell U. Med. Coll., 1957-89, Livingston Farrand prof. pub. health, 1972-89, prof. emeritus pub. health and medicine, 1989—, chmn. dept. pub. health, 1972-92; chmn. human ecology study sect. NIH, 1961-65; chmn. med. adv. com. Vis. Nurse Svc., N.Y., 1963—; mem. med. control bd. Health Ins. Plan Greater N.Y., 1964—; mem. Gov.'s Health Adv. Coun., N.Y., 1974-79. Author: (with R. Merton, P. Kendall) The Student Physician, 1957, (with Goss) Comprehensive Medical Care and Teaching, 1967, (with Goodrich and Olendzki) Welfare Medical Care: An Experiment, 1969; mem. editorial bd. Medical Care, 1969-70, Jour. Med. Edn, 1975-79; editor-in-chief Milbank Meml. Fund Quar.: Health and Society, 1972-76. Bd. dirs. N.Y.C. Vis. Nurse Svc., The Osborn Retirement Community, Health Ins. Plan Greater N.Y., 1983-93, Helen Keller Internat.; trustee Cornell U., 1982-87. Lt. USNR, 1944-46, PTO. Fellow ACP, APHA (governing coun. 1968-69), AAAS, Am. Coll. Preventive Medicine; mem. AMA, N.Y. Acad. Medicine (chmn. com. med. edn. 1968-71, v.p. 1978-80), Am. Sociol. Assn., Harvey Soc., Internat. Sociol. Assn., Internat. Epidemiol. Assn., N.Y.C. Pub. Health Assn. (pres. 1956), Inst. Medicine Nat. Acad. Scis. (sr. mem.), Sigma Xi, Alpha Omega Alpha. Home: 155 Stuyvesant Ave Rye NY 10580-3112

READER, JOSEPH, physicist; b. Chgo., Dec. 1, 1934. BS, Purdue U., 1956, MS, 1957; PhD in Physics, U. Calif., 1962. Rsch. assoc. physics Argonne Nat. Lab., 1962-63; staff physicist Nat. Inst. Standards and Tech., Gaithersburg, Md., 1963—. Recipient Gold medal Dept. Commerce, 1989. Fellow Am. Phys. Soc., Optical Soc. Am. (William F. Meggers award 1992). Achievements include research in experimental atomic physics, optical spectroscopy, hyperfine structure, electronic structure of highly ionized atoms, wave length standards, and ionization energies of atoms and ions. Office: Natl Inst Of Standards & Tech Gaithersburg MD 20899

READING, ANTHONY JOHN, physician; b. Sydney, Australia, Sept. 10, 1933; s. Abe Stanley and Esma Daisy R.; m. Elisabeth Ann Hoffman, July 27, 1975; children—Wendy Virginia Elisabeth, Sarah Alexandra Jane. M.B., B.S., U. Sydney, 1956; M.P.H., Johns Hopkins U., 1961, Sc.D., 1964. Intern Sydney Hosp., 1957-58; resident in psychiatry Johns Hopkins Hosp., Balt., 1965-68; asst. prof. psychiatry and medicine Johns Hopkins U. Sch. Medicine, Balt., 1968-73, assoc. prof. psychiatry, 1973-75, dir. psychiat. liaison service, 1974-75; dir. comprehensive alcoholism program Johns Hopkins Hosp., 1972-75; prof., chmn. dept. psychiatry and behavioral medicine U. South Fla. Coll. Medicine, 1975—, assoc. dean, 1993—. Mem. AMA, AAAS, Am. Psychosomatic Soc., Am. Psychiat. Assn. Home: 1171 Shipwatch Cir Tampa FL 33602-5787 Office: 3515 E Fletcher Ave Tampa FL 33613-4706

READING, JAMES EDWARD, transportation executive; b. Milw., June 26, 1924; s. James Edwards and Helen Marie (Boehm) R.; m. Ada Irene Kelly, May 24, 1944; children—Wendy Irene, James David, Christopher Kelly, Mary Katherine, Kevin Sinclair. Student, San Diego State U., 1942, Ga. Inst. Tech., 1944. With Union-Tribune Pub. Co., San Diego, 1942-59, dist. mgr., 1953-58; circulation promotion mgr. Union-Tribune Pub. Co., 1958-59; adminstrv. asst. to v.p. Copley Newspapers, La Jolla, Calif., 1959-60; dir. advt. and public relations San Diego Transit System, 1960-67; dir. mktg. Calif. Motor Express, 1967-68; asst. to exec. v.p. Am. Transit Assn., Washington, 1968; v.p. Nat. City Mgmt. Co.; resident mgr. Regional Transit Service, Rochester, N.Y., 1968-74; asst. gen. mgr. ops. Regional Transit Dist., Denver, 1974-77; gen. mgr. Central Ohio Transit Authority, Columbus, 1977-85; dir. Santa Clara County Transp. Agy., San Jose, Calif., 1985-90; ind. cons. San Diego, 1990—; guest lectr. numerous univs. Served with U.S. Army, 1943-46, ETO. Named Public Relations Man of Yr. Public Relations Club, San Diego, 1962; recipient Urban Mass Transp. Adminstrs. award for outstanding pub. service, 1980, 82. Mem. Pub. Rels. Soc. Am. (past pres. 4 chpts.), Am. Pub. Transit Assn. (bd. dirs., past v.p., elected Hall of Fame 1995), Transp. Rsch. Bd., Am. Soc. Pub. Adminstrs., Am. Pub. Works Assn., Am. Legion, Rotary, Press Club of Rancho Bernardo (v.p.), Tau Kappa Epsilon. Republican. Roman Catholic. Home: 11728 Caminito Corriente San Diego CA 92128-4548

READY, ROBERT JAMES, financial company executive; b. Bridgeport, Conn., June 26, 1952; s. John Edward and Anne (Salata) R.; m. Margaret S. Neale, Aug. 23, 1975; children: Carolyn, Christopher and Steven (twins). AS, Housatonic Community Coll., 1972; BS, Babson Coll., 1974. CLU; chartered fin. cons.; cert. ins. cons. Agt. John Hancock Mut. Life Ins. Co., Hamden, Conn., 1975-77; broker Beardsley, Brown & Bassett Inc., Bridgeport, Conn., 1977-80; agt. Aetna Life and Casualty Ins. Co., Trumbull, Conn., 1980-83; v.p. Crestview Fin. Services Inc., Westport, Conn., 1983—, Crestview Securities Inc., Westport, Conn., 1983—, Crestview Investment Advisors Inc., Westport, Conn., 1983—. Mem. Nat. Assn. Life Underwriters, Conn. Assn. Life Underwriters, Bridgeport Life Underwriters (bd. dirs. 1977), Nat. Assn. Health Underwriters, Conn. Assn. Health Underwriters, Am. Soc. CLU and Chartered Fin. Cons., New Haven County CLU and Chartered Fin. Cons., Bridgeport Jaycees. Roman Catholic. Avocations: golf, tennis. Office: The Crestview Fin Group 431 Post Rd E Ste 1 Westport CT 06880-4403

READY, WILLIAM ANDREW, mergers, acquisitions and management consultant; b. Oakland, Calif., May 30, 1943; s. Thomas James and Cathrynn Maryann (Reinheimer) R.; m. Carroll Ann Beilke, Feb. 5, 1944; children: Robyn, Patrick. BA, Stanford U., 1965, MBA, 1968. Group v.p. Church's Fried Chicken, San Antonio, Tex., 1973-76; gen. mgr. Foster Farms Restaurants Inc., Modesto, Calif., 1976-79; pres., chief ops. officer Ky. Fried Chicken U.S.A., Louisville, 1979-83, Hickory Farms, Toledo, 1983-85; chief exec. officer, dir. Profitwatch Systems Inc., Indpls., 1985—; also bd. dirs. MBA Internat., Indpls.; founder, pres., CEO Markets USA, Louisville, 1987—, Investment Finders USA, Louisville, 1988—; bd. dirs. Steward & Loyd, Indpls.; trustee Heidelberg Coll., Tiffin, Ohio, 1983—; chmn., pres. The Phoenix Group, 1991—; mem. bd. adv. Stanford U. Water Polo Found. Mem. IBBA, IBC, MWBBA, Am. Mgmt. Assn. Republican. Presbyterian. Avocations: reading, gardening, stock market/investments, travel. Address: 255 W Broadway Louisville KY 40202-2111

REAGAN, BARBARA BENTON, economics educator. B.S. with honors, U. Tex., 1941; M.A. in Stats., Am. U., 1947; M.A. in Econs., Harvard U., 1949, Ph.D. in Econs., 1952. Econ. researcher Dept. Agr., 1942-47; sr. project leader Agrl. Research Service, Washington, 1949-55; prof. econs. Tex. Woman's U., Denton, 1959-67; prof. econs. So. Meth. U., Dallas, 1967-90, prof. emeritus, 1990—, chmn. dept., 1984-90; dir. interdisciplinary research project So. Meth. U., 1969-70, dir. undergrad. studies econs. dept., 1972-75, assoc. dean Univ. Coll., 1975, asst. to pres. for student acad. services, 1975-76, pres. faculty senate, 1981-82, mem. exec. com., 1981-84; dir. Region IX Fed. Home Loan Bank, 1981-85; mem. Dallas Morning News Bd. Economists, 1982-88; dir. Agrl. Rsch. Svc. Project, Dallas, 1970-71; mem. adv. bd. econs. USA Wharton Econometric Forecasting Assocs., 1983-85; reviewer NSF; disting. vis. prof. econs. Kenyon Coll., spring, 1979; bd. dirs. 1st Am. Savs. Bank, 1990—, North Tex. Mesbic, 1991-93, Tex. Guaranteed Student Loan Corp., 1991—, sec., exec. com., chmn. policy com., 1992-93, chmn. bd., 1993-95. Author: Economic Foundations of Labor Supply of Women, 1981; co-editor, contbg. author: Women in the Workplace: Implications of Occupational Segregation, 1976; editor, contbg. author: Issues in Federal Statistical Needs Relating to Women, 1979; bd. editors: Jour. Econ. Lit., 1977-79, Jour. Econ. Edn., 1984-92; referee profl. jours. contbr. articles to profl. publs. Mem. Nat. Adv. Food and Drug Coun., 1968-71; mem. adv. com. Nat. Rsch. Inst. on Family, 1973-76; nat. coord. on issues in fed. statis. needs for women Census Bur. Conf., 1978; mem. Tex. adv. bd. Tex Coastal Mgmt. Program, 1977-78; mem. adv. com. White House Conf. on Balance Nat. Growth and Econ. Devel., 1977-78; bd. dirs. League for Ednl. Advancement in Dallas, 1972-75; trustee, mem. instrnl. TV com. Pub. Comm. Found. North Tex., 1973-76; mem. North Tex. Coun. Govts.' Manpower Coun., 1972-74; mem. adv. bd. Women's Ctr. Dallas, 1975-79, 82-85, 95—, pres. 1981, bd. dirs. 1990-92; bd. dirs. Dallas Urban League, 1975-79, co-chmn. com. on skills bank, 1977-79; Leadership Am., 1989-90. Ferguson fellow Harvard U., 1947-49; named Outstanding Tchr., So. Meth. U. 1972; recipient Women's Ctr. Dallas award as one of Dallas Outstanding Women, 1980,So. Meth. U. M award 1972, Willis M. Tate award as outstanding faculty mem., 1982, Laurel award AAUW, 1983, Headliner award Dallas Press Club, 1985, 86, Disting. Alumna award Mary Baldwin Coll., 1986. Mem. Am. Econ. Assn. (chmn. sessions 1977, 80, chmn. com. on status of women in econs. profession 1974-78), Southwestern Social Sci. Assn. (exec. com. 1977-80, pres. 1978-79), Assn. Am. Colls. (faculty rep. 1984), Dallas Economists Club, Dallas C. of C. (com. on urban affairs 1975), Phi Beta Kappa (pres. So. Meth. U. chpt. 1975-76), Town and Gown Club (pres. 1986-87), The Dallas Summit (exec. com. 1990-92). Home: 10 Duncannon Ct Dallas TX 75225-1809 Office: So Meth U Dept Econs Dallas TX 75275
America's productivity can be improved greatly by making better use of its human resources. Equality of opportunity needs to become a reality.

REAGAN, GARY DON, state legislator, lawyer; b. Amarillo, Tex., Aug. 23, 1941; s. Hester and Lois Irene (Marcum) R.; m. Nedra Ann Nash, Sept. 12, 1964; children: Marc, Kristi, Kari, Brent. AB, Stanford U., 1963, JD, 1965. Bar: N.Mex. 1965, U.S. Dist. Ct. N.Mex., 1965, U.S. Supreme Ct. 1986. Assoc. Smith & Ransom, Albuquerque, 1965-67; ptnr. Smith, Ransom, Deaton & Reagan, Albuquerque, 1967-68, Williams, Johnson, Houston, Reagan & Porter, Hobbs, N.Mex., 1968-77, Williams, Johnson, Reagan, Porter & Love, Hobbs, 1977-82; sole practice, Hobbs, 1982—; city atty. City of Hobbs, 1978-80, City of Eunice, N.M., 1980—; mem. N.Mex. State Senate, 1993-96; instr. N.Mex. Jr. Coll. and Coll. of S.W., Hobbs, 1978-84; N.Mex. commr. Nat. Conf. Commrs. Uniform State Laws, 1993-96; mem. adv. mem. N.Mex. Constl. Revision Commn., 1993-95. Mayor, City of Hobbs, 1972-73, 76-77, city commr., 1970-78; pres., dir. Jr. Achievement of Hobbs, 1974-85; pres., trustee Landsun Homes, Inc., Carlsbad, N.Mex., 1972-84; trustee Lydia Patterson Inst., El Paso, Tex., 1972-84, N.Mex. Conf. United Meth. Ch., 1988—, Coll. of S.W., Hobbs, 1989—; chmn. County Democratic Com., 1983-85. Mem. ABA, State Bar N.Mex. (coms. 1989—, v.p. 1992-93, pres. 1994-95), Lea County Bar Assn. (pres. 1976-77), Hobbs C. of C. (pres. 1989-90), Rotary (pres. Hobbs 1985-86), Hobbs Tennis (pres. 1974-75). Home: 200 E Eagle Dr Hobbs NM 88240-5323 Office: 501 N Linam St Hobbs NM 88240-5715

REAGAN, HARRY EDWIN, III, lawyer; b. Wichita, Kans., Sept. 9, 1940; s. Harry E. II and Mary Elizabeth (O'Steen) R.; m. Marvene R. Rogers, June 17, 1965; children: Kathleen, Leigh, Mairen. BS, U. Pa., 1962, JD, 1965. Bar: Pa. 1965, U.S. Dist. Ct. (ea. dist.) Pa. 1965, U.S. Ct. Appeals (3d cir.) 1965. From assoc. to ptnr. Morgan, Lewis & Bockius, Phila., 1965—. Chmn. Northhampton Twp. Planning Commn., Bucks County, Pa., 1974-79; mem. Warwick Twp. Planning Commn., 1980-95, chmn., 1994; supr. Warwick Twp., 1996—; Pa. Relays ofcl. Mem. ABA (labor sect.), Pa. Bar Assn. (labor sect.), Phila. Bar Assn. (labor sect.), Indsl. Rels. Assn. (pres. Phila. chpt. 1990-91). Republican. Presbyterian. Avocations: coaching rugby, skiing, raising horses, bicycling, Pa. Relays official. Home: 2930 Wilkinson Rd Rushland PA 18956 Office: Morgan Lewis & Bockius 2000 One Logan Sq Philadelphia PA 19103

REAGAN, JANET THOMPSON, psychologist, educator; b. Monticello, Ken., Sept. 15, 1945; d. Virgil Joe and Carrie Mae (Alexander) Thompson; m. Robert Barry Reagan, Jr., Aug. 7, 1977; children: Natalia Alexandria, Robert Barry. B.A. in Psychology, Berea Coll., 1967; Ph.D. in Psychology, Vanderbilt U., 1972. Mgr. research and eval. Nashville Mental Health Center, 1971-72; mgr. eval. Family Health Found., New Orleans, 1973-74; asst. prof. dept. health systems mgmt. Tulane U., New Orleans, 1974-77; dir. eval. Project Heavy West, Los Angeles, 1977-78; asst. prof. health adminstrn. Calif. State U.-Northridge, 1978-83, assoc. prof., director health adminstrn., 1983-87, prof., dir. health adminstrn., 1987—; cons. in field. Mem. Am. Pub. Health Assn., Am. Coll. Health Care Adminstrn., Assn. Health Svcs. Rsch., Am. Coll. Health Care Execs. (com. on higher edn. 1987, chmn. 1991), Assn. Univ. Programs in Health Adminstrn. (task force on undergrad. edn. 1985-90, chmn. 1988-90, mem. bd. dirs. 1995), Psi Chi, Phi Kappa Phi. Mem. editorial adv. bd. Jour. of Long Term Care Adminstrn.; contbr. to books, articles to profl. jours., papers to profl. assns. Home: 9354 Encino Ave Northridge CA 91325-2414 Office: Calif State U Dept Health Sci Northridge CA 91330

REAGAN, JOSEPH BERNARD, retired aerospace executive; b. Somerville, Mass., Nov. 26, 1934; s. Joseph B. and Helen Lowry R.; m. Dorothy Hughes; children: Patrick, Michael, Kevin, Kathleen, Brian, John, Maureen. BS in Physics, Boston Coll., 1956, MS in Physics, 1959; PhD in Space Sci., Stanford U., 1975; postgrad. exec. mgmt., Pa. State U., State College, 1981. Staff scientist, rsch. scientist, sr. scientist, scientist Lockheed Rsch. & Devel. Div., Palo Alto, Calif., 1959-75, mgr., 1975-84, dir., 1984-86, dep. gen. mgr., 1986-88, v.p., asst. gen. mgr., 1988-90; v.p. gen. mgr., 1991-96; bd. dirs. Southwall Technologies Inc., Palo Alto. Contbr. articles to profl. jours. Bd. dirs. Tech. Mus., San Jose. Capt. U.S. Army, 1956-64. Recipient Career Achievement in Sci. award Boston Coll. Alumni Assn., 1993. Fellow AIAA (outstanding engr. San Francisco chpt. 1988); mem. Am. Geophys. Union. Republican. Roman Catholic. Avocations: computer and woodworking hobbies. Home and Office: 13554 Mandarin Way Saratoga CA 95070-4847

REAGAN, LAWRENCE PAUL, JR., systems engineer; b. Honolulu, Nov. 5, 1957; s. Lawrence Paul Sr. and Laura Louise (Sears) R.; m. Ann Marie Decker, Apr. 15, 1989; children: Lawrence P. III, Andrew Scott, Kelly Rene. BS in Mech. & Aerospace Engring., Ill. Inst. Tech., 1979; MS in Acquisition & Contract Mgmt., West Coast U., Santa Barbara, Calif., 1986. Product engr. R.G. Ray Corp., Schaumburg, Ill., 1978-80; launch integration mgr. USAF Hqrs. Space Divsn., L.A. AFB, 1980-84; chief Titan program mgmt. USAF Aerospace Test Group, Vandenberg AFB, Calif., 1984-89; chief joint communication br. USAF Pentagon, Washington, 1989-91; sr. sys. engr. Dynamics Rsch. Corp., Arlington, Va., 1992—; CEO Jacob's Well, Inc., Lexington Park, Md., 1993—. Contbr. papers to profl. publs. Named Outstanding Young Engr., Air Force Assn. Mem. AIAA, Soc. Logistics Engring., Air Force Assn. Home: PO Box 22 Lusby MD 20657-0022 Office: Dynamics Rsch Corp 1755 Jeff Davis Hwy Ste 802 Arlington VA 22202-3509

REAGAN, NANCY DAVIS (ANNE FRANCIS ROBBINS), volunteer, wife of former President of United States; b. N.Y.C., July 6, 1923; d. Kenneth and Edith (Luckett) Robbins; step dau. Loyal Davis; m. Ronald Reagan, Mar. 4, 1952; children: Patricia Ann, Ronald Prescott; stepchildren: Maureen, Michael. BA, Smith Coll.; LLD (hon.), Pepperdine U., 1983; LHD (hon.), Georgetown U., 1987. Contract actress, MGM, 1949-56; films include The Next Voice You Hear, 1950, Donovan's Brain, 1953, Hellcats of the Navy, 1957; Author: Nancy, 1980; formerly author syndicated column on prisoner-of-war and missing-in-action soldiers and their families; author: (with Jane Wilkie) To Love a Child, (with William Novak) My Turn: The Memoirs of Nancy Reagan, 1989. Civic worker, visited wounded Viet Nam vets., sr. citizens, hosps. and schs. for physically and emotionally handicapped children, active in furthering foster grandparents for handicapped children program; hon. nat. chmn. Aid to Adoption of Spl. Kids, 1977; spl. interest in fighting alcohol and drug abuse among youth: hosted first ladies from around the world for 2d Internat. Drug Conf., 1985; hon. chmn. Just Say No Found., Nat. Fedn. of Parents for Drug-Free Youth, Nat. Child Watch Campaign, President's Com. on the Arts and Humanities, Wolf Trap Found. bd. of trustees, Nat. Trust for Historic Preservation, Cystic Fibrosis Found., Nat. Republican Women's Club; hon. pres. Girl Scouts of Am. Named one of Ten Most Admired Am. Women, Good Housekeeping mag., ranking #1 in poll, 1984, 85, 86; Woman of Yr. Los Angeles Times, 1977; permanent mem. Hall of Fame of Ten Best Dressed Women in U.S.; recipient humanitarian awards from Am. Camping Assn., Nat. Council on Alcoholism, United Cerebral Palsy Assn., Internat. Ctr. for Disabled; Boys Town Father Flanagan award; 1986 Kiwanis World Service medal; Variety Clubs Internat. Lifeline award; numerous awards for her role in fight against drug abuse. Address: Century City Fox Plaza 2121 Ave of the Stars 34th Fl Los Angeles CA 90024*

REAGAN, REGINALD LEE, biologist, clinical pathologist; b. Broadford, Pa., July 19, 1910; s. James Blaine and Helen (McLaughlin) R.; PhD, U. Md., 1956; m. Marie Ann Johnson, Mar. 5, 1932 (dec. 1980); children: Nelda (Mrs. Dan Cullivan) (dec.), Helen (Mrs. Bill Savage), Bill Olsen (dec.), Elsa (Mrs. Leo Sullivan). Joined U.S. Army, 1928, advanced through grades to maj., 1946; Rockefeller Found. Research assoc. Rockefeller Inst., N.Y.C., 1936-40; faculty U. Md., College Park, 1946-61, assoc. prof., 1948-52, prof. med. virology, 1952-61; chief virologist Jen-Sal Lab., Kansas City, Mo., 1961-62; biologist Nat. Cancer Inst., Bethesda, Md., 1962-80. Mem. N.Y. Acad. Sci., Soc. Exptl. Biology and Medicine, Electronmicroscopic Soc., Ret. Officers Assn., Soc. Clin. Pathologists, AAUP. Author: One Man's Research, 1980; contbr. over 300 articles to profl. jours. Home: care Savage P30 Marullo Calle Dorado PR 00646

REAGAN, RONALD WILSON, former President of United States; b. Tampico, Ill., Feb. 6, 1911; s. John Edward and Nelle (Wilson) R.; m. Jane Wyman, Jan. 25, 1940 (div. 1948); children: Maureen E., Michael E.; m. Nancy Davis, Mar. 4, 1952; children: Patricia, Ronald. AB, Eureka Coll., 1932, MA (hon.), 1957. Actor GE Theatre, 1954-62; host TV series Death Valley Days, 1962-66; gov. State of Calif., 1967-74; businessman, rancher, commentator on public policy, 1975-80, Pres. of U.S., 1981-89. Sports announcer, motion picture and TV actor, 1932-66. Author: Where's The Rest of Me?, Speaking My Mind: Selected Speeches, 1989, An American Life: The Autobiography, 1990. Mem. Calif. State Rep. Ctrl. Com., 1964-66; del. Rep. Nat. Conv., 1968, 72; chmn. Rep. Gov. Assn., 1968-73; mem. presdl. Commn. CIA Activities Within U.S., 1975; bd. dirs. Com. Present Danger, Washington, 1977—; cand. for Rep. nomination for Pres., 1976. Served as capt. USAAF, 1942-45. Recipient Great Am. of Decade award, Va. Young Am. for Freedom, Man of Yr. Free Enterprise award, San Fernando Valley Bus. & Profl. award, 1964, Am. Legion award, 1965, Horation Alger award, 1969, George Washington Honor medal, Freedoms Found. Valley Forge award, 1971, Disting. Am. award; inducted into Nat. Football Found. Hall of Fame, Am. Patriots Hall of Fame. Mem. SAG (pres. 1947-52, 59), Am. Fedn. Radio & TV Artists, Lions, Friars, Tau Kappa Epsilon. Republican. Address: Century City Fox Plaza 2121 Avenue Of The Stars 34th Fl Los Angeles CA 90024*

REAGAN, THEODORE JOHN, geologist, exploration consultant, oil and gas mineral investment evaluator; b. Oceanside, Calif., Sept. 16, 1927; s. Walter William and Eugenia (Felix) R.; m. Lorraine Coldewey, Apr. 6, 1936; children: Claire R. Reagan Pelegrin, Ryan, Claudia Rene Bynum. BS in Geology, Tex. A&M U., 1952. Staff geologist Union Sulphur and Oil Inc., Houston, Midland and Corpus Christi, Tex., 1954-57; part owner, v.p. T.L.R. Inc., Corpus Christi, 1957-65; part owner, pres. Petroquest Oil and Gas Inc., Corpus Christi, 1958-87; geol. oil and gas exploration cons. Smithville, Tex., 1987—; exploration dir. Petroquest Oil and Gas Inc., 1965-87. 1st lt. U.S. Artillary, 1952-54. Fellow Am. Assn. Petroleum Geologists, Corpus Christi Geol. Soc., Oil and Gas Industries Libr. (pres. 1983). Achievements include research and discovery in oil and gas fields-Karren Beauchamp Miocenc and Frio fields, Goliad County, Tex., Princess Louise gas field, San Patrico County, Tex., Cotten Vicksburg field, Nueces County, Tex. 1976, New Waverley Cockfield and Vegua oil and gas field, San Jacinto County, Tex., 1978. Avocations: golf, gardening, fishing.

REAL, MANUEL LAWRENCE, federal judge; b. San Pedro, Calif., Jan. 27, 1924; s. Francisco Jose and Maria (Mansano) R.; m. Stella Emilia Michalik, Oct. 15, 1955; children: Michael, Melanie Marie, Timothy, John Robert. B.S., U. So. Calif., 1944, student fgn. trade, 1946-48; LL.B., Loyola Sch. Law, Los Angeles, 1951. Bar: Calif. 1952. Asst. U.S. Atty.'s Office, Los Angeles, 1952-55; pvt. practice law San Pedro, Calif., 1955-64; U.S. atty. So. Dist. Calif., 1964-66; judge U.S. Dist. Ct. (cen. dist.) Calif., L.A., 1966—. Served to ensign USNR, 1943-46. Mem. Am., Fed., Los Angeles County bar assns., State Bar Calif., Am. Judicature Soc., Chief Spl. Agts. Assn., Phi Delta Phi, Sigma Chi. Roman Catholic. Club: Anchor (Los Angeles). Office: US Dist Ct 312 N Spring St Los Angeles CA 90012-4701*

REALS, WILLIAM JOSEPH, pathologist, academic administrator, educator; b. Hot Springs, S.D., June 22, 1920; s. Reuben Joseph and Gertrude Cecilia (Harrigan) R.;m. Norma Rosalie Monahan, May 6, 1944; children: William J. Jr., John F., Elaine A., Mary C., Thomas C. BS, Creighton U., 1944, MD, MS in Medicine, 1945. Diplomate Am. Bd. Pathology (trustee 1973-80). Intern Creighton Meml./St. Joseph Hosp., Omaha, 1945-46; resident Creighton Meml./St. Joseph Hosp.; resident Creighton U. Sch. Medicine, Omaha, 1946-49, instr. in pathology, 1949-50; dir. labs. St. Joseph Med. Ctr., Wichita, Kans., 1953-80; prof. pathology, dean U. Kans. Med. Ctr., Wichita, 1980-91, vice chancellor, 1988—; cons. Office Pathology, VA, Washington, 1963-79, Under-sec. Def., Rsch. and Engring., Washington, 1975-79, Office Surgeon Gen., USAF, Washington, 1980—. Author: Aerospace Pathology, 1973; editor: Poems of Alice Henry Boone, 1980; contbr. numerous articles to profl. jours. Trustee Inst. Logopedics, Wichita, 1986, Kans. Newman Coll., Wichita, 1988, Kans. region NCCJ, 1988—. Brig. gen. USAF, 1950-80. Recipient Alumni Achievement citation Creighton U., 1986. Fellow ACP, Coll. Am. Pathologists (pres. 1970-73), Royal Coll. Pathologists Australia, Aerospace Med. Assn.; mem. Can. Assn. Pathologists (hon.), Most Venerable Order Hosp. of St. John of Jerusalem, Cosmos Club (Washington), Army-Navy Club (Washington), Alpha Omega Alpha. Home: 706 N Stratford St Wichita KS 67206-1455 Office: U Kans Sch Medicine 1010 N Kansas St Wichita KS 67214-3124

REAM, JAMES TERRILL, architect, sculptor; b. Summit, N.J., Sept. 8, 1929; s. Merrill Jay and Catherine Ada (Terrill) R.; m. Joyce Kimball Johnson, June 9, 1953 (div. Dec. 1976); children—Claudia, Sarah, Benjamin, m. Nancy Ann Buford, Jan. 1, 1980; stepchildren—Kathleen, Ann Maguire. BArch, Cornell U., 1953; postgrad., Pratt Inst., 1953-54, U. Rome, 1956-57. Registered architect. Assoc. W. C. Muchow Assocs., Denver, 1959-62; prin. Ream, Quinn & Assocs., Denver, 1962-66; v.p. design John Carl Warnecke & Assocs., San Francisco, 1966-69; prin., pres. James Ream & Assocs., Inc., San Francisco, 1969-78, Robbins and Ream Inc., San Francisco, 1978-83; prin. James Ream Architect, San Francisco, 1983—. Prin. archtl. works include Denver Convention Ctr., Currigan Hall, Pasadena Conf. Ctr., Stapleton Plaza Hotel, Vail Transp. Ctr. Bd. dirs. San Francisco Planning and Urban Rsch. Assn., 1977—; chmn. bd. dirs. San Francisco Heritage, 1984-91, pres., 1983-84. Served to 1st lt. USAF, 1954-56. Recipient citation for design in steel Am. Iron and Steel Inst., 1975; Honor award Am. Concrete Inst., 1975; Nat. Design award Prestressed Concrete Inst., 1983; Honor award for design in steel Am. Inst. Steel Constrn., 1970. Fellow AIA (honor award western region 1969, fellowship in design 1979, honor award for design excellence 1983, design cons. San Jose Arena). Democrat. Avocations: opera, theater, hiking, tennis. Office: 3385 Clay St San Francisco CA 94118-2006

REAMAN, GREGORY HAROLD, pediatric hematologist, oncologist; b. Akron, Ohio, Sept. 9, 1947; s. Harold J. and Margaret U. (D'Alfonso) R.; m. Susan J. Pristo, Sept. 7, 1974; children: Emily Margaret, Sarah Elizabeth. BS in Biology, U. Detroit, 1969; MD, Loyola U., Chgo., 1973. Diplomate Nat. Bd. Med. Examiners, Am. Bd. Pediatrics. Pediatric intern Loyola U. Med. Ctr., 1973-74; resident in pediatrics Montreal Children's Hosp., McGill U., 1974-76; clin. assoc. pediatric oncology br. Nat. Cancer Inst., NIH, Bethesda, Md., 1976-78, investigator pediatric oncology br., 1978-79; assoc. dept. hematology/oncology, attending physician Children's Nat. Med. Ctr., Washington, 1979-87, chmn. dept. hematology/oncology, 1987—; asst. prof. pediatrics Sch. Medicine and Health Scis., George Washington U., 1979-82, assoc. prof. pediatrics, 1982-87, prof. pediatrics, 1987—; mem. immunology devices panel FDA; assoc. chmn. Children's Cancer Group; bd. dirs., mem. med. affairs com., chmn., strategic planning com. Children's Oncology Scs. of Met. Washington. Mem. editorial bd. Cancer Physicians Data Query, Nat. Cancer Inst.; reviewer Cancer Treatment Resports, Blood, Jour. Clin. Oncology; contbr. articles to profl. publs. Trustee Nat. Childhood Cancer Found., Arcadia, Calif.; bd. dirs. Am. Cancer Soc., Atlanta; trustee, chmn. patient care and profl. edn. coms. Leukemia Soc. Am. Lt. comdr. USPHS, 1976-79, Res., 1979—. Folger Summer scholar Am. Cancer Soc.; recipient Spl. Fellowship Rsch. award Leukemia Soc. Am., 1980-82; grantee DHHS, Nat. Cancer Inst., 1987—. Mem. Soc. Pediatric Rsch., Am. Fedn. Clin. Rsch., Am. Soc. Clin. Oncology, Am. Assn. Cancer Rsch., Am. Soc. Pediatric Hematology/Oncology, Children's Cancer Group, Washington Blood Club, Alpha Omega Alpha. Democrat. Roman Catholic. Home: 7306 Brennon Ln Chevy Chase MD 20815-4064 Office: Children's Nat Med Ctr 111 Michigan Ave NW Washington DC 20010-2970

REAMER, SHIRLEY JEAN, minister; b. South Bend, Ind., Aug. 15, 1935; d. John Lewis and Vivian Leora (Hammer) Helvey; m. Thomas Charles Reamer, June 22, 1956; children: Thomas Darwin, Trent Alan, Terry Michael, Traci Sue, Tricia Ann. Grad. high sch., South Bend, 1953; ThD, Shalom Bible Coll. and Sem., West Des Moines, Iowa, 1992. Ordained to ministry Full Gospel Fellowship, 1974. Dir. children's ministry Calvary Temple, South Bend, 1972-73; evangelist Full Gospel Fellowship, 1976—; founder, pastor Maranatha Temple, South Bend, 1981-83; founder, pres. Women's Aglow Fellowship, Michiana, Ind., 1976-79; founder, dir. Prison Ministry-Aglow, Westville, Ind., 1976-77; founder, dir. Soup Kitchen/Care Ctr., Maranatha Temple, 1982—, Supplied Facilities for Ctr. for Homeless, 1984-87, dir. City March, 1989; mem. United Religious Community Task Force, South Bend, 1985. Author: Ministerial Ethics, 1984, Teaching Syllabus, 1985, Recruits for Christ, 1987, Teaching Syllabus, Genesis, The Beginning, 1994. Recipient Spirit of Am. Women award J.C. Penneys, South Bend, 1988; named one of 16 Best Pastors, Charisma Mag., 1988. *Life, when valued like our most treasured possessions, will be held as sacred and will always be found on a lighted path to direct the way of another.*

REAMS, BERNARD DINSMORE, JR., lawyer, educator; b. Lynchburg, Va., Aug. 17, 1943; s. Bernard Dinsmore and Martha Eloise (Hickman) R.; m. Rosemarie Bridget Boyle, Oct. 26, 1968; children: Andrew Dennet, Adriane Bevin. BA, Lynchburg Coll., 1965; MS, Drexel U., 1966; JD, U. Kans., 1972; PhD, St. Louis U., 1983. Bar: Kans. 1973, Mo. 1986. Instr., asst. librarian Rutgers U., 1966-69; asst. prof. law, librarian U. Kans., Lawrence, 1969-74; mem. faculty law sch. Washington U., St. Louis, 1974-95, prof. law, 1976-95, prof. tech. mgmt., 1990-95, librarian, 1974-76, acting dean univ. libraries, 1987-88; prof. law, assoc. dean, dir. Law Libr. St. John's U. Sch. Law, Jamaica, N.Y., 1995—. Author: Law For The Businessman, 1974, Reader in Law Librarianship, 1976, Federal Price and Wage Control Programs 1917-1979: Legis. Histories and Laws, 1980, Education of the Handicapped: Laws, Legislative Histories, and Administrative Documents, 1982, Housing and Transportation of the Handicapped: Laws and Legislative Histories, 1983, Internal Revenue Acts of the United States: The Revenue Act of 1954 with Legislative Histories and Congressional Documents, 1983 Congress and the Courts: A Legislative History 1978-1984, 1984, University-Industry Research Partnerships: The Major Issues in Research and Development Agreements, 1986, Deficit Control and the Gramm-Rudman-Hollings Act, 1986, The Semiconductor Chip and the Law: A Legislative History of the Semiconductor Chip Protection Act of 1984, 1986, American International Law Cases, 2d series, 1986, Technology Transfer Law: The Export Administration Acts of the U.S., 1987, Insider Trading and the Law: A Legislative History of the Insider Trading Sanctions Act, 1989, Insider Trading and Securities Fraud, 1989, The Health Care Quality Improvement Act of 1989: A Legislative History of P.L. No. 99-660, 1990; The National Organ Transplant Act of 1984: A Legislative History of P.L. No. 98-507, 1990, United States and International Aviation Law Reports, 1993, A Legislative History of Individuals with Disabilities Education Act, 1994, Federal Legislative Histories: An Annotated Bibliography and Index to Officially Published Sources, 1994; co-author: Segregation and the Fourteenth Amendment in the States, 1975, Historic Preservation Law: An Annotated Bibliography, 1976, Congress and the Courts: A Legislative History 1787-1977, 1978, Federal Consumer Protection Laws, Rules and Regulations, 1979, A Guide and Analytical Index to the Internal Revenue Acts of the U.S., 1909-1950, 1979, The Numerical Lists and Schedule of Volumes of the U.S. Congressional Serial Set: 73d Congress through the 96th Congress, 1984, Human Experimentation: Federal Laws, Legislative Histories, Regulations and Related Documents, 1985, American Legal Literature: A Guide to Selected Legal Resources, 1985, The Constitution of the United States: A Guide and Bibliography, 1987, The Congressional Impeachment Process and the Judiciary, 1987, Tax Reform 1986: A Legislative History of the Tax Refrom Act of 1986, 1988, The Constitutions of the States: A State by State Guide and Bibliography, 1988, Executive and Professional Employment Contracts, 1988, The Legislative History of the Export Trading Company Act of 1982 Including the Foreign Trade Antitrust Improvements Act, 1989, Federal Deficit Control, 1989, The Legislative History of the Export Trading Company Act of 1982 Including the Foreign Trade Antitrust Improvements Act, 1989, United States-Canada Free Trade Act: A Legislative History, 1990, Electronic Contracting Law, 1991, Trade Reform Legislation 1988: A Legislative History of the Omnibus Trade and Competitiveness Act of 1988, 1992, Disability Law in the United States, 1992, Bankruptcy Reform Amendments, 1992, The Law of Hospital and Health Care Administration: Case and Materials, 1993, The Civil Rights Act of 1991: A Legislative History, 1994, The North American Free Trade Agreement, 1994, Catalonia, Spain, Europe, and Latin America: Regional Legal Systems and their Litrature, 1995. Fellow Am. Bar Foun.; recipient Thornton award for excellence Lynchburg Coll., 1986, Joseph L. Andrews Bibliog. award, 1995; named to Hon. Order Ky. Cols., 1992. Fellow Am. Bar Found.; mem. ABA, Am. Law Inst., ALA, Am. Soc. Law and Medicine, Nat. Health Lawyers Assn., Am. Assn. Higher Edn., Spl. Librs. Assn., Internt. Assn. Law Libssn. Coll. and Univ. Attys., Order of Coif, Phi Beta Kappa, Sigma Xi, Beta Phi Mu, Phi Delta Phi, Phi Delta Epsilon, Kappa Delta Pi, Pi Lambda Theta. Office: St Johns U Sch Law 8000 Utopia Pky Jamaica NY 11439

REANEY, GILBERT, musician, educator; b. Sheffield, Eng., Jan. 11, 1924; came to U.S., 1960; s. Lawrence and Mabel (Crookes) R. BA with honors, Sheffield U., 1948, BMus, 1950, MA, 1951; postgrad., U. Paris, 1950-52. Researcher, tchr. Reading (Eng.) U., 1953-56, Birmingham (Eng.) U., 1956-59; vis. prof. musicology U. Hamburg, Fed. Republic Germany, 1960; assoc. prof. music dept. UCLA, 1960-62, prof., 1963—; founder, dir. London Medieval Group, 1958—; cons. panel BBC, 1958-60; guest lectr. Eng., Germany, U.S. Author: Early 15th Century Music, 7 vols., 1955-83, (with A. Gilles and J. Maillard) Philippe de Vitry, Ars Nova, 1964, International Inventory of Musical Sources, 2 vols., 1966-69, Machaut, 1971, (with Gilles) Franconis de Colonia Ars Cantus mensurabilis, 1974; gen. editor: Corpus Scriptorum de Musica, 1966—, Johannes Hothby, Opera Omnia de Musica Mensurabili, 1983, (with H. Ristory) Johannes dictus Balloce, Abreviatio Magistri Franconis, etc., 1987; asst. editor: Musica Disciplina, 1956-76, co-editor: (with F. D'Accone), 1989—. With Brit. Army, 1943-46. Guggenheim fellow, 1964-65, Nat. Humanities Found. sr. fellow, 1967-68. Mem. Am. Musicol. Soc., Internat. Musicol. Soc., Royal Mus. Assn. (Dent medal 1961), Plainsong & Medieval Music Soc. Home: 1001 3rd St Santa Monica CA 90403 Office: UCLA Musicology Dept Los Angeles CA 90025-1623

REANEY, JAMES CRERAR, dramatist, poet, educator; b. South Easthope, Ont., Can., Sept. 1, 1926; s. James Nesbitt and Elizabeth Henrietta (Crerar) R.; m. Colleen Thibaudeau, Dec. 29, 1951; children: James Stewart, Susan Alice. B.A., U. Toronto, 1948, M.A., 1949, Ph.D., 1957; D.Litt., Carleton U., 1975. Asst. prof. English U. Man., 1949-60; prof. English U. Western Ont., London, 1960—. (Recipient Massey award for the Killdeer 1960, Chalmers award for best Can. play The St. Nicholas Hotel 1975); Author: Killdeer, 1960 (Massey award), Poems, 1972, Colours in the Dark, 1969, Masks of Childhood, 1972, Listen to the Wind, 1972, Apple Butter and Other Plays for Children, 1973; plays include The St. Nicholas Hotel, 1975 (Chalmers award for best Can. play), Sticks and Stones: The Donnellys Part I, 1975, The Donnellys Part II, 1976, Handcuffs: The Donnellys Part III, 1977, 14 Barrels from Sea to Sea, 1977, The Dismissal, 1978, Wacousta, 1980, King Whistle, 1982, I the Parade, 1983, The House by the Churchyard, 1985, Alice Through the Looking-Glass, 1994, Serinette (opera libretto), 1986, Crazy to Kill (opera libretto), Performance Poems, 1991; novels for children include: The Boy with an R on his Hand, 1963, Take the Big Picture, 1986, Box Social & Other Stories, 1996; editor, pub.: Alphabet, 1960-70; contbr. articles to profl. jours. Decorated Order of Can. Fellow Royal Soc. Can.; mem. Playwrights Union Can., Can. Poetry League. Mem. New Democratic Party. Home: 276 Huron St, London, ON Canada Office: U We Ont, Dept English, London, ON Canada N6A 3K7 also: John Miller Lit Agt, 14 Earl St, Toronto, ON Canada M4Y 1M3

REAP, JAMES B., judge; b. Oct. 17, 1930; s. James S. and Jessie Burnett R.; m. Nancy Leigh Jenkins, Sept. 21, 1957; children: James J., Michael H., Jessica Leigh. BA cum laude, Weslyan U., 1952; JD, Harvard U., 1957; diploma, U.S. Naval War Coll., Armed Forces Staff Coll., Nat. War Coll., Armed Forces Pub. Info. Sch., U.S. Naval Sch. of Justice. Bar: N.Y. 1957, U.S. Dist. Ct. (ea. and so. dists.) N.Y. 1957, U.S. Ct. Mil. Appeals 1957, U.S. Ct. Internat. Trade 1957, U.S. Supreme Ct., U.S. Ct. of Claims. Commd. USN, 1951, advanced through grades to rear admiral, 1990; ptnr. Kent Hazzard et al, 1957-77, Campbell, Hyman and Reap, 1977-79; chief judge White Plains City Ct., 1980-92; U.S. adminstrn. law judge, 1993—. Merit badge counselor Boy Scouts of Am. Recipient N.Y. State Conspicuous Svc. medal, Disting. Svc. award Jaycees, Presdl. Meritorious Svc. medal, 1978, Presdl. Legions of Merit, 1984, 85. Mem. ABA, N.Y. Bar Assn., N.Y. Assn. City Ct. Judges, Nat. Trial Ct. Judges Assn., Am. Judges Found., Assn. of Adminstrv. Law Judges, Westchester County Bar Assn., Univ. Club, Legal Aid Soc., Am. Legion, USN Inst., Smithsonian Inst., Am. Acad. Polit. and Social Sci., Naval Res. Assn., Militia Assn. of N.Y., N.Y. Commandery Navy Order U.S.A., Naval Acad. Found., Havillands Manor Assn., Chi Psi. Office: 399 Knollwood Rd White Plains NY 10603

REAP, SISTER MARY MARGARET, college administrator; b. Carbondale, Pa., Sept. 8, 1941; d. Charles Vincent and Anna Rose (Ahern) R. BA, Marywood Coll., Scranton, Pa., 1965; MA, Assumption Coll., Worcester, Mass., 1972; PhD, Pa. State U., 1979. Elem. tchr. St. Ephrem's,

Bklyn., 1966-67; secondary tchr. South Catholic High, Scranton, Pa., 1967-69, Maria Regina High Sch., Uniondale, N.Y., 1969-72; mem. faculty Marywood Coll., Scranton, Pa., 1972-86, dean, 1986-88, pres., 1988—; tchr. Mainland China, Wuhan, 1982, Marygrove Coll., Detroit, 1979; bd. dirs. Moses Taylor Hops., Scranton Prep. Sch.; bd. dirs., exec. com. Lourdesmont Sch. Contbr. articles to profl. jours. Recipient bilingual fellowship Pa. State U., 1976-79, Local Chpt. Svc. award UN, 1984, Woman of Yr. awrd Boy Scouts Am., 1993; named Northeast Woman, Scranton Times, 1986, Outstanding Alumna, Pa. State Coll. Edn., 1989. Mem. Pa. Assn. for Colls. and Univs. (exec. com.), Coun. for Ind. Colls. and Univs., Am. Assn. Cath. Colls., Phi Delta Kappa (Educator of Yr. award 1990). Office: Marywood Coll Office of the President Scranton PA 18509-1598

REARDEN, CAROLE ANN, clinical pathologist, educator; b. Belleville, Ont., Can., June 11, 1946; d. Joseph Brady and Honora Patricia (O'Halloran) R. BSc, McGill U., 1969, MSc, MDCM, 1971. Diplomate Am. Bd. Pathology, Am. Bd. Immunohematology and Blood Banking. Resident and fellow Children's Meml. Hosp., Chgo., 1971-73; resident in pediatrics U. Calif., San Diego, 1974, resident then fellow, 1975-79, asst. prof. pathology, 1979-86, dir. histocompatability and immunogenetics lab., 1979-94, assoc. prof., 1986-92, prof., 1992—, head divsn. lab. medicine, 1989-94; dir. med. ctr. U. Calif. Thornton Hosp. Clin. Labs., San Diego, 1993—; prin. investigator devel. monoclonal antibodies to erythroid antigens, recombinant autoantigens; dir. lab. exam. com. Am. Bd. Histocompatibility and Immunogenetics. Contbr. articles to profl. jours. Mem. Mayor's Task Force on AIDS, San Diego, 1983. Recipient Young Investigator Rsch. award NIH, 1979; grantee U. Calif. Cancer Rsch. Coordinating Com., 1982, NIH, 1983. Mem. Am. Soc. Investigative Pathology, Acad. Clin. Lab. Physicians and Scientists, Am. Soc. Hematology, Am. Assn. Blood Banks (com. organ transplantation and tissue typing 1982-87), Am. Soc. Histocompatibility and Immunogenetics. Office: U Calif San Diego Dept Pathology 0612 9500 Gilman Dr La Jolla CA 92093-5003

REARDON, FRANK EMOND, lawyer; b. Providence, May 22, 1953; s. J. Clarke and Dorothy (Emond) R.; m. Deborah Walsh, Sept. 30, 1978; children: Kathleen Elizabeth, Brendan Francis, William James, Sean Patrick. BA, Holy Cross Coll., Worcester, Mass., 1975; JD, Suffolk U., 1978; MS, Harvard U., 1981. Bar: Mass. 1978, R.I. 1978, U.S. Dist. Ct. Mass. 1980, U.S. Dist. Ct. R.I. 1980, U.S. Supreme Ct. 1986. Counsel Nat. Assn. Govtl. Employment and Internat. Brotherhood Police Officers, Cranston, R.I., 1978-81; asst. gen. counsel Brigham and Women's Hosp., Boston, 1981-84; litigation counsel Risk Mgmt. Found. Harvard Med. Instns., Cambridge, Mass., 1984-87; ptnr. Hassan and Reardon, Boston, 1987—; chmn. bd. dirs. St. Monica's Nursing Home, 1984-89, Med. Area Fed. Credit Union, 1984-89. Contbr. articles to profl. jours. Chmn. fin. com. Town of Needham, Mass.; mem. pres.'s council Coll. Holy Cross, 1985—. Beuilacqua scholar, 1978. Mem. ABA, Mass. Bar Assn. (chmn. health law sect. 1987—), Assn. Trial Lawyers Am., Am. Soc. Law and Medicine (cmty. rep. children's hosp. ethics com.). Democrat. Roman Catholic. Avocations: tennis, sailing, golf, writing. Home: 44 Sargent St Needham MA 02192-3434 Office: Hassan & Reardon 535 Boylston St Boston MA 02116-3720

REARDON, JAMES LOUIS, education educator, consultant; b. Vinton, Iowa, June 29, 1943; s. James Harold and Hazel Alice (Pieper) R.; m. Antonia Anita Boni, July 3, 1971. BSBA, U. Iowa, 1964, MA in Edn., 1966; EdD, U. LaVerne, 1985. Cert. tchr., Calif. Supr. tchr. edn. U. Calif., Riverside, 1971—, coord. intern credential program, 1994; co-dir. Inland Area History-Social Sci. Project, Riverside, 1990-94; cons. We. Assn. Schs. and Colls., State Dept. Edn. Expanded Accreditation, Sacramento, 1990-92; reviewer Charles Merrill Pubs., Columbus, Ohio, 1988-91; convenor Tech. Edn. Program Area Com., Riverside, 1990; edn. specialist Nat. Assn. Trade and Tech. Schs., Washington, 1983—. Recipient People Who Make a Difference award, Riverside Press, 1989. Mem. Inland Empire Coun. for the Social Studies (treas. 1986—, Leadership in Social Studies Edn. award 1993), Calif. Coun. for the Social Studies (mem. editl. bd. 1985—), Nat. Coun. for the Social Studies, Network for Secondary Edn. Profs. (pres. 1985-86). Home: 1513 Lynne Ct Redlands CA 92373-7143 Office: U Calif 2105 Sproul Hall Riverside CA 92521

REARDON, LOUISE ARLEEN, medical school administrator; b. Fall River, Mass., June 21, 1923; d. John Brackett and Catherine (Ironside) Bartlett; m. Malcolm B. Reardon, Oct. 25, 1940 (dec. 1953); children: John B., David W. (dec.). BA, Boston U., 1976. Stenographer USAF, Rapid City, S.D., 1951-54; stenographer, asst. to contr. USAF, Falmouth, Mass., 1955-73; adminstr. Harvard Med. Sch., Boston, 1976—. Bd. dirs. Old South Ch., Boston; mem. Women's State-Wide Legis. Network, Boston, 1985—. Mem. AAUW (Boston br., pres. 1983-85), Falmouth Bus. and Profl. Women (pres. 1968-70), Coll. Club of Boston (bd. dirs.), Order of Ea. Star. Home: 59 Bay State Rd Boston MA 02215-1813 Office: Harvard Med Sch Resource Devel Office 25 Shattuck St Boston MA 02115-6027

REARDON, PEARL RANCE, real estate executive, writer; b. Savanna La Mar, Westmoreland, Jamaica, Apr. 17, 1941; came to U.S., 1968; d. Hugh Lawrence Rance and Ada Louise (Mullings) Watson; m. Michael I. Phillips, June 9, 1962 (div. Sept. 1977); children: Karim Irving, Felita Alessandra; m. Michael John Reardon, May 24, 1980. Student, Howard Community Coll., 1974-77; MFA in Creative Writing, Am. U., 1996. Cert. real estate broker Grad. Real Estate Inst. Sr. sec. Nat. Coun. Cath. Men, Washington, 1968-69; exec. sec. Nat. Acad. Sci, Washington, 1969-71; sr. sec. Pres.'s Commn. on Population, Washington, 1971-72; exec. sec. Westinghouse Health System, Columbia, Md., 1972-76; adminstrv. group mgr. Price, Williams & Assocs., Silver Spring, Md., 1976-78; assoc. broker Merrill Lynch Realty, Silver Spring, 1977-81; pres. and CEO Pearl Properties, Silver Spring, 1982-93; v.p. Croton Mgmt. Svcs., Washington, D.C., 1994—. Organizer Peoples Nat. Party, Linstead, Jamaica, 1966; founding mem. Jamaica Nat. Assn., Washington, 1969, sec. 1969-73. Mem. Nat. Assn. Realtors, D.C. Bd. Realtors, Authors Guild, Dramatists Guild. Avocations: writing, music, piano, reading, dancing, crafts. Office: Croton Mgmt Svcs 110 Gallatin St NW # 1 Washington DC 20011-3270

REASON, J. PAUL, naval officer; b. Washington, Mar. 22, 1941; s. Joseph Henry and Bernice (Chism) R.; m. Dianne Lillian Fowler, June 12, 1965; children: Rebecca, Joseph. BS, U.S. Naval Acad., 1965; MS, USN Postgrad. Sch., 1970. Cert. nuclear propulsion engr. Commd. ens. USN, 1965, advanced through grades to vice adm., 1996; naval aide to pres. The White Ho., Washington, 1976-79; exec. officer USS Miss., 1979-81; comdg. officer USS Coontz, 1981-83, USS Bainbridge, 1983-86; comdr. Naval Base, Seattle, 1986-88, Cruiser-Destroyer Group 1, 1988-90, Naval Surface Force Atlantic, 1991-94; dep. chief naval ops. plans, policy and ops. Dept. Navy, Washington, 1994—. Decorated DSM, Legion of Merit, other mil. awards. Avocations: fishing, tennis. Office: DCNO Plans Policy & Ops (N3/N5) Dept of Navy 2000 Navy Pentagon Washington DC 20350-2000

REASONER, BARRETT HODGES, lawyer; b. Houston, Apr. 16, 1964; s. Harry Max and Macey (Hodges) R.; m. Susan Hardig; children: Matthew Joseph, Caroline Macey. BA cum laude, Duke U., 1986; Grad. Dipl., London Sch. Econs., 1987; JD with honors, U. Tex., 1990. Bar: Tex. 1990, U.S. Dist. Ct. (so. and no. dists.) Tex. 1993, U.S. Ct. Appeals (5th cir.) 1993. Asst. dist. atty. Harris County Dist. Atty.'s Office, Houston, 1990-92; assoc. Gibbs & Bruns, L.L.P., Houston, 1992—. Mem. Am. Judicature Soc. (bd. dirs. 1994—), State Bar of Tex., Houston Bar Assn. (legal lines com. 1994—), Houston Young Lawyers Assn. (pub. schs./pub. edn. com. 1994—), Order of Barristers. Episcopalian. Home: 6139 Cedar Creek Dr Houston TX 77057-1801

REASONER, HARRY MAX, lawyer; b. San Marcos, Tex., July 15, 1939; s. Harry Edward and Joyce Majorie (Barrett) R.; m. Elizabeth Macey Hodges, Apr. 15, 1963; children: Barrett Hodges, Elizabeth Macey Reasoner Stokes. BA in Philosophy summa cum laude, Rice U., 1960; JD with highest honors, U. Tex., 1962; postgrad., U. London, 1962-63. Bar: Tex., D.C., N.Y. Law clk. U.S. Ct. Appeals (2d cir.), 1963-64; assoc. Vinson & Elkins, Houston, 1964-69, ptnr., 1970—, mng.ptnr., 1992—; vis. prof. U. Tex. Sch. Law, 1971, Rice U., 1976, U. Houston Sch. Law, 1977; chair adv. group U.S. Dist Ct. (so. dist.) Tex.; mem. adv. com. Supreme Ct. Tex. Author: (with Charles Alan Wright) Procedure: The Handmaid of Justice, 1965; author: (with others) American Economic Policy in the 1980s, 1994. Life trustee U. Tex. Law Sch. Found.; trustee Southwestern Legal Found., 1990—, Baylor Coll. Medicine, 1992—; chair Tex. Higher Edn. Coordinating Bd., 1991; bd. govs. Rice U., 1994—; exec. bd. dirs. Greater Houston Partnership, 1992—; mem. exec. coun. Ex-Student's Assn. U. Tex., 1992—; gov. Houston Forum, 1992—; bd. dirs. Central Houston, Inc., 1993—. Rotary Found. fellow 1962-63; recipient Disting. Alumnus award for cmty. svc. U. Tex. Law Alumni Assn., 1995. Fellow Am. Coll. Trial Lawyers, Internat. Acad. Trial Lawyers, Internat. Soc. Barristers, ABA Found., Tex. Bar Found.; mem. ABA (chmn. antitrust sect. 1989-90), Houston Bar Assn., Assn. Bar City N.Y., Am. Law Inst., Chancellors, Houston Com. Fgn. Rels., Houston Philos. Soc., Philos. Soc. Tex., Am. Bd. Trial Advocates, Century Assn. N.Y.C., Houston Country Club, Rotary Club, Ramada Tex. Club, Eldorado Country Club (Calif.), Castle Pines Golf Club (Castle Rock, Colo.), Cosmos Club of Washington, Galveston Artillery Club, Phi Beta Kappa, Phi Delta Phi. Democrat. Baptist. Office: Vinson & Elkins 2800 First City Tower 1001 Fannin St Houston TX 77002-6760

REASONER, STEPHEN M., federal judge; b. 1944. BA in Econs., U. Ark., 1966, JD, 1969. Mem. firm Barret, Wheatley, Smith & Deacon, Jonesboro, Ark., 1969-88; from judge to chief judge U.S. Dist. Ct. (ea. dist.) Ark., Little Rock, 1988—; bd. dirs. U. Ark. Law Rev.; mem. judicial coun. 8th cir., 1990-93. Trustee Craighead-Jonesboro Pub. Libr., 1972—, chmn. 1984-88; bd. dirs. Jonesboro C. of C., 1981-84, Ark. IOLTA, 1987—, Abilities Unltd., 1974-81; mem. St. Marks Episcopal Ch. Vestry, 1976-79, sr. warden, 1979. With USAR, 1969-73. Mem. ABA, Am. Counsel Assn., Am. Judicature Soc., Ark. Bar Assn. (exec. com., ho. of dels. 1984-87), Craighead County Bar Assn. (pres. 1983-84). Avocation: flying. Office: Courthouse 600 West Capital St Rm 501 Little Rock AR 72201*

REASONER, WILLIS IRL, III, lawyer; b. Hamilton, Ohio, Dec. 24, 1951; s. W. Irl Jr. and Nancy Jane (Mitchell) R.; m. Lana Jean Mayes, Apr. 19, 1975 (div. Sept. 1985); 1 child, Erick; m. Joan Marie Mogil, Dec. 30, 1986; children: Scott, Sally. BA in History, Ind. U., 1974; JD cum laude, U. S.C., 1978. Bar: Ohio 1978, U.S. Dist. Ct. (so. dist.) Ohio 1978, U.S. Dist. Ct. (no. dist.) Ohio 1979, U.S. Ct. Appeals (6th cir.) 1988, U.S. Ct. Appeals (1st cir.) 1991. Assoc. Porter, Wright, Morris & Arthur, Columbus, Ohio, 1978-83; ptnr. Baker & Hostetler, Columbus, 1983-95, Habash, Reasoner & Frazier, 1995—. Mem. ABA, Ohio Bar Assn., Columbus Bar Assn. Home: 1101 Riva Ridge Blvd Columbus OH 43230-3808 Office: Habash, Reasoner & Frazier 395 E Broad St Ste 210 Columbus OH 43215-4213*

REASOR, RODERICK JACKSON, industrial engineer; b. Hampton, Va., Apr. 8, 1953; s. Emmett Jackson and Cora (Keller) R.; m. Anita Marie Knibb, June 29, 1974; children: Rebecca Eileen, Matthew Ryan, Christopher James, Laura Kathleen. BS, Va. Poly. Inst. & State U., 1976, MS, 1981, PhD in Indsl. Engring. and Ops. Rsch., 1990. Registered profl. engr., Va. Indsl. engr. Tenn. Eastman Co., Kingsport, Tenn., 1977-83; program mgr. Mgmt. Systems Labs., Blacksburg, Va., 1983-86; instr. IEOR Va. Poly. Inst. & State U., Blacksburg, 1986-89, asst. prof. indsl. and systems engring., dir. lab., 1989-95; sr. indsl. engr. Eastman Chem. Co., Kingsport, Tenn., 1995—; cons. in field. Author: (with others) Occupational Ergonomics, 1995; referee jours.; contbr. articles to proceedings. Deacon, elder 1st Christian Ch., Kingsport, Tenn., 1979-83, vice chmn. bd., 1982, sec. bd., 1981, bible sch. supt., 1982-83, chmn. coms., 1979-83; vol. econ. discussion series for high sch. srs. Kingsport (Tenn.) C. of C., 1983; judge annual product fair Jr. Achievement Kingsport, 1983; vice chmn. bd. Blacksburg Christian Ch., 1985-88, elder, 1988—, treas., 1989-90, chmn. bd., 1991-92; bd. dirs. Woodbine Homes Assn., Blacksburg, 1990-91, v.p., 1991-92, pres., 1992-93. Grantee ITT Teves, 1991-92, NSF, 1991-93, Computer Aided Mfg. Internat., 1991-92, Barden corp., 1989-90, Aluminum Co. Am., 1984-85. Mem. Am. Soc. Engring. Edn. (sec.-treas. 1991-92, editor newsletter 1992-93, program chmn. 1993-94, chmn. indsl. engring. divsn. 1994-95), Inst. Indsl. Engrs. (sr., pres. Tri-Cities Tenn. chpt. 1979-83, Award of Excellence 1983, adv. bd. chmn., dir., program chmn. 1985-89, Pride award 1988, bd. dirs. 1988-89, chpt. devel. chmn. 1990-93, asst. dir. dist. III 1990-92, Excelence award 1990, 91), Coll.-Industry coun. Material Handling Edn. (chmn. acad. programs and activities com. 1994—, adv. bd. 1994—), Inst. Ops. Rsch. and Mgmt. Scis. (session chmn. fall ann. meeting 1989), Kiwanis (pub. affairs com. 1982-83), Alpha Pi Mu. Home: 1104 Hillsboro Cir Kingsport TN 37660 Office: Eastman Chem Co PO Box 1973 Kingsport TN 37662

REATH, GEORGE, JR., lawyer; b. Phila., Mar. 14, 1939; s. George and Isabel Duer (West) R.; children from a previous marriage: Eric (dec. 1995), Amanda; m. Ann B. Rowland, 1990. BA, Williams Coll., 1961; LLB, Harvard U., 1964. Bar: Pa. 1965, U.S. Dist. Ct. (ea. dist.) Pa. 1965. Assoc. Dechert Price & Rhoads, Phila., 1964-70, Brussels, 1971-74; atty. Pennwalt Corp., Phila., 1974-78, mgr. legal dept., asst. sec., 1978-87, sr. v.p.-law, sec., 1987-89; sr. v.p., gen. counsel, sec. Elf Atochem N.Am., Inc. (formerly Pennwalt Corp.), Phila., 1990-92; sr. v.p. Legal Triage Svcs., Inc., Phila., 1993—; bd. dirs. Internat. Bus. Forum, Inc., 1978-91. Trustee Children's Hosp., Phila., 1974—, sec., 1980-81, vice chmn., 1984—; bd. mgrs. Phila. City Inst. Libr., 1974—, treas., 1981-88, pres., 1989—; bd. dirs. Phila. Festival Theatre for New Plays, 1983-94, Ctrl. Phila. Devel. Corp., 1987-93; bd. dirs. Bach Festival Phila., 1990—, v.p., 1992-93; bd. dirs. Crime Commn. Delaware Valley, 1st vice chmn., 1992-94, chmn., 1994-96. Mem. ABA, Pa. Bar Assn., Am. Soc. Corp. Secs., Phila. Bar Assn., Penllyn Club, Winter Harbor Yacht Club, Phi Beta Kappa.

REAVES, BENJAMIN F., academic administrator. BA, Oakwood Coll., 1955; MDiv, Andrews U., 1966, MA, 1972; DMin, Chgo. Theol. Sem., 1974; diploma inst. for ednl. mgmt., Harvard U., 1987. Ordained to ministry. Pastor, evangelist various chs., Ill., Ind. and Ohio, 1956-68; tchr. adult edn. programs Chgo. Bd. Edn., 1968-72; pastor for Coll. Youth Pioneer Meml. Ch. Andrews U., 1972-73, assoc. prof. preaching and urban ministry, 1973-77; chmn. dept. religion and theology, prof. preaching Oakwood Coll., 1977-85, pres., 1985—; case worker dept pub. aid Cook County, 1968-72; vis. prof. Chgo. cluster Theol. Sems., 1973-77; conductor workshops homiletics and liturgics U.S. Army Bd. Chaplains, 1977-85; speaker, lectr. in field. Contbr. articles to profl. jours. Counselor Vietnam vets. drug abuse case VA Westside Hosp., Chgo., 1968-72; coordinator convocation on black music and grad. programs Urban Ministry, 1973-77; adv. bd. Andrews U., Loma Linda U.; exec. com. south cen. conf., so. union conf. 7th Day Adventist; mem. United Negro Coll. Fund, Council for the Advancement Pvt. Colls. Ala.; developer various community programs. Mem. Acad. Homiletics, Nat. Assn. for Equal Opportunity in Higher Edn. Lodge: Rotary. Office: Oakwood Coll Office of Pres Huntsville AL 35896

REAVES, FRANKLIN C., secondary school educator; b. Mullins, S.C., Aug. 7, 1942; s. Fred and Vestena (Nance) Reaves; m. Algenia Reaves; children: Kathy J., Jacquelyn C., Frankie D., Anthony, Ron, Randy, Dexter, Brandon. BS, Fayetteville (N.C.) State U., 1968; MS, N.C. A&T State U., 1974, N.C. A&T State U., 1982; PhD, U. Santa Barbara, Calif., 1990. Cert. Am. history tchr., adminstr., career edn., N.C. Lectr. Columbus County Schs., Whiteville, N.C. Pastor St. Mary African Meth. Episcopal Ch., Marion S.C. Mem. NEA, ASCD, N.C. Assn. Educators (pres. Columbus County), N.C. Assn. Edn. (black caucus), Nat. Vocat. Assn., N.C. Vocat. Assn., Internat. Platform Assn., Operation Help the Econ. Linkage of the Poor (nat. pres.), Marion County Concern Citizens Movement (chmn.). Home: PO Box 534 Mullins SC 29574-0534

REAVES, JOHN DANIEL, lawyer, playwright, actor; b. Camp Hill, Ala., Mar. 14, 1939; s. William Newell and Katherine (Rawlinson) R.; m. Wendy Wick; children: Paul Newell, Caroline Rawlinson. BS, Auburn U., 1961; LLB, U. Va., 1964. Bar: Ala. 1965, D.C. 1972, U.S. Supreme Ct. 1977. Law clk. to Hon. Richard T. Rives U.S. Ct. Appeals (5th cir.), 1964-65; asst. prof. law U. Ga., 1965-71; fellow Fed. Jud. Ctr., Washington, 1971-72; atty. Bur. Competition, FTC, Washington, 1972-73; legal advisor to Hon. Elizabeth Dole, commr. FTC, Washington, 1973-77; ptnr. Baker & Hostetler, Washington, Montedomico, Hamilton & Altar, Washington; vis. prof. law George Washington U., Washington, 1975. mem. editorial bd. Va. Law Rev.; founder Ga. Law Rev., 1966; writer, performer H.L. Mencken: Reveries of an Iconoclast, 1981; appeared in The Kingfish, 1979. Bd. dirs. Woolly Mammoth Theatre Co., 1992—. Mem. D.C. Bar, Ala. State Bar Assn., Cosmos Club (Washington). Office: Montedomico, Hamilton & Altar 5301 Wisconsin Ave Ste 400 Washington DC 20015*

REAVES, MARY JENNINGS, health facility administrator; b. Rock Hill, S.C., July 16, 1939; d. John Adam and Richelene (Sandifer) Jennings; m. Titus Reaves, Sr.; children: Sylvia R. Norman, Corliss R. Baxter, Titus Reaves, Jr. Diploma, Columbia (S.C.) Hosp., 1961. Coord. nursing Richland Meml. Hosp., Columbia, supr. nursing, head nurse Ob-Gyn, quality assurance coord. Mem. Nat. Assn. Quality Assurance Profls., Columbia Hosp. Alumni Assn., S.C. Nurses Assn., ANA.

REAVES, RAY DONALD, civil engineer; b. Jacksonville, Ala., Aug. 6, 1935; s. William Ozzie and Josephine (Jackson) R.; m. Annette Baird, Dec. 18, 1959; children: Tanya Ann Walker, Ronald Ray. BS in Civil Engring., Auburn (Ala.) U., 1960; MBA, U. Utah, 1976; postgrad., U. Mo., Kansas City. Registered profl. engr., Okla.; diplomate Am. Acad. Environ. Engrs. Commd. 2d lt. USAF, 1961, advanced through grades to col., 1981; comdt. Airlift Ops. Sch., Scott AFB, Ill., 1980-82; dep. base comdr. Little Rock AFB, 1982-83; base comdr. Kunsan Air Base, Korea, 1983-84, Tinker AFB, Oklahoma City, 1984-85; dir. environ. mgr. Oklahoma City Air Logistics Ctr., Tinker AFB, 1985-89; ret. USAF, 1989; mgr. environ. engring. Oklahoma County, Oklahoma City, 1989-95, Okla. county engr., 1995—; Bus. Tech. Delegation Citizen to Citizen ambassador to Russia and Ukraine, 1992. Mem. ASCE, NSPE, Okla. Soc. Profl. Engrs. (citizen ambassador to Russia and Ukraine 1992), Midwest City C. of C., Rotary, Masons, Shriners. Avocations: golf, boating, tinkering.

REAVEY, WILLIAM ANTHONY, III, lawyer; b. Springfield, Mass., Dec. 27, 1944; s. William A. Jr. and Deborah M. (Clancy) R.; Jacqueline R. Beauvais, Sept. 2, 1967; children: Patrick, Kevin, Brian, Michael. BS, USAF Acad., 1966; MA, Yale U., 1968, JD, 1976. Bar: Calif. 1976. Assoc. Latham & Watkins, Newport Beach, Calif., 1976-81; ptnr. Aylward, Kintz & Stiska, San Diego, 1981-87, Lillick & McHose, San Diego, 1987-90, Pillsbury, Madison & Sutro, San Diego, 1991—; ptnr Hillyer & Irvin, San Diego, CA. Bd. dirs. Am. Liver Found., San Diego, 1991, Kind Found., San Diego, 1992, San Diego Comml. Indsl. Coun. Bldg. Industry Assn., 1992. Capt. USAF, 1966-73, Vietnam. Decorated Bronze Star. Mem. ABA. Roman Catholic. Avocations: fishing, back-packing, biking. Home: 10515 Livewood Way San Diego CA 92131-2203 Office: Hillyer & Irvin 550 West C St 16th fl San Diego CA 92101*

REAVIS, LIZA ANNE, semiconductor executive; b. N.Y.C., July 27, 1959; d. William Ralph and Juliette (Bustillo y Zelaya) Bartlett; m. Paul H. Reavis, May 25, 1985. BA in Internat. Rels., Rice U., 1981; MBA, Georgetown U., 1988. Project asst. Latham, Watkins & Hills, Washington, 1982-83; assoc. mgr. countertrade Sears World Trade, Washington, 1983-85; export asst. Weadon, Dibble & Rehm, Washington, 1985-86; assoc. cons. Vanguard Communications Corp., Palo Alto, Calif., 1988-90; bus. mgr. Teleport Communications Corp., San Francisco, 1990-94; sr. fin. analyst Nat. Semicondr. Corp., 1995—. Contbr. Project Open Hand, San Francisco, Calif. Wheelchair Vets. Assn., Am. Assn. for AIDS Rsch., San Francisco, 1990—; mem. Golden Gate Nat. Recreation Area, San Francisco, 1990—. Recipient TCG Ann. Hero award; Presdl. scholar. Mem. Women in Tech., Acad. Polit. Sci., Club des Hiboux (sec. 1979-80), Commonwealth Club, Sierra Club, Cousteau Soc., Phi Beta Kappa, Beta Gamma Sigma, Pi Delta Phi. Avocations: international cultures and politics, classical ballet, poetry, piano. Home: 6931 Geary Blvd San Francisco CA 94121-1620 Office: Nat Semicondr Corp 2900 Semiconductor Dr Mail Stop C1245 Santa Clara CA 95052-8090

REAVLEY, THOMAS MORROW, federal judge; b. Quitman, Tex., June 21, 1921; s. Thomas Mark and Mattie (Morrow) R.; m. Florence Montgomery Wilson, July 24, 1943; children—Thomas Wilson, Marian, Paul Stuart, Margaret. B.A., U. Tex., 1942; J.D., Harvard, 1948; LL.D., Austin Coll., 1974, Southwestern U., 1977, Tex. Wesleyan, 1982; LL.M., U. Va., 1983; LLD, Pepperdine U., 1993. Bar: Tex. 1948. Asst. dist. atty. Dallas, 1948-49; mem. firm Bell & Reavley, Nacogdoches, Tex., 1949-51; county atty. Nacogdoches, 1951; with Collins, Garrison, Renfro & Zeleskey, 1951-52; mem. firm Fisher, Tonahill & Reavley, Jasper, Tex., 1952-55; sec. state Tex., 1955-57; mem. firm Powell, Rauhut, McGinnis & Reavley, Austin, Tex., 1957-64; dist. judge Austin, 1964-68; justice Supreme Ct., Tex., 1968-77; counsel Scott & Douglass, 1977-79; judge U.S. Ct. Appeals (5th cir.), Austin, 1979-90; now sr. judge U.S. Ct. Appeals (5th cir.), Austin, TX, 1990—; lectr. Baylor U. Law Sch., 1976-94; adj. prof. U. Tex. Law Sch., 1958-59, 78-79, 88-95. Chancellor S.W. Tex. conf. United Meth. Ch., 1972-93, chancellor emeritus, 1993—. Lt. USNR, 1943-45. Club: Mason (33 deg.). Home: 24 Woodstone Sq Austin TX 78703-1159 Office: US Ct Appeals 903 San Jacinto Blvd # 434 Austin TX 78701-2450

REBACK, JOYCE ELLEN, lawyer; b. Phila., July 11, 1948; d. William and Sue (Goldstein) R.; m. Itzhak Brook, Aug. 2, 1981; children: Jonathan Zev, Sara Jennie. BA magna cum laude, Brown U., 1970; JD with honors, George Washington U., 1976. Bar: D.C. 1976, U.S. Dist. Ct. D.C. 1976, U.S. Ct. Appeals (D.C. cir.) 1976, U.S. Ct. Appeals (3d cir.) 1983, U.S. Ct. Appeals (Fed. cir.) 1985. Assoc. Fulbright & Jaworski, Washington, 1976-84, ptnr., 1984-87; legal cons. IMF, Washington, 1987—. Contbr. articles to profl. jours. Mem. ABA, D.C. Bar Assn., Phi Beta Kappa. Jewish. Office: Internat Monetary Fund 700 19th St NW Washington DC 20431-0001

REBANE, JOHN T., lawyer; b. Bamberg, Germany, Oct. 29, 1946; s. Henn and Anna (Inna) R.; m. Linda Kay Morgan, Sept. 22, 1972; children: Alexis Morgan, Morgan James. BA, U. Minn., 1970, JD, 1973. Bar: Minn. 1973. Atty. Land O'Lakes, Inc., Arden Hills, Minn., 1973-80, assoc. gen counsel, 1983, v.p., gen. counsel, 1984—; sec. Cenex Land O'Lakes Agronomy Co.; sec., dir. Land O' Lakes Internat. Devel. Corp. Mem. ABA, Minn. Bar Assn., Hennepin County Bar Assn., Nat. Coun. Farm Coop. (exec. com. chmn.). Office: Land O'Lakes Inc PO Box 116 Minneapolis MN 55440-0116

REBAR, ROBERT WILLIAM, obstetrician, gynecologist, educator; b. Stillwater, Okla., Apr. 22, 1947; s. John and Blanche (Fried) R.; m. Margo Storm Freeborn, July 7, 1969; children: Bryan Matthew, Jeannette Heather, Darren Wade. BS, U. Mich., 1969, MD, 1972. Diplomate Am. Bd. Ob-Gyn, cert. spl. competence in reproductive endocrinology. Intern Parkland Meml. Hosp., Dallas, 1972-73, resident in ob-gyn, 1973=74; sr. resident in ob-gyn U. Calif. San Diego Med. Ctr., 1976-78; asst. prof. dept. reproductive medicine U. Calif., San Diego, 1978-82, assoc. prof. div. reproductive endocrinology, dept. reproductive medicine, 1982-84; prof., head sect. reproductive endocrinology and infertility, dept. ob-gyn Northwestern U., Chgo., 1984-88; George B. Riley prof. dept. ob-gyn U. Cin., 1988—, chmn. dept., 1988—; clin. assoc. physician, NIH, 1974-76, mem. reproductive endocrinology study sect., 1986-89; mem. NIH population rsch. com., 1992-96. Co-editor: Principles and Practice of Endocrinology and Metabolism, 1990, Gynecology and Obstetrics: A Longitudinal Approach, 1992; co-editor: Infertility, Evaluation and Treatment, 1995; mem. editorial bd. Jour. Clin. Endocrinology and Metabolism, 1985-88, Obstetrics and Gynecology, 1993-96. Asst. surgeon USPHS, 1974-76. Fellow Am. Coll. Obstetrics and Gynecology; mem. Endocrine Soc., Am. Soc. Reprodn. Medicine (program com. 1989-91), Am. Gynecol. Obstetric Soc., Soc. Gynecol. Investigation, Pacific Coast Fertility Soc. (Wyeth award 1972, 82), Phi Beta Kappa, Alpha Omega Alpha. Home: 195 Sunny Acres Dr Cincinnati OH 45255-3902 Office: U Cin Coll of Medicine Dept Ob-Gyn PO Box 670526 Cincinnati OH 45267-0526

REBAY, LUCIANO, Italian literature educator, literary critic; b. Milan, Italy, Apr. 23, 1928; came to U.S., 1955; s. Angelo and Pierina (Doniselli) R.; m. Martha Virginia Krauss, Aug. 2, 1952; children: Alexandra, Ilaria. Maturita classica Liceo Manzoni, Milan, 1946; Licence es lettres, U. Aix-en-Provence, France, 1951; Ph.D., Columbia U., 1960. Instr. Italian Columbia U., N.Y.C., 1957-60, asst. prof., 1960-63, assoc. prof., 1963-65, prof., 1965-73, Giuseppe Ungaretti prof. Italian lit., 1973—; chmn. Italian Dept. Columbia U., 1970-73; dir. Ctr. Italian Studies, 1985-88; cons. to scholarly jours.; mem. Nat. Bd. Translators, Columbia U. Transl. Ctr. Author: Le origini della poesia di Giuseppe Ungaretti, 1962, Invitation to Italian Poetry, 1969, Alberto Moravia, 1970, Giuseppe Ungaretti, Gli scritti egiziani, 1909-1912, 1980, Montale, Clizia e l'America, 1982; editor: Giuseppe Ungaretti, Saggi e interventi, 1974, Jean Paulhan-Giuseppe Ungaretti, Correspondance, 1921-68, 1989, Montale per amico, 1994. Guggenheim fellow, 1966-67; Am. Council Learned Socs. fellow, 1970-71; NEH fellow, 1980-81; Am. Philos. Soc. research grantee, 1970, 75. Mem. MLA, Am.

Assn. Tchrs. of Italian, Associazione Internazionale per gli Studi di Lingua e Letteratura Italiana. Office: Columbia U Dept Italian New York NY 10027

REBEC, GEORGE VINCENT, neuroscience researcher, educator, administrator; b. Harrisburg, Pa. Apr. 6, 1949; s. George Martin and Nadine (Bosko) R. AB, Villanova U., 1971; MA, U. Colo., 1974, PhD, 1975. Postdoctoral fellow U. Calif., San Diego, 1975-77; asst. prof. Ind. U., Bloomington, 1977-81, assoc. prof., 1981-85, prof. psychology, 1985—, dir. program in neural sci., 1985—; mem. rsch. rev. com. NIMH. Author: (with P.M. Groves) Introduction to Biological Psychology, 1988, 92; contbr. articles to profl. jours. Recipient Eli Lilly Teaching award, 1978, Pres.' award Ind. U., 1990; grantee NIDA, 1979—, NSF, 1985—. Fellow AAAS; mem. Soc. for Neurosci. (chmn. Ind. U. chpt.), Internat. Brain Rsch. Orgn., Am. Psychol. Soc., Assn. Neurosci. Depts. and Programs (treas.). Roman Catholic. Avocation: sports. Office: Ind U Program in Neural Sci Dept Psychology Bloomington IN 47405

REBEIZ, CONSTANTIN A., plant physiology educator; b. Beirut, July 11, 1936; came to U.S., 1969, naturalized, 1975; s. Anis C. and Valentine A. (Choueyri) R.; m. Carole Louise Conness, Aug. 18, 1962; children: Paul A., Natalie, Mark J. B.S., Am. U., Beirut, 1959; M.S., U. Calif. - Davis, 1960, Ph.D., 1965. Dir. dept. biol. scis. Agrl. Research Inst., Beirut, 1965-69; research assoc. biology U. Calif. - Davis, 1969-71; assoc. prof. plant physiology U. Ill., Urbana-Champaign, 1972-76, prof., 1976—. Contbr. articles to sci. publs. plant physiology and biochemistry. Recipient Beckman research awards, 1982, 85, Funk award, 1985, John P. Trebellas Research Endowment, 1986, Sr. Rsch. award Univ. Ill., 1994; named One of 100 Outstanding Innovators, Sci. Digest, 1984-85. Mem. Am. Soc. Plant Physiologists, Comite Internat. de Photobiologie, Am. Soc. Photobiology, AAAS, Lebanese Assn. Advancement Scis. (exec. com. 1967-69), Sigma Xi. Achievements include research on pathway of chlorophyll biosynthesis, chloroplast devel., bioengring. of photosynthetic reactors; pioneered biosynthesis of chlorophyll in vitro; duplication of greening process of plants in test tube, demonstration of operation of multibranched chlorophyll biosynthetic pathway in nature; formulation and design of laser herbicides, insecticides and cancer chemotherapeutic agents. Home: 301 W Pennsylvania Ave Urbana IL 61801-4918 Office: U Ill 240A Pabl Urbana IL 61801 *Meaningful scientific discoveries are those that help humans achieve a better understanding of themselves, of their environment or of the universe at large, as well as those that contribute to the betterment of the human spiritual, psychological and physical condition.*

REBENACK, JOHN HENRY, retired librarian; b. Wilkinsburg, Pa., Feb. 10, 1918; s. Charles Lewis and Carrie (Fielding) R.; m. Dorothy Merle Treat, Oct. 31, 1942 (dec. Apr. 1971); children: Charles Edwin, Christine (Mrs. Clair N. Hayes III); m. Frances Strabley Krieger, May 6, 1972. A.B., U. Pitts., 1942; B.S. in L.S, Carnegie Library Sch., 1947. Reference asst. Carnegie Library, Pitts., 1947-50; librarian Salem (Ohio) Pub. Library, 1950-53, Elyria (Ohio) Library, 1953-57; asst. librarian Akron (Ohio) Public Library, 1957-65, asso. librarian, 1965-67, librarian-dir., 1967-80; dir. U.S. Book Exchange, Inc., 1972. Mem. United Community Council, Citizens' Com. Pub. Welfare, 1965-66, chmn. group work and recreation div., 1963-66, v.p., 1967-68, pres. conf. of execs., 1975-76; mem. steering com., planning div. United Way; mem. Akron Mayor's Task Force on Human Relations, 1962; mem. library com. President's Com. on Employment of Handicapped, 1967-80, chmn., 1973-80, mem. sch. library manpower adv. com., 1967-73; mem. coll. adv. com. U. Akron, 1972-85; mem. adv. council on fed. programs State Library of Ohio, 1975-79; Bd. visitors Grad. Sch. Library and Info. Sci., U. Pitts., 1968-74; mem. exec. bd. Gt. Trail council Boy Scouts Am., 1977-80; bd. dirs. Summit County unit Am. Cancer Soc., 1976—, pres., 1979-81; bd. dirs. Ohio div., 1981-91, chmn. pub. info. com., 1989-90, exec. com. 1988-91. With AUS, 1942-45. Recipient Newton D. Baker citation, 1968. Mem. ALA (chmn. personnel adminstrv. sect. 1966-67, chmn. bldgs. and equipment sect. 1971-73, chmn. legislation assembly 1976-77), Ohio Library Assn. (exec. bd. 1957-60, chmn. adult edn. round table 1963, chmn. legis. com. 1965-66, 70-72, 76-80, pres. 1966-67, Librarian of Year 1979, named to Hall of Fame 1989), Ohio Library Found. (privileged mem. 1980, privileged dir. 1988—), Carnegie Library Sch. Assn. (pres. 1961-63), U. Pitts. Grad. Sch. Library and Info. Sci. Alumni Assn. (exec. com. 1978-79, Disting. Alumnus award 1980), Am. Assn. UN (v.p. Akron chpt. 1960), Beta Phi Mu. Congregationalist. Clubs: Torch (pres. 1968-69), Kiwanis (pres. Akron 1978-79). Home: 2095 Brookshire Rd Akron OH 44313-5323

REBENFELD, LUDWIG, chemist, educator; b. Prague, Czechoslovakia, July 10, 1928; came to U.S., 1939, naturalized, 1946; s. Carl and Martha (Scheib) R.; m. Ellen Vogel, July 27, 1956. BS, Lowell Tech. Inst., 1951; MA, Princeton, 1954, PhD, 1955; D Textile Sci. (hon.), Phila. Coll. Textiles and Sci., 1980, Liberec Tech U., Czech Republic, 1993. Rsch. fellow, sr. scientist Textile Rsch. Inst., Princeton, N.J., 1951-59, assoc. rsch. dir., also edn. program dir., 1960-66, v.p. edn. and rsch., 1966-70, pres., 1971-92, pres. emeritus and rsch. assoc., 1993—; vis. lectr., assoc. prof., prof. chem. engring. Princeton U., 1964—; life trustee Phila. Coll. Textiles and Sci. Editor Textile Rsch. Jour., 1992—. Recipient Distinguished Achievement award Fiber Soc., Harold DeWitt Smith Meml. medal ASTM. Fellow Am. Inst. Chemists, Brit. Textile Inst. (hon., Inst. medal), Inst. Textile Sci. Can.; mem. AAAS, Am. Chem. Soc., Am. Assn. Textile Chemists and Colorists (Olney medal 1987), Fiber Soc. (governing coun., sec.-treas. 1962-84), Nat. Coun. Textile Edn., Sigma Xi, Phi Psi. Home: 49 Pardoe Rd Princeton NJ 08540-2617 Office: Textile Rsch Inst PO Box 625 601 Prospect Ave Princeton NJ 08540-4034

REBER, STANLEY ROY, insurance company executive; b. Phila., Dec. 28, 1943; s. Louis A. and Rose (Dubin) R.; m. Rose Marie J. Apostolico, June 21, 1970; children: Douglas, Matthew, Jessica. BA in Econs., U. Pa., 1965, MA in Econs., 1967; PhD in Econs., U. Chgo., 1970; postgrad., Harvard U., 1989. V.p. Chase Econometrics Assocs., Inc., N.Y.C., 1971-73; dir. bus. analysis The Conf. Bd., N.Y.C., 1974-75; exec. v.p. Tex. Am. Bank, Ft. Worth, 1975-85; sr. v.p. Provident Mut. Life Ins., Phila., 1985-88, exec. v.p., 1988—; now v.p., chief investment officer Provident Mutual Life Insur., Berwyn; pres. Market St. Fund, Phila., 1986—, Provident Mut. Family of Funds, 1990—; bd. dirs. Cortland Trust, Newbold's Asset Mgmt., Inc., Sigma Am. Corp. Overseer U. Pa. Sch. Nursing, 1987—; exec. com. Pa. Economy League, Phila., 1987—; bd. dirs. Presbyn. Med. Ctr. Phila., 1989—, YMCA of Phila., 1990—. Mem. Nat. Assn. Bus. Economists (bd. dirs. 1987-88), Union League Club. Republican. Jewish. Avocations: jogging, skiing, tennis, bicycling, reading. Home: 926 Black Rock Rd Gladwyne PA 19035-1405 Office: Provident Mut Life Ins Co 1050 Westlakes Berwyn PA 19312*

REBERG, ROSALIE BRACCO, elementary education educator; m. Larry Alan Reberg, Aug. 16, 1975; children: Camden Ashleigh, Jacob Alan. BA, Holy Names Coll., 1971; MA with distinction, Calif. State U., Stanislaus, 1994. Elem. edn. tchr. Stanislaus Union Sch. Dist., Modesto, Calif., 1974—; classroom mgmt. mentor tchr., Stanislaus Union Sch. Dist., 1988-89; presenter Eisenhut Elem. Sch., Modesto, 1992, 93. CCD aide St. Joseph's Catholic Ch., Modesto, 1986; team mother Modesto Youth Soccer Assn., 1989, Bal Passi Youth Baseball, 1991. Mem. TESOL, Nat. Tchrs. Assn., Calif. Tchrs. Assn., Stanislaus Union Tchrs. Assn. Democrat. Avocations: reading, computers. Office: Eisenhut Elem Sch 1809 Sheldon Dr Modesto CA 95350-0420

REBIK, JAMES MICHAEL, otolaryngologist; b. Marshalltown, Iowa, July 10, 1953; s. Hubert James and Donna Jean (Grandgeorge) R.; m. Sue Ellyn Primmer, Dec. 22, 1979; children: Christopher James, Kristin Leigh, Robert James, Jonathan Michael. BA summa cum laude, U. No. Iowa, 1981; DO, Kirksville Coll. Osteo. Med., 1985. Diplomate in otorhinolaryngology and facial plastic surgery Am. Osteo. Bd. Ophthalmology and Otorhinolaryngology; diplomate Nat. Bd. Med. Examiners for Osteo. Physicians and Surgeons; lic. physician, Mo., Iowa, Minn., Tex. Intern Kirksville (Mo.) Osteo Med. Ctr., 1985-86, resident otorhinolaryngology/oro-facial plastic surgery, 1986-90; otolaryngologist Landstuhl (Germany) Army Regional Med. Ctr., 1990-92; chief otolaryngology-head and neck surgery svc. Reynolds Army Community Hosp., Ft. Sill, Okla., 1992-94; with Primary Med. Clinic, Midland, Tex., 1996—. Maj. M.C. U.S. Army, 1990-94. Recipient 1st degree brown belt Gup U.S. Tang Soo Do Moo Duk Kwan Fedn., 1979. Fellow Soc. Mil. Otolaryngologists; mem. AMA, Am. Osteo. Assn., Am. Coll. Ophthalmology and Otolaryngology-Head and Neck Surgery, Assn. Mil. Surgeons U.S., Am. Acad. Otolaryngic Allergy, Am. Acad. Otolaryngology-Head and Neck Surgery, Christian Soc. Otolaryngology-Head and Neck Surgery, Freeborn County Med Soc., Minn. Med. Assn., Pan-Am. Assn. Otorhinolaryngology-Head and Neck Surgery, Tex. Osteo. Med. Assn., Mensa. Baptist. Avocations: jogging, medieval and World War II history, baroque and classical music. Home: 610 Hillside Dr Big Spring TX 79720 Office: Westwood Med Ctr Profl Bldg Ste 100 4214 Andrews Hwy Midland TX 79703

RECABO, JAIME MIGUEL, lawyer; b. Manila, Philippines, Oct. 6, 1950; came to U.S., 1969; s. Matthew M. and Luisa (De Leon) R.; children: James M., Danielle M.; m. Maureen Susan Ward, Dec. 1980; children: Matthew J., Maura E., Joseph A., Olivia M. BA, Fordham U., 1973, JD, 1988; MBA in Fin., St. John's U., 1977. Bar: N.Y. 1989, N.J. 1989, Conn. 1989. Bus. office mgr. Eger Nursing Home Inc., S.I., N.Y., 1974-77; sr. acct. Kingsbrook Jewish Med. Ctr., Bklyn., 1977-78; asst. compt. Jewish Home & Hosp. for the Aged, Bronx, N.Y., 1978-79; dir. fiscal svcs. Frances Schervier Home & Hosp., Bronx, 1979-86; exec. v.p. finance & legal affairs Franciscan Health System N.Y., Bronx, 1986-89; mgmt. cons., health and immigration atty. N.Y.C., 1989—. Bd. dirs. Frances Schervier Home & Hosp., Bronx, 1987-90, Bklyn. United Meth. Ch. Home, 1991—; vice-chmn. NYAHSA Contrs. Com., N.Y.C., 1985-86, N.Y. Archdiocese Contrs. Coun., N.Y.C., 1980-83. Mem. ABA, Am. Immigration Lawyers Assn., N.J. Bar Assn., N.Y. Bar Assn., Conn. Bar Assn., Healthcare Fin. Mgmt. Assn., Nat. Health Lawyers Assn. Roman Catholic. Office: 34 Palmer Ave Bronxville NY 10708-3404

RECCHIA, RICHARD D., automotive sales executive; b. 1939. MBA, Wayne State U. Gen. sales mgr. Chrysler Corp., Detroit, 1953-78; pres. Fiat Motors of N. Am., Inc., Newark, N.J., 1978-81, R.D.R. Svcs., Inc., L.A., 1981-82; exec. v.p., COO Mitsubishi Motor Sales of Am., Cypress, Calif., 1982—. Office: Mitsubishi Motor Sales of Amer 6400 Katella Ave Cypress CA 90630-5208*

RECH, JEAN MAY, management consultant; d. George S. May. Various George S. May Intl Co Del, Park Ridge, Ill., 1962—; also bd. dirs. Office: George S May Intl Co Del 303 S Northwest Hwy Park Ridge IL 60068*

RECHARD, OTTIS WILLIAM, mathematics and computer science educator; b. Laramie, Wyo., Nov. 13, 1924; s. Ottis H. and Mary (Bird) R.; m. Dorothy Lee Duble, Nov. 19, 1943; children—Katherine L. (Mrs. Larry V. Baxter), Carol G. (Mrs. David P. Reiter), Nancy L. (Mrs. William Moore), Elizabeth A. B.A., U. Wyo., 1943; postgrad., U. Calif., Los Angeles, 1943; M.A., U. Wis., 1946, Ph.D., 1948. Instr. U. Wis., 1948; instr., asst. prof. Ohio State U., 1948-51; staff mem. Los Alamos (N.Mex.) Nat. Lab., 1951-56; prof., dir. computing ctr. Wash. State U., Pullman, 1956-68; prof., chmn. dept. computer sci. Wash. State U., 1963-76, prof., dir. systems and computing, 1968-70; prof. math. and computer scis. U. Denver, 1976-95, prof. emeritus, 1995—, dir. computing services, 1976-79; vis. prof., chmn. dept. computer sci. U. Wyo., 1986-87; cons. NSF, Idaho Nuclear Corp., Los Alamos Nat. Lab.; program dir. computer sci. program NSF, 1964-65, chmn. adv. panel on instl. computing facilities, 1969-70. Mem. Los Alamos Sch. Bd., 1954-56; mem. Pullman Sch. Bd., 1967-74; Trustee, past pres. Westminster Found., Synod Wash.-Alaska. Served to 1st lt. USAAF, 1943-45. Decorated Order of Leopold II Belgium). Fellow AAAS; mem. Assn. for Computing Machinery, Am. Math. Soc., Math. Assn. Am., IEEE Computer Soc., Soc. Indsl. and Applied Math., AAUP, Phi Beta Kappa, Sigma Xi, Phi Kappa Phi. Presbyn. (elder). Club: Rotarian. Home: RR 3 Box 369 Calder ID 83808 also: 6980 E Girard Ave Apt 405 Denver CO 80224-2915

RECHARD, PAUL ALBERT, consulting civil engineering company executive; b. Laramie, Wyo., June 4, 1927; s. Ottis H. and Mary R. (Bird) R.; m. Mary Lou Roper, June 26, 1949; children: Robert Paul, Karen Ann. BS, U. Wyo., 1948, MS, 1949, CE, 1955. Registered land surveyor, Wyo.; registered profl. engr., Wyo., Utah, Mont., Colo., Calif., Nebr., S.D., N.Mex.; cert. profl. hydrologist Am. Inst. Hydrology; diplomate Am. Acad. Environ. Engrs. Hydraulic engr. U.S. Bur. Reclamation, Cody, Wyo. and Billings, Mont., 1949-54; dir. water resources Natural Resource Bd., Cheyenne, Wyo., 1954-58; prin. hydraulic engr. Upper Colorado River Commn., Salt Lake City, 1958-64; dir. Water Resources Research Inst., U. Wyo., Laramie, 1964-81, mem. faculty dept. civil engring., 1964-82, prof., 1964-82; pres. Western Water Cons., Laramie, 1980—, Hydrology Assocs., Laramie, 1978-80; owner Paul A. Rechard, P.E., Laramie, 1964-78. Editor: Compacts, Treaties and Court Decrees Affecting Wyoming Water, 1956. Contbr. articles to tech. publs. Pres., Thayer Sch. PTA, Laramie, 1965; mem. Laramie City Planning Commn., 1974-80. Served with USNR, 1945-46. Recipient Wyo. Eminent Engr. award Tau Beta Pi, 1993. Fellow ASCE (life mem., pres. Wyo. sect. 1968); mem. Am. Soc. Testing Materials, NSPE, Am. Geophys. Union, Nat. Water Well Assn., Wyo. Engring. Soc. (pres. 1976, hon.), Am. Water Works Assn., Am. Water Resources Assn., U.S. Com. on Irrigation and Drainage, U.S. Com. on Large Dams, Sigma Xi (pres. Wyo. chpt. 1973), Phi Kappa Phi (pres. Wyo. chpt. 1969), Gamma Sigma Delta, Sigma Tau (pres. Wyo. chpt. 1948, selected Wyo. Eminent Engr. 1993). Republican. Presbyterian. Lodges: Lions (pres. Laramie 1968), Masons. Home: 316 Stuart St Laramie WY 82070-4866 Office: Western Water Cons Inc 611 Skyline Rd Laramie WY 82070-8909

RECHCIGL, JACK EDWARD, soil and environmental sciences educator; b. Washington, Feb. 27, 1960; s. Miloslav and Eva (Edwards) R.; m. Nancy Ann Palko, Sept. 30, 1983; children: Gregory John, Kevin Thomas, Lindsey Nicole. BS, U. Del., 1982; MS, Va. Poly. Inst. and State U., 1983, PhD, 1986. Asst. prof. soil sci. U. Fla. Agrl. Rsch. and Edn. Ctr., Ona, 1986-91, assoc. prof. soil and environ. scis., 1991-96; prof. soil and environ. scis., 1996—. Editor: Soil Amendments and Environmental Quality, 1995, Soil Amendments: Impact on Biotic Systems, 1995; assoc. editor: Jour. Environ. Quality, 1994—; editor-in-chief: (book series) Agriculture and Environment; contbr. chpts. to books, articles to Environ. Quality, Soil Sci., Soil Fertility, Water Quality. Recipient rsch. achievement award U. Fla., 1991; rsch grantee TVA, 1984-86, Allied Signal, 1987—, So. Fla. Water Mgmt. Dist., 1987-90, Fla. Inst. Phosphate Rsch., 1990—, USDA, 1992—. Mem. Am. Soc. Agronomy, Soil Sci. Soc. Am., Sigma Xi, Gamma Beta Phi, Gamma Sigma Delta, Phi Sigma. Achievements include research leading to the reduction of fertilizer recommendations in Florida, thereby helping to improve water quality; utilization of industrial organic and inorganic wastes (ex. phosphogypsum and granular biosolids) as potential fertilizers in agriculture. Home: 13511 4th Plz E Bradenton FL 34202 Office: Fla Agrl Rsch and Edn Ctr RR 1 Box 62 Ona FL 33865-9706

RECHCIGL, MILOSLAV, JR., government official; b. Mlada Boleslav, Czechoslovakia, July 30, 1930; s. Miloslav and Marie (Rajtrova) R.; came to U.S., 1950, naturalized, 1955; m. Eva Marie Edwards, Aug. 29, 1953; children: John Edward, Karen Marie. BS, Cornell U., 1954, M of Nutrition Sci., 1955, PhD, 1958. Teaching asst. Cornell U., Ithaca, N.Y., 1953-57, grad. rsch. asst., 1957-58, rsch. assoc., 1958; USPHS rsch. fellow Nat. Cancer Inst., 1958-60, chemist enzymes and metabolism sect., 1960-61, rsch. biochemist, tumor host rels. sect., 1962-64, sr. investigator, 1964-68; grants assoc. program NIH, 1968-69; spl. asst. for nutrition and health to dir. Regional Med. Programs Svc., Health Svcs. and Mental Health Adminstrn., HEW, 1969-70, exec. sec. nutrition program adv. com. Health Svcs. and Mental Health Adminstrn., 1969-70; nutrition adviser AID, Dept. State, Washington, 1970—, chief Rsch. and Instl. Grants div., 1970-73, exec. sec. rsch. and instl. grants coun., 1970-74, exec. sec. AID rsch. adv. com., 1971-83, AID rep. USC/FAR com., 1972-82, asst. dir. Office Rsch. and Instl. Grants, 1973-74, acting dir., 1974-75, dir. interregional rsch. staff, 1975-78, devel. studies program, 1978, chief rsch. and methodology div., 1979-82, rsch. mgmt. and rev. dir. Office of the Sci. Advisor, 1982-91, Office of Rsch., 1992-94, rsch. and methodology specialist, Bur. for Program and Policy Coordination, 1994—; del. White House Conf. on Food, Nutrition and Health, 1969, Agrl. Rsch. Policy Adv. Com. Conf. on Rsch. to Meet U.S. and World Food Needs, 1975; cons. Office Sec. Agr., 1969-70, Dept. Treasury, 1973, Office Technol. Assessment, 1977, FDA, 1979, NAS, NRC, 1985-93. Author: The Czechoslovak Contribution to World Culture, 1964, Czechoslovakia Past and Present, 1968, (with Z. Hruban) Microbodies and Related Particles: Morphology, Biochemistry and Physiology, 1969, Russian edit., 1972, Enzyme Synthesis and Degradation in Mammalian Systems, 1971, (with Eva Rechcigl) Biographical Directory of the Members of the Czechoslovak Society of Arts and Sciences in America, 3d edit., 1972, 4th edit., 1978, 5th edit., 1983, 6th edit., 1988, 7th edit., 1992, Food, Nutrition and Health: A Multidisciplinary Treatise Addressed to the Major Nutrition Problems from a World Wide Perspective, 1973, Man, Food and Nutrition: Strategies and Technological Measures for Alleviating the World Food Problem, 1973, World Food Problem: A Selective Bibliography of Reviews, 1975, Carbohydrates, Lipids and Accessory Growth Factors, 1976, Nutrient Elements and Toxicants, 1977, Nitrogen, Electrolytes, Water and Energy Metabolism, 1979, Nutrition and the World Food Problem, 1979, Educators with Czechoslovak Roots: A U.S. and Canadian Faculty Roster, 1980, Physiology of Growth and Nutrition, 1981, Nutritional Requirements, 1977, Diet, Culture Media and Food Supplements, 4 vols., 1977, Nutritional Disorders, 3 vols., 1978, Handbook of Nutritional Requirements in a Functional Context, 2 vols., 1981, Handbook of Agricultural Productivity, 2 vols., 1981, Handbook of Nutritive Value of Processed Food, 2 vols., 1982, Handbook of Foodborne Diseases of Biological Origin, 1983, Handbook of Naturally Occurring Food Toxicants, 1983, Handbook of Nutritional Supplements, 2 vols, 1983, U.S. Legislators with Czechoslovak Roots from Colonial Times to Present, 1987, others; co-editor: Internat. Jour. of Cycle Research, 1969-74, Jour. Applied Nutrition, 1970-82; series editor: Comparative Animal Nutrition, 1976-81; editor-in-chief: (series) Nutrition and Food, 1977—; mem. editorial bd.: Nutrition Reports Internat., 1977-80; translator: Chemical Abstracts, 1959-61; contbr. articles to sci. jours. Organizer, mem. council Montrose Civic Assn., Rockville, Md.; mem. ethnic affairs com., Montgomery County, Md., 1990-92, vice chair, 1991-92. Recipient Josef Hlavka Commemorative medal Czechoslovak Acad. Scis., 1991; NAS grantee, 1962. Fellow AAAS, Am. Inst. Chemists (councilor 1972-74, program chmn. 1974 ann. meeting, mem. pram com. 1980 meeting), Internat. Coll. Applied Nutrition, Intercontinental Biog. Assn.. Washington Acad. Scis. (del. 1972—); mem. Am. Inst. Nutrition (com. Western Hemisphere Nutrition Congress 1971, 74, program com. 1979-82), Am. Soc. Biol. Chemists, Am. Chem. Soc. (joint bd.-council com. on internat. activities 1975-76), D.C. Inst. Chemists (pres. 1972-74, councilor 1974-80), Am. Inst. Biol. Scis., Soc. for Exptl. Biology and Medicine, Am. Soc. Animal Sci., Internat., Am. socs. cell biology, Soc. for Developmental Biology, Am. Assn. for Cancer Research, Soc. for Biol. Rhythm, Am. Pub. Health Assn., N.Y. Acad. Scis., Chem. Soc. Washington (symposium com. 1970, 71), Internat. Coll. Applied Nutrition, Internat. Soc. for Research on Civilization Diseases and Vital Substances, Soc. for Geochemistry and Health, Soc. for Internat. Devel., Internat. Platform Assn., Am. Assn. for Advancement Slavic Studies, Czechoslovak Soc. Arts and Scis. in Am. (hon., dir.-at-large 1962—, dir. publs. 1962-68, 70-74, v.p. 1968-74, pres. 1974-78, 94—, pres. collegium 1978—), History of Sci. Soc., Soc. Research Adminstrs., Sigma Xi, Phi Kappa Phi, Delta Tau Kappa (hon.). Clubs: Cosmos, Cornell (Washington). Home: 1703 Mark Ln Rockville MD 20852-4106 Office: AID-Bur for Program & Policy Coord Washington DC 20523

RECHTIN, EBERHARDT, retired aerospace executive, educator; b. East Orange, N.J., Jan. 16, 1926; s. Eberhardt Carl and Ida H. (Pfarrer) R.; m. Dorothy Diane Denebrink, June 10, 1951; children: Andrea C., Nina, Julie Anne, Erica, Mark. B.S., Calif. Inst. Tech., 1946, Ph.D. cum laude, 1950. Dir. Deep Space Network, 1958-67; asst. dir. Calif. Inst. Tech. Jet Propulsion Lab., 1960-67; dir. Advanced Rsch. Projects Agy., Dept. Def., 1967-70, prin. dep. dir. def. rsch. and engring., 1970-71, asst. sec. def. for telecom., 1972-73; chief engr. Hewlett-Packard Co., Palo Alto, Calif., 1973-77; pres., CEO Aerospace Corp., El Segundo, Calif., 1977-87; pres.-emeritus Aerospace Corp., El Segundo, 1988; prof. U. So. Calif., 1988-94, emeritus prof., 1994—. Served to lt. USNR, 1943-56. Recipient maj. awards NASA, Dept. Def., USN, Disting. Alumni award Calif. Inst. Tech., 1984, NEC C&C prize, Japan, 1992. Fellow AAAS, AIAA (Robert H. Goddard Astronautics award 1991), IEEE (Alexander Graham Bell award 1977); mem. NAE, Tau Beta Pi. Home: 1665 Cataluna Pl Palos Verdes Peninsula CA 90274

RECHY, JOHN FRANCISCO, author; b. El Paso, Tex.; s. Roberto Sixto and Guadalupe (Flores) R. B.A., U. Tex., El Paso; student, New Sch. Social Research. Instr. creative writing UCLA, Occidental Coll., U. So. Calif. Author: City of Night, 1963, Numbers, 1967, this Day's Death, 1969, The Vampires, 1971, The Fourth Angel, 1973, The Sexual Outlaw, 1977, Rushes, 1979, Bodies and Souls, 1983, Marilyn's Daughter, 1988, The Miraculous Day of Amalia Gõmez, 1991, Our Lady of Babylon, 1996; (plays) Momma As She Became-Not As She Was, 1968, Rushes, 1978, Tigers Wild, 1986; contbr.: short stories and articles to Tex. Observer, The Nation, Village Voice, London mag., Saturday Rev., N.Y. Times Book Rev., L.A. Times, Washington Post Book World, Phila. Inquirer, Contemporary Fiction, Big Table, others; also anthologies Chicano Voices, Black Humor, Urban Reader, Evergreen Rev. Reader, New Am. Story, The Moderns, Rediscoveries, Men on Men, others; trans.: stories and articles for Tex. Quar., Evergreen Rev. Served with AUS. Recipient Longview Found. award for short story The Fabulous Wedding of Miss Destiny; Nat. Endowment for Arts grantee, 1976. Mem. Authors Guild, Tex. Inst. Letters, PEN, Nat. Writers Union.

RECK, ANDREW JOSEPH, philosophy educator; b. New Orleans, Oct. 29, 1927; s. Andrew Gervais and Katie (Mangiaracina) R.; m. Elizabeth Lassiter Torre, June 17, 1987. B.A., Tulane U., 1947, M.A., 1949; Ph.D., Yale U., 1954; student, U. St. Andrews, Scotland, 1952-53, U. Paris, summers 1962, 64. Instr. English U. Conn., 1949-50; instr. philosophy Yale, 1951-52, 55-58; mem. faculty Tulane U., 1958—, prof. philosophy, 1964—, chmn. dept., 1969-89, dir. Master Liberal Arts program, 1984—; Thomasfest lectr. Xavier U., Cin., 1970; Suarez Lectr. Spring Hill Coll., 1971; Niebuhr lectr. Elmhurst (Ill.) Coll., 1976; vis. prof. Fordham U., 1979; vis. scholar Hastings Ctr. (N.Y.), 1981; Woodruff lectr. Emory U., 1982; Fairchild lectr. U. So. Miss., 1982, 87: Matchette Found. lectr. Cath. U. Am., 1991, 95; Sr. Scholar Inst. Humane Studies, Menlo Park, Calif., 1982; vis. scholar Poynter Ctr., Ind. U., Bloomington, 1983; Tulane U. faculty rep. to bd. adminstrs. Tulane Ednl. Fund., 1988-91. Author: Recent American Philosophy, 1964, Introduction to William James, 1967, New American Philosophers, 1968, Speculative Philosophy, 1972; editor: George Herbert Mead Selected Writings, 1964, 2d edit., 1981, Knowledge and Value, 1972, (with T. Horvath, T. Krittek and S. Grean) American Philosophers' Ideas of Ultimate Reality and Meaning, 1993; co-editor Ultimate Reality and Meaning, Interdisciplinary Studies in the Philosophy of Understanding, 1990—; mem. adv. editl. bd. Internat. Jour. World Peace, Trans. Charles Peirce Soc., Santayana edit. So. Jour. Philosophy; editor History of Philosophy Quar., 1993—. Served with AUS, 1953-55. Howard fellow, 1962-63, Liberty Fund grantee, 1982, Newcomb fellow, 1991-93; Fulbright scholar, 1952-53; Am. Coun. Learned Socs. grantee, 1961-62, Am. Philos. Soc. grantee, 1972, Huntington Libr. grantee, 1973, La. Ednl. Quality State Found. grantee, 1994—, U.S. Info. Agy. grantee, Brazil, 1993. Mem. Am. Philos. Assn. (program com. eastern divsn. 1969, adv. com. to program com. eastern divsn., 1994—, nominating com. western divsn. 1975-76, 81-82, mem. ad hoc com. on history 1992—), Southwestern Philos. Soc. (exec. com. 1965-69, v.p. 1971-72, pres. 1972-73), So. Soc. Philosophy and Psychology (treas. 1968-71, pres. 1976-77), Am. Coun. Learned Socs. (Am. studies adv. com. 1972-76), Coun. for Internat. Exch. Scholars (philosophy screening com. 1974-77), Metaphys. Soc. Am. (councillor 1971-75, pres. 1977-78, program com. 1989-90, chair program com. 1995-96), Soc. Advancement Am. Philosophy (exec. com. 1980-83), Charles S. Peirce Soc. (sec.-treas. 1985-86, v.p. 1986-87, pres. 1987-88), Internat. Soc. for Study of Human Ideas of Ultimate Reality and Meaning (bd. dirs. 1989—), La. Endowment for Humanities (bd. dirs. 1990—), Phi Beta Kappa (pres. Alpha of La. 1966-67), Alpha Sigma Lambda (hon. Theta chpt. of La.). Home: 6125 Patton St New Orleans LA 70118-5832 Office: Tulane U Dept Philosophy New Orleans LA 70118

RECK, JOEL M(ARVIN), lawyer; b. Worcester, Mass., Sept. 27, 1941; s. Saul I. and Sylvia (Levine) R.; m. Rachel E. Feinsilver, June 9, 1963; children: Daniel C., Deborah R. BA cum laude, Bowdoin Coll., 1963; JD, Harvard U., 1966. Bar: Mass. 1967. Ptnr., chmn. real estate dept. Brown, Rudnick, Freed & Gesmer, Boston, 1968—; chmn. Wayland (Mass.) Zoning Bd., 1979-82; trustee Mass. Continuing Legal Edn., Inc., Boston, 1988—. Mem. exec. com. Combined Jewish Philanthropies, Boston, 1982—; sec. Nat. Jewish Commn. on Rels. Adv. Coun., N.Y.C., 1992-93; pres. Jewish Community Rels. Coun., Boston, 1987-90; mem. Mass. Gov.'s Entrepreneurial Adv. Coun., Boston, 1986-90. Mem. ABA, Lawyers Alliance for World Security (mem. exec. com. Mass. law), Real Estate Fin. Assn. (clk. 1992-94),

Pension Real Estate Assn. (mem. govt. affairs com. 1991—), Mass. Bar Assn., Boston Bar Assn. (pres.-elect 1995-96, chmn. real estate sect. 1985-87), Mass. Conveyancers Assn. (mem. exec. com. Boston chpt. 1986), Abstract Club (mem. exec. com. Boston chpt. 1990). Avocations: sailing, skiing, jogging. Office: Brown Rudnick Freed Gesmer One Financial Center Boston MA 02111-1000

RECKER, THOMAS EDWARD, fraternal organization administrator; b. Livonia, Mich., Feb. 28, 1960; s. Peter Edward and Patricia Ann (Heidenwolf) R. BA in Ednl. Psychology, U. Mich., 1982; MA in Coll. Student Personnel, Bowling Green State U., 1985. Asst. exec. dir. Grand Chpt. of Phi Sigma Kappa, Indpls., 1985-87, exec. dir., 1987-90; exec. v.p. Grand Chpt. of Phi Sigma Kappa and Phi Sigma Kappa Found., Indpls., 1990—. Mem. Am. Soc. Assn. Execs., Assn. Frat. Advisers, Frat. Execs. Assn. Office: Phi Sigma Kappa Frat 2925 E 96th St Indianapolis IN 46240-1368

RECKLEIN, LINDA SUE, library administrator; b. St. Louis, Feb. 19; d. Clifford H. and Billie M. (Bader) Lincks; m. Dan S. Recklein, Sept. 4 1993; 1 stepchild, Allison Faith. BA in Psychology cum laude, U. Mo., St. Louis, 1972; MLS, U. Mo., 1977. Supr., para-profl. St. Louis County Libr., 1972-80; mgr. info. ctr., info. specialist Ralston Purina Co., St. Louis, 1980—; mem. bus. adv. bd. cons. group Gale Rsch., Detroit, 1990—; team mem. spl. librs. delegation Citizen Ambassador Program of People to People Internat., Russia and Czech Republic, 1995. Distbr. campaign lit. for Dem. and Rep. parties; vol. phone support at campaign hdqs.; vol. solicitor ARC Corp. Assocs. Ann. Fund, 1994. Recipient Cert. of Leadership, YWCA, 1991; named Outstanding Young Woman of Am., 1981. Mem. NAFE, AAUW, Soc. Competitive Intelligence Profls., Spl. Librs. Assn. (chpt. bd. dirs. 1983-84), Women in Bus. Network (treas. 1982-83), Am. Mgmt. Assn., St. Louis Regional Library Network (edn. com., info-lib lunchtime topics task force 1984-86). Roman Catholic. Avocations: photography, travel, gardening, running, cooking. Home: 637 Laven Del Ln Saint Louis MO 63122-1115 Office: Ralston Purina Co Checkerboard Sq Saint Louis MO 63164

RECORD, PHILLIP JULIUS, newspaper executive; b. Fort Worth, Jan. 12, 1929; s. Phillip Cross and Frances Virginia (McElwee) R.; m. Patricia Ann Edwards, Sept. 29, 1954; children: Christopher Phillip, Gregory Edwards, Timothy James. B.A. in Journalism, U. Notre Dame, 1950. Gen. reporter Lubbock Avalanche-Jour., Tex., 1950-54; copy editor, reporter Fort Worth Star-Telegram, 1954-67, asst. city editor, 1967-68, city editor evening edit., 1968-76, mng. editor, 1976-80, assoc. exec. editor, 1980-91, spl. asst. to pub., ombudsman, 1991—; dir. Freedom Info. Found. Tex., 1987-93; mem. mass comms. com. Tex. Tech. U., chmn., 1990-92. Mem. conciliation/arbitration bd. Cath. Diocese of Ft. Worth, 1994—, chair, 1996—, publs. adv. com., 1982—; founding mem. Ft. Worth Theatre; mem. Friends of Ft. Worth Pub. Libr.; bd. dirs. Tarrant County Mental Health Assn., 1990—. With U.S. Army, 1950-52. Recipient 3d ann. Ethics award Tex. Christian U., 1991, numerous other awards for reporting, photography and headline writing; named to Tex. Tech U. Mass Comms. Hall of Fame. Mem. ABA (nat. commn. on pub. understanding about law 1984-90, commn. on partnership programs 1990-93), Investigative Reporters and Editors Inc., Soc. Profl. Journalists (pres. 1983-84, bd. dirs. Found. 1980—, v.p. Found., 1991-94, bd. chair 1994—, Wells Key 1991), Creative Thinking Assn., Orgn. News Ombudsmen (dir. 1994—, v.p. 1995-96, pres. 1996—), Petroleum Club. Avocation: tennis. Home: 6144 Walla Ave Fort Worth TX 76133-3557 Office: Fort Worth Star-Telegram 400 W 7th St Fort Worth TX 76102-4701 *As a journalist, I strive to be a servant of the truth and a servant of the people. As a follower of Jesus, I try to live my life as he would. But, being human, I fail frequently. But I try and I care. I think that makes me OK in God's eyes.*

RECORDS, RAYMOND EDWIN, ophthalmologist, medical educator; b. Ft. Morgan, Colo., May 30, 1930; s. George Harvey and Sara Barbara (Louden) R.; 1 child, Lisa Rae. BS in Chemistry, U. Denver, 1956; MD, St. Louis U., 1961. Diplomate Am. Bd. Ophthalmology. Intern St. Louis U. Hosp. Group, 1961-62; resident in ophthalmology U. Colo. Med. Ctr., Denver, 1962-65; instr. ophthalmology, 1965-67, asst. prof., 1967-70; prof. ophthalmology U. Nebr. Coll. Medicine, Omaha, 1970-93, prof. emeritus, 1993, dept. chmn., 1970-89. Author: Physiology of Human Eye (Med. Writers award 1980), 1979. Author, editor: Biomedical Foundations of Ophthalmology, 1982. Med. dir. Nebr. Lions Eye Bank, 1970-81. Fellow Am. Acad. of Ophthalmology (outstanding contbn. award 1978); mem. Nev. Med. Assn., Clark County Med. Soc., Omaha Ophthal. Soc. (pres. 1981-82), Assn. Rsch. in Vision and Ophthalmology. Home: 21919 Riverside Cir Elkhorn NE 68022-1708 Office: 1640 Alta Dr # 1 Las Vegas NV 89106-4171

RECTOR, FLOYD CLINTON, JR., physiologist, physician; b. Slaton, Tex., Jan. 28, 1929; s. Floyd Clinton and Faye Elizabeth (Tucker) R.; m. Marjory L. Bullen, May 27, 1950; children—Lynn, Ruth, Janet. BS, Tex. Tech. Coll., 1950; MD, U. Tex. Southwestern Med. Sch., 954. Instr. U. Tex. Southwestern Med. Sch., Dallas, 1958-59; asst. prof. medicine U. Tex. Southwestern Med. Sch., 1959-63, assoc. prof., 1963-66, prof., 1966-73; prof. medicine and physiology, sr. scientist Cardiovascular Research Inst.; dir. div. nephrology U. Calif., San Francisco, 1973-89, chmn. dept. medicine, 1989—. Editor: (with B.M. Brenner) The Kidney, 1976, 81, 85, 90-91, 94. Served with USPHS, 1956-58. NIH grantee, 1973—. Mem. Am. Soc. Nephrology, Am. Soc. Clin. Investigation, Am. Assn. Physicians, Am. Physiol. Soc. Office: U Calif PO Box 0120 San Francisco CA 94143

RECTOR, JOHN MICHAEL, lawyer, association executive; b. Seattle, Aug. 15, 1943; s. Michael Robert and Bernice Jane (Allison) R.; m. Mary Kaaren Sueta Jolly, Feb. 8, 1977 (div. 1995). BA, U. Calif., Berkeley, 1966; JD, U. Calif., Hastings, 1969; PharmD (hon.), Ark. State Bd. Pharmacy, 1991. Bar: Calif. 1970, U.S. Supreme Ct. 1974. Trial atty. civil rights div. Dept. Justice, 1969-71; dep. chief counsel judiciary com. U.S. Senate, 1971-73, counsel to Sen. Birch Bayh, 1971-77, chief counsel, staff dir., 1973-77; confirmed by U.S. Senate as assoc. adminstr. to Law Enforcement Assistance Adminstn. and adminstr. of Office Juvenile Justice Dept. Justice, 1977-79; spl. counsel to U.S. Atty. Gen., 1979-80; dir. govt. affairs Nat. Assn. Retail Druggists, Washington, 1980-85; sr. v.p. govt. affairs, gen. counsel Nat. Assn. Retail Druggists, 1986—; chmn. adv. bd. Nat. Juvenile Law Center, 1973-77; mem. Hew panel Drug Use and Criminal Behavior, 1974-77; mem. cons. panel Nat. Commn. Protection Human Subjects of Biomed. and Behavioral Research, 1975-76; mem. bd. Nat. Inst. Corrections, 1977-79; chmn. U.S. Interdepartmental Council Juvenile Justice, 1977-79; mem. bd. com. civil rights and liberties Am. Democratic Action, 1976-80, Pres.'s Com. Mental Health-Justice Group, 1978; com. youth citizenship ABA, 1978-84; mem. Pharm. Industry Adv. Com.; exec. dir., treas. polit. action com. Nat. Pharmacists Assn., 1981—; exec. dir. Retail Druggist Legal Legis. Def. Fund, 1985—, founder, chmn. Washington Pharmacy Industry Forum; mem. numerous fed. narcotic and crime panels and coms.; owner Second Genesis, an antique and furniture restoration co. Mem. editorial bd. Managed Care Law; contbr. articles to profl. jours. Exec. com. small bus. and fin. couns. Dem. Nat. Com.; dir. Dem. Leadership Coun.'s Network, 1989—, bd. advisers, 1992—; bd. dirs. Small Bus. Legis. Coun., 1987—; bd. dirs. Nat. Bus. Coalition for Fair Competition, 1984—. Perry E. Towne scholar, 1966-67; mem. U.S. Atty. Gen.'s Honors Program, 1968-71; recipient Children's Express Juvenile Justice award, 1981. Mem. Calif. Bar Assn., Nat. Health Lawyers Assn., Am. Soc. Assn. Execs. (govt. affirs sect.), Washington Coun. Lawyers, Assn. of Former Senior Senate Aides, Vinifera Wine Growers Assn. Va. (life), Health R Us, Am. League of Lobbyists, Theta Chi. Democrat. Avocation: collecting antique furniture, books and documents. Home: 205 Daingerfield Rd Alexandria VA 22314 Office: Nat Assn Retail Druggists 205 Daingerfield Rd Alexandria VA 22314-2833

RECTOR, MILTON GAGE, social work educator, former association executive; b. Fallon, Nev., Jan. 3, 1918; s. William L. and Virginia E. (Renfro) R.; m. Harriet Louise Phibbs, Aug. 1, 1940; children: Brian Eugene (dec.), Barbara Elaine (dec.), Dianne Eileen, Bruce Alan. B.A., U. So. Calif., 1940; postgrad., U. Calif.-Berkeley, Columbia U. With Los Angeles County Probation Dept., 1940-46, probation officer charge forestry camp for delinquent boys, 1943-46; with Nat. Council Crime and Delinquency, 1946-82, cons. Western region, 1946-52, dir. parole services, 1952-55, asst. exec. dir., 1955-59, exec. dir., 1959-82, pres., 1972-82; vis. prof. Grad. Sch. Social Work U. Utah, 1982-84; Mem. President's Adv. Com. on Delinquency and Youth Crime, 1960-66; Cons. to U.S. Senate subcom. investigation delinquency, 1953; organized Nat. Conf. Parole, 1956; bd. dirs. Am. Correctional Assn., 1959-73, Osborne Assn., 1960-75, Nat. Study Service, 1960-76, U. Md. Inst. Criminal Justice, 1972-78, Center for Correctional Justice, 1972-78, SUNY-Albany Criminal Justice Inst., Acad. Jud. Edn., 1970-75, Law in Am. Society Found.; chmn. bd. dirs. Joint Commn. Correctional Manpower and Tng., 1965-70; cons. Pres.'s Crime Commn., 1965-68; U.S. rep. UN Social Def. Sect., 1965-75; U.S. del. UN World Congress on Crime and Delinquency, Stockholm, 1965, Kyoto, Japan, 1970; mem. Nat. Commn. on Reform Fed. Criminal Laws, 1969-70, N.Y.C. Criminal Justice Coordinating Council, 1967-73, Nat. Commn. on Criminal Justice Standards and Goals, 1971-73, Inst. on Jud. Adminstrn.-Am. Bar Assn. Commn. on Juvenile Justice Standards, 1973-76; mem. adv. com. on correctional edn. Edn. Commn. of States, 1975-77. Contbr. numerous articles profl. jours., procs., Nat. Council Crime and Delinquency; syndicated columnist: Of Crime and Punishment. Served to lt. (j.g.) USNR, 1944-46; comdr. Res. Recipient August Volmer award Am. Criminological Soc., 1971; Meritorious Service award Nat. Council Juvenile and Family Ct. Judges, 1962; John Howard award John Howard Assn., 1974; award John Jay Coll. Criminal Justice, 1979; Karl Menninger award Fortune Soc., 1979; Harold DeWolf award Offender Aid and Restoration U.S.A. Inc., 1980; award Nat. Forum on Criminal Justice, 1981; Margaret Mead award Internat. Halfway House Assn., 1982; award for enhancement profl. edn. U. Utah Grad. Sch. Social Work, 1983. Home: 27 James Buchanan Dr Cranbury NJ 08512-4847 *My life work in the field of juvenile and criminal justice and its insights into the depths of man's inhumanity to man have enabled me to serve in a ministry for the reform of a system which at times seems impervious to reform, and thus continues to deny the attainment of social justice in my country.*

RECTOR, ROBERT WAYMAN, mathematics and engineering educator, former association executive; b. San Jose, Calif., Jan. 28, 1916; s. Joseph Jones and Eva (Hembree) R.; m. Margaret Eileen Hayden, Aug. 25, 1940; children: Cleone Rector Black, Robin Rector Krupp, Bruce Hayden. B.A., San Jose State U., 1937; M.A., Stanford U., 1939; Ph.D., U. Md., 1956. Instr. Compton (Calif.) Coll., 1939-42; asso. prof. math. U.S. Naval Acad., 1946-56; staff mathematician Space Tech. Labs., Los Angeles, 1956-61; asso. dir. computation center Aerospace Corp., El Segundo, Calif., 1961-65; v.p. Informatics, Inc., Van Nuys, Calif., 1965-70, Cognitive Systems, Inc., Beverly Hills, Calif., 1970-71; asso. dir. continuing edn. engring. and math. UCLA, 1971-73, 81-92; dean Coll. Engring. and Computer Sci. West Cost U., L.A., 1992—; Exec. dir. Am. Fedn. Info. Processing Socs., Montvale, N.J., 1973-79; spl. asst. White House Conf. Library and Info. Services, 1979; v.p. Conf. and Meeting Assistance Corp., East Greenwich, R.I., 1980—. Bd. govs.: Pacific Jour. Math, 1957-92. Mem. Los Angeles Mayor's Space Adv. Com., 1964-73, Calif. Mus. Found. (aviation and space hist. research com. 1984—). Served with USNR, 1942-46. Mem. Math. Assn. Am., Assn. Computing Machinery, Naval Res. Assn., Res. Officers Assn., Ret. Officers Assn. Home: 10700 Stradella Ct Los Angeles CA 90077-2604

REDBONE, LEON, singer, musician. Albums include: On the Track, 1975, Double Time, 1976, Champagne Charlie, 1977, From Branch to Branch, 1981, Red to Blue, 1985, Christmas Island, 1988, No Regrets, 1988, Sugar, 1990, Up a Lazy River, 1992, Whistling in the Wind, 1994.

REDDA, KINFE KEN, chemist, educator; b. Senafe, Eritrea (Africa), Mar. 21, 1948; arrived in Can., 1973; came to U.S., 1979; s. Guangul and Demekech (Zewde) R.; m. Abeda Hindeya, 1978 (div. 1983); 1 child, Fre; m. Lul Haile, 1989; children: Aman, Aaron, Semhal. BS in Pharmacy, Haile Selassie U., Addis Ababa, Ethiopia, 1970; PhD in Medicinal Chemistry, U. Alberta, Edmonton, Can., 1978. Lic. pharmacist, Ethiopia. Postdoctoral fellow U. Alberta, Edmonton, Can., 1977-78, Dalhousie U., Halifax, Can., 1978-79; asst. prof. U. Puerto Rico, San Juan, 1980-85; assoc. prof. Fla. A&M U., Tallahassee, 1985-89, prof., 1989—; nat. grant reviewer Nat. Inst. Drug Abuse, Rockville, Md., 1985-88; dir. space life sics. tng. program NASA, Kennedy Space Ctr., Tallahassee, 1987-95; dir. NIH minority biomed. rsch. support program, Fla. A&M U., Tallahassee, 1988—. Chief editor: Cocaine, Marijuana and Designer Drugs Chemistry, Pharamacology and Behavior, 1989; contbr. articles to profl. jours; patentee synthesis of new biologically active compounds Tetrahydropyridines, 1979—. Mem. NAACP (Tallahassee chpt.), Tallahassee Urban League, Harambe Festival, Tallahassee. Recipient Inventor's medal, Canadian Patents & Developments, Ottawa, Can., 1978, grant Nat. Inst. Health, Bethesda, Md., 1985—, NASA, Washington, 1987—. Mem. numerous nat. and internat. profl. orgns. Democrat. Mem. Coptic Christian Ch. Avocations: jogging, swimming, reading, travel, spectator sports. *Sincere and voluntary service to others is the deepest form of human kindness.*

REDDAN, HAROLD JEROME, sociologist, educator; b. N.Y.C., Dec. 4, 1926; s. Harold B. and Catherine G. (Kelly) R.; m. Margaret M. Byrne, Oct. 11, 1952; children: Harold James, Patricia Anne, James Joseph, Kathleen Mary. B.A., St. Francis Coll., 1950; M.S., St. Johns U., 1957, Ph.D., 1961. Social investigator N.Y.C. Dept. Welfare, 1950-58; assoc. prof. sociology St. Johns U., 1958-69; lectr. sociology Kings County Hosp. Center Sch. of Nursing, N.Y.C., 1961-66; family counselor, 1961—; adj. assoc. prof. Manhattan Coll., 1968-69, prof. sociology, head dept. managerial scis., 1969-73; adj. sociology faculty Nassau Community Coll., 1971—, Mercy Coll.; adj. prof. L.I. corr. facility, 1980-84; adminstrv. cons. Molloy Coll., 1973-74; adj. prof. sociology and bus. adminstrn. C.W. Post Coll., 1974-80; mem. behavioral scis. faculty, police sci. program N.Y. Inst. Tech., 1974-75; adj. prof. sociology SUNY, Farmingdale; provost Molloy Coll., 1975-78, v.p. for planning and spl. programs, 1978-79; ednl. cons., 1979—. Author: Sociology, 1971, Arco GRE Tests, 1985. Dir. Jamaica VI Peace Corps Tng. Program, 1965; Coordinator New Hyde Park Citizens for Kennedy, 1960, campaign mgr. 1st Assembly Dist., 1962-64. Served with AUS, 1945-46. Mem. Am. Sociol. Assn., Am. Acad. Polit. and Social Sci., Am. Acad. Mgmt., Assn. Psychiat. Treatment Offenders, VFW, Garden City Park Hist. Soc. (pres. 1960-63), Delta Mu Delta, Delta Sigma Pi, Zeta Sigma Pi, Alpha Kappa Delta. Democrat. Home: 96 5th St New Hyde Park NY 11040-4108

REDDEL, CARL WALTER, education adminstration; b. Gurley, Neb., May 31, 1937; s. Walter Julius and Friedora Regina (Sorge) R.; m. Colette Marie Antoinette Mansuy, Oct. 26, 1963; children: Eric, Damien. BSED, Drake U., 1959; MA in Russian studies, Syracuse U., 1962; PhD in Russian history, Ind. U., 1973, cert. Russian studies, 1973. Lectr. U. Md., Toul-Rosieres, France, 1963-66; instr. U.S.A.F. Acad., Colo. Springs, Colo., 1967-68, 71-72, asst. prof., 1972-73, assoc. prof., 1973-80; prof., head dept. history, post-doctoral fellow U. Edinburgh, Edinburgh, Scotland, 1981-82; prof., head dept. history U.S. Air Force Acad., 1982—; nat. coord., regional World History Assn., Phila., 1990—; bd. editors, mem. Joun. Slavic Military, London, 1988—; series editor Military Hist. Symposium Series, Colo. Springs, 1993—. Editor: Transformation in Russian and Soviet Military History, 1990; contbr. articles to profl. jours. Mem. Rotary Internat., 1994—. With U.S. Air Force, 1962—. Recipient Young Faculty exchange Internat. Rsch. Exchanges Bd., Moscoe, 1975; Danforth fellowship Danforth Found., 1959-61. Mem. Am. Historical Assn., Am. Assn. Advancement of Slavic Studies, World History Assn., Rocky Mountain World History Assn., Cen. Slavic Assn. Lutheran. Home: 4504 Bell Flower Dr Colorado Springs CO 80917 Office: U S A F Acad Dept History Colorado Springs CO 80840

REDDELL, DONALD LEE, agricultural engineer; b. Tulia, Tex., Sept. 28, 1937; s. Kimball Tuscola and Winonah (Claiborne) R.; m. Minnie Ellen Cox, Jan. 27, 1957; children: Revis Diane, Cheryl Reneé, Stephen Patrick. BS, Tex. Tech U., 1960; MS, Colo. State U., 1967, PhD, 1969. Registered profl. engr., Tex. Jr. engr. High Plains Underground Water Conservation Dist. No. 1, Lubbock, Tex., 1960-61, agrl. engr., 1961-63, engr., 1963-65; NSF trainee civil and agrl. engring. dept. Colo. State U., Ft. Collins, 1965-69; asst. prof. agrl. engring. dept. Tex. A&M U., College Station, 1969-72, assoc. prof. agrl. engring. dept., 1972-77, prof. agrl. engring. dept., 1977-89, prof. and head agrl. engring. dept., 1989-93, prof., 1993—. Author: Numerical Simulation of Dispersion in Groundwater Aquifers, 1970; assoc. editor: Jour. Environ. Quality, 1979-85, Energy in Agr. (The Netherlands), 1981-85; contbr. articles to profl. jours. Recipient Outstanding Jour. Paper award ASCE Jour. Irrigation and Drainage, 1989. Fellow Am. Soc. Agrl. Engrs. (pres. Tex. sect. 1979-80, ASAE Paper award 1977, 82, Agrl. Engr. of Yr. award Tex. sect. 1975, Disting. Young Agrl. Engr. of Yr. award SW region chpt. 1977); mem. Am. Geophys. Union, NSPE. Achievements include co-development of the Laplace Transform Finite Difference, Laplace Transform Finite Element, Laplace Transform Boundary Element, Laplace Transform Solute Transport techniques for modeling groundwater flow, eliminating the need for discretizing time in numerical simulations; development of Method of Characteristics used to describe solute transport in ground water, of automatic advance rate feedback furrow irrigation system. Home: 3808 Courtney Cir Bryan TX 77802-3407 Office: Tex A&M U Agrl Engring Dept College Station TX 77843

REDDEN, JAMES ANTHONY, federal judge; b. Springfield, Mass., Mar. 13, 1929; s. James A. and Alma (Cheek) R.; m. Joan Ida Johnson, July 13, 1950; children: James A., William F. Student, Boston U., 1951; LL.B., Boston Coll., 1954. Bar: Mass., 1954, Oreg., 1955. Pvt. practice Mass., 1954-55; title examiner Title & Trust Ins. Co., Oreg., 1955; claims adjuster Allstate Ins. Co., 1956; mem. firm Collins, Redden, Ferris & Velure, Medford, Oreg., 1957-73; treas. State of Oreg., 1973-77; atty. gen., 1977-80; U.S. dist. judge, now sr. judge U.S. Dist. Ct. Oreg., Portland, 1980—. Chmn. Oreg. Pub. Employee Relations Bd.; mem. Oreg. Ho. of Reps., 1963-69, minority leader, 1967-69. With AUS, 1946-48. Mem. ABA, Mass. Bar Assn., Oreg. State Bar. Office: US Dist Ct 612 US Courthouse 620 SW Main St Portland OR 97205-3037

REDDEN, LAWRENCE DREW, lawyer; b. Tallassee, Ala., Dec. 16, 1922; s. A. Drew and Berta (Baker) R.; m. Christine U. Cunningham, Dec. 20, 1943. A.B., U. Ala., 1943, LL.B., 1949. Bar: Ala. bar 1949. Since practiced in Birmingham; asst. U.S. atty. No. Dist. Ala., 1949-52; partner firm Rogers, Howard, Redden & Mills, 1952-79, Redden, Mills & Clark, 1979—; Civilian aide for Ala. to sec. army, 1965-69; Mem. Ala. Democratic Exec. Com., 1966-74. Editor-in-chief: Ala. Law Rev, 1948. Trustee Ala. Law Sch. Found.; adv. council Cumberland Law Sch. Served with AUS, 1943-46; maj. gen. Res. ret. Decorated D.S.M.; recipient Outstanding Civilian Service medal Dept. Army, 1970. Fellow Am. Coll. Trial Lawyers, Internat. Soc. Barristers; mem. ABA, Am. Judicature Soc., Ala. Bar Assn. (pres. 1972-73), Birmingham Bar Assn. (past pres.), Ala. Law Inst. (mem. coun.), U. Ala. Law Sch. Alumni Assn. (past pres.), Phi Beta Kappa, Alpha Tau Omega, Omicron Delta Kappa. Baptist. Home: 2513 Beaumont Cir Birmingham AL 35216-1301

REDDEN, NIGEL A., performing company executive; b. Nicosia, Cyprus, Nov. 12, 1950; s. Normand William and Annabel (Austin) R.; m. Arlene Shuler; children: William Austin, Julia Austin. B.A. in Art History, Yale U., 1972. Asst. dir. Italo-American Med. Edn. Found., Rome, 1975-76; press rep. Am. Dance Festival, New London, Conn., 1976; dir. performing arts Walker Art Ctr., Mpls., 1976-82; dir. dance programs Nat. Endowment for the Arts, Washington, 1982-86; gen. mgr. Spoleto Festival USA, Charleston, S.C., 1986-91; exec. dir. Santa Fe (N.Mex.) Opera, 1992-95; exec. prodr. Lincoln Ctr. Festival, N.Y.C., 1995; gen. mgr. Spoleto Festival USA, Charleston, S.C., 1995—; cons., panelist Visual Arts program Nat. Endowment for Arts, 1978, Inter-Arts program, 1979-82, N.W. Area Found., Mpls., 1981-82, MacArthur Found., Chgo., 1983-84; pres. New Music Alliance, Mpls., 1979-80, Am. Music Theater Festival, 1992-94; cons. Tenn. Bicentennial Commn., 1991—, Lincoln Ctr. for Performing Arts, 1994-95. Mem. Century Club. Office: Spoleto Festival USA PO Box 157 Charleston SC 29402

REDDEN, ROGER DUFFEY, lawyer; b. Washington, Dec. 19, 1932; s. Layman J. and Elizabeth (Duffey) R.; m. Gretchen Sause, July 14, 1962. A.B., Yale Coll., 1954; LL.B., U. Md., 1957. Bar: Md. 1958, U.S. Dist. Ct. Md. 1958, U.S. Ct. Appeals (4th cir.) 1958, U.S. Supreme Ct. 1965. Law clk. to judge U.S. Ct. Appeals (4th cir.), 1957-58; assoc. Smith, Somerville & Case, Balt., 1959-63, ptnr., 1965-68; asst. atty. gen. State of Md., 1964-65; ptnr. Piper & Marbury, Balt., 1969—; bd. dirs. Peoples Water Svc. Co.; draftsman Md. State Dept. Legis. Reference, 1958; counsel Md. Savs. and Loan Study Commn., 1960-61; mem. Gov.'s Commn. to revise testamentary laws of Md., 1965-70; mem. standing com. on rules of practice and procedure Md. Ct. Appeals, 1969-73, 88-91, Md. code revision com., 1970—, Appellate Jud. Nominating Commn., 1975-79, Commn. to study Md. Tax Ct., 1978-79, Gov.'s Task Force on Energy, 1991-95; chmn. Task Force on Permits Simplification, 1979-81. Editor in chief Md. Law Rev., 1956-57; contbr. articles to legal jours. Served with U.S. Army, 1958-59, 61-62. Fellow Am. Bar Found., Md. Bar Found.; mem. Md. State Bar Assn. (chmn. probate and estate law sect. 1966-68, chmn. long range planning com. 1972-73, chmn. com. on laws 1988-89, council sect. adminstrv. law 1980-82, council sect. bus. law 1978-81), Balt. City Bar Assn. (chmn. com. on continuing legal edn. 1976-77, chmn. com. on judiciary 1978-79, chmn. com. on by-laws 1981-82), ABA, Jud. Conf. U.S. Ct. Appeals for 4th Cir. (conf. study com. 1982-83). Democrat. Episcopalian. Office: Piper & Marbury 36 S Charles St Baltimore MD 21201-3020

REDDER, THOMAS H., newspaper publishing executive; b. Detroit, 1948. Student, U. Mich., Mich. State U. V.p. info. systems Newsday, Inc., Melville, N.Y. Mem. Data Processing Mgrs. Assn., Newspaper Systems Group. Office: Newsday Inc 235 Pinelawn Rd Melville NY 11747-4226

REDDICLIFFE, STEVEN, editor-in-chief periodical. Office: North America Publishing Inc 1211 Avenue of the Americas New York NY 10036*

REDDIN, GEORGE, religious organization administrator. Dir. Lifeword Broadcast Ministries, Conway, Ark. Office: Lifeword Broadcast Ministries PO Box 6 Conway AR 72033-0006

REDDING, BARBARA J., nursing administrator, occupational health nurse; b. Youngstown, Ohio, Jan. 5, 1938; d. Richard Howard and Helen N. (Price) Sterling; m. Philip L. Redding, Nov. 7, 1957; children: Cheryl L., Jeffrey A., Scott P. Diploma in nursing, Miami Valley Hosp., Dayton, Ohio, 1959; AA in Sociology, Miami U., Oxford, Ohio, 1984; postgrad., U. Cin. RN, Ohio; cert. EMT, CPR, BLS. Office nurse Dr. Stewart Adam, Dayton; primary nurse Miami Valley Hosp; adminstr. employee health Armco Steel Co., L.P., Middletown, Ohio; v.p. Redding Ins. Agy., Inc., Middletown, Ohio, 1993—. Instr. CPR, ARC. Mem. NAFE, Am. Assn. Occupational Health Nurses, Ind. Ins. Agts. Am., Inc. Home: 4501 Riverview Ave Middletown OH 45042-2938

REDDING, EVELYN A., dean, nursing educator; b. Gulfport, Miss., Mar. 13, 1945; d. Arthur Edward and Rebecca (Morris) R. BSN, U. Ala., 1967; MS, Fla. State U., 1971; EdD, Okla. State U., 1974; cert. PNP, Tex. Women's U., 1974; MSN, Wichita State U., 1980. Psychiat. nurse Camp Ponderosa, Mentone, Ala., 1967; dir. health svcs. Community Action Agy., Head Start, Dadeville, Ala., 1967-68; pediatric nurse All Children's Hosp., St. Petersburg, Fla., 1968-69; instr. Sch. Nursing A&M U., Tallahassee, 1969-71; coord. mater and child health Western Ky. U., Bowling Green, 1971-72; dir. grad. program U. Tex. Health Sci. Ctr., Houston, 1974-78; prof., assoc. dean Coll. Nursing U. Tulsa, 1978-81; dean, prof. Coll. Nursing U. Southwestern La., Lafayette, 1981—; presenter in field. Contbr. articles to profl. jours. Mem. policy adv. bd. Northwest Fla. Family Planning Project, 1969-71, Nurses Coalition for Action in Politics; mem. exec. com. Hospice of Acadiana, 1982-85, pres., bd. dirs., 1984; cons. big Bend Comprehensive Svcs. Clinic, Tallahassee, 1970-71; cons. family planning nurse practitioner program Planned Parenthood Ctr., Houston, 1975-78; cons. grad. edn., nurse clinician program Madigan Army Med. Ctr., Washington, 1975; pres. Dirs. Nursing Edn. and Nursing Svc. Acadiana, 1982-83; docent intern Gilcrease Mus.; chairperson Tulsa Area Dirs. Nursing Svc. and Nursing Edn. Mem. AAUW (cultural affairs and community com.), ANA, Nat. League for Nursing, ANA Coun. Nurse Researchers, Soc. for Rsch. Nursing Edn., La. State Nurses Assn. (program com. dist. IV 1986), Okla. Nurses Assn. (nurse edn. com. dist. 2 1978-79, by-laws com. 1978-80), Tex. Nurses Assn. (chairperson task force for profl. self-determination 1976-78), Coun. Adminstrs. Nursing Edn. La. (presenter 1987-88), Sigma Theta Tau, Omicron Nu. Avocations: bike riding, reading, fishing, yard work. Home: 125 Alyene Dr Lafayette LA 70506-6811 Office: U Southwestern La Coll Nursing PO Box 42490 Lafayette LA 70504-2490

REDDING, PETER STODDARD, manufacturing company executive; b. Bklyn., June 27, 1938; s. Kenneth Benckert and Frances Elizabeth (Hasselman) R.; m. Mary Lorelei LeBrun, Feb. 4, 1961; children: Shelagh, Mark, Todd, Jill. BA, U. Md., 1960; M in Decision Scis., Ga. State U., 1974. Dept. mgr. trainee J.C. Penney Co., 1960-62; sales rep. Standard Register Co., Washington, 1962-66, asst. dist. sales mgr., Washington, 1966-68, Atlanta, 1968-69, dist. sales mgr., Atlanta, 1969-76, regional sales mgr. Pacific region, Orinda, Calif., 1976-79, asst. to pres., Dayton, Ohio, 1979-81, v.p. mktg., 1981-87, sr. v.p., 1987-90, exec. v.p. adminstrn., 1990. exec. v.p., gen. mgr. Forms Div., 1990-94, exec. v.p., COO, 1994, pres., CEO, 1994—; trustee The Children's Med. Ctr., Dayton, Human Race Theatre, Vitoria Theater Assn., Dayton Country Club, Country Club of the North, Orinda Country Club, Racquet Club, Rotary; bd. mem. standard register Soc. Bank, So. Ohio Divsn. Republican. Roman Catholic. Home: 4966 Ashwyck Pl Dayton OH 45429-1902 Office: Standard Register Co 600 Albany St Dayton OH 45408-1405

REDDING, ROGERS WALKER, physics educator; b. Louisville, July 15, 1942; s. George Walker and Carolyn Lorraine (Rogers) R.; m. Jennie Ruth Fincher, Sept. 6, 1966 (div.); children: Jeffrey Walker, Jonathan Hull; m. Shirley Rubrecht, Aug. 24, 1991. BS, Georgia Tech., 1965; PhD, Vanderbilt U., 1969. Research assoc. Nat. Bur. Standards, Washington, 1969-70; from asst. prof. to assoc. prof. North Tex. State U. (name now U. North Tex.), Denton, 1970-78, prof. physics, 1978-94, dept. chmn., 1980-87, dir. Tex. Acad. Math. and Sci., 1987-89, assoc. dean arts and scis., 1990-94; prof. physics, dean Coll. Arts and Scis. No. Ky. U., Highland Heights; disting. vis. prof. USAF Acad., 1989-90. Author: Exploring Physics, 1984; contbr. articles to profl. jours. Mem. Am. Phys. Soc., Am. Assn. Physics Tchrs., AAAS, Optical Soc. Am. Democrat. Lodge: Kiwanis. Avocations: handball, jogging, referee college football, little league coach. Home: 10501 Cheshire Ridge Florence KY 41042 Office: No Ky U Coll Arts & Scis Highland Heights KY 41099

REDDY, ERAGAM PREMKUMAR, medical educator; b. Madanapalli, India, Jan. 2, 1944; married; 2 children. BS in Chemistry, Botany, Zoology, Osmania U., India, 1962, MS in Chemistry, 1965, PhD in Molecular Biology, 1971. Rsch. scholar Indian Coun. Sci. and Indsl. Rsch., Hyderabad, 1965-72; NIH postdoctoral fellow UCLA, 1972-73; Fogarty Internat. postdoctoral fellow Nat. Cancer Inst., 1974-75; head viral immunology program Microbiol. Assocs., Bethesda, Md., 1975-78; vis. scientist Lab. Cellular and Molecular Biology, Nat. Cancer Inst., 1978-82, chief molecular genetics sect., 1982-84; rsch. leader dept. molecular oncology Hoffman-LaRoche, Inc., Nutley, N.J., 1984-85; full mem. Roche Inst. Molecular Biology, Nutley, 1985-86; prof. The Wistar Inst., Phila., 1986-91; Wister prof. pathology U. Pa., Phila., 1987-91; dep. dir. Wistar Inst., Phila., 1991-92; dir. Fels Inst. for Cancer Rsch. and Molecular Biology, Phila., 1992—; bd. dirs. Nat. Inst. Environ. Health Scis., NIH, 1990-95, mem. cell biology, physiology study sect.-2, 1984-89; invited participant nat. and internat. sci. meetings, workshops and symposia; Laura H. Carnell prof. medicine Temple U., Phila., 1993—. Editor: Oncogene, 1987—, The Oncogene Handbook, 1988; assoc. editor Jour. Cellular Biochemistry, 1994. Adv. com. State of N.J. Commn. on Cancer Rsch., 1987—; adv. com. on cell and developmental biology Am. Cancer Soc., 1984. Recipient Sci. Achievement award Am. Cancer Soc., 1993. Mem. AAAS, Internat. Assn. for Comparative Rsch. on Leukemia and Related Diseases. Office: Fels Inst Cancer Rsch 3420 N Broad St Philadelphia PA 19140

REDDY, GOPAL BAIREDDY, engineering educator; b. Palwai, India, May 11, 1950; came to U.S., 1974; s. B. Soogi and B. Govindamma Reddy; m. Shanti Baireddy, June 27, 1981; children: Kasthuri, Madhuri, Sumana, Bhargava. BE, Osmania U., Hyderabad, India, 1974; MS, Tex. Tech. U., 1976; PhD, N.C. State U., 1986. Lectr. U. N.C., Charlotte, 1976-78, 81-83; pool officer Coun. Sci. and Indsl. Rsch., Hyderabad, 1980-81; asst. prof. Fairleigh Dickinson U., Teaneck, N.J., 1986-90, Trenton (N.J.) State Coll., 1990-91; assoc. prof. U. Houston, 1991—; cons. in field. Contbr. articles to Internat. Jour. Heat and Mass Transfer, Internat. Jour. Energy Rsch., Computers in Edn., Internat. Jour. Ambient Energy. Mem. ASME (dir. coll. rels. 1987-90, Outstanding Contribution award 1989), Am. Soc. Engring. Edn. (Outstanding Campus Rep award 1989), Soc. Mfg. Engring., Tau Beta Pi. Home: 35 Fernglen Dr The Woodlands TX 77380-1557 Office: U Houston College Park Houston TX 77204-4083

REDDY, HELEN MAXINE, singer; b. Melbourne, Australia, Oct. 25, 1941; came to U.S., 1966; d. Max David and Stella Campbell (Lamond) R.; m. Jeff Wald, Nov. 1, 1966 (div.); children: Traci Donat, Jordan; m. Milton Robert Ruth (div. 1996). Student, UCLA Extension. Ind. entertainer, rec. artist, actress, 1966—; pres. entertainment prodn. co. Helen Reddy, Inc., 1983—. Rec. artist, composer I Am Woman, 1973 (Grammy award 1973); rec. artist: Delta Dawn, 1978, Crazy Love, I Don't Know How To Love Him, Peaceful, Keep On Singing, You and Me Against The World, Angie Baby, 1978, Leave Me Alone, 1978; star NBC Summer Show, 1973, permanent host Midnight Special; actress: (films) Airport, 1975, Pete's Dragon, 1977; (theatre) Blood Brothers, 1994, 95 (Broadway and England). Active Nat. Women's Polit. Caucus, Women's Ctr., Alliance for Women in Prison; commr. Calif. Dept. Parks and Recreation. Recipient Image award NAACP, 1974, Humanitarian award B'nai B'rith, N.Y., 1975, Maggie award People Helping People, L.A., 1976, numerous Gold and Platinum Album awards Rec. Industry Assn. Am.; named Woman of Yr., L.A. Times, 1975; honoree for her advocacy for women's health issues and AIDS, Weizmann Inst. of Sci. Founders Event, 1993. Mem. NOW.

REDDY, JANARDAN K., medical educator; b. Moolasaal, India, Oct. 7, 1938. MB, BS, Osmania U., Hyderabad, India, 1961; MD in Pathology, All India Inst. Med. Scis., 1965. Lic. physicain, Mo., Kans., Ill.; diplomate Am. Bd. Pathology. Rotating house officer Osmania Gen. Hosp., 1961-62; instr. pathology Kakatiya Med. Coll., Warangal, India, 1962-63, asst. prof., 1965-66; resident fellow pathology U. Kans. Med. Ctr., 1966-68, rsch. fellow pathology, 1968-70, asst. prof., 1970-73, assoc. prof., 1973-76, prof., 1976; prof. pathology Northwestern U. Med. Sch., Chgo., 1976—; dir. med. scientist tng. program Northwestern U. Med. Sch., 1990-93, chmn. pathology, 1993—; dir. anatomic pathology Northwestern Meml. Hosp., 1978-81, mem. med. staff, 1976—; mem. Northwestern U. Cancer Ctr., 1976—; mem. med. staff VA Lakeside Hosp., 1990—; group leader Chem.Carcinogenesis Rsch. Group, Northwestern U. Cancer Ctr., 1990—, assoc. dir. cancer edn., 1991—; mem. Task Force on an Environ. Sci./Policy Initiative, Northwestern U., 1991—; chmn. NIH clin. scis. study sect., 1990-91; mem. NIH spl. study sect., 1992; mem. com. on comparative toxicity of naturally occurring carcinogens, 1993—; mem. Nat. Toxicology Program Rev. Com., 1992—; mem. monograph com. WHO, Internat. Agy. on Cancer Rsch., Lyon, France, 1994. Mem. editl. bds. Jour. Histochemistry and Cytochemistry, 1973-76, Exptl. Pathology, 1982—, Toxicologic Pathology, 1983—, Internat. Jour. Pancreatology, 1986—, Lab. Investigation, 1988—, Carcinogenesis, 1989—, The Jour. Northwestern U. Cancer Ctr., 1990—, Gene Expression, 1990—, Internat. Jour. Toxicology, Occupational and Environ. Health, 1992—, Life Sci. Advanced, Oncology, 1991—; assoc. editor Jour. Toxicology and Environ. Health, 1984—, Cancer Rsch., 1985-90. Grantee Joseph Mayberry Endowment Fund, Cancer Rsch. Found., 1991-93, NIEHS, 1995—, NIGMS, 1992-97, NIDDK, 1995—, NIGMS, 1992-97; merit scholar Osmania U., 1954-61, Govt. of Andhra Pradesh merit scholar, 1963-65; WHO Yamagiwa-Yoshida Internat. Cancer fellow in Japan, 1985; recipient NIH merit award, 1987, UN Devel. Programme-Tokten award, 1988, Fletscher scholar award, 1991; named George H. Joost Outstanding Basic Sci. Tchr., 1995. Mem. AAAS, Assn. Scientists of Indian Origin in Am. (pres. 1983-84, sr. scientist award 1991), Soc. Toxicology (v.p. molecular toxicology speciality sect. 1990-91, pres. 1991-92, pres. carcinogenesis specialty sect. 1990-91, Kenneth P. Dubois award 1990), Am. Pancreatic Assn., Am. Assn. Pathologists (mem. program com. 1989-93), Am. Assn. Cancer Rsch. (mem. program com. 1990-91), Internat. Acad. Pathology, Am. Soc. Cell Biology, Histochem. Soc., Soc. Exptl. Biology and Medicine, Biochem. Soc. London, Soc. Toxicology Pathologists, Internat. Assn. Pancreatology, N.Y. Acad. Scis. Home: 1212 Asbury Ave Evanston IL 60202 Office: Northwestern U Med Sch Dept Pathology Ward 6-204 303 E Chicago Ave Chicago IL 60611-3008

REDDY, KAMBHAM RAJA, plant physiology educator; b. Ambuvari Palli, India, July 1, 1953; came to U.S., 1988; s. Kambi Kambham and Ammannamma (Reddy) R.; m. Anasuya Kambham, Feb. 9, 1982; 1 child, Sasank. BSc, S.V. U., Tirupati, India, 1975, MSc in Botany, 1977, PhD in Botany, 1984. Curator in botany S.V. U., 1977-88; asst. prof. plant physiology Miss. State U., 1988—; vis. scientist Govt. of India, 1988. Contbg. author: Climate Change and Agriculture: Analysis of Potential International Impacts, 1995; contbr. articles to profl. jours. Mem. Agronomy Soc. Am., Crop Sci. Soc. Am., Biol. Sys. Simulation Work Group, Gamma Sigma Delta (Rsch. award of merit 1995). Achievements include development of new theories and concepts in plant growth regulation and incorporated into a cotton model GOSSYM/COMAX, used by cotton producers, consultants and researchers across the cotton belt. Home: PO Box 3648 Mississippi State MS 39762-3648 Office: Mississippi State U PO Box 5367 Mississippi State MS 39762-5367

REDDY, KRISHNA NARAYANA, artist, educator; b. Chittoor, India, July 15, 1925; s. Narayana B. and Laksmamma R.; m. Judith Blum, June 30, 1967; 1 child, Aparna. Diploma in Fine Arts, Internat. U. Santiniketan, India, 1947; cert. in Fine Arts, Slade Sch. Fine Arts, U. London, 1952; student of Zadkine in sculpture, Academie Grande Chaumière, Paris, 1952-55; student of Marino Marini in sculpture, Academia di Belle Arti di Brera, Milan, 1956-57; specialist in Gravure, Internat. Ctr. for Graphics, Atelier 17, Paris, 1953-55; D.Litt. (hon.), S.V. Univ., India, 1984. Asst. dir. Internat. Ctr. for Graphics, Atelier 17, Paris, 1957-64, prof., co-dir., 1964-76; prof. art, dir. graphics and printmaking program, dept. art and art edn. N.Y. U., N.Y.C., 1977—; lectr. art Arundale Montessori Tchrs. Tng. Center, 1948-49; dir. art dept. Coll. Fine Arts, Kalakshetra, Madras, India, 1947-49; vis. prof. Yale U. Summer Sch. Music and Art, 1978, Am. U., 1964, Kala Inst. Graphics, Berkeley, Calif., 1979, U. Calif., Santa Cruz, 1979; Andrew Mellon vis. prof. Cooper Union Sch. Art and Architecture, 1977; prof. U. Wis., Madison, 1973, U. Calif., Davis, 1970-71; guest prof. Yale U. Summer Sch. Music and Art, 1973. Retrospective exhbns., Bronx Mus. Arts, 1981-82, Indian Council for Cultual Relations, Ministry of Culture and India Nat. Acad. Fine Arts, 1984-85, Museo del Palacio de Bellas Artes, Mexico City, 1988-89. Recipient Gagan-Abani Puraskar Nat. award Viswa-Bharati, 1983; named Featured Guest Artist Printmaker of Yr., Northwest Print Council Ann. Meeting, 1985. Title of Padma Shree awarded by Pres. of India, 1972. Home: 80 Wooster St New York NY 10012-4347 Office: NYU Dept Art and Art Edn New York NY 10003

REDDY, NAGENDRANATH K., biochemist, researcher; b. Bangalore, India, Nov. 18, 1937; came to U.S., 1968; s. K. Rami and K. (Gnanamma) R.; m. Saraswati K., May 11, 1967; children: Kalpana, Sandip. BS, SRI Venkateswara U., Andhra, India, 1957; MS, U. Saugor, Madhya Pradesh, India, 1959; PhD, Indian Inst. Sci., Bangalore, 1971. Jr. research asst. Nat. Dairy Research Inst., Bangalore, 1959-60; sr. research asst. Indian Inst. Sci., Bangalore, 1965-68; research assoc. Roswell Park Meml. Inst., Buffalo, 1968-73; asst. prof. U. Cin., 1975-80; asst. prof. research biochemistry U. So. Calif., L.A., 1980-90; biochemist Sci. Svcs. Bur., L.A., 1990—. Editor: Fibrinolysis, 1980; patentee fibrinolytic enzyme from snake venom; contbr. articles to profl. jours. Recipient Research Career Devel. award NIH, 1978. Mem. AAAS, Am. Soc. Biol. Chemists. Avocation: internet surfing. Home: 3402 S Punta Del Este Dr La Puente CA 91745-6634

REDDY, PRATAP CHANDUPATLA, cardiologist, educator, researcher; b. Laxmipur, Andhra Pradesh, India, Apr. 12, 1944; came to U.S., 1969; s. Chandra C. and Butchamma (Kota) R.; m. Shobha Katangur, May 15, 1971; children: Ashutosh, Kirthi. MBBS, Osmania U., Hyderabad, India, 1968. Diplomate Am. Bd. Internal Medicine, Am. Bd. Cardiovascular Diseases. Resident in internal medicine St. Vincent Med. Ctr., S.I., N.Y., 1969-73; fellow in cardiology Maimonide Med. Ctr., Bklyn., 1973-74; rsch. assoc. USPHS Hosp., S.I., 1974-76; asst. prof. medicine U. Ky., Lexington, 1976-81, dir. cardiac electrophysiology, 1976-84, assoc. prof., 1981-84; prof. medicine La. State U. Med. Ctr., Shreveport, 1984—, assoc. dir. cardiology, 1984—, dir. cardiac electrophysiology program, 1984—; attending cardiologist VA Med. Ctr., Shreveport, La. Editor: Tachycardia, 1984; contbr. articles to profl. jours. Named Kentucky Colonel Gov. Ky., 1983. Fellow ACP, Am. Coll. Cardiology; mem. AMA, Am. Heart Assn. (v.p. La. affiliate 1988-89, pres. 1991-92, mem. coun. clin. cardiology), Cen. Soc. for Clin. Rsch., N.Am. Soc. Pacing and Electrophysiology. Office: La State U Med Sch 1530 Kings Hwy Shreveport LA 71103-4229

REDDY, THIKKAVARAPU RAMACHANDRA, electrical engineer; b. Nellore, India, June 4, 1944; came to the U.S., 1979; s. Thikkavarapu Kota and Saraswathi T. (Sivareddy) R.; m. Padmavathi Reddy Kakuturu Thikkavarapu, Aug. 17, 1973; children: Lavanya T., Samatha T. BSEE, Osmania U., 1968; diploma in computer sci., Coll. Engring., Madras, India, 1978. Cert. profl. engr., chartered engr. Supervising engr. APSE Bd., Hyderabad, India, 1969-79; elec. design engr. Sargent & Lundy, Chgo., 1979-80; engr. Bechtel Corp., San Francisco, 1980-82; supr. Bechtel Corp., Athens, Ala., 1989-92; sr. project engr. EGS, Inc., Huntsville, Ala., 1983-84; sr. start-up engr. Gilbert Commonwealth Co., Reading, Pa., 1984-86; cons. Quantum Resources, Decatur, Ala., 1986-87; prin. engr. Ebasco Svcs. Inc., N.Y.C., 1987-89; pres. LSP Internat. Inc., Huntsville, 1992—; guest lectr. gen. interest and wide range of engring. issues. Author: Qualification of Electrical Distribution Components, 1984, Thermal Aging Techniques of Organic Materials, 1984, and others; contbr. articles to profl. jours. Mem. NSPE (outstanding profl. award 1991, Profl. Engr. of Yr. 1996), IEEE (meritorious svc. award 1985), C. of C., Ala. Soc. Profl. Engrs., Commonwealth Engrs. Coun., Project Mgmt. Inst., Am. Telugu Assn. (life), TANA (life), Internat. Platform Assn. Avocations: journalism, watching TV, table tennis, community service, anthropology. Home: 1213 Willowbrook Dr SE Apt 7 Huntsville AL 35802-3800

REDDY, YENAMALA RAMACHANDRA, metal processing executive; b. Polavaram, Andhra, India, Feb. 12, 1939; came to U.S., 1974; s. Y. Venkata and Y. Lakshamamma Reddy; m. Y. Uma Reddy, May 30, 1965; children: Y. Sharath, Y. Jay. BME, S.V. U., Andhra, 1961; M in Tech., IIT, Bombay, 1966, PhD, 1970. Lic. profl. engr., Wis. Asst. prof. IIT, Bombay, 1966-69; research and devel. mgr. Jyoti Pumps, Baroda, 1973-74; chief engr. Patterson Pumps, Toccoa, Ga., 1974-80; pres. R.B. Pump Co., Baxley, 1980—, U.B. Cons., Ga., 1980—. Contbr. articles to tech. jours. Postdoctoral fellow U. of Tech., Loughborough, Eng., 1970-73. Mem. Am. Soc. of Mech. Engrs. Office: R B Pump Co 1 Dixie Dr # 557 Baxley GA 31513

REDEKER, ALLAN GRANT, physician, medical educator; b. Lincoln, Nebr., Sept. 10, 1924; s. Fred Julius and Fern Frances (Grant) R.; m. Andrea K. Siedschlag, June 16, 1979; children by previous marriage—Martha, James, Thomas. B.S., Northwestern U., Chgo., 1949, M.D., 1952. Intern Hollywood Presbyn. Hosp., Los Angeles, 1952-53; resident in internal medicine Hollywood Presbyn. Hosp., 1953-54; asst. prof. medicine U. So. Calif., 1959-62, assoc. prof., 1962-69, prof., 1969—; mem. Nat. Digestive Diseases Adv. Bd., 1985-88; mem. U.S.-Japan Med. Sci. Program, U.S. Dept. State, 1978—; bd. dirs. Am. Liver Found. Contbr. numerous articles to research jours. Served with AUS, 1943-46. Recipient Research Career Devel. award NIH, 1962-69; research fellow Giannini Found., 1956-58. Mem. Assn. Am. Physicians, Am. Soc. Clin. Investigation, Am. Gastroent. Assn. Home: 9323 Samoline Ave Downey CA 90240-2716 Office: 7601 Imperial Hwy Downey CA 90242-3456

REDENBACH, SANDRA IRENE, educational consultant; b. Boston, Nov. 18, 1940; d. David and Celia (Wish) Goldstein; m. Gunter L. Redenbach, Mar. 16, 1963 (div. 1980); 1 child, Cori-Lin; m. Kenneth L. Gelatt, June 25, 1989. BA, U. Calif., Davis, 1972; MEd in Ednl. Leadership, St. Mary's Coll., Moraga, Calif., 1995. Cert. tchr., Calif. Tchr. Solano County Juvenile Hall, Fairfield, Calif., 1968-70, St. Basil's Sch., Vallejo, Calif., 1970-73, St. Philomenes Sch., Sacramento, 1973; tchr., assoc. dean Vet.'s Spl. Edn. Program, U. Calif., Davis, 1973-75, Woodland (Calif.) Jr. High Sch., 1973-76, Lee Jr. High Sch., Woodland, 1976-79, Woodland High Sch., 1979-87; founder, coord., tchr. Ind. Learning Ctr., Woodland, 1987-94; dir. curriculum and instrn. Dixon (Calif.) Unified Sch. Dist., 1994—; teaching asst., lectr. U. Calif., Davis, 1985-86; pres., cons. Esteem Seminar Programs and Pubs., Davis, 1983—; cons., leader workshop. Author: Self-Esteem: The Necessary Ingredient for Success, 1991; author tng. manual: Self-Esteem: A Training Manual, 1990-91, Innovative Discipline: Managing Your Own Flight Plan, 1994, Autobiography of a Dropout: Dear Diary, 1996. Active Dem. Club of Davis, 1976-79; human rights chair Capitol Svc. Ctr., Sacramento, 1987-92. Martin Luther King scholar, 1986; Nat. Found. for Improvement of Edn. grantee, 1987-88. Mem. Assn. Calif. Sch. Adminstrs., Woodland Edn. Assn. (pres. 1980-83, Outstanding Educator 1992, 93), Phi Delta Kappa (pres. 1992-93). Jewish. Avocations: singing, acting, dancing, travel, theatre. Home: 313 Del Oro Ave Davis CA 95616-0416 Office: Esteem Seminar Programs & Publs 313 Del Oro Ave Davis CA 95616-0416

REDFERN, JOHN D., manufacturing company executive; b. 1935. Grad. Queen's U., Kingston, Ont., 1958, DEng (honoris causa), Carleton U., 1992. With Lafarge Can. Inc. (formerly Can. Cement Lafarge Ltd.), Montreal, 1977—, pres., chief exec. officer, 1977-84, chmn., 1985—; chmn. bd. parent co. Lafarge Corp., Reston, Va., 1985-88, vice-chmn., 1989— Office: Lafarge Can Inc, 606 Cathcart Ste 800, Montreal, PQ Canada H3B 1L7

REDFORD, DONALD BRUCE, historian, archaeologist; b. Toronto, Ont., Can., Sept. 2, 1934; s. Cyril Fitzjames and Kathleen Beryl (Coe) R.; m. Susan Pirritano, Jan. 30, 1982; children: Alexander, Aksel; children by previous marriage: Christopher, Philip. B.A., U. Toronto, 1957, M.A., 1958; Ph.D., Brown U., 1965. Lectr. Brown U., 1960-61; lectr. U. Toronto, 1961-64, asst. prof. Egyptian history and language, 1965-67, asso. prof., 1967-69, prof., 1969—; site supr. Brit. Sch. Archaeol. Excavations, Jerusalem, 1964-67; dir. Soc. Study Egyptian Antiquities Expdn. to, Karnak, Egypt, 1970-72, Akhenaten Temple Project, Luxor, Egypt, 1972—; research asso. Univ. Museum, U. Pa., Royal Ont. Mus.; vis. prof. Ben Gurion U., Beersheva, Israel, 1986, U. Pa., 1995-96. Author: History and Chronology of the Egyptian 18th Dynasty, 1967, A Study of the Biblical Joseph Story, 1970, Papyrus and Tablet, 1973, The Akhenaten Temple Project, vol. I, 1977, Akhenaten, the Heretic King, 1984; Annals, King-Lists and Daybooks, 1986, The Akhenaten Temple Project, vol. II, 1988, Egypt, Canaan and Israel in Ancient Times, 1992. Killam grantee, 1975-79; Smithsonian Fgn. Currency grantee, 1973-76, 1979, Social Scis. Humanities Research Council Can. grantee, 1980—. Fellow Royal Soc. Can. Discovered Temple of Akhenaten at Luxor, 1976. Office: U Toronto, Dept Near Eastern Studies, Toronto, ON Canada M5S 1A1

REDFORD, ROBERT (CHARLES ROBERT REDFORD), actor, director; b. Santa Monica, Calif., Aug. 18, 1937; m. Lola Van Wegenen (div.); children: Shauna, Jamie, Amy. Student, U. Colo., Pratt Inst. Design, Am. Acad. Dramatic Arts; LHD (hon.), U. Colo., 1987; D (hon.), U. Mass., 1990. Owner ski resort Sundance, Provo, Utah. Stage appearances include: Tall Story, The Highest Tree, Sunday in New York, Barefoot in the Park; Films include: (actor) War Hunt, 1961, Situation Hopeless But Not Serious, 1965, Inside Daisy Clover, 1965, The Chase, 1966, This Property Is Condemned, 1966, Barefoot in the Park, 1967, Butch Cassidy and the Sundance Kid, 1969, Tell Them Willie Boy is Here, 1969, Little Fauss and Big Halsey, 1970, The Hot Rock, 1972, Jeremiah Johnson, 1972, The Way We Were, 1973, The Sting, 1973 (Academy award nominee), The Great Gatsby, 1974, The Great Waldo Pepper, 1975, Three Days of the Condor, 1975, A Bridge Too Far, 1977, The Electric Horseman, 1979, Brubaker, 1980, The Natural, 1984, Out of Africa, 1985, Legal Eagles, 1986, Havana, 1990, Sneakers, 1992, Indecent Proposal, 1993, Up Close and Personal, 1996; (actor, exec. prodr.) Downhill Racer, 1969, The Candidate, 1972, All The President's Men, 1976; (exec. prodr.) Promised Land, 1988, Some Girls, 1988, The Dark Wind; (exec. prodr., narrator) Yosemite: The Fate of Heaven, 1989, Incident at Ogala, 1992; (dir.) Ordinary People, 1980 (Academy and Golden Globe Awards, Best Director); (dir., prodr.) The Milagro Beanfield War, 1988, Quiz Show, 1994; (dir., prodr., narrator) A River Runs Through It, 1993. Recipient Audubon medal, 1989, Dartmouth Film Soc. award, 1990; Cecil B. Demille Golden Globe Award for Lifetime Achievement, 1994. *

REDGRAVE, LYNN, actress; b. London, Eng., Mar. 8, 1943; d. Michael Scudemore and Rachel (Kempson) R.; m. John Clark, Apr. 2, 1967; children: Benjamin, Kelly, Annabel. Ed., Queensgate Sch., London, Central Sch. Speech and Drama, London. Stage debut as Helena in Midsummer Night's Dream, 1962; theatrical appearances include The Tulip Tree, Andorra, Hayfever, Much Ado About Nothing, Mother Courage, Love for Love, Zoo, Zoo, Widdershins Zoo, Edinburgh Festival, 1969, The Two of Us, London, 1970, Slag, London, 1971, A Better Place, Dublin, 1972, Born Yesterday, Greenwich, 1973, Hellzapoppin, N.Y., 1976, California Suite, 1977, Twelfth Night, Stratford Conn. Shakespeare Festival, 1978, The King and I, St. Louis, 1983, Les Liaisons Dangereuses, L.A., 1989, The Cherry Orchard, L.A., 1990, Three Sisters, London, 1990; Broadway appearances include Black Comedy, 1967, My Fat Friend, 1974, Mrs. Warren's Profession (Tony award nomination), 1975, Knock, Knock, 1976, St. Joan, 1977, Sister Mary Ignatius Explains It All, 1985, Aren't We All?, 1985, Sweet Sue, 1987, A Little Hotel on the Side, 1992, The Masterbuilder, 1992, Shakespeare For My Father (Tony and Drama Desk nominations, Elliot award 1993), 1993, also nat. tour, 1993; film appearances include Tom Jones, Girl With Green Eyes, Georgy Girl (Recipient N.Y. Film Critics award, Golden Globe award, Oscar nomination for best actress 1967), The Deadly Affair, Smashing Time, The Virgin Soldiers, Last of the Mobile Hotshots, Don't Turn the Other Cheek, Every Little Crook and Nanny, Everything You Always Wanted to Know About Sex, The National Health, The Happy Hooker, The Big Bus, Sunday Lovers, Morgan Stuart's Coming Home, Getting It Right; TV appearances include: The Turn of the Screw, Centennial, 1978, The Muppets, Gauguin the Savage, Beggarman Thief, The Seduction of Miss Leona, Rehearsal for Murder, 1982, Walking On Air, The Faintheart Feminist (BBC-TV), 1984, My Two Loves, 1986, The Old Reliable, 1988, Jury Duty 1989, Whatever Happened to Baby Jane, 1990, Fighting Back (BBC-TV), 1992, Calling the Shots (Masterpiece Theatre), 1993; guest appearances include Carol Burnett Show, Evening at the Improv and Steve Martin's Best show Ever, Circus of the Stars; co-host nat. TV syndication Not for Women Only, 1977—; nat., TV spokesperson Weightwatchers, 1984-92; TV series include House Calls, 1981, Teachers Only, 1982, Chicken Soup, 1989; albums: Make Mine Manhattan, 1978, Cole Porter Revisited, 1979; video: (for children) Meet Your Animal Friends, Off We Go, Off We Go Again: audio book readings include, Pride and Prejudice, The Shell Seekers, The Blue Bedroom, The Anastasia Syndrome, The Women in His Life, Snow In April, Gone With The Wind, 1994; author: This is Living, 1990. Named Runner-up Actress, All Am. Favorites, Box Office Barometer 1975; recipient Sarah Siddons award as Chgo.'s best stage actress of 1976, 94. Mem. The Players (pres. 1994). Office: care John Clark PO Box 1207 Topanga CA 90290-1207*

REDGRAVE, VANESSA, actress; b. London, Jan. 30, 1937; d. Michael and Rachel (Kempson) R.; m. Tony Richardson, Apr. 28, 1962 (div.); children: Natasha Jane, Joely Kim, Carlo. Student, Central Sch. Speech and Drama, London, 1955-57. Prin. theatrical roles include Helena in Midsummer Night's Dream, 1959, Stella in Tiger and the Horse, 1960, Katerina in The Taming of the Shrew, 1961, Rosalind in As You Like It, 1961, Imogene in Cymbeline, 1962, Nina in The Seagull, 1964, Miss Brodie in The Prime of Miss Jean Brodie, 1966; other plays include Cato Street, 1971, Threepenny Opera, 1972, Twelfth Night, 1972, Antony and Cleopatra, 1973, Design for Living, 1973, Macbeth, 1975, Lady from the Sea, 1976, 78, 79, The Aspern Papers, 1984, The Seagull, 1985, Chekhov's Women, 1985, The Taming of the Shrew, Ghosts, 1986, Touch of the Poet, 1988, Orpheus Descending, 1989, A Madhouse in Goa, 1989, Three Sisters, 1990, When She Danced, 1991, Heartbreak House, 1991, Maybe, 1993, Brecht in Hollywood, 1994, Vita and Virginia, 1994—; film roles include Leonie in Morgan-A Suitable Case for Treatment, 1965 (Best Actress award Cannes Film Festival 1966), Sheila in Sailor from Gibraltar, 1965, Anne-Marie in La Musica, 1965, Jane in Blow-Up, 1967, Guinevere in Camelot, 1967, Isadora in Isadora Duncan, 1968 (Best Actress award Cannes Film Festival); other films include The Charge of the Light Brigade, 1968, The Seagull, 1968, A Quiet Place in the Country, 1968, Daniel Deronda, 1969, Dropout, 1969, The Trojan Women, 1970, The Devils, 1970, The Holiday, 1971, Mary, Queen of Scots, 1971, Murder on the Orient Express, 1974, Winter Rates, 1974, 7 per cent solution, 1975, Julia, 1977 (Academy award Best Supporting Actress, Golden Globe award), Agatha, 1978, Yanks, 1978, Bear Island, 1979, Playing for Time, 1980, My Body My Child, 1981, Wagner, 1982, The Bostonians, 1984 (Oscar nomination Best Actress, Golden Globe nomination), Wetherby, 1985, Steaming, 1985, Prick Up Your Ears, 1987, Comrades, 1987, Consuming Passions, 1988, Diceria dell'Untore, 1989, The Ballad of the Sad Café, 1990, Howard's End, 1992 (Oscar nomination Best Supporting Actress), Great Moments in Aviation, 1993, Crime and Punishment, 1993, The House of the Spirits, 1994, Mother's Boys, 1994, A Month by the Lake, 1995, Little Odessa, 1995; TV film and miniseries appearances include Snow White and the Seven Dwarfs, 1985, Three Sovereigns for Sarah, 1985, Peter the Great, 1986, Second Serve, 1986 (Emmy award, Golden Globe award), A Man for

All Seasons, 1988, Young Catherine, 1990, Whatever Happened to Baby Jane, 1990, Playing for Time (Emmy award), The Wall, 1992, Down Came A Blackbird, 1994; Author: Pussies and Tigers, 1964, (autobiography) Vanessa, 1991, Vanessa Redgrave: An Autobiography, 1994. Bd. govs. Central Sch. Speech and Drama, 1963—. Decorated comdr. Order Brit. Empire; recipient 4 times Drama award Evening Standard, 1961-91, Best Actress award Variety Club Gt. Brit., 1961, 66, Best Actress award Brit. Guild TV Producers and Dirs., 1966, Laurence Olivier award Best Actress for The Aspern Papers, 1984, London Standard Drama award Best Actress for The Seagull, 1985, New York Film Critics Circle award Best Supporting Actress for Prick Up Your Ears, 1988, Evening Standard award Best Actress for When She Danced, 1991, Ace award Best Supporting Actress movie/miniseries for Young Catherine, 1992, Variety Club of Great Britain award, 1992, Best Actress Nat. Film Critics (USA) New Delhi Internat. Film Festival for The Bostonians, Laurence Olivier award Actress of the Yr. in a Revival for A Touch of the Poet; fellow Brit. Film Inst., 1988.

REDHEAD, PAUL AVELING, physicist; b. Brighton, Eng., May 25, 1924; m. Doris Packman, 1948; children: Janet, Patricia. BA with honors in Physics, Cambridge (Eng.) U., 1944, MA, 1948, PhD, 1969. Sci. officer dept. naval ordnance Brit. Admiralty, 1944-45, svcs. electronics rsch. lab., 1945-47; rsch. officer NRC Can., Ottawa, Ont., 1947-69; dir. planning group NRC Can., 1970-72, dir.-gen. planning, 1972-73, dir. div. physics, 1973-86, chmn. com. of lab. dirs., 1981-86, sec. sci. and tech. policy com., 1986-89, researcher emeritus, 1989—. Author: Physical Basis of Ultrahigh Vacuum, 1968, 2d edit., 1993; editor: Jour. Vacuum Scis. and Tech., 1969-74; contbr. numerous articles to profl. jours. Fellow IEEE, Royal Soc. Can., Am. Phys. Soc., Am. Vacuum Soc. (past pres., Medard W. Welch award 1975); mem. Can. Assn. Physicists (medal for achievement in physics 1989). Patentee in field. Home: 1958 Norway Crescent, Ottawa, ON Canada K1H 5N7 Office: Nat Rsch Coun Can, Inst Microstructural Scis, Ottawa, ON Canada K1A OR6

REDHEFFER, RAYMOND MOOS, mathematician, educator; b. Chgo., Apr. 17, 1921; s. Raymond L. and Elizabeth (Moos) R.; m. Heddy Gross Stiefel, Aug. 25, 1951; 1 son, Peter Bernard. S.B., MIT, 1943, S.M., 1946, Ph.D., 1948; DSc (hon.), U. Karlruhe, 1991. Rsch. assoc. MIT Radiation Lab., 1942-45, Rsch. Lab. of Electronics, 1946-48; instr. Harvard U., Radcliffe Coll., 1948-50; mem. faculty UCLA, 1950—, prof. math., 1960—; guest prof. Tech. U. Berlin, 1962, Inst. for Angewandte Math., Hamburg, 1966, Math. Inst. U. Karlsruhe, 1971-72, 81, 88, 91, 95; U.S. sr. scientist Alexander von Humboldt Found., Karlsruhe, 1976, 85. Author: (with Ivan Sokolnikoff) Mathematics of Physics and Modern Engineering, 1958, (with Charles Eames) Men of Modern Mathematics, 1966, (with Norman Levinson) Complex Variables, 1970, Differential Equations, Theory and Applications, 1991, Introduction to Differential Equations, 1992; film author, animator, 1972-74; contbr. articles to profl. jours. Pierce fellow Harvard U., 1948-50; sr. postdoctoral fellow NSF, Göttingen, Germany, 1956; Fulbright rsch. scholar Vienna, 1957, Hamburg, 1961-62; recipient Disting. Teaching award UCLA Alumni Assn., 1969. Mem. Deutsche Akademie der Naturforscher (Leopoldina), Sigma Xi. Home: 176 N Kenter Ave Los Angeles CA 90049-2730 Office: UCLA Dept Mathematics 6224 Math Sci Bldg Los Angeles CA 90024

REDIG, DALE FRANCIS, dentist, association executive; b. Arcadia, Iowa, Mar. 24, 1929; s. Philip F. and Clara (Bohnenkamp) R.; m. Diane Marie Murphy, June 13, 1953; children: Mary Catherine, John Francis, Ann Bennett. Student, U. Iowa, 1949-51, DDS, 1955, MS, 1965. Pvt. practice specializing in pediatric dentistry Des Moines, 1955-61; mem. faculty U. Iowa Coll. Dentistry, Iowa City, 1961-69; assoc. prof. pedodontics U. Iowa Coll. Dentistry, 1968-69, head dept., 1964-69; Fulbright lectr. U. Baghdad, 1963-64; dean Sch. Dentistry U. Pacific, San Francisco, 1969-78; exec. dir. Calif. Dental Assn., Sacramento, 1978—; bd. dirs. CDA Holding Co., chmn., 1993—; mem. dental health rsch. and edn. adv. com. USPHS, 1972-74; UN devel. program cons. to Quatar Ministry of Health, 1991. Dir dental div. Des Moines United Campaign, 1958; bd. dirs. Des Moines Health Ctr., 1956-61, pres., 1961; bd. dirs. Am. Fund for Dental Health, 1976-84, pres., 1980-83; regent U. Pacific, 1986—, chmn. bd. dirs., 1994; mem. adv. bd. Golden Gate U., 1992—; bd. dirs. Sacramento Theater Co., 1994—; mem. corp. cabinet Sacramento AIDS Found., 1994—. With USAAF, 1946-49. Mem. ADA (ednl. cons. Vietnam 1968, mem. coun. on dental edn. 1974-78), Am. Soc. Dentistry for Children, Am. Acad. Pediatric Dentistry (bd. dirs. 1972-75), Am. Coll. Dentists, Internat. Coll. Dentists, Am. Soc. Constituent Dental Execs. (pres. 1989-90). Office: Calif Dental Assn PO Box 13749 Sacramento CA 95853-4749

REDIKER, ROBERT HARMON, physicist; b. Bklyn., June 7, 1924; s. Moe J. and Estelle (Rosenwasser) R.; m. Barbara June Zenn, May 26, 1980; children by previous marriage: Richard J., Donald E. SB, MIT, 1947, PhD, 1950. Research asso. physics MIT, 1950-51; staff Lincoln Lab., Lexington, Mass., 1951-52, 53-57; asst. group leader semi-conductor physics Lincoln Lab., 1957-59, group leader applied physics, 1959-66; prof. dept. elec. engring. MIT, 1966-76, adj. prof., 1976-82, sr. research scientist, 1982—; asso. head optics div. Lincoln Lab., 1970-72, head optics div., 1972-80, sr. staff, 1980-91; sr. v.p. advanced R&D Cynosure Inc., 1992—; research assoc. physics Ind. U., 1952-53; Vice pres. Newton Lower Falls Improvement Assn., 1968-71; Mem. spl. group optical masers Def. Dept., 1966-73, working group D (lasers), 1973-76, working group C (electro-optics), 1979-92, mem. adv. group on electron devices, high energy laser rev. group, 1973-75; mem. ad hoc com. on materials and processes for electron devices Nat. Acad. Scis., 1970-72; mem. evaluation panel Nat. Bur. Standards, 1975-78; mem. panel on Office of Naval Research Opportunities in Physics, 1988, 91. Author. Served with Signal Corps AUS, 1943-46. Fellow IEEE (chmn. com. solid state devices 1961-63, sec. treas. group electron devices 1965-66, vice chmn. 1967, awards bd. 1976-79, chmn. Liebmann awards com. 1977-78, David Sarnoff award 1969), Am. Phys. Soc., Optical Soc. Am.; mem. Nat. Acad. Engring., Sigma Xi, Alpha Epsilon Pi. Jewish. Patentee in field. Home: 151 Coolidge Ave Watertown MA 02172-2863 Office: MIT Rm 36-487 Cambridge MA 02139

REDING, JOHN A., lawyer; b. Orange, Calif., May 26, 1944. AB, U. Calif., Berkeley, 1966, JD, 1969. Bar: Calif. 1970, U.S. Dist. Ct. (no., ctrl. ea. and so. dists.) Calif., U.S. Claims Ct., U.S. Supreme Ct. Mem. Crosby, Heafey, Roach & May P.C., Oakland, Calif., mem. exec. com. Mem. ABA (sects. on litigation, intellectual property, and natural resources, energy and eviron. law, coms. on bus. torts, internat. law, trial practice and torts and insurance), Am. Intellectual Property Law Assn., State Bar Calif. (sect. on litigation), Alameda County Bar Assn., Bar Assn. San Francisco, Assn. Bus. Trial Lawyers. Office: Crosby Heafey Roach & May PC PO Box 2084 Oakland CA 94604-2084

REDING, NICHOLAS LEE, chemical company executive; b. Algona, Iowa, Nov. 7, 1934; s. Louis Clair and Alice Rosanne (Steil) R.; m. Patricia Jane Finnegan, Aug. 2, 1958; children: Nancy Allison, Scott Nicholas. BSChemE, Iowa State U., 1956; grad. exec. program, Stanford U., 1975. With Monsanto Co., 1956—; v.p., mng. dir. Monsanto Agrl. Products Co., St. Louis, 1976-78; group v.p., mng. dir. Monsanto Agrl. Products Co., 1978-81, exec. v.p., 1981—; pres. Monsanto Agrl. Co., St. Louis, 1986-90; exec. v.p. environ., safety, health and mfg. Monsanto Co., St. Louis, 1990—, now vice chmn.; mem. mgmt. com. parent co., bd. dirs. Internat. Multifoods Corp., 1986—; bd. dirs. NutraSweet Co., G.D. Searle & Co., Internat. Environ. Bur., The Keystone Ctr. Bd. dirs., exec. com. United Way greater St. Louis, 1982—, St. Louis Country Day Sch., 1986-90; bd. dirs. St. Louis Children's Hosp., 1986-91, St. Louis Mcpl. Theatre Assn., 1989—, St. Louis Zoo, 1990—; chancellor's coun. U. Mo., St. Louis, 1988—; mem. Conf. bd. coun. on Environ. Affairs. Recipient award for excellence in agrl. mktg. Nat. Agri-Mktg. Assn., 1982. Mem. Nat. Agrl. Chem. Assn. (chmn. exec. com. 1980-81, bd. dirs. 1986-91), Alpha Zeta (hon.), St. Louis Club, Bellerive Country Club, Bogey Club. Methodist. Office: Monsanto Co 800 N Lindbergh Blvd Saint Louis MO 68167-7843*

REDISH, EDWARD FREDERICK, physicist, educator; b. N.Y.C., Apr. 1, 1942; s. Jules and Sylvia (Coslow) R.; m. Janice Copen, June 18, 1967; children: A. David, Deborah. AB, Princeton U., 1963; PhD, MIT, 1968. CTP fellow U. Md., College Park, 1968-70, asst. prof., 1970-74, assoc. prof., 1974-79, prof., 1979—, chair dept. phys. astronomy, 1982-85; vis. prof. Ind. U., Bloomington, 1985-86, U. washington, Seattle, 1992-93; vis. fgn. collaborator CEN, Saclay, France, 1973-74; co-dir. U. Md. Project in Physics and Ednl. Tech., 1983—, Comprehensive Unified Physics Learning Environment, 1989—; mem. Nuclear Sci. Adv. Com., Dept. of Energy/NSF, 1987-90; mem. program adv. com. Ind. U. Cyclotron Facility, 1985-89, chmn., 1986-89; mem. Internat. Commn. on Physics Edn., 1993-96. Author: (software) Orbits, 1989, The M.U.P.P.E.T. Utilities, 1994, The Comprehensive Unified Physics Learning Environment, 1994; editor: (conf. procs.) Computers in Physics Instrn., 1990; contbr. over 60 articles to profl. jours. Named Sr. Resident Rsch. Assoc., NAS-NRC, 1977-78; recipient Inst. medal Ctrl. Rsch. Inst. for Physics, 1979, Leo Schubert award Wash. Acad. Sci., 1988, Educator award Md. Assn. Higher Edn., 1989, Glover award Dickinson Coll., 1991, Forman award Vanderbilt U., 1996. Fellow AAAS, Am. Phys. Soc., Wash. Acad. Sci., Am. Assn. Physics Tchrs. Office: U Md Dept Physics College Park MD 20742-4111

REDLICH, FREDRICK CARL, psychiatrist, educator; b. Vienna, Austria, June 2, 1910; married; 2 children. MD, U. Vienna, 1935. Intern Allgem Krankenhaus, Vienna, 1935-36; resident Univ. Psychiat. Clin. U. Vienna, 1936-38; asst. physician State Hosp. Iowa, 1938-40; resident Neurol. Unit Boston City Hosp., 1940-42; from instr. to assoc. prof. psychiat. Yale U., New Haven, Conn., 1942-50, exec. officer, 1947-50, prof. psychiat., chmn. dept., 1950-67, assoc. provost med. affairs, dean, 1967-72, prof. psychiat. Sch. Medicine, 1972-77, dir. Behavioral Sci. Study Ctr., 1973-77, emeritus prof. psychiat. and neuropsychiat., 1977—; assoc. chief of staff edn. VA Med. Ctr., Brentwood, 1977-82; mem. staff Neuropsychiat. Inst. UCLA, 1982—; tchg. fellow Harvard Med. Sch., 1941-42; dir. Conn. Mental Health Ctr., 1964-67; cons. NIMH and Office Surgeon Gen., U.S. Army. Fellow Am. Psychiat. Assn., Am. Orthopsychiat. Assn., AAAS; mem. Inst. Medicine-NAS, Am. Psychosomatic Soc. Office: UCLA Dept of Psychiatry Neuropsychiat Inst. Los Angeles CA 90024*

REDLICH, NORMAN, lawyer, educator; b. N.Y.C., Nov. 12, 1925; s. Milton and Pauline (Durst) R.; m. Evelyn Jane Grobow, June 3, 1951; children: Margaret Bonny-Claire, Carrie Ann, Edward Grobow. AB, Williams Coll., 1947, LLD (hon.), 1976; LLB, Yale U., 1950; LLM, NYU, 1955; LLD (hon.), John Marshall Law Sch., 1990. Bar: N.Y. 1951. Practiced in N.Y.C., 1951-59; assoc. prof. law NYU, 1960-62, prof. law, 1962-74, assoc. dean Sch. Law, 1974-75, dean Sch. Law, 1975-88, dean emeritus, 1992—, Judge Edward Weinfeld prof. law, 1982—; counsel Wachtell, Lipton, Rosen & Katz, N.Y.C., 1988—; editor-in-chief Tax Law Rev., 1960-66; mem. adv. com. Inst. Fed. Taxation, 1963-68; exec. asst. corp. counsel, N.Y.C., 1966-68, 1st asst. corp. counsel, 1970-72, corp. counsel, 1972-74; asst. counsel Pres. Commn. on Assassination Pres. Kennedy, 1963-64; mem. com. on admissions and grievances U.S. 2d Circuit Ct. Appeals, 1978—, chmn., 1978-87. Author: Professional Responsibility: A Problem Approach, 1976, Constitutional Law, Cases and Materials, 1983, rev. edit., 1996, Understanding Constitutional Law, 1995; contbr. articles in field. Chmn. commn. on law and social action Am. Jewish Congress, 1978—, chmn. governing coun., 1996; mem. Borough Pres.'s Planning Bd. Number 2, 1959-70, counsel N.Y. Com. to Abolish Capital Punishment, 1958-77; mem. N.Y.C. Bd. Edn., 1969; mem. bd. overseers Jewish Theol. Sem., 1973—; trustee Law Ctr. Found. of NYU, 1975—, Freedom House, 1976-86, Vt. Law Sch., 1977—, Practicing Law Inst., 1980—; trustee Lawyers Com. for Civil Rights Under Law, 1976—, co-chmn., 1979-81; bd. dirs. Legal Aid Soc., 1983-88, NAACP Legal Def. Fund, 1985—, Greenwich House, 1987—. Decorated Combat Infantryman's Badge. Mem. ABA (coun. legal edn. and admissions to bar 1981—, vice chmn. 1987-88, chmn. 1989-90, equal opportunities in legal profession 1986-92, ho. of dels. 1991—), Assn. of Bar of City of N.Y. (exec. com. 1975-79, professionalism com. 1988-92). Office: 51 W 52nd St Fl 30 New York NY 10019-6119

REDMAN, BARBARA KLUG, nursing educator; b. Mitchell, S.D.; d. Harlan Lyle and Darlien Grace (Bock) Klug; m. Robert S. Redman, Sept. 14, 1958; 1 child, Melissa Darlien. BS, S.D. State U., 1958; MEd, U. Minn., 1959, PhD, 1964; LHD (hon.), Georgetown U., 1988; DSc (hon.), U. Colo., 1991. RN. Asst. prof. U. Wash., Seattle, 1964-69; assoc. dean U. Minn., Mpls., 1969-75; dean Sch. Nursing U. Colo., Denver, 1975-78; VA scholar VA Cen. Office, Washington, 1978-81; postdoctoral fellow Johns Hopkins U., Balt., 1982-83; exec. dir. Am. Assn. Colls. Nursing, Washington, 1983-89, ANA, Washington, 1989-93; prof. nursing Johns Hopkins U., Balt., 1993-95; dean, prof. Sch. Nursing U. Conn., Storrs, 1995—; vis. fellow Kennedy Inst. Ethics, Georgetown U., 1993-94; fellow in med. ethics Harvard Med. Sch., 1994-95. Author: Process of Patient Education, 1968—; contbr. articles to profl. jours. Bd. dirs. Friends of Nat. Libr. of Medicine, Washington, 1987—. Recipient Disting. Alumnus award S.D. State U., 1975, Outstanding Achievement award U. Minn., 1989. Fellow Am. Acad. Nursing; mem. Am. Ednl. Rsch. Assn., Internat. Patient Edn. Coun. (pres. 1988-89). Home: 12425 Bobbink Ct Potomac MD 20854-3005 Office: U Conn 231 Glenbrook Rd Storrs CT 06269-2026

REDMAN, CHARLES EDGAR, diplomat; b. Waukegan, Ill., Dec. 24, 1943; s. Edgar Bell and Helen Louise (Baker) R.; m. Eileen Kowal, July 31, 1971; children: Melissa, Vanessa, Christina. BS, USAF Acad., 1966; MA, Harvard U., 1968. Commd. 2d lt. USAF, 1966, advanced through grades to capt., 1969; spl. asst. to asst. chief staff intelligence USAF, Washington, 1974, resigned; joined Fgn. Svc., Dept. State; staff asst. Ops. Ctr., Bur. European Affairs, Dept. State, 1974-76; polit. officer Am. Embassy, Paris, 1976-79; dep. dir. Office Sec. Gen., NATO Internat. Staff, Brussels, 1979-82; polit. officer Am. Embassy, Algiers, 1982-84; dep. dir. Office European Security and Polit. Affairs, NATO, Washington, 1984-85; dep. spokesman Bur. Pub. Affairs, Washington, 1985-87, spokesman, 1986-89; asst. sec. pub. affairs Bur. Pub. Affairs, 1987-89; U.S. amb. to Sweden, 1989-93, U.S. amb. to Germany, 1994—. Office: American Embassy PSC 117 APO AE 09080*

REDMAN, DALE E., diversified financial services company executive, title company executive; b. 1947. B in Acctg., La. State U., 1968. CPA. With Ernst & Whinney CPA's, Baton Rouge, La., 1968-80; exec. v.p., cfo United Co. Fin. Corp., Baton Rouge, La., 1980—; mem. sec., treas. United Gen. Title Ins. Co., v. chmn. United Co. Lending corp. Office: United Co Lending Corp 4041 Essen Ln Baton Rouge LA 70809-2129*

REDMAN, ERIC, lawyer; b. Palo Alto, Calif., June 3, 1948; s. M. Chandler and Marjorie Jane (Sachs) R.; children: Ian Michael, Graham James. AB, Harvard U., 1970, JD, 1975; BA, Oxford U., 1972, MA, 1980. Bar: Wash. 1975, U.S. Dist. Ct. (we. dist.) Wash. 1975, D.C. 1979, U.S. Ct. Appeals (9th cir.) 1981, U.S. Supreme Ct. 1983. Asst. U.S. senator W.G. Magnuson, Washington and Seattle, 1968-71, 74-75; assoc. Preston, Thorgrimson et al, Seattle, 1975-78, ptnr., 1979-82; ptnr. Heller, Ehrman, White & McAuliffe, Seattle, 1983—. Author: Dance of Legislation, 1973; also book revs., articles. Office: Heller Ehrman White & McAuliffe 6100 Columbia Ctr 701 5th Ave Seattle WA 98104-7016

REDMAN, MONTE N., bank executive. Sr. v.p., CFO, dir. Astoria Fin. Corp., New Hyde Park, N.Y. Office: Astoria Fin Corp 1 Astoria Federal Plz New Hyde Park NY 11040*

REDMAN, PETER, finance company executive; b. Phila., Feb. 9, 1935; s. Hamilton Matthew and Martha (Lawson) R.; m. Julie Anne Burr, June 9, 1984; children: Kirsten, Heidi, Gretchen, Britt. B.A. in Econs., Middlebury Coll., 1958. Sr. group ins. rep. Conn. Gen. Life Ins. Co., Hartford, 1962-65; v.p. Conn. Bank & Trust Co., Hartford, 1965-73; v.p. Midlantic Nat. Bank, Newark, 1973-75, 4th Nat. Bank, Wichita, Kans., 1975-78; v.p., gen. mgr. Cessna Internat. Fin. Corp. (subs. Cessna Aircraft Co.), Wichita, 1978-82, now pres., dir.; pres., gen. mgr., Cessna Fin. Corp., Wichita, 1982—, also dir. Served to 1st lt. U.S. Army, 1958-62. Republican. Episcopalian. Home: 721 Preston Trl Wichita KS 67230-1504 Office: Cessna Fin Corp PO Box 308 Wichita KS 67201-0308*

REDMAN, TIMOTHY PAUL, English language educator, author, chess federation administrator; b. Elmhurst, Ill., June 26, 1950; s. William Charles and Eileen Marie (Keenan) R. B.A., Loyola U., Chgo., 1973; M.A., U. Chgo., 1974, Ph.D., 1987. Instr. Loyola U., Rome, 1977, Ill. Inst. Tech., Chgo., 1980-84; lectr. English dept. Loyola U., Chgo., 1982-84; lectr. U. Wis., Parkside, 1984-85; instr. Ohio State U., Lima, 1985-87, asst. prof., 1987-89; asst. prof. U. Tex., Dallas, 1989-91, assoc. dean, coll. master, 1991-92, assoc. prof., 1991—. Author: Ezra Pound and Italian Fascism, 1991; editor: Official Rules of Chess, 3d edit., 1987. Whiting fellow, 1981-82, NEH fellow, 1992-93. Mem. MLA, U.S. Chess Fedn. (past pres.), Nat. Coun. Tchrs. English, PEN U.S.A. West. Roman Catholic. Home: 3034 Brookshire Dr Plano TX 75075-7644 Office: U Tex at Dallas Sch Arts & Humanities JO31 PO Box 830688 Richardson TX 75083-0688 also: US Chess Fedn 186 US Highway 9W New Windsor NY 12553-7624

REDMON, BOB GLEN, insurance company executive; b. Snyder, Okla., July 30, 1931; s. Ed Ray and Gertrude (Lett) R.; m. Harriet Ann Nicholas, Mar. 12, 1953; children: Patricia, Pamela, Susanne. Student, Phoenix Coll., 1949-51. Ins. adjuster various ins. cos. L.A., 1952-62, Phoenix, 1952-62; branch claims mgr. Western Ins. Cos., Phoenix, 1962-71; pres. B.G. Redmon & Assocs., Inc., Phoenix, 1971—; risk mgmt. cons. Bashas' Markets, Chandler, Ariz., 1976—. Sgt. USAF, 1951-52. Recipient Robert Charles Meml. award Ariz. Pond Blue Goose Internat., 1972. Mem. Ariz. Ins. Claims Assn. (pres. 1961), Self-Insurers Inst. Am., Early V8 Ford Club Am. Avocations: Am. history, Irish history. Home: 8655 N Farview Dr Scottsdale AZ 85258-2040 Office: B G Redmon & Assocs Inc (SRT) 2255 N 44th St Ste 220 Phoenix AZ 85008-3278

REDMOND, DONALD EUGENE, JR., neuroscientist, educator; b. San Antonio, June 17, 1939; s. Donald Eugene and Viola (Kellum) R.; m. Patricia Welder Robinson, Dec. 22, 1972; 1 child, Andy J. BA, So. Meth. U., 1961; MD, Baylor U., 1968; MAH, Yale U., 1987. Diplomate Am. Bd. Psychiatry and Neurology. With Lab. of Clin. Sci., NIMH, Bethesda, Md., 1973-74; assoc. chief clin. neurosci. unit Conn. Mental Health Ctr., New Haven, 1974-87; asst. prof. psychiatry Yale U., New Haven, 1974-77; assoc. prof. psychiatry Yale U., 1978-87, prof. psychiatry, dir. neurobehavior lab., 1987—, dir. neural transplant program for neurol. diseases, 1987—; pres. St. Kitts Biomed. Rsch. Found., St. Kitts, W.I., 1983—, Axion Rsch. Found., Hamden, Conn., 1985—; prof. neurosurgery, 1993—. Contbr. articles to profl. jours.; patentee in field. With USPHS, 1972-74. Recipient Rsch. Scientist award NIMH, 1980— Founds. Fund prize, 1981; grantee NIMH, 1974-91, Nat. Inst. Neurol. Diseases and Stroke, 1986—, others. Mem. Am. Psychiat. Assn., Am. Coll. Neuropsychopharmacology, Am. Soc. Neural Transplantation (coun. mem. 1994—), Internat. Med. Soc. Motor Disturbances. Office: Neurobehavior Lab PO Box 3333 New Haven CT 06510-0333

REDMOND, DOUGLAS MICHAEL, diversified company executive; b. Central Islip, N.Y., May 13, 1954; s. Ronald George and Josephine Bernadette (Donelon) R.; m. Millie Vidal, Oct. 13, 1985; children: Douglas Michael Jr., Brandon Richard, Chelsea Lynn. BA in Bus., SUNY, Oneonta, 1976; MS, SUNY, Stony Brook, 1984. Ops. mgr. Whitman Labs Ltd., Petersfield, Eng., 1981-82; line supr. Estee Lauder Inc., Melville, N.Y., 1976-78; materials supr. Estee Lauder Inc., Melville, 1978-79, prodn. control mgr., 1979-81, materials mgr., 1980-81; cons. Estee Lauder Internat., N.Y.C., 1982-83; dir. materials Estee Lauder Internat., Melville, 1983-86, dir. mfg. svcs., 1986-88, exec. dir., 1988-92, v.p. supply, 1992-94; prin. Redmond Enterprises, Inc., East Islip, N.Y., 1987—, Global Decisions, Inc., 1991—, Oxygene Internat., Ltd., 1994—, pres. CBG Mercantile, Ltd, Inc., 1994—. Active in Bush campaign Rep. Com., Babylon, N.Y., 1988. Mem. Am. Prodn. and Inventory Control Soc. Roman Catholic.

REDMOND, JAMES RONALD, zoology educator, researcher; b. Cin., July 14, 1928; s. Matthew J. and Elizabeth (True) R.; m. Eleanor Hausfeld, Aug. 13, 1949; children: Cleve R., Jill A. BS, U. Cin., 1949; PhD, UCLA, 1954. Asst. prof. biology U. Fla., Gainesville, 1956-62; assoc. prof. zoology Iowa State U., Ames, 1962-67, prof., 1967-93, acting chmn. dept., 1983-84; prof. emeritus, 1993—; vis. asst. prof. U. Wash., Seattle, 1960; chief scientist Alpha Helix Nautilus Expdn., NSF, Philippines, 1975. Contbr. numerous articles to sci. jours., chpts. to books; contbr. zoology revs. Ency. Brit., 1986-89. With U.S. Army, 1954-56. NIH grantee, 1957-72. Fellow AAAS; mem. Am. Soc. Zoologists, Western Soc. Naturalists, Bermuda Biol. Sta. for Rsch. (corp.), Phi Beta Kappa, Sigma Xi, Phi Eta Sigma, Phi Kappa Phi. Avocations: travel, photography, electronics. Office: Dept Zoology and Genetics Iowa State U Ames IA 50011

REDMOND, JULIE CHRISTINE, elementary education educator; b. Niskayuna, N.Y., Nov. 8, 1969; d. John Edward and Patricia Wanda (Zmyewski) R. BS cum laude, Coll. of St. Rose, Albany, N.Y., 1991, MS in Edn., 1994. Cert. N-6 elem. tchr., Am. sign lang., N.Y. Dir., instr. Town of Rotterdam, N.Y., 1990-91; head tchr. Rensselaer Poly. Inst., Troy, N.Y., 1991-93; substitute tchr. Mohonasen Ctrl. Sch., Rotterdam, 1993—, Schalmont Ctrl. Sch., Schenectady, 1993—; instr. YMCA, Schenectady, 1994—. Mem. ASCD, Nat. Assn. for Edn. Young Children, People for Ethiical Treatment Animals, Out-of-Control Ski Club, Kappa Delta Phi. Democrat. Home: 726 Cramer Ave Schenectady NY 12306-3004

REDMOND, PATRICIA, radiologist, educator; b. N.Y.C., May 10, 1946; d. William Patrick and Mary (Boland) R.; m. Leonard Berliner, Aug. 13, 1982; children: Alanna, Ryan. BA cum laude, Fordham U., 1968; student, SUNY, Bklyn., 1968-70; MD, NYU, 1972. Diplomate Am. Bd. Radiology. Resident diagnostic radiology NYU-Bellevue Med. Ctr., 1972-76, fellow in abdominal imaging, 1976; asst. attending in radiology NYU Med. Ctr. and Bellevue Hosp., N.Y.C., 1976-81; chief gastrointestinal radiology NYU Hosp., N.Y.C., 1977-81; attending radiologist, asst. dir. radiology S.I. (N.Y.) Hosp., 1981-84, dir. radiology, 1984—; pres. Seaview Radiology, 1987—, S.I. Radiol. Assocs., P.C., 1985—; pvt. practice, S.I., 1985—; instr. NYU Med. Ctr., 1976-77, asst. prof., 1977-81, clin. asst. prof., 1981—; med. dir. The Women's Health Exch., S.I. U. Hosp., 1992—; presenter in field. Contbr. articles to med. jours. Mem. N.Y. Med. Polit. Action Com., Albany, 1985—; advisor, mem. sci. coun. S.I. chpt. Nat. Found. for Ileitis and Colitis. Mem. AMA, Am. Med. Women's Assn., Radiol. Soc. N.Am., Am. Profl. Practice Assn., Am. Assn. Women Radiologists, Am. Coll. Phys. Execs., Women's Med. Assn. N.Y.C., N.Y. C. of C., N.Y. Postgrad. and Univ. Hosp. Alumni Assn., Bellevue Hosp. Alumni Assn., NAFE, Phi Beta Kappa. Office: SI U Hosp 475 Seaview Ave Staten Island NY 10305-3436

REDMOND, PAUL ANTHONY, utility executive; b. Lakeview, Oreg., 1937. BSEE, Gonzaga U., 1965. Asst. elec. engr. Wash. Water Power Co., Spokane, 1965-67, maintenance engr., 1967-69, supt. contract constrn., 1969-73, constrn. and maintenance supt., 1973-75, mgr. constrn. and maintenance, 1975-77, asst. to pres., 1977-78, v.p., asst. to pres., 1978-79, sr. v.p. ops., 1979-80, exec. v.p., 1980-82, pres., 1982-88, chief oper. officer, 1982-84, chief exec. officer, 1984—, chmn. bd., 1985—, also bd. dirs.; former pres. Wash. Irrigation & Devel. subs. Wash. Water Power Co., Spokane, now chmn., pres., chief exec. officer, 1985—; bd. dirs. Security Pacific Bank Washington, Spokane Indsl. Park Inc., Limestone Co. Inc., Devel. Assocs. Inc., Pentzer Corp., Water Power Improvement Co., Wash. Irrigation and Devel. Co., Itron Inc. Lt. col. USNG. Office: Wash Water Power Co PO Box 3727 Spokane WA 99220-3727*

REDMOND, ROBERT FRANCIS, nuclear engineering educator; b. Indpls., July 15, 1927; s. John Felix and Marguerite Catherine (Breinig) R.; m. Mary Catherine Cangany, Oct. 18, 1952 (dec. May 1988); children: Catherine, Robert, Kevin, Thomas, John; m. Carole Moon Jacobs, Apr. 9, 1994. B.S. in Chem. Engring, Purdue U., 1950; M.S. in Math, U. Tenn., 1955; Ph.D. in Physics, Ohio State U., 1961. Engr. Oak Ridge Nat. Lab., 1950-53; scientist, adviser-cons. Battelle Meml. Inst., Columbus, Ohio, 1953-70; prof. nuclear engring. Ohio State U., Columbus, 1970-92; assoc. dean. Coll. Engring. Ohio State U., dir. Engring. Experiment Sta., 1977-92, acting dean, 1990-92, prof. emeritus mech. engring., assoc. dean emeritus, 1992—. Contbr. articles to profl. jours. V.p. Argonne Univs. Assn., 1976-77, trustee, 1972-80; mem. Ohio Power Siting Commn., 1978-82; trustee Edison Welding Inst., 1988-92. With AUS, 1945-46. Mem. Am. Nuclear Soc. (chmn. Southwestern Ohio sect.), AAAS, Nat. Regulatory Rsch. Inst. (bd. dirs. 1988-92), Trans. Rsch. Ctr., Am. Soc. Engring. Edn., Sigma Xi, Tau Beta Pi. Home: 4621 Nugent Dr Columbus OH 43220-3047 Office: Ohio State U Coll Engring Columbus OH

REDMONT, BERNARD SIDNEY, university dean, journalism educator; b. N.Y.C., Nov. 8, 1918; s. Morris Abraham and Bessie (Kamerman) R.; m. Joan Rothenberg, Mar. 12, 1940; children: Dennis Foster, Jane Carol. B.A., CCNY, 1938; M.J., Columbia U., 1939; D.H.L., Fla. Internat. U., 1980.

Reporter, book reviewer Bklyn. Daily Eagle, 1936-38; free lance corr. Europe, 1939, Mexico City, 1939-40; telegraph editor, editorial writer Herkimer (N.Y.) Evening Telegram, 1941-42; newswriter U.S. Office of Inter-Am. Affairs (Washington shortwave radio newscasts to Latin Am.), 1942-43, dir. News div., 1944-46; staff corr., bur. chief U.S. News & World Report, Buenos Aires and Paris, 1946-51; columnist Continental Daily Mail, Paris, 1951-53; chief corr. English Lang. World News Service Agence France-Presse, Paris, 1953-65; European corr. Paris news bur. chief Westinghouse Broadcasting Co., Paris, 1961-76; corr., bur. chief CBS News, Moscow, 1976-79; corr. CBS News, Paris, 1979-81; prof. journalism, dir. broadcast journalism program, dean Boston U. Coll. Communication, 1982-86, dean emeritus, prof. journalism, 1986—, mem. adv. bd. Latin Am. journalism program, 1989—; cons. Exec. Svc. Corps. of New Eng., 1991—, Internat. Exec. Svc. Corps, 1992—. Author: Risks Worth Taking: The Odyssey of a Foreign Correspondent, Univ. Press of Am., 1992. Served with USMCR, 1943-44. Decorated Purple Heart, chevalier Legion of Honor (France); recipient award for advancement of journalism Columbia U., 1986, Townsend Harris medal for life achievement, 1991, Yankee Quill award for disting. contbns. to betterment of journalism, 1995; Pulitzer travel fellow. Mem. Overseas Press Club (award best radio reporting from abroad 1968, 73), Soc. Profl. Journalists, Nat. Press Club, Anglo-American Press Assn. of Paris (pres. 1961, treas. 1970-73, sec. 1974-76). Unitarian. *Life has more meaning when it affirms, with grace, the Yang and the Yin, reconciling opposites--independence, yet cooperative effort and community caring; courage and hard work, yet moderation and generosity; hatred of injustice, yet kindness, fairness and compassion.*

REDNER, RICHARD, food products executive. Pres., CEO Redners Markets, Inc., Reading, Pa., 1970—. Office: Redners Markets Inc RD 2 Box 2430 Reading PA 19605*

REDO, DAVID LUCIEN, investment company executive; b. Lakewood, Ohio, Sept. 1, 1937; s. Joseph L. and Florence M. (Morse) R.; m. Judy L. Ijams, Aug. 4, 1962; children: Jenny, Mark. BSEE, U. Calif., Berkeley, 1961; MBA, U. Santa Clara, 1967. Registered investment advisor. Asst. engring. mgr. AT&T, N.Y.C., 1968-71; pension fund mgr. Pacific Telephone, San Francisco, 1971-77; mng. dir. The Fremont Group (formerly Bechtel Investments Inc.), San Francisco, 1977—; pres., CEO Fremont Investment Advisors, Inc., San Francisco, 1986—; bd. dirs. The Fremont Group (formerly Bechtel Investments, Inc.) San Francisco, J.P. Morgan Securities Asia, Singapore, Sequoia Ventures Inc., San Francisco, Fremont Investment Advisors, Sit/Kim Internat. Investments. Bd. trustees U. Calif., Berkeley, 1988—; chmn. investment com. U. Calif. Found., 1988—. Mem. Sentinel Pension Inst. (bd. advisors), Fin. Execs. Inst., Treas. Club of San Francisco, Internat. Assn. of Fin. Planners. Avocations: golf, traveling, reading, walking. Office: Fremont Investment Advisors 50 Beale St Ste 100 San Francisco CA 94105-1813

REDO, S(AVERIO) FRANK, surgeon; b. Bklyn., Dec. 28, 1920; s. Frank and Maria (Guida) R.; m. Maria Lappano, June 27, 1948; children—Philip, Martha. B.S., Queens Coll., 1942; M.D., Cornell U., 1950. Diplomate: Am. Bd. Thoracic Surgery, Am. Bd. Surgery (pediatric surgery). Intern in surgery N.Y. Hosp., N.Y.C., 1950-51; asst. resident surgeon N.Y. Hosp., 1951-56, resident surgeon, 1956-57, asst. attending surgeon, 1958-60, assoc. attending surgeon, 1960-66, surgeon in charge pediatric surgery, 1960, attending surgeon, 1966—; practice medicine specializing in surgery; clin. asso. prof. surgery Cornell U. Med. Coll., 1963-72, prof., 1972—. Author: Surgery in the Ambulatory Child, 1961, Principles of Surgery in the First Six Months of Life, 1976, Atlas of Surgery in the First Six Months of Life, 1977; contbr. articles to profl. jours. Served to capt. USAAF, 1942-46. Fellow A.C.S., Am. Coll. Chest Physicians; mem. Harvey Soc., Pan Am. Med. Assn., Soc. Univ. Surgeons, Am. Acad. Pediatrics, Am. Fedn. for Clin. Research, Internat. Cardiovascular Soc., Am. Surg. Assn., Am. Assn. Thoracic Surgery, Soc. for Surgery Alimentary Tract, Am. Soc. Artificial Internat. Organs, Am. Acad. Pediatrics, Assn. Advancement Med. Instrumentation, Soc. Thoracic Surgeons, Internat. Soc. Surgery, N.Y. Gastroent. Soc., N.Y. Acad. Sci., N.Y. Cardiovascular Soc., N.Y. Acad. Medicine, N.Y. Soc. Thoracic Surgery, N.Y. Pediatric Soc., Med. Soc. County N.Y., Queens Coll. Alumni Assn. (gov. 1962—), Sigma Xi. Patentee in field. Home: 435 E 70th St New York NY 10021-5342 Office: 525 E 68th St New York NY 10021-4873 *My life is based on the principles of doing as much for others as possible and doing no harm; to offer advice only when asked; to apply myself unstintingly, but not selfishly, to my work; to learn from my mistakes; to strive for perfection; and to always have a project and a dream.*

REDRUELLO, ROSA INCHAUSTEGUI, municipal department executive; b. Havana, Cuba, Dec. 6, 1951; came to U.S., 1961, naturalized, 1971; d. Julio Lorenzo and Laudelina (Vazquez) Inchaustegui; m. John Robert Redruello, Dec. 14, 1972; 1 child, Michelle. AA, Miami-Dade Community Coll., 1972; BS, Fla. Internat. U., 1974. Cert. systems profl. With Fla. Power & Light Co., Miami, 1975-81, records analyst, 1981-84, sr. records analyst, 1984-87, office mgr. Miami Beach Sanitation Dept., 1987—; exec. Mcpl. Dept., 1986-89; police officer patrol divsn. Miami Police Dept., 1989-91, narcotics divsn., 1991—; mem. spl. task force Drug Enforcement Adminstrn. HDTA Group 1, 1994-96; cons. United Bus. Records, Miami, 1985—. Editor South Fla. Record newsletter, 1983-86; editor, producer Files Mgmt. video tape, 1984-85. Rotary Club scholar, 1970. Mem. Assn. Records Mgrs. and Adminstrs. (chpt. chmn. bd. 1985—, chpt. mem. of yr. 1985), Assn. for Info. and Image Mgmt., Exec. Female, Nuclear Info. and Records Mgmt. Assn. (Appreciation award 1985). Republican. Roman Catholic. Avocations: swimming, jazzercise, reading. Office: Miami Beach Police Dept 1100 Washington Ave Miami FL 33139-4612

REDSTONE, LOUIS GORDON, architect; b. Poland, Mar. 16, 1903; came to U.S., 1923; s. Abraham Aaron and Anna (Gordon) Routenstein; m. Ruth R. Rosenbaum, June 25, 1939; children: Daniel Aaron, Eliel Gordon. BS in Architecture, U. Mich., 1929; MArch, Cranbrook Acad. Arts, 1948. Pvt. practice architecture Israel, 1933-37; founder Louis G. Redstone Assocs. Inc. (architects/engrs./planners), Detroit, 1937-85; pres., chmn. Redstone Assocs. Inc. (architects/engrs./planners), 1985-96; cons. Redstone and Tiseo Architects, 1996—; Del. internat. congresses, Caracas, Tokyo, Moscow and, Buenos Aires; exec. com. Pan Am. Fedn. Architects, 1955-70; juror archtl. and artists exhbns., profl. adviser archtl. competitions sponsored by Dow Chem. Co.; mem. Mich. Commn. on Art in State Bldgs., 1975-82; moderator Internat. Sculpture Conf., Washington, 1990. Author: Art in Architecture, 1968, New Dimensions in Shopping Centers and Stores, 1973, The New Downtown-Rebuilding Business Districts, 1976, Hospitals and Health Care Facilities, 1978, Institutional Buildings, 1980, Public Art-New Directions, 1981, Masonry in Architecture, 1984, From Israeli Pioneer to American Architect, 1989; contbr. articles to profl. mags. and newspapers; one-man shows include Macomb County Art Ctr., Mt. Clemens, Mich., 1992, T'Marra Gallery, Ann Arbor, 1991-93, Livonia (Mich.) Art Ctr., 1993, Detroit Inst. Art, 1993, Cranbrook Acad. Art, 1994; represented in permanent collections Long Beach (Calif.) Mus. Art, Detroit Inst. Art, Cranbrook Acad. Art. Trustee Mich. Found. for Arts; co-chmn. Bus. Consortium for Arts Sculpture Exhbns., Southfield, Mich. Recipient Patron award Mich. Found. for Arts, 1977, Detroit's Disting. Recognition award City Coun., 1993, Disting. Vol. Svc. award City of Southfield, 1993, Mich. Gov.'s Civic Leader award, 1993. Fellow AIA (pres. Detroit 1965, Gold medal outstanding contbn. to profession, Significant Lifetime Achievement award Detroit chpt. 1993), Mich. Soc. Architects (Robert F. Hastings award for outstanding achievement 1983), Engring. Soc. Detroit, Royal Acad. Fine Arts Netherlands (hon.); mem. Royal Acad. Fine Arts, San Fernando, Spain (corr. academician). Home: 19303 Appoline St Detroit MI 48235-1216 Office: Redstone and Tiseo Architects 29201 Telegraph Rd Ste 400 Southfield MI 48034-7647 *The architect must be a positive force in creating surroundings that enhance and fulfill all human needs, in which the arts become an integral part of man's daily environment. He must implement this approach by studying the specific needs and requirements of those who will use the building. These needs must then be satisfied within an aesthetically designed and functional enclosure that is in harmony with its surroundings. This basic concept must not be limited in application to individual buildings; it must be extended to the wider horizon of the total urban environment.*

REDSTONE, SUMNER MURRAY, entertainment company executive; b. Boston, May 27, 1923; s. Michael and Belle (Ostrovsky) R.; m. Phyllis Gloria Raphael, July 6, 1947; children: Brent Dale, Shari Ellin. B.A., Harvard U., 1944, LL.B., 1947; LLD (hon.), Boston U., 1994. Bar: Mass. 1947, U.S. Ct. Appeals (1st cir.) 1948, U.S. Ct. Appeals (8th cir.) 1950, U.S. Ct. Appeals (9th cir.) 1948, D.C. 1951, U.S. Supreme Ct. 1952. Law sec. U.S. Ct. Appeals for 9th Circuit, San Francisco, 1947-48; instr. law and labor mgmt. U. San Francisco, 1947; spl. asst. to U.S. Atty. Gen., Washington, 1948-51; ptnr. Ford, Bergson, Adams, Borkland & Redstone, Washington, 1951-54; pres., CEO Nat. Amusements Inc., Dedham, Mass., 1967—, chmn. bd., 1986-87; chmn. bd. Viacom Internat. Inc., N.Y.C., 1987—; prof. Boston U. Law Sch., 1982, 85-86; bd. dirs. TV Acad. Arts and Scis. Found.; vis. prof. Brandeis U., Waltham, Mass.; lectr. Harvard Law Sch., Cambridge, Mass.; Judge on Kennedy Libr. Found., (sel. comm. John F. Kennedy Profile in Courage award). Chmn. met. divsn. NE Combined Jewish Philanthropies, Boston, 1963; mem. exec. bd. Combined Jewish Philanthropies of Greater Boston; mem. corp. New Eng. Med. Ctr., 1967—, Mass. Gen. Hosp. Corp.; trustee Children's Cancer Rsch. Found.; founding trustee Am. Cancer Soc.; chmn. Am. Cancer Crusade, State of Mass., 1984-86; Art Lending Libr.; sponsor Boston Mus. Sci.; chmn. Jimmy Fund Found., 1960; v.p., mem. exec. com. Will Rogers Meml. Fund; bd. dirs. Boston Arts Festival; bd. overseers Dana Farber Cancer Ctr., Boston Mus. Fine Arts; mem. presdl. adv. com. on arts John F. Kennedy Libr. Found., also judge ann. John F. Kennedy Profile in Courage Award com. 1st lt. AUS, 1943-45. Decorated Army Commendation medal; named 1 of 10 Outstanding Young Men in New Eng., Boston Jr. C. of C., 1958; recipient William J. German Human Rels. award Am. Jewish Com. Entertainment/Comm. Divsn., 1977, Silver Shingle award Boston U. Law Sch., 1985, Variety New Eng. Humanitarian award, 1989, Golde Plate award Am. Acad. Achievement 32d Ann. Salute to Excellence Program, Bus. Excellence award U. So. Calif. Sch. Bus. Adminstrn., 1994, The Stephen S. Wise award The Am. Jewish Congress, 1994, The Legends in Leadership award Emory U., 1995, Allan K. Joens Lifetime Achievement award Am. Cancer Soc., 1995, Man of Yr. award MIPCOM, the Internat. Film and Programme Market for TV, Video, Cable and Satellite, 1995, Humanitarian award Variety Club Internat., 1995; named Communicator of Yr., B'nai B'rith Comm./Cinema Lodge, 1980, Man of Yr., Entertainment Industries Divsn. of UJA Fedn., 1988, Pioneer of Yr., Motion Picture Pioneers, 1991, Grad. of Yr., Boston Latin Sch., 1989, Honoree 7th ann. fundraiser Montefiore Med. Ctr., 1995, Hall of Fame award Broadcasting and Cable mag., 1995. Mem. ABA, Nat. Assn. Theatre Owners (chmn. bd. dirs. 1965-66, exec. comm. 1995—), Theatre Owners Am. (asst. pres. 1960-63, pres. 1964-65), Motion Picture Pioneers (bd. dirs.), Boston Bar Assn., Mass. Bar Assn., Harvard Law Sch. Assn., Am. Judicature Soc., Masons, Univ. Club, Harvard Club. Home: 98 Baldpate Hill Rd Newton MA 02159-2825 Office: Nat Amusements Inc PO Box 9126 Dedham MA 02027-9126

REDWAY, ALAN ARTHUR SYDNEY, Canadian legislator, lawyer; b. Toronto, Ont., Can., Mar. 11, 1935; s. Alan Edwin Sydney and Phyllis May (Turner) R.; m. Mary Louise Harvey, Apr. 21, 1962; children: Kimberley Ann, Andrea Elizabeth. B. Commerce, U. Toronto, 1958; LLB, Osgoode Hall, Toronto, 1961; Diploma of Applied Arts and Scis. (hon.), Centennial Coll., Toronto, 1985. Bar: Ont. 1963; apptd. Queen's Counsel, 1977. Ptnr. Frost & Redway, Toronto, 1966-84, Redway Cooney & Roherty, Toronto, 1984-87, Redway & Butler, Toronto, 1987-89, 92—; M.P. Ho. of Commons, Ottawa, Ont., 1984-93, min. state for housing, 1989-91, chmn. spl. rev. com. on Employment Equity Act, 1991-92; vice chmn. Aboriginal affairs com., 1992-93. Recipient Hon. Diploma of Applied Arts and Tech., Centennial Coll., Toronto, 1985. Mem. Leaside Lions Club (pres. 1971-72). Progressive Conservative. Avocations: cross country skiing, gardening. Office: Ste 4086, 3080 Yonge St, Toronto, ON Canada M4N 3N1

REDWINE, RICHARD H., manufacturing executive, light; b. 1938. V.p. Kimble Glass, Inc., Vineland, N.J., 1968—. Office: Kimble Glass Inc 537 Crystal Ave Vineland NJ 08360-3200*

REDWINE, ROBERT PAGE, physicist, educator; b. Raleigh, N.C., Dec. 3, 1947; s. Robert Word and Hazel Virginia (Green) R.; m. Jacqueline Nina Hewitt, Nov. 22, 1986; children: Keith Hewitt, Jonathan Hewitt. AB, Cornell U., 1969; PhD, Northwestern U., 1973. Rsch. assoc. Los Alamos (N.Mex.) Nat. Lab, 1973-77, staff sci., 1977-79; rsch. assoc. U. Berne, Switzerland, 1974-75; asst. prof. physics MIT, Cambridge, Mass., 1979-82, assoc. prof., 1982-89, prof., 1989—, dir. lab. nuclear sci., 1992—; cons. Los Alamos Nat. Lab., 1980—. Contbr. articles to profl. jours. Fellow AAAS, Am. Phys. Soc. Office: MIT Lab Nuclear Sci Bldg 26-505 Cambridge MA 02139

REECE, E. ALBERT, obstetrician, gynecologist, perinatologist; b. Spanishtown, Jamaica, Jan. 3, 1950; came to U.S., 1969; s. Wilfred Anderson Reece and Daisy Lucinda (Price) Reece Batten; m. Sharon Andrea Blake, July 28, 1974; children: Kelie, Brynne, Sharon-Andrea II. BS with honors, L.I. U., 1973; MD, NYU, 1978; ob/gyn specialty diploma, Columbia U., 1982; maternal-fetal subspecialty diploma, Yale U., 1984. Diplomate Am. Bd. Ob-Gyn.; bd. cert. maternal-fetal medicine. Intern, resident Columbia U., Presbyn. Med. Ctr., N.Y.C., 1978-82; materal-fetal medicine fellow Yale U. Sch. Medicine, 1982-84; asst. prof. ob-gyn Yale U. Sch. Medicine, New Haven, 1984-87, assoc. prof. ob-gyn, 1987-90; prof., chmn. ob-gyn Temple U. Sch. Medicine, Phila., 1991—. Co-editor Diabetes Mellitus in Pregnancy: Principles and Practice, 1st edit., 1988, 2nd edit., 1995, Medicine of the Fetus and Mother, 1992, A Study Guide for Medicine of the Fetus and Mother, 1992, A Handbook of Medicine of the Fetus and Mother, 1995; co-author: Fundamentals in Obstetric and Gynecologic Ultrasonography, 1993; contbr. articles, abstract to profl. jours. in excess of 250. Mem. sci. adv. com. March of Dimes, 1993—; mem. sci. adv. bd. NIH-DC Infant Mortality Initiative, 1993—; mem. adv. com. Nat. Inst. Child Health and Human Diseases, NIH, 1994—; trustee Reading Rehab. Hosp., 1992—; mem. bioeffects com. AIUM, 1992-95. Grantee March of Dimes, 1985-87, Friedman Found., 1990-92, William Penn Found., 1989-93, Am. Diabetes Assn., 1991-93, NIH, 1992—. Fellow Am. Coll. Ob-Gyn., Coll. Physicians Phila.; mem. Am. Diabetes Assn. (coun. on diabetes in pregnancy), Am. Inst. Ultrasound in Medicine, Hellenic Perinatal Soc. Greece (hon.), Nat. Med. Assn. (exec. com. 1987-88, chmn. ob-gyn. sect. 1991-93), New Haven Obstet. Soc., Soc. for Gynecol. Investigation, Soc. Perinatal Obstetricians (leader diabetes spl. interest 1992-94, bd. mem. 1995—), Phila. Perinatal Soc. (program chair 1993—), Phila. Obstet. Soc. (mem. coun. 1992-94). Seventh-Day Adventist. Office: Temple U Sch Medicine 3401 N Broad St # 70pd Philadelphia PA 19140-5103

REECE, GERALDINE MAXINE, elementary education educator; b. L.A., May 13, 1917; d. Charles Kenneth and Bertha (Austin) Ballou; m. Thomas Charles Bauman, Aug. 16, 1942 (div. Oct. 1971); children: Thomas Charles Bauman, Jr., Kathleen Marie Bauman Messenger, Stephen Kenneth Bauman; m. Wilbert Wallingford Reece, Nov. 3, 1973 (dec. 1988). AA, L.A. City Coll., 1942; BA, U. So. Calif., L.A., 1966. Specialist tchr. in reading, elem. edn. Tchr. Archdiocese of L.A., Altadena, Calif., 1962-66; master tchr. Alhambra (Calif.) City and H.S., 1966-79, writer multicultural component early childhood edn. program. Author poetry. Mem. San Gabriel Child Care Task Force, 1984-86; mem. steering com. West San Gabriel Valley Cmty. Awareness Forum, 1985-87; past pres. women's divsn., bd. dirs. San Gabriel C. of C., 1989-90; mem. sch. site and facilities com. Sch. Dist. Unification, San Gabriel, 1992-93; mem. task force Episcopal Parish/Healing Our Cities, San Gabriel, 1992-93; docent San Gabriel Mus., 1989, 92-93. Recipient Exceptional Svc. awards Am. Heart Assn., West San Gabriel Valley, 1990, 91, 93, 94, 95, Dedicated Svc. award San Gabriel C. of C., 1989, Outstanding and Dedicated Cmty. Svc. award Fedn. Cmty. Coord. Couns., San Gabriel, 1986, 87, others, Woman of Yr. award City of San Gabriel, 1994, Diamond Homer trophy Famous Poet Soc., 1995. Mem. AAUW (Money Talks sect. chairperson 1981, 82, corr. sec./treas. Alhambra-San Gabriel 1982-83, 83-85), Calif. Ret. Tchrs. Assn. (past pres. 1989-91, Outstanding Svc. plaque 1994), Nat. Soc. DAR (3rd vice regent 1994, 95), Pasadena Women's City Club, St. Francis Guild, San Gabriel Ret. Tchrs. (pres. 1985-89), San Gabriel Hist. Assn., San Gabriel Cmty. Coord. Coun. (pres. 1986),. Democrat. Episcopalian. Avocations: reading, Bridge, writing poetry, stitchery.

REECE, JOE WILSON, engineering company executive; b. Elkin, N.C., Mar. 1, 1935; s. Thad Marshall and Anita (Hobson) R.; m. Nancy Lee Fletcher, Aug. 25, 1955; children: James Thad, Joel Wade; m. Ellen Frances West, Nov. 21, 1992; 1 child, Joe Wilson Jr. B in Nuclear Engring., N.C. State U., 1957, MS, 1961; PhD, U. Fla., 1963. Registered profl. engr., Ala. Instr. engring. mechanics N.C. State U., Raleigh, 1958-61; asst. prof. mech. engring. Auburn (Ala.) U., 1963-67, assoc. prof., 1967-76, prof., 1976-85; dep. dir. operating reactors div. U.S. Nuclear Regulatory Commn., 1976-78; pres. Reece Engring. Assocs., 1985—; cons. U.S. Army Missile Command, Combustion Engring. Co., Westinghouse, others. Campus drive chmn. Auburn United Fund, 1969, chmn. bd., 1971. Named Disting. Classroom Tchr. N.C. State U. Sch. Engring., 1961, Outstanding Faculty mem. Auburn U. Sch. Engring., 1965, 73. Mem. Am. Soc. Engring. Edn. (pres. SE sect. 1977), ASME, Ala. Acad. Sci., Scabbard and Blade, Sigma Xi, Phi Kappa Phi, Tau Beta Pi, Phi Eta Sigma, Sigma Pi Sigma, Theta Tau, Pi Tau Sigma. Methodist (lay leader 1967, chmn. trustees 1972). Club: Civitan (Auburn) (pres. 1968). Home: 402 N Carolina Ave Boonville NC 27011-9701

REECE, JULIETTE M. STOLPER, community health and mental health nurse; b. Muskogee, Okla., Oct. 4, 1926; d. Joseph Harry and Marie (Duquesne) Stolper; m. Warren Crane, Apr. 12, 1947; children: Warren Crane, Judith Gayle Crane Cox Fitzpatrick, Janice M. Crane Sharp, Cathy L. Crane Hubble; m. Roy M. Reece Jr., July 16, 1970 (dec.). Diploma, Muskogee Gen. Hosp., 1947; BS in Psychology, Cameron Coll., Lawton, Okla., 1993, postgrad., 1993; student, U. Okla. Cert. pub. health nurse. ICU nurse Southwestern Hosp., Lawton, 1976-77; psychiat. nurse Taliaferro Community Mental Health Ctr., 1977-86; cons. nurse Cedar Crest Manor, Lawton, 1985-86, dir. nursing svc., 1986-87; asst. head nurse Reynolds Family Practice Clinic, Ft. Sill, Okla., 1987-91, head nurse, 1991—, also diabetes educator, 1991—; patient/staff edn. coord. dept. family practice Reynolds Army Cmty. Hosp., Ft. Sill, 1996—; vis. mem. Pub. Health Nursing Study Group, USSR, 1979. Vol. for Am. Cancer Soc., Am. Heart Assn., Am. Diabetes Assn., Am. Lung Assn., Am. Assn. Diabetes Educators, Assn. Western Okla. Diabetes Educators, ARC, Easter Seal Programs; tchr. classes for home health care aides, ARC; tchr. med. terminology to hosp. receptionists. Recipient nursing grants. Home: 1601 NW Pollard Ave Lawton OK 73507-2048 Office: Reynolds Family Practice Clinic # 4 Thomas St Bldg # 4300 Fort Sill OK 73503

REECE, MARILYN KING, college dean; b. Cullman, Ala., July 7, 1949; d. John McCarley and Florence Augusta (Freeman) King; m. John Robert Williamson, Aug. 23, 1970 (div. 1987); children: Joan King, Rachel King; m. David Donald Reece, Apr. 15, 1995. BA, U. Ala., Tuscaloosa, 1971, MA, 1972. Instr. English, N.E. Ala. C.C., Rainsville, 1973-89, dean extended day, 1989—. Mem. MLA, NEA, Nat. Coun. Tchrs. English, Conf. on Coll. Composition and Comm., Ala. Assn. for Women in Edn. Democrat. Office: NE Ala CC PO Box 159 Rainsville AL 35986-0159

REECE, MAYNARD FRED, artist, author; b. Arnolds Park, Iowa, Apr. 26, 1920; s. Waldo H. and Inez V. (Latson) R.; m. June Carman, Apr. 7, 1946; children: Mark A., Brad D. Privately educated. Artist Meredith Pub. Co., Des Moines, 1938-40; artist, asst., mus. dir. Iowa Dept. History and Archives, Des Moines, 1940-50. Artist: Fish and Fishing, 1963, Waterfowl of Iowa, 1943; watercolor Trout, Saturday Evening Post (award of Distinctive Merit 1962); watercolors 73 Fish, Life mag. (cert. of merit 1955); print of Water's Edge Canada Geese for Am. Artist Collection, Am. Artist Mag., 1985; author, artist: The Waterfowl Art of Maynard Reece, 1985. Chmn. Gov.'s Com. Conservation of Outdoor Resource, 1963-64; trustee Iowa Natural Heritage Found., Des Moines, 1979—; hon. trustee Ducks Unltd., Inc., 1983—; trustee J.N. "Ding" Darling Conservation Found., Inc., Des Moines, 1962—. Served with AUS, 1943-45. Recipient awards for duck stamps and others Dept. Interior, 1948, 51, 59, 69, 71; recipient award Govt. Bermuda, 1963, award Iowa Conservation Commn., 1972, 77, 80, 81, award Fish and Game Commn., Little Rock, 1982, 88, award Tex. Parks and Wild Life Dept., 1983, award Nat. Fish & Wildlife Found., 1988, award Wash. State Dept. Wildlife, 1989; named Artist of Yr. Ducks Unltd. Inc., 1973; chosen Master Artist 1989, Leigh Yawkey Woodson Art Mus., Wausau, Wis., 1989. Mem. Nat. Audubon Soc., Nat. Wildlife Fedn., Izaak Walton League Am. (hon. pres. 1974-75). Home and Office: 5315 Robertson Dr Des Moines IA 50312-2133

REECE, MONTE MEREDITH, lawyer, judge; b. Jackson, Tenn., May 29, 1945; s. Jerrel Rexford Sr. and Marjorie (Ricks) R.; m. Melanie Fleshman; children: Hugh, Bryan, Andrew, Jerrel, Rebecca. Student, La. State U., 1963-64, 66, La. Coll., 1964-65; LLB, Western State U., 1974. Atty. English & Marotta A.P.C., Downey, Calif., 1974-78; pvt. practice, 1978—; magistrate judge U.S. Dist. Ct. (ea. dist.) Calif., South Lake Tahoe, 1983—; judge pro tem El Dorado County Mcpl. Ct., South Lake Tahoe, 1983—; cons. assembly judiciary com., Sacramento, 1993. Advisor Tahoe Human Svcs., South Lake Tahoe, 1986—; pres. Sudden Infant Death syndrome, South Lake Tahoe, 1988—. With USNR, 1968-70, Vietnam. Mem. Fed. Magistrate Judges Assn., El Dorado County Search and Rescue (pres. 1989—), Lions (pres. 1985—, Lion of Yr. 1988-89). Avocations: golf, antique furniture restoration. Office: US Dist Ct PO Box 20000 3330 Lake Tahoe Blvd Ste 10 South Lake Tahoe CA 96150-7911

REECE, ROBERT WILLIAM, zoological park administrator; b. Saginaw, Mich., Jan. 21, 1942; s. William Andrews and Mary Barbara (Murphy) R.; m. Jill Whetstone, Aug. 21, 1965; children: William Clayton, Gregory Scott, Mark Andrews. B.S., Mich. State U., 1964; postgrad., U. West Fla., 1969-71, U. South Fla., 1974-76. Dir. Northwest Fla. Zool. Gardens, Pensacola, Fla., 1970-72; zool. dir. Lion Country Ga., Stockbridge, 1972-73; asst. dir. Salisbury Zoo, Md., 1976-77; dir. zoology Wild Animal Habitat, Kings Island, Ohio, 1977-92; exec. dir. The Wilds Internat. Ctr. for Preservation of Wild Animals, Columbus, Ohio, 1992—. Assoc. editor: Sci. Jour. Zoo Biology, 1982—. Lt. USN, 1964-69, Korea. Profl. fellow Am. Assn. Zool. Parks and Aqariums; mem. Cin. Wildlife Rsch. Fedn., Am. Soc. Mammalogists, Animal Behavior Soc., Captive Breeding Specialist Group, Species Survival Commn., Internat. Union for Conservation of Nature and Natural Resources. Republican. Episcopalian. Home: 11784 Canterbury Ave Pickerington OH 43147-8490 Office: The Wilds 1400 International Rd Cumberland OH 43732

REECE, THOMAS L., manufacturing executive. Pres., CEO Dover Corp., N.Y.C. Office: Dover Corp 280 Park Ave New York NY 10017*

REECE-PORTER, SHARON ANN, global education educator; b. Cin., Nov. 28, 1953; d. Edward and Claudia (Ownes) Reece; divorced, 1981; children: Erika Lynn, Melanie Joyce. BS in Consumer Sci., Edgecliff Coll., 1975; cert. clerical computer, So. Ohio Coll., 1984; MEd in Gen. Edn., SUNY, Buffalo, 1994; postgrad. in Adult Edn. Global Studies, Nova U., 1994—; EdD in Global Edn. (hon.), Australian Inst. Coordinated Rsch., Victoria, 1995. Cert. tchr., Ohio. Dept. supr., asst. buyer Mabley & Carew, Cin., 1975-76; claims adjuster Allstate Ins. Co., Cin., 1976-78; sales merchandiser Ekco Houseware, Cin., 1979-80; sales rep. Met. Life Inc., Cin., 1981-83; info. processing specialist GPA/Robert Half/Word Source, Cin., Dallas, 1985-87; tchr. adult edn. Princeton City Schs., Cin., 1984-90; with Rainbow Internat. Non-Profit Adult Ednl. Rsch. Ctr., Buffalo, 1990—; edn. specialist rsch. found. SUNY, Buffalo, 1993; prof. computer sci. So. Ohio Tech. and Bus. Coll., Cin., 1986-90; computer software tng. cons., 1987-89; part-time tchr. adult GED classes Adult Learning Ctr. Buffalo Bd. Edn., 1994-95; participant Am. Forum for Global Edn. Tutor U.S. div. Internat. Laubach Literacy, Clermont County, Ohio, 1984. Fellow Australian Inst. for Coordinated Rsch. (life); mem. NAFE, ASTD, Internat. DOS Users Group, Am. Ednl. Rsch. Assn., Nat. Assn. Women Bus. Owners, World Assn. Women Entrepreneurs, Assn. Baha'i Studies in Australia, Boston Computer Soc., Cin. Orgn. Data Processing Educators and Trainers, Internat. Platform Assn., Cin. C. of C. (cert. minority supplier devel. coun.). Baha'i. Home: 173 Palmdale Dr Buffalo NY 14221-4006 Office: Rainbow Internat A Global Edn Inst 7954 Transit Rd Ste 253 Buffalo NY 14221-4117

REED, ADAM VICTOR, psychologist, engineer; b. Torun, Poland, Jan. 11, 1946; came to U.S., 1959, naturalized, 1965; s. Henry Kenneth and Eva (Tenenbaum) R.; B.S. in E.E., M.I.T., 1967, M.S. in Biology and M.S. in E.E., 1970; Ph.D., U. Oreg., 1974; m. Barbara Irene Birnbaum, Dec. 26, 1982; 1 child, Halina Brooke. Research programmer Artificial Intelligence Lab., M.I.T., Cambridge, 1965; research engr. Hewlett Packard Co., Palo Alto, Calif., 1966-67; mem. research staff Riverside Research Inst., N.Y.C., 1970-71; postdoctoral fellow, adj. asst. prof. Rockefeller U., N.Y.C., 1974-

78; asst. prof., vis. lectr. psychology Grad. Faculty Social and Polit. Sci., New Sch. Social Research, N.Y.C., 1977-82; mem. tech. staff Lucent Techs. (formerly, AT&T Bell Labs.), 1981—; peer rev. referee NSF, others. Sci. and tech. adv. Libertarian Party v.p. candidate Tonie Nathan, 1972; mem. Marlboro Twp. Bd. Edn., N.J., 1994—. NDEA Title IV fellow, 1967-70; NSF fellow, 1970-73; NIMH Research Service fellow, 1974-77. Mem. N.Y. Acad. Sci., IEEE, Am. Psychol. Assn., Soc. Engring. Psychologists, Assn. Computing Machinery, Am. Soc. Cybernetics, AAAS, Sigma Xi, Tau Beta Pi, Eta Kappa Nu. Libertarian. Achievements include patents in field; first implementation of steepest descent, first statistically adaptive user interface, first switch-based facsimile server; research on experimental psychology-response signals method; contbr. articles to profl. jours.

REED, ALAN L., lawyer; b. Dec. 8, 1933. BA, Williams Coll., 1955; LLB, Harvard U., 1961. Bar: Pa. 1962. Ptnr. Morgan, Lewis & Bockius, Phila. Mem. ABA (chmn. sect. pub. utility, comm. and transp. law 1987-88). Office: Morgan Lewis & Bockius 2000 One Logan Sq Philadelphia PA 19103-6993*

REED, ALFRED, retired composer, conductor; b. N.Y.C., Jan. 25, 1921; s. Carl Mark and Elizabeth (Strasser) Friedman; m. Marjorie Beth Deley, June 20, 1941; children: Michael Carlson, Richard Judson. Student, Juilliard Sch. Music, 1946-48; MusB, Baylor U., 1955, MusM, 1956; MusD, Internat. Conservatory of Music, Lima, Peru, 1968. Exec. editor Hansen Publs., N.Y.C., 1955-66; prof. music U. Miami (Fla.) Sch. Music, 1966-93. Composer, arranger, N.Y.C., 1941-60; condr. Tri-State Music Festival, Okla., 1956-57, 60-66, 70, 73, Midwest Nat. Band Clinic, 1960-91, Bemidji (Minn.) Summer Music Camp, 1970-71, 75, Mid-East Instrumental Music Conf., Pitts., 1957-60, Can. Music Educators Assn., Edmonton, Alta., 1975; composer: Russian Christmas Music, 1944, Symphony for Brass and Percussion, 1952, Rhapsody for Viola and Orch, 1956, Choric Song, 1966, Titania's Nocturne, 1967, A Festival Prelude, 1962, Passacaglia, 1968, Music for Hamlet, 1973, Armenian Dances, 1974-75, Punchinello, Overture to a Romantic Comedy, 1974, Testament of an American, 1974, First Suite for Band, 1975, Othello, A Symphonic Portrait in Five Scenes, 1976, Prelude and Capriccio, 1977, Second Symphony, 1978, Siciliana Notturno, 1978, Second Suite for Band, 1978, The Enchanted Island, 1979, The Hounds of Spring, 1980, Third Suite for Band, 1981, Queenston Overture, 1982, Viva Musica!, 1983, A Little Concert Suite, 1983, El Camino Real, 1985, Centennial!, 1985, Three Revelations from the Lotus Sutra, 1985, Golden Jubilee, 1986, A Christmas Celebration, 1986, Praise Jerusalem!, 1987, Third Symphony, 1988, Eventide, 1988, Golden Eagle, 1989, Curtain Up!, 1990, A Springtime Celebration, Hymn Variants, 1991, With Trumpets and Drums, 1991, Concertino for Marimba and Winds, 1991, 4th Symphony, 1992, Fourth Suite for Band, 1993, Evolutions, A Concert Overture, 1993, 5th Symphony, 1994, Fifth Suite for Band, 1995, also others. Served with AUS, 1942-46. Mem. ASCAP, Am. Bandmasters Assn., Am. Fedn. Musicians, Nat. Band Assn., Music Educators Nat. Conv. Home: 1405 Ancona Ave Miami FL 33146-1903 *As a composer, my desire has always been to achieve both a depth and intensity of communication between myself, my music and my audiences that would enable me to express something of value as regards myself and my time that, hopefully, would give rise to a deeply felt response on the part of my fellow human beings. I suppose this is true of the arts in general, and all artists, regardless of their medium of expression, but music, for me at least, has been the supreme expression of all time, for all men.*

REED, A(LFRED) BYRON, retired apparel and textile manufacturing company; b. Indpls., June 30, 1916; s. Alfred Lumpkin and Myrtle (Wood) R.; m. Mary Ellen Myers, Sept. 1, 1950; 1 child, Charles W. B.S., Butler U., 1939; postgrad., U. Chgo., 1946-47. Asst. brokerage mgr. Conn. Gen. Life Ins. Co., Chgo., 1939-41; sales mgr., mktg. mgr., asst. gen. mgr. Vassar Co., Chgo., 1946-57; gen. mgr. women's div. Munsingwear, Inc., Mpls., 1958-66; pres., chief exec. officer Munsingwear, Inc., 1966-79, chmn., 1979-81, also dir.; dir., trust com., exec. com. 1st Nat. Bank Mpls., Hoerner Waldorf Co., St. Paul, 1973-77, Murphy Motor Freight; mem. mgmt.-labor textile adv. com. U.S. Dept. Commerce. Chmn. Nat. Alliance Businessmen, Mpls., 141972; mem. Adv. Council U.S.-Japan Econ. Relations, Washington, also exec. com.; adviser Council Fin. Aid to Edn.; chmn. U.S. Savs. Bond Drive, 1975-76; Bd. dirs. Better Bus. Bur. Mpls., 1973-74, Minn. Pvt. Coll. Fund, Mpls. YMCA; trustee Butler U. Served to lt. USNR, 1942-46. Mem. Am. Apparel Mfrs. Assn. (chmn. bd. dirs., exec. com.), U.S. C. of C. (internat. policy com., internat. trade subcom.), Mpls. C. of C. (dir.), Minneapolis Club, Minikahda Club, Mission Viejo Country Club, Indian Wells Country Club, Phi Delta Theta. Republican. Episcopalian. Home: 76-750 Iroquois Dr Indian Wells CA 92210-9019

REED, ALFRED DOUGLAS, university director; b. Bristol, Tenn., July 18, 1928; s. Roy Theodore and Elizabeth Brown (Tuft) R.; m. Emily Joyce Freeman, Mar. 18, 1950; children: Roy Frederick, Robert Douglas, David Clark, Timothy Wayne, Joseph William. AB, Erskine Coll., Due West, S.C., 1949. Reporter Citizen-Times, Asheville, N.C., 1949-51, city editor, 1953-60, mng. editor, 1962-63, assoc. editor, 1963-66, capital corr., 1959-66; asst. editor The Presbyn. Jour., Weaverville, N.C., 1951-52; assoc. editor Shelby (N.C.) Daily Star, 1961-62; dir. pub. info. Western Carolina U., Cullowhee, N.C., 1966—; cons. Devel. Office, East Carolina U., Greenville, 1980; bd. dirs. Wachovia Bank and Trust Co., Sylva, N.C., 1969—. Author: Prologue, 1968, Decade of Development, 1984, Our Second Century, 1992, Fulfillment of Promise, 1994; exec. editor: Western, The Mag. of Western Carolina University, 1991—. Mem. Asheville City Bd. Edn., 1958-62; vice chmn. bd. dirs. Sta. WCQS FM, Western N.C. Pub. Radio Inc., Asheville, 1978-88; bd. dirs. Cherokee Hist. Assn., 1985—, Western N.C. Assn. Comtys., 1985—, Jackson County Fund of N.C. Comty. Found., 1991-93; mem. Hunter Libr. Adv. Bd., 1991—, Pack Place Adv. Coun., Asheville, 1991—. Recipient Paul A. Reid Disting. Svc. award Western Carolina U., 1980. Mem. Coun. for Advancement and Support Edn., Pub. Rels. Assn. Western N.C. (bd. dirs., treas.), Coll. News Assn. Carolinas (bd. dirs. 1968-71, 80-82), N.C. Press Assn. (assoc.), Smoky Mountain Host Assn. (bd. dirs., 1st v.p. 1988—). Democrat. Presbyterian. Avocations: travel, stamps, gardening. Home: 310 University Hts Cullowhee NC 28723-9691 Office: Western Carolina U Dir Pub Info 420 Robinson Cullowhee NC 28723

REED, ANDRE DARNELL, professional football player; b. Allentown, Pa., Jan. 29, 1964. Grad., Kutztown State. Wide receiver Buffalo Bills, N.Y., 1985—. Pro Bowl Selection, 1988-93, Played in Super Bowl XXV, 1990, XXVI, 1991, XXVII, 1992, XXVIII, 1993. Office: Buffalo Bills 1 Bills Dr Orchard Park NY 14127-2237

REED, BERENICE ANNE, art historian, artist, government official; b. Memphis, Jan. 1, 1934; d. Glenn Andrew and Berenice Marie (Kallaher) R. BFA, St. Mary-of-the-Woods Coll., Ind., 1955; MFA in Painting and Art History, Istituto Pio XII, Villa Schifanoia, Florence, Italy, 1964. Cert. art tchr., Tenn. Comml. artist Memphis Pub. Co., 1955-56; arts adminstr., educator pub. and pvt. instns., Washington, Memphis, 1957-70; arts adminstr. Nat. Park Svc., 1970-73; mem. staff U.S. Dept. of Energy, Washington, 1973-81, U.S. Dept. Commerce, Washington, 1983-84, Exec. Office of the Pres., Office of Mgmt. and Budget, Washington, 1985; with fin. mgmt. svc. U.S. Treasury Dept., Washington, 1985—; cons. on art and architecture in recreation AIA, 1972-73; artist-in-residence St. Mary-of-the-Woods Coll., Ind., 1965; guest lectr. instr. Nat. Sch. Fine Arts, Tegucigalpa, Honduras, 1968; mem. exec. com. Parks, Arts and Leisure Project, Washington, 1972-73; researcher art projects, Washington, 1981-83. Developer (video) In Your Intere$t, 1992. Bd. dirs. Am. Irish Bicentennial Com., 1974-76; advisor Royal Oak Found. Recipient various awards for painting. Mem. Soc. Woman Geographers, Nat. Soc. Arts and Letters, Ctr. for Advanced Study in Visual Arts, Art Barn Assn. (bd. dirs. 1973-83). Roman Catholic. Avocations: photography, performing arts. Home: PO Box 34253 Bethesda MD 20827-0253 Office: Dept Treasury Fin Mgmt Svc 401 14th St SW Washington DC 20227-0001

REED, BILL, purchasing agent. Pres. CPG Pepsi Bottlers Inc. (formerly Consol. Purchasing Group), Atlanta, Ga. Office: CPG Pepsi Bottlers Inc 2849 Paces Ferry Rd NW Atlanta GA 30339-3769*

REED, CHARLES ALLEN, anthropologist; b. Portland, Oreg., June 6, 1912; s. C. Allen and Gladys (Donohoe) R.; m. Lois Wells, Aug. 18, 1951; children: C. Allen, Robin M., Brian W. Student, Whitman Coll., 1929-30; B.S., U. Oreg., 1937; Ph.D., U. Calif. at Berkeley, 1943. Instr. biology U. Oreg., 1936-37; lectr. anatomy U. Calif. Med. Sch. at Berkeley, 1943; instr. biology Reed Coll., 1943-46; asst. prof. zoology U. Ariz., 1946-49; asst. prof., assoc. prof. zoology U. Ill. Sch. Pharmacy, 1949-54, 55-61; research assoc. anthropology U. Chgo., 1954-55; assoc. prof. biology Yale U., 1961-66; prof. biology and anthropology U. Ill., Chgo., 1966-67; prof. anthropology U. Ill., 1967—, acting head dept., 1967-70; Mem. Catlow Caves archeol. expdn. U. Oreg., 1937; Iraq-Jarmo archeol. expdn. Oriental Inst. U. Chgo., 1954-55; Iranian prehistoric project Oriental Inst., 1960; U. Istanbul-Chgo. Prehistoric project, Turkey, 1970, U. Ill. archeol. expedition to Sinai, 1986; curator mammals and reptiles Peabody Mus., Yale, 1961-66; dir. Yale prehistoric expdn. to Nubia, 1962-65; research asso. vertebrate anatomy Field Mus. Natural History, Chgo., 1966—; mem. U.S. com. Nat. Acad. Scis. for Internat. Union for Quaternary Research, 1967-74. Editor: Origins of Agriculture, 1977; Contbr. articles to profl. jours. Recipient Pomerance award for sci. excellence in archaeology Archaeol. Inst. Am. Fellow Am. Assn. Anthropologists (life), Asso. Current Anthropology, AAAS (life); mem. Am. Soc. Mammalogists (life), Am. Soc. Ichthyologists and Herpetologists (life), Am. Assn. Phys. Anthropology, Am. Soc. Zoologists, Am. Soc. Anatomists, Soc. Study Evolution, Soc. Vertebrate Paleontology, Am. Assn. Quaternary Research, Explorers Club, Chgo. Acad. Scis. (bd. sci. govs.), Chgo. Anthrop. Soc. (pres. 1979-81), Phi Beta Kappa, Sigma Xi (life). Home: 151 N Kenilworth Ave Oak Park IL 60301 Office: U Ill Chgo Dept Anthropology Chicago IL 60607

REED, CHARLES BASS, academic administrator; b. Harrisburg, Pa., Sept. 29, 1941; s. Samuel Ross and Elizabeth (Johnson) R.; m. Catherine A. Sayers, Aug. 22, 1964; children: Charles B. Jr., Susan Allison. BS, George Washington U., 1963, MA, 1964, EdD, 1970; postgrad. Summer Inst. for Chief State Sch. Officers,, Harvard U. Grad Sch. Edn., 1977; D of Pub. Svc. (hon.), George Washington U., 1987; LLD (hon.), Stetson U., 1987; LittD (hon.), Waynesburg Coll., 1988; LHD (hon.), St. Thomas U., 1988. From asst. prof. to assoc. prof. George Washington U., Washington, 1963-70; asst. dir. Nat. Performance-Based Tchr. Edn. Project, Am. Assn. Colls. for Tchr. Edn., Washington, 1970-71; assoc. for planning and coordination Fla. Dept. Edn., Tallahassee, 1971-75, dir. Office Ednl. Planning, Budgeting, and Evaluation, 1975-79; edn. policy coord. Exec. Office of Gov., Tallahassee, 1979-80, dir. legis. affairs, 1980-81, dep. chief of staff, 1981-84, chief of staff, 1984-85; chancellor State Univ. System Fla., Tallahassee, 1985—; bd. dirs. Fla. Progress Corp., Capital Health Plan; chmn. bd. dirs. Regional Tech. Strategies, Inc. Mem. Coun. for Advancement and Support of Edn., Coun. on Fgn. Rels., Bus.-Higher Edn. Forum, Coun. of 100. Recipient Disting. Alumni award George Washington U., 1987. Mem. Am. Assn. State Colls. and Univs., Am. Assn. for Higher Edn., Am. Coun. on Edn., Fla. Assn. Colls. and Univs., Edn. Commn. of States (exec. com. 1984-87, exec. com. for campus compact project, Disting. Svc. award 1982), So. Regional Ednl. Bd. (vice-chmn. 1988-90, exec. com.), Assn. Governing Bds. of Univs. and Colls., Nat. Assn. Sys. Heads, Golden Key. Democrat. Roman Catholic. Office: State U System Fla Office of Chancellor 325 W Gaines St Tallahassee FL 32399-1950

REED, CHARLES C., marketing professional, insurance company executive; m. Lorna Young, Aug. 8, 1959. BA in Econs., Stanford U., MBA. Dir. mktg. H.F. Ahmanson & Co.; exec. v.p., dir. mktg. Great Western Fin. Corp.; exec. v.p. Alexander & Alexander Calif., Inc.; dir. Transam. Investors, DiGiorgio Corp., San Francisco, 1985-90. Chmn. bd. dirs. L.A. C. of C.; past. chmn., dir. Ind. Colls. So. Calif., Ctrl. City Assn. L.A., LA 200 Partnership, Calif. Mus. Found.; past committeeman Rep. Party Calif. Office: Alexander & Alexander Calif Ste 700 801 S Figueroa St Los Angeles CA 90017

REED, CHRISTOPHER ROBERT, civil engineer; b. Charleston, W.Va., Feb. 12, 1948; s. Clarence Milton and Anne (Schaffner) R.; m. Mary Dandridge Kennedy, Mar. 4, 1983. Student W.Va. Inst. Tech., 1966-70, 76-77, Ga. State U., 1973-74. Designer, Sverdrup & Parcel, Charleston, 1970-72; asso. project engr. Mayes, Sudderth & Etheredge, Atlanta, 1973-76; project mgr. Sverdrup & Parcel, Washington, 1976-79; estimator Deleuw, Cather/Parsons, Washington, 1979-80; project mgr. Parsons Brinckerhoff, McLean, Va., 1980-85; assoc. Lolederman Assocs., Inc., Rockville, Md., 1985-86; assoc. Post Buckley Schuh and Jernigan Inc., Arlington, Va., 1986-89; assoc., dir. mcpl. engring. Lolederman Assocs., Inc., Rockville, 1989-90; mgr. CRS Donohue and Assocs. Inc., Fairfax, Va., 1990-92; asst. dist. location and design mgr. VDOT, Fairfax, 1992-95, dist. location and design engr., 1995—. Mem. Constrn. Specifications Inst., Inst. Transp. Engrs., Am. Assn. Cost Engrs., Am. Ry. Engring. Assn., Soc. Am. Mil. Engrs., Am. Pub. Transit Assn., ASTM, Capital Yacht Club (sec. 1988-89, vice commodore 1990, commodore 1991), Corinthian Yacht Club (fleet capt. 1992, rear commodore, 1993). Home: 320 Culpeper St Warrenton VA 22186-3001 Office: 3975 Fair Ridge Dr Fairfax VA 22033-2924

REED, CLARENCE RAYMOND, retired association executive; b. Shamokin, Pa., Sept. 23, 1932; s. Benton Howard and Gerda Maude (Hoover) R.; m. Joan Ann Engle, June 25, 1955; children: Ann Elizabeth, Susan Engle. B.A., U. Pa., 1954, M.B.A. with distinction, 1958; grad., Stonier Grad. Sch. Banking, 1969. With Prudential Ins. Co. Am., 1954; with Robert Morris Assos., Phila., 1958-95; asst. sec. Robert Morris Assos., 1959-60, sec.-treas., 1960-74, exec. mgr., 1961-74, exec. v.p., 1974-95, mem. exec. com., 1980-95, pres., 1995—, also dir., 1995; mem. faculty loan mgmt. seminar Ind. U., 1971-72; Chmn. Shares in Edn., 1968. Pres. Council Springfield (Pa.) Twp. Home and Sch. Assns., 1969-70. Served with AUS, 1954-56. Mem. Credit Assn. Delaware Valley, Am. Soc. Assn. Execs., Am. Mgmt. Assn., Cen. Home and Sch. Assn. (pres. 1966-67), Wharton M.B.A. Alumni Assn., Exchequer Club (chancellor 1984-85/Washington). Presbyterian (fin. sec. 1970, 79, ruling elder 1972-74, 83-85, chmn. 50th anniversary com. 1974, trustee 1977-79). Home: 15 Long Rd Berwyn PA 19312-1211

REED, CYNTHIA KAY, minister; b. Amarillo, Tex., July 10, 1952; d. Carlos Eugene and Marjorie Marie (Daughetee) R. B of Music Edn., McMurry Coll., Abilene, Tex., 1976; MDiv, Perkins Sch. Theol., Dallas, 1991. Ordained to ministry Meth. Ch., 1989; cert. dir. music. Dir. music and Christian edn. Oakwood United Meth. Ch., Lubbock, Tex., 1978-84; dir. music and Christian edn. 1st United Meth. Ch., Childress, Tex., 1976-78, Littlefield, Tex., 1984-86; intern min. 1st United Meth. Ch., Lubbock, 1989-90, assoc. min., 1990-91; min. Meadow and Ropesville United Meth. Chs., 1991-93, Earth (Tex.) United Meth. Ch., 1993—; extern chaplain Meth. Hosp., Lubbock, 1989—, Walk to Emmaus Renewal Movement, Lubbock, 1990—. Com. mem. Life Gift-Organ Donation, Lubbock, 1991; mem. Arthritis Found., Lubbock, 1991. Georgia Harkness scholar Div. Ordained Ministry, 1989. Mem. Christian Educators & Musicians Fellowship, Am. Guild Organists.

REED, D. GARY, lawyer; b. Covington, Ky., June 4, 1949; m. Mary Elizabeth Goetz, May 20, 1972; children: Mark, Stacey. BA, Xavier U., 1971; JD, Catholic U. Am., 1974. Bar: Ohio 1974, Ky. 1975, U.S. Ct. Appeals (6th cir.) 1975, U.S. Dist. Ct. (so. dist.) Ohio 1974, U.S. Dist. Ct. (ea. dist.) Ky. 1977, U.S. Dist. Ct. (we. dist.) Ky. 1980. Law clk. to judge U.S. Dist. Ct. (so. dist.) Ohio, Cin., 1974-75; assoc. Dinsmore & Shohl, Cin., 1976-82, ptnr., 1982-90; dir. legal svcs. Choice Care, Cin. Contbg. author: Woodside, Drug Product Liability, vol. 3, 1987. Mem. ABA, Ky. Bar Assn., Ohio Bar Assn., Nat. Health Lawyers Assn., No. Ky. C. of C. (Leadership award 1988), Greater Cin. Coun. for Epilepsy (treas., bd. dirs. 1990—), Leadership No. Ky. Alumni Assn. Office: Choice Care 655 Eden Park Dr Cincinnati OH 45202-6000

REED, DANNY LAWRENCE, manufacturing research and development specialist; b. Roanoke, Va., Dec. 3, 1940; s. Barney Isaac and Etta Tamer (Booth) R.; m. Judy Anne Mitchell, Aug. 17, 1962; children: Janet Michele, Danny Lawrence II. BSCE, U. Tenn., 1963, MS in Engring. Sci., 1965, PhD in Engring. Sci., 1967. Sr. structures engr. Gen. Dynamics Ft. Worth Co., 1967-76, supr., chief, mgr., 1976-82, dir. mfg. devel., 1982-92; lean aircraft initiative Lockheed Martin, 1992-94; mem. rsch. staff Inst. for Def. Analyses, Alexandria, Va., 1994—; total quality mgmt. facilitator, corp. recruiter, 1978-90; corp. mgmt. seminar, 1985; chmn. bd. dirs. Computer-Aided Mfg. Internat., Arlington, Tex., 1986-91; mem. mgmt. program. Pa. State U., State Coll., 1978; mem. process action team Air Force-Measures of Success, Wright-Paterson AFB, Ohio, 1990. Contbr. over 20 publs. to profl. jours. NDEA fellow U. Tenn., 1963-66. Mem. AIAA (tech. com. on mgmt. 1985—), Aerospace Industries Assn. (mfg. com. 1976-92), Soc. Mfg. Engrs., Soc. Mech. Engring., Sigma Xi. Mem. Ch. of Christ. Achievements include numerous technical and management presentations in field. Office: Inst for Def Analyses 1801 N Beauregard St Alexandria VA 22311-1733

REED, DARWIN CRAMER, health care consultant; b. Artesia, N.Mex., July 24, 1915; s. Darwin W. and Candace (Cramer) R.; m. Martha Gene Thalmann, Aug. 15, 1940; children—Geney Catherine Reed Fuller, Darwin Kim. A.B., Wichita U., 1937; M.D., Washington U., St. Louis, 1941; M.S., U. Pa., 1954. Diplomate: Am. Bd. Urology. Intern St. Francis Hosp., Wichita, Kans., 1941-42; resident St. Francis Hosp., 1946-48, U. Pa. Hosp., Phila., 1952-54, Med. Coll. Va. Hosp., 1954-55; practice medicine Wichita, 1948-52; partner Wichita Urology Group, Kans., 1955-70; dean Coll. Health Related Professions, Wichita State U., 1970-73, v.p. for health edn., 1973-77; prof. surgery, vice chancellor U. Kans. Sch. Medicine, Wichita, 1975-78; sr. v.p. Wesley Med. Center, Wichita, 1978-86; pres. Health Strategies, Inc., 1980-86; exec. dir. Greater Wichita Community Found., 1986-88; program cons. Kans. Health Found., 1989-93; pres. Cramer Reed & Assocs., 1993-95; v.p. sr. initiatives, Columbia-Wesley Med. Ctr., 1995—; mem. Kans. Bd. Healing Arts, 1964-67; chmn. dean's com. Wichita VA Hosp., 1975-78. Chmn. bd. trustees Wichita State U., 1966-68. Lt. col. M.C., USAAF, 1942-46. Fellow A.C.S.; mem. AMA, Pan Am. Med. Assn., Am. Urologic Assn., Am. Cancer Soc. (pres. Kans. div. 1960-61, 65-66). Methodist. Home: 7520 E 21st St N Apt 22 Wichita KS 67206-1086

REED, DAVID ANDREW, foundation executive; b. Butler, Pa., Feb. 24, 1933; s. Sherman W. and Caroline (Janner) R.; m. Virginia Rogers, Dec. 1, 1956; children: Kristine Lynn, Katherine Louise, Elizabeth Anne, Amy Janner. A.B., Allegheny Coll., 1955; M.S., U. Pitts., 1961. Diplomate: Sch. Pub. Health, Columbia U. Adminstrv. resident Titusville (Pa.) Hosp., 1959, Cin. Gen. Hosp., 1960-61; asst. adminstr. Warren (Pa.) Gen. Hosp., 1961-62, Western Pa. Gen. Hosp., Pitts., 1962-63; with Cin. Gen. Hosp., 1963-69, adminstr., 1964-69; asso. prof. hosp. adminstrn. U. Cin. Coll. Medicine, 1966-69; preceptor program med. and hosp. adminstrn. U. Pitts. Grad. Sch. Pub. Health, 1966-69; pres. Lenox Hill Hosp., N.Y.C., 1969-78; v.p., chief exec. officer Good Samaritan Hosp., Phoenix, 1978-82; pres. SamCor/Samaritan Health Service, Phoenix, 1982-89; pres., chief exec. officer The Samaritan Found., Phoenix, 1989, St. Joseph Health System, Orange, Calif., 1990—; now ptnr. DAR Cons. Grp., Dana Point; instr.; past pres. Greater Cin. Hosp. Council, Phoenix Regional Hosp. Council; bd. govs. Greater N.Y. Hosp. Assn.; chmn. Am. Hosp. Assn., also trustee; cons. Hosp. Devel. and Research Inst. Contbr. articles to profl. jours. Bd. dirs. Urban League Cin. Served with AUS, 1955-57. Fellow Am. Coll. Hosp. Adminstrs.; mem. Hosp. Adminstrs. Club N.Y.C. (pres.), Hosp. Assn. N.Y., Phi Gamma Delta. Presbyterian. Clubs: Paradise Valley Country, Pacific Golf, Marbella Country, Center. Office: DAR Cons Grp 24681 La Plaza Se 240 Dana Point CA 92629*

REED, DAVID BENSON, bishop; b. Tulsa, Feb. 16, 1927; s. Paul Spencer and Bonnie Frances (Taylor) R.; m. Susan Henry Riggs, Oct. 30, 1954 (div.); children: Mary, Jennifer, David, Sarah, Catherine; m. Catherine Camp Luckett, Apr. 15, 1984. A.B., Harvard U., 1948; M.Div., Va. Theol. Sem., 1951, D.D., 1964; D.D., U. of South, 1972, Episc. Theol. Sem., Ky., 1985. Ordained priest Episcopal Ch., 1952; missionary priest in Panama and Colombia, 1951-58; with Nat. Ch. Exec. Office, 1958-61; mission priest S.D., 1961-63; bishop of Colombia, 1964-72, Ecuador, 1964-70; bishop coadjutor Diocese of Ky., Louisville, 1972-74; bishop of Ky. Diocese of Ky., 1974-94; asst. bishop of Conn. Episcopal Diocese of Conn., Hartford, 1994-95; 1st pres. Anglican Council Latin Am., 1969-72; chmn. standing commn. on ecumenical relations Episcopal Ch., 1979-82; pres. Ky. Coun. Chs., 1988-91; mem. governing bd. Nat. Coun. of Chs. of Christ in U.S.A., 1982-91, mem. exec. com., 1985-91, sec., 1988-91; Anglican co-chmn. Anglican Orthodox Theol. Cons., 1984-94. Bd. dirs. Alliant Health Systems (formerly Norton Kosair Children's Hosp.), Louisville, 1979-94; trustee U. of the South, 1972—, regent, 1979-82; chmn. Louisville United Against Hunger, 1980-84, 86-87; chmn. Presiding Bishop's Com. on Interfaith Rels., 1991—. Mem. Harvard Club of Western Ky. (pres. 1992-94). Democrat. Home: 5226 Moccasin Trl Louisville KY 40207-1634

REED, DAVID FREDRICK, artist; b. San Diego, Jan. 20, 1946; s. David Fredrick II and Beverly (Behl) R.; m. Lillian Ball, June 28, 1986; 1 child previous marriage, John. Student, Skowhegan (Maine) Sch. Painting and Sculpture, 1966, N.Y. Studio Sch., 1966-67; BA, Reed Coll., 1968. One-man shows include Max Protetch Gallery, N.Y.C., 1977, 79, 83, 85, 86, 88, 89, 91, 92, 95, Asher/Faure Gallery, L.A., 1988, Galerie Rolf Ricke, Cologne, Germany, 1991, 93, San Francisco Art Inst., 1992, Kölnischer Kunstverein, Cologne, Germany, 1995. Rockefeller Found. fellow, 1966, John Simon Guggenheim Meml. Found. fellow, 1988, Nat. Endowment Arts Visual Arts fellow, 1991; grantee Roswell (N.Mex.) Mus. and Art Ctr., 1969.

REED, DAVID GEORGE, entrepreneur; b. Alameda, Calif., July 19, 1945; s. David Francis and Anna Amelia Vangeline (Paulson) R.; m. Marianne Louise Watson, Apr. 7, 1971 (div. June 1975); m. Michele Ann Hock, June 28, 1989; 1 child, Casey Christine Michele. AA in Bus. Adminstrn., Diablo Valley Coll., Pleasant Hill, Calif., 1965; BA in Design and Industry, San Francisco State U., 1967, MBA in Mktg., 1969; cert. res. police officer, Los Medanos Coll., Pittsburg, Calif., 1977. Owner Western Furs, Ltd., Walnut Creek, Calif., 1963-72; mgmt. cons. Controlled Interval Scheduling, Rolling Hills Estates, Calif., 1972-73; owner Dave Reed's Texaco, Concord, Calif., 1973-76; mgmt. cons. Mgmt. Scheduling Systems, Houston, 1974-76, Thomas-Ross Assocs., Mercer Island, Wash., 1972-82; plant mgr. Bonner Packing, Morgan Hill, Calif., 1981; mfg. engr. Systron Donner, Concord, 1982-84, Beckman Instruments, San Ramon, Calif., 1984-90; owner Dave Reed & Co. Water Ski Sch., White Water Rafting, Chiloquin, Oreg., 1987—, Dave Reed & Co., design, market, mfg. Contender boats, Chiloquin, Oreg., 1976—; lectr. wildlife mgmt. Dave Reed & Co., Chiloquin, 1965—, lectr. mgmt. seminars, 1982—; coach Japanese Water Ski Team, Bluff Water Ski Club, Tokyo, 1984; fin. mgr. Japanese investors Dave Reed & Co., Chiloquin, 1986—, design and supply solar electric power sys., 1994—. Res. dep. sheriff Contra Costa County Sheriff's Dept., Martinez, Calif., 1977-80. With U.S. Army, 1969-71, Vietnam. Recipient Gold medal internat. freesytle wrestling Sr. Olympics, Fullerton, Calif., 1983. Mem. Am. Water Ski Assn. (Calif. state water ski champion 1977, 86, western region water ski champion 1977, silver medal nat. water ski championships 1977), Bay Area Tournament Assn. (chmn. 1968—), Diablo Water Ski Club (bd. dirs. 1968—). Republican. Avocations: water skiing, snow skiing, surfing, camping, fly fishing. Home: PO Box 336 Chiloquin OR 97624-0336

REED, DONALD ANTHONY, executive; b. New Orleans, Nov. 22, 1935; s. Roscoe and Mildred (Fauria) R. BS, Loyola U., 1957; MSLS, U. So. Calif., 1958, JD, 1968. Instr. U. Beverly Hills, L.A.; libr. Woodburg U., L.A.; instr. L.A. Valley Coll., Calif. Inst. of Arts, L.A.; founder, pres. Coun. Film Orgns., L.A., 1980—, Acad. of Family Films, L.A., 1980—, The Count Dracula Soc., L.A., 1962—, Acad. Sci. Fiction Fantacy & Horror Films, L.A., 1972—; cons. in field. Author: The Vampire on the Screen, 1964, The Outlawry of War in Outer Space, 1966, Admiral Leahy at Vichy France, 1968, Robert Redford, 1975, Science Fiction Film Awards, 1981. Recipient The Saturn award, 1978, Count Dracula Soc. award, 1964. Mem. Acad. Magical Arts, Sons of the Desert, Beta Phi Mu (pres. 1958-60), Phi Alpha Theta, Phi Kappa Alpha. Democrat. Roman Catholic. Avocations: comic operas of Gilbert and Sullivan, Count Dracula books and films, Calvin Coolidge, Abbott and Costello, dir. Bryan Singer. Office: Acad Sci Fiction Fantasy & Horror 334 W 54th St Los Angeles CA 90037

REED, DONALD JAMES, biochemistry educator; b. Montrose, Kans., Sept. 26, 1930; married, 1949; 6 children. BS, Coll. of Idaho, 1953; MS, Oreg. State U., 1955, PhD in Chemistry, 1957. Asst. Oreg. State U., Corvallis, 1953-55, asst., then assoc. prof., 1962-72, prof. biochemistry, 1972-90, prof. toxicology program, dist. prof. biochemistry, 1990, dir. environ. health sci. ctr., 1981—, acting chair dept. biochemistry, 1994-95; assoc. biochemist cereal investigations western regional rsch. lab., agr. rsch. svc. USDA, Calif., 1957-58; asst. prof. chemistry Mont. State U., Bozeman, 1958-62; mem. toxicology study sect. NIH, 1971-75, ad hoc rev. com. Nat. Cancer Inst., 1975-87, sabbatical scientist, 1984-85; mem. environ. sci. rev. panel health rsch. EPA, 1981, environ. health sci. rev. com. Nat. Inst. Environ. Health Sci., 1982-85; mem. Burroughs Wellcome Toxicology Scholar Award Selection Com., 1984-87; vis. prof. MRC Toxicology Unit, Carshalton, Eng., 1984; mem. task group health criteria, internat. program chem. safety WHO, 1986,biochem. & carcinogenesis rev. com. Am. Cancer Soc., 1984—; cons. U. Calif., San Francisco, 1985-90; mem. nat. adv. environ. health scis. coun. NIH, 1992—; mem. health review com. Health Effects Inst., 1993—. Assoc. editor Jour. Toxicology and Environ. Health, 1980-84, Toxicology and Applied Pharmacology, 1981-84, Cancer Rsch., 1987-95; editor Cell Biology and Toxicology, 1988—. USPHS Spl. Rsch. fellow NIH, 1969-70, Eleanor Roosevelt Am. Cancer Soc. Internat. Cancer fellow Karolinska Inst., 1976-77; Burroughs Wellcome Travel grantee, 1984, 92; MERIT award NIH, 1986, Discovery award Med. Rsch. Found., 1988, Burroughs Wellcome Vis. Prof. in the Basic Med. Scis. award U. Ariz., 1988-89, Sam Kuna Lectr. award Rutgers U., 1989, F.A. Gilfillan Meml. award for Dist. Scholarship in Sci., 1990. Mem. Am. Soc. Biol. Chemistry, Am. Soc. Pharmacology and Exptl. Therapeutics, Am. Assn. Cancer Rsch., Internat. Union Toxicology (dir. 1992—, 1st v.p. 1995—), Soc. Toxicology (pres. 1991-93), Sigma Xi (rsch. award), Phi Kappa Phi. Achievements include research in biological oxidations, environmental toxicology, biochemical anticancer drugs, protective mechanisms of glutathione functions, vitamin E status. Office: Oreg State U Environ Health Scis Ctr Agrl and Life Scis Bldg Rm 1011 Corvallis OR 97331-7302

REED, EDWARD CORNELIUS, JR., federal judge; b. Mason, Nev., July 8, 1924; s. Edward Cornelius Sr. and Evelyn (Walker) R.; m. Sally Torrance, June 14, 1952; children: Edward T., William W., John A., Mary E. BA, U. Nev., 1949; JD, Harvard U., 1952. Bar: Nev. 1952, U.S. Dist Ct. Nev. 1957, U.S. Supreme Ct. 1974. Atty. Arthur Andersen & Co., 1952-53; spl. dep. atty. gen. State of Nev., 1967-79; judge U.S. Dist. Ct. Nev., Reno, 1979—, chief judge, now sr. judge. Former vol. atty. Girl Scouts Am., Sierra Nevada Council, U. Nev., Nev. Agrl. Found., Nev. State Sch. Adminstrs. Assn., Nev. Congress of Parents and Teachers; mem. Washoe County Sch. Bd., 1956-72, pres. 1959, 63, 69; chmn. Gov.'s Sch. Survey Com., 1958-61; mem. Washoe County Bd. Tax Equalization, 1957-58, Washoe County Annexation Commn., 1968-72, Washoe County Personnel Com., 1973-77, chmn. 1973; mem. citizens adv. com. Washoe County Sch. Bond Issue, 1977-78, Sun Valley, Nev., Swimming Pool Com., 1978, Washoe County Blue Ribbon Task Force Com. on Growth, Nev. PTA (life); chmn. profl. div. United Way, 1978; bd. dirs. Reno Siver Sox, 1962-65. Served as staff sgt. U.S. Army, 1943-46, ETO, PTO. Mem. ABA (jud. adminstrn. sect.), Nev. State Bar Assn. (adminstrv. com. dist. 5, 1967-79, lien law com. 1965-78, chmn. 1965-72, probate law com. 1963-66, tax law com. 1962-65), Am. Judicature Soc. Democrat. Baptist. Office: US Dist Ct 5147 US Courthouse 300 Booth St Reno NV 89509-1316

REED, ELIZABETH MAY MILLARD, mathematics and computer science educator, publisher; b. Shippensburg, Pa., July 1, 1919; d. Jacob Franklin and Isabelle Bernadine (Dorn) Millard; m. Jesse Floyd Reed, Aug. 5, 1961; 1 child, David Millard. BA, Shepherd Coll., 1941; MA, Columbia U., 1948; postgrad., W.Va. U., U. Hawaii, Columbia U., NSF Summer Insts., Oakland U., 1974-85. Cert. assoc. in tchr. edn., W.Va. Math. tchr. Hedgesville (W.Va.) High Sch., 1941-47, Martinsburg (W.Va.) High Sch., 1948-51, George Washington High Sch. and Territorial Coll. Guam, Agana, 1952-54, Valley Stream (N.Y.) Meml. Jr. High Sch., 1954-55, Rye (N.Y.) High Sch., 1955-57, Elkins (W.Va.) Jr. High Sch., 1971-87; dir. admissions Davis and Elkins Coll., 1957-67, asst. prof. math., 1968-71, adj. prof., 1987—, lectr. geography, 1971-73; pres. Three Reeds Studios, Elkins, 1989—; Vets. Upward Bound, 1989-94; statis. clk. Lord, Abbett & Co., N.Y.C., 1947-48; customer rep. Kay, Richards & Co., Winchester, Va., 1951-52; mem. adj. grad. faculty W.Va. U., Morgantown, 1984-89; mem. adj. faculty Evans Coll. U. Charleston, W.Va., 1989-90; presenter regional and state computer workshops, W.Va. Author: Computer Literacy at Elkins Junior High School, 1983; project dir. (video) Women: Professionally Speaking, 1988. Dir. pilot project Project Bus., Jr. Achievement, Elkins, 1972-78; organizer Randolph County Math. Field Day, Elkins, 1977; initiator Comprehensive Achievement Monitoring, Elkins, 1980; treas. Humanities Found. W.Va., Charleston, 1983-85, pres., 1985-87; vice-moderator quadrant II Presbytery of W.Va. Recipient Presdl. award for Excellence in Tchg. Math. in W.Va., NSF, 1985. Mem. AAUW (pres. W.Va. divsn. 1977-79, editor 1983—, pres. Elkins br. 1988-94), W.Va. Coun. Tchrs. of Math., Nat. Coun. Tchrs. of Math., W.Va. Item Writing Workshop-Math. 9-12 (writer 1985-86). Avocations: travel, photography, reading mysteries, sewing, needlepoint. Home & Office: 4 Lincoln Ave Elkins WV 26241-3669

REED, EVA SILVER STAR, chieftain; b. Vinita, Okla., Nov. 29, 1929; d. Robert Elbert Jones and Anna Mae (Campfield) Reed; m. Johnnie Silver Eagle Reed, June 10, 1946 (dec. Sept. 1982); children: Patty Deeanne, Lorrie Ann, Billy John. Sec. United Lumbee Nation of N.C. and Am., Fall River Mills, Calif., 1979-82; nat. head chieftain United Lumbee Nation of N.C. and Am., Fall River Mills, 1982—, also bd. dirs.; bd. dirs., sec. Chapel of Our Lord Jesus, Exeter, Calif., 1974—, Native Am. Wolf Clan, Calif., 1977—; tchr. Indian beading and crafts, Calif., 1977—. Author, compiler: Over the Cooking Fires, 1982, Lumbee Indian Ceremonies, 1982, United Lumbee Deer Clan Cook Book, 1988; editor: (newspaper) United Lumbee Nation Times, 1981—. Mem. parent com. Title IV & Johnson O'Malley Indian Edn. Program, Tulare/Kings County, 1976-80, Shasta County, Calif., 1982-84. Recipient United Lumbee Nation of N.C. and Am.'s Silver Eagle award, 1991, also various awards for beadwork Intermountain Fair, Shasta County, 1982-95. Avocations: writing, Indian beadwork, basket making, Indian crafts. Office: United Lumbee Nation of NC & Am PO Box 512 Fall River Mills CA 96028

REED, FRANK FREMONT, II, retired lawyer; b. Chgo., June 15, 1928; s. Allen Martin and Frances (Faurot) R.; m. Jaquelin Silverthorne Cox, Apr. 27, 1963; children: Elizabeth Matthiessen Mason, Laurie Matthiessen Stern, Mark Matthiessen, Jeffrey, Nancy, Sarah. Student Chgo. Latin Sch.; grad. St. Paul's Sch., 1946; A.B., U. Mich., 1952, J.D., 1957. Bar: Ill., 1958. Assoc. Byron, Hume, Groen & Clement, 1958-61, Marks & Clerk, 1961-63; pvt. practice law, Chgo., 1963-78; dir. Western Acadia (Western Felt Works), 1960-75, chmn. exec. com., 1969-71. Rep. precinct capt. 1972-78; candidate for 43d ward alderman, 1975; bd. dirs., sec. Chgo. Found. Theater Arts, 1959-64; vestryman St. Chrysostom's Ch., 1975-79, mem. ushers guild, 1964-79, chmn., 1976-78; bd. dirs. North State, Astor, Lake Shore Dr. Assn., 1975-78, pres. 1977-78; bd. dirs. Community Arts Music Assn. of Santa Barbara, 1984-93, treas. 1988-93; bd. dirs. Santa Barbara Arts Coun., 1987-89. Cpl. AUS, 1952-54. Mem. ABA, Ill. Bar Assn., Phi Alpha Delta, Racquet Club, Wausaukee Club (sec., dir. 1968-71, 92-) (Chgo.); Birnam Wood Golf Club (Santa Barbara, Calif.). Episcopalian. Author: History of the Silverthorn Family, 4 vols., 1982, Allen Family of Allen's Grove, 1983, Goddard and Ware Ancestors, 1987, Faurot Family, 1988. Contbr. articles to The Am. Genealogist, 1972-73, 76-77. Home: 1944 E Valley Rd Santa Barbara CA 93108-1428

REED, FRANK METCALF, bank executive; b. Seattle, Dec. 22, 1912; s. Frank Ivan and Pauline B. (Hovey) R.; student U. Alaska, 1931-32; BA, U. Wash., 1937; m. Maxine Vivian McGary, June 11, 1937; children: Pauline Reed Mackay, Frank Metcalf. V.p. Anchorage Light & Power Co., 1937-42; pres. Alaska Electric & Equipment Co., Anchorage, 1946-50; sec., mgr. Turnagain, Inc., Anchorage, 1950-56; mgr. Gen. Credit Corp., Anchorage, 1957; br. mgr. Alaska SBA, Anchorage, 1958-60; sr. v.p. First Interstate Bank of Alaska, Anchorage, 1960-87, also dir., corp. sec.; dir. First Interstate Corp. of Alaska, First Nat. Bank of Fairbanks; pres., dir. Anchorage Broadcasters, Inc.; past pres., chmn. Microfast Software Corp.; dir., treas. R.M.R. Inc.; dir. Anchorage Light & Power Co., Turnagain, Inc., Alaska Fish and Farm, Inc., Life Ins. Co. Alaska. Pres., Anchorage Federated Charities, Inc., 1953-54; mem. advisory bd. Salvation Army, 1948-58; mem. Alaska adv. bd. Hugh O'Brian Youth Found., 1987-91; trustee Anchor Age Endowment Fund, 1988—, chmn., 1991; mem. City of Anchorage Planning Commn., 1956; mem. City of Anchorage Coun., 1956-57; police commr. Ter. of Alaska, 1957-58; chmn. City Charter Commn., 1958; mem. exec. com. Greater Anchorage, Inc., 1955-65; pres. Sch. Bd., 1961-64; mem. Gov.'s Investment adv. com., 1970-72; mem. Alaska State Bd. Edn.; mem. citizens adv. com. Alaska Meth. U.; chmn. Anchorage Charter Commn., 1975; chmn. bldg. fund dr. Cmty. YMCA, 1976—; sec.-treas. Breakthrough, 1976-78 ; bd. dirs Alaska Treatment Ctr., 1980-87, pres. 1985-86; trustee Marston Found., Inc., 1978, exec. dir. 1988. Served as lt. USNR, 1942-46. Elected to Hall Fame, Alaska Press Club, 1969; named Outstanding Alaskan of Year Alaska C. of C., 1976, Alaskan of Yr., 1990, Outstanding Vol. in Philanthropy Alaska chpt. Nat. Soc. Fundraising Execs, 1991. Mem. Am. Inst. Banking, Am. (exec. council 1971-72) Alaska (pres. 1970-71) bankers assns., Nat. Assn. State Bds. Edn. (sec.-treas. 1969-70), Anchorage C. of C. (pres. 1966-67, dir.), Pioneers of Alaska, Navy League (pres. Anchorage council 1961-62). Clubs: Tower (life), San Francisco Tennis. Lodges: Lions (sec. Anchorage, 1953-54, dir. 1988, pres., 1962-63), Elks. Home: 1361 W 12th Ave Anchorage AK 99501-4252

REED, GEORGE FORD, JR., investment executive; b. Hollywood, Calif., Dec. 26, 1946; s. George Ford and Mary Anita Reed; B.A. in Econs. with honors, U. So. Calif., 1969, M.A., 1971; m. Kathryn Nixon, 1981. Analyst planning and research Larwin Group, Beverly Hills, Calif., 1971-72; with Automobile Club So. Calif., Los Angeles, 1972-76, supr. mgmt. info., research and devel., 1973-74, mgr. fin. and market analysis, 1975-81, group mgr. fin. analysis and forecasting, 1981-86; pres. Reed Asset Mgmt. Co., Inc., Los Angeles, 1986—; instr. bus. and econs. Los Angeles Community Coll. Mem. population task force Los Angeles C. of C., 1974; mem. Gov. Calif. Statewide Econ. Summit Conf., 1974. Served with U.S. Army, 1969. Mem. Assn. Corp. Real Estate Execs., Fin. Execs. Inst., Nat. Assn. Bus. Economists, Western Regional Sci. Assn., Am. Mgmt. Assn., Am. Fin. Assn., So. Calif. Planners Assn., Rotary Internat., Omicron Delta Epsilon. Home: 1001 S Westgate Ave Los Angeles CA 90049-5905 Office: 10940 Wilshire Blvd Ste 1530 Los Angeles CA 90024-3915

REED, GLEN ALFRED, lawyer; b. Memphis, Sept. 24, 1951; s. Thomas Henry and Evelyn Merle (Roddy) R.; m. Edith Jean Renick, June 17, 1972; children: Adam Christopher, Alec Benjamin. BA, U. Tenn., 1972; JD, Yale U., 1976. Bar: Ga. 1976. Project dir. Tenn. Research Coordinating Unit, Knoxville, 1972-73; assoc. Alston Miller & Gaines, Atlanta, 1976-77; assoc. Bordurant Miller Hishon & Stephenson, Atlanta, 1978-81, ptnr., 1981-85; ptnr., King & Spalding, Atlanta, 1985—. Author: Practical Hospital Law, 1979. legal adv. Ga. Gov.'s Commn. on Healthcare, 1994; Gen. counsel Assn. Retarded Citizens-Atlanta, 1979—, pres., 1992—; vice-chmn. CARE Atlanta adv. bd., 1992-94, pres., 1994—; v.p. Ga. Network for People with Developmental Disabilities, 1991-92; bd. dirs. Ctrl. Health Ctr., 1989—, Vis. Nurse Health System, 1991—, Sch. Pub. Health Emory U., Atlanta, 1993—. Mem. ABA, Ga. Bar Assn., Acad. Hosp. Attys. (bd. dirs. 1991—), Ga. Acad. Hosp. Attys. (pres. 1991-92), Nat. Health Lawyers Assn., Phi Beta Kappa. Methodist. Office: King & Spalding 191 Peachtree St NE Atlanta GA 30303-1740

REED, GRANT, phamaceutical executive. CEO LaRoche Holdings. Office: 1100 Johson Ferry Rd NE Atlanta GA 30342

REED, HELEN I., medical, surgical nurse; b. Radford, Va., Aug. 3, 1967; d. Billy Wayne and Beverly Gayle (Sparks) R. Cert. Practical Nursing, Radford City Sch. Nursing, 1986; BSN, Radford U., 1990. RN, Va.; cert. med.-surg. nurse ANCC; cert. ACLS provider, CPR instr. Student nurse intern Radford Cmty. Hosp., 1989-90, staff nurse, 1990—; substitute instr. Radford City Sch. Practical Nursing, med. unit continuing edn. coord., preceptor to new staff. Jr. vol. Radford Cmty. Hosp., 1981-85. Nette Whitehead nursing scholar, John Nye scholar, jr. vol. scholar. Mem. ANA, NSNA. Methodist. Office: Radford Community Hosp Acute Care Ctr 700 Randolph St Radford VA 24141-2430

REED, ISHMAEL SCOTT (EMMETT COLEMAN), writer; b. Chattanooga, Feb. 22, 1938; s. Bennie Stephen (stepfather) and Thelma (Coleman) R.; m. Priscilla Rose, 1960 (div. 1970); children: Timothy, Brett; m. Carla Blank; 1 child, Tennessee Maria. Co-founder Yardbird Pub. Co. Inc., Berkeley, 1971, editorial dir., 1971-75; editor Yardbird Reader, 1972-76; co-founder Reed, Cannon & Johnson Comm. Co., Berkeley, 1973—, Before Columbus Found., Berkeley, 1976—; editor-in-chief Y'Bird mag., 1978-80; co-founder Ishmael Reed and Al Young's Quilt, Berkeley, 1980—; co-editor Quilt mag., 1981—; co-founder East Village Other, 1965, Advance, 1965; tchr. St. Mark's in the Bowery prose workshop, 1966; guest lectr. U. Calif., Berkeley, 1968—, U. Wash., 1969-70, SUNY, Buffalo, 1975, 79, Yale U., 1979, Dartmouth Coll., 1980-81, Sitka Cmty. Assn., 1982, U. Ark., Fayetteville, 1982, Columbia U., 1983, Harvard U., 1987; assoc. fellow Calhoun Coll., Yale U., 1982—, Harvard Signet Soc., 1987—; regents lectr. U. Calif., Santa Barbara, 1988; mem. usage panel Am. Heritage Dictionary. Author: (novels) The Free-Lance Pallbearers, 1967, Yellow Back Radio Broke-Down, 1969, Mumbo Jumbo, 1972 (Nat. Book award nomination 1973), The Last Days of Louisiana Red, 1974 (Richard and Hinda Rosenthal Found. award Nat. Inst. Arts and Letters 1975), Flight to Canada, 1976, The Terrible Twos, 1982, Reckless Eyeballing, 1986, Cab Calloway Stands In for The Moon, 1986, The Terrible Threes, 1989, Japanese By Spring, 1993; (poetry) Catechism of d neoamerican hoodoo church, 1970, Conjure: Selected Poems 1963-70, 1972 (Nat. Book award nomination 1973, Pulitzer prize nomination 1973), Chattanooga, 1973, A Secretary to the Spirits, 1978, Ishmael Reed: New and Collected Poems, 1989; (essays) Shrovetide in Old New Orleans, 1978, God Made Alaska for the Indians, 1981, Airing Dirty Laundry, 1993; (play) (with Carla Blank and Suzushi Hanayagi) The Lost State of Franklin, 1976; editor: The Rise, Fall, and...? of Adam Clayton Powell, 1967, 19 Necromancers from Now, 1970 (Calif. Assn. Eng. Tchrs. certificate of merit 1972), Yardbird Lives!, 1978, Calafia: The California Poetry, 1979, Writin' Is Fightin': Thirty-seven Years of Boxing on Paper, 1988; exec. prodr.: (TV pilot) Personal Problems. Chmn. Berkeley Arts Commn., 1980, 81; bd. dirs. chmn. Coordinating Council Lit. Mags., 1975-79, adv. bd. chmn., 1977-79. Recipient John Simon Guggenheim Meml. Found. award for fiction, 1974, Lewis Michaux award, 1978, ACLU award, 1978, Pushcart prize, 1979; Wis. Arts Bd. fellow, 1982; Nat. Endowment for Arts writing fellow, 1974; Guggenheim fellow, 1975. Mem. Author's Guild Am., PEN, Celtic Found.

REED, JAMES DONALD, journalist, author; b. Jackson, Mich., Oct. 7, 1940; s. Clair and Esther (Bryden) R.; m. Christine Flowers, June 14, 1969; children: Phoebe C., Alicia M., Gabrielle A. Student, Albion Coll., 1958-60; BA, Mich. State U., 1962; postgrad., SUNY-Stony Brook, 1967-69; MFA, U. Mont., 1970. Mem. faculty dept. creative writing U. Mass., 1970-75; dir. M.F.A. program, 1974; staff writer Sports Illustrated, N.Y.C., 1975-80; assoc. editor Time mag., 1980-90; sr. writer People mag., N.Y.C., 1990-91, sr. editor, 1991-93; sr. assoc. editor spl. issues, 1993—. Author: (poetry) Expressways, 1970, Fatback Odes, 1973; (fiction) Free Fall, 1980; (with Christine Reed) Exposure, 1987. Guggenheim fellow, 1971. Office: People Mag Time Life Bldg Rockefeller Ctr New York NY 10020

REED, JAMES ELDIN, consultant, educator; b. Walla Walla, Wash., Mar. 13, 1945; s. Eldin Wallace and Mary Ellen (White) R.; m. Deborah Jane Addis, Apr. 14, 1983. AB, Ripon Coll., 1967; AM, Harvard U., 1968, MTS, 1971, PhD, 1976. Tchg. fellow Harvard U., Cambridge, Mass., 1972-77; founder, pres. Addis & Reed Cons., Inc., Boston, 1977-94; chmn. ARC Internat., Boston, 1995—; rsch. assoc., adj. prof. Fletcher Sch. Law and Diplomacy, Medford, Mass., 1994—; v.p., pres. Assn. Mgmt. Cons., Boston, 1985-89. Author: The Missionary Mind, 1983; editor: (newsletter) American Canada Watch, 1995—; contbr. numerous articles, papers, and revs. to profl. publs. Cons. House Agr. Com. Washington, 1978; invited witness Senate Judiciary Com., Washington, 1990. Woodrow Wilson fellow, 1967-68; vis. scholar Harvard U., 1993-94. Mem. Am. Hist. Assn., Can. Inst. Internat. Affairs, Boston Athenaeum, Harvard Club of Boston, Phi Beta Kappa. Unitarian. Achievements include study of traditional Far East policy of U.S. Home: 25 Holly Ln Brookline MA 02167 Office: ARC Internat PO Box 85 Chestnut Hill MA 02167

REED, JAMES WESLEY, social historian, educator; b. New Orleans, Oct. 17, 1944; married. BA, U. New Orleans, 1967; AM, Harvard U., 1968, PhD, 1974. Research fellow in history Schlesinger Library, 1973-75; prof. history Rutgers U., New Brunswick, N.J., 1975—; dean Rutgers Coll., Rutgers U., New Brunswick, 1985-94. Author: From Private Vice to Public Virtue: The Birth Control Movement and American Society Since 1930, 1978. Office: Rutgers U Dept of History Van Dyke Hall New Brunswick NJ 08903-5059

REED, JAMES WHITFIELD, physician, educator; b. Pahokee, Fla., Nov. 1, 1935; s. Thomas Reed and Chineater (Grey) Whitfield; married; children: David M., Robert A., Mary I., Katherine E. BS, W.Va. State Coll., 1954; MD, Howard U., 1963. Diplomate Am. Bd. Internal Medicine, Am. Bd. Endocrinology and Metabolism. Commd. U.S. Army, 1963; advanced through grades to col., 1981; resident in internal medicine Madigan Army Med. Ctr., Tacoma, Wash., 1966-69, chief endocrinology and metabolism, 1971-76, chief dept. clin. rsch., 1976-78; chief dept. medicine Eisenhower Army Med. Ctr., Augusta, Ga., 1978-81; assoc. prof. internal medicine edn. for FP program U. Tex. at Dallas, 1981-84; prof. medicine Morehouse Sch. Medicine, Atlanta, 1985—, chmn. dept., 1985-92, chmn. grad. med. edn., 1992—, activity chmn., 1986-88; postdoctoral fellow in endocrinology and metabolism U. Calif. Med. Ctr., San Francisco, 1969-71; dir. endocrinology, fellow Madigan Army Med. Ctr., 1976-78; dir. internal medicine residency program Eisenhower Army Med. Ctr., 1978-81, chmn. directorate of clin. investigation, 1978-81, dir. endocrinology fellowship program; med. cons. Tuskgee (Ala.) VA Hosp., 1985—; mem. nat. high blood pressure edn. com. NHLBI/NIH, Nat. Diabetes Mellitus Adv. Coun., Nat. Diabetes Adv. Bd., NHLBI working Com. on Hypertension and Diabetes; chmn. Sub Com. Special Population and Situations, chmn. subcom., mem. exec. com. Joint Nat. Commn. for Detection Evaluation and Treatment of High Blood Pressure. Author: Black Man's Guide to Good Health, 1994; contbr. articles to profl. publs. Med. advisor, chmn. March of Dimes, Pierce County, Tacoma, 1976-78; pres. Charles Drew Sickle Cell and Health Bd., Tacoma, 1976-78; mem. task force on cardiovascular risk reduction Am. Heart Assn. Decorated Legion of Merit; recipient Disting. Alumni award Nat. Assn. for Equal Opportunity in Higher Edn., 1988, Nat. Alumnus of Yr. award W.Va. State Coll., 1987; inducted into ROTC Hall of Fame, W.Va. State Coll., 1987. Fellow ACP; mem. Assn. Profs. Medicine, Endocrine Soc., Internat. Soc. Hypertension in Blacks (v.p. 1986, pres. 1992—), Assn. of Program Dirs. in Internal Medicine, Am. Heart Assn. Task Force on Cardiovascular Risk, Alpha Phi Alpha. Democrat. Avocations: bowling, skiing. Home: 380 Mcgill Pl NE Atlanta GA 30312-1069 Office: Morehouse Sch Medicine 720 Westview Dr SW Atlanta GA 30310-1458 *One cannot control the circumstance of one's birth, but with keen alertness and honest hard work there are no limits to what one can achieve. So hitch your wagon to a star and never lose sight of it.*

REED, JESSE FRANCIS, entrepreneur, artist, inventor, theologian, business consultant; b. Federalsburg, Md., June 6, 1925; s. Homer F. and Lola Irene (Stevens) R.; BFA, Montclair Coll., 1950; DD, Gnostic Sem., 1968; m. Mary Grace Mayo, July 9, 1944; 1 son, Gary. Owner, Reed's Frozen Foods, Paterson, N.J., 1950-59; pres. A.E. Inc., N.Y.C., 1959-72, Intercontinental Bus. Rsch. & Devel. Inc., San Francisco, 1959-72, chmn. bd., pres. Dallas and Washington, 1972—, Intercontinental Oil & Ore Inc., Carson City, Nev. and Dallas, 1972—; chmn. bd., pres. COSMO U.S.A., Inc., Dallas and Washington, 1974—, Internat. Art Exchange Ltd., Dallas and Los Angeles, 1980—; chmn. bd. Gnosis (Self Discovery and Identification Sys.), 1980—. Chmn. bd. Internat. Arts Soc., Inc., Dallas, 1981—; dir. XTR Corp. Bd. dirs. Am. Art Alliance, Inc., Internat. Fine Art, Inc., Worldwide Art Exchange, Inc., IBR&D, Inc. Gnostic Ch. Served with USN, 1942-46. Recipient various Art Show awards in Tex., Calif., N.J., N.Y., Ga., Fla., Wash., Ill., Hawaii, Minn., Nev., N.Mex., Oreg., Mo., Can., Eng., France, Belgium, Norway, Sweden, Denmark, Switzerland, Australia, N.Z. Mem. Screen Writers Guild, Cattlemen's Assn. Inventor protein converter (controlled environ. food prodn. chain) , visual edn. system to translate all ednl. disciplines into their pictorial presentations, modular prefabricate bldg. systems, BIO-HAB (a self energizing life-support system employing; bio chemical, wind, solar, voltaic-cell, energy to powerheat-cool and feed humans and animals), solar energy systems, hydroponic systems, plasma energy systems, electric vehicle systems, subliminal learning systems, precious metal recovery/assaying systems, currency system based upon precious metal art creations, estate protection systems, health systems. Office: PO Box 12488 Dallas TX 75225-0488

REED, JOAN-MARIE, special education educator; b. St. Paul, Sept. 8, 1960; d. William Martin Reed and Diana-Marie (Miller) Reed Moss. BA, U. Minn., 1982, BS, 1983; MEd, Tex. Woman's U., 1986. Cert. tchr., Tex. Tchr. emotionally disturbed Birdville Ind. Sch. Dist., Ft. Worth, 1984-86; tchr. emotionally disturbed Goose Creek Ind. Sch. Dist., Baytown, Tex., 1986-92, ctr. leader, 1992-93, dept. chairperson, 1987-91; tchr. emotionally disturbed Conroe (Tex.) Ind. Sch. Dist., 1993-94, Willis (Tex.) Ind. Sch. Dist., 1994-95, Jefferson County Pub. Schs., 1995—; Co-editor: New Teacher Handbook, 1986-87, Behavior Improvement Program Handbook, 1987-88. Mem. NEA, Coun. for Exceptional Children. Congregationalist. Avocations: reading, classical literature, traveling, walking, biking.

REED, JODY ERIC, professional baseball player; b. Tampa, Fla., June 26, 1995. Student, Manatee Jr. Coll.; BA, Fla. State U., 1985. With Milw. Brewers, Boston Red Sox, 1987-92, L.A. Dodgers, 1993; 2d baseman San Diego Padres, 1995—. Achievements include mem. Am. League East Divsn. Champions, 1988, 90. Office: Boston Red Sox 4 Yawkey Way Boston MA 02215

REED, JOEL LESTON, diversified manufacturing company executive; b. Enid, Okla., Jan. 21, 1951; s. Arrel Leston and Velma Jo (Kesner) R.; m. Alicia Kay Biller, Nov. 28, 1970 (dec.); m. Ann Denise Timmersman, June 6, 1981; children: Benjamin Joel, Elizabeth Ann, Peter David. BS in Acctg., Okla. State U., 1972, MS in Acctg., 1973. CPA, Okla, Colo. Successively staff acct., sr. acct., mgr. Deloitte Haskins & Sells, Denver, 1973-81; contr., treas. Ensource Inc., Englewood, Colo., 1981-82, v.p., CFO, 1983-84; CFP Wagner & Brown, Midland, Tex., 1984-89, pres., CEO, 1993-94; ptnr. Batchelder & Ptnrs., Inc., La Jolla, Calif., 1994—; pres., CEO Insilco Corp., 1989-93. Contbr. articles to profl. jours. Mem. AICPA (oil and gas com., Elijah Watt Sells award 1973), Colo. Soc. CPAs, Am. Petroleum Inst., Ind. Petroleum Assn. Am., Porsche Car Club Am., Beta Alpha Psi. Home: 1608 Stanolind Ave Midland TX 79705-8651*

REED, JOHN ALTON, lawyer; b. Washington, June 29, 1931; s. John Alton and Emma Powers (Ball) R.; m. Louisa Wardman, June 6, 1953; children: Donna, Joanne, Deborah. AB, Duke U., 1954, LLB, 1956. Bar: Fla. 1956. Assoc. firm Fowler-White, Tampa, Fla., 1956-57; partner firm Rush, Reed & Marshall, Orlando, Fla., 1957-67; judge Fla. 4th Dist. Ct. Appeal, 1967-73, chief judge, 1971-73; judge U.S. Dist. Ct. for Middle Dist. Fla., Orlando, 1973-84; ptnr., chmn. dept. litigation Lowndes, Drosdick, Doster, Kantor & Reed, Orlando, 1985—; mem. com. on standard civil jury instructions Fla. Supreme Ct. Bd. visitors Duke U. Law Sch., 1983—. Mem. Am., Orange County, Fla. bar assns., Am. Judicature Soc. Republican. Episcopalian. Home: 1020 Mayfield Ave Winter Park FL 32789-2613 Office: PO Box 2809 215 N Eola Dr Orlando FL 32802*

REED, JOHN CHARLES, chemical engineer; b. Springfield, Ill., Dec. 3, 1930; s. Ralph Albert and Haldeen (Vandeveer) R.; m. Mary Helen Simpson, June 25, 1966; children: Katherine June Griffin, Kare Joy Griffin, Stephanie Lynn Reed. BSChemE, U. Ill., 1953; MSChemE, U. Del., 1954; PhD, U. Wis., 1961. Registered profl. engr., Ill., Okla. Chem. engr. Esso Rsch. and Engring., Linden, N.J., 1960-62; sr. engr. Pan Am. Petroleum Corp., Tulsa, 1962-69; assoc. prof. U. Tulsa, 1969-71; supr., tech. advisor, sr. pub. svc. adminstr. Ill. EPA, Springfield, 1971—. With U.S. Army, 1954-56. Mem. AICE (Winston Churchill fellowship 1970), Am. Chem. soc., Am. Soc. of Cost Engrs. Home: 317 W Franklin St Edinburg IL 62531-9412 Office: Ill EPA PO Box 19276 Springfield IL 62794-9276

REED, JOHN FRANCIS (JACK REED), congressman, lawyer; b. Providence, Nov. 12, 1949; s. Joseph Anthony and Mary Louise (Monahan) R. BS, U.S. Mil. Acad., 1971; M in Pub. Policy, Harvard U., 1973, JD cum laude, 1982. Bar: D.C. 1982, R.I. 1983. Commd. 2d. lt. U.S. Army, 1971, served with 82d Airborne Div., 1973-77; asst. prof. U.S. Mil. Acad., West Point, N.Y., 1977-79; resigned U.S. Army, 1979; assoc. Sutherland, Asbill & Brennan, Washington, 1982-83, Edwards & Angell, Providence, 1983-89; mem. R.I. Senate, 1984-90, 102nd-104th Congresses from 2d R.I. dist., 1990—; mem. judiciary com., mem. econ. and ednl. opportunity com., regional whip for New Eng. Dem. del.; vice chair N.E.-Midwest Congl. Coalition. Author: (with others) American National Security, 1981. Recipient Disting. Svc. award AARP, 1989, John Fogarty award, 1990, Disting. Legislator award United Way Southeastern New Eng., 1988. Mem. ABA, R.I. Bar Assn., D.C. Bar Assn., Environ. and Energy Study Inst., Phi Kappa Phi. Democrat. Roman Catholic. Avocations: reading, hiking. Office: US

Ho of Reps 1510 Longworth HOB Washington DC 20515 also: Dist Office 100 Midway Rd Ste 5 Cranston RI 02920-5707*

REED, JOHN FRANKLIN, instrument manufacturing company executive; b. Winfield, Mo., Aug. 10, 1917; s. Claude F. and Inez (Crenshaw) R.; m. Ann M. Walter, Aug. 31, 1940; children: John Franklin, James D., Thomas W., William C., Robert D. B.S. in Mining Engring, Mo. Sch. Mines and Metallurgy, 1940. Indsl. engr. Tenn. Coal Iron R.R. Co., 1940-42; time study methods engr. McDonnell Aircraft Corp., 1943; prodn. planner, chief estimator Fairchild Aircraft Co., 1944; joined Manning, Maxwell & Moore, Inc., Stratford, Conn., 1944; works mgr. Manning, Maxwell & Moore, Inc., Tulsa, Shaw Box, Crane and Hoist div., Muskegon, Mich., 1951-57; gen. mgr. Instrument and Gauge div., 1957-59, v.p., gen. mgr., 1959, exec. v.p., 1959-62, pres., chief exec. officer, dir., 1962-65; pres., dir. Manning, Maxwell and Moore of Can., Ltd., Galt, Ont., 1962-65; pres., chief oper. officer Hupp Corp., Cleve., 1965-67, pres., dir., 1967-68; pres., chief exec. officer, dir. Hercules Galion Products, Inc., Ohio, 1968-69; pres., chief exec., dir. Canrad Inc., Newark, 1969—; chmn. Canrad Inc., 1976-86; mem. exec. com. Canrad-Hanovia Inc., 1984-89, also bd. dirs., 1984-89; bd. dirs. Rhein Med., Tampa, Fla., Am. Health Capital, Irving, Tex. Mem. Royal Poinciana Golf. Presbyterian. Home: 745 Willowhead Dr Naples FL 33940-3543

REED, JOHN HATHAWAY, former ambassador; b. Fort Fairfield, Maine, Jan. 5, 1921; s. Walter and Eva Ruth (Seeley) R.; m. Cora Mitchell Davison, Mar. 24, 1944; children—Cheryl, Ruth. B.S., U. Maine, 1942, LL.D. (hon.), 1960; LL.D. (hon.), Ricker Coll.; grad., Harvard Naval Supply Sch., 1944. Officer Reed Farms, Inc., Fort Fairfield, Maine, 1948—; pres. Aroostook Raceway, Inc., 1958-59; adv. com. Fort Fairfield br. No. Nat. Bank of Presque Isle; mem. Nat. Transp. Safety Bd., Washington, 1967-75, chmn., 1969-75; ambassador to Sri Lanka Colombo, 1975-77; dir. govt. rels. Assoc. Builders & Contractors, Inc., Washington, 1978-81; ambassador to Sri Lanka and Republic of Maldives, 1982-85; cons. Dept. State, 1985-90; pvt. practice cons. Washington, 1990—; chmn. Nat. Govs. Conf. Rep., 1966; rep. Fort Fairfield to Maine Legislature, 1954-56; mem. Senate, 1957-59, pres., 1959-60; gov. State of Maine, 1960-67. Pres. bd. Community Gen. Hosp., Fort Fairfield, 1952-54, No. Maine Fair, 1953-59; trustee Ricker Coll., 1953-60, Oak Grove Sch., Vassalboro, Maine; bd. advisors Coll. of Democracy, 1986—, chmn., 1991—. Served to lt. (j.g.) USNR, 1942-46. Mem. Am. Fgn. Svc. Assn., Coun. Am. Abassadors, Soc. Sr. Aerospace Execs. Inc. (bd. dirs. 1987—, pres. 1988-91), Nat. Inst. Former Govs. (bd. dirs. 1992—), Am. Legion, VFW, Grange, Maine Assn. Agrl. Fairs (pres. 1956), Mil. Order of Carabao, Capitol Hill Club, Driving Club (Ft. Fairfield) (pres. 1950-53), Rotary, Masons, KP. Republican. Congregationalist. Office: 410 O St SW Washington DC 20024-2239

REED, JOHN HOWARD, school administrator; b. Bloomfield, Mo., July 14, 1934; s. Floyd John and Lena Joyce (Howard) R.; m. Weymuth Heuiser; children: Cathy, David. BS cum laude, SE Mo. State U., 1956; M., U. Mo., 1959; edn. specialist, SE Mo. State U., 1977; PhD, So. Ill. U., 1983. Cert. supt., prin., tchr. Tchr., coach Scott County R-6 Schs., Sikeston, Mo., 1956-63; supr. student tchr. SE Mo. State U., Cape Girardeau, 1963-75; prin. Scott County R-3 Schs., Oran, Mo., 1975-76; supt. schs. Scott County R-2 Schs., Chaffee, Mo., 1976-79; bus. mgr. SE Mo. State U., Cape Girardeau, 1980-83; dean, pres. Sikeston C.C., 1983-86; supt. Marion County Sch. Dist. 1, Centralia, Ill., 1986-88; head New Life Montessori Sch., Shreveport, La., 1989-90, Belleview Schs., Westminster, Colo., 1990—. Editor: History of Missouri National Guard, 1963. Bd. dirs., sec. Scott County Bd. Edn., Benton, Mo., 1970-79. Lt. col. U.S. Army, 1960-63. Mem. Rotary (sec. 1976-78), Phi Alpha Theta (pres. 1976-78). Baptist. Avocation: history. Home: 8175 Green Ct Westminster CO 80030-4101 Office: Belleview Schs 3455 W 83rd Ave Westminster CO 80030-4005

REED, JOHN SHEDD, former railway executive; b. Chgo., June 9, 1917; s. Kersey Coates and Helen May (Shedd) R.; m. Marjorie Lindsay, May 4, 1946; children: Ginevra, Keith, Helen, Peter, John Shedd. Student, Chgo. Latin Sch., Hotchkiss Sch.; BS in Indsl. Adminstrn., Yale U., 1939; grad., Advanced Mgmt. Program, Harvard U., 1955. With A.T. & S.F. Ry., 1939-83; test dept. asst., successively spl. rep. to gen. supt. transp. Chgo.; transp. insp. Amarillo, Tex.; trainmaster Slaton, Tex., Pueblo, Colo.; supt. Mo. div., Marceline, Mo.; asst. to v.p. Chgo., 1957-59, exec. asst. to pres., 1957-59, v.p. finance, 1959-64, v.p. exec. dept., 1964-67, pres., 1967-78, chief exec. officer, 1968-82, chmn. bd., 1973-83; pres. Santa Fe Industries, Inc., 1968-78, chmn. bd. dirs., CEO Santa Fe So. Pacific Corp., 1987, chmn., 1987-88. Dir. Nat. Merit Scholarship Corp., 1996, past chmn.; trustee Shedd Aquarium, Chgo., 1996, past pres. With USNR, 1940-45. Mem. Chgo. Club, Old Elm Club, Shoreacres Club, Onwentsia Club (Lake Forest). Home: 301 W Laurel Ave # 112 Lake Forest IL 60045-1180 Office: 224 S Michigan Ave Rm 200 Chicago IL 60604-2507

REED, JOHN SHEPARD, banking executive; b. Chgo., Feb. 7, 1939; divorced; 4 children; m. Cindy McCarthy, 1994. BA and BS, Washington and Jefferson Coll., MIT, 1961; MS, Sloan Sch. MIT, 1965. With Citicorp/Citibank, 1965—, chmn., CEO, 1984—; bd. dirs. Philip Morris Inc., Monsanto Co.; mem. Bus. Coun.; mem. policy com., Bus. Roundtable; chmn. Coalition of Svc. Inds., svcs. policy adv. com. to the U.S. Trade Rep. Mem. bd. MIT, Meml. Sloan-Kettering Cancer Ctr., Rand Corp., Spencer Found., Am. Mus. Nat. History. Served with C.E. U.S. Army, Korea, 1962-64.

REED, JOHN THEODORE, publisher, writer; b. Camden, N.J., July 5, 1946; s. Theodore and Marion Theresa (Simonsick) R.; m. Margaret Ogden Tunnell, May 31, 1975; children: Daniel Tunnell, Steven Tunnell, Michael Tunnell. BS in Mil. Sci., U.S. Mil. Acad., West Point, N.Y., 1968; MBA, Harvard U., 1977. Salesman Pritchett & Co., Pine Hill and Collingswood, N.J., 1972-74; property mgr. Fox & Lazo Inc., Cherry Hill, N.J., 1974-75; writer Harcourt Brace Jovanovich, Boston, 1976-86; bank exec. Crocker Nat. Bank, San Francisco, 1977-78; writer, pub. Danville, Calif., 1977—. Author, pub.: Apartment Investing Check Lists, 1978, Aggressive Tax Avoidance for Real Estate Investors, 1981, 15th edit., 1996, How to Manage Residential Property for Maximum Cash Flow and Resale Value, 1995, 4th edit., 1991, How to Use Leverage to Maximize Your Real Estate Investment Return, 1984, 86, How to Increase the Value of Real Estate, 1986, Office Building Acquisition Handbook, 1982, 85, 87, Residential Property Acquisition Handbook, 1991, How To Buy Real Estate for at Least 20% Below Market Value, 1993, Coaching Youth Football Defense, 1994, John T. Reed's Real Estate Investor's Monthly Newsletter, 1986—, Coaching Youth Football, 1995. Served to 1st lt. U.S. Army, 1968-72, Vietnam. Mem. Nat. Assn. Real Estate Editors, Am. Baseball Coaches Assn., Am. Football Coaches Assn., Nat. Youth Sports Coaches Assn., Nat. Fedn. Interscholastic Coaches Assn. Avocations: reading, baseball, youth and high sch. coaching, activities with family. Home: 342 Bryan Dr Danville CA 94526-1258 Office: John T. Reed Pub 342 Bryan Dr Danville CA 94526-1258

REED, JOHN W., religious organization administrator. Pres. Min. and Missionaries Benefit Bd. of the ABC inthe USA. Office: Min & Miss Benefit Board 475 Riverside Dr New York NY 10115-0122

REED, JOHN WESLEY, lawyer, educator; b. Independence, Mo., Dec. 11, 1918; s. Novus H. and Lilian (Houchens) R.; m. Dorothy Elaine Floyd, Mar. 5, 1961; children: Alison A., John M. (dec.), Mary V., Randolph F., Suzanne M. AB, William Jewell Coll., 1939, LLD, 1995; LLB, Cornell U., 1942; LLM, Columbia U., 1949, JSD, 1957. Bar: Mo. 1942, Mich. 1953. Assoc. Stinson, Mag, Thomson, McEvers & Fizzell, Kansas City, Mo., 1942-46; assoc. prof. law U. Okla., 1946-49; assoc. prof. U. Mich., 1949-53, prof., 1953-64, 68-85, Thomas M. Cooley prof., 1985-87, Thomas M. Cooley prof. emeritus, 1987—; dean, prof. U. Colo., 1964-68; dean, prof. Wayne State U., Detroit, 1987-92, prof. emeritus, 1992—; vis. prof. NYU, 1949, U. Chgo., 1960, Yale U., 1963-64, Harvard U., 1982, U. San Diego, 1993; dir. Inst. Continuing Legal Edn., 1968-73; reporter Mich. Rules of Evidence Com., 1975-78, 83-84. Author: (with W.W. Blume) Pleading and Joinder, 1952; (with others) Introduction to Law and Equity, 1953, Advocacy Course Handbook series, 1963-81; editor in chief Cornell Law Quar., 1941-42; contbr. articles to profl. jours. Pres. bd. mgrs. of mins. and missionaries benefit bd. Am. Bapt. Chs. U.S.A., 1967-74, 82-85, 88-94; mem. com. visitors JAG Sch., 1971-76; trustee Kalamazoo Coll., 1954-64, 68-70. Recipient Harrison Tweed award Assn. Continuing Legal Edn. Adminstrs., 1983, Samuel E. Gates award Am. Coll. Trial Lawyers, 1985, Roberts P. Hudson award State Bar Mich., 1989. Fellow Internat. Soc. Barristers (editor jour. 1980—); mem. ABA (mem. coun. litigation sect.), Assn. Am. Law Schs. (mem. exec. com. 1965-67), Am. Acad. Jud. Edn. (v.p. 1978-80), Colo. Bar Assn. (mem. bd. govs. 1964-68), Mich. Supreme Ct. Hist. Soc. (bd. dirs. 1991—), Sci. Club Mich., Order of Coif. Office: U Mich Sch Law Ann Arbor MI 48109-1215

REED, JOSEPH RAYMOND, civil engineering educator, academic administrator; b. Pitts., Aug. 15, 1930; s. David Raymond and Mary (O'Neil) R.; m. Mary Morris Leggett, Mar. 19, 1960; children: Michelle Edwards, Stephanie Anne Reed Wilkinson, David Shepard Reed. BS in Civil Engring., Pa. State U., 1952, MS in Civil Engring., 1955; PhD in Civil Engring., Cornell U., 1971. Registered profl. engr., Tex. Asst. engr. George H. McGinness Assocs., Pitts., 1953-55; constrn. liaison officer USAF, Dallas, 1956-59; civil engring. faculty Pa. State U., University Park, 1959-64; rsch. asst. Cornell U., Ithaca, N.Y., 1964-67; prof. civil engring. Pa. State U., 1967-95; prof. emeritus Cornell U., Ithaca, N.Y., 1996; cons. Westvaco, Tyrone, Pa., 1981, Ketron, Inc., Phila., 1982-83, McGraw-Hill Book Co., N.Y.C., 1984-91, MacMillan Pub. Co., N.Y.C., 1987, others; acad. officer dept. civil engring. Pa. State U., 1989-95. Chmn. Stormwater Authority, State College, Pa., 1974-78; coach State Little League, Teener League (All-Star team state championship 1986) and Am. Legion Baseball, State College, 1978-89. Capt. USAF, 1956-59, USAFR, 1959-71. Sci.-Faculty fellow NSF, 1966-67; recipient Adviser Leadership award Tau Beta Pi Assn., 1986. Mem. ASCE, Internat. Assn. Hydraulic Rsch., Elks, Scottish Rite, Sigma Xi, Tau Beta Pi, Chi Epsilon, Phi Sigma Kappa (v.p. 1952). Presbyterian. Avocations: golf, bowling, youth baseball. Home: 1394 Penfield Rd State College PA 16801-6419 Office: Pa State U Dept Civil Engring 212 Sackett Bldg University Park PA 16802-1408 *Everyone will probably be a teacher at some point in their lives, be it as a professional, a parent, a coach, a supervisor, etc. An effective philosophy to follow is to teach the way you would like to be taught.*

REED, JOSEPH VERNER, JR., diplomat; b. N.Y.C., Dec. 17, 1937; s. Joseph V. and Permelia (Pryor) R; m. Marie Maude Byers, Dec. 19, 1959; children: Serena, Electra. BA, Yale U., 1961. With office of pres. The World Bank, Washington, 1959-61; asst. to pres. IBRD, 1961-63; asst. to dir. Chase Manhattan Bank, 1963-68, v.p., exec. asst. to chmn., 1969-81; U.S. amb. to Morocco, 1981-85; amb. to ECOSOC of UN, N.Y.C., 1985-87; undersec. gen. UN, 1987-89; U.S. chief of protocol, The White Ho., Washington, 1989-91; U.S. rep. to UN Gen. Assembly, 1992—; under-sec. gen. UN spl. rep. pub. affairs, 1992—. Mem. Coun. on Fgn. Rels., Met. Club, Links club, River Club. Republican. Episcopalian. Home: 73 Sterling Rd Greenwich CT 06831-2627 Office: Under-Sec-Gen UN Rm S-3045A New York NY 10017

REED, JOSEPH WAYNE, American studies educator; b. St. Petersburg, Fla., May 31, 1932; s. Joseph Wayne and Gertrude (Cain) R.; m. Lillian Craig (Kit), Dec. 10, 1955; children: Joseph McKean, John Craig, Katherine Hyde. BA, Yale U., 1954, MA, 1958, PhD, 1961. Rsch. asst. Yale Libr., 1956-57; instr. English Wesleyan U., Middletown, Conn., 1960-61, asst. prof., 1961-67, assoc. prof., 1967-71, prof., 1971—, chmn. dept., 1971-73, 75-76, 85-86, prof. English and Am. studies, 1987; vis. lectr. Yale U., New Haven, 1974; lectr. U.S. dept. State and USIS, Can., India, Nepal, 1974; coord. cultural exch., New Delhi, Bombay, 1992; coord. music and writing workshop U. Va., Georgetown U., others. Author: English Biography in the Early Nineteenth Century, 1801-38, 1966, Faulkner's Narrative, 1973, Three American Originals: John Ford, William Faulkner, Charles Ives, 1984, American Scenarios, 1989, rev. edit., 1990; editor: Barbara Bodichon's American Diary, 1972, (with W.S. Lewis) Horace Walpole's Family Correspondence, 1975, (with F.A. Pottle) Boswell, Laird of Auchinleck, 1977, 2d edit., 1994; one-man shows include Portal Gallery, London, 1971, USIS Libr., New Delhi, 1974, 92, Addison/Ripley Gallery, Washington, 1987, 92, 95. Chmn. Wesleyan Sesquicentennial, 1982; chmn. bd. trustees Yale Libr. Assocs., 1984—. Lt. (j.g.) USNR, 1954-56. Mem. Elizabethan Club, The Johnsonians (chmn. 1988). Democrat. Episcopalian. Home: 45 Lawn Ave Middletown CT 06457-3135

REED, KATHLYN LOUISE, occupational therapist, educator; b. Detroit, June 2, 1940; d. Herbert C. and Jessie R. (Krehbiel) R. BS in Occupational Therapy, U. Kans., 1964; MA, Western Mich. U., 1966; PhD, U. Wash., 1973; MLS, U. Okla., 1987. Occupational therapist in psychiatry Kans. U. Med. Center, Kansas City, 1964-65; instr. occupational therapy U. Wash., Seattle, 1967-70; assoc. prof. dept. occupational therapy U. Okla. Health Scis. Ctr., Oklahoma City, 1973-77, prof., 1978-85; chmn. dept. occupational therapy U. Okla. Health Scis. Ctr., 1973-85; libr. edn. info. svcs. Houston Acad. Medicine Tex. Med. Ctr. Libr., 1988—; cons. to Okla. State Dept. Health, 1976-77, Children's Convalescent Ctr., Oklahoma City, 1977-80, Oklahoma City pub. schs., 1980-81; vis. scholars program Tex. Woman's U., 1991-94, adj. prof. Sch. Occupational Therapy, Tex. Woman's U., 1992—. Author: (with Sharon Sanderson) Concepts of Occupational Therapy, 1980, 2d edit., 1983, 3rd edit., 1992, Models of Practice in Occupational Therapy, 1983, Quick Reference to Occupational Therapy, 1991, (with Julie Pauls) Quick Reference to Physical Therapy, 1996. Vol. crisis counselor Open Door Clinic, Seattle, 1968-72; mem. exec. bd. Seattle Mental Health Inst., 1971-72; Mem. Citizen Participation Liaison Council, Seattle, 1970-72. Recipient Award of Merit, Can. Assn. Occupational Therapists, 1988. Fellow Am. Occupational Therapy Assn. (Merit award 1983, Slagle lecture award 1985, Svc. award 1985); mem. ALA, World Fedn. Occupational Therapists, Coun. Exceptional Children, Okla. Occupational Therapy Assn. (pres. 1974-76), Tex. Occupational Therapy Assn., Med. Libr. Assn. (Rittenhouse award 1987, Acad. Health Info. Professions), Nat. Rehab. Assn., Am. Occupational Therapy Found., Assn. Advancement Rehab. Tech., Sensory Integration Internat., Sigma Kappa (Colby award 1994). Democrat. Home: 6699 De Moss Dr Houston TX 77074-5003

REED, KEITH ALLEN, lawyer; b. Anamosa, Iowa, Mar. 5, 1939; s. John Ivan and Florence Lorine (Larson) R.; m. Beth Illana Kesterson, June 22, 1963; children: Melissa Beth, Matthew Keith. BBA, U. Iowa, 1960, JD, 1963. Bar: Ill. and Iowa 1963. Ptnr. Seyfarth, Shaw, Fairweather & Geraldson, Chgo., 1963—. Co-author: Labor Arbitration in Healthcare, 1981; co-editor: Federal Employment Law and Regulations, 1989; co-contbr. articles to Am. Hosp. Assn. publs., 1986-89. Trustee Meth. Hosp. Chgo., 1985—, Trinity Ch. North Shore, Wilmette, Ill., 1983—; mem. ad hoc labor adv. com. Am. Hosp. Assn., Chgo., 1980—; bd. dirs. Lyric Opera Chgo. Ctr. for Am. Artists, pres., 1983-86. Mem. ABA (dir. health law forum 1979-82), Chgo. Bar Assn. (labor and employment law com. 1978—), Union League Club Chgo. (bd. dirs. 1985-88), Sunset Ridge Country Club (Northbrook, Ill.). Republican. Methodist. Avocations: music, community theater, tennis, golf. Office: Seyfarth Shaw Fairweather & Geraldson 55 E Monroe St Ste 4200 Chicago IL 60603-5803

REED, KENNETH G., petroleum company executive; b. 1917; married. Ed., U. Tex. With Amerada Petroleum Corp., Tulsa, 1948-70; sr. v.p. Amerada Petroleum Corp., 1967-70; exec. v.p. internat. operations Amerada Hess Corp., N.Y.C., 1970; pres., chief exec. officer APEXCO, Inc., Tulsa, 1971-77; pres., chief exec. officer Natomas Internat. Corp., 1977, also dir.; exec. v.p. energy, dir. Natomas Co., San Francisco, 1977-83, vice chmn., pres., 1983—; pres., dir. Natomas Energy Co., 1979—; chmn., chief exec. officer Overseas Petroleum Ltd., San Francisco, 1984—; dir. Natomas N.Am. Inc., 1st Nat. Bank & Trust Co., Tulsa, Oneok Inc., Tulsa. Home: 7 BC Rocky Pl Condominium 1400 Poly Dr Billings MT 59102-1737 Office: 100 N 27th St Ste 440 Billings MT 59101-2054

REED, LEONARD NEWTON, secondary school educator; b. Alva, Okla., Feb. 27, 1952; s. Leonard S. and Vevian M. (Chew) R. BA, Northwestern Okla. State U., 1970, MA, 1980; postgrad., No. Ariz. U., 1982-89; cert. ESL, U. Phoenix, 1992. Cert. social sci. tchr., Ariz., Okla., ESL, Ariz. Social sci. tchr. Chinle (Ariz.) Unified Sch. Dist., 1974—; night staff Navajo C.C., 1988—; student coun. advisor Chinle Unified Sch. Dist., 1975-76, 78-83, 84-93. Mem. com. Apache County (Ariz.) Dem. Party, 1980-88, 93-95; state del. Ariz. Dem. Party, 1980; mem. Nat. Gay and Lesbian Task Force, 1976—. Mem. NEA (gay and lesbian caucus 1988—, rural and small caucus, 1986—, Ariz. Edn. Assn. (bd. dirs. 1984-88, 89-90, human rels. com. 1987-94, 95—, chair, human rels. com. 1992-94, treas. N.E. adv. coun., Bill Hodge award 1989), Ariz. Student Coun. Advisors Assn., Chinle Edn. Assn. (past pres. 1979, 81, treas.), CHS (social sci. dept. chair 1981-84, 85-93). Home: PO Box 1678 Chinle AZ 86503-1678 Office: Chinle Unified Sch Dist # 24 PO Box 587 Chinle AZ 86503-0587

REED, LESTER JAMES, biochemist, educator; b. New Orleans, Jan. 3, 1925; s. John T. and Sophie (Pastor) R.; m. Janet Louise Gruschow, Aug. 7, 1948; children—Pamela, Sharon, Richard, Robert. B.S., Tulane U., 1943; D.Sc. (hon.), 1977; Ph.D., U. Ill., 1946. Rsch. asst. NDRC, Urbana, Ill., 1944-46; rsch. assoc. biochemistry Cornell U. Med. Coll., 1946-48; faculty U. Tex., Austin, 1948—; prof. chemistry U. Tex., 1958—, Ashbel Smith prof., 1984—; rsch. sci. Clayton Found. Biochem. Inst., 1949—, assoc. dir., 1962-63, dir., 1963—. Contbr. articles profl. jours. Recipient ASBMB-Merk award Am. Soc. for Biochemistry, 1994. Mem. NAS, Am. Acad. Arts and Scis., Am. Soc. for Biochemistry and Molecular Biology (Merck award 1994), Am. Chem. Soc. (Eli Lilly & Co. award in biol. chemistry 1958), Phi Beta Kappa, Sigma Xi. Home: 3502 Balcones Dr Austin TX 78731-5802 Office: U Tex Biochem Inst Experimental Sci Bldg 442 Austin TX 78712

REED, LORRIE C., education educator, research consultant; b. Waukegan, Ill., June 15, 1951; d. Oscar Robert and Juanita (Fields) Allen Montgomery; m. James Raymond Reed III, Mar. 20, 1971; 1 child, Tamara Lyn Reed. BSEd, So. Ill. U., 1975; MSEd, U. Ill., Springfield, 1980; PhD, Loyola U., 1995. Tchr. English Murphysboro Twp. (Ill.) H. S., 1975-77; data processing programmer, analyst Ill. Dept. Trans., Springfield, 1977-79, personnel analyst, 1979-80; edn. cons. Ill. State Bd. Edn., Chgo., 1980-86; assoc. prin. Crete-Monee (Ill.) H. S., 1986-89; dir. curriculum, personnel Sch. dist. 88, Bellwood, Ill., 1989-91; prin. Sch. dist 163, Park Forest, Ill., 1991-95; asst. prof. edn. adminstrn. Chgo. State U., 1995—; adv. bd. West Cook County Adminstrs. Acad., 1989-91; steering com. Proviso Twp. Curriculum, Maywood, Ill., 1989-91. Mem. ASCD, Am. Ednl. Rsch. Assn., Nat. Coun. Profs. Ednl. Adminstrn., Nat. Coun. Measurement Edn., Ill. Adminstrs. Acad. (assoc. 1992), Ill. Principals' Assn., Phi Delta Kappa, Zeta Phi Beta.

REED, LOWELL A., JR., federal judge; b. Westchester, Pa., 1930; s. Lowell A. Sr. and Catherine Elizabeth (Pauly) R.; m. Diane Benson; children: Jeffrey Barton, Lowell Andrew, Diane Reed Marsh. BBA, U. Wis., 1952; JD, Temple U., 1958. Bar: Pa. 1959, U.S. Dist. Ct. (ea. dist.) Pa. 1961, U.S. Ct. Appeals (3d cir.) 1962, U.S. Supreme Ct. 1970. Corp. trial counsel PMA Group, Phila., 1958-63; assoc. Rawle & Henderson, Phila., 1963-65, gen. ptnr., 1966-88; judge U.S. Dist Ct., Phila., 1988—; lectr. law Temple U., 1965-81, faculty Acad. Advocacy, 1988—, Pa. Bar Inst., 1972—. Contbr. articles to profl. jours. Elder Abington (Pa.) Presbyn. Ch.; past. mem. Pa. Senate Select Com. Med. Malpractice; past pres., bd. dirs. Rydal Meadowbrook Civic Assn.; bd. dirs. Abington Sch. Bd., 1971, World Affairs Coun. Phila., 1983-88; trustee Abington Health Care Corp., 1983-88, 90-93. Lt. comdr. USNR, 1952-57. Recipient Alumni Achievement award Temple U. 1988. Mem. ABA, Pa. Bar Assn., Phila. Bar Assn. (chmn. medico legal com. 1975, constl. bicentennial com. 1986-87, commn. on jud. selection and retention 1983-87), Temple Am. Inn of Ct. (pres. 1990-93, master of bench), Am. Judicature Soc., Temple U. Law Alumni Assn. (exec. com. 1987-90), Hist. Soc. U.S. Supreme Ct., Hist. Soc. U.S. Dist. Ct. Ea. Dist. Pa. Republican. Office: US Dist Ct 11614 US Courthouse Independence Mall W Philadelphia PA 19106

REED, MICHAEL A., agricultural products supplier; b. 1947. Grad., U. Mo., 1969, JD, 1976. With Poole, Reed and Croessmann, Springfield, Mo., 1977-80, Tindle Mills, Springfield, 1980-83, Vigortone Ag Products, Inc., Cedar Rapids, Iowa, 1983-85; with PM AG Products Inc., Homewood, Ill., 1985—, now pres. With USAF, 1970-74. Office: PM AG Products Inc 17475 Govanna St Homewood IL 60430-4610*

REED, MICHAEL HAYWOOD, lawyer; b. Phila., Jan. 17, 1949; s. Soloman Taylor and Vivian (Haywood) Reed; m. Yalta Gilmore, Aug. 12, 1978; children: Alexandra Haywood, Michael Haywood Jr. BA in Polit. Sci., Temple U., 1969; JD, Yale U., 1972. Bar: Pa. 1972, U.S. Dist. Ct. (ea. dist.) Pa. 1972, U.S. Dist. Ct. (ea. dist.) Mich. 1982, U.S. Supreme Ct. 1982, U.S. Ct. Appeals (3d cir.) 1985. Assoc. Pepper, Hamilton & Scheetz, Phila., 1972-80, ptnr., 1980—; co-adj. prof. law Rutgers U., Camden, N.J., 1983, 85; adj. prof. sch. law Temple U., Phila., 1989; mem. Pa. Judicial Inquiry and Rev. Bd., 1990-93; mem. steering com. Ea. Dist. Pa. Bankruptcy Conf., 1992—. Contbr. articles to profl. jours. Advisor Post 913 Law Explorers, Phila., 1974-84; trustee Acad. Natural Scis., Phila., 1988—, Episcopal Hosp., Phila., 1986—; bd. advisors Pub. Interest Law Ctr., Phila., 1992—; exec. bd. Com. of Seventy, Phila., 1985—. Recipient cert. of honor Alumnus of Yr. Coll. of Arts & Scis. Temple U., 1995. Fellow Am. Coll. Bankruptcy; mem. ABA (chmn. subcom. mass tort and environ. claims, bus. bankruptcy com. 1991—, bus. bankruptcy com. 1991—, bus. bankruptcy com. sect. bus. law), Nat. Bar Assn., Pa. Bar Assn. (ho. of dels. 1985—, chmn. minority bar com. 1988-90, bd. govs. 1993—, co-chair 1994 ann. meeting, Spl. Achievement award 1989, Cert. of Honor award 1995), Barristers Assn. Phila. (1st v.p. 1974-76), Alpha Phi Alpha, Yale Club (Phila.). Democrat. Baptist. Avocations: racquetball, film, theatre, biking, piano. Home: 225 N 23rd St Philadelphia PA 19103-1005 Office: Pepper Hamilton & Scheetz 3000 Two Logan Sq 18th Arch St Philadelphia PA 19103

REED, MILLARD C., academic administator; b. Hannibal, Mo., Nov. 19, 1933; s. Harlow and Mary Agnes R.; m. Barbara Jean Cunningham, Nov. 26, 1953; children: Stephen, Deborah, Paul, John. AB, Olivet Nazarene Coll., 1955; MDiv, Eden Theol. Sem., 1961; postgrad., U. Chgo., 1961-63; D of Ministry, Vanderbilt U., 1979. Pres. Trevecca Nazarene Coll., Nashville. Author: Let Your Church Grow: Proclaiming the Spirit, Take Care Man: Family Love in All Dimensions, Biblical PReaching for Contemporary Man, How to Live the Holy Life. Chaplain Nashville Optimist Club, Rotary Club, Billy Graham exec. com. Nashville Crusade; bd. dirs. Nashville Coop. Ministry, Tenn. Preparatory Sch., Czar Palaver Club. Office: Trevecca Nazarene Coll 333 Murfreesboro Rd Nashville TN 37210-2834

REED, NANCY BOYD, English language and elementary education educator; b. Lodi, Calif., Oct. 10, 1946; d. Leo H. and Anna Gwen (Coombes) Boyd; m. Maurice Allen Reed, Dec. 22, 1966; 1 child, Scot Alastair. AA Recreational Adminstrn. with honors, Delta Coll., 1974; BA Recreational Adminstrn. with honors, Calif. State U., Sacramento, 1976, MA in Edn., English Lang. Devel., 1988; cert. computers in edn., U. Calif., Davis, 1984. Cert. multiple subject, phys. edn., computers in edn. teaching. Tchr. 4th grade Hagginwood Sch., Sacramento, 1980-81; tchr. 4th/5th grade impacted lang. Noralto Sch., Sacramento, 1981-88, bilingual resource tchr., 1988-91, tchr. English lang. devel., 1991—; mentor tchr. North Sacramento Sch. Dist., Sacramento, 1992-95; fellow, tchr./cons. No. Calif. Math. Project, U. Calif., Davis, 1985—. Dir. Jasmine Flower Dancers, Sacramento, 1984—; comty. rep. Am. Host Found., Sacramento, 1976—. Named Outstanding Educator Capitol Svc. Ctr., 1992, Tchr. of Yr., Noralto Sch., North Sacramento Sch., 1996; scholar Fridtjof-Nansen-Akademie, Ingleheim, Germany, 1993, Adenauer Found., Berlin, 1982, 93. Mem. NEA, Nat. Vis. Tchrs. Assn. (bd. dirs. 1994—), Nat. Assn. Bilingual Edn., Nat. Coun. Tchrs. Math., Calif. Tchrs. Assn. (state coun. rep. 1995—), North Sacramento Edn. Assn. (sec. 1986-88, v.p. 1988-90, pres. 1990-92, outstanding educator 1992). Avocations: travel, photography, camping. Home: 5309 Colusa Way Sacramento CA 95841-2301 Office: North Sacramento Sch Dist 670 Dixieanne Ave Sacramento CA 95815-3023

REED, PAMELA, actress; b. Tacoma, Wash., Apr. 2, 1949; d. Vernie Reed; m. Sandy Smolar. BA in Drama, U. Wash. Prin. stage roles include Getting Through the Night, Ensemble Studio Theatre, N.Y.C., 1976, Curse of the Starving Class, N.Y. Shakespeare Festival, Pub. Theatre, 1978, The November People (Broadway debut), Billy Rose Theatre, 1978, All's Well That Ends Well, N.Y. Shakespeare Festival, Delacorte Theatre, 1978, Getting Out, Phoenix Theatre, Marymount Manhattan Theatre, N.Y.C., 1978, Seduced, Am. Place Theatre, N.Y.C., 1979, Sorrows of Stephen, N.Y. Shakespeare Festival, Pub. Theatre, 1979, Fools, Eugene O'Neill Theatre, N.Y.C., 1981, Criminal Minds, Theatre Guinevere, N.Y.C., 1984, Fen, N.Y. Shakespeare Festival, Pub. Theatre, 1984, Aunt Dan and Lemon, N.Y. Shakespeare Festival, Pub. Theatre, 1985, Mrs. Warren's Profession, Roundabout Theatre, N.Y.C., 1985, Haft Theatre, 1986; film appearances include The Long Riders, 1980, Melvin and Howard, 1980, Eyewitness, 1981, Young Doctors in Love, 1982, The Right Stuff, 1983, The Goodbye People, 1984, The Best of Times, 1986, The Clan of the Cave Bear, 1986,

Rachel River, 1989, Chattahoochee, 1990, Cadillac Man, 1990, Kindergarten Cop, 1990, Passed Away, 1992, Junior, 1994; TV series appearances include The Andros Targets, 1977, Tanner, 1988, The Dark Horse (HBO), 1988, Grand, 1990, The Home Court, 1995—; TV films include Inmates: A Love Story, 1981, I Want to Live, 1983, Heart of Steel, 1983, Scandal Sheet, 1985, Born Too Soon, 1993, Mary Hemingway miniseries, 1988, Caroline? (Hallmark Hall of Fame), 1989. Office: ICM 8942 Wilshire Blvd Beverly Hills CA 90211-1934*

REED, PATSY BOSTICK, university administrator, nutrition educator; b. Holland, Tex., Dec. 1, 1936; d. William T. and Evelyn R. (Smith) Bostick; m. F. Dewitt Reed, Sept. 6, 1958. BS, U. Tex., 1959, MS, 1967, PhD, 1969. Tchr. pub. schs., Austin and Port Arthur, Tex., 1959-65; postdoctoral fellow U. Va., Charlottesville, 1969-70; research chemist U. Heidelberg, W.Ger., 1970-72; assoc. prof. nutrition Idaho State U., Pocatello, 1973-79; prof. nutrition, adminstr. No. Ariz. U., Flagstaff, 1979-94, dean Coll. Design and Tech., 1981-85; asst. v.p. acad. affairs U. N.C., Asheville, 1985-87, v.p. acad. affairs, 1987-94, chancellor, 1994—. Author: Nutrition: An Applied Science, 1980. Mem. AAAS, Am. Chem. Soc., Am. Dietetic Assn., Phi Kappa Phi, Sigma Xi. Office: U NC 1 University Hts Asheville NC 28804-3229

REED, PAUL ALLEN, artist; b. Washington, Mar. 28, 1919; s. Charles Miler and Lula Rachael (Annadale) R.; m. Esther Kishter, July 10, 1939; children—Jean Reed Roberts, Thomas, Robert. Student, San Diego State Coll., 1936, Corcoran Sch. Art, 1937. Asst. art dir. USAF mag., N.Y.C., 1942-44; artist B.D. Adams Advt. Agy., Montclair, N.J., 1944-48; asst. art dir. M.F. Dreher Advt. Agy., N.Y.C., 1948-50; free lance graphics designer Washington, 1950-62; graphics dir. U.S. Peace Corps, Washington, 1962-71; asst. prof. Corcoran Sch. Art, Washington, 1971-81. Exhibited in one man shows at, Corcoran Gallery Art, 1966, Washington U., 1967, Ariz. State U., 1971, Phoenix Art Mus., 1977; represented in more than 50 permanent collections at Hirshhorn Mus., Nat. Mus. Am. Art, N.C. Mus. Art, Corcoran Gallery, San Francisco Mus. Art, Detroit Inst. Art, others; artist in residence, Phoenix Art Mus., 1976; vis. artist Ariz. State U., Tempe, 1980. Home: 3541 N Utah St Arlington VA 22207-4444

REED, RAYMOND DERYL, architect; b. Alturas, Calif., Mar. 29, 1930; s. Russell Jacob and Nita Ferne (Wilcox) R.; m. Patricia Reinerth, Apr. 30, 1954; children—Kathryn, Russell, Ann, Andrea. B.Arch., Tulane U., 1953; M.Arch., Harvard U., 1958. Chmn. architecture and interior design dept. U. Southwestern La., 1958-64; head dept. architecture Iowa State U., 1964-70, dir. grad. research in architecture, 1970-73; mem. faculty Tex. A&M U., 1973—, prof. architecture, 1973—; dean Tex. A&M U. (Coll. Architecture and Environ. Design), 1973-80; dir. Internat. Ctr. for Cybernetics and Informatics, 1990. Author: Sustainable Architecture, 1988, rev. edit, 1990; contbr. numerous articles on energy conservation and post petroleum architecture to research publs. Served with USNR, 1953-58. Mem. AIA, Nat. Council Archtl. Registration Bds., Am. Collegiate Schs. Architecture, Tex. Soc. Architects, La. Architects Soc. Home: 1601 Wolf Pen Ct College Station TX 77840-3169 Office: Tex A&M U Dept Architecture College Station TX 77843

REED, REX, author, critic; b. Ft. Worth, Oct. 2, 1938; s. Jimmy M. and Jewell (Smith) R. BA, La. State U., 1960. Film critic Holiday mag., Women's Wear Daily, 1968-71; music critic Stereo Rev., 1968-75; syndicated columnist Chgo. Tribune-N.Y. Daily News Syndicate, 1971—; film critic N.Y. Daily News, 1971-75; now columnist N.Y. Observer, N.Y.C.; critic At the Movies, public TV series, 1986. Appeared in film Myra Breckenridge, 1970, Superman, 1978; author: Do You Sleep in the Nude?, 1968, Conversations in the Raw, 1969, Big Screen, Little Screen, 1971, People Are Crazy Here, 1974, Valentines and Vitriol, 1977, Travolta to Keaton, 1979; author: (novel) Personal Effects, 1986. Office: NY Observer 54 E 64th St New York NY 10021-7326

REED, REX RAYMOND, retired telephone company executive; b. Peterson, Iowa, Mar. 19, 1922; s. Charles Bernard and Dagmar Helen (Heick) R.; m. Rita Compton, Dec. 3, 1944; children: Julie, Nancy, Linda; m. Mary Connors, June 13, 1992. Student, Morningside Coll., 1940-41, Iowa State U., 1941-43, 46-47, U. Notre Dame, 1943-44; B.S. in Gen. Engring, Iowa State U., 1947. With Northwestern Bell Telephone Co. (various locations), 1947-60, 61-66; employee info. mgr., pub. relations dept. Northwestern Bell Telephone Co. (various locations), Omaha, 1957-58; gen. comml. mgr., comml. dept. Northwestern Bell Telephone Co. (various locations), Fargo, N.D., 1958-60; asst. v.p. personnel and employment Northwestern Bell Telephone Co. (various locations), 1961-62; asst. v.p. personnel Northwestern Bell Telephone Co. (various locations), Nebr. area, 1962-64; asst. v.p. personnel and labor relations Northwestern Bell Telephone Co. (various locations), 1964-66; with AT&T Corp., N.Y.C., 1960-61, 66-84; dir. labor relations, personnel dept. AT&T Corp., 1966-71, v.p. labor relations, 1971-83, sr. v.p. labor relations, 1984; ret., 1984; dir. Ind. Bell Telephone Co., Ill. Bell Telephone Co., First Investors Corp N.Y.C. Mem. Madison (N.J.) Bd. Edn., 1969-70, pres., 1971-75; Trustee Menninger Found., Topeka, 1979—, Morristown (N.J.) Meml. Hosp., 1977—; bd. dirs. Nat. Urban Coalition, 1981-84. Served with USMC, 1943-46; to capt. 1951-53. Mem. Bus. Roundtable (chmn. labor-mgmt. com. 1976-77), Labor Policy Assn. (chmn. 1979-83), Inst. Collective Bargaining (bd. dirs. 1976-84), Orgn. Resources Counselors, Morris County Golf Club (Morristown, N.J., pres. bd. govs. 1991-92). Home: 1381 Fairway Oaks Kiawah Island SC 29455

REED, RICHARD JOHN, retired meteorology educator; b. Braintree, Mass., June 18, 1922; s. William Amber and Gertrude Helen (Volk) R.; m. Joan Murray, June 10, 1950; children: Ralph Murray, Richard Cobden, Elizabeth Ann. Student, Boston Coll., 1940-41, Dartmouth Coll., 1943-44; BS, Calif. Inst. Tech., 1945; ScD, MIT, 1949. Research staff mem. MIT, Cambridge, 1950-54; asst. prof. dept. atmospheric scis. U. Wash., Seattle, 1954-58, assoc. prof., 1958-63, prof., 1963-91, prof. emeritus, 1991—; cons. U.S. Weather Service, Suitland, Md., 1961-62, European Ctr. for Medium Range Weather Forecasts, Reading, Eng., 1985-86; exec. scientist NRC, Washington, 1968-69; trustee Univ. Corp. for Atmospheric Research, Boulder, Colo., 1987-92. Served to lt. (j.g.) USN, 1942-46. Fellow AAAS, Am. Meteorol. Soc. (pres. 1972, Meisinger award 1964, Second Half Century award 1972, Charles Franklin Brooks award 1983, Carl-Gustaf Rossby Rsch. medal 1989), Am. Geophys. Union; mem. NAS. Democrat. Unitarian. Office: U Wash Box 351640 Dept Atmospheric Scis Seattle WA 98195-1640

REED, ROBERT DANIEL, publisher; b. Pottsville, Pa., May 24, 1941; s. Robert Daniel R.; children: Robert Duane, Alan Andrija, Tanya. Purchasing mgr. Ogden Tech. Labs., Sunnyvale, Calif., 1962-69; mktg. mgr. Plaza Press, Sunnyvale, 1969-94; pub. R & E Pubs., Saratoga, Calif., 1966-94; founder Bob Reed Studios; ptnr. Reed's Mktg. Svcs.; co-founder Ceasefire USA; founder, pres. Green PR Internat. Mktg. Cons.; pres. Robert D. Reed Pubs. Author: We Care Cookbook, 1974; pub. over 1150 books on human rights, ethnic history edn., criminology, AIDS, Alzheimers disease, teen suicide, also how-to, trade, and humor books; co-author 50 books on poverty, hunger, homelessness, abuse, sexual assault. With U.S. Army, 1959-61. Mem. Ctr. for Dem. Instns., Nat. Fedn. Ind. Bus., Calif. Inventors Coun., Smithsonian Instn., Soc. for Scholarly Pub., World Future Soc. Inventor electro mech.-electronics devices, creative humor products. Home: 750 La Playa #647 San Francisco CA 94121 *Spend your life doing what you like to do, by putting all your efforts into it. Don't be afraid to take a chance. Remember, if life gets dull-Risk it a bit.*

REED, ROBERT MONROE, publishing executive b. Sheldon, Iowa, Feb. 18, 1932; s. Carl A. and Hazel A. (Dockendorf) R.; m. Maxine Kathryn Gordon, June 7, 1954; children—Robert G., Richard K., Deri L. B.A., U. Iowa, 1956; M.A., U. Mich., 1958. Prodn. mgr. Sta. WETV, Atlanta, 1958-60; program mgr. Sta. WHA-TV, Madison, Wis., 1960-62; founder, gen. mgr. Sta. KHET-TV, Honolulu, 1962-69; exec. dir. PBS Video, Washington, 1969-76; gen. mgr. Sta. KUED-TV, Salt Lake City, 1976-78; exec. v.p. Nat. Video Clearinghouse, Inc., Syosset, N.Y., 1978-88; pres. Reed-Gordon Books Inc., 1988—; asst. prof. U. Wis.-Madison, 1960-62; assoc. prof. U. Hawaii, 1962-69; cons HEW, Dept. Army, Toronto Bd. Edn., NSF, others. Author: American Telecommunications Market, 1982; Career Opportunities: TV/Video, 1982, 86, 90, Ency. of TV, Cable and Video, 1992, Dictionary of TV, Cable and Video, 1994, The Potluck Dinner That Went Astray, 1996; pub.: The Video Source Book, ann. 1978-89; Video Tape/Disc Guides, ann. 1978-88; contbr. articles to profl. jours. Chmn., Honolulu Council Chs., 1965; troop leader Boy Scouts Am., Honolulu, 1966. With USN, 1949-52; Korea. Mem. Nat. Assn. Ednl. Broadcasters, Assn. Ednl. Communications Tech., Rocky Mountain Corp. Pub. Broadcasting (dir. 1977-79), Pacific Mountain Network (dir. 1976-79), Pub. Broadcasting Service (dir. 1978-79). Presbyterian. Lodge: Masons. Home: 285 Burr Rd East Northport NY 11731-5201

REED, ROBERT PHILLIP, lawyer; b. Springfield, Ill., June 14, 1952; s. Robert Edward and Rita Anne (Kane) R.; m. Janice Leigh Kloppenburg, Oct. 8, 1976; children: Kevin Michael, Matthew Carl, Jennifer Leigh, Rebecca Ann. AB, St. Louis U., 1974; JD, U. Ill., 1977. Bar: Ill. 1977, U.S. Dist. Ct. (ctrl. dist.) Ill. 1979, U.S.Ct. Appeals (7th cir.) 1983, U.S. Dist. Ct. (so. dist.) Ill. 1992, Colo. 1993. Intern Ill. Legislature, Springfield, 1977-78; assoc. Traynor & Hendricks, Springfield, 1979-80; ptnr. Traynor, Hendricks & Reed, Springfield, 1981-88; pvt. practice Springfield, 1988—; pub. defender Sangamon County, Ill., Springfield, 1979-81; hearing examiner Ill. State Bd. Elections, Springfield, 1981-88; spl. asst. atty. gen. State of Ill., Springfield, 1983—; instr. Lincoln Land Community Coll., Springfield, 1988. Trustee Springfield Pk. Dist., 1985-89. Mem. Assn. Trial Lawyers Am., Comml. Law League Am., Ill. State Bar Assn., Colo. Bar Assn., Attys. Title Guaranty Fund, Inc., Phi Beta Kappa. Roman Catholic. Office: 1129 S 7th St Springfield IL 62703-2418

REED, ROSALIE, horse trainer; b. San Diego, May 5, 1954; d. Lester Woodrow Reed and Pearl (Peterson) Hampton. Trainer Fletcher Hills Ranch, San Diego, 1970-74, Willow Glen Farm, El Cajon, Calif., 1974-77, Moreno Valley Ranch, Lakeside, Calif., 1978-80, Mill Creek Farm, Malibu, Calif., 1980-81, L.A. Equestrian Ctr., 1981—; Judge Appaloosa Horse Club Nat. Show, Syracuse, N.Y.., Appaloosa Horse Club. Can. Author: Handbook of Hunter Seat Equitation, 1977, Handbook of Saddle Seat Equitation, 1977; contbr. to profl. publs. Inducted San Diego Hall of Champions, 1978; winner 8 world championships, Appaloosa Horse Club, 1972-76, 7 nat. championships, 1972-76; demonstrator 1984 Summer Olympics, L.A. Mem. ASCAP, Am. Horse Show Assn. (judge), Internat. Arabian Horse Assn. (judge), Pacific Coast Horse Show Assn., Calif. Profl. Horsemen's Assn., Equestrian Trails Internat. Avocations: singing, songwriting, skydiving. Office: LA Equestrian Ctr 480 W Riverside Dr Burbank CA 91506-3209

REED, SALLY D., foundation executive; b. Lynwood, Calif., May 20, 1955; d. William H. and Sally Frances (Hayes) Gibson. A.A., Cooke County Coll., 1975; B.S.Ed., Southwestern U., 1978. Tchr. civics Killeen High Sch., Tex., 1978-81; dir. devel. Nat. Conservative Polit. Action Com., Alexandria, Va., 1981-83; founder, chmn. Nat. Council for Better Edn., Alexandria, Va., 1983—. Pres., Conservative Youth Found., Alexandria, 1984—, Profl. Educators Guild, 1984—. Author: NEA: Propaganda Front of the Radical Left, 1983; A Parent's Survival Guide to the Public Schools, 1985. Republican. Roman Catholic.

REED, SHERMAN KENNEDY, chemical consultant; b. Chgo., Apr. 11, 1919; s. Frank Hynes and Helen Louise (Kennedy) R.; m. Octavia Bailey, Oct. 11, 1943; children: Martin Bailey, Holly Anne, Julie Marie Reed. B.S. with honors, U. Ill., 1940; Ph.D., Cornell U., 1949. Asst. instr. chemistry Cornell U., 1940-43; asst. research scientist Manhattan Project, N.Y.C., 1942-46; asst. prof. Bucknell U., Lewisburg, Pa., 1946-50; with FMC Corp., 1950—, mgr., asst. dir. research, 1950-60, divisional dir. research and devel., central research dir., 1960-76, v.p., 1976-82; cons. FMC Corp., Chgo., 1983—; dir. Avicon, Inc., 1970-82; pres., dir. FMC Gold Corp.; mng. dir. COGAS Devel. Co., 1975—; dir. Indsl. Research Inst., N.Y.C., Franklin Inst., Phila., 1976-83; chmn. bd. Franklin Research Ctr., Phila., 1976-83. Fellow Am. Inst. Chemists; mem. Am. Chem. Soc., AAAS, Assn. Research Dirs. (pres. 1973). Republican. Clubs: Union League (Phila.); Nassau (Princeton, N.J.). Home and Office: 14 Sailfish Rd Vero Beach FL 32960-5279

REED, STANLEY FOSTER, editor, writer, publisher, lecturer; b. Bogota, N.J., Sept. 28, 1917; s. Morton H. and Beryl (Turner) R.; m. Stella Swingle, Sept. 28, 1940 (div. 1978); children: Nancie, Beryl Ann, Alexandra; m. Shirley Weihman, Sept. 28, 1985 (dec. Feb. 1988); m. Catherine Case Commander, Dec. 16, 1989 (div. 1991). Student, George Washington U., 1939-40, Johns Hopkins, 1940-41; MBA, Loyola U., Md., 1981. Registered profl. engr., D.C. With Bethlehem Steel Corp., Balt., 1940-41; cons. engr., 1942-44; founder, pres. Reed Research, Inc., Washington, 1945-62; pres. Reed Research Inst. Creative Studies, Washington, from 1951; founder, chmn. LogEtronics, Inc., 1955; founder, pres., chmn. Tech. Audit Corp., 1962; assoc. Mgmt. Analysis Corp., 1978-81; sr. cons. Hay Assocs., Phila., 1980-83; entrepreneur in residence Coll. Charleston; co-chmn. semi-ann. Merger Week Northwestern U.; lectr. numerous U.S. and fgn. groups and instns. including Union Theol. Sem., U. Pa., Pa. State U., U. Colo., Georgetown U., Rensselaer Poly. Inst., Am. U., Claremont Coll., So. Meth. U., Pace U., Wayne State U., U. Oreg., U. Conn., St. John's U., Pepperdine U., Loyola Coll. of Md., San Francisco State U., U. Pitts., U. R.I., Marquette U., Vanderbilt U., Boston U., U. Cin., Gustavus Adolphus Coll., U. Mo., Mich. State U., Lehigh U., Calif. Inst. Tech., Denver U., George Washington U., Elmhurst Coll.; vis. fellow Wilton Pk. Conf., Eng., 1968. Author: The Art of M&A: A Merger/Aquisition/Buyout Guide, 1989, The Toxic Executive, 1993; editor: The International Deals Dictionary, 1994; founder, editor, pub.: Mergers and Acqusitions mag., 1965—, Dirs. and Bds. mag., 1976—; founder, editor, pub.: Campaigns and Elections mag., 1979—; founder, pub. Export Today mag., 1985; contbr. articles to leading jours., chpts. to books; patentee. Bd. dirs. Nat. Patent Coun., 1970—; founder, chmn. ann Merger Week, Washington, 1973-77, Northwestern U., 1977-87. Mem. Soc. Naval Architects and Marine Engrs. (life), Am. Econ. Assn., Dictionary Soc. of N.Am., Am. Student Action Partnership (chmn. adv. bd.), N.Y. Yacht Club, Internat. Club (Washington). Home: 330 Concord St Charleston SC 29401-1549 Office: 9 Liberty St Charleston SC 29401-1400

REED, SUELLEN KINDER, state education administrator. BA in History, Polit. Sci.and Secondary Edn., Hanover Coll.; MA in Elem. Edn. and History, Ball State U., PhD in Adminstrn. and Supervision; postgrad., Fla. Atlantic U., U. Scranton, Purdue U., Earlham Coll., Ind. U.; Ind. State U. Cert. secondary tchr., elem. tchr., gifted and talented tchr., administr., supr., Fla., Ind., supt., Ind. Tchr. 5th and 6th grades Rushville (Ind.) Consol. Sch. Corp., 1967-70, asst. supt., 1987-91, supt., 1991-93; tchr. Shelbyville (Ind.) High Sch., 1970-71; tchr. 6th, 7th and 8th grade social studies, curriculum Broward County (Fla.) Sch. Corp., 1971-76; tchr. Rushville Jr. High Sch., 1976-77; asst. prin. Rushville Elem. Sch., 1977-79; prin. Frazee Elem. Sch., Connersville, Ind., 1979-87; asst. supt. Rushville Consolidated Schs., 1987-90, supt., 1991-93; supt. pub. instrn., chairperson bd. edn., CEO dept. edn. State of Indiana, Indpls., 1993—. Mem. ASCD (nat. and Ind. chpts.), Internat. Reading Assn., Nat. Assn. Elem. Sch. Prins. (assoc.), Ind. Assn. Pub. Sch. Supts., Ind. Assn. Elem. and Mid. Sch. Prins. (assoc.), Ind. Assn., Network Woman Adminstrs., Indpls. Zoo, Indpls. Art Mus., Bus. and Profl. Women of Rushville, Altrusa Club Connersville (chmn. internat. rels. 1979-87), Connersville Area Reading Coun., Smithsonian, Rushville County Players, Rotary (Rushville chpt.), Monday Cir., Delta Kappa Gamma (past pres., Phi Lambda Theta, Phi Delta Kappa (Conner Prairie). Office: Superintendent Edn Dept 229 State Office Bldg Indianapolis IN 46204-2212

REED, THOMAS LEE, II, minister, elementary education educator; b. Kansas City, Jan. 9, 1964; s. Thomas Lee and Kathleen E. (Green) R. BA in Preaching, Okla. Christian, 1986; BS in Edn., Mo. Southern State Coll., Joplin, 1994. Cert. elem. edn. Assoc. min Ch. of Christ, Nevada, Mo., 1986-89; music min. Plymouth, Ind., 1989; assoc. min. Nevada, Mo., 1990—; clin. tchr. 3rd grade Mo. Sch. Dist., Joplin, 1992; practicum tchr. Early Childhood Devel. Ctr. MSSC, Joplin, Mo., 1993; student tchr. 4th grade Web City (Mo.) Sch. Dist., 1994; music dir., 1981-89, 90—, youth min., 1984, religious edn., 1986—, Ch. of Christ, Nev., Mo. Recipient Key Charitable Fund scholarship, 1993, Selected for Acad. fellowship Mo. So. State Coll., Oxford U., Eng., 1994. Mem. Assn. Childhood Edn. Internat., Phi Eta Sigma. Mem. Churches of Christ. Avocations: music composition, writing, vocal performance, drawing, painting.

REED, TONY NORMAN, aviation company executive; b. Odessa, Tex., Apr. 12, 1951; s. Norman W. and Naoma N. (Johnson) R.; m. Gwen Stanphill, Mar. 29, 1973; 3 children. Pres. Trinity Aviation, Trinity Communication, Tyler, Tex., 1986-90; v.p. internat. mktg. Cardinal Aerospace, Inc., Independence, Mo., 1990-92; v.p. comml. programs Multinat. Enterprises, Inc., N.Y.C., 1992—; internat. sales profl. Puritan-Bennett Aero Systems, Inc., Lenexa, Kans., 1993—; bd. dirs. Missionary Aviation Svcs., Tyler. Mem. Aircraft Owners and Pilots Assn. Home: PO Box 1085 Blue Springs MO 64013-1085

REED, TRAVIS DEAN, public relations executive; b. Trinity, Tex., Sept. 27, 1930; s. Travis and Alma (Rains) R.; m. Caroline M. McDonald, June 15, 1957; children: Anne Reed Adams, Lisa Reed Lettau. Student, Tex. A&M U., 1948-51, U. Houston, 1951-53. Reporter Houston Post, 1951-53; Washington Bur. corr. McGraw-Hill Pub. Co., 1955-61, Boston Herald-Traveler, 1961-62; with Newhouse News Svc., Washington, 1962-79, chief corr., 1964-67, editor, 1967-79; pub. rels. cons. Washington, 1979—. 1st lt. U.S. Army, 1953-55. Mem. Nat. Press Club, Federal City Club, Gridiron Club. Home: 37277 Branchriver Rd Purcellville VA 22132 Office: T Dean Reed Co Madison Office Bldg 1155 15th St NW Ste 1003 Washington DC 20005-2706

REED, V. KEITH, pension fund administrator; b. 1944. Profit and loss analyst Sears Roebuck & Co., Kansas City, Mo., 1963-73; adminstr. Mt. of David Crippled Children's Hosp., Bethlehem, Israel, 1973-78, Indian Creek Nursing Ctr. Mo., Kansas City, 1978-81; with Boilermakers Blksm Nat. Pension Tr., Kansas City, Kans., 1981—, exec. adminstr., 1986—. Office: Boilermakers Blksm Natl Pns Tr 754 Minnesota Ave Ste 522 Kansas City KS 66101-2725

REED, VANESSA REGINA, secondary school educator; b. Grenada, Miss., Oct. 4, 1965; d. Willie Mann and Elma Lee (Finley) R. BS in Social Sci. Edn., Miss. Valley State U., 1987; MA in History, Jackson State U., 1988; postgrad., Miss. State U., Meridian, 1991, 92. Cert. tchr. social sci. History tchr. Jackson (Miss.) State U., 1987-88; social studies tchr. Magnolia Mid. Sch., Meridian, 1988-93; U.S. history tchr. Kate Griffin Jr. H.S., Meridian, 1993—. Sunday sch. tchr. Mt. Olive Bapt. Ch., children's ministry dir.; mem. Heroines of Jericho. Mem. NAACP, Nat. Coun. Social Studies, Sigma Gamma Rho, Miss. Valley State U. Nat. Alumni Assn., Am. Fedn. Tchrs., Meridian Am. Fedn. Tchrs. Democrat. Avocations: traveling, geneology, reading. Office: Kate Griffin Jr HS 2814 Davis St Meridian MS 39301-5655

REED, VASTINA KATHRYN (TINA REED), child psychotherapist; b. Chgo., Mar. 5, 1960; d. Alvin Hillard and Ruth Gwendolyn (Thomas) R.; 1 child, Alvin J. BA in Human Svcs. magna cum laude, Nat.-Louis U., Chgo., 1988; MA, Ill. Sch. Profl. Psychology, 1991. Tchr. early childhood edn. Kendall Coll. Lab. Sch., Evanston, Ill., 1983-85, Rogers Park Children's Learning Ctr., Chgo., 1983-85; child life therapist Mt. Sinai Hosp., Chgo., 1988; child psychotherapist Nicholas Barnes Therapeutic Day Sch., Chgo., 1989-90. Den leader Boy Scouts Am., Chgo., 1989-92, scoutmaster troop 267, 1992—. Recipient Cub Scouter award Boy Scouts Am., 1990, Scoutmaster award of merit, 1993, 94, Scouters Vet. award, 1994, Scouters Key Tng. award, 1995, Scoutmasters Key award, 1996, Okpik Cold Weather Camping cert., 1994-95. Mem. APA, Nat. Orgn. for Human Svc. Edn., Order of the Arrow, Phi Theta Kappa, Kappa Delta Pi. Democrat. Roman Catholic. Avocations: camping, cruising, music, archery, air rifle shooting. Home: 1872 S Millard Ave Chicago IL 60623-2542

REED, VINCENT EMORY, federal education official; b. St. Louis, Mar. 1, 1928; s. Artie David and Velma Veander (Body) R.; m. Frances Bullitt, Sept. 20, 1952. B.S. in Edn., W.Va. State Coll., 1952, H.L.D. (hon.), 1977; M.A., Howard U., Washington, 1965; D.P.A. (hon.), Southeastern U., Washington, 1976; postgrad., Wharton Sch., U. Pa., 1969; Ph.D. (hon.), Georgetown U., 1977; L.H.D. (hon.), Strayer Coll., Harris-Stowe U., 1983, Slippery Rock U., 1990; LLD (hon.), U. D.C., 1984. Football coach W.Va. State Coll., 1955; mem. staff D.C. Pub. Schs., 1962—, asst. supt. secondary schs., 1971-74, assoc. supt. state office, 1974-75, supt. schs., 1975-80; asst. sec. for elem. and secondary edn. U.S. Dept. Edn., 1981—. Author articles, book revs. Dir. Home Fed. Savs. and Loan Assn.; bd. dirs. D.C. Goodwill Industries, Washington YMCA, 12 Neediest Kids; vol. worker S.E. Boys' Club, S.E. Youth Football Assn. Served as 1st lt. AUS, 1953-55, Korea. Named All-Am. Football Player Pitts. Courier, 1951, to W.Va. ROTC Hall of Fame, 1981; recipient Superior Service award D.C. Bicentennial Assembly, 1976; Outstanding Achievement award W.Va. State Coll., 1976; Alumnus of Yr., 1976; named to Athletic Hall of Fame, 1983; Outstanding Community Service award NAACP, 1977; Scouter of Yr. award Washington, 1981; Human Relations award NCCJ, 1981; Man of Yr. award YMCA, 1984; Excellent Role Models for Edn. award Colgate-Palmolive; Martin Luther King, Jr. Civil Rights for Edn. award Com. Civil Rights and Urban Affairs; many others. Mem. Nat. Assn. Secondary Sch. Prins., Am. Assn. Sch. Personnel Adminstrs., Nat. Assn. Sch. Security Officers, Am. Soc. Bus. Ofcls., NAACP, NEA., D.C. PTA, Washington Sch., Club, Phi Delta Kappa, Kappa Alpha Psi. Baptist. Clubs: Pigskin, Kiwanis. Home: 7115 16th St NW Washington DC 20012-1537 Office: Washington Post Company 1150 15th St NW Washington DC 20071-0001

REED, W. FRANKLIN, lawyer; b. Louisville, Dec. 30, 1946; s. William Ferguson and Stella Elizabeth (Richardson) R.; m. Sharon Ann Coss, June 16, 1973; children: Jonathan Franklin, William Brian, Carrie Ann. BA, Williams Coll., 1968; JD, Columbia U., 1971. Bar: N.Y. 1972, U.S. Dist. Ct. (so. dist.) N.Y. 1975, U.S. Ct. Appeals (2d cir.) 1975, Pa. 1982, U.S. Dist. Ct. (we. dist.) 1983. Assoc. Milbank, Tweed, Hadley & McCloy, N.Y.C., 1971-82, Reed Smith Shaw & McClay, Pitts., 1982-83; ptnr. Reed, Smith, Shaw & McClay, Pitts., 1984—. Mem. ABA, Pa. Bar Assn., Allegheny Bar Assn., Carnegie 100, Williams Coll. Alumni Soc. W. Pa. (sec. 1983—), Rivers Club (Pitts.), St. Clair Country Club (Upper St. Clair, Pa.), Duquesne Club (Pitts.), Phi Beta Kappa. Democrat. Presbyterian. Avocations: fishing, golf. Home: 525 Miranda Dr Pittsburgh PA 15241-2039 Office: Reed Smith Shaw & McClay 435 6th Ave Pittsburgh PA 15219-1809

REED, WALLACE ALLISON, physician; b. Covina, Calif., May 19, 1916; s. Wallace Allison and Mary Julia (Birdsall) R.; m. Maria Eva Wiemers, Jan. 20, 1938; children: Ellen E., Barbara R. (Mrs. David Maurice Knize), Wallace J., Michael E., Kathryn L., Vicki T. A.B., UCLA, Los Angeles, 1937; postgrad., U. Cologne, 1937-38; U. Freiburg, Breisgau, 1938-39; M.D., U. So. Calif., 1944. Diplomate: Am. Bd. Anesthesiology. Intern Santa Fe Coast Lines Hosp., Los Angeles, 1943-44; resident Los Angeles County Gen. Hosp., 1946-47, asst. to head dept. anesthesiology, 1946-47; clin. instr. surgery U. So. Calif. Sch. Medicine, 1946-47; practice medicine, specializing in anesthesiology Phoenix, 1948-89; hon. staff mem. Good Samaritan Hosp., St. Joseph Hosp., Maricopa County Gen. Hosp.; mem. hon. staff Children's Hosp.; co-founder John L. Ford, M.D., Surgicenter, 1970; vice pres. Maricopa Found. for Med. Care, 1970-74, pres., 1975-76; mem. House Ways and Means Adv. Com.; adv. coun. Nat. Health Inst., 1975-76; mem. accreditation coun. for ambulatory health care Joint Commn. on Accreditation of Hosps., 1975-79; vice-chmn. Accreditation Assn. for Ambulatory Health Care, 1979-81, pres., 1981-83; mem. panel for study Nat. Health Ins., Congl. GAO; chmn. bd. Alterna Care Corp., 1984-87, now chmn. bd. emeritus; mem. adv. bd. Kind Inst., 1994-95. Bd. dirs. South Phoenix Montessori Sch., pres. bd., 1971-75; bd. dirs. Ctrl. Ariz. Health Sys. Agy., 1975-78; exec. dir. Surgictr. of Pheonix, 1987—. Capt. M.C., AUS, 1944-46. Recipient Pinal award Ariz. Psychiat. Soc., 1967-68, Gerard B. Lambert Merit award for innovative ideas that improve patient care; John L. Ford M.D., 1972. Fellow Am. Coll. Anesthesiologists; mem. Am. Soc. Anesthesiologists, Ariz., Maricopa County socs. anesthesiologists, AMA, Acad. Anesthesiology (pres. 1969, dir. 1966-72), Soc. for Advancement Free-Standing Ambulatory Surg. Care (pres. 1974-75, dir.), Soc. for Ambulatory Anesthesia (bd. dirs. 1985-87), Ariz. Med. Assn. (dir. 1972-78), Maricopa County Med. Soc. (pres. 1964, dir., Salsbury medal 1967, 71, Thomas Dooley medal 1970), Central Ariz. Physicians Service Assn. (pres. 1982-83), Am. Assn. Founds. for Med. Care (dir. 1970-74), Guedel Assn. (pres. 1972), Seed Money for Growth Found. (pres. 1984—). Methodist. Home: 4716 N Dromedary Rd Phoenix AZ 85018-2939 Office: 1040 E Mcdowell Rd Phoenix AZ 85006-2622

REED, WALTER GURNEE DYER, lawyer; b. N.Y.C., July 11, 1952; s. Stanley Forman and Harriet Tailer (Dyer) R.; m. Cynthia Ann Stewart, Sept. 6,1986. BA magna cum laude, Harvard Coll., 1974; JD, Columbia U., 1977. Bar: N.Y. 1978, R.I. 1983. Assoc. Milbank, Tweed, Hadley & McCloy,

N.Y.C., 1977-81; assoc. Edwards & Angell, Providence, 1981-83, ptnr., 1983—. Bd. dirs. Children's Mus. R.I., Pawtucket, 1984-91, Providence Athenaeum, 1991-94, Preservation Soc. Newport County, 1995—. Scholar Kent U., Stone scholar. Mem. ABA, R.I. Bar Assn. (chmn. com. on corp. law 1991-93), N.Y.C. Lawyers Assn., Spouting Rock Beach Assn., Hope Club, Agawam Hunt Club. Democrat. Congregationalist. Home: 14 Cooke St Providence RI 02906-2006 Office: Edwards & Angell 2700 Hospital Trust Towers Providence RI 02903

REED, WILLIAM EDWARD, government official, educator; b. Columbia, La., July 15, 1914; s. William Reed and Virginia (Barnes) R.; m. Mattye Marie Scott, Aug. 27, 1942; children: Edwarda Marie (Mrs. Lucien L. Johnson), Carol Ann, Beverlyn Bernetiae. B.S., So. U., 1937; M.S., Iowa State U., 1941; Ph.D., Cornell U., 1946. County agrl. agt. Agr. and Home Econs. Extension Service, La. State U., 1937-41; lectr. soil sci. and chemistry So. U., 1942-47; agrl. research specialist U.S. Econ. Mission to Liberia, 1947-49; dean agr. Agrl. and Tech. Coll. N.C., 1949-61; mem. U.S. del. Russia; rep. ICA in Togo, 1961; asst. dir. AID Mission to Nigeria, 1961-68; mem. U.S. del. to UN Conf. on Application Sci. and Tech., 1963; dep. dir. AID Mission to Ethiopia, 1968-72; fgn. service officer in residence N.C. A. & T. State U., Greensboro, 1972-74; spl. asst. to chancellor for internat. programs N.C. A. & T. State U., 1974-76, asso. dean research and spl. projects, 1976-78, dir. internat. programs, 1978-84; cons. in field, 1984—. State rep. Sisters Cities Internat. Mem. Nat. Planning Assn., Am. Fgn. Svc. Assn., Sigma Xi, Phi Kappa Phi, Beta Kappa Chi, Sigma Pi Phi, Gamma Sigma Delta, Beta Epsilon (trustee Boulé Found. 1964—). Episcopalian. Home: 2711 Mcconnell Rd Greensboro NC 27401-4534

REED, WILLIAM G., JR., paper company executive; b. 1939. Grad., Duke U.; MBA, Harvard U., 1969. Mgmt. trainee Simpson Investment, Seattle, 1963-66, gen. mgr. engineered wood products divsn., 1966, vice chmn., 1970-71, chmn., 1971, now CEO; mgmt. trainee Weyerhaeuser Co., Federal Way, Wash., 1967-69; chmn. Simpson Timber Co. (subs. Simpson Investment), 1969—. Served USMC, 1961-63. Office: Simpson Investment 1201 3rd Ave Ste 4900 Seattle WA 98101-3000*

REED, WILLIAM H., federal agency administrator. Dir. Def. Contract Audit Agy. Dept. Def., Washington, 1986—. Office: Dept of Defense Defense Contract Audit Agency Cameron Sta Alexandria VA 22304*

REED, WILLIS, professional basketball team executive, former head coach; b. Hico, La., June 25, 1942; s. Willis and Inell R.; m. Geraldine Oliver (div.); children: Carl, Veronica. Student, Grambling Coll., 1960-64. Center, forward N.Y. Knickbockers, NBA, 1964-74; coach N.Y. Knickerbockers, NBA, 1977-79, Creighton U., Omaha, 1981-85; asst. coach Atlanta Hawks, N.B.A., 1985-88, Sacramento Kings, NBA, 1988; head coach New Jersey Nets, NBA, 1988-89, v.p. basketball and bus. dev., 1989-90, sr. v.p., 1990—, now exec. v.p. basketball, gen mgr. Author: (with Phil Pepe) The View from the Rim, 1971. Mem. Nat. Basketball Assn. All-Star team, 1965-71, 73; mem. World Championship team, 1970, 73; recipient Most Valuable Player awards for playoffs and all-star games, 1970; named Nat. Basketball Assn. Rookie of Yr., 1965, NBA Playoffs Most Valuable Player, 1970, 73; named to Naismith Meml. Hall of Fame, 1981. Office: NJ Nets 405 Murray Hill Pky East Rutherford NJ 07073-2136

REEDER, CECELIA PAINTER, English educator; b. Tampa, Fla., Oct. 9, 1936; d. William Painter and Cecelia (Bachman) Hendry; children: Susan Reeder Shipp, William J. BEd, U. Miami, 1958; MA in Gifted Edn., U. South Fla., 1983. Cert. elem./gifted-talented tchr., K-12, English 7-9, Fla. Elem. tchr. Dade County Bd. Pub. Inst., Miami, Fla., 1958-70, 83-86, tchr., English, 1986-89; tchr. gifted English and Social Studies 7th and 8th grades Richmond Heights Mid. Sch., Miami, Fla., 1989-94; substitute tchr. pub. schs., tutor elem. edn.; part-time tchr. gifted English 6th and 7th grades Homestead (Fla.) Mid. Sch., 1995—; part-time tchr. gifted English and geography grades 6-7 Homestead Mid. Sch. Recipient Assoc. Master Tchr. award State of Fla., 1986. Home: 1520 NW 10th St Homestead FL 33030-3872

REEDER, CHARLES BENTON, economic consultant; b. Columbus, Ohio, Oct. 31, 1922; s. Charles Wells and Lydia (Morrow) R.; m. Carol Lincoln, June 25, 1949 (div. June 1972); 1 son, Charles; m. Beverly Lawrence, Nov. 11, 1972; adopted children: Keith, Sue. BS, Ohio State U., 1945, PhD, 1951; MBA, Harvard U., 1947. Econ. analyst Cleve. Elec. Illuminating Co., 1947-48; instr. Ohio State U., Columbus, 1948-51; econ. analyst, asst. economist Armstrong Cork. Co., Lancaster, Pa., 1951-55; assoc. economist E. I. DuPont de Nemours & Co., Inc., Wilmington, Del., 1955-70; chief economist E.I. DuPont de Nemours & Co., Inc., Wilmington, Del., 1970-85; pres. Charles Reeder Assocs., 1986—; bd. dirs. Sentinel Group Mut. Funds, Montpelier, Vt. Author: The Sobering Seventies, 1981. Bd. dirs. Greater Wilmington Devel. Coun., 1963-84; treas. Del. Coun. on Econ. Edn., 1958-85, Bank of Del., Wilmington, 1975-92. 1st lt. Q.M.C., AUS, 1943-46. Recipient Silbert award Sterling Nat. Bank of N.Y., 1982. Fellow Nat. Assn. Bus. Economists (pres. 1966-67); mem. Nat. Bur. Econ. Research (past bd. dirs.). Methodist. Clubs: Wilmington, Greenville Country. Home: 16 Brendle Ln Wilmington DE 19807-1300 Office: 16 Brendle Ln Ste 4 Wilmington DE 19807-1300

REEDER, ELLEN DRYDEN, museum curator; b. Balt., Apr. 11, 1947; d. Oliver Howard and Nancy Hardcastle (Fisher) R. BA, Wellesley U., 1969; MA, Princeton U., 1972, PhD, 1974. Curator archaeological collection John Hopkins U., Balt., 1974-78; asst. prof. art George Washington U., Washington, 1978-84; assoc. curator ancient art Walters Art Gallery, Balt., 1984-86, curator ancient art, 1986—; mem. at large mng. com. Am. Sch. Classical Studies, Athens, Greece, 1987—, adv. bd. U.S. Ctr. Lexicon Iconographicum Mythologiae Classicae, New Brunswick, N.J., 1986—. Author: The Archaeological Collection of the Johns Hopkins University, 1984; author, editor: Hellenistic Art in the Walters Art Gallery, 1988, mem. editl. bd., 1985—; author, editor: Pandora: Women in Classical Greece, 1995; contbr. articles to profl. jours. Trustee Calvert Sch., Balt., 1990—. Woodrow Wilson fellow, 1969, Princeton Nat. U. fellow, 1969-74. Mem. Archaeol. Inst. Am., Coll. Art Assn., Phi Beta Kappa Assocs. (bd. dirs. 1993—, sec.-treas. 1994—), Phi Beta Kappa. Office: Walters Art Gallery 600 N Charles St Baltimore MD 21201-5118

REEDER, F. ROBERT, lawyer; b. Brigham City, Utah, Jan. 23, 1943; s. Frank O. and Helen H. (Heninger) R.; m. Joannie Anderson, May 4, 1974; children: David, Kristina, Adam. JD, U. Utah, 1967. Bar: Utah 1967, U.S. Ct. Appeals (10th cir.) 1967, U.S. Ct. Mil. Appeals 1968, U.S. Supreme Ct. 1972, U.S. Ct. Appeals (D.C. and 5th cirs.) 1979. Shareholder Parsons, Behle & Latimer, Salt Lake City, 1968—, bd. dirs., 1974-92. Bd. dirs. Holy Cross Found., 1981-90, chmn., 1987-90; bd. dirs. Holy Cross Hosp., 1990-93, treas., 1986-87, vice chmn., 1987-93; bd. dirs. Holy Cross Health Svcs. Utah, 1993-94, treas., 1993-94; bd. dirs., vice chmn. Salt Lake Regional Med. Ctr., 1995—; trustee Univ. Hosp. Found., 1995; hon. col. Salt Lake City Police, Salt Lake County Sheriff. Served with USAR, 1967-73. Mem. ABA, Utah State Bar, Salt Lake County Bar (ethic adv. com. 1989-94), Cottonwood Country Club (bd. dirs. 1978-82, 83-86, pres. 1981-82), Rotary. Office: Parsons Behle & Latimer PO Box 45898 Salt Lake City UT 84145-0898

REEDER, FRANKLIN S., federal agency administrator. BA in Internat. Rels., U. Pa.; student, George Washington U. Various positions Treasury and Defense Depts., Washington, 1961-70; dep. dir. house info. sys. U.S. Ho. of Reps., Washington, 1977-80; dir. info. policy staff Office of Mgmt. and Budget, Washington, dep. asst. dir. gen. mgmt., asst. dir. gen. mgmt., dep. assoc. dir. vet. affairs and personnel; dir. office of adminstrn. Exec. Office of Pres., Washington, 1995—; mem. career Sr. Exec. Svc., 1984-95; adj. faculty U. Md., George Washington U.; mem. Nat. Adv. Bd. Ctr. Informatics Law John Marshall Law Sch., Chgo.; U.S. del., chair pub. mgmt. com. Orgn. Econ. Coop. and Devel. Office: Office Dir Mgmt Adminstrn Old Exec Office Bldg Washington DC 20503

REEDER, JEFFREY K., retail executive; b. 1952. BS in Econs., Purdue U., 1974. With Marsh Super Market, Yorktown, Ind., 1967-75, Fleming Foods, Houston, 1975-77; with Gerlands Food Fair Inc., Houston, 1977—, v.p.-treas., CFO. Office: Gerlands Food Fair Inc 3131 Pawnee St Houston TX 77054-3302*

REEDER, JOE ROBERT, federal official; b. Tacoma, Nov. 28, 1947; s. William Thomas and Marilyn Ruth (Parker) R.; m. Katharine Randolph Boyce, Jan 1, 1983; children: Rachael Anne, Aubrilyn, Julia, Kelsey. BS, U.S. Mil. Acad., West Point, N.Y., 1970; JD, U. Tex., 1975; LLM, Georgetown U., 1981. Bar: Tex. 1975, D.C. 1979, U.S. Dist. Ct. (so. dist.) Tex 1975, U.S. Ct. Appeals (5th cir.) 1989, U.S. Ct. Claims 1979, U.S. Dist. Ct. D.C. 1982, U.S. Ct. Appeals (Fed. cir.) 1984, U.S. Supreme Ct. 1988, U.S. Ct. Appeals (4th cir.) 1988, Md. 1989, U.S. Dist. Ct. (Md. dist) 1989, U.S. Dist. Ct. (no. dist.) Tex. 1991, U.S. Dist. Ct. (so. dist.) Tex. 1991. Commd. 2d lt. U.S. Army, 1970, advanced through grades to maj., 1985; law clk. to presiding justice U.S. Dist. Ct. (so. dist.) Tex., 1976; trial atty. litigation div. U.S. Army, Pentagon, D.C., 1976-78; trial atty. contract appeals div. U.S. Army, Pentagon, 1978-79; assoc. Patton, Boggs & Blow, Washington, 1979-82, ptnr., 1983-93; under sec. of U.S. Army U.S. Dept. Def., Washington, 1993—; chmn. bd. Panama Canal Commn., 1994—. Mem. ABA (assoc. editor pub. contract law jour. 1985-93), ATLA, Am. Law Inst., Fed. Bar Assn., D.C. Bar Assn., Tex. Bar Assn., Bar Assn. 5th Fed. Circuit, Bd. Contract Appeals Bar Assn., Rotary. Episcopalian. Home: 106 W Rosemont Ave Alexandria VA 22301 Office: Under Sec of Army 102 Army Pentagon Washington DC 20310-0102

REEDER, OLIVER HOWARD, paint products manufacturing executive; b. Balt., Sept. 19, 1916; s. Charles Howard and Nannie Dryden (Kensett) R.; m. Nancy Hardcastle Fisher, Apr. 18, 1942; children: Nancy Fisher, Ellen Dryden. A.B., Princeton U., 1939. With Balt. Copper Paint Co., Balt., 1939—; tech. dir., treas. Balt. Copper Paint Co., 1939-47, pres., 1947—, chmn., 1959—; v.p. Balt. Copper Paint div. Glidden-Durkee Div. SCM Corp., 1969—; pres. Jotun-Balt. Copper Paint Co., Inc., 1974-76, v.p., 1976-81. Pres. Hosp. for Consumptives of Md., 1968-84, trustee, 1951-95, trustee emeritus, 1995—; trustee Gilman Sch., Balt., 1948-65, Walters Art Gallery, 1978-83, U.S. Frigate Constellation Found., 1976-89; trustee Johns Hopkins Hosp., 1957-87, trustee emeritus, 1987—, vice chmn. bd., 1986-87; trustee Md. Hosp. Laundry, 1970-89, pres., 1975-84. Fellow Am. Inst. Chemists; mem. Am. Chem. Soc., Soc. Naval Architects and Marine Engrs., Phi Beta Kappa, Sigma Xi. Home: 1300 Dulaney Valley Rd Baltimore MD 21286-1308

REEDER, ROBERT HARRY, retired lawyer; b. Topeka, Dec. 3, 1930; s. William Harry and Florence Mae (Cochran) R. AB Washburn U., 1952, JD, 1960. Bar: U.S. Dist. Ct. Kans. 1960, Kans. 1960, U.S. Supreme Ct. 1968. Rsch. asst. Kans. Legis. Council Rsch. Dept., Topeka, 1955-60; asst. counsel Traffic Inst., Northwestern U., Evanston, Ill., 1960-67, gen. counsel, 1967-92; exec. dir. Nat. Com. on Uniform Traffic Laws and Ordinances, Evanston, 1982-90. Co-author: Vehicle Traffic Law, 1974; The Evidence Handbook, 1980. Author: Interpretation of Implied Consent by the Courts, 1972. Served with U.S. Army, 1952-54. Mem. Com. Alcohol and Other Drugs (chmn. 1973-75). Republican. Methodist.

REEDS, ROGER, church administrator. Dir. Sunday School and Church Training Dept. of the Nat. Assn. of Free WillBaptists, Antioch, Tenn. Office: Natl Assn of Free Will Baptists PO Box 5002 Antioch TN 37011-5002

REEDY, CATHERINE IRENE, science and health educator, library/media specialist; b. Suffolk County, N.Y., Dec. 27, 1953; d. Edward and Catherine (Spindler) Grafenstein. AA, Suffolk C.C., Selden, N.Y., 1980; BA in Social Sci., summa cum laude, Dowling Coll., Oakdale, N.Y., 1983, MS in Edn., 1986. Media specialist, tchr. coord. for sci. and health St. Ignatius Sch., Hicksville, N.Y., 1983—, dir. sci. lab. and media ctr. Contbr. poetry to Beyond the Stars, 1996, Walk Through Paradise, 1995, Best Poems of 1996. Recipient Editor's Choice award Nat. Soc. Poetry, 1995, Nat. Lib. Poetry, 1995. Mem. ASCD, AAUW, N.Y. Acad. Scis., N.Y. Sci. Tchrs. Assn., Nat. Assn. Univ. Women, Nat. Poet Soc., Internat. Soc. Poets, Alpha Zeta Nu (1st sec.), Phi Theta Kappa, Phi Alpha Sigma, Kappa Delta Pi (pres. Xi Chi chpt. 1985-87). Home: 15 Nikia Dr Islip NY 11751-2630 Office: St Ignatius Sch 30 E Cherry St Hicksville NY 11801-4302

REEDY, EDWARD K., research operations administrator. Assoc. dir. Georgia Tech. Rsch. Inst., Atlanta, Ga.; dir. rsch. ops. Georgia Tech. Rsch. Inst., Atlanta. Office: Ga Tech Rsch Inst Rsch Ops Centennial Rsch Bldg #225 Atlanta GA 30332

REEDY, GEORGE EDWARD, educator, author, lecturer; b. East Chicago, Ind., Aug. 5, 1917; s. George Edward and Mary (Mulvaney) R.; m. Lillian Greenwald, Mar. 22, 1948 (dec.); children: Michael Andrew, William James; m. Ruth Brial Wissman, May 7, 1988. B.A. in Sociology, U. Chgo., 1938; D.J.C., Nashota Sem., 1981; LHD, Lycoming Coll., 1991. Reporter Phila. Inquirer, summer 1937; Congl. corr. U.P., 1938-41, 46-51; staff cons. armed services preparedness subcom. U.S. Senate, 1951-52, staff dir. minority policy com., 1953-54, staff dir. majority policy com., 1955-60; spl. asst. to Vice Pres. Lyndon B. Johnson, 1961-63; press sec. to Pres. Johnson, 1964-65; pres. Struthers Research and Devel. Corp., Washington, 1966-68; v.p. planning Struthers Wells Corp., N.Y.C., 1966-68; spl. cons. to President Lyndon B. Johnson, 1968-69; writer, lectr., cons., 1969—; dean, Nieman prof. Coll. Journalism, Marquette U., Milw., 1972-77, Nieman prof., 1977-90, prof. emeritus, 1991—; mem. Pres.'s Commn. on White House Fellowships, 1993; former fellow Woodrow Wilson Internat. Ctr. for Scholars, Smithsonian Instn., Washington; fellow in communication Duke U., 1973-74; lectr. S.Am., Cen. Am., Asia, India, 1975-84. Author: Who Will Do Our Fighting for Us?, 1969, The Twilight of the Presidency, 1970, The Presidency in Flux, 1973, Lyndon B. Johnson, A Memoir, 1982; The U.S. Senate: Paralysis or Search for Consensus, 1986, The Twilight of the Presidency, Johnson to Reagan, 1987, From the Ward to the White House, The Irish in American Politics, 1991; numerous articles on govt. and politics in mags. and newspapers. Mem. Pres.'s Nat. Adv. Commn. Selective Svc., 1966-67, Marine Sci., Engring. Resources, 1967-68, Pres.'s Commn. on White House Fellowships, 1993; mem. diocesan coun. Washington Diocese, Episcopal Ch. With USAAF, 1942-45. Mem. Alpha Sigma Nu. Office: Marquette U Coll Communications Milwaukee WI 53233

REEDY, JERRY EDWARD, editor, writer; b. Aberdeen, S.D., Feb. 4, 1936; s. Robert Emmett and Helen Mary (Issenhuth) R.; m. Susan Mary Rogers, June 22, 1968; children: Megan Marie, Erin Elizabeth, Matthew Robert-Emmett, Thomas Walter. AB, U. Notre Dame, 1958; MA, U. S.D., 1961. Area editor Red Wing (Minn.) Daily Republican Eagle, 1959-60; with Better Homes & Gardens mag. Meredith Pub. Co., Des Moines, 1961-69; assoc. editor Better Homes & Gardens mag. Meredith Pub. Co., 1966-67, spl. assignments editor, 1967-69; editor in chief, contbg. author Odyssey Mag., Chgo., 1969-78; free-lance editor, writer and photographer for nat. mags. and maj. met. daily newspapers, 1978—; travel editor Better Homes and Gardens Brides Book, 1983-84; instr. English, U. S.D., 1960-61; instr. mag. writing Drake U., 1966-68, Barat Coll., 1976-77. Author: Great American Indian Leaders, Notable Quotables, Family Adventure Guide and Road Atlas, God, Country, Notre Dame: The Autobiography of Theodore M. Hesburgh, 1990, (with Rev. Theodore Hesbough); editor: Travels with Ted and Ned, 1992; contbr. to Ency. Brit., 1980, World Book, 1984, Family Vacation Atlas, 1986 and various nat. mags. Pres. Com. on Cmty. Life, Chgo., 1976-78; chmn. bd. dirs. The Shelter, 1980-85. Recipient certs. of excellence Chgo. Comm. Collaborative, 1976, Addy Gold 1st pl. award for mags. Am. Advt. Fedn., 1976, 1st pl. awards of excellence for overall quality and for photojournalism Chgo. Assn. Bus. Communicators, 1977. Mem. Am. Soc. Journalists and Authors (pres. Chgo. chpt. 1995-96), Midwest Writers. Roman Catholic. Home and Office: 3542 N Pine Grove Ave Chicago IL 60657-1877

REEF, ARTHUR, industry business consultant; b. N.Y.C., Sept. 21, 1916; s. Herman and Eva (Van Panich) R.; m. Betty Olsen, Aug. 1995; children from previous marriage: Jennifer, Nancy. B.A., CCNY, 1937; postgrad., U. Pa., 1937-38, Am. U., 1941-42, Sorbonne, U. Paris, 1949. With Ruder & Finn. Internat., N.Y.C., 1955-57, Barnet & Reef, N.Y.C., 1957-64; with AMAX, Inc., Greenwich, Conn., 1964-81, sr. v.p. and dir. office communications and pub. affairs; sr. cons. to exec. office AMAX, Inc., Greenwich and N.Y.C., 1981-87; dir. AMAX Australia Ltd.; trustee, chmn. U.S. com. Internat. Inst. Communications, 1979-81; bd. mem. World Environ. Ctr. N.Y., 1974-79, Ctr. for the Study of the Presidency; trustee Am. Coun. of Young Polit. Leaders; councillor Am.-Australian Bi-Centennial Commn. Fellow Inst. Mining and Metallurgy London, Acad. Internat. Bus.; mem. French Am. C. of C. (former councillor), Chaine des Rotisseurs (chevalier), Am. Food and Wine Inst., Fgn. Policy Assn. (assoc.), Overseas Press Club Am. (chmn. fgn. journalism com. 1958-63). Home: 2000 S Ocean Blvd Apt 608 Delray Beach FL 33483-6413

REELING, PATRICIA GLUECK, library educator, educational consultant; b. Cin., June 6, 1939; d. Arthur William and Bertha Louise Glueck; m. Glenn Eugene Reeling, Aug. 18, 1962; children: Craig Patrick, Aimee Reeling Berger. BA, Edgecliff Coll., Cin., 1960; MA, Ind. U., 1961; DLS, Columbia U., 1969. Reference libr. Ohio State U., Columbus, 1961-62; asst. to dir. Boston Coll. Librs., 1962-63; assoc. prof. Sch. Comm., Info. and Libr. Studies Rutgers U., New Brunswick, N.J., 1970—, chmn. dept. libr. and info. studies, 1984-89; ednl. cons. Reeling Assocs., Somerset, N.J., 1969—; evaluator Mid. States Assn. Commn. on Higher Edn., Phila., 1975—; vis. prof. Emporia State U., Denver, 1991—. Editor: Education for the Library/Information Profession: Strategies for the Mid-90s, 1993; editor column Govt. Info., RQ, 1983-85; contbr. articles to profl. jours. Mem. depository libr. coun. to pub. printer U.S. Govt. Printing Office, Washington, 1982-85; mem. network rev. bd. N.J. State Libr., Trenton, 1989-90. Recipient 1st Leadership award N.J. State Libr., 1987; grantee Rutgers U., 1983. Mem. ALA (life, mem. or chmn. numerous coms. 1961—, James Bennett Childs award 1988, Libr. Edn. Centennial Honor Role award 1988), AAUP (officer Rutgers coun. chpts. 1967—), Assn. for Libr. and Info. Sci. Edn. (mem. or chmn. various coms. 1964—), Documents Assn. N.J. (pres. 1981-82, archivist 1983—), N.J. Libr. Assn. (various coms. 1964—, Disting. Svc. award coll. and univ. sect. 1984), Beta Phi Mu (officer Omicron chpt. 1961—). Home: 131 Drake Rd Somerset NJ 08873-2317 Office: Rutgers U Sch Comm Info Libr Studies Alexander Library College Ave New Brunswick NJ 08901-1071

REEMELIN, ANGELA NORVILLE, dietitian consultant; b. Pitts., Apr. 28, 1945; d. Richard Gerow and Kathleen Taylor (Brannen) Norville; m. Philip Barrows Reemelin, Nov. 17, 1973; children: Richard Barrows, Kathleen Easson. BS, U. Tenn., 1967; dietetic intern, Emory U., 1968. Cert. water safety instr. Adminstr. dietitian Servomation of Atlanta, 1968-70; food svc. dir. ARA Food Svcs., Norfolk, Va., 1970-80; cons. Jacksonville, Fla., 1980—; cons. William T. Hall Convalescent Home, Portsmouth, Va., 1975-79. Recipient Outstanding Young Dietitian award Tidewater Dietetic Assn., 1974; Best of Show in sewing FFWC State Arts Festival, 1985, 86, 87. Mem. ARC (30 yr. Vol. award), ADA, Am. Soc. Hosp. Food Svc. Adminstrs., Jr. Womans Club Orange Park (pres. 1986-87, v.p., fundraiser, membership chair, Outstanding Dist. Pres. 1987), U. Tenn. Alumni Assn. (pres. 1982-84, bd. govs. 1984-85), Omicron Nu. Roman Catholic. Avocations: tennis, swimming, sewing, exercising. Home: 601 Lorn Ct Orange Park FL 32073-4228

REEP, EDWARD ARNOLD, artist; b. Bklyn., May 10, 1918; s. Joseph and Elsie (Abramson) R.; m. Karen Patricia Stevens, Dec. 9, 1942; children—Susan Kay, Cristine Elyse, Janine J., Mitchell Jules. Student, Art Center Coll. Design, 1936-41. Instr. painting and drawing Art Center Coll. Design, Los Angeles, 1946-50, Chouinard Art Inst., Los Angeles, 1950-69; prof. painting, chmn. dept., artist in residence E. Carolina U., 1970-85, prof. emeritus, 1985—; cons. editor Van Nostrand Reinhold Pub. Co.; ofcl. war artist-corr. WWII, Africa and Italy. Author: The Content of Watercolor, 1968, A Combat Artist in World War II, 1987; shows include Whitney Mus. Am. Art Ann., N.Y.C., 1946-48, Los Angeles County Mus. Ann., 1946-60, Corcoran Gallery Art Biennial, Washington, 1949, Nat. Gallery Art, Washington, 1945, Mus. Modern Art, N.Y.C.; represented in permanent collections Los Angeles County Mus., U.S. War Dept., Grunwald Graphic Arts Collection, UCLA, Nat. Mus. Am. Art, Washington, Lytton Collection, Los Angeles, State of Calif. Collection, Sacramento. Guggenheim fellow, 1945-46; Nat. Endowment for Arts grantee, 1975. Mem. AAUP, Nat. Watercolor Soc. (past pres.), Watercolor USA Honor Soc. Democrat. Home: 9021 Crowningshield Dr Bakersfield CA 93311-1901 *I once was consumed by the desire to become an artist. I feel no differently today. There is work ahead. If I had set goals for myself I no longer can recall what they may have been; I go along painting as well or as inventively as I can. Never have I sacrificed living life as I feel I must for my art. My work is a reflection of my life—experiences real and imagined.*

REES, CHARLES H. G., retired financial officer, investor, consultant; b. Trenton, N.J., Mar. 6, 1922; s. Albert H. and Helen (Gallagher) R.; m. Nancy Thomas, Oct. 30, 1954; children: Liberty, Camilla, Nancy, Hilleary. BA, Princeton U., 1948. Salesman John A. Roebling's Sons Co., Trenton, 1948-50; staff officer CIA, Washington, 1951-54; assoc. J.H. Whitney & Co., N.Y.C., 1954-59; gen. ptnr. Whitcom Investment Co., N.Y.C., 1967-85; with Whitney Comm. Corp., N.Y.C., 1960-85, pres., 1982-85. Trustee Riverside Rsch. Inst., N.Y.C. Capt. U.S. Army, 1942-46, 50-51. Decorated Bronze Star. Mem. Brook Club, Pilgrims of N.Y.C., Ivy Club, Nassau Club (Princeton, N.J.), Misquamicut Club, Watch Hill (R.I.) Yacht Club, Stonington Country Club, Wadawanuck Club (Stonington). Republican. Home: 215 Farmholme Rd Stonington CT 06378

REES, CLIFFORD HARCOURT, JR. (TED REES), association executive, retired air force officer; b. Newport News, Va., Dec. 11, 1936; s. Clifford Harcourt Sr. and Mary Evelyn (Brooks) R.; m. Joan Elizabeth Mittong, July 26, 1958; children—Clifford Harcourt III, Steven M., Daniel B., William B. BS in Fgn. Svc., Georgetown U., 1958; MS in Polit. Sci., Auburn U., 1969; grad., Air War Coll., Montgomery, Ala., 1978. Commd. 2d lt. U.S. Air Force, 1958; advanced through grades to lt. gen., 1988; later comdr. 421st Tactical Fighter Squadron, Udorn Royal Thai AFB, 1974-75; chief, house liaison office U.S. Ho. Reps., Washington, 1978-80; asst. col. assignments Randolph AFB, 1980-82; vice-comdr. Air Force Manpower and Personnel Ctr., 1982; dep. dir. legis. liaison Office Sec. Air Force, 1982-84, dir. legis. liaison, 1984-86; comdr. USAF Air Defense Weapons Ctr., Tyndall AFB, Fla., 1986-88; vice comdr. in chief USAF in Europe, Ramstein AB, Federal Republic of Germany, 1988-92; ret. USAF in Europe, 1992; founder, pres. Rees Group Cons.; pres. Air Conditioning and Refrigeration Inst., Arlington, Va., 1993—; U.S. rep. to v.p. Internat. Coun. Mil. Sports, Brussels, 1982-94. Decorated D.S.M. with one oak leaf cluster, DFC with one oak leaf cluster, Legion of Merit with one oak leaf cluster, Meritorious Svc. medal with one oak leaf cluster, Air medal with 11 oak leaf clusters USAF, Das Grosse Verdienstkreuz Mit Stern, Pres. Fed. Republic Germany, 1993; named Commander Order of Meritorious Svc. Mil. Sports Coun., 1993. Mem. Delta Phi Epsilon (v.p. membership 1957-58, nat. pres. 1984-86). Methodist. Home: 2487 Oakton Hills Dr Oakton VA 22124-1530 Office: Air Conditioning & Refrigeration Inst 4301 Fairfax Dr Ste 425 Arlington VA 22203-1627

REES, DAVID WAYNE, lawyer; b. Tucson, May 25, 1952; s. Paul G. and Donna V. (Smith) R.; m. Suzanne Jeanette Greenwalt, Aug. 13, 1977 (Oct. 1991); children: Melissa B., Roxanne J. BA, U. Ariz., 1977, JD, 1977. Bar: Ariz. 1977, U.S. Ct. Appeals (9th cir.) 1977. Assoc. Pima Cmty. Coll., Tucson, 1978-81; atty. pvt. practice, Tucson, 1977—. Bd. dirs. Drug Prevention Orgn., Tucson, 1981-91. Fellow Am. Trial Lawyers Assn., Ariz. Bar Found. (tchr./instr. 1990—); mem. Am. Bd. Trial Advocates (advocate), Ariz. Trial LAwyers Assn. (sustaining mem. 1977—). Democrat. Methodist. Avocations: fishing, hunting, teaching, cmty. svc. Office: 145 E University Blvd Tucson AZ 85705-7738

REES, FRANK WILLIAM, JR., architect; b. Rochester, N.Y., June 5, 1943; s. Frank William and Elizabeth R. (Miller) R.; m. Joan Mary Keevers, Apr. 1, 1967; children: Michelle, Christopher. BS in Architecture, U. Okla., 1970; postgrad., Harvard U., Boston, 1979, 90; OPM, Harvard U., 1990. Registered architect, 36 states; cert. Nat. Coun. Archtl. Registration Bds. Sales mgr. Sta. KFOM, Oklahoma City, 1967-70; project architect Benham-Blair & Affiliates, Oklahoma City, 1970-75; pres., founder Rees Assocs., Inc., Oklahoma City, 1975—; pres., CEO Rees Assocs. Inc., Dallas, 1995—; pres., chmn. bd. Weatherscan Radio Network, Oklahoma City, 1973-78; chmn. bd. Weatherscan Internat., Oklahoma City, 1972-78; pres. Frontier Communications, Oklahoma City, 1980-84; chmn. architecture bd. U. Okla., Norman, 1988-91. Past pres. Lake Hefner Trails, Oklahoma City, Hosp. Hospitality House, Oklahoma City, Oklahoma City Beautiful; mem. Leadership Oklahoma City. Mem. AIA, Am. Assn. Hosp. Architects, Am. Healthcare

Assn., Tex. Hosp. Assn., World Pres. Orgn., Nat. Assn. Sr. Living Industries. Home: 1104 Stone Gate Dr Irving TX 75063-4676 Office: Ste 200 3102 Oak Lawn Dallas TX 75219-4241

REES, JAMES CONWAY, IV, historic site administrator; b. Richmond, Va., May 5, 1952. BA, Coll. William & Mary, 1974; MPA, George Washington U., 1978. Reporter, photographer Newport News Daily-Press, 1974; coord. radio and television programming The Coll. William & Mary, 1974-78; mng. editor The William & Mary Mag., 1978-82; promotions dir. Va. Shakespeare Festival, 1980; dir. annual giving and pub. info. The Coll. William & Mary, 1978-80, dir. annual support and corp. rels., 1980-81, dir. capital support, 1981-82; asst. dir. devel. Nat. Trust Historic Preservation, 1982-83, assoc. dir. devel., 1983; dir. devel. and comms. Historic Mount Vernon, 1983-85, assoc. dir., 1985-94, resident dir., 1994—; exec. v.p. Mount Vernon Inn, Inc., 1994—; Mem. bd. dirs. Va. Shakespeare Festival, Washington Area Chpt. WIlliam and Mary Alumni Soc. Mem. Nat. Trust for Historic Preservation, Friends of the Nat. Symphony, WETA Pub. Television. Mem. Am. Film Inst., Va. Assn. Mus. (pres. 1991-94). Methodist. Home: 710 A St NE Washington DC 20002 Office: Mount Vernon Ladies Assn Mount Vernon VA 22121

REES, JOHN ROBERT, physicist; b. Peru, Ind., Feb. 17, 1930; s. Alton Edwin and Mary Katherine (Morse) R.; m. Marian Janet Heimert, Jan. 28, 1956; children: Carol Ellen, John Alton. AB, Ind. U., 1951, MS, 1953, PhD, 1956. Rsch. fellow Harvard U., Cambridge, Mass., 1956-65; chief accelerator br. high energy physics program AEC, Washington, 1967-69; mem. staff Stanford Linear Accelerator Ctr., Palo Alto, Calif., 1965-75; dir. Positron-Electron Project, Palo Alto, 1975-80; prof. Stanford U., Palo Alto, 1980—; assoc. dir. Stanford Linear Accelerator Ctr., Palo Alto, 1980-93; project mgr., assoc. dir. Superconducting Super Collider, Dallas, 1991-93. Fellow Am. Phys. Soc. Office: Stanford Linear Accelerator Ctr PO Box 4349 Stanford CA 94305

REES, MORGAN ROWLANDS, engineer, educator; b. Kingston, Pa., Jan. 17, 1940; s. William Arthur and Anna Fae (Mericle) R.; m. Janet Marsello, May 15, 1965; 1 child, Bradley Alan. BS in Civil Engring., Worcester Poly. Inst., 1961, MS in Civil Engring., 1969; M Pub. Adminstrn., U. So. Calif., Washington, 1988, D Pub. Adminstrn., 1993. Registered profl. engr., Mass. Mgmt. trainee Bell Telephone of Pa., Scranton, 1961-62; appraisal engr. Am. Appraisal Co., N.Y.C., 1964-67; hydraulic rsch. engr. Worcester (Mass.) Poly. Inst., 1967-69; coastal engr. New Eng. Corps Engrs., Waltham, Mass., 1969-73, chief regulatory br., 1973-81; chief regulatory policy sect. Hqrs. Army C.E., Washington, 1981-82; asst. regulatory affairs U.S. Army Civil Works, Washington, 1982-86, dep. asst. sec., 1986-95; prin. Rees Engring. and Environ. Svcs., Alexandria, Va., 1995—; civil engring. dept. adv. com. Worcester Poly. Inst., 1988—. Jr. warden St. Luke's Ch., Worcester, 1974-79; v.p. Collingwood Citizen's Assn., Alexandria, Va., 1983-84. 1st lt. U.S. Army, 1962-64. Named to Athletic Hall of Fame Worcester Poly. Inst., 1984. Mem. ASCE, Soc. Am. Mil. Engrs., Sr. Exec. Assn., Am. Assn. Port Authorities. Avocations: jogging, reading, home remodeling.

REES, NORMA S., academic administrator; b. N.Y.C., Dec. 27, 1929; d. Benjamin and Lottie (Schwartz) D.; m. Raymond R. Rees, Mar. 19, 1960; children—Evan Lloyd, Raymond Arthur. B.A., Queens Coll., 1952; M.A., Bklyn. Coll., 1954; Ph.D., NYU, 1959. Cert. speech-language pathology, audiology. Prof. communicative disorders Hunter Coll., N.Y.C., 1967-72; exec. officer, speech and hearing scis. grad. sch. CUNY, N.Y.C., 1972-74, assoc. dean for grad. studies, 1974-76, dean grad. studies, 1976-82; vice chancellor for acad. affairs U. Wis., Milw., 1982-85, from 1986, acting chancellor, 1985-86; vice chancellor for acad. policy and planning Mass. Bd. Regent for Higher Edn., Boston, 1987-90; pres. Calif. State U., Hayward, 1990—; bd. dirs. Am. Assn. State Colls. and Univs., 1995—, Coun. of Postsecondary Accreditation, Washington, 1985-94; chmn. Commn. Recognition of Postsecondary Accreditation, 1994—. Contbr. articles to profl. jours. Trustee Citizens Govtl. Rsch. Bur., Milw., 1985-87; active Task Force on Wis. World Trade Ctr., 1985-87; bd. dirs. Greater Boston YWCA, 1987-90; mem. Mayor's Cabinet Ednl. Excellence, Oakland, Calif.; mem. steering com. Econ. Devel. Adv. Bd. Alameda County, 1995—. Fellow Am. Speech-Lang-Hearing Assn. (honors); mem. Am. Coun. Edn. (com. internat. edn. 1991-93), Am. Assn. Colls. and Univs. (chair task force on quality assessment 1991-92, mem. steering com. of coun. of urban met. colls. & univs. 1992—), Nat. Assn. State Univs. and Land Grant Colls. (exec. com. divsn. urban affairs 1985-87, com. accreditation 1987-90). Office: Calif State Univ-Hayward 25800 Carlos Bee Blvd Hayward CA 94542-3000

REES, PATRICIA GLINES, occupational health nurse, consultant, educator; b. Santa Maria, Calif., Aug. 28, 1945; d. Jack Holloway and Frances Ruth (Baril) Glines; m. Nov. 28, 1970 (div. July 1989); children: Eric Michael, Jennifer Lynne. BSN with honors, U. Calif., San Francisco, 1968; MSN, Clarkson Coll., Omaha, 1994. RN, Nebr., Calif.; cert. occupational health nurse; cert. BLS, CPR, first aid instr., hearing conservationist. Staff nurse Marin Gen. Hosp., Marin County, Calif., 1968-70; sch. health nurse Novato (Calif.) Unified Sch. Dist., 1968-70; obstetrics office nurse Oxon Hill, Md., 1971-72; vol. sch. health svcs. Sullivan Sch., Yokosuka, Japan, 1976-80; sch. health nurse, client svcs. rep. Vis. Nurse Assn., Omaha, 1987-89; occupational health nurse Armour Swift-Eckrich, Omaha, 1989-91; program mgr. Advantage Health Sys., Inc., Kansas City, Mo., 1991—; preceptor U. Nebr. Med. Ctr., Omaha, 1994-95; vol./instr. ARC, Omaha, 1989—; presenter in field. Co-author: Cumulative Trauma Disorders, 1991, Case Management, 1994, Work Injury Management, 1996; contbr. articles to profl. jours. Mem. Nebr. Safety Coun., Omaha, 1989-91, U.S. Swimming, Omaha, 1981-89. Pres.'s scholar U. Calif., San Francisco, 1967-68. Mem. APHA, Am. Assn. Occupational Health Nurses, Nebr. Assn. Occupational Health Nurses (edn. com. 1989—), Clarkson Honor Soc. (pres. 1994-96), Sigma Theta Tau, Alpha Xi Delta. Avocations: travel, miniatures, stitchery. Home: 1311 Beechwood Ave Papillion NE 68133-2509

REES, ROGER, actor, educator; b. Aberystwyth, Wales, May 5, 1944; s. William John and Doris Louise (Smith) R. Educated, Camberwell Sch. Art, Slade Sch. Fine Art. Instr. theatre Columbia U., N.Y.C., 1981-82; Hoffman chair prof. Fla. State U., Tallahassee, 1986; assoc. dir. Bristol Old Vic Theatre Co., 1986—. Made theatre debut in Hindle Wakes, Wimbledon, Eng., 1964; other theatre appearances include The Cherry Orchard, Pitlochry, Scotland, 1965, The Merchant of Venice, Aldwych Theatre, London, also The Island of the Mighty, 1971-72; Candida, Neptune Theatre, Halifax, N.S., 1973; Paradise, Theatre Upstairs, London, also Moving Clocks Go Slow, 1975, The Alchemist, London, 1977, Macbeth, Warehouse Theatre, London, also Factory Birds, 1977, The Way of the World, Aldwych Theatre, 1978, The Suicide, various theatres, London, 1980, The Adventures of Nicholas Nickleby, Aldwych Theatre, London and Plymouth Theatre, N.Y.C., 1981 (Tony award for Best Actor 1982), The Real Thing, Strand Theatre, London, 1983, Cries from the Mammoth House, Royal Court Theatre, London, 1983, Double-Double, Watford Palace and Fortune Theatres, London, 1986, Archangels Don't Play Pinball, Bristol Old Vic Theatre Co., Theatre Royal, London, 1986, Hapgood, Aldwych Theatre, 1988; appeared with Royal Shakespeare Co. in The Taming of the Shrew, 1967, As You Like It, 1967, Julius Caesar, 1968, The Merry Wives of Windsor, 1968, Pericles, 1969, Twelfth Night, 1969, 70, 76, Henry VIII, 1969, The Winter's Tale, 1969, 70, The Plebeians Rehearse the Uprising, 1970, Major Barbara, 1970, Much Ado About Nothing, 1971, Othello, 1971, Romeo and Juliet, 1976, Macbeth, 1976, The Comedy of Errors, 1976, Cymbeline, 1979, Hamlet, 1984, Love's Labours Lost, 1984, Indiscretions, 1995 (Tony nominee - Lead Actor in a Play) tour London Assurance, various U.S. cities, 1974-75, tour Is There Honey Still For Tea?, The Three Sisters, Twelfth Night, various U.K. cities, 1978; toured U.K. cities with Cambridge Theatre Co., 1973-74, in Twelfth Night, Aunt Sally or the Triumph of Death, She Stoops to Conquer, Fear and Misery in the Third Reich, Jack and the Beanstalk, 1975, in The Importance of Being Earnest, The Birthday Party; appeared in film Star 80, 1983; appeared in TV film A Christmas Carol, 1984, The Ebony Tower, Great Performances, PBS, 1987, Charles and Diana: Unhappily Ever After, 1992; recurring role as Robin Colcord on TV series Cheers, NBC. Office: Charles Burrows Charles Prodns 5555 Melrose Ave Los Angeles CA 90038-3149

REESE, ALFERD GEORGE, retired army civilian logistics specialist; b. Granville, N.D., Apr. 5, 1934; s. Ferdinand Emil and lola May (Boulds) R.; m. Donna Mae Berger, 1955 (div. 1972); children: Rick, Denise, Roxanna; m. Nelda Cecilia Pena, May 31, 1985; children: Nancy, Joyce, Alfred, Jeffrey, Jessica, James, Alicia. AS, Humphreys Coll., 1963; BS, U. State of N.Y., Albany, 1983; MPA, U. Colo., Colorado Springs, 1985; postgrad., Ga. State U., 1987-88; PhD, Columbia Pacific U., 1994. Inspector, mechanic Sharp Army Depot, Lathrop, Calif., 1958-66; equipment specialist various stations U.S. Army Aviation Systems Command, 1966-84; supervisory equipment specialist U.S. Army Aviation Systems Command, Atlanta, 1984-88; supervisory logistics specialist U.S. Army Aviation Systems Command, St. Louis, 1988-93. Mem. com. Boy Scouts Am., Fed. Republic Germany, 1979-81. With USAF, 1953-57. Mem. Army Aviation Assn. Assn. (USAEUR Dept. Army Civilian of Yr. 1980, 81), Ctr. for the Study of the Presidency, Acad. Polit. Sci., Am. Soc. for Pub. Adminstrn., Nat. Rifle Assn. Avocations: golf, skiing, photography, painting. Home: 1590 Fairmount Dr Florissant MO 63033-2645

REESE, ANN N., financial executive. Formerly tres. Mobil Europe; asst. treas. ITT Corp., 1987-89, v.p., 1989-92, sr. v.p., treas., 1992—, exec. v.p., CFO. Office: ITT Corp 1330 Avenue Of The Americas New York NY 10019*

REESE, CHARLES EDGAR, columnist; b. Washington, Ga., Jan. 29, 1937; s. Edgar Ernest and Neoma (Moody) R.; m. Gretchen Elise Krughoff, May 16, 1965 (div. July 1984); children: Benjamin, Alice, Theodore. PhD (hon.), Webber Coll., 1989. Caption writer Planet Newspictures Ltd., London, 1956-57; reporter Pensacola (Fla.) News-Jour., 1957-67; account exec. Dodson, Craddock & Born, Pensacola, 1967-69, Fry, Hammond & Born, Pensacola, 1971-72; chief bur. media svcs. State of Fla. Dept. of Commerce, Tallahassee, 1969-71; asst. metro editor Orlando Sentinel, 1972-75, asst. to pub., 1975-78, columnist, mem. editorial bd., 1978—. Author: Great Gods of the Potomac, Common Sense for the 80s. Active Hist. Commn., Pensacola, 1968; bd. dirs. Holocaust Meml., Orlando, 1985-90. With USAR, 1959-65. Named Best Columnist, Fla. Press Club, 1984, Fla. Soc. Newspaper Editors. Mem. SCV. Democrat. Avocations: pistol shooting, hunting, sketching. Office: Orlando Sentinel 633 N Orange Ave Orlando FL 32801-1300

REESE, DOUGLAS WAYNE, geologist; b. Omaha, June 27, 1963; s. Larry Wayne and Sandra Kay (Bullerdick) R. BA in Geology, Case Western Res. U., 1987. Geologist, technician Mason de Verteuil Geotech. Svcs., Columbus, Ohio, 1987—, lab. supr., 1990—; owner D.R. Info. Sys., Reynoldsburg, Ohio. Mem. ASTM, ACLU, Am. Assn. Petroleum Geologists, Amnesty Internat., Electronic Frontier Found. Avocations: computers, investing, golf. Home: 1650 Hallworth Ct Columbus OH 43232-7400 Office: DLZ Corp 6121 Huntley Rd Columbus OH 43229 also: DR Info Sys 6326 E Livingston Ave # 199 Reynoldsburg OH 43068-2795

REESE, ERROL LYNN, academic administrator, dentist; b. Fairmont, W.Va., May 3, 1939; s. Edgar B. and Elizabeth (Carpenter) R.; m. Julia Hinebaugh, June 8, 1963; children: Daniel, Elizabeth. BS, Fairmont State Coll., 1960; DDS, W.Va. U., 1963; cert. of tng., U. Detroit, 1968, MS, 1968. Grad. asst. Sch. Dentistry U. Detroit, 1966-68; asst. prof. Sch. Dentistry U. Md., Balt., 1968-73, assoc. prof. Sch. Dentistry, 1978, prof. Sch. Dentistry, 1978—, from assoc. dean to dean Sch. Dentistry, 1973-90, pres., 1990-94. Capt. U.S. Army, 1963-66. Mem. ADA, Am. Assn. Dental Schs. (pres. 1989-90), Am. Acad. History of Dentistry, Nat. Found. Dentistry for Handicapped, Acad. Gen. Dentistry Found. Office: U Md Dental Sch 666 W Baltimore St Baltimore MD 21201-1627

REESE, FRANCIS EDWARD, retired chemical company executive, consultant; b. Monaca, Pa., Nov. 3, 1919; s. Francis Edward and Vivian Iris (Hancuff) R.; m. Katherine Mary McBrien, June 29, 1946; 1 son, Francis Edward III. B.S. in Chem. Engring, Purdue U., 1941. Registered profl. engr., Pa. With Monsanto Co., St. Louis, 1941; research engr. plastics div. Monsanto Co., 1941-48, chief devel. engring. plastics div., 1948-53, asst. engr. plastics div., 1953-56, dir. engring. plastics div., 1956-59, asst. gen. mgr. plastics div., 1959-61, asst. gen. mgr. hydrocarbons div., 1961-65, asst. gen. mgr., hydrocarbons and polymers div., 1965-66, gen. mgr. internat. div., 1966-68, corp. v.p., 1968-74, gen. mgr., hydrocarbons and polymers div., 1968-71, gen. mgr. polymers and petrochems. div., 1971-73, gen. mgr. internat. div., 1973-74, dir., 1973-84, group v.p., 1974-79, sr. v.p., 1979-84; pres. FTR Assocs., Inc.; mem. engring. found. adv. coun. U. Tex. Fellow AAAS, Am. Inst. Chem. Engrs.; mem. Am. Chem. Soc., Nat. Soc. Profl. Engrs., Soc. Chem. Industry, Tau Beta Pi, Phi Lambda Upsilon. Home: Rydal Park 271W 1515 The Fairway Rydal PA 19046-1628 Office: 100 Old York Rd Ste 1202A Jenkintown PA 19046-3613

REESE, HARRY EDWIN, JR., electronics executive; b. Balt., Oct. 27, 1928; s. Harry Edwin and Margery Lee (Stroud) R.; m. Elizabeth Syra Pfeiffer, Oct. 15, 1955; children: Clifford Owen, Susan Syra, Peter Eyre. BSEE, Tufts U., 1950; MS in Stats., Villanova U., 1960. Engr. Philco Corp., Phila., 1950-54; project engr. Burroughs Corp., Paoli, Pa., 1956-59, dept. mgr., 1959-65; dept. mgr. GE Co., King of Prussia, Pa., 1965-69; group staff mgr. Burroughs Corp., Paoli, Pa., 1969-75; gen. mgr. Burroughs Corp., Plainfield, N.J., 1975-82; corp. staff dir. Burroughs Corp., Detroit, 1982-83; v.p. quality assurance Am. Electronic Labs., Inc., Lansdale, Pa., 1984-90, ret., 1990. Chmn. Charlestown Twp. Planning Commn., Pa., 1973-75. With U.S. Army, 1954-56. Fellow IEEE (life, pres. Reliability Soc. 1969-70, gen. chmn. Rams symposium 1968, chmn. bd. 1969, Centennial medal 1984); mem. Nat. Mgmt. Assn. (life, chmn. formation com. Am. Electronics Labs. chpt. 1985, Leadership award 1973, 86), Lake Hopatcong Yacht Club (treas., rear commodore), Masons, Rotary (Paul Harris fellow, treas.). Republican. Episcopalian. Avocations: carpentry, architecture, boating, antiques, travel. Home: 17 Bass Rock Rd Hopatcong NJ 07843-1901

REESE, HAYNE WARING, psychologist; b. Comanche, Tex., Jan. 14, 1931; s. Tom F. and Marion (Waring) R.; m. Patsy Atwood, Aug. 24, 1957 (div. Apr. 1967); children: Anne, William, Margaret; m. Nancy Mann, Dec. 16, 1967; 1 child, Bradley. Student, So. Meth. U., 1949-50; B.A., U. Tex., 1953, M.A., 1955; Ph.D., U. Iowa, 1958. Asst. prof. U. Buffalo, 1958-62; assoc. prof. SUNY-Buffalo, 1962-66, prof., 1966-67; prof. U. Kans., Lawrence, 1967-70; Centennial prof. psychology W.Va. U., Morgantown, 1970—, dir. grad. tng. in life-span devel. psychology, 1973—; mem. initial rev. groups div. research grants NIH, Washington, 1974-78, 79-84. Author: Perception of Stimulus Relations, 1968; co-author: Life-Span Developmental Psychology, 1977, Child Development, 1979; editor: Advances in Child Development and Behavior, 22 vols., 1969-94; co-editor: Life-Span Developmental Psychology, 7 vols., 1973-94; assoc. editor: Jour. Exptl. Child Psychology, 1975-83, editor, 1983—. Served with U.S. Army, 1954. Fellow AAAS, Am. Psychol. Soc.; mem. AAUP, Soc. for Rsch. in Child Devel., Psychonomic Soc., Assn. for Behavior Analysis, Ea. Psychol. Assn., Internat. Soc. for Study Behavioral Devel. Office: W Va U Dept Psychology PO Box 6040 Morgantown WV 26506-6040

REESE, JOHN ROBERT, lawyer; b. Salt Lake City, Nov. 3, 1939; s. Robert McCann and Glade (Stauffer) R.; m. Francesca Marroquin Gardner, Sept. 5, 1964 (div.); children—Jennifer Marie Gardner, Justine Francesca; m. Robin Ann Gunsul, June 18, 1988. AB cum laude, Harvard U., 1962; LLB, Stanford U., 1965. Bar: Calif. 1966, U.S. Dist. Ct. (no. dist.) Calif. 1966, U.S. Ct. Appeals (9th cir.) 1966, U.S. Dist. Ct. (cen. dist.) Calif. 1974, U.S. Supreme Ct. 1976, U.S. Dist. Ct. (ea. dist.) Calif. 1977, U.S. Ct. Appeals (6th cir.) 1982, U.S. Ct. Appeals (8th cir.) 1985, U.S. Ct. Appeals (10th cir.) 1992, U.S. Ct. Appeals (Fed. cir.) 1994. Assoc. McCutchen, Doyle, Brown & Enersen, San Francisco, 1965-74, ptnr., 1974—; adj. asst. prof. law Hastings Coll. of Law, 1991; lectr. U. Calif., Berkeley, 1987, 92. Mem. editorial, adv. bds. Antitrust Bull., Jour. Reprints for Antitrust Law and Econs. Bd. dirs. Friends of San Francisco Pub. Libr., 1981-87; bd. vis. Stanford U., 1983-86. Capt. U.S. Army, 1966-68. Decorated Bronze Star. Mem. ABA, State Bar Calif., San Francisco Bar Assn., U.S. Supreme Ct. Hist. Soc., Ninth Jud. Cir. Hist. Soc., Calif. Acad. Appellate Lawyers, Order of the Coif. Avocations: aviculture, gardening. Home: 9 Morning Sun Dr Petaluma CA 94952-4780 Office: McCutchen Doyle Brown & Enersen 3 Embarcadero Ctr San Francisco CA 94111-4003

REESE, JOHN TERENCE, professional bridge player, writer; b. Epsom, Surrey, Eng., Aug. 28, 1913; s. John and Anne Maria (Hutchings) R.; m. Alwyn Sherrington, Jan. 23, 1970. Student, Bradfield Coll., Berkshire, Eng.; grad., New Coll., Oxford U., Eng. Worldwide profl. bridge player, 1955-96; bridge corr. The London Evening News, 1948-96, The Observer newspaper, 1949-96, The Lady Mag., 1954-96, The London Evening Standard, 1981-96; world champion bridge player, 1955; mem. world team Olympiad, 1980, World Pairs Olympiad, 1962, world par champion, 1961, European champion, 1948, 49, 54, 63; winner all top Brit. championships, including Gold Cup 8 times, Masters Pairs 7 times, also others; an originator of ACOL sys. in the 1930's; considered at one time top-ranking player in world. Author or co-author over 100 books on bridge, poker, backgammon, casino gambling, and canasta, including Reese on Play, 1948, 2d edit., 1975 (transl. into 5 langs.), The Expert Game, 1958, 2d edit., 1973, Teach Yourself Bridge, 1980, 2d edit., 1992; contbr. numerous articles on bridge to mags. and periodicals worldwide. Mem. English Bridge Union (hon. life). Avocation: golf. Home and Office: Flat 5 23 Adelaide Crescent Hove, East Sussex BN3 2JG, England *Died Jan. 28, 1996.*

REESE, MONTE NELSON, agricultural association executive; b. Mooreland, Okla., Mar. 31, 1947; s. James Nelson and Ruby Edith (Bond) R.; m. Treisa Lou Bartow, May 25, 1968; children: Bartow Allan, Monica Lynnelle. BS in Agrl. Econs., Okla. State U., 1969. Staff asst. Wilson Cert. Foods, Oklahoma City, 1969-71; assoc. farm dir. Sta. WKY Radio and TV, Oklahoma City, 1971-73; radio-TV specialist Tex. A&M U., College Station, 1973; dir. agrl. devel. Oklahoma City C. of C., 1973-76; asst. exec. dir. Am. Morgan Horse Assn., Westmoreland, N.Y., 1976-77; v.p. pub. affairs Farm Credit Banks of Wichita, Kans., 1977-87; exec. dir. Coffey County Econ. Devel., Burlington, Kans., 1987-88; farm dir. Mid-Am. Ag Network, Wichita, 1988-89; CEO Cattlemen's Beef Promotion and Rsch. Bd., Englewood, Colo., 1989-96; exec. dir. Cattlemen's Beef Promotion & Rsch. Bd., Englewood, CO, 1996—. Lt. col. USAR, 1969—. Home: 982 S Dearborn Way Apt 2 Aurora CO 80012-3878 Office: Cattlemen's Beef Promotion and Rsch Bd PO Box 3316 Englewood CO 80155

REESE, WILLIAM ALBERT, III, psychologist; b. Tabor, Iowa, Nov. 23, 1932; s. William Albert and Mary-Evelyn Hope (Lundeen) R.; B.A., U. Washington Reed Coll., 1955; M.Ed., U. Ariz., 1964, Ph.D., 1981; m. Barbara Diane Windermere, Dec. 22, 1954; children: Judy, Diane, William IV, Sandra-Siobhan, Debra-Anne, Robert-Gregory, Barbara-Joanne. Diplomate Am. Bd. Christian Psychology. Clin. Psychology cons. Nogales Pub. Schs., Nogales-Tucson, Ariz., 1971-79; clin. psychologist Astra Found., N.Y.C., 1979-86, chief psychology svc., neuropsychiatry, 1980-89; chief psychologist Family Support Ctr. Community-Family Exceptional Mem. Svcs., Sonoita, Ariz., 1986-89, Psychol. Svc. Ctr., Mount Tabor, Iowa, 1989-95, Calif. Ctr., 1995—; dir. religious Marriage and Family Life Wilderness Ctr., Berchtesgaden, W.Ger., summer 1981-82; exec. sec. Astra Ednl. Found., 1975-79, bd. dirs., 1979—, EEO officer, 1978—. Served with USAF, 1967-71: Vietnam. Decorated Bronze Star. Fellow in cons. psychology and holistic medicine Clin. Services Found., Ariz., 1979—. Fellow Am. Psychol. Soc.; mem. Calif. Psychol. Assn., Ariz. Psychol. Assn., Am. Counseling Assn., Iowa Psychol. Assn. Clubs: Los Padres Wilderness Center, Outdoor, Sierra, Skyline Estates Golf and Country (Tucson), K.C. Author: Developing a Scale of Human Values for Adults of Diverse Cultural Backgrounds, 1981, rev. edit., 1988. Office: Psychol Service Ctr Integrated Med Ctr-Wellness Clin 225 Crossroads Blvd Ste 417 Carmel CA 93923-8649 also: Box 1089 Bellevue NE 68005-1089

REESE, WILLIAM LEWIS, philosophy educator; b. Jefferson City, Mo., Feb. 15, 1921; s. William Lewis and Lillian Amelia (Fisher) R.; m. Louise Weeks, June 11, 1945; children: Claudia, Patricia, William Lewis III. A.B., Drury Coll., 1942; B.D., U. Chgo., 1945, Ph.D., 1947; postdoctoral, Yale U., 1955-56. Asst. prof. philosophy Drake U., 1947-49, asso. prof. philosophy, 1949-57, head dept., 1954-57; asso. prof. philosophy Grinnell Coll., 1957-60; vis. prof. philosophy Iowa State U., 1958; prof. philosophy, chmn. dept. U. Del., Newark, 1960-67, dir. seminar in philosophy of sci., 1960-66; H. Rodney Sharp prof. philosophy U. Del., 1965-67; prof. philosophy SUNY-Albany, 1967—, chmn. dept., 1968-74, 84; Tully Cleon Knoles lectr. U. Pacific, 1962; Del. U.S. Nat. Commn. for UNESCO, 1963; gen. mem. 4th East-West Philosophers Conf., 1964. Author, contbr.: Studies in C.S. Peirce, 1952, (with Charles Hartshorne) Philosophers Speak of God, 1953, The Ascent from Below, 1959, 2d edit., 1987, (with Eugene Freeman) Process and Divinity, 1964, Dictionary of Philosophy and Religion: Eastern and Western Thought, 1980, 2d edit., 1996; gen. editor: Philosophy of Science, The Delaware Seminar, vols. 1, 2, 1963, vol. 3, 1967; editor: Philosophy and World Religions: The Reader's Adviser, vol. 4, 1988; contbg. editor: Philosophical Interrogations, 1964; co-editor: Metaphilosophy, 1967-75; editl. bd.: State of N.Y. Press, 1968-78; contbr. articles to profl. jours. Recipient Ford Found. Study award Argentina, 1967; Fulbright lectr. Argentina, summer 1971; Inst. Humanistic Studies fellow, 1977—. Mem. AAUP, Am. Philos. Assn., Metaphysical Soc. Am. (sec.-treas. 1962-65). Mem. Christian Ch. (Disciples of Christ). Home: Font Grove Rd Slingerlands NY 12159 Office: SUNY Dept Philosophy Albany NY 12222 *To have before one always the realistic sense that if one has been successful in one way one has failed in others, and that one's failures surely outnumber one's successes.*

REESE, WILLIAM WILLIS, banker; b. N.Y.C., July 8, 1940; s. Willis Livingston Meiser and Frances Galletin (Stevens) R.; BA, Trinity Coll., 1963; MBA, JD, Columbia U., 1970. Admitted to N.Y. bar, 1972; rsch. analyst Morgan Guaranty Trust Co., N.Y.C., 1971-73, investment rsch. officer, 1973-77, asst. v.p., 1977-86, v.p., 1986— . Bd. dirs. N.Y.C. Ballet, 1975-87, Counseling and Human Devel. Ctr., 1977-89, 3d St. Music Sch. Settlement, 1976—; trustee Millbrook Sch., 1972-91. Served with USAF, 1963-67. Mem. Am., Inter-Am., N.Y. State (sec. com. on internat. law 1973-76), Dutchess County bar assns., N.Y. Soc. Security Analysts, Certified Fin. Analysts, Assn. Bar City N.Y., Union, Club, Racquet and Tennis Club, Rockaway Hunt Club, Soldiers', Sailors' & Airmen's Club (bd. dirs. 1991—), Mt. Holyoke Lodge. Republican. Episcopalian. Home: 910 Park Ave New York NY 10021-0255 Office: Morgan Guaranty Trust Co 522 Fifth Ave New York NY 10036

REESER, RACHEL ANNE EVERSON, graphic designer; b. Shreveport, La., Nov. 16, 1964; d. Robert Higgins and Marian Louise (Wimberly) Everson; m. Kirk Allen "Korky" Reeser, Feb. 1, 1994. BS, Okla. State U., 1986. Mgr. Fabric, Floors & Such, Oklahoma City, Okla., 1986-87; advt. dir. Pipkin Cameras & Video, Oklahoma City, 1987-88; asst. nat. advt. mgr. Morgan Bldgs. & Spas, Dallas, 1988-89; sr. art dir. Avrea/Pugliese, Coconut Grove, Dallas, 1989-91; pres., creative dir. Freestyle Studio, Inc., Dallas, 1991—. Mem. Dallas Soc. Illustrators (bd. dirs. 1992-94, Merit award 1993), Dallas Soc. Visual Comms. Avocations: painting, tennis. Office: Freestyle Studio 8150 N Central Expy Ste 1000 Dallas TX 75206-1805 Address: PO Box 823554 Dallas TX 75382-3554

REETZ, GARY, medical facility administrator; b. 1947. Grad., Mich. State U., 1970. With Deloitte & Touche CPA's, Detroit, 1970-78, St. John Hosp., Detroit, 1978-83, Peat Marwick & Mitchell CPA's, Detroit, 1983-85, The Healthsource Group Inc., Flint, Mich., 1985-88; with Genesys Regional Med. Ctr., Flint, 1988—, now v.p. fin. Office: Genesys Reg Med Ctr 302 Kensington Ave Flint MI 48503-2000*

REETZ, HAROLD FRANK, JR., industrial agronomist; b. Wat., Ill.; s. Harold Frank and Evelyn Evedeen (Russell) R.; m. Christine Lee Kaiser, Aug. 25, 1973; children: Carrie, Wesley, Anthony. BS in Agrl. Sci., U. Ill., 1970; MS in Agronomy, Purdue U., 1972, PhD in Agronomy, 1976. Rsch. specialist Purdue U., West Lafayette, Ind., 1974-82; regional dir. Potash & Phosphate Inst., Monticello, Ill, 1982--; cons. Control Data Corp., Mpls., 1978-82, Internat. Harvester Co., Chgo., 1979-82, Monsanto Agrl. Chem. Co., St. Louis, 1981-82. Author: Crop Simulation Model, CORNCROPS, 1976, several crops mgmt. computer programs; contbr. articles to profl. jours. Chmn. Ill. Com. for Agrl. Edn., 1987-89; mem. Ill. Groundwater Adv. Coun., 1988—; mem. Ill. Fertilizer Rsch. and Edn. Coun., Ill. Dept. Agr., 1989—; chmn. Ill. Cert. Crop Adviser State Bd., 1992-94; mem. Monticello Unit 25 Bd. Edn., 1989-93. Recipient Hon. mem. Hon. State Farmer Ill. Assn. FFA, Urbana, 1987; IFCA Spl. Recognition award Ill. Fertilizer and Chem. Assn., 1988. Fellow Crop Sci. Soc. Am., Am. Soc. Agronomy; mem. Soil Sci. Soc. Am. (divsn. chmn. editl. bd., chmn. nat. cert. crop adviser exec. com. 1996—), Ill. Assn. Vocat. Agrl. Tchrs. (hon. life 1989—). Methodist. Avocations: photography, travel, computers.

REEVE, CHRISTOPHER, actor; b. N.Y.C., Sept. 25, 1952; s. Franklin D. and Barbara (Johnson) R.; children: Matthew, Alexandra; m. Dana Morosini, 1 son, Will. BA, Cornell U., 1974; student, Juilliard Sch., N.Y.C.; studies with, Austin Pendleton, Sandra Seacat. Performed in theaters including Boothbay (Maine) Playhouse, The Williamstown (Mass.) Theatre, San Diego Shakespeare Festival, The Loeb Drama Center; appeared on Broadway with Katherine Hepburn, A Matter of Gravity, 1976, Fifth of July, 1980, The Winter's Tale, 1989; films include Gray Lady Down, 1978, Superman, 1978, Somewhere in Time, 1980, Superman II, 1980, Deathtrap, 1982, Monsignor, 1982, Superman III, 1983, The Bostonians, 1984, The Aviator, 1984, Street Smart, 1987, Superman IV, 1987, Switching Channels, 1988, Noises Off, 1992, The Remains of the Day, 1993, Morning Glory, 1993, Speechless, 1994, The Rhinehart Theory, 1994, Village of the Damned, 1995; appeared in over 110 plays including My Life, 1977, The Greeks, Williamstown Theatre Festival prodn., 1981, The Aspern Papers, London prodn., 1984, Marriage of Figaro, 1985, Summer and Smoke, Los Angeles prodn., 1988, also The Royal Family, Holiday, Richard Corey, Mesmer, Cherry Orchard; appeared in John Brown's Body (Stephen Vincent Benet), Williamstown Theatre Festival, 1989; TV appearances include: (series) Love of Life, 1968-76; (movies) Anna Karenina, 1985, The Great Escape II: The Untold Story, 1988, The Rose and the Jackal, 1990, Bump in the Night, 1991, Death Dreams, 1991, Mortal Sins, 1992, Nightmare in the Daylight, 1992, The Sea Wolf, 1993, Above Suspicion, 1995, The Black Fox, 1995.

REEVE, FRANKLIN D., literature educator, writer; b. Phila., Sept. 18, 1928. AB, Princeton U., 1950; PhD, Columbia U., 1958; AM (hon.), Wesleyan, 1964. Instr., asst. prof. Columbia U., N.Y.C., 1952-61; assoc. prof., prof. Wesleyan U., Middletown, Conn., 1962-66, adj. prof., 1970-87, prof., 1988—; bd. dirs., sec. Poets House, N.Y.C., Translation Ctr., N.Y.C.; vis. scholar, Moscow, 1961; mem. adv. panel Vt. Ctr. for the Book; vis. prof. Oxford (Eng.) U., 1964, Columbia U., 1988; vis. lectr. Yale U., New Haven, 1972-84; cons. in field. Author: Aleksandr Blok: Between Image and Idea, 1962, Robert Frost in Russia, 1964, The Russian Novel, 1966, The Red Machines, 1968, In the Silent Stones, 1968, Just Over the Border, 1969, The Brother, 1971, The Blue Cat, 1972, White Colors, 1974, The White Monk, 1989, (edited with Jay Meek) After the Storm, 1991, Concrete Music, 1992, A Few Rounds of Old Maid and Other Stories, 1995; editor: Winged Sprits, 1995. Recipient Lit. award Am. Acad.-Nat. Inst., 1970, Lifetime Golden Rose award New Eng. Poetry Soc., 1994. Office: Wesleyan U Lit Dept Wesleyan Sta Middletown CT 06459

REEVE, JOHN NEWTON, molecular biology and microbiology educator; b. Wakefield, W. Yorkshire, Eng., June 21, 1947; came to U.S., 1979; s. Arthur Newton and Lilian Elsworth (Tallant) R.; m. Patricia Margaret Watson, Sept. 21, 1967; children: Simon Arthur, Daniel John. BS with 1st class honors, U. Birmingham, Eng., 1968; PhD, U. B.C., Vancouver, Can., 1971. Rsch. scientist U. Ariz., Tucson, 1971-73, Nat. Inst. Med. Rsch., Mill Hill, London, 1973-74; rsch. dir. Max-Planck Inst., Berlin, 1974-79; prof. Ohio State U., Columbus, 1979—, chair dept. microbiology, 1985—; cons. Battelle Rsch. Lab., Columbus, 1982-87, Govt. of Bulgaria, Sofia, 1987, Promega Corp., Madison, Wis., 1990, Procter and Gamble Co., Cin., 1990; mem. sci. adv. bd. BioTrol. Inc., Chaska, Minn., 1986-90; Disting. vis. prof. U. Adelaide, Australia, 1984, U. Wyo., Laramie, 1988, U. Calcutta, India, 1989, Frei U., Berlin, 1991, U. Karachi, Pakistan, 1995, U. Concepcion, Chile, 1995. Named Disting. Rsch. Scholar Ohio State U., 1989. Mem. Am. Soc. for Microbiology (lectr. Found. for Microbiology 1987-88, 94-96). Office: Ohio State U Dept of Microbiology 484 W 12th Ave Columbus OH 43210-1214

REEVE, LORRAINE ELLEN, biochemist, researcher; b. Cato, Wis., Aug. 12, 1951; d. Robert K. and Lila M. (Breneman) R.; m. Dennis L. Kiesling, July 21, 1990. BS, U. Wis., 1973, MS, 1978, PhD, 1981. Postdoctoral scholar U. Mich., Ann Arbor, 1981-86; project scientist Cleve. Clinic Found., 1986-88; sr. rsch. scientist R.P. Scherer Corp., Troy, Mich., 1988-89, Mediventures, Inc., Dearborn, Mich., 1989-92; prin. investigator Mediventures, Inc., Dearborn, 1992-94; project mgr. MDV Technologies, Inc. (formerly Mediventures, Inc.), Dearborn, 1994—. Contbr. articles to profl. jours. Mem. Founders Soc. Detroit Inst. Art, 1989—, Nat. Trust for Historic Preservation, 1991—. Mem. AAAS, N.Y. Acad. Sci. Achievements include patents for topical drug delivery, ophthalmic drug delivery, drug delivery by injection and body cavity drug delivery all with thermo-irreversible and thermoreversible gels, ablatable mask of polyoxyalkylene polymer and ionic polysaccharide gel for laser reprofiling of the cornea; European patent pending for drug delivery with thermoreversible gels. Home: PO Box 2962 Ann Arbor MI 48106-2962 Office: MDV Techs Inc 15250 Mercantile Dr Dearborn MI 48120-1207

REEVE, RONALD CROPPER, JR., manufacturing executive; b. Logan, Utah, Jan. 29, 1943; s. Ronald Cropper and Aldus (Moser) R.; m. Susan Leticia Gardner, July 4, 1966 (div. June 1975); children: Heather Renee, Michael Scott; m. Deborah Lynn Crooks, Dec. 31, 1976 (div. Apr. 1986); 1 child, Thomas Adam; m. Barbara Ruttan Avery, June 20, 1992; 2 stepchildren: Bryan Keith Avery, Allison Kathleen Avery. BS in Physics, Ohio State U., 1967; MBA in Mktg., Xavier U., 1972. Successively devel. engr., research engr., product planner Specialty Materials dept. Gen. Electric Co., Worthington, Ohio, 1969-73; successively product mgr., mktg. mgr., gen. mgr. Air Products & Chems., Inc., Lancaster, Ohio, 1974-79; founder, pres., chmn. Advanced Robotics Corp., Columbus, Ohio, 1979-84; founder, pres. R.C. Reeve, Inc., Westerville, Ohio, 1983—; founder, chief exec. officer Edison Welding Inst., Columbus, 1984-87; chief exec. officer Control Systems and Equipment Co., Inc., Columbus, 1987-90, CYBO Robots, Inc., 1988—, Check Guarantee Inc., Columbus, 1989-92, Indpls., 1991-92, Robot One Inc., Indpls. Tech. adv. bd. Franklin U., Civil Engring. Rsch. Found., dir. Internat. Assn. of Automation and Robotics in Constrn. Served with USAF, 1968-69. Named Small Businessman of Year, SBA, 1981. Mem. Am. Welding Soc., Am. Soc. Metals, Soc. Mfg. Engrs., Robot Inst. Am., Internat. Inst. Welding, Welding Inst., Robotics Internat., Hoover Yacht Club, Worthington Hill Country Club. Patentee diamond crystal structure. Home: 1460 Briarcliffe Dr Powell OH 43065-9060 Office: CYBO Robots Inc Indianapolis IN 46241

REEVES, ALEXIS SCOTT, journalist; b. Atlanta, Feb. 4, 1949; d. William Alexander and Marian (Willis) Scott; m. Marc Anthony Lewis, Sept. 14, 1968 (div. 1973); m. David Leslie Reeves, Mar. 16, 1974; children: Cinque Scott, David Leslie, Jr. Student Barnard Coll., 1966-68; student Spelman Coll., 1989-90, Regional Leadership Inst., 1992. Reporter, asst. city editor, cable TV editor, mgr. video edit., v.p. community affairs Atlanta Jour. & Constn., Atlanta, 1974-93; dir. Diversity for Cox Enterprises Inc., 1993—; vis. instr. summer program for minority journalists, Berkeley, Calif., 1980, 81, 84, 85, 87 Grady High Sch., Atlanta, 1982-83; journalist-in-residence Clark Coll., Atlanta, 1983. Researcher, writer: The History of Atlanta NAACP, 1983 (NAACP award, 1984). Recipient Disting. Urban Journalism award Nat. Urban Coalition, 1980. Michele Clark fellow Columbia U. Sch. Journalism, 1974. Named one of 100 Top Black Bus. & Profl. Women, 1986; recipient Acad. Achievement award YWCA, 1989. Mem. Nat. Assn. Media Women (Media Woman of Yr. award, 1983, Media Woman of Yr. nat. award 1983, pres. Atlanta chpt. 1985-87), Atlanta Assn. Black Journalists (Commentary Print award 1983), Nat. Assn. Black Journalists, Sigma Delta Chi (bd. dirs. 1980-84, treas. 1985-88). Moderator, First Congl. Ch., 1982-92. Office: Cox Enterprises Inc PO Box 105357 1400 Lake Hearn Dr NE Atlanta GA 30348

REEVES, BARBARA ANN, lawyer; b. Buffalo, Mar. 29, 1949; d. Prentice W. and Doris Reeves; m. Richard C. Neal; children: Timothy R. Neal, Stephen S. Neal (dec.), Robert S. Neal, Richard R. Neal. Student, Wellesley Coll., 1967-68; B.A. (NSF fellow, Lehman fellow), New Coll., Sarasota, Fla., 1970; J.D. cum laude, Harvard U., 1973. Bar: Calif. 1973, D.C. 1977. Law clk. U.S. Ct. Appeals, 9th Circuit, Portland, Oreg., 1973-74; assoc. firm Munger, Tolles and Rickershauser, L.A., 1977-78; trial atty. spl. trial sect. Dept. Justice (Antitrust div.), 1974-75; spl. asst. to asst. atty. gen. Antitrust div. Dept. Justice, Washington, 1976-77; chief antitrust div. L.A. field office, 1978-81; ptnr. Morrison & Foerster, L.A., 1981-94, Fried, Frank, Harris, Shriver & Jacobson, L.A., 1995—; mem. exec. com. state bar conf. of dels. L.A. Delegation, 1982-91; del. 9th Cir. Jud. Conf., 1984-88; mem. Fed. Ct. Magistrate Selection Com., 1989; bd. dirs. Pub. Counsel, 1988-92, Western Ctr. Law and Poverty, 1992—; lectr. in field. Editor: Federal Criminal Litigation, 1994; contbg. author: International Antitrust, 1995; contbr. articles to profl. jours. Mem. ABA (litigation sect., antitrust sect.), Am. Arbitration Assn. (arbitrator, mediator, mem. adv. panel large complex case program), L.A. County Bar Assn. (antitrust sect. officer 1980-81, litigation sect. officer 1988-93 trustee 1990-92, chair alternative dispute resolution sec. 1992-95, L.A. County Ct. ADR com.). Home: 1410 Hillcrest Ave Pasadena CA 91106-4503 Office: Fried Frank Harris Shriver & Jacobson 725 S Figueroa St Ste 3890 Los Angeles CA 90017-5438

REEVES, BARRY LUCAS, aerophysics research engineer; b. St. Louis, Jan. 11, 1935; s. Raymond O. and Frances M. (Lucas) R.; m. Marilyn Alva Riester, May 8, 1954; children: Katherine, Michael, Janet. BS, Washington U., St. Louis, 1956, MS, 1958, PhD, 1960. Rsch. assoc. McDonnell Aircraft Corp., St. Louis, 1959-60; postdoctoral rsch. fellow Calif. Inst. Tech., Pasadena, 1960-64; staff scientist Avco Corp., Wilmington, Mass., 1964-68, sr. staff scientist, 1968-74, sr. cons. scientist, 1974-86; prin. scientist Textron Corp., Wilmington, Mass., 1986—; cons. Space Gen. Corp., L.A., 1962-63, Nat. Engring. and Sci. Co., Pasadena, 1963-64, Aerojet Corp. Azusa, Calif., 1964; contr. engring. symposiums; reviewer Jour. Fluid Mechanics, Physics of Fluids, Jour. Applied Mech., Internat. Jour. Heat and Mass Transfer, Jour. Spacecraft and Rockets, AIAA Jour. Contbr. over 30 articles to profl. jours. Mem. Snow Mountain Farms Assn., Vt., 1982—. Fellowship Convair Aircraft Corp., 1958, NSF, 1959, 60; postdoctoral rsch. fellow Air Force Office Sci. Rsch., 1960, 61; rsch. grantee Guggenheim Aero. Lab., Calif. Inst. Tech., Pasadena, 1962-63. Mem. Am. Inst. Physics, Smithsonian Assocs. (assoc.), Nat. Trust for Historic Preservation, Sigma Xi, Tau Beta Pi, Pi Tau Sigma (former v.p., treas.). Home: 10 Hillcrest Pky Winchester MA 01890-1427 Office: Textron Systems Divsn 201 Lowell St Wilmington MA 01887-4113

REEVES, CHARLES HOWELL, classics educator; b. Schenectady, Nov. 23, 1915; s. Howell H. and Justina (Smith) R.; m. Lucille Jane Pritchard, Dec. 22, 1945; children—Jane L. Reeves McGee, Frances E. Reeves Herring, Helen Ann Reeves Hanks, Ruth M. Reeves Connell, Justina P., Charles Howell. A.B., Union Coll., Schenectady, 1937; Ph.D. in Classics, U. Cin., 1947. Instr. classics Ind. U., 1946-49; asst. prof. classics Johns Hopkins, 1949-52; asso. prof., then prof. classics U. Okla., 1952-66; prof. classics Case Western Res. U., 1966-86, prof. emeritus, 1986—, chmn. dept., 1966-77. Author articles on Greek tragedy. Served to lt. USNR, 1942-45. Mem. Am. Philol. Assn., Am. Inst. Archaeology, Classical Assn., Middle West and South, Soc. Ancient Greek Philosophy, Virgilian Soc., N. Am. Patristics Soc., Phi Beta Kappa. Home: 1791 Cadwell Ave Cleveland OH 44118-1606 Office: Case Western Res U Dept Classics Cleveland OH 44106

REEVES, DANIEL EDWARD, professional football coach; b. Rome, Ga., Jan. 19, 1944; m. Pam Reeves; children: Dana, Laura, Lee. Grad., U. S.C. Running back Dallas Cowboys, NFL, 1965-72, player-coach, 1970-71, asst. coach, 1972, 74-80; head coach Denver Broncos, NFL, 1981-92, also v.p.; head coach N.Y. Giants, 1993—. Player NFL Championship Game, 1966, 67, 70, 71; recipient NFL Coach of the Year award, 1993; named to S.C. Hall Fame. Office: care New York Giants Giants Stadium East Rutherford NJ 07073 also: Denver Broncos 13665 E Davies Pl Englewood CO 80112-4004*

REEVES, DANIEL MCDONOUGH, video artist; b. Washington, Aug. 1, 1948; s. Suzanne Sticha Reeves; m. Debra Schweitzer, 1979 (div. 1986); m. Linda Garwood, Apr. 20, 1987; 1 child, Adele Grace. AS, Ithaca Coll., BA, 1979. Exec. prodr. Shakti Prodns., N.Y.C., 1980—. Artist Eingang/The Way In, 1990-94, Smothering Dreams, 1982 (Three Emmy awards); exec. prodr., creator Obsessive Becoming, 1995; creator, prodr. Forty-Nine Bodhisa Tivas, 1996—. With USMC, 1966-68, Vietnam. Rockefeller fellow, 1995; recipient Blue ribbon Am. Film Inst., 1983. Buddhist. Avocations: computer graphics programs, poetry, writing, music, hiking. Home and Office: 799 Greenwich St # 6S New York NY 10014

REEVES, DIANNE L., artist; b. Milw., Apr. 8, 1948; d. John J. and Bernice M. (Hendricksen) Kleczka; m. Robert A. McCoy, Oct. 15, 1983 (div. June 1988). BFA, U. Wis., Milw., 1968; student, Mus. Fine Arts, Houston, 1974-77, 83, Glassell Sch. Art, Houston, 1980-83. Instr. papermaking Glassell Sch. Art, 1984-85. Exhibited in solo shows at Women and Their Work Gallery, Austin, Tex., 1988, Moreau Galleries/Hamms Gallery, Notre Dame, Ind., 1991, The Martin Mus. of Art, Waco, Tex., 1996; internat. exhbns. include Leopold-Hoesch Mus., Duren, Germany, 1991, 92, 93, galleries in Netherlands and Basel, Switzerland; exhibited in numerous group exhbns.; author: (ltd. edit.) From Fiber to Paper, 1991. Bd. dirs., sec. Friends of Dard Hunter, Inc., 1993-94. NEA/Tex. fellow Mid-Am. Arts Alliance/NEA, 1986; recipient awards for art work. Mem. Internat. Assn. Hand Papermakers and Paper Artists (co-chair nominating com. 1993-94), Women and Their Work, Inc., Sierra Club, Tex. Fine Arts Assn., Austin Visual Arts Assn. Avocations: archaeology/anthropology, camping, reading, travel, environmental issues. Home and Studio: 1103 S 3rd St Austin TX 78704

REEVES, DONNA ANDREWS, golfer; b. Boston, Apr. 12, 1967; d. James Barclay and Helen Louise (Munsey) Andrews; m. John A. Reeves, Nov. 13, 1993. BBA, U. N.C., 1989. Qualified golfer LPGA Tour, Fla., 1990; winner Ping-Cellular One Golf Tounament, Portland, Oreg., 1993, Ping-Welch's Golf Tournament, Tucson, Ariz., 1994, Dinah Shore Major Golf Tournament, Palm Springs, Calif., 1994. Office: LPGA 2570 Volusia Ave Daytona Beach FL 32114-1119*

REEVES, FRANK BLAIR, architect, educator; b. Beaumont, Tex., June 5, 1922; s. William Garland and Hazel Ann (Blackburn) R.; m. Mary Nell Gibson, Aug. 3, 1948; 1 son, William Gibson. B.Arch., U. Tex., 1948; postgrad., Archtl. Assn., London, 1945; M.Arch., U. Fla., 1953. Assoc. architect Stone and Pitts (Architects), Beaumont, Tex., 1946-49; mem. faculty dept. architecture U. Fla., 1949-87, now prof. emeritus, dir. grad. program in archtl. preservation, 1970-87; supervising architect Hist. Am. Bldgs. Survey, 1958-71; cons. archtl. preservation, 1960—; co-founder Preservation Inst., Nantucket; mem. adv. bd. Nat. Ctr. Preservation Tech. and Tng., 1993—. Contbr. articles to Jour. AIA. Mem. Fla. Bicentennial Commn., 1972-76. Served with U.S. Army, 1943-46. Named Beinecke-Reeves Disting. Chair in Archtl. Preservation, 1994. Fellow AIA (Fla. Assn. spl. citation for preservation 1976, AIA Found. Octagon com. 1991—); mem. Nat. Trust Hist. Preservation (trustee emeritus, Louise DuPont Crowninshield award 1987), Fla. Trust Hist. Preservation (trustee emeritus), Delta Tau Delta. Democrat. Methodist.

REEVES, GEORGE MCMILLAN, JR., comparative literature educator, educational administrator; b. Spartanburg, S.C., Oct. 18, 1921; s. George McMillan and Bina Fay (Garvey) R.; m. Francine Helene Wickman, Jan. 27, 1950 (div. 1962); m. 2d Mary Carolyn Honeycutt, Apr. 14, 1964; children: George McMillan III, Marianne Elizabeth, Miriam Katherine, Alison Adams. B.S., Wofford Coll., 1942; M.A., U. Ala., 1948; Doctorat D'Universite, Sorbonne U. Paris, 1953; cert. in meteorology, NYU, 1943; DLitt (hon.), Wofford Coll., 1992. Asst. prof. English Presbyn. Coll., Clinton, S.C., 1948-50; from instr. to prof. English and comparative lit. U. S.C., Columbia, 1953-68, chmn. comparative lit. program, 1966-72, assoc. dean Grad. Sch., 1968-72, head dept. fgn. langs., 1972-74, dean Grad. Sch., 1974-94, interim provost, 1990-92, asst. to pres., 1992-93, dep. provost, 1993-94, dean emeritus, cons. to office of provost, 1994—; cons. to: The Explicator, Columbia, 1957-65; mem. vis. teams So. Assn. Colls. and Schs., Atlanta, 1970—, SREB Small Grants program, Atlanta, 1980—; mem. exec. bd. Conf. So. Grad. Schs., 1983-86; mem. awards com. Drug Sci. Found., 1985-88; chmn. bd. Greenville, S.C. Higher Edn. Ctr., 1990-92. Author: Thomas Wolfe et L'Europe, 1955; editor: Gustave Flaubert: Poesies de Jeunesse Inedites, 1968; editor and translator: The Time of William Faulkner, 1971 (MLA Scholars Library award 1971). Mem. Columbia Mus. Art and Sci., 1957—. Served to capt. USAAF, 1946-42, ETO. Fulbright scholar Sorbonne, Paris, 1951-52. Mem. MLA, S. Atlantic MLA (chmn. comparative lit. sect. 1970-71), AAUP, Phi Beta Kappa. Democrat. Lutheran. Club: Quail Hollow Swim and Racquet (pres.) (1979-80). Home: 1436 Mohawk Dr West Columbia SC 29169-6201 Office: U SC Office of Provost Columbia SC 29208-0001

REEVES, JOHN MERCER, II, international trade finance professional; b. Sanford, N.C., July 26, 1954; s. Charles Mercer Jr. and Sarah Frances (Crosby) R.; m. Jo Ann Funderburke, Dec. 30, 1978; children: Caroline Elizabeth, Rebekah Ann, John M. III. BCE, N.C. State U., 1977, MCE, 1978; MBA, Duke U., 1983. Engr. Nello L. Teer Co., Durham, N.C., 1973-83; mgmt. cons. Matthews Young & Assocs., Chapel Hill, N.C., 1983-85; pvt. practice option trader Durham, 1985-86; founder Med. Products Search, Inc., Durham, 1986-87; pvt. practice mgmt. cons. Chapel Hill, 1988; pvt. practice real estate developer Durham, 1990-92; merger and acquistion intermediary Allen Comml. Svcs., Raleigh, N.C., 1992-94; founder, pres. First Exim Fin. Ltd., Charlotte, N.C., 1994; bd. dirs. Digital Recorders Inc., Research Triangle Park, N.C., World, Horizon Fin. Svcs., Hastings, England. Mem. com. Durham C. of C. Named Paul Harris fellow Rotary Internat., 1990. Mem. S.W. Durham Rotary Club (bd. dirs. 1983-87). Republican. Presbyterian. Avocations: racket ball, tennis, gardening. Office: 1st Exim Fin Ltd 343 W Main St Durham NC 27701-3215

REEVES, KEANU, actor; b. Beirut, Sept. 2, 1964. Stage appearances: Wolf Boy (debut), For Adults Only, Romeo and Juliet; films: Flying, 1986, Youngblood, 1986, River's Edge, 1987, Permanent Record, 1988, The Night Before, 1988, The Prince of Pennsylvania, 1988, Dangerous Liaisons, 1988, Blll and Ted's Excellent Adventure, 1989, Parenthood, 1989, I Love You to Death, 1990, Tune in Tomorrow, 1990, Bill and Ted's Bogus Journey, 1991, Point Break, 1991, My Own Private Idaho, 1991, Bram Stoker's Dracula, 1992, Much Ado About Nothing, 1993, Little Buddha, 1994, Even Cowgirls Get the Blues, 1994, Speed, 1994, Johnny Mnemonic, 1995, A Walk in the Clouds, 1995; TV films: Letting Go, 1985, Act of Vengeance, 1986, Young Again, 1986, Babes in Toyland, 1986, Under the Influence, 1986, Brotherhood of Justice, 1986; TV special: Save the Planet, 1990. *

REEVES, LUCY MARY, retired secondary school educator; b. Pewamo, Mich., July 2, 1932; d. Lavaldin Edgar and Marian S. (Lee) Hull; m. Walter Emery Reeves, Jan. 21, 1922. BS, Western Mich. U., Kalamazoo, 1965; postgrad., Western Mich. U., 1965-75. Tchr. Country Sch. One Room, Matherton, Mich., 1956-57, Ionia, Mich., 1957-58, Belding, Mich., 1958-62, Saranac, Mich., Belding, Mich., 1965; tchr. Belding (Mich.) Area Schs., 1965-89; ret. Mem. NEA, Mich. Edn. Assn., Belding Area Edn., Profl. Businesswomen's Assn. Avocations: computers, reading, travelling, sewing.

REEVES, MICHAEL STANLEY, public utility executive; b. Memphis, Oct. 2, 1935; m. Patricia Ann Board, June 27, 1959; children: Michael, Michelle. Student Iowa State U., 1954-56; B.A., Roosevelt U., 1964; M.B.A., Northwestern U., 1972. With People Gas Light and Coke Co., Chgo., 1956—, supr., 1967-69, asst. supt., 1969-72, supt., 1972-75, gen. supt., 1975-77, v.p. mktg. and customer relations, 1977-87, exec. v.p., 1987—. Bd. dirs., chmn. Better Bus. Bur. Chgo., No. Ill.; mem. Local Initiatives Support Corp. Chgo. Adv. Com.; trustee Shedd Aquarium, Abraham Lincoln Centre; bd. dirs. Peoples Energy Corp., 1991, Children's Meml. Hosp. Served with U.S. Army. Mem. Chgo. Assn. Commerce and Industry, Am. Gas Assn., Am. Assn. Blacks in Energy, Am. Heart Assn. (Met. Chgo. bd. govs.), Chgo. Econ. Club. Club: University (Chgo., mem. bd. dirs.). Office: Peoples Energy Corp 122 S Michigan Ave 2nd fl Chicago IL 60603

REEVES, PATRICIA RUTH, heavy machinery manufacturing company executive; b. Bklyn., Mar. 26, 1931; d. Maurice G. and Ethel Helen (Kessler) Der Brucke m. Cedric E. Reeves, June 22, 1952. BA, Adelphi U., 1952. Chief of records sect. Hydrocarbon Rsch., Inc., N.Y.C., 1952-65; lead sec. C.F. Braun & Co., Murray Hill, N.J., 1965-69; exec. sec. Wilputte Corp., Murray Hill, N.J., 1969-75, adminstrv. asst., 1975-79, sales coord., 1979-81, pers. adminstr., 1981-82; sales coord. Krupp Wilputte Corp., Murray Hill, N.J., 1982-84; pers. adminstr. Somerset Techs., Inc., N.J., 1984-85, pers. mgr., 1985-95; pres. Human Resources Svcs., Watchung, N.J., 1995—. Pres. Mountain Jewish Community Ctr., Warren, N.J., 1976-77, bd. dirs., 1972-81. Mem. NAFE, AAUW, Women's NetWork Ctrl. N.J. (v.p., editor newsletter 1981-83, coord. career assistance 1984-85, membership chair 1986-89), Am. Soc. Pers. Adminstrs. (membership chair 1986-88, sec. 1986-88), Soc. Human Resources Mgmt. (sec. Ctrl. N.J. chpt. 1986-88, v.p. 1988-89, pres. 1989-90, sec.-treas. N.J. State Coun. 1990-92, sec.-treas. Area I bd. 1993-95, dir mem. at large, 1996, co-chair N.J. Conf., 1994-95, chair chpt. awards 1996, sr. advisor 1996). Home and Office: Human Resources Svcs 89 Knollwood Dr Watchung NJ 07060-6245

REEVES, PEGGY LOIS ZEIGLER, accountant; b. Orangeburg, S.C., May 12, 1940; d. Joseph Harold and Lois Vivian (Stroman) Zeigler; m. Donald Preston Reeves, Sept. 9, 1961. Degree in Secretarial Sci., Coker Coll., 1960. Sec. Ladson Beach, CPA, Orangeburg, 1960-61; acctg. clk. Milliken & Co., Laurens, S.C., 1962-67, sec., 1967-73, mgmt. trainee, 1973, plant contr., 1973-74, 76-81; cost acctg. supr. Milliken & Co., Spartanburg, S.C., 1974-76, 81—. Chair bd. dirs. Enoree (S.C.)-Lanford Fire Dist., 1982—, treas., 1988—; mem. Coker Coll. Alumni Bd., 1996—. H.L. Jones scholar Coker Coll., 1959-60. Mem. Inst. Mgmt. Accts. (sec. 1991-94, v.p. membership 1994-95, v.p. adminstrn. and fin. 1995-96, pres.-elect 1996—), Profl. Secs. Internat. (v.p., rec. sec., Sec. of Yr. 1973). Baptist. Avocations: reading, collecting plates and antiques.

REEVES, RALPH B., III, publisher, editor; b. Raleigh, N.C., Apr. 2, 1947; s. Ralph Bernard Reeves Jr. and Frances Rhoda (Campbell) M.; m. Caroline Holton Green, Apr. 24, 1971 (div. 1986); children: Ralph B. IV, Daniel MacQuarrie. AB in History, U. N.C., 1970. Field coord. FMI Mgmt. Group, Raleigh, N.C., 1972-76; gen. mgr., v.p. The Leader Newspaper, Rsch. Triangle Pk., N.C., 1976-78; pres., pub., founder Spectator Pubs. Inc., Raleigh, N.C., 1978—, Triad Bus., Greensboro, N.C., 1986-88, Triangle Bus., Raleigh, 1985-91, Spectator Pub., N.C. Architect, 1981-84. Editor: Mr. Spectator, 1978—. 1st v.p. Mordecai Square Hist. Soc., Raleigh, 1980-83; pres. Hilltop Home, 1982-84; chmn. Downtown Adv. Com., 1983-85; mem. Bus. Adv. Com. for N.C. Sec. of State, Raleigh, 1992—; bd. dirs. N.C. State U. Friends of Libr., Nike Carolina Classic Golf Tournament. Gov's Bus. award in the Arts and Humanities, 1986, Benjamin Fine award, 1991, AABP award Triangle Bus., 1st place award Feature Writing, 1991. Mem. Fifty Group, U. N.C. Dean's Club, English Speaking Union (past pres. RTP br. 1988—), Carolina Co. Club, Sphinx Club. Democrat. Episcopalian. Avocations: golf, history, travel. Home: 1707 Mcdonald Ln Raleigh NC 27608-2111 Office: Spectator Pubs Inc 1318 Dale St Ste 200 Raleigh NC 27605-1275

REEVES, ROBERT GRIER LEFEVRE, geology educator, scientist; b. York, Pa., May 30, 1920; s. Edward LeGrande and Helen (Baker) R.; m. Elizabeth Bodette Simmons, June 11, 1942; children: Dale Ann, Edward Boyd. Student, Yuba Coll., 1938-40; B.S., U. Nev., 1949; M.S., Stanford U., 1950, Ph.D., 1965. Registered profl. engr., Tex. Geophysicist, geologist U.S. Geol. Survey, 1949-69; with assignments as project chief iron ore deposits of Nev., tech. adviser Fgn. Aid Program; vis. prof. econ. geology U. Rio Grande do Sul, Brazil; staff geologist for research contracts and grants and profl. staffing Washington; prof. geology Colo. Sch. Mines, Golden, 1969-73; staff scientist Earth Resources Observation Systems Data Center, U.S. Geol. Survey, Sioux Falls, S.D., 1973-78; prof. geology U. Tex.-Permian Basin, Odessa, 1978-85, chmn. earth scis., 1978-82; dean Coll. Sci. and Engring. U. Tex. Permian Basin, 1979-84; cons. geologist, engr. ptnr. Orion, Ltd., Midland, Tex., 1984-87, cons. engr., geologist, 1987—; leader People to People Econ. Geology Trip to Brazil and Peru, 1985; co-leader Am. Geol. Inst. Internat. Field Inst. to Brazil, 1966; vis. geol. scientist Boston Coll., Boston U., 1967; sr. Fulbright lectr. U. Adelaide, Australia, 1969. Contbr. articles profl. jours. Served to maj. Signal Corps AUS, 1941-46, ETO. Recipient Outstanding Service award U.S. Geol. Survey, 1965. Fellow Geol. Soc. Am., Soc. Econ. Geologists; mem. Am. Inst. Mining, Metall. and Petroleum Engrs. (sec. Washington 1964), Am. Soc. Photogrammetry (editor-in-chief Manual of Remote Sensing), Soc. Ind. Profl. Earth Scientists. Home and Office: 4025 Lakeside Dr Odessa TX 79762-7203

REEVES, ROSSER SCOTT, III, retired investment company executive; b. N.Y.C., Aug. 20, 1936; s. Rosser and Elizabeth (Street) R.; m. Colin McRae Squibb, Dec. 14, 1963; 1 dau., Elizabeth Robinson. Acad. degree with honors, Westminster Sch., 1954; postgrad., Yale, 1954-55; BS with honors in architecture, U. Va., 1961. Assoc. real estate firm Douglas L. Elliman & Co., N.Y.C., 1961-62; investment banker Lazard Freres & Co., N.Y.C., 1962-67; founder, mng. partner R.S. Reeves & Co., N.Y.C., 1967-68; sr. mng. partner Bacon, Stevenson & Reeves, N.Y.C., 1968-70; chmn. bd. Quantum Corp., N.Y.C., 1970-75; pres. Rosser Reeves Holdings, Ltd.,

N.Y.C., 1975—; pres., chief exec. officer dir. Rosser Reeves, Inc., N.Y.C., 1976—; pres. Charlie O Co., 1980-82; pres., chief exec. officer Tiderock Corp., Little Rock, Ark., 1990—; founder, CEO The Recovery Found., 1992—; mem. N.Y. Stock Exch., 1967-69; mng. ptnr. Wall St. Leasing Assn., 1968-70; chmn. bd. Internat. Subsea Devel. Corp., N.Y.C., 1969-75, Mil. Armament Corp., N.Y.C., 1969-75. Trustee Youth Consultation Service, N.Y.C., 1968-72; bd. dirs. Ark. Symphony Orch., 1982-85. Mem. Scarab. Clubs: Union League (N.Y.C.), Racquet and Tennis (N.Y.C.), N.Y. Stock Exchange Lunch (N.Y.C.); Little Rock (Ark.). Home: 1412 Pickering Dr Little Rock AR 72211-1618

REEVES, VAN KIRK, lawyer; b. N.Y.C., May 14, 1939; arrived in France, 1967; s. William Harvey and Caroline (Buck) R.; m. Ann Murchison, June 24, 1967; children: Daisy Fiona, Evander James. BA, Harvard U., 1961, JD, 1964. Ptnr. Coudert Frères, Paris, 1973-95, Coudert Bros., N.Y.C., 1973-95, Porter & Reeves, Paris, 1995—. Author: The Structure and Financing of Art Transactions, 1994; co-author: (with Dr. J. Boll) Auction Sales and Conditions, 1991. Bd. mem., v.p. Internat. Coun. Muss. Found., Paris, 1972-95; bd. suprs. Am. Tax Inst., London, 1978; bd. mem. Fabergé Arts Found., Washington, 1992. Mem. Inst. Internat. Bus. Law and Practice (corr. mem.). Avocations: projects for the preservation of cultural heritage, hiking. Home: 8 Cité Nicolas Poussin, 240 Blvd Raspail, 75014 Paris France Office: Porter & Reeves, 5 Rue Cambon, 75001 Paris France

REEVES, WILLIAM BOYD, lawyer; b. Easley, S.C., Mar. 24, 1932; s. William C. and Elise B. (Brooks) R.; m. Rose Mary Weil, Sept. 7, 1957 (dec. Nov. 1977); 1 dau., Gabrielle; m. Gladys Frances Brown, Nov. 24, 1978; children: Stephanie, William. B.A., Furman U., 1954; LL.B., Tulane U., 1959. Bar: La. 1959, Ala. 1960, U.S. Supreme Ct 1971. Law clk. to U.S. Dist. Judge, So. Dist. Ala., 1959-61; assoc. firm Armbrecht, Jackson & DeMouy, 1961-65; ptnr. Armbrecht, Jackson, DeMouy, Crowe, Holmes & Reeves, Mobile, 1965—. Chancellor St. Lukes Episcopal Ch. and Sch., 1973—. Served to capt. U.S. Army, 1954-56. Fellow Am. Coll. Trial Lawyers, Am. Coll. Legal Medicine, Internat. Soc. Barristers; mem. ABA., Ala. State Bar, La. State Bar, Mobile Bar Assn. (pres. 1981), Internat. Assn. Ins. Counsel, Maritime Law Assn. U.S. (exec. coun. 1988-90), Ala. Defense Lawyers Assn. (past pres.), Southeastern Admiralty Law Inst. (past pres.), Nat. Bd. Trial Advocates, Am. Bd. Trial Advocates (pres. Ala. chpt. 1986-87), Athelstan Club, Mobile Country Club, Internat. Trade Club, Bienville Club, Propeller Club, Mason. Home: 3755 Rhonda Dr S Mobile AL 36608-1733

REFIOR, EVERETT LEE, labor economist, educator; b. Donnellson, Iowa, Jan. 23, 1919; s. Fred C. and Daisy E. (Gardner) R.; m. Marie Emma Culp, Sept. 12, 1943; children: Gene A., Wendell F., Paul D., Donna M.; m. Betty Pottenger Phelps, Nov. 27, 1993. BA, Iowa Wesleyan Coll., 1942; postgrad., U. Glasgow, 1945; MA, U. Chgo., 1955; PhD, U. Iowa, 1962. Instr. econs. and bus. Iowa Wesleyan Coll., 1947-50; teaching asst. U. Iowa, 1950-51; research asst. Bur. of Labor and Mgmt., 1951-52, instr. mgmt. and social sci., 1954-55; assoc. prof. econs. Simpson Coll., 1952-54; asst. prof. econs. U. Wis. at Whitewater, 1955-62, assoc. prof., 1962-64, prof., 1964-83, prof. emeritus, 1983—, chmn., 1966-75. Lyricist (hymns) Eternal Love, 1980, Divine Order, 1980, If We But Dare, 1984, Humanity, 1989, others. Found. pres. Whitewater chpt. World Federalists Assn., 1960-68, 76-78, 86-92, midwest regional pres., 1969-71, 75-87, nat. bd., 1968-89, 92—; del. World Congress, Ottowa, 1970, Brussels, 1972, Paris, 1977, Tokyo, 1980, Phila., 1987, San Francisco, 1995; exec. com. Assn. World Citizens, 1980—; sec. World Govt. Orgns. Coalition, 1987-96; mem. Gov.'s Commn. on UN 1971-89, state coord. Campaign for UN Reform, 1984-96, nat. pres., 1996—; mem. Wis. Conf. bd. Social Concerns, Meth. Ch., 1961-68, 70-76; Dem. precinct com. Whitewater, 1966-96; chmn. Walworth County Dem. Party, 1975-78, Wis. Dem. Platform Com., 1978—; bd. dirs. Alcohol Problems Coun. Wis., 1976—. Mem. Indsl. Rels. Rsch. Assn. (adv. bd. Wis. chpt. 1964-78, acad. v.p. 1978-83), Peace Action, Population Inst., Fedn. Am. Scientists, South Ctrl. Wis. UN Assn. (pres. 1979-80, v.p. 1995—), Kiwanis (pres. local club 1987-88). Methodist (lay speaker). Home: 205 N Fremont St Whitewater WI 53190-1322 *Life is too precious to be spent on ourselves. We show love for our Creator by what we do for others. Happiness is a by-product.*

REFO, PATRICIA LEE, lawyer; b. Alexandria, Va., Dec. 31, 1958. BA with high honors and high distinction, U. Mich., 1980, JD cum laude, 1983. Bar: Ill. 1983, U.S. Dist. Ct. (no. dist.) Ill. 1988, U.S. Ct. Appeals (7th cir.) 1989, U.S. Ct. Appeals (11th cir.) 1990, U.S. Ct. Appeals (5th cir.) 1992, Fed. Trial Bar (no. dist.) Ill. 1993. Ptnr. Jenner & Block, Chgo., 1991—; mem. faculty Nat. Inst. Trial Advocacy, 1989—; bd. advisors Lender Liability News, Chgo., Legal Club; lectr. ALI/ABA and Practicing Law Inst. on Various subjects including trial advocacy and lender liability. Co-author: Class Action Controversies, 1989, Notice to Members of the Class, IICLE Class Actions Handbook, 1986. Dir. Legal Clinic for the Disabled, 1994—, Chgo. Lawyers' Com. Civil Rights Under Law, 1987-91, Cabrini Green Legal Aid Clinic, 1987-91. Mem. ABA (chair sect. litigation 1990 annual meeting, co-chair sect. litigation Pro Bono com. 1990-93, dir. divsns. sect. litigation 1993-94, sec. sect. litigation 1994—). Office: Jenner & Block 1 E IBM Plz Fl 47 Chicago IL 60611-3608

REGALADO, RAUL L., airport parking executive; b. L.A., Jan. 31, 1945; s. Raul and Antonia (Estavillo) R.; m. Helen Sutcliffe; children: Stephanie, Jennifer. BS, Embry-Riddle Aero. U., 1972. Mgr. airport City of Klamath Falls, Oreg., 1972-74, City of Fresno, Calif., 1974-79, Orange County, Santa Ana, Calif., 1979-80; dir. aviation San Jose (Calif.) Airport, 1980-89; aviation cons. Raul Regalado & Assocs., Huntington Beach, Calif., 1989-91; dep. dir. aviation Houston Dept. Aviation, 1991-95; pres. airport properties APCOA, Inc., Vancouver, Wash., 1995—. Capt. U.S. Army, 1966-71, col. USAR (retired). Decorated Legion of Merit, Bronze Star, DFC, Air medal with 49 oak leaf clusters, Meritorious Svc. medal, Army Commendation medal with 3 oak leaf clusters. Mem. Am. Assn. Airport Execs., Calif. Assn. Airport Execs. (pres. 1980-81), Airport Operators Coun. Internat. (bd. dirs. 1986-88), Vietnam Helicopter Pilots Assn., Army Aviation Assn. Am., Aero. Club No. Calif. (bd. dirs. 1982-91, pres. 1987-89), Quiet Birdmen.

REGAN, DAVID, brain researcher, educator; b. Scarborough, Eng., May 5, 1935; arrived in Can., 1976; s. Randolph and Muriel Frances (Varley) R.; m. Marian Pauline Marsh, Aug. 15, 1959; children: Douglas Lawrence, Howard Michael. BSc, London U., 1957, MSc, 1958, PhD, 1964, DSc, 1974. Lectr. physics London U., 1960-65; reader neurosci. Keele U., Eng., 1965-75; prof. psychology Dalhousie U., Can., 1976-80, prof. physiology, 1980-84, assoc. prof. medicine, 1978-84, prof. medicine, 1984-87, prof. ophthalmology, 1980-87, prof. otolaryngology, 1980-84, Killam rsch. prof., 1978-82; prof. engring. Rutgers U., 1985-86; prof. psychology York U., Can., 1987—, prof. biology; prof. ophthalmology U. Toronto, Ont., Can., 1987—; retained inventor Wilkinson-Graviner Group, Eng., 1970-75; cons. Westinghouse, Pitts., 1980-86; co-dir. human performance in space lab. Inst. for Space and Terrestrial Sci., York U., 1989—, disting. rsch. prof., 1991—; indsl. rsch. chair aviation vision Natural Sci. and Engring. Rsch. Coun. Can./Can. Aviation Electronics, 1993. Author: Human Evoked Potentials, 1972, Human Brain Electrophysiology, 1989; editor: Spatial Vision, 1989, Binocular Vision, 1989, Vision Research, 1992; contbr. more than 250 articles to profl. jours.; holder 8 patents. Recipient Forman prize for med. rsch. Dalhousie U., 1983; rsch. grantee NIH, NRC, Air Force Office Sci. Rsch., Nat. Scis. and Engring. Rsch. Coun. Can., Med. Rsch. Coun.; Killam fellow, 1990. Fellow Royal Soc. Can., Optical Soc. Am.; mem. Exptl. Psychology Soc., Soc. Clin. Electroretinography, Assn. Rsch. in Vision and Ophthalmology, Royal Coll. Sci. (London, assoc.), Am. Acad. Optometry (Prentice medal 1990). Avocations: cricket, walking, modern European history. Office: York U Dept Psychology, 4700 Keele St, North York, ON Canada M3J 1P3

REGAN, DONALD PAUL, finance company executive; b. 1946. BS in Acctg., Calif. State U., 1968, MS in Acctg., 1972. CPA. With Peat Marwick, Mitchell & Co., 1970-73; v.p. Hemming Morse Inc., San Mateo, Calif., 1971—. Office: Hemming Morse Inc 160 Bovet Rd San Mateo CA 94402*

REGAN, DONALD THOMAS, financier, writer, lecturer; b. Cambridge, Mass., Dec. 21, 1918; m. Ann G. Buchanan, July 11, 1942. BA, Harvard U., 1940; LLD (hon.), Hahnemann Med. Coll. Hosp., 1968, U. Pa., 1972, Pace U., 1973; DHL (hon.), Colgate U. With Merrill Lynch, Pierce, Fenner & Smith Inc. (and predecessor), 1946-81, sec., dir. adminstrv. div., 1960-64, exec. v.p., 1964-68, pres., 1968-70, chmn., chief exec. officer, 1971-80; chmn. bd., chief exec. officer Merrill Lynch & Co. Inc., 1973-81; sec. Dept. of Treasury, Washington, 1981-85; White House chief of staff Washington, 1985-87; vice chmn., dir. N.Y. Stock Exchange, 1972-75. Author: A View from the Street, 1972, For the Record, 1988. Trustee Charles E. Merrill Trust, 1961-80; chmn. bd. trustees U. Pa., 1974-78, life trustee, 1978-80; mem. policy com. Bus. Roundtable, 1978-80; trustee Com. for Econ. Devel., 1978-80. Served to lt. col. USMCR, World War II. Laureat Bus. Hall of Fame, 1981. Clubs: Army-Navy, Burning Tree. Office: 240 Mclaws Cir Williamsburg VA 23185-5650

REGAN, ELLEN FRANCES (MRS. WALSTON SHEPARD BROWN), ophthalmologist; b. Boston, Feb. 1, 1919; d. Edward Francis and Margaret (Moynihan) R.; AB, Wellesley Coll., 1940; MD, Yale U., 1943; m. Walston Shepard Brown, Aug. 13, 1955. Intern, Boston City Hosp., 1944; asst. resident, resident Inst. Ophthalmology, Presbyn. Hosp., N.Y.C., 1944-47, asst. ophthalmologist, 1947-56, asst. attending ophthalmologist, 1956-84; instr. ophthalmology Columbia Coll. Physicians and Surgeons, 1947-55, asso. ophthalmology, 1955-67, asst. clin. prof., 1967-84. Mem. Am. Ophthal. Soc., AMA, Am. Acad. Ophthalmology, N.Y. Acad. Medicine, N.Y. State Med. Soc., Mass. Med. Soc., River Club. Office: PO Box 632 Tuxedo Park NY 10987-0632

REGAN, JOHN BERNARD (JACK REGAN), community relations executive, senator; b. Chgo., Feb. 2, 1934; s. Andrew J. and Frances (O'Born) R.; m. Rosemary E. Seger, Aug. 17, 1980. BA, So. Ill. U., 1960. V.p. Collins Bros., Las Vegas, Nev., 1971-76; pres. Terra, Inc., Las Vegas, 1973-80; owner Jack's Place, Las Vegas, 1980-95; govt. and mil. affairs liaison C.C. So. Nev., North Las Vegas, 1984-95; dist. dir. Nat. Coun. for Community Rels., 1984-86; nat. treas. Nat. Coun. Mktg. and Pub. Rels., 1986-88; state dir. Internat. Coun. of Shopping Ctrs., Nev., 1976. State assemblyman Nev. State Legis., Carson City, 1988-90, 92-93, state senator 1994—; chmn. Am. Legis. Exch. Coun., 1990-93; trade, travel and tourism com. mem. Nat. Coun. of State Legis., 1990-93, com. on Devel. Disabilties; active Las Vegas Habitat for Humanity. With USN, 1951-55. Recipient Lion of Yr. award Las Vegas Lions Club, 1978, Paragon award Nat. Coun. for Community Rels., 1985. Mem. Thunderbird Chpt. Air Force Assn. (pres. 1989-90, named hon. Thunderbird, Nighthawk, stealth fighter), North Las Vegas C. of C. (v.p. 1986). Democrat. Jewish. Avocations: reading, community service, coin collecting. Home: 1650 Cookson Ct Las Vegas NV 89115-6948

REGAN, JUDITH THERESA, publishing executive; b. Leominster, Mass., Aug. 17, 1953; d. Leo James and Rita Ann (Imprescia) R.; children: Patrick, Lara. BA, Vassar Coll., 1975. Sr. editor, v.p. Simon & Schuster, N.Y.C., 1989-94; pres., pub. Regan Books, N.Y.C., 1994—; TV prodr. Entertainment Tonight, N.Y.C., Geraldo, N.Y.C.; prodr. 20th Century Fox Films, Fox TV; corr. Full Disclosure, Fox TV; pub. Regan Books, Harper Collins. Author: The Art of War for Women; editor numerous books including And the Beat Goes On (Sonny Bono), 1991, The Way Things Ought to Be (Rush Limbaugh), 1992, Shampoo Planet and Life After God (Douglas Coupland), 1992, She's Come Undone (Wally Lamb), 1992, Rogue Warrior (Richard Marcinko), 1992, Feminine Force: Release the Power Within You to Create the Life You Deserve (Georgette Mosbacher), 1993, Private Parts (Howard Stern), 1993, I Can't Believe I Said That (Kathie Lee Gifford), 1994. Office: Regan Books 1211 Avenue Of The Americas New York NY 10036-8701

REGAN, MURIEL, librarian; b. N.Y.C., July 15, 1930; d. William and Matilda (Riebel) Blome; m. Robert Regan, 1966 (div. 1976); 1 child, Jeanne Booth. BA, Hunter Coll., N.Y.C., 1950; MLS, Columbia U., 1952; MBA, Pace U., N.Y.C., 1982. Post libr. US Army, Okinawa, 1952-53; researcher P.F. Collier, N.Y.C., 1953-57; asst. libr. to libr. Rockefeller Found., N.Y.C., 1957-67; dep. chief libr. Manhattan Community Coll., N.Y.C., 1967-68; libr. Booz Allen & Hamilton, N.Y.C., 1968-69, Rockefeller Found., N.Y.C., 1969-82; prin. Gosage Regan Assocs., Inc., N.Y.C., 1980-95; pub. svcs. libr. Carlsbad (N.Mex.) Pub. Libr., 1995—; dir. N.Y. Met. Reference and Rsch. Libr. Agy., 1988-95, Coun. Nat. Libr. and Info. Assns., 1991-95; cons. Librs. Info. Ctrs. Mem. SLA (pres. 1989-90), Archons of Colophon, Altrusa, N.Y. Libr. Club. Avocations: cats, reading, playing piano, traveling. Home: 604 N Lake St Carlsbad NM 88220 Office: Carlsbad Pub Libr 101 S Halagueno St Carlsbad NM 88220

REGAN, PETER FRANCIS, III, physician, psychiatry educator; b. Bklyn., Nov. 11, 1924; s. Peter Francis Jr. and Veronica (Tierney) R.; m. Laurette Patricia O'Connor, June 18, 1949; children: Peter, Stephen, William, Elizabeth, John, Carol. MD, Cornell U., Ithaca, N.Y., 1949. Diplomate Am. Bd. Psychiatry and Neurology, Nat. Bd. Med. Examiners. Intern in medicine N.Y. Hosp., 1949-50; asst. resident psychiatry Payne Whitney Psychiat. Clinic, 1950, 53-54, resident, 1954-56; asst. prof. psychiatry Cornell U. Med. Coll., 1956-58; prof., head dept. psychiatry U. Fla. Coll. Medicine, chief psychiat. svc. Univ. Teaching Hosp., 1958-64; prof. psychiatry SUNY, Buffalo, 1964-84, v.p. health affairs, 1964-67, exec. v.p. univ., 1967-69, exec. v.p., acting pres. univ., 1969-70, vice chancellor acad. programs, 1970-71; assoc. chief staff for edn. Buffalo VA Med. Ctr., 1979-84; prof. psychiatry U. Tex. Health Sci. Ctr., San Antonio, 1984-87, assoc. dean Sch. Medicine, 1986-87; assoc. chief staff for edn. San Antonio VA Med. Ctr., 1984-86, chief staff, 1986-87; dep. assoc. chief med. dir. for acad. affairs VA Cen. Office, Washington, 1987-88, assoc. chief med. dir. for acad. affairs, 1988-92; prof. emeritus / sen. cons. dept. psychiatry SUNY, Buffalo, N.Y., 1992—; project dir. Ctr. for Ednl. Rsch. and Innovation, OECD, 1972-74. Author: (with F. Flach) Chemotherapy in Emotional Disorders, 1960, (With E. Pattishall) Behavioral Science Contributions to Psychiatry; contbr. articles to profl. jours. Capt. M.C. AUS, 1951-52. Fellow Am. Psychiat. Assn., Am. Coll. Psychiatrists (bd. regents 1986-95, 2d v.p. 1988, 1st v.p. 1989, pres.-elect 1990, pres. 1991); mem. AMA, Alpha Omega Alpha. Home: 900 Delaware Ave # 504 Buffalo NY 14209-2012 Office: SUNY Dept Psychiatry 462 Grider St Buffalo NY 14215-3075

REGAN, PHILIP RAYMOND, professional baseball coach; b. Otsego, Mich., Apr. 6, 1937. Student, Western Mich. U. Baseball player Detroit Tigers, 1956-65, L.A. Dodgers, 1965-68, Chgo. Cubs, 1968-72, Chgo. White Sox, 1972-73; head coach Grand Valley State Coll., Mich., 1973-82; scout, minor league pitching instr. Seattle Mariners, 1983-84, pitching coach, 1984-86; pitching coach Cleve. Indians, 1994; scout L.A. Dodgers, 1987-93; head baseball mgr. Balt. Orioles, 1995; mgr. Albuquerque Dukes, 1996—. Office: Albuquerque Dukes 1601 Stadium SE Albuquerque NM 87106*

REGAN, ROBERT CHARLES, English language educator; b. Indpls., Mar. 13, 1930; s. Francis Bernard and Alma Ophelia (McBride) R.; m. Katherine Jeanclos, Aug. 11, 1989; children by previous marriage: Christopher, Alison, Amelia. B.A., Centenary Coll., 1951; M.A., Harvard U., 1952; Ph.D., U. Calif., Berkeley, 1965. Instr. English, Centenary Coll., 1956-57; asst. prof. English, U. Va., 1963-67; Fulbright-Hays lectr. Am. civilization U. Montpellier, France, 1967-68; assoc. prof. English, U. Pa., Phila., 1968-82, prof., 1982—, undergrad. chmn. dept. English, 1978-80, 81-83, 89-90, dir. Penn-in-London program; lectr. Internat. Communications Agy., Morocco, Algeria, Jordan, 1980; vis. prof. King's Coll., London, 1983-84. Author: Unpromising Heroes; Mark Twain and His Characters, 1966, Poe: A Collection of Critical Essays, 1967; mng. editor: Am. Quar., 1969-72; contbr. articles to lit. jours. Served with USNR, 1952-56, 61-62. Woodrow Wilson fellow, 1962-63; Am. Philos. Soc. research grantee, 1970. Democrat. Episcopalian. Office: U Pa Dept English Philadelphia PA 19104

REGAN, SYLVIA, playwright; b. N.Y.C., Apr. 15, 1908; d. Louis and Esther (Albert) Hoffenberg; m. James J. Regan, Feb. 11, 1931 (div. June 1936); m. 2d Abraham Ellstein, Nov. 7, 1940 (dec. Mar. 1963). Student pub. schs. Broadway actress N.Y.C., 1927-31; with pub. relations and promotion dept. Theatre Union and Orson Welles Mercury Theatre, N.Y.C., 1932-39; playwright, 1940—. Author: Morning Star, 1940, The Golden Door, 1951; musical Great to be Alive, 1951; The Fifth Season, 1953; libretto for grand opera The Golem, N.Y.C., 1962; Zelda, 1969. Sec. Sydney Epstein Meml. Fund for Strang Cancer Clinic, N.Y.C., 1948-68. Recipient citition Fedn. Women Zionists of Gt. Britain and Ireland, 1953. Mem. Dramatists Guild, Authors League of Am., Am. Jewish Hist. Soc., Nat. Council Jewish Women (citation of merit 1953). Democrat. Home: 55 E 9th St New York NY 10003-6311

REGAN, TIMOTHY JAMES, grain company executive; b. Atchison, Kans., July 31, 1956; s. Vincent James and Phyllis (Brull) R.; m. Veronica Sue Kasten, June 25, 1977; children: Katrina Sue, Brian James. BS, Kans. State U., 1978. Corp. acct. Lincoln Grain Co., Atchison, 1978-80; acctg. supr. Pillsbury Co., St. Joseph, Mo., 1980; br. account mgr. Pillsbury Co., St. Joseph, 1980-82, Omaha, 1982; internal auditor Pillsbury Co., Mpls., 1983; regional account mgr. Pillsbury Co., Huron, Ohio, 1983-84; regional account mgr. Scoular Grain Co., Omaha, 1984-87, controller, 1987-91, v.p., mem. exec. com., 1990—, CFO, 1991—; Fin. advisor Grace Abbott Sch. PTO, Omaha, 1987, treas., 1990-91. Fin. adviser Grace Abbott Sch. PTO, Omaha, 1987, treas., 1990-91; dir. Cath. Charities, 1994—; coach Little League Baseball and Soccer. Mem. KC, Elks. Republican. Roman Catholic. Avocations: jogging, basketball, coaching little league baseball and soccer. Home: 2009 S 182d Cir Omaha NE 68130-2748 Office: Scoular Co 2027 Dodge St Omaha NE 68102-1227

REGAN, WILLIAM JOSEPH, JR., energy company executive; b. Bronx, N.Y., Mar. 7, 1946; s. William Joseph and Eleanor F. (Malone) R.; m. Mary Lee Wynn; children—Katrina Lee, Thomas Wynn, James William. B.S., U.S. Air Force Acad., 1967; M.B.A., U. Wis.-Madison, 1969, Ph.D., 1972. Asst. prof. Wayne State U., Detroit, 1971-75; with Nat. Bank Detroit, 1975-77; sr. bus. planner Am. Natural Resources Co., Detroit, 1977-78, dir. fin. planning, 1978-82, v.p., treas., 1982-85; v.p. corp. fin. United Svcs. Automobile Assn., San Antonio, 1986-88, sr. v.p., treas., 1988-95; v.p., treas. Entergy Corp., New Orleans, 1995—. Mem. English Turn Golf Club, The City Energy Club. Republican. Roman Catholic. Home: 104 English Turn Dr New Orleans LA 70131

REGAZZI, JOHN HENRY, retired corporate executive; b. N.Y.C., Jan. 4, 1921; s. Caesar B. and Jennie (Moruzzi) R.; m. Doris Mary Litzau, Feb. 16, 1946; children: Mark, Dale. B.B.A., Pace Coll., 1951. C.P.A., N.Y. Mgr. Price Waterhouse, N.Y.C., 1946-62; comptroller ABC, N.Y.C., 1962-70; sr. v.p., CFO Avnet, Inc., N.Y.C., 1970-93; retired, 1993. Contbr. articles to profl. jours. Pres. bd. River Dell Regional High Sch., Oradell, N.J., 1962-65; trustee, treas. Oradell Pub. Library, 1970-79; councilman Borough of Oradell, 1979-88. Served as staff sgt. USAF, 1942-45. Mem. Fin. Execs. Inst., Am. Inst. CPA's, Nat. Assn. Accts., Nat. Assn. Corp. Treas. Republican. Roman Catholic. Lodge: Lions. Home: 8980 King John Ct Las Vegas NV 89129

REGAZZI, JOHN JAMES, III, publishing executive; b. Bklyn., June 8, 1948; s. John James Jr. and Theresa Cecil (Fiore) R.; m. Marie Louise Ford, May 30, 1971; children: John James IV, Thomas Paul, Michael Rees. BS, St. John's U., Queens, N.Y., 1970; MA, U. Iowa, 1972; MS, Columbia U., 1974; PhD, Rutgers U., 1983. Systems mgr. No. Ill. U., De Kalb, Ill., 1974-76; dir. pub. Found. Ctr., N.Y.C., 1976-79; assoc. prof. Rutgers U., New Brunswick, N.J., 1979-81; v.p. The H.W. Wilson Co., N.Y.C., 1981-88; pres., chief exec. officer Engring. Info., Inc., N.Y.C., 1988—; chmn. Article Express Internat., 1992-94; bd. dirs. ICSTI; adj. prof. SUNY, Albany, Columbia U., Rutgers U. Author: Guide to Periodicals in Religion, 1974. Mem. AAAS, IEEE, ALA, Am. Assn. Pubs. (bd. dirs. N.Y.C. chpt. 1987-88), Nat. Info. Standards Orgn. (vice chmn. 1989-90), Nat. Fedn. of Abstracting and Info. Svcs. (bd. dirs. 1980-81, 88), Assn. Computing Machinery, N.Y. Acad. Sci. Avocation: tennis. Office: Engring Info Inc 1 Castle Point Terrace Hoboken NJ 07030

REGEIMBAL, NEIL ROBERT, SR., retired journalist; b. Mpls., Mar. 16, 1929; s. Louis Odlin and Marie Elizabeth (O'Neill) R.; m. Mary Elizabeth Sutton, Aug. 18, 1950; children—Neil Robert, James Michael, Claire Marie, Stephen Louis, Mary Suzanne, Elizabeth Anne. B.S. in Journalism, U. Md., 1951. With AP, Washington, 1949-50; asso. editor Takoma (Md.) Jour., 1950-51; reporter Washington Times-Herald, 1951-54, Washington Post, 1954; Washington corr. Chilton Publs., 1954-71, Wash. bur. chief, v.p., 1975-91; dir. publ. relations Motor Vehicle Mfrs. Assn., Detroit, 1971-74; Washington editor Oil and Gas Jour., Washington; ret., 1991. Recipient Tom Campbell Editorial Achievement award, 1968, 69, 71, 78, Jesse H. Neal Editorial Achievement award, 1982, 84. Mem. White House Corrs. Assn., Sigma Delta Chi. Republican. Roman Catholic. Club: Nat. Press. Home and Office: 13811 Marianna Dr Rockville MD 20853-2737

REGELBRUGGE, ROGER RAFAEL, steel company executive; b. Eeklo, Belgium, May 22, 1930; came to U.S., 1953, naturalized, 1961; s. Victor and Rachel (Roesbeke) R.; m. Dorcas Merchant; children: Anita, Marc, Laurie, Jon, Craig, Kurt, Christiane, Lauren, Roger Rafael Jr. B.Sc. in Mech. Engring, State Tech. Coll., Ghent, 1951; B.Sc. in Indsl. Engring, Gen. Motors Inst., Flint, Mich., 1955; M.Sc. in Mech. Engring, Mich. State U., 1964. Supr. product engring. dept. Gen. Motors Corp., Antwerp, 1955-58; chief devel. engr., then gen. mgr. Airmaster div. Hayes Industries Inc., Jackson, Mich., 1958-66; with Koehring Co., 1966-74; group v.p. internat. ops. Koehring Co., Milw., 1969-74; exec. v.p. Korf Industries, Inc., Charlotte, N.C., 1974-77; chmn., pres., CEO, Georgetown Industries, Inc. (formerly Korf Industries, Inc.), 1977-95; chmn., CEO GS Industries Inc., 1995—; chmn. bd. Georgetown Steel Corp., Georgetown Investment Corp., Georgetown Fin. Corp., Georgetown Wire Co., Tree Island Industries; chmn. GS Technologies, GST Operating Co.; bd. dirs. Steel Mfrs. Assn., Am. Iron and Steel Inst.; chmn., CEO Fla. Wire and Cable, Inc. N.C. adv. bd. Fuqua Sch. Bus. Duke U.; mem. Charlotte Chamber Bd. Advisors; mem. adv. coun. Coll. Engring. U. Notre Dame; trustee Belmont (N.C.) Abbey Coll. Mem. ASME, Am. Soc. Automotive Engrs., Charlotte Athletic Club, Carmel Country Club, Tower Club (Charlotte), Georgetown Club (Washington). Roman Catholic. Office: GS Industries Inc Ste 200 1901 Roxborough Rd Charlotte NC 28211-3482

REGENBOGEN, ADAM, lawyer, judge; b. Steyer, Austria, June 12, 1947; s. William and Pauline (Firestein) R.; m. Paula Ruth Rothenberg, June 27, 1970 (div. Oct. 1993); children: Stacy, Candice. BA, Temple U., 1969; MSW, U. Pa., 1972; JD, Temple U., 1980. Bar: N.Y. 1983. Social worker VA, Coatesville, Pa., 1974-78; supr. VA, Northport, N.Y., 1978-80, quality assurance dir., 1980-87; dir. quality assurance N.Y. State Office Mental Health, Willard, 1987-91; atty. N.Y. State Workers Compensation Bd., Binghamton, 1992—; pvt. practice N.Y., 1983—. Organizer/incorporator Ithaca (N.Y.) Reform Temple, 1992; organizer Parents Without Partners, Ithaca, 1992. Recipient Pro Bono Svc. award Suffolk County Bar Assn., 1986. Mem. ABA, Broome County Bar Assn. Home: 9 Oak Brook Dr Ithaca NY 14850 Office: Workers Compensation Bd 44 Hawley St Binghamton NY 13901

REGENSTEIN, LEWIS GRAHAM, conservationist, author, lecturer, speech writer; b. Washington, Feb. 21, 1943; s. Louis and Helen Lucile (Moses) R.; divorced; children: Anna Lucile, Daniel Louis. Cert. of European studies, Inst. Am. Univs., Aix-en-Provence, France, 1964; B.A. in Polit. Sci., U. Pa., 1965; M.A. in Polit. Sci., Emory U., 1975. Intelligence officer, analyst C.I.A., Washington, 1966-71; wildlife editor Environ. Quality mag., 1973; real estate agt., 1984—; v.p. Help Our Planet Earth; bd. dirs. The Monitor Consortium, 1977—, pres., 1979-81; bd. dirs. Washington Humane Soc., 1978-84, Interfaith Coun. for Protection Animals and Nature, 1982-88, Atlanta Outdoor Activities Coun., Ctr. for Respect of Life and Environment, 1989—, Earth Save Found., 1989—. Author: The Politics of Extinction: the Story of the World's Endangered Wildlife, 1975, America the Poisoned: How Deadly Chemicals are Destroying Our Environment, Our Wildlife— And Ourselves, 1982, paperback edit., 1983, How to Survive in America the Poisoned, 1987, Replenish the Earth: The Teachings of Religion on Protecting Animals and Nature, 1991, Cleaning Up America the Poisoned: How to Survive Our Polluted Society, 1993; co-author: (jokebook) Sex, Wealth, and Power: How to Live Without Them, 1990; contbr. Environmental Encyclopedia, 1993; mem. editorial bd. the Westminster Schs., 1991—; contbr. numerous articles and book revs. on environ. and nat. security to maj. newspapers; author text of comml. record album; writes speeches and humor for corp. execs. and polit. leaders. Alumni exec. bd. The Lovett Sch., 1986—; co-chmn. Mayor's Environ. Task Force City of Atlanta, 1994—; dir. Piedmont Park Conservancy, Atlanta; steering com. Global Forum Ga., 1991. Home and Office: 3691 Tuxedo Rd NW Atlanta GA 30305-1061

REGENSTEINER, ELSE FRIEDSAM (MRS. BERTOLD REGENSTEINER), textile designer, educator; b. Munich, Apr. 21, 1906; came to U.S., 1936, naturalized, 1942; d. Ludwig and Hilda (Nelson-Bachhofer) Friedsam; m. Bertold Regensteiner, Oct. 3, 1926; 1 dau., Helga Regensteiner Sinaiko-Botts. Tchrs. degree, Deutsche Frauenschule, Munich, 1925; student, U. Munich, Inst. Design, Chgo. Instr. Hull House, Chgo., 1941-45, Inst. Design, Chgo., 1942-46; asst. prof. Sch. Art Inst. Chgo., 1945-57, prof., 1957-71, prof. emeritus, 1971—; textile designer for industry; partner Reg Wick Studios, 1945-80; also lectr.; Cons. Am. Farm Sch., Thessaloniki, Greece, 1972-78. Exhibited one man shows throughout U.S., 1946—; represented in permanent collection, Art Inst. Chgo., Cooper-Hewitt Mus., N.Y.C.; Author: The Art of Weaving, 2d edit, 1981, 3d edit., 1986, German edit., 1987, Program for a Weaving Study Group, 1974, Weaver's Study Course- Sourcebook for Ideas and Techniques, 1982, 2d edit., 1987, Geometric Design in Weaving, 1986; contbr. articles to profl. mags. Recipient 1st prize for drapery and upholstery Internat. Textile Exhbn., 1946; five citations merit Am. Inst. Decorators, 1947, 48, 50; Regensteiner award Midwest Weavers Assn., 1980; Award of Merit in Textiles, The Textile Arts Ctr., Chgo., 1994. Fellow Collegium Craftsmen of Am. Crafts Coun.; mem. Am. Crafts Coun., Handweavers Guild Am. (bd. dirs. 1970-78). Address: 1416 E 55th St Chicago IL 60615-5409

REGENSTREIF, S(AMUEL) PETER, political scientist, educator; b. Montreal, Que., Can., Sept. 9, 1936; s. Albert Benjamin and Miriam Lillian (Issenman) R.; children: Anne Erica, Mitchell Chester, Jeffrey Gershon, Gail Aviva. BA, McGill U., 1957; PhD, Cornell U., 1963. Mem. faculty U. Rochester, 1961—, prof. polit. sci., 1971—; coordinator Can. studies program, 1967—; editl. cons. Toronto Star, 1968-82, Chgo. Sun-Times, 1988-89; polit. cons. Bunting Warburg, Toronto, 1973-90, Coopers & Lybrand, Ltd., 1981-89, Loewen, Ondaatje, McCutcheon, 1991â-94; prin. Policy Concerts Inc., Toronto; broadcaster CKO Radio Network, 1983-89; pvt. polit. cons. Author: The Diefenbaker Interlude: Parties and Voting in Canada, 1965; syndicated columnist: Toronto Star, 1963-82; contbr. articles to profl. jours. Served to lt. Canadian Army, 1957. Ford. Found. fellow, 1960; Can. Council fellow, 1960, 65; Canadian Royal Commn. on Bilingualism and Biculturalism grantee, 1964-66; recipient Edward Peck Curtis award U. Rochester, 1979. Mem. AAAS, Am. Polit. Sci. Assn., Can. Polit. Sci. Assn., Assn. Can. Studies in U.S., Phi Beta Kappa. Jewish. Clubs: Faculty, Tennis. Home: 30 Glen Ellyn Way Rochester NY 14618-1502 Office: Univ Rochester Dept Polit Sci Rochester NY 14627

REGER, LAWRENCE LEE, trade association administrator; b. Lincoln, Nebr., June 23, 1939; s. Lawrence John and Bertha (Hergenrader) R. Student, U. Nebr., 1961; LL.B., Vanderbilt U., 1964. Bar: Nebr 1964. Asso. firm Crosby, Guenzel & Binning, Lincoln, 1964-70; gen. counsel Nat. Endowment Arts, 1970-72, dir. program devel. and coordination, 1972-78; dir. Am. Assn. Mus., Washington, 1978-86; pres. Nat. Instn. for Conservation of Cultural Property, Washington, 1988—; mem. visual arts vis. com. U. Del., 1995—; mem. cultural property adv. com. USIA, 1996—. Chmn. Nat. Humanities Alliance, 1982-86; bd. dirs. Nat. Musical Arts, 1990—. Home: 1937 39th St NW Washington DC 20007 Office: Inst Conserv Cultural Prop Ste 602 3299 K St NW Apt 602 Washington DC 20007-4415

REGES, MARIANNA ALICE, marketing executive; b. Budapest, Hungary, Mar. 23, 1947; came to U.S., 1956, naturalized, 1963; d. Otto H. and Alice M. R.; m. Charles P. Green, Feb. 15, 1975; children: Rebecca, Charles III. AAS with honors, Fashion Inst. Tech., N.Y.C., 1967; BBA magna cum laude, Baruch Coll., 1971, MBA in Stats., 1978. Media rsch. analyst Doyle, Dane, Bernbach Advt., N.Y.C., 1967-70; rsch. supr. Sta. WCBS-TV, N.Y.C., 1970-71; rsch. mgr. Woman's Day mag., N.Y.C., 1971-72; asst. media dir. Benton & Bowles Advt., N.Y.C., 1972-75; mgr. rsch. and sales devel. NBC Radio, N.Y.C., 1975-77; sr. rsch. mgr. Ziff-Davis Pub. Co., N.Y.C., 1977-84; media mgr. Bristol-Myers Squibb Co., 1984—; mem. Spanish Radio Adv. Coun., N.Y.C., 1986-88; mem. Pan-European TV Audience Rsch. Mgmt. Com., 1988—. Mem. Vt. Natural Resources Council, 1977—; advisor Baruch Coll. Advt. Soc., 1975—. Mem. Am. Mktg. Assn., Am. Advt. Fedn., Media Rsch. Dirs. Assn., Radio and TV Rsch. Coun., Advt. Rsch. Found., Nature Conservancy, Vt. Natural Resources Coun., World Future Soc., Beta Gamma Sigma. Home: 626 E 20th St New York NY 10009-1509 Office: Bristol-Myers Squibb Co 345 Park Ave New York NY 10154-0004

REGGIO, GODFREY, film director; b. New Orleans, 1940. Dir. (films) Koyaanisqatsi, 1983, Powaqqatsi, 1988 (Best Film, Sao Paolo Film festival), Anima Mundi, 1992. Mem. Christian Bros., 1954-68; founder Inst. for Regional Edn., Santa Fe, N.Mex., 1972. Home: c/o Inst for Regional Edn PO Box 2404 Santa Fe NM 87504*

REGGIO, VITO ANTHONY, management consultant; b. Rochester, N.Y., Dec. 17, 1929; s. Salvatore and Carrie Angela (LoRe) R.; m. Mary Ann Dolores Pippie, Sept. 28, 1957; children: Salvatore, Angela. BS, Purdue U., 1952; postgrad. sch. modern langs., Middlebury Coll., 1948; postgrad. fellowship, U. Ky., U. Tenn. and U. Ala., 1952-53. Jr. engr. Rochester (N.Y.) Gas and Electric Co., 1950; designer/drafter Globe Constrn. Co., Rochester, 1951; rsch. analyst Commonwealth of Ky., Frankfort, 1952; orgn. & methods analyst, then wage adminstrn. specialist USN Dept. Indsl. Rels., Indpls., 1955-56; cons. mgmt. engr. to project mgr. to account exec. Bus. Rsch. Corp., Chgo., 1956-60; sr. cons. econ. feasibilities Ebasco Svcs., Inc., Chgo., 1960-63, dir. pers. mgmt. cons. dept., 1970-77; regional mgr., orgn. and pers. mgmt. svcs. EBS Mgmt. Cons., Chgo., 1963-65, nat. dir. orgn. and pers. mgmt. svcs., 1965-70; pres., bd. dirs. Reggio and Assocs., Inc., Chgo., 1977—; mng. dir. Pay Data Svc., 1977—; bd. dirs. Pay Data Svcs., Chgo. Contbr. papers to profl. publs. With U.S. Army, 1953-55. Named Solco Cultural Soc. fellow, Rochester, N.Y., 1948. Mem. Am. Compensation Assn., Am. Mgmt. Assn., Chgo. Compensation Assn., Soc. Human Resources Profls., Soc. Human Resources Mgmt., Human Resources Mgmt. Assn. Chgo., Western Soc. Engrs. Office: Reggio and Assocs Inc 550 W Jackson Blvd Chicago IL 60661-5716

REGINA, MARIE ANTOINETTE, parochial school educator; b. Wilkinsburg, Pa., Jan. 10, 1958; d. Albert Edward and Katherine Ann (Mediate) R. BS in Early Childhood/Elem. Edn., California (Pa.) State Coll., 1980; MS in Reading, California U. of Pa., 1986. Cert. tchr. early childhood, elem. and reading. Tchr. grade 3 St. REgis Cath. Sch., Trafford, Pa., 1980-88; early childhood tchr. Little Peoples Ednl. Workshop, Forest Hills, Pa., 1984; Klubmates and early childhood tchr. Kinder Care, North Huntingdon, Pa., 1985-86; tchr. social studies McKeesport (Pa.) Ctrl. Cath. Sch., 1984-88, reading tchr. grade 6, 1988—; reading presch. tchr. Happy Home Day Care, North Huntingdon, 1992; dir. for ages 3, 4, 5 YMCA of Penn Hills, Pa., 1993; cons. World Book, North Huntingdon, 1993—; pvt. tutor. Mem. Internat. Reading Assn., Keystone State Reading Assn., Westmoreland Reading Coun., Cath. Alumni Club of Pitts. Roman Catholic. Avocations: volleyball, walking, water aerobics, cooking, arts and crafts. Home: 13327 Dean Dr N Huntingdon PA 15642-1811 Office: McKeesport Ctrl Cath Sch 2412 Versailles Ave Mc Keesport PA 15132

REGINATO, ROBERT JOSEPH, soil scientist; b. Palo Alto, Calif., Apr. 13, 1935; s. Guiseppe Primo and Carolina Theresa (Boccignone) R.; m. Donna Marie LeStum, Aug. 26, 1956; children: Richard Lynn, David Lewis, Christopher Michael, Michael Jeffrey. B.S., U. Calif., Davis, 1957; M.S., U. Ill., 1959; Ph.D., U. Calif., Riverside, 1973. Rsch. asst. U. Calif., Davis, 1956-57, U. Ill., Urbana, 1957-59; soil scientist U.S. Water Conservation Lab., USDA-Agrl. Rsch. Svc., Phoenix, 1959-89 , rsch. leader, 1980-89; assoc. dir. Pacific W. Area USDA Agrl. Rsch. Svc., Albany, Calif., 1989-91, dir., 1991-96; assoc. adminstr. ARS, Washington, 1996—; vis. scientist U. Calif., Davis, 1977-78; USDA collaborator U. Ariz., Tucson, 1959-89. Contbr. over 180 articles to tech. jours. Active Roosevelt coun. Boy Scouts Am., 1960-76. Fellow Am. Soc. Agronomy, Soil Sci. Soc. Am.; mem. Am. Geophys. Union, Internat. Soil Sci. Soc., Western Soil Sci. Soc., Sigma Xi, Alpha Zeta, Kappa Sigma. Roman Catholic. Office: USDA Agrl Rsch Svc Jamie Whitten Bldg Rm 302-A 14th & Independence Ave SW Washington DC 20250

REGIS, NINA, librarian, educator; b. Corinth, Miss., Oct. 19, 1928; d. W.C. and Mary Isabelle (Rushing) Hanner; m. George Regis, Sept. 5, 1949 (dec. Jan. 6, 1990); 1 child, Simonne Marie. BA, Bridgewater (Mass.) State U., 1971, MEd, 1975; MALS, U. South Fla., 1981. Cert. libr., tchr.. Genealogical libr., asst. researcher to curator New Bedford (Mass.) Pub. Libr., 1963-71; assoc. libr. New Eng. Hist. Geneal. Soc., Boston, 1972-73; media specialist, libr. Brevard County Schs., Port Malabar Elem. Sch., Palm Bay, Fla., 1978-90; libr., faculty Brevard Community Coll., Palm Bay, 1990—. Developed and organized libraries, 1968, 80, 91—. Mem. ALA, Fla. Assn. C.C.s, Libr. Assn. of Brevard County, Internat. Platform Assn., Phi Kappa Phi, Beta Phi Mu. Avocations: creative writing, genealogical research. Office: Brevard Community Coll Fla Advanced Tech Ctr 250 Grassland Rd SE Palm Bay FL 32909-2206

REGISTER, ULMA DOYLE, nutrition educator; b. West Monroe, La., Feb. 4, 1920; s. John William and Lillian (Reagan) R.; m. Helen Louise Hite, June 15, 1942; children: Rebecca, Dorothy, Deborah. BS, Madison Coll., 1942; MS, Vanderbilt U., 1944; PhD, U. Wis., 1950. Postdoctoral fellow Tulane Sch. Med., New Orleans, 1950-51; instr. biochemistry Loma Linda (Calif.) U., 1951-53, asst. prof., 1953-58, assoc. prof., 1959-67, prof. nutrition, 1967—, chmn. dept. nutrition, 1967-84; ret., 1985; part time prof., 1985-95; pres. Calif. Nutrition Coun., 1973. Co-author: Food for Us All, 1981, It's Your World Cookbook, 1981; contbr. numerous articles to sci. jours. Served to 1st lt. U.S. Army, 1944-47. Mem. Am. Inst. Nutrition, Am. Dietetic Assn., Calif. Nutrition Council (pres. 1973), Am. Soc. Clin. Nutrition. Republican. Adventist. Home: 11448 Benton St Loma Linda CA 92354-3679 Office: Loma Linda U Nutrition Sch Public Health Loma Linda CA 92350

REGN FRAHER, BONNIE, construction company executive; b. Neptune, N.J., Mar. 29, 1957; d. Alfred Wesley and Jennie Jeanette (Osinga) R.; m. William James Fraher III, July 25, 1995. BA, U. Calif., Santa Cruz, 1978; EdS, Rutgers U., 1982, MA, 1983. Cert. tchr. of the handicapped, cert. elem. tchr. Tchr. Search Day Program, Wanamassa, N.J., 1978-87; v.p. Fin-Addict Charters, Wall, N.J., 1987-93, Archtl. Woodworking, Bradley Beach, N.J., 1994-95; v.p., dir. fin. William Cook Custom Homes, Wall, 1987-95; v.p. Archtl. Woodworking, 1993-95; tchr. Palm Beach County Sch. Dist., 1995-96. Mem. sisterhood Temple Beth Torah. Mem. Autism Soc. Am., Long Branch Ski Club. Avocation: writing (short story pub.).

RÉGNIER, MARC CHARLES, lawyer, corporate executive; b. Rockland, Ont., Can., Apr. 24, 1939; s. Lucien and Joséphine (Mattar) R.; m. Claudette Picard, July 29, 1989; 1 child, Mathieu. BA, U. Ottawa, Ont., 1960, LLB, 1964. Bar: Que. 1969. Spl. asst. combines br. Dept. Justice, Ottawa, 1960-66; sollicitor, sec. Celanese Can. Ltd., Montréal, Que., Can., 1966-72; sec., legal counsel Microsystems Internat., Montréal, 1972-75; sr. group counsel No. Telecom Ltd., Montréal, 1974-75; sr. v.p., gen. counsel Avenor Inc. (formerly Can. Pacific Forest Products Ltd.), Montréal, 1976—; bd. dirs. Avenor Maritimes Inc., Dalhousie, N.B., Can., Pacific Forest Products Ltd., Vancouver, B.C., Can. Bd. dirs. Montréal Internat. Music Competition, Montréal Symphony Orch., Festival de Theatre des Ameriques, Fondation Hôpital St.-Luc, Montréal. Mem. Can. Bar Assn., Que. Bar Assn., Law Soc. Upper Can., Assn. Can. Gen. Counsel (pres. 1987-88), Club St.-Denis, CARE Can. Avocations: music, travel, fishing. Office: Avenor Inc, 1250 René-Lévesque Blvd West, Montreal, PQ Canada H3B 4Y3

REGNIER, RICHARD ADRIAN, lawyer; b. Portland, Oreg., Aug. 23, 1931; s. Augustus Jerome and Marietta (Howland) R.; m. Maria Teresa Arguindegui, Oct. 12, 1957; children: Richard Adrian Jr., Lisa Marina, Augustus Jerome II, Teresa Lynn; m. Georgianna Pennington, Aug. 5, 1993. Student, Harvard U., 1949-50; BS, U.S. Mil. Acad., 1955; LLB, U. Calif., Berkeley, 1962. Bar: Calif. 1963, U.S. Dist. Ct. (so. dist.) Calif. 1963, U.S. Supreme Ct. 1968. Commd. 2d lt. USAF, 1955, advanced through grades to capt., res., 1959; dep. dist. atty. Ventura County, Calif., 1963-65; assoc. Ferguson, Regnier & Paterson, Oxnard, Calif., 1965-68, ptnr., 1968-90; pvt. practice Oxnard, Calif., 1990—; instr. criminal law and evidence Ventura County Jr. Coll. and Ventura County Sheriff's Acad., 1963-65; judge pro tem Superior Ct. Ventura County, 1971—. Speaker Right to Life League So. Calif., Ventura County, 1973—; campaign chmn. MacIntyre for Assesor, Ventura County, 1986. Named Extraordinary Minister of Holy Eucharist, Archbishop of Los Angeles, Ventura, 1971—. Mem. ABA, Am. Bd. Trial Advocates, Calif. Bar Assn. (group ins. com. 1973-76), Ventura County Bar Assn. (exec. com. 1987-89), Assn. Trial Lawyers Am., Calif. Trial Lawyers Assn. (recognition of experience certs. various areas), Ventura County Trial Lawyers Assn. (pres. 1971, 86, lectr. trial law), Am. Judicature Soc., Ventura County Legal Aid Assn. (pres. 1968), Am. Arbitration Assn. (arbitrator 1966—), Nat. Bd. Trial Adv. (diplomate, cert.), Saticoy Country Club (pres. 1992). Republican. Lodges: Rotary (pres. 1982-83, Paul Harris fellow 1986), K.C. Avocations: golf, running, weight lifting, skiing. Office: Law Offices Richard Regnier 301 N A St Oxnard CA 93030-4901

REGO, ANTHONY C., food products executive; b. 1940. Officer Rego West, Cleve., 1964-88; mem. exec. com. Rini Rego Warehouse Co., Inc., 1980—; now chmn., CEO, dir. Riser Foods (merged with Rego West), Cleve. Office: Riser Foods Inc 5300 Richmond Rd Cleveland OH 44146*

REGULA, RALPH, congressman, lawyer; b. Beach City, Ohio, Dec. 3, 1924; s. O.F. and Orpha (Walter) R.; m. Mary Rogusky, Aug. 5, 1950; children: Martha, David, Richard. B.A., Mt. Union Coll., 1948, LL.D., 1981; LL.B., William McKinley Sch. Law, 1952; LL.D., Malone Coll., 1976. Bar: Ohio 1952. Sch. adminstr. Stark County Bd. Edn., 1948-55; practiced law Navarre, from 1952; mem. Ohio Ho. of Reps., 1965-66, Ohio Senate, 1967-72, 93rd-104th Congresses from 16th Ohio dist., 1973—; chmn. appropriations subcom. on the interior; ptnr. Regula Bros.; Mem. Pres.'s Commn. on Fin. Structures and Regulation, 1970-71. Mem. Ohio Bd. Edn., 1960-64; hon. mem. adv. bd. Walsh Coll., Canton, Ohio; Trustee Mt. Union Coll., Alliance, Ohio, Stark County Hist. Soc., Stark County Wilderness Soc. Served with USNR, 1944-46. Recipient Community Service award Navarre Kiwanis Club, 1963; Meritorious Service in Conservation award Canton Audubon Soc., 1965; Ohio Conservation award Gov. James Rhodes, 1969; named Outstanding Young Man of Yr. Canton Jr. C. of C., 1957, Legis. Conservationist of Yr. Ohio League Sportsmen, 1969. Republican. Episcopalian. Office: US Ho of Reps 2309 Rayburn HOB Washington DC 20515

REHART, BURTON SCHYLER, journalism educator, freelance writer; b. Pacific Grove, Calif., July 24, 1934; s. Burton Schyler Sr. and Ruth Evelyn (Whitaker) R.; m. Catherine Loverne Morison, Apr. 14, 1962 (div. Aug. 1983); children: William, Anne Marie, Catherine Evelyn; m. Felicia Rose Cousart, June 30, 1984 (div. Aug. 1995); m. Shirlee Jan Mynatt, July 20, 1996. BA in Journalism, Fresno (Calif.) State Coll., 1957; MA in History, Calif. State U., Fresno, 1966; cert., Coro found., 1961, Stanford U., summer 1975. Cert. adult edn. tchr., Calif. Reporter Bakersfield Californian, 1955; reporter, photographer Fresno Bee, 1957, Madera (Calif.) Daily Tribune, 1960-61, Ventura (Calif.) Free Press, 1961-62; from instr. to prof. journalism Calif. State U., Fresno, 1963—, prof. journalism, 1979—, chmn. dept. journalism, 1992-94. Author: M. Theo. Kearney-Prince of Fresno, 1988, (with others) Fresno in the 20th Century, 1986; editor, chmn. editorial bd. Fresno City, County Hist. Soc. Jour.; contbr. articles to profl. jours. Asst. foreman Fresno County Grand Jury, 1969. With U.S. Army, 1958-60. Mem. Soc. Profl. Journalists (pres. 1987-89), World Future Soc. (writer), Phi Kappa Phi (pres. 1977-78, Calif. State U. Fresno chpt.). Democrat. Episcopalian. Avocations: model ship building, photography, writing local history. Home: 1557 E Roberts Ave Fresno CA 93710-6433 Office: Calif State U Dept Journalism Shaw and Cedar Avenues Fresno CA 93740-0010

REHG, KENNETH LEE, linguistics educator; b. East St. Louis, Ill., Nov. 21, 1939; s. Theophil Albert and Kathryn Louise (George) R.; 1 child, Laura Le'olani. BA, U. Ill., 1962; MA, So. Ill. U., 1965; PhD, U. Hawaii, 1986. Tng. officer Internat. Ctr. for Lang. Studies, Washington, 1966-67; lang. officer U.S. Peace Corp, Saipan, Micronesia, 1967-70; asst. rschr. social sci. rsch. inst. U. Hawaii, Honolulu, 1974-83, asst. prof., 1984—; cons. Micronesian govt., 1973-76, Samoa Dept. Edn., Pago Pago, 1978, U.S. Geol. Survey, Menlo Park, Calif., 1979-81, Japan Nat. Mus. Ethnology, Osaka, 1986; participant Fulbright-Hays Study Group, Ea. Indonesia, 1991. Author: Ponapean Reference Grammar, 1981; co-author: Kitail Lokaiahn Pohnpei, 1969, Ponapean-English Dictionary, 1979; mng. editor Oceanic Linguistics; contbr. articles to profl. jours. Rsch. fellow U. Hawaii, 1981-82; recipient Excellence in Teaching award Hawaii Tchrs. ESL, 1984, Mortar Bd., 1990. Mem. Linguistic Soc. Am., Linguistic Soc. Hawaii. Office: U Hawaii Dept Linguistics Moore Hall 569 1890 E West Rd Honolulu HI 96822-2318

REHM, JACK DANIEL, publishing executive; b. Yonkers, N.Y., Oct. 10, 1932; s. Jack and Ann (McCarthy) R.; m. Cynthia Fenning, Oct. 18, 1958; children: Lisabeth R., Ann M., Cynthia A., Jack D. Jr. BSBA, Coll. of the Holy Cross, 1954. Advt. sales trainee, asst. account exec. Batten, Barton, Durstine & Osborne, N.Y.C., 1954-59; mgr. Suburbia Today, N.Y.C., 1959-62; with advt. sales dept. Better Homes and Gardens Meredith Corp., N.Y.C., 1962-66; mgr. advt. sales Meredith Corp., Phila., 1966-67; mgr. advt. sales Meredith Corp., N.Y.C., 1967-69, advt. sales dir. Better Homes and Garden mag., 1969-73, v.p., pub. dir. mag. div., 1973-75, v.p., pub. Better Homes and Gardens, pub. dir. mag. div., 1975-76, v.p. pub. group, gen. mgr., mag. pub., 1976-80; pres. pub. group Meredith Corp., Des Moines, 1980-86, exec. v.p. corp. svcs., 1986-88, pres., chief oper. officer, 1988—, pres., chief exec. officer, 1989—, chmn., pres., chief exec. officer, 1992—, also bd. dirs.; bd. dirs. Norwest Bank Iowa, N.A., Vernon Co., Newton, Iowa, Internat. Multifoods, Mpls., Equitable of Iowa Cos., Am. Coun. for Capital Formation. Bd. govs. Drake U., 1988—; trustee Coll. Holy Cross, Worcester, Mass.; mem. bus. com. Mus. Modern Art, N.Y.C., Greater Des Moines Com., Inc.; chmn. Des Moines Devel. Corp., 1993-94; active Iowa Bus. Coun.; mem. mag. and print com. USIA. With U.S. Army, 1956-57. Mem. Mag. Pubs. Am. (bd. dirs. 1981—, chmn. 1983-85, Publisher of Yr. 1988), Pine Valley Golf Club, Scarsdale Golf Club, Wakonda Golf Club. Roman Catholic. Avocation: golf. Home: 3131 Fleur Dr Apt 1001 Des Moines IA 50321-1751 Office: Meredith Corp 1716 Locust St Des Moines IA 50309-3038*

REHM, JOHN BARTRAM, lawyer; b. Paris, Nov. 23, 1930; s. George and Mary (Torr) R.; m. Diana Mary Aed, Dec. 19, 1959; children: David Bartram, Jennifer Aed. AB, Harvard U., 1952; LLB, Columbia U., 1955; M.T.S., Wesley Sem., 1990. Bar: N.Y. 1955, D.C. 1969, U.S. Dist. Ct. D.C. 1971, U.S. Ct. Internat. Trade 1980, U.S. Supreme Ct. 1988. Assoc. Willkie, Owen, Farr, Gallagher & Walton, N.Y.C., 1955-56; atty.-advisor U.S. Dept. State, Washington, 1956-62, asst. legal advisor for econ. affairs, 1962-63; gen. counsel Office of Spl. Trade Rep., Washington, 1963-69; ptnr. Busby, Rivkin, Sherman, Levy & Rehm, Washington, 1969-77, Busby, Rehm and Leonard, Washington, 1977-87, Dorsey & Whitney, Washington, 1988—. Democrat. Episcopalian. Home: 5005 Worthington Dr Bethesda MD 20816-2748 Office: Dorsey & Whitney 1330 Connecticut Ave NW Washington DC 20036-1704

REHM, LEO FRANK, civil engineer; b. Milw., Jan. 8, 1916; s. Joseph V. and Theresa (Binder) R.; m. Irene R. Kegel, Aug. 24, 1940; children: Judith Ann LeDoux, Cecelia C. Nelson. B.C.E., Marquette U., 1938. Civil engr. Consoer, Townsend & Quinlan, Chgo., 1938-43; asso. Consoer Townsend & Assocs. (Cons. Engrs.), Chgo., 1946-53; gen. partner Consoer Townsend & Assocs. (Cons. Engrs.), 1953-74, mng. partner, 1974-76; pres. PRC Consoer Townsend, Chgo., 1976-83, pres. emeritus, 1983-85; v.p. PRC Engring., Inc., Chgo., 1976-85; chmn. bd. Environ. Engring., Inc., 1976-83, Consoer Townsend Harris Internat., Inc., 1976-83; dir., v.p. Planning Research Corp., 1976-80; Mem. planning and adv. bd. Village of River Forest (Ill.), 1964-76; mem. exec. senate Marquette U., Milw., 1978—; mem., chmn. adv. council Marquette U. (Coll. Engring.), 1976-89. Mem. bldg. bd. appeals Village of River Forest, Ill., 1977-87, pres.'s adv. council Rosary Coll., River Forest, 1986-91, Exec. Svc. Corps Chgo. With U.S. Army, 1943-46. Recipient Disting. Engring. Alumnus award Marquette U. Coll. Engring., 1975; Alumnus of Yr. award Marquette U., 1983. Mem. Am. Public Works Assn., Am. Water Resources Assn., Am. Water Works Assn., Water Environ. Fedn., Inter-Am. Assn. San. Engring., NSPE, Western Soc. Engrs., Ill. State C. of C. (bd. dirs. 1981-85), VFW, KC, Country Club of Naples. Roman Catholic.

REHME, ROBERT G., film company executive; b. Cin., May 5, 1935; s. Gordon W. and Helen H. (Henkel) R.; m. Kay Yazell, Jan. 9, 1964; children: Robin, Tracy. Ed., U. Cin. Theatre mgr. RKO Theatres, Cin.; advt. mgr. Cin. Theatre Co., 1961; publicist United Artists Pictures, 1965-67; dir. advt. and publicity United Artists Pictures and Paramount Pictures, 1967-69; pres., CEO Avco Embassy Pictures Corp., Los Angeles, 1978-81; pres. distbn. and mktg. Universal Pictures Corp., 1981-82; pres. motion picture group MCA Universal, 1982-83; chief exec. officer New World Pictures, Los Angeles, 1983-89; prin. Neufeld/Rehme Prodns., 1989—; pres. Acad. Motion Picture Arts and Scis., 1992-93. Mem. Am. Film Inst. (trustee), Acad. Motion Picture Arts and Scis. Democrat. Presbyterian. Club: Variety. Office: Paramount Pictures 5555 Melrose Ave Los Angeles CA 90038-3149

REHMUS, CHARLES MARTIN, law educator, arbitrator; b. Ann Arbor, Mich., June 27, 1926; s. Paul A. and Amy D. (Martin) R.; m. Carolyn Brown, Dec. 21, 1948 (div. July 1982); children—Paul, James, Jon, David; m. Laura Carlson, Sept. 4, 1982. A.B., Kenyon Coll., 1947; M.A., Stanford U., 1951, Ph.D., 1955. Commr. Fed. Mediation and Conciliation Service, San Francisco, 1952-58; staff dir. Presdl. R.R. Commn., Washington, 1959-61; prof. polit. sci. U. Mich., Ann Arbor, 1962-80, dir. Inst. Labor and Indsl. Relations, 1962-76; chmn. Mich. Employment Relations Commn., Detroit, 1976-80; dean N.Y. State Sch. Indsl. and Labor Relations, Cornell U., Ithaca, 1980-86; prof. law U. San Diego, 1988—. Author: Final-Offer Arbitration, 1975, The Railway Labor Act at Fifty, 1977, Labor and American Politics, 1967, rev. edit., 1978, The National Mediation Board, 1984, Emergency Strikes Revisited, 1990. Chmn. 4 Presdl. emergency bds. at various times. Served to lt. USNR, 1943-45; PTO. Mem. Internat. Inst. Labor Studies (bd. govs. 1984-92), Indsl. Rels. Rsch. Assn. (exec. bd. 1984-88), Nat. Acad. Arbitrators (bd. govs. 1979-82, v.p. 1993-95).

REHNQUIST, WILLIAM HUBBS, United States supreme court chief justice; b. Milw., Oct. 1, 1924; s. William Benjamin and Margery (Peck) R.; m. Natalie Cornell, Aug. 29, 1953; children: James, Janet, Nancy. BA, MA, Stanford U., 1948; MA, Harvard U., 1949; LLB, Stanford U., 1952. Bar: Ariz. Law clk. to former justice Robert H. Jackson, U.S. Supreme Ct., 1952-53; with Evans, Kitchel & Jenckes, Phoenix, 1953-55; mem. Ragan & Rehnquist, Phoenix, 1956-57; ptnr. Cunningham, Carson & Messenger, Phoenix, 1957-60, Powers & Rehnquist, Phoenix, 1960-69; asst. atty.-gen. office of legal counsel Dept. of Justice, Washington, 1969-71; assoc. justice U.S. Supreme Ct., 1971-1986, chief justice, 1986—; mem. Nat. Conf. Commrs. Uniform State Laws, 1963-69. Author: Grand Inquests: The Historic Impeachments of Justice Samuel Chase and President Andrew Johnson, 1992; contbr. articles to law jours., nat. mags. Served with USAAF, 1943-46, NATOUSA. Mem. Fed., Am. Maricopa (Ariz.) County bar assns., State Bar Ariz., Nat. Conf. Lawyers and Realtors, Phi Beta Kappa, Order of Coif, Phi Delta Phi. Lutheran. Office: Supreme Ct US #1 1st St NE Washington DC 20543*

REHORN, LOIS M(ARIE), nursing administrator; b. Larned, Kans., Apr. 15, 1919; d. Charles and Ethel L. (Canaday) Williamson; m. C. Howard Smith, Feb. 15, 1946 (dec. Aug. 1980); 1 child, Cynthia A. Huddleston; m. Harlan W. Rehorn, Aug. 25, 1981. RN, Bethany Hosp. Sch. Nursing, Kansas City, Kans., 1943; BS, Ft. Hays Kans. State U., Hays, 1968, MS, 1970. RN, N.Mex. Office nurse, surg. asst. Dr. John H. Luke, Kansas City, Kans., 1943-47; supr. nursing unit Larned (Kans.) State Hosp., 1949-68, dir. nursing edn., 1968-71, dir. nursing, 1972-81, ret., 1981. Named Nurse of Yr. DNA-4, 1986. Mem. Am. Nurses Assn., Kans. Nurses Assn. (dist. treas.), N.Mex. Nurses Assn. (dist. pres. 1982-86, dist. bd. dirs. 1992-94). Home: 1436 Brentwood Dr Clovis NM 88101-4602 *Keep within you a place where dreams may grow. The fountain of understanding is the willingness to listen.*

REIBEL, KURT, physicist, educator; b. Vienna, Austria, May 23, 1926; came to U.S., 1938; s. Michael and Regina (Pak) R.; m. Eleanor Elvira Mannino, June 10, 1954; children—Leah, Michael, David. B.A., Temple U., Phila., 1954; M.S., U. Pa., Phila., 1956, Ph.D., 1959. Jr. research assoc. in physics Brookhaven Nat. Lab., 1957-59; research assoc. U. Pa., Phila., 1959-61; asst. prof. Ohio State U., Columbus, 1961-64, assoc. prof., 1964-70, prof. physics, 1970-92, prof. emeritus, 1992—; vis. scientist CERN, Geneva, Switzerland, 1968-69, 75-76. Author research papers on nuclear and elementary particle physics. NSF fellow, 1954-56. Mem. Am. Phys. Soc., AAUP, Fedn. Am. Scientists, Union Concerned Scientists, Sigma Xi. Jewish. Office: Ohio State U Dept Physics 174 W 18th Ave Columbus OH 43210-1106

REIBMAN, JEANETTE FICHMAN, retired state senator; b. Ft. Wayne, Ind., Aug. 18, 1915; d. Meir and Pearl (Schwartz) Fichman; m. Nathan L. Reibman, June 20, 1943; children: Joseph M. Edward D., James E. AB, Hunter Coll., 1937; LLB, U. Ind., 1940; LLD, Lafayette Coll., 1969; hon. degree, Lehigh U., 1986, Wilson Coll., 1974, Cedar Crest Coll., 1977, Moravian Coll., 1990. Bar: Ind., 1940, U.S. Supreme Ct. 1944. Pvt. practice law Ft. Wayne, 1940; atty. U.S. War Dept., Washington, 1940-42, U.S. War Prodn. Bd., Washington, 1942-44; mem. Pa. Ho. of Reps., 1956-66, Pa. State Senate, Harrisburg, 1966-94; chmn. com. on edn. Pa. State Senate, 1971-81, minority chmn., 1981-90, majority caucus adminstr., 1992-94; mem. Edn. Commn. of the States. Trustee emeritus Lafayette Coll.; bd. mem. Pa. Higher Edn. Assistance Agy., Pa. Coun. on Arts, Camphill Schs. Recipient Disting. Dau. of Pa. award and medal Gov. Pa., 1968, citation on naming of Jeanette F. Reibman Adminstrn. Bldg., East Stroudsburg State Coll., 1972, Early Childhood Learning Ctr. Northampton Community Coll., 1992, Pub. Svc. award Pa. Psychol. Assn., 1977, Jerusalem City of Peace award Govt. Israel, 1977; named to Hunter Coll. Alumni Hall of Fame, 1974; U. Ind. Law Alumni fellow, 1993. Mem. Hadassah (Myrtle Wreath award 1976), Sigma Delta Tau, Delta Kappa Gamma, Phi Delta Kappa, Order Ea. Star. Democrat. Jewish. Office: 711 Lehigh St Easton PA 18042-4325

REIBSTEIN, RICHARD JAY, lawyer; b. Phila., Mar. 12, 1951; s. Albert Simon and Alma (Wilf) R.; m. Susan Barbara Fisch, May 18, 1975. BA with distinction, U. Rochester, 1973; JD with honors, George Washington U., 1976. Bar: Pa. 1976 (nonresident inactive), N.Y. 1979, N.J. 1979, U.S. Dist. Ct. (so. dist.) N.Y. 1979, U.S. Dist. Ct. (ea. dist.) N.Y. 1979, N.J. 1979, U.S. Ct. Appeals (3d cir.) 1980, U.S. Ct. Appeals (2d cir.) 1982, U.S. Supreme Ct. 1983. Staff atty. Dept. Labor, Washington, 1976; counsel NLRB, Washington, 1976-78; assoc. Seham, Klein & Zelman (formerly Surrey, Karasik, Morse & Seham), N.Y.C., 1978-81; assoc. Epstein Becker & Green, P.C., N.Y.C., 1981-86, ptnr., 1986-91; ptnr. McDermott, Will & Emery, N.Y.C., 1992—. Co-author: Negligent Hiring, Fraud, Defamation, and Other Emerging Areas of Employer Liability, 1988, Employer's Guide to Workplace Torts, 1992; contbr. articles to legal jours. Mem. ABA (devel. of law under NLRA com., sect. labor and employment law 1976—), N.Y. State Bar Assn. Democrat. Office: McDermott Will & Emery 1211 Avenue Of The Americas New York NY 10036-8701

REICH, ABRAHAM CHARLES, lawyer; b. Waterbury, Conn., Apr. 17, 1949; s. Samuel and Esther (Gurvitz) R.; m. Sherri Engelman, Aug. 15, 1971; children: Spencer, Alexander. BA, U. Conn., 1971; JD, Temple U., 1974. Bar: Pa. 1974, U.S. Supreme Ct. 1979. Assoc. Fox, Rothschild, O'Brien & Frankel, Phila., 1974-81, ptnr., 1981—. Mem. Phila. Bar Assn. (chairperson profl. responsibility com. 1983-84, chairperson bench-bar com. 1985, chairperson profl. guidance com. 1987-88, bd. govs. 1987-89, chair bd. govs. 1989, vice chancellor 1993, chancellor-elect 1994, chancellor 1995). Home: 2224 Mt Vernon St Philadelphia PA 19130-3115 Office: Fox Rothschild O'Brien Frankel 2000 Market St Ste 10 Philadelphia PA 19103-3201

REICH, ALAN ANDERSON, foundation administrator; b. Pearl River, N.Y., Jan. 1, 1930; s. Oswald David and Alma Carolyn (Anderson) R.; m. Gay Ann Forsythe, Dec. 19, 1954; children: James, Jeffrey, Andrew, Elizabeth. B.A., Dartmouth Coll., 1952; diploma in Slavic Studies, Oxford U., 1953; M.A., Russian Inst., Middlebury Coll., 1953; M.B.A., Harvard U., 1959; LLD (hon.), Gallaudet Coll., 1981, Dartmouth Coll., 1992. Exec. Polaroid Corp., Cambridge, Mass., 1960-70; dep. asst. sec. ednl. and cultural affairs Dept. State, Washington, 1970-75; spl. asst. to sec. HEW, 1976-77; dep. asst. sec. commerce, dir. Bur. East-West Trade, Dept. Commerce, 1977-78; pres. U.S. Council for Internat. Yr. of Disabled Persons, Washington, 1978-81, Nat. Orgn. Disability, Washington, 1982—, Bimillennium Found., 1982—, Disability 2000 CEO coun., 1991—. Chmn. Sudbury (Mass.) Community United Fund, 1962, 66; mem. U.S. del. WHO Gen. Assembly, 1970; pres. Nat. Paraplegia Found.; chmn. bd. dirs. Paralysis Cure Research Found., bd. dirs. of the Healing Community, chmn. People-to-people Com. for Handicapped; Impact Found., 1986—; chmn. World Com. on Disability, 1985—. Served to 1st lt. inf. AUS, 1953-57. Named to U.S. Army Inf. OCS Hall of Fame, 1994; recipient Sevier award for svc. to handicapped, 1994. Mem. Paralyzed Vets. Am., Cosmos Club, Achilles Club (London), Beta Theta Pi. Republican. Methodist. Home: 6017 Copely Ln Mc Lean VA 22101-2507 Office: Nat Orgn on Disability 910 16th St NW Ste 600 Washington DC 20006-2903

REICH, ALLAN J., lawyer; b. Chgo., July 9, 1948; s. H. Robert and Sonya (Minsky) R.; m. Lynne Susan Roth, May 23, 1971; children: Allison, Marissa, Scott. BA, Cornell U., 1970; JD cum laude, U. Mich., 1973. Bar: Ill. 1973, U.S. Dist. Ct. (no. dist.) Ill. 1973. Ptnr. McDermott, Will & Emery, Chgo., 1973-93; ptnr., chairperson corp./securities group D'Ancona & Pflaum, Chgo., 1993—. Bd. dirs., pres. Young Men's Jewish Council, Chgo., 1974-84, Coun. for Jewish Elderly, 1986—, v.p., mem. exec. com., 1989—; mem. men's council Mus. Contemporary Art, Chgo., 1983-90, pres. 1988-89; trustee Mus. of Contemporary Art, Chgo., 1988-89; v.p., mem. Chgo. exec. bd. Am. Jewish Com., 1989—; mem. adv. bd. Columbia Dance Ctr., 1992—. Mem. ABA, Chgo. Bar Assn. Clubs: Standard (Chgo.); Northmoor Country (Highland Park, Ill.). Home: 936 Skokie Ridge Dr Glencoe IL 60022-1434 Office: D'Ancona & Pflaum 30 N La Salle St Chicago IL 60602-2508

REICH, BERNARD, telecommunications engineer; b. N.Y.C., Jan. 7, 1926; s. Adolph and Rose (Gluck) R.; m. Sylvia Greenberg, June 15, 1947; children: Robin Reich Murphy, Richard. BS in Physics, CCNY, 1948; postgrad., Rutgers U., 1954. Electronic engr., supervisory electronic engr. U.S. Army Electronics R & D Command, Ft. Monmouth, N.J., 1948-81; unit mgr. Semcor, Farmingdale, N.J., 1981-88; telecommunications engr. Telos Corp., Shrewsbury, N.J., 1988—; chmn. spl. working group on semicondrs. and microelectronics NATO, Brussels, 1959-80, chmn. group experts on electronic parts, 1972-80; adv. editor Microelectronics and Reliability, 1970—. Contbr. over 100 articles to tech. jours.; patentee in field. Mem. Juvenile Conf. Com., Ocean Twp., N.J., 1964—; pres. Manor at Wayside Condominium Assn., Ocean Twp., 1990-91. Sgt. U.S. Army, 1945-46, ETO. Recipient decoration for meritorious civilian svc. U.S. Army Electronics R & D Command, 1981. Fellow IEEE (chartered.), IEE (Eng.). Avocations: walking, grandparenting. Home: 45 Gimbel Pl Ocean NJ 07712-2565 Office: Telos Corp 656 Shrewsbury Ave Shrewsbury NJ 07701-4915

REICH, BERNARD, political science educator; b. Bklyn., Dec. 5, 1941; s. Moe and Rosalyn (Hartglass) R.; m. Madelyn Sue Ingber, June 16, 1963; children—Barry, Norman, Michael, Jennifer. BA cum laude with spl. honors, CCNY, 1961; MA, U. Va., 1963, PhD, 1964. Asst. prof. polit. sci. and internat. affairs George Washington U., Washington, 1964-70, assoc. prof., 1970-76, prof., 1976—, chmn. dept. polit. sci., 1976-82, 88-91; vis. prof. U. Va., 1969, 94, Sch. Advanced Internat. Studies Johns Hopkins U., 1978-80; vis. rsch. assoc. Tel Aviv U., 1971-72. Author: Quest for Peace: United States-Israel Relations and the Arab-Israel Conflict, 1977, The U.S. and Israel: Influence in the Special Relationship, 1984, Israel: Land of Tradition and Conflict, 1985, 93, Historical Dictionary of Israel, 1992, Securing the Covenant: United States-Israel Relations After the Cold War, 1995; editor, co-author: Government and Politics of the Middle East and North Africa, 1980, 86, 95; editor, co-author: Israel Faces the Future, 1986, The Powers in the Middle East, 1987, Israeli National Security Policy: Political Actors and Perspectives, 1988, Political Leaders of the Contemporary Middle East and North Africa: A Biographical Dictionary, 1990, Israeli Politics in the 1990's Key Domestic and Foreign Policy Factors, 1991, Arab-Israeli Conflict and Conciliation: A Documentary History, 1995, An Historical Encyclopedia of the Arab-Israeli Conflict, 1996; co-author: United States Foreign Policy and the Middle East/North Africa: A Bibliography of Twentieth-Century Research, 1990, Asian States' Relations with the Middle East and North Africa: A Bibliography, 1950-93, 94, U.S. Foreign Relations with the Middle East and North Africa: A Bibliography, 1994; mem. adv. bd. editors Middle East Jour., 1977—, Jour. Israel Affairs, 1994—, Terrorism, 1987-93, Fgn. Svc. Jour., 1987-90; contbr. articles to profl. jours. Bd. govs. Middle East Inst. Fulbright research scholar, UAR, 1965; NSF postdoctoral fellow, 1971-72. Mem. Internat. Inst. Strategic Studies, Middle East Studies Assn., Phi Beta Kappa. Home: 13800 Turnmore Rd Silver Spring MD 20906-2134 Office: George Washington U Dept Polit Sci Washington DC 20052

REICH, CHARLES WILLIAM, nuclear physicist; b. Oklahoma City, Sept. 12, 1930; s. Fred William And Gertrude Evelyn (Veal) R.; m. Juana Sue Woods, June 8, 1952; children: Paul William, Jane Kristen, Donna Karen. BS in Physics, U. Okla., 1952; MA in Physics, Rice U., 1954, PhD in Physics, 1956. Physicist, group leader Atomic Energy Div. Phillips Petroleum Co., Idaho Falls, Idaho, 1956-66; group leader, sect. chief Idaho Nuclear Corp., Idaho Falls, 1966-71; sect. chief Aerojet Nuclear Corp., Idaho Falls, 1971-76; prin. scientist, sect. chief EG&G Idaho, Inc., Idaho Falls, 1976-82, sci., engring. fellow, 1982-92, fellow emeritus, 1992—; guest scientist Niels Bohr Inst., Copenhagen, 1964-65; U.S. rep., coord. coordinated rsch. program IAEA, 1977-86; mem. transplutonium program com. U.S. Dept. Energy, 1978—; chmn. decay data subcom. Cross Sects. Evaluation Working Group, 1974-86; mem. task force on decay heat predictions nuclear data com. Nuclear Energy Agy., 1988-90; mem. sci. framework writing com. State of Idaho Dept. Edn., 1994. Contbr. articles to profl. jours. Recipient H.A. Wilson rsch. award Rice Inst., 1956; predoctoral fellow NSF, 1954-55. Fellow Am. Phys. Soc. (editl. bd. Phys. Rev. C 1978, 82-84); mem. N.Y. Acad. Scis., Sigma Xi, Phi Beta Kappa. Mem. Ch. Nazarene. Office: Idaho Nat Engring Lab PO Box 1625 Idaho Falls ID 83415-2114

REICH, DAVID LEE, library director; b. Orlando, Fla., Nov. 25, 1930; s. P.F. and Opal Katherine (Wood) Reichelderfer; m. Kathleen Johanna Weichel, Aug. 2, 1954 (div. Sept. 1964); 1 son, Robert Weichel. Ph.B. magna cum laude, U. Detroit, 1961; A.M. in L.S. (Carnegie Library Sci. Endowment scholar), U. Mich., 1963. Tchr. English Jefferson Davis Jr. Sch., San Antonio, 1961-62; dir. engring. library Radiation Inc., Melbourne, Fla., 1963-64; asst. to dir. libraries Miami-Dade Jr. Coll., Miami, Fla., 1964-65; dir. learning resources Monroe County Community Coll., Monroe, Mich., 1965-68; dep. dir. Dallas Pub. Library, 1968-73; dep. chief librarian The Chgo. Pub. Library, 1973-74, commr., 1975-78; dir. Bd. Library Commrs., Commonwealth of Mass., Boston, 1978-80; exec. sec. New Eng. Library Bd., Augusta, Maine, 1980-82; dir. Lakeland Pub. Library, Lakeland, Fla., 1983—; vice chmn. New Eng. Library Bd., 1979-80; libr. cons. Macomb County C.C., Warren, Mich., 1967; chmn. adv. com. to libr. tech. asst. program El Centro Coll., Dallas, 1969-71; mem. inter-task working group Goals for Dallas, 1968-70, mem. Dallas Area Libr. planning coun., 1970-73; mem. adv. coun. dept. libr. sci. No. Ill. U., 1975-78; v.p., pres.-elect Tampa Bay Libr. Consortium, 1985-86, pres., 1986-87. Co-author: The Public Library in Non-traditional Education, 1974; Contbr. articles to library jours. Bd. dirs. The Villas II Homeowners Assn., 1994-96. Sgt. U.S. Army, 1952-55. Recipient Disting. Alumnus award U. Mich., 1978; William B. Calkins Found. scholar Orlando, 1963. Mem. ALA (coun.-at-large 1968-72, 75-79), S.E. Libr. Assn., Fla. Libr. Assn. (sec.-treas. coll. and spl. librs. divsn. 1965, steering com. mcpl. librs. caucus 1983-84, chmn. 1984-85, exec. bd. 1984-87), Soc. Fla. Archivists (exec. bd. 1994-96, sec. 1966-67), Fla. Pub. Libr. Assn. (pres. 1987-88, exec. bd. 1988-89, 94-95, editor newsletter 1992-93, 96—, chmn. libr. adminstrn. divsn. 1992, friends and trustees divsn. 1993, 95), Alumni Assn. U. Mich. (pres. Libr. Sch. alumni 1973). Home: 3929 Old Road 37 Villa 134 Lakeland FL 33813-1058 Office: Lakeland Pub Libr 100 Lake Morton Dr Lakeland FL 33801-5347

REICH, HERB, editor; b. N.Y.C.; s. Herman S. and Hattie (Davis) R.; m. Gerri Toog, Aug. 7, 1960; children: Amanda Suri, Elizabeth Jo. B.A., Bklyn. Coll., 1950; M.A., Bklyn. Coll. and Kings County Hosp., 1951; postgrad., Columbia U., 1951-54. Author sketches and lyrics Tamiment Revues (Pa.), 1951; staff writer NBC-TV, N.Y.C. and Los Angeles, 1955-57; research coordinator Inst. for Motivational Research, Croton-on-Hudson, N.Y., 1958-59; research dir. Scientist and Engr. Technol. Inst., N.Y.C., 1960-64; mng. editor SETI Pubs. Inc., N.Y.C., 1961-64; sr. editor Odyssey Press, N.Y.C., 1964-65; editorial dir. Profl. and Tech. Programs Inc., N.Y.C., 1966-72; dir. Behavioral Sci. Book Service, N.Y.C., 1966-72; dir. behavioral scis. program Basic Books Inc., N.Y.C., 1973-79; editor intersci. div. John Wiley & Sons. Inc., N.Y.C., 1979-87, sr. editor profl. and trade divsn., 1987-95; pres. H&G Reich, Publ., Hastings Hdsn., N.Y., 1980—; publ., rsch., advt. and polit. cons.; rschr., statistician, rsch. cons. Am. Found. for Blind, Pepsi Cola Co., Nowland and Co., Comms. and Media Rsch. Svcs.; freelance TV writer. Mng. editor: Odyssey Science Library Ency. of Engring., Signs and Symbols, 1965, Dictionary of Physics and Mathematics Abbreviations, Signs and Symbols, 1965, Dictionary of Electronics Abbreviations, Signs and Symbols, 1965, Dictionary of Computers and Control Systems Abbreviations, Signs and Symbols, 1965; contbr. Random House Dictionary of the English Language, 1967, rev. edit., 1987, The Greatest Revue Sketches, 1982, Ency. of Psychology, 2d edit., 1994; TV writer: Broadway Open House, 1951, Milton Berle Texaco Star Theatre, 1952, All-Star Revue, 1952, Mel Torme Show, 1952, Red Buttons Show, 1954, Jerry Lester Show, 1954, Jan Murray Time, 1955, Wayne and Schuster Hour, 1957. Co-founder, vice chmn. Mt. Vernon United for Better Edn., N.Y., 1970-73; mem. Westchester County Democratic Com., 1972-76; exec. com. Mt. Vernon Dem. City Com., 1973-76; mem. supt.'s adv. com. Hastings Schs., Hastings-on-Hudson, N.Y., 1981-82. Recipient Gold award of excellence for radio advt. Advt. Club of Westchester, 1980; recipient Gold and Bronze awards of excellence for radio advt. Advt. Club of Westchester, 1981. Mem. AAAS, APA, N.Y. Acad. Scis., Alpha Phi Omega.

REICH, JACK EGAN, insurance company executive; b. Chgo., June 17, 1910; s. Henry Carl and Rose (Egan) B.; m. Jean Grady, Apr. 30, 1935; children: Rosemary (Mrs. Jerry Semler), Judith (Mrs. Dan Hoyt). Student, Purdue U., 1928-31; LLD (hon.), Butler U., 1973; PhD (hon.), Marian Coll., 1983; LLD (hon.), Ind. U., 1986; PhD (hon.), Purdue U., 1993. With Inland Steel Co., East Chicago, Ind., 1925-31; field dir. gross income tax and employment security divs. State of Ind., 1933-40; field dir. Ind. C. of C., 1940-52, exec. v.p., 1952-62; pres., chmn. bd. Indpls. Water Co., 1962-67; chmn. bd. emeritus Am. United Life Ins. Co.; mem., past pres. Assn. Ind. Life Ins. Cos. Bd. dirs., past pres. Greater Indpls. Progress Com.; mem. exec. com., past chmn. Ind. Legal Found.; bd. dirs. Ind. Colls. of Ind. Found., Wishard Meml. Found., Indpls. Downtown Inc.; bd. dirs., past campaign chmn., past pres. United Way Cen. Ind.; past mem. bd. lay trustees St. Mary-of-Woods Colls.; mem. adv. bd. St. Vincent Hosp.; bd. regents, past pres. Ind. Acad.; past local and state pres., nat. v.p. Jaycees. Mem. Ind. C. of C. (bd. dir., past chmn. and exec. v.p.), Econ. Club (past pres.), Columbia Club, Indpls. Athletic Club, Indpls. Press Club, Meridian Hills Country Club, Skyline Club (chmn.), Ind. Soc. Club (Chgo.), Pi Kappa Alpha. Home: 7404 N Pennsylvania St Indianapolis IN 46240-3067 Office: Am United Life Ins Co 1 American Sq PO Box 368 Indianapolis IN 46206

REICH, KENNETH IRVIN, journalist; b. Los Angeles, Mar. 7, 1938; s. Herman and Ruth Alberta (Nussbaum) R.; m. Nov. 14, 1970; children: Kathleen, David. B.A., Dartmouth Coll., 1960; M.A. (Woodrow Wilson fellow), U. Calif., Berkeley, 1962. With UPI, Sacramento, 1962-63, Life mag., 1963-65; with Los Angeles Times, 1965—, polit. writer, 1972-77, 1984 Olympics writer, 1977-84, investigative reporter ins. law, ins. politics & fin. sports, 1985-92; lectr. in field. Author: Making it Happen, Peter Ueberroth and the 1984 Olympics, 1985, Covering Earthquakes, Volcanos and Other Issues Relating to Geology, 1992—; contbr. articles to mags. Daniel Webster Nat. Honor scholar Dartmouth Coll., 1956-60. Mem. Dartmouth Alumni Club (chpt. officer 1991—, dist. enrollment dir. 1992-95, meml. chmn. Dartmouth Class of 1960 1993-95, class sec. 1995—). Office: Times-Mirror Sq Los Angeles CA 90053

REICH, MERRILL DRURY, intelligence consultant, writer; b. Washington, Aug. 28, 1930; s. Merrill Dale Reich and Evelyn Merle Wright; m. Georgia Ann Ewing, Aug. 28, 1953; 1 child, Alexandra Therese. BA in History, Govt., Rollins Coll., 1954; postgrad., U. Vienna, 1954-55, Naval War Coll., 1973-74; MA in Mgmt., Cen. Mich. U., 1981. Commd. ensign USN, 1955, advanced through grades to capt., ret., 1982; dir. systems mgmt. BDM Corp., Columbia, Md., 1982-92; cons. Crytec, Inc., 1992-95. Fulbright scholar, 1954-55. Mem. Nat. Trust for Hist. Preservation, U.S. Naval Inst., Naval War Coll. Found., Assn. Former Intelligence Officers, Navy Cryptologic Vets. Assn., Fulbright Assn., New Eng. Hist. Geneal. Soc., Omicron Delta Kappa, Pi Gamma Mu, Phi Kappa Tau. Republican. Avocations: genealogy, lapidary, antiques, swimming, sailing. Home: 514 Kirkwood Ln Camden SC 29020

REICH, MICHAEL, economics educator; b. Poland, Oct. 18, 1945; came to U.S., 1949; s. Melvin and Betty (Mandelbaum) R.; m. Nancy J. Chodorow, 1977; children: Rachel, Gabriel. BA, Swarthmore Coll., 1966; PhD, Harvard U., 1974. Asst. prof. Boston U., 1971-74; asst. prof. U. Calif., Berkeley, 1974-81, acting assoc. prof., 1981-82, assoc. prof., 1982-89, prof., 1989—; rsch. dir. Nat. Ctr. for the Workplace, 1993—. Author: Segmented Work, Divided Workers, 1982, Racial Inequality, 1981, The Capitalist System, 1986, Social Structurs of Accumulation, 1994; editor: Indsl. Rels. Jour., 1986—; contbr. articles to profl. jours. Mem. Am. Econ. Assn., Indsl. Rels. Rsch. Assn., Phi Beta Kappa, Sigma Xi. Office: Dept of Econs U Calif 611 Evans Hall Berkeley CA 94720

REICH, MORTON MELVYN, marketing communications company executive; b. Phila., Aug. 11, 1939; s. Morris and Lillian (Rabinowitz) R.; m. Geraldine Joan Krassan, May 31, 1964; children: Hope, Marla. Student, Charles Morris Price Sch. Advt. and Journalism, 1961-62, Temple U., 1963-68. Asst. dir. pub. relations Goodwill Industries, Phila., 1962-63; dir. promotion and information services Yellow Cab Co., Phila., 1963-66; dir. corp. employee communications Philco-Ford Co., Phila., 1966-68; exec. dir. J.M. Korn & Son Inc., Phila., 1968-75; pres. Richard Yeager Assos., Moorestown, 1975—, Reich, Robinson, Inc., Phila., 1975-76; sr. v.p. Kalish & Rice, Phila., 1976-79; exec. dir. owner Mktg. Communications Mgmt., Phila., from 1979; now pres. The Reich Group (formerly Mktg. Communications mgmt.), Phila.; tchr. Charles Morris Price Sch.; lectr. in field. Contbr. articles to profl. jours. Served with USN, 1957-60. Recipient Disting. Alumni award Charles Morris Price Sch., 1973, Creative Marketing award Readers Digest, 1974, Nat. Jr. C. of C. award, 1972. Mem. Phila. Jr. C. of C. (dir. 1962-65), Advt. Chairmen Phila. Fellowship Commn., others. Home: 6N Woodleigh Dr Cherry Hill NJ 08003 Office: Reich Group 1635 Market St Fl 200 Philadelphia PA 19103-2217

REICH, NATHANIEL EDWIN, physician, poet, author, artist, educator; b. N.Y.C., May 19, 1907; s. Alexander and Betty (Feigenbaum) R.; m. Joan Finkel, May 22, 1943; children: Andrew, Matthew. B.S., NYU, 1927; student, Marquette U. Coll. Medicine, 1927-29; M.D., Rush Med. Coll., U. Chgo., 1932. Diplomate Am. Bd. Internal Medicine. Intern, resident pathologist City Hosp., N.Y.C., 1931-33; emeritus attending physician Kingsbrook Jewish Med. Center Hosp.; vis. physician Kings County Hosp., Bklyn.; attending physician State U. Hosp.; faculty SUNY Downstate Med. Center, 1938—, asso. clin. prof. medicine, 1952-74, clin. prof., 1974-77, emeritus prof., 1977—; vis. prof. San Marcos U. Coll. Medicine, Lima, Peru, 1968, U. Afghanistan, 1970, U. Indonesia, 1972, U. Sri Lanka, 1975; asst. attending physician N.Y. Postgrad. Hosp., Columbia U., 1940; cons. Dept. H and HS; cardiac cons. U.S. R.R. Retirement Bd., 1965—; program cons. Acad. Family Physicians, 1973, N.Y. State Disability Determinations; lectr. univs., Rome, Moscow, Rijeka, Haiti, Jerusalem, Cairo, Athens, Bangkok, Bucharest, Manila, Lisbon, Beijing, Shanghai, Romania, Taiwan, Cairo, Athens, Tunis, Triente, Madras, Dakar, Senegal, Durban, Witwatersrand, Capetown, Natal, Lima, Buenos Aires, Rio de Janeiro, Quito; 1st Am. physician invited to lecture in USSR, 1956; lectr. univs. U. Madras (India), 1969, Spain, 1971, Auckland, N.Z., Sydney, Australia, Senegal, Portugal; lectr. Japan Med. Assn., Philippine Heart Assn., Royal Thai Air Force Med. Svc., China Med. Assn., Shanghai, 1978, Nat. Taiwan U., Taipei, 1978, Beijing Cardiac Inst., 1986; chmn. internat. cardiology sect. Congress Chest Diseases, Cologne, Germany, 1956; impartial specialist U.S. Fed. Employees; cons. N.Y. State Bur. Disability Determinations, N.Y.C., Office Vocat. Rehab., Dept. Health and Human Svcs., 1965—; chief med. examiner SSS, 1942-44 (Presdl. commendation). One-man shows include L.I. U., 1961, NYU Loeb Ctr., 1962, 72, 74, Greer Gallery, 1962, 64, St. Charles, La., 1964, Nyack, N.Y., 1986, Prospect Park Ctrl. Art Show, 1966, Art Inst. Boston, 1970, 76, George Wiener Gallery, 1972; exhibited in group shows at Little Studio, 1952, Mus. Modern Art, Paris, 1970, Bodley Gallery, 1965, 69, Nyack, N.Y., 1987, others; represented in permanent collections at Huntington Hartford collection N.Y. Cultural Ctr., 1969, Washington County Mus. of Fine Arts, Hagerstown, md.; author 3 textbooks on cardiology; author chpts. in 3 encys.; author: A Renaissance Man at Large; author: (collected poems) Reflections, 1993. Served from 1st lt. to maj. M.C., AUS, 1944-47. Recipient St. Gaudens award, 1923, 1st prize Art Assn. AMA, 1948, 1st prize Art Assn. Literary Soc., 1949, Disting. Achievement award Boys' H.S. Alumni Assn., 1988, Am. Poetry Assn. Hon. mention World of Poetry, 1990; named Best New Poets of 1989, 94, 95. Fellow ACP, Royal Soc. Medicine (London), Am. Coll. Cardiology, Am. Coll. Angiology (med. honor award 1956, 59), Am. Coll. Legal Medicine (founder), Am. Coll. Chest Physicians (chmn. exhibits com. 1961, cardiovascular rehab. com. 1965, coronary disease com. 1968, pres. N.Y. state chpt. 1970); mem. N.Y. State Med. Soc. (vice chmn. space med. sect. 1967, 75, chmn. chest sect. 1972), Internat. Soc. Internal Medicine, World Med. Assn., Am. Heart Assn. (coun. on thrombosis), N.Y. Heart Assn., N.Y. Cardiol. Soc. (exec. bd., pres.), Explorers Club (4 explorations described in jour. 1966—), Temple Club (v.p.), Doctors Club Bklyn. (vice chmn. bd. govs.), Circumnavigators. Home: 1620 Avenue I Brooklyn NY 11230-3050

REICH, PAULA JUDY, nursing educator; b. Troy, N.Y., Jan. 27, 1942; d. Samuel and Dora (Luskin) Bendick; m. Lawrence W. Reich, Nov. 1, 1964; children: Ronna, Heather, Sheara. AAS in Nursing, Queens Coll., 1961; BSN, St. John's U., Queens, N.Y., 1964; MS in Curriculum and Instrn., SUNY, Albany, 1975; MS in Nursing, Adelphi U., 1982. RN, N.Y. Staff nurse obstetrics Flushing Hosp., Queens, 1962-63; staff nurse ob/gyn. Queens Gen. Hosp., 1963-64; sr. staff nurse pediatrics Mt. Sinai Hosp., N.Y.C., 1964-65; supr. ob-gyn. Nassau Hosp., Mineola, N.Y., 1965-67; staff nurse obstetrics St. Peters Hosp., Albany, 1968-73; dir. Tri Cities Childbirth Instrn., Albany, 1973-78; mem. faculty dept. nursing Adelphi U., Garden City, N.Y., 1978-79, SUNY, Farmingdale, 1978—; clin. instr. Albany Jr. Coll., 1977-78; cons. maternal/child continuing edn. Adelphi U., 1984; dir. nursing continuing edn. SUNY, Farmingdale, 1985-91, dir. LPN/ADN nursing ract, 1990-94. V.p. bd. dirs. Suffolk Network Adolescent Pregnancy, Suffolk County, N.Y., 1985-90. Mem. Suffolk Perinatal Coalition. Avocations: sailing, travel, reading. Office: SUNY Farmingdale Dept Nursing Rt 110 Melville NY 11735

REICH, PAULINE CAROLE, international business consultant, educator, author; b. Kew Gardens, N.Y., Nov. 13, 1946; d. Stanley Garfield and Elsa Olga (Doctor) R. Cert. in critical langs. program, Princeton U., 1967; BA, CCNY, 1968; MA, CUNY, 1972; JD, N.Y. Law Sch., 1985; grad., Coro Found. Pub. Affairs Leadership Program, 1981. Bar: N.J., U.S. Ct. Internat. Trade, U.S. Ct. Appeals (Fed. cir.). Cons. Pan Pacific, Inc., Bayside, N.Y., 1988-90, Japan Pacific Group, N.Y.C., 1990-93, Asia Pacific Group, Great Neck, N.Y., 1994—; prof. Waseda U. Sch. Law, Tokyo, 1995—. Contbr. book chpts. and articles to profl. jours. Japan Found. fellow, 1973, Princeton Found. fellow, 1966-67, Carnegie Found. fellow, 1966-67, Nat. Def. Edn. Act. fellow, 1966; elected East Coast Dir. Ind. Scholars Asia, 1981-86. Mem. ABA (sect. of internat. law and practice, labor and employment law, dispute resolution sect., co-chair Pacific rim com., Asia-Pacific law com.), Japan Soc., Am. C. of C. in Japan (legal svcs. com.), Am. Arbitration Assn. (arbitration panel), U.S. Coun. for Internat. Bus. (arbitration panel), Assn. for Asian Studies (com. on Asian law). Avocations: international travel, underwater photography, genealogy. Office: Waseda U Sch Law, 1-6-1 Nishi-Waseda, Shinjuku-ku Tokyo Japan

REICH, ROBERT BERNARD, federal official, political economics educator; b. Scranton, Pa., June 24, 1946; s. Edwin Saul and Mildred Dorf (Freshman) R.; m. Clare Dalton, July 7, 1973. BA, Dartmouth Coll., 1968, MA (hon.), 1988; MA, Oxford (Eng.) U., 1970; JD, Yale U., 1973. Asst. solicitor gen. U.S. Dept. Justice, Washington, 1974-76; dir. policy planning FTC, Washington, 1976-81; mem. faculty John F. Kennedy Sch. Govt. Harvard U., Cambridge, Mass., 1981—; sec. Dept. of Labor, Washington, 1993—; chmn. biotech. sect. U.S. Office Tech. Assessment, Washington, 1990-91. Author: The Next American Frontier, 1983, Tales of a New America, 1987, The Work of Nations, 1991; co-author: The Power of Public Ideas, 1987; contbg. editor The New Republic, Washington, 1982-93; chmn. editorial bd. The Am. Prospect, 1990-93. Mem. governing bd. Common Cause, Washington, 1981-85; bd. dirs. Bus. Enterprise Trust, Palo Alto, Calif., 1989-93; trustee Dartmouth Coll., Hanover, N.H., 1989-93. Rhodes scholar, 1968; recipient Louis Brownlow award ASPA, 1983.

REICH, ROBERT SIGMUND, retired landscape architect; b. N.Y.C., Mar. 22, 1913; s. Ulysses S. and Adele G. R.; m. Helen Elizabeth Adams, May, 1945; children—Barbara, Betsy, Bob, Bill. B.S., Cornell U., 1934, Ph.D.,

1941; postgrad., U. So. Calif., 1951. Instr. landscape design Cornell U., 1936-39, 40-41; instr. land design U. Conn., 1939-40; Instr. Land Design La. State U., 1941-46, asst. prof. landscape architecture, 1946-49, asso. prof., 1949-60, prof., 1960—, Alumni prof., 1967—, head dept. landscape architecture, 1964-79, dir. Sch.Landscape Architecture, 1979-83; prof. Landscape Architecture, 1992—; instr. Shrivenham (Eng.) Am. U., 1946, Biarritz (France) Am. U., 1947; vis. lectr. Tulane U., 1958-67; judge, instr. Nat. Council Garden Clubs, 1956—; mem. task force on parks, recreation and tourism Goals for La. Program; mem. com. to establish Chicot State Park Arboretum, Ville Plate, La., 1964, mem. steering com., 1964-75; examiner La. Bd. Examination for Landscape Architects, 1957-77. Co-author: Landscape and You, 1953. Mem. com. to establish City/Parish Beautification Commn., 1961-82; mem. area and facilities com. Baton Rouge Recreation and Parks Commn., 1957-83; bd. dirs. Hubbard Edn. Trust, Weston, Mass., 1967—; adv. com. Friends of Frederick Law Olmsted Papers, 1983—. With U.S. Army, 1942-45; in charge alter arrangements U. United Meth. Ch., 1945—. Recipient Teaching award of merit Gamma Sigma Delta, 1963, Baton Rouge Green Individual Honor award, 1996. Fellow Am. Soc. Landscape Architects (trustee 1968-71, 83-86, 3d v.p. 1971-73, Medal 1992); mem. S.W. Park and Recreation Tng. Inst. (dir. 1975-77, award of merit 1968), Phi Kappa Phi, Pi Alpha xi, Omicron Delta Kappa, Sigma Lambda Alpha. Home: 333 E Boyd Dr Baton Rouge LA 70808-4507 Office: La State U Sch Landscape Architecture Coll Design Bldg Baton Rouge LA 70803

REICH, ROSE MARIE, retired art educator; b. Milw., Dec. 24, 1937; d. Valentine John and Mary Jane (Grochowski) Kosmatka; m. Kenneth Pierce Reich, July 13, 1968; 1 stepson, Lance Pierce. BA, Milw. Downer Coll., 1959; MA, U. Wyo., 1967. Art tchr. Oconomowoc (Wis.) Area Schs., 1959-93, ret., 1993. Mem. Oconomowoc Edn. Assn., NEA (life), Wis. Edn. Assn., AAUW (v.p. membership 1989—), Delta Kappa Gamma (past pres.). Roman Catholic. Avocations: Newfoundland dogs, needlework, designing stationery, Polish paper cutting, restoring old church statues and mannequins. Home: 3717 N Golden Lake Rd Oconomowoc WI 53066-4104

REICH, SEYMOUR DAVID, lawyer, former fraternal organization executive; b. Bklyn., Apr. 23, 1933; s. James and Esther (Reich) R.; m. Helyn Brenner; children: Keith E., Leslie B., Jaime Reich Amiram. BA, U. Pa., 1954; LLB, Harvard U., 1957. Sr. ptnr. Dreyer and Traub, N.Y.C.; now ptnr. Gallet, Dreyer & Berkey, LLP. Pres. B'nai Brith Internat., 1986-90; chmn. Conf. of Pres.'s Major Am. Jewish Orgn., 1989-90. Mem. Phi Beta Kappa. Office: Gallet, Dreyer, & Berkey 845 3rd Ave New York NY 10022*

REICH, STEVE, composer; b. N.Y.C., Oct. 3, 1936; m. Beryl Korot; children: Ezra, Michael. Studies in percussion with Roland Kohloff, 1950-53; BA in Philosophy with honors, Cornell U., 1957; studies in composition with Hall Overton, 1957-58; studies with Bergsma and Persichetti, Julliard Sch. Music, 1958-61; MA in Music, Mills Coll., 1963; studies in composition with Darius Milhaud and Luciano Berio; studies in drumming, Inst. for African Studies, U. Ghana, 1971; student, Am. Soc. for Ea. Arts, Seattle and Berkeley, 1973, 74, Cantillation of Hebrew Scriptures, N.Y.C. and Jerusalem, 1976-77. Organized ensemble Steve Reich and Musicians, 1966; performed throughout the world, 1971—; recs. with various cos. including Columbia Records, Disques Shandar, Hungaraton, Angel, ECM, Deutsche Grammophon, Nonesuch, Phillips, Virgin Classics, Argo. Composer, performer: (albums) Come Out, 1967, It's Gonna Rain, 1969, Violin Phase, 1969, Four Organs, 1970, Phase Patterns, 1970, Drumming, 1971, Four Organs, 1973, Six Pianos, 1973, Music for Mallet Instruments, Voices, and Organ, 1973, Music for Eighteen Musicians, 1978, Octet, 1980, Music for a Large Ensemble, 1980,Violin Phase, 1980, Tehillim, 1982, The Desert Music, 1984, Sextet, 1986, Six Marimbas, 1986, Electric Counterpoint, 1987, Different Trains, 1988 (Grammy award 1989), The Four Sections, 1987, The Cave, 1994, City Life, 1995, Proverb, 1996, others; composer: Vermont Counterpoint, Variations for Winds, Strings and Keyboards, Eight Lines for Chamber Orchestra, Piano Phase, Clapping Music, Pendulum Music, Music for Pieces of Wood, other works performed by major orchs. and ensembles; commd. to compose for Holland Festival, 1978, Radio Frankfurt, 1979, San Francisco Symphony, 1980, Rothko Chapel, 1981, West German Radio, Cologne, 1984, Fromm Music Found., 1985, Richard Stoltzman, 1985, Bklyn. Acad. Music, 1987, Kronos Quartet, 1988, St. Louis Sympnony, 1987, The Cave commd. by Vienna Festival, Holland Festival, Festival d'Automne à Paris, Theatre de la Monnaie, Brussels, Hebbel Theatre, Berlin, South Bank Centre/Serious Speakout, London and the Brooklyn Acad. Music, Next Wave Festival, 1993. Recipient Koussevitzky Found. award, 1981; Rockefeller Found. grantee 1975, 78, 81, 90, Nat. Endowment for the Arts grantee, 1974, 76, 91, N.Y. State Council on the Arts grantee, 1974; Guggenheim fellow, 1978. Office: care IMG Artists 22 E 71st St New York NY 10021

REICH, YARON Z., lawyer; b. Bklyn., June 1, 1950. BA, Columbia U., 1975, JD, 1978; LLM in Taxation, NYU, 1984. Bar: Pa. 1978, N.Y. 1979. Law clk. to Hon. Arlin M. Adams U.S. Ct. Appeals (3d cir.), 1978-79; ptnr. Cleary, Gottlieb, Steen & Hamilton, N.Y.C. Spl. issue editor Columbia Law Review, 1977-78. Mem. Assn. Bar City of N.Y. (taxation of corps. com.) N.Y. State Bar Assn. (exec. com. tax sect. 1990-92). Office: Cleary Gottlieb Steen & Hamilton 1 Liberty Plz New York NY 10006-1404*

REICHARD, HUGO MANLEY, English literature educator; b. South Plainfield, N.J., Jan. 21, 1918; s. Bernard and Emma (Klein) R.; m. Virginia Evelyn Kougias, Aug. 28, 1943; children—Enid Evelyn Reichard Satariano, Claude Manley, Eric George. B.A., U. Mich., 1939; M.A., Harvard U., 1948, Ph.D., 1951. Instr. English lit. Duke U., 1951-56; mem. faculty Purdue U., 1956-88, prof. English lit., 1970-88, prof. emeritus, 1988—. Author articles in field. Served with AUS, 1941-46. Decorated Bronze Star. Mem. MLA, Johnson Soc. Central Region (pres. 1979-80). Office: Purdue U Heavilon Hall English Dept West Lafayette IN 47907

REICHARD, JOHN FRANCIS, educational consultant; b. Abington, Pa., June 2, 1924; s. Francis Radcliffe and Katharine (Butler) R.; m. Ruth Naomi Nachod, Aug. 5, 1950; children: Scot, John Nicholas. BA, Wesleyan U., 1949, postgrad., 1949-50; postgrad., Glasgow U., Scotland, 1950-51. Instr. English/humanities Wesleyan U., Middletown, Conn., 1951-52, Ohio Wesleyan U., Delaware, 1952-54; internat. campus adminstr. U.S. Nat. Student Assn., Cambridge, Mass., 1954; exec. dir. Internat. Student Assn. Greater Boston, 1955-60; pres. Phila. Coun. for Internat. Visitors, 1960-73; internat. coord. Phila. 76, 1973-75; exec. dir. Global Interdependence Ctr., 1975-79; exec. v.p. NAFSA: Assn. of Internat. Educators, Washington, 1980-92; internat. edn. cons., Bethesda, Md., 1992—. Bd. Internat. Devel. Conf.; mem. internat. program com. USDA Grad. Sch. Counselor Meridian House Internat.; travel adv. com. U.S. Travel Svc., 1963-64; pres. Nat. Coun. Internat. Visitors, 1963-65; organizer, co-chmn. Internat. Yr. of Child, UNICEF, Phila., 1977-78; internat. adv. bd. Bryn Mawr Coll., 1975-79; chmn. schools com. Phila. steering com. on alumni affairs Wesleyan U., 1968-76; adv. bd. Hariri Found.; mem. Nat. Liaison Com. on Fgn. Student Admissions. Contbr. articles to profl. jours. Served with USAAF, 1943-46. Winchester fellow Wesleyan U., 1949; Fulbright scholar Glasgow U., 1950-51; recipient Tribute of Appreciation, U.S. Dept. State, 1973, 92, Svc. award Coun. on Internat. Ednl. Exch., 1991. Mem. Am. Coun. on Edn. (secretariat, commn. on internat. edn. 1980-92), Internat. Ednl. Exch. Liaison Group (chmn. 1982-84), Test of English as a Fgn. Lang. (policy coun.), Fulbright Alumni Assn. (v.p. 1978-80), Cosmos Club, Phi Beta Kappa. Democrat. Home: 4974 Sentinel Dr Apt 301 Bethesda MD 20816-3571

REICHARD, WILLIAM EDWARD, lawyer, consultant; b. Lorain, Ohio, Dec. 6, 1938; s. Russell E. and Regina C. (Bartinique) R.; m. Patricia J. Mooney, Apr. 20, 1963; children: Ann E. Reichard McHugh, John B., William M., Margaret C., Kathryn M., Patrick M., Elizabeth J., Daniel C., Michael C. BS in Physics, Coll. Holy Cross, 1961; JD, NYU, 1968. Bar: Ohio 1968, Fla. 1975, U.S. Dist. Ct. (no. dist.) Ohio 1968. Law clk. to Hon. William J. Thomas U.S. Dist. Ct. (no. dist.) Ohio, Cleve., 1968-69; atty. Spieth, Bell, McCurdy & Newell, Cleve., 1969-73; ptnr. Conway, Patton, Bouhall & Reichard, Cleve., 1973—; bd. dirs. Sachem, Inc., Austin, Tex., Alloy Engring. Co., Berea, Ohio. Trustee Magnificat H.S., Rocky River, Ohio, 1985—, St. Ignatius H.S., Cleve., 1995—. Mem. Fla. Bar Assn., Ohio Bar Assn., Cleve. Bar Assn., Cuyahoga County Bar Assn., Westwood Country Club. Republican. Roman Catholic. Avocations: tennis, golf, wine collecting. Home: 18560 High Pkwy Rocky River OH 44116 Office: Conway Patton Bouhall & Reichard 1990 Huntington Bldg Cleveland OH 44115

REICHARDT, PAUL BERNARD, dean, chemistry educator; b. St. Louis, Aug. 15, 1943; s. Bernard George and Elaine Charlotte (Schmudde) R.; m. Cordelia Morris Hufnagel, Apr. 27, 1968; children: Laura, Rebecca, Daniel. BS, Davidson Coll., 1965; PhD in Organic Chemistry, U. Wis., 1969. Post-doctoral rsch. assoc. Yale U., New Haven, 1969-71, instr., 1971; asst. prof. Ohio State U., Columbus, 1971-72; asst. prof. chemistry U. Alaska, Fairbanks, 1972-75, assoc. prof. chemistry, 1975-81, prof. chemistry, 1981—, dean coll. natural scis., 1991—; head dept. chemistry U. Alaska, Fairbanks, 1978-82, 88-90, interim dean coll. natural scis., 1990-91, interim provost, 1993-94; interim dir. U. Alaska Mus., 1992-93; mem. Gov.'s Sci. & Engring. Adv. Com., 1986-90, Alaska 2000 Sci. Standards Com., 1992-93. Contbr. articles to profl. jours., chpts. to books and monographs. Named one of Outstanding Young Men of Am., Jaycees, 1980; recipient Inspirational Tchr. award U. Alaska at Fairbanks Alumni Assn., 1982. Mem. AAAS, Am. Chem. Soc., Internat. Soc. Chem. Ecology, Phi Beta Kappa, Sigma Xi (pres. local chpt. 1994-95), Phi Kappa Phi. Presbyterian. Avocations: fishing, camping, hiking. Office: University of Alaska Coll Natural Scis 358 Natural Scis Bldg Fairbanks AK 99775-5940

REICHART, STUART RICHARD, lawyer; b. N.Y.C., Nov. 18, 1924; s. Stanley and Rae (Wein) R.; m. Joan Feirtag, Mar. 28, 1981. LLB, Bklyn. Law Sch., 1948; LLM, NYU, 1951. Bar: N.Y. 1949, D.C. 1971, U.S. Supreme Ct. Adminstrv. judge Armed Services Bd. Contract Appeals, Washington, 1966-72; asst. gen. counsel for procurement USAF, Washington, 1972-75, dep. gen. counsel, 1975-78, gen. counsel, 1978-81; of counsel Fried, Frank, Harris, Shriver & Jacobson, Washington, 1982-90; ind. cons., 1991—; instr. govt. procurement Ohio State U., U. Dayton, U. Md., 1960-70. Contbr. legal articles on govt. procurement to profl. jours. Served with AUS, 1942-45; served to col. USAF, 1951-71. Decorated Legion of Merit, D.F.C., Air medal with silver oak leaf cluster, Purple Heart; recipient Disting. Civilian Service medals Dept. Air Force, 1979, Dept. Def., 1982, Stuart R. Reichart award USAF, 1982. Mem. ABA, Fed. Bar Assn. Lodge: Masons. Avocations: bridge, tennis, golf. Home and Office: 8000 Grand Teton Dr Potomac MD 20854-4074 also: 16873C Isle of Palm Dr Delray Beach FL 33484-6941

REICHARTZ, W. DAN, hotel executive; b. 1946. Exec. Hilton Hotels Corp., N.Y.C., 1965-76, 85-86; pres., treas. Va. Hot Springs Inc., Hot Springs Telephone Co. & Devel. Co., 1976-85; pres., CEO Caesars Palace, Las Vegas, 1987—. Office: Caesars Palace 3570 Las Vegas Blvd S Las Vegas NV 89109-8924*

REICHE, FRANK PERLEY, lawyer, former federal commissioner; b. Hartford, Conn., May 8, 1929; s. Karl Augustus and LaFetra (Perley) R.; m. Janet Taylor, Sept. 26, 1953; children: Cynthia Reiche Schumacker, Dean S. AB, Williams Coll., 1951; LLB, Columbia U., 1959; MA, George Washington U., 1959; LLM in Taxation, NYU, 1966. Bar: N.J. 1960, D.C. 1981. Assoc. Stryker, Tams & Dill, Newark, 1959-61; assoc. Smith, Stratton, Wise & Heher, Princeton, N.J., 1962-64, ptnr., 1964-79; commr. Fed. Election Commn., Washington, 1979-85; chmn. Fed. Election Commn., 1982; ptnr. Katzenbach, Gildea & Rudner, Lawrenceville, N.J., 1986-93; pvt. practice law Princeton, N.J., 1993—. Trustee Westminster Choir Coll., Princeton, 1974-86, Ctr. Theol. Inquiry, Princeton, 1991—, Wells Coll., Aurora, N.Y., 1994—; mem. planned giving com. Williams Coll., Williamstown, Mass., 1973-87, nat. chmn. planned giving, 1983-87. Lt. USN, 1952-56. Mem. ABA, D.C. Bar Assn., N.J. Bar Assn., Am. Coll. Trust and Estate Counsel (N.J. state chair 1995—). Republican. Presbyterian. Clubs: Washington Golf and Country, Capitol Hill.

REICHEK, JESSE, artist; b. Bklyn., Aug. 16, 1916; s. Morris and Celia (Bernstein) R.; m. Laure Guyot, May 16, 1950; children—Jonathan, Joshua. Student, Inst. Design, Chgo., 1941-42; diploma, Academie Julian, Paris, 1951. Instr. dept. architecture U. Mich., Ann Arbor, 1946-47; prof. Inst. Design Ill. Inst. Tech., Chgo., 1951-53; prof. dept. architecture U. Calif., Berkeley, 1953-87, prof. emeritus, 1987—; cons. Nat. Design Inst. Ford Found. project, Ahmedabad, India, 1963, San Francisco Redevel. Agy. Embarcadero Center, 1966—; lectr. Nat. Inst. Architects, Rome, 1960, U. Florence, 1960, U. Naples, 1960, Israel Inst. Tech., 1960, Greek Architects Soc., Athens, 1960, U. Belgrade, 1960, MIT, 1965, U. N.Mex., 1964, Am. Cultural Center, Paris, 1960, 64, Gujarat Inst. Engrs. and Architects, 1963, U. Colo., 1961, Harvard, 1962, U. Minn., 1962, U. Coll. London, 1967, Inst. Contemporary Arts, London, 1967, Ecole Nationale des Beaux-Arts, 1967; artist in residence Tamarind Lithography Workshop, 1966, Am. Acad. in Rome, 1971-72; research prof. Creative Arts Inst. U. Calif., 1966-67; artist in residence IBM Los Angeles Sci. Center, 1970-71. Exhibited one man shows at, Galerie Cahiers d'Art Paris, 1951, 59, 68, U. Calif. at Berkeley, 1954, Betty Parsons Gallery, N.Y.C., 1958, 59, 63, 65, 67, 69, 70, Molton Gallery, London, 1962, Am. Culture Center, Florence, Italy, 1962, Bennington Coll., 1963, U. N.Mex., 1966, U. So. Calif., 1967, Axiom Gallery, London, 1968, Yoseido Gallery, Tokyo, 1968, Los Angeles County Mus. Art, 1971; exhibited in group shows, Bklyn. Mus., 1959, Mus. Modern Art, N.Y.C., 1962, 65, 69, Knox-Albright Art Gallery, 1962, Art Inst. Chgo., 1963, Cin. Art Mus., 1966, Balt. Art Mus., 1966, Yale Art Gallery, 1967, Grand Palais, Paris, 1970, Nat. Mus. Art, Santiago, Chile, 1970, art and tech. exhibit, Los Angeles County Mus. Art, 1971, Maeght Found., St. Paul de Vence, France, 1971, Mus. Modern Art, Paris, 1971; represented in permanent collections, Mus. Modern Art, Art Inst. Chgo., Bibliotheque Nationale, Paris, Victoria & Albert Mus., London, Los Angeles County Art Mus., Grunwald Graphic Arts Found., U. Calif. at Los Angeles, San Diego Mus. Art, Amon Carter Mus., Fort Worth; Author: Jesse Reichek-Dessins, 1960, La Monte de la Nuit, 1961, Fontis, 1961, Etcetera, 1965, Le Bulletin Des Baux, 1972; e.g., 1976. Served to capt. C.E. AUS, 1942-46. Home: 5925 Red Hill Rd Petaluma CA 94952-9437

REICHEK, MORTON ARTHUR, retired magazine editor, writer; b. N.Y.C., Nov. 2, 1924; s. Meyer and Katherine (Rabinowitz) R.; m. Sybil Green, June 13, 1953; children: Amy, Marjorie (dec.), James. BS, NYU, 1948; postgrad., Am. U., 1948-50. Press officer, editor U.S. Fish & Wildlife Svc., Washington, 1948-49, U.S. Br. Labor Statistics, Washington, 1949-51, U.S. Nat. Prodn. Authority, Washington, 1951-52; Washington corr. McGraw-Hill Mags., 1952-63, Newhouse Newspapers, 1963-65; assoc. editor Forbes, N.Y.C., 1965-66; assoc. editor Bus. WeeK, N.Y.C., 1966-76, sr. editor, writer, 1978-88; dir. editorial svcs. Gulf & Western. Industries, Inc., N.Y.C., 1976-78; U.S. rep. NATO journalist program U.S. Dept. State, France, 1957; adj. lectr. Columbia U. Graduate Sch. Journalism, N.Y.C., 1981. Contbr. articles to N.Y. Times Mag., New Republic, others. Staff sgt. U.S. Army, 1943-46, China-Burma-India. Journalist fellow Carnegie-Mellon U. Grad. Sch. Indsl. Adminstrn., 1979; grantee NEH, 1980. Mem. Nat. Press. Club, Nat. Soc. Journalists and Authors, Nat. Book Critics Circle. Jewish. Avocations: tennis, computers, music. Home: 1 Worchester Dr Cranbury NJ 08512-4723 Home (winter): 14388 Emerald Lake Dr Apt 1 Delray Beach FL 33446-3382

REICHEL, WALTER EMIL, advertising executive; b. Irvington, N.J., Dec. 12, 1935; s. Walter Edwin and Flora Maria (Pfister) R.; m. Priscilla Tedesco, Feb. 1, 1969; 1 son, Bradley Joseph. B.A., Columbia, 1959; M.A., N.Y. U., 1971, M. Philosophy, 1989, postgrad., 1989—. With Benton & Bowles, N.Y.C., 1959-67; v.p. Benton & Bowles, 1965-67, asso. media dir., 1965-67; with Ted Bates & Co., Inc. N.Y.C., 1967-87; sr. v.p. Ted Bates & Co., Inc., N.Y.C., 1973-82; exec. dir. media and programs Ted Bates & Co., Inc., 1974-82, exec. v.p., 1982-87, dir.; cons., 1987-91; mng. ptnr. A.S. Link Inc., N.Y.C., 1991—. Mem. Advt. Rsch. Found. Home: 449 1/2 Henry St Brooklyn NY 11231-3011 Office: 805 3rd Ave New York NY 10022-7513

REICHERT, BRUCE ROBERT, travel industry executive; b. Chgo., Dec. 7, 1942; s. Walter Frederick and Helen (Wellman) R.; m. Marcia Pion-Bobadilla. BSC in Acctg., DePaul U., 1973; MBA, Roosevelt U., 1976. Fin. dir. Milton Bradley Ltd., London, 1974-76; mgr. cost devel. Rockwell Corp., Pitts., 1976-77; controller, plastics div. ITT Corp., Madison Heights, Mich., 1978-80; mgr. fin. control ITT Corp., N.Y.C., 1980-82, mgr. cost control, 1982-84; controller Summagraphics, Fairfield, Conn., 1984-86; pres. Mgmt. Controls Corp., Fairfield, 1986-91, Leisure Group Ltd., Milford, Conn., 1991—; bd. dirs. Leisure Group Ltd., URW, Inc.; chmn. bd. Worldhotel Co. Author: U.S. Lady, 1966, One-Up Production, 1986, Autofact '87, 1987, Flow Dynamics, 1987; editor Spotlight on Cost newsletter, 1985; columnist Paper Age MAg. Served with U.S. Army, 1966-69. Home: 15C Heritage Sound Milford CT 06460 Office: Leisure Group Ltd 344 W Main St Milford CT 06460-2561

REICHERT, DAVID, lawyer; b. Cin., Nov. 23, 1929; s. Victor E. and Louise F. (Feibel) R.; m. Marilyn Frankel, May 31, 1959; children—James G., Steven F., William M. B.A., Bowling Green State U., 1951; J.D., U. Cin., 1954. Bar: Ohio 1954, U.S. Supreme Ct. 1963. Ptnr. firm Porter, Wright, Morris & Arthur, formerly sr. ptnr. Reichert, Strauss & Reed and predecessors, Cin.; dir. numerous corps. Monthly columnist: Scrap Age mag, 1966-74; bd. editors: U. Cin. Law Rev, 1953-54. Pres. brotherhood Rockdale Temple, Cin., 1960-61, temple treas., 1973-75, v.p., 1975-79, pres., 1979-81; mem. Amberley Village Planning Commn. & Zoning Bd. Appeals, 1972-79, Ohio Solid Waste Adv. Group, 1974; treas. Contemporary Arts Ctr., Cin., 1973-75, pres., 1976-77, trustee, 1982-88; trustee Cin. Art Mus., 1978-93, v.p., 1992-93, chmn. vis. com. for contemporary art, 1990-92; trustee Jewish Publ. Soc., 1980-86, Cin. Sculpture Coun., 1984-87; mem. acquisitions com. Miami U. Art Mus., 1982-85. Mem. Cin. Print and Drawing Cir. (pres. 1974-76), The Literary Club (sec. 1988-91, v.p. 1991-92, pres. 1992-93), Losantiville Country Club (bd. govs. 1985-92, sec. 1986-90, pres. 1990-92), Omicron Delta Kappa, Sigma Tau Delta, Phi Delta Phi, Zeta Beta Tau. Office: Porter Wright Morris & Arthur 250 E 5th St Ste 2200 Cincinnati OH 45202-4103

REICHERT, JACK FRANK, manufacturing company executive; b. West Allis, Wis., Sept. 27, 1930; s. Arthur Andrew and Emily Bertha (Wallinger) R.; m. Corrine Violet Helf, Apr. 5, 1952; children: Susan Marie, John Arthur. Cert. mktg., U. Wis., Milw., 1957; AMP, Harvard U., 1970; LLD (hon.), Marian Coll., 1994. Various mktg. positions GE, 1948-57; with Brunswick Corp., Lake Forest, Ill., 1957-95; pres. Mercury Marine div. Brunswick Corp., 1972-77; corp. v.p. Brunswick Corp., Lake Forest, 1974-77, group v.p. Marine Power Group, 1974-77, pres., COO, 1977-93; CEO Brunswick Corp., 1982-95; chmn. bd. dirs. Brunswick Corp., Lake Forest, Ill., 1983-95; dir. Brunswick Corp., 1977—; bd. dirs. The Dial Corp., Phoenix. Trustee Carroll Coll., Waukesha, Wis., 1972; indsl. chmn. Fond du Lac United Fund, 1977. With C.E. U.S. Army, 1951-53. Named Disting. Alumnus of the Yr., U. Wis., Milw. 1979, Top Chief Exec. Officer in Multi-Industry Group, Fin. World Mag., 1984; recipient Gold award in leisure industry Wall St. Transcript, 1983, 86, Bronze award in multi-industry category Wall St. Transcript, 1985, Leisure Industry Silver award, 1988. Mem. Am. Mgmt. Assn., U. Wis.-Milw. Alumni Assn., Knollwood Club, Harvard Club, Mid-Am. Club, Beta Gamma Sigma (hon.). Presbyterian. Avocations: golf, reading. Home: 580 Douglas Dr Lake Forest IL 60045-3342 Office: Brunswick Corp 1 N Field Ct Lake Forest IL 60045-4810 *To meet with any success, one must have a sense of urgency to get things done.*

REICHERT, LEO EDMUND, JR., biochemist, endocrinologist; b. N.Y.C., Jan. 9, 1932; s. Leo and Anne (Holsten) R.; m. Gerda Sihler, July 20, 1957; children: Leo, Christine, Linda, Andrew. B.S., Manhattan Coll., N.Y.C., 1955; Ph.D., Loyola U., Chgo., 1960. Asst. prof. biochemistry Emory U. Med. Sch., Atlanta, 1960-66; assoc. prof. Emory U. Med. Sch., 1966-72, prof., 1972-79; prof., chmn. dept. biochemistry Albany (N.Y.) Med. Coll., 1979-88, prof. biochemistry, 1988—; dir. human and animal hormone isolation and distbn. program (NIH), Emory U. Med. Sch., 1960-75; mem. med. adv. bd. Nat. Pituitary Agy., 1971-74; com. on glycoprotein hormones Nat. Hormone and Pituitary Program, 1968-86; mem. reproductive biology study sect. NIH, 1971-75; mem. adv. panel on cellular physiology NSF, 1983-86, div. of integrative and neuro biology, 1992; mem. WHO Expert Adv. Panel on Biol. Standardization, 1984—, Nat. Bd. Med. Examiners, Part I, 1989-91. Mem. editl. bd. Endocrinology, 1967-75, Molecular and Cellular Endocrinology, 1977-83, 90-94, Biology of Reproduction, 1968-70, 86-90, Andrology, 1983-86, Molecular Andrology, 1989—; contbr. more than 250 articles to profl. jours.; patentee in field. Served with USMC, 1950-52. List among 75 endocrinologists, 1000 scientists most cited, 1965-78. Mem. AAAS, Am. Soc. Biol. Chemists, Endocrine Soc. (Ayerst award 1970), Andrology Soc. (coun. 1983-87), Soc. for Study of Reprodn. Home: 10 Laurel Dr Albany NY 12211-1618 Office: Albany Med Coll Dept Biochemistry Albany NY 12208

REICHERT, NORMAN VERNON, financial services consultant; b. Berwyn, Ill., Apr. 17, 1921; s. John G. and Valeria (Hoffman) R.; m. Wilma Eleanor Catey, Feb. 5, 1944; children: Susan, Norman Vernon. BS, Northwestern U., 1943; MBA, Harvard Bus. Sch., 1944. CPA, Ill. Acct. Arthur Young & Co., Chgo., 1946-50; central fin. staff, controller styling div. Ford Motor Co., Dearborn, Mich., 1950-61; treas. Philco Ford Corp., Phila., 1961-69; asst. treas. United Air Lines, Inc., Chgo., 1969-72; v.p. fin. Trailer Train Co., Railbox Co., Railgon Co., Chgo., 1972-83; v.p. fin., treas. U.S. Windpower, Inc., San Francisco, 1983-86; pres. Blackhawk Fin., 1986—. Served to lt. USNR, 1943-46. Mem. AICPA, Fin. Execs. Inst., Navy League U.S., Exptl. Aircraft Assn., Union League Chgo., Knollwood Club (Lake Forest), Olympic Club San Francisco, Beta Alpha Psi, Sigma Alpha Epsilon. Home and Office: 921 Grandview Ln Lake Forest IL 60045-3913 *Each day we must start over. One cannot live on yesterday's accomplishments, but instead, must establish new goals. Last year's champion is soon forgotten as we focus on the current achiever. This is the way I try to approach each new day. And, at the end of each day, I evaluate my performance against my goals for that day.*

REICHGOTT JUNGE, EMBER D., state legislator, lawyer; b. Detroit, Aug. 22, 1953; d. Norbert Arnold and Diane (Pincich) R.; m. Michael Junge. BA summa cum laude, St. Olaf Coll., Minn., 1974; JD, Duke U., 1977; MBA, U. of St. Thomas, 1991. Bar: Minn. 1977, D.C. 1978. Assoc., Larkin, Hoffman, Daly & Lindgren, Bloomington, Minn., 1977-84; counsel Control Data Corp., Bloomington, Minn., 1984-86; atty. The Gen. Counsel, Ltd., 1987—; mem. Minn. State Senate, 1983—, chmn. legis. com. on econ. status of women, 1984-86, vice chmn. senate edn. com., 1987-88, senate majority whip, 1990-94, chmn. property tax div. senate tax com., 1991-92, chmn. senate judiciary com., 1993-94; senate asst. majority leader, 1995—, chmn. spl. subcom. on Ethical Conduct; instr. polit. sci. St. Olaf. Coll., Northfield, Minn., 1993; dir. Citizens Ind. Bank, St. Louis Park, Minn., 1993—. Host (cable TV monthly series) Legis. Report, 1985-92. Trustee, bd. dirs. N.W. YMCA, New Hope, Minn., 1983-88; Greater Mpls. Red Cross, 1988—, United Way Mpls., 1989—. Youngest woman ever elected to Minn. State Senate, 1983; recipient Woman of Yr. award North Hennepin Bus. and Prof. Women, 1983, Award for Contbn. to Human Svcs., Minn. Social Svcs. Assn., 1983, Clean Air award Minn. Lung Assn., 1988, Disting. Svc. award Mpls. Jaycees, 1984, Minn. Dept. Human Rights award, 1989, Myra Bradwell award Minn. Women Lawyers, 1993, Disting. Alumnae award Lake Conf. Schs., 1993; named One of Ten Outstanding Young Minnesotans, Minn. Jaycees, 1984, Policy Advocate of Yr. NAWBO, 1988, Woman of Achievement Twin West C. of C., 1989, Marvelous Minn. Woman, 1993. Mem. Minn. Bar Assn. (bd. govs. 1992—, Pro Bono Publico Atty. award 1990), Hennepin County Bar Assn., Corporate Counsel Assn. (v.p. 1989—), Minn. Dem. Farmer-Labor Party (state co-chair Clinton/Gore Presdl. Campaign 1992, 96, del. nat. Dem. conv. 1984, 92). Home: 7701 48th Ave N Minneapolis MN 55428-4515

REICHL, RUTH MOLLY, restaurant critic; b. N.Y.C., Jan. 16, 1948; d. Ernst and Miriam and (Brudno) R.; m. Douglas Wilder Hollis, Sept. 5, 1970 (div. 1985); married. BA, U. Mich., 1968, MA in History of Art, 1970. Chef, owner The Swallow Restaurant, Berkeley, Calif., 1973-77; food writer, editor New West mag., San Francisco, 1978-84; editor restaurant column L.A. Times, 1984-93, food editor, 1990-93; restaurant critic N.Y. Times, 1993—. Author: Mmmm: A Feastiary, 1972, The Contest Book, 1977; contbr. articles to profl. jours. Office: NY Times 229 W 43rd St New York NY 10036-3913

REICHLIN, SEYMOUR, physician, educator; b. N.Y.C., May 31, 1924; s. Henry and Celia (Rosen) R.; m. Elinor Thurman Dameshek, June 24, 1951; children: Seth David, Douglas James, Ann Elise. Student, CCNY, 1940-41; AB, Antioch Coll., 1945; MD, Washington U., St. Louis, 1948; PhD, U. London, 1954. Intern N.Y. Hosp., 1948-49; asst. resident Barnes Hosp., St. Louis, 1949-50, N.Y. Hosp., 1950-51; chief resident Barnes Hosp., 1951-52; research fellow physiology dept. Maudsley Hosp., London, Eng., 1952-54;

instr. psychiatry Washington U., 1954-55, asst. prof. psychiatry and medicine, 1955-60; pvt. practice clin. endocrinology, St. Louis, 1955-60, Rochester, 1961-69, Hartford, Conn., 1969-71, Boston, 1972—; asso. prof. medicine U. Rochester, 1960-66, prof., 1966-69; prof., head dept. med. and pediatric spltys. Sch. Medicine U. Conn., 1969-71, prof., head dept. physiology, 1971-72; prof. medicine Tufts U., 1972-96; rsch. prof. U. Ariz., 1994—; sr. physician New Eng. Med. Ctr., 1972-93, sr. endocrinologist, 1993-96; cons. Genesee and Rochester Gen. Hosp., 1960-69, Hartford Hosp., 1970—, New Britain (Conn.) Gen. Hosp., 1970-72; mem. endocrinology study sect. HIH, 1966-70; mem. adv. panel FDA, 1977-79; mem. coun. Nat. Inst. Kidney, Diabetes, Digestive Diseases, 1987-90. Mem. editl. bd. Endocrinology, 1969-74, New Eng. Jour. Medicine, 1976-79, Jour. Psychoneuroendocrinology, 1979—, Brain, Brhavior and Immunity, 1990—; contbr. articles to profl. jours., also monographs. Bd. dirs. Founds. Fund, New Haven, 1968-70; med. adv. bd. Med. Found., Boston, adv. bd. MacArthur Found., 1988. Served with AUS, 1943-44. Commonwealth Fund fellow, 1952-54, Lowell M. Palmer fellow, 1954-56. Master ACP; fellow AAAS, Am. Acad. Arts and Scis.; mem. Ctrl. Soc. Clin. Rsch., Am. Soc. Clin. Investigation, Assn. Am. Physicians, Am. Physiol. Soc., Endocrine Soc. (Eli Lilly award 1972, pres. 1975-76), Brit. Soc. Endocrinology, Am. Psychosomatic Soc., Am. Thyroid Assn., Internat. Brain Orgn., Assn. for Rsch. in Nervous and Mental Disease (pres. 1976), Pituitary Soc. (pres. 1994-95), Alpha Omega Alpha. Home: X-9 Ranch Vail AZ 85641 also: U Ariz Coll Medicine Tucson AZ 85724

REICHMAN, FREDRICK THOMAS, artist; b. Bellingham, Wash., Jan. 28, 1925; s. Frederick and Ilma Lucia (Yearing) R.; m. Michela Madelene Robbins, Sept. 24, 1955; children: Alexandra Ilma, Matthew Nathaniel. BA cum laude, U. Calif., Berkeley, 1950, MA in Art, 1952; postgrad., San Francisco Art Inst., 1946-47. Instr. art San Francisco Art Inst., 1952, U. Calif., Davis, 1963-66, Dominican Coll., San Rafael, Calif., summer 1974, Calif. Coll. Arts and Crafts, Oakland, 1976, U. Calif. extension, San Francisco, 1966—; lectr. U. Calif., Berkeley, 1953; dir. children's art classes Jr. Center Art and Sci., Oakland, 1953-64, 66-77. One-man exhbns. include Rose Rabow Galleries, San Francisco, 1958, 61, 63, 65, 69, 73, 75, San Francisco Mus. Modern Art, 1969, Benson Gallery, Bridgehampton, N.Y., 1966-72, Silvan Simone Gallery, L.A., 1971-73, Santa Barbara (Calif.) Mus. Art, 1974, Rose Rabow Galleries-James Willis Gallery, San Francisco, 1976, Gallery Paule Anglim, San Francisco, 1979-81, Chikyudo Gallery, Tokyo, 1980, Espace Doyoo, Tokyo, 1982, Ki-Do-Ai-Raku, Tokyo, 1982, Maeitetsu-Marukoshi, Kanazawa, Japan, 1982, The New Gallery, Taos, N.Mex., 1982, Charles Campbell Gallery, San Francisco, 1984, 86, David Barnett Gallery, Milw., 1985, 89, Artform Gallery, 1985, The New Gallery, Houston, 1985, Mekler Gallery Inc., L.A., 1988, Ruth Siegel Gallery, N.Y., 1991, U. Calif., Santa Cruz, Ann Porter Sesnon Art Gallery, 1991, Galerie B. Haasner, Germany, 1990, 92, 94, 96, Harcourts Contemporary, San Francisco, 1992, 95, Louis Newman Galleries, Beverly Hills, Calif., 1992, 93, 94, Horwitch Newman Gallery, Scottsdale, 1995; 2-man show, Iannetti-Lanzone Gallery, San Francisco, 1989, Miyagi Mus. Art, Sendai, Japan, 1982, R.B. Stevenson Gallery, La Jolla, 1995; 3-man show, Milw. Art Mus., 1982, group exhbns. include, Esther Robles Gallery, L.A., 1961, Whitney Mus. Am. Art traveling exhbn., 1962-63, Expo '70, Osaka, Japan, 1970, Oakland Mus., 1971, Joslyn Art Mus. traveling exhbn., 1973-74, San Francisco Mus. Modern Art, 1974, Martha Jackson Gallery, N.Y.C., 1978, New Gallery, 1981, Forum Gallery, N.Y.C., 1984, Smith Andersen Gallery, Palo Alto, 1986, Ruth Siegel Gallery, N.Y.C., 1986, Kultorvert Galerie, Copenhagen, 1986, Richmond (Calif.) Art Ctr., 1987, Nat. Mus. Am. Art, Washington, 1989, Arte 7, San Francisco, 1990, Harcourts Contemporary, San Francisco, 1991, Kouros Gallery, N.Y.C., 1993, Berkeley Art Ctr., 1993, Estudio Moyo Coyatzin, San Jose, Costa Rica; represented in permanent collections throughout U.S., including Nat. Mus. Am. Art, San Francisco Mus. Modern Art, Oakland Mus., Univ. Art Mus., Berkeley, Santa Barbara Mus. Art, Milw. Art Mus., Ulrich Mus. Art, Wichita, Fine Arts Museums San Francisco, Okla. Art Center, Oklahoma City, Bank Am. World Hdqrs., San Francisco, Achenbach Found., San Francisco, Mills Coll. Art Gallery, Oakland, U. Calif., San Francisco; works rep. art publs.; commns. include stage set for, San Francisco Mime Troupe, The Exception to the Rule, 1965; mural, Boche Pediatrics Outpatient Clinic, Stanford U. Med. Sch., 1961, San Francisco Civic Center, 1968. Served with USNR, 1943-45. Recipient Purchase prize San Francisco Art Festival, 1964, One-Man Show award, 1968; Irving prize Am. Wit and Humor U. Calif., Berkeley, 1951; Taussig traveling fellow U. Calif., Berkeley, 1952; profiled in 50 West Coast Artists by Henry Hopkins, 1981, Art in the San Francisco Bay Area 1945-80 by Thomas Albright, 1985. *There is a unique energy that exists on the Pacific Coast. It is different from our eastern seaboard, different from Europe and the Orient—yet it comes out of all these sources to create inspiration and fresh insights. The light and the land, the atmosphere that exist here, have their own particular ambience. I feel a part of this energy.*

REICHMAN, JOEL H., retail executive. With The GAP, San Francisco, 1971-76, Slak Shak Inc., Boston, 1971-76; with Designs, Inc., 1976-85, exec. v.p., 1985-93, dir., 1987; pres., COO Designs Inc., Chestnut Hill, Mass., 1993-94; pres., CEO, 1994—. Office: Designs Inc 1244 Boylston St Chestnut Hill MA 02167-2115

REICHMAN, LEE BRODERSOHN, physician; b. N.Y.C., June 25, 1938; s. Theodore and Elinore (Brodersohn) R.; m. Rose Ehrinpreis, Oct. 9, 1965; children: Daniel Mark, Deborah Gar. AB, Oberlin Coll., 1960; MD, NYU, 1964; MPH, Johns Hopkins U., 1971. Intern Bellevue Hosp., I Med. Div., N.Y.C., 1964-65, resident, 1967-68; resident Harlem Hosp. Ctr., N.Y.C., 1968-69; fellow in pulmonary medicine Harlem Hosp. Ctr., 1969-70; dir. Bur. Tb, Bur. Chronic Disease, N.Y.C. Health Dept., 1971-73, asst. commr. health, 1973-74; assoc. prof. medicine N.J. Med. Sch., Newark, 1974-78, prof. medicine, 1978—; dir. pulmonary div. U. Medicine and Dentistry N.J.-N.J. Med. Sch. Univ. Hosp., 1974-92; exec. dir. N.J. Med. Sch. Nat. Tuberculosis Ctr., 1993—; cons. CDC, Atlanta, 1970—; prin. investigator pulmonary complications of HIV Infection, Nat. Heart Lung Blood Inst., 1987-95, Model TB Ctr. for Disease Control and Prevention, 1993—, Nat. Rsch. Consortium (CDC), 1994—. Contbr. articles to profl. jours. Bd. dirs. Art Ctr. No. N.J., 1979-86; chmn. N.J. Commn. on Smoking of Health, 1986-87; mem. N.J. TB Adv. Coun., 1976—, chmn. 1991-93; chair Nat. Coalition for Elemination of Tuberculosis, 1992—; mem. N.J. Clean Air Coun., 1987. With USPHS, 1965-67. Recipient Nat. Heart Lung and Blood Inst., Pulmonary Acad. career award, 1975-80, Preventive Pulmonary Acad. career award, 1987-92, Tb Acad. career award, 1993—. Fellow ACP, Am. Coll. Chest Physicians (gov. 1984-90, pres. N.J. chpt. 1982-84), Acad. Medicine of N.J.; mem. Am. Thoracic Soc., Internat. Union Against Tb and Lung Disease (exec. com. 1982-92, vice chair exec. com. 1989-91), Am. Lung Assn. (nat. bd. dirs. 1980-94, pres. elect 1991-92, pres. 1992-93, past pres. 1993-94), N.J. Thoracic Soc. (pres. 1982-84), Am. Lung Assn. N.J. (bd. dirs. 1976—, pres. 1984-86). Office: 65 Bergen St Ste Gb1 Newark NJ 07107-3001

REICHMAN, NANCI SATIN, oil company owner; b. Tulsa, July 7, 1939; d. Jack Harold and Tybie Mary (Davis) Satin; m. Louis Reichman, Dec. 25, 1960 (dec. Feb. 1972); children: David Michael, Jill Satin; life ptnr. Phillip M. Citrin. Student, Sarah Lawrence Coll., Bronxville, N.Y., 1957-59; cert. Jungian psychology, C.G. Jung Inst., Evanston, Ill., 1988. Fashion model Miss Jackson's, Tulsa, 1969-70; pres. LIR Investments, Tulsa, 1972-78; pres., dir. devel. Tymar Oil Co., Tulsa and Santa Fe, N.Mex., 1990—; owner ind. oil prodn. Chgo., 1972—; audio tape lectr for various workshops. Pres. C.G. Jung Inst., Evanston, Ill., 1980-81, 81-82, 84-85, also mem. adv. bd.; v.p. Tulsa Jr. Philharm., 1968; sec. Tulsa Ballet, 1968; mem. Women's Forum N.Mex., 1996—; bd. dirs. Found. Santa Fe Cmty. Coll., 1995—. Avocations: poetry writing, travel, reading, philanthropy. Home: 653 Canyon Rd # 4 Santa Fe NM 87501

REICHMAN, OMER JAMES, ecology educator; b. Tampa, Fla., Jan. 4, 1947; m. Jessica Hagemann, 1982. BA, Tex. Tech. U., 1968, MS, 1970; PhD, No. Ariz. U., 1974. Instr. biology No. Ariz. U., 1972-74; rsch. ecologist Mus. No. Ariz., 1975-81; from asst. prof. to prof. Kans. State U., Manhattan, 1981—; coord. Konza Prairie Rsch. Nat. Area Kans. State U., 1990—; Fellow U. Utah, 1974-75; ecol. program dir. NSF, 1990-91; trustee Biosis Corp., 1992—. Mem. AAAS, Ecol. Soc. Am. (coun. 1993—), Am. Soc. Mammalogists (bd. dirs. 1988—), Am. Soc. Nature, Sigma Xi, Animal Behavior Soc. Office: Kansas St Univ Konza Prairie Research Nat Area Div of Bio Ackert Hall Manhattan KS 66506 Office: Kans State U Div Biology Ackert Hall Manhattan KS 66506*

REICHMANIS, ELSA, chemist; b. Melbourne, Victoria, Australia, Dec. 9, 1953; came to U.S., 1962; d. Peteris and Nina (Meiers) R.; m. Francis Joseph Purcell, June 2, 1979; children: Patrick William, Elizabeth Anne, Edward Andrew, Thomas Alexander. BS in Chemistry, Syracuse U., 1972, PhD in Chemistry, 1975. Postdoctoral intern Syracuse (N.Y.) U., 1975-76, Chaim Weizmann rsch. fellow, 1976-78; mem. tech. staff AT&T Bell Labs., Murray Hill, N.J., 1978-84, supr. radiation sensitive materials and applications, 1984-94, head organic and polymer materials, 1994-95; head polymer and organic materials Lucent Techs., Bell Labs., New Providence, N.J., 1996—; mem. panel on advanced materials. Japanese Tech. Evaluation Prog., NSF, Washington, 1986, mem. com. to survey materials. rsch. opportunities and needs for electronic industry, Nat. Rsch. Coun., 1986, Nat. Materials Adv. Bd., 1993—. Editor: The Effects of Radiation on High Tech Polymers, 1989, Polymers in Microlithography, 1989, Irradiation of Polymer Materials, 1993, Microelectronics Technology: Polymers for Advanced Imaging and Packaging, 1995; patentee in field; contbr. numerous articles to profl. jours. Recipient Soc. of Women Engrs. Achievement award, 1993. Mem. AAAS, Nat. Acad. Engring. (elected mem.), Am. Chem. Soc. (mem.-at-large 1986-90, sec. 1991-92, vice chair 1993, chair-elect 1994, chair 1995, polymer materials sci. and engring divsn. 1991—), Soc. for Photo-optical Engrs. Avocations: music, reading, needlepoint. Office: Bell Labs Lucent Techs 600 Mountain Ave # ID 260 New Providence NJ 07974-2008

REICHSTETTER, ARTHUR CHARLES, banker; b. Providence, June 14, 1946; s. Edward Arthur and Joyce Marie (Scull) R.; children: Daniella Lynn, Hans Francis and Karl Arthur (twins). B.S., U. R.I., 1972; M.B.A., Dartmouth Coll., 1974. Assoc. 1st Boston Corp., N.Y.C., 1974-76, asst. v.p., 1976-78, v.p., 1978-82; mng. dir. The First Boston Corp., N.Y.C., 1982-93, Merrill Lynch & Co., N.Y.C., Md., 1993—. Served to 1st lt. U.S. Army, 1967-69.

REICIN, RONALD IAN, lawyer; b. Chgo., Dec. 11, 1942; s. Frank Edward and Abranita (Rome) R.; m. Alyta Friedland, May 23, 1965; children—Eric, Kael. B.B.A., U. Mich., 1964, M.B.A., 1967, J.D. cum laude, 1967. Bar: Ill. 1967, U.S. Tax Ct. 1967; CPA, Ill. Mem. staff Price Waterhouse & Co., Chgo., 1966; ptnr. Jenner & Block, Chgo., 1967—. Bd. dirs. Nat. Kidney Found., Ill., 1978—, v.p., 1992-95, pres., 1995—; bd. dirs. Ruth Page Found., 1985—, v.p., 1990—; bd. dirs. Scoliosis Assn. Chgo., 1981-90, Kohl Children's Mus., 1991-95. Mem. Chgo. Bar Assn., Internat. Conf. Shopping Ctrs., ABA, Ill. Bar Assn., Chgo. Mortgage Attys. Assn., Phi Kappa Phi, Beta Gamma Sigma, Beta Alpha Psi. Clubs: Executive, Legal (Chgo.). Home: 1916 Berkeley Rd Highland Park IL 60035-2725 Office: Jenner & Block 1 E IBM Plz 41st Fl Chicago IL 60611-3586

REICKERT, ERICK ARTHUR, automotive executive; b. Newport, Tenn., Aug. 30, 1935; s. Frederick Arthur and Reva M. (Irish) R.; m. Diane Lois Comens, June 10, 1961 (div. Jan. 1979); children: Craig A., Laura L.; m. Heather Kathleen Ross, Sept. 1, 1982. BSEE, Northwestern U., 1958; MBA, Harvard U., 1965. Various positions Ford Motor Co., Dearborn, Mich., 1965-73, exec. dir. small car planning, 1979-84; v.p. export ops. Ford Motor Co., Brentwood, Eng., 1973-79; v.p. advance product devel. Chrysler Motors, Detroit, 1984-86, v.p. program mgmt., 1986-87; chmn., mng. dir. Chrysler Mexico, 1987-89; chmn., CEO Acustar Inc., Troy, Mich., 1990-91; v.p. power train ops. Chrysler Corp., Auburn Hills, Mich., 1991-92; pres., CEO New Venture Gear Inc., Troy, 1992—; bd. dirs. Truck Components Inc., Rockford, Ill., 1994-95. Bd. dirs. Jr. Achievement of S.E. Mich., Detroit, 1992—, Children's Ctr., Detroit, 1993—; regent for S.E. Mich., Northwestern U., Evanston, Ill., 1994—. Mem. Soc. Automotive Engrs., Engring. Soc. Detroit, Harvard Bus. Sch. Club of Detroit. Avocations: photography, travel, sailing, skiing. Office: New Venture Gear Inc 1650 Research Dr Ste 300 Troy MI 48083-2100

REID, ANTONIO (L. A. REID), musician, songwriter. With musical group The Deele; songwriter with Kenny Edmonds, also occasionally with Darryl Simmons. Songs include Girlfriend, 1987, Rock Steady, 1987, Two Occasions, 1987, Don't Be Cruel, 1988, Love Saw It, 1988, Lover In Me, 1988, Every Little Step, 1988 (Grammy award nomination for R&B Song of Yr. 1989), Dial My Heart, 1988, Way You Love Me, 1988, Secret Rendezvous, 1988, Superwoman, 1988, Roses Are Red, 1988, Can't Stop, 1989, My Kinda Girl, 1989, It's No Crime, 1989, On Our Own, 1989, Ready or Not, 1989, Tender Lover, 1989, Giving You the Benefit, 1990, I'm Your Baby Tonight, 1990. Office: Kear Music care Carter Turner & Co 9229 W Sunset Blvd West Hollywood CA 90069-3402

REID, BELMONT MERVYN, brokerage house executive; b. San Jose, Calif., May 17, 1927; s. C. Belmont and Mary Irene (Kilfoyl) R. BS in Engring., San Jose State U., 1950, postgrad.; m. Evangeline Joan Rogers, June 1, 1952. Pres., Lifetime Realty Corp., San Jose, 1969-77, Lifetime Fin. Planning Corp., San Jose, 1967-77; founder, chmn. bd. Belmont Reid & Co., Inc., San Jose, 1960-77; pres., registered investment advisor JOBEL Fin. Inc., Carson City, Nev., 1980—; pres., chmn. bd. Data-West Systems, Inc., 1984-85. County chmn. 1982-85, Carson City Rep. Cen. Com., treas., 1979-81; chmn. Carson City Gen. Obligation Bond Commn., 1986—; rural county chmn. Nev. Rep. Cen. Com., 1984-88; mem. Carson City Charter Rev. Com., 1986-91, chmn., 1988-91. With USN, 1945-46, 51-55. Decorated Air medals. Mem. Nat. Assn. Securities Dealers, Mcpl. Securities Rulemaking Bd., Carson City C. of C. (pres. 1986-87, bd. dir. 1982-88), Capital Club of Carson City, Rotary (chpt. sec. 1983-84, 86-87, pres. 1988-89, Paul Harris fellow). Home: 610 Bonanza Dr Carson City NV 89706-0201 Office: 711 E Washington St Carson City NV 89701-4063

REID, CHARLES ADAMS, III, lawyer; b. Plainfield, N.J., Apr. 21, 1947; s. Charles Adams Jr. and Gertrude C. (Egan) R.; m. Teresa Keenan, May 11, 1974. BA, Colgate U., 1969; JD, Columbia U., 1974. Bar: N.Y. 1974, U.S. Dist. Ct. (ea. and so. dists.) N.Y. 1975, U.S. Dist. Ct. N.J. 1976, U.S. Ct. Appeals (3d cir.) 1983, U.S. Ct. Appeals (fed. cir.) 1989, U.S. Ct. Appeals (2d cir.) 1991. Law clk. to hon. John R. Bartels U.S. Dist. Ct. (ea. dist.) N.Y., Bklyn., 1974-75; assoc. Coudert Bros., N.Y.C., 1975-77, Shanley & Fisher, Newark, 1977-82; ptnr. Shanley & Fisher, Newark and Morristown, N.J., 1983—. Mem. planning bd. Peapack-Gladstone, N.J., 1984-88, chmn., 1987-88; bd. dirs. Morris Ctr. YMCA, Cedar Knolls, N.J., 1986-93. Served with U.S. Army, 1970-72, Vietnam. Mem. ABA (litigation sect.), N.J. Bar Assn., Morris County Bar Assn., Essex County Bar Assn., Morristown Club, Park Avenue Club (Florham Park). Home: PO Box 398 Gladstone NJ 07934-0398 Office: Shanley & Fisher PC 131 Madison Ave Morristown NJ 07960-6086

REID, CHARLES MURRY, insurance company executive. CEO, pres. United Guaranty Corp., Greensboro, N.C., 1981—. Office: United Guaranty Corp 230 N Elm St Greensboro NC 27401-2436*

REID, CHARLES PHILLIP PATRICK, academic administrator, researcher, educator; b. Columbia, Mo., Jan. 8, 1940; s. Charles Henry and Fern Elnora (Chorlton) R.; m. Miriam Davis, July 17, 1961; children: Clayton Patrick, Miriam. BSF, U. Mo., 1961; MF, Duke U., 1966, PhD, 1968. Asst. prof. dept. forest and wood scis. Colo. State U., Ft. Collins, 1969-73, assoc. prof. dept. forest and wood scis., 1973-77, prof. dept. forest and wood scis., 1977-86; prof., chmn. dept. forestry U. Fla., Gainesville, 1986-92, interim dir. Sch. Forest Resources and Conservation, 1991-92; prof., dir. Sch. Renewable Natural Resources U. Ariz., Tucson, 1992—; vis. faculty mem. dept. botany Sheffield (Eng.) U., fall 1973; vis. scientist div. of soils Commonwealth Sci. and Indsl. Rsch. Orgn., Glen Osmond, South Australia, 1976-77; sr. Fulbright fellow dept. microbiology U. Innsbruck, Austria, 1985-86; chmn. working group on root physiology and symbiosis Internat. Union Forestry Rsch. Orgns., 1984-88. Contbr. articles to profl. jours. Copres. Barton Elem. Parent Tchr. Orgn., Ft. Collins, 1979-80; bd. dirs. Vol. Clearing House, Ft. Collins, 1974-76, Fla. 4-H Found., Gainesville, 1988-89. Lt. (j.g.) USNR, 1961-64, comdr. USNR, ret. Mem. AAAS, Ecol. Soc. Am., Soc. Am. Foresters, Nat. Assn. Profl. Forestry Schs. and Colls. (exec. com. 1994—), Sertoma (treas., bd. dirs. Ft. Collins chpt. 1972-75), Rotary. Republican. Episcopalian. Office: U Ariz Sch Renewable Natural Resources Bioscience East Tucson AZ 85721

REID, CLARICE DELORES, physician; b. Birmingham, Ala., Nov. 21, 1931; d. Noah Edgar, Sr., and Willie Mae (Brown) Wills; m. Arthur Joseph Reid, Jr., June 11, 1955; children: Kevin, Sheila, Jill, Clarice A. BS, Talladega Coll., 1952; cert. and Degree Med. Tech., Meharry Med. Coll., 1954; MD, U. Cin., 1959. Med. technologist Jewish Hosp., Cin., 1954-55, 57-59; intern, Jewish Hosp., Cin., 1959-60; resident, Jewish Hosp. and Children's Hosp., Cin., 1960-62; practice medicine specializing in pediatrice, Cin., 1962-68; dir. pediatric edn. Jewish Hosp., Cin., 1968-69, chmn. dept. pediatrics, 1969-70; dep. dir. sickle cell disease, USPHS, Rockville, Md., 1973-76; chief sickle cell disease NIH, Bethesda, Md., 1976-94, dir. divsn. blood disease and resources; nat. coordinator sickle cell disease program, 1994—; med. cons. USPHS, Rockville, 1971-73. Contbr. chpts. to books; editor proceedings, 1977. Named Outstanding Student, Meharry Med. Coll., 1954, Pres.' award, 1980; recipient NIH Dir.'s award, 1979, Pres. Meritorious Exec. award, 1991; charter mem. sr. Exec. Service, 1979. Mem. Acad. Pediatrics, Nat. Med. Assn., Am. Soc. Hematology. Roman Catholic. Club: Links. Home: 9715 Fernwood Rd Bethesda MD 20817-1554 Office: DHHS Nat Heart Lung & Blood Inst Blood Diseases and Resources 6701 Rockledge Dr Bethesda MD 20892-7950

REID, DANIEL JAMES, public relations executive; b. Grand Rapids, Mich., Sept. 7, 1960; s. Robert Alexander and Janette Helen (Hickey) R.; m. Meredith Christine Ryan, Apr. 30, 1994. BA, Mich. State U., 1983. Sr. account exec. Burson-Marsteller, Chgo., 1983-88; group dir. Ogilvy & Mather, Chgo., 1988-90; sr. ptnr., nat. dir. Fin. Rels. Bd., Inc., Chgo., 1990—; prodr. Stas. WLAV-WTWN, Grand Rapids, 1980-81. Contbr. articles to profl. publs. and newspapers. Recipient Bronze Anvil award Pub. Rels. Soc. Am., 1984, creative excellence award U.S. Film Festival, 1984, 87, gold award Fin. World mag., 1990-94, numerous others. Mem. Nat. Investor Rels. Inst., Union League Club Chgo. Republican. Roman Catholic. Office: Fin Rels Bd Inc 875 N Michigan Ave Chicago IL 60611-1803

REID, DAVID EVANS, pipeline company executive; b. St. Thomas, Ont., Can., Jan. 10, 1943; s. Murray Reid and Betty Evans; m. Nancy Blake, Dec. 6, 1969; children: Lindsay, Graeme. BSc with honors, Queen's U., Kingston, Ont., 1965; MASc, Toronto (Ont.) U., 1967. Registered profl. engr., Ont., Alta. Various positions in head and field offices TransCanada PipeLines, Toronto and Winnipeg, Man., 1967-89; v.p. ops. TransCanada PipeLines, Toronto, 1989-90; v.p. for engring. TransCanada PipeLines, Calgary, Alta., 1990—. Mem. Assn. Profl. Engrs. in Province Ont., Assn. Profl. Engrs., Geologists and Geophysicists Alta., Glencoe Golf and Country Club, Glencoe Club. Office: TransCanada PipeLines Ltd, 111 5th Ave SW, Calgary, AB Canada T2P 4K5

REID, DONNA JOYCE, small business owner; b. Springfield, Tenn., June 25, 1954; d. Leonard Earl Reid and Joyce (Robertson) Kirby; m. Kenneth Bruce Sadler, June 26, 1976 (div. Apr. 1980); m. John Christopher Moulton, Oct. 18, 1987 (div. Dec. 1992); m. Peter Leatherland, Apr. 3, 1993. Student, Austin Peay State U., Clarksville, Tenn., 1972-75. Show writer, producer WTVF-TV (CBS affiliate), Nashville, 1977-83, promotion producer, 1983-85, on-air promotion mgr., 1985-86; gen. mgr. Steadi-Film Corp., Nashville, 1986-90; co-owner Options Internat., Nashville, 1990—. Big sister Buddies of Nashville, 1981-87. Named to Honorable Order of Ky. Cols. John Y. Brown, Gov., 1980; recipient Significant Svc. award ARC, 1982, Clara Barton Communications award, 1983. Mem. NAFE, Nat. Assn. TV Arts and Scis, Nat. Film Inst., Nat. Assn. Broadcasters, Internat. Platform Assn. Methodist. Avocations: reading, outdoor sports. Office: Options Internat Inc 913 18th Ave S Nashville TN 37212-2102

REID, EDWARD SNOVER, III, lawyer; b. Detroit, Mar. 24, 1930; s. Edward S. Jr. and Margaret (Overington) R.; m. Carroll Grylls, Dec. 30, 1953; children: Carroll Reid Highet, Richard Gerveys, Jane Reid McTique, Margaret Reid Boyer. B.A., Yale U., 1951; LL.B. magna cum laude (Sheldon fellow), Harvard U., 1956. Bar: Mich. 1957, N.Y. 1958, D.C. 1982, Gaikokuho jimu-bengoshi, Tokyo 1991. Asso. Davis, Polk & Wardwell, N.Y.C., 1957-64; partner Davis, Polk & Wardwell, 1964-95, sr. counsel, 1996—; dir. Gen. Mills, Inc., 1974-89. Mem. N.Y.C. Bd. Higher Edn., 1971-73; trustee Bklyn. Inst. Arts and Scis., 1966-93, chmn., 1974-79; trustee Bklyn. Mus., 1973-93, 94—; bd. dirs. Bklyn. Bot. Garden Corp., 1977-92, Bargemusic Ltd., 1990-93. Lt. USMC, 1951-53. Mem. ABA, N.Y. State Bar Assn., Assn. of Bar of City of N.Y., Am. Law Inst., Internat. Bar Assn., Inter-Pacific Bar Assn., Heights Casino Club, Rembrandt Club, Century Assn. Club, Yale Club, L.I. Wyandanch Club, Quoque Beach Club, Shinnecock Yacht Club. Home: 1 Pierrepont St Apt 5-a Brooklyn NY 11201-3361 Office: Davis Polk & Wardwell 2-1 Marunouchi 450 Lexington Ave New York NY 10017

REID, GEORGE KELL, biology educator, researcher, author; b. Fitzgerald, Ga., Mar. 23, 1918; s. George Kell and Pauline (Bowles) R.; m. Eugénie Louise Chazal, July 23, 1949 (div. Dec. 1978); children: George Philip (dec.), Deborah Louise. BS, Presbyn. Coll., Clinton, S.C., 1940; MS, U. Fla., 1949, PhD, 1952. Instr. U. Fla., Gainesville, 1949-52; asst. prof. Coll. William and Mary, Williamsburg, Va., 1952-53, Tex. A&M U., College Station, 1953-56, Rutgers U., New Brunswick, N.J., 1956-60; prof. Eckerd Coll., St. Petersburg, Fla., 1960-83, prof. emeritus, 1983—; pvt. practice cons., writer Boca Raton, Fla., 1988—; rsch. scientist Va. Inst. Marine Sci., Gloucester, 1953; rsch. biologist Tex. Game and Fish. Commn., Rockport, 1954-56; cons. in field, 1955—. Author: Ecology of Cedar Key Fishes, 1954, Ecology of Inland Waters and Estuaries, 1961, (co-author) rev. edit., 1976, Pond Life, 1967, rev. edit., 1992, Ecology of Intertidal Zones, 1967; co-author: Bioscience, 1967; contbr. articles to profl. jours. and popular periodicals. Mem. City Environ. Com., St. Petersburg, 1975. 1st lt. U.S. Army, 1942-46. Recipient numerous grants NIH, NSF, Explorers Club, others, 1953—. Fellow AAAS; mem. Am. Soc. Limnology and Oceanography, Am. Inst. Biol. Scis., Fla. Acad. Sci. (pres. 1963-64), Ecol. Soc. Am. (chmn. aquatic ecology sec. 1964-66), Sigma Xi, Phi Sigma, Chi Beta Phi, Sigma Chi. Presbyterian. Achievements include pioneering in fish community ecology research in Gulf of Mexico localities; research in population dynamics in mangrove ecosystems, Wetland utilization, early literature on natural history of Florida. Home: 6079 Town Colony Dr Apt 1022 Boca Raton FL 33433-1911

REID, HARRY, senator; b. Searchlight, Nev., Dec. 2, 1939; s. Harry and Inez Reid; m. Landra Joy Gould; children—Lana, Rory, Leif, Josh, Key. AS, Southern Utah State U., 1959; LLD (hon.), U. So. Utah, 1984; BA, Utah State U., 1961; JD, George Washington U., 1964. Senator, chmn. dem. policy com. 104th Congress U.S. Senate, Washington. *

REID, HOCH, lawyer; b. Chanute, Kans., Dec. 27, 1909; s. James W. and Anna (Hoch) R.; m. Mona McMillan, July 3, 1937; children: Wallis H., Luanna Reid. A.B., Amherst Coll., 1931; LL.B., Columbia U., 1934. Bar: N.Y. 1935. Practiced in N.Y.C., 1935—; ptnr. Valicenti, Leighton, Reid & Pine, 1942-75, Burke & Burke, Daniels, Leighton & Reid, 1976-78; ptnr. Townley & Updike, 1978-86, retired ptnr., 1986-95; mem. staff Navy Price Adjustment Bd., 1944-46. Author: How to Use Investment Company Shares in Estate Planning, 1972, Paying Up for Services, 1976. Trustee Village of Pleasantville, N.Y., 1961-63; chmn. Pleasantville Library Bd., 1955-61; mem. Mt. Pleasant Pub. libr. bd., 1982-86; mem. social policy com., planning com. on aging Fedn. Protestant Welfare Agys., N.Y.C., 1970-86; mem. com. agrl. missions Nat. Council Chs., 1962-91, chmn., 1962-76; bd. dirs. Bethel Methodist Homes, Ossining, N.Y., 1948-82, pres., 1962-75, hon. dir., 1982—; bd. dirs. Agrl. Missions, Inc., 1950-91, pres., 1962-76; bd. dirs., mem. exec. com. Japan Internat. Christian U. Found., 1965-91; pres., trustee Open Space Inst., 1969-72; trustee Natural Area Council, 1975-85. Mem. ABA, Assn. Bar City N.Y., Sawmill River Audubon Soc. (pres. 1984-86), Nature Conservancy, World Affairs Coun. (Hartford), Mark Twain Meml. Congregationalist. Home: Duncaster 60 Loeffler Rd Bloomfield CT 06002-2275

REID, HUBERT M., computer software company executive, electronics executive; b. 1953. BBA in acctg., Howard U., Washington, 1975. Audit, tax mgr. Touche Ross & Co., Washington, 1979-80; with Ward Corp., Rockville, Md., 1980-84; sr. v.p., fin., sec., treas. OAO Corp, Greenbelt, Md., 1984—. Office: OAO Corp 7500 Greenway Center Dr Greenbelt MD 20770-3502*

REID, INEZ SMITH, lawyer, educator; b. New Orleans, Apr. 7, 1937; d. Sidney Randall Dickerson and Beatrice Virginia (Bundy) Smith. BA, Tufts U., 1959; LLB, Yale U., 1962; MA, UCLA, 1963; PhD, Columbia U., 1968. Bar: Calif. 1963, N.Y. 1972, D.C. 1980. Assoc. prof. Barnard Coll. Columbia U., N.Y.C., 1972-76; gen. counsel youth div. State of N.Y., 1976-77; dep. gen. counsel HEW, Washington, 1977-79; inspector gen. EPA, Washington, 1979-81; chief legis. and opinions, dep. corp. counsel Office of Corp. Counsel, Washington, 1981-83; corp. counsel D.C., 1983-85; counsel Laxalt, Washington, Perito & Dubuc, Washington, 1986-90, ptnr., 1990-91; counsel Graham & James, 1991-93, Lewis, White & Clay, P.C., 1994-95; assoc. judge D.C. Ct. Appeals, 1995—. William J. Maier, Jr. vis. prof. law W.Va. U. Coll. Law, Morgantown, 1985-86. Author: Together Black Women, 1972; contbr. articles to profl. jours. and publs. Bd. dirs. Homeland Ministries Bd. United Ch. of Christ, N.Y.C., 1978-83, vice chmn., 1981-83; chmn. bd. govs. Antioch Law Sch., Washington, 1979-81; chmn. bd. trustees Antioch U., Yellow Springs, Ohio, 1981-82; bd. trustees Tufts U., Medford, Mass., 1988—, Lancaster (Pa.) Sem., 1988—; bd. govs. D.C. Sch. Law, 1990—, chmn., 1991-95. Recipient Emily Gregory award Barnard Coll., 1976, Arthur Morgan award Antioch U., 1982, Service award United Ch. of Christ, 1983, Disting. Service (Profl. Life) award Tufts U. Alumni Assn., 1988. Office: DC Ct Appeals 500 Indiana Ave NW 6th Fl Washington DC 20001-2131

REID, IRVIN D., academic official. Dean bus. adminstrn. U. Tenn., Chattanooga, until 1989; pres. Montclair State Coll., Upper Montclair, N.J., 1989—. Office: Montclair State Coll Office of Pres Upper Montclair NJ 07043

REID, JACK POWELL, oil company executive; b. Sublette, Kans., Sept. 1, 1936; s. Eldon Gene and Leona M. (Powell) R.; m. Jane B. Logan, June 7, 1958; children: Willie Donald, Tonilou Michelle. BSChemE, U. Kans., 1958. Chief process engr. Refineria Panama, Republic of Panama, 1961-66; process supt. Conoco, Artesia, N.Mex., 1966-67; refinery mgr. Conoco-Navajo, Artesia, 1967-74; gen. mgr. Navajo Refining Co., Artesia, 1974-76, chief operating officer, 1976-82, pres., 1982—; bd.d irs. Holly Corp., Dallas. Avocation: golfing. Office: Navajo Refining Co PO Box 159 Artesia NM 88211*

REID, JACKSON BROCK, psychologist, educator; b. Honea Path, S.C., Sept. 18, 1921; s. Alexander Mack and Ann Orr (Brock) R.; m. Avis Boykin Long, Jan. 12, 1947; step-children: Jules Heywood Long, Barbara Banning Long. B.S., The Citadel, 1942; postgrad., Ariz. State Coll., Flagstaff, 1948; Ph.D., UCLA, 1951, postgrad., summer 1951. Cert., lic. psychologist, Tex. Asst. prof. ednl. psychology U. Tex., Austin, 1951-55; assoc. prof. U. Tex., 1955-59, prof., 1959-93, prof. emeritus, 1993—, assoc. dean for grad. studies in edn., 1965-73; coordinator ESEA programs U.S. Office Edn., 1969—, chmn. dept. ednl. psychology, 1972-84; cons. in field. Served to capt. U.S. Army, 1942-47. Office Edn. grantee, 1966-73. Fellow Am. Psychol. Assn. (exptl. and ednl. divs.); mem. AAAS, Am. Ednl. Research Assn., Interam. Soc. Psychology, AAUP, Southwestern Psychol. Assn. (sec.-treas. 1965-66, pres. 1967-68), Tex. Psychol. Assn., Ret. Officers Assn., Nat. Psoriasis Found., ACLU, Common Cause, Fund for Peace, Planned Parenthood of Am., Sigma Xi. Clubs: U. Tex. Faculty Center; Lighthouse Resort and Club (Sanibel Island, Fla.). Research, publs. in learning theory, behavioral effects of radiation and drugs, child and adolescent behavior, programmed instn., computer-assisted instrn., 1951. Office: U Tex Dept Ednl Psychology Austin TX 78712 *The principal goal in my career has been to preserve psychology as an academic discipline devoted to objective inquiry into the etiology of behavior on the basis of logically directed empirical investigation as opposed to rationalistic - mystical - doctrinaire approaches.*

REID, JAMES DOLAN, mathematics educator, researcher; b. Augusta, Ga., June 24, 1930; s. Richard and Katherine (O'Leary) R.; m. Anne Carmody Donohue, Jan. 7, 1959; children: James Jr., Margaret, Gerald. BS, Fordham Coll., 1952, MA, 1954; PhD, U. Wash., 1960; MA (hon.), Wesleyan U., 1972. Asst. prof. Syracuse (N.Y.) U., 1960-61, 1963-65, assoc. prof., 1965-69; research assoc. Yale U., New Haven, 1961-62; asst. prof. Amherst (Mass.) Coll., 1962-63; assoc. prof. math. Wesleyan U., Middletown, Conn., 1969-70, prof., 1970—, chmn. math. dept., 1970-73, 85-88, cons. ednl. studies program, 1980—; vis. prof. U. Würzburg, Fed. Republic Germany, 1989. Contbr. numerous articles on algebra (Abelian groups) to profl. jours. Mem. Bd. Edn., Regional Sch. Dist. #17, 1983-87. With USN, 1954-56. Mem. Am. Math. Soc., Irish Math. Soc., Math. Assn. of Am. Home: PO Box 444 New Harbor ME 04554-0444 Office: Wesleyan U Dept Math Middletown CT 06459

REID, JAMES SIMS, JR., automobile parts manufacturer; b. Cleve., Jan. 15, 1926; s. James Sims and Felice (Crowl) R.; m. Donna Smith, Sept. 2, 1950; children: Sally, Susan, Anne (dec.), Jeanne. AB cum laude, Harvard U., 1948, JD, 1951. Bar: Mich., Ohio 1951. Pvt. practice law Detroit, 1951-52, Cleve., 1953-56; with Standard Products Co., Cleve., 1956—, dir., 1959, pres., 1962-89, chmn., chief exec. officer, 1989—. Trustee John Carroll U., 1967—, chmn., 1987-91, Musical Arts Assn. of Cleve. Orch., 1973—. Office: Standard Products Co 2130 W 110th St Cleveland OH 44102-3510

REID, JOHN MITCHELL, biomedical engineer, researcher; b. Mpls., June 8, 1926; s. Robert Sherman and Meryl (Mitchell) R.; m. Virginia Montgomery, Dec. 31, 1949 (div.); children: Donald, Kathryn, Richard; m. Shadi Wang, June 30, 1983. BS, U. Minn., 1950, MS, 1957; PhD, U. Pa., 1965. Engring. assoc. U. Minn., Mpls., 1950-54; rsch. engr. St. Barnabas Hosp., Mpls., 1954-57; assoc. U. Pa., Phila., 1957-66; rsch. asst. prof. U. Wash., Seattle, 1966-72; rsch. engr. Providence Hosp., 1972-74; dir. bioengring. Inst. of Applied Physiology & Medicine, 1973-81; Calhoun prof. Drexel U., Phila., 1981-94, prof. emeritus, rsch. prof., 1994; adj. prof. radiology Thomas Jefferson Med. Sch., Phila., 1982—; affiliate prof. U. Washington, 1995—; cons. Inst. Applied Physiology and Medicine, Seattle. Contbr. over 100 articles to profl. jours.; 5 U.S. patents on devel. of ultrasonic med. imaging. Scoutmaster Boy Scouts Am., Mpls., 1955-57, Phila., 1960-65, cub and scoutmaster, Seattle, 1965-70. With USN, 1950-52, World War II. Recipient Pioneer award Soc. of Vascular Technologists, 1994; grantee NIH. Fellow IEEE, Am. Inst. Ultrasound in Medicine (bd. govs., Pioneer award), Acoustical Soc. Am., Engring. in Medicine and Biology Soc. (Lifetime Achievement award 1993), Am. Inst. Med. and Biol. Engrs. Home: 16711 254 Ave SE Issaquah WA 98027-7262 also: Inst Applied Physiology and Medicine 701 16th Ave Seattle WA 98122-4525

REID, JOHN PHILLIP, law educator; b. Weehawken, N.J., May 17, 1930; s. Thomas Francis and Teresa Elizabeth (Murphy) R. B.S.S., Georgetown U., 1952; LL.B., Harvard U., 1955; M.A., U. N.H., 1957; J.S.D., NYU, 1962. Bar: N.H. 1955. Law clk. U.S. Dist. Ct. N.H., 1956; instr. NYU, N.Y.C., 1960-62, asst. prof. law, 1962-64, assoc. prof., 1964-65, prof. Sch. Law, 1966—. Author: Chief Justice: The Judicial World of Charles Doe, 1967, A Law of Blood: The Primitive Law of the Cherokee Nation, 1970, In a Defiant Stance, 1977, Ina Rebellious Spirit, 1979, Law for the Elephant: Property and Social Behavior on the Overland Trail, 1980, In Defiance of the Law, 1981, Constitutional History of the American Revolution: The Authority of Rights, 1986, Constitutional History of the American Revolution: The Authority to Tax, 1987, The Concept of Liberty in the Age of the American Revolution, 1988, The Concept of Representation in the Age of the American Revolution, 1989, Constitutional History of the American Revolution: The Authority to Legislate, 1991, Constitutional History of the American Revolution: The Authority of Law, 1993, Policing the Elephant: Crime, Punishment, and Social Behavior on the Overland Trail, 1996. Fellow Guggenheim Found., 1980, Huntington Library-NEH, 1980, 84; hon. fellow Am. Soc. Legal History, 1986. Republican. Roman Catholic. Office: NYU Law Sch 40 Washington Sq S New York NY 10012-1005

REID, JOSEPH BROWNING, architect; b. Flint Hill, Va., June 24, 1924; s. Charles Garrison and Grace Pearl (Bradley) R.; m. Maria Aida Amadounian, July 5, 1957; children: Charles, Avedis, Robert. Student, U. Va., 1948; BS in Forestry with highest honors, N.C. State U., 1952; postgrad., Columbia U., 1955; cert. in architecture, Cooper Union, 1960. Registered architect, N.Y., Va., Md., Pa., D.C.; cert. Nat. Coun. Archtl. Registration Bds.; lic. interior designer, D.C. Staff architect Charles Luckman & Assocs., N.Y.C., 1956-63; sr. architect Clive Entwistle & Assocs., N.Y.C., 1963-64; sr. assoc. Perkins & Will, Washington, 1964-74; v.p. John Carl Warnecke FAIA, Washington, 1974-82; founding ptnr. Kemnitzer Reid & Haffler, Washington, 1982-89; prin. Einhorn Yaffee Prescott, Washington, 1989—; advisOr interior design program Marymount Coll., 1982-85; profl. coord. off-campus work program for architecture students Va. Poly. Inst., 1975-81; lectr. No. Va. C.C.; a juror for residential awards Washingtonian mag., 1986; advisor, organizer archtl. awards program Washington Mayor's Award Program. With Mcht. Marine, 1942-47. Recipient Disting. Svc. cert. USO, Washington, 1976, Presdl. Design award Nat. Endowment for Arts, 1987, Hist. Preservation Honor award, 1988, Design award Washington Metro chpt. Am. Soc. Interior Designers, 1989, 2 awards GSA, 1992; Hilda Johnson Cox scholar N.C. State U., 1950. Mem. AIA (sr. dir. Washington Met. chpt. 1979-80, treas. 1981-82, sec. 1982-83, v.p. 1983-84, pres. 1984-85, cert. of deep appreciation 1984, cert. of appreciation 1984), Constrn. Specifications Inst. (bd. dirs. 1979-81, 91-92, citation for disting. svc. 1982, nat. honor awards 1992), Soc. Archtl. Adminstrs. (co-founder Washington chpt.), Phi Eta Sigma, Alpha Zeta, Xi Sigma Pi, Alpha Sigma Pi. Democrat. Methodist. Avocations: surf fishing, Greek history, travel in Greece. Home: 6926 Tyndale St Mc Lean VA 22101-5070 Office: Einhorn Yaffee Prescott Arch 1000 Potomac St NW # 1 Washington DC 20007-3501

REID, JOSEPH LEE, physical oceanographer, educator; b. Franklin, Tex., Feb. 7, 1923; s. Joseph Lee and Ruby (Cranford) R.; m. Freda Mary Hunt, Apr. 7, 1953; children: Ian Joseph, Julian Richard. BA in Math., U. Tex., 1942; MS, Scripps Instn. Oceanography, 1950. Rsch. staff Scripps Instn. Oceanography, La Jolla, Calif., 1957-74; prof. oceanography Scripps Instn. Oceanography, La Jolla, 1974-91, ret., 1991; dir. Marine Life Rsch. Group, 1974-87; assoc. dir. Inst. Marine Resources, 1975-82; cons. Sandia Nat. Labs., Albuquerque, 1980-86. Author: On the Total Geostrophic Circulation of the South Pacific Ocean: Flow Patterns, Tracers and Transports, 1986, On the Total Geostrophic Circulation of the North Atlantic Ocean: Flow Patters, Tracers and Transports, 1994; contbr. articles to profl. jours. Lt. USNR, 1942-46, ETO, PTO. Lt. USNR, 1942-46, ETO, PTO. Recipient award Nat. Oceanographic Data Ctr., Washington, 1984, Albatross award Am. Miscellaneous Soc., 1988, Alexander Agassiz medal NAS, 1992, The Henry Stommel Rsch. award Am. Meteorology Soc., 1996. Fellow AAAS, Am. Geophys. Union (pres. Ocean Scis. sect. 1972-74, 84-86); mem. Am. Meteorol. Soc., Oceanography Soc. Home: 1105 Cuchara Dr Del Mar CA 92014-2623

REID, LANGHORNE, III, merchant banker; b. Dallas, Apr. 3, 1950; s. Langhorne Jr. and Mary Anne (Beasley) R.; m. Sally Wolf, Dec. 26, 1972 (div. Aug. 1977); m. Eve Catherine Murphy, Sept. 6, 1986; 1 child, Claire Hart Reid. BA in Psychology, U. Tex., Austin, 1972, JD, 1975; MBA, U. Pa., 1977. Bar: Tex. 1975. V.p. Dillon, Read & Co., Inc., N.Y.C., 1977-82; mng. dir. Drexel Burnham Lambert Inc., N.Y.C., 1982-87; co-dir. mergers and acquisitions Paine Webber Group, N.Y.C., 1987-89; ptnr. Gordon Investment Inc., N.Y.C., 1989-93; pres. Beacon Advisors, Inc., Dallas, 1993—; bd. dirs. Windmill Holdings; pres. Partnership Svcs., 1992-93. Trustee, treas. Animal Med. Ctr., N.Y.C., 1981—. Mem. Tex. Bar Assn., River Club N.Y. Home: 4307 University Blvd Dallas TX 75205 Office: Beacon Advisors Inc Box 285 25 Highland Park Village Ste 100 Dallas TX 75205

REID, LOREN DUDLEY, speech educator; b. Gilman City, Mo., Aug. 26, 1905; s. Dudley Alver and Josephine (Tarwater) R.; m. Mary Augusta Towner, Aug. 28, 1930; children: Jane Ellen, John Christopher, Stephen Dudley Towner, Don Anthony. A.B., Grinnell Coll., 1927; A.M., State U. Iowa, 1930, Ph.D., 1932. Tchr. Vermillion (S.D.) High Sch., 1927-29; instr. State U. Iowa, 1931-33; tchr. Westport High Sch., Kansas City, Mo., 1933-35; English instr. U. Mo., 1935-37, asst. prof., 1937-39; asst. prof. and later assoc. prof. of speech Syracuse U., 1939-44; prof. of speech U. Mo., 1944—, sesquicentennial prof., 1990, chmn. dept. speech, 1947-52; vis. prof. speech U. So. Calif., summer, 1947; summer lectr. La. State U., 1949, Mich., 1950, 56; summer lectr. State U. Iowa, 1952, Denver, 1960, Oklahoma, 1962; vis. prof. U. Utah, summer 1952, San Diego State Coll., summer 1954, U. So. Calif., summer 1954; European staff U. Md., 1952-53, summer, 1955, 1961-62, London; European staff U. Mich., summer 1957, State U. Iowa, summer 1958; Carnegie vis. prof. U. Hawaii, 1957, La. State U., 1985; vis. lectr. Kyoto (Japan) Sangyo U., 1987. Author: Charles James Fox: An Eighteenth Century Parliamentary Speaker, 1932, Course Book in Public Speaking, (with Gilman and Aly) Speech Preparation, 1946, Fundamentals of Speaking, 1951, Teaching Speech in High School, 1952, Teaching Speech, rev. edit., 1960, 4th edit., 1971, First Principles of Public Speaking, 1960, rev. edit., published in 1962, Studies in American Public Address, 1961, Speaking Well, 4th edit., 1982, Hurry Home Wednesday (Mo. Writers Guild award), Finally It's Friday, 1981, Professor on the Loose, 1992, Reflections, 1995. Recipient Alumni Achievement award Grinnell Coll., 1962. Fellow Royal Hist. Soc.; mem. Speech Assn. Am. (exec. sec. 1945-51, pres. 1957, Disting. Svc. award 1981), N.Y. State Speech Assn. (pres. 1942-44, Spl. award for outstanding svc. 1967), Cen. States Speech Assn. (exec. sec. 1937-39, Disting. Svc. award 1979), Speech and Theatre Assn. Mo. (Disting. Svc. award 1982), AAUP, Conf. on Brit. Studies. U. Mo. Club (pres. 1947). Democrat. Episcopalian. Home: 200 E Brandon Rd Columbia MO 65203-3566

REID, LORENE FRANCES, middle school educator; b. St. Louis, May 28, 1946; d. Frank Bernard and Marcella Marie (Froechtenigt) Niemeyer; m. Patrick Joseph Reid, Aug. 11, 1967; 1 child, Christina Marie. BA in Spanish, Maryville U., 1968; MED in Secondary Edn., U. Mo., St. Louis, 1990; PhD in Edn., St. Louis U., 1995. Cert. Spanish, social studies, ESL tchr., Mo. Spanish tchr. Rosary H.S., Spanish Lake, Mo., 1968-69, Taylor Sch., Clayton, Mo., 1969-70, Roosevelt H.S., St. Louis, 1988-89, Cleve. Jr. Naval Acad., St. Louis, 1989-90, Thomas Dunn Meml. Adult Edn., St. Louis, 1992—; social studies tchr. St. Luke's Sch., Richmond Heights, Mo., 1981-88; ESL tchr. Grant Mid. Sch., St. Louis, 1990-92, Fanning Mid. Sch., St. Louis, 1992—; tutor Sylvan Learning Ctr., Crestwood, Mo., 1990-92; mem. St. Louis Ednl. Leadership Inst., 1994—. Mem. Cmty. Leadership Program for Tchrs., St. Louis, 1993-94. Recipient Emerson Electric Excellence in Teaching award, 1994; named Tchr. of Yr., St. Louis Pub. Schs., 1994-95; named as one of 60 tchrs. recognized by Disney Channel Salutes the Am. Tchr., 1995-96. Mem. ASCD, Am. Ednl. Rsch. Assn., Tchrs. English to Spkrs. of Other Langs., Nat. Coun. Tchrs. English, Midam. Tchs. English to Spkrs. of Other Langs., Phi Delta Kappa.

REID, LYLE, judge; b. Brownsville, Tenn., June 17, 1930; m. Elizabeth W.; children: Betsy, Martha Lyle. BSBA, U. Tenn., JD, 1956. Asst. state atty. gen. State of Tenn., Nashville, 1961-63; county atty. Haywood County, Brownsville, Tenn., 1964-86; atty. Reid & Banks, Brownsville, Tenn., 1963-66; assoc. judge Tenn. Ct. Criminal Appeals, Tenn., 1987-90; chief justice Tenn. Supreme Ct., Nashville, 1990-94; deputy commr. Dept. Commerce & Ins., Tenn. With USAF, Korea. Mem. ABA, Am. Bar Found., Tenn. Bar Assn. Democrat. Methodist. Office: Tenn Supreme Ct 321 Supreme Ct Bldg 401 7th Ave N Nashville TN 37219-1407

REID, LYNNE MCARTHUR, pathologist; b. Melbourne, Australia, Nov. 12, 1923; d. Robert Muir and Violet Annie (McArthur) R. M.D., U. Melbourne, 1946; M.D. (hon.), Harvard U., 1976. Reader in exptl. pathology London U., 1964-67, prof. exptl. pathology, 1967-76; dean Cardiothoracic Inst., 1973-76; pathologist-in-chief Children's Hosp., Boston, 1976-89, pathologist-in-chief emeritus, 1990—; S. Burt Wolbach prof. pathology Harvard Med. Sch., Boston, 1976—. Fellow Royal Coll. Physicians (U.K.), Royal Australian Coll. Physicians, Royal Coll. Pathologists, Royal Coll. Radiologists (hon.), Royal Soc. Medicine, Royal Inst. Gt. Britain, Pathol. Soc. Gt. Britain and Ireland, Thoracic Soc., Assn. Clin. Pathologists, Brit. Thoracic Soc., Fleischner Soc., Can. Thoracic Soc., Neonatal Soc., Am. Thoracic Soc., Am. Soc. Pathologists, Fedn. Am. Socs. Exptl. Biology. Office: 300 Longwood Ave Boston MA 02115-5724

REID, MARILYN JOANNE, state legislator, lawyer; b. Chgo., Aug. 14, 1941; d. Kermit and Newell Azile (Hahn) N.; m. M. David Reid, Nov. 26, 1966 (div. Mar. 1983); children: David, Nelson. Student, Miami U., 1959-61; BA, U. Ill, 1963; JD, Ohio No. U., 1966. Bar: Ohio 1966, Ark. 1967, U.S. Dist. Ct. 1967. Trust adminstr. First Nat. Bank, Dayton, Ohio, 1966-67; assoc. Sloan & Ragsdale, Little Rock, Ohio, 1967-69; ptnr. Reid and Reid, Dayton, 1969-76, Reid & Buckwalter, Dayton, 1975—; mem. Ohio Ho. of Reps., 1993—; mem. Judiciary and Criminal Justice com., vice chmn. ins. com., Vets. com., Pub. utilities com. Mem. Ohio adv. bd. U.S. Commn. Civil Rights; chmn., treas. various polit. campaigns, 1975—; trustee Friends Libr. Beavercreek (Ohio); bd. dirs. Beavercreek YMCA, 1985-88; active Mt. Zion United Ch. of Christ. Mem. ABA, Ohio Bar Assn., Greene County Bar Assn., Beavercreek C. of C. (pres. 1986-87), Dayton Panhellenic Assn. (pres. 1982), Altrusa (v.p. Greene County 1978-79, pres. 1979-80), Lioness (pres. Beavercreek 1975), Rotary, Kappa Beta Pi, Gamma Phi Beta (v.p. 1974-75). Republican. Mem. Ch. Christ. Avocations: tennis, skiing, boating, bridge. Office: Reid & Buckwalter 3866 Indian Ripple Rd Dayton OH 45440-3448

REID, MICHAEL J., international management consultant and educator; b. Chgo., Aug. 13, 1938; s. Robert and Dorothy (Wolfson) R.; m. Arlene Elaine Tufano, June 2, 1963; children: Cameron, Krista, Eaton. Student advt. design, U. Ill. Coll. Fine Art, 1956-58; Student med. illustration, U. Ill. Coll. Medicine, 1958-60; student, Ill. Inst. Tech., 1960-62, BS, 1962. Pres. Michael Reid Design Inc., Chgo., 1964-79; program designer, productivity lectr., 1979-85; exec. v.p. TTI Inc., Greenbrae, Calif., 1985-88; nat. tng. dir. Ctr. for Mgmt. Design, Greenbrae, 1988-90; chief exec. officer The Reid Cons. Partnership, San Francisco, 1990—; bd. dirs., designer-developer for mgmt. edn., process reengring. and project programs strategy formulation, Matrix mgmt. coaching; mgmt. cons. USA and internationally; instr. visual design Art Inst. Chgo. Contbr. designs to profl. jours. Mem. Am. Inst. Graphic Arts, Soc. Typographic Arts, 27 Chgo. Designers.

REID, RALPH WALDO EMERSON, management consultant; b. Phila., July 5, 1915; s. Ralph Waldo Emerson and Alice Myrtle (Stuart) R.; m. Ruth Bull, Dec. 7, 1946; 1 child, Robert. Student, Temple U., 1932-34. BS, Northwestern U., 1936; MA, U. Hawaii, 1938; PhD, Harvard U., 1948. Cert. mgmt. cons. Asst. to v.p. Northwestern U., Evanston, Ill., 1938-40; chief mcpl. govt. br., spl. asst. govt. sect. Supreme Comdr. Allied Powers, 1946-47; spl. asst. Under Sec. of Army, 1948-49; chief Far Eastern affairs div. Office Occupied Areas, chief econs. div. Office Civil Affairs and Mil. Govt., Dept. of Army, 1950-53; asst. to dir. U.S. Bur. of Budget, Washington, 1953-55, asst. dir., 1955-61; resident mgr. A.T. Kearney Inc., Washington, 1961-72, mng. dir., Tokyo, 1972-81, cons., Alexandria, Va., 1981—; former dir. Nihon Regulator Co., Tokyo, Yuasa-Ionics Ltd., Tokyo, Japan DME, Tokyo. Served to comdr. USNR, 1941-46, PTO. Decorated Commendation Ribbon, USN; Order of Rising Sun 3d class (Japan); recipient Exceptional Civilian Service award U.S. Army, 1954. Mem. Inst. Mgmt. Consultants, Am. Polit. Sci. Assn. Republican. Am. Baptist. Clubs: Cosmos, Capitol Hill (Washington); Union League (Chgo.). Home: 412 Monticello Blvd Alexandria VA 22305-1616 Office: A T Kearney Inc PO Box 1405 Alexandria VA 22313-1405

REID, RICHARD A., data processing. Pres. Am. Mgmt. Systems. Office: 66 Van Gordon St Denver CO 80228

REID, ROBERT CLARK, chemical engineering educator; b. Denver, June 11, 1924; s. Frank B. and Florence (Seerley) R.; m. Anna Marie Murphy, Aug. 26, 1950; children: Donald M., Ann Christine. BS, Colo. Sch. Mines, 1946-48; MS, Purdue U., 1950; ScD, MIT, 1954. Prof. chem. engring. MIT, Cambridge, from 1954; now prof. emeritus chem. engring. MIT; Olaf A. Hougen prof. chem. engring. U. Wis., 1980-81. Author: (with J.M. Prausnitz and B.E. Poling) Properties of Gases and Liquids, 1966, 4th edit., 1987, (with M. Ohara) Modeling Crystal Growth Rates from Solution, 1973, (with M. Modell) Thermodynamics and Its Applications, 1974, 2d edit., 1983; Contbr. articles to profl. jours. Recipient Warren K. Lewis award, 1976; Chem. Engring. award Am. Soc. Engring. Edn., 1977; research fellow Harvard U., 1963-64. Mem. Am. Inst. Chem. Engrs. (Ann. lectr. 1967, council 1969-71, editor jour. 1970-76, Founders award 1986), Nat. Acad. Engring., Blue Key, Sigma Alpha Epsilon, Tau Beta Pi. Home: 22 Burroughs Rd Lexington MA 02173-1908 Office: MIT 16-512C Cambridge MA 02139

REID, ROBERT LELON, college dean, mechanical engineer; b. Detroit, May 20, 1942; s. Lelon Reid and Verna Beulah (Custer) Cook; m. Judy Elaine Nestell, July 21, 1962; children: Robert James, Bonnie Kay, Matthew Lelon. ASE, Mott C.C., Flint, Mich., 1961; BChemE, U. Mich., 1963; MME, So. Meth. U., 1966, PhDME, 1969. Registered profl. engr., Tenn., Tex., Wis. Asst. rsch. engr. Atlantic Richfield Co., Dallas, 1964-65; assoc. staff engr. Linde Div., Union Carbide Corp., Tonawanda, N.Y., 1966-68; from asst. to assoc. prof. U. Tenn., Knoxville, 1969-75; assoc. prof. Cleve. State U., 1975-77; from assoc. to full prof. U. Tenn., Knoxville, 1977-82; prof., chmn. U. Tex., El Paso, 1982-87; dean Coll. Engring. Marquette U., Milw., 1987—; summer prof. NASA Marshall Space Ctr., Huntsville, Ala., 1970, EXXON Prodn. Rsch., Houston, 1972, 73, NASA Lewis Space Ctr., Cleve., 1986; cons. Oak Ridge Nat. Lab., 1974-75, TVA, 1978, 79, State of Calif., Sacramento, 1985, Tex. Higher Edn. Coordinating Bd., Austin, 1987. Contbr. 80 articles on heat transfer and solar energy to books, jours. and procs. Grantee NSF, DOE, TVA, NASA, DOI, 1976-87; named Engr. of Yr. Engring. Socs. El Paso, 1986. Fellow ASME (Centennial medallion 1980, chmn. cryogenics com. 1977-81, chmn. solar energy divsn. 1983-84, chmn. Rio Grande sect. 1985-87); mem. ASHRAE, Engrs. and Scientists Milw. (bd. dirs. 1988-93, v.p. 1989-90, pres. 1991-92). Lutheran. Avocations: travel, classic car restoration. Office: Marquette U Coll Engring PO Box 1881 Milwaukee WI 53201-1881

REID, ROBERT NEWTON, retired lawyer, mortgage and financial consultant; b. Ottawa, Ill., Mar. 28, 1908; s. Robert Joseph and Mae (Newton) R. Ph.B., U. Chgo., 1929, J.D., 1930. Bar: Ill. 1930, U.S. Supreme Ct. 1949, Md. 1961, D.C. 1961. Practiced in Chgo., 1930-39; with Follansbee, Shorey & Schupp, 1933-39; govt. atty. FCA, Washington, 1939-42; atty., counsel RFC, Fed. Nat. Mortgage Assn., 1942-49; asst. gen. counsel Fed. Nat. Mortgage Assn., 1949-50, gen. counsel, 1950-70, spl. counsel, 1970-73, v.p., 1950-59, 68-73, dir., 1954-59, cons., 1973-95; retired, 1995. Mem. bd. advisors Washington Studio Sch., 1985-95. Served from 2d lt. to lt. col. Judge Adv. Gen. Corps USAR, 1942-46. Decorated Legion of Merit. Mem. ABA (life), Fed. Bar Assn. D.C. Bar Assn. (life), Am. Judicature Soc., Supreme Ct. Hist. Soc., Res. Officers Assn. (life), Am. Legion (life), SAR (life), Ret. Officers Assn. (life), Mil. Order of World Wars (life), Nat. Assn., Uniformed Svcs., English Speaking Union, Delta Sigma Phi (life), Phi Alpha Delta. Clubs: Nat. Lawyers (life), University (life) (Washington). Lodge: Masons (life). Home: University Club 1135 16th St NW Washington DC 20036-4801

REID, SARAH LAYFIELD, lawyer; b. Kansas City, Mo., Sept. 22, 1952; d. Jim Tom and Sarah Pauline (Clark) R.; m. David Harris Gikow, June 12, 1983; children: Stephen Nathaniel, Emily Pauline. AB, Bryn Mawr Coll., 1974; JD, Harvard U., 1977. Bar: N.Y. 1978, U.S. Dist. Ct. (so. and ea. dists.) N.Y. 1978, U.S. Ct. Appeals (11th cir.) 1981, U.S. Ct. Appeals (2d cir.) 1982, U.S. Supreme Ct. 1988, U.S. Ct. Appeals (3d cir.) 1990. Assoc. Kelley Drye & Warren, N.Y.C., 1977-85, ptnr., 1986—, co-head securities litigation practice group, 1995—. Mem. ABA, N.Y. State Bar Assn., Fed. Bar Coun., Assn. of Bar of City of N.Y. (mem. task force on women in the profession). Office: Kelley Drye & Warren 101 Park Ave New York NY 10178

REID, SIDNEY WEBB, English educator; b. Neptune, N.J., Nov. 24, 1943; s. Sidney Webb and Mary Cook (Bennett) R.; m. Judith Wright, Aug. 22, 1969; 1 child, Laura. BA, Duke U., 1965; MA, U. Va., 1966, PhD, 1972. Grad. tchg. fellow U. Va., Charlottesville, 1968-70; asst. prof. English, Kent (Ohio) State U., 1970-75, assoc. prof., 1975-84, prof., 1984—, dir. Inst. Bibliography and Editing, 1985—; vis. fellow Clare Hall, Cambridge (Eng.) U., 1992-93, life mem., 1993—. Textual editor Bicentennial Edition of Charles Brockden Brown, 6 vols., 1977-87; editor-in-chief: (Cambridge edits. of Joseph Conrad) The Secret Agent, 1990, Almayer's Folly, 1994. NDEA fellow U. Va., 1965-68; Rsch. grantee NEH, 1977-84. Office: Kent State University Inst Bibliography-Editing 1118 Library Kent OH 44242

REID, SUE TITUS, law educator; b. Bryan, Tex., Nov. 13, 1939; d. Andrew Jackson Jr. and Loraine (Wylie) Titus. BS with honors, Tex. Woman's U., 1960; MA, U. Mo., 1962, PhD, 1965; JD, U. Iowa, 1972. Bar: Iowa 1972, U.S. Ct. Appeals (D.C. cir.) 1978, U.S. Supreme Ct. 1978. From instr. to assoc. prof. sociology Cornell Coll., Mt. Vernon, Iowa, 1963-72; assoc. prof., chmn. dept. sociology Coe Coll., Cedar Rapids, Iowa, 1972-74; assoc. prof. law. U. Wash., Seattle, 1974-76; exec. assoc. Am. Sociol. Assn., Washington, 1976-77; prof. law U. Tulsa, 1978-88; dean, prof. Sch. Criminology, Fla. State U., Tallahassee, 1988-90; prof. pub. adminstrn. and policy Fla. State U., 1990—; acting chmn. dept. sociology Cornell Coll., 1965-66; vis. assoc.

prof. sociology U. Nebr., Lincoln, 1970; vis. disting. prof. law and sociology U. Tulsa, 1977-78, assoc. dean 1979-81; vis. prof. law U. San Diego, 1981-82; mem. People-to-People Crime Prevention Del. to People's Republic of China, 1982; George Beto Vis. Prof. criminal justice Sam Houston U., Huntsville, Tex., 1984-85; lecture/study tour of Criminal Justice systems of 10 European countries, 1985; cons. Evaluation Policy Rsch. Assocs., Inc., Milw., 1976-77, Nat. Inst. Corrections, Idaho Dept. Corrections, 1984, Am. Correctional Inst., Price-Waterhouse. Author: (with others) Bibliographies on Role Methodology and Propositions Volume D - Studies in the Role of the Public School Teacher, 1962, The Correctional System: An Introduction, 1981, Crime and Criminology, 7th edit., 1994, Criminal Justice, 1987, 3d edit., 1993, 4th edit. Brown and Benchmark, 1996, Criminal Law, 1989, 3d edit., 1995; editor: (with David Lyon) Population Crisis: An Interdisciplinary Perspective, 1972; contbr. articles to profl. jours. Recipient Disting. Alumni award Tex. Woman's U., 1979; named One of Okla. Young Leaders of 80's Oklahoma Monthly, 1980. Mem. Am. Soc. Criminology, Acad. Criminal Justice Scis., Soc. Criminal Jus. Assn. Avocations: walking, swimming, reading, sewing, cooking. Office: Fla State Univ Dept Pub Adminstrn Tallahassee FL 32306

REID, TERENCE C. W., corporation executive; b. Johannesburg, Republic of South Africa, Oct. 28, 1941; arrived in Canada, 1964; s. Edward Harold and Constance Mary (Jenner) R.; m. Carole Julie Davies; children: Alison, Michael, Christopher. Diploma in law, Witwatersrand U., Johannesburg, 1962; MBA, Toronto U., 1966. Articled clk. Bowen's Co., Johannesburg, 1959-64; various positions to vice chmn. Wood Gundy Inc., Toronto and Montreal, 1966—; Dir. Kinross Gold Corp. Office: CIBC Wood Gundy Securities, Inc, BCE Pl/PO Box 500, Toronto, ON Canada M5J 2S8

REID, TIMOTHY, business organization executive; b. Toronto, Ont., Can., Feb. 21, 1936; s. Escott and Ruth (Herriot) R.; m. Julyan Fancott, Oct. 11, 1962; children: Dylan, Vanessa. BA with honors, U. Toronto, 1959; MA, Yale U., 1960; MLitt, Oxford U., Eng., 1965; grad. Advanced Mgmt. Program, Harvard U., 1983. Half back Hamilton (Ont., Can.) Tiger Cats Football Club, 1962; asst. to pres. York U., Toronto, 1963-67; mem. provincial parliament Ont. Legislature, 1967-71; prin. adminstr. OECD, Paris, 1972-74; asst. dep. minister Govt. of Can., Ottawa, 1974-85; dean faculty of bus. Ryerson Poly. Inst., Toronto, 1985-89; commr. Ont. Securities Commn., 1987-89; pres. Can. C. of C., Ottawa, 1989—; bd. dirs., co-chair bus. Can. Labor Market and Productivity Ctr., 1989—. Rhodes scholar, 1960. Mem. Can. Exec. Svc. Orgn. (bd. dirs. 1992—). Office: Can Chamber of Commerce, 55 Metcalfe St # 1160, Ottawa, ON Canada K1P 6N4

REID, WILLIAM HILL, mathematics educator; b. Oakland, Calif., Sept. 10, 1926; s. William Macdonald and Edna Caroline (Hill) R.; m. Elizabeth Mary Kidner, May 26, 1962; 1 child, Margaret Frances. BS, U. Calif., Berkeley, 1949, MS, 1951; PhD, Cambridge U., Eng., 1955, ScD (hon.), 1968; AM (hon.), Brown U., 1961. Lectr. Johns Hopkins U., Balt., 1955-56; NSF fellow Yerkes Observatory, Williams Bay, Wis., 1957-58; asst. prof. Brown U., Providence, 1958-61, assoc. prof., 1961-63; assoc. prof. U. Chgo., 1963-65, prof., 1965-89, prof. emeritus, 1989—; prof. Ind. U.-Purdue U., Indianapolis, 1989—; cons. research labs. Gen. Motors Corp., Warren, Mich., 1960-73. Author: (with P.G. Drazin) Hydrodynamic Stability, 1981; contbr. articles to profl. jours. Served with U.S. Mcht. Marine, 1945-47, with AUS, 1954-56. Fulbright research scholar Australian Nat. U., 1964-65. Fellow Am. Phys. Soc., Cambridge Philos. Soc.; mem. Am. Math. Soc., Am. Meteorol. Soc., Sigma Xi. Home: 7554 Ballinshire N Indianapolis IN 46254-9772 Office: Ind U-Purdue U Dept Math Scis 402 N Blackford St Indianapolis IN 46202-3272

REID, WILLIAM JAMES, social work educator; b. Detroit, Nov. 14, 1928; s. James Macknight and Sophie Amelia (Schneider) R.; m. Anne E. Fortune, May 22, 1988; children by previous marriage—Valerie, Steven. B.A., U. Mich., 1950, M.S.W., 1952; D.S.W., Columbia U., 1963. Caseworker-in-charge Family Service of Westchester, Mt. Kisco, N.Y., 1956-59; asst. prof. social work U. Chgo., 1962-65, prof., 1968-75, George Herbert Jones prof., 1975-80; prof. Sch. Social Welfare, SUNY, Albany, 1980—; dir. Center for Social Casework Research, Community Service Soc., N.Y.C., 1965-68. Author: Brief and Extended Casework, 1969, Task-Centered Casework, 1972, Task-Centered Practice, 1977, The Task-Centered System, 1978, Models of Family Treatment, 1981, Research in Social Work, 1981, 2d edit., 1989, Family Problem Solving, 1985, The Role-Sharing Marriage, 1986, Advances in Clinical Social Work Research, 1990, Task Strategies, 1992, Qualitative Research in Social Work, 1994, Generalist Practice: A Task-Centered Approach, 1994. Served with U.S. Army, 1952-56. Recipient excellence in rsch. award Nat. Assn. Social Workers, 1990. Mem. Phi Beta Kappa. Office: 135 Western Ave Albany NY 12203-1011

REID, WILLIAM JAMES, retired physicist, educator; b. Abbeville, S.C., Nov. 2, 1927; s. William James and Mary Lelia (Shelley) R.; m. Nancy Louise Edwards, Nov. 25, 1964; children: Laura Louise, William James III, Sandra Shelley. AB in Chemistry, Erskine Coll., 1949; MS in Chemistry, Duke U., 1958; PhD in Physics, Clemson U., 1967. Instr. Erskine Coll., Due West, S.C., 1949-51, field rep., 1951-52; svc. mgr. Reid Motor Co., Abbeville, S.C., 1954-57; asst. prof. Erskine Coll., Due West, 1957-62, assoc. prof., 1966-68; prof., head physics dept. Jacksonville (Ala.) State U., 1968-91, head dept. phys. scis. and engring., 1991-94, ret., 1994; pres. faculty senate Jacksonville State U., 1971-72, 76-77, 88-89. Contbr. various articles to profl. jours. With U.S. Army, 1945-46, 1st lt. S.C. NG, 1948-56. Recipient Disting. Svc. award Jr. C. of C. Abbeville, S.C., 1960; named Kiwanian of Yr., Jacksonville, 1975. Mem. Am. Phys. Soc., Am. Assn. Physics Tchrs., Ala. Acad. Sci., Rotary Club Clemson, Sigma Xi, Phi Lambda Upsilon, Sigma Pi Sigma, Omicron Delta Kappa, Alpha Mu Gamma, Pi Kappa Phi. Methodist. Home: 3240 Six Mile Hwy Central SC 29630-9021

REID-CRISP, WENDY, publishing executive; m. Ewing Walker; 1 child, Max Crisp. BA in Eng., Whitman Coll., 1965. Editor-in-chief Savvy Mag.; founder, pub. New Chapter Press, N.Y.C.; editor-in-chief Small Press; nat. dir. Nat. Assn. Female Execs., founder, editor Profl. Libr. bus. books for women, liaison other women's orgns.; lectr. profl. women's issues, 1988—. Author: Give Me One Good Reason: Why Living Takes Up So Much Of Our Time, 1992. Bd. dirs. United Meth. Comms., 1984—.

REIDENBAUGH, LOWELL HENRY, retired sports editor; b. Lititz, Pa., Sept. 7, 1919; s. Harry Martin and Marian Marie (Nies) R.; m. Ruth Elizabeth Cameron, Nov. 23, 1944; children: Karen Lee (Mrs. William Rogers), Kathy Jean (Mrs. William J. Schuchman). A.B., Elizabethtown (Pa.) Coll., 1941. Gen. reporter Lancaster (Pa.) Intelligencer Jour., 1941-42; sports writer Phila. Inquirer, 1944-47; mem. staff The Sporting News, St. Louis, 1947-89; mng. editor The Sporting News, 1962-79, sr. editor, 1980-83, corp. editor, 1983-89. Author: National League History, 1976, The Super Bowl Book, 1981, Cooperstown, Where Baseball's Legends Live, 1983, Take Me Out to the Ballpark, 1983, The Sporting News, First 100 Years, 1985, The 50 Greatest Games, 1986, History 33d Va. Infantry Regiment, CSA, 1987, 25 Greatest Pennant Races, 1987, 25 Greatest Teams, 1988, History 27th Va. Infantry Regiment, CSA, 1993. Served with AUS, 1942-43.

REIDENBERG, LOUIS MORTON, lawyer; b. Phila., Dec. 1, 1939; s. Bernard and Beatrice (Rauer) R.; children: Daniel J., Jeffrey B. BBA, U. Miami, Fla., 1961; JD, U. Minn., 1965. Bar: Minn. 1965. Law clk. Minn. Supreme Ct., St. Paul, 1965-66; assoc. Katz, Burstein & Galbraith, Mpls., 1966-70; ptnr. Burstein & Reidenberg, Mpls., 1970-71; pvt. practice Mpls., 1971-78, 81-83; ptnr. Reidenberg & Eagon, Mpls., 1978-81, Reidenberg & Jaycox, Bloomington, Minn., 1983-85, Reidenberg & Ormond, Mpls., 1985-87; pvt. practice Mpls., 1988-91; ptnr. Reidenberg & Arrigoni, Mpls., 1991—; lectr. Minn. Continuing Legal Edn., 1976, 75, 76, 77, 83, 86, Minn. Inst. Legal Edn., 1987. Mem. Am. Acad. Matrimonial Lawyers, Minn. State Bar Assn. (mem. family law com.), Hennepin County Bar Assn. (family law com. 1971-83). Office: Reidenberg & Arrigoni 625 Pillsbury Ctr 200 S 6th St Minneapolis MN 55402

REIDENBERG, MARCUS MILTON, physician, educator; b. Phila., Jan. 3, 1934; s. Leon and Adeline Reidenberg; m. June Wilson, July 14, 1957; children: Bruce, Joel, Julie. Student, Cornell U., 1951-54; MD, Temple U., 1958. Diplomate Am. Bd. Internal Medicine. Intern Community Gen. Hosp., Reading, Pa., 1958-59; resident Temple U. Hosp., Phila., 1962-65; from instr. to assoc. prof. Temple U. Med. Sch., Phila., 1962-75; assoc. prof. Cornell U. Med. Coll., N.Y.C., 1975-76, prof. pharmacology, head div. clin. pharmacology, 1976—, prof. medicine, 1980—, acting assoc. dean, 1981-82, asst. dean, 1988—; attending physician N.Y. Hosp., 1980—; vis. physician Rockefeller U. Hosp., N.Y.C., 1980—; mem. project adv. group FDA, Rockville, Md., 1977-82; vice chmn. Joint Commn. on Prescription Drug Use, Washington, 1977-80; mem. study sect. NIH, Bethesda, Md., 1980-86; del. U.S. Pharmacopeal Conv., 1975-80. Author: Renal Function and Drug Action, 1971; editor various books; editor Clin. Pharmacology and Therapeutics, 1985—; contbr. articles to profl. jours. Served to lt. M.C., USNR, 1960-62. Recipient Research Career Devel. award NIH, 1970, Julius Sturmer award Phila. Coll. Pharmacy and Sci., 1982. Fellow ACP; mem. Am. Soc. Clin. Investigations, Assn. Am. Physicians, Am. Soc. Clin. Pharmacology and Therapeutics (pres. 1984-85, Rawls Palmer award 1981), Am. Soc. Pharmacology and Exptl. Therapeutics (award 1983), Internat. Union Pharmacology (vice chmn. sect. clin. pharmacology 1984-87, chmn. 1987-89). Office: Cornell U Med Coll Dept Clin Pharmacology 1300 York Ave New York NY 10021-4805

REIDER, MARTHA CRAWFORD, industrial immunologist; b. Red Bank, N.J., Apr. 29, 1954; d. Harry Edward and Ernestine (Bird) Crawford; m. Michael John Reider, Sept. 22, 1979. BA in Biol. Scis., Ohio No. U., 1976; postgrad., Kennedy-Western U., 1993—. Product devel. scientist E.I. Du-Pont de Nemours and Co., Newark, Del., 1976-82, supr. animal facility, 1982-84, rsch. immunologist, 1984-87, mfg. process scientist, 1987-89, quality assurance supr. testing and release, 1989-90; co-founder, v.p. mfg. Strategic Diagnostics Inc., Newark, 1990—; co-founder, dir. quality assurance TSD Biosvcs., Newark, 1991—; mem. product quality com., mem. customer focus group, human resources com.; facilitator for multiple pers. tng. programs. Contbr. articles to profl. conf. procs. Water safety and CPR/first aid trainer/instr. ARC, 1977—, bd. dirs. Del. br., Wilmington; instr. aquatics YMCA Del., Newark, 1988—. Mem. ASTD, NAFE, Am. Soc. Quality Control (cert. quality auditor), Soc. Human Resources Mgmt., Am. Mgmt. Assn., Beta Beta Beta. Methodist. Avocations: American sign language, teaching swimming. Office: Strategic Diagnostics Inc 128 Sandy Dr Newark DE 19713

REIDINGER, RUSSELL FREDERICK, JR., fish and wildlife scientist; b. Reading, Pa., June 19, 1945. BS, Albright Coll., 1967; PhD in Zoology, U. Ariz., 1972. Asst. prof. biology Augustana Coll., 1971-74; rsch. physiologist The Philippines, 1974-78; asst. mem., wildlife biologist Monell Chem. Senses Ctr., 1978-86; dir. Denver Wildlife Rsch. Ctr. U.S. Dept. Agr., Denver, 1987-93; dir. Ctr. Excellence Nat. Resources Mgmt. Lincoln U., Jefferson City, Mo., 1993—; vis. prof. dept. zoology U. Philippines, 1975-78; cons. Bangladesh Agr. Rsch. Coun., USAID, 1977, Ministry Agrl. Devel. & Agrarian Reform, Nicaragua, 1981, CID, Uganda, 1996. Mem. Am. Soc. Mammalogists, Wildlife Soc., Nat. Animal Damage Control Assn. Office: Lincoln U Dept Ag Nat & Home Econ Jefferson City MO 65102-0029

REID-ROBERTS, DAYL HELEN, mental health counselor; b. Rochester, N.Y., Oct. 15, 1941; d. Russell Harrison and Elizabeth Spencer (Page) Ferrey; m. David Alan Reid, July 16, 1960 (div. 1982); children: Deborah Elizabeth, Patricia Anne, David Alan Jr., Matthew Stephen; m. David Gillies Roberts, Aug. 9, 1985. BA, Salisbury (Md.) State U., 1988, MEd, 1990. Lic. profl. counselor. Clinician Community Svcs. Bd., Eastern Shore, Nassawadox, Va., 1990—; clinician substance abuse svc. Community Svcs. Bd., Eastern Shore, Onancock, Va., 1990—; clinican, mental social worker, psychiat. Northampton Accomack Meml. Hosp., Nassawadox, 1992-93; v.p. Humanitec, Inc., Accomac, Va., 1993—; instr. philosophy, psychology Ea. Shore Cmty. Coll., 1995—; asst. dir. Literacy Coun. of No. Va., Annandale, 1980-85. Contbr. articles to profl. jours. Treas., co-founder Ea. Shore Literacy Coun., 1986. Mem. Am. Counseling Assn., Am. Psychologists Assn. (student), Phi Sigma Tau, Kappa Delta Phi. Republican. Presbyterian. Avocations: reading, needlepoint, house renovation, antiques, bridge. Home: The Oliver House Onancock VA 23417 Office: Humanitec Inc Front St PO Box 580 Accomac VA 23301-0580

REIDY, CAROLYN KROLL, publisher; b. Washington, May 2, 1949; d. Henry August and Mildred Josephine (Mencke) Kroll; m. Stephen Kroll Reidy, Dec. 28, 1974. BA, Middlebury Coll., 1971; MA, Ind. U., 1974, PhD, 1982. Various positions to mgr. subs. rights Random House, Inc., N.Y.C., 1975-83, assoc. pub., 1987-88; dir. subs. rights William Morrow & Co., N.Y.C., 1983-85; v.p., assoc. pub. Vintage Books, N.Y.C., 1985-87, pub., 1987-88; pub. Anchor Books, Doubleday & Co., N.Y.C., 1988; pres., pub. Avon Books, N.Y.C., 1988-92; pres., pub. trade div. Simon & Schuster, N.Y.C., 1992—. Bd. dis. NAMES Project, 1994—. Mem. Women's Media Group, Pubs. Lunch Club. Office: Simon & Schuster 1230 Avenue Of The Americas New York NY 10020-1513

REIDY, GERALD PATRICK, federal organization executive, arbitrator, mediator, fact-finder; b. N.Y.C., Apr. 25, 1929; s. Patrick Joseph and Kathleen Theresa (Holohan) R.; m. Patricia Hope Johnston, Nov. 28, 1953; children: Anne Marie Reidy Borenstein, James M., Susan P., Patricia Reidy Conrad, Daniel E., Thomas J., John G. BS, Fordham Coll., 1949, JD, 1952; LLM in Labor Law, Georgetown U., NYU, 1958; MBA, Iona Coll., 1969. Spl. agent FBI, Phila., Washington, N.Y.C., 1954-65; mgr. indsl. rels., asst. dir. pers. Canada Dry Corp., N.Y.C., 1965-68; dir., adminstr. pers. Bunker Ramo Corp., Trumbull, Conn., 1968-71; dir. pers. The Roosevelt Hosp., N.Y.C., 1971-73; regional dir. U.S. Dept. Labor, Boston, 1973-77, fact-finder, mediator, arbitrator, 1977-78; asst. dir. labor rels. Boston Pub. Libr., 1978-83; regional adminstr. OSHA U.S. Dept. Labor, N.Y.C., 1983-87; dir. Office of Constrn. and Maritime Compliance Assistance OSHA U.S. Dept. Labor, Washington, 1987-91, dir. Office of Constrn. and Civil Engring. Safety Standards OSHA, 1991-95; dir. Office of Constrn. Stds. and Compliance Assistance OSHA, 1995—. Lt. USAF, 1952-54. Mem. Internat. Soc. for Fall Protection, Soc. of Former Spl. Agents FBI, Design Loads on Structures During Constrn. Standards Com. Republican. Roman Catholic. Avocations: fishing, walking seashore, reading, gourmet cooking. Office: OSHA US Dept Labor #N3621 200 Constitution Ave NW # N3621 Washington DC 20210-0001

REIDY, RICHARD ROBERT, publishing company executive; b. Patchogue, N.Y., May 9, 1947; s. Joseph Robert and Irene (Jennings) R.; m. Carolyn Alyce Armstrong, Mar. 21, 1970; children: Dawn Patricia, Shawn Patrick, Christopher Keith. Student, Suffolk County Community Coll., 1966-68, L.I. Tech. Sch., 1969-70, Scottsdale Community Coll., 1983-84, 85-86. Lic. real estate agt., Ariz. Restaurant owner Reidy's, Patchogue, 1973-77; design draftsman Sverdrop & Parcel, Tempe, Ariz., 1978-79, Sullivan & Masson, Phoenix, 1979-81; pres. Success Pub. Co., Scottsdale, Ariz., 1983—; with U.S. Postal Dept., 1980—. Editor, owner, pub.: Who's Who in Arizona, 1984-85, 89-90. Chief Scottsdale YMCA, 1983-84; eucharistic minister St. Daniel the Prophet Cath. Ch., Scottsdale, 1985—; mem. World Wide Marriage Encounter, 1986—; pres. Coronado High Sch. Band Boosters, 1988-89. Mem. Scottsdale C. of C., Phoenix Better Bus. Bur. Office: Success Pub Co PO Box 3431 Scottsdale AZ 85271-3431

REIDY, THOMAS ANTHONY, lawyer; b. Bronx, N.Y., Sept. 30, 1952; s. John Alexander and Elinor Ann (Tracey) R.; m. Victoria Mary Moxham, Mar. 12, 1977; children: J. Benjamin, Jacob T., Thomas A. II. BA with honors, Lehigh U., 1974; JD, U. Va., 1978. Bar: Ohio 1978, U.S. Dist. Ct. (so. dist.) Ohio 1980. Assoc. Moritz, McClure, Hughes, Kerscher & Price, Columbus, Ohio, 1978-80; assoc. Porter, Wright, Morris & Arthur, Columbus, 1980-87, ptnr., 1987-92; v.p. human resources and employment counsel The Longaberger Co., Dresden, Ohio, 1993-94, gen. counsel, 1994—; First v.p. Easter Seals Soc. Ctrl. Ohio, Columbus, 1990-92. Office: Longaberger Co PO Box 73 Dresden OH 43821-0073

REIF, (FRANK) DAVID, artist, educator; b. Cin., Dec. 14, 1941; s. Carl A. and Rachel L. (Clifton) R.; m. Ilona Jekabsons, July 30, 1966; 1 child, Megan Elizabeth. BFA, Art Inst. Chgo., 1968; MFA, Yale U., 1970. Asst. prof. art U. Wyo., Laramie, 1970-74, assoc. prof., 1974-81, prof., 1981—; assoc. prof. U. Mich., Ann Arbor, 1980-81; acting head dept. art U. Wyo., Laramie, 1986-87; selection cons. Ucross Found. Residency Program, Wyo., 1983—; exhibit juror Artwest Nat., Jackson, Wyo., 1986; panelist Colo. State U., Ft. Collins, 1981; lectr. U. Mich., 1980; apptd. Wyo. Arts Coun., 1993—. One-man shows include U. Wyo. Art Mus., 1993, Dorsky Galleries, N.Y.C., 1980, No. Ariz. U., 1977, 87, U. Mich., 1980, 81, One West Ctr. Contemporary Art, Ft. Collins, 1991; exhibited in group shows at First, Second and Third Who. Biennial Tour, 1984-88, U.S. Olympics Art Exhbn., L.A., 1984, Miss. Mus. Art and NEA Tour, 1981-83, L.A. Invitational Sculpture Tour Exhbn., 1991-92, Nicolaysen Art Mus., Casper, Wyo., 1994. Apptd. chair Wyo. Arts Coun. With USAR, 1963-69. Recipient F.D. Pardee award Yale U., 1970; Best Sculpture award Joslyn Art Mus. Omaha, 1978; Nat. Endowment Arts grantee, 1978-79, Wyo. Basic Rsch. grantee, 1983-84, 86-87. Mem. Coll. Art Assn., Internat. Sculpture Ctr. Democrat. Home: 3340 Aspen Ln Laramie WY 82070-5702 Office: U Wyo Dept Art PO Box 3138 Laramie WY 82071-3138

REIF, ERIC PETER, lawyer; b. Pitts., Nov. 2, 1942; s. Ernest Carl and Bernice Elizabeth (Thompson) R.; m. Donna Deeter, June 13, 1970; children: Roger Michael, Brian Peter. BA, U. Mich., 1963, JD, 1967. Bar: Mich. 1968, Pa. 1969, U.S. Dist. Ct. (ea., we. and mid. dists.) Pa. 1969. Law clk. to presiding justice Mich. Ct. Appeals, Lansing, 1967-68; trial lawyer Reed, Smith, Shaw & McClay, Pitts., 1968—, ptnr. litigation, 1979—; now ptnr. Pretragallo, Bosick & Gordon, Pitts. Mem. ABA, Pa. Bar Assn., Allegheny County Bar Assn., Acad. Trial Lawyers Allegheny County. Democrat. Presbyterian. Club: Longue Vue (Verona, Pa.). Avocations: running, skiing, boating, travel. Home: 14 Windsor Rd Pittsburgh PA 15215-1813 Office: Petragallo, Bosick & Gordon 1 Oxford Centre38th Fl Pittsburgh PA 15219*

REIF, LOUIS RAYMOND, lawyer, utilities executive; b. Buffalo, July 4, 1923; s. John Dennis and Sadie (Wilkenson) R.; m. Nancy C. Heuer, Apr. 12, 1958; children: Tracey Lynn, Christopher Louis. Student, Mich. State U., 1941-42, The Citadel, 1943; A.B., U. Buffalo, 1948; J.D., U. Mich., 1951. Bar: N.Y. 1953. Pvt. practice Chgo., 1951-52, Buffalo, 1953—; atty. Continental Ill. Nat. Bank, Chgo., 1951-52, Iroquois Gas Corp., Buffalo, 1952-53; asst. sec. Iroquois Gas Corp., 1953-58, v.p., 1958-63, sr. v.p., 1963-71, pres., 1971—, also bd. dirs.; v.p. Nat. Fuel Gas Co., N.Y.C., 1960-74, pres., 1974, pres., chief exec. officer, 1975-87, chmn., chief exec. officer, 1988—; asst. to chmn. Del. North Cos., Buffalo, 1988, chief oper. officer, 1989—, also bd. dirs., 1989; bd. dirs. Goldome Bank; chmn. N.Y. Gas Group, 1973—; chmn. 17th World Gas Conf., Internat. Gas Union, 1986-88. Pres., dir. Buffalo Better Bus. Bur., 1970; trustee SUNY-Buffalo Found. Served with C.E. AUS, 1943-46, ETO. Mem. ABA, N.Y. Bar Assn., Fed. Power Bar Assn., Erie County Bar Assn., Barrister Soc., Am. Gas Assn. (chmn. dir. 1984-85, Disting. Svc. award 1986), Nat. Alliance Businessmen (dir., chmn. 1967-68), Buffalo C. of C. (dir. 1973—), chmn. nat. affairs com. 1969—), Buffalo Club (bd. dirs 1988, pres. 1991-92), Phi Alpha Delta. Office: Nat Fuel Gas Distbn Corp 10 Lafayette Sq Buffalo NY 14203-1824

REIFF, JAMES STANLEY, addictions physician, psychiatric physician, osteopathic physician, surgeon; b. Chgo., Mar. 17, 1935; s. Nathan Edgar and Freda Matilda (Imhoff) R.; m. Sharon Ann Kraybill, June 9, 1956 (div. Apr. 1970); children: Gregory James, James Stanley II, Cynthia Diane, Jeffery Cameron. B.A. in Chemistry, Goshen Coll., 1957; D.O., Chgo. Coll. Osteo. Medicine, 1961. Biochemist Miles/Ames Pharm. Co., Elkhart, Ind., 1955-57; gen. practice medicine, Michigan City, Ind., 1962-69; addictions physician Oaklawn Psychiat. Ctr., Elkhart, Ind. 1974-84; clin. team leader, addictions team Oaklawn Ctr., Elkhart, 1980-83. Alcohol Anonymous Cen. Service Area Inc., 1984-87; med. dir., Life Recovery Cen., Elkhart, 1987-90; med. dir., Substance Abuse Coun. St. Joe County, Mich., 1990-95; med. dir. Am. Plasma Mgmt., Inc., Kalamazoo and East Lansing, Mich., 1991—; staff psychiatrist Community Mental Health Svcs. St. Joe County, 1993—; bd. dirs. Home for Runaway Kids - Victory House, Elkhart, Ind., 1974-76, 12 Step House Meth. Ch.-Halfway House, Elkhart, 1974-77; bd. dirs., treas. Caldwell Home Corp.-Social Rehab. Ctr. for Alcoholism, Elkhart, 1984-87; bd. dirs. Hope House, Jonesville, Mich.; organist First Presbyn. Ch., Sturgis, Mich., 1993—. Mem. AMA, Am. Osteopathic Assn., Am. Soc. Addiction Medicine (com. on addiction medicine in correctional facilities 1993—), Am. Med. Soc. on Alcoholism, Soc. Correctional Physicians, Nat. Coun. on Alcoholism and Drug Dependence in Mich., Mich. State Med. Soc., St. Joe County Med. Soc., Am. Osteopathic Assn. Avocations: organ and piano playing. Home: 1301 E Congress St Sturgis MI 49091-2326 Office: Cmty Mental Health St Joe County 210 S Main St Three Rivers MI 49093

REIFF, PATRICIA HOFER, space physicist, educator; b. Oklahoma City, Mar. 14, 1950; d. William Henry and Maxine Ruth (Hoffer) R.; m. Thomas Westfall Hill, July 4, 1976; children: Andrea Hofer Hill, Adam Reiff Hill, Amelia Reiff Hill. Student, Wellesley Coll., 1967-68; BS, Okla. State U., 1971; MS, Rice U., 1974, PhD, 1975. Cert. secondary tchr., Okla., Tex. Rsch. assoc. space physics and astronomy dept. Rice U., Houston, 1975, asst. prof. space physics and astronomy dept., 1978-81, assoc. chmn. space physics and astronomy dept., 1979-85, assoc. rsch. sci., 1981-87, sr. rsch. scientist, 1987-90; resident rsch. assoc. Marshall Space Flight Ctr., Huntsville, Ala., 1975-76; adj. asst. prof. Rice U., 1976-78, disting. faculty fellow, 1990-92, prof. 1992—; mem. sci. team Atmosphere Explorer Mission, Dynamics Explorer Mission, Global Geospace Sci. Mission, ESA/Cluster Mission; prin. investigator The Public Connection NASA; cons. Houston Mus. Natural Sci., 1986—; adv. com. on atmospheric scis. NSF, Washington, 1988-92; mem. stategic implementation study panel NASA, Washington, 1989-91; mem. space sci. adv. com. NASA, 1993—; univ. rep. U. Space Rsch. Assn., Washington, 1993— (mem. nom. com.); exec. com. George Observatory, Houston, 1989-92, others. Designer Cockrell Sundial/Solar Telescope, 1989; editor EOS (sci. newspaper), 1986-89; contbr. articles to profl. jours. Trustee, Citizens' Environ. Coalition, Houston, 1978—, pres. 1980-85; mem. air quality com. Houston/Galveston Area Coun., 1980-83, Green Ribbon Com., City of Houston, 1981-83; active coms. Macedonia United Meth. Ch., 1988—. Named rsch. fellow NAS/NRC., 1975, an Outstanding Young Woman Am., 1977, '80, to Houston's Women on the Move, 1990; recipient grant NSF, Houston, 1990-92, NASA, 1993, 94. Mem. Am. Geophys. Union (fin. com. 1980-82, editor search com. 1992, awards com.), Am. Meteorol. Soc. (coun. 1985-88), Cosmos Club, Wellesley Club, Internat. Union of Geodesy and Geophysics (del. 1975, 81, 83, 89, 91, 93, 95, chair working group 2F, 1991-95). Avocations: organic gardening, beef ranching. Office: Rice U Dept Space Physics 6100 S Main St Houston TX 77251-1892

REIFFEL, LEONARD, physicist, scientific consultant; b. Chgo., Sept. 30, 1927; s. Carl and Sophie (Miller) R.; m. Judith Eve Blumenthal, 1952 (div. 1962); children—Evan Carl, David Lee; m. Nancy L. Jeffers, 1971. B.Sc., Ill. Inst. Tech., 1947, M.Sc., 1948, Ph.D., 1953. Physicist Perkin-Elmer Corp., Conn., 1948; engring. physicist U. Chgo. Inst. Nuclear Studies, 1948-49; with Ill. Inst. Tech. Research Inst., Chgo., 1949-65, dir. physics research, 1956-63, v.p., 1963-65; cons. to Apollo program NASA Hdqrs., 1965-70, pvt. practice cons., 1970—; tech. dir. manned space flight expts. bd. NASA, 1966-68; chmn. bd. Instructional Dynamics, Inc., 1966-81, Interand Corp., 1969-91, Telestrator Industries, Inc., 1970-73; sci. editor Sta. WBBM-CBS radio, Chgo.; sci. cons./commentator WBBM-TV, 1971-72; host Backyard Safari, 1971-73; sci. feature broadcaster WEEI-CBS radio, Boston, 1965-75; syndicated newspaper columnist World Book Ency. Sci. Service, Inc. (later Universal Sci. News, Inc.), 1966-72, Los Angeles Times Syndicate, 1972-76; sci. cons. CBS Network, 1967-71; chmn. Exelar Corp., Chgo., 1991—; chmn. bd., pres., CEO Amerare Corp., Chgo., 1992-95; mem. bd of overseers Armour Coll. Ill. Inst. Tech., 1995—; cons. Korean Govt. on establishment atomic energy rsch. program; mem. adv. com. isotope and radiation devel. AEC; com. rsch. reactors NAS, 1958-64; cons. U.S. Army, 1976—. Author: (book) The Contaminant, 1979; author numerous sci. papers. Bd. dirs. Student Competitions on Relevant Engring. Named Outstanding Young Man of Year Chgo. Jr. C. of C., 1954, 61; recipient Merit award Chgo. Tech. Socs., 1968; Peabody award for radio edn., 1968; IR-100 award for inventing Telestrator CBS Chalkboard, 1970; award for coverage space events Aviation Writers Assn., 1971; IR-100 award for invention underwater diver communications system, 1972, IR-100 award for DISCON video teleconferencing systems, 1985, Third Annual High Tech Entrepreneur award, 1986; also for invention Audiografix, 1973; Disting. Alumni Achievement award Ill. Inst. Tech., 1974, named to Hall of Fame IIT, 1984. Fellow Am. Phys. Soc.; mem. AAAS, Chgo. Literary Club, Sigma Xi, Tau Beta Pi, Eta Kappa Nu. Patentee in field; responsible for world's 1st indsl. nuclear reactor, 1956. Home: 602 W Deming Pl Chicago IL 60614-2618

REIFLER, CLIFFORD BRUCE, psychiatrist, educator; b. Chgo., Dec. 28, 1931; s. Eugene Alan and Harriet (Offer) R.; m. Barbara Karnuth, Sept. 11,

1954; children: Margery Sue, Cynthia Jean, Angela Harriet. AB, U. Chgo., 1951; BS, Northwestern U., 1953; MD, Yale U., 1957; MPH, U. N.C., 1967. Intern Univ. Hosps., Ann Arbor, Mich., 1957-58; resident in psychiatry Strong Meml. Hosp., Rochester, N.Y., 1958-61; mem. faculty U. N.C. Med. Sch., 1963-70, assoc. prof. psychiatry, 1969-70, assoc. prof. mental health Sch. Pub. Health, 1969-70, sr. psychiatrist, chief mental health sect., student health svc., 1963-70; prof. health svcs., psychiatry and community and preventive medicine U. Rochester Med. Sch., 1970-94, dir. univ. health svc., 1970-80, 81-94, prof. emeritus of psychiatry and health svcs., dir. emeritus, 1994—, interim v.p. student affairs, 1980-81, sr. assoc. dean for clin. affairs Sch. Medicine and Dentistry, acting chmn. dept. health svcs., 1983-85; med. dir. Strong Meml. Hosp., 1983-85; bd. dirs. Genesee Valley Group Health Assn., 1972-82; cons. in field; vis. prof. of psychiatry, Harvard U. Med. Sch., 1987; Dana L. Farnsworth hon. cons. Harvard U. Health Service, 1987. Co-author: Mental Health on the Campus-A Field Study, 1973; co-author: The Alternative Services: Their Role in Mental Health, 1975, Old Folks at Home-A Field Study of Nursing and Board-and-Care Homes, 1976; exec. editor Jour. Am. Coll. Health, 1983—; mem. editorial bd. Jour. of Coll. Student Psychotherapy, 1986—; contbr. profl. jours. Bd. dirs. Am. Coll. Health Found., 1994—, chair 1995—; bd. dirs. Rochester Meml. Soc., 1971-74; mem. med. adv. com., bd. dirs. Planned Parenthood Rochester and Monroe County, 1973-74; mem. devel. com. Seneca Zool. Soc., 1990-95, chair 1993-95, trustee, 1991—; mem. mem. com. Rochester Philharm. Orch. Inc., 1981-83. With M.C., USAF, 1961-63. Fellow Am. Coll. Health Assn. (pres. 1976-77, Edward Hitchcock award 1981, Ruth C. Boynton award 1988), Am. Psychiat. Assn. (life), Am. Coll. Physician Execs. (disting.); mem. N.Y. State Coll. Health Assn. Home: 143 Palmerston Rd Rochester NY 14618-1247 Office: U Health Svc 250 Crittenden Blvd Box 617 Rochester NY 14642-8617

REIFSNIDER, KENNETH LEONARD, metallurgist, educator; b. Balt., Feb. 19, 1940; s. David Leonard and Daisy Pearl (Hess) R.; m. Loretta Lieb, June 15, 1963; children—Eric Scott, Jason Miles. BA, Western Md. Coll., 1963; BS in Engring., Johns Hopkins U., 1963, MS in Engring., 1965, PhD, 1968. Jr. instr. John Hopkins U., Balt., 1966-67; asst. prof. Va. Poly. Inst. and State U., Blacksburg, 1968-72, assoc. prof., 1972-75, prof., 1975-83, Reynolds Metals prof. engring. sci. and mechanics, 1983-90, Alexander Giacco prof., 1990—, also chmn. materials engring. sci. Ph.D. program, 1974-92, chmn. adminstrn. bd. Ctr. Composite Materials and Structures, 1984, 1994—; dir. Va. Inst. for Material Systems, 1988—; engr. Lawrence Livermore Nat. Lab., 1981; cons. in materials sci. NATO, 1969, 75. Mem. troop 44 com. Boy Scouts Am., Blacksburg, Va. Recipient Va. Acad. Sci. J. Shelton Horsley award, 1978, Va. Poly. Inst. Alumni award, 1982, Disting. Rsch. award Am. Soc. Composites, 1992. Fellow ASTM (founder Jour. of Composites Tech. and Rsch., vice chmn. standing com. on publs., award of merit 1982); mem. ASME, Council on Engring. Editor, co-editor, author books, book chpts., articles for profl. publs.

REIFSNYDER, CHARLES FRANK, lawyer; b. Ottumwa, Iowa, Sept. 6, 1920; s. Charles L. and Lena (Emery) R.; A.B., George Washington U., 1944, LL.B., 1946; m. Sally Ann Evans, Dec. 27, 1948; children: Daniel Alan, Jeremy Evans; m. Nancy Lee Laws, Mar. 4, 1960; 1 child, Frank Laws. Admitted to D.C. bar, 1945; sec. Judge T. Alan Goldsborough, U.S. Dist. Ct., Washington, 1945; law clk. Chief Judge Bolitha J. Laws, U.S. Dist. Ct., 1946-47; asst. U.S. atty., Washington, 1947-51; spl. asst. to Atty. Gen. U.S., 1950-51; assoc. Hogan & Hartson, Washington, 1951-58, ptnr., 1959-85; chmn. personnel security rev. bd. Energy Rsch. and Devel. Adminstrn. (formerly AEC). Trustee, Legal Aid Agy. (now Pub. Defender Svc.), Washington, 1960-67; bd. dirs. Nat. Jud. Coll., Reno, 1968-70. Fellow Inst. Jud. Adminstrn., N.Y.C., 1967-68. Fellow Internat. Soc. Barristers, Am. Bar Found.; mem. Am. (chmn. spl. com. coordination jud. improvements 1971-74, mem. spl. com. atomic energy law 1969-73, chmn. div. jud. adminstrn. 1967-68, del. 1968-69), Fed., Fed. Energy (pres. 1981-82, chmn. com. natural gas 1967-68), D.C. (dir. 1955-56) bar assns., Am. Arbitration Assn., (nat. panel arbitrators), Am. Judicature Soc. (dir. 1972-76), Am. Law Inst., Phi Delta Phi, Sigma Nu. Episcopalian. Clubs: Met., Barristers, Lawyers (Washington), Gibson Island (Md.) Yacht Squadron, Annapolis (Md.) Yacht, Farmington Country (Charlottesville, Va.). Home: Skywater Rd-Box 30 Gibson Island MD 21056

REIFSNYDER, WILLIAM EDWARD, meteorologist; b. Ridgway, Pa., Mar. 29, 1924; s. Howard William and Madolin (Boyer) R.; m. Marylou Bishop, Dec. 19, 1954 (dec. July 1990); children: Rita, Cheryl, Gawain. B.S. in Meteorology, NYU, 1944; M.F., U. Calif., Berkeley, 1949; Ph.D., Yale U., 1954. Cert. cons. meteorologist. Meteorologist Pacific S.W. Forest and Range Expt. Sta., 1952-55; mem. faculty Yale U., 1955-90, prof. emeritus, 1990—, prof. forest meteorology and biometeorology, 1967-90; vis. scientist Max Planck Inst. for Meteorology, Hamburg, U. Munich, Environ. Rsch. Labs., Nat. Oceanic and Atmospheric Adminstrn.; cons. World Meteorol. Orgn., UN Univ., Internat. Coun. Rsch. in Agroforestry. Author: Hut Hopping in the Austrian Alps, Footloose in the Swiss Alps, The High Huts of the White Mountains, Radiant Energy in Relation to Forests, Weathering the Wilderness, Adventuring in the Alps; editor-in-chief Agrl. and Forest Meteorology; editor: Meteorology and Agroforestry. Bd. dirs. Am. Youth Hostels. Service with USAAF, 1943-47. Fellow AAAS; mem. Conn. Acad. Sci. and Engring. (corr.), Am. Meteorol. Soc. (Outstanding Achievement in Biometeorology award), Soc. Am. Foresters, Internat. Soc. Biometeorology (v.p.). Home: HC81 (Lama) Box 3 Questa NM 87556 Office: Sch Forestry and Environ Studies Yale U New Haven CT 06511

REIG, JUNE WILSON, writer, director, producer; b. Schenectady, N.Y., June 1, 1933; d. Wallace John and Lillian Lucy (Gay) Wilson; m. Robert Maxwell, Nov. 26, 1969. BA summa cum laude, N.Y. State U., 1954; MA in Dramatic Arts, NYU, 1962. Instr. NYU, 1962-67; producer NYU Theater, 1963-67; writer, producer, dir. NBC, N.Y.C., 1963-73; writer-dir. NBC TV News & Public Affairs, 1966; pres. Bunny/Chord Prodns., N.Y.C., 1972—. Author: Diary of the Boy King Tut-Ankh-Amen, 1978; writer, dir. (TV film spl.) Stuart Little, 1966 (Peabody award Prix Jeunesse); writer (TV spl.) The Reluctant Dragon, 1968 (Brotherhood award), (music spls.) The Heart of Christmas, 1965, An Afternoon at Tanglewood (Peabody award); writer, dir., producer (TV spls.) Rabbit Hill, 1966 (ALA award) Bill Cosby As I See It, 1970 (Ohio State award) A Day With Bill Cosby, 1971, Jennifer & Me, 1972; (TV daily series) Watch Your Child - The Me Too Show, 1973 (Action for Children's TV Achievement award); prodr., writer (TV spl.) Little Women, the ballet, 1976, Tut, the Boy King, 1978 (Peabody award); films in permanent collection of Mus. Broadcasting, N.Y.C. Recipient Prix Jeunesse, 1966, Christopher award, 1970, Emmy award nomination, 1966, 76. Mem. Writers Guild Am., Dirs. Guild Am., Nat. Acad. TV Arts and Scis., NYU Alumni Assn., Internat. Soc. Animal Rights, Friends of Animals, Audubon Soc. Club: Alan Devoe Bird (Old Chatham, N.Y.). Avocations: photography, music, animals. Office: Bunny/Chord Prodns Inc Ste 1405 119 W 57th St New York NY 10019-2401 *Whether I am working on a teleplay or book, I write about things I believe children are interested in: feelings, aspirations, caring, animals, loving. As I see it, too much of the fare for young people gives them a distorted view of how much violence there is in the world, and I want to counteract that impression. I want to write about things that create a sense of worth, warm security, and an absence of unnecessary anxiety. When I do write about the darker things that happen in life, it is to help the young person understand himself and the world a little better.*

REIGHARD, HOMER LEROY, physician; b. Martinsburg, Pa., Dec. 1, 1924; s. David F. and Cora E. (Steel) R.; m. Barbara Jane Suttell, Dec. 14, 1951; children: Carol, Janet, Paul. B.S., Franklin and Marshall Coll., 1945; M.D., Temple U., 1948; M.P.H., Harvard U., 1961. Intern Temple U. Hosp., Phila., 1948-49; physician-in charge accidents dispensary Temple U. Hosp., 1949-50; med. officer CAA, Washington, 1953-59; practice medicine Bethesda, Md., 1953-60; chief med. standards div. FAA, 1959-61, spl. asst. to civil air surgeon, 1962-63, dep. fed. air surgeon, 1963-75, fed. air surgeon, 1975-84; cons. in aviation medicine, 1984—, workplace anti-drug programs, 1987—. Bd.dirs. Aviation Rsch. & Edn. Found., 1985-92. Served with M.C, USAF, 1950-53. Recipient Meritorious Service award FAA, 1970, Disting. Career Service award, FAA, 1984. Fellow Aerospace Med. Assn. (Harry G. Moseley flight safety award 1977); mem. Phi Beta Kappa. Developer passenger screening system to identify potential hijackers. Home: 10215 Hatherleigh Dr Bethesda MD 20814-2223

REIGLE, JAMES D., manufacturing executive; b. 1926. BS in Commerce, Ohio U., 1949. With Regal Ware Inc., 1949—, asst. gen. mgr., 1955-62, v.p. sales and mgmt., 1962-65, pres., 1965—, now pres., chmn. bd. Office: Regal Ware Inc 1675 Reigle Dr Kewaskum WI 53040*

REIGROD, ROBERT HULL, manufacturing executive; b. N.Y.C., Mar. 26, 1941; s. David and Beatrice (Simon) R.; divorced; children: Sandra, Donald. BA in Anthropology, Calif. State U., Long Beach, 1973. Account exec. Ira Haupt & Co., N.Y.C., 1961-64; regional adminstrv. mgr. Brother Internat. Corp., Los Angeles, 1964-70; regional sales mgr. Brother Internat. Corp., Irvine, Calif., 1970-77, gen. mgr. west region, 1977-82; v.p. Brother Internat. Corp., 1982-86; dir., sr. v.p. Brother Internat. Corp., Somerset, N.J., 1986—; pres. Brother Internat. de Mexico, S.A. de C.V., 1992—. Trustee Leukemia Soc. Am., 1982-84; bd. dirs. Irvine Children's Fund, 1988-90. Mem. Japan Soc. South Fla. (dir. 1994—, trustee). Office: Brother Internat Corp 3333 W Comml Blvd Fort Lauderdale FL 33309

REIKEN, STEVEN ROSS, biomedical engineer; b. Bklyn., Feb. 20, 1964; s. Jerome and Marilyn Helene (Cohen) R. BS, Tufts U., 1986; MS, Mich. State U., 1988, PhD, 1991. Rsch. assoc. Mich. State U., East Lansing, 1986-91, asst. prof., 1992; postdoctoral assoc. Wash. State U., Pullman, 1991-93; rsch. fellow Mass. Gen. Hosp./Harvard Med. Sch./Shriners Burns Inst., Boston, 1993—. Contbr. articles to profl. jours. Dow Chem. Co. tchg. fellow, 1991, Coll. Engring. fellow Mich. State U., 1988. Mem. AIChE, Am. Chem. Soc., Sigma Xi. Democrat. Jewish. Achievements include patent for membrane based biosensor with receptor tailored to specific antigens. Avocations: scuba diving, ultimate frisbee, skiing. Office: Shriners Burns Inst 1 Kendall Sq Ste 1400 W Cambridge MA 02139-1562

REILAND, LOWELL KEITH, sculptor; b. Wahpeton, N.D., May 11, 1948; s. Peter Paul And Evelyn Ruth (Huss) R. Student, N.D. State U., 1966-68; BA, BS, Moorhead State U., 1971; MFA, Cornell U., 1974. Intern teaching Anglo-Am. Sch., Stockholm, 1971; artist-in-residence Pulpit Rock Artist's Community, Woodstock, Conn., 1974-76; asst. to Richard Lippold, Archtl. Sculptor, N.Y.C., 1970, 75, 77; artist-in-residence Moorhead (Minn.) State U., 1978; artist N.Y.C., 1976-92; lectr.-at-large N.D. State U., Fargo, 1988; lectr. art Conn. Assn. Psychiatrists Ann. Meeting, New Haven, 1985, New Sch., N.Y.C., 1986, Plains Art Mus., Moorhead, 1988, philosophy N.D. State U., Fargo, 1988, Westchester C.C., Westerly Pub. Libr., 1992, Lyman Allyn Art Mus., 1993; participant bronze casting invitational U. Conn., Storrs, 1982. Exhibited at Sarah Y. Rentschler Gallery, N.Y.C., 1979-83, Soho Ctr. for Visual Artists, N.Y.C., 1987, DiLaurenti Gallery, N.Y.C., 1987, Aldrich Mus., Contemporary Art, Ridgefield, Conn., 1988, Plains Art Mus., Moorhead, 1988, Bayly Art Mus. of U. Va., Charlottesville, Travel: Studio Sch., N.Y.C., 1990, Wichita (Kans.) Art Mus., 1990, Lyman Allyn Art Mus., 1993-94, Virginia Lynch Gallery, R.I., 1994, 96; prin. works include City of Fargo, 1978, Moorhead State U., 1978, collection Clara M. Eagle Mus., Murray, Ky., 1984, collection Palace of the Sultan of Brunei, 1985; contbr. articles to profl. jours. Recipient Art award/prize Am. Acad. and Inst. Arts and Letters, N.Y.C., 1986; artist's grantee Pollock/Krasner Found., N.Y.C., 1987-88, Change, Inc., 1989, exhbn. grantee Artist's Space, N.Y.C., 1985; grantee, resident Art League Schleswig-Holsteinisches Kunstlerhaus, Selk, Fed. Republic Germany, 1990. Avocations: studies Cen., S.Am. and Asian primative arts, studies Italian Renaissance art. Home and Studio: Lowell Reiland Sculpture Indsl Trust Co Bldg 14 High St Westerly RI 02891-1854

REILEY, T. PHILLIP, systems analyst; b. Ft. Lewis, Wash., May 5, 1950; s. Thomas Phillip and Anne Marie (Russick) R. BSc in Biophysics, Pa. State U., 1973; postgrad. in Bus. Adminstrn., Rutgers U.; MBA, NYU, 1991. Cert. prodn. and inventory mgmt., cert. integrated resource mgmt. Inventory supr. Leland Tube Co., South Plainfield, N.J., 1973-76; prodn. inventory control supr. Bomar Crystal Co., Middlesex, N.J., 1976-79; prodn. control mgr. Codi Semicondr. Inc., Linden, N.J., 1979-81; mfg. systems analyst Western Union Info. Systems, Mahwah, N.J., 1981-85; sr. systems analyst Nabisco Brands Biscuit Div., Parsippany, N.J., 1985-95, tech. cons., 1994—. Mem. Am. Prodn. and Inventory Control Soc. (past chmn. ednl. com. Raritan Valley chpt.), N.Y. Acad. Scis., Mensa, Coun. Logistics Mgmt., Am. Inst. Mgmt. Accts. Republican. Home: 56 Carlton Club Dr Piscataway NJ 08854-3114 Office: Nabisco Brands 100 Deforest Ave East Hanover NJ 07936-2813

REILING, HENRY BERNARD, business educator; b. Richmond, Ky., Feb. 5, 1938; s. Henry Bernard and Lucille Frances (Fowler) R.; m. Carol-Lina Maria Schuetz, June 4, 1962; children: Christina Lucille, Maria Hays, Carol-Lena Alexis. B.A., Northwestern U., 1960; M.B.A., Harvard U., 1962; J.D., Columbia U., 1965. Bar: N.Y. 1965. Mem. faculty Columbia U. Bus. Sch., 1965-76, prof., 1974-76; vis. prof. Stanford U. Bus. Sch., 1974-75; vis. asso. prof. Harvard U. Bus. Sch., 1972-73, prof., 1976—, Eli Goldston prof. bus. adminstrn., 1978—; bd. dirs. Levitz Furniture Inc. Contbr. bus. and law jours. Trustee Riverside Ch., N.Y.C., 1976-77; mem. vis. com. Northwestern U. Coll. Arts and Scis., 1989—. Recipient Alumnus Merit award Northwestern U., 1996. Mem. ABA, N.Y. Bar Assn., Bar Assn. City N.Y., Am. Fin. Assn., Fin. Mgmt. Assn., Nat. Tax Assn., Tax Inst. Am., Union Club (N.Y.C.), Beta Gamma Sigma (hon.). Home: 28 Meriam St Lexington MA 02173-3600 Office: Harvard U Bus Sch Boston MA 02163

REILLEY, JAMES CLARK, artist, cartoonist, small business owner; b. Detroit, Nov. 4, 1919; s. James Aloyisus and Lillian May (Cole) R.; m. Beatrice C. Clemente, May 10, 1952; children: James A. (dec.), Anthony Francis, Beatrice Anita. Grad., Art Inst. of Pitts., 1948. Artist Banner Advt., Phila., 1948-49; layout artist Lit Bros. Dept. Store, Phila., 1949; comic book illustrator John Prentice, Long Island, N.Y., 1950; artist DuPont Co., Wilmington, Del., 1950-59; artist/owner Jim Reilley Studio, Wilmington, 1959-94; ret. Sgt. USAAF, 1942-45. Inducted to Penns Grove H.S. Personal Achievement Hall of Fame, 1996. Roman Catholic. Avocations: fishing, music, sports. Home: 110 N Broad St Penns Grove NJ 08069-1269

REILLY, DANIEL PATRICK, bishop; b. Providence, May 12, 1928; s. Francis E. and Mary (Burns) R. Student, Our Lady of Providence Sem., 1943-48, Grand Seminaire, St. Brieuc, France, 1948-53, Harvard U., 1954-55, Boston Coll., 1955-56; D (hon.), Providence Coll.; D. (hon.), St. Michael's Coll.; D (hon.), Holy Apostles Coll. and Sem., Salve Regina Coll., Our Lady of Providence Coll., Sacred Heart U., Assumption Coll., 1995, Anna Maria Coll., 1995, Holy Cross Coll., 1996. Ordained priest Roman Catholic Ch., 1953; asst. pastor Cathedral Saints Peter and Paul, Providence, 1953-54; asst. chancellor Diocese of Providence, 1954-56, sec. to bishop, 1956-64, chancellor, 1964-72, adminstr., 1971-72, vicar gen., 1972-75; became monsignor, 1964, consecrated bishop, 1975; bishop of Norwich, Conn., 1975-94; installed bishop of Worcester, Mass., 1994—; Conn. state chaplain K.C., 1976-94; Episcopal moderator Nat. Cath. Cemetery Corp., 1977-87; ad hoc mem. to aid ch. in Ea. Europe NCCB/U.S. Cath. Conf., adminstrv. com. mem., 1976-86, 92—; pro-life com. mem. NCCB, 1989-92, chmn. 10th anniversary peace pastoral com., 1992-93, chmn. internat. policy com., 1993; mem. Priestly Life and Ministry Commn., 1991-94; past pres. New Eng. Consultation Ch. Leaders; drafting com. mem. U.S. Cath. Conf. Pastoral Letter on Peace, 1983, mem. com. on cons.; active Holy See Pontifical Coun.-Cor Unum, 1984-89. Trustee Cath. Mut. Relief Soc., Omaha, 1979—, St. John's Sem., Brighton, Mass., 1987—, Am. Coll., Louvain, Belgium, St. Mary's Sem., Balt.; bd. dirs. United Way Southeastern Conn., 1976-94, Conn. Drug and Adv. Coun., 1978-80; chmn. bd. Cath. Relief Svcs., 1978-86; mem. fin. and budget com. U.S. Cath. Conf., 1985-87; chancellor Holy Apostles Coll. and Sem., Cromwell, Conn., 1982-94; pres. Conn. Interfaith Housing, 1975-94; cons. Pontifical Coun. Justice and Peace, 1995. Mem. Rotary. Home: 2 High Ridge Rd Worcester MA 01602-1432 *If you would make a true success of your life for time and for eternity, never forget that it will be achieved by your willingness to make countless efforts that will be known only to God.*

REILLY, DAVID HENRY, university dean; b. Paterson, N.J., Nov. 7, 1936; s. David Henry and Ethel Taylor (Alt) R.; m. Jean Lockwood, July 2, 1960; children—David Scott, Chris Robert, Sandra Jean. B.A., U. Vt., 1959; Ed.M., Rutgers U., 1962, Ed.D., 1965. Diplomate: Am. Bd. Profl. Psychology. Remedial reading instr. Drake Sch. of N.J. Neuro-Psychiat. Inst., Princeton, 1959-62; jr. fellow psychol. services at inst. Drake Sch. of N.J. Neuro-Psychiat. Inst., summer 1962-63; research asst. N.J. Bur. Research Neurology and Psychiatry; also sch. psychologist Woodbridge (N.J.) sch. system, 1962-63; clin. psychologist, then research asso. N.J. Bur. Research Neurology and Psychiatry, 1963-64, 65; sch. and research psychologist Woodbridge sch. system, 1964-65; post doctoral fellow clin. child psychology Devereux Found., Devon, Pa., 1965-66; mem. faculty U. N.C., Chapel Hill, 1966-74; prof. psychology U. N.C., 1974—, chmn. dept. sch. psychology program, 1966-74; dean U. N.C. (Sch. Edn.), Greensboro, 1974-86; dean Coll. of Grad. and Profl. Studies The Citadel, Charleston, 1992—; Mem. N.C. Bd. Examiners Practicing Psychologists, 1973—, treas., 1975, chmn., 1976. Contbr. articles to profl. jours. Research grantee NIMH, 1963; Fulbright Vis. scholar Republic of Cyprus, 1986-87, USSR, 1990. Fellow Am. Psychol. Assn.; mem. Southeastern Psychol. Assn., N.C. Psychol. Assn. (pres. 1980-81), N.C. Assn. Coll. Tchr. Edn. (pres. 1981), N.C. Sch. Psychology Assn. (pres. 1976-77). Home: 306 Mimms Ave Charleston SC 29409

REILLY, EDWARD ARTHUR, lawyer; b. N.Y.C., Dec. 17, 1943; s. Edward Arthur and Anna Marguerite (Sautter) R.; children: M. Teresa, Edward A. A.B., Princeton U., 1965; J.D., Duke U., 1968. Bar: N.Y. 1969, N.C. 1971, Fla. 1979, Conn. 1983. Asst. dean law sch. Duke U., 1970-72; assoc. Shearman & Sterling, N.Y.C., 1972-80, ptnr., 1980-87; ptnr. Harlow, Reilly, Derr & Stark, Research Triangle Park, N.C., 1988-90; counsel Morris & McVeigh, N.Y.C., 1991-93, ptnr., 1993—. Lt. USNR, 1968-80. Decorated Chevalier de l'Ordre des Arts et des Lettres, French Govt.-Ministry of Culture and Comm., 1992. Fellow Am. Coll. Trust & Estate Counsel; mem. N.Y. State Bar Assn., Fla. Bar Assn., Conn. Bar Assn. Episcopalian. Office: Morris & McVeigh 767 3rd Ave New York NY 10017-2023

REILLY, EDWARD FRANCIS, JR., former state senator, federal agency administrator; b. Leavenworth, Kans., Mar. 24, 1937; s. Edward F. and Marian C. (Sullivan) R.; BA, U. Kans., 1961. V.p. Reilly & Sons, Inc., Leavenworth, 1967-92; pres. Yllier Lake Estates, Inc., Easton, Kans., 1965-89; mem. Kans. Ho. of Reps., 1963-64; mem. Kans. State Senate, 1964-92, asst. majority leader, 1977-80, vice-chmn. govtl. orgn., chmn. ins. subcom., chmn. fed. and state affairs com. Mem. Nat. Commn. on Accreditation of Law Enforcement Agys.; chmn. U.S. Parole Commission Dept. of Justice, Md., 1992—; commr. ex officio U.S. Sentencing Commn., Washington; del. to Republican Nat. Conv., Miami Beach, Fla., 1968; chmn. Leavenworth County Radio Free Europe Fund, 1972; bd. dirs. St. John's Hosp., Leavenworth, 1970-79, sec.; bd. dirs. Leavenworth Assn. for Handicapped, 1968-69, ARC, Leavenworth chpt., Kans. Blue Cross/Blue Shield, 1969-72; apptd. by Pres. Reagan Nat. Hwy. Safety Adv. Com.; active Trinity Nat. Leadership Roundtable, Cath. Campaign Am., Kans. Adv. Bd. Juvenile Offenders, Nat. Com. Cmty. Corrections. Recipient Community Leaders of Am., 1971, 85, 86, Hallpac Pub. Svc. award, 1988, Am. Police Hall of Fame award, 1990, Good Samaritan award Order of Michael the Arch Angel Police Legion, 1990, Commendation award mayor and city commn. of Leavenworth, Kans., 1990, Carnegie Hero Fund Commn. award and medallion, 1991, Silver Angel award Kans. Cath. Conf., 1992; named Outstanding Young Men Am., 1965-76. Mem. Nat. Inst. Corrections (adv. bd.), Am. Paroling Authorities Internat., Am. Correctional Assn., Am. Probation and Paroling Assn., Leavenworth C. of C. (hon. dir. 1970-73), Assn. U.S. Army (Henry Leavenworth award 1960), Kansas City (Kans.) C. of C., Leavenworth Hist. Soc. (dir. 1968-73), John Carroll Soc., Native Sons of Kansas City, Ancient Order of Hibernians, U.S. Supreme Ct. Hist. Soc., Kiwanis (dir. 1969-70, Connelly award 1991, Legion of Honor award 1996), K.C., Elks, Eagles, Order of Malta. Republican. Roman Catholic.

REILLY, EDWARD J., public relations executive. Ptnr. Robinson Lake Lerer & Montgomery Sawyer Miller Group, N.Y.C. Office: Robinson Lake Lerer & Montgomer Sawyer Miller Group 75 Rockefeller Plz New York NY 10019*

REILLY, FRANK KELLY, business educator; b. Chgo., Dec. 30, 1935; s. Clarence Raymond and Mary Josephine (Ruckrigel) R.; m. Therese Adele Bourke, Aug. 2, 1958; children: Frank Kelly III, Clarence Raymond II, Therese B., Edgar B. B.B.A., U. Notre Dame, 1957; M.B.A., Northwestern U., 1961, U. Chgo., 1964; Ph.D., U. Chgo., 1968; LLD (hon.), St. Michael's Coll., 1991. Chartered fin. analyst. Trader Goldman Sachs & Co., Chgo., 1958-59; security analyst Tech. Fund, Chgo., 1959-62; asst. prof. U. Kans., Lawrence, 1965-68, assoc. prof., 1968-72; prof. bus., assoc. dir. div. bus. and econ. research U. Wyo., Laramie, 1972-75; prof. fin. U. Ill., Champaign-Urbana, 1975-81; Bernard J. Hank prof. U. Notre Dame, Ind., 1981—, dean Coll. Bus. Adminstrn., 1981-87; bd. dirs., chmn. First Interstate Bank No. Ind., Brinson Global Fund Inc., Assn. Investment Mgmt. and Rsch., Inst. Chartered Fin. Analysts (also vice chair), NIBCO Corp., Internat. Bd. CFPs, Greenwood Trust Corp., Ft. Dearborn Income Securities. Author: Investment Analysis and Portfolio Management, 1979, 4th edit., 1994, Investments, 1982, 4th edit., 1995; co-editor: Ethics and the Investment Industry, 1989; editor: Readings and Issues in Investments, 1975, High Yield Bonds: Analysis and Risk Assessment, 1990; assoc. editor Fin. Mgmt., 1977-82, Quar. Rev. Econs. and Bus, 1979-87, Fin. Rev., 1979-87, 92—, Jour. Fin. Edn., 1981—, Jour. Applied Bus. Rsch., 1986—, Fin. Svcs. Rev., 1989—, Internat. Rev. Econs. and Fin., 1992—, European Jour. Fin., 1994—. Arthur J. Schmidt Found. fellow, 1962-65; U. Chgo. fellow, 1963-65. Mem. Midwest Bus. Adminstrn. Assn. (pres. 1974-75), Am. Fin. Assn., Western Fin. Assn. (exec. com. 1973-75), Ea. Fin. Assn. (exec. com. 1979-84, pres. 1982-83), Midwest Fin. Assn. (pres. 1993-94), Fin. Analysts Fedn., Fin. Mgmt. Assn. (pres. 1983-84, chmn. 1985-91, bd. dirs.), Acad. Fin. Svcs. (pres. 1990-91), Inst. Chartered Fin. Analysts (coun. of examiners, rsch. and edn. com., edn. steering com., C. Stewart Shepard award 1991), Internat. Assoc. Fin. Planners (ednl. resource com., bd. dirs.), Assn. of Investment Mgmt. and Rsch., Investments Analysts Soc. Chgo. (bd. dirs. 1988-89), Beta Gamma Sigma. Roman Catholic. Office: U Notre Dame Coll Bus Adminstrn Notre Dame IN 46556 *Any success I have enjoyed is due to the talents God has given me and my belief that I have an obligation to maximize the output from those talents by hard work, while never forgetting that my family comes first because they have always provided me with the love and support necessary for success and happiness.*

REILLY, GEORGE, lawyer; b. Waukegan, Ill., Nov. 29, 1934; s. James M. and Hilda Clara (Van Hieresele) R.; m. Dadee Bruce, Dec. 23, 1957; children: Laurene Beth, Theresa Ann. BA, Ill. Coll., 1956; MS, S.D. State U., 1958; JD, U. Minn., 1964. Bar: Minn. 1964, U.S. Dist. Ct. Minn. 1964, U.S. Ct. Appeals (8th cir.) 1965. Assoc. Leonard, Street and Deinard, Mpls., 1964-70, ptnr., 1973-82, mng. ptnr., 1983-91, ptnr., chair of bus. divsn., 1991-96; chief dep. atty. gen. State of Minn., St. Paul, 1971-72; chief counsel Minn. Housing and Fin. Agy., St. Paul, 1972-80. Campaign chair Spannaus for Atty. Gen. com., 1974, 78, Spannaus for Gov., 1982. Mem. ABA, Minn. State Bar Assn., Citizens League, Variety Childrens Assn. (pres.). Democrat. Avocations: travel, sports. Office: Leonard Street & Deinard 150 S 5th St Ste 2300 Minneapolis MN 55402-4223

REILLY, GEORGE LOVE ANTHONY, history educator; b. Montclair, N.J., Oct. 17, 1918; s. James Joseph and Anna F. (Love) R.; m. Ethel M. Ehrlich, Aug. 29, 1953; children—Mary Anne, Elizabeth Ruthe, Georgette Louise. A.B. cum laude, Seton Hall U., 1940; A.M., Harvard U., 1942; Ph.D., Columbia U., 1951. Instr. Caldwell (N.J.) Coll., 1946-48, Rutgers U., New Brunswick, N.J., 1948-51; mem. faculty Seton Hall U., South Orange, N.J., 1951—; prof. history Seton Hall U., 1960—, chmn. dept., 1961—; faculty Irish Studies seminar Columbia U., 1974—. Author: Camden and Amboy Railroad in New Jersey Politics, 1951, Sacred Heart in Bloomfield, 1953, A Century of Catholicism, 1956, Neighbors in New Jersey, 1963, History of Seton Hall University, 1980; co-author: Shepherds of Newark, 1978, also articles.; Adv. editor: Cath. Hist. Rev, 1957-61; mem. editorial bd. Avocate, Newark, 1968—. Served to capt. F.A. AUS, 1942-45. Mem. Nat. Geog. Soc., Am., Am. Cath. hist. assns., Conf. on Brit. Studies, Victorian Studies Assn., N.J. Hist. Soc. Democrat. Roman Catholic. Club: Harvard (N.J.). Home: 273 Scotland Rd South Orange NJ 07079-2040

REILLY, JEANETTE P., clinical psychologist; b. Denver, Oct. 19, 1908; d. George L. and Marie (Bloedorn) Parker; A.B., U. Colo., 1929; M.A., Columbia U., 1951, Ed.D., 1959; m. Peter C. Reilly, Sept. 15, 1932; children: Marie Reilly Heed, Sara Jean Reilly Wilhelm, Patricia Reilly Davis. Lectr. psychology Butler U., Indpls., 1957-58, 60-65; cons. child psychologist

Mental Hygiene Clinic, Episcopal Community Services, Indpls., 1959-65; cons. clin. psychologist VA Hosp., Indpls., 1965-66; Christian Theol. Sem., 1968-70; pvt. practice clin. psychology, Indpls., 1967-89; cons. clin. psychologist St. Vincent's Hosp., 1973-86; adv. cons. middle mgmt. group Indpls. City Council, 1980-81. Mem. women's aux. council U. Notre Dame, 1953-65; trustee Hanover (Ind.) Coll., 1975-91; bd. dirs. Community Hosp. Found., Indpls., 1978-92, Regional Cancer Hosp. Bd., 1988-90, Indpls. Mus. Art, 1987-93; mem. Ind. Bd. Examiners in Psychology, 1969-73; mem. Com. for Future of Butler U., 1985-86. Mem. Am. Psychol. Assn., Am. Personnel and Guidance Assn., Am. Vocat. Assn., Ind. Psychol. Assn., Central Ind. Psychol. Assn., Ind. Personnel and Guidance Assn., Nat. Registry Psychologists in U.S.A. Office: 3777 Bay Road N Dr Indianapolis IN 46240-2973

REILLY, JOHN B., lawyer; b. Bangor, Maine, Sept. 12, 1947; s. Louis J. and Evelyn I. (Lindsay) R.; m. Susan P. Viselli, May 13, 1978; children: Carolyn, Bridget. BA, U. R.I., 1970; JD cum laude, Suffolk U., 1976. Bar: R.I. 1976, U.S. Dist. Ct. R.I. 1976, U.S. Claims Ct. 1980, U.S. Supreme Ct. 1983, U.S. Ct. Appeals (1st and 2d cirs.) 1984, Mass. 1985, U.S. Dist. Ct. Mass. 1985, U.S. Ct. Appeals (3rd cir.) 1985, U.S. Dist. Ct. Conn. 1995. Sole practice, Providence, 1976-81, Warwick, R.I., 1981-83; sr. ptnr. John Reilly & Assocs. predecessor firms, Warwick, 1984-89. Mem. Def. Rsch. Inst., Gov's Automobile Ins. Reform Task Force, 1992-93. Mem. troop council Narragansett coun. Boy Scouts Am., Warwick, 1982-88. Mem. ABA, R.I. Bar Assn., Trucking Ind. Def. Assn., Pi Sigma Alpha, Phi Kappa Psi. Home: 80 Paterson Ave Warwick RI 02886-9110 Office: John Reilly & Assoc Ste 330 Summit W 300 Centerville Rd Warwick RI 02886

REILLY, JOHN E., automotive executive. Exec. v.p. Mid Altantic Motors, Balt., 1963-80; chmn. bd. American Isuzu Motors Inc., La Puente, Calif., 1980—. Office: American Isuzu Motors Inc 13181 Crossroads Pky N La Puente CA 91746-3419*

REILLY, MARGARET MARY, retired therapist; b. N.Y.C.; d. Thomas Michael and Margaret Mary (Lane) R. AB, Coll. of New Rochelle, 1933; MSW, Fordham U., 1966. Case worker, case supr., sr. case supr., dir. N.Y.C. Dept. Social Svc., 1947-77; therapist Cath. Charities Counselling Svc., N.Y.C., 1980-94; ret. Mem. NASW, Acad. Cert. Social Workers. Roman Catholic. Avocations: travel, opera. Home: 309 E Mosholu Pky N Bronx NY 10467-4840

REILLY, MICHAEL K., mining executive; b. 1933. With Zeigler Coal Holding Co., Fairview Heights, Ill., 1963—; now CEO Zeigler Coal Holding Co., East Saint Louis, Ill. Office: Zeigler Coal Holding 50 Jerome Ln Fairview Heights IL 62208-2015*

REILLY, PETER C., chemical company executive; b. Indpls., Jan. 19, 1907; s. Peter C. and Ineva (Gash) R.; AB, U. Colo., 1929; MBA, Harvard U., 1931; DSc (hon.), Butler U; m. Jeanette Parker, Sept. 15, 1932; children: Marie (Mrs. Jack H. Heed), Sara Jean (Mrs. Clarke Wilhelm), Patricia Ann (Mrs. Michael Davis). With accounting dept. Republic Creosoting Co., Indpls., 1931-32; sales dept. Reilly Tar & Chem. Corp. (became Reilly Industries, Inc. 1989), N.Y.C., 1932-36, v.p., Eastern mgr., 1936-52; v.p. sales, treas. both cos., Indpls., 1952-59, pres., 1959-73, chmn. bd., 1973-75, vice chmn., 1975-82, chmn., 1982-90, chmn. exec. com. 1990—; dir. Environ. Quality Control Inc. Dir. Goodwill Industries Found.; past bd. dirs. United Fund Greater Indpls., Indpls. Symphony Orch., Jr. Achievement Indpls., bd. govs.; mem. adv. council U. Notre Dame Sch. Bus. Adminstrn., 1947—; mem. adv. coun., past bd. dirs. Winona Meml. Hosp.; life mem. Boy Scouts Am., Crossroads of Am. Coun.; mem. adv. coun. Walther Cancer Inst.; Recipient Sagamore of Wabash award; named Disting. Eagle Scout Boy Scouts Am. Mem. Chem. Spltys. Mfg. Assn. (life; treas. 1950-60, past bd. dirs.), Chem. Mfrs. Assn. (past bd. dirs.), Am. Chem. Soc., Soc. Chem. Industry (past dir. Am. sect.). Clubs: Union League, Harvard, Chemist (N.Y.C.); Larchmont (N.Y.) Yacht; Indianapolis Athletic, Pine Valley Golf (N.J.), Meridian Hills Country (past bd. dirs.), Columbia (Indpls.); Rotary (Paul Harris award), One Hundred (past bd. dirs.); Crooked Stick Golf. Home: 3777 Bay Rd N Indianapolis IN 46240 Office: Reilly Industries Inc 300 N Meridien St Ste 1500 Indianapolis IN 46204-1763

REILLY, PHILIP RAYMOND, medical research administrator; b. Albany, N.Y., Oct. 3, 1947. MD, Yale U., New Haven, 1981. Diplomate Am. Bd. Clin. Genetics. Intern Boston City Hosp., 1983-85, resident, 1983-85; staff Mass. Gen. Hosp., Boston; dir. Eunice Kennedy Shriver Ctr. for Mental Retardation, Waltham, Mass. Mem. Am. Assn. for the Advancement of Sci., Am. Soc. of Human Genetics. Office: Eunice Kennedy Shriver Ctn 200 Trapelo Rd Waltham MA 02154-6332

REILLY, ROBERT FREDERICK, valuation consultant; b. N.Y.C., Oct. 3, 1952; s. James J. and Marie (Griebel) K.; m. Janet H. Steiner, Apr. 16, 1975; children: Ashley Lauren, Brandon Christopher, Cameron Courtney. BA in Econs., Columbia U., 1974, MBA in Fin., 1975. CPA, Ohio, Ill.; cert. mgmt. acct., CFA; cert. real estate appraiser; cert. gen. appraiser Ill., Va., Utah; accredited sr. appraiser, cert. rev. appraiser. Sr. cons. Booz, Allen & Hamilton, Cin., 1975-76; dir. corp. planning Huffy Corp., Dayton, Ohio, 1976-81; v.p. Arthur D. Little Valuation, Inc., Chgo., 1981-85; ptnr., nat. dir. of valution svcs. Deloitte & Touche, Chgo., 1985-91; mng. dir. Willamette Mgmt. Assocs., Chgo., 1991—; adj. prof. accounting U. Dayton Grad. Sch. Bus., 1977-81; adj. prof. fin. econs., Elmhurst (Ill.) Coll., 1982-87; adj. prof. fin. Ill. Inst. Tech. Grad. Sch. Bus., Chgo., 1985—; adj. prof. taxation U. Chgo. Grad. Sch. Bus., 1985-87. Co-author: Valuing Small Businesses and Professional Practices, 1993, Business Valuation Video Course, 1993, Valuing a Business, 1995; editor, columnist Small Bus. Taxation, 1989-90, Bus. Valuation Rev., 1989-90, Jour. of Real Estate Acctg. and Taxation, 1991-93, Ohio CPA Jour., 1984-86, 91—, Jour. Property Taxation Mgmt., 1993—, Jour. Am. Bankruptcy Inst., 1993—; contbr. more than 200 articles to profl. jours. Mem. AICPA, Nat. Assn. Real Estate Appraisers (cert.), Am. Soc. Appraisers (mem. bd. examiners 1985-89), Nat. Assn. Accts. (chpt. dir. 1976—), Inst. Property Taxation, Soc. Mfg. Engrs., Ill. Soc. CPAs, Ohio Soc. CPAs (chpt. dir. 1978-81), Accreditation Coun. Accountancy (accredited in fed. income tax), Bus. Valuation Asn., Chgo. Soc. Investment Analysts, Inst. CFAs, Am. Bankruptcy Inst., Am. Econ. Assn., Nat. Assn. Bus. Economists. Home: 310 Algonquin Rd Barrington IL 60010-6109 Office: 8600 W Bryn Mawr Ave Chicago IL 60631-3505

REILLY, THOMAS, humanities educator; b. Hollymount, Mayo, Ireland, Dec. 16, 1941; arrived in Eng., 1967; s. Patrick and Josephine (Sheridan) R.; m. Feb. 22, 1977; children: Anna, Siobhán. BA, U. Coll. Dublin, Ireland, 1967; MSc, Royal Free Hosp., London, 1971; PhD, Liverpool (Eng.) Poly., 1975; M.I. Biology, Inst. Biology, London, 1977. Clerical officer Dublin Corp., 1960-65; tchr., athletic coach Govt. of Cameroun, 1968-70; technician Med. Rsch. Coun., London, 1971; rsch. asst. Liverpool Poly., 1972-75, lectr., then prin. lectr., reader, 1975-88, prof. sports sci., 1988—; dir. sch. Liverpool John Moores U., 1991-95; head grad. sch. Liverpoort John Moores U., 1995—; vis. prof. Tsikuba (Japan) U., 1977; vis. coach Nigerian Sports Coun., 1976; vis. rsch. assoc. U. Calif. Berkeley, 1980; invited spkr. 2d World Congress on Sci. and Football, The Netherlands, 1991, 3d World Congress on Sci. and Football, Cardiff, 1995; contbd. consensus statement on nutrition for soccer F.I.F.A., Zürich, 1994. Editor: Sports Fitness and Sports Issues, 1981, Physiology of Sports, 1990, Science and Football, 1988, Science and Football 11, 1993, Science and Soccer, 1996; editor Jour. Sports Sci., 1983—. Organizer Hollymount Internat. Rd. Race, Mayo, Ireland, 1976—; coord. acclimation strategy Brit. Olympic Assn., London, 1993—, chair exercise physiology steering group, 1992—. Mem. Brit. Assn. Sport and Exercise Sci. (chmn. 1994—), Internat. Steering Group on Sci. and Football (chmn. 1987—), European Coll. Sport Sci. (founder). Roman Catholic. Avocations: soccer, Gaelic football, running, squash, orienteering. Office: Liverpool John Moores U, 2 Rodney St/Grad Sch, Liverpool England

REILLY, WILLIAM FRANCIS, publishing company executive; b. N.Y.C., June 8, 1938; s. William F. and Genevieve Reilly; m. Ellen Chapman, Nov. 19, 1966; children: Anthony Chapman and Jane Wasey (twins). AB cum laude, U. Notre Dame, 1959; MBA, Harvard U., 1964. Mgr. fin. analysis W.R. Grace & Co., N.Y.C., 1964-67, asst. to pres., 1969-71, CEO Bekaert Textile Divsn., 1971-74; pres., CEO Herman's World of Sporting Goods, Carteret, N.J., 1974-77; v.p., pres. W.R. Grace and Co., 1978; pres., CEO Home Ctr. Div., 1979-80; pres. Macmillan, Inc., N.Y.C., 1980-90; chmn., CEO K-III Comm. Corp., N.Y.C., 1990—. 1st lt. U.S. Army, 1959-61. Home: 7 Sutton Sq New York NY 10022 Office: K-III Comm Corp 745 5th Ave New York NY 10151

REILLY, WILLIAM THOMAS, lawyer; b. Passaic, N.J., Feb. 25, 1949; s. Thomas Edwin and Edna May (Dorritie) R.; m. Sheila Mary Brogan, Aug. 1, 1981; children: Kathleen Anne, Brendan Thomas, Timothy John. BS, Boston Coll., 1971; JD, Harvard U., 1974. Bar: N.J. 1974, U.S. Dist. Ct. N.J. 1974, U.S. Supreme Ct. 1979, U.S. Ct. Appeals (3rd cir.) 1984. Assoc. McCarter & English, Newark, 1974-81, ptnr., 1982--. Trustee United Hosps. Med. Ctr., Newark, 1983-89, One-to-One/N.J., Inc., 1990—, chmn., 1993—. Mem. ABA, N.J. State Bar Assn., Harvard Law Sch. Assn., Eastward Ho Country Club. Avocation: golf. Home: 302 Kensington Dr Ridgewood NJ 07450-1822 Office: McCarter & English Four Gateway Ctr 100 Mulberry St Newark NJ 07102-4004

REIMAN, DONALD HENRY, English language educator; b. Erie, Pa., May 17, 1934; s. Henry Ward and Mildred Abbie (Pearce) R.; m. Mary Warner, 1958 (div. 1974); 1 child, Laurel Elizabeth Reiman Henneman; m. Hélène Liberman Dworzan, Oct. 3, 1975. A.B., Coll. of Wooster, 1956, Litt.D., 1981; M.A., U. Ill., 1957, Ph.D., 1960. Instr. English, Duke U., Durham, N.C., 1960-62, asst. prof., 1962-64; assoc. prof. U. Wis., Milw., 1964-65; adj. assoc. prof. grad. program in English CUNY, 1967-68; adj. prof. Columbia U., N.Y.C., 1969-70, sr. rsch. assoc. in English, 1970-73; vis. prof. St. John's U., Jamaica, N.Y., 1974-75; editor Shelley and His Circle, Carl H. Pforzheimer Library, N.Y.C., 1965-86, N.Y. Pub. Libr., 1986-92; with Carl & Lily Pforzheimer Found., 1992—; vis. lectr. U. Ill., 1963; vis. prof. U. Wash., Seattle, 1981, NYU, 1992; Lyell reader in bibliography Oxford U., 1988-89; adj. prof. English U. Del., 1992—; cons. Harvard U. Press, Yale U. Press, Princeton U. Press, Johns Hopkins U. Press, Garland Pub. Inc., W.W. Norton, Oxford U. Press, others. Author: Shelley's The Triumph of Life, A Critical Study, 1965, 2d edit., 1979, Percy Bysshe Shelley, 1969, 2d edit., 1990, (with D.D. Fischer) Byron on the Continent, 1974, English Romantic Poetry, 1800-1835, 1979, Romantic Texts and Contexts, 1987, Intervals of Inspiration: The Skeptical Tradition and the Psychology of Romanticism, 1988, The Study of Modern Manuscripts, 1993; editor: Shelley and His Circle, Vols. V-VI, 1973, Vols. VII-VIII, 1986, The Romantics Reviewed: Contemporary Reviews of English Romantic Writers, 9 vols., 1972, (with S.B. Powers) Shelley's Poetry and Prose: A Norton Critical Edition, 1977, The Romantic Context: Poetry, 128 vols., 1976-79, (with M.C. Jaye and B.T. Bennett) The Evidence of the Imagination, 1978; gen. editor: Manuscripts of the Younger Romantics; I The Esdaile Notebook: A Facsimile, 1985, II The Mask of Anarchy: Facsimiles, 1985, III Hellas, 1985, V The Harvard Shelley Poetic Manuscripts, 1991, VIII Fair-Coply Manuscripts of Shelley's Poems, 1996; editor-in-chief: The Bodleian Shelley Manuscripts, 1984—, I Peter Bell The Third and the Triumph of Life, 1986, VII Shelley's Last Notebook and Other MSS, 1990, (with M.J. Neth) The Hellas Notebook, XVI, 1994; mem. editl. com. adv. bd. Keats-Shelley Jour., 1968-73, Milton and the Romantics, 1975-80, Studies in Romanticism, 1977—, Romanticism Past and Present, 1980-86, Text, 1981—, Nineteenth-Century Literature, 1986—, Nineteenth-Century Contexts, 1987-90; contbr. articles to encyclopedias, books and profl. jours. Active Common Cause. Am. Coun. Learned Socs. fellow, 1963-64, Wesleyan Ctr. Advanced Studies fellow, 1963-64, NEH fellow, 1978; grantee Am. Coun. Learned Socs., 1961, NEH, 1983—. Mem. AAUP, MLA (life), Modern Humanities Rsch. Assn. (life), Wordsworth-Coleridge Assn. Am. (founder), Byron Soc. (Am. com. 1973—), Keats-Shelley Assn. Am. (bd. dirs., treas. 1973-91, v.p. 1991—, Disting. Scholar award 1987), Bibliog. Soc. Am., Soc. Textual Scholarship (exec. com. 1981-93), Coleridge in Somerset Assn., Charles Lamb Soc., Assn. Documentary Editing, N.Am. Soc. Study of Romanticism, Assn. Literary Scholars and Critics. Democrat. Presbyterian. Office: NY Pub Libr Fifth Ave at 42nd St Rm 226 New York NY 10018

REIMANN, WILLIAM PAGE, artist, educator; b. Mpls., Nov. 29, 1935; s. Hobart and Dorothy (Sampson) R.; m. Helen Vera Sadowy, June 3, 1961; children: Christopher, Katherine. BA, Yale U., 1957, BFA, 1959, MFA in Sculpture, 1961. Instr. Old Dominion U., Norfolk, Va., 1961-62; asst. prof. Old Dominion U., 1962-64; asst. prof. design Harvard U., 1964-67, lectr., 1969-75, sr. preceptor in visual studies, 1975—, head tutor dept. visual studies, 1986-94. Recent major commns. include Tropicana Corp., Bradenton, Fla., Southwest Bell Telephone Co., Houston, Gen. Mills Corp., Mpls., Shell Oil Co., Houston, 1st Ch. of Christ, Scientist, Boston; designated artist Radnor (Pa.) Twp. Gateway Enhancement Project, Boston Redsox Baseball Club; represented in permanent collections, Mus. Modern Art, N.Y.C., Nat. Gallery Art, Washington, Whitney Mus. Am. Art, Boston Mus. Fine Art, Rockefeller U., Yale U., Harvard U., also numerous pvt. collections. Recipient 2 Gold medals U.S. Master's Rosing Nat. Championships, 1995, 4 Gold medals F.I.S.A. world Vets.' Rowing Competitions. Mem. Cambridge Boat Club (bd. dirs.). Home: 1 Gerrys Landing Cambridge MA 02138-5511 Office: Carpenter Ctr Visual Arts 24 Quincy St Cambridge MA 02138-3804

REIMER, BENNETT, music educator, writer; b. N.Y.C., June 19, 1932; s. George and Sarah (Talkofsky) R.; children: Jan Ellen, Terry. BM, State Tchr.'s Coll. (now SUNY-Fredonia), 1954; MM, U. Ill., 1955, EdD, 1963. Asst. prof. music edn. U. Ill., Urbana, 1960-65; Kulas prof., chmn. dept. music edn. Case Western Res. U., Cleve., 1965-78; John W. Beattie prof., chmn. dept. Northwestern U., Evanston, Ill., 1978—. Author: A Philosophy of Music Education, 1970, 2d edit., 1989, Developing the Experience of Music, 1985; editor: Toward an Aesthetic Education, 1971, The Arts, Education and Aesthetic Knowing, 1992, On the Nature of Musical Experience, 1992; co-author: The Experience of Music, 1972, Silver Burdett Music Grades 1-8, 1974, 4th edit., 1985; contbr. over 100 articles on music and arts edn. to profl. jours. Mem. Music Educators Nat. Conf., Music Edn. Research Council, Edn. Aesthetic Awareness (bd. dirs.). Office: Northwestern U Sch Music Evanston IL 60208

REIMER, JAN RHEA, mayor; b. Edmonton, Alta., Can., May 23, 1952; married; 2 children. BA, U. Alta., 1973. Councillor for Ward 2 City Coun. of Edmonton, 1980-89, chair various standing coms.; mayor City of Edmonton, 1989-95; former chair City of Edmonton Task Force Econ. Devel., Inter-Mcpl. Task Force Out-of-Sch. Care, River Valley Steering Com., Mayor's Task Force Safer Cities; chair Safer Cities Initiatives Com., No. Alta. Mayors' Caucus; mem. Bd. Edmonton Power; Edmonton rep. Big City Mayors' Caucus, Can.; mem. Winter Cities Secretariat; organizer Edmonton Region Mayors and Reeves Caucus. Co-author: N.U.T.S. & B.O.L.T.S.: A Self-Help Guide for Community Groups. Pres. Mcpl. Non-Profit Housing Corp.; organizer Toxic Round-Up, Blue Box, various other environ. programs; mem. Bd. Edmonton Pub. Libr., Edmonton Met. Regional Planning Commn., Mayor's Task Force Citizen Participation, Inter-Mcpl. Task Force Waste Mgmt.; citizen coord. Calder Action Com., Edmonton; mem. bd. govs. Royal Alexandra Hosp.; bd. dirs. Edmonton Social Planning Coun., Econ. Devel. Edmonton. Address: 10114 87th St, Edmonton, AB Canada T5H 1N4

REIN, BERT WALTER, lawyer; b. Bklyn., Feb. 7, 1941; s. Moe and Florence (Fishman) R.; m. Jennifer Christine Bulson, July 11, 1966 (dec. Mar. 1989); children: Joanna, Benjamin, Samantha; m. Barbara Jean Kahn, Oct. 18, 1992. BA, Amherst Coll., 1961; LLB, Harvard U., 1964. Bar: D.C. 1965, U.S. Dist. Ct. D.C. 1965, U.S. Ct. Appeals (D.C. cir.) 1968, U.S. Ct. Appeals (2d cir.) 1973, U.S. Ct. Appeals (8th cir.) 1974, U.S. Ct. Appeals (4th cir.) 1976, U.S. Ct. Appeals (11th cir.) 1982, U.S. Supreme Ct. 1982. Law ck. to Justice John M. Harlan U.S. Supreme Ct., Washington, 1966-67; assoc. Kirkland & Ellis, Washington, 1967-69, ptnr., 1973-83; spl. asst. U.S. Dept. State, Washington, 1969-70, dep. asst. sec., 1970-73; ptnr. Wiley, Rein & Fielding, Washington, 1983—; bd. dirs., chmn. govt. and regulation affairs com. U.S. C. of C., 1986-90; bd. dirs. Nat. Chamber Litigation Ctr.; advisor Reagan Dept. Justice Transition, Washington, 1980; mem. adv. com. U.S. Sentencing Commn., 1988-89; edn. gen. counsel Comty. Learning and Info. Network, 1992—. Contbr. articles to profl. publs. Capt. USAR, 1964-68. Mem. ABA, Am. Law Inst., Internat. Trade Commn. Trial Lawyers Assn. (pres. 1990-91), Internat. Aviation Club. Republican. Jewish. Home: 6423 Shadow Rd Chevy Chase MD 20815-6613 Office: Wiley Rein & Fielding 1776 K St NW Washington DC 20006-2304

REIN, CATHERINE AMELIA, financial services executive, lawyer; b. Lebanon, Pa., Feb. 7, 1943; d. John and Esther (Scott) Shultz. BA summa cum laude, Pa. State U., 1965; JD magna cum laude, NYU ., 1968. Bar: N.Y. 1968, U.S. Supreme Ct. 1971. Assoc. Dewey, Ballantine, Bushby, Palmer & Wood, N.Y.C., 1968-74; with Continental Group, Stamford, Conn., 1974-85, sec., sr. atty., 1976-77, v.p., gen. counsel, 1980-85; sec., asst. gen. counsel Continental Diversified Ops., 1978-80; v.p. human resources Met. Life Ins. Co., N.Y.C., 1985-88, sr. v.p. human resources, 1988-89, exec. v.p. corp. and profl. svcs. dept., 1989—; bd. dirs Bank of NY., Gen. Pub. Utilities, Corning Inc., Nat. Urban League, Inroads, N.Y.C. Trustee Nat. Urban League, NYU Sch. Law Found. Mem. ABA, Assn. of Bar of City of N.Y. Episcopalian. Avocations: decorating, restoration, cooking. Home: 21 E 22nd St Apt 8B New York NY 10010-5335 Office: Met Life Ins Co 1 Madison Ave New York NY 10010-3603

REIN, STANLEY MICHAEL, lawyer; b. St. Paul, Apr. 15, 1946; s. Clayton George Rein and Rose Gertrude (Mintz) Brown; m. Linda. R. Arnold; children: Gabriel Todd, Leah Suzanne. BA, U. Minn., 1968; JD cum laude, Harvard U., 1973. Bar: Minn. 1973, U.S. Tax Ct. 1973. Assoc. Dorsey & Whitney, LLP, Mpls., 1973-78; ptnr. Dorsey & Whitney PLLP, Mpls., 1979—. Mem. planned giving adv. coun. ARC Mpls. chpt., 1986, 88, planned giving adv. com. Minn. Pub. Radio, 1988-89; bd. dirs. South Metro Airport Action Council, Mpls., 1986, 87. With U.S. Army, 1968-70, Vietnam. Fellow Am. Coll. of Trust and Estate Counsel; mem. Minn. Bar Assn. (probate and trust law sect.), Hennepin County Bar Assn. (probate and trust law sect.), Phi Beta Kappa. Jewish. Avocations: tennis, reading, travel. Office: Dorsey & Whitney LLP 220 S 6th St Minneapolis MN 55402-4502

REINBOLD, DARREL WILLIAM, energy engineering specialist; b. Louisville, Nov. 13, 1960; s. Paul William and Betty Lou (Buechler) R.; m. Theresa Marie Morris, June 17, 1989; children: Jessica Marie, Elizabeth Ashley. Cert. heating, air condit., refrig., Pleasure Ridge Pk. Vocat. Sch., Louisville, 1978; AAS, U. Louisville, 1987, BS in Occupational Edn., 1987; cert. universal technician, Esco Inst., 1994. Lic. journeyman HVAC mechanic, Ky. Apprentice pipe fitter A & A Mech., Louisville, 1978-80; heating, ventilation, air conditioning technician Prudential Heating and Air Conditioning, Louisville, 1980-87; heating, ventilation, air conditioning mechanic U. Louisville, 1988-89; svc. sys. specialist Honeywell Inc., Louisville, 1989-93; air conditioning estimator Ware Energy, Louisville, 1993—. Mem. baseball team U. Louisville, 1980-81. Mem. Assn. of Energy Engrs. Avocations: fishing, skiing. Home: 3219 LaVel Ln Louisville KY 40216-1217 Office: Ware Energy 4005 Produce Rd Louisville KY 40218

REINBOLT, MARY JO, occupational health nurse; b. Detroit, Sept. 11, 1938; d. Frank O'Brien Connolly and Josephine Grace Dyer Lynch; m. Gerald S. Gorcyca, May 28, 1960 (div. Dec. 1984); children: Deborah Mayfield, David, Paul, Lynn Babcock; m. Ray C. Reinbolt, June 1, 1992. ADN, Oakland U., Highland Lakes, Mich., 1980; postgrad., U. Detroit Mercy, 1994—. Cert. 1st responder for confined space injuries. Nursing supr. Medico's, Detroit, 1980-81; staff nurse neurology Mt. Carmel Hosp., Detroit, 1981-82; staff nurse emergency Oakland Gen. Hosp., Madison Heights, Mich., 1982-94; staff nurse/supr. Am. Home Nursing, Ferndale, Mich., 1985-88; dir. pharmacy patients Caremark, Livonia, Mich.; occupl. health nurse Chrysler Corp., Trenton, Mich., 1994—; mem. ergonomics com., safety rescue team Chrysler Corp. Staff worker Rep. Ctrl. Com., Lansing, Mich., 1992, Royal Oak, Mich., 1993, Dem. Ctrl. Com., Madison Heights, 1994; vol. nurse Shriners Crippled Children, Mich., 1992; vol. St. Patrick's Sr. Citizen Coalition. Mem. Am. Assn. Occupl. Health Nurses, Am. Assn. Healthcare Execs., Am. Assn. Individual Investors. Republican. Roman Catholic. Avocations: cross country skiing, sewing, reading, boating, home repair. Home: 24542 W Chicago Redford MI 48239-1652

REINECKE, MANFRED G., chemistry educator; b. Milw., May 19, 1935; s. Fritz Wilhelm and Erna (Rittmeyer) R.; m. Marlene Zwisler, June 15, 1957; children: Kurt, Kryn, Claire. BS in Chemistry, U. Wis., 1956; PhD in Organic Chemistry, U. Calif., 1960. Asst. prof. U. Calif., Riverside, 1959-64; asst. prof. Tex. Christian U., Ft. Worth, 1964-68, assoc. prof., 1968-73; vis. prof. U. Tubingen, Fed. Republic of Germany, 1971-72; prof. Tex. Christian U., Ft. Worth, 1973—; vis. prof. U. British Columbia, Vancouver, Can., 1987; chmn. health professions adv. com. Tex. Christian U., 1974-91; mem. sci. adv. bd. Univera Phytoceuticals, Inc.; cons. in field. Contbr. more than 70 articles on natural product, organic chemistry and chem. edn. to profl. jours. Recipient W.T. Doherty award Ft. Worth, Dallas sect. Am. Chem. Soc., 1984; Nat. Sci. Found. Teaching fellow, 1971-72, NAS fellow, 1979, 90. Mem. Am. Chem. Soc. (chmn. Ft. Worth, Dallas sect. 1976), So. Assn. Advisors Health Professions (bd. dirs. 1986-89), Alpha Epsilon Delta (dir. SW region 1985—). Office: Tex Christian Univ Dept Of Chemistry Fort Worth TX 76129

REINECKE, ROBERT DALE, ophthalmologist; b. Ft. Scott, Kans., Mar. 26, 1929; s. George Alfred and Bessie Irene (Newell) R.; m. Mary Jeannetta Portwood, Oct. 5, 1952; 1 child, Karen Denise. O.D., Ill. Coll. Optometry, 1951; A.B., U. Kans., 1955, M.D., 1959. Diplomate: Am. Bd. Ophthalmology. Research fellow ophthalmology Harvard U. Med. Sch., 1957, 58; intern U. Kans. Med. Center, 1959-60; resident in ophthalmology Mass. Eye and Ear Infirmary, Boston, 1961-63; asst. in ophthalmology Mass. Eye and Ear Infirmary, 1963-69; asst. prof. ophthalmology Harvard U. Med. Sch., 1967-69; mem. faculty Albany (N.Y.) Med. Sch., 1970-81, prof. ophthalmology, 1970-81, chmn. dept., 1970-81; prof. ophthalmology Jefferson Med. Coll., Phila., 1981—; chmn. dept. Jefferson Med. Coll., 1981-85; ophthalmologist-in-chief Wills Eye Hosp., 1981-85, dir. Foerderer Eye Movement Ctr., 1985—; bd. dirs. Conrad Berens Internat. Eye Film Library, 1970-80; exec. com. N.Y. State Bd. Medicine, 1978-80, chmn., 1980-81; com. vision NRC, 1976-81, chmn., 1979-80; Alumni lectr. Georgetown U. Med. Sch., 1970; Proctor lectr. U. Calif. Med. Sch., San Francisco, 1977; Schoenberg lectr. N.Y. Acad. Medicine, 1979; Spaeth lectr. Coll. Physicians, 1982; Bajandas lectr., 1989. Contbr. numerous articles to med. jours. USPHS summer fellow, 1956, 58; Fight for Sight fellow, summers 1957, 60; recipient Senior Honor award Am. Acad. Ophthalmology, 1986. Fellow Am. Acad. Ophthalmology (sec. govt. rels. 1980-86, pres. 1989); mem. ACS, AMA, Am. Bd. Ophthalmology (bd. dirs. 1984-87), Assn. Rsch. Vision and Ophthalmology (trustee sect. on eye movements, strabismus and amblyopia 1986-91), Am. Acad. Ophthalmology (sec. for program 1986-87), Pa. Med. Soc., N.Y. State Ophthal. Assn., Am. Assn. Pediatric Ophthalmology (pres. 1975-76), Phila. County Med. Soc. (chmn. med. econ. com. 1994-95), Pa. Acad. Ophthalmology (pres. 1991), Pa. Med. Soc., Coll. of POhysicians, Ophthalmic Club of Phila. Office: Wills Eye Hosp 9th and Walnut St Philadelphia PA 19107-5127

REINER, BERT LEO, consumer product engineering/manufacturing consultant; b. Dresden, Germany, May 30, 1937; came to U.S., 1949; s. Horace W. and Gertrude (Katz) R.; m. Sandra J. Winkler, June 25, 1960; children: Helaine, Eric, Dana. BME, Resselaer Poly. Inst., 1960. Design engr. Sikorsky Aircraft Div., Stratford, Conn., 1960-62; project engr. Soundscriber Corp., New Haven, Conn., 1962-63; chief engr. A.C. Gilbert Co., New Haven, 1963-66; dir.Far East Mfg. Ideal Toy Co., Jamaica, N.Y., 1967-69; v.p. engring. Coleco IndustriesInc., Hartford, Conn., 1964-88; sr. v.p. Coleco Industries Inc., West Hartford, Conn., 1985-88; pres. Reiner Assocs. Inc., Wallingford, Conn., 1988—. Patentee in field. Mem. ASME, IEEE, Am. Assn. Profl. Cons., Soc. Plastics Engrs. (sr.). Avocations: bonsai, stamp and coin collecting, skiing, racquetball. Office: Reiner Assocs Inc 21 Blakeslee Rd Wallingford CT 06492-5212

REINER, CARL, actor, writer, director; b. Bronx, N.Y., Mar. 20, 1922; s. Irving and Bessie (Mathias) R.; m. Estelle Lebost, Dec. 24, 1943; children: Robert, Sylvia A., Lucas. Student, Sch. Fgn. Service, Georgetown U., 1943. Appeared on Broadway and with road co.: Call Me Mister, 1947-48; on Broadway in:Inside U.S.A, 1948-49, Alive and Kicking, 1950; TV actor, 1950—; appeared: YourShow of Shows, 1950-54, Caesar's Hour, 1954-58 (Emmy award 1956, 57); master ceremonies: Keep Talking, 1958-59; writer-actor: Dinah Shore Show, 1960; producer,writer: The Dick Van Dyke Show (Emmy awards as writer 1962, 63, 64, as producer1965, 66), The New Dick Van Dyke Show, Enter Laughing, written 1958, directed 1967,The Comics, 1968; dir.: (films) Enter Laughing, The Comic, 1967, The Comic, 1969,

Where's Poppa, 1970, Oh, God!, 1977, The One and Only, 1978, The Jerk, 1979, Dead Men Don't Wear Plaid, 1982, The Man With Two Brains, 1983, All of Me, 1984, Summer Rental, 1985, Summer School, 1987, Bert Rigby, You're a Fool, 1989, Sibling Rivalry, 1990, Fatal Instinct, 1993; appeared in: movie Happy Anniversary, 1959, The Gazebo, 1960, Gidget Goes Hawaiian, 1961, It's a Mad, Mad, Mad, Mad World, 1963, The Russians Are Coming, 1966, The End, 1978, Dead Men Don't Wear Plaid, 1982; writer, dir.: Something Different, 1967; writer: Sid Caesar, Imogene Coca, Carl Reiner, Howard Morris Special (Emmy award, 1967); producer: TV series Good Heavens, 1976 (recipient Emmy award 1957, 58, 62, 63); Author: (novel) All Kinds of Love, 1993, (novel) Continue Laughing, 1995; author: short stories: screenplay The Thrill of It All; (with Mel Brooks) albums The 2000 Year Old Man, The 2001 Year Old Man, The 2013 Year Old Man; exec. producer: film Heaven Help Us, 1976; dir. The Man with Two Brains, 1983. Served with AUS, 1942-46. recipient Guest Actor in a Comedy Series Emmy award for Mad About You, 1995. Recipient greatest number of Emmys (12) for any individual. Office: care George Shapiro Shapiro-West 141 S El Camino Dr Beverly Hills CA 90212-2731

REINER, ROB, actor, writer, director; b. N.Y.C., Mar. 6, 1947; s. Carl and Estelle (Lebost) R.; m. Penny Marshall, 1971 (div.), m. Michele Singer, May 19, 1989. Student, UCLA. Co-founder Castle Rock Entertainment, Beverly Hills, Calif. Actor: (TV series) All In the Family, 1971-78 (Emmy award 1974, 78), (TV movie) Thursday's Game, 1974 (films) Throw Momma From the Train, 1987, Postcards From the Edge, 1990, The Spirit of '76, 1990, Sleepless in Seattle, 1993, Bullets Over Broadway, 1994, Mixed Nuts, 1994, Bye Bye, Love, 1995 (theatre) The Roast, 1980; actor, writer: (films) Halls of Anger, 1970, Where's Pappa?, 1970, Summertree, 1971, Fire Sale, 1971; actor, co-writer: (film) Enter Laughing, 1967; actor, co-writer, prodr. (TV) More Than Friends, 1978, Million Dollar Infield, 1982; actor, co-writer, dir. (film) This Is Spinal Tap, 1984; dir. (films) The Sure Thing, 1985, Stand By Me, 1986; dir. prodr. (films) The Princess Bride, 1987, When Harry Met Sally, 1989, Misery, 1990, A Few Good Men, 1992, North, 1994, The American President, 1995; co-creator (TV series) The Super, 1972; co-creator, actor (TV series) Free Country. Mem. SAG, AFTRA, Dir. Guild Am., Writers Guild Am. Office: Castle Rock Entertainment 335 N Maple Dr Ste 135 Beverly Hills CA 90210-3858

REINERT, JAMES A., entomologist, educator; b. Enid, Okla., Jan. 26, 1944; s. Andrew J. and Emma Reinert; m. Anita Irwin; children: Travis J., Gina N., Mindy K., Melanie B., Gregory W., Teresa J. BS, Okla. State U., 1966; MS, Clemson U., 1968, PhD, 1970. Asst. state entomologist U. Md., College Park, 1970; asst. prof. entomology to prof. entomology Ft. Lauderdale Rsch. and Edn. Ctr., U. Fla., 1970-84; resident dir., prof. entomology Rsch. and Ext. Ctr., Tex. A&M U. Sys., Dallas, 1984-94; prof. entomology Tex. A&M Univ. System, Dallas, 1994—. Contbr. over 275 articles to profl. jours. NDEA fellow, 1968; recipient Porter Henegar Meml. award., So. Nurserymen's Assn., 1982. Mem. Inter-Turfgrass Soc., Entomol. Soc. Am., Fla. Entomol. Soc. (v.p. 1983, pres. 1984, Entomologist of Yr. 1985), Fla. State Hort. Soc. (v.p. 1982), S.C. Entomol. Soc., Rsch. Ctr. Adminstrs. Soc. (v.p. 1994, state rep. 1991-92, sec. 1993), Dallas Agr. Club (bd. dirs. 1989, v.p. 1990, pres. 1991). Roman Catholic. Home: 3805 Covinton Ln Plano TX 75023-7731 Office: Tex A&M Univ Rsch and Ext Ctr 17360 Coit Rd Dallas TX 75252-6599

REINERT, NORBERT FREDERICK, patent lawyer, retired chemical company executive; b. Hamilton, Ohio, Apr. 12, 1928; s. Fred F. and Jennie A. R.; m. Ida Elizabeth Barickman, Jan. 26, 1956; children: Matthew W., Paul H. B.Ch.E., Ohio State U., 1951; LL.B., Cleve.-Marshall Law Sch., 1959. Bar: Ohio 1959, D.C. 1961. Patent agt. Standard of Ohio, Cleve., 1957-59; patent lawyer Standard of Ohio, 1959-60, E.I. duPont de Nemours & Co., Wilmington, Del., 1960-91; dir. investor relations E.I. duPont de Nemours & Co., 1981-84, mng. counsel, 1985-91; v.p., gen. counsel Endo Labs, Inc. subs. DuPont, Garden City, N.Y., 1971-73; exec. v.p. Endo Labs, Inc. subs. DuPont, 1973-77, pres., 1977-81; pvt. practice patent law, 1991—. Served with Chem. Corps AUS, 1955-56. Mem. Am. Patent Law Assn., Tau Beta Pi. Republican. Roman Catholic. Home: PO Box 311 Mendenhall PA 19357-0311

REINERT, PAUL CLARE, university chancellor emeritus; b. Boulder, Colo., Aug. 12, 1910; s. Francis John and Emma (Voegtle) R. A.B., St. Louis U., 1933, A.M., 1934; Ph.D., U. Chgo., 1944; LL.D. (hon.), St. Ambrose Coll., 1951, Xavier U., 1954, Washington U., 1955, Colo. Coll., 1956, Loyola U., 1957, U. Mo., 1957, John Carroll U., 1961, U. Notre Dame, 1964, St. Joseph's Coll., 1964; Ped.D. (hon.), Bradley U., 1956; L.H.D. (hon.), Manhattan Coll., 1963; Litt.D. (hon.), McKendree Coll., 1966, St. Norbert Coll., 1975; LL.D. (hon.), St. Anselm's Coll., 1967, Coll. Mt. St. Joseph of Ohio, 1970, Loyola U., New Orleans, 1973, So. Ill. U., 1973, Creighton U., 1976; L.H.D. (hon.), Lindenwood Colls., 1972, DePaul U., 1973, Carroll Coll., 1974, St. Francis Coll., 1974, Canisius Coll., 1975, Brandeis U., 1975, Wittenberg U., 1976, Ursuline Coll., 1976, U. Portland, 1977, Tarkio Coll., 1977; P.C.S. (hon.), Regis Coll., 1977; Ed.Adm.D. (hon.), Drury Coll., 1973, numerous others. Entered Soc. of Jesus, 1927, ordained priest, 1940; instr. classical langs. and English Creighton U. High Sch., Omaha, Neb., 1934-37; instr. edn. and registrar St. Mary's Coll., St. Marys, Kan., 1938-41; prof. edn. St. Louis U., 1950—; dean St. Louis U. (Coll. Arts and Scis.), 1944-48, dir. summer sessions, 1945-48, v.p., 1948, pres., 1949-74, chancellor, 1974-90, chancellor emeritus, 1990—; chmn. St. Louis Edn. TV Commn., 1955-57; Mem. President's Com. Edn. Beyond High Sch., 1956-57; co-chmn. Mayor's Commn. Equal Employment Opportunities, 1963-65; mem. Pres. Nixon's Task Force on Edn., 1968-69; bd. dirs. St. Louis Civic Alliance for Housing, 1969-71. Author: The Urban Catholic University, 1970, To Turn the Tide, 1972. Bd. dirs. Assn. Am. Colls., 1970—, chmn., 1972; trustee Ednl. Testing Service, 1969—; bd. dirs. Midwest Research Inst., 1962—; pres. Midtown, Inc., 1972—; mem. Mo. Commn. for Humanities, 1975—; trustee Regis Coll.; bd. overseers St. Meinrad Coll. Mem. N. Central Assn. Colls. and Secondary Schs. (pres. 1956-57), Nat. Cath. Ednl. Assn. (pres. coll. and univ. dept. 1956-58, v.p. 1964-65, pres. 1968-70, exec. bd. 1956-65), Am. Council Edn. (dir. 1965-68), Assn. Urban Univs. (pres. 1950-51), Nat. Council Ind. Colls. and Univs. (pres. 1973), Cath. Commn. on Intellectual and Cultural Affairs, NEA, Assn. for Higher Edn., Ind. Colls. and Univs. Mo. (pres. 1974), Jesuit Edn. Assn. (pres. 1966-70), Phi Beta Kappa, Phi Delta Kappa. Address: Saint Louis U 221 N Grand Blvd Saint Louis MO 63103-2006

REINERTSEN, JAMES LUTHER, internist; b. Pietermaritzburg, South Africa, 1947. MD, Harvard U., 1973. Diplomate Am. Bd. Internal Medicine. Intern San Francisco Gen. Hosp., 1973-74; resident internal medicine U. Calif., 1974-76; resident in rheumatology NIH, Bethesda, Md., 1976-78; with Meth. Hosp., Mpls.; pvt. practice HealthSys. Minn., Mpls. Mem. ACP, ARA, Alpha Omega Alpha. Office: Healthsys Minn PO Box 650 Minneapolis MN 55440

REINERTSEN, NORMAN, retired aircraft systems company executive; b. Bklyn., Mar. 27, 1934; s. Berthin and Malene Katherine (Dahl) R.; m. Elizabeth T. O'Shea, Aug. 30, 1958; children: Michael, Christopher, Katherine. BEE, CCNY, 1960; postgrad., Harvard U., 1982. Registered profl. engr., Calif. Various positions Grumman Aerospace Corp., 1960-75; gen. mgr. Grumman Aerospace Corp. (Great River ops.), 1975-77; v.p. automotive Grumman Allied Industries, Melville, N.Y., 1977-83; sr. v.p. vehicle div. Grumman Allied Industries, 1983-94; sr. v.p. Olson Bodies, Inc., 1977-79; exec. v.p. Grumman Flexible, Delaware, Ohio, 1979-82; pres. Grumman Olson, Mellville, 1983-85; sr. v.p. Vehicle div. Grumman Allied, 1985-87; v.p. quality ops. Northrop Grumman, 1987-94; ret., 1994. With U.S. Army, 1955-57. Mem. Air Force Assn., Northport Yacht Club. Home: 7 Oleander Dr Northport NY 11768-3438

REINES, FREDERICK, physicist, educator; b. Paterson, N.J., Mar. 16, 1918; s. Israel and Gussie (Cohen) R.; m. Sylvia Samuels, Aug. 30, 1940; children: Robert G., Alisa K. M.E., Stevens Inst. Tech., 1939, M.S., 1941; Ph.D., NYU, 1944; D.Sc. (hon.), U. Witwatersrand, 1966; D. Engring. (hon.), Stevens Inst. Tech., 1984. Mem. staff Los Alamos Sci. Lab., 1944-59; group leader Los Alamos Sci. Lab. (Theoretical div.), 1945-59; dir. (AEC expts. on Eniwetok Atoll), 1951; prof. physics, head dept. Case Inst. Tech., 1959-66; prof. physics U. Calif., Irvine, 1966-88, dean phys. scis., 1966-74, Disting. prof. physics, 1987-88, prof. emeritus, 1988—; Centennial lectr. U. Md., 1956; Disting. Faculty lectr. U. Calif., Irvine, 1979; L.I. Schiff Meml. lectr. Stanford U., 1988; Albert Einstein Meml. lectr. Israel Acad. Scis. and Humanities, Jerusalem, 1988; Goudschmidt Meml. lectr., 1990; co-discoverer elementary nuclear particles, free antineutrino, 1956. Contbr. numerous articles to profl. jours.; contbg. author: Effects of Atomic Weapons, 1950. Mem. Cleve. Symphony Chorus, 1959-62. Recipient J. Robert Oppenheimer Meml. prize, 1981, Nat. Medal Sci., 1983, medal U. Calif., Irvine, 1987, Michelson Morley award, 1990; co-recipient Rossi prize Am. Astron. Soc., 1990; Guggenheim fellow, 1958-59, Sloan fellow, 1959-63, Franklin medal Franklin Inst., 1992, Nobel Prize in Physics, 1995. Fellow Am. Phys. Soc. (W.K.H. Panofsky prize 1992), AAAS; mem. NAS, Am. Assn. Physics Tchrs., Argonne U. Assn. (trustee 1965-66), Am. Acad. Arts and Scis., Russian Acad. Sci. (fgn. mem.), Phi Beta Kappa, Sigma Xi, Tau Beta Pi. Office: U Calif Dept Physics Campus Dr Irvine CA 92717

REING, ALVIN BARRY, special education educator, psychologist; b. Bklyn., July 10, 1930; s. Louis B. and Sylvia (Weinstein) R.; m. Barbara R. Reing, Aug. 18, 1957 (dec. June 1992); children: Lynne Laufer, Phyllis Klein, Sheryl Abramson, Naomi. BA, CUNY, Bklyn., 1952; MA, CUNY, 1955; PhD, NYU, 1969; certs. guidance and sch. psychology, Yeshiva U., 1962. Lic. psychologist, N.Y.; tchr., counselor. Borough guidance coord. Bd. Edn., Bklyn.; prof. edn. CUNY, Bklyn.; pvt. practice. Text author; contbr. articles to profl. jours. rsch. dir. Corinthian Med. and Health Svcs. Orgn. Fellow Am. Assn. Mental Retardation; mem. APA, NYSPA, ABPDC, CEC, PBK. Home: 2814 Avenue X Brooklyn NY 11235-1904

REINGOLD, HAIM, mathematics educator; b. Lodz, Poland, Mar. 16, 1910; came to U.S., 1930, naturalized, 1942; s. Shmaryahu and Esther (Rudnianski) R.; m. Leah Jacobson, Apr. 16, 1942 (dec. Mar. 1964); children—Edward M., Arthur L.; m. Badonna Levinson, Nov. 16, 1966; 1 son, David A. Student, NYU, 1931; A.B., U. Cin., 1933, M.A., 1934, Ph.D. in Math, 1938. Teaching asst. U. Cin., 1936-38; head dept. math. Our Lady of Cin. Coll., 1938-42; supr. math. Ill. Inst. Tech., 1942-43, asst. prof., 1943-47, assoc. prof., 1947-56, prof., 1956-75, prof. emeritus, 1975—, chmn. dept. math., 1951-75; adj. prof. math. Ind. U. Northwest, 1975-82; vis. prof. Purdue U.-Calumet (Ind.), 1982-84; prof., chmn. dept. math. Mundelein Coll., 1984-91; sr. prof. Loyola U., Chgo., 1991. Author: (with Andres, Miser) Basic Mathematics for Engineers, 1944, Basic Mathematics for Science and Engineering, 1955. Mem. Am. Math. Soc., Math. Assn. Am., Am. Soc. Engring. Edn. (chmn. math. div. 1955-56, mem. council 1957-59), AAAS, Soc. Engring. Sci., Sigma Xi (chpt. pres. 1966-67). Jewish. Home: 1329 E 55th St Chicago IL 60615-5301

REINGOLD, NATHAN, historian; b. N.Y.C., Mar. 23, 1927; s. Benjamin and Fanny R.; m. Ida Hornstein, Jan. 1, 1955 (dec. 1988); children: Matthew H., Nicholas F.; m. Ellen Miles, Nov. 28, 1992. B.A., NYU, 1947, M.A., 1948; Ph.D., U. Pa., 1951. Staff mem. Nat. Archives, Washington, 1951-59; history of sci. specialist Library of Congress, Washington, 1959-66; editor Papers of Joseph Henry, Smithsonian Instn., Washington, 1966-85; sr. historian Nat. Mus. Am. History, 1985—, historian emeritus, 1993; vis. prof. Johns Hopkins U., 1993-95; adj. fellow Woodrow Wilson Internat. Ctr. for Scholars, 1975; planning com. program on knowledge in Am. soc. Am. Acad. Arts and Scis., 1970-83; com. on history applied math. in World War II, Math. Assn. Am., 1979; adv. bd. archives History Am. Psychology, 1970; mem. oversight com. for history and philosophy sci. program NSF, 1981; Allen lectr. history of math. Rensselaer Poly. Inst., 1981. Contbr. sects. to books, numerous articles to profl. jours. Editorial bd. Hist. Studies of Phys. Scis., 1968-79, N.Y. History, 1973-77; editorial adv. bd. Social Studies of Sci., 1974-80, Isis, 1971-75. Council mem. Rockefeller Archive Ctr., Rockefeller U., 1973-82, 85-91, spl. con. governing council, 1983-84; pres. commn. on documentation Internat. Union History and Philosophy of Sci., 1981; panel for history and philosophy sci. NSF, 1976-78. Recipient Centennial medal Nat. Acad. Scis., 1963. Sesquicentennial medal Coast and Geodetic Survey, 1956; scholar: N.Y. State Regents, 1945-47, NYU, 1945-48; sr. fellow Yale, 1960-61; research grantee Am. Philos. Soc., 1962-63, NSF, 1965-66, 67-72, NEH, 1973-78, Lounsbery Found., 1982-83. Mem. Assn. for Documentary Editing (bd. publs. 1980-81), Soc. for History Tech. (adv. council 1962-65), History Sci. Soc. (council 1964-67), Phi Beta Kappa (selection com. sci. book award 1966-69). Jewish. Club: Cosmos (Washington). Office: Nat Mus Am History Smithsonian Instn Washington DC 20560

REINHARD, CHRISTOPHER JOHN, merchant banking, venture capital executive; b. Bridgeport, Conn., Nov. 11, 1953; s. Warren John and Marian Louise (Dutter) R.; m. Maureen Francis, Sept. 24, 1977; 1 child, Griffin John. BS, Babson Coll., 1976, MBA, 1977. Sr. fin. analyst Gen. Motors Corp., Detroit and N.Y.C., 1977-81; asst. sec. Wheelabrator-Frye Inc., N.H., 1981-83; asst. sec., asst. treas. The Signal Cos., Inc., La Jolla, Calif., 1983-86; mng. dir., v.p. The Henley Group, Inc., La Jolla, 1986-90; mng. dir. Fisher Sci. Group, Inc., La Jolla, 1986-90; mng. dir., v.p. Wheelabrator Tech. Inc., Henley Mfg. Corp., 1987-90; founder, pres. Colony Group Inc., Rancho Santa Fe, 1990—, Reinhard Assocs., Rancho Santa Fe, 1990-95; v.p., chief fin. officer Advanced Access, Inc., San Diego, 1995—; pres. Direct Feedback, Inc., 1990, Dairy Queen Ventures, 1990—, Winsor Sport Fencing, 1993—; v.p., founder, CFO Collateral Therapeutics Inc., 1995—; gen. ptnr. Cabrillo Ventures, 1995—. Mem. Boston Athenaeum, N.Y. Athletic Club, San Diego Polo Club, Rancho Santa Fe Polo Club, Duquesne Club. Office: 9395 Cabot Dr San Diego CA 92126-4310

REINHARD, JAMES RICHARD, judge; b. Pollock, Mo., July 7, 1929; s. Virgil and Meltha (Anspach) R.; m. Shari L. Horton, Dec. 30, 1958; 1 child, James K. Student, N.E. Mo. State U., 1947-50; AB, U. Mo., 1951, JD, 1953. Bar: Mo. 1953. Prosecuting atty. Sullivan County (Mo.), 1955-57; prosecuting atty. Monroe County (Mo.), 1959-65; spl. asst. atty. gen. State of Mo., 1967-68; judge 10th Jud. Circuit, 1973-77; judge Mo. Ct. Appeals (ea. dist.), St. Louis, 1977—, chief judge, 1984-85; pvt. practice Milan, Mo., 1955-57, Paris, Mo., 1957-73. Bd. regents N.E. Mo. State U., Kirksville, 1965-73, pres., 1967-73. Sgt. U.S. Army, 1953-55. Mem. ABA, 10th Jud. Bar Assn. (pres. 1972), Mo. Bar Assn. (bd. govs. 1965-69), Met. Bar Assn. St. Louis, Lawyers Assn. St. Louis, Mo. Bd. Cert. Ct. Reporter Examiner (vice chmn. 1988-90), Mo. Press-Bar Commn. (vice chmn. 1992—), Judicial Fin. Commn. (chmn. 1990-94). Home: 5 Hamlin Heights Dr Hannibal MO 63401-1903 Office: Mo Ct Appeals Ea Dist 111N N 7th St Saint Louis MO 63101-2133

REINHARD, KEITH LEON, advertising executive; b. Berne, Ind., Jan. 20, 1935; s. Herman L. and Agnes V. R.; m. Rose-Lee Simons, Nov. 7, 1976; children: Rachel, Elizabeth; children by previous marriage: Christopher, Timothy, Matthew, Geoffrey, Jacqueline. Student public schs., Berne. Comml. artist Kling Studios, Chgo., 1954-56; mgr. tech. communications dept. Magnavox Co., Ft. Wayne, Ind., 1957-60; creative/account exec. Biddle Co., Bloomington, Ill., 1961-63; exec. v.p., dir. creative services, pres. Needham, Harper & Steers, Inc., Chgo., from 1964; then chmn., chief exec. officer Needham, Harper & Steers/USA, Chgo.; also dir. Needham, Harper & Steers, Inc.; chmn., chief exec. officer DDB Needham Worldwide Inc., N.Y.C., 1986—, chmn. exec. com., 1989—. Episcopalian. Office: DDB Needham Worldwide Inc 437 Madison Ave New York NY 10022-7001*

REINHARD, SISTER MARY MARTHE, educational organization administrator; b. McKeesport, Pa., Aug. 29, 1929; d. Regis C. and Leona (Reese) R. AB, Notre Dame Coll.; MA, U. Notre Dame. Asst. prin. Regina High Sch., Cleve., 1960-62, prin., 1963-64; prin. Notre Dame Acad., Chardon, Ohio, 1965-72; pres. Notre Dame Coll. of Ohio, Cleve., 1973-88; dir. devel. Sisters of Notre Dame Ednl. Ctr., Chardon, 1989—. Trustee, mem. exec. com. NCCJ, Cleve., 1987; bd. dirs. Centerior Energy; mem. coun. Geauga United Way Svcs., 1990—, vice-chair fund raising, 1991-94, vice-chair planning 1995—; mem. adv. bd. Kent State U., Geauga campus, 1991-94; trustee Leadership Geauga 1995—. Recipient Fidelia award Notre Dame Coll., 1989, Woman of Yr. award 1990; Humanitarian award Cleve. chpt. NCCJ, 1990; named one of 100 most influential women in Cleve. Women's City Club, 1983, one of 79 most interesting people in Cleve. The Cleve. mag., 1979. Roman Catholic. Home and Office: 13000 Auburn Rd Chardon OH 44024-9330

REINHARD, PHILIP G., federal judge; b. LaSalle, Ill., Jan. 12, 1941; s. Godfrey and Ruth R.; married Virginia Reinhard; children: Bruce, Brian, David, Philip. BA, U. Ill., Champaign, 1962, JD, 1964. Asst. state atty. Winnebago County, 1964-67; atty. Hyer, Gill & Brown, 1967-68; state atty. Winnebago County, 1968-76; judge 17th Jud. Cir., 1976-80, Appellate Ct., 1980-92, U.S. Dist. Ct. (no. dist.) Ill., 1992—. Mem. Ill. Bar Assn., Winnebago County Bar Assn., Am. Acad. Judicial Edn. Office: US Courthouse 211 South Court St Rm 215 Rockford IL 61101*

REINHARDT, BENJAMIN MAX, lawyer, arbitrator, mediator; b. N.Y.C., Dec. 29, 1917; s. Meyer and Miriam (Fischer) R.; mn. Marlaena M. Chubey, May 23, 1971; children: Dennis, Dixie. BA, Harvard U., 1940; JD magna cum laude, Southwestern U., L.A., 1956. Bar: Calif. 1956, U.S. Supreme Ct. 1960. Pvt. practice Van Nuys, Calif., 1957-87, Palm Desert, Calif., 1987—; chief legal counsel Northridge (Calif.) Hosp. Found., 1965-75; atty. Calif. Psychol. Assn., San Francisco, 1965-70; tchr. law Los Angeles County Bd. Edn., L.A., 1965-73; instr. law U. So. Calif., L.A., 1963-69, Coll. of Desert, Palm Desert, Calif., 1992-94; arbitrator Superior Ct. Calif., Palm Springs, 1994—; atty. Sr. T.V., Indian Wells, Calif., 1992—. Mem. Palm Desert Police Adv. Com., 1993—; mem. adv. bd. Ret. Sr. Vol. Program, Palm Desert, 1994—; instr. law Elderhostel, Indian Wells, Calif., 1993—. Capt. U.S. Army, 1941-46. Mem. State Bar Calif., Desert Bar Assn. Republican. Avocations: golf, reading. Office: 73880 Grapevine St Palm Desert CA 92260-5561

REINHARDT, JOHN EDWARD, former international affairs specialist; b. Glade Spring, Va., Mar. 8, 1920; s. Edward Vinton and Alice (Miller) R.; m. Carolyn Lillian Daves, Sept. 2, 1947; children: Sharman W. Reinhardt Lancefield, Alice N. Reinhardt Jeffers, Carolyn C. Reinhardt Fenstermaker. A.B., Knoxville Coll., 1939; M.S., U. Wis., 1947, Ph.D., 1950. Prof. English Va. State Coll., Petersburg, 1950-56; cultural affairs officer USIS, Manila, 1956-58; dir. Am. Cultural Ctr., Kyoto, Japan, 1958-63; cultural attache USIS, Tehran, Iran, 1963-66; dep. asst. dir. Office East Asia and Pacific, USIA, Washington, 1966-68, 70-71, asst. dir. Office for Africa, 1968-70; ambassador to Nigeria, 1971-75, asst. sec. state for pub. affairs, 1975-77; dir. USIA, Washington, 1977-78, U.S. Internat. Communication Agy., Washington, 1978-81; acting dir. Smithsonian Mus. African Art, Washington, 1981-83; asst. sec. for history and art Smithsonian Instn., Washington, 1983-84; dir. directorate internat. activities Smithsonian Instn., 1984-87; prof. polit. sci. U. Vt., Burlington, 1987-90, prof. emeritus, 1990—. Served as officer AUS, 1942-46. Mem. MLA, Am. Fgn. Svc. Assn. (v.p. 1969-71). Methodist. Clubs: Cosmos, International (Washington).

REINHARDT, STEPHEN ROY, federal judge; b. N.Y.C., Mar. 27, 1931; s. Gottfried and Silvia (Hanlon) R.; children: Mark, Justin, Dana. B.A. cum laude, Pomona Coll., 1951; LL.B., Yale, 1954. Bar: Calif. 1958. Law clk. to U.S. Dist. Judge Luther W. Youngdahl, Washington, 1956-57; atty. O'Melveny & Myers, L.A., 1957-59; partner Fogel Julber Reinhardt Rothschild & Feldman (L.C.), L.A., 1959-80; judge U.S. Ct. Appeals (9th cir.), L.A., 1980—; Mem. exec. com. Dem. Nat. Com., 1969-72, nat. Dem. committeeman for Calif., 1976-80; pres. L.A. Recreation an dParks Commn., 1974-75; mem. Coliseum Commn., 1974-75; mem. L.A. Police Commn., 1974-78, pres., 1978-80; sec., mem. exec. com. L.A. Olympic Organizing com., 1980-84; bd. dirs. Amateur Athletic Found. of L.A., 1984-92; adj. prof. Loyola Law Sch., L.A., 1988-90. Served to 1st lt. USAF, 1954-56. Mem. ABA (labor law coun. 1975-77).

REINHARDT, WILLIAM PARKER, chemical physicist, educator; b. San Francisco, May 22, 1942; s. William Oscar and Elizabeth Ellen (Parker) R.; m. Katrina Hawley Currens, Mar. 14, 1979; children: James William, Alexander Hawley. BS in Basic Chemistry, U. Calif., Berkeley, 1964; AM in Chemistry, Harvard U., 1966, PhD in Chem. Physics, 1968; MA (hon.), U. Pa., 1985. Instr. chemistry Harvard U., 1967-69, asst. prof. chemistry, 1969-72, assoc. prof., 1972-74; prof. U. Colo., Boulder, 1974-84, chmn. dept. chemistry, 1977-80; prof. chemistry U. Pa., Phila., 1984-91, chmn. dept., 1985-88, D. Michael Crow prof., 1987-91; prof. chemistry U.Wash., Seattle, 1991—, assoc. chmn. undergrad. program, 1993—; vis. fellow Joint Inst. for Lab. Astrophysics of Nat. Bur. Stds. and U. Colo., 1972, 74, fellow, 1974-84; dir. Telluride Summer Rsch. Ctr., 1986-89, treas., 1989-93; com. on atomic, molecular and optical scis. NRC, 1988-90; vis. scientist Nat. Inst. Stds. and Tech., summers 1993, 94, 96. Mem. editl. bd. Phys. Rev. A., 1979-81, Chem. Physics, 1985-94, Jour. Chem. Physics, 1987-89, Jour. Physics B. (U.K.), 1992—, internat. Jour. Quantum Chemistry, 1994—; rschr. theoretical chem. physics, theoretical atomic and molecular physics for numerous publs. Recipient Camille and Henry Dreyfus Tchr. Scholar award, 1972; Alfred P. Sloan fellow, 1972; J.S. Guggenheim Meml. fellow, 1978; Coun. on Rsch. and Creative Work faculty fellow, 1978. Fellow AAAS, Am. Phys. Soc.; mem. Am. Chem. Soc., Phi Beta Kappa, Sigma Xi (nat. lectr. 1980-82), Phi Lambda Upsilon (Fresenius award 1977). Office: U Wash Dept Chemistry Box 1700 Seattle WA 98195

REINHART, DIETRICH THOMAS, university president, history educator; b. Mpls., May 17, 1949; s. Donald Irving and Eleanor Therese (Noonan) R. BA in History, St. John's U., Collegeville, Minn., 1971; AM in History, Brown U., 1976, PhD in History, 1984. Benedictine monk St. John's Abbey, 1971—; assoc. prof. history St. John's U., 1981—, dean of the coll., 1988-91, pres., 1991—; dir. liturgy St. John's Abbey, 1983-88. Bd. dirs. Minn. Pvt. Coll. Coun., 1991—, George A. MacPherson Fund, 1991—, Hill Monastic Manuscript Library, 1991—, Inst. for Ecumenical and Cultural Rsch., 1991—, First Am. Nat. Bank St. Cloud., 1992—; bd. overseers St. John's Prep. Sch., 1990—. Home: St John's Abbey Collegeville MN 56321 Office: St John's U Office of Pres Collegeville MN 56321

REINHART, KELLEE CONNELY, journalist; b. Kearney, Nebr., Dec. 15, 1951; d. Vaughn Eugene and Mary Jo (Mullen) Connely; m. Stephen Wayne Reinhart, June 15, 1974; children: Keegan Connely, Channing Mullen. B.A., U. Ala., 1972, M.S., 1974. Advt. copywriter Stas. WTBC-AM, WUOA-FM, 1970-72; asst. mgr. Ala. Press Assn., 1972-74; asst. to the editor Antique Monthly mag., 1974-75, mng. editor, 1975-77; editorial dir. Antique Monthly and Horizons mags., 1977-89; dir. univ. rels. U. Ala. System, Tuscaloosa, 1989—. Editor: Wild Birds of America: The Art of Basil Ede, 1991. Bd. dirs. Ala. Humanities Found., Ala. Writers Forum. Recipient Druids Arts award, 1995. Mem. Soc. Profl. Journalists, Am. Soc. Mag. Editors, Newcomen Soc. U.S., Art Table. Office: 401 Queen City Ave Tuscaloosa AL 35401-1551

REINHART, MARY ANN, medical board executive; b. Jackson, Mich., Aug. 14, 1942; d. Herbert Martin and Josephine Marie (Keyes) Conway; m. David Lee Reinhart, Dec. 28, 1963; children: Stephen Paul, Michael David. MA, Mich. State U., 1983, PhD, 1985. Rsch. asst. Mich. State U., East Lansing, 1979-82, 85, teaching asst. dept psychology, 1982-84, asst. prof. Office Med. Edn. R&D, Coll. Human Medicine, 1985-88; assoc. exec. dir. Am. Bd. Emergency Medicine, East Lansing, 1988-95, dep. exec. dir., 1995—; cons. Am. Bd. Emergency Medicine, 1985-88; chairperson collegewide evaluation com. Coll. Human Medicine, Mich. State U., East Lansing, 1985-88; adj. asst. prof. Office Med. Edn. Rsch. and Devel., Coll. Human Medicine, 1988—. Reviewer Annals of Emergency Medicine, 1987-95, Acad. Emergency Medicine, 1995—. Bd. dirs. Neahtawanta Rsch. and Edn. Ctr., Traverse City, Mich., 1991—. Mem. APA (divsn. indsl./orgnl. psychology, health psychology), Phi Kappa Phi. Achievements include application of chart stimulated recall method of assessment in a national medical recertification examination; development and implementation of national longitudinal study of emergency medicine residents and emergency physicians. Office: Am Bd Emergency Medicine 3000 Coolidge Rd East Lansing MI 48823-6319

REINHART, PETER SARGENT, corporate executive, lawyer; b. Mineola, N.Y., May 17, 1950; s. Charles Woodham and Martha Way (Sargent) R.; m. Susan Stockwell, Aug. 29, 1970 (div. Jan. 1976); 1 child, Amy Lynn; m. Gale McElroy, Oct. 16, 1976 (div. May 1985); 1 child, James Gharrett; m. Carol O. Gaffney, Jan. 4, 1992. BA, Franklin and Marshall Coll., 1971; JD, Rutgers U., 1975. Bar: N.J. 1975. Atty. Pillsbury and Russell, Atlantic Highlands, N.J., 1975-78; corp. counsel K. Hovnanian Enterprises, Inc., Red Bank, N.J., 1978-81, sr. v.p., gen. counsel, 1981—; also bd. dirs.; pres. Inst. Multi-Family Housing, Plainsboro, N.J., 1989—. Trustee, mem. editorial bd. Housing N.J. mag., 1991—. Trustee Community Assns. Inst., Arlington, Va., pres. N.J. chpt., 1988; trustee Assn. for Children of N.J., Newark, 1988-93, Keep Middlesex Moving, New Brunswick, 1990-93, Bayshore Community Hosp., Holmdel, N.J., 1992—, v.p., 1995; pres. Greater Red Bank

Jaycees, 1978-79; v.p. Monmouth coun. Boy Scouts Am., Oakhurst, N.J., 1987-94, pres., 1994—; v.p. Garden State Games, Edison, N.J., 1991-94; mem. Coun. Affordable Housing, Trenton, N.J., 1993—. Named to Community Assns. Inst. Hall of Fame, 1988; named Jaycee of Yr. Greater Red Bank Jaycees, 1977. Mem. N.J. State Bar Assn., N.J. Shore Builders Assn. (pres. 1989-90, Builder of Yr. 1987, Hall of Fame 1991), Ea. Monmouth C. of C. (trustee 1992—), Nat. Assn. Indsl. and Office Parks (bd. dirs. 1990-92), N.J. Builders Assn. (v.p. 1992-94, pres. 1995—, Builder of Yr., 1995, Atlantic Highlands Rep. Club (pres. 1978), Shore Athletic Club (Oakhurst, N.J.). Avocations: road racing, marathon running. Home: 2 Bayhill Rd Leonardo NJ 07737-1801 Office: Hovnanian Enterprises Inc 10 Hwy 35 PO Box 500 Red Bank NJ 07701

REINHARZ, JEHUDA, academic administrator, history educator; b. Haifa, Israel, Aug. 1, 1944; came to U.S., 1961; s. Fred and Anita (Weigler) R.; m. Shulamit Rothschild, Nov. 26, 1967; children—Yael, Naomi. B.S., Columbia U., 1967; B.R.E., Jewish Theol. Sem., 1967; M.A., Harvard U., 1968; Ph.D., Brandeis U., 1972; LHD, Hebrew Union Coll., 1995; DHL, The Jewish Theol. Sem. of Am., 1996. Prof. modern Jewish history U. Mich., Ann Arbor, 1972-82; Richard Koret prof. modern Jewish history Brandeis U., Waltham, Mass., 1982—, dir. Tauber Inst. Study of European Jewry, 1984-94; provost, sr. v.p. for acad. affairs Brandeis U., Waltham, Mass., 1992-94; pres. Brandeis U., Waltham, Mass., 1994—; mem. internat. acad. bd. Annenberg Rsch. Inst., 1986-90; bd. dirs. Yad Chaim Weizmann, 1990—, Internat. Editl. Bd. Pardès, 1996—; pres. Israel Prize, 1990, Akiba award, Am.-Jewish Com., 1996. Author: Fatherland or Promised Land: The Dilemma of the German Jew 1893-1914, 1975, Chaim Weizmann: The Making of a Zionist Leader, 1985 (Present Tense Literary award 1985, Kenneth B. Smilen Literary award 1985, Nat. Jewish Book award 1986, Shazar prize in history Israel, 1988), (in Hebrew) Hashomer Hazair in Germany, 1931-39, 1989, Chaim Weizmann: The Making of a Statesman, 1993 (Nat. Jewish Book award 1994); also numerous articles in French, German, Hebrew and English; gen. editor: Studies in Jewish History, 1984, European Jewish History, 1985; co-editor: The Jew in the Modern World, 1980, 2d edit. 1995, Mystics, Philosophers and Politicians, 1982, Israel in the Middle East 1948-83, 1984, The Jewish Response to German Culture, 1985, The Jews of Poland Between Two World Wars, 1989, The Impact of Western Nationalisms, 1992, Zionism and Religion, Hebrew edit., 1994, Essential Papers on Zionism, 1996; editor: The Letters and Papers of Chaim Weizmann, 1918-20, 1977, Dokumente zur Geschichte des deutschen Zionismus, 1882-1933, 1981, Living with Antisemitism, 1987. Bd. govs. United Israel Appeal/Jewish Agy., 1994; mem. bd. dir., exec. com. Am. Joint Distbn. Com., 1994; mem. acad. com. U.S. Holocaust Mus., 1990—. Fellow Leo Baeck Inst., Royal Hist. Soc., Am. Acad. Jewish Rsch., Am. Acad. Arts and Scis.; mem. Yad Vashem Soc. (adv. bd. 1983), Nat. Coun. Shazar Ctr., Assn. for Jewish Studies (sec. 1986-88, treas./sec., 1988-94), Commn. on Israel-Diaspora Rels. Home: 66 Beaumont Ave Newton MA 02160 Office: Brandeis U Office of Pres Waltham MA 02254-9110

REINHERZ, HELEN ZARSKY, social services educator; b. Boston, Aug. 4, 1923; d. Zachary and Anna (Cohen) Zarsky; m. Samuel E. Reinherz, Aug. 29, 1943; 1 son, Ellis. A.B. magna cum laude, Wheaton Coll., 1944; M.S., Simmons Coll., 1946; S.M., Harvard U., 1962, Sc.D., 1965. Social worker Newton Family Service, Mass., 1946-49, Mass. Gen. Hosp., Boston, 1949-51; supr. psychiat. social work State Hosp., Waltham, Mass., 1958-61; faculty mem. Simmons Coll., Boston, 1965—, prof. methods research, 1972—, dir. research Sch. Social Work, 1968—, dir. PhD program, 1993—; prin. investigator Identifying Children at Risk, 1976-84, Adaption in Adolescence, 1987-93, Early Adulthood Rsch. Project, 1993—; rsch. cons. Dept. Mental Health, 1970-80; prin. investigator Study Adolescent Drug Abuse, 1971-73; chmn. Gov.'s Adv. Coun. on Mental Health and Retardation, 1972; mem. adv. com. Mental Health Manpower to Fed. Govt., 1980-82. Author: (with H. Wechler, D. Dobbins) Social Work Research in the Human Services, 1976, (with M. Heywood, J. Camp) A Community Response to Drug Abuse, 1976; cons., assoc. editor: Jour. Prevention, 1980-91; mem. fed. adv. com. Rsch. in Prevention Rev., 1984-87; editorial bd. Jour. Early Adolescence; contbr. 55 articles to profl. jours. Recipient Maida H. Solomon award Simmons Coll. Alumni, 1961; NIH tng. fellow, 1961-65; Grant Found. grantee, 1963; Med. Found. grantee, 1967-69; NIMH grantee, 1975-84, 87—. Fellow Am. Orthopsychiat. Assn.; mem. Acad. Cert. Social Workers, Am. Pub. Health Assn., Council Social Work Edn., Harvard Sch. Pub. Health Alumni Assn. (sec.-treas. 1965-68), Phi Beta Kappa, Delta Omega. Home: 17 Corey Rd Malden MA 02148-1116 Office: Simmons Sch Social Work 51 Commonwealth Ave Boston MA 02116-2348 *As a teacher and researcher my efforts have been directed towards encouraging students to formulate the right questions about human problems as a first step to understanding and change.*

REINHOLD, JUDGE (EDWARD ERNEST REINHOLD, JR.), actor; b. Wilmington, Del.. Student, Mary Washington Coll., N.C. Sch. of the Arts. Actor: (feature films) Running Scared, 1979, Stripes, 1981, Thursday the Twelfth, 1982, Pandemonium, 1982, Fast Times at Ridgemont High, 1982, Gremlins, 1984, Beverly Hills Cop, 1984, Roadhouse, 1985, Ruthless People, 1986, Head Office, 1986, Off Beat, 1986, Beverly Hills Cop II, 1987, Vice-Versa, 1988, Rosalee Goes Shopping, 1990, Daddy's Dyin'...Who's Got the Will, 1990, Zandalee, 1991, Beverly Hills Cop III, 1994, The Santa Clause, 1994; (TV episodes) Wonder Woman, Magnum P.I., Seinfeld, 1993 (Emmy nomination, Guest Actor - Comedy Series, 1994); (TV movies) The Survival of Dana, 1979, Brothers and Sisters, A Step Too Slow, The Wilmar Eight, Booker, Promised a Miracle. Mem. Screen Actors Guild, AFTRA. Office: care ICM 8942 Wilshire Blvd Beverly Hills CA 90211*

REINHOLD, RICHARD LAWRENCE, lawyer; b. Buffalo, Feb. 24, 1951; s. Richard J. and Ann J. R.; m. Beth Stacey Grossman, May 11, 1991; 1 child: Elizabeth Jane. AB, Cornell U., 1973; JD, SUNY, Buffalo, 1976. Bar: N.Y. 1977, Fla. 1977. Assoc. Hodgson, Russ, Andrews, Woods & Goodyear, Buffalo, 1976-81; with office of tax legis. counsel U.S. Dept. Treasury, Washington, 1982-84; ptnr. Cahill Gordon & Reindel, N.Y.C., 1985—. Contbr. articles to profl. jours. Fellow Am. Coll. of Tax Counsel; mem. N.Y. State Bar Assn. (chair tax sect. 1996—), Internat. Fiscal Assn., Tax Club. Office: Cahill Gordon & Reindel 80 Pine St New York NY 10005-1702

REINHORN, ANDREI M., civil engineering educator, consultant; b. Bucharest, Romania, Oct. 23, 1945; s. Moritz A. and Dina (Rosenfeld) R.; m. Tova A. Waldman, Oct. 15, 1968; children: Michael, Gad. BSc, Technion - Israel Inst. Tech., Haifa, 1968, DSc, 1978. Registered profl. engr., N.Y., Israel. Structural engr. Milstein & Singer, Cons. Engrs., Tel Aviv, 1972-73; structural engr. Haifa, 1973-79, Buffalo, 1980-85; vis. asst. prof. U. Buffalo, 1979-81, asst. prof., 1981-86, assoc. prof., 1986-90, prof., 1990—; chmn. dept. civil engring. U. Buffalo, Buffalo, 1996—; cons. Niagara Machine & Tolls, Buffalo, 1982—, WSF Industries, Buffalo, 1983—, Walt Disney World, Lake Buenavista, Fla., 1986, Westinghouse, 1987-89, West Valley Nuclear Site, 1989, Princeton U., 1992, LeMessurier Cons., 1992, Dames & Moore, 1990-92, County of L.A., 1993; investigator Nat. Ctr. Earthquake Engring. Rsch., 1986—. Inventor, patentee press brake deflection compensation structure, automatic diagnostic sys. for elec. cir. breakers; contbr. over 250 articles to profl. jours., chpts. to books and conf. procs. Pres. W.E.S.T. Age Group Swim Club, Buffalo, 1985. Served to capt. Israel Def. Force, 1968-72. Rsch. grantee NSF, 1983-84, 86-95, 94—, Nalge/Snyder Industries, 1987. Fellow ASCE (faculty advisor 1981-83, bd. dirs. 1986-96, pres. Buffalo sect. 1993-94, Outstanding Svc. award 1982, 83); mem. N.Y. State Profl. Engring. Assn. (Engring. Educator of Yr. award 1991, Hist. Achievement award 1995), Am. Concrete Inst., Earthquake Engring. Rsch. Inst., Nat. Ctr. for Earthquake Engring. Rsch. Avocations: photography, skiing, bicycling. Home: 12 Troy View Ln Buffalo NY 14221-3522 Office: SUNY Buffalo Dept Civil Engring 231 Ketter Hall Amherst NY 14260

REINIGER, DOUGLAS HAIGH, lawyer; b. Mt. Kisco, N.Y., Nov. 8, 1948; s. Haigh McDiarmid and Virginia (Munson) R.; m. Margaret Vrablic, Aug. 31, 1968 (div. Jan. 1983); 1 child, Brian Christopher; m. Anne Fanning, Aug. 5, 1984. BA, Iona Coll., 1970; MSW, Fordham U., 1974, JD, 1980. Bar: N.Y. 1981, U.S. Dist. Ct. (so. dist.) N.Y. 1982, U.S. Dist. Ct. (ea. dist.) N.Y., U.S. Supreme Ct 1986. Psychiat. aide St. Vincent's Psychiat. Hosp., Harrison, N.Y., 1968-69; child care worker Cardinal McCloskey Home for Children, White Plains, N.Y., 1969-71, social worker, 1971-75, dir. legal affairs, 1975-81; sole practice N.Y.C., 1981-83; ptnr. Rosin & Reiniger, N.Y.C., 1983—; assoc. prof. Sch. Social Work Columbia U., N.Y.C., 1991—, coord. law minor program, Sch. Social Work, 1994—; lectr. appellate divsn. N.Y. Supreme Ct., N.Y.C., 1985, Fedn. Protestant Welfare, N.Y.C., 1987-91, Ct. Apptd. Spl. Advs., N.Y.C., 1987-94, Practicing Law Inst., N.Y.C., 1988. Mem. ABA (family law sect., com. on adoption, com. on custody 1992—), N.Y. State Bar Assn. (lectr. 1988, 91, family law sect., com. on family ct., com. on adoption), Assn. Bar City N.Y. (lectr. 1995, com. on family law and family ct. 1985-88, com. on juvenile justice 1989-91, com. on children and the law 1993—), Am. Acad. Adoptive Attys. (lectr. 1995-96), N.Y. State Foster and Adoptive Parents Assn. (bd. dirs. 1992—, lectr. 1992-95), N.Y. County Lawyers' Assn. (lectr. 1994-95). Roman Catholic. Office: Rosin & Reiniger 630 3d Ave New York NY 10017-6705

REINING, BETH LAVERNE (BETTY REINING), public relations consultant, journalist; b. Fargo, N.D.; d. George and Grace (Twiford) Reimche; student N.D. State Coll., U. Minn., Glendale Community Coll., Calif. State Coll., Carson; 1 dau., Carolyn Ray Toohey Hiett; m. Jack Warren Reining, Oct. 3, 1976 (div. 1984). Originated self-worth seminars in Phoenix, 1970-76; owner Janzik Pub. Relations, 1971-76; talk show reporter-hostess What's Happening in Ariz., Sta. KPAZ-TV, 1970-73; writer syndicated column People Want to Know, Today newspaper, Phoenix, 1973; owner JB Communications, Phoenix, 1976-84; owner, pres. Media Communications, 1984—; freelance writer; tchr. How to Weigh Your Self-Worth courses Phoenix Coll., Rio Solado Community Coll., Phoenix, 1976-84; instr. pub. rels. Scottsdale (Ariz.) Community Coll., 1987; muralist, works include 25 figures in med. office. Founder Ariz. Call-A-Teen Youth Resources, Inc., pres., 1975-76, v.p., 1976-77, now bd. dirs. Recipient awards including 1st pl. in TV writing Nat. Fedn. Press Women, 1971-88, numerous state awards in journalism Ariz. Press Women, 1971-76, Good Citizen award Builders of Greater Ariz., 1961. Mem. Ariz. Press Women (1st place award 1988), No. Ariz. Press Women (pres. 1983), Nat. Fedn. Am. Press Women, Pub. Relations Soc. Am., Phoenix Pub. Relations Soc., Nat. Acad. TV Arts and Scis., Phoenix Valley of Sun Convention Bur., Verde Valley C. of C. (bd. dirs., tourism chmn. 1986-87, Best Chair of Yr. award 1986), Phoenix Metro C. of C. Cottonwood C. of C. (chmn. of Yr. award, 1986). Inventor stocking-tension twist footlet, 1962. Club: Phoenix Press. Office: PO Box 10509 Phoenix AZ 85064-0509

REININGHAUS, RUTH, artist; b. N.Y.C., Oct. 4, 1922; d. Emil William and Pauline Rosa (Lazarik) R.; m. George H. Morales, Feb. 20, 1944; children: George James, Robert Charles; m. Allan Joseph Smith, May 28, 1960. Student, Hunter Coll., NYU, Nat. Acad. Sch. of Design, 1960-61, Frank Reilly Sch. of Art, 1963, Art Students League, 1968. Instr. art Banker's Trust, N.Y.C., 1971-77, 79—, Kittredge Club for Women, N.Y.C., 1967-77. Exhibited in group shows at Berkshire Art Mus., 1970s, Hammer Galleries, Inc., N.Y.C., 1974, Far Gallery, N.Y.C., 1974, Mufalli Gallery, N.Y. and Fla., 1983-90, Pen and Brush Club, 1985—, Petrucci Gallery, Saugerties, N.Y., 1988-94, Pastel Soc. Am., 1988—, John Lane Gallery, Rhinebeck, N.Y., 1992—, Regianni Gallery, N.Y.C., 1994, Catherine Lorillard Wolfe Club, Salmagundi Club, Allied Arts Am., Heidi Newhoff Gallery, N.Y.C., Hudson Valley Art Assn., Knickerbocker Artists, N.Y.C., Pastel Soc. Am., others. Recipient Robert Lehman award, 1960s, 3d prize in oils Murray Hill Art Show, 1968, Coun. Am. Artists award, 1985, Internat. award Oil Pastel Assn., 1987; scholar Nat. Acad., 1962, Frank Reilly Sch. Art, 1963, NYU, 1968; subject NBC TV show You Are an Artist, 1950s. Fellow Am. Artists Profl. League (Claude Parsons Meml. award 1974), Hudson Valley Art Assn.; mem. Pastel Soc. Am. (bd. dirs. 1988-90, J. Giffuni purchase award 1988, Flora B. Giffuni pres.' award 1990), Allied Artists Am. (assoc.), Soc. Illustrators (hon. 1983-87), Nat. Arts Club, Reciprocal, Artists Fellowship, Washington Sq. Outdoor Art Assn. (bd. dirs. 1983-90, Talens award 1963, Richtone Artists award 1968), Salmagundi Club N.Y. (pres. 1983-87, curator 1989—, Baker Brush award 1969, scholar 1969, Philip Isenberg award 1974, 89, 90, 92, 95, hon. mention 1983, 84, Salmagundi Club prize 1985, Franklin B. Williams Fund prize 1987, Tom Picard award 1987, Mortimer E. Freehof award 1988, John N. Lewis award 1988, Salmagundi Club medal of honor 1989, John N. Lewis award 1989, Samuel T. Shaw award 1990, Thomas Moran award 1990, Helen S. Coes award 1990, hon. mention 1991, Alice B. McReynolds award 1991, Salmagundi award 1991, Alphaeus Cole Meml. award 1991), Catharine Lorillard Wolfe Art Club (bd. dirs. 1987—, Anna Hyatt Huntington award 1978), Coun. Am. Artists (award 1985, hon. mention 1991, Catharine Lorillard Wolfe award for pastel 1992, cash award 1993), Pen and Brush Club (Helen Slotman award 1986, OPA Internat. award 1987, Gene Alden Walker award 1988, Pen and Brush Solo award 1992, hon. mention 1991), Knickerbocker Artists (Flora B. Giffuni PSA Pres.' award 1990), Oil Pastel Assn. (Pen and Brush award 1987, Strathmore award 1989, Salmagundi Club award 1991), Am. Artists Profl. League (Claude Parson's Meml. award 1974, 2nd prize in oils 1992, 3d prize oils 1993, Pres. award 1994), Alpha Delta Pi. Lutheran. Avocations: travel, tech. illustration, oil and pastel painting, collecting antique music boxes and watches. Home: 222 E 93rd St Apt 26A New York NY 10128-3758

REINISCH, BODO WALTER, electrical engineering educator; b. Beuthen, Germany, Nov. 26, 1936; came to U.S., 1965; s. Kurt and Alice Ada (Walleiser) R.; m. Gerda Seidenschwand, June 1, 1963; children: Karin, Ulrike. MS, U. Freiburg, Germany, 1963; PhD, Lowell Tech. Inst., 1970. Rsch. asst. Ionosphären Inst., Breisach, Germany, 1961-63, physicist, 1963-65; physicist Lowell (Mass.) Tech. Inst., 1965-75; dir. Ctr. for Atmospheric Rsch. U. Mass., Lowell, 1975—, assoc. prof. elec. engring., 1980-83, prof., 1983—, dept. head, 1988-94; cons. Royal Meteorol. Inst., Brussels, 1970-71; guest prof. physics U. Linz, Austria, 1978-79. Contbr. over 100 articles to Radio Sci., Jour. Geophys. Rsch., Advances of Space Rsch., others. Mem. sch. com. German Saturday Sch., Boston, 1979—. Grantee USAF, NASA, NSF, others; awarded Bundesverdienstkreuz by Pres. of Germany, 1987; Univ. Prof. U. Mass., Lowell, 1987-90; recipient Outstanding Achievement award U. Mass., Lowell, 1986, 87, 88. Sr. mem. IEEE; mem. Am. Geophys. Union, Internat. Union Radio Sci. (mem. COSPAR/URSI Task Force on Internat. Reference Ionosphere, internat. vice chmn. com. G 1993—), Sigma Pi Sigma, Sigma Chi. Achievements include development of global network of "digisonde" sounders; established HF Doppler observations for ionospheric drift studies; 2 patents. Office: U Mass Ctr Atmospheric Rsch 450 Aiken St Lowell MA 01854-3602

REINISCH, JUNE MACHOVER, psychologist, educator; b. N.Y.C., Feb. 2, 1943; d. Mann Barnett and Lillian (Machover) R. BS cum laude, NYU, 1966; MA, Columbia U., 1970, PhD with distinction, 1976. Asst. prof. psychology Rutgers U., New Brunswick, N.J., 1975-80; assoc. prof. psychology Rutgers U., New Brunswick, N.J., 1980-82, adj. assoc. prof. psychiatry, 1981-82; prof. psychology Ind. U., Bloomington, 1982-93, dir. Kinsey Inst. Rsch. in Sex, Gender, and Reprodn., 1982-93; prof. clin. psychology Sch. Medicine, Indpls., 1983-93; dir. emeritus Kinsey Inst., 1993—; dir., prin. investigator Prenatal Devel. Projects, Copenhagen, 1976—, sr. rsch. fellow, trustee The Kinsey Inst., 1993—; pres. R2 Sci. Comms., Inc., Ind., N.Y., 1985—; vis. sr. rschr. Inst. for Preventive Medicine, Copenhagen Health Svcs., Kommunehospitalet, Copenhagen, 1994—; cons. SUNY. Author: The Kinsey Institute New Report on Sex, 1990, pub. 8 fgn. edits.; editor books Kinsey Inst. series; syndicated newspaper columnist: The Kinsey Report; contbr. rsch. reports, revs., articles to profl. jours.; appeared on TV shows including PBS, Discovery, Oprah Winfrey, Sally Jessy Rafael, Good Morning Am., Today Show, CBS This Morning; guest host TV shows including CNBC Real Personal, TalkLive, also fgn. appearances. Founders day scholar NYU, 1966; NIMH trainee, 1971-74; NIMH grantee, 1978-80, Ford Found. grantee, 1973-75, Nat. Inst. Edn. grantee, 1973-74, Erikson Ednl. Found. grantee, 1973-74, grantee Nat. Inst. Child Health and Human Devel., 1981-88, Nat. Inst. on Drug Abuse, 1989-95; recipient Morton Prince award Am. Psychopath. Assn., 1976, Silver medal for 9th Dr. S.T. Huang-Chan Meml. Lectr. Hong Kong U., 1988, Dr. Richard J. Cross award Robert Wood Johnson Med. Sch., 1991, Award First Internat. Conf. on Orgasm, New Delhi, 1991, Disting. Alumnae award Tchrs. Coll. Columbia U., 1992. Fellow AAAS, APA, Am. Psychol. Soc., Soc. for Sci. Study Sex; mem. Internat. Acad. Sex Rsch. (charter), Internat. Soc. Psychoneuroendocrinology, Internat. Soc. Rsch. Aggression, Internat. Soc. Devel. Psychobiology, Am. Assn. Sex. Educators, Counselors and Therapists, Sigma Xi. Office: SUNY HSCB PBL Box 120 450 Clarkson Ave Brooklyn NY 11203-2012 also: The Kinsey Inst Prenatal Devel Project Ind U Bloomington IN 47405

REINKE, DORIS MARIE, retired elementary education educator; b. Racine, Wis., Jan. 12, 1922; d. Otto William Reinke and Louise Amelia Goehring. BS, U. Wis., Milw., 1943; MS, U. Wis., Whitewater, 1967. Tchr. kindergarten Elkhorn (Wis.) Area Sch. Sys., 1943-69, bldg. prin., 1968-70, summer sch. dir., 1974-75, grade 2 tchr., 1970-84, primary dept. chmn., 1971-84, administrv. asst., supervising tchr., 1957-83, student tchr., 1984, ret., 1984; oriented experience tchr. Program Area Sch. Sys., Elkhorn, 1966; pres. Elkhorn Edn. Assn., 1949-50; rep. dist. State Kindergarten Conf., Oshkosh, Wis., 1966; participant early edn. conf. State Early Edn. Conf., Eagle River, Wis., 1968. Columnist Mature Life Styles newspaper; monthly columnist Beacon, 1994—; contbr. weekly newspaper column Webster Notes, 1989; Walworth County Diary Monthly column in The Week, 1991—; author Doris' Corner newsletter Walworth County Geneal. Soc., 1992—. Bd. dirs. Food Pantry, Elkhorn, 1985-88, 96, RSVP Vol. Food Pantry, Elkhorn, 1985-95; del. dist. constn. conv. Evang. Luth. Ch. Am., Beloit, Wis., 1987; com. mem. Luth. Ch., Elkhorn, 1987; chmn. sch. centennial, Elkhorn, 1987; mem. Elkhorn Hist. Preservation Com., 1991—; archivist Sugar Creek Luth. Ch., 1992—. Recipient Wis. Edn. Research, West Bend, Wis., 1966, Outstanding Elem. Tchrs., Wash., 1973, Wis. Dept. Edn., Madison, 1980, Local History award State Hist. Soc. Wis., 1993. Mem. Nat. Ret. Tchrs. Assn., Walworth County Ret. Tchrs. Assn. (v.p. 1988, pres . 1990), Walworth county Hist. Soc. (treas. 1985-89, v.p. 1990-91, pres. 1991-96), Walworth County Geneal. Soc. (bd. dirs. 1991-92), Alpha Delta Kappa (state pres. 1968-70, 76-78). Avocations: reading, baseball, bird watching, traveling. Home: 516 N Wisconsin St Elkhorn WI 53121-1119

REINKE, JOHN HENRY, clergyman, educational administrator; b. Covington, Ky., Sept. 14, 1915; s. Henry Tilden and Helena (Ungeheuer) R. B.A., Loyola U., 1937, M.A., 1942, postgrad., 1947-54; postgrad., UCLA, 1948-49. Ordained priest Roman Cath. Ch., 1945; instr. psychology Loyola U., Chgo., 1947-54, vice chancellor, 1975-76, chancellor, 1976—; instr. psychology Xavier U., Cin., 1954-56, asst. prof., 1956-59; dir. guidance Loyola Acad., Wilmette, Ill., 1959-60, headmaster, 1960-65, pres., 1965-75; instr. music therapy Ind. U., Bloomington, summers 1958-60; trustee Regis Coll., Denver, 1973—, Xavier U., 1973—, Hadley Sch. for Blind, Winnetka, 1971—; chancellor emeritus Loyola U. of Chgo., Chgo., 1993—. Mem. Nat. Cath. Ednl. Assn., Nat. Sch. Public Relations Assn., Conf. Religious Dirs. Edn., Chgo. Art Inst., Field Mus., Nat. Assn. Ind. Schs., Jesuit Adminstrs. Assn., Nat. Cath. Guidance Conf. Clubs: Mid-Am, Internat, Plaza. Lodge: K.C. 1st U.S. priest to appear as soloist with maj. symphony orch., Cin., 1956, 57, 60. Office: Loyola U 820 N Michigan Ave Chicago IL 60611-2103

REINKE, RALPH LOUIS, retired academic administrator; b. Elmhurst, Ill., June 22, 1927; s. Louis Fred and Malinda Marie (Beckmann) R.; m. Lois Hermine Borneman, Aug. 28, 1948 (dec. Mar. 1984); children: Janice Reinke Eisenloeffell, Stephan, Sharon Reinke Holaway; m. Carole Louise Redlehs, June 14, 1986. Student, U. Ill., 1945-46; BS, Concordia Tchrs. Coll., River Forest, Ill., 1949; MA, Northwestern U., 1952; postgrad., U. Chgo., 1956-63; LittD, Concordia Sem., 1972. Prin. St. John Elem. Sch., Houston, 1949-56; assoc. prof. psychology and edn. Concordia U., River Forest, 1956-68; pres., chief exec. officer Concordia Pub. House, St. Louis, 1968-86; pres. Concordia Coll., Seward, Nebr., 1986-90; ret., 1990. Author: Christian Spelling Series, 2d edit, 1971. Mem. sch. bd. selecting com., Oak Park, Ill., 1965-67, chmn. lit. commn. Mo. Synod Luth. Ch., 1967-69. with USNR, 1944-46. Mem. Am. Assn. Ednl. Rschrs., Am. Mgmt. Assn., Protestant Ch. Owned Pubs. Assn. (dir. 1969-84, pres. 1982-84), St. Louis Printing Assn. (bd. dirs. 1975-77), Am. Assn. Indsl. Mgmt. (bd. dirs. 1981-85), Assn. Ind. Colls. and Univs. of Nebr. (pres. 1988-89), Concordia Univ. (bd. dirs. 1992—), Luth. Edn. Assn. (pres. 1967-69), Rotary, Phi Delta Kappa. Lutheran. *Life is a most precious and finite gift of God to man. Those who would lead must make a commitment to devote their full energies and intellects to the improvement of the quality of life of their fellowmen. In the highest sense, leadership is the integrity to heed the quiet voice of conscience from within in the quest of that quality.*

REINKE, WILLIAM JOHN, lawyer; b. South Bend, Ind., Aug. 7, 1930; s. William August and Eva Marie (Hein) R.; m. Sue Carol Colvin, 1951 (div. 1988); children: Sally Sue Taelman, William A., Andrew J.; m. Elizabeth Beck Lockwood, 1991. A.B. cum laude, Wabash Coll., 1952; J.D., U. Chgo., 1955. Bar: Ind. 1955. Assoc. Barnes & Thornburg and predecessors, South Bend, Ind., 1957-61, ptnr., 1961—, former chmn. compensation com., former mem. mgmt. com.; chmn. Constrn. Law Practice Group; trustee Stanley Clark Sch., 1969-80, pres. 1977-80; mem. adv. bd. Salvation Army, 1973—, pres., 1990-92; bd. dirs. NABE Mich. chpt., 1990-94, pres. 1993-94, Isaac Walton League, 1970-81, United Way 1978-81; pres. South Bend Round Table, 1963-65; trustee First Meth. Ch., 1967-70. Served with U.S. Army, 1955-57. Recipient Outstanding Local Pres. award Ind. Jaycees, 1960-61, Boss of Yr. award, 1969, South Bend Outstanding Young Man award, 1961. Mem. ABA, Ind. State Bar Assn., St. Joseph County Bar Assn., Ind. Bar Found. (patron fellow), Am. Judicature Soc., Def. Rsch. Inst., Ind. Soc. Chgo., Summit Club (past gov., founders com.), Rotary (bd. dirs. 1970-73, 94—). Home: 51795 Waterton Square Cir Granger IN 46530-8317 Office: Barnes & Thornburg 600 1st Source Bank Ctr 100 N Michigan St South Bend IN 46601-1630

REINKER, NANCY CLAYTON COOKE, artist; b. Owensboro, Ky., July 6, 1936; d. Billie Clayton and Barbara Jane (Mitchell) Cooke; m. Dale Bruce Reinker, Sept. 29, 1956; children: Shahn Elizabeth, Laura Beth, Karen Christian. Student, Kent State U., 1954-55, Cleve. Art Inst., 1956-57; studied sculpture with Stanley Bleifeld, 1979-80; student, Silvermine Sch. of Art, 1988-89. Owner Nettle Creek Shops of Westport and Cos Cob, Conn., 1974-86, Cross River Design Studio, 1986-89. One woman shows at Hayes Gallery, 1992 Silvermine Guild Arts Ctr., 1992, Art Place, 1993, Westport Art Ctr., 1994, also in numerous nat. and internat. exhbns. Chmn. Cultural Events Commn., Weston, Conn., 1993-94; pres. Inst. for Visual Artists, New Canaan, Conn., 1992-93; v.p., pres. Art Place Gallery, Southport, Conn., 1991-92, 94. Named to 1992 Cir. of Excellence, Soc. Nat. Art Patrons, 1992; recipient 1st prize Spectrum, 1992, 93, 94. Mem. ASID, Silvermine Guild of Artists (trustee 1994—), New Haven Paint and Clay (Merit award 1993), Nat. Assn. Women Artists, Conn. Women Artists (Painting award 1991), Greenwich Art Soc. (Randolph Chitwood award 1994), Women's Caucus for Art, Chi Omega. Home and Studio: 87 Valley Forge Rd Weston CT 06883-1913

REINMUTH, JAMES E., college dean. Dean Coll. Bus. Adminstrn. U Oreg., Eugene. Office: Dean Business Administration U Oregon Eugene OR 97403

REINMUTH, OSCAR MACNAUGHTON, physician, educator; b. Lincoln, Nebr., Oct. 23, 1927; s. Oscar William and Catharine Anne (MacNaughton) R.; m. Patricia Dixon, June 19, 1951 (div. Jan. 1977); children—David Dixon, Diane MacNaughton, Douglas Stewart; m. Audrey Longridge Holland, June 26, 1980. B.S., U. Tex., Austin, 1948; M.D. (F.B. Hanes research fellow 1950-51), Duke U., 1952. Intern Duke Hosp., 1952-53; asst. resident in medicine Yale U. Med. Ctr., 1953-54, NIH research trainee, 1954-55; asst. resident in neurology Boston City Hosp., 1955-56, chief resident, teaching fellow in neurology Harvard U. Neurol. unit, 1956-57; NIH spl. trainee, clin. asst. Nat. Hosp., London, 1957-58; from asst. prof. to prof. neurology U. Miami (Fla.) Med. Sch., 1958-77; prof. neurology and behavioral neuroscience, chmn. dept. U. Pitts. Med. Sch., 1977-93, prof. emeritus, 1994—; prof. neurology U. Ariz. Med. Sch., Tucson, 1993—; mem. research tng. com. A and C NIH, 1966-73. Served with AUS, 1946-47. Recipient Mosby award, 1952. Fellow ACP, Am. Acad. Neurology (1st v.p. 1973-76), Am. Neurol. Assn. (1st v.p. 1977-78, 2d v.p. 1976-77), Am. Heart Assn. (fellow stroke coun., vice chmn. 1978-79, chmn. 1980-82, editor pubs. 1975-78, editor-in-chief Stroke jour. 1987-91, Award of Merit 1992). Home: 5545 N Entrada Quince Tucson AZ 85718-4709 Office: U Med Ctr Dept Neurology 1501 N Campbell Ave Tucson AZ 85724-5023

REINOEHL, RICHARD LOUIS, writer, artist; b. Omaha, Oct. 11, 1944; s. Louis Lawrence and Frances Margaret (Robinson) R.; m. Linda Dale Iroff, Feb. 28, 1982; 1 child, Joy Margaret Iroff-Reinoehl. BS in Sociology, Portland State U., 1970; MSW, U. Minn., Duluth, 1977; postgrad., Cornell U.,

1984-88. Acting dir. Vanguard Group Homes, Virginia, Minn., 1976-77; dir. Minn. Chippewa Tribe Group Home, Duluth, 1978, Human Devel. Consortium, Minn., N.Y., Ohio, 1978—; faculty Social Work Program U. Wis., Superior, 1981-84; adv. bd. Computers in Social Svcs. Network, 1982-85; mem. Com. on Internat. Social Welfare Edn., 1982-86, Am. Evaluation Assn., 1986-89; affiliate scholar Oberlin Coll., 1991—. Editor: Computer Literacy in Human Services Education, 1990, Computer Literacy in Human Services, 1990, Men of Achievement, 16th edit., 1993; mem. editorial bd. Computers in Human Svcs., 1983—, assoc. editor, 1996; contbr. numerous articles to profl. jours. Mem. Legis. Task Force Regional Alcoholism Bd., 1972-73, Assn. Drug Abuse, Prevention and Treatment, 1973-74, Minn. Pub. Health Assn., 1976-78, Minn. Social Svc. Assn., 1976-83, Wis. Coun. Social Work Edn., 1983-84, N.Y. State Coun. Family Rels., 1986-89, Nat. Coun. Family Rels., 1986-89; exec. bd. Duluth Community Action Program, 1982-83; Dem. precinct chair, Portland, Oreg., 1972-74; precinct vice-chair Dem. Farmer-Labor Party, Duluth, 1979-81, chair, 1981-83, 2d vice-chair exec. bd., 1981-83. Mem. NASW (exec. com., chair program com. Arrowhead Region Minn. chpt., 1980-81, co-chair task force on computers in social work, 1981-82), Acad. Cert. Social Workers, Cornell U. Sailing Club (pres. 1990). Avocations: canoeing, sailing. Office: Human Devel Consortium Inc 46180 Butternut Ridge Rd Oberlin OH 44074-9778 *It's noteworthy that the most sought-after items in a society cannot be bought or sold. Included are wisdom, respect, generosity, truthfulness, and the love of family and friends.*

REINS, RALPH ERICH, automated service company executive; b. Detroit, Sept. 18, 1940; s. Erich John and Florence (Franz) R.; m. Victoria Louise Kolts, Sept. 14, 1963; children—Ann Marie, Christine Louise. B.S.I.E., U. Mich., 1963. Asst. supt. Chevrolet Motor div., Gen. Motors Corp., Detroit, 1963-72; v.p., pres. hwy. product ops. Rockwell Internat., Troy, Mich., 1972-85; sr. v.p. ITT Corp., Bloomfield Hills, Mich., 1985-89; chmn. of the bd., pres., chief exec. officer Mack Trucks, Inc., Allentown, Pa., 1989-90; pres. United Tech. Automotive, Dearborn, Mich., 1990-91; exec. v.p., pres. automotive sector Allied Signal Corp., 1991-94; pres., CEO Envirotest Sys. Corp., Phoenix, 1995-96, A.P. Parts Internat., Toledo, 1996—. Mem. Roeper Sch. Bd. Trustees; mem. found. bd. Oakland U. Mem. Soc. Automotive Engrs., Bloomfield Hills Country Club. Republican. Avocations: golf; hunting; fishing. Home: 29612 Durham Dr Perrysburg OH 43551 Office: A P Parts Internat 543 Matzinger Rd PO Box 965 Toledo OH 43697-0965

REINSCH, WILLIAM ALAN, government executive, educator; b. Evanston, Ill., Jan. 15, 1946; s. Bert and Kathleen (Penn) R.; m. Susan Polley Reinsch, Jan. 3, 1970; children: Andrew, Christian. BA, Johns Hopkins U., 1968; MA in Internat. Rels., Johns Hopkins U.-Sch. Advanced Internat. Studies, 1969. Legis. asst. Congressman Gilbert Gude, Washington, 1973-76, Congressman Richard Ottinger, Washington, 1976; chief legis. asst. Senator John Heinz, Washington, 1977-91; legis. asst. Senator John D. Rockefeller IV, Washington, 1991-93; cons., under sec. for export adminstrn. Dept. Commerce, Washington, 1994—; tchr. Landon Sch., Bethesda, Md., 1968-73; adj. assoc. prof. U. Md. U. Coll. Grad. Sch. Mgmt. and Tech., College Park, Md., 1990—; acting staff dir. Environmental Study Conf. U.S. Ho. Reps., 1976. Contbr. articles to profl. jours. Pres. St. Mark Elderly Housing Corp., Rockville, Md. Mem. Phi Beta Kappa, Omicron Delta Kappa, Alpha Delta Phi. Democrat. Presbyterian. Office: Dept Commerce Rm 3898B Washington DC 20230

REINSCHMIEDT, ANNE TIERNEY, nurse, lawyer, rancher; b. Washington, Mar. 6, 1932; d. Edward F. and Frances (Palmer) Tierney; m. Edwin Ruben Reinschmiedt, Sept. 20, 1959 (div. 1961); 1 child, Kathleen Frances Tierney. BS, Cen. State U., Edmond, Okla., 1975; JD, Oklahoma City U. Sch. Law, 1991. RN, Calif., Okla.; lic. residential care facility adminstr., nursing home adminstr. Nurse San Jose (Calif.) Hosp., 1952-55; owner, operator Hominy Studio, 1960-62; dir. nurses, lab and x-ray, technician, adminstr. Hominy (Okla.) City Hosp., 1961-63; nurse Jackson County Dept. Health, Altus, Okla., 1963-65; adminstr. Propp's Inc., Oklahoma City, 1965-80; nursing homes cons. Propps & Self, Oklahoma City, 1965—; pres. Shamrock Health Care Ctr., Bethany, Okla., 1981—; operator Lakeview Lodging Residential Care Facility, 1981—; adult edn. instr., med. aide technicians East Central U., Ada, Okla., 1987-89; cons. residential care facilities, 1985—. Author: Recovery Room Procedures, 1958. Mem. Jackson County (Okla.) Draft Bd., 1965-70. Lt. USN, 1955-60. Mem. ANA, Nat. Assn. Residential Care Facilities (sec., bd. dirs. 1983-85), Okla. Bar Assn., Okla. Assn. Residential Care Facilities (founding pres. 1981-87, bd. dirs. 1981—), Beta Sigma Phi, Phi Alpha Delta (vice justice, exec. bd. 1988-90). Republican. Roman Catholic. Avocations: reading, horses, astrology, ceramics, golf. Office: Shamrock Health Care PO Box 848 Bethany OK 73008-0848

REINSDORF, JERRY MICHAEL, professional sports teams executive, real estate executive, lawyer, accountant; b. Bklyn., Feb. 25, 1936; s. Max and Marion (Smith) R.; m. Martyl F. Rifkin, Dec. 29, 1956; children: David Jason, Susan Janeen, Michael Andrew, Jonathan Milton. BA, George Washington U., 1957; JD, Northwestern U., 1960. Bar: D.C., Ill. 1960; CPA, Ill.; cert. specialist real estate securities, rev. appraiser; registered mortgage underwriter. Atty. staff regional counsel IRS, Chgo., 1960-64; assoc. law firm Chapman & Cutler, 1964-68; ptnr. Altman, Kurlander & Weiss, 1968-74; of counsel firm Katten, Muchin, Gitles, Zavis, Pearl & Galler, 1974-79; gen. ptnr. Carlyle Real Estate Ltd. Partnerships, 1971, 72; chmn. bd. Balcor Co., 1973-87; mng. ptnr. TBC Films, 1975-83; chmn. Chgo. White Sox, 1981—, Chgo. Bulls Basketball Team, 1985—; ptnr. Bojer Fin., 1987—; lectr. John Marshall Law Sch., 1966-68; former bd. dirs. Shearson Lehman Bros., Inc., Project Academus of DePaul U., Chgo., Sports Immortals Mus., 1987-89, Com. Commemorate U.S. Constn., 1987; bd. dirs. La Salle Nat. Bank, La Salle Nat. Corp.; bd. overseers Inst. for Civil Justice, 1996—; lectr. in real estate, sports and taxation. Author: (with L. Herbert Schneider) Uses of Life Insurance in Qualified Employee Benefit Plans, 1970. Co-chmn. Ill. Profls. for Senator Ralph Smith, 1970; mem. Chgo. region bd. Anti-Defamation League, 1986—; trustee Ill. Inst. Tech., 1991—; mem. Ill. Commn. on African-Am. Males, 1992—; bd. dirs. Chgo. Youth Success Found., 1992—, Corp. for Supportive Housing, 1995—; nat. trustee Northwestern U., 1993—; bd. govs. Hugh O'Brian Youth Found.; mem. internat. adv. bd. Barrow Neurol. Found., 1996—. Recipient Hallmark award Chgo. Baseball Cancer Charities, 1986, Corp. Superstar award Ill. chpt. Cystic Fibrosis Found., 1988, Sportsman of Yr. award, 1994, Chicagoan of Yr. award Chgo. Park Dist., 1990, Kellogg Excellence award, 1991, Cmty. Hero award Interfaith Organizing Project, 1991, Operation Push Bridgebuilder award, 1992, Alumni Merit award Northwestern U., 1992, Ellis Island Medal of Honor award Nat. Ethnic Coalition of Orgns., 1993, Lifetime Achievement award March of Dimes, 1994, Hallmark Hall of Fame Civic award Ind. Sports Charities, 1994, Am. Spirit award USAF, 1995, Alpha Epsilon Pi Arthur and Simiteich Outstanding Alumnus award, 1995; inductee B'nai B'rith Nat. Jewish Am. Sports Hall of Fame, 1994. Mem. ABA, FBA, Ill. Bar Assn., Chgo. Bar Assn., Nat. Sports Lawyers Assn., Nat. Assn. Rev. Appraisers and Mortgage Underwriters, Northwestern U. Law Sch. Alumni Assn. (bd. dirs.), Comml. Club Chgo., Order of Coif, Omega Tau Rho. Office: Chgo White Sox 333 W 35th St Chicago IL 60616

REINSTEIN, JOEL, lawyer; b. N.Y.C., July 23, 1946; s. Louis and Ruth Shukovsky; children: Lesli, Louis, Mindy. B.S.E., U. Pa., 1968; J.D. cum laude, U. Fla., 1971; LL.M. in Taxation, NYU, 1974. Bar: Fla. 1971, U.S. Tax Ct. 1973, U.S. Dist. Ct. (so. dist.) Fla. 1976. Atty., office of chief counsel IRS, 1971-74; ptnr. Capp, Reinstein, Kopelowitz and Atlas, P.A., Ft. Lauderdale, Fla., 1975-85; dir., ptnr. Greenberg, Traurig, Hoffman, Lipoff, Rosen & Quentel, P.A., Ft. Lauderdale, 1985-92; gen. counsel Internat. Magnetic Imaging, Inc., Boca Raton, Fla., 1992-94; prin. Law Offices of Joel Reinstein, Boca Raton, 1993—; lectr. Advanced Pension Planning, Am. Soc. C.L.U.s; lectr. in field. Mem. Fla. Bar Assn. (tax sect.), ABA (tax sect., adj. mem. com. employee benefits), Order of Coif, Phi Kappa Phi, Phi Delta Phi. Mem. editorial bd. U. Fla. Law Rev., 1970-71; contbr. articles to profl. jours. Office: The Plaza 5355 Town Center Rd Ste 801 Boca Raton FL 33486-1069

REINSTEIN, PAUL MICHAEL, lawyer; b. N.Y.C., Jan. 19, 1952; s. Joseph and Edith (Ambaras) R.; m. Gila Ann Moldoff, Apr. 16, 1978; children: Meira, Rachel, Aryeh, Joseph. BA, Yeshiva Coll., 1973; JD, Yale U., 1976. Bar: N.Y. 1977. Assoc. Fried Frank Harris Shriver & Jacobson, N.Y.C., 1976-83, ptnr., 1983—. Mem. ABA, N.Y. State Bar Assn. Home: 282 Maple St West Hempstead NY 11552-3206 Office: Fried Frank Harris et al 1 New York Plz New York NY 10004*

REINTHALER, RICHARD WALTER, lawyer; b. N.Y.C., Feb. 27, 1949; s. Walter F. and Maureen C. (Tully) R.; m. Mary E. Maloney, Aug. 8, 1970; children: Brian, Scott, Amy. BA in Govt. magna cum laude, U. Notre Dame, 1970, JD summa cum laude, 1973. Bar: N.Y. 1974, U.S. Dist. Ct. (so. and ea. dists.) N.Y. 1974, U.S. Ct. Appeals (2d cir.) 1974, U.S. Ct. Appeals (9th cir.) 1976, U.S. Ct. Appeals (5th cir.) 1978, U.S. Ct. Appeals (11th cir.) 1981, U.S. Supreme Ct. 1977. Assoc. White & Case, N.Y.C., 1973-81, ptnr., 1981-95; ptnr. Dewey Ballantine, N.Y.C., 1995—; mem. adv. group U.S. Dist. Ct. (ea. dist.) N.Y., 1992—, chairperson subgroup on ethics, 1993—. Contbr. articles to profl. jours. Served to 1st lt. U.S. Army, 1974. Mem. ABA (2d cir. chmn. discovery com. 1982-87, program coord. 1986, ann. meeting litigation sect., vice chmn. com. on fed. procedure 1988-89, co-chmn. com. on profl. responsibility 1989-92, vice chmn. securities litigation com. 1993-94, vice chair Hong Kong meeting 1995), N.Y. State Bar Assn., Assn. of Bar of City of N.Y. (mem. com. to enhance diversity in the profession 1990—, mem. Orison S. Marden Meml. Lectrs. com. 1994—, spl. com. on mergers, acquisitions and corp. control contests, 1995—), Scarsdale Golf Club (Hartsdale, N.Y., bd. govs. 1994—), Capital Hill Club (Washington). Republican. Roman Catholic. Avocations: golf, tennis. Office: Dewey & Ballantine 1301 Ave of the Americas New York NY 10019

REIS, ARTHUR ROBERT, JR., men's furnishings manufacturer; b. N.Y.C., Dec. 8, 1916; s. Arthur M. and Claire (Raphael) R.; m. Muriel Henle, Sept. 25, 1953; children: Arthur, Diane, Pamela. B.A., Princeton U., 1939. Joined Pan. Am. Airways, 1940, asst. to v.p., 1943; joined Robert Reis & Co., N.Y.C., 1946, pres., 1947-79; ptnr. Energy Applications Assocs., 1980-82; mem. departmental disciplinary com. Appellate Ct. N.Y., 1994; supr. cons. Nat. Exec. Svcs. Corps. Mem. N.Y. State Com. on Refugee Relief Act of 1953; trustee, mem. exec. com. Storm King Sch., Cornwall-on-Hudson, N.Y. Served from pvt. to capt. Air Transport Command USAAF, 1943-46; asst. chief of staff Central Pacific Wing. Decorated B.S.M. Mem. Young Pres.' Orgn. (co-founder), N.Y.C. of C. (exec. com.), Princeton Club of N.Y. (bd. govs.). Home: 1136 5th Ave New York NY 10128-0122

REIS, DON, publishing executive; b. N.Y.C., Nov. 19, 1927; m. Barbara Weinberg, 1947; children: Robert, Richard. AB, Princeton U., 1947; MA, NYU, 1955. Rsch. editor Bantam Books, 1952-55, edn. editor, 1955-66; editor-in-chief Washington Square Press Divsn. Simon & Schuster, 1966-68; v.p., editorial dir. Ednl. Directions Inc., Westport, Conn., 1968-85; mng. editor Barron's Ednl. Series, 1985-87; gen. and ednl. editor Barron's, 1987-93; sr. cons. editor Barron's, Hauppauge, N.Y., 1993—; editorial dir. Reis Assocs., Forest Hills, N.Y., 1993—. Author (with A. Butman and D. Sohn) Paperback Books in the Schools, 1962; editor The Collected Essays of Aldous Huxley, 1958. Home: 57 Summer St Forest Hills NY 11375-6035 Office: Barron's Edn Series Inc 250 Wireless Blvd Hauppauge NY 11788-3924

REIS, DONALD JEFFERY, neurologist, neurobiologist, educator; b. N.Y.C., Sept. 9, 1931; s. Samuel H. and Alice (Kiesler) R.; m. Cornelia Langer Noland, Apr. 13, 1985. A.B., Cornell U., 1953, M.D., 1956. Intern N.Y. Hosp., N.Y.C., 1956; resident in neurology Boston City Hosp.-Harvard Med. Sch., 1957-59; Fulbright fellow, United Cerebral Palsy Found. fellow London and Stockholm, 1959-60; rsch. assoc. NIMH, Bethesda, Md., 1960-62; spl. fellow NIH, Nobel Neurophysiology Inst., Stockholm, 1962-63; asst. prof. neurology Cornell U. Med. Sch., N.Y.C., 1963-67; assoc. prof. neurology and psychiatry Cornell U. Med. Sch., 1967-71, prof., 1971—, First George C. Cotzias Disting. prof. neurology, 1982—; mem. U.S.-Soviet Exch. Program; mem. adv. coun. NIH; bd. sci. advisers Merck, Sharpe & Dohm, Sterling Rsch. Group; cons. Eli Lilly, Servier Pharms.; bd. dirs. China Seas, Inc., Charles masterson Burke Rsch. Found. Contbr. articles to profl. jours.; mem. editorial bd. various profl. jours. Recipient CIBA Prize award Am. Heart Assn. Fellow AAAS, ACP; mem. Am. Physiol. Soc., Am. Neurol. Assn., Am. Pharmacol. Soc., Am. Assn. Physicians, Telluride Assn., Am. Soc. Clin. Investigation, Century Assn., Ellis Island Yacht Club (commadore), Phi Beta Kappa, Sigma Xi, Alpha Omega Alpha. Home: 190 E 72nd St New York NY 10021-4370 also: 73 Water St Stonington CT 06378-1433 Office: 1300 York Ave New York NY 10021-4805

REIS, JOSEPHINE GOODALE MILLS, YMCA association executive; b. Upper Montclair, N.J., Jan. 15, 1908; d. Irving Parker and Sophia (Goodale) Mills; m. L. Sanford Reis, Jan. 15, 1932; children: Curtis, Barbara Goodale Reis Johnson. BA, Cornell U., 1929. With trust dept. City Bank Farmers Trust Co., N.Y.C., 1929-34; pres. YWCA, Ridgewood, N.J., 1960-63; nat. bd. dirs., chair teen adv. com. YWCA U.S.A., 1964-76, mem. world svc. coun. Contbr. poetry to the Saturday Rev. Lit. Asst. dir. vol. svcs. ARC, Bklyn., 1942-45; hon. mem. YWCA, Ridgewood, N.J.; past mem. trustee nominating com. Cornell U. Recipient Army-Navy E award Armed Forces, 1945. Mem. AAUW, LWV, NOW, Coll. Club (hon., pres. 1957-59), Mortar Bd., Penthama. Democrat. Avocations: tennis, golf, travel. Home: 4200 Shell Rd Sarasota FL 34242-1238

REIS, JUDSON PATTERSON, investment manager; b. Bryn Mawr, Pa., July 31, 1942; s. Maurice J. and Wiley W. (Patterson) R.; m. Judith Morse (div.); children: Judson P. Jr., C. Parker; m. Kathryn Ann Fortuin, June 16, 1972; children: Mark B., Nicholas D., A. Curtis. BA cum laude, Washington and Lee U., 1964; MBA with distinction, Harvard U., 1966. Assoc. Morgan Stanley & Co., Inc., N.Y.C., 1966-72, v.p., 1973, prin., 1974, mng. dir., 1975-88; exec. v.p., mng. dir. Kleinwort Benson N.A., N.Y.C., 1988-91; pres. Sire Mgmt. Corp., N.Y.C., 1991—; mng. gen. ptnr. Sire Ptnrs., L.P., 1991—; bd. dirs. Kleinwort Benson Ltd., London; Morris vis. prof. bus. adminstrn. Colgate Darden Grad. Sch. Bus. U. Va., 1987-88, 1989—. Treas. Caputo for Congress com., N.Y.C., 1977; treas. Caputo for Lt. Gov. com., 1978; bd. dirs. Pilobolus Dance Co.; pres. bd. trustees Showhegan Sch. Painting and Sculpture. Republican. Clubs: University (N.Y.C.), Farmington Country, Charlottesville, Va., Bond, Links (N.Y.C.); Bridgehampton (N.Y.). Home: 43 W 13th St PHR New York NY 10011 Office: Sire Ptnrs LP 630 5th Ave New York NY 10111-0001

REIS, MURIEL HENLE, lawyer, broadcast executive/television commentator; b. N.Y.C.; d. Frederick S. and Mary (Meyers) Henle; m. Arthur Reis Jr., Sept. 25, 1953; children: Arthur Henle, Diane Mary, Pamela Robin. BA, Vassar Coll., 1946; LLB, Columbia U., 1949. Assoc. MS-I Isaacs, N.Y.C., 1950-52; asst. gen. counsel ABC, N.Y.C., 1952-54; from asst. gen. counsel to assoc. gen. counsel Metromedia Inc., N.Y.C., 1956-86; v.p. WNEW, N.Y.C., 1974-86; v.p., legal affairs Fox TV Sta. Inc., N.Y.C., 1986—, on-air legal commentator, 1995—. Mem. Assn. of Bar of City of N.Y., Internat. Soc. Radio and TV Execs. Home: 1136 Fifth Ave New York NY 10128-0122 Office: Fox TV Sta Inc 205 E 67th St New York NY 10021-6048

REISBERG, BARRY, geropsychiatrist, neuropsychopharmacologist; b. Bklyn., Dec. 3, 1947; s. Harry and Claire (Cohen) R.; m. Rosalie DePaola, Feb. 23, 1974 (dec. Oct. 1975); m. Nancy A. Minich, May 7, 1988. BA, CUNY, Bklyn., 1968; MD, N.Y. Med. Coll., 1972. Diplomate Am. Bd. Psychiatry and Neurology, Am. Bd. Geriatric Psychiatry. Intern N.Y. Med. Coll./Met. Hosp., N.Y.C., 1972-75, resident in psychiatry, 1972-75; fellow dept. psychiatry Middlesex Hosp. Med. Sch. U. London, 1975; staff psychiatrist Franklin D. Roosevelt VA Hosp., Montrose, N.Y., 1975-78; staff psychiatrist Neuropsychopharmacology Rsch. Unit NYU Med. Ctr., N.Y.C., 1978-80, clin. dir. Aging and Dementia Rsch. Ctr., 1978—; adj. prof. Ctr. for Studies in Aging McGill U., Montreal, Que., Can., 1993—; clin. instr. dept. psychiatry N.Y. Med. Coll., Valhalla, 1975-78; asst. prof. NYU Sch. Medicine, N.Y.C., 1978-84, assoc. prof., 1984-90, prof., 1990—; rsch. collaborator, vis. clinician Brookhaven Nat. Labs., Upton, N.Y., 1979-80; dir. clin. core NIMH Clin. Rsch. Ctr., 1989—, Nat. Inst. Aging Alzheimer's Disease Ctr., 1990—; dir. Zachary and Elizabeth M. Fisher Alzheimer's Disease Edn. and Resources Program NYU Med. Ctr., 1995—; med. and sci. adv. bd. Alzheimer's Assn., Chgo., 1993—; cons. psychiatrist N.Y. VA Hosp., 1980-89; chmn. work group WHO, Copenhagen, 1984; mem. aging sect. NIH, 1986-90; vis. prof. Palmerston North Postgrad. Med. Soc., New Zealand, 1991. Author: Brain Failure, 1981; editor: Alzheimer's Disease, 1983; (with others) Diagnosis and Treatment of Senile Dementia, 1989; mem. editl. bd. Jour. Am. Aging Assn., 1985—, Alzheimer's Disease and Associated Disorders, 1985—, Jour. Geriat. Psychiatry and Neurology, 1986—, Am. Jour. Alzheimer's Care, 1986—, Internat. Psychogeriat., 1989—, Am. Jour. Geriat. Psychiatry, 1992—, Integrative Psychiatry, 1994—; contbr. over 150 articles to med. and sci. jours. Fellow NSF, 1963, Coun. on Internat. Ednl. Exch.-Japan Soc., Tokyo, 1968; grantee NIH, 1979-81, 82-85, 87, 90, 92—, NIMH, 1983-85. Mem. Internat. Psychogeriat. Assn. (bd. dirs. 1985-93, treas. 1993-95, pres.-elect 1995—), Am. Aging Assn. (bd. dirs. 1990—), Alzheimer's and Related Disorders Soc. India (hon.), Am. Assn. Geriat. Psychiatry (sec. 1991-92, bd. dirs. 1992-96), Am. Coll. Neuropsychopharmacology. Office: NYU Med Ctr Aging and Dementia Rsch Ctr 550 1st Ave New York NY 10016-6481 *Our studies have demonstrated that Alzheimer's disease (AD) recapitulates normal human development inversely in terms of cognition, functioning and in other ways. These findings have profound implications, e.g. a better understanding of AD can improve understanding of normal human development and behavior and vice versa.*

REISBERG, LEON ELTON, education educator; b. Dallas, Sept. 1, 1949; s. Morris Abraham and Gertrude (Turner) R.; m. Iris Fudell, July 3, 1973 (div. 1986); children: Joshua Fudell, Leah Fudell; m. Donna Brodigan, July 11, 1993. BS in Edn., U. Tex., Austin, 1971; MEd, U. Ark., Fayetteville, 1972; EdD, U. Kans., Lawrence, 1981. Tchr. Oklahoma City Sch. Dist., 1972-75, Putnam City Sch. Dist., Oklahoma City, 1975-78, U. Kans. Med. Ctr., Kansas City, 1978-79; asst. prof. Pacific Luth. U., Tacoma, 1981-88; tchr. Tacoma (Wash.) Sch. Dist., 1989-90; assoc. prof. edn. Pacific Luth. U., 1988-94; chmn. dept. spl. edn. Pacific Luth. U., Tacoma, 1986-93, chmn. profl. edn. adv. bd., 1992-94, assoc. dean sch. edn., 1993—, prof., 1995—; project dir., Consulting Spl. Edn. Personnel Tng. Project, Tacoma, 1983-86; chmn. Profl. Edn. Adv. Bd. Cons. editor Learning Disability Quar., 1981-89, Acad. Therapy, 1988-90, Intervention, 1990—; contbr. articles to profl. publs. Mem. Coun. Exceptional Children, Coun. Learning Disabilities (Pacific Rim region rep. 1993-96), Assn. Trainer Spl. Edn. Pers. (chmn. 1991), Phi Kappa Phi. Democrat. Jewish. Office: Pacific Luth U Sch Edn Tacoma WA 98447 *Personal philosophy: Research and professional interests in promoting the inclusion of students with disabilities in regular classrooms.*

REISCH, MICHAEL STEWART, social work educator; b. N.Y.C., Mar. 4, 1948; s. Joseph and Charlotte (Rosenberg) R.; m. Amy Jane Lewis, May 21, 1972; children: Jennifer, Nikki. BA in History with highest honors, NYU, 1968; PhD in History with distinction, SUNY, Binghamton, 1975; MSW with honors, CUNY, 1979. Youth worker Washington-Heights-Inwood YM-YWHA, N.Y.C., 1965-66; editor, columnist Heights Daily News, Bronx, N.Y., 1966-68; rsch./teaching asst. SUNY, Binghamton, 1970-72; unit dir., program cons. Child Study Assn.-Wel Met, Inc., N.Y.C., 1970-72; asst. dir. youth div. Mosholu-Montefiore Community Ctr., Bronx, 1972-73; project dir. Silberman Found./N.Y. Assn. Deans, N.Y.C., 1973-74; asst. dean Sch. Social Welfare, asst. prof. SUNY, Stony Brook, 1974-79; assoc. prof., then assoc. prof. Sch. Social Work U. Md., Balt., 1979-86; dir. Sch. Social Work, prof. social work/pub. adminstrn. San Francisco State U., 1986-95; prof. social welfare U. Pa., Phila., 1995—; cons. and spkr. in field. Co-author: From Charity to Enterprise, 1989 (Social Sci. Book of Month); editor, author various books in field; contbr. articles to profl. publs., chpts. to books. Cons. to numerous local, state, and fed. polit. campaigns, 1971—; mem. Gov.'s Adv. Coun. Human Resources, Md., 1983-86; pres. Welfare Advs., Md., 1983-86; campaign mgr. Rep. Barbara Mikulski, Balt., 1982; bd. dirs. Coleman Advs. for Children and Youth, 1987-95, San Francisco Internat. Program, 1987-95, Calif. Social Work Edn. Ctr., 1991-95, Ctr. for S.E. Asian Refugee Resettlement, 1992-95, Am. Jewish Congress, N. Calif., 1994-95, Coun. Internat. Programs, 1995—; chair Children's Budget Task Force City of San Francisco, 1989-92; mem. Mayor's Adv. Coun. on Drug Abuse, San Francisco, 1988-91; mem. steering com. Poverty Action Alliance, 1993-95. Woodrow Wilson Found. fellow, 1972-73. Mem. NASW (del. 1990-92, 94-96, chair peace and justice com. 1992—), Coun. on Social Work Edn. (com. on status of women 1989-92, bd. dirs. 1993—, chair commn. on ednl. policy 1994—), Am. Hist. Assn., Nat. Assn. Deans/Dirs. of Schs. and Social Work (sec. 1993-95), Calif. Assn. Deans/Dirs. of Schs. of Social Work (pres. 1992-94). Avocations: travel, hiking, cooking, swimming, creative writing.

REISER, MORTON FRANCIS, psychiatrist, educator; b. Cin., Aug. 22, 1919; s. Sigmund and Mary (Roth) R.; m. Lynn B. Whisnant, Dec. 19, 1976; children: David E., Barbara, Linda. B.S., U. Cin., 1940, M.D., 1943; grad., N.Y. Psychoanalytic Inst., 1960. Diplomate Am. Bd. Psychiatry and Neurology. Intern King's County Hosp., Bklyn., 1944; resident Cin. Gen. Hosp., 1944-49; practice medicine, specializing in psychiatry Cin., 1947-52, Washington, 1954-55, N.Y.C., 1955-69; mem. faculty Cin. Gen. Hosp., also U. Cin. Coll. Medicine, 1949-52, Washington Sch. Psychiatry, 1953-55; faculty Albert Einstein Coll. Medicine, Yeshiva U., N.Y.C., 1955-69; prof. psychiatry Albert Einstein Coll. Medicine, Yeshiva U., 1958-69, dir. research dept. psychiatry, 1958-65; chief div. psychiatry Montefiore Hosp. and Med. Center, N.Y.C., 1965-69; chmn. dept. psychiatry Yale Med. Sch., 1969—, prof., 1969-78, chmn. dept., 1969-86, Charles B.G. Murphy prof., 1978-86, Albert E. Kent prof., 1986-90, Albert E. Kent prof. emeritus, 1990—; cons. Walter Reed Army Inst. Research, 1957-58, High Point Hosp., Port Chester, N.Y., 1957-69; com. WHO, 1963; mem. profl. adv. com. Jerusalem Mental Health Center, 1972—; mem. clin. program projects rev. com. NIMH, 1970—, chmn., 1973-74. Author: (with H. Leigh) The Patient: Biological, Psychological, and Social Dimensions of Medical Practice, 1980, Mind, Brain, Body: Toward a Convergence of Psychoanalysis and Neurobiology, 1984; (with H. Leigh) The Patient, 3d edit., 1992; Memory in Mind and Brain: What Dream Imagery Reveals, 1990; editor: American Handbook of Psychiatry, vol. IV, 1975; editor in chief Psychosomatic Medicine, 1962-72; mem. editorial bd. AMA Archives of Gen. Psychiatry, 1961-71, (with H. Leigh) Psychiatry Medicine and Primary Care, 1978; contbr. articles to profl. jours. and books. Fellow Am. Coll. Psychiatrists, Am. Psychiat. Assn. (Seymour Vestermark award 1986); mem. Am. Soc. Clin. Investigation, Am. Psychosomatic Soc. (pres. 1960-61), Am. Fedn. Clin. Research, Am. Assn. Chairmen Depts. Psychiatry (exec. com. 1971—, pres. 1975-76), Acad. Behavioral Medicine Research (exec. council 1978), Am. Psychoanalytic Assn. (pres.-elect 1980-82, pres. 1982-84), Internat. Psycho-Analytical Assn., Assn. Psychophysiol. Study of Sleep, Internat. Coll. Psychosomatic Medicine (pres. 1975), Psychiat. Research Soc., A. Graeme Mitchell Undergrad. Pediatric Soc., Benjamin Rush Soc., Rapaport-Klein Study Group, World Psychiat. Assn. (organizing com. sect. psychosomatic medicine 1967), Sigma Xi, Phi Eta Sigma, Pi Kappa Epsilon, Alpha Omega Alpha. Home: 200 Todd St Hamden CT 06518-1511 Office: 255 Bradley St New Haven CT 06510-1105

REISER, PAUL, actor, comedian; b. N.Y.C., Mar. 30, 1957; m. Paula Reiser. BFA in Music, SUNY, Binghampton, 1977. comedian various nightclubs and venues including Catch a Rising Star, N.Y.C., The Comic Strip, N.Y.C., The Improv, N.Y.C., 1979—. Performances include (feature films) Diner, 1982, Beverly Hills Cop, 1984, Aliens, 1986, Beverly Hills Cop II, 1987, Cross My Heart, 1987, Crazy People, 1990, The Marrying Man, 1991, Bye Bye, Love, 1995, (TV series) The Investigator, HBO, The Comedy Zone, (TV spls.) Paul Reiser: Out on a Whim, HBO, 1987, (TV pilots) Diner, CBS, Just Married, ABC, (TV movies) Sunset Limousine, 1987, You Ruined My Life, 1987, The Tower, 1993; regular (TV series) My Two Dads, NBC, 1987-1991, Mad About You, NBC, 1992— (Emmy nomination, Lead Actor - Comedy Series, 1994); guest star various talk shows including The Tonight Show, Late Night with David Letterman; author: Couplehood, 1994. Office: UTA 9560 Wilshire Blvd 5th fl Beverly Hills CA 90212*

REISER, WALTER FREDERICK, athletic director, athletic trainer; b. N.Y., Apr. 8, 1961; s. Edward Eugene and Anne Lorraine (Bassett) R.; m. Kathleen Mary Urbanowicz, July 30, 1988. BS, Springfield Coll., 1983, MEd, 1984; Cert. in Supervision, Georgian Court Coll., 1994. Part-time asst. trainer New Eng. Patriots (NFL), Foxbough, Mass., 1983; asst. athletic trainer Springfield (Mass.) Coll., 1983-84; health-phys. edn. instr./trainer Rumson (N.J.)-Fair Haven Regional H.S., 1984-88, dir. athletics/athletic trainer, 1987—. Mem. Nat. Athletic Trainers Assn., Nat. Interscholastic Athletic Adminstrs., Shore Conf. Athletic Trainers (chairperson 1988-94), Monmouth County Dirs. Athletics (sec. 1992-94, pres.-elect 1994—). Avocations: golf, running, fitness. Home: 6 Maindraid Ct Neptune NJ 07753-7685 Office: Rumson Fair Haven Regional 74 Ridge Rd Rumson NJ 07760-1851

REISERT, CHARLES EDWARD, JR., real estate executive; b. New Albany, Ind., Apr. 5, 1941; s. Charles Edward Sr. and Jane. W. (Willcox) R.; m. Mary Lynn Nunemacher, Nov. 9, 1963; children: Perry G., Heidi L. BS in Edn., Ind. U., 1963, MA, 1968. Cert. residential specialist, residential broker. Tchr. Ind. Pub. Schs., 1963-67; mgr. Ind. Bell Tel. Co., Indpls., 1967-70; trust officer Ind. Nat. Bank, Indpls., 1970-72; ptnr. R.F.R. Prodns. Inc., Zionsville; dir. Wichita (Kans.) Art Assn., 1972-73; realtor Century 21 Reisert, Baker, Walker & Assocs., Jeffersonville, Ind., 1973—. Mem. Ind. Real Estate Commn., 1982-90, chmn., 1990; pres. bd. dirs. Clark County Youth Shelter, 1987—; bd. dirs., past pres. United Way Clark County; bd. dirs. New Hope, Inc., Sagamore of Wabash; mem. Leadership So. Ind., Leadership Louisville; trustee Jeffersonville Twp. Pub. Libr. Mem. So. Ind. Realtors Assn., (past pres. Realtor of Yr.) Nat. Assn. Realtors, Ind. Assn. Realtor (bd. dirs.), Realtors Nat. Mktg. Inst., So. Ind. C. of C. (past bd. dirs., Profl. of Yr.), Rotary (past pres., Paul Harris fellow). Roman Catholic. Home: 2005 Utica Pike Jeffersonville IN 47130-5003 Office: Century 21 Reisert Baker Walker & Assocs 1302 E 10th St Jeffersonville IN 47130-4231

REISIN, EFRAIN, nephrologist, researcher, educator; b. Cordoba, Argentina, Feb. 25, 1943; came to U.S., 1979; s. Maximo and Elisa Reisin; m. Ilana Hershkovitz, Sept. 6, 1971; children: Eyal, Thalia Alexis. MD, Nat. U., Cordoba, 1966. Intern internal medicine Nat. U. Cordoba-Clinicas Hosp., 1966; resident Jimenes Diaz Found., Madrid, 1966-68; resident Chaim Sheba Med. Ctr., Tel Hashomer, Israel, 1968-71, fellow in nephrology, 1971-74, staff physician nephrology, 1974-77; rsch. fellow in hypertension Health Sci. Ctr., Winnipeg, Man., Can., 1977-78; vis. scientist in hypertension Nat. Health Welfare Can., Winnipeg, Man., 1978-79; Ochsner vis. scientist in hypertension Ochsner Found. Hosp., New Orleans, 1979-82; from asst. prof. to assoc. prof. medicine La. State U., New Orleans, 1982-89, prof. medicine, 1989—; dir. dept. nephrology Med. Ctr. Charity Hosp., New Orleans, 1985—; panelist Consensus Conf., NIH, Bethesda, Md., 1991. Author numerous articles and book chpts. on hypertension and nephrology; conducted 1st research study documenting positive effects of weight reduction in treatment of hypertension, 1978 (citation classic Inst. Sci. Info. 1988). 1st lt. Israel Army, 1971-72. Grantee Nat. Health and Welfare Can., 1978-79, Am. Heart Assn., 1980-81, also several pharm. cos., 1984—. Fellow ACP, Am. Coun. High Blood Pressure Rsch., Am. Heart Fund, Am. Coll. Clin. Pharmacology (counselor south ctrl. regional chpt. 1991-92), Am. Fedn. Clin. Rsch., So. Soc. for Clin. Investigation; mem. Internat. Soc. Nephrology, Internat. Soc. Hypertension, Am. Soc. Nephrology, Am. Soc. Hypertension, Coun. Nephrology, Am. Heart Assn., Inter-Am. Soc. Hypertension, Orleans Parish Med. Soc. Avocations: tennis, reading, movies. Office: La State U Sch Medicine 1542 Tulane Ave New Orleans LA 70112-2825

REISINGER, GEORGE LAMBERT, management consultant; b. Pitts., Aug. 28, 1930; s. Eugene Merle and Pauline Jane (Lambert) R.; m. Judith Ann Brush, Nov. 24, 1967; children—Douglas Lambert, Christine Elizabeth. B.S. in Bus. Adminstrn., Central Coll., 1953; postgrad., Cleveland-Marshall Law Sch., 1962-67. Asst. personnel mgr. Continental Can Co., Houston, 1958-60; mgr. labor relations The Glidden Co., Cleve., 1960-67; dir. employee relations Mobil Oil Corp., N.Y.C., Caracas, Dallas, Denver, 1967-78; sr. v.p. Minton & Assocs., Denver, 1978-82; v.p., ptnr. Korn-Ferry Internat., Denver, 1982-86; pres. The Sigma Group, Inc., Denver, 1986—. Bd. dirs. Ponderosa Hills Civic Assn., 1977-80, Arapahoe County Youth League, Parker Action Team for Drug Free Colo.; pres. Douglas County Youth League; bd. dirs., steering com. Rocky Mountain Lions Eye Inst. With USAF, 1953-58. Mem. Am. Soc. Pers. Adminstrs., N.Y. Pers. Mgmt. Soc., Colo. Soc. Pers. Adminstrn., Am. Soc. Profl. Cons., Rocky Mountain Inst. Fgn. Trade and Fin., Employment Mgmt. Assn. Republican. Methodist. Clubs: Denver Petroleum, Pinery Country, Republican 1200. Home: 7924 Deertrail Dr Parker CO 80134-8262 Office: Sigma Group Internat Ste 125 6551 S Revere Pkwy Ste 125 Englewood CO 80111-6410

REISINGER, SANDRA SUE, journalist, lawyer; b. Washington Court House, Ohio, Feb. 27, 1946; d. Dale E. and Elinor Jean (McMurray) R. BS, Ohio State U., 1968, MA, 1969; JD, U. Dayton (Ohio), 1980. Bar: Ohio 1980. Teaching asst. Ohio State U., 1968-69; with Dayton Daily News, 1969-81, asst. mng. editor, 1976-81; mng. editor The Miami (Fla.) News, 1981-89, Broward Miami (Fla.) Herald, 1989-93, dep. mng. editor, 1994—; adj. prof. Sinclair (Ohio) C.C., 1971-74, U. Dayton, Ohio, 1980-81. Mem. ABA, AP Mng. Editors Assn. (bd. dirs. 1987-82, exec. com. 1987-94, pres. 1992). Office: The Miami Herald Pub Co One Herald Plz Miami FL 33132-1693

REISMAN, ARNOLD, retired management science educator; b. Lodz, Poland, Aug. 2, 1934; came to U.S., 1946, naturalized, 1955; s. Isadore and Rose (Joskowitz) R.; m. Mar. 12, 1955 (div. 1978); children—Miriam Jennie, Ada Jo, Deborah Fawn, Nina Michelle; m. Ellen Kronheim, Aug. 3, 1980. B.S., UCLA, 1955, M.S., 1957, Ph.D., 1963. Registered profl. engr., Calif., Wis., Ohio. Design engr. Los Angeles Dept. Water and Power, 1955-57; assoc. prof. Calif. State U., Los Angeles, 1957-66; prof. U. Wis., Milw., 1966-68; prof. ops. research Case-Western Res. U., Cleve., 1968-95; chmn. dept., 1982-87, ret., 1995; vis. prof. Hebrew U., Jerusalem, 1975; affiliate faculty Japan-Am. Inst. Mgmt. Sci., Honolulu, 1975—; vis. prof. U. Hawaii, Honolulu, 1971; asso. research engr. Western Mgmt. Sci. Inst., UCLA, 1964-65; coordinator programs between Inst. Mgmt. Scis. and AAAS, 1971—; examiner N. Central Assn. Colls., Univs. and Secondary Schs., 1971; v.p. Univ. Assos., Inc., Cleve., 1968-75; expert witness solicitor gen. Dept. Labor, 1969-70, U.S. Equal Opportunities Commn., 1976-79, Office of Atty. Gen., State of Ohio, 1981; cons. to asst. sec. HEW, 1971-72, Office Program Planning and Evaln., U.S. Office Edn., 1972-73; cons. Project Hope, 1981-82, Pan Am. Health Orgn., 1981—, Minister of Health, Barbados, 1989—, IRS Div. Research, 1985, UN Devel. Programme, 1988; cons. in gen. field systems analysis to numerous corps. and instns.; invited lectr. USSR Acad. Scis., 1989, Hungarian Acad. Sci.s, 1989. Author: Managerial and Engineering Economics, 1971, Systems Approach and The City, 1972, Industrial Inventory Control, 1972, Health Care Delivery Planning, 1973, Systems Analysis in Health Care Delivery, 1979, Materials Management for Health Services, 1980, Computer System Selection, 1981, Management Science Knowledge: Its Creation, Generalization and Consolidation, 1992; co-author: Welcome Tomorrow, 1982; series editor: Operations Management; assoc. editor: Socio Economic Planning Sciences; contbr. numerous articles to profl. jours. U.S. del. to Internat. Fedn. Ops. Research Socs., Conv., Dublin, Ireland, 1972; Review Bd. mem. Lake Erie Regional Transp. Authority, 1974-75; mem. del. assembly Jewish Community Fedn. Cleve., 1974-76; mem. Shaker Heights (Ohio) Citizens adv. com., 1972-84; bd. dirs., founder Greater Cleve. Coalition on Health Care Cost Effectiveness.; Trustee Hillel Found. Named Cleve. Engr. of Yr., 1973; NSF fellow, 1963. Fellow AAAS (council), Soc. Advanced Med. Systems; mem. Ops. Rsch. Soc. Am., Inst. Mgmt. Scis., ASME, Pan Am. Health Orgn., Am. Soc. Engring. Edn., AAUP, Am. Inst. Indsl. Engrs., N.Y. Acad. Scis., Nat. Soc. Profl. Engrs., Sigma Xi, Phi Delta Kappa. Home: 18428 Parkland Dr Cleveland OH 44122-3451

REISMAN, BERNARD, theology educator; b. N.Y.C., July 15, 1926; s. Herman and Esther Sarah (Kavesh) R.; m. Elaine Betty Sokol, Aug. 26, 1951; children: Joel Ira, Sharon Fay, Eric K., Robin Sue. B in Social Sci, CCNY, 1949; M in Social Sci. and Adminstrn., Western Res. U., 1951; LHD, Hebrew Coll., Boston, 1995; DHL (hon.), Gratz Coll., Phila., 1995. Agy. dir. Jewish Community Ctr., Chgo., 1951-67; prof. Brandeis U., Waltham, Mass., 1969—, dir. Hornstein program in Jewish communal svc., 1971-93, Klutznick prof. Contemporary Jewish Studies, 1993—; lectr. in field; vis. prof. Baerwald Sch. Social Work, Hebrew U., Jerusalem, 1978, Ctr. Jewish Edn. in Diaspora, 1978; sr. cons. Josephtal Found., Jerusalem, 1978; cons. European coun. Am. Joint Distbn. Com., 1978, Inst. for Jewish Life, N.Y.C., 1972-76; rsch. assoc. on future of religion Nat. Coun. Chs., 1972-73; Arnulf Pins meml. lectr. Hebrew U., Jerusalem, 1983, 84. Author: Reform Is a Verb, 1972, The Jewish Experimental Book: Quest for Jewish Identity, 1978, The Chavurah: A Contemporary Jewish Experience, 1977. Mem. Conf. Jewish Communal Svc. (chmn. publs. com. 1980—), Nat. Jewish Family Ctr., Am. Jewish Com. (1st chmn. acad. adv. com. 1979-82, 75th Anniversary award 1981), Am. Jewish Hist. Soc. (acad. coun. 1979—), Assn. for Jewish Studies. Home: 28 Fairway Dr Newton MA 02165-1713 Office: Brandeis Univ Hornstein Prog in Jewish Communal Svc Waltham MA 02254

REISMAN, FREDRICKA KAUFFMAN, education educator; b. Rochester, N.Y., Sept. 22, 1930; d. Samuel Hopkins and Rosalind (Lessen) Kauffman; 1 dau., Lisa Reisman Halterman. Student, Barnard Coll., 1951; B.A., Syracuse U., 1952, M.S., 1963, Ph.D., 1968. Lectr. Syracuse U., 1967-69; adj. assoc. prof. ednl. psychology Maria Regina Coll., Syracuse, N.Y., 1968; asst. prof. elem. edn. U. Ga., Athens, 1969-74; assoc. prof. U. Ga., 1974-79, prof. and chair early childhood middle sch. and elem. edn., prof. math. edn. and spl. edn., 1979-83; vis. prof., dept. human behavior and devel.; coordinator tchr.-scholar program Drexel U., Phila., 1984-85, dir. divsn. instrn. and program, head tchr. preparation, 1991—, prof., dir. tchr. preparation, cert. officer, 1986—; vis. prof. U. Calif., Riverside, Marianne Frostig Center Ednl. Therapy, Los Angeles; cons. diagnostic teaching math.; mem. program approval com. Pa. State Dept. Edn., 1984—, tchr. cert. com., 1984—. Author: Guide to the Diagnostic Teaching of Arithmetic, 1972, 3d edit., 1982, Diagnostic Teaching of Elementary School Mathematics: Methods and Content, 1977, 2d edit., 1981, (with S. H. Kaufman) Teaching Mathematics to Children with Special Needs, 1980, Sequential Assessment in Mathematics, 1985, Elementary Education: A Basic Text, 1987; contbr. articles to profl. jours. Recipient outstanding faculty citizen recognition Am. Assn. Higher Edn., 1994. Mem. Nat. Coun. Tchrs. Math., Am. Psychol. Assn., Internat. Assn. Applied Psychology, Soc. for Rsch. in Child Devel., Sch. Sci. and Math. Assn., ASCD, Assn. for Tchr. Educators, Am. Edn. Rsch. Assn., Sigma Xi, Pi Lambda Theta, Phi Delta Kappa.

REISMAN, ROBERT E., physician, educator; b. Buffalo, Nov. 1, 1932; s. Harry S. and Jessie (Goldberg) R.; m. Rena Estry, Sept. 5, 1954; children: Jeanne, Linda, Nancy, David. M.D., SUNY-Buffalo, 1956; Dr.h.c., U. Montpellier (France), 1982. Diplomate Am. Bd. Internal Medicine (bd. dirs. 1984-86), Am. Bd. Allergy and Clin. Immunology (bd. dirs. 1981-86, chmn. 1985, mem. residency rev. com. for allergy and immunology, 1988-93, chmn. 1990-91). Intern Buffalo Gen. Hosp., 1956-57, resident in medicine, 1957-59; practice medicine specializing in allergy and clin. immunology Buffalo, 1961—; clin. prof. pediatrics and medicine SUNY, Buffalo, 1978—; co-dir. Allergy Research Lab., Buffalo Gen. Hosp., 1970-90 ; mem. panel on allergenic extracts Bur. Biologics, FDA. Served with U.S. Army, 1968-69. Master ACP; fellow Am. Acad. Allergy (pres. 1980-81). Home: 113 Carriage Cir Buffalo NY 14221-2163 Office: 295 Essjay Rd Williamsville NY 14221-8216 also: 85 High St Buffalo NY 14203-1149

REISMAN, WILLIAM M., lawyer, educator; b. 1939. LL.B., Hebrew U., 1963; LL.M., Yale U., 1964, J.S.D., 1965. Bar: Conn. 1964. Assoc. prof. Yale U. Law Sch., New Haven, 1969-72, prof., 1972-82, Hohfeld prof. jurisprudence, 1982—; mem. Inter-Am. Commn. on Human Rights, 1990-95, chmn., 1994-95; vice-chmn. Policy Scis. Ctr., Inc., 1992—. Author: Nullity and Revision, 1971, Art of the Possible: Diplomatic Alternatives in Middle East, 1970, Puerto Rico and the International Process, 1974, Folded Lies: Bribery, Crusades and Reforms, 1979, (with Weston) Toward World Order and Human Dignity, 1976, (with McDougal) International Law in Contemporary Perspective, 1981, (with McDougal) Internaitonal Law Essays, 1981, (with McDougal) Power and Policy in Quest of Law: Essays in Honor of Eugene V. Rostow, 1985, (with Schreiber) Jurisprudence: Understanding and Shaping Law, 1986, (with Willard) International Incidents: The Law that Counts in World Politics, 1988, (with James E. Baker) Regulating Covert Action: Practices, Contexts and Policies of Covert Coercion Abroad in International and American Laqw, 1991, Systems of Control in International Adjudication and Arbitration: Breakdown and Repair, 1992, (with Westerman) Straight Baselines in International Maritime Boundary Delimitation, 1992, (with C. Antoniou) The Laws of War, 1994. Fulbright grantee, 1966-67. Office: Yale U Law Sch PO Box 208215 New Haven CT 06520-8215

REISMANN, HERBERT, engineer, educator; b. Vienna, Austria, Jan. 26, 1926; s. Henrik and Olga (Pokorny) R.; m. Edith Falber, Aug. 14, 1952; children—Sandra Jean, Barbara Anne. BS in Aero. Engring., Ill. Inst. Tech., 1947, MS, 1949; PhD in Engring., U. Colo., 1962. Project engr. Convair, Ft. Worth, 1951-53; prin. structures engr. Republic Aviation Corp., Hicksville, N.Y., 1954-56; chief engr. systems analysis, chief solid mechanics Martin Marietta Corp., 1957-64; prof., dir. aerospace engring. SUNY, Buffalo, 1964—; Cons. NASA, Bell Aero Systems Corp. Co-author: Elastokinetics, 1974, Elasticity, 1980; author: Elastic Plates, 1988; contbr. articles to profl. jours. Assoc. fellow AIAA (award best tech. paper 1962, oustanding aerospace achievement award 1987); mem. ASME, Internat. Assn. Bridge and Structural Engring., AAUP, Sigma Xi, Tau Beta Pi. Home: 71 Chaumont Dr Buffalo NY 14221-3511 Office: SUNY-Buffalo 605 Furnas Hall Buffalo NY 14260

REISNER, MILTON, psychiatrist, psychoanalyst; b. N.Y.C., Jan. 30, 1934; s. Maximillian and Dora Reisner; m. Linda Ellis, Mar. 3, 1959 (div. 1975); children: Margaret Ann, Amanda Lee. BA, NYU, 1954; MD, Downstate Med. Ctr., 1958. Diplomate Am. Bd. Forensic Examiners, Nat. Bd. Med. Examiners, N.Y. State Bd. Psychiat. Examiners. Resident in psychiatry Kings County Hosp., Bklyn., 1959-62; sr. psychiatrist Manhattan VA Hosp., N.Y.C., 1962-66; assoc. dir. psychiatry Westchester Community Mental Health Bd., White Plains, N.Y., 1966-69; dir. psychiatry Westchester Mental Health Bd., White Plains, 1969-74; pvt. practice N.Y.C., 1976—; cons. Cath. Charities, N.Y.C., 1965-66, H.I.P., N.Y.C., 1973-74, NYU Med. Ctr., 1963-68. Contbr. articles to profl. jours. Lt. j.g. USPHS, 1958-59. Fellow Am. Soc. Psychoanalytic Physicians; mem. Am. Assn. Psychoanalytic Physicians (pres. 1985-86, 87-88, Plaque 1988), Nat. Arts Club, Phi Beta Kappa. Achievements include research in mirroring as a technique for treating delusions. Office: 200 E 84th St New York NY 10028-2906

REISS, ALBERT JOHN, JR., sociology educator; b. Cascade, Wis., Dec. 9, 1922; s. Albert John and Erma Amanda (Schueler) R.; children: Peter C., Paul Wetherington, Amy. Student, Mission House Coll., 1939-42; Ph.B., Marquette U., 1944; M.A., U. Chgo., 1948, Ph.D., 1949; LL.D. (hon.), CUNY, 1980; Docteur (honoris causa), U. Montreal, 1985. Instr. sociology U. Chgo., 1947-49, asst. prof., 1949-52; asso. dir. Chgo. Community Inventory (U. Chgo.), 1948-51, acting dir., 1951-52; asso. prof. sociology Vanderbilt U., 1952-58, prof., 1954-58, chmn. dept., 1952-58; prof. sociology and dir. Iowa Urban Community Research Center, State U. Iowa, 1958-60; prof. sociology, dir. survey research labs. U. Wis., 1960-61; prof. sociology, dir. U. Mich. Center for Research on Social Orgn., Ann Arbor, 1961-70, chmn. dept., 1970; prof. sociology Yale U., 1970—, prof. social sci. Inst. Social and Polit. Sci., 1970-87, William Graham Sumner prof., 1977—, chmn. dept., 1972-80, 85-89; chmn. Census Com. on Enumeration Areas, Chgo., 1950-52, Nashville, 1952-58; mem. tech. adv. com. Chgo. Plan Commn., 1951-52; cons. USAF Human Resources Research Inst., 1952-54. Author: A Survey of Probation Needs and Services in Illinois, 1947, (with Paul K. Hatt) Reader in Urban Sociology, 1951, (with Evelyn R. Kitagawa) Mobility of Chicago Workers, 1951, Social Characteristics of Rural and Urban Communities, 1950 (with Otis Dudley Duncan), 1956, Cities and Society, 1958, Occupational and Social Status, 1960, The Police and the Public, 1971, (with J. Roth) Understanding and Preventing Violence, 1993. Served as pvt., meteorology program A.C., AUS, 1943-44. Recipient Disting. Alumnus award Lakeland Coll., 1990, Beccaria Gold medal, 1990. Fellow Am. Sociol. Assn. (chmn. methodology sect. 1960, coun. and exec. com. 1962-65), Sociol. Rsch. Assn. (pres. 1969), Am. Statis. Assn.; mem. NAS (chmn.), Ohio Valley Sociol. Soc. (pres. 1966), Am. Soc. Criminology (pres. 1983-84), Soc. for Study Social Problems (pres. 1968), Social Rsch. (pres. 1949), Internat. Soc. Criminology (sci. commn. 1982-89, pres. sci. commn. 1985-89, pres. 1990-95). Home: 600 Prospect St Apt 7A New Haven CT 06511-2116 Office: Yale U Dept Sociology PO Box 208265 New Haven CT 06520-8265

REISS, ALVIN, writer; b. Ft. Sill, Okla., Oct. 31, 1932; s. Clarence Gustav Alvin and Mabel Alma (Craig) R.; m. Audrey Spencer, Sept. 1, 1951 (div. 1974); children—Belinda, Karen. Student, U. Oreg., 1950-51, So. Oreg. Coll., 1969. With Union Pacific and Denver & Rio Grande, 1951-61, chief clk., 1955-61; with KBOY-FM, Medford, Oreg., 1961-68; FM program dir. KBOY-FM, 1966-68; news dir. KYJC, Medford, 1969-73; staff writer Medford Mail Tribune, 1969—; dir. Rogue Valley Writers Conf. So. Oreg. State Coll., 1992, 93, 94. Screenwriter, Larry Lansburgh Films, Inc., 1972 (recipient John Masefield Meml. award Poetry Soc. Am. 1970, regional award for playwriting, Oreg. 1965, Ala. 1963); author: (plays) The Smallest Giant, 1963, River Children, 1983, Nines and Lunch, 1986, The Last Beach Ball, 1995, also stories and poetry; contbg. writer: Matinee at the Bijou, 1984-85. Recipient Fiction prize West Wind Review, 1986, 2d prize Oreg. State Poetry Assn., 1987, 1st prize Oreg. State Poetry Assn., 1988. Mem. Am. Theater Critics Assn. (exec. com. 1983-86, adv. council 1986), Internat. Assn. Theatre Critics, Poetry Soc. Am., Jacksonville Art Alliance (poetry instr., dir. 1983), Mensa, Dramatists Guild, Authors League Am., Sigma Delta Chi (pres. So. Oreg. chpt. 1977-78). Home: PO Box 597 115 F St Jacksonville OR 97530 Office: c/o Archer King Ltd 10 Columbus Cir New York NY 10019-1203

REISS, DALE ANNE, accounting executive, investment company executive; b. Chgo., Sept. 3, 1947; d. Max and Nan (Hart) R.; m. Jerome L. King, Mar. 5, 1978; 3 children: Matthew Reiss, Mitchell, Stacey King. BS, Ill. Inst. Tech., 1967; MBA, U. Chgo., 1970. CPA, Ill., Mich., Mo. Cost acct. First Nat. Bank, Chgo., 1967; asst. controller City Colls. of Chgo., 1967-71; dir. fin. Chgo. Dept. Pub. Works, 1971-73; prin. Arthur Young & Co., Chgo., 1973-80; sr. v.p., controller Urban Investment & Devel. Co., Chgo., 1980-85, mng. ptnr. E & Y Kenneth Leventhal Ernst & Young LLP, Chgo., 1985—; bd. dirs. Ill. Inst. Tech., Urban Land Inst., The Chgo. Network; adv. bd. Kellogg Real Estate, Northwestern U. Mem. Fin. Execs. Inst., AICPA, Chgo. Network. Clubs: Econ. of Chgo., Metropolitan, Chgo. Yacht. Office: E & Y Kenneth Leventhal 1 N Franklin St Ste 2100 Chicago IL 60606-3421

REISS, HOWARD, chemistry educator; b. N.Y.C., Apr. 5, 1922; s. Isidor and Jean (Goldstein) R.; m. Phyllis Kohn, July 25, 1945; children: Gloria, Steven. A.B. in Chemistry, NYU, 1943; Ph.D. in Chemistry, Columbia U., 1949. With Manhattan Project, 1944-46; instr., then asst. prof. chemistry Boston U., 1949-51; with Central Research Lab., Celanese Corp. Am., 1951-52, Edgar C. Bain Lab. Fundamental Research, U.S. Steel Corp., 1957, Bell Telephone Labs., 1952-60; asso. dir., then dir. research div. Atomics Internat., div. N.Am. Aviation, Inc., 1960-62; dir. N.Am. Aviation Sci. Center, 1962-67, v.p. co., 1963-67; v.p. research aerospace systems group N.Am. Rockwell Corp., 1967-68; vis. lectr. chemistry U. Calif. at Berkeley, summer 1957; vis. prof. chemistry UCLA, 1961, 62, 64, 67, prof., 1968-91, prof. emeritus, 1991—; vis. prof. U. Louis Pasteur, Strasbourg, France, 1986, U. Pa., 1989; vis. fellow Victoria U., Wellington, New Zealand, 1989; cons. to chem.-physics program Air Force Cambridge Rsch. Cambridge Rsch. Labs., 1950-52; chmn. editor proc. Internat. Conf. Nucleation and Interfacial Phenomena, Boston; mem. Air Force Office Sci. Rsch. Physics and Chemistry Rsch. Evaluation Groups, 1966—, Oak Ridge Nat. Lab. Reactor Chemistry Adv. Com., 1966-68; adv. com. math. and phys. scis. NSF, 1970-72, ARPA Materials Rsch. Coun., 1968—; chmn. site rev. com. NRC Associateships Program, Naval Rsch. Lab., 1989. Author: The Methods of Thermodynamics, 1965; author articles; editor in field.; editor: Progress in Solid State Chemistry, 1962-71, Jour. Statis. Physics, 1968-75, Jour. Colloid Interface Sci; mem. editorial adv. bd. Internat. Jour. Physics and Chemistry of Solids, 1955, Progress in Solid State Chemistry, 1962-73, Jour. Solid State Chemistry, 1969, Jour. Phys. Chemistry, 1970-73, Ency. of Solid State, 1970, Jour. Nonmetals, 1971—, Jour. Colloid and Interface Sci., 1976-79, Langmuir, 1985—. Guggenheim Meml. fellow, 1978. Fellow AAAS, Am. Phys. Soc. (exec. com. div. chem. physics 1966-69); mem. NAS, Am. Chem. Soc. (chmn. phys. chemistry sect. N.J. sect. 1957, Richard C. Tolman medal 1973, Kendall award in colloid and surface chemistry 1980, J.H. Hildebrand award in theoretical and exptl. phys. chemistry of liquids 1991, Van Arkel hon. chair in chemistry U. Leiden, The Netherlands, 1994), Phi Beta Kappa, Sigma Xi, Phi Lambda Upsilon. Office: U Calif Dept Chemistry and Biochemistry Los Angeles CA 90024

REISS, IRA LEONARD, sociology educator, writer; b. N.Y.C., Dec. 8, 1925; s. Philip and Dorothy (Jacobs) R.; m. Harriet Marilyn Eisman, Sept. 4, 1955; children: David, Pamela, Joel. BS cum laude, Syracuse U., 1949; MA, Pa. State U., 1951, PhD, 1953. Instr. in sociology Bowdoin Coll., Brunswick, Maine, 1953-55; asst. prof. sociology Coll. William and Mary, Williamsburg, Va., 1955-59; asst. prof. Bard Coll., Annandale-On-Hudson, N.Y., 1959-61; assoc. to full prof. U. Iowa, Iowa City, 1961-69; prof. U. Minn., Mpls., 1969—; rsch. evaluator U.S. Dept. Edn. and Nat. Inst. Child Health and Human Devel., Washington, 1966-78; rsch. dir. Family Study Ctr., U. Minn., 1969-74; ednl. advisor Kimberly-Clark Corp., Neenah, Wis., 1971-75; chair planning com. and bd. dirs. Inst. for Child, Adolescent Sexual Health, 1992-93; lectr. at 200 univs., 150 profl. mtgs., 100 civic groups, 1953—; vis. prof. Uppsala Univ., Sweden, 1975-76. Author: Premarital Sexual Standards in America, 1960, The Social Context of Premarital Sexual Permissiveness, 1967, Family Systems in America (4 edits.), 1971, 76, 80, 88, Journey into Sexuality: An Exploratory Voyage, 1986, An End to Shame: Shaping Our Next Sexual Revolution, 1990; editor 3 textbooks; contbr. over 100 articles to jours. and chpts. to textbooks in field. Mem. ACLU, 1948—, Planned Parenthood, 1960—, Nat. Abortion Rights Action League 1975—, Amnesty Internat., 1984—.With U.S. Army, 1944-46, ETO. Mem. Midwest Sociol. Soc. (pres. 1971-72), Am. Sociol. Assn. (chair family sect. 1975-76), Nat. Coun. on Family Rels. (pres. 1979-80, Reuben Hill award 1980, E.W. Burgess award 1984), Polish Acad. Sexual Sci. (hon., Internat. Sexual Sci. award 1989), Soc. for Sci. Study Sex (pres. 1980-81, Disting. Sci. Achievement award 1982, Alfred Kinsey award 1990), Internat. Acad. Sex Rsch. (pres. 1984-85), Am. Assn. Sex Educators, Counselors and Therapists (leadership award 1993). Democrat. Jewish. Avocations: good conversations with family and friends. Home: 5932 Medicine Lake Rd Minneapolis MN 55422-3328 Office: U Minn Dept Sociology 1031 Social Scis 267 19th Ave S Minneapolis MN 55455-0499

REISS, JEROME, lawyer; b. Bklyn., Dec. 7, 1924; s. William and Eva (Stein) R.; m. Naomi Betty Plutzik, June 15, 1947 (div.); children: Robert Scott, Harlan Morgan, Andrea Ellen, Samantha Glynis. BA, Bklyn. Coll., 1948; JD, Harvard U., 1951. Bar: N.Y. 1951, D.C. 1967. Staff atty. civil br. Legal Aid Soc., 1951-54; asst. corp. counsel City of N.Y., 1954-58; assoc. Max E. Greenberg, 1958-67; sr. ptnr. Max E. Greenberg, Trayman, Cantor, Reiss & Blasky, 1967-80, Max E. Greenberg, Cantor & Reiss, N.Y.C., 1980-88, Thelen, Marrin, Johnson & Bridges, N.Y.C., 1989—; lectr. on constrn. law; Small Claims Ct. arbitrator, 1960-88; bd. advisors Fed. Pub., Inc. Gen. counsel Artist Fellowship, Inc. Cpl. USAAF, 1943-46. Mem. ABA, Am. Judges Assn. (founding fellow), Am. Coll. Constrn. Lawyers, Internat. Bar Assn., Mcpl. Assist. Corp. of City of N.Y. (bd. dirs.), Jacob K. Javits Convention Ctr. Oper. Corp. (bd. dirs.). Contbr. articles to profl. jours., chpts. in books.

REISS, JOHN BARLOW, lawyer; b. London, Aug. 29, 1939; came to U.S., 1963; s. James Martin and Margaret Joan (Ping) R.; m. Mary Jean Maudsley, Aug. 6, 1967 (div. 1978); m. Kathleen Strouse, Aug. 2, 1979; 1 child, Juliette Blanche. BA with honors, Exeter U., Devon, Eng., 1961; AM, Washington U., St. Louis, 1966, PhD, 1971; JD, Temple U., 1977. Bar: Pa. 1977, N.J. 1977, U.S. Dist. Ct. N.J. 1977, D.C. 1980, U.S. Supreme Ct. 1981, U.S. Dist. Ct. D.C. 1982. Economist Commonwealth Econ. Com., London, 1962-63; asst. prof. Allegheny Coll., Meadville, Pa., 1967-71; assoc. prof. Stockton State Coll., Pomona, N.J., 1971-75; asst. health commr. State of N.J., Trenton, 1975-79; dir. office of health regulation U.S. Dept. HHS, Washington, 1979-81; assoc. Baker & Hostetler, Washington, 1981-82; assoc. Dechert Price & Rhoads, Phila., 1982-86, ptnr., 1986-93, asst. chair health law group, 1984-91, chmn. health law group, 1991-93; ptnr. Saul, Ewing, Remick & Saul, Phila., 1993—, chmn. health law dept., 1995—. Mem. editl. bd. Topics in Hosp. Law, 1985-86, Hosp. Legal Forms Manual, 1985—, Jour. Health Care Tech., 1984-86; contbr. Hosp. Contracts Manual, 1983—; contbr. articles to profl. jours., chpts. to books. Bd. dirs. Gateway Sch. Little Children, Phila., 1986—, ECRI, Plymouth Meeting, Pa., 1994—; mem. vestry All Saints Ch., Wynnewood, Pa., 1993; mem. The Union League of Phila., 1995—. Pub. Health Svc. fellow, 1979-81, English Speaking Union fellow, 1963-66, Econ. Devel. Adminstr. fellow Washington U., 1966-67. Mem. Nat. Health Lawyers Assn., N.J. Soc. Hosp. Attys., Phila. Bar Assn., Am. Hosp. Assn., Union League of Phila., N.J. Hosp. Assn., Brit. Am. C. of C. of Greater Phila. (bd. dirs. 1991). Avocations: gardening, house restoring, reading, philately. Home: 415 Wister Rd Wynnewood PA 19096-1808 Office: Saul Ewing Remick & Saul 3800 Centre Sq W Philadelphia PA 19102

REISS, JOHN C., bishop; b. Red Bank, N.J., May 13, 1922; s. Alfred and Sophia (Telljohan) R. Student, Immaculate Conception Sem., 1941-46; B.A., Seton Hall U., 1947; S.T.L., Catholic U., 1947, J.C.D., 1953. Ordained Priest Roman Catholic Ch., 1947. Asst. chancellor Diocese of Trenton, 1954, sec., master ceremonies, 1953-62, vice chancellor, 1956-62, officialis,

1962-80, aux. bishop, 1967-80, bishop, 1982—. Mem. Trenton Mayor's Adv. Commn. on Civil Rights, 1962-68. Home: 901 W State St Trenton NJ 08618-5327 Office: 901 W State St Trenton NJ 08618-5327*

REISS, MARTIN HAROLD, engineering executive; b. Long Beach, N.Y., Aug. 16, 1935; s. Arthur and Mary (Schreckinger) R.; m. Rhea Cohen, June 24, 1956; children—Mitchell, Randi, Robyn. B.S., MIT, 1956; M.S., Ohio State U., 1959; M.S., MIT, 1961. Staff member MIT Inst. Lab., Cambridge, 1959-61; tech. dir. Raytheon Co., Sudbury, Mass., 1961-65; pres. Alarmtronics Engring., Newton, Mass., 1965-73, Gamewell Corp., Medway, Mass., 1973-83, chmn. bd., 1983-90; dir. Cerberus Techs., Inc., Waltham, Mass., 1990-93, pres., Rolf, Jensen & Assoc., 1993—; sustaining fellow MIT, 1981—; bd. overseers WPI Fire Scis., Worchester, Mass., 1985—, chmn., 1989—; dir. Practicorp, Newton, 1984-88; dir., treas. Nat. Fire Protection Research Found., Quincy, Mass., 1982—; dir. Nat. Fire Protection Assn., Quincy, 1991—, vice chair, 1996—. Patentee in field. Trustee Mass. Bay Community Coll., Wellesley, 1980-90, chmn. bd., 1985-86. Served to capt. USAF, 1956-59. Fellow Soc. Fire Protection Engrs. (bd. dirs. 1988-94); mem. Nat. Elec. Mfg. Assn. (sect. chmn. 1983-85, Man of Yr. award 1985), Automatic Fire Alarm Assn. (pres. 1978-80, Man of Yr. award 1985, bd. dirs. 1980-93). Office: Rolf Jensen & Assoc 55 William St Wellesley MA 02181-4003

REISS, MICHAEL, medical oncologist, researcher; b. Addis Ababa, Ethiopia, Sept. 22, 1950; came to U.S., 1982; s. Willy and Lies (Gerzon) R.; m. Elisabeth Meta Souget, Mar. 15, 1977; children: Kim, Daniel J. Student, U. Amsterdam Med. Sch., The Netherlands, 1968-73; MD, U. Amsterdam, 1976. Cert. Bd. Internal Medicine, The Netherlands; fed. licensing exam.; lic. physician Conn. Clk., subintern U. Amsterdam Hosps. and Affiliated Hosps., 1974-76; rsch. assoc. Cen. Lab. Netherlands Red Cross Blood Trans. Lab. for Immunology, U. Amsterdam, 1976-77; intern in internal medicine Med. Coll. Ohio, Toledo, 1977-78; resident in internal medicine U. Hosp. Binnengasthuis, Amsterdam, 1978-82; rotation in med. oncology Netherlands Cancer Inst., Amsterdam, 1980; postdoctoral fellow in med. oncology Yale U. Sch. Medicine, 1982-85, instr. in med. oncology, 1985-87, asst. prof. dept. internal medicine Yale Comp. Cancer Ctr., 1987-91, assoc. prof. dept. internal medicine Yale Comp. Cancer Ctr., 1991—; attending physician Yale New Haven Hosp., 1985—; med. oncologist Yale Comprehensive Breast Care Ctr., 1989—, co-dir., 1992—; dir. breast cancer rsch. program Yale Cancer Ctr., 1995—; chmn. rsch. com. sect. med. oncology Yale U. Sch. Medicine, 1986—, fellowship com. sect. med. oncology, 1986—, cancer edn. com. Yale Comprehensive Cancer Ctr., 1989—, funds and fellowships com., 1991-95; mem. instnl. grant rev. com. Am. Cancer Soc., 1988-94; invited mem. Sec.'s Spl. Conf. on Breast Cancer, NIH, 1993; reviewer Netherlands Cancer Found. Rsch. Grants. Reviewer: Cancer Rsch., Blood, Jour. Cell Physiology, Cancer Comms., European Jour. Cancer Clin. Oncology; contbr. articles to profl. jours. 2d lt. Dutch Army, 1975-77. Recipient Swebilius Cancer Rsch. award, 1985-86; clin. fellow Queen Wilhelmina Cancer Found., Amsterdam, 1982-84; rsch. grantee numerous orgns. Mem. AAAS, Am. Assn. for Cancer Rsch., Am. Soc. Clin. Oncology, Am. Soc. Cell Biology, Am. Fedn. for Clin. Rsch. Avocations: complexity theory, computers, fishing, cycling, music.

REISS, PAUL JACOB, college president; b. Lake Placid, N.Y., Aug. 10, 1930; s. Julian J. and Daisy M. (Smith) R.; m. Rosemary A. Donohue, June 25, 1955; children: Catherine, Paul, Gregory, Mark, Julia, David, Steven, Martha, John. B.S., Holy Cross Coll., 1952; M.A., Fordham U., 1954; Ph.D., Harvard U., 1960. Tutor Harvard U., 1954-57; instr., asst. prof. Marquette U., 1957-63, chmn. dept. sociology, 1961-63; asso. prof. sociology Fordham U., Bronx, N.Y., 1963-75, prof., 1976-85, chmn. dept. sociology and anthropology, 1964-68; dean Fordham U. (Liberal Arts Coll.), 1968-69, v.p. acad. affairs, 1969-75, exec. v.p., 1975-85; pres. St. Michael's Coll., Colchester, Vt., 1985—. Editor: Sociological Analysis: A Journal in the Sociology of Religion, 1961-68; contbr. articles to profl. jours. Exec. dir. Julian Reiss Found., Lake Placid, N.Y.; trustee Wadhams Hall Sem. Coll.; bd. dirs. Lake Placid Sinfonietta, Greater Burlington Indsl. Commn., Nat. Assn. Ind. Colls. and Univs., Assn. Cath. Colls. and Univs.; chmn. Vt. World Trade Office. Fellow Am. Sociol. Assn.; mem. Assn. for Sociology of Religion (pres.), Assn. Vt. Ind. Colls. (pres.), Vt. Higher Edn. Coun. (pres.), Vt. Bus. Roundtable, Vt. World Trade Office (pres.). Democrat. Roman Catholic. Home: St Michael's Coll Colchester VT 05439

REISS, STEVEN ALAN, lawyer, law educator; b. N.Y.C., Dec. 18, 1951; s. Louis and Ruth (Harrow) R.; m. Mary A. Mattingly; children: Alexandra Mattingly Reiss, Tyler Brennan Reiss. BA, Vassar Coll., 1973; JD, Stanford (Calif.) U., 1976. Bar: N.Y., D.C., Calif. Law clk. to John Minor Wisdom U.S. Ct. Appeals for 5th Cir., New Orleans, 1976-77; law clk. to justice William J. Brennan U.S Supreme Ct., Washington, 1977-78; assoc. Miller, Cassidy, Larroca & Lewin, Washington, 1978-80; vis. prof. Georgetown U. Law Ctr., Washington, 1981; asst. prof. Law Sch., NYU, 1981-83, assoc. prof., 1984-87, prof., 1987-91; ptnr. Weil, Gotshal & Manges, N.Y.C., 1990—. Editor-in-chief White Collar Crime Reporter, 1987-91, contbg. editor, 1991—. Trustee Vassar Coll. Poughkeepsie, N.Y., 1978-82; bd. dirs. NYU Cmty. Fund, 1984-87, Concert Artists Guild, 1991-94; gen. counsel Brennan Ctr. for Justice, 1996—. Mem. N.Y. State Bar Assn., D.C. Bar Assn., Calif. Bar Assn., Assn. of Bar of City of N.Y. (fed. legis. com. 1981-87), 2d Jud. Conf. (reporter 1984—). Home: 25 E 86th St New York NY 10028-0553 Office: Weil Gotshal & Manges 767 5th Ave New York NY 10153

REISS, SUSAN MARIE, editor, writer; b. Washington, Sept. 14, 1963; m. Paul L. Roney Jr., May 25, 1991. BA in English Lit., U. Va., 1985; MA in English, George Mason U., 1989. Editorial asst. Water Pollution Control Fedn., Alexandria, Va., 1985-87; freelance writer, editor Arlington, Va., 1987-90; staff writer George Mason U., Fairfax, Va., 1988-90; staff writer Optical Soc. Am., Washington, 1990-91, news editor, 1991-93, mng. editor, 1993—. Newsletter editor: Arlington County Tennis Assn., 1990-91; contbr. articles to profl. jours. and mags. Mem. Nat. Press Club, Washington Ind. Writers, D.C. Sci. Writers Assn., N.Y. Acad. Scis., Sigma Tau Delta (founding mem. U. Va. chpt.). Avocations: tennis, piano, cross-country skiing. Home: 6814 30th Rd N Arlington VA 22213-1602 Office: Optical Soc Am 2010 Massachusetts Ave NW Washington DC 20036-1023

REISS, TIMOTHY JAMES, comparative literature educator, writer; b. Stanmore, Eng., May 14, 1942; came to U.S., 1964, 84; s. James Martin and Margaret Joan (Ping) R.; m. Patricia J. Penn Hilden, 1988; children from previous marriage: Matthew James, Suzanna Jean, Justin Timothy. B.A. hons., Manchester U., Eng., 1964; M.A., U. Ill., 1965, Ph.D., 1968. Instr. French U. Ill., Urbana, 1967-68; instr., then asst. prof. Yale U., New Haven, 1968-73; assoc. prof., then prof. comparative lit. U. Montreal, Can., 1973-84, dir. comparative lit., 1976-81; prof. comparative lit., French and philosophy Emory U., Atlanta, 1983-86, Samuel Candler Dobbs prof. French and comparative lit., 1986-87; prof. comparative lit. NYU, 1987—, chmn., 1987-94; vis. prof. U. Toronto, 1976-77, U. B.C., Vancouver, 1979, NYU, N.Y.C., 1982, U. Montreal, 1984-87, Grad. Ctr. CUNY, 1985, SUNY, Binghamton, 1988-89. Author: Toward Dramatic Illusion, 1971, Tragedy and Truth, 1980, Discourse of Modernism, 1982, The Uncertainty of Analysis, 1988, The Meaning of Literature, 1992 (Morris D. Forkosch Intellectual History prize); editor: Science, Language and the Perspective Mind, 1973; (with others) Opening Up the Disciplines, 1982, Tragedy and the Tragic, 1983, Sisyphus and Eldorado: Magical and Other Realisms in Caribbean Literature, 1996. Morse fellow, 1971-72; Am. Counc. Learned Socs. travel grantee, 1976, fellow, 1986-87; Can. Council fellow Oxford, Eng., 1977-78; rsch. fellow U. Montreal, 1979-80; Social Scis. and Humanities Rsch. Coun. of Can.; sr. fellow Oxford, Eng., 1983-84; Emory U. faculty fellow, 1986-87; Guggenheim fellow, 1990-91. Fellow Royal Soc. Can., Acad. Literary Studies; mem. MLA, Am. Comparative Lit. Assn., Renaissance Soc. Am., C. S. Peirce Soc., Can. Assn. Comparative Lit. (v.p. 1981-83), Internat. Comparative Lit. Assn., Can. Soc. Research in Semiotics. Office: NYU Dept Comparative Lit 19 University Pl New York NY 10003-4501

REISSE, R.A., research physicist; b. Phila., Apr. 9, 1946; married, 1976; 2 children. BA, Wesleyan U., 1967; MS, U. Md., 1970, PhD in Physics, 1976. Rsch. assoc. dept. physics U. Md., 1976-77; mem. tech. staff physics Sperry Rand Corp., 1977-81; rsch. asst. prof. Ariz. Rsch. Labs & Santa Catalina Lab U. Ariz., Tucson, 1981-82; with CGR Med. Corp., Balt., 1982-85; mem. staff ITE Inc., Beltsville, Md., 1985-88; mentor Techs. Inc., Rockville, Md., 1988-91; prin. scientist Sci. Inquiries Inc., 1991—. Mem. Am. Phys. Soc., Optical Soc. Am. Office: Science Inquiries Catonsville MD 21228*

REISSNER, ERIC (MAX ERICH REISSNER), applied mechanics researcher; b. Aachen, Germany, Jan. 5, 1913; came to U.S., 1936, naturalized, 1945; s. Hans and Josephine (Reichenberger) R.; m. Johanna Siegel, Apr. 19, 1938; children: John E., Eva M. Dipl. Ing., Technische Hochschule, Berlin, 1935, Dr. Ing., 1936; Ph.D., MIT, 1938; Dr. Ing. (hon.), U. Hannover, Germany, 1964. Mem. faculty MIT, Cambridge, 1939-69, prof. math., 1949-66; prof. applied math. MIT, 1966-69; prof. applied mechanics U. Calif., San Diego, 1970-78, prof. emeritus, 1978—; aero. rsch. scientist NACA, Langley Field, 1948, 51, Ramo, Wooldridge, 1954, 55, Lockheed, Palo Alto, 1956, 57; vis. prof. U. Mich., Ann Arbor, 1949, U. Calif., San Diego, 1967. Cons. editor Addison-Wesley Pub. Co., 1949-60; mng. editor Jour. Math. and Physics, 1945-67; assoc. editor Quar. Applied Math., 1946-95, Studies Applied Math., 1970—, Internat. Jour. Solids and Structures, 1983-95; contbr. chpts. to books, articles to profl. jours. Recipient Clemens Herschel award Boston Soc. Civil Engrs., 1956, Theodore von Karman medal ASCE, 1964; Guggenheim fellow, 1962. Fellow ASME (hon. mem. 1991; Timoshenko medal 1973, ASME medal 1988), AIAA (Structures and Materials award 1984), Am. Acad. Arts and Scis., Am. Acad. Mechanics; mem. NAE, Internat. Acad. Astronautics, Am. Math. Soc., Gesellschaft für Angewandte Mathematik und Mechanik (hon.). Office: U Calif San Diego Dept Applied Mechs Eng S La Jolla CA 92093-0411

REISTER, RAYMOND ALEX, retired lawyer; b. Sioux City, Iowa, Dec. 22, 1929; s. Harold William and Anne (Eberhardt) R.; m. Ruth Elizabeth Alkema, Oct. 7, 1967. AB, Harvard U., 1952, LLB, 1955. Bar: N.Y. 1956, Minn. 1960. Assoc. Paul, Weiss, Rifkind, Wharton & Garrison, N.Y.C., 1955-56; ptnr. Dorsey & Whitney, Mpls., 1959-92; ret., 1993; instr. U. Minn. Extension Divsn., 1964-66. Editor (with Larry W. Johnson): Minnesota Probate Administration, 1968. Trustee Mpls. Soc. Fine Arts, 1981-87; v.p. Minn. Hist. Soc., 1994—. 1st lt. U.S. Army, 1956-59. Mem. Am. Coll. Trust and Estate Counsel (regent 1980-86), ABA, Minn. Bar Assn., Hennepin County Bar Assn., Mpls. Club, Harvard Club Minn. (pres. 1969-70). Home: 93 Groveland Ter Minneapolis MN 55403-1142 Office: Dorsey & Whitney 220 S 6th St Minneapolis MN 55402-4502

REISTER, RUTH ALKEMA, lawyer, business executive; b. Grand Rapids, Mich., May 30, 1936; d. Henry and Lena (Land) Alkema; m. Raymond A. Reister, Oct. 7, 1967. B.A., U. Mich., 1958, J.D., 1964; grad. Program in Bus. Adminstrn., Harvard U., 1959, postgrad. Program in Mgmt. Devel., 1976. Bar: Minn., Mich. 1964, U.S. Supreme Ct. 1976. Trust officer Northwestern Nat. Bank, Mpls., 1964-70; asst. counsel, asst. v.p., sec. Fed. Res. Bank, Mpls., 1970-81; asst. sec., bd. govs. Fed. Res. System, 1977; dep. under sec. U.S. Dept. Agr., Washington, 1981-83; pres. First Bank Systems Agrl. Credit Corp., Mpls., 1983-84; pres. Groveland Corp., Mpls., 1986—; dir. Herman Miller, Inc., Zealand, Mich., 1984—. Bd. dirs. United Way, ARC, Jones Harrison Home, Mpls., Gustavus Adolfus Coll., 1995—; chmn. Jones-Harrison Found. Mem. Harvard Bus. Sch. Club Minn., Minn. Women's Econ. Round Table (pres. 1980-81). Republican.

REISTLE, CARL ERNEST, JR., petroleum engineer; b. Denver, June 26, 1901; s. Carl E. and Leonora I. (McMaster) R.; m. Mattie A Muldrow, June 23, 1922; children: Bette Jean (Mrs. George F. Pierce), Mattie Ann (Mrs. James Tracy Clark), Nancy L. (Mrs. Travis Parker), Carl Ernest III. B.S., U. Okla., 1922; postgrad., Harvard Sch. Bus. Adminstrn., 1948. Petroleum chemist U.S. Bur. Mines, 1922-29, petroleum engr., 1929-33; chmn. East Tex. Engring. Assn., 1933-36; engr. in charge Humble Oil & Refining Co., 1936-40, chief petroleum engr., 1940-45, gen. supt. prodn., 1945-46, mgr. prodn. dept., 1946-51, dir., 1948-51, dir. in charge prodn. dept., 1951-55, v.p., 1955-57, exec. v.p., 1957-61, pres., 1961-63, chmn. bd., chief exec. officer, 1963-66, ret., 1966, cons., 1966-69; dir. Eltra Corp.; dir., chmn. exec. com. Olinkraft, Inc., 1967-78. Contbr. numerous articles to profl. jours. Bd. dirs. Tex. Tech Coll., Lubbock, 1966-69, U. Okla. Research Inst., Norman. Recipient Anthony F. Lucas Gold medal Am. Inst. Mining, Metall. and Petroleum Engrs., 1958. Mem. Am. Petroleum Inst., Am. Inst. Mining, Metall. and Petroleum Engrs. (pres. 1956), Sigma Xi, Tau Beta Pi, Sigma Tau, Alpha Chi Sigma. Club: River Oaks Country. Home: 3196 Chevy Chase Dr Houston TX 77019-3208 Office: 601 Jefferson St Ste 975 Houston TX 77002

REISZ, HOWARD FREDERICK, JR., seminary president, theology educator; b. Balt., May 13, 1939; s. Howard Frederick and Katheryn M. (Gwynn) R.; m. Mabel (May) Martha Martin, June 6, 1965; children: Lisa Katherine, Heather Lyn. AB magna cum laude in English lit., Gettysburg (Pa.) Coll., 1961; BD, Luth. Theol. Sem., Gettysburg, 1965; AM in Systematic Theology, U. Chgo., 1967, PhD in Systematic Theology, 1977. Ordained to ministry Luth. Ch., 1969. Co-resident head undergrad. women's resident halls U. Chgo., 1965-69, 72-73, lectr. new collegiate divsn., 1969; assoc. Luth. campus pastor Pa. State U., State College, 1969-72; asst. pastor Trinity Luth Ch., 1969-72; pastor to univ. Wittenberg U., Springfield, Ohio, 1973-78; Luth. denominational counselor Harvard Div. Sch., 1980-92; sr. pastor Univ. Luth. Ch., Cambridge, Mass., 1978-92; pres., prof. theology Luth. Theol. So. Sem., Columbia, S.C., 1992—; instr. grad. student seminars Div. Sch., U. Chgo., summer 1968; lectr. new collegiate divsn. U. Chgo., 1969; tchr. dept. religion Wittenberg U., Springfield, Ohio, 1974-78; Luth. counselor Harvard Div. Sch., 1980-92; tchr. ann. theology Seminars So. Sem., 1993—; leader monthly theology discussion group for area Luth. mins., 1983-92; tchr. ann. non-credit seminars MIT, 1979-92; tchr. courses Diakonia, Lay Theology Sch., Boston, 1987-88; lectr.-spkr. nat. and regional events., 1992—; exec. bd. divsn. edn. and schs. Evang. Luth. Ch. Am., 1991—; bd. mem. Mass. Coun. Chs., Boston, 1985-92; mem. adv. bd. Word & World Jour., Mpls., 1982—; chair Luth. Orientation Com., Boston, 1980-92; mem. Coun. for Theol. Edn. in N.E., Com. on Svcs. to Students in Non-Luth. Sems., 1980-92; mem. staff associated with Campus Min. Com. New Eng. Synod, 1978-87, 91-92; mem. Luth. Roman Cath. Dialogue New Eng., 1984-92, Luth.-Episcopal Dialogue New Eng., 1989-92; chair New Eng. Synod Continuing Edn., 1989-92; ecumenical officer for Mass., 1988-92; sec. bd. Nat. Luth. Campus Ministry, Inc., 1991—; mem. exec. com. bd. Divsn. Higher Edn. and Schs., Evang. Luth. Ch. Am., 1991—; bd. mem. Mass. Coun. Chs., 1985-92; bishop's staff person Boston Ch. Leader's Covenant Group, 1988-92; ecumenical officer Evang. Luth. Ch. Am. Synod Bishop, 1988-92; mem. bd. ministry Harvard U., 1981-84, 86-90, 90-93, chair, 1989-91; founding mem. adv. com. Harvard Weekly Meal Program for Hungry, 1982-93, chair adv. bd., 1985-92; sec. Harvard Square Clergy, 1984-92; v.p. United Ministry at Harvard/Radcliffe, 1991-92. Contbr. articles to profl. jours. Mem. Mayor's Adv. Com. on Homelessness, Cambridge, Mass., 1987-89; vol. magician Children's Hosp., Columbia, S.C., 1993—; mem. Spl. Task Force for Cambridge Emergency Sheltering, 1987, Mayor's Adv. Com. on Homlessness, Cambridge, 1987-89, Cambridge/Somerville Com. on Homelessness, 1986-91, Cambridge Clergy for Affordable Housing, 1990-92; chair Harvard Square Affordable Housing, 1989-90; lectr. Cambridge Hospice, 1985-88, pastor resource, 1991-92; advisor, host pastor Emergency Winter Shelter Univ. Luth. Ch., 1983-92; mem. Liferaft network Harvard U., 1984-92; mem. Greater Columbia Cmty. Rels. Coun., 1994—; performer monthly charity magic shows Boston area hosps. and in Columbia, S.C. Recipient Fellowship Luth. Theol. Sem., Gettysburg, Underwood grad. fellowship Danforth Found., 1972-73, Leadership award Shelter, Inc., Cambridge, Mass., 1986, Nat. Disting. Svc. award Luth. Campus Ministry, 1990, Joseph Sittler award, 1992. Mem. Am. Acad. Religion, Ctr. for Process Studies, Bread for the World, Luth. Peace Fellowship, N.Am. Paul Tillich Soc. (bd. dirs. 1982-87, 89-92, pres. 1990-92, v.p. 1989-90, sec.-treas., editor newsletter 1984-87), Internat. Brotherhood of Magicians, Soc. Am. Magicians (local hosp. show chair 1978-92), Am. Acad. Religion, Boston Mins. Club, Rotary, Phi Beta Kappa, Eta Sigma Phi. Avocations: professional magic, poetry, art. Home: 4202 N Main St Columbia SC 29203 Office: Luth Theol So Sem 4201 N Main St Columbia SC 29203

REITAN, DANIEL KINSETH, electrical and computer engineering educator; b. Duluth, Minn., Aug. 13, 1921; s. Conrad Ulfred and Joy Elizabeth R.; m. Marian Anne Stemme, July 18, 1946; children: Debra Leah, Danielle Karen. BSEE, N.D. State U., 1946; MSEE, U. Wis., 1949, PhD, 1952. Registered profl. engr., Wis. Control engr. Gen. Electric Co., Schenectady, N.Y., 1946-48; transmission line engr. Gen. Telephone Co., Madison, Wis., 1949-50; mem. faculty Coll. Engring. U. Wis., Madison, 1952-85; prof. elec. and computer engring. Coll. Engring. U. Wis., 1962-85; cons. Energy Industries, 1985-95; dir. power systems simulation lab. Coll. Engring. U. Wis., 1968-84, also dir. wind power research Energy Ctr.; cons. Nat. Inst. Sci. and Tech. (formerly U.S. Nat. Bur. Standards). Contbr. articles to profl. jours.; patentee in field. Served with U.S. Army, World War II. Recipient Outstanding Tchr. award Polygon Engring. Council., Gov.'s citation for service to State of Wis. Fellow IEEE (Centennial medal and cert. for outstanding achievement 1984, Centennial medal and cert. dept. ECE U. Wis., 1991, IEE power Engring., Computer Control Indsl. Applications and Edn. Soc.), Conf. Internat. des Grand Reseaux Electriques a Haute Tension, Am. Soc. Engring. Edn., Wis. Acad. Scis., Am. Wind Energy Assn., Sigma Xi, Tau Delta Pi, Tau Beta Pi, Eta Kappa Nu, Kappa Eta Kappa. Lutheran. *I believe that in one's career professionalism and perseverance are key factors in success. In one's personal life, the family should be the center, but not the circumference, about which all activities revolve.*

REITAN, PAUL HARTMAN, geologist, educator; b. Kanawha, Iowa, Aug. 18, 1928; s. John Olsen and Anna (Meldahl) R.; m. Reidun Engebretsen, Sept. 28, 1962; children: Kirsten Berit, Eric Hartmann. A.B. (Salisbury fellow), U. Chgo., 1953; Ph.D. (Fulbright fellow), U. Oslo, Norway, 1959. Instr. U. Ill., Chgo., 1955; geologist U.S. Geol. Survey, 1953-56; state geologist Geol. Survey of Norway, 1956-60; asst. prof. mineralogy Stanford U., 1960-66; mem. faculty SUNY, Buffalo, 1966—; now prof. dept. geology SUNY, dean, 1975-79; cons. U. Calif.-Davis, Am. Geol. Inst.; guest scientist Centre for Geol. Sci., Acad. Sci., Warsaw, Poland, Geol. Survey Prague, Czechoslovakia., Geol. Survey, Norway, Nat. Geophys. Rsch. Inst. and Geol. Survey, India. Author: (with Davis and Pestrong) Geology, 1976; contbr. articles to profl. jours. Served with U.S. Army, 1946-49. NATO sr. fellow in sci., 1972; G. Unger Vetlesen fellow, 1973; Fulbright sr. lectr., India, 1986; Norwegian Marshall Fund grantee, 1986, 93. Fellow Geol. Soc. Am., Mineral. Soc. Am., Soc. Econ. Geology, Geol. Soc. India; mem. AAAS, Internat. Assn. Geochemistry and Cosmochemistry, Royal Norwegian Soc. Scis. and Letters (fgn.), Norsk Geologisk Forening (life), Sigma Xi. Home: 120 Walton Dr Buffalo NY 14226-4556 Office: SUNY Buffalo NY 14260-3050

REITEMEIER, RICHARD JOSEPH, physician; b. Pueblo, Colo., Jan. 2, 1923; s. Paul John and Ethel Regina (McCarthy) R.; m. Patricia Claire Mulligan, July 21, 1951; children: Mary Louise, Paul, Joseph, Susan, Robert, Patrick, Daniel. A.B., U. Denver, 1944; M.D., U. Colo., 1946; M.S. in Internal Medicine, U. Minn., 1954. Diplomate: Am. Bd. Internal Medicine (gov. 1971-79, chmn. 1978-79, rep. to Federated Council Internal Medicine 1977-80, 83-84, accreditation council grad. med. edn. 1979-85, chmn. 1982-83). Intern Corwin Hosp., Pueblo, 1946-47; resident Henry Ford Hosp., Detroit, 1949-50, Mayo Found., Rochester, Minn., 1950-53; cons. internal medicine and gastroenterology Mayo Clinic, Rochester, 1954-87; chmn. dept. internal medicine Mayo Clinic (Mayo Clinic and Mayo Med. Sch.), 1967-74, prof., 1971—; bd. govs. Mayo Clinic, 1970-74; bd. dirs. Sisters of Mercy Health System, St. Louis, 1986-92; mem. governing bd. Am. Bd. Med. Specialties, 1983-86; sci. and med. dir. Ludwig Inst. Cancer Rsch., 1987-88; cons. Kaiser Family Med. Found., 1989-90; med. dir. Phoenix Alliance Inc., 1990-93. Author: (with C. G. Moertel) Advanced Gastrointestinal Cancer, Clinical Management and Chemotherapy, 1969; contbr. numerous articles to med. jours. Trustee Mayo Found., 1970-74; trustee St. Mary's Hosp., Rochester, 1976-82. Served with U.S. Army, 1947-49. Recipient Alumni award U. Colo. Sch. Medicine; Irving Cutter award Phi Rho Sigma, 1986. Master ACP (regent 1979-82, gov. for Minn. 1975-79, pres. 1983-84, Alfred Stengel Meml. award 1990); fellow Am. Gastroenterol. Assn., AMA, Am. Clin. and Climatol. Assn., Am. Fedn. Clin. Rsch., Am. Soc. Clin. Oncology, Coun. Med. Splty. Socs., Inst. Medicine, Am. Assn. Cancer Rsch., Am. Assn. Study Liver Disease, Nat. Bd. Med. Examiners (treas. 1987-89), Alpha Omega Alpha. Republican. Roman Catholic. Home: 707 12th Ave SW Rochester MN 55902-2027 Office: 200 1st Ave SW Rochester MN 55902-3129

REITEN, RICHARD G., natural gas industry executive; b. 1939. BA, U. Wash., 1962. With Simpson Timber Co., Seattle, 1962-64, St. Regis Paper Co., Tacoma, 1964-66, Hearin Products, Inc., Portland, Oreg., 1966-71; with Di Giorgio Corp., San Francisco, 1971-79, pres. bldg. material group; with Nicoli Co., Portland, 1979-87; dir. Oreg. Econ. Devel. Dept., Salem, 1987-89; pres. Portland Gen. Corp., 1989-92; pres. Portland Gen. Electric Co., 1992-95, pres., COO, 1996—. Office: Northwest Natural Gas Co One Pacific Square 13th Flr 220 Northwest Second Portland OR 97209

REITER, GLENN MITCHELL, lawyer; b. N.Y.C., Feb. 1, 1951; s. Bernard Leon and Helene (Edson) R.; m. Marilyn Beckhorn, Sept. 5, 1976; children: Benjamin, Diana, Julie. BA, Yale U., 1973, JD, 1976. Bar: N.J. 1976, Pa. 1977, D.C. 1978, N.Y. 1979. Law clk. to judge U.S. Ct. Appeals, Phila., 1976-77; assoc. Schnader, Harrison, Segal & Lewis, Phila., 1977-78; assoc. Simpson, Thacher & Bartlett, N.Y.C., 1978-84, ptnr., 1984—; resident ptnr. Simpson, Thacher & Bartlett, London, 1986-90. Mem. Phi Beta Kappa.

REITER, JOSEPH HENRY, lawyer, retired judge; b. Phila., Mar. 21, 1929; s. Nicholas and Barbara (Hellmann) R.; m. Beverlee A. Bearman, Nov. 8, 1993. AB, Temple U., 1950, LLB, 1953. Bar: D.C. 1953, Pa. 1954. Atty. advisor U.S. Army, 1955-61; asst. U.S. atty. Ea. Dist. Pa., 1961-63, asst. U.S. atty. in charge of civil div., 1963-69; chief organized crime and racketeering strike force Western N.Y. State, U.S. Dept. Justice, 1969-70, sr. trial atty. tax div. 1970-72, regional dir. office of drug abuse law enforcement, 1972-73; dep. atty. gen., dir. Drug Law Enforcement Office of Pa., 1973-77; ptnr. Stassen, Kostos and Mason, Phila. 1978-85, Kostos Reiter & Lamer, 1985-89; judge Armed Svcs. Bd. of Contract Appeals, Falls Church, Va., 1989-95; of counsel Kostos & Lamer, Phila., 1995—; mem. adv. com. Joint State Commn. on Procurement; lectr. in field. Contbr. articles to profl. jours. Mem. Citizens Crime Commn. Pa. With U.S. Army, 1953-55. Recipient Meritorious Svc. award U.S. Atty. Gen. Clark, 1967, Spl. Commendation Asst. U.S. Atty. Gen. Tax Div., 1969, Outstanding Performance award U.S. Atty. Gen. Richardson, 1973. Mem. ABA, Fed. Bar Assn., D.C. Bar Assn., Pa. Bar Assn., Phila. Bar Assn., Am. Legion, Vesper Club, Downtown Club. Office: Kostos & Lamer 1608 Walnut St Ste 1300 Philadelphia PA 19103

REITER, MICHAEL A., lawyer, educator; b. Pitts., Nov. 15, 1941. BS, U. Wis., 1963, MS, 1964, JD, 1967, PhD, 1969. Bar: Wis. 1967, Ill. 1975, U.S. Supreme Ct. 1975. Ptnr. Holleb & Coff, Chgo., 1987—; adj. prof. law Northwestern U., Chgo., 1977—; mem. faculty Nat. Inst. Trial Advocacy, 1980—. Office: Holleb & Coff 55 E Monroe St Ste 4100 Chicago IL 60603-5803

REITER, ROBERT EDWARD, banker; b. Kansas City, Mo., Dec. 27, 1943; s. Robert Vincent and Helen Margaret (Petrus) R.; m. Mary J. Darby, June 20, 1964; children: Mollie K., Jennifer M., Ellen R., Robert E. Jr. BA, Rockhurst Coll., 1964; JD, St. Louis U., 1967; LLM, U. Mo., Kansas City, 1969. Bar: Mo. 1967. Assoc. atty. Burke, Jackson & Millin, Kansas City, 1967-69; personal trust adminstr. City Nat. Bank and Trust Co., Kansas City, 1969-71; estate planning officer United Mo. Bank of Kansas City, 1971-73, v.p., 1973-80, sr. v.p., 1980-85, exec. v.p., 1985—; pres., corp. bd. Seton Ctr., Kansas City, 1992-95. Contbr. articles to profl. jours. Bd. of Counselors St. Joseph Health Ctr., Kansas City, 1977-85; pres. St. Joseph Health Ctr. Adv. Coun., Kansas City, 1985-86; sec. United Mo. Polit. Action Com., Kansas City, 1987-88. Grantee St. Louis U. Sch. of Law, 1964-67. Mem. Mo. Bar Assn., Kansas City Bar Assn. (chmn. employee benefits com. 1989-90), Employee Benefit Inst. (adv. bd. 1986—, chmn. 1989), Estate Planning Soc. Kansas City (pres. 1985-86), Serra Club of Kansas City (v.p. 1987-89). Avocation: coaching youth soccer. Home: 1024 W 70th St Kansas City MO 64113-2004 Office: UMB Bank NA 1010 Grand Blvd PO Box 419692 Kansas City MO 64141-6692

REITER, STANLEY, economist, educator; b. N.Y.C., Apr. 26, 1925; s. Frank and Fanny (Rosenberg) R.; m. Nina Sarah Breger, June 13, 1944; children: Carla Frances, Frank Joseph. A.B., Queens Coll., 1947; M.A., U. Chgo., 1950, Ph.D., 1955. Rsch. assoc. Cowles Commn., U. Chgo., 1949-50; mem. faculty Stanford U., 1950-54, Purdue U., 1954-67; prof. econs. and math. Northwestern U., 1967—, now Morrison prof. econs. and math. Coll. Arts and Scis., Morrison prof. managerial econs. and decision scis. Kellogg Grad. Sch. Mgmt.; dir. Ctr. for Math. Studies in Econs. and Mgmt. Sci.; cons. in field. Trustee Roycemore Sch., Evanston, Ill., 1969-71, treas., 1970-

71. Served with inf. AUS, 1943-45. Decorated Purple Heart. Fellow Econometric Soc., AAAS; mem. Soc. Indsl. and Applied Math., Inst. Mgmt. Scis., Ops. Rsch. Soc. Am., Am. Math. Soc., Math. Assn. Am., Am. Acad. of Arts and Scis. Home: 2138 Orrington Ave Evanston IL 60201-2914 Office: Northwestern U Ctr for Math Studies 2001 Sheridan Rd Evanston IL 60201-2925

REITH, CARL JOSEPH, apparel industry executive; b. Peoria, Ill., Jan. 11, 1914; s. Joseph and May (Kolb) R.; m. Jennie S. Habbinga, Apr. 3, 1936; 1 child, Joyce Elaine. Grad. high sch. Office staff sales Peoria Creamery Co., Ill., 1932; with Kroger Co., 1934-60; successively asst. br. acct., office mgr., acct. Kroger Co., Terre Haute, Ind., Atlanta; adminstr., coord. tng. and mgmt. devel. programing Kroger Co. (Gen. Offices), Cin.; gen. merchandising mgr. Kroger Co. (St. Louis br.), 1946-50; br. mgr. Kroger Co., Indpls., 1950-55; div. v.p. Kroger Co., Cin., 1955-57; regional v.p. Kroger Co., 1957-60; pres., chief exec. officer Colonial Stores, Inc., 1960-67; bd. dir., pres. Oxford Industries, 1967-78, now dir. Adv. bd. Salvation Army, Atlanta.; bd. dirs. Atlanta Coll. Art; trustee Robert Woodruff Art Ctr. Mem. Indiana Chain Store Council (pres., v.p. 1951-55), Ind. C. of C. (bd. 1954-55), Indpls. C. of C. (bd. 1950), Ga. C. of C. (indsl. devel. council), Atlanta C. of C. (v.p., bd. dir. 1964-67), Augusta (Ga.) Nat. Golf Club, Piedmont Driving Club, Capital City Club, Peachtree Golf Club, Masons, Shriners, Rotary. Home: 3747 Peachtree Rd NE Apt 1708 Atlanta GA 30319-1366 Office: Oxford Industries Inc 222 Piedmont Ave NE Atlanta GA 30308-3306

REITINGER, THOMAS ANTHONY, hospital administrator; b. Freeport, Ill., July 12, 1944; married. BA, U. Wis., 1967; MA, Washington U., 1971. Adm. resident Jewish Hosp. St. Louis, 1970-71; asst. admin. St. John's Regional Health Ctr., Springfield, Mo., 1971-73, assoc. dir., 1973-75; exec. dir. Waupun (Wis.) Meml. Hosp., 1975-77, Fort Atkinson (Wis.) Meml. Hosp., 1977-83; v.p. St. Joseph's Hosp., Milw., 1983-84, sr. v.p., 1984-86, exec. v.p., COO, 1986-90, pres., CEO, 1990-93; pres., CEO Mercy Hosp. Med. Ctr., Des Moines, 1993—. Home: 5554 Beechwood Ter West Des Moines IA 50266-6620 Office: Mercy Hosp Med Ctr 400 University Des Moines IA 50313

REITMAN, IVAN, film director, producer; b. Komarmo, Czechoslovakia, Oct. 27, 1946; came to Can., 1951; s. Leslie and Clara R.; m. Genevieve Robert, Sept. 12, 1976; children: Jason, Catherine, Caroline. MusB, McMaster U., 1969. Judge FOCUS Nissan-Datsun, N.Y.C., 1981-83. Theatrical prodr.: The Magic show, 1974, The National Lampoon Show, 1975, Merlin, 1983 (also dir.); Films include: (dir., exec. prodr.) Cannibal Girls, 1973; (prodr.) They Came From Within (aka Shivers), 1975, Death Weekend (aka The House by the Lake), 1977, Blackout, 1978, National Lampoon's Animal House, 1978, Heavy Metal, 1981, Stop! Or My Mom Will Shoot, 1992, Space Jam, 1996, Private Parts, 1996; (prodr., dir.) Foxy Lady, 1971, Meatballs, 1979, Stripes, 1981, Ghostbusters, 1984, Legal Eagles, 1986, Twins, 1988, Ghostbusters II, 1989, Kindergarten Cop, 1990, Dave, 1993, Junior, 1994; (exec. prodr.) Rabid, 1976, Spacehunter: Adventures in the Forbidden Zone, 1983, Big Shots, 1987, Casual Sex?, 1988, Feds, 1988, Beethoven, 1992, Beethoven's 2nd, 1993, Commandments, 1996; TV Series: (prodr., dir.) Delta House, 1978; TV film exec. prodr. The Late Shift, 1996. Mem. Dirs. Guild Am. Office: CAA 9830 Wilshire Blvd Beverly Hills CA 90212-1804*

REITMAN, JERRY IRVING, advertising agency executive; b. Phila., Jan. 9, 1938; s. Benjamin and Ruth (Eisenberg) R.; m. Monica Birgitta Hall, Oct. 27, 1968; children—Jennifer Sharon, Sarah Beth. B.S. in Fin., Pa. State U., 1961. Exec. v.p., chief exec. officer Brit. Pubs., N.Y.C. and London, 1965-69; pres., pub. Acad. Media, Sherman Oaks, Calif., 1969-73; v.p. Pubs. Clearing House, Port Washington, N.Y., 1973-78; exec. v.p. Ogilvy & Mather, N.Y.C., 1978-81; with Scali, McCabe, Sloves, Inc., N.Y.C., 1981-86; pres. Scali, McCabe, Sloves Direct, N.Y.C.; chmn. bd. The Reitman Group, 1986-87; exec. v.p. The Leo Burnett Co., Chgo., 1986-96; pres., CEO Internat. Data Response Corp., Chgo., 1996&; dir. Scandinavian Airlines System Pub./Distbn. Svcs.; mem. adv. bd. Ill. Dept. Trade and Tourism, 1988—; internat. awards chmn., bd. dirs. John Caples Internat., 1989—; mem. Internat. Direct Mktg. Symposium, Zurich, Switzerland. Author: A Common Sense Approach to Small Business, 1968, Beyond 2000: The Future of Direct Marketing, 1994; contbr. articles to profl. jours. Trustee Locust Valley Libr. Assn., N.Y., 1982—; exec. com. mem. Pub. Hall of Fame, 1987—; bd. govs. Children's Miracle Network, 1992—; bd. dirs. Children's Meml. Found. Telethon, The Direct Mktg. Ednl. Found., exec. dir., 1996—. Recipient Key to City, New Orleans, 1959, Silver Apple award N.Y. Direct Mktg. Club, 1989; Anderson scholar, 1961. Fellow Psychiat. Re-Edn. Assn.; mem. Direct Mktg. Assn. (bd. mem. ethics com. 1984), Creative Guild (dir. 1984), Internat. Direct Mktg. Assn. (bd. dirs. 1981-82), Publ. Hall of Fame (exec. com. 1988—), Direct Mktg. Club N.Y. (pres. 1983-84), Beta Gamma Sigma, Delta Sigma Pi. Avocations: tennis; old car restoration; classical woodworking. Home: 2204 N Leavitt St Chicago IL 60647-3204 Office: Internat Data Response Corp 1735 N Paulina St Chicago IL 60622

REITMAN, ROBERT STANLEY, manufacturing and marketing executive; b. Fairmont, W.Va., Nov. 18, 1933; s. Isadore and Freda A. (Layman) R.; m. Sylvia K. Golden, Dec. 24, 1955; children: Scott Alan, Alayne Louise. BS in Acctg., W.Va. U., 1955; JD, Case Western Res. U., 1958. Bar: Ohio 1958. Mem. firm Burke, Haber & Berick, Cleve., 1958-60; ptnr. Burke, Haber & Berick, 1960-68; exec. v.p., vice chmn. Tranzonic Cos. (formerly AAV Cos.), Pepper Pike, Ohio, 1968-70; pres., vice-chmn. Tranzonic Cos. (formerly AAV Cos.), 1970-73, chief exec. officer, pres., vice chmn., 1973-82, pres., chmn., chief exec. officer, 1982—; bd. dirs. Soc. Nat. Bank, Weirton Steel Corp., mem. Bus. adv.Com. Mandel Ctr. for non-profit Organ. Case Western Reserve U., 1995, vis. com. Weatherhead Sch. of Bus. Case Western Reserve U., 1995. Mem. Republican fin. com., Cuyahoga County, 1968-78; mem. Com. for Econ. Growth for Israel, Cleve., 1977-80, pres., 1978-80; mem. adv. coun. Cleve. Mus. Nat. History, 1982-85, Cleve. Opera, 1977—; del. Coun. of Jewish Fedns., N.Y.C., 1981—; gen. co-chmn. Jewish Welfare Fund, Cleve., 1975-78, 81-85, gen. vice chmn., 1985-89, gen. chmn., 1989-91; sect. and div. chmn., team capt. United Way Svcs., 1974—, mem. del. assembly, 1976-85, trustee, 1977-83, 84-90, 91—, v.p., 1985-88, chmn. nominating. com., 1988-90, campaign chmn., 1993, chair fund raising planning com., 1994—; mem. employment com. Jewish Vocat. Svc., Cleve., 1974-83; bd. dirs. Capital for Israel, Inc., N.Y.C., 1986-87; nat. vice chmn. United Jewish Appeal, 1987-92, nat. allocations chmn., 1987-90, trustee, 1988-94, chair retirement fund com., 1994—; trustee B'nai B'rith Hillel Found., 1975-81, Cleve. Jewish News, 1976-79, Ednl. TV Sta. WVIZ, Cleve., 1976—, vice chmn. 1986-90, chmn. bd., 1990—; trustee, pres. Bus. Volunteerism Coun., 1994-; trustee Jewish Community Fedn. Cleve., 1983—, treas., 1991-94, v.p., 1995, Jewish Edn. Ctr. of Cleve., 1993—, Cleve. Zool. Soc., 1972—, pres., 1979-87, chmn., 1987-92, chmn. emeritus, 1992—, chmn. JDC-Brookdale Inst. of Gerontology and Human Devel., 1995; trustee Am. Jewish Joint Distbn. Com., 1988—, United Israel Appeal, 1987-94, Mt. Sinai Med. Ctr., Cleve., 1976—, chmn., 1982-85; trustee Cleve. State U. Devel. Found., 1986-89, Greater Cleve. Roundtable, 1991—; pres., trustee The Wilds, 1995. Mem. ABA, Cleve. Growth Assn., The 50 Club Cleve., Case Western Res. Univ. Sch. of Law Soc. Benchers, Am. Kennel Club (regional del. 1960-75), Western Res. Kennel Club (officer, trustee 1959-75), Beechmont Club (fin. com. 1972-80, house com. 1974), Pepper Pike Club, Union Club, Masons, B'nai Brith, Zeta Beta Tau, Tau Epsilon Rho. Avocations: golf, swimming, pure-bred dogs. Office: Tranzonic Cos 30195 Chagrin Blvd # 224E Cleveland OH 44124-5703

REITSEMA, HAROLD JAMES, aerospace engineer; b. Kalamazoo, Jan. 19, 1948; s. Robert Harold and Bernice Jean (Hoogsteen) R.; m. Mary Jo Gunnink, Aug. 6, 1970; children: Ellen Celeste, Laurie Jean. BA, Calvin Coll., 1972; PhD, N.Mex. State U., 1977. Rsch. assoc. U. Ariz., Tucson, 1977-79, sr. rsch. assoc., 1979-82, vis. scientist, 1987—; sr. mem. tech. staff Ball Aerospace, Boulder, Colo., 1982-85, prin. systems engr., 1985-88, program mgr., 1988-89, staff cons., 1989—; cons. Aerospace Tech., 1987—. Contbr. articles to Astrophys. Jour., Aston. Jour., Nature, Sci., Icarus. Bd. dirs. EE Barnard Obs., Golden, Colo., 1984-91. Fellow AIAA (assoc., tech. com. chair 1991, Engr. of Yr. Colo. region 1990); mem. Am. Astron. Soc. (planetary sci. com. 1991-94), Internat. Astron. Union. Achievements include discovery of Larissa, fifth satellite of Neptune; co-discovery of Telesto, seventeenth satellite of Saturn; patents for Optically-coupled Shaft Angle Encoder. Home: 4795 Hancock Driver Boulder CO 80303 Office: Ball Aerospace 1600 Commerce St Boulder CO 80301-2734

REITZ, BRUCE ARNOLD, cardiac surgeon, educator; b. Seattle, Sept. 14, 1944; s. Arnold B. and Ruth (Stillings) R.; m. Nan Norton, Oct. 3, 1970; children: Megan, Jay. BS, Stanford U., 1966; MD, Yale U., 1970. Diplomate: Am. Bd. Surgery, Am. Bd. Thoracic Surgery. Intern Johns Hopkins Hosp., Balt., 1970-71, cardiac surgeon-in-charge, 1982-92; resident Stanford U. Hosp., (Calif.), 1971-72, 74-78; clin. assoc. Nat. Heart Lung Blood Inst., NIH, Bethesda, Md., 1972-74; asst. prof. Stanford U. Sch. Medicine, 1977-81, assoc. prof., 1981-82; prof. surgery Johns Hopkins U. Sch. Medicine, Balt., 1982-92; prof., chmn. Sch Medicine Stanford (Calif.) U., 1992—. Developer heart-lung transplant technique, 1981. Office: Stanford U Sch Medicine Dept Cardiothoracic Surgery Stanford CA 94305

REITZ, CURTIS RANDALL, lawyer, educator; b. Reading, Pa.; s. Lester S. and Magdalene A. (Crouse) R.; m. Virginia R. Patterson, Dec. 19, 1953 (div.); children—Kevin R., Joanne E., Whitney A.; m. Judith N. Renzulli, Sept. 18, 1983. B.A., U. Pa., 1951, LL.B., 1956. Bar: Pa. 1957, U.S. Supreme Ct. 1959. Law clk. to Chief Justice Earl Warren U.S. Supreme Ct., 1956-57; mem. faculty law U. Pa., Phila., 1957—; asst. prof. law U. Pa., 1957-60, assoc. prof., 1960-63, prof., 1963—, provost, v.p., 1970-71, Algernon Sydney Biddle prof. law, 1985—. Trustee Internat. House Phila.; bd. mgrs. Glen Mills Schs., Pa. Served to 1st lt. U.S. Army, 1951-53. Mem. Am. Law Inst., Nat. Conf. Commrs. on Uniform State Laws, Order of Coif. Office: U Pa Law Sch 3400 Chestnut St Philadelphia PA 19104-6204

REITZ, RICHARD ELMER, physician; b. Buffalo, Sept. 18, 1938; s. Elmer Valentine and Edna Anna (Guenther) R.; m. Gail Pounds, 1960 (div. 1990); children: Richard Allen, Mark David; m. Myrnna Mecenario, 1991. BS, Heidelberg Coll., 1960; MD, SUNY-Buffalo, 1964. Intern Hartford (Conn.) Hosp., 1964-65, resident in medicine, 1966-67; asst. resident in medicine Yale U., 1965-66; vis. rsch. assoc. NIH, Bethesda, Md., 1967-68; rsch. fellow in medicine Harvard Med. Sch., Mass. Gen. Hosp., Boston, 1967-69; dir. clin. investigation ctr. Naval Regional Med. Ctr., 1969-71; dir. Endocrine Metabolic Ctr., Oakland, Calif., 1973-92; med. dir. Corning Nichols Inst.; asst. prof. medicine U. Calif.-San Francisco, 1971-76; chmn. dept. medicine John Muir MEd. Ctr., 1975-77; assoc. clin. prof. medicine U. Calif.-Davis, 1976-86; clin. prof. med. 1986—; chief endocrinology Providence Hosp., Oakland, Calif., 1972-92. Contbr. articles to profl. jours., chpt. to book. Mem. scholarship com., Bank of Am., San Francisco, 1983. Served to comdr. USNR, 1969-71. Mem. Endocrine Soc., Am. Soc. Bone and Mineral Rsch., Am. Fedn. Clin. Rsch., Am. Fertility Soc., Am. Soc. Internal Medicine, AAAS, Am. Assn. Clin. Endocrinologists, Am. Coll. Endocrinology. Democrat. Office: Corning Nichols Inst 3100 Summit St Oakland CA 94609-3410

REITZ, WILLIAM, supermarket company executive; b. 1933. With Scott's Foodlane Inc., Ft. Wayne, Ind., 1954-70, Reitz #1, Ft. Wayne, 1970-78, SV Ventures, Ft. Wayne, 1978—; now co-gen. mgr. SV Ventures. Office: SV Ventures 4118 N Clinton St Fort Wayne IN 46805*

REJAI, MOSTAFA, political science educator; b. Tehran, Iran, Mar. 11, 1931; came to U.S., 1954; s. Taghi and Forough (Lashgari) R. AA, Pasadena City Coll., 1957; BA, Calif. State U., L.A., 1959, MS, 1961; PhD, UCLA, 1964. Teaching fellow UCLA, 1963-64; asst. prof. polit. sci. Miami U., Oxford, Ohio, 1964-67, assoc. prof., 1967-70, prof., 1970-83, Disting. prof., 1983—; vis. scholar Ctr. for Internat. Affairs, Harvard U., 1972, Hoover Instn. on War, Revolution and Peace, Stanford U., 1973, Inst. Internat. Studies, Iran, 1974-75; vis. prof. Western Coll., Oxford, 1971, 72. Author: World Military Leaders: A Collective and Comparative Analysis, 1966, The Strategy of Political Revolution, 1973, The Comparative Study of Revolutionary Strategy, 1977, Comparative Political Ideologies, 1984; (with Kay Phillips) Leaders of Revolution, 1979, World Revolutionary Leaders, 1983, Loyalists and Revolutionaries: Political Leaders Compared, 1988, Demythogizing an Elite: American Presidents in Empirical, Comparative, and Historical Perspectives, 1993, Political Ideologies: A Comparative Approach, 1991, 2d edit., 1995; editor, contbr.: Democracy: The Contemporary Theories, 1967, Decline of Ideology?, 1971; editor: Mao Tse-Tung on Revolution and War, 1969, rev. edit., 1970; assoc. editor Jour. Polit. and Mil. Sociology, 1973—; contbr. articles to profl. jours., book chpts. Recipient Outstanding Teaching award Miami U., 1970. Mem. Am. Polit. Sci. Assn. (polit. psychology sect.), Am. Sociol. Assn. (polit. soc. sect.), Internat. Polit. Sci. Assn., Internat. Soc. Polit. Psychology, Internat. Studies Assn., Inter-Univ. Seminar on Armed Forces and Soc., Conf. for Study Polit. Thought, Midwest Polit. Sci. Assn., So. Polit. Sci. Assn., Wesetern Polit. Sci. Assn., Pi Gamma Mu, Pi Sigma Alpha. Office: Miami U Dept of Political Science Oxford OH 45056

REKATE, ALBERT C., physician; b. Buffalo, June 12, 1916; s. Gustave E. and Fannie (Hummell) R.; m. Elizabeth Foster, June 12 1943 (dec. 1985); 1 child, Suzanne (Mrs. R. Willis Post); m. Linda Ann Holt, Aug. 1, 1992. M.D., U. Buffalo, 1940. Diplomate Am. Bd. Internal Medicine. Intern E.J. Meyer Meml. Hosp., 1940-41, med. resident, 1941-44; asst. prof. medicine SUNY-Buffalo, 1954-61, assoc. prof., 1961-65, prof., 1965-86, prof. emeritus, 1986—, dir. rehab. medicine, 1965-72, acting dean Sch. Health Related Professions, 1965-66; assoc. dean SUNY-Buffalo (Sch. Health Related Professions), 1966-74; acting chmn. dept. rehab. medicine SUNY-Buffalo, 1972-75; assoc. dir. medicine E.J. Meyer Meml. Hosp., 1957-63, head dept. rehab. medicine, 1964-69, dir. primary rehab. center, 1965-69, acting head cardiology, 1966-69, dir., 1970-72; bd. dirs. Buffalo Hearing and Speech Ctr., 1973—; mem. adv. bd. Coastal Empire Mental Health Ctr., S.C., 1980-81, bd. dirs., 1981-93; mem. dean's adv. coun. U. Buffalo Sch. Medicine and Biomed. Scis., 1995—. Contbr. articles to profl. jours. Served with M.C. AUS, World War II. Mem. Am. Heart Assn., Western N.Y. Heart Assn. (pres. 1954-55), Assn. Am. Med. Colls., N.Y. State Heart Assembly, N.Y. Acad. Scis., Med. Union (pres. 1974-75), Buffalo Acad. Medicine (pres. 1969-70), Erie County Med. Soc., Med. Alumni Assn. U. Buffalo (pres. 1960-61), Beaufort-Jasper Mental Health Assn. (dir. 1980-86). Home: PO Box 3164 Hilton Head Island SC 29928-0164 Office: 462 Grider St Buffalo NY 14215-3075

REKSTIS, WALTER J., III, lawyer; b. San Diego, 1945. BBA, U. Cin., 1968, JD, 1972. Bar: Ohio 1972. Ptnr. Squire, Sanders & Dempsey, Cleve. Office: Squire Sanders & Dempsey 4900 Society Ct 127 Public Sq Cleveland OH 44114-1216

REKTORIK-SPRINKLE, PATRICIA JEAN, Latin language educator; b. Robstown, Tex., Feb. 19, 1941; d. Julius and Elizabeth Lollie (Ermis) Rektorik; m. Edgar Eugene Sprinkle, June 22, 1963; children: Julie Anne, Mark. BA in English and Latin, Our Lady of the Lake Coll., San Antonio, 1963, MA, 1967; doctoral student, Tex. A&M U., 1968-74, U. North Tex., 1987—. Cert. secondary tchr., Tex. Latin and English tchr. Ysleta Independent Sch. Dist., El Paso, Tex., 1963-64, El Paso Independent Sch. Dist., 1964-65; instr. Our Lady of the Lake Coll., 1965-66; rhetoric and composition instr. Tex. A&M U., College Station, 1968-69, 72-74, Harford Community Coll., Bel Aire, Md., 1970-71; Latin tchr. Denton (Tex.) Pub. Schs., 1974—; mem. residents adv. com. Tex. Acad. Math. and Sci., Denton, 1987-88; chmn. Latin reading competition Nat. Jr. Classical League, Miami, Ohio, 1988-93; mem. methodology com. Am. Classical League, 1993-95; dir. Tex. State Jr. Classical League Conv., 1996; presenter workshops in field; mem. Tex. State Textbook Adv. Com., 1989-90. Costume designer Denton Cmty. Theater, 1984; choir dir. Immaculate Conception Ch., Denton, 1985-87; chmn. costume competition Tex. State Jr. Classical League, 1987—, exec. bd. sponsor, 1981—. Arthur Patch McKinlay scholar, 1986, 91. Mem. Am. Classical Assn., Classical Assn. of the Mid-West and South, Metroplex Classics Assn. (constl. adv. com. 1988), Classics Assn. Southwestern U.S. (pres. 1987-88), Tex. Classics Assn., Tex. Fgn. Lang. Assn. (chmn. hon. mem. 1988-89, chmn. local arrangements 1977). Roman Catholic. Office: Billy Ryan High Sch 5101 E McKinney St Denton TX 76208-4630

RELIAS, JOHN ALEXIS, lawyer; b. Chgo., Apr. 2, 1946; s. Alexis John and Marie Helen (Metos) R.; m. Linda Ann Pontious, Nov. 27, 1971; children: Anne, Alexandra. BA, Northwestern U., Evanston, 1968; LLB, Northwestern U., Chgo., 1972. Bar: Ill., 1972, U.S. Dist. Ct. (no. dist.) Ill. 1972, U.S. Ct. Appeals (9th cir.) 1981, U.S. Ct. Appeals (7th cir.) 1983. Assoc. Vedder, Price, Kaufman & Kammholz, Chgo., 1972-78; ptnr. Vedder, Price, Kaufman & Kammholz, 1979-94, Franczek, Sullivan, Mann, Crement, Hein & Relias, Chgo., 1994—. Mem. bd. edn. Wilmette (Ill.) Sch. Dist. 39, 1989—, pres., 1992-93, 1995-96. Mem. Nat. Assn. Sch. Attys., Ill. Assn. Sch. Attys., Chgo. Bar Assn., Order of the Coif, Phi Beta Kappa. Greek Orthodox. Home: 2500 Kenilworth Ave Wilmette IL 60091-1337 Office: Franczek Sulian Mann Crement Hein & Relias 300 S Walker Dr Chicago IL 60606

RELKIN, ALLEN, commodities executive; b. 1944. With Philipp Bros., N.Y.C., 1966-88, group v.p.; with Centrotrade Mineral Metals Inc., N.Y.C., 1988—, now pres., CEO. Office: Centrotrade Mineral Metals Inc 330 Madison Ave Fl 25 New York NY 10017-5001*

RELL, M. JODI, state official; b. Norfolk, Va.. Student, Old Dominion U., Western Conn. State U. Mem., dep. minority leader Conn. Ho. Reps., 1984-94; lt. gov. State of Conn., 1995—. Past vice chmn. Brookfield Rep. Town Com.; trustee YMCA Western Conn. Mem. Nat. Order Women Legislators (past nat. pres., former v.p., treas., corr. sec.), Brookfield Rep. Women's Club (past pres.), Brookfield Bus. and Profl. Women's Club. Address: 125 Long Meadow Hill Rd Brookfield CT 06804-1339 Office: Office Lt Governor State Capitol Rm 304 Hartford CT 06106

RELLE, FERENC MATYAS, chemist; b. Gyor, Hungary, June 13, 1922; came to U.S., 1951, naturalized, 1956; s. Ferenc and Elizabeth (Netratics) R.; m. Gertrud B. Tubach, Oct. 9, 1946; children: Ferenc, Ava, Attila. B-SChemE, Jozsef Nador Poly. U., Budapest, 1944, MS, 1944. Lab. mgr. Karl Kohn Ltd. Co., Landshut, W.Ger., 1947-48; resettlement officer IRO, Munich, 1948-51; chemist Farm Bur. Coop. Assn., Columbus, Ohio, 1951-56; indsl. engr. N.Am. Aviation, Inc., Columbus, 1956-57; rsch. chemist Keever Starch Co., Columbus, 1957-65; rsch. chemist Ross Labs. div. Abbott Labs., Columbus, 1965-70, rsch. scientist, 1970-89; cons. in field. Chmn. Columbus and Central Ohio UN Week, 1963; pres. Berwick Manor Civic Assn., 1968; trustee Stelios Stelson Found., 1968-69; deacon Brookwood Presbyn. Ch., 1963-65, 92-93, trustee, 1990-91. Mem. Am. Chem. Soc. (alt. councilor 1973, chmn. long range planning com. Columbus sect. 1972-76, 78-80), Am. Assn. Cereal Chemists (chmn. Cin. sect. 1974-75), Ohio Acad. Sci., Arpad Acad., Internat. Tech. Inst. (adv. dir. 1977-82), Nat. Intercollegiate Soccer Ofcls. Assn., Am. Hungarian Assn., Hungarian Cultural Assn. (pres. 1978-81), Ohio Soccer Ofcls. Assn., Columbus Männerchor, Germania Singing and Sport Soc., Civitan (gov. Ohio dist. 1970-71, dist. treas. 1982-83, pres. Eastern Columbus 1963-64, 72-73, gen. sec. for Hungary 1991-92, Eastern European Growth Mgr., 1993-94, amb. at large, 1994—, established 1st Civitan club in Hungary 1991, Ukraine 1992, Slovakia 1994, Internat. Gov. of Yr. award 1971, Internat. Honor Key 1992, master club builder award 1992, various other awards), World Fedn. of Hungarian Engrs. Home and Office: 3487 Roswell Dr Columbus OH 43227-3560

RELMAN, ARNOLD SEYMOUR, physician, educator, editor; b. N.Y.C., June 17, 1923; s. Simon and Rose (Mallach) R.; m. Harriet Morse Vitkin, June 26, 1953; children: David Arnold, John Peter, Margaret Rose. A.B., Cornell U., 1943; M.D., Columbia U., 1946; LLD (hon.), U. Pa.; ScD (hon.), Med. Coll. Wis., Union U., Med. Coll. Ohio, CUNY; DMSc (hon.), Brown U.; DLH (hon.), SUNY; LittD (hon.), Temple U. Diplomate Am. Bd. Internal Medicine. House officer New Haven Hosp., Yale, 1946-49; NRC fellow Evans Meml., Mass. Meml. hosps., 1949-50; practice medicine, specializing in internal medicine Boston, 1950-68, Phila., 1968-77; asst. prof., prof. medicine Boston U. Sch. Medicine, 1950-68; dir. Boston U. Med. Services, Boston City Hosp., 1967-68; prof. medicine, chmn. dept. medicine U. Pa.; chief med. services Hosp. of U. Pa., 1968-77; editor New Eng. Jour. Medicine, Boston, 1977-91, editor emeritus, 1991—; sr. physician Brigham and Women's Hosp., Boston, 1977—; prof. medicine and social medicine Harvard Med. Sch., 1977-93, prof. medicine and social medicine emeritus, 1993—; cons. NIH, USPHS.; mem. bd. registration in medicine Commonwealth of Mass., 1995—. Editor: Jour. Clin. Investigation, 1962-67, (with F.J. Ingelfinger and M. Finland) Controversy in Internal Medicine, Vol. 1, 1966, Vol. 2, 1974; contbr. articles to profl. jours. Trustee Columbia U., 1990—; bd. dirs. Hastings Ctr., 1981-83. Recipient Columbia Alumni Gold medal, 1980, Disting. Svc. award Am. Coll. Cardiology, 1987, McGovern award Cosmos Club Washington, 1991, John Peters award Am. Soc. Nephrology, 1992. Fellow ACP (master, John Phillips medal 1985), Am. Acad. Arts and Scis.; mem. AMA, Assn. Am. Physicians (coun., pres. 1983-84, Kober medal 1993), Am. Physiol. Soc., Mass. Med. Soc., Inst. Medicine of NAS (coun. 1979-82), Am. Soc. Clin. Investigation (past pres.), Am. Fedn. Clin. Rsch. (past pres.), Phi Beta Kappa (senator 1991—), Alpha Omega Alpha. Office: Brigham and Women's Hosp Dept of Medicine 75 Francis St Boston MA 02115-6110

RELSON, MORRIS, patent lawyer; b. N.Y.C., Apr. 14, 1915; s. Benjamin and Minnie R.; m. Rita L. Rubenstein, Apr. 5, 1941; children—Katherine D., David M., Peter J. BSEE, CCNY, 1935; MA in Math, George Washington U., 1940; JD, NYU, 1945. Bar: N.Y. 1945, U.S. Supreme Ct. 1950. Elec. engr. Nat. Park Svc., Washington, 1936-37; patent examiner U.S. Patent Office, 1937-41; patent agt. and atty. Sperry Gyroscope Co., Gt. Neck, N.Y., 1941-48; ptnr. Darby & Darby P.C., and predecessor, N.Y.C., 1948—; vol. spl. master U.S. Dist Ct. for So. Dist N.Y., 1979-80. Contbr. articles to legal jours. Mem. ABA (patent, trademark and copyright sect.), IEEE, Am. Patent Law Assn., N.Y. Patent Law Assn. (pres. 1976-77, bd. dirs. 1970-78), N.Y. Acad. Sci., Phi Beta Kappa, Sigma Xi., Sigma Pi Sigma. Patentee in field. Home: 27 Tain Dr Great Neck NY 11021-4422 Office: Darby & Darby 805 Third Ave New York NY 10022-7513

REMAK, JEANNETTE ELIZABETH, quality control executive; b. Queens, N.Y., Nov. 23, 1952; d. Bela Alexander and Helen (Almassy) R. Student, N.Y. Inst. Photography, 1971-72; student, Sch. Visual Arts, N.Y.C., 1972-73, CUNY, 1973-76. Cert. photo finishing engr. Photo Mktg. Assn. Prodn. mgr. Rembrandt Color Labs., Jamaica, N.Y., 1976-80; builder, operator Fast Photo, N.Y.C., 1980-83; prodn. mgr. Jackson Photo, N.Y.C., 1983-86; quality control and prodn. mgr. Universal Photo, N.Y.C., 1986—. Paintings exhibited at Internat. Art Challenge Art Show, Calif., 1987; paintings included in (book) American Artists an Illustrated Survey, 1990, USAF Mus., Wright-Patterson AFB, Ohio, the Pentagon, Washington. Contbg. mem. USAF Art Program. Mem. Soc. Photofinishing Engrs., Am. Soc. Aviation Artists, Am. Soc. Sci. Fiction Fantasy Artists, Challenger Ctr. for Edn. (sponsor).

REMAR, ROBERT BOYLE, lawyer; b. Boston, Nov. 19, 1948; s. Samuel Roy and Elizabeth Mary (Boyle) R.; m. Victoria A. Greenhood, Nov. 11, 1979; children: Daniel A.G., William B.G. BA, U. Mass., 1970; JD, Boston Coll., 1974. Bar: Ga. 1974, Mass. 1975, U.S. Ct. Appeals (5th cir.) 1978, U.S. Ct. Appeals (11th cir.) 1981, U.S. Ct. Appeals (2d cir.) 1995, U.S. Supreme Ct. 1981. Staff atty. Ga. Legal Svcs. Program, Savannah, 1974-76, Western Mass. Legal Svcs., Greenfield, 1976-77; sr. staff atty. Ga. Legal Svcs. Program, Atlanta, 1977-82; ptnr. Remar & Graettinger, Atlanta, 1983—, Kirwan, Parks, Chesin & Remar PC, Atlanta, 1993—; bd. dirs., exec. com. ACLU, N.Y.C., pres. Ga. chpt., 1985-87, gen. counsel, 1980-83; hearing officer Ga. Pub. Svc. Commn., Atlanta, 1985—; adj. prof. Ga. State U., Atlanta, 1984—, spl. asst. atty. gen., 1990—; bd. experts Lawyers Alert, Boston, 1985-94. Mem. Ga. Energy Regulatory Reform Commn., Gov. of Ga., 1980-82, Ga. Consumer Adv. Bd., 1981-82; pres. Ga. Consumer Ctr. Inc., 1988-91; bd. dirs., exec. com. Ga. Resource Ctr.; v.p. Ga Ctr. Law Pub. Inst., 1991-94. Mem. ABA (chmn. individual rights access to civil justice com.), ATLA, Ga. Bar Assn. (chmn. individual rights sect. 1981-83, co-chmn. consumer rights and remedies com. 1979-83, chmn. death penalty re. com. 1993—, mem. legis. adv. com. 1994—), Gate City Bar Assn., Lawyers Club Atlanta, Lamar Inn of Ct. (master of the bench). Democrat. Avocations: golf, gardening. Home: 1714 Meadowdale Ave NE Atlanta GA 30306-3114 Office: Kirwan Parks Chesin & Remar 75 14th St Atlanta GA 30309

REMBAR, CHARLES (ISAIAH), lawyer, writer; b. Oceanport, N.J., Mar. 12, 1915; s. Louis S. and Rebecca (Schneider) Zaremba; m. Billie Ann Olsson, Feb. 23, 1944; children: Lance Richard, James Carlson. A.B., Harvard U., 1935; LL.B., Columbia U., 1938. Bar: N.Y. 1938. Atty. govt. agencies, 1938-42, 45; law sec. N.Y. Supreme Ct., 1946; practice law N.Y.C.,

1947—. Author: The End of Obscenity, 1968, Perspective, 1975, The Law of the Land, 1980; Editor: Columbia Law Rev. 1936-38; Contbr. articles to various periodicals. With USAAF, 1942-45. Recipient George Polk Meml. award for outstanding book of 1968, 1969. Mem. Assn. Bar City N.Y. (chmn. spl. com. on communications 1972-78), Authors League, P.E.N. Clubs: Century Assn. (N.Y.C.), Harvard (N.Y.C.). Office: Rembar & Curtis 19 W 44th St New York NY 10036

REMBE, TONI, lawyer; b. Seattle, Apr. 23, 1936; d. Armin and Doris (McVay) R.; m. Arthur Rock, July 19, 1975. Cert. in French Studies, U. Geneva, 1956; LL.B., U. Wash., 1960; LLM in Taxation, NYU, 1961. Bar: N.Y., Wash., Calif. Assoc. Chadbourne, Parke, Whiteside & Wolff, N.Y.C., 1961-63; assoc. Pillsbury, Madison & Sutro, San Francisco, 1964-71, ptnr., 1971—; dir. Potlatch Corp., San Francisco, Pacific Telesis, San Francisco, Am. Pres.. Cos., Ltd., Oakland, Calif., Transamerica Corp., San Francisco. Pres. Van Loben Sels Charitable Found., San Francisco; trustee Am. Conservatory Theatre, San Francisco. Fellow Am. Bar Found.; mem. ABA, Am. Judicature Soc., State Bar Calif., Bar Assn. San Francisco, Commonwealth Club of Calif. (govs. of the club). Office: Pillsbury Madison & Sutro 235 Montgomery St San Francisco CA 94104*

REMENICK, SEYMOUR, artist, educator; b. Detroit, Apr. 3, 1923; s. Oscar and Luba (Shackman) R.; m. Diane Kathryn Thommen, Aug. 30, 1950; children: Richard Vincent, Catherine Ann. Student, Tyles Sch. Fine Arts, Phila., 1940-42, 46, Hans Hofmann Sch., N.Y.C., 1946-48, Pa. Acad. Fine Arts, 1948. Instr. Pa. Acad. Fine Arts, Phila., 1977—;, 1977-96. Exhibited one-man shows: Davis Gallery, N.Y.C., annually, 1954-62, Peridot Gallery, N.Y.C., annually, 1967-71, Pearl Fox Gallery, Pa., 1969, 73, 76, Gross McCleaf Gallery, Phila., 1981, Gallery K, Washington, 1983, (retrospective) Rosemont Coll., Pa., 1983; group shows: 3d Biennial Exhbn., Italy, 1955, Am. Painting, Rome, 1955, Paris exhbn., 1956, 57, Pa. Acad. Fine Arts, 1957, 59, 64, 68, Festival of Arts, Spoleto, 1959, Nat. Acad., 1960, 63, 66, Phila. Mus. Art. Served with U.S. Army, 1942-45, ETO. Recipient Tiffany Found. award NAD, N.Y.C., 1955; recipient Altman Landscape Prize, 1960, Hallmark Purchase award Hallmark Co., 1960. Mem. NAD (academician 1983). Home: 812 Catharine St Philadelphia PA 19147-3902

REMER, DONALD SHERWOOD, chemical engineer, engineering economist, cost estimator, educator, administrator; b. Detroit, Mich., Feb. 16, 1943; s. Nathan and Harriet R.; m. Louise Collen, Dec. 21, 1969; children: Tanya, Candace, Miles. BS, U. Mich., 1965; MS, Calif. Inst. Tech., 1966, PhD, 1970. Registered profl. engr., Calif., Mich., La. Tech. service engr., chem. raw materials div. coordinator, sr. running plan coordinator, task team mgr. Exxon, Baton Rouge, 1970-75; assoc. prof. engring. Harvey Mudd Coll., Claremont, Calif., 1975-79, prof., 1980—, Oliver C. Field prof. engring., dir. Energy Inst., 1981-83; cons., mem. tech. staff, mgr. planning analysis Jet Propulsion Lab., Calif. Inst. Tech., 1976—; co-founder, ptnr. Claremont Cons. Group, 1979—; mem. adv. council Nat. Energy Found., N.Y.C., 1981-85; mem. Inst. Mgmt. Cons., 1988-89. Case study editor Am. Soc. Engring. Edn., Inst. Indsl. Engrs., Engring. Economist, 1977-89; mem. editorial bd. Jour. Engring. Costs and Prodn. Econs., 1985-91, Internat. Jour. Prodn. Econs., 1992—; contbr. articles to profl. jours. Shelter mgr. ARC, Baton Rouge, 1965-70. Recipient Outstanding Chem. Engr. award U. Mich., 1965, First Place Pub. Relations award Am. Inst. Chem. Engring., 1975, Outstanding Alumni Fund Achievement award Calif. Inst. Tech., 1976, Outstanding Young Man of Am. award, 1976, NASA award, 1983, Best Paper of the Year in Jour. Parametrics, Internat. Soc. Parametric Analysts, 1991-92, Centennial award certificate Am. Soc. Engring. Edn., 1993; named Outstanding Research Seminar Speaker Occidental Research Corp., 1976. Mem. Am. Soc. Engring. Mgmt. (bd. dirs. 1981-83), Toastmasters Club (pres. Claremont-Pomona chpt. 1978).

REMER, VERNON RALPH, travel consultant; b. Urbana, Iowa, July 14, 1918; s. Ralph William and Kittie (Weisbard) R.; m. Jane V. Bush, Sept. 19, 1941; children—Richard Charles, Linda Jane (Mrs. A.D. Bleiberg). B.S., U. Iowa, 1939. With Central Life Assurance Co., Des Moines, Iowa, 1939-78; sr. v.p. Central Life Assurance Co., 1972-77; travel cons., 1977—; pres. Urbana Savs. Bank, 1944-64, dir., 1944-67. Precinct committeeman Republican party, 1952-60; mem. Polk County Rep. Central Com., 1953-56. Fellow Life Office Mgmt. Assn.; mem. Life Ins. Mktg. and Research Assn. (dir. 1971-74, chmn. agy. mgmt. conf. com. 1971—), Am. Soc. Travel Agts. (diploma), Sigma Nu. Congregationalist. Clubs: Masons, Des Moines. Home: 13018 Pomard Way Poway CA 92064-1108

REMICK, FORREST JEROME, JR., former university official; b. Lock Haven, Pa., Mar. 16, 1931; s. Forrest Jerome Sr. and Ruth Betsy (Saiers) R.; m. Grace Louise Grove, June 7, 1953; children: Beth Ann Remick Gillio, Eric Forrest. BSME, Pa. State U., 1955, MSME, 1958, PhD in ME, 1963; diploma, Oak Ridge (Tenn.) Sch. Reactor Tech., 1956. Engr. Bell Telephone Labs., Whippany, N.J., 1955-56; dir. nuclear reactor facility Pa. State U., University Park, 1959-65, dir. Inst. Sci. Engring., 1967-79, acting dir. Ctr. Air Environ. Studies, 1976-78, dir. intercoll. research programs, 1979-85, asst. v.p. research, grad. studies, 1979-84, assoc. v.p. research, 1985-89; dir. Curtiss Wright Nuclear Research Lab., Quehanna, Pa., 1960-65; chief tng. sect. dept. tech. assistance IAEA, Vienna, Austria, 1965-67; mem. Nat. Nuclear Accrediting Bd., Inst. Nuclear Power Ops., Atlanta, mem. adv. coun., 1995—; mem. Sci. Adv. Com. Idaho Nat. Engring. Lab., Idaho Falls, 1984-89, Reactor Safety Adv. Com., Savannah River Lab., Aiken, S.C., 1986-89, chmn., 1989; mem. Adv. Com. on Reactor Safeguards, Washington, 1982, vice chmn., 1987-88, chmn., 1989; commr. U.S. Nuclear Regulatory Commn., 1989-94, cons., 1994—; bd. dirs. Pub. Svc. Enterprise Group, Pub. Svc. Electric and Gas; mem. adv. bd. Applied Rsch. Lab., Pa. State U., 1994—. Served to sgt. U.S. Army, 1951-52. Named Outstanding Engring. Alumnus, Pa. State U., 1993; recipient Thomas P. Hamrick award for contbns. to tng. of nuclear facility pers., 1995. Fellow Am. Nuclear Soc. (bd. dirs. 1995—, meml. lectr. award 1971, disting. speaker award 1983); mem. ASME, Am. Soc. Engring. Edn., Nuclear Accrediting Bd. Republican. Lutheran. Home and Office: 305 E Hamilton Ave State College PA 16801-5413

REMICK, OSCAR EUGENE, academic administrator; b. Ellsworth, Maine, Aug. 24, 1932; s. Horace and Blanche (Rich) R.; m. Emma L. Lorance, Dec. 18, 1959; children: Mark Stephen, John Andrew, Paul Thomas. A.B., Ea. Coll., 1954; B.D. magna cum laude, Ea. Bapt. Theol. Sem., 1957; M.A., U.Pa., 1957; Ph.D., Boston U., 1966; student, Columbia U., 1959-61, Andover Newton Theol. Sem., 1957-58, Heidelberg (Germany) U., 1958-59; postdoctoral study, India, 1967; D.D., Assumption Coll., 1971, Allegheny Coll., 1974, Ea. Bapt. Theol. Sem., 1993; LL.D. (hon.), Alma Coll., 1987, Davis and Elkins Coll., 1991; HHD (hon.), Carroll Coll., 1991. Ordained to ministry Presbyn. Ch. (U.S.A.), 1957. Ordained minister United Presbyn. Ch. U.S.A.; minister United Baptist Ch., Topsham, Maine, 1961-63; part-time instr. philosophy Bates Coll., 1962-63; minister First Congregational Ch., Paxton, Mass., 1963-66; asst. prof. philosophy and theology Assumption Coll., 1966-67, assoc. prof., 1967-71, prof. religious studies, 1969-71, v.p., acad. dean, coordinator acad. affairs, 1968-71; co-dir. ecumenical Inst. Religious Studies, 1967-71; Minister theol. studies First Baptist Ch., Worcester, Mass., 1966-71; pres. Chautauqua (N.Y.) Instn., 1971-77; lectr. State U. N.Y., 1972-77, prof. philosophy, dean for arts and humanities, dir. internat. edn., 1977-80; theologian-in-residence First Presbyn. Ch., Jamestown, N.Y., 1974-80; pres. Alma (Mich.) Coll., 1980-87, prof. philosophy and religion, 1980-87; pres., prof. philosophy Westminster Coll., New Wilmington, Pa., 1987—; bd. dirs. Integra North Bank, Titusville, Pa. Author: Value in the Thought of Paul Tillich; Christianity and Other Major Religions, 1968, India and Hinduism, 1968, Responding to God's Call, 1970, The Hidden Crisis in Education, 1971. Pres. Worcester Area Coun. Chs., 1970-71; mem., chmn. Mich. Coun. for the Arts, 1981-87; mem. N.Y. State Coun. on the Arts, 1983-87; mem., chmn. Pa. Coun. on Arts, 1990—; mem. Hoyt Inst. for Arts; bd. dirs. Found. for Ind. Colls. Inc., Jameson Hosp.; bd. dirs., chmn. Pa. Assn. Colls. and Univs.; mem. exec. com., chmn. Pa. Commn. for Ind. Colls. and Univs.; mem. exec. com., chmn. Assn. Presbyn. Colls. and Univs., 1992—. Mem. Am. Philos. Assn., Soc. Advancement Continuing Edn. for Ministry, Am. Assn. for Advancement of Humanities, Paul Tillich Soc. N.Am., Deutsche Paul-Tillich-Gesellschaft, Am. Assn. Higher Edn., Soc. Sci. Study Religion, Am. Acad. Religion, N.Am. Acad. Ecumenists, Soc. for Arts, Religion and Contemporary Culture, Assn. Presbyn. Colls. and Univs. (exec. com., vice chmn.), Nat. Assn. Ind. Colls. and Univs. (commn. on fins., higher edn.), Lawrence County C. of C. (past pres.). Home: 521 S New Castle St New Wilmington PA 16142-1426 Office: Westminster Coll South Market St New Wilmington PA 16172-0001 *The striving for excellence cannot be limited to a single discipline, task, or job. It involves a commitment of such intensity that the quest for excellence must be regarded as a way of life. I have taken a great deal of inspiration from both great artists and athletes whose achievements tell us that even if excellence cannot be readily defined, there is no way it can be approximated or achieved without self-discipline, dedication and commitment.*

REMINE, WILLIAM HERVEY, JR., surgeon; b. Richmond, Va., Oct. 11, 1918; s. William Hervey and Mabel Inez (Walthall) ReM.; m. Doris Irene Grumbacher, June 9, 1943; children: William H., Stephen Gordon, Walter James, Gary Craig. B.S. in Biology, U. Richmond, 1940, D.Sc. (hon.), 1965; M.D., Med. Coll. Va., Richmond, 1943; M.S. in Surgery, U. Minn., Mpls., 1952. Diplomate Am. Bd. Surgery. Intern Doctor's Hosp., Washington, 1944; fellow in surgery Mayo Clinic, Rochester, Minn., 1944-45, 47-52; instr. surgery Mayo Grad. Sch. Medicine, Rochester, Minn., 1954-59, asst. prof. surgery, 1959-65, assoc. prof. surgery, 1965-70, prof. surgery, 1970-83, prof. surgery emeritus, 1983—; surg. cons. to surgeon gen. U.S. Army, 1965-75; surg. lectr., USSR, 1987, 89, Japan, 1988, 90, Egypt, 1990; lectr. Soviet-Am. seminars, USSR, 1987, 89. Sr. author: Cancer of the Stomach, 1964, Manual of Upper Gastro-intestinal Surgery, 1985; editor: Problems in General Surgery, Surgery of the Biliary Tract, 1986; mem. editorial bd. Rev. Surgery, 1965-75, Jour. Lancet, 1968-77; contbr. 200 articles to profl. jours. Served to capt. U.S. Army, 1945-47. Recipient St. Francis surg. award St. Francis Hosp., Pitts., 1976, disting. service award Alumni Council, U. Richmond, 1976. Mem. ACS, AAAS, Am. Assn. History of Medicine, AMA, Am. Med. Writers Assn., Am. Soc. Colon and Rectal Surgeons, Soc. Surgery Alimentary Tract (v.p. 1983-84), Am. Surg. Assn., Assn. Mil. Surgeons U.S., Internat. Soc. Surgery, Digestive Disease Found., Priestley Soc. (pres. 1968-69), Central Assn. Physicians and Dentists (pres. 1972-73), Central Surg. Assn., Soc. Med. Cons. Armed Forces, Mayo Clinic Surg. Soc. (chmn. 1964-66), Soc. Head and Neck Surgeons, Soc. Surg. Oncology, So. Surg. Assn., Western Surg. Assn. (pres. 1979-80), Minn. State Med. Assn., Minn. Surg. Soc. (pres. 1966-67), Zumbro Valley Med. Soc., Sigma Xi; hon. mem. Colombian Coll. Surgeons, St. Paul Surg. Soc., Flint Surg. Soc., Venezuelan Surg. Soc., Colombian Soc. Gastroenterology, Dallas So. Clin. Soc., Ga. Surg. Soc., Soc. Postgrad. Surgeons Los Angeles County, Japanese Surg. Soc., Argentine Surg. Digestive Soc., Bassanese Surg. Assn. (Italy), Tex. Surg. Soc., Omicron Delta Kappa, Alpha Omega Alpha, Beta Beta Beta, Kappa Sigma. Methodist. Avocations: hunting, fishing, golf, photography, boating, music. Home: Sawgrass Players Club 8212 Seven Mile Dr Ponte Vedra Beach FL 32082-3129

REMINGER, RICHARD THOMAS, lawyer; b. Cleve., Apr. 3, 1931; s. Edwin Carl and Theresa Henrietta (Bookmyer) R.; m. Billie Carmen Greer, June 26, 1954; children: Susan Greer, Patricia Allison, Richard Thomas. A.B., Case-Western Res. U., 1953; J.D., Cleve.-Marshall Law Sch., 1957. Bar: Ohio 1957, Pa. 1978, U.S. Supreme Ct. 1961. Personnel and safety dir. Motor Express, Inc., Cleve., 1954-58; mng. ptnr. Reminger & Reminger Co., L.P.A., Cleve., 1958-90; mem. nat. claims couns. adv. bd. Comml. Union Assurance Co., 1980-90; lectr. transp. law Fenn Coll., 1960-62; lectr. bus. law Case Western Res. U., 1962-64; lectr. products liability U. Wirtschaft at Schloss Gracht, Erfstadt-Liblar, Germany, 1990-91, Bar Assn. City of Hamburg, Germany, 1990; mem. faculty Nat. Inst. for Trial Advocacy, 1992. Mem. joint com. Cleve. Acad. Medicine-Greater Cleve. Bar Assn.; trustee Cleve. Zool. Soc., mem. exec. com., 1984-89, v.p., 1987-89; trustee Andrew Sch., 1984-96, Huron Road Hosp., Meridia Huron Hosp., Cleve., Cleve. Sch. for Blind, 1987-88, Cerebral Palsy Assn., 1984-87; trustee Good Samaritan Hosp., Palm Beach, Fla., 1992—, bd. govs., 1992—. With AC, USNR, 1950-58. Named Man of Yr. Cleve.-Marshall Law Sch., 1989. Mem. ABA (com. on law and medicine, profl. responsibility com. 1977-90), FBA, ATLA, Fedn. Ins. and Corp. Counsel, Internat. Ins. Law Soc., Internat. Bar Assn., Ohio Bar Assn. (coun. dels. 1987-90, internat. law com. 1990-91), Pa. Bar Assn., Cleve. Bar Assn. (chmn. med.-legal com. 1978-79, prof. liability com. 1977-90), Transp. Lawyers Assn., Cleve. Assn. Civil Trial Attys., Am. Soc. Hosp. Attys., Soc. Ohio Hosp. Attys., Ohio Assn. Civil Trial Attys., Am. Judicature Soc., Def. Rsch. Inst., Maritime Law Assn. U.S., Am. Coll. Law and Medicine, 8th Jud. Bar Assn. (life Ohio dist.), Internat. Ins. Law Soc., Oil Painters Am. (assoc.), Internat. Soc. Marine Painters (profl. mem.), Lost Tree Property Owners Assn., Mayfield Country Club (pres. 1980-82), Union Club, Hermit Club (pres. 1973-75), Lost Tree Club (bd. govs. 1991-94), Everglades Club (Fla.), Kirtland Counry Club, Rolling Rock Club (Pa.).

REMINGTON, DEBORAH WILLIAMS, artist; b. Haddonfield, N.J., June 25, 1935; d. Malcolm Van Dyke and Hazel Irwin (Stewart) R. BFA, San Francisco Art Inst., 1957. Adj. prof. art Cooper Union, N.Y.C., 1973—, NYU, 1994—. One-woman shows include Dilexi Gallery, San Francisco, 1962, 63, 65, San Francisco Mus. Art, 1964, Bykert Gallery, N.Y.C., 1967, 69, 72, 74, Galerie Darthea Speyer, Paris, 1968, 71, 73, 92, Pyramid Gallery, Washington DC, 1973, 76, zola-Leiberman Gallery, Chgo., 1976, Hamilton Gallery, N.Y.C., 1977, Portland (Oreg.) Ctr. for Visual Arts, 1977, Michael Berger Gallery, Pitts., 1979, Mary Ryan Gallery, N.Y.C., 1982, Ramon Osuna Gallery, Washington D.C., 1983, Newport Harbor Art Mus., 1983, Oakland (Calif.) Mus., 1984, Jack Shainman Gallery, N.Y.C., 1987, Shoshana Wayne Gallery, Los Angeles, 1988; group shows include Whitney Mus. Am. Art, N.Y.C., 1965, 67, 72, San Francisco Mus. Art, 1956, 60, 61, 63, 64, 65, Lausanne Mus., Switz., 1966, Fondation Maeght, St. Paul de Vence, France, 1968, Smithsonial Inst., Washington, D.C., 1968, Art. Inst., Chgo., 1974, Inst. Contemporary Art, Boston, 1975, Nat. Gallery Modern Art, Lisbon, Portugal, 1981, Toledo Mus. Art, 1975, The 6 Gallery, 1954-57, Natsoulas Noveloso Gallery, Davis, Calif., 1990, 1st Trienalle des Ameriques Maubeuge, France, 1993, and numerous others; represented in permanent collections of Whitney Mus. Am. Art, Nat. Mus. Am. Art, Washington, Art Inst., Chgo., Centre d'Art et de Culture Georges Pompidou, Paris,Carnegie Mus., Pitts. Recipient Hassam and Speicher Purchase award Am. Acad. and Inst. Arts and Letters, 1988; NEA fellow, 1979-80; Tamarind Inst. fellow, 1973; Guggenheim fellow, 1984. Home and Office: 309 W Broadway New York NY 10013-2226 *Be aware of yourself, aware of what makes you distinctive from others, and make those individual characteristics part of your work, whatever that may be. Read philosopy. Develop your own. This gives you ballast when the pendulum swings too far in one direction.*

REMINGTON, PAUL JAMES, mechanical engineer, educator; b. Plainfield, N.J., Mar. 19, 1943; s. Elmer Joseph and Genevieve Leona (Kehoe) R.; m. Lynne Louise Harris, Aug. 21, 1965; children: Christopher, Alexander. BSME, MSME, MIT, 1966, PhD, 1970. Prin. engr. Bolt Beranek & Newman Inc., Cambridge, Mass., 1969—; adj. prof. mech. engring. Boston U., 1995; vis. lectr. Tufts U., Medford, Mass., 1979; vis. scientist Tech. U. Berlin, 1990; organizer 3rd Internat. Workshop on Rlwy. and Tracked Transit System Noise, 1981. Contbr. chpts. to: Handbook of Machine Design, 1986, Transportation Noise Reference Book, 1987, Handbook of Acoustics, 1995, also articles to profl. publs. Recipient Cert. of Recognition, NASA, 1976, Excellence in Presentation award Soc. Automotive Engrs., 1984. Fellow Acoustical Soc. Am. (assoc. editor jour. 1982—, nominee Biennial award 1977); mem. ASME, Tau Beta Pi, Pi Tau Sigma (pres. 1964-65). Achievements include development of basic understanding of rolling noise generation, development of approaches for controlling wheel/rail noise from trains. Avocations: hiking, downhill and cross-country skiing, tennis, cabinet making. Office: BBN Sys and Technologies 10 Moulton St Cambridge MA 02138-1119

REMLEY, THEODORE PHANT, JR., counseling educator, lawyer; b. Eustis, Fla., Feb. 7, 1947; s. Theodore Phant Sr. and Era Annie (Forehand) R. BA, U. Fla., 1969, EdS, 1971, PhD, 1980; JD, Catholic U., 1980. Bar: Va. 1981, Fla. 1982; lic. profl. counselor, Va., Miss., La. Exec. dir. Am. Counseling Assn., Alexandria, Va., 1990-94; prof. counseling U. New Orleans, 1994—. Contbr. articles to profl. jours., chpts. to books. Mem. Am. Counseling Assn., Am. Assn. State Counseling Bds. Democrat. Roman Catholic. Home: 3800 Camp St New Orleans LA 70115-2629 Office: Dept Edn Leadership Counseling & Founds U New Orleans New Orleans LA 70148

REMNICK, DAVID J., journalist; b. Hackensack, N.J., Oct. 29, 1958; s. Edward C. and Barbara (Seigel) R.; m. Esther B. Fein; children: Alexander, Noah. AB, Princeton U., 1981. Reporter The Washington Post, 1982-91; staff writer The New Yorker, N.Y.C., 1992—; vis. fellow Coun. Fgn. Rels., N.Y.C., 1992-94. Author: Lenin's Tomb: The Last Days of the Soviet Empire, 1993 (Pulitzer Prize for gen. non-fiction 1994, George Polk award 1994). Recipient Livingston award, 1991, Helen Bernstein award N.Y. Pub. Libr., 1994. Home: 322 W 72nd St New York NY 10023-2676 Office: The New Yorker 20 W 43rd St New York NY 10036-7400*

REMONDI, JOHN F., student aid administrator. Treas. Nellie Mae, Inc., Braintree, Mass. Office: Nellie Mae Inc 50 Braintree Hill Park Braintree MA 02184-8724

REMPEL, GARRY LLEWELLYN, chemical engineering educator, consultant; b. Regina, Sask., Can., Aug. 20, 1944; s. Henry Jacob and Grace Violet (Pullman) R.; m. Flora Tak Tak Ng, Sept. 20, 1975. BSc with 1st class honours, U. B.C., Vancouver, Can., 1965, PhD in Catalysis, 1968. Nat. Rsch. Coun. Can. postdoctoral fellow Imperial Coll. Sci. and Tech., London, 1968-69; asst. prof. chem. engring. U. Waterloo, 1969-73, assoc. prof., 1973-80, prof., 1980—, chmn. dept., 1988—, mem. faculty dept. chemistry, 1976—, cons. Inst. for Polymer Rsch., 1984—, bd. dirs. Waterloo Ctr. for Process Devel., 1988-90; vis. scientist Inst. for Catalysis Rsch., Nat. Ctr. Sci. Rsch., Lyon, France, 1978; vis. rsch. fellow dept. chemistry U. Chgo., 1978-79; dir. applied scis. divsn. Royal Soc. Can.; mem. grant selection com. in chem. and metall. engring. Natural Scis. and Engring. Rsch. Coun., 1992-95; mem. sci. program com. Ont. Ctr. for Materials Rsch., 1991-95, acad. leader polymers and plastic program mgmt. com., 1992-95; cons. Polysar Rubber Corp., Sarnia, Ont., 1981-95, Rempel Rsch. Inc., Waterloo, 1981, Ortho McNeil Inc., Toronto, 1992—, Bayer Rubber Inc., Sarnia, 1995—. Contbr. over 120 articles to profl. jours.; patentee for novel catalyst sys. and methods of preparation, polymer hydrogenation processes, oxidation of polythionates, gas consumption measuring sys., amine modified hydrogeneration of nitrile rubber, nitrile rubber hydrogenation, hydrogenation of nitrile rubber, catalytic hydrogenation of nitrile rubber, catalytic solution hydrogenation of nitrile rubber. Grantee Nat. Scis. and Engring. Rsch. Coun., 1987-88, 90, 92-95, Polysar Ltd., 1987-88, Province of Ont. URIF, 1987-88, 90-92, 93, Nova Husky, 1989-91, Polysar Rubber Corp., 1989-92, 95, Ortho McNeil Inc., 1992-93; recipient Best Rsch. Paper award U. Waterloo Dept. Chem. Engring., 1988, 93, Univ.-Industry Rsch. Partnership award Conf. Bd. Can., 1995. Fellow Royal Soc. Can. (Thomas W. Eadie medal 1993), Chem. Inst. Can.; mem. AIChE, Can. Soc. for Chem. Engring. (award in indsl. practice 1994), Am. Chem. Soc., Soc. Chem. Industry. Office: U Waterloo, Dept Chem Engring, Waterloo, ON Canada N2L 3G1

REMSEN, CHARLES CORNELL, III, microbiologist, educator, research administrator; b. Newark, N.J., May 16, 1937; s. Charles Cornell Jr. and Elizabeth Havens (Atwood) Remsen; children: David Pratt, Linda Remsen Brandenburg, Stephen Dwyer, Andrew Walker; m. Margaret Ellis Fairchild, June 19, 1976; stepchildren: Elizabeth Hoffman Herzog, Jennifer Hoffman Jonas. BS in Food Chemistry and Microbiology, Delaware Valley Coll. Sci. and Agr., 1960; MS in Microbiology, Syracuse U., 1963, PhD in Microbiology, 1965. Rsch. asst. Schering Pharm., Bloomfield, N.J., 1959-60; rsch. asst. dept. preventive medicine Upstate Med. Ctr., Syracuse, N.Y., 1961-63; grad. teaching asst. Syracuse U., 1962-63, grad. rsch. asst., 1963-65; NIH post-doctoral fellow dept. gen. biology Swiss Fed. Inst. Tech., Zurich, Switzerland, 1965-67; asst. scientist Woods Hole (Mass.) Oceanographic Inst., 1967-71, assoc. scientist, 1971-75; rsch. assoc. in microbial ecology Marine Biol. Labs., Woods Hole, 1973-74; assoc. prof. dept. zoology/microbiology, assoc. scientist Ctr. Great Lakes Studies U. Wis., Milw., 1975-83, prof., sr. scientist, 1983—, coord. zoology/microbiology, 1976-84, acting dir. Ctr. Great Lakes Studies, Great Lakes Rsch. Facility, 1987-89, interim dir., 1989-92, dir., 1992—; mem. editorial bd. Jour. of Bacteriology, 1969-77; external examiner McGill U. Grad. Sch., 1971-73; chmn. joint com. for biol. oceanography MIT-WHOI PhD Program, 1971-74; mem. internat. adv. bd. ScienceQuest. Author: (with others) The Encyclopedia of Microscopy and Microtechnique, 1973, Effect of the Ocean Environment on Microbial Activities, 1974, The Phytosynthetic Bacteria, 1978, Responses of Marine Organisms to Pollutants, 1984, Structure of Photosynthetic Prokaryotes, 1991; contbr. articles to profl. jours. Del. Coun. on Ocean Affairs. Recipient NIH Foreign Postdoctoral fellowship, 1965-67, Disting. Svc. award Jour. of Bacteriology, 1977. Mem. Nat. Assn. Marine Labs. (exec. com.), Am. Geophys. Union, Am. Soc. for Microbiology, Internat. Assn. for Great Lakes Rsch., Coun. Great Lakes Rsch. Mgrs. (internat. joint commn.), N.E. Assn. Marine Labs. (co-v.p.), N.E. Assn. Marine and Great Lakes Labs., Nature Conservancy (bd. trustees Wis. chpt. 1987, exec. com. 1989—, sec. 1989—), Sigma Xi. Achievements include research in relating the structure of chemolithotrophs to their ecological niche, and to their response to the environment, methane-oxidizing bacteria and how these microorganisms fit into the overall carbon cycle in the Great Lakes, the study of sediment samples from Lakes Superior, Michigan and Huron in order to determine the extent and rate of organic matter diagenesis in sediments, the exchange of gases (CO2, CH4, O2) with overlying waters and ultimately the atmosphere, the ecological role and significance of chemosynthesis and photosynthesis in sublacustrine hydrothermal vents and gas fumaroles. Office: University of Wisconsin Mil Ctr for Great Lakes Studies Milwaukee WI 53201

REMSEN, JAMES VANDERBEEK, JR., biologist, museum curator; b. Newark, Sept. 21, 1949; s. James V. and Elizabeth (Willox) R.; m. Catherine Cummins, Nov. 12, 1988; 1 child, Kenneth William. BA, Stanford U., 1971, MA, 1971; PhD, U. Calif., Berkeley, 1978. Asst. dir., curator birds, prof. La. State U. Mus. Natural Sci., Baton Rouge, 1978—. Author: Annotated List of the Birds of Bolivia, 1989, (monograph) Community Ecology of Neotropical Kingfishers, 1990; contbr. numerous articles to sci. jours. Fellow Am. Ornithologists Union; mem. AAAS. Doliornis remseni species of bird named after him. Home: 545 Pecan Dr Saint Gabriel LA 70776-5513 Office: La State U Mus Natural Sci Baton Rouge LA 70803

REMY, RAY, chamber of commerce official; b. San Francisco. B in Polit. Sci., Claremont Men's Coll. (now Claremont McKenna Coll.); M in Pub. Adminstrn., U. Calif., Berkeley. Adminstrv. intern City of Berkeley, 1962-63; with So. Office League of Calif. Cities, 1963, then asst. to exec. dir. and mgr., to 1969; exec. dir. So. Calif. Assn. Govt., 1969-76; appointed dep. mayor City of L.A., 1976-84; pres. L.A. Area C. of C., 1984—; president Los Angeles Area C. of C. Bd. dirs. Mus. Sci. and Industry; past chmn. bd. councilors U. So. Calif. Sch. Pub. Adminstrn., L.A.; vice chmn. bd. dirs. Rose Inst. for State and Local Govt.; vice chmn. bd. trustees Claremont (Calif.) McKenna Coll., Calif. Trust for Environment, Bay Delta Adv. Coun.; pres. Inst. for Local Self Govt.; bd. dirs. Rebuild L.A.; chmn. Calif. Trade and Goods Movement Study; mem. bus. adv. com. U.S. Dept. Transp. Recipient numerous awards including Fletcher Bowron award, Donald Stone award, Mus. of Sci. and Industry Fellowship award, others. Mem. Nat. Acad. Pub. Adminstrn., Jr. Statesmen Found., Am. Soc. Pub. Adminstrn. (past pres.). Office: LA Area C of C PO Box 3696 350 S Bixel St Los Angeles CA 90051-1696*

RENARD, KENNETH GEORGE, civil engineer; b. Sturgeon Bay, Wis., May 5, 1934; s. Harry Henry and Margaret (Buechner) R.; m. Virginia Rae Heibel, Sept 8, 1956; children: Kenlynn T., Craig G., Andrew T. BCE, U. Wis., 1957, MCE, 1959, PhD in Civil Engring., U. Ariz., 1972. Registered profl. civil engr., Ariz. Hydraulic engr. Agrl. Rsch. Svc., USDA, Madison, Wis., 1957-59; resident engr. Agrl. Rsch. Svc., USDA, Tombstone, Ariz., 1959-64; rsch. hydraulic engr. Agrl. Rsch. Svc., USDA, Tucson, 1964-72, rsch. leader, 1972-87, rsch. hydraulic engr., 1987—; adj. prof. agrl. and biosys. engring. U. Ariz., Tucson, 1990—. Contbr. articles to profl. jours. Fellow ASCE (pres. Ariz. sect. 1981, exec. com. irrigation and drainage divsn. 1987—, chair 1990, mgmt. group D 1991—, editor Jour. Irrigation and Drainage Engring. 1983-85, John C. Park award 1987, Arid Lands Hydraulic Engr. award 1992), Soil Conservation Soc. Am. (pres. Ariz. sect. 1975, Conservationist of Yr. 1983), Am. Geophys. Union; mem. Lions (pres. Tombstone chpt. 1963). Roman Catholic. Home: 4822 E Paseo Del Bac Tucson AZ 85718-6708 Office: USDA Agrl Rsch Svc 2000 E Allen Rd Tucson AZ 85719-1520

RENAUD, BERNADETTE MARIE ELISE, author; b. Ascot Corner, Que., Can., Apr. 18, 1945; d. Albert and Aline (Audet) R.; m. Pierre La Brosse,

1973. Diploma, Présentation de Marie, Granby, Que., 1962-64. Librarian asst. Schs. of Waterloo, Que., 1964-67; tchr. primary schs. Schs. of Waterloo, 1967-70; adminstrv. sec. Assn. Medi-Tech-Sci., Montreal, Que., 1972-76. Author: Emilie La Baignoire A Pattes, 1976 (Can. Coun. Children's Lit. prize 1976, Assn. Advancement of Scis. and Technics of Documentation award 1976); adaptations of 8 children's classics, 1977; 20 Short Stories for Young Children, 1978, 79, 80, Le Chat de l'Oratoire, 1978, Emilie la baignoire à pattes album, 1978, La maison tête de pioche, 1979, La rèvolte de la courte pointe, 1979; mem. adminstrv. bd.: Communication-Jeunesse, 1977-82, Consil culturel de la Montèrègie, 1987-90; author: La dèpression de l'ordinateur, 1981, Une boîte Magique Très Embètante, 1981, The Cat in the Cathedral, 1983, La grande question de Tomatelle, 1982, The Computer Revolts, 1984, Comment on fait un livre?, 1983; author (book and movie) Bach et Bottine, 1986 (awards for movie, 17 awards across the world, transl. into 7 langs., and subtitled into 8 langs.); (novel) Un Homme Comme Tant d'Autres, tome I 1992, tome II, 1993, tome III, 1994; (short movie for Nat. Film Bd. of Can.) Quand l'accent devient grave, 1989; dir., coord. Écrirè pour la jeunesse project, 1990.

RENBARGER, LARRY D., prefabricated housing manufacturing executive. Pres., CEO Shelter Components Corp., Elkhart, Ind. Office: Shelter Components Corp 27217 County Road 6 Elkhart IN 46514-5601*

RENCIS, JOSEPH JOHN, engineering educator, mechanical/civil engineer; b. Denville, N.J., May 19, 1958; s. Joseph John and Leila Jean (Colin) R.; m. Minerva Vasquez, Sept. 14, 1991; 1 child, Christina. AAS in Archtl. & Bldg. Constrn. Engring., Milw. (Wis.) Sch. Engring., 1978, BS in Archtl. & Bldg. Constrn. Engring., 1980; MS in Theoretical & Applied Mechanics, Northwestern U., 1982; PhD in Engring. Mechanics, Case Western Res. U., 1985. Registered profl. engr., Mass. Engring. technician U.S. Army Armament Rsch., Devel. and Engring. Ctr., Picatinny Arsenal, N.J., summer 1979; instr., grader dept. archtl. & bldg. constrn. engring. tech. Milw. (Wis.) Sch. Engring., 1979-80; rsch. asst. dept. civil engring. Northwestern U., Evanston, Ill., 1980-81; rsch. and tchg. asst. dept. civil engring. Case Western Res. U., Cleve., 1982-85; grad. student rschr. Flight Dynamics Lab. Wright-Patterson AFB, Dayton, Ohio, summer 1984; instr. engring. tech. dept. Cuyahoga C.C., Cleve., 1984; asst. prof. mech. engring. dept. Worcester (Mass.) Poly. Inst., 1985-90, assoc. prof. mech. engring. dept., 1990-95, asso. prof., Russel M. Searle disting. instr. mech. engring., 1994—; engring. cons. Brooks Sci., Inc., Cambridge, Mass., 1986-89; ASEE-NASA faculty fellow NASA-Lewis Rsch. Ctr., Cleve., summers 1989, 90; rsch. assoc. Phillips Lab., Geophysics Directorate, Space Sys. Tech. br., Hanscom AFB, Mass., summer 1991; mem. adv. bd. for engring. tech. Sussex County Vocat. Tech. H.S., Sparta, N.J., 1994—. Editl. bd. mem. Boundary Elements Commn., Computational Mechanics Publs., Southampton, U.K., 1989—; editl. bd. mem. Engring. Analysis with Boundary Elements, Elsevier Applied Sci., London, U.K., 1993—; contbr. articles to profl. jours. Recipient Class of 1980 Outstanding Alumni award Milw. (Wis.) Sch. Engring., 1990, Citizen of the Yr. award West Boylston (Mass.) Sch. Sys., 1992; Walter P. Murphy fellow Northwestern U., Evanston, 1980-81. Mem. ASME (sec. Ctrl. Mass. sect. 1988-89, vice-chair 1989-90, chair 1990-92), ASCE (structural divsn. com. on electronic computation, subcom. on personal computers and work stas. 1986-91), Internat. Soc. for Boundary Elements (sci. steering com. 1989—), Am. Soc. Engring. Edn., Am. Acad. Mechanics, Internat. Assn. for Boundary Element Methods, Pi Tau Sigma, Tau Omega Mu. Roman Catholic. Achievements include pioneering work on error estimation and self-adaptive mesh refinement technique for Boundary Element Method; research on iterative/direct equation solving strategies for Boundary Element Method. Home: 8 Merlin Ct Worcester MA 01602 Office: Worcester Poly Inst Mech Engring Dept 100 Institute Rd Worcester MA 01609

RENDA, DOMINIC PHILLIP, airline executive; b. Steubenville, Ohio, Dec. 25, 1913; s. Joseph J. and Catherine (Roberta) R.; m. Delores E. Noland, July 12, 1980; children: Dominique Patricia, Dominic Phillip, Patrick Blake. B.S. in Bus. Adminstrn; J.D., Ohio State U., 1938. Bar: Ohio 1938. Practice law Steubenville, 1938-41; adminstrv. asst. to mem. Congress, 1941-42; with Western Air Lines, Inc., Los Angeles, 1946-68; asst. sec. Western Air Lines, Inc., 1947, v.p. legal, 1954-65, sr. v.p. legal, corp. sec., 1958-68; pres. Air Micronesia, Inc., Los Angeles, 1968-73; sr. v.p. internat. and pub. affairs Continental Air Lines, Inc., 1968-73; exec. v.p., dir., mem. exec. com. Western Air Lines, 1973-76, pres., mem. exec. and nominating coms., 1976-81, chief exec. officer, mem. mgmt. resources and compensation com., 1979-81, chmn. bd., 1981, emeritus chmn., 1982-85; dir. Bank of Montreal, Calif.; Mem. bus. adminstrn. adv. council Coll. Adminstrv. Sci., Ohio State U., 1974-82; bd. councilors Sch. Internat. Relations, U. So. Calif., 1967-82. Trustee Peace Found., Ponape, Caroline Islands, 1976-84; chmn. devel. com. Marymount High Sch., 1977-82. Served to lt. comdr. USNR, 1942-46. Mem. Calif., Ohio state bars, ABA, Los Angeles County Bar Assn. (past trustee), Calif. C. of C. (dir.), Phi Alpha Delta (pres. Los Angeles 1965-66). Clubs: Los Angeles Chancery (pres. 1966-67), Bel-Air Country, Calif.

RENDA, RANDOLPH BRUCE, university dean emeritus; b. Tokat, Turkey, Mar. 31, 1926; came to U.S., 1945, naturalized, 1956; s. Abdurrahman and Adviye (Adams) R.; m. Martha McDowell Hill, Aug. 30, 1948; children: William, Susan, Bennett, Lyle, Bruce. B.S., Purdue U., 1952, M.S., 1957, Ph.D. (Proctor and Gamble fellow), 1959. Project engr. Nat. Castings Co., Indpls., 1951-53; instr. mfg. processes Purdue U., Lafayette, Ind., 1953-55; instr. mech. engring. Purdue U., 1955-59; asst. prof. U. Ky., 1959-60, Swarthmore (Pa.) Coll., 1960-61; assoc. prof. U. Ky., 1961-65; prof., chmn. mech. engring. U. Louisville, 1966-72; assoc. dean, dir. U. Louisville (Inst. Indsl. Research), 1972-74; dean Sch. Engring. and Tech., Purdue U. at Indpls., 1974-94; dean, prof. emeritus, 1994—; Cons. Spindletop Research, Inc., Lexington, Ky., Besmar Assos., Knoxville, Pratt & Whitney Co., West Hartford, Conn., Glove Valve Co., Delphi, Ind. Trustee St. Francis Sch., Louisville, 1968-70. Mass. Inst. Tech. summer fellow, 1960; NSF fellow, 1961; NASA/Case Inst. summer fellow, 1964, 65. Mem. ASME (pres. 1969), Louisville Engring. Socs. Coun., Am. Soc. Engring. Edn., Nat. Soc. Profl. Engrs., Ky. Soc. Profl. Engrs., Soc. Engring. Sci., Sigma Xi, Sigma Tau, Pi Tau Sigma. Clubs: Rotarian, Columbia. Home: 8639 Bay Colony Dr Indianapolis IN 46234-2912

RENDA, ROSA A., special education educator; b. Jamaica, N.Y., Nov. 3; d. Liborio and Josephine (Finamore) Lombardo; m. Philip F. Renda, Mar. 30, 1980; children: Felicia-Anne, Philip Jr., Heather. BA, Molloy Coll., 1971; MEd, St. John's U., Jamaica, N.Y., 1973; postgrad., L.I. U., 1977. Tchr., asst. prin. St. Rose of Lima, Massapequa, N.Y., 1967-73, Acad. of St. Joseph, Brentwood, N.Y., 1973-79; tchr. Sewanhaka H.S., Floral Park, N.Y., 1979-81, Queen of the Rosary Acad., Amityville, N.Y., 1981-86; tchr. Blessed Trinity, Ocala, Fla., 1987-93, math. coord., 1993-94; S.E.D. tchr. Emerald Ctr., Ocala, Fla., 1994; tchr. adult edn. for the emotionally/mentally disturbed Marion Citrus Mental Health, Ocala, 1994—. Author: Teaching Metrics, 1975. Vol. Nassau County Rep. Club, Hempstead, N.Y., 1974-76. Mem. ASCD, NEA, Nat. Coun. Tchrs. Math., Nat. Cath. Edn. Assn., Nassau/Suffolk Math. Tchrs., Women of the Moose, Columbiettes, K.C. Aux. Roman Catholic. Avocations: reading, swimming, gourmet cooking.

RENDALL, STEVEN FINLAY, language educator, editor, translator, critic; b. Geneva, Ill., May 2, 1939; s. Harvard John and Jessie Evangeline (Galbraith) R.; children from previous marriage: Matthew, Ruby Larisch; m. Lisa Dow Neal, May, 1992; 1 child, Josephine Dow Neal. BA summa cum laude in Philosophy, U. Colo., 1961; postgrad., Univ. de Lille, 1961-62, Johns Hopkins U., 1962-67; PhD, Johns Hopkins U., 1967. From asst. prof. romance langs. to assoc. prof. romance langs. U. Oreg., Eugene, 1967-79, prof. romance langs., 1979—; guest prof. Universität Konstanz, 1981; leader NEH summer seminar, 1987. Author: Distinguo: Reading Montaigne Differently, 1992; editor: Montaigne, 1984, Of History, 1994; translator: The Practice of Everyday Life, 1984, History and Memory, 1992, Astrea, 1995, Hitler, 1996, Torments of Love, 1996, Shipwreck with Spectator, 1996; co-editor: Comparative Literature, 1990—, assoc. editor 1978—, asst. editor, 1972-78, acting editor, 1980, 85-86; mem. editl. bd., adv. com. Montaigne Studies, 1989—; contbr. 35 articles to profl. jours., 37 book revs. Rsch. on Translation SUNY, Binghamton, 1993, Camargo Found. fellow, 1988, Alexander von Humboldt-Stiftung Rsch. fellow, 1980-82, 95, NEH fellow, 1977, Danforth fellow, 1962-67, Gilman fellow, 1964-67, Woodrow Wilson fellow, 1962-63; Fulbright scholar, 1961-62. Mem. Modern Lang. Assn., Phi Beta Kappa. Home: 3217 N 25th St Tacoma WA 98406-6115 Office: U Oregon 223 Friendly Hall Eugene OR 97403

RENDELL, EDWARD GENE, mayor, lawyer; b. N.Y.C., Jan. 5, 1944; s. Jesse T. and Emma (Sloat) R.; B.A. in Polit. Sci., U. Pa., 1965; J.D., Villanova (Pa.) U., 1968; m. Marjorie Osterlund, July 10, 1971; 1 son, Jesse Thompson. Admitted to Pa. bar, 1968, U.S. Supreme Ct., 1981; asst. dist. atty., chief homicide unit Office Dist. Atty. Phila., 1968-74; dep. spl. prosecutor Phila., 1976; dist. atty. Phila., 1978-86; mayor City of Phila., 1992—. Served as 2d lt. USAR, 1968-74. Recipient Man of Year award VFW, 1980, Am. Cancer League, 1981; Disting. Public Service award Pa. County Detectives Assn., 1981. Mem. Am. Bar Assn., Pa. Dist. Attys. Assn. (legis. chmn. 1979—), Phila. Bar Assn., United Jewish Orgns., Jewish War Vets, Democrat. Club: B'nai B'rith. Office: Office of the Mayor 215 City Hall Philadelphia PA 19107-3201*

RENDELL, MARJORIE O., federal judge; m. Edward G. Rendell. BA, U. Pa., 1969; postgrad., Georgetown U., 1970-71; JD, Villanova U., 1973; LLD (hon.), Phila. Coll. Textile and Sci., 1992. Ptnr. Duane, Morris & Heckscher, Phila., 1972-93; judge U.S. Dist. Ct. (ea. dist.) Pa., 1994—; asst. to dir. annual giving Dept. Devel., U. Pa., 1973-78; mem. adv. bd. Chestnut Hill Nat. Bank/East Falls Adv. Bd.; mem. alternative dispute resolution com. mediation divsn. Ea. Dist. Pa. Bankruptcy Conf. Active Acad. Vocal Arts, Market St. East Improvement Assn., Pa.'s Campaign for Choice, Phila. Friends Outward Bound; vice chair Ave. of Arts, Inc.; vice chair bd. trustees Vis. Nurse Assn. Greater Phila. Mem. ABA, Am. Bankruptcy Inst., Pa. Bar Assn., Phila. Bar Assn. (bd. dirs. young lawyers sect. 1973-78), Phila. Bar Found. (bd. dirs.), Forum Exec. Women, Internat. Women's Forum, Phi Beta Kappa. Office: US Courthouse 601 Market St Rm 3114 Philadelphia PA 19106-1510

RENDELL-BAKER, LESLIE, anesthesiologist, educator; b. St. Helens, Eng., Mar. 27, 1917; came to U.S., 1957, naturalized, 1963; s. Frank Nelder and Ada (Gill) Rendell-B.; m. Rosemary Carr Hogg, Aug. 17, 1946; children: Sheila Diane, Helen Rosemary, Frances Nelda. BS, MB, Guy's Hosp. Med. Sch., London, 1941. Diplomate: Am. Bd. Anesthesiology. Resident anesthesia Brit. Army of Rhine Hosps., 1945-46, Guy's Hosp., London, 1946-48; sr. asst. (assoc. prof.) anesthesiology Welsh Nat. Sch. Medicine, Cardiff, 1948-57; Fulbright asst. prof. anesthesiology U. Pitts., 1955-56; from asst. prof. to assoc. prof. Sch. Medicine Case Western Res. U., Cleve., 1957-62; dir. dept. anesthesiology Mt. Sinai Hosp., N.Y.C., 1962-79; prof., chmn. dept. anesthesiology Mt. Sinai Sch. Medicine, CUNY, 1966-79; prof. dept. anesthesiology Sch. Medicine Loma Linda (Calif.) U., 1979—; Chmn. sect. com. Z79 standards for anesthesia and respiratory equipment Am. Nat. Standards Instn., 1962-68, vice chmn., 1969-81, mem. exec. com. med. devices standards mgmt. bd., 1973-79, bd. dirs., 1976-79; chmn. classification panel on anesthesiology devices FDA, 1972-76. Author: (with W.W. Mushin) Principles of Thoracic Anesthesia, 1953, (with W.W. Mushin and Thompson) Automatic Ventilation of the Lungs, 3d edit., 1980; editor: Problems with Anesthetic and Respiratory Therapy Equipment, 1982, Maintenance, Cleaning and Sterilization of Anesthetic Equipment, 1993, Future Directions in Anesthesia Apparatus, 1993, The History and Evolution of Pediatric Anesthesia Equipment, 1992; author (with others) The Care of Anesthesia Equipment, 1992. Served to capt. Royal Army Med. Corps, 1942-46. Fellow Royal Coll. Anaesthetists; fellow Royal Soc. Medicine, Assn. Anaesthetists Gt. Britain and Ireland; mem. Am. Soc. Anesthesiologists (chmn. com. equipment and standardization 1962-68), Am. Soc. for Testing and Materials (chmn. subcom. D10-34 1981-91), Assn. Advancement Med. Instrumentation , AAAS. Inventor baby endotracheal connector, pediatric face masks and equipment. Home: 630 Beauregard Cres Redlands CA 92373-5602 Office: Loma Linda U Sch Medicine Dept Anesthesiology 11234 Anderson St Loma Linda CA 92354-2804

RENDL-MARCUS, MILDRED, artist, economist; b. N.Y.C., May 30, 1928; d. Julius and Agnes (Hokr) Rendl. BS, NYU, 1948, MBA, 1950; PhD, Radcliffe Coll., 1954; m. Edward Marcus, Aug. 10, 1956. Economist, GE, 1953-56, Bigelow-Sanford Carpet Co., Inc., 1956-58; lectr. econs. evening sessions CCNY, 1953-58; rsch. investment problems in tropical Africa, 1958-59; instr. econs. Hunter Coll. CUNY, 1959-60; lectr. econs. Columbia U., 1960-61; rsch. econ. devel. Nigeria, West Africa, 1961-63; sr. economist Internat. div. Nat. Indsl. Conf. Bd., 1963-66; asst. prof. Grad. Sch. Bus. Adminstrn., Pace Coll., 1964-66; assoc. prof. Borough of Manhattan C.C., CUNY, 1966-71, prof., 1972-85; vis. prof. Fla. Internat. U., 1986; prin. MRM Assocs., Rendl Fine Art; corp. art econ. and contemporary art cons.; fine arts appraiser; artist Allied Social Sci. Assn. Conf., Boston, 1994; participant Internat. Econ. Meeting, Amsterdam, 1968, Prague, Czech Republic, 1993, Brussels, 1994, Econs. of Fine Arts in Age of Tech., 1984, Internat. Economic Assn. N.Am., Laredo, Tex., 1987-88, London, 1994, Soc. Southwestern Economists, San Antonio, 1988, New Orleans, 1989, Dallas, 1989, Houston, 1991, Dallas, 1994, S.W. Soc. Economists, San Antonio, 1992, Dallas, 1994, San Diego, 1990, 92, Reno, 1991, Western Econ. Assn. Internat., 1990, Ind. U. Pa., 1990, London, 1992-93, Ariz. Sr. Acad., Tucson, 1995. Exhibited New Canaan Art Show, 1982-85, Am. Soc. of Bus. and Behavioral Scis, Las Vegas, 1996, New Canaan Soc. for Arts Ann., 1983, 85, New Canaan Arts, 1985, Silvermine Galleries, 1986, Stamford Art Assn., 1987, Women in the Arts at Phoenix Gallery, Group Show, N.Y.C., 1988, Parkview Point Gallery, Miami Beach, Fla., 1982-89, Art Complex, New Canaan, Miami Beach, 1985—; group shows include Lever House, N.Y.C., 1990, Cork Gallery, Lincoln Ctr., N.Y.C., 1990, Women's Caucus for Art, San Antonio, 1990, Artist's Equity, Broome St. Gallery, N.Y.C., 1991, Greater Hartford Architecture Conservancy, 1991; symposium participant Sienna, Italy, 1988, South Fla. Art Ctr., Miami Beach, 1990, 92-93, Wadsworth Atheneum, Hartford, Conn., 1994-95, Annual Barnum Festival, 1995, Discovery Mus., Bridgeport, Conn., 1995. Bd. dirs. N.Y.C. Coun. on Econ. Edn., 1970—; mem. program planning com. Women's Econ. Roundtable, N.Y.C.; participant Eastern Econ. Assn., Boston, 1988, Art and Personal Property Appraisal, NYU, 1986-88. Recipient Disting. Svc. award CUNY, 1985; Dean Bernice Brown Cronkhite fellow Radcliffe Coll., 1950-51, Anne Radcliffe Econ. Rsch. Sub-Sahara Africa fellow, 1958-59. Fellow Gerontol. Assn.; mem. Internat. Schumpeter Econs. Soc. (founding), Am. (vice chmn. ann. meeting 1973), Met. (sec. 1954-56) econ. assns., Indsl. Rels. Rsch. Assn., Audubon Artists and Nat. Soc. Painters in Casein (assoc. 1987-88) Allied Social Sci. Assn. (vice chmn. conv. 1973, artist Boston nat. conv. 1994), AAUW, N.Y.C. Women in Arts, Allied Social Sci. Assn. (artist 1994), Women's Econ. Roundtable, Greater Hartford Architecture Conservancy, NYU Grad. Sch. Bus. Adminstrn. Alumni (sec. 1956-58), Radcliffe Club, Women's City Club (art and landmarks com.). Author: (with husband) Investment and Development of Tropical Africa, 1959, International Trade and Finance, 1965, Monetary and Banking Theory, 1965; Economics, 1969; (with husband) Principles of Economics, 1969; Economic Progress and the Developing World, 1970; Economics, 1978, Fine Art with Many Equilibrium Prices, 1995; also monographs and articles in field. Econ. and internat. rsch. on industrialization less developed areas, internat. debtor nations and workability of buffer stock schemes, pricing fine art; columnist economics of art, Art As An Investment, Money Substitute, or Consumer Durable Good Art Valuation; When Is A Price of Fine Art The Price?, Prices and Varied Appraisals, Fine Art with Many Equilibrium Prices: Price Distortion-A Segmented Market in Fine Art, Am. Soc. of Bus. and Behavioral Sci. (Las Vegas Ann. Meeting 1996); editor Women in the Arts Found. Newetter, 1986-92; contbr. Coalition Womens Art Orgs., 1986-92, other profl. publs. Home: PO Box 814 New Canaan CT 06840-0814 Office: Art Complex PO Box 814 New Canaan CT 06840-0814 also: 7441 Wayne Ave Miami FL 33141

RENDU, JEAN-MICHEL MARIE, mining executive; b. Tunis, Tunisia, Feb. 25, 1944; s. Paul C. and Solange M. (Krebs) R.; m. Karla M. Meyer, Aug. 18, 1973; children: Yannick P., Mikaël P. Ingénieur des Mines, Ecole des Mines St. Etienne, France, 1966; MS, Columbia U., 1968, D. Engring. Sci., 1971. Mgr. ops. rsch. Anglovaal, Johannesburg, Republic of South Africa, 1972-76; assoc. prof. U. Wis., Madison, 1976-79; assoc. Golder Assocs., Denver, 1979-84; dir. tech. and sci. systems Newmont Mining Corp., Danbury, Conn., 1984-88; v.p. Newmont Gold Co., Denver, 1988—. Author: An Introduction to Geostatistical Methods of Mineral Evaluation, 1978, 81; contbr. tech. papers to profl. jours. Recipient Jackling award medal SMME, 1994. Fellow South African Inst. of Mining and Metallurgy (corr. mem. of coun.); mem. N.Y. Acad. Sci., Internat. Assn. for Math. Geology, Soc. Mining Engrs., Sigma Xi. Roman Catholic. Office: Newmont Gold Co 1700 Lincoln St Denver CO 80203-4501

RENEAU, DANIEL D., university administrator. Prof., head dept. biomed. engring. La. Tech. U., Ruston, 1973-80, v.p. acad. affairs, 1980-87, pres., 1987—. Office: La Tech U Tech Station RR 6 Ruston LA 71270

RENEBERG, RICHARD (RICHEY RENEBERG), professional tennis player; b. Phoenix, Oct. 5, 1965; m. Marget Reneberg, Nov. 16, 1991. Student, SMU, 1985-87. Ranked 10th U.S. Tennis Assn., 1991, ranked 8th U.S. Tennis Assn., 1993. Named All-American NCAA, 1985, 86, 87; winner of U.S. Open Men's Double Title (with Jim Grabb), 1992; mem. U.S. Davis Cup Team, 1993, (with Jared Palmer) Australian Open Men's Doubles Title, 1995, 8 U.S. Junior Titles, 2 Profl. Singles Titles.

RENEE, LISABETH MARY, art educator, artist; b. Bklyn., July 28, 1952; d. Lino P. and Elizabeth M. (Dines) Rivano; m. John S. Witanowski, May 15, 1982. Student, U. Puget Sound, 1972-74; BA in Art, SUNY, Buffalo, 1977; MFA, L.I. U., 1982; EdD, U. Ctrl. Fla., 1996. Cert. art tchr., Fla. Adj. faculty L.I. U., Greenvale, N.Y., 1980-82, Rollins Coll., Winter Park, Fla., 1982; art tchr. Phyllis Wheatley Elem. Sch., Apopka, Fla., 1983-85, McCoy Elem. Sch., Orlando, Fla., 1985-86, Lake Howell H.S., Winter Park, Fla., 1986-93; adj. faculty U. Ctrl. Fla., 1994-95, vis. instr., 1995-96; gallery dir., instr. West Campus Valencia (Fla.) C.C., 1996—; adj. faculty Valencia C.C., 1995-96; dir. So. Artists' Registry, Winer Park, 1984-87; cons. Fla. Dept. Edn., 1989-90, mem. curriculum writing team for arts end. program; mem. com. Fla. Bd. Edn. Task Force for Subject Area Subtest of Fla. Tech. Cert. Exam.; visual arts dir. Very Spl. Arts Ctr. Fla. Fest, 1996; presenter at profl. confs. Author: The Phenomenological Significance of Aesthetic Communion, 1996; editor: Children and the Arts in Florida, 1990. Visual arts dir. Very Spl. Arts Ctrl. Fla. Festival, 1995; mem. local Sch. Adv. Coun., Winter Park, 1992. Recipient Tchr. Merit award Walt Disney World Co., 1990; grantee Found. for Advancement of Cmty. Throught Schs., 1991, Divsn. Blind Svcs. Invision, 1995, Tangelo Park Project, 1995; ACE scholar Arts Leadership Inst., 1993-95. Mem. NEA, ASCD, Nat. Art Edn. Assn., Fla. Art Edn. Assn. (regional rep. 1989-94), Seminole County Art Edn. Assn., Coll. Art Assn., Caucus on Social Theory and Art Edn., Women's Caucus for Art, Phi Kappa Phi, Kappa Delta Pi. Home: 20 Cobblestone Ct Casselberry FL 32707-5410 Office: Valencia CC West Campus Humanities Dept MC 4011 Orlando FL 32803

RENEGAR, DELILAH A., chiropractor, educator; b. Great Falls, Mont., May 16, 1963; d. Clarence Arthur and Ruth Eloise (Campbell) R.; m. James Stephen Bowman, Oct. 5, 1991. BA in Psychology, U. Ctrl. Fla., 1985; BS in Human Biology, Nat. Coll. Chiropractic, Lombard, Ill., 1986, DC, 1988. Assoc. physician Wymore Chiropractic, Winter Park, Fla., 1989-90; prin. DuPage Chiropractic, Lisle, Ill., 1990—; lectr. chiropractic Nat. Coll. Chiropractic, Lombard, 1993—; cons. physician Oak Brook Terrace (Ill.) Police, 1992—. Precinct committeeperson Lisle Twp., 1992-94. Mem. NOW (v.p. DuPage County 1992-93), Lisle Jaycees (v.p. 1994—), Rotary Club Lisle, Lisle Women's Club. Avocations: reading, rollerblading. Office: DuPage Chiropractic Assocs 1045 Burlington Ave Lisle IL 60532-1887

RENEHAN, ROBERT FRANCIS XAVIER, Greek and Latin educator; b. Boston, Apr. 25, 1935; s. Francis Xavier and Ethel Mary (Sullivan) R.; m. Joan Lee Axtell-Damerow, Sept. 9, 1966; children—Martin, Sharon, Stephen, Judith, John. A.B., Boston Coll., Chestnut Hill, Mass., 1956; A.M., Harvard, 1958, Ph.D., 1963. Instr. Greek and Latin U. Calif. at Berkeley, 1963-64; instr. Harvard U., 1964-65; asst. prof. Boston Coll., 1966-69, assoc. prof., 1969-71, prof., 1971-77, chmn. dept. classical studies, 1969-77; prof. Greek and Latin U. Calif. at Santa Barbara, 1976—, chmn. dept., 1984-88, 93—. Author: Greek Textual Criticism, 1969, Leo Medicus, 1969, Greek Lexicographical Notes, 1975, 2d series, 1982, Studies in Greek Texts, 1975; assoc. editor Classical Philology, 1976—, Am. Jour. Philology, 1987-95; sr. mem. editl. bd. Classical Antiquity, 1980-87; contbr. articles to profl. jours. Nat. Endowment for Humanities Sr. fellow, 1972-73. Mem. Am. Philol. Assn., Soc. for Ancient Medicine. Office: Dept of Classics Univ of Calif Santa Barbara CA 93106

RENEKER, MAXINE HOHMAN, librarian; b. Chgo., Dec. 2, 1942; d. Roy Max and Helen Anna Christina (Anacker) Hohman; m. David Lee Reneker, June 20, 1964 (dec. Dec. 1979); children: Sarah Roeder, Amy Johannah, Benjamin Congdon. BA, Carleton Coll., 1964; MA, U. Chgo., 1970; DLS, Columbia U., 1992. Asst. reference libr. U. Chgo. Libraries, 1965-66; classics libr. U. Chgo. Libr., 1967-70, asst. head acquisitions, 1970-71, personnel libr., 1971-73; personnel/bus. libr. U. Colo. Libr., Boulder, 1978-80; asst. dir. sci. and engring. div. Columbia U., N.Y.C., 1981-85; assoc. dean of univ. librs. for pub. svcs. Ariz. State U. Libr., Tempe, 1985-89; dir. instrnl. and rsch. svcs. Stanford (Calif.) Univ. Librs., 1989-90; dir. info. svcs., dir. Dudley Knox Libr. Naval Postgrad. Sch., Monterey, Calif., 1993—; acad. libr. mgmt. intern Coun. on Libr. Resources, 1980-81; chmn. univ. librs. sect. Assn. Coll. and Rsch. Librs., 1989-90. Contbr. articles to profl. jours. Rsch. grantee Coun. on Library Resources, Columbia U., 1970-71, fellow, 1990-92. Mem. ALA, Am. Soc. Info. Sci., Sherlockian Scion Soc., Phi Beta Kappa, Beta Phi Mu. Home: 740 Dry Creek Rd Monterey CA 93940-4208 Office: Naval Postgrad Sch Dudley Knox Libr 411 Dyer Rd Monterey CA 93943-5198

RENFREW, CHARLES BYRON, oil company executive, lawyer; b. Detroit, Oct. 31, 1928; s. Charles Warren and Louise (McGuire) R.; m. Susan Wheelock, June 28, 1952 (div. June 1984); children: Taylor Allison Ingham, Charles Robin, Todd Wheelock, James Bartlett; m. Barbara Jones Orser, Oct. 6, 1984; 5 stepchildren. AB, Princeton U., 1952; JD, U. Mich., 1956. Bar: Calif. 1956. Assoc. Pillsbury, Madison & Sutro, San Francisco, 1956-65, ptnr., 1965-72, 81-82; U.S. dist. judge No. Dist. Calif., San Francisco, 1972-80; dep. atty. gen. U.S. Washington, 1980-81; instr. U. Calif. Boalt Hall Sch. Law, 1977-80; v.p. law Chevron Corp. (formerly Standard Oil Co. Calif.), San Francisco, 1983-93, also bd. dirs.; ptnr. LeBoeuf, Lamb, Greene & McRae, San Francisco, 1994—; mem. exec. com. 9th Cir. Jud. Conf., 1976-78, congl. liaison com. 9th Cir. Jud. Council, 1976-79, spl. com. to propose standards for admission to practice in fed. cts. U.S. Jud. Conf., 1976-79; chmn. spl. com. to study problems of discovery Fed. Jud. Ctr., 1978-79; mem. council on role of cts. U.S. Dept. Justice, 1978-83; mem. jud. panel Ctr. for Pub. Resources, 1981—; head U.S. del. to 6th UN Congress on Prevention of Crime and Treatment of Offenders, 1980; co-chmn. San Francisco Lawyers Com. for Urban Affairs, 1971-72, mem., 1983—; bd. dirs. Internat. Hospitality Ctr., 1961-74, pres., 1967-70; mem. adv. bd. Internat. Comparative Law Ctr., Southwestern Legal Found., 1983-93; trustee World Affairs Council No. Calif., 1984-87, 94—, Nat. Jud. Coll., 1985-91, Grace Cathedral, 1986-89. Contbr. articles to profl. jours. Bd. fellow Claremont U., 1986-94; bd. dirs. San Francisco Symphony Found., 1964-80, pres., 1971-72; bd. dirs. Coun. Civic Unity, 1962-73, pres., 1971-72; bd. dirs. Opportunity Through Ownership, 1969-72, Marin County Day Sch., 1972-74, No. Calif. Svc. League, 1975-76, Am. Petroleum Inst., 1984—, Nat. Crime Prevention Coun., 1982—; alumni trustee Princeton U., 1976-80; mem. vis. com. u. chgo. Law Sch., 1977-79, u.Mich. Law Sch., 1977-81; bd. visitors J. Reuben Clark Law Sch., Brigham Young U., 1981-83, Stanford Law Sch., 1983-86; trustee Town Sch. for Boys, 1972-80,pres. 1975-80; gov. San Fransciso Symphony Assn., 1974—; mem. nat. adv. bd. Ctr. for Nat. Policy, 1982—; bd. dirs. Nat. Coun. Crime and Deliquency, 1981-82,NAACP Legal Def. and Edn. Fund, 1982—; parish chancellor St. Luke's Episcopal Ch., 1968-71, sr. warden, 1974-76; mem. exec. coun. San Francisco Deanery, 1969-70; mem. diocesan coun. Episcopal Diocese of Calif., 1970; mem. adv. coun. Epsicopal Ch. Found., 1974—; chmn. Diocesan Conv., 1977, 78, 79. Served with USN, 1946-48, 1st lt. U.S. Army, 1952-53. Fellow Am. Bar Found.; mem. ABA (coun. mem. sect. antitrust law 19778-82, vice c hmn. sect. antitrust law 1982-83), San Francisco Bar Assn. (past bd. dirs.), Assn. Gen. Counsel, State Bar Calif., Am. Judicature Soc., Am. Coll. Trial Lawyers (pres. 1995—), Am. Law Inst., Coun. Fgn. Rels., Order of Coif, Phi Beta Kappa, Phi Delta Phi. Office: LeBoeuf Lamb Greene & MacRae 4th fl One Embarcadero Ctr San Francisco CA 94111

RENFREW, MALCOLM MACKENZIE, chemist, educator; b. Spokane, Wash., Oct. 12, 1910; s. Earl Edgar and Elsie Pauline (MacKenzie) R.; m. Carol Joy Campbell, June 26, 1938. B.S., U. Idaho, 1932, M.S., 1934, D.Sc., 1976; Ph.D., U. Minn., 1938. Asst. physics U. Idaho, 1932-33, Asst.

chemistry, 1933-35; Asst. chemistry U. Minn., 1935-37, duPont fellow, 1937-38; research chemist plastics dept. duPont Co., 1938-44, supr. process devel., 1944-46, supr. product devel., 1946-49; head chem. research dept., research labs. Gen. Mills, Inc., 1949-52, dir. chem. research, 1952-53, dir. chem. research and devel., 1953-54; dir. research and devel. Spencer Kellogg & Sons, Inc., 1954-58; phys. sci. div. head, prof. chemistry U. Idaho, 1959-73, prof., 1973-76, emeritus, 1976—; dir. U. Idaho (Coll. Chem. Cons. Service), 1969-76; on leave as sr. staff asso. Adv. Council Coll. Chemistry, Stanford, 1967-68; mem. materials adv. bd. Nat. Acad. Scis.; exec. v.p. Idaho Research Found., 1977-78, patent dir., 1978-88. Editor: Safety in the Chemical Laboratory, Vol. IV, 1981, (with Peter Ashbrook), Safe Laboratories: Principles and Practices for Design and Remodeling, 1991; safety editor: Jour. Chem. Edn, 1977-91; Contbr. to tech. and trade publs. on plastics, coatings, safety, chem. edn. Recipient Excellence in Teaching award Chem. Mfrs. Assn., 1977, Outstanding Achievement award U. Minn., 1977; named to U. Idaho Hall of Fame, 1977. Fellow AAAS, Am. Inst. Chemists; mem. Am. Chem. Soc. (councilor 1948, 59, 67-89 , chmn. paint varnish and plastics div. 1949, chmn. chem. mktg. and econs. div. 1958-59, chmn. chem. health and safety div. 1982, James Flack Norris award 1976, Chem. Health and Safety award 1985, Mosher award 1986), Am. Inst. Chem. Engrs., Soc. Chem. Industry, Phi Beta Kappa, Sigma Xi, Phi Kappa Phi, Sigma Pi Sigma, Phi Gamma Delta (disting. Fiji 1986). Presbyterian. Home: 1271 Walenta Dr Moscow ID 83843-2426

RENFRO, ANNA STURGIS, principal; b. Gastonia, N.C., Mar. 30, 1957; d. Harry L. and Iris (Fouché) Sturgis; m. Don Hugh Renfro Jr., July 19, 1980. MusB, Mars. Hill Coll., 1979; math. cert., Wingate Coll., 1984; MEd, Queens Coll., Charlotte, N.C., 1990; adminstrn. cert., U. N.C., Charlotte, 1991. Choral dir. T.C. Roberson High Sch., Skyland, N.C., 1979-80; primary reading asst. Alderman Elem. Sch., Wilmington, N.C., 1980-81; chpt. I reading asst. Parkwood Mid. Sch., Monroe, N.C., 1981-82; 5th grade tchr. Southview Acad., Wadesboro, N.C., 1984-85; math. tchr. Anson Jr. High Sch., Wadesboro, 1985-87; math. tchr., dept. chmn. Highland Jr. High Sch., Gastonia, N.C., 1987-92; asst. prin. Cramerton (N.C.) Jr. High Sch., 1992-93, Crammerton (N.C.) Jr. High Sch., 1993-94, Springfield Elem. Sch., Stanley, N.C., 1993-94; prin. Cramerton Jr. H.S., 1994—. Editorial advisor Scholastic MATH Mag., 1986-90. Recipient awards NASA, NSTA, NCTM, Kennedy Space Ctr., 1989. Mem. ASCD, NEA, N.C. Assn. Educators, Nat. Coun. Tchrs. Math., N.C. Coun. Tchrs. Math., Delta Omicron. Avocation: golf. Home: 2212 Monticello Dr Gastonia NC 28056-6568 Office: Cramerton Jr High Sch 236 8th Ave Cramerton NC 28032-1228

RENGARAJAN, SEMBIAM RAJAGOPAL, electrical engineering educator, researcher, consultant; b. Mannargudi, Tamil Nadu, India, Dec. 12, 1948; came to U.S., 1980; s. Srinivasan and Rajalakshmi (Renganathan) Rajagopalan; m. Kalyani Srinivasan, June 24, 1982; children: Michelle, Sophie. BE with honors, U. Madras, India, 1971; MTech, Indian Inst. Tech., Kharagpur, 1974; PhD in Elec. Engring., U. N.B., Fredericton, Can., 1980. Mem. tech. staff Jet Propulsion Lab., Pasadena, Calif., 1983-84; asst. prof. elec. engring. Calif. State U., Northridge, 1980-83, assoc. prof., 1984-87, prof., 1987—; vis. rschr. UCLA, 1984-93, vis. prof., 1987-88; cons. Hughes Aircraft Co., Canoga Park, Calif., 1982-87, NASA-Jet Propulsion Lab., Pasadena, 1987-90, 92-94, Ericsson Radar Electronics, Sweden, 1990-92, Martin Mariette, 1995; guest rschr. Chalmers U., Sweden, 1990, UN Devel. Program, 1993, Rome Lab., USAF, summer 1995. Contbr. sci. papers to profl. publs. recipient Outstanding Faculty award Calif. State U., Northridge, 1985, Disting. Engring. Educator or Yr. award Engrs. Coun., L.A., 1995, Meritorious Performance and profl. Promise award, 1986, 88, Merit award San Fernando Valley Engrs., Coun., 1989, cert. of recognition NASA, 1991, 92; Nat. Merit scholar Govt. India, 1965-71. Fellow Inst. Advancement Engrs., IEEE (L.A. chpt. sec., treas. antennas and propagation soc. 1981-82, vice chmn. 1982-83, chmn. 1983-84), Internat. Union Radio Sci. (U.S. nat. com.), The Electromagnetics Acad. Avocations: swimming, camping, jogging, tennis. Office: Calif State U 18111 Nordhoff St Northridge CA 91330-0001 *Personal philosophy: I wish to contribute to the society through my work in science and technology.*

RENICK, KYLE, artistic director; b. St. Louis, Apr. 24, 1948; s. Mark Allen and Annabelle (Myers) R. B.A. magna cum laude, Tufts U., 1970. Sr. fund acct. New Eng. Mchts. Nat. Bank, Boston, 1970-73; fund acct. Fidelity Mgmt. and Research Corp., Boston, 1973; bus. mgr. American Place Theatre, N.Y.C., 1973-78; producing dir. WPA Theatre, N.Y.C., 1977-82, artistic dir., 1982—; pres. WPA Prodns., Inc., N.Y.C., 1987—; trustee Alliance of Resident Theatres-N.Y., 1982-92; cons. N.Y. State Council on Arts, 1982-85, Nat. Endowment for Arts, 1986. Producer Steel Magnolias, 1987, The Lady In Question, 1989; contbr. articles to profl. publs. Recipient spl. award for outstanding achievement Drama Desk Assn., 1983. Mem. N.Y. Zool. Soc., Soc. Preservation Film Music, Phi Beta Kappa. Club: The Players (N.Y.C.), The Packard Club. Avocations: early music; record collecting. Home: 2 Bethune St Apt 4B New York NY 10014-1860 Office: WPA Theatre 519 W 23rd St New York NY 10011-1102

RENK, CAROL ANN, secondary education educator; b. Elizabeth, Pa., May 19, 1937; d. Benjamin Franklin and Anna Jeannette (Carnahan) Smart; m. Ralph Charles Renk, Oct. 5, 1961 (dec. May 1965); 1 child, Tracy Renk Caldwell. BS in Biol. Scis., U. Pitts., 1959, MEd, 1970. Cert. secondary edn. biol. and social scis. Tchr. Quaker Valley Schs., Leetsdale, Pa., 1959-60, Pitts. City Schs., 1960-94; liaison tchr. South Hills H.S., 1984-86. Coach Pleasant Hills (Pa.) Area Recreation Assn., 1970-73. NSF grantee, 1965. Mem. Pitts. Fedn. Tchrs., Am. Legion, Allegheny Club, Alpha Delta Kappa (state, local office 1969-73), Beta Beta Beta, Alpha Psi Omega, Delta Zeta (sec. 1958-59). Republican. Methodist. Home: 349 Tara Dr Pittsburgh PA 15236-4318

RENN, ERIN MCCAWLEY, museum administrator; b. Fort Sheridan, Ill., Oct. 23, 1934; d. John Clifford and Frances (Lenfestey) McCawley; divorced; children: Cecilia Frances Renn, Tracy Renn Mattox. BS in History and Art, Fla. State U., 1956, MA in European History and Humanities, 1967, PhD in Early 19th Century European History, 1970; post-doctoral study, Brown U., 1974. Adj. asst. prof. Wheeling (W.Va.) Coll., 1970-77, Bethany (W.Va.) Coll., 1970-77; staff asst. LeMoyne Art Found., Tallahassee, Fla., 1977-78; asst. prof. Valdosta (Ga.) State Coll., 1978-79; lectr. U. Md., Japan, Okinawa, the Azores, Spain, Germany, England, 1979-84; coord. grad. program in East Anglia U. Md., 1982-84; site adminstr. Deutschheim State Historic Site, Mo., 1984—; cons. 1840's Korthauer House and Mus. Project Bensenville (Ill.) Hist. Commn., 1990—, German Inn and Garden, Conner Prairie, Fishers, Inc., Naperville Settlement, Ill., Zoar Cmty., Ohio, travelling exhibit Cole Camp, 1992. Author: (books) The Breads, Cakes, Cookies, Sweets and Special Foods of a Missouri German Christmas, 1991, Weihnachtsgebäck, -konfect, und -speisen—The Breads, Cakes, Cookies, Sweets and Special Foods of a Midwest German Christmas, 1994; contbr. chpts. to books and articles to jours. in field. Mem. bd. dirs. Mo. Folklore Soc., 1988-91, 92—, pres. 1991-92, Mo. Mus. Assocs., 1988092, Mo. Alliance for Historic Preservation, 1989—, Hermann Area C. of C., 1985-86, Hermann Fine Arts Coun., 1987—; chair street entertainment Hermann Maifest Coun., 1988, 89; program chair Gasconade County Hist. Soc., 1992-93. Recipient Ford Found. Asian Studies grantee Fla. State U., 1964, Rsch. grantee Mil. Hist. Inst. Valdosta State Coll., Carlisle Barracks, Pa., 1979, Mil. Hist. Inst., 1979; U. Rsch. fellow Fla. State U., 1967-68, Dissertation fellow Coll. of Arts and Scis., 1968-69. Mem. Am. Assn. Mus., Am. Assn. State and Local History, Am. Livestock Breeds Conservancy, German Am. Heritage Soc., German Am. Soc., Carondelet Hist. Soc., Soc. German Am. Studies, German Studies Assn., Midwest Mus. Conf., Midwest Open Air Mus. Coord. Coun., Midwest Registrars Com., Assn. for Living Historical Farms and Agrl. Mus., Vernacular Architecture Forum. Avocations: reading, music, travel. Office: Deutschheim State Hist Site 109 W 2nd St Hermann MO 65041-1045

RENNELS, MARSHALL LEIGH, neuroanatomist, biomedical scientist, educator; b. Marshall, Mo., Sept. 2, 1939; s. Ivory P. and Alfrieda S. Rennels; m. Margaret Ann Baker, Dec. 28, 1971. B.S., Eastern Ill. U., 1961; M.A., U. Tex.-Galveston, 1964, Ph.D., 1966. Asst. prof. anatomy U. Md., Balt., 1966-71; assoc. prof., 1971-79, prof., 1979—, dir. MD/PhD Program, 1989—. Contbr. articles to sci. jours. Mem. AAAS, Am. Assn. Anatomists, Soc. Neurosci., Soc. Cerebral Blood Flow and Metabolism. Office: U Md Sch Medicine Dept Anatomy Baltimore MD 21201

RENNER, GERALD ANTHONY, journalist; b. Phila., June 5, 1932; s. Walter C. and Marie (Watson) R.; m. Jacquelyn Breen, Sept. 7, 1957; children: Margaret, Anne Victoria, Mary X., Andrea, John. BS, Georgetown U., 1959. Reporter UPI, Washington, 1956, Reading (Pa.) Eagle, 1959-65; assoc. info. dir. Nat. Conf. Cath. Bishops, Washington, 1965-67; dir. pub. rels. NCCJ, N.Y.C., 1967-69; exec. dir. regional NCCJ, Ill., Md., 1969-76; mng. editor Religious News Svc., N.Y.C., 1976-79, editor, dir., 1979-84; religion writer Hartford (Conn.) Courant, 1985—. With USN, 1951-55. Office: Hartford Courant Co 285 Broad St Hartford CT 06155-2510

RENNER, ROBERT GEORGE, federal judge; b. Nevis, Minn., Apr. 2, 1923; s. Henry J. and Beatrice M. (Fuller) R.; m. Catherine L. Clark, Nov. 12, 1949; children: Robert, Anne, Richard, David. BA, St. John's U., Collegeville, Minn., 1947; JD, Georgetown U., 1949. Bar: Minn. 1949. Pvt. practice Walker, 1949-69; U.S. atty. Dist. of Minn., 1969-77, U.S. magistrate, 1977-80, U.S. dist. judge, 1980—. Mem. Minn. Ho. of Reps., 1957-69. Served with AUS, 1943-46. Mem. ABA, Fed. Bar Assn. Roman Catholic. Office: US Dist Ct 748 US Courthouse 316 Robert St N Saint Paul MN 55101-1423

RENNER, SIMON EDWARD, steel company executive; b. Florence, S.C., Feb. 5, 1934; s. Simon Samson and Ruby (Pickett) R.; m. Katherine May Schneider, May 10, 1958; children: Katherine Leah, J. Eric, Philip E., S. Todd. BS, Yale U., 1956; diploma, Carnegie Mellon U., 1972. Gen. mgr. specialty steel Jones & Laughlin Steel Corp., Pitts, 1973-74; gen. mgr. basic steel Jones & Laughlin Steel Corp., Pitts., 1974-75, v.p. prodn., 1975-77, pres. eastern div., 1977-79, corp. v.p., 1979-86; pres. LTV R.R.'s, 1986-94; v.p. LTV Steel, 1994—; pres. LTV R.R.s, 1994—. Vice pres. Allegheny Trails council, Boy Scouts Am.; pres. Quigley High Sch. Bd. End., Baden, Pa., 1982. Capt. USMC, 1956-59. Mem. Am. Iron and Steel Inst. (chmn. mfg. com. 1980-82), Assn. Iron and Steel Engrs., Am. Short Line RR Assn. (bd. dirs.). Republican. Clubs: Duquesne (Pitts.); Allegheny Country (Sewickley, Pa.); Harvard-Yale-Princeton. Home: 104 Willow Rd Sewickley PA 15143 Office: LTV RRs 3600 2d Ave 25 W Prospect Ave Cleveland OH 44115-1000

RENNERFELDT, EARL RONALD, farmer, rancher; b. Epping, N.D., July 10, 1938; s. Carl John and Margaret E. (Long) R.; m. Lois Ann Thune, Sept. 12, 1959; children: Charysse Renee, Carter Ryan. Student, NDSSS, Wahpeton, N.D., 1958. Farmer/rancher Williston, N.D. Mem. N.D. Ho. of Reps., Bismarck, 1991—; mem. Lake Sacajawea Planning Bd., Williston, N.D., 1992; mem. Am. Legis. Exch. Coun., 1991-92; adv. bd. N.D. State U. Exptl.. Sta.; bd. dirs. Mercy Med. Found. With U.S. Army, 1962-64. Recipient Harvest Bowl award N.D. State U., 1988; named Outstanding Young Farmer C. of C., 1972. Mem. Am. Legion, N.D. Grain growers, N.D. Durum Growers, Williston C. of C., N.D. Stockmen's Assn., Elks. Republican. Evangelical Free Ch. Avocations: antiques, golf. Home and Office: 1704 Rose Ln Williston ND 58801-4362

RENNERT, IRA LEON, heavy manufacturing executive; b. 1934. BA, Bklyn. Coll., 1954; MBA, NYU, 1956. Credit analyst M. Lowenstein Corp., N.Y.C., 1956-57; salesman Underwood Corp., N.Y.C., 1957-58; registered rep. Francis I. Dupont & Co., N.Y.C., 1958-60; established I.L. Rennert & Co., Inc. (formerly Rubin, Rennert & Co., Inc.), N.Y.C., 1960-64; cons. N.Y.C., 1964-75; pres. Consolidated Sewing Machine Corp., N.Y.C., 1975—; pres., ceo Renco Group, Inc., N.Y.C., 1980—; ceo WCI Steel Inc., Warren, Ohio, 1988—; chmn. bd. Am. Gen. Corp., South Bend, Ind., 1992. Office: Renco Group 30 Rockefeller Plaze New York NY 10112*

RENNERT, OWEN MURRAY, physician, educator; b. N.Y.C., Aug. 8, 1938; s. David Rennert and Frieda (Weinsteiner) Sommer; m. Sandra Serota, Mar. 22, 1964; children: Laura, Rachel, Ian. BS, BA, U. Chgo., 1957, MD, 1961, MS in Biochemistry, 1963. Diplomate Am. Bd. Pediatrics, Am. Bd. Genetics, Am. Bd. Med. Genetics. Assoc. prof. pediatrics U. Fla., Gainesville, 1968-71, prof. pediatrics and biochemistry, 1971-78; prof. biochemistry, prof. and head dept. pediatrics U. Okla., Oklahoma City, 1977-88; chief pediatrics service and head genetics, endocrinology and metabolics Okla. Children's Mem. Hosp., Oklahoma City, 1977-88; prof., chmn. dept. pediatrics Georgetown U. Sch. Medicine, Washington, 1988—. Co-author: Metabolism of Trace Metals in Man: Developmental Biology and Genetic Implications (2 vols.), 1983; contbr. articles to profl. jours. Bd. dirs. Children's Med. Research, Oklahoma City, 1984-88. Served to sr. surgeon USPHS, 1964-66. Named Clin. Scientist of Yr., Am. Assn. Clin. Scientists, 1978. Mem. Am. Pediatric Soc., Am. Acad. Pediatrics, Soc. Pediatric Research, Am. Coll. Clin. Nutrition, Biochem. Soc., Am. Soc. Molecular Biology and Biochemistry. Office: Georgetown U Childrens Med Ctr Dept Pediatrics 3800 Reservoir Rd NW Washington DC 20007-2196 also: Georgetown U Sch Medicine 3900 Reservoir Rd NW Washington DC 20007-2187

RENNIE, JOHN COYNE, aerospace company executive; b. Boston, May 30, 1937; s. John Christopher and Mary Elizabeth (Coyne) R.; m. Carol Jane Hornbeck, July 12, 1958; children: John P., Kathleen M., Carol L., Steven M., Michele H. BS in Engring., U.S. Naval Acad., 1958; MS in Engring. Mgmt., Northeastern U., Boston, 1971; diploma, Harvard Bus. Sch., 1975. Cert. exptl. test pilot. Sr. systems engr. Raytheon Co., Bedford, Mass., 1967-68; chmn., CEO, bd. dirs. Pacer Systems, Inc., Billerica, Mass., 1968—; bd. dirs. Prospect Assocs., Inc., Rockville, Md. Author, editor: Exportise, 1983, 4th edit., 1993; patentee in field. Pres. Smaller Bus. Assn. New Eng., Waltham, Mass., 1982-84; chmn. Profl. Svcs. Coun., Washington, 1987-88, Mass. Bus. Alliance for Edn., 1989—; pres. Small Bus. Found. Am., Boston, 1985—. Named Small Bus. Person of Yr. New Eng., SBA, 1983, Small Bus. Exporter of Yr. Mass. 1985. Mem. Nat. Small Bus. United (dir., pres. 1992-93), Nat. Security Indsl. Assn. (v.p. 1985—), U.S. Naval Acad. Alumni Assn. (trustee 1983—), Mass. Industry-Edn. Partnership Com. (chmn. 1987-88), U.S. C. of C. (dir. 1984-89), City Club. Democrat. Roman Catholic. Avocations: stamp collecting, golf, reading. Home: 18 Harvard Dr Bedford MA 01730-1020 Office: Pacer Systems Inc 900 Technology Park Dr Billerica MA 01821-4125

RENNIE, PAUL STEVEN, science administrator, biochemist; b. Toronto, Ont., Can., Feb. 9, 1946; m. Carol Andrews, 1968; 1 child, Jan. BSc, U. Western Ont., 1969; PhD in Biochemistry, U. Alta., 1973. Rsch. assoc. U. Alta., 1975-76, asst. prof. medicine, 1976-79, assoc. prof., 1979; rsch. scientist B.C. Cancer Agy., 1979-92, dir. rsch., 1992—; prof. surgery U. B.C., 1986—. Med. Rsch. Coun. rsch. fellow Imperial Cancer Rsch. Fund, 1973-75; rsch. scholar Nat. Cancer Inst. Can., 1976-79. Mem. Can. Soc. Clin. Investigation, Biochem. Soc., Endocrine Soc. Achievements include research on biochemical control of growth in androgen responsive organs and neoplasms; genetic markers in breast cancer. Office: B C Cancer Agy, 600 W 10th Ave, Vancouver, BC Canada V5Z 4E6

RENNINGER, MARY KAREN, librarian; b. Pitts., Apr. 30, 1945; d. Jack Burnell and Jane (Hammerly) Gunderman; m. Norman Christian Renninger, Sept. 3, 1965 (div. 1980); 1 child, David Christian. B.A., U. Md., 1969, M.A., 1972, M.L.S., 1975. Tchr. English West Carteret High Sch., Morehead City, N.C., 1969-70; instr. in English U. Md., College Park, 1970-72; head network services Nat. Libr. Svc., Libr. of Congress, Washington, 1974-78, asst. for network support, 1978-80; mem. fed. women's program com. Libr. of Congress, Washington, 1978-80; chief libr. divsn. Dept. Vets. Affairs, Washington, 1980-90; chief serial and govt. publs. divsn. Libr. of Congress, Washington, 1991—, mem. fed. libr. com., 1980-90, mem. exec. adv. bd., 1985-90; mem. USBE pers. subcom., 1982-84; bd. regents Nat. Libr. of Medicine, 1986-90, mem. outreach panel, 1988-89; fed. libr. task force for 1990 White House Conf. on Librs., 1986-90; liaison to The White House Conf. Med. Libr. Assn., 1989-90. Recipient Meritorious Svc. award Libr. of Congress, 1974, Spl. Achievement award, 1976, Performance award VA, ann. 1982-89, Adminstr.'s Commendation, 1985, Spl. Contbn. award, 1986. Mem. ALA (Govt. Documents Roundtable), Libr. Tech. Assn., Med. Libr. Assn. (govt. rels. com. 1985—), D.C. Libr. Assn., Soc. Applied Learning Tech., Med. Interactive Videodisc Consortium, Govt. Documents Roundtable, Knowledge Utilization Soc., Nat. Multimedia Assn. Am., U.S. Tennis Assn., Phi Beta Kappa, Alpha Lambda Delta, Beta Phi Mu. Home: 840 College Pky Rockville MD 20850-1931 Office: Libr of Congress Ser and Govt Pub Divsn LM 133 Washington DC 20540

RENO, JANET, federal official, lawyer; b. Miami, Fla., July 21, 1938; d. Henry and Jane (Wood) R. A.B. in Chemistry, Cornell U., 1960; LL.B., Harvard U., 1963. Bar: Fla. 1963. Assoc. Brigham & Brigham, 1963-67; ptnr. Lewis & Reno, 1967-71; staff dir. judiciary com. Fla. Ho. of Reps., Tallahassee, 1971-72; cons. Fla. Senate Criminal Justice Com. for Revision Fla.'s Criminal Code, spring 1973; adminstrv. asst. state atty. 11th Jud. Circuit Fla., Miami, 1973-76, state atty., 1978-93; ptnr. Steel Hector and Davis, Miami, 1976-78; atty. gen. Dept. Justice, Washington, 1993—; mem. jud. nominating commn. 11th Jud. Circuit Fla., 1976-78; chmn. Fla. Gov.'s Council for Prosecution Organized Crime, 1979-80. Recipient Women First award YWCA, 1993. Mem. ABA (Inst. Jud. Adminstrn. Juvenile Justice Standards Commn. 1973-76), Am. Law Inst., Am. Judicature Soc. (Herbert Harley award 1981), Dade County Bar Assn., Fla. Pros. Atty.'s Assn. (pres. 1984-86). Democrat. Office: Dept Justice 10th & Constitution Ave NW Washington DC 20530

RENO, JENNIFER, principal. Prin. Western Hills Elem. Sch., Lawton, Okla. Recipient Elem. Sch. Recognition award U.S. Dept. Edn., 1989-90. Office: Western Hills Elem Sch 5402 NW Kinyon Ave Lawton OK 73505-4653

RENO, JOHN F., communications equipment company executive; b. Peoria, Ill., June 15, 1939; s. John Henkle and Alice Hanna (Findley) R.; m. Suzanne McKnight, Apr. 18, 1964; children: David, Anne. AB, Dartmouth Coll., 1961; MBA, Northwestern U., 1963. Ptnr. G.H. Walker & Co., Boston, 1968-74; divsn. pres. Dynatech Cryomedical Co., Burlington, Mass., 1974-79; corporate v.p. Dynatech Corp., Burlington, 1979-82, group v.p., 1982-87, pres., COO, 1987-93, pres., CEO, 1993—; bd. dirs. Millipre Corp., Bedford, Mass. Trustee Boston Mus. of Sci., 1992—; bd. dirs. Boston Ptnrs. in Edn., CEOs for Fundamental Change in Edn., Cambridge, Mass. Named Entrepreneur of Yr., Inc. mag., 1995. Avocation: oil painting. Office: Dynatech Corp 3 N.E. Executive Park Burlington MA 01803

RENO, JOSEPH HARRY, retired orthopedic surgeon; b. Allentown, Pa., Mar. 5, 1915; s. Harvey Luther and Olive May (Wilson) R.; m. Maude Olivia Mutchler, June 27, 1942; children: Joseph David, Sally Jo, Diana Jane, Deborah Marion. Student, Temple U., 1934-37, MD, 1941. Intern. Chester (Pa.) Hosp., 1941-42; residency Tex. Scottish Rite Hosp. for Crippled Children, Dallas, 1942-43, 44-45, Robert Packer Hosp., Sayre, Pa., 1943-44; assoc. Homer Stryker, M.D., Kalamazoo, 1945-46; pvt. practice Bethlehem, Pa., 1946-71, Flagstaff, Ariz., 1971-93; team physician Lehigh U., Bethlehem, 1946-70, No. Ariz. U., Flagstaff, 1971-77, Ariz. State U., Tempe, 1977-84; chief surg. staff Flagstaff Hosp., 1975. Contbr. articles to profl. jours.; prodr. surg. films for Am. Acad. Ortho. Surgeons and others, 1952-70. Pres. Coconino County Easter Seal Soc., 1973; bd. dirs., med. advisor Ariz. Easter Seal Soc., 1974-84. Recipient Pioneer award Ariz. Med. Assn., 1981, Cert. of Appreciation, Pa. Dept. Health Crippled Children's Div., 1971; Dr. Joseph Reno Sports Medicine award named in honor, No. Ariz. State U. and Blue Cross Blue Shield, 1986. Fellow Am. Acad. Ortho. Surgeons, Am. Assn. for Surgery of Trauma, Am. Coll. Sports Med., Am. Coll. Surgeons (chmn. Lehigh Valley subcom. on trauma 1954-66, Ea. Pa. chpt. pres. 1969); mem. NRA, Am. Bd. Ortho. Surgery (cert., diplomate 1948), Coconino County Med. Soc. (pres. 1976), Western Ortho. Assn., Babcock Surg. Soc., Phi Chi, Alpha Tau Omega. Home: 621 Beal Rd Flagstaff AZ 86001-3008

RENO, ROGER, lawyer; b. Rockford, Ill., May 16, 1924; s. Guy B. and Hazel (Kinnear) R.; m. Janice Marie Odelius, May 17, 1952; children: Susan Marie, Sheri Jan Reno-Rudolph, Michael Guy. Student, Kenyon Coll., 1943-44, Yale U., 1944, U. Wis., 1946; A.B., Carleton Coll., 1947; LL.B., Yale U., 1950. Bar: Ill. 1950. Practiced in Rockford, 1950; assoc. firm Reno, Zahm, Folgate, Lindberg & Powell, 1950-56, partner, 1956-84, of counsel, 1984—; chmn. Amcore Fin. Inc., 1982-95; atty. Rockford Bd. Edn., 1955-64. Past pres., bd. dirs. Childrens Home Rockford; trustee Swedish-Am. Hosp. Assn., 1967-77, Keith Country Day Sch. Served to 1st lt. USAAF, 1943-46. Mem. ABA, Ill. Bar Assn., Winnebago County Bar Assn. (pres. 1979-80). Republican. Methodist. Club: Forest Hills Country (Rockford). Home: 2515 Chickadee Trl Rockford IL 61107 Office: Reno Zahm Folgate Lindberg & Powell Amcore Fin Plaza Rockford IL 61104

RENO, RUSSELL RONALD, JR., lawyer; b. Gary, Ind., Nov. 28, 1933; s. Russell Ronald Sr. and Katherine Narcissus (White) R.; m. Mary Ellen Klock, Jan. 30, 1956; children: Mary Hall, Russell III, William, Elizabeth. AB, Haverford Coll., 1954; JD, U. Pa., 1957. Bar: Md. 1957, D.C. 1983. Assoc. Venable, Baetjer & Howard, Balt., 1958-66, ptnr., 1966—; asst. atty. gen. State of Md., Balt., 1962-64. Author: Maryland Real Estate Law-Practice, 1983. Bd. dirs. Balt. Choral Arts Soc., 1966—; trustee Goucher Coll., Balt., 1978—; chancellor Episcopal Diocese of Md., Balt., 1985—; bd. mgrs. Haverford Coll., 1990—. Fellow Am. Bar Found., Md. Bar Found.; mem. ABA, Md. State Bar Assn., Am. Coll. Real Estate Lawyers, Hamilton St. Club, Wednesday Law Club. Home: 706 W Joppa Rd Baltimore MD 21204-3810 Office: Venable Baetjer & Howard 2 Hopkins Plz Baltimore MD 21201-2930

RENOUF, EDDA, artist; b. Mexico City, June 17, 1943; d. Edward and Catharine (Smith) R.; m. Alain Middleton, Sept. 20, 1977; 1 child, Mélisande. B.A., Sarah Lawrence Coll., 1965; M.F.A., Columbia U., 1971. One-woman exhbns. include Yvon Lambert Gallery, Paris, 1972, 74, 76, 78, 80, 82, 84, 93, Konrad Fischer Gallery, Düsseldorf, Fed. Republic Germany, 1974, 79, Blum-Helman Gallery, N.Y.C., 1978, 80, 82, 85, 87-89, U. Mich. Mus. Art, 1995; group exhbns. included 8th Paris Biennale, 1973, Mus. Modern Art, N.Y.C., 1973, 90, Stedelijk Mus., Amsterdam, 1974, Whitney Mus. Am. Art, N.Y.C., 1979, 85, Centre Georges Pompidou, Paris, 1979, Met. Mus. Art, N.Y.C., 1982, 87, Serpentine Gallery, 1984, Galerie Denise René, Paris, 1985, The Tel Aviv Mus., 1986, Mus. Fridericianum, Kassel, Fed. Republic of Germany, 1988, Mus. d'Art Moderne de Lille, France, 1992, Bibliothèque Nationale, Paris, 1992, Nat. Gallery Art, Washington, 1993, 94, Harvard U. Straus Gallery, 1996; represented in permanent collections, Mus. Modern Art, Whitney Mus. Am. Art, Met. Mus. Art, Centre Georges Pompidou, Chgo. Art Inst., Phila. Art Mus., Yale U. Art Gallery, Met. Mus. Art, Neuberger Mus., Australian Nat. Gallery, Cin. Mus. Art, St. Louis Art Mus., Tel Aviv Mus., La. Mus., Denmark, Walker Art Ctr., Nat. Gallery Art, Washington, Biblioteque Nationale Paris; subject of articles in art publs. Nat. Endowment Arts grantee, 1978-79, Pollock-Krasner Found. Inc. grantee, 1990-91. Address: 37 Rue Volta, 75003 Paris France

RENOUF, HAROLD AUGUSTUS, business consultant; b. Sandy Point, St. George's Bay, Nfld., Can., June 15, 1917; s. John Robert and Louisa Maud R.; m. Dorothy Munro, June 16, 1942; children: Janet, Ann Petley-Jones, Robert, Susan. B.Commerce, Dalhousie U., 1938, LL.D. (hon.), 1981. N.S.C.A., Halifax, 1942 C.M.A., 1950. With H.R. Doane and Co., Halifax, N.S., Can., 1938-75, ptnr., 1942-75; ptnr. in charge H.R. Doane and Co., New Glasgow, N.S., Can., 1947-62; ptnr. in charge mgmt. services H.R. Doane and Co., Halifax, 1963-67, chmn., 1967-75; dir. Associated Acctg. Firms Internat., N.Y.C., 1967-75; commr. Anti-Inflation Bd., Ottawa, Ont., 1975-77, chmn., 1977-79; chmn. Petroleum Monitoring Agy., Ottawa, 1980-82, VIA Rail Can. Inc., Montreal, Que., 1982-85; ret., 1993; bd. dirs. N.S. Mcpl. Fin. Corp.; pres. Can. Inst. Chartered Accts., 1974-75. Contbr. articles to profl. publs. Chmn. adv. commn. Dalhousie U. Grad. Sch. Bus. Adminstrn., 1978-86. Decorated Queen's medal, 1977, officer Order of Can., 1979; recipient Commemorative medal for 125th anniversary of Can. Confederation, 1992; named to Acctg. Hall of Fame St. Mary's Univ., N.S., 1993. Fellow Inst. Chartered Accts. N.S.; mem. Soc. Mgmt. Accts., Dalhousie U. Alumni Assn. (hon. chmn. 1987-89), Halifax Club, Saraguay Club (treas. 1972-75), Waegwaltic Club. Liberal. Mem. United Ch. Can. Home: 6369 Coburg Rd Apt 1605, Halifax, NS Canada B3H 4J7

RENOUX, ANDRÉ, science educator; b. Courbevoie, France, Oct. 27, 1937; s. Robert and Jeanne (Noël) R.; divorced; children: Vincent, Nathalie. Lic. Sci., Faculty Scis., 1958, Dr 3rd cycle, 1961, Drs, 1965. Asst. Faculty Scis., Paris, 1959-61, master asst., 1961-66; prof. sci. Faculty Scis., Tunis, 1966-69; prof. Faculty Scis., Brest, France, 1969-80, U. Paris, 1980—; gen. conf. chmn. European Aerosol Conf., Blois, France, 1994. Editl. bd. Idojaras, 1979—, Pollution Atmospherique, 1979—, Aerosol Sci. & Tech., 1992—; contbr. over 200 articles to sci. publs. Gen. sec. Syndicat d'initiative, Brest, 1973-77; mem. Cons. Com. Univs., France, 1973-80. Mem. Com. Regional Anti-Pollution Brest (pres. 1973-80), Soc. France (prs. 1987-91), Am. Assn.

Aerosol Rsch., Gesellschaft Aerosolforschung, Hungarian Meteorol. soc. (hon.), French Aerosol. Rsch. Com. Pres.). Avocations: tennis, opera. Home: 11 Sq de L'eau Vive, 94000 Créteil France Office: Lab Phys Aerosols, U Paris, 94000 Créteil France

RENQUEST, RICHARD A., religious organization executive. Pres. Am. Baptist Men, Valley Forge, Pa. Office: Am Baptist Men PO Box 851 Valley Forge PA 19482-0851

RENSE, PAIGE, editor, publishing company executive; b. Iowa, May 4, 1929; m. Kenneth Noland, Apr. 10, 1994. Student, Calif. State U., L.A. Editor-in-chief Architectural Digest, L.A., 1970—. Recipient Nat. Headliner award Women in Communications, 1983, pacifica award So. Calif. Resources Coun., 1978, editl. award Dallas Market Ctr., 1978, golden award Chgo. Design Resources Svc., 12982, Agora award, 1982, outstanding profl. in comms. award, 1982, trailblazers award, 1983, disting. svcs. award Resources Coun., Inc., 1988; named woman of yr. L.A. Times, 1986, Muses, 1986, woman of internat. accomplisment, 1991; named to Interior Design Hall of Fame. Office: Architectural Digest 6300 Wilshire Blvd Fl 11 Los Angeles CA 90048-5202

RENSHAW, AMANDA FRANCES, retired physicist, nuclear engineer; b. Wheelwright, Ky., Dec. 10, 1934; d. Taft and Mamie Nell (Russell) Wilson; divorced; children: Linda, Michael, Billy. BS in Physics, Antioch Coll., 1972; MS in Physics, U. Tenn., 1982, MS in Nuclear Engring., 1991. Rsch. asst. U. Mich., Ann Arbor, 1970-71; teaching asst. Antioch Coll., Yellow Springs, Ohio, 1971-72; physicist GE, Schenectady, N.Y., 1972-74, Union Carbide Corp., Oak Ridge, Tenn., 1974-79; rsch. assoc. Oak Ridge Nat. Lab., 1979-91, mgr. strategic planning, 1991-92, liaison for environ. scis., 1993-96; ret., 1996; asst. to counselor for sci. and tech. Am. Embassy, Moscow, 1990; asst. to dir. nat. acid precipitation assessment program Office of Pres. U.S., 1993-94. Contbr. articles to profl. jours. Mem. AAUW, Am. Assn. Artificial Intelligence, Am. Nuclear Soc. (Oak Ridge chpt.), Soc. Black Physicists. Avocations: reading, travelling. Home: 1850 Cherokee Bluff Dr Knoxville TN 37920-2215

RENSI, EDWARD HENRY, restaurant chain executive; b. Hopedale, Ohio, Aug. 15, 1944; s. Ernest Henry and Virginia Marie (Gill) R.; m. F. Anne Bossick, Oct. 9, 1965. Student, Ohio State U., 1962-66. Ind. paint contractor, 1963; salesman Hillcrest Dairy, Steubenville, Ohio, 1964, Borden's Dairy, Columbus, Ohio, 1965, Shoe Corp. Am., Columbus, 1966; with McDonald's Corp., Oak Brook, Ill., 1966—; v.p. McDonald's Corp., 1976-78, sr. v.p. ops., tng. and product devel., 1978-80, sr. exec. v.p., chief operating officer, 1980-84; pres. McDonald's U.S.A., 1984—. Mem. nat. adv. bd. dirs. Children's Oncology Svcs., Oak Brook. Office: McDonald's Corp 1 Kroc Dr Oak Brook IL 60521-2275

RENSON, JEAN FELIX, psychiatry educator; b. Liège, Belgium, Nov. 9, 1930; came to U.S., 1960; s. Louis and Laurence (Crahai) R.; m. Gisèle Bouillenne, Sept. 8, 1956; children: Marc, Dominique, Jean-Luc. MD, U. Liege, 1959; PhD in Biochemistry, George Washington U., 1971. Diplomate Am. Bd. Psychiatry. Asst. prof. U. Liège, 1957-60; rsch. fellow U. Liege, 1966-72; clin. assoc. prof. dept. psychiatry U. Calif., San Francisco, 1978—; vis. asst. prof. Stanford U., Palo Alto, Calif., 1972-77. Assoc. editor: Fundamentals of Biochemical Pharmacology, 1971. NIH fellow, 1960-66. Democrat. Avocations: neurosciences, music.

RENT, CLYDA STOKES, academic administrator; b. Jacksonville, Fla., Mar. 1, 1942; d. Clyde Parker Stokes Sr. and Edna Mae (Edwards) Shuemake; m. George Seymour Rent, Aug. 12, 1966; 1 child, Cason Lynley Rent Helms. BA, Fla. State U., 1964, MA, 1966, PhD, 1968; LHD (hon.), Judson Coll., 1993. Asst. prof. Western Carolina U., Cullowhee, N.C., 1968-70; asst. prof. Queens Coll., Charlotte, N.C., 1972-74, dept. chair, 1974-78, dean Grad. Sch. and New Coll., 1979-84, v.p. for Grad. Sch. and New Coll., 1984-85, v.p. acad. affairs, 1985-87, v.p. community affairs, 1987-89; pres. Miss. U. for Women, Columbus, 1989—; bd. dirs. Trustmark Nat. Bank, Trustmark Corp.; cons. Coll. Bd. N.Y.C., 1983-89; sci. cons. N.C. Alcohol Rsch. Authority, Chapel Hill, 1976-89; bd. mem. So. Growth Policies Bd., 1992-94; mem. adv. bd. Nat. Women's Hall of Fame; rotating chair Miss. Instns. Higher Learning Pres.' Coun., 1990-91; commn. govtl. rels. Am. Coun. Edn., 1990-93; adv. bd. Miss. Power and Light, 1994—. Mem. editl. rev. bd. Planning for Higher Education, 1995; author rsch. articles in acad. jours.; speeches pub. in Vital Speeches; mem. editl. bds. acad. jours. Trustee N.C. Performing Arts Ctr., Charlotte, 1988-89, Charlotte County Day Sch., 1987-89; bd. visitors Johnson C. Smith U., Charlotte, 1985-89; exec. com. bd. dirs. United Way Allocations and Rev., Charlotte, 1982-88; bd. advisors Charlotte Mecklenburg Hosp. Authority, 1985-89; bd. dirs. Jr. Achievement, Charlotte, 1983-89, Miss. Humanities Coun., Miss. Inst. Arts and Letters, Miss. Symphony, Miss. Econ. Coun.; chair Leadership Miss. and Collegiate Miss.; chmn. bd. dirs. Charlotte/Mecklenburg Arts and Sci. Coun., 1987-88; Danforth assoc. Danforth Found., St. Louis, 1976-88, Leadership Am., 1989; golden triangle adv. bd. Bapt. Meml. Hosp.; pres. So. Univs. Conf., 1994-95; mem. commn. govt. rels. Am. Coun. Edn., 1990-93. Recipient Grad. Made Good award Fla. State U., 1990, medal of excellence Miss. U. for Women, 1995; named Prof. of Yr., Queens Coll., 1979, One of 10 Most Admired Women Mgrs. in Am., Working Women mag., 1993, One of 1000 Women of the 90's, Mirabella mag., 1994; Ford Found. grantee, 1981; Paul Harris fellow, 1992. Mem. Am. Assn. State Colls. and Univs. (bd. dirs. 1994-96), Sociol. Soc., So. Assn. Colls. and Schs. (mem. commn. on colls. 1996), N.C. Assn. Colls. and Univs. (exec. com. 1988-89), N.C. Assn. Acad. Officers (sec.-treas. 1987-88), Soc. Internat. Bus. Fellows, Miss. Assn. Colls. (pres. 1992), Newcomen Soc. U.S., Internat. Women's Forum, Univ. Club, Rotary. 1st female pres. of Miss. U. for Women (1st pub. coll. for women in Am.). Office: Miss U Women Pres Office Box W 1600 Columbus MS 39701-9998

RENTSCHLER, WILLIAM HENRY, publisher, columnist, writer, corporate executive; b. Hamilton, Ohio, May 11, 1925; s. Peter Earl and Barbara (Schlosser) R.; AB, Princeton U., 1949; m. Sylvia Gale Angevin, Dec. 20, 1948; children: Sarah Yorke, Peter Ferris, Mary Rentschler Alley, Phoebe Rentschler Cole; m. Martha Guthrie Snowdon, Jan. 20, 1967; 1 child, Hope Snowdon. Reporter, Cin. Times-Star, 1946; chmn. The Daily Princetonian, 1948; reporter, asst. to exec. editor Mpls. Star & Tribune, 1949-53; 2d v.p. No. Trust Co., Chgo., 1953-56; pres. Martha Washington Kitchens, Inc., and Stevens Candy Kitchens, Inc., 1957-68; investor closely-held cos.; bus. and mktg. cons., 1970—; chmn., chief exec. officer Medart, Inc., Greenwood, Miss., 1981-87, Roper Whitney Corp., Rockford, Ill., 1985-87; editor, pub. News/Voice Newspapers, Inc., Highland Park, Lake Bluff, Ill., 1983-91. editor/pub. San Francisco Progress, 1986-88; editor in chief and chmn., founder VOICE Pub. USA, Ltd., 1995—; columnist Chgo. Life Mag., 1994—, Chgo. Sun-Times, 1995—; commentator WBEZ-FM, Nat. Pub. Radio, Chgo., 1995—. Spl. adviser Pres.'s Nat. Program for Vol. Action, 1969; chmn. Ill. Low Tech./High Return Adv. Bd., 1986; exec. com. Nat. Council Crime and Delinquency; bd. dirs. Better Boys Found., Citizens Info. Svc.; pres. John Howard Assn., 1985-87; Rep. candidate U.S. Senate, 1960, 70; chmn. Ill. Citizens for Nixon, 1968; pres. Young Reps. Ill., 1957-59; exec. com. United Rep. Fund Ill., 1963-69; former trustee Rockford Coll., Goodwill Industries, Coun. on Fgn. Rels.; mem. San Francisco mayor's Fiscal Adv. Com., Blue Ribbon Com. on Bus., 1987-88, Com. of 100, Voices for Ill. Children, Chgo. Mayor Daly's Task Force on Youth Devel., 1993-94. Recipient 1st Ann. Buddy Hackett award for svc. to young men, 1968, Voice for Children award Coleman Advs., San Francisco, 1987, Peter Lisagor award for Exemplary journalism, 1989, 90, 92, John Howard Assn. Media award, 1990, Nat. Media award Nat. Coun. Crime and Delinquency, 1990; Pulitzer prize nominee, 1985, 87, 88, 89, 90. Mem. Onwentsia Club, Economic Club, Sky-Line Club (Chgo.). Home: 1088 Griffith Ave Lake Forest IL 60045-1319

RENTZ, TAMARA HOLMES, software consultant; b. Austin, Tex., Nov. 23, 1964; d. Thomas Michael and Elizabeth Dianne (Ames) Holmes; m. Christopher Michael Rentz, Sept. 21, 1991. BS in Speech/Orgnl. Comm., U. Tex., 1987. Cert. meeting facilitator; notary public State of Tex. Mgr. PC Sta., Inc., Austin, 1985-86; telecom. advisor Internat. Talent Network, Austin, 1986-87; mktg. rep. Wm. Ross & Co., Austin, 1987; life ins. rep. A.L. Williams, Austin, 1987-88; exec. sec. Adia Temporaries/SEMATECH, Austin, 1988; tng. adminstr. SEMATECH, Austin, 1988-89, data coord. equipment improvement program, 1989-90, user group program mgr., 1992-93; pres. Innovative Bus. Solutions, Austin, 1994—. Mem. Austin Software Coun. Avocations: weight lifting, golf. Home and Office: 4004 Love Bird Ln Austin TX 78730-3522

RENTZEPIS, PETER M., chemistry educator; b. Kalamata, Greece, Dec. 11, 1934; m. Alma Elizabeth Keenan; children—Michael, John. B.S., Denison U., 1957, D.Sc. (hon.), 1981; M.S., Syracuse U., 1959, Ph.D. (hon.), 1980; Ph.D., Cambridge U., 1963; DSc (hon.), Carnegie-Mellon U., 1983, Tech. U. Greece, Athens, Greece, 1995. Mem. tech. staff, rsch. labs. Gen. Electric Co., Schenectady, 1960-62; mem. tech. staff AT&T Bell Labs., Murray Hill, N.J., 1963-73, head phys. and inorganic chemistry rsch. dept., 1973-85; Presdl. prof. chemistry U. Calif., Irvine, 1986—, Presdl. chair, 1985—, regent lectr., 1984; vis. prof. Rockefeller U., N.Y.C., 1971, MIT, Cambridge, to 1975; vis. prof. chemistry U. Tel Aviv; adj. prof. U. Pa., Phila.; with Ctr. Biol. Studies, SUNY-Albany, 1979—; adj. prof. chemistry and biophysics Yale U., New Haven, 1980—; mem. numerous adv. bodies; lectr. Robert A. Welch Found., 1975; faculty lectr. Rensselaer Poly. Inst., Troy, N.Y., 1978; IBM lectr. Williams Coll., 1979; lectr. disting. lecture series U. Utah, 1980; Xerox lectr. N.C. State U., 1980; Frank C. Whitmore lectr. in chemistry Pa. State U., 1981; Dreyfus disting. scholar lectr., 1982; regent lectr. U. Calif., 1982, UCLA, 1985; Harry S. Ganning disting. lectr. U. Alta., Can., 1984; mem. IUPAC Commn. on Molecular Structure and Spectroscopy; chmn. 1981 Internat. Conf. on Photochemistry and Photobiology; bd. dirs. KRIKOS Sci. and Tech. Resources for Greece; mem. com. on kinetics Nat. Acad. Scis., NRC; chmn. fast reaction chemistry U.S. Fgn. Applied Sci. Assessment Ctr.; with NATO Advanced Study Insts., 1984—; dir. Quanex Corp. Assoc. editor Chem. Physics, Jour. Lasers and Chemistry, Jour. Biochem. and Biophys. Methods; editorial bd. Biophys. Jour., Jour. Chem. Intermediates; contbr. articles, papers to profl. publs.; patentee in field. Recipient Scientist of Yr. award, 1977, award for significant contbns. to field of biochem. instrumentation ISCO, 1979, award for leadership in sci. and edn. AHEPA, Disting. Alumni award SUNY, 1982, H.S. Ganning award U. Alta., 1984; Camille and Henry Dreyfus disting. scholar Williams Coll., 1982; AAAS fellow, 1985; alumni scholar Denison U., 1978. Fellow N.Y. Acad. Scis. (A Cressy Morrison award 1978), Am. Phys. Soc. (chmn. chem. physics divsn. 1979-80, exec. com. 1980-82, chmn. nominating com. 1981, Irving Langmuir award 1973); mem. NAS, Nat. Acad. Greece, Am. Chem. Soc. (exec. com. divsn. phys. chemistry to 1978, Peter Debye award phys. chemistry 1982), Inter-Am. Photochem. Soc. (nominating coun., chmn. phys. divsn. Laser Conf. prize 1989), Sigma Xi. Office: U Calif Dept Chemistry Irvine CA 92717

RENVALL, JOHAN, ballet dancer; b. Stockholm. Dancer Royal Swedish Ballet; with Am. Ballet Theater, N.Y.C., 1978—, soloist, 1980-87, prin. dancer, 1987—. Appeared in numerous ballet co-prodns. including La Bayadere, Coppelia, Etudes, The Rite of Spring, Romeo and Juliet, SinFonietta, The Sleeping Beauty, La Sylphide, Undertow; guest appearances with Royal Swedish Ballet; created role of the Young Fighter in The Informer (Agnes de Mille); appeared in film Dance; choreographer Persnickety, 1987, Tango, Jacob's Pillow Dance Festival, 1990, Romeo and Juliet, 1992. Recipient Silver medal Varna Internat. Ballet Competition, 1978. Office: Am Ballet Theatre 890 Broadway New York NY 10003-1211

RENWICK, EDWARD S., lawyer; b. L.A., May 10, 1934. AB, Stanford U., 1956, LLB, 1958. Bar: Calif. 1959, U.S. Dist. Ct. (cen. dist.) Calif. 1959, U.S. Ct. Appeals (9th cir.) 1963, U.S. Dist. Ct. (so. dist.) Calif. 1973, U.S. Dist. Ct. (no. dist.) Calif. 1977, U.S. Dist. Ct. (ea. dist.) Calif. 1981, U.S. Supreme Ct. 1985. Ptnr. Hanna and Morton, L.A.; mem., bd. vis. Stanford Law Sch., 1967-69; mem. environ. and natural resources adv. bd. Stanford Law Sch. Bd. dirs. Calif. Supreme Ct. Hist. Soc. Fellow Am. Coll. Trial Lawyers, Am. Bar Found.; mem. ABA (mem. sect. on litigation, antitrust law, bus. law, chmn. sect. of nat. resources, energy and environ. law 1987-88, mem. at large coord. group energy law 1989-92, sect. rep. coord. group energy law 1995—, Calif. del. legal com., interstate oil compact com.), Calif. Arboretum Assn. (trustee 1986-92), L.A. County Bar Assn. (chmn. natural resources law sect. 1974-75), The State Bar of Calif., Assn. Atty.- Mediators, Chancery Club (pres. 1992-93), Phi Delta Phi. Office: Hanna & Morton 600 Wilshire Blvd Fl 17 Los Angeles CA 90017-3212

RENWICK, KEN, retail executive. CEO All-Phase Electric Supply, Benton Harbor, Mich. Office: All Phase Electric Supply 875 Riverview Dr Benton Harbor MI 49022

RENZETTI, ATTILIO DAVID, physician; b. N.Y.C., Nov. 11, 1920; s. Attilio and Anna (Accardi) R.; m. Mabel Lucille Woodruff, May 24, 1947; children: Patricia Ann, Laurence, Pamela Sorensen, David. AB, Columbia Coll., 1941, MD, 1944. Diplomate: Am. Bd. Internal Medicine (chmn. subsplty. bd. pulmonary disease 1970-72). Intern, resident Bellevue Hosp., N.Y.C., 1944-45, 47-49, 51-52; fellow cardiopulmonary physiology Bellevue Hosp., 1949-51; asst. prof. medicine U. Utah, 1952-53, State U. N.Y., Syracuse, 1953-57; assoc. prof. SUNY, 1957-60; asst. prof. Johns Hopkins U., 1960-61; assoc. prof. U. Md., 1960-61, U. Utah, Salt Lake City, 1961-67; prof. U. Utah, 1967-90, emeritus, 1990—. Editorial bd.: Am. Rev. Respiratory Disease, 1964-67; Contbr. articles to med. jours. Pres. Utah TB and Health Assn., 1965-66; bd. dirs. Am. Lung Assn., 1965-74, 78-81. With M.C. AUS, 1945-47. Mem. Am. Thoracic Soc. (pres. 1975-76). Home and Office: 1801 London Plane Rd Salt Lake City UT 84124-3531

REOCK, ERNEST C., JR., retired government services educator, academic director; b. Belleville, N.J., Oct. 13, 1924; s. Ernest C. and Helen Rutan (Evans) R.; m. Jeanne Elizabeth Thomason, Jan. 25, 1953; children: Michael, Thomas, Kathleen. BS, Swarthmore Coll., 1945; AB, Rutgers U., 1948, MA, 1950, PhD, 1959. Rsch. assoc. bur. govt. rsch. Rutgers U., New Brunswick, N.J., 1950-59, asst. prof., dir., 1960-63, assoc. prof., dir., 1963-68, prof., dir., 1968-92; cons. N.J. Constnl. Conv., New Brunswick, 1966, N.J. State and Local Revenue and Expenditure Commns., 1986-88. Author: Handbook for New Jersey Assessors, 1962, School Budget Caps in New Jersey, 1981 (Govtl. Rsch. Assn. award 1983); editor: New Jersey Legislative District Data Book, 1972-92. Chmn. Middlesex County Charter Study Commn., New Brunswick, 1973-74; cons. various mcpl. charter commns., 1965-93. Lt. USN, 1943-46, 51-53. Mem. Am. Soc. Pub. Adminstrn. (Pub. Adminstr. of Yr. 1982), Am. Ednl. Fin. Assn. Avocations: sailing, swimming. Home: 7 Kendall Rd Kendall Park NJ 08824-1010 Office: Rutgers U Ctr Govt Svcs PO Box 5079 New Brunswick NJ 08903

REPHAN, JACK, lawyer; b. Little Rock, Mar. 16, 1932; s. Henry and Mildred (Frank) R.; m. Arlene Clark, June 23, 1957; children: Amy Carol, James Clark. BS in Commerce, 1954; LLB, U. Va., 1959. Bar: Va. 1959, D.C. 1961. Assoc. Kanter & Kanter, Norfolk, Va., 1959-60; law clk. to Judge Sam E. Whitaker, U.S. Ct. Claims, Washington, 1960-62; assoc. Pierson, Ball & Dowd, Washington, 1962-64; ptnr. Danzansky, Dickey, Tydings, Quint & Gordon, Washington, 1964-77; mem. Braude, Margulies, Sacks & Rephan, Washington, 1977-87; ptnr. Porter, Wright, Morris & Arthur, Washington, 1987-88, Sadur, Pelland & Rubinstein, Washington, 1988-93; counsel Hofheimer, Nusbaum, McPhaul & Samuels, Norfolk, Va., 1993—; mem. nat. panel arbitrators Am. Arbitration Assn.; lectr. joint com. continuing legal edn. State Bar Va. Contbr. articles to legal jours. Pres. Patrick Henry PTA, Alexandria, Va., 1968-69; treas. John Adams Mid. Sch. PTA, Alexandria, 1970-71; pres. Seminary Ridge Citizens Assn., 1976-77; Dem. candidate for Alexandria City Com., 1969. 1st lt. AUS, 1955-57. Mem. ABA (chmn. subcom. on procurement of jud. remedies pub. contract sect. 1973-74), Va. Bar Assn. (govt. sect. constrn. law 1979—, vice chmn. 1980-81, chmn. 1981-82), D.C. Bar Assn., Kiwanis (pres. Landmark Club 1969), Westwood Country Club (v.p. 1977-78), Belle Haven Country Club, Cavalier Golf and Yacht Club. Jewish. Home: 3978 Ocean Hills Ct Virginia Beach VA 23451-2631 Office: 1700 Dominion Towers PO Box 3460 Norfolk VA 23514-3460

REPINE, JOHN E., internist, educator; b. Rock Island, Ill., Dec. 26, 1944; married, 1969, 88; 6 children. BS, U. Wis., 1967; MD, U. Minn., 1971. Instr., then assoc. prof. internal medicine U. Minn., Mpls., 1974-79; asst. dir divsn. exptl. medicine Webb-Waring Lung Inst., Denver, 1979-89, prof. medicine, pres. and dir., 1989—; prof. medicine U. Colo., Denver, 1979—, prof. pediatrics, 1981-96; James J. Waring prof. Webb-Waring Lung Inst., Denver, 1996—; mem. rsch. com., co-chmn. steering com. Aspen Lung Conf., 1980, chmn., 1981; assoc. dean for student advocacy Nat. Heart and Lung Inst., 1990—. Young Pulmonary Investigator grantee Nat. Heart & Lung Inst., 1974-75; recipient Basil O'Connor Starter Rsch. award Nat. Found. March of Dimes, 1975-77. Mem. AAAS, Am. Assn. Immunologists, Am. Fedn. Clin. Rsch., Am. Heart Assn. (established investigator award 1976-81), Am. Thoracic Soc., Am. Soc. Clin. Investigators, Assn. Am. Physicians. Achievements include research in role of phagocytes and oxygen radicals in lung injury and host defense (ARDS). Office: Webb-Waring Lung Inst 4200 E 9th Ave Denver CO 80220-3706

REPLINGER, JOHN GORDON, architect; b. Chgo., Nov. 9, 1923; s. Roy Lodawick and Dorothy Caroline (Thornstrom) R.; m. Dorothy Thiele, June 26, 1945; children: John Gordon Jr., Robert Louis, James Alan. B.S. in Architecture with highest honors, U. Ill., Urbana, 1949, M.S. in Architecture, 1952. Registered architect, Ill. Designer-draftsman L. Morgan Yost (Architect), Kenilworth, Ill., 1949-50; instr. U. Ill., 1951-53, asst. prof. architecture, 1953-57, assoc. prof. architecture, 1957-61, prof. architecture, 1961-85, prof. housing research and devel., 1972-85, prof. emeritus, 1985—, assoc. head dept. for acad. affairs, 1970-71; practice architecture Urbana, 1951—. Served with USAAF, 1943-45. Decorated Air medal with oak leaf clusters; recipient Sch. medal AIA, 1949, List of Tchrs. Ranked as Excellent by Their Students award U. Ill., 1976, 77, 78, 82, 83; Allerton Am. travelling scholar, 1948. Mem. Nat. Trust Hist. Preservation. Home and Office: 403 Yankee Ridge Ln Urbana IL 61801-7113

REPLOGLE, DAVID ROBERT, publishing company executive; b. Chgo., Feb. 24, 1931; s. Homer Mock and Helen (Fluke) R.; m. Jeanne Lonnquist, Nov. 4, 1954; children: William T., Bruce R., Stewart D., James M., John B. A.B., Dartmouth Coll., 1953; postgrad., Princeton U., 1957-58. V.p., gen. mgr. Doubleday & Co., Inc., N.Y.C., 1958-70; pres., chmn. bd. G. & C. Merriam Co., Springfield, Mass., 1970-75; pres. Praeger Publishers, N.Y.C., 1970-75; exec. v.p., dir. Houghton Mifflin Co., Boston, 1975-91; chmn. DR&A Inc., Hingham, Mass., 1992—. Trustee L.I. Replogle Found., Chgo., 1982—. Served to lt. USNR, 1953-57. Mem. Cohasset Golf Club. Home: 84 Gammons Rd Cohasset MA 02025-1406 Office: DR&A Inc 75 Terry Dr Ste 223 Hingham MA 02043-1518

REPLOGLE, WILLIAM H(ENRY), II, lawyer; b. LaPorte, Ind., Mar. 19, 1946; s. William Henry and Lucille Jeanette (Schoettler) R.; m. Joyce Ann Pankonin, Jan. 8, 1977; children: Kathryn Ann, Michael Scott, Patrick William. BS, Indiana U., 1968, JD, 1971. Bar: Oreg. 1971, U.S. Dist. Ct. Oreg. 1971. Law clerk Oreg. Tax Court, Salem, 1971-72; assoc. Joss, Bosch & Burns, Portland, Oreg., 1973-74, Pattulo, Gleason & Scarborough, Portland, 1974-76; house counsel Pacific N.W. Bell, Portland, 1976-79; assoc. Schwabe, Williamson & Wyatt, Portland, 1979-84, ptnr., 1984-94; ptnr. Meyers, Radler, Replogle & Bohy, Tigard, Oreg., 1994—. Chmn. Halfway House City Club of Portland, 1980-81, rsch. bd., 1982-83; divsn. chmn. United Way, Portland, 1984; bd. dirs. Vol. Bur. Portland, 1987-89, Quadriplegics United Against Dependency, bd. dirs. 1990—, pres. 1994—. Mem. ABA, Oreg. State Bar (mem. discipline rules com. 1976-79, pub. svc. and info. com. 1973-76), Multnomah Bar Assn. (mem. professionalism com. 1989-92, judicial screening com., 1993-96), Blue Goose Internat., Oswego Lake Country Club (bd. dirs.). Avocations: basketball, bicycling, golf, running, swimming. Office: Meyers Radler Replogle & Bohy Pacific Four Bldg Ste 200 6745 SW Hampton Tigard OR 97223

REPP, RONALD STEWART, insurance company executive; b. Phila., Dec. 12, 1944; s. Carl George Jr. and Pauline Francis (Hunley) R.; m. Nancy Elaine Hannigan, Sept. 16, 1967; children: Christopher Robert, Justin Ronald. Grad. high sch., Pitts.; cert., Am. Coll., Bryn Mawr, Pa., 1973, Am. Inst., Malvern, Pa., 1977. CLU, CPCU, assoc. in risk mgmt. Admistr. Liberty Mut. Ins. Group, Pitts., 1963-65, sales rep., 1967-70, sales supr., 1970-72, sales mgr., 1972-78; spl. agt. The Prudential, Pitts., 1966-67; account exec. Ind. Ins. Svc. Corp., Canton, Ohio, 1978-83, v.p., 1983-90, sr.v.p., 1990—; mem. adv. bd. dirs. Silver Lake Estates. Contbr. articles to profl. jours. Staff sgt. U.S. Army, 1964-65. Mem. Soc. CPCUs, Soc. CLUs, Ind. Ins. Agts. Assn., Akron City Club (chmn. mem. com. 1992-94), Bay Point Yacht Club, Akron Cruising Club (bd. trustees), Silver Lake Country Club. Lutheran. Avocation: sailing. Home: 3103 Silver Lake Blvd Silver Lake OH 44224-3130 Office: Ind Ins Svc Corp 236 3rd St SW Canton OH 44702-1622

REPPEN, NORBJORN DAG, electrical engineer, consultant; b. Hadsel, Norway, May 10, 1940; came to U.S., 1966; s. Harald and Bergit (Bakke) R.; m. Grete Elisabeth Holm, July 25, 1964; children: Dag, Anne, Erik Harald. Degree in elec. engring., Norwegian Inst. Tech., 1965. Registered profl. engr., N.Y. Application engr. GE, Schenectady, N.Y., 1966-69; application engr. Power Techs., Inc., Schenectady, 1969-73, sr. engr., 1973-84, sr. cons., 1984-91, unit mgr., 1991—; bd. dirs. Hydro Techs., Inc., Schenectady, Power Techs., Inc., Schenectady. Bd. dirs. 1st Unitarian Soc. Schenectady, 1984-87, 93. Fellow IEEE. Avocations: sailing, cross country skiing.

REPPERT, RICHARD LEVI, lawyer; b. Phila., Nov. 6, 1948; s. William Downing and Angela R. (Schmid) R.; m. Faith Simpson, Dec. 30, 1972 (div. Aug. 1992); 1 child, Richard Jacob; m. Jeanette T. deHaven, Apr. 10, 1994. BA, Lehigh U., 1970; JD, Villanova U., 1974. Bar: Ohio 1974, U.S. Dist. Ct. (no. dist.) Ohio 1974, Pa. 1993. Assoc. Thompson, Hine and Flory, Cleve., 1974-82, ptnr., 1982-89; ptnr. Jones, Day, Reavis & Pogue, Cleve., 1989—. Mem. ABA, Am. Coll. Real Estate Lawyers, Nat. Assn. Office and Indsl. Pks., Ohio State Bar Assn., Cleve. Bar Assn., Mortgage Bankers Assn. Greater Cleve. Office: Jones Day Reavis & Pogue 901 Lakeside Ave E Cleveland OH 44114-1116*

REPPERT, STEVEN MARION, pediatrician, scientist, educator; b. Sioux City, Iowa, Sept. 4, 1946; s. Ray Fred and Norma Grace (Coppock) R.; m. Mary Alice Herman, Dec. 28, 1968; children—Jason Steven, Katherine Mary, Christina Marie. BS, U. Nebr., Lincoln, 1973; MD with distinction, U. Nebr.-Omaha, 1973, MA (hon.), Harvard U., 1993. Diplomate Nat. Bd. Med. Examiners. Intern, Mass. Gen. Hosp., Boston, 1973-74, resident in pediatrics, 1974-76, asst. in pediatrics, 1979-80, asst. pediatrician, 1980-85, dir. lab. devel. chronobiology, 1983—, assoc. pediatrician, 1985—; pvt. practice medicine specializing in pediatrics, Boston, 1973-88; clin. assoc. NIH, Bethesda, Md., 1976-79; instr. pediatrics Harvard Med. Sch., Boston, 1979-81, asst. prof., 1981-85, assoc. prof., 1985-93, prof. 1993—; vis. scientist Lab. Molecular Neurobiology Mass. Gen. Hosp., 1989-90. Mem. adv. com. Charles H. Hood Found., 1993—. Editor: Development of Circadian Rhythmicity and Photoperiodism in Mammals, 1989; co-editor: Suprachiasmatic Nucleus: The Mind's Clock, 1991; contbr. articles to sci. jours, chpts. to books. Regents scholar U. Nebr., 1971; Pfizer Labs. Med. scholar, 1971; Charles King Trust research fellow, 1981-83; Grantee NIH, 1981—, Nat. Found/March of Dimes, 1981-88; recipient E. Mead Johnson award, 1989, NIH Merit award, 1992. Mem. Am. Physiol. Soc., Am. Soc. for Clin. Investigation, Endocrine Soc., Soc. for Pediatric Research, Soc. for Neurosci., Soc. for Research on Biol. Rhythms (adv. com.), Am. Heart Assn. (established investigator 1985-90), Lepidopterists Soc., Cambridge Entomol. Club, Alpha Omega Alpha. Democrat. Avocation: natural history of saturniid moths. Office: Mass Gen Hosp 32 Fruit St Boston MA 02114-2620

REPPETO, WILLIAM M., III, lawyer; b. Dallas, Jan. 8, 1966; s. William M. Jr. and Mary Elizabeth (Carpenter) R.; m. Deveri Marie Darilek, Aug. 22, 1992. BA, U. Tex., 1988; JD, So. Meth. U., 1992. Bar: Tex., U.S. Dist. Ct. (we. dist.) Tex. Atty. Gordon Hollon, Boerne, Tex., 1992, Bobbitt & Holter, Boerne, Tex., 1993-94, Reppeto & Geistweidt, Boerne, Tex., 1994—. Dir. police activities City of Boerne, 1994—. Mem. Kendall County Bar Assn. (officer, dir. 1994—), Rotary (officer, dir. 1994—). Republican. Methodist. Avocations: physical fitness, fly fishing, travel, western art, golf. Office: Reppeto & Geistweidt 106 W Blanco Boerne TX 78006

REPPUCCI, NICHOLAS DICKON, psychologist, educator; b. Boston, May 1, 1941; s. Nicholas Ralph and Bertha Elizabeth (Williams) R.; m. Christine Marlow Onufrock, Sept. 10, 1967; children: Nicholas Jason, Jonathan Dickon, Anna Jin Marlow. BA with honors, U. N.C., 1962; MA, Harvard U., 1964, PhD, 1968. Lectr., rsch. assoc. Harvard U., Cambridge, Mass., 1967-68; asst. prof. Yale U., New Haven, 1968-73, assoc. prof., 1973-76; prof. psychology U. Va., Charlottesville, 1976—, dir. grad. studies in psychology, 1984-95; originator biennial conf. on community rsch. and action, 1986. Assoc. editor Law and Human Behavior, 1986—; mem. editl. bd. Am. Jour. Cmty. Psychology, 1974-83, 88-91; author: (with J. Haugaard) Sexual Abuse of Children, 1988; editor: (with J. Haugaard) Prevention in Community Mental Health Practice, (with E. Mulvey, L. Weithorn and J. Monahan) Mental Health, Law and Children, 1984; contbr. over 100 articles to profl. publs., chpts. in books. Adv. bd. on prevention Va. Dept. Mental Health, Mental Retardation and Substance Abuse Svcs., Richmond, 1986-92. Disting. scholar in psychology Va. Assn. Social Sci., 1991. Fellow APA (chair task force on pub. policy 1980-84), Am. Psychol. Soc., Soc. for Community Rsch. and Action (pres. 1986), Phi Beta Kappa. Office: U Va Dept Psychology Charlottesville VA 22903

REPPY, WILLIAM ARNEILL, JR., law educator; b. Oxnard, Calif., Mar. 14, 1941; s. William Arneill and Margot Louise Reppy; m. Susan Westerberg, Sept. 30, 1967 (div. 1973); m. Juliann Tenney, Nov. 28, 1975. B.A. with great distinction, Stanford U., 1963, J.D. with great distinction, 1966. Bar: Calif. 1966, N.C. 1971, U.S. Supreme Ct. 1971. Law clk. to Justice William Douglas, U.S. Supreme Ct., Washington, 1967-68; assoc. Tuttle & Taylor, Los Angeles, 1968-71; prof. law Duke U., Durham, N.C. 1971—; cons. Calif. Law Revision Com., Palo Alto, 1979-83; mem. Condominium Statutes Commn., Raleigh, N.C., 1980—. Author: Community Property in California, 1980; Community Property-Gilbert Law Summaries, 1983; co-author: Community Property in U.S., 2d edit., 1982, Texas Matrimonial Property Law, 1983. Mem. editorial bd. Community Property Jour., 1973—. Recipient Nathan Abbot award Stanford U., 1966. Mem. Am. Law Inst., Order of Coif, Phi Beta Kappa. Republican. Office: Duke Univ Sch Law Durham NC 27706*

REQUARTH, WILLIAM HENRY, surgeon; b. Charlotte, N.C., Jan. 23, 1913; s. Charles William and Amelia (George) R.; m. Nancy Charlton, 1948 (div. 1966); children—Kurt, Betsy, Jeff, Jan, Tim, Suzanna; m. Connie Harper, 1977. A.B., Millikin U., 1934; M.D., U. Ill., 1938, M.S., 1939. Diplomate: Am. Bd. Surgery. Intern St. Luke's Hosp., Chgo., 1938-39; resident Cook County Hosp., Chgo., 1940-42, 46-48; pvt. practice medicine, specializing in surgery Decatur, Ill., 1950—; clin. prof. surgery U. Ill. Med. Sch., from 1962, now emeritus; Mem. Chgo. Bd. Trade. Author: Diagnosis of Abdominal Pain, 1953, The Acute Abdomen, 1958; also contbg. author chpts. books. Chmn. trustees Millikin U.; chmn. James Millikin Found.; bd. dirs. Decatur Meml. Hosp. Served to comdr. USNR, 1941-46. Mem. ACS, Cen. Surg. Assn., Western Surg. Assn., Chgo. Surg. Soc., Ill. Surg. Soc. (pres. 1970-71), Am. Soc. Surgery Hand (founder), Am. Soc. Surgery Trauma, Soc. Surgery Alimentary Tract, Warren Cole Soc., Societe Internationale Chirurgie, Nat. Pilots Assn. (pres. 1960-61), Soaring Soc. Am., Sportsman Pilot Assn. (pres. 1966-67), Aerobatic Club Am., Internat. Aerobatic Club. Home: 1860 S Spitler Dr Decatur IL 62521-4417 Office: 158 W Prairie Ave Decatur IL 62523-1230

RESCH, JOSEPH ANTHONY, neurologist; b. Milw., Apr. 29, 1914; s. Frank and Elizabeth (Zetsch) R.; m. Rose Catherine Ritz, May 25, 1939; children—Rose, Frank, Catherine. Student, Milw. State Tchrs. Coll., 1931-34; B.S., U. Wis., Madison, 1936, M.D., 1938. Intern St. Francisco Hosp., LaCrosse, Wis., 1938-39; gen. practice medicine Holmen, Wis., 1939-40; med. fellow in neurology U. Minn., 1946-48, clin. instr. neurology, 1948-51, clin. asst. prof., 1951-55, clin. assoc. prof., 1955-62, assoc. prof., 1962-65, prof., 1965-84, prof. emeritus, 1984—, head dept. neurology, 1976-82, asst. v.p. health sci., 1970-79, prof. lab. medicine and pathology, 1979-84; practice medicine specializing in neurology Mpls., 1948-62. Contbr. articles and abstracts to profl. jours., chpts. in books. Served to lt. col. M.C. U.S. Army, 1940-46; col. Med. Res. 1946-53. Mem. Hennepin County Med. Soc., Minn. Med. Assn., AMA, Minn. Soc. Neurol. Scis., Central Assn. Electroencephalographers, Am. Acad. Neurology, Am. Neurol. Assn., Am. Assn. Neuropathologists, Am. EEG Soc., Sonoma County Med. Assn., Am. Epilepsy Soc. Home: 900 River Beach Rd The Sea Ranch CA 95497

RESCH, RICHARD J., furniture manufacturing executive; b. 1938. Grad., MIT, Milw.; MBA, Harvard U. With Hudson Pulp & Paper, N.Y.C., 1959-64; with Krueger Internat. Inc., Green Bay, Wis., 1964—, now pres./CEO. Office: Krueger Internat Inc 1330 Bellevue St Green Bay WI 54302-2119*

RESCHER, NICHOLAS, philosophy educator; b. Hagen, Westphalia, Germany, July 15, 1928; came to U.S. 1938, naturalized 1944; s. Erwin Hans and Meta Anna (Landau) R.; m. Dorothy Henle, Feb. 10, 1968; children: Mark, Owen, Catherine; 1 child from a previous marriage, Elizabeth. BS in Math., Queens Coll., 1949; PhD, Princeton U., 1951; LHD (hon.), Loyola U.-Chgo., 1970, Lehigh U., 1993; Dr. honoris causa U. Córdoba, Argentina, 1992, U. Konstanz, Germany, 1995. Instr. philosophy Princeton U., N.J., 1951-52; assoc. prof. philosophy Lehigh U., Bethlehem, Pa., 1957-61; Univ. prof. philosophy U. Pitts., 1961—, vice chmn. Ctr. for Philosophy of Sci., 1988—; trustee St. Edmunds Acad., Pitts., 1980-85; nonresident mem. Corpus Christi Coll., Oxford; disting. vis. lectr. Oxford, Salamanca, Munich, Konstanz. Author: The Coherence Theory of Truth, 1973, Scientific Progress, 1978, The Limits of Science, 1985, Luck, 1995, others; exec. editor: Am. Philos. Quarterly; mem.editl. bd. 15 jours.; contbr. over 250 articles to profl. jours. Sec. gen. Internat. Union of History and Philosophy of Sci. (UNESCO), 1969-75. Served with USMC, 1952-54. Recipient Alexander von Humboldt Humanities prize 1983. Mem. Am. Philos. Assn. (past pres.), Royal Asiatic Soc., G.W. Leibniz Soc. Am. (past pres.), C.S. Peirce Soc. (past pres.), Inst. Internat. de Philosophie, Academie Internationale de Philosophie des Sciences. Roman Catholic. Avocation: reading history and biography. Home: 5818 Aylesboro Ave Pittsburgh PA 15217-1446 Office: Univ of Pitts Dept Philosophy 1012 Cathedral Pittsburgh PA 15260

RESCHKE, MICHAEL W., real estate executive; b. Chgo., Nov. 29, 1955; s. Don J. and Vera R. (Helmer) R.; m. Kim P. Shaw, July 17, 1977; children: Michael W. Jr., Tiffanie G. BS summa cum laude with univ. honors, No. Ill. U., 1977; JD summa cum laude, U. Ill., 1980. Bar: Ill. 1980; CPA, Ill. Assoc. Winston & Strawn, Chgo., 1980-82; pres., CEO The Prime Group, Inc., Chgo., 1982—, also chmn. bd. dirs.; chmn. bd. dirs. Prime Retail, Inc., NASDAQ: PRME and PRMEP; bd. dirs. Prime Residential, Inc., NASDAQ: PRES. Mem. Chgo. Devel. Coun., 1987. Mem. ABA, Ill. Bar Assn., Urban Land Inst., Chgo. Club, Econ. Club Chgo., Nat. Realty Com. (mem. chmn.'s roundtable 1992—), Nat. Assn. Real Estate Investment Trusts, Order of Coif, Phi Delta Phi, Beta Alpha Psi. Office: The Prime Group 77 W Wacker Dr Ste 3900 Chicago IL 60601-1629

RESCIGNO, RICHARD JOSEPH, editor; b. N.Y.C., Apr. 13, 1946; s. Vincent James and Rose (Sofia) R.; m. Carol Sue Conyne, Apr. 22, 1978; children: Timothy, Daniel. BA in English Lit., Fairleigh Dickinson U., 1967; MS in Journalism, Columbia U., 1968. Reporter The Hudson Dispatch, Union City, N.J., 1967; reporter, copy editor The Bergen Record, Hackensack, N.J., 1971-75; reporter, copy editor, asst. city editor Newsday, Melville, N.Y., 1975-81; sr. editor, news editor, asst. mng. editor, mng. editor Barron's, The Dow Jones Bus. and Fin. Weekly, N.Y.C., 1981—. With U.S. Army, 1968-70. Avocations: foreign languages, travel, sports. Office: Barron's 200 Liberty St New York NY 10281

RESCORLA, ROBERT ARTHUR, psychology educator; b. Pitts, May 9, 1940; s. Arthur R. and Mildred J. (Jenkins) R.; m. Shirley Steele; children: Eric, Michael. BA, Swarthmore Coll., 1962; PhD, U. Pa., 1966; MA, Yale U., 1974. Successively asst. prof., assoc. prof., prof. Yale U., New Haven, 1966-80; prof. psychology U. Pa., Phila., 1981—, James Skinner prof. sci., 1986—, dean of coll. Sch. of Arts and Scis., 1994—. Author: Pavlovian Second-Order Conditioning, 1980; editor: Animal Learning and Behavior, 1995—; contbr. articles to profl. jours. Mem. APA (pres. div. 3 1985, Disting. Sci. Contbn. award 1986), Am. Psychol. Soc. (William James fellow 1988), NAS, AAAS (pres. sect. J, psychology 1988-89), Soc. Exptl. Psychologists (Warren medal 1991), Psychonomic Soc. (mem. governing bd. 1979-85, chmn. publ. bd. 1985-86), Ea. Psychol. Assn. (bd. dirs. 1983-86, pres. 1986-87). Office: U Pa Dept Psychology 3815 Walnut St Philadelphia PA 19104-3604

RESEK, ROBERT WILLIAM, economist; b. Berwyn, Ill., July 2, 1935; s. Ephraim Frederick and Ruth Elizabeth (Rummele) R.; m. Lois Doll, July 9, 1960; 1 child, Richard Alden. BA, U. Ill., 1957; AM, Harvard U., 1960, PhD, 1961. Vis. scholar MIT, Cambridge, 1967-68; asst. prof. econs. U. Ill., Urbana, 1961-65, assoc. prof., 1965-70, prof., 1970—; dir. Bur. Econ. and Bus. Rsch., 1977-89, acting v.p. for acad. affairs, 1987-89, v.p. for acad. affairs, 1989-94; prof. Inst. Govt. and Pub. Affairs, 1994—; vis. prof. U. Colo., 1967, 74, 75, 76, 82, Kyoto (Japan) U., 1976; cons. GM, 1964-66, U.S. Congress Joint Econ. Com., 1978-80, ABA, 1980-82; vis. scholar UCLA, 1994-95; co-dir. Midwest Economy: Issues and Policy, Midwest Govs. Conf., 1981; bd. dirs. Midwest U. Consortium Internat. Activities, v.p., 1991-94. Co-author: Environmental Contamination by Lead and Other Heavy Metals—Synthesis and Modeling, 1978, Special Topics in Mathematics for Economists, 1976, A Comparative Cost Study of Staff Panel and Participating Attorney Panel Prepaid Legal Service Plans, 1981; editor: Illinois Economic Outlook, 1982-87, Illinois Economic Statistics, 1981; co-editor: The Midwest Economy: Issues and Policy, 1982, Frontiers of Business and Economic Research Management, 1983, Illinois Statistical Abstract, 1987. Woodrow Wilson fellow, 1957; Social Sci. Rsch. Coun. grantee, 1964; NSF fellow, 1967-69, grantee, 1974-77; U.S. Dept. State scholar, Japan, 1976. Mem. Assn. Univ. Bus. and Econ. Rsch. (mem. exec. com. 1977-89, v.p. 1978-82, pres. 1982-83), Econometric Soc., Beta Gamma Sigma, Phi Kappa Phi. Home: 201 E Holmes St Urbana IL 61801-6612 Office: Univ Ill 211 IGPA 1007 W Nevada St Urbana IL 61801-3812

RESHOTKO, ELI, aerospace engineer, educator; b. N.Y.C., Nov. 18, 1930; s. Max and Sarah (Kalisky) R.; m. Adina Venit, June 7, 1953; children: Deborah, Naomi, Miriam Ruth. B.S., Cooper Union, 1950; M.S., Cornell U., 1951; Ph.D., Calif. Inst. Tech., 1960. Aero. research engr. NASA-Lewis Flight Propulsion Lab., Cleve., 1951-56; head fluid mechanics sect. NASA-Lewis Flight Propulsion Lab., 1956-57; head high temperature plasma sect. NASA-Lewis Research Center, 1960-61, chief plasma physics br., 1961-64; asso. prof. engring. Case Inst. Tech., Cleve., 1964-66, dean, 1986-87; prof. engring. Case Western Res. U., 1966-88, chmn. dept. fluid thermal and aerospace scis., 1970-76, chmn. dept. mech. and aerospace engring., 1976-79, Kent H. Smith prof. engring., 1989—; Susman vis. prof. dept. aero. engring. Technion-Israel Inst. Tech., Haifa, Israel, 1969-70; cons. United Technologies Research Ctr., United Research Corp., Dynamics Tech. Inc., Micro Craft Tech., Martin-Marietta Corp., Rockwell Internat.; mem. adv. com. fluid dynamics NASA, 1961-64; mem. aero. adv. com. NASA, 1980-87, chmn. adv. subcom. on aerodynamics, 1983-85; chmn. U.S. Boundary Layer Transition Study Group, NASA/USAF, 1970—; U.S. mem. fluid dynamics panel AGARD-NATO, 1981-88; chmn. steering com. Symposium on Engring. Aspects Magneto-hydro-dynamics, 1966, Case-NASA Inst. for Computational Mechanics in Propulsion, 1985-92, USRA/NASA ICASE Sci. Coun., 1992; Joseph Wunsch lectr. Technion-Israel Inst. Tech., 1990. Contbr. articles to tech. jours. Chmn. bd. govs. Cleve. Coll. Jewish Studies, 1981-84. Guggenheim fellow Calif. Inst. Tech., 1957-59. Fellow ASME, AAAS, AIAA (Fluid and Plasma Dynamics award 1980, Dryden lectr. in rsch. 1994), Am. Phys. Soc., Am. Acad. Mechanics (pres. 1986-87); mem. NAE, AAUP, Ohio Sci. and Engring. Roundtable, Sigma Xi, Tau Beta Pi, Pi Tau Sigma. Office: Case Western Reserve Univ University Cir Cleveland OH 44106

RESIKA, PAUL, artist; b. N.Y.C., Aug. 15, 1928. Student, Sol Wilson, N.Y.C., 1940-44, Hans Hofmann Sch., 1945-47, Venice, Italy, 1950-53. adj. prof. art Cooper Union, 1966-78; instr. Art Students League, 1968-69; faculty Skowhagen Sch. Painting and Sculpture, 1973, 76; chmn. M.F.A. program Parsons Sch. Design, 1978-89. Artist-in-residence, Dartmouth Coll., 1972; one-man shows include George Dix Gallery, N.Y.C., 1948, Peridot Gallery, N.Y.C., 1965, 67, 68, 69, 70, Washburn Gallery, N.Y.C., 1971, 73, Hopkins Ctr. Dartmouth Coll., 1972, Graham Gallery, N.Y.C., 1976, 77, 79, 81, 83, 85, Longpoint Gelelry, Provincetown, Mass., 1979, 81, 95, 89, 92, 25-yr. survey Artists Choice Mus., 1985, Merideth Long Gallery, Houston, 1986, Kornbluth Gallery, Fairlawn, N.J., 1986, Crane Kalman Gallery, London, 1986, Graham/Modern Gallery, 1987-88, 90, Salander-O'Reilly Galleries, N.Y.C., 1993, 94, 95 Am. Acad. Arts and Letters, 1994, Walker-Kornbluth Gallery, Fairlawn, 1995, Vered Gallery, East Hampton, N.Y., 1995, Longpoint Gallery, Provincetown, 1995; represented in permanent collections U. Nebr. Art Gallery, Indpls. Mus. Art, Chase Manhattan Bank, N.Y.C., Neuberger Mus., SUNY, Pruchase, U. Wyo., Laramie, Met. Mus. Art N.Y., Colby Coll., NAD, Owensboro (Ky.) Mus. Art, U. Ariz., William Benton Mus. Art, Hood Museum, Darthmouth Coll., Hanover, N.H., Tucson Mus. Art, U. Conn., Crackow Mus. Art, Poland, Parish Art Mus., Southampton, N.Y., Heckscher Mus., Huntington, N.Y., Mills Coll. Mus., Oakland, Calif., pvt. collections. Recipient award Am. Acad. Arts and Letters, 1977, Altman prize NAD, 1982, 91; Louis Comfort Tiffany grantee, 1959; Ingram Merrill grantee, 1969; Guggenheim fellow, 1984. Mem. NAD, Am. Acad. Arts and Letters. Office: care Salander-O'Reilly Galleries 20 E 79th St New York NY 10021-0106

RESKE, STEVEN DAVID, lawyer; b. Mpls., May 31, 1962; s. Albert Edgar Reske and Florence Altland Marxen. BA with distinction, St. Olaf Coll., Northfield, Minn., 1985; JD cum laude, Boston U., 1988. Bar: Ill. 1988, Minn. 1989, U.S. Dist. Ct. Minn. 1991, U.S. Ct. Appeals (5th cir.) 1989, (7th and 8th cir.) 1992, U.S. Supreme Ct. 1993. Intern U.S. Senator Durenberger, Washington, 1981-82, Abbott-Northwestern Hosp., Mpls., 1984, U.S. Dist. Ct. Judge Magnuson, St. Paul, 1986; summer assoc. Faegre & Benson, Mpls., 1987, assoc. (on leave), 1989—; assoc. Sidley & Austin, Chgo., 1988; law clk. U.S. Ct. Appeals, 5th Cir. Judge, Shreveport, La., 1988-89. Author CD Rev., 1993—; contbr. articles to profl. jours.; editor Am. Jour. Law and Medicine, 1987-88. Recipient Am. Jurisprudence award Boston U. Sch. Law, 1987, Edward F. Hennessey scholar, 1987, G. Joseph Tauro scholar, 1986. Mem. ABA.

RESNICK, ALAN HOWARD, health care and optics executive; b. Boston, Nov. 1, 1943; s. Max Lawrence and Natalie (Levine) R.; m. Janice M. Mark, Jan. 26, 1948; children: Stephen Seth, Helaine Elise, Eileen, Michelle. BS, Tufts U., 1965; MBA, Columbia U., 1967. Fin. analyst E.I. DuPont de Nemours & Co., Wilmington, Del., 1967-73; various positions Bausch & Lomb Inc., Rochester, N.Y., 1973—, treas., 1986—; mem. adv. bd. Allendale Ins. Co., Johnston, R.I., 1987. Bd. dirs. Rochester Monroe County chpt. ARC, 1988—, Park Ridge Hosp., 1990—. Jewish. Avocation: stamp collecting. Office: Bausch & Lomb Inc 1 Bausch & Lomb Pl Rochester NY 14604

RESNICK, ALICE ROBIE, state supreme court justice; b. Erie, Pa., Aug. 21, 1939; d. Adam Joseph and Alice Suzanne (Spizarny) Robie; m. Melvin L. Resnick, Mar. 20, 1970. PhB, Siena Heights Coll., 1961; JD, U. Detroit, 1964. Bar: Ohio 1964, Mich. 1965, U.S. Supreme Ct. 1970. Asst. county prosecutor Lucas County Prosecutor's Office, Toledo, 1964-75, trial atty., 1965-75; judge Toledo Mcpl. Ct., 1976-83, 6th Dist. Ct. Appeals, State of Ohio, Toledo, 1983-88; instr. U. Toledo, 1968-69; justice Ohio Supreme Ct., 1989—; co-chairperson Ohio State Gender Fairness Task Force. Trustee Siena Heights Coll., Adrian, Mich., 1982—; organizer Crime Stopper Inc., Toledo, 1981—; mem. Mayor's Drug Coun.; bd. dirs. Guest House Inc. Mem. ABA, Toledo Bar Assn., Lucas County Bar Assn., Nat. Assn. Women Judges, Am. Judicature Soc., Toledo Women's Bar Assn., Ohio State Women's Bar Assn. (organizer), Toledo Mus. Art, Internat. Inst. Toledo. Roman Catholic. Home: 2407 Edgehill Rd Toledo OH 43615-2321 Office: Supreme Ct Office 30 E Broad St Fl 3 Columbus OH 43215-3414

RESNICK, DONALD IRA, lawyer; b. Chgo., July 19, 1950; s. Roland S. and Marilyn B. (Weiss) R.; m. Jill Allison White, July 3, 1977; children: Daniel, Allison. BS with high honors, U. Ill., 1972; JD, Harvard U., 1975. Bar: Ill. 1975, U.S. Dist. Ct. (no. dist.) Ill. 1975. Assoc. Arvey, Hodes, Costello & Burman, Chgo., 1975-80, ptnr., 1981-83; sr. ptnr. Nagelberg & Resnick, Chgo., 1983-89, Levenstein & Resnick, Chgo., 1989-91; co-chmn. real estate dept. Jenner & Block, Chgo., 1992—; gen. counsel Real Estate Consortium. Bd. dirs. Ill. chpt. Real Estate/Investment Assn., Chgo., 1986—. Mem. ABA. Club: Birchwood (Highland Park, Ill.). Office: Jenner & Block 1 E Ibm Plz Chicago IL 60611

RESNICK, IDRIAN NAVARRE, foundation administrator; b. Wichita, Kans., Apr. 24, 1936; s. Herbert and Virginiae Miriam (Goldsmith) Speer; m. Jane Letham Riley (div. 1980); children: Michael Mosi, David Shaka; m. Kathleen Margaret Pelich (div. 1993); stepchildren: Robert Andrew, Kathleen Mary, Janice Margaret; m. Louise La Montagne, 1996. BA, Clark U., 1958; MA, Boston U., 1961, PhD, 1966. Lectr. dept. econs. Boston U., 1962-63; asst. prof. econs. Howard U., Washington, 1963-64; lectr. econs. U. Dar es Salaam, Tanzania, 1964-67; vis. prof. econs. Princeton (N.J.) U., 1967-68; asst. prof. econs. Columbia U., N.Y.C., 1968-70; sr. economist Ministry Econ. Planning, Dar es Salaam, 1970-72; exec. dir. Econ. Devel. Bur., New Haven, 1974-81; pres. Resnick Devel. Services, New Haven, 1982—; exec. dir. Assn. Am. Indian Affairs, N.Y.C., 1985-89, Action for Corp. Accountability, New Haven, 1991-94; prof. Cornell U., Ithaca, N.Y., 1982-84; cons. Govt. of Nicaragua, Managua, 1979-81, Govt. of the Netherlands, The Hague, 1977, Govt. of Somalia, Mogodishu, 1985. Author: The Long Transition: Building Socialism in Tanzania, 1981, Controlling Consulting, 1989; editor: Tanzania: Revolution by Education, 1968; video producer (in the Lakota lang.) AIDS, 1989; contbr. articles to profl. jours. Organizer Namibia Com., New Haven, 1977-79, Conn. Task Force on Cen. Am., 1985; mem. Pledge of Resistance, U.S., 1985—; vol. adviser AIDS Interfaith Network, New Haven, 1990. Nat. Edn. scholar U.S. Govt., 1959-62; Albert Schweitzer Resh fellow Columbia U., 1969-70. Avocations: chess, theatre, travel, tennis, golf, photography, woodworking, classical music. Home: 16 Old Pawson Rd Branford CT 06405

RESNICK, JEFFREY LANCE, federal magistrate judge; b. Bklyn., Mar. 5, 1943; s. Bernard and Selma (Monheit) R.; m. Margery O'Connor, May 27, 1990. BA, U. Conn., 1964; LLB, U. Conn., West Hartford, 1967. Bar: Conn. 1967, N.Y. 1968, U.S. V.I. 1968, D.C. 1979, U.S. Ct. Appeals (3d cir.) 1979. Assoc. Office of J.D. Marsh, Christiansted, St. Croix, V.I., 1967-69; asst. atty. gen. Dept. Law, Christiansted, 1969-73; ptnr. James & Resnick, Christiansted, 1973-89; magistrate judge U.S. Dist. Ct. V.I., Christiansted, 1989—. Active V.I. Bridge Team, 1971—. Jewish. Avocations: writing poetry and palindromes. Office: US District Court 3013 Est Golden Rock Christiansted VI 00820-4256

RESNICK, MYRON J., retired insurance company executive, lawyer; b. Louisville, July 13, 1931; s. Harry C. and Sybil G. (Glick) R.; m. Alicia M. Ward, Dec. 16, 1967; children—Hugh, Clay, David. B.S. in Econs., U. Pa., 1953; J.D., U. Mich., 1956. Various positions Allstate Ins. Co., Northbrook, Ill., 1959-88, sr. v.p., treas. bd. dirs., 1959-95; chmn. bd. Federated Ins. Co. Ltd. (U.K.), Sale, Cheshire, Eng., 1979-81; dir. Allstate Ins. Co. Ltd. (U.K.), Sale; pres. Allstate Investment Mgmt. Co. Mem. Chgo. exec. com. Anti-Defamation League, 1975—; bd. dirs. Chgo. Urban League, 1987—, St. Scholastica High Sch., Chgo., 1977-79; trustee George Williams Coll., Downers Grove, Ill., 1981-93, chmn. bd. trustees, 1991-93; trustee Aurora U., 1993—; bd. advisors Inst. Law and Econs. U. Pa., 1994—. With U.S. Army, 1956-58. Mem. ABA (resource devel. coun.), Chgo. Bar Assn., Ill. Bar Assn., Assn. Life Ins. Counsel, Chgo. Mortgage Attys. Assn. (bd. dirs. 1965-75), Reform Club (London).

RESNICK, PAUL R., research chemist; b. N.Y.C., Apr. 7, 1934; married, 1966; 1 child. BA, Swarthmore Coll., 1955; PhD in Organic Chemistry, Cornell U., 1961. Fellow U. Calif., Berkeley, 1960-62; from chemist to sr. rsch. chemist E.I. DuPont De Nemours & Co., Inc., 1962-74, rsch. assoc., 1974-85, rsch. fellow, 1985-88, sr. rsch. fellow, 1988-91, DuPont fellow, 1991—. Recipient Am. Chem. Soc. award for Creative Work in Flourine Chemistry, 1995. Mem. Am. Chem. Soc. (Award for Creative Work in Fluorine Chemistry 1995). Office: DuPont Fluoroproducts PO Drawer Z Fayetteville NC 28302-1770

RESNICK, ROBERT, physicist, educator; b. Balt., Jan. 11, 1923; s. Abraham and Anna (Dubin) R.; m. Mildred Saltzman, Oct. 14, 1945; children—Trudy, Abby, Regina. A.B., Johns Hopkins U., 1943, Ph.D. (Pres.'s Fund scholar 1946-49), 1949. Physicist NACA, Cleve., 1944-46; asst. prof., assoc. prof. physics U. Pitts., 1949-56; assoc. prof., prof. physics Rensselaer Poly. Inst., Troy, N.Y., 1956-93; prof. emeritus, 1993—; chmn. interdisciplinary sci. curriculum Rensselaer Poly. Inst., Troy, N.Y., 1973-88, Edward P. Hamilton Disting. prof. sci., 1975-93; hon. research fellow Harvard U., 1964-65; Fulbright prof. Peru, 1971; hon. vis. prof. Peoples Republic of China, 1981, 85; mem. Commn. on Coll. Physics, 1960-68; commencement speaker Rensselaer Poly. Inst., 1993. Author: A Manual for Laboratory Physics, 1954, (with D. Halliday) Physics, 1960, 3d edit., 1978, 4th edit., 1991, extended version, 1986, 2d edit. extended version, 1991, Introduction to Special Relativity, 1968, (with R. Eisberg) Notes on Quantum Theory, 1968, Notes on Modern Physics, 1969, Quantum Physics of Atoms, Molecules, Solids, Nuclei and Particles, 1974, 2d edit., 1985, (with D. Halliday) Fundamentals of Physics, 1970, 4th edit., 1993, extended version, 1988, 2d edit., 1993, (with others) Student Study Guide for Physics, 1970, 5th edit., 1993, Basic Concepts in Relativity and Early Quantum Theory, 1972, 2d edit., 1985, Basic Concepts in Relativity, 1991; author: (with others) Sourcebook for Programmable Calculators, 1978, (with E. Derringh) Solutions to Physics Problems, 1980, 4th edit., 1992, (with K. Brownstein) Tests for Physics, 1987; books translated into numerous fgn. langs; mem. adv. bd., project staff: Physical Science for Non-Scientists, 1964-678, pub., 1968; co-dir.: Project Physics Demonstration Experiments, 1962-70; pub. project, 1970, Workshop on Apparatus for College Physics, 1964-65, 66, Videotapes in Physics Instruction, 1975-78, 1978; dir. project Physics Demonstration and Laboratory Apparatus Workshop, 1960-61; pub. project, 1961; adv editor: John Wiley & Sons, Inc., 1967-89, Macmillan Pubs., 1990-94; mem. U.S. adv. bd. Quantum joint USSR/USA sci. mag., 1989-93. Recipient Disting. Svc. citation Am. Assn. Physics Tchrs., 1967, Hans Christian Oersted medal, 1974, Esso award for outstanding teaching, 1953, Disting. Faculty award Rensselaer Poly. Inst., 1971; named to Hall of Fame, Balt. City Coll., 1989; Robert Resnick Ctr. for Physics established at Rensselaer Poly. Inst., 1993, Robert Resnick Ann. Sci. Lectr. series endowed, 1993. Fellow AAAS, Am. Phys. Soc.; mem. AAUP, Am. Assn. Physics Tchrs. (v.p. 1986, pres.-elect 1987, pres. 1988), Am. Soc. Engring. Edn., Am. Inst. Physics (governing bd. 1987-90), Textbook Author Assn. (coun. 1990-93), Phi Beta Kappa, Sigma Xi. Rsch. publs. in aerodynamics, nuclear physics, atomic physics, upper atmosphere physics, history of physics, physics edn. Home: 13 Oxford Rd Troy NY 12180-7053

RESNICK, STEWART ALLEN, diversified company executive; b. Jersey City, Dec. 24, 1936; s. David and Yetta (Goldmaker) R.; children from previous marriage: Jeffrey Brian, Ilene Sue, William Jay; m. Lynda Rae Harris, Nov. 26, 1972; children: Jonathon Charles Sinay, Jason Daniel Sinay. BS, UCLA, 1959, LLB, 1962. Chmn., owner Roll Internat. Corp., L.A., 1958—; chmn. The Franklin Mint, Franklin Center, Pa., 1985—; chmn., owner Teleflora, L.A., Paramount Citrus Co., L.A., Paramount Farming Co., L.A. Bd. trustees Bard Coll., N.Y.C.; acquistions com. Nat. Gallery, Washington; co-chmn. mktg. dept., adv. bd., mem. Mgmt. Edn. Coun., The Wharton Sch., U. Pa.; exec. com. mem. Mayor's Alliance for a Safer L.A. Avocations: health and fitness related activities. Office: The Franklin Mint US Rt 1 Media PA 19091

RESNIK, HARVEY LEWIS PAUL, psychiatrist; b. Buffalo, Apr. 6, 1930; s. Samuel andCelia (Greenberg) R.; m. Audrey Ruth Frey, Aug. 30, 1964 (dec. 1993); children: Rebecca Gabrielle, Henry Seth Maccabee, Jessica Ruth. B.A. magna cum laude, U. Buffalo, 1951; M.D., Columbia, 1955; grad., Phila. Psychoanalytic Inst., 1967. Diplomate: Am. Bd. Psychiatry and Neurology. Intern Phila. Gen. Hosp., 1955-56, resident in surgery, 1956-57; resident in psychiatry Jackson Meml. Hosp., Miami, Fla., 1959-61; fellow U. Pa. Hosp., 1961-62, mem. staff, 1962-67; instr. Sch. Medicine, U. Pa., 1962-66; instr. med. hypnosis Sch. Medicine, U. Pa. (Grad. Sch. Medicine), 1963-65; clin. dir. psychiatry E. J. Meyer Meml. Hosp., Buffalo, 1967; dir. psychiatry E. J. Meyer Meml. Hosp., 1968; assoc. prof. psychiatry Sch. Medicine, SUNY at Buffalo, 1967, prof., 1968-70, dep. chmn. dept. psychiatry, 1968-69; chief Nat. Center for Studies of Suicide Prevention, NIMH, 1969-74, chief mental health emergencies sect., 1974-76; with Reproductive Biology Research Found., St. Louis, 1971; clin. prof. psychiatry Sch. Medicine, George Washington U., 1969—; dir. Human Behavior Found., 1975—; lectr. Sch. Medicine, Johns Hopkins, 1969-74; adj. prof. Johns Hopkins U. Sch. Pub. Health, 1981-82; prof. cmty. health Fed. City Coll., 1971-75; med. dir. Human Behavior Found., 1975—, Johns Hopkins U. Compulsive Gambling Ctr. (now Washington Ctr. for Pathol. Gambling); mem. dir. Univ. Alcohol and Substance Abuse Program, 1986—; CEO Assoc. Mental Helath Profls.; instr. Delaware Valley Group Therapy Inst.; vis. prof. Katholieke U., Leuven, Belgium, 1986—; cons. to Sec.-Gen. Ministry of Health, Belgium, 1986-95, NATO, 1986-87, also fellow Ten Kerselaere Psycho-Geriatric Hosp.; bd. dirs. Internat. Helath Ctr., Belgium, Human Behavior Found.; cons. various hosps. and orgns. Author: Suicidal Behaviors: Diagnosis and Management, 1968, 2d edit., 1994, (with M. E. Wolfgang) Treatment of the Sexual Offender, 1971, Sexual Behaviors: Social, Clinical and Legal Aspects, 1972, (with B. Hathorne) Suicide Prevention in the Seventies, 1973, (with H.L. Ruben) Emergency Psychiatric Care, 1974, (with others) The Prediction of Suicide, 1974, Emergency and Disaster Management, 1976; (with J.T. Mitchell) Emergency Response to Crisis, 1981; Editor: Bull. Suicidology, 1969-74; Contbr. (with others) articles on hypnosis, sexual offenders, marriage and sexual dysfunction treatment, suicide, death and dying, emergency psychiatric care. Mem. Addictions Adv. Bd. Prince Georges County, 1980-85. Served to capt. USAF, 1957-59, ETO-Middle East; capt. USNR; ret. Decorated officer in the Order King Leopold, Belgium, 1990. Fellow Am. Coll. Psychiatrists, Am. Psychiat. Assn. (life); mem. Med-Chi of Md., Prince Georges County Med. Assn., Phila. Psychoanalytic Soc., Columbia Med. Alumni Assn. (bd. dirs. 1993-95), Phi Beta Kappa, Beta Sigma Rho (grand vice warden 1963), Cosmos Club (Washington). Jewish. Office: Air Rights Ctr # 1300W 7315 Wisconsin Ave Bethesda MD 20814-3202 also: Univ Profl Ctr 4700 Berwyn House Rd # 201 College Park MD 20740-2474

RESNIK, LINDA ILENE, marketing and information executive, consultant; b. Dallas, Oct. 26, 1950; d. Harold and Reatha (Gordon) R. BJ in Broadcast Journalism, U. Mo., 1971; MA in Journalism, U. North Tex., 1977, MBA in Mktg., 1980. News and documentary producer Sta. KDFW-TV, Dallas, 1971-73; mktg.-info. officer Dallas County Community Coll. Dist., 1973-79; dir. mktg. The Learning Channel, Washington, 1980-82; dir. Nat. Narrowcast Service, Pub. Broadcasting Service, Washington, 1982-85; exec. dir. Am. Soc. Info. Sci., Washington, 1985-89, White House Conf. on Libr. and Info. Svcs., Washington, 1990—; mem. adv. com. ALA Library/Book Fellows Project; fellow Ctr. for Info. and Communication Scis., Ball State U.; mem. U.S. exec. com. U. of the World; mktg., tng. and telecommunications cons. to edni. assns., others. Writer and editor college-level study guides; scriptwriter college credit TV courses. Youth activities coordinator YMCA, Dallas, 1975-78; spl. event organizer Am. Cancer Soc., Dallas, 1976-77; com. leader Goals for Dallas, 1978-80. Recipient Best TV Feature Story award AP, Tex., 1973. Mem. Am. Soc. Assn. Execs., Am. Soc. Info. Sci. (pub. bull. 1985-89), Women in Cable, Info. Inst., Am. Mktg. Assn., Washington Met. Cable Club. Avocations: travel, racquet sports, reading, theater. Office: 3533 Piedmont Dr Plano TX 75075-6254

RESNIK, PETER L., lawyer; b. New Britain, Conn., Feb. 4, 1945; m. Kathleen Ann Murphy; children: Rebecca, Elizabeth, Benjamin. BA, Yale U., 1967; JD cum laude, Boston U., 1970. Bar: Mass. 1970. Ptnr. McDermott, Will & Emory, Boston. Editor: Boston U. Law Rev., 1968-70. Mem. ABA, Mass. Bar Assn. Office: McDermott Will & Emery 75 State St Ste 1700 Boston MA 02109-1807

RESNIK, REGINA, operatic singer; b. N.Y.C., Aug. 30, 1924; d. Sam and Ruth R.; m. Harry W. Davis, July 18, 1946; 1 son, Michael Philip; m. Arbit Blatas, 1975. B.A., Hunter Coll., 1942. condr. seminars on opera New Sch. for Social Research. Debut as Lady Macbeth, 1942; soprano debut Met. Opera Co., N.Y.C., 1944; mezzo-soprano debut, Met. Opera Co., N.Y.C., 1946; regular guest, Vienna Staatsoper, La Scala, Milan, Covent Garden, Salzburg, Deutsche Opera, Berlin, Teatro Colon, Buenos Aires, Bayreuth Festival, Germany, Munich Staatsoper, Chgo., Phila., San Francisco, others; co-dir., starred in: Carmen, Hamburg Opera, 1971, Electra, 1971, Falstaff at Nat. Opera Poland, 1975; starred in broadway prodn. Cabaret, 1987-88 (nominated for Tony award), prize-winning documentary Ghetto of Venice, PBS, 1983-87; has recorded extensively. Decorated comdr. French Acad. Arts, Scis. and Letters; recipient awards including U.S. Pres.'s medal, 40th Anniversary medal San Francisco Opera, 1982; named Kammersänger in Austria. Office: Am Guild Musical Artists 1727 Broadway New York NY 10019-5214

RESNIK, ROBERT, medical educator; b. New Haven, Dec. 7, 1938; s. Nathan Alfred and Elsie (Hershman) R.; m. Lauren Brahms, Oct. 29, 1966; children: Andrew Scott, Jamie Layne. BA, Yale U., 1960; MD, Case Western Res. U., 1965. Intern in internal medicine Mt. Sinai Hosp., Cleve., 1965-66; resident in ob-gyn. Yale U. Sch. Medicine, 1966-70; asst. prof. Sch. Medicine U. Calif., San Diego, 1974-78, assoc. prof., 1978-82, prof. reproductive medicine, 1982—, chmn. dept., 1982-95, dean clin. affairs, 1988-90, dean admissions, 1995—; cons. Nat. Heart, Lung and Blood Inst. NIH, Washington, 1987; mem. exec. com. Coun. Residency Edn. Ob-Gyn, Washington, 1988-94, residency rev. com., 1988-94. Editor: (textbook) Maternal-Fetal Medicine: Principles and Practice, 1984, 3d edit., 1994; contbr. numerous articles to profl. jours. Major U.S. Army, 1970-72. Rsch. grantee Nat. Found., NIH. Fellow Am. Coll. Obstetrics and Gynecology, Pacific Coast Obstet. and Gynecol. Soc.; mem. Soc. Gynecologic Investigation (coun. 1983-88), Perinatal Rsch. Soc. (pres. 1985), Am. Gynecologic and Obstet. Soc., San Diego Gynecol. Soc. (pres. 1982), Yale Club. Office: U Calif Sch Medicine Dept 0621 9500 Gilman Dr La Jolla CA 92093-0621

RESO, ANTHONY, geologist, earth resources economist; b. London, Eng., Aug. 10, 1934; s. Harry and Marion (Gerth) R.; came to U.S., 1940, naturalized, 1952. AB, Columbia Coll., N.Y.C., 1954; MA, Columbia U., 1955; postgrad. U. Cin., 1956-57; PhD (fellow) Rice U., 1960; postgrad. Grad. Sch. Bus. U. Houston, 1964-68. Instr. geology Queens Coll., Flushing, N.Y., 1954; geologist Atlantic Richfield Corp., Midland, Tex., 1955-56; asst. prof. geology and curator invertebrate paleontology Pratt Mus., Amherst (Mass.) Coll., 1959-62; staff rsch. geologist Tenneco Oil Co., Houston, 1962-86; geol. mgr. Peak Prodn. Co., Houston, 1986—, v.p., 1988—. Cons. in geol. rsch. Tenn. Gas and Oil Co., 1960-61; lectr. U. Houston, 1962-65; vis. prof. Rice U., 1980; mem. bd. advisers Gulf Univs. Rsch. Corp., Galveston, Tex., 1967-75, chmn., 1968-69; dir. Stewardship Properties, Houston, 1968—. Recipient rsch. grants Am. Assn. Petroleum Geologists, 1958, 59, Geol. Soc. Am., 1958, Eastman Fund, 1962; NSF fellow, 1959. Fellow Geol. Soc. Am. (com. investments 1984-95, chmn. 1985-92, budget com. 1993-95, Disting. Svc. award 1996), AAAS; mem. Am. Assn. Petroleum Geologists (life, com. convs. 1977-83, chmn. 1980-83, gen. chmn. nat. conv. 1979, com. on investments 1982-88, chmn. com. group ins. 1986-88, treas. 1986-88; Disting. svc. award 1985, found. trustee assoc. 1991), Paleontol. Soc., SEPM Soc. for Sedimentary Geology (com. on investments 1990—, chmn. 1992-95), Paleontol. Rsch. Instn., Tex. Acad. Sci., Houston Geol. Soc. (v.p. 1973-75, pres. 1975-76, chmn. constn. revision com. 1981, Disting. svc. award 1985), English-Speaking Union U.S. (dir. Houston chpt. 1978—, v.p. 1982-88, 94—, mem. scholarship com. 1988—, chmn. 1991—), Varsity C Club, Sigma Xi, Sigma Gamma Epsilon, Beta Theta Pi. Episcopalian. Contbr. profl. jours. Home: 1801 Huldy St Houston TX 77019-5767 Office: care Peak Prodn Co PO Box 130785 Houston TX 77219-0785

RESOR, STANLEY ROGERS, lawyer; b. N.Y.C., Dec. 5, 1917; s. Stanley Burnet and Helen (Lansdowne) R.; m. Jane Lawler Pillsbury, Apr. 4, 1942 (dec.); children: Stanley R., Charles P., John L., Edmund L., William B., Thomas S., James P. BA, Yale U., 1939, LLB, 1946. Bar: N.Y. 1947. Assoc., then ptnr. firm Debevoise & Plimpton, N.Y.C., 1946-65, 71-73, 79-87, of counsel, 1988-90; undersec. Dept. Army, 1965, sec., 1965-71, ambassador negotiations for Mut. and Balanced Force Reductions in Central Europe, 1973-78; undersec. for policy Dept. Def., 1978-79. Fellow Yale Corp., 1979-86. Served to maj. AUS, 1942-45. Decorated Silver Star, Bronze Star, Purple Heart; recipient George C. Marshall award Assn. U.S. Army, 1974, Sylvanus Thayer award Assn. Graduates of U.S. Mil. Acad., 1984. Mem. ABA, Assn. of Bar of City of N.Y. (chmn. com. internat. arms control and security affairs 1983-86), Atlantic Coun. (bd. dirs.), Arms Control Assn. (chmn. bd.), UN Assn. U.S.A. (nat. coun.), Coun. Fgn. Rels., Lawyers Alliance for World Security (bd. dirs.), Internat. Inst. Strategic Studies. Republican. Episcopalian. Home: 809 Weed St New Canaan CT 06840-4023 Office: Debevoise & Plimpton 875 3rd Ave New York NY 10022-6225

RESTANI, JANE A., federal judge; b. San Francisco, Feb. 27, 1948; d. Roy J. and Emilia C. Restani. BA, U. Calif., Berkeley, 1969; JD, U. Calif., Davis, 1973. Bar: Calif., 1973. Trial atty. U.S. Dept. Justice, Washington, 1973-76, asst. chief comml. litigation sect., 1976-80, dir. comml. litigation sect., 1980-83; judge U.S. Ct. Internat. Trade, N.Y.C., 1983—. Mem. Order of Coif. Office: US Ct Internat Trade 1 Federal Plz New York NY 10278-0001*

RESTER, ALFRED CARL, JR., physicist; b. New Orleans, July 11, 1940; s. Alfred Carl and Willietta (Voth) R.; m. Blanche Sue Bing, June 20, 1964 (div. Jan. 20, 1985); children: Andrea Dawn, Karen Alane; m. Sherry Alice Warren, Dec. 12, 1985. BS, Miss. Coll., 1962; MS, U. N.Mex., 1964; PhD, Vanderbilt U., 1969. Postdoctoral fellow U. Delft, Netherlands, 1969-70, scientist first class, 1970-71; guest prof. U. Bonn (Germany) Dept. Physics, 1972-74; asst. prof. Emory U., Dept. Physics, Atlanta, 1975-76; assoc. prof. Tenn. Tech. U., Dept. Physics, Cookeville, Tenn., 1976-77; vis. assoc. prof. U. Fla., Dept. Physics, Gainesville, 1978-81; assoc. rsch. scientist U. Fla. Space Astronomy Lab., Gainesville, 1981-88; dir. U. Fla. Inst. for Astrophysics and Planetary Exploration, Alachua, 1988-93; pres., CEO Constellation Tech. Corp., St. Petersburg, Fla., 1992—; cons. Lockheed Ga., Marietta, 1976, Oak Ridge (Tenn.) Nat. Lab., 1976-77. Editor: High Energy Radiation Background in Space, 1989; contbr. articles to profl. jours. Recipient Antarctica Svc. medal NSF-USN, 1988; grantee various fed. agys. Mem. AAAS, Am. Phys. Soc., Am. Astron. Soc., Sigma Xi Sci. Rsch. Soc. Avocations: writing fiction, fishing, nature walks. Office: Constellation Tech Corp 9887 4th St N Ste 100 Saint Petersburg FL 33702

RESTIVO, JAMES JOHN, JR., lawyer; b. Pitts., Aug. 15, 1946; s. James J. and Dorothy (Ardolino) R.; m. Gail Sharon Hackenburg, July 11, 1970; 4 children. BA in History, U. Pa., 1968; JD, Georgetown U., 1971. Bar: Pa. 1971, U.S. Dist. Ct. (we. and ea. dists.) Pa. 1971, U.S. Ct. Appeals (3d cir.) 1971, U.S. Supreme Ct. 1979. Ptnr. Reed, Smith, Shaw & McClay, Pitts., 1979—, head litigation group, 1986—. Mem. editl. staff Georgetown Law Rev., 1970-71. Bd. dirs. Greater Pitts. C. of C. Mem. ABA, Acad. Trial Lawyers Allegheny County, Allegheny County Bar Assn., Pa. Economy League (Western divsn.), Def. Rsch. Inst. Home: 209 Deer Meadow Dr Pittsburgh PA 15241-2253 Office: Reed Smith Shaw & McClay 435 6th Ave Pittsburgh PA 15219-1809

RESWICK, JAMES BIGELOW, former government official, rehabilitation engineer, educator; b. Ellwood City, Pa., Apr. 16, 1922; s. Maurice and Katherine (Parker) R.; children: James Bigelow, David Parker (dec.), Pamela Reswick; m. Irmtraud Orthlies Hoelzerkopf, Dec., 27, 1973. SBME, MIT, 1943; SM, Mass. Inst. Tech., 1948, ScD, 1952; DEng (hon.), Rose Poly. Inst., 1968. Asst. prof., then assoc. prof., head machine design and graphics div. MIT, 1948-59; Leonard Case prof. engring., dir. Engring. Design Ctr., Case Western Res. U., 1959-70; prof. biomed. engring. and orthopaedics U. So. Calif., also dir. of rsch. dept. orthopaedics, 1970-80; assoc. dir. tech. Nat. Inst. Handicapped Rsch., U.S. Dept. Edn.; dir. VA Rehab. R & D Evaluation Unit VA Med. Ctr., Washington, 1984-88; dir. rsch. scis. Nat. Inst. on Disability and Rehab. Rsch. U.S. Dept. Edn., Washington, 1989-94; engring. cons. on automatic control, product devel., automation and bio-med. engring. Mem. com. prosthetics R & D Nat. Acad. Scis., 1962—; chmn. design and devel. com.; mem. bd. rev. Army R & D Office, 1965—; mem. applied physiology and biomed. engring. study sect. NIH, 1972—. Author: (with C.K. Taft) Introduction to Dynamic Systems, 1967; also articles.; Editor: (with F.T. Hambrecht) Functional Electrical Stimulation, 1977; series on engring. design, 1963—. Chmn. Mayor's Commn. for Urban Transp., Cleve., 1969. Served to lt. (j.g.) USNR, 1943-46, PTO. Decorated officer Yugoslav Flag with golden wreath medal (Yugoslavia), 1990; recipient Product Engring. Master Designer award, 1969, Isabelle and Leonard H. Goldenson award United Cerebral Palsy Assn., 1973; NSR sr. postdoctoral fellow Imperial Coll., London, 1957. Fellow IEEE, Am. Inst. Med. and Biological Engring. (founder); mem. ASME (honor award for best paper 1956, sr. mem.), Am. Soc. Engring. Edn., Instrument Soc. Am., Biomed. Engring. Soc. (sr. mem., pres. 1973, dir.), Am. Acad. Orthopedic Surgeons (asso.), Inst. Medicine of Nat. Acad. Scis., Nat. Acad. Engring., Internat. Soc. Orthotics and Prosthetics, Orthopaedics Research Soc., Rehab. Engring. Soc. N.Am. (founding pres.), Sigma XI. Patentee in field. Home: 1003 Dead Run Dr Mc Lean VA 22101-2120

RESZKA, ALFONS, computer systems architect; b. Imielin, Poland, Dec. 17, 1924; s. Alfons and Maria (Galazka) R.; m. Betty Reszka; children: Ann, Elizabeth, Alfred, Catherine. B.S., U. London, 1954; M.S.E.E., Northwestern U., 1960, Ph.D., 1976. Engr. Brit. Jeffrey Diamond, Wakefield, Eng., 1954-55; lectr. Bradford Tech. Coll., Eng., 1955-56; engr. A.C. Nielson, Chgo., 1956-59; with Teletype Corp., Skokie, Ill., 1959-80, project dir., 1969-75, sr. staff engr., 1975-80; cons. computer architecture, computer networks and data base mgmt. systems Bell Labbs., Naperville, Ill., 1980-85; prof. info. sci. North Central Coll., Naperville, 1983-86; computer systems cons. ARC, Wheaton, Ill., 1986—. Patentee in electronics. Mem. IEEE, Computer Soc., Tech. Com. of Computer Architecture. Home: 1090 Creekside Dr Wheaton IL 60187-6173 Office: ARC 1090 Creekside Dr Wheaton IL 60187-6173

RETALLACK, GREGORY JOHN, geologist, educator; b. Hobart, Australia, Nov. 8, 1951; came to U.S., 1977; s. Kenneth John Retallack and Moira Wynn (Dean) Gollan; m. Diane Alice Johnson, May 21, 1981; children: Nicholas John, Jeremy Douglas. B.A., Macquarie U., Sydney, 1973; B.Sc. with honors, U. New Eng., 1974, Ph.D., 1978. Vis. asst. prof. Northern Ill. U., Dekalb, 1977-78; vis. scholar Ind. U., Bloomington, 1978-81; asst. prof. U. Oreg., Eugene, 1981-86, assoc. prof., 1986-92, prof., 1992—. Author: Geological Excursion Guide to the Sea Cliffs North of Sydney, 1978, Late Eocene and Oligocene Paleosols from Badlands National Park, South Dakota, 1983, Soils of the Past, 1990, Miocene Paleosols and Ape Habitats in Pakistan and Kenya, 1991; contbr. numerous articles in field to profl. jours. Grantee NSF, 1979—, Wenner-Gren Found., 1983. Mem. Geol. Soc. Am., Geol. Soc. Australia, Bot. Soc. Am., Paleontol. Soc. (pres. Pacific sect. 1986), Oreg. Acad. Sci. (pres. 1986), Soc. Econ. Paleontologists and Mineralogists, Sigma Xi (pres. U. Oreg. chpt. 1983-84). Home: 2715 Elinor St Eugene OR 97403-2513

RETHEMEYER, ROBERT JOHN, social studies educator; b. St. Louis, Jan. 20, 1948; s. John Henry and Olivia Antonia (Fallbeck) R.; m. Kay Lynn Jones, Aug. 22, 1971; children: Robin Lynn, Rustin John. BS in Edn., Cen. Mo. State Coll., 1970; M in Sch. Adminstrn., Cen. Mo. State U., 1973, EdS in Supt., 1985. Tchr. 7th grade social studies Smith-Hale Jr. H.S., Kansas City, Mo., 1970-78, asst. prin., 1978-80, tchr. 7th and 8th grade social studies, 1980—, summer sch. prin., 1981—; chmn. bldg. dept. Cons. Sch. Dist. 1, Kansas City, 1982—, alt. sch. com., 1993—. Mem. NEA, Nat. Coun. for Social Studies, Phi Delta Kappa. Home: 1026 SE Timbercreek Ln Lees Summit MO 64081-3003 Office: Smith-Hale Jr H S 8925 Longview Rd Kansas City MO 64134-4110

RETHORE, BERNARD GABRIEL, diversified company executive; b. Bklyn., May 22, 1941; s. Francis Joseph and Katharine Eunice (MacDwyer) R.; BA, Yale U., 1962; MBA, U. Pa., 1967; m. Marilyn Irene Watt, Dec. 1, 1962; children: Bernard Michael, Tara Jean, Kevin Watt, Alexandra Marie, Rebecca Ann, Christopher Philip, Abigail Lyn. Assoc., McKinsey & Co., Inc., Washington, 1967, then sr. assoc., 1973; v.p./gen. mgr. Greer div. Microdot, Inc., Darien, Conn., 1973-77, v.p. ops. connector group, 1977-78, pres. bus. devel. group, 1978-82, pres. fastening systems and sealing devices groups, 1982-84, pres. Microdot Industries, 1984-87, pres., chief exec. officer, 1988; pres. Microdot Europe Ltd., 1984-88; sr. v.p. Phelps Dodge Corp., Phoenix, 1989-95; group exec. Phelps Dodge Industries, 1989-90, pres., 1990-95; pres., CEO, bd. dirs. BW/IP Internat. Inc., 1995—; bd. dirs. Blue Cross/Blue Shield of Conn., 1989-90, Maytag Corp., 1994—; cons. U.S. Govt., UN; mem. Global Adv. Coun., Am. Grad. Sch. Internat. Mgmt., 1990—, chmn., 1991-94. Mem. dean's adv. bd. Wharton Sch. Bus., U. Pa., 1972-80; chmn. Emmaus adv. bd. Fairfield Prep. Sch.-Lauralton Hall Acad., 1981-85; elected mem. bd. fin. Town of Westport, Conn., 1986-90; trustee Ballet Arizona, 1989-95, vice chmn. 1991-95; bd. dirs. Boys Hope of Phoenix, 1989-95; trustee Phoenix Country Day Sch., 1992—; trustee Am. Grad. Sch. Internat. Mgmt., 1994—. Served to capt., inf., AUS, 1962-65. Decorated Bronze Star. Mem. Nat. Assn. Mfrs. (bd. dirs. 1994-95), Yale Club (N.Y.C.), Union League (Chgo.), Ariz. Club (Scottsdale). Home: 6533 E Maverick Rd Paradise Valley AZ 85253-2632 Office: BW/IP Internat Inc 200 Oceangate Blvd Ste 900 Long Beach CA 90802

RETSINAS, NICOLAS P., federal official. BA in Economics, NYU; M in City Planning, Harvard U. Exec. dir. Housing and Mortgage Corp., R.I., 1987-93; asst. sec. for Housing-Fed. Housing Commr., Washington, 1993—; dir. policy for Gov. R.I., 1991; adj. asst. prof. urban studies Brown U. Mem. Nat. Coun. State Housing Authorities (past sec.), Nat. Community Devel. Assn. (past pres.). Office: Fed Housing Finance Bd 451 7th St SW Washington DC 20410*

RETTIG, RICHARD ALLEN, social sciences educator, policy analyst, administrator; b. Seattle, Sept. 14, 1936; s. Roy Edward and Mildred Januara (Hegdahl) Rettig; m. Angie L. Magnusson, Aug. 10, 1968; children: Kirsten, Mark, Jerry. U.S. Bur. Budget, Washington, 1967-68, N.J. Dept. Higher Edn., Trenton, N.J., 1968-69; Asst. prof. Cornell U., Ithaca, N.Y., 1969-71; assoc. prof. Ohio State U., 1971-75; sr. social scientist RAND Corp., Washington, 1975-81; prof. social sci. Ill. Inst. Tech., Chgo., 1981-86, chmn. dept., 1981-85, dir. M.P.A. program, 1981-86; Inst. Med. of NAS, Washington, 1987-95; sr. social scientist RAND corp., 1995—. Author: Cancer Crusade: The Story of the National Cancer Act, 1977; editor: (with Norman G. Levinsky) Kidney Failure and the Federal Government, 1991, (with Laurence E. Earley and Richard A. Merrill) Food and Drug Administration Advisory Committees, 1992, (with Adam Yarmolinsky) Federal Regulation of Methadone Treatment, 1995; mem. editorial bd. Am. Jour. Kidney Diseases; contbr. articles to profl. jours. Fellow AAAS. Home: 5411 42nd St NW Washington DC 20015-2913 Office: The RAND Corp 2100 M St NW Washington DC 20037-1207

RETZ, WILLIAM ANDREW, naval officer; b. Blauvelt, N.Y., June 3, 1940; s. Andrew Macmillan and Katherine (Deyoe) R.; m. Julia Irene Patterson, Sept. 23, 1989; children: Andrew, Gregory, Mark, Alyse Reavis, Mark Rogers. Student, Tex. A&M U., 1957; BS in Mech. Engring., U. N.Mex., 1963; MS, George Washington U., 1970; grad., Naval War Coll., 1972. Commd. ensign USN, 1963, advanced through grades to rear adm., 1991; patrol officer river div. 511 USN, Vietnam, 1968-69; flag sec. to comdr. Amphibious Group Two USN, Norfolk, Va., 1972-74, exec. officer USS Ainsworth, 1974-76, commanding officer USS Stump, 1980-82, commodore Destroyer Squadron 22, 1985-87; dep. for ops. U.S. Cen. Command USN, Tampa, Fla., 1987-90; comdr. Naval Base Pearl Harbor, 1992-94, Naval Surface Group Mid. Pacific, 1992-94; commanded and closed Naval Base Phila., 1994-95; ret. USN, 1995. Active Episcopal Ch., Honolulu. Decorated Navy Dist. Svc. medal, Legion of Merit, Def. Disting. Svc. medal, Meritorious Svc. medal, Bronze star. Mem. U.S. Naval Inst. Avocations: running, sailing.

RETZER, KENNETH ALBERT, mathematics educator; b. Jacksonville, Ill., Nov. 6, 1933; s. Samuel Stark and Cora Edith (Martin) R.; m. Dorcas Anne Schroeder, Apr. 18, 1953 (dec. Aug. 1990); children: Martin Wayne, Kent Arnold, Sheryl Kaye; m. Wei Dong, Feb. 14, 1991; 1 child, Roger Dong Retzer. AB, Ill. Coll., 1954; MEd, U. Ill., 1957, PhD, 1969. Cert. tchr., Ill., 1954-57; cert. sch. adminstrn., Ill., 1957—. Tchr. Saunemin (Ill.) Twp. High Sch., 1954-58, asst. supt., 1955-58; prof. math. Ill. State U., Normal, 1959-89, Abilene (Tex.) Christian U., 1989—; asst. chmn. math. dept. Ill. State U., Normal, 1969-71; vis. prof. U. Ga., Athens, 1973, Tex. A&M U., College Station, 1984, U. Hawaii-Maui, Kahului, 1990, 91; cons. Arabian Am. Oil Co., Dhahran, Saudi Arabia, 1984, Ill. State Bd. Edn., Springfield, 1983-88; rsch. fellow U. Western Sydney, Australia, 1993; lectr. Zhejiang U., Hangzhou, China, Northwest Normal U., Lanzhou, China, Gansu Edn. U., Lanzhou, Lanzhou Normal U., Zhangye Normal U., China, summer 1994. Contbr. articles to profl. jours. in the U.S., Can., China. Mem. NEA, AAUP, Nat. Coun. Tchrs. Math., Sch. Sci. and Math. Assn., Math. Assn. Am., Rsch. Coun. on Diagnostic and Prescriptive Math., Ill. Coun. Tchrs. Math. (Max Beberman award 1988), Tex. Coun. Tchrs. Math., Big County Coun. Tchrs. Math., Ill. Assn. Higher Edn., Pi Mu Epsilon, Phi Delta Kappa. Mem. Church of Christ. Avocations: travel, photography, hiking, reading, Christian studies. Home: 58 Bay Shore Ct Abilene TX 79602-4202 Office: Abilene Christian Univ Math Dept ACU Box 8012 1600 Campus Ct Abilene TX 79699-8012

RETZLER, KURT EGON, diversified management company executive, hospitality, travel and marketing company executive; b. Bechkerek, Mar. 31, 1927; came to U.S., 1950, naturalized, 1954; s. Joseph J. and Melinda (Beno) R.; m. Rali Tjotis, Aug. 3, 1957; children: Jo Elaine, Kurt Steven. B.B.A. with distinction, U. Mich., 1955, M.B.A. with distinction, 1956. C.P.A., Mich., Minn. C.P.A. Arthur Andersen & Co., Detroit, 1956-63; asst. controller Carlson Cos., Inc., Mpls., 1963-65; v.p., controller Carlson Cos., Inc., 1965-74, v.p., 1974—, v.p. corp. acquisitions and devel., 1974—, mem. fin. com., 1974—; bd. dirs. TGI Fridays, Inc., Dallas, Carlson Travel Network, Radisson Hotel Corp., Carlson Properties, Inc., Country Kitchen Internat., Inc. Treas. PTA, Golden Valley, Minn., 1967. Served with AUS, 1951-53. Mem. Financial Execs. Inst. (dir. Twin Cities chpt. 1969-70, treas. 1971-72), Nat. Assn. Accountants, Am. Inst. C.P.A.'s, Minn. Assn. C.P.A.'s, Am. Accounting Assn., Assn. for Corp. Growth, Beta Gamma Sigma, Phi Kappa Phi, Beta Alpha Psi. Home: 1100 Heritage Ln Wayzata MN 55391-9133 Office: Carlson Cos Inc Carlson Pkwy PO Box 59159 Minneapolis MN 55459-8214

REUBEN, ALVIN BERNARD, entertainment executive; b. Harrisburg, Pa., Aug. 11, 1940; s. Maurice and Lillian (Katzef) R.; m. Barbara Ann Harrison, Mar. 18, 1967; 1 dau., Mindee Jill. B.S. in Commerce, Rider U., 1962. Buyer Pomeroy's div. Allied Stores Corp., Harrisburg, 1962-67; sales rep. Random House, Inc., N.Y.C., 1967-74; dir. mktg. Ballantine Books, Inc. (div. Random House), N.Y.C., 1974-76; v.p. sales Simon & Schuster, N.Y.C., 1976-79, sr. v.p. sales Pocket Books div., 1979-81, sr. v.p. mktg., 1981-82, pres. promotional pub. group, 1982-83, exec. v.p. electronic pub. div., 1983-85; exec. v.p. Prentice Hall div. Simon & Schuster, 1985-86; sr. v.p. mktg., sales and distbn. Vestron, Inc., 1986-89; sr. v.p. St. Martin's Press, N.Y.C., 1989-91; sr. v.p. sales, mktg. Sony Music Video, N.Y.C., 1991-92; sr. v.p. spl. markets Sony Music, N.Y.C., 1992-95; sr.v.p. video and interactive sales and distbn. BMG Entertainment, 1995—; instr. edn. in pub. program, grad. program SUNY; active problem solving seminar Pubs. Weekly, N.Y.C., 1980. With USAFR, 1963-69. Mem. Tau Kappa Epsilon. Home: 54 High Point Rd Westport CT 06880-3911 Office: 1540 Broadway New York NY 10036-4098

REUBEN, DON HAROLD, lawyer; b. Chgo., Sept. 1, 1928; s. Michael B. and Sally (Chapman) R.; m. Evelyn Long, Aug. 27, 1948 (div.); children: Hope Reuben Paul, Michael Barrett, Timothy Don, Jeffrey Long, Howard Ellis; m. Jeannette Hurley Haywood, Dec. 13, 1971; stepchildren: Harris Hurley Haywood, Edward Gregory Haywood. BS, Northwestern U., 1949, JD, 1952. Bar: Ill. 1952. With firm Kirkland & Ellis, Chgo., 1952-78, sr. ptnr., until 1978; sr. ptnr. Reuben & Proctor, Chgo., 1978-86, Isham, Lincoln & Beale, Chgo., 1986-88; sr. counsel Winston & Strawn, 1988-94; of counsel Altheimer & Gray, Chgo., 1994—; spl. asst. atty. gen. State of Ill., 1963-64, 69, 84; counsel spl. session Ill. Ho. of Reps., 1964, for Ill. treas. for congl., state legis. and jud. reapportionment, 1963; spl. fed. ct. master, 1968-70; dir. Lake Shore Nat. Bank., 1973-93, Heitman Fin., 1993—; mem. citizens adv. bd. to sheriff County of Cook, 1962-66, mem. jury instrns. com., 1963-68; rules com. Ill. Supreme Ct., 1963-73; mem. pub. rels. com. Nat. Conf. State Trial Judges; mem. com. study caseflow mgmt. in law div. Cook County Cir. Ct., 1979-88; mem. adv. implementation com. U.S. Dist. Ct. for No. Dist. Ill., 1981-82; mem. Chgo. Better Schs. Com., 1968-69, Chgo. Crime Commn., 1970-80; mem. supervisory panel Fed. Defender Program.; lectr. on libel, slander, privacy and freedom of press; gen. counsel Tribune Co., 1965-88, Chgo. Bears Football Club, 1965-88, Catholic Archdiocese of Chgo., 1975-86. Bd. dirs. Lincoln Park Zool. Soc., 1972-84 ; trustee Northwestern U., 1977—; mem. vis. com. U. Chgo. Law Sch., 1976-79. Mem. Ill. Bar Assn., Chgo. Bar Assn. (chmn. subcom. on propriety and regulation of contingent fees com. devel. law 1966-69, subcom. on media liaison 1980-82, mem. com. on profl. info. 1980-82), ABA (standing com. on fed. judiciary 1973-79, standing com. on jud. selection, tenure and compensation 1982-85), Am. Law Inst., Am. Judicature Soc., Fellows Am. Bar Found., Am. Coll. Trial Lawyers (Rule 23 com. 1975-82, judiciary com. 1987-91), Am. Arbitration Assn. (nat. panel arbitrators), Internat. Acad. Trial Lawyers, Union League Club (Chgo.), Tavern Club, Mid-Am. Club, Law Club, Casino Club, The Springs Club, Desert Riders of Palm Springs, The Chgo. Club, Phi Eta Sigma, Beta Alpha Psi, Beta Gamma Sigma, Order of Coif. Home: 20 Jill Ter Rancho Mirage CA 92270-2635 Office: Altheimer & Gray 10 S Wacker Dr 40th Fl Chicago IL 60606-7407

REUBER, GRANT LOUIS, banking insurance company executive; b. Mildmay, Ont., Can., Nov. 23, 1927; s. Jacob Daniel and Gertrude Catherine (Wahl) R.; m. Margaret Louise Julia Summerhayes, Oct. 21, 1951; children: Rebecca, Barbara, Mary. BA, U. Western Ont., 1950; AM, Harvard U., 1954, PhD, 1957; LLD (hon.), Wilfred Laurier U., 1983, Simon Fraser U., 1985; LLD, U. Western Ont., 1985; LLD (hon.), McMaster U., 1994; postgrad., Cambridge U., 1954-55. Mem. research dept. Bank Can., Ottawa, 1950-52; mem. Can. Dept. Finance, Ottawa, 1955-57; asst. prof. econ. U. Western Ont., London, 1957-59, assoc. prof., 1959-62, prof., head dept., 1963-69, dean faculty Social Sci., 1969-74, mem. bd. govs., 1974-78, acad. v.p., provost, 1975-78, chancellor, 1988-92; sr. v.p., chief economist Bank of Montreal, Que., Can., 1978-79; exec. v.p. Bank of Montreal, 1980-81, dep. chmn., dep. chief exec. officer, 1981-83, dir., mem. exec. com., 1981-89, pres., chief operating officer, 1983-87, dep. chmn., 1987-89; dep. minister fin. Can., 1979-80; chmn. Can. Deposit Ins. Corp., 1993—; mem. Royal Commn. Banking and Fin., Toronto, 1962-63; chmn. Ont. Econ. Coun., 1973-78; cons. Can. Internat. Devel. Agy., 1968-69; hon. rsch. assoc. in econs. Harvard U., 1968-69; cons. devel. ctr. OECD, 1969-73; bd. dirs. Opinac Energy Corp.; mem. adv. com. U. Western Ont. Sch. Bus.; lectr. U. Chgo. Sch. Bus., 1992-93; econ. advisor to prime min. of Lithuania, 1991-92. Author: Private Foreign Investment in Development, 1973, Canada's Political Economy, 1980; contbr. articles to profl. jours. Pres. Can. Ditchley Found., 1991—; vice chmn. Can. Merit Scholarship Found., 1994—. Decorated officer Order of Can. Fellow Royal Soc. Can.

REUBISH, GARY RICHARD, English language educator; b. Breckenridge, Minn., Jan. 6, 1946; s. Irving Earl and Genevieve Loretta (Miller) R. AA, N.D. State Coll. Sci., Wahpeton, 1969; BS, Valley City State Coll., 1971. Cert. tchr., N.D. Tchr. English Wolford (N.D.) Pub. Sch., 1971-72, Lake Benton (Minn.) Pub. Sch., 1972-76, Wahpeton (N.D.) Pub. Sch., 1976—. With USAF, 1965-71. Mem. NEA, N.D. Edn. Assn., Wahpeton Edn. Assn. Home: 10 Dak Ave 11 Wahpeton ND 58075 Office: Wahpeton Mid Sch 1209 Loy Ave Wahpeton ND 58075-5069

REUDINK, DOUGLAS OTTO JOHN, communications company executive, researcher; b. West Point, Nebr., May 6, 1939; s. Raymond A. and Pearl Marie (Stolzman) R.; m. Jamie Karin Allinger, Aug. 27 1961; children: Mark, Michael, Matthew. B.A., Linfield Coll., 1961; Ph.D., Oreg. State U., 1965. Mem. tech. staff Bell Labs., Holmdel, N.J., 1965-72, head satellite research, 1972-78, dir. radio research, 1978-84; dir. computer and robotics research AT&T Bell Labs, Holmdel, N.J., 1984-86; dir. labs. Boeing Electronics Co., Seattle, 1986-89; dir. electronics techs. Boeing Aerospace and Electronics, 1989-91; dir. wireless planning U.S. West NewVector Group, Bellevue, Wash., 1991-95; pres., CEO Metawave Comm. Corp., Bellevue, 1995—; advisor Voice of Am., Washington, 1983—, NASA, Washington, 1980-86. Mem. editorial bd. Jour. Space Communication and Broadcasting, Netherlands, 1982-86; contbr. chpts. to books, numerous articles to tech. jours.; patentee in field. Vice pres. Sea Girt Bd. Edn., N.J., 1980-86. NDEA fellow, 1961-64. Fellow IEEE (best paper award 1972); mem. AIAA, Internat. Sci. Radio Union. Lutheran. Home: 13916 SE 47th St Bellevue WA 98006-3048 Office: Metawave Comm Corp 8700 148th Ave Redmond WA 98052

REUM, JAMES MICHAEL, lawyer; b. Oak Park, Ill., Nov. 1, 1946; s. Walter John and Lucy (Bellegay) R. BA cum laude, Harvard U., 1968, JD cum laude, 1972. Bar: N.Y. 1973, D.C. 1974, U.S. Dist. Ct. (so. dist.) N.Y. 1974, Ill. 1979, U.S. Dist. Ct. (no. dist.) Ill. 1982. Assoc. Davis Polk & Wardwell, N.Y.C., 1973-78; assoc. Minority Counsel Com. on Judiciary U.S. Ho. of Reps., Washington, 1974; ptnr. Hopkins & Sutter, Chgo., 1979-93, Winston & Strawn, Chgo., 1994—. Midwest advance rep. Nat. Reagan Bush Com., 1980; nominee commr. Securities and Exchange Comm., Pres. Bush, 1992. Served to SP4 USAR, 1969-75. Recipient Harvard U. Honorary Nat. Scholarship, 1964-72. Mem. ABA, Monte Carlo Country Club (Monaco), Chgo. Club, Univ. Club (N.Y.C.). Republican. Home: 12 E Scott St Chicago IL 60610 Office: Winston & Strawn 35 W Wacker Dr Chicago IL 60601-1614

REUM, W. ROBERT, manufacturing executive; b. Oak Park, Ill., July 22, 1942; m. Sharon Milliken. BA, Yale U., 1964; JD, U. Mich., 1967; MBA, Harvard U., 1969. Dir. investment analysis City Investing Co., N.Y.C., 1969-72; v.p. corp fin. Mich. Nat. Corp., Bloomfield Hills, Mich., 1972-78; v.p., treas. White Motor Corp., Cleve., 1978-79; v.p. fin., chief fin. officer Lamson & Sessions, Cleve., 1980-82; v.p. fin., chief fin. officer The Interlake Corp., Oak Brook, Ill., 1982-88, exec. v.p., 1988-90, chmn., pres., chief exec. officer, 1991—; dir. Amsted Industries, Inc., Chgo., Duplex Products, Inc., Sycamore, Ill.; mem. nat. adv. bd. Chem. Bank, N.Y.C. Contbr. articles to Harvard Bus. Rev. Bd. trustees Mfrs. Alliance, Washington. Mem. Chgo. Golf Club, Chgo. Club, Dunham Woods Riding Club (Wayne, Ill.), Rolling Rock Club (Ligonier, Pa.). Office: Interlake Corp 550 Warrenville Rd Lisle IL 60532-4308

REUMAN, ROBERT EVERETT, philosophy educator; b. Foochow, China, Feb. 16, 1923; s. Otto G. and Martha Lydia (Bourne) R.; m. Dorothy Ann Swan, Sept. 2, 1949; children: Martha Claire, David Alan, Jonathan Robert, Ann Evalyn, Elizabeth Linda. A.B., Middlebury Coll., 1945; M.A., U. Pa., 1946, Ph.D., 1949. Asst. instr. U. Pa., 1946-48; instr. Temple U., 1947-49; mem. Friends' Ambulance Service Unit, China, 1949-51, chmn., 1950-51; dir. Quaker Student House, Freiburg im Breisgau, Fed. Republic Germany, 1951-53; instr. Lafayette Coll., 1953-54, asst. prof., 1954-56; mem. faculty Colby Coll., Waterville, Maine, 1956—, prof. philosophy, 1969—, chmn. social sci. div., 1975-78, chmn. dept. philosophy and religion, 1975-78; Dana prof. philosophy Colby Coll., 1986-91, ret., 1991. Author: Mauern, 1965, (with others) Anatomy of Anti-Communism, 1969; pamphlet Walls, 1966; contbr. articles to profl. jours. New Eng. regional chmn. Danforth Assocs., 1963-64; Quaker internat. affairs rep., Germany, 1964-66; bd. dirs. Am. Friends of Le College Cevenol, 1973-85; mem. Maine Humanities Coun., 1980-85, mem. exec. com., 1981-84. With Civilian Pub. Svc., 1943-46. Harrison fellow, 1945-46; Colby Coll. grantee, 1972, 79, 82. Mem. Am. Philos. Assn., AAUP, Soc. for Values in Higher Edn. Democrat. Unitarian-Quaker.

REUSCHLEIN, HAROLD GILL, university dean; b. Burlington, Wis., Dec. 2, 1904; s. Joseph Felix and Frances (Gill) R.; m. Marcella Christien, Apr. 24, 1930; 1 dau., Mary Frances. A.B., U. Iowa, 1927; LL.B., Yale, 1933; J.S.D., Cornell, 1934; LL.D., Dominican Coll., 1955, Dickinson Sch. Law, 1970, LaSalle Coll., 1971, Creighton U., 1975, St. Mary's U., 1984; L.H.D., Villanova U., 1972. Bar: Wis. 1936, U.S. Supreme Ct. 1944, Pa. 1955. Instr. history N.Y. U., 1930-32; asst. gen. counsel Fidelity Mut. Life Ins. Co., 1934; prof. law Georgetown U., 1934-46, U. Notre Dame, 1946-47, Syracuse U., 1947-48, U. Pitts., 1948-53; dean Sch. Law, Villanova U., 1953-72, dean emeritus, 1984; Ryan Distinguished prof. law St. Mary's U., 1972-84; vis. prof. Case Western Res. U., 1967-68. Author: The Schools of Corporate Reform, 1950, Jurisprudence-Its American Prophets, 1951, Cases on Unincorporated Business, 1952, Cases on Agency and Partnership, 1962, Handbook of Law of Agency and Partnership, 1990. Choirmaster, organist First Meth. Episcopal Ch., New Haven, 1927-33, Ch. St. Bernard of Clarivaux, Pitts., 1948-53; dir. Pub. Health Law Project, U. Pittsburgh. Served as col. Judge Adv. Gen. Dept., World War II; chief Office Legislative Service Hdqrs. AAF. Awarded Legion of Merit; Decorated Papal Knight of the Holy Sepulchre, Knight St. Gregory the Great. Mem. ABA, Wis. Bar Assn., Pa. Bar Assn., Cosmos Club (Washington), Order of Coif, Pi Kappa Alpha, Pi Gamma Mu. Roman Catholic. Home: Riddle Village Williamsburgh Bldg # 106 Media PA 19063

REUSCHLEIN, ROBERT WILLIAM, accountant, researcher; b. Madison, Wis., Jan. 8, 1950; s. Earl Vincent and Rosemary Markham R. BSEE, U. Wis., 1972; MBA, Oregon State U., 1977. Surveyor and draftsman Ctrl. Wis. Builders, Madison, 1971-72; estimator Dyson Constrn., Madison, 1972; pub. acct. Earl V. Reuschlein & Assocs., Madison, 1973-74; mgmt. intern Portland (Oreg.) Gen. Elec., 1976; controller Doorcraft, Inc., Harrisburg, Oreg., 1977-79; pub. acct. C.F. Rogers CPA, Eugene, Oreg., 1980; lobbyist Dem. Party of Oregon, Salem, 1981-85; rschr. Earlwal, Ltd., Eugene, 1986-93; acct., pres. Earlwal, Ltd., Madison, Wis., 1993—; mem. Citizen Involvement Com., City of Springfield, Oreg., 1979; founding dir. Neighborhood Econ. Devel. Corp., Eugene, 1979-81; dir. Eugene Peace Works, 1991-93; gen. mgr. Jomblee, Inc., Madison, 1995—; internat. peace econs. U. Oreg., 1987, 89; lectr. Econ. Conversion Conf., Miami, Fla., 1990. Author: Peace Economics, 1986, Strength Through Peace, 1989; columnist Peace Economics in Oreg. Peace Worker, 1989— (columns also played on Radio for Peace Internat., Costa Rica, 1993); developer Natural Global Warming Theory, 1991. Mem. Dem. Exec. Com., Oreg., 1981-87; del. Dem. Nat. Conv., San Francisco, 1984; chmn. 4th Congl. Dist. Dems., Oreg., 1982-87, Eugene Peace Works, 1992-93; program dir. Prairie Soc. Unitarian Ch., 1995—. Mem. AICPA, Wis. Inst. CPAs, Madison Progressive Inst., World Federalists (bd. dirs. local chpt.). Avocations: running, volleyball, campaigning, lecturing, dancing. Office: Earlwal Ltd 6515 Grand Teton Plz Ste 120 Madison WI 53719

REUSCHLING, THOMAS LYNN, academic administrator, consultant; b. Conneaut, Ohio, Dec. 28, 1942; s. Fred Leonard and Florice Lucille (Corlew) R.; m. Dorothy Ellen Ford, Sept. 8, 1962; children: Renee, Tracy. BA, Hiram (Ohio) Coll., 1964; MBA, Kent State U., 1966; D. Bus. Adminstrn., U. Colo., 1970. Asst. prof. Kent State U., 1969-73; dir. Sch. Bus. U. No. Iowa, Cedar Falls, 1973-78; dean Sch. Bus. U. Richmond, Va., 1978-88; pres. St. Andrews Presbyn. Coll., Lauringburg, N.C., 1988-94, Fla. So. Coll., Lakeland, 1994—. Pres. Jr. Achievement of Richmond, 1985-86, Carolina Intercollegiate Athletic conf., 1993-94; bd. dirs. United Way of Richmond, 1987-88, United Way of Ctrl. Fla., 1995—. NDEA fellow U. Colo., 1966-69. Avocations: basketball, traveling, reading. Office: Fla So Coll 111 Lake Hollinsworth Dr Lakeland FL 33801-5698 Address: PO Box 1125 Laurinburg NC 28353-1125

REUSS, ROBERT PERSHING, telecommunications executive, consultant; b. Aurora, Ill., Mar. 23, 1918; s. George John and Mary Belle (Gorrie) R.; m. Mildred Louise Daly, Dec. 22, 1940 (dec. May 1985); children: Lynn Ann (Mrs. David Bohmer), Robert Cameron; m. Grace K. Brady, Aug. 28, 1986. BS, U. Ill., 1939; postgrad., Harvard U., 1943; MBA, U. Chgo., 1950; D Bus. Adminstrn., Blackburn Coll., 1976. Staff AT&T, 1955-58, asst. compt., 1958-59; v.p. Ill. Bell Tel. Co., 1959-72, dir., 1970-72; pres., chief exec. officer, dir. Centel Corp., Chgo., 1972-76, chmn., 1977-88; cons. Chgo., 1988-93, Sprint Corp., 1993—; bd. govs. Midwest Stock Exch., 1978-82; bd. dirs. Tellabs, Inc. Trustee Rush-Presbyn.-St. Luke's Med. Ctr., Chgo., Blackburn Coll., 1953-83, Aurora U., 1986—, Lyric Opera, 1987—; bd. dirs. U. Ill. Found., 1979—. Lt. (s.g.) USNR, 1943-46, PTO. Mem. Chgo. Assn. Commerce & Industry (bd. dirs. 1971-78), Comml. Club, Chgo. Club, Chgo. Golf Club, Ocean Club, Country Club of Fla., Phi Kappa Phi. Presbyterian (deacon, trustee). Office: 40 Shuman Blvd Ste 240 Naperville IL 60563-8465

REUSS VON PLAUEN, PRINCE-ARCHBISHOP HEINRICH XXVI, metropolitan, nursing, legal consultant, psychologist, educator; b. Greiz, Plauen, Germany, Feb. 3, 1942; s. Prince Heinrich XXV and Princess Maria (Obrenovic-Brankovic) Reuss von Plauen. BSN, U. der Heiligen Dreifeltigkeit, Fed. Republic Germany, 1968, PhD, STD (hon.), 1974, JD, 1984; BA, San Francisco State U., 1970, MS, 1980; LLD (hon.), South East U., Hong Kong, 1973; MSN, San Jose State U., 1989. Therapist The Counselling Centre, Calif., Germany, Hong Kong, 1968-74, adminstr., 1972-73; prof. psychiat. nursing and law Order of St. John, Calif., Germany, 1974-78; adminstr. Hospice of the Holy Spirit, Calif., Colo., 1981-84; prof. nursing and law Order of St. John/U. Heiligen Dreifeltigkeit, Austria, Germany, 1981-84; nursing cons. Order of St. John of Jerusalem, Calif., Germany, 1964—; chmn. Hospice of the Holy Spirit, Germany, 1974—; rector Holy Trinity Seminary, 1974—; bd. dirs. Hospice of St. John, Denver. Contbr. articles on law, ethics, nursing practices, therapy and theology. Decorated prince-grand master Order St. Thomas the Apostle, Ea. Cath. Order of the Holy Sepulchre, knight grand cross Order Royal Crown Balearica (Spain), Order St. Agatha (Spain), Order of Black Eagle, Order St. Constantine (Greece), bailiff grand cross Knights of the Holy Sepulchre (Germany), knight grand cross of justice Order St. George (Eng.), Order St. John of Knights of Malta, grand prelate Sovereign Hospitaller Order St. John of Knights of Malta. Avocations: fencing, pistol shooting, archery, equestrian. Address: Eastern Cath Archdiocese (Chaldean-Syrian) PO Box 3337 Daly City CA 94015-0337 *The purpose of the Church is to serve and to love Christ's flock, especially the poor, needy, sick and the dying, in accordance with the Holy Scriptures. The Church must maintain the Apostolic Traditions and Canons of the Historic Church, in order to bring mankind up to God's level, not bring God down to mankind's level.*

REUTER, CAROL JOAN, insurance company executive; b. Bklyn., June 1, 1941; d. Michael John and Elizabeth Lucille (Garmer) R. BA, St. John's U., 1962. Pres., CEO N.Y. Life Found., N.Y.C., 1979-89, sec., 1989-90, pres., 1990-96, CEO, 1996—; also bd. dirs.; asst. v.p. N.Y. Life Ins. Co., N.Y.C., 1984-89, corp. v.p., 1990-95, v.p., 1995—. Mem., former chmn. contbns. coun. Conf. Bd., N.Y. Contbns. Adv. Group; mem. corp. adv. coun. ARC; mem. corp. adv. com. United Negro Coll. Fund.; mem. corp. assocs. United Way of Am. Named Acad. of Women's Achievers, YWCA, 1987. Republican. Roman Catholic. Office: NY Life Ins Co 51 Madison Ave New York NY 10010-1603

REUTER, FRANK THEODORE, history educator; b. Kankakee, Ill., Mar. 18, 1926; s. Frank Theodore and Evelyn Marie (Scott) R.; m. Kathleen Ann Pester, June 16, 1951; children: Mark, Stephen, Christopher, Ann, Katherine. B.S., U. Ill., 1950, M.A., 1959, Ph.D., 1960. Instr. West Liberty (W. Va.) State Coll., 1960-62; asst. prof. Texas Christian U., Fort Worth, 1962-66; assoc. prof. Texas Christian U., 1966-71; prof. history Tex. Christian U., 1971-92; dean Texas Christian U. (Grad. Sch.), 1970-75, chmn. dept. history, 1980-83; prof. emeritus Tex. Christian U., 1992—. Author: West Liberty State College: The First 125 Years, 1963, Catholic Influence on American Colonial Policies, 1898-1904, 1967, Trials and Triumphs: George Washington's Foreign Policy, 1983; co-author: Injured Honor: The Chesapeake-Leopard Affair, 1996. Served with USNR, 1944-46. U. Durham Rsch. fellow, 1991. Mem. Orgn. Am. Historians, Am. Hist. Assn., Soc. Historians Early Republic, Soc. Historians Am. Fgn. Relations, Phi Beta Kappa, Phi Alpha Theta. Roman Catholic. Home: 3617 Winifred Dr Fort Worth TX 76133-2126 Office: Tex Christian U History Dept Fort Worth TX 76129

REUTER, JAMES WILLIAM, lawyer; b. Bemidji, Minn., Sept. 30, 1948; s. John Renee and Monica (Dugas) R.; m. Patricia Carol Creelman, Mar. 30, 1968; children: Kristine, Suzanne, Natalee. B.A., St. John's U., 1970; J.D., William Mitchell Coll. of Law, 1974. Bar: Minn. 1974, U.S. Dist. Ct. Minn. 1975, U.S. Ct. Appeals (8th cir.) 1985; cert. civil trial specialist. Editor, West Pub. Co., St. Paul, 1970-73; assoc. Terpstra & Merrill, Mpls., 1974-77; ptnr. Barna, Guzy, Merrill, Hynes & Giancola, Ltd., Mpls., 1977-89, ptnr. Lindquist & Vennum, Mpls., 1989—. Recipient Cert. award Nat. Inst. Trial Advocacy, 1978. Mem. ABA (intellectual property, torts and insur practice, and civil litigation sects.), Assn. Trial Lawyers Am., Minn. Bar Assn. (civil litigation and computer sects.), Hennepin County Bar Assn. (ethics com.), Anoka County Bar Assn. (pres. 1981-82). Avocations: skiing; golf; camping; reading. Office: Lindquist & Vennum 4200 IDS Ctr 80 S 8th St Minneapolis MN 55402-2100

REUTER, STEWART RALSTON, radiologist, lawyer, educator; b. Detroit, Feb. 14, 1934; s. Carl H. and Grace M. R.; m. Marianne Ahfeldt, June 6, 1966. B.A., Ohio Wesleyan U., 1955; M.D., Case Western Res. U., 1959; J.D., U. San Francisco, 1980. Diplomate: Am. Bd. Radiology. Bar: Tex. 1981. Intern U. Calif., San Francisco, 1959-60, resident in radiology, 1960-63; instr. radiology Stanford (Calif.) U., 1963-64; asst. prof. U. Mich., Ann Arbor, 1966-69, prof., 1972-76; assoc. prof. U. Calif., San Diego, 1969-72; prof. U. Calif., San Francisco and Davis, 1976-80; prof., chmn. dept. radiology Health Scis. Ctr., U. Tex., San Antonio, 1980—. Co-author: Gastrointestinal Radiology, 3d edit., 1986; mem. editorial bd. Am. Jour. Roentgenology, 1975-91, Iatrogenics, 1990-93; contbr. articles to profl. jours. Picker fellow, 1964-66. Fellow Am. Coll. Radiology, Am. Coll. Legal Medicine (bd. govs. 1985-91, 92-94, sec. 1994, pres.-elect 1995, pres. 1996); mem. ABA, Assn. Univ. Radiologists, Am. Roentgen Ray Soc., Tex. Radiol. Assn. (trustee 1989-92, pres. 1994), Soc. Cardiovascular and Interventional Radiologists (pres. 1979), Soc. Gastrointestinal Radiologists, Tex. Bar Assn. Home: 3923 Morgans Crk San Antonio TX 78230-1945 Office: U Tex Health Sci Ctr Dept Radiology 7703 Floyd Curl Dr San Antonio TX 78284-6200

REUTHER, DAVID LOUIS, children's book publisher, writer; b. Detroit, Nov. 2, 1946; s. Roy Louis and Fania (Sonkin) R.; m. Margaret Alexander Miller, July 21, 1973; children: Katherine Anna, Jacob Alexander. BA with honors, U. Mich., 1968. Tchr. Lewis-Wadhams Sch., Westport, N.Y., 1969-71; asst. dir. Children's Book Council, N.Y.C., 1971-73; editor children's books Macmillan Publishing Co., N.Y.C., 1973-76; sr. editor Four Winds Press-Scholastic Inc., N.Y.C., 1976-82; sr. v.p., editor-in-chief Morrow Jr. Books, N.Y.C., 1982—; co-founder Baseball Ink, Inc., 1986-90; mem. Nat. Sci. Tchrs. Assn.-Children's Book Coun. Joint Com., 1982-85; joint com. mem. Am. Bookseller Assn., 1990-93; treas. Childrens Book Coun., 1986, chmn., 1993-94. Author: with Roy Doty) Fun To Go, A Take-Along Activity Book, 1982, Save-the-Animals Activity Book, 1982, (with John Thorn and Pete Palmer) The Hidden Game of Baseball, 1984, Total Baseball, 1989, The Whole Baseball Catalog, 1990, Total Baseball II, 1991; editor: (with John Thorn) The Armchair Quarterback, 1982, The Armchair Aviator, 1983, The Armchair Mountaineer, 1984, The Armchair Book of Baseball, 1985, The Armchair Angler, 1986, The Armchair Book of Basesball II, 1987, The Armchair Traveler, 1988. Mem. ALA, Authors Guild, Soc. Children's Book Writers. Home: 271 Central Park W New York NY 10024-3020 Office: William Morrow & Co 1350 Avenue Of The Americas New York NY 10019-4702

REUTHER, WALTER, horticulture educator; b. Manganoui County, North Is., New Zealand, Sept. 21, 1911; came to U.S., 1919; s. Arthur W.G. and Martha (Krüger) R.; m. Flora Astbury Nelson, Aug. 4, 1935; children: David Walter, Charles Arthur. BS in Chemistry, U. Fla., 1933; PhD in Plant Physiology, Cornell U., 1940. Asst. horticulturist Agrl. Experiment Sta., U. Fla., Gainesville, 1933-37; rsch. asst. in pomology Cornell U., Ithaca, N.Y., 1937-40; asst. prof. pomology Cornell U., Ithaca, 1940; assoc. horticulturist, then prin. horticulturist USDA, Orlando, Fla., 1941-55; head dept. horticulture U. Fla., Gainesville, 1955-56; prof., chmn. dept. horticulture, researcher Citrus Ctr., U. Calif., Riverside, 1956-66, prof., horticulturist, 1966-72, 74-79; coord. regional rsch. Inst. Nat. Investigations in Agriculture, Valencia, Spain, 1972-74; prof. emeritus U. Calif., Riverside, 1979—; cons. Del Monte Corp., 1962-72, Govt. of Greece, 1963, 64, Rockefeller Found., 1965, 66-67, 69, UN, 1970, 75, 77, Govt. of Spain, 1972-74, Govt. of Brazil, 1975, 81, Govt. of Indonesia, 1977-78, 84, Govt. of Republic of China, 1979, Govt. of Honduras, 1980, Govt. of Mex., 1982, Govt. of Colombia, 1982. Editor: The Citrus Industry, 1967-90; contbr. 130 articles to profl. jours. Fellow Am. Soc. Hort. Sci. (pres. 1962-63, chmn. bd. dirs. 1963-64). Democrat. Avocations: reading, gradening, walking. Home: 12751 Gateway Park Rd Ste 322 Poway CA 92064-2064 Office: U Calif Dept Botany and Plant Sci Riverside CA 92521

REUTIMAN, ROBERT WILLIAM, JR., lawyer; b. Mpls., June 4, 1944; s. Robert William and Elsbeth Bertha (Doering) R.; m. Virginia Lee Traxler, June 25, 1983; children: Robert James, Joseph Lee. BA magna cum laude, U. Minn., 1966, JD, 1969. Bar: Minn. 1969, U.S. Ct. Mil. Appeals 1969, U.S. Dist. Ct. Minn. 1973, U.S. Ct. Appeals (8th cir.) 1976, U.S. Tax. Ct. 1979. Mem. Armstrong, Phleger, Reutiman & Vinokour, Ltd., Wayzata, Minn., 1973-76; ptnr. Phleger & Reutiman, Wayzata, 1976-81; pvt. practice Wayzata, 1981—. Chmn. Spring Pk. Planning Commn., 1978. Capt. U.S. Army, 1969-73. Decorated Army Commendation medal. Mem. ABA, Minn. Bar Assn., Hennepin County Bar Assn., Am. Arbitration Assn. (panel of arbitrators), Phi Beta Kappa. Lutheran. Avocations: fishing, rose growing. Home: 11610 3rd Ave N Plymouth MN 55441-5919 Office: 305 Rice St E Wayzata MN 55391-1615

REUTTER, EBERHARD EDMUND, JR., education and law educator; b. Balt., May 28, 1924; s. Eberhard Edmund and Irene Louise (Loewer) R.; m. Bettie Marie Lytle, Aug. 16, 1947; 1 son, Mark Douglas. B.A., Johns Hopkins U., 1944; M.A., Columbia U., 1948, Ph.D., 1950. Dir., Tokyo Army Edn. Program Sch., 1945-47; head math. dept. Barnard Sch., N.Y.C., 1947-49; mem. faculty Tchrs. Coll., Columbia U., 1950—, prof., 1957—; vis. prof. U. Alaska, 1960, 66, U. P.R., 1954, U. So. Calif., 1960; speaker, cons. Coordinator spl. edn. projects NAACP Legal Def. Fund, 1965-68. Author: The School Administrator and Subversive Activities, 1951, Schools and the Law, 5th edit., 1981, (with W.S. Elsbree) Staff Personnel in the Public Schools, 1954, (with R.R. Hamilton) Legal Aspects of School Board Operation, 1958, (with W.S. Elsbree) Principles of Staff Personnel Administration in Public Schools, 1959, (with L.O. Garber) The Yearbook of School Law, 1967, 68, 69, 70, Legal Aspects of Control of Student Activities by Public School Authorities, 1970, The Law of Public Education, 4th edit., 1994, The Courts and Student Conduct, 1975, The Supreme Court's Impact on Public Education, 1982; also articles, chpts. in books. Chmn. citizens adv. com. Emerson (N.J.) Bd. Edn., 1954-57. Served from pvt. to 1st lt. inf. AUS, 1943-46. Recipient Marion A. McGhehey award for outstanding service in field edn. law, 1986. Mem. Nat. Orgn. Legal Problems of Edn. (pres. 1967), AAUP, Am. Assn. Sch. Adminstrs., NEA, Am. Assn. Sch. Personnel Adminstrs., Internat. Personnel Mgmt. Assn., Phi Beta Kappa, Kappa Delta Pi, Phi Delta Kappa. Home: 316 Grand Blvd Emerson NJ 07630-1157 Office: Columbia Univ Tchrs Coll New York NY 10027

REVEAL, ARLENE HADFIELD, librarian, consultant; b. Riverside, Utah, May 21, 1916; d. Job Oliver and Mabel Olive (Smith) Hadfield; children: James L., Jon A. BS with hons., Utah State U., 1938; grad. in librarianship San Diego State U., 1968; M in Libr. and Info. Sci., Brigham Young U., 1976. Social case worker Boxelder County Welfare, Brigham City, Utah, 1938-40; office mgr. Dodge Ridge Ski Corp., Long Barn, Calif., 1948-65, Strawberry Inn, Strawberry, Calif., 1950-65, Pinecrest Permittees Assn., 1955-66; adminstrv. asst. Mono County Office of Edn., Bridgeport, Calif., 1961-67; catalog libr. La Mesa-Spring Valley Sch. Dist., La Mesa, Calif., 1968-71; libr. Mono County Libr., Bridgeport, Calif., 1971—; chmn. Mountain Valley Library System, 1987-89. Author: Mono County Courthouse, 1980. Active Devel. Disabilities Area Bd. # 12, 1974—, chmn., 1990-92. Recipient John Cotton Dana award H.W. Wilson Co., 1974; named Bridgeport Citizen of Yr., 1993. Mem. Delta Kappa Gamma (pres. Epsilon Alpha chpt. 1984-88), Beta Sigma Phi (treas. Xi Omicron Epsilon chpt. 1981, 83-85, 91—, pres. 1982, 85, 89), Beta Phi Mu. Lodge: Rebekah (treas. 1973-90). Home: 185 Main St Bridgeport CA 93517-0532 Office: Mono County Free Libr 94 N School St Bridgeport CA 93517-0398

REVEAL, ERNEST IRA, III, lawyer; b. Chgo., Oct. 19, 1948; s. Ernest Ira Jr. and Hazel (Holt) R.; m. Katherine Trennerry, Nov. 24, 1979; children: Genevieve, Adrienne, Danielle. BA, Cornell U., 1970; JD, U. Mich., 1973. Bar: Minn. 1973, U.S. Dist. Ct. Minn. 1973, U.S. Ct. Appeals (8th cir.) 1974, U.S. Dist. Ct. S.D. 1976, U.S. Ct. Claims 1976, U.S. Ct. Appeals (7th cir.) 1984, U.S. Dist. Ct. (so. dist.) Calif. 1991, U.S. Ct. Appeals (9th cir.) 1991, U.S. Supreme Ct., 1991. Assoc. Robins, Kaplan, Miller & Ciresi, Mpls., 1973-79, ptnr., 1979—. Author: Public Sector Labor Law, 1983. Mem. Civil Svc. Commn., St. Paul, Minn., 1976. Mem. ABA, Minn. Bar Assn. (past chair labor law and employment law sect.), Cornell Club of Minn. (past pres.), Assn. Trial Lawyers Am. Democrat. Presbyterian. Avocations: sports, reading. Office: Robins Kaplan Miller & Ciresi 600 Anton Blvd Ste 1600 Costa Mesa CA 92626-7147

REVEIZ, FUAD, professional football player; b. Bogota, Colombia, Feb. 24, 1963. Student, U. Tenn. Placekicker Minn. Vikings. Named to NFL Pro Bowl Team, 1994; tied record for most field goals made in NFL, 1994. Office: Minn Vikings 9520 Viking Dr Eden Prairie MN 55344

REVEL, JEAN-PAUL, biology educator; b. Strasbourg, France, Dec. 7, 1930; came to U.S., 1953; s. Gaston Benjamin and Suzanne (Neher) R.; m. Helen Ruth Bowser, July 27, 1957 (div. 1986); children: David, Daniel Neher, Steven Robert; m. Galina Avdeeva Moller, Dec. 24, 1986; 1 stepchild, Karen. BS, U. Strasbourg, 1949; PhD, Harvard U., 1957. Rsch. fellow Cornell U. Med. Sch., N.Y.C., 1958-59; from instr. to prof. Harvard Med. Sch., Boston, 1959-71; prof. Calif. Inst. Tech., Pasadena, 1971—; AB Ruddock chair in biology Calif. Inst. Tech., 1978—; mem. sch. advisors bd. Nat. Insts. Aging, Balt., 1977-80; mem. ad hoc adv. biology NSF, Washington, 1982-83; mem. Nat. High Voltage Microscopy Adv. Group, Bethesda, Md., 1983, Nat. Rsch. Resources Adv. Coun., 1986-90. Author: (with E.D. Hay) Fine Structure of Developing Avian Cornea, 1969; editor: Cell Shape and Surface Architecture, 1977, Science of Biological Specimen Preparation, 1986; mem. editl. bd. Jour. Cell Biology, 1969-72, Internat. Rev. Cytology, 1970, Cell and Tissue Rsch., 1979—, Molecular and Cell Biology, 1983-91; editor in chief Jour. Microscopy Soc. Am. Fellow AAAS (leader biol. scis. sect. 1991-92, Gordon conf. cell adhesion); mem. Am. Soc. Cell Biology (pres. 1972-73), Electron Micros. Soc. Am. (pres. 1988, Disting. Scientist award 1993), Soc. Devel. Biology. Avocations: watercolors, photography. Office: Calif Inst Tech # 156-29 Pasadena CA 91125

REVELEY, WALTER TAYLOR, III, lawyer; b. Churchville, Va., Jan. 6, 1943; s. Walter Taylor and Marie (Eason) R.; m. Helen Bond, Dec. 18, 1971; children: Walter Taylor, George Everett Bond, Nelson Martin Eason, Helen Lanier. AB, Princeton U., 1965; JD, U. Va., 1968. Bar: Va. 1970, D.C.

1976. Asst. prof. law U. Ala., 1968-69; law clk. to Justice Brennan U.S. Supreme Ct., Washington, 1969-70; fellow Woodrow Wilson Internat. Ctr. for Scholars, 1972-73; internat. affairs fellow Coun. on Fgn. Rels., N.Y.C., 1972-73; assoc. Hunton & Williams, Richmond, Va., 1970-76, ptnr., 1976—, mng. ptnr., 1982-91; lectr. Coll. William and Mary Law Sch., 1978-80. Author: War Powers of the President and Congress: Who Holds the Arrows and Olive Branch, 1981; mem. editorial & mng. bds. Va. Law Rev., 1966-68; contbr. articles to profl. jours. Trustee Princeton U., 1986—, Presbyn. Ch. (U.S.A.) Found., 1991—, Va. Hist. Soc., 1991—, Union Theol. Sem., 1992—, Andrew W. Mellon Found., 1994—, Va. Mus. Fine Arts, 1995—; bd. dirs. Fan Dist. Assn., Richmond, Inc., 1976-80, pres., 1979-80; bd. dirs. Richmond Symphony, 1980-92, pres., 1988-90, pres. symphony coun., 1994—; bd. dirs. Presbyn. Outlook Found. and Book Svc., 1985—, pres., 1992—; bd. dirs. Va. Mus. Found., 1990—; elder Grace Covenant Presbyn. Ch. Mem. ABA, Va. Bar Assn., D.C. Bar Assn., Richmond Bar Assn., Am. Soc. Internat. Law, Am. Judicature Soc., Am. Bar Found., Princeton Assn. Va. (bd. dirs. 1981—, pres. 1983-85), Edn. Lawyers (chmn. Va. State Bar sect. 1992-95), Raven Soc., Knickerbocker Club (N.Y.C.), Country Club Va., Downtown Club, Order of Coif, Phi Beta Kappa, Omicron Delta Kappa. Home: 2314 Monument Ave Richmond VA 23220-2604 Office: Hunton & Williams Riverfront Pla East Tower 951 E Byrd St Richmond VA 23219-4040

REVELL, GRAEME, composer. Film scores include Dead Calm, 1989, Spontaneous Combustion, 1990, Child's Play 2, 1990, Until the End of the World, 1991, The Hand That Rocks the Cradle, 1991, Love Crimes, 1992, Traces of Red, 1992, Body of Evidence, 1993, Hear No Evil, 1993, The Crush, 1993, Hard Target, 1993, Boxing Helena, 1993, The Crow, 1994, Ghost in the Machine, 1994, The Basketball Diaries, 1995. Office: 5093 N Pkwy Calabasas Calabasas CA 91302

REVELLE, CHARLES S., environmental engineer, geophysicist, systems analysis and economics educator; b. Mar. 26, 1938; m. Penelope ReVelle; 2 children. BChemE, Cornell U., 1961, PhD, 1967. Chemist Nat. Starch and Chem. Co., Plainfield, N.J., 1961; rsch. engr., instr. dept. sanitary engring. Cornell U., 1962, environ. systems engring. fellow, 1963-67, asst. prof. dept. environ. systems engring., 1967-71; on leave to Johns Hopkins U. 1968-69; asst. prof. Johns Hopkins U., Balt., 1971, assoc. prof., 1971-75, prof. program in systems analysis and econs. for pub. decision making, dept. geography and environ. engring., 1975—; part-time vis. scholar Inst. Water Resources, U.S. Army Corps of Engrs., Ft. Belvoir, Va., 1993—; vis. prof. dept. geography U. Iowa, 1976; invited lectr. Oxford U., Eng., 1974, U. Genoa, 1975, 82, U. Bristol, U.K., 1975, U. Stirling, Scotland, 1975, Internat. Inst. for Applied Systems Analysis, Vienna, Austria, 1980, U. N.C., Chapel Hill, 1984, Ohio State U., 1987, others; del. Univ. Coun. on Water Resources, 1984—; mem. com. on water resources of water scis. and tech. bd. NAE/NAS, 1985-87, subcom. on instl. rsch., 1986; advisor water resources rsch. com. ASCE, 1989; cons. in field; presenter papers at numerous profl. meetings. Co-author: (with Penelope ReVelle) Sourcebook on the Environment: The Scientific Perspective, 1974, The Environment: Issues and Choices for Society, 1981, 3d edit., 1988 (with Penelope ReVelle) The Global Environment: Securing a Sustainable Future, 1992; mem. edtl. bd. Geog. Analysis, 1987-91, European Jour. Ops. Rsch., 1991—; assoc. editor Mgmt. Sci.; contbr. over 130 articles to profl. jours. Recipient Robert B. Pond Sr. Excellence in Teaching award Johns Hopkins U., 1990; Fulbright-Hays fellow Erasmus U., The Netherlands, 1975; rsch. grantee City of Balt., 1975-76, 81-82, Nat. Bur. Standards, 1977, Office of Water Rsch. and Tech., 1977-81, U.S. Dept. Energy, 1980-82, N.J. Dept. Energy, 1980-81, Dept. Navy, 1985-87. Mem. Am. Geophys. Union, Arms Control Assn., Inst. Mgmt. Scis., Ops. Rsch. Soc. Am., Internat. Regional Sci. Assn., Phi Kappa Phi, Sigma Xi. Research in: (1) siting of emergency and other public sector facilities; (2) water quality and water resources systems; (3) forestry and natural area preservation models. Office: Johns Hopkins U Dept Geography & Environ Engring Ames Hall Baltimore MD 21218 *"Our challenge is to begin to erect the structure that preserves the earth we inherited."*

REVELLE, DONALD GENE, manufacturing and health care company executive, consultant; b. Cape Girardeau, Mo., July 16, 1930; s. Lewis W. and Dorothy R.; m. Jo M. Revelle, Aug. 1, 1954; children—Douglas, David, Daniel, Dianne. BA, U. Mo., 1952; JD, U. Colo., 1957; grad., Harvard U. Bus. Sch., 1971. Dir. employee relations Westinghouse Corp., Pitts., 1957-65; asst. to v.p. Diebold Corp., 1966; v.p. human resources TRW Corp., Cleve., 1967-84; sr. v.p. human resources Black and Decker Co., Towson, Md., 1984-86; exec. v.p. corp. rels. Montefiore Acad. Med. Ctr., Bronx, 1987—; univ. lectr.; cons. Duerba Ship, Blue Cross N.Y., Windsor Hosp., Salvation Army. Contbr. articles to profl. jours. Mem. sch. bd. State of N.Y. Lt. USNR, 1952-54. Mem. ABA (labor law com.), Colo. Bar Assn., Fed. Bar Assn., Human Resource Planning Soc., MBA Assn. Methodist. Home: 1004 Chestnut Ridge Dr Lutherville Timonium MD 21093-1725 Office: Montefiore Acad Med Ctr 111 E 210th St Bronx NY 10467-2490

RE VELLE, JACK B(OYER), statistician, consultant; b. Rochester, N.Y., Aug. 2, 1935; s. Mark A. and Myril (Bubes) Re V.; m. Brenda Lorraine Newcombe, Aug. 2, 1968; 1 child, Karen Alyssa. BS in Chem. Engring., Purdue U., 1957; MS in Indsl. Engring. and Mgmt., Okla. State U., 1965, PhD in Indsl. Engring. and Mgmt., 1970. Commd. 2d lt. USAF, 1957, advanced through grades to major, 1968, resigned, 1968; adminstrv. asst. Gen. Dynamics, Ft. Worth, 1970-71; cons. engr. Denver, 1971-72; chmn. decision scis. U. Nebr., Omaha, 1972-77; dean Sch. Bus. and Mgmt. Chapman U., Orange, Calif., 1977-79; sr. staff engr. McDonnell Douglas Space Systems, Huntington Beach, Calif., 1979-81; head mfg. tng. and devel. Hughes Aircraft Co., Fullerton, Calif., 1981-82, sr. statistician, 1982-86; corp. mgr. R & D Hughes Aircraft Co., L.A., 1986-88, corp. chief statistician, 1988-93; leader continuous improvement Hughes Missile Systems Co., Tucson, Ariz., 1994—; mem. bd. examiners Malcolm Baldridge nat. quality award Nat. Inst. Stds. and Tech., U.S. Dept. Commerce, Washington, 1990, 93; judge Ariz. Quality Alliance, Phoenix, 1994—, Rochester Inst. Tech.-USA Today Quality Cup Competition, 1994—, Def. Contract Mgmt. Command-Commdrs. Cup; cons. to various pub. and pvt. orgns.; presenter in field; lectr. at seminars. Author: Safety Training Methods, 1980, The Two-Day Statistician, 1986, The New Quality Technology, 1988, Policy Deployment, 1993, (with others) Quest for Quality, 1986, Mechanical Engineers Handbook, 1986, Production Handbook, 1987, Handbook of Occupational Safety and Health, 1987, A Quality Revolution in Manufacturing, 1989, Quality Engineering Handbook, 1991; co-author: Quantitative Methods for Managerial Decisions, 1978, The Executive's Handbook on Quality Function Deployment, 1994, From Concept to Customer, 1995, (software package) TQM ToolSchool, 1995. Bd. dirs. Assn. for Quality and Participation, Cin., 1985-86. Fellow Inst. for the Advancement Engring., 1986; recipient Disting. Econs. Devel. award Soc. Mfg. Engrs., 1990. Fellow Am. Soc. for Quality Control (co-chair total quality mgmt. com. 1990-92), Am. Soc. Safety Engrs. (nat. accreditation project dir. 1978-80), Inst. Indsl. Engrs. (regional v.p. 1982-84, treas. 1992-93, sr. v.p. 1993-94). Office: Hughes Missile Systems Co Old Nogales Hwy Tucson AZ 85734

REVENS, JOHN COSGROVE, JR., state senator, lawyer; b. Providence, Jan. 29, 1947; s. John C. and Rita M. (Williams) R.; AA, C.C. of R.I., 1966; BA, Providence Coll., 1969; JD, Suffolk U., 1973; m. Susan L. Shaw, Aug. 31, 1974; children: Leigh Elizabeth, Marcie Greene, Emily May. Mem. R.I. Ho. of Reps., 1968-74, sec. house steering com., 1971-74, mem. edn. and welfare com., 1968-70; admitted to R.I. bar, 1973; pres. firm Revens, Lanni, Revens & St. Pierre, Warwick, R.I., 1977—; mem. R.I. Senate, 1974-89, 1991—, mem. jud. and labor coms., 1974, chmn. jud. com., 1980-83, majority whip, 1977-80, Senate majority leader, 1983-89; Senate pres. pro tempore, 1993-95; dir. New Eng. Bd. Higher Edn., 1975-83, chmn., 1977-81; chmn. R.I. Children's Code Commn., 1979-83; bd. dirs. C.C. of R.I. Found., Vols. of Warwick Schs., R.I. Acad. Decathlon Assn.; mem. Commn. on Jud. Tenure and Discipline, 1982-84, Family Ct. Bench Bar Com., 1980-82, Women and Infants Hosp. Corp., 1983—; commr. Uniform State Laws, 1982-84. Mem. R.I. Bar Assn., Kent County Bar Assn., Am. Arbitration Assn. (panel of arbitrators 1980—), K.C. Democrat. Roman Catholic. Office: 946 Centerville Rd Warwick RI 02886-4398

REVER, GEORGE WRIGHT, psychiatrist, health facility administrator; b. Balt., May 18, 1928; s. William Benjamin and Amy Blanche (Wright) R.; m. Bridget Valerie Hanley, 1961 (dec. 1988); children: Kurt, Maeve Rever Raedle; m. Ann Roe, Feb. 4, 1994. BS, U. Md., 1950; MD, U. Md., Balt., 1957. Rotating intern Mercy Hosp., Balt., 1957-58; resident psychiatry and neurology VA Hosp., Boston, 1958-60; fellow Harvard Med. Sch., Cambridge, Mass., 1960-64, clin. instr. psychiatry, 1964—; psychiatrist divsn. legal medicine Cambridge Ct., 1960-71; pvt. practice Cohasset, Mass., 1963-90, Easton, Md., 1990-93; psychiatric cons. Travelers Aid Soc., Boston, 1966-74; psychiatrist Eunice Kennedy Shriver Ctr., Waltham, Mass., 1967-90; fellow child psychiatry Mass. Gen. Hosp., Boston, 1960-61, 62-63, fellow community mental health, 1963-64, staff psychiatrist, 1964-90, dir. child psychiatry tng. program neuropsychiatry devel. disabilities sect., 1967-90, asst. pediatrician, 1969-71, psychiat. cons. social svc. dept., 1970-74, psychiatrist Chelsea Health Ctr., 1974-77, hon. psychiatrist, 1991—; med. dir. Brockton (Mass.) Family and Community Rsch., 1979-90; child and adolescent psychiatrist Wicomico County Health Dept., Salisbury, Md., 1990-91, Queen Anne County Mental Health, Centreville, Md., 1990-92; child and adolescent psychiatrist Talbot County Mental Health, Easton, 1990-92, med. dir., 1992—; psychiatric cons. Benedictine Sch., Ridgely, Md., 1990—; part-time fellow child psychiatry Mass. Gen. Hosp., Boston, 1961-62, James Jackson Putnam Children's Ctr., Roxbury, Mass., 1961-62; cons. Am. Heritage Dictionaries, 1992. Editl. cons. The Am. Jour. of Child and Adolescent Psychiatry, 1994—. Sgt. U.S. Army, 1950-52, Korea. Decorated Bronze Star medal; Recipient Talbot County Assn. Retarded Citizens award, 1993. Mem. AMA, Am. Acad. Child and Adolescent Psychiatry, Am. Psychiatric Assn., Md. Psychiatric Soc., Med. and Chirurg. Faculty Md., Talbot County Med. Soc. Home: 104 W Chestnut St PO Box D Saint Michaels MD 21663-2980

REVERDIN, BERNARD J., lawyer; b. Baden, Switzerland, June 21, 1919; came to U.S., 1948, naturalized, 1954; s. Jean and Germaine Reverdin; children: Caroline Reverdin Flanagan, Brigitte Reverdin Sarasin, Nathalie. LLB, U. Geneva, 1942; postgrad., Harvard Law Sch., 1949. Bar: Switzerland 1945, N.Y. 1955. Atty., legal asst. Geneva Govt., 1945-48; assoc. Sullivan & Cromwell, N.Y.C., 1949-51; assoc., ptnr. Lovejoy, Wasson, Lundgren & Ashton, N.Y.C., 1951-84; ptnr., counsel Hunton & Williams, N.Y.C., 19846-88; ptnr. Eaton & Van Winkle, N.Y.C., 1988—; dir. subs. of European corps. Contbr. articles to profl. jours.; lectr. in field. V. p., treas., bd. dirs. Friends of Cuttington Coll., Liberia; v.p. LCM Found. on European Affairs Inc. Mem. N.Y. State Bar Assn. (chair com. internat. trust and estate 1988-90), Am. Fgn. Law Assn. (past pres.), Consular Law Soc. (past pres.), Internat. Law Assn., Swiss Soc. N.Y., German Am. Law Assn. Home: 11 Beech Hill Rd Huntington NY 11743 Office: Eaton & Van Winkle 600 3rd Ave Fl 39 New York NY 10016-2001

REVERE, VIRGINIA LEHR, clinical psychologist; b. Long Branch, N.J.; d. Joseph and Essie Lehr; m. Robert B. Revere; children: Elspeth, Andrew, Lisa, Robert Jr. PhB, U. Chgo., 1949, MA, 1959, PhD, 1971. Lic. cons. clin. psychologist, Va. Intern, staff psychologist Ea. Mental Health Reception Ctr., Phila., 1959-61; instr. Trenton (N.J.) State Coll., 1962-63; staff psychologist Trenton State Hosp., 1964-65, Bucks County Psychiat. Ctr., Phila., 1965-67; assoc. prof. Mansfield (Pa.) State U., 1967-77; clin. rsch. psychologist St. Elizabeth Hosp., Washington, 1977-81, tng. psychology coord., 1981-83, staff psychologist, 1985-91; child psychologist Community Mental Health Ctr., Washington, 1983-85; pvt. practice Alexandria, Va., 1980—; cons., lectr. in field. Author: Applied Psychology for Criminal Justice Professionals, 1982; contbr. articles to profl. jours. Recipient Group Merit award St. Elizabeth's Hosp., 1983, Community Svc. award D.C. Psychol. Assn., 1978, Outstanding Educator award, 1972; traineeship NIH, USPHS, Chgo., 1963-65; fellow Family Svcs. Assn., 1958-59. Mem. APA, No. Va. Soc. Clin. Psychologists, Va. Acad. Clin. Psychologists. Home: 9012 Linton Ln Alexandria VA 22308-2733 Office: 5021 Seminary Rd Ste 110 Alexandria VA 22311-1923

REVES, JOSEPH GERALD, anesthesiology educator; b. Charleston, S.C., Aug. 14, 1943; s. George Everett and Frances (Masterson) R.; m. Virginia Cathcart, Jan. 05, 1945; children: Virginia Masterson, Christine Frances, Elizabeth Cathcart. BA, Vanderbilt U., 1965; MD, Medical Coll. S.C., 1969; MS, U. Ala., Birmingham, 1973. Lic. anesthesiologist S.C., Ala., Md., N.C.; Diplomate Am. Coll. Anesthesiology, Am. Bd. Anesthesiology. Rsch. asst., dept. pharmacology Med. Coll. S.C., 1965, 66 (summers); intern U. Ala. Hosp. and Clinics, Birmingham, Ala., 1969-70, resident in anesthesiology, 1970-72; post-doctoral, dept. anesthesia and physiology U. Ala. Med. Sch., 1972; instr., dept anesthesiology U. Ala. Hosp. and Clinics, 1973; dept. tng. staff, anesthesiology Nat. Naval Med. Ctr., Bethesda, Md., 1973-75; clin. instr., dept. anesthesiology George Washington U. Sch. Med., Washington, 1973-75; assoc. prof., dept. anesthesiology U. Ala. Hosp. and Clinics, 1975-78; dir., div. anesthesiology rsch. U. Ala., 1977-84, prof. anesthesiology, 1978-84; clin. anesthesia coord. UAB Cardiac Transplant Program, Birmingham, 1982-84; prof. anesthesiology, dir. cardiothoracic anesthesia Duke U. Med. Ctr., Durham, N.C., 1984-1991; dir., Duke Heart Ctr., Duke Med. Ctr., Durham, N.C., 1987—; interim chmn., dept. anesthesiology Duke U. Med. Ctr., 1990-91, prof. and chmn., dept. anesthesiology, 1991—; cons. Hoffman-LaRoche, Somatogen, Abbott/Oximetric. Contbr. to numerous profl. jours., refereed jours., chpts. in books, published scientific reviews, selected abstracts, editorials, films, audio visual presentations, letters, positions and background papers; author: Acute Revascularization of the Infracted Heart, 1987, Common Problems in Cardiac Anesthesia, 1987, Intravenous Anesthesia and Analgesia, 1988, Anesthesiology Clinics of North America, 1988, Anesthesia, 1990, International Anesthesiology Clinics, 1991; Cardiac Anesthesia, Privileges and Practice, 1994; editor: Anesthesia and Analgesia, 1984—, cardiovascular sect. editor 1991—; editorial bd. Society Cardiovascular Anesthesia Monograph Series (chmn. 1986-89), Current Opinion in Anaesthesia 1987—, American Antec Newsletter 1989—; co-editor in chief: Current Opinion in Anaesthesiology 1990—. Dir. Clairmont Ave Hist. Preservation Com. 1976-78; Am. Heart Assn. (Durham chpt. pres. 1988-90, com. mem. anesthesiology, radiology and surgery rsch. study com. 1988-91). Grantee NIH 1991—, Janssen Pharmaceutica 1991-93, Anaquest 1989-92, Diprivan Ednl. grant ICI Pharmaceuticals Group 1991-92. Fellow Am. Coll. Cardiology; mem. AMA, Durham County Medical Soc., Internat. Soc. on Oxygen Transport to Tissue, N.C. Soc. Anesthesiologist (edn. com. 1992—), N.C. State Medical Soc., Birmingham Vanderbilt Club (bd. dirs. 1975-80, 1st v.p. 1979, pres. 1980), Southern Med. Assn. (chmn. elect. anesthesiology sect. 1976-77, chmn. 1977-78, chmn. 1988-89), Southern Soc. Anesthesiologists (v.p. 1978-79, pres. elect 1979-80, pres. 1980-81), Soc. Cardiovascular Anesthesiologists (pres. 1979-80), Assn. Univ. Anesthetists (elected to mem. 1980), Assn. Cardiac Anesthesiologists (elected to mem. 1982, pres. 1990), Soc. for Neuroleptanalgesia (bd. dirs. 1988), U. Ala. Birmingham Nat. Alumni Soc. (dist. dir., bd. dirs. 1991-93), Internat. Anesthesia Rsch. Soc. (bd. Trustees 1992—), Am. Soc. Anesthesiologists (com. sub-specialty representation 1980—, subcommittee on clin. circulation 1992—, com. geriatric anesthesia 1992—), Sigma Xi, Alpha Omega Alpha. Achievements include research on effects of age on neurologic response to cardiopulmonary bypass; cerebral blood flow and metabolism during cardiac surgery; automated delivery system of intravenous anesthetic drugs; pathophysiology of cardiopulmonary bypass. Office: Duke U Med Ctr Dept Anesthesiology PO Box 3094 Durham NC 27715-3094

REVOILE, CHARLES PATRICK, lawyer; b. Newark, Jan. 15, 1934; s. Charles Patrick and Olga Lydia (Zecca) R.; m. Sally Cole Gates, Nov. 8, 1963. B.A., U. Md., 1957, LL.B., 1960. Bar: Md. 1962, U.S. Dist. Ct. Md. 1962, U.S. Supreme Ct. 1970, U.S. Ct. Claims 1976, U.S. Ct. Appeals (fed. cir.) 1982. Legis. counsel Nat. Canners Assn., Washington, 1960-64; asst. counsel Deco Electronics Inc., Washington, 1964-67; div. counsel Westinghouse Electric, Leesburg, Va., 1967-71; v.p., gen. counsel Stanwick Corp., Arlington, Va., 1971-85, sr. v.p., gen. counsel, sec. CACI Internat. Inc., 1985-92, bd. dirs., 1992—, chmn. compensation com., 1996—; ret. lawyer and cons., 1993—; mem. regional adv. coun. NASD, 1989-92; lectr., panelist, advisor. Active in Md. Ednl. Found., College Park, 1974—; assoc. Nat. Symphony Orchestra, Washington, 1972-93, Smithsonian Instn., 1980-93, M Club Found., 1985—; lawyer, lobbyist various non profit orgns., Washington, 1984—; mem. exec. com. ann. bus. campaign Gallaudet U., 1989-91; chmh. various coms. Kemeer Open Championships, 1980-86; exec. com. 1995 USGA Sr. Open, 1997 USGA Open Championships; gen. counsel, mem. exec. com. 1995 and 1996 Kemper Open Championship. Mem. Md. Bar Assn., Wash. Corp. Counsels Assn., Am. Corp. Counsels Assn., U.S. Golf Assn., Mid. Atlantic Golf Assn. (exec. com. 1989—, v.p.). Republican. Roman Catholic. Club: Congl. Country (com. chmn. 1966-92, bd. govs. 1987-93, Bethesda, Md.), Avondale Golf (Pymble, Australia). Home: 4112 Culver St Kensington MD 20895-3624

REVSINE, LAWRENCE, accounting educator, consultant; b. Chgo., May 29, 1942; s. Victor and Pauline (Berger) R.; m. Barbara Sue Epstein, 1963; children: Pamela, David. B.S., Northwestern U., 1963, M.B.A., 1965, Ph.D., 1968. C.P.A., Ill. Staff acct. Peat, Marwick, Mitchell & Co., Chgo., 1963-64; asst. prof. U. Ill., Urbana, 1968-70, assoc. prof., 1970-71; assoc. prof. acctg. Northwestern U., 1971-74, prof., 1975-79, Eric L. Kohler prof. acctg., 1979-86, John and Norma Darling disting. prof. fin. acctg., 1986—, chmn. dept. acctg. and info. systems, 1985-93; vis. prof. U. Wis., Madison, 1974-75; cons. in field. Author: Replacement Cost Accounting, 1973, Accounting in An Inflationary Enviroment, 1977, (with others) Statement on Accounting Theory and Theory Acceptance, 1977; contbr. articles to profl. jours.; editorial cons.: Acctg. Rev., 1977-80, mem. editorial bd., 1971-74, Jour. Acctg. and Pub. Policy, 1982—, Jour. Acctg. and Bus., 1986—. Recipient commendation for teaching excellence Northwestern U. Grad. Mgmt. Assn., 1981, 82, 86, 91; recipient Tchr. of Yr. award Northwestern U. Grad. Mgmt. Assn., 1983; Ford Found. doctoral fellow, 1966-68; Peat, Marwick, Mitchell Found. grantee, 1978. Mem. AICPAs, Am. Acctg. Assn. (chmn. com. on concepts and standards-external fin. reports 1974-76, disting. overseas lectr. 1991, outstanding educator 1992, chmn. fin. reporting issues conf. com. 1994), Ill. Soc. CPAs (outstanding educator 1993, fin. acctg. standards adv. coun. 1992-95), Beta Alpha Psi, Beta Gamma Sigma. Office: Northwestern U Kellogg Grad Sch Mgmt Evanston IL 60208

REVZEN, JOEL, conductor. BS, MS, The Juilliard Sch. Music; studies with Jorge Master, Jean Martinon,Margaret Hills, Abraham Kaplan. Music dir., condr. Prince William Symphony Orch., Lake Ridge, Va.; mem. Fargo-Moorhead Symphony, Fargo, N.D., Berkshire Opera Co.; former dean St. Louis Conservatory Music. Recipient Grammy award for recording with Soprano Arleen Anger, 1993; named guest conductor of Kirov Opera, St. Petersburg, Russia, 1994, 95. Office: Fargo Moorhead Symphony 810 4th Ave S Moorhead MN 56560-2800

REWAK, WILLIAM JOHN, academic administrator, clergyman; b. Syracuse, N.Y., Dec. 22, 1933; s. William Alexander and Eldora Venetia (Carroll) R. BA, Gonzaga U., 1957, MA in English, 1958; MA in Theology, Regis Coll., Toronto, Ont., Can., 1965; PhD in English, U. Minn., 1970. Joined S.J., 1951, ordained priest Roman Cath. Ch., 1964. Tchr. English Bellarmine Coll. Prep. Sch., 1958-61; asst. prof. English Santa Clara (Calif.) U., 1970-71, pres., 1976-88; rector Jesuit Community, 1971-76; pres. Spring Hill Coll., Mobile, Ala., 1989—; bd. dirs. Gulf Coast Broadcasting Inc., Badger-Stonewall Ins. Co., Marine Environ. Scis. Consortium. Contbr. articles to theol. and critical jours., poetry, short stories to lit. jours. Bd. dirs. Mobile Bay Area Partnership for Youth, Mercy Med. Ctr.; mem. Ala. Ind. Colls., Coun. for Advancement Pvt. Colls. in Ala.; bd. trustees Loyola U. New Orleans. Mem. MLA, Coll. English Assn., Bienville Club. Democrat. Home and Office: Spring Hill Coll Office of Pres 4000 Dauphin St Mobile AL 36608-1780

REWCASTLE, NEILL BARRY, neuropathology educator; b. Sunderland, Eng., Dec. 12, 1931; arrived in Can., 1955; s. William Alexander and Eva (Coapes) R.; m. Eleanor Elizabeth Barton Boyd, Sept. 27, 1958; 4 children. MB, ChB in Medicine cum laude, U. St. Andrews, Scotland, 1955; M.A., U. Toronto, 1962, FRCPC in gen. pathology, 1962, FRCPC in neuropathology, 1968. Rotating intern U. Vancouver, 1955-56; resident in pathology Shaughnessy Hosp., Vancouver, 1956-57, U. Toronto, Ont., Can., 1957-60; fellow Med. Rsch. Coun. Can., 1960-64; demonstrator dept. pathology U. Toronto, Ont., Can., 1964-65, lectr., acting head neuropathology, 1965-69, assoc. prof., 1969-70, prof. div. neuropathology, 1970-81, head div. neuropathology, 1969-81; prof., head dept. pathology U. Calgary, Alta., Can., 1981-91, prof., 1981—; dir. dept. histopathology Foothills Hosp., Calgary, 1981-91, pathologist, 1981—, cons. neuropathology, 1981—. Recipient Queen Elizabeth Silver Jubilee medal, 1977. Fellow: Royal Coll. Physicians (cert.); mem. Can. Assn. Neuropathologists (sec. 1965-69, pres. 1976-79). Office: Foothills Hosp Dept Histopathology, 1403 29th St NW, Calgary, AB Canada T2N 2T9

REX, CHRISTOPHER DAVIS, classical musician; b. Orlando, Fla., Feb. 1, 1951; s. Charles Gordon Rex and Betty Helen (MacCauslin) Soubricas; m. Martha Anne Wilkins, Nov. 30, 1985; 1 child, Caroline Bethea. MusB, Curtis Inst. of Music, Phila., 1972; postgrad., The Juilliard Sch., 1972-73. Cellist Lyric Opera and Grand Opera, Phila., 1970-75, Phila. Orchestra, 1972-79, Georgian Chamber Players, Atlanta, 1984—; cello tchr. Gettsburg (Pa.) Coll., 1972-73, New Sch. of Music, Phila., 1969-74, Ga. State U., 1980-83; cellist, tchr. Eastern Music Festival, Greensboro, N.C., 1969-74; prin. cello Atlanta Symphony Orchestra, 1979—; concert soloist Hillyer Internat. Inc., N.Y.C., 1984—; bd. dirs. Ga. Cello Soc., Inc., Atlanta, Georgian Chamber Players, Atlanta; acting prin. during Europe Tour Cello of N.Y. Philharm., 1988; premiered Double Concerto for Violin, Cello, and Orch. N.Y. Philharm., 1994. Editor: (mus. transcription) Pictures at an Exhibition (Moussorgsky), 1987. Recipient First prize Young Artist Competition Am. Fedn. of Music Clubs, 1979. Mem. Phila. Musical Soc., Atlanta Fedn. of Music. Presbyterian. Avocations: art, watercolor painting. Home: 1237 Woods Cir NE Atlanta GA 30324-2725 Office: Atlanta Symphony Orch Woodruff Arts Ctr Atlanta GA 30309

REX, DAVID LAWRENCE, proejct manager; b. Elizabeth, N.J., Oct. 26, 1935; s. Harland Earl and Kathryn Elizabeth (Murphy) R.; m. Ann Ivy Dipple, Sept. 26, 1964; children: Harland Edward, Bradley David. BS in Mech. Engring., U. Wis., Madison, 1958. Registered profl. engr., Tex. Project engr. Bechtel Corp., San Francisco, 1961-67; sr. project engr. Arabian Am. Oil Co., Dhahran, Saudi Arabia, 1967-83; project mgr. Creole Prodn. Svcs. Inc., Houston, 1983-85, Frederic R. Harris, Suez, Egypt, 1986-88; constrn. mgr. Morton Thiokol Inc., Karnack, Tex., 1988; project mgr. Bechtel Corp., Houston, 1988-92, Morrison Knudsen, Cleve., 1992-94; sales engr. McCracken & Assocs., Bristol, Tenn., 1994-95; sales rep. Touch Controls, Inc., Oceanside, Calif., 1996—. Capt. USAFR, 1958-61. Mem. Nat. W Club, Kingsport Bicycle Assn., Rep. Nat. Com., Airport Christian Ch., Disciples of Christ, Beta Theta Pi. Home: 780 Hamilton Rd Apt C4 Blountville TN 37617-6417

REX, LONNIE ROYCE, religious organization administrator; b. Caddo, Okla., May 11, 1928; s. Robert Lavern and Lennie Cordy (Gilcrease) R.; m. Betty Louise Sorrells, Apr. 8, 1949; children: Royce DeWayne, Patricia Louise, Debra Kaye. MusB, Oklahoma City U., 1950; DD (hon.), Am. Bible Inst., 1970. Advt. mgr. Oral Roberts Evang. Assn., Tulsa, 1955-57; bus. mgr. T.L. Osborn Found., Tulsa, 1957-69; gen. mgr. Christian Crusade, Tulsa, 1969-80; sec.-treas. David Livingstone Missionary Found., Tulsa, 1970-80, pres., 1980—; dep. dir. gen. Internat. Biog. Assn.; bd. dirs. Intra-Ch. Pension Fund, Bethany, Okla.; speaker internat. confs. Eng., Hungary, Korea, Singapore, Spain, N.Y.C. Author: Never a Child, 1989. Mem. Internat. PHC Loan Fund; bd. dirs. Armand Hammer United World Coll. of Am. West, 1993—. Recipient Merit award Korea, 1975, Moran medal Republic of Korea, Humanitarian award Senator Hugh Scott, 1983, Svc. to Mankind award Internat. Biog. Congress, Spain, 1987, Internat. Lions Club award; named Outstanding Humanitarian of Yr., Am. Biog. Inst., 1987, Man of Yr., 1990, 1993; knighted in Moscow, 1993. Mem. Knights of Malta (Sword of Svc. 1996), Phi Beta Kappa. Home: 6919 S Columbia Ave Tulsa OK 74136-4328 Office: David Livingstone Missionary Found 6555 S Lewis Ave Tulsa OK 74136-1010 *In my work among the starving in Ethiopia, I walked into a tent of over 100 mothers, lying on mats, who had given birth during the last three days. It was silent! Morbid silence! That haunting silence lives with me since that moment. I asked why? I was informed the babies did not have the strength to cry. I'm thankful my children could cry.*

REXROTH, NANCY LOUISE, photographer; b. Washington, June 27, 1946; d. John Augustus and Florence Bertha (Young) R. B.F.A., Am. U., 1969; M.F.A. in Photography, Ohio U., Athens, 1971. Asst. prof. photography Antioch Coll., Yellow Springs, Ohio, 1977-79, Wright State U., Dayton, Ohio, 1979-82. Author: Iowa, 1976, The Platinotype, 1977, 1976. Nat. Endowment Arts grantee, 1973; Ohio Arts Council, 1981. Mem. Am. Massage Therapy Assn. Democrat. Home and Office: 2631 Cleinview Ave Cincinnati OH 45206-1810

REY, MARGRET ELIZABETH, writer; b. Hamburg, Germany, May 16, 1906; came to U.S., 1940; d. Felix and Gertrude (Rosenfeld) Waldstein; m. Hans A. Rey (dec. 1977). Art degree, Art Acad., Hamburg, Germany, 1929, Bauhaus, Dessau, Germany, 1931, Acad. Art, Dusseldorf, Germany, 1932. Children's author Houghton Mifflin Co., Boston, 1941—, Harper & Row, N.Y.C., 1945—; script cons. Curgeo, Montreal, Quebec, Can., 1977-83; adj. prof. Brandeis U., Waltham, Mass., 1978-84. Author: Pretzel, 1944, Spotty, 1945, Billy's Picture, 1948; co-author: Curious George, 1941, Curious George Takes a Job, 1947, Curious George Rides a Bike, 1952, Curious George Gets a Medal, 1957, Curious George Flies a Kite, 1958, Curious George Learns the Alphabet, 1963, Curious George Goes to the Hospital, 1966. Founder, trustee The Curious George Found., Cambridge, Mass., 1991—; bd. dirs. Phillips Brooks House, Harvard U., Cambridge, Mass., 1989—. Mem. World Wildlife, Smithsonian, Mus. Fine Arts, Audobon Soc., Defenders of Wildlife. Democrat. Avocations: reading, gardening. Home: 14 Hilliard St Cambridge MA 02138-4922

REY, NICHOLAS ANDREW, ambassador; b. Warsaw, Poland, Jan. 23, 1938; m. Louisa Machado; 3 children. BA, Princeton U.; MA, Johns Hopkins U. From economist to dir. exec. secretariat, staff asst. to sec. Dept. Treasury, 1963-66; v.p. Drexel, Harriman, Ripley, Inc., 1968-70; staff mem. Pres.'s Commn. Internat. Trade and Investment Policy, 1970-71; mng. dir. Merrill Lynch Capital Markets, 1971-87, Bear, Stearns & Co., Inc., 1987-92; vice chair Polish-Am. Fund, 1990-92; with Productivity Consulting Firm, 1992-93; U.S. amb. to Poland, 1993—; Bd. dirs. Resource Found.; mem. Coun. Fgn. Rels., 1972—, N.Y. Stock Exchange; chmn. adv. com. Internat. Capital Markets; mem. internat. com. Security Industry Assn., 1987-92; participant sem. on fin. markets Soviet-N.Y. Stock Exchange, Moscow, 1990; mem. econ. devel. com., transitional corp. and Third World devel. subcom., 1980; mem. internat. Montary Fund study on access to capital markets Internat. Bank for Reconstrn. and Devel., 1978-79; mem. dept. treasury Clinton-Gore Transition Team; mem. fgn. portfolio investment adv. com. Dept. Treasury, 1979-80. Mem. Human Rights Commn., Larchmont, N.Y., 1984-92. With USAR, 1962-68. Office: Am Embassy Warsaw Unit 1340 APO AE 09213-1340

REYES, ANDRE, ballet dancer; b. San Francisco; s. Benjamin and Josefa Reyes. Student, Santa Clara Ballet Sch., Sch. Am. Ballet, Am. Ballet Theatre Sch., San Francisco Ballet Sch. With San Francisco Ballet, 1981-95; prin. dancer Pacific Northwest Ballet, 1995—. Appeared in televised performances of Cinderella, 1985 (Dance in Am. Series), To the Beatles, 1984 (Smuin), Stravinsky Pinao Pieces, 1984 (Smuin), Stravinsky Piano Pieces, 1984 (Smuin), Symphony in 3 Movements (Gladstein); guest artist Ballet Philippines 20th Anniversary Gala; guest artist San Francisco Symphony's Pops Series, San Francisco Arts For Life benefit gala, San Francisco Opera. Office: 5612 Greenwood Ave N Seattle WA 98103 also: Pacific Northwest Ballet 301 Mercer St Seattle WA 98109-4600

REYES, EDWARD, pharmacology educator; b. Albuquerque, May 5, 1944; s. Salvador and Faustina (Gabaldon) R.; m. Shirley Ann Trott, Aug. 15, 1970; children: David Joshua, Elizabeth Ann, Steven Mark. BS in Pharmacy, U. N.Mex., 1968; MS in Pharmacology, U. Colo., 1970, PhD in Pharmacology, 1974. Asst. prof. pharmacy U. Wyo. Sch. of Pharmacy, Laramie, 1974-75; asst. prof. pharmacology Dept. Pharmacology, U. N.Mex., Albuquerque, 1976-85, assoc. prof. pharmacology, 1985—; dir. minority biomed. rsch. support program U. N.Mex. Sch. of Medicine, Albuquerque, 1994—; referee Pharmacology Biochemistry Behavior, San Antonio, 1986—; adv. com. mem. NIMH Minority Neuro Sci. Fellowship, Washington, 1991—. Author: (with others) Alcohol and Drug Abuse Review, 1991; contbr. articles to profl. jours. Scoutmaster Boy Scouts Am., Albuqueque, 1986-94; vis. scientist N.Mex. Acad. of Sci., Las Vegas, 1988—; youth preacher Rio Grande Bapt. Ch., Albuqueque, 1980—. Grantee Nat. Inst. of Alcohol Abuse and Alcoholism, NSF. Mem. Rsch. Soc. on Alcoholism, Western Pharmacology Soc., Soc. for Neurosci. (chair minority edn. tng. and profl. adv. 1987-94), Soc. for Advancement of Chicanos and Native Ams. Achievements include rsch. that the in utero adminstration of alcohol produces an increase in liver and brain Y-glutamyl transpeptidase activity; isolated GTP from brain of rats. Office: Univ NMex Sch Medicine 915 Camino de Salud NE Albuquerque NM 87131

REYES, JOSE ANTONIO, SR., minister; b. Canovanas, P.R., May 24, 1940; s. Dionisio Reyes and Antonia (Rodriguez) R.; m. Olfa R. Martinez, May 30, 1964; 1 child, Jose A. BA in Edn., U. P.R., 1962; MA, Sch. Theology, Cleveland, Tenn., 1984; D Ministry, Logos Sch., 1985. Ordained to ministry Ch. of God of Prophecy, 1969. Youth dir. Ch. of God of Prophecy, Rio Piedras, P.R., 1956-58, pastor, 1963-68; mission rep. for Latin Am. Ch. of God of Prophecy, Cleveland, Tenn., 1969-75, internat. radio speaker, 1969—, internat. asst. gen. overseer, 1981—; pres. Hispanic Nat. Religious Broadcasting, Parsippany, 1985-88; v.p. Nat. Orgn. Advancement of Hispanic, 1983-86; com. mem. Hispanic Task Force of Am. Bible Soc., 1985-87; mem. Hispanic Commn., Nat. Assn. Evangelicals, Carol Stream, Ill., 1988—; exec. com. Nat. Religious Broadcasters, 1990-93, bd. dirs., 1990—; founding mem. Alliance Nat. Evang. Ministries, 1993—; pres. ref. com. Latin Am. Christian Comm., 1992—; mem. exec. com. Washington for Jesus, 199—; founding mem. Israel Christian adv. coun., 1996. Author: The Hispanics in USA - A Challenge, An Opportunity for the Church, 1984; author 10 Bible Study Guides on books of the Bible, 1985-90. Recipient Excellence in Hispanic Program Producer award Nat. Religious Broadcasters, 1988, Excellence in Ministry award Internat. Ministry Com., 1990. Mem. Spanish Voice of Salvation Sponsorship Club (pres.). Republican. Home: 3816 Northwood Dr NW Cleveland TN 37312-3805 *Equalling our Lord is an impossible task, but imitating Him is our supreme duty.*

REYES, LILLIAN JENNY, lawyer; b. Covington, Ky., June 23, 1955; d. Luis and Lillian Ann (Barroso) R.; m. Robert Timothy Joyce, May 16, 1986. BA magnum cum laude, U. Miami, Fla., 1977; JD with honors, U. Fla., 1980. Bar: Fla. 1980, U.S. Dist. Ct. (mid. dist.) Fla. 1981, U.S. Ct. Appeals (11th cir.) 1981. Assoc. Carlton, Fields, Ward, Emmanual, Smith & Cutler, Tampa, Fla., 1980-87; ptnr. Joyce & Reyes, Tampa, 1987—. Bd. dirs. Suncoast counsel Girl Scouts Am., 1981-83; bd. dirs., past chmn. aging rsch. unit, chmn. ombudsman counsel project, community rsch. devel. bd., pub. affairs com., legis. breakfast com. Jr. League Tampa. Recipient George W. Milan award U. Fa. Law Rev.; named Ms. Clearwater, Fla., Miss Am. Pageant, 1973, princess Orange Bowl Com., 1977. Mem. Fla. Bar Assn., Hillsborough County Bar Assn. (probate and guardianship rules com. 1981-87, asst. chmn. law week 1984-85, bd. dirs. young lawyers sect. 1985-87, law week chmn. 1987-88, bd. dirs. 1987—), Assn. Trial Lawyers Am., Fla. Trial Lawyers Assn., Bay Area Legal Svcs. Vol. Lawyers Program, U. Fla. Law Rev. Alumni Assn. Democrat. Roman Catholic. Avocations: acting, travel. Office: Joyce & Reyes 101 E Kennedy Blvd Ste 3875 Tampa FL 33602

REYES, NICHOLAS CARLOS, photographer; b. Wichita Falls, Tex., Feb. 22, 1953; s. Charles and Ramona Reyes; m. Mickie Felix, Apr. 15, 1972; 1 child, Aimee Nicole. Midwestern U., 1975; postgrad., Art Inst. Ft. Lauderdale, 1976. Photographer Times & Record News, Wichita Falls, 1974-76, U.S. Govt., various locations, 1976-84; owner, photographer Photography By Reyes, Wichita Falls, 1983—; photographer NFL, 1994—, Fox TV, 1994—; restorer John Kennedy pictures Sam Rayburn Libr. Photos exhibited at Wichita Falls Mus. and Art Ctr., 1988 (Best in Exhibit award), White House, 1990; works included Big Click of Texas Picture Book. Photographer poster child Multiple Dystrophy Assn., Wichita Falls, 1987, 88. With USAF, 1971-73. Recipient Best Photo of Wichita Falls, City of Wichita Falls, 1987. Mem. Profl. Photographers Am. Democrat. Roman Catholic. Home: 1508 Buchanan St Wichita Falls TX 76309-2208 Office: Photography by Reyes 1506 Buchanan St Wichita Falls TX 76309-2208

REYES, ROSE MARIE, nursing educator; b. San Antonio, Sept. 27, 1940; d. Rudolfo Davila and Maria de la Luz (Acosta) Lagunas; m. Maximilian Ortegon Reyes, Nov. 23, 1961; children: Cheryl Yvette, Karen Renee Reyes Vieira, Max Eric. Student, San Antonio C.C., 1958-59, AA, 1980; diploma, Bapt. Meml. Hosp. Sch. Nursing, San Antonio, 1961; grad. in Instrn. Health Occupations, Tex. A&M U., 1982; BS in Health Professions, S.W. Tex. State U., 1987, postgrad. RN, cert. instr. vocat. nursing, Tex.; cert. neonatal care. Charge nurse dept. pediatrics Bexar County Hosp., San Antonio, 1961-62; charge nurse depts. pediatrics and med.-surg. Bapt. Meml. Hosp., San Antonio, 1962-65; clin. nurse specialist dept. pediatrics Brooke Army Med. Ctr., San Antonio, 1965-66; charge nurse newborn nursery S.W. Tex. Meth. Hosp., San Antonio, 1967-70, from charge nurse to head nurse and relief supr. newborn nursery and neonatal ICU, 1970-80; instr. vocat. nursing San Antonio Sch. Dist., 1980-88, migrant health nurse, 1988-90; instr. vocat. nursing, program team leader, chair curriculum com. Bapt. Meml. Hosp. Sch. Vocat. Nursing, San Antonio, 1990—; edn. coun. chair Bapt. Meml. Hosp. Sch., 1996. Mem. adoption com. Luth. Social Svcs., San Antonio, 1993—; active King of Kings Luth. Ch. Recipient Nurses Assn. Ob-Gyn. award. Mem. Tex. Assn. Vocat. Nursing Educators (membership com. 1990—), Luth. Women's Missionary League (treas.). Avocations: reading, travel, history, music. Office: Bapt Meml Hosp Sch Vocat Nursing 511 Richmond San Antonio TX 78215-2008

REYNA, LEO J., psychologist, educator, editor; b. N.Y.C., Oct. 26, 1918; s. Samuel J. and Alegria (Azuz) R.; B.A., U. Mo., 1943, M.A., U. Iowa, 1944, Ph.D., 1946; lic. psychologist, Fla., Mass.; m. Priscilla Deane Trick (dec.); children—Stephen, Christopher, Susan, Patrick, Alix. Lectr., sr. lectr. U. Witwatersrand, Johannesburg, South Africa, 1946-50; asst. prof. to prof., Boston U., 1950-78; prof. psychology Nova U., Ft. Lauderdale, Fla., 1978—, founding dir. PhD program clin. psychology; mem. faculty extension divsn. Harvard U., 1959-76; program devel. assoc. Judge Rotenberg Ednl. Ctr., Providence, R.I., 1994—; cons. Johannesburg Child Guidance Ctr., VA hosps., Boston, Bedford and Brockton, Mass., Northport VA Hosp. (N.Y.), Tufts U. Med. Sch., Worcester Youth Guidance Ctr. (Mass.), U. Va. Med. Sch., Temple U. Med. Sch., Boston Med. Found., Epilepsy Found. Mass., R.I. Div. Vocat. Rehab., Cambridge Psychiat. Day Ctr., others; founding mem., adv. bd., mem. exec. com. trustee Cambridge Ctr. Behavioral Studies, 1980—; founding mem. African studies program Boston U.; founding mem. mailman family ctr. Nova U.; lab. devel. Boston U. grantee NSF, 1956-57, Research grantee USPHS, 1957-61, 64-67. Mem. Am. Psychol. Assn., Am. Psychol. Soc., Eastern Psychol. Assn., Mass. Psychol. Assn., No. Calif. Assn. Behavior Analysis, Behavior Therapy and Research Soc. (dir.), Assn. for Advancement of Behavior Therapy, Nat. Inst. for Psychotherapies, Internat. Assn. Behavior Analysis, AAUP, Sigma Xi. Co-author: Conditioning Therapies, 1964; co-editor: Behavior Therapy in Psychiatric Practice, 1976; co-founder, assoc. editor Jour. Behavior Therapy and Exptl. Psychiatry, 1970—; contbr. articles in field to profl. publs. Home: 1961 SW 82nd Ave Fort Lauderdale FL 33324-5402 also: 2550 Dana St Berkeley CA 94704-2878 Office: Nova U Sch Psychology College Ave Fort Lauderdale FL 33314 also: 22 Mason Ter Brookline MA 02146-2604

REYNIK, ROBERT J., materials scientist, research administrator; b. Bayonne, N.J., Dec. 25, 1932; s. Mary Reynik; m. Georgiana M. Walker, Apr. 12, 1959; children: Michael, Christopher, Jonathan, Katherine, Steven, Kevin. BS in Math. and Physics, U. Detroit, 1956; MS in Elec. Engring., U. Cin., 1960, PhD in Phys. Chemistry, 1963. Rsch. assoc. Sch. Metallurgical Engring. U. Pa., Phila., 1963-64, asst. prof., 1964-67; assoc. prof. Drexel U., Phila., 1967-70; assoc. dir. engring. materials program NSF, Washington, 1970-71, dir. engring. materials program, 1971-74, dir. metallurgy program, 1974-82, head metallurgy, polymers, ceramics and electronics material, 1983-90, head office spl. programs in materials, 1990-94; sr. staff scientist divsn. materials rsch. NSF, Arlington, Va., 1994—; exec. sec. and cognizant program dir. US-USSR Internat. Agreement in Sci. and Tech., Washington, 1974-79; NSF liaison rep. Nat. Materials Adv. Bd., Washington, 1985-94; coord. integration of rsch. and edn. Office of the Asst. Dir., Math. & Phys. Scis. Directorate, 1996—; dir. electrometallurgy and materials, corrosion, program US-USSR internat. agreement sci. and tech., 1974-80; mem. First U.S. Metall. Del. People's Republic China, 1978; vis. prof. materials sci. and engring. U. Pa., 1982-83; tech. coord. Sci. & Tech. Ctrs. in Material Sci. & Engring., 1990-94; co-chair Fed. Coord. Coun. for Sci., Engring. and Tech. joint com. edn. and tng. Office of Sci. and Tech. Policy, 1992-93; co-chair task group edn. and tng. Aeronautics Materials and mfg. Techs. Working Groups Nat. Sci. and Tech. coun., Office of Vice Pres. of U.S., 1994; tech. mgr. rsch. grants mfg. devel. and mfg. Tech. Reinvestment Project, Fed. Govt., 1994-96. Fellow Am. Soc. Materials Internat. (fellow 1993, mem.-at-large materials sci. coun. 1990—, golf medal selection com.); mem. AAAS, AIME (chair govt. pub. affairs com. 1994—, chair all inst. govt. affairs com.), Am. Chem. Soc., Am. Phys. Soc., Am. Assn. Engring. Socs. (honors and awards com.), The Metals, Minerals and Materials Soc. (mem. and chmn. various coms.), Materials Rsch. Soc., Sr. Exec. Assn., Sigma Xi (past chpt. pres., exec. counselor), Tau Beta Pi. Office: Nat Sci Found Divsn Materials Rsch 4201 Wilson Blvd Arlington VA 22203-1803

REYNOLDS, A. WILLIAM, manufacturing company executive; b. Columbus, Ohio, June 21, 1933; s. William Morgan and Helen Hibbard (McCray) R.; m. Joanne D. McCormick, June 12, 1953; children: Timothy M., Morgan Reynolds Brigham, Mary Reynolds Miller. AB in Econs., Harvard U., 1955; MBA, Stanford U., 1957. Pres. Crawford Door Co., Detroit, 1959-66; staff asst. to treas TRW Inc., Cleve., 1957-59, asst. to exec. v.p. automotive group, 1966-67, v.p. automotive aftermarket group, 1967-70, exec. v.p. indsl. and replacement sector, 1971-81, exec. v.p. automotive worldwide sector, 1981-84; pres. GenCorp, Akron, Ohio, 1984-85, pres., chief exec. officer, 1985-87, chmn., CEO, 1987-94, chmn., 1994-95; bd. dirs. Eaton Corp., Cleve., Boise (Idaho) Cascade Corp., Boise Cascade Office Products Corp., Itasca, Ill., Stant Corp., Richmond, Ind., Fed. Res. Bank Cleve., now chmn.; mem. dean's adv. coun. Stanford (Calif.) U. Grad. Sch. Bus., 1981-88. Chmn. United Way-Red Cross of Summit County, Ohio, 1987; trustee Univ. Hosps. of Cleve., 1984—, chmn., 1987-94. Mem. SAE, Bus. Roundtable (policy com.), Coun. on Fgn. Rels., Kirtland Country Club, Union Club, Rolling Rock Club, John's Island Club, Pepper Pike Club. Episcopalian. Avocations: hunting, fly fishing, skiing, golf. Office: GenCorp Inc 175 Ghent Rd Akron OH 44333-3330

REYNOLDS, ALAN ANTHONY, economist, speaker, consultant; b. Abilene, Tex., Apr. 11, 1942; s. Alan DeForrest and Rosine (McDougall) R.; m. Karen Kane, Feb. 27, 1965; children: John Alan, Melissa Maurine. BA, UCLA, 1965; postgrad., Sacramento State Coll., 1967-71. Dept. mgr. J.C. Penny Co., Sacramento, 1965-71; assoc. editor Nat. Review, N.Y.C., 1972-75; sr. economist Argus Rsch. Corp., N.Y.C., 1976; v.p., economist First Nat. Bank, Chgo., 1977-80; v.p., chief economist Polyconomics Inc., Morristown, N.J., 1981-89; dir. econ. rsch. Hudson Inst., Indpls., 1994—; sr. v.p. H.C. Wainright & Co. Econs., Boston; cons. Leading Authorities, Washington; rsch. dir. Kemp Tax Reform Commn., 1995. Contbr. Wall St. Jour., Washington Times, Forbes, Nat. Rev., Internat. Economy. Mem. Mont Pelerin Soc., Nat. Tax Assn. (mem. fed. tax com.). Office: Hudson Inst PO Box 26-919 5395 Emerson Way Indianapolis IN 46226-1475

REYNOLDS, ALBERT BARNETT, nuclear engineer, educator; b. Lebanon, Tenn., Feb. 1, 1931; s. George Lazenby and Marion (Barnett) R.; m. Helen Buck, Sept. 6, 1954; children—Albert Jr., Charlotte, Marion. Student, U. of South, 1948-51; S.B. in Physics, MIT, 1953, S.M. in Nuclear Engring., 1955, Sc.D. in Chem. Engring., 1959. Physicist-mgr. Gen. Electric Co., San Jose, Calif., 1959-68; prof. nuclear engring. U. Va., Charlottesville, 1968—, chmn. dept. nuclear engring. and engring. physics, 1991-92; cons. NRC, Washington, 1970-84, U.S. Dept. Energy, 1987-89; fields of rsch. include liquid metal reactor safety, electric cable aging, boron neutron capture therapy, radiation detection for nuclear test ban treaty. Author: Bluebells and Nuclear Energy, 1996; co-author: Fast Breeder Reactors, 1981; contbr. numerous articles to profl. jours. Fellow Am. Nuclear Soc. (exec. com. div. nuclear reactor safety 1980-83, chair Va. sect. 1986-87); mem. ASME, IEEE, Am. Soc. Engring. Edn., Sigma Xi, Tau Beta Pi. Home: 1502 Holly Rd Charlottesville VA 22901-3132 Office: U Va Dept Mech Aerospace & Nuclear Engring Charlottesville VA 22903

REYNOLDS, BENEDICT MICHAEL, surgeon; b. N.Y.C., Sept. 12, 1925; s. Benedict and Delia (Coan) R.; m. Alice Marie Hodnett, May 3, 1952; children: Benedict, John, Ann Marie, Mary Alice, Daniel. Student, Columbia U., 1942-43, U. Rochester, 1943-44; MD, NYU, 1948. Diplomate: Am. Bd. Surgery, Pan Am. Med. Assn. Intern Bellevue Med. Center, N.Y.C., 1948-49; surg. resident Bellevue Med. Center, 1951-55; asst. in surgery N.Y. U., N.Y.C., 1953-55; instr. surgery Albert Einstein Coll. Medicine, Bronx, N.Y., 1955-56; asst. prof. surgery Albert Einstein Coll. Medicine, 1956-58, clin. asst. prof., 1958-71, vis. prof. surgery, 1977; prof. surgery N.Y. Med. Coll., N.Y.C., 1971—; practice medicine specializing in surgery Bronx, 1955—; dir. surgery Misericordia Hosp. Med. Center, Bronx, 1962-83, Fordham Hosp., 1964-76; chmn. dept. surgery Lincoln Hosp., Bronx, 1976-82; attending surgeon Met. Hosp., N.Y.C., 1972—; cons. Community Gen. Hosp. of Sullivan County, 1972—. Contbr. articles in field to med. jours. Served with USN, 1943-45, 49-51. Fellow N.Y. Acad. Medicine, A.C.S.; mem. AMA, N.Y. State Med. Soc., N.Y. Acad. Sci., Soc. Surgery Alimentary Tract, N.Y. and Bklyn. Regional Chpt. on Trauma, Internat. Soc. Lymphology, N.Y. Surg. Soc., Am. Gastroent. Assn. Roman Catholic. Home: 150 Overhill Rd Bronxville NY 10708-5136 Office: 1578 Williams Bridge Rd Bronx NY 10461-3000

REYNOLDS, BILL See ARCHER, WILLIAM REYNOLDS, JR.

REYNOLDS, BURT, actor, director; b. Waycross, Ga., Feb. 11, 1936; s. Burt R.; m. Judy Carne (div. 1965); m. Loni Anderson, Apr. 29, 1988 (div. 1994). Ed., Fla. State U., Palm Beach Jr. Coll. Owner ranch, Jupiter, Fla. Actor numerous stage prodns. including The Rainmaker; movie appearances include: Angel Baby, 1961, Armored Command, 1961, Operation CIA, 1965, Navajo Joe, 1967, Impasse, 1969, 100 Rifles, 1969, Sam Whiskey, 1969, Skullduggery, 1970, Shark, 1970, Deliverance, 1972, Fuzz, 1972, Everything You've Always Wanted to Know about Sex But Were Afraid to Ask, 1972, Shamus, 1973, The Man Who Loved Cat Dancing, 1973, White Lightning, 1973, The Longest Yard, 1974, At Long Last Love, 1975, W.W. and the Dixie Dance Kings, 1975, Hustle, 1975, Lucky Lady, 1975, Silent Movie, 1976, Nickelodeon, 1976, Smokey and the Bandit, 1977, Semi-Tough, 1977, Hooper, 1978, Starting Over, 1979, Rough Cut, 1980, Smokey and the Bandit II, 1980, Cannonball Run, 1981, Paternity, 1981, The Best Little Whorehouse in Texas, 1982, Best Friends, 1982, Stroker Ace, 1983, The Man Who Loved Women, 1983, City Heat, 1984, Cannonball Run II, 1984, Stick, 1985, Uphill All The Way, 1986, Rent A Cop, 1987, Heat, 1987, Malone, 1987, Switching Channels, 1988, Physical Evidence, 1989, Breaking In, 1989, Modern Love, 1990, Cop and a Half, 1993, also voice in All Dogs Go To Heaven, 1989; dir., actor: Gator, 1976, The End, 1978, Sharkey's Machine, 1981; TV appearances include: Branded, 1964; regular appearances on Gunsmoke, 1962-65; star series Hawk, 1966, Dan August, 1970-71, B.L. Stryker, 1989, ABC Saturday Mystery Movie, 1988, Evening Shade, 1990-94. Recipient Emmy award as Outstanding Lead Actor in a Comedy Series ("Evening Shade") Nat. Acad. TV Arts and Scis., 1991. Mem. Dirs. Guild Am. Office: William Morris Agency 151 El Camino Beverly Hills CA 90212*

REYNOLDS, CALVIN, management consultant, business educator; b. N.Y.C., Oct. 2, 1928; s. Charles Edward and Edna (Klockgeter) R.; m. E. Juana Jaynes, Aug. 22, 1955 (div. 1984); m. Mary Virginia Gregg, May 4, 1985; children: Dwight, Neal J. BS in Bus., Columbia U., 1952, MS in Bus., 1959. Dir. ops. Europe Uniroyal Internat., Geneva, 1956-67; v.p. Nat. Fgn. Trade Coun., N.Y.C., 1967-74; sr. v.p. Orgn. Resources Counselors, N.Y.C., 1975-92; sr. counselor Orgn. Resources Counselors, Ossining, N.Y., 1993—; pres. Calvin Reynolds and Assocs., Inc., Ossining, N.Y., 1993—; dir. Yokogawa-ORC, Tokyo, Am. Compensation Assn.; pres. Indsl. Rels. Counselors. Contbr. articles to profl. jours. Wharton Sch. U. Pa. sr. fellow, 1993-94. Mem. Inst. for Internat. Human Resource Mgmt. Republican. Congregationalist. Avocations: golf, music, reading. Home and Office: Calvin Reynolds & Assocs Inc 52 Underhill Rd Ossining NY 10562-5118

REYNOLDS, CARL CHRISTIANSEN, government official; b. Wellsville, Utah, Sept. 8, 1934; s. Joseph William and Theresa (Christiansen) R.; m. Sharon Zollinger, Feb. 15, 1963; children: Rose Marie, Jeffrey Wayne. BS, Utah State U., 1957. Lab. technician Thiokol Chem. Corp., Brigham City, Utah, 1960-62; investigator FDA, Denver, 1962-66; resident investigator FDA, Albuquerque, 1966-72; supervisory investigator FDA, Dallas, 1972-77; dir. investigations FDA, Orlando, Fla., 1977-89; dist. dir. FDA, Detroit, 1989-95; dir. office field programs FDA, Washington, 1995—. Mem. council exec. bd. Boy Scouts Am., Albuquerque, 1967-72, mem. nat. com. Dallas, 1982-86, dist. com., Orlando and Dallas, 1972-87. Served with U.S. Army, 1957-59. Recipient Award of Merit Boy Scouts Am., 1975, Silver Beaver award, 1986. Mem. Assn. Food and Drug Officials. Republican. Mormons. Avocations: camping, computer programming, electronics.

REYNOLDS, CAROLYN MARY, elementary education educator; b. Bklyn., May 17, 1936; d. Wesley and Christine (Cardieri) Russo; m. Richard Martin Reynolds, Apr. 12, 1958; children: Donna Marie Reynolds Dewey, Richard Edward. BS, Adelphi U., 1968; MA, SUNY, Stony Brook, 1971. Cert. tchr., N.Y. Tchr. Rocky Point (N.Y.) Sch., 1956-57, Little Flower Sch., Wading River, N.Y., 1957-59, Shoreham (N.Y.)-Wading River Sch. Dist., 1969—; mem. sch. consolidation task force Shoreham-Wading River Sch. Dist., 1992-93, mem. supt. search com., 1995, mem. dist. shared decision making team, 1995-96; supervising tchr. St. Joseph Coll., 1991, 95, Dowling Coll., Oakdale, N.Y., 1992, C.W. Post Coll., Southampton, N.Y., SUNY, Stonybrook; coord. constructivist course, Shoreham, N.Y., 1990—. Editor tchr. union publ. VOX, 1989-90 (award 1990). Leader Girl Scouts U.S., Rocky Point, N.Y., 1956. Noyes Found. fellow; NSF grantee. Mem. ASCD, Nat. Coun. Tchrs. English, N.Y. State United Tchrs., Shoreham-Wading River Tchrs. Assn. (co-pres., sec., negotiator tchrs. contract), United Fedn. Tchrs. (10 Yr. pin for leadership), Internat. Reading Assn. (coun. pres. 1980—). Home: 50 Highland Down Shoreham NY 11786-1122

REYNOLDS, CLARK WINTON, economist, educator; b. Chgo., Mar. 13, 1934; m. Nydia O'Connor Viales. AB, Claremont (Calif.) Men's Coll., 1956; student, MIT, 1956-57, 58; student divinity sch., Harvard U., 1957-58; MA, U. Calif., Berkeley, 1961, PhD in Econs., 1962. Asst. prof. Occidental Coll., L.A., 1961-62; from asst. to assoc. prof. dept. edn. and econ. growth Yale U., New Haven, 1962-67; sr. fellow The Brookings Inst., Washington, 1975-76; prof. econs., prin. investigator, founding dir. Ams. program Stanford (Calif.) U., 1967—; vis. prof. Nat. U. Mex., Chapingo, 1966, El Colegio de Mex., Mexico City, 1964, 65, 79; vis. lectr. in econs. Stockholm U. Econs., 1968; vis. rsch. scholar Internat. Inst. for Applied Systems Analysis, Laxenburg, Austria, 1978; advisor N.Am. forum Stanford U., 1990—. Author: The Mexican Economy, 1970; co-editor: Essays on the Chilean Economy, 1965, (with C. Tello) U.s.-Mexican Relations: Economic and Social Aspects, Las Relaciones Mexico Estados Unidos, 1983, Dynamics of North American Trade, 1991, North American Labor Market Interdependence, 1992, Open Regionalism in the Andes, 1996. Dir. Monticello West Found., 1980—. Woodrow Wilson Found. fellow, 1956-57, Rockefeller Found. fellow, 1957-58, Doherty Found. fellow, 1960-61, Inst. Internat. Studies fellow Stanford U., 1990—; grantee Social Sci. Rsch. Coun., Ford Found., Hewlett Found., Rockefeller Found., Mellon Found., MacArthur Found., Tinker Found. Office: Stanford U Food Rsch Inst Encina Hall W Rm 305/306 Stanford CA 94305-6084

REYNOLDS, COLLINS JAMES, III, foundation administrator; b. N.Y.C., Feb. 28, 1937; s. Collins James and Alta Roberta (Carr) R.; m. Harriet Virginia Blackburn (div. 1965); children: Collins James IV, Quentin Scott; m. Carol Ann Miller, June 24, 1967; children: Justin Blake, Carson Jonathan. Student govt. and econs., Harvard U., George Washington U. Data processing supr. missile and space vehicle div. Gen. Electric, Phila., 1961; contract adminstr. Allison div. Gen. Motors, Indpls., 1962-65; country dir. Peace Corps, Mauritania, 1966-67; dir. Peace Corps, Sierra Leone, 1971-74; dir. div. ops. Gen. Learning Corp., Time Inc., Washington, 1968-71; trustee, sec., treas., exec. dir. Center for Research and Edn., Denver, 1974-79; Carter Presdl. appointee, assoc. dir. Internat. Devel. Coop. Agy., AID, 1980; dir. mktg. Am. TV & Communications Corp., Time Inc., Denver, 1980-81; founder, chmn. bd., pres. Omnicom, Inc., Denver, 1981-87; Bush Presdl. appointee, sr. exec. svc., assoc. dir. mgmt. Peace Corps, 1989-92; dir. comms. divsn. Am. Water Works Assn., 1994—; cons., UN Secretariat, Econ. Devel. Adminstrn., OECD, USAID, USDA; project dir. Model Cities Edn. Plan, HUD, Gen. Learning, Balt., Dept. Labor/HEW Remedial Edn. and Job Placement Program, Transcentury Corp., Washington; program mgr. Ft. Lincoln New Town Sch. System, Washington; supervising dir. VISTA, Boston, N.Y.C., Atlanta; dir. adminstrn. Job Corps, Kansas City. Founder, editor, pub.: The Bridge; patentee in field. Served as aviator USMCR, 1956-60. Home: 1615 Krameria St Denver CO 80220-1552

REYNOLDS, DAVID G(EORGE), physiologist, educator; b. South Chicago Heights, Ill., Nov. 25, 1933; s. Gilbert J. and Louise C. (Roescheisen) R.; m. Carol J. Adams, Nov. 8, 1958 (div. 1981); children: Stephen D., Douglas S.; m. Julia M. Davis, Aug. 26, 1987. BA, Knox Coll., 1955; MS, U. Ill., 1957; PhD, U. Iowa, 1963. Commd. 2d lt. M.C., U.S. Army, 1957, advanced through grades to lt. col., 1971; chief basic scis. Med. Field Sci. Sch., Fort Sam Houston, Tex., 1957-60, 1963-65; chief gastroenterology Walter Reed Army Inst. Research, Washington, 1965-72, dir. surgery, 1972-77; ret., 1977; prof. surgery, dir. surg. research U. Iowa Hosp., Iowa City, 1977-87, U. South Fla., Tampa, 1987-90; prof. surgery, dir. exptl. surgery, dir. divsn. surg. scis. U. Minn., Mpls., 1991—. Co-editor: Advances in Shock Research, 1983; others; contbr. numerous articles, chpts., abstracts to profl. publs. Active youth athletics, Iowa City. Mem. AAAS, Am. Physiol. Soc., Assn. Acad. Surgery, Shock Soc. (pres. 1986-87), Soc. Exptl. Biology and Medicine. Home: 110 Bank St SE Apt 504 Minneapolis MN 55414-3902 Office: U Minn Dept Surgery Minneapolis MN 55455

REYNOLDS, DAVID PARHAM, metals company executive; b. Bristol, Tenn., June 16, 1915; s. Richard S. and Julia L. (Parham) R.; m. Margaret Harrison, Mar. 25, 1944 (dec. 1992); children: Margaret A., Julia P., Dorothy H. Student, Princeton U. With Reynolds Metals Co., Louisville, 1937—, salesman, 1937-41, asst. mgr. aircraft parts div., 1941-44, asst. v.p., 1944-46, v.p., 1946-58, exec. v.p., 1958-69, exec. v.p., gen. mgr., 1969-75, vice chmn., chmn. exec. com., 1975-76, chief exec. officer, 1976-86, chmn. bd., 1986-88, chmn. emeritus, 1988—; former chmn. bd. dirs. Eskimo Pie Corp. Trustee emeritus Lawrenceville (N.J.) Sch., U. Richmond. Mem. AIA (hon.), Primary Aluminum Inst., Aluminum Assn. (past chmn.). Office: Reynolds Metals Co 6601 W Broad St Richmond VA 23230-1701

REYNOLDS, DEBBIE (MARY FRANCES REYNOLDS), actress; b. El Paso, Tex., Apr. 1, 1932; m. Eddie Fisher, Sept. 26, 1955 (div. 1959); children—Carrie, Todd; m. Harry Karl, Nov., 1960 (div. 1973); m. Richard Hamlett (separated). Active high sch. plays; screen debut Daughter of Rosie O'Grady; motion pictures include: June Bride, 1948, The Daughter of Rosie O'Grady, 1950, Three Little Words, 1950, Two Weeks With Love, 1950, Mr. Imperium, 1951, Singin' in the Rain, 1952, Skirts Ahoy!, 1952, I Love Melvin, 1953, The Affairs of Dobie Gillis, 1953, Give a Girl a Break, 1953, Susan Slept Here, 1954, Athena, 1954, Hit the Deck, 1955, The Tender Trap, 1955, The Catered Affair, 1956, Bundle of Joy, 1956, Tammy and the Bachelor, 1957, This Happy Feeling, 1958, The Mating Game, 1959, Say One for Me, 1959, It Started With a Kiss, 1959, The Gazebo, 1959, The Rat Race, 1960, Pepe, 1960, The Pleasure of His Company, 1961, The Second Time Around, 1961, How the West Was Won, 1962, My Six Loves, 1963, Mary, Mary, 1963, The Unsinkable Molly Brown, 1964, Goodbye Charlie, 1964, The Singing Nun, 1966, Divorce American Style, 1967, How Sweet It Is!, 1968, What's the Matter with Helen?, 1971, Charlotte's Web, (voice only) 1973, That's Entertainment!, 1974, The Bodyguard, 1992, Heaven and Earth, 1993; star TV program The Debbie Reynolds Show, 1969; star Broadway show Irene, 1973-74, Annie Get Your Gun, Los Angeles, San Francisco, 1977, Woman of the Year, 1984, The Unsinkable Molly Brown, 1989-90 (nat. tour); author: If I Knew Then, 1963, Debbie-My Life, 1988; creator exercise video Do It Debbie's Way, 1984. Prin. Debbie Reynolds's Hotel/Casino and Hollywood Motion Picture Mus., Las Vegas, 1993—. Named Miss Burbank, 1948. Office: Debbie Reynolds Studios care Margie Duncan 6514 Lankershim Blvd North Hollywood CA 91606-2409

REYNOLDS, DONALD MARTIN, art historian, foundation administrator, educator; b. Kansas City, Mo., Jan. 11, 1931; s. James Martin and Mary Helen (Hughes) R.; m. Nancy Zlobik, June 5, 1970. Student, Amarillo Coll., 1949-51; BA, Assumption Sem., San Antonio, 1955, Columbia U., 1968; MA, Columbia U., 1970, PhD, 1975. Announcer KGNC Radio/TV, Amarillo, Tex., 1949-51; account exec. Monte Rosenwald & Assocs., Amarillo, Tex., 1957-59; copy writer, account rep., account supr. J. Walter Thompson, N.Y.C., C.Am., 1959-61; mgr. Ctrl. Am., Young & Rubicam Advt., N.Y.C., Panama, 1961-62; advt. mgr., mktg. dir. Colgate-Palmolive Co. Western Hemisphere Divsn., 1962-64; founder, dir. Image, Internat. Mktg. Agy., N.Y.C., 1964-66; mus. educator in charge Dept. Pub. Edn. Met. Mus. of Art, 1977-79; curator of parks Dept. Parks and Recreation, N.Y.C., 1986-88; founder, coord. Ann. Symposium on Pub. Monuments, N.Y.C., 1991—; founder, dir. The Monuments Conservancy, Inc., N.Y.C., 1992—; adj. prof. art history Columbia U., N.Y.C., 1973—; adj. prof. art history Fairfield (Conn.) U., 1981—; adj. asst. prof. art history Hunter Coll., 1972-81; asst. prof. art history Coll. Mt. St. Vincent and Manhattan Coll., 1973-77. Author: The Ideal Sculpture of Hiram Powers, 1977, Manhattan Architecture, 1988, Eng., French edits., The Architecture of New York City: Histories and Views of Important Structures, Sites, and Symbols, 1984, paper, 1988, rev. edit., 1994, Monuments and Masterpieces: Histories and Views of Public Sculpture in New York City, 1988, Nineteenth-Century Art, 1985, also fgn. langs. edits., Nineteenth Century Architecture, 1992, Masters of American Scultpure, the Figurative Tradition from the American Renaissance to the Millennium, 1993; editor, compiler: The Impact of Non-European Civilizations on the Art of the West: Selected Lectures of Rudolf Wittkower, 1989; contbg. author The Macmillan Ency. of Architects, 1982. Trustee Brookgreen Gardens, S.C., Brookgreen Gardens Mus., S.C. With U.S. Army, 1955-61. Mem. Nat. Sculpture Soc., Coll. Art Assn., Authors Guild. Office: PO Box 608 Cooper Sta New York NY 10003

REYNOLDS, EDWARD, book publisher; b. N.Y.C., Apr. 25, 1926; s. Edward and Dorothea Curtis (Jordan) R.; m. Joan Gale, Sept. 13, 1953; children—Edward, Peter Winsor, James Lyman, Joseph Warren. A.B., Harvard U., 1950, M.B.A., 1953. With United Aircraft Can. Ltd., Montreal, 1953-60; v.p. fin. and adminstn. Mitre Corp., Bedford, Mass., 1960-66; sr. v.p. fin. and adminstrn. Houghton Mifflin Co., Boston, 1967-76; dir. fin. New England Med. Ctr. Hosp., Boston, 1978-79; v.p. fin. and adminstrn. John Wiley & Sons, Inc., N.Y.C., 1980-83, sr. v.p. fin. and adminstrn., 1983-86; pres., chief exec. officer Innovative Scis., Inc., Stamford, Conn., 1987-90, treas., 1991—, also bd. dirs. With USNR, 1944-46. Clubs: Union League, Cruising of Am. Office: Innovative Scis Inc 975 Walnut St Cary NC 27511-4216

REYNOLDS, ERNEST WEST, physician, educator; b. Bristow, Okla., May 11, 1920; s. Ernest West and Florence (Brown) R. B.S., U. Okla., 1942, M.D., 1946, M.S., 1952. Diplomate: Am. Bd. Internal Medicine. Intern Boston City Hosp., 1946-47; resident Grady Meml. Hosp., Atlanta, 1949-50; practice medicine Tulsa, Okla., 1953-54; prof. medicine U Mich., 1965-72; prof. medicine, dir. cardiology U. Wis., 1972—; dir. Kellogg Found. Comprehensive Coronary Care Project, 1967-72; chmn. NIH Cardiovascular Study Sect. A, 1972-73. Mem. editorial bd.: Am. Heart Jour; Contbr. articles to profl. jours. Served to capt. AUS, 1947-49. Mem. Am. Heart Assn. (fellow council clin. cardiology); mem. Central Soc. Clin. Research. Home: 17 Red Maple Trl Madison WI 53717-1515 Office: U Wis 600 Highland Ave Madison WI 53792-0001 *In the academic environment, research oriented toward the solution of human problems is more productive in career advancement than the pursuit of applications of new technology. In the private sector applied research which solves real problems rather than copies or improves existing technology is met with surprising sales success and few failures.*

REYNOLDS, FRANK EVERETT, religious studies educator; b. Hartford, Conn., Nov. 13, 1930; s. Howard Wesley and Caroline Mills Roys R.; m. Mani Bloch, Mar. 28, 1959 (dec. 1993); children: Roy Howard, Andrew Everett, Roger Frank. Student, Princeton U., 1948-51; B.A., Oberlin U., 1952; B.D., Yale Div. Sch., 1955; M.A., U. Chgo., 1963, Ph.D., 1971. Ordained to ministry Am. Baptist Ch., 1955. Program dir. Student Christian Ctr., Bangkok, Thailand, 1956-59; minister to fgn. students U. Chgo. Ecumenical Ministries, 1961-64; instr. U. Chgo., 1967-69, asst. prof. then assoc. prof., 1969-79, prof. history of religions and Buddhist studies, 1979—; program dir. Inst. for the Advanced Study of Religions, 1992—; co-dir. Liberal Arts and Study of Religions Project, 1985-90, NEH Sangitiyavasama Transl. Porject, 1991-93. Author: Guide to Buddhist Religion, 1981; (with others) Two Wheels of Dhamma, 1971, Religions of the World, 3d edit., 1993; editor, co-translator: 3 Worlds According to King Ruang, 1981; co-editor: Anthropology and the Study of Religion, 1984, Cosmology and Ethical Order, 1985, Myth and Philosophy, 1990, Beyond the Classics: Religious Studies and Liberal Education, 1990, Discourse and Practice, 1992, Religion and Practical Reason, 1994; co-editor History of Religion Jour., 1977—; assoc. editor Jour. Religion, 1976—, Jour. Religious Ethics, 1981—. Jacob Fox Found. fellow, 1952, Danforth Found. fellow, 1960, 64; sr. rsch. grantee Fulbright Commn., 1973-74, NEH, 1978-79. Mem. Am. Coun. Learned Socs. (com. on history of religions 1985-94), Am. Soc. Study Religion, Am. Acad. Religion (chmn. com. on history of religions 1994—), Assn. Asian Studies (co-editor monograph series 1978-86), Internat. History of Religions, Internat. Assn. Buddhist Studies, Law and Soc. Home: 5433 S Blackstone Ave Chicago IL 60615-5406 Office: U Chgo Swift Hall 1025 E 58th St Chicago IL 60637-1509

REYNOLDS, FRANK MILLER, retired government administrator; b. Tulsa, Jan. 8, 1917; s. Frank Miller and Grace (Shields) R.; m. Barbara G. MacWilliams, Dec. 7, 1946; children: Susan G., Ellen M., Frank M. A.B., LL.B., U. Okla., 1939; LL.M., George Washington U., 1942; B.S., Georgetown Sch. Fgn. Service, 1946. Bar: Okla. 1940. Mem. firm Flippo & Reynolds, Tulsa, 1940; elec. engr. Bur. Ships, Dept. of Navy, 1942-43; with office Gen. Counsel Dept. of Navy, 1946; chief negotiator, dep. dir. contract div. Office Naval Research, 1947-54; dep. dir., dir. resources div. Office Asst. Sec. Def., 1954-57; asst. sec. Inst. for Defense Analyses, 1957-61; sec., treas. Logistics Management Inst., Washington, 1961-65; v.p. Logistics Management Inst., 1966-76; dir. adminstrv. affairs Uniformed Services U. Health Scis., Bethesda, Md., 1976-78; dir. resource mgmt. Uniformed Services U. Health Scis., 1978-82, exec. sec. bd. regents, 1978-83; dir. patient relations Sibley Meml. Hosp., 1983-84, cons., 1984-87; professorial lectr. mgmt. research George Washington U. Sch. Engring., 1956—; cons. Nat. Exec. Service Corps., United Srs. Health Coop., 1984—. Served with radio div. Naval Research Lab., 1944-46. Mem. Okla. Bar Assn., Congl. Country Club, Delta Upsilon. Home: 9107 River Rd Potomac MD 20854-4627

REYNOLDS, GARY KEMP, librarian; b. Phila., June 2, 1944; s. Thomas Clifford and Lillian Olive (Thompson) R.; m. Regina Romano, May 16, 1970; 1 child, Elizabeth Alexandra Marie. BA in History with honors, Pa. State U., 1973, BA in East Asian Studies magna cum laude, 1973; MA in E.Asian Studies, U. Mich., 1975, MLS, 1976. Reference libr. George Washington U., Washington, 1977-80; info. rsch. specialist congl. rsch. svc. Libr. of Congress, Washington, 1980—. Reviewer manuscripts for profl. jours.; contbr. articles to profl. publs. Sgt. USAF, 1962-66. Mem. Phi Beta Kappa, Phi Kappa Phi, Phi Alpha Theta, Mensa. Republican. Episcopalian. Avocations: painting, Oriental arts and antiques, science fiction. Home: 7472 Convent Wood Ct Annandale VA 22003 Office: Libr of Congress Washington DC 20540

REYNOLDS, GENE, television producer, director; b. Cleve., Apr. 4, 1925; m. Bonnie Jones. Actor motion pictures including Thank You, Jeeves, 1936, In Old Chicago, 1937, Boys Town, 1938, They Shall Have Music, 1939, Edison the Man, 1940, Eagle Squadron, 1942, The Country Girl, 1954, The Bridges at Toko-Ri, 1955, Diane, 1955; exec. producer TV series Room 222, 1969-74, Anna and the King, 1972, Karen, 1975; producer TV pilot The Ghost and Mrs. Muir, 1968-70, Roll Out!, 1973-74; exec. producer Lou Grant, 1977-82 (Emmy award 1979, 80); producer TV series M*A*S*H, 1972-76, exec. producer from 1976; producer, dir. TV movie People Like Us, 1976; dir. In Defense of Kids, 1983, Doing Life, 1986. Recipient Emmy award Nat. Acad. TV Arts and Scis. 1970, 74, 75, 76; Dirs. Guild award for TV comedy (2); (with others) Peabody award for M*A*S*H. Mem. Dirs. Guild Am. Office: care Broder Kurland Webb Agy 9242 Beverly Blvd # 200 Beverly Hills CA 90210-3710

REYNOLDS, GENEVA B., special education educator; b. Saginaw, Mich., Nov. 2, 1953; d. Roger and Alrine (Braddock) Rucker; m. Montie Reynolds, Aug. 1, 1981; children: Monte, Marcus. BS, Chgo. State U., 1992. Cert. educable mental handicap and learning disability, social/emotional disturbed. Adminstrv. specialist USAF, 1973-77, command and control specialist, 1977-81; info. supt. USAFR, Chgo., 1981—; head tchr. South Ctrl. Cmty. Svcs., Chgo., 1986—. SM sgt. USAF, 1973-81, USAFR, 1981—. Mem. Coun. for Exceptional Children, Kappa Delta Pi. Democrat. Baptist. Avocations: reading, computers, going to plays.

REYNOLDS, GEORGE THOMAS, physics educator, researcher, consultant; b. Trenton, May 27, 1917. B.Sc. in Physics and Math., Rutgers U., 1939; M.A. in Physics, Princeton U., 1942, Ph.D. in Physics, 1943. Research physicist Princeton (N.J.) U., 1943-44, asst. prof., 1946-51, assoc. prof., 1951-59, prof., 1959-78, Class of 1909 prof. physics, 1978-87, emeritus, 1987—, dir. high energy physics program, 1948-70, dir. sci. in human affairs program, 1963-67, dir. Ctr. Environ. Studies, 1970-73, mem. council on environ. studies, 1970-73, 80-87, prin. investigator biophysics program, 1964-87; mem. univ. research bd. Princeton (N.J.), 1980-86; assoc. faculty Princeton Environ. Inst., 1996—; physicist Manhattan Project, 1944-46; mem. NSF Adv. Com. for Planning and Instl. Relations, 1971-74; mem. vis. adv. com. dept. applied sci. Brookhaven Nat. Lab., 1971-74; mem. corp. Marine Biol. Lab., Woods Hole, Mass., 1968—, chmn. radiation com., 1973-77; mem. ad hoc adv. panel for environ. problems Dept. Energy Div. Biomed. and Environ Research; vis. prof. Imperial Coll.-U. London, 1955-56, Open U. (U.K.), 1981-82; cons. in field; mem. adv. panel for radiation physics Nat. Bur. Standards, 1962-64; seminar assoc. Columbia U. Sem. on Tech. and Social Change, 1966-85; mem. study panel on physics edn. Nat. Acad. Scis., 1970-72; cons. NSF div. Policy Research and Analysis, 1985-88. Bd. editors: Rev. Sci. Instruments, 1955-58; contbr. chpts. to books, numerous jour. articles. Chmn. adv. council for research and grad. edn. Rutgers U., New Brunswick, N.J., 1969-72, trustee, 1974-86, 89—. Served to lt. (j.g.) USNR, 1944-46. Recipient cert. appreciation Army-Navy, 1948; Guggenheim fellow U. London, 1955-56; Churchill fellow Cambridge (Eng.) U., 1973-74; vis. sr. research fellow Oxford (Eng.), 1981-82; Royal Soc. guest research fellow, 1985. Fellow AAAS, Am. Phys. Soc.; mem. Biophys. Soc., Am. Geophys. Union, IEEE, Am. Soc. Photobiology, Phi Beta Kappa, Sigma Xi (local pres. 1962-63). Office: Princeton U Dept Physics Joseph Henry Labs Jadwin Hall PO Box 708 Princeton NJ 08544

REYNOLDS, GLENN FRANKLIN, medicinal research scientist; b. Rahway, N.J., July 16, 1944; s. Frank Vanderbilt and Estelle (Ohlott) R.; m. Marianne DelliSanti, Nov. 25, 1967; children William Matthew, David Glenn, Wendy Joy. Student, Rutgers U., 1962-63, Union Coll., 1963-65; BS in Chemistry, Phila. Coll. Pharmacy and Sci., 1967. Rsch. scientist Merck & Co., Rahway, 1967-70, staff chemist, 1970-77, rsch. chemist, 1977-86, sr. rsch. assoc., 1991—; Merck recruiter Fairleigh Dickinson U., 1980, Howard U., 1980, U. N.C., 1981, Rutgers U., 1985. Inventor Proscar; contbr. articles to profl. jours.; patentee in field. Named Inventor of Yr. Intellectual Property Owners, 1993. Mem. Am. Chem. Soc., Masons (Lafayette lodge #27). Presbyterian. Avocations: computer science, biking, skiing, reading. Home: 252 Edgewood Ave Westfield NJ 07090-3918 Office: Merck & Co Inc PO Box 2000 126 E Lincoln Ave 121/267C Rahway NJ 07065

REYNOLDS, GLENN HARLAN, law educator; b. Birmingham, Ala., Aug. 27, 1960; s. Charles Harlan Reynolds and Glenda Lorraine (Teal) Childress. BA, U. Tenn., 1982; JD, Yale U., 1985. Bar: Tenn. 1985, D.C. 1986. Law clk. U.S. Ct. Appeals, Nashville, 1985-86; assoc. Dewey, Ballantine, Bushby, Palmer & Wood, Washington, 1986-89; assoc. prof. law U. Tenn., Knoxville, 1989—. Author: Outer Space: Problems of Law and Policy, 1989. Recipient Outstanding Svc. award Space Cause, Washington, 1990. Mem. AAAS, Nat. Space Soc. (chair legis. com. 1989-93, CEO 1994-95, Space Pioneer award 1991). Office: U Tenn 1505 Cumberland Ave Knoxville TN 37916-3199

REYNOLDS, HARRY LEE, track and field athlete; b. Akron, Ohio, June 8, 1964. Student, Butler County C.C., Kans., Ohio State U., 1988. Springer Foot Locker AC. Winner NCAA, USA/Mobil and several other major European meets; recipient Bronze medal World Championships; ranked No. 1 for 1987 Track and Field News. Office: USA Track and Field PO Box 120 Indianapolis IN 46204

REYNOLDS, HARRY LINCOLN, physicist; b. Port Chester, N.Y., Mar. 31, 1925; s. Harry Benson and Lydia (Wilde) R.; m. Katherine Haile, 1950; children: Patricia Reynolds Cabral, Margaret Benson Neufeld. B.S., Rensselaer Poly. Inst., 1947; Ph.D., U. Rochester, 1951. Sr. scientist Oak Ridge Nat. Lab., 1951-55; physicist Lawrence Livermore Nat. Lab., 1955-65; asst. program mgr. NASA Manned Spacecraft Center, Houston, 1965; asso. dir. nuclear test, nuclear design and nuclear explosives programs Lawrence Livermore Nat. Lab., Calif., 1965-80, spl. asst. to dir., 1980-81; dep. asso. dir. advanced concepts Los Alamos Nat. Lab., 1981-85; dir. advanced concepts Rockwell Internat. Corp., Seal Beach, Calif., 1985-94; cons. in field. Contbr. articles to profl. jours. Trustee Valley Meml. Hosp., Livermore, 1980-81; mem. Army Sci. Bd., 1982-88. Served with U.S. Navy, 1944-46. AEC fellow, 1947-49. Fellow Am. Phys. Soc. Home: 801 Via Somonte Palos Verdes Peninsula CA 90274-1631

REYNOLDS, HELEN ELIZABETH, management services consultant; b. Minerva, N.Y., Aug. 30, 1925; d. Henry James and Margurite Catherine (Gallagher) McNally; m. Theodore Laurence Reynolds, Feb. 27, 1948; children: Laurence McBride, David Scott, William Herbert. BA, SUNY, Albany, 1967; MA, Union Coll., Schenectady, N.Y., 1971. Grad. Realtors Inst., N.Y. Owner, mgr. Schafer Studio, Schenectady, 1970-73; co-owner, v.p. Reynolds Chalmers Inc., Schenectady, 1971—; pres. HR Mgmt. Cons., Schenectady, 1994—; program coord. Schenectady County, 1980-81; adminstr. Wellspring House of Albany, N.Y., 1981-94; cons., examiner N.Y. State Civil Service, Albany, 1971-81; mem. adv. council SBA, Washington, 1978-80. Mem. planning bd. Town of Niskayuna, N.Y., 1977-81, town councilwoman, 1986-94; co-chair Gt. N.E. Festival on the Mohawk River, 1989, 90; bd. dirs. HAVEN, Schenectady YWCA; mem. Schenectady Indsl. Devel. Agy., N.Y. State Commn. on The Capital Region, 1994—, Acad. of Women of Achievement, Schenectady, 1994, Libr. of Congress. Named Woman Vision, 1986, 87, Today's Woman, 1987, Schenectady YWCA. Mem. Antique and Classic Boat Soc. (bd. dirs. 1974-89, Disting. Svc. award 1979, Founders award 1989), Assn. Adminstrs. Ind. Housing (pres. 1986-88, 92-94), Zonta (pres. 1981-82), Nat. Trust for Historic Preservation, Adirondack Mus., Antique Boat Mus., Schenectady Mus., League of Schenectady Symphony Orch., Union Coll. Alumni Assn., Charlotte Harbor Yacht Club, Charlotte County Art Guild. Avocations: photography, reading, writing, skiing, canoeing. Home: 1365 Van Antwerp Rd Apt J104 Niskayuna NY 12309-4441 Office: 104 SW Leland St Port Charlotte FL 33952

REYNOLDS, HERBERT YOUNG, physician, internist; b. Richmond, Va., Aug. 20, 1939; s. George Audney and Pearle Maupin (Young) R.; m. Anne Browning Leavell, July 11, 1964; children: Nancy, George, William Stuart. BA in English, U. Va., 1961, MD, 1965; MA (hon.), Yale U., 1979. Diplomate Am. Bd. Internal Medicine, Am. Bd. Allergy and Immunology. Intern in medicine The N.Y. Hosp., Cornell Med. Ctr., N.Y.C., 1965-66, asst. physician, fellow in medicine, 1966-67; clin. assoc., lab. clin. investigation Nat. Inst. Allergy and Infectious Diseases, NIH, Bethesda, Md., 1967-70, chief clin. assoc. lab. clin. investigation, 1968-69; sr. investigator lab. of clin. investigation Nat. Inst. Allergy and Infectious Diseases, NIH, 1971-76; chief resident, instr. medicine U. Hosp. U. Wash., Seattle, 1970-71; assoc. prof. internal medicine, head pulmonary div. Sch. Medicine Yale U., New Haven, 1976-79, prof., 1979-88; J. Lloyd Huck prof. medicine, chmn. dept. Pa. State U.-Milton S. Hershey Med. Ctr., 1988—; mem. exec. com. Coll. Medicine Pa. State U.-Hershey Med. Ctr., 1988—, mem. exec. bd. U. Hosp., 1988, mem. fin. bd. acad. enrichment fun, 1988-95, mem. dean's adv. com., 1988-96, others; cons. in infectious diseases Nat. Naval Med. Ctr. NIH, Bethesda, 1971-76, mem. clin. rsch. com., 1971-76, chmn., 1974-76, med. bd., 1974-76, pulmonary disease adv. com. divsn. of lung diseases Nat. Heart, Lung and Blood Inst., 1978-82, mem. sci. counselors bd., 1984-88, mem. data and safety monitoring bd. registry of patientss with deficiency of Alpha-1 Antitrypsin, 1989-96. Assoc. editor, mem. editl. bd. Lung, 1978-96, Am. Jour. Medicine, 1979-89, Jour. Clin. Investigation, 1980-86, Am. Rev. Respiratory Disease, 1980-87, Jour. Applied Physiology, 1981-89, Resident Physician, 1981-95; contbr. over 260 articles and revs. to profl. jours. Mem. parent com. Troop 1 Boy Scouts Am., Madison, 1979-82; bd. dirs. Neighborhood Music Sch., Guilford, Conn., 1978-87, Music at Gretna, 1994—; bd. dirs. Harrisburg Symphony, 1996—; active All Saints Episc. Ch., Hershey; mem. pulmonary infections com. Cystic Fibrosis Found., Bethesda, 1980-86; mem. coun. sci. advisors Parker B. Francis Found., Kansas City, Kans., 1983-87; mem. internat. com. World Orgn. for Sarcoidosis and other Granulomatous Disorders, 1987-95; bd. dirs., mem. coun. Am. Lung Assn., 1989-93, bd. govs. 1990-93, various com. positions, 1990—; coach Guilford Soccer League, 1985-88. Surgeon USPHS, 1967-70. John Edward Nobel fellow, 1961-65; named Outstanding Med. Specialist in USA, Town and Country Mag., 1989, The Best Med. Specialists, Town & Country mag., 1995, One of 400 Best Drs. in U.S. Good Housekeeping Mag., 1991, named in The Best Doctors in America, 1st edit. 1992-93, 2d edit. 1994-95. Fellow ACP (coun. subsplty. socs. 1989—), Am. Coll. Chest Physicians (program com. 1978-84), Infectious Disease Soc. Am., Coll. Physicians Phila.; mem. Am. Thoracic Soc. (sec.-treas. 1987-88, bd. dirs. 1989-93, v.p. 1988-89, pres. 1992-93), Am. Soc. Clin. Investigation, Assn. Am. Physicians, Am. Assn. Immunologists, Am. Fedn. Clin. Rsch., Am. Clin. and Climatological Soc., Interurban Clin. Club (emeritus 1989), Assn. Profs. Medicine, Country Club of Hershey, Farmington Country Club, Raven Soc., Phi Beta Kappa, Alpha Omega Alpha. Republican. Avocations: tennis, violin. Home: 226 E Caracas Ave Hershey PA 17033-1309 Office: Pa State U Milton S Hershey Med Ctr 850 University Dr Hershey PA 17033

REYNOLDS, JACK MASON, manufacturing company executive; b. East Orange, N.J., Jan. 27, 1927; s. Frederick Lynn and Bernice (Mason) R.; m. Rhea Evans, June 14, 1949; children: Jeff, Jennifer Reynolds Brickley, Mark. B.S., U.S. Mcht. Marine Acad., 1948. With Bendix Corp., Southfield, Mich., 1948-83, exec. v.p. automotive group, 1979-80, pres. automotive group, 1980-83; pres. automotive sector, exec. v.p. Allied-Signal Inc., Morristown, N.J., 1983-89; dir. NBD Bancorp Inc. Bd. dirs. Detroit Renaissance, 1983-89, Citizens Rsch. Coun. of Mich., 1983-89, Detroit Econ. Growth Corp., 1983-89, Detroit Symphony Orch., 1983-89. With USNR, 1944-48. Mem. Soc. Automotive Engrs., Renaissance (Detroit) Club. Home: PO Box 744 Cooperstown NY 13326-0744

REYNOLDS, JACK W., retired utility company executive; b. Magazine, Ark., Feb. 28, 1923; s. Robert H. and Effie (Files) R.; m. Alberta Barkett, Nov. 13, 1949; children: John, David, Steven, Thomas, Laurie. B.S. in Phys. Sci., Okla. State U., 1943, B.S. in Indsl. Engring., 1947. With B.F. Goodrich Co., Akron, Ohio, 1947-75, dir. union relations, 1969-70, dir. indsl. rels., 1970-75; v.p. pers. Consumers Power Co., Jackson, Mich., 1975-78, sr. v.p. pers. and pub. affairs, 1978-81, exec. v.p. energy supply, 1981-88; pres. Mich. Gas Storage Co., Jackson, 1981-88, Plateau Resources, Ltd., Jackson, 1988; now ret. Served to 1st lt. C.E. U.S. Army, 1943-46, CBI. Republican. Methodist. Clubs: Jackson Country.

REYNOLDS, JAMES, management consultant; b. Detroit, Mar. 22, 1941; s. Richard James and Esther (Nikander) R.; m. Joanne M.J. B.A. in Econs., NYU, 1965, postgrad., 1965-66. Cons. to pres. Rothrock, Reynolds & Reynolds Inc., N.Y.C., 1966-70; sr. v.p. health, med. div. Booz, Allen & Hamilton, N.Y.C., 1970-80; pres. Reynolds & Co. (mgmt. cons.), San Francisco, N.Y.C., Washington, 1981—; developer 1978, orgn. concepts for multihosp. systems, 1983, managed care contracting strategies, 1988, value chain analysis in the health field, 1994, leading the transition to Integrated Healthcare Sys.; bd. dirs. Booz, Allen & Hamilton, 1977-79; chmn. bd. J.X. Reynolds Fine Arts, Ltd., 1979—; bd. dirs. Health Center Mgmt. Inst.; lectr. Harvard Sch. Pub. Health; faculty mem. Am. Coll. of Healthcare Execs.; bd. dirs. Health Center Mgmt. Inst., Richmond, Va., 1977; mem. health adv. bd. Hunter Coll., 1980—. Editorial bd. Physicians Fin. News. Recipient NYU Founders award, 1965. Mem. Am. Pub. Health Assn., Am. Mgmt. Assn., Assn. Am. Med. Colls., Am. Hosp. Assn., Hosp. Mgmt. Systems Soc., Hosp. Fin. Mgmt. Assn., Asia Soc., Phi Beta Kappa, Mus. Modern Art, Met. Mus. Art, Met. Opera Guild (N.Y.C.). Episcopalian. Home and Office: Reynolds Co 333 E 51st St New York NY 10022-6702 also: 2500 3 Mile Run Rd Perkasie PA 18944-2020

REYNOLDS, JEAN EDWARDS, publishing executive; b. Saginaw, Mich., Dec. 11, 1941; d. F. Perry and Kathrine (Edwards) R.; m. Cary Wellington, Sept. 10, 1975 (div. 1982); children, Bradley, Abigail, Benjamin. BA, Wells Coll., 1963; postgrad., CCNY, 1965-67. Asst. editor, sr. editor trade book div. Prentice-Hall, Englewood Cliffs, N.J., 1963-66; dir. children's books Prentice-Hall, Englewood Cliffs, 1966-69, McCall Pub. Co., N.Y.C., 1969-71; sr. v.p., editorial dir. Franklin Watts Inc., N.Y.C., 1971-75; pres. Pet Projects Inc., Ridgefield, Conn., 1975-81; editor in chief young people's publs. Grolier Inc., Danbury, Conn., 1981-89; pres. The Millbrook Press, Brookfield, Conn., 1989—; bd. dirs. Wellington Leisure Products, Atlanta, Kiper Enterprises, Oswego, N.Y.; chairperson Conn. Ctr. for the Book, 1991-94. Bd. dirs. Jewish Home for the Elderly, Fairfield, Conn., 1989-90, Book Industry Study Group, 1991—, The Wooster Sch., Danbury, Conn., 1992—, Temple Shearith Israel, Ridgefield, Conn., 1994—; pres. Jewish Fedn. Greater Danbury, 1991-93. Mem. ALA, Children's Book Coun.,

Mensa, Assn. for Sch. Librs. Internat. (bd. dirs. 1993-94). Jewish. Avocations: skiing, tennis, sailing, needlework, SCUBA. Home: 33 Corntassle Rd Danbury CT 06811-3208 Office: The Millbrook Press Inc 2 Old New Milford Rd Brookfield CT 06804-2426

REYNOLDS, JOHN FRANCIS, insurance company executive; b. Escanaba, Mich., Mar. 29, 1921; s. Edward Peter and Lillian (Harris) R.; m. Dorothy Gustafson, May 1, 1946; children—Lois, Margaret, Michael. B.S., Mich. State U., 1942. Claims and assoc. surety mgr. Hartford Ins. Co., Escanaba, Mich. and Chgo., 1946-55; asst. v.p., bond mgr. Wolverine Ins. Co., Battle Creek, Mich., 1955-64, v.p. underwriting, 1964-69; Midwest zone underwriting mgr. Transamerica Ins. Co. (Wolverine Ins. Co.), Battle Creek, Mich., 1969-74; pres., gen. mgr. Can. Surety Co. subs. Transamerica Ins. Co., Toronto, Ont., Canada, 1974-75; v.p. midwestern zone mgr. Transamerica Ins. Group, Battle Creek, Mich., 1975-83; pres., chief operating officer Transamerica Ins. Group, Los Angeles, 1983-84, chmn., chief exec. officer, 1984-85; apptd. spl. dep. ins. commr., dep. conservator Cadillac Inc. Co., 1989; pres. Underwriting Exec. Council Midwest, 1967; dir. Underwriters Adjustment Bur., Toronto, 1974, Underwriters Labs. of Canada, Montreal, 1974; chmn. Mich. Assn. Ins. Cos., Lansing, 1976, Mich. Basic Property Ins. Assn., Detroit, 1973. Commr. City of Battle Creek, 1967-69; dir. Urban League, Battle Creek, 1969, 70, dir. Mich. Ins. Fedn., Lansing, 1975-83. Served to sgt. U.S. Army, 1942-45; New Guinea. Roman Catholic. Avocations: golf; fishing.

REYNOLDS, JOHN HAMILTON, physicist, educator; b. Cambridge, Mass., Apr. 3, 1923; s. Horace Mason and Catharine (Coffeen) R.; m. Ann Burchard Arnold, July 19, 1975; children from previous marriages: Amy, Horace Marshall, Brian Marshall, Karen Leigh, Petra Catharine. AB, Harvard U., 1943; MS, U. Chgo., 1948, PhD, 1950; D. honoris causa, U. Coimbra, Portugal, 1987. Rsch. asst. Electroacoustic Lab., Harvard U., 1941-43; assoc. physicist Argonne Nat. Lab., 1950; physicist U. Calif. at Berkeley, 1950—, prof. physics, 1961-88; chmn. dept. physics U. Calif., Berkeley, 1984-86, faculty rsch. lectr., 1974; prof. emeritus U. Calif.-Berkeley, Berkeley, 1989—. Contbr. articles to profl. jours. Lt. USNR, 1943-46. Recipient Wetherill medal Franklin Inst., 1965, Golden Plate award Am. Acad. Achievement, 1968, Exceptional Sci. Achievement award NASA, 1973; Guggenheim fellow U. Bristol, Eng., 1956-57, Los Alamos Nat. Lab., 1987, NSF fellow U. São Paulo, Brazil, 1963-64; Fulbright-Hays rsch. grantee U. Coimbra, Portugal, 1971-72; U.S.-Australia Coop. Sci. Program awardee U. Western Australia, 1978-79, Berkeley citation, 1988. Fellow AAAS, Am. Acad. Arts and Scis., Am. Phys. Soc., Am. Geophys. Union, Geochem. Soc., Calif. Acad. Scis. (hon.), Meteoritical Soc. (Leonard medal 1973); mem. NAS (J. Lawrence Smith medal 1967), Faculty Club (Berkeley), Phi Beta Kappa. Democrat. Office: U Calif Dept Physics Berkeley CA 94720

REYNOLDS, JOHN W., federal judge; b. Green Bay, Wis., Apr. 4, 1921; s. John W. and Madge (Flatley) R.; m. Patricia Ann Brody, May 26, 1947 (dec. Dec. 1967); children: Kate M. Reynolds Lindquist, Molly A., James B.; m. Jane Conway, July 31, 1971; children: Jacob F., Thomas J., Frances P., John W. III. PhB, U. Wis., 1946, LLB, 1949. Bar: Wis. 1949. Since practiced in Green Bay, dist. dir. price stblzn., 1951-53, U.S. commr., 1953-58, atty. gen. of Wis., 1958-62; gov. State of Wis., 1963-65; U.S. dist. judge Ea. Dist. Wis., Milwa., 1965-71, chief judge, 1971-86, sr. judge, 1986—. Served with U.S. Army, 1942-46. Mem. State Bar Wis., Am. Law Inst., Fed. Judges Assn., Former Govs. Assn. Office: US Dist Ct 296 US Courthouse 517 E Wisconsin Ave Milwaukee WI 53202

REYNOLDS, JOSEPH HURLEY, lawyer; b. Wilmington, Del., July 22, 1946; s. Peter G. and Elizabeth (Yorks) R.; m. Margaret Jack, Sept. 29, 1969; children: Joseph B., Alicia K., Charles Y. BA, Lehigh U., 1968, MA, 1972; JD, Union U., 1976. Bar: N.Y. 1976, D.C. 1985. Law clk. to hon. judge Dominick Gabriell N.Y. Ct. of Appeals, Albany, 1976-78; assoc. Nixon, Hargrave, Devans & Doyle, Rochester, N.Y., 1978-85; ptnr. Nixon, Hargrave, Devans & Doyle, Washington, 1985—. Office: Nixon Hargrave Devans Doyle One Thomas Circle Washington DC 10005

REYNOLDS, LEWIS DAYTON, administrator, pastor; b. Charleston, W.Va., July 26, 1937; s. James Shelby and Sybil Catherine (Lanham) R.; m. Ann Kathryn Combs, Aug. 25, 1962; children: John Mark, Daniel Adam. BBA, Marshall U., 1959; BTh, Aurora U., 1961; MDiv, Evang. Theol. Sem., Naperville, Ill., 1962. Ordained to ministry Advent Christian Ch., 1962. Pastor Mendota (Ill.) Advent Christian Ch., Mendota, Ill., 1961-64, Clendenin (W.Va.) Advent Christian Ch., Clendenin, W.Va., 1964-72, New Covenant Fellowship, Penfield, N.Y., 1972-89; gen. overseer Elim Fellowship, Lima, N.Y., 1989—; mem. bd. adminstrn. Nat. Assn. Evangelists, Wheaton, Ill., 1989—, Pentecostal Fellowship N.Am. (now Pentecostal/Charismatic Chs. N.Am.), Virginia Beach, 1989—; bd. dirs. Elim Bible Inst., Lima; mem. steering com. N.Am. Renewal Svcs., Virginia Beach, 1990—. Editor Elim Herald mag. Mem. Phi Eta Sigma. Republican. Home: 1701 Dalton Rd Apt 503 Lima NY 14485-9542

REYNOLDS, LLOYD GEORGE, economist, educator; b. Wainwright, Alberta, Can., Dec. 22, 1910; came to U.S., 1934, naturalized, 1940; s. George F. and Dorothy (Carl) R.; m. Mary F. Trackett, June 12, 1937; children: Anne Reynolds Skinner, Priscilla Reynolds Roosevelt, Bruce Lloyd. A.B., U. Alberta, 1931, LL.D., 1958; A.M., McGill U., 1933; Ph.D., Harvard, 1936. Instr. econs. Harvard, 1936-39; asso. polit. economy Johns Hopkins, 1939-41, asso. prof., 1941-45; asso. prof. econs. Yale, 1945-47, prof. econs., 1947-52, Sterling prof. econs., 1952-81, chmn. dept. econs., 1951-59; prof. emeritus, 1981—; dir Econ. Growth Center, 1961-67; vis. fellow All Souls Coll., Oxford, 1967-68; Mem. adv. bd. Pakistan Inst. Devel. Econs., 1965-73; cons. to Social Sci. Research Center, U. P.R., 1951-65; dir. Nat. Bureau Econ. Research, 1958-81; Research dir. labor studies 20th Century Fund, 1940-43; research sec., com. on employment Social Sci. Research Council, 1941-42; co-chmn. appeals com. N.W.L.B., 1943-45; cons. Bur. of Budget, 1945-47; Guggenheim fellow, 1954-55, 1966-67; dir. program in econs. and bus. adminstrn. Ford Found., 1955-57. Author: The British Immigrant in Canada, 1935, Control of Competition in Canada, 1940, Labor and National Defense, 1941, An Index to Trade Union Publications, 1945, Labor Economics and Labor Relations, 1949, The Structure of Labor Markets, 1951, The Evolution of Wage Structure, 1956, Economics: A General Introduction, 1963, Wages, Productivity and Industrialization in Puerto Rico, 1965, The Three Worlds of Economics, 1971, Agriculture in Development Theory, 1975, Image and Reality in Economic Development, 1977, The American Economy in Perspective, 1981, Economic Growth in the Third World, 1850-1980, 1985; contbr. articles to profl. jours. Fellow Am. Acad. Arts and Scis.; mem. Indsl. Rls. Rsch. Assn. (pres. 1955), Am. Econ. Assn. (v.p. 1959, exec. com. 1952-54), Am. Acad. Polit. Sci., Am. Statis. Assn., Phi Beta Kappa. Clubs: Graduates (New Haven) (pres. 1961-64); Harvard (Boston); Century (N.Y.C.); Cosmos (Washington); Mill Reef (Antigua). Home: 4000 Cathedral Ave NW Washington DC 20016-5249 Office: Yale University Economics Dept New Haven CT 06520

REYNOLDS, LOUISE MAXINE KRUSE, retired school nurse; b. Waynesboro, Va., May 28, 1935; d. Emil Herman and Cora Lee (Hammer) Kruse; m. Elbert B. Reynolds Jr., June 13, 1964; children: David Emil, Jane Marie. Diploma, Rockingham Meml. Hosp., 1956; student, Madison Coll., Tex. Tech U. RN, Tex., Va, cert. sch. nurse. Head nurse orthopedic, opthalmology dept. surgery Duke U., Durham, N.C., 1961-62; head nurse surg. fl. Waynesboro (Va.) Hosp., 1962-64; sch. nurse Lubbock (Tex.) Ind. Sch. Dist., 1974-94, ret., 1994. Mem. Va. Nurses Assn. (dist. sec., chair), Tex. Assn. Sch. Nurses (sec., treas. dist. 17, program chair 1989 state conv.).

REYNOLDS, LYNNE WARREN, special education educator, speech pathologist; b. Richmond, Va., June 6, 1940; d. Edward Paul Jr. and Margie (Meads) Warren; m. Thomas Grover Reynolds III, June 23, 1962; children: Thomas G. IV, Marguerite Agee. BS, U. Va., 1962, postgrad., 1963-65; MEd, R.I. Coll., 1973; EdD, Heed U., 1985. Cert. tchr., spl. edn. tchr., N.Y., Mass., R.I., Va.; lic. speech and lang. pathologist, N.Y. Tchr. spl. edn. Nelson County Pub. Schs., Lovingston, Va., 1962-63, Albemarle County Pub. Schs., Charlottesville, Va., 1963-66; tchr. spl. edn., program coord. Plainville (Mass.) Pub. Schs., 1967-73; pvt. practice speech-lang. pathology, edn. cons. Kingston, N.Y., 1973-85; edn. cons. Edn. for Relocation, Neunen and Eindhoven, Netherlands, 1986-91; tchr. spl. edn. W.S. Hart Union High Sch. Dist., Santa Clara, Calif., 1991-92; ind. edn. cons. Smyrna, Ga., 1992—; sec., chmn. mental health and mental retardation com. Ulster County Community Svcs. Bd., Kingston, 1978-85; mem. N.Y. State com. UN Yr. of Child, 1983-84; mem. community svcs. adv. bd. Spl. Edn. Svcs. Santa Clarita, Calif., 1991-92; mem. People to People citizen amb. del. on learning disabilities to Russia & Estonia; presenter seminars to parent, educator and profl. groups; presenter tng. workshops. Author classroom tchrs.' handbook: HELP, 1969. Mem. Chaminade Singers, 1966-73; sec., chmn. Indsl. Devel. Commn., Town of Plainville, 1969-73, mental health svcs. coord., 1970-73; dir. nautographer ann. synchronized swimming show Zena Recreation Park, N.Y., 1975-84; mem. learnint disabilities delegation to Russia and Estonia: People to People Citizen Amb. Program, 1993; active Internat. Women's Club Eindhoven, 1985-90; guest performer Alliance Theatre Christmas House, 1993-95, Atlanta Symphony Open House; vol. Sci. Trek Sci. Mus., 1992-94; mem. E. Cobb Quilters Guild, 1993—, sec. 1994, 1st v.p. 1995—, pres. 1996; vol. Alliance Children's Theatre of Atlanta, 1993—, Georgia Olympic Quilt Project, 1993—. Recipient Profl. Svc. Recognition award Girl Scouts U.S., Plainville, 1971, Recognition award Girl Scouts U.S., Plainville, 1971, Recognition of Svc. award Ulster County Mental Health Assn., 1983, 84, Award for Svc. Ulster County Cmty. Svcs. Bd., 1985, Vol. of Yr. Sci. Trek Sci. Mus., 1993, Outstanding Me. Alliance Childrens Theatre, 1994. Mem. Coun. Exceptional Children (div. communication disorders, div. learning disabilities, coun. ednl. diagnostic svcs., coun. behavioral disorders), Orton Dyslexia Soc., Assn. for Citizens with Learning Disabilities (chpt. bd. dirs. 1976-85, state bd. dirs. 1978-84, chair memberships com.), N.Y. Speech, Lang. and Hearing Assn., Assn. Ednl. and Psychol. Cons., Assn. Ednl. Therapists, Zeta Tau Alpha. Avocations: music, theater, reading, quilting, needlework.

REYNOLDS, MARGARET JENSEN, quality assurance professional; b. Miami, Fla., Nov. 15, 1950; d. Arden Edward Jensen and Elizabeth Emma (Stevenson) Galliher; m. Lawrence S. Stewart, Jr., June 2, 1969 (div. Aug. 1990); 1 child, Lawrence S. Stewart Jr.; m. Thomas L. Reynolds, July 17, 1993. BS, Auburn U., 1972; MS, U. So. Miss., 1991. Chemist Am. So. Dyeing & Finishing Corp., Opa Locka, Fla., 1972-74; sr. chemist Morton Internat., Moss Point, Miss., 1976-91, quality cert. coord., TQM facilitator, 1991—; treas. Dog River Fed. Credit Union, Moss Point, 1981-83. Vestry St. John's Episcopal Ch., Ocean Springs, Miss., 1989-91; mem. City/County Taxation Commn., Miss. Econ. Coun., Jackson, 1985-86. Mem. Am. Soc. Quality Control (cert., treas. 1994—, auditor 1993-94), AAUW (br. v.p. 1980-82, br. pres. 1984-87, Miss. state Edn. Found. chair 1984-86, crisis in higher edn. forum chair 1986). Home: 10805 Eagle Nest Rd Ocean Springs MS 39564-8339 Office: Morton Internat 5724 Elder Ferry Rd Moss Point MS 39563-9506

REYNOLDS, MARSHALL T., bank executive, holding company executive, investor. Printer Chapman Printing Co. Inc., Huntington, W. Va., 1958-64; chmn. bd. dirs. The Harrah and Reynolds Corp., Huntington, W. Va., 1964—; prin. Banc One W. Va. Corp., Huntington, W. Va., 1993—; now pres., chmn. bd. Champion Ind. Office: Champion Industries 2450-90 1st Ave Huntington WV 25703*

REYNOLDS, MARSHALL TRUMAN, printing company executive; b. Logan, W.Va., Feb. 21, 1937; s. Douglas Vernon and Dorothy Lee (Dingess) R.; m. Shirley Ann Earwood, Mar. 24, 1968; children: Jack Marine, Douglas Vernon. Student, Marshall U., 1956-58. Sales mgr. Chapman Printing Co., Huntington, W.Va., 1960-61, gen. mgr., 1961-64; pres., gen. mgr. Chapman Printing Co., Huntington, Parkersburg and Charleston, W.Va., Lexington, Ky., 1964—; chmn. bd. McCorkle Machine & Engring., Huntington, KY-OWVA Corrugated Container, Huntington, Stationers, Inc., Huntington, Charleston, Radisson Hotel, Huntington, Huntington Indsl. Corp., Champion Industries Inc., Am. Babbit Bearing Inc.; bd. dirs. Guyan Machinery, Huntington, United Huntington Industries, Persinger Supply Co., Prichard, W.Va., First Guaranty Bank, Hammond, La., Banc One WV Corp., Charleston, W.Va. Bd. dirs. W.Va. Roundtable, Huntington, 1989—, W. Va. Bus. Found., Huntington, 1989—, Boys and Girls Club, Huntington, 1989—, Huntington United Way, 1989—; mem. Gov.'s Task Force on Children, Youth and Families, 1989—; guest lectr. various high schs. on free enterprise. Named Outstanding Small Businessman of Yr., Huntington Jaycees, 1983, Business Man of Yr. Jaycess, 1988. Mem. Huntington C. of C., Western Star Lodge (Guyandotte, W.Va.). Republican. Baptist. Avocation: raising cattle. Home: 1130 13th St Huntington WV 25701-3632 Office: Chapman Printing Co 2450-90 1st Ave Huntington WV 25703

REYNOLDS, MARY TRACKETT, political scientist; b. Milw., Jan. 11, 1913; d. James P. and Mary (Nachtwey) Trackett; m. Lloyd G. Reynolds, June 12, 1937; children: Anne Reynolds Skinner, Priscilla Reynolds Roosevelt, Bruce; m. Yoke San Lee. BA, U. Wis., 1935, MA, 1935; postgrad. (Rebecca Green fellow), Radcliffe Coll., 1935-36; PhD (U. fellow, Barnard fellow), Columbia U., 1939. Rsch. asst. Littauer Sch. Harvard U., 1938-39; instr. Queens Coll., 1939-40; instr. Hunter Coll., 1941-42, lectr., 1945-47; assoc. in polit. sci. Johns Hopkins U., 1942-43; lectr. Conn. Coll., 1947-48, asst. prof., 1948-50; rsch. assoc. in econs. Yale U., 1961-67, vis. lectr. in English, 1973-82; meml. lectr. Joyce Centennial, 1982; assoc. fellow Berkeley Coll., 1982—. Author: Interdepartmental Committees in the National Administration, 1940, Joyce and Nora, 1964, Source Documents in Economic Development, 1966, Joyce and D'Annunzio, 1976, Joyce and Dante: The Shaping Imagination, 1982, Mr. Bloom and the Lost Vermeer, 1989, James Joyce: New Century Views, 1993; bd. editors James Joyce Quar., 1985—, James Joyce Studies Ann., 1990—. Rsch. asst. Pres.'s Com. Adminstrn. Mgmt., 1936; sr. economist Nat. Econ. Com., 1940; adminstrn. asst. Glenn L. Martin Aircraft Co., Balt., 1942-43; editorial asst. pub. adminstrn. com. Social Sci. Rsch. Coun., 1944-45; cons. Nat. Def. Adv. Commn., 1949, Nat. Mcpl. Assn., 1956, Orgn. Econ. Cooperation and Devel., Paris, 1964, U.S. State Dept.-AID 1965. Mem. MLA, AAUP, LWV, Am. Polit. Sci. Assn., Dante Soc. Am., Internat. James Joyce Found. (bd. trustees 1995—), Conn. Acad. Arts and Scis. (coun. 1988-89), Elizabethan Club (sec.-treas. 1984-89, bd. incorporators 1986-89), Sulgrave Club (Washington), Grolier Club, Appalachian Mountain Club, Phi Beta Kappa. Home: 4000 Cathedral Ave NW Apt 147B Washington DC 20016-5249 Office: Yale Sta PO Box 604 New Haven CT 06520

REYNOLDS, MEGAN BEAHM, primary and elementary education educator; b. Lima, Ohio, Aug. 29, 1955; d. Walter Clarence and Jo Ann (Wood) Beahm; m. Dale Myron Reynolds, Aug. 28, 1976 (div. July 1983); 1 child, Emily Jo Reynolds. BS, Tenn. Wesleyan Coll., 1977; postgrad., U. Tenn., 1986-88. Cert. elem. and early edn. tchr., Tenn. Tchr. adult basic edn. Athens (Tenn.) City Schs., 1977-78; asst. dir. Child Shelter Home, Cleveland, Tenn., 1978; tchr. kindergarten First Bapt. Presch./Kindergarten, Cleveland, 1978-80; teller, bookkeeper C & C Bank Monroe County, Sweetwater, Tenn., 1982-83; substitute elem. tchr. Knox County Schs., Knoxville, Tenn., 1983-85, elem. tchr., 1985-87, tchr. kindergarten, 1987—; career ladder III Knox County Schs., Knoxville, 1993; mem. adv. bd., grade-level chairperson Norwood Elem. Sch., Knox County Schs., 1990-93, mem. adopt a sch. com., 1992-93, S team rep., 1991-92. Editor Norwood Elem. Yearbook, 1989-90. Parent helper Girl Scouts U.S., 1986-90; neighborhood collector Am. Heart Assn., 1987—; v.p. Norwood Elem./Knox County Schs. PTO, 1991-92; Norwood rep. Ft. Kid, 1990-91; youth counselor Middlebrook Pike Meth. Ch., mem. Costa Rica missions team; active participant Vols. of Am. Mem. NEA, Tenn. Edn. Assn., Knox County Edn. Assn., Knox County Assn. Young Children, Children and Adults with Attention Deficit Disorder (presch. Summer intervention program, parent/sch. comms. program 1995—). Methodist. Avocations: reading, outdoor activities, travel, family activities, church and community volunteering. Home: 8525 Savannah Ct Knoxville TN 37923 Office: Norwood Elem Sch 1909 Merchants Dr Knoxville TN 37912-4714

REYNOLDS, NANCY BRADFORD DUPONT (MRS. WILLIAM GLASGOW REYNOLDS), sculptor; b. Greenville, Del., Dec. 28, 1919; d. Eugene Eleuthere and Catherine Dulcinea (Moxham) duPont; m. William Glasgow Reynolds, May 18, 1940; children: Kathrine Glasgow Reynolds, William Bradford, Mary Parminter Reynolds Savage, Cynthia duPont Reynolds Farris. Student, Goldey-Beacom Coll., Wilmington, Del., 1938. One-woman shows include Rehoboth (Del.) Art League, 1963, Del. Art Mus., Wilmington, Caldwell, Inc., 1975, Wilmington Art Mus., 1976; exhibited group shows Corcoran Gallery, Washington, 1943, Soc. Fine Arts, Wilmington, 1937, 38, 40, 41, 48, 50, 62, 65, NAD, N.Y.C., 1964, Pa. Mil. Coll., Chester, 1966, Del. Art Ctr., 1967, Met. Mus. Art, N.Y.C., 1977, Lever House, N.Y.C., 1979; sculpture work Brookgreen Gardens, S.C.; represented in permanent collections Wilmington Trust Co., E.I. duPont de Nemours & Co., Children's Home, Inc., Claymont, Del., Children's Bur., Wilmington, Stephenson Sci. Ctr., Nashville, Lutheran Towers Bldg., Travelers Aid and Family Soc. Bldg., Wilmington, bronze fountain head Longwood Gardens, Kennett Square, Pa., bronze statue Brookgreen Gardens, Murrells Inlet, S.C.; contbr. articles to profl. jours. Organizer vol. svc. Del. chpt. ARC, 1938-39; chmn. Com. for Revision Del. Child Adoption Law, 1950-52; pres., bd. dirs. Children Bur. Del.; pres., trustee Children's Home, Inc.; del., past regent Gunston Hall Plantation, Lorton, Va.; mem. adv. com. Longwood Gardens, Kennett Sq., Pa.; garden and grounds com. Winterthur (Del.) Mus.; mem. rsch. staff Henry Francis DuPont Winterthur Mus., 1955-63; mem. archtl. com. U. Del., Newark. Recipient Confrerie des Chevaliers du Tastevin Clos de Vougeot-Bourgogne France, 1960; Hort. award Garden Club Am., 1964, medal of Merit, 1976; Dorothy Platt award Garden Club of Phila., 1980; Alumni medal of merit Westover Sch., Middlebury, Conn. Mem. Pa. Hort. Soc., Wilmington Soc. Fine Arts, Mayflower Descs., Del. Hist. Soc., Colonial Dames, League Am. Pen Women, Nat. Trust Hist. Preservation. Garden Club of Wilmington (past pres.), Garden Club of Am. (past asst. zone 4 chmn.), Vicmead Hunt Club, Greenville Country Club, Chevy Chase Club (Washington), Colony Club (N.Y.C.). Episcopalian. Address: PO Box 3919 Greenville DE 19807-0919

REYNOLDS, NANCY REMICK, editor, writer; b. San Antonio, July 15, 1938; d. Donald Worthington and Edith (Remick) R.; m. Brian Rushton, June 25, 1983; 1 child, Ehren T. Park. Student, Sch. Am. Ballet, 1951, 53-61, Juilliard Sch. Music, 1957, Martha Graham Sch. Contemporary Dance, N.Y.C., 1959, U. Sorbonne, Paris, 1962; BA in Art History, Columbia U., 1965; postgrad., Goethe Inst., Prien, 1972, U. Chgo. and Sarah Lawrence Coll., 1974-77. Dancer N.Y.C. Ballet, 1956-61; editor Praeger Pubs., N.Y.C., 1965-71; dir. rsch. book Choreography by George Balanchine: A Catalogue of Works, N.Y., 1979-82 (pub. 1983); dir. rsch. pub. TV spl. Balanchine, N.Y., 1983-84; assoc. editor Internat. Ency. of Dance, 1991—; dir. rsch. The George Balanchine Found., N.Y.C., 1994—; co-pub. Twentieth-Century Dance in Slides, 1978—. Author: Repertory in Review: Forty Years of the New York City Ballet, 1977 (De la Torre Bueno prize 1977), The Dance Catalog: A Complete Guide to Today's World of Dance, 1979, co-author: In Performance,1980, Dance Classics, 1991 (rec. for teen age N.Y. Pub Libr.); editor: Movement and Metaphor: Four Centuries of Ballet (Lincoln Kirstein), 1970, Dance as a Theatre Art: Source Readings in Dance History from 1581 to the Present (Selma Jeanne Cohen), 1974, School of Classical Dance (V. Kostrovitskaya and A. Pisarev), 1978; contbr. (book) Ballet: Bias and Belief, "Three Pamphlets Collected" and Other Dance Writings of Lincoln Kirstein, 1983, also numerous articles and revs. to Dancing Times, Ballet News, Playbill, ArtsLine, Dancemag., Town & Country, Connoisseur, N.Y. Times, Ency. Britannica., others. Ford Found. Travel and Study grantee, 1974; Mary Duke Biddle Found. grantee, 1990. Mem. Dance Critics Assn. (pres. 1986-87), Soc. Dance History Scholars, Soc. for Dance Rsch., Am. Soc. for Theatre Rsch., European Assn. Dance Historians, Internat. Fedn. for Theatre Rsch. in affiliation with Societe Internat. des Bibliotheques et Musees des Arts du Spectacle. Home: 9 Prospect Park W Brooklyn NY 11215-1758

REYNOLDS, NICHOLAS S., lawyer; b. Grosse Point, Mich., June 16, 1944. BS, Wilkes Coll., 1968; JD with honors, George Washington U., 1971. Bar: Va. 1971, D.C. 1973. Ptnr. Winston & Strawn, Washington. Mem. ABA (chmn. atomic energy com. sect. pub. utility, comm. and transp. law 1980—). Office: Winston & Strawn 1400 L St NW Washington DC 20005-3509*

REYNOLDS, NORMAN, production designer, art director. Prodn. designer: (films) The Little Prince, 1974, Mr. Quilp, 1975, (with Leslie Dilley and John Barry) Star Wars, 1977 (Academy award best art direction 1977), (with Dilley, Harry Lange, and Alan Tomkins) The Empire Strikes Back, 1980 (Academy award nomination best art direction 1980), (with Dilley) Raiders of the Lost Ark, 1981 (Academy award best art direction 1981), (with Fred Hole and James Schoppe) Return of the Jedi, 1983 (Academy award nomination best art direction 1983), Return to Oz, 1985, Young Sherlock Holmes, 1985, Empire of the Sun, 1987 (Academy award nomination best art direction 1987), Avalon, 1990, Mountains of the Moon, 1990, Alien 3, 1992, Alive, 1993; art dir.: (films) The Incredible Sarah, 1976 (Academy award nomination best art direction 1976). Office: care Spyros Skouras Sanford Skouras Gross & Assocs 1015 Gayley Ave Fl 3 Los Angeles CA 90024-3424

REYNOLDS, NORMAN EBEN, lawyer; b. Muskogee, Okla., Dec. 1, 1919; s. Norman Eben and Elizabeth (Boyd) R.; m. Margaret Maxey Cooper, Nov. 21, 1953; children: Norman Eben III, Margaret Boyd, Nancy Elizabeth, Robert Cooper. A.B., U. Okla., 1941, LL.B., 1947. Bar: Okla. 1942, U.S. Supreme Ct. 1961. Ptnr. Reynolds, Ridings, Vogt & Morgan, Oklahoma City, 1947-89, of counsel, 1989—; dir. Oharco Corp.; mem. Okla. Ho. of Reps., 1949-55; spl. legal cons. Gov. Okla., 1959-63; spl. justice Okla. Supreme Ct., 1961. Pres. trustees Heritage Hall, 1970. Served to capt. AUS, 1942-46. Named Outstanding Young Man in Oklahoma City, 1951. Mem. Comml. Law League Am. (past nat. sec., Pres.'s Cup for disting. svc. 1980), ABA (co-chmn. nat. conf. lawyers and collection agys. 1979), Okla. Bar Assn., Okla. County Bar Assn. (most Outstanding Voluntary Pub. Svc. ann. award 1989), Am. Judicature Soc., Mil. Order World Wars, Phi Beta Kappa (past pres. alumni assn., Phi Beta Kappa of Yr. 1993), Sigma Alpha Epsilon (past pres. alumni assn.), Sooner Dinner Club (Oklahoma City) (pres. 1969), Kiwanis (Oklahoma City), Men's Dinner Club. Episcopalian (sr. warden 1971, chmn. com. to build Canterbury Living Ctr., pres. Episc. Retirement Community, Inc. 1981-94). Club: Sooner Dinner (Oklahoma City) (pres. 1969). Lodge: Kiwanis (Oklahoma City) (pres. 1968). Home: 2212 NW 56th St Oklahoma City OK 73112-7702 Office: Reynolds Ridings Vogt & Morgan 2200 First Nat Ctr Oklahoma City OK 73102

REYNOLDS, R. JOHN, university administrator; b. Milw., Dec. 3, 1936; s. Edward R. and Elizabeth (Wickenhauser) R.; m. Carol G. Lucas, Dec. 15, 1956; children: John D., Katherine A. BEd, U. Wis., Whitewater, 1961; MA, No. Mich. U., 1967; PhD, So. Ill. U., 1971. Bus. instr. Green Bay (Wis.) Tech. Inst., 1964-65; dir. vocat. tng. No. Mich. U., Marquette, 1965-68; v.p. Tech. Edn. Corp., St. Louis, 1968-69, prof., 1969-71; acting dean, chmn dept. So. Ill. U., Carbondale, 1969-71, 74-80, 81-82; assoc. acad. dean N.H. Coll., Manchester, 1971-74; head. bus. and econs. dept. Lake Superior State U., Sault Ste. Marie, Mich., 1981-82; pres. Nat. Coll., Rapid City, S.D., 1982-84, Huron (S.D.) U., 1984—; cons. various colls. and schs. Contbr. articles to profl. jours. Pres. Dakotaland Mus., Huron, 1986—. Named Researcher of Yr. Ill. Bus. Edn. Assn., 1971. Office: Huron U Office of Pres 8th And Ohio Huron SD 57350

REYNOLDS, RALPH DUANE, oncologist, educator; b. Powhatan Point, Ohio, Feb. 22, 1934; s. Ray Campbell and Edna Louise (Corbett) R.; m. Gertrude Elaine Manifold, June 15, 1957 (div. 1982); children: Daniel Ralph, Barry Duane, Ronald Arthur; m. Norita Rose Sholly, Nov. 6, 1982; children: Nancy Lee, Susan. BS, Muskingum Coll., 1956; MD, Ohio State U., 1960. Diplomate Am. Bd. Internal Medicine. Commd. 2d lt. USAF, 1959, advanced through grades to col., 1972, served in various locations including Vietnam, 1959-82, ret., 1982; intern Madigan Gen. Hosp., Tacoma, Wash., 1960-61; resident, then chief med. resident Wilford Hall Med. Ctr., San Antonio, 1961-64, fellow in hematology, oncology, 1964-65; chief hematology-oncology svc. David Grant Med. Ctr., Fairfield, Calif., 1965-82; med. dir. Ellis Fischel Cancer Ctr., Columbia, Mo., 1982-87; assoc. dir. oncology Adria Labs., Columbus, Ohio, 1987—; clin. prof. medicine U. Calif.-Davis, Sacramento, 1967-82, U. Mo. Sch. Medicine, Columbia, 1982-87; prin. investigator Nat. Cancer Inst., Bethesda, Md., 1967-87; dir. med. edn. David Grant Med. Ctr., 1969-81; sr. scientist, dir. clin. rsch. Cancer Rsch. Ctr., Columbia, 1982-87; sr. dir. cancer R&D U.S. Bioscience, 1993—. Patentee high-dose cancer therapy; author, editor: Cancer and the Heart, 1986; contbr. articles on cancer therapy and diagnosis to profl. publs. Treas. Meth. Ch., San Antonio, 1964-65; pres. Little League and Babe Ruth Baseball, Vacaville, Calif., 1970-73; commr. Babe Ruth Baseball, Trenton, 1977-87. Decorated Legion of Merit, Bronze Star medal; recipient Med. Rsch. in Cancer award Surgeon Gen., 1982; named Man of Yr. Babe Ruth

Baseball, Trenton, 1982; grantee NIH, 1986. Fellow ACP (region pres. 1981-82, Physician of Yr. Air Force region 1981); mem. AMA, Soc. Air Force Physicians (bd. govs. 1977-79), Am. Soc. Clin. Oncology, Am. Soc. Hematology. Presbyterian. Avocations: baseball, history.

REYNOLDS, RANDOLPH NICKLAS, aluminum company executive; b. Louisville, Nov. 22, 1941; s. William Gray and Mary (Nicklas) R.; m. Susan Van Reypen, Aug. 6, 1964; children: Randolph Nicklas, Ralph Seymour, Robert Gray. BA in Bus., Bellarmine Coll., 1966; postgrad., U. Louisville, 1967-68. With Reynolds Metals Co., Richmond, Va., 1969—, market dir. chems., 1975-77, gen. mgr. chem., 1977-78, pres. Reynolds Aluminum Internat. Svcs. divsn., 1978-85, v.p., exec. v.p. info., 1985-94, vice chmn., 1994—; v.p. Reynolds Internat., Inc., Richmond, 1978-79, pres., 1979—; pres. Reynolds Internat. Svc. Co., Southfield, Mich., 1987—; pres. Malakoff (Tex.) Industries, 1981—; bd. dirs. Reynolds Metals Co. and 36 subs. Bd. sponsors Coll. William and Mary. Democrat. Episcopalian. Home: 8605 River Rd Richmond VA 23229-8301 Office: Reynolds Metals Co 6601 W Broad St Richmond VA 23230-1701*

REYNOLDS, RICHARD CLYDE, physician, foundation administrator; b. Saugerties, N.Y., Sept. 2, 1929; s. Thomas Watson and Myrtle Edith (Myer) R.; m. Mary Jane Beck, July 7, 1954; children—Karen Sue, Stephanie Ann, Wayne Thomas. B.Sc., Rutgers U., 1949; M.D., Johns Hopkins U., 1953; D.Sc. (hon.), Hahnemann U., 1988, N.Y. Med. Coll., 1992; DSc, Uniformed Svcs. U. Health Sci., 1995. Diplomate Am. Bd. Internal Medicine. Intern Johns Hopkins Hosp., Balt., 1953-54; asst. resident Johns Hopkins Hosp., 1954-55, 57-58, fellow in infectious disease, 1958-59; practice medicine specializing in internal medicine Frederick, Md., 1959-68; mem. faculty U. Fla. Coll. Medicine, 1968-78, prof. medicine, prof., chmn. dept. community health and family medicine, 1970-78; prof. medicine, prof. environ. and community medicine, dean U. Medicine and Dentistry N.J., Robert Wood Johnson Med. Sch., 1978-87; sr. v.p. acad. affairs U. Medicine and Dentistry N.J., 1984-87; exec. v.p. Robert Wood Johnson Found., 1987—; mem. Liaison Com. on Med. Edn., 1982-87. Co-author: The Health of a Rural County: Perspectives and Problems, 1976, Patient Wishes and Physician Obligations, 1978; co-editor: On Doctoring: Stories, Poems, Essays, 1991, 2d edit., 1995; contbr. articles to med. publs. Sr. asst. surgeon USPHS, 1955-57. Mem. ACP, AMA. Office: Robert Wood Johnson Found PO Box 2316 Princeton NJ 08543-2316

REYNOLDS, ROBERT EDGAR, academic administrator, physician; b. Pontiac, Mich., June 3, 1938; s. Arthur James and Jean Lucille (Thompson) R.; m. Barbara Fisher, June 11, 1961 (div. May 1980); children: Jennifer Robin, Lisa Anne; m. Erika Renate Forte, July 25, 1981; children: Timothy Williams, Julia Renate. BA, Yale U., 1960; MD, Harvard U., 1964; MPH, Johns Hopkins U., 1967, DrPH, 1970. Med. dir. Chonic Disease Hosp., Balt. City Hosps., 1968-70; assoc. prof. medicine and community medicine, assoc. dean Med. Coll. Ga., Augusta, 1970-73; med. dir. br. hosps. Rush Presbyn. St. Lukes Med. Ctr., Chgo., 1973-81, assoc. prof. internal medicine, prof. preventive medicine, 1973-81, med. dir., 1975-81; assoc. dean, assoc. prof. medicine Johns Hopkins U. Sch. Medicine, Balt., 1981-88; sr. assoc. v.p. for health scis., prof. medicine U. Va. Health Sci. Ctr., Charlottesville, 1988—; prof. health evaluation scis. U. Va., Charlottesville, 1995—; sec.-treas. Med. Adminstrs. Conf., 1979-80, pres., 1981. Served to capt. USAR, 1965-73. Fellow ACP, Am. Coll. Preventive Medicine; mem. AMA, Assn. Am. Med. Colls. (assoc., chmn. group on instln. planning 1988-89), Found. for Health Svcs. Rsch. (nat. adv. com.), Assn for Health Svc. Rsch., Nat. Libr. Medicine (biomedical rev. com. 1992—), Computer-based Patient Record Inst. (bd. dirs. 1992—). Office: U Va Med Ctr Charlottesville VA 22908

REYNOLDS, ROBERT GREGORY, toxicologist, management consultant; b. Chgo., July 29, 1952; s. Robert G. and Loys Delle (Kever) R.; m. Phyllis Thurrell, May 1983. BS in Nutrition and Food Sci., MIT, 1973, postgrad. in toxicology, 1973-78; postgrad. in mgmt. Sloan Sch. Mgmt., 1977-78. Mng. editor The Graduate Mag., MIT, 1975-78; v.p. Internat. Contact Bur., Ft. Lauderdale, Fla., 1977—; staff toxicologist, asst. to v.p. mktg. Enviro Control, Inc., Rockville, Md., 1978-79; dir. tech. resources Borriston Rsch. Labs., Inc., Temple Hills, Md., 1979-80; dir. mktg. Northrop Svcs., Inc., Rsch. Triangle Park, N.C., 1980-88, mgr. bus. devel., NSI Tech. Svcs.Corp., 1988-89; mgr. proposal mgmt. Roy F. Weston, Inc., West Chester, Pa., 1989-90; project dir. Human Health Scis., 1990-91; pres. Spectrum Assocs., Uwchland, Pa., 1991—; mgmt. cons., 1981—; dir. bus. devel. Groundwater Tech., Inc., Chadds Ford, Pa., 1992-93; v.p. fed. programs ETG Environ. Inc., Blue Bell, Pa., 1993-94; dir. govt. bus. devel. OHM Corp., Findlay, Ohio, 1994—; toxicol. cons. Energy Resources Co., Inc., Cambridge, 1976-77. NSF fellow, 1973. Mem. Am. Def. Preparedness Assn., Soc. Am. Mil. Engrs. Episcopalian. Contbr. chpts. to textbook, lab. manual, sci. jours. and govt. publs. Home: 455 Fox Run Rd Findlay OH 45840 Office: OHM Corp PO Box 551 Findlay OH 45839-0551

REYNOLDS, ROBERT HARRISON, retired export company executive; b. Mpls., Sept. 6, 1913; s. Clarence H. and Helen (Doyle) R.; m. Gladys Marie Gaster, Apr. 7, 1934; 1 child, Shirley Anne (Mrs. Frank S. Potestio); m. Viola E. Shimel, June 26, 1982. Export sales mgr., rolled products sales mgr. Colo. Fuel & Iron Corp., Denver, 1938-46; pres. Rocky Mountain Export Co., Inc., Denver, 1941-93. Mem. Denver Club (life). Home: 13850 E Marina Dr Aurora CO 80014-5509 Office: 12331 E Cornell Ave Aurora CO 80014-3323

REYNOLDS, ROBERT HUGH, lawyer; b. St. Louis, Jan. 3, 1937; s. Leslie A. and Rebecca (McWaters) R.; m. Carol Jemison, Apr. 8, 1961; children: Stephen H., Cynthia C., Laura M. BA, Yale U., 1958; JD, Harvard U., 1964. Assoc. Barnes & Thornburg, Indpls., 1964-70, ptnr., 1970—, chmn. bus. dept., 1983-91; chmn. internat. practice group, 1992—. Co-chmn., editor Comml. Real Estate Financing for Ind. Attys., 1968; vice-chmn., co-editor Advising Ind. Businesses, 1974; chmn., editor Counseling Ind. Businesses, 1981, The Purchase and Sale of a Business, 1987. Bd. dirs. Crossroads Am. Coun. Boy Scouts Am., 1970—, v.p., 1971-75, pres., 1987-89; v.p. Area 4 Ctrl. Region Boy Scouts Am., 1989-92, pres., 1992-93, pres. Ctrl. Region, 1993-96, Nat. Exec. Bd., 1993—; bd. dirs. Family Svc. Assn. Indpls., 1974-81, pres., 1978-80; bd. dirs. Family Svc. Am., 1979-88, Greater Indpls. Fgn. Trade Zone, 1987—, Indpls. Conv. and Visitors Assn., 1989—, Indpls. Econ. Devel. Corp., 1983—, exec. com., sec.; mem. Greater Indpls. Progress Com., 1986—, exec. com., vice chmn. (Charles L. Whistler award); disting. adviser, trustee Children's Mus. Indpls., 1988-96, chmn., 1992-94; mem. Indpls. Downtown Inc., 1993—; bd. gov. Legacy Fund, 1992—; bd. dirs. Noyes Mem. Found., 1986—, Japan-Am. Soc. Ind., 1988—, pres., 1994—, Terralex, co-chmn. N.Am., 1996—. Fellow Ind. Bar Found., Indpls. Bar Found.; mem. ABA, Ind. Bar Assn. (chmn. corp., banking and bus. law sect. 1981-82, chmn. internat. sect. 1994—), Internat. Bar Assn., Indpls. Bar Assn., Greater Indpls. C. of C. (bd. dirs. 1987—), Econ. Club Indpls. (bd. dirs. 1995—). Republican. Clubs: Univ., Skyline (Indpls.). Lodge: Kiwanis. Office: Barnes & Thornburg 1313 Merchants Bank Bldg 11 S Meridian St Indianapolis IN 46204-3506

REYNOLDS, ROBERT JOEL, economist, consultant; b. Indpls., May 13, 1944; s. Joel Burr and Betty (Schimpf) R.; m. Lucinda Margaret Lewis, May 27, 1979; children: Joel, Sarah. BSBA in Fin., Northwestern U., 1965, PhD in Econs., 1970. Asst. prof. econs. U. Idaho, Moscow, 1969-73, assoc. prof., 1973-75; asst. dir, sr. economist econ. policy office Dept. Justice, Washington, 1973-81; sr. economist, v.p. ICF Inc., Washington, 1981-87, sr. v.p., 1987-91; exec. v.p., prin. Econsult Corp., Washington, 1991—; vis. assoc. prof. U. Calif., Berkeley, 1976-77, Cornell U., Ithaca, N.Y., 1981. Reviewer: NSF, Rand Jour. of Econs., Internat. Econ. Rev., Internat. Jour. Indsl. Orgn., Jour. Indsl. Econs., Am. Econ. Rev.; mem. editorial bd. Managerial and Decision Econs.; contbr. numerous papers to profl. jours. Recipient Dow Jones award Wall St. Jour., 1965; AT&T grantee, 1971-72, Brookings Instl. grantee, 1968-69; NDEA fellow, 1965-69. Mem. AAAS, IEEE (computer sect.), SIAM, Am. Math. Assn., Am. Econ. Assn., Econometric Soc., Royal Econ. Soc., Am. Statis. Assn., European Assn. for Rsch. in Indsl. Econs., Soc. for the Promotion of Econ. Theory, Math. Assn. Am. Congregationalist. Home: PO Box 59712 Potomac MD 20859-9712 Office: Econsult Corp 901 15th St NW Ste 370 Washington DC 20005-2327

REYNOLDS, ROGER LEE, composer; b. Detroit, July 18, 1934; s. George Arthur and Katherine Adelaide (Butler) R.; m. Karen Jeanne Hill, Apr. 11, 1964; children: Erika Lynn, Wendy Claire. BSE in Physics, U. Mich., 1957, MusB, 1960, MusM, 1961. Assoc. prof. U. Calif. San Diego, La Jolla, 1969-73, prof., 1973—, founding dir. Ctr. Music Expt. and Related Rsch., 1972-77; vis. prof. Yale U., New Haven, 1981; sr. rsch. fellow ISAM, Bklyn. Coll., 1985; George Miller prof. Amherst (Mass.) Coll., 1988; Rothschild composer in residence Peabody Conservatory of Music, 1992-93. Author: MIND MODELS: New Forms of Musical Experience, 1975, A Searcher's Path: A Composer's Ways, 1987, A Jostled Silence: Contemporary Japanese Musical Thought, 1992-93; contbr. numerous articles and revs. to profl. jours. Bd. dirs. Am. Music. Ctr., Meet the Composer, Fromm Found. Harvard U.; mem. bd. govs. Inst. Current World Affairs. Recipient citation Nat. Inst. Arts and Letters, 1971, NEA awards, 1975, 78, 79, 86, Pulitzer prize for music, 1989; sr. fellow Inst. Studies in Am. Music, 1985, fellow Rockefeller Found., Guggenheim Found.; Fulbright scholar. Office: U Calif San Diego Dept Music 0326 La Jolla CA 92093

REYNOLDS, SCOTT WALTON, academic administrator; b. Summit, N.J., July 15, 1941; s. Clark Leonard and Shirley (Hill) R.; m. Margaret Ann Johnson, July 5, 1969; children: Jane, Amy, David. B.A., Trinity Coll., Hartford, Conn., 1963; M.B.A., Harvard U., 1965. Mng. dir. corp. staff Bankers Trust Co., N.Y.C., 1967-94; asst. to the pres. St. Peter's Coll., Jersey City, 1994—. Chmn. fund campaign Montclair (N.J.) ARC, 1974; chmn. bus. and fraternal group Montclair Bicentennial Com., 1976; bd. fellows Trinity Coll., 1982-88, trustee, 1992—, sec., exec. com., 1993—. 1st lt. U.S. Army, 1965-67. Recipient 150th Anniversary award Trinity Coll., 1978, Alumni medal for Excellence, 1988, Pres.' Leadership medal, 1993. Mem. Montclair Jaycees (treas. 1973), Trinity Coll. Alumni Assn. N.Y. (pres. 1972-73). Episcopalian. Club: Harvard (N.Y.C.). Office: St Peters Coll 2641 John F Kennedy Blvd Jersey City NJ 07306-5943

REYNOLDS, STEPHEN CURTIS, hospital administrator; b. Little Rock, May 1, 1946; married. BA, Ark. State U., 1968; MA, Washington U., 1972. Adminstrv. resident Baptist Meml. Health Care System, Memphis, 1971-72, adminstrv. asst., 1972-75, asst. v.p., 1975-80, v.p., 1980-86, sr. v.p., 1986-89, exec. v.p., 1992; exec. v.p. Baptist Meml. Hosp., Memphis, 1990-92, pres., 1992—. With Armed Forces, 1968-70. Mem. Tenn. Hosp. Assn. (chmn., 1989-90, bd. dirs. 1986-91). Home: 461 Princeton Wood Cv Memphis TN 38117-1907 Office: Bapt Meml Hosp 899 Madison Ave Memphis TN 38103-3405*

REYNOLDS, THOMAS A., JR., lawyer; b. Chgo., Aug. 30, 1928. AB, Georgetown U., 1948; JD, U. Mich., 1951. Bar: Ill. 1954. Ptnr. Winston & Strawn, Chgo. Mem. ABA, Ill. State Bar Assn., Chgo. Bar Assn. Office: Winston & Strawn 35 W Wacker Dr Chicago IL 60601-1614*

REYNOLDS, THOMAS A., III, lawyer; b. Evanston, Ill., May 12, 1952. BSBA, Georgetown U., 1974; JD, Emory U., 1977. Bar: Ill. 1977, U.S. Dist. Ct. (no. dist.) Ill. 1978, U.S. Ct. Appeals (7th cir.) 1979, U.S. Dist. Ct. (no. dist. trial bar) Ill. 1983. Ptnr. Winston & Strawn, Chgo. Office: Winston & Strawn 35 W Wacker Dr Chicago IL 60601-1614

REYNOLDS, THOMAS HEDLEY, academic administrator; b. N.Y.C., Nov. 23, 1920; s. Wallace and Helen (Hedley) R.; m. Jean Fine Lytle, Apr. 24, 1943; children: Thomas Scott, David Hewson, John Hedley, Tay. Grad., Deerfield (Mass.) Acad., 1938; A.B., Williams Coll., 1942, LL.D. (hon.), 1978; M.A. in History, Columbia U., 1947, Ph.D. in History, 1953; LL.D., U. Maine, 1968, Bowdoin Coll., 1969, Colby Coll., 1969; DHL (hon.), Bates Coll., 1990, Middlebury Coll., 1992. Instr. history Hunter Coll., 1947-48; staff historian ARC, Washington, 1948-49; mem. faculty Middlebury Coll., 1949-67, chmn. dept. history, 1957-67, dean of coll., 1964-67; pres. Bates Coll., Lewiston, Maine, 1967-89, U. New Eng., Biddeford, Maine, 1991-95; mem. Edn. Commn. of States, 1969-80; mem. Higher Edn. Coun., 1971—, Commn. on Maine's Future, 1975—; dir. New Eng. Bd. Higher Edn., 1976—, mem. exec. com., 1977—; chmn. Gov.'s Commn. on Status of Edn. in Maine, 1983—. Bd. advisors AIDS project; bd. dirs. SALT, Inc.; mem. Vt. Hist. Sites Commn., 1964-66; mem. New Eng. Colls. Fund, pres., 1971-72; chmn. Com. on Jud. Responsibility and Disability, 1982—; trustee WCBB Ednl. TV, 1974—; bd. dirs. Nat. Assn. Ind. Colls. and Univs., 1977. Capt. AUS, 1942-46; col. Res. Mem. Am. Hist. Assn., Am. Antiquarian Soc., AAUP, Maine Hist. Soc., Vt. Hist. Soc., Maine Ptnrs. Alliance for Progress. Office: U New Eng 11 Hills Beach Rd Biddeford ME 04005-9526

REYNOLDS, VALRAE, museum curator; b. San Francisco, Dec. 18, 1944; d. Ralph Stanley and Valberta May (Eversole) R.; m. Richard Lee Huffman, Sept. 14, 1974; children: Elizabeth Anne, Margaret Lee. BA in Fine Arts with honors, U. Calif., Davis, 1966; MA, NYU, 1969. Asst. curator Asian collections Newark (N.J.) Mus., 1969-70, curator Asian collections, 1970—; cons. SITES Exhibition, 1988; lectr., presenter in field. Editor: Newark Mus. Quar., 1976, Tibetan Jour., 1976, Asia Soc., 1977, Arts of Asia, 1989, Explore Tibet, 1992; contbr. over 36 articles and revs. to profl. jours.; prodr. multimedia prodns. in field. Grantee NEA, NEH, 1972-74, 82-83, 85-86, 88-91, 89-92, J. Paul Getty grantee, 1986, 89-91, Travel grantee Asian Cultural Coun., 1989. Mem. Assn. Asian Studies (chmn. art history sect. Mid-Atlantic regional conf. 1973), China Inst. Am. (art com.), Japan Soc. (art com.). Home: 229 Baltic St Brooklyn NY 11201-6403 Office: Newark Mus PO Box 540 49 Washington St Newark NJ 07102-3109

REYNOLDS, WARREN JAY, retired publisher; b. Chgo., Mar. 10, 1918; s. Bradford Jay and Bessie Pearl (Bon Durant) R.; m. Mary Ellen Seaman, June 29, 1940 (dec. Sept. 1995); children: William, Nancy, David, Linda. BA, DePauw U., 1939. Retail salesman Gen. Foods Corp., Chgo., 1939-41; advt. salesman Capper Publs., Chgo., 1941-42, 45-47; with Parade Publs., Inc., N.Y.C., 1947—; pub., dir. Parade Publs., Inc. (Parade Mag.), 1967-83; pub. emeritus Parade Publs., Inc., 1983—. Served to lt. comdr. USN, 1942-45. Recipient Alumnus of Yr. award DePauw U., 1968. Republican. Club: Venice Yacht (Fla.). Home: 312 Yacht Harbor Dr Osprey FL 34229-9151 Office: 711 3rd Ave New York NY 10017-4014

REYNOLDS, WILLIAM BRADFORD, lawyer; b. Bridgeport, Conn., June 21, 1942; s. William Glasgow and Nancy Bradford (DuPont) R.; m. Marguerite Lynn Morgan, June 27, 1964 (div. Feb. 1987); children: William Bradford Jr., Melissa Morgan, Kristina DuPont, Wendy Riker; m. Clare Alice Conroy, Aug. 29, 1987; 1 child, Linda Matisan. BA, Yale U., 1964; LLB, Vanderbilt U., 1967. Bar: N.Y. 1968, D.C. 1973, U.S. Supreme Ct. 1971. Assoc. Sullivan and Cromwell, N.Y.C., 1967-70; asst. to Solicitor Gen. U.S. Dept. Justice, Washington, 1970-73; ptnr. Shaw, Pittman, Potts & Trowbridge, Washington, 1973-81; asst. atty. gen. Civil Rights div. U.S. Dept. Justice, Washington, 1981-88, counselor to Atty. Gen., 1987-88; ptnr. Ross & Hardies, 1989-91, Dickstein, Shapiro & Morin, 1991-94, Collier, Shannon, Rill & Scott, 1994—; chmn. Archtl. Transp. Barriers Compliance Bd., 1982-84. Editor-in-chief Vanderbilt Law Rev., 1966. Disting. scholar Free Congress Found., 1989-93, Disting. fellow Nat. Legal Ctr. for Pub. Interest, Washington, 1989-90. Mem. ABA, Fed. Bar Assn., D.C. Bar Assn., Order of Coif. Republican. Episcopalian.

REYNOLDS, WILLIAM CRAIG, mechanical engineer, educator; b. Berkeley, Calif., Mar. 16, 1933; s. Merrill and Patricia Pope (Galt) R.; m. Janice Erma, Sept. 18, 1953; children—Russell, Peter, Margery. B.S. in Mech. Engring., Stanford U., 1954, M.S. in Mech. Engring., 1955, Ph.D. in Mech. Engring., 1957. Faculty mech. engring. Stanford U., 1957—, chmn. dept. mech. engring., 1972-82, 89-93, Donald Whittier prof. mech. engring., 1986—, chmn. Inst. for Energy Studies, 1974-81; staff scientist NASA/Ames Rsch. Ctr., 1987—. Author: books, including Energy Thermodynamics, 2d edit, 1976; contbr. numerous articles to profl. jours. NSF sr. scientist fellow Eng., 1964, Otto Laporte awd., Am. Physical Soc., 1992. Fellow ASME, Am. Phys. Soc. Am. Acad. Arts Sci.; mem. AAUP, AIAA, Nat. Acad. Engring, Stanford Integrated Mfg. Assn. (co-chmn. 1990-94), Sigma Xi, Tau Beta Pi. Achievements include research in fluid mechanics and applied thermodynamics. Office: Stanford U Dept Mechanical Engineering Stanford CA 94305

REYNOLDS, WILLIAM FRANCIS, mathematics educator; b. Boston, Jan. 31, 1930; s. William Leo and Grace Regina (Devlin) R.; m. Pauline Jane Fitzgerald, Aug. 5, 1962; children—Nancy, Jane. A.B. summa cum laude, Holy Cross Coll., 1950; A.M., Harvard, 1951, Ph.D., 1954. Instr. Holy Cross Coll., Worcester, Mass., 1954-55; instr. Mass. Inst. Tech., Cambridge, 1955-57; asst. prof. math. Tufts U., Medford, Mass., 1957-60, assoc. prof., 1960-67, prof., 1967—, Walker prof. math., 1970—. Contbr. articles to math. jours. Mem. Am. Math. Soc., Math. Assn. Am., Sigma Xi. Achievements include research on modular and projective representations of finite groups. Home: 3 Preble Gardens Rd Belmont MA 02178-3460 Office: Dept Math Tufts U Medford MA 02155

REYNOLDS, WILLIAM HENRY, film editor; b. Elmira, N.Y., June 14, 1910. Grad., Princeton Univ. Swing gang laborer Fox Film Corp., 1934; asst. editor Paramount, 1936-37, editor, 1937-42; editor Twentieth Century-Fox, 1947-62; free-lance editor, 1962—. Asst. editor: (films) The Farmer Takes a Wife, 1935, The Gay Deception, 1935, Big Brown Eyes, 1936, Her Master's Voice, 1936, Palm Springs, 1936, Spendthrift, 1936, John Meade's Woman, 1937, Honeymoon in Bali, 1939, A Night at Earl Carroll's, 1940, Typhoon, 1940; editor: (films) (with Otto Lovering) 52nd Street, 1937, (with Lovering) Algiers, 1938, So Ends Our Night, 1941, Moontide, 1942, Carnival in Costa Rica, 1947, Give My Regards to Broadway, 1948, The Street with No Name, 1948, You Were Meant for Me, 1948, Come to the Stable, 1949, Mother Is a Freshman, 1949, Halls of Montezuma, 1951, The Day the Earth Stood Still, 1951, The Frogmen, 1951, Take Care of My Little Girl, 1951, The Outcasts of Poker Flat, 1952, Red Skies of Montana, 1952, Beneath the 12-Mile Reef, 1953, Dangerous Crossing, 1953, The Kid from Left Field, 1953, Desiree, 1954, Three Coins in the Fountain, 1954, Daddy Long Legs, 1955, Good Morning, Miss Dove, 1955, Love Is a Many-Splendored Thing, 1955, Bus Stop, 1956, Carousel, 1956, In Love and War, 1958, Beloved Infidel, 1959, Blue Denim, 1959, Compulsion, 1959, Wild River, 1960, Tender Is the Night, 1961, Fanny, 1961 (Academy award nomination best film editing 1961), (with Gene Milford, Eda Warren, and Folmar Blangsted) Taras Bulba, 1962, Kings of the Sun, 1963, Ensign Pulver, 1964, The Sound of Music, 1965 (Academy award best film editing 1965), Our Man Flint, 1966, The Sand Pebbles, 1966 (Academy award nomination best film editing 1966), Star!, 1968, Hello, Dolly!, 1969 (Academy award nomination best film editing 1969), The Great White Hope, 1970, What's the Matter with Helen?, 1971, (with Peter Zinner) The Godfather, 1972 (Academy award nomination best film editing 1972), Two People, 1973, The Sting, 1973 (Academy award best film editing 1973), The Great Waldo Pepper, 1975, (with Danford Greene) The Master Gunfighter, 1975, The Seven-Percent Solution, 1977, The Turning Point, 1977 (Academy award nomination best film editing 1977), Old Boyfriends, 1979, A Little Romance, 1979, (with Lisa Fruchtman, Gerald Greenberg, and Tom Rolf) Heaven's Gate, 1980, Nijinsky, 1980, Making Love, 1982, Author! Author!, 1982, Yellowbeard, 1983, (with Raja Gosnell) The Lonely Guy, 1984, The Little Drummer Girl, 1984, (with Herve De Luze) Pirates, 1986, Dancers, 1987, (with Richard A. Cirincione and Stephen A. Rotter) Ishtar, 1987, A New Life, 1988, Rooftops, 1989, Taking Care of Business, 1990, Newsies, 1992; prodr.: (films) (with Richard Widmark) Time Limit, 1957. Office: The Gersh Agency 232 N Canon Dr Beverly Hills CA 90210-5302

REYNOLDS, WILLIAM LEROY, lawyer, educator; b. Balt., July 26, 1945; s. Austin Leroy and Doris (Hill) R.; m. Theodora Hoe, Sept. 3, 1966; children: William, Megan, Sarah. A.B., Dartmouth Coll., 1967; J.D., Harvard U., 1970. Bar: Md. 1972, U.S. Supreme Ct. 1975. Clk. to judge U.S. Dist. Ct. Md., 1970-71; asst. prof. law U. Md., 1971-74, assoc. prof., 1974-77, prof., 1977—; of counsel Piper & Marbury, Balt., 1992—; bd. dirs. Md. Jud. Inst. Author: Judicial Process in a Nutshell, 1980, 2d edit., 1991, Understanding the Conflict of Laws, 1984, 2d edit., 1993, Cases and Materials on Conflict of Laws, 1990. Mem. Am. Law Inst., Md. State Bar Assn., Am. Judicature Soc. Clubs: Serjeants' Inn, Wranglers (Balt.); St. Regis Yacht (Paul Smiths, N.Y.), Hamilton St. Office: U Md Sch Law 500 W Baltimore St Baltimore MD 21201-1786

REYNOLDS, W(YNETKA) ANN, academic administrator, educator; b. Coffeyville, Kans., Nov. 3, 1937; d. John Ethelbert and Glennie (Beanland) King; m. Thomas H. Kirschbaum; children—Rachel Rebecca, Rex King. BS in Biology-Chemistry, Kans. State Tchrs. Coll., Emporia, 1958; MS in Zoology, U. Iowa, Iowa City, 1960, PhD, 1962; DSc (hon.), Ind. State U., Evansville, 1980; LHD (hon.), McKendree Coll., 1984, U. N.C., Charlotte, 1988, U. Judaism, L.A., 1989, U. Nebr., Kearney, 1992; DSc (hon.), Ball State U., Muncie, Ind., 1985, Emporia (Kans.) State U., 1987; PhD (hon.), Fu Jen Cath. U., Republic of China, 1987; LHD (hon.), U. Nebr., Kearney, 1992, Colgate U., 1993; LHD, No. Mich. U., 1995. Asst. prof. biology Ball State U., Muncie, Ind., 1962-65; asst. prof. anatomy U. Ill. Coll. Medicine, Chgo., 1965-68, assoc. prof. anatomy, 1968-73, research prof. ob-gyn, from 1973, prof. anatomy, from 1973, acting assoc. dean acad. affairs Coll. Medicine, 1977, assoc. vice chancellor, dean grad. coll., 1977-79; provost, v.p. for acad. affairs, prof. ob-gyn. and anatomy Ohio State U., Columbus, 1979-82; chancellor Calif. State Univ. system, Long Beach, 1982-90, prof. biology, 1982-90; bd. dirs. Abbott Labs., Maytag, Owens-Corning, Humana, Inc.; clin. prof. ob/gyn. UCLA, 1985-90; chancellor CUNY, 1990—; mem. Nat. Rsch. Coun. Undergrad. Sci. Edn., 1993—; co-chair Fed. Task Force on Women, Minorities and Handicapped in Sci. and Tech., 1987-90, Pacesetter Program Reform for Secondary Sch. Coll. Bd., 1992—; adv. bd. Congl. Black Caucus Inst. Sci., Space and Tech., 1987-91; Calif. Labor Employment and Tng. Corp., 1993—; Contbr. chpts. to books, articles to profl. jours; assoc. editor Am. Biology Tchr., 1964-67. Active numerous civic activities involving edn. and the arts; mem. nat. adv. bd. Inst. Am. Indian Arts, 1992—; bd. dirs. Lincoln Ctr. Inst., 1993—, UAW Calif., Calif. Econ. Devel. Corp., 1984-90; trustee Internat. Life Scis. Inst.-Nutrition Found., 1987—, Southwest Mus., L.A. County High Sch. for Arts Found., 1985-90. Recipient Disting. Alumni award Kans. State Tchrs. Coll., 1972, Calif. Gov.'s Award for the Arts for an Outstanding Individual in Arts in Edn., 1989, Prize award Cen. Assn. Obstetricians and Gynecologists, 1968; NSF Predoctoral fellow, 1958-62, Woodrow Wilson Hon. fellow, 1958. Fellow ACOG; mem. AAAS, Perinatal Rsch. Soc., Soc. Gynecol. Investigation (sec./treas. 1980-83, pres. 1992-93), Nat. Assn. Systems Heads (pres. 1987-88), Sigma Xi. Office: CUNY Office of the Chancellor 535 E 80th St New York NY 10021-0767

REYNOLDSON, WALTER WARD, state supreme court chief justice; b. St. Edward, Nebr., May 17, 1920; s. Walter Scorer and Mabel Matilda (Sallach) R.; m. Janet Aline Mills, Dec. 24, 1942 (dec. 1986); children: Vicki (Mrs. Gary Kimes), Robert; m. Patricia A. Frey, June 3, 1989. BA, State Tchrs. Coll., 1942; JD, U. Iowa, 1948; LLD (hon.), Simpson Coll., 1983, Drake U., 1987. Bar: Iowa 1948. Justice Iowa Supreme Ct., 1971-78, chief justice, 1978-87, sr. judge, 1989-93; of counsel Reynoldson Law Firm, Osceola, Iowa, 1993—; adj. prof. law Drake U., 1989-93; county atty., Clarke County, Iowa, 1953-57. Contbg. author: Trial Handbook, 1969. Pres. Nat. Ctr. for State Cts., 1984-85. Served with USNR, 1942-46. Recipient Osceola Community Svc. award, 1968. Mem. Iowa Bar Assn. (chmn. com. on legal edn. and admission to bar 1964-71), ABA, Am. Judicature Soc. (bd. dirs. 1983-87, Herbert Harley award 1990), Iowa Acad. Trial Lawyers, Conf. Chief Justices (pres. 1984-85), Am. Coll. Trial Lawyers. Office: Reynoldson Law Firm 200 W Jefferson St Osceola IA 50213-1206

REYNOLDS-SAKOWSKI, DANA RENEE, science educator; b. Centralia, Ill., June 28, 1968; d. David Lavern and Betty Lou (Shelton) Reynolds; m. Jason Bielas Sakowski, Oct. 8, 1994. BS in Edn., U. No. Colo., 1991, postgrad., 1994—. Tchr. life sci. and math. Ken Caryl Mid. Sch., Littleton, Colo., 1991-92; tchr. sci. Moore Mid. Sch., Arvada, Colo., 1992-93; tchr. life sci. Moore Mid. Sch., Arvada, 1993—. Mem. Nat. Wildlife Fedn., Colo. Assn. Sci. Tchrs., Colo. Biology Tchrs. Assn., Sierra Club, World Wildlife Fund, Nat. Parks and Conservation Assn., Natural Resources Defense Coun. Avocations: camping, writing poetry, hiking, singing. Office: Moore Mid Sch 8455 W 88th Ave Arvada CO 80005-1620

REZAK, RICHARD, geology and oceanography educator; b. Syracuse, N.Y., Apr. 26, 1920; s. Habib and Radia (Khoury) R.; m. Hifa Hider, July 1, 1944 (div. Mar. 1965); 1 child, Christine Sara; m. Anna Lucile Nesselrode, Mar. 18, 1965. MA, Washington U., St. Louis, 1949; PhD, Syracuse U., 1957. Geologist U.S. Geol. Survey, Denver, 1952-58; rsch. assoc. Shell Devel. Co., Houston, 1958-67; assoc. prof. oceanography Tex. A&M U., College Station, Tex., 1967-71; prof. Tex. A&M U., College Station, 1971-91, prof. emeritus, 1991—; mem. edit. bd. Geo-MArine Letters, N.Y.C., 1981—;

coun. SEPM, Tulsa, Okla., 1968-69; mem. govs. adv. panel Offshore Oil & Chem. Spill Response, Austin, Tex., 1984-85. Co-author: Reefs and Banks of the Northwest Gulf of Mexico, 1985; co-editor: Contributions on the Geological Oceanography of the Gulf of Mexico, 1972, Carbonate Microfabrics, 1993; contbr. articles to profl. jours. Comdr. USNR, 1942-64. Rsch. grantee various fed. agys., 1968-90. Mem. Lions (Melvin Jones fellow). Episcopalian. Home: 3600 Stillmeadow Dr Bryan TX 77802-3324 Office: Tex A&M U Dept Oceanography College Station TX 77843

REZIN, JOYCE JUNE, pediatric nurse practitioner; b. Kalamazoo, Apr. 29, 1936; d. Stephen Palc and Alexandra Kwiatkowski Salerno; m. Joseph Gerald Rezin, Feb. 15, 1958; children: Michael, William, Valerie. BSN, San Diego State U., 1971; MS, U. LaVerne, 1991. Cert. pediatric nurse practitioner; RN, Calif. Staff nurse med./surg. St. Vincent's Hosp., L.A., 1957-58; staff nurse surgery City of Hope Med. Ctr., Duarte, Calif., 1958-59; sch. nurse Sweetwater Union H.S. Dist., Chula Vista, Calif., 1973-84, San Diego Unified Sch. Dist., 1984—; guest lectr. San Diego State U. Sch. Pub. Health, 1994, 95. Vol. nurse Otay Cmty. Clinic, Chula Vista, 1978-79; CPR instr., ARC, Chula Vista, 1977-81, 95; sch. nurse governance team mem. San Diego Unified Sch. Dist., 1991-94. Named Woman of Achievement, Southland Bus. and Profl. Woman's Club, 1987. Fellow Nat. Assn. Pediatric Nurse Assocs. and Practitioners (bd. dirs. San Diego chpt. 1984-85, 95—); mem. Calif. Sch. Nurse Orgn. (bd. dirs. San Diego/Imperial counties chpt. 1981-86), Nat. Assn. Sch. Nurses. Roman Catholic. Avocations: travel, reading. Home: 10747 Viacha Dr San Diego CA 92124-3418 Office: San Diego City Schs Child Devel Program 4100 Normal St San Diego CA 92103-2653

REZNECK, DANIEL ALBERT, lawyer; b. Troy, N.Y., Apr. 26, 1935; s. Samuel and Elizabeth (Fishburne) R.; m. Beverly Ann Macht, Mar. 7, 1971; children: Jonathan Noah, Abigail Rebecca. BA, Harvard U., 1956, JD, 1959. Bar: N.Y. 1959, D.C. 1961. Rsch. asst. Harvard U. Law Sch., Cambridge, Mass., 1959-60; law clk. to Justice William J. Brennan U.S. Supreme Ct., Washington, 1960-61; asst. U.S. atty. Dept. Justice, Washington, 1961-64; assoc. Arnold & Porter, Washington, 1964-68, ptnr., 1969-95; gen. counsel D.C. Fin. Responsibility and Mgmt. Assistance Authority, Washington, 1995—; adj. prof. law Georgetown U., Washington, 1963—; mem. D.C. Commn. on Jud. Disabilities and Tenure, 1979-86, D.C. Bd. Profl. Responsibility, 1994—; trustee D.C. Pub. Defender Svc., 1981-87. Contbr. articles to profl. jours. Named Young Lawyer of Yr. for D.C., 1971. Fellow Am. Coll. Trial Lawyers, Am. Bar Found.; mem. ABA, D.C. Bar (pres. 1975-76, pres. Bar Found. 1994—), Bar Assn. D.C., Asst. U.S. Attys. Assn., D.C. B'nai Brith. Jewish. Avocations: American history; reading; writing. Home: 2852 Albemarle St NW Washington DC 20008-1036 Office: DC Fin Respons/Mgmt Asst Au Ste 900 1 Thomas Cir NW Washington DC 20005

REZNIK, ALAN A., petroleum engineering educator; b. Pitts., Sept. 25, 1939; s. Lawrence S. and Rose (Fairman) R.; m. Marion Bergstein, Sept. 8, 1963; children—Amy Jean, Robert I.S. B.S., U. Pitts., 1963, M.S., 1964, Ph.D., 1971. Research scientist Continental Oil Co., Ponca City, Okla., 1964-66; instr. chem. and petroleum engring. dept. U. Pitts., 1966-67; instr. dept. civil engring. Technion-Israel Inst. Tech., Haifa, 1967-68; sr. research assoc. Calgon Corp., Pitts., 1969; engring. supr. U.S. Bur. Mines, Pitts., 1973-75; assoc. prof. chem. and petroleum engring. U. Pitts., 1975—, dir. petroleum engring. program, 1981-92 ; cons. and lectr. in field. Assoc. editor Jour. Petroleum Sci. and Engring., 1986-93 . Contbr. articles to profl. jours. Recipient U. Pitts. Outstanding Sr. award, 1963; U.S. Dept. Energy grantee, 1976-78, Gulf Oil Found. grantee, 1979, U.S. Dept. Energy grantee, 1978-79, 80-82, 85-86. Mem. Soc. Petroleum Engrs. of AIME, Am. Chem. Soc. (sec.-treas. 1975-76), Sigma Xi, Sigma Tau, Sigma Gamma Epsilon. Democrat. Jewish. Clubs: Train Collectors Assn. (Strassburg, Pa.), Israel Numesmatic Soc. (Pitts., founder, dir. 1969-78), Antique Toy Collectors Am. Office: U Pitts Chem & Petroleum Engring Dept 1249 Benedum Hall Pittsburgh PA 15261-2212

RHA, CHOKYUN, biomaterials scientist and engineer, researcher, educator, inventor; b. Seoul, Republic of Korea, Oct. 5, 1933; came to U.S., 1956; d. Sea Zin and Young Soon (Choi) R.; m. Anthony John Sinskey, Aug. 22, 1969; children: Tae Minn Song, Tong Ik Lee Sinskey. BS in Life Scis., MIT, 1962, MS in Food Tech., 1964, MSChemE, 1966, ScD in Food Sci., 1967. Sr. rsch. engr. Anheuser-Busch, Inc., St. Louis, 1967-69; asst. prof. food and biol. process engring. U. Mass., Amherst, 1969-73; assoc. prof. food process engring. MIT, Cambridge, 1974-82, assoc. prof. biomaterials sci. and engring., 1982-90, prof. biomaterials sci. and engring., 1990—; prin. BioInfo. Assocs., Boston, 1980—; mem. sci. adv. bd. Genzyme, Cambridge, 1985—; pres. Rha-Sinskey Assocs., Boston, 1972—, XGen, Inc., Boston, 1992—; bd. dirs. Am. Flavor Inc., Boston. Mem. editorial bd. Carbohydrate Polymers, Food Hydrocolloids; author, editor: Theory, Determination and Control of Physical Properties of Food Materials, 1975; editor Biomaterials Sci. and Engring.; contbr. over 120 articles and sci. papers to sci. jours. Mem. AICE, Inst. Food Technologists, Soc. of Rheology, Sigma Xi. Achievements include patents for Encapsulated Active Material System, for Process for Encapsulation and Encapsulated Active Material System, for Hydrocarbon and Non-Polar Solvents Gelled with a Lipophilic Polymer Carbohydrate Derivative, for process of making powdered cellulose laurate, for method of making soybean beverages, for chewing gum, for method of utilizing an exocellular polysaccharide isolated zoogloea ramigera, for glucan compositions and process for preparation thereof, for liquid-liquid extractions, many others. Office: MIT 77 Massachusetts Ave # 56-137 Cambridge MA 02139-4301

RHA, Y. B., electronics executive. With Kamsung Group, Korea, 1972-91; president Samsung Semiconductor Inc., San Jose, Calif., 1991—. Office: Samsung Semiconductor Inc 3655 N 1st St San Jose CA 95134-1707*

RHAME, THOMAS GENE, army officer; b. Winnfield, La., Jan. 27, 1941; s. Thomas Elton and Mary Sue (Blair) R.; m. Linda Ann Saunders, Jan. 21, 1961; children: Rebecca Jean Rhame Barton, Thomas Gregory. BS, La. State U., 1963; MBA, Syracuse U., 1970. Commd. 2d lt. U.S. Army, 1963, advanced through grades to lt. gen., 1993; co. comdr., advisor 1st Cavalry Div., Republic of Vietnam, 1967-71; student Armed Forces Staff Coll., Norfolk, Va., 1975; bn. comdr. 2d Armored Div., Ft. Hood, Tex., 1976-78; advisor Calif. N.G. 40th Inf. Div., L.A., 1979-80; student Army War Coll., Carlisle, Pa., 1981; brigade comdr. 3d Inf., Kitzingen, Fed. Republic Germany, 1981-83; chief of staff 3d Armored Div., Frankfurt, Fed. Republic Germany, 1983; community comdr., asst. div. comdr. U.S. Army Europe, Hanau, Fed. Republic Germany, 1985-86; dep. chief of staff for pers. U.S. Army Staff, Washington, 1986-89; comdr. 1st Inf. Div., Ft. Riley, Kans., 1989-91; Operation Desert Storm chief U.S. Mil. Tng. Mission, U.S. Cen. Command, Riyadh, Saudi Arabia, 1991-93; dir. Def. Security Assistance Agy., Washington, 1993—. Mem. Transatlantic coun. Boy Scouts Am., Fed. Republic Germany, 1985-86; bd. dirs. Soc. Big Red One, 1989-91. Decorated Legion of Merit, Bronze Star (3), Silver Star (2), M.S.M. (3), Army D.S.M. (2), Def. D.S.M., Air Medal, Army Commendation Medal; named to La. State Hall of Disting. Grads., 1991. Mem. Assn. U.S. Army. Republican. Baptist. Avocations: stamp collecting, hunting, fishing.

RHAME, WILLIAM THOMAS, land development company executive; b. Wantagh, N.Y., Aug. 14, 1915; s. Frank Phipps and Eleanora May Sanger (Davis) R.; m. Thelma Scorgie, Aug. 12, 1939 (div. 1964); children—Frank Scorgie, Frederick Taylor. B.A., U. Cin., 1936; M.B.A., Harvard, 1938, D.C.S., 1942. Mem. faculty Harvard Grad. Sch. Bus. Adminstrn., 1938-40; partner Robert Heller & Assos., Cleve., 1940-45; bus. cons. N.Y.C., 1945-48; pres. Texstar Corp., San Antonio, 1948-65, Merger Consultants of Am., Inc., 1965—; partner Investment Realty Co.; chmn. finance com., dir. ICN Pharms., Inc., Irvine, Calif., 1960-76; dir. T.O. Corp., Hallmark Realty Corp., Mountain Top Estates Inc. Pres. Guadalupe Com. Center, 1956-57, The Argyle, 1957-58; chmn. bd. dirs. Mind Sci. Found. Mem. Phi Beta Kappa, Sigma Alpha Epsilon, Sigma Sigma, Tau Kappa Alpha, San Antonio Country Club, Argyle Club. Republican. Episcopalian. Home: 4001 N New Braunfels Ave San Antonio TX 78209-6349 Office: 1635 NE Loop 410 San Antonio TX 78209-1625

RHEIN, MURRAY HAROLD, management consultant; b. N.Y.C., June 7, 1912; s. Aaron and Celia (Hagler) R.; m. Miriam Eisenstadt, Dec. 22, 1940; children: Alan A., Barbara (Mrs. Allan D. Kramer). B.A., U. Ark., 1932, postgrad., 1932-33. Jr. exec. R.H. Macy & Co., N.Y.C., 1934-39; with Platt & Munk Co., N.Y.C., 1940-78, sales mgr., 1958-64, exec. v.p., 1964-67, pres., 1967-77; v.p. Questor Edn. Products Co., 1969-78; with M & M Rhein (mgmt. consultants to pub. industry), 1978—. Pub.: The Little Engine that Could. Served with USCGR, 1943-46. Jewish (trustee, v.p. temple).

RHEINBOLDT, WERNER CARL, mathematics educator, researcher; b. Berlin, Sept. 18, 1927; came to U.S., 1956; s. Karl L. and Gertrud (Hartwig) R. Dipl Math, U. Heidelberg, Fed. Republic Germany, 1952; Dr rer nat, U. Freiburg, Fed. Republic Germany, 1955. Mathematician Computer Lab., Nat. Bur. Standards, Washington, 1957-59; asst. prof. math., dir. Computer Ctr., Syracuse (N.Y.) U., 1959-62; dir. Computer Sci. Ctr., U. Md., College Park, 1962-65, prof. math. and computer sci., 1965-78, dir. applied math. program, 1974-78; A.W. Mellon prof. math. U. Pitts., 1978—; cons. various orgns., 1965—; cons. editor Acad. Press, Inc., N.Y.C., 1987—; mem. adv. panel NSF, Army Rsch. Office, Office Naval Rsch., NASA. Author: (with J. Ortega) Iterative Solution of Nonlinear Equations in Several Variable, 1970; Methods of Solving Systems on Nonlinear Equations, 1974, Numerical Analysis of Parametrized Equations, 1985; also over 130 articles. With German Army, 1943-45. Recipient Av. Humboldt Disting. Scientist award, Alexander von Humboldt Found., Germany; grantee NSF, 1965—, Office Naval Rsch., 1972—. Fellow AAAS; mem. Am. Math. Soc., Soc. for Indsl. and Applied Math. (editor 1964—, v.p. publs. 1976, pres. 1977-78, coun. 1979-80, trustee, 1982, chmn. bd. trustees 1985-90). Office: U Pitts Dept Math and Stats 612 Thackeray Building Pittsburgh PA 15260-4146

RHEINSTEIN, PETER HOWARD, government official, physician, lawyer; b. Cleve., Sept. 7, 1943; s. Franz Joseph Rheinstein and Hede Henrietta (Neheimer) Rheinstein Lerner; m. Miriam Ruth Weissman, Feb. 22, 1969; 1 child, Jason Edward. BA with high honors, Mich. State U., 1963, MS, 1964; MD, Johns Hopkins U., 1967; JD, U. Md., 1973. Bar: Md., D.C.; diplomate Am. Bd. Family Practice. Intern USPHS Hosp., San Francisco, 1967-68; resident in internal medicine USPHS Hosp., Balt., 1968-70; practice medicine specializing in internal medicine Balt., 1970—; instr. medicine U. Md., Balt., 1970-73; med. dir. extended care facilities CHC Corp., Balt., 1972-74; dir. drug advt. and labeling div. FDA, Rockville, Md., 1974-82, acting dep. dir. Office Drugs, 1982-83, acting dir. Office Drugs, 1983-84, dir. Office Drug Standards, 1984-90; dir. medicine staff, Office Health Affairs FDA, 1990—; chmn. Com. on Advanced Sci. Edn., 1978-86, Rsch. in Human Subjects Com., 1990-92; adj. prof. forensic medicine George Washington U., 1974-76; WHO cons. on drug regulation Nat. Inst. for Control Pharm. and Biol. Products, People's Republic of China, 1981—; advisor on essential drugs WHO, 1985—; FDA del. to U.S. Pharmacopeial Conv., 1985-90. Co-author: (with others) Human Organ Transplantation, 1987; spl. editorial advisor Good Housekeeping Guide to Medicine and Drugs, 1977—; mem. editorial bd. Legal Aspects Med. Practice, 1981-89, Drug Info. Jour., 1982-86, 91—; contbr. articles to profl. jours. Recipient Commendable Svc. award FDA, 1981, Group award of merit, 1983, 88, Group Commendable Svc. award 1989, 92, 93, 95, Commr.'s Spl. citation, 1993. Fellow Am. Coll. Legal Medicine (bd. govs. 1983-93, treas., chmn. fin. com. 1985-88, 90-91, chmn. publs. com. 1988-93, jud. coun. 1993—; Pres.'s awards 1985, 86, 89, 90, 91, 93), Am. Acad. Family Physicians; mem. AMA, ABA, Drug Info. Assn. (bd. dirs. 1982-90, pres. 1984-85, 88-89, v.p. 1986-87, chmn. ann. meeting 1991, 94, steering com. Ams. 1991—, Outstanding Svc. award 1990), Fed. Bar Assn. (chmn. food and drug com. 1976-79, Disting Svc. award 1977), Med. and Chirurgical Faculty Md., Balt. City Med. Soc., Johns Hopkins Med. and Surg. Assn., Am. Pub Health Assn., Md. Bar Assn., Math. Assn. Am., Soc. Indsl. and Applied Math., Mensa (life), U. Md. Alumni Assn. (life), Johns Hopkins U. Alumni Assn. (life), Chartwell Golf and Country Club, Annapolis Yacht Club, Johns. Hopkins Club, Delta Theta Pi. Avocations: boating, electronics, physical fitness, real estate investments. Home: 621 Holly Ridge Rd Severna Park MD 21146-3520 Office: FDA Office of Health Affairs Dir Medicine Staff 5600 Fishers Ln Rockville MD 20857-0001

RHETT, HASKELL EMERY SMITH, foundation executive, educator; b. Evanston, Ill., Aug. 29, 1936; s. Haskell Smith and Eunice Campbell (Emery) R.; m. Roberta Teel Oliver, Sept. 9, 1961 (div. 1973); children: Kathryn Emery, Cecily Coffin; m. Anita Leone, May 30, 1983 (div. 1993). AB, Hamilton Coll., 1958; MA, Cornell U., 1967, PhD, 1968. Asst. to the pres. Hamilton Coll., Clinton, N.Y., 1961-64; rsch. asst. Cornell U., Ithaca, N.Y., 1964-66; rsch. assoc. U. London, 1966-67; dir. program devel. Ednl. Testing Svc., Princeton, N.J., 1967-73; asst. chancellor N.J. Dept. Higher Edn., Trenton, 1973-85; v.p. The Coll. Bd., N.Y.C., 1985-90; pres. The Woodrow Wilson Nat. Fellowship Found., Princeton, 1990—. Author: Going to College in New Jersey, 1978; contbg. author: Government's Role in Supporting College Savings, 1990. Commr. N.J. Pub. Broadcasting Authority, Trenton, 1983-85; mem. Nat. Task Force on Student Aid Problems, Washington, 1974-75; mem. Gov.'s Adv. Panel on Higher Edn. Restructuring, State of N.J., 1994; trustee Dominican Coll., San Rafael, Calif., 1990—; del. Dem. Nat. Conv., Miami, 1972; sr. warden Trinity Episcopal Ch., Princeton, 1988-92, vestryman, 1979-82, dep. Gen. Conv., Detroit, 1988, Phoenix, 1991; mem. standing com. Episcopal Diocese of N.J., 1992—; trustee Trenton State Coll., 1992—, vice-chmn. 1995—, Gov. Dummer Acad., Mass., 1993—, Heartland Edn. Cmty., Ohio, 1992—. Nat. Def. fellow U.S. Govt., 1966-67, Eliot-Winant fellow Brit.-Am. Assocs., 1982, Harvard U. fellow, 1985, faculty fellow Wilson Coll., Princeton U., 1993—. Mem. Am. Assn. for Higher Edn., Nat. Assn. State Scholarship and Grant Programs (pres. 1976-78), Nassau Club, Cornell Club (N.Y.), Springdale Golf Club. Avocations: tennis, golf, sailing, classic automobiles. Home: 64 River Dr Titusville NJ 08560-1726 also: PO Box 53 Blue Hill Falls ME 04615 Office: The Woodrow Wilson Nat Fellowship Found CN 5281 Princeton NJ 08543-5281

RHETT, JOHN TAYLOR, JR., government official, civil engineer; b. Fort Benning, Ga., Feb. 20, 1925; s. John Taylor and Bessie (Grier) R.; m. Helen Watson, Nov. 5, 1949; children—Elizabeth, John Taylor III. B.S. in Mil. Engring., U.S. Mil. Acad., 1945; M.E. in Civil Engring., U. Calif.-Berkeley, 1952; M.S. in Internat. Relations, George Washington U., 1965. Registered civil engr., Fla., D.C. Commd. 2d lt. U.S. Army, 1942, advanced through grades to col., 1967; chief engring. U.S. Army Constrn. Agy., Vietnam, 1968-69; dist. engr. C.E., U.S. Army, Louisville, Ky., 1969-72; resident mem. Rivers and Harbors Bd., C.E., U.S. Army, 1972-73; ret. U.S. Army, 1973; dep. asst. adminstr. water program ops. EPA, Washington, 1973-79; fed. insp. Alaska Natural Gas Transp. System, Washington, 1979-86; self-employed cons. Arlington, Va., 1986—. Decorated Legion of Merit; recipient Gold medal EPA, 1976, Disting. Career award EPA, 1979. Fellow ASCE; mem. Am. Acad. Environ. Engrs. (diplomate), Soc. Mil. Engrs. Presbyterian.

RHI, SANG-KYU, lawyer, educator; b. Namwon, Cheon-buk, Republic Korea, July 1, 1933; s. Byong-Choon and Pil-Soon (Huh) R.; m. Hyo-Sook Kim, June 4, 1956; children: Eun-Sook, Jihn-u, Eun-Yong, Jihn-Soo. LLB, Chongchy Coll., 1955; LLM, So. Meth. U., 1961; postgrad., Nottingham (Eng.) U., 1966-67; LLD (hon.), Harding U., 1992. Legislating officer Office Legislation, Republic Korea, 1961-67; pres. Korea Environ. Law Assn., Seoul, 1977-83; vice min. Ministry Edn., Republic Korea, 1980; lawyer Rhi Law Offices, Seoul, 1981—; prof. Coll. Law Korea U., Seoul, 1982-94; rep. Korea Legal Ctr., Seoul, 1989—. Author: American Administrative Law, 1962, Administrative Law, 1965, Law of Administrative Remedy, 1985, State Liability and Compensation, 1995. 1st Lt. Republic Korea army, 1957-58. Recipient Presdl. commendation Govt. Korea, 1963, Red-Stripe Keunjeong medal, 1971. Mem. Seoul Bar Assn. (chmn. legis. com. 1989-91, Commendation Merit 1990), Korea Bar Assn. (exec. dir. 1991-93, bd. dirs. 1994—), Inter-Pacific Bar Assn. (coun. mem. 1995—), Internat. Bar Assn., Lawasia (coun. mem. 1995—). Avocations: golf, classical music. Home: 2-201 Asia Athletes Apt, 86 Jamshil 7-dong, Songpa-ku, Seoul 138-227, Republic of Korea Office: Rhi Law Offices Ste 1153, KCCI BLDG 45 Namdaemunro 4ka, Seoul 100-743, Republic of Korea

RHIEW, FRANCIS CHANGNAM, physician; b. Korea, Dec. 3, 1938; came to U.S., 1967, naturalized, 1977; s. Byung Kyun and In Sil (Lee) R.; m. Kay Kyungja Chang, June 11, 1967; children: Richard C., Elizabeth. BS, Seoul Nat. U., 1960, MD, 1964. Intern, St. Mary's Hosp., Waterbury, Conn., 1967-68; resident in radiology and nuclear medicine L.I.U.-Queens Hosp. Ctr., N.Y., 1968-71; instr. radiology W. Va. U. Sch. Medicine, Morgantown, 1971-73; mem. staff Mercy Hosp. and Moses Taylor Hosp., Scranton, Pa., 1973—, also dir. nuclear medicine; clin. instr., Temple U., 1987—; pres. Radiol. Consultants, Inc., 1984—. Served with M.C., Korean Army, 1964-67. Recipient Minister of Health and Welfare award, 1963; certified Am. Bd. Nuclear Medicine. Mem. AMA, Soc. Nuclear Medicine, Radiol. Soc. N.Am., Am. Coll. Nuclear Medicine, Am. Coll. Radiology, Am. Inst. Ultra Sound, Country Club Scranton, Pres.'s Club U. Scranton, Elks. Home: 14 Lakeside Dr Clarks Summit PA 18411-9419 Office: 746 Jefferson Ave Scranton PA 18510-1624

RHIND, JAMES THOMAS, lawyer; b. Chgo., July 21, 1922; s. John Gray and Eleanor (Bradley) R.; m. Laura Haney Campbell, Apr. 19, 1958; children: Anne Constance, James Campbell, David Scott. Student, Hamilton Coll., 1940-42; A.B. cum laude, Ohio State U., 1944; LL.B. cum laude, Harvard U., 1950. Bar: Ill. bar 1950. Japanese translator U.S. War Dept., Tokyo, Japan, 1946-47; congl. liaison Fgn. Operations Adminstrn., Washington, 1954; atty. Bell, Boyd & Lloyd, Chgo., 1950-53, 55—, ptnr., 1958-92, of counsel, 1993—; Bd. dirs. Kewaunee Scientific Corp., Statesville, N.C., Lindberg Corp., Rosemont, Ill., Microseal Corp., Zion, Ill., Griffith Labs., Inc., Alsip, Ill. Commr. Gen. Assembly United Presbyn. Ch., 1963; life trustee Ravinia Festival Assn., Hamilton Coll., Clinton, N.Y., U. Chgo.; Northwestern Univ. Assocs.; chmn. Cook County Young Republican Orgn., 1957; Ill. Young Rep. nat. committeeman, 1957-58; v.p., mem. bd. govs. United Rep. Fund Ill., 1965-84; pres. Ill. Childrens Home and Aid Soc., 1971-73, life trustee; bd. dirs. E.J. Dalton Youth Center, 1966- 69; governing mem. Orchestral Assn., Chgo.; mem. Ill. Arts Council, 1971-75; mem. exec. com. div. Met. Mission and Ch. Extension Bd., Chgo. Presbytery, 1966-68; trustee Presbyn. Home, W. Clement and Jessie V. Stone Found., U. Chgo. Hosps. Served with M.I. AUS, 1943-46. Mem. ABA, Ill. Bar Assn., Chgo. Bar Assn. (bd. mgrs. 1967-69), Fed. Bar Assns., Chgo. Council on Fgn. Relations, Japan Am. Soc. Chgo., Legal Club Chgo., Law Club Chgo., Phi Beta Kappa, Sigma Phi. Clubs: Chicago, Glen View (Ill.), Commercial (Chgo.), Mid-Day Club (Chgo.), Economic (Chgo.). Home: 830 Normandy Ln Glenview IL 60025-3210 Office: Bell Boyd & Lloyd 3 First National Pla 70 W Madison St Ste 3200 Chicago IL 60602-4207

RHINE, JOHN E., lawyer; b. Eldorado, Ill., Nov. 12, 1952; s. R.L. and Iris Faye (Harlow) R.; m. Susan L. Edwards, Dec. 28, 1974; children: Oliver Sampson, Tison Hausser, Julia Eva. BA, So. Ill. U., 1974; JD magna cum laude, U. Ill., 1977. Bar: Ill. 1977, U.S. Dist. Ct. (so. dist.) Ill. 1979, U.S. Ct. Appeals (7th cir.) 1985. Law clk. to justice Ill. Supreme Ct., Springfield, 1977-78; pvt. practice law Mt. Carmel, Ill., 1978-79; ptnr. Rhine & Vargo, Mt. Carmel, 1979—; bd. dirs. Nat. Land & Mineral Co., Inc., Starlight TV Corp., chmn., 1989-94; vis. prof. law Moscow State Inst. Internat. Rels., 1993, 95. Adv. coun. mineral lands mgmt. U. Evansville (Ind.), 1984-88; active Mr. Carmel Planning Commn., 1986-88; del. Moscow Conf. on Law and Econs., 1990; bd. dirs. Voices Ill. Children, chmn. bd. dirs., 1993—. Mem. Ill. Bar Assn. (mineral law subcom. 1984, law office econs. sect. coun. 1986-93, chmn. 1991-92, mineral law sect. coun. 1993—). Presbyterian. Office: Rhine & Vargo 616 N Market St Mount Carmel IL 62863-1459

RHINEHEART, GARY, mortgage company executive; b. 1943. Pres. Sunshine Mortgage Corp., Smyrna, Ga. With USAF, 1967-70. Office: Sunshine Mortgage Corp 2401 Lake Park Dr Ste 300 Smyrna GA 33080*

RHINELANDER, ESTHER RICHARD, secondary school educator; b. Honolulu, Aug. 31, 1940; d. William Wise and Elizabeth (Chilton) Richard; m. Harvey James Rhinelander, July 24, 1965; 1 child, Lori. BEd, U. Hawaii, 1963, profl. cert., 1964. Tchr. music Kamehameha Sch., Honolulu, 1965—, Kamehameha Sch. for Girls, Honolulu, 1964, Waianae High and Intermediate Sch., Honolulu, 1965; dir. Waiokeola Ch. Choir, Honolulu, 1964-67, Kawaiahao Ch. Choir, Honolulu, 1980-87; judge song contest Kamehameha Schs., 1972, 88; judge choral composition contest Hawaii Found. on Culture and Arts, Honolulu, 1984, 85; pianist Kahikuonalani Ch., Honolulu, 1987—, Ch. Choral Ensemble, 1987—; tchr. Sunday Sch., 1988—. Mem., asst. accompanist Honolulu Opera Guild, 1955-59. Mem. Am. Choral Dirs. Assn., Soc. Gen. Music Tchrs. (sec. 1989-90), Music Educators Nat. Conf., Hawaii Music Educators Assn. Democrat. Mem. United Ch. of Christ. Avocations: reading, gardening, baking. Office: Highlands Child Care Ctr 757 Ho'omalu St Pearl City HI 96782

RHINES, PETER BROOMELL, oceanographer, atmospheric scientist; b. Hartford, Conn., July 23, 1942; s. Thomas B. and Olive (Symonds) R.; m. Marie Louise Lenos, Oct. 12, 1968; (div. 1983); m. Linda Jean Mattson; 1 child, Andrew Nelson. B.S., M.S., M.I.T., Cambridge U., 1964; Ph.D., Trinity Coll., Cambridge U., Eng., 1967. Asst. prof. oceanography M.I.T., Cambridge, 1968-71; rsch. asst. dept. applied math. and theoretical physics Cambridge U., Eng., 1971-72; scientist Woods Hole Oceanographic Inst., Woods Hole, Mass., 1972-84; prof. oceanography and atmospheric scis. U. Wash., Seattle, 1984—; vis. fellow Christ's Coll., Cambridge, Eng., 1979-80, 1983. Recipient de Florez research award MIT, 1963; NSF fellow, 1963-64; Guggenheim fellow, 1979-80; Queen's fellow in marine scis., Australia, 1988; A.E. Sloan Research scholar MIT, 1960-63; Marshall scholar Cambridge, 1964-67; Green scholar U. Calif., San Diego, 1981. Fellow Am. Geophys. Union, Am. Meterol. Soc.; mem. Nat. Acad. Scis. Avocations: guitar, walking, studying the global environment. Home: 5753 61st Ave NE Seattle WA 98105-2037 Office: Sch Oceanography U Wash WB-10 Seattle WA 98195

RHINES, WALDEN C., information system specialist; b. 1948. With Tex. Instruments, Dallas, 1972-93, exec. v.p. semiconductor group; with Mentor Graphics Corp., Wilsonville, Oreg., 1993—, now CEO, pres. Office: Mentor Graphics Corp 8005 SW Boeckman Rd Wilsonville OR 97070-9733*

RHINESMITH, STEPHEN HEADLEY, international management consultant; b. Mineola, N.Y., Dec. 13, 1942; s. Homer Kern and Winifred Headley (Long) R.; m. Kathleen Alys Law, Aug. 28, 1965; children: Chrisopher Law, Colin Headley. BA (Baker scholar), Wesleyan U., 1965; M in Pub. and Internat. Affairs, (Heinz fellow), U. Pitts., 1966, PhD (NDEA fellow), 1972. Dir. internat. svcs. McBer and Co., Cambridge, Mass., 1969-71; pres. AFS Intercultural Programs, N.Y.C., 1972-80, 87-89, Holland Am. Cruises, N.Y.C., 1980-82, Moran, Stahl, Boyer, N.Y.C., 1982-84, Rhinesmith & Assocs. Inc., N.Y.C., 1984—; named amb., coord. Pres.'s U.S.-Soviet Exch. Initiative, 1986-87; chmn. dept. orgnl. sociology Moscow State U., 1991—. Author: Bring Home the World: A Management Guide for Community Leaders of International Programs, 1975, 85; A Manager's Guide to Globalization: Six Skills for Success in a Changing World, 1993, 2d edit., 1996. Mem. ASTD (chair 1994), Met. Club (Washington). Office: 1 Devonshire Pl PH10 Boston MA 02109

RHO, EDWARD, information systems professional; b. Naples, Italy, Nov. 10, 1941; s. Pasquale and Rosa (Esposito) Rho; m. Lorraine Therese Craveira. BS equivalency, U. Naples, Taranto, Italy, 1964; postgrad., various schs., 1986-90. Programmer, analyst Cross & Brown, N.Y.C., 1967-69; project leader, sr. programmer, analyst Honfed Bank, 1970-81; d.p. cons., project mgr., sr. programmer, analyst Fin. Banking, Ins. and other orgns., Honolulu, 1981-83; cons., project mgr. MTL, Inc., Honolulu, 1983-84; data base analyst, chief analyst, project mgr. Universo Assicurazioni, Bologna, Italy, 1984-86; sr. programmer, analyst, project leader Allied Forces So. Europe/NATO, Naples, Italy, 1986-88; data base analyst, sr. systems analyst, acting task mgr. Planning Rsch. Corp./Hickam AFB, Aiea, Hawaii, 1989; sr. systems analyst, project leader, quality assurance rep. U.S. Dept. Def., Am. Express Bank, Ltd., Merchants Nat. Bank, Honolulu, 1989-90; data processing systems analyst V, project mgr. State of Hawaii/Exec. Br. Budget and Fin. Dept., 1990-91, data processing systems analyst VI, project mgr./sect. chief, 1991—. Designer, developer computer software. Mem. Hist. Hawaii Found., Friends of Italy Soc. of Hawaii, Sacred Heart League. Home: 47-409 Lulani St Kaneohe HI 96744-4718 Office: State of Hawaii Dept Budget Info and Comm Svcs Divsn 1151 Punchbowl St Honolulu HI 96813-1940

RHOADES, JOHN SKYLSTEAD, SR., federal judge; b. 1925; m. Carmel Rhoades; children: Mark, John, Matthew, Peter, Christopher. AB, Stanford U., 1948; JD, U. Calif., San Francisco, 1951. Prosecuting atty. City of San Diego, 1955-56, dep. city atty., 1956-57; pvt. practice San Diego, 1957-60; ptnr. Rhoades, Hollywood & Neil, San Diego, 1960-85; judge U.S. Dist. Ct. (so. dist.) Calif., San Diego, 1985—. With USN, 1943-46. Office: US Dist Ct 940 Front St San Diego CA 92101-8705

RHOADES, MARYE FRANCES, paralegal; b. Ft. Defiance, Va., Jan. 29, 1937; d. Silas Caswell Sr. and Mary Ann Frances (James) Rhodes; m. Minter James Rowe, May 1964 (div. 1968); children: Margaret Frances Omar, James Robert; m. Robert Charles Rhoades Jr., July 25, 1980. Student, Coll. W.Va., 1956-58, 68, U. Charleston, 1962-63, 74, 89, Antioch U., 1972-73; grad., Mike Tyree Sch. Real Estate, 1984, Evans Coll. Legal Studies, 1990. Educator Nicholas County Sch. System, Summersville, W.Va., 1958-61; edit. staff, columnist, staff writer, reporter, photographer Beckley Newspapers Corp., 1962-76; Educator Raleigh County Bd. Edn., Beckley, W.Va., 1967-68; exec. editor, columnist Local News Jour., Whitesville, W.Va., 1976-77; libr. bookmobile, asst. ref. libr., outreach coord. Raleigh County Pub. Libr., Beckley, 1977-78; agt. Combined Ins. Co., Chgo., 1978-79; legal sec., paralegal W.Va. Legal Svcs. Inc., Beckley, 1979-82; paralegal Applachian Rsch and Defense Fund Inc., Beckley, 1982-83; exec. dir., owner Rhoades and Rowe, Beckley, 1983-85; paralegal patinet advocate Comty. Health Sys. Inc., Beckley, 1986-96; pvt. practice Mac Arthur, W. Va., 1996—. Contbr. articles to mags. State bd. dirs., pub. resl. LWV, Beckley; pub. rels., various coms. Raleigh County Dem. Women, Beckley; sec., pub. rels. Orchard Valley Women's Club, Crab Orchard, W.Va.; trustee Fraternal Order Ealges; pub. rels., various coms. Loyal Order Moose, Beckley, Beckley Profl. Bus. Women; com. mem. Nat. Coalition to Save the New River; sales rep. So. U.S. Rep. to U.S. Mil. Acad., West Point, N.Y.; mem. Am. Legion Aux., Mullens, W.Va. Mem. NEA, Classroom Tchrs. Assn., Nat. Paralegal Assn., Nat. Fedn. Paralegals Assn., Nat. Ind. Paralegals Assn., Nat. Com. Save Soc., Sec. Medicare, Nat. Legal Aid and Def. Assn., Nat. Orgn. Social Security Claimants Reps., State Soc. Sec. Task Force, Nat. Vets. Legal Svcs. Project Inc., W.Va. U. Alumni Assn., Community AIDS Edn. Com., W.Va. Edn. Assn. Democrat. Pentacostal Holiness. Avocations: creative arts and music, walking, NASCAR, doll collecting. Home: PO Box 416 Mac Arthur WV 25873-0416

RHOADES, RODNEY ALLEN, physiologist, educator; b. Greenville, Ohio, Jan. 5, 1939; s. John H. and Floris L. Rhoades; m. Judith Ann Brown, Aug. 6, 1961; children: Annelisa, Kirsten. BS, Miami U., 1961, MS, 1963; PhD, Ohio State U., 1966. Asst. prof. Pa. State U., State College, 1966-72, assoc. prof., 1972-75; rsch. scientist NIH, Bethesda, Md., 1975-76; prof. Ind. U. Sch. Medicine, Indpls., 1976-81, prof., chmn., 1981—; dir. Indpls. Ctr. for Advanced Rsch. Author: Physiology, 1984; contbr. articles to profl. jours. Recipient NASA fellow, 1964-66, Rsch. Career Devel. award NIH, 1975-80. Mem. Am. Physiol. Soc., Am. Heart Assn., Am. Thoracic Soc., Biophysics Soc., Sigma Xi. Home: 1768 Spruce Dr Carmel IN 46033-9025 Office: Ind U Sch Medicine 635 Barnhill Dr Indianapolis IN 46202-5126

RHOADS, GEORGE GRANT, medical epidemiologist; b. Phila., Feb. 11, 1940; s. Jonathan Evans and Teresa (Folin) R.; m. Frances Ann Secker, June 5, 1965; children: Thomas C., James E. MD, Harvard U., 1965; MPH, U. Hawaii, 1970. Intern Hosp. of U. Pa., Phila., 1965-66, resident in internal medicine, 1966-68; resident in preventive medicine U. Hawaii Sch. Pub. Health, 1968-71; epidemiologist Japan-Hawaii Cancer Study, Honolulu, 1974-75; assoc. prof. U. Hawaii, Honolulu, 1974-79, chair dept. pub. health sci., 1978-81, dir. gen. preventive medicine, 1978-81, prof. pub. health, 1979-82; chief epidemiology br. Nat. Inst. Child Health and Human Devel./NIH, Bethesda, Md., 1982-89; prof., dir. grad program in pub. health U. Medicine and Dentistry N.J.-Robert Wood Johnson Med. Sch., Piscataway, 1989—. Contbr. more than 130 articles on the epidemiology of non-infectious diseases to profl. jours. Recipient Dirs. award NIH, 1987, EEO award NICHD, 1984. Fellow Am. Coll. Physicians; mem. Am. Epidemiol. Soc. Mem. Soc. of Friends. Achievements include research on the protective effect of high density Lipoprotein in the blood against development of heart attacks. Office: Environ and Occupl Health Scis Inst PO Box 1179 681 Frelinghuysen Rd Piscataway NJ 08855-1179

RHOADS, GERALDINE EMELINE, editor; b. Phila., Jan. 29, 1914; d. Lawrence Dry and Alice Fegley (Rice) R. A.B., Bryn Mawr Coll., 1935. Publicity asst. Bryn Mawr (Pa.) Coll., 1935-37; asst. Internat. Students House, Phila., 1937-39; mng. editor The Woman mag., N.Y.C., 1939-42; editor Life Story mag., 1942-45, Today's Woman mag., N.Y.C., 1945-52, Today's Family Mag., N.Y.C., 1952-53; lectr. Columbia U., 1954-56; assoc. editor Readers Digest, 1954-55; producer NBC, 1955-56; assoc. editor Ladies Home Jour., 1956-62, mng. editor, 1962-63; exec. editor McCall's mag., 1963-66; editor Woman's Day mag., 1966-82, editorial dir., 1982-84; editorial dir. Woman's Day Resource Center, 1984-89; v.p. Woman's Day mag., 1972-77, 78-84, CBS Consumer Publs., 1977-84; cons. Woman's Day, N.Y.C., 1989-91; editorial cons., dir. Nat. Mag. Awards, 1991-94. Author: (with others) Woman's Day Help Book, 1988. Recipient award for profl. achievement Diet Workshop Internat., 1977; Elizabeth Cutter Morrow award YWCA Salute to Women in Bus., 1977; Recipient Econ. Equity award Women's Equity Action League, 1982; March of Dimes Women Editor's citation, 1982. Mem. Nat. Press Club (dir.), Fashion Group (bd. govs. 1977-79, 87-88, chmn. bd. govs. 1978-80, treas. bd. govs. 1983-85, bd. dirs. Found. 1980-81), Am. Soc. Mag. Editors (chmn. exec. com. 1971-73), N.Y. Women in Comms. (Matrix award 1975), Advt. Women in N.Y. (bd. govs. 1983-85, 2d v.p. 1985-87, 1st v.p. 1987-89, bd. dirs. 1989-90, Pres.'s award 1987), Women's Forum (bd. dirs. 1985-87), YWCA Acad. Women Achievers, Women's City Club of N.Y., Literacy Vols. of N.Y.C. (bd. dirs. 1986-93), Turtle Bay Assn. (bd. dirs. 1989-92), Bryn Mawr Coll. Alumni Assn. (bd. dirs. 1989-94), Bryn Mawr Club of N.Y.C. (bd. dirs. 1994—). Home: # 21M 185 W End Ave Apt 21M New York NY 10023-5549

RHOADS, JAMES BERTON, archivist, former government official, consultant, educator; b. Sioux City, Iowa, Sept. 17, 1928; s. James Harrison and Mary (Keenan) R.; m. S. Angela Handy, Aug. 12, 1947; children: Cynthia Patrice Neven, James Berton, Marcia Marie MacKellar. Student, Southwestern Jr. Coll., 1946-47, Union Coll., Lincoln, Neb., 1947-48; BA, U. Calif.-Berkeley, 1950, MA, 1952; PhD, Am. U., 1965. With GSA-Nat. Archives and Records Service, Washington, 1952-79; asst. archivist for civil archives GSA-Nat. Archives and Records Service, 1965, dept. archivist U.S., 1966-68, archivist U.S., 1968-79; chmn. Nat. Archives Trust Fund Bd., 1968-79; chmn. adminstrv. com. Fed. Register, 1968-79; chmn. Nat. Hist. Publs. and Records Commn., 1968-79; mem. Fed. Council on Arts and Humanities, 1970-79; pres. Rhoads Assos. Internat., 1980-84; dir. grad. program in archives and records mgmt. Western Wash. U., Bellingham, 1984-94, prof. history, 1987—, dir. Ctr. for Pacific N.W. studies, 1994—; prof. emeritus, 1994—. Trustee Woodrow Wilson Internat. Center for Scholars, 1969-79; v.p. Intergovtl. Coun. UNESCO Info. Program, 1977-79; mem. adv. bd. Wash. State Hist. Records, 1990—. Recipient Meritorious and Disting. Service awards GSA, 1966, 68, 79. Fellow Soc. Am. Archivists (pres. 1974-75); mem. Internat. Coun. Archives (pres. 1976-79), Am. Antiquarian Soc., Am. Coun. Learned Socs. (com. Soviet-Am. archival coop. 1986-91), Mass. Hist. Soc. (corr.), Wash. State Hist. Soc. (trustee 1986-95), Acad. Cert. Archivists (pres. 1992-94). Office: Western Wash U Ctr Pacific NW Studies Bellingham WA 98225

RHOADS, JONATHAN EVANS, surgeon; b. Phila., May 9, 1907; s. Edward G. and Margaret (Ely Paxson) R.; m. Teresa Folin, July 4, 1936 (dec. 1987); children: Margaret Rhoads Kendon, Jonathan Evans Jr., George Grant, Edward Otto Folin, Philip Garrett, Charles James; m. Katharine Evans Goddard, Oct. 13, 1990. BA, Haverford Coll., 1928, DSc (hon.), 1962; MD, Johns Hopkins U., 1932; D. Med. Sci., U. Pa., 1940, LLD (hon.), 1960; DSc (hon.), Swarthmore Coll., 1969, Hahnemann Med. Coll., 1978, Duke U., 1979, Med. Coll. Ohio, 1985; DSc (Med.) (hon.), Med. Coll. Pa., 1974, Georgetown U., 1981, Yale U., 1990; LittD (hon.), Thomas Jefferson U., 1979. Intern Hosp. of U. Pa., 1932-34, fellow, instr. surgery, 1934-39; asso. surgery, surg. research U. Pa. Med. Sch., Grad. Sch. Medicine, 1939-47, asst. prof. surg. research, 1944-47, asst. prof. surgery, 1946-47, assoc. prof., 1947-49; J. William White prof. surg. research U. Pa., 1949-51; prof. surgery Grad. Sch. Medicine, U. Pa., 1950—; prof. surgery and surg. research U. Pa. Sch. Med., 1951-57, prof. surgery, 1957-59; provost U. Pa., 1956-59, provost emeritus, 1977—, John Rhea Barton prof. surgery, chmn. dept. surgery, 1959-72, prof. surgery, 1972—, asst. dir. Harrison dept. surg. research, 1946-59, dir., 1959-72; chief surgery Hosp. U. Pa., 1959-72, chmn. med. bd., 1959-61; dir. surgery Pa. Hosp., 1972-74; surg. cons. Pa. Hosp., Germantown (Pa.); mem. staff Hosp. of U. Pa.; mem. bd. pub. edn., City of Phila., 1965-69; co-chmn. Phila. Mayor's Commn. on Health Aspects of Trash to Steam Plant, 1986, chief justice Pa. Com. on Phila. Traffic Ct.; former mem. bd. mgrs. Haverford Coll., chmn., 1963-72, pres. corp., 1963-78, emeritus bd. mgrs. 1989—; bd. mgrs. Friends Hosp. of Phila.; trustee Coriell Inst. Med. Rsch., 1957-90, v.p. sci. affairs, 1964-76, life trustee, 1990—; trustee GM Cancer Rsch. Found.; chmn. bd. trustees Measey Found.; trustee emeritus Bryn Mawr Coll.; mem. com. in charge Westtown Sch., 1962-94; treas. Germantown Friends Sch.; cons. Bur. State Services, VA, 1963; cons. to divsn. med. scis. NIH, 1962-63; nat. adv. gen. medical scis. council USPHS, 1963; adv. council Life Ins. Med. Research Fund., 1961-66; Pres. Phila. div., 1955-56; chmn. adv. commn. on research on pathogenesis of cancer Am. Cancer Soc., 1956-57, del., 1956-61, dir. at large, 1965—, pres., 1969-70, past officer dir., 1970-77, hon. life mem., 1977—; chmn. surgery adv. com. Food and Drug Adminstrn., 1972-74; chmn. Nat. Cancer Adv. Bd., 1972-79; Mem. Am. Bd. Surgery, 1963-69, sr. mem., 1969—. Author, co-editor: Surgery: Principles and Practice, 1957, 61, 65, 70; author: (with J.M. Howard) The Chemistry of Trauma; mem. editl. bd. Jour. Surg. Rsch., 1960-71, Oncology Times, 1979—; co-editor: Accomplishments in Cancer research, 1979-94; editor Jour. Cancer, 1972-91, editor emeritus, 1991—; editl. bd. Annals of Surgery, 1947-77, emeritus, 1977-95, sr. 1995—, chmn. 1971-73; editl. adv. bd. Guthrie Bull., 1986—; contbr. articles to med. jours., chpts. to books. Trustee John Rhea Barton Surg. Found. Recipient Roswell Park medal, 1973, Papanicolaou award, 1977, Phila. award, 1976, Swanberg award, 1987, Benjamin Franklin medal Am. Philos. Soc., Medal of the Surgeon Gen. of U.S., Disting. Alumnus award U. Pa., 1993, Russell W. Richie award Friends Hosp. Phila., 1994, Presdl. award Nat. Assn. Psychiat. Health Systems, 1994; hon. Benjamin Franklin fellow Royal Soc. Arts; Patient Care Pavilion at Hosp. U. Pa. named in honor of Jonathan Evans Rhoads, 1994. Fellow Am. Med. Writers Assn., Am. Philos. Soc. (sec. 1963-66, pres. 1977-84), ACS (regent, chmn. bd. regents 1967-69, pres. 1971-72), Royal Coll. Surgeons (Eng.) (hon.), Royal Coll. Surgeons Edinburgh (hon.), Deutsches Gesellschaft für Chirurgie (corr.), Assn. Surgeons India (hon.), Royal Coll. Physicians and Surgeons Can. (hon.), Coll. Medicine South Africa (hon.), Polish Assn. Surgeons (hon.), Royal Coll. Surgeons in Ireland (hon.), AAAS (sec. med. sci. sect. 1980-86); mem. Hollands Maatschappij der Wetenschappen (fgn.), Am. Public Health Assn., Assn. Am. Med. Colls. (chmn. council acad. socs. 1968-69, disting. service mem. 1974—), Fedn. Am. Socs. Exptl. Biology, Am. Assn. Surgery Trauma (Fitts lectr., 1995), Am. Soc. Clin. Nutrition, Am. Trauma Soc. (founding mem., chmn. bd. dirs. 1986-94), AMA (co-recipient Goldberger award 1970, Dr. Rodman and Thomas G. Sheen award 1980), Pa. Med. Soc. (mem. jud. coun. 1991-94, vice chmn. 1994-96, chmn. 1996—, Disting. Svc. award 1975), Phila. County Med. Soc. (pres. 1970, Strittmater award 1968), Coll. Physicians Phila. (v.p. 1954-57, pres. 1958-60, Disting. Svc. award 1987), Phila. Acad. Surgery (pres. 1964-66), Phila. Physiol. Soc. (v.p. 1945-46), Am. Surg. Assn. (pres. 1972-73, Disting. Service medal, trustee found., vice chmn. 1992-94), Pan Pacific Surg. Assn. (v.p. 1975-77), So. Surg. Assn., The Internat. Surg. Group (pres. 1958), Internat. Fedn. Surg. Colls. (v.p. 1972-78, pres. 1978-81, hon. pres. 1987—), Fellows of Am. Studies, Soc. of U. Surgeons, Soc. Clin. Surgery (pres. 1966-68), Am. Assn. for Cancer Research, Am. Chem. Soc., Am. Physiol. Soc., Coun. Biology Editors, Internat. Soc. Surgery (hon.) N.Y. Acad. Scis., Surg. Infection Soc. (pres. 1984-85), Surgeons Travel Club (pres. 1976, hon. mem.), Am. Inst. Nutrition, World Med. Assn., Am. Acad. Arts and Scis., Inst. of Medicine (sr.), Soc. for Surgery Alimentary Tract (pres. 1967-68), Southeastern Surg. Congress, Soc. Surg. Chmn. (pres. 1966-68), Buckingham Mountain Found. (sec., treas., pres., 1996—), James IV Soc. (hon.), Phi Beta Kappa, Alpha Omega Alpha, Sigma Xi. Clubs: Rittenhouse, Union League, Philadelphia; Cosmos (D.C.). Achievements include demonstration that protein malnutrition could retard callus formation in experimental fractures and that positive nitrogen balance could be induced in protein deficient patients who could not take things by mouth. Office: 3400 Spruce St Philadelphia PA 19104

RHOADS, NANCY GLENN, lawyer; b. Washington, Oct. 15, 1957; d. Donald L. and Gerry R. R.; m. Robert A. Koons, June 23, 1984. BA, Gettysburg Coll., 1980; JD, Temple U., 1983. Bar: Pa., U.S. Dist. Ct. (ea. dist.) Pa. 1983. Rsch. asst. Prof. Mikochick, Phila., 1982-83; law clk. Phila. Ct. of Common Pleas, 1983-85; assoc. Post and Schell P.C., Phila., 1985-90, Sheller, Ludwig and Badey, Phila., 1990—. Co-author: Aging and the Aged: Problems, Opportunities, Challenges, 1980. Vol. Spl. Olympics. Mem. Phila. Bar Assn. (med. legal com.), Phi Beta Kappa, Phi Alpha Theta, Pi Delta Epsilon, Eta Sigma Phi. Avocations: classical piano, horticulture, swimming. Home: Gwynedd Knoll 1374 Tanglewood Dr North Wales PA 19454-3671 Office: Sheller Ludwig and Badey 1528 Walnut St Third Fl Philadelphia PA 19102-3604

RHOADS, PATRICIA MARY (GRUENEWALD), securities consultant; b. St. Louis, Mar. 17, 1953; m. Harvey D. Rhoads; children: Kevin G. Gruenewald, Grant A. BSBA, U. Mo., St. Louis, 1975; MA in Computer Data Mgmt., Webster U., 1985. Mgr. estates and legal securities Edward D. Jones & Co., St. Louis, 1978-80, mgr. money market fund processing, 1980-84, mgr. mut. fund processing, 1983-84, mgr., gen. prin. funds processing and daily passport cash trust, 1984-88, mgr. trade processing, 1989-93; ind. contractor Bridgeton, Mo., 1994—; mem. broker/dealer adv. com. Investment Co. Inst., Washington, 1987-88; mem. retail adv. bd. Chgo. Stock Exch., 1990-93; ind. contractor Coopers and Lybrand Internat., Rep. of Latvia, 1994. Bd. dirs. CORO, St. Louis, 1990-91; mem. day care svcs. panel United Way, 1990-94, mem. admissions com., 1993—; candidate for Bridgeton City Coun., 1995. Mem. NAFE, Bus. and Profl. Women of Troy.

RHOADS, PAUL KELLY, lawyer; b. La Grange, Ill., Sept. 4, 1940; s. Herbert Graves and Mary Margaret (Gurrie) R.; m. Katheryn Virginia Reissaus, Sept. 14, 1963; children: Elizabeth R. Saline, Katheryn R. Meek, Julia S. BA, Washington & Lee U., 1962; JD, Loyola U., Chgo., 1967. Bar: Ill. 1967, U.S. Dist. Ct. (no. dist.) Ill. 1967, U.S. Tax Ct. 1980. Trust officer 1st Nat. Bank Chgo., 1963-69; with Schiff Hardin & Waite, Chgo., 1969—, ptnr., 1973—; bd. dirs. McKay Enterprises, Chgo., Haymarsh Corp., Glen Ellyn, Ill., Philanthrophy Roundtable, Indpls. Author: Starting a Private Foundation, 1993; contbr. articles to profl. jours. and chpts. to books. Trustee Ill. Inst. Tech., 1985-95, Western Springs (Ill.) Hist. Soc., 1983-92; bd. dirs. Cyrus Tang Scholarship Found., 1984-91; bd. overseers Ill. Inst. Tech. Chgo.-Kent Coll. Law, 1985-95; pres., bd. dirs. Grover Hermann Found., Chgo., 1984—; sec., bd. dirs. Western Springs Svc. Club, 1976-86; sec. Vandivort Properties, Inc., Cape Girardeau, Mo.; mem. adv. com. estate, tax and fin. planning Loyola U., 1986-92; adv. com. Thomas A. Roe Inst. for Econ. Policy Studies, Heritage Found., 1989—. Mem. Ill. State Bar Assn., Chgo. Bar Assn., Union League, Salt Creek Club (Hinsdale, Ill.) (pres. 1982, bd. dirs. 1981-83), Portage Lake Yacht Club (Onekama, Mich.) (commodore 1988, bd. dirs. 1985-89), Manistee (Mich.) Golf and Country Club. Republican. Avocations: sailing, golf, tennis. Office: Schiff Hardin & Waite 233 S Wacker Dr Chicago IL 60606-6306

RHOADS, STEVEN ERIC, political science educator; b. Abington, Pa., May 12, 1939; s. John Reginald and Barbara Ann (Dugan) R.; m. Diana Cabanis Akers, May 17, 1944; children—Christopher, Nicholas, John. B.A., Princeton U., 1961; M.P.A., Cornell U., 1965, Ph.D., 1972. Mem. staff Office Mgmt. and Budget, Washington, 1965-66; asst. prof. dept. govt. and fgn. affairs U. Va., Charlottesville, 1970-76, assoc. prof., 1977-86, prof. 1986—. Served to lt. (j.g.) USN, 1961-63. Fellow NEH, Inst. Ednl. Affairs, Earhart Found., Bradley Found., Olin Found. Mem. Am. Polit. Sci. Assn., Assn. Pub. Policy and Mgmt. Author: Policy Analysis in the Federal Aviation Administration, 1974; Valuing Life: Public Policy Dilemmas, 1980; The Economist's View of the World: Government, Markets and Public Policy, 1985, Incomparable Worth: Pay Equity Meets the Market, 1993; contbr. articles to profl. publs. Home: 3190 Dundee Rd Earlysville VA 22936-9621 Office: U Va Dept Govt and Fgn Affairs Cabell Hall 232 Charlottesville VA 22903

RHODE, ALFRED SHIMON, business consultant, educator; b. Vienna, Austria, July 31, 1928; s. Aron and Olga (Schwarz) Rothkirch; came to U.S., 1940, naturalized, 1949; m. Phyllis Mazur, Dec. 28, 1959; children: Yael, Tamar, Yvette, Liane. BCE, CUNY, 1950; MEA, George Washington U., 1959; PhD, Am. U., 1973. Engr., Bur. of Reclamation, Sacramento, 1950-52; various engring. positions U.S. Govt., 1954-63; head logistics rsch. Navy Supply Systems Command, Washington, 1963-68; head support forces, manpower and logistics br. Navy Program Planning Office, Washington, 1968-75; sr. v.p. nat. security analysis and warfare support group Info. Spectrum, Inc., Arlington, Va., 1976-89, cons., 1989-92; professorial lectr. George Washington U., Washington, 1969-75; adj. faculty Sch. Bus. Adminstrn. George Mason U., Fairfax, Va., 1990—; pretrial screener Office State's Atty., Montgomery County, Md. Contbr. articles to profl. jours. Served to capt. USAF, 1952-54. Congl. fellow, 1962. Registered profl. engr., Md. Fellow Mil. Ops. Rsch. Soc. (1st v.p., dir.); mem. Inst. Ops. Rsch. and Mgmt. Scis. (chmn. mil. applications sect.), Washington Ops. Rsch. Sci. Coun., Internat. Inst. Strategic Studies. Home: 8305 Fox Run Potomac MD 20854-2576

RHODE, DEBORAH LYNN, law educator; b. Jan. 29, 1952. BA, Yale U., 1974, JD, 1977. Bar: D.C. 1977, Calif. 1981. Law clk. to judge U.S. Ct. Appeals (2d cir.), N.Y.C., 1977-78; law clk. to Hon. Justice Thurgood Marshall U.S. Supreme Ct., D.C., 1978-79; asst. prof. law Stanford (Calif.) U., 1979-82, assoc. prof., 1982-85, prof., 1985—; dir. Inst. for Rsch. on Women and Gender, 1986-90, Keck Ctr. of Legal Ethics and The Legal Profession, 1994—; trustee Yale U., 1983-89; chmn. profl. responsibility sect. Am. Assn. Law Schs., co-chmn. ABA com. profl. responsibility. Author several books; contbr. articles to profl. jours. Office: Stanford U Law Sch Crain Quadrangle Stanford CA 94305

RHODE, EDWARD ALBERT, veterinary medicine educator, veterinary cardiologist; b. Amsterdam, N.Y., July 25, 1926; s. Edward A. and Katherine (Webb) R.; m. Dolores Bangert, 1955; children: David E., Peter R., Paul W., Robert M., Catherine E. DVM, Cornell U., 1947. Diplomate Am. Coll. Veterinary Internal Medicine. Prof. emeritus vet. medicine U. Calif., Davis, 1964—, chmn. dept. vet. medicine, 1968-71, assoc. dean instrn. Sch. Vet. Medicine, 1971-77, 78-81, dean sch. Vet. Medicine, 1982-91. Mem. AAAS, Nat. Acad. Practices, Am. Coll. Vet. Internal Medicine, Am. Vet. Medicine Assn., Basic Sci. Coun., Am. Heart Assn., Am. Acad. Vet. Cardiology, Am. Physiol. Soc., Calif. Vet. Medicine Assn. Office: U Calif Sch Vet Medicine Davis CA 95616

RHODEN, MARY NORRIS, educational center director; b. Greenville, S.C., Jan. 3, 1943; d. Tony and Carrie Thelma (Reuben) Norris; 1 adopted child, Scottie Brooks-Rhoden. BS in Biology, Allen U., Columbia, S.C., 1966; postgrad., Atlanta U., 1967-68. Dir., tchr. MSR Learning Ctr., Riverdale, Ga., 1989—. Author poetry. Vol. Buffalo Soldiers Monument Commn., Ft. Leavenworth, Kans., 1991—; developed letters for nat. campaign to petition Congress, Postmaster Gen. to issue Buffalo Soldiers Stamp. Recipient Cert. Appreciation NAACP, Greenville, S.C., 1979, Wheat St. Bapt. Ch., Atlanta, 1989. Mem. Alpha Kappa Alpha, Alpha Kappa Delta. Democrat. African Meth. Episcopal Ch. Avocations: jogging, writing, swimming, skating, skiing. Office: MSR Learning Ctr 7037 Shangrila Trl Riverdale GA 30296-2138

RHODEN, WILLIAM GARY, lawyer; b. Aiken, S.C., June 20, 1955; s. Thomas Gary and Catherine (Moseley) R.; m. Paula Jean Henderson, Aug. 8, 1981. BS in Psychology, U. S.C., Aiken, 1977; JD, U. S.C., 1980. Bar: S.C. 1981, U.S. Dist. Ct. S.C. 1982, U.S. Ct. Appeals (4th cir.) 1985. Lab. asst. psychology dept. U. S.C., Aiken, 1975-77; asst. dir. Greer (S.C.) YMCA, 1977-78; law clk. U.S. Atty. Office, Greer, 1977-78; intern U.S. Justice Dept., Columbia, S.C., 1980-81; staff atty. Office of Atty. Gen. State of S.C., Florence, 1981; asst. atty. gen. Office of Atty. Gen. State of S.C., Charleston, S.C., 1981-83; asst. solicitor 7th Jud. Cir., Spartanburg, S.C., 1984-86; pvt. practice Gaffney, S.C., 1986—. Bd. dirs. Cherokee Children's Home, S.C. Peach Festival. Mem. ABA, Cherokee County Bar Assn. (sec.-treas. 1988-96, pres. 1996—), Rotary (Paul Harris fellow), Phi Alpha Delta. Avocations: tennis, golf, racquetball. Home: 119 College Dr Gaffney SC 29340-3002 Office: 221 E Floyd Baker Blvd PO Box 1937 Gaffney SC 29342

RHODES, ALFRED WILLIAM, former insurance company executive; b. Manchester, Eng., Dec. 20, 1922; came to U.S., 1930, naturalized, 1943; s. William Henry and Agnes Anna (King) R.; m. Joan Helen LaVine, Oct. 12, 1947; children: Alfred William, Ellen Jeanne, Thomas John, Phyllis Irene, Kenneth James. BS, Hofstra U., 1947; AMP, Harvard U., 1967. With John Hancock Mut. Life Ins. Co., Boston, 1942-85; regional supr. John Hancock Mut. Life Ins. Co., 1953-54, field v.p., 1954-69, 2d v.p., 1969-71, v.p., 1971-74, sr. v.p., 1974-85; ret., 1985. Past pres. Needham (Mass.) Youth Soccer Program; host family Mass. chpt. Am. Field Service, 1971-72, pres., 1972-75; mem. Town of Needham Finance Com., 1973-80. Served with AUS, 1943-46. Decorated Bronze Star. Mem. AARP (instr. and counselor tax counseling for the elderly), Nat. Assn. Life Underwriters, Gen. Agts. and Mgrs. Conf., Life Underwriter Tng. Coun. (past trustee), Life Ins. Mktg. and Rsch. Assn. (past bd. dirs.), CLUs, Club Med, Sandpiper Golf Club. Episcopalian. Home: 1761 SE Adair Rd Port Saint Lucie FL 34952-5739

RHODES, ANN L(OUISE), theatrical producer, invester; b. Ft. Worth, Oct. 17, 1941; d. Jon Knox and Carol Jane (Greene) R.; student Tex. Christian U., 1960-63. V.p. Rhodes Enterprises Inc., Ft. Worth, 1963-77; owner-mgr. Lucky R Ranch, Ft. Worth, 1969—, Ann L. Rhodes Investments, Ft. Worth, 1976—; pres., chmn. bd. ALR Enterprises, Inc., Ft. Worth, 1977-93; pres. ALR Prodns., Inc., 1993—. Bd. dirs. Tarrant Coun. Alcoholism, 1973-78, hon. bd. dirs., 1978—; bd. dirs. N.W. Tex. coun. Arthritis Found., 1977-84; adv. bd. Stage West, 1987—, Hip Pocket Theatre, 1994—; bd. dirs. Circle Theater, 1987-94, Arts Coun. of Ft. Worth and Tarrant County, 1991-94; bd. govs. Ft. Worth Theatre, 1989—; mem. pro-arts bd. TCU Coll. Fine Arts & Communications, 1994; exec. com. Tarrant County Rep. Party, 1964-69; bd. dirs. Live Theatre League Tarrant County, 1993—. Recipient various svc. awards, including Patron of Yr. award Live Theatre League Tarrant County, 1992-93. Mem. Jr. League Ft. Worth, Addison and Randolph Clark Soc. Tex. Christian U., Alpha Psi Omega, Kappa Kappa Gamma. Episcopalian. Office: Ste 908 Ridglea Bank Bldg Fort Worth TX 76116

RHODES, CHARLES HARKER, JR., lawyer; b. Chgo., May 24, 1930; s. Charles Harker and Claire (Hepner) R.; m. Mae Ellen Svoboda, Apr. 19, 1952; children: Charles Harker, James Albert, Edward Joseph. BA, U. Chgo., 1948, JD, 1951. Bar: Ill. 1951. Assoc. Schatz & Busch, Chgo., 1951-53; assoc. Sonnenschein Nath & Rosenthal, Chgo., 1953-60, ptnr., 1961—; dir. Ill. Inst. for Continuing Legal Edn., Springfield, 1977-84, 86-88; pres. Ill. Bar Automated Rsch., 1975-85. Trustee Nat. Ctr. for Automated Info. Rsch., N.Y.C., 1976-94; pres. B.R. Ryall YMCA, Glen Ellyn, Ill., 1967. Fellow Am. Bar Found. (devel. com. 1988—), Chgo. Bar Found. (pres. 1977-80), Ill. Bar Found. (fellows chmn. 1990-91); mem. ABA (mem. tort and ins. practice sect., long range planning com. 1991-92, mem. pub. editorial bd. com. 1993—), Ill. State Bar Assn. (bd. govs. 1975-79, chmn. liaison com. Atty. Registration and Disciplinary Commn. 1992-93), Chgo. Bar Assn. (libr., bd. mgrs. 1969-72), Am. Arbitration Assn. (arbitrator), Nat. Conf. Bar Founds. (trustee, pres. 1987-88), Met. Club Chgo. Republican. Presbyterian. Avocations: world travel, photography. Home: 267 N Montclair Ave Glen Ellyn IL 60137-5508 Office: Sonnenschein Nath & Rosenthal 233 S Wacker Dr Ste 8000 Chicago IL 60606-6404

RHODES, CHARLES KIRKHAM, physicist, educator; b. Mineola, N.Y., June 30, 1939; s. Walter Cortlyn and Evelyn (Kirkham) R.; m. Mary M. Cannon, Oct. 23, 1976; children: Lisa, Gregory, Edward, Elizabeth. B.E.E., Cornell U., 1963; M.E.E., M.I.T., 1965, Ph.D. in Physics, 1969. Research asst. Chalmers U., Gothenburg, Sweden, 1963; research asso. radiation lab. Columbia U., 1969; staff specialist Control Data Corp., Melville, N.Y., 1969-70; physicist Lawrence Livermore Lab./U.Calif., 1970-75; lectr. dept. applied sci. U. Calif., Davis, 1971-75; program mgr. Molecular Physics Center, Stanford Research Inst. and cons. prof. dept. elec. engring. Stanford U., 1975-78; prof. physics U. Ill.-Chgo., 1978-82, research prof. physics, 1982—; cons. atomic and molecular physics, laser research. Editor: Excimer Lasers, 1979, 2d edit., 1984. NSF fellow, 1963-68. Fellow Am. Phys. Soc., Optical Soc. Am.; mem. Joint Council on Quantum Electronics, IEEE (sr.; editor spl. issue 1979), European Phys. Soc., Sigma Xi, Phi Kappa Phi, Tau Beta Pi, Eta Kappa Nu. Home: 237 E Delaware Pl Apt 10A Chicago IL 60611-1713 Office: Univ Ill at Chgo Dept Physics Mail Code 273 845 W Taylor St Chicago IL 60607-7059

RHODES, DONALD ROBERT, musicologist, retired electrical engineer; b. Detroit, Dec. 31, 1923; s. Donald Eber and Edna Mae (Fulmer) R.; children: Joyce R. Bridges, Jane E., Roger C., Diane R. Herran. BEE, Ohio State U., 1945, MEE, 1948, PhD, 1953. Research assoc. Ohio State U., Columbus, 1945-54; research engr. Cornell Aero. Lab., Buffalo, 1954-57; head basic research dept. Radiation, Inc., Orlando, Fla., 1957-61; sr. scientist Radiation, Inc., Melbourne, Fla., 1961-66; Univ. prof. N.C. State U., Raleigh, 1966-94, univ. prof. emeritus, 1994—. Author: Introduction to Monopulse, 1959, 2d edit., 1980, Synthesis of Planar Antenna Sources, 1974, A Reactance Theorem, 1977. Co-founder Central Fla. Community Orch., Winter Park, 1961, pres., 1961-62. Recipient Benjamin G. Lamme medal Ohio State U., 1975; Eminent Engr. award Tau Beta Pi, 1976; named to N.C. State U. Acad. Outstanding Tchrs., 1980. Fellow AAAS, IEEE (John T. Bolljahn award 1963, pres. Antennas and Propagation Soc. 1969); mem. Am. Musicological Soc. Home: 625 Cardinal Gibbons Dr Apt 101 Raleigh NC 27606-3255 Office: PO Box 7911 Raleigh NC 27695

RHODES, FRANK HAROLD TREVOR, university president emeritus, geologist; b. Warwickshire, Eng., Oct 29, 1926; came to U.S. 1968, naturalized 1976; s. Harold Cecil and Gladys (Ford) R.; m. Rosa Carlson, Aug. 16, 1952; children: Jennifer, Catherine, Penelope, Deborah. BSc, U. Birmingham, 1948, PhD, 1950, DSc (hon.), 1963; LLD (hon.), Wooster Coll., 1976, Nazareth Coll. Rochester, 1979, Skidmore Coll., 1989, U. Mich., 1990, Clemson U., 1991, Dartmouth Coll., 1993; LHD (hon.), Colgate U., 1980, Johns Hopkins U., 1982, Wagner Coll., 1982, Hope Coll., 1982, Rensselaer Poly. Inst., 1982, LeMoyne Coll., 1984, Pace U., 1986, Alaska Pacific U., 1987, Hamilton Coll., 1987, SUNY, 1992, Canisius Coll., 1994, Ithaca Coll, 1995; DSc (hon.), U. Wales, Eng., 1981, Bucknell U., 1985, U. Ill., 1986, Reed Coll., 1988, Elmira Coll., 1989, U. Southampton, 1989, U. Sydney (Aus.), 1995, U. Durham (Eng.), 1995, Millsaps Coll., 1996; DLitt (hon.), U. Nev., 1982; EdD (hon.), Ohio State U., 1992; D. Univ. (hon.), U. Stirling (Eng.), 1994. Post-doctoral fellow, Fulbright scholar U. Ill., 1950-51, vis. lectr. geology, summers 1951, 52; lectr. geology U. Durham, 1951-54; asst. prof. U. Ill., 1954-55, assoc. prof., 1955-56; dir. U. Ill. field sta., Wyo., 1956; prof. geology, head geology dept. U. Wales, Swansea, 1956-68, dean faculty of sci., 1967-68; prof. geology and mineralogy Coll. Lit., Sci. and Arts, U. Mich., 1968-77, dean, 1971-74, v.p. for acad. affairs, 1974-77; pres., prof. geology Cornell U., Ithaca, N.Y., 1977-95; Gurley lectr. Cornell U., 1960; Bownocker lectr. Ohio State U., 1966; Case lectr. U. Mich., 1976; dir. NSF, Am. Geol. Inst., Summer Field Inst., 1963; Australian vice-chancellors' visitor to Australian univs., 1964; vis. fellow Clare Hall, Cambridge, summer 1982; Bye fellow Robinson Coll., Cambridge, summers 1986, 87; Am. Fulbright Disting. fellow, Kuwait, 1987; scholar in residence, Bellagio study and conf. ctr., 1995. Author: The Evolution of Life, 1962, 2d edit., 1976, Fossils, 1963, Geology, 1972, Evolution, 1974, Language of the Earth, 1981; author numerous articles and monographs on sci. and edn. Trustee Carnegie Found. for Advancement Teaching, 1978-86, vice chmn., 1983-85, chmn. 1985-86; trustee The Freedom Forum, 1983-93; trustee Com. for Econ. Devel., 1984-93; bd. trustees Andrew W. Mellon Found., 1984—; bd. dirs. KMI Continental, Inc., 1979-86, Tompkins County Trust Co., 1984—, Gen. Electric Co., 1984—, NBC, 1986—, Am. Council on Edn., 1983-88, vice chair, 1985-86, chair, 1986-88, H. John Heinz III Ctr. for Sci., Econs., and the Environ., 1996—, v.p. Dyson Charitable Trust, 1996—; bd. overseers Meml. Sloan Kettering Cancer Ctr., 1979-91; chmn. adv. bd. Freedom Forum Media Studies Ctr., 1984-93; mem. Nat. Sci. Bd., 1987—, chair, 1994-96, Internat. Exec. Svce. Corps. Council, 1984-95; v.p. Dyson Charitable Trust, 1996—. Recipient Clark Kerr medal U. Calif., Berkeley, 1995; NSF sr. vis. rsch. fellow, 1965-66. Fellow Geol. Soc. London (council 1963-66, Bigsby medal 1967); mem. Palaeontol. Assn. (v.p. 1963-68), Brit. Assn. Advancement Sci., Geol. Soc. Am., Am. Assn. Petroleum Geologists, Soc. Econ. Paleontologists and Mineralogists, Phi Betta Kappa (hon.). Office: Cornell U Office of Pres Emeritus 3104 Snee Hall Ithaca NY 14853

RHODES, GARY LYNN, food company executive; b. Kalamazoo, July 1, 1941; s. Jay Richard and Vivian Mabel (Stevens) R.; m. Lova Lydia Kuhlmann, May 9, 1964; children: Todd Alan, Eric Richard. BSME, Purdue U., 1964. Plant supt. Gen. Foods Corp., Houston, 1967-74, mgr. engring., 1974-76; mgr. engring. Borden Foods, Plymouth, Wis., 1976-77, plant mgr., 1977-79; v.p. ops. Fisher Cheese Co., Wapakoneta, Ohio, 1979-83, pres., 1983-87; pres., chief exec. officer Maplehurst, Inc., Indpls., 1987-92; CEO Sodiaal North Am. Corp., Harleysville, Pa., 1992—. Republican. Methodist. Lodge: Masons. Avocation: flying. Office: Sodiaal N Am Corp 832 Harleyville Pike Harleysville PA 19438

RHODES, GERALDINE BRYAN, secondary school administrator; b. Asheville, N.C., Dec. 7, 1941; d. Robert Gerald and Myrtle (Bartlett) B.; m. Gayle Dean Rhodes, May 27, 1967; children: Jennifer Ellen, Leah Rebecca. BM, So. Meth. U., 1967; MA, Columbia U., 1987, MEd, 1988, postgrad., 1988—. Permanent tchr. cert., N.Y. Music tchr. Dallas Ind. Sch. Dist., 1967-69, Yamaha Music Sch., Poughkeepsie, N.Y., 1971-75, Hudson Valley Philharmonic Music Sch., Poughkeepsie, 1986-88; music tchr. Poughkeepsie Day Sch., 1987-90, dir. music edn., 1990-92; tchr. fine arts Ctrl. Tex. Coll., Youngsan U.S. Army Base, Seoul, 1992-94; music tchr. Arlington Ctrl Schs, Poughkeepsie, NY, 95—; tchr., cons. Dutchess Arts Camp, Poughkeepsie, 1986-92, Hollingworth Pre-sch., Columbia U., N.Y.C., 1987-88; tchr., dir. Inter-generation Chorus N.Y. State Coun. Arts, Poughkeepsie, 1988-92. Mem. Music Educators Nat. Congress, N.Y. State Sch. Music Assn., Am. Orff Schulwerk Assn. Republican. Episcopalian. Office: Arlington Ctrl Schs 120 Dutchess Turnpike Poughkeepsie NY 12603

RHODES, IDA ELIZABETH, human services professional; b. Ansonia, Conn., May 26, 1942; d. Samuel Lee and Beersheba Queen (London) R. AS in Human Svcs., South Ctrl. C.C., 1977; BS in Human Svcs., N.H. Coll., 1982. Asst. housing dir., counselor Urban League Greater New Haven (Conn.), 1978-83; mental health worker Conn. Mental Health Ctr., New Haven, 1984-86; social worker trainee Bridgeport (Conn.) Community Mental Health, 1986-87; psychiatric social worker asst. Bridgeport (Conn.) Community Mental Health, New Haven, 1987-88, Conn. State Mental HEalth Ctr., New Haven, 1988-89; resident advocate, social worker Conn. AIDS Residence Program, New Haven, 1989-90; social worker NIH AIDS Rsch. Program, Hill Health Ctr., New Haven, 1990; corrections psychiatric treatment worker State of Conn. Dept. Corrections, Bridgeport, 1990—; membership coord. Community Housing Resource Bd., Dept. Housing & Urban Devel. & New Haven Bd. Realtors, 1979-80; asst. coord. N.H. Coll. Student Community Svc. Group, 1980-82. Author of poems. Mem. East Coast Affirmative Action Com., 1978-79; v.p. Urban League Guild-Urban League Greater New Haven, Inc., 1979-83; mem. Mayor's Task Force on AIDS, New Haven, 1989-90; sec., bd. dirs. Afro-Am. Hist. Soc., New Haven, 1979; nominated honoree Women in Leadership-YWCA, New Haven, 1983. Avocations: writing poetry, reading, singing, ch. and community activities. Address: PO Box 7733 New Haven CT 06519-0733

RHODES, JAMES T., electric power industry executive; b. 1941. BS, N.C. State U., 1963; MS, Cath. U., 1968; PhD, Purdue U., 1972. Nuclear physicist Va. Electric & Power Co., 1971-72, supr. nuclear fuel, 1972-75, dir. nuclear fuel, 1975-78, dist. mgr., 1978-80, mgr. nuclear tech. svcs., 1980-81, v.p. adminstrv. svcs., 1981-84, v.p. pers. then sr. v.p. fin., 1984-89, pres., CEO, 1989—. Office: Va Electric & Power Co PO Box 26666 Richmond VA 23261*

RHODES, JOHN BOWER, management consultant; b. Pitts., July 8, 1925; s. John Bower and Mary Lucile (Lewis) R.; m. Joan Ann Black, June 11, 1955; children: John Bower, III, Mark Lewis, Lydia Black. B.S. in Mech. Engring, Princeton U., 1946; postgrad., N.Y. U. Law Sch., 1953-55. With internat. ops. California Texas Oil Co., N.Y.C., 1946-59; mgr. ops. in California Texas Oil Co., Arabia, 1947-50, Calif. Tex. Oil Co., India, 1955-59; mng. officer Europe Booz, Allen & Hamilton Internat. NV, Zurich, Switzerland, 1959-63, Dusseldorf, Fed. Republic of Germany, 1963-68; v.p. internat. affairs Booz, Allen & Hamilton Inc., N.Y.C., 1968-70, vice chmn., 1970-90, of counsel, 1990—. Mgr. N.Y. Inst. for Edn. of Blind, 1976—. Served with USMC, 1943-45, 51-52. Mem. Internat. C. of C. (U.S. council), Council Fgn. Relations, Orgn. Econ. Coop. and Devel. Clubs: Princeton, N.Y. Yacht, Colonial, Nantucket (Mass.) Yacht. Office: Booz Allen Hamilton Inc 101 Park Ave New York NY 10178

RHODES, JOHN JACOB, lawyer, former congressman; b. Council Grove, Kans., Sept. 18, 1916; s. John Jacob and Gladys Anne (Thomas) R.; m. Mary Elizabeth Harvey, May 24, 1942; children: John Jacob 3d, Thomas H., Elizabeth C. Rhodes Reich, James Scott. BS, Kans. State U., 1938; LLB, Harvard U., 1942. Bar: Kans. 1942, Ariz. 1945, D.C. 1965. Mem. 83d-97th congresses from 1st Dist. Ariz., chmn. Republican policy com. 89th-93d congresses, house minority leader, 1973-81; of counsel Hunton & Williams, Washington; mem. bd. overseers Hoover Instn., 1984-92; chmn. platform com. Nat. Rep. Conv., 1972, permanent chmn., 1976, 80. Mem. Ariz. Bd. Pub. Welfare, 1951-52. Served with AUS, World War II; Col., ret. Mem. Mesa C. of C. (pres. 1950), SAR, Am. Legion, Ariz. Club, Mesa Golf and Country Club, Capitol Hill Club, Met. Club, Burning Tree Club (Bethesda, Md.), Pinetop Country Club, Masons (33 deg., Grand Cross), KP, Elks, Moose, Rotary, Beta Theta Pi (internat. pres. 1984-87). Republican. Methodist. Office: Hunton & Williams 2000 Pennsylvania Ave NW Washington DC 20006-1812

RHODES, LAWRENCE, artistic director; b. Mt. Hope, W.Va., Nov. 24, 1939. Studied with Violette Armand. Joined Ballet Russe de Monte Carlo, 1958-60; from dancer to prin. dancer Joffrey Ballet, N.Y.C., 1960-64; prin. dancer Harkness Ballet, 1964-68, dir., prin. dancer, 1968-70; tchr. dance dept. NYU, 1978—, prin. ballet tchr., 1981—, chmn. dance dept., 1981-91; prin. dancer, ballet master, choreographer, tchr., artistic dir. Les Grands Ballets Canadiens, Montreal, 1989—; guest artist Het Nationale Ballet, Amsterdam, 1970-71, Pa. Ballet, 1971-76, Feld Ballet, N.Y.C., 1973-75. Danced with Makarova, Hayden and Fracci; danced for Butler, Joffrey, Ailey, Lubovitch, Harkarvy, Nault, Van Dantzig and Mac Donald; featured dancer in film A Dancer's Vocabulary, PBS's Dance Am. series, CBS's Camera Three. Office: Les Grands Ballets Canadiens, 4816, rue Rivard, Montreal, PQ Canada H2J 2N6

RHODES, MARLENE RUTHERFORD, counseling educator, educational consultant; b. St. Louis; d. Odie Douglas and Helen (Ward) Rutherford; m. David L. Rhodes, Nob. 18, 1961; children: Jay David, Michael Stanford, John David, Mark Stanford. BS in Psychology cum laude, Washington U., St. Louis, 1973, MA in Counseling Edn., 1975; postgrad., St. Louis U., 1987—. Registered med. record libr. Caseworker I and II, Mo. Div. Family Svcs., St. Louis, 1961-65, supr. caseworker II's, 1965-70; personal effectiveness trainer women's program U. Mo., St. Louis, 1974-77; assoc. prof. counseling, chair counseling St. Louis C.C. at Forest Park, 1975—, chmn. dept., 1993—, dir. step up coll. program, 1990-93; developer, coord. crisis intervention facilitation tng. St. Louis Pub. Schs., 1987-88; ednl. project cons. Project Achievement, Ralston Purina Co., 1993-94; developer, presenter over 80 ednl. project consultations for area colls., profl. orgns. and bus. groups, 1975—. Author: Crisis Intervention Facilitation Training Manual, 1988. Chmn. Ft. Louis Friends of Arts, 1984—; coord. for coun. of elders for Better Family Life Orgn., 1995—; com. co-chmn. for black dance and unity ball Better Family Inc., St. Louis, 1990—; panelist for counseling support svcs. for families United Way Greater St. Louis, 1993—; mem. fin. com. St. Thomas Archdiocese, 1995—; bd. dirs. Bishop Hearly Cath. Sch. Recipient Disting. Svc. as Am. Educator award Alpha Zeta chpt. Iota Phi Lambda, 1990, role model award St. Louis Pub. Schs., 1993, cert. of achievement Nat. Orgn. for Victim Assistance, 1993. Mem. NEA (co-coord. polit. action com. St. Louis 1985-90, bargaining negotiator 1987—), ACA (nat. chair orgn., adminstrn. and mgmt. com. 1994-95), Assn. Multicultural Counseling and Devel. (nat. pres. 1994-95), Nat. Assn. for Multicultural Counseling and Devel. (rep. for 13 states 1990-92, pres. 1994-95, Exemplary Svc. award 1992, 94), Mo. Assn. Multicultural Counseling and Devel. (chpt. pres. 1977-78). Democrat. Roman Catholic. Avocations: reading, scrabble, chess, African dance, ping pong. Home: 5935 Pershing Ave Saint Louis MO 63112-1513 Office: St Louis CC at Forest Park 5600 Oakland Ave Saint Louis MO 63110-1316

RHODES, MARY, mayor; m. Donald A. Rhodes; children: Bryan, Randy. Grad., Youngstown Hosp. Assn. Mem. council. City of Corpus Christi, Tex., mayor, 1991—. Mem. LWV, Bus. and Profl. Womens Assn. Presbyterian. Office: Office of the Mayor PO Box 9277 1201 Leopard St Corpus Christi TX 78401-2162*

RHODES, PETER EDWARD, label company executive; b. Rochester, N.Y., Sept. 25, 1942; s. Robert A. and Anne (Ward) R.; m. Cassandra Durkee, May 26, 1962 (div. Sept. 1991); children: Tamara, Amy, Brian. B.S., Rochester Inst. Tech., 1964, M.B.A., 1970. With Touche Ross & Co., Rochester, 1962-69; sr. auditor Touche Ross & Co., to 1969; with Xerox Co., Rochester, 1969, Fay's Drug Co., Inc., Liverpool, N.Y., 1970-87; exec. v.p. Fay's Drug Co., Inc., 1974-87, also dir.; exec. v.p. Syracuse Label Co., Inc., Liverpool, 1987—, also bd. dirs.; dir. Byrne Dairy Inc. Mem. N.Y. State Soc. C.P.A.s, Am. Inst. C.P.A.s, Fin. Execs. Inst. Club: Belevue Country.

RHODES, RICHARD LEE, writer; b. Kansas City, Kans., July 4, 1937; s. Arthur and Georgia Saphronia (Collier) R.; m. Linda Iredell Hampton, Aug. 30, 1960 (div. 1974); children: Timothy James, Katherine Hampton; m. Mary Magdalene Evans, Nov. 26, 1976 (div. 1988); m. Ginger Kay Untrif, Oct. 3, 1993. BA cum laude, Yale U., 1959; LHD (hon.), Westminster Coll., Fulton, Mo., 1988. Author: The Inland Ground, 1970, The Last Safari, 1970, The Ungodly, 1973, The Ozarks, 1974, Holy Secrets, 1978, Looking for America, 1979, Sons of the Earth, 1981, The Making of the Atomic Bomb, 1987, Farm, 1989, A Hole in the World, 1990, Making Love, 1992, Nuclear Renewal, 1993, How to Write, 1995, Dark Sun, 1995; contbr. articles to nat. mags. Trustee Andrew Drumm Inst., Independence, Mo., 1991—. Recipient Nat. Book Critics Cir. award for nonfiction, Nat. Book award for nonfiction, 1987, Pulitzer prize, 1988; Guggenheim fellow, 1974-75, fellow Nat. Endowment for Arts, 1978-79, Ford Found., 1981-83, Sloan Found., 1985, 89, 91, 92, MacArthur Found., 1990-91. Office: Janklow & Nesbit Assoc 598 Madison Ave New York NY 10022-1614

RHODES, RONDELL HORACE, biology educator; b. Abbeville, S.C., May 25, 1918; s. Leslie Franklin and Pearl Lee (Clinkscales) R.; B.S., Benedict Coll., Columbia, S.C., 1940; M.S., U. Mich., 1950; Ph.D., N.Y.U., 1960. Instr. biology Lincoln U., Jefferson City, Mo., 1947-49; asst. prof. Tuskegee (Ala.) Inst., 1950-55; teaching fellow N.Y.U., 1955-61; mem. faculty Fairleigh Dickinson U., Teaneck, N.Y., 1961—, prof. biol. scis., 1968-88, prof. emeritus, 1988—; chmn. dept., 1966-70, 73-76, 79-82. Served with AUS, 1942-46. Mem. AAAS, Am. Inst. Biol. Scis., Am. Soc. Zoologists, AAUP, Nat. Assn. Biology Tchrs., N.Y. Acad. Scis., Sigma Xi. Democrat. Episcopalian. Home: 122 Ashland Pl Apt 5H Brooklyn NY 11201-3910 Office: Fairleigh Dickinson U Teaneck NJ 07666

RHODES, SAMUEL, violist, educator; b. Long Beach, N.Y., Feb. 13, 1941; s. Bernard and Martha (Ephraim) R.; m. Hiroko Yajima, Dec. 30, 1968; children—Amy, Harumi. B.A., Queen's Coll., CUNY, 1963; M.F.A., Princeton U., 1967; D.F.A. (hon.), Mich. State U., 1984; MusD (hon.), Jacksonville U., 1986, San Francisco Conservatory, 1996. Mem. faculty Juilliard Sch., N.Y.C., 1969—, Mich. State U., East Lansing, 1977-85, SUNY-Purchase, 1982-86; violist Marlboro Festival, 1960-68, 78-81, 91—, Galimir String Quartet, 1961-68, Juilliard String Quartet, 1969—; mem. faculty Tanglewood Music Ctr., 1988—. Office: Juilliard Sch Music Lincoln Ctr New York NY 10023

RHODES, WILLIAM REGINALD, banker; b. N.Y.C., Aug. 15, 1935; s. Edward R. and Elsie R.; divorced; 1 child, Elizabeth. BA in History, Brown U., 1957. Sr. officer internat. banking group-Latin Am. and Caribbean Citibank, N.A., N.Y.C., 1977-80, sr. corp. officer Latin Am. and Caribbean, 1980-84, chmn. restructuring com., 1984-90, group exec., 1986-90, also chmn. bank adv. coms. for Brazil, Argentina, Peru, and Uruguay, 1982-90, co-chmn. bank adv. com. for Mexico, 1982-90, sr. exec.-internat., 1990-91; vice chmn. Citicorp, N.Y.C., 1991—; vice chmn. Inst. Internat. Fin., Met. Mus. Bus. Com.; mem. exec. com. Bretton Woods Com., U.S.-Russia Bus. Coun.; past chmn. adv. com. Export-Import Bank of U.S.; chmn. U.S. Sect., Venezuela-U.S. Bus. Coun., External Adv. bd. for Columbia U. Program in Econ. Policy Mgmt.; active U.S.-Egyptian Pres. Coun.; bd. dirs. Citicorp/Citibank; Pvt. Export Funding Corp. Trustee Brown U.; chmn. Northfield-Mt. Hermon Sch.; bd. dirs. N.Y. Hosp., N.Y.C. Partnership; bd. overseers of Watson Inst. for Internat. Studies; active Lincoln Ctr. Corporate Leadership Com. Decorated comdr. Nat. Order of the Southern Cross, Brazil, chevalier Legion of Honor, France, Orden de Mayo, Argentina, officer Order Francisco Miranda 1st and 3rd classes, Order Merito en el Trabajo 1st class, Venezuela. Mem. Americas Soc. (bd. dirs.), Coun. of Ams. (trustee), Inst. for EastWest Studies (bd. dirs.), Bankers Assn. for Fgn. Trade (past pres.), Coun. Fgn. Rels., Venezuelan-Am. C. of C. (past pres.), Bankers Roundtable. Avocations: reading history, jogging, swimming. Office: CitiBank 399 Park Ave New York NY 10022-4614

RHODES, YORKE E(DWARD), organic chemistry educator; b. Elizabeth, N.J., Mar. 25, 1936; s. Yorke Edward and Helen (Pyper) R.; m. Mechthilde Weggenmann, May 24, 1975; children—Yorke Edward III, Christopher A., Matthias Raabe, Timothy A. B.S., U. Del., 1957, M.S., 1959; Ph.D., U. Ill., 1963. Chemist, Thiokol Chem. Corp., Elkton, Md., 1959; lectr. Yale U., New Haven, 1964-65; asst. prof. chemistry NYU, N.Y.C., 1965-71, assoc. prof., 1971—, asst. dean Coll. Arts and Sci., 1987-89, dir. NYU-Stevens Dual Degree Program in Sci. and Engring., 1988—; vis. prof. Universitat Freiburg, Fed. Republic Germany, 1972-73, Technische Universitat Munich, Fed. Republic Germany, 1977, Université Grenoble, 1987; named Humboldt vis. prof. tech. U. Munich, 1978; Dept. State sci. exchange visitor Zagreb, Yugoslavia, and Prague, Czechoslovakia, 1977. Contbr. articles to profl. pubs. Englewood Democratic committeeman, N.J., 1968-72. NIH fellow Yale U., 1964-65; NASA summer faculty fellow Jet Propulsion Labs., Pasadena, Calif., 1980, 81. Mem. Am. Chem. Soc., Royal Chem. Soc., Planetary Soc., N.Y. Acad Scis., Sigma Xi. Avocations: opera; photography; travel; gardening; railroads. Office: NYU Dept Chemistry 100 Washington Sq E New York NY 10003-6656

RHODIN, THOR NATHANIEL, educational administrator; b. Dec. 9, 1920; m. Elspeth Lindsay, Sept. 21, 1949; children: Robert, Ann, Lindsay, Jeffrey. BS in Chemistry, Haverford Coll., 1942; AM in Chem. Physics, Princeton U., 1945, PhD in Chem. Physics, 1946. Rsch. asst. Manhattan Project, Princeton U., 1944-46; rsch. assoc. James Franck Inst., Chgo., 1946-51; jr. faculty dept. chemistry U. Chgo., 1946-51; rsch. assoc. E.I. duPont de Nemours & Co., Inc., Wilmington, Del., 1951-58; assoc. prof. applied engring. physics Cornell U., Ithaca, N.Y., 1958-65, prof. applied engring. physics, 1965-91, acting assoc. dean grad. rsch. and edn. Coll. Engring., 1988-89, assoc. dean and dir. continuing edn. Coll. Engring., 1989-90, dir. master of engring. program, chmn. grad. profl. program, 1988-90, assoc. dir. Mario Einaudi Ctr. for Internat. Studies, 1991-94; prof. emeritus applied and engring. physics Cornell U., 1991—; vis. prof. materials sci. and solid state physics MIT, 1973, Japan Soc. for Promotion of Sci., U. Tokyo, 1976, U. Osaka, 1992; cons. Kodak, IBM, duPont; referee reviewer of proposals and pubs. Am. Chem. Soc., Am. Phys. Soc., NSF, Surface Sci. Surface Sci. Letters; co-prin. investigator synchorotron radiation beamline (U16-B), Nat. Synchrotron Light Source, Brookhaven Nat. Lab., 1985—. Editor: Stress-Corrosion Fracture, 1959; co-editor: Nature of the Surface Chemical Bond, 1979, Proceedings Microphysics of Beams, Adsorbates and Surfaces, 1989; author: Chemistry and Physics of Surfaces and Interfaces, 1992; adv. editor Surface Sci., Physics Status Solidi(a), Progress in Surface Sci., Langmuir Surface Chemistry Jour.; contbr. over 150 articles to profl. jours. NSF sr. fellow, 1964-65, NATO sr. fellow, 1975; named Disting. Vis. Faculty, NATO Adv. Study Inst. on Electron Structure and Reactivity of Metal Surfaces, Namur, Belgium, 1971-75; Humboldt Sr. Scientist Inst. of Phys. Chemistry, Maximillian U., Munich, 1985; others. Fellow Am. Phys. Soc., Am. Vacuum Soc.; mem. Am. Chem. Soc., Am. Soc. for Materials Rsch. Office: Cornell Univ 217 Clark Hall Ithaca NY 14853-2501

RHODY, RONALD EDWARD, banker, communications executive; b. Frankfort, Ky., Jan. 27, 1932; s. James B. and Mary M. (Clark) R.; m. Patricia Schupp, Apr. 23, 1955; children: Leslie K., Mary M., Virginia K., Ronald C. Student, Georgetown Coll., Ky., 1950-52, U. Ky., 1953-55. Accredited pub. relations Pub. Relations Soc. Am. Pub. relations dir. Kaiser Aluminum & Chem. Corp., Ravenswood, W.Va., 1959-62, N.Y.C., 1962-67; corporate v.p. Kaiser Aluminum & Chem. Corp., Oakland, Calif., 1967-83; sr. v.p. corp comm. Bank of Am. NT&SA, San Francisco, 1983—, exec. v.p., 1992-94; CEO Rhody, Inc., 1994—. Contbr. articles to profl. jours. Mem. exec. steering com. St. Mary's Coll., Moraga, Calif.; mem. adv. bd. U. Tex. Sch. Journalism and Mass Communications; chmn. media adv. coun., Media Inst., Washington. Named Pub. Relations Profl. of Yr. Pub. Relations News, 1981. Mem. Pub. Relations Soc. Am. (pres.'s adv. council Rex Harlow award), Internat. Assn. Bus. Communicators (Gold Quill award 1980), Pub. Relations Roundtable San Francisco (bd. govs., awards 1980, 85). Clubs: San Francisco Press; International (Washington); Nat. Press (Washington). Office: 712 Bancroft Rd Walnut Creek CA 94598-1531

RHONE, DOUGLAS PIERCE, pathologist, educator; b. Bloomsburg, Pa., Mar. 27, 1940; s. Wilbur Clayton and Marian Faye (Shaffer) R.; m. Leta Daiva Budelskis, Sept. 27, 1969; children: Jennifer Ann, Todd Brader. BS, Ill. Benedictine U., 1965; MD, MS in Pathology, U. Ill., 1969. Diplomate Am. Bd. Pathology. Attending pathologist Ill. Masonic Med. Ctr., Chgo., 1976, chmn. dept. pathology, 1976—; asst. prof. pathology U. Ill. Coll. Medicine, Chgo., 1976-80, assoc. prof. pathology, 1980—; dir. residency pathology Ill. Masonic Med. Ctr., Chgo., 1976-90, U. Ill. Metro. Hosps., Chgo., 1990—; assoc. dir. med. affairs, 1992-95, Ill. Masonic Med. Ctr. Pathologists, S.C., Chgo., 1977—, Lab. Cons., Ltd., Chgo., 1977—. Contbr. articles to profl. jours. Maj. U.S. Army, 1974-76. Recipient Raymond B. Allen award U. Ill. Coll. Medicine, 1979, 80, 95, C. Thomas Bombeck award, 1991. Fellow Am. Soc. Clin. Pathologists (Sheard-Sanford Rsch. award 1969), Coll. Am. Pathologists; mem. Chgo. Pathology Soc., Ill. Soc. Pathologists. Roman Catholic. Avocations: antiquities, gardening, oil painting, classical music and opera, Russian history and culture. Home: 222 S Spring Ave La Grange IL 60525-2243 Office: Ill Masonic Med Ctr Dept Pathology 836 W Wellington Ave Chicago IL 60657

RHONE, SYLVIA, recording industry executive; b. Philadelphia, PA, Mar. 11, 1952; d. James and Marie (Christmas) R.; 1 daughter, Quinn. M.A., Wharton Sch. of Comm., U. of Pa., 1974. Dir. nat. black music promotion Atlantic Records, New York, N.Y., 1985-88; Sr. V.P. Atlantic Records, New York, N.Y., 1988-91; chair/CEO EastWest Records America, New York, N.Y., 1991—; chair Elektra Entertainment, N.Y.C., N.Y., 1994—. Mem., bd. dirs. Alvin Ailey Am. Dance Theatre, The RIAA, Rock n' Roll Hall of Fame, Jazz at Lincoln Ctr., R&B Found. Became 1st black female recording industry executive when appointed to Sr. V.P. at Atlantic in 1988. Office: Elektra Enterntainment 75 Rockefeller Plz New York NY 10016

RHOTON, ALBERT LOREN, JR., neurological surgery educator; b. Parvin, Ky., Nov. 18, 1932; s. Albert Loren and Hazel Arnette (Van Cleve) R.; m. Joyce L. Moldenhauer, June 23, 1957; children: Eric L., Albert J., Alice S., Laural A. BS, Ohio State U., 1954; MD cum laude, Washington U., St. Louis, 1959. Diplomate Am. Bd. Neurol. Surgery (bd. dirs. 1985-91, vice chmn. 1991). Intern, Columbia Presbyn. Med. Ctr., N.Y.C., 1959; resident in neurol. surgery Barnes Hosp., St. Louis, 1961-65; cons. neurol. surgery Mayo Clinic, Rochester, Minn., 1965-72; chief div. neurol. surgery U. Fla., Gainesville, 1972-80, R.D. Keene prof. and chmn. dept. neurol. surgery, 1980—; developer microsurg. tng. ctr.; guest lectr. Neurol. Socs. Switzerland, Japan, Venezuela, France, Columbia, Middle East, Brazil, Japan, Mex., Can., Costa Rica, Uruguay, Korea, Australia, Egypt, Argentina, Hong Kong, UK, Turkey; invited faculty and guest lectr. Harvard U., Washington U., Emory, U., UCLA, U. Calif., San Francisco, U. Miami, U. Okla., U. So. Calif., U. Mich., Northwestern U., U. Chgo., U. Pa., Johns Hopkins U., Ohio State U., Temple U., Duke U., Cornell U., NYU, U. Cin., Tulane U., Vanderbilt, U. Minnesota, U. Md., U. Pa., Albany Med. Coll., Cleve. Clin. Found., St. Louis U., Henry Ford Med. Found., Med. Coll. N.Y., Jefferson Med. Coll., Hahnamann Med. Coll., U. P.R., U. Calif., Irvine, U. Hong Kong, La. State U., U. Ky., U. Louisville, Singapore Nat. U. Recipient Disting. Faculty award U. Fla., 1981, Alumni Achievement award Washington U. Sch. Medicine, 1985, Jones award for outstanding spl. med. exhibit of yr. Am. Assn. Med. Illustrators, 1969; grantee NIH, VA, Am. Heart Assn.; awarded hon. memberships neurosurg. socs. of Brazil, Japan, Mex., Can., Uruguay, Venezuela, Tex., Okla., Wis., Ga., Rocky Mountain. Mem. ACS (bd. govs. 1978-84), Congress Neurol. Surgeons (pres. 1978, honored guest 1993), Nat. Found. Brain Rsch. (bd. dirs. 1990-94), Nat. Coalition for Rsch. in Neurol. Disorders (bd. dirs. 1990-94), Fla. Neurosurgical Soc. (pres. 1978), Am. Assn. Neurol. Surgeons (chmn. vascular sect., treas. 1983-86, v.p. 1987-88, pres. 1989-90, exec. com. 1993), Soc. Neurol. Surgeons (treas. 1975-81, pres. 1993), So. Neurol. Soc. (v.p. 1976), Alachua County Med. Soc. (exec. com. 1978), AMA (Billings Bronze medal for sci. exhibit 1969), Fla. Med. Assn., Am. Surg. Assn., Soc. Univ. Neurosurgeons, Am. Heart Assn. (stroke coun., Outstanding Achievement award 1971), North Am. Skull Base Soc. (pres. 1993-94), Am. Acad. Neurol. Surgery, Neurol. Soc. Am., Acoustic Neuroma Assn. (med. adv. bd. 1983—, chmn. 1992—), Trigeminal Neurol. Assn. (med. advisor bd. 1992—). Designed over 200 microsurgery instruments. Author: Orbit and Sellar Region, 1996; contbr. numerous articles to profl. jours.; mem. editorial bd. Neurosurgery, Jour. Microsurgery, Surgical Neurology, Jour. Fla. Med. Assn., Am. Jour. Otology, Skull Base Surgery.

Home: 2505 NW 22nd Ave Gainesville FL 32605-3819 Office: U Fla Shands Hosp Gainesville FL 32610

RHYAN, JEANETTE DELORES, physical education educator; b. Clarinda, Iowa, June 26, 1952; d. Warren DeLos and Delores Elenore (Goecker) Renander; m. James William Rhyan, Aug. 5, 1978. BS, Dana Coll., 1974. Cert. secondary tchr., Ariz. Tchr. phys. edn. and sci. Moe (Victoria) High Sch., Australia, 1974-76; tchr. phys. edn. and health and social studies Holbrook (Ariz.) Jr. High Sch., 1977—. Mem. AAHPERD, Ariz. Assn. Jr. High Student Couns. (sec. 1984-85, v.p. 1985-86, pres. 1986-87), Order Ea. Star, Delta Kappa Gamma. Republican. Lutheran. Avocations: travel, crafts, music, collecting reindeers. Office: Holbrook Sch Dist 3 PO Box 640 1001 N 8th Ave Holbrook AZ 86025

RHYNE, CHARLES SYLVANUS, lawyer; b. Charlotte, N.C., June 23, 1912; s. Sydneyham S. and Mary (Wilson) R.; m. Sue Cotton, Sept. 16, 1932 (dec. Mar. 1974); children: Mary Margaret, William Sylvanus; m. Sarah P. Hendon, Oct. 2, 1976; children: Sarah Wilson, Elizabeth Parkhill. BA, Duke U., 1934, LLD, 1958; JD, George Washington U., 1937, DCL, 1958; LLD, Loyola U., Calif., 1958, Dickinson Law Sch., 1959, Ohio No. U., 1966, De Paul U., 1968, Centre, 1969, U. Richmond, 1970, Howard U., 1975, Belmont Abbey, 1982. Bar: D.C. 1937. Pvt. practice Washington; sr. ptnr. Rhyne & Rhyne; gen. counsel Nat. Inst. Mcpl. Law Officers, 1937-88, of counsel; prof. govt. and aviation law George Washington U., 1948-53; prof. govt. Am. U., 1939-44; gen. counsel Fed. Commn. Jud. and Congl. Salaries, 1953-54; spl. cons. Pres. Eisenhower, 1957-60; Dir. Nat. Savs. & Trust Co., 1941-76, ACCIA Life Ins. Co., 1966-84; Mem. Internat Commn. Rules Judicial Procedures, 1959-61, Pres.'s Commn. on UN, 1969-71; spl. ambassador, personal rep. of Pres. U.S. to UN High Commr. for Refugees, 1971-73. Author: Civil Aeronautics Act, Annotated, 1939, Airports and the Courts, 1944, Aviation Accident Law, 1947, Airport Lease and Concession Agreements, 1948, Cases on Aviation Law, 1950, The Law of Municipal Contracts, 1952, Municipal Law, 1957, International Law, 1971, Renowned Law Givers and Great Law Documents of Humankind, 1975, International Refugee Law, 1976, Law and Judicial Systems of Nations, 1978, Law of Local Government Operations, 1980, Working for Justice in America and Justice in the World, 1996; editor Mcpl. Atty., 1937-88; contbr. articles to profl. jours. Trustee George Washington U., 1957-67, Duke U., 1961-85, now trustee emeritus. Recipient Freedoms Found. award for creation Law Day-U.S.A., 1959; Alumni Achievement award George Washington U., 1960; Nat. Bar Assn. Stradford award, 1962; 1st Whitney M. Young award, 1972; Harris award Rotary, 1974; U.S. Dept. State appreciation award, 1976; Nansen Ring for refugee work, 1976, 1st Peacemaker award Rotary Internat., 1988. Mem. ABA (pres. 1957-58, chmn. ho. dels. 1956-58, chmn. commn. world peace through law 1958-66, chmn. com. aero. law 1946-48, 51-54, chmn. internat. and comparative law sect. 1948-49, chmn. UN com., chmn. commn. on nat. inst. justice 1972-76, nat. chmn. Jr. Bar Conf. 1944-45, ABA Gold Medal 1966), D.C. Bar Assn. (pres. 1955-56, Disting. Svc. award, Grotius Peace award 1958), Inter-Am. Bar Assn. (v.p. 1957-59), Am. Bar Found. (pres. 1957-58, chmn. fellows 1958-59), Internat. Bar (founder patron 1947, v.p. 1957-58), Am. Judicature Soc. (dir. life), Am. Law Inst. (life), Am. Soc. Internat. Law (life), World Peace Through Law Ctr. (pres. 1963-89), World Jurist Assn. (life, pres. 1989-91, hon. pres. for life), Nat. Aero. Assn. (bd. dirs. 1945-47), Washington Bd. Trade, Duke U. Alumni Assn. (chmn. nat. coun. 1955-56, pres. 1959-60), Barristers, Met. Club (life), Nat. Press Club, Congl. Country Club (life), Nat. Lawyers Club (life), Univ. Club, Order of Coif (life), Scribes, Delta Theta Phi (life), Omicron Delta Kappa. Home and Office: 1404 Langley Pl Mc Lean VA 22101-3010

RHYNE, JAMES JENNINGS, condensed matter physicist; b. Oklahoma City, Nov. 14, 1938; s. Jennings Jefferson and Clyde Margaret (Russell) R.; m. Susan Margaret Watson, May 26, 1990; children: Nancy Marie, Edward Paxton. BS in Physics, U. Okla., 1959; MS in Physics, U. Ill., 1961; PhD in Physics, Iowa State U., 1965. Rsch. scientist Naval Ordnance Lab., White Oak, Md., 1965-75; rsch. physicist Nat. Inst. of Stds. and Tech., Gaithersburg, Md., 1975-90; prof. physics U. Mo., Columbia, 1991—, dir. Rsch. Reactor Ctr., 1991—. Adv. editor Jour. of Magnetism and Mag. Materials, 1990—; editl. bd. Jour. Applied Physics, 1986-89; co-editor procs. Fellow Am. Phys. Soc. Home: 2704 Westbrook Way Columbia MO 65203 Office: U Mo Rsch Reactor Ctr Columbia MO 65211

RHYNE, VERNON THOMAS, III, electrical engineer, consultant; b. Gulfport, Miss., Feb. 18, 1942; s. Vernon T. and Elizabeth (Brame) R.; m. Glenda Pevey, June 5, 1961; children: Amber Ruth, Tommy. BSEE, Miss. State U., 1962; MEE, U. Va., 1964; PhD, Ga. Inst. Tech., 1967. Registered profl. engr., Tex. Mem. tech. staff NASA Langley Rsch. Ctr., Hampton, Va., 1962-65; prof. elec. engring. Tex. A&M U., College Station, 1967-83; v.p. R&D MCC, Austin, Tex., 1983-94; mgr. strategic programs, semiconductor products sector Motorola, Austin; patent cons., expert witness, N.Y.C., Houston, L.A., 1975—. Author: Fundamentals of Digital Systems Design, 1973 (Terman award Am. Soc. Engring. Edn. 1980). Pres. bd. trustees Eanes Ind. Sch. Dist., Austin, 1987-90, trustee, 1990—. Fellow IEEE (bd. dirs. 1990-95, treas. 1994-95), Accreditation Bd. for Engring. and Tech. Baptist. Home: 3410 Day Star Cv Austin TX 78746-1433 Office: Motorola MD: TX30/OE14 6501 William Cannon Dr W Austin TX 78735

RHYNEDANCE, HAROLD DEXTER, JR., lawyer, consultant; b. New Haven, Feb. 13, 1922; s. Harold Dexter and Gladys (Evans) R.; 1 son by previous marriage: Harold Dexter III; m. Ruth Cosline Hakanson. BA, Cornell U., 1943, JD, 1949; grad., U.S. Army Command and Gen. Staff Coll., 1961, U.S. Army War Coll., 1970. Bar: N.Y. 1949, D.C. 1956, U.S. Tax Ct. 1950, U.S. Ct. Mil. Appeals 1954, U.S. Supreme Ct. 1954, U.S. Ct. Appeals (D.C. cir.) 1956, (2d cir.) 1963, (3rd cir.) 1965, (4th cir.) 1973, (5th cir.) 1968, (7th cir.) 1973, (9th cir.) 1964, U.S. Temporary Emergency Ct. Appeals 1975, U.S. Dist. Ct. D.C. 1956, U.S. Dist. Ct. (so. and ea. dist.) N.Y. 1963. Pvt. practice Buffalo, Eggertsville, N.Y., 1949-50; examiner/gen. atty. ICC, Washington, 1950-51; atty.-adviser subversive activities control bd. ICC, 1951-52; trial atty., spl. asst. to atty. gen., asst. U.S. atty. U.S. Dept. Justice, Washington, 1953-62; trial atty., asst. gen. counsel, gen. counsel FTC, Washington, 1962-73; exec. sec. of adv. coun. on rule and procedures FTC; counsel Howrey & Simon, Washington, 1973-76; mng. atty., asst. gen. counsel, corp. counsel Washington Gas Light Co., 1977-87; counsel Conner & Wetterhahn, 1987-90; cons. Fairview, N.C., 1990—; mem. Jud. Conf. (D.C. Cir.), 1967—; chmn. legal and regulatory subcom. Solar Energy Com., Am. Gas Assn., Washington, 1978-84; lectr. George Washington U. Law Ctr., 1974; faculty moderator Def. Strategy Seminar Nat. War Coll., 1973. V.p., bd. dirs. Peninsula Symphony Assn., Palos Verdes Peninsula, Calif., 1989-94; bd. dirs. Help-The-Homeless-Help-Themselves, Inc., Palos Verdes Peninsula, 1991-93. 1st lt. U.S. Army, 1943-46, PTO; col. AUS, 1982—. Mem. ABA, Fed. Bar Assn., D.C. Bar Assn., Bar Assn. of D.C., Washington Met. Area Corp. Counsel Assn. (bd. dirs. 1981-84), Cornell Lawyers Club D.C. (pres. 1959-61), The Selden Soc. (London), Biltmore Forest Country Club (Asheville, N.C.), Leadership Asheville Forum (N.C.), The Am. Legion, Res. Officers Assn. (life), Mil. Order Carabao, U.S. Army War Coll. Alumni Assn. (life), Cornell Alumni Assn., Sigma Chi, Phi Delta Phi. Republican. Episcopalian. Home and Office: Eagles View 286 Sugar Hollow Rd Fairview NC 28730-9559

RIACH, DOUGLAS ALEXANDER, marketing and sales executive, retired military officer; b. Victoria, B.C., Can., Oct. 8, 1919; s. Alex and Gladys (Provis) R.; came to U.S., 1925, naturalized, 1942; BA, UCLA, 1948; postgrad. in mktg. Fenn Coll., 1959, Grad. Sch. Sales Mgmt. and Mktg., 1960, U.S. Army Command and Gen. Staff Coll., 1966, Armed Forces Staff Coll., 1968, Indsl. Coll. of the Armed Forces, 1970-71; m. Eleanor Montague, Mar. 28, 1942; 1 child, Sandra Jean. With Gen. Foods Corp., 1948-80, terr. sales mgr., San Francisco, 1962-80; with Food Brokers, San Francisco Bay area, 1980-90; exec. v.p. Visual Market Plans Inc., Novato, Calif., 1984-87; ter. mgr. Ibbotson, Berri, DeNola Brokerage, Inc., Emeryville, Calif., 1990—. Served to capt. inf. AUS, 1941-46, ETO; to col. inf. USAR, 1946-79, from comdr. 2d inf. brigade Calif. State mil. res., 1984-87 to brigadier gen. (ret.) 1990. Decorated Legion of Merit, Bronze Star with V device and oak leaf cluster, Purple Heart, Combat Infantry Badge, Croix de Guerre avec Palme (France and Belgium), Fouragerre (Belgium), Combattant Cross-Voluntaire (France), Combattant Cross-Soldier (France), Medaille-Commemorative de la Liberee (France), Medaille-Commemorative Francais (France), Medaille-War Wounded (France), Medaille-Commemorative Belgique (Belgium), Medaille-de la Reconnaissance (Belgium), Medaille du Voluntaire (Belgium), Cross of Freedom (Poland), Royal Commemorative War Cross (Yugoslavia); named knight Order of the Compassionate Heart (internat.), knight commdr. Sovereign Mil. Order, Temple of Jerusalem (knights templar), CDR Commandery of Calif. (knights templar 1992-94), comdr. Commandery of St. Francis; knight commdr. sovereign Order of St. John of Jerusalem (knights hospitaller), knight commdr. Polonia Restituta, knight comdr. Cross with Star Sovereign Order of St. Stanislaus; named to U.S. Army Inf. Hall of Fame, 1982; recipient Calif. Medal of Merit and cluster, Commendation medal. Mem. Long Beach Food Sales Assn. (pres. 1950), Assn. Grocers Mfrs. Reps. (dir. 1955), Am. Security Coun. (nat. adv. bd. 1975—), Res. Officers Assn. (San Francisco Presidio pres. 1974-76, v.p. 1977-82, v.p. dept. Calif. 1979, exec. v.p. 1980, pres. 1981, nat. councilman 1981-82), Nat. Assn. Uniformed Svcs., Exchange Club (v.p. Long Beach 1955), St. Andrews Soc. Queens Club San Francisco, Combat Infantry Assn., Assn. U.S. Army, Am. Legion, Assn. Former Intelligence Officers, Presidio Soc., Navy League, Ret. Officers Assn., Mil. Order Purple Heart, DAV, Psychol. Ops. Assn., Nat. Guard Assn. Calif., State Def. Force Assn. Calif., Merchandising Execs. San Francisco (dir. 1970-75, sec. 1976-77, v.p. 1978-79, pres. 1980, bd. dirs. 1981-89), Commonwealth of Club Calif. (nat. def. sect. vice chmn. 1964-66, chmn. 1967-72), Elks, Masons (master, lodge 400, Shrine, Islam Temple, 32d degree Scottish Rite, sojouner chpt. #277). Republican. Presbyterian. Home: 2609 Trousdale Dr Burlingame CA 94010-5706

RIASANOVSKY, NICHOLAS VALENTINE, historian, educator; b. Harbin, China, Dec. 21, 1923; came to U.S., 1938, naturalized, 1943; m. Arlene Ruth Schlegel, Feb. 15, 1955; children—John, Nicholas, Maria. B.A., U. Oreg., 1942; A.M., Harvard U., 1947; D.Phil., Oxford (Eng.) U., 1949. Mem. faculty U. Iowa, 1949-57; mem. faculty U. Calif., Berkeley, 1957—, prof. history, 1961—, Sidney Hellman Ehrman prof. European history, 1969—; trustee Nat. Council Soviet and E. European Research, 1978-82; mem. Kennan Inst. Acad. Council, 1986-89; vis. research prof. USSR Acad. Scis., Moscow, 1969, Moscow and Leningrad, 1974, 79. Author: Russia and the West in Teaching of the Slavophiles: A Study of Romantic Ideology, 1952, Nicholas I and Official Nationality in Russia, 1825-1855, 1959, A History of Russia, 1963, 5th edit., 1993, The Teaching of Charles Fourier, 1969, A Parting of Ways: Government and the Educated Public in Russia, 1801-1855, 1976, The Image of Peter the Great in Russian History and Thought, 1985, The Emergence of Romanticism, 1992, Collected Writings 1947-94, 1993; co-editor: California Slavic Studies, 1960—; editl. bd. Russian rev., Zarubezhnaia Periodicheskaia Pechat' Na Russkom Iazyke; contbr. articles to profl. jours. Served to 2d lt. AUS, 1943-46. Decorated Bronze Star; recipient Silver medal Commonwealth Club Calif., 1964; Rhodes scholar, 1947-49; Fulbright grantee, 1954-55, 74, 79; Guggenheim fellow, 1969; sr. fellow Nat. Endowment Humanities, 1975; Fulbright sr. scholar, sr. fellow Ctr. Advanced Studies in Behavioral Scis., 1984-85; sr. fellow Woodrow Wilson Internat. Ctr. for Scholars, 1989-90. Mem. AAAS, Am. Assn. Advancement Slavic Studies (pres. 1973-76, Disting. Contbr. award 1993), Am. Hist. Assn. (award for Scholarly Distinction 1995).

RIBA, NETTA EILEEN, secondary school educator; b. Bronx, N.Y., Apr. 6, 1944; d. Jack and Anne (Parnes) Browner; m. Benjamin Riba, July 22, 1975; children: Rebecca, Joseph. BS, Queens Coll., 1965, MS, 1968. Cert. tchr., N.Y. Math. tchr. Bayside (N.Y.) H.S., 1965-68, Flushing (N.Y.) H.S., 1968-75, Harry S Truman H.S., Bronx, 1975-95, Christopher Columbus H.S., Bronx, 1996—. Vol. guide N.Y. Zool. Soc., Bronx, 1973-75; leader Rockland County Coun. Girl Scouts USA, 1985-88. Mem. Nat. Coun. Tchrs. Math. Jewish. Avocations: animal behavior, sewing. Office: Christopher Columbus HS 925 Astor Ave Bronx NY 10469

RIBACK, ESTELLE POSNER, art dealer; b. Bklyn., June 8, 1934; d. Max Jacob and Rose (Rosen) Posner; m. Arnold O. Riback, June 17, 1956; children: Phillip Scott, Stephen Craig, Debra Lyn. BS in Psychology, Tufts U., 1956; MS in Elem. Edn., Hofstra U., 1964; MA in Art History, NYU, 1981, cert. art appraiser, 1993. Cert. elem. tchr., N.Y. Tchr. reading improvement Glen Cove (N.Y.) Pub. Schs., from 1964; ptnr., v.p. Artlego, N.Y.C., 1980-83; devel. officer East Harlem Tutorial Program, N.Y.C., 1985-86; asst. to dir. devel. Ams. Soc., N.Y.C., 1986-89; pres., ptnr. Manley-Riback, Inc., N.Y.C., 1989—. Pres., bd. dirs. Azzizz Theatre, Inc., Bklyn., 1993-95, chmn. benefit com., 1993-94, chmn. fundraising, 1993-95; former mem. Hebrew Sch. of Congregation Tifereth Israel Bd. Edn., Glen Cove; former chmn. major gifts Suffolk region Hadassah Med. Orgn., former v.p. for fundraising Huntington chpt. Mem. Soc. for Advancement of Judaism, Westhampton Yacht Squadron, Psi Chi, Alpha Xi Delta. Democrat. Avocations: tennis, sailing, bridge, travel, collecting art and artifacts. Home and Office: 201 E 79th St Apt 19D New York NY 10021-0846

RIBBANS, GEOFFREY WILFRID, Spanish educator; b. London, Apr. 15, 1927; came to U.S. 1978; s. Wilfrid Henry and Rose Matilda (Burton)R.; m. Magdalena Willmann, Apr. 21, 1956; children: Madeleine Elizabeth, Helen Margaret, Peter John. BA with 1st class hons., Kings Coll., U. London, 1948, MA, 1953. Asst. lectr. U. Sheffield, Eng., 1954-56; lectr. U. Sheffield, 1956-61, sr. lectr. Spanish, 1961-63; Gilmour prof. Spanish U. Liverpool, Eng.; 1963-78 Mellon prof. Spanish, U. Pitts., 1970-71; Wm. R. Kenan Jr. U. prof. Spanish Brown U., Providence, 1978—, chmn. dept., 1981-84; editor Bull. Hispanic Studies, 1964-78; vis. prof. U. Salamanca, Spain, 1995. Author: Catalunya I Valencia al Segle XVIII, 1955, 2d edit., 1993, Niebla y Soledad: Aspectos de Unamuno y Machado, 1971, Galdos: Fortunata y Jacinta, 1977 (Spanish transl. 1988); editor: Antonio Machado, Soledades, Galerias, Otros Peomas, 1984, 13th edit., 1996, Campos de Castilla, 1989, 5th edit., 1994, History and Fiction in Galdo's Narratives, 1993, 2d edit., 1995; contbr. numerous articles to profl. jours. Hispanic studies in his honour, Liverpool, 1992. Mem. MLA, Internat. Assn. Hispanists (v.p. 1974-80), Internat. Assn. Galdós Scholars (pres. 1988-89). Office: Brown U Dept Hispanic Studies PO Box 1961 Providence RI 02912-1961

RIBBLE, JOHN CHARLES, medical educator; b. Paris, Tex., July 26, 1931; s. Elbert Alfred and Dorothy (Pyeatt) R.; m. Anne Blythe Hoerner; 1 stepchild Helen Blythe Strate Kielty. MD, U. Tex., 1955. Diplomate Am. Bd. Internal Medicine. Asst. prof. medicine Cornell U., N.Y.C., 1962-66, assoc. prof. pediatrics, 1966-78, assoc. dean, 1974-78; assoc. dean Med. Sch., U. Tex., Houston, 1978-86, dean, 1986-95; vis. scholar The Health Inst. New Eng. Med. Ctr., Boston, 1995-96; mem. Nat. Adv. Coun. Gen. Med. Scis. NIH, Bethesda, Md., 1988-91. Episcopalian. Home: 6200 Willers Way Houston TX 77057-2808 Office: U Tex Med Sch 6431 Fannin St Houston TX 77030-1501

RIBBLE, RONALD GEORGE, psychologist, educator, writer; b. West Reading, Pa., May 7, 1937; s. Jeremiah George and Mildred Sarah (Folk) R.; m. Catalina Valenzuela (Torres), Sept. 30, 1961; children: Christina, Timothy, Kenneth. BSEE cum laude, U. Mo., 1968, MSEE, 1969, MA, 1985, PhD, 1986. Cert. psychologist, Tex. Enlisted man USAF, 1956-60, advance through grades to lt. col., 1976; rsch. dir. Coping Resources, Inc., Columbia, Mo., 1986; pres., co-owner Towers and Rushing Ltd., San Antonio, 1986—; referral devel. Laughlin Pavilion Psychiat. Hosp., Kirksville, Mo., 1987; program dir. Psychiat. Insts. of Am., Iowa Falls, Iowa, 1987-88; lead psychotherapist Gasconade County Counseling Ctr., Hermann, Mo., 1988; lectr. U. Tex., San Antonio, 1989—, Trinity U., San Antonio, 1995—; assessment clinician Afton Oaks Psychiat. Hosp., San Antonio, 1989-91; psychologist Olmos Psychol. Svcs., Inc., San Antonio, 1991-93; vol. assessor Holmgreen Children's Shelter, San Antonio, 1992-93; condr. seminars, revs. for maj. pubs. Author: Apples, Weeds, and Doggie Poo, 1995; contbr. essays to psychol. reference books and poetry to anthologies periodicals, lyrics to popular music; columnist Feelings, 1993—; public access TV appearances, 1991—. Del. Boone County (Mo.) Dem. Conv., 1984; vol. announcer pub. radio sta., Columbia, 1993; contbg. mem. Dem. Nat. Com., 1983—, Presdl. Congl. Task Force, 1994; vol. counselor Cath. Family and Children's Svc., San Antonio, 1989-91; chpt. advisor Rational Recovery Program for Alcoholics, San Antonio, 1991-92; mem. Pres. Leadership Cir., 1994-95. Recipient Roberts Meml. Prize in Poetry, 1995. Mem. APA, AAUP, NEA, ACLU, Am. Coll. Forensic Examiners, Internat. Soc. for Study of Individual Differences, Internat. Platform Assn. (Poetry award 1995), Bexar County Psychol. Assn., Air Force Assn., Ret. Officers Assn, People for the Am. Way, Poetry Soc. Am., Acad. Am. Poets. Roman Catholic. Avocations: running and fitness, poetry, singing, pub. speaking. Home: 14023 N Hills Village Dr San Antonio TX 78249-2531 Office: U Tex Divsn Cultural and Sci San Antonio TX 78249 also: Towers and Rushing Ltd San Antonio TX 78249

RIBICOFF, ABRAHAM A., lawyer, former senator; b. New Britain, Conn., Apr. 9, 1910; s. Samuel and Rose (Sable) R.; m. Ruth Siegel, June 28, 1931 (dec.); children: Peter, Jane; m. Lois Mathes, 1972. Student, NYU; LL.B. cum laude, U. Chgo., 1933. Bar: Conn. 1933, N.Y. 1981, U.S. Ct. Appeals (D.C. cir.) 1982, U.S. Supreme Ct. 1981. Mem. Conn. Ho. of Reps., 1939-42; mcpl. judge Hartford, Conn., 1942-43, 45-47; chmn. Conn. Assembly Mcpl. Ct. Judges, 1942; mem. 81st—82d congresses from 1st Conn. Dist., mem. com. fgn. affairs; gov. Conn., 1955-61; sec. HEW, 1961-62; mem. U.S. Senate from Conn., 1963-81, mem. fin., joint econ. coms., chmn. govt. affairs com.; spl. counsel firm Kaye, Scholer, Fierman, Hays & Handler, N.Y.C. and Washington, 1981—; dir. Hartford Ins. Group, United Television, Inc. Author: Politics: The American Way, 1967, America Can Make It, 1972, The American Medical Machine, 1972. Democrat. Office: 425 Park Ave New York NY 10022-3506

RIBLE, MORTON, management consultant, manufacturing executive, lawyer; b. Los Angeles, July 30, 1938; s. Ulysses Floyd and Ruth (Morton) R.; m. Ann Martin, June 22, 1963; children: Kimberly, Kristen. AB cum laude, Princeton U., 1961; JD, Stanford U., 1964; MBA, U. So. Calif., 1973. Bar: Calif. 1964. Ptnr. Darling, Mack, Hall & Call, Los Angeles, 1965-69; v.p., gen. counsel, sec. The Leisure Group Inc., Los Angeles, 1969-76; sr. v.p., gen. counsel, dir. Calif. Life Corp., Los Angeles, 1976-78; v.p., gen. counsel, sec. Pacific S.W. Airlines, San Diego, 1978-85, v.p. human resources and adminstrn., 1985-87; v.p., gen. counsel, sec. PS Group Inc., San Diego, 1978-87; sr. v.p., gen. counsel, chief adminstrv. officer AM Internat., Inc., Chgo., 1988-94; chmn. San Diego Travel Group, Inc., 1994—, Simpact Inc., San Diego, 1994—. Bd. dirs. San Diego C. of C., 1983-86, Rancho Santa Fe (Calif.) Community Found., 1981-89; pres. Palos Verdes (Calif.) Community Arts Assn., 1976-77; trustee Rancho Santa Fe Youth Inc., 1980-82. Mem. ABA, Calif. Bar Assn. Avocations: running, skiing. Address: PO Box 945 Rancho Santa Fe CA 92067

RIBMAN, RONALD BURT, playwright; b. N.Y.C., May 28, 1932; s. Samuel M. and Rosa (Lerner) R.; m. Alice S. Rosen, Aug. 27, 1967; 2 children. BBA, U. Pitts., 1954, MLitt, 1958, PhD, 1962. Asst. prof. English lit. Otterbein Coll., 1962-63. Author plays including: Harry, Noon and Night, 1965, The Journey of the Fifth Horse, 1966 (Obie award Best Play, 1965-66), The Ceremony of Innocence, 1967, Passing Through From Exotic Places (includes The Son Who Hunted Tigers in Jakarta, Sunstroke, The Burial of Esposito), 1969, Fingernails Blue as Flowers, 1971, A Break in the Skin, 1972, The Poison Tree, 1976 (Straw Hat award Best New Play, 1973), Cold Storage, 1977 (Elizabeth Hull-Kate Warriner award Dramatists Guild 1977), Buck, 1983 (Playwrights USA award 1984), The Cannibal Masque, 1987, A Serpent's Egg, 1987, Sweet Table at the Richelieu, 1987, The Rug Merchants Of Chaos, 1991, Dream of the Red Spider, 1993, (screenplays) The Final War of Olly Winter, 1967 (Emmy award nomination 1967), The Angel Levine, 1969, Seize The Day, 1986; (miniseries) The Sunset Gang, 1991. With AUS, 1954-56. Rockefeller Found grantee, 1966, 68; Guggenheim fellow, 1970; Nat. Endowment Arts fellow, 1974, 86-87; Rockefeller Found. awardee for contbn. to Am. Theatre, 1975. Office: care Samuel Gelfman BDP & Assocs 10637 Burbank Blvd North Hollywood CA 91601 Address: 152 Stone Meadow South Salem NY 10590

RIBNER, HERBERT SPENCER, physicist, educator; b. Seattle, Apr. 9, 1913; s. Joseph Herman and Rose Esther (Goldberg) R.; m. Lelia Carolyn Byrd, Oct. 29, 1949; children—Carol Anne, David Byrd. B.S., Calif. Inst. Tech., 1935; M.S., Washington U., St. Louis, 1937; Ph.D., Washington U., 1939. From physicist to dir. lab. Brown Geophys. Co., Tex., 1939-40; from physicist to head stability sect. Langley Lab., NACA, Va., 1940-49; cons. to head boundary layer sects. Lewis Lab. NACA, Cleve., 1949-54; research assoc. Inst. aerospace studies U. Toronto, Ont., Can., 1955-56; asst. prof. U. Toronto, 1956-57, assoc. prof., 1957-59, prof., 1959-78, prof. emeritus, 1978—; vis. prof. U. Southampton, 1960-61; staff scientist NASA Langley Research Ctr., 1975-76, disting. rsch. assoc., 1979—; chmn. sonic boom panel Internat. Civil Aviation Orgn., 1969-70; adviser com. on hearing, bioacoustics and mechanics Nat. Acad. Scis., 1972-74. Contbr. over 100 articles to profl. jours. Recipient Can. 125th Commemorative medal, 1993, Pub. Svc. medal NASA, 1994. Fellow AIAA (Aero-Acoustics award 1976, Dryden lectr. 1981), Royal Soc. Can., Am. Phys. Soc., Acoustical Soc. Am., Can. Aero. and Space Inst. (Turnbull lectr. 1968); mem. Can. Acoustical Assn. (chmn. 1966-68). Office: U Toronto Inst Aerospace Studies 4925 Dufferin St, Downsview, ON Canada M3H 5T6

RICARD, JOHN H., bishop, educator; b. Baton Rouge, Feb. 29, 1940; s. Maceo and Albanie (St. Amant) R. BA, St. Joseph Sem., 1962, MA, 1968; MS, Tulane U., 1970. Ordained priest Roman Cath. Ch., 1968. Pastor Holy Redeemer Ch., Washington, 1972-75, Holy Comforter Ch., Washington, 1975-84; ordained titular bishop of Rucuma, 1984; aux. bishop Balt., 1984; assoc. prof. Cath. U. Am., Washington, 1973—; mem. priest's senate Archdiocese of Washington, 1974—, mem. shc. bd., 1976—. Chmn. Com. on Social Devel. and World Peace, Domestic Social Devel., 1992-95; pres. Catholic. Relief Svcs. USCC, 1995—; mem. Pontifical Coun., COR UNUM, 1996—. Mem. Secretariat of Black Caths. Office: St Francis Xavier Rectory 1501 E Oliver St Baltimore MD 21213-2910

RICARDI, LEON JOSEPH, electrical engineer; b. Brockton, Mass., Mar. 21, 1924; s. Philip Julius and Eva Isabel (DuBois) R.; m. Angelena Marie Giorgio, Jan. 19, 1947; children: Eva Marie, John Philip, Richard Christopher. B.S. in Elec. Engring, Northeastern U., 1949, M.S., 1952, Ph.D., 1969. Engr. Andrew Alford Cons. Engrs., Boston, 1950-51; project engr. Gabriel Labs., Needham, Mass., 1951-54; group leader, head Tech. Adv. Office, MIT-Lincoln Lab., Lexington, Mass., 1954-84; pres. L.J. Ricardi, Inc., El Segundo, Calif., 1984-95, Creative Engring., Manhattan Beach, Calif., 1996—; part-time tchr. Northeastern U., Boston, 1969-80; cons. U.S. Air Force, 1965-85. Served with USAF, 1943-45. Fellow IEEE. Roman Catholic. Office: Creative Engring 865 Manhattan Beach Manhattan Beach CA 90266 *Listen as much as possible but never fail to speak when you feel that you are right and what you have to say is more than of average importance.*

RICARDO-CAMPBELL, RITA, economist, educator; b. Boston, Mar. 16, 1920; d. David and Elizabeth (Jones) Ricardo; m. Wesley Glenn Campbell, Sept. 15, 1946; children: Barbara Lee, Diane Rita, Nancy Elizabeth. BS, Simmons Coll., 1941; MA, Harvard U., 1945, PhD, 1946. Instr. Harvard U., Cambridge, Mass., 1946-48; asst. prof. Tufts U., Medford, Mass., 1948-51; labor economist U.S. Wage Stabilization Bd., 1951-53; economist Ways and Means Com. U.S. Ho. of Reps., 1953; cons. economist, 1957-60; vis. prof. San Jose State Coll., 1960-61; sr. fellow Hoover Instn. on War, Revolution, and Peace, Stanford, Calif., 1968-95, sr. fellow emerita, 1995—; lectr. health svc. adminstrn. Stanford U. Med. Sch., 1973-78; bd. dirs. Watkins-Johnson Co., Palo Alto, Calif., Gillette Co., Boston; mgmt. bd. Samaritan Med. Ctr., San Jose, Calif. Author: Voluntary Health Insurance in the U.S., 1960, Economics of Health and Public Policy, 1971, Food Safety Regulation: Use and Limitations of Cost-Benefit Analysis, 1974, Drug Lag: Federal Government Decision Making, 1976, Social Security: Promise and Reality, 1977, The Economics and Politics of Health, 1982, 2d edit., 1985; co-editor: Below-Replacement Fertility in Industrial Societies, 1987, Issues in Contemporary Retirement, 1988; contbr. articles to profl. jours. Commr. Western Interstate Commn. for Higher Edn. Calif., 1967-75, chmn., 1970-71; mem. Pres. Nixon's Adv. Coun. on Status Women, 1969-76; mem. task force on taxation Pres.'s Coun. on Environ. Quality, 1970-72; mem. Pres.'s Com. Health Services Industry, 1971-73, FDA Nat. Adv. Drug Com., 1972-75; mem. Econ. Policy Adv. Bd., 1981-90, Pres. Reagan's Nat. Coun. on Humanities, 1982-89, Pres. Nat. Medal of Sci. com., 1988-94; bd. dirs. Ind. Colls. No. Calif., 1971-87; mem. com. assessment of safety, benefits, risks Citizens Commn. Sci., Law and Food Supply, Rockefeller U., 1973-75; mem. adv. com. Ctr. Health Policy Rsch., Am. Enterprise Inst. Pub. Policy Rsch., Washington, 1974-80; mem. adv. coun. on social security Social Security Adminstrn., 1974-75; bd. dirs. Simmons Coll. Corp., Boston, 1975-80; mem. adv. coun. bd. assocs. Stanford Librs., 1975-78; mem. coun. SRI Internat., Menlo Park, Calif., 1977-90. Mem. Am. Econ. Assn., Mont Pelerin Soc. (bd. dirs. 1988-92, v.p. 1992-94), Harvard Grad. Soc. (coun. 1991), Phi Beta

Kappa. Home: 26915 Alejandro Dr Los Altos Hills CA 94022-1932 Office: Stanford U Hoover Instn Stanford CA 94305-6010

RICARDS, JUNE ELAINE, nursing consultant, administrator; b. Nebr., June 3, 1939; d. Carl F. and Merle E. (Block) Middendorf; children: Elaine R. Hertz, Kristine K. Hineline. Diploma, Lincoln Gen. Hosp., 1960; BSN, Calif. State U., Bakersfield, 1980. Cert. nurse operating room, nurse adminstrn. Asst. dir. nursing svc. Kern Med. Ctr., Bakersfield, 1976-80; mgr. surg. svcs. St. Vincent Hosp., Billings, Mont., 1980-84; sr. coord. consultation Assn. Operating Room Nurses, Denver, 1984-87; dir. surg. svcs. Boone Hosp. Ctr., Columbia, Mo., 1989-92; nurse cons. Higman Healthcare, St. Petersburg, Fla., 1992-94, Baxter Healthcare, Chgo., 1994—. Mem. ANA, Am. Coll. Healthcare Execs., Assn. Operating Room Nurses, Sigma Theta Tau.

RICART, FRED, automotive company executive. CEO Ricart Automotive, Groveport, Ohio. Office: Ricart Automotive 4255 S Hamilton Rd Groveport OH 43227

RICART, RHETT C., retail automotive executive; b. 1956. Grad., Ohio State U., 1977. Prin. Ricard Ford, Groveport, Ohio, 1977—, pres., CEO, 1988—. Office: Ricart Ford Inc 4255 S Hamilton Rd Groveport OH 43125-9332 Office: Ricart Automotive 4255 S Hamilton Rd Groveport OH 43125*

RICCARDS, MICHAEL PATRICK, academic administrator; b. Hillside, N.J., Oct. 2, 1944; s. Patrick and Margaret (Finelli) R.; m. Barbara Dunlop, June 6, 1970; children: Patrick, Catherine, Abigail. BA, Rutgers U., 1966, MA, 1967, MPhil, 1969, PhD, 1970. Spl. asst. to chancellor Dept. Higher Edn., Trenton, N.J., 1969-70; from asst. prof. to assoc. prof. SUNY, Buffalo, 1970-77; dean U. Mass., Boston, 1977-82; provost, prof. Hunter Coll.-CUNY, 1982-86; pres. St. John's Coll., Santa Fe, 1986-89, Shepherd Coll., Shepherdstown, W.Va., 1989-95, Fitchburg (Mass.) State Coll., 1995—. Author: The Making of the American Citizenry, 1973, A Republic If You Can Keep It, 1987, The Ferocious Engine of Democracy, 2 vols., 1995; co-editor: Reflections on American Political Thought, 1973. Chmn. N.Mex. Endowment for Humanities, 1989; mem. nat. adv. com. Ctr. for Study of Presidency, 1987—; mem. bd. trustees Albuquerque Acad.; mem. Coun. Humanities W.Va. Fulbright fellow 1973, Huntington Libr. fellow 1974, NEH fellow Princeton U. 1976-77. Home: 123 Apple Tree Hill Fitchburg MA 01420 Office: Fitchburg State Coll Fitchburg MA 01420

RICCI, GIOVANNI MARIO, finance company executive, government consultant; b. Barga, Lucca, Italy, Aug. 7, 1929; s. Ettore and Jolanda (Bardoni) R.; m. Lia Cheli, Feb. 14, 1949 (div. 1970); children: Ettore, Franco, Cristiana; m. Angela Carbognin, Oct. 21, 1973; children: Mariangela, Rebecca. Ed. Italian schs.; D. honoris causa in Theology, 1983. Fin. advisor Seychelles Republic, 1974—; journalist, corr. ANSA (Italian News Agy.), 1980—; chmn., CEO sales, restructuring, mergers and indsl. mgmt. GMR Group A.G.; founder, hon. chmn. Fondazione Ricci, Pascoli, Italy, 1990—. Office: GMR Group, Via Nassa 21, CH-6901 Lugano Switzerland

RICCI, ROBERT RONALD, manufacturing company executive; b. N.Y.C., Jan. 11, 1945; s. George and Mary Pauline (Barbieri) R.; m. Sandra Piccione, Jan. 18, 1948; children: Jason, Sean. AAS, S.I. Community Coll., 1972; BBA, Bernard Baruch Coll., 1974, MBA, 1976. Sales mgr. G.A.F. Photo, Elizabeth, N.J., 1974-76; v.p. Photo Drive Thru, Pennsauken, N.J., 1976-80; head nat. accounts Berkey Photo, Phila., 1980-85; dir. nat. account sales Qualex, Inc., Durham, N.C., 1988-92, v.p. sales east, 1993-95; v.p. new acct. devel. sales National, 1995—; pres. Sanjasean, Inc., Marlton, N.J., 1978-86. Served with USN, 1966-70. Mem. Photo Mktg. Assn. Republican. Roman Catholic. Avocations: photography, carpentry, computers. Home: 1001 Clingmans Pl Raleigh NC 27614-8199 Office: Qualex Inc 3404 N Duke St Durham NC 27704-2130

RICCI, RUGGIERO, violinist, educator; b. San Francisco, July 24, 1918; s. Pietro Ricci and Emma Bacigalupi; m. Ruth Rink, 1942; m. Valma Rodriguez, 1957; m. Julia Whitehurst Clemenceau, 1978; 5 children. Pupil, Louis Persinger, Mischel Piastro, Paul Stassevitch, Georg Kulenkampff. Began career as child prodigy; N.Y. debut Manhattan Symphony, 1929; performed concert engagements throughout world including unaccompanied violin recitals, 1st European tour, 1932, specializes in violin solo, introduced Ginastera, von Einem and Veerhoff violin concerti, U.S. premiere Paganini, 6th violin concerto; prof. music Ind. U., 1971-74, Juilliard Sch., 1974-79, U. Mich., Ann Arbor, 1982-87; prof. Mozarteum, Salzburg, Austria, 1989—. Recordings include The GreatViolinist Series, The Making of a Legend, Vols. 3, 4, Portrait of an Artist, Vol. 4, Vol. 6, Ruggiero Ricci, Virtuoso Recital. Served with USAAF, 1942-45. Decorated Knight Order of Merit Italy. Mem. Royal Acad. Music (hon.). Made first complete recording of Paganini's Caprices. Office: Intermusica Stephen Lumsden, 16 Duncan Terr, London N1 8B2, England also: One-Eleven Ltd c/o Albany Music Distrs Inc P O Box 5011 Albany NY 12205 also: c/o Jonn Gingrich Mgmt Inc P O Box 1515 New York NY 10023

RICCIARDI, ANTONIO, prosthodontist, educator; b. Jersey City, June 5, 1922; s. Frank and Eugenia (Izzo) R.; m. Lucy DePalma, June 21, 1945; children: Eugenia, Lynda. Student Upsala Coll., 1941-42, BA in Chemistry, 1951; DDS, Temple U., 1958. Diplomate Am. Bd. Oral Implantology, Am. Bd. Implant Dentistry. Purchasing agt. Dade Bros., Newark, Airport, 1951-52; asst. work mgr. Cooper Alloy Steel Co., Hillside, N.J., 1954; chemist White's Pharm. Co., Union, N.J., 1954; practice gen. dentistry, Westfield, N.J., 1958—; dentist Westfield Public Schs., 1958-60; mem. staff Mountainside Hosp., Montclair, N.J., St. Elizabeth's Hosp., Elizabeth, N.J.; implant staff John F. Kennedy Hosp., Edison, N.J., chief of prosthetics, 1980—; clin. chmn. implant study Columbia U. Sch. Oral Surgery and Dentistry; implant cons. Columbia Presbyn. Sch. Oral Surgery and Dentistry, N.Y.C.; cons. Implants Internat., N.Y.C., 1971—; pres. Universal Dental Implements, Inc., 1979—. Pres. Nat. Gymnastics Clinic, Sarasota, Fla., 1968—; v.p. rebound tumbling center Welmarick Inc.,Plainfield, 1958—. Gymnastics ofcl. Eastern Coll. Conf., 1954—. Served to lt. col. USMCR, figter pilot, 1942-48, jet fighter pilot, 52-54, Korea. Fellow Acad. Gen. Dentistry, Royal Soc. Health (Eng.), Internat. Coll. Oral Implantology (founding mem.), Am. Acad. Gen. Dentistry, Am. Acad. Implant Dentistry (program chmn. nat. conv. 1974, sec. 1976, pres. N.E. sect. 1978, chmn. ethics com. 1980, ethics chmn. 1981, credentialling mem. 1985—), Acad. Dentistry Internat., Am. Acad. Implant Dentistry, Fedn. Dentistry Internat.; hon fellow Italian and German implant socs.; mem. Inst. Endosseous Implants, Inst. for Advance Dental Research, ADA, Middlesex County Dental Assn., Union County and Plainfield Dental Soc. Fedn. Prosthodontics Orgns., Internat. Research Com. on Oral Implantology (pres. U.S. chpt.), Am. Acad. Oral Implantology, Nat. Gymnastics Judges Assn. (pres. Eastern div.; named to Gymnastic Hall of Fame 1978), Delta Sigma Delta. Writer, lectr. on implantology. Address: 1450 Fernwood Rd Mountainside NJ 07092-2503

RICCIARDI, LAWRENCE R., food products company executive, lawyer. BA, Fordham U., 1962; JD, Columbia U., 1965; course in executive program, Stamford U., 1978. Bar: N.Y. 1967. Assoc. Gilbert, Segall & Young, 1965-69; counsel Overseas Pvt. Invest Corp/US Dept. State Internat. Devel., 1969-73; internat. counsel Am. Express, 1973-75; gen. counsel Internat. Banking Corp., 1975-77, Travel Related Svcs., 1977-89; exec. v.p., gen. counsel RJR Nabisco, Inc., N.Y.C., 1989-93, pres., 1993-1995; sr. v.p. & gen. counsel IBM, Armonk, N.Y., 1995—. Mem. Assn. of Bar of City of N.Y. Office: IBM Old Orchard Rd Armonk NY 10504*

RICCIARELLI, KATIA, soprano; b. Rovigo, Italy, Jan. 18, 1946; m. Pippo Baudo, 1986. Grad. summa cum laude, Benedetto Marcello Conservatory, Venice, Italy. Operatic debut as Mimi in La Boheme, Mantua, Italy, 1969, also Covent Garden, London, 1974, I Due Foscari, Lyric Opera, Chgo., 1972; appeared in Suor Angelica, La Scala, Milan, 1976, La Boheme, Met. Opera Co., N.Y.C., 1975; other roles include Donizetti's Caterina Cornaro, Maria de Rohan and Lucrezia Borgia, and Bellini's Imogene, Elisabeth de Valois in Don Carlos, Covent Garden, 1989; numerous appearances in maj. opera houses throughout U.S. and Europe including San Francisco Opera, Paris Opera, Verona Festival; leading roles in Anna Bolena; recs. include I Due Foscari, Turandot, Carmen, Aida, Un Ballo in Maschera, Falstaff, Il Trovatore, La Boheme, Tosca, Pavarotti and Ricciarelli Live, Duetti d'Amore with Jose Carreras; also appears as Desdemona in Franco Zeffirelli's video Otello. Office: ICM Artists Ltd 40 W 57th St New York NY 10019-4001 Office: Via Magellana 2, I-20097 Corsica Italy

RICCIO, JANET MARIE, advertising executive; b. Bridgeport, Conn., Oct. 1, 1957; d. Victor Salvatore and Joyce (Reichert) R. BA, Boston U., 1979. Traffic mgr. Shailer Davidoff Rogers, Inc., Fairfield, Conn., 1980-81; account exec. Savitt Tobias Balk, Inc., N.Y.C., 1981-83; v.p., account supr. Rosenfeld Sirowitz & Lawson, Inc., N.Y.C., 1983-86; sr. v.p., mgmt. supr. Laurence, Charles, Free & Lawson, Inc., N.Y.C., 1986-87; v.p. new bus. devel. Corinthian Communications, Inc., 1987-88; v.p., gen. mgr. Della Femina McNamee WCRS; Hartford, Conn., 1988-89; sr. v.p. regional dir. Arnold Fortuna Lawner & Cabot, Hartford, 1989—. Active Hartford Stage, Conn. Forum, Jr. Achievement. Mem. AAUW, NAFE. Roman Catholic. Avocations: travel, music, cooking, movies, reading.

RICCO, DONNA, fashion designer. Pres. Donna Ricco Inc., N.Y.C. Office: Donna Ricco Inc 253 W 35th St 9th Fl New York NY 10001

RICE, (ETHEL) ANN, publishing executive, editor; b. South Bend, Ind., July 3, 1933; d. Walter A. and Ethylan Maude (Worden) R. A.B., Nazareth Coll., Kalamazoo, 1955. Editorial asst. Ave Maria mag., Notre Dame, Ind., 1955-63, asst. editor, 1963-64; asst. editor Today mag., Notre Dame, 1963-64, Scott, Foresman & Co., Chgo., 1964-67; editor U. Notre Dame Press, 1967-74, exec. editor, 1974—. Democrat. Roman Catholic. Office: U Notre Dame Press Notre Dame IN 46556

RICE, ANNE, author; b. New Orleans, Oct. 14, 1941; d. Howard and Katherine (Allen) O'Brien; m. Stan Rice, Oct. 14, 1961; children: Michele (dec.), Christopher. Student, Tex. Woman's U., 1959-60; BA, San Francisco State Coll., 1964, MA, 1971. Author: Interview with the Vampire, 1976, The Feast of all Saints, 1980, Cry to Heaven, 1982, The Vampire Lestat, 1985, The Queen of the Damned, 1988, The Mummy or Ramses the Damned, 1989, The Witching Hour, 1990, Tale of the Body Thief, 1992, Lasher, 1993, Taltos, 1994, Memnoch the Devil, 1995; (as A.N. Roquelaure) The Claiming of Sleeping Beauty, 1983, Beauty's Punishment, 1984, Beauty's Release: The Continued Erotic Adventures of Sleeping Beauty, 1985, Memnoch the Devil, Servant of the Bone, 1996; (as Anne Rampling) Exit to Eden, 1985, Belinda, 1986; screenwriter: Interview with a Vampire, 1994. Office: care Alfred A Knopf Inc 201 E 50th St New York NY 10022-7703*

RICE, ANNIE L. KEMPTON, medical, surgical and rehabilitation nurse; b. West Fairlee, Vt., Oct. 26, 1932; d. James Warren and Lena May (Bower); m. Abbott Eames Rice, Aug. 29, 1959; children: James W., Beverly A., Abbott Jr., David K. Diploma, Mary Hitchcock Sch. Nursing, Hanover, N.H., 1955; student, U. R.I., 1956-57; BSN, Boston U., 1959; postgrad., St. Anthlems Coll., Manchester, N.H. RN. Staff nurse spl. care unit R.I. Hosp., 1955; staff nurse New Eng. Deaconess Hosp., Boston, 1957; head nurse Jordan Hosp, Plymouth, Mass., 1960; staff nurse ICU/emergency Lakes Region Hosp., Laconia, N.H., 1968; staff nurse Pine Hill Nurses Registry, Nashua, N.H., 1976; charge nurse Greenbriar Terr., Nashua, 1985—. Past mem. Arthritis Found. Mem. Mary Hitchcock Sch. Nursing Alumnae, Boston U. Alumnae, Ea. Star, Grange, Women's Club. Home: 28 Sunland Dr Hudson NH 03051-3209

RICE, ARGYLL PRYOR, Hispanic studies and Spanish language educator; b. Va.; d. Theodorick Pryor and Argyll (Campbell) R. BA, Smith Coll., 1952; MA, Yale U., 1956, PhD, 1961. Spanish instr. Yale U., New Haven, 1959-60, 61-63; asst. prof. Spanish, Conn. Coll., New London, 1964-67, assoc. prof., 1967-72, prof., 1972—, chair dept. Hispanic Studies, 1971-74, 77-84. Author: Emilio Ballagas: poeta o poesia, 1967, Emilio Ballagas, Latin American Writers III; editor in chief Carlos A. Sole, Charles Scribner's Sons, 1989. Mem. MLA, Am. Assn. Tchrs. of Spanish and Portuguese, New Eng. Coun. Latin Am. Studies, U.S. Tennis Assn. (New England hall of fame), Phi Beta Kappa. Avocations: music, tennis. Home: 292 Pequot Ave Apt New London CT 06320-4437

RICE, CATHY SUE HARRISON, educational administrator; b. Vidalia, Ga., Oct. 8, 1951; d. Charles Curtis and Bonnie Faye (Smith) Harrison; m. Jerry Clifford Rice, Nov. 23, 1983; 1 child, James West Page. BS in Elem. Edn., Ga. So. U., 1972, MEd in Elem. Edn., 1980, EdS in Early Childhood Edn., 1993. Cert. L-5 adminstrn. and supervision. Tchr. Claxton (Ga.) Elem. Sch., 1973-74, Brooklet (Ga.) Elem. Sch., 1974-76, Dearing (Ga.) Elem. Sch., 1976-78, Glyndale Elem. Sch., Brunswick, Ga., 1978-94; instrnl. specialist Burroughs-Mollette Elem. Sch., Brunswick, 1994—; speaker S.E. Regional Math. Conf., 1993, Ga. At Risk Conf., 1994; presider Ga. Math. Conf., 1993. Pres. Brunswick Exchangettes, 1986, v.p., 1992, sec., 1994. Mem. ASCD, Delta Kappa Gamma (program chmn. 1993—), Phi Delta Kappa. Baptist. Avocations: reading, camping, boating, playing golf, fishing. Home: 107 Mackqueen Dr Brunswick GA 31525 Office: Burroughs Molette Elem Sch 1900 Lee St Brunswick GA 31520-6340

RICE, CHARLES DUNCAN, university official; b. Aberdeen, Scotland, Oct. 20, 1942; came to U.S., 1969; s. James Inglis and Jane Meauras (Scroggie) R.; m. Susan Ilene Wunsch, July 5, 1967; children: James Duncan, Samuel Duncan, Jane Emma. MA with 1st class honors, U. Aberdeen, 1966; PhD, U. Edinburgh, Scotland, 1969. Lectr. history U. Aberdeen, 1966-69; asst. prof. history Yale U., New Haven, 1970-76, assoc. prof., 1976-79; prof. history Hamilton Coll., Clinton, N.Y., 1979-85, dean, 1979-85; prof. history, dean faculty of arts and sci. NYU, 1985-95, vice chancellor, 1991—. Author: Rise and Fall of Black Slavery, 1975, The Scots Abolitionists, 1982; assoc. editor: Slavery and Abolition, 1979-86; contbr. articles and revs. in field. Trustee The Peddie Sch., Hightstown, N.J., 1973-82, 86—. C. & J. Henry Fund fellow, 1965-66, Am. Coun. Learned Socs. fellow, 1969-70, Morse fellow, 1976-75. Home: 29 Washington Sq W Apt 15C New York NY 10011-9199 Office: NYU/Vice Chancellor 70 Washington Sq S New York NY 10012

RICE, CHARLES EDWARD, bank executive; b. Chattanooga, Tenn., Aug. 4, 1936; s. Charles Edward and Louise (Goodson) R.; m. Dianne Tauscher; children: Danny, Celeste, Michelle. B.B.A., U. Miami, 1958; M.B.A., Rollins Coll., Winter Park, Fla., 1964; grad., Advanced Mgmt. Program, Harvard U., 1975. Vice pres., then pres. Barnett Bank, Winter Park, 1965-71; exec. v.p. Barnett Banks Fla., Inc., Jacksonville, 1971-73, pres., from 1973, chief exec. officer, 1979—, now also chmn., bd. dirs.; bd. dirs. Sprint Corp., CSX Corp. Trustee Univ. of Miami, Rollins Coll. Office: Barnett Banks Inc 50 N Laura St Jacksonville FL 32202-3664*

RICE, CLARE I., electronics company executive; b. Rice Lake, Wis., Nov. 3, 1918; s. Chris Nilson and Ingeborg (Haug) R.; m. Virginia M. Bateman; children: Karen Bateman, Carol Rice Brannon, David Alan; m. Elaine Spurrier. B.S. in Elec. Engring, U. Wis., 1943; B.S. in Law, St. Paul Coll. Law, 1950; D.Engring., Rose-Hulman Inst. Tech., 1979. Registered profl. engr., Minn., D.C. Supr. aircraft radio engring. Northwest Airlines, Inc., Mpls., 1946-51; staff engr. Aero. Radio, Inc., Washington, 1951-53; aviation sales mgr., gen. mgr. Bendix Avionics Div., Balt., 1953-62; pres. Sunbeam Electronics, Inc., Ft. Lauderdale, Fla., 1962-66; v.p. Nova U., Ft. Lauderdale, 1966-68; asst. v.p., v.p., sr. v.p. Collins Radio Co., pres. Collins Avionics group Rockwell Internat. Corp., Cedar Rapids, Iowa, 1968-83; dir. Rockwell-Collins Internat., Inc., Dallas. Chmn. United Way, Cedar Rapids, 1973-74; trustee Coe Coll., 1979-83, Hoover Presdl. Libr.; bd. dirs. St. Luke's Hosp., 1976-82, Mchts. Nat. Bank, 1977-83; chmn. Mcpl. Airport Commn., Cedar Rapids, 1980-84; charter mem. Aviation Hall of Fame; capt. Hon. Dep. Sheriffs Assn., 1987—; pres. Cmty. Assn. Rancho Bernardo Heights, 1988-91; dir. Rancho Bernardo Cmty. Found. Lt. comdr. USNR, 1943-46. Recipient Disting. Svc. citation U. Wis., 1979, 84; Pioneer award Milw. Sch. Engring., 1981. Sr. mem. IEEE; mem. Iowa Mfrs. Assn. (bd. dirs. 1975-81), Gen. Aviation Mfrs. Assn. (dir. 1970-81, chmn. 1979), U. Wis. Alumni Assn. (chmn. 1981-82, pres. 1980-81, Disting. Service award 1984). Republican. Presbyn. Clubs: Wings (N.Y.C.); Nat. Aviation (Washington); Rancho Bernardo Heights Country. Lodge: Royal Order of Jesters (dir. 1979). Home: 12201 Fairway Pointe San Diego CA 92128-3230

RICE, DARREL ALAN, lawyer; b. Denver, Jan. 8, 1947; s. Dale Harvey and Dorothy (Enewold) F.; m. Jeffrey Lynn Taylor, May 31, 1970; children: Ashley, Justin, Chandler. BSIE, U. Ark., 1969; JD, So. Meth. U., 1972. Bar: Tex. 1972. Assoc. Butler & Binion, Houston, 1972-75, Winstead, McGuire, Sechrest & Minick, P.C., Dallas, 1975-78; shareholder Winstead Sechrest & Minick, P.C., Dallas, 1978—. Trustee 1st Presbyn. Ch. Found., Dallas, 1982-94; adv. dir. Spl. Camps for Spl. Kids, Dallas, 1987-90, bd. dirs., mem. exec. com., 1990—; bd. dirs. Tex. Bus. Law Found., 1989—; bd. dirs., mem. exec. com. Dallas CASA, 1989—; mem. exec. bd. So. Meth. U. Law Sch., 1991—. Mem. ABA, Tex. Bar Assn., State Bar Tex. (chmn. legal opinions com. 1989-92, mem. coun. bus. law sect. 1992-94), Dallas Bar Assn., Tex. Assn. Bank Counsel, Tower Club. Office: Winstead Sechrest & Minick PC 5400 Renaissance Tower 1201 Elm St Dallas TX 75270

RICE, DAVID EUGENE, JR., trade association administrator, lawyer, consultant; b. Greenwood, S.C., July 1, 1916; s. David Sr. and Mamie Elizabeth (Johnson) R.; m. Virginia E. Dunning, Dec. 24, 1947 (div. 1955); m. Beryl Lena Carter, June 5, 1971. BA, Ohio State U., 1937; JD, Northwestern U., 1941; LLM, Yale U., 1950. Bar: Md., 1946. Assoc. prof. Lincoln U., St. Louis, Mo., 1946-48; Sterling fellow Yale Law Sch., New Haven, 1948-50; dean Tex. So. U. Sch. Law, Houston, 1950-55; savs. officer Ill. Fed. Savs. and Loan Assn., Chgo., 1956-65; assoc. dir. Chgo. Small Bus. Opportunity Corp. (name now CEDCO), Chgo., 1965-67; dir. project outreach Nat. Bus. League, Washington, 1967-68, asst. to pres. and dir. constituency affairs, 1969-83, v.p. constituency affairs, 1984-86, exec. v.p., 1987—; liaison Nat. Student Bus. League, Washington, 1975-92; dean Cert. Insts.: Nat. Bus. League, Washington, 1977-87; resident hist./archivist Nat. Bus. League, Washington, 1981—. Editor: National Bar Journal, 1947-48; contbr. articles to profl. jours. Chmn. rules com. D.C. Black Rep. Coun., Washington, 1985—; active D.C. Black Rep. Scholarship Fund, Inc., 1985—; mem. subcom. trade and commerce D.C.-Dakar Capital Cities Friendship Coun., 1986—; active Mighty Men of Valor; mem. Kool achiever awards screening com. Nabisco Nat. Leadership Visitation Program; trustee Met. African Meth. Episcopal Ch., 1986—, chair leadership retreat, 1990, mem. loan negotiating com. With CIC, AUS, 1943-45, Corps Mil. Police, 1945-46. Mem. NAACP, Nat. Bar Assn., Nat. Bus. League (life), Minority Trade Assn. Roundtable of SBA, Coun. of 100, U.S./African Bus. Exch., Yale Law Alumni Assn., Northwestern U. Law Alumni Assn., Ohio State U. Alumni Assn., Pigskin Club, Kappa Alpha Psi. Republican. Avocations: piano, tennis, walking, reading, writing. Office: Nat Bus League 1511 K St NW # 432 Washington DC 20005-1401

RICE, DENIS TIMLIN, lawyer; b. Milw., July 11, 1932; s. Cyrus Francis and Kathleen (Timlin) R.; children: James Connelly, Tracy Ellen. A.B., Princeton U., 1954; J.D., U. Mich., 1959. Bar: Calif. 1960. Practiced in San Francisco, 1959—; assoc. firm Pillsbury, Madison & Sutro, 1959-61, Howard & Prim, 1961-63; prin. firm Howard, Rice, Nemerovski, Canady, Falk & Rabkin, 1964—; dir. Gensler & Assocs., Inc., San Francisco; chmn., mng. com. San Francisco Inst. Fin. Svcs., 1983-92. Councilman, City of Tiburon, Calif., 1968-72, mayor, 1970-72; dir. Marin County Transit Dist., 1970-72, 77-81, chmn., 1979-81; supr. Marin County, 1977-81, chmn., 1979-80; commr. Marin Housing Authority, 1977-81; mem. San Francisco Bay Conservation and Devel. Commn., 1977-83; bd. dirs. Planning and Conservation League, 1981, Marin Symphony, 1984-92, Marin Theatre Co., 1987—, Marin Conservation League, 1995—, Digital Village Found., 1995—; mem. Met. Transp. Commn., 1980-83; mem. bd. visitors U. Mich. Law Sch. 1st lt. AUS, 1955-57. Recipient Freedom Found. medal, 1956. Fellow Am. Bar Found.; mem. ABA (fed. regulation of securities com., chair Asia-Pacific Bus. Law Com.), State Bar Calif., San Francisco Bar Assn., Am. Judicature Soc., Bankers Club, Tiburon Peninsula Club, Nassau Club, Olympic Club, Order of Coif, Phi Beta Kappa, Phi Delta Phi. Home: 1850 Mountain View Dr Belvedere Tiburon CA 94920-1810 Office: 3 Embarcadero Ctr Ste 700 San Francisco CA 94111-4065

RICE, DONALD BLESSING, business executive, former secretary of air force; b. Frederick, Md., June 4, 1939; s. Donald Blessing and Mary Celia (Santangelo) R.; m. Susan Fitzgerald, Aug. 25, 1962; children: Donald Blessing III, Joseph John, Matthew Fitzgerald. BSChemE, U. Notre Dame, 1961, DEng (hon.), 1975; MS in Indsl. Adminstrn., Purdue U., 1962, PhD in Mgmt. and Econs., 1965, D. Mgmt. (hon.), 1985; LLD (hon.), Pepperdine U., 1989; LHD (hon.), West Coast U., 1993; D in Pub. Policy (hon.), Rand Grad. Sch., 1995. Dir. cost analysis Office Sec. Def., Washington, 1967-69, dep. asst. sec. def. resource analysis, 1969-70; asst. dir. Office Mgmt. and Budget, Exec. Office Pres., 1970-72; pres., CEO The Rand Corp., Calif., 1972-89; sec. USAF, 1989-93; pres., COO Teledyne, Inc., L.A., 1993—; bd. dirs. Teledyne, Inc., Vulcan Materials Co., Wells Fargo Bank, Wells Fargo & Co.; mem. Nat. Sci. Bd., 1974-86; chmn. Nat. Commn. Supplies and Shortages, 1975-77; mem. Nat. Commn. on U.S.-China Relations; mem. nat. adv. com. oceans and atmosphere Dept. Commerce, 1972-75; mem. adv. panel Office Tech. Assessment, 1976-79; adv. council Coll. Engring., U. Notre Dame, 1974-88; mem. Def. Sci. Bd., 1977-83, sr. cons., 1984-88; U.S. mem. Trilateral Commn.; dir. for sec. def. and Pres. Def. Resource Mgmt. Study, 1977-79. Author articles. Served to capt. AUS, 1965-67. Recipient Sec. Def. Meritorious Civilian Service medal, 1970, Def. Exceptional Civilian Svc. medal, 1993, Forrestal award, 1992; Ford Found. fellow, 1962-65. Fellow AAAS; mem. Council Fgn. Relations, Inst. Mgmt. Scis. (past pres.), Tau Beta Pi. Office: Teledyne Inc 2049 Century Park E 15th Fl Los Angeles CA 90067

RICE, DONALD SANDS, lawyer, entrepreneur; b. Bronxville, N.Y., Mar. 25, 1940; s. Anton Henry and Lydia Phipps (Sands) R.; m. Edgenie Higgins, Aug. 27, 1966; children: Alice Higgins, Edgenie Reynolds. AB magna cum laude, Harvard U., 1961, LLB cum laude, 1964; LLM in Taxation, NYU, 1965. Bar: N.Y. 1964, U.S. Ct. Claims 1965, U.S. Supreme Ct. 1981. Law clk. to judge U.S. Ct. Claims, 1965-67; assoc. Barrett, Smith, Schapiro & Simon, N.Y.C., 1967-71; ptnr. Barrett, Smith, Schapiro, Simon & Armstrong, N.Y.C., 1971-86; vice chmn. bd. The Bowery Savs. Bank, N.Y.C., 1986-88; also bd. dirs. The Bowery Savs. Bank; ptnr. Chadbourne & Parke, N.Y.C., 1988-96; mng. dir. and prin. Ravitch Rice & Co. LLC, N.Y.C., 1996—; lectr. Nat. Assn. Real Estate Investment Trusts, Bank Adminstrs. Inst., Bank Tax Inst., 1971-86; chmn., bd. dirs. Corp. of Yaddo, 1986—; co-chmn. Soviet-Am. Banking Law Working Group, 1991—; v.p., treas., bd. dirs. Soviet Bus. and Comml. Law Edn. Found., 1991—; vol. lectr. Fin. Svcs. Vol. Corps Mongolian Bank Tng. Program, 1993, Georgetown Internat. Law Inst., NYU Sch. Continuing Edn., Russian Trade Fair-U.S. Dept. Commerce, 1994; mem. real estate adv. bd. to N.Y. State Comptr., 1987-93. Bd. dirs. African Med. Rsch. Found., 1978—; trustee Marimed Found., 1984—, Chapin Sch., 1980-91, The Hackley Sch., 1974-81, St. Philip's Episcopal Ch., Mattapoisett, Mass., 1987—; trustee Nat. Com. Am. Fgn. Policy, 1994—, v.p. 1996—. Mem. ABA, Internat. Bar Assn., Coun. Fgn. Rels., N.Y. State Bar Assn. (chmn. fin. instns. com. tax sect. 1984-86), Bar Assn. of City of N.Y., Century Assn., Harvard Club, N.Y. Yacht Club, River Club. Home: 1120 Fifth Ave New York NY 10128-0144 Office: Ravitch Rice & Co LLC 156 West 56th St Ste 902 New York NY 10019

RICE, DOROTHY PECHMAN (MRS. JOHN DONALD RICE), medical economist; b. Bklyn., June 11, 1922; d. Gershon and Lena (Schiff) Pechman; m. John Donald Rice, Apr. 3, 1943; children: Kenneth D., Donald B., Thomas H. Student, Bklyn. Coll., 1938-39; BA, U. Wis., 1941; DSc (hon.), Coll. Medicine and Dentistry N.J., 1979. With hosp. and med. facilities USPHS, Washington, 1960-61; med. econs. studies Social Security Adminstrn., 1962-63; health econs. br. Community Health Svc., USPHS, 1964-65; chief health ins. rsch. br. Social Security Adminstrn., 1966-72, dep. asst. commr. for rsch. and statistics, 1972-75; dir. Nat. Ctr. for Health Stats., Rockville, Md., 1976-82; prof. Inst. Health & Aging U. Calif., San Francisco, 1982-94, prof. emeritus, 1994—; developer, mgr. nationwide health info. svcs.; expert on aging, health care costs, disability, and cost-of-illness. Contbr. articles to profl. jours. Recipient Social Security Adminstrn. citation, 1968, Disting. Service medal HEW, 1974, Jack C. Massey Found. award, 1978. Fellow Am. Public Health Assn. (domestic award for excellence 1978, Sedgwick Meml. medal, 1988), Am. Statis. Assn.; mem. Inst. Medicine, Assn. Health Svcs. Rsch. (President's award 1988), Am. Econ. Assn., Population Assn. Am., LWV. Home: 13895 Campus Dr Oakland CA 94605-3831 Office: U Calif Sch Nursing Calif San Francisco CA 94143-0646

RICE, EDWARD EARL, former government official, author; b. Saginaw, Mich., Feb. 6, 1909; s. William Edward and Katherine Marie (Meyer) R.; m. Mary June Kellogg, Oct. 26, 1942. Student, U. Wis., 1926-28; BS, U. Ill.,

1930, postgrad., 1934-35; postgrad., U. Mex., 1931, Coll. Chinese Studies, also pvt. tutors, Beijing, 1935-37. Joined Fgn. Svc., Dept. State, 1935; lang. attache Beijing, 1935-37; vice consul Canton, China, 1938-40; consul Foochow, China, 1940-42; 2d sec. Am. Embassy, Chungking, China, 1942-45; asst. chief div. Chinese affairs Dept. State, 1946-48, asst. chief div. Philippine affairs, 1948-49; 1st sec., consul Am. Embassy, Manila, 1949-51; consul gen. Stuttgart, Fed. Republic Germany, 1952-56; fgn. svc. insp. Dept. State, 1956-58, dep. dir. pers., 1959, mem. plicy planning coun., 1959-61, dep. asst. sec. of state for Far Ea. affairs, 1962-63; consul gen., min. Hong Kong, 1964-67; diplomat in residence with rank of prof. U. Calif., Berkeley, 1968-69, rsch. assoc. Ctr. for Chinese Studies, 1969—; vis. prof. Marquette U., 1973; advisor U.S. del. 3d, 4th and 5th sessions Econ. Commn. for Asia Far East, 1948-49. Author: Mao's Way, 1972, Wars of the Third Kind, 1988. Recipient Gold medal for non-fiction Commonwealth Club, 1973. Mem. Beta Gamma Sigma. Home: 1819 Lagoon View Dr Belvedere Tiburon CA 94920-1807 Office: U Calif Ctr for Chinese Studies Berkeley CA 94720

RICE, EUGENE FRANKLIN, JR., history educator; b. Lexington, Ky., Aug. 20, 1924; s. Eugene Franklin and Lula (Piper) R.; m. Charlotte Bloch, Aug. 26, 1952 (dec. Oct. 1982); children: Eugene, John, Louise. BA, Harvard U., 1947, MA, 1948, PhD, 1953; postgrad., Ecole Normale Superieure, 1951-52. Instr. Harvard U., Cambridge, Mass., 1953-55; asst. prof. Cornell U., Ithaca, N.Y., 1955-59, assoc. prof., 1959-63; prof. Cornell U., Ithaca, 1963-64; prof. Columbia U., N.Y.C., 1964-74, William R. Shepperd prof., 1974—; chmn. dept. history Columbia U., 1970-73; advisor in history Random House, Knopf, N.Y.C., 1964-90; chmn., founder seminar Columbia U. Seminar Homosexualities. Author: The Renaissance Idea of Wisdom, 1958, The Foundations of Early Modern Europe, 1970, The Epistles of Lefevre d'Etaples, 1972, St. Jerome in the Renaissance, 1985; contbr. articles to profl. jours. Staff sgt. U.S. Army, 1943-45, ETO. Guggenheim Found. fellow Inst. for Advanced Study, 1959-60, 62-63, NEH fellow, 1974-75. Mem. Am. Hist. Assn. (v.p. rsch. 1979-81), Renaissance Soc. Am. (exec. dir. 1966-88), Soc. for Reformation Rsch. Democrat. Home: 560 Riverside Dr Apt 12J New York NY 10027-3214 Office: Columbia U Dept Of History New York NY 10027

RICE, FERILL JEANE, writer, civic worker; b. Hemingford, Nebr., July 4, 1926; d. Derrick and Helen Agnes (Moffatt) Dalton; m. Otis LaVerne Rice, Mar. 7, 1946; children: LaVeria June McMichael, Larry L. Student, U. Omaha, 1961. Dir. jr. and sr. choir Congl. Ch., Tabor, Iowa, 1952-66; tchr. Fox Valley Tech. Inst., Appleton, Wis., 1970-77; activity dir. Family Heritage Nursing Home, Appleton, Wis., 1972-75; dir. activity Peabody Manor, Appleton, Wis., 1975-76. Editor: Moffatt and Related Families, 1981; asst. editor (mag.) Yester-Year, 1975-76; contbr. articles to profl jours. Chmn. edn. Am. Cancer Soc., Fremont County, 1962, 63, 64; founder, 1st pres. Mothers Club Nishna Valley chpt. Demolay for Boys. Mem. DAR, Internat. Carnival Glass Assn., Heart Am. Carnival Glass Assn., Nat. Cambridge Collectors, Heisey Collectors Am., Iowa Fedn. Women's Clubs (Fremont county chmn. 1964, 65, 66, 67, 7th dist. chmn. libr. svcs. 1966-67), Tabor Women's Club (pres. 1962, 63, 64), Jr. Legion Aux. (founder, 1st dir. 1951-52), Fenton Art Glass Collectors Am. (co-founder 1977, sec., editor newsletter 1976-86, editor/sec. 1988-93, pres./editor 1993-95, treas. 1995—), Mayflower Soc., John Howland Soc., Ross County Ohio Geneal. Soc., Iowa Geneal. Soc., Dallas County Mo. Geneal. Soc., Imperial Collectors Am., Clay County (Ind.) Geneal. Soc., Owen County (Ind.) Geneal. Soc., Fenton Finders of Wis. (chpt. #1 pres. 1988-90). Republican. Methodist. Lodges: Order Ea. Star (worthy matron 1956, 64), Rainbow for Girls (bd. dirs. 1964), Internat. Order Job's Daus. (honored queen 1945). Home: 302 Pheasant Run Kaukauna WI 54130-1802 Office: Rice Enterprises & Rice & Rice 1665 Lamers Dr # 305 Little Chute WI 54140-2519

RICE, FRANCES MAE, pediatrician, family practitioner; b. Oakland, Calif., Apr. 19, 1931; d. George Henry and Clare Evelyn (Youngman) Rice. AB cum laude, U. Calif., Berkeley, 1953, MPH, 1964; MD, U. Calif., San Francisco, 1957. Intern U. Calif. Hosp., San Francisco, 1957-58; resident U. Calif. Hosp., 1959-61; pediatric and family physician HMO, Hanford, Calif., 1974-75; clin. pediatrician Kern County Health Dept., Bakersfield, Calif., 1975-76; physician Kern Med. Group, Inc., Bakersfield, 1976-83; pvt. practice pediatrics Shafter, Calif., 1983-89; physician Kern County Health Dept., Bakersfield, 1989, Mercy Medicenter, Bakersfield, 1990-91, K.C.E.O.C. Family Clinic, Bakersfield, 1993—. USPHS fellow, 1963-64. Fellow Royal Soc. Medicine; mem. AMA, N.Y. Acad. Sci., Calif. Med. Assn. Avocation: hiking. Home: 5909 Lindbrook Way Bakersfield CA 93309 Office: KCEOC Family Health Clinic 1611 1st St Bakersfield CA 93304

RICE, FREDERICK COLTON, environmental management consultant; b. Exeter, N.H., Aug. 8, 1938; s. Frederick Nott and Mary (Colton) R.; m. Joan Alis Lambrecht, June 25, 1962; children: Frederick Lambrecht, Janelle Alis. BS, U.S. Mil. Acad., 1960. Registered environ. assessor. Commd. 2d lt. U.S. Army, 1960, advanced through grades to maj., 1967, resigned, 1970; supr. Pacific Bell, San Bruno, Calif., 1970-71; area mgr. Sta-Power Industries, San Francisco, Phoenix and Balt., 1971-73; v.p. Getty Synthetic Fuels, Signal Hill, Calif., 1974-83; dir. land resources The Irvine Co., Newport Beach, Calif., 1983-84; pres. F. C. Rice & Co., Inc., Orange, Calif., 1984-88; nat. tech. dir. HDR Engring., Inc., Irvine, 1988-89; So. Calif. mgr. R. W. Beck and Assocs., Irvine, 1990-91; pres. F.C. Rice & Co., Laguna Hills, Calif., 1991-92; project dir. Roy F. Weston, Inc., Wilmington, Mass., 1993-95; pres. F.C. Rice & Co. Inc., Hampton, N.H., 1995—. Contbr. articles to profl. jours. Mem. nat. referee com. Am. Youth Soccer Orgn., Tustin, Calif., 1978-79; admissions rep., U.S. Mil. Acad. Admissions Office, 1975-87, area coord., Orange County, Calif., 1987-92, So. Calif. coord., 1992-93. Mem. Solid Waste Assn. N.Am. (so. Calif. chpt. bd. dirs. 1989-91, chmn. landfill gas com. 1979-80, resource recovery com. 1981-83, control tech. com. 1988-89, landfill gas divsn. 1991-93, Profl. Achievement award 1994), Internat. Solid Waste Assn., West Point Soc. Orange County (pres. 1975-76, bd. govs. 1975-93, Duty, Honor, Country award 1987), West Point Soc. New Eng. (sec., bd. govs. 1996—), U.S. Mil. Acad. Assn. Grads. (trustee-at-large 1992-95, societies com. 1991—, chmn. mem. subcom. 1994-95). Republican. Roman Catholic. Avocations: skiing, golf, backpacking. Home: 15 Heather Ln Hampton NH 03842-1118 Office: FC Rice & Co Inc 15 Heather Ln Hampton NH 03842

RICE, GARY RUSSELL, special education educator; b. Franklin, Pa., Oct. 11, 1951; s. Robert Russell and Della Elizabeth Rice. Grad. cum laude, Cleve. State U., 1973. Cert. polit. sci. tchr., learning disabilities, behavioral disorders, Ohio. Substitute tchr. Lakewood, Rocky River, Westlake (Ohio) Schs., 1973-77; instr. West Side Inst. Tech., Cleve., 1977-78; spl. edn. tchr. Parma (Ohio) City Sch. Dist., 1978—; learning disabilities tutor, Lakewood, 1974-75; guitar conservator Rock and Roll Hall of Fame and Mus., Cleve. Asst. scoutmaster, leader Boy Scouts Am., Cleve.; Sunday sch. tchr. local ch., Cleve.; spkr. to various groups on Spl. Children, the Holocaust and Native Americans; charter mem. U.S. Holocaust Meml. Mus. Recipient Outstanding Spl. Educator award Parma PTA Spl. Edn. com., 1985, Thanks to Tchrs. award Sta. TV-8 WJW, Cleve., 1994. Mem. Parma Edn. Assn., Cleve. Fedn. Musicians, DeMolay Masons, Shriners. Avocations: music, photography.

RICE, GEORGE LAWRENCE, III (LARRY RICE), lawyer; b. Jackson, Tenn., Sept. 24, 1951; s. George Lawrence Jr. and Judith W. (Pierce) R.; m. Joy Gaia, Sept. 14, 1974; children: George Lawrence IV, Amy Colleen. Student, Oxford U., 1972-73; BA with honors, Southwestern Coll., 1974; JD, Memphis State U., 1976; Nat. Coll. Advocacy, ATLA, 1978. Bar: Tenn. 1977, U.S. Supreme Ct. 1980. Assoc. Rice, Rice, Smith, Bursi, Veazey, 1976-81, ptnr., 1981—, acting sr. ptnr., 1995. Author: Divorce Practice in Tennessee, 1987, Divorce Lawyer's Handbook, 1989, (video) Divorce What You Need to Know When it Happens to You, 1990, Tactics in Divorce Practice American Journal of Family Law, 1989; The Complete Guide to Divorce Practice, American Bar Association, 1993, Visual Persuasion, Practice Tips Series, AIDS and Clients; bd. editors Matrimonial Strategist, 1994-96, mem. editl. bd. Active Supreme Ct. Child Support Guidelines Commn., 1989, Family Law Revision Commn., 1990-91. Mem. Timberwolves Paintball Team. Named One of Best Lawyers in Am. Mem. ABA (conv. lectr. 1993, 94), ATLA, Tenn. Bar Assn. (chmn. family law sect. 1987-88), Memphis Bar Assn. (founding chmn. family law sect.), Tenn. Trial Lawyers Assn. Office: Rice Rice Smith Bursi Veazey & Amundsen 44 N 2nd St Fl 10 Memphis TN 38103-2220

RICE, JAMES ROBERT, engineering scientist, geophysicist; b. Frederick, Md., Dec. 3, 1940; s. Donald Blessing and Mary Celia (Santangelo) R.; m. Renata Dmowska, Feb. 28, 1981; children by previous marriage: Douglas, Jonathan. B.S., Lehigh U., 1962, Sc.M., 1963, Ph.D., 1964. Postdoctoral fellow Brown U., Providence, 1964-65, asst. prof. engring., 1965-68, assoc. prof., 1968-70, prof., 1970-81, Ballou prof. theoretical and applied mechanics, 1973-81; McKay prof. engring. sci. and geophysics Harvard U., Cambridge, Mass., 1981—. Recipient awards for sci. publs. ASME, awards for sci. publs. ASTM, awards for sci. publs. U.S. Nat. Com. Rock Mechanics, Timoshenko medal Am. Soc of Mechanical Engineers, 1994, Francis J. Clamer medal Franklin Institute, 1995. Fellow ASME, AAAS; mem. NAS, NAE, ASCE, Am. Geophys. Union, Fgn. Mem. Royal Soc. Research contbns. to solid mechanics, materials sci. and geophysics. Office: Harvard U Div Applied Sci Cambridge MA 02138

RICE, JERRY LEE, professional football player; b. Starkville, Miss., Oct. 13, 1962; m. Jackie Rice; 1 child, Jaqui. Student, Miss. State Valley U. Football player San Francisco 49ers, 1985—. Named MVP, Super Bowl XXIII, 1989, Sporting News NFL Player of Yr., 1987, 90; named to Sporting News Coll. All-Am. team, 1984, Sporting News All-Pro team, 1986-92, Pro Bowl team, 1986-93, 95, Pro Bowl MVP, 1995. Holder NFL career records for most touchdown receptions (131), most touchdowns (139); most consecutive games with one or more touchdowns (13), 1987; NFL single-season record for most touchdown receptions (22), 1987; shares NFL single-game record for most touchdown receptions (5), 1990. Office: care San Francisco 49ers 4949 Centennial Blvd Santa Clara CA 95054-1229*

RICE, JERRY MERCER, biochemist; b. Washington, Oct. 3, 1940; s. John Earle Rice and Leona (Mercer) Greiner; m. Mary Jane Janocha, Jan. 10, 1978; children: Stacey Lynn, Stephen Mark. BA, Wesleyan U., 1962; PhD, Harvard U., 1966. Commd. officer USPHS, 1966; rsch. scientist Nat. Cancer Inst., Bethesda, Md., 1966-81, chief Lab. of Comparative Carcinogenesis, Frederick, Md., 1981-94, 96; assoc. dir. Frederick Cancer Rsch. and Devel. Ctr., Nat. Cancer Inst., Frederick, Md., 1994-95, acting dir. divsn. cancer etiology, 1994-95; sr. scientist WHO, 1996—; chief Unit of Carcinogen Identification and Evaluation Internat. Agy. for Rsch. on Cancer, Lyons, France, 1996—; lectr. univs., profl. groups, med. socs. Editor: Perinatal Carcinogenesis, 1979. Co-editor: Organ and Species Specificity in Chemical Carcinogenesis, 1983, Perinatal and Multigeneration Carcinogenesis, 1989; contbr. rsch. articles and revs. in mechanisms of chem. carcinogenesis to profl. jours. Mem. Am. Soc. Microbiology, Am. Assn. Cancer Research, Internat. Soc. of Differentiation, Teratology Soc., Phi Beta Kappa, Sigma Xi. Avocation: viticulture. Home: 3213 Coquelin Ter Bethesda MD 20815-4840 Office: Internat Org Rsch Cancer, 150 Cours Albert Thomas, 69372 Cedex 08 Lyon France

RICE, JOHN RISCHARD, computer scientist, researcher, educator; b. Tulsa, June 6, 1934; s. John Coykendal Kirk and Margaret Lucille (Rischard) R.; m. Nancy Ann Bradfield, Dec. 19, 1954; children: Amy Lynn, Jenna Margaret. BS, Okla. State U., 1954, MS, 1956; PhD, Calif. Inst. Tech., 1959. Postdoctoral fellow Nat. Bur. Standards, Washington, 1959-60; rsch. mathematician GM Rsch. Labs., Warren, Mich., 1960-64; prof. Purdue U., West Lafayette, Ind., 1964-89; head dept. computer sci. Purdue U., West Lafayette, 1983-96, disting. prof., 1989—; editor-in-chief ACM Trans. Math. Software, N.Y.C., 1975-93; chmn. ACM-Signum, N.Y.C., 1977-79; dir. Computing Rsch. Bd., Washington, 1987-94; chair Computing Rsch. Assn., Washington, 1991-93. Author: The Approximation of Functions, 1964, Vol. 2, 1969, Numerical Methods, Software and Analysis, 1983; author and editor: Mathematical Software, 1971; editor: Intelligent Scientific Software Systems, 1991. Fellow AAAS, ACM (George Forsythe Meml. lectr. 1975); mem. IFIP (working group 2.5, vice chmn. 1977-91), Soc. Indsl. and Applied Math., Nat. Acad. Engring., Pji Kappa Phi. Home: 112 E Navajo St West Lafayette IN 47906-2153 Office: Purdue U Computer Sci Dept West Lafayette IN 47907

RICE, JOHN THOMAS, architecture educator; b. New London, Conn., Feb. 4, 1931; s. Clarence Benjamin and Emily (Gudal) R. BS in Engring., U. Conn., 1952; MSME, Newark Coll. Engring., 1954; D.Sc. in Engring., Columbia U., 1962. Registered profl. engr., N.Y. Test equipment designer propeller div. Curitss-Wright Corp., Caldwell, N.J., 1952-54; stress analyst Wright Aeronautical div. Curtiss-Wright Corp., Woodridge, N.J., 1954-59; chief structural mechanics Gen. Dynamics/Electric Boat, Groton, Conn., 1962-64; asst. prof. mech. engring. Pratt Inst., Bklyn., 1964-66, assoc. prof., 1966-74, prof., 1974—, chmn. dept. mech. engring., 1981-90. Mem. ASME (chmn. mech. engring. dept. heads com. region II 1987-89, chmn. profl. devel. region II 1989-93, mem. exec. com. met. sect. 1990—, vice chmn. 1991-92, chmn. 1992-93, sec. region II 1993—), Pi Tau Sigma, Tau Beta Pi. Office: Pratt Inst Dept of Architecture 200 Willoughby Ave Brooklyn NY 11205-3817

RICE, JON RICHARD, state health officer, physician; b. Grand Forks, N.D., July 10, 1946; s. Harry Frazer and Marian (Lund) R.; m. Robera Jane Lindbergh, June 7, 1969; children: Kristen, Jennifer. BA, U. N.D., 1969, BS, 1970; MD, U. Tex., San Antonio, 1972; MS in Health Adminstrn., U. Colo., 1991. Intern U.S. Naval Hosp., San Diego, 1972-73; resident U. N.D. Sch. Medicine, Minot, 1975-77; physician Valley Med., Grand Forks, 1977-93; state health officer N.D. Dept. Health, Bismarck, 1993—. Contbg. author: Pilots, Personality and Performance. Lt. USN, 1972-75. Recipient Outstanding Vol. award Dakota Heart Assn., 1989, YMCA, 1992, Outstanding Health Care Provider Grand Forks C. of C., 1992. Mem. AMA, Am. Acad. Family Physicians, Am. Coll. Physician Execs., Rotary, Alpha Omega Alpha. Office: ND Dept Health 600 E Boulevard Ave Bismarck ND 58505-0200

RICE, JONATHAN C., educational television executive; b. St. Louis, Feb. 19, 1916; s. Charles M. and May R. (Goldman) R.; m. Kathleen Feiblman, Aug. 6, 1946 (dec. June 1964); children: Jefferson Charles, Kit (dec.), May Nanette. AB, Stanford U., 1938. War photographer, reporter Acme Newspix/NEA Svc., PTO of WWII, 1941-43; picture book editor Look Mag., N.Y.C., 1947-48; news/spl. events dir. Sta. KTLA-TV, L.A., 1948-53; program mgr. Sta. KQED-TV, San Francisco, 1953-67, dir. program ops., 1967-78, asst. to pres., 1978-90, bd. dirs., 1990—; cons. NET, PBS, Corp. for Pub. Broadcasting, Ford Found., TV Lima Peru, Sta. WGBH-TV, Boston, Sta. WNET-TV, N.Y.C., French TV, Europe Eastern Edn. TV, Dept. Justice, 1955-90; lectr. Stanford U., 1958-77. Editor: Look at America, The South, Official Picture Story of the FBI, 1947. Bd. dirs. NATAS, San Francisco, Planned Parenthood, San Francisco and Marin County, Calif. Maj. USMC, 1943-47, PTO. Recipient George Foster Peabody award, 1956, Thomas Alva Edison award for best station, N.Y.C., 1960, Gov.'s award NATAS, 1972-73, Ralph Lowell award Corp. for Pub. Broadcasting, 1972; Jonathan Rice Studio named in his honor, 1986. Avocations: rowing, bicycling, cooking, photography, travel. Home: 1 Russian Hill Pl San Francisco CA 94133-3605

RICE, JOSEPH ALBERT, banker; b. Cranford, N.J., Oct. 11, 1924; s. Louis A. and Elizabeth J. (Michael) R.; m. Katharine Wolfe, Sept. 11, 1948; children: Walter, Carol, Philip, Alan. B.Aero. Engring., Rensselaer Poly. Inst., 1948; M.Indsl. Engring., NYU, 1952, MA, 1968. With Grumman Aircraft Engring. Corp., 1948-53; with IBM, N.Y.C., 1953-65, mgr. ops., real estate, constrn. divs., 1963-65; dep. group exec. N.Am. comml. telecommunications group, pres. telecommunications div. ITT, N.Y.C., 1965-67; sr. v.p. Irving Trust Co., N.Y.C., 1967-69, exec. v.p., 1969-72, sr. exec. v.p., 1972-73, vice chmn., 1973-74, pres., from 1974, chmn., 1984-88; exec. v.p. Irving Bank Corp., 1971-74, vice chmn., 1974-75, pres., 1975-83, chmn. bd., CEO, 1984-88; bd. dirs. Avon Products, Inc., Apache Corp. Trustee John Simon Guggenheim Meml. Found., Hist. Hudson Valley, Insts. Religion and Health. Mem. Coun. Fgn. Relations, N.Y. Acad. Scis., University Club, Links, Sky Club.

RICE, JOSEPH LEE, III, lawyer; b. Bklyn., Feb. 24, 1932; s. Joseph Lee Jr. and Frances (Plunkett) R.; m. Franci Blassberg, Jan. 4, 1992; children: Kimberley, Daniel, Lee Ann. BA, Williams Coll., Williamstown, Mass., 1954; LLB, Harvard U., 1960. Assoc. Sullivan & Cromwell, N.Y.C., 1960-66; v.p. Laird Inc., N.Y.C., 1966-68, McDonnell & Co., N.Y.C., 1968-69; founding ptnr. Gibbons, Green & Rice, N.Y.C., 1969-78; founder, chmn., CEO Clayton, Dubilier & Rice, Inc., N.Y.C., 1978—. Trustee, Williams Coll., 1988—. Lt. USMC, 1954-57. Mem. Bronxville Field Club, Maidstone Club, The Links Club, River Club, Univ. Club. Office: Clayton Dubilier & Rice Inc 375 Park Ave New York NY 10152

RICE, JOY KATHARINE, psychologist, educational policy studies and women's studies educator; b. Oak Park, Ill., Mar. 26, 1939; d. Joseph Theodore and Margaret Sophia (Bednarik) Straka; m. David Gordon Rice, Sept. 1, 1962; children: Scott Alan, Andrew David. B.F.A. with high honors, U. Ill., Urbana, 1960; M.S., U. Wis., Madison, 1962, U. Wis., Madison, 1964; Ph.D., U. Wis., Madison, 1967. Lic. clin. psychologist. USPHS predoctoral fellow dept. psychiatry Med. Sch. U. Wis., Madison, 1964-65, asst. dir. Counseling Ctr., 1966-74, dir. Office Continuing Edn. Svcs., 1972-78, prof. ednl. policy studies and women's studies, 1974-95, clin. prof. psychiatry, 1995—; pvt. practice psychology Psychiat. Svcs., S.C., Madison, 1967—; mem. State Wis. Ednl. Approval Bd., Madison, 1972-73; mem. Adult Edn. Commn., U.S. Office Career Edn., Washington, 1978. Author: Living Through Divorce, A Developmental Approach to Divorce Therapy, 1985, 2d edit., 1989; edit. bd. Lifelong Learning, 1979-86; cons. editor Psychology of Women Quar., 1986-88, assoc. editor, 1989-94; cons. editor Handbook of Adult and Continuing Education, 1989; contbr. articles to profl. jours. Knapp fellow U. Wis.-Madison, 1960-62, teaching fellow, 1962-63; recipient Disting. Achievement award Ednl. Press Assn. Am., 1992. Fellow APA (exec. bd. Psychology of Women divsn. 1994—); mem. Nat. Assn. Women in Edn. (editl. bd. jour. 1984-88, cons. editor Initiatives 1988-91), Internat. Coun. Psychologists, Am. Assn. Continuing and Adult Edn. (meritorious svc. award 1978-80, 82), Wis. Psychol. Assn., Phi Delta Kappa. Avocations: interior design, collecting art, gardening, travel. Home: 4230 Waban Hl Madison WI 53711-3711 Office: 2727 Marshall Ct Madison WI 53705

RICE, JULIAN CASAVANT, lawyer; b. Miami, Fla., Dec. 31, 1923; s. Sylvan J. and Maybelle (Casavant) R.; m. Dorothy Mae Haynes, Feb. 14, 1958; children—Scott B., Craig M. (dec.), Julianne C., Linda D., Janette M. Student, U. San Francisco, 1941-43; JD cum laude, Gonzaga U., 1950. Bar: Wash. 1950, Alaska 1959, U.S. Tax Ct. 1988. Pvt. practice law Spokane, 1950-56, Fairbanks, Alaska, 1959—; prin. Law Office Julian C. Rice (and predecessor firms), Fairbanks, 1959; bd. dirs. Key Bank of Alaska, Anchorage; founder, gen. counsel Mt. McKinley Mut. Savs. Bank, Fairbanks, 1965—, chmn. bd., 1979-80; v.p., bd. dirs., gen. counsel Skimmers, Inc., Anchorage, 1966-67; gen. counsel Alaska Carriers Assn., Anchorage, 1960-71, Alaska Transp. Conf., 1960-67. Mayor City of Fairbanks, 1970-72. Served to maj. USNG and USAR, 1943-58. Decorated Bronze Star, Combat Infantryman's Badge. Fellow Am. Bar Found. (life); mem. ABA, Wash. Bar Assn., Alaska Bar Assn., Transp. Lawyers Assn., Spokane Exchange Club (pres. 1956). Office: 1008 16th Ave Ste 102 Fairbanks AK 99701-6038 Office: PO Box 70516 Fairbanks AK 99707-0516

RICE, KAY DIANE, elementary education educator, consultant; b. Redding, Calif., Mar. 21, 1952; d. Ray H. and Patricia Barton (Stabler) Quibell; m. 1976 (div. 1982); 1 child, Brooke Elise; m. F. Scott Rice, June 29, 1985. AA in Gen. Edn., Shasta Coll., Redding, 1972; BA in Liberal Studies, Calif. State U., Chico, 1975; EdM in Policy and Govt., U. Wash., 1991. Cert. tchr., Calif., Wash., cert. prin., Wash. Tchr. grade 3 Anderson (Calif.) Schs., 1976-79; tchr. grades 1, 2, and 3 Redding (Calif.) Elem. Schs., 1979-81, tchr. grade 1, 1981-83, tchr. grade 5, 1986-87; tchr. grade 2 Bellevue (Wash.) Pub. Schs., 1987-88; tchr. grade 4 Lake Wash. Sch. Dist., Kirkland, Wash., 1988-89; tchr. grades 3-4 Bellevue (Wash.) Pub. Schs., 1989-90; prin. intern Bellevue (Wash.) and Mercer Island (Wash.) Schs., 1990-91; tchr. grades K-1 Bellevue (Wash.) Pub. Schs., 1991-93, tchr. grades 1-2, 1993-96; mem. adv. com. Ednl. Program Com., Bellevue Pub. Schs., 1992-94, mem. Early Childhood Assessment Project, 1993-95; presenter in field. Vol. ZEST Sch. Dist. Vol. Program, Bellevue, 1991-93; vol. asst. children's choir First Presbyn. Ch., Bellevue, 1992-93, vol. asst. youth handbells, 1993-95. Recipient Pres.'s Merit award, Parent Student Tchr. Assn., 1988, U.S. Presdl. EPA award, 1987; Bellevue Schs. Found. grantee, 1987, Danforth Edn. Leadership grantee Bellevue Pub. Schs., 1990-91, Ednl. Travel Study grantee Shunju Club, Japanese Bus. People Wash., 1994. Mem. ASCD, NEA, AAUW (hospitality com. 1982), PTSA, Wash. Orgn. for Reading Devel., Ea. Star (adult advisor to Rainbow for Girls 1978-80, Grand Cross of Color 1981), PEO. Avocations: cooking, outdoor sports, reading. Home: 6818 205th Ave NE Redmond WA 98053-4721 Office: Bellevue Pub Schs PO Box 90010 Bellevue WA 98009-9010

RICE, KENNETH LLOYD, environmental services executive, educator; b. St. Paul, June 17, 1937; m. Eliza Beth Lyman VanKat, May 11, 1963 (dec. 1992); children: Anne Louise, Kenneth L. Jr., Elizabeth Ellen, Stephen James. BBA, U. Wis., 1959; postgrad., N.Y. Inst. Finance, 1960-64; completed 71st Advanced Mgmt. Program, Harvard U., 1975. Trainee corp. finance Irving J. Rice & Co., St. Paul, 1959-64; asst. branch mgr. DB Marron & Co. Inc., St. Paul, 1964-65; mgr. corp. finance JW Sparks & Co. Inc., St. Paul, 1965-69, The Milw. Co., St. Paul, 1969-70; dir. finance Cedar Riverside Assocs. Inc., Mpls., 1970-71; prin. Kenneth L. Rice & Assocs., St. Paul, 1971-88; chmn., CEO investment banking Allegro Tech. Corp., St. Paul, 1988-92; prof. mgmt. and environ. econs. Budapest (Hungary) U. Econs. Scis., 1992—; chmn., edtl. bd. New Horizons Magazine, Hungary, 1995—; Minn. del. World Trade Ctrs. Assn., Budapest, Hungary, 1987; dir. Hungarian U.S. Fulbright Commn., 1995—. Founder Chimera Theatre, St. Paul, 1969; pres. Liberty Pla. Non-Profit Housing Project, St. Paul, 1975-77; judge Leadership Fellows Bush Found., St. Paul, 1985-90; co-chmn. Parents Fund, Macalester Coll., St. Paul, 1985-87; Hungary hon. rep. State of Minn. Trade Office. Bush Leadership fellow, 1974. Mem. Environ. Mgmt. and Law Assn. Hungary, Harvard Bus. Club (local bd. dirs. 1978-83), Harvard Club of Hungary (v.p. 1994—), Am. C. of C. in Hungary (dir. 1995—, chmn. edn. com. 1993—), Masons, KT, Shriners. Presbyterian.

RICE, LACY I., JR., lawyer; b. Martinsburg, W.Va., Dec. 29, 1931; s. Lacy Isaac and Anna (Thorn) R.; m. Linda Watkins, Mar. 2, 1957; children: Anne W., Lacy I. III, William T. BA, Princeton U., 1953; LLB, U. Va., 1956. Bar: W.Va. 1956, U.S. Dist. Ct. (no. Dist.) W.Va. 1956, U.S. Cir. Ct. Appeals (3d and 4th cirs.) 1968. Ptnr. Lacy I. Rice Sr. law firm & Rice, Hannis & Rice & successors, Martinsburg, 1956-89; sr. ptnr. Bowles, Rice, McDavid, Graff & Love, Martinsburg, 1989—; pres. Old Nat. Bank of Martinsburg, 1978, chmn. bd.; chmn., CEO One Valley Bank-East N.A.; vice chmn. One Valley Bancorp, Inc.; bd. dirs. Continental Brick Co., C&P Telephone Co., W.Va. Mem. W.Va. Bar Assn. (pres. 1984-85). Home: 600 N Tennessee Ave Martinsburg WV 25401-9281 Office: PO Drawer 1419 105 W Burke St Martinsburg WV 25401

RICE, LESTER, electronics company executive; b. Detroit, Feb. 23, 1927; s. Carvel Lester and Irene R.; m. Barbara Helen Winston, June 27, 1957; children—Scott W., Jody I., Jeffrey C., Judy A., Timothy D. B.S.E.E., U. Mich., 1951. Gen. sales mgr. Westinghouse Semicondr. Div., Youngwood, Pa., 1951-68; pres. Airco Speer Elec. div. Airco Inc., Bradford, Pa., 1968-80; vice chmn., dir. KOA Speer Electronics, Inc., Bradford, 1980—; bd. dirs. DeFond No. Am. Inc.; chmn. bd. Lester Rice, Inc., Bradford, 1980—. Adv. bd. U. Pitts. With USN, 1945-46. Mem. IEEE, Electronics Industries Assn. (bd. govs.), Am. Legion, Masons. Republican. Home: 2 Vista Avenue Ext Bradford PA 16701-2759 Office: PO Box 547 Bradford PA 16701-0547

RICE, LINDA JOHNSON, publishing executive; b. Chgo., Mar. 22, 1958; d. John J. and Eunice Johnson; m. Andre Rice, 1984. BA Journalism, Univ. Southern California, Los angeles, 1980; MBA, Northwestern Univ., Evanston, 1988. With Johnson Pub. Co., 1980—, past v.p. and asst. to pub., pres., 1987—, also chief oper. officer. *

RICE, LOIS DICKSON, former computer company executive; b. Portland, Maine, Feb. 28, 1933; d. David A. and Mary D. Dickson; m. Alfred B. Fitt, Jan. 7, 1978 (dec. 1992); children: Susan, John Rice. A.B. magna cum laude, Radcliffe Coll., 1954; postgrad. (Woodrow Wilson fellow), Columbia U., 1954-55; LL.D. (hon.), Brown U., 1981, Bowdoin Coll., 1984. Dir. counseling services Nat. Scholarship Service and Fund for Negro Students, N.Y.C., 1955-59; with The Coll. Bd., N.Y.C. and Washington, 1959-81; v.p. The Coll. Bd., Washington, 1973-81; sr. v.p. govt. affairs, bd. dirs. Control Data Corp., 1981-91; guest scholar The Brookings Inst., Washington,

1991—; bd. dirs. McGraw Hill Inc., Bell Atlantic, Washington, Hartford Steam Boiler Inspection and Ins. Co., Internat. Multifoods, Shawmut Nat. Corp., UNUM Corp.; overseer Tuck Sch. Mgmt. Dartmouth Coll., 1990-94; mem. Pres. Fgn. Intelligence adv. bd., 1993—; trustee George Washington U., 1992-94. Contbr. articles on edn. to profl. publs.; editor: Student Loans: Problems and Policy Alternatives, 1977. Mem. Gov.'s Commn. on Future of Postsecondary Edn. in N.Y. State, 1976-77; mem. Carnegie Coun. on Higher Edn., 1975-80; bd. dirs. Potomac Inst., 1977-92, German Marshall Fund, 1984-94, Joint Ctr. Polit. and Econ. Studies, 1991-94, Harry Frank Guggenheim Found., 1990—, Reading is Fundamental, 1991—; trustee Radcliffe Coll., 1969-75, Stephens Coll., Mo., 1976-78, Beauvoir Sch., Washington, 1970-76, Children's TV Workshop, 1970-73; chmn. adv. bd. to dir. NSF, 1981-89, chair 1986-89. Recipient Disting. Service award HEW, 1977. Mem. Cosmos Club, Phi Beta Kappa. Episcopalian. Home: 2332 Massachusetts Ave NW Washington DC 20008-2801 Office: The Brookings Instn 1775 Massachusetts Ave NW Washington DC 20036-2188

RICE, MICHAEL LEWIS, business educator; b. Ann Arbor, Mich., Jan. 7, 1943; s. Edwin Stevens and Elaine (Ivey) R.; m. Eileen Lynn Barnard, July 7, 1961. BS, Fla. State U., 1971, MBA, 1972; PhD, U. N.C., 1975. Asst. prof. U. N.C., Chapel Hill, 1974-80; assoc. prof. Wake Forest U., Winston-Salem, N.C., 1980-83; prof., dean U. Alaska, Fairbanks, 1983-91, vice chancellor adminstrv. svcs., 1991—. Contbr. numerous articles on fin. topics. Pres. United Way of Tanana Valley, Fairbanks, 1986-91. Mem. Am. Mgmt. Assn., Am. Mktg. Assn., Am. Econs. Assn., Am. Assembly Collegiate Schs. Bus., Western Assn. Collegiate Schs. Bus. (sec.-treas.), Rotary (bd. officer Fairbanks 1986-92, pres. 1992-93). Avocations: flying, amateur radio. Office: U Alaska Vice Chancellor Adminstrv Svcs Fairbanks AK 99775-7900

RICE, NANCY MARIE, nursing consultant; b. Murphy, N.C., Aug. 3, 1940; d. Berlon and Elizabeth Beryl (Ammons) Lovingood; m. Lewis T. Rice, Jan. 23, 1976; 1 child, Elizabeth Robertson Flowers. Diploma, Grady Meml. Hosp., Atlanta, 1961; BA, U. West Fla., Pensacola, 1973; MS, Fla. State U., Tallahassee, 1979. Cert. cmty. health nurse, nursing adminstr.; diplomate Am. Bd. Quality Assurance and Utilization Review Physicians. Staff nurse Riegel Community Hosp., Trion, Ga., 1961; pub. health nurse Escambia County Health Unit, Pensacola, 1962-63, Santa Rosa County Health Unit, Milton, Fla., 1963-73; pub. health nursing supr. I Leon County Health Unit, Tallahassee, Fla., 1973-77; pub. health nurse Broward County Health Unit, Ft. Lauderdale, Fla., 1977-78; nursing cons. social and econ. svcs. Tallahassee, 1978-79; HMO program specialist social and econ. scvs. program office DHRS Dist. X, Ft. Lauderdale, 1979; pub. health nurse, supr. II Sarasota (Fla.) County Health Unit, 1979-81; health program specialist health program office DHRS Dist X, Ft. Lauderdale, Fla., 1981-83; nursing cons. Dept. Labor, Div. Workers' Compensation, Tallahassee, 1983—. Recipient Cert. of Svc. State of Fla., 10 yr., 20 yr., 25 yrs., 30 yrs., Cert. of Appreciation, 1976, Leon County-Tallahassee Community Action Program. Mem. Am. Nurses Assn., Fla. Nurses Assn., Eta Sigma Gamma. Home: PO Box 13731 Tallahassee FL 32317-3731

RICE, NORMAN B., mayor; b. 1943. With govt. City of Seattle, 1978—, city councilman, 1978-89, mayor, 1990—; pres. U.S. Conf. of Mayors, 1995. Office: Office of the Mayor Municipal Bldg 12th Fl 600 4th Ave Seattle WA 98104-1826

RICE, PATRICIA OPPENHEIM LEVIN, special education educator, consultant; b. Detroit, Apr. 5, 1932; d. Royal A. and Elsa (Freeman) Oppenheim; m. Charles L. Levin, Feb. 21, 1956 (div. Dec. 1981); children: Arthur David, Amy Ragen, Fredrick Stuart; m. Howard T. Rice, Dec. 16, 1990 (div. Apr. 1994). AB in History, U. Mich., 1954, PhD, 1981; MEd, Marygrove Coll., 1973. Tchr. reading and learning disabled, cons., Detroit, 1967-76, Marygrove Coll.; coord. spl. edn., Marygrove Coll., 1976-86; adj. prof. Oakland U., 1987-90, U. Miami, 1989-95; edn., curriculum cons. Lady Elizabeth Sch., Jávea (Alicante) Spain, 1988-91; dir. Oppenheim Tchr. Tng. Inst., Detroit; v.p. Mashpelah Cemetary Bd., Ferndale, Mich., 1978—; mem. adv. bd. Eton Acad., Birmingham, Mich., 1991-93; internat. conf. presenter; workshop presenter Dade City Schs., 1992—. Mem. Mich. regional bd. ORT, 1965-68, 86—; mem. youth svcs. adv. com. S.E. Mich. chpt. ARC Bd., 1973-79; mem. Met. Mus., N.Y.C., Seattle Art Mus., Smithsonian Instn.; v.p. women's aux. Children's Hosp. Mich.; bd. dirs. women's com. United Cmty. Svcs., 1968-73; judge Dade County Schs. for Tchr. Grants, 1996; women's com. Detroit Grand Opera Assn., 1970-75; mem. coms. Detroit Symphony Orch., Detroit Inst. Arts; torch drive area chmn. United Found., 1967-70; bd. dirs. Greater Miami Opera Guild Bd., 1994—, Men's Opera Guild Bd., 1996—, Miami City Ballet Dade Guild, 1996—, Opera Ball com., 1992, Lincoln Rd. Walk, chair, 1996, Diabetes Rsch. Inst. & Found. Love & Hope Com., Fla. Concert Assn. Cresendo Soc., 1993—, Hope Ball com., 1996; mem. Miami City Ballet Guild Bd., 1996—, Villa Maria Angel, 1996—, Men's Opera Guild Bd., 1996—. Mem. NAACP, Detroit Inst. of Art Founders, Navy League (mem. Miami Coun.), Internat. Reading Assn., Nat. Coun. Tchrs. of English, Assn. Supervision and Curriculum Devel., Nat. Assn. Edn. of Young Children, Mich. Assn. Children with Learning Disabilities (edn. v.p., exec. bd. 1976-80), Coun. Exceptional Children, Williams Island Club, Westview Country Club (mem. house com.), Turnberry Isle Clubs (signiture), Phi Delta Kappa, Pi Lambda Theta.

RICE, PAUL JACKSON, lawyer, educator; b. East St. Louis, Ill., July 15, 1938; s. Ray Jackson and Mary Margaret (Campbell) R.; m. Carole Jeanne Valentine, June 6, 1959; children: Rebecca Jeanne Ross, Melissa Ann Hansen, Paul Jackson Jr. BA, U. Mo., 1960, JD, 1962; LLM, Northwestern U., 1970; student, Command and Gen. Staff Coll., 1974-75, Army War Coll., 1982-83. Bar: Mo. 1962, Ill. 1969, U.S. Dist. Ct. (no. dist.) Ill. 1970, U.S. Supreme Ct. 1972, U.S. Ct. Appeals (D.C. cir.) 1991, D.C. 1993. Commd. 1st lt. U.S. Army, 1962, advanced through grades to col., 1980; asst. judge advocate 4th Armored Div., Goeppingen, Fed. Repulic Germany, 1966-69; dep. staff judge advocate 1st Cavalry Div., Republic Vietnam, 1970-71; inst., prof. The Judge Adv. Gen. Sch., Charlottesville, Va., 1971-74, commdt., dean, 1985-88; br. chief Gen. Law Br., Pentagon, 1975-78; chief adminstrv. law div. Office Judge Adv. Gen., Pentagon, Washington, 1978-79; staff judge adv. 1st Inf. Div., Ft. Riley, Kans., 1979-82, V Corps U.S. Army, Frankfurt, Fed. Republic Germany, 1983-85, USACAC, Ft. Leavenworth, Kans., 1989-90; faculty Indsl. Coll. Armed Forces, 1988-89; chief counsel Nat. Hwy. Traffic Safety Adminstrn., Washington, 1990-93; ptnr. Arent Fox Kintner Plotkin & Kahn, Washington, 1993—. Contbr. articles to profl. jours. Granted Legal Svc. award State of Hessen, Weisbaden, Fed. Republic Germany, 1985, Cert. Merit U. Mo. Alumni Assn., 1987. Mem. ABA, Fed. Bar Assn. (pres. local chpt. 1986-88), Mo. Bar Assn., Ctr. For Law and Nat. Security, U. Va. Sch. Law (1985-89), Lion Tamers, Phi Delta Phi. Methodist. Avocations: writing, reading, sports. Home: 7835 Vervain Ct Springfield VA 22152-3107 Office: Arent Fox Kintner Plotkin & Kahn 1050 Connecticut Ave NW Washington DC 20036-5303

RICE, REGINA KELLY, marketing executive; b. Yonkers, N.Y., July 11, 1955; d. Howard Adrian and Lucy Virginia (Butler) Kelly; m. Mark Christopher Rice, Sept. 11, 1981; children: Amanda Kelly, Jaime Brannen. BS in Community Nutrition, Cornell U., 1948. Account exec. J. Walter Thompson Co., N.Y.C., 1978-79; sr. account exec. Ketchum, MacLeod & Grove, N.Y.C., 1979-80; supr. Burson Marstellar, Hong Kong, 1981-83; v.p., dep. dir. food and beverage unit, creative dir. N.Y. office Hill and Knowlton, N.Y.C., 1983-91; mktg. cons. Rice & Rohr, N.Y.C., 1991-93; sr. v.p., dir. consumer mktg. practice Manning, Selvage & Lee, N.Y.C., 1993—. Writer Fast and Healthy Mag., 1991. Mem. Pub. Rels. Soc. Am., Women Execs. in Pub. Rels. Roman Catholic. Avocations: aerobics, baking. Home: 18 Westminster Dr Croton On Hudson NY 10520-1008 Office: Manning Selvage & Lee 79 Madison Ave New York NY 10016-7802

RICE, RICHARD CAMPBELL, retired state official, retired army officer; b. Atchison, Kans., Dec. 11, 1933; s. Olive Campbell and Ruby Thelma (Rose) R.; m. Donna Marie Lincoln, Aug. 4, 1956; children: Robert Alden, Holly Elizabeth. BS in History, Kans. State U., 1955; MA in Social Studies, Eastern Mich. U., 1965; grad. U.S. Army Command and Gen. Staff Coll., 1968, U.S. Army War Coll., 1977, FBI Nat. Exec. Inst., 1990, grad. program for sr. execs. in state and local govt., Harvard U., 1985. Commd. 2d lt. U.S. Army, 1955; advanced through grades to col., 1976; with Joint Chiefs of Staff, Washington, 1975-76; faculty U.S. Army War Coll., Carlisle Barracks, Pa., 1977-79; chief of staff Hdqrs. 3d ROTC Region, Ft. Riley, Kans., 1982-83; ret. 1983; dir. Mo. State Emergency Mgmt. Agy., Jefferson City, 1983-85, dir. Mo. Dept. Pub. Safety, Jefferson City, 1985-93; trustee Mo. State Employees Retirement System, 1990-93; bd. visitors Nat. Emergency Mgmt. Inst., 1991-92. Grad. Leadership, Mo., 1991; mem. Coordinating Coun. Health Edn., Mo.'s Children and Adolescents., Mo. Jail and Prison Overcrowding Task Force, Gov.'s Domestic Violence Task Force, Gov.'s Conf. Health Needs Children, Gov.'s Commn. on Crime, Gov.'s Adv. Coun. on Driving While Intoxicated, Mo. Children's Svcs. Commn., Blue Ribbon Commn. on Svcs. to Youth, Campaign to Protect Our Children; mem. policy com. Mo. Youth Initiative; chmn. Gov.'s Cabinet Coun. for Justice Adminstrn., Mo. Statistical Analysis Ctr. adv. bd., adv. bd. Mo. Criminal Hist. Records; bd. dirs. Mo. Law Enforcement Meml. Found, Gt. Rivers coun. Boy Scouts Am., 1993—; peer rev. cons. Nat. Inst. of Justice; chmn. Alliance for Uniform Hazmat Transp. Procedures, 1991-93. Decorated Legion of Merit, Bronze Star (3), Meritorious Service medal (4), Air medal (2), Joint Service Commendation medal, Army Commendation medal (2); Republic of Vietnam Cross of Gallantry with Silver Star; recipient Conspicuous Svc. medal State of Mo. Mem. Nat. Eagle Scout Assn., Assn. U.S. Army, Soc. First Div., Am. Legion, VFW, Disabled Am. Vets., AMVETS, Mil. Order of World Wars, Nat. Soc., Sons Am. Revolution, The Retired Officers Assn., Nat. Criminal Justice Assn. (bd. dirs. 1987-93), Rotary (Paul Harris fellow), St. Andrews Soc., Theta Xi. Republican. Avocation: sailing.

RICE, RICHARD LEE, retired architect; b. Raleigh, N.C., May 4, 1919; s. Robert Edward Lee and Grace Lucille (Betts) R.; m. Cora Belle Stegall, Apr. 12, 1946; children—Richard Lee, Westwood Carter, David Sinclair. BS in Archtl. Engring., N.C. State U., 1941; grad., U.S. Army Command and Gen. Staff Coll., 1961. Assoc. Cooper-Shumaker, Architects, Raleigh, 1946-47; prin. Richard L. Rice, Architects, Raleigh, 1947-48; assoc. Cooper, Haskins & Rice and predecessor firm, Raleigh, 1948-52, ptnr., 1953-54; ptnr. Haskins & Rice, Architects, Raleigh, 1954-85; prin. Haskins, Rice, Savage & Pearce, Architects, 1985-91, pres., 1985-91; v.p. N.C. Design Found., 1973; pres. N.C. Archtl. Found., 1975; mem. Raleigh Arts Commn., 1978-82, Raleigh Hist. Properties Commn., 1990-92, Raleigh Hist. Dists. Commn., 1991-92. Archtl. works include renovations, Raleigh Meml. Auditorium, 1964, 78, 91 (SE Regional AIA award of merit 1964), Auditorium, 4 high schs. and 13 elem. schs., Raleigh Civic Ctr., stack addition Wilson Libr. U. N.C., Chapel Hill, 1977, Reidsville, N.C. Jr. High Sch.; assoc. architect Raleigh Radisson Hotel, 1980, One Hanover Sq. Office Bldg., 1985, Two Hannover Sq. Office Bldg., 1990, additions and renovations to Raleigh Meml. Auditorium, 1989, 3 indsl. plants, 7 bldgs., Wake Tech. C.C., 50 chs. Pre.s Wake County (N.C.) Hist. Soc., 1973-74; mem. N.C. Gov.'s Com. for Facilities for Physically Handicapped, 1970-73; arbitrator Am. Arbitration Assn. With inf. and C.E. U.S. Army, 1941-46, ETO; col. USAR; ret. Decorated Silver Star.; Legion of Merit; Bronze Star; Purple Heart. Fellow AIA (pres. N.C. chpt. 1970, Disting. Svc. award N.C. chpt. 1975); mem. Raleigh Council Architects (pres. 1950), Nat. Trust for Hist. Preservation, N.C. State Art Soc., Res. Officers Assn. U.S., Ret. Officers Assn. U.S. (pres. Triangle chpt. 1983), N.C. State U. Gen. Alumni Assn. (pres., chmn. bd. 1960-61, pres. Class 1941, 1986-91), Carolina Country Club, Lions, Torch Club (pres. 1982-83), Phi Eta Sigma, Phi Kappa Phi. Democrat. Baptist.

RICE, ROBERT H., principal; b. Coatesville, Pa., June 14, 1937; s. Samuel W. and Iva (Simpson) R.; m. Judith Bugar, May 27, 1961; 1 child, Laura Anne. BS, West Chester U., 1959; MA, Villanova U., 1965; EdD, Temple U., 1984. Tchr. West Chester (Pa.) Sch. Dist., 1960-65, guidance counselor, 1965-68; guidance counselor Wallingford (Pa.)/Swarthmore Sch. Dist., 1968-71, prin., 1971—; site vis. U.S. Dept. Edn. Blue Ribbon Schs. Award Program, Ill., N.J., 1992-93. With U.S. Army, 1960-65. Recipient Elem. Sch. Recognition award U.S. Dept. Edn., 1989-90. Mem. Nat. Assn. Elem. Prins., Del. County Prins. Assn., Pa. Prins. Assn. Home: 914 N Hill Dr West Chester PA 19380-4319 Office: Wallingford/Swarthmore Sch Dist 20 S Providence Rd Wallingford PA 19086-6224

RICE, ROGER DOUGLAS, television executive, artist; b. Spokane, Wash., Feb. 20, 1921; s. Leland L. and Bernice B. (Metcalf) R.; m. Molly Herron, Feb. 22, 1946; children: Stephannie Lee, Roger Douglas. B.S., U. Wash., 1944. With KING Radio, Seattle, 1947-51, 53-54; sta. mgr. KTVW-TV, Seattle, Tacoma, 1954-55; gen. sales mgr. WIIC-TV, Pitts., 1955-66; gen. mgr. WIIC-TV, 1966-68; v.p., gen. mgr. Cox Broadcasting Corp. KTVU, San Francisco, Oakland, Calif., 1968-74; pres., chief exec. officer TV Bur. Advt., N.Y.C., 1974-88; also abstract artist. Chmn. U.S./Japan Cultural Exchange, 1974; mem. Japan-U.S. Friendship Commn.; bd. dirs. Advt. Council. Mem. Nat. Assn. Broadcasters (bd. dirs. TV code rev. bd. 1971-74). Clubs: Pres. Com. of 25 (v.p.), Thunderbird Country (bd. dirs., Rancho Mirage, Calif.).

RICE, RONALD JAMES, hospital administrator; b. Springfield, Mo., Feb. 5, 1944; s. Glen Elwood and Alice Jeanett (Robinson) R. BSBA, Cen. Mo. State U., 1966, MABA, 1969, Specialist, 1972. Lic. nursing home adminstr.; lic. risk mgr. Unit mgr. Bapt. Med. Ctr., Kansas City, Mo., 1970-71; dir. unit mgmt. Ind. Health Ctr., Independence, Mo., 1971-72; adminstrv. officer Meth. Hosp., Jacksonville, Fla., 1972-73, dir. personnel, 1973-74; assoc. adminstr. Humana Hosp. Orange Park (Fla.), 1974-77; adminstr. Cathedral Rehab. Hosp., Jacksonville, 1977-79, Marion County Gen. Hosp., Hamilton, Ala., 1979-80, Nassau Gen. Hosp., Fernandina Beach, Fla., 1980-85, Reception Med. Ctr., Lake Butler, Fla., 1985-91; regional adminstr. health svcs. Dept. Corrections, Gainesville, Fla., 1991—; cons. Clay Meml. Hosp., Green Cove Springs, Fla., 1976-77, Allied Health Care, Jacksonville, 1989. Mem. Polit. Action Com., Fla. Hosp. Assn., 1990, Coun. on Crime and Delinquency, Gainesville, 1990, Human Resources Com., Orlando, 1991. With U.S. Army, 1967-69. Decorated Army Commendation medal. Fellow Am. Coll. Health Care Execs.; mem. am. acad. Med. Adminstrs., Am. Coll. Health Care Adminstrs., Am. Soc. Personnel Adminstrs., Fla. Hosp. Assn., Rotary (pres. 1984-86). Democrat. Unity Sch. Christianity. Avocations: boating, auto collecting model, antique juke box collecting, reading. Home: 1744 Horton Dr Orange Park FL 32073-2757

RICE, RONALD MAX, superintendent. Supt. Ames Community Sch. Dist., Ames, Iowa. Recipient State Finalist for Nat. Supt. of Yr. award, 1992. Office: Ames Community Sch Dist 120 S Kellogg Ave Ames IA 50010-6719

RICE, SHARON MARGARET, clinical psychologist; b. Detroit, Sept. 4, 1943; d. William Christopher and Sylvia Lucille (Lawecki) R.; m. John Robert Speer, Aug. 14, 1977 (dec. Mar. 1994). AB, Oberlin Coll., 1965; MA, Boston U., 1968, PhD, 1977. Clin. psychologist Los Angeles County Juvenile Probation, L.A., 1969-75, Las Vegas (Nev.) Mental Health Ctr., 1976-81, Foothills Psychol. Assn., Upland, Calif., 1981—; pvt. cons., Claremont, Calif., 1984—. NIMH grantee, 1967-69; recipient Good Apple award Las Vegas Tchrs. Ctr., 1978-80. Mem. APA, Calif. Psychol. Assn., Internat. Soc. for Study of Dissociation, Inst. Noetic Scis., Sigma Xi. Avocations: dog breeding and showing. Office: Foothills Psychol Assn 715 N Mountain Ave # G Upland CA 91786-4364

RICE, STANLEY TRAVIS, JR., poet, English language educator; b. Dallas, Nov. 7, 1942; s. Stanley Travis and Margaret Nolia (Cruse) R.; m. Anne O'Brien, Oct. 14, 1961; children: Michele (dec.), Christopher. BA, San Francisco State U., 1963, MA, 1965. Asst. prof. San Francisco State U., 1965-71, assoc. prof., 1971-76, prof. English and creative writing, 1977-88, asst. dir. Poetry Ctr., 1964-72, chmn. dept. creative writing, 1980-88, ret. Author: Some Lamb, 1975, Whiteboy, 1976 (Edgar Allen Poe award Acad. Am. Poets 1977), Body of Work, 1983, Singing Yet: New and Selected Poems, 1992, Fear Itself, 1995; one-man show of paintings Gallerie Simone Stern, New Orleans, La., 1992. Nat. Endowment Arts grantee, 1966, writing fellow, 1972; recipient Joseph Henry Jackson award San Francisco Found., 1968.

RICE, STEPHEN LANDON, engineering educator; b. Oakland, Calif., Nov. 23, 1941; s. Landon Frederick and E. Genevieve (Hunt) R.; m. Penny Louise Baum, Dec. 29, 1965; children: Andrew Landon, Katherine Grace. BS, U. Calif., Berkeley, 1964, MEngring., 1969, PhD, 1972. Registered profl. engr., Fla. Design engr. Lawrence Berkeley Lab., 1964-69; asst. prof. U. Conn., Storrs, 1972-77, assoc. prof., 1977-82, prof., 1982-83; prof., chmn. U. Ctrl. Fla., Orlando, 1983-88; assoc. dean, rsch. dir. U. Central Fla., Orlando, 1988—; interim asst. v.p. acad. affairs U. Ctrl. Fla., Orlando, 1995—; program evaluator ASME/ABET, N.Y.C., 1988-93; NASA predoctoral fellow, 1969-72; U.S. del. to Internat. Rsch. Group, Orgn. for Econ. Cmty. Devel., 1993—. Inventor impact wear apparatus, 1975. Named Outstanding Young Faculty Dow/ASEE, 1975, Eminent Engr., Tau Beta Pi, 1988; Fulbright rsch. scholar U. South Pacific, 1978-79; participant Fulbright exch. program for adminstrs. in internat. edn., Germany, 1995. Fellow ASME; mem. Am. Soc. Engring. Edn., Orlando C. of C. (mem. Goals 2000 1988-92), Theta Delta Chi. Avocations: sailing, tennis. Office: U Ctrl Fla Office of Dean 1 University Blvd Orlando FL 32816-0450

RICE, STUART ALAN, chemist, educator; b. N.Y.C., Jan. 6, 1932; s. Harry L. and Helen (Rayfield) R.; m. Marian Ruth Coopersmith, June 1, 1952; children—Barbara, Janet. BS, Bklyn. Coll., 1952; MA, Harvard, 1954, PhD, 1955. Jr. fellow Harvard, 1955-57; faculty U. Chgo., 1957—, prof. chemistry, 1960-69, Louis Block prof. phys. scis., 1969—, chmn. dept. chemistry, 1971-76, Frank P. Hixon disting. service prof., 1977—, dean phys. scis. div., 1981-95, dir. Inst. Study Metals, 1981-95; mem. Nat. Sci. Bd., 1980-86; nat. Phi Beta Kappa lectr., 1994-95. Author: Polyelectrolyte Solutions, 1961, Statistical Mechanics of Simple Liquids, 1965, Physical Chemistry, 1980; bd. dirs.; also numerous articles. Bull. Atomic Scientists. Guggenheim fellow, 1960-61; Falk-Plautt lectr. Columbia U., 1964; Riley lectr. Notre Dame U., 1964; NSF sr. postdoctoral fellow, 1965-66; USPHS spl. postdoctoral fellow U. Copenhagen, 1970-71; Univ. lectr. chemistry U. Western Ont., 1970; Seaver lectr. U. Soc. Calif., 1972; Noyes lectr. U. Tex., Austin, 1975; Foster lectr. SUNY, Buffalo, 1976; Frank T. Gucker lectr. Ind. U., 1976; Fairchild lectr. Calif. Inst. Tech., 1979; Baker lectr. Cornell U. 1985-86; Centenary lectr. Royal Soc. Chemistry, 1986-87, Nat. Phi Beta Kappa lectr., 1994-95. Fellow Am. Philos. Soc.; mem. Am. Chem. Soc. (award Pure Chemistry 1963, Leo Hendrik Baekland award 1971, Peter Debye award 1985, Hildebrand award 1987), Nat. Acad. Sci., Am. Acad. Sci., Am. Phys. Soc., AAAS, Faraday Soc. (Marlowe medal 1963), N.Y. Acad. Scis. (A. Cressy Morrison prize 1955), Danish Acad. Sci. and Letters (fgn.).

RICE, SUSAN E., federal agency official; m. Ian Cameron. BA in History, Stanford U., 1986; MPhil, Oxford U., 1988, DPhil, 1990. Mgmt. cons. McKinsey and Co., Toronto, Ontario, Can., 1991-93; dir. internat. orgns. and peacekeeping NSC, Washington, 1993-95, spl. asst. to pres., sr. dir. African affairs, 1995—; mem. subcom. employment opportunities U.S. Ho. of Reps., 1981, 82. Asst. to dir. The Black Student Fund, Washington, 1986; legal asst. NAACP Legal Defense Fund, Washington, 1986, Mid-Peninsula Support Network for Battered Women, Mountain View, Calif., 1983-84; co-founder, dir., The Free South Africa Fund, Stanford, Calif., 1986-87; fgn. policy aide Dem. Pres. Campaign, Boston, 1988;. Harry S. Truman scholar, 1984, Rhodes scholar, 1986; recipient Walter Frewen Lord prize, Royal Commonwealth Soc., 1990, Assn. prize, Chatham House-British Internat. Studies, 1992. Mem. Phi Beta Kappa. Avocations: tennis, basketball, cooking, writing poetry, traveling. Office: African Affairs Directorate Nat Security Coun 1600 Pennsylvania Ave NW Washington DC 20500

RICE, SUSAN F., zoological park executive; b. Chgo., Dec. 10, 1939. BA, St. Mary's Coll., 1961; MPA, UCLA, 1976; EdD, Pepperdine U., 1986. Pres. YWCA, Santa Monica, Calif., 1978, League of Women Voters Calif., San Francisco, 1979-81; sr. fundraising profl. adminstr., instr. Santa Monica (Calif.) Coll., 1978-81; dir. govtl. rels. UCLA Alumni Assn., 1981-82; dir. devel. UCLA Grad. Sch. Mgmt., 1982-89; dep. dir. mktg. and devel., dir. major gifts Spl. Olympics Internat., Washington, 1989-90; v.p. devel. Bus. Exec. Nat. Security, Washington, 1991-92; pres., CEO Greater L.A. Zoo Assn., 1992—. Co-author: Women, Money and Political Clout in Women as Donors, Woman as Philanthropists, 1994. Bd. dirs. St. Mary's Coll. Alumnae Assn., Notre Dame, Ind., 1982-84, Santa Monica Coll. Assocs., 1984-94, Internat. Human Rights Law Group, 1990-92; trustee, chair pers. compensation com. L.A. Mus. Nat. History Found., 1982-89; treas. Women's Commn. Refugee Women, 1990—; vice chmn. pers. commn. Santa Monica Coll. Dist., 1985-89. Recipient Disting. Alumna award St. Mary's Coll., 1986, Humanitarian award, NCCJ-L.A., 1995. Mem. Nat. Soc. Fundraising Execs. (bd. dirs 1995—, v.p. GLAC). Office: Greater Los Angeles Zoo Assn 5333 Zoo Dr Los Angeles CA 90027-1451

RICE, VICTOR ALBERT, manufacturing executive, heavy; b. Hitchin, Hertfordshire, Eng., Mar. 7, 1941. With Ford Motor Co., U.K., 1957-64, Cummins Engines, U.K., 1964-67, Chrysler Corp., U.K., 1968-70; comptroller N. European ops. Perkins Engines Group Ltd., Peterborough, U.K., subsequently Group's dir. fin., Group dir. sales, and dep. mng. dir. ops., 1970-75; comptroller world-wide Varity Corp. (formerly Massey-Ferguson Ltd.), Toronto, Ont., Can., 1975-77; v.p. staff ops. Varity Corp., Toronto, Ont., Can., 1977-78, pres., chief operating officer, 1978-80; chmn., chief exec. officer Varity Corp., Buffalo, N.Y., 1980—, also bd. dirs. Mem. Chief Execs. Orgns., World Pres. Orgns., Toronto Club, Toronto Golf Club, Country Club of Buffalo, Buffalo Club. Office: Varity Corp 672 Delaware Ave Buffalo NY 14209-2202*

RICE, WILLIAM EDWARD, newspaper columnist; b. Albany, N.Y., July 26, 1938; s. Harry Edward, Jr. and Elizabeth (Lally) R.; m. Carol Timmon, June 3, 1978 (div.); m. Jill Van Cleave, Aug. 20, 1983. BA in History, U. Va., 1960; MS with honors, Columbia U., 1963. Reporter, editorial writer, critic Washington Post, 1963-69; student LeCordon Bleu, Paris, 1969-70; dir. L'Ecole de Cuisine, Bethesda, Md., 1971-72; freelance writer, restaurant critic Washingtonian Mag., 1971-72; exec. food editor Washington Post, 1972-80; editor-in-chief Food and Wine Mag., N.Y.C., 1980-85; food and wine columnist Chgo. Tribune, 1986—; Dining In columnist Gentlemen's Quarterly, 1987-89; chmn. restaurant awards com. James Beard Found., 1993—. Author: Feasts of Wine and Food, 1986; editor: (with others) Where to Eat in America, 1978, 2d edit., 1980, 3d edit., 1987. Served with USN, 1960-62. Recipient Vesta award as outstanding newspaper food editor, 1979, Ordre du Merite Agricole (France), 1983. Home: 840 N Sheridan Rd Chicago IL 60657 Office: Chgo Tribune Co Po Box 25340 435 N Michigan Ave Chicago IL 60611-4001

RICE, WILLIAM PHIPPS, investment counselor; b. Bronxville, N.Y., Mar. 27, 1944; s. Anton Henry Jr. and Lydia Phipps (Sands) R.; m. Lynn Lucas Rice, May 21, 1972; children: William Phipps Jr., Paige Sands Rice. BA cum laude, Kenyon Coll., 1966. Analyst Spencer Trask & Co., N.Y.C., 1960-67; v.p., portfolio mgr. Endowment Mgmt. and Rsch. Corp., Boston, 1969-77, Ft. Hill Investors Mgmt. Corp., Boston, 1977-83; pres., founder Anchor Capital Advisors Inc., Boston, 1983—, Anchor/Russell Capital Advisors, Boston, 1989—; bd. dirs. Claw Island Foods. Pres., trustee Mass. Bible Soc., Boston, 1985-89; trustee of donations Episcopal Ch. Diocese of Mass., Boston, 1989—. With U.S. Army, 1967-69. Mem. Assn. for Investment Mgmt. and Rsch., Assn. Investment Mgmt. Sales Execs., Boston Security Analysts Soc., Boston C. of C. Avocations: skiing, boating, woodworking. Home: PO Box 1599 Duxbury MA 02331-1599 Office: Anchor Capital Advisors Inc 1 Post Office Sq Boston MA 02109-2103

RICH, ADRIENNE, writer; b. Balt., May 16, 1929; d. Arnold Rice and Helen Elizabeth (Jones) R.; m. Alfred H. Conrad (dec. 1970); children: David, Paul, Jacob. AB, Radcliffe Coll., 1951; LittD (hon.), Wheaton Coll., 1967, Smith Coll., 1979, Brandeis U., 1987, Coll. Wooster, Ohio, 1988, CCNY, Harvard U., 1990, Swarthmore Coll., 1992. Tchr. workshop YM-WHA Poetry Ctr., N.Y.C., 1966-67; vis. lectr. Swarthmore Coll., 1967-69; adj. prof. writing divsn. Columbia U., 1967-69; lectr. CCNY, 1968-70, instr., 1970-71, asst. prof. English, 1971-72, 74-75; Fannie Hurst vis. prof. creative lit. Brandeis U., 1972-73; prof. English Douglass Coll., Rutgers U., 1976-79; Clark lectr., disting. vis. prof. Scripps Coll., 1983-84; A.D. White prof.-at-large Cornell U., 1981-87; disting. vis. prof. San Jose State U., 1984-85; prof. English and feminist studies Stanford U., 1986-93; Marjorie Kovler vis. lectr. U. Chgo., 1989. Author: (poetry) Collected Early Poems, 1950-1970, 1993, Diving into the Wreck, 1973, The Dream of a Common Language, 1978, A Wild Patience Has Taken Me This Far, 1981, Your Native Land, Your Life, 1986, Time's Power, 1989, An Atlas of the Difficult World, 1991, Dark Fields of the Republic, 1995; (prose) Of Woman Born: Motherhood as Experience and Institution, 1976, 10th anniversary edit., 1986, On Lies, Secrets and Silence, 1979, Blood, Bread and Poetry, 1986, What Is Found There: Notebooks on Poetry and Politics, 1993. Mem. nat. adv. bd. Bridges, Boston Women's Fund, Sisterhood in Support of Sisters in South Africa. Recipient Yale Series of Younger Poets award, 1951, Ridgely Torrence

Meml. award Poetry Soc. Am., 1955, Nat. Inst. Arts and letters award in poetry, 1961, Bess Hokin prize Poetry mag., 1963, Eunice Tietjens Meml. prize, 1968, Shelley Meml. award, 1971, Nat. Book award, 1974, Fund for Human Dignity award Nat. Gay Task Force, 1981, Ruth Lilly Poetry prize, 1986, Brandeis U. Creative Arts medal for Poetry, 1987, Nat. Poetry Assn. award, 1989, Elmer Holmes Bobst award arts and letters NYU, 1989, others. Mem. PEN, Am. Acad. Arts and Letters (dept. of lit. 1990—), Nat. Writers Union, Am. Acad. Arts and Scis. Office: care W W Norton Co 500 5th Ave New York NY 10110

RICH, ALAN, music critic, editor, author; b. Boston, June 17, 1924; s. Edward and Helen (Hirshberg) R. A.B., Harvard, 1945; M.A., U. Calif-Berkeley, 1952. Alfred Hertz Meml. Traveling fellow in music Vienna, Austria, 1952-53; Asst. music critic Boston Herald, 1944-45, N.Y. Sun, 1947-48; contbr. Am. Record Guide, 1947-61, Saturday Rev., 1952-53, Mus. Am., 1955-61, Mus. Quar., 1957-58; tchr. music U. Calif. at Berkeley, 1950-58; program and music dir. Pacifica Found., FM radio, 1953-61; asst. music critic N.Y. Times, 1961-63; chief music critic, editor N.Y. Herald Tribune, 1963-66; music critic, editor N.Y. World Jour. Tribune, 1966-67; contbg. editor Time mag., 1967-68; music and drama critic, arts editor N.Y. mag., 1968-81, contbg. editor, 1981-83; music critic, arts editor Calif. (formerly New West mag.), 1979-83, contbg. editor, 1983-85; gen. editor Newsweek mag., N.Y.C., 1983-87; music critic L.A. Herald Examiner, 1987-89, L.A. Daily News, 1989-92, L.A. Weekly, 1992—; tchr. New Sch. for Social Rsch., 1972-75, 77-79, U. So. Calif. Sch. Journalism, 1980-82, Calif. Inst. Art, 1982-94, UCLA, 1990-91; artist-in-residence Davis Ctr. for Performing Arts CUNY, 1975-76. Author: Careers and Opportunities in Music, 1964, Music: Mirror of the Arts, 1969, Listeners Guides to Classical Music, Opera, Jazz, 3 vols., 1980, The Lincoln Center Story, 1984, Play-by-Play: Bach, Mozart, Beethoven, Tchaikovsky, 4 vols., 1995, American Pioneers, 1995, Play-by-Play: Handel, The Romantics, 2 vols., 1996; author: (interactive CD-ROM computer programs): Schubert's Trout Quintet, 1991, So I've Heard: Bach and Before, 1992, So I've Heard: The Classical Ideal, 1993, So I've Heard: Beethoven and Beyond, 1993; contbr. articles to entertainment mags. Recipient Deems Taylor award ASCAP, 1970, 73, 74. Mem. Music Critics Circle N.Y. (sec. 1961-63, chmn. 1963-64), N.Y. Drama Critics Circle, Am. Theatre Critics Assn., Music Critics Assn., PEN. Home: 2925 Greenfield Ave Los Angeles CA 90064-4019

RICH, ALEXANDER, molecular biologist, educator; b. Hartford, Conn., Nov. 15, 1924; s. Max and Bella (Shub) R.; m. Jane Erving King, July 5, 1952; children: Benjamin, Josiah, Rebecca, Jessica. A.B. magna cum laude in Biochem. Scis, Harvard U., 1947, M.D. cum laude, 1949; Dr. (hon.), Fed. U. Rio de Janeiro, 1981; PhD honoris causa, Weizmann Inst. Sci., Rehovot, Israel, 1992; DSc (hon.), Eidgenössische Technische Hochschule, Zurich, Switzerland, 1993. Research fellow Gates and Crellin Labs., Calif. Inst. Tech., Pasadena, 1949-54; chief sect. phys. chemistry NIMH, Bethesda, Md., 1954-58; vis. scientist Cavendish Lab., Cambridge (Eng.) U., 1955-56; asso. prof. biophysics MIT, Cambridge, 1958-61; prof. biohpysics MIT, 1961—, William Thompson Sedgwick prof. biophysics, 1974—; Fairchild disting. scholar Calif. Inst. Tech., Pasadena, 1976; mem. AAAS (coun. mem. 1967-71), Biophysical Soc (coun. mem. 1960-69), com. career devel. awards NIH, 1964-67, mem. postdoctoral fellowship bd., 1955-58; mem. com. exobiology space sci. bd. NAS, 1964-65; mem. U.S. nat. com. Internat. Orgn. Pure Applied Biophysics, 1965-67; mem. vis. com. dept. biology Weizmann Inst. Sci., 1965-66, co-chmn. sci. and adv. com. 1987-91; mem. vis. com. biology dept. Yale U.1963; mem. life scis. com. NASA, 1970-75, mem. lunar planetary missions bd., 1968-70; mem. biology team Viking Mars Mission, 1969-80; mem. corp. Marine Biol. Lab., Woods Hole, Mass., 1965-77, 87—; mem. sci. rev. com. Howard Hughes Med. Inst., Miami, Fla., 1978-90; mem. vis. com. biology div. Oak Ridge Nat. Lab., 1972-76; chmn. com. on USSR and Ea. Europe Exch. Bd. NAS, 1973-76; mem. Internat. Rsch. and Exchs. Bd. Am. Coun. Learned Socs., N.Y.C., 1973-76, mem. panel judges N.Y. Acad. Sci. ann. book award for children's sci. books, N.Y.C.,1973-90; chmn. nominating com. Am. Acad. Arts and Sci., 1974-77, adv. bd., acad. forum NAS, 1975-82; mem. sci. adv. bd. Stanford Synchrotron Radiation Project, 1976-80, Mass. Gen. Hosp., Boston, 1978-83; mem. U.S. Nat. Sci. Bd., 1976-82; mem. bd. govs. Weizmann Inst. Sci., 1976—; mem. research com. Med. Found., Boston, 1976-80; mem. U.S.-USSR Joint Commn. on Sci. and Tech., Dept. State, Washington, 1977-82; sr. cons. Office of Sci. and Tech. Policy, Exec. Office of Pres., Washington, 1977-81; mem. council Pugwash Confs. on Sci. and World Affairs, Geneva, 1977-82; chmn. basic research com. Nat. Sci. Bd., Washington, 1978-82; mem. U.S. Nat. Com. for Internat. Union for Pure and Applied Biophysics, NAS, 1979-83; mem. nominating com. NAS, 1980; bd. dirs. Med. Found., Boston, 1981-90; mem. vis. com. for Div. Med. Sci., Harvard U., 1981-87; mem. exec. com. of council, 1985-88, mem. govt.-univ.-industry research round table, 1984-87; chmn. sci. adv. com. dept. molecular biology Mass. Gen. Hosp., Boston, 1983-87; mem. governing bd. NRC, 1985-88; mem. nat. adv. com. Pew Scholars program Pew Meml. Trust, 1986-88; mem. com. on USSR and Eastern Europe Nat. Research Council, Washington, 1986—; mem. external adv. com. Ctr. for Human Genome Studies, Los Alamos Nat. Lab., N.Mex., 1989—, Nat. Critical Techs. Panel, Office of Sci. & Tech. Policy, Exec. Office of Pres., Washington, 1990-91; mem. vis. com. NASA Ctr. Exobiology, La Jolla, Calif., 1992—; fgn. mem. Russian Acad. Scis., Moscow, 1994—; vis. prof. Collège de France, Paris, 1987. Editor: (with Norman Davidson) Structural Chemistry and Molecular Biology, 1968;mem. editorial bd. Biophys. Jour, 1961-63, Currents Modern Biology, 1966-72, Science, 1963-69, Analytical Biochemistry, 1969-81, Bio-Systems, 1973-86, Molecular Biology Reports, 1974-85, Procs. NAS, 1973-78, Jour. Molecular and Applied Genetics, 1980-84, DNA, 1981-89, EMBO Jour., 1988-90, Jour. Biotech., 1987—, Genomics, 1987—, Proteins, Structure, Function and Genetics, 1986-91, Jour. Molecular Evolution, 1983—; Springer Series on Molecular Biology, 1980-88; editorial advisory bd. Jour. Molecular Biology, 1959-66, Accounts of Chemical Research, 1980-82, Jour. Biomolecular Strucure and Dynamics, 1983—, PAABS Revista, 1972-77, Biopolymers, 1963-74; contbr. articles to profl. jours. Served with USN, 1943-46. Recipient Skylab Achievement award NASA, 1974, Theodore von Karmin award Viking Mars Mission, 1976, Presdl. award N.Y. Acad. Scis., 1977, Jabotinsky medal Jabotinsky Found., 1980, James R. Killian Faculty Achievement award MIT, 1980, Lewis S. Rosenstiel Basic Biomed. Rsch. award Brandeis U., 1983, Nat. Sci. medal, 1995; NRC fellow, 1949-51; Guggenheim Found. fellow, 1963; mem. Pontifical Acad. Scis. The Vatican, 1978. Fellow AAAS; mem. NAS (chmn. biotech., program, com. on scholarly comm. with China 1986—, exec. com. 1985—, com. on sci. comm. and nat. security 1982—), Am. Chem. Soc. (exec. com. div. biol. chemistry 1962, Linus Pauling award 1995), Biophys. Soc. (coun. 1960-69), Am. Soc. Biol. Chemists, Am. Crystallographic Soc., Internat. Soc. for Study of Origin of Life, French Acad. Scis. (fgn.), European Molecular Biology Orgn. (assoc.), Japanese Biochem. Soc. (hon.), Physicians for Social Responsibility (nat. adv. bd. 1983—), Am. Philos. Soc., Inst. of Medicine (sr. mem. 1990), Phi Beta Kappa, Alpha Omega Alpha. Office: MIT Dept Biology 77 Massachusetts Ave Rm 68-233 Cambridge MA 02139-4301

RICH, ARTHUR LOWNDES, music educator; b. Woodcliff, N.J., May 7, 1905; s. Frank Joseph and Ruth (Lowndes) R.; m. Helen Wall, July 26, 1934; children: Arthur Lowndes, Ruth Anne. A.B., Rutgers U., 1926; A.M., Columbia U., 1928; Ph.D., NYU, 1940; diploma, Julliard Sch. Music, 1928; licentiate, Royal Schs. Music (Royal Acad. Music, Royal Coll. of Music), London, 1939; spl. study, Harvard, 1943, Christiansen Choral Sch., 1948; 52. Prof. music Catawba Coll., Salisbury, N.C., 1928-43; dir. music Belhaven Coll., Jackson, Miss., 1943-44, Mercer U., Macon, Ga., 1944—; Roberts prof. music Mercer U., 1945-74, prof. emeritus, dir. concert series and cultural affairs, 1974—; Choral condr., adjudicator, Ga. and S.E.; music critic Macon News; corr. Mus. Am.; pres. Tudor Apts., Biscayne Apts., Inc. Author: Lowell Mason, the Father of Singing Among the Children, 1945; Contbr. articles to ednl., music jours., reference books. Bd. dirs. Macon Arts Council, Middle Ga. Symphony Orch. Life hon. mem. Community Concert Assn. (dir.); mem. Mark Twain Soc. (hon.), Am. Assn. Coll. and Univ. Concert Mgrs., Nat. Assn. Schs. Music, Phi Mu Alpha Sinfonia Soc., Macon Morning Music Club (hon.), Macon Federated Music Club (hon.). Lodge: Rotary. Home: 369 Candler Dr Macon GA 31204-2450

RICH, BEN ARTHUR, lawyer, educator; b. Springfield, Ill., Mar. 27, 1947; s. Ben Morris and Betty Lorraine (Ingalls) R.; m. Caroline Rose Castle, Oct. 4, 1984 (div. Nov. 1988); m. Kathleen Mills, Aug. 17, 1991. Student, U. St. Andrews, Scotland, 1967-68; BA, DePauw U., 1969; JD, Washington U., 1973; postgrad., U. Colo. Bar: Ill. 1973, N.C. 1975, Colo. 1984. Rsch. assoc. U. Ill. Coll. Law, Urbana, 1973-74; staff atty. Nat. Assn. Attys. Gen., Raleigh, N.C., 1974-76; prin. Hollowell, Silverstein, Rich & Brady, Raleigh, 1976-80; dep. commr. N.C. Indsl. Commn., Raleigh, 1980-81; counsel N.C. Meml. Hosp., Chapel Hill, 1981-84; assoc. univ. counsel U. Colo. Health Scis. Ctr., Denver, 1984-86; gen. counsel U. Colo., Boulder, 1986-89, spl. counsel to the regents, 1989-90; asst. clin. prof. U. Colo. Sch. Medicine, 1992-94; asst. prof. U. Colo. Health Scis. Ctr., 1995—, asst. dir. program in healthcare ethics, humanities and law, 1995—; asst. prof. attendent U. Colo. Sch. Medicine, 1986-91, adj. instr. Sch. Law, 1988—, vis. assoc. prof., 1990-91; lectr. U. Denver Coll. Law. Contbr. articles to jours., chpt. to book. Mem. Am. Coll. Legal Medicine (assoc.-in-law 1987), Am. Philos. Assn., Soc. for Health and Human Values, Am. Soc. Medicine and Ethics (health law tchrs. sect.), Toastmasters Internat. (pres. Raleigh chpt. 1978). Unitarian. Avocations: sailing, jogging, tennis. Home: 222 S Elm St Denver CO 80222-1133 Office: Univ Colo Health Scis Ctr Box 245 Denver CO 80262

RICH, BETTY AN, early childhood educator; b. Montclair, N.J., July 18, 1931; d. William Proctor and Elizabeth Andrews (Ross) McElroy; children: Stuart Lloyd Rich, Betsy Baxter Rich. BS in Edn., Towson State U., 1953; MEd, Lesley Coll., 1989. Cert. early childhood educator, N.H. Spl. educator Orthopedic Unit, Mt. Rainier, Md., 1953-56; 2d grade tchr. Woodman Park Sch., Dover, N.H., 1956-59; organizer, facilitator Head Start, Claremont, N.H., 1965, tchr., 1966; kindergarten tchr. Charlestown (N.H.) Primary Sch., 1968-74, Bluff Sch., Claremont, 1974-89, Kindergarten Ctr., Claremont, 1989—; founder, chair Area Bridging Com. for Children, Claremont, 1989—; lectr. profl. confs., 1990—. Mem. adv. bd. Tech. Coll. Day Care, Claremont, 1992—, Tech. High Sch. Day Care, Claremont, 1990—. Named to Honor Roll of Tchrs. Assn. Sci. Tech. Ctrs., 1988. Mem. Nat. Assn. for Edn. Young Children, NEA, N.E. Soc. for Modern Group Studies (exec. adminstr. 1992—), Sugar River Tchrs. Assn., N.H. Assn. for Edn. Young Children (award for excellence 1992). Episcopalian. Avocations: amateur herbalist, naturalist. Home: RD 2 Box 30 Bible Hill Rd E Claremont NH 03743-9302 Office: Claremont Kindergarten Ctr 10 Vine St Claremont NH 03743

RICH, CLAYTON, university administrator; b. N.Y.C., May 21, 1924; s. Clayton Eugene and Leonore (Elliot) R.; m. Mary Bell Hodgkinson, Dec. 19, 1953 (div. May 2, 1974); 1 son, Clayton Greig.; m. Rosalind Rich, Apr. 1987. Grad., Putney Sch., 1942; student, Swarthmore Coll., 1942-44; M.D., Cornell U., 1948. Diplomate Am. Bd. Internal Medicine. Intern Albany (N.Y.) Hosp., 1948-49, asst. resident, 1950-51; research asst. Cornell U. Med. Coll., 1949-50; asst. Rockefeller U., 1953-58, asst. prof., 1958-60; asst. prof. medicine U. Wash. Sch. Medicine, 1960-62, assoc. prof., 1962-67, prof., 1967-71, assoc. dean, 1968-71; chief radioisotope service VA Hosp., Seattle, 1960-70; assoc. chief staff VA Hosp., 1962-71, chief staff, 1968-70; v.p. med. affairs, dean Sch. Medicine; prof. medicine Stanford U., 1971-79, Carl and Elizabeth Naumann prof., 1977-79; chief staff Stanford U. Hosp., 1971-77, chief exec. officer, 1977-79; sr. scholar Inst. Medicine, Nat. Acad. Sci., Washington, 1979-80; Mem. gen. medicine B study sect. NIH, 1969-73, chmn., 1972-73; mem. spl. med. adv. group VA, 1977-81; provost U. Okla. Health Scis. Ctr., Oklahoma City, 1980—, v.p. for health scis., 1983—; also exec. dean, prof. U. Okla. (Coll. Medicine), 1980-83. Editorial bd.: Calcified Tissue Research, 1966-72, Clin. Orthopedics, 1967-72, Jour. Clin. Endocrinology and Metabolism, 1971-72; Contbr. numerous articles to med. jours. Bd. dirs. Children's Hosp. at Stanford, Stanford U. Hosp., 1974-79; chmn. Gordon Research Conf. Chemistry, Physiology and Structure of Bones and Teeth, 1967; bd. dirs. Okla. Med. Research Found.; bd. dirs. Leadership Oklahoma City, 1981—, v.p., 1985—; bd. dirs. Okla. Blood Inst., 1982—, Oklahoma City Chpt. ARC, 1983—. Served to lt. USNR, 1951-53. Fellow ACP; mem. Assn. Am. Physicians, Western Assn. Physicians, Am. Soc. Mineral and Bone Research (adv. bd. 1977-80), Am. Soc. Clin. Investigation, Assn. Am. Med. Colls. (exec. council 1975-79), Inst. of Medicine, Western Soc. Clin. Research (v.p. 1967-68), Endocrine Soc., Assn. Acad. Health Ctrs. (bd. dirs. 1984—), Sigma Xi, Alpha Omega Alpha. Office: Provost Office U Okla PO Box 26901 Oklahoma City OK 73126

RICH, DANIEL HULBERT, chemistry educator; b. Fairmont, Minn., Dec. 12, 1942; married, 1964; 2 children. BS, U. Minn., 1964; PhD in Organic Chemistry, Cornell U., 1968. Rsch. assoc. organic chemist Cornell U., 1968; rsch. chemist Dow Chem. Co., 1968-69; rsch. assoc., organic chemist Stanford U., 1969-70; asst. prof. pharm. chemistry U. Wis., Madison, 1970-75, assoc. prof., 1975-81, prof. dept. medical chemistry, 1981—, prof. dept. organic chemistry, 1988—, Ralph F. Hirschmann prof. medicinal and organic chemistry, 1994—; cons. biorganic natural product study sect., NIH, 1980—, mem., 1981—. Recipient H.I. Romnes award, 1980, Vincent du Vigneaud award, 1990, Hitchings award for innovative methods in drug design, 1992, Alexander von Humboldt award, 1993, E. Volwiler award Am. Assn. Colls. Pharmacy, 1995; fellow NIH, 1968. Fellow AAAS, Am. Chem. Soc. (Ralph F. Hirschmann award in peptide chemistry 1993, divsn. medicinal chemistry award 1991), Am. Assn. Pharm. Sci. (rsch. achievement award 1992), Am. Assn. Coll. Pharmacy (Volwiler award 1995). Achievements include research in synthesis in peptides and hormones, inhibition of peptide receptors and proteases, characterization, synthesis and mechanisms of action of peptide natural products. Office: U Wis Dept Med Chemistry 425 N Charter St Madison WI 53706-1508

RICH, DAVID BARRY, city official, auditor, accountant, entertainer; b. Bronx, N.Y., July 3, 1952; s. Steven and Gizella (Kornfeld) R.; m. Biverly Hayag, Dec. 6, 1995; 1 child, Suzanne Stephanie. BS in Health Adminstrn., Ithaca Coll., 1976; postgrad. in acctg., Bryant and Stratton Coll., Buffalo, 1977. Office mgr. Rubin Gorewitz, CPA, N.Y.C., 1977-78; auditor State of Ariz., Phoenix, 1979-83; internal auditor City of Phoenix, 1983-84; sales use tax auditor City of Mesa (Ariz.), 1984—; pres. Clovis Acctg. Inc., Mesa, 1980-94; rep. H.D. Vest Investment Inc., Irving, Tex., 1984-94; owner D.B. Rich Enterprises Import/Export, Mesa, 1992—; stage name Barry Rich, Stand-up Comedy, 1994—. Treas., bd. dirs. Missing Mutts Inc., Tempe, Ariz., 1986-88. With USAF, 1971-76. Fellow Nat. Assn. Tax Preparers; mem. Toastmasters (treas. Mesa 1986-87), Phi Beta Kappa. *The world is one big neighborhood and we are all neighbors. If we will survive as a planet we must work together as friends. We must treat all people as our equals.*

RICH, DOROTHY KOVITZ, educational administrator, author. BA in Journalism and Psychology, Wayne U.; MA, Columbia U.; EdD, Catholic U. Founder, pres. The Home and Sch. Inst., Inc., Washington, 1964—; adv. coun. Nat. Health Edn. Consortium; adv. com. Ctr. for Workplace Prep. and Quality Edn., U.S. C. of C.; mem. readiness to learn task force U.S. Dept. Edn., urban edn. team Coun. Gt. City Schs.; legislative nat. initiatives including work on Family/Sch. Partnership Act, 1989; formulator New Partnerships for Student Achievement program, 1987; creator MegaSkills Edn. Ctr. The Home and Sch. Inst. Inc., 1990; designer MegaSkills Leader Tng. for Parent Workshops, 1988, MegaSkills Essentials for the Classroom, 1991, learning and working program for sch.-to-work initiatives, 1996, New MegaSkills Bond Tchr./Parent Partnership, 1994. Author: MegaSkills in School in Life: The Best Gift You Can Give Your Child, 1988, rev. edit., 1992, 12 tng. books; TV appearances include The Learning Channel, NBC Today Show, Good Morning Am.; subject of videos: Families and Schools: Teaming for Success, Survival Guide for Today's Parents. Recipient Am. Woman Leader award, Citation U.S. Dept. Edn., Nat. Gov.'s Assn., Alumni Achievement award in edn. Cath. U., 1992, Golden Apple award for MegaSkills Tchrs. Coll., Columbia U., 1996; grantee John D. and Catherine T. MacArthur Found.; named Washingtonian of Yr. Mem. Cosmos Club. Office: MegaSkills Edn Ctr Home and Sch Inst Inc 1500 Massachusetts Ave NW Washington DC 20005-1821

RICH, FRANK HART, critic; b. Washington, June 2, 1949; s. Frank Hart Rich and Helene Bernice (Aaronson) Fisher; m. Alexandra Rachelle Witchel, 1991; children from previous marriage: Nathaniel Howard, Simon Hart. B.A. in Am. History and Lit. magna cum laude, Harvard U., 1971. Co-editor Richmond (Va.) Mercury, 1972-73; sr. editor, film critic New Times mag., N.Y.C., 1973-75; film critic N.Y. Post, N.Y.C., 1975-77; film and TV critic Time mag., N.Y.C., 1977-80; chief drama critic N.Y. Times, N.Y.C., 1980-93; columnist N.Y. Times Sunday Mag., N.Y.C., 1993; Op-Ed columnist N.Y. Times, N.Y.C., 1994—. Author: (with others) The Theatre Art of Boris Aronson, 1987. Office: The NY Times 229 W 43rd St New York NY 10036-3913

RICH, GILES SUTHERLAND, federal judge; b. Rochester, N.Y., May 30, 1904; s. Giles Willard and Sarah Thompson (Sutherland) R.; m. Gertrude Verity Braun, Jan. 10, 1931 (dec.); 1 child, Verity Sutherland Grinnell (Mrs. John M. Hallinan); m. Helen Gill Field, Oct. 10, 1953. SB, Harvard, 1926; LLB, Columbia, 1929; LLD (hon.), John Marshall Law Sch., Chgo., 1981, George Washington U., 1989, Franklin Pierce Law Ctr., 1993. Bar: N.Y. 1929, U.S. Patent Office 1934. Pvt. practice N.Y.C., 1929-56; ptnr. specializing patent and trademark law Williams, Rich & Morse, 1937-52, Churchill, Rich, Weymouth & Engel, 1952-56; assoc. judge U.S. Ct. Customs and Patent Appeals, 1956-82; cir. judge U.S. Ct. Appeals (Fed. cir.), 1982—; lectr. patent law Columbia, 1942-56, N.Y. Law Sch., 1952; adj. prof. Georgetown U. Law Sch., 1963-69. Contbr. articles to profl. jours. Recipient Jefferson medal N.J. Patent Law Assn., 1955, Kettering award Patent Trademark and Copyright Inst. George Washington U., 1963, Founder's Day award for disting. govt. svcs., 1970, Freedom Found. award Am. Inst. Chemists, 1967, Eli Whitney award Conn. Patent Law Assn., 1972, Columbia U. Sch. Law medal for Excellence, 1994, Licensing Execs. Soc. of U.S.A. and Can. award, 1994. Mem. ABA, Assn. of Bar of City of N.Y., Am. Intellectual Property Law Assn., N.Y. Patent Law Assn. (pres. 1950-51), Rochester Patent Law Assn. (hon. life), L.A. Patent Law Assn. (hon.), San Francisco Patent Law Assn. (hon. life). Clubs: Harvard (Washington), Cosmos. Office: US Ct Appeals Fed Cir 717 Madison Pl NW Washington DC 20439-0001

RICH, HARRY E., financial executive; b. Wichita, Kans., Mar. 5, 1940; s. Hubert E. and Lorene (Sadler) R.; m. Elfreda Elizabeth Babcock, Aug. 8, 1964; children—Lisa G., Carey E., Ashley H. B.A., Harvard U., 1962, M.B.A., 1968. Pres. instrumentation div. Baxter Travenol, Deerfield, Ill., 1977-78; group v.p. Mallinckrodt, Inc., St. Louis, 1978-83; sr. v.p., chief fin. officer Brown Group, Inc., St. Louis, 1983-88, exec. v.p., chief fin. officer, 1988—, also dir.; bd. dirs. Boatmen's Nat. Bank St. Louis, Gen. Am. Capital Co. divsn. Gen. Am. Life Ins. Co. Bd. dirs. Repertory Theatre, 1984—, pres. bd. dirs.,1988-90; treas. V.P. Fair Found., 1985-88; bd. trustees Mary Inst., 1986-90, Mary Inst./St. Louis Country Day Sch., 1990—. Lt. USN, 1962-66. Avocations: tennis, jogging, sailing. Home: 101 Fair Oaks Saint Louis MO 63124-1579 Office: Brown Group Inc 8300 Maryland Ave Saint Louis MO 63105-3645

RICH, J(AY) PETER, lawyer; b. Santa Monica, Calif., July 28, 1953; s. Jay Baum and Claire Louise (Niessen) R.; m. Elizabeth Ann Higdon, Dec. 27, 1980; children: Jennifer Jeanne, Natalie Amanda, Megan Elizabeth. AB summa cum laude, UCLA, 1974; JD, Harvard U., 1977. Bar: Calif. 1977, U.S. Dist. Ct. (ctrl. dist.) Calif. 1978, U.S. Ct. Appeals (9th cir.).. Assoc. Memel, Jacobs, et al, L.A., 1978-84, ptnr., 1984-87; ptnr. McDermott, Will & Emery, L.A., 1987—; pres., bd. dirs. Univ. Religious Conf. UCLA, L.A., 1986-89, dir., 1989—; mem., bd. govs. Unicamp UCLA, L.A., 1986—. Author: Alternative Forms of Healthcare Delivery Systems: HMOs and PPOs, 1983, State Laws and Regulations Governing Preferred Provider Organizations, 1986; contbr. chpts. to books and articles to profl. jours. Mem. Hillcrest Country Club, Phi Beta Kappa. Avocations: golf, basketball, coaching youth soccer, military history, cinema. Office: McDermott Will & Emery 2049 Century Park E Ste 3400 Los Angeles CA 90067-3208

RICH, JOHN, film and television producer, director; b. Rockaway Beach, N.Y., July 6, 1925; s. Louis and Jennie (Rich) R.; children: Catherine Lee, Anthony Joseph, Robert Lawrence. AB, U. Mich., 1948, MA, 1949. Exec. prodr. TV series MacGyver, 1984-93; dir. (films) Wives and Lovers, 1963, The New Interns, 1964, Roustabout, 1964, Boeing-Boeing, 1965, Easy Come, Easy Go, 1967, (TV) Academy Awards, The Dick Van Dyke Show, All in the Family, other series include Bob Newhart, Barney Miller, Benson, Dear John, Murphy Brown, Hudson Street. Served to capt. USAAF, 1943-46. Recipient Outstanding Comedy Direction awards Acad. TV Arts and Scis. for The Dick Van Dyke Show, 1963, All in the Family, 1972, 73; Sesquicentennial award U. Mich., 1967; Dirs. Guild Am. award for most outstanding directorial achievement, 1972, Robert B. Aldrich award, 1992; Golden Globe awards for All in the Family, 1972, 73, Emmy award as prodr., 1973, Christopher award for Henry Fonda as Clarence Darrow, 1974. Mem. Dirs. Guild Am. (bd. dirs., founding trustee DGA-Prodrs. Pension Plan, chmn. 1964-65, 68-69, 92-93, 95-96), Phi Beta Kappa, Phi Kappa Phi.

RICH, JOHN MARTIN, humanities educator, researcher; b. Tuscaloosa, Ala., Dec. 14, 1931; s. Emanuel Morris and Bertha (Rose) R.; m. Martha Elaine Schur, June 6, 1955 (div. June 1966); children—Jeffrey Brian, Suzanne Elon; m. Joyce Ann Stegemoller, Aug. 28, 1967 (div. Mar. 1985); m. Audrey Faye Arnold, Aug. 1, 1987. B.A., U. Ala., 1954, M.A., 1955; Ph.D., Ohio State U., 1958. Grad. asst. Ohio State U., Columbus, 1955; asst. instr. edn. Ohio State U., 1956-58; asst. prof. edn. U. Tenn.-Martin, 1958-60; assoc. prof. edn. Coll. SUNY-Oneonta, 1960-61; from asst. prof. to assoc. prof. Iowa State U., Ames, 1961-66; assoc. prof. social and philos. studies U. Ky., Lexington, 1966-69; prof. cultural founds. edn. U. Tex., Austin, 1969-96, prof. emeritus, 1996—, chmn. dept. cultural founds. edn., 1969-75; vis. lectr. Nat. Kaohsiung (Taiwan) Normal U., 1993. Author: (books) Education and Human Values, 1968, Humanistic Foundations of Education, 1971, Portuguese translation, 1975, Korean translation, 1985, Challenge and Response, 1974, New Directions in Educational Policy, 1974, Discipline and Authority in School and Family, 1982, Professional Ethics in Education, 1984, Innovative School Discipline, 1985, Foundations of Education, 1992; co-author: Theories of Moral Development, 1985 (named an Outstanding Book of 1985-86 Choice mag.), 2d edit., 1994, Helping and Intervention, 1988, Competition in Education, 1992, The Success Ethic, Education, and the American Dream, 1996; editor: Readings in the Philosophy of Education, 1966, 2d edit., 1972, Conflict and Decision, 1972, Innovations in Education, 6th edit., 1992; co-editor, editl. adv. bd. Ednl. Studies, 1970-74, 77-80, 89-91; bd. contbg. editors Rev. Edn., 1977-85; editl. bd. Focus on Learning, 1980-84, Educational Foundations, 1985-91; bd. cons. Jour. Rsch. and Devel. in Edn., 1982-96, Ednl. Theory, 1991-95; contbr. articles to profl. jours., U.S., Can., Eng., Australia. Recipient Faculty Research Assignment award Univ. Research Inst., Austin, Tex., 1983-84; vis. scholar U. London, 1977; Univ. Research Inst. grantee, 1981-82, 84-85. Mem. North Central Philosophy of Edn. Soc. (pres. 1966-67), Ohio Valley Philosophy of Edn. Soc. (pres. 1967-68), Philosophy of Edn. Soc. (exec. bd. 1967-68, 80-82, Cert. Significant Svc.), Am. Ednl. Studies Assn. (exec. council 1972-74, pres. 1975-76). Home: 1801 Lavaca St Apt 8M Austin TX 78701-1307 Office: U Tex Edn Bldg 406 Austin TX 78712

RICH, JOSEPH JOHN, accountant; b. Detroit, Sept. 5, 1944; s. John H. and Edna R. (Swallow) R.; m. Carolyn A. Atkinson, Nov. 3, 1962 (div. Dec. 19, 1983); children: Marcella, Loren; m. Darlene E. Kornfehl, Aug. 2, 1985. A of Commerce, Alpena Community Coll.; A in Ins. Law, Am. Edn. Inst. Pres. Tax Svcs., Inc., Portland, Mich., 1965—; claim specialist State Farm Ins., Marshall, Mich., 1966-80; owner Someplace Else Travel Ctr., Portland, 1990—, The Expresso Experience, 1995—; Accredited bus. acct. Author: Insurance Guide for Theatres, 1977, Accounting for Non-Profit Theatres, 1976. Chmn. Ionia (Mich.) County Commn., 1986-90; mem. Ionia Social Svcs. Bd., 1992, Ionia Planning Commn., 1986, Portland Area Mcpl. Authority, 1992. Named one of Outstanding Young Men in Am., 1981. Mem. Portland Kiwanis Club, Ind. Accts. Assn. of Mich. Republican. Avocations: theatre, travel. Office: Tax Svcs Inc 200 W Bridge St Portland MI 48875-1153

RICH, JUDE T., management consulting firm executive; b. Atlantic City, Aug. 4, 1943; s. Samuel John and Mary Elizabeth (Miller) R.; m. Mary Theresa Bosies, Apr. 28, 1979; children: Victoria Elizabeth, Jessica Anne; children from previous marriage: Denise Marie, Jude T. Jr., Dina Marie. BS in Econs. cum laude, Rutgers U., 1966, MBA cum laude, 1974. Coll. recruiter Johnson & Johnson, New Brunswick, N.J., 1966-68; pers. mgr. NL Industries, N.Y.C., 1968-72; pers. dir. RCA, N.Y.C., 1972-74; ptnr., human resources practice head McKinsey & Co., N.Y.C., 1974-84; chmn. Sibson & Co., Princeton, N.J., 1984—; dir. Assn. Mgmt. Cons. Firms. Co-author: (rsch. publ.) Productivity in the Public Schools, 1982; contbr. articles to profl. jours. Pres. Gramercy Spire Assn., N.Y.C., 1980-82; bd. dirs. Recording for Blind. Mem. Human Resource Planning Soc., Assn. of Mgmt. Cons. (bd. dirs.), Univ. Club.. Episcopalian. Avocations: sailing, scuba, military history. Office: Sibson & Co Inc 504 Carnegie Ctr Princeton NJ 08543-5211*

RICH, KENNETH MALCOLM, executive search and management consultant; b. Newark, N.J., Aug. 17, 1946; s. Lucien Ludwell and Grace (Hardy) R.; m. Sandra Ann Arrington; children: Stephen Montgomery, Khristine Nicole. AB in Chemistry, Lafayette Coll., 1967; MBA in Fin., Mktg., U. Chgo., 1969; cert. in acctg., NYU, 1979. Assoc., corp. fin. Kuhn, Loeb & Co., N.Y.C., 1969-73; special asst. to the asst. sec. policy, devel. and rsch. HUD, Washington, 1973-74; mng. dir. fgn. investments The Dornbush Co., Atlanta, 1974; resident v.p. Citibank, N.A., N.Y.C., Athens and Dubai, U.A.E., 1975-78; mng., cons. div. Peat, Marwick, Mitchell & Co., N.Y.C., 1978-80; mng., strategic planning Gen. Elec. Credit Corp., Stamford, Conn., 1981-83; ptnr. Paul Ray Berndtson Inc., N.Y.C., 1983—; mem. mktg. com. Paul R. Ray & Co., Inc., N.Y.C., 1985-88, chmn. fin. svcs. practice com., 1989-92, mem. fin. svcs. practice com., 1989—, chmn. investment com., 1995-96; mem. stk. com., bd. dirs. practice group; also bd. dirs. Paul Ray Berndtson Inc., N.Y.C., 1989-96; trustee Lafayette Coll., Easton, Pa., 1970-75. Chief umpire Ridgefield (Conn.) Little League, 1980-89; mem. Lafayette Leadership Coun., 1993—; bd. dirs. Juvenile Diabetes Found. Internat., 1993—, exec. com., 1995—, chair nominating com., 1995—, mem. long range planning com., 1995. Standard Oil of N.J. fellow U. Chgo., 1967-69; named one of N.Am.'s top exec. recruiters The New Career Makers (by John Sibbald), 1994. Mem. Assn. Exec. Search Cons. (bd. dirs. 1994—, chair regional affairs com. 1995—). Presbyterian. Avocations: reading, music, cross training. Home: 67 St Johns Rd Ridgefield CT 06877-5524 Office: Paul Ray Berndtson Inc 101 Park Ave New York NY 10178 *At the end of the day, all anyone really has is his integrity. That is why I place such a high value on honesty, sincerity, empathy, and generosity. But unless you have a sense of humor, no one will ever notice your other virtues.*

RICH, LEE, entertainment industry executive; b. Cleve.; m. Ilene Graham; children by previous marriage: Jessica, Miranda. B.A., Ohio U., hon. degree in communications, 1982; LL.D. (hon.), Southwestern U., 1983. Advt. exec., resigned as sr. TV v.p. Benton & Bowles to become pres. Mirisch Rich TV, 1965-67; with Leo Burnett Agy., 1967-69; pres., co-owner Lorimar Prodns., Culver City, Calif., 1969-86; chmn., chief exec. officer MGM/UA Communications Co., Beverly Hills, Calif., 1986-95; chmn. bd. Lee Rich Prodns., Burbank; co-chmn. Eagle Point Prodn., Culver City, Calif., 1995—. Prodr: (TV movie) Sybil, (films) Helter Skelter, Green Eyes, Eric, The Homecoming, The Blue Knight, Skag, Two of a Kind, (TV series) Dallas, The Waltons (Emmy awards), Eight is Enough, Knots Landing, Falcon Crest; film prodr.: Being There, The Big Red One, The Postman Always Rings Twice, Who Is Killing the Great Chefs of Europe, Victory, S.O.B., Hard to Kill, 1990, Passenger 57, 1992, Innocent Blood, 1992, Little Panda, 1994, Just Cause, 1994. Recipient Disting. Citizenship award Southwestern U. Sch. Law, 1983. Office: Eagle Point Prodn 10202 W Washington Blvd Culver City CA 90232-9999

RICH, MICHAEL DAVID, research corporation executive, lawyer; b. Los Angeles, Jan. 23, 1953; s. Ben Robert and Faye (Mayer) R.; m. Debra Paige Granfield, Jan. 12, 1980; children: Matthew, William. AB, U. Calif., Berkeley, 1973; JD, UCLA, 1976. Bar: Calif., 1976. Law clk. to judge U.S. Dist. Ct., Boston, 1976; staff mem. RAND, Santa Monica, Calif., 1976-85, dir. resource mgmt. program, 1980-85, dep. v.p., 1986, v.p. nat. security rsch. and dir. Nat. Def. Rsch. Inst., 1986-93; sr. v.p. RAND, 1993-95, exec. v.p., 1995—. Author numerous classified and unclassified reports and articles. Immediate past pres., bd. dirs. WISE Sr. Svcs. Mem. Internat. Inst. Strategic Studies, Council Fgn. Relations. Office: RAND PO Box 2138 1700 Main St Santa Monica CA 90401-3208

RICH, MICHAEL JOSEPH, lawyer; b. N.Y.C., June 19, 1945; s. Jesse and Phyllis (Sternfeld) R.; m. Linda Christine Kubis, July 19, 1969; children: David Lawrence, Lisa Diane. BA, Gettysburg Coll., 1967; JD, Am. U., 1972. Bar: Del. 1973, U.S. Dist. Ct. Del. 1973, U.S. Supreme Ct. 1976, Pa. 1981. Law clk. Del. Supreme Ct., Georgetown, 1972-73; assoc. Tunnell & Raysor, Georgetown, 1973-76; ptnr. Dunlap, Holland & Rich, P.A., Georgetown, 1976-80; gen. counsel Pearlette Fashions, Inc., Lebanon, Pa., 1981-83; assoc. Morris, Nichols, Arsht & Tunnell, Georgetown, 1983-86, ptnr., 1987-91; ptnr. Twilley, Street, Rich, Braverman & Hindman, P.A., Dover, Del., 1991-95; state solicitor, 1995—; mem. Bd. Bar Examiners, Del., 1986—, chair, 1996—; minority counsel Del. Ho. of Reps., Dover, 1977-79; mem. Del. Gov's Magistrate Commn., 1980, 83-86; sec. Del. Gov's. Jud. Nominating Commn., 1986-89. Bd. dirs. People's Place II, Inc., Milford, Del., 1973-77; pres. Bi-County United Way, Inc., Milford, 1977-78; mem. Partnership Greater Milford Commn., 1987-89, Friends Milford Library. Served to 1st lt. U.S. Army, 1967-69, Vietnam. Dean's fellow Am. U., 1971-72. Mem. ABA, Am. Judicature Soc., Del. Bar Assn. (pres. 1990-91), Sussex County Bar Assn. (pres. 1987-89). Republican. Office: Dept Justice 820 N French St Wilmington DE 19801-3509

RICH, PHILIP DEWEY, publishing executive; b. Nashua, N.H., Feb. 1, 1940; s. John Parker and Olive Frances (Hussey) R.; m. Leslie Ann Burke, June 14, 1974 (div. 1982). AB magna cum laude, Harvard U., 1961; MA, NYU, 1962; postgrad., Princeton U., 1962. Editor Houghton Mifflin Co., Boston, 1964-73; asst. mng. editor UpCountry Mag. Berkshire Eagle, Pittsfield, Mass., 1976-77; editor Book Creations Inc., Canaan, N.Y., 1977-80, editor-in-chief, 1980-91, v.p., exec. editor, 1991-92; cons. editor Berkshire Ho. Publs., Lee, Mass., 1992-93; mng. editor Berkshire Ho. Publs., Stockbridge, Mass., 1993—. Office: Berkshire House Pubs Ste 5 480 Pleasant St Lee MA 01238

RICH, R(OBERT) BRUCE, lawyer; b. N.Y.C., Oct. 28, 1949; s. John J. and Sylvia (Berkenblit) R.; m. Melissa Jo Saxe; children—Megan, Alexander. A.B., Dartmouth Coll., 1970; J.D., U. Pa., 1973. Bar: N.Y. 1974, U.S. Dist. Ct. (so. and ea. dists.) N.Y. 1974, U.S. Ct. Appeals (2d cir.) 1980, U.S. Supreme Ct. 1980, U.S. Ct. Appeals (D.C. cir.) 1985. Assoc. firm Weil, Gotshal & Manges, N.Y.C., 1973-81, ptnr., 1981—. Contbg. author: Cultivating the Wasteland: Can Cable Put the Vision Back in TV?, 1983, The International Libel Handbook, 1995. Contbr. articles to profl. jours. Bd. advisers Communications and the Law, Westport, Conn., 1983—. Mem. ABA (antitrust law sect., forum com. on communications law), Assn. Bar City N.Y. (com. on trade regulation 1982-85, communications law com. 1985-88), Phi Beta Kappa. Office: Weil Gotshal & Manges 767 5th Ave New York NY 10153

RICH, ROBERT C., manufacturing executive; b. 1944. BA, Brigham Young U., 1969; MBA, Northwestern U., 1971. Fin. analyst, supr. Ford Motor Co., Dearborn, Mich., 1971-75; divsn. contr. Pullman, Inc., Chgo., 1975-81; v.p. fin. men's apparel group Hartmarx Corp., Chgo., 1981-87; v.p. fin. Tonka Corp., Minnetonka, Minn., 1987-88; sr. v.p. Masterbrand Industries, 1988-92; exec. v.p. ops. Master Lock Co., Milw., 1993—. Office: Master Lock Co 2600 N 32nd St Milwaukee WI 53210-2506

RICH, ROBERT E., SR., frozen foods company executive; married. Grad., U. Buffalo, 1935. Owner Wilber Farms Dairy, 1935; founder, chmn. bd. dirs. Rich Products Corp., Buffalo, 1944—. Office: Rich Products Corp 1 West Ferry St Buffalo NY 14213*

RICH, ROBERT E., JR., food products company executive; b. 1941. Student, Williams Coll.; MBA, U. Rochester. Pres., bd. dirs. Rich Products Corp., Buffalo; also vice-chmn. bd. dirs. Buffalo Sabres Hockey Club. Office: Rich Products Corp 1145 Niagara St Buffalo NY 14213-1713 also: Buffalo Sabres Meml Auditorium 140 Main St Buffalo NY 14202-4110*

RICH, ROBERT EDWARD, lawyer; b. Corbin, Ky., Feb. 4, 1944; s. Edward Bluch and Marjorie Brooks (Wentworth) R.; m. Janet Sue Shearer, May 14, 1966; children: Susan M., Christopher R., David E., Sarah M. AB, U. Ky., 1966; JD, Harvard U., 1969. Bar: Ohio 1970. Jud. clk. U.S. Ct. Appeals for 6th Cir., Louisville, 1969-70; assoc. Taft, Stettinius & Hollister, Cin., 1970, ptnr., 1978—. V.p. Lighthouse Youth Svcs., Inc., Cin., 1985; trustee Ky. Youth Assn., State YMCA, Frankfort, Ky., 1990; pres. Ctr. for Hope, Inc., Mt. Health, Ohio, 1991, Cin. Bar Found., 1991. Mem. ABA, Cin. Bar Assn. Republican. Presbyterian. Home: 215 Hilltop Ln Wyoming OH 45215-4121 Office: 1800 Star Bank Ctr 425 Walnut St Cincinnati OH 45202-3957

RICH, ROBERT F., political sciences educator, academic administrator; married; 3 children. BA in Govt. with high honors, Oberlin Coll., 1971; student, Free U. of Berlin, 1971-72; MA in Polit. Scis., U. Chgo., 1973, PhD in Polit. Scis., 1975. Project dir., asst. rsch. scientist Ctr. for Rsch. on Utilization Sci. Knowledge, Inst. Social Rsch., U. Mich., lectr. dept. polit. sci., 1975-76; asst. prof. politics and pub. affairs Princeton U., 1976-82, coord. domestic and urban policy field Woodrow Wilson Sch., 1979-81; assoc. prof. polit. sci., pub. policy and mgmt. Sch. Urban and Pub. Affairs, Carnegie-Mellon U., 1982-86; prof. polit. sci., health resources mgmt., medical humanities and social svcs., community health, prof. Inst. Environ. Studies U. Ill., Urbana, 1986—, dir. Inst. Govt. and Publ. Affairs; acting head med. humanities and social scis. program U. Ill., Urbana-Champaign, 1988-90, prof. Inst. for Environ. Studies; fellow Johns Hopkins U. Ctr. for Study of Am. Govt., Washington, 1993-95; cons. Carnegie-Mellon U., 1986—, MacArthur Found., NIMH, 1988-89, Food, Drug and Law Inst., HHS, 1989, others. Author: Social Science Information and Public Policy Making: The Interaction Between Bureaucratic Politics and the Use of Survey Data, 1981; co-author: Government Information Management: A Counter-Report of the Commission on Federal Paperwork, 1980; editor: Translating Evaluation into Policy, 1979, The Knowledge Cycle, 1981, Knowledge, Creation, Diffusion, Utilization, 1979-88, 88-91; co-editor: Competitive Approaches to Health Policy Reform, 1993, Health Care Policy, Federalism and the Role of the States, 1996; assoc. editor Society, 1984-88, Evaluation Rev., 1985-89; mem. editorial adv. rev. bd. Policy Studies Rev. Series, 1980-83; mem. editorial bd. Evaluation and Change, 1979-82; mem. editorial adv. bd. Law and Human Behavior, 1983-87; contbr. numerous articles to profl. jours., book chpts. Recipient Emil Limbach Teaching award Carnegie-Mellon U., Sch. Urban and Pub. Affairs, 1985; fellow German Acad. Exch. Program, Fed. Republic Germany, 1971-72, Nat. Opinion Rsch. Ctr. fellow, 1972-73, German Govt. fellow, 1974, Russel Sage Found. Rsch. fellow, 1974-75; vis. scholar Hastings Ctr. for Society, Ethics and Life Scis., 1982. Mem. APA (task force on victims of crime and violence 1982-84), Soc. for Traumatic Stress Studies (bd. dirs. 1980—), World Fedn. for Mental Health (chmn. com. on mental health needs of victims 1985—, vice chmn. 1981-83, Robert F. Rich rsch. ann. award established in his honor, sci. com. on mental health needs of victims 1983), Howard R. Davis Soc. for Knowledge Utilization and Planned Change (pres. 1986-89), Polit. Sci. 400, Policy Studies Assn. (Aaron Wildnusky award 1994), Phi Beta Kappa, Sigma Xi, Phi Kappa Phi. Office: U Ill Inst Govt & Pub Affairs 1007 W Nevada St # 204 Urbana IL 61801-3812 also: 921 W Van Buren St # C 191 Chicago IL 60607-3542

RICH, ROBERT REGIER, immunology educator, physician; b. Newton, Kans., Mar. 7, 1941; s. Eldon Stahly and Margaret Joy (Regier) R.; m. Susan Jepson Solliday, Mar. 22, 1974; children from previous marriage: Kenneth Eldon, Cathryn Louise. A.B., Oberlin Coll., 1962; M.D., U. Kans., 1966. Diplomate Am. Bd. Internal Medicine (bd. dirs. 1990-93), Am. Bd. Allergy and Immunology (bd. dirs. 1987-93, chmn. 1991); cert. spl. qualification Diagnostic Lab. Immunology. Intern, resident in internal medicine U. Wash., Seattle, 1966-68; clin. asso., chief clin. asso., sr. staff fellow NIH, Bethesda, Md., 1968-71; research asso. Harvard Med. Sch., Boston, 1971-73; asst. in medicine Peter Bent Brigham Hosp., 1972-73; asst. prof., assoc. prof. microbiology, immunology and internal medicine Baylor Coll. Medicine, Houston, 1973-78, prof., 1978-95, Disting. Svc. prof., 1995—, head immunology sect., 1978—, chief clin. immunology, 1979-91, v.p., dean rsch., 1990—; investigator Howard Hughes Med. Inst., Bethesda, Md., 1977-91; mem. immunobiology study sect. NIH, 1977-81; mem. med. staff Harris County Hosp. Dist., Meth. Hosp., Houston; mem. transplantation biology and immunology com. Nat. Inst. Allergy and Infectious Disease, 1982-86, chmn., 1984-86; mem. nat. ctr. grants com. Arthritis Found., 1983-86, chmn., 1984-86, nat. rsch. com., 1984-89, chmn., 1986-89, ho. of dels., 1985-91; mem. rsch. adv. com. Nat. Multiple Sclerosis Soc., 1989-94, chmn., 1993-94. Assoc. editor: Jour. Immunology, 1978-82, sect. editor, 1991—; assoc. editor: Jour. Infectious Diseases, 1984-88; adv. editor: Jour. Exptl. Medicine, 1980-84; mem. editl. bd. Jour. Clin. Immunology, 1989—, Clin. and Exptl. Immunology, 1995—; editor-in-chief Clin. Immunology: Principles and Practice; contbr. articles to profl. jours. Served with USPHS, 1968-70. Recipient Research Career Devel. award NIH, 1975-77, Merit award NIH, 1987. Fellow ACP, Am. Acad. Allergy, Asthma, and Immunology (chmn. basic and clin. immunology interest sect. 1992-93, chmn. profl. edn. coun. 1996—), Infectious Diseases Soc. Am.; mem. AMA, AAAS, Am. Bd. Internal Medicine (diplomate, bd. dirs. 1990-93), Am. Bd. Allergy and Immunology (diplomate, bd. dirs. 1987-93), Assn. Am. Physicians, Am. Soc. Clin. Investigation, Am. Soc. Histocompatibility and Immunogenetics, Am. Assn. Immunologists (chmn. pub. affairs com. 1994—), Am. Assn. Investigative Pathology, Transplantation Soc., Am. Soc. Microbiologists, So. Soc. Clin. Investigation, Am. Fedn. Clin. Rsch., Am. Clin. Climatological Assn., Harris County Med. Soc., Tex. Med. Assn., Clin. Immunology Soc. (coun. 1990—, pres. 1995), Alpha Omega Alpha, Sigma Xi. Office: Baylor Coll Medicine One Baylor Pla Houston TX 77030

RICH, ROBERT STEPHEN, lawyer; b. N.Y.C., Apr. 30, 1938; s. Maurice H. and Natalie (Priess) R.; m. Myra N. Lakoff, May 31, 1964; children: David, Rebecca, Sarah. AB, Cornell U., 1959; JD, Yale U., 1963. Bar: N.Y. 1964, Colo. 1973, U.S. Tax Ct. 1966, U.S. Supreme Ct. 1967, U.S. Ct. Claims 1968, U.S. Dist. Ct. (so. dist.) N.Y. 1965, U.S. Dist. Ct. (ea. dist.) N.Y. 1965, U.S. Dist. Ct. Colo. 1980, U.S. Ct. Appeals (2d cir.) 1964, U.S. Ct. Appeals (10th cir.) 1978; conseil juridique, Paris, 1968. Assoc. Shearman & Sterling, N.Y.C., Paris, London, 1963-72; ptnr. Davis, Graham & Stubbs, Denver, 1973—; adj. faculty U. Denver Law Sch., 1977—; adv. bd. U. Denver Ann. Tax Inst., 1985—; adv. bd. global bus. and culture divsn. U. Denver, 1992—, Denver World Affairs Coun., 1993—; bd. dirs. Clos du Val Wine Co. Ltd., Danskin Cattle Co., Areti Wines, Ltd., Taltarni Vineyards, Christy Sports, Copper Valley Assn., pres.; bd. dirs. several other corps.; mem. Colo. Internat. Trade Adv. Coun., 1985—, tax adv. com. U.S. Senator Hank Brown; mem. Rocky Mountain Dist. Export Coun. U.S. Dept. Commerce, 1993—. Author treatises on internat. taxation; contbr. articles to profl. jours. Bd. dirs. Denver Internat. Film Festival, 1978-79, Alliance Française, 1977—; actor, musician N.Y. Shakespeare Festival, 1960; sponsor Am. Tax Policy inst., 1991—; trustee, sec. Denver Art Mus., 1982—; mem. adv. bd. Denver World Affairs Coun., 1993—. Capt., AUS, 1959-60. Fellow Am. Coll. Tax Counsel (bd. regents 10th cir. 1992—); mem. ABA, Internat. Bar Assn., Colo. Bar Assn., N.Y. State Bar Assn., Assn. of Bar of City of N.Y., Asia-Pacific Lawyers Assn., Union Internationale des Avocats, Internat. Fiscal Assn. (pres. Rocky Mt. br. 1992—, U.S. regional v.p. 1988—), Japan-Am. Soc. Colo. (bd. dirs., 1989—, pres. 1991-93), Confrerie des Chevaliers du Tastevin, Meadowood Club, Denver Club, Cactus Club Denver, Yale Club, Denver Tennis Club. Office: PO Box 61429 Denver CO 80206-8429

RICH, S. JUDITH, public relations executive; b. Chgo., Apr. 14; d. Irwin M. and Sarah I. (Sandock) R. BA, U. Ill., 1960. Staff writer, reporter Economist Newspapers, Chgo., 1960-61; asst. dir. pub. rels. and communications Coun. Profit Sharing Industries, Chgo., 1961-62; dir. advt. and pub. rels. Chgo. Indsl. Dist., 1962-63; account exec., account supr., v.p., sr. v.p., exec. v.p. and nat. creative dir. Edelman Pub. Rels. Worldwide, Chgo., 1963-85; exec. v.p., dir. Ketchum Pub. Rels. Worldwide, Chgo., 1985-89, exec. v.p., exec. creative dir. USA, 1990—; frequent spkr. on creativity and brainstorming. workshop facilitator, spkr. in field. Mem. pub. rels. adv. bd. U. Chgo. Grad Sch. Bus., Roosevelt U., Chgo., DePaul U., Chgo., Gov.'s State U. Mem. Pub. Rels. Soc. Am. (Silver Anvil award, judge Silver Anvil awards), Counselors Acad. of Pub. Rels. Soc. Am. (exec. bd.), Chgo. Publicity Club (8 Golden Trumpet awards). Avocations: theatre, swimming, cycling, racquetball. Home: 2500 N Lakeview Ave Chicago IL 60614-1836 Office: Ketchum Pub Rels # 3400 205 N Michigan Ave Chicago IL 60601-5925

RICH, WALTER GEORGE, railroad transportation executive; b. Oneonta, N.Y., Jan. 9, 1946; s. George C. and Dorretta (Gregg) R.; m. Karine Schmook, July 14, 1990; children: Derik, Stephanie. BA, Syracuse (N.Y.) U., 1968, JD, 1971. Gen. mgr. Delaware Otsego Corp., Oneonta, 1966-68, v.p., gen. mgr., 1968-71; pres. Delaware Otsego Corp., Cooperstown, N.Y., 1971—, N.Y. Susquehanna & Western Rwy., Cooperstown, 1980—; bd. dirs. Delaware Otsego Corp., Copperstown, Norwich (N.Y.) Aero Products, Inc., Security Mut. Life Ins. Co. of N.Y.; bd. dirs. (apptd. by Gov. Cuomo) N.Y. Pub. Transp. Safety Bd., 1993—; v.p. Ea. region/bd. dirs. Am. Shortline R.R. Assn. Commr. of elections Delaware County, 1971-78; trustee Glimmerglass Opera, Cooperstown, 1986—; mem. N.Y. Gov. George Pataki's transition team, 1994; bd. dirs. N.Y. Bus. Devel. Corp., 1995. Mem. Nat. Rwy. Hist. Soc., Newcomen Soc., Eastern Gen. Mgrs. Assn. (pres. 1985, sec. 1986—), Lexington Group in Transp., N.Y. Athletic Club (N.Y.C.), Ft. Orange Club (Albany), Union League Club (Phila.). Episcopalian. Republican. Office: Del Otsego Corp 1 Railroad Ave Cooperstown NY 13326-1110

RICH, WAYNE ADRIAN, retired lawyer; b. Piner, Ky., Aug. 8, 1912; s. Shirley S. and Edna Jane (Mann) R.; m. Ellen Peters, Sept. 4, 1937 (dec. Dec., 1966); children—Wayne A., Ellen Randolph Williams; m. Frances Runyan, Oct. 4, 1968; 1 stepchild, Charles Hamilton West. A.B., U. Cin., 1935; J.D., Harvard U., 1938. Bar: W.Va., U.S. Supreme Ct., U.S. Tax Ct. Sole practice law, Charleston, W.Va., 1938-77, ret., 1977—; dir. City Nat. Bank, Charleston, 1956-77, pres., 1967-68, chmn. bd., trust officer, 1968-77. Mem. Kanawha Juvenile Council, Charleston, 1955-62; bd. dirs. Kanawha Welfare Council, 1957-63; trustee Greater Kanawha Valley Found., 1968-77; mem. City Council, Charleston, 1955-59, Mcpl. Planning Commn., Charleston, 1962-77; mem. W.Va. adv. council SBA, 1962-63. Served to comdr. USN, 1943-46. Mem. W.Va. State Bar Assn., Kanawha County Bar Assn. (v.p. 1953, 59), Tau Kappa Alpha, Omicron Delta Kappa, Sigma Chi. Republican. Presbyterian. Club: Kingsmill Golf (Williamsburg). Avocation: golf. Home: 12 Ensign Spence Williamsburg VA 23185-5561

RICH, WILLIS FRANK, JR., banker; b. Ft. Dodge, Iowa, July 26, 1919; s. Willis Frank and Agnes Reed (Paterson) R.; m. Jo Ann Rockwell, Apr. 12, 1947; children: Ronald Rockwell, Roxanne, Andrew Paterson. B.A., Princeton U., 1941. Credit analyst Northwestern Nat. Bank, Mpls., 1947-52; asst. cashier Northwestern Nat. Bank, 1952-55, asst. v.p., 1955, v.p., 1955-57; pres. N.W. Nat. Bank, Bloomington-Richfield, Minn., 1952-58; v.p., cashier N.W. Nat. Bank, 1957-60, v.p. div. A, 1960-68, sr. v.p. nat. and internat. divs., 1968-73; exec. v.p. N.W. Nat. Bank, Mpls., 1973-81, vice chmn. bd. dirs., chief credit officer, 1981-84; fin. cons., 1984—; dir. Advance Acceptance Corp. Pres. Viking coun. Boy Scouts Am., 1970-71, trustee found., 1971-86; mem. exec. bd. Minn. Cmty. Rsch. Coun., 1969-77; dir. Minn. Zoo, 1987-95; trustee St. Martin's Found., 1986-90; vestry mem. St. Martin's-By-The-Lake Ch. With AUS, 1941-46. Decorated Bronze Star. Mem. Robert Morris Assocs. (nat. pres. 1977-78). Episcopalian. Clubs: Woodhill, Swan Lake Country. Home: 4770 Manitou Rd Excelsior MN 55331-9400

RICHARD, ALFRED LOUIS, marketing professional; b. Santiago, Chile, Sept. 9, 1943; came to U.S., 1975; s. Jorge and Sara Rosa (Waugh) R.; m. Regina Eliana Nuñez, Jan. 23, 1966 (div. 1975); children: Alfredo, Alejandro, Jaime Andres; m. Millie Rose Carrasco, Dec. 17, 1976; 1 child, Sebastian Edward Richard. BS in Mech. Engring., U. Santiago, 1969. Parts and svc. mgr., Ctrl. Am. and Caribbean Ford Motor Co. Tractor Divsn., Costa Rica, 1971-75; field sales mgr. South Am. Ford Motor Co. Tractor Divsn., Ft. Lauderdale, Fla., 1975-79; nat. mktg. mgr. Spain Ford Motor Co. Tractor Divsn., Barcelona, 1979-80; Argentina mktg. mgr. Ford Motor Co. Tractor Divsn., Buenos Aires, 1980-81; tractor office dir. Ford Motor Co. Tractor Divsn., Valencia, Venezuela, 1982-85; sales dir. Latin Am./Mexico Ford New Holland, Ft. Lauderdale, 1985-93; mktg. dir. internat. divsn. Tokheim Corp., Ft. Wayne, Ind., 1993; sales, mktg. dir. South Am., Asia Pacific, Africa, Mid. East Tokheim Corp., Ft. Wayne, 1993—. Mem. Pine Valley Country Club. Roman Catholic. Avocations: golf, tennis, boating. Home: 10806 Sandpiper Cv Fort Wayne IN 46845-1572 Office: Tokheim Corp PO Box 360 Fort Wayne IN 46801-0360

RICHARD, ALISON FETTES, anthropology educator; b. Great Britain, Mar. 1, 1948. BA, Cambridge U., 1969; PhD, London U., 1973. Asst. prof. anthropology Yale U., New Haven, 1972-76, assoc.prof. anthropology, 1976-85, prof. anthropology, 1985—, provost prof., 1994—; dir. Yale Peabody Mus. Natural History, 1990-94. Bd. dirs. Yale-New Haven Health Svcs., 1994—, World Wildlife Fund, 1995—. Mem. Am. Primatological Soc., Am. Assn. Phys. Anthropologists, Am. Anthrop. Assn., Brit. Ecol. Soc., Primate Soc. Gt. Britain, Zool. Soc. London, Cambridge Philosophical Soc. Office: Office of the Provost Yale U New Haven CT 06520-8118

RICHARD, ANN BERTHA, nursing administrator; b. Hartford, Conn., Mar. 21, 1944; d. Victor Charles and Theresa (Gasper) R.; children: Elena Skrinak, Judith Dunn. Diploma, Capital City Sch. Nursing, Washington, 1965; BSN summa cum laude, U. Hartford, Bloomfield, Conn., 1982; MS, U. Conn., 1986. RN, Conn.; cert. nurse adminstr., med.-surg. nurse. Staff nurse D.C. Gen. Hosp., Washington, 1965-66; staff nurse Hartford Hosp., 1972-73, asst. head nurse, 1973-74, head nurse, 1974-83, nutritional support clinician, 1983-85; total nursing care project cons. Hosp. of St. Raphael, New Haven, 1986-88, assoc. dir. gen. surg. nursing and spltys., 1986-88; v.p. for patient svcs. Manchester (Conn.) Meml. Hosp., 1988—. Contbr. chpt. to book. Passini scholar, 1985. Mem. ANA (nuring adminstrn. coun. 1986—), Conn. Nurses Assn. (govt. rels. com. 1984-88, bd. dirs. 1990-94), Conn. Orgn. Nurse Execs. (nominating com. 1986-88), Am. Coll. Healthcare Execs., Conn. Hosp. Assoc. (chairperson nurse exec. conf. 1993-95, bd. dirs. 1995—), Sigma Theta Tau (program com. 1986-88, nominating com. 1988-89), Alpha Chi, Conn. League Nursing (bd. dirs. 1990-92), Nat. League Nursing, N.E. Orgn. Nurse Execs. Office: Meml Hosp 71 Haynes St Manchester CT 06040-4112

RICHARD, EDWARD H., manufaturing company executive, former municipal government official; b. N.Y.C., Mar. 15, 1937; s. Henry and Ida Richard; B.A., Antioch Coll., 1959. Pres., chmn. bd. dirs. Magnetics Internat. Inc., Maple Heights, Ohio, 1967-86, exec. v.p. Stearns Magnetics S.A., Brussels, Belgium, 1974-77; prin. Edward H. Richard & Assocs., Cleve., 1967-92; pres., treas. David Round & Son, Inc., Cleve; exec. adminstrv. asst. to mayor City of Cleve., 1979-87, dir. dept. pub. utilities, 1981-89, dep. to mayor, chief adminstrv. officer, 1986-89; dir. airports and port control City of Cleve., 1988-90; pres., CEO David Round & Son, Inc., Solon, Ohio, 1989—; chmn. Cleve. dist. adv. council Small Bus. Adminstrn., 1975-79; former mem. nat. adv. council Dept. Treasury; cons. and advisor in field; del. world trade fairs. Former trustee Regional Econ. Devel. Council, Met. Cleve. Jobs Council, Cleve. Devel. Found., Cleve. Better Bus. Bur.; former trustee Hiram House, Antioch U., former treas., 1972-77; N.E. Ohio Regional Sewer Dist., Greater Cleve. Domed Stadium Corp., Greater Cleve. Conv. and Vis. Bur.; former trustee, vice-chmn. Cleve. Center Econ. Edn.; former pres. Bratenahl Condominium Assn.; mem., chmn. fin. com. Bratenahl Bd. Edn., 1971-75. Office: PO Box 39456 Solon OH 44139-0456

RICHARD, ELLEN, theater executive; b. Bridgeport, Conn., Dec. 12, 1957; d. Laurent and Anne (Markham) R. Bus. mgr. Atlas Scenic Studio, Bridgeport, 1977-82; theater mgr. Stamford (Conn.) Ctr. for Arts, 1980-83; bus. mgr. Westport (Conn.) Country Playhouse, 1982-84; gen. mgr. Roundabout Theatre Co. Inc., N.Y.C., 1983—. Mem. N.Y. Cycling Club. Republican. Avocations: cycling, skiing. Office: Roundabout Theatre Co 1530 Broadway New York NY 10036-4002

RICHARD, GERALD LAWRENCE, soil scientist; b. Brush, Colo., Oct. 26, 1931; s. Donald Lehman and Gladys Lucile (Eikenbary) R.; m. Phyllis Darlene Hansen, Dec. 28, 1952; children: Donald Lawrence, Dale Kendall, Lori Ann Fosmire, Julie Lynn Young. BS in Agronomy, Colo. State U., 1956. Cert. profl. soil scientist. Soil scientist Soil Conservation Svc., Wheatland, Wyo., 1957, Torrington and Cheyenne, Wyo., 1959-65; work unit conservationist Soil Conservation Svc., Laramie, Wyo., 1965; area soil scientist Soil Conservation Svc., Bellefonte, Pa., 1965-71; asst. state soil scientist Soil Conservation Svc., Spokane, Wash., 1971-78; sr. soil scientist Soil Conservation Svc./U.S. Agy. for Internat. Devel., Lashkar Gah, Afghanistan, 1978-79; soil scientist/land use interpreter Soil Conservation Svc./U.S. Agy. for Internat. Devel., Kathmandu, Nepal, 1979-80; dep. co-mgr./soil scientist Soil Conservation Svc./Western Carolina U., Kathmandu, 1980-82, team leader resource conservation project, 1982-85; state soil scientist Soil Conservation Svc., Boise, Idaho, 1985-89; cons. soil scientist Spokane, 1989—. Contbr. articles to profl. publs. 1st lt. U.S. Army, 1957-59. Mem. Am. Soc. of Agronomy, Soil Sci. Soc. Am., Soil and Water Conservation Soc. (pres. keystone chpt. Pa. 1971), Washington Soc. of Profl. Soil Scientists.

Democrat. Methodist. Avocations: woodworking, fishing, travel. Home: 2709 S Post Spokane WA 99203

RICHARD, HAROLD IRVIN, agricultural business executive; b. Lodi, Ohio, Mar. 13, 1935; s. Charles Irvin and Thelma (Grier) R.; m. Nancy Hutchinson, Oct. 4, 1959; children—David Scott, Julia Lynn, Douglas Alan, Bryce Noel. B.Sc., Ohio State U., 1959. Owner, mgr. Dowler Farm, Ashville, Ohio, 1959-74; European dir. Am. Soybean Assn., Brussels, Belgium, 1975-79; pres. Farmers Commodity Corp., West Des Moines, 1979-84, Agri Industries, West Des Moines, 1984-85; v.p. Ill. Futures Co., Chgo., 1982—; dir. Farmers Export Co., Kansas City, Mo., 1984—; chmn. bd. Farmers Commodity Corp., West Des Moines, 1984—, Agri Fin. Services, West Des Moines, 1984—. Served with U.S. Army, 1953-55, Korea. Mem. Nat. Feed & Grain Dealers (dir. 1985—), Iowa Farm Bur., Nat. Futures Assn. (arbitration com. 1983—), Commodity Futures Trading Commn. (arbitration commn. 1985—). Republican. Mem. Reformed Ch. Club: Des Moines Country. Avocations: Golf; raquetball; travel. Home: 14266 Wildwood Dr Des Moines IA 50325-7702 Office: Farmers Commodities 2829 Westown Pky Ste 240 West Des Moines IA 50266-1314*

RICHARD, MARK M., government official, lawyer; b. N.Y.C., Nov. 16, 1939; s. Louis and Rae (Karnefsky) R.; m. Sheila Levitan, Aug. 6, 1960; children: Cara, Alisa, Daniel. B.A., Bklyn. Law Sch., 1961, J.D., 1967. Bar: N.Y. 1968, D.C. Trial atty. fraud sect., criminal div. Dept. Justice, Washington, 1967-75; exec. sec. Atty. Gen.'s White Collar Crime Com., Washington, 1975-76; chief fraud sect., criminal div. Dept. Justice, Washington, 1976-79, dept. asst. atty. gen. criminal div., 1979—; mem. econ. crime com. ABA, Washington, 1977-79. Recipient Legal award Assn. Fed. Investigators, 1981, Meritorious Exec. award Pres. of U.S., 1980, Legal award Assn. Fed. Prosecutors, 1981; fellow Harvard U., 1989. Mem. N.Y. State Bar Assn., D.C. Bar. Home: 912 Burnt Crest Ln Silver Spring MD 20903-1340 Office: Dept Justice Criminal Divsn 10th Constitution Ave NW Washington DC 20570

RICHARD, OLIVER GONZARD, III (RICK RICHARD), gas company executive; b. Lake Charles, La., Oct. 11, 1952; s. Oliver Gonzard and Mary Jean (Turvey) R.; m. Donna Margaret Guzman, July 6, 1974; 1 child, David Turvey. B.A., La. State U., 1974, J.D., 1977; M.L.T., Georgetown U., 1981. Bar: La. 1977, U.S. Dist. Ct. (ea. dist.) La. 1977, U.S. Dist. Ct. (we. dist.) La. 1977, U.S. Dist. Ct. (mid. dist.) La. 1977, U.S. Supreme Ct. 1981. Assoc., Sanders, Downing, Kean & Cazedessus, Baton Rouge, 1977; legis. asst. to U.S. Senator J. Bennett Johnston, Washington, 1977-81; ptnr. Hayes Durio & Richard, Lafayette, La., 1981-82; mem. FERC, Washington, 1982-85; v.p., gen. counsel Tenngasco Corp. div. Tenneco, 1985-87, v.p. regulatory and competitive analysis, 1987-95; chmn., pres., CEO Columbia Gas Sys., Inc., Wilmington, Del., 1995—. Fellow Council Econ. Regulation; mem. ABA, Omicron Delta Kappa. Democrat. Roman Catholic. Office: 20 Montchanin Rd Wilmington DE 19807*

RICHARD, PATRICIA ANTOINETTE, physician, dentist; b. Bridgeport, Conn., June 15, 1950; d. Mr. and Mrs. Richard. DMD, U. Conn., 1976; MD, Hahnemann U., 1980. Cert. sr. FAA med. examiner. Intern in internal medicine St. Vincents Med. Ctr., Bridgeport, Conn., 1980-81; resident in surgery U. Med. and Dentistry, Rutgers U., Camden, N.J., 1983-84; resident in internal medicine U. Hosp., Jacksonville, Fla., 1984-85; sr. resident in internal medicine Hartford (Conn.) Hosp., 1985-86; emergency medicine physician St. Francis Hosp., Hartford, 1985-87, U. Conn.-John Dempsey Hosp., Farmington, 1986-88, Bristol (Conn.) Hosp., 1986-87; pvt. practice in medicine and dentistry, biotech. R&D cons. Fairfield, Conn., 1987—; mem. medico-legal com. Fairfield County Med. Assn., 1994—, Fairfield County Ctr. for Trauma and Internal Medicine, Temporomandibular Joint Disorders, Aviation Medicine and Biotech., R&D, 1993—. Reviewer Patient Care Med. Jour., 1987-88. Mem. Rep. Senatorial Inner Cir., Washington, 1992; perpetual mem. Franciscan Benefactors Assn., Mt. Vernon, N.Y., 1994; mem. Lourdes Prayer League, Shrine of Our Lady of Snows, Belleville, Ill., 1995. Recipient Rep. Presidential award Bd. of Govs.-Rep. Presidential Task Force, 1994. Mem. AIAA, AMA, ADA, Aerospace Med. Assn., Am. Bd. Forensic Examiners. Achievements include 3 patents in fields of hematology, metabolism, endocrinology, pharmacology and orthopedics. Office: 1735 Post Rd PO Box 702 Fairfield CT 06430

RICHARD, PATRICK, science research administrator, nuclear scientist; b. Crowley, La., Apr. 28, 1938; married; two children. BS, U. Southwestern La., 1961; PhD, Fla. State U., 1964. Rsch. assoc. prof. nuclear physics U. Wash., 1965-68; from asst. prof. to prof. physics U. Tex., Austin, 1968-72; dir. J.R. MacDonald Lab. physics dept., prof. physics Kansas State U., 1972—; cons. Columbia Sci. Rsch. Inst., 1969-71. Mem. Am. Phys. Soc. Office: Kans State U J R MacDonald Lab Physic Dept Cardwell Hall Manhattan KS 66506 Office: Kans State U Physics Dept Cardwell Hall Manhattan KS 66506*

RICHARD, PAUL, art critic; b. Chgo., Nov. 22, 1939. BA, Harvard U., 1961; student, U. Pa. Art critic Washington Post, 1967—. Office: Washington Post Co 1150 15th St NW Washington DC 20071-0001

RICHARD, SCOTT F., portfolio manager; b. Chgo., Dec. 13, 1946; s. Jerome and Sue (Selig) Richard; m. Susan L. Diamond, June 15, 1969 (div. May 1983); children: Rebecca, Michael; m. Roberta C. Meyerson, Oct. 1, 1983. BS, MIT, 1968; D Bus. Adminstrn., Harvard U., 1972. Prof. fin. Carnegie-Mellon U., Pitts., 1972-87; v.p. fixed income rsch., co-dir. rsch. and model devel. Goldman, Sachs & Co., N.Y.C., 1987-92; portfolio mgr. Miller, Anderson & Sherrerd, West Conshohocken, Pa., 1992—, ptnr., 1993—; vis. prof. fin. MIT, Cambridge, Mass., 1986-87; advt. bd. Jour. of Portfolio Mgmt., 1989—, Jour. of Fixed Income, 1991—. Author: (with A.H. Meltzer and A. Cukierman) Political Economy, 1991; assoc. editor: Jour. of Fin., 1983-88, Jour. Fin. Econs., 1976-83, Mgmt. Sci., 1977-78; contbr. articles to profl. jours. Mem. Am. Econs. Assn., Am. Fin. Assn., The Econometric Soc., Inst. Mgmt. Sci. Office: Miller Anderson & Sherrerd One Tower Bridge West Conshohocken PA 19428

RICHARD, SUSAN MATHIS, public relations executive; b. Detroit, June 21, 1949; d. Robert Louis and Maybelle Ann (Kromm) Engel; m. Paul Carl Mathis, May 12, 1973 (div. 1982); m. Robert Stephen Richard, Oct. 26, 1985. BA, U. Mich., 1971. Cert. tchr., Mich. Tchr. Carl Brablec High Sch., Roseville, Mich., 1971-73; anchorperson, producer Sta. WNCC-Cable TV, East Lansing, Mich., 1973-76; press asst. Ford-Dole Presdl. Campaign, Washington, 1976; TV and radio reporter Cox Communications, Washington, 1977-81; dep. dir. media rels. White House, Washington, 1981-84, spl. asst. to Pres., dir. media rels., 1985-87; mgr. pub. rels. Walt Disney World, Lake Buena Vista, Fla., 1987-88; v.p. industry communications Nat. Cable TV Assn., Washington, 1989; dep. assoc. adminstr. for pub. affairs Nat. Aeros. and Space Adminstrn., 1990-93; v.p. comm. The Personal Comm. Industry Assn., 1993—; mem. exec. com. Radio-TV Corrs. Galleries, Washington, 1978-81. Dir. promotions Action for Children's TV, East Lansing, 1975; mem. Strategic Planning Adv. Coun. of the Orange County (Fla.) Pub. Schs., 1988; communications dir. Bush-Quayle Fla. Campaign, 1988. Named Outstanding Young Working Woman, Lansing C. of C., 1975, Outstanding Working Woman, Washington Woman mag., 1985. Mem. AAUW (bd. dirs. Lansing chpt. 1974), Nat. Assn. Execs., Am. Soc. Assn. Execs. (Pub. Rels. trophy 1994), Radio-TV News Dirs. Assn., Fla. Youth and Family Svcs. Network (bd. dirs. 1988), Acad. TV Arts and Scis. (pub. rels. com. 1989), Women in Aerospace, Women in Wireless, U. Mich. Alumni Assn. (bd. dirs. 1983-85), Gamma Phi Beta Alumnae Assn. Episcopalian. Avocations: doll houses, decorating.

RICHARDI, RALPH LEONARD, airline executive; b. Jersey City, Oct. 10, 1947; s. Nicholas Frank and Genevieve (Miele) R.; m. Cathy A. Himmelberger, Apr. 11, 1981. BS in Indsl. Mgmt., Fairleigh Dickinson U., 1969, MBA, 1976; cert. advanced mgmt. program, Harvard U., Boston, 1991. Indsl. engr. Ford Motor Co., Mahwah, N.J., 1969-72, Chase Manhattan Bank, N.Y.C., 1974-76; indsl. engr. Am. Airlines, Dallas-Ft. Worth, 1976-80, dir. indsl. engring., 1980-83, dir. quality of work life, 1983-85, asst. v.p. labor rels., 1985-87; gen. mgr. reservations Am. Airlines, L.A., 1987-88; gen. mgr. San Francisco Airport Am. Airlines, 1988-89, v.p. Dallas-Ft. Worth Airport, 1989-95; pres. Simmons Airlines/Am. Eagle, 1995—. Vice chmn. fund drives United Way, Dallas-Ft. Worth Airport, 1989-91. Avocation: golf. Address: 6103 Mimosa Ln Dallas TX 75230-5041 Office: Am Airlines Inc PO Box 619616 Dallas TX 75261-9616

RICHARDS, ARTHUR V., lawyer, corporate executive; b. 1939; married. B.B.A., St. John's U., 1963, LL.B., 1966. With Melville Corp., Harrison, N.Y., 1969—, asst. sec., 1970-77, sec., gen. atty., 1977-89. v/p., gen. counsel, corp. sec. Office: Melville Corp 1 Theall Rd Rye NY 10580-1404

RICHARDS, BERNARD, investment company executive; b. N.Y.C., July 12, 1927; s. Charles and Sadie (Rubin) R.; m. Arlene Kaye, Dec. 23, 1948; children: Carol Leslie, Patricia Ellen, Lori Gale. BBA, Baruch Coll., 1949. CPA, N.Y. Acct. Eisner & Lubin, N.Y.C., 1949-53, S.D. Leidesdorf, N.Y.C., 1953-56; from controller to treas. to v.p. fin. to pres. Slattery Group Inc., N.Y.C., 1956-87; pres. Slattery Investors Corp., N.Y.C., 1988—; chmn. bd. dirs. Slattery Assocs., Inc., N.Y.C., 1968-87. Trustee Temple Sinai, Roslyn, N.Y., 1987-89; bd. dirs. Variety Boys Club, Queens, N.Y., 1972—; bd. dirs. N.Y.C. Indsl. Devel. Bd., 1973-76; pres., bd. dirs. Baruch Coll. Fund, N.Y.C., 1975—, Man Yr., 1972. Recipient Heavy Constrn. award United Jewish Appeal, 1980, Pres.'s medal Baruch Coll., 1989; named Oustanding Alumnus of Yr. Baruch Coll., 1979, Man of Yr. United Jewish Appeal, 1980, March of Dimes, 1983; Wood fellow Baruch Coll., 1979. Mem. AICPA, N.Y. State Soc. CPAs, Moles, Beavers (bd. dirs. 1982—), Shelter Rock Tennis Club. Republican. Jewish. Avocations: tennis, travel, cycling, swimming, hiking. Home: 18 Applegreen Dr Old Westbury NY 11568-1203 Office: Slattery Investors Corp 1 Hollow Ln Ste 311 New Hyde Park NY 11042-1215

RICHARDS, CAROL ANN RUBRIGHT, editor, columnist; b. Buffalo, Sept. 24, 1944; d. Jesse Bailey and Emma Amanda (Fisher) Rubright; m. Clay F. Richards, Aug. 12, 1967; children: Elizabeth Amanda, Rebecca Diana. BA, Syracuse U., 1966. Reporter Rochester (N.Y.) Times-Union, 1966; legis. corr. Gannett News Svc., Albany, N.Y., 1967-73; White House corr. Gannett News Svc., Washington, 1974-76, regional/nat. editor, 1979-84; founding editor USA Today, Arlington, Va., 1982, mem. editl. bd., 1985-87; dep. editor editl. page Newsday, Melville, N.Y., 1987—. Pres. Washington Press Club, 1981-82. Mem. Nat. Press Club. Episcopalian. Home: 352 Scudder Ave Northport NY 11768 Office: Newsday 235 Pinelawn Rd Melville NY 11747-4250

RICHARDS, CHARLES A., government official; b. Irvona, Pa., May 6, 1940; s. Charles A. Sr. and Genevieve H. (Peterson) R.; m. Mary Gale Davis, May 10, 1980; children: Amy, Antonina. BS in Edn., Indiana U. Pa., 1963. Tchr. history Woodbridge Twp, N.J., 1963-68; nat. rep. Am. Fedn. Tchrs., Washington, 1968-74, asst. to pres., dir. organizing, 1974-82; dir. field activities Pub. Employee Dept. AFL-CIO, Washington, 1982-92; nat. labor coord. Clinton/Core Campaign, Little Rock, 1992; labor coord. Presdl. Transistion Team Clinton/Gore, Washington, 1992-93; dep. asst. sec. U.S. Dept. Labor, Washington, 1993—. Coach Little League. Avocations: skiing, reading. Office: US Dept Labor 200 Constitution Ave NW Washington DC 20210-0001

RICHARDS, CHARLES FRANKLIN, JR., lawyer; b. Evergreen Park, Ill., Jan. 30, 1949; s. Charles Franklin and Mary Corinne (Joyce) R.; m. Maureen Patricia Duffy, June 17, 1972 (div. Mar. 1989); m. Deborah Ann Murphy, May 20, 1991; children: Patrick, Corrine, Meghan, Shannon. BA, St. Mary's of Minn., 1971; JD, U. Ill., 1974. Bar: Minn. 1974, U.S. Dist. Ct. Minn. 1974, Ariz. 1985, U.S. Dist. Ct. Ariz. 1985, U.S. Ct. Appeals (9th cir.) 1985; cert. civil trial adv. Nat. Bd. Trial Advocacy. Asst. city atty. City of Rochester, Minn., 1974-76; assoc., then ptnr. O'Brien, Ehrick, Wolf, Deaner & Downing, Rochester, 1976-85; assoc., shareholder Gallagher & Kennedy, PA, Phoenix, 1985-94; pvt. practice, Phoenix, 1994—; judge pro tem Ariz. Ct. Appeals, 1994. Contbr. articles to legal publs. Bd. dirs. St. Mary's Hosp., Rochester, 1983-85; del. Dem. Nat. Conv., San Francisco, 1984. Mem. ABA, ATLA, State Bar Ariz. (exec. coun. 1994—, civil jury instrns. com. 1994—, co-editor Trial Practice Newsletter 1990—), Ariz. Assn. Def. Counsel, Ariz. Trial Lawyers Assn., Maricopa County Bar Assn. (CLE com. 1988-91), Minn. Bar Assn. Roman Catholic. Avocations: golf, bicycling, hiking, reading, astronomy. Office: 5308 N 12th St Ste 401 Phoenix AZ 85014-2903

RICHARDS, CONSTANCE ELLEN, nursing school administrator, consultant; b. Exeter, N.H., June 21, 1941; d. Edward Nowell and Mary Isabel (Bean) R. RN diploma, Concord (N.H.) Hosp., 1964; BSN, U. Cin., 1971, MA in Pub. Adminstrn., 1973, MS in Comprehensive Health Planning, 1973. RN, Mass. Nurse ICU/Opening CCU Syracuse (N.Y.) Meml. Hosp., 1964; instr. ICU and CCU Crouse-Irving Meml. Hosp., Syracuse, 1967; instr. cardiovascular, orthopedic and surg. The Christ Hosp., Cin., 1973; instr. med.-surg. nursing Md. Gen. Hosp., Balt., 1978; night supr. Manor Care Ruxton, Towson, Md., 1980; adult health svcs. mgr. Exeter Vis. Nurses Assn., 1982; dir. insvc. edn. Bethany Hosp., Framingham, Mass., 1983; assoc. prof. nursing Mass. Bay C.C., 1985; instr. insvc. edn. Brockton-West Roxbury (Mass.) VA Hosp., 1986; staff nurse Charles River Hosp., Wellesley, Mass., 1987; night supr. Blair House, Milford, Mass., 1988; staff nurse psychogeriatrics Worcester State Hosp., 1989; with Agys. Internat. Health Talent Tree, Olsten Health Care Svcs., 1990; with indsl. svcs. program, CNA trng. program Northampton State Hosp., 1992; nursing asst., state tester ARC, 1992-93; pres. Caring Hands, Inc., 1993—; DON Excel Health Svcs., Inc., 1993—; instr. LPN evening program Greater Lowell Regional Vocat. Tech. Sch., 1992-94; adv. bd. Excel Health Svcs., Tewksbury, Mass., 1993-94; pres. Spltap Arts, Lowell, Mass., 1993-94. Author: Freddie the Foot, 1982. Mem. Lowell Hist. Soc., 1994, Women's Network, Lowell, 1994, Crime Watch Group Edn. Component, Lowell, 1994. Mem. ANA, Mass. Nurses Assn., Nat. League Nurses. Democrat. Roman Catholic. Avocations: writing, poetry, minature dollhouses, painting, church group. Home: 30 Hungton St Lowell MA 01852 Office: Caring Hands Inc 353 Lodes Pond Shutesbury MA 01072

RICHARDS, CORY, demographic think-tank executive. V.p. for pub. policy Alan Guttmacher Inst. Wash. Office, Washington, D.C. Office: Alan Guttmacher Inst Washington Office 1120 Connecticut Ave Ste 460 Washington DC 20036*

RICHARDS, CRAIG M., wholesale distribution executive; b. 1950. BA, Brigham Young Univ., 1975. Audit staff Arthur Andersen & Co., 1975-77; dir. fin. reporting Marriott Corp., 1978-86; dir. fin. analysis, v.p. project finance Bear Stearns, N.Y., 1986-92; CEO Baker & Taylor. Office: Ste 500 2709 Water Ridge Pkwy Charlotte NC 28217

RICHARDS, DANIEL WELLS, company executive; b. Taylor, Pa., Dec. 16, 1928; s. Daniel Wells and Bernice (Robling) R.; m. Helen Reilly, Feb. 10, 1979; children: Kenneth, Deborah, Thomas. BA, Dickinson Coll., 1950; postgrad., U. Pitts., 1953-54. Mgr. advt. prodn. Miller Machine Co., Pitts., 1954-55; mgr. sales promotion Gen. Paper Co., Pitts., 1955-57; advt. and product mgr. Harris Seybold Co., Cleve., 1957-67; v.p. mktg. Colwell Systems Inc., Champaign, Ill., 1967-86, pres., 1986-91; Disting. lectr., exec. in residence Ill. State U., 1991-93; pres. D.W. Richards & Assocs., Champaign, 1994—. Mem. Urbana (Ill.) City Council, 1975-77; budget dir. Ill. Humanities Council, 1980-84; bd. dirs. United Way Champaign County, 1987—, Sinfonia da Camert, 1987—. Served to lt. U.S. Army, 1950-53. Unitarian. Home and Office: 1704 Coventry Dr Champaign IL 61821-5242

RICHARDS, DAVID A. J., lawyer, educator; b. 1944. AB, Harvard U., 1966, JD, 1971; PhD (Knox Meml. fellow), Oxford U., Eng., 1970. Bar: N.Y., 1972. Assoc. Cleary, Gottlieb, Steen & Hamilton, N.Y.C., 1971-74; assoc. prof. Fordham U., N.Y.C., 1974-77; vis. prof. philosophy Barnard Coll., N.Y.C., 1974-77; assoc. prof. law NYU, 1977-79, prof. of law, 1979—. Author: A Theory of Reasons for Action, 1971, The Moral Criticism of Law, 1977, Sex, Drugs, Death and the Law, 1982 (named best book in criminal justice ethics, 1982), Toleration and the Constitution, 1986, Criminal Legal Education. Rockefeller grantee Austinian Soc. and Ctr. for Study of Law and Soc., Berkeley, Calif., 1974; Mellon fellow Aspen Inst. for Humanistic Studies. Mem. Soc. for Philosophy and Pub. Affairs (bd. dirs. N.Y. chpt. 1975-76), Austinian Soc. (pres. 1974). Club: Tuesday Evening. Office: NYU Law Sch 40 Washington Sq S New York NY 10012-1099*

RICHARDS, DAVID ALAN, lawyer; b. Dayton, Ohio, Sept. 21, 1945; s. Charles Vernon and Betty Ann (Macher) R.; m. Marianne Catherine Del Monaco, June 26, 1971; children: Christopher, Courtney. BA summa cum laude, Yale U., 1967, JD, 1972; MA, Cambridge U., 1969. Bar: N.Y., 1973. Assoc. Paul, Weiss, Rifkind, Wharton & Garrison, N.Y.C., 1972-77, Coudert Bros., N.Y.C., 1977-80, ptnr., 1981-82; ptnr., head real estate group Sidley & Austin, N.Y.C., 1983—; gov. Anglo-Am. Real Property Inst. U.S./U.K., 1983-88, sec., 1988, chair, 1993; mem. Chgo. Title N.Y. Realty Adv. Bd., 1992—. Contbr. articles to profl. jours. Trustee Scarsdale Pub. Libr. , 1984-89, pres., 1988-89. Fellow Am. Bar Found.; mem. ABA (real property, probate and trust sect., coun. 1982-88, chair 1991-92), Am. Coll. Real Estate Lawyers (chmn. amicus curiae brief com. 1985-88, gov. 1987-93), Internat. Bar Assn., Assn. of Bar of City of N.Y. (real property com. 1978-80, 84-87), Shenorock Shore Club (Rye, N.Y.). Democrat. United Ch. of Christ. Home: 18 Forest Ln Scarsdale NY 10583-6464 Office: Sidley & Austin 875 3rd Ave New York NY 10022-6225

RICHARDS, DAVID GLEYRE, German educator; b. Salt Lake City, July 27, 1935; s. Oliver L. and Lilian Marie (Powell) R.; m. Annegret Horn, Sept. 3, 1959 (div. 1992); 1 child, Stephanie Susanne. BA, U. Utah, 1960, MA, 1961; PhD, U. Calif.-Berkeley, 1968. Asst. prof. German SUNY, Buffalo, 1968-74, assoc. prof., 1974-84, prof., 1984—. Author: Georg Buchners Woyzeck, 1975, George Buchner and the Birth of the Modern Drama, 1976, The Hero's Quest for the Self: An Archetypal Approach to Hesse's Demian and other Novels, 1987; editor: (with H. Schulte) Crisis and Culture in Post-Enlightenment Germany: Essays in Honor of Peter Heller, 1993, Exploring the Divided Self: Hermann Hesse's Steppenwolf and the Critics, 1996. SUNY grantee, 1973; NEH grantee, 1977-78, Fulbright Commn. grantee, 1980; Rsch. Found. of SUNY fellow, 1982. Mem. MLA, Am. Assn. Tchrs. German. Democrat. Avocation: photography. Office: SUNY Buffalo Dept Modern Langs & Lits 910 Clemens Hall Buffalo NY 14260

RICHARDS, DAVID KIMBALL, investor; b. Portland, Maine, May 14, 1939; s. Robert Ladd and Janice (Kimball) R.; m. Carol Ann Liebich, May 27, 1967; children: Adam, Peter. A.B. cum laude, Harvard U., 1961, M.B.A., 1965; B.A., Wadham Coll., Oxford, Eng., 1963. Research analyst H.C. Wainwright & Co., N.Y.C., 1965-71, ptnr., 1971-73; sr. v.p., dir. Capital Research & Mgmt. Co., Los Angeles, 1973-85; v.p. Income Fund of Am., Los. Angeles, 1976-85; pres. Fundamental Investors Co., Los Angeles, 1982-85; vice chmn. Primecap Mgmt., Pasadena, Calif., 1985-91; pvt. investor, 1991—. Republican. Home: 109 Esparta Way Santa Monica CA 90402-2137

RICHARDS, EDGAR LESTER, psychologist, educator; b. Albany, N.Y., Apr. 20, 1942; s. Edgar Lester and Gertrude Veronica (Halpin) R.; B.S. in Biology, Siena Coll., 1966, M.S. in Edn., 1968; M.A., U. Pa., 1975; C.A.S., Wesleyan U., 1976; M.Phil., Columbia U., 1977, Ph.D., 1981; m. Ruth Anne Farrar, Dec. 21, 1968; children—Edgar Lester, Christopher Hartington, James Gerald, Ruth Anne. Tchr. secondary sch. biology Stillwater Central Sch. Dist. (N.Y.), 1966-71; NSF grantee, 1969, 70; adminstrv. asst. to supt. City Sch. Dist., Watervliet, N.Y., 1971-72, supt. schs., 1972-74; research and devel. assoc. Ctr. for Sch. Study Councils Grad. Sch. Edn., U. Pa., Phila., 1974-75; research scientist N.Y. State Psychiat. Inst., 1975-77; asst. dir. for research and devel. Nat. Bd. Med. Examiners, Phila., 1977-78; research and evaluation coordinator Research for Better Schs., Inc., Phila., 1979-80, coordinator field support services, 1980-81, specialist in evaluation and devel., 1981-82; adj. asst. prof. Grad. Sch. Edn., Fordham U., N.Y.C., 1985-86, 88, adj. assoc. prof., 1990—; asst. supt. schs. Mahopac Central Sch. Dist. (N.Y.), 1982—; cons. Nat. Tng. and Evaluation Center, N.Y.C., 1977-79, N.Y.C. Bd. Edn., 1977-79, Research for Better Schs., Inc., 1974-75, 84. Cert. secondary sch. biology and gen. sci. tchr., sch. dist. adminstr., secondary prin., N.Y. State; cert. secondary sch. biology, chemistry, and gen. sci. tchr., prin., Mass. Mem. Am. Assn. Sch. Adminstrs., Am. Assn. Sch. Pers. Adminstrs., Am. Ednl. Research Assn., Am. Psychol. Assn., Assn. for Supervision and Curriculum Devel., Nat. Council on Measurement in Edn., Phi Delta Kappa. Democrat. Roman Catholic. Author: Career Education Linking Agents: Perspectives and Roles, 1981, Career Education Program Design, 1981, Perceptions of the Preparation of Youth for Work: Report of a Three State Survey, 1980, Sharing Career Education Resources with Schools: An Exploratory Study of Employer Willingness, 1980; contbr. articles to profl. jours. Home: 26 Nevins Rd Mahopac NY 10541-3034 Office: Mahopac Pub Schs Dist Cen Office Mahopac NY 10541

RICHARDS, FRED TRACY, finance company executive; b. Waverly, N.Y., Feb. 8, 1914; s. Parke and Lois (Tracy) R.; m. Gladys Bucher Albright, Aug. 1, 1942 (div. 1973); children: Fred Tracy, John Harvey; m. Jean Hunter, June 16, 1973. B.S. in Engring. with honors, Princeton U., 1935. Supr. maintenance way, spl. purchasing agt. Pa. R.R. Co., Phila., 1935-47; supr. materials Dept. Interior and Office Def. Transp., 1941-42; chmn. bd., chief exec. officer Central Supply Co. Va. Inc., Phila., 1947-55; asst. to chmn. Avco Corp., Greenwich, Conn., 1955-79; pres. Richards Resources, Inc., 1979—. Pres., bd. dirs. U.S.O., N.Y., 1973-80; v.p. Nat. Exec. Service Corps, N.Y.C., 1981-86. Served to lt. col. C.E. AUS, 1942-46. Mem. Soc. Mayflower Descs. State N.Y., S.R., The Pilgrims, Princeton Club (N.Y.C.). Home: 100 Putnam Park Greenwich CT 06830-5777

RICHARDS, FREDERIC MIDDLEBROOK, biochemist, educator; b. N.Y.C., Aug. 19, 1925; s. George and Marianna Richards; m. Heidi Clarke, 1948 (div. 1955); children: Sarah, Ruth Gray; m. Sarah Wheatland, 1959; 1 child, George Huntington. BS, MIT, 1948; PhD, Harvard U., 1952; DSc (hon.), U. New Haven, 1982. Rsch. fellow in phys. chemistry Harvard Med. Sch., Cambridge, Mass., 1952-53; NRC postdoctoral fellow Carlsberg Lab., Denmark, 1954; NSF fellow Cambridge U., Eng., 1955; asst. prof. biochemistry Yale U., New Haven, Conn., 1955-59, assoc. prof., 1959-62, prof., 1963-89, Henry Ford II prof. molecular biophysics, 1967-89, Sterling prof. molecular biophysics, 1989-91, Sterling prof. emeritus, 1991—, chmn. dept. molecular biology and biophysics, 1963-67, chmn. dept. molecular biophysics and biochemistry, 1969-73; dir. Jane Coffin Childs Meml. Fund Med. Rsch., 1976-91; mem. Nat. Adv. Rsch. & Resources Coun., 1983-87; mem. corp. Woods Hole Oceanographic Inst., 1977-83, 84-90; mem. bd. advisors Whitney Marine Lab., 1979-84, Purdue U. Magnetic Resonance Lab., 1980-84, Biology divsn. Argonne Nat. Lab., 1982-84, Brookhaven Nat. Lab., Nat. Synchrotron Light Source; mem. sci. adv. bd. structural biology Howard Hughes Med. Inst., 1988-89, adv. bd., 1989-92; mem. sci. adv. bd. Donaghue Found. Med. Rsch., 1991-92. Mem. editorial bd. Jour. Biol. Chemistry, 1963-69, 82-84, Jour. Molecular Biology, 1973-75, Advances in Protein Chemistry, 1963—; contbr. articles on protein and enzyme chemistry to profl. jours. Sgt. U.S. Army, 1944-46. Recipient Pfizer-Paul Lewis award in enzyme chemistry, 1965, Kai Linderstrom-Lang prize in protein chemistry, 1978, Sci. medal State of Conn., 1995; Guggenheim fellow, 1967-68. Fellow AAAS, Am. Acad. Arts and Scis.; mem. NAS, Am. Philos. Soc., Am. Soc. Biochemistry and Molecular Biology (Merck award 1988), Protein Soc. (Stein and Moore award 1988), Internat. Union Pure and Applied Biophysics (mem. coun. 1975-81), Am. Soc. Biol. Chemists (pres. 1979-80), Biophys. Soc. (pres. 1972-73), Am. Chem. Soc., Am. Crystallographic Assn., Conn. Acad. Sci. and Engring. Avocation: sailing. Home: 69 Andrews Rd Guilford CT 06437-3715 Office: Yale U Dept Molecular Biophysics 260 Whitney Ave PO Box 208114 New Haven CT 06520-8114

RICHARDS, GALE LEE, communication educator; b. Long Run, W.Va., July 31, 1918; s. Robert Amaziah and Edna Jane (Scott) R.; m. Barbara Lee Neely, Apr. 19, 1944; children: Robin Lee, Wendell Scott, Jeffrey Marshall. B.A. (Pixley scholar), U. Akron, O., 1940; M.A. (C.S. Knight Meml. scholar), U. Ia., 1942, Ph.D., 1950. Instr. speech U. Akron, 1941-42; asst. prof. speech Drake U., 1947-48; asst. prof. English U. Nev., 1948-52; asst. prof. speech U. Wash., 1952-58; assoc. prof. speech U. So. Calif., 1958-65; prof. communication Ariz. State U., Tempe, 1965—, chmn. dept. speech and theatre, 1965-73; Pub. relations cons. Red Feather campaign United Fund, Los Angeles, 1955-58; mgmt. and tng. cons. various profl. and comml. orgns., 1955—. Cons. editor: Western Speech, 1957-61, 62-65, 69-72, Jour. of Communication, 1961-67; Contbr. articles profl. jours. Bd. dirs. Phoenix Little Theatre. Served to lt. USNR, 1942-45, PTO. Recipient Distinguished Alumni award Radio Sta. WSUI, 1942. Mem. Speech Communication Assn. (adminstrv. coun., legis. coun., chair commn. on Am. Parliamentary procedures, 1988, emeritus 1991), Internat. Communication Assn. (adminstrv. coun.), Am. Inst. Parliamentarians, Western States Communication Assn. (2d v.p. 1956, 71, pres. Execs. club 1975, Disting. Svc. award 1989), Ariz. Communication and Drama Assn. (pres. 1967, editor jour. 1984-87), Blue Key, Phi Kappa Phi, Delta Sigma Rho. Democrat. Presbyterian. Home: 614 E Bishop Dr Tempe AZ 85282-2325

RICHARDS, HERBERT EAST, minister emeritus, commentator; b. Hazleton, Pa., Dec. 30, 1919; s. Herbert E. and Mabel (Vannaucker) R.; m. Lois Marcey, Jan. 1, 1942; children: Herbert Charles, Marcey Lynn, Robyn Lois, Fredrick East, Mark Allen. AB, Dickinson Coll., 1941; BD, Drew U., 1944; MA, Columbia, 1944; DD, Coll. of Idaho, 1953; postgrad., Union Theol. Sem., 1941-48, Bucknell U., 1943-44. Accredited news reporter Nat. Assn. Broadcasters. Ordained to ministry Methodist Ch., 1944; pastor in Boiling Springs, Pa., 1937-40, West Chester, Pa., 1940-41, Basking Ridge, N.J., 1941-47; mem. faculty Drew U. and Theol. Sem., 1944-51, assoc. prof. homiletics and Christian criticism, chmn. dept., asst. dean, 1947-51; spl. lectr. religion Howard U., 1947; minister 1st Meth. Cathedral, Boise, Idaho, 1951-69, 1st United Meth. Ch., Eugene, Oreg., 1969-78; minister Tabor Heights United Meth. Ch., Portland, Oreg., 1978-86, minister emeritus, 1986—; weekly radio broadcaster Sta. KBOI, Sta. KIDO, 1941—; weekly TV broadcaster CBS, 1945—, ABC, 1969—, NBC, 1973; pres. Inspiration, Inc., TV Found., 1965—, TV Ecology, 1973; producer Life TV series ABC, 1974-85, also BBC, Eng., Suise Romande, Geneva; chmn. Idaho bd. ministerial tng. Meth. Conf., 1954-60, TV, Radio and Film Commn., 1954-62, Oreg. Coun. Public Broadcasting, 1973; del. Idaho Conf. Meth. Gen. Conf., 1956, Jurisdictional Conf., 1956, World Meth. Coun., 1957, 81, World Meth. Conf., 1981, mem. Gen. Conf., 1956-60, Jurisdictional Conf., 1956, 60; meml. chaplain Idaho Supreme Ct., 1960; chaplain Idaho Senate, 1960-68; mem. Task Force on TV and Ch., 1983. Author: In Time of Need, 1986; contbr. articles to religious publs.; composer: oratorios Prophet Unwilling, 1966, Meet Martin Luther, 1968, Dear Jesus Boy, 1973. Mem. Commn. on Centennial Celebration for Idaho, 1962-63; committeeman Boy Scouts Am.; bd. dirs. Eugene chpt. ARC, 1954-73; trustee Willamette U., Cascade Manor Homes; adv. bd. Medic-Alert Found. Recipient Alumni citation in religious edn. Dickinson Coll., 1948, Golden Plate award Am. Acad. Achievement, 1965, Jason Lee Mass Media TV award, 1983; named Clergyman of Yr., Religious Heritage Am., 1964. Mem. AAUP, CAP (chaplain Idaho wing, lt. col.), Am. Acad. Achievement (bd. govs. 1967—), Am. Found. Religion and Psychiatry (charter gov.), Greater Boise Ministerial Assn. (pres.), Eugene Ministerial Assn. (pres. 1978), Masons (33 degree, editor Pike's Peak Albert That Is), Shriners, Elks, Rotary (editor Key and Cog, pres. dist. 510 Pioneer Club), Kappa Sigma (Grand Master of Beta Pi). Home: 10172 SE 99th Dr Portland OR 97266-7227 Office: Tabor Heights United Meth Ch 6161 SE Stark St Portland OR 97215-1935 *When a person presses his face against the window pane of life, he becomes as a child waiting for his father's return; simple, trusting and infinitely wiser. In our present time of growth/conflict, such a face-pressing is essential to get us safely from where we are to where we ought to be.*

RICHARDS, HILDA, academic administrator; b. St. Joseph, Mo., Feb. 7, 1936; d. Togar and Rose Avalynne (Williams) Young-Ballard. Diploma nursing St. John's Sch. Nursing, St. Louis, 1956; BS cum laude, CUNY, 1961; MEd, Columbia U., 1965, EdD, 1976; MPA, NYU, 1971. Dep. chief dept. psychiatry Harlem Rehab. Ctr., N.Y.C., 1969-71; prof., dir. nursing Medgar Evers Coll., CUNY, N.Y.C., 1971-76, prof., assoc. dean, 1976-79; dean Coll. Health and Human Service, Ohio U., Athens, 1979-86; provost, v.p. for acad. affairs Indiana U., Pa., 1986-93; chancellor Ind. U. N.W., Gary, 1993—; bd. dirs. Sta. 56-TV; active N.W. Satir Inst., Execs. Coun. N.W. Ind., ACE Commn. on Minorities in Higher Edn., AASCU Com. on Diversity and Social Change. Author: (with others) Curriculum Development and People of Color: Strategies and Change, 1983; editor Black Conf. on Higher Edn. Jour., 1989-93. Bd. dirs. Avanta Network, 1984—, Urban League N.W. Ind., 1993, N.W. Ind. Forum, 1993, Bank One Regional Bd., Merrillville, Ind., 1994, The Meth. Hosps., Inc., Gary.Merrillville, 1994, Lake Area United Way, 1994, Boys and Girls Clubs N.W. Ind.; life mem. Gary chpt. NAACP; exec. com. Pa. Black Conf. on Higher Edn., 1988-93. Recipient Rockefeller Found. award Am. Council Edn., Washington, 1976-77, Black Achiever award Black Opinion Mag., 1989, Athena award Bus. and Profl. Women's Club Ind., 1991; Martin Luther King grantee NYU, N.Y.C., 1969-70, Gunt Found. grantee Harvard Inst. Ednl. Mgmt., Cambridge, Mass., 1981. Fellow Am. Acad. Nursing; mem. ANA (Outstanding Woman of Color award 1990), AAHE, AAUW, APHA, Am. Assn. State Colls. and Univs., Nat. Assn. Allied Health Profls., Am. Assn. Univ. Adminstrs., Assn. Black Nursing Faculty in Higher Edn. (bd. dirs. 1989—), Pa. Nurses Assn., Assn. Black Women in Higher Edn., Inc., Nat. Black Nurses Assn. (bd. dirs., 1st v.p. 1984—, editor jour. 1985—, Spl. Recognition award 1991, Disting. African-Am. Nurse Educator award Queens County chpt., 1991), Nat. Assn. Women in Edn., Am. Coun. Edn. (exec. com. coun. fellows), Internat. Assn. Univ. Pres., N.W. Rotary, N.W. Kiwanis, Phi Delta Kappa, Sigma Theta Tau, Zonta Club of Ind. County. Democrat. Avocations: needlepoint, travel. Home: 7807 Hemlock Ave Gary IN 46403-2164 Office: Ind U NW Office of Chancellor 3400 Broadway Gary IN 46408-1197

RICHARDS, HUGH TAYLOR, physics educator; b. Baca County, Colo., Nov. 7, 1918; s. Dean Willard and Kate Bell (Taylor) R.; m. Mildred Elizabeth Paddock, Feb. 11, 1944; children: David Taylor, Thomas Martin, John Willard, Margaret Paddock, Elizabeth Nicholls, Robert Dean. BA, Park Coll., 1939; MA, Rice U., 1940, PhD, 1942. Research assoc. Rice U., Houston, 1942; scientist U. Minn., Mpls., 1942-43, U. Calif. Sci. Labs., Los Alamos, N.Mex., 1943-46; research assoc. U. Wis., Madison, 1946-47, mem. faculty, 1947-52, prof., 1952-88, prof. emeritus, 1988—, physics dept. chairperson, 1960-63, 66-69, 85-88; assoc. dean Coll. Letters and Sci., U. Wis, 1963-66. Author: Through Los Alamos 1945: Memoirs of a Nuclear Physicist, 1993; contbr. articles to profl. jours. Fellow Am. Phys. Soc.; mem. Am. Assn. Physics Tchrs. Unitarian-Universalist. Achievements include neutron measurements first A-Bomb test; fission neutron (and other) spectra by new photo-emulsion techniques; mock fission neutron source; spherical electrostatic analyzer for precise reaction energy measurements; negative ion sources for accelerators (He ALPHATROSS, SNICS); accurate proton, deuteron, and alpha particle scattering and reaction cross sections; systematics mirror nuclei; isospin violations in nuclear reactions. Home: 1902 Arlington Pl Madison WI 53705-4002 Office: Univ of Wis Dept Of Physics Madison WI 53706

RICHARDS, J. SCOTT, rehabilitation medicine professional. BA in Psychology cum laude, Oberlin Coll., 1968; Cert. in Elem. Edn., Wayne State U., 1969; MS in Resource Ecology, U. Mich., 1973; PhD in Psychology, Kent State U., 1977. Elem. tchr. Detroit Pub. Schs., 1968-71; rsch. asst. Inst. Fisheries Rsch., 1971-73; teaching asst. Kent State U., 1973-74; psychology intern, 1973-77; dir. psychology and instr. dept. rehab. medicine, co-dir. pain control program SRC, with depts. psychiatry and psychology U. Ala., Birmingham, 1977—, from asst. to assoc. prof. dept. rehab. medicine, 1980-90, prof., 1990—, dir. tng. med. rehab. rsch. tng. ctr., 1985-87, dir. rsch. and dir. of Psychology, Dept. of Physical Med. & Rehab., 1987—, co-dir. UAB Spinal Cord Injury Care System, 1989—; cons. Ctrs. Disease Control, Nat. Inst. Disability & Rehab. Rsch. Contbr. articles to profl. jours. Fellow APA. Office: U Ala Sch Medicine Dept Phys Med & Rehab 1717 6th Ave S Rm 530 Birmingham AL 35233*

RICHARDS, JAMES CARLTON, microbiologist, business executive; b. Storm Lake, Iowa, Aug. 19, 1947; s. Jack M. and June G. Richards; m. Lois Ruth Rebbe, July 22, 1974 (div. Sept. 1986); 1 child, Kimberly Ann; m. Susan M. Wos, Aug. 27, 1988; children: Derek Anthony, Kristin Marie. BS in Microbiology, U. Ill., 1970; PhD in Microbiology, So. Ill. U., 1977. Postdoctoral fellow Pa. State U. Med. Ctr., Hershey, Pa., 1977-79; sr. scientist E.I. duPont de Nemours, Wilmington, Del., 1979-85; program mgr. Amoco, Naperville, Ill., 1985-86; dir. bus. Gene-Trak Systems, Framingham, Mass., 1986-90; mng. dir. Carlton BioVenture Ptnrs., Sudbury, Mass., 1990—; pres., CEO, bd. dirs. Symbollon Corp., Sudbury, Mass., 1991-95; pres., CEO, bd. dirs. IntelliGene, Ltd., Sudbury, Mass., 1995—, Jerusalem, Israel, 1995—; invited lectr. on genetic analysis. Contbr. chpt. to books, articles to sci. jours.; patentee in field. Deacon United Ch. of Christ, Framingham, 1988—. Mem. AAAS, Am. Soc. for Microbiology, Am. Chem. Soc., Inst. Food Technologists, N.Y. Acad. Scis., Clin. Ligand Soc., Sigma Xi, others. Avocations: golf, travel, jogging, gardening, skiing. Home and office: 44 Codman Dr Sudbury MA 01776-1745

RICHARDS, JAMES E., pharmaceutical executive. Chmn. bd., ceo Tenn. Wholesale Drug Co., Nashville, Tenn., 1940—. Office: Tennessee Wholesale Drug Co 200 Cumberland Bnd Nashville TN 37228-1804*

RICHARDS, JAMES M., career officer; b. Baytown, Tex., Jan. 16, 1947. BS in Indsl. Tech., Tex. A & M, 1969; MS in Syss. Mgmt., U. So. Calif., 1978; student, Army Command and Gen. Staff Coll., 1980-81. Commd. 2nd lt. USAF, 1969, advanced through grades to brig. gen., 1992; OV-10 forward air controller USAF, Quang Tri combat base, Pleiku air base, Vietnam, 1971; B-52 pilot 441st bomb squadron, bomber scheduling , wing exec. officer USAF, Mather AFB, Calif., 1972-77; action officer, exec. officer, dep. dir. plans and policy USAF, Washington, 1977-80; B-52 instr. pilot, flight comdr., squadron opers. officer 668th bomb squadron USAF, Griffiss AFB, N.Y., 1981-83; comdr. 524th bomb squadron USAF, Wurtsmith AFB, Mich., 1983-84; chief strategic aircraft divsn. HQ USAF, Washington, 1985-87; comdr. 416th bombardment wing USAF, Griffiss AFB, N.Y., 1988-90; asst. dep. chief of staff, plans and resources USAF, Offutt AFB, Nebr., 1990-92; comdr. 92nd bomb wing USAF, Fairchild AFB, Wash., 1992-93; dir. long range power projection, SOF, airlift and tng. programs USAF, Washington, 1993-96, dir. global reach programs, 1996—. Decorated Legion of Merit with two oak leaf clusters, Disting. Flying Cross with two oak leaf clusters, air medal with 14 oak leaf clusters, Republic of Vietnam Gallantry Cross with palm. Office: SAF/AQQ 1060 Air Force Pentagon Washington DC 20330-1060

RICHARDS, JAY CLAUDE, commercial photographer, news service executive, historian; b. Glen Ridge, N.J., Apr. 6, 1954; s. Jacob Tilghman and Joan Louise (Walsh) R. Student, Tenn. Wesleyan Coll., Athens, 1972-73. Various positions armed security work, 1973-75; reporter, photographer Press Publs.: The News, Belvidere, N.J., 1977—; pres. J.C. Richards Assocs., Harmony Twp., N.J., 1980—; owner Poor Richards' Brit. Gun Shop, Harmony Twp., 1976—; photography judge Warren County 4-H, Belvidere, 1990—; press officer Warren County Office Emergency Mgmt., Belvidere, 1989—. Author: Penn, Patriots and the Pequest: The History of Pre-Victorian Belvidere, 1716-1845, 1995, Flames Along the Delaware, 1996; photographer (video) From Flax to Linen, 1993, Belvidere: N.J.'s Best Kept Secret, 1994, Heritage Festival TV commls.; contbr. photographs to mags., calendars, coll. catalogs. Mem. Hazardous Materials Adv. Coun., Warren County, N.J.; mem. Joint Emergency Mgmt. Coun., Belvidere/White Twp., N.J.; mem. Warren County Arts Adv. Coun. Named Hon. Mem. Boy Scout Troop 141, Belvidere, 1993; recipient Outstanding Cmty. Svc. award Am. Legion Post 131, 1994. Mem. Nat. Press Photographers Assn., Soc. Profl. Journalists, Res. Officers Assn. U.S., Sr. Army Res. Comdrs. Assn., U.S. Naval Inst. Episcopalian. Avocations: militaria collecting, gourmet cooking, gardening, herbal medicine. Home and Office: 3110 Belvidere Rd Phillipsburg NJ 08865-9515

RICHARDS, JEANNE HERRON, artist; b. Aurora, Ill., Apr. 8, 1923; d. Robert Watt and Ida (Herron) R. B.F.A., U. Iowa, 1952, M.F.A., 1954. instr. art State U. Iowa, 1955-56; instr. U. Nebr., 1957-59, asst. prof., 1959-63; instr. Ascension Acad., Alexandria, Va., 1967-68. One-woman shows include U. Nebr. Art Galleries, Lincoln, 1959, U. Ill., Champaign-Urbana, 1969, group shows include Library of Congress, 1947-61, Corcoran Gallery, Washington, 1974; represented in permanent collections Lessing J. Rosenwald Collection, Library of Congress, Nat. Mus. Am. Art, Smithsonian Instn. Served with USNR, 1943-46. Fulbright grantee, 1954-55. Mem. Soc. Am. Graphic Artists, Soc. Washington Printmakers, Gamma Phi Beta. Address: 9526 Liptonshire Dr Dallas TX 75238-2727

RICHARDS, JERRY LEE, academic administrator, religious educator; b. Lawrenceville, Ill., Nov. 4, 1939; s. Russell O. and Elvessa A. (Goodman) R.; m. Susan Richards, Apr. 25, 1986; children: Mark, Renee, Teresa, Angela. B.A., Lycoming Coll., 1965; B.D., Evang. Congregational Sch. Theology, 1967; M.Div., Garrett Theol. Sem., 1968; D.Ministry, St. Paul Sch. Theology, 1975. Ordained to ministry Meth. Ch., 1968. Pastor chs. Pa., 1960-65, Williamsport, Iowa, 1965-70; mem. faculty Iowa Wesleyan U., Mt Pleasant, 1970-85; prof. religion, dir. responsible social involvement Iowa Wesleyan U., Mt. Pleasant, 1975-85, v.p. for acad. affairs, 1975-82, pres., 1982-85; dir. gift planning U. Wis., Eau Claire, 1985—. Pres. Mental Health Inst. Aux., Mt. Pleasant, 1976. Mem. Phi Alpha Theta. Office: U Wis Office of Devel 215 Schofield Hall Eau Claire WI 54701

RICHARDS, JOSEPH EDWARD, artist; b. Des Moines, Oct. 10, 1921; s. Earl L. and Ivanore M. (Shelledy) R.; m. Elizabeth Anne Morrow, Mar. 23, 1943. Student Am. Acad. Art, Chgo., 1946-49, Art Inst. Chgo., 1949-50, Pa. Acad. Fine Arts, 1950-52. Exhbns. include: Butler Inst. Am. Art, Youngstown, Ohio, 1976, 77, 78, 81, Tex. Fine Arts Assn./Laguna Gloria Art Mus., Austin, Tex., 1977, NAD, N.Y.C., 1978, Silvermine Guild Artists, New Cannan, Conn., 1978, 79, Pa. Acad. Fine Arts, Phila., 1978, 80, 94, Va. Mus., Richmond, 1979, O.K. Harris Gallery, N.Y.C., 1982, 89, 92, 94, O.K. Harris West Gallery, Scottsdale, Ariz., 1981, 82, Robert Kidd Galleries, Birmingham, Mich., 1984, Soghor, Leonard & Assocs. Gallery, N.Y.C., 1985, O.K. Harris South, Miami, Fla., 1986, Butler Inst. Am. Art, Youngstown, Ohio, 1987, Tortue Gallery, Santa Monica, Calif., 1988, Art Expo, Tokyo, 1990, Art Now Gallery, Gothenburg, Sweden, 1990, Louis Stern Gallery, Beverly Hills, Calif., 1991, Bobbitt Visual Arts Ctr. Albion (Mich.) Coll., 1991. Represented in private and corp. collections in U.S., Can., Europe. Recipient Disting. Artists award Va. Mus. Fine Art, 1979. Fellow Pa. Acad. Fine Arts. Home: PO Box 374 Hillsdale NY 12529-0374

RICHARDS, KEITH, musician; b. Dartford, Kent, Eng., Dec. 18, 1943; s. Bert and Doris Richards; m. Anita Pallenberg; children: Marlon, Angela; m. Patti Hansen, Dec. 18, 1983; children: Theodora, Alexandra. Student, Sidcup Art Sch. Lead & rhythm guitarist, vocalist, Rolling Stones, 1962—; films include: Sympathy for the Devil, 1970, Gimme Shelter, 1970, Ladies and Gentlemen, the Rolling Stones, 1974, Let's Spend the Night Together, 1983, film mus. dir. (with Chuck Berry, Eric Clapton and friends) Hail! Hail! Rock & Roll, 1987; composer (with Mick Jagger) numerous songs and ablums, 1964—, including (albums) The Rolling Stones, Now!, 1964, Aftermath, 1966, Flowers, 1967, Beggars Banquet, 1968, Let It Bleed, 1969, Sticky Fingers, 1971, Hot Rocks, 1972, Exile on Main Street, 1972, Goat's Head Soup, 1973, It's Only Rock and Roll, 1974, Metamorphosis, 1975, Black and Blue, 1976, Some Girls, Emotional Rescue, 1980, Tatoo You, 1981, Still Life, 1982, Under Cover, 1983, Dirty Work, 1986, Steel Wheels, 1989, Flashpoint, 1991, Voodoo Lounge, 1994 (Grammy award Best Rock Album), Stripped, 1995; (songs) Wild Horses, Angie, Start Me Up, Honky Tonk Woman, Jumpin' Jack Flash, (I Can't Get No) Satisfaction, Before They Make Me Run, Miss You, Happy, Shattered, Paint It Black, Waiting On a Friend, Ruby Tuesday, You Can't Always Get What You Want, Brown Sugar, Tumbling Dice, Faraway Eyes, Mixed Emotions, Rock and a Hard Place, Highwire, Love is Strong; producer (soundtrack album) Hail! Hail! Rock 'N Roll, 1987; solo albums: Talk Is Cheap, 1988, Keith Richards & The X-Pensive Winos Live At The Hollywood Palladium, Dec. 15, 1988, 1991, Main Offender, 1992. Recipient Living Legend award Internat. Rock; inducted into Rock and Roll Hall of Fame, 1989. Address: care Raindrop Svcs 1776 Broadway New York NY 10019-2002*

RICHARDS, LACLAIRE LISSETTA JONES (MRS. GEORGE A. RICHARDS), social worker; b. Pine Bluff, Ark.; d. Artie William and Geraldine (Adams) Jones; m. George Alvarez Richards, July 26, 1958; children: Leslie Rosario, Lia Mercedes, Jorge Ferguson. BA, Nat. Coll. Christian Workers, 1953; MSW, U. Kans., 1956; postgrad. Columbia U., 1960. Diplomate Clin. Social Work, Am. Bd. of Examiners in Clin. Social Work, Nat. Assn. Social Workers; cert. gerontologist. Psychiat. supervisory, teaching, community orgn., adminstrv. and consultative duties Hastings Regional Ctr., Ingleside, Nebr., 1956-60; supervisory, consultative and adminstrv. responsibilities for psychiat. and geriatric patients VA Hosp., Knoxville, Iowa, 1960-74, field instr. for grad. students from U. Mo., EEO counselor, 1969-74, 78-90, com. chmn., 1969-70, Fed. women's program coordinator, 1972-74; sr. social worker Mental Health Inst., Cherokee, Iowa, 1974-77; adj. asst. prof. dept. social behavior U. S.D.; instr. Dept. of Psychiatry U. S.D Sch. of Medicine, 1988-96, Augustana Coll., 1981-86; outpatient social worker VA Med. and Regional Office Center, Sioux Falls, S.D., 1978-96; med., surg. & intensive care social worker, 1990-92, surg. & intermediate care social worker, 1992-96; EEO counselor. Mem. Knoxville Juvenile Adv. Com., 1963-65, 68-70, sec., 1965-66, chmn., 1966-68; sec. Urban Renewal Citizens' Adv. Com., Knoxville, 1966-68; mem. United Methodist Ch. Task Force Exptl. Styles Ministry and Leadership, 1973-74, mem. adult choir, mem. ch. and society com.; counselor Knoxville Youth Line program; sec. exec. com. Vis. Nurse Assn., 1979-80; canvasser community fund drs., Knoxville; mem. Cherokee Civil Rights Commn.; bd. dirs., pub. relations, membership devel. and program devel. cons. YWCA, 1983-85; bd. dirs. Family Svc. Agy., 1989-90, Food Svcs. Ctr. Inc., 1992-95; mem. S.D. Symphonic Choir, 1991—. Named S.D. Social Worker of Yr., 1983. Mem. NAACP (chmn. edn. com. 1983-85), AAUW (sec. Hastings chpt. 1958-60), Nat. Assn. Social Workers (co-chmn. Nebr. chpt. profl. standards com. 1958-59), Acad. Cert. Social Workers, S.D. Assn. Social Workers (chmn. minority affairs com., v.p. S.E. region 1980, pres. 1980-82 exec. com. 1982-84, mem. social policy and action com.), Nebr. Assn. Social Workers (chmn. 1958-59), Seventh Dist. S.D. Med. Soc. Aux., Coalition on Aging., Nat. Assn. Social Workers (qualified clin. social worker 1991—), Methodist (Sunday sch. tchr. adult div.; mem. commn. on edn.; mem. Core com. for adult edn.; mem. Adult Choir; mem. Social Concerns Work Area); mem. 1st Evangelical Free Ch., 1995—. Home: 1701 E Ponderosa Dr Sioux Falls SD 57103-5019

RICHARDS, LISLE FREDERICK, architect; b. Merrick, N.Y., Dec. 28, 1909. B.Arch., U. So. Calif., 1934. Draftsman H.C. Nickerson, 1935, Lawrence Test, 1936-40, Raimond Johnson, 1937; with Richards & Logue (architects); practice as L.F. Richards Santa Clara, Calif., 1947-78. Prin. works include Labor Temple, San Jose, Calif., 1948, Swimming Center, Santa Clara, 1949, C.W. Haman Sch, Santa Clara, 1952, Scott Lane Sch, Santa Clara, 1953, W.A. Wilson Sch, Santa Clara, 1954, Westwood Sch, Santa Clara, 1955, Civic Center, Santa Clara, 1962, Santa Clara Internat. Swim Center, 1970. Mem. Santa Clara County Appeals Bd., 1952; mem. Santa Clara Code Com., 1954. Fellow AIA (pres. Coast Valleys chpt. 1956, pres. Calif. Council 1958, Disting. Service award 1959, Disting. Service citation Santa Clara Valley chpt. 1982, Testimonial Appreciation 1990). Home: 4985 Ponderosa Ter Campbell CA 95008-5751 *As I look back on the past seventy years—what a wonderful and terrible time it has been to live.*

RICHARDS, LLOYD GEORGE, theatrical director, university administrator; b. Toronto, Ont., Can.; came to U.S., 1923; s. Albert George and Rose Isabella (Coote) R.; m. Barbara Davenport, Oct. 11, 1957; children: Scott, Thomas. Student, Wayne U., 1943-44. Head actor tng. NYU Sch. Arts, N.Y.C., 1966-72; artistic dir. Nat. Playwrights Conf., Eugene O'Neill Meml. Theatre Ctr., Waterford, Conn., 1969—; prof. theatre and cinema Hunter Coll., N.Y.C., 1972-79; dean Yale U. Sch. Drama, New Haven, 1979-91; artistic dir Yale Repertory Theatre, New Haven, 1979-91; prof. emeritus Sch. Drama, 1991—; artistic dir. Yale Repertory Theater, 1979-91; pres. Theater Devel. Fund; head actor tng. Sch. Arts NYU, 1966-72; lectr., cons. in field; bd. dirs. Theatre Comm. Group, U.S. Bicentennial World Theatre Festival; mem. various profl. adv. groups, task forces; mem. playwrights selection com. Rockefeller Found.; mem. new Am. plays program com. Ford Found.; mem. com. on profl. theater tng. Nat. Endowment Arts. Actor on radio, TV and theater, 1943—; including Broadway plays The Egghead, 1957, Freight, 1956; disc jockey, Detroit; dir. for: radio, TV, film and theater, including Broadway plays A Raisin in the Sun, 1958, The Long Dream, 1960, The Moon Besieged, 1962, I Had a Ball, 1964, The Yearling, 1966, Paul Robeson, 1977-78, Ma Rainey's Black Bottom, 1984, Fences, 1987 (Tony award 1987), Joe Turner's Come and Gone, 1986, The Piano Lesson, 1990, Two Trains Running, 1992; and TV prodns. include: segment of Roots: The Next Generation, 1979, Bill Moyers' Jour, 1979, Robeson, 1979, Hallmark Piano Lesson 95. Served with USAAF, 1943-44. Recipient Pioneer award AUDELCO, 1986-87, Frederick Douglas award, 1986-87, Golden Plate award, 1987, Nat. Medal of Arts, 1993. Mem. Soc. Stage Dirs. and Choreographers (pres.), Actors Equity Assn., AFTRA, Dirs. Guild Am. Office: 18 W 95th St New York NY 10025-6708

RICHARDS, MAX DE VOE, management educator, consultant, researcher, author; b. Nova, Ohio, May 23, 1923; s. Paul Leroy and Dorothy Charlotte (Daniels) Richards; m. Winona Marie Petersen, Mar. 3, 1950 (div. Dec. 1974); children: Cassandra, Elizabeth; m. Ruth Sara Nixon, Nov. 12, 1977. M.B.A., Harvard U., 1947; Ph.D., U. Ill., 1955. Indsl. engr. Nat. Tube div. U.S. Steel Co., 1948-49; instr. mgmt. U. Ill., Urbana, 1949-54; assoc. prof., head dept. mgmt. U. Wichita, Kans., 1954-56; assoc. prof., head div. mgmt. Pa. State U., University Park, 1956-64, prof., head dept. mgmt., 1964-67, 78-81, prof., asst. dean, dir. grad. programs Coll. Bus. Adminstrn., 1966-77; disting. prof. mgmt. Rollins Coll., Winter Park, Fla., 1981-85; organizational and strategic mgmt. cons., program speaker, U.S., internationally, 1954—; bd. dirs. Inst. for Adminstrv. Research, 1967-69; evaluator Middle States Accrediting Assn., Newark, 1973—. Author: Organizational Goal Structures, 1978, Intermediate and Long Term Credit Small Corporations, 1980, Setting Strategic Goals and Objectives, rev. edit., 1986; co-author: Management Decisions and Behavior, 2d edit. 1973; editor: Readings in Management, 7th edit. 1986. Ford Found. faculty fellow, 1965-66; Social Sci. Research Council fellow, 1966. Fellow Acad. Mgmt. (dir. 1961-68, v.p., program chmn. 1965-66, pres. 1966-67, chmn. policy and planning div. 1975, dir. div. 1974-78); mem. Strategic Mgmt. Soc. (editorial bd. 1983—), Order of Artus, Sigma Iota Epsilon (trustee 1968), Beta Gamma Sigma, Beech Mountain Club (N.C.), Tuscawilla Country Club (Winter Springs, Fla.), Elks. Home: 1117 Winged Foot Cir W Winter Spgs FL 32708-4201 Office: Crummer Grad Sch Bus Rollins Coll Winter Park FL 32789

RICHARDS, MERLON FOSS, retired diversified technical services company executive; b. Farmington, Utah, May 18, 1920; s. Ezra Foss and Mertie Malinda (Hunt) R.; m. Caryle Jane Vandenberg, July 18, 1945 (dec. 1994); children: Craig M., Cathy Jean, Cynthia Jane, Julie Ann. BS, U. Utah, 1942; MBA, Harvard U., 1947. CPA, Ill. Pub. acct. Arthur Andersen & Co., Chgo., 1947-52; asst. treas. to exec. v.p. Land-Air, Inc., Chgo., 1952-59; from v.p. to vice chmn., chief exec. officer DynCorp (formerly Dynalectron Corp.), Washington, 1959-85, bd. dirs., mem. exec. com., 1971-88; consulting fin. officer Indsl. Tng. Corp., Herndon, Va., 1988-89; former dir. over 20 DynCorp subs.; mem. adv. bd. Sycom Inc., 1986-88; dir. Riggs Nat. Bank, 1979-81. Chmn., vice chmn. membership Potomac dist. Nat. Capital Area coun. Boy Scouts Am., 1989—; pub. affairs dir. Washington region LDS Ch., 1984-94; mem. fin. com. Interfaith Conf. of Met. Washington, 1992—. Maj. F.A., U.S. Army, 1941-54, ETO. Decorated Bronze Star, Silver Star. Mem. Pi Kappa Alpha. Republican. Home and Office: 4701 Willard Ave Apt 436 Chevy Chase MD 20815-4262

RICHARDS, MICHAEL, actor, comedian; b. 1949; 1 child. TV appearences include Fridays, 1980-82, Marblehead Manor, 1987, Seinfeld, 1990— (Emmy award, Outstanding Supporting Actor in a Comedy Series, 1993, 94); films include Young Doctors in Love, 1982, Transylvania 6-5000, 1985, UHF, 1989, Problem Child, 1990, Coneheads, 1993, Unstrung Heroes, 1995. Office: APA 9000 Sunset Blvd/Ste 1200 Los Angeles CA 90069*

RICHARDS, NORMAN BLANCHARD, lawyer; b. Melrose, Mass., May 27, 1924; s. Henry Edward and Annie Jane (Blanchard) R.; m. Diane Maionchi, July 9, 1977; children—Terri, Jeffrey. B.S., Bowdoin Coll., 1945; J.D., Stanford U., 1951. Bar: Calif. bar 1951. Mem. firm McCutchen Doyle Brown & Enersen, San Francisco, 1951—; partner McCutchen Doyle Brown & Enersen, 1960—; mem. faculty Tulane Admiralty Law Inst., Hastings Coll. Advocacy. Bd. visitors Stanford Law Sch. With USN, 1943-46. Fellow Am. Coll. Trial Lawyers; mem. ABA, Calif. State Bar, San Francisco Bar ASsn., Maritime Law Assn. U.S. Home: 85 Platt Ave Sausalito CA 94965-1897 Office: McCutchen Doyle Brown & Enerson 3 Embarcadero Ctr San Francisco CA 94111-4003

RICHARDS, PATRICIA FAE, elementary education educator; b. St. Louis, Mich., June 30, 1950; d. Paul Gerald and Ellen Elizabeth (Anderson) Flowers; m. David Joseph Richards, Apr. 15, 1988; children: Mark David, Emily Elizabeth. BA, Cen. Mich. U., 1971, MA in Gen. Edn., 1978. Elem. tchr. Carson City (Mich.) Elem., 1971-88, chpt. 1 tchr., 1988—; union sec. Carson City, 1973-74, region 9 del., 1974-75; rep. Young Author's Conf., Montcalm County, Mich., 1980. Fellow Am. Legion Aux., Womens Club of Carson City. Avocations: camping, photography, gardening. Home: 9484 Mount Hope Rd Carson City MI 48811-9724 Office: Carson City Crystal Schs 115 E Main Carson City MI 48811

RICHARDS, PAUL A., lawyer; b. Oakland, Calif., May 27, 1927; s. Donnell C. and Theresa (Pasquale) R.; m. Ann Morgans, May 20, 1948 (dec. 1984); 1 child, Paul M. BA, U. Pacific, 1950; JD, U. San Francisco, 1953. Bar: Nev. 1953, U.S. Dist. Ct. Nev. 1953, U.S. Supreme Ct. 1964, U.S. Ct. Claims 1976, U.S. Ct. Appeals (9th cir.) 1982. Pvt. practice, Reno, 1953—, prin. Paul A. Richards, Ltd.; prof. environ. law Sierra Nevada Coll., 1970-80. Mem. Washoe Dem. Central Com., 1959-74, chmn., 1964-66, vice chmn., 1966-68; trustee Sierra Nevada Coll., 1970-82, Ducks Unltd., 1964-72; trustee emeritus, 1974—; mem. Fed. Land Law Commn., Nev., 1973-80; bd. dirs. Reno Rodeo Assn., 1963, pres., 1979. Served with U.S. Navy, 1945-46. Recipient Pres.'s Buckle and award Reno Rodeo Assn., 1979. Mem. Nev. Bar Assn., Washoe County Bar Assn., Am. Legion. Democrat. Roman Catholic. Club: Press. Lodge: Elks, Masons. Office: 248 S Sierra St Reno NV 89501-1908

RICHARDS, PAUL GRANSTON, geophysics educator, seismologist; b. Cirencester, Eng., Mar. 31, 1943; came to U.S., 1965; s. Albert George and Kathleen Margaret (Harding) R.; m. Jody Margaret Porterfield, June 1, 1968; children: Mark, Jessica, Gillian. BA, Cambridge (Eng.) U., 1965; MS, Calif. Inst. Tech., Pasadena, 1966, PhD, 1970. Prof. geol. scis. Columbia U., N.Y.C., 1971—, chmn. dept. geol. scis., 1980-83. Co-author: Quantitative Seismology, 2 vols., 1980. Guggenheim Found. fellow, 1977-78, MacArthur Found. fellow, 1981-86. Fellow Royal Astron. Soc.; mem. Am. Geophys. Union (Macelwane award 1976), Coun. Fgn. Rels. Episcopalian. Office: Lamont-Doherty Earth OBS Palisades NY 10964

RICHARDS, PAUL LINFORD, physics educator, researcher; b. Ithaca, N.Y., June 4, 1934; s. Lorenzo Adolph and Zilla (Linford) R.; m. Audrey Jarratt, Aug. 24, 1965; children: Elizabeth Anne, Mary-Ann. AB, Harvard U., 1956; PhD, U. Calif., Berkeley, 1960. Postdoctoral fellow U. Cambridge (Eng.), 1959-60; mem. tech. staff Bell Telephone Labs., Murray Hill, N.J., 1960-66; prof. physics U. Calif., Berkeley, 1966—; faculty sr. scientist Lawrence Berkeley Lab., 1966—; advisor NASA, 1975-92, Conductus Inc., Mountain View, Calif., 1988—; hon. prof. Miller Inst. Rsch. in Phys. Scis., Berkeley, 1969-70, 87-88; vis. prof. Ecole Normale Superieure, Paris, 1984, 92; vis. astronomer Paris Obs., 1984. Contbr. over 300 articles to profl. jours. Guggenheim Meml. Found. fellow, Cambridge, Eng., 1973-74; named Calif. Scientist of Yr. Mus. Sci., L.A., 1981; recipient sr. scientist award alexander von Humboldt Found., Stuttgart, Fed. Republic Germany, 1982; Berkeley Faculty Rsch. lectr. 1991. Fellow NAS, Am. Phys. Soc., Am. Acad. Arts and Scis. Avocations: vineyardist, wine making.

RICHARDS, REUBEN FRANCIS, natural resource company executive; b. Aug. 15, 1929; s. Junius A. and Marie R. (Thayer) R.; m. Elizabeth Brady, Nov. 28, 1953; children: Reuben Francis, Timothy T., Andrew H. AB, Harvard U., 1952. With Citibank, N.A., N.Y.C., 1953-82, exec. v.p., 1970-82; chmn. Terra Industries Inc., N.Y.C., 1982—; bd. dirs. Ecolab, Inc., St. Paul, Potlatch Corp., San Francisco, Minorco, Luxembourg, Santa Fe Energy Resources, Inc., Houston, Engelhard Corp., Iselin, N.J.; chmn., pres., CEO Minorco (U.S.A.) Inc. With USNR, 1948-50. Office: Minorco Inc 30 Rockefeller Plz Ste 4212 New York NY 10112

RICHARDS, RILEY HARRY, insurance company executive; b. North Judson, Ind., Oct. 6, 1912; s. Harry J. and Chestie (Johnson) R.; m. Eloise Quinn Smith, May 4, 1940; children: Roy, Lynne. AB, U. Calif., Berkeley, 1934; MBA, Harvard U., 1937. Chartered fin. analyst. Fin. analyst Savs. Bank Trust Co. N.Y.C., 1937-40, SEC, Washington, Phila., 1940-45; accountant U.S. Steel Corp., Pitts., 1945-47; with Equitable Life Ins. Co. Iowa, Des Moines, 1947-77; v.p. finance Equitable Life Ins. Co. Iowa, 1961-73, v.p., sec., treas., 1973-76, sr. v.p., sec.-treas., 1976-77; dir., mem. exec. com. Equitable of Iowa Cos., 1977-84; pres. Westminster House, Inc., 1989-96; dir. F.M. Hubbell Sons & Co., 1977-85. Mem. Des Moines Plan and Zoning Commn., 1959-70, chmn., 1968-69; mem. bd. pensions U.P. Ch. in U.S.A., 1960-72, chmn. finance com., 1963-72; trustee United Presbyn. Found., 1979-87, vice chmn., 1981-83, chmn., 1983-87; bd. regents Life Officers Investment Seminar, 1969-70; trustee Thompson Trust, 1976—, Frederick M. Hubbell Estate, 1977-85. Mem. Am. Coun. Life Ins. (chmn. fin. sect. 1970), Iowa Soc. Fin. Analysts (pres. 1965-67), Sigma Alpha Epsilon. Republican. Club: Des Moines. Lodges: Masons, Rotary. Home: 2880 Grand Ave Apt 311 Des Moines IA 50312-4274

RICHARDS, ROBERT A. (BOB RICHARDS), accounting executive, management consulting executive; b. 1931. Diploma, U. Wash., 1953. With IRS, Seattle, 1953-64, Peat Marwick, Mitchell & Co., Seattle, 1964-71; pvt. practice, 1971-79; v.p. Branch Richards and Co., Seattle, 1979—. Office: Branch Richards and Co 2201 6th Ave Ste 1009 Seattle WA 98121*

RICHARDS, ROBERT W., mortgage company executive; b. 1943. With Source One Mortgage Svcs. Corp., Farmington, Mich., 1971—, now chmn. bd.; now chmn. bd. Mortgage Auth. Inc. subs. Source One Mortgage Svcs. Corp., Farmington, Mich. Office: Source One Mortgage Svcs Corp 27555 Farmington Rd Farmington MI 48334-3314*

RICHARDS, ROBERT WADSWORTH, civil engineer, consultant; b. Beacon, N.Y., Jan. 26, 1921; s. Parke and Lois Richmond (Tracy) R.; m. Cynthia Elizabeth Pigot, May 31, 1952; children: Sarah Palmer Richards Graves III, Robert Wadsworth, Tracy Leigh Richards Purdy. BS, Princeton U., 1943, MCE, 1944. Registered profl. engr., Ga. Instr. civil engring. Swarthmore (Pa.) Coll., 1944-45; rsch. engr. The Budd Co., Phila., 1945-50; assoc. charge Atlanta office Howard, Needles, Tammen & Bergendoff, 1950-88; cons. engr. Tech. & Creative Writing, 1988—. Contbr. articles to tech. and bus. jours. Named Eminent Engr., Tau Beta Pi. Fellow ASCE; mem. Am. Soc. Engring. Edn. (life), Princeton Campus Club. Home and Office: 1051 Winding Branch Ln Atlanta GA 30338-3947

RICHARDS, ROY, JR., wire and cable manufacturing company executive. Chmn., CEO, dir. Southwire Co., Carrollton, Ga. Office: Southwire Co Inc PO Box 1000 Carrollton GA 30119*

RICHARDS, STANFORD HARVEY, advertising agency executive, design studio executive; b. Phila., Nov. 8, 1932; s. Jack and Ruth (Stein) R.; m. Betty Jo Pugh, July 12, 1957; children—Grant Leonard, Bradford Craig. Student, Pratt Inst., 1950-53. Creative dir. Bloom Advt., Dallas, 1954-55; owner Stan Richards & Assocs., Dallas, 1955-75; owner, pres. The Richards Group, Inc., Dallas, 1975—, also bd. dirs.; instr. E. Tex. State U., Commerce, 1976-77; assoc. bd. mem. Cox Sch. Bus., So. Meth. U., Dallas, 1980-84, 88—. Author: Hobo Signs, 1965. Trustee Dallas Symphony, 1978, Dallas Ballet, 1978; bd. dirs. Episcopal Sch., Dallas, 1981—, Dallas Arboretum, 1984-86, The Sci. Pl., 1987-90; mem. Dallas Citizens Council, adv. council Salvation Army Adult Rehab. Ctr., 1986—, adv. bd. Dallas County Salvation Army, 1987—; exec. com. United Way, 1990—; bd. dirs. YMCA, 1990—. Recipient alumni achievement award Pratt Inst., Bklyn., 1985. Club: Aerobic Activity Ctr. Avocations: deep sea fishing, running, skiing. Office: The Richards Group 8750 N Central Expy Ste 1200 Dallas TX 75231-6437*

RICHARDS, STEPHEN HAROLD, engineering educator; b. Austin, Tex., July 19, 1952; s. Harold Richards Jr. and Janice Valerie (Mahone) Jackson; m. Mary Kathryn King Coleman, Aug. 15, 1974 (div. July 1981); 1 child, Adam King. BSCE, U. Tex., 1976; MCE, Tex. A&M U., 1977; PhDCE, U. Tenn., 1989. Registered profl. engr., Tenn., Tex. Rsch. asst. Tex. Transp. Inst., Tex. A&M U., 1976-77, engring. rsch. assoc., 1977-81, asst. rsch. engr., 1982-84; asst. dir. transp. ctr. U. Tenn., Knoxville, 1984-87, acting dir. transp. ctr., 1987-89, dir. transp., 1989—, assoc. prof. civil engring., 1989—; traffic engring. cons., 1976—; engr., mgr. Walton & Assocs./Cons. Engrs., Inc., Houston, 1981-82; lectr. in civil engring. U. Houston, 1982, Tex. A&M U., 1978-81, 83-84; instr. Tex. Engring. Extension Svc., Tex. A&M U., 1978-84; Dwight D. Eisenhower Fellowship Rev. Com., Tenn. State U., 1993, N.C. A&T Univ., 1992; Bicentennial planning Com. U. Tenn., 1993, dir. program for minority student recruitment into transp. careers, 1992—, coll. engring. awards com., 1991—, chmn. spl. events traffic planning com., 1985—. Contbr. numerous articles to profl. jours. Mem. Cumberland Gateway Com., 1993—; edn. com. Southeastern Transp. Ctr., 1992—; exec. dir. Southeastern Consortium of U. Transp. Ctrs., 1992—; chmn. Knoxville Transp. Authority, 1992-94, vice-chmn., 1990-92, commr., 1989-93; rep. Coun. of Univ. Transp. Ctrs. U. Tenn., 1987—, bd. dirs. 1992—; adv. com. Ga. State u. Transp. Ctr., 1989—; traffic control device subcom. Transp. Rsch. Bd., 1989-91, traffic control devices, 1991—, many other coms. Hwy. Safety fellowship Fed. Hwy. Adminstrn., U.S. Dept. Transp., 1976-77. Mem. ASCE, Inst. of Transp. Engrs. (chmn. tech. com. Tenn. sect. 1988—, area coord. Tex. sect. 1982-84, guidelines for driveway design and location), Transp. Rsch. Bd., Soc. Profl. Engrs., Am. Road and Transp. Builders Assn. (edn. com. 1988—), Phi Kappa Phi, Chi Epsilon. Office: U Tenn Knoxville Transt Ctr 200 Henley St Ste 309 Knoxville TN 37996-4133

RICHARDS, SUZANNE V., lawyer; b. Columbia, S.C., Sept. 7, 1927; d. Raymond E. and Elise C. (Gray) R. AB, George Washington U., 1948, JD with distinction, 1957, LLM, 1959. Bar: D.C., 1958. Sole practice, Washington, 1974—; lectr. in family and probate law. Recipient John Bell Larner award George Washington U., 1958; named Woman Lawyer of the Yr., Women's Bar Assn. D.C., 1977. Mem. Bar Assn. D.C. (pres. 1989-90), Women's Bar Assn. (pres. 1977-78), Trial Lawyers Assn. of D.C. (bd. govs. 1978-82, 85—, treas. 1982-85), D.C. Bar, Fed. Bar Assn., Nat. Assn. Women Lawyers, ABA (mem. ho. dels. 1988-90), D.C. Jud. Conf. Office: 1701 K St NW Washington DC 20006-1503

RICHARDS, THOMAS SAVIDGE, utility company executive; b. Dansville, Pa., July 8, 1943; s. Thomas Beddoe and Mary (Savidge) R.; m. Betty Stalter Richards, Aug. 4, 1969; children: Ted, Matthew. BS, Bucknell U., 1965; JD, Cornell U., 1972. Bar: N.Y. 1973. Assoc. Nixon, Hargrave, Devans & Doyle, Rochester, N.Y., 1972-79; ptnr. Nixon, Hargrave, Devans & Doyle, Rochester, 1979-91; gen. counsel Rochester (N.Y.) Gas & Electric Corp., 1991-93, sr. v.p. fin., gen. counsel, 1993-95, sr. v.p. energy svcs., 1995-96; bd. dirs. Eltrex Industries, Inc., Rochester, Rochester Econ. Devel. Corp. Mem. exec. bd. Boy Scout Am., Otetiana Coun., Rochester; mem. governing bd. Colgate Rochester Divinity Sch.; chmn. bd. dirs. Greater Rochester Housing Partnership; dir. Highland Hosp., Rochester, Rochester Pub. Libr., Vis. Nurse Found., Rochester. Lt. USN, 1965-69. Mem. ABA, N.Y. State Bar Assn., Monroe county Bar Assn. Office: Rochester Gas & Elec Corp 89 East Ave Rochester NY 14649

RICHARDS, VINCENT PHILIP HASLEWOOD, librarian; b. Sutton Bonington, Nottinghamshire, Eng., Aug. 1, 1933; emigrated to Can., 1956, naturalized, 1961; s. Philip Haslewood and Alice Hilda (Moore) R.; m. Ann Beardshall, Apr. 3, 1961; children: Mark, Christopher, Erika. A.L.A., Ealing Coll., London, 1954; B.L.S. with distinction, U. Okla., 1966. Cert. profl. librarian, B.C. Joined Third Order Mt. Carmel, Roman Catholic Ch., 1976; with Brentford and Chiswick Pub. Libraries, London, 1949-56; asst. librarian B.C. (Can.) Pub. Library Commn., Dawson Creek, 1956-57; asst. dir. Fraser Valley Regional Library, Abbotsford, B.C., 1957-67; chief librarian Red Deer (Alta., Can.) Coll., 1967-77; dir. libraries Edmonton (Alta.) Pub. Library, 1977-89; libr. and book industry cons. Ganges, Can., 1990—; pres. Faculty Assn. Red Deer Coll., 1971-72, bd. govs., 1972-73. Contbr. articles to profl. jours., 1954—. Vice pres. Jeunesses Musicales, Red Deer, 1969-70; bd. dirs. Red Deer TV Authority, 1975-76, Alta. Found. Lit. Arts, 1984-86; mem. Reform Party Can. Served with Royal Army Ednl. Corps, 1951-53. *Dedication to public service, in spite of its frustrating aspects, diversity of experience, people and places, and the avoidance of over-specialization are great contributors to an enjoyable working life.*

RICHARDS, WALTER DUBOIS, artist, illustrator; b. Penfield, Ohio, Sept. 18, 1907; s. Ralph DuBois and Ruby Mildred (Smith) R.; m. Glenora Case, June 20, 1931; children: Timothy, Henry Tracy. Grad., Cleve. Sch. Art, 1930. With Sundblom Studios, Chgo., 1930-31, Tranquillini Studios, Cleve., 1931-36, Charles E. Cooper Studios, N.Y.C., 1936-50. Freelance artist, 1950—; executed paintings and illustrations for leading indsl. corps., nat. mags.; designed: U.S. postage stamps including Frederick Douglas 25 cent stamp; block of 4 stamps on beautification of Am.; Am. bald eagle-Mus. Natural History with commemorative; Cape Hatteras Nat. Parks Centennial block of four stamps; Paul Lawrence Dunbar Am. Poets commemorative; block of 4 stamps on Am. trees, 1978, blocks of 4 stamps on Am. architecture, 1979, 80, 81, 82; co-designer anti-pollution block of four stamps; James Hoban stamp, 1981, Timberline Lodge 50th Anniversary U.S. commemorative stamp, 1987; exhibited, Cleve. Mus. Art, Art Inst., Chgo., Met. Mus., N.Y.C., Pa. Acad. Fine Arts, Bklyn. Mus., N.A.D., Whitney Mus., 200 Years Watercolor Painting, Met. Mus., 1966, 200 Years Am. Illustration, N.Y. Hist. Soc., 1976; represented in permanent collection, Whitney Mus., New Britain Mus. Am. Art, Cleve. Mus. Art, William A. Farnsworth Library and Art Mus., West Point Mus., Worcester (Mass.) Art Mus., Yale U. Art Gallery-New Haven, Conn. Bd. dirs. Rowayton Art Center, Historic New Orleans Collection, 1989. Recipient highest award in lithography Cleve. Mus. Art, ann. 1935-38; Spl. Honor USAF, 1964; ann. Environ. Improvement award, 1983; named to Rocky River (Ohio) High Sch. Hall of Fame, 1991. Mem. Am. Watercolor Soc. (2d v.p. 1965-67), Conn. Watercolor Soc., NAD, Soc. of Illustrators, Fairfield Watercolor Group (pres., founder), Westport Artists. Address: Po Box 1134 87 Oak St New Canaan CT 06840

RICHARDS, WANDA JAMIE, education educator; b. Brownwood, Tex., Jan. 11, 1930; d. William Steven and Mary (Effie) Rodgers; m. Kenneth E. Graham, Mar. 29, 1949 (div. Jan. 3, 1963); 1 child, Kenneth Jr.; m. Neill Richards, Mar. 15, 1972 (dec. Dec. 2, 1982). BA, Eastern N.Mex. U., 1962; MA, Colo. State Coll., 1964; EdD, U. No. Colo., 1966. Tchr. spl. edn. Pub. Sch., Roswell, N.Mex., 1961-63; dept. head spl. edn. Eastern N.Mex. U., Portales, 1965-69; curriculum researcher N.Mex. State U., Las Cruces, 1969-71; dir. edn. Inst. of Logopedics, Wichita, Kans., 1971-72; owner W. J. Enterprises, Kans., 1973-89; pres., treas. W.J.G. Enterprise Corp., Sedona, Ariz., 1990—; pres.'s coun. on spl. edn. Fed. Govt., Washington, 1967-69; planning cons. in field. Contbr. articles to profl. jours. Mem. Citizens for Quality Edn., Sedona, 1991, C. of C., Sedona, 1990-91, Humane Soc., Sedona, 1991. Recipient Fellowship in Spl. Edn., Fed. Govt. Pub. Law 85962, 1963-65; named Faculty Woman of Yr., Eastern New Mex. U., 1967. Republican. Home: 30 Sedona St Sedona AZ 86351-7752

RICHARDS-KORTUM, REBECCA RAE, biomedical engineering educator; b. Grand Island, Nebr., Apr. 14, 1964; d. Larry Alan and Linda Mae (Hohnstein) Richards; m. Philip Ted Kortum, May 12, 1985; children: Alexander Scott, Maxwell James. BS, U. Nebr., 1985; MS, MIT, 1987, PhD, 1990. Assoc. U. Tex., Austin, 1990—. Named Presdl. Young Investigator NSF, Washington, 1991; NSF presdl. faculty fellow, Washington, 1992; recipient Career Achievement award Assn. Advancement Med. Instrumentation, 1992, Dow Outstanding Young Faculty awd., Am. Soc. for Engineering Education, 1992. Mem. AAAS, Am. Soc. Engring. Edn. (Outstanding Young Faculty award 1992), Optical Soc. Am., Am. Soc. Photobiology. Achievements include research in photochemistry, photobiology, applied optics and bioengring. Office: U Tex Dept Elec & Computer Engring Austin TX 78712

RICHARDSON, ANN BISHOP, foundation executive, lawyer; b. New Rochelle, N.Y., Dec. 15, 1940; d. Erwin Julius and Mary Frances (Stuart) Heilemann; m. James K. Bishop, Jr., Nov. 30, 1960 (div. 1972); children: Timothy William, Lynn Patricia, Melanie Elizabeth; m. John P. Richardson, Apr. 16, 1972 (div. 1994). BA summa cum laude, Georgetown U., 1977; JD, George Washington U., 1984; cert. Oxford U., Eng., 1986. Bar: Md. 1988, DC 1989. Student counselor Amideast, Beirut, 1967-68, program specialist 1970-73; adminstrv. asst. UN Devel. Program, Yaounde, Cameroon, 1968-70; adminstrv. mgr. Antioch Sch. Law, Washington, 1977-79; chief adminstrv. officer for internat. ops. Peace Corps, Washington, 1980-84; dir. adminstrn. and fin. African Devel. Found., Washington, 1984-87; atty. Karr and McLain, Washington, 1987-92; v.p., gen. counsel Time Dollar, Inc., Washington, 1992—; adj. prof. law D.C. Sch. Law, Washington, 1994—. Mem. Neighbors, Inc., Washington, 1976—. Recipient spl. achievement award Peace Corps, 1981, 82, African Devel. Found., 1986. Mem. ABA, ACLU, D.C. Bar Assn., Assn. Am. Women Univ. Grads., Soc. for Internat. Devel. Phi Beta Kappa. Office: Time Dollar Inc 5500 39th St NW Washington DC 20015-2904

RICHARDSON, ANNE HAZARD, volunteer agency adminstrator; b. Providence, R.I., Dec. 5, 1929; d. Thomas P. and Nancy (Cope) H.; m. Elliot L. Richardson; children: Henry, Nancy, Michael. BA in History magna cum laude, Radcliffe Coll.; postgrad., Am. U.; LLD (hon.), Lawrence U., 1992. Extensive vol. and pub. svc. work, including support for performing arts and programs promoting literacy and reading; chmn. cmty. adv. bd. Second Genesis; bd. overseers Harvard U. recipient Helen Homans Gilbert award for disting. vol. svc. from the Arthur and Elizabeth Schlesinger Libr. on the History of Women in Am., Radcliffe Coll., 1991; mem., former chmn. bd. dirs. Reading Is Fundamental. Office: Smithsonian Inst Reading Is Fundamental 600 Maryland Ave SW Washington DC 20560

RICHARDSON, ARLINE ANNETTE, accountant, comptroller; b. N.Y.C., Aug. 20, 1939; d. Charles Sidney and Kathleen Gertrude (Sinclair) Hunt; m. David Edward Richardson, Sept. 13, 1958; children: Valerie-Jayne, LaVerne; stepchildren: James, David, Carl. AA, Bronx (N.Y.) C.C., 1976; BBA, CUNY, 1979, MPA, 1984. Mgr. patient accounts Jewish Home and Hosp. for Aged, N.Y.C., 1960-80; chief bookkeeper Edwin Gould Svcs. for Children, N.Y.C., 1980-81; staff acct. N.Y. Hosp., N.Y.C., 1981-84; mgr. Met. Transp. Authority, N.Y.C., 1984-92; compt. The Computer Lab., Morrisville, N.C., 1993—. Vol. cmty. tax aide, N.Y.C., 1979-83; tutor Henderson (N.C.) Mid. Sch., 1993—; vol. Maria Parham Hosp., 1993—; active Leadership Vance, 1996. Recipient Mitchell-Titus award, 1979. Mem. Am. Assn. Ret. Persons (assoc. dist. coord., instr. tax-aide program North Ctrl. N.C. 1993—), Henderson Bus. and Profl. Women's Club (leadership vance 1996), Beta Gamma Sigma, Phi Theta Kappa (Mitchell-Titus award 1979). Home: 1614 Peace St Henderson NC 27536-3549 Office: The Computer Lab 2700 Gateway Centre Blvd Morrisville NC 27560-9137

RICHARDSON, ARTEMAS P(ARTRIDGE), landscape architect; b. Phila., May 24, 1918; s. Eugene Stanley and Jessica (Ripple) R.; m. Frederica McAfee, Sept. 2, 1945; children: Steven, David, Ann, Vida, Stanley. BA in Fine Arts, Williams Coll., 1940; student, Pa. State U., 1940-42; BS in Landscape Architecture, Iowa State U., 1947. Registered landscape architect, Conn., Fla., Md., Mass., Miss., N.Y., Ohio, R.I., Tenn. Asst. landscape architect McCloud & Scatchard, Lilitz, Pa., 1947-48; asst. landscape architect Olmsted Bros., Brookline, Mass., 1949-50, ptnr., 1950-61; ptnr. Olmsted Assocs., Brookline, 1961-64, pres, treas., 1964-80; owner The Olmsted Office, Fremont, N.H., 1980—; lectr. Harvard U., Cambridge, 1961; mem., chair Bd. Registration Landscape Architects, Mass., 1968-77. Illustrator: Trees for Every Purpose, 1980. Mem., chair Planning Bd., Needham, Mass., 1956-62, Conservation Commn., Fremont, 1982—, chair, 1984—; mem. N.H. Gov.'s Task Force on Community Trees, Concord, 1989-91. Lt. USNR, 1942-46, ETO. Fellow Am. Soc. Landscape Architects, Boston Soc. Landscape Architects (pres. 1952-56); mem. N.H. Landscape Assn. (bd. dirs. 1984-87), Granite State Landscape Architects (vice chair 1990-91), Herb Soc. Am. (life), Scarab, Rotary (pres. local club 1965-66, dist. trustee 1968-69, dist. gov. 1970-71, bd. dirs. R.I. 1978-80), Delta Phi, Tau Sigma Delta, Pi Gamma Alpha. Avocations: photography, woodworking, gardening. Home: 106 North Rd Fremont NH 03044-3100 Office: The Olmsted Office 106 North Rd Fremont NH 03044-3100

RICHARDSON, A(RTHUR) LESLIE, former medical group consultant; b. Ramsgate, Kent, Eng., Feb. 21, 1910; s. John William and Emily Lilian (Wilkins) R.; came to U.S., 1930, naturalized, 1937; student spl. courses U. So. Calif., 1933-35; m. B. Kathleen Sargent, Oct. 15, 1937. Mgr., Tower Theater, Los Angeles, 1931-33; accountant Felix-Krueper Co., Los Angeles, 1933-35; indsl. engr. Pentland, Inc., Los Angeles, 1935-37; purchasing agt. Gen. Petroleum Corp. Los Angeles, 1937-46; adminstr. Beaver Med. Clinic, Redlands, Calif., 1946-72, exec. cons. 1972-75, 95; sec.-treas. Fern Properties, Inc., Redlands, 1955-75, Redelco, Inc., Redlands, 1960-67; pres. Buinco, Inc., Redlands, 1956-65; vice chmn. Redlands adv. bd. Bank of Am., 1973-80; exec. cons. Med. Adminstrs. Calif., 1975-83. Pres., Redlands Area Community Chest, 1953; volunteer exec. Internat. Exec. Service Corps; mem. San Bernardino County (Calif.) Grand Jury, 1952-53. Bd. dirs. Beaver Med. Clinic Found., Redlands, 1961—, sec.-treas., 1961-74, pres., 1974-75, chmn. bd. dirs. 1992—. Served to lt. Med. Adminstrv. Corps., AUS, 1942-45. Recipient Redlands Civic award Elks, 1953. Fellow Am. Coll. Med. Practice Execs. (life, disting. fellow 1980, pres. 1965-66, dir.); mem. Med. Group Mgmt. Assn. (hon. life; mem. nat. long range planning com. 1963-68, pres. western sect. 1960), Kiwanis (pres. 1951), Masons. Episcopalian. Home: 1 Verlie Dr Redlands CA 92373-6943 *Personal philosophy: Do unto others as you would have them do unto you.*

RICHARDSON, ARTHUR WILHELM, lawyer; b. Glendale, Calif., Apr. 3, 1963; s. Douglas Fielding and Leni (Tempelaar-Lietz) R. AB, Occidental Coll., 1985; student, London Sch. Econs., 1983; JD, Harvard U., 1988. Bar: Calif. 1989. Assoc. Morgan, Lewis and Bockius, L.A., 1988-90; staff lawyer U.S. SEC, L.A., 1990-92, br. chief, 1992-96, sr. counsel, 1996—. Contbr. Harvard Civil Rights/Civil Liberties Law Rev. Mem. ABA, Calif. Bar Assn., L.A. County Bar Assn., Harvard/Radcliffe Club So. Calif., Town Hall Calif., L.A. World Affairs Coun., Sierra Club, Phi Beta Kappa. Presbyterian. Home: 2615 Canada Blvd Apt 208 Glendale CA 91208-2077 Office: US SEC 11th Fl 5670 Wilshire Blvd Los Angeles CA 90036-3648

RICHARDSON, BRUCE LEVOYLE, dentist; b. Corvallis, Oreg., Jan. 28, 1950; s. Richard LeVoyle Richardson and Bonney Willard (Blair) Williams; m. Rhonda Kay Stratton, Sept. ll, 1976; children: Zachary LeVoyle, Nicklis Emery Christopher, Jessica Christine. BS, U. Oreg., 1972; DDS, U. Oreg., Portland, 1977. Pvt. practice Newport, Oreg., 1977—. Chmn. Lincoln County Extension Citizens Adv. Com., 1980-82; trustee Pacific Communities Hosp. Found., 1991; bd. dirs. Lincoln County YMCA, 1983—, chmn. advance gifts campaign, 1984, active current support campaign, 1985, mem. bldg. com., 1985—. Fellow Nat. Acad. Gen. Dentistry (mem. long-range planning com. 1986-88, mem. ann. meeting coun. 1991—, Mastership award 1987); mem. Oreg. Dental Assn. (mem. ho. dels. 1983-87, trustee 1984-87, v.p. 1987-88, pres. 1989—, Oreg. Young Dentist award 1990), Advanced Periodontic Study Club, Lincoln County Study Club, Newport C. of C., Rotary. Republican. Methodist. Avocations: whitewater rafting, camping, fishing, biking, raising cattle. Home: 333 NW Beaver Valley Dr Seal Rock OR 97376-9523 Office: 123 SE Douglas St Newport OR 97365

RICHARDSON, CAMPBELL, lawyer; b. Woodland, Calif., June 18, 1930; s. George Arthur and Mary (Hall) R.; m. Patricia Packwood, Sept. 3, 1958 (dec. Oct. 1971); children: Catherine, Sarah, Thomas; m. Carol Tamblyn, June 1975 (div. Dec. 1977); m. Susan J. Lienhart, May 3, 1980; 1 child, Laura. AB, Dartmouth Coll., 1952; JD, NYU, 1955. Bar: Oreg. 1955, U.S. Dist. Ct. Oreg. 1957. Ptnr. Stoel Rives LLP, Portland, 1964—. Co-author: Contemporary Trust and Will Forms for Oregon Attorneys; contbr. articles to profl. jours. Mem. Portland/Metro Govt. Boundary Commn., 1976; mem. Oreg. Adv. Com. to U.S. Commn. on Civil Rights, 1976-84; bd. dirs. Ctr. for Urban Edn., Portland, 1980-84, Dorchester Conf., Inc., Bend, Oreg., 1982, Friends of the Zoo, 1993—; chmn. planned giving com. St. Vincent Med. Found., 1988—; planned giving com. Oregon Health Scis. Found., 1994—; trustee Met. Family Svc. Found., 1990—. Served with U.S. Army, 1955-57. Mem. ABA, Oreg. Bar Assn., Multnomah County Bar Assn., Estate Planning Coun. Portland (pres. 1978), Am. Coll. Trust and Estate Counsel, City Club, Multnomah Athletic Club (Portland). Republican.ican. Home: 1500 SW 5th Ave Apt 1701 Portland OR 97201-5430 Office: Stoel Rives LLP 900 SW 5th Ave Ste 2300 Portland OR 97204-1232

RICHARDSON, CHARLES CLIFTON, biochemist, educator; b. Wilson, N.C., May 7, 1935; s. Barney Clifton and Florence Elizabeth (Barefoot) R.; m. Ute Ingrid Hanssum, July 29, 1961; children—Thomas Clifton, Matthew Wilfrid. B.S.M., Duke U., 1959, M.D., 1960; A.M. (hon.), Harvard U., 1967. Intern dept. medicine Duke U., Durham, N.C., 1960-61; postdoctoral fellow dept. biochemistry Stanford U. Med. Sch., Calif., 1961-63; asst. prof. biol. chemistry Harvard Med. Sch., Boston, 1964-67, assoc. prof., 1967-69, prof. biol. chemistry, 1969—, chmn. dept. biol. chemistry, 1978-87, Edward S. Wood prof., 1979—; mem. physiol. chemistry study sect. NIH, 1970-74; mem. Fachbeirat of Max-Planck Inst. für Moleculare Genetik, Berlin, Fed. Republic Germany, 1980-89; mem. sci. adv. com. Genetics Inst., Cambridge, Mass., 1986—; mem. Nat. Bd. Med. Examiners, 1973-76; mem. nucleic acids and protein adv. com., Am. Cancer Soc. Inst., 1975-78; mem. vis. com. Boston Biomed. Rsch. Found., 1985—; assoc. Helicon Found., San Diego, Calif., 1983—; bd. dirs. Amersham Life Sci., Inc. Editor: Ann. Rev. Biochemistry, 1983—(assoc. editor 1973-82) ; mem. editorial bd. Jour. Biol. Chemistry, 1968-73, 84-88, Jour. Molecular Biology, 1976-79. Recipient Career Devel. award NIH, 1967-76, Merit award, 1986. Fellow Am. Acad. Arts and Scis., Inst. of Medicine; mem. Nat. Acad. Scis., Am. Chem. Soc.

(Eli Lilly Co. biol. chem. award 1968), Am. Soc. Biol. Chemsits (mem. nominating com. 1974-75, 1983-84), Am. Cancer Soc. (coun. for rsch. and clin. investigation 1989-92), Am. Soc. Biochemistry and Molecular Biology (Merck award in biochemistry and molecular biology 1996).

RICHARDSON, CURTIS JOHN, ecology educator; b. Gouverneur, N.Y., July 27, 1944; s. Nilie John and Rose Marie (LaPierre) R.; m. Carol Bartlett, Aug. 22, 1972; children: John, Suzanne. BS in Biology, SUNY, Cortland, 1966; PhD in Ecology, U. Tenn., 1972. Asst. prof. resource ecology Sch. Natural Resources U. Mich., Ann Arbor, 1972-77; asst. prof. plant ecology U. Mich., Biologican Station, Mich., summer 1973; assoc. prof. resource ecology Sch. Forestry and Environ. Studies Duke U., Durham, N.C., 1977-87, prof. resource ecology, 1988—, dir. Wetland Ctr., 1990—; sr. rsch. fellow in applied ecology and forestry U. Edinburgh, Scotland, 1982; mem. sci. adv. bd. Nat. Wetland Rsch. Plan, U.S. EPA, Washington, 1991, chmn. Nat. Wetland EMAP rev. panel, 1992; panel mgr. competitive grants program water quality USDA, Washington, 1990-91. Mem. AAAS, Am. Inst. Biol. Scis., Am. Soc. Agronomy, Ecol. Soc. Am., Soc. Wetland Scientists (v.p. 1986-87, prs. 1987-88, assoc. editor 1987-93). Avocations: jogging, hiking, fishing. Office: Duke U Wetland Ctr Nichols Sch Environ LSRC Research Dr Durham NC 27708-0333 Home: 717 Anderson St Durham NC 27706

RICHARDSON, DANIEL RALPH, lawyer; b. Pasadena, Calif., Jan. 18, 1945; s. Ralph Claude and Rosemary Clare (Lowery) R.; m. Virginia Ann Lorton, Sept. 4, 1965; children: Brian Daniel, Neil Ryan. BS, Colo. State U., 1969; MBA, St. Mary's Coll. of Calif., 1977; JD, JFK U., 1992. Bar: Calif. Systems engr. Electronic Data Systems, San Francisco, 1972-73; programmer/analyst Wells Fargo Bank, San Francisco, 1973-74; systems analyst Crown-Zellerbach Corp., San Francisco, 1974; programming mgr. Calif. Dental Svc., San Francisco, 1974-75, Fairchild Camera and Inst., Mountain View, Calif., 1975-77; sr. systems analyst Bechtel Corp., San Francisco, 1977; pres. Richardson Software Cons., Inc., San Francisco, 1977—; pvt. practice San Francisco, 1993—; instr. data processing Diablo Valley Coll., Concord, Calif., 1979-80. Author: (book) System Development Life Cycle, 1976, (computer software) The Richardson Automated Agent, 1985. Asst. scoutmaster Boy Scouts Am., Clayton, Calif., 1983-91; soccer coach Am. Youth Soccer League, Clayton, 1978-83. 1st lt. USAF, 1966-72. Mem. ABA, State Bar Calif., Computer Law Assn., Acad. Profl. Cons. and Advisers (cert. profl. cons.), Assn. Systems Mgrs., San Francisco C. of C., San Francisco Better Bus. Bur. Avocations: travel, reading, writing, computer repair. Office: 870 Market St #400 San Francisco CA 94102

RICHARDSON, DAVID BACON, writer, journalist; b. Maplewood, N.J., July 13, 1916; s. Percy Bacon and Elizabeth (Jones) R.; m. Ruth Cummings (dec.); children: Hilary C., Julia R. Neilson, Francesca Richardson-Allen; m. Anne Phelan Werner, Oct. 8, 1994. BA, Ind. U., 1940; postgrad. press fellow, Princeton U., 1953-54. Sports reporter Daily Courier, Orange, N.J., 1934-36; mng. editor, editor-in-chief Ind. Daily Student, 1939-40; editorial staff N.Y. Herald Tribune, N.Y.C., 1940-41; combat corres. Yank, The Army Weekly, PTO, 1942-45; corr. Time Mag., India, 1945-46, Fed. Republic Germany, 1947-50, U.K., 1950-52, Mideast, 1952-53, Mex., 1954-56; bur. chief S.Am. U.S. News & World Report, Buenos Aires, 1959-64; chief domestic news burs. U.S. News & World Report, Washington, 1964-73; chief European corr. U.S. News & World Report, Rome, 1974-81; chief nat. corr. U.S. News & World Report, Washington, 1981-82; freelance writer Washington, 1983—; lectr. in field, 1986—. Contbr. to books The Best From Yank, 1945, Yank, the GI Story of the War, 1947. V.p., bd. dirs. Iona Sr. Svcs., 1993-96; pres., bd. dirs. Greenbriar Condo., Washington, 1984-87; comms. adviser Samaritan Ministry, 1989—. Decorated Legion of Merit, Bronze Star; recipient Valor medal Nat. Headliners Club, Disting. Alumni Svc. award Ind. U. Mem. Coun. Fgn. Rels., Washington Inst. Fgn. Affairs, Overseas Writers Assn., Soc. Profl. Journalists, Merrill's Marauders Assn. (mil. liaison officer 1995—), Internat. Combat Camera Assn., Cosmos Club. Episcopalian. Home and Office: #1014 E 4201 Cathedral Ave NW Washington DC 20016-4901

RICHARDSON, DAVID JOHN, ballet dancer, educator; b. Middletown, N.Y., Mar. 2, 1943; s. Fred and Helen (Anderson) R. Grad., high sch., Pine Bush, N.Y. Dancer Am. Ballet Theatre, N.Y.C., 1961-63, ballet master, 1983—; dancer N.Y.C. Ballet, 1963-83, asst. ballet master, 1976-83. Repertoire includes (with N.Y.C. Ballet) Jerome Robbins' The Goldberg Variations, George Balanchine's The Four Temperaments, Firebird, Episodes, Antony Tudor's Dim Lustre; staged various ballets including Circus Polka, Paris Opera Ballet, 1974, San Francisco Ballet, 1979, Royal Danish Ballet, 1984, Le Tombeau de Couperin, Paris Opera Ballet, 1975, Coppelia, Asami Maki Ballet, Tokyo, 1981, The Leaves Are Fading, Star Dancers Ballet, Tokyo, 1991, Bruch Violin Concert No. 1, Scottish Ballet, 1993; staged annual performances of George Balanchine's The Nutcracker, Stamford City Ballet, Pa. Ballet, 1988, Pittsburgh Ballet Theatre, 1990, Miami City Ballet, 1992; TV credits include Choreography by Balanchine Parts I and II, PBS, Coppelia, PBS, A Tribute to George Balanchine, PBS, The Nutcracker, CBS, Edward Villella's Little Women, NBC, Lee Theodore's Kiss Me, Kate, NBC, (children's choreographer) Baryshnikov at the White House. Office: Am Ballet Theater 890 Broadway New York NY 10003-1211

RICHARDSON, DAVID WALTHALL, cardiologic educator, consultant; b. Nanking, China, Mar. 22, 1925; s. Donald William and Virginia (McIlwaine) R.; m. Frances Lee Wingfield, June 12, 1948; children—Donald, Sarah, David. B.S., Davidson Coll., 1947; M.D., Harvard U., 1951. Diplomate Am. Bd. Internal Medicine, Am. Bd. Cardiology. Intern, resident Yale New Haven Hosp., Conn., 1951-53; resident, fellow Med. Coll. Va., Richmond, 1953-56, assoc. prof. to prof. medicine, 1962-95, prof. emeritus, 1995—, chmn. div. cardiology, 1972-87; interim chmn. dept. medicine, 1973-74; chief cardiology, assoc. chief staff for rsch. VA Hosp., Richmond, 1956-61, dir. cardiology tng. program, 1990-95; vis. scientist Oxford U., Eng., 1961-62; vis. prof. U. Milan, Italy, 1972-73. Contbr. articles to profl. jours. Moderator Hanover Presbytery, Presbyterian Ch. U.S., Richmond, 1970; chmn. events com. NHLBI Cardiac Arrhythmia Suppression Trial, 1983-92. Served with USN, 1944-46. Fellow. Am. Coll. Cardiology (gov. VA. 1970-72), Am. Heart Assn. (coun. clin. cardiology and high blood pressure rsch.); mem. Am. Soc. Clin. Investigation, Am. Clin. and Climatol. Assn. Home: 5501 Queensbury Rd Richmond VA 23226-2121

RICHARDSON, DEAN EUGENE, retired banker; b. West Branch, Mich., Dec. 27, 1927; s. Robert F. and Helen (Husted) R.; m. Barbara Trytten, June 14, 1952; children: Ann Elizabeth, John Matthew. AB, Mich. State U., 1950; JD, U. Mich., 1953; postgrad., Stonier Grad. Sch. Banking, 1965. With Indsl. Nat. Bank, Detroit, 1953-55; with Mfrs. Nat. Bank, Detroit, 1955-90; v.p. adminstrn. Mfrs. Nat. Bank, 1964-66, sr. v.p., 1966-67, exec. v.p., 1967-69, pres., 1969-73, chmn. bd. dirs., 1973-89, chmn. exec. com., 1989-90; chmn. bd. Mfrs.-Detroit Internat. Corp., 1973-90; chmn. exec. com. Mfrs. Nat. Bank, 1989-90; bd. dirs. Detroit Edison Co., Tecumseh Products Co., AAA of Mich. Served with USNR, 1945-46. Mem. Mich. Bar Assn., Detroit Bar Assn., Masons, KT, Detroit Athletic Club Country Club Detroit. Episcopalian. Office: Comerica Bank Bldg 20180 Mack Ave Grosse Pointe MI 48236-1839

RICHARDSON, DON ORLAND, agricultural educator; b. Auglaize County, Ohio, May 12, 1934; s. Dana Orland and Mary Isabell (Bowersock) R.; m. Shirley Ann Richardson (div. 1982); children: Daniel, Bradley, Eric, Laura. BS, Ohio State U., 1956, MS, 1957, PhD, 1961. Asst. prof. to prof. U. Tenn., Knoxville, 1963—, head Animal Sci. Dept., 1982-88, dean Agrl. Exptl. Sta., 1988—. Mem. Am. Dairy Sci. Assn., Am. Soc. Animal Sci., Coun. Agrl. Sci. and Tech., Holstein Assn. Am., Rotary Club Knoxville. Office: Tenn Agrl Exptl Sta 103 Morgan Hall PO Box 1071 Knoxville TN 37901-1071

RICHARDSON, DONN CHARLES, business and marketing educator; b. Indpls., Mar. 3, 1940; s. George Covey and Edythe Francis (Chesterfield) R.; m. Carolyn Jean Hassan, Nov. 8, 1969; children: Bradley George, Jason Arthur, Christopher Charles. BA in Journalism and Polit. Sci., Butler U., 1962; MA in Mass Comm., Ohio State U., 1969. Staff editor Cin. Bell Mag. Cin. (Ohio) Bell, 1969-73; mgmt. newsletter editor, spl. projects mgr. US West Comms., Denver, 1973-76; Colo. pub. rels. and outreach dir. US West Comms., Boulder, 1976-84, Colo. employee comm. mgr., 1984-85, market mgr. market planning, 1986-88; fed. govt. market mgr. US West Comms., Englewood, Colo., 1989-94; pres. Richardson Info. Resources, Boulder, Colo., 1994—; cons. Northglenn (Colo.) Recreation Ctr., 1982; presenter in field. Author, pub.: The Quick Consultant's Guide to Public Speaking; contbr. articles to profl. jours. Pres. Shannon Estates Homeowners Assn., Boulder, 1978-80; pub. rels. dir. Boulder (Colo.) Mental Health Ctr. Benefit, 1980; publicity dir. FC Boulder (Colo.) Soccer Club, 1991-94. Capt. USAF, 1963-69. Mem. Internat. Assn. Bus. Communicators (dist. profl. devel. chair 1982-84, chpt. v.p. 1985, internat. pub. rels. chair 1985-86, accredited bus. communicator), Pub. Rels. Soc. Am. (accredition judge 1989, accredited pub. rels. profl.). Avocations: youth recreation coaching, traveling. Home: 1212 Cavan St Boulder CO 80303-1602

RICHARDSON, DOUGLAS FIELDING, lawyer; b. Glendale, Calif., Mar. 17, 1929; s. James D. and Dorothy (Huskins) R.; m. Leni Tempelaar-Lietz, June 26, 1959; children—Arthur Wilhelm, John Douglas. A.B., UCLA, 1950; J.D., Harvard U., 1953. Bar: Calif. 1953. Assoc. O'Melveny & Myers, Los Angeles, 1953-68, ptnr., 1968-86, of counsel, 1986—. Author: (with others) Drafting Agreements for the Sale of Businesses, 1971, Term Loan Handbook, 1983. Bd. govs. Town Hall of Calif., L.A., 1974-87, sec., 1977, v.p., 1978-79, pres., 1984, mem. adv. coun., 1987—, chmn. sect. on legis. and adminstrn. of justice, 1968-70, pres. Town Hall West, 1975, mem. exec. bd., 1973-93; bd. dirs. Hist. Soc. Calif., 1976-82, pres., 1980-81; bd. dirs. Alliance Francaise de Pasadena, treas., 1993-95. Mem. ABA (com. on devels. in bus. financing, com. state regulation of securities, com. corp. law and acctg., com. employee benefits and exec. compensation of sect corp. banking and bus. law.), Calif. Bar Assn., Los Angeles County Bar Assn. (chmn. com. Law Day 1968, exec. com. comml. law sect. 1974-78, exec. com. corp. law sect. 1975-86), Kiwanis, Phi Beta Kappa. Republican. Presbyterian (elder). Clubs: California, Harvard So. Calif. Home: 1637 Valley View Rd Glendale CA 91202-1340 Office: O'Melveny & Myers 400 S Hope St Los Angeles CA 90071-2801

RICHARDSON, EDWARD R., state agency administrator; b. Pensacola, Fla., Jan. 24, 1939; s. Edward H. and Doria (Parker) R.; m. Nell C.; children: Merit Lynn Richardson Smith, Laura Leigh. BS, Auburn U., 1962, MEd, 1967, EdD, 1972. Sci. tchr. Montgomery Pub. Schs., Montgomery, Ala., 1962-64; prin. Montgomery Pub. Schs., 1967-70, Andalusia High Sch., Andalusia, Ala., 1972-80; asst. prof. Auburn U., Montgomery, 1980-82; supt. Auburn City Schs., Auburn, Ala., 1982-95, state of Ala., Montgomery, 1995—; bd. mem. So. Regional Edn. Bd., Atlanta, 1989—; co-dir. Ala. Mgmt. Inst. Sch. Leaders, Montgomery, 1980-82. Ednl. advisor Gov. Guy Hunt, Montgomery, 1987—; active Landmarks Found., Montgomery, 1968-69. Named Supt. of Yr., State PTA, Montgomery, 1986-87, Educator of Yr., Andalusia Jaycees, 1973-74. Mem. Ala. Assn. Secondary Sch. Adminstrs. (pres. 1978-79), Ala. Assn. Sch. Adminstrs. (pres. 1986-87), Rotary (Auburn chpt. pres. 1987-88), Capitol Lions Club (pres. 1968-69), Phi Delta Kappa (Auburn U. chpt. pres. 1971-72). Republican. Methodist. Avocations: tennis, reading, gardening. Home: 1309 Gatewood Dr Apt 1204 Auburn AL 36830-2836 Office: Ala Dept of Edn 5303 Gordon Persons Bldg PO Box 302101 Montgomery AL 36130-2101

RICHARDSON, ELLIOT LEE, lawyer; b. Boston, July 20, 1920; s. Edward P. and Clara (Shattuck) R.; m. Anne F. Hazard, Aug. 2, 1952; children: Henry, Nancy, Michael. AB cum laude, Harvard U., 1941, LLB cum laude, 1947, LLD (hon.), 1971; other hon. degrees. Bar: Mass. 1949, D.C. 1980. Law clk. Judge Learned Hand, U.S. Ct. Appeals (2d cir.), N.Y., 1947-48, Supreme Ct. Justice Felix Frankfurter, 1948-49; assoc. Ropes, Gray, Best, Coolidge & Rugg, Boston, 1949-53, 55-56; asst. to Mass. Senator Leverett Saltonstall, 1953-54; acting counsel to Mass. Gov. Christian A. Herter, 1956; asst. sec. legis. HEW, 1957-59; U.S. atty. for Mass., 1959-61, spl. asst. to atty. gen. U.S., 1961; ptnr. Ropes & Gray, Boston, 1961-64; lt. gov. Mass., 1965-67, atty. gen. Mass., 1967-69, under sec. state, 1969-70; sec. HEW, 1970-73; sec. def., 1973, atty. gen. U.S., 1973; fellow Woodrow Wilson Internat. Ctr. for Scholars, Washington, 1974-75; ambassador Ct. St. James's, London, 1975-76; sec. commerce, 1976-77; ambassador-at-large, spl. rep. of pres. Law of Sea Conf., Washington, 1977-80; sr. ptnr. Milbank, Tweed, Hadley & McCloy, Washington, 1980-92; personal rep. SG of UN for Nicaraguan Elections, 1989-90; spl. rep. of Pres. of U.S. for multilateral assistance in The Philippines, 1989-94; bd. dirs. Oak Industries, BNFL Inc.; mem. adv. bd. Am. Flywheel Systems; former dir. John Hancock Life Ins. Co. Author: The Creative Balance, 1976; contbr. numerous articles to profl. jours. and others. Former trustee Radcliffe Coll., Mass. Gen. Hosp.; hon. trustee Roger Tory Peterson Inst.; pres. World Affairs Coun., Boston; dir. Mass. Bay United Fund, past chmn. Greater Boston United Fund Campaign; mem. bd. overseers Harvard Coll.; chmn. overseers com. to visit John F. Kennedy Sch. Govt., Harvard U.; mem. overseers com. to visit Harvard U. Law Sch.; bd. dirs. U.S. Coun. Internat. Bus., Urban Inst.; chmn. Coun. on Ocean Law, Hitachi Found., Japan-Am. Soc. Washington; co-chmn. Nat. Coun., UN Assn. U.S.; chmn. overseers com. to visit Harvard Med. Sch. and Sch. Dental Medicine; vice chmn. Citizens Network Fgn. Affairs; mem. Compt. Gen.'s cons. panel; chmn. quality rev. bd. GAO; mem. adv. com. for commemoration World War II, Dept. Def.; bd. dirs. Am. Acad. Diplomacy. Served to 1st lt. inf. U.S. Army, 1942-45. Decorated Bronze Star, Purple Heart with oak leaf cluster, Légion d'Honneur; recipient Jefferson award Am. Inst. Pub. Svc., Thomas Hart Benton award Kansas City Art Inst., Emory R. Buckner medal Fed. Bar Coun., Penn Club award, Albert Lasker Spl. Pub. Svc. award, Neptune award, Meritorious Pub. Svc. award USCG, Harry Truman Good Neighbor award, Spkr. Thomas P. O'Neill Jr. award for pub. svc., Sam Rayburn award, F.D. Roosevelt Freedom medal, and other awards. Fellow AAAS, Am. Bar Found., Mass. Bar Found.; mem. ABA, ASPA, D.C. Bar Assn., Mass. Bar Assn., Harvard U. Alumni Assn. (former elected dir.), Coun. on Fgn. Rels., Am. Law Inst., Am. Soc. Internat. Law, Bretton Woods Com., Am. Acad. Diplomacy, Am. Acad. Social Ins., Internat. Law Assn., Nat. Acad. Pub. Adminstrn., Coun. on Excellence in Govt., DAV, VFW, Am. Legion, Alfalfa Club, F Street Club. Office: Milbank Tweed Hadley McCloy 1825 I St NW Ste 1100 Washington DC 20006-5403

RICHARDSON, ERNEST RAY (ROCKY RICHARDSON), housing program supervisor; b. Dermott, Ark., Sept. 5, 1932; s. Louis Jr. and Leila Mae (Purdom) R.; m. Deloris Cobb, Mar. 25, 1955 (div. Apr. 1964); children: Victor Ray, Rodney Lynn, Regenia Ann; stepchildren, Denise Nelson, Darrin Hicks; m. Doretha Tolbert, Apr. 1964 (div. June 1978); m. Shirley Ann Johnson, June 8, 1978; 1 child, Kimberly Ann; stepchildren: Janet, Kay, and Jerome Pate. BA in Bus. Adminstrn., Franklin U., 1975; AA in Real Estate, Parkland Coll., 1980; postgrad., Lewis U., 1980-83. Cert. real estate broker, Ill. Dir. edn. & tng. Champaign County Opportunities Industrialization Ctr., Champaign, Ill., 1968-70, exec. dir., pers. dir., 1970-73; fin. specialist City of Urbana, Ill., 1975-79; fin. specialist City of Joliet, Ill., 1979-82, dir. neighborhood svcs. divsn., 1982-87; exec. pers. dir. Aurora (Ill.) Housing Authority, 1987-89; housing program supr. City of Modesto, Calif., 1979—; mem. adv. com. Ctrl. Valley Opportunities Ctr., Inc. Modesto, 1992-96; vice chmn. mgmt. devel. com., City of Modesto, 1993-94, mem. mgmts. continuous improvement com., 1995, 96; mem. funds allocation rev. com. Nat. Opportunities Industrialization Ctr., 1971-72. Sgt. USAF, 1951-67. Mem. nat. Assn. Real Estate Appraisers (pres.-elect Ill. chpt. 1984-85, pres. Ill. chpt. 1985-86, Ill. chpt. Mem. of the Yr., 1988), Am. Legion, Modesto Kiwanis Club. Avocations: income tax business and real estate appraisal, walking, reading, travel. Home: 309 Yuba Ridge Ln Modesto CA 95354-3369 Office: City of Modesto Ofc Housing/Neighborhoods 940 11th St Modesto CA 95354-2319

RICHARDSON, EVERETT VERN, hydraulic engineer, educator, administrator, consultant; b. Scottsbluff, Nebr., Jan. 5, 1924; s. Thomas Otis and Jean Marie (Everett) R.; m. Billie Ann Kleckner, June 23, 1948; children—Gail Lee, Thomas Everett, Jerry Ray. B.S., Colo. State U., 1949, M.S., 1960, Ph.D., 1965. Registered profl. engr., Colo. Hydraulic engr. U.S. Geol. Survey, Wyo., 1949-52; hydraulic engr. U.S. Geol. Survey, Iowa, 1953-56; rsch. hydraulic engr. U.S. Geol. Survey, Ft. Collins, Colo., 1956-63, project chief, 1963-68; prof. civil engring., adminstr. engring. rsch. ctr. Colo. State U., Ft. Collins, 1968-82, prof. in charge of hydraulic program, 1982-88, prof. civil engring., 1988-94, prof. emeritus, 1994—, dir. hydraulic lab. engring. rsch. ctr., 1982-88, dir. Egypt water use project, 1977-84, dir. Egypt irrigation improvement project, 1985-90; dir. Egypt Water Rsch. Ctr. Egypt Water Rsch. Ctr. Project, Ft. Collins, 1988-89; sr. assoc. Ayers Assocs. Inc. (formerly Resource Cons./Engrs., Inc.), Ft. Collins, Colo., 1989-93, Ayres Assocs., Ft. Collins, Colo., 1994—; dir. Consortium for Internat. Devel., Tucson, Ariz., 1972-87; cons. in field. Editor: Highways in the River Environment, Fed. Hwy. Adminstrn., 1975, 90, Evolutionary Scour at Bridges, Fed. Hwy. Adminstrn., 1991n 93n 95; contbr. articles to profl. jours., chpts. in books. Mem. Ft. Collins Water Bd., 1969-84; mem. N.Y. State Bridge Safety Assurance Task Force, 1988-91. Decorated Bronze Star, Purple Heart; Combat Infantry Badge, U.S. Govt. fellow MIT, 1962-63. Fellow ASCE (J.S. Stevens award 1961, chair task force com., chair tech com. bridge scour rsch. 1990-96, hydraulics divsn. excellence award, 1993); mem. Internat. Congress for Irrigation and Drainage (bd. dirs.), Sigma Xi, Chi Epsilon, Sigma Tau. Home: 824 Gregory Rd Fort Collins CO 80524-1504 Office: Ayres Assocs PO Box 270460 Fort Collins CO 80527-0460

RICHARDSON, F. C., academic administrator; b. Memphis, Sept. 22, 1936; m. Bernice Tanner. AB in Biology, Rust Coll., 1960; MS in Biology, Atlanta U., 1964; PhD in Botany, U. Calif., Santa Barbara, 1967. Asst. prof. botany Ind. U. N.W., Gary, 1967-71, assoc. prof., 1971-82, prof., 1982-84, chair dept. biology, 1971-72, chair div. arts and scis., 1972-84; prof. Jackson (Miss.) State U., 1984-85, v.p. for acad. affairs, 1984-85; v.p. for acad. affairs Moorhead (Minn.) State U., 1985-89; prof. SUNY Coll. at Buffalo, 1989, pres., 1989—; cons., evaluator North Ctrl. Assn., 1987-89; mem. commn. on elem. schs. Mid. States Assn., 1990—; mem. Commn. on Minorities in Higher Edn., Am. Coun. on Edn.; mem. task force on outcomes and accountability Coun. on Postsecondary Edn., 1991—. Mem. editorial bd. Negro Ednl. Rev., 1977—, exec. editor, 1981—; contbr. numerous articles to profl. jours. Mem. fellowship selection com. for Martin Luther King, Jr. Fellowship Program, Woodrow Wilson Nat. Fellowship Found., Chgo., 1969-74; bd. dirs. Lake County Assn. for Retarded Citizens, 1969-75; chair Ind. U. N.W./Community Adv. Bd. for Spl. Svcs., 1970-74; mem. Gary Air Pollution Control Adv. Bd., 1970-84, chair; chair steering com. for creation of Gary Neighborhood Svcs., Inc., 1970-71, bd. dirs., 1971-84; mem. N.W. Ind. Clean Air Coordinating Com., N.W. Ind., 1970-73, Comprehensive Health Planning Coun., 1971-75, Com. on Sci. and Tech. R&D, State of Minn., 1987, Moorhead Chamber Edn. Task Force, 1987-88; mem. Gary Bd. Health, 1972-82, sec., 1976-79, pres., 1979-82; bd. dirs. Meth. Hosps., Gary, 1973-84, Med. Ctr. of Gary, Inc., 1975-81, Greater Buffalo Devel. Found., 1989—, Buffalo Soc. Natural Scis., 1989—, Western N.Y. Tech. Devel. Ctr., Inc., 1991—, Buffalo Fine Arts Acad., 1991—; mem. Lake area planning and allocation com. United Way, 1981-83, chair Lake area campaign exec. group, 1982-83, bd. dirs. United Way Buffalo and Erie County, 1990—; mem. local organizing com. World Univ. Games 1993, 1989—; mem. bd. govs. NCCJ of Western N.Y., 1989—. Univ. scholar Atlanta U., 1962-64; fellow NSF, 1966, U. Calif., 1967-68. Mem. Am. Inst. Biol. Scis., Bot. Soc. Am., Internat. Soc. Plant Morphologists, Am. Assn. State Colls. and Univs. (SCAN team 1986). Home: 152 Lincoln Pky Buffalo NY 14222-1012 Office: SUNY Coll at Buffalo Office of Pres 1300 Elmwood Ave Buffalo NY 14222-1004

RICHARDSON, FRANK H., retired oil industry executive; b. Mar. 15, 1933. BS, South Dakota Sch. Mines, 1955. With Shell Oil Co., Houston, 1955-93, exec. v.p., 1983-88, pres., CEO, 1988-93. Address: 2001 Kirby Dr Ste 504 Houston TX 77019-6033

RICHARDSON, GORDON BANNING, insurance company executive, investment consultant; b. N.Y.C., May 19, 1937; s. Ogden Barker and May Thistle (Shirres) R.; m. Judy Carolyn Williams, May 7, 1966; children: Gordon Banning II, Randall S. Student Ashbury Coll., Ottawa, Ont., Can., 1956, Tex. A&M, 1971; BS in Bus. Adminstrn., Boston U., 1962; CLU, Am. Coll., 1974; AEP, NAEDC, 1995. Owner, pres. Ins. Assocs., Caldwell, Tex., 1968—. Recipient Hon. State Farmer award Future Farmers Am., 1975. Mem. Tex. Assn. Life Underwriters (pres. 1989-90), Confederate Air Force (sponsor), Million Dollar Round Table (life), Sigma Alpha Epsilon, Mass Beta Upsilon (life). Baptist. Lodge: Lions (dist. gov. 1981-82).

RICHARDSON, HERBERT HEATH, mechanical engineer, educator, institute director; b. Lynn, Mass., Sept. 24, 1930; s. Walter Blake and Isabel Emily (Heath) R.; m. Barbara Ellsworth, Oct. 6, 1973. SB, SM with honors, MIT, 1955, ScD, 1958. Registered profl. engr., Mass., Tex. Research asst., research engr. Dynamic Analysis and Control Lab. MIT, 1953-57, instr. Dept. Mech. Engring., 1957-58, mem. faculty, 1958-84, prof. mech. engring., 1968-85, head dept., 1974-82, assoc. dean engring., 1982-84; Disting. prof. engring. Tex. A&M U., 1984—; Regents prof. Tex. A&M U. System, College Station, 1993—; dean, vice chancellor engring. Tex. A&M U. Sys., 1984-85; dep. chancellor, dean, dir. Tex. Engring. Expt. Sta. Tex. A&M U., 1985-91; chancellor Tex. A&M U. System, College Station, 1991-93, assoc. vice chancellor engring., 1993—, assoc. dean engring., 1993—; dir. Tex. Trans. Inst., Tex. A&M Univ. Sys., 1993—; with Ballistics Rsch. Lab. Abderdeen Proving Ground, Md., 1958; chief scientist U.S. Dept. Transp., 1970-72; bd. dirs. Foster-Miller Inc., Mass., Ten X Inc., Tex. Utilities Co.; chmn. adv. com. for engring. NSF, 1987-89, adv. com. basic energy scis. U.S. Dept. Energy, 1987-91. Author: Introduction to System Dynamics, 1971; contbr. articles to profl. publs. Trustee S.W. Rsch. Inst. Officer U.S. Army, 1968. Recipient medal Am. Ordnance Assn., 1953, Gold medal Pi Tau Sigma, 1963, Meritorious Service award and medal Dept. Transp., 1972. Fellow AAAS, ASME (Moody award fluid engring. divsn. 1970, Centennial medallion 1983, Rufus Oldenberger medal 1984, Meritorious Svc. medal 1986, Disting. Svc. award 1986, hon. mem. 1987); mem. NAE (coun. 1986-92, com. on engring. edn.), Am. Soc. Engring. Edn. (Disting. Svc. medal 1993), N.Y. Acad. Sci., Inst. Transp. Engrs., Nat. Rsch. Coun. (gov. bd. 1986-92, chmn. transp. rsch. bd. 1988-89), Sigma Xi, Tau Beta Pi. Office: Tex A&M U Sys CE TTI Bldg MS 3135 College Station TX 77843-3135

RICHARDSON, HOLLIS MALCOLM, electrical engineer, researcher; b. Fortson, Ga., June 19, 1908; s. Philip Woodson and Exa Estelle (Martin) R.; m. Jane Caroline Brueser, Sept. 4, 1937; children; Robert Hollis, Carol Vade. BS in Elect. Engring., Ga. Inst. Tech., 1931. Test and appl. engr. Radio Corp Am., Harrison, N.J., 1932-36; electronic sales engr. Westinghouse lamp divsn., Bloomfield, N.J., 1937-39; sr. project engr. microwave radio system Western Union Telegraph Co., N.Y.C., 1940-67; elec. and electronic engr. Picatinny Arsenal, Dover, N.J., 1967-78; retired, 1978. Author: What Makes the Earth Tick?, 1990 (Key to Borough of Morris Plains); speaker to toastmasters groups, service clubs, other orgns. on the Macroatomic Theory (his development) and other related subjects. Pres., program chmn. Drop-in Ctr. Sr. Group, United Meth. Ch., Morristown, N.J., 1982-92; mem. speakers bur., think tank Retired Sr. Vol. Program, Morris Plains, 1980—. Mem. Morris Mus. Astron. Soc., Am. Geophys. Union, Toastmasters Internat., Phi Kappa Phi, Sigma Xi. Republican. Avocations: contract bridge, gardening, public speaking. Home: 32 Dogwood Rd Morris Plains NJ 07950-1919

RICHARDSON, IRENE M., health facility administrator; b. Columbia, Tenn., Oct. 22, 1938; d. John Frank and Beatrice (Hill) Murphy; m. Joseph Richardson, Dec. 27, 1960; children: Pamela, Joseph, John, Karen. BS, Ramapo Coll., Mahwah, N.J., 1981; MBA, Farleigh Dickinson U., 1987; nursing diploma summa cum laude, St. Thomas Sch. of Nursing, Nashville, 1959. RN, N.J.; cert. sr. profl. in human resources. Clin. instr. St. Thomas Hosp., Nashville; coord. edn., staff nurse St. Clare's Hosp., Denville, N.J.; pres. Cygnus Assocs., Inc., Kinnelon, N.J., 1986-95; dir. edn. and tng. Northwest Covenant Med. Ctr. (formerly St. Clares Riverside), Denville, N.J., 1995—. Author: RN Job Satisfaction. Recipient U.S. Pub. Health Svc. scholarship. Mem. Am. Soc. for Health Care Edn. and Tng., Soc. for Health Care Edn. and Tng. N.J. (bd. dirs.), Women's Svc. Orgn. (pres. 1995-96). Home: 65 Fayson Lake Rd Kinnelon NJ 07405-3129

RICHARDSON, J. DAVID, surgeon; b. Morehead, Ky., 1945. MD, U. Ky., 1970. Diplomate Am. Bd. Surgeons, Am. Bd. Vascular Surgery, Am. Bd. Thoracic Surgery, Am. Bd. SCC. Intern U. Ky. Med. Ctr., Lexington, 1970, resident, 1971-72; resident U. Tex., San Antonio, 1972-76; surgeon Norton Kosair Children's Hosp., Louisville, Ky., 1977—; prof. surgery U. Louisville, 1979—. Fellow ACS; mem. AMA, AAST, SSAT, Alpah Omega Alpha. Office: U Louisville Dept Surgery 530 S Jackson St Louisville KY 40292*

RICHARDSON, JANE, librarian; b. Sept. 16, 1946; d. Robert Clark and Evagene (Davis) Richardson; m. Frank Velasques Martinez Jr., May 28, 1966 (div. July 1970); 1 child, Robert Louis Martinez; m. William John Lorance, Feb. 14, 1983 (div. 1996). BA in History, U. Wyo., 1971; MLibr,

U. Wash., 1972. Reference and fine arts libr. Clark County Libr., 1973; dept. head Clark County Libr. Dist., 1974-77; br. supr./adminstr. Newport Beach (Calif.) Pub. Libr., 1978-82; on-call libr. Santa Ana and Newport Beach Pub. Librs., Calif. State U., Fullerton, 1984; br. adminstr. Las Vegas-Clark County Libr. Dist., 1985—. Mem. Freedom to Read Found. Mem. ALA, Popular Culture Assn., Nev. Libr. Assn., Mountain Plains Libr. Assn., So. Calif. On-Line Users Group, Newport Beach Profl. and Tech. Employees Assn. Office: Las Vegas-Clark County Libr 833 Las Vegas Blvd N Las Vegas NV 89101-2030

RICHARDSON, JEROME JOHNSON, food service company executive; b. 1936; married. AB, Wofford Coll., Spartanburg, S.C., 1959. Profl. football player Balt. Colts, 1959-61; pres. Spartan Food Systems Inc., Spartanburg, S.C., 1962-86, Spartan Food Systems div. TWS, Spartanburg, 1986-89; pres., chief exec. officer Spartan Food Systems Inc., Spartanburg, 1989—, chmn., 1990—; pres., chief exec. officer Denny's, Inc., 1988, chmn., 1989—; pres., chief exec. officer Canteen Corp., 1989—; pres. TWS, Spartanburg, 1987-89, pres., chief exec officer, 1989—, also bd. dirs.; pres., chief exec. officer TWH, Spartanburg, 1989—; chmn., dir. Flagstar Cos.; now owner/founder Carolina Panthers; bd. dirs. Isotechnologies Inc., Sonat Inc., Spartan Mills. Bd. dirs. NCAA Found. Address: Canteen Corp 222 N La Salle St Chicago IL 60601-1003*

RICHARDSON, JOAN, reporter. Edn. reporter Detroit Free Press. Office: Detroit Free Press 321 W Lafayette Blvd Detroit MI 48226-2705

RICHARDSON, JOHN, retired international relations executive; b. Boston, Feb. 4, 1921; s. John and Hope (Hemenway) R.; m. Thelma Ingram, Jan. 19, 1945; children: Eva Selek Teleki, Teren de Cossy, Hope Gravelly, Catherine Munch, Hetty L. A.B., Harvard U., 1943, J.D., 1949. Bar: N.Y. 1949. Assoc. Sullivan & Cromwell, N.Y.C., 1949-55; with Paine, Webber, Jackson & Curtis, N.Y.C., 1955-69, gen. ptnr., 1958-61, ltd. ptnr., 1961-69; pres., chief exec. officer Free Europe, Inc. (Radio Free Europe), 1961-68; asst. sec. for ednl. and cultural affairs Dept. State, 1969-77, also acting asst. sec. state for pub. affairs, 1971-73; exec. dir. for social policy Ctr. for Strategic and Internat. Studies; research prof. internat. communication Sch. Fgn. Service, Georgetown U., Washington, 1977-78; pres., chief exec. officer Youth for Understanding, Inc., 1978-86, bd. dirs., 1986—, vice chmn., 1989—; counselor U.S. Inst. of Peace, 1987-90; spl. advisor Aspen Inst. Humanistic Studies, 1977-80. Mem. Coun. Fgn. Rels., 1957—, Citizens Commn. on S.E. Asian Refugees, 1978—; founder Polish Med. Aid Project, 1957-61; co-founder, chmn. bd. Am. Com. to Aid Poland, 1989-95; pres. Internat. Rescue Com., 1960-61, bd. dirs., 1958-61, 78—; chmn. N.Y.C. Met. Mission United Ch. of Christ, 1966-69, Am. Coun. for UN U., 1977-87, Consortium for Internat. Citizens Exch., 1980-84; bd. dirs. Coun. for Advancement of Citizenship, 1991, Delphi Internat., 1991—, chmn., 1995—, Freedom House, 1963-69, pres., 1977-84; chmn. Nat. Endowment for Democracy, 1984-88, 91-92, bd. dirs., 1984-92, chmn. emeritus, 1992—; bd. dirs. Kennedy Ctr. for Performing Arts, 1970-77, Inter-Am. Found., 1970-77, East-West Ctr., 1975-77, Fgn. Policy Assn., 1958-68, 77-86, Japan-U.S. Friendship Commn., 1976-77, Am. Forum, 1977—, Social Sci. Found., U. Denver, 1992—, Meridian House Internat., 1978-83, Atlantic Coun. U.S., 1982-84, Fgn. Student Svc. Coun., 1978-82. With U.S. Army, World War II. Decorated Bronze Star with v device, Order of the Sacred Treasure, Gold and Silver Star, Japan; Commdr.'s. Cross, Order of Merit Fed. Republic Germany. Home: # 1104 9707 Old George Town Rd Bethesda MD 20814-1727

RICHARDSON, JOHN CARROLL, lawyer, tax legislative consultant; b. Mobile, Ala., May 3, 1932; s. Robert Felder and Louise (Simmons) R.; m. Cicely Tomlinson, July 27, 1961; children: Nancy Louise, Robert Felder III, Leslie. BA, Tulane U., 1954; LLB cum laude, Harvard U., 1960. Bar: Colo. 1960, N.Y. 1965, D.C. 1972. Assoc. Holland & Hart, Denver, 1960-64; legal v.p. Hoover Worldwide Corp., N.Y.C., 1964-69; v.p., gen. counsel Continental Investment Corp., Boston, 1969; dep. tax legis. counsel U.S. Dept. Treasury, Washington, 1970-71, tax legis. counsel, 1972-73; ptnr. Brown, Wood, Ivey, Mitchell & Petty, N.Y.C., 1973-79, LeBoeuf, Lamb, Leiby & MacRae, N.Y.C., 1979-88, Morgan, Lewis & Bockius, N.Y.C., 1988-93; ret., 1993; tax legis. cons., Orford, N.H., 1993—; adj. prof. Law Sch. Fordham U., 1990-94. Served to lt. comdr. USN, 1954-57. Mem. ABA (chmn. com. adminstrv. practice tax sect. 1984-86), N.Y. State Bar Assn. (exec. com. tax sect. 1975-84), D.C. Bar Assn., Am. Coll. Tax Counsel, N.Y. Athletic Club, Royal Automobile Club.

RICHARDSON, JOHN EDMON, marketing educator; b. Whittier, Calif., Oct. 22, 1942; s. John Edmon and Mildred Alice (Miller) R.; m. Dianne Elaine Ewald, July 15, 1967; 1 child, Sara Beth. BS, Calif. State U., Long Beach, 1964; MBA, U. So. Calif., 1966; MDiv, Fuller Theol. Sem., 1969, D of Ministry, 1981. Assoc. prof. mgmt. Sch. Bus. and Mgmt. Pepperdine U., Malibu, Calif., 1969—. Author: (leader's guides) Caring Enough to Confront, 1984, The Measure of a Man, 1985; editor: Ann. Editions: Marketing, 1987—, Bus. Ethics, 1990—. Lay counselor La Canada (Calif.) Presbyn. Ch., 1978-84, mem. lay counseling task force, 1982-84. Mem. Am. Mgmt. Assn., Soc. Bus. Ethics, Christian Writers Guild, Fuller Sem. Alumni Cabinet (pres. 1982-85), Am. Mktg. Assn., Beta Gamma Sigma. Avocations: fishing, woodworking, tennis, photography. Office: Pepperdine U Sch Bus and Mgmt 400 Corporate Pt Culver City CA 90230-7615

RICHARDSON, JOHN THOMAS, academic administrator, clergyman; b. Dallas, Dec. 20, 1923; s. Patrick and Mary (Walsh) R. B.A., St. Mary's Sem., Perryville, Mo., 1946; S.T.D., Angelicum U., Rome, Italy, 1951; M.A., St. Louis U., 1954. Prof. theology, dean studies Kenrick Sem., St. Louis, 1951-54; lectr. Webster Coll., 1954; dean Grad. Sch. DePaul U., Chgo., 1954-60, exec. v.p., dean faculties, 1960-81, pres., 1981-93; prof. DePaul U. Coll. Law, Chgo., 1955; chancellor DePaul U., Chgo., 1993—. Trustee DePaul U., Chgo., 1954—. Home: 2233 N Kenmore Ave Chicago IL 60614-3504 Office: De Paul U 1 E Jackson Blvd Chicago IL 60604-2201

RICHARDSON, JOHN VINSON, JR., library science educator; b. Columbus, Ohio, Dec. 27, 1949; s. John Vinson Sr. and Hope Irene (Smith) R.; m. Nancy Lee Brown, Aug. 22, 1971. BA, Ohio State U., 1971; MLS, Vanderbilt U., 1972; PhD, Ind. U., 1978. Asst. prof. UCLA, 1978-83, assoc. prof., 1983—, editor The Libr. Quar., 1994—; fellow advanced rsch. Inst. U. Ill., 1991; pres. Info. Transfer, Inglewood, Calif., 1988—; mem. editl. bd. Ref. Svcs. Rev., Ann Arbor, Mich., 1991—, Jour. Govt. Info., Oxford, Eng., 1975—, Index to Current Urban Documents, Westport, Conn., 1987—, U. Calif. Press Catalogues and Bibliographies series, 1993—; vis. fellow Charles Stuart U. NSW Australia, 1990; vis. scholar ALISE Russia Project, St. Petersburg and Moscow, 1996; vis. disting. scholar OCLC Inc., Dublin, Ohio, 1996-97; chmn. Calif. Pacific Ann. Conf. Com. on Archives and History, 1992-96. Author: Spirit of Inquiry, 1982, Gospel of Scholarship, 1992, Knowledge-based Systems for General Reference Work, 1995; editor elect The Libr. Quar., 1994-95, editor, 1995—. Mem. UCLA Grad. Coun., 1992—, chair, 1995—; mem. U. Calif. systemwide coord. com. on grad. affairs, 1993—; pres. Wesley Found., L.A., 1981-87; lay del. Cal-Pac Conf. United Meth. Ch., 1985, 86, 92—, chair conf. commn. on archives and history, 1992—. Rsch. grantee Coun. on Libr. Resources, 1985, 90, Assn. Libr. and Info. Sci. Educators rsch. grantee, 1984, 87; Harold Lancour scholar Beta Phi Mu, 1986; recipient Louise Maxwell award Ind. U. Alumni Assn., 1995. Mem. ALA (Justin Winsor prize 1990, Ref. and Adult Svcs. divsn. Outstanding Paper award 1992), AAAS, Assn. Libr. and Info. Sci. Educators (rsch. paper prize 1986, 91, Best Info. Sci. book 1995), Am. Statis. Assn., Sigma Xi. Democrat. Avocations: wine tasting,reading, fgn. travel, lilac point Siamese. Office: UCLA GSE&IS/DLIS PO Box 951520 300 Circle Dr N Ste 204 Los Angeles CA 90095-1520 *By our common action, we can bend the flow of history.*

RICHARDSON, JOSEPH HILL, physician, medical educator; b. Rensselaer, Ind., June 16, 1928; s. William Clark and Vera (Hill) R.; m. Joan Grace Meininger, July 8, 1950; children: Lois N., Ellen M., James K. MS in Medicine Northwestern U., 1950, MD, 1953. Intern, U.S. Naval Hosp., Great Lakes, Ill., 1953-54; fellow in medicine Cleve. Clinic, 1956-59; individual practice medicine specializing in internal medicine and hematology, Marion, Ind., 1959-67, Ft. Wayne, Ind., 1967—; assoc. clin. prof. medicine, Ind. U. Sch. Medicine, 1993—; med. dir. emeritus The Med. Protective Co., Ft. Wayne, 1995—. Served to lt. MC USNR, 1953-56. Diplomate Am. Bd. Internal Medicine. Fellow ACP, AAAS; mem. AMA, Masons. Contbr. articles to med. jours. Home and Office: 8726 Fortuna Way Fort Wayne IN 46815-5725

RICHARDSON, LAUREL WALUM, sociology educator; b. Chgo., July 15, 1938; d. Tyrrell Alexander and Rose (Foreman) R.; m. Herb Walum, Dec. 27, 1959 (div. 1972); children: Benjamin, Joshua; m. Ernest Lockridge, Dec. 12, 1981. AB, U. Chgo., 1955, BA, 1956; PhD, U. Colo., 1963. Asst. prof. Calif. State U., Los Angeles, 1962-64; postdoctoral fellow Sch. Medicine Ohio State U., Columbus, 1964-65, asst. prof. sociology, 1970-75, assoc. prof., 1975-79, prof. sociology, 1979—; asst. prof. sociology Denison U., Granville, Ohio, 1965-69; mem. editorial bd. Jour. Contemporary Ethnography, Symbolic Interaction, Gender & Soc., Qualitative Sociology, Sociol. Quar. Author: Dynamics of Sex and Gender, 1977, 3d edit. 1988, The New Other Woman, 1985, Die Neve Andere, 1987, A Nova Outra Mulher, 1987, Writing Strategies: Reaching Diverse Audiences, 1990, Gender and University Teaching: A Negotiated Difference, 1995; editor: Feminist Frontiers, 1983, 4th edit., 1997; author more than 100 rsch. articles and papers. Ford Found. fellow, 1954-56; NSF dissertation fellow, 1960-62; post doctoral fellow Vocat. Rehab., Columbus, 1964; grantee Ohio Dept. Health, 1986-87, Nat. Inst. Edn., 1981-82, NIMH, 1972-74, NSF, 1963-64, NEH, 1992; recipient Disting. Affirmative Action award Ohio State U., 1983. Mem. Am. Sociol. Assn. (com. on coms. 1980-81, com. on pub. info. 1987—), North Ctrl. Sociol. Assn. (pres. 1986-87), Sociologists for Women in Soc. (coun. mem. 1978-80), Ctrl. Ohio Sociologists for Women in Soc. (past pres.), Women's Poetry Workshop, Soc. for Study of Symbolic Interaction (publs. com.). Democrat. Avocations: hiking, poetry, reading, antiques. Office: Ohio State Univ Dept of Sociology 190 N Oval Mall Columbus OH 43210-1321

RICHARDSON, LAWRENCE, JR., Latin language educator, archeologist; b. Altoona, Pa., Dec. 2, 1920; married. B.A., Yale U., 1942, Ph.D. in Classics, 1952. Instr. classics Yale U., New Haven, 1946-47, instr. to assoc. prof., 1955-66; prof. Duke U., Durham, N.C., 1966-78, James B. Duke prof. Latin, 1978-91, prof. emeritus, 1991—; field archeologist Am. Acad. Rome, 1952-55, Mellon prof., 1980-81; mem. Inst. Advanced Study, 1967-68. Author: Pompeii: An Architectural History, 1988, A New Topographical Dictionary of Ancient Rome, 1992; contbr. articles to profl. jours. Guggenheim fellow, 1958-59; Am. Council Learned Socs. fellow, 1967-68, 72-73; NEH fellow, 1979-80. Mem. German Archeol. Inst. (corr.), Am. Philol. Assn., Archeol. Inst. Am. Office: Duke U West Campus Dept Classical Studies Durham NC 27708

RICHARDSON, LILY PENDARVIS, retired occupational health nurse; b. Columbia, N.C., Feb. 23, 1939; d. Theophilus Pendarvis and Comeller (Bowser) Johnson; m. Napoleon Richardson, Apr. 4, 1959; children: Donald Felton, Napoleon Jr. BS cum laude, N.C. A&T U., 1961. RN, D.C. Charge nurse L. Richardson Hosp., Greensboro, N.C., 1961-63; charge nurse medicine Georgetown U. Med. Ctr., Washington, 1963-64; charge nurse of nursery D.C. Gen. Hosp., Washington, 1964-67; occupational health nurse, occupational health adminstr. FBI, Washington, 1967-94; adminstr. nursing program FBI, 1994; part time instr. practical nurses Dudley High Sch., Greensboro, 1962; cons. Establishing Health Units, 1990-94, Med. Standard Task Force, Washington, 1993, Bloodborne Pathogen Task Force, 1993. Active cmty. svc. Rosemary Hills Sch., Silver Spring, Md., 1992-94, sch. bd., 1993; blood pressure screener, counselor at several cmty. chs. and cmty. health ctrs.; mail worker Health Reform Com., Washington, 1993-94. Mem. NAACP, Nat. Black Nurses Assn., Black Nurses Greater Washington D.C. ARea (rec. sec. 1985—), Met. Washington Assn. Occupational Health Nurses, Teloca Nursing Alumni (parliamentarian 1970—), A&T Alumni, Sigma Theta Tau (Mutau chpt. internat. charter, Gamma Beta chpt. 1 of 100 Extraordinary Nurses 1994). Home: 2212 Ross Rd Silver Spring MD 20910-2336

RICHARDSON, MARGARET MILNER, federal agency administrator, lawyer; b. Waco, Tex., May 14, 1943; d. James W. and Margaret Wiebusch Milner; m. John L. Richardson, July 22, 1967; 1 child, Margaret Lawrence. AB in Polit. Sci., Vassar Coll., 1965; JD with honors, George Washington U., 1968. Bar: Va. 1968, D.C. 1968, U.S. Dist. Ct. D.C. 1968, U.S. Ct. Appeals (4th, 5th, D.C. and Fed. cirs.) 1968, U.S. Claims Ct. 1969, U.S. Tax Ct. 1970, U.S. Supreme Ct. 1971. Clk. U.S. Ct. Claims, Washington; with Office Chief Counsel IRS, Washington, 1969-77; with Sutherland, Asbill and Brennan, Washington, 1977-80, ptnr., 1980-93; commr. IRS, Washington, 1993—; mem. commr.'s adv. group IRS, 1988-90, chair, 1990; mem. fed. tax adv. group Prentice Hall. Contbr. articles to profl. jours. Assisted Clinton 1992 gen. election campaign; served as team leader Justice Dept./Civil Rights Cluster during Presdl. Transition. Mem. ABA, D.C. Bar Assn. (tax sect.), Va. State Bar Assn., Fed. Bar Assn. (coun. taxation), Fin. Women's Assn. N.Y. Avocations: foreign travel, collecting antiques, needlepoint, gardening. Office: IRS 1111 Constitution Ave NW Washington DC 20224-0001

RICHARDSON, MARTHA, nutrition analyst; b. Noble, La., Apr. 22, 1917; d. Alexander M. and Olive (Barlow) R.; A.B., U. Mo., 1938, Ph.D., 1953; M.S., Kans. State U., 1939. Dietitian, William Newton Meml. Hosp., Winfield, Kans., 1940-42, Molly Stark Sanatorium, Canton, Ohio, 1942-47; asst. dir. residence halls, instr. home econs. U. Mo., 1947-50, instr. home econs., 1951-53; head of foods and nutrition U. Utah, 1953-55; nutrition analyst Agrl. Research Service, Washington, 1955-80. Named Disting. Alumna, U. Mo., 1968. Fellow AAAS; mem. Am. Dietetic Assn., Am. Home Econs. Assn., Am. Med. Writers Assn., Am. Inst. Food Techologists, Am. Chem. Soc. Am. Assn. Cereal Chemists, Am. Forestry Assn., AAUW, N.Y. Acad. Scis., Sigma Xi, Gamma Sigma Delta, Phi Upsilon Omicron, Sigma Delta Epsilon. Contbr. articles to profl. jours. Home: 18700 Walkers Choice Rd Apt 302 Gaithersburg MD 20879-2552

RICHARDSON, MARY LOU, psychotherapist; b. Topeka, Oct. 4, 1953; d. Darrell and Beverly Nutter; m. Kenneth T Richardson Jr. children: Shad Martin, Cheralyn Pasbrig, Kenneth T Richardson III, Russ Richardson. Cert. addictions counselor, Ariz.; cert. Nat. Assn. of Alcolism and Drug Abuse Counselors. Counselor Compcare Alcoholism Ctr. The Meadows Treatment Ctr., Phoenix, 1986-88; co-dir. Phoenix Cons. & Counseling Assocs., Ariz., 1989—; founder and adminstr. The Orion Found., Ariz.; project mem. The Hutoomkhum Com. and Support Program, Hopi Reservation, Ariz.; cons. Baywood Hosp., 1988-89; faculty instr. The Recovery Source, 1989-90; chair Nat. Conv. Women, 1992. Author: Women's Acts of Power, 1991-93, Relationship Recover, 1992—, Women's Empowerment, 1992—, Body, Mind & Spirit, 1994—. Mem. Am. Mental Health Counselors, Am. Counseling Assn., Nat. Assn. Alcoholism & Drug Abuse Counselors, Nat. Reciprocity Consortium. Avocations: writing, sculpting, dancing. Office: Phoenix Cons & Counseling Assocs 5333 N 7th St Ste A202 Phoenix AZ 85014

RICHARDSON, MARY WELD, company executive; b. Port Washington, N.Y., Dec. 8, 1946; d. Weld and Florence (McBeth) R. BA, Columbia U., 1970; MA in Psychology, Sonoma State U., Calif., 1992. Ops. dir. restaurant divsn. Newhall Land & Farming Co., Valencia, Calif., 1976-80; regional tng. specialist World Savs. and Loan Assn., Oakland, Calif., 1982-89; tng. specialist San Francisco Fed. Savs. and Loan, 1989-92; sr. ptnr. WorkLife Resources, Kenwood, Calif., 1990—; tng. and orgn. effectiveness specialist Sola Optical, Petaluma, Calif., 1995—; tng. cons. Redwood Conflict Resolution Svc., Santa Rosa, Calif., 1993—, SSU Cons. Group, Santa Rosa, 1990-93. Author: Client Centered Learning, 1993. Mediator RECOURSE, Santa Rosa, 1990—; family group facilitator Choices for Cnahge, Santa Rosa, 1992-95; facilitator Am. Corps.-The Sonoma Project, 1993-95, Sonoma County AIDS Found., 1994—. Mem. Nat.SOc. Performance and Instruction (chpt. pres. 1993-94). Office: WorkLife Resources PO Box 886 842 Warm Springs Rd Kenwood CA 95452-0886

RICHARDSON, MAURICE M., manufacturing executive; b. 1933. Exec. v.p., COO Engraph Inc. (now Sonoco Engraph), Atlanta, 1983—; now pres., ceo. Office: Sonoco Engraph 2635 Century Pky NE Atlanta GA 30345-3112*

RICHARDSON, MELVIN MARK, state legislator, broadcast executive; b. Salt Lake City, Apr. 29, 1928; s. Mark and Mary (Lundquist) R.; m. Dixie Joyce Gordon, 1952; children: Pamela, Mark, Lance, Todd, Kristi. Grad., Radio Operational Engring. Sch., Burbank, Calif., 1951. Radio announcer, program dir. Sta. KBUH, Brigham City, Utah, 1951-54; mgr. Sta. KLGN, Logan, Utah, 1954-58; announcer, sports dir. Sta. KID Radio/TV, Idaho Falls, Idaho, 1958-86; mgr., program dir. Sta. KID-FM/AM, Idaho Falls, 1986; mem. Idaho Ho. of Reps., 1988-92, Idaho Senate, 1992—; cons., dir. INEL Scholastic Tournament, Idaho Nat. Engring. Lab.; speaker in field. Host: Mel's Sports Scene, Thirty Minutes, Channel Three Reports, Probes, Probing America. Dir. Assn. Idaho Cities, Ricks Coll. Booster Club, Bonneville County Crime Stoppers, Idaho Falls Child Devel. Ctr.; active Idaho Centennial Commn., Anti-Lottery Com., Gov.'s Conf. on Children; commr. Bonneville County Parks and Recreation Commn.; mayor City of Ammon, Idaho, 1966-72; candidate from Idaho Dist. # 2 for U.S. Congress. Sgt. USAR, 1951-57. Named Man of Yr., Ricks Coll., 1980. Mem. Idaho Broadcasters Assn. (bd. dirs.). Republican. Mem. LDS Ch. Home and Office: 3725 Brookfield Ln Idaho Falls ID 83406-6803

RICHARDSON, MIDGE TURK, magazine editor; b. Los Angeles, Mar. 26, 1930; d. Charles Aloysius and Marie Theresa (Lindekin) Turk; m. Hamilton Farrar Richardson, Feb. 8, 1974. BA, Immaculate Heart Coll., L.A., 1951, MA, 1956; postgrad., U. Calif., Santa Barbara, Duquesne U., U. Pitts. Mem. Immaculate Heart Community, Roman Catholic Ch., 1948-66; asst. to dean Sch. Arts, NYU, 1966-67; coll. editor Glamour mag., N.Y.C., 1967-74; editor-in-chief Co-Ed mag.; also editorial dir. Forecast and Co-Ed mags., N.Y.C., 1974-75; editor-in-chief Seventeen mag., N.Y.C., 1975—; lectr. Tishman seminars Hunter Coll., N.Y.C., 1975-77. Host, guest TV and radio programs.; Author: The Buried Life: A Nun's Journey, 1971, Gordon Parks: A Biography for Children, 1971; also articles. Bd. dirs. YMCA, N.Y.C., 1972-73, Timothy Dwight Sch., 1979-83, Girl Scout council Greater N.Y., 1979-82; life trustee Internat. House. Recipient award Outstanding Women in Pub., 1982; winner ASME Nat. Mag. award for fiction, 1984. Mem. Am. Soc. Mag. Editors, Fashion Group. Democrat. Clubs: River, Meadow. Office: Seventeen Mag 200 Madison Ave New York NY 10016-3903

RICHARDSON, MIRANDA, actress; b. Lancashire, Eng., 1958. Studied, Drama Program Bristol. Stage performances London: Moving, All My Sons, Who's Afraid of Virginia Woolf, The Life of Einstein, A Lie of the Mind; others include The Changling, Mountain Language; TV appearances: The Hard World, Sorrel and Son, A Woman of Substance, Underworld, Death of the Heart, (series) Black Adder II, Sweet as You Are, (miniseries) Die Kinder; films: Dance with a Stranger, 1985, The Innocent, 1986, Empire of the Sun, 1987, Eat the Rich, 1987, Twisted Obsession, 1990, The Bachelor, 1991, Enchanted April, 1992, Damage, 1992, The Crying Game, 1992 (Acad. award nominee for best supporting actress), Fatherland, HBO, 1994 (Golden Globe award), Tom & Viv, 1994 (Acad. award nominee for best actress 1995). Office: care Susan Smith & Assocs 121 N San Vicente Blvd Beverly Hills CA 90211*

RICHARDSON, NATASHA JANE, actress; b. May 11, 1963; d. Tony Richardson and Vanessa Redgrave; m. Liam Neeson, July 3, 1994; 1 son: Micheál Richard Antonio. Acting debut on stage at Leeds (England) Playhouse, 1983; appearences include (plays) A Midsummer's Night Dream, Hamlet, 1985, The Seagull, 1985, High Society, 1987, Anna Christie, 1993 (Tony award nominee 1993, Drama Desk award), (films) Every Picture Tells a Story, 1984, Gothic, 1987, A Month in the Country, 1987, Patty Hearst, 1988, Fat Man and Little Boy, 1989, The Handmaid's Tale, 1990, The Comfort of Strangers, 1991, The Favor, The Watch and the Very Big Fish, 1992, Past Midnight, Widows' Peak, 1994, Nell, 1994, (TV) In a Secret State, 1984, The Copper Beaches, 1984, Ghosts, 1986, Suddenly Last Summer, 1992, Hostages, 1993, Zelda, 1993. Recipient Most Promising Newcomer award Plays & Players, 1986; named Best Actress by London Theatre Critics, Plays & Players, 1990, Evening Standard Best Actress, 1990.

RICHARDSON, NOLAN, university athletic coach. Head coach U. Arkansas Razorbacks, 1985—. Coach NCAA championship team 1994, NCAA 2nd place team, 1995; recipient Naismith award for Best NCAA Divsn. IA coach, 1994. Office: Univ Arkansas Broyles Athletic Ctr Fayetteville AR 72701*

RICHARDSON, PATRICIA, actress; b. Bethesda, Md., Feb. 23, 1951; d. Laurence Baxter and Elizabeth (Howard) R.; m. Raymond Baker, June 20, 1982; children: Henry, Roxanne, Joseph. BFA, So. Meth. U., 1972. Appearences include (Broadway) Gypsy, Loose Ends, The Wake of Jamie Foster; (off-Broadway) The Collected Works of Billy the Kid, The Frequency, Vanities, The Coroner's Plot, Hooters, Company, Fables for Friends, The Miss Firecracker Contest, Cruise Control; (regional theatre) King Lear, The Killing of Sister George, Relatively Speaking, The Importance of Being Earnest, Of Mice and Men, The Philadelphia Story, Room Service, Fifth of July, About Face; (nat. tours) Gypsy, Vanities; (films) Gas, 1972, You Better Watch Out, Lost Angels, 1988, In Country, 1988; (TV) Double Trouble, 1984, Eisenhower & Lutz, 1988, FM, 1989-90, Home Improvement, 1991— (Lead Actress in a Comedy Series Emmy award nominee, 1994, Golden Globe award nominee, 1993, 94). Office: William Morris Agy care Jonathon Howard 151 S El Camino Dr Beverly Hills CA 90212-2704*

RICHARDSON, PETER DAMIAN, mechanical engineering educator; b. West Wickham, Eng., Aug. 22, 1935; came to U.S., 1958; s. Reginald W. and Marie S. (Ouseley) R. B.Sc. in Engring, Imperial Coll., U. London, 1955, A.C.G.I., 1955, Ph.D. (Unwin scholar), 1958, D.I.C., 1958; D.Sc. in Engring, U. London, 1974, D.Sc. in Physiology, 1983. Demonstrator dept. mech. engring. Imperial Coll., U. London, 1955-58; vis. lectr. Brown U., Providence, 1958-59; research asso. Brown U., 1959-60, asst. prof. engring., 1960-65, asso. prof., 1965-68, prof., 1968-84, prof. engring. and physiology, 1984—, chmn. faculty, 1987-88; chmn. exec. com. Center Biomed. Engring., 1972—; cons. to industry, U.S. govt. agys; on leave at U. London, 1967, U. Paris, 1968, Orta Dogu Teknik Universitesi, Ankara, Turkey, 1969, Medizinischen Fakultat, RWTH, Aachen, Germany, 1976, U. Paris XIII, 1991. Co-author: Principles of Cell Adhesion, 1995; contbr. articles to profl. pubs. Recipient Sr. Scientist award Alexander Von Humboldt Found., 1976; named Laureate in Medicine, Jung Found., 1987. Fellow ASME, Royal Soc., Am. Inst. Med. Biol. Engring.; mem. Am. Soc. Engring. Edn., Am. Soc. Artificial Internal Organs (past assoc. editor jour.), European Soc. Artificial Organs., Biomed. Engring. Soc. Office: Brown U Box D 79 Waterman St Providence RI 02912-9079

RICHARDSON, RALPH ERNEST, publisher; b. Bristol, Conn., Nov. 1, 1927; s. Ralph Augustus and Estelle (Platt) R.; m. Shirley Collette Laffey, June 11, 1983; m. Ellen Adele Lee, Feb. 7, 1953 (div.); children—Martha Lee, Sarah Platt, Amy Treadwell, Samuel Heller. B.A., Wesleyan U., 1951. Sales mktg. staff, Time Inc., Detroit, 1953-59; pres. Mactier Pub. Co., N.Y.C., 1960-71; mng. dir. EPN SA, Brussels, Belgium, 1971-72; cons. N.Y.C., 1973-77; pub. Thomas Pub. Co., N.Y.C., 1978—. Club: Confrerie des Chevaliers du Tastevin (France). Office: Thomas Pub Co 5 Penn Plz New York NY 10001 also: Indsl Equipment News 5 Penn Plz New York NY 10001-1810

RICHARDSON, RALPH HERMAN, lawyer; b. Detroit, Oct. 12, 1935; s. Ralph Onazime and Lucinda Ollie (Fluence) R.; m. Arvie Y., June 1, 1956 (div. 1961); children: Cassandra, Tanya, Arvie Lynn; m. Julia A., Sept. 16, 1962 (div. 1982); children: Traci, Theron. BA, Wayne State U., 1964, JD, 1970. Bar: Mich., U.S. Ct. Appeals (6th cir.), Supreme Ct. U.S., 1970. Postal transp. clk. U.S. P. O., Detroit, 1954-56; clk. pub. aid worker City Detroit, 1956-65; sr. labor relations rep. Ford Motor Co., Ypsilanti, Mich., 1965-70, wage admins., 1966, labor relations rep., 1967; atty. Brown Grier, Richardson P.C., Detroit, 1970-71; atty Richardson, Grier P.C., Detroit, 1971-73; ptnr. Stone, Richardson P.C., Detroit, 1973—; bd. dirs. Legal Aid, Defender Assn. Detroit, 1985-86. Mem. bd. dirs. YMCA Fisher Branch; Boy Scouts Am.; apptd. to Bd. Appeals for Hosp. Bed Reduction by Gov. State of Mich., 1982, apptd. Spl. Asst. Atty. Gen., by Frank J. Kelley, Atty Gen. for the State Mich., May 23, 1984, apptd. to Task Oriented Com. to review the issue in-home child care by Detroit City Council Mem., Maryann Mahaffey. With U.S. Army, 1964. Mem. NAACP (life), Am. Arbitration Assn., Legal Aid Defender Assn., Mich. State Bar Fellows, Optimists, Masons, Shriners (imperial legal advisor, gen. counsel 1994-96), Phi Alpha Delta, Kappa Alpha Psi. Democrat. Office: Stone Richardson PC 2910 E Jefferson Ave Detroit MI 48207-4208

RICHARDSON, RICHARD COLBY, JR., leadership and policy studies educator, researcher; b. Burlington, Vt., Sept. 10, 1933; s. Richard Colby and Florence May (Barlow) R.; m. Patricia Ann Barnhart, Dec. 21, 1954; children—Richard Colby III, Michael Donald, Christopher Robin. BS, Castleton State Coll., 1954; MA, Mich. State U., 1958; PhD, U. Tex., 1963; Litt.D. (hon.), Lafayette Coll., 1973. Instr., counselor Vt. Coll., Montpelier, 1958-61; dean instrn. Forest Park Community Coll., St. Louis, 1963-67; pres. Northampton County Area Community Coll., Bethelehem, Pa., 1967-77; chmn. dept. higher edn. and adult edn. Ariz. State U., Tempe, 1977-84, prof. edn. leadership and policy studies, 1984—. Jr. author: The Two Year College: A Social Synthesis, 1965; sr. author: Governance for the Two-Year College, 1972, Functional Literacy in the College Setting, 1981, Literacy in the Open Access College, 1983, Fostering Minority Acess and Achievement in Higher Education, 1987, Achieving Quality and Diversity, 1991. Bd. dirs. Easton Hosp., 1973-77, v.p., 1975-77; exec. council Minsi Trails council Boy Scouts Am., Bethelehem, 1973-77. Named Disting. Grad., Coll. Edn., U. Tex., Austin, 1982; recipient Outstanding Research Publ. award Council Univ. and Colls.-Am. Assn. Community and Jr. Colls., 1983, Disting. Service award, 1984. Mem. Am. Assn. Higher Edn. (charter life, dir. 1970-73), AAUP, Assn. for Study of Higher Edn. (bd. dirs. 1984), Am. Assn. Community and Jr. Colls. (dir. 1980-83). Democrat. Home: 5654 E Wilshire Dr Scottsdale AZ 85257-1950 Office: Ariz State U Tempe AZ 85287

RICHARDSON, RICHARD JUDSON, political science educator; b. Poplar Bluff, Mo., Feb. 16, 1935; s. Jewell Judson and Naomi Fern (Watson) R.; m. Sammie Sue Cullum, Dec. 29, 1961; children: Jon Mark, Anna Cecile, Ellen Elizabeth, Megan Leigh. BS, Harding Coll., 1957; cert., U. Dublin, 1958; MA, Tulane U., 1961, PhD, 1967. Instr. Tulane U., 1962-65; asst. prof. polit. sci. Western Mich. U., Kalamazoo, 1965-67; assoc. prof. Western Mich. U., 1967-69; vis. assoc. prof. U. Hawaii, 1967-68; asso. prof. U. N.C., Chapel Hill, 1969-72, prof., 1972-77, Burton Craige prof., 1977—, assoc. chmn. dept., 1972-73, chmn. dept., 1975-80, 85-90, chmn. curriculum in justice, 1990-95, assoc. v.p. acad. affairs univ. gen. adminstrn., 1991-92; adj. prof. Duke U., Durham, 1972-74; provost, vice chancellor acad. affairs U. N.C., 1995—; cons. in field. Author: (with Kenneth Vines) The Politics of Federal Courts, 1971, (with Darlene Walker) People and the Police, 1973, (with Marian Irish, James Prothro) The Politics of American Democracy, 1981. Del. County Dem. Conv., 1972, 83; vice chmn. Dem. Party Precinct, 1983-85; chmn. bldg. fund YMCA, 1976; chmn. Carolina Challenge for endowment U. N.C., Chapel Hill, 1979-80; chmn. U. N.C. Bicentennial Observance, 1991-94; chmn. United Way, 1983, pres., 1985; pres. PTA County Coun., 1984. Recipient Edward S. Corwin award Am. Polit. Sci. Assn., 1967, Tanner Disting. Teaching award U. N.C., 1972, Univ. award for Outstanding Teaching, 1981, Thomas Jefferson award, 1987, Alumni Faculty Disting. Svc. award, 1994, James Johnston Disting. Teaching award, 1993; Edgar Stern fellow, 1959-61; NEH grantee, 1970. Mem. N.C. Polit. Sci. Assn. (pres. 1978-79), Am. Polit. Sci. Assn., So. Polit. Sci. Assn., ACLU (bd. dirs. local chpt. 1985-88, state bd. dirs. 1988-89), Order of Janus, Order of the Long Leaf Pine, Order of Golden Fleece, Order of the Grail. Home: 1135 River Rd Pittsboro NC 27312-8108 Office: U NC Dept Polit Sci Chapel Hill NC 27514

RICHARDSON, RICHARD THOMAS, retired banker; b. Hackensack, N.J., Dec. 16, 1933; s. Rolande Herbert and Rose Hortense (Collina) R.; m. Melinda Davis Murphy; children: Lisa Richardson Charles, Heidi Davis, Peter Thomas. B.S., Yale U., 1955. With Chem. Bank, N.Y.C., 1960-92, v.p., 1969-74; v.p., gen. mgr. Chem. Bank, London, 1974-77; sr. v.p., head audit div. Chem. Bank, N.Y.C., 1977-80, sr. v.p., head Middle East, Africa, 1980-87, mng. dir., head instl. banking-internat., 1987-92; dir. Wiremold Co., West Hartford, Conn., 1980—; dir. Fosterlane Holdings Corp., Wilmington, Del., Mitsui Trust Bank (U.S.A.), N.Y.C. Trustee Internat. Coll., Beirut, Lebanon, 1986-93, N.J. Ctr. for Visual Arts, Summit, 1993-94. Mem. Yale Club (N.Y.C.), Beacon Hill Club (Summit, N.J.).

RICHARDSON, ROBERT, cinematographer. Cinematographer: (films) Salvador, 1986, Platoon, 1986 (Academy award nomination best cinematography 1986), Wall Street, 1987, Dudes, 1988, Eight Men Out, 1988, Talk Radio, 1988, Born on the Fourth of July, 1989 (Academy award nomination best cinematography 1989), City of Hope, 1991, The Doors, 1991, JFK, 1991 (Academy award best cinematography 1991), A Few Good Men, 1992, Heaven and Earth, 1993, Natural Born Killers, 1994, (TV spl.) To the Moon, Alice, 1990; cameraman: (films) Repo Man, 1984, Making the Grade, 1984. Office: care Spyros Skouras Sanford Skouras Gross & Assocs 1015 Gayley Ave Fl 3 Los Angeles CA 90024-3424

RICHARDSON, ROBERT ALLEN, lawyer, educator; b. Cleve., Feb. 15, 1939; s. Allen B. and Margaret C. (Thomas) R.; m. Carolyn Eck Richardson, Dec. 9, 1968. BA, Ohio Wesleyan U., 1961; LLB, Harvard U., 1964. Bar: Ohio 1964, Hawaii 1990. Ptnr. Caffee, Halter & Griswold, Cleve., 1968-89; counsel Mancini, Rowland & Welch (formerly Case & Lynch), Maui, Hawaii, 1990—; lectr., affirmative action officer, atty. Maui (Hawaii) C.C., 1989—; counsel Maui C. of C., Kahului, Maui, Hawaii, 1994—. Pres. trustee Big Bros., Big Sisters of Maui, 1990-94; v.p., trustee, pres. Ka Hole A Ke Ole Homeless Resource Ctr., 1990—; trustee Maui Acad. Performing Arts, Maui Symphony, Maul Counseling Svc., Kapalua Music Festival. Mem. Rotary Club of Maui, Maui Country Club, Roufant Club (advocate), Cleve. Skating Club. Home: 106 Poohina Rd Kula HI 96790 Office: Mancini Rowland & Welch 33 Lono Ave Kahului HI 96732

RICHARDSON, ROBERT CARLETON, engineering consultant; b. Grand Junction, Colo., Mar. 17, 1925; s. Carleton O. and Mabel Grace (Davy) R.; m. Ruby Lucille Morrison, Jan. 11, 1947 (dec.); children: Robert James, Lori Dianne Richardson Dismont. Student, U. Colo., Boulder, 1943-44, U. Calif., 1946-47, I.C.S., Scranton, Pa., 1947-50, Calif. State U., Long Beach, 1983, John F. Kennedy U., Martinez, Calif., 1967. Chief engr./gen. mgr. Gilmore Fabricators, Oakland, Calif., 1948-56; nat. sales mgr. Gilmore Steel Contrs., Oakland, 1957-72; v.p. engring. R&D Davis Walker Corp., L.A., 1972-86; tech. dir. Ivy Steel divsn. MMI, Houston, 1986-93; engring. cons. R.C. Richardson & Assocs., Sun Lakes, Ariz., 1993—; engring. instr. Calif. State U., Long Beach, 1983-85; pres. Nat. Cons. Industry Bd., San Francisco, 1984; chmn. bd. Wire Reinforcement Inst., Leesburg, Va., 1978, 82; mem. bd. dirs. ASCC, 1982-84. Chpt. author: Manual of Standard Practice, 1988-90, Structural Detailing Manual, 1990-94. With USMC, 1943-45. Recipient Outstanding Achievement award Wire Reinforcement Inst., 1993; named Boss of the Yr., Women in Constrn., Oakland, 1964, 65. Mem. ASTM, Structural Engrs. Assn. of Calif., Am. Concrete Inst. (chair 439-A 1991—), Marines Meml. Assn., Earthquake Engring. Rsch. Inst. Republican. Achievements include research on high strength steel reinforcement; research on fatigue of wire reinforcement under dynamic loads; research on crack behavior of shear reinforcement in concrete beams and girders. Avocations: swimming, walking, golf, fishing, hunting. Home and Office: 10930 E San Tan Blvd Sun Lakes AZ 85248

RICHARDSON, ROBERT CHARLWOOD, III, management consultant, retired air force officer; b. Rockford, Ill., Jan. 5, 1918; s. Robert Charlwood, Jr. and Lois (Farman) R.; m. Anne Waln Taylor, Sept. 13, 1952; children: Anne Newbold, Robert Charlwood, Lydia Farman. B.S., U.S. Mil. Acad., 1939; grad., Nat. War Coll., 1956. Commd. 2d lt. U.S. Army, 1939; advanced through grades to brig. gen. USAF, 1960; squadron comdg. officer Ascension Island, 1942-43; (Army Air Force Bd.), Orlando, Fla., 1943-44; assigned U.K. and France, 1944-45; comdg. officer 365th Fighter Group, 9th Air Force, 1945-46; assigned joint war plans com. Joint Chiefs Staff, NATO, 1946-49, Washington and Paris, 1949-54; U.S. mil. rep. European Def. Community, 1954-55, comdg. officer 83d and 4th Fighter Wing, Tactical Air Command, 1956-58, assigned plans div. Hdqrs. USAF, 1958-61, mil. rep. NATO Council Paris, 1962-64, dep. chief staff for sci. and tech. Air Force Systems Command, 1964-66; dep. comdr., field command Def. Atomic Support Agy. Sandia Base, 1966-67, ret., 1967; sr. assoc. Schriever & McKee Assos., Inc., 1967-70; policy cons., pres. Encabulator Corp., 1970-80; pres. Global Activities Ltd.; v.p. Cons.'s Internat. Inc., 1973-77; dep. dir. High Frontier Inc., 1981—; pres. Exim Corp., 1977-82. Contbr. numerous articles on atomic warfare, NATO, strategy and concepts. Bd. dirs., sec./treas. Am. Cause, 1975-80, Security and Intelligence Fund, 1977-90; exec. dir. Am. Fgn. Policy Inst., 1976-86; bd. dirs., sec.-treas. Space Transp. Assn., 1991—. Decorated Legion of Merit with oak leaf cluster, Air medal, Army Commendation medal; Croix de Guerre with silver star France). Home: 212 S St Asaph St Alexandria VA 22314-3744

RICHARDSON, ROBERT DALE, JR., English language educator; b. Milw., June 14, 1934; s. Robert Dale and Lucy Baldwin (Marsh) R.; m. Elizabeth Hall, Nov. 7, 1959 (div. 1987); m. Annie Dillard, Dec. 10, 1988; children: Elisabeth, Anne, Rosy. AB magna cum laude in English, Harvard U., 1956, PhD in English Lit., 1961. Instr. English Harvard U., Cambridge, Mass., 1961-63; asst. prof. English U. Denver, 1963-68, assoc. prof., 1968-72, prof., 1972-87, Lawrence C. Phipps prof. humanities, 1979-82, chmn. dept., 1968-73, pres. Univ. senate, 1972-73, assoc. dean grad. studies, 1975-76; prof. English, U. Colo., Boulder, 1987; vis. prof. letters Wesleyan U., Middletown, Conn., 1989-94; vis. prof. Harvard U., summer 1976, CUNY, 1978, Sichuan U., 1983; vis. fellow Huntington Libr., 1973-74; vis. instr. Yale U., 1988; bd. dirs. David R. Godine Pub. Author: Literature and Film, 1969, Henry Thoreau: A Life of the Mind, 1986 (Melcher award 1986), Emerson: The Mind on Fire, 1995 (Parkman prize 1995), Myth and Literature in the American Renaissance, 1978; (with Burton Feldman) The Rise of Modern Mythology 1680-1860, 1972. Trustee Meadville-Lombard Theol. Sch., 1981-87. Guggenheim fellow, 1990. Mem. MLA, Rocky Mountain MLA, Am. Studies Assn., Soc. Eighteenth Century Studies, Melville Soc., Author's Guild, Thoreau Soc., Emerson Soc., Assn. Lit. Scholars and Critics. Democrat. Unitarian.

RICHARDSON, ROBERT JANECEK, library director; b. Savannah, Ga., July 30, 1945; s. William Blakely and Mildred Ann (Salcedo) R.; m. Janice Amelia Neder, June 10, 1967; children: Robert Jr., Mary Neder Salcedo. AA, Mid. Ga. Coll., 1965; BA, West Ga. Coll., 1967; MSc, Fla. State U., 1971. Tchr. social studies Dublin (Ga.) City Schs., 1967-70; libr., instr. Ga. Coll., Milledgeville, 1971-78; asst. libr. dir. Chattahoochee Valley Regional Libr., Columbus, Ga., 1979-80; libr. dir. Young Harris (Ga.) Coll., 1980—; mem. peer rev. team So. Assn. Colls. and Schs., Atlanta, 1983—; cons. Ga. Mil. Coll. Libr., Milledgeville, 1986, 95. Mem. adminstrv. coun. Sharp Meml. Meth. Ch., Young Harris, 1984-88; trustee Towns County Libr., Hiawassee, Ga., 1980-84, 92—, chmn. 1995—; bd. dirs. Towns-Union Credit Union, Young Harris, 1986—. Mem. Ga. Libr. Assn. (pres. 1989-91, Nix-Jones Svc. award 1993), Ga. Assn. Media Assts. (state advisor 1983-89), Ga. Assn. Instrnl. Tech. (svc. award for continued involvement and support of Joint Annual Libr. Media Conf. 1995). Democrat. Methodist. Avocations: camping, gardening. Office: Young Harris Coll 1 Duckworth Blvd Young Harris GA 30582

RICHARDSON, R(OSS) FRED(ERICK), insurance executive; b. Renfrew, Ont., Can., Feb. 4, 1928; came to U.S., 1980; s. Garfield Newton and Grace Mary (MacLean) R.; m. Betty Blanche Betts, Feb. 4, 1972; children by previous marriage—Sheri Joan, Robert John, Paul Frederick. BA in Math. and Physics with honors, Queens U., 1950. CLU. Actuarial asst. Empire Life Ins. Co., Kingston, Ont., Can., 1950-55; sec. Maritime Life Ins. Co., Halifax, N.S., Can., 1955-59, dir. sales, 1959-65, chief exec. officer, 1967-72; mng. dir., chief exec. officer Abbey Life Ins. Co., U.K., 1972-80; group gen. mgr. Hartford Europe Group, 1975-80; sr. v.p., dir. worldwide life ins. ops. Hartford Ins. Group, Conn., 1980-83, dir. worldwide life ins. ops., 1983-88; pres., chief operating officer Hartford Life Cos., 1983-88; pvt. ins. cons. Boca Raton, Fla., 1988; pres., chief exec. officer Crown Life Ins. Co., 1988-93; cons. INSCE, Boca Raton, 1993—. Fellow Soc. Actuaries; mem. Inst. Actuaries Gt. Britain. Home and Office: 17047 Boca Club Blvd Apt 165B Boca Raton FL 33487-1253

RICHARDSON, ROY, management consultant; b. Chgo., Mar. 22, 1931; s. John George and Margaret Beattie (Henderson) R.; B.A. in Psychology, Macalester Coll., 1952; M.A. in Labor and Indsl. Relations, U. Ill., 1953; Ph.D. in Indsl. Relations, U. Minn., 1969; m. Mary C. Westphal, May 16, 1970; children: Beth Barnett, Jessica, Adam, Roman, Alexis. With Honeywell, Inc., Mpls., 1956-70, corp. manpower mgr., 1967-70; mgr. manpower devel. and tng. Internat. Harvester, Chgo., 1970-73; dir. personnel U. Minn., 1973-75; v.p. human resources Onan Corp., Mpls., 1975-82; v.p. human resources Graco Corp., Mpls., 1982-84, v.p. human resources and corp. devel., 1985-91; v.p. Human Resources and Quality Mgmt. Systems, 1992-94; pres. Intergrated Mgmt. Systems, 1994—; pres. Pers.l Surveys, Inc., Mpls., 1978-80; dir., chmn. exec. com. Kotz Grad. Sch. Mgmt., St. Paul, 1984-90. V.p. Mpls. Urban League, 1962-64. Recipient Disting. Citizens award City of Mpls., 1964; U. St. Thomas, Mpls. exec. fellow. Mem. Soc. for Human Resource Mgmt., U. Minn. Indsl. Rels. Alumni Soc. (dir. 1979-85, pres. 1981), Am. Soc. Quality Ctrl. Republican. Episcopalian. Club: Ford's Colony Country. Author: Fair Pay and Work, 1971.

RICHARDSON, RUDY JAMES, toxicology and neurosciences educator; b. May 13, 1945. B.S. magna cum laude, Wichita State U., 1967; Sc.M., Harvard U., 1973, Sc.D., 1974. Diplomate Am. Bd. Toxicology. Research geochemist Columbia U., N.Y.C., summer 1966; NASA trainee SUNY, Stony Brook, 1967-70; research biochemist Med. Research Council, Carshalton, Eng., 1974-75; asst. prof. U. Mich., Ann Arbor, 1975-79, assoc. prof., 1979-84, prof. toxicology, 1984—, assoc. prof. neurotoxicology neurology dept., 1987—, acting dir. dept. Toxicology, 1993; dir., 1994—; vis. scientist Warner-Lambert Co., Ann Arbor, 1982-83; vis. prof. U. Padua, Italy, 1991; cons. NAS, Washington, 1978-79, 84, Office Tech. Assessment U.S. Congress, 1988-90, Nat. Toxic Substance Disease Registry, 1990—; mem. sci. adv. panel on neurotoxicology EPA, 1987-89; chmn. work group on neurotoxicity guidelines Orgn. for Econ. Coop. and Devel., 1990, Nat. Inst. Orgnl. Safety and Health, 1990, 94. Contbr. articles to profl. jours., chpts. to books; mem. editorial bd. Neurotoxicology, 1980—, Toxicology and Indsl. Health, 1986—, Toxicology and Applied Pharmacology, 1989—. Mem. Mich. Lupus Found., Ann Arbor, 1979—. Grantee NIH, 1977-86, EPA, 1977-86; invited speaker Gordon Conf., Meriden, N.H., 1984, Cholinesterase Congress, Bled, Yugoslavia, 1983. Mem. AAAS, Soc. Toxicology (pres. neurotoxicology sect. 1987-88, councillor 1988-89), Soc. for Neurosci., Am. Diabetes Assn., Am. Chem. Soc., Internat. Soc. Neurochemistry, Internat. Brain Rsch. Orgn. Achievements include co-discoverer (with B.R. Dudek) of lymphocyte neurotoxic esterase (NTE); development of lymphocyte NTE as biomarker of exposure to neuropathic organophosphates; refinement of NTE assay for use in neurotoxicity testing. Office: U Mich Toxicology Program M 7525 Sph # 2 Ann Arbor MI 48109

RICHARDSON, SYLVIA ONESTI, physician; b. San Francisco, Sept. 12, 1920; d. Silvio J. and Johanna (Kristoffy) Onesti; m. William R. Richardson, Sept. 8, 1951 (dec. 1994); children: William Charles, Christopher Lee. B.A., Stanford, 1940; postgrad., U. Wash., 1940-41; M.A., Columbia U., 1942; M.D., McGill U., 1948; D.Litt. (hon.), Emerson Coll. Intern Children's Meml. Hosp., Montreal, 1948-49; resident Children's Med. Center, Boston, 1949-50; instr. spl. edn. Columbia, 1942-43; supr. hearing handicapped New Rochelle (N.Y.) Pub. Schs., 1942-43; clin. fellow in medicine Boston Children's Med. Center, 1949-51, dir. speech clinic, 1950-52, asso. physician, 1951-52, research fellow in surgery, 1954-55; instr. speech dept. Boston U., 1950-52, San Diego State Coll., 1952-54; teaching fellow in medicine Harvard U., 1951-52; cons. dept. child health and maternal welfare State of Mass., 1951-52; asst. clin. prof. pediatrics State U. N.Y., Downstate Med. Center, Bklyn., 1957-58; asso. prof. pediatrics and psychiatry, dir. child study center U. Okla. Sch. Medicine, 1958-65; asst. clin. prof. pediatrics U. Cin. Sch. Medicine, 1965-67, asso. prof., 1967-80; dir. learning disabilities program Center for Developmental Disorders, 1966-80; disting. prof. communication scis. and disorders, clin. prof. pediatrics U. South Fla., 1980—; cons. dept. child health and maternal welfare State of Okla., 1957-65; spl. cons. Nat. Inst. Nervous Diseases and Blindness, 1960-62; spl. cons. on mental retardation Okla. State Dept. Pub. Welfare, 1963-65; cons. Bur. State Services, USPHS, Bur. Edn. Handicapped, U.S. Office Edn. Editor: Children's House mag, 1966-67; mem. editorial bd. Jour. Learning Disbailities, Topics in Lang. Disorders. Mem. Okla. gov.'s com. White House Conf., 1960, White House Conf. on Children, 1970; Okla. citizen's com. Adequate Higher Edn., 1958-62. Recipient award for mental health planning Gov. of Okla., 1966; Distinguished Service award Internat. Assn. Children with Learning Disabilities, 1969; Old Master award Purdue U., 1972; named Okla. Woman of the Year, 1964; Talisman Service award Ohio Assn. Children with Learning Disabilities, 1974; Newell Kephart award for services to exceptional children, 1976. Fellow Am. Speech and Hearing Assn. (mem. exec. council 1957-59, chmn. elect ho. of dels. 1965, pres. 1973, honor award 1988), Royal Soc. Health, Internat. Assn. Rsch. in Learning Disabilities, Multidisciplinary Acad. for Clin. Edn., Internat. Assn. for Logopedics and Phoniatrics; mem. AMA, Mass. Speech and Hearing Assn. (co-founder, pres. 1950-52), Okla. Speech and Hearing Assn. (exec. council), Orton Dyslexia Soc. (bd. dirs. 1978-84, pres. 1984-88, Samuel T. Orton award 1992), Ohio Speech and Hearing Assn., Oklahoma County Council Mentally Retarded Children (bd. dirs. 1960-65), Oklahoma County Mental Health Assn. (profl. adv. bd. 1961-65), Okla. Hearing Soc. (v.p., bd. dirs. 1959-61), Soc. Research in Child Devel., Assn. Children with Learning Disabilities (chmn. profl. adv. bd.), Council Exceptional Children, Cin. Pediatric Soc. Home: 4141 Bayshore Blvd Apt 1701 Tampa FL 33611-1802

RICHARDSON, THOMAS HAMPTON, design consulting engineer; b. St. Louis, Nov. 25, 1941; s. Claude Hampton and Pearl Lily (Burks) R.; m. Lois Louise Atteberry June 8, 1963; children: Shelley Ann, David Hampton, Stephanie Lynn. BTEE, Wash. U., St. Louis, 1974. Registered profl. engr., Mo., Ill., Ind., Kans., Iowa, Fla., Ky., Miss. Elec. project designer Fruco Engrs. Inc., St. Louis, 1967-68; mgr., mech./elec. engr. MBA Engrs. Inc., St. Louis, 1968-74, Kenneth Balk and Assoc., St. Louis, 1974-76; instr. elec. engring. Wash. U., St. Louis, 1976; v.p., chief engr. John F. Steffen Assoc., St. Louis, 1976-79; prin. ptnr. Keeler, Webb and Richardson, St. Louis, 1979-94; pres./owner The Richardson Engring. Group, St. Louis, 1979—. Contbr. articles to profl. jours. Recipient Internat. Lgt. Des. award Illuminating Engr. Soc. St. Louis 1985, Edwin F. Guth award of Merit Illuminating Engr. Soc. N.Am. 1986. Mem. NSPE, ASHRAE, Am. Cons. Engr. Coun., Illuminating Engring. Soc. Past pres.), Soc. for Mkt. Profl. Svcs. (v.p.), Profl. Svcs. Mgmt. Assn. (bd. dirs.), Mo. Soc. Profl. Engrs. (govt. rels. com.), Nat. Fire Protection Assn., Green Turtle Bay Yacht Club, Grand Lake Yacht Club, Ky. Lake Club. Avocations: sailing, flying, horses, photography. Office: The Richardson Engring 7227 Devonshire Saint Louis MO 63119

RICHARDSON, W. FRANKLYN, minister. Gen. sec. Nat. Bapt. Conv. USA, Mt. Vernon, N.Y., 1994; pastor Grace Bapt. Ch., Mt. Vernon, 1994—. Address: 52 S 6th Ave Mount Vernon NY 10550-3005

RICHARDSON, WALTER JOHN, architect; b. Long Beach, Calif., Nov. 14, 1926; s. Walter Francis and Ava Elizabeth (Brown) R.; m. Marilyn Joyce Brown, June 26, 1949 (div. 1982); children: Mark Steven, Glenn Stewart; m. Mary Sue Sutton, Dec. 4, 1982. Student, UCLA, 1944-45, Long Beach City Coll., 1946; BA, U. Calif., Berkeley, 1950. Registered architect, Ala., Ariz., Calif., Colo., Fla., Hawaii, Ill., Kans., Md., Mass., Nev., N.J., N.Y., Okla., Oreg., Tex., Utah, Vt., Va., Wash. Draftsman Wurster, Bernardi, Emmons, San Francisco, 1950-51, Skidmore, Owings & Merrill, San Francisco, 1951; designer Hugh Gibbs Architect, Long Beach, 1952-58; ptnr. Thomas & Richardson Architects, Long Beach, Costa Mesa, 1958-70; pres. Walter Richardson Assocs. Architects, Newport Beach, Calif., 1970-74; chmn. bd. Richardson, Nagy, Martin Architects and Planners, Newport Beach, 1974—. Co-author: The Architect and the Shelter Industry, 1975. Chmn. Planning Commn., City of Orange, Calif., 1967-68. With USAF, 1945. Recipient over 200 Gold Nugget Design awards Pacific Coast Builders Conf., San Francisco, 1969-94, 12 Builders Choice Design awards Builder Mag.; named Architect of Yr. Profl. Builder mag., 1986. Fellow AIA (pres. Orange County chpt. 1970, chmn. nat. housing com. 1976, 7 design awards); mem. Nat. Assn. Home Builders, Nat. Coun. Archtl. Registration Bds., Alpha Tau Omega. Republican. Avocations: photography, downhill skiing, travel, tennis. Office: Richardson Nagy Martin 4611 Teller Ave Ste 100 Newport Beach CA 92660-2104

RICHARDSON, WILLIAM BLAINE, congressman; b. Pasadena, Calif., Nov. 15, 1947; m. Barbara Flavin, 1972. BA, Tufts U., Medford, Mass., 1970; MA, Fletcher Sch. Law and Diplomacy, 1971. Mem. staff U.S. Ho. of Reps., 1971-72, Dept. State, 1973-75; mem. staff fgn. relations com. U.S. Senate, 1975-78; exec. dir. N. Mex. State Democratic Com., 1978, Bernalillo County Democratic Com., 1978; businessman Santa Fe, N. Mex., 1978-82; mem. 98th-103rd Congresses from 3rd N.Mex. dist., Washington, 1982—; democratic chief dep. majority whip 103d Congress; ranking minority mem. Resources Com. on Nat. Pks., Forests and Lands; mem. Select Com. on intelligence, Helsinki Commn. Vice chair Dem. Nat. Com.; active Big Bros.-Big Sisters, Santa Fe. Mem. Santa Fe Hispanic C. of C., Santa Fe C. of C., Council Fgn. Relations, NATO 2000 Bd., Congl. Hispanic Caucus, Am. G.I. Forum. Office: 2209 Rayburn House Office Bldg Bldg Washington DC 20515-0001*

RICHARDSON, WILLIAM CHASE, foundation executive; b. Passaic, N.J., May 11, 1940; s. Henry Burtt and Frances (Chase) R.; m. Nancy Freeland, June 18, 1966; children: Elizabeth, Jennifer. BA, Trinity Coll., 1962; MBA, U. Chgo., 1964, PhD, 1971. Rsch. assoc., instr. U. Chgo., 1967-70; asst. prof. health services U. Wash., 1971-73, assoc. prof., 1973-76, prof., 1976-84, chmn. dept. health services, 1973-76, assoc. dean Sch. Pub. Health, 1976-81, acting dean, 1977, 78, dean Grad. Sch., vice provost, 1981-84; exec. v.p., provost, prof. dept. family and community medicine Pa. State U., 1984-90; pres. Johns Hopkins U., Balt., 1990-95, pres., prof. emeritus, 1995, prof. dept. health policy, mgmt., 1990-95, prof. emeritus, 1995—; pres., CEO W.K. Kellogg Found, Battle Creek, Mich., 1995—; cons. in field; bd. dirs. Kellogg Co., CSX Corp., Mercantile Bankshares Corp., Mercantile-Safe Deposit & Trust Co. Author: books, including Ambulatory Use of Physicians Services, 1971, Health Program Evaluation, 1978; contbr. articles to profl. jours. Mem. external adv. com. Fred Hutchinson Cancer Rsch. Ctr. Kellogg fellow, 1965-67. Fellow Am. Public Health Assn.; mem. Inst. Medicine, Nat. Acad. Scis. Office: WK Kellogg Found One Michigan Ave E Battle Creek MI 49017

RICHARDSON, WILLIAM F., lawyer; b. Harvey, Ill., Apr. 20, 1948; s. Donald and Dorothy (Warren) R. BS, U. Ill., 1970, JD, 1973. Bar: Ill. 1973. Ptnr. Peterson and Ross, Chgo., 1973-94, Blatt, Hammesfahr & Eaton, Chgo., 1994—. Mem. ABA. Office: Blatt Hammesfahr & Eaton 333 W Wacker Dr Ste 1900 Chicago IL 60606-1226

RICHARDSON-MELECH, JOYCE SUZANNE, secondary school educator, singer; b. Perth Amboy, N.J., Nov. 15, 1957; d. Herbert Nathaniel and Fannie Elaine (Franklin) Richardson; m. Gerald Melech, July 28, 1990. MusB, Westminster Choir Coll., 1979, MusM, 1981. Cert. music tchr., N.J. Musical play dir. Perth Amboy H.S., 1989-92, asst. band dir., 1984-94; music tchr. Perth Amboy Bd. Edn., 1981—, gifted and talented music tchr., 1992—; vocal soloist N.Y. Philharm. and Westminster Symphonic Choir, 1977, United Moravian Ch., N.Y.C., 1980-81, Ctrl. Jersey Concert Orch., Perth Amboy, 1994—. Participant Perth Amboy Adult Cmty. Theatre, 1983. Mem. Am. Fedn. Tchrs., Am. Fedn. Musicians (local 373), Music Educators Nat. Conf., Ctrl. Jersey Music Educators, Alpha Phi Omega. Democrat. Mem. African Meth. Episcopal Zion Ch. Avocations: needlepoint, cross-stitch, knitting, sewing, crocheting. Home: 148 Carson Ct Somerset NJ 08873-4790 Office: Samuel Shull Sch 380 Hall Ave Perth Amboy NJ 08861-3402

RICHART, JOHN DOUGLAS, investment banker; b. Urbana, Ill., Jan. 16, 1947; s. Frank Edwin and Elizabeth Norma (Goldthorp) R.; m. Nan Jackson, June 27, 1970. BS in Engring., U. Mich., 1967, MS in Engring., 1968; MBA, Harvard U., 1973. V.p. Donaldson, Lufkin and Jenrette Securities Corp., N.Y.C., 1973-82; mng. dir. Chase Investment Bank div. Chase Manhattan Bank, N.A., N.Y.C., 1982-89; 1st v.p. mgr. mergers and acquisitions Australia and New Zealand Banking Group, N.Y.C., 1989-91; pres. Richart & Co., Upper Montclair, N.J., 1991—. Lt. (j.g.) USCG, 1968-71. Mem. Harvard Bus. Sch. Club N.Y., Montclair Golf Club, Bradford Bath and Tennis Club, PGA West. Republican. Avocations: golf, platform tennis. Home: 15 Bradford Way Cedar Grove NJ 07009-1933 also: 54-981 Southern Hls La Quinta CA 92253-5634 Office: Richart & Co Ste 379 551 Valley Rd Montclair NJ 07043-1850

RICHBURG, KATHRYN SCHALLER, nurse, educator; b. Picayune, Miss., Nov. 29, 1949; m. Edward Richburg Sr., June 24, 1972; children: William II, Kathryn. Diploma, Gilfoy Sch. Nursing, 1970; BSN, U. Miss. Med. Ctr., 1972. Cert. in nursing adminstrn., nursing continuing edn., infection control; cert. healthcare quality profl. Oper. rm. nurse, instr. ARC, 1970-82; infection control nurse U.S. Naval Hosp., Guam, 1982-83; nurse epidemiologist, utilization review coord. Nemours Children's Hosp., Jacksonville, Fla., 1983-86; utilization review coord. SunCare HMO, Jacksonville,

Fla., 1986-87; program mgr. Trident Tech. Coll. Dept. Continuing Edn., Charleston, S.C., 1987-89; program mgr., acting dir. dept. continuing edn. Med. U. S.C., Charleston, 1989-90; edn. coord. quality mgmt. VA Med. Ctr., Charleston, 1990-93; quality assurance risk mgr. U.S. Naval Hosp., Yokosuka, Japan, 1993-95; health promotion dept. head U.S. Naval Hosp., Yokosuka, 1995—. Mem. S.C. Nurses Assn. (chmn. conv. com. 1992, mem. continuing edn. provider unit 1990-92), Trident Nurses Assn. (del. 1990-92, mem. planning com. Rsch. Day 1991, 92), Nat. Assn. Healthcare Quality.

RICHBURG, KEITH BERNARD, journalist, foreign correspondent; b. Detroit, May 19, 1958; s. Walter Arthur and Katie Lee (Clemons) R. BA in Polit. Sci., U. Mich., 1980; MSc in Internat. Rels., London Sch. Econs., 1984. Met. staff reporter Washington Post, 1980-83, nat. staff corr., 1984-86; S.E. Asia bur. chief Washington Post, Manila, 1986-90; Africa bur. chief Washington Post, Nairobi, Keyna, 1991-94; Hong Kong bur. chief Washington Post, 1995—. Recipient fgn. reporting award Nat. Assn. Black Journalists, 1993, UN reporting award Korn-Ferry, 1993, George Polk award for fgn. reporting L.I. U., 1994; Harry S Truman scholar Truman Found., 1978. Mem. Am. Friends London Sch. Econs., U. Mich. Alumni Assn., Phi Beta Kappa. Home and Office: Washington Post (Fgn Desk) 1150 15th St NW Washington DC 20071-0001

RICHELSON, HARVEY, lawyer, educator; b. N.Y.C., Sept. 5, 1951; s. Nathan Eli and Rose (Michalofsky) R. BS in Bus., U. Ariz., 1973; JD, Southwestern U., L.A., 1977; Diploma in Postgrad. Studies Taxation, U. San Diego, 1986, LLM in Taxation cum laude, 1988. Bar: Calif. 1978, Ariz. 1978, U.S. Dist. Ct. (ctrl. dist.) Calif. 1978, U.S. Tax Ct. 1978, U.S. Dist. Ct. (so. dist.) Calif. 1988, U.S. Ct. Appeals (9th cir.) 1986. Pvt. practice Ventura, Calif., 1978-79; ptnr. Hughes & Richelson, Thousand Oaks, Calif., 1979-84; corp. counsel Consolidated Energy Sys., Inc., Thousand Oaks, 1986-91; pvt. practice Thousand Oaks, 1984—; prof. bus. law Moorpark (Calif.) C.C., 1981-93, Calif. C.C., 1981; pres. Consul-Tax Corp., Inc., 1979-81. Screenwriter (theatrical movie) Punk Vacation, 1986. Exec. dir. Scrub Oaks Self-Help Housing, 1984-86, trustee, 1983-88; mem. citizens adv. com. City of Thousand Oaks, 1984-85. Recipient Am. Jurisprudence Book award, West Pub. Co., 1976. Mem. Calif. State Bar Assn., Ariz. State Bar Assn., L.A. County Bar Assn. Office: Ste 424 223 E Thousand Oaks Blvd Thousand Oaks CA 91360

RICHELSON, PAUL WILLIAM, curator; b. Montpelier, Idaho, Sept. 27, 1939; s. Paul Newton and June (Quayle) R. BA, Yale U., 1961; MFA, Princeton U., 1967, PhD, 1974. Asst. prof. Lawrence U., Appleton, Wis., 1970-77, U. Denver, 1977-84; asst. dir., curator Trisolini Gallery of Ohio U., Athens, 1984-87; chief curator Grand Rapids (Mich.) Mus., 1987-91; curator of Am. art Mobile Mus. Art, Mobile, Ala., 1991—. Author: (book) Studies in the Personal Imagery Collection of 20th Prints Ohio University, 1985, (catalogue) The Golden Age 19th Century Prints by David Roberts, 1988, Lee Loring: A Southern Sophisticate, 1992, Modernism and American Painting of the 1930s, 1993, ThirtySomething, 1994, Alabama Impact: Contemporary Artists with Alabama Ties, 1995, Louise Lyons Heistis (1965-1951): A Retrospective, 1995, The French Connection: Jean Simon Chaudron Returns To Mobile, 1996. Lt. (j.g.) USN, 1961-63. Fulbright-Hays fellow to Italy, 1967-69; Mus. Purchase Plan grantee Nat. Endowment for the Arts, 1991. Mem. Southeastern Museums Conf. Home: 6427 Grelot Rd Apt 405 Mobile AL 36695-2630 Office: Mobile Museum of Art PO Box 8426 Mobile AL 36689-0426

RICHENBURG, ROBERT BARTLETT, artist, retired art educator; b. Boston, July 14, 1917; s. Frederick Henry and Spray (Bartlett) R.; m. Libby Chic Peltyn, Nov. 11, 1942 (dec. 1977); 1 child, Ronald P.; m. Margaret Kerr, Feb. 9, 1980; stepchildren: William Blakeley Kerr, David Garrett Kerr, Margaret Frances Kerr. Student, Boston U., George Washington U., Corcoran Sch. Art, Art Students League N.Y., Ozenfant Sch. Fine Arts, Hans Hofmann Sch. Art. Tchr. painting Schrivenham Am. U., Eng., 1945; instr. Coll. City N.Y., 1947-52, Cooper Union, 1954-55; instr., dir. Bklyn.-Queens Central YMCA, 1947-51; instr. NYU, 1960-61, Pratt Inst., Bklyn., 1951-64; assoc. prof. art Cornell U., Ithaca, N.Y., 1964-67; prof. art Hunter Coll., N.Y.C., 1967-70, Aruba (Netherlands Antiles) Research Center, 1970; prof. art Ithaca Coll., 1970-83, mem. council on arts; panelist various orgns. One-man shows Hendler Gallery, Phila., N.Y. Artists Gallery, Tibor DeNagy Gallery, Hansa Gallery, N.Y., Dwan Gallery, Los Angeles, Santa Barbara Mus. (Calif.), Dayton Art Inst., Dana Arts Center Colgate U., Ithaca Coll. Mus. Art, Grad. Sch. Bus. Cornell U., others; exhibited in group shows Mus. Modern Art, Solomon Guggenheim Mus., N.Y.C., Chrysler Art Mus., Yale Art Gallery, Whitney Mus., N.Y.C., Univ. Art Mus., Austin, Tex., Balt. Mus., Cocoran Mus. Art, Washington, Bklyn. Mus., Knox Albright Mus., Buffalo, Larry Aldrich Mus., Seattle Art Mus., Boston Mus. Fine Arts, numerous others; represented in permanent collections Chrysler Mus. Art, Norfolk Mus. Art, Coll. of William and Mary, Whitney Mus., Phila. Mus. Art, Pasadena Mus. Fine Art, Mus. Modern Art, Univ. Art Mus., U. Calif.-Berkeley, U. Tex. Art Mus., Austin, Ithaca Coll. Mus., Hirschorn Mus., Smithsonian Instn., Washington, many others. Served with AUS, 1942-45. Mem. Am. Assn. U. Profs., Coll. Art Assn., Internat. Platform Assn., Art Students League N.Y. (life). Club: (N.Y.C.). Home: 1006 Springs Fireplace Rd East Hampton NY 11937-1432

RICHENS, KIMBERLEE MARIE, real estate property manager, appraiser; b. Marion, Ohio, May 12, 1957; d. Rudolph Richard and Margaret Charlott (Carroll) Mucheck; m. Tim Richens, Dec. 10, 1978; 1 child, Jessica Elizabeth. Residential mgr. cert., IREM, 1984; cert., Am. Schs., Anaheim, Calif., 1992. Licensed Real Estate Appraiser. Property mgr. Forest City Mgmt. Inc., Cleveland, 1979—; real estate appraiser Grand Terrace, Calif., 1992—. Inventor sun enhancer, 1993; contbr. articles to profl. jours. Mem. Inst. Real Estate Mgmt., Nat. Assn. Real Estate Appraiser, San Bernardino Ch. of C., Grand Terrace C. of C. Democrat. Roman Catholic. Avocations: boating, Tai-Chi, hiking, dogs, gardening. Home: 22636 Lark St Grand Terrace CA 92313-5714 Office: Forest City Mgmt Inc 11750 Mount Vernon Ave Grand Terrace CA 92313

RICHERSON, HAL BATES, physician, internist, allergist, immunologist, educator; b. Phoenix, Feb. 16, 1929; s. George Edward and Eva Louise (Steere) R.; m. Julia Suzanne Bradley, Sept. 5, 1953; children: Anne, George, Miriam, Julia, Susan. BS with distinction, U. Ariz., 1950; MD, Northwestern U., 1954. Diplomate Am. Bd. Internal Medicine, Am. Bd. Allergy and Immunology, Bd. Diagnostic Lab. Immunology; lic. physician, Ariz., Iowa. Intern Kansas City (Mo.) Gen. Hosp., 1954-55; resident in pathology St. Luke's Hosp., Kansas City, 1955-56; trainee in neuropsychiatry Brooke Army Hosp., San Antonio, 1956; resident in medicine U. Iowa Hosps., Iowa City, 1961-64, fellow in allergy and immunology, 1964-66; fellow in immunology Mass. Gen. Hosp., Boston, 1968-69, instr. internal medicine, 1964-66, asst. prof., 1966-70, assoc. prof., 1970-74, prof., 1974—, acting dir. divsn. allergy/applied immunology, 1970-72, dir. allergy and clin. immunology sect., 1972-78, dir. divsn. allergy and immunology, 1978-91; gen. practice, asst. to Gen. Surgeon Ukiah, Calif., 1958; gen. practice medicine Holbrook, Ariz., 1958-61; vis. lectr. medicine Harvard U. Sch. Medicine, Boston, 1968-69; vis. prof., rsch. scientist U. London and Brompton Hosp., 1984; prin. investigator Nat. Heart, Lung and Blood Inst., 1971—, mem. pulmonary diseases adv. com., 1983-87; prin. investigator Nat. Inst. Allergy and Infectious Diseases, 1983-94; dir. Nat. Inst. Allergy and Infectious Diseases' Asthma and Allergic Diseases Ctr., U. Iowa, 1983-94; mem. VA Merit Rev. Bd. in Respiration, 1981-84; mem. com. NIH Gen. Clin. Rsch. Ctrs., 1989-93; mem. rev. reserve NIH, 1993—; mem. bd. sci. advisors Merck Inst., 1990-94; presenter lectures, seminars, continuing edn. courses; mem. numerous univ., coll. and hosp. coms., 1970—; cons. Merck Manual, 1982, 87, 92. Contbr. numerous articles and revs. to profl. jours., chpts. to books; reviewer Sci., Jour. Immunology, Jour. Allergy and Clin. Immunology, Am. Rev. Respiratory Disease, New Eng. Jour. Medicine, Ann. Internal Medicine. Served to capt. U.S. Army, 1956-58. NIH fellow 1968-69. Fellow ACP, Am. Acad. Allergy; mem. AMA (mem. residency and rev. com. for allergy and immunology; mem. accreditation com. for grad. med. edn. 1980-85, vice-chmn. 1984-85), AAAS, Iowa Med. Soc., Iowa Thoracic Soc. (chmn. program com. 1964-65, 69-71, pres. 1972-73, mem. exec. com. 1972-74), Am. Thoracic Soc. (bd. dirs. 1981-82, councilor assembly on allergy and immunology 1980-81, mem. nominating com. 1988-90), Iowa Clin. Med. Soc., Am. Fedn. Clin. Rsch., Am. Assn. Immunologists, Ctrl. Soc. Clin. Rsch. (chmn. sect. on allergy-immunology 1980-81, mem. coun. 1981-84), Alpha Omega Alpha. Avocations: reading, swimming, handball, scuba diving. Home: 331 Lucon Dr Iowa City IA 52246-3300 Office: U Iowa Hosps and Clinics Dept Internal Medicine SE 630 Gen Hosp Iowa City IA 52242

RICHERT, PAUL, law educator; b. Elwood, Ind., Aug. 31, 1948; s. Clarendon George and Margaret Ann (Cummins) R.; m. Catherine George Stanton, June 24, 1972; children: John Cummins, William Stanton. AB, U. Ill.-Urbana, 1970, MS, 1971; JD, Tulane U., 1977. Bar: Ohio 1977. Asst. law librarian U. Akron, 1977-78, law librarian, asst. prof. law, 1978-83, assoc. prof., 1983-87, prof. law, 1987—; cons. to cts. Served with U.S. Army, 1971-74. Mem. Am. Assn. Law Libraries, Akron Bar Assn., ABA. Mem. United Churches of Christ. Editor: Ohio Appellate Decision on Fiche, 1981; indexer Publs. Clearing House Bull., vols. 1-4. Home: 2030 Ganyard Rd Akron OH 44313-6050 Office: U Akron Sch of Law Libr 150 University Ave Akron OH 44304-1502

RICHETTE, LISA AVERSA, judge; b. Phila., Sept. 11, 1928; d. Domenico and Maria (Giannini) Aversa; m. Lawrence J. Richette, Apr. 15, 1958 (div. Apr. 1971); 1 child, Lawrence Anthony II. BA summa cum laude, U. Pa., 1949; LLB, Yale U., 1952. Bar: Pa. 1954. Rsch. assoc. Yale U. Law Sch., 1952, instr., 1952-54; asst. dist. atty. Dist. Atty.'s Office, Phila., 1954-64, chief family ct. div., 1956-64; judge Ct. Common Pleas, Phila., 1972—; lectr. Temple U. Law Sch., 1972—, adj. prof. law, 1972—; adj. prof. sociology dept. St. Joseph's U.; clin. prof. law Villanova (Pa.) U. Law Sch., 1970-72. Author: The Throwaway Children, 1969. Co-founder, bd. dirs. Big Sisters, Phila. YWCA, Nat. Commn. Child Abuse; pres. Phila. Health and Welfare Coun., 1958-60. Decorated Star of Solidarity (Italy); recipient Disting. Dau. of Pa. award Commonwealth Pa., 1991, St. Thomas More Lawyer of Yr. award, 1994. Mem. Phila. Bar Assn. (vice chmn. chancellor's commn. on drug abuse 1972-75), Justinian Soc., U. Pa. Women's Alumna Soc. (pres. 1966-70), Mortar Bd., Phi Beta Kappa, Phi Alpha Theta. Office: Criminal Justice Ctr 1301 Filbert St Rm 1407 Philadelphia PA 19107-3201

RICHEY, CHARLES ROBERT, federal judge; b. Logan County, Ohio, Oct. 16, 1923; s. Paul D. and Miriam (Blaine) R.; m. Agnes Mardelle White, Mar. 25, 1950; children: Charles R. Jr., William Paul. BA, Ohio Wesleyan U., 1945, LLD, 1996; LLB, Case-Western Res. U., 1948. Bar: Ohio 1949, D.C. 1951, U.S. Supreme Ct. 1952, Md. 1964. Legis. counsel, former congresswoman Frances P. Bolton, Ohio, 1948-49; practice in Washington and Chevy Chase, Md., 1950-71; founding partner firm Richey & Clancy, Washington and Chevy Chase, Md., 1964-71; gen. counsel Md. Pub. Service Commn., 1967-71; judge U.S. Dist. Ct. D.C., 1971—; sat by designation as mem. U.S. Ct. Appeals for D.C., 1972-75, 77-85; mem. Temporary U.S. Emergency Ct. Appeals, 1983-84, Commn. on Criminal Law and Adminstrn. of Probation Sys. of Jud. Conf. U.S., 1954-55; adj. prof. trial advocacy-practice Georgetown Law Ctr., 1975-94, mem. adv. bd. CLE Program, 1979-85; mem. faculty Nat. Coll. State Judiciary, 1973-75, Fed. Jud. Ctr., 1976-86, U.S. Atty. Gen.'s Advocacy Inst., Washington, 1977-85, 96; spl. counsel councilman redistricting Montgomery County Govt., 1965-66; vice chmn. Charter Revision Commn., 1967-68; lectr. ABA and ATLA ann. meetings, CLE programs of Am. Law Inst., ABA, Practicing Law Inst. and other Bar and civic groups throughout U.S.; mem. Jud. Coun., D.C. Cir., 1988-94; co-chair D.C. 1st and 3d cirs. Sentencing Insts., 1984, D.C. 3d and 7th cirs. Sentencing Insts., 1992. Author: Manual on Employment Discrimination and Civil Rights Actions, 1994, Prisoner Litigation in the United States Courts, 1995; contbr. articles to profl. jours. Legal counsel Boys' Clubs Greater Washington, 1966-71; affiliate mem. D.C. Urban Renewal Council and Citizens Housing Commn., 1961-64; chmn. parents assn. Sidwell Friends Sch., Washington, 1968-70; mem. Montgomery County Bd. Appeals, 1965-67, chmn., 1966-67; trustee Immaculata Coll., Washington, 1970-73, Suburban Hosp. Bethesda, Md., 1967-71; pres. PTA, Potomac, Md., 1966-67. Recipient Outstanding and Dedicated Pub. Svc. award Montgomery County, Md., 1966, 68, Cert. Disting. Citizenship award Gov. Md., 1971, Ann. Award of Merit by Adminstrv. Law Judges of U.S., 1979, Outstanding U.S. Fed. Trial Judge, ATLA, 1979, Humanitarian of Yr. award, Howard U. Law Sch. Alumni Assn., 1979, Supreme Ct. Justice Howard Hitz Burton award, Cleveland Club of Washington, 1990, Judge H. Carl Moultrie award for Jud. Excellence, D.C. Area Trial Lawyers Assn., 1990, Outstanding Spkr. award Fla. Bar Assn., 1991, Ben A Arneson Disting. Pub. Career award Ohio Wesleyan U., 1994, Case Western Res. U. Law Sch. medal, 1994. Fellow Am. Bar Found. (life); mem. ABA (ho. of dels. 1981-85, chmn. com. on alcohol and drug abuse 1973-76, chmn. com. on sentencing probation and parole 1975-77, mem. coun. criminal justice sect. 1976-80, chmn. nat. adv. com. Project ADVoCATE 1976-80, chmn. nat. conf. fed. trial judges 1980-81, officer and mem. exec. com. 1975-85, mem. coun. jud. adminstrv. divsn. 1980-81), ATLA (faculty Nat. Coll. Advocacy 1975-77), Am. Judicature Soc., Bar Assn. D.C., Md. Bar Assn., Supreme Ct. Hist. Soc. (founding), Edward Bennett Williams Am. Inn. of Ct. (master, charter), Charlotte E. Ray Am. Inn of Ct. (master, charter), Soc. of Benchers of Case Western Res. U. Sch. Law, Omicron Delta Kappa, Delta Sigma Rho, Pi Delta Epsilon, Phi Delta Phi, Phi Gamma Delta (gen. counsel 1960-63). Methodist. Club: Nat. Lawyers (Washington). Lodge: Masons (33rd degree). Home: 8101 Connecticut Ave Apt C-501 Chevy Chase MD 20815-2810 Office: US Dist Ct US Courthouse 3rd & Constitution Ave NW Washington DC 20001

RICHEY, CLARENCE BENTLEY, agricultural engineering educator; b. Winnipeg, Manitoba, Can., Dec. 28, 1910; s. Raus Spears and Emily Cornelia (Bentley) R.; m. Marguerite Anne Jannusch, Dec. 27, 1936; children: David Volkman, Stephen Bentley. BS in Agrl. Engring., Iowa State U., 1933; BS in Mech. Engring., Purdue U., 1939. Registered agrl. engr., Calif. Instr. agrl. engring. Purdue U., West Lafayette, Ind., 1936-41; asst. prof. dept. agrl. engring. Ohio State U., Columbus, 1941-43; head devel. engr. Electric Wheel Co., Quincy, Ill., 1943-46; project engr. Harry Ferguson, Inc., Detroit, 1946-47; sr. project engr. Dearborn Motors Corp., Detroit, 1947-54; supt., chief rsch. engr. Ford Tractor Divsn., Birmingham, Mich., 1954-62; chief engr. Fowler (Calif.) divsn. Massey-Ferguson Ltd., 1964-69; product mgmt. engr. Massey-Ferguson Ltd., Toronto, Ont., Can., 1970-71; assoc. prof. agrl. engring. Purdue U., West Lafayette, 1971-76, prof. emeritus, 1976—; farm equipment cons. Ford Found., Allahabad, India, 1963. Author: (autobiography) Fifty Years of Engineering Farm Equipment, 1989; editor-in-chief: Agricultural Engineer's Handbook, 1961; contbr. bulls. and articles to profl. jours. Fellow Am. Soc. Agrl. Engrs. (Cyrus Hall McCormick Gold medal 1977); mem. Lafayette Kiwanis. Achievements include patent for farm equipment; holder or co-holder of 79 patents. Home: 2217 Delaware Dr West Lafayette IN 47906-1917

RICHEY, MARVIN E(LDEN), electrical engineer, administrator; b. Wichita, Kans., Nov. 21, 1946; s. Marvin Elden Sr. and Barbara Jean (Carterette) R.; m. Linda Louise Wheeler, Oct. 15, 1966 (div. Sept. 1977); m. Janice Ellen Doyle, Nov. 21, 1990; children: Brittany, Sean, Amy, Rachel. BBA, Nat. U., San Diego, 1991, MBA, 1992. Registered profl. elec. engr., Nev. Elec. project mgr. Intercontinental Engring., Riverside, Mo., 1971-78; engr. IV Princeton (N.J.) U., 1980-89; engr. specialist I EG&G, Morgantown, W.Va., 1978-80; sr. engr. EG&G, Las Vegas, Nev., 1989-94; dir. elec. engring. Design Engring. Assocs., Las Vegas, 1994-95; pres. Argus Engring., 1995—; dir. R & D U-Products, Internat., Las Vegas, 1989—. Cons. Aid for Aids Nev., Las Vegas, 1990-92. Recipient Nuclear Weapons award for Excellence, U.S. Dept. Energy and U.S. Dept. Def., Las Vegas, 1991, 94. Mem. Assn. Energy Engrs. (sr.). Achievements include the designing of coin-operated games. Avocations: restoring classic cars, woodworking. Home: 745 Yacht Harbor Dr Las Vegas NV 89128 Office: Design Engring Assocs 2880 Meade Ave Las Vegas NV 89102

RICHEY, PHIL HORACE, former manufacturing executive, consultant; b. Detroit, July 30, 1923; s. Lawrence Kennedy and Hazel Annsonia (Stuckey) R.; children: Karen L. Richey Forrester, Ann C. Richey Zepke; stepchildren: Gregory F. Lloyd, Charles E. Lloyd III.; m. Mary Elizabeth McCulloch, June 30, 1984; stepchildren: Julie Ann McCulloch Beal, Mary Elizabeth McCulloch, Claire May Thompson. B.A. with distinction, U. Mich., 1948. With Detrex Chem. Industries Inc., Detroit, 1948-56; group v.p. Detrex Chem. Industries Inc., 1962-71; with Allied Research Products Co., 1956-59, v.p. fin., 1958-59; with U.S. Chem. Milling Co., Manhattan Beach, Calif., 1959-61; v.p. U.S. Chem. Milling Co., 1960-61; with Olin Corp., Stamford, Conn., 1971-81; corp. v.p., pres. Winchester group, 1977-81; mgmt. cons., 1981—; bd. dirs. Assn. Chems. and Svcs., Inc. 1st lt. AUS, 1942-46. Mem. Phi Kappa Phi, Beta Gamma Sigma. Home and Office: 342 Winamar Ave La Jolla CA 92037-6549

RICHEY, RONALD KAY, insurance company executive, lawyer; b. Erie, Kans., June 16, 1926; s. Earle Jacob and Mary Wintress (Oakleaf) R.; m. Florence E. Kane, Nov. 24, 1949; children: Linda, Robert, Chris. B.A., Washburn U., 1949, LL.B., 1951. Bar: Kans. 1951, Ill. 1958, Okla. 1965. Vice pres. Central Plains Ins. Group, Hutchinson, Kans., 1955-57; legis. mgr. Am. Mut. Ins. Alliance, Chgo., 1957-64; exec. v.p. Globe Life and Accident Ins. Co., Oklahoma City, 1964-78, chmn. bd., 1978—, chief exec. officer, 1978-82; pres. Torchmark Corp., Birmingham, Ala., 1982-85, pres., chief operating officer, 1985-86, chmn. bd., chief operating officer, 1986—, also bd. dirs.; bd. dirs. Liberty Nat. Life Ins. Co., Birmingham, United Am. Inst. Co., Dallas; chmn. bd. VESTA Ins. Group, Inc., Birmingham, United Group of Funds, TMK/United Funds, Inc., Waddell & Reed Funds, Inc., Shawnee Mission, Kans. Served with U.S. Army, 1944-46. Mem. ABA, Am. Coun. Life Ins. Assn. (bd. dirs.), Okla. Bar Assn., Health Ins. Assn. Am., Oklahoma City C. of C. (bd. dirs.), Shoal Creek Golf and Country Club, Old Overton Club (Vestavia Hills, Ala.), Rancho La Quinta Country Club (Calif.). Republican. Clubs: Quail Creek Golf and Country (Oklahoma City); Oaktree Golf and Country (Edmond, Okla.); Shoal Creek Golf and Country (Birmingham). Office: Torchmark Corp 2001 3rd Ave S Birmingham AL 35233-2101

RICHIE, JEROME PAUL, surgeon, educator; b. San Antonio, 1944. MD, U. Tex., 1969. Surg. intern UCLA, 1969-70, resident in gen. surgery, 1970-71, resident in urology, 1971-75, lectr. surg. urology, 1974-75; asst. clin. prof. U. Calif., San Diego, 1975-77; asst. prof. urology Harvard U., 1977-80, assoc. prof., 1980-86, prof., 1986—, Elliott C. Cutler prof. surgery, 1987—, chmn. program in urology, 1987—; chief urol. oncology Brigham and Women's Hosp., Boston, 1977—; cons. Dana Farber Cancer Ctr., Boston, 1977—. Lt. comdr. M.C., USN, 1975-77. Mem. ACS, Am. Assn. Gerito-Urinary Surgeons, Am. Urol. Assn., Assn. Acad. Surgery, Am. Soc. (Clin.) Oncology, Am. Surg. Assn. Office: Brigham & Womens Hosp 45 Francis St # 3 Boston MA 02115-6105

RICHIE, LEROY C., lawyer, automotive executive; b. Buffalo, N.Y., Sept. 27, 1941; s. Leroy C. and Mattie A. (Allen) R.; m. Julia Thomas Richie, June 10, 1972; children: Leroy, Lamont, Loren, Brooke, Darcy. BA magna cum laude, CCNY, 1970; JD, NYU, 1973. Bar: Mich. 1985, N.Y. 1974, U.S. Ct. Appeals (2nd cir.) 1974. Atty. White & Case, N.Y.C., 1973-78; dir. Fed. Trade Commn. N.Y. Regional Office, N.Y.C., 1978-83; asst. gen. counsel Chrysler Corp., Highland Park, Mich., 1983-84; assoc. gen. counsel Chrysler Corp., Highland Park, 1984-86, v.p., gen. counsel of Automotive Legal Affairs, 1986—; chmn. Vis. Nurses Assn., Detroit, 1988-90, Highland Park (Mich.) Devel. Corp., 1988—; chmn. bd. trustees Marygrove Coll., Detroit, 1994—; treas. Nat. Jud. Coll., Reno. With U.S. Army, 1961-64, Germany. Fellowship award, Arthur Garfield Hayes Civil Liberties, NYU, 1972. Mem. Am. Corporate Counsel Assn. (bd. dirs. Mich. chpt. 1987—), Detroit Bar Assn. Office: Chrysler Motors Corp 1000 Chrysler Dr Auburn Hills MI 48326-2766*

RICHIE, LIONEL B., JR., singer, songwriter, producer; b. Tuskegee, Ala., June 20, 1949; s. Lyonel B. Sr. and Alberta (Foster) R.; m. Brenda Harvey, 1975. BS in Econs., Tuskegee U., 1971, MusD (hon.), 1985; MusD (hon.), Boston Coll., 1986. Pres. Brockman Music, L.A. Mem. group The Mystics (name changed to The Commodores), 1969-81; writer, producer songs for Commodores including: Easy, Three Times a Lady (Am. Music award 1979, People's Choice award for best song 1979), Still (People's Choice award for best song 1980), Sail On, Lady (Nat. Music Pubs. award 1980, 81, People's Choice award for best composer 1981); songwriter, producer album for Kenny Rogers; albums (with The Commodores) include Midnight Magic, Machine Gun, Movin' On, Commodores, Caught in the Act, Hot on the Tracks, Natural High, Heroes, (solo albums) Lionel Richie, Can't Slow Down, 1984 (Grammy award Album of Yr. 1985), Dancing on the Ceiling, 1986, Back to Front, 1992; producer, composer: (songs) Truly (Grammy award 1982, 2 Am. Music awards 1983, People's Choice award Best Song, 1983), All Night Long (Nat. Music Pubs. award 1984, 3 Black Gold awards 1984, Am. Music award 1984, Hello (2 Am. Music awards 1985), Say You, Say Me (ASCAP Pop award 1987, Am. Music award 1987, Oscar award Best Song 1986, Golden Globe award Best Song 1986), Dancing on the Ceiling (3 Am. Music awards 1987), (duet with Diana Ross) Endless Love (Grammy award 1982, 2 Am. Music awards 1982, Am. Movie award 1982, Rojo award Gold Status in Hong Kong 1982, People's Choice award Best Song 1982), (sung by Kenny Rogers) Lady, (with Michael Jackson) We Are The World, 1985 (Grammy awards Best Song, Record of Yr. 1986, People's Choice award Best Song 1986). Recipient Best Young Artist in Film award, 1980, 2 NAACP image awards, 1983, Favorite Male Vocalist Pop/Rock award Am. Music Acad., 1987, Favorite Male Vocalist Soul/R&B award Am. Music Acad., 1987; named Man of Yr. Children's Diabetes Found., 1984, Alumnus of Yr. United Negro Coll. Fund, 1984, Favorite Male Singer People mag. Readers Poll, 1985, Entertainer of Yr., NAACP, 1987. Mem. ASCAP (Writer of Yr. 1984, 85, 86, Pub. of Yr. 1985).

RICHIE, RODNEY CHARLES, critical care and pulmonary medicine physician; b. Big Springs, Tex., Aug. 17, 1946; s. Howard Mouzon and Gloria (Hollingshead) R.; m. Sara Lee Dilley, July 13, 1968; children: Megan Kathryn, Paul Nathan. BA in Chemistry, So. Meth. U., 1968; MD cum laude, Baylor Coll., 1972. Diplomate in Internal Medicine, Pulmonary, Crit. Care and Ins. Medicine. Resident in medicine Baylor Affiliated Hosps., Houston, 1973-75, chief med. resident, 1975, fellow in pulmonary medicine, 1976-77; pvt. practice, pres. Waco (Tex.) Lung Assocs., 1977—; med. dir. Tex. Life Ins., Waco, 1985—. Chmn. med. staff Hillcrest Bapt. Med. Ctr., Waco, 1993; chmn. bd. dirs. GH Pape Found., Waco, 1993. Fellow Am. Coll. Chest Physicians; mem. ACP, AMA, Am. Thoracic Soc., Tex. Club Internists. Episcopalian. Avocations: snow skiing, writing, reading. Home: 3509 Lake Heights Dr Waco TX 76708-1005 Office: Waco Med Group 2911 Herring Ave Ste 212 Waco TX 76708-3244

RICHIE, SHARON I., army nursing officer; b. Phila., Dec. 14, 1949; d. William Joseph and Helen Lucille (Oglesby) R.; m. Paul Henri, Jan. 1, 1986. BS, Wagner Coll., 1971; MS, U. Tex. Grad. Sch. Nursing, San Antonio, 1976; postgrad. George Washington U., 1987—;student Army War Coll., 1987-88. Commd. 2d lt. U.S. Army, advanced through grades to col., 1988; clin. staff nurse Walter Reed Army Med. Ctr., Washington 1971-74; hosp. pschiat. nurse cons., head nurse 5th Gen. Hosp., Landstuhl, Germany, 1976-77; psychiat. clin. nurse specialist Alcholism Treatment Facility, Stuttgart, Germany, 1977-79; cons. alcohol and drug abuse nursing U.S. Army Surg. Gen., The Pentagon, Washington, 1980, also clin. liaison officer; asst. dir. edn. and rehab. Office Drug and Alcohol Abuse Prevention, Dept. Def., Pentagon, 1980-82; White House fellow, 1982-83; asst. chief nurse evenings/nights Letterman Army Med. ctr., San Francisco, 1983-84, chief ambulatory nursing service, 1984-85, dir. quality assurance, dept. nursing, 1985-86; PROFIS chief nurse, 8th Evacuation Hosp., Fort Ord, Calif., 1984-86; asst. chief nurse Kimbrough Army Hosp., Ft. Meade, Md., 1986, chief dept. nursing, 1986-87; chief clin. nursing svc. Walter Reed Army Med. Ctr., Washington, 1988-90; chief dept. nursing Letterman Army Med. Ctr., San Francisco, 1990-91; dir. med. directorate U.S. Army Recruiting Command, Ft. Sheridan, Ill., 1991; dir Health Svcs. Directorate U.S. Army Recruiting Command, Ft. Knox, Ky., 1991-93; chief nurse S.E. Regional Health Svcs. Support Area and dir. Nursing Eisenhower Army Med. Ctr., Fort Gordon, Ga., 1993—; cons. Regional Commrs. Pres's Commn. on White House Fellow, 1985-86, sec. White House Fellow Assn. and Found. Bd. Named Alumni of Yr., Wagner Coll., S.I., 1983; White House fellow, 1982; recipient Meritorious medal sec. Def., 1982, A Prefix U.S. Army Surgeon Gen., 1992, Legion of Merit 1993, Presdl. Svc. Badge (white house) 1993. Mem. Nat. Black Nurses Assn., Am. Nurses Assn., Am. Nurses Found., Assn. U.S. Army, Assn. U.S. Mil. Surgeons, Sigma Theta Tau. Clubs: Presidio Officers (co chmn. council 1985-86), Army and Navy Club, Rocks (Washington) (former v.p.). Avocations: weight lifting, collecting miniature camels, indoor gardening. Home: 3019 Bransford Rd Augusta GA 30909-3090 Office: Eisenhower Army Med Ctr Dept Nursing Augusta GA 30905

RICHKIN, BARRY ELLIOTT, financial services executive; b. N.Y.C., Apr. 14, 1944; s. Harry and Celia (Goldberg) R. BA, Bklyn. Coll., 1964. CLU, cert. in personal fin. planning, NASD. Auditor First Nat. Bank of N.Y.,

N.Y.C., 1968-70; sr. supr. ABC, N.Y.C., 1970-73; account rep. Met. Life Ins. co., Atlanta, 1973-74; rep. Mixon-Baker Fin. Svcs., Atlanta, 1974-78; owner Barry Richkin Fin. Svcs., Roswell, Ga., 1978—; owner Barry Richkin Philatelics, Roswell, 1991—; cons., owner Benefit Cons. Group, Roswell, 1989—; cons., pres., bd. dirs. Am. Health Network, Roswell, 1982—. Author: Guide to Preferred Provider Organizations, 1986. Mem. Am. Soc. CLU and ChFC, Am. Philatelic Soc., Manuscript Soc., U.S. Postal Hist. Soc., Conn. Hist. Soc. Avocations: manuscripts, philatelics, jogging. Office: Barry Richkin Fin Svcs 600 Houze Way Bldg C-6 Roswell GA 30076-1435

RICHLER, MORDECAI, writer; b. Montreal, Que., Can., Jan. 27, 1931; s. Moses Isaac and Lily (Rosenberg) R.; m. Florence Wood, July 27, 1959; children: Daniel, Noah, Emma, Martha, Jacob. Student, Sir George Williams U., 1948-50. vis. prof. Carleton U., Ottawa, Ont., 1972-74; assoc. judge for Can., Book-of-the-Month Club, 1974-88, also mem. editorial bd., N.Y. Author: (novels) The Acrobats, 1954, Son of a Smaller Hero, 1955, A Choice of Enemies, 1957, The Apprenticeship of Duddy Kravitz, 1959, Stick Your Neck Out, 1963, Cocksure, 1967, St. Urbain's Horseman, 1971, Joshua Then and Now, 1980, Solomon Gursky Was Here, 1990, (essays) Notes on an Endangered Species, 1974, Home Sweet Home, 1984, Oh Canada!, Oh Quebec! A Lament for a Divided Nation, 1992, (stories) The Street, 1975, (nonfiction) Oh Canada! Oh Quebec! Requiem for a Divided Country, 1992, This Year in Jerusalem, a memoir, 1994; children books Jacob Two-Two Meets The Hooded Fang, 1975, Jacob Two-Two and the Dinosaur, 1987; film The Apprenticeship of Duddy Kravitz, 1974 (Acad. award nomination 1974, Writers Guild of Am. award 1974), Joshua, Then and Now, 1985, Jacob Two-Two's First Spy Case, 1995; editor: The Best of Modern Humor, 1983, Writers on World War II, 1991; contbr. articles to profl. jours. Recipient Gov.-Gen.'s award for lit., 1968, 71, Paris Rev. Humour prize, 1968, Commonwealth Writer's prize, 1990; Guggenheim fellow, 1961; various Can. Coun. fellowships. Mem. Montreal Press Club. Home: Apt 80 C, 1321 Sherbrooke St W, Montreal, PQ Canada H3Y 1J4

RICHLIN, W. GAR, investment banking executive, lawyer; b. N.Y.C., July 7, 1945; s. Padie and Sylvia (Salzman) R.; m. Margaret Goodman, June 7, 1967; children: Kimberly A., Jenny R. AB with honors, Wesleyan U., 1967; JD, Georgetown U., 1971. Law clk. to Hon. Harrison L. Winter, U.S. Ct. Appeals, 1971-72; assoc. Piper & Marbury, Balt., 1972-79, ptnr., 1979-89; mgr., gen. counsel Alex Brown & Sons Inc., Balt., 1989-91, head investment banking, mgr., 1991—, also bd. dirs. Home: 11425 High Hay Dr Columbia MD 21044-1027 Office: Alex Brown & Sons Inc 135 E Baltimore St Baltimore MD 21202-1607

RICHMAN, ALAN, magazine editor; b. Bronx, N.Y., Nov. 12, 1939; s. Louis and Sonia (Carity) R.; m. Kelli Shor, June 21, 1964; children: Lincoln Seth Shor, Matthew Mackenzie Shor. B.A., Hunter Coll., 1960. Reporter Leader-Observer (weekly newspaper), N.Y.C., 1960-61; asst. editor Modern Tire Dealer (publ.), N.Y.C., 1962-64; assoc. editor ASTA Travel News, N.Y.C., 1964-65; pub. relations rep. M.J. Jacobs, Inc. (advt. agy.), N.Y.C., 1965-66; mng. editor Modern Floor Coverings, N.Y.C., 1966-68; editor Bank Systems & Equipment, N.Y.C., 1968-79, Health Care Products News, N.Y.C., 1976; asso. pub. Bank Systems & Equipment, 1969-71, co-pub., 1971-73, pub., 1973-79; editorial dir. Nat. Jeweler, N.Y.C., 1979-81; editor Health Foods Bus.: editorial dir. Army/Navy Store and Outdoor Merchandiser, 1981-88, The Pet Dealer, 1983-88; editor Cabinet Mfg. and Fabricating KBC Publs., 1988—; program dir. Cabinet Mfg. Fair, 1989—; adj. faculty NYU, 1989—, Brookdale Community Coll., 1992—, Bergen County Community Coll., 1994—. Exec. editor: Kitchen and Beth Design News, 1992-93; editor-in-chief Wood Digest, PTN Pub. Co., 1992-94; editor: Whole Foods, 1994—; author: Czechoslovakia in Pictures, 1969, A Book on the Chair, 1968. Served with AUS, 1961-62. Recipient Jesse H. Neal certificate merit Am. Bus. Press, 1973. Mem. Internat. Platform Assn.

RICHMAN, ARTHUR SHERMAN, sports association executive; b. N.Y.C., Mar. 21, 1926; s. Samuel Abraham and Clara (Ganbarg) R.; m. Martha Landgrebe, Nov. 9, 1979. Student, Bklyn. Coll., 1942-44. Baseball writer, columnist N.Y. Mirror, N.Y.C., 1943-63; acct. exec. Grey Pub. Rels., N.Y.C., 1963-65; dir. promotions, pub. rels., traveling sec., spl. asst. to gen. mgr. N.Y. Mets, Flushing, 1965-89; sr. v.p. N.Y. Yankees, Bronx, 1989—. Contbr. articles to profl. and popular jours. Leader baseball groups USO/U.S. Dept. Def., Vietnam, Thailand, Japan, Korea, Philippines, Guam, Hawaii and Greenland, 1965-74;. Recipient Ben Epstein Good Guy award N.Y. Baseball Writers, 1983, Long and Meritorious Svc. award Major League Baseball Scouts, 1984, Good Guy award N.Y. Press Photographers, 1988, Gerage Sisler Long and Meritorious Svc. award St. Louis Browns Hist. Soc., 1996; electo to Bklyn. Coll. Atletic Hall of Fame, 1984, St. Louis Browns Baseball Media Hall of Fame, 1986; inducted into Nat. Jewish Am. Sports Hall of Fame, 1996. Mem. Assn. Profl. Baseball Players Am. (v.p. 1986—). Jewish. Office: NY Yankees Yankee Stadium E 161st St & River Ave Bronx NY 10451

RICHMAN, DAVID PAUL, neurologist, researcher; b. Boston, June 9, 1943; s. Harry S. and Anne (Goodkin) R.; m. Carol Mae von Bastian, Aug. 31, 1969; children—Sarah Ann, Jacob Charles. A.B., Princeton U., 1965; M.D., Johns Hopkins U., 1969. Diplomate Am. Bd. Psychiatry and Neurology. Intern, asst. resident in medicine Albert Einstein Coll. Medicine, N.Y.C., 1969-71; resident in neurology Mass. Gen. Hosp., Boston, 1971-73, chief resident in neurology, 1973-74; instr. neurology Harvard Med. Sch., Boston, 1975-76; asst. prof. neurology U. Chgo., 1976-80, assoc. prof. dept. neurology, mem. immunology and neurobiology coms., 1981-85, prof. dept. neurology and com. on immunology, 1985-91, Straus prof. neurol. scis., 1988-91; prof., chair dept. neurology U. Calif., Davis, 1991—; mem. com. Nat. Inst. Aging, NIH, 1984-85, mem. immunogical scis. study sect., 1986-90. Mem. AAAS, Am. Assn. Immunologists, Am. Acad. Neurology, Am. Neurol. Assn., Phi Beta Kappa, Sigma Xi. Office: U Calif Davis Neurology Dept Davis CA 95616-8603

RICHMAN, FREDERICK ALEXANDER, lawyer; b. Pasadena, Calif., Oct. 18, 1945; s. Matthew and Ruth (Beckman) R.; m. Judith R., Oct. 24, 1971; children—Robert, David. A.B. cum laude, Harvard U., 1967; J.D. cum laude, NYU, 1970. Bar: Calif. 1971. Assoc. firm O'Melveny & Myers, Los Angeles, 1970-77; ptnr. O'Melveny & Myers, 1978—. Mem. ABA, Calif. Bar Assn., Los Angeles County Bar Assn. Office: O'Melveny & Myers 1999 Avenue Of The Stars Fl 7 Los Angeles CA 90067-6022*

RICHMAN, GERTRUDE GROSS (MRS. BERNARD RICHMAN), civic worker; b. N.Y.C., May 16, 1908; d. Samuel and Sarah Yetta (Seltzer) Gross; B.S., Tchrs. Coll. Columbia U., 1948, M.A., 1949; m. Bernard Richman, Apr. 5, 1930; children—David, Susan. Vol. worker Hackensack Hosp., 1948-70; mem. bd. dirs. YM-YWHA, Bergen County, N.J., 1950-75, bd. mem. emeritus, 1975—; chmn. Leonia Friends of Bergen County Mental Health Consultation Center, 1959; founder, hon. pres. Bergen County Serv-A-Com., affiliated with women orgns. Div. Nat. Jewish Welfare Bd.; v.p. N.J. sect. Nat. Jewish Welfare Bd., 1964-71; hon. trustee women's div. Bergen County United Jewish Community; mem. adv. council Bergen County Office on Aging, 1968-83, reappointed, 1984—; mem. Hackensack Bd. Edn., 1946-51; mem. pub. relations com. Leonia Pub. Schs., 1957-58; N.J. del. White House Conf. on Aging, 1971; trustee Mary McLeod Bethune Scholarship Fund; v.p. Bergen County nat. women's com. Brandeis U., 1966-67. Recipient citation Nat. Council Jewish Women and YWCA in Bergen County, 1962; citation Nat. Jewish Welfare Bd., 1964, Harry S. Feller award N.J. Region, 1965; 14th Ann. Good Scout award Bergen council Boy Scouts Am., 1977; Woman Vol. of Distinction, Bergen County council Girl Scouts, 1979; Human Relations award Bergen County sect. Nat. Council Negro Women, 1982; recipient Gov.'s award, 1988, Cert. of Commendation County Exec. and the Bergen County Bd. of Chosen Freeholders, 1989; honored at testimonial United Jewish Community Bergen County, 1987; Senior Advocate award Divsn. on Aging, 1993. Mem. Kappa Delta Pi.

RICHMAN, HAROLD ALAN, social welfare policy educator; b. Chgo., May 15, 1937; s. Leon H. and Rebecca (Klieman) R.; m. Marlene M. Forland, Apr. 25, 1965; children: Andrew, Robert. AB, Harvard U., 1959; MA, U. Chgo., 1961, PhD, 1969. Asst. prof., dir. Ctr. for Study Welfare Policy, Sch. Social Svc., U. Chgo., 1967-69, dean, prof. social welfare policy, 1969-78, Hermon Dunlap Smith prof., 1978—, dir. of ctr., 1978-81, dir. Children's Policy Rsch. Project, 1978-84, dir. Chapin Hall Ctr. for Children, 1985—, chmn. univ. com. on pub. policy studies, 1974-77; chmn. Univ. Lab. Schs., 1985-88; cons. to gov. State of Ill., Edna McConnell Clark Found., 1984-95, Lilly Endowment, 1987-90, Ford Found., 1987-89; co-chair roundtable on comprehensive cmty. initiatives, Chgo., 1993—. Chmn. editorial bd. Social Svcs. Rev., 1970-79; contbr. articles to profl. jours. Bd. dirs. Chgo. Com. Fgn. and Domestic Policy, 1969-78, S.E. Chgo. Commn., 1970—, Jewish Fedn. Met. Chgo., 1970-75, Ill. Facilities Fund, 1989-94, Welfare Coun. Met. Chgo., 1970-72, Erikson Inst. Early Childhood Edn., 1972-79, Nat. Urban Coalition, 1975-86, Family Focus, 1980-89, Jewish Coun. Urban Affairs, 1982-87, Ctr. for Study Social Policy, 1983-92, Nat. Family Resource Coalition, 1990-93, Pub./Pvt. Ventures, 1992—, Benton Found., 1994—; bd. dirs. Israel Ctr. on Children, chmn., 1995—. Capt. USPHS, 1961-63. White House fellow, Washington, 1965-66; recipient Disting. Svc. citation U.S. Dept. Health, Edn. & Welfare, 1970, Quantrell award U. Chgo., 1990. Mem. White House Fellows Assn. (v.p. 1976-77), Am. Pub. Welfare Assn. (bd. dirs. 1989-92). Home: 5715 S Dorchester Ave Chicago IL 60637-1726 Office: U Chgo Chapin Hall Ctr for Children 1313 E 60th St Chicago IL 60637-2745

RICHMAN, HOWARD, surgeon; b. N.Y.C., Oct 11, 1927; s. Morton and Beatrice (Antel) R.; m. Barbara Renee Richman, Dec. 1947 (dec. 1958); children—Leslie Francine, Michael Edward; m. 2d Thelma Miriam Richman, Nov. 1969 (dec. 1980); m. 3d Barbara Susan Richman, Oct. 1985. B.A., NYU, 1949, M.D., 1953. Intern, NYU/Bellevue Med. Ctr., 1953-54, resident, 1954-58 practice medicine, specializing in surgery, N.Y.C., 1975-93; dir. surgery S. Staten Is. U. Hosp., N.Y., 1993—; chief of surgery N.Y. Infirmary/Beekman Downtown Hosp., N.Y.C., 1975—; prof. clin. surgery NYU Med. Center, 1960—. Contbr. articles to profl. jours. Served with USAF, 1946-47. Fellow ACS, AMA, Am. Bd. Surgery, Internat. Coll. Surgeons, N.Y. Acad. Sci. Democrat. Jewish. Club: NYU. Office: Staten Island Univ Hosp Dept Surgery South 375 Seguine Ave Staten Island NY 10309

RICHMAN, JOAN F., television consultant; b. St. Louis, Apr. 10, 1939; d. Stanley M. and Barbara (Friedman) R. B.A., Wellesley (Mass.) Coll., 1961. Asst. producer Sta. WNDT, N.Y.C., 1964-65; researcher CBS News, N.Y.C., 1961-64, researcher spl. events unit, 1965-67; mgr. rsch. CBS News (Rep. and Dem. nat. convs.), N.Y.C., 1968; assoc. producer CBS News, N.Y.C., 1968, producer spl. events, 1969-72; sr. producer The Reasoner Report, ABC News, N.Y.C., 1972-75; exec. producer Sports Spectacular CBS, N.Y.C., 1975-76; exec. producer CBS Evening News weekend broadcasts CBS News, N.Y.C., 1976-81, v.p., dir. spl. events, 1982-87, v.p. news coverage, 1987-89; fellow Inst. Politics, John F. Kennedy Sch. Govt., Harvard U., 1990. Mem. nat. patrons com. Opera Theatre St. Louis. Recipient Emmy award for CBS News space coverage Nat. TV Acad. Arts and Scis., 1970-71; Alumnae Achievement award Wellesley Coll., 1973. Mem. Coun. on Fgn. Rels., Wellesley Coll. Alumnae Assn. (pres. class of 1961, 1966-70). Home: 14 Tinicum Creek Rd Erwinna PA 18920-9246

RICHMAN, JOEL ESER, lawyer, mediator, arbitrator; b. Brockton, Mass., Feb. 17, 1947; s. Nathan and Ruth Miriam (Bick) R.; m. Elaine R. Thompson, Aug. 21, 1987; children: Shawn Jonah, Jesse Ray. BA in Psychology, Grinnell Coll., 1969; JD, Boston U., 1975. Bar: Mass. 1975, U.S. Dist. Ct. MAss. 1977, U.S. Supreme Ct. 1980, U.S. Ct. Appeals (1st cir.) 1982, Hawaii 1985, U.S. Dist. Ct. Hawaii 1987. Law clk. Richman & Perenyi, Brockton, Mass., 1973-75, atty., 1975-77; atty. pvt. practice, Provincetown, Mass., 1977-82, Paia, Hawaii, 1985—; arbitrator Am. Arbitration Assn., Paia, 1992—, mediator, 1994—. Pres. Jewish Congregation Maui (Hawaii), 1989—, bd. dirs., 1984-89; referee State of Hawaii High Sch. Wrestling, 1985—; bd. dirs. Pacific Primate Ctr., 1991—, pres., 1994—. Avocations: windsurfing, softball, T'ai Chi. Office: P O Box 46 Paia HI 96779-1083

RICHMAN, JOHN MARSHALL, lawyer, business executive; b. N.Y.C., Nov. 9, 1927; s. Arthur and Madeleine (Marshall) R.; m. Priscilla Frary, Sept. 3, 1951; children: Catherine Richman Wallace, Diana H. BA, Yale U., 1949; LLB, Harvard U., 1952. Bar: N.Y. 1953, Ill. 1973. Assoc. Leve, Hecht, Hadfield & McAlpin, N.Y.C., 1952-54; mem. law dept. Kraft, Inc., Glenview, Ill., 1954-63; gen. counsel Sealtest Foods div. Kraft, Inc., Glenview, 1963-67, asst. gen. counsel, 1967-70, v.p., gen. counsel, 1970-73, sr. v.p., gen. counsel, 1973-75, sr. v.p. adminstrn., gen. counsel, 1975-79, chmn. bd., chief exec. officer, 1979; chmn. bd., chief exec. officer Dart & Kraft, Inc. (name changed to Kraft, Inc. 1986), Glenview, 1980; chmn. Kraft Gen. Foods, Glenview, Ill., 1988-89; counsel Wachtell, Lipton, Rosen & Katz, Chgo., 1990—; bd. dirs. BankAm. Corp. and Bank of Am. Nat. Trust and Savs. Assn., R.R. Donnelley & Sons. Co., USX Corp.; mem. Bus. Coun. Trustee Chgo. Symphony Orch.; trustee Northwestern U.; trustee Johnson Found.; bd. dirs. Evanston Hosp. Corp., Chgo. Coun. on Fgn. Rels., Lyric Opera Chgo. Mem. Comml. Club, Econ. Club, Chgo. Club, Casino Club (Chgo.); Union League Club (N.Y.C.); Westmoreland Country Club (Wilmette, Ill.); Old Elm Club (Ft. Sheridan, Ill.); Lost Tree Club (N. Palm Beach, Fla.), Shoreacres, Lake Bluff, Ill. Congregationalist. Office: Wachtell Lipton et al 227 W Monroe St Ste 4825 Chicago IL 60606-5018

RICHMAN, MARC HERBERT, forensic engineer, educator; b. Boston, Oct. 14, 1936; s. Samuel and Janet (Gordon) R.; m. Ann Raeshel Yoffa, Aug. 31, 1963. BS, MIT, 1957, ScD, 1963; MA, Brown U., 1967. Registered profl. engr., Conn., Mass., R.I.; cert. forensic examiner. Cons. engr., 1957—; engr. shipbldg. div. Bethlehem Steel Corp., Quincy, Mass., 1957; instr. metallurgy MIT, Cambridge, 1957-60, research asst. dept. metallurgy, 1960-63; instr. metallurgy div. univ. extension Commonwealth of Mass., 1958-62; asst. prof. engring. Brown U., Providence, 1963-67, assoc. prof., 1967-70, prof., 1970—, dir. central electron microscopy facility Materials Research program, 1971-86, dir. undergrad. program in engring., 1991—; pres. Ednl. Aids of Newton Inc., Providence, 1968-71, Marc H. Richman Inc., Providence, 1981—; guest scientist Franklin Inst., Phila., 1959; vis. prof. U. R.I., Kingston, 1970-71; biophysicist dept. medicine Miriam Hosp., Providence, 1974-87; biogengr. dept. orthopaedics R.I. Hosp., 1979-93. Author: Introduction to Science of Metals, 1967; also articles; editor Soviet Physics: Crystallography, 1970-94; mem. editorial adv. bd. Metallography, 1970—; mem. editorial adv. bd. Jour. Forensic Engring., 1985-88. Maj. Ordnance Corps, U.S. Army, 1963. Served to maj. Ordnance Corps, U.S. Army, 1963. Recipient Engr. of Yr. award R.I. Soc. Profl. Engrs., 1993. Fellow Nat. Acad. Forensic Engrs. (cert.), Am. Coll. Forensic Examiners (cert.), Am. Inst. Chemists, Inst. Materials (U.K.); mem. ASCE, AIME, NSPE, ASEE (Outstanding Young Faculty award 1969), NAFE (bd. cert. diplomate in forensic engring.), Am. Acad. Forensic Scis., Am. Soc. Metals (sec.-treas. 1965-68, chmn. R.I. chpt. 1968-69, Albert Sauveur Meml. award 1968, 69), Providence Engring. Soc. (pres. 1991-92, Freeman award for engring. achievement 1989), B'nai B'rith, Sigma Xi, Tau Beta Pi. Home: 291 Cole Ave Providence RI 02906-3452 Office: Brown U Divsn Engring Box D Providence RI 02912 also: One Richmond Sq Providence RI 02906

RICHMAN, MARTIN FRANKLIN, lawyer; b. Newark, Feb. 23, 1930; s. Samuel L. and Betty E. (Goldstein) R.; stepson Doris (Bloom) R.; m. Florence E. Reif, May 6, 1962; children—Judith, Andrew. B.A. magna cum laude, St. Lawrence U., 1950; LL.B. magna cum laude, Harvard U., 1953. Bar: N.Y. 1953, D.C. 1981. Law clk. to Judge Calvert Magruder and Chief Justice Earl Warren, 1955-57; assoc., mem. firm Lord Day & Lord, Barrett Smith (and predecessors), N.Y.C., 1957-66, 69-94; of counsel Kirkpatrick & Lockhart, LLP, N.Y.C., 1994—; dep. asst. atty. gen. Office Legal Counsel, Dept. Justice, Washington, 1966-69; Public mem. Adminstrv. Conf. U.S., 1970-76; bd. dirs. Community Action for Legal Services, 1977-80. Trustee St. Lawrence U., 1979-95, trustee emeritus, 1995—, vice chmn. bd., 1988-95; bd. dirs. Friends of Law Libr. of Congress, 1992—. Recipient Alumni citation St. Lawrence U., 1972. Fellow Am. Bar Found., N.Y. Bar Found.; mem. ABA (chmn. sect. adminstrv. law 1983-84), N.Y. State Bar Assn. (ho. of dels. 1981-84), Assn. of Bar of City of N.Y. (sec. and mem. exec. com. 1976-79, chmn. com. fed. legislation 1972-75, com. lawyer's pro bono obligations 1977-81), Am. Law Inst. Office: Kirkpatrick & Lockhart Kirkpatrick & Lockhart LLP New York NY 10020-1104

RICHMAN, MARVIN JORDAN, real estate developer, investor, educator; b. N.Y.C., July 13, 1939; s. Morris and Minnie (Graubart) R.; m. Amy Paula Rubin, July 31, 1966; children: Mark Jason, Keith Hayden, Susanne Elizabeth, Jessica Paige. BArch, MIT, 1962; M Urban Planning, NYU, 1966, postgrad., 1967-69; MBA, U. Chgo., 1977; U.S. Dept. State fellow U. Chile, 1960. Architect, planner Skidmore, Owings & Merrill, N.Y.C., 1964, Conklin & Rossant, N.Y.C., 1965-67; ptnr. Vizbaras & Ptnrs., N.Y.C., 1968-69; v.p. Urban Investment & Devel. Co., Chgo., 1969-79, sr. v.p., 1979; pres. bd. dirs. First City Devels. Corp., Beverly Hills, Calif., 1979-80; pres. Olympia & York (U.S.) Devel. (West), 1987-89, Olympia & York Calif. Equities Corp., L.A., 1981-87, Olympia & York Calif. Devel. Corp., 1981-87, Olympia & York Hope St. Mgmt. Corp., 1982-87, Olympia & York Homes Corp., 1983-89, Olympia & York Calif. Constrn. Corp., 1986-89, The Richman Co., L.A., 1989—, pres. Richman Real Estate Group, Salt Lake City, 1995—; dean Sch. Bus. and Mgmt. Woodbury U., Burbank, Calif., 1993—; lectr. NYU, 1967-69, UCLA, 1989-90, Nat. Humanities Inst., other univs. Adv. NEA. Bd. advisors UCLA Ctr. Fin. and Real Estate. With USAF, 1963-64. Registered architect; lic. real estate broker. Mem. AIA, Am Planning Assn., Internat. Coun. Shopping Ctrs., L.A. World Affairs Coun., Urban Land Inst., Nat. Assn. Office and Indsl. Parks, Chief Exec.'s Round Table, Air Force Assn., Lambda Alpha.

RICHMAN, PAUL, semiconductor industry executive, educator; b. N.Y.C., Nov. 17, 1942; s. Harry and Molly (Armel) R.; m. Ellen Margaret Kleiman, July 3, 1966; children: Lee Stuart, Alyson Michelle, Daniel Noah. B.S.E.E., MIT, 1963; M.S.E.E., Columbia U., 1964. V.p. R & D Standard Microsystems Corp., Hauppauge, N.Y., 1971-76, pres., 1976-81, pres., chief exec. officer, 1981-83, pres., chmn. bd., chief exec. officer, 1983—; co-founder Toyo Microsystems Corp., Tokyo, 1987—; pres. The Consortium for Tech. Licensing, Ltd., Nissequogue, N.Y., 1994—; vis. prof. elec. engring. SUNY, Stony Brook, 1976-85; dir. MOSAID Tech., Inc., Ottawa, Ont., Can. Author: Characteristics and Operation of MOS Field Effect Devices, 1967, MOS Field Effect Transistors and Integrated Circuits, 1974; inventor: COPLAMOS tech. Recipient ann. award for achievement in electronics, Electronics Mag., 1978; named one of 30 most Important Contbrs. in the world to devel. integrated cir. tech., Elec. Engring. Times/Elec. Buyers' News/V.L.S.I. Systems Design, 1988. Fellow IEEE (award for outstanding tech. achievement 1980).

RICHMAN, PETER, electronics executive; b. N.Y.C., Nov. 7, 1927; s. Emil H. and Janet (Seidler) R.; m. Vivian Hoffman, July 29, 1951; children: Meredith, Jeremy. BS, MIT, 1946; MS, NYU, 1953. Asst. chief engr. Reeves Instrument Corp., Garden City, N.Y., 1948-58; chief engr. Epsco, Inc., Cambridge, Mass., 1959-60; v.p., co-founder Rotek Instrument Corp., Watertown, Mass., 1960-64; v.p. Weston-Rotek, Lexington, Mass., 1964-67; cons. electronics engr. Lexington, 1967—; bd. dirs. Thermo Voltek Corp; founder, pres. KeyTek Instrument Corp., 1975-93; mem. NRC/NAS/Nat. Acad. Engring. Evaluation Panel for electricity divsn. Nat. Bur. Standards; mem. sci. adv. groups for several indsl. and sci. orgns. Patentee in precision electronic instrumentation; pioneer in precision dc and audio-frequency measurements, surge electrostatic discharge generation and electrostatic discharge measurements; contbr. articles to profl. jours. Mem. bd. overseers Boston Mus. Sci. Fellow IEEE; mem. Electromagnetics Acad., Instrument Soc. Am. (sr.), Sigma Xi, Tau Beta Pi.

RICHMAN, PETER MARK, actor, painter, writer; b. Phila., Apr. 16, 1927; s. Benjamin and Yetta Dora (Peck) R.; m. Theodora Helen Landess, May 10, 1953; children: Howard Bennett, Kelly Allyn, Lucas Dion, Orien, Roger Lloyd. BS in Pharmacy, Phila. Coll. Pharmacy and Sci., 1951; student of Lee Strasberg, N.Y.C., 1952-54; mem., Actors' Studio, N.Y.C., 1954—. Registered pharmacist, Pa., N.Y. Appeared in little theater, Phila., 1946-51, on stage radio and in live TV, Phila., N.Y.C., and Los Angeles, 1948-65, including Have I Got a Girl for You (pre-Broadway tryout), Biltmore Theater, L.A., 1962, The Deputy, Ctr. Theater Group, L.A., 1965; appeared at Grove Theater, Nuangola, Pa., 1952, Westchester Playhouse, 1953, Drury Lane, Chicago, 1957, Strand, N.J., 1957, Capri, 1959, Ogonquit (Maine) Playhouse, 1955-62, Matunuck, R.I., 1955, Falmouth, Mass., 1953-55, Westport, Conn., 1955, Harrison, Maine, 1962, Dennis, Mass., 1955-62, Phila. Playhouse in the Park, 1962-63; Broadway plays include End as a Man, 1953, Hatful of Rain,Broadway and Nat. Tour, 1956-57, Masquerade, 1959; off-Broadway plays include End as a Man, 1953, The Dybbuk, 1954, The Zoo Story (400 performances), 1960-61; Rainmaker, Private Lives, Angel Street, Arms and the Man, Funny Girl, Hold Me, Equus, Night of the Iguana, Blithe Spirit, Twelve Angry Men, Henry Fonda Theatre, L.A., 1985, Babes in Toyland, Calif. Mus. Theater, 1988, Ray Bradbury's Next in Line, L.A., 1992, an numerous others; writer, performer (one man show) 4 Faces, 1995, and others; motion pictures include Friendly Persuasion, 1956, The Strange One, 1956, Black Orchid, 1958, The Dark Intruder, 1965, Agent for HARM, 1965, For Singles Only, 1967, Judgement Day (formerly The Third Hand), 1988, Friday the 13th, Part 8 (Jason Takes Manhattan), 1989, Naked Gun 2 1/2 (The Smell of Fear), 1991; appeared on TV series as Nick Cain in Cain's Hundred, 1961-62, as David in David Chapter III for CBC, 1966, as Duke Page in series Longstreet, 1971-72, as Andrew Laird in series Dynasty, 1981-84, as Channing Capwell in series Santa Barbara, 1984, voice of God series Heroes of the Bible, 1979, voice of the Phantom in animated series Defenders of the Earth, 1986, as Madros in Berlin series My Secret Summer (formerly Mystery of the Keys), 1991; guest star over 500 TV shows, including Hotel, Dallas, Hart to Hart, Fantasy Island, Murder She Wrote, T.J. Hooker, Three's Company, Knight Rider, Star Trek: The Next Generation, Matlock, Beverly Hills 90210, others; starred in TV movies House on Greenapple Road, 1968, McCloud, 1969, Yuma, 1970, Nightmare at 43 Hillcrest (Wide World of Entertainment), 1974, Mallory, 1975, The Islander, 1978, Greatest Heroes of the Bible, 1979, Blind Ambition, 1979, The PSI Factor, 1981, Dynasty, 1981, Dempsey, 1983, City Killer, 1984, Bonanza, The Next Generation, 1988; one-man shows (paintings) Am. Masters Gallery, L.A., 1967, Orlando Gallery, L.A., 1966, McKenzie Gallery, L.A., 1969, 73, Hopkins Gallery, L.A., 1971, Goldfield Gallery, L.A., 1979, Galerie des Stars, L.A., 1988, Crocker Mus., Sacramento, Calif., 1967, others; group shows include Bednarz Gallery, L.A., 1968, Dohan Gallery, L.A., 1966, Celebrity Art Exhibits, 55-city tour, 1964-65, Parkhurst Gallery, Seal Beach, Calif., 1991; 1996; March thur May, inaugural exhibition of the Henley Gallery Chapman U., Orange, Calif., (a 30-yr retrospective, A life in Art), representted in permanent collections U.S. and abroad; playwright: Heavy What Hangs Over? , 1971, a Metal for Murray, 1991 4 Faces, 1995; dir. plays Apple of His Eye, 1954, Glass Menagerie, 1954; featured in book Actor as Artists, 1992, Guide to Artists in Southern California, 1994.n. Trustee Motion Picture and TV Fund. Served with USN, 1945-46. Recipient Silver Medallion award Motion Picture TV Fund, 1990, Sybil Brand Humanitarian award Jeffrey Found., 1990, Critics Choice Performance award, 1996. Mem. SAG, AFTRA, Actors Equity Assn., Assn. Can. TV and Radio Artists, Acad. Motion Picture Arts and Scis, Acad. TV Arts and Scis. Office: c/o Budd Moss Shapiro Lichtmann Agy 8827 Beverly Blvd Los Angeles CA 90048 *I have always been grateful to be able to work in more than one medium. In a way they are all related, each solidifying and nurturing the other. I have a strong belief in God...and spiritual values. This, along with my marriage, children, and family life, has helped me enormously to express my own individuality as an artist.*

RICHMAN, PHYLLIS CHASANOW, newspaper critic; b. Washington, Mar. 21, 1939; d. Abraham and Helen (Lieberman) C.; m. Alvin Richman, June 5, 1960 (div. 1984); children—Joseph, Matthew, Libby. B.A., Brandeis U., 1961; postgrad., U. Pa., 1961-63, Purdue U., 1966-70. Restaurant critic Washington Post, 1976—, exec. food editor, 1980-88, food critic, 1988—. Author: Barter, 1976, Best Restaurants, 1980, 82, 85, 89. Mem. Washington Ind. Writers (adv. bd.). Home: 2118 O St NW Washington DC 20037-1007 Office: Washington Post 1150 15th St NW Washington DC 20071-0001

RICHMAN, STEPHEN EDWARD, lawyer; b. Phila., Aug. 3, 1956; s. Sidney and Bernice Audrey (Eubank) R.; m. Cynthia Ann James, Apr. 21, 1989; children: Catherine Therese, Samuel Ethan. BA with high hons., U. Fla., 1978; JD cum laude, Hastings Coll. of Law, 1982. Assoc. O'Connor & Cavanagh, Phoenix, 1982-95, sr. mem., 1995—. Trustee Ariz. Theatre Co., Phoenix, 1993—. Mem. State Bar of Ariz. (sec. constrn. law sect. 1994—), Ariz. Builders Alliance (mem. legal adv. coun. 1990—), Ariz. Contractors Assn. (mem. legal adv. coun. 1990—), Thurston Soc., Phi Beta Kappa. Avocations: running, scuba diving, theatre, computers. Office: Ste 1100 1 E Camelback Rd Phoenix AZ 85012

RICHMAN, STEPHEN ERIK, lawyer; b. Austin, Tex., Mar. 10, 1945; s. Allen A. and Erika (Zimmerman) R.; m. Frances Ellen Sharpe, Aug. 29,

1971; children: Joshua Eric, Wendy Michelle. BA magna cum laude, Amherst Coll., 1967; JD cum laude, Harvard U., 1970. Bar: Wis. 1972. Assoc. Webster Sheffield, N.Y.C., 1970-72; assoc. Quarles & Brady, Milw., 1972-78, ptnr., 1978—. Pres. Milw. Youth Symphony Orch., 1985-87; mem. exec. com. Milw. Jewish Fedn., 1990—, Milw. Symphony Orch., 1992—; bd. dirs. Jewish Cmty. Found., Milw., 1992—. Mem. ABA, Nat. Assn. Bond Lawyers, State Bar Wis., Phi Beta Kappa. Home: 709 E Carlisle Ave Milwaukee WI 53217-4835 Office: Quarles & Brady 411 E Wisconsin Ave Milwaukee WI 53202-4409

RICHMAN, STEPHEN I., lawyer; b. Washington, Pa., Mar. 26, 1933; m. Audrey May Gefsky. BS, Northwestern U., 1954; JD, U. Pa., 1957. Bar: Pa. 1958, U.S. Dist. Ct. (we. dist.) Pa. With McCune Greenlee & Richman, 1960-63, Greenlee Richman Derrico & Posa, 1963-84, ptnr. Richman, Smith Law Firm, P.A., Washington, 1985—; bd. dirs. Three Rivers Bank; lectr. U. South Fla. Sch. Medicine, Mine Safe Internat. Chamber of Mines of Western Australia, W.Va. U. Med. Ctr. Grand Rounds, Am. Coll. Chest Physicians, Pa. Thoracic Soc., Am. Thoracic Soc., The Energy Bur., Coll. of Am. Pathologists, Allegheny County Health Dept., APHA, Internat. Assn. Ind. Accident Bds. and Commns., Indsl. Health Found., Nat. Coun. Self-Insurers Assn., Am. Iron and Steel Inst., Can. Thoracic Soc., I.L.O./N.I.O.S.H., Univs. Associated for Rsch. and Edn. in Pathology, Am. Ceramics Soc., Nat. Sand Assn.; mem. adv. com. U.S. Dist. Ct. Western Dist. Pa., 1994—; lectr. in field. Author: Meaning of Impairment and Disability, Chest, 1980, Legal Aspects for the Pathologist, in Pathology of Occupational and Environmental Lung Disease, 1988, A Review of the Medical and Legal Definitions of Related Impairment and Disability, Report to the Department of Labor and the Congress, 1986, Medicolegal Aspects of Asbestos for Pathologists, Arch. Pathology and Laboratory Medicine, 1983, Legal Aspects of Occupational and Environmental Disease, Human Pathology, 1993, Impairment and Disability in Pneunoconiosis, State of the Art Reviews in Occupational Medicine-The Mining Industry, 1993, other publs. and articles; author House Bills 2103 and 885 co-author Act 44 amending Pa. Workmen's Compensation Act. Mem. legal com. Indsl. Health Found., Pitts.; bd. dirs. Pitts. Opera Soc., 1994—, Pitts. Jewish Fedn., 1994—; dir. Jewish Family and Children's Svc., Pitts. Mem. ABA (vice chair workers compensation and employers liability law com., toxic and hazardous substance and environ. law com., lectr.), ATLA, Pa. Bar Assn. (former mem. coun. of worker's compensation sect., lectr., contbg. author bar assn. quarterly 1992, 93), Pa. Chamber Bus. and Industry (workers' compensation com., chmn. subcom. on legis. drafting, lectr.). Home: 820 E Beau St Washington PA 15301 Office: Washington Trust Bldg Ste 200 Washington PA 15301

RICHMOND, ANTHONY HENRY, sociologist, emeritus educator; b. Ilford, Essex, Eng., June 8, 1925; s. Henry James and Ellen Bertha (Hankin) R.; m. Freda Williams, Mar. 29, 1952; 1 dau., Glenys Catriona Richmond Troth. BSc in Econs., London Sch. Econs., 1949; MA, U. Liverpool (Eng.), 1951; PhD, U. London, 1965. Rsch. officer U. Liverpool, 1949-51; lectr. dept. social study U. Edinburgh, Scotland, 1952-63; reader in sociology Bristol (Eng.) Coll. Sci. and Tech., 1963-65; prof. sociology York U., Toronto, Ont., Can., 1965-89; prof. emeritus, sr. scholar York U., Toronto, 1989—; dir. York U. (Inst. Behavioral Rsch.), 1979-82; social rsch. cons.; vis. prof. Australian Nat. U., Canberra, 1971, 77, St. Antony's Coll., Oxford, Eng., 1984-85. Author: Colour Prejudice in Britain, 1954, 2d edit., 1971, The Colour Problem: A Study of Racial Relations in Britain, Africa and the West Indies, 1955, rev. edit., 1961, Post-War Immigrants in Canada, 1967, (with others) Immigrant Integration and Urban Renewal in Toronto, 1973, Migration and Race Relations in an English City, 1973, (with W. E. Kalbach) Factors in the Adjustment of Immigrants and Their Descendants, 1980, Immigration and Ethnic Conflict, 1988, Caribbean Immigrants: A Demoeconomic Analysis, 1989, Global Apartheid: Refugees, Racism and the New World Order, 1994; editor: Readings in Race and Ethnic Relations, 1972, (with D. Kubat) Internal Migration: The New World and the Third World, 1976; contbr. chpts. to books, articles to profl. jours. Recipient research grants and scholarships. Fellow Royal Soc. Can.; mem. Can. Sociology and Anthropology Assn., Can. Population Soc. Mem. Soc. of Friends. Avocations: classical music, photography. Office: York U, Dept Sociology, 4700 Keele St, North York, ON Canada M3J 1P3

RICHMOND, DAVID WALKER, lawyer; b. Silver Hill, W.Va., Apr. 20, 1914; s. David Walker and Louise (Finlaw) R.; m. Gladys Evelyn Mallard, Dec. 19, 1936; children: David Walker, Nancy L. LL.B., George Washington U., 1937. Bar: D.C. 1936, Ill. 1946, Md. 1950. Partner firm Miller & Chevalier, Washington; lectr. fed. taxation. Contbr. to profl. jours. Served from ensign to lt. comdr. USNR, 1942-46. Decorated Bronze Star; recipient Disting. Alumni Achievement award George Washington U., 1976. Fellow Am. Bar Found., Am. Coll. Trial Lawyers, Am. Coll. Tax Counsel; mem. ABA (chmn. taxation sect. 1955-57, ho. of dels. 1958-60), Am. Law Inst., Lawyers' Club of Washington, Union League (Chgo.), Bird Key Yacht Club (Sarasota), Masons. Republican. Methodist. Home: 988 Boulevard Of The Arts Sarasota FL 34236-4872 Office: 655 15th St NW Washington DC 20005-5701

RICHMOND, EERO, composer, music librarian; b. Tacoma, Wash., Jan. 5, 1938; s. Orin August and Esther Maija (Johnson) R. BA in Music, U. Wash., 1961, MLS, 1966. Music libr. N.Y.C. Pub. Libr., 1966-68, head music cataloger, 1969-80; dir. info. svcs. Am. Music Ctr., N.Y.C., 1982-93, head music cataloger, 1994-95, coord. info. svcs., 1995—; pianist Slavic Arts Ensemble, N.Y.C., 1985—, Inoue Chamber Ensemble, N.Y.C., 1993—. Composer musical works performed throughout U.S., Europe, South Am., Japan; contbr. articles to profl. jours. Mem. ASCAP, Internat. Soc. for Contemporary Music (v.p. 1986-90), Sibelius Soc. (v.p. 1985—), Phi Mu Alpha Sinfonia, Beta Phi Mu. Democrat. Lutheran. Avocations: travel (especially Berlin), reading. Office: Am Music Ctr 30 W 26th St # 1001 New York NY 10010-2011

RICHMOND, ERNEST LEON, research engineer, consultant; b. Catskill, N.Y., Sept. 11, 1914; s. Leon J. and Beulah B. (Garling) R.; m. Constance R. Vroom, Oct. 9, 1943. B of Mech. Engring. cum laude, Clarkson U., 1942; postgrad., N.J. Inst. Tech., 1950-60, Rutgers U., 1950-60. Registered profl. engr., N.J. Test engr. Mack Trucks, Inc., Plainfield, N.J., 1936-45; from asst chief to chief engr. Worthington Corp., Plainfield Works, 1945-58; rsch. engr. Ethicon, Inc. (div. Johnson & Johnson), Somerville, N.J., 1958-75, ret., 1975; consulting engr. Dunellen, N.J., 1975—; seminar speaker Worthington Corp. Speakers' Bur., Plainfield, 1950-58. Author design papers; patentee in field. Vol. United Fund, Plainfield, 1940-50, Cancer Fund, Plainfield, 1940-50, Heart Fund, Plainfield, 1940-50; coach YMCA Ch. Basketball League, Plainfield, 1960-65, chmn. exec. com., 1964-65. Mem. ASME, NSPE, Am. Electroplaters and Surface Finishers Soc. Republican. Presbyterian. Avocations: civil war history, golf, working with young people. Office: PO Box 314 Dunellen NJ 08812-0314

RICHMOND, GAIL LEVIN, law educator; b. Gary, Ind., Jan. 9, 1946; d. Herbert Irving and Sylvia Esther (Given) Levin; children: Henry, Amy. AB, U. Mich., 1966, MBA, 1967; JD, Duke U., 1971. Bar: Ohio 1971, U.S. Claims Ct. 1986, U.S. Ct. Mil. Appeals, 1994; CPA, Ill. Acct. Arthur Andersen & Co., Chgo., 1967-68; assoc. Jones, Day, Cleve., 1971-72; asst. prof. Capital U. Law Sch., Columbus, Ohio, 1972-73, U. N.C. Law Sch., Chapel Hill, 1973-78; vis. asst. prof. U. Tex. Law Sch., Austin, 1977-78, Nova U. Law Ctr., Ft. Lauderdale, Fla., 1979-80; assoc. prof. Nova U. Law Ctr., Ft. Lauderdale, 1980-81, assoc. prof., assoc. dean, 1981-85, prof., assoc. dean., 1985-93, 95—, prof., acting dean, 1993-95. Author: Federal Tax Research, 5th edit., 1996; contbr. articles to profl. jours. Pres. Greater Ft. Lauderdale Tax Coun., 1987-88; chair Law Sch. Admission Coun. Audit Com., 1991-93; chair Assn. Am. Law Schs. Audit Com., 1992; trustee Law Sch. Admission Coun., 1994-97. Mem. ABA, Am. Assn. Atty.-CPAs (dir. Fla. chpt. 1992-95), Assn. Am. Law Schs. (mem. audit com. 1990-92, chair sect. adminstrn. of law schs. 1996, pres. S.E. chpt. 1993-94, sec. S.E. chpt. 1995—), Broward County Women Lawyers Assn. Democrat. Jewish. Avocation: reading. Office: Nova Southeastern U Shepard Broad Law Ctr 3305 College Ave Fort Lauderdale FL 33314-7721

RICHMOND, HAROLD NICHOLAS, lawyer; b. Elizabeth, N.J., Apr. 5, 1935; s. Benjamin I. and Eleanor (Turbowitz) R.; m. Elaine Zemel, June 16, 1957 (div. Nov. 1972); children: Bonnie J. Ross, Michele Weinfeld; m. Marilyn A. Wenrich, Aug. 26, 1973; children: Eric L., Kacy L. BA, Tulane U., 1957; LLB, NYU, 1961, LLM in Taxation, 1965. Estate tax examiner IRS, Newark, 1963-65; tax mgr. Puder & Puder/Touche Ross & Co., CPAs, Newark, 1965-73; ptnr. Sodowick Richmond & Crecca, Newark, 1973-84; prin. Harold N. Richmond, West Orange, N.J., 1984-86; ptnr. Wallerstein Hauptman & Richmond, West Orange, 1986-91, Hauptman & Richmond, West Orange, 1992—. With U.S. Army, 1959-60. Mem. ABA (tax sect. closely held bus. com., real property and probate sect.), N.J. Bar Assn. (tax, real property and probate sects.), Essex County Bar Assn. (chmn. tax com. 1989, real property and probate sect.). Avocations: running, tennis. Office: Hauptman & Richmond 200 Executive Dr West Orange NJ 07052-3303

RICHMOND, JAMES ELLIS, restaurant company executive; b. Chgo., Feb. 16, 1938; s. Kenneth E. and Irene M. (Anderson) R.; m. Karen Ann Ryder, Oct. 6, 1956; children: Scott, Brian, Ann, Susan. BBA, Case Western Res. U., 1960. CPA, Ohio. Sr. auditor Ernst & Ernst, Cleve., 1960-64; treas. Cook United, Inc., Cleve., 1964-75; treas. Fairmont Foods Co., Houston, 1975-80, v.p. ops., 1980-82; v.p., treas. U-tote-M, Inc., 1982-84; mktg. exec. Circle K Convenience Stores, 1984-86; v.p. Consol. Products, Inc., Indpls., 1986—. Lutheran. Home: 13088 Tarkington Common Carmel IN 46033-9352 Office: Consol Products Inc 36 S Pennsylvania St Indianapolis IN 46204-3634

RICHMOND, JAMES G., lawyer; b. Sacramento, Feb. 20, 1944; s. James Gibbs and Martha Ellen (Glidden) R.; m. Lois Marie Bennett, Oct. 22, 1988; 1 child, Mark R. BS in Mgmt., Ind. U., 1966, postgrad., 1966-69, JD, 1969. Bar: Ind. 1969, Ill. 1991, U.S. Dist. Ct. (no. dist.) Ind. 1971, U.S. Dist. Ct. (so. dist.) Ind., 1969, U.S. Ct. Appeals (7th cir.) 1975, U.S. Tax Ct. 1980. Spl. agent FBI, 1970-74; spl. agent Criminal Investigation Divsn. IRS, 1974-76; asst. U.S. atty. no. dist. U.S. Atty. Office, Ind., 1976-80; assoc. Galvin, Stalmack & Kirschner, Hammond, Ind., 1980-81; pvt. practice Highland, Ind., 1981-83; ptnr. Goodman, Ball & Van Bokkelen, Highland, Ind., 1983-85; U.S. atty. no. dist. State of Ind., Hammond, 1985-91; spl. counsel to dep. atty. gen. of the U.S. U.S. Dept. Justice, Washington, 1990-91; mng. ptnr. Coffield, Ungaretti and Harris, Chgo., 1991-92, ptnr., 1995—; exec. v.p., gen. counsel Nat. Health Labs., 1992-95; practitioner in residence Ind. U. Sch. Law, Bloomington, 1989. Fellow Am. Coll. Trial Lawyers. Republican. Avocation: fishing. Office: Coffield Ungaretti & Harris 3500 Three First National Plz Chicago IL 60602-4283

RICHMOND, JULIUS BENJAMIN, retired physician, health policy educator emeritus; b. Chgo., Sept. 26, 1916; s. Jacob and Anna (Dayno) R.; m. Rhee Chidekel, June 3, 1937 (dec. Oct. 9, 1985); children: Barry J., Charles Allen, Dale Keith (dec.); m. Jean Rabow, Jan. 11, 1987. BS, U. Ill., 1937, MS, MD, 1939; DSc (hon.), Ind. U., 1978, Rush-Presbyn.-St. Luke Med. Ctr., 1978, U. Ill., 1979, Georgetown U., 1980, Syracuse U., 1986, U. Ariz., 1991; DMS (hon.), Med. Coll. Pa., 1980; D in Pub. Svc. (hon.), Nat. Coll. Edn., Evanston, Ill., 1980; LHD (hon.), Tufts U., 1986. Intern Cook County Hosp., Chgo., 1939-41, resident, 1941-42, 46; resident Mcpl. Contagious Disease Hosp., Chgo., 1941; mem. faculty U. Ill. Med. Sch., Chgo., 1946-53, prof. pediatrics, 1950-53; dir. Inst. Juvenile Research Inst. Juvenile Rsch., Chgo., 1952-53; prof., chmn. dept. pediatrics Coll. Medicine, SUNY at Syracuse, 1953-65, dean med. faculty, chmn. dept. pediatrics, 1965-70; prof. child psychiatry and human devel., prof., chmn. dept. preventive and social medicine Harvard Med. Sch., 1971-77, prof. health policy, 1981-88, dir. divsn. health policy rsch. and edn., 1983-88, prof. health policy emeritus, 1988—; also faculty Harvard Sch. Pub. Health; psychiatrist-in-chief Children's Hosp. Med. Center, Boston, 1971-77, adv. on child health policy, 1981—; dir. Judge Baker Guidance Center, Boston, 1971-77; asst. sec. health and surgeon gen. HHS, 1977-81; mem. Pres.'s Commn. on Mental Health, 1977. Author: Pediatric Diagnosis, 1962, Currents in American Medicine, 1969. Nat. dir. Project Head Start; dir. Office Health Affairs OEO, 1965-66. Served as flight surgeon USAAF, 1942-46. Recipient Agnes Bruce Greig Sch. award, 1966, Parents Mag. award, 1966, Disting. Service award Office Econ. Opportunity, 1967, Family Health Mag. award, 1977, Myrdal award Assn. For Evaluation Rsch., 1977, award for disting. sci. contbn. Soc. for Research in Child Devel., 1979, Dolly Madison award Inst. on Clin. Infants Programs, 1979, Public Health Disting. Service award HEW, 1980, Illini Achievement award U. Ill. Alumni Assn., 1982, Community Service award Health Planning Council Greater Boston, 1985, Lemuel Shattuck award Mass. Pub. Health Assn., 1985, 1st Ann. Ronald McDonald Children's Charities award for Outstanding Contbns. to Child Health and Welfare, 1986, Sedgwick award APHA, 1992. Fellow Am. Orthopsychiat. Assn. (Ittleson award 1994), Am. Psychiat. Assn. (disting.); mem. Am. Acad. Child Psychiatry (hon.), New Eng. Coun. Child Psychiatry (assoc.), Inst. Medicine of NAS (1st Ann. Gustav O. Lienhard award 1986), AMA (AMA-ERF award in health edn. 1988), Am. Pediatric Soc. (John Howland award 1990), Am. Acad. Pediatrics (C. Anderson Aldrich award 1966, ann. award sect. on community pediatrics 1977, Outstanding Contbn. award sect. community pediatrics 1978), Soc. Pediatric Rsch., Am. Psychosomatic Soc., APHA (Martha May Eliot award 1970, Sedgwick Medal 1992), Sigma Xi, Alpha Omega Alpha, Phi Eta Sigma.

RICHMOND, MARILYN SUSAN, lawyer; b. Bethesda, Md., Oct. 19, 1949; d. Carl Hutchins Jr. and Elizabeth Adeline (Saeger) R. BA with honors, U. Fla., 1971; JD, Georgetown U., 1974. Bar: Md. 1974, D.C. 1975. Atty. Office of Gen. Counsel, FTC, Washington, 1974-77, antitrust atty. Bur. of Competition, 1977-81; counsel, consumer subcom. of com. on commerce, sci. and transp. U.S. Senate, Washington, 1981-85; assoc. Heron, Burchette, Ruckert & Rothwell, Washington, 1985-87, ptnr., 1987-90; dep. asst. sec. for govtl. affairs U.S. Dept. Transp., Washington, 1990-91, acting asst. sec. for govtl. affairs, 1991-92; cons. Raffaelli, Spees, Springer & Smith, Washington, 1993-94; asst. exec. dir. govt. rels. APA Practice Directorate, 1995—; lectr. Brookings Instn. Ctr. for Pub. Policy Edn., Washington, 1985-88. Active Lawyers for Bush-Quayle, Washington, 1988. Mem. ABA (antitrust, adminstrv. law sect., vice chair transp. industry com. antitrust sect. 1992-95), Trade Assn. (vice chair com. antitrust sect. 1995). Republican. Methodist. Avocations: horseback riding, tennis. Home: Apt 503 I 2725 Connecticut Ave NW Washington DC 20008-5305

RICHMOND, MITCHELL JAMES (HAMMER ROCK RICHMOND), professional basketball player; b. Ft. Lauderdale, Fla., June 30, 1965; m. Juli Richmond; children: Phillip Mitchell, Jerin Mikell. Bachelor in Social Sci., Kansas State U., 1988. Guard Golden State Warriors, 1988-91, Sacramento Kings, 1991—. Hon. bd. dirs. NCPCA (Spl. Friend award); established Solid As A Rock Scholarship Found., Ft. Lauderdale, 1992. Selected Rookie of the Yr., 1989, Rookie of the Month 3 times, Dec., Jan., March; named NBA Player of the Week, Mar. 25, 1991; selected to NBA All-Star Team, 1993, 94, 95. Avocations: bowling, video games. Office: Sacramento Kings One Sports Parkway Sacramento CA 95834

RICHMOND, PATRICIA NORTHRUP, elementary art educator; b. Rochester, N.y., May 18, 1950; d. Richard and Louise Northrup; m. John Richmond, Mar. 1989. BA, Alma Coll., St. Thomas, Ont., Can., 1968; MEd, Loyola U., Chgo., 1973; postgrad., Coll. William and Mary, 1974, U. Ctrl. Fla., 1990. Cert. tchr. art K-12. Media-action tchr. Henry Lomb Sch., Rochester, N.Y., 1973-75; art tchr. Berkeley Elem. Sch., Williamsburg, Va., 1975-78; dir. children's programs Project on Domestic Violence Salvation Army Emergency Lodge, Chgo., 1978-79; play facilitator Chiswick Family Rescue, London, 1980-81; tchr. Northwestern Meml. Hosp., Chgo., 1982-83; arts adminstr. Focus Inc., Detroit, 1983-86; art tchr. Detroit Pub. Schs., 1986-89, Volusia County Schs., Deland, Fla., 1989—; GED tchr. Met. Correctional Ctr., Chgo., 1978-79; cons., play facilitator Dublin (Ireland) Women's Aid, 1981, Belgium Fedn. Women's Refuges, Leuven, Hasselt, Michelen, 1981; substitute tchr. Chgo. Bd. Edn., 1982-83; workshop tchr., cons. Levine Inst., Detroit; art educator drop out prevention program RESS Discovery Summer Program, Crooms Sch. of Choice, Sanford, Fla., 1992; adj. instr. U. Ctrl. Fla. Daytona Beach campus, Orlando, summers 1994, 95; mem. Ctr. Creative Studies, Detroit, 1987-89. Exhibited in group shows at Pewabic Pottery Student/Faculty Show, summer 1987, Detroit Art Tchrs. Assn. Mich. Gallery, 1988; curator art exhbn. U. Ctrl. Fla. Art for Elem. Edn. Majors Exhbn., 1994. Host family Friendship Force Greater Daytona Beach, Friendship Force New Smyrna Beach, Fla., 1993—, Am. Field Svc., Daytona Beach, 1994-95. Recipient grant Children's Program for Victims of Domestic Violence, McCormick Corp., Chgo., 1978, 79, Arts in Edn. grant Mich. Arts Coun., Detroit, 1984, 85, 86, Golden Apple award Palm Ter. Elem. Sch., Daytona Beach, 1994. Mem. Nat. Art Edn. Assn., Arts for a Complete Edn., Fla. Art Tchrs. Assn., Volusia Art Educator's Assn., Detroit Puppetry Guild (pres. 1987-89), Detroit Art Tchrs. Assn. (bd. mem. 1985-89), Fla. Craftsman Coun., Fla. Art Edn. Assn., Puppeteers of Am. Avocation: travel. Home: 4043 S Waterbridge Cir Port Orange FL 32119-9616 Office: Palm Ter Elem Sch Art Dept 1825 Dunn Ave Daytona Beach FL 32114-1250

RICHMOND, RICHARD THOMAS, journalist; b. Parma, Ohio, May 16, 1933; s. Arthur James and Frances Marie (Visosky) R.; m. Charlotte Jean Schwoebel, Dec. 19, 1933; children: Kris Elaine, Leigh Alison, Paul Evan. AB, Washington U., St. Louis, 1961. Bur. mgr. UPI News Pictures, St. Louis, 1957-62; asst. picture editor Post-Dispatch, St. Louis, 1962-64, editor color sect., 1964-80, columnist, 1971—, editor calendar sect., 1983-94; asst. entertainment editor, 1995; v.p. Golden Royal Enterprises, St. Louis, 1976-78; pres. Oroquest Press, St. Louis, 1977-80; dir. U.S. Mortgage & Investment Corp., Hilton Head Island, N.C., 1977-81; pres. Magalar Mining, Texarkana, Ark., 1979-83. Co-author: Treasure Under Your Feet, 1974, In the Wake of the Golden Galleons, 1976, Diabetes: The Facts That Will Let You Regain Control of Your Life, 1986. Avocation: undersea treasure hunting. Home: 307 Lebanon Ave Belleville IL 62220-4126 Office: St Louis Post-Dispatch 900 N Tucker Blvd Saint Louis MO 63101-1099

RICHMOND, ROBERT LINN, management consultant; b. Columbus, Ohio, Apr. 10, 1920; s. Loren Magee and Ruth Winifred (Shannon) R.; m. Ruth Felton Morrison, Dec. 6, 1943; children: Robert Morrison, Bates Carleton. BSBA, Ohio State U., 1942. CPA, cert. internal auditor. Sr. auditor Keller, Kirschner, Martin & Clinger (C.P.A.s), Columbus, Ohio, 1946-52; div. v.p., gen. auditor B.F. Goodrich Co., Akron, Ohio, 1952-78; pres., chief operating officer Inst. Internal Auditors, Altamonte Springs, Fla., 1979-81; cons. mgmt. controls systems Naples, Fla., 1981—; bd. regents Cert. Internal Auditor Exams., 1976-78. Editor: Internal Auditor, 1963-68. Speaker seminars and meetings.; Active Little Hoover Commn. Task Force, Summit County, Ohio, 1969-70; mem. Citizens Com., Silver Lake, Ohio, 1968-70. Served to capt., Signal Corps U.S. Army, 1942-45. Mem. AICPA (spl. adv. com. on internal acctg. control 1977-79, auditing standards adv. coun. 1978-81), Ohio Soc. CPAs, Inst. Internal Auditors (hon., Cadmus Meml. award 1978), Citrus Club, Masons, Shriners, Kiwanis (Kiwanian of Yr. award 1985). Republican. Episcopalian. Home: 1300 Gulf Shore Blvd N Apt 610 Naples FL 33940-4904 Office: 660 9th St S Ste 34A Naples FL 33940-6720

RICHMOND, ROBERTA THOMPSON, elementary education educator; b. Tampa, Fla., Feb. 12, 1946; d. Robert Shaw and Peggy (McMichael) Thompson; m. Jim Edward Richmond, June 22, 1968; children: Austin Lee, Ramsey Thompson. BS in Edn., U. Ga., 1968; MAT, Emory U. Tchr. English David Reese Elem. Sch., Sacramento, 1969; tchr. drama Mather Heights, Sacramento, summer 1969; tchr. 6th grade Rehoboth Elem. Sch., Atlanta, 1970-73; tchr. 4th grade Kincaid Elem. Sch., Marietta, Ga., 1973-74; tchr. lang. arts Branford (Fla.) High Sch., 1976; tchr. 4th and 5th grades Suwannee West Elem. Sch., Live Oak, Fla., 1977—; coord., instr. sci. and math. for 4th and 5th grade tchrs., Suwannee West Elem. Sch., 1992-93, 94, mem. art adv. com. 1990-91. Tchr. Sunday sch. Melody Christian Life Ch., Live Oak, 1989-91; bd. dirs. Suwannee County Found. for Excellence, 1994—; pres., dir. Camp Dovewood Christian Camp for Girls, 1977—. Emory U. scholar, 1973. Mem. Am. Camping Assn., Horsemanship's Assn., Christian Camping Internat., Jr. League of Atlanta, Women's Club (Branford, v.p. 1974-78), Emory U. Alumni Assn. (Columbia, Fla., sec. 1975-78), Alpha Delta Kappa (chmn. altruistic com., chaplain 1989-91). Democrat. Avocations: music, ballet, drama, horseback riding, reading.

RICHMOND, SAMUEL BERNARD, management educator; b. Boston, Oct. 14, 1919; s. David E. and Freda (Braman) R.; m. Evelyn Ruth Kravitz, Nov. 26, 1944; children: Phyllis Gail, Douglas Emerson, Clifford Owen. AB cum laude, Harvard U., 1940; MBA, Columbia U., 1948, PhD, 1951. Mem. faculty Columbia U., 1946-76, assoc. prof., 1957-60, prof. econ. and statistics, 1960-76; assoc. dean Grad. Sch. Bus. Columbia U., 1971-72, acting dean, 1972-73; dean prof. mgmt. Owen Grad. Sch. Mgmt. Vanderbilt U., Nashville, 1976-86, Ralph Owen prof. mgmt., 1984-88, Ralph Owen prof. mgmt. emeritus, 1988—, dean emeritus, adj. prof., 1988—; vis. prof. U. Sherbrooke, Que., 1967, U. Buenos Aires, Argentina, 1964, 65, Case Inst. Tech., Cleve., 1958-59, Fordham U., N.Y.C., 1952-53; dir. IMS Internat. Inc., N.Y.C., 1978-88, 1st Am. Corp., Nashville, 1981-86, Winners Corp., Nashville, 1983-89, Corbin Ltd., N.Y.C., 1970-85, Ingram Industries Inc., Nashville, 1981-92; cons. to maj. comml., ednl., profl. and govtl. orgns. Author: Operations Research for Management Decisions, 1968, Statistical Analysis, 1957, 2d. edit., 1964, Regulation and Competition in Air Transportation, 1961; talk show host Nashville Bus. Edit., WDCN-TV, 1984-86. Trustee Ramapo Coll., N.J., 1975-76; bd. dirs. Jewish Fedn. Nashville and Middle Tenn., Temple Ohabai Shalom, Nashville; trustee Endowment Fund Jewish Fedn. Nashville and Middle Tenn. 1st lt. USAAF, 1943-45. Recipient Honor award CAB, 1971, Alumni award for outstanding svc. Grad. Sch. Bus., Columbia U., 1973. Mem. Am. Statis. Assn. (chmn. adv. com. rsch. to CAB 1966-74, dir. 1965-67), Am. Econ. Assn., Inst. Mgmt. Sci., Ops. Rsch. Soc. Am., Beta Gamma Sigma. Home: 5404 Camelot Rd Brentwood TN 37027-4113 Office: Vanderbilt U Owen Grad Sch Mgmt Nashville TN 37203

RICHMOND, WILLIAM PATRICK, lawyer; b. Cicero, Ill., Apr. 5, 1932; s. Edwin and Mary (Allgier) R.; m. Elizabeth A., Jan. 9, 1954 (div.); children: Stephen, Janet, Timothy; m. Magda, June 8, 1992. AB, Albion Coll., 1954; JD, U. Chgo., 1959. Bar: Ill. 1959, N.Y. 1985. Assoc. Sidley & Austin, Chgo., 1960-67, ptnr., 1967—. Served with U.S. Army, 1954-56. Fellow Am. Coll. Trial Lawyers; mem. ABA, Soc. Trial Lawyers, Chgo. Bar Assn. Republican. Methodist. Clubs: Mid-Day; Legal; Ruth Lake Country (Hinsdale, Ill.). Home: 4 Tartan Ridge Burr Ridge IL 60521-8904 Office: Sidley & Austin 1 First Nat Plz Chicago IL 60603

RICHSTEIN, ABRAHAM RICHARD, lawyer; b. N.Y.C., Apr. 18, 1919; s. Morris and Ida (Stupp) R.; m. Rosalind Bauman; children: Eric, Jonathan. B.S., CCNY, 1939; J.D., Fordham U., 1942; LL.M. in Internat. Law, NYU, 1956; M.S. in Internat. Affairs, George Washington U., 1966; diploma, Command and Gen. Staff Coll., 1958, Nat. War Coll., 1966. Bar: N.Y. 1942, U.S. Supreme Ct 1956, U.S. Ct. of Mil. Appeals, 1956, U.S. Dist. Ct. S.D., N.Y., 1957, D.C. 1977. Enlisted as pvt. U.S. Army, 1942, advanced through grades to col., 1966; served with Mil. Intelligence, U.S. 9th Army U.S. Army, Europe, 1944; legal staff U.S. War Crimes Commn. U.S. Army, Ger., 1946; staff officer UN Command (U.S. Army), Far East, 1951-53; mil. law judge (Hdqrs. First Army), 1954-57; chief internat. affairs Office Judge Adv., Hdqrs. US Army Europe U.S. Army, 1960-63; chief plans office Office Judge Adv. Gen., Washington, 1963-64; Judge Adv. Hdqtrs. U.S. Army Combat Devels. Command, 1964-66; ret., 1969; asst. gen. counsel AID, State Dept., 1969-81; gen. counsel ACDA, Washington, 1981-83; mem. faculty Nat. War Coll., 1966-68; adj. prof. Def. Intelligence Coll., Washington, 1989-91; joint staff planner, policy and planning directorate Joint Chiefs Staff, Washington, 1968-69. Mem. editorial bd. Mil. Law and Law of War Rev., 1960-63, Fed. Bar News Jour., 1988-89; book rev. editor: Fordham U. Law Rev., 1941-42. Decorated Bronze Star.; recipient AID Superior Honor award, 1980, ACDA Meritorious Honor award, 1983. Mem. Am. Soc. Internat. Law. Home: 8713 Mary Lee Ln Annandale VA 22003-3659

RICHSTONE, BEVERLY JUNE, psychologist; b. N.Y.C., June 8, 1952; d. Max and Rosalyn Richstone. BA summa cum laude, Queens Coll., 1975; MEd, U. Miami, 1978; PsyD, Nova U., 1982. Lic. clin. psychologist. Clin. fellow Harvard Med. Sch., 1982-83; staff psychologist Met. State Hosp., Waltham, Mass., 1983-85; asst. attending psychologist McLean Hosp., Belmont, Mass., 1983-84; asst. psychologist Cambridge Hosp./N. Charles Mental Health Rsch./Tng. Found., Cambridge, Mass., 1984-85; assoc. dir. Coastal Geriatric Svcs., Hingham, Mass., 1985-86, Alpha Geriatric Svcs., Hingham, 1986-87; rsch. assoc. Harvard Sch. Pub. Health, Boston, 1992-94; instr. psychology Harvard Med. Sch., Boston, 1983-84; consulting psychologist Coastal Geriatric Svcs., Hingham, 1985. Contbg. author: The New Our Bodies, Ourselves, 1992. Cmty. advisor Mass. Office Disability, Boston, 1992—. Mem. APA, Phi Beta Kappa.

RICHTER, BURTON, physicist, educator; b. N.Y.C., Mar. 22, 1931; s. Abraham and Fanny (Pollack) R.; m. Laurose Becker, July 1, 1960; children: Elizabeth, Matthew. B.S., MIT, 1952, Ph.D., 1956. Research assoc. Stanford U., 1956-60, asst. prof. physics, 1960-63, assoc. prof., 1963-67, prof., 1967—, Paul Pigott prof. phys. sci., 1980—, tech. dir. Linear Accelerator Ctr., 1982-84, dir. Linear Accelerator Ctr., 1984—; cons. NSF, Dept. Energy; bd. dirs. Varian Corp., Litel Instruments; Loeb lectr. Harvard U., 1974; DeShalit lectr. Weizmann Inst., 1975. Contbr. over 300 articles to profl. publs. Recipient E.O. Lawrence medal Dept. Energy, 1975; Nobel prize in physics, 1976. Fellow Am. Phys. Soc. (pres. 1994), AAAS; mem. NAS, Am. Acad. Arts and Scis. Achievements include research in elementary particle physics. Office: Stanford Linear Accel Ctr PO Box 4349 Stanford CA 94309-4349

RICHTER, DEBBIE KAY, artist; b. Riverside, Calif., Feb. 15, 1952; d. Charles Ray and Normajeane (Nicodemus) Dickey; m. Kurt E. Richter, Apr. 14, 1984; 1 child, Christopher Michael. AA, Riverside City Coll., 1971; BA, U. Calif., Riverside, 1975; culinary degree, Williams Sonoma, 1977. Ops. mgr. Brown Interpacific, Tustin, Calif., 1977-80; purchasing mgr. Anderson Winn, Burbank, Calif., 1980-84; artist DKR Inc., Kent, Wash., 1984—. Works exhibited in Manahatten Arts, 1993, Ency. Living Artists, 1993, 94, 95; publisher Gango Editions, Portland, Oreg. Republican. Lutheran. Avocations: cooking, gardening, decorating.

RICHTER, DONALD PAUL, lawyer; b. New Britain, Conn., Feb. 15, 1924; s. Paul John and Helen (Racoske) R.; m. Jane Frances Gumpright, Aug. 10, 1946; children: Christopher Dean, Cynthia Louise. A.B., Bates Coll., 1947; LL.B., Yale U., 1950. Bar: N.Y. 1951, Conn. 1953. Assoc. Winthrop, Stimson, Putnam & Roberts, N.Y.C., 1950-52; ptnr. Murtha, Cullina, Richter and Pinney, Hartford, Conn., 1954-94, counsel, 1994—. Trustee Bates Coll., 1962-94, Manchester (Conn.) Meml. Hosp., 1963-94, Hartford Sem., 1973-85; trustee Suffield Acad., 1974—, pres., 1982-89; bd. dirs. Met. YMCA Greater Hartford, 1970-94, pres., 1976-81, trustee, 1994—; mem. nat. coun. YMCA, 1978-82; bd. dirs. Church Homes, 1967-81; trustee, v.p., Silver Bay Assn., 1971—. With USNR, 1943-46. Fellow Am. Coll. Trust and Estate Counsel; mem. ABA, Conn. Bar Assn., Univ. Club, Hartford Club, Rotary (Paul Harris fellow 1996), Phi Beta Kappa, Delta Sigma Rho. Congregationalist. Home: 140 Boulder Rd Manchester CT 06040-4508 Office: Murtha Cullina Richter & Pinney City Place I 185 Asylum St Hartford CT 06103-3402

RICHTER, GEORG, book publishing executive. Pres. Bantam Doubleday Dell Books for Young Readers, N.Y.C. Office: Bantam Doubleday Dell Books 1540 Broadway New York NY 10036-4039

RICHTER, JUDITH ANNE, pharmacology educator; b. Wilmington, Del., Mar. 4, 1942; d. Henry John and Dorothy Madelyn (Schroeder) R. BA, U. Colo., 1964; PhD, Stanford U., 1969. Postdoctoral fellow Cambridge (Eng.) U., 1969-70, U. London, 1970-71; asst. prof. pharmacology Sch. Medicine Ind. U., Indpls., 1971-78, assoc. prof. pharmacology and neurobiology, 1978-84, prof., 1984—; vis. assoc. prof. U. Ariz. Health Sci. Ctr., Tucson, 1983; mem. biomed. rsch. rev. com. Nat. Inst. on Drug Abuse, 1983-87. Mem. editorial bd. Jour. Neurochemistry, 1982-87; contbr. numerous articles to sci. jours. Scholar Boettcher Found., 1960-64; fellow Wellcome Trust, 1969-71. Mem. AAAS, Am. Soc. for Pharmacology and Exptl. Therapeutics (exec. com. neuropharmacology div. 1989-91), Am. Soc. for Neurochemistry, Internat. Soc. for Neurochemistry, Soc. for Neurosci., Women in Neurosci., Assn. Women in Sci., Phi Beta Kappa, Sigma Xi. Achievements include research in neuropharmacology, especially barbiturates and neurobiology of mutant mice and dopaminergic systems. Office: Ind U Sch Medicine 791 Union Dr Indianapolis IN 46202-4887

RICHTER, MICHAEL THOMAS, professional hockey player; b. Phila., Sept. 22, 1966. Student, U. Wisconsin. With N.Y. Rangers, 1985—; goalie U.S. Nat. Team, 1987-88, U.S. Olympic Team, 1987-88. Recipient WCHA Rookie of the Yr. award, 1985-86; named MVP, All-Star Game, 1994. Played in NHL All-Star Game, 1992-93, Stanley Cup Championship, 1994. Office: NY Rangers 4 Pennsylvania Plz New York NY 10001*

RICHTER, PETER CHRISTIAN, lawyer; b. Opava, Czechoslovakia, June 13, 1944; came to U.S., 1951; s. Hanus and Alzbeta (Kindlarova) R.; m. Leslie Diane Rousseau, Nov. 25, 1967; children: Timothy Jason, Lindsey Berta. BS, U. Oreg., 1967, JD, 1971. Bar: Oreg. 1971, U.S. Dist. Ct. 1972, U.S. Ct. Appeals (9th cir.) 1972, U.S. Supreme Ct. 1983. Assoc. Veatch, Lovett & Stiner, Portland, Oreg., 1971-73; with Miller, Nash, Wiener, Hager & Carlsen, Portland, 1973—; adj. prof. law trial advocacy Northwestern Sch. of Law, Lewis and Clark Coll., Portland, 1986—; pro tempore judge Multnomah County Cir. Ct., Portland, 1985—, Oreg. State Bar Trial Advocacy Seminars, 1988—. Author: (handbook) Oregon State Bar, 1987, 88, 89; co-author: (chpt. in book) Oregon State Bar Damage Manual, 1985, 90; editor, program planner Sales: The Oregon Experience, 1989. Trustee, bd. dirs. Parry Ctr. for Children, Portland, 1990; former bd. dir. Boy Scouts of Am., Columbia Pacific Coun., Portland, Nat. Conf. Christians and Jews, Portland, 1983. With Oreg. Army N.G., 1967-75. Recipient Cert. of Appreciation Northwestern Sch. of Law, 1990. Fellow Am. Bar Found. (mem. trial techniques com.); mem. ABA (trial techniques com.), Fed. Bar Assn. (Oreg. chpt.), Am. Bd. Trial Advocates (advocate), Oreg. Bar Assn. (lectr. trial advocacy seminars 1988—, mem. jud. adminstn. com, bus. lit. sec. exec. comm.), Multnomah Bar Assn. (bd dirs.), Oreg. Assn. Def. Counsel (cert. of appreciation 1987, 89) Inns of Ct., Multnomah Athletic Club, Arlington Club. Avocations: squash, tennis, skiing, golf, reading. Office: Miller Nash Wiener Hager & Carlsen 111 SW 5th Ave Portland OR 97204-3604

RICHTER, RICHARD PAUL, academic administrator; b. Bryn Mawr, Pa., Mar. 6, 1931; s. Manuel DeWitt and Emma Margaret (Theilacker) R.; m. Margot Denithorne, Sept. 5, 1953; children: Karen Lee, Kurt Richard. BA, Ursinus Coll., 1953, LLD (hon.), 1976; MA, U. Pa., 1957; cert., Inst. Ednl. Mgmt., Harvard U., 1974; DHL (hon.), Tohoku Gakuin U., Sendai, Japan, 1986, Muhlenberg Coll., 1989. Editor Provident Mut. Life Ins. Co., Phila., 1956-58; supr. employee communications Phila. Gas Works divsn. UGI Corp., 1958-65; alumni dir. Ursinus Coll., Collegeville, Pa., 1965-67, asst. to pres., 1967-69, v.p. adminstrv. affairs, 1969-76, pres., 1976-94; pres. emeritus, 1995—; instr. in English Ursinus Coll., Collegeville, Pa., 1965-73, asst. prof. English, 1973-86; prof. of coll. Ursinus Coll., Collegville, Pa., 1986-94; chmn. Commn. for Ind. Colls. and Univs. Pa., 1984, Found. for Ind. Colls. of Pa., Harrisburg, 1985; past chmn. Coun. for Higher Edn. United Ch. of Christ; bd. dirs. CenterCore. Contbtr. articles, poems to various publs. Chmn. CMMC, Inc. Montgomery Hosp., Norristown, Pa. Recipient Gold Quill award Am. Assn. Indsl. Editors, 1964, Lindback award for excellence in tchg. Ursinus Coll., 1973, Silver Beaver award Boy Scouts Am., 1985, Muhlenberg Leadership award Hist. Soc. Trappe, Pa., 1994, Francis J. Michelini award for outstanding svc. Assn. Ind. Colls. and Univs. of Pa., 1996, Arthur V. Ciervo award Coll. and Univ. Pub. Rels. Assn. of Pa., 1996. Mem. Pa. Assn. Colls. and Univs. (bd. dirs.), Del. Valley Assn. Communicators (past treas.), Pa. Folklife Soc., Montgomery County Hist. Soc. Home: 236 6th Ave Collegeville PA 19426-2510 Office: Ursinus Coll PO Box 1000 Collegeville PA 19426-1000

RICHTER, W. D., screenwriter, director, producer; b. New Britain, Conn., Dec. 7, 1945; s. Walter Oswald and Hedwig (Duch) R.; m. Susan Booth, June 22, 1968. BA, Dartmouth Coll., 1968; postgrad., U. So. Calif., 1968-70. Freelance writer, producer, director, 1973—. Screenwriter: Slither, 1973, Peeper, 1975, Nickelodeon, 1976, Invasion of the Body Snatchers, 1978, Dracula, 1979, Brubaker, 1980 (Academy award nomination best original screenplay 1980), All Night Long, 1981, Big Trouble in Little China, 1986, Needful Things, 1993; prodr., dir.: (films) Buckaroo Banzai, 1984, Late for Dinner, 1991. Mem. Writers Guild Am., Dirs. Guild Am. Office: The Shapira/Lichtman Agency 8827 Beverly Blvd Los Angeles CA 90048-2405

RICHTOL, HERBERT HAROLD, science foundation program director; b. Bklyn., Aug. 13, 1932; s. Israil and Pearl (Boshnack) R.; m. Iris Gloria Klar, Aug. 11, 1956; children: Nancy Anne, Susan Gail, Elise Carol, Michael Bruce. BS, St. Lawrence U., 1954; PhD, NYU, 1961. Instr. Queens (N.Y.) Coll., 1960-61; chemistry prof. Rensselaer Poly. Inst., Troy, N.Y., 1961-85, dean undergrad. coll., 1985-94; program dir. Divsn. Undergrad. Edn. NSF, Arlington, Va., 1994—. Contbr. articles to profl. jours. Bd. dirs. Temple Beth El, Troy, 1980-85. Served with U.S. Army, 1954-56. Mem. Am. Chem. Soc., AAAS, Am. Assn. Higher Edn., Woodrow Wilson Soc., Sigma Xi. Democrat. Jewish. Avocations: theater, squash. Home: 850 North Randolph St Arlington VA 22203 Office: NSF Divsn Undergrad Edn 4201 Wilson Blvd Arlington VA 22230-0001*

RICK, CHARLES MADEIRA, JR., geneticist, educator; b. Reading, Pa., Apr. 30, 1915; s. Charles Madeira and Miriam Charlotte (Yeager) R.; m. Martha Elizabeth Overholts, Sept. 3, 1938 (dec.); children: Susan Charlotte Rick Baldi, John Winfield. B.S., Pa. State U., 1937; AM, Harvard U., 1938, Ph.D., 1940. Asst. plant breeder W. Atlee Burpee Co., Lompoc, Calif., 1936, 37; instr., jr. geneticist U. Calif., Davis, 1940-44; asst. prof., asst. geneticist U. Calif., 1944-49, asso. prof., asso. geneticist, 1949-55, prof., geneticist, 1955—; chmn. coordinating com. Tomato Genetics Coop., 1950-82; dir. CMR Tomato Genetics Resource Ctr., 1975—; mem. genetics study sect. NIH, 1958-62; mem. Galapagos Internat. Sci. Project, 1964; mem. genetic biology panel NSF, 1971-72; mem. nat. plant genetics resources bd. Dept. Agr., 1975-82; Gen. Edn. Bd. vis. lectr. N.C. State U., 1956; Faculty Research lectr. U. Calif., 1961; Carnegie vis. prof. U. Hawaii, 1963; vis. prof. Universidade São Paulo, Brazil, 1965; vis. scientist U. P.R., 1968; centennial lectr. Ont. Agr. Coll. U. Guelph, Ont., Can., 1974; adj. prof. Univ. de Rosario, Argentina, 1980; univ. lectr. Cornell U., 1987; mem. Plant Breeding Research Forum, 1982-84. Contbr. numerous articles in field to books and sci. jours. Recipient award of distinction Coll. Agr. and Environ. Scis., U. Calif., Davis, 1991, Disting. Svc. award Calif. League Food Processors, 1993, Alexander von Humboldt award Alexander von Humboldt Found., 1993; grantee NSF, USPHS/NIH, Rockefeller Found., 1953-83; Guggenheim fellow, 1948, 50, Pa. State U. Alumni fellow, 1991; C.M. Rick Tomato Genetics Resource Ctr. at U. Calif., Davis named in his honor, 1990. Fellow Calif. Acad. Sci., AAAS (Campbell award 1959), Indian Soc. Genetics and Plant Breeding (hon.), Am. Soc. Horticultural Sci.; mem. Nat. Acad. Scis., Bot. Soc. Am. (Merit award 1976), Am. Soc. Hort. Sci. (M.A. Blake award 1974, Vaughan Research award 1946), Mass. Hort. Soc. (Thomas Roland medal 1983), Soc. Econ. Botany (named Disting. Econ. Botanist 1987), Nat. Council Comml. Plant Breeders (Genetic and Plant Breeding award 1987), Am. Genetics Assn. (Frank N. Meyer medal 1982). Office: U Calif Davis CA 95616

RICKARD, NORMAN EDWARD, office equipment company executive; b. Rochester, N.Y., Apr. 6, 1936; s. Norman E. and Florentine (Jensen) R.; m. Patricia Chester, Jan. 19, 1963 (dec. March 7, 1966); children: Anne, Margaret; m. Carol Miller, Apr. 6, 1968 (div. March 24, 1981); children: Sarah, Catherine, Elizabeth; m. Margaret S., June 6, 1981; stepchildren: Lee Ann, Sarah W. BA, St. John Fisher Coll., 1958; MBA, St. John's U., 1962; postgrad. study, NYU, 1962-64. Instr. St. John's U., N.Y.C., 1962-63; various fin. functions Oxford Paper Co., Rumford, Maine and N.Y.C., 1963-66; various positions planning, fin. Xerox Corp., Rochester, N.Y., 1966-71; controller, N.E. region Xerox Corp. U.S. Mktg., White Plains, N.Y., 1971-73; dir. internat. fin. Xerox Corp., Stamford, Conn., 1974-75; controller Xerox Corp., Rank Xerox, London, 1975-78; v.p. planning & control Xerox Corp., Worldwide Mfg., Stamford, 1978-81; dir. Xerox Corp., Stamford, 1981-87, v.p. quality, 1987-92; pres. Xerox Bus. Svcs., 1992—; co-chairperson, mem. conf. bd. Total Quality Mgmt. Ctr., bd. dirs.; bd. dirs. Vt. Pure Bottling, Am. Direct; sr. examiner Malcolm Baldridge Nat. Quality Award, 1992-93. Trustee St. John Fisher Coll. With U.S. Army, 1958-60. Mem. Assn. for Quality and Participation (bd. dirs. 1991-94), Whippoorwill Country Club, Stratton Mounty Country Club, Manchester Country Club. Republican. Roman Catholic. Office: Xerox Corp PO Box 1600 800 Long Ridge Rd Stamford CT 06902-1227

RICKARD, RUTH DAVID, retired history and political science educator; b. Fed. Republic Germany, Feb. 20, 1926; came to U.S., 1940; d. Carl and Alice (Koch) David; m. Robert M. Yaffe, Oct. 1949 (dec. 1959); children: David, Steven; m. Norman G. Rickard, June 1968 (dec. 1988); 1 stepson, Douglas. BS cum laude, Northwestern U., 1947, MA, 1948. Law editor Commerce Clearing House, Chgo., 1948; instr. history U. Ill., Chgo., 1949-51; instr. extension program U. Ill., Waukegan, 1960-67; instr. history Waukegan Schs., 1960-69; original faculty, prof. western civilization, polit. sci. Coll. of Lake County, Grayslake, Ill., 1969-92; mem. Inter-Univ. Seminar on Armed Forces and Soc.; mem. Hospitality Info. Svc. for Diplomatic Residents and Families affiliate Meridian Internat. Ctr. Author: History of College of Lake County, 1987 (honored by city of Waukegan 1987), (poem) I Lost My Wings, 1989, Au Revoir from Emeritusdom, 1993, Where are the Safety Zones, 1994; spkr. on various ind. radio and TV programs; contbr. articles to profl. jours. Mem. Econ. Devel. Com., Waukegan, 1992-93. Scholar Freedoms Found. Am. Legion, Valley Forge, Pa., 1967. Mem. AAUW (pres. Waukegan chpt. 1955-57, scholarship named for her 1985), LWV (charter, v.p. Waukegan chpt.), Nat. Press Club D.C. (co-writer/editor NPC History), Phi Beta Kappa. Avocations: writing, travel, reading, theater.

RICKARDS, LEONARD MYRON, oil company executive; b. Canton, N.C., Aug. 17, 1927; s. James Cooper and Ethel Naomi (Trull) R.; m. Pauline Hope Murray, Feb. 28, 1953; children—Tim Paul, Lisa Diane. BS, U. Kans., 1950; postgrad., European Inst. Bus. Adminstrn., Fountainbleau, France, 1974. With Phillips Petroleum Co., Bartlesville, Okla., 1950—; sr. v.p. Europe-Africa Phillips Petroleum Co., London, 1973-76; mgr. N.Am. exploration and prodn. div. Phillips Petroleum Co., Bartlesville, 1976-77, v.p. N.Am., 1977-80, sr. v.p. exploration and production, 1980-85, exec. v.p., bd. dirs., 1985-89, ret., 1989. Served with U.S. Coast Guard, 1945-46. Mem. Am. Assn. Petroleum Geologists, Am. Petroleum Inst. (past, bd. dirs.), Okla. Soc. Profl. Engrs., Sigma Tau, Tau Beta Pi, Theta Tau.

RICKART, CHARLES EARL, mathematician, educator; b. Osage City, Kans., June 28, 1913; s. Charles Day and Ola May (Brewer) R.; m. Annabel Esther Erickson, Mar. 31, 1942; children: Mark Charles, Eric Alan, Thomas Melvin. B.A., U. Kans., 1937, M.A., 1938; Ph.D., U. Mich., 1941. Peirce instr. math. Harvard U., 1941-43; mem. faculty Yale U., 1943—, prof. math., 1959-83, chmn. dept., 1959-65, Percey F. Smith prof. math., 1963-83, prof. emeritus, 1983—. Author: General Theory of Banach Algebras, 1960, Natural Function Algebras, 1979, Structuralism and Structures, 1995. Mem. AAAS, AAUP, Conn. Acad. Arts and Scis., Am. Math Soc., Math . Assn. of Am. Home: 88 Notch Hill Rd Apt 173 North Branford CT 06471-1846 Office: Yale U Dept Math New Haven CT 06520

RICKEL, ANNETTE URSO, psychology educator; b. Phila.; d. Ralph Francis and Marguerite (Calcaterra) Urso; m. Peter Rupert Fink, July 21, 1989; 1 child, John Ralph. BA, Mich. State U., 1963; MA, U. Mich., 1965, PhD, 1972. Lic. psychologist, Mich. Faculty early childhood edn. Merrill-Palmer Inst., Detroit, 1967-69; adj. faculty U. Mich., Ann Arbor, 1969-75; asst. dir. N.E. Guidance Ctr., Detroit, 1972-75; asst. prof. psychology Wayne State U., Detroit, 1975-81; vis. assoc. prof. Columbia U., N.Y.C., 1982-83; assoc. prof. psychology Wayne State U., 1981-87, asst. provost, 1989-91, prof. psychology, 1987—; Am. Coun. on Edn. fellow Princeton and Rutgers Univs., 1990-91; dir. mental health and devel. Nat. Com. for Quality Assurance, Washington, 1995-96; clin. prof. dept. Psychiatry Georgetown U., Washington, 1995—; AAAS and APA Congl. Sci. fellow on Senate Fin. Subcom. on Health and Pres.'s Nat. Health Care Reform Task Force, 1992-93. Cons. editor Am. Jour. of Community Psychology; co-author: Social and Psychological Problems of Women, 1984, Preventing Maladjustment..., 1987; author: Teenage Pregnancy and Parenting, 1989; contbr. articles to profl. jours. Mem. Pres.'s Task Force on Nat. Health Care Reform, 1993; bd. dirs. Children's Ctr. of Wayne County, Mich., The Epilepsy Ctr. of Mich., Planned Parenthood League, Inc. Grantee NIMH, 1976-86, Eloise and Richard Webber Found., 1977-80, McGregor Fund, 1977-78, 82, David M. Whitney Fund, 1982, Katherine Tuck Fund, 1985-90; recipient Career Devel. Chair award, 1985-86; Congl. Sci. fellow AAAS, 1992-93. Fellow APA (div. pres. 1984-85); mem. Midwestern Psychol. Assn., Mich. Psychol. Assn., Soc. for Rsch. in Child Devel., Soc. for Rsch. in Child and Adolescent Psychopathology, Internat. Assn. of Applied Psychologists, Sigma Xi, Psi Chi. Roman Catholic.

RICKELS, KARL, psychiatrist, physician, educator; b. Wilhelmshaven, Germany, Aug. 17, 1924; came to U.S., 1954, naturalized, 1960; s. Karl E. and Stephanie (Roehrhoff) R.; m. Rosalind Wilson, June 27, 1964; children: Laurence Arthur, Stephen W., Michael R. M.D., U. Muenster, 1951. Intern Dortmund (Germany) Hosp., 1951-52; postgrad. tng. U. Erlangen, U. Frankfurt, City Hosp. Kassel, 1952-54; resident in psychiatry Mental Health Inst., Cherokee, Iowa, 1954-55, Hosp. U. Pa., Phila., 1955-57; from instr. to assoc. prof. U. Pa., Phila., 1957-69; prof. psychiatry U. Pa., 1969—, prof. pharmacology, 1976—, Stuart and Emily B.H. Mudd prof. human behavior, 1977—, chief mood and anxiety disorders program, 1964—; chmn. com. on studies involving human beings U. Pa., Phila., 1985—; chief psychiatry Phila. Gen. Hosp., 1975-77. Editor, author 7 books; contbr. over 500 articles to profl. publs. Fellow Am. Coll. Neuropsychopharmacology (charter), Am. Coll. Clin. Pharmacology, Am. Psychiat. Assn., Coll. Physicians Phila., Collegium INternat. Neuro-Psychopharmacologicum; mem. Arbeits Gemeinschaft Neuro-Psychopharmacology, Internat. Soc. Investigation of Stress, European Coll. Neuropsychopharmacology (corr.). Home: 1324 Youngsford Rd Gladwyne PA 19035-1231 Office: U Pa Dept Psychiatry 803 Sci Ctr 3600 Market St Philadelphia PA 19104-2611

RICKER, WILLIAM EDWIN, biologist; b. Waterdown, Ont., Can., Aug. 11, 1908; s. Harry Edwin and Rebecca Helena (Rouse) R.; m. Marion Torrance Cardwell, Mar. 30, 1935; children—Karl Edwin, John Fraser, Eric William, Angus Clemens. B.A., U. Toronto, 1930, M.A., 1931, Ph.D., 1936; D.Sc. (hon.), U. Man., 1970; LL.D., Dalhousie U., 1972. Sci. asst. Fisheries Research Bd. Can., Nanaimo, B.C., 1931-38; editor publs. Fisheries Research Bd. Can., Nanaimo, 1950-62, biol. cons. to chmn. and staff, 1962-63; acting chmn. Fisheries Research Bd. Can., Ottawa, 1963-64; chief scientist Fisheries Research Bd. Can., Nanaimo, 1964-73; jr. scientist Internat. Pacific Salmon Fisheries Commn., New Westminster, B.C., 1938-39; asst. prof., assoc. prof., prof. zoology Ind. U., 1939-50; dir. Ind. Lake and Stream Survey Ind. Dept. Conservation, 1939-50; vol., contract investigator Pacific Biol. Sta., Nanaimo, 1973-95. Contbr. articles to profl. jours. Decorated officer Order of Can., 1986; named Eminent Ecologist Ecol. Soc. Am., 1990; recipient Murray Newman award Vancouver Aquarium, 1995. Fellow Royal Soc. Can. (Flavelle medal 1970), AAAS; mem. Wildlife Soc. (awards 1956, 59), Profl. Inst. Pub. Service Can. (gold medal 1966), Am. Fisheries Soc. (award of excellence 1969), Can. Soc. Zoologists (F.E.J. Fry medal 1983), Am. Soc. Limnology and Oceanography (pres. 1959), Arctic Inst. N.Am., Can. Soc. Wildlife and Fishery Biologists, Entomol. Soc. B.C., Internat. Assn. Limnology, Marine Biol. Assn. India, Ottawa Field-Naturalists Club, Wilson Ornithol. Club, Explorers Club, Sigma Xi. Home: 3052 Hammond Bay Rd, Nanaimo, BC Canada V9T 1E2

RICKERD, DONALD SHERIDAN, foundation executive; b. Smiths Falls, Ont., Can., Nov. 8, 1931; s. Harry M. and Evaline Mildred (Sheridan) R.; m. Julie Rekai, Dec. 14, 1968; 1 child, Christopher. Student, St. Andrews U., Scotland, 1951-52; BA, Queen's U., Can., 1953; LLD, Queen's U., 1985; BA (Rotary Found. fellow), Oxford U., Eng., 1955, MA, 1963; DCL, Mount Allison U., Can., 1985; LLD, Trent U., Can., 1986; LLB, York U., Can., 1991. Bar: Ont. 1959; apptd. Queen's Counsel, 1978. Assoc. Fasken & Calvin, Toronto, 1957-61; registrar, lectr. history, asst. prof. law Faculty of Adminstrv. Studies York U., Toronto, 1961-68; pres. Donner Can. Found., Toronto, 1968-89, W.H. Donner Found., Inc., N.Y.C., 1971-87, Max Bell Found., Toronto, 1989—; chmn. bd. dirs. Draeger Can. Ltd.; bd. dirs. ICWI Found., Kingston, Jamaica. Former chmn. Coun. Ontario Coll. Art, Toronto; bd. dirs., chmn. Ctrl. Hosp.; mem. Royal Commn. concerning activities of Royal Canadian Mounted Police, 1977-81; former bd. govs. Upper Can. Coll., Toronto, trustee, vice chmn. bd. trustees, Queen's U.; former mem. bd. regents Mt. Allison U. Decorated Order of Can. Mem. Can. Bar Assn., County of York Law Assn., Toronto Lawyers Club, Bd. Trade Met. Toronto, Univ. Club. Office: Max Bell Found. PO Box 105, 79 Wellington St W, Toronto, ON Canada M5K 1G8

RICKERSON, JEAN MARIE, video producer, journalist, photographer; b. Takoma Park, Md., Dec. 29, 1956; d. Charles Marvin and Rita Ann (Smith) Blackburn; m. Ronald Wayne Rickerson, Oct. 18, 1989; children: Drew Elliott, Ella. BS, U. Md., 1978. Pres. Videofax Inc., Bethesda, Md., 1982-90; founder, dir. Found. for Acad. Excellence Inc., Bethesda, 1985-90; video prodr. Applied Measurement Systems Inc., Bremerton, Wash., 1990—; pres. Photo Graphics Inc., Bremerton, 1992—. Contbr. articles and photographs to profl. jours; writer, prodr., dir. videotape SEAFAC, 1992, USNS Hayes, 1993, High Gain Array Test Module, 1993, Advanced Mine Detection Sonar, 1995, BQH-9 Signal Data Recording Set, Submarine Acoustic Maintenance Program, 1996, Intermediate Scale Measurement System, 1996. Avocations: skiing, camping, gardening, scuba diving. Office: Applied Measurement Sys Inc 645 4th St Ste 202 Bremerton WA 98337-1402

RICKERT, JONATHAN BRADLEY, foreign service officer; b. Washington, July 23, 1937; s. Van Dusen and Margaret Eleanor (Bradley) R.; m. Ulla Gerd Margareta Granstrand, June 20, 1969; children: Ulla Margaret, Jonathan Bernt. AB cum laude, Princeton U, 1959; diploma Russian lang., U.S. Army Lang. Sch., 1962; student, Harvard U., 1976-77; MA, George Washington U., 1982. Rotational jr. officer Exec. Sec. State Dept., 1963-65; consular officer Embassy, London, 1965-66; staff aide to amb., polit. officer Embassy, Moscow, 1966-68; exchanges officer Office Soviet and Eastern European Exchanges State Dept., 1969-70, with Romanian Lang. Tng. FSI, 1971; consular officer Embassy Bucharest, 1971-73, polit. officer, 1973-74; spl. asst. to U.S. Rep. U.S. Delegation MBFR, Vienna, 1974-76; polit./labor officer Embassy Port Spain, 1977-80; desk officer Trinidad, Guyana, Suriname, acting dep. dir. Office Caribbean Affairs State Dept., 1980-82, desk officer Romania, Office Eastern European and Yugoslav Affairs, 1982-84, with Bulgarian Lang. Tng., 1984-85; dep. chief mission Embassy Sofia, 1985-88; chief European Assignments divsn. State Dept., 1988-90; legis. asst. to Sen Bob Packwood, 1990-91; dep. chief mission Embassy Bucharest, 1991-95; dir. Office of N. Cen. European Affairs State Dept., 1995—. With U.S. Army, 1961-62. Mem. Am. Fgn. Svc. Assn. Episcopalian.

RICKETTS, GARY EUGENE, animal scientist; b. Willard, Ohio, Aug. 2, 1935; s. Franklin Edward and Berthalda Marie (Albright) R.; m. Audrey May Wheeler, Sept. 14, 1958; children—Dawn, John, Mark. B.S., Ohio State U., 1957, M.S., 1960, Ph.D., 1963. Livestock extension specialist dept. animal sci. U. Ill., Urbana-Champaign, 1964-86, sheep extension specialist and extension program leader, 1986—. Contbr. articles to profl. jours. and livestock publs. Active Little League Baseball, 8 yrs.; leader 4-H Club, 11 yrs. Served with Army N.G., 1958-64. Recipient Beef Booster award Ill. Red Angus Assn., 1973, G.R. Carlisle Ext. award, 1979, 95, Outstanding Leadership and Recognition award Ill. Sheep Industry, 1984, Sustained Excellence award in ext. Ill. Coop. Ext. Svc., 1984, J.C. Spitler award Epsilon Sigma Phi, 1984, State Disting. Svc. award, 1995, Guy Green award Am. Corriedale Assn., 1992. Mem. Am. Soc. Animal Sci. (Young Scientist award Midwest sect. 1971, Extension award 1984), Am. Registry Profl. Animal Scientists. Republican. Methodist. Home: 2506 S Cottage Grove Ave Urbana IL 61801-6820 Office: 128 ASL 1207 W Gregory Dr Urbana IL 61801-3838

RICKETTS, THOMAS ROLAND, bank executive; b. Detroit, Mar. 4, 1931; s. Samuel Charles and Lillian May (Schwab) R.; m. Priscilla Anne Irving, Aug. 10, 1957; children: Robert T., Karen L. B.B.A., U. Mich., 1953, J.D., 1956. Bar: Mich. 1956. With Standard Fedn. Bank, Troy, Mich., 1956—; branch mgr. Standard Fed. Savs. Bank, Troy, Mich., 1958-62, v.p. advertising, pub. relations, personnel, 1962-70, sr. v.p., treas., 1970-72, exec. v.p., chief adminstrv. officer, 1972-73, pres., chief adminstrv. officer, 1973-74, pres., mng. officer, 1974-81, chmn. bd., pres., mng. officer, 1981—, also bd. dirs.; pres. Savs. Instns. Mktg. Soc. Am., 1968, bd. dirs., 1965-69; pres. Mich. Savs. and Loan League, 1976, bd. dirs. 1975-78; mem. adv. com. Fed. Savs. and Loan Ins. Corp., 1989. Trustee Olivet Coll., 1973-87, Savs. and Loan Found., 1978-82, Detroit Symphony Orch., 1980—, Citizens Rsch. Coun. Mich., 1981—; bd. dirs. United Found., Detroit, 1978—, Detroit-Wayne County Port Authority, 1984-88, Detroit Econ. Growth Corp., 1984—, Detroit Econ. Growth Fund, 1984—; bd. dirs. New Detroit, Inc., 1978—, chmn. minority econ. devel. com., 1979-81, mem. housing com., 1978-83; chmn. Mich. Infrastructure Coalition. 1993-87; mem. Gov.'s Commn. on Jobs and Econ. Devel., 1983-90. Mem. State Bar Mich., U.S. League of Savs. Instn. (govt. affairs com. 1976-93, bd. dirs. 1983-86), Mich. League of Savs. Instn. (legis. and legis. policy coms. 1971-93), Econ. Club Detroit (Bd. dirs. 1989-93). Office: Std Fed Bank 2600 W Big Beaver Rd Troy MI 48084-3323*

RICKEY, GEORGE WARREN, artist, sculptor, educator; b. South Bend, Ind., June 6, 1907; s. Walter J. and Grace (Landon) R.; m. Edith Leighton, May 24, 1947 (wid. June 1995); children: Stuart Ross, Philip J.L. Ed., Trinity Coll., Glenalmond, Scotland, 1921-26; B.A., Balliol Coll., Oxford U., 1929, M.A., 1940; postgrad., Académie Lhote, Paris, 1929-30, Inst. Fine Arts, NYU, 1945-46, State U. Iowa, 1947, Inst. Design, Chgo., 1948-49; hon. doctorates, Union Coll., Schenectady, 1973, Ind. U., 1974, Kalamazoo Coll., 1977, York U., Can., 1978, Tulane U., 1983, Rensselaer Polytechnic Inst., Troy, N.Y., 1990. Tchr. Groton Sch., 1930-33; artist-in-residence Olivet Coll., 1937-39, Kalamazoo Coll., 1939-40, Knox Coll., 1940-41; head dept. art Muhlenberg Coll., 1941-42, 46-48; assoc. prof. design Ind. U., Bloomington, 1949-55; prof. Tulane U., New Orleans, 1955-61, head dept., 1955-59; prof. art Sch. Architecture Rensselaer Poly. Inst., Troy, N.Y., 1962-65. Sculptor, DAAD Art Program, Berlin, Germany, 1968-69, 71-72. Exhibited Denver Mus., 1945, 48, Met. Mus. Art, 1951, Pa. Acad. Ann., 1952-54, Whitney Mus., 1952-53, 64, Mus. Modern Art, 1959, Albright-Knox Gallery, 1965, Mus. Modern Art Internat. Council, 1965, Stedelijk Mus., Amsterdam, Holland, 1965, Mus. Tel Aviv, 1965, St. Louis Bicentennial Sculpture Exhbn., 1965, Dag Hammerskjold Plaza, N.Y.C., 1977, Pier and Ocean, Hayward Gallery, London, 1980, Whitney Mus., 1983, Neuer Berliner Kunstverein, 1987, Am. Fedn. Arts, 1991, Found. Maeght, France, 1992, other U.S. and fgn. galleries; one man shows: John Herron Art Mus., Indpls., 1953, Delgado Mus., New Orleans, 1955, Kraushaar Gallery, 1955, 1959, Amerika Haus, Hamburg, Germany, 1957, Santa Barbara Mus., 1960, Kunstverein, Düsseldorf, Fed. Republic Germany, 1962, Kunsthalle, Hamburg, 1962, Inst. Contemporary Arts, Boston, 1964, Corcoran Gallery, Washington, 1966, UCLA, 1971, Kestner Gesellschaft, Hannover, 1973, Nationalgalerie, Berlin, 1973-74, Amerika Haus, Berlin, 1979, Guggenheim Mus., 1979, Montreal Musée d'Art Contemporain, 1981, Nat. Sculpture Trust, Glasgow, Scotland, 1982, Sculpture Park, Yorkshire, Eng., 1982, Fairweather Hardin Gallery, 1982, Tulane U. Art Gallery, New Orleans, 1983, Bauhaus Archiv., Berlin, Fed. Republic Germany, 1984, Josef Albers Mus., Bottrop, Fed. Republic Germany, 1984, George Rickey in South Bend, 1985, Neuer Berliner Kunstverein, Berlin, 1986, Neuberger Mus., Purchase, N.Y., 1987, Veranneman Found., Holland, 1988, Mus. Boymans-van Beuningen, Rotterdam, Holland, 1989, Gallery Kasahara, Osaka, Japan, 1989, Artcurial, Paris, 1990, Katonah Mus. Art, 1991, Berlinische Galerie, Berlin, 1992, Foundation Maeght, Vence, France, 1992, UCLA Wright Art Gallery, L.A., 1993, Harenberg Verlag, Dortmund, Germany, 1994, numerous others; represented in permanent collections: Dallas Mus., Kunsthalle, Hamburg, Whitney Mus., Mus. Modern Art, Albright-Knox Gallery, Tate Gallery, London, U. Glasgow, U. Heidelberg, Nationalgalerie, Berlin, Corcoran Gallery of Arts, Washington, Louisiana Mus., Humlebaek, Denmark, Auckland City Art Gallery, New Zealand, Tokyo City Hall, Japan, City of Nurnberg, Germany, Nat. Mus. Fine Art, Osaka, Japan, New Theatre, Rotterdam, Parliament Bldg., Dusseldorf, Fed. Republic Germany, Hara Mus., Tokyo, Berlinische Galerie, Berlin, others, also pvt. collections; executed commns. Ft. Worth City Hall, 1974, Fed. Courthouse, Honolulu, 1976, Tech. U., Ulm, Germany, 1977, Ruhr U., Bochum, Ger., 1978, K.B. Plaza, New Orleans, 1978, Central Trust Center, Cin., 1979, Nat. City Ctr., Cleve., 1980, Pitts. Nat. Steel Ctr., 1982, Gerald Ford Library, Ann Arbor, Mich., 1982, Musée de Grenoble, France, 1991, Nat. Gallery, Washington, 1992, Martin Gropius Bau, Berlin, 1992, Nat. Mus. of Fine Arts, Osaka, 1993, Met. Mus. of Art, N.Y.C., 1994; author: Constructivism: Origins and Evolution, 1967, 95; contbr. to publs. in field. Decorated Order of Merit 1st Class, Germany, 1993; recipient Fine Arts medal AIA, 1972, Skowhegan medal for sculpture Skowhegan Sch. Painting and Sculpture, 1973, Ind. Arts. Commn. award for sculpture, 1975, Creative Arts Award medal Brandeis U., 1979; Guggenheim fellow, 1960-62. Mem. Am. Acad. Arts and Letters (Gold medal for sculpture 1995), Coll. Art Assn., Akademie der Kunste (Berlin). Episcopalian. Club: Century Assn. (N.Y.C.).

RICKLES, DONALD JAY, comedian, actor; b. L.I., N.Y., May 8, 1926; s. Max S. and Etta (Feldman) R.; m. Barbara Sklar, Mar. 14, 1965; children: Mindy Beth, Lawrence Corey. Grad., Am. Acad. Dramatic Arts, N.Y.C. Appeared in TV shows The Don Rickles Show, 1971-72, C.P.O. Sharkey, 1976-77, Foul-Ups, Bleeps and Blunders, 1984, Daddy Dearest, 1993; appeared in movies Run Silent, Run Deep, 1958, The Rabbit Trap, 1959, The Rat Race, 1960, Where It's At, 1969, Innocent Blood, 1992, Kelly's Heroes, 1992, Casino, 1995, Toy Story, 1995, others; appeared as comedian at Tropicana Hotel, Las Vegas, Nev., Harrah's Club, Reno and Lake Tahoe, Nev., Trump Taj Mahal, Atlantic City, numerous other nightclubs; numerous appearances TV variety shows; rec. albums include Don Rickles Speaks. Served with USN, 1943-45. Named Entertainer of Yr., Friars Club, 1974. Jewish. Avocation: golfing. Office: care Shefrin Co 800 S Robertson Blvd Los Angeles CA 90035-1606

RICKMAN, ALAN, actor; b. London, 1946. Student, Royal Acad. of Dramatic Arts. Stage appearances: Measure for Measure, Mephisto, Les Liaisons Dangereuses, 1985, 87 (Tony award Best Actor 1987), Tango at the End of Winter, 1991, Desperately Yours (also director), 1980; TV: Romeo and Juliet, Masterpiece Theatre-Therese Raquin, Smiley's People, Barchester Chronicles; films: Die Hard, 1988, The January Man, 1989, Robin Hood: Prince of Thieves, 1989, Quigley Down Under, 1990, Truly, Madly, Deeply, 1991, Closet Land, 1991, Close my Eyes, 1991, Bob Roberts, 1992, Mesmer, 1994, An Awfully Big Adventure, 1995, Sense and Sensibility, 1995.

RICKMAN, TOM, screenwriter, director; b. Sharpe, Ky., Feb. 8, 1940; s. Marshall and Mattie Colleen (Johnston) R. BA, Murray State Coll., 1965; MA, U. Ill., 1969. Fellow Am. Film Inst., Beverly Hills, Calif., 1969-71; founder, dir. Squaw Valley (Calif.) Screenwriters Workshop, 1975—; resource advisor Sundance (Utah) Inst., 1981—, trustee, 1981-88; instr. grad. course in screenwriting U. So. Calif., L.A., 1987. Writer, dir. (short film) What Fixed Me, 1971 (Best Film award Nat. Student Assn. 1971), (feature film) The River Rat, 1984, (TV movie) Shannon's Deal: Wrongful Death, 1991; writer (feature films) The Laughing Policeman, 1973, W.W. and the Dixie Dancekings, 1975, Coal Miner's Daughter, 1980 (Academy award nomination best adapted screenplay 1980), Everybody's All-American, 1988; co-writer (feature films) Kansas City Bomber, 1972, The White Dawn, 1974, Hooper, 1978; author (play) The Collaborators, 1981. Served with USMC, 1958-61.

RICKS, DONALD JAY, agricultural economist; b. Lansing, Mich., Sept. 14, 1936; s. Glenn L. and Evelyn N. R.; m. Joanne M. Burr, Aug. 24, 1968; children: Mark, Craig. B.S. with highest honors, Mich. State U., 1958, M.S., 1960; Ph.D., Oreg. State U., 1965. Instr. econs. Oreg. State U., 1962-63, asst. in agrl. econs., 1963-64; asst. prof. agrl. econs. Mich. State U., 1964-70, assoc. prof., 1970-76, prof., 1976—, extension mktg. economist, 1973—, project leader, extension mktg., 1976-82; chmn. Fed. Cherry Adminstrv. Bd.; mem. Mich. Apple Com. Contbr. numerous articles to various publs. Recipient State Extension Team award, 1971, Man of Yr. award Nat. Cherry Industry, 1989. Mem. Am. Agrl. Econs. Assn., Extension Specialists Assn., Mich. Assn. County Agts. (Outstanding Extension Specialist award 1982), Mich. Extension Specialists Assn. (Outstanding Extension Specialist award 1989), Phi Kappa Phi, Epsilon Sigma Phi, Phi Eta Sigma, Alpha Zeta. Home: 953 Barry Rd Haslett MI 48840-9116 Office: Room 23 Agr Hall Mich State U East Lansing MI 48823

RICKS, MARY F(RANCES), academic administrator, anthropologist; b. Portland, Oreg., July 6, 1939; d. Leo and Frances Helen (Corcoran) Samuel; m. Robert Stanley Ricks, Jan. 7, 1961; children: Michael Stanley, Allen Gilbert. BA, Whitman Coll., 1961; MA, Portland State U., 1977, MPA, 1981, PhD, 1995. Asst. to dir. auxiliary services Portland State U., 1975-79, instnl. researcher, 1979-85, dir. instnl. research and planning, 1985—, rsch. assoc. prof., 1994—. Contbr. articles and presentations to profl. socs. Vol. archeologist BLM-USDI, Lakeview, Oreg., 1983—. Fellow Soc. Applied Anthropology; mem. Soc. Am. Archaeology, Soc. Coll. and U. Planning, Pacific N.W. Assn. Instnl. Rsch. and Planning (pres. 1990-91), Assn. Oreg. Archaeologists (v.p. 1988-90), Assn. Instl. Rsch., City Club of Portland, Sigma Xi. Home: 5466 SW Dover Loop Portland OR 97225-1033 Office: Portland State U Office Instnl Rsch/Planning PO Box 751 Portland OR 97207-0751

RIDDELL, MATTHEW DONALD RUTHERFORD, consulting environmental engineer; b. Toronto, Ont., Can., Mar. 13, 1918; s. Matthew Rutherford and Edith (Downs) R.; m. Dorothy Jane Williams, Oct. 2, 1948; children: James, David, Ann. S.B., Harvard U., 1940, M.S. in San. Engring., 1946. Registered profl. engr., Ill., Mich., Wis. With Greeley & Hansen, Chgo., 1946—; ptnr. Greeley & Hansen, 1957-85, cons., 1986—; mem. water resources tech. adv. com. Northeastern Ill. Planning Commn., 1968—. Pres., bd. dirs. Glenview (Ill.) Pub. Library, 1970-71. Served with USNR, 1941-46. Named Chgo. Civil Engr. of Year, 1975. Mem. ASCE, Am. Acad. Environ. Engrs. (trustee 1969-75, pres. 1980-81), Am. Water Works Assn., Central States Water Pollution Control Assn., Am. Pub. Works Assn., Inst. Water Resources (pres. 1979-80, hon. 1986), Phi Beta Kappa, Delta Omega, Tau Beta Pi. Clubs: Union League (Chgo.). Home: 1215 Elm St Glenview IL 60025-2809 Office: 100 S Wacker Dr Chicago IL 60606-4006

RIDDELL, RICHARD ANDERSON, naval officer; b. Cambridge, Md., Nov. 20, 1940; s. Edward Leo and Katherine Francis (Insley) R.; m. Anne Price Fortney, May 10, 1986; children: Joel Anderson, Amy Kirsten. BS, U.S. Naval Acad., 1962. Commd. ensign USN, 1962, advanced through grades to rear adm., 1991; exec. officer USS Spadefish USN, Norfolk, Va., 1973-76; comdg. officer USS Nautilus USN, New London, Conn., 1976-80, dep. comdr. submarine squadron 2, 1980-81; spl. asst to dir. naval nuclear propulsion program Dept. Navy USN, Washington, 1981-84, dep. dir. strategic policy div. Dept. Navy, 1984-86; comdr. submarine squadron 1 USN, Pearl Harbor, Hawaii, 1986-88, chief of staff Pacific submarine force, 1988-90; dir. strategic submarine div. Dept. Navy USN, Washington, 1990-92; comdr. Submarine Group 9/Comdr. Naval Base, Seattle, 1992-94; dir. spl. programs, dir. test evaluation, tech. requiements Dept. Navy, The Pentagon, Washington, 1994—. Mem. U.S. Naval Inst. Office: The Pentagon Spl Programs OPNAV Navy Dept 5D660 Washington DC 20350-2000

RIDDELL, RICHARD HARRY, retired lawyer; b. Seattle, Nov. 29, 1916; s. Charles F. and Kathryn (Wykoff) R.; m. Dolores Gloyd, Feb. 10, 1970; children by previous marriage: Dorothea R. Alleyne, Wendy, Kathryn R. Reeves, Mark W. A.B., Stanford, 1938; LL.B., Harvard, 1941. Bar: Wash. 1941. Ptnr. Riddell, Williams, Bullitt and Walkinshaw and predecessor firms, Seattle, 1941-92; ret., 1992. Chmn. Seattle Transit Commn., 1971. Fellow Am. Coll. Trial Lawyers; mem. ABA, County Bar Assn. (pres. 1963-64), Wash. State Bar Assn. (pres. 1976-77), Seattle Tennis Club, Spanish Trail Golf Club. Home: 7833 Rancho Mirage Dr Las Vegas NV 89113-1239

RIDDER, BERNARD HERMAN, JR., newspaper publisher; b. N.Y.C., Dec. 8, 1916; s. Bernard Herman and Nell (Hickey) R.; m. Jane Delano, Feb. 24, 1939; children: Laura, Paul A., Peter, Robin, Jill. B.A., Princeton U., 1938. Advt. dir. Duluth News-Tribune, 1941-42, gen. mgr., 1947-52, pub., 1952-72; pub. St. Paul Dispatch-Pioneer Press, 1959-73; pres. Ridder Publs., Inc., 1969—; chmn. bd. Knight-Ridder Newspapers, 1979-83; dir. AP, 1954-64, Seattle Times;. Served from ensign to lt. USNR, 1942-45. Recipient Journalism award U. Minn., also Regents award. Mem. U.S. Golf Assn. (mem. exec. com. 1958-64), Inland Daily Press Assn. (pres. 1954). Clubs: Royal and Ancient Golf (St. Andrews, Scotland); Somerset Country (St. Paul); Augusta Nat. Golf (Ga.), Gulf Stream Golf (Delray Beach, Fla.). Office: St Paul Pioneer Press NW Publ Inc 345 Cedar St Saint Paul MN 55101-1014

RIDDER, ERIC, newspaper publisher; b. Hewlett, L.I., N.Y., July 1, 1918; s. Joseph E. and Hedwig (Schneider) R.; m. Ethelette Tucker, 1939 (div.); children: Eric, Susan; m. Madeleine Graham, 1955 (dec. Nov. 1991). Student, Harvard U., 1936-37. Entire career in newspaper work; dir. Seattle Times Co., Knight-Ridder Newspapers, Inc. Trustee South St. Seaport Mus. Republican. Roman Catholic. Clubs: Seawanhaka-Corinthian Yacht (N.Y.C.), Piping Rock (N.Y.C.), N.Y. Yacht (N.Y.C.), India House (N.Y.C.); Royal Swedish Yacht. Home: Piping Rock Rd Locust Valley NY 11560-2208 Office: 2 World Trade Ctr Fl 27 New York NY 10048-2798

RIDDER, PAUL ANTHONY, newspaper executive; b. Duluth, Minn., Sept. 22, 1940; s. Bernard H. and Jane (Delano) R.; m. Constance Louise Meach, Nov. 6, 1960; children: Katherine Lee Pennoyer, Linda Jane, Susan Delano Cobb, Paul Anthony, Jr. B.A. in Econs., U. Mich., 1962. With Aberdeen (S.D.) Am. News, 1962-63; With Pasadena (Calif.) Star News, 1963-64; with San Jose (Calif.) Mercury News, 1964-86, bus. mgr., 1968-75, gen. mgr., 1975-77, pub., 1977-86, pres., 1979-86; pres. Knight-Ridder Newspaper Div., Miami, Fla., 1986—; pres. Knight-Ridder, Inc., Miami, 1989—, also bd. dirs.; bd. dirs. Seattle Times, Knight-Ridder, Inc., Newspaper First. Bd. dirs. United Way; mem. adv. bd. Ctr. for Econ. Policy Devel. Stanford U., U. Mich.; mem. pres.' adv. bd. U. Mich. Named Calif. Pub. of Yr., 1983, Newspaper Exec. of Yr., Ad Week, 1991. Mem. Fla. C. of C. (bd. dirs., coun. of 100), Cypress Point Club, Indian Creek Club, Pine Valley Golf Club.

RIDDERHEIM, DAVID SIGFRID, hospital administrator; b. Providence, Apr. 26, 1936; married. BA, Brown U., 1958; MA, U. Minn., 1960. Adminstrv. res. St. Luke's Hosp., Cleve., 1959-60, adminstrv. asst., 1960; assoc. adminstr. Parkview Meml. Hosp., Ft. Wayne, Ind., 1963-77, adminstr., 1977-84, exec. v.p., 1984-91, pres., 1989-91; pres., CEO Parkview Health System, Ft. Wayne, Ind., 1991—; adj. educator in field. Contbr. articles to profl. jours. Mem. Ind. Hosp. Assn. (community svc.). Home: 8508 Gerig Rd Leo IN 46765-9619 Office: Parkview Health System 2200 Randallia Dr Fort Wayne IN 46805-4638*

RIDDICK, DANIEL HOWISON, obstetrics and gynecology educator, priest; b. Lynchburg, Va., Dec. 12, 1941; s. Joseph Henry and Nancy Eloise (Gordon) R.; m. Louisa McIntosh Spruill, June 9, 1963; children: Ellen, Daniel. BA, Duke U., 1963, MD, 1967, PhD in Physiology, 1969. Diplomate Am. Bd. Ob-Gyn, Am. Bd. Reproductive Endocrinology; ordained priest Episc. Ch., 1969. Asst. prof. physiology Duke U., Durham, N.C., 1973-74; asst. prof. ob-gyn U. Conn. Sch. Medicine, Farmington, 1974-76, dir. reproductive endocrinology and infertility, 1974-85, assoc. prof. ob-gyn, 1976-81, prof. ob-gyn, 1981-85; prof., chmn. ob-gyn dept. U. Vt., Burlington, 1985—, assoc. dean grad. med. edn., 1987-88. Editor: Reproductive Endocrinology in Clinical Practice, 1987; editor: (with others) Pathology of Infertility, 1987. Mem. ACOG, Am. Fertility Soc. (pres. 1992-93), Am. Gynecol. and Obstet. Soc. Avocation: sheep-raising. Home: 680 Mayo Rd Huntington VT 05462-9410 Office: Fletcher Allen Health Care Dept of Obstetrics & Gynecology 111 Colchester Ave Burlington VT 05401-1473

RIDDICK, FRANK ADAMS, JR., physician, health care facility administrator; b. Memphis, June 14, 1929; s. Frank Adams and Falba (Crawford) R.; m. Mary Belle Alston, June 15, 1952; children: Laura Elizabeth Dufresne, Frank Adams III, John Alston. BA cum laude, Vanderbilt U., 1951, MD, 1954. Diplomate: Am. Bd. Internal Medicine (bd. govs. 1973-80). Intern Barnes Hosp., St. Louis, 1954-55, resident in medicine, 1957-60; fellow in metabolic diseases Washington U., St. Louis, 1960-61; staff Ochsner Clinic (Ochsner Found. Hosp.), New Orleans, 1961—; head sect. endocrinology and metabolic disease Ochsner Clinic (Ochsner Found. Hosp.), 1976-83, asst. med. dir., 1968-72, assoc. med. dir., 1972-75, med. dir., 1975-92; clin. prof. Tulane U., New Orleans, 1977—; trustee Alton Ochsner Med. Found., 1973—, CEO, 1991—; chmn. bd. Ochsner Health Plan, 1983-92; pres. Orleans Svc. Corp., 1976-80, South La. Med. Assocs., New Orleans, 1978—; dir. Brent House Corp., New Orleans, 1980—; chmn. Accreditation Coun. on Grad. Med. Edn., 1986-87, v.p. nat. resident matching program, 1986-90, mem. accreditation coun. on med. edn., 1988-90. Trustee St. Martin's Protestant Epis. Sch., Metairie, La., 1970-84; bd. govs. Isidore Newman Sch., New Orleans, 1987-93. Recipient Disting. Alumnus award Castle Heights Mil. Acad., 1979; recipient teaching award Alton Ochsner Med. Found., 1969, Physician Exec. award Am. Coll. Med. Group Adminstrs., 1984, Disting. Alumnus award Vanderbilt U. Sch. Med., 1988. Fellow ACP, Am. Coll. Physician Execs. (pres. 1987-88); mem. AMA (ho. dels. 1971-92, chmn. coun. on med. edn. 1983-85, coun. on jud. and ethical affairs 1995—), NAS Inst. Medicine, Am. Soc. Internal Medicine (trustee 1970-76, disting. internist award), Endocrine Soc., Am. Diabetes Assn., Soc. Med. Adminstrs. (pres. 1995—), Am. Group Practice Assn. (pres. 1992-94), Boston Club, New Orleans Country Club, Cosmos Club. Home: 1923 Octavia St New Orleans LA 70115-5651 Office: Ochsner Clinic 1514 Jefferson Hwy New Orleans LA 70121-2429

RIDDIFORD, LYNN MOORHEAD, zoologist, educator; b. Knoxville, Tenn., Oct. 18, 1936; d. James Eli and Virginia Amalia (Berry) Moorhead; m. Alan Wistar Riddiford, June 20, 1959 (div. 1966); m. James William Truman, July 28, 1970. AB magna cum laude, Radcliffe Coll., 1958; PhD, Cornell U., 1961. Rsch. fellow in biology Harvard U., Cambridge, Mass., 1961-63, 65-66, asst. prof. biology, 1966-71, assoc. prof., 1971-73; instr. biology Wellesley (Mass.) Coll., 1963-65; assoc. prof. zoology, U. Wash., Seattle, 1973-75, prof., 1975—; mem. study sect. tropical medicine and parasitology NIH, Bethesda, Md., 1974-78; mem. Competitive Grants panel USDA, Arlington, Va., 1979, 89, 95; mem. regulatory biology panel NSF, Washington, 1984-88; mem. governing coun. Internat. Ctr. for Insect Physiology and Ecology, 1985-91, chmn. program com., 1989-91; chmn. adv. com. SeriBiotech, Bangalore, India, 1989; mem. bio. adv. com. NSF, 1992-95. Contbr. articles to profl. jours. Mem. editorial bd. profl. jours. NSF fellow, 1958-60, 61-63; grantee NSF, 1964—, NIH, 1975—, Rockefeller Found., 1970-79, USDA, 1978-82, 89—; fellow John S. Guggenheim, 1979-80, NIH, 1986-87. Fellow AAAS, Am. Acad. Arts and Scis., Royal Entomol. Soc., Entomol. Soc. Am.; mem. Am. Soc. Zoologists (pres. 1991), Am. Soc. Biochem. and Molecular Biology, Entomol. Soc. Am., Am. Soc. Cell Biology, Soc. Devel. Biology. Methodist. Home: 16324 51st Ave SE Bothell WA 98012-6138 Office: U Wash Dept Zoology Box 351800 Seattle WA 98195-1800

RIDDLE, CHARLES ADDISON, III, state legislator, lawyer; b. Marksville, La., June 8, 1955; s. Charles Addison Jr. and Alma Rita (Gremillion) R.; m. Margaret Susan Noone, Mar. 24, 1978; children: Charles Addison IV, John H., Michael J. BA, La. State U., 1976, JD, 1980. Bar: La. 1980, U.S. Dist. Ct. (mid. and we. dists.) La. 1983, U.S. Ct. Appeals (5th cir.) 1988, U.S. Supreme Ct. 1991, U.S. Ct. Vets. Appeals 1994. Assoc. Riddle & Bennett, Marksville, 1980; pvt. practice Marksville, 1981—; mem. La. Ho. of Reps., Baton Rouge, 1992—. Elected La. State Dem. Cen. com., Avoyelles Parish, 1983-87, Parish Exec. Demo. Com. 1987-91. Mem. Avoyelles Bar Assn. (pres. 1987-88), Bunkie Rotary (bd. dirs.), Marksville Lions, Marksville C. of C. (pres. 1988-92). Office: 208 E Mark St Marksville LA 71351-2416

RIDDLE, DONALD HUSTED, former university chancellor; b. Bklyn., Jan. 22, 1921; s. William Ewing and Ruth (Husted) R.; m. Leah Dunlap Gallagher, June 20, 1942; children: Susan Lee and Judith Lee (twins). AB magna cum laude, Princeton U., 1949, MA (Woodrow Wilson fellow), 1951, PhD (Ford Found. fellow), 1956; LLD (hon.), Am. U., 1980, John Jay Coll. Criminal Justice, 1990. Asst. prof. dept. govt. Hamilton Coll., 1952-58; dir. rsch., assoc. prof., prof. politics Eagleton Inst. Politics, Rutgers U., 1958-65; dean faculty John Jay Coll. Criminal Justice, CUNY, 1965-68, pres., 1968-76; chancellor U. Ill. - Chgo., 1976-83, chancellor emeritus, 1983—; staff asst. Conn. Commn. on State Govt. Orgn., 1949; staff mem. Survey Field Services, Dept. Interior, 1950; staff U.S. Senator Paul H. Douglas, 1955-56; cons. N.Y. State Spl. Com. on Constl. Revision and Simplification, 1958. Author: The Truman Committee: A Study in Congressional Responsibility, 1964; Editor, co-author: The Problems and Promise of American Democracy, 1964, Contemporary Issues of American Democracy, 1969; Editor: American Society in Action, 1965. Mem. bd. edn., Princeton, N.J., 1962-64; mem. Mayors Criminal Justice Coordinating Council, N.Y.C., 1968-73; life mem. U. Ill. Pres. Council. Served to 1st lt. USAAF, 1942-46. Recipient Presdl. medal John Jay Coll. Criminal Justice, 1979. Mem. Acad. Criminal Justice Scis. (pres. 1970-71; hon. life, Presdl. Disting. award for contbg. to criminal justice edn. 1979), Phi Beta Kappa, Phi Sigma Alpha.

RIDDLE, JAMES DOUGLASS, academic administrator; b. Austin, Tex., Oct. 8, 1933; s. Prebble Elmer and Jewel Lee (Nalley) R.; m. Marilyn Brown Moore, Sept. 8, 1956; children: Mary Elizabeth, Margaret Allison, Charles Douglass. BA in History and Govt., Southwestern U., 1958; MDiv in Theology and Social Ethics, Boston U. Sch. Theology, 1962; postgrad., Boston U., 1962-65; D Ministry, San Francisco Theol. Sem., 1991. Ordained to ministry Meth. Ch., 1963, transferred to United Ch. of Christ, 1966. Copastor The First Parish Ch., Lincoln, Mass., 1963-67; sr. pastor The Community Ch., Chapel Hill, N.C., 1967-80, First Ch. of First Congl. United Ch. of Christ, Springfield, Mass., 1980-89; v.p. devel. Am. Internat. Coll., Springfield, 1989—; teaching fellow, lectr. in human rels. Boston U. Sch. Bus., 1960-64; mem. Chapel Hill-Carrboro Bd. Edn., Chapel Hill, 1975-80. Mem. governing bd. Nat. Coun. Chs., 1969-72, commn. on faith and order, 1969-72, com. on future ecumenical structure, 1971-72; chmn. commn. on ecumenical study and svc. United Ch. of Christ, 1969-75, del. gen. synod, mem. exec. coun., 1969-75; pres. N.C. Legal Def. Fund, 1969-80, Orange-Chatham Counties Community Action Agy., 1970-76, Chapel Hill-Carrboro Inter-Ch. Coun. Housing Corp., 1969-77; mem. bd. Community Care Mental Health Ctr., 1980-90, chair, 1985-88; chair Downtown Ministry Project, 1981-84; mem. governing bd. Greater Springfield Coun. Chs., 1980-86, Downtown Econ. Devel. Corp., Springfield Cen., 1981—, StageWest Regional Theatre Co., 1982-92, Springfield YMCA, 1982-87, City of Springfield 350th Anniversary, 1984-87, Springfield Adult Edn. Coun., 1984—; corporator Zone Arts Ctr., 1986—; mem., chmn. Hampden Assn. ch. & ministry Com. United Ch. of Christ, 1990—. Named Person of Yr. NOW, 1987; recipient 350th Anniversary Medallion, City of Springfield, 1986. Mem. ACLU, Coun. for Advancement and Support of Edn., Nat. Soc. Fund Raising Execs., Estate Planning Coun. Hampden County, New Eng. Devel. Rsch. Assn., Acad. Religion and Mental Health, Congl. Christian Hist. Soc. (mem. bd. 1987—), Assn. Humanistic Psychology, Common Cause, The Reality Club of Springfield, Springfield Rotary. Democrat. Avocations: backpacking, sailing, travel, cooking. Office: Am Internat Coll 1000 State St Springfield MA 01109-3151

RIDDLE, MARK ALAN, child psychiatrist; b. Huntingburg, Ind., Feb. 18, 1948; s. James G. and Louise (Burgdorf) R.; m. Clarine Carol Nardi, Aug. 15, 1971; children: Carl, Julia. BA, Ind. U., 1970, MS, 1973, MD, 1977. Intern in pediatrics Ind. U. Med. Ctr., Indpls., 1977-78; resident in psychiatry Sch. Medicine Yale U., New Haven, 1978-81; fellow in child psychiatry Yale Child Study Ctr., New Haven, 1981-83; asst. prof. child psychiatry Sch. Medicine Yale U., New Haven, 1983-89, assoc. prof. child psychiatry, 1989-93; dir. divsn. child and adolescent psychiatry Johns Hopkins Med. Inst., 1993—. Assoc. editor Jour. Child and Adolescent Psychopharmacology; contbr. articles to profl. jours. Mem. med. com. Tourette Syndrome Assn., 1989—. Mem. Am. Acad. Child and Adolescent Psychiatry (editorial bd. Jour.). Home: 10607 Millet Seed Hl Columbia MD 21044-4150

RIDDLE, STURGIS LEE, minister; b. Stephenville, Tex., May 26, 1909; s. Lee and Linda (McKinney) R.; m. Elisabeth Pope Sloan, Oct. 14, 1939. B.A. magna cum laude, Stanford U., 1931; student, Gen. Theol. Sem., N.Y.C., 1931-32; B.D. cum laude, Episcopal Theol. Sch., Cambridge, Mass., 1934; D.D., Seabury Western Theol. Sem., Evanston, Ill., 1957. Ordained deacon P.E. Ch., 1934, priest, 1935; Episcopal chaplain U. Calif., 1934-37; instr. church Div. Sch. of Pacific, 1934-37; rector Caroline Ch., Setauket, L.I., 1937-40; asst. minister St. Thomas Ch., N.Y.C., 1940-46; rector St. James Ch., Florence, Italy, 1947-49; dean Am. Cathedral of Holy Trinity, Paris, France, 1949-74; dean emeritus Am. Cathedral of Holy Trinity, 1974—; exchange preacher Trinity Ch., N.Y.C., 1956-57, 62, St. Bartholomew's Ch., N.Y.C., 1958, 63, 73, St. John's Cathedral, Denver, 1959, Grace Cathedral, San Francisco, 1960, Nat. Cathedral, Washington, 1961, Trinity Ch. Boston, 1964, St. Andrew's Cathedral, Honolulu, 1965, St. John's Ch., Washington, 1966, 67, 68, 70, 73, St. Thomas' Ch., N.Y., 1968, 73, St. Paul's Cathedral, Boston, 1969; clerical dep. Europe to Gen. Conv. P.E. Ch., 1949-60, 64, 70. Author: One Hundred Years, 1950; contbg. Author: We Believe in Prayer, 1958, That Day with God, 1965. Hon. gov. Am. Hosp. in Paris; fellow Morgan Library, N.Y.C., trustee bd. fgn. parishes; chmn. Friends of the Am. Cathedral in Paris. Decorated Legion of Honor France; grand cross and grand prelate Sovereign Order St. John of Jerusalem Knights of Malta; grand cross Ordre du Milice de Jesus Christ; Patriarchal Order Mt. Athos. Mem. Nat. Inst. Social Sci., Am. Soc. French Legion of Honor, Phi Beta Kappa. Clubs: Union, University, Pilgrims, Spouting Rock Beach Assn. Home: 870 5th Ave New York NY 10021-4953

RIDDLE, VERYL LEE, lawyer; b. Campbell, Mo., Dec. 6, 1921; s. Elvis Lloyd and Etter Whitehead (Wood) R.; m. Mary J. Riggs, Jan. 15, 1941 (div. 1967); children—Kay Riddle Campbell, Jo Riddle McCarver, Janet Lee Riddle, Veryl Lee, Jr.; m. Janet Lewis, Nov. 24, 1985. Student, Southeast Mo. U., 1939-41; student, U. Buffalo, 1942, 45-46; J.D., Washington U., St. Louis, 1948. Bar: Mo. 1948, U.S. Dist. Ct. (ea. and we. dists.) Mo. 1949, U.S. Ct. Appeals (8th cir.) 1949, U.S. Supreme Ct. 1969, U.S. Ct. Appeals

(7th cir.) 1970, U.S. Ct. Appeals (5th cir.) 1974, U.S. Ct. Appeals (3d cir.) 1975. Investigator Dept. Justice, N.Y.C., Buffalo and El Paso, Tex., 1942-43; U.S. atty. Eastern Dist. Mo. Dept. Justice, St. Louis, 1967-69; ptnr. Riddle, Baker & O'Herin, Malden, Mo., 1948-67; sr. ptnr. Bryan Cave, St. Louis, 1969—; pros. atty. Dunklin County, Mo., 1950-53; chmn. merit selection panel for U.S. Magistrate, St. Louis, 1983-84. Del., Nat. Democratic Conv., Chgo., 1956, Los Angeles, 1960. Served with U.S. Army, 1943-45. Recipient Disting. Alumni award Washington U. Sch. Law, 1993. Fellow Am. Coll. Trial Lawyers, Internat. Acad. Trial Lawyers; mem. Acad. Mo. Squires. Baptist. Clubs: Bellerive Country, Noonday, Round Table (St. Louis). Office: Bryan Cave 211 N Broadway Saint Louis MO 63102-2733

RIDDOCH, GREGORY LEE, professional baseball manager; b. Greeley, Colo., July 17, 1945; s. William Perry and Ruth C. (Gregory) R.; m. Linda Marcella Andre, Mar. 2, 1968; children: Rory David, Raliegh Davin. BBA, U. No. Colo., 1968; MA in Ednl. Adminstrn., Colo. State U., 1983. Minor league baseball player Cin. Reds, 1967-71, minor league mgr., 1973-80; scout Cin. Reds, Colo., Kans., Nebr., Wyo., 1981-83; asst. dir. player devel. and scouting Cin. Reds, 1984, dir. minor leagues, 1985; dir. instrn. San Diego Padres, 1986, coach, 1987-90, mgr., 1990—; substitute tchr. Greeley (Colo.) Sch. Dist., 1971-83; speaker in field. Writer videotapes: Tony Gwynn Fielding, 1989, Tony Gwynn Hitting, 1989. Vol. March of Dimes, Greeley, 1970—, Children's Hosp., San Diego, 1986—, Say No to Drugs, 1986—; fundraiser UNICEF, Greeley, 1970—. Named Mgr. of Yr., N.W. League, 1975-78; mgr. winning team State Spl. Olympics Boys Basketball Champions, 1975. Mem. Profl. Baseball Players Assn., NEA. Avocations: hunting, fishing, stained glass, jogging. Home: 1711 Glen Meadows Dr Greeley CO 80631-6831

RIDE, SALLY KRISTEN, physics educator, scientist, former astronaut; b. L.A., May 26, 1951; d. Dale Burdell and Carol Joyce (Anderson) R.; m. Steven Alan Hawley, July 26, 1982 (div.). BA in English, Stanford U., 1973, BS in Physics, 1973, PhD in Physics, 1978. Teaching asst. Stanford U., Palo Alto, Calif.; researcher dept. physics Stanford U.; astronaut candidate, trainee NASA, 1978-79, astronaut, 1979-87; on-orbit capsule communicator STS-2 mission Johnson Space Ctr. NASA, Houston; on-orbit capsule communicator STS-3 mission NASA, mission specialist STS-7, 1983, mission specialist STS-41G, 1984; sci. fellow Stanford (Calif.) U., 1987-89; dir. Calif. Space Inst. of U. Calif. San Diego, La Jolla, 1989—; prof. Physics U. Calif. San Diego, La Jolla, 1989—; mem. Presdl. Commn. on Space Shuttle, 1986, Presdl. Com. of Advisors on Sci. and Tech., 1994—. Author: (with Susan Okie) To Space and Back, 1986, (with T.O'Shaughnessy) Voyager: An Adventure to the Edge of the Solar System, 1992, The Third Planet: Exploring the Earth From Space, 1994. Office: U Calif San Diego Calif Space Inst 0221 La Jolla CA 92093-0221

RIDENHOUR, JOSEPH CONRAD, textile company executive; b. Rowan County, N.C., Aug. 12, 1920; s. Martin Luther and Mary Virginia (Schaeffer) R.; m. Julia Claire Thorne, Dec. 21, 1943; 1 child, Janis Claire. Student, Duke U., 1938-40; L.H.D., Lenoir Rhyne Coll., 1974. Asst. sec. Cannon Mills Co., Kannapolis, N.C., 1953-63; asst. v.p. Cannon Mills Co., 1959-60, v.p., 1960-71, sr. v.p., dir. mktg., 1971-82, vice chmn. bd., 1981-83, also dir. Mem. Kannapolis Bd. Edn., 1954-65; sec. Home Mission Found., N.C. synod United Lutheran Ch. in Am., 1953-68, dir., 1953—, pres., 1968—; mem. bd. Luth. Theol. So. Sem., 1964-85. Served with arty AUS, World War II, ETO. Home and Office: Oaklynn 420 Idlewood Dr Kannapolis NC 28083-3630

RIDEOUT, EDNA BAKER, artist; b. Billings, Mont., Sept. 29, 1918; d. Frederick Hubbard and Edna Beers (Baker) Ballou; m. Horton Burbank Rideout, May 26, 1951; children: Douglas Burbank Rideout, Nancy Penelope Rideout, Thomas Ballou Rideout. BA, U. Wash., 1940, MA, 1949. Cert. secondary tchr., Wash. Art editor Croftonian Crofton House Sch., Vancouver, B.C., Can., 1935-36; art tchr. Neah Bay (Wash.) High Sch., 1940-41, Winlock (Wash.) High Sch., 1942-44, Seattle Pub. Schs., 1945-47, 49-51, Fish and Wildlife Svc. Pribilof Islands, St. George Island, Alaska, 1951-53; dir. Visual Art Sch., Edmonds, Wash., 1972-74; sec. Gallery North, Edmonds, 1974-76; artist, 1953—. Watercolors included in nat. juried exhbns., 8 juried mem. and regional exhbns., 36 nat. juried shows in 7 yrs., invitational exhbns. sponsored by Bellevue, Wash. Art Mus., North West Water Color Soc., Arts Olympia; works included in In Harmony with Nature, 1990; 2 ink drawings used as cover designs for Alaska Timber Econ. Studies texts. Recipient Masterfield award Fla. Soc. Exptl. Artists, 2 purchase awards Watercolor U.S.A., Ajomari/Arches/Rives award Watermedia Mont., 1st pl. award Artstravaganza Nat., 3rd pl. award Navarro Coun. of Arts, Judge's Spl. award North Coast Collage Soc. Mem. Nat. Collage Soc. (sec. 1994), Women Painters of Wash. (program dir. 1992-93), North West Watercolor Soc. (asst. program dir. 1989-91), Soc. Exptl. Artists Fla., Pa. Watercolor Soc., North West Collage Soc. (sec. 1995—), East Side Assn. Fine Arts, Gallery North (hon.), Planetary Soc. Avocations: photography, hiking, observing nature, studying outer space. Home: 18616 92nd Ave NE Bothell WA 98011-2207

RIDEOUT, PATRICIA IRENE, operatic, oratorio and concert singer; b. St. John, N.B., Can., Mar. 16, 1931; d. Eric Aubrey and Florence May (Chase) R.; m. Rolf Edmund Dissmann, Sept. 3, 1955 (dec. 1975); m. Leonard R. Rosenberg, May 25, 1987. Ed., U. Toronto Opera Sch., Royal Conservatory Music, 1952-55. Tchr. voice Queen's U., Kingston, Ont., 1980-86, Royal Conservatory Music, Toronto, 1980-91. Singer Can. Opera Co., Toronto, 1954-85; leading roles in operas, Stratford, Ont., Vancouver, B.C., Guelph, Ont., 1956-85, CBC, 1958-90. Mem. Actors Equity Assn., Assn. Radio and TV Artists, Toronto Heliconian Club. Unitarian.

RIDEOUT, PHILIP MUNROE, publishing company executive; b. Boston, June 24, 1936; s. Allen MacDonald and Allene Lucille (Holman) R.; m. Sylviane R.L. Eldin, Aug. 7, 1959; 1 dau., Nicole MacDonald. B.A., Williams Coll., 1958. With Addison-Wesley Pub. Co., 1961-77; gen. mgr. W.A. Benjamin, Inc., Menlo Park, Calif., 1972-77; gen. mgr. health scis. div. Addison-Wesley Co., Menlo Park, 1975-77; pres. Cummings Pub. Co., Inc., Menlo Park, 1968-77; v.p. Coll. Mktg. Group, Inc., 1977-78; v.p., editor-in-chief Larousse U.S.A., Inc., N.Y.C., 1979-85; v.p., pub. Keystone Publs., N.Y.C., 1986-91; CEO Monroe Allen Pubs. Inc., N.Y.C., 1991—; bd. dirs. Monroe Allen Pubs., Inc., 1990—. Served with U.S. Army, 1958-61. Decorated Disting. Svc. medal. Mem. S.A.R. Home: 67-25 Dartmouth St Forest Hills NY 11375-4058 Office: 370 W 58th St New York NY 10019-1828

RIDEOUT, WALTER BATES, English educator; b. Lee, Maine, Oct. 21, 1917; s. Walter John and Helen Ruth (Brickett) R.; m. Jeanette Lee Drisko, Aug. 2, 1947; children: Linda Carolyn, Richard Bates, David John. A.B., Colby Coll., 1938; M.A., Harvard U., 1939, Ph.D., 1950. Teaching fellow English Harvard U., 1946-49, asst. prof., summer 1954, prof., summer 1969; from instr. to assoc. prof. English Northwestern U., Evanston, Ill., 1949-63, dir. program Bell System execs., 1957-58, 59-61; prof. English U. Wis., Madison, 1963—, Harry Hayden Clark prof. English, 1972—, chmn. dept., 1965-68, sr. vis. prof. Inst. Research in Humanities, 1968-69; vis. prof. U. Hawaii, summer 1977; Disting. lectr. English Kyoto Am. Studies Summer Seminar, Kyoto, Japan, 1981. Author: The Radical Novel in the United States, 1900-1954, 1956; editor: (with Howard Mumford Jones) Letters of Sherwood Anderson, 1953, (with James K. Robinson) A College Book of Modern Verse, 1958, A College Book of Modern Fiction, 1961, The Experience of Prose, 1960, I. Donnelly-Caesar's Column, 1960, (with G.W. Allen and J.K. Robinson) American Poetry, 1965, Sherwood Anderson: Collection of Critical Essays, 1974. Recipient MidAm. award Soc. for Study of Midwestern Lit., Mich. State U., 1983, Outstanding Educator award, 1993; fellow Newberry Libr., 1951, Guggenheim fellow, 1957; Fulbright grantee to Kyoto, 1981. Mem. ACLU, MLA (mem. nat. exec. council 1970-73), Phi Beta Kappa. Home: 1306 Seminole Hwy Madison WI 53711-3728 Office: Dept English U Wis 600 N Park St Madison WI 53706-1403

RIDER, JOHN ALLEN, II, business educator, paralegal; b. Gage, Okla., Mar. 11, 1928; s. George Henry Rider and Laurenna Agnes Meek; m. Audrey Claudine Baker, July 16, 1961; children: Michelle Renee Rider Brown, John Allen III. BS, Northwestern Okla. State U., 1952; MA, U. Wyoming, 1956; EdD, U. Nebr., 1966; postgrad., U. Ky. Cert. profl. tchr., Tenn., Iowa. Court reporter, stenographer USN, 1946-48; dep. ct. clk., ct. reporter Ellis County, Okla., 1948-49; tchr. bus. Rozel (Kans.) Rural High Sch., 1952-53, Norwich (Kans.) High Sch., 1953-54, Bluff City (Kans.) High Sch., 1954-56; instr. Black Hills State Coll., Spearfish, S.D., 1956-58; tchr. bus. Balboa (C.Z.) High Sch., 1958-60; instr. Northwestern Coll., Orange City, Iowa, 1958-60, chair divsn. edn., 1962-64; asst. prof. Northwestern State Coll., Alva, Okla., 1962-63; teaching asst. U. Nebr., Lincoln, 1963-64; head bus. edn. program, assoc. prof. U. N.Mex., Albuquerque, 1966-70; prof. West Tex. State U., Canyon, 1970-74; chair prof. occupational edn. divsn. Coffeyville (Kans.) Community Jr., 1974-75; assoc. prof. East Tenn. State U., Johnson City, 1975-94, coord. bus. edn. program, 1985-94; ret., 1994; cons. various bus.; bd. dirs. Enid Literacy Coun., tutor. Active Johnson City Literacy Coun., v.p./tutor trainer, 1978-80; relief worker, registrar Mid-Am. yearly meeting Friends Ch., Wichita, 1981; cons. yearly meeting N.C. Soc. Friends, 1987. Recipient Meritorious award West Tex. Bus. Tchr., 1970-74, Outstanding Edn. Grad. award Northwestern Okla. State U. Alumni Assn., 1995; named Tchr. of Yr., Dist. 16 Tex. Bus. Edn. Assn., 1973. Mem. NEA (life), Am. Vocat. Assn. (life), Nat. Bus Edn., Nat. Assn. Tchr. Edn. (life, bus. and office edn.), Tex. State Edn. Assn., Tenn. Bus. Edn. Assn. (treas., pres.-elect, pres., past pres., Educator of Yr. 1986), So. Bus. Edn., Kiwanis (Johnson City exec. bd. 1975-80, 92), Am. Legion (King's Mt. post), SAR (former sec., pres. Panhandle-Plains chpt., Tex. soc.), Holt County (Mo.) Hist. Soc. (charter, life). Republican. Avocations: genealogy, history, photography. Home: 3002 N Grant Enid OK 73702-1619

RIDER, SHERRI EILEEN, critical care nurse, educator; b. Wichita, Kans., Feb. 26, 1954; d. Bernard James Malone and Judy Ann (Jones) Hoffman; m. Terry Kendall Rider, Nov. 19, 1977; 1 child, Stephanie Marie. BSN, Wichita State U., 1986, M of Health Sci., 1992. RN, Kans.; cert. BLS instr., Kans., ACLS instr., Kans. Charge nurse emergency rm. Osteopathic Hosp., Wichita, 1977; charge nurse, relief charge nurse ICU, critical care unit Osteopathic Hosp. (name changed to Riverside Hosp.), Wichita, 1977—; cardiac rehab. coord. Riverside Hosp., Wichita, 1983-84, 87-89, orientation coord., 1989, continuing edn. facilitator, 1984—; patient care coord. ICU/critical care unit Riverside Health Sys., Wichita, 1993—; clin. instr. Kans. Newman Coll., Wichita, fall 1993, 94. Severe weather spotter Nat. Weather Svc., Wichita, 1993-95. Mem. AACCN (vols. in participation 1993, treas. local chpt. 1993-94), Kans. Health Care Edn. Coun., Midwest Nursing Rsch. Soc., Kans. Assn. Nursing Continuing Edn. Providers, Alpha Eta. Lutheran. Avocations: climatology, astronomy, railroading, crochet, cross-stitch. Office: Riverside Health System 2622 W Central Wichita KS 67203

RIDGE, MARTIN, historian, educator; b. Chgo., May 7, 1923; s. John and Ann (Lew) R.; m. Marcella Jane VerHoef, Mar. 17, 1948; children: John Andrew, Judith Lee, Curtis Cordell, Wallace Karsten. AB, Chgo. State U., 1943; AM, Northwestern U., 1949, PhD, 1951. Asst. prof. history Westminster Coll., New Wilmington, Pa., 1951-55; from asst. prof. to prof. San Diego State Coll., 1955-66; prof. history Ind. U., Bloomington, 1966-79, Calif. Inst. Tech., 1980-95; vis. prof. UCLA, summer 1963, Northwestern U., summer 1959; editor Jour. Am. History, 1966-77; sr. research assoc. Huntington Library, 1977—; bd. dirs. Calif. Hist. Landmarks Commn., 1954-64; cons. in field; Tanner lectr. Mormon Hist. Assn., 1991; Whitsett Meml. lectr., Calif. State U., 1992. Author: Ignatius Donnelly: Portrait of a Politician, 1962, 91, The New Bilingualism: An American Dilemma, 1981, Frederick Jackson Turner: Wisconsin's Historian of the Frontier, 1986, Atlas of American Frontiers, 1992, My Life East and West, 1994; co-author: California Work and Workers, 1963, The American Adventure, 1964, America's Frontier Story, 1969, Liberty and Union, 1973, American History after 1865, 1981, Westward Expansion, 1982; editor: Children of Ol'Man River, 1988, Westward Journeys, 1989, History, Frontier and Section, 1993. Served with U.S. Maritime Service, 1943-45. William Randolph Hearst fellow, 1950; fellow Social Sci. Research Council, 1952; fellow Guggenheim Found., 1965; fellow Am. Council Learned Socs., 1960; Newberry fellow, 1964; Huntington fellow, 1974; Annenberg scholar U. So. Calif., 1979-80; recipient Best Book award Phi Alpha Theta, 1963, Gilberto Espinos prize N.Mex. Historical Review, 1989, Ray Allan Billington prize Western History Assn., 1991. Mem. Am. Hist. Assn. (v.p. Pacific Coast br. 1994, pres. 1995, Best Book award 1963), Orgn. Am. Historians, Western History Assn. (v.p. 1985-86, pres. 1986-87), So. History Assn., Agrl. History Soc., Social Sci. History Soc., Hist. Soc. So. Calif. (pres. 1994—). Democrat. Address: Huntington Library San Marino CA 91108

RIDGE, THOMAS JOSEPH, governor, former congressman; b. Munhall, Pa., Aug. 26, 1945; m. Michele Moore, 1979. B.A., Harvard U., 1967; J.D., Dickinson Coll. Law, Carlisle, Pa., 1972. Bar: Pa. 1972. Sole practice Erie, Pa., 1972-82; mem. 98th-103rd Congresses from Pa. 21st dist., Washington, D.C., 1983-1995; mem. Banking, Fin., Urban Affairs com., subcoms. Econ. Growth and Credit Formation, Housing and Community Devel., Veteran's Affairs com.; former dist. atty. Erie County; mem. subcom. Hosps. and Healthcare, Oversight and Investigation, Post Office and Civil Svc. com., subcom. Census and Population, Civil Svc.; former legal instructor Erie County; gov. State of Penn., 1995—. Served with inf. U.S. Army, 1968-70, Vietnam. Office: Office of the Gov 245 Main Capitol Bldg Harrisburg PA 17120

RIDGEWAY, JAMES FOWLER, journalist; b. Auburn, N.Y., Nov. 1, 1936; s. George L. and Florence (Fowler) R.; m. Patricia Carol Dodge, Nov. 1966; 1 son, David Andrew. A.B., Princeton U., 1959. Assoc. editor New Republic, Washington, 1962-68, contbg. editor, 1968-70; editor Hard Times, 1968-70, Elements, 1974-78; assoc. editor Ramparts, 1970-75; assoc. fellow Inst. for Policy Studies, 1973-77; mem. Pub. Resource Center, 1977—; staff writer Village Voice, 1973—. Author: The Closed Corporation, 1969, Politics of Ecology, 1970, The Last Play, 1973, New Energy, 1975, (with Alexander Cockburn) Smoke, 1978, Political Ecology, 1979, Energy-Efficient Community Planning, 1979, Who Owns the Earch, 1980, Powering Civilization, 1983, Blood in the Face, 1991, The March to War, 1991, (with Jean Casella) To Cast A Cold Eye, 1991, The Haiti Files, 1994, (with Jasmina Udovicki) Yugoslavia's Ethnic Nightmare, 1995, (with Sylvia Plachy) Red Light, 1996. Served with Army N.G., 1959. Home: 3103 Macomb St NW Washington DC 20008-3325

RIDGLEY, SHERRY E., lawyer; b. Klamath Falls, Oreg., Apr. 21, 1952; d. William Wesley and Iva Lee (Redi) R. BA, U. So. Calif., 1975; JD, Loyola Law Sch., 1978. Bar: Calif. 1978, Fed. Tax Ct. 1980. Ptnr. Nagata, Conn & Ridgley, L.A., 1983-87, Musick, Peeler & Garrett, L.A., 1987-89, 92—; of counsel Jones, Day, Reavis & Pogue, L.A., 1989-91. Mem. ABA, L.A. County Bar Assn., Women Lawyers Assn. Address: 3625 Del Amo Blvd Torrance CA 90503

RIDGLEY, THOMAS BRENNAN, lawyer; b. Columbus, Ohio, Apr. 29, 1940; s. Arthur G. and Elizabeth (Tracy) R.; m. Nancy Vaughan, June 27, 1964; children: Elizabeth, Jennifer, Kathryn. BA, Princeton (N.J.) U., 1962; JD with honors, U. Mich., 1965. Bar: Pa. 1965, Ohio 1968, U.S. Dist. Ct. (so. and no. dists.) Ohio, U.S. Dist. Ct. (ea. dist.) Pa., U.S. Ct. Appeals (6th, 3d and 10th cirs.), U.S. Supreme Ct. Assoc. Dechert, Price and Rhoades, Phila., 1965-67; ptnr. Vorys, Sater, Seymour and Pease, Columbus, 1967—. Author: Interstate Conflicts and Cooperation, 1986, (with others) Fending Off Corporate Raiders, 1987. Bd. dirs., mem. exec. com. United Way of Franklin County, Columbus, 1986—, Cmty. Shelter Bd., 1992—. Fellow Am. Coll. Trial Lawyers. Office: Vorys Sater Seymour & Pease 52 E Gay St Columbus OH 43215-3108

RIDGWAY, BRUNILDE SISMONDO, archaeology educator; b. Chieti, Italy, Nov. 14, 1929; came to U.S., 1953, naturalized, 1963; d. Giuseppe G. and Maria (Lombardo) Sismondo; m. Henry W. Ridgway Jr., Sept. 6, 1958; children: Conrad W., Eric R., Kevin P., Christopher L. Laurea in Lettere Classiche, Messina U., Italy, 1953; MA in Classical Archaeology, Bryn Mawr Coll., 1954, PhD, 1958; HHD, Georgetown U., 1992; LLD, Union Coll., 1992. Asst. prof., head dept. classics Hollins (Va.) Coll., 1960-61; Asst., then instr. archaeology Bryn Mawr (Pa.) Coll., 1957-60, mem. faculty, 1961—, prof. classical archaeology, 1970—, Rhys Carpenter prof. archaeology, 1977-93, prof. emerita, 1993—; dir. Summer Sch. in Greece Am. Sch. Classical Studies, Athens, 1967, 71; Disting. Andrew Mellon vis. prof. U. Pitts., 1978; disting. vis. prof. George Washington U. Art Dept. 1986; E. Whitehead prof. Am. Sch. Classical Studies, Athens, Greece, 1988; Cecil H. and Ida Green vis. prof. classics dept. U. B.C., Vancouver, Can., 1990; H.L. Hooker Disting. vis. prof. McMaster U., Hamilton, Can., 1992; vis. prof. Archeol. Inst. Australia, Athens, Australia, 1992; Hanes-Willis vis. prof. dept. Art., U. N.C., Chapel Hill, 1995; vis. prof. Aarhus U., Denmark, 1995; ann. mem. Inst. Advanced Study, Princeton, N.J., 1967-68; Thomas Spencer Jerome lectr. U. Mich., Ann Arbor and Am. Acad. in Rome, 1981-82; guest curator Allentown Art Mus., Pa., 1979; Geddes-Harrower Chair, U. Aberdeen, Scotland, fall term 1989. Author: The Severe Style in Greek Sculpture, 1970; Classical Sculpture, 1972; The Archaic Style in Greek Sculpture, 1977, 2d rev. edit., 1993; (with G.F. Pinney) Aspects of Ancient Greece, 1979; Fifth Century Styles in Greek Sculpture, 1981; Roman Copies of Greek Sculpture, The Problem of the Originals, 1984; (with C.J. Eiseman) The Porticello Shipwreck: A Mediterranean Merchant Vessel of 415-385 B.C., 1987; Hellenistic Sculpture I: The Styles of ca. 331-200 B.C., 1990; (with others) Greek Sculpture in the Art Mus., Princeton U.: Greek Originals, Roman Copies and Variants, 1994; contbr. articles to profl. jours., (others), editor-in-chief Am. Jour. Archaeology, 1977-85; editor: (with others) Ancient Anatolia, 1986. Recipient Christian R. and Mary F. Lindback Found. award for disting. teaching, 1981, Gold medal Coun. for Advancement and Support Edn., 1989; named Pa. Prof. of Yr., 1989; Guggenheim fellow, 1974-75; Kress Sr. fellow Ctr. Advanced Study in Visual Arts, Nat. Gallery of Art , 1986. Mem. Archaeol. Inst. Am. (life, Disting. Archeol. Achievement Gold medal 1988), Internat. Assn. Classical Archaeology, German Archaeol. Inst. (corr.), Am. Philos. Soc. Home: 601 Montgomery Ave Bryn Mawr PA 19010-3529 Office: BrynMawr Coll Dept Archaeology 101 N Merion Ave Bryn Mawr PA 19010-2859

RIDGWAY, DAVID WENZEL, educational film producer, director; b. Los Angeles, Dec. 12, 1904; s. David Nelson and Marie (Wenzel) R.; AB UCLA, 1926; MBA, Harvard U., 1928; m. Rochelle Devine, June 22, 1955. With RKO Studios, Hollywood, Calif., 1930-42; motion picture specialist WPB, Washington, 1942-43; prodn. mgr., producer Ency. Brit. Films, Wilmette, Ill., 1946-60; dir. film activities, exec. dir. Chem. Edn. Material Study, U. Calif. at Berkeley, 1960-90, dir., 1990—; producer, on-screen interviewer Am. Chem. Soc. TV series Eminent Chemists, 1981; advisor TV project Mech. Universe, Calif. Inst. Tech., 1985 also Am. Inst. Biol. Scis.; introduced CHEM study films to People's Republic of China, 1983. Lt. comdr. USNR, 1943-46. Recipient Chris award for prodn. CHEM Study Ednl. Films in Chemistry, Film Coun. Greater Columbus, 1962-63; Bronze medal, Padua, Italy, 1963; CINE Golden Eagle awards, 1962-64, 73; Gold Camera award for film Wondering About Things, U.S. Indsl. Film Festival, 1971; diploma of honour Internat. Sci. Film Assn. Festival, Cairo, 1st prize Am. Biol. Photog. Assn. for film MARS: Chemistry Looks for Life, 1978. Mem. Soc. Motion Pictures and TV Engrs. (chmm. San Francisco sect. 1970-72), Am. Chem. Soc., Am. Sci. Film Assn. (trustee 1974-81), Delta Upsilon, Alpha Kappa Psi. Clubs: Faculty (U. Calif.), Bohemian (San Francisco), Harvard (San Francisco). Author: (with Richard J. Merrill) The CHEM Study Story, 1969; also articles in ednl. jours. Home: 1735 Highland Pl Berkeley CA 94709-1074 Office: U Calif Lawrence Hall of Sci Berkeley CA 94720-5200
Personal philosophy: If someone draws a circle to keep you out, you draw a circle to take him in. Consider your integrity your most valued asset.

RIDGWAY, ROZANNE LEJEANNE, executive, former diplomat; b. St. Paul, Aug. 22, 1935; d. H. Clay and Ethel Rozanne (Cote) R.; m. Theodore E. Deming. BA, Hamline U., 1957, LLD (hon.), 1978; hon. degrees, U. Helsinki, George Washington U., Elizabethtown Coll.; hon. degree, Albright Coll., Coll. of William and Mary, Hood Coll. Career diplomat U.S. Fgn. Svc., 1957-89, amb. at large for oceans and fisheries, 1975-77; amb. to Finland, 1977-80; counselor of the Dept. State, Washington, 1980-81; spl. asst. to sec. state, 1981; amb. to German Dem. Republic, 1982-85; asst. sec. state Europe and Can., 1985-89; pres. The Atlantic Coun. U.S., Washington, 1989-92, co-chair, 1993—; chair Baltic-Am. Enterprise Fund, 1994—; bd. dirs. 3M Corp., RJR Nabisco, Union Carbide Corp., Bell Atlantic, Citicorp, Citibank, Emerson Electric Co., The Boeing Corp., Sara Lee Corp., Nat. Geog. Soc., Internat. Bd. Advisors, New Perspective Fund. Trustee Hamline U.; bd. dirs. Am. Acad. Diplomacy, Ptnrs. for Democratic Change, Catalyst, Aspen Inst., Brookings Instn. Recipient Profl. awards Dept. State, Presdl. Disting. Performance award, Joseph C. Wilson internat. rels. achievement award, 1982, Sharansky award Union Couns. Soviet Jewry, 1989, Grand Cross of the Order of the Lion, Finland, 1989; named Person of Yr., Nat. Fisheries Inst., 1977, Knight Comdr. of the Order of Merit, Fed. Republic Germany, 1989, U.S. Presdl. Citizens Achievement medal, 1989. Fellow Nat. Acad. Pub. Adminstrn.; mem. Met. Club, Army-Navy Country Club. Office: The Atlantic Coun of The US 910 17th St NW Ste 1000 Washington DC 20006-2601

RIDINGS, DOROTHY SATTES, foundation admministrator; b. Charleston, W.Va., Sept. 26, 1939; d. Frederick L. and Katharine E. (Backus) Sattes; m. Donald Jerome Ridings, Sept. 8, 1962; children: Donald Jerome Jr., Matthew Lyle. Student, Randolph-Macon Woman's Coll., 1957-59; BSJ, Northwestern U., 1961; MA, U. N.C.-Chapel Hill, 1968; D.Pub. Svc. (hon.), U. Louisville, 1985; LHD (hon.), Spalding U., 1986. Reporter Charlotte Observer, N.C., 1961-66; instr. U. N.C. Sch. Journalism, 1966-68; freelance writer Louisville, 1968-77; news editor Ky. Bus. Ledger, Louisville, 1977-80, editor, 1980-83; communications cons., editor, 1983-86; mgmt. assoc. Knight-Ridder Inc., Charlotte, N.C., 1986-88; pres., pub. The Bradenton (Fla.) Herald, 1988-96; pres., CEO, Coun. on Founds., Washington, 1996—; adj. prof. U. Louisville, 1982-83; v.p. Nat. Mcpl. League, 1985-86; bd. dirs. com. on Constl. Sys., Nat. Com. Against Discrimination in Housing, 1982-87, Com. for Study of Am. Electorate, 1982—; bd. dirs. Ind. Sector, 1983-88, 92—; mem. exec. com. Leadership Conf. Civil Rights, 1982-86. Pres. LWV U.S., 1982-86, 1st v.p., 1980-82, human resources dir., 1976-80, chair edn. fund, 1982-86, 1st vice chair, 1980-82, trustee, 1976-80, pres. Louisville/Jefferson County, 1974-76, bd. dirs., 1969-76; trustee Louisville Presbyn. Theol. Sem., 1992—, Ford Found., 1989—, Manatee C.C., 1992-96; bd. dirs. Benton Found., Fla. Press Assn., 1994-96, Leadership Ky., 1984-87, Leadership Louisville, 1983-86, Louisville YWCA, 1978-80, Jr. League Louisville, 1972-74; mem. ABA Accreditation Com., 1987-93, Gov.'s Coun. Ednl. Reform, 1984-85; chair Prichard Com. Acad. Excellence, 1985-86; mem. Gov.'s Commn. Full Equality, 1982-83; mem. state adv. coun. U.S. Commn. Civil Rights, 1975-79; mem. steering com. Task Force for Peaceful Desegregation, 1974-75; elder 2d Presbyn. Ch., 1972-75, 78-81; mem. adv. coun. on ch. and soc. United Presbyn. Ch. in USA, 1978-84; mem. bd. visitors U. N.C., 1996. Recipient Disting. Alumna award U. N.C., 1995, Leadership award Nat. Assn. Cmty. Leadership Orgns., 1986, Alumnae Achievement award Randolph-Macon Woman's Coll., 1985, Disting. Citizen award Nat. Mcpl. League, 1983. Office: Council on Foundations 1828 L St NW Washington DC 20036

RIDINGS, SUSAN ELIZABETH, social worker; b. Bethlehem, Pa., July 6, 1949; d. Charles Frederick Schmidt and Eleanor Martin Jenico; m. Edward Haslam Ridings, Aug. 28, 1971; children: Alexis Katherine, Adam Edward. BSW, Pa. State U., 1971. Caseworker Pa. Dept. Welfare, Phila., 1973-78; bus. mgr. Vallemont Surg. Assocs., Lewistown, Pa., 1987—. Pres. bd. dirs. Cmty. Counseling Ctr., Lewistown, 1986-88, Mifflin County Children and Youth Svcs., Lewistown, 1990—; bd. dirs. Mifflin-Juniata Assn. of the Blind, Lewistown, 1987-91, v.p., 1994—; pres.-elect Lewistown Hosp. Aux., 1989, pres., 1991-93, pres., 1996—; bd. dirs. Mifflin County 2000, 1995, chmn. Goal 8 Com.; mem. Mifflin County Sch. Dist. steering com.; rec. sec. P.A.H.A., 1994—; legis. chairperson State P.A.H.A., 1994—; trustee Mifflin County Libr. Assn., 1988-91, Lewistown Hosp., 1991—; co-founder Teen Parenting Program, Lewistown, 1985; mem. Lewistown Hosp. Found.; founding mem. Teen Pregnancy Coalition, 1995. Mem. AAUW (programming v.p. 1994-96, Outstanding Woman 1985), Pa. Assn. Hosp. Auxs. (chair ctrl. regional legis., record exec. ctrl. region, legis. chair state bd.), Alpha Omicron Pi. Avocations: reading, gardening, needlework, playing piano. Home: 1 Pine Ln Lewistown PA 17044-2626 Office: Vallemont Surgical Assocs 100 Stine Dr Lewistown PA 17044-1339

RIDLEN, SAMUEL FRANKLIN, agriculture educator; b. Marion, Ill., Apr. 24, 1916; s. Will and Leoma Josephine (Sneed) R.; m. Helen Louise Camp, Apr. 17, 1946; children: Judith Elaine, Barbara Jo, Mark Ellis. BS, U. Ill., 1940; MS, Mich. State U., 1957. Agr. instr. Westville (Ill.) Twp. High Sch., 1940-43; gen. mgr. Honegger Breeder Hatchery, Forrest, Ill., 1953-56; assoc. prof. poultry sci. U. Conn., Storrs, 1957-58; from asst. prof. to prof. poultry extension U. Ill., Urbana-Champaign, 1946-86, prof. emeritus poultry extension, 1986—, asst. head dept. animal scis., 1978-86. Author: An Idea and An Ideal-Nabor House Fraternity 1939-1989, 1989; poultry editorial cons. Successful Farming, Wonderful World Ency., 1960;

poultry editor Am. Farm Youth, 1949-53, Ill. Feed Folks, 1949-53. Founding mem., charter mem. Nabor House Frat. Recipient Superior Svc. award U.S. Dept. Agr., 1982, Paul A. Funk Recognition award Coll. Agr., U. Ill., 1983, numerous others. Fellow Poultry Sci. Assn.; mem. World's Poultry Sci. Assn., Ill. State Turkey Growers Assn., Ill. Poultry Industry Coun., Ill Egg Market Devel. Coun. (adv. mem.), Ill. Animal Industry Coun., Coun. for Agr. Sci. and Tech., Ill. Alumni Assn. (life), DAV (life), Alpha Tau Alpha, Epsilon Sigma Phi, Gamma Sigma Delta (pres. 1982-83). Home: 1901 Lakeside Dr # C Champaign IL 61821-5967

RIDLEY, BETTY ANN, educator, church worker; b. St. Louis, Oct. 19, 1926; d. Rupert Alexis and Virginia Regina (Weikel) Steber; m. Fred A. Ridley, Jr., Sept. 8, 1948; children: Linda Drue Ridley Archer, Clay Kent. BA, Scripps Coll., Claremont, Calif., 1948. Christian sci. practitioner, Oklahoma City, 1973—; tchr. Christian sci., 1983—; mem. Christian Sci. Bd. Lectureship, 1980-85. Trustee Daystar Found.; mem. The First Ch. of Christ Scientist, Boston, Fifth Ch. of Christ Scientist, Oklahoma City. Mem. Jr. League Am. Home: 7908 Lakehurst Dr Oklahoma City OK 73120-4324 Office: Suite 100-G 3000 United Founders Blvd Oklahoma City OK 73112 *What makes life a continuing joy and free of all fear is to know that God who is the only Creator is infinitely good. He is our Father and our Mother, our Judge and our best friend. He is our great Physician, caring for us tenderly and uninterruptedly. We have but to know this and live according to His law in order to enjoy His blessings.*

RIDLEY, CLARENCE HAVERTY, lawyer; b. Atlanta, June 3, 1942; s. Frank Morris Jr. and Clare (Haverty) R.; m. Eleanor Horsey, Aug. 22, 1969; children: Augusta Morgan, Clare Haverty. BA, Yale U., 1964; MBA, Harvard U., 1966; JD, U. Va., 1971. Bar: Ga. 1971. Assoc. King & Spalding, Atlanta, 1971-77, ptnr., 1977—; bd. dirs. Haverty Furniture Cos., Inc., mem. exec. com., 1992—, vice chmn. bd. dirs., 1996—. Author: Computer Software Agreements, 1987, 2d edit., 1993; exec. editor Va. Law Rev., 1970-71. Chmn. St. Joseph's Hosp. Found., Atlanta, 1986-89; trustee St. Joseph's Health Svcs., 1987—, chmn. fin. com., 1992-96, vice chmn. bd. trustees, 1996—. Roman Catholic. Home: 2982 Habersham Rd NW Atlanta GA 30305-2854 Office: King & Spalding 191 Peachtree St Atlanta GA 30303

RIDLOFF, RICHARD, real estate executive, lawyer, consultant; b. N.Y.C., July 18, 1948; s. Sol and Daisey (Metz) R.; m. Caren Sara Berger, Mar. 27, 1977; children: Michael Joshua, Daniel Joseph. BA cum laude, Queens Coll., 1969; JD, Cornell U., 1972. Bar: N.Y. 1973. Assoc. counsel MONY, N.Y.C., 1972-79; sr. v.p., gen. counsel, sec. MONY Real Estate Investors, N.Y.C., 1979-85; v.p. investments MONY Fin. Svcs., N.Y.C., 1985-87; pres. MONY Realty Ptnrs. Inc., Glen Point, N.J., 1985-91; v.p. for investment mgmt. MONY Real Estate Investment Mgmt., N.Y.C., 1988-91; exec. v.p. Tibor Pivko and Co., Clifton, N.J., 1991-94; pres., dir. Growth & Income Inc., 1993-94; spl. projects dir. Kimco Realty Corp., 1995-96; pres. The Richardson Co., 1996—; bd. dirs. Growth & Income Inc.; mem. adv. commn. on real property ins. to Calif. Sen. Com. on Ins. Claims and Corps., 1986-92; adv. com. N.Y. chpt. Nat. Assn. Corp. Real Estate Execs., 1990. Author: A Practical Guide to Construction Lending, 1985; editor Real Estate Financing Newsletter, 1980-85 ; contbr. articles to profl. jours. Mem. secondary sch. interviewing com. Cornell U., Ithaca, N.Y., 1981—; chmn. fed. legis. com. Nat. Assn. Real Estate Investment Trusts, Washington, 1981-82. Mem. ABA (mem. real property com., fin. sect. real property, probate and trustlaw 1979—), N.Y. Bar Assn., Oakwood-Princeton Park Civic Assn., Omicron Delta Epsilon, Pi Sigma Alpha, Alpha Epsilon Pi.

RIDOUT, DANIEL LYMAN, III, physician, educator; b. Salisbury, Md., June 13, 1953; married. BA in Music, Dartmouth Coll., 1975; MD, U. Cin., 1979. Diplomate Nat. Bd. Med. Examiners, Am. Bd. Internal Medicine, Am. Bd. Gastrointestinal Bd.; lic. physician, Pa., Del; cert. ACLS, Advanced Trauma and Life Support. Intern then resident U. Pa. Hosp., Phila., 1979-82, chief med. resident, clin. instr. internal medicine, 1982-83, clin. instr., 1983-84, attending physician, teaching staff, 1986—; attending physician Crozer-Chester Med. Ctr., Upland, Pa., 1988—; pvt. practice, Upland, 1986—; chief gastrointestinal divsn. VA Hosp., Coatesville, Pa., 1987-89. Contbr. articles to profl. jours. Recipient Achievement and Svc. in Medicine award Afro-Am. Hist. Soc. Del., 1989. Mem. AMA, Am. Profl. Practice Assn., Am. Soc. Gastrointestinal Endoscopy, Pa. Med. Soc., Del. County Med. Soc. (bd. dirs.), Am. Soc. Internal Medicine, Med. Soc. Eastern Pa., Phila. County Med. Soc., Phila. Coll. Physicians, New Castle County Med. Soc. Office: Crozer Chester Med Ctr Profl Office Bldg 1 Medical Blvd Upland PA 19013

RIEBE, NORMAN JOHN, contractor; b. Michigan City, Ind., Mar. 9, 1903; s. William J. and Hattie (Fink) R.; m. Gwendolyn Ester Main (dec. 1924); children: Norman W., Harriet M. Kirchner; m. Eddie Lou Growden, 1978. PhD in Constrn., DSc (hon.). Registered profl. engr., Ind., Ark. Ariz. Draftsman, die designer Haskel and Barker Car Co.; with Steel Fabricating Corp., 1924-26; chief engr. Stefco Steel Co., 1926-36; pvt. practice Michigan City, Ind., 1936-40; v.p. R.E. McKee, Gen. Contractor, Los Alamos, N.Mex., 1947-52; v.p., gen. mgr. C.H. Leavell & Co., El Paso, 1952-61. Contbr. articles to profl. jours. Active Yuma County Bd. Adjustment; past vestryman Episc. Ch. Col. U.S. Army, 1932-62. Decorated Legion of Merit. Mem. Soc. Am. Mil. Engrs. (life), Ret. Officers Assn. (life), Associated Gen. Contractors (past pres. El Paso chpt. 1960), Am. Arbitration Assn., Am. Ordnance Assn. (past pres.), Masons, Shriners, Knights Templar. Republican. Avocation: raising peafowl and peaches. Home and Office: 14141 S Avenue 4 E Yuma AZ 85365-9339

RIEBEL, JOAN STROM, social services administrator; b. Madelia, Minn., Oct. 30, 1942; d. Percy Carroll and Marcella Theresa (Rohe) Strom; m. Leland John Riebel, June 12, 1965; children: John, Andrew. BA, Coll. of St. Benedict, 1964; MSW, U. Minn., 1978. Tchr. Our Lady of Peace High Sch., St. Paul, 1964-65; social worker Cath. Charities, Rockford, Ill., 1965-68, Ramsey County Human Svcs., St. Paul, 1968-78; adminstr. of HHS grant U. Minn., Mpls., 1978-80; pvt. practice cons. and psychotherapist Mpls., 1980-84; exec. dir. Family Alternatives, Inc., Mpls., 1985—; mem. Legis. Task Force on Foster Care, St. Paul, 1990—; mem. Gov.'s Commn. on Children's Mental Health, St. Paul, 1988-90; chair social work adv. com. Coll. St. Benedict, St. Joseph, Minn., 1989-92; pres. N.Am. Foster Family-based Treatment Assn., Mpls., 1988-90; co-chair subcom. Nat. Commn. on Foster Care/Child Welfare League Am., Washington, 1990-92. Author: (chpt.) Sexual Abuse of Children: A Prevention Strategy, 1980. Mem. 4th Ward, Dist. 65A Caucus, St. Paul, 1978-90; pres. St. Joan of Arc Ch. Coun., Mpls., 1990—. Recipient Recognition award Nat. Foster Parent Assn., 1989, Benedictan Svc. award Coll. St Benedict, 1989, Outstanding Alumna award U. Minn., 1992. Mem. NASW, Am. Group Psychotherapy Assn., Nat. Assn. Foster Parents, Orthopsychiat. Assn. Avocations: reading, travel, fishing, renovating. Office: Family Alternatives Inc 416 E Hennepin Ave # 218 Minneapolis MN 55414-1006

RIEBMAN, LEON, electronics company executive; b. Coatsville, Pa., Apr. 22, 1920; s. Abraham Benjamin and Bertha (Aisikovitz) R.; m. Claire Jay Edeson, Feb. 27, 1944; children: Barbara Lynne, Robert Alvin. B.E.E., U. Pa., 1943, M.S., 1947, Ph.D., 1951. Sr. engr. Philco, Phila., 1946; research asso., part-time instr. U. Pa., 1948-51; a founder, pres. Am. Electronic Labs., Colmar and Lansdale, Pa., 1950—; dir. Ampal, Old York Rd. Bank. Served to lt. (j.g.) USNR, 1943-46. Recipient State of Israel Bond award, 1968, Atwater Kent award, 1943. Fellow IEEE; mem. Am. Technion (pres. Phila. chpt.), Sigma Xi., Tau Beta Pi, Etta Kappa Nu, Pi Mu Epsilon. Patentee in field. Home: 1380 Barrowdale Rd Jenkintown PA 19046-2418 Office: Am Electronic Labs Inc 305 Richardson Rd Lansdale PA 19446-1480

RIECHMANN, FRED B., retired newspaper publisher; b. Evansville, Ind., Oct. 30, 1915; s. George Edward and Helen (Umbach) R.; m. Pauline Ashby, Nov. 11, 1939; children—Fredrica Ann Riechmann Wellborn, Paul F. Student, U. Evansville, 1931-33; M.E., U. Cin., 1938. Registered profl. engr., Ohio. Bookkeeper Nat. City Bank, Evansville, 1933-35; product exec. Servel Inc., Evansville, 1935-59; v.p., treas. Miller Block Co., Evansville, 1960-70; pres., dir. Evansville Courier, 1970-87. Served to maj. Ordnance Dept., U.S. Army, 1941-46. Republican. Lutheran. Home: Apt B 510 SE Riverside Dr Evansville IN 47713-1044

RIECKE, HANS HEINRICH, architect; b. Münster, Westfalia, Germany, Mar. 30, 1929; came to U.S., 1955; s. Hans Joachim and Hildegard (Schwarze) R.; m. Elvira Maria Magdalena Kaatz, Nov. 30, 1954; children: Christine, Annette, Monica, Ralph, Heidi. Student architecture, Technische Hochschule, Hannover, Fed. Republic. Germany, 1953; BA in Architecture, U. Calif., Berkeley, 1957. Registered architect, Calif., Hawaii. Draftsman Orinoco Mining Co., Puerto Ordaz, Venezuela, 1954-55, H.K. Ferguson Co., San Francisco, 1956-57; architect, ptnr. Hammarberg and Herman, Oakland, Calif., 1957-74; prin. Hans Riecke, Architect Inc., Kahului, Maui, Hawaii, 1974-78, Riecke Sunnland Kono Architects Ltd, Kahului, Maui, Hawaii, 1978—. Bd. dirs. Kihei Community Assn., Maui, Hawaii, 1975-77, Seabury Hall, Makawao, Maui, 1980-82; chmn. Mayor's Com. on Housing, County of Maui, 1984. Recipient Merit award Pacific Coast Builders Con., Kahului, Hawaii, 1990. Fellow AIA (pres. Maui chpt. 1990); mem. Am. Arbitration Assn. (panel of arbitrators 1980). Avocations: biking, gardening. Office: Riecke Sunnland Kono Architect PO Box 1627 Kahului HI 96732-7627

RIECKEN, HENRY WILLIAM, psychologist, research director; b. Bklyn., Nov. 11, 1917; s. Henry William and Lilian Antoinette (Nieber) R.; m. Frances Ruth Manson, Aug. 7, 1955; children—Mary Susan, Gilson, Anne. A.B., Harvard U., 1939, Ph.D., 1950; M.A., U. Conn., 1941. Social sci. analyst Dept. Agr., 1941-46; teaching fellow Harvard U., 1947-49, lectr. social psychology, research assoc. clin. psychology, 1949-54; assoc. prof. then prof., sr. mem. lab. research social relations U. Minn., 1954-58; program dir. social sci. research NSF, Washington, 1958-59; head Office Social Sci., Washington, 1959-60, asst. dir. social scis., 1960-64, assoc. dir. sci. edn., 1964-66; v.p. Social Sci. Research Council, N.Y.C., 1966-69; pres. Social Sci. Research Council, 1969-71; prof. behavioral scis. U. Pa., Phila., 1972-85, prof. emeritus, 1985—; assoc. dir. for planning Nat. Library Medicine, Bethesda, Md., 1985-87; fellow Ctr. Advanced Study Behavioral Scis., Stanford, Calif., 1971-72; Paterson Meml. lectr. U. Minn., 1970; Jensen lectr. Duke U., 1973; mem. adv. com. to dir. NIH, 1966-70, chmn. internat. ctrs. com., 1968-73; pres. Am. Psychol. Found., 1971-73; vice chmn., chmn. com. nat. needs for biomed. and behavioral rsch. pers. NRC, 1975-80; mem. commn. sociotech. systems Nat. Acad. Scis., 1976-79; adj. prof. psychiatry U. Tex. Med. Br., 1988—. Author: The Volunteer Work Camp, 1952, When Prophecy Fails, 1956, Social Experimentation, 1974, Experimental Testing of Public Policy, 1976; contbr. articles to profl. jours. Bd. dirs. Found. Child Devel. (formerly Assn. Aid Crippled Children), N.Y.; trustee W.T. Grant Found., N.Y. Served with USAAC, 1943-45. Fellow Am. Psychol. Assn. (Harold M. Hildreth award 1971), Am. Acad. Arts and Scis.; mem. Am. Assn. Pub. Opinion Research, Sociol. Research Assn. (pres. 1966), Nat. Acad. Scis., Inst. Medicine. Clubs: Harvard (N.Y.C.); Cosmos (Washington). Office: Kezar Assocs Washington DC

RIEDEBURG, THEODORE, management consultant; b. Milw., June 7, 1912; s. Theodore and Elva Pauline (Wolf) R.; m. Margaret Anna Louise Oertel, Dec. 24, 1937 (dec.); children: Theodore, Charles Howard; m. Ruth Jones Keith, May 3, 1980. BS, Marquette U., 1934, MS, 1936. Dist. sales mgr. Philip Morris & Co., 1937-42; asst. mgr. fumigants dept. Dow Chem. Co., Midland, Mich., 1942-45; sales mgr. agrichems. Westvaco Chem., N.Y.C., 1945-50; mng. dir. Theodore Riedeburg Assocs., N.Y.C., 1950-80; ind. forensic chemist-pesticides St. Simons Island, Ga., 1980—. Contbr. articles to profl. jours. Pres. Citizens League White Plains, N.Y., 1962; chmn. St. Simone Island Beautification Coun., 1995-96. Fellow Soc. Profl. Mgmt. Cons. (past pres.); mem. Am. Arbitration Assn., Nat. Bur. Profl. Mgmt. Cons. (exec. adv. bd. 1989), Chemists Club (N.Y.C.). Home: 2507 Demere Rd Apt 2 Saint Simons Island GA 31522 Office: PO Box 21158 Saint Simons Island GA 31522

RIEDEL, ALAN ELLIS, manufacturing company executive, lawyer; b. Bellaire, Ohio, June 28, 1930; s. Emil George and Alberta (Shafer) R.; m. Ruby P. Tignor, June 21, 1953; children: Ralph A., Amy L., John T. AB magna cum laude, Ohio U., 1952, LLD (hon.), 1994; JD, Case Western Res. U., 1955; grad., Advanced Mgmt. Program, Harvard, 1971. Bar: Ohio 1955, Tex. 1968. Assoc. Squire, Sanders & Dempsey, Cleve., 1955-60; gen. counsel Cooper Industries Inc. (formerly Cooper Bessemer Co.), Mt. Vernon, Ohio, 1960-63, sec., 1963-68, 1963-68, v.p. indsl. rels., 1968-73; sr. v.p. adminstrn. Cooper Industries, Inc., Houston, 1973-92; dir. Cooper Industries Inc., Houston, 1981-94, vice chmn., 1992-94; bd. dirs. Standard Products Co., Cleve., Arkwright Mut. Ins. Co., Waltham, Mass., Belden Inc., St. Louis, First Knox Nat. Bank Corp.; bd. dirs. Gardner Denver Machinery Inc., Quincy, Ill., chmn. bd. dirs., 1994—. Former chmn. bd. dirs. Jr. Achievement of S.E. Tex.; former chmn. bd. trustees Ohio U. Endowment Found. Mem. Order of Coif, Phi Beta Kappa, Omicron Delta Kappa, Delta Tau Delta. Home: 803 Creek Wood Way Houston TX 77024-3023

RIEDEL, BERNARD EDWARD, retired pharmaceutical sciences educator; b. Provost, Alta., Can., Sept. 25, 1919; s. Martin and Naomi E. (Klingaman) R.; m. Julia C. McClurg, Mar. 5, 1944 (dec. Mar. 1992); children: Gail Lynne, Dwain Edward, Barry Robert. BS in Pharmacy, U. Alta., Edmonton, 1943, MS in Pharmacology, 1949; PhD in Biochemistry, U. Western Ont., 1953; DSc (hon.), U. Alta., 1990. Lectr., asst. prof. Faculty of Pharmacy U. Alta., Edmonton, 1946-49, asst. prof. then assoc. prof., 1953-58, prof., 1959-67, exec. asst. to v.p., 1961-67; dean, prof. Faculty Pharm. Scis. U. B.C., Vancouver, 1967-84, coordinator Health Scis. Centre, 1977-84; mem. sci. adv. com. Health Rsch. Found. of B.C., 1991—. Contbr. numerous articles on pharmacology to profl. jours. Elder Ryerson United Ch.; mem. exec. bd. Boy Scouts Can., Edmonton Region, Alta.; mem. Cancer Control Agy. of B.C., trustee 1979-86, v.p., 1984, pres. 1985-86; bd. dirs. B.C. Lung Assn., 1988—, v.p., 1989, pres., 1990-91; chmn., bd. dirs. B.C. Organ Transplant Soc., 1986-89. Wing comdr. RCAF, 1943-46, 49-67. Recipient Gold medal in Pharmacy, 1943; Centennial medal, 1967, 75th Anniversary medal U. B.C., 1990; Can Forces decoration, 1965; Commemorative medal for 125th Anniversary of the Confedn. of Can., 1992. Mem. Alta. Pharm. Assn. (hon. life), Can. Pharm. Assn. (hon. life), Assn. of Faculties of Pharmacy of Can. (hon. life, chmn. 1959, 69), Can. Biochem. Soc., Pharmacol. Soc. Can., Can. Assn. of Univ. Tchrs., Can. Soc. Hosp. Pharmacists, B.C. Coll. Pharmacists (hon. life), U. B.C. Profs. Emeriti Divsn. Alumni Assn. (pres. 1993—). Home: 8394 Angus Dr, Vancouver, BC Canada V6P 5L2

RIEDEL, JUANITA MAXINE, writing educator; b. Overbrook, Kans., Nov. 17, 1918; d. Albert Ernest and Gladys Jennie (Hadsell) Smith; m. Richard Joseph Riedel, May 16, 1943 (dec. Aug. 1988); children: Nancy Riedel Basford, Linda Riedel Haynes. BE, U. Kans., 1944. Instr. creative writing Jackson (Mich.) C.C., 1979-86; instr. Creative Writers Workshop, Jackson, 1982—. Author: Words--Power and the Pattern, 1981, Church on Main Street, Jackson, MI, 1984, Wahroonga, 1994, Sidewalks, 1995; editor numerous books. Mem. AAUW (pres. 1976-78, grantee 1980), Beta Sigma Phi (various offices 1949—), 1st United Meth. Ch. Republican. Home: 3149 Halstead Blvd Jackson MI 49203-2553

RIEDL, JOHN ORTH, university dean; b. Milw., Dec. 9, 1937; s. John O. and Clare C. (Quirk) R.; m. Mary Lucille Priestap, Feb. 4, 1961; children: John T., Ann E., James W., Steven E., Daniel J. BS in Math. magna cum laude, Marquette U., Milw., 1958; MS in Math., U. Notre Dame, 1960, PhD in Math., 1963; postgrad., Northwestern U., 1963. Asst. prof. math. Ohio State U., Columbus, 1966-70, assoc. prof., 1970—, asst. dean Coll. Math. and Phys. Sci., 1969-74, assoc. dean, 1974-87, acting dean, 1984-86, spl. asst. to provost, 1987, dean, dir. Mansfield (Ohio) Campus, 1987—, coord. dean regional campus, 1988—; panelist sci. edn. NSF, 1980-91; cons. Ohio Dept. Edn., 1989, Ohio bd. regents subsidy cons., 1991, 95. Pres., v.p., exec. com. Univ. Cmty. Assn., Columbus, 1970-78; mem. edn. commn. St. Peter's Schs., Mansfield, 1989-95; trustee Rehab. Svc. North Ctrl. Ohio, Mansfield, 1990—, v.p., 1993-94, pres., 1995—; pres. Ohio Assn. Regional Campuses, 1993-95. NSF grad. fellow, 1960, 61, 62; recipient Faculty Svc. award Nat. U. Continuing Edn. Assn., 1988, Creative Programming award, 1988. Mem. Math. Assn. Am. (chair com. on minicourse 1981-87), Rotary Internat. Democrat. Roman Catholic. Avocations: fishing, woodworking, handball, gardening. Home: 745 Clifton Blvd Mansfield OH 44907-2284 Office: Ohio State U 1680 University Dr Mansfield OH 44906-1547

RIEDLINGER, BRIAN A., principal. Prin. Jean Gordon Elem. Sch., New Orleans. Recipient Elem. Sch. Recognition award U.S. Dept. Edn., 1989-90. Office: Jean Gordon Elem Sch 6101 Chatham Dr New Orleans LA 70122-2743

RIEDLSPERGER, MAX ERNST, history educator; b. San Luis Obispo, Calif., July 7, 1937; s. Helmuth Georg and Jean (Bennett) R.; m. Deanna Beckmann, Feb. 12, 1966; 1 child, Gretchen. AB, Wabash Coll., 1959; MA, U. Mich., 1961; PhD, U. Colo., 1969. Tchr. Eastern High Sch., Detroit, 1961-63, Bay de Noc C.C., Escanaba, Mich., 1963-66; teaching assoc. U. Colo., Denver, 1966-67; instr. Colo. Women's Coll., Denver, 1967-68; asst. prof. Calif. Poly. State U., San Luis Obispo, 1969-72, assoc. prof., 1977-82, prof., 1983—, chmn. history dept., 1985-91; dir. internat. programs Calif. State U., Heidelberg, Fed. Republic Germany, 1983-84. Author: Lingering Shadow of Nazism, 1978; contbr. articles to profl. publs., chpts. to books. Bd. dirs. San Luis Obispo Mozart Festival, 1979-83, 84-85, v.p., 1985-86. Austrian Ministry of Edn. fellow, 1968-69; grantee Am. Coun. Learned Socs., 1972, NEH, 1976, U.S. Dept. Edn., 1986-88. Mem. Am. Hist. Assn., German Studies Assn. Democrat. Avocations: swimming, skiing, tennis, music. Office: Calif Poly State U Dept History San Luis Obispo CA 93407

RIEDY, MARK JOSEPH, finance educator; b. Aurora, Ill., July 9, 1942; s. Paul Bernard and Kathryn Veronica R.; m. Erin Jeanne Lynch, Aug. 29, 1964; children: Jennifer Erin, John Mark. BA in Econs. maxima cum laude, Loras Coll., 1964; MBA, Washington U., St. Louis, 1966; PhD, U. Mich., 1971. Asst. prof. bus. adminstrn. U. Colo., Boulder, 1969-71; sr. staff economist Council of Econ. Advisers, Washington, 1971-72; spl. asst. to chmn. Fed. Home Loan Bank Bd., Washington, 1972; v.p., dir. research PMI Investment Corp., San Francisco, 1973; v.p., chief economist Fed. Home Loan Bank of San Francisco, 1973-77; exec. v.p., chief operating officer Mortgage Bankers Assn. of Am., Washington, 1978-84; pres., chief operating officer Fed. Nat. Mortgage Assn., Washington, 1985-86, cons., 1986-87; pres., chief operating officer J.E. Robert Cos., Alexandria, Va., 1987-88; pres., chief exec. officer Nat. Coun. Community Bankers, Washington, 1988-92, also bd. dirs.; Ernest W. Hahn prof. real estate fin. U. San Diego, 1993—; mem. adv. coun. Credit Rsch. Ctr., Purdue U., 1981-82; bd. dirs. Fed. Nat. Mortgage Assn., Am. Residential Mortgage Corp., Continental Savs. Bank, Accubanc Mortgage Corp., Neighborhood Bancorp, Noble Broadcast Group, Drayton Ins. Cos., Perpetual Savs. Bank, Ctr. for Fin. Studies; mem. San Diego Mayor's Renaissance Commn. Vice chmn. St. Vincent De Paul Village. Woodrow Wilson scholar, 1964; Nat. Def. scholar, 1964-66; U.S. Steel Found. fellow, 1966-68; Robert G. Rodkey Found. fellow, 1966-69; Earhart Found. fellow, 1968-69. Mem. Am. Econ. Assn., Am. Fin. Assn., Nat. Assn. Bus. Economists, Am. Soc. Assn. Execs., Urban Land Economics, Lambda Alpha Internat., Alpha Kappa Psi (hon.). Office: U San Diego Sch Bus Adminstrn 5998 Alcala Park San Diego CA 92110-2492

RIEFER, GLORIA JOYCE, educational consultant; b. Canton, Ohio, Dec. 8, 1940; d. Alexander and Mary Anne Sollie; children: Lisa Leigh, Mark Turner. BS in Edn., Malone Coll., 1971; MS in Edn. Adminstrn., U. Akron, 1975. Cert. elem. tchr., elem. prin. Elem. tchr. North Canton (Ohio) Schs., 1971-75, prin., 1975-94; cons. grants and spl. projects Summit County Office Edn., Cuyahoga Falls, Ohio, 1994—; owner Joy's Flower Shop. Recipient Adminstrv. Leadership award Martha Holden Jennings Found., 1980-81. Mem. Nat. Assn. Elem. Adminstrs., Ohio Assn. Elem. Adminstrs. (zone dir. 1983-87, Red Feather awards 1983-87), North Canton Adminstrs. Assn. (pres. 1981, sec. 1985), Coll. Club Canton (chmn. Mature Women's grant com. 1975), Order Eastern Star (Canton chpt. star point 1968, 91), Phi Delta Kappa (scholarship com. 1983). Republican. Home: 6111 Pilot View Cir Louisville OH 44641-9253 Office: Summit County Office Edn 420 Washington Ave Cuyahoga Falls OH 44221-2042

RIEFF, PHILIP, sociologist; b. Chgo., Dec. 15, 1922; s. Gabriel and Ida (Hurwitz) R.; m. Alison Douglas Knox, Dec. 31, 1963; 1 son by previous marriage, David. BA, U. Chgo., 1946, MA, 1947, PhD, 1954. Teaching fellow U. Chgo., 1946, instr., 1947-52; asst. prof. Brandeis U., Waltham, Mass., 1952-57; fellow Ctr. for Advanced Study in Behavior Scis., Palo Alto, Calif., 1957-58; assoc. prof. sociology U. Calif., Berkeley, 1958-61; prof. U. Pa., Phila., 1961—, Univ. prof. sociology, 1965-67, Benjamin Franklin Prof. Sociology, 1967-93, prof. emeritus, 1993—; prof. psychiatry Med. Coll. Pa., Phila., 1993—; chief editorial cons. Beacon Press, Boston, 1952-58; vis. assoc. prof. Harvard U., 1960; vis. fellow Ctr. for Study of Dem. Instns., Santa Barbara, Calif., 1963-64; Gauss lectr. Princeton U., 1975; Terry lectr. Yale U., 1976-77; prof. psychiatry and preventive medicine, Med. Coll. Pa., 1993—; vis. professorial lectr. Naval Acad., 1993. Author: Freud: The Mind of the Moralist, 1959, rev. edit., 1961, The Triumph of the Therapeutic: Uses of Faith After Freud, 1966, Fellow Teachers, 1973, The Feeling Intellect, 1990; editor The Collected Papers of Sigmund Freud (10 vols.), 1961; assoc. editor Am. Sociol. Rev., 1958-61; founding editor Jour. Am. Acad. Arts and Scis., 1956-59, Daedalus. Chief cons. planning dept. Nat. Coun. Chs., 1961-64. Named Fulbright Prof. U. Munich, 1959-60, Guggenheim fellow, 1970, Sometime fellow All Souls Coll., Oxford. Fellow Royal Soc. Arts London; mem. Libr. Co. Phila., Am. Sociol. Assn., Soc. Sci. Study Religion (mem. coun.), Societe Europeene de Culture, Garrick Club of London. Office: Med Coll Pa Dept Psychiatry 3200 Henry Ave Philadelphia PA 19129-1137

RIEFLER, DONALD BROWN, financial consultant; b. Washington, Nov. 10, 1927; s. Winfield W. and Dorothy (Brown) R.; m. Patricia Hawley, Oct. 12, 1957; children: Duncan, Linda, Barbara. BA, Amherst Coll., 1949. With J.P. Morgan & Co. Inc., N.Y.C., 1952-91; v.p. Morgan Guaranty Trust Co. of N.Y., 1962-68, sr. v.p., 1968-77, chmn. market risk com., 1977-91; fin. mkts. cons., 1991—; bd. dirs. Niagara Mohawk Power Corp., Bank of Tokyo Trust Co. With U.S. Army, 1950-52. Mem. John's Island Club, Riomar Country Club, Country Club of the Rockies (Edwards, Colo.). Home: 512 Bay Dr Vero Beach FL 32963-2107 Office: J P Morgan 109 Royal Palm Way Palm Beach FL 33480-4249

RIEGEL, BYRON WILLIAM, ophthalmologist; b. Evanston, Ill., Jan. 19, 1938; s. Byron and Belle Mae (Huot) R.; BS, Stanford U., 1960; MD, Cornell U., 1964; m. Marilyn Hills, May 18, 1968; children—Marc William, Ryan Marie, Andrea Elizabeth. Intern, King County Hosp., Seattle, 1964-65; asst. resident in surgery U. Wash., Seattle, 1965; resident in ophthalmology U. Fla., 1968-71; pvt. practice medicine specializing in ophthalmology, Sierra Eye Med. Group, Inc., Visalia, Calif., 1972—; mem. staff Kaweah Delta Dist. Hosp., chief of staff, 1978-79. Bd. dirs., asst. sec. Kaweah Delta Dist. Hosp., 1983-90. Served as flight surgeon USN, 1966-68. Co-recipient Fight-for-Sight citation for research in retinal dystrophy, 1970. Diplomate Am. Bd. Ophthalmology, Nat. Bd. Med. Examiners. Fellow ACS, Am. Acad. Ophthalmology; mem. Calif. Med. Assn. (del. 1978-79), Tulare County Med. Assns., Calif. Assn. Ophthalmology (v.p. 3d party liaison 1994-96), Am. Soc. Cataract and Refractive Surgery, Internat. Phacoemulsification and Cataract Methodology Soc. Roman Catholic. Club: Rotary (Visalia). Home: 3027 W Keogh Ct Visalia CA 93291-4228 Office: 2830 W Main St Visalia CA 93291-4331

RIEGEL, JOHN KENT, corporate lawyer; b. Olean, N.Y., Sept. 24, 1938; s. Forrest M. and Lena (Zilkofsky) R.; m. Betty Ann Eden, Mar. 16, 1968; children: John Kent, Geoffrey. BA, Alfred U., 1961; LLB, Syracuse U., 1963. Bar: N.Y. 1963, Md. 1971. Military lawyer USMC, 1964-68; atty. advisor USN, Washington, 1968-71; asst. atty. gen. State of Md., Annapolis, 1971-72, gen. counsel dept. agriculture, 1972-74; atty. regulatory law ICI Ams. Inc., Wilmington, Del., 1974-76, atty. law dept., 1976-85; gen. counsel ICI Specialty Chems./ICI Ams. Inc., Wilmington, 1985-86; v.p., gen. counsel ICI Ams. Inc., Wilmington, 1986-93, also bd. dirs., exec. com., 1986—, pres., gen counsel, 1993—; now pres. ICI North America, Wilmington, DE. Bd. overseers Widener U. Sch. Law, 1987—; bd. trustees Med. Ctr. Del., 1987—; bd. dirs. Child Care Connection, 1991-94. Mem. ABA, N.Y. State Bar Assn., Am. Corp. Counsel Assn. (bd. dirs. Del. Valley chpt. 1987-90, pres. 1989), European-Am. C. of C. (bd. dirs. 1995—). Office: ICI Americas Inc 3411 Silverside Rd Wilmington DE 19810-4812*

RIEGEL, KURT WETHERHOLD, environmental protection executive; b. Lexington, Va., Feb. 28, 1939; s. Oscar Wetherhold and Jane Cordelia (Butterworth) R.; children: Tatiana Suzanne, Samuel Brent Oscar, Eden Sonja Jane. BA, Johns Hopkins U., 1961; PhD, U. Md., 1966; PMD, Harvard U., 1977. Asst. prof. astronomy UCLA, 1966-74; prof. astronomy U. Calif. Extension, Los Angeles, 1968-74; mgr. energy conservation program Fed.

Energy Adminstrn., Washington, 1974-75; chief tech. and consumer products energy conservation Dept. Energy, Washington, 1975-78, dir. consumer products div., conservation and solar energy, 1978-79; assoc. dir. environ. engring. and tech. EPA, 1979-82; head Astronomy Ctrs. NSF, 1982-89; dir. Environ. Protection Office USN, 1989-94; dir. environ. tech. USN, Washington, 1994—; cons. Aerospace Corp., El Segundo, Calif., 1967-70, Rand Corp., Santa Monica, Calif., 1973-74; vis. fellow U. Leiden, Netherlands, 1972-73; Mem. Casualty Council Underwriters Labs., Nat. Radio Astron. Observatory Users Com., 1968-74. Contbr. articles to profl. jours. Mem. AAAS, Am. Phys. Soc., Sierra Club, Audubon Soc., Internat. Radio Sci. Union, Am. Astron. Soc., Internat. Astron. Union, Assn. of Scientists and Engrs. Home: 3019 N Oakland St Arlington VA 22207-5320

RIEGEL, T. E., manfacturing executive, light; b. 1942. Degree, Southwest Mo. State U., 1965. With O'Sullivan Industries, Inc., Lamar, Mo., 1965—, now exec. v.p. Office: O'Sullivan Industries Inc 1900 Gulf St Lamar MO 64759-1849*

RIEGER, MITCHELL SHERIDAN, lawyer; b. Chgo., Sept. 5, 1922; s. Louis and Evelyn (Sampson) R.; m. Rena White Abelmann, May 17, 1949 (div. 1957); 1 child, Karen Gross Cooper; m. Nancy Horner, May 30, 1961 (div. 1972); stepchildren: Jill Levi, Linda Hanan, Susan Perlstein, James Geoffrey Felsenthal; m. Pearl Handelsman, June 10, 1973; stepchildren: Steven Newman, Mary Ann Malarkey, Nancy Halbeck. A.B., Northwestern U., 1944; J.D., Harvard U., 1949. Bar: Ill. 1950, U.S. Dist. Ct. (no. dist.) Ill. 1950, U.S. Supreme Ct. 1953, U.S. Ct. Mil. Appeals 1953, U.S. Ct. Appeals (7th cir.) 1954. Legal asst. Rieger & Rieger, Chgo., 1949-50, assoc., 1950-54; asst. U.S. atty. No. Dist Ill., Chgo., 1954-60; 1st asst. No. Dist Ill., 1958-60; assoc. gen. counsel SEC, Washington, 1960-61; ptnr. Schiff Hardin & Waite, Chgo., 1961—; instr. John Marshall Law Sch. Chgo., 1952-54. Contbr. articles to profl. jours. Mem. Chgo. Crime Commn., 1984-94, life mem., 1995—; pres. Park View Home for Aged, 1969-71; Rep. precinct committeeman, Highland Park, Ill., 1964-68; bd. dirs. Spertus Mus. Judaica, 1987-91, vis. com., 1991—. Fellow Am. Coll. Trial Lawyers; mem. ABA, FBA (pres. Chgo. chpt. 1959-60, nat. v.p. 1960-61), Chgo. Bar Assn., Ill. Bar Assn., Am. Judicature Soc., 7th Circuit Bar Assn., Standard Club, Law Club Chgo., Vail Racquet Club, Phi Beta Kappa. Jewish. Avocations: photography; skiing; sailing. Home: 4950 S Chicago Beach Dr Chicago IL 60615-3207 Office: Schiff Hardin & Waite 7200 Sears Towers Chicago IL 60606

RIEGER, PHILIP HENRI, chemistry educator,; b. Portland, Oreg., June 24, 1935; s. Otto Harry and Carla (Oertli) R.; m. Anne Bioren Lloyd, June 18, 1957; 1 child, Christine Lloyd. B.A., Reed Coll., 1956; Ph.D., Columbia U., 1962. Prof. chemistry Brown U., Providence, 1962—. Contbr. articles to profl. jours. Mem. Am. Chem. Soc. (chmn. R.I. sect. 1978), Royal Soc. Chemistry, New Eng. Assn. Chemistry Tchrs. Epscopalian. Home: 119 Congdon St Providence RI 02906-1462 Office: Brown U Dept Chemistry Box H Providence RI 02912

RIEGER, STEVEN ARTHUR, state legislator, business consultant; b. Pullman, Wash., May 14, 1952; s. Samuel and Olga (Skoblikoff) R.; m. Karen Jean Gibson, July 5, 1992. AB, Harvard U., 1974, MBA, 1976. Asst. to v.p. Crowley Maritime Corp., Seattle, 1976-79; asst. v.p. Seattle-Northwest Securities Corp., Anchorage, 1980-81; spl. asst. Alaska State Legislature, Juneau, 1981-82; v.p. William Kent Co., Anchorage, 1983-84; mem. Alaska Ho. Reps., Juneau, 1985-91; pres. S. Rieger & Co., Anchorage, 1991-92; mem. Alaska State Senate, Juneau, 1993—. Bd. dirs. AWAIC women's shelter. Republican. Avocations: running, skiing, outdoor activities. Office: Alaska State Legislature Box V Capitol Juneau AK 99811

RIEGERT, PETER, actor; b. N.Y.C., Apr. 11, 1947. BA in English, U. Buffalo. Appearences include (theatre, Off-Broadway) Minnie's Boys, (debut), Dance With Me, 1975, Sexual Perversity in Chicago, 1976, Censured Scenes From King Kong, 1980, Isn't It Romantic, 1981, La Brea Tar Pits, 1984, A Hell of a Town, 1984, A Rosen By Any Other Name, 1986, (Broadway) The Nerd, 1987, (films) National Lampoons Animal House, 1978, Americathon, 1978, Chilly Scenes of Winter, 1982, National Lampoon Goes to the Movies, 1982, The Big Carnival, 1983, Local Hero, 1983, The City Girl, 1984, A Man in Love, 1987, The Stranger, 1987, Crossing Delancy, 1988, That's Adequate, 1990, A Shock to the Systems, 1990, The Object of Beauty, 1991, Oscar, 1991, Passed Away, 1992, Utz, 1993, The Mask, 1994; TV series) Middle Ages, 1992, (TV movies) Ellis Island, 1984, News at Eleven, 1986, Barbarians at the Gate, 1993 (Emmy award nominee 1993), Gypsy, 1993.

RIEGERT, ROBERT ADOLF, law educator, consultant; b. Cin., Apr. 21, 1923; s. Adolf and Hulda (Basler) R.; m. Roswitha Victoria Bigalke, Oct. 28, 1966; children: Christine Rose, Douglas Louis. BS, U. Cin., 1948; LLB cum laude, Harvard U., 1953; Doctoris Juris Utriusque magna cum laude, U. Heidelberg, Germany, 1966; postgrad., U. Mich., Harvard U., Yale U., MIT. Bar: D.C. 1953, Cts. Allied High Commn. Germany 1954. Mem. Harvard Legal Aid Bur., 1952-53; sole practice Heidelberg, 1954-63; vis. assoc. prof. So. Meth. U. Law Sch., Dallas, 1967-71; prof. law Cumberland Law Sch., Samford U., Birmingham, Ala., 1971—; dir. Cumberland Summer Law Program, Heidelberg, 1981—; Disting. vis. prof. Salmon P. Chase Coll. Law, 1983-84. Author: (With Robert Braucher) Introduction to Commercial Transactions, 1977, Documents of Title, 1978; contbr. articles to profl. jours. Chmn. subcom. on com. laws Ala. Pattern Jury Instruction Com. Served to 1st lt. USAAF, 1943-46. Grantee Dana Fund for Internat. and Comparative Law, 1979; grantee Am. Bar Found., 1966-67; German Acad. Exchange, 1953-55, mem. Harvard Legal Aid Bur., Salmon P. Chase Coll. law scholar, 1950; Pres.'s scholar U. Cin., 1941. Mem. ABA (com. on new payment systems), Internat. Acad. Comml. and Consumer Law, Am. Law Inst., Ala. Law Inst. (coun.), Assn. Am. law Schs. (chmn. exec. com., sect. internat. legal exchs.), Ala. Pattern Jury Instrns. Com., German Comparative Law Assn., Acad. Soc. German Supreme Cts., Army-Navy Club (Washington). Office: Samford U Cumberland Law Sch Birmingham AL 35229

RIEGSECKER, MARVIN DEAN, pharmacist, state senator; b. Goshen, Ind., July 5, 1937; s. Levi and Mayme (Kauffman) R.; m. Norma Jane Shrock, Aug. 3, 1958; children: Steven Scott, Michael Dean. BA in Pharmacy, U. Colo., 1967. Pharmacist Parkside Pharmacy, Goshen, Ind., 1967-73; pharmacist, mgr. Hooks Drugs, Inc., Goshen, 1973-94; coroner Elkhart County, Goshen, 1977-84; mem. Ind. Senate, Indpls., 1988—; pharmacist Walgreens, Goshen, 1994—; bd. dirs. Goshen Gen. Hosp., 1985-94. Rep. commr. Elkhart County, 1985-88; bd. commrs. pres., 1987-88; past adv. bd. dirs. Oaklawn Hosp.; past chmn. Michiana Area Coun. of Govts. Mem. Ind. Pharm. Assn., Elkhart County Pharm. Assn., Exch. Club. Republican. Mennonite. Avocation: jogging. Home: 1814 Kentfield Way Goshen IN 46526-4010 Office: Ind Senate Statehouse 4-D N 200 W Washington St Indianapolis IN 46204-2728

RIEHECKY, JANET ELLEN, writer; b. Waukegan, Ill., Mar. 5, 1953; d. Roland Wayne and Patricia Helen (Anderson) Polsgrove; m. John Jay Riehecky, Aug. 2, 1975; 1 child, Patrick William. BA summa cum laude, Ill. Wesleyan U., 1975; MA in Communication, Ill. State U., 1978; MA in English, Northwestern U., 1983. Tchr. English Blue Mound (Ill.) High Sch., 1977-80, West Chicago (Ill.) High Sch., 1984-86; editor The Child's World Pub. Co., Elgin, Ill., 1987-90; freelance writer Elgin, 1990—. Author: Dinosaur series, 24 vols., 1988, UFOs, 1989, Saving the Forests, 1990, The Mystery of the Missing Money, 1996, The Mystery of the UFO, 1996, Irish Americans, 1995, others. Recipient Summit award for best children's nonfiction Soc. Midland Authors, 1988. Mem. Soc. Am. Magicians, Children's Reading Round Table, Soc. Children's Book Writers and Illustrators, Mystery Writers of Am., Phi Kappa Phi. Democrat. Baptist. Avocations: reading, hiking, dinosaur hunting.

RIEKE, ELIZABETH ANN, federal agency administrator; b. Buffalo, July 10, 1943; divorced; children: Frederick Martin, Eowyn Ann. BA in Polit. Sci. summa cum laude, Oberlin Coll., 1965; JD with highest distinction, U. Ariz., 1981. Rsch. asst. S.W. Environ. Svc., Tuscon, 1976-79; law clk. Snell & Wilmer (formerly Bilby, Shoenhari, Warnock & Dolph), Tuscon, 1979; law clk. Office of Solicitor Divsn. Conservation and Wildlife, Dept. Interior, Washington, 1980; law clk. to Hon. William C. Canby Jr. U.S. Ct. Appeals (9th cir.), 1981-82; dep. legal counsel Ariz. Dept. Water Resources, 1982-85, chief legal counsel, 1985-87, dir., 1991-93; assoc. Jennings, Strouss & Salmon, Phoenix, 1987-89, ptnr., 1989-91; asst. sec. for water and sci. Dept. Interior, Washington, 1993—; now dir. Natural Resouces Law Ctr Univ. Colorado, Boulder; adj. prof. Ariz. State U., Phoenix, 1989; speaker in field. Recipient Disting. Alumnus award U. Ariz., 1986. Office: Univ. Colorado Sch. Law Campus 401 Boulder CO 80309-0401*

RIEKE, PAUL VICTOR, lawyer; b. Seattle, Apr. 1, 1949; s. Luvern Victor and Anna Jane (Bierstedt) R.; m. Judy Vivian Farr, Jan. 24, 1974; children: Anna Katharina, Peter Johann. BA, Oberlin Coll., 1971; postgrad. U. Wash., 1971, Shoreline C.C., 1972-73; JD, Case Western Res. U., 1976. Bar: Wash. 1976, U.S. Dist. Ct. (we. dist.) Wash. 1976, U.S. Tax Ct. 1978. Assoc. Hatch & Leslie, Seattle, 1976-82, ptnr., 1982-91; ptnr. Foster, Pepper & Shefelman, 1991—. Exec. notes editor Case Western Res. U. Law Rev., 1975-76. Mem. exec. bd. dist. council N. Pacific dist. Am. Luth. Ch., Seattle, 1978-83, council pres. 1983, Am. Luth. Ch. pub. bd., 1984-87; v.p. Northwest Wash. Synod of Evangelical Luth. Ch. Am., Seattle, 1988-90, mem. Synod Coun., 1990-92, del. ELCA Nat. Assembly, 1991, ELCA Northwest Synod Regional Rep., 1992-96, region one coun. pres., 1994-96. Mem. ABA, Wash. State Bar Assn., Seattle-King County Bar Assn., Order of Coif. Democrat. Lodge: Seattle Downtown Central Lions. Home: 321 NE 161st St Seattle WA 98155-5741 Office: Foster Pepper & Shefelman 34th Fl 1111 3rd Ave Seattle WA 98101

RIEKE, WILLIAM OLIVER, foundation director, medical educator, former university president; b. Odessa, Wash., Apr. 26, 1931; s. Henry William and Hutoka S. (Smith) R.; m. Joanne Elynor Schief, Aug. 22, 1954; children: Susan Ruth, Stephen Harold, Marcus Henry. B.A. summa cum laude, Pacific Luth. U., 1953; M.D. with honors, U. Wash., 1958. Instr. anatomy U. Wash. Sch. Medicine, Seattle, 1958; asst. prof. U. Wash. Sch. Medicine, 1961-64, adminstrv. officer, 1963-66, assoc. prof., 1964-66; prof., head dept. anatomy Coll. Medicine U. Iowa, Iowa City, 1966-71; dean protem Coll. Medicine U. Iowa (Coll. Medicine), 1969-70, chmn. exec. com., 1969-70; vice chancellor for health affairs, prof. anatomy U. Kans. Med. Center, Kansas City, 1971-73; exec. vice chancellor, prof. anatomy U. Kans. Med. Center, 1973-75; affiliate prof. biol. structure U. Wash. Sch. Medicine, Seattle, 1975—; pres. Pacific Lutheran U., Parkland, Wash., 1975-92; pres. emeritus, 1992—; exec. dir. Ben B. Cheney Found., 1992—; Mem. interdisciplinary gen. basic sci. test com. Nat. Bd. Med. Examiners, 1968-72, chmn. anatomy test com., 1972-75, mem. at large, 1975-79; spl. cons. NIH, 1970-72; mem. adv. com. Inst. Medicine, Nat. Acad. Scis., 1974-76; mem. Commn. on Colls., NW Assn. Schs. and Colls., 1979-84. Editor: Procs. 3d Ann. Leucocyte Culture Conf, 1969; editorial bd.: Am. Jour. Anatomy, 1968-71. Bd. dirs. Luth. Ednl. Council N. Am., 1980-83, pres., 1982-83; chmn. Wash. Friends Higher Edn., 1983-91. Named one of Most Effective Coll. or Univ. Pres., Bowling Green State U. Rsch. Study, 1986, Disting. Alumnus Pacific Luth. U., 1970, Disting. Alumnus Pi Kappa Delta, 1977, Disting. Alumnus U. of Washington Med. Alumni, 1989; decorated Knight First Class Royal Norwegian Order of Merit, 1989; named to Cashmere H.S. Wall of Fame, 1995. Lutheran (mem. ch. council 1967-70). Home: 13905 18th Ave S Tacoma WA 98444-1006 Office: Ben B Cheney Found 1st Interstate Plz Ste 1600 Tacoma WA 98402

RIELLY, JOHN EDWARD, educational association administrator; b. Rapid City, S.D., Dec. 28, 1932; s. Thomas J. and Mary A. (Dowd) R.; m. Elizabeth Downs, Dec. 28, 1957 (marriage annulled 1976); children: Mary Ellen, Catherine Ann, Thomas Patrick, John Downs; m. Irene Diedrich, Aug. 1, 1987. B.A., St. John's U., Collegeville, Minn., 1954; postgrad. (Fulbright scholar), London Sch. Econs. and Polit. Sci., 1955-56; Ph.D., Harvard U., 1961. Faculty dept. govt. Harvard U., 1958-61; with Alliance for Progress programs Dept. State, Washington, 1961-62; fgn. policy asst. to Sen. then Vice Pres. Hubert Humphrey, Washington, 1963-69; cons. office European and internat. affairs Ford Found., N.Y.C., 1969-70; sr. fellow Overseas Devel. Council, Washington, 1970-71; exec. dir. Chgo. Council on Fgn. Relations, 1971-74, pres., 1974—; cons. NSC; mem. adv. bd. Grad. Sch. Arts and Scis., Harvard U.; bd. dirs. Am. Coun. on Germany, Nat. Com. on U.S.-China Rels., China Coun. of Asia Soc., Am. Ditchley Found., Trilateral Commn., commn. on U.S.-Brazilian Rels.; past pres. Nat. Coun. Comty. World Affairs Orgns. Contbr. articles to profl. jours.; editor: American Public Opinion and U.S. Foreign Policy, 1975, 2d edit., 1979, 83, 87, 91, 95; editl. bd. Fgn. Policy Quar., 1974—. Former trustee St. John's U. Mem. Am. Polit. Sci. Assn., Council on Fgn. Relations, N.Y.C. Home: 2021 Kenilworth Ave Wilmette IL 60091-1519 Office: 116 S Michigan Ave Chicago IL 60603-6001

RIEMENSCHNEIDER, ALBERT LOUIS, engineering educator; b. Cody, Nebr., May 18, 1936; s. Albert L. and Agnes E. (Schilling) R.; m. Norma Mae Geisler, June 24, 1962 (dec.); children: Richard L., David F., Barbara J. BSEE, S.D. Sch. Mines and Tech., 1959, MSEE, 1962; PhD, U. Wyo., 1969. Registered profl. engr., S.D. Engr. Sperry Utah Corp., Salt Lake City, 1959-60; design engr. Dakota Steel & Supply Co., Rapid City, S.D., 1960-61; instr. U. Wyo., Laramie, 1961-67; chief engr. Dunham Assocs., Rapid City, 1974-80; grad. tchg. asst. S.D. Sch. Mines and Tech., Rapid City, 1961-62, asst. prof., 1967-73, assoc. prof., 1973-74, 80-84, prof., dept. head, 1983-95, prof., 1995—; cons. ALR Engring., RE/SPEC, Inc., Rapid City, 1987—. Mem. IEEE, Am. Soc. Engring. Edn., Nat. Soc. Profl. Engrs. Democrat. Lutheran. Lodge: Elks. Avocations: electronics, computers, hunting, fishing. Home: 4051 Corral Dr Rapid City SD 57702-9228 Office: South Dakota Sch of Mines 501 E Saint Joseph St Rapid City SD 57701-3901

RIEMENSCHNEIDER, DAN LAVERNE, religious organization administrator; b. Pontiac, Mich., July 21, 1952; s. Henry LaVerne and Sarah Lou R.; m. Rebecca Joy Fruth, June 26, 1976; 1 child, Derek Henri. BA in Social Work, Mich. State U., 1974, PhD in Family Ecology, 1985; MA in Religion Edn., Asbury Seminary, Wilmore, Ky., 1976. Min. of Edn. Spring Arbor (Mich.) Free Meth. Ch., 1977-85; asst. prof. social work and family sci. Spring Arbor Coll., 1985-87; exec. dir. dept. edn. Free Meth. Ch. of North Am., Indpls., 1987—; chmn. Samaritan Counseling Ctr., Jackson, Mich., 1985-87. Bd. dirs. Mich. Council on Family Relations, Lansing, Mich., 1985-87. Mem. Nat. Council Family Relations, Nat. Assn. Evangelicals, Nat. Christian Edn. Assn. (bd. dirs.), Nat. Task Force on Family (bd. dirs.). Office: Free Meth World Hdqrs PO Box 535002 770 N High School Rd Indianapolis IN 46214-3756

RIEMENSCHNEIDER, PAUL ARTHUR, physician, radiologist; b. Cleve., Apr. 17, 1920; s. Albert and Selma (Marting) R.; m. Mildred McCarthy, May 12, 1945; children: Barbara Anne, Nancy Emelia, David Andrew, Paul Albert, Mary Elizabeth, Sarah Bache. BS magna cum laude, Baldwin-Wallace Coll., 1941; MD, Harvard U., 1944. Diplomate Am. Bd. Radiology (trustee 1973-85), Nat. Bd. Med. Examiners. Prof., chmn. dept. radiology SUNY, Syracuse, 1945-64; chief diagnostic radiology Santa Barbara (Calif.) Cottage Hosp., 1964-89, bd. dirs., 1984-90; vis. prof. in residence SUNY, Syracuse, 1983—; Radiology Soc. of No. Am. Internat. vis. prof. of Radiology, Univ. Malaya, 1990-91. Co-editor: N.Y. State Jour. Medicine, 1960-64; mem. editorial adv. bd. Yearbook of Cancer, 1960-64; contbr. articles to profl. jours. Mem. appropriations com. Santa Barbara Found., 1984-93; vestryman All Saints Episc. Ch., 1970-76, sr. warden, 1973; bd. dirs. ARC, Santa Barbara, 1968-72, Am. cancer Soc., Santa Barbara, 1967-70, Casa Dorinda Retirement Residence, 1975-76, 89-96, pres., 1993-96; bd. dirs. Wood Glen Hall Retirement Residence, 1980—, sec., 1987; bd. dirs. Cancer Found. Santa Barbara, 1966-82, 89-95, chmn. equipment com., 1973-82. Lt. comdr. USNR, 1945-46, 54-56. Recipient Alumni Merit award Baldwin-Wallace Coll., 1985. Fellow Am. Coll. Radiology (cancer com. 1952-54, council 1956-64, bd. chancellors 1967-73, chmn. commn. standards in radiologic practice 1968-71, v.p. 1972, pres. 1974, chmn. com. manpower 1972-86, chmn. com. manpower in armed svcs. 1975-86, Gold medal 1982); mem. AMA, Calif. Med. Assn., Santa Barbara County Med. Soc. (chmn. med. sch. com. 1967-71), Am. Roentgen Ray Soc. (mem. publs. com. 1965-75, chmn. 1970-75, exec. council 1970-75, 77-82, chmn. program com. 1977-79, pres.-elect 1977-79, pres. 1979, Gold medal award 1986), South Coast Radiol. Soc. (pres. 1967), Assn. Univ. Radiologists (sec. 1960, pres. 1961, com. resident tng. 1984-88), Radiol. Soc. N.Am. (Gold medal award 1990), Am. Soc. Neuroradiology, Soc. Pediatric Radiology, Eastern Radiol. Soc. (pres.-elect 1987, pres. 1988-89), Calif. Radiol. Soc., So. Calif. Radiol. Soc., Detroit Roentgen Soc. (hon.), Bluegrass Radiol. Soc. (hon.), Pacific N.W. Radiol. Soc. (hon.), Alpha Omega Alpha. Republican. Clubs: Birnamwood Golf (Santa Barbara); Skaneateles Country (N.Y.). Avocations: tennis, swimming. Home: 112 Olive Mill Rd Santa Barbara CA 93108-2424

RIEMKE, RICHARD ALLAN, mechanical engineer; b. Vallejo, Calif., Oct. 11, 1944; s. Allan Frederick and Frances Jewell (O'Brien) R. BA in Physiology, U. Calif., Berkeley, 1967, MA in Physiology, 1971, PhD in Engring. Sci., 1977. Postdoctoral fellow U. So. Calif., Los Angeles, 1977-78; rsch. engr. Del Mar Avionics, Irvine, Calif., 1979; staff fellow NIH, Bethesda, Md., 1980; adv. engr. Idaho Nat. Engrin. Lab., Idaho Falls, 1980—. Served with U.S. Army, 1969-75. Mem. AAAS, ANS, Am. Soc. Mech. Engrs., Biomed. Engring. Soc., Soc. Computer Simulation, Soc. Math. Biology, Soc. Engring. Sci., Order of Golden Bear, Alpha Sigma Phi. Republican. Roman Catholic. Avocations: swimming, surfing. Home: 1727 Grandview Dr # 4 Idaho Falls ID 83402-5016 Office: Lockheed Martin Ida Techs Inc Idaho Nat Engring Lab Idaho Falls ID 83415-3880

RIENNE, DOZIE IGNATIUS, structural engineer; b. Awka, Nigeria, July 22, 1954; s. James O. and Joy I. Rienne; m. Charlotte Roberts, Feb. 6, 1982; children: Tonnia, Chovia, Brittany. BS in Engring Tech., Constrn. Mgmt, Okla. State U., 1988; postgrad. in Civil Engring., LaSalle U. Project mgr. DF Young Constrn. Co., Dallas, 1981-84; constrn. mgr. VB Cons. Group, Oklahoma City, 1984-88; programs dir. Riennes Corp., Chickasha, Okla., 1989—. Editor: The Role of the Construction Managers, 1992, The Code Plus Built Homes, 1992. Mem. Am. Plywood Assn. (cert., profl. builder and remodeler). Office: Riennes Constrn Co 1524 S 1st St Chickasha OK 73018-5908

RIENNER, LYNNE CAROL, publisher; b. Pitts., Aug. 3, 1945; d. David and Molly (Rice) R. B.A., U. Pa., 1967. Exec. v.p., assoc. publisher, editorial dir. Westview Press Inc., Boulder, Colo., 1975-84; pres. Lynne Rienner Pub. Inc., Boulder, Colo., 1984—; pub. cons. various orgns.; lectr. U. Denver Pub. Inst., 1981-84, 93; panelist nat. meetings. Bd. dirs. Boulder Breast Cancer Coalition, 1993-95. Mem. Assn. Am. Pubs. (bd. dirs. 1992-96, exec. coun. of profl. and scholarly pub. divsn. 1996—). Office: Lynne Rienner Pub Inc 1800 30th St Ste 314 Boulder CO 80301-1026

RIEPE, DALE MAURICE, philosopher, writer, illustrator, educator, Asian art dealer; b. Tacoma, June 22, 1918; s. Rol and Martha (Johnson) R.; m. Charleine Williams, 1948; children: Kathrine Leigh Riepe Herschlag, Dorothy Lorraine. B.A., U. Wash., 1944; M.A., U. Mich., 1946, Ph.D., 1954; postgrad. (Rockefeller-Watamull-McInerny fellow), U. Hawaii, Banaras and Madras, India, Tokyo and Waseda, Japan, 1949. Instr. philosophy Carleton Coll., 1948-51; asst. prof. U. S.D., 1952-54; asso. prof. U. N.D., 1954-59, prof., 1959-62, chmn. dept., 1954-62; prof., chmn. C.W. Post Coll., 1962-63; prof. philosophy SUNY, Buffalo, 1963—; chmn. dept. social scis., assoc. dean SUNY (Grad. Sch.), 1964—; exchange lectr. U. Man., 1955; vis. lectr. Western Wash. U., 1961; instr. marine electricity Naval Tng. Program, Seattle, 1943-45; mem. nat. screening bd. South Asia, Fulbright Selection, 1968-70, Asia, 1970-72; chmn. Fulbright Selection Com. for Asia, 1972, 82; vis. Fulbright lectr. Tokyo U., 1957-58, vis. lectr. Delhi U., 1967; exchange lectr. Moscow State U., 1979, Beijing Higher Edn. Inst., 1984; docent Albright-Knox Art Gallery; cons. Ctr. for Sci., Tech. and Devel., Council of Sci. adn Indsl. Rsch., Govt. India, 1978—, Inst. Fang Studies, 1987—; del. Cuban-N.Am. Philosophy Conf., Cuban Inst. Social Sci., 1982, Fang Centennial, Taiwan Nat. U., Taipeh, 1987, Hungarian-Am. Philos. Conf., Budapest, 1988; sports columnist The Town Crier. Author: The Naturalistic Tradition in Indian Thought, 1961, The Philosophy of India and its Impact on American Thought, 1970, Indian Philosophy Since Independence, 1979, The Owl Flies by Day, 1979, Asian Philosophy Today, 1981, Objectivity and Subjectivism in the Philosophy of Science, 1985, Philosophy and Revolutionary Theory, 1986, also articles in field.; editor: Phenomenology and Natural Existence, 1973, Philosophy and Political Economy; co-editor: The Structure of Philosophy, 1966, Contributions of American Sankritists in the Spread of Indian Philosophy in the United States, 1967, Radical Currents in Contemporary Philosophy, 1970, Reflections on Revolution, 1971, Philosophy at the Barricade, 1971, Contemporary East European Philosophy, 1971, Essays in East-West Dialogue, 1973, Explorations in Philosophy and Society, 1978; illustrator The Quick and the Dead, 1948; editorial com. Chinese Studies in History, 1970—, Chinese Studies in Philosophy, 1970—; publs. bd. Conf. for Asian Affairs; Editor various series.; editl. bd. Philos. Currents and Revolutionary World, 1972-86, Soviet Studies in Philosophy, 1979-87, Marxist Dimensions, 1987—,. Actice ACLU; mem. com. overseers Chung-an U., Korea; bd. dirs. Evergreen Coll. Cmty. Orgn., 1988—; bd. dirs. Friends of Evergreen Coll. Libr., 1992—; active Henry Gallery, Frye Gallery, Palm Springs Desert Mus., Seattle Art Mus., Phila. Mus. Art; mem. Capital Mus. and Art Soc., Wash. State Hist. Soc. Fulbright scholar India, 1951-52; Fulbright lectr. U. Tokyo, 1957-58; U. Mich. fellow, 1945-48, Carnegie Corp. fellow Asian Studies, 1960-61; Am. Inst. Indian Studies research fellow, 1966-67; grantee 4th East-West Philosophers Conf., 1964; Penrose fund Am. Philos. Soc., 1963; SUNY Research Found., 1965, 66, 67, 69, 72, 73, Bulgarian Acad. Sci., 1975, London Sch. Oriental and African Studies grantee, 1971. Fellow Royal Asiatic Soc., Far Eastern Inst. (Tokyo); mem. AAAS, Internat. Hegel-Vereinigung, Conf. Asian Affairs (sec. 1995), Am. Oriental Soc., Am. Philos. Soc., Indian Inst. Psychology, Philosophy and Psychical Rsch. (hon. adviser), Soc. for Am. Philosophy (chmn. 1960), Am. Inst. Indian Studies (trustee 1965-66), Soc. for Creative Ethics (sec.), Am. Archaeol. Soc., Am. Assn. Asian Studies, Am. Math. Soc., Am. Aesthetics Soc., Internat. Soc. Aesthetics, Am. Soc. Comparative and Asian Philosophy, Asiatic Soc. (Calcutta), Soc. for Philos. Study Dialectical Materialism (founding sec.-treas. 1962—), Soc. for Philos. Study Marxism (publs. sec. 1973-86), Union Am. and Japanese Profls. Againstar Omnicide (treas. U.S. sec. 1978—), Internat. House of Japan, Internat. Philosophers for Prevention Nuclear Omnicide, United Univ. Profs. of SUNY-Buffalo (v.p.), Johnson Soc., Kokusai Bunka Shinkokai, Tumwater Valley Golf, Alpha Pi Zeta. Office: SUNY 605 Baldy Hall Buffalo NY 14261

RIEPE, JAMES SELLERS, investment company executive; b. Bryn Mawr, Pa., June 25, 1943; s. Henry Brunt and Marjorie (Sellers) R.; m. Gail Nelms Petty, Sept. 14, 1968; children: Christina, James, Jr. B.S., Wharton Sch., U. Pa., 1965, M.B.A., 1967. Mem. audit staff Coopers & Lybrand, C.P.A.s, Phila., 1967-69; asst. to pres. Wellington Mgmt. Co., Phila., 1969-72; v.p. Wellington Mgmt. Co., 1972-75; exec. v.p. Vanguard Group, Inc., Valley Forge, Pa., 1975-82; dir. Vanguard Group, Inc., 1979-82; mng. dir., mem. mgmt. com. T. Rowe Price Assocs., Inc., Balt., 1982—; pres. T. Rowe Price Investment Services, 1982—; chmn. TRP Trust Co., 1982—, TRP Retirement Plan Svcs., 1982—; dir. Rhône-Poulenc Rorer; bd. dirs. Balt. Equitable Soc. Trustee, former chmn. Balt. Mus. Art; trustee U. Pa., mem. exec. com., mem. exec. com. health sys.; pres. Gilman Sch., 1994—. Mem. NASD (gov.), Investment Co. Inst. (gov.), Greenspring Valley Hunt Club, Caves Valley Golf Club. Office: T Rowe Price Assocs Inc 100 E Pratt St Baltimore MD 21202-1009

RIERSON, ROBERT LEAK, broadcasting executive, television writer; b. Walnut Cove, N.C., Sept. 5, 1927; s. Sanders C. and Anna (Cox) R.; m. Barbara Eugenia McLeod, Sept. 23, 1950 (dec. Feb. 1988); children: Barbara Elaine, Richard Troy. Student, Duke U., 1945-46, Davidson Coll., 1946-47; BS in Speech cum laude, Northwestern U., 1948. Program dir., program ops. mgr. WBT Radio and WBTV, Charlotte, N.C., 1948-66; program mgr. WJBK-TV, Detroit, 1966-69, WTOP-TV, Washington, 1969-71; dir. broadcasting WCBS-TV, N.Y.C., 1971-73; pres. Rierson Broadcast Consultants, N.Y.C., 1973-75; program exec. Grey Advt., N.Y.C., 1975-77; v.p., dir. programming Dancer-Fitzgerald-Sample, N.Y.C., 1977-80; exec. producer Corinthian Prodns., N.Y.C., 1980-82; dir. news programming CNN TV, Atlanta, 1982—. Producer-creator TV show ABCs of Democracy, 1965; producer, writer TV show George Washington's Mt. Vernon, 1970; creator, writer TV series 24 Days of Christmas, 1978. Bd. dirs. Mich. Coun. Chs., Detroit, 1968-69, ARC, Charlotte, 1960-62; 1st v.p. Charlotte Oratorio Singers, 1960-66. Lt. USNR, 1952-54. Recipient Edn. award Charlotte Jr. Woman's Club, 1961, George Washington Honor medal Freedoms Found., 1970; named Young Man of Yr., 1960. Mem. Nat. Assn. Radio-TV Program Execs. (charter mem., bd. dirs. 1964—), Radio-TV News Dirs. Assn., Order of Long Leaf Pine. Republican. Mem. Moravian Episcopal Ch. Avocations: reading, travel, movies. Home: 3068 Vinings Ridge Dr NW Atlanta GA 30339-3771 Office: Turner Program Svcs 1 Cnn Ctr NW Atlanta GA 30303-2705

RIES, EDWARD RICHARD, petroleum geologist, consultant; b. Freeman, S.D., Sept. 18, 1918; s. August and Mary F. (Graber) R.; student Freeman Jr. Coll., 1937-39; A.B. magna cum laude, U. S.D., 1941; M.S., U. Okla., 1943, Ph.D. (Warden-Humble fellow), 1951; postgrad. Harvard, 1946-47; m. Amelia D. Capshaw, Jan. 24, 1949 (div. Oct. 16, 1956); children: Rosemary Melinda, Victoria Elise; m. Maria Wipfler, June 12, 1964. Asst. geologist Geol. Survey S.D., White River area, 1941; geophys. interpreter Robert Ray Inc., Western Okla., 1942; jr. geologist Carter Oil Co., Mont., Wyo., 1943-44, geologist Mont., Wyo., Colo., 1944-49; sr. geologist Standard Vacuum Oil Co., Assam, Tripura and Bangladesh, India, 1951-53, sr. regional geologist N.V. Standard Vacuum Petroleum, Maatschappij, Indonesia, 1953-59, geol. adviser for Far East and Africa, White Plains, N.Y., 1959-62; geol. adviser Far East, Africa, Oceania, Mobil Petroleum Co., N.Y.C., N.Y., 1962-65; geol. adviser for Europe, Far East, Mobil Oil Corp., N.Y.C., 1965-71, sr. regional explorationist Far East, Australia, New Zealand, Dallas, 1971-73, Asia-Pacific, Dallas, 1973-76, sr. geol. adviser Rsch. Geology, 1976-79, assoc. geol. advisor Geology-Geophysics, Dallas, 1979-82, sr. geol. cons., 1982-83; ind. internat. petroleum geol. cons. Europe, Africa, Sino-Soviet and S.E. Asia, 1986—. Grad. asst., teaching fellow U. Okla., 1941-43, Harvard, 1946-47. Served with AUS, 1944-46. Mem. AAAS, Am. Assn. Petroleum Geologists (assoc. editor 1978-83, 50 Yr. Mem. Svc. award 1993), Geol. Soc. Am., Am. Geol. Inst., Nat. Wildlife Fedn., Nat. Audubon Soc., N.Y. Acad. Sci., Soc. Exploration Geophysicists, Wilderness Soc., Am. Legion, Phi Beta Kappa, Sigma Xi, Phi Sigma, Sigma Gamma Epsilon. Republican. Mennonite. Club: Harvard (Dallas). Author numerous domestic and internat. proprietary and pub. hydrocarbon generation and reserve evaluations, reports and profl. papers. Home and Office: 6009 Royal Crest Dr Dallas TX 75230-3434

RIES, MARTIN, artist, educator; b. Washington, Dec. 26, 1926; s. Martin Frank and Kathryn (Stretch) R.; m. Dianys d'Arcy Frobisher, June 8, 1953; children: d'Arcy, Von, Gannett, Nicole. BFA, Am. U., 1950; MA in Art History, Hunter Coll., 1968, postgrad. in mus. adminstrn., 1968. Asst. dir. pub. rels. Nat. Congl. Com., Washington, 1951; asst. dir. Hudson River Mus., 1957-67; advisor Westchester Cultural Ctr., 1965-66; curator instnl. art exhibits, prof. art L.I. U., Bklyn., 1967-94. One-man shows include Atelier Gallery, N.Y.C., 1968, Paul Gallery, Tokyo, 1968, Atelier Terre d'Ocre, France, 1973, Unicorn Gallery, Soho, N.Y., 1976, Ganesh Gallery, Lenox, Mass., 1978, Belanthi Gallery, Bklyn., 1984, Stamford Mus., Stamford, Conn., 1987, Raja Idris Gallery, Melbourne, Australia, 1989, Robb St. Gallery, Bairnsdale, Australia, 1989, Salena Gallery, L.I.U.; exhibited in group shows Smithsonian Inst., 1952, Mus. of Modern Art, N.Y.C., 1956, SUNY-Albany, 1967, Casa de la Cultura Ecuatoriana in Cuayaquil, Ecuador, 1979, Hammer Gallery, N.Y.C., 1980, Muestra Internacional de Obra Grafica, Spain, 1982, Aaron Berman Gallery, N.Y.C., 1983, Kenkeleba Gallery, N.Y.C., 1985, Inst. of Contemporary Art, London, 1988; contbr. editor Arts Mag., 1974-75; contbr. articles, revs., catalog introductions, and artists' statements to publs. Art editor Greenwich Village News, 1976-77. With Intelligence and Reconnaissance, U.S. Army, 1945-46. Mem. Artists Representing Environ. Art (bd. dirs.), Assn. Internationale des Critiques d'Art (Am. sect.), Am. Soc. Contemporary Artists (bd. dirs.). Home: 36 Livingston Rd Scarsdale NY 10583-6845

RIES, STANLEY K., plant physiologist, university educator; b. Kenton, Ohio, Sept. 6, 1927; s. Edwin John and Gertrude (Hanna) R.; m. Mary Isabelle Kinsel, June 19, 1949; children: Carol, Don, Kathleen. BS, Mich. State Coll., East Lansing, 1950; PhD, Cornell U., 1954. Rsch. asst. Cornell U., Ithaca, N.Y., 1950-53; asst. prof. Mich. State U., East Lansing, 1953-58; assoc. prof. Mich. State U., 1958-65, prof., 1965—; cons. agrl. bus., 1954—, several chem. cos., 1960—. Contbr. articles to profl. publs. With USAF, 1945-46. Fellow AAAS, ASHS; mem. Phi Kappa Phi, Sigma Xi. Achievements include patents for Cucumber Harvester, Tomato Harvester; discovery of two natural plant growth regulators. Home: 1529 Cahill Dr East Lansing MI 48823-4724 Office: Mich State U Dept Horticulture East Lansing MI 48824

RIES, WILLIAM CAMPBELL, lawyer; b. Pitts., Apr. 8, 1948; s. F. William and Dorothy (Campbell) R.; m. Mallory Burns, Oct. 26, 1968; children: William Sheehan, Sean David. AB, Cath. U. Am., 1970; JD, Duquesne U., 1974; cert. Grad. Sch. Indsl. Adminstrn., Carnegie Mellon U., 1980. Bar: Pa. 1974, U.S. Dist. Ct. (we. dist.) Pa. 1974, U.S. Supreme Ct. 1979. Atty., then mng. counsel trust and investment svc. Mellon Bank, N.A., Pitts., 1974-90; ptnr. Dickie, McCamey and Chilcote, Pitts., 1990—; mem. adv. com. decedents' estates and trust law Pa. Joint State Govt. Commn., 1981—; adj. prof. Duquesne U., 1984—. Pres. McCandless Twp. Civic Assn., Pitts., 1981—, McCandless Town Coun., chair pub. safety com., vice chair fin com.; sec. McCandless Indsl. Devel. Auth.; liaison McCandless zoning hearing bd. Fellow Am. Bar Found.; mem. ABA (chmn. fiduciary svcs. subcom.), Pa. Bar Assn., Allegheny County Bar Assn., Pitts. Estate Planning Coun., Joint State Govt. Commn., Am. Bankers Assn. (co-chmn. nat. conf. lawyers and corp. fiduciaries, chmn. trust counsel com.), Pa. Bankers Assn. (trust com., trust legis. com.), Rivers Club, Treesdale Golf and Country Club. Republican. Avocations: golf, sailing, cross-country skiing, fitness. Home: 9602 Fawn Ln Allison Park PA 15101-1737

RIESE, ARTHUR CARL, environmental engineering company executive, consultant; b. St. Albans, N.Y., Jan. 2, 1955; s. Walter Herman and Katherine Ellen (Moore) R. BS in Geology, N.Mex. Inst. Mining and Tech., 1976, MS in Chemistry, 1978; PhD in Geochemistry, Colo. Sch. Mines, 1982. Lic. geologist, N.C.; registered profl. geologist, N.C., S.C., Ark., Fla., Tenn., Wyo. Asst. petroleum geologist N.Mex. Bur. Mines and Mineral Resources, Socorro, 1973-76; geologist Nord Resources, Inc., Albuquerque, 1975; rsch. asst. N.Mex. Inst. Mining and Tech., Socorro, 1976-78; vis. faculty Colo. Sch. Mines, 1978-81; rsch. geochemist Gulf R & D Co., Houston, 1982-84; sr. planning analyst/mgr. tech. planning Atlantic Richfield Co., L.A., 1984-87; sr. v.p. Harding Assocs. and Harding Lawson Assocs., Denver, 1987—; mem. affiliate faculty U. Tex., Austin, 1983—; speaker, conf. chmn. in field. Numerous patents in field. Panel participant N.Mex. First, Gallup, 1990. Recipinet Engrng. Excellence award Cons. Engrs. Coun. Colo., 1991, 95. Mem. Am. Inst. Hydrology (cert. profl. hydrogeologist 1988), Am. Inst. Profl. Geologists (cert. geol. scientist 1988). Office: Harding Lawson Assocs 2400 MCI Tower 707 17th St Denver CO 80202-3404

RIESENFELD, STEFAN ALBRECHT, law educator, consultant; b. Breslau, Ger., June 8, 1908; came to U.S., 1934, naturalized, 1940; s. Conrad Ernst and Margarethe (Landecker) R.; m. Phyllis B. Thorgrimson, Dec. 23, 1943; children—Peter William, Stefan Conrad. J.U.D., U. Breslau, 1932, U. Milan, 1934; LL.B., U. Calif.-Berkeley, 1937; S.J.D., Harvard U., 1940; B.S., U. Minn., 1943; D.h.c., U. Cologne (Ger.), 1970, Humboldt U., Berlin. Bar: Minn. 1939, U.S. Supreme Ct. 1978. Prof. law U. Minn., Mpls., 1938-52; prof. law U. Calif.-Berkeley, 1952—, Emanuel S. Heller prof., 1954-75, prof. emeritus, 1975—; prof. law U. Calif., Hastings Coll. Law, San Francisco, 1975—; cons. to U.S. Bd. Econ. Warfare, 1942, UN antitrust com., 1952; counselor on internat. law Dept. Def., 1955, Dept. State, 1977-82; mem. Adv. Com. on Bankruptcy Rules, 1961-72; vis. prof. various U.S. and fgn. univs.; cons. Calif. law revision commn., 1970-81, Legal Ref. Bur. of Hawaii, 1968-74. Served with USN, 1943-46. Recipient Silver medal Dept. State, 1979, 84; Verdienstkreuz, Fed. Republic of Germany, 1975. Mem. ABA, Nat. Bankruptcy Conf., Am. Acad. Arts and Scis., Am. Soc. Internat. Law, Internat. Law Assn. (Am. br.), Soc. Legal History. Lutheran. Author: Protection of Fisheries Under International Law, 1943, Modern Social Legislation, 1950, (with Hetland, Maxwell and Warren) California Secured Land Transactions, 4th edit., 1992, Creditors' Remedies and Debtors' Protection, 4th edit., 1986, (with Abbot) Parliamentary Participation in Treaty-Making, 1993. Home: 1129 Amador Ave Berkeley CA 94707-2632 Office: U Calif Berkeley Law Sch Boalt Hall Berkeley CA 94720

RIESENFELD, STEFAN CONRAD, finance company executive; b. Mpls., July 10, 1948; s. Stefan A. and Phyllis B. R.; m. Christine Wolf; May 23, 1990. BS in Physics, Calif. Inst. Tech., 1970; MA in Econs., Stanford U., 1975, MBA, 1975. Programmer Burroughs Corp., Pasadena, Calif., 1970-73; asst. v.p. Chem. Bank, London, 1975-80; treas. System Devel. Corp./Unisys, Santa Monica, Calif., 1980-83; exec. asst. to pres. Burroughs Corp./Unisys, Detroit, 1983-84, dir. corp. devel., 1984-86; v.p. corp. devel. Unisys Corp., Blue Bell, Pa., 1986-89; v.p., treas. Unisys Corp., Blue Bell, 1989—. Mem. Fin. Execs. Inst. Office: Unisys Corp Township Ln Union Mtg Rads Blue Bell PA 19422

RIESER, JOSEPH A., JR., lawyer; b. Pitts., Aug. 28, 1947; s. Joseph Alexander and Ruth Margaret (Piper) R.; m. Susan Jean Irving, Feb. 28, 1976; 1 child, Alexander H.I. AB, Princeton U., 1969; JD, Harvard U., 1974, MPP, 1974. Bar: Pa. 1974, D.C. 1976, U.S. Supreme Ct. 1979. Assoc. Reed Smith Shaw & McClay, Pitts. and Washington, 1974-82; ptnr. Reed Smith Shaw & McClay, Washington, 1983—. Chmn. nat. alumni assn. Kennedy Sch. Govt., Cambridge, Mass., 1979-82; bd. dirs. Harvard U. Alumni Assn., 1982-84; gen. counsel 1984 Dem. Nat. Conv., Washington, 1983-84; gen. counsel Nat. Dem. Party, Washington, 1985-89; spl. counsel Clinton/Gore '92, Inc.; mem. Clinton-Gore 1992 Presdl. Transition Team. Mem. D.C. Bar (chmn. bus. related taxes com. 1989-92, tax policy steering com., chmn. D.C. Bar Nat. Fed. Tax Inst. 1991, 92, chmn. state and local taxes com. 1994—), Harvard-Yale-Princeton Club, Cosmos Club. Presbyterian. Home: 3517 Davis St NW Washington DC 20007-1426 Office: Reed Smith & McClay Ste 1100-East Tower 1301 K St NW Washington DC 20005

RIESER, LEONARD MOOS, college administrator, physics educator; b. Chgo., May 18, 1922; s. Leonard Moos and Margaret (Wallerstein) R.; m. Rosemary Littledale, July 16, 1944; children: Leonard, Timothy Savage, Abigail Wild; 1 adopted child, Kenneth Willis. S.B., U. Chgo., 1943; Ph.D., Stanford, 1952; A.M. (hon.), Dartmouth, 1963. Research asst., then research assoc. Stanford, 1949-52; mem. faculty Dartmouth, 1952—, prof. physics, 1960—, dir. grad. study, 1961-66, dean arts and scis., provost, 1967-71, v.p., dean of faculty, 1971-80, provost, 1979-82, dir. Dickey Endowment, 1982—; Pres. New Eng. Conf. Grad. Edn., 1965; mem. com. grants Research Corps, N.Y., 1961-66; chmn. bd. Bull. Atomic Scientists, 1985—; vis. scholar MacArthur Found., 1990. Trustee Hampshire Coll., 1984—, Latin Am. Students in Am. Univs., 1990—. Served with AUS, World War II. Mem. AAAS (chmn. com. sci. edn. 1965, bd. dirs. 1967-75, pres. 1973, chmn. bd. 1974, chmn. com. new directions 1975—, chmn. com. sci. freedom), Interciencia Assn. (v.p. 1976-80, pres. 1980-84), Am. Assn. Physics Tchrs., Am. Phys. Soc., Sigma Xi., Phi Beta Kappa. Home: Elm St Norwich VT 05055 Office: Baker Library Dartmouth Coll Hanover NH 03755

RIESKE, GORDON, food products executive; b. 1937. With Price Waterhouse, L.A., 1966-71, Memorex Corp., L.A., 1971-77; v.p., COO, now sr. v.p., COO Wilsey Foods Inc., La Puente, Calif., 1977—. Office: Wilsey Foods Inc PO Box 3636 Industry CA 91744*

RIESS, GORDON SANDERSON, management consultant; b. Salonika, Macedonia, Greece, Feb. 25, 1928; came to U.S., 1932; s. Lewis William and Dorothy Onward (Sanderson) R.; m. Priscilla Rich, June 2, 1951; children: Mark C., Kimberly A., Blake G. AB with highest honors, Whitman Coll., 1949; MBA cum laude, Harvard U., 1951. Cert. mgmt. cons.; registered profl. cons.; accredited profl. cons. Mgmt. trainee Ford Internat. Div., N.Y.C., 1951-53; asst. fin. mgr. Ford Motor Co., Mid. East, Alexandria, Egypt, 1953-57; gen. sales mgr. Ford Motor Co., Rome, Italy, 1957-60; regional fin. mgr. Ford Motor Co., Scandinavia, Copenhagen, Denmark, 1960-62; gen. mgr. Ford Motor Co., European, Brussels, Belgium, 1962-67; v.p. Internat. Paper Co., Zurich, Switzerland, 1967-71; exec. v.p. Cinema Internat. Corp., London, 1971-75; chmn., pres. Stewart-Riess Labs. Inc., Tarzana, Calif., 1976-83; pres., CEO Intercontinental Enterprises Ltd., Beverly Hills, Calif., 1983—; chmn. Vis. Nurse Found., L.A., 1985-87, bd. dirs., chmn. Vis. Nurse Assn., L.A., 1976—; bd. dirs. Beverly Found., Pasadena, Calif., 1990—; vice-chmn. of bd., Whitman Coll., Walla Walla, Wash., 1985—. Inventor/patentee pre-fillable hypodermic syringe. Chmn. Inter-Community Sch. Zurich, 1968-71; trustee Am. Sch. London, 1972-75; vice chmn. Krafterliner Mfgs. Assn., Zurich, 1968-71; bd. dirs. Vols. in Tech. Assistance, Arlington, Va., 1986-93; bd. overseers Muhlenberg Coll., 1993—; internat. bd. Czechoslovak Mgmt. Ctr., 1992—. Sgt. U.S. Army, 1946-47. R.H. Macy scholar, Harvard Bus. Sch., 1949. Mem. Am. Assn. Profl. Cons., Am. Cons. League, L.A. World Affairs Coun., Hollywood Radio & Television Soc., Inst. Mgmt. Cons., Lic. Execs. Soc. Avocations: skiing, scuba diving. Office: Intercontinental Ent Ltd 256 S Robertson Blvd Ste 3194 Beverly Hills CA 90211-2898

RIESS, J. M., gas and oil industry executive; b. 1942. BSBA, Drake U., 1964. With The Gates Rubber Co., Denver, 1965—, pres., ceo, now coo, 1994—. Office: The Gates Rubber Co PO Box 5887 900 S Broadway Denver CO 80209-4010*

RIESSER, GREGOR HANS, arbitrage investment adviser; b. Riga, Latvia, Apr. 13, 1925; came to U.S., 1948; s. Hans Edward and Gilda (Von Scherf) R.; m. Joanna Gray (dec. Aug. 1991); children: Cindy Laughlin, William Riesser; m. Edith Naparst, Dec. 19, 1992; stepchildren: Nicole Naparst, Harold Naparst. MS in Chemistry, U. Geneva, Switzerland, 1949; PhD, U. Calif., Berkeley, 1952. Rsch. chemist Shell Chem. Co., Houston, 1952-70, catalysis bus. ctr., 1970-73; sr. staff chemist Shell Devel. Co., Houston, 1973-84; speaker on long-term options, scores and primes, arbitrages, dual funds and the stock market; mem. bd. arbitrators NASD. Featured in Forbes, Houston Post, Houston Chronicle. Mem. Am. Assn. Individual Investors, Houston Computer Investment Assn. (dir. 1990—), Quant Award). Unitarian. Home and Office: 2309A Nantucket Dr Houston TX 77057-2956

RIESZ, PETER CHARLES, marketing educator, consultant; b. Orange, N.J., Apr. 30, 1937; s. Kolman and Ellen (Wachs) R.; m. Elizabeth Strider Dunkman, Dec. 28, 1968; children—Sarah Kathleen. B.S., Rutgers Coll., 1958; M.B.A., Columbia U., 1963, Ph.D., 1971. Asst. prof. U. Iowa, Iowa City, 1968-73, assoc. prof., 1973-80, prof. mktg., 1980—, chmn. dept. mktg., 1981-84, 85-87, Williams prof. tchg., 1994—; vis. prof. Boston U., 1974-75, Duke U., Durham, N.C., 1984-85; cons. in field. Contbr. articles to profl. jours. Recipient Teaching Excellence award HON Industries, 1989; named MBA Prof. of Yr., 1990; Old Gold fellow U. Iowa, 1972. Mem. Am. Chem. Soc., Am. Mktg. Assn. Democrat. Presbyterian. Avocations: photography. Home: 2411 Tudor Dr Iowa City IA 52245-3638 Office: U Iowa Dept of Teaching Iowa City IA 52242

RIFENBURGH, RICHARD PHILIP, investment company executive; b. Syracuse, N.Y., Mar. 3, 1932; s. Russell D. and Edna (MacKenzie) R.; m. Doris Anita Hohn, June 24, 1950; children: David, Susan, Robert. Student, Wayne State U. With Mohawk Data Scis. Corp., Herkimer, N.Y., 1964-74, pres., 1970-74, chmn., 1974; chmn. Moval Mgmt. Corp., Herkimer, 1968—; CEO, GCA Corp., Andover, Mass., 1986-87; gen. ptnr. Hambrecht and Quist Venture Ptnrs., 1987-90; chmn. Miniscribe Corp., Longmont, Colo., 1988-91, Ironstone Group Inc., 1988-91; dir. Libr. Bur. Inc., Herkimer, 1976-95; chmn. St. G Crystal Ltd., Jeannette, Pa., 1985—; bd. dirs. Concurrent Computer Corp.; dir. Glasstech Inc., 1995—; chmn. Ross Cosmetics Distbn. Ctrs., Inc. (now named Tristar Corp.), 1992—. With USAF, 1951-55. Address: Moval Mgmt Corp Ste 133 2637 E Atlantic Blvd Pompano Beach FL 33062-4939

RIFKIN, ARNOLD, film company executive; m. Rita George; two children. BA, U. Cin. Founder Rifkin-David, 1974-80; merged to form Rifkin/David/Kimble/Parseghian, 1980-81, DHKPR, 1981-84; head motion picture dept. Triad Artists, Inc., 1984-92; sr. v.p., worldwide head motion picture divsn. William Morris Agy., Beverly Hills, Calif., 1992—; lectr. UCLA. Office: William Morris Agy 151 S El Camino Dr Beverly Hills CA 90212-2704*

RIFKIN, HAROLD, physician, educator; b. N.Y.C., Sept. 10, 1916; s. Jack and Rose (Zuckoff) R.; m. Beatrice Weiss, Nov. 25, 1945; children—Janet, Matthew, Phyllis. B.A., U. Mo., 1935; M.D., Dalhousie U., 1940. Diplomate Am. Bd. Internal Medicine. Intern Jewish Hosp., Bklyn, 1940-41; resident in internal medicine Montefiore Hosp., N.Y.C., 1942-43, 46-47; practice medicine specializing in internal medicine and diabetes N.Y.C., 1947—; clin. prof. medicine Albert Einstein Coll. Medicine, N.Y.C., 1974-93, disting. univ. prof. of medicine emeritus, 1993—; prof. clin. medicine NYU Sch. Medicine, 1975—; chief of diabetes svc. emeritus Montefiore Med. Ctr., N.Y.C., 1993—; cons. emeritus Lenox Hill Hosp., N.Y.C., 1992—. With U.S. Army, 1943-46. Fellow ACS, N.Y. Acad. Medicine, N.Y. Acad. Scis.; mem. AMA, Internat. Diabetes Fedn. (chmn. N.Am. region 1985—, assoc. editor-in-chief Bull. 1985—, v.p. 1988—, hon. pres. 1994—), Am. Diabetes Assn. (bd. dirs. 1973—, pres. 1985-86), N.Y. Diabetes Assn. (past pres., bd. dirs. 1970—), N.Y. County Med. Soc., N.Y. State Med. Soc., Am. Soc. Clin. Rsch., Harvey Soc. Home: 885 Park Ave New York NY 10021-0325

RIFKIN, LEONARD, metals company executive; b. N.Y.C., Apr. 10, 1931; s. Irving W. and May (Goldin) R.; m. Norma Jean Smith, Aug. 22, 1954 (dec. Jan. 1983); children: Daniel Mark, Richard Sheldon, Martin Stuart; m. Ariel Kalisky, Jan. 14, 1984. B.S., Ind. U., Bloomington, 1952. Pres. Omni Source Corp., Fort Wayne, Ind., 1960—. Served with U.S. Army, 1956-58. Office: Omni Source Corp 1610 N Calhoun St Fort Wayne IN 46808-2762*

RIFKIN, NED, museum director; b. Florence, Ala., Nov. 10, 1949; s. Arthur Robert and Ina Blanche (Steinberg) R.; m. Diann Carole Kleinman, Mar. 4, 1976; children: Moses Kleinman, Amos Kleinman. BA, Syracuse U., 1972; MA in Art History, U. Mich., 1973, PhD in Art History, 1976. Asst. prof. dept. art U. Tex., Arlington, 1977-80; curator, asst. dir. New Mus. Contemporary Art, N.Y.C., 1980-84; curator contemporary art Corcoran Gallery Art, Washington, 1984-86; chief curator exhbns. Hirshhorn Mus. and Sculpture Garden, Washington, 1986-90, chief curator, 1990-91; dir. High Mus. Art, Atlanta, 1991—.

RIFKIND, ARLEEN B., physician, researcher; b. N.Y.C., June 29, 1938; d. Michael C. and Regina (Gottlieb) Brenner; m. Robert S. Rifkind, Dec. 24, 1961; children: Amy, Nina. BA, Bryn Mawr Coll., 1960; MD, NYU, 1964. Intern Bellevue Hosp., N.Y.C., 1964-65, resident, 1965; clin. assoc. Endocrine br. Nat. Cancer Inst., 1965-68; research assoc., asst. resident physician Rockefeller U., 1968-71; asst. prof. medicine Cornell U. Med. Coll., N.Y.C., 1971-82, assoc. prof. medicine, 1983—, asst. prof. pharmacology, 1973-78, assoc. prof., 1978-82, prof., 1983—; chmn. Gen. Faculty Council Cornell U. Med. Coll., 1984-86; mem. Nat. Inst. Environ. Health Scis. Rev. Com., 1981-85, chmn., 1985-86; mem. toxicology study sect. Nat. Inst. Health, 1989-91, chmn. 1991-93; bd. sci. counselors USPHS Agy. for Toxic Substances and Disease Registry, 1991-95, adv. com. FDA Ranch Hand., Spl. Studies Relating to the Possible Long-Term Health Effects of Phenoxy Herbicides and Contaminents, 1995—. Mem. editorial bd. Drug Metabolism and Disposition, 1994—, Toxicology and Applied Pharmacology; contbr. articles to profl. jours. Chmn. Friends of the Library, Jewish Theol. Sem. Am., 1984-86; trustee Dalton Sch., 1986-92; mem. Environ. Health and Safety Coun. Am. Health Found., 1990—. Recipient Andrew W. Mellon Tchr.-Scientist award, 1976-78; USPHS spl. fellow, 1968-70, 71-72. Mem. Endocrine Soc., Am. Soc. Clin. Investigation, Am. Soc. Pharmacology and Exptl. Therapeutics, AAAS, Internat. Soc. Study Xenobiotics, Soc. Toxicology. Office: Cornell U Med Coll Dept Pharmacology 1300 York Ave New York NY 10021-4805

RIFKIND, ROBERT S(INGER), lawyer; b. N.Y.C., Aug. 31, 1936; s. Simon H. and Adele (Singer) R.; m. Arleen Brenner, Dec. 24, 1961; children: Amy, Nina. BA, Yale U., 1958; JD, Harvard U., 1961. Bar: N.Y. 1961, U.S. Supreme Ct. 1965. Asst. to solicitor gen. Dept. Justice, 1965-68; assoc. firm Cravath, Swaine & Moore, N.Y.C., 1962-65, 68-70; ptnr. Cravath, Swaine & Moore, 1971—. Trustee Dalton Sch., N.Y.C., 1975-83, hon. trustee, 1983—, pres., 1977-79; trustee The Loomis Inst., 1987-95, Citizens Budget Commn.; bd. dirs. Charles H. Revson Found., 1991—, Jewish Theol. Sem. Am., 1983—, Benjamin N. Cardozo Sch. Law, 1984-89; pres. Am. Jewish Com., 1994—. Recipient Stanley M. Isaacs Human Rels. award Am. Jewish Com., 1983. Fellow Am. Coll. Trial Lawyers, N.Y. Bar Found.; mem. ABA, Coun. Fgn. Rels., Am. Law Inst., Assn. of Bar of City of N.Y., Phi Beta Kappa. Democrat. Office: Cravath Swaine & Moore Worldwide Pla 825 8th Ave New York NY 10019-7416

RIGALI, JUSTIN F., archbishop; b. L.A., Apr. 19, 1935; s. Henry Alphonsus and Frances Irene (White) R. B in Sacred Theology, Cath. U. Am., 1961; Lic. in Canon Law, Gregorian U., Rome, 1963, D in Canon Law, 1964; LHD (hon.), St. Louis U., 1995. Ordained priest Apr. 25, 1961. Titular archbishop of Bolsena, 1985-94; sec. Congregation for Bishops Holy See, Vatican City, 1989-94, sec. Coll. of Cardinals, 1990-94; archbishop Archdiocese of St. Louis, 1994—. Office: Archdiocese of St Louis 4445 Lindell Blvd Saint Louis MO 63108

RIGBY, PAUL CRISPIN, artist, cartoonist; b. Melbourne, Australia, Oct. 25, 1924; came to U.S., 1977; s. James Samuel and Violet Irene (Wood) R.; m. Marlene Anne Cockburn, Nov. 16, 1956; children: Nicole, Pia, Peter, Paul, Danielle. Student, Brighton Tech. Sch., Australia, Art Schs., Victoria, Victoria Nat. Gallery, Australia. Free lance artist, 1940-42; illustrator West Australian News, Ltd., 1948-52; editorial cartoonist Daily News Australia, 1952-69; daily cartoonist London Sun and News of the World, 1969-74; editorial cartoonist New York Post, 1977-84, 93—, New York Daily News, 1984-93. Illustrator numerous books; represented in exhbns. of painting in, Australia, Europe and U.S.A.; Contbr. work to numerous publs., U.S., Europe, Asia. Served with Royal Australian Air Force, 1942-46. Decorated knight comdr. Order of St. John, Knights of Malta; recipient Walkley award Australia, 1960, 61, 63, 66, 69; N.Y. Press Club award for art, 1981, 83, Page One award for excellence in journalism Newspaper Guild, 1982, 83, 84, 85. Mem. Ch. of Eng. Clubs: Rolls Royce Owners, Royal Freshwater Bay Yacht; Friars, Players (N.Y.C.). Home: 72 Kenyon Rd Hampton CT 06247-1123 Office: NY Post 210 South St New York NY 10002-7807

RIGBY, PERRY GARDNER, medical center administrator, educator, former university dean, physician; b. East Liverpool, Ohio, July 1, 1932; s. Perry Lawrence and Lucille Ellen (Orin) R.; m. Joan E. Worthington, June 16, 1957; children: Martha, Peter, Thomas, Matthew. B.S. summa cum laude, Mt. Union Coll., 1953, D.Sc. hon., 1976; M.D., Western Res. U., 1957. Diplomate: Am. Bd. Internal Medicine. Intern in medicine U. Va. Hosp., Charlottesville, 1957-58, asst. resident in medicine, 1958-60; research fellow in hematology Mass. Meml. Hosp., Boston, 1960-62; clin. asst. in medicine Boston City Hosp., 1961-62; research assoc. in medicine Mass. Meml. Hosp., Boston U. Med. Ctr., 1961-62; asst. prof. internal medicine and anatomy U. Nebr., Omaha, 1964-66, assoc. prof. internal medicine and anatomy, 1966-69, prof. internal medicine, 1969-78, prof. anatomy, 1969-74, prof. med. edn., 1973-74, head sect. hematology Eugene C. Eppley Inst. for Research in Cancer and Allied Diseases, 1964-68, dir. hematology div., 1968-74, asst. dean for curriculum Coll. Medicine, 1971-72, assoc. dean for acad. affairs, 1972-74, dir. office ednl. services, 1972-74, acting assoc. dean for allied health professions, 1973-74, vice chmn. dept. med. and ednl. adminstrn., 1974, dean, 1974-78, chmn. dept. med. and ednl. adminstrn., 1974; prof. internal medicine La. State U., Shreveport, 1978—, assoc. dean acad. affairs Sch. Medicine, 1978-81, acting dean, 1981-82, dean, 1982-85; chancellor La. State U., 1985-94; dir. Health Care Systems La. State U., New Orleans, 1994—; mem. clin. bd. Univ. Hosp. La. State U., 1978—, chmn. clin. bd., 1978—, program dir. biomed. research support grant program, 1980-81; chmn. dean's com. VA Hosp., 1978—; mem. courtesy staff Immanuel Med. Ctr.; bd. dirs. Health Planning Council of Midlands, Omaha, 1976-78; cons. WHO, Kabul, Afghanistan, 1976. Bd. dirs. Fontenelle Forest, Omaha, 1976-78; bd. dirs. River Cities High Tech. Group, Shreveport, 1982—. Served as capt. M.C. U.S. Army, 1962-64. Markle scholar, 1965. Fellow ACP; mem. Am. Fedn. Clin. Research (councillor 1971), AMA (del.), Am. Soc. Hematology, N.Y. Acad. Scis., Am. Assn. Med. Colls. (council of deans of Midwest-Gt. Plains 1974-78, chmn. Midwest-Gt. Plains 1976), Am. Assn. Cancer Research, AAAS, Am. Heart Assn., Central Soc. Clin. Research, Internat. Soc. Hematology, Health Edn. Media Assn., Am. Assn. Physicians' Assts., So. Soc. Clin. Investigation, Shreveport C. of C. (dir. 1982—), Sigma Xi, Alpha Omega Alpha, Phi Rho Sigma. Office: La State U Med Ctr Resource Ctr 433 Bolivar St New Orleans LA 70112-2223

RIGDON, IMOGENE STEWART, nursing educator, associate dean; b. St. Joseph, Mo., Apr. 2, 1937; d. George Francis and Mary Elizabeth (Byrne) Stewart; m. Michael Allen Rigdon, Nov. 1, 1973; 1 child, Mary Lisa. BSN, Marillac Coll., 1961; MSN, Cath. U. Am., 1973; PhD, U. Utah, 1985. Cert. clin. specialist in adult psychiat.-mental health nursing Am. Nurses Assn. Asst. dir. nursing St. Anthony Hosp., Oklahoma City, 1974-76; regional teaching nurse III Shands Teaching Hosp., Gainsville, Fla., 1977-78; asst. prof. U. Fla., Gainsville, 1978-82; teaching fellow U. Utah Coll. Nursing, Salt Lake City, 1983-85; clin. specialist U. Hosp., Salt Lake City, 1985; asst. prof. U. Utah Coll. Nursing, Salt Lake City, 1985-87, vol. aux. faculty, assoc. prof., 1987-95; dean, assoc. prof. St. Mark's Westminster Sch. Nursing, Salt

Lake City, 1987-95; assoc. dean for acad. affairs, assoc. prof. U. Utah Coll. Nursing, Salt Lake City, 1996—; mem. Advanced Practice task force, 1990—, Utah Nursing Resoources task force, 1988-90, Utah Stat Be. Regents' com. on Nursing Edn., 1988-89, Psychiat-Metnal health Nursing Conf. Group; mem. Advanced Psychiat.-Mental Health Nursing Adv. Com. to the State Bd. Nursing, 1986-89; mem. Intermountain Health Care Home Health Av. Com., 1988; group leader grief edn. groups Holy Cross Grief Ctr. and the Sharing Place, 1990-95; others. Contbr. chpts. to books and articles to profl. jours. Bd. mem. Holy Cross Bereavement Program Adv. Coun., 1989-94; mem. Utah Com. for Am.-Soviet Rels., 1988—; bd. trustees Widowed Persons Svc., 1995—; chair Salt Lake County Alcohol & Drug Planning Allocation Coun., 1994—. Capt. USAFR, 1972-82. Mem. AAUW, Am. Assn. Colls. Nursing, Nat. League Nursing, Am. Orthopsychiatric Assn., Soc. for Edn. and Rsch. in Psychiat. Nursing, Coun. Clin. Specialists in Psychiat.-Mental Health Nursing, Utah Nurses' Assn. (Utah health agenda task force 1988-89, gov. bd. 1986-89, dist. 1 treas. 1985-87), Mental Health Assn., Sierra Club, ACLU, Amnesty Internat., Sigma Theta Tau (Kappa chpt., Iota Iota chpt.). Democrat. Roman Catholic. Avocations: guitar playing, cross country skiing, gardening, walking. Home: 3196 Millcreek Canyon Rd Salt Lake City UT 84109-3112 Office: U Utah Coll of Nursing 25 S Medical Dr Salt Lake City UT 84122

RIGG, CHARLES ANDREW, pediatrician; b. Hamilton, Vic., Australia, Oct. 18, 1926; came to U.S., 1963; s. Arthur Oscar and Mary Eileen (Wingrove) R. B in Medicine, Surgery with honors, Sydney U., 1951. Staff adolescent medicine Children's Hosp., Boston, 1964-65; chief dept. adolescent medicine Children's Hosp., Washington, 1967-80, Boston City Hosp., 1981-83; med. dir. Outer Cape Health, Provincetown, Mass., 1983-88; pediatrician, med. dir. Medicenter Five, Harwich, Mass., 1988-95, pediatrician, 1995—; from asst. prof. to assoc. prof. child health George Washington U. Med. Sch., 1967-80; cons. Nat. Naval Med. Ctr., Bethesda, Md., 1973-80, Walter Reed Army Med. Ctr., Washington, 1973-80; assoc. prof. pediatrics Boston U. Med. Sch., 1981-83; courtesy staff medicine Children's Hosp., Boston, 1983—. Editor: Adolescent Medicine Present and Future Concepts, 1980; contbr. articles to profl. jours. Lt. col. USAR, 1985-91. Decorated Army Commendation medal; model tng. program in adolescent medicine grantee Maternal and Child Health Svcs.-U.S. Govt., 1967-80, Comprehensive Health Svcs. Adolescent Ctr. grantee Mass. Dept. Pub. Health, 1981-83. Fellow Am. Acad. Pediatrics, Royal Australasian Coll. Physicians, Soc. Adolescent Medicine (charter, treas., chmn., legis. com.); mem. Royal Sydney Golf Club, City Tavern Club Washington. Episcopalian. Avocations: hist. preservation, gardening, theater, music, walking. Office: Medicenter Five 525 Long Pond Dr Harwich MA 02645-1227

RIGG, DIANA, actress; b. Doncaster, Yorkshire, Eng., July 20, 1938; d. Louis and Beryl (Helliwell) R.; m. Menahem Gueffen, July 6, 1973 (div. Sept. 1976); m. Archibald Hugh Stirling, Mar. 25, 1981 (div.); 1 child, Rachael Atlanta. Grad., Fulneck Girls' Sch., Pudsey, Yorkshire; student, Royal Acad. Dramatic Art, London; D (hon.), Stirling U., Eng., 1988, Leeds U., Eng., 1992. Stage debut as Natella Abashwilli in The Caucasian Chalk Circle, Theatre Royal, York, Eng., 1957; joined Royal Shakespeare Co., Stratford-on-Avon, 1959, debut as Andromache in Troilus and Cressida, 1960; London debut as Philippe Trincant in The Devils, London, 1961; numerous repertory appearances; joined Nat. Theatre, 1972; appeared in Jumpers, Macbeth, 1972, The Misanthrope, 1973, Pygmalion, 1974, Phaedra Britannica, 1975, Night and Day, 1978, Collette, 1982, Heartbreak House, 1983, Little Eyolf, 1985, Antony and Cleopatra, 1985, Wildlife, 1986, Follies, 1987, Love Letters, 1990, All for Love, 1991, Putting It Together, 1992, Berlin Bertie, 1992, Medea, 1992 (Tony award, Broadway prod., 1994); film appearances include A Midsummer Night's Dream, The Assassination Bureau, On Her Majesty's Secret Service, Julius Caesar, The Hospital, Theatre of Blood, A Little Night Music, The Great Muppet Caper, Evil Under the Sun, A Good Man in Africa; co-starred as Emma Peel in Brit. TV series The Avengers, 1965-67; star TV series Diana, 1973-74; numerous TV movies including This House of Brede, 1975, Hedda Gabler, 1981, Little Eyolf, 1982, Witness for the Prosecution, 1982, King Lear, 1983, Bleak House, 1984, A Hazard of Hearts, 1987, Worst Witch, 1987, Unexplained Laughter, 1989, Mother Love (Broadcasting Guild Award), 1989, Citizen Cohn, 1994; host PBS series Mystery, 1989—; author: No Turn Unstoned, 1982, U.S. edit., 1983. Decorated comdr. Brit. Empire; created dame, 1994; recipient Tony award nomination as best actress in Abelard and Heloise and The Misanthrope; Plays and Players award for Phaedra Britannica and Night and Day; Variety Club Gt. Britain award for best actress for Evil Under the Sun; Brit. Acad. Film and TV Arts award for best TV actress in Mother Love, 1989. Mem. United Brit. Artists (co-founder, dir. 1982—). Office: care London Mgmt, 235 Regent St, London W1A 2JT, England also: c/o Lionel Larner, Ltd 119 W 57th St New York NY 10019*

RIGGINS-EZZELL, LOIS, museum administrator; b. Nashville, Nov. 18, 1939; d. Percy Leon and Lula Belle Prather (Traughber) Von Schmittou; 1 son, Nicholas. B.S., Belmont Coll., 1968; postgrad., U. Western Ky., 1969-72, George Washington U., 1978. Cert. tchr., Ky., Tenn. Tchr. Ky. Pub. Schs., Adairville, 1962-71; tour supr. Tenn. State Capitol, Nashville, 1972-74; curator of extension services Tenn. State Mus., Nashville, 1975-77, curator edn., 1977-81, exec. dir., 1981—. Chmn. Nashville Flight of Tenn. Friendship Force, Caracas, Venezuela, 1977, Tenn. Am. Revolution Bicentennial Arts Competition, 1976, Gov.'s Quicentennial Com., 1991-92; bd. dirs. Tenn. State Mus. Found., Inc., 1981—, Zool. Soc. Mid. Tenn., 1986-88, So. Folk Cultural Revival Project, 1986-93, Tenn. Pres. Trust, 1989—, Hist. Coun., Girl Scouts U.S.; mem. commning. com. USS Tenn., 1990; keynote speaker nat. forums Corp. Philanthropy Report, Chgo., Atlanta, 1991. Named Woman for Lears, Lears Mag., 1990, Tenn. Woman of Distinction, 1993. Mem. Southeastern Mus. Conf. (edn. com., rep. to Am. Assn. Mus. council, publs. advt. com. 1983), Inter Mus. Council of Nashville (chmn. edn. 1980-81), Am. Assn. Mus., Am. Assn. State and Local History (edn com. 1988-90), Am. Fedn. Art., Art Dirs. Forum. Office: Tenn State Mus 505 Deaderick St Nashville TN 37243-1120

RIGGIO, LEONARD, book publishing executive; b. 1941. Merchandise mgr. NYU Bookstore, N.Y.C., 1962-65; pres., CEO, bd. dirs. Barnes & Noble Bookstores, Inc., 1965—; chmn. bd., CEO, pres., treas. Barnes & Noble Inc., N.Y.C., 1986—; chmn. bd., prin. beneficial owner Software Etc. Stores, Inc., Mpls., MBS Textbook Exchange, Inc., Columbia, Mo. Office: Barnes & Noble Inc 122 5th Ave New York NY 10011-5605 Address: MBS Textbook Exchange Inc 2711 W Ash St Columbia MO 65203-4613

RIGGIO, STEPHEN, book store chain executive; married; 3 children. BA in Anthropology, Bklyn. Coll., 1974. Buying, mktg. areas Barnes & Noble Bookstores, Inc., N.Y.C., 1974-78, gen. mdse. mgr., 1978-81, head direct mail bus., 1981-86, exec. v.p. merchandising, 1986-90, exec. v.p., chief oper. officer, 1990—; originator Children With Special Needs collection books about and for children with learning disabilities. Bd. dirs. N.Y. chpt. Assn. Help Retarded Children. Office: Barnes & Noble Bookstores Inc 122 5th Ave Fl 4 New York NY 10011-5605*

RIGGLEMAN, JAMES DAVID, professional baseball team manager; b. Ft. Dix, N.J., Dec. 9, 1952. Degree in Physical Edn., Frostburg State U. Minor league baseball player, 1974-81, minor league baseball mgr., 1982-88, 91-92; dir. player devel., then coach St. Louis Cardinals, 1988-90; mgr. San Diego Padres, 1993-94, Chicago Cubs, 1995—. Office: Wrigley Field 1060 W Addison St Chicago IL 60613-4397

RIGGS, ANDY J., JR., newspaper publishing executive. V.p. prodn. The Daily News, N.Y.C. Office: The Daily News 220 E 42nd St Fl 817 New York NY 10017-5806

RIGGS, ARTHUR JORDY, retired lawyer; b. Nyack, N.Y., Apr. 3, 1916; s. Oscar H. and Adele (Jordy) R.; m. Virginia Holloway, Oct. 15, 1942 (dec.); children: Arthur James (dec.), Emily Adele Riggs Freeman, Keith Holloway, George Bennett; m. Priscilla McCormack, Jan. 16, 1993. AB, Princeton U., 1937; LLB, Harvard U., 1940. Bar: Mass. 1940, Tex. 1943; cert. specialist in labor law to 1992. Assoc., Warner, Stackpole, Stetson & Bradlee, Boston, 1940-41; staff mem. Solicitors Office U.S. Dept. Labor, Washington and Dallas, 1941-42; mem. Johnson, Bromberg, Leeds & Riggs, Dallas, 1949-81; of counsel Geary & Spencer, Dallas, 1981-91. Mem. ABA, State Bar Tex., Phi Beta Kappa. Avocations: Maya archeology, photography, scuba diving. Home and Office: 4116 Amherst Ave Dallas TX 75225-6901

RIGGS, BENJAMIN CLAPP, JR., building products manufacturing company executive; b. Boston, Sept. 29, 1945; s. Benjamin Clapp and Norma (Campanaro) R.; m. Cheryl Pusey, July 3, 1970 (div. 1987); children: Sonia Campanaro, Anne Elizabeth; m. Lee Thornton Ainsworth, Feb. 25, 1989. BA, Boston U., 1968. Commd. ens. U.S. Navy, 1969, advanced through grades to capt., 1990, served as pilot and aero. engr., 1969-76, now res.; exec. v.p. Resource Mgmt. Corp., Boston, 1976-78; br. mgr. Reynolds Aluminum Co., Mt. Kisco, N.Y., 1978-80; mktg. dir. Am. Abrasive Metals Co., Irvington, N.J., 1980-83; v.p., gen. mgr. Glen-Gery Corp., River Edge, N.J., 1984-90; dir. Resource Mgmt. Co., Oakland, N.J., 1990—; pres. HAPCO div. Kearney-Nat., Abington, Va., 1992-93; CEO, mng. dir. Resource Mgmt. Co., Bristol, Tenn., 1993—; pres., CEO P&K Pole Products, Inc., Newark, 1996—. Mem. Res. Officers Assn. Republican. Episcopalian. Avocations: sailing, ocean cruising, tennis, skiing, writing. Office: P&K Pole Products 84 Foundry St Newark NJ 07105

RIGGS, BYRON LAWRENCE, JR., physician, educator; b. Hot Springs, Ark., Mar. 24, 1931; s. Byron Lawrence and Elizabeth Ann (Patching) R.; m. Janet Templeton Brewer, June 24, 1955; children: Byron Kent, Ann Templeton. B.S., U. Ark., 1953, B.S. in Medicine, 1955, M.D., 1955; M.S. in Medicine, U. Minn., 1962. Diplomate: Am. Bd. Internal Medicine. Intern Letterman Army Hosp., San Francisco, 1955-56; resident in internal medicine Mayo Grad. Sch. Medicine Hosp., Rochester, Minn., 1958-61; asst. to staff Mayo Clinic and Found., Rochester, 1961, mem. staff internal medicine and metabolism, 1962—; mem. faculty U. Minn. Med. Sch., Rochester, 1962—, assoc. prof., 1970-72, prof., 1972—; Purvis and Roberta Tabor prof. med. rsch. Mayo Clinic and Med. Sch., Rochester, 1974—, chmn. divsn. endocrinology and metabolism, 1974-84; mem. gen. medicine B study sect. NIH, 1979-82; nat. adv. bd. NIAMS/NIH, 1987-91, disting. investigator Mayo Found., 1991—. Contbr. articles to med. jours. Dist. investigator Mayo Found., 1991—. Served with M.C. AUS, 1956-58. Recipient Mayo Found. postgrad. travel award, 1961; Kappa Delta award Am. Acad. Orthopedic Surgery, 1972; traveling fellow Royal Soc. Medicine, 1973. Fellow ACP; mem. AMA, AAAS, Assn. Am. Physicians, Am. Soc. Clin. Investigation, Endocrine Soc. (Rorer Clin. Investigator award 1989), Am. Fedn. Clin. Rsch. (councillor Midwest sect. 1969-71), Am. Soc. for Bone and Mineral Rsch. (pres. 1985-86, Bartter Clin. Investigation award 1990, Career Recognition award, 9th Workshop on Vitamin D rsch.), Ctrl. Soc. Clin. Rsch. (councillor). Home: 432 10th Ave SW Rochester MN 55902-2911 Office: Mayo Clinic 200 1st St SW Rochester MN 55905-0001

RIGGS, DONALD EUGENE, librarian, university dean; b. Middlebourne, W.Va., May 11, 1942; m. Jane Vasbinder, Sept. 25, 1964; children: Janna Jennifer, Krista Dyonis. BA, Glenville State Coll., 1964; MA, W.Va. U., 1966; MLS, U. Pitts., 1968; EdD, Va. Poly. Inst. and State U., 1975. Head librarian, tchr. sci. Warwood (W.Va.) High Sch., 1964-65; head librarian, audiovisual dir. Wheeling (W.Va.) High Sch., 1965-67; sci. and econs. librarian California State Coll. of Pa., 1968-70; dir. library and learning center Bluefield State Coll., 1970-72; dir. libraries and media services Bluefield State Coll., Concord Coll., Greenbrier Community Coll., and So. campus W.Va. Coll. of Grad. Studies, 1972-76; dir. libraries U. Colo., Denver, Met. State Coll., and Community Col. of Denver—Auraria Campus, 1976-79; univ. librarian Ariz. State U., 1979-88, dean univ. libraries, 1988-90; prof. info. and libr. sci., dean univ. libr. U. Mich., Ann Arbor, 1991—; adj. prof. Calif. State Coll., 1968-70, W.Va. U., 1970-72, U. Colo., 1977-79, U. Ariz., 1985; fed. rels. coord. Am. and W.Va. Libr. Assns., 1970-75; chmn. bd. dirs. Ctrl. Colo. Libr. Sys., 1976-79; chmn. Colo. Coun. Acad. Librs., 1977-78; mem. exec. bd. Colo. Alliance Rsch. Librs., 1978-79; cons. to librs.; fgn. assignments in Xi'an, People's Republic of China, 1988, Guadalajara, Mex., 1990, Budapest, Hungary, 1991, 95, Hong Kong, 1992, 94, San Juan, P.R., 1993, Melbourne, Australia, 1994, Empatory, Republic Crimea, Ukraine, 1996, London, 1996; del. Users Coun. Online Computer Libr. Ctr., Dublin, Ohio, 1987-91, pres.-elect, 1990-91, chair artificial intelligence and expert systems nat. group, 1987-88; bd. govs. Rsch. Librs. Group, Inc., Mountain View, Calif., 1991-92; vice chmn. mgmt. com. William L. Clements Libr., 1991—. Editor: W.Va. Librs., 1973-75, Libr. Hi Tech, 1993—, Coll. & Rsch. Librs., 1996—; founding editor: Libr. Adminstrn. and Mgmt., 1987-89; assoc. editor: Southeastern Libr., 1973-75; contbg. editor: Libraries in the Political Process, 1980, Options for the 80's, 1982, Library and Information Technology: At the Crossroads, 1984; contbg. author, editor: Library Leadership: Visualizing the Future, 1982; author: Strategic Planning for Library Managers, 1984, (with Helen Gothberg) Time Management in Academic Libraries, 1986, (with Gordon Sabine) Libraries in the 90's: What the Leaders Expect, 1988, Creativity, Innovation and Entrepreneurship in Libraries, 1989, Library Communication: The Language of Leadership, 1991, (with Rao Aluri) Expert Systems in Libraries, 1990, Cultural Diversity in Libraries, 1994; editl. bd. Am. Librs., 1987-89, Jour. Libr. Adminstrn., 1987—, Coll. and Rsch. Librs., 1990-96. Trustee Mesa (Ariz.) Pub. Library, 1980-86, chmn., 1985-86; mem. Ariz. State Library Adv. Council, 1981-84; bd. dirs. Documentation Abstracts, Inc., 1986-90. Recipient Alumnus of Yr. award Glenville State Coll., 1992; named Outstanding Young Educator, Ohio County Schs., 1966; Coun. on Libr. Resources grantee, 1985; sr. fellow UCLA, 1989. Mem. ALA (councilor-at-large 1982-86, 89-93, chmn. coun.'s resolutions com. 1985-86, pub. com. 1988-92, Hugh Atkinson award 1991), Ariz. Libr. Assn. (pres. coll. and univ. divsn. 1981-82, pres. 1983-84, Spl. Svc. award 1986, Disting. Svc. award 1990), Colo. Libr. Assn. (pres. 1978-79), W.Va. Libr. Assn. (pres. 1975-76), Assn. Coll. and Rsch. Librs. (pres. Tri-State chpt. 1972-74, pres. Ariz. chpt. 1981-82), So. Libr. Assn. (chmn. coll. and univ. sect. 1982-83), Assn. Rsch. Librs. (100th meeting planning com. 1982, mgmt. of rsch. libr. resources com. 1990-93, rsch. collections com. 1993-96), AMIGOS Bibliograph Coun. (trustee 1986-90, chmn. bd. trustees 1988-89), Libr. Adminstrn. and Mgmt. Assn. (bd. dirs. 1987-89, pres.-elect 1993-94, pres. 1994-95), Libr. Info. and Tech. Assn. (bd. dirs. 1989-93), Ctr. for Rsch. Librs. (councilor 1989-93), Ctr. for Rsch. Librs. (councilor 1979—), Mountain Plains Libr. Assn. (bd. dirs. 1987-90, pres.-elect 1990-91), Beta Phi Mu, Chi Phi, Phi Delta Kappa, Phi Kappa Phi. Office: U Mich Hatcher Grad Libr Office of Dean Ann Arbor MI 48109-1205

RIGGS, DOUGLAS A., lawyer; b. Rigby, Idaho, Aug. 20, 1944; s. Ursel and Elsie Groom Riggs; m. Heidi Bankart Eddy, Dec. 27, 1985; 1 child, Nathan Whittlesey. BS, Brigham Young U., 1966; MS, W.Va. U., 1967; JD, Cornell U., 1973. Bar: Alaska 1974, D.C. 1985. Assoc. Johnson, Christensen & Schamberg Inc., Anchorage, 1974-75; gen. counsel Alaska State Housing Authority, Anchorage, 1975-76, exec. dir., 1976-77; spl. counsel to the gov. State of Alaska, Washington, 1977-79; counsel Citizens for Mgmt. for Alaska Lands Inc., Washington, 1979; sole practice Anchorage, 1979-80; ptnr. Bogle & Gates, Anchorage, 1980-83; spl. asst. to pres. for pub. liaison The White House, Washington, 1983-85; gen. counsel U.S. Dept. Commerce, Washington, 1985-87; v.p. corp. planning, communications and external affairs, mem. corp. mgmt. com. Pitney-Bowes, Inc. World Hdqrs., Stamford, Conn., 1988-93, v.p. comms., planning, sec., gen. counsel, corp. mgmt. com., 1993—; now v.p. corp. comms. Pitney-Bowes, Inc., Stamford, CT. Counsel Senator Frank H. Murkowski campaign, Anchorage, 1980; mem. exec. com. Senator Ted Stevens re-election campaign, Anchorage, 1982-83. Served to sgt. U.S. Army, 1967-70. Mem. Alaska Bar Assn., D.C. Bar Assn. Republican. Home: 18 Weir Farm Ln Ridgefield CT 06877-6000 Office: Pitney Bowes Inc 1 Elm Croft Rd Stamford CT 06926-0700*

RIGGS, FRANK, congressman; b. Louisville, Ky., Sept. 5, 1950; m. Cathy Anne Maillard; three children: Ryan, Matthew, Sarah Anne. BA, Golden Gate U. With Veale Investment Properties, until 1987; co-founder (with wife) Duncan Enterprises; mem. 102nd Congress 1st Calif. Dist., 1991-92, mem. 104th Congress, 1995—. With U.S. Army, 1972-75. Republican. Office: US House Reps 1714 Longworth Office Bldg Washington DC 20515-0501*

RIGGS, FRANK LEWIS, foundation executive; b. Indpls., Apr. 1, 1937; s. Frank Lloyd Riggs and Marie Loretta (Shaner) Ellis; m. Gail Evelyn Kershner, July 28, 1960 (div. 1987). BS in Bus. Adminstrn., U. Ariz., 1961, EdD, 1976; MBA, George Washington U., 1964. Mktg. adminstr. TRW Systems, L.A., 1964-67; assn. exec. Electric League Ariz., Phoenix, 1967-68; pub. affairs adminstr. Ariz. Regional Med. program Coll. of Medicine, U. Ariz., Tucson, 1968-73; dir. community affairs Tucson Med. Ctr., 1973-82; dir. pub. rels. Good Samaritan Med. Ctr., Phoenix, 1982-85; pres. The Lew Riggs Co., Phoenix, 1985-88; chief exec. officer Tucson Osteo. Med. Found., Tucson, 1988—; adj. prof. U. Ariz. Coll. Edn., Tucson, 1976-79; cons. to hosps. and physicians in group practice nationally; presenter in field. Editor: Public Relations Handbook, 1982; co-author booklets; contbr. articles to profl. jours. Chmn. pub. rels. Nat. Arthritis Found., Atlanta, 1985-87; participant Ariz. Strategic Planning and Econ. Devel., 1991-92. Lt. col. USAFR, 1987. Recipient Silver Anvil award Pub. Rels. Soc. Am., Golden Mike award Am. Legion Aux., MacEachern citation Acad. Hosp. Pub. Rels., Pres.'s citation Pub. Rels. Soc. Mem. Nat. Assn. Osteo. Founds. (pres. 1991—), Student Osteo. Med. Assn. (found. bd. dirs. 1990—), Acad. Hosp. Pub. Rels. (treas. 1980-81), Rotary. Republican. Methodist. Home: 5050 E South Regency Cir Tucson AZ 85711-3040 Office: Tucson Osteo Med Found 4280 N Campbell Ave Ste 200 Tucson AZ 85718-6585

RIGGS, FRED WARREN, political science educator; b. Kuling, China, July 3, 1917; (parents Am. citizens); s. Charles H. and Grace (Frederick) R.; m. Clara-Louise Mather, June 5, 1943; children: Gwendolyn, Ronald (dec.). Student, U. Nanking, China, 1934-35; BA, U. Ill., 1938; MA, Fletcher Sch. Law and Diplomacy, 1941; PhD, Columbia U., 1948. Lectr. CUNY, 1947-48; rsch. assoc. Fgn. Policy Assn., 1948-51; asst. dir. Pub. Adminstrn. Clearing House, N.Y.C., 1951-55; Arthur F. Bentley prof. govt. Ind. U., 1956-67; dir. Social Sci. Rsch. Inst. U. Hawaii, 1970-73, prof. polit. sci., 1967-87, prof. emeritus, 1987—; vis. asst. prof. Yale U., 1955-56; vis. lectr. Nat. Officials Tng. Inst., Korea, 1956; vis. prof. U. Philippines, 1958-59, MIT, 1965-66, CUNY, 1974-75; vis. scholar Inst. Soc. Studies, The Hague, 1972; sr. specialist East-West Ctr. U. Hawaii, 1962-63. Author: Pressures on Congress: A Study of the Repeal of Chinese Exclusion, 1950, reprinted, 1973, Formosa under Chinese Nationalist Rule, 1952, reprinted, 1972, The Ecology of Public Administration, 1961 (pub. in Portuguese, 1964), Administration in Developing Countries: The Theory of Prismatic Society, 1964 (pub. in Korean, 1966, Portuguese, 1968), Thailand: The Modernization of a Bureaucratic Polity, 1966, Organization Theory and International Development, 1969, Administrative Reform and Political Responsiveness: A Theory of Dynamic Balancing, 1971, Prismatic Society Revisited, 1973 (pub. in Korean, 1987), Applied Prismatics, 1978, (with Daya Krishna) Development Debate, 1987; author: (with others) Contemporary Political Systems: Classifications and Typologies, 1990, Handbook of Comparative and Development Public Administration, 1991, Terminology: Applications in Interdisciplinary Communication, 1993, Parliamentary vs. Presidential Government, 1993, Public Administration in the Global Village, 1994, International Studies Notes, 1994, Comparing Nations: Concepts, Strategies, Substance, 1994, Handbook of Bureaucracy, 1994; co-author, editor: Frontiers of Development Administration, 1971, Tower of Babel: On the Definition and Analysis of Concepts in the Social Sciences, 1975; mem. editorial bd. Pub. Adminstrn. Review, various other jours.; contbr. articles to profl. jours. Dir. INTERCOCTA project Internat. Social Sci. Coun., 1970-93; chair UNESCO com. INTERCONCEPT project, 1977-79; chair com. conceptual and terminol. analysis Comm. on Conceptual and terminologicsl Analysis, Internat. Polit. Sci. Assn., Internat. Sociol. Assn. and Internat. Social Sci. Coun., 1973-79; co-chair N.AM. roundtable on cooperation Social Sci. Info. Mpls., 1979; chair lexicographic terminology com. Dictionary Soc. N.Am., 1983-86. Decorated Order of White Elephant, King of Thailand, 1986; fellow com. comparative politics Social Sci. Rsch. Coun., 1957-58, Ctr. Advanced Study in Behavioral Scis., 1966-67; honoree Eastern Regional Orgn. Pub. Adminstrn. Conf., 1983. Mem. COVICO (co-chair com. on viable constitutionalism), Am. Polit. Sci. Assn., Am. Soc. Pub. Adminstrn. (chair comparative adminstrn. group 1960-71, Dwight Waldo award 1991), Internat. Studies Assn. (chair comparative interdisciplinary studies sect. 1970-74, v.p. 1970-71, co-chair com. on ethnicity, nationalism and migration 1995—), Internat. Polit. Sci. Assn., Internat. Sociol. Assn., Assn. Asian Studies (chair com. rsch. materials S.E. Asia 1969-73). Home: 3920 Lurline Dr Honolulu HI 96816-4006 Office: U Hawaii Political Science Dept 2424 Maile Way Honolulu HI 96822-2223

RIGGS, GINA GINSBERG, educational association administrator; b. Berlin, Germany, Mar. 29, 1921; came to U.S., 1945; d. Hugo Herz and Elisabeth Herrmanns; m. Sidney Ginsberg, Dec. 24, 1954 (dec. (Sept. 1974); children: Matt, Jill; m. Sheldon K. Riggs, June 5, 1976 (dec. Oct. 1985). Sales mgr. Consolidated Bus. Systems, N.Y.C., 1950-54; exec. dir. Gifted Child Soc., Glen Rock, N.J., 1968—; project dir. Parent Info. Network for Gifted; con. Nat. Rsch. Ctr. on Gifted and Talented. Contbr. articles to profl. publs. Charter mem. Leadership N.J., 1989—. Recipient cert. of merit U.S. Office Edn., 1980. Avocations: internat. peace, artificial intelligence. Home: 59 Glen Gray Rd Oakland NJ 07436 Office: Gifted Child Soc Inc 190 Rock Rd Glen Rock NJ 07452

RIGGS, GREGORY LYNN, lawyer; b. Columbus, Ohio, Apr. 21, 1948; s. Roy Albert and Edith Myrtle (Riggins) R.; m. Janet Kaye Adams, June 26, 1982; children: Caroline Ashley, Kristen Nicole. BA, U. NC., 1971, Oxford U., 1976; JD, Emory U., 1979. Atty. Delta Air Lines, Atlanta, 1979-84, sr. atty., 1984-92, asst. gen. counsel, 1992-94, assoc. gen. counsel, 1994—. Office: Delta Air Lines Inc Law Dept Hartsfield Internat Airport Atlanta GA 30320

RIGGS, HENRY EARLE, academic administrator, engineering management educator; b. Chgo., Feb. 25, 1935; s. Joseph Agnew and Gretchen (Walser) R.; m. Gayle Carson, May 17, 1958; children: Elizabeth, Peter, Catharine. BS, Stanford U., 1957; MBA, Harvard U., 1960. Indsl. economist SRI Internat., Menlo Park, Calif., 1960-63; v.p. Icore Industries, Sunnyvale, Calif., 1963-67, pres., 1967-70; v.p. fin. Measurex Corp., Cupertino, Calif., 1970-74; prof. engring. mgmt. Stanford U., Calif., 1974-88, Ford prof., 1986-88, v.p. for devel., 1983-88; pres. Harvey Mudd Coll., Claremont, Calif., 1988—; bd. dirs. Mutual Funds of capital Rsch. Group, Internat. Tech. Author: Accounting: A Survey, 1981, Managing High-Tech Companies, 1983, Financial and Cost Analysis, 1994; contbr. articles to Harvard Bus. Rev. Bd. dirs. Mt. Baldy Coun. Boy Scouts Am., 1993—. Baker scholar Harvard Bus. Sch., Boston, 1959; recipient Gores Teaching award Stanford U., 1980. Mem. Stanford U. Alumni Assn. (bd. dirs. 1990-94, chmn. 1993), Calif. Club, Pauma Valley Club, Sunset Club, Phi Beta Kappa, Tau Beta Pi. Congregationalist. Office: Harvey Mudd Coll Kingston Hall #201 Claremont CA 91711

RIGGS, JOHN ALAN, federal government official; b. Chgo., Feb. 19, 1943; s. Joseph Archie and Verna Anne (Christophel) R.; m. Judith Assmus, Mar. 8, 1975; 1 child, Michael Joseph. BA, Swarthmore Coll., 1964; MPA, Princeton U., 1966. Dir. peace corps tng. Princeton (N.J.) U., 1966; program officer Agy. for Internat. Devel., Saigon, Vietnam, 1966-71; capital devel. officer Agy. for Internat. Devel., Rio de Janeiro, Brazil, 1972; legislative asst. U.S. Ho. of Reps., Washington, 1973; campaign mgr. Sharp for Congress, Muncie, Ind., 1974; adminstrv. asst. U.S. Ho. of Reps., Washington, 1975-80; staff dir. House Fossil Fuels Subcom., Washington, 1981-86, House Energy and Power Subcom., Washington, 1987-93; dep. asst. sec. for policy U.S. Dept. Energy, Washington, 1993—; vis. lectr. U. Pa., Phila., 1989-93. Adult leader Boy Scouts Am., Washington, 1986-94; mem adv. com. Johns Hopkins Internat. Energy Program, Washington, 1986-93, alumni coun. Swarthmore (Pa.) Coll., 1993—. Recipient Superior Honor award U.S. Agy. for Internat. Devel., Washington, 1971. Home: 5230 Watson St NW Washington DC 20016 Office: Dept of Energy Policy 1000 Independence Ave SW Washington DC 20585-0001

RIGGS, LORRIN ANDREWS, psychologist, educator; b. Harput, Turkey, June 11, 1912; parents Am. citizens; s. Ernest Wilson and Alice (Shepard) R.; m. Doris Robinson, 1937 (dec.); children: Douglas Rikert, Dwight Alan; m. Caroline Cressman, 1994. A.B., Dartmouth Coll., 1933; M.A., Clark U., 1934, Ph.D., 1936. NRC fellow biol. scis. U. Pa., 1936-37; instr. U. Vt., 1937-38, 39-41; with Brown U., 1938-39, 41—, from asst. to assoc. prof., 1938-51, prof., 1951—, L. Herbert Ballou prof., 1960-68, E.J. Marston Univ. prof., 1968-77, prof. emeritus, 1977—; Guggenheim fellow U. Cambridge, 1971-72. Author sci. articles on vision, physiol. psychology. Recipient Kenneth Craik award Cambridge U., 1979, Prentice medal Am. Acad. Optometry, 1973. Mem. AAAS (chmn., v.p. sect. 1 1964), APA (div. pres. 1962-63, Disting. Sci. Contn. award 1974), Eastern Psychol. Assn. (pres. 1975-76), Optical Soc. Am. (Tillyer medal 1969, Ives medal 1982), Nat. Acad. Scis., Am. Physiol. Soc., Internat. Brain Rsch. Orgn., Soc. for

Neurosci., Soc. Exptl. Psychologists (Howard Crosby Warren medal 1957), Assn. Rsch. in Vision and Ophthalmology (pres. 1977, Friedenwald award 1966), Am. Acad. Arts and Scis., Am. Psychol. Soc. (William James fellow 1989), Sigma Xi (chpt. pres. 1962-64). Home: Kendal at Hanover # 104 80 Lyme Rd Hanover NH 03755-1225

RIGGS, MICHAEL DAVID, magazine editor, writer; b. Frankfort, Ky., Apr. 30, 1951; s. Homer David and Helen Marion (Webber) R.; m. Elizabeth Susan Borman, Apr. 24, 1983; children: David B., William B. AB, Washington U., 1973. Chief trader Thomte & Co., Boston, 1975-77; tech. writer Saddlebrook Corp., Cambridge, Mass., 1977-79; assoc. editor Mini-Micro Systems Mag., Boston, 1979-80; editor High Fidelity Mag., N.Y.C., 1980-89; exec. editor Stereo Review Mag., N.Y.C., 1989-95; editor-in-chief Audio Mag., N.Y.C., 1995—. Author: Understanding Audio and Video, 1989. Mem. Audio Engrng. Soc., Am. Society of Magazine Editors., Boston Audio Soc. Office: Audio Mag 1633 Broadway New York NY 10019-6708

RIGGS, RITA, costume designer; b. Boone County, Ark., Sept. 2, 1930; d. J. Almus and Ida V. (Keeling) Riggs; m. Charles S. Sharp, May 9, 1982 (dec. Sept. 1982). AA in Theatre Prodn., Santa Ana Coll., 1950; BA in Theatre Prodn., U. Ariz., 1952, MFA, 1954. Freelance designer Norman Lear's Tandem Prodns., L.A., 1970-80; costumer designer, pres. Rita Riggs Inc. Design Studio, L.A., 1980—; owner The Loft design studio, L.A., 1967—, Eureka Springs Train Sta., Ark., 1980—. Costume designer for numerous film, TV and theatrical prodns., including Divorce American Style, Seconds, The Professionals, The Model Shop, Petulia, The Lawyer, Happy Ending, Cold Turkey, Pro, Cinderella Liberty, Bite the Bullet, Electra Glide in Blue, Domino Principle, Night Moves, All in The Family, Sanford and Son, Maude, The Jeffersons, Good Times, One Day at a Time, Nancy Walker, All's Fair, Mary Hartman, Mary Hartman, Cattle Annie & Little Britches, The Idol Maker, Yes Giorgio, An Officer and A Gentleman, Deal of the Century, Women of Valor, Off Limits, Mr. North, Texasville, Broadway Bound, A Part of the Family, A Thing Called Love, The Last Outlaw, The Hunted. Home: 100 North Irving Blvd Los Angeles CA 90004 Office: The Loft Costume Studio 5971 West Third St Los Angeles CA 90036 Office: Rita Riggs Inc 5971 W 3d St Los Angeles CA 90036

RIGGS, SONYA WOICINSKI, elementary school educator; b. Newhall, Calif., Oct. 9, 1935; d. Jack Lewis Woicinski and Mittie Mozelle (Bennett) Gillett; m. Eugene Garland Riggs, Dec. 21, 1956; children: Georgia Ann, Madeline Sue, Dana Eugene. BS in Elem. Edn., U. Tex., 1970; MEd in Reading Edn., S.W. Tex. State U., 1980. Cert. elem. tchr., Tex.; cert. reading specialist K-12. Sec. state govts., Nebr./Tex., 1955-57; piano instr. Elgin, Tex., 1961-66; tchr. 1st grade Elgin Elem. Sch., Elgin, 1967-69, tchr. Music 3rd/4th grades, 1971-72, tchr. 4th grade, 1972-73; pres. El Tesoro internacionale, 1973-74; sec. region office Planned Parenthood/World Population, Austin, 1975-76; tchr. 8th-12th grades Giddings (Tex.) State Sch., 1976-78; tchr. 4th/5th grades Thorndale (Tex.) Ind. Sch. Dist., 1979-80; tchr. remedial reading Brazosport Ind. Sch. Dist., Freeport, Tex., 1980-81; tchr. 6th grade reading and chpt. I Bastrop (Tex.) Mid. Sch., 1981-94, Bastrop Intermediate, 1994—. Contbr. articles to Shih Tzu Reporter, 1993 French Bulldog Ann., French Bullytin, Boston Quar., Golden Retriever World; contbr. poetry to anthologies Garden of Life, 1996, Best Poems of 1996, 1996. Mem. Elgin Band Boosters, 1970-83, sec., 1976. Mem. Assn. Tex. Profl. Educators (campus rep. 1996-97), Austin Kennel Club (bd. dirs. 1990-91, 95—, sec. 1996-97), Am. Shih Tzu Club (edn. and rescue com. mem. south ctrl. regional hearing com.), French Bulldog Club Am. (rescue com.), Mission City Ring Stewards Assn., Internat. Soc. Poets, Austin Writers League. Avocations: exhibiting dogs to Am. Kennel Club championships, writing poetry, playing piano, drawing, painting.

RIGGS, TIMOTHY ALLAN, museum curator; b. New Haven, Conn., Feb. 15, 1942; s. Douglas Shepard and Robin (palmer) R.; divorced; 1 child, Emma; m. Carolyn P. Coolidge, June 25, 1995. BA, Swarthmore Coll., 1964; MA, Yale U., 1966, PhD, 1971. Rschr. Print Coun. Am., 1970-73; asst. curator Worcester (Mass.) Art Mus., 1973-76, curator prints and drawings, 1976-84; asst. dir. Ackland Art Mus., Chapel Hill, N.C., 1984—, acting dir., 1986, 94; adj. prof. U. N.C., Chapel Hill, 1984—. Contbr. catalogs. Mem. Print Coun. Am. (bd. dirs. 1981-84), Historians Netherlandish Art. Office: Ackland Art Mus U NC Chapel Hill CB # 3400 S Columbia St near Franklin St Chapel Hill NC 27599-3400

RIGGSBY, DUTCHIE SELLERS, education educator; b. Montgomery, Ala., Oct. 26, 1940; d. Cleveland Malcolm and Marcelia (Bedsole) Sellers; m. Ernest Duward Riggsby, Aug. 25, 1962; 1 child, Lyn. BS, Troy (Ala.) State Coll., 1962, MS, 1965; postgrad., George Peabody Coll., 1963; EdD, Auburn U., 1972. Cert. tchr., Ala., Ga.; cert. libr., Ga. Tchr. Montgomery Pub. Sch.s, 1962-63, Troy City Schs., 1963-67; instr. Auburn (Ala.) U., 1968-69; asst. prof. Columbus (Ga.) Coll., 1972-77, assoc. prof., 1978-83, prof., 1983—; coord. Instrnl. Tech. Sch. Edn., 1996—; vis. prof. U. P.R., Rio Piedras, 1972, 73; cons. schs. Columbus and Ft. Benning, Ga., 1980; leader various workshops, 1989, 93—; software reviewer Nat. Sci. Tchrs. Assn. Photographer: (book) Families, Professionals and Exceptionality, 1986, (textbook) Counseling Parents of Exceptional Children, 1986; contbr. more than 80 articles on state, regional, nat., and internat. programs to profl. jours., 1968—; reviewer instrnl. materials. Educator internal aerospace CAP, Maxwell AFB, 1980-90; dir. Air and Space Camp for Kids, 1990—. Recipient STAR Tchr. award Nat. Sci. Tchrs. Assn., Washington, 1968. Mem. Assn. for Ednl. Comms. and Tech. (non-periodical publs. com. 1994-96, awards com. 1994-96), Nat. Congress on Aviation and Space Edn. (dir. spl. promotions 1986-90), World Aerospace Edn. Orgn., Ga. Assn. Instrnl. Tech. (bd. dirs. 1982-84), Phi Delta Kappa (pres. Chattahochee Valley chpt. 1986-87, Svc. award 1989, Svc. Key award 1993). Baptist. Avocations: photography, mining for gemstones. Home: 1709 Ashwood Ct Columbus GA 31904-3009 Office: Columbus Coll Sch Edn 4225 University Ave Columbus GA 31907-5679

RIGGSBY, ERNEST DUWARD, science educator, educational development executive; b. Nashville, June 12, 1925; s. James Thomas and Anna Pearl (Turner) R.; m. Dutchie Sellers, Aug. 25, 1964; 1 child, Lyn-Dee. BS, Tenn. Polytech. Inst., 1948; BA, George Peabody Coll. Tchrs., 1952, George Peabody Coll. Tchrs., 1953; MA, George Peabody Coll. Tchrs., 1956, EdS, 1961, EdD, 1964. Vis. grad. prof. U. P.R., Rio Piedras, George Peabody Coll., 1963-64; prof. Auburn (Ala.) U., Troy (Ala.) State U., Columbus (Ga.) Coll.; pres. Ednl. Developers, Inc., Columbus, Ga.; vis. grad. prof. George Peabody Coll., 1963-64; vis. lectr. Fla. Inst. Tech., summers 1967-77. Contbr. articles to profl. jours. Col., USAF, 1944-85. Named to Aerospace Crown Cir., 1984; elected to Aerospace Edn. Hall of Fame, 1982. Fellow AAAS; mem. Nat. Sci. Tchrs. Assn., World Aerospace Edn. Assn. (v.p. for the Ams.). Home: Columbus Coll Columbus GA 31907-5645

RIGHTER, WALTER CAMERON, bishop; b. Phila., Oct. 23, 1923; s. Richard and Dorothy Mae (Bottomley) R.; m. Nancy Ruth DeGroot, Aug. 22, 1992; children: Richard, Rebecca. BA, U. Pitts., 1948; MDiv, Berkeley Div. Sch., New Haven, 1951, DD, 1972; DCL, Iowa Wesleyan U., 1982; DD, Seabury Western Sem., 1984. Ordained priest Episcopal Ch., 1951, consecrated bishop, 1972; lay missioner St. Michael's Ch., Rector, Pa., 1947-48; priest-in-charge All Saints Ch., Aliquippa, Pa., 1951-54, St. Luke's, Georgetown, Pa., 1952-54; rector Ch. of Good Shepherd, Nashua, N.H., 1954-71; bishop Diocese of Iowa, Des Moines, 1972-89; asst. bishop Dio. of Newark, 1989-91; interim rector St. Elizabeth's, Ridgewood, N.J., 1991; mem. exec. coun. Protestant Episcopal Ch. U.S.A., 1979-85; spl. adv. NH Cursillo, 1994-96. Mem. N.H. com. White House Conf. on Youth, 1962, Regional Crime Commn., Hillsboro County, N.H., 1969-71; trustee Nashua Libr., 1968-71, Seabury Western Sem., 1986-89; founding trustee The Morris Fund, Des Moines; planning com. Town of Alstead, N.H., 1993-96. Fellow Coll. Preachers, Washington Cathedral.

RIGHTS, GRAHAM HENRY, minister; b. Winston-Salem, N.C., Jan. 14, 1935; s. Douglas LeTell and Cecil Leona (Burton) R.; m. Sybil Critz Strupe, Sept. 7, 1963; children: Susan Elizabeth, John Graham. BA, U. N.C., 1956; BD, Yale U., 1959; postgrad., Moravian Theol. Sem., 1959-60, U. Edinburgh, Scotland, 1965-66; DD (hon.), Wofford Coll., 1989. Ordained to ministry Moravian Ch., 1960. Pastor Union Ch., Managua, Nicaragua, 1960-63, Managua Moravian Ch., 1960-65, Mayodan (N.C.) Moravian Ch., 1966-72, Messiah Moravian Ch., Winston-Salem, 1972-81; exec. dir. Bd. World Mission Moravian Ch., Bethlehem, Pa., 1981-83; pres. exec. bd. so. province Moravian Ch., Winston-Salem, 1983-95; pres. exec. bd. world-wide Moravian Ch., 1991-94; pastor First Moravian Ch., Greensboro, N.C., 1995—. Author: On the Roof of the World, 1961. Trustee Moravian Coll., Bethlehem, 1983-95, Moravian Theol. Sem., Bethlehem, 1983-95; bd. dirs. Crisis Control Ministry, Forsyth County, 1976—, Pastoral Care Found., N.C. Bapt. Hosp., 1990—, Ecumenical Inst., 1995—, Salemtowne Retirement Comty., 1996—, Moravian Ch. Found., 1988—. Home: 208 S Elam Ave Greensboro NC 27403 Office: 304 S Elam Ave Greensboro NC 27403

RIGOLOT, FRANÇOIS, French literature educator, literary critic; b. Château-du-Loir, Sarthe, France, May 21, 1939; s. Paul and Madeleine (Overnoy) R.; m. Carol Nolan, Sept. 5, 1970; children—Sophie, Stephanie. Diplôme, Hautes Etudes Commerciales, Paris, 1961; MA in Econs., Northwestern U., 1963; Ph.D. in French, U. Wis.-Madison, 1969. Asst. prof. U. Mich, Ann Arbor, 1969-74; bicentennial preceptor Princeton U., N.J., 1974-77, assoc. prof. dept. romance langs. and lits., 1977-79, prof., 1979-81, Meredith Howland Pyne prof. French lit., chmn. dept., 1984-91; chair Renaissance studies Princeton U., 1993—; prof. French Middlebury (Vt.) Coll., 1973; dir. NEH seminar for coll. tchrs., Princeton, 1981, 84, 86, 88, 90; vis. prof. Johns Hopkins U., 1981; vis. mem. Inst. for Advanced Study, Princeton, 1982-83; dir. seminar The Folger Inst., Washington, 1987; prof. Inst. d'Etudes Françaises, Avignon, 1989, 95; ofcl. lectr. Alliance Française, 1994-95. Author: Les Langages de Rabelais, 1972, Poétique et Onomastique, 1977, Le Texte de la Renaissance, 1982 (Gilbert Chinard Lit. prize 1984), Les Métamorphoses de Montaigne, 1988; editor: Complete Works of Louise Labé, 1986, Journal de Voyage of Montaigne, 1992; co-editor: A New History of French Literature, 1989 (MLA James Russell Lowell prize 1990), De la Littérature Française, 1993; collaborator: Sémantique de La Poésie, 1979. Recipient Médaille de la ville de Bordeaux, Médaille de la ville de Tours, 1992, Officier des Plames Académiques, 1993, Howard T. Behrman award for Disting. Achievement in the Humanities, 1993; NEH fellow, 1979-80, Guggenheim Found. fellow, 1982-83. Mem. Acad. Literary Studies, Am. Assn. Tchrs. French, Renaissance Soc. Am., MLA, Assn. Internat. des Etudes Françaises. Home: 81 Pretty Brook Rd Princeton NJ 08540-7537 Office: Princeton U East Pyne Dept Romance Langs and Lits Princeton NJ 08544-5264

RIGOR, BRADLEY GLENN, bank executive; b. Cheyenne Wells, Colo., Aug. 9, 1955; s. Glenn E. and Lelia (Teed) R.; m. Twyla G. Helweg, Sept. 4, 1983; children: Camille, Brent, Tiffany, Lauren. BS in Mktg., Ft. Hays State U., 1977; JD, Washburn U., 1980. Bar: Kans. 1980, U.S. Dist. Kans., 1980, U.S. Tax Ct. 1981, U.S. Ct. Appeals (10th cir.) 1982, U.S. Supreme Ct. 1986, Colo. 1990, Tex. 1991, U.S. Dist. Ct. Colo. 1991, Mo. 1993; cert. trust and fin. advisor. Ptnr. Zuspann & Rigor, Goodland, Kans., 1980-82; city atty. Goodland, 1981-82; asst. county atty. Wallace County, Sharon Springs, Kans., 1982-84, county atty., 1984; city atty. Sharon Springs, 1983-84; judge Mcpl. Ct., Goodland, 1988-93; ptnr. Fairbanks, Rigor & Irvin, P.A., Goodland, 1982-93; v.p., mgr. personal trusts Merchantile Bank, St. Joseph, Mo., 1993—. Mem. Kans. Bar Assn., Tex. Bar Assn., Mo. Bar Assn., Colo. Bar Assn., St. Joseph Bar Assn. Republican. Baptist. Office: Mercantile Bank St Joseph 415 Francis St PO Box 308 Saint Joseph MO 64501-1704

RIGOUTSOS, ISIDORE, computer scientist; b. Athens, Greece, Feb. 6, 1963; came to U.S., 1985; s. Ioannis and Fragkiska (Rafiopoulos) R. BS magna cum laude, Nat. U. Athens, 1984; MS, U. Rochester, 1987, NYU, 1989; PhD, NYU, 1992. Computational biology rschr. IBM Corp., Yorktown Heights, N.Y., 1992—. Fellow Fulbright Found., 1985-90. Mem. IEEE Computer Soc., AAAS, Assn. Computing Machinery. Roman Catholic. Avocation: photography. Office: IBM TJW Rsch Ctr PO Box 704 Yorktown Heights NY 10598

RIGSBEE, STEPHEN REESE, risk management executive; b. Durham, N.C., Mar. 11, 1956; s. William Alton and Shirley (Morgan) R.; m. Lisa Lou Sloan, Dec. 10, 1992. AB, Duke U., 1978; AM in Econs., U. Chgo., 1982, MBA, 1984. With Allstate Life Ins. Co., Northbrook, Ill., 1978-81; sr. v.p., dir. rsch. GNP Fin., Chgo., 1984-87; pres. Quantitative Risk Mgmt. Group, Chgo., 1987—. Co-author: Handbook of Mortgage Backed Securities, 1988, Asset/Liability Management, 1991, 96; contbr. articles to profl. jours. Mem. Chgo. Coun. on Fgn. Rels. Mem. Am. Fin. Assn., Beta Gamma Sigma. Republican. Home: 7th Fl 2314 N Lincoln Park W Chicago IL 60614-3455 Office: Quantitative Risk Mgmt Group 39 S La Salle St Ste 700 Chicago IL 60603-1606

RIGSBY, CAROLYN ERWIN, music educator; b. Franklinton, La., Apr. 11, 1936; d. Sheldon Aubrey and Edna Marie (Fussell) Erwin; m. Michael Hall Rigsby, May 30, 1959; 1 child, Laura Elaine Rigsby Boyd. B in Music Edn., Northwestern State U., La., 1958; MEd, Nicholls State U., 1970. Cert. vocal music tchr. k-12. Music tchr. Terrebonne Parish Sch., Houma, La., 1958-81, 81-83; music coord. Terrebonne Parish Sch., Houma, 1983-84; music tchr. Pasadena (Tex.) Ind. Sch. Dist., 1988—. Mem. Tex. Music Educators Assn., Packard Autombile Classics, Lone Star Packard Club, Delta Kappa Gamma (pres. 1988-90). Republican. Methodist. Avocations: Bay Area chorus, golf, gardening. Home: 16014 Mill Point Dr Houston TX 77059-5216

RIGSBY, LEE SCOTT, chemist, consultant; b. Ashland, Ky., Sept. 16, 1947; s. Leo Samuel and Gertrude (Woled) R.; m. Judith Eileen Greene, July 6, 1969; 1 child, Noel Scott Rigsby. BS in Chemistry, Marshall U., 1979; MBA, Xavier U., 1991. Shift supr. Armco Steel Corp., Ashland, 1974-77; lab. mgr. Tri-State Testing Co., Inc., Ashland, 1977-79, v.p., 1979-80; mgr. tech. svcs. Ashland Coal Inc., Huntington, W.Va., 1981-86; dir. tech. divsn. Standard Labs. Inc., Ashland, 1986-92; pres. Vanguard Solutions, Inc., Ashland, 1992—. Contbr. articles to profl. jours. Mem. ASTM (com. chmn. 1994), Am. Soc. for Quality Control (com. chmn. 1994), Am. Chem. Soc., Soc. Mining Engrs. Achievements include patents in field. Avocations: bicycling, golf, music. Office: Vanguard Solutions Inc 2104 13th St Ashland KY 41101-3520

RIHANI, SARMAD ALBERT (SAM RIHANI), civil engineer; b. Beirut, Lebanon, Feb. 22, 1954; s. John Albert and Loreen Salim (Schoucair) R.; m. Ina Lee Hand, July 12, 1975; children: Cedar, Paul, Michael. BSCE, Oreg. State U., 1977. Registered profl. engr., D.C., Va., Mo., Oreg., Calif. Designer Butler Mfg. Co., Kansas City, Mo., 1977-79; applications analyst United Computing Systems, Overland Park, Kans., 1979-80; mgmt. info. systems supr. Zamil Steel Bldgs. Co., Saudi Arabia, 1980-81, sr. structural engr., 1981-82, design mgr., 1982-84, engrng. mgr., 1984-87, bldg. products mgr., 1987-89; gen. mgr. multistory bldg. system Butler Mfg. Co., Kansas City, Mo., 1989-91; v.p. project mgmt. and engrng. Beaman Corp., Greensboro, N.C., 1991-92, bd. dirs.; divsn. svc. mgr. Varco-Pruden Bldgs., Little Rock, Ark., 1992-94; mng. dir. Options For Sr. America Corp., Rockville, Md., 1994—; bd. dirs. Engrs. Coun., Saudi Arabia, 1988-89. Am. Field Svc. scholar, 1970. Mem. ASCE (pres. Saudi Arabia 1988, bd. dirs. 1989, appreciation award 1989), Nat. Soc. Profl. Engrs., Am. Lebanese League (bd. dirs. 1990), Tau Beta Pi. Republican. Roman Catholic. Avocations: personal computers, reading, tennis, skiing.

RIKE, SUSAN, public relations executive; b. N.Y.C., Aug. 29, 1952; d. George Carson and Mildred Eleanor (Geehr) R. BA cum laude, Bklyn. Coll., 1975. Editl. asst. Artforum Mag., N.Y.C., 1975-77; co-owner Say Cheese, Bklyn., 1977-80; editl. asst. The Star, N.Y.C., 1980-82; acct. sec. Robert Marston and Assocs., N.Y.C., 1983-84; asst. acct. exec. Marketshare, N.Y.C., 1984; acct. exec. Doremus Pub. Rels. BBDO Internat., N.Y.C., 1984-86; pres. Susan Rike Pub. Rels., Bklyn., 1986—. Democrat. Avocations: travel, music festivals and concerts, literature. Office: Susan Rike Pub Rels 335 State St Ste 3C Brooklyn NY 11217-1719

RIKER, WALTER F., JR., pharmacologist, physician; b. N.Y.C., Mar. 8, 1916; s. Walter F. and Eleanore Louise (Scafard) R.; m. Virginia Helene Jaeger, Nov. 28, 1941; children: Donald K., Walter F., Wayne S. BS, Columbia U., 1939; MD, Cornell U., 1943; D.Sc. (hon.), Med. Coll. Ohio, 1980. Instr. pharmacology Cornell U. Med. Coll., N.Y.C., 1944-47; instr. medicine Cornell U. Med. Coll., 1945-46, asst. prof. pharmacology, 1947-50, assoc. prof., 1950-56, prof., chmn. dept. pharmacology, 1956-83, Revlon chair pharmacology and toxicology, 1980-83, prof. emeritus, 1983—; mem. study sect. NIH, 1956-63, 65-68; mem. Nat. Inst. Gen. Med. Scis. Council., 1963-64, Nat. Inst. Environ. Health Scis. Council, 1971-75, Pres.'s Sci. Adv. Com. on Toxicology, 1964-65; vis. prof. pharmacology U. Kans. Med. Coll., 1953; mem. Unitarian Service Med. Exchange Program, Japan, 1956; mem. sci. adv. com. Pharm. Mfrs.'s Assn. Found., 1966-87; adj. mem. Roche Inst. Molecular Biology, 1972-80; med. advisor on drugs Nat. Football League, 1973-84; adv. com. Irma T. Hirschl Found., N.Y.C., 1973—; bd. sci. advisors Sterling Drug, 1973-76; dir. Richardson-Vicks Inc., 1979-85. Recipient Teaching award Cornell U. Med. Coll., 1968, 78, citation Pharm. Mfrs.'s Assn. Found., 1972, 87, Award of Distinction Cornell U. Med. Coll. Alumni Assn., 1981, Maurice R. Greenberg Svc. award N.Y. Hosp./Cornell U. Med. Ctr., 1990; Sterling Drug vis. professorship established in honor at Cornell U. Med. Coll., 1979; named Hon. Fellow, Am. Coll. Clin. Pharmacology, 1987. Fellow AAAS, N.Y. Acad. Medicine, Harvey Soc.; mem. Am. Soc. Pharmacology and Exptl. Therapeutics (chmn. membership com. 1956-59, councillor 1959-62, bd. publs. trustees 1962-64, chmn. bd. publs. trustees 1962-70, chmn. com. ednl. and profl. affairs 1972-74, John Jacob Abel award 1951, Publs. citation 1970, Torald Sollman award 1986, Oscar B. Hunter award 1990), Japanese Pharmacology Soc., Am. Soc. Clin. Pharmacology and Therapeutics, N.Y. Acad. Scis., Sigma Xi, Alpha Omega Alpha. Office: Cornell U Med Coll 1300 York Ave New York NY 10021-4805

RIKER, WILLIAM KAY, pharmacologist, educator; b. N.Y.C., Aug. 31, 1925; s. Walter Franklin and Eleanore Louise (Scafard) R.; m. Carmela Louise DePamphilis, Dec. 21, 1947 (dec. 1981); children: Eleanor Louise, Gainor, Victoria; m. Leena Mela, Aug. 13, 1983. B.A., Columbia U., 1949; M.D., Cornell U., 1953. Intern 2d Cornell med. div., Bellevue Hosp., 1953-54; practice medicine, specializing in pharmacology Phila., 1954-69, Portland, Oreg., 1969—; instr., asst. prof. dept. pharmacology U. Pa. Sch. Medicine, 1954-61; spl. fellow dept. physiology U. Utah Sch. Medicine, 1961-64; assoc. prof., prof., chmn. dept. pharmacology Woman's Med. Coll., Phila., 1964-69; prof., chmn. dept. pharmacology U. Oreg. Sch. Medicine, U. Oreg. Health Scis. Center, 1969-91, prof. emeritus, 1991—, asst. dean. for admissions, 1986-89; mem. neurol. disorders program project com. NIH, 1975-79. Editor: Jour. Pharmacology and Exptl. Therapeutics, 1969-72; contbr. articles to biomed. jours. Served with USNR, 1943-46. Recipient Christian R. and Mary F. Lindback Found. award for disting. teaching, 1968; Pa. Plan scholar, 1957-61; Nat. Inst. Neurol. Diseases and Blindness spl. fellow, 1961-64; USPHS-NIH research grantee, 1958-83. Mem. Am. Soc. Pharmacology and Exptl. Therapeutics (sec.-treas. 1978-81, pres. 1985-86), Western Pharmacol. Soc. (pres. 1976), Japanese Pharmacol. Soc., Assn. Med. Sch. Pharmacologists (sec. 1976-78), Epilepsy Assn. Am., Pharm. Mfrs. Assn. Found. (chmn. pharmacology-morphology adv. com., sci. adv. com. 1976-92), Cosmos Club. Home: 4326 SW Warrensway Portland OR 97221

RIKKERS, LAYTON FREDERICK, surgeon; b. Fond du Lac, Wis., Jan. 31, 1944; s. Judson John and Dorothy (Layton) R.; m. Diane Lynn Foster, Aug. 20, 1966; children: Steven, Kristin. BS, U. Wis., 1966; MD, Stanford U. Sch. Medicine, 1970. Diplomate Nat. Bd. Med. Examiners, Am. Bd. Surgery. Intern U. Utah Sch. Medicine, Salt Lake City, 1970-71, surgical residency, 1971-76; instr. surgery Emory U. Sch. Medicine, Atlanta, 1976-77; from asst. prof. surgery to acting chmn. div. gen. surgery U. Utah Sch. Medicine, Salt Lake City, 1977-84; prof., chmn. dept. surgery U. Nebr. Med. Ctr., Omaha, 1984-96; chmn. dept. surgery U. Wis., Madison, 1996—; interim dean Coll. Medicine, U. Nebr. Coll. Medicine, 1991-93, M.M. Musselman prof. surgery, 1990—; cons. Omaha Vet. Adminstrv. Ctr., 1984-86, NIH, 1992, Gov.'s Blue Ribbon Coalition on Health Care, Nebr., 1993-94. Editor: Surgical Clinics of North America, 1990; contbr. articles to profl. jours. Mem. Am. Surgical Assn., Am. Coll. Surgeons (com. chair 1993-95), Am. Bd. Surgery (clin. chmn. 1994-95), Soc. Clin. Surgery (pres.-elect 1994-95). Episcopalian. Avocations: hiking, reading, skiing, travel. Office: U Wis H4/710 Clin Sci Ctr 600 Highland Ave Madison WI 53792-0001

RIKLI, DONALD CARL, lawyer; b. Highland, Ill., June 16, 1927; s. Carl and Gertrude Louise (Stoecklin) R.; m. Joan Tate, Oct. 10, 1953; children: Kristine, David. AB, Ill. Coll., 1951; JD, U. Ill., 1953. Bar: Ill. 1953, U.S. Dist. Ct. (so. dist.) Ill. 1961, U.S. Ct. Appeals (7th cir.) 1968, U.S. Supreme Ct. 1974. Pvt. practice law Highland, 1953—; atty. City of Highland, 1956-59; lectr. in field. Author: The Illinois Probate System, 1974, 75, 77, 78; bd. editors Illinois Real Property I, 1966, 71, Lawyers World, 1970-72, Law Notes, 1981-83, The Compleat Lawyer, 1985-87; contbr. over 60 articles to profl. jours. Mem. consistory United Ch. of Christ, 1960-62, 93-95. With U.S. Army, 1945-47. Fellow Am. Coll. Trust and Estate Counsel, Ill. Bar Found., Am. Bar Found.; mem. ABA (sec. chairperson gen. practice sect. 1990-91, Ho. of Dels. 1991-93, mem. coun. gen. practice sect. 1981-93, Sole Practitioner of Yr. 1990), Ill. Bar Assn. (chmn. Bill of Rights com. 1967-68, coun. estate planning probate and trust sect. 1976-81, sec. 1980-81), Madison County Bar Assn. (pres. 1966-67), Am. Acad. Estate Planning Attys. (bd. govs. 1994-95). Home: 1312 Old Trenton Rd Highland IL 62249-2028 Office: 914 Broadway Highland IL 62249-1897

RIKLIS, MESHULAM, manufacturing and retail executive; b. Turkey, Dec. 2, 1923; came to U.S., 1947, naturalized, 1955; s. Pinhas and Betty (Guberer) R.; children: Simona Riklis Ackerman, Marcia Riklis Hirschfeld, Ira Doron, Kady Zadora Riklis, Kristofer Riklis. Student, U. Mexico, 1947; BA, Ohio State U., 1950, MBA, 1968. Co-dir. youth activities and mil. tng. Hertzlia High Sch., Tel-Aviv, 1942; tchr. Hebrew Talmud Torah Sch., Mpls., 1951; research dept. Piper, Jaffray & Hopwood, 1951-53, sales rep., 1953-56; vice chmn. McCrory Corp., N.Y.C., 1960-69, vice chmn. exec. com., from 1970, chmn., 1975-85, dir., former pres.; with Rapid-Am. Corp., N.Y.C., 1956—, chmn., 1956—, pres., chief exec. officer, 1957-73, chmn., chief exec. officer, 1973-76, chmn., pres., chief exec. officer, 1976—; E-II Holdins, 1988-90. Served Brit. 8th Army, 1942-46. Mem. Pi Mu Epsilon. Jewish. Office: McCrory Corp 667 Madison Ave 12th Fl New York NY 10021 also: Riklis Family Corp 2901 Las Vegas Blvd S Las Vegas NV 89109-1930*

RIKON, MICHAEL, lawyer; b. Bklyn., Feb. 2, 1945; s. Charles and Ruth (Shapiro) R.; m. Leslie Sharon Rein, Feb. 11, 1968; children: Carrie Rachel, Joshua Howard. BS, N.Y. Inst. Tech., 1966; JD, Bklyn. Law Sch., 1969; LLM, NYU, 1974. Bar: N.Y. 1970, U.S. Dist. Ct. (so. and ea. dists.) N.Y. 1971, U.S. Ct. Appeals (2d cir.) 1972, U.S. Supreme Ct. 1973, U.S. Ct. Appeals (5th and 11th cirs.) 1981. Asst. corp. counsel City of N.Y., 1969-73; law clk. N.Y. State Ct. Claims, 1973-80; ptnr. Rudick and Rikon, P.C., N.Y.C., 1980-88; pvt. practice, N.Y.C., 1988-94; ptnr. Goldstein, Goldstein and Rikon, P.C., N.Y.C., 1994—. Contbr. articles to profl. jours. Pres. Village Greens Residents Assn., 1978-79; chmn. bd. Arden Heights Jewish Ctr., Staten Island, N.Y., 1976-77; pres. North Shore Republican Club, 1977; mem. community bd. Staten Island Borough Pres., 1977. Mem. ABA, ATLA, TLPJ Found., N.Y. State Bar Assn. (spl. com. of condemnation law), Suffolk County Bar Assn., N.Y. County Lawyers Assn. Republican. Jewish. Avocations: collecting stamps, photography, collecting miniature soldiers. Home: 133 Avondale Rd Ridgewood NJ 07450-1301 Office: 80 Pine St New York NY 10005

RIKOSKI, RICHARD ANTHONY, engineering executive, electrical engineer; b. Kingston, Pa., Aug. 13, 1941; s. Stanley George and Nellie (Gober) R.; m. Giannina Batchelor Petrullo, Dec. 18, 1971 (div. 1979); children: Richard James, Jennifer Anne. BEE, U. Detroit, 1964; MSEE, Carnegie Inst. Tech., 1965; PhD, Carnegie-Mellon U., 1968; postdoctoral student, Case-Western Res. U./NASA, 1971. Registered profl. engr., Ill., Mass., Pa. Engr. 1st communication satellite systems Internat. Tel. & Tel., Nutley, N.J., 1961-64; engr. Titan II ICBM program Gen. Motors, Milw., 1964; trainee NASA, 1964-67; instr. Carnegie-Mellon U., Pitts., 1966-68; asst. prof. U. Pa., Phila., 1968-74; assoc. prof., dir. hybrid microelectronics lab., chmn. ednl. TV com. IIT, Chgo., 1974-80, chmn. ednl. TV com., 1974-80; rsch. engr. nuclear effects ITT Rsch. Inst., Chgo., 1974-75; pres. Tech. Analysis Corp., Chgo., 1980—; engr. color TV colorimetry Hazeltine Rsch., Chgo., 1969; engr. Metroliner rail car/roadbed ride quality dynamics analysis U.S. Dept. Transp., ENSCO, Inc., Springfield, Va., 1970; pres. Tech. Analysis Corp., Chgo., 1978-91; contractor analysis of color TV receiver safety hazards U.S. Consumer Product Safety Commn., 1977, analysis heating effect in aluminum wire Beverly Hills Supper Club Fire, Covington, Ky., 1978; engr. GFCI patent infringement study 3M Corp., St. Paul, 1979-81; elec. systems analyst Coca-Cola Corp., Atlanta, 1983-91; fire investigator McDonald's Corp., Oak Brook, Ill., 1987-90; engrng. analyst telephone switching ctrs. ATT, Chgo., 1990-91; expert witness numerous other govtl.

and corp. procs. Author: Hybrid Microelectronic Circuits, 1973; editor: Hybrid Microelectronic Technology, 1973; contbr. articles to profl. jours. Officer Planning Commn., Beverly Shores, Ind., 1987-93, trustee town coun., 1992—, police liason 1993—; mem. Chgo. Coun. Fgn. Rels., USAF SAC Comdrs. Disting. Vis. Program; adv. coun. Nat. Park Svc. Ind. Dunes Nat. Lake Shore, 1993—. NASA fellow, 1964-67, 70. Mem. IEEE (sr. ednl. activities bd. N.Y.C. 1970-74, USAB career devel. com. 1972-74, editor Soundings 1973-75, Cassette Colloquia 1973-74, del. Popov Soc. Tech. Exch. USSR, mgr. Dial Access Tech. Edn. program 1972), Assn. for Media Based Continuing Engring. Edn. (bd. dirs.), Nat. Fire Protection Assn., Sigma Xi, Tau Beta Pi, Eta Kappa Nu. Republican. Avocations: sailing, travel. Home: One E Lakefront Dr Beverly Shores IN 46301-0444 Office: Tech Analysis Corp 3600 N Lake Shore Dr Chicago IL 60613-4656

RILES, WILSON CAMANZA, educational consultant; b. Alexandria, La., June 27, 1917; m. Mary Louise Phillips, Nov. 13, 1941; children: Michael, Narvia Riles Bostick, Wilson, Phillip. B.A., No. Ariz. U., 1940; M.A., 1947, LL.D., 1976; LL.D., Pepperdine Coll., 1965, Claremont Grad. Sch., 1972, U. So. Calif., 1975, U. Akron, 1976, Golden Gate U., 1981; L.H.D., St. Mary's Coll., 1971, U. Pacific, 1971, U. Judaism, 1972. Tchr. elem. schs., adminstr. pub. schs. Ariz., 1940-54; exec. sec. Pacific Coast region Fellowship of Reconciliation, Los Angeles, 1954-58; with Calif. Dept. Edn., 1958-83, dep. supt. pub. instrn., 1965-70, supt. pub. instruction, 1971-83; pres. Wilson Riles & Assocs., Inc., 1983—; dir. emeritus Wells Fargo Bank, Wells Fargo Co. Past mem. editorial adv. bd.: Early Years mag. Ex-officio mem. bd. regents U. Calif., 1971-82; ex-officio trustee Calif. State Univs. and Colls., 1971-82; nat. adv. council Nat. Schs. Vol. Program; former mem. council Stanford Research Inst.; former mem. adv. council Stanford U. Sch. Bus.; former mem. adv. bd. Calif. Congress Parents and Tchrs.; former trustee Am. Coll. Testing Program; former mem. Edn. Commn. of States; past 2d v.p. Nat. PTA.; former trustee Found. Teaching Econs.; former mem. Joint Council Econ. Edn.; former mem. Nat. Council for Children and TV. With USAF, 1943-46. Recipient Spingarn medal NAACP, 1973. Mem. Assn. Calif. Sch. Adminstrs., Cleve. Conf., NAACP (Spingarn medal 1973), Nat. Acad. Pub. Adminstrn., Phi Beta Kappa. Office: 400 Capitol Mall Ste 1540 Sacramento CA 95814-4408 *Is growing up in rural Louisiana during the depression as an orphan, poor and black, attending a segregated school, a handicap? I have never thought so. Maybe it's because of the superb teachers who never let me feel sorry for myself. As I recall, some did not even have college degrees, but they believed I could learn. Because they did, it never occurred to me that I couldn't. Forrest Paul Augustine, the principal, admonished us to get as much education as we could because, "that is one thing no one can ever take away from you". I chose education as a career because those humble public schools gave me a chance. I want all boys and girls to have a chance, too.*

RILEY, ANN J., state legislator, technology specialist; b. Memphis, Oct. 27, 1940; m. Ray T. Riley, Apr. 28, 1962. BSBA, U. Albuquerque, 1985; MBA, Webster U., 1988; cert. in pub. policy, Harvard U., 1994. Loan officer Ravenswood Bank, Chgo., 1970-74; mgr. dist. sales Security Lockout, Chgo., 1974-77; owner AR Fasteners, Albuquerque, 1977-82; tech. transfer agt. Sandia Nat. Labs., Albuquerque, 1983—; mem. N.Mex. Senate, Santa Fe, 1993—; resolutions chair energy com. Nat. Order of Women Legis. Nat. Conf. State Legislators. Bd. dirs. All Faiths Receiving Home. Albuquerque, 1989-92, Law Enforcement Acad., Santa Fe, 1991-92; active Leadership Albuquerque, 1991, state federal task force U.S. Office Sci. & Tech., 1995. Flemming fellow Am. U. Ctr. for Policy Alternatives, 1996. Democrat. Avocations: running, bicycling, politics, reading. Home: 10301 Karen Ave NE Albuquerque NM 87111-3633

RILEY, ANTHONY WILLIAM, German language and literature educator; b. Radcliffe-on-Trent, Eng., July 23, 1929; s. Cyril Frederick and Winifred Mary (White) R.; m. Maria Theresia Walter, July 16, 1955; children: Christopher, Katherine, Angela. B.A. with honors, U. Manchester, Eng., 1952; Dr. Phil., U. Tübingen, Fed. Republic Germany, 1958. Lectr. U. Tübingen, 1957-59, 60-62; asst. lectr. Queen Mary Coll., U. London, Eng., 1959-60; asst. prof. German lang. and lit. Queen's U., Kingston, Ont., Can., 1962-65; asso. prof. Queen's U., 1965-68, prof., 1968-92; emeritus prof. Queen's U., Kingston, Ont., Can., 1993—; head dept. German lang. and lit. Queen's U., 1967-76, acting head dept., 1979-80, 86-87; vis. prof. U. Munich, 1996. Author: Elisabeth Langgässer Bibliographie mit Nachlassbericht, 1970; also articles on Elisabeth Langgässer, Alfred Döblin, Thomas Mann, Herman Hesse, Frederick Philip Grove, Joseph Wittig; co-editor: The Master Mason's House (F.P. Grove), 1976, Echoes and Influences of German Romanticism, 1987, Muse and Reason, The Relation of Arts and Sciences 1650-1850, 1994; co-translator, co-editor: Fanny Essler, 2 vols. (Grove), 1984; editor: Der Oberst und der Dichter/Die Pilgerin Aetheria (Alfred Doblin), 1978, Der unsterbliche Mensch/Der Kampf mit dem. Engel (Alfred Doblin), 1980, Jagende Rosse/Der Schwarze Vorhang (Alfred Doblin), 1981, Wadzeks Kampf mit der Dampfturbine (Alfred Doblin), Kleine Schriften I (1902-1921) (Doblin), 1985, Kleine Schriften II (1922-24) (Doblin), 1990, Schicksalsreise (Döblin), 1993. Served with Brit. Army, 1947-49. Summer fellow Weil Inst. for Studies in Religion and the Humanities, Cin., 1965; Can. Council Leave fellow, 1969-70, 76-77, 83-84. Fellow Royal Soc. Can. (sec. acad. humanities and social scis. 1992-95); mem. Can. Assn. Univ. Tchrs. German (v.p. 1973-75, pres. 197-576, Hermann Boeschenstein medal 1987, Konrad Adenauer rsch. award Alexander von Humboldt Found. 1989), deutsche Schillergesellschaft, Internat. Alfred Döblin-Gesellschaft (v.p. 1984-95), Internat. Assn. for German Studies, Elisabeth Langgässer-Gesellschaft (Darmstadt). Home: 108 Queen Mary Rd, Kingston, ON Canada K7M 2A5

RILEY, CARROLL LAVERN, anthropology educator; b. Summersville, Mo., Apr. 18, 1923; s. Benjamin F. and Minnie B. (Smith) R.; m. Brent Robinson Locke, Mar. 25, 1948; children: Benjamin Locke, Victoria Smith Evans, Cynthia Winningham. A.B., U. N.Mex., 1948, Ph.D., 1952; M.A., UCLA, 1950. Instr. U. Colo., Boulder, 1953-54; asst. prof. U. N.C., Chapel Hill, 1954-55; asst. prof. So. Ill. U., Carbondale, 1955-60, assoc. prof., 1960-67, prof., 1967-86, Disting. prof., 1986-87, Disting. prof. emeritus, 1987—, chmn. dept., 1979-82, dir. mus., 1972-74; rsch. assoc. lab. anthropology Mus. N.Mex., 1987—; rsch. collaborator Smithsonian Instn., 1988—; adj. prof. N.Mex. Highlands U., 1989—. Author: The Origins of Civilization, 1969, The Frontier People, 1982, expanded edit., 1987, Rio del Norte, 1995, Bandelier, 1996; editor: Man Across the Sea, 1971, Southwestern Journals of Adolph F. Bandelier, 4 vols., 1966, 70, 75, 84, Across the Chichimec Sea, 1978, others; contbr. numerous articles to profl. jours. Served in USAAF, 1942-45. Decorated 4 battle stars; grantee Social Sci. Research Council, NIH, Am. Philos. Soc., Am. Council Learned Socs., NEH, others. Home and Office: 1106 6th St Las Vegas NM 87701-4311

RILEY, DANIEL EDWARD, air force officer; b. Flint, Mich., Aug. 18, 1915; s. Daniel Edward and Elva (Kirby) R.; m. Margaret E. Marengo, Nov. 28, 1938; children—Dennis M., Patricia A., Daniel R. B. Aero. Engring., U. Detroit, 1940; M.B.A., U. Mich., 1951; postgrad., Indsl. Coll. of Armed Forces, 1959. Commd. 2d lt. USAAF, 1936; advanced through grades to maj. gen. USAF, 1968; chief of plans and ops. (7290th Procurement Squadron at), Rhein/Main Air Base, Germany, 1951-1952; dep., later chief of procurement and prodn. div. (Hdqrs. USAF in), Europe; also comdr. (7290th Procurement Squadron), 1952-54; dep. chief of staff materiel (Directorate of Procurement and Prodn., Hdqrs. USAF), 1954-58; program dir. (MACE missile Air Research and Devel. Command), Wright-Patterson AFB, Ohio, 1959-60; program dir. SAC C&C Systems AFSC, 1961-63; vice comdr. (Electronics Systems div. AFSC), Bedford, Mass., 1965; comdr. (Air Force Contract Mgmt. Div.), Los Angeles, 1965-69; asst. dir. (Def. Supply Agy.), Washington, 1969-70; asst. to pres. Novatronics Inc., Pompano Beach, Fla., 1976-77. Decorated Legion of Merit with 2 oak leaf clusters. Mem. Air Force Assn., Ret. Officer Assn., Embry-Riddle Aero U. Bd. of Visitors, Indsl. Coll. Armed Forces Assn., Mil. Order World Wars, Lindbergh Fund, Halifax River Yacht Club, Beta Gamma Sigma, Phi Kappa Phi. Home: 1566 Poplar Dr Ormond Beach FL 32174-3414

RILEY, DANIEL JOSEPH, lawyer, educator; b. Amarillo, Tex., Jan. 14, 1947; s. Roy Weldon and Joette Aline (Winger) R.; m. Glenda Joy Hoel, Apr. 15, 1947; children: Carla Annette, Ragan Patrick. BA cum laude, U. Tex., 1969, JD summa cum laude, 1971. Bar: Tex. 1971, U.S. Ct. Fed. Claims 1974, U.S. Supreme Ct. 1979, U.S. Ct. Appeals (fed. cir.) 1982. Ptnr. Baker & Botts LLP, Washington, 1977—; adj. prof. grad. sch. U. Dallas, 1983—. Assoc. editor U. Tex. Law Rev., 1970. Mem. constitution rev. com. State of Tex., Austin, 1978. Mem. ABA (uniform state procurement code com. 1980), Nat. Contract Mgmt. Assn. (bd. advisors), Tex. Bar Found., Tex. Bar Assn., Dallas Bar Assn., Order of Coif, Phi Beta Kappa. Republican. Home: 712 W Braddock Rd Alexandria VA 22302 Office: Baker & Botts LLP 1299 Pennsylvania Ave NW Washington DC 20004

RILEY, DAWN C., special education educator, educational philosopher, researcher; b. Rochester, N.Y., Mar. 18, 1954; d. John Joseph Jr. and June Carol (Cleveland) R. BA in Edn., Polit. Sci., SUNY, 1976; MEd, in Special Edn., summa cum laude, U. Ariz., 1980; PhD, Univ. Calif., Berkeley, 1994. Cert. multiple subject credential (K-Coll.), specialist credential (K-12), Calif., coun. of educators for deaf; elem. permanent credential, N.Y. Elem. sch. tchr., 4th grade Escola Americana do Rio de Janeiro, Brazil, 1975; pvt. practice, comml. artist Rochester, 1972-80; elem. tchr. Rochester City Sch. Dist., 1976-78; rsch. asst., summer vestibule program The Nat. Tech. Inst. for Deaf, 1976-79; tchr. English, 7th-12th grades The Calif. Sch. for Deaf, 1980-94; rsch. asst. to Dr. Richard J. Morris The Univ. Ariz., 1978-80; rsch. asst., Calif. new tchr. support project The Far West Lab. for Ednl. R & D., San Francisco, 1989; chair high sch. English dept. The Calif. Sch. for Deaf, 1990—; coord. & devel. Practical Lang. in Applied Settings Program, 1981-82; chair Computer Curriculum Com., 1982-84, Critical and Creative Thinking Skills Com., 1983-84; coord. Gifted and Talented Program, 1983—. Recipient Kate Navin O'Neill Grad. scholar Univ. of Calif., Berkeley, 1989; University fellow, 1978-80, Evelyn Lois Corey fellow, 1990; Recipient Sustained Superior Accomplishment award Calif. Dept. Edn., 1991. Mem. AAUW, Nat.Coun. Tchrs. of English, Am. Ednl. Rsch. Assn., Am. Assn. Colls. for Tchr. Edn., Philosophy of Edn. Soc., John Dewey Soc., Phi Beta Kappa. Home: 3015 58th Ave Oakland CA 94605-1123 Office: Calif Sch for the Deaf 39350 Gallaudet Dr Fremont CA 94538-2308

RILEY, DOROTHY COMSTOCK, judge; b. Detroit, Dec. 6, 1924; d. Charles Austin and Josephine (Grima) Comstock; m. Wallace Don Riley, Sept. 13, 1963; 1 child, Peter Comstock. BA with honors in Polit. Sci., Wayne State U., 1946, LLB, 1949; LLD (hon.), Alma Coll., 1988, U. Detroit, 1990. Bar: Mich. 1950, U.S. Dist. Ct. (ea. dist.) Mich. 1950, U.S. Supreme Ct. 1957. Atty. Wayne County Friend of Ct., Detroit, 1956-68; ptnr. Riley & Roumell, Detroit, 1968-72, 73-76; judge Wayne County Cir., Detroit, 1972, Mich. Ct. Appeals, Detroit, 1976-82; assoc. justice Mich. Supreme Ct., Detroit, 1982-83, 85—, chief justice, 1987-91; mem. U.S. Jud. Conf. Commn. on State-Fed. Ct. Rels.; chmn. tort reform com. Conf. of Chief Justices; bd. dirs. Nat. Ctr. for State Cts., Thomas J. Cooley Law Sch. Co-author manuals, articles in field. Mem. steering com. Mich. Children Skillman Found., 1992; mem. multistate profl. responsibility exam. com. Nat. Conf. Bar Examiners, 1992. Recipient Disting. Alumni award Wayne U., 1990; Headliner award Women of Wayne, 1977; Donnelly award, 1946; Law Enforcement Commendation medal Nat. Soc. Sons of Am. Revolution, 1991; inducted in Mich. Women's Hall of Fame, 1991. Mem. ABA (family law sect. 1965—, vice chmn. gen. practice sect. com. on juvenile justice 1975-80, mem. jud. adminstrn. sect. 1973—, standing com. on fed. ct. improvements, mem. judges adv. com. of standing com. on ethics and profl. responsibility 1992), Am. Judicature Soc., Fellows Am. Bar Found., Mich. State Bar Found., State Bar Mich. (civil liberties com. 1954-58), Detroit Bar Assn. (pub. rels. com. 1955-56, author Com. in Action column, Detroit Lawyers 1955, chmn. friend of ct. and family law com. 1974-75), Nat. Women Judges Assn., Nat. Women Lawyers Assn., Women Lawyers Assn. Mich. (pres. 1957-58), Mich. Sup. Ct. Hist. Soc., Karyatides, Pi Sigma Alpha. Republican. Roman Catholic. Avocations: reading, gardening. Office: Mich Supreme Ct 500 Woodward Ave Fl 20 Detroit MI 48226-3423

RILEY, GEORGIANNE MARIE, lawyer; b. Chgo., Feb. 5, 1953. BA in Psychology, Drake U., 1974, JD, 1978. Bar: Ill., 1978. Chief counsel Ill. Indsl. Commn., Chgo., 1979-83; dep. chief counsel Ill. Dept. Transp., Chgo., 1983-89; counsel Chem. Waste Mgmt., Oakbrook, Ill., 1989-91, sr. counsel, 1991-92; gen. counsel, v.p., sec. Rust Indsl. Svcs., Westchester, Ill., 1993—. Office: Waste Mgmt Inc 3003 Butterfield Rd Oak Brook IL 60521-1107

RILEY, GRESHAM, museum administrator. Pres. Mus. Am. Art, Pa. Acad. Fine Arts, Phila. Office: Mus Am Art Pa Acad Fine Arts 118 N Broad St Philadelphia PA 19102

RILEY, HAROLD JOHN, JR., manufacturing executive; b. Syracuse, N.Y., Nov. 13, 1940; s. Harold John and Esther Emma (Denmark) R.; m. Diane Marie Slattery, June 15, 1963; children—Beth Ann, Thomas, Patrick. B.S. in Indsl. Engring., Syracuse U., 1961; postgrad., Harvard Bus. Sch., 1985. Mfg. tng. program Gen. Elec. Co., various locations, 1961-63; various mfg. assignments Crouse-Hinds Co., Syracuse, 1963-74; gen. mgr. Midwest Elec., Chgo., 1974-77; v.p., gen. mgr. Crouse Hinds Distbn. Equipment Div., Earlysville, VA., 1977-79; v.p. Crouse-Hinds Co., Syracuse, 1979-82; exec. v.p. Cooper Industries Inc., Houston, 1982-92, pres., chief oper. officer, 1992-95, pres., CEO, 1995—, also bd. dirs.; bd. dirs. Wyman-Gordon Co., North Grafton, Mass. Bd. dirs. Jr. Achievement Southeast Tex., Houston Ctrl., Houston Symphony. Mem. Mfrs. Alliance for Productivity Improvement, The Bus. Roundtable, Houston Club, Lakeside Country Club, Farmington Country Club. Republican. Roman Catholic. Home: 3669 Chevy Chase Dr Houston TX 77019-3009 Office: Cooper Industries Inc PO Box 4446 Houston TX 77210-4446

RILEY, HARRIS DEWITT, JR., pediatrician, educator; b. Clarksdale, Miss., Nov. 12, 1924; s. Harris DeWitt and Louise (Allen) R.; m. Margaret Barry, Sept. 16, 1950; children: Steven Allen, Mark Barry, Margaret Ruth. B.A., Vanderbilt U., 1945, M.D., 1948. Intern Balt. City Hosps., Johns Hopkins Hosp., 1948-49; resident in pediatrics Babies and Children's Hosp., Univ. Hosp., Cleve., 1949-50, Vanderbilt U. Hosp., 1950-51; instr., fellow in pediatrics Vanderbilt U. Med. Sch., 1953-57; prof. pediatrics, chmn. dept. U. Okla. Med. Sch., 1958—; med. dir. Children's Meml. Hosp., 1972—; disting. prof. pediatrics U. Okla., 1976; prof. pediatrics Vanderbilt U. Sch. of Medicine, Nashville, 1991—. Served as capt. M.C. USAF, 1951-53. Office: Vanderbilt Children Hosp Vanderbilt U Med Ctr Nashville TN 37232

RILEY, HELENE MARIA KASTINGER, Germanist; b. Vienna, Austria, Mar. 11, 1939; came to U.S., 1959; d. Josef and Helene (Friedl) Kastinger; m. Edward R. Riley, Nov. 6, 1957 (div. May 1970); children: India Helene, John Edward, Jesse Dale, Michael Rutledge; m. Darius G. Ornston, May 11, 1983. Grad., bus. coll., Vienna, 1955; BA in Music, North Tex. State U., 1970; MA in Germanics, Rice U., 1973, PhD in Germanics, 1975. Teaching asst. Rice U., Houston, 1971-75; asst. prof. German Yale U., New Haven, Conn., 1975-78, head summer lang. inst., 1979-81, assoc. prof., 1979-85; chmn. Dept. Fgn. Langs. Wash. State U., Pullman, 1981-82; head Dept. Langs. Clemson (S.C.) U., 1985-86, prof., 1985-95, Alumni Disting. prof., 1996—; guest prof. Middlebury (Vt.) Coll., 1976; speaker in field. Author: Achim von Arnim, 1979, Virginia Woolf, 1983, Clemens Brentano, 1985, Die Weibliche Muse, 1986, Max Weber, 1991, others; contbr. numerous articles to profl. jours. Recipient German-Am. Friendship award Consul Gen. of the German Fed. Republic, 1989; grantee Griswold Found., 1975-76, 78, S.C. Dept. Edn., 1986, NEH, 1986, Provost's award Clemson U., 1989, Hilles Fund, 1976, 79, 82, S.C. Humanities Coun., 1996; NDEA fellow, 1972, 73, Rice fellow, 1971, 74, Morse fellow, 1977-78, Deutscher Akademischer Austausch-Dienst fellow, 1979, Yale U. sr. faculty fellow, 1981-82, Holland Fund fellow, 1982, Deutsche Forschungsgemeinschaft fellow, 1982, Mesda fellow, 1993. Fellow Davenport Coll., Yale U.; mem. AAUP (v.p. 1987-88, pres. 1988-89), MLA, Am. Assn. Tchrs. German, So. Comparative Lit. Assn., others. Democrat. Avocations: reading, writing, sports, needlecraft, painting. Office: Clemson U Dept Langs 717 Strode Twr Clemson SC 29634-1515

RILEY, HENRY CHARLES, banker; b. Newton, Mass., Mar. 23, 1932; s. Charles Matthew and Marion Anna (Armstrong) R.; m. Patricia Ann Buchanan, Mar. 3, 1962; children: Lauren Elizabeth, Carolyn Ann, Julie Louise. A.B., Yale U., 1954; M.B.A., Boston Coll., 1965. With BayBank Harvard Trust Co., Cambridge, Mass., 1958-89, treas., sec., 1967-70, v.p., treas., 1970-72, sr. v.p., sec., 1972-82; exec. v.p. BayBank Harvard Trust Co., 1982-87; mng. dir. community banking BayBank Systems Inc., Waltham, Mass., 1987-90; exec. v.p., dir. community banking BayBank Boston, 1990-92; exec. v.p. BayBank Systems, Inc., Waltham, 1992—; bd. dirs. BayBank FSB, Nashua, N.H., BayBank N.H., Derry. Trustee, treas. Longy Sch. Music, 1970-92; bd. dirs. Richard Warren Surg. Rsch. and Ednl. Fund Inc., 1984—; bd. dirs., pres. Cambridge Econ. Devel. Corp., 1982-87; corporator, past asst. treas. Mt. Auburn Hosp.; past mem. exec. bd. Gettysburg Coll. Parents Assn.; past treas. St. John's Episcopal Ch., sr. warden, Westwood, Mass., 1982-85; mem. St. Paul's Cathedral chpt., Boston, 1990-93. With USNR, 1956-57. Mem. Am. Bankers Assn. (chmn. 1991-92, exec. com. br. adminstrv. divsn. 1992, chmn. nat. retail banking conf. 1990), Nat. Br. Adminstrs. Roundtable, Boston Coll. Sch. Mgmt. Alumni Assn. (past dir., pres.), Harvard Sq. Bus. Assn. (past dir.), Cambridge C. of C. (past dir., past treas., v.p. 1975-87), Rotary (club dir. 1976-80, pres. 1979-80), Yale Club (Boston), Harvard Club (Boston), Dennis Yacht Club (mem. bd. govs., treas. 1993-94), The Meadows Country Club (Sarasota, Fla.). Episcopalian. Home: 33 York Way Westwood MA 02090-2633 Office: BayBank Systems Inc One BayBank Technology Pl Waltham MA 02154-7438

RILEY, JACK, actor, writer; b. Cleve., Dec. 30, 1935; s. John A. and Agnes C. (Corrigan) R.; m. Ginger Lawrence, May 18, 1975; children: Jamie, Bryan. BS in English, John Carroll U., 1961. Mem.: Rolling Along of 1960, Dept. Army Travelling Show; co-host: Baxter & Riley, Sta.-WERE, Cleve., 1961-65; numerous TV appearances, including: as Mr. Carlin on Bob Newhart Show, CBS-TV, 1972-78; Occasional Wife, 1966, Mary Tyler Moore, 1972, Barney Miller, 1979, Diff'rent Strokes, 1979, Hart to Hart, 1980, Love Boat, 1984, Night Court, 1985-91, St. Elsewhere, 1986, Babes, 1991, Evening Shade, 1992, Family Matters, 1993, Hangin' with Mr. Cooper, 1993, Dave's World, 1994, Married with Children, 1994, The Boys are Back, 1995; appeared in feature films including Catch-22, 1969, McCabe and Mrs. Miller, 1970, Long Goodbye, 1972, Calif. Split, 1974, World's Greatest Lover, 1978, High Anxiety, 1978, Butch and Sundance: The Early Years, 1979, History of the World, Part I, 1981, Frances, 1983, To Be or Not To Be, 1983, Finders Keepers, 1984, Spaceballs, 1987, Rented Lips, 1987, Gleaming the Cube, 1988, C.H.U.D. II, 1988, The Player, 1992, Dangerous Woman, 1993, T-Rex, 1995; plays West Coast premier of Small Craft Warnings, 1975, Los Angeles revival of 12 Angry Men, 1985, Zeitgeist, 1990, House of Blue Leaves, at Cleve. Playhouse and tour Ea. Europe, 1993; TV writer: Don Rickles Show, 1968, Mort Sahl Show, 1967; writer commls. for, Blore & Richman Inc., Los Angeles, 1966-84; numerous radio commls. and TV voice-overs, Rugrats (cartoon series), 1993. Served with U.S. Army, 1958-61. Mem. Screen Actors Guild, Actor's Equity, AFTRA, Writers Guild Am., Acad. Motion Picture Arts and Scis., Acad. TV Arts and Scis. Office: care Ho of Reps 9911 W Pico Blvd Ste 1060 Los Angeles CA 90035-2712*

RILEY, JERLENA, church administrator. Fin. dir. Ch. of God of Prophecy Admin. Com. Office: Church of God of Prophecy PO Box 2910 Cleveland TN 37320-2910

RILEY, JOHN GRAHAM, economics educator; b. Christchurch, New Zealand, Dec. 8, 1945; came to U.S., 1969; s. Charles Graham and Patricia (White) R.; m. Rita Jane Stulin, July 5, 1971 (div. 1981); m. Beverly Fong Lowe, Oct. 16, 1982; 1 child, Alexandra Lowe Riley. BS, U. Canterbury, Christchurch, 1967, M in Commerce, 1969; PhD, MIT, 1972. Instr. Boston Coll., 1971-72, asst. prof., 1972-73; asst. prof. econs. UCLA, 1973-76, assoc. prof., 1976-80, prof., 1980—, chmn. dept., 1992-96. Assoc. editor Am. Econs. Rev., 1983-85, co-editor, 1985-87; contbr. numerous articles to profl. jours. Co-chair Ch. and Synagogue Assocs., Inc., 1991—. Erskine fellow U. Canterbury, 1987; NSF grantee, 1975-89. Fellow Econometrics Soc. Office: UCLA Dept Econs 2263 Bunche Hall Los Angeles CA 90095-1477

RILEY, JOHN WINCHELL, JR., consulting sociologist; b. Brunswick, Maine, June 10, 1908; s. John Winchell and Marjorie Webster (Prince) R.; m. Matilda White, June 19, 1931; children: John Winchell III, Lucy Ellen. AB, Bowdoin Coll., 1930, LLD, 1972; MA, Harvard U., 1933, PhD, 1936. Mem. faculty Marietta Coll., 1933-35, Wellesley Coll., 1935-37, Douglass Coll., 1937-45; mem. faculty Rutgers U., 1945-60, prof. sociology, chmn. dept., 1945-60; v.p., dir. social research Equitable Life Assurance Soc. of U.S., N.Y.C., 1960-68, v.p. corp. relations, 1968—, sr. v.p. corp. relations, 1968-72, sr. v.p. social research, 1972-73, cons., 1973—; mem. faculty Harvard U., 1955; cons. Market Rsch. Co. Am., 1940-45, Columbia Broadcasting Co., 1945-50, Ford Motor Co., 1965, Am. Coun. Life Ins., 1973-90, WHO, 1984—, Internat. Fedn. Aging, 1983—, Scripps Found., 1987—, Max Planck, 1989, numerous others; sr. cons. Matthew Greenwald & Assocs ., 1990—, Project Age and Structural Change Nat. Inst. Aging, 1994—; vis. scholar Ctr. for Advanced Study in Behavioral Sci., 1978-79; mem. adv. bd. Carnegie Corp. Aging Soc. project, 1982—, U. Mich. Inst. Gerontology, 1987—, U. So. Calif. Intergenerational Project, 1990; lectr. in field. Author: (with Bryce Ran, Marcia Lifshitz) The Student Looks at His Teacher, 1950 (with Wilbur Schramm) The Reds Take A City, 1951 (with Matilda W. Riley, Jackson Toby) Sociological Studies in Scale Analysis, 1954 (with Matilda W. Riley, Marilyn Johnson) Aging and Society, Vol. II, 1969; editor: The Corporation and Its Public, 1963; contbr. Our Aging Soc., 1986, Nationalization of the Social Sciences, 1987, Ency. of Aging, 1990, The Changing Contract Among Generations, 1993, others. Former trustee Am. Found. Blind, Inst. Edn. Devel., Nat. Urban League, Boethner Rsch. Inst.; trustee Industrywide Network Social Rural and Rural Efforts; mem. capital campaign com. Bowdoin Coll., 1984; rsch. adv. bd. The Am. Coll., 1989—. With OWI, Psychol. Warfare Divsn., AUS, 1944, Far Ea. Rsch. Group, USAF, 1950-51. Recipinet Stuart A. Rice Merit award, 1990, numerous other awards for profl. excellence. Fellow AAAS; mem. Sociol. Research Assn. (pres. 1964-65), Oliver Wendall Holmes Assn. (former trustee), Am. Sociol. Assn. (sec. 1950-55, Disting. Career award for practice 1983), Eastern Social Soc., Osborne Assn. (former trustee), Am. Assn. Pub. Opinion Research (pres. 1961-62, Disting. Career award 1983), Market Research Council, Am. Assn. Internat. Aging (former trustee), Am. Sociol. Found. (incorporator, mem. adv. com. 1987—), D.C. Sociol. Soc. (co-pres. 1984-85). Home and Office: 4701 Willard Ave Apt 1607 Chevy Chase MD 20815-4630

RILEY, JOSEPH HARRY, retired banker; b. Pitts., May 13, 1922; s. Joseph John and Frances P. (Wacker) R.; m. Anna Belle Hepler, May 2, 1957 (dec. May 1994); 1 child, Michelle Patricia. B.C.S., Benjamin Franklin U., 1950; postgrad., Grad. Sch. Banking, Rutgers U., 1954. With Crestar Bank, N.A. (name formerly Nat. Savs. & Trust Co.), Washington, 1947—; exec. v.p. Crestar Bank, N.A. (name formerly Nat. Savs. & Trust Co.), 1970-73, sr. exec. v.p., 1973-76, pres., 1976-80, chmn., pres., 1980-84, also bd. dirs. Treas. Heroes; bd. dirs. Anthony Francis Lucas Spindletop Found., Anson Mills Found., Jr. Achievement Washington, Boys Club Greater Washington; bd. dirs., pres. Kiwanis Found.; past pres. Met. Washington Bd. Trade. Served with USMCR, 1942-46, 50-51. Mem. D.C. Bankers Assn. (past pres.), Am. Bankers Assn., Mortgage Bankers Assn., Washington Conv. and Visitors Bur. (past pres.), Soc. Friendly Sons St. Patrick (past pres.), Congl. Country Club (Washington), Univ. Club (Washington), Met. Club (Washington), Burning Tree Club, Rolling Rock Club (Ligonier, Pa.). Home: 10116 Iron Gate Rd Potomac MD 20854-4728 Office: 1445 New York Ave NW Washington DC 20005-2158 *If one guideline stood out in my life it would be my belief in contributing. I feel you should voluntarily offer to give of yourself in any endeavor in which you are a participant whether it be business, community or social. If you fail to make such an effort you have forfeited the right to complain regardless of the final result.*

RILEY, KEVIN M., principal. Prin. Gretna (Nebr.) Jr. Sr. High Sch. Recipient Blue Ribbon award U.S. Dept. Edn., 1990-91. Office: Gretna Jr-Sr High Sch 805 S County Rd Gretna NE 68028-4777

RILEY, LAWRENCE JOSEPH, bishop; b. Boston, Sept. 6, 1914; s. James and Ellen (Ryan) R. A.B., Boston Coll., 1936, LL.D., 1965; S.T.B., Gregorian U., 1939; S.T.D., Catholic U. Am., 1948; LL.D., Stonehill Coll., 1957. Ordained priest Roman Cath. Ch., 1940. Prof., rector St. John's Sem., Boston, 1941-66; prof. Emmanuel Coll., 1965-66; chaplain Harvard Cath. Club, 1950-54; vice officialis Met. Tribunal, Archdiocese of Boston, 1950-76; sec. to archbishop of Boston, 1951-58; aux. bishop Archdiocese of Boston, 1972-90; aux. bishop emeritus Archdiocese of Boston, 1990—; asst. at Pontifical Throne, 1986—; vicar gen. emeritus Archdiocese of Boston; pastor emeritus Most Precious Blood Parish, Hyde Park, Mass. Decorated Knight Comdr. with star Holy Sepulchre of Jerusalem; decorated Knight Order of Star of Italian Solidarity. Mem. Cath. Theol. Soc. Am. (past pres.), Mariological Soc. Am., Canon Law Soc. Am., Dante Alighieri Soc. Mass. (past v.p.), Nat. Cath. Edn Assn., Fellowship of Cath. Scholars, Pope John XXIII Med.-Moral Ctr. Address: 43 Maple St Hyde Park MA 02136-2755

RILEY, MATILDA WHITE (MRS. JOHN W. RILEY, JR.), sociology educator; b. Boston, Apr. 19, 1911; d. Percival and Mary (Cliff) White; m. John Winchell Riley, June 19, 1931; children: John Winchell III, Lucy Ellen Riley Sallick. BA, Radcliffe Coll., 1931, MA, 1937, DSc (hon.), 1994; DSc, Bowdoin Coll., 1972; LHD (hon.), Rutgers U., 1983. Rsch. asst. Harvard U., Cambridge, Mass., 1932; v.p. Market Rsch. Co. Am., 1938-49; chief cons. economist WPB, 1941; rsch. specialist Rutgers U., 1950, prof., 1951-73, dir. sociology lab., chmn. dept. sociology and anthropology, 1959-73, emeritus prof., 1973—; Daniel B. Fayerweather prof. polit. econ. and sociology Bowdoin Coll., 1974-78, prof. emeritus, 1978—; assoc. dir. Nat. Inst. on Aging, 1979-91, sr. social scientist, 1991—; mem. faculty Harvard U., summer 1955; staff assoc., dir. aging and society Russell Sage Found., 1964-73, staff sociologist, 1974-77; chmn. com. on life course Social Sci. Rsch. Coun., 1977-80; sr. rsch. assoc. Ctr. for Social Scis., Columbia U., 1978-80; adv. bd. Carnegie Aging Soc. Project, 1985-87; mem. Commn. on Coll. Retirement, 1982-86; vis. prof. NYU, 1954-61; cons. Nat. Coun. on Aging, Acad. Ednl. Devel.; mem. study group NIH, 1971-79, Social Sci. Rsch. Coun. Com. on Middle Years, 1973-77; chmn. NIH Task Force on Health and Behavior, 1986-91; cons. WHO, 1987—; Winkelman lectr. U. Mich., 1984, Selo lectr. U. No. Calif., 1987, Boettner lectr. Am. Coll., 1990, Claude Pepper lectr. Fla. State U., 1993, Disting. lectr. Southwestern Social Scis. Assn., 1990, Standing lectr. SUNY, 1992, Inaugural lectr. Cornell U., 1992; lectr. Internat. Inst. of Sociology, Plenary, 1993, Inter-Univ. Consortium Pol. and Social Rsch., U. Mich., 1993, Duke U., 1993. Author: (with P. White) Gliding and Soaring, (with Riley and Toby) Sociological Studies in Scale Analysis, 1954, Sociological Research, vols. I, II, 1964, (with others) Aging and Society, vol. I, 1968, vol. II, 1969, vol. III, 1972, (with Nelson) Sociological Observation, 1974, Aging from Birth to Death: Interdisciplinary Perspectives, 1979, (with Merton) Sociological Traditions from Generation to Generation, 1980, (with Abeles and Teitelbaum) Aging from Birth to Death: Sociotemporal Perspectives, 1982, (with Hess and Bond) Aging in Society, 1983; editor: (with M. Ory and D. Zablotsky) AIDS in an Aging Society: What We Need to Know, 1989; co-editor: Perspectives in Behavioral Medicine: The Aging Dimension, 1987, (with J. W. Riley) The Quality of Aging, 1989, The Annuals, 1989; sr. editor: Structural Lag, 1994; editorial com.: Ann. Rev. Sociology, 1978-81, Social Change and the Life Course, vol. 1, Social Structures and Human Lives, (with B. Huber and B. Hess) Sociological Lives, vol. II, 1988, (with R. Kahn and Anne Foner) Structural Lag, 1994; contbr. chpts. to books, articles to profl. jours. Former trustee The Big Sisters Assn. Recipient Lindback Rsch. award Rutgers U., 1970, Social Sci. award Andrus Gerontology Ctr., U. So. Calif., 1972, Radcliffe Alumnae award, 1982, Commonwealth award 1984, Kesten Lecture award U. So. Calif., 1987, Sci. Achievement award Washington Acad. Scis., 1989, Disting. Sci. award, 1989, Disting. Creative award Gerontol. Soc. Am., 1990, Presdl. Meritorious award, 1990, Stuart Rice award Columbia Sociol. Soc., 1992, Kent award Gerontol. Soc. Am., 1992; fellow Advanced Study in Behaviorial Scis., 1978-79; Matilda White Riley award in rsch. and methodology established in her honor Rutgers U., 1977; Matilda White Riley prize established Bowdoin Coll., 1987; Matilda White Riley House dedicated Bowdoin Coll., 1996. Fellow AAAS (chmn. sect. on social and econ. scis. 1977-78); mem. NAS, Inst. Medicine of NAS (sr.), Acad. Behavioral Medicine Rsch., Am. Sociol. Assn. (exec. officer 1949-60, v.p. 1973-74, pres. 1986, 91, chmn. sect. on sociology of aging 1989, Disting. Scholar in Aging 1988, Career award 1992), Am. Assn. Public Opinion Rsch. (sec.-treas. 1949-51, Disting. Svc. award 1983), Eastern Sociol. Soc. (v.p. 1968-69, pres. 1977-78, Dis. Career award 1986), Soc. for Study Social Biology (bd. dirs. 1986-92), Am. Acad. Arts and Scis., D.C. Sociol. Soc. (co-pres. 1983-84), Sociol. Rsch. Assn., Internat. Orgn. Study Human Devel., Am. Philos. Soc. (membership lectr. 1987), Phi Beta Kappa, Phi Beta Kappa Assocs. Home: 4701 Willard Ave Apt 1607 Chevy Chase MD 20815-4630 Office: NIH Nat Inst on Aging 7201 Wisconsin Ave Bethesda MD 20814-4810

RILEY, MICHAEL JOSEPH, government official; b. Rochester, N.H., Mar. 14, 1943; s. Matthew Howard and Agnes Riley; m. Nancy Sarah Mason, July 25, 1970; children: Shawn, Paul, James, Sarah. B.S., U.S. Naval Acad., 1965; M.B.A., U. So. Calif., Los Angeles, 1972; D. Bus. Adminstrn. in Fin., Harvard U., 1977. Acct. Teradyne, Boston, 1972-73; asst. controller Northeast Utilities, Berlin, Conn., 1976-83; treas. Mich. Bell Telephone Co., Detroit, 1983-85; sr. v.p. fin., chief fin. officer United Airlines, Elk Grove Village, Ill., 1985-87; v.p. fin. Lee Enterprises, Inc., Davenport, Iowa, 1987-93; CFO, sr. v.p. U.S. Postal Svc., Washington, 1993—; lectr. fin. U. Conn., 1977-81, U. Mich., 1985. Author: (with Dwight B. Crane) NOW Accounts: Strategy for Financial Institutions, 1978. Lt. USN, 1965-70, Vietnam. Mem. Fin. Execs. Inst. (pres. Mississippi Valley chpt. 1991, com. on govt. liaison 1993—), Fin. Mgmt. Assn. (dir. 1983-85). Office: US Postal Svc 475 Lenfant Plz SW Washington DC 20260-5000

RILEY, NANCY MAE, retired vocational home economics educator; b. Grand Forks, N.D., May 1, 1939; d. Kenneth Wesley and Jeanne Margaret Olive (Hill) R. BS in Edn., Miami U., 1961; postgrad., Ohio U., 1964-69; MA, Marietta Coll., 1989. Cert. high sch. tchr. Tchr. home econs. Malta-McConnelsville (Ohio) High Sch., 1961-67; tchr. home econs. Waterford (Ohio) High Sch., 1968-92; advisor Malta-McConnelsville Future Homemakers, 1961-66, Waterford Future Homemakers Am., 1968-92; advisor to state officer Ohio Future Homemakers Am., McConnelsville, 1963, Waterford, 1976. Leader Girl Scouts Am., McConnelsville, 1962-66, camp counselor, 1962-76; fair judge Waterford Cmty. Fair, Waterford, 1970-85. Mem. NEA, Am. Vocat. Assn. (life), Ohio Edn. Assn. (life, del. 1979), Ohio Vocat. Assn. (life), DAR, Daus. Union Vets. (del. 1992—, tent pres. 1993-94, dist. pres. 1996), Daus. of War of 1812 (pres. 1991—, state sec. 1995—), Ohio Geneal. Soc., Order Ea. Star (worthy matron 1967-68, dep. grand matron 1978), White Shrine Jerusalem (worth high priestess 1979-81, 83). Republican. Baptist. Avocations: ceramics, genealogy, camping, reading, handcrafts. Home: PO Box 137 Waterford OH 45786-0137

RILEY, PATRICIA GRACE, maternal, child nurse manager; b. Berwyn, Ill., Dec. 6, 1936; d. James Ramsay and Janet White (Wright) Philip; m. Peter Gerald Riley, June 29, 1957; children: Thomas, Janet, James, Mary Kathleen. Diploma, Ill. Masonic Med. Ctr., Chgo., 1957; BS, Coll. St. Francis, Joliet, Ill., 1984; MS, Memphis State U., 1987. RN, Ill. Staff nurse newborn nursery Mac Neal Hosp., Berwyn, Ill., 1957-70, 72-76; staff nurse maternal-child Bryn Mawr (Pa.) Hosp., 1970-72; staff nurse maternal-children Good Samaritan Hosp., Downers Grove, Ill., 1976-77; asst. head nurse nursery Mac Neal Hosp., 1977-80; nurse mgr. newborn nursery Bapt. Hosp. East, Memphis, 1981-93, nurse mgr. mother-baby unit, 1993—; instr. BLS Bapt. Hosp. East, 1986—; phone cons. Birth Right, Memphis, 1987-92; expert witness, 1994. Mem. AWHONN (cert.). Roman Catholic. Office: Bapt Meml Hosp East 6019 Walnut Grove Rd Memphis TN 38120-2113

RILEY, PATRICK JAMES, professional basketball coach; b. Rome, N.Y., Mar. 20, 1945; s. Leon R.; m. Chris Riley; children: James Patrick, Elisabeth. Grad., U. Ky., 1967. Guard San Diego Rockets, 1967-70; guard L.A. Lakers, 1970-75, asst. coach, 1979-81, head coach, 1981-90; head coach N.Y. Knicks, 1991-95; guard Phoenix Suns, 1975-76; broadcaster L.A. Lakers games Sta. KLAC and Sta. KHJ-TV, 1977-79, NBC Sports, 1990-91; player NBA Championship Team, 1972, coach, 1982, 85, 87, 88; head coach Miami (Fla.) Heat, 1995—. Author: The Winner Within: A Life Plan for Team Players, 1993. Named NBA Coach of Yr., 1990, 93. Holder NBA record most playoff wins (137). Office: Miami Heat Miami Arena Miami FL 33136-4102*

RILEY, PETER JAMES, lawyer; b. Teaneck, N.J., June 7, 1956; s. John Bernard and Mary Ann (Lannig) R.; m. Laura Willson Latham, June 12, 1982; children: Peyton Lannig, Rachel Malone. BBA, U. Tex., 1978; JD, So. Meth. U., 1981. Bar: Tex. 1981, U.S. Dist. Ct. (no. dist.) Tex. 1981. Sr. shareholder Thompson & Knight, Dallas, 1981—. Mem. ABA, Dallas Bar Assn, Tower Club, Brook Hollow Golf Club. Republican. Presbyterian. Avocation: golf. Home: 6606 Glendora Ave Dallas TX 75230-5220 Office: Thompson & Knight 3300 1st City Ctr Dallas TX 75201

RILEY, RANDY JAMES, banker; b. Waukegan, Ill., May 5, 1950; s. Francis James and Florence Josephine (Belec) R.; m. Joanne M. Lehtola (div.); 1 child, Tara Lynn; m. Marge Witte Hagen. Student, Elmhurst Coll., 1969-70, U. Wis. Grad. Sch. Banking, 1975-76, U. Colo. Sch. of Bank Mktg., 1984-85. Mgmt. trainee Am. Nat. Bank, Waukegan, 1971-73; v.p. 1st Nat. Bank, Eagle River, Wis., 1973-85, M&I Western State Bank, Oshkosh, Wis., 1985-88; sr. v.p. Community Nat. Bank, Titusville, Fla., 1988-89, Citrus Bank, N.A., Vero Beach, Fla., 1989—; treas. Brevard Small Bus. Assistance Coun., Indian River Chamber Small Bus. Task Force, 1990, Legis. Task Force, 1992, vice-chmn. 1994. Pres. Eagle River C. of C., 1981, Oshkosh Comml. Devel. Corp., 1987; pres., founder Eagle River Cmty. Theatre, 1983, Headwater's Performing Arts, Eagle River, 1983; affordable housing subcom. mem. Indian River County; bd. dirs., treas. Jr. Achievement, 1992, vice-chmn., 1993, chmn., 1995. Mem. Am. Inst. Banking, Robert Morris Assocs., Lions (v.p. Oshkosh club 1987), Elks, Kiwanis (v.p. 1992, pres. 1993., lt. gov. Fla. dist. 1996). Avocations: golf, skiing, sailing. Home: 965 4th Ln Vero Beach FL 32962-1586 Office: Citrus Bank NA 1717 Indian River Blvd Vero Beach FL 32960-0867

RILEY, RICHARD WILSON, federal official; b. Greenville, S.C., Jan. 2, 1933; s. Edward Patterson and Martha Elizabeth (Dixon) R.; m. Ann Osteen Yarborough, Aug. 23, 1957; children: Richard Wilson, Anne Y., Hubert D., Theodore D. B.A., Furman U., 1954; J.D., U. S.C., 1959. Bar: S.C. 1960. Ptnr. Riley & Riley, Greenville, 1959-78, Nelson, Mullins, Riley & Scarborough, Greenville and Columbia, S.C., 1987-93; gov. State of S.C., 1979-87; sec. U.S. Dept. Edn., Washington, 1993—; spl. asst. to subcom. U.S. Senate Jud. Com., 1960; mem. S.C. Ho. of Reps., 1963-66, S.C. Senate senate from Greenville-Laurens Dist., 1966-76. Lt. (j.g.) USNR, 1954-56. Recipient Harold W. McGraw, Jr. Prize in Education, McGraw-Hill, 1989; James Bryant Conant Award, Edn. Comm. of the States, 1995. Mem. S.C., Greenville bar assns., Furman U. Alumni Assn. (pres. 1968-69), Phi Beta Kappa. Rotarian. Office: US Dept Edn Washington DC 20202-0001

RILEY, ROBERT BARTLETT, landscape architect; b. Chgo., Jan. 28, 1931; s. Robert James and Ruth (Collins) R.; m. Nancy Rebecca Mills, Oct. 5, 1956; children: Rebecca Hill, Kimber Bartlett. PhB, U. Chgo., 1949; BArch, MIT, 1954. Chief designer Kea, Shaw, Grimm & Crichton, Hyattsville, Md., 1959-64; prin. partner Robert B. Riley (A.I.A.), Albuquerque, 1964-70; campus planner, asso. prof. architecture, dir. Center Environ. Research and Devel., U. N.Mex., 1966-70; prof. landscape architecture and architecture U. Ill., Urbana-Champaign, 1970—, head dept. landscape architecture, 1970-85; vis. prof. Harvard U., 1996—; sr. fellow landscape architecture studies Dumbarton Oaks/Harvard U., 1992—; mem. rev. panel landscape architects Fed. Civil Service-Nat. Endowment Arts. Assoc. editor Landscape mag., 1967-70; editor Landscape Jour., 1987—. Served with USAF, 1954-58. Nell Norris fellow U. Melbourne, Australia, 1977; project fellow Nat. Endowment Arts, 1985. Fellow Am. Soc. Landscape Architects (Nat. Honor award 1979); mem. Coun. of Educators in Landscape Architecture (pres. 1984-85, chmn. bd. dirs. 1985-86, Outstanding Educator award 1992, Pres.'s award 1994), AIA (Design award Md. 1962, N.Mex. 1968, Environ. Svc. award N.Mex. 1970), Environ. Design Rsch. Assn. (chmn. bd. 1990-91), Phi Beta Epsilon. Unitarian. Home: 407 E Mumford Dr Urbana IL 61801-6231 Office: Univ Ill 101 Temple Buell Hall 611 E Lordo Taft Dr Champaign IL 61820

RILEY, ROBERT EDWARD, financial services company executive; b. Boston, Feb. 19, 1930; s. Edward Gerard and Nina Loretta (Wolfe) R.; m. Ann Elizabeth McCourt, Nov. 10, 1956 (div. 1972); children: Robert Edward, David, Thomas; m. Carol Lee Anthony, June 22, 1974; children: Michael, Brian. A.B., Holy Cross Coll., 1951; M.B.A., Harvard U., 1953. Pres., chief exec. officer Putnam Mgmt. Co., Boston, 1970-80, Marsh & McLennan Asset Mgmt. Co., Boston, 1974-81; sr. v.p. Am. Express Co., N.Y.C., 1981-84; sr. v.p. group pensions Prudential Ins. Co. Am., Newark, 1984-85; pres. Prudential Asset Mgmt. Co., Newark, 1985-86; exec. v.p. Prudential Investment Corp., Newark, 1986-94; chmn. Prudential Realty Group, Newark, 1986-90; chmn., CEO Prudential Residential Svcs. Co., Boston, 1990-93, Prudential Reins. Co., 1993-94; pres., COO Dreyfus Corp., 1995; pres., CEO Leggat McCall Properties, 1995—; bd. dirs. Chgo. Title and Trust Co. Assoc. trustee Holy Cross Coll.; overseer Tufts U. Sch. medicine; bd. dirs. John F. Kennedy Libr.; corporator New Eng. Deaconess Hosp. Lt. comdr. USNR, 1953-56, Korea. Named Chief Exec. Officer of Yr. Fin. World Mag., 1975, 79. Republican. Roman Catholic. Clubs: Union (Boston); Univ. (N.Y.C.). Avocations: boating, skiing, ice hockey. Office: Prudential Ctr Ste 4365 10 Post Office Sq Boston MA 02109

RILEY, SCOTT C., lawyer; b. Bklyn., Oct. 5, 1959; s. William A. and Kathleen (Howe) R.; m. Kathleen D. O'Connor, Oct. 6, 1984; children: Matthew, Brendan. BA, Seton Hall U., South Orange, N.J., 1981; JD, Seton Hall U., Newark, 1984. Bar: N.J. 1985, U.S. Dist. Ct. N.J. 1985. Assoc. Dwyer, Connell & Lisbona, Montclair, N.J., 1985-87; assoc. gen. counsel, v.p. Consolidated Ins. Group, Wilmington, Del., 1987-91; counsel Cigna Ins. Group, Phila., 1991-94; assoc. gen. counsel KWELM Cos., N.Y.C., 1994—. Mem. ABA (com. on environ. ins. coverage), Fedn. of Ins. and Corp. Counsel, Excess and Surplus Lines Claims Assn., N.J. State Bar Assn. Office: KWELM Companies 599 Lexington Ave New York NY 10022

RILEY, STEPHEN THOMAS, historian, librarian; b. Worcester, Mass., Dec. 28, 1908; s. John and Mary (Ward) R.; m. Alice Amelia Riehle, July 2, 1949. A.B., Clark U., 1931, A.M., 1932, Ph.D. in Am. History, 1953, L.H.D. (hon.), 1981; grad., U. Pa. Army Specialized Tng. Program, 1943-44. Asst. librarian Mass. Hist. Soc., Boston, 1934-47; librarian Mass. Hist. Soc., 1947-62, dir., 1957-76, dir. emeritus, 1977—; mem. Mass. Revolutionary War Bi-Centennial Commn., 1965-91, Mass. Gov.'s Commn. on Need of New Mass. Archives Bldg., 1974, Mass. Archives Adv. Com., 1978-91; mem. adminstrv. bd. Adams Family Papers, 1956-91, George Washington Papers, 1969-91, Daniel Webster Papers, 1966-89; mem. vis. com. Boston Coll. Library, 1964, 67-68, Harvard U. History Dept., 1962-68, Harvard U. Press, 1965-71; cons. N.Y. State Hist. Assn., 1978, Va. Hist. Soc., 1981. Author: The Massachusetts Historical Society, 1791-1959, 1959, Stephen Thomas Riley: The Years of Stewardship, 1976; editor: (with Edward W. Hanson) The Papers of Robert Treat Paine, Vol. I 1746-1756, Vol. II 1757-1774, 1992; contbr. articles and revs. to hist. jours. Bd. dirs. Freedom Trail, Boston, 1965-91; trustee Clark U., 1963-74, hon. trustee, 1974—. Served with U.S. Army, 1942—44; USAAF, 1944-45. Fellow AAAS; mem. Archives Am. Art (adv. com. New Eng. br. 1972-91), Am. Antiquarian Soc., Am. Bostonain Soc., Colonial Soc. Mass. (v.p. 1980-91), Mass. Hist. Soc., New Eng. Hist. Geneal. Soc. (corr. sec. 1973-81), Weston (Mass.) Hist. Soc. (pres. 1977-84), Odd Vols. (Boston, v.p. 1979-83), Grolier Club (N.Y.C.), Odd Vols. Club (v.p. 1979-83), Phi Beta Kappa. Democrat. Roman Catholic. Home: 334 Wellesley St Weston MA 02193-2620 Office: 1154 Boylston St Boston MA 02215-3695

RILEY, TERRY, composer, musician; b. Colfax, Calif., June 24, 1935. Student, San Francisco State Coll., 1955-57; MA, U. Calif., Berkeley, 1961. mem. creative assoc. program SUNY, Buffalo, 1969; mem. faculty Mills Coll., 1972-87. Plays keyboards and soprano saxophone; performer, tchr. North Indian vocal music; composer, performer U.S., Europe, 1963—; guest Swedish Radio and Acad. Music, 1967; compositions include In C, 1964, The Keyboard Studies, 1965, Dorian Reeds, 1966, Untitled Organ, 1966, Poppy Nogood and the Phantom Band, 1968, A Rainbow in Curved Air, 1969, Music with Balls, 1969, Genesis (ballet), 1970, Persian Surgery Dervishes, 1971, Shri Camel, 1976, G-Song for string quartet, 1980, Songs from the Old Country, 1980-81, Song of the Emerald Runner, 1983, Songs for Ten Voices of the Two Prophets, 1983, The Medicine Wheel for piano, voice, synthesizer, sitar, and tabla, 1983, Cadenza on the Night Plain for string quartet, 1984, The Harp of New Albion for solo piano, 1985, Salome Dances for Peace, parts I and II, for string quartet, 1985, 86, The Room of Remembrance for vibraphone, marimba, piano, and soprano saxophone, 1987, Chanting the Light of Foresight for saxophone quartet, 1987, The Crows Rosary for keyboard and string quartet, 1988, The Jade Palace Orchestral Dances for large symphony orch., 1989, Cactus Rosary for mixed instruments, 1990, The Sands concerto for string quartet and orch., 1991, June Buddhas concerto for chorus and orch., 1991, The Saint Adolf Ring, 1992, 4 Wölfli sketches for chamber ensemble, 1992, Embroidery, Eastern Man, Chorale of the Blessed Day, Ritmos and Melos for piano, violin, percussion, 1993, El Hombre for String Quartet and Piano, 1993, Ascencion for solo guitar, 1993, Chorus 193 for large mixed vocal ensemble, 1993, The Heaven Ladder, others. Nat. Endowment Arts grantee, 1977; Guggenheim fellow, 1979; Koussevitzky Music Found. grantee, 1991.

RILEY, THOMAS JOSEPH, anthropologist; b. Portland, Maine, Nov. 2, 1943; s. Joseph Gerard and Virginia C. (Cunningham) R.; m. Karma Jean Ibsen, July 10, 1967 (div. 1985); children: Kirsten, Katherine, Erin; m. Carol Ann, Nov. 21, 1989; 1 child, Julia Wade. BA, Boston Coll., 1965; MA, U. Hawaii, 1970, PhD, 1973. Asst. prof. NYU, 1972-74; from asst. prof. to prof. anthropology U. Ill., Urbana, 1974—, assoc. dean Grad. Coll., 1983-86, head dept. anthropology, 1986-93; chair univ. senate coun., 1995—; acad. adv. bd. SALT Ctr., Portland, 1980—. Co-author: Prehistoric Agriculture, 1972; mem. editl. bd. Ency. of World Cultures, 1993-96; contbr. over 70 articles to profl. jours. Chair bd. Devel. Svcs. Ctr., Champaign, 1986-89, Human Rels. Area Files at Yale U., 1995—, v.p. 1996—; sec. bd. C-U Independence, Champaign, 1987—; bd. dirs. Disabled Citizens Found., Champaign, 1988—, Ill. Assn. Retarded Citizens, Chgo., 1988-94, Champaign County Mental Health Bd., 1993—, Ill. State Hist. Sites Adv. Coun., 1986-89. NSF fellow, 1978-79; NSF grantee 1978—. Fellow Am. Anthropology Assn., Ill. Archeol. Survey; mem. Soc. Am. Archaeology, AAAS, Soc. Archeol. Scis. (treas. 1982-83), Sigma Xi (chpt. v.p. 1987-88, chpt. pres. 1988-91). Roman Catholic. Home: 2503 Melrose Dr Champaign IL 61820-7608 Office: U Ill Dept Anthropology 109 Davenport Hall Urbana IL 61801

RILEY, TOM JOSEPH, lawyer; b. Cedar Rapids, Iowa, Jan. 9, 1929; s. Joseph Wendell and Edna (Kyle) R.; m. Nancy Evans, Jan. 21, 1952; children: Pamela Chang, Peter, Lisa Thirnbeck, Martha Brown, Sara Brown, Heather Mescher. BA, U. Iowa, 1950, JD, 1952. Bar: Iowa 1952, U.S. Dist. Ct. (no. dist.) Iowa 1952, U.S. Ct. Appeals (8th cir.) 1960, U.S. Supreme Ct. 1966. Assoc. Simmons, Perrine, Allbright & Ellwood, Cedar Rapids, 1952-60, ptnr., 1960-80; pres. Tom Riley Law Firm, P.C., Cedar Rapids, 1980—; adj. prof. trial advocacy Coll. Law, U. Iowa, Iowa City, 1979. Author: Proving Punitive Damages, 1981, The Price of a Life, 1986. Mem. Iowa Ho. of Reps., 1960-64, Iowa Senate, 1965-74. First lt. USAF, 1952-54. Named Outstanding Freshman Legislator, Des Moines Press and Radio Club, 1961. Fellow Iowa Acad. Trial Lawyers (bd. govs. 1982-91); mem. Cedar Rapids Country Club, U. Athletic Club, Iowa City, Des Moines Club, Masons. Republican. Presbyterian. Avocations: tennis, sailing, downhill skiing. Home: 5300 Lakeside Rd Rural Route Marion IA 52302 Office: 4040 1st Ave NE Cedar Rapids IA 52402-3143

RILEY, VICTOR J., JR., financial services company executive; b. Buffalo, Aug. 29, 1931; s. Victor J. and Gwenevieve Riley; m. Marilyn A. Felrath, Aug. 8, 1954; children—Victor J. III, Karen, Patricia, Kevin, Shawn, Mary Katherine. BA in Econs., U. Notre Dame; LLD, Coll. St. Rose, 1983. With trust div. 1st Nat. Bank Miami, Fla., 1955-62; mgr. Miami office Bowles, Andrews & Towne, 1962-64; trust officer Nat. Comml. Bank (now Key Bank N.A.), Albany, N.Y., 1964-73; pres., chief exec. officer KeyCorp (formerly Key Banks Inc.), Albany, from 1973—, now chmn., pres., chief exec. officer, also bd. dirs.; also dir.; chmn. bd. Key Bank N.A., Albany, 1984—, Ctr. Econ. Growth; dir. Albany Med. Ctr., Interstate Banking Commn. for State of N.Y., 1986—. Hon. chmn. Capital Dist. Cerebral Palsy Telethon, Albany, 1981-87; bd. dirs. Pop Warner Football League; chmn. various fund raising drives. Served with U.S. Army, 1953-55. Apptd. civilian aide to Sec. Army, 1985—. Decorated Knight of Malta. Mem. N.Y. State Bankers Assn. (long-range planning com.), Interstate Banking Com. State N.Y. Republican. Roman Catholic. Avocations: travel, fishing, cooking. Home: 5 Hemlock Ln East Greenbush NY 12061-2035 Office: KeyCorp 127 Public Square Cleveland OH 44114*

RILEY, WILLIAM, corporate executive, writer; b. Indpls., June 30, 1931; s. Leo Michael and Edna (Wilhelm) R.; m. Laura Etz, Apr. 20, 1957. AB, U. Notre Dame, 1952; LLB, Yale U., 1955. V.p., dir., chmn. Ivy Corp., Atlanta, 1960-80; chmn. Moore-Handley, Inc., Birmingham, Ala., 1981—; bd. dirs. Tru-Die, Inc., Franklin Pk., Ill., Fabco-Air, Inc., Gainesville, Fla. Author: (with Laura Riley) Guide to the National Wildlife Refuges, 1979 (Pulitzer prize nominee). Trustee The Raptor Trust, Basking Ridge, N.J., 1980—; bd. dirs. Nat. Wildlife Refuge Assn., Potomac, Md., 1985-94, Hawk Mountain Sanctuary Assn., Kempton, Pa., 1989—, Nat. Audubon Soc., N.Y.C., 1990-94. With U.S. Army, 1957-58. Mem. Met. Club of N.Y.C. Office: 745 5th Ave Ste 1803 New York NY 10151-0002

RILEY, WILLIAM B., JR., plastic surgeon; b. Chattanooga, Aug. 2, 1941. MD, U. N.C., 1967. Diplomate Am. Bd. Plastic Surgery. Intern Stanford (Calif.) U., 1967-68; resident in gen. surgery U. Ariz., Tucson, 1971-73; resident in plastic surgery Royal Melbourne (Australia) Hosp., 1973-74, Emory U. Affiliated Hosps., Atlanta, 1974-75, U. Miami Affiliated Hosps., 1975-76; active staff Ft. Bend Hosp., Sugar Land, 1984; staff Meml. Southwest Hosp., Houston, 1987—; clin. prof. surgery U. Tex., Houston, 1991—; pvt. practice Plastic Surgery Specialists, Houston, 1977—; courtesy staff Hermann Hosp., Houston, 1977—, St. Luke's Hosp., Houston, 1987—. Mem. AMA. Office: Plastic Surgery Specialists Ste 110 4665 Sweetwater Blvd Houston TX 77479-3000

RILEY, WILLIAM FRANKLIN, mechanical engineering educator; b. Allenport, Pa., Mar. 1, 1925; s. William Andrew and Margaret (James) R.; m. Helen Elizabeth Chilzer, Nov. 5, 1945; children—Carol Ann, William Franklin. B.S. in Mech. Engring., Carnegie Inst. Tech., 1951; M.S. in Mechanics, Ill. Inst. Tech., 1958. Mech. engr. Mesta Machine Co., West Homestead, Pa., 1951-54; research engr. Armour Research Found., Chgo., 1954-61; sect. mgr. IIT Research Inst., Chgo., 1961-64, sci. adviser, 1964-66; prof. Iowa State U., Ames, 1966-78, Disting. prof. engring., 1978-88, prof. emeritus, 1989—; ednl. cons. Bihar Inst. Tech., Sindri, India, 1966, Indian Inst. Tech., Kanpur, summer 1970. Author: (with A.J. Durelli) Introduction to Photmechanics, 1965; (with J. W. Dally) Experimental Stress Analysis, 1991; (with D. Young, K. McConnell and T. Rogge) Essentials of Mechanics, 1974; (with A. Higdon, E. Ohlsen, W. Stiles and J. Weese) mechanics of Materials, 4th edit., 1985; (with J. Dally and K. McConnell) Instrumentation for Engineering Measurements, 1993; (with L.W. Zachary) Introduction to Mechanics of Materials, 1989, (with L.D. Sturges) Engineering Mechanics-Statics and Dynamics, 1993, 2d edit., 1996; also numerous articles and tech. papers. Served to lt. col. USAAF, 1943-46. Fellow Soc. for Exptl. Mechanics (hon. mem.); mem. Soc. for Exptl. Stress Analysis (hon., M.M. Frocht award 1977). Home: 1518 Meadowlane Ave Ames IA 50010-5547

RILEY-DAVIS, SHIRLEY MERLE, advertising agency executive, marketing consultant, writer; b. Pitts., Feb. 4, 1935; d. William Riley and Beatrice Estelle (Whittaker) Byrd; m. Louis Davis; 1 child, Terri Judith. Student U. Pitts., 1952. Copywriter, Pitts. Mercantile Co., 1954-60; exec. sec. U. Mich., Ann Arbor, 1962-67; copy supr. N.W. Ayer, N.Y.C., 1968-76, assoc. creative dir., Chgo., 1977-81; copy supr. Leo Burnett, Chgo., 1981-86; freelance advt. and mktg. cons., 1986—; advt. and mktg. coord. Child and Family Svc., Ypsilanti, Mich., 1992—; vis. prof. Urban League Black Exec. Exch. Program; print, radio, and TV commercials; bd. dirs. Sr. Housing Bur., Ann Arbor; mem. adv. bd. Cmty. Diabetes, past bd. mem. People's Hope for Housing, Ypsilanti, Mich. Recipient Grand and First prize N.Y. Film Festival, 1973, Gold and Silver medal Atlanta Film Festival, 1973, Gold medal V.I. Film Festival, 1974, 50 Best Creatives award Am. Inst. Graphic Arts, 1972, Clio award, 1973, 74, 75, Andy Award of Merit, 1981, Silver medal Internat. Film Festival, 1982, Corp. Mgmt. Assistance Program award, 1986, Good Sam award 1981, Svc. Advt. Creativity of Distinction cert., 1981; Senatorial scholar. Bd. dirs. Housing bur. for Srs. of the U. Mich. Med. Ctr., 1995—. Mem. Women in Film, Facets Multimedia Film Theatre Orgn. (bd. dirs.), Greater Chgo. Coun. for Prevention of Child Abuse (past bd. dirs.), Internat. Platform Assn. Democrat. Roman Catholic. Avocations: dance, poetry, design, writing, volunteering. Office: 118 S Washington St Ypsilanti MI 48197-5427

RILEY-SCOTT, BARBARA POLK, retired librarian; b. Roselle, N.J., Nov. 21, 1928; d. Charles Carrington and Olive Bond P.; AB, Howard U., 1950; BS, N.J. Coll. Women, 1951; MS, Columbia U., 1955; m. George Emerson Riley, Feb. 23, 1957 (dec.); children: George E., Glenn C., Karen O.; m. William I. Scott, Oct. 6, 1990. Asst. librarian, Fla. A&M U., 1951-53; with Morgan State Coll., 1955; with Dept. Def., 1955-57, S.C. State Coll., 1957-59, U.Wis., 1958-59; asst. librarian Atlanta U., 1960-68; asst. dir. Union County Anti Poverty Council, 1968; librarian Union County Tech. Inst., Scotch Plains, N.J., 1968-82, Plainfield campus Union County Coll., 1982-95; ret., 1995. Mem. Roselle Bd. Edn., 1976-78; bd. dirs. Union County Anti

Poverty Council, 1969-72; mem. Roselle Human Relations Commn., 1971-73, Plainfield Sci. Center, 1974-76, Union County Psychiat. Clinic, 1980-83, Pinewood Sr. Citizens Council, 1981-85; bd. dirs. Project, Women of N.J. 1985-93, Pinewood Sr. Citizen Housing, 1981-85, Black Women's History Conf., 1985-92, pres., 1989-91. Mem. N.J. Library Assn., Council Library Tech., ALA (Black caucas), N.J. Coalition of 100 Black Women, African Am. Women's Polit. Caucus, N.J. Black Librarians Network (bd. dirs.), Links, Inc. (North Jersey chpt.), Black Women's History Conf., Alpha Kappa Alpha. Mem. A.M.E. Ch. Club: Just-A-Mere Lit. Home: 114 E 7th Ave Roselle NJ 07203-2028

RILL, JAMES FRANKLIN, lawyer; b. Evanston, Ill., Mar. 4, 1933; s. John Columbus and Frances Eleanor (Hill) R.; m. Mary Elizabeth Laws, June 14, 1957; children: James Franklin, Roderick M. AB cum laude, Dartmouth Coll., 1954; LLB, Harvard, 1959. Bar: D.C. bar 1959. Legis. asst. Congressman James P. S. Devereux, Washington, 1952; pvt. practice Washington, 1959-89; assoc. Steadman, Collier & Shannon, 1959-63; ptnr. Collier, Shannon & Rill, 1963-69, Collier, Shannon, Rill & Scott, 1969-89; asst. atty. gen., antitrust div. U.S. Dept. Justice, Washington, 1989-92; ptnr. Collier, Shannon, Rill & Scott, Washington, 1992—; pub. mem. Adminstrv. Conf. of U.S., 1992-94; coun. prin. Coun. for Excellence in Govt.; mem., advisor panel Office of Tech. Assessment of Multinat. Firms and U.S. Tech. Base. Contbr. articles to profl. jours. Trustee Bullis Sch., Potomac, Md. Served to 1st lt. arty. AUS, 1954-56. Mem. ABA (founder antitrust law sect. spl. com., mem. coun., past chmn. sect. of antitrust law), D.C. Bar Assn., Phi Delta Theta, Met. Club, Loudon Valley Club. Home: 8215 Meadowbrook Ln Bethesda MD 20815-3001 Office: Collier Shannon Rill & Scott 3050 K St NW Ste 400 Washington DC 20007-5108

RILLING, DAVID CARL, surgeon; b. Phila., Oct. 10, 1940; s. Carl Adam and Elizabeth Barbara (Young) R.; m. Karina Sturman, Mar. 25, 1972; children: Jonathan David, Alexander Valentine, Claudia Carla. BS with honors in Biology, Dickinson Coll., Carlisle, pa., 1962; MD, Hahnemann U., 1966. Diplomate Am. Bd. Surgery. Intern Hosp. of U. Pa., Phila., 1966-67; resident Abington (Pa.) Meml. Hosp., 1967-68, 70-73; surgeon Pennridge Surg Assocs., Sellersville, Pa., 1973—; active staff Grand View Hosp., Sellersville, Pa., chmn. dept. surgery, 1985-89, pres. med. staff, 1995. Lt. col. U.S. Army, 1968-70, Vietnam, USARMC. Decorated Bronze Star medal, Nat. Def. Svc. medal, Vietnam Svc. medal. Fellow Am. Coll. Surgeons; mem. AMA, Soc. Clin. Vascular Surgery, Pa. Med. Soc., Bucks County Med. Soc., Vietnam Vascular Registry. Avocations: paleontology, tennis, skiing. Office: Pennridge Surg Assocs 670 Lawn Ave Sellersville PA 18960-1571

RILLING, JOHN ROBERT, history educator; b. Wausau, Wis., Apr. 28, 1932; s. John Peter and Esther Laura (Wittig) R.; m. Joanne Marilyn McCrory, Dec. 21, 1953; children—Geoffrey Alan, Andrew Peter. B.A. summa cum laude, U. Minn., 1953; A.M., Harvard U., 1957, Ph.D., 1959. Asst. prof. history U. Richmond, Va., 1959-62, assoc. prof. history, 1962-68, prof. history, 1968—, chmn. dept. history, 1977-83; chmn. Westhampton Coll. dept. history, 1965-71; pres. Faculty Senate of Va., 1975-77. Elder Ginter Park Presbyn. Ch., 1973-83. Served with U.S. Army, 1953-55. Woodrow Wilson fellow, 1955-59; Harvard U. Travelling fellow, 1958; Coolidge fellow, 1955-56; Folger Library fellow, 1960; recipient U. Richmond Disting. Educator award, 1975, 76, 77, 80, 87, Prof. of Yr. finalist Coun. for the Advancement and Support of Edn., 1981 Mem. Am. Hist. Assn., Econ. History Soc., Conf. Brit. Studies, Phi Beta Kappa, Omicron Delta Kappa (prof. of yr. 1995). Contbr. articles to profl. jours. Avocations: hiking, bicycling, enology. Home: 1507 Wilmington Ave Richmond VA 23227-4429 Office: U Richmond Dept History Richmond VA 23173

RIMA, INGRID HAHNE, economics educator; d. Max F. and Hertha G. (Grunsfeld) Hahne; m. Philip W. Rima; children: David, Eric. BA with honors, CUNY, 1945; MA, U. Pa., 1946, PhD, 1951. Prof. econs. Temple U., Phila., 1967—. Author: Development of Economic Analysis, 1967, 5th edit., 1996, Labor Markets Wages and Employment, 1981, The Joan Robinson Legacy, 1991, The Political Economy of Global Restructuring, Vol. I, Production and Organization, Vol. II, Trade and Finance, 1993, Measurement, Quantification and Economic Analysis, 1994, Labor Markets in a Global Economy, 1996. Fellow Ea. Econ. Assn.; mem. Am. Econ. Assn., History of Econs. Soc. (pres. 1993-4), Phi Beta Kappa. Office: Temple U Broad & Montgomery Ave Philadelphia PA 19122

RIMEL, REBECCA WEBSTER, foundation executive. BS, U. Va., 1973; MBA, James Madison U., 1983. RN, Va. Head nurse, emergency dept. U. Va. Hosp., Charlottesville, 1973-74, coord. med. out-patient dept., 1974-75, nurse practitioner dept. neurosurgery, 1975-77, instr. in neurosurgery, 1975-80, asst. prof., 1981-83; program mgr. health Pew Charitable Trusts, Phila., 1983-84; asst. v.p. Glenmede Trust Co., Pew Charitable Trusts, Phila., 1984-85; v.p. for programs Pew Charitable Trusts, Phila., 1985-88, exec. dir., 1988-94; pres., 1994—; mem. Coun. on Founds., Washington; prin. investigator dept. neurosurgery U. Va., 1981-85; adv. com. for U.S. Olympics on Boxing, 1983-86; adv. coun. Nat. Inst. of Neurol. Disorders & Strokes, 1988-91, also bd. dirs.; bd. dirs. Nat. Environ. Edn. and Tng. Found., Inc., Washington, Thomas Jefferson Meml. Found., Ind. Sector, Washington. Contbr. articles and abstracts to profl. jours., chpts. in books. Recipient Disting. Nursing Alumni award U. Va., 1988; Kellogg Nat. fellow, 1982. Mem. APHA, ANA, Va. State Nurses Assn. (membership and credentials com. 1982-86), Am. Acad. Nursing, Am. Assn. Neurosurg. Nurses, Emergency Dept. Nurses Assn.

RIMER, JOHN THOMAS, foreign language educator, academic administrator, writer, translator; b. Pitts., Mar. 2, 1933; s. John T. and Naomi (Bowser) R.; m. Laurence E. Mus., Apr. 18, 1964; children: John, Mark. B.A., Princeton U., 1954; M.A., Columbia U., 1969, Ph.D., 1971. Asst. cultural officer USIA, Laos, Japan; then dir. Am. Cultural Ctr. Kobe, Japan, 1958-67; assoc. prof., then prof. Japanese lang. and lit. Washington U., St. Louis, 1973-83, chmn. dept. Chinese and Japanese, 1973-83; chief Asian div. Library of Congress, Washington, 1983-86; chmn. Hebrew and East Asian langs. and lits. U. Maryland, College Park, 1986-91; chmn. East Asian langs. and lits. U. Pitts., 1991—; mem. Am. adv. bd. Japan Found., 1984—. Author: Toward a Modern Japanese Theatre, 1974, Traditions in Modern Japanese Fiction, 1978; translator: stories Mori Ogai, 2 vols., 1977, Mask and Sword: Two Plays for the Contemporary Japanese Theatre, 1980, On the No Drama, 1983, Pilgrimages, 1988, A Reader's Guide to Japanese Literature, 1988; editor: Multiple Meanings, 1987; editor, contbr.: Culture and Identity, Japanese Intellectuals during the Interwar Years, 1990, Shisendo, 1991, Youth and Other Stories by Mori Ogai, 1994, Kyoto Encounters, 1995, A Hidden Fire: Russian and Japanese Cultural Encounters, 1868-1929, 1995. Served with U.S. Army, 1955-58. NEH fellow France, 1976-77; NEH grantee, 1979-81. Mem. Social Sci. Research Council (joint com. on Japan studies 1979-83). Episcopalian. Home: 1400 N Negley Ave Pittsburgh PA 15206-1118 Office: U Pitts Dept East Asian Langs and Lits 1501 CL Pittsburgh PA 15260

RIMERMAN, IRA STEPHEN, banker; b. N.Y.C., Apr. 28, 1938; s. Samuel David and Dorothy (Hoffman) R.; m. Iris Jacqueline, Mar. 10, 1962; children: Traci, Randi-Sue, Judith. BA in Indsl. Engring., Syracuse U., 1960; MBA, U. Pa., 1961; profl. degree indsl. engring., Columbia U., 1968. Tech. data processor ITT, Paramus, N.J., 1962-65, CBS, N.Y.C., 1965-67, Allied Chem., N.Y.C., 1967-69, Computer Usage Corp., N.Y.C., 1969-71; data processing mgr. Citicorp, N.Y.C., 1971; CFO Citicorp subs. Citicorp, Columbus, Ohio, 1971-73; dir., v.p. econ. devel. ctr. Citicorp, N.Y.C., 1974-75, chief of staff, v.p. N.Y. banking group, 1975-76; bus. mgr., v.p. consumer bus. Citicorp, Hong Kong, 1976-81; div. head bank cards Citibank USA div. Citicorp, N.Y.C., 1981-85, group exec. comsumer svc. internat., 1985-87, group exec. card products, 1987-89, sr. v.p. adminstrn., 1989—, sr. v.p., 1992—; sr. account mgr. for Citicorp Wharton Bus. Sch. U. Pa., Phila., 1986—. Trustee The Cmty. Synagogue, 1982-88; bd. dirs. Vis. Nurse Svc., N.Y., treas., 1987—, chmn. fin. com., 1988—; bd. dirs. Beth Israel Med. Ctr., 1989—; mem. Wharton Grad. Exec. Bd., 1989-95; bd. dirs. Wharton Entrepreneurial Ctr., 1990—. Mem. Am. Inst. Indsl. Engrs., Film Soc. N.Y. (bd. dirs. 1996—), Wharton Alumni Assn. (bd. dirs. 1976-89), Hong Kong Club. Democrat. Jewish. Avocations: swimming, reading. Home: 63 Sands Point Rd Sands Point NY 11050-1645 Office: Citicorp Center 23rd Fl Zone 1 153 E 53rd St New York NY 10043

RIMMER, JACK, retired chemical company executive; b. N.Y.C., Mar. 1, 1921; s. Sigmund and Esther (Grumet) R.; m. Mae Haskin, Oct. 31, 1942; children: Phyllis Ellen, Carole Ruth, Ann Rhoda. B.S. in Chemistry, Bklyn. Coll., 1946. Prodn. mgr. Winthrop Labs., Rensselaer, N.Y., 1946-57; dir. ops. B.T. Babbitt, Inc., Albany, N.Y., 1957-61; with W.R. Grace & Co., N.Y.C., 1961-85; exec. v.p. W.R. Grace & Co., 1980-85, also dir.; pres. The Grey Group, 1988; bd. dirs. W.R. Grace & Co., Dearborn Chem. Co., Dearborn-U.K. Ltd., E.J. Killam Assocs., Teroson K.K. (Japan), The Grey Group; lectr. Georgetown U.; instr. Hudson Valley Tech. Inst., Northwood Univ. V.p., trustee Arts-in-Edn. Found. of N.J.; trustee Bklyn. Coll. Found. Score; bd. dirs. Armory Art Ctr. With USN, 1944-46. Mem. Am. Chem. Soc., Am. Inst. Chem. Engrs., World Trade Assn. Home: 123 Lakeshore Dr North Palm Beach FL 33408-3614

RIMMEREID, ARTHUR V., bishop. Bishop N.W. Minn. Synod Evang. Luth. Ch., Moorhead.

RIMOIN, DAVID LAWRENCE, physician, geneticist; b. Montreal, Nov. 9, 1936; s. Michael and Fay (Lecker) R.; m. Mary Ann Singleton, 1962 (div. 1979); 1 child, Anne; m. Ann Piilani Garber, July 27, 1980; children: Michael, Lauren. BSc, McGill U., Montreal, 1957, MSc, MD, CM, 1961; PhD, Johns Hopkins U., 1967. Asst. prof. medicine, pediatrics Washington U., St. Louis, 1967-70; assoc. prof. medicine, pediatrics UCLA, 1970-73, prof., 1973—, chief med. genetics, Harbor-UCLA Med. Ctr., 1970-86; dir. dept. pediatrics, dir. Med. Genetics and Birth Defects Ctr., 1986—; Steven Spielberg chmn. pediatrics Cedars-Sinai Med. Ctr., L.A., 1989—; chmn. coun. Med. Genetics Orgn., 1993. Co-author: Principles and Practice of Medical Genetics, 1983, 90; contbr. articles to profl. jours., chpts. to books. Recipient Ross Outstanding Young Investigator award Western Soc. Pediatric Research, 1976, E. Mead Johnson award Am. Acad. Pediatrics, 1976. Fellow ACP, AAAS, Am. Coll. Med. Genetics (pres. 1991—); mem. Am. Fedn. Clin. Rsch. (sec.-treas. 1972-75), Western Soc. Clin. Rsch. (pres. 1978), Western Soc. Pediatric Rsch. (pres. 1995), Am. Bd. Med. Genetics (pres. 1979-83), Am. Soc. Human Genetics (pres. 1984), Am. Pediatric Soc., Soc. Pediatric Rsch., Am. Soc. Clin. Investigation, Assn. Am. Physicians, Johns Hopkins Soc. Scholars, Inst. Medicine. Office: Cedars-Sinai Med Ctr 8700 Beverly Blvd Los Angeles CA 90048-1804

RIMPEL, AUGUSTE EUGENE, JR., management and technical consulting executive; b. St. Thomas, V.I., Aug. 25, 1939; s. Auguste Eugene and Leah Eudora (Harris) R. B.A. magna cum laude, Inter-Am. U. P.R., 1957; M.S. in Ch.E., M.I.T., 1961; Ph.D., Carnegie Inst. Tech., 1964; M.B.A., Columbia U., 1964-65; m. Maria Czernetski, Sept. 23, 1966; children: Nicole, Christopher. Research chem. engr. Am. Cyanamid Co., Stamford, Conn., 1961-62; with Arthur D. Little, Inc., Cambridge, Mass., 1965-75, sr. staff mem., 1973-75; commr. of commerce, spl. advisor to gov. for econ. affairs Govt. U.S. V.I., St. Thomas, 1975-78; mem. corp. spl. staff Arthur D. Little, Inc., Cambridge, 1978-81, also v.p. Arthur D. Little Internat., Inc.; v.p. Booz-Allen and Hamilton, Inc., 1981-83; v.p., ptnr., Price Waterhouse, 1983—. Bd. dirs. Caribbean/Lat. Am. Action, 1979-94; mem. U.S. del. World Bank Conf. on Caribbean Econ. Devel., 1977-78; mem. subcoms. on internat. econ. devel. U.S. C. of C., 1980-83; V.I. rep. White Ho. Conf. on Balanced Nat. Growth and Econ. Devel., 1978; bd. dirs. travel adv. bd. U.S. Dept. Commerce, 1977-78; pres. Caribbean Tourism Assn., 1977-78; bd. dirs., mem. exec. com. Caribbean Tourism Research Center, 1976-78. Mem. Am. Inst. Chem. Engrs., Am. Chem. Soc., Am. Inst. Chemists, Soc. Internat. Devel., Sigma Xi. Office: 1616 N Ft Myer Dr Arlington VA 22209-3100

RIMROTT, FRIEDRICH PAUL JOHANNES, engineer, educator; b. Halle, Germany, Aug. 4, 1927; emigrated to Can., 1952; s. Hans and Margarete (Hofmeister) R.; m. Doreen McConnell, Apr. 7, 1955; children: Karla, Robert, Kira, Elizabeth-Ann. Dipl. Ing., U. Karlsruhe, Germany, 1951; MASc, U. Toronto, Ont., Can., 1955; PhD, Pa. State U., 1958; Dr Ing., Tech. U., Darmstadt, Germany, 1961; P.Eng., Ontario Prov., 1954; C.Eng., U.K., 1987; D.Eng. (hon.), U. Victoria, 1992. Asst. prof. engring. mechanics Pa. State U., 1958-60; mem. faculty dept. mech. engring. U. Toronto, 1960—, assoc. prof., 1962-67, prof., 1967-93, prof. emeritus, 1993—; vis. prof. Tech. U. Vienna, Austria, 1969-70, 86, Tech. U. Hanover, Germany, 1970, U. Bochum, Germany, 1971, U. Wuppertal, Germany, 1987, 89, U. Lanzhou, People's Republic of China, 1989, Otto-von-Guericke-U. Magdeburg, 1992, 93, 94, 95, 96; mng. dir. German Lang. Sch. (Metro Toronto) Inc., 1967-91; pres. 15th Internat. Congress Theoretical and Applied Mechanics, 1980; pres. CSME Mech. Engring. Forum, 1990. Author: Introductory Attitude Dynamics, 1988, Introductory Orbit Dynamics, 1989 (with K.Y. Yeh) Orbital Mechanics Introduction, Chinese edit., 1993, (with B. Tabarrok) Variational Methods and Complementary Formulations in Dynamics, 1994; editor: (with J. Schwaighofer) Mechanics of the Solid State, 1968, (with L.E. Jones) Proceedings CANCAM 67, 1968, (with J.T. Pindera, H.H.E. Leipholz, D.E. Grierson) Experimental Mechanics in Research and Development, 1973, (with W. Eichenlaub) Was Du ererbt, 1978, (with B. Tabarrok) Theoretical and Applied Mechanics, 1980. Mem. Can. Council on Multiculturalism, 1972-79. NRC postdoctoral fellow, 1959, Alexander von Humboldt sr. fellow, 1962, NRC sr. rsch. fellow, 1969-70; recipient Can. Congress Applied Mechanics award, 1989, Alexander von Humboldt Rsch. prize, 1994. Fellow ASME, Instn. Mech. Engrs., Engring. Inst. Can., Can. Soc. Mech. Engring. (pres. 1974-75), Can. Aero. and Space Inst.; mem. Can. Congress Applied Mechanics (ctrl. com., chmn. congress com. 1967, 69, 71, 77), Can. Metric Assn. (pres. 1971-72), Soc. German Engrs. (Germany), Soc. for Applied Math. and Mechanics (Germany) (dir. 1971-79). Home: 6 Thurgate Cres, Thornhill, ON Canada L3T 4G3 Office: U Toronto, Dept Mech Engring, Toronto, ON Canada M5S 3G8

RIMSZA, SKIP, mayor; b. Chgo.; m. Kim Gill; children: Brian, Jenny. Mem. Phoenix City Coun., 1990-94; vice mayor City of Phoenix, 1993, mayor, 1994—; former pres. Bd. Realtors. Mem. several cmty. bds. Office: Office of the Mayor 200 W Washington St Phoenix AZ 85003

RIN, ZENGI, economic history educator; b. Yuanlin, Taiwan, Sept. 15, 1935; arrived in Japan, 1962; s. Sankei and Sango (Ko) R.; m. Shien Gi, Dec. 28, 1969; children: Kotatsu, Jobun, Joan. BA, Zhong Xing U., Taiwan, 1960; MA, Kyoto U., 1965, postgrad., 1965-68. From asst. prof. to prof. economic history Nagoya Gakuin U., Seto, 1968—; vis. scholar, Harvard U., Cambridge, 1979-80, Peking U., 1985. Author: Introduction to Economic History, 1981, General Economic History, 1984, Lectures on Asian Economic History, 1987, The Current in the Economic History, 1992, A Brief Economic History of Asia, 1994. Mem. Japan Assn. for Asian Polit. and Econ. Studies, Socio-Econ. History Soc. Japan, Bus. History Soc. Japan. Home: 1263-4 Shimokirido Arai, Owariasahi Aichi 488, Japan Office: Nagoya Gakuin U, 1350 Kamishinano-cho, Seto Aichi 480-12, Japan

RINALDINI, LUIS EMILIO, investment banker; b. Cambridge, Eng., July 29, 1953; came to U.S., 1964; s. Luis Maria and Fanny Josefina (Lopez) R.; m. Elaine Nash McHugh, June 22, 1974 (div. 1987); m. Julie Sayre Short, Aug. 1, 1987. BSE, Princeton U., 1974; MBA, Harvard U., 1980. Architect Johnson Burgee Architects, N.Y.C., 1974-78; assoc. Lazard Freres & Co. LLC, N.Y.C., 1980-85, mng. dir., 1986—. Mem. Piping Rock Club (Locust Valley, N.Y.), Meadowbrook Club (Jericho, N.Y.), Lyford Cay Club (Bahamas), Raquet and Tennis Club (N.Y.C.). Home: 124 E 64th St New York NY 10021-7307 Office: Lazard Freres & Co LLC 30 Rockefeller Plz New York NY 10020

RINAMAN, JAMES CURTIS, JR., lawyer; b. Miami, Fla., Feb. 8, 1935; s. James Curtis and Ruth Marie (Rader) R.; m. Gloria Margaret Kaspar; children: James, Mark, Christine, Karen. BA, U. Fla., 1955, JD, 1960. Bar: Fla. 1960, U.S. Dist. Ct. (so. dist.) Fla. 1960, U.S. Ct. Appeals (5th cir.) 1960, U.S. Supreme Ct. 1963, U.S. Dist. Ct. (mid. dist.) Fla. 1967, U.S. Dist. Ct. (no. dist.) Fla. 1981, U.S. Ct. Appeals (11th cir.) 1981, U.S. Ct. Claims 1991, U.S. Ct. Mil. Appeals 1994. With Marks, Gray, Conroy & Gibbs, P.A., Jacksonville, Fla., 1960—; gen. counsel Fla. Bd. Architecture, 1965-79, City of Jacksonville, 1970-71, Jacksonville C. of C., 1973-76, 90; adj. prof. Coll. Architecture, U. Fla., 1975-90. Pres. Jacksonville Cmty. Coun. Inc., 1985. Leadership Jacksonville, Inc., 1987; mem. Jacksonville Transp. Authority, 1971-80, Jacksonville BRAC Commn., 1993-95. Jacksonville Cecil Field Devel. Commn., 1994-96; chmn. N.E. Fla. chpt. ARC, 1996. With U.S. Army, 1955-57, Fla. NG, 1957-92. ret. brig. gen., 1992. Named to U. Fla. Hall of Fame. Fellow Am. Coll. Trial Lawyers, Am. Bar Found., Fla. Bar Found. (bd. dirs. 1982-87, 88, Disting. Svc. award 1983, 86, Medal of Honor 1988); mem. ABA (ho. of dels. 1982-86), Jacksonville Bar Assn. (pres. 1972-73), The Fla. Bar (pres. 1982-83), Def. Rsch. Inst. (so. regional v.p. 1980-83, bd. dirs. 1976-78, 83-87), Am. Judicature Soc. (Herbert Harley award 1987), Fla. Coun. Bar Pres. (Outstanding Past Pres. award 1989), Lawyers for Civil Justice (pres. 1989-91, chmn. bd. dirs. 1991-94), Vol. Lawyers Resource Ctr. of Fla., (pres. 1984-89, chmn. bd. dirs. 1989-93), So. Conf. of Bar (pres. 1982—), Nat. Conf. of Bar, Assn. Def. Trial Attys. (internat. pres., nat. pres. 1976-77), Internat. Assn. Def. Counsel, Jacksonville Assn. Def. Counsel, Fla. Defense Lawyers Assn. (pres. 1973), Fla. C. of C., Jacksonville C. of C. (chmn. 1994), Meninack Civic Club (pres. 1986), Jacksonville Commodores League, Fla. Blue Key, San. Jose Country Club, River Club, Univ. Club, Phi Gamma Delta (bd. trustees ednl. found. 1995—), Phi Alpha Delta. Republican. Methodist. Office: Marks Gray Conroy & Gibbs 1200 Riverplace Blvd Ste 800 Jacksonville FL 32207-9046 also: PO Box 447 Jacksonville FL 32201-0447

RINDEN, DAVID LEE, editor; b. Lake Mills, Iowa, Aug. 1, 1941; s. Oscar Henry and Iva (Stensrud) R.; m. Gracia Elizabeth Carlson, Sept. 11, 1966; children: Jonathan, Elizabeth, Amy. BA, Moorhead State U., 1964; diploma, Luth. Brethren Sem., 1966; postgrad., Seattle Pacific U., 1973. Ordained to ministry Luth. Ch., 1967. Pastor Bethesda Luth. Ch., Eau Claire, Wis., 1968-72, Maple Pk. Luth. Ch., Lynnwood, Wash., 1972-79; v.p. Ch. of the Luth. Brethren, Fergus Falls, Minn., 1991—; editor Faith & Fellowship, Fergus Falls, Minn., 1979—; exec. dir. ch. svcs. Ch. of the Luth. Brethren, Fergus Falls, 1979—; chmn. com. on commitment Ch. of Luth. Brethren, Fergus Falls, 1981-82, com. on role of women in ch., 1984-86, chmn. com. on 90th anniversary, 1989—, chmn. bd. publs., 1968-78. Editor: Explanation of Luther's Small Catechism, 1988; author: Biblical Foundations, 1981. Founding com. JAIL, Inc., Fergus Falls, 1991; pres. bd. dirs. Fergus Falls Fed. Community Credit Union, 1987—. Mem. Fergus Falls Ministerial Assn. (sec. 1989-90, v.p. 1991-92, pres. 1992-93), Kiwanis (pres. 1994-95, lt. gov. 1996-97). Home: 701 W Channing Ave Fergus Falls MN 56537-3218 Office: Ch of the Luth Brethren 1007 Westside Dr # 655 Fergus Falls MN 56537-2646

RINDER, GEORGE GREER, retired retail company executive; b. Chgo., Feb. 3, 1921; s. Carl Otto and Jane (Greer) R.; m. Shirley Laurine Latham, Dec. 21, 1946; children: Robert Latham, Carl Thomas, Susan Jane Sitrick. M.B.A., U. Chgo., 1942. C.P.A., Ill. With Gen. Electric Co., 1941-42; with Marshall Field & Co., Chgo., 1946-86; asst. to gen. mgr. Marshall Field & Co., 1959-62, v.p., comptroller, 1962-67, v.p. finance, 1967-71, exec. v.p. fin., 1971-74, exec. v.p., 1974-78, sr. exec. v.p., 1978-81, vice chmn., 1981-86, dir., 1972-83; ret., 1986. Nat. trustee McCormick Theol. Sem.; mem. coun. Grad. Sch. Bus., U. Chgo. Served to capt. AUS, 1942-46. Recipient Alumni Svc. citation U. Chgo., 1990, Alumni Svc. medal U. Chgo., 1995. Mem. Fin. Execs. Inst., Phi Beta Kappa, Delta Upsilon, Beta Gamma Sigma. Clubs: Chicago (Chgo.), University (Chgo.), Economic (Chgo.); Hinsdale (Ill.) Golf.). Home: 169 Pheasant Hollow Dr Burr Ridge IL 60521-5050

RINDERKNECHT, ROBERT EUGENE, internist; b. Dover, Ohio, Apr. 27, 1921; s. Henry Carl and Mary Dorothy (Walter) R.; m. Janice Marie Rausch, Oct. 14, 1966; children: Mary Ellen, William A., Janis E. BS, Case Western Reserve U., 1943, MD, 1945. Diplomate Am. Bd. Internal Medicine. Intern Grasslands Hosp., Valhalla, N.Y., 1945-46; resident U. Hosps. Cleve., 1948-49, VA Hosp., Cleve., 1949-51; internist pvt. practice, Dover, Ohio, 1951-79; ret., 1979; trustee Physicians Ins. Co. Ohio, Columbus, 1978-79. Pres. Tuscarawas County (Ohio) Heart Br., 1962-64, 75-77, East Ctrl. Ohio Heart Assn., Canton, 1967-69. Fellow ACP; mem. Masons, Shriners, Elks. Republican. Presbyterian. Home: 114 Dewitt Loop Daphne AL 36526-7740

RINDFUSS, RONALD RICHARD, sociology educator; b. Buffalo, Dec. 11, 1946; married Aug. 1968; 2 children. BA, Fordham U., 1968; PhD, Princeton U., 1974. Rsch. asst. Nat. Fertility Study, Office Population Rsch., Princeton U., 1971-73; rsch. assoc. Ctr. Demography and Ecology U. Wis., Madison, 1973-76; asst. prof. sociology U. N.C., Chapel Hill, 1976-79, assoc. prof., 1979-84; prof. sociology U. N.C., 1984—; dir. Carolina Population Ctr., Chapel Hill, 1992—; cons. in field. Contbr. numerous articles to profl. jours.; assoc. editor Social Forces, 1976—; cons. editor Am. Jour. Sociology, 1977-80; contbg. editor Sociol Biology, 1974; referee for numerous jours. NIH traineeship, 1968-71. Mem. Am. Sociol. Assn. (chmn. sociology of population sect. 1989-90, mem. pubs. com. 1983-84), Population Assn. Am. (pres. 1991, mem. Mindel C. Sheps award com. 1990, bd. dirs. 1984-87), Internat. Union for Sci. Study Population, Nat. Coun. on Family Rels., So. Regional Demographic Group, So. Sociol. Soc., Coun. on Family Rsch. Office: Carolina Population Ctr. CB # 8120 University Sq 123 W Franklin St Chapel Hill NC 27516-2524

RINDLAUB, JOHN WADE, advertising agency executive; b. Lancaster, Pa., July 26, 1934; s. Willard Weaner and Jean (Wade) R.; m. Laurette Lukens, June 22, 1956; children: John Wade, Curtis Clay, David Landis. BA, Yale U., 1956. Copywriter, supr. Young & Rubicam, N.Y.C., 1956-68; v.p., creative dir. Toronto, 1968-71; assoc. creative dir. N.Y.C., 1971-73; creative dir. Stockholm and Frankfurt, Fed. Republic Germany, 1973-77; mng. dir. Holter, Young & Rubicam, Oslo, 1977-78; assoc. dir. mktg. Young & Rubicam, N.Y.C., 1978-80, sr. v.p., mgr. creative services, 1980-84, assoc. creative dir., 1984-88, sr. v.p., dir. corp. rels., 1988-90, dir. industry and govt. rels., 1990—. Mem. Yale Club, Riverside Yacht Club. Episcopalian. Home: 8 Hill Lane Ave Riverside CT 06878-2500 Office: Young & Rubicam 285 Madison Ave New York NY 10017-6401

RINE, SUSAN, principal. Prin. Centennial Elem. Sch. Office: Centennial Elem Sch 38501 Centennial Rd Dade City FL 33525-1635

RINEARSON, PETER MARK, journalist, author, software developer; b. Seattle, Aug. 4, 1954; s. Peter Morley and Jeannette Irene (Love) R.; m. Jill Chan, Sept. 15, 1991. Student, U. Wash., 1972-78. Editor Sammamish Valley News, Redmond, Wash., 1975-76; reporter Seattle Times, 1976-78, govt. and polit. reporter, 1979-81, aerospace reporter, 1982-84, Asian corr., 1985-86; pres. Alki Software Corp., Seattle, 1990—, Raster Ranch, Ltd., 1995—. Author: Word Processing Power with Microsoft Word, 4th edit., 1991, Microsoft Word Style Sheets, 1987, Quick Reference Guide to Microsoft Word, 1988, Microsoft Word Companion Disk, 1988, Masterword, 1990, 91, 92, (with Bill Gates and Nathan Myhrvold) The Road Ahead, 1995. Recipient Spl. Paul Myhre award-series Penney-Mo. Newspaper awards, 1983, Disting. Writing award Am. Soc. Newspaper Editors, 1984, Pulitzer prize for feature writing, 1984, Lowell Thomas Travel Writing award, 1984, John Hancock award,1985, semi-finalist NASA Journalist-in-Space Project, 1986; U.S.-Japan Leadership Program fellow Japan Soc., 1988. Office: 300 Queen Anne Ave N # 410 Seattle WA 98109-4599

RINEHART, CHARLES R., savings and loan association executive; b. San Francisco, Jan. 31, 1947; s. Robert Eugene and Rita Mary Rinehart; married; children: Joseph B., Kimberly D., Michael P., Scott. BS, U. San Francisco, 1968. Exec. v.p. Fireman's Fund Ins. Cos., Novato, Calif., 1969-83; pres., CEO Avco Fin. Services, Irvine, Calif., 1983-89, H.F. Ahmanson & Co., Irwindale, Calif., 1989—; chmn., CEO Home Savs. of Am., Irwindale; mem. Fannie Mae Nat. Adv. Coun., Thrift Instn. Adv. Coun.; bd. dirs. Fed. Home Loan Bank San Francisco, L.A. World Affairs Coun. Mem. adv. com. Drug Use is Life Abuse; mem. Tustin Pub. Sch. Found. Camp com. Served to 2d lt. U.S. Army, 1968-69. Fellow Casualty Actuarial Soc.; mem. Am. Mgmt. Assn., Am. Acad. Actuaries. Republican. Roman Catholic. Avocations: athletics, gourmet cooking, model trains. Office: Ho Savs Am/H F Ahmanson & Co 4900 Rivergrade Rd Irwindale CA 91706-1404

RINEHART, JONATHAN, public relations executive; b. N.Y.C., Apr. 19, 1930. BA in Internat. Rels., Yale U., 1952. Corr., bur. chief, chief mil. corr. Time Mag., 1956-62; dep. chief corrs., gen. editor Newsweek, 1962-65; sr. v.p. public rels. Ea. Airlines, 1965-73; pres. Jonathan Rinehart Group, Inc., 1974-77; pres. Adams & Rinehart, 1977-87, chmn., CEO, 1987-92; chmn. Ogilvy Pub. Rels. Group, 1987-92, Ogilvy Adams & Rinehart, 1992—; also bd. dirs. Ogilvy & Mather Worldwide; chmn. Powell Tate, New York. Office: Powell Tate 520 Madison Ave 33 fl New York NY 10022*

RINES, JOHN RANDOLPH, automotive company executive; b. Balt., Aug. 3, 1947; s. John William and Betty (Singer) R.; m. Peggy J. Daugaard, Sept. 19, 1969 (dec. 1978); m. Katherine M. Duff, Nov. 29, 1980; children: Jacqueline D., Eleanor W. BS in Econs., Colo. State U., 1970; MBA, U. Va., 1977. With GM, 1970-75, 77—; fin. analyst GM, Detroit, 1977-78, dir. product programs, 1978-80, asst. to pres., 1980-81, gen. dir. fin., 1981-82; exec. dir. GM, Sao Paulo, Brazil, 1982-84; dir. fin. Buick/Oldsmobile/Cadillac group GM, Flint, Mich., 1984-85; gen. mgr. motors holding div. and GM auction GM, Detroit, 1985-91, gen. mgr. parts ops., 1991—; pres. GM Acceptance Corp., Detroit, 1992—. Trustee Arts Found. Mich., Detroit. Mem. Grosse Pointe (Mich.) Club, Old Club (Harsen's Island), Birmingham Athletic Club. Office: GM 3044 W Grand Blvd Detroit MI 48202-3091

RINES, S. MELVIN, investment banker; b. Berlin, N.H., Aug. 26, 1924; s. William James and Gladys Olive (Estes) R.; m. Mary Jo Marcy, Feb. 27, 1954; children: Pamela Marcy, Jeffrey William, David Melvin. BA, U. N.H., 1947; OD, No. Ill. Coll., 1950. Asst. v.p. Kidder, Peabody & Co., Inc., N.Y.C., 1970, v.p.,, 1972—, shareholder, 1973—; mng. dir. Kidder, Peabody & Co. Inc., 1986—, sr. v.p., mng. dir., 1986-95; adj. prof. Am. U., Washington, 1986—. Co-editor: The Supranationals, 1986; contbr. articles to profl. jours. Mem. Bretton Woods Com., Washington, 1987—; trustee U. N.H. Found., 1994—, exec. bd. Whittemore Sch. Bus. and Econs., 1995—. Lt., fighter pilot USN, 1943-46, 50-54, Korea. Mem. Boston Exec. Assn. (pres. 1970-71). Republican. Clubs: Downtown (pres. 1974-81), Bond (Boston) (pres. 1976-77); Met. (Washington); DTA (N.Y.). Avocations: tennis, skiing, sailing, swimming, riding. Home: 21 Sudbury Rd Weston MA 02193-1332 Office: Paine Webber Inc 100 Federal St Boston MA 02110

RINEY, HAL PATRICK, advertising executive; b. Seattle, July 17, 1932; s. Hal Patrick and Inez Marie R.; m. Elizabeth Kennedy; children: Benjamin Kennedy, Samantha Elizabeth. BA, U. Wash., Seattle, 1954. From art dir./writer to v.p., creative dir. BBDO, Inc., San Francisco, 1956-72; exec. v.p., creative dir. Botsford Ketchum, San Francisco, 1972-76; sr. v.p., mng. dir., creative dir. Ogilvy & Mather, San Francisco, 1976-81; exec. v.p. Ogilvy & Mather West, 1981-86; chmn. Hal Riney & Ptnrs., Inc., San Francisco, 1986—. Recipient 5 Lion d'Or du Cannes awards, 17 Clio awards, 15 Addy awards, Grand Prix du Cannes; named to Creative Hall of Fame. Mem. Am. Assn. Advt. Agys., San Francisco Advt. Club, San Francisco Soc. Communicating Arts, Wild Goose Club, Meadow Club, St. Francis Yacht Club. Home: 1 Los Pinos Nicasio CA 94946-9701 Office: Hal Riney & Ptnrs Inc 735 Battery St San Francisco CA 94111-1501

RING, ALICE RUTH BISHOP, physician; b. Ft. Collins, Oct. 11, 1931; d. Ernest Otto and Mary Frances (Drohan) Bishop; m. Wallace Harold Ring, July 26, 1956 (div. 1969); children: Rebecca, Eric, Mark; m. Robert Charles Deifenbach, Sept. 10, 1977. BS, Colo. State U., 1953; MD, U. Colo., 1956; MPH, U. Calif., Berkeley, 1971. Physician cons. Utah State Div. HEalth, Salt Lake City, 1960-65; med. dir., project head start Salt Lake City Community Action Program, 1965-70; resident Utah State Div. Health, 1969-71; asst. assoc. reg. health dir. U.S. Pub. Health Svc., San Francisco, 1971-75; med. cons. U.S. Pub. Health Svc., Atlanta, 1975-77, dir. primary care, 1977-84; dir. div. diabetes control Ctrs. Disease Control, Atlanta, 1984-88; dir. WHO Collabor Ctr., Atlanta, 1986-91; dir. preventive medicine residency Ctrs. Disease Control, Atlanta, 1988-94; exec. dir. Am. Bd. Preventive Medicine, 1993—; trustee Am. Bd. Preventive Medicine, 1990-92 (diplomate); lectr. Emory U. Sch. Pub. Health, 1988-94. Co-author: Clinical Diabetes, 1991. Bd. dirs. Diabetes Assn. Atlanta, 1985-90, med. adv. com., 1990-94. Fellow Am. Coll. Preventive Medicine (bd. dirs. 1990-94); mem. APHA, AMA (grad. med. edn. adv. com. 1993—), Assn. Tchrs. Preventive Medicine, Am. Acad. Pediatrics, Sigma Xi. Office: Am Bd Preventive Medicine 9950 Lawrence Ave Schiller Park IL 60176-1310

RING, ALVIN MANUEL, pathologist; b. Detroit, Mar. 17, 1933; s. Julius and Helen (Krolik) R.; m. Cynthia Joan Jacobson, Sept. 29, 1963; children—Jeffrey, Melinda, Heather. BS, Wayne State U., 1954; MD, U. Mich., 1958. Intern Mt. Carmel Hosp., Detroit, 1958-59; resident in pathology Michael Reese Hosp., Chgo., 1960-62; asst. pathologist Kings County Hosp., Bklyn., 1962-63; assoc. pathologist El Camino Hosp., Mountain View, Calif., 1963-65; chief pathologist, dir. labs. St. Elizabeth's Hosp., Chgo., 1965-72, Holy Cross Hosp., Chgo., 1972-87, Silver Cross Hosp., Joliet, Ill., 1990—; instr. SUNY, 1962-63, Stanford U., 1963-65; asst. prof. pathology U. Ill., Chgo., 1966-69, assoc. prof., 1969-78, prof., 1978—; adj. clin. prof. No. Ill. U., 1981-87; adj. prof. med. edn. U. Ill. Coll. Medicine, 1988—; chmn. histotech. Nat. Accrediting Agy. for Clin. Lab Scis., 1977-81; mem. spl. adv. com. Health Manpower, 1966-71; pres. Spear Computer Users Group, 1981-82; mem. adv. com. Mid-Am. chpt. ARC, 1979-85; pres. Pathology and Lab Cons., Inc., 1985—; adj. prof., med. dir. Med. Tech., Moraine Valley C.C., 1994—; originator, coord. pathology, med. decision-making courses Nat. Ctr. for Advanced Med. Edn., 1981—, others. Author: Laboratory Correlation Manual, 1968, 82, 86, Laboratory Assistant Examination Review Book, 1971, Review Book in Pathology, Anatomic, 1986, Review Book in Pathology, Clinical, 1986; mem. editorial bd. Lab. Medicine, 1975-87; contbr. articles to med. jours. Fellow Coll. Am. Pathology (insp. 1973—), Am. Soc. Clin. Pathology; mem. AMA, Ill. Med. Soc., Chgo. Med. Soc. (alt. councilor 1980-85, mem. adv. com. on health care delivery), Ill. Pathol. Soc., Chgo. Pathol. Soc. (pres. 1986-88, exec. com. 1985-89, program. com. 1987—), Am. Assn. Blood Banks, Assn. Brain Tumor Rsch. (cons.), Exec. Svc. Corps (exec. cons. 1988—), Phi Lambda Kappa. Home: 100 Graymoor Ln Olympia Fields IL 60461-1213 Office: Silver Cross Hosp 1200 Maple Rd Joliet IL 60432-1439

RING, HERBERT EVERETT, management executive; b. Norwich, Conn., Dec. 19, 1925; s. Herbert Everett and Catherine (Riordan) R.; m. Marilyn Elizabeth Dursin, May 21, 1955 (dec. Jan. 1994); children: Nancy Marie, Herbert Everett. BA, Ind. No. U., 1971, MBA, 1973; AMP, Harvard U., 1981. V.p. ops. Ogden Foods, Inc., Toledo, 1963-74; sr. v.p. Ogden Foods, Inc., Boston, 1974-75; v.p. concessions SportSvc. Corp., Buffalo, 1976-78, sr. v.p., 1978-80, pres., 1980-83, bd. dir.; pres. Universal Mgmt. Concept Counseling, Sylvania, Ohio, 1983—; prin. Hysen Group II, Livonia, Mich., 1991-95; counselor L.A. Olympic Concessions Food Svc., 1984, Phila. Meml. Stadium, 1985, Del. North Cos. Internat. London Eng., 1985-86, Chgo. Stadium Corp., 1989-92, Buffalo Sabres N.Y., 1992, Fine Host Inc. Greenwich Ct., 1993, Delaware North of Australia Ltd., 1994, Temp DNC Health Support Ltd., Wellington, New Zealand, 1995; bd. dirs. Greenfield Restaurant Co., Inc., Letheby and Christopher Ltd., Reading, Berkshire, Eng., Air Terminal Svcs., Inc., The Aud Club, Inc., Bluegrass Turf Svc., Inc., Concession Suppliers, Inc., Cosel Drive-In Theatre, Inc., G&H Sports Concessions, Inc., Hazel Park Parking, Inc. Mem. Toledo Mus. Art., 1985-92. Sgt. Air Corps U.S. Army, 1944-46, ETO, USAF, 1950-51. Mem. Internat. Assn. of Auditorium Mgrs., N.W. Ohio Restaurant Assn. (bd. dirs. 1990-93), Am. Culinary Fedn. Inc., Harvard Bus. Club (Detroit). Roman Catholic. Home and Office: 5540 Radcliffe Rd Sylvania OH 43560-3740

RING, JAMES EDWARD PATRICK, mortgage banking consulting executive; b. Washington, Feb. 12, 1940; s. Edward Patrick and Eleanor (Sollers) R.; m. Kathleen Murphy, Aug. 10, 1979; children: Christopher James, Daniel Edward Patrick. Student, Holy Cross Coll., Worcester, Md., 1958-59; BSEE, U.S. Naval Acad., 1963; MBA in Fin., Wharton Sch. Bus., U. Pa., 1972. Lic. securities broker, comml. pilot. Fin. analyst Exec. Office of the President, Washington, 1972-74; sr. budget analyst Bd. Govs. Fed. Res. System, Washington, 1974-77; dir. fin. planning Fed. Home Loan Mortgage Ins., Washington, 1977-83; dir. mktg. Ticor Mortgage Ins., Falls Church, Va., 1983-84, G.E. Mortgage Ins., Mc Lean, Va., 1985-86; sr. v.p. First Chesapeake Mortgage, Beltsville, Md., 1986-88; v.p. G.E. Capital Mortgage Corp., McLean, 1988-94; cons. Mortgage Dynamics, McLean, 1994—. Vol. Big. Bros. Am., Washington, 1973-81; pres. U.S. Naval Acad. Class of 1963 Found., 1983-96. Lt. USN, 1963-69. Mem. Wharton Club (Washington), U.S. Naval Acad. Alumni Assn., Army-Navy Country Club. Republican. Roman Catholic. Home: 1716 Stonebridge Rd Alexandria VA 22304-1039 Office: 1355 Beverly Rd Ste 300 Mc Lean VA 22101-5723

RING, JAMES WALTER, physics educator; b. Worcester, N.Y., Feb. 24, 1929; s. Carlyle Conwell and Lois (Tooley) R.; m. Agnes Elizabeth Muir, July 18, 1959; 1 son, Andrew James. AB, Hamilton Coll., 1951; PhD (Root fellow), U. Rochester, 1958. Asst. prof. physics Hamilton Coll., Clinton, N.Y., 1957-62, assoc. prof., 1962-69, prof., 1969—, Winslow prof., 1975—, chmn. dept. physics, 1968-80, 87-88, 91-92, radiation safety Officer, 1964-84, engring. liaison officer, 1969—; attached physicist Atomic Energy Rsch. Establishment, Harwell, Eng., 1965-66; vis. physicist Phys. Chemistry Lab., Oxford (Eng.) U., 1973; vis. fellow Ctr. for Energy and Environ. Studies, Princeton U., 1981; vis. scientist Lab. for Heating and Air Conditioning, Danish Tech. U., Copenhagen, 1987. Contbr. articles to profl. jours. and books in physics, chemistry, solar energy, environ. sci., health physics and engring. Recipient prize Acad. Edn./Devel., 1980; NSF grantee, 1959-66; NSF sci. faculty fellow, 1965-66. Mem. AAUP (chpt. pres. 1987-92), Am. Phys. Soc., Am. Assn. Physics Tchrs., Interant. Solar Energy Soc., Internat. Soc. Indoor Air Quality and Climate, Phi Beta Kappa, Sigma Xi. Achievements include solar house design and testing, indoor air studies in radon dangers and thermal comfort, and a study of the use of solar energy by the Romans during the Roman Empire. Office: Hamilton Coll Dept Physics Clinton NY 13323

RING, LEONARD M., lawyer; b. Taurage, Lithuania, May 11, 1923; came to U.S., 1930, naturalized, 1930; s. Abe and Rose (Kahn) R.; m. Donna R. Cecrle, June 29, 1959; children—Robert Steven, Susan Ruth. Student, N.Mex. Sch. Mines, 1943-44; LLB, DePaul U., 1949, JD; LLD (hon.), Suffolk U., 1990. Bar Ill. 1949. Spl. asst. atty. gen. State Ill., Chgo., 1967-72; spl. atty. Ill. Dept. Ins., Chgo., 1967-73; spl. trial atty. Met. San. Dist. Greater Chgo., 1967-77; lectr. civil trial, appellate practice, tort law Nat. Coll. Advocacy, San Francisco, 1971, 72; mem. com. jury instrns. Ill. Supreme Ct., 1967—; nat. chmn. Attys. Congl. Campaign Trust, Washington, 1975-79. Author: (with Harold A. Baker) Jury Instructions and Forms of Verdict, 1972. Editorial bd. Belli Law Jour., 1983—; adv. bd. So. Ill. U. Law Jour., 1983—. Contbr. chpts. to books including Callaghan's Illinois Practice Guide, Personal Injury, 1988 and chpt. 6 (Jury Selection and Persuasion) for Masters of Trial Practice, also numerous articles to profl. jours. Trustee, Roscoe Pound-Am. Trial Lawyers Found., Washington, 1978-80; chmn. bd. trustees Avery Coonley Sch., Downers Grove, Ill., 1974-75. Served with U.S. Army, 1943-46. Decorated Purple Heart. Fellow Am. Coll. Trial Lawyers, Internat. Acad. Trial Lawyers, Internat. Soc. Barristers, Inner Circle Advs.; mem. Soc. Trial Lawyers, Am. Judicature Soc., Appellate Lawyers Assn. (pres. 1974-75), Assn. Trial Lawyers Assn. (nat. pres. 1973-74), Ill. Trial Lawyers Assn. (pres. 1966-68), Trial Lawyers for Pub. Justice (founder, pres. 1990-91), Chgo. Bar Assn. (bd. mgrs. 1971-73, 2d v.p. 1993), ABA (coun. 1983—, chair tort and ins. sect. 1989—, fed. jud. standing com. 7th cir. 1991—), Ill. Bar Assn., Kans. Bar Assn. (hon., life), Lex Legion Bar Assn. (pres. 1976-78), Met. Club, Plaza Club, Meadow Club, River Club, Monroe Club. Home: 6 Royal Vale Dr Ginger Creek Oak Brook IL 60521 Office: Ill Supreme Ct 111 W Washington St Ste 1333 Chicago IL 60602-2707

RING, MICHAEL WILSON, lawyer; b. Phoenix, Feb. 14, 1943; s. Clifton A. and Leona (Wilson) R. BA, U Wash., 1964; JD, U. Calif., Berkeley, 1968. Bar: Calif. 1969. Assoc. Sheppard, Mullin, Richter & Hampton, L.A., 1968-76, ptnr., 1976-87; ptnr. Mayer, Brown & Platt, L.A., 1987-92, Sonnenschein Nath & Rosenthal, L.A., 1992—. Mem. ABA, L.A. County Bar Assn., Am. Coll. Real Estate Lawyers, Urban Land Inst. (assoc.), Internat. Coun. Shopping Ctrs. (assoc.), L.A. Hdqrs. City Assn. Home: 3658 Mountain View Ave Los Angeles CA 90066-3129 Office: Sonnenschein Nath & Rosenthal 601 S Figueroa St Ste 1500 Los Angeles CA 90017-5720

RING, RENEE E., lawyer; b. Frankfurt, Germany, May 29, 1950; arrived in U.S., 1950; d. Vincent Martin and Etheline Bergetta (Schoolmeesters) R.; m. Paul J. Zofnass, June 24, 1982; Jessica Renee, Rebecca Anne. BA, Catholic U. Am., 1972; JD, U. Va., 1976. Bar: N.Y. 1977. Assoc. Whitman & Ransom, N.Y.C., 1976-83; assoc. Carro, Spanbock, Fass, Geller, Kaster & Cuiffo, N.Y.C., 1983-86, ptnr., 1986; ptnr. Finley Kumble Wagner et. al., N.Y.C., 1987; of counsel Kaye, Scholer, Fierman, Hays & Handler, N.Y.C., 1988; ptnr. Kaye Scholer Fierman Hays & Handler LLP, N.Y.C., 1989—. Mem. exec. com. Lawyers for Clinton, Washington, 1991-92; team capt. Clinton Transition Team, Washington, 1992-93; mem. Nat. Lawyers Coun. Dem. Nat. Com., 1993—. Mem. ABA, N.Y. Women's Bar Assn. Democrat. Roman Catholic. Office: Kaye Scholer Fierman Hays & Handler 425 Park Ave New York NY 10022-3506

RING, TERRY WILLIAM, company executive, environmentalist; b. Lewiston, Idaho, Nov. 11, 1955; s. Robert L. and Irene M. (Sullivan) R. BA, Boise State U., 1979. Pres. Silver Creek Outfitters, Inc., Ketchum, Idaho, 1980—. Bd. dirs. Idaho Nature Conservancy, Ketchum, 1982—, chmn., 1986-2; bd. dirs. The Peregrine Fund, Boise, Idaho, 1994—. Mem. Nature Conservancy (Oak Leaf Awd. 1993). Home: PO Box 1096 Sun Valley ID 83353-1096 Office: Silver Creek Outfitters Inc 500 N Main St Ketchum ID 83340

RINGEL, DEAN, lawyer; b. N.Y.C., Dec. 12, 1947; m. Ronnie Sussman, Aug. 24, 1969; children: Marion, Alicia. BA, Columbia Coll., 1967; JD, Yale U., 1971. Bar: N.Y. 1972, U.S. Ct. Appeals (6th cir.) 1972, U.S. Ct. Appeals (2d and D.C. cirs.) 1974, U.S. Supreme Ct. 1976, U.S. Ct. Appeals (10th cir.) 1982. Law clk. to Judge Anthony J. Celebrezze U.S. Ct. Appeals (6th cir.), 1971-72; assoc. Cahill Gordon & Reindel, N.Y.C., 1972-79; ptnr. Cahill, Gordon & Reindel, N.Y.C., 1979—. Mem. ABA (vice chmn. com. on freedom of speech and press 1978-79), Assn. of Bar of City of N.Y. (commn. com., fed. litig.), N.Y. State Bar (chmn. antitrust com., sect. comml. and fed. litig.), Pub. Edn. Assn. (trustee). Office: Cahill Gordon & Reindel 80 Pine St New York NY 10005-1702

RINGEL, ELEANOR, film critic; b. Atlanta, Nov. 3, 1950; d. Herbert Arthur and Sara (Finklestein) R.; m. John Gillespie, Nov. 18, 1989. BA magna cum laude, Brown U., 1972. With Alliance Theatre, 1974, S.C. Open Road Ensemble, 1974-75, N.Y. Shakespeare Festival, 1975-78, Children's TV Workshop, 1975-77; obituary writer Atlanta Jour., 1978; critic, editor Atlanta Jour.-Constitution Film, 1978—. Named Best Local Critic Atlanta Mag., 1990, Best of Cox Newspapers Critisims, 1987, Finalist Citations Critisims, 1984-85, Merit award, 1981. Mem. Nat. Soc. Film Critics (elected 1994). Home: 235 1/2 E Wesley Rd NE Atlanta GA 30305-3774 Office: Atlanta Journal Constitution Entertainment Desk 72 Marietta St NW Atlanta GA 30303-2804

RINGEL, ROBERT LEWIS, university administrator; b. N.Y.C., Jan. 27, 1937; s. Benjamin Seymour and Beatrice (Salis) R.; m. Estelle Neuman, Jan. 18, 1959; children—Stuart Alan, Mark Joseph. B.A., Bklyn. Coll., 1959; M.S., Purdue U., 1960, Ph.D., 1962. cert. speech pathologist. Rsch. scientist, laryngeal rsch. lab. Ctr. Health Scis., UCLA, 1962-64; asst. prof. communication disorders U. Wis., 1964-66; mem. faculty Purdue U., 1966—, prof., head dept. audiology and speech sci., 1970-73, dean Sch. Humanities, Social Sci. and Edn. (Sch. Liberal Arts), 1973-86, v.p., dean Grad. Sch., 1986-90, exec. v.p. for acad. affairs, 1991—; vis. prof. Inst. Neurology and Nat. Hosps. Coll. Speech Scis., U. London, 1985; cons. NIH, NEH, Bur. Edn. Handicapped of U.S. Office Edn.; bd. dirs. Indpls. Ctr. for Advanced Rsch., 1988-92. Author sci. articles; contbr. to monographs and textbooks. Bd. dirs. Lafayette Home Hosp., 1978-87, Lafayette Symphony Orch., 1983-85. Recipient Research Career Devel. award Nat. Inst. Dental Research, 1967-70, Award for highest merit for sci. article Jour. Speech and Hearing Research, 1979, Disting. Alumnus award Bklyn. Coll., 1985. Fellow Am. Speech and Hearing Assn. (v.p. Found. 1990—); mem. AAUP, Nat. Assn. State Univs. and Land Grant Colls. (exec. com. 1988-91, rsch. policy and grad. edn., exec. com. coun. on acad. affairs 1991—, com. on instnl. coop., exec. com. provosts instn. coop. com. 1991—), Sigma Xi (v.p. 1986—). Office: Purdue Univ Off Exec VP for Acad Affairs West Lafayette IN 47907-1073

RINGEN, CATHERINE OLESON, linguistics educator; b. Bklyn., June 3, 1943; d. Prince Eric and Geneva Muriel (Leigh) Oleson; m. Jon David Ringen, Nov. 22, 1969; children: Kai Mathias, Whitney Leigh. Student, Cornell U., 1961-63; BA, Indiana U., 1970, MA, 1972, PhD, 1975. Vis. lectr. U. Minn., Mpls., 1973-74; asst. prof. U. Iowa, Iowa City, 1975-79, assoc. prof., 1980-87, prof., 1988—, chair linguistics, 1987-93. Author: Vowel Harmony: Theoretical Implications, 1988; contbr. articles to profl. jours. Sr. Fulbright prof. Trondheim, Norway, 1980, Poznan, Poland, 1994-95. Mem. AAAS, Linguistic Soc. Am., Phi Beta Kappa. Office: U Iowa Dept Linguistics Iowa City IA 52242

RINGER, JAMES MILTON, lawyer; b. Orlando, Fla., July 9, 1943; s. Robert T. and Jessie M. (Rowe) R.; m. Jaquelyn Hope, Apr. 10, 1965; children—Carolyn Hope, James Matthew. A.B., Ohio U., 1965; J.D., Cornell U., 1968. Bar: N.Y. 1968, U.S. Dist. Ct. (no. dist.) N.Y. 1968, U.S. Dist. Ct. (so. and ea. dists.) N.Y. 1972, U.S. Ct. Appeals (2d cir.) 1972, U.S. Ct. Claims 1976, U.S. Dist. Ct. (we. dist.) N.Y. 1978, U.S. Ct. Appeals (4th cir.) 1981, U.S. Ct. Appeals (9th cir.) 1983. Assoc. Rogers & Wells, N.Y.C., 1968-78, ptnr., 1978—; instr. bus. law U. Alaska, 1970-71. Editor Cornell Law Rev., 1967-68. Served to lt. JAGC, USNR, 1969-72. Republican. Episcopalian. Office: Rogers & Wells 200 Park Ave New York NY 10166-0005

RINGER, JEROME, public relations executive; b. L.A., Mar. 1, 1935; s. Arthur and Alice (Olds) R.; m. Shirley A. O'Neal, Jan. 5, 1955; children: Julie Ann Webster, Kellie Lynn Burns. BSBA, Calif. State U., Northridge, 1967. Reporter Glendale (Calif.) News, 1956-58; pub. relations Northrop, Van Nuys and Thousand Oaks, Calif., 1956-64; pub. relations and advt. mgr. Walter Kidder Webber A/C Div., Burbank, Calif., 1964-67; account exec. Smith Klitton Advt. Agy., Santa Monica, Calif., 1967-68; asst. to pres. Cubic Corp., San Diego, 1968-94, dir. investor rels., 1994—; pub. rels. trustee U. San Diego, 1985—; teaching assoc. pub. rels. U. Calif., San Diego, 1984-94; bd. dirs. Jr. Achievement, San Diego, 1971-90. Pres. San Diego chpt. Nat. Football Found., 1972—; bd. dirs. U.S. Olympic Tng. Sight Task Force, San Diego, 1986-92. Sgt. U.S. Army, 1954-56. Named Profl. of Yr. Pub. Relations Club, 1986. Mem. Press Club of San Diego (pres., Best Com. Rels. Program award 1975, 78, 80, Man of Yr. 1986), Fin. Analyst Soc., Aviation Space Writers Assn., Pub. Rels. Soc. Am. (bd. dirs.), U. So. Calif. Trojan Club (San Diego). Avocations: jogging, sports, gardening, helping youth. Office: Cubic Corp 9333 Balboa Ave San Diego CA 92123-1515

RINGGOLD, FAITH, artist; b. N.Y.C., Oct. 8, 1930. B.S., CCNY, 1955; M.A., 1959; DFA (hon.), Moore Coll. Art, Phila., 1986, Coll. Wooster, Ohio, 1987, Mass. Coll. Art, Boston, 1991, CCNY of CUNY, 1991, DSc (hon.), Brockport (N.Y.) State U., 1992, Calif. Coll. Arts. and Crafts, Oakland, Calif., 1993, RISD, 1994. Art tchr. N.Y. Pub. Schs., 1955-73; lectr. Bank St. Coll. Grad. Sch., N.Y.C., 1970-80; prof. art U. Calif., San Diego, 1984—. Solo exhbns. include Spectrum Gallery, N.Y.C., 1967, 70, 10 year retrospective, Voorhees Gallery, Rutgers U., 1973, Summit Gallery, N.Y.C., 1979, 20 year Retrospective, Studio Mus. in Harlem, N.Y.C., 1984, Bernice Steinbaum Gallery, N.Y.C., 1987-88, Balt. Mus., Deland (Fla.) Mus., Faith Ruggold 25 Yr. Survey Fine Arts Museum L.I., Hempstead, 1990-93; exhibited in group shows at Meml. Exhibit for MLK, Mus. Modern Art, N.Y.C., 1968, Chase Manhattan Bank Collection, Martha Jackson Gallery, N.Y.C., 1970, Am. Women Artists, Gedok, Kunstalle, Hamburg, Ger., 1972, Jubilee, Boston Mus. Fine Arts, 1975, Major Contemporary Women Artists, Suzanne Gross Gallery, Phila., 1984, Committed to Print Mus. Modern Art, N.Y.C., 1988, The Art of Black Am. in Japan, Terada Warehouse, Tokyo, Made in the USA, Art in the 50s and 60s U. Calif. Berkeley Art Mus., Craft Today Poetry of the Physical, Am. Craft Mus., N.Y.C., Portraits and Homage to Mothers Hecksher Mus. Huntington, 1987; works in collections at Chase Manhattan Bank, N.Y.C., Philip Morris Collection, N.Y.C., Children's Mus., Bklyn., Newark Mus., The Women's House of Detention, Rikers Island, N.Y., The Studio Mus., N.Y.C., High Mus., Atlanta, Guggenheim Mus., Met. Mus. Art, Boston Mus. Fine Arts, MOMA. Author: Tar Beach, 1991, Aunt Harriet's Underground Railroad in the Sky, 1992; contbr. articles to profl. jours. Recipient AAUW travel award to Africa, 1976, Caldecott honor award, Coretta Scott King award best illustrated children's books Tar Beach, 1991; John Simon Guggenheim Meml. Found. Fellowship (painting), 1987, N.Y. Found. for Arts award (painting), 1988, Nat. Endowment Arts award (sculpture) 1978, (painting) 1989, La Napoule Found. award (painting in So. of France) 1990, Arts Internat. award (travel to Morocco) 1992. Office: Marie Brown Assocs 625 Broadway New York NY 10012-2611

RINGLE, BRETT ADELBERT, lawyer; b. Berkeley, Calif., Mar. 17, 1951; s. Forrest A. and Elizabeth V. (Darnall) R.; m. Sue Kinslow, May 26, 1973. B.A., U. Tex., 1973, J.D., 1976. Bar: Tex. 1976, U.S. Dist. Ct. (no. dist.) Tex. 1976, U.S. Supreme Ct. 1980, U.S. Ct. Appeals (5th cir.) 1984. Ptnr., Shank, Irwin & Conant, Dallas, 1976-86, Jones, Day, Reavis & Pogue, Dallas, 1986—; adj. prof. law So. Meth. U., Dallas, 1983. Author: (with J. W. Moore and H. I. Bendix) Moore's Federal Practice, Vol. 12, 1980, Vol. 13, 1981, (with J. W. Moore) Vol. 1A, 1982, Vol. 1A Part 2, 1989. Mem. Dallas Bar Assn. Home: 3514 Gillon Ave Dallas TX 75205-3220 Office: Jones Day Reavis & Pogue 2001 Ross Ave PO Box 660623 Dallas TX 75266

RINGLEE, ROBERT JAMES, consulting engineering executive; b. Sacramento, Apr. 23, 1926; s. Francis and Marie N. R.; m. Helen Laura Carleton, Aug. 27, 1949; children—Sarah N., Jane C., Robert K. B.S.E.E., U. Wash., 1946, M.S.E.E., 1948; Ph.D. in Mechanics, Rensselaer Poly. Inst., 1964. Registered profl. engr., N.Y. With advanced engring. program Gen. Electric Co., 1948-51, advanced devel. engr., power transformer dept., 1951-55, supr. power transformer design, 1955-60, sr. analytical engr., 1960-65, mgr. system and equipment reliability, 1965-69; prin. engr. dir. Power Technologies, Inc., Schenectady, 1969-86; prin cons. Power Technologies, Inc., 1986-93; TAG assoc. Power Techs., Inc., 1993-94; assoc. cons., 1994—. Contbr. articles to profl. publs. Mem. Schalmont Bd. Edn., 1966-70, pres., 1968-69. Served with USNR, 1944-46. Recipient Managerial award Gen. Electric Co., 1953. Fellow IEEE (3 prize paper awards), AAAS; mem. Internat. Conf. on High Voltage Power Systems (expert advisor, Attwood Assoc.), Adirondack Mountain Club (pres. 1990-93, acting exec. dir. 1994). Democrat. Unitarian. Patentee. Home: 315 Juniper Dr Schenectady NY 12306-1705 Office: PO Box 1058 Schenectady NY 12301-1058

RINGLER, JAMES M., cookware company executive; b. 1945. BS, U. Buffalo, 1967, MBA, 1968. Mgr., cons. Arthur Andersen & Co., 1968-76; v.p. appliance group Tappan Co., Mansfield, Ohio, 1976-78, gen. v.p., mgr. appliance div., 1978-87, pres., chief operating officer, 1987—, also bd. dirs.; pres., COO Premark Internat., Inc., Deerfield, Ill. Office: Premark Internat Inc 1717 Deerfield Rd Deerfield IL 60015-3977*

RINGLER, JEROME LAWRENCE, lawyer; b. Detroit, Dec. 26, 1948. BA, Mich. State U., 1970; JD, U. San Francisco, 1974. Bar: Calif. 1974, U.S. Ct. Appeals (9th cir.) 1974, U.S. Dist. Ct. (no. dist.) Calif. 1974, U.S. Dist. Ct. (ctrl. dist.) Calif. 1975, U.S. Dist. Ct. (so. dist.) Calif. 1981. Assoc. Parker, Stansbury et al, L.A., 1974-76; assoc. Fogel, Feldman, Ostrov, Ringler & Klevens, Santa Monica, Calif., 1976-80, ptnr., 1980—; arbitrator L.A. Superior Ct. Arbitration Program, 1980-85. Mem. ATLA, ABA, State Bar Calif., L.A. County Bar Assn. (litigation sect., exec. com. 1994—), L.A. Trial Lawyers Assn. (bd. govs. 1981—, treas. 1988, sec. 1989, v.p. 1990, pres.-elect 1991, pres. 1992, Trial Lawyer of the Yr. 1987), Calif. Trial Lawyers Assn., Am. Bd. Trial Advs. (assoc. 1988, adv. 1991), Inns of Ct. (master). Avocations: skiing, tennis. Office: Fogel Feldman Ostrov et al 1620 26th St #100 S Santa Monica CA 90404-4040

RINGLER, LENORE, educational psychologist; d. Albert Haendel and Ida (Brafstein) Haendel; 1 son, Adam. BA, Bklyn. Coll.; MA, Queens Coll., 1954; PhD, NYU, 1965. Tchr., then reading specialist N.Y.C. Bd. Edn.; prof. NYU, 1965—, chair dept. ednl. psychology, 1974-79; ednl. cons. Psychol. Corp., Council on Interracial Books for Children, N.Y.C. Bd. Edn. Author: Skills Monitoring System-Reading, 1977, A Language-Thinking Approach to Reading, 1984; author reading series for Holt Rhinehart & Winston, 1989; contbr. articles to profl. jours. Mem. Citizens Com. for Children; mem. Commn. on Reading Nat. Acad. Edn., 1983-85. Grantee U.S. Office Edn., 1968-69, Newspapers in Edn., 1990. Mem. Am. Psychol. Assn., Am. Ednl. Rsch. Assn., Internat. Reading Assn. (past pres. Manhattan coun.), Nat. Reading Conf. (v.p. 1982-84, pres. 1984-85), Pi Lambda Theta (rsch. fellow 1963-64), Kappa Delta Pi. Office: NYU 239 Greene St Rm 400 New York NY 10003

RINGO, JAMES JOSEPH, mortgage company executive; b. Akin, Ill., Sept. 15, 1935; s. James William and Mildred Fern (Frye) R.; m. Daphne Ivy Phillips, Aug. 17, 1957 (div. Feb. 1968); children: James John, Johnny Jack, Mary Jane. Student, Fla. State U., 1961-63, U. Md., 1956-70; AS, Miami-Dade Coll., 1980. Master sgt. USAF, 1952-73; branch mgr. Fed. Land Bank, Miami, Fla., 1973-74; comml. credit mgr. 1st State Bank, Miami, 1974-80; v.p. City Fed. Savs., Somerset, N.J., 1980-84, Carteret Savs. Bank,

Cedar Knolls, N.J., 1984-85, Centrust Savs. Bank, Deerfield, Fla., 1985-86, Southeast Bank, Miami, 1986-87, Am. Savs. Fla., Miami, 1987—; pres. James Ringo & Assocs., Miami, 1986—; sr. cons. James Ringo & Assocs., Miami, 1986—. Burgher Guard, Holland Soc. of N.Y., 1982—. Decorated Air medal, Vietnam, Commendation medals, Korea and Vietnam. Mem. Holland Soc. N.Y. (burgher guard 1982—, genealogy com.), Lions (pres., sec., treas. Miami Springs chpt. 1974—). Republican. Methodist. Home: 6460 Milk Wagon Ln Miami Lakes FL 33014-6080

RINGWALD, LYDIA ELAINE, artist, poet; b. L.A., Oct. 8, 1949; d. Siegfried Carl Ringwald and Eva M. (Macksoud) Mack; m. Hal von Hofe, July 31, 1972 (div. 1978). BA, Scripps Coll., 1970; student, Ruprecht-Karl Univ., Heidelberg, Germany, 1971; MA in Comparative Lit., U. Calif., Irvine, 1972; studied with William Bailey, Yale Art Sch., 1972-74; postgrad., U. Conn., 1976. Instr. English and German Cerritos (Calif.) Coll., 1975-83; instr. German Golden West Coll., Huntington Beach, Calif., 1976-83; instr. English Saddleback Coll., Mission Viejo, Calif., 1976-81, Long Beach (Calif.) City Coll., 1976-83; curator exhbns. Cultural Affairs Satellite Dept., L.A., 1994; cons., lectr. in field. Solo exhbns. include Great Western Bank, 1989, Atlantis Gallery, 1992, L.A. Pub. Libr., Sherman Oaks, Calif., 1993, Sumitomo Bank, 1993, Phoenix Gallery, 1994; group exhbns. include Long Beach (Calif.) Arts, 1988-89, Installations One, 1989, 90, Heidelberger Kunstverein, Heidelberg, Germany, 1990, Barbara Mendes Gallery, L.A., 1991, Folktree Gallery, 1991-92, Armand Hammer Mus., 1992, Jansen-Perez Gallery, L.A., 1993; author: Blessings in Disguise: Life is a Gift; Accept it with Both Hands, 1990, Blau: Kaleidescope einer Farbe, 1992. Mem. Internat. Friends Transformative Arts, Humanistic Arts Alliance, Nat. Mus. Women in Arts, L.A. Mcpl. Art Gallery, Mus. Contemporary Art, L.A. County Mus., U. Calif. Irvine Alumni Assn., Scripps Coll. Alumni Assn., Inst. Noetic Scis., Philosophical Rsch. Soc. Avocations: modern dance, ballet, music, piano. Home and Office: Creative Realities 2801 Coldwater Canyon Dr Beverly Hills CA 90210-1305

RINK, LAWRENCE DONALD, cardiologist; b. Indpls., Oct. 14, 1940; s. Joe Donald and Mary Ellen (Rand) R.; m. Eleanor Jane Zimmerly, Aug. 10, 1963; children: Scott, Virginia. BS, DePauw U., 1962; MD, Ind. U., 1966. Diplomate Am. Bd. Internal Medicine, Am. Bd. Cardiology, Critical Care Medicine. Clin. asst. prof. Ind. U. Med. Sch., Indpls., 1973-79, clin. assoc. prof., 1979-85; clin. prof. med. Ind. Univ. Med. Sch., Indpls., 1985—; cardiologist Internal Medicine Assocs., Bloomington, Ind., 1974-95, pres.; dir. cardiac rehab. Bloomington Hosp., 1976—, dir. cardiology, 1983—; pres., chief med. officer Unity Physician Group, Bloomington, 1995—; physician Ind. U. Basketball Team, 1979—; dir. med. edn. Bloomington Hosp., 1976—; med. dir. Track and Field Pan Am. Games, 1987; U.S. Olympic Physician Olympic Sports Festival, 1989, World Univ. Games, 1990, Olympic Games, Barcelona, 1992, World Univ. Games, Fukuoka, Japan, 1995; N. Am. continent rep. Fed. Internat. Student Univ. Sports. Bd. dirs. J.O. Ritchie Soc., Ind. U. Med. Sch. Bd. dirs., dean's coun. Ind. U. Med. Sch., 1992—. Recipient Quality of Life award Major Bloomington, 1978; named Most Outstanding Flight Surgeon, USN, 1968. Fellow Am. Coll. Cardiology, Am. Heart Assn., Am. Soc. Critical Care, Am. Coll. Sports Medicine; mem. AMA, Ind. U. Med. Alumnae Assn. (pres. 1986-87, exec. alumna coun.). Avocations: reading, writing, golf, tennis. Office: Internal Medicine Assn 719 S Rogers St Bloomington IN 47403-2335

RINK, WESLEY WINFRED, banker; b. Hickory, N.C., June 14, 1922; s. Dewey Lee and Mabel E. (Yount) R.; m. Doreen M. Warman, Sept. 7, 1946; children: Rebecca S., Christopher L. B.S. in Accountancy, U. Ill., 1947, M.S., 1948. Acct., Glidden Co., Chgo., 1948-58; adminstrv. mgr. Central Soya Co., Chgo., 1958-65; v.p., comptroller State Nat. Bank, Evanston, Ill., 1965-71; exec. v.p., dir. Pioneer Trust & Savs. Bank, Chgo., 1971-76; corp. v.p. Exchange Bancorp., Inc., Tampa, 1977-82; sr. v.p. NCNB Nat. Bank Fla., Tampa, 1982-86; fin cons. Temple Terrace, Fla., 1986—; dir. 1st Bank of the Villages, Lady Lake, Fla. Served to capt. USAAF, 1942-46. Home: 523 Garrard Dr Tampa FL 33617-3819 Office: 5140 E Fowler Ave PO Box 16828 Temple Terrace FL 33687-6828

RINKER, RUBY STEWART, foundation administrator; b. Dayton, Ohio, June 11, 1936; d. Encle Stewart and Addie (Hamilton) Stewart-Smith; children: William Bertram Klawonn, Elizabeth Lynn Dennis, William Stewart-Bradley Klawonn. Human relations counselor Palm Beach County Sch. System, West Palm Beach, Fla., 1974-84; adminstrv. asst. Bohmfalk Estate, Palm Beach, Fla., N.Y.C, Newport, R.I., 1984—; hon. counselor U.S. Naval Acad., U.S. Air Force Acad. Trustee Bohmfalk Charitable Found. Mem. Phi Delta Kappa. Home: 561 Island Dr Palm Beach FL 33480-4746

RINSCH, CHARLES EMIL, insurance company executive; b. Vincennes, Ind., June 28, 1932; s. Emil and Vera Pearl (White) R.; m. Maryann Elizabeth Hitchcock, June 18, 1964; children: Christopher, Daniel, Carl. BS in Stats., Ind. U., 1953; MS in Bus., Butler U., 1959; MBA, Stanford U., 1960. Budget analyst Chrysler Corp., Indpls., 1955-57; sr. fin. analyst Ford Motor Co., Indpls., 1957-59; budget dir. Nat. Forge Co., Warren, Pa., 1960-61; div. controller and asst. to v.p., fin. Norris Industries, L.A., 1961-65; v.p., treas., sec. Teledyne Inc, L.A., 1965-88; pres., chief exec. officer Argonaut Group Inc., L.A., 1988—. Cubmaster Pack 721, Boy Scouts Am., L.A., 1987-88, treas. 1981-87; mem. dean's adv. coun. Ind. U. Sch. Bus. 1st lt. U.S. Army, 1953-55. Mem. Acad. Alumni Fellows Ind. U. Sch. Bus., L.A. Treas.'s Club. Avocations: photography, travel. Home: 19849 Greenbriar Dr Tarzana CA 91356-5428 Office: Argonaut Group Inc Ste 1175 1800 Avenue Of The Stars Los Angeles CA 90067-4213

RINSCH, MARYANN ELIZABETH, occupational therapist; b. L.A., Aug. 8, 1939; d. Harry William and Thora Analine (Langlie) Hitchcock; m. Charles Emil Rinsch, June 18, 1964; children: Christopher, Daniel, Carl. BS, U. Minn., 1961. Registered occupational therapist, Calif. Staff occupational therapist Hastings (Minn.) State Hosp., 1961-62, Neuropsychiat. Inst., L.A., 1962-64; staff and sr. occupational therapist Calif. Children's Svcs., L.A., 1964-66, head occupational therapist, 1966-68; researcher A. Jean Ayres, U. So. Calif., L.A., 1968-69; pvt. practice neurodevel. and sensory integraton Tarzana, Calif., 1969-74; pediat. occupational therapist neurodevel. & sensory integration St. Johns Hosp., Santa Monica, Calif., 1991-95; pvt. practice, cons. Santa Monica-Malibu Unified Sch. Dist., 1994—. Mem. alliance bd. Natural History Mus., L.A. County, 1983—; cub scouts den mother Boy Souts Am., Sherman Oaks, Calif., 1986-88, advancement chair Boy Scout Troop 474, 1989-92; mem. vol. League San Fernando Valley, Van Nuys, Calif., 1985-93; trustee Viewpoint Sch., Calabasas, Calif., 1987-90, Valley Women's Ctr., 1990-91. Mem. Am. Occupational Therapy Assn., Calif. Occupational Therapy Assn. Home: 19849 Greenbriar Dr Tarzana CA 91356-5428

RINSKY, JOEL CHARLES, lawyer; b. Bklyn., Jan. 29, 1938; s. Irving C. and Elsie (Millman) R.; m. Judith L. Lynn, Jan. 26, 1963; children: Heidi M., Heather S., Jason W. BS, Rutgers U., 1961, LLB, 1962, JD, 1968. Bar: N.J. 1963, U.S. Dist. Ct. N.J. 1963, U.S. Supreme Ct. 1967, U.S. Ct. Appeals (3d cir.) 1986; cert. civil trial atty., N.J. Sole practice Livingston, N.J., 1964—. Dem. committeeperson Millburn-Short Hills, N.J., 1982-96, vice chmn., 1983-87; trustee Student Loan Fund, Millburn, 1983-91. Fellow Am. Acad. Matrimonial Lawyers; mem. N.J. Bar Assn., Essex County Bar Assn. (exec. com. sect. family law). Jewish. Avocations: tennis, running, chess, golf, piano. Home: 23 Winthrop Rd Short Hills NJ 07078-1411 Office: 66 W Mt Pleasant Ave Livingston NJ 07039-2930

RINSKY, JUDITH LYNN, foundation administrator, educator consultant; b. Sept. 12, 1941; d. Allen A. and Sophie (Schwartz) Lynn; m. Joel C. Rinsky, Jan. 29, 1963; children: Heidi Mae Schnapp, Heather Star Maxon. Jason Wayne. BA in Home Econs., Montclair State U., 1963. Notary pub., N.J. Tchr. home econs. Florence Ave. Sch., Irvington, N.J., 1963-66; substitute tchr. Millburn-Short Hills Sch. System, Millburn Twp., N.J., 1978-82, 90—; sr. citizen coord. Millburn-Short Hills Sch. System, 1982-87; respite care coord. Essex County Divsn. on Aging, East Orange, N.J., 1988-90; pvt. practice educator Short Hills, N.J., 1990—; bd. mem. adv. com. gerontology Seton Hall U., 1984-90; coord. Mayor's Adv. Bd. Sr. Citizens, Millburn-Short Hills, 1982-87. Pres. Deerfield Sch. PTA, 1979-80, Millburn H.S. PTA, 1983-85; co-chmn. dinner dance Charles T. King Student Loan Fund, 1981; active Handicapped Access Study Com., 1983-85; bd. dirs. Coun. on Health and Human Svcs., 1985-90, 94—; acting dir. B'nai Israel Nursery Sch., 1994. Mem. Lake Naomi Assn. (chmn. sailing com. 1981), N.J. Home Econs. Assn., Am. Home Econs. Assn., Rotary (pres. Millburn chpt. 1992-93, bd. dirs. 1992—, advisor Millburn interact club 1987—, chair Internat. Interact dist. 7470 1993-95, advisor 1995—). Home and Office: 23 Winthrop Rd Short Hills NJ 07078-1411

RINSLAND, ROLAND DELANO, university official; b. Low Moor, Va., Apr. 11, 1933; s. Charles Henry and Lottie (Parks) R.; A.B. with distinction, Va. State U., 1954; A.M., Tchrs. Coll., Columbia U., 1959, profl. diploma, 1960, Ed.D., 1966. Asst. to dean of men Va. State Coll., Petersburg, 1952-54; asst. purchasing agt. Glyco Products Co., Inc., N.Y.C., 1956-57; asst. office of registrar Tchrs. Coll., Columbia U., N.Y.C., 1957-66, tchr. cert. advisor, 1959—, registrar, 1966-71, asst. dean for student affairs, also registrar, dir. office doctoral studies, 1971—; mem. Tchrs. Coll. Devel. Council, 1974-76, 91-95; rep., presenter of degrees Tchrs. Coll., Japan, 1989, 91, 93, 94. Served to 1st lt. AUS, 1954-56. Designated Important and Valuable Human Resource of USA Am. Heritage Research Assn. First Am. Bicentenium. Mem. N.Y. State Personnel and Guidance Assn., Am. Coll. Personnel Assn., Nat. Soc. Study Edn., Am. Ednl. Research Assn., Middle States, Am. assns. collegiate registrars and admission officers (inter-assn. rep. to state edn. depts. on tchr. cert. 1973-74, mem. com. on orgn. and adminstrn. registrars activities 1973, 74-76), Assn. Records Execs. and Adminstrs. (charter mem., by-laws and program chmn. 1969), Am. Acad. Polit. and Social Sci., Am. Assn. Higher Edn., Assn. Instl. Research, Internat. Assn. Applied Psychology, Soc. Applied Anthropology, Am. Assn. Counseling and Devel., Assn. Study of Higher Edn., AAAS, N.Y. Acad. Scis., Met. Opera Guild, NEA (Leah B. Sykes award for life mem.), Scabbard and Blade, Kappa Phi Kappa, Phi Delta Kappa, Kappa Delta Pi. Home: 25 W 68th St New York NY 10023-5302 Office: 525 W 120th St New York NY 10027-6625

RINTA, CHRISTINE EVELYN, nurse, air force officer; b. Geneva, Ohio, Oct. 4, 1952; d. Arvi Alexander and Catharina Maria (Steenbergen) R. BSN, Kent State U., 1974; MSN, Case Western Res. U., 1979. CNOR. Staff nurse in oper. rm. Euclid (Ohio) Gen. Hosp., 1974-76, oper. rm. charge nurse, 1977-79; commd. 1st lt. USAF, 1979, advanced through grades to lt. col.; staff nurse oper. rm. Air Force Regional Hosp., Sheppard AFB, Tex., 1979-82; staff nurse oper. rm., asst. oper. rm. supr. Regional Med. Ctr. Clark, Clark Air Base, Philippines, 1982-83; chief, nurse recruiting br. 3513th Air Force Recruiting Squadron, North Syracuse, N.Y., 1983-87; nurse supr. surg. svcs. 432d Med. Group, Misawa Air Base, Japan, 1987-89; course supr./instr. oper. rm. nursing courses 3793d Nursing Tng. Squadron, Keesler Med. Ctr., Keesler AFB, Miss., 1989-92; asst. dir., then dir. oper. rm. and ctrl. sterile supply Keesler Med. Ctr., Keesler AFB, Miss., 1992-93; comdr., enlisted clin. courses flight 383d Tng. Squadron, Sheppard AFB, Tex., 1993-94; comdr., officer clin. courses flight 383rd Tng. Squadron, Sheppard AFB, Tex., 1994-95; comdr. enlisted courses flight 383rd Tng. Squadron, Sheppard AFB, Tex., 1995—. Decorated Air Force Commendation medal, Air Force Achievement medal, Meritorious Svc. medal. Mem. ANA, Ohio Nurses Assn., Assn. Operating Rm. Nurses, Air Force Assn., Sigma Theta Tau. Home: 14 Pilot Point Dr Wichita Falls TX 76306-1000 Office: 383d Tng Squadron 939 Missile Rd Ste 3 Sheppard AFB TX 76311-2262

RINZEL, DANIEL FRANCIS, lawyer; b. Hartford, Wis., Dec. 30, 1942; s. Arthur Zeno and Marie Rose (Lorenz) R.; m. Kathleen Marie Saunders, Aug. 31, 1968 (div. 1987); children—Daniel, Laura, Joseph. B.A., Marquette U., 1965; J.D., U. Wis., 1968. Bar: Wis. 1968, D.C. 1982. Staff atty. Wis. Legis. Council, Madison, 1968-69; trial atty. U.S. Dept. Justice, Washington, 1969-79; chief criminal sect. U.S. Dept. Justice, 1979-83, dep. asst. atty. gen., 1984; staff dir., chief counsel U.S. Senate Permanent Subcom. on Investigations, 1984-86, chief counsel for minority, 1986-94; ptnr. Leonard, Ralston, Stanton & Remington, 1995—; adj. faculty Columbia Sch. Law Cath. U. Am., 1989—. Supr., Dane County Bd. Suprs., Wis., 1968-69. Recipient Atty. Gen.'s Disting. Service award U.S. Dept. Justice, 1983. Mem. Wis. Bar Assn., D.C. Bar Assn. Republican. Roman Catholic.

RINZLER, ALLAN, consulting company executive; b. Atlanta, May 18, 1941; s. Harry and Florence (Raab) R.; m. Brenda Joan Schear, Aug. 19, 1962; children: Harley S., S. Barrett. Student, Emory U., 1959-61, Emory U., 1962-65, Ohio State U., 1961-62; BA, Emory U., 1964, LLB, 1965. CPA; bar: Ga. 1964, U.S. Dist. Ct. Ga. 1965, U.S. Ct. Appeals 1965. Tax sr. Arthur Andersen & Co., Atlanta, 1965-68; v.p. fin. Super Food Svcs., Inc., Dayton, Ohio, 1968-69; v.p. treas. Schearbrook Land and Livestock, Inc., Dayton, 1969-72; pres., chief exec. officer Rinzler and Assocs., Inc., Dayton, 1972—; bd. dir. Chapel Electric Co., Dayton 1982—, Dynamic Industris Inc., Detroit 1983-88, DECOR Corp., Columbus 1984-86, So. Calif. Savs., 1984. Trustee Wright State U., Dayton, 1985-94, vice chmn. bd., 1991-92, bd. trustees chmn., 1992-93; bd. dirs., pres. Hillel Acad. Dayton; trustee Friends Clambake Found., Gov. coun., 1988-90. Mem. Ga. Bar Assn., Ga. Soc. CPAs, Meadowbrook Country Club (treas. 1987-88), Gainey Ranch Golf Club, Racquet Club, Beta Gamma Sigma. Jewish. Avocations: golf, bridge. Office: Rinzler & Assocs Inc 1230 Talbott Tower Dayton OH 45402

RIOPELLE, ARTHUR JEAN, psychologist; b. Thorp, Wis., Apr. 22, 1920; s. Wilfred Gaspar and Ann Marie (Schroeder) R.; m. Mary Jane Astell, May 2, 1942; children—Mary Ann, James Michael, Jean Elizabeth. B.S., U. Wis., 1941, M.S., 1948, Ph.D., 1950. Asst. prof., then assoc. prof. Emory U., 1950-57; dir. psychology div. U.S. Army Med. Research Lab., Ft. Knox, Ky., 1957-59; dir. Yerkes Labs. Primate Biology, Orange Park, Fla., 1959-62, Delta Regional Primate Research Ctr., Covington, La., 1962-71; prof. psychology La. State U., Baton Rouge, 1972—, Boyd prof., 1977-89, Boyd prof. emeritus, 1989—; mem. NRC panel on manganese, Com. on Med. and Biol. Effects of Environ. Pollutants. Editor Jour. Gen. Psychology, 1978-95; asst. editor Animal Behavior, 1962-65; cons. editor Jour. Genetic Psychology and Genetic Psychology Monograph, 1978-95; contbr. chpts. to books. La. Bd. Examiners of Psychologists, 1972-75; mem. panel on Air Force tng. Nat. Acad. Sci.-NRC, 1955-56; primate research study sect. Am. Inst. Biol. Scis.-NASA, 1959-63; chmn. sub-com. on man Lunar Receiving Lab. Study, 1970-71; chmn. U.S.-Japan Conf. Primate Research, 1963-64; chmn. sub-com. primate standards Inst. Lab. Animal Resources, NRC, 1964-69. Served with USAAF, 1942-46, ETO. Mem. Am. Psychol. Assn., Am. Physiol. Soc., So. Soc. Philosophy and Psychology, Internat. Primatological Soc., AAAS, Psychonomic Soc., Southeastern Psychol. Assn., Sigma Xi, Phi Kappa Phi, Sigma Chi. Home: 9710 Highland Rd Baton Rouge LA 70810-4031 Office: La State U Dept Psychology Baton Rouge LA 70803

RIORDAN, GEORGE NICKERSON, investment banker; b. Patchogue, N.Y., May 16, 1933; s. E. Arthur and Constance E. (Whelden) R.; m. Ann Wiggins, Jan. 4, 1958; children—Susan M., Peter G. B.S., Cornell U., 1955; M.B.A., Harvard U., 1960. Vice-pres. Lehman Bros., N.Y.C., 1960-71; mng. dir. Blyth Eastman Paine Webber, Los Angeles and N.Y.C., 1971-81, Prudential-Bache Securities, Los Angeles, 1981-88, Bear Stearns & Co., Inc., L.A., 1988-89, Dean Witter Reynolds Inc., 1989-91; bd. dirs. MacNea Schwendler Corp., L.A., Pancho's Mexican Buffet, Inc., Ft. Worth, Lewis Galoob Toys, Inc. Served to capt. USAF, 1955-57. Mem. Calif. Club, Quoque Field Club, Athenaeum Club, Valley Hunt Club (Pasadena, Calif.). Office: 3300 Hyland Ave Costa Mesa CA 92626-1503

RIORDAN, JAMES QUENTIN, retired company executive; b. Bklyn., June 17, 1927; s. James A. and Ruth M. (Boomer) R.; m. Gloria H. Carlson, June 23, 1951; children: Harris, Susan, James, Ruth. BA, Bklyn. Coll., 1945; LLB, Columbia U., 1949. Bar: N.Y. 1951, U.S. Supreme Ct. 1954. Atty. Winthrop, Stimson, Putnam & Roberts, N.Y.C., 1949-51; mem. staff Ways and Means sub-com., Washington, 1951-52; atty. tax div. Justice Dept., Washington, 1952-55; atty. Chadbourne, Parke, Whiteside & Wolff, N.Y.C., 1955-57; various positions to vice chmn., chief fin. officer Mobil Corp., 1957-89; pres. Bekaert Corp., 1989-92; ret., 1992; bd. dirs. Dow Jones & Co., Inc., The Bklyn. Union Gas Co., Tri-Continental Corp. and other J & W Seligman mutual funds, Pub. Broadcasting Svc. Bd. dirs. Com. Econ. Devel., Tax Foun., Inc.; trustee Bklyn. Mus. Mem. Rembrandt Club (N.Y.C.), Blind Brook Club, Sailfish Point (Fla.). Office: 675 3rd Ave New York NY 10017-5704

RIORDAN, JOHN FRANCIS, oil and gas corporate executive; b. Medina, N.Y., Jan. 12, 1936; s. Francis J. and Harriet (Stork) R.; m. Judith Kathryn Wokna, Feb. 5, 1967; children: Michael, Timothy, Allison. B.A. in Chemisty, Niagara U., 1958; M.B.A., SUNY-Buffalo, 1975. Chemist Durez div. Occidental Chem. Corp., North Tonawanda, N.Y., 1958-61, field sales rep., 1961-67; product mgmr. Durez div. Occidental Chem. Corp., North Tonawanda, N.Y., 1967-75; dir. corp. devel. Occidental Chem. Corp., Grand Island, N.Y., 1965-76; v.p., gen. mgr. internat. Occidental Chem. Corp., Niagara Falls, N.Y., 1976-78, v.p., gen. mgr. ECD, Hooker Chems. Plastic Corp., 1978-80, v.p. employee rels. Hooker Corp., Houston,, 1980-81, pres. ICG, Hooker Corp., 1981-85; exec. v.p. Occidental Chem. Corp., Niagara Falls, 1985-86; exec. v.p. NGL Group Cities Service Oil & Gas Corp., Tulsa, 1986-88; pres. MidCon Corp., Lombard, Ill., 1988, chief exec. officer, 1990—; exec. v.p. Occidental Petroleum Corp., 1990—; dir. Occidental Petroleum Corp. Roman Catholic. Office: MidCon Corp 701 E 22nd St Lombard IL 60148-5009*

RIORDAN, RICHARD J., mayor; b. Flushing, N.Y., 1930; m. Eugenia Riordan; 6 children (2 dec.); m. Jill Riordan. Attended, U. Calif., Santa Clara; grad., Princeton U., 1952; JD, U. Mich., 1956. With O'Melveny & Myers, L.A.; owner, operator Original Pantry Cafe; founder Total Pharmaceutical Care, Tetra Tech; mayor L.A., 1993—. Co-founder LEARN, 1991; sponsor Writing to Read computer labs Riordan Found.; active Eastside Boys and Girls Club. Lt. U.S. Army, Korea. Office: Los Angeles City Hall 200 N Spring St Los Angeles CA 90012-4801*

RIOS, ALBERTO ALVARO, English educator; b. Nogales, Ariz., Sept. 18, 1952; s. Alberto Alvaro and Agnes (Fogg) R.; m. Maria Guadalupe Barron, Sept. 8, 1979; 1 child, Joaquin. BA in Lit. & Creative Writing with honor, U. Ariz., 1974, BA in Psychology with honors, 1975, MFA in Creative Writing, 1979. Asst. prof. English Ariz. State U., Tempe, 1982-85, assoc. prof., 1985-89, prof., 1989-94, regent's prof., 1995—, dir. creative writing program, 1986-89, 92—; mem. editorial bd. New Chicano Writing, 1990—; corr. editor Manoa, 1989—; bd. dirs. Librs. of Congress/Ariz. Ctr. for the Book, 1988—, vice chair, 1989—. Author: Elk Heads on the Wall, 1979, Sleeping on Fists, 1981, Whispering to Fool the Wind, 1982, The Iguana Killer, 1984, Five Indiscretions, 1985, The Lime Orchard Woman, 1988, The Warrington Poems, 1989, Teodoro Luna's Two Kisses, 1990 (Pulitzer prize nomination), Pig Cookies, 1995; editor Ploughshares, 1991-92, adv. editor, 1992—; poetry editor Colorado Review, 1993; editl. bd. New Chicana/Chicano Writing, 1990—, Equinox, 1992—; contbr. poems and stories to numerous jours. and anthologies. Guggenheim fellow, 1988-89; recipient Western States Book award for Fiction, Walt Whitman award Acad. Am. Poets, Pushcart Prize, 1986, 88, 89, 93, Community Appreciation award Chicanos Por La Causa, 1988, Gov.'s Arts award State of Ariz., 1991; named Author of Yr. Mountain Plains Libr. Assn., 1991; NEA fellow; Ariz. State U. grantee. Office: Ariz State U Dept English Tempe AZ 85287-0302

RIOS, EVELYN DEERWESTER, columnist, musician, artist, writer; b. Payne, Ohio, June 25, 1916; d. Jay Russell and Flossie Edith (Fell) Deerwester; m. Edwin Tietjen Rios, Sept. 19, 1942 (dec. Feb. 1987); children: Jane Evelyn, Linda Sue Rios Stahlman. BA with honors, San Jose State U., 1964, MA, 1968. Cert. elem., secondary tchr., Calif. Lectr. in music San Jose State U., 1969-75; bilingual cons., then assoc. editor Ednl. Factors, Inc., San Jose, 1969-76, mgr. field research, 1977-78; writer, editor Calif. MediCorps Program, 1978-85; contbg. editor, illustrator The Community Family Mag., Wimberly, Tex., 1983-85; columnist The Springer, Dripping Springs, Tex., 1985-90; author, illustrator, health instr. textbooks elem. schs., 1980-82. Choir dir. Bethel Luth. Ch., Cupertino, Calif., 1965-66, Bethel Luth. Ch., 1968-83; dir. music St. Aban's Ch., Bogota Colombia; organist Holy Spirit Episcopalian Ch., Dripping Springs, Tex., 1987-94; music dir. Cambrian Park (Calif.) Meth. Ch., 1961-64; chmn. Dripping Springs Planning and Zoning Commn., 1991-93. Mem. AAUW, Am. Guild Organists (dean 1963-64), Phi Kappa Phi (pres. San Jose chpt. 1973-74). Episcopalian. Avocations: weaving, stitching, painting. Home and Office: 23400 FM 150 Dripping Springs TX 78620

RIOUX, CLAUDE, economics educator; b. Tracadie, N.B., Can., Sept. 4, 1955; s. Joseph and Yvonne (Mercure) R.; m. Sylvaine Gesseaume, July 26, 1982; children: Marie, Camille, Mathilde. B Social Sci., U. Moncton, N.B., 1977, MSc in Econs., 1978; D Econs. Sci., U. Dijon, France, 1982. Prof. dept. econs. and mgmt. U. Que. (Can.), Rimouski, 1981—, head dept., 1991-95. Office: University of Quebec, 300 Allee des Ursulines, Rimouski, PQ Canada G5L 3A1

RIPKEN, CALVIN EDWIN, JR. (CAL RIPKEN), professional baseball player; b. Havre de Grace, Md., Aug. 24, 1960. Player minor league teams Bluefield, Miami, Charlotte, Rochester, 1978-81; player Balt. Orioles, 1978—. Recipient Rookie of Yr. award Internat. League, 1981, Rookie of Yr. award Baseball Writers Assn., Am. League, 1982, Silver Slugger award, 1983-86, 89, 91, 93-94, Gold Glove award, 1991-92; named Am. League Rookie of the Yr., The Sporting News, 1982, Player of the Yr., 1983, 91, Am. League MVP, 1983, 91, Major League Player of Yr., The Sporting News, 1983, 91; named to Am. League All-Star Team, 1983-96. Holder major league record for consecutive games played; broke Lou Gehrig's record of 2131 consecutive games played, 1995; maj. league record home runs by shortstop; highest single season fielding percentage (.996), 1990; most consecutive errorless games at shortstop (95). Office: care Balt Orioles Oriole Pk at Camden Yards 333 W Camden St Baltimore MD 21201-2435*

RIPLEY, ALEXANDRA BRAID, author; b. Charleston, S.C., Jan. 8, 1934; m. Leonard Ripley, 1958 (div. 1963); m. John Graham, 1981; children Elizabeth, Merrill. BA in Russian, Vassar Coll., 1955. Former tour guide, travel agent, underwear buyer; former manuscript reader, publicity director N.Y.C. Author: Charleston, 1981, On Leaving Charleston, 1984, The Time Returns: A Novel of Friends and Mortal Enemies in Fifteenth Century Florence, 1985, New Orleans Legacy, 1987, Scarlett: The Sequel to Margaret Mitchell's Gone With the Wind, 1991, From Fields of Gold, 1994. Office: care Janklow-Nesbit Assoc 598 Madison Ave New York NY 10022-1614

RIPLEY, JOHN WALTER, academic administrator; b. Welch, W.Va., June 29, 1939; m. Molin B. Ripley, May 9, 1964; children: Stephen B., Mary D., Thomas H., John M. BSEE, U.S. Naval Acad., 1962; MS, Am. U., 1976. Commd. 2d lt. USMC, 1962, advanced through grades to col., 1984, ret., 1992; polit./mil. planner Office of Joint Chiefs of Staff, Washington; asst. prof. history Oreg. State U., Corvallis, 1972-75; dir. divsn. English and history U.S. Naval Acad., Annapolis, Md., 1984-87; commanding officer Naval ROTC unit Va. Mil. Inst., Lexington, 1990-92; chancellor So. Va. Coll., Buena Vista, 1992—; lectr. in field. Decorated Navy Cross, Legion of Merit (2), Silver Star, Bronze Star (2), Purple Heart. Mem. Phi Alpha Theta. Office: Southern Virginia College One College Hill Dr Buena Vista VA 24416

RIPLEY, RANDALL BUTLER, political scientist, educator; b. Des Moines, Jan. 24, 1938; s. Henry Dayton and Aletha (Butler) R.; m. Grace A. Franklin, Oct. 15, 1974; children: Frederick Joseph, Vanessa Gail. B.A., DePauw U., 1959; M.A., Harvard, 1961, Ph.D., 1963. Teaching fellow Harvard, 1960-62; mem. staff Brookings Inst., Washington, 1963-67; research asst. Brookings Inst., 1963-64, research asso., 1964-67; intern Office of Democratic Whip, U.S. Ho. of Reps., Washington, 1963; assoc. prof. dept. polit. sci. Ohio State U., Columbus, 1967-69, prof., 1969—, chmn., 1969-91, dean Coll. Social and Behavioral Scis., 1992—; lectr. Cath. U., Washington, 1963-64; professorial lectr. Am. U., Washington, 1964-67; vis. prof. U. Okla., 1969-91. Author: Public Policies and Their Politics, 1966, Party Leaders in the House of Representatives, 1967, Majority Party Leadership in Congress, 1969, Power in the Senate, 1969, The Politics of Economic and Human Resource Development, 1972, Legislative Politics U.S.A, 1973, American National Government and Public Policy, 1974, Congress: Process and Policy, 1975, 4th edit., 1988, Policy-making in the Federal Executive Branch, 1975, Congress, the Bureaucracy, and Public Policy, 1976, 5th edit., 1991, National Government and Policy in the United States, 1977, A More Perfect Union, 1979, 4th edit., 1989, Policy Implementation and Bureaucracy, 1982, 2d edit., 1986, CETA: Politics and Policy, 1973-82, 1984, Policy Analysis in Political Science, 1985, Readings in American Government and Politics, 1989, 2d edit. 1993, Congress Resurgent, 1993; contbr. articles to profl. jours. Bd. govs. Stratford Festival, Ont., Can., 1994—. Woodrow Wilson fellow, 1959-60; Danforth fellow, 1959-63; recipient Sumner prize Harvard, 1963. Mem. Am. Polit. Sci. Assn. (sec. 1978), Midwest Polit. Sci. Assn., Phi Beta Kappa. Democrat. Home: 2685 Berwyn Rd Columbus OH 43221-3207

RIPPE, PETER MARQUART, museum administrator; b. Mpls., Dec. 16, 1937; s. Henry Albert and Zelda (Marquart) R.; m. Maria Boswell Wornom, Aug. 10, 1968. BA, U. Puget Sound, 1960; MA, U. Del., 1962. Dir. Confederate Mus., Richmond, Va., 1962-68; exec. dir. Harris County Heritage Soc., Houston, 1968-79, Roanoke Mus. Fine Arts (Va.), 1979-89, P. Buckley Moss Mus., Waynesboro, Va., 1989—; mem. Roanoke Arts Commn., 1983-90. Fellow Old Deerfield Found., 1958, H.F. duPont Winterthur Mus., 1960-62, chmn. Blue Ridge TV, Roanoke; bd. dirs. Augusta-Staunton-Waynesboro Visitors Bur. Mem. Am. Assn. Mus. (chmn. small mus. com. 1981-83, sr. examiner, 1983—, councillor-at-large 1985-88), Tex. Assn. Mus. (pres. 1975-77, Tex. award 1979), Va. Assn. Mus. (pres. 1983-84), Southeast Mus. Conf. (chmn. awards com. 1986-89), Rotary (Waynesboro chpt.), Waynesboro Club. Democrat. Lutheran. Home: 149 Brook Ct Waynesboro VA 22980-5559 Office: P Buckley Moss Mus 2150 Rosser Ave Waynesboro VA 22980-9406

RIPPEL, CLARENCE W., academic administrator. Acting pres. Lincoln U. Office: Lincoln U Office of President 281 Masonic Ave San Francisco CA 94118-4416

RIPPEL, HARRY CONRAD, mechanical engineer, consultant; b. Phila., Feb. 19, 1926; s. Philip and Emma (Metzger) R.; m. Dorothy Ann Tartala, Nov. 20, 1948; children—Linda Jean, Richard Peter. B.M.E., Drexel U., Phila., 1952, M.S., 1957. Registered profl. engr., Pa. With Franklin Research Center, div. Franklin Inst., Phila., 1952-87, Inst. fellow, 1978—; cons. in tribology, 1987—; resident consultant Rotor Bearing Tech. & Software Inc., 1987—; mem. Com. on Sci. and the Arts, Franklin Inst., Phila. Author manuals and articles in field. Sunday sch. tchr., layreader St. James Episcopal Ch., Phila.; bd. dirs. Turbo Rsch. Found. With AUS, WWII, ETO. Decorated Bronze Star. Fellow ASME, Soc. Tribologists and Lubrication Engrs.; mem. Sigma Xi, Pi Tau Sigma. Home: 1434 Sharon Park Dr Sharon Hill PA 19079-2218 Office: Rotor Bearing Tech & Software Inc Lee Park 1100 E Hector St Conshohocken PA 19428-2374

RIPPEL, JEFFREY ALAN, library director; b. Moberly, Mo., June 19, 1945; s. Charles Kenneth and Mildred Agnes (Dodge) R.; m. Mary Elizabeth Burton, Oct. 25, 1969; children: Sarah, Andrew. BA, Fla. State U., 1967; MLS, U. Tex., 1973. Cert. county librarian, Tex., profl. librarian, S.C. Br. librarian Waco (Tex.) Pub. Library, 1974-76; dir. Victoria (Tex.) Pub. Library, 1976-78; dep. dir. Greenville (S.C.) County Library, 1978-81; dir. Longview (Tex.) Pub. Library, 1981-88, Lubbock (Tex.) City-County Library, 1988—. Contbr. articles to profl. jours. Bd. dirs. Lubbock Area Coalition for Literacy. Capt. USAF, 1967-72. Mem. ALA, Tex. Library Assn., Lubbock Area Library Assn. (past pres.). Home: 2627 22nd St Lubbock TX 79410-1615 Office: Lubbock City-County Libr 1306 9th St Lubbock TX 79401-2798

RIPPER, RITA JO (JODY RIPPER), strategic planner, researcher; b. Goldfield, Iowa, May 8, 1950; d. Carl Phillip and Lucille Mae (Stewart) Ripper; BA, U. Iowa, 1972; MBA, NYU, 1978. Contracts and fin. staff Control Data Corp., Mpls., 1974-78; regional mgr. Raytheon Corp., Irvine, Calif., 1978-83; v.p. Caljo Corp., Des Moines, Iowa, 1980-84; asst. v.p. Bank of Am., San Francisco, 1984-88; pres. The Northhaven Co., 1988—, The Boardroom Adv. Group, 1990—. Am. United; vol. Cancer, Heart, Lung Assns., Edina, N.Y.C., Calif., 1974-78, 84—. Mem. Amnesty Internat., Internat. Mktg. Assn., World Trade Ctr. Assn., Acctg. Soc. (pres. 1975-76), World Trade Club, Intertel, Mensa, Beta Alpha Psi (chmn. 1977-78), Phi Gamma Nu (v.p. 1971-72) Presbyterian. Club: Corinthian Yacht. Home and Office: 501 Oak Lane Dr West Des Moines IA 50265-5146 also: The Northhaven Co PO Box 25145 West Des Moines IA 50265 also: The Boardroom Adv Group 537 Newport Center Dr # 277 Newport Beach CA 92660-6937

RIPPETEAU, DARREL DOWNING, architect; b. Clay Center, Nebr., Jan. 14, 1917; s. Claude LaVerne and Eva (Downing) R.; m. Donna Doris Hiatt, Jan. 8, 1939 (dec. 1988); children: Bruce Estes, Darrel Downing, Jane Upson Heffron; m. Joyce Spencer, May 18, 1991. B.A. in Architecture, U. Nebr., 1941. Staff architect FHA, Omaha, 1941-42; project mgr., mng. ptnr. Sargent-Webster-Crenshaw & Folley, Archs. and Engrs., Watertown, Buffalo, Syracuse, N.Y., Burlington, Vt, Bangor, Maine, 1946-81; treas., dir. Empire Forest System, Albany, N.Y., 1984-89; ret., 1990; bd. dirs. Archtl. Corp. Atlanta, Key Bank No. N.Y., Watertown, Assn. Island Recreational Corp.; commr. N.Y. State Coun. Architecture, 1975-85; mem. N.Y. State Forest Practice Bd., 1980—, chmn., 1994-96; nat. adv. bd. mem. Remington Art Mus., Ogdensburg, N.Y., 1983-95. Prin. works include Justice Bldg, Albany, N.Y. State Office Bldg Watertown, Toomey Abbott Towers Syracuse, State U. N.Y. Cortland, U.S. P.O. Facility Syracuse. Mem. nat. fin. com. Rep. Party, 1971-73; bd. dirs. The Antique Boat Mus., Clayton, N.Y., 1973—, Glenn Curtiss Mus., Hammondsport, N.Y. Maj. U.S. Army, 1942-46; lt. col. Corps of Engrs. Recipient North Country citation St. Lawrence U., Canton, N.Y., 1971; Sears-Roebuck scholar, 1936-37; U. Nebr. Dept. Architecture grantee, 1940-41; Nebr. master U. Nebr., 1971; Disting. Alumni award Coll. of Architecture Alumni Assn., U. Nebr., 1996. Fellow AIA (nat. dir. 1969-73, trustee AIA Found. 1970-73); mem. Greater Watertown C. of C. (past pres.), N.Y. State Assn. Indsl. Devel. Agys. (past v.p.), N.Y. State Assn. Architects (pres. 1968-69, polit. action com. 1980—, James Kideney award 1987), Bldg. Rsch. Inst., Res. Officers Assn. (past pres.), Am. Tree Farm Assn., Jefferson County Hist. Soc. (dir. 1974-78), OX-5 Aviation Pioneers (chpt. pres.), Assn. U.S. Army (chpt. pres. 1985-86). Republican. Presbyterian. Home: 1011 NW 3rd Ave Delray Beach FL 33444-2938 Home and Studio: River Oaks 45650 Landon Rd Wellesley Is NY 13640-2112

RIPPEY, DONALD TAYLOR, education educator; b. Aztec, N.Mex., Jan. 1, 1927; s. Charles Elwell and Lydia (Hulburt) R.; m. Margaret Simonton, Dec. 18, 1968 (div.); children: John, Jane Parson; m. Gwen Oglesby Rippey; children: Gary, Albert, Kim, Kelly Hall. BA, U. N.Mex., 1950, MA, 1952; EdD, U. No. Colo., 1963. Cert. tchr., adminstr. N.Mex., Wash. Tchr. Roswell (N.Mex.) Jr. High Sch., 1950-53; prin. Washington Elem. Sch., Roswell, 1953-61; dir. Roswell Community Coll., 1958-62; pres. Columbia Basin Coll., Pasco, Wash., 1962-66, El Centro Coll., Dallas, 1966-76; prof. edn. adminstrn. U. Tex., 1976-90, W.K. Kellogg prof., 1990-94, prof. emeritus, 1994—; acting pres. U. Tex.-Permian Basin, Odessa, 1982-83; exec. dir. Nat. Coun. C.C. Bus. Ofcls., 1988-94. Author: Some Called It Camelot, 1987; (monograph) What is Student Development, 1981; contbr. articles on tech. and devel. edn. to profl. jours.; mem. editorial bd. Jour. Devel. Edn., 1979-95. Chmn. bd. dirs. Dallas Young Adult Inst., 1969-74; pres. Benton/Franklin Mental Health Assn., Pasco, 1964, Dallas Council on Alcoholism, 1973. Served as cpl. USAF, 1944-46, PTO. Recipient Appreciation award Ala. Dept. Postsecondary Edn., 1986, Disting. Service award Council Colls. and Univs., Washington, 1987, Master Tchr. award Nat. Inst. award Staff and Organizational Devel., 1989. Mem. Phi Delta Kappa. Methodist. Avocations: reading, traveling, hunting, fishing. Home: 6110 Mountainclimb Dr Austin TX 78731-3824 Office: Univ of Tex at Austin Dept of Edn Adminstrn Univ Station Austin TX 78712

RIPPLE, KENNETH FRANCIS, federal judge; b. Pitts., May 19, 1943; s. Raymond John and Rita (Holden) R.; m. Mary Andrea DeWeese, July 27, 1968; children: Gregory, Raymond, Christopher. AB, Fordham U., 1965; JD, U. Va., 1968; LLM, George Washington U., 1972, LLD (hon.), 1992. Bar: Va. 1968, N.Y. 1969, U.S. Supreme Ct. 1972, D.C. 1976, Ind. 1984, U.S. Ct. Appeals (7th cir.), U.S. Ct. Mil. Appeals, U.S. Dist. Ct. (no. dist.) Ind. Atty. IBM Corp., Armonk, N.Y., 1968; legal officer U.S. Supreme Ct., Washington, 1972-73, spl. asst. to chief justice Warren E. Burger, 1973-77; prof. law U. Notre Dame, 1977—; judge U.S. Ct. Appeals (7th cir.), South Bend, 1985—; reporter Appellate Rules Com., Washington, 1978-85; commn. on mil. justice U.S. Dept. Def., Washington, 1984-85; cons. Supreme Ct. Ala., 1983, Calif. Bd. Bar Examiners, 1981; cons. Anglo-Am. Jud. Exch., 1977, mem., 1980; adv. com. Bill of Rights to Bicentennial Constn. Commn., 1989; mem. adv. com. on appellate rules Jud. Conf. U.S., 1985-90, chmn., 1990-93; chmn. adv. com. on appellate judge edn. Fed. Jud. Ctr., 1996—. Author: Constitutional Litigation, 1984. Mem. bd. visitors Sch. Law, Brigham Young U., 1989-92. Served with JAGC, USN, 1968-72. Mem. ABA, Am. Law Inst., Phi Beta Kappa. Office: US Ct of Appeals 208 US Courthouse 204 S Main St South Bend IN 46601-2122 also: Fed Bldg 219 S Dearborn St Ste 2660 Chicago IL 60604-1803

RIPPLEY, ROBERT, wholesale distribution executive; b. 1968. BS in Bus. pub. adminstn., U. Mo., 1972. Exec. v.p., CEO Affiliated Food Stores Inc., Tulsa, Okla., 1989—. Office: Affiliated Food Stores Inc 4433 W 49th St Tulsa OK 74107-7313*

RIPPON, THOMAS MICHAEL, art educator, artist; b. Sacramento, Apr. 1, 1954; s. Samuel Joseph Jr. and June Evelyn (Garnet) R.; m. Sarah Sterrett, Dec. 22, 1980; children: Adam Michael, Peter Thomas. MFA, Art Inst. Chgo., 1979. Instr. Columbia Coll., Chgo., 1978-79; asst. prof. Montana State U., Bozeman, 1980, Calif. State U., Sacramento, 1981; assoc. prof. Tenn. Tech. U., Cookeville, 1982-87; asst. prof. U. Nev., Reno, 1987-89; assoc. prof. U. Montana, Missoula, 1989—, chair dept. art, 1990—; artist in residence U. Nevada, Reno, 1988; vis. prof. U. Calif., Davis, 1989; lectr. in field, 1973—. Solo exhbns. include Quay Gallery, San Francisco, 1975, 77, 81, 85, Rochester (Minn.) Art Ctr., 1979, Betsy Rosenfield Gallery, Chgo., 1980, 82, 84, Drake U., Des Moine, Iowa, 1985, Cross Creek Gallery, Malibu, Calif., 1987, 88, Judith Weintraub Gallery, Sacramento, 1990, 91, Huntington (W.Va.) Mus. Art, 1991, Kohler Art Ctr., Sheboygan, Wis., 1992, Yellowstone Art Ctr., Billings, Mont., 1993, Missoula Mus. Arts, 1994, Holter Mus. Art, Helena, Mont., 1995, others; group exhbns. include San Francisco Mus. Modern Art, 1972, Davis (Calif.) Art Ctr., 1973, Oakland Mus., 1974, Evanston (Ill.) Art Ctr., 1974, Fendrick Gallery, Washington, 1975, Campbell Mus., Camden, N.J., 1976, Montana State U., Bozeman, 1976, De Young Mus., San Francisco, 1978, Am. Craft Mus., N.Y.C., 1978, 81, Phila. Mus. Modern Art, 1980, Craft and Folk Mus., L.A., 1980, Indpls. Mus. Art, 1982, Impressions Today Gallery, Boston, 1982, Elements Gallery, N.Y.C., 1983, Tampa (Fla.) Mus., 1983, Hyde Park Art Ctr., Chgo., 1983, 85, Traver-Sutton Gallery, Seattle, 1984, Erie (Pa.) Art Mus., 1985, Fay Gold Gallery, Atlanta, 1986, Seattle Art Mus., 1987, Candy Store Art Gallery, Folsom, Calif., 1987, Crocker Art Mus., Sacramento, 1988, Lang Gallery Scripps Coll., Claremont, Calif., 1988, Sherley Koteen & Assoc., Washington, 1989, 90, Eve Mannes Gallery, Atlanta, 1989, Art Gallery Western Australia, 1989, Joanne Rapp Gallery, Scottsdale, 1990, Missoula Mus. of Arts, 1991, 92, Sutton West Gallery, Missoula, 1992, Yellowstone Art Ctr., 1992, Natsoulas Gallery, Davis, Calif., 1993, many others; represented in pvt. collections; pub. collections include San Francisco Mus. Art, L.A. County Mus. Art, Sheldon Meml. Collection U. Nebr., Mus. Fine Arts, Salt Lake City, Ch. Fine Arts Collection U. Nev., Reno, Kanzawa-Shi, Hokkoku Shinbun, Kyoto, Japan, Renwick Gallery Smithsonian Institution, Contemporary Art Mus., Honolulu, J.B. Speed Art Mus., Louisville, Ky., U. Iowa, Ames, Missoula Mus. Arts, others. Recipient Kingsley Art Club award Crocker Art Mus., Sacramento, 1971, Crocker-Kingsley award, 1972; NEA fellow, 1974, 81, Nelson Raymond fellow Art Inst. Chgo., 1979. Office: Univ of Montana Dept Of Art Missoula MT 59812

RIPSTEIN, CHARLES BENJAMIN, surgeon; b. Winnipeg, Man., Can., Dec. 13, 1913; came to U.S., 1949; s. Hyman Mendel and Bertha (Benjamin) R.; m. Barbara Adelman, Dec. 26, 1950; children: Ellen Joan, Linda Hope. B.S., U. Ariz., 1936; M.D., C.M., McGill U., 1940. Diplomate: Am. Bd. Surgery, Am. Bd. Thoracic Surgery, Am. Bd. Colon and Rectal Surgery. Intern medicine Royal Victoria Hosp., Montreal, 1940-41; residency in surgery Royal Victoria and Montreal Gen. hosps., 1945-48; demonstrator surgery McGill U., 1948-49; asso. prof. surgery SUNY, Bklyn., 1949-52; prof. surgery SUNY, 1952-54; prof. surgery, also exec. officer dept. surgery Albert Einstein Coll. Medicine, Yeshiva U., 1954-58, prof. clin. surgery, 1958—; clin. prof. surgery U. Miami Sch. Medicine, 1972; chief divs. gen. and thoracic surgery Bronx Mcpl. Hosp. Center, N.Y.C., 1954-58; dir. surg. service Beth-El Hosp., Bklyn., 1958—; dir. surgery Brookdale Hosp. Center, Bklyn.; cons. in surgery Maimonides Hosp., Bklyn., Bronx VA Hosp., surgeon Miami Heart Inst.; attending surg. Lebanon Hosp.; clin. prof. surgery U. Miami, Fla.; cons. cardiac surgery Health Ins. Plan N.Y.; vis. prof. surgery U. Tel Aviv, 1969-70. Author chpt. on cardiac surgery in textbook. Served as squadron leader RCAF, 1941-45. Fellow ACS, Royal Coll. Surgeons (Can.), N.Y. Acad. Medicine, Am. Coll. Chest Physicians; mem. AMA, Soc. Univ. Surgeons, Am. Assn. Thoracic Surgery, Am. Heart Assn., N.Y. Surg. Soc., Alpha Omega Alpha, Zeta Beta Tau. Home: 500 Bayview Dr Apt 932 Miami FL 33160-4749

RIRIE, CRAIG MARTIN, periodontist; b. Lewiston, Utah, Apr. 17, 1943; s. Martin Clarence and VaLera (Dixon) R.; m. Becky Ann Ririe, Sept. 17, 1982; children: Paige, Seth, Theron, Kendall, Nathan, Derek, Brian, Amber, Kristen. AA, San Bernadino Valley Coll., 1966; DDS, Creighton U., 1972; MSD, Loma Linda U., 1978. Staff mem. Flagstaff (Ariz.) Med. Ctr., 1974—; pvt. practice dentistry specializing in periodontics Flagstaff, 1974—; assoc. prof. periodontics No. Ariz. U., Flagstaff, 1979—, chmn. dept. dental hygiene, 1980-81; med. research cons. W.L. Gore, Flagstaff, 1983—. Contbr. articles to profl. jours. Vice pres. bd. dirs. Grand Canyon coun. Boy Scouts Am., 1991—. Lt. col. USAFR. Health professions scholarship Creighton U., Omaha, 1969-71; recipient Mosby award Mosby Pub. Co., 1972; research fellowship U. Bergen, Norway, 1978-79. Mem. ADA, Am. Acad. Periodontology (cert.), Western Soc. Periodontology (chmn. com. on rsch. 1982—, bd. dirs. 1983—), No. Ariz. Dental Soc. (pres. 1994-96), Am. Acad. Oral Implantologists, Internat. Congress Oral Implantologists, Ariz. Dental Assn., Am. Cancer Soc. (bd. dirs.), Flagstaff C. of C., Rotary. Republican. Mem. LDS Ch. Avocations: skiing, tennis, golf. Home: 1320 N Aztec St Flagstaff AZ 86001-3004 Office: 1050 N San Francisco St Flagstaff AZ 86001-3259

RIS, HANS, zoologist, educator; b. Bern, Switzerland, June 15, 1914; came to U.S., 1938, naturalized, 1945; s. August and Martha (Egger) R.; m. Hania Wislicka, Dec. 26, 1947 (div. 1971); children: Christopher Robert, Annette Margo; m. Theron Caldwell, July 14, 1980. Diploma high sch. teaching, U. Bern, 1936; Ph.D., Columbia, 1942. Lectr. zoology Columbia U., 1942; Seessel fellow in zoology Yale U., 1942; instr. biology Johns Hopkins U., 1942-44; asst. Rockefeller Inst., N.Y.C., 1944-46; assoc. Rockefeller Inst., 1946-49; assoc. prof. zoology U. Wis., Madison, 1949-53; prof. U. Wis., 1953-84, prof. emeritus, 1984—; hon. prof. Peking U., Beijing, 1995—. Fellow AAAS; mem. Am. Acad. Arts and Scis., Nat. Acad. Scis., Electron Microscopy Soc. Am. (Disting. Investigator award 1983), Am. Soc. for Cell Biology (E.B. Wilson award 1993). Achievements include research on mechanisms of nuclear division, chromosome structure, nuclear envelope, cell ultrastructure, electron microscopy. Office: U Wis Zoology Rsch 1117 W Johnson St Madison WI 53706-1705

RIS, HOWARD C., JR., nonprofit public policy organization administrator. BA in Math., Duke U., 1970, postgrad., 1972; MLA, SUNY, Syracuse, 1974. Sr. assoc. Roy Mann Assocs., Inc., Cambridge, Mass., 19774-76; sr. planner Mass. Office Coastal Zone Mgmt., Boston, 1976-78; program mgr. New Eng. River Basins Commn., Boston, 1980-81; dep. dir. Union Concerned Scientists, Inc., Cambridge, 1981-84, exec. dir., 1984—; bd. dirs. Ris Paper Corp., Inc.; founding dir. Profls.' Coalition for Nuclear Arms Control, Internat. Network Engrs. and Scientists for Global Responsibility. Mem. Energy and Transp. Task Force, President's Coun. on Sustainable Devel., New Eng. Bus. Coun.; mem. adv. bd. Living on Earth Prodns. Office: Union of Concerned Scientists 2 Brattle Sq Cambridge MA 02238

RIS, WILLIAM KRAKOW, lawyer; b. Dubuque, Iowa, June 11, 1915; s. Rinehart F. and Anna W. (Krakow) R.; m. Patty S. Nash, Dec. 28, 1940; children: Frederic N., William Krakow Jr. AB, U. Colo., 1945, LLB, 1939. Bar: Colo. 1939. Practice in Denver, 1939-43, 46-86; with firm Wood, Ris & Hames, P.C., 1948-86, of counsel, 1986—; mem. Commn. on Jud. Qualifications, 1973-77, chmn., 1977. Served with AUS, 1943-46. Fellow Am. Bar Found., Am. Coll. Trial Lawyers (bd. regents 1982-83); mem. Colo. Bar Assn. (pres. 1962-63), Denver Law Club (pres. 1956-57), Order of Coif. Episcopalian. Home: Unit 114 2800 S University Blvd Denver CO 80210 Office: 1775 Sherman St Ste 1600 Denver CO 80203-4317

RISCH, JAMES E., lawyer; b. Milw., May 3, 1943; s. Elroy A. and Helen B. (Levi) R.; m. Vicki L. Choborda, June 8, 1968; children—James E., Jason S., Jordan D. B.S. in Forestry, U. Idaho, 1965, J.D., 1968. Dep. pros. atty. Ada County, Idaho, 1968-69, chief dep. pros. atty., 1969-70, pros. atty., 1971-75; mem. Idaho Senate, 1974-88, 95—, majority leader, 1977-82, pres. pro tem, 1983-88, asst. majority leader, 1996—; ptnr. Risch Goss & Insinger, Boise, Idaho, 1975—; prof. law Boise State U., 1972-75. Chmn. George Bush Presdl. Campaign, Idaho, 1988; mem. Gen. Coun. Idaho Rep. Party, 1991-95. Mem. ABA, Idaho Bar Assn., Boise Bar Assn., Am. Judicature Soc., Nat. Dist. Attys. Assn. (bd. dirs. 1977), Idaho Pros. Attys. Assn. (pres. 1976), Ducks Unlimited, Nat. Rifle Assn., Nat. Cattlemans Assn., Idaho Cattlemans Assn., Am. Angus Assn., Idaho Angus Assn., Boise Valley Angus Assn., Phi Delta Theta, Xi Sigma Pi. Republican. Roman Catholic. Avocations: hunting; fishing; skiing; horseback riding; tennis. Home: 5400 S Cole Rd Boise ID 83709-6401 Office: Risch Goss & Insinger 407 W Jefferson St Boise ID 83702-6049

RISCH, MARTIN DONALD, marketing-management consulting company executive; b. Bklyn., Oct. 7, 1929; s. Rene and Lillian (Grant) R.; m. Joan Nattrass, Dec. 26, 1955; children: Lillian, David. BA, Colgate U., 1951; MBA, Harvard U., 1955. Dir. mktg. devel. Riegel Paper Co., N.Y.C., 1950-60, Fitchburg (N.Y.) Paper Co., 1960-64; dir. planning speciality paper div. Litton Industries, Fitchburg, 1965-69, 70-71, v.p. planning paper printing div., 1971-76; pres. Lincoln Assocs., Lexington, Mass., 1976—. 1st lt. USAF, 1951-53, Korea. Mem. TAPPI, Graphic Arts Tech. Found., Packaging Internat., Harvard Club, Oak Hill Country Club. Home: 71 Winter St Lincoln MA 01773-3502 Office: Lincoln Assocs 35 Bedford St Ste 4 Lexington MA 02173-4400

RISDEN, NANCY DIKA, mathematics educator; b. Englewood, N.J., Sept. 14, 1948; d. John and Dorothy Louise (Eisberg) Macris; m. Dennis Richard Risden, Apr. 6, 1974; children: Jeannine, Steven, David. BS, Ursinus Coll., Collegeville, Pa., 1970; MA, Montclair State Coll., Upper Montclair, N.J., 1976. Cert. postgrad. prof. tchr. secondary math., Va., N.J. Tchr. math. West Essex Regional Mid. Sch., North Caldwell, N.J., 1970-71, South Jr. H.S., Bloomfield, N.J., 1971-79; substitute tchr. Oldham County Mid. Sch., Oldham County, Ky., 1981-82; instr. math. Watterson Coll., Louisville, 1984; tchr. math. Duke U. Hosp. Sch., Durham, N.C., 1988-90; substitute tchr. York County Pub. Schs., Yorktown, Va., 1991-93; tchr. math. Tabb Mid. Sch., Yorktown, 1993—. Treas. Mangum Primary Sch. PTA, Durham County, 1988-89; cookie chmn. Girl Scouts U.S., Durham County, 1989; den leader cub scouts Boy Scouts Am., Durham County, 1988-91, com. chairperson pack 104, Yorktown, Va., 1991-95. Mem. NEA, Va. Edn. Assn., York County Edn. Assn., Nat. Coun. Tchrs. Math., Va. Mid. Sch. Assn., Order Ea. Star N.J. (Worth Matron 1975-76, Grand Adah 1976-77). Presbyterian. Avocations: needlework, church choir. Home: 113 Daphne Dr Yorktown VA 23692-3220 Office: Tabb Middle School 300 Yorktown Rd Yorktown VA 23693-3504

RISEBROUGH, DOUG, professional hockey team executive; b. 1954; m. Marilyn Risenbrough; children: Allison, Lindsay. Former player Montreal (Que.) Canadiens, for 8 years; former player Calgary (Alta., Can.) Flames, for 5 years, former asst. coach, 1987-89, asst. gen. mgr., 1989-90, head coach, 1990-92; General Manager Calgary (Alt., Can.) Flames, 1992—. Office: Calgary Flames, PO Box 1540 Sta M, Calgary, AB Canada T2P 3B9*

RISELEY, MARTHA SUZANNAH HEATER (MRS. CHARLES RISELEY), psychologist, educator; b. Middletown, Ohio, Apr. 25, 1916; d. Elsor and Mary (Henderson) Heater; BEd, U. Toledo, 1943, MA, 1958; PhD, Toledo Bible Coll., 1977; student Columbia U., summers 1943, 57; m. Lester Seiple, Aug. 27, 1944 (div. Feb. 1953); 1 child, L. Rolland, III; m. Charles Riseley, July 30, 1960. Tchr. kindergarten Maumee Valley Country Day Sch., Maumee, Ohio, 1942-44; dir. recreation Toledo Soc. for Crippled Children, 1950-51; tchr. trainable children Lott Day Sch., Toledo, 1951-57; psychologist, asst. dir. Sheltered Workshop Found., Lucas County, Ohio, 1957-62; psychologist Lucas County Child Welfare Bd., Toledo, 1956-62; tchr. educable retarded, head dept. spl. edn. Maumee City Schs., 1962-69; pvt. practice clin. psychology, 1956—; instr. spl. edn. Bowling Green State U., 1962-65; instr. Owens Tech. Coll., 1973-78; interim dir. rehab. services Toledo Goodwill Industries, summer 1967, clin. psychologist Rehab. Center, 1967—; staff psychologist Toledo Mental Health Center, 1979-84. Dir. camping activities for retarded girls and women Camp Libbey, Defiance, Ohio, summers 1951-62; group worker for retarded women Toledo YWCA, 1957-62; guest lectr. Ohio State U., 1957. Health care profl. mem. Nat. Osteoporosis Found., 1988—. Mem. Ohio Assn. Tchrs. Trainable Youth (pres. 1956-57), NW Ohio Rehab. Assn. (pres. 1961-62), Toledo Council for Exceptional Children (pres. 1965), Greater Toledo Assn. Mental Health, Nat. Assn. for Retarded Children, Ohio Assn. Tchrs. Slow Learners, Am. Assn. Mental Deficiency, Am. Soc. Psychologists in Marital and Family Counseling, Psychology and Law Soc. Am. (assoc.), Ohio, NW Ohio (sec.-treas. 1974-77, pres. 1978-79), Am. Theater Orgn. Soc., Ohio Psychol. Assn. (continuing edn. com. 1978—), NEA, AAUW, Am. Soc. Psychologists in Pvt. Practice (nat. dir. 1976—), State Assn. Psychologists and Psychol. Assts., Bus. and Profl. Women's Club, (pres. 1970-72), Ohio Fedn. Bus. and Profl. Women's Clubs (dist. sec. 1970-71, dist. legis. chmn. 1972-74), Toledo Art Mus., Women's Aux. Toledo Bar Assn., League Women Voters (pres. Toledo Lucas County 1991-93), Y Matrons (pres. 1993—), Toledo Area Theater Orgn. Soc. (sec. 1991—), Zonta Internat. (local pres. 1973-74, 78-79, area dir. 1976-78, Maumee River Valley Woman of Yr. for svc. to community and Zonta, 1992), Maumee Valley Hist. Soc., MBLS PEO (chpt. pres. 1950-51), Toledo Council on World Affairs, Internat. Platform Assn. Baptist. Home and Office: 2816 Wicklow Rd Toledo OH 43606-2833

RISEN, WILLIAM MAURICE, JR., chemistry educator; b. St. Louis, July 22, 1940. ScB, Georgetown U., 1962; PhD, Purdue U., 1967. Asst. prof. chemistry Brown U., Providence, 1967-72, assoc. prof. chemistry, 1972-75, prof. chemistry, 1975—, chmn. chemistry dept., 1972-80, chmn. of faculty, 1993-94; cons. in field. Contbr. over 100 articles to profl. jours. Grantee in field. Mem. Am. Chem. Soc., Am. Phys. Soc., Am. Ceramic Soc. Office: Brown U Dept of Chemistry 324 Brook St Providence RI 02912-9019

RISHE, MELVIN, lawyer; b. Chgo., June 16, 1940. BS, Roosevelt U., 1963; JD, De Paul U., 1967. BAr: Ill. 1967, D.C. 1974, U.S. Supreme Ct. 1974, U.S. Claims Ct. 1974, U.S. Ct. Appeals (D.C. cir.) 1974. Dep. gen. counsel Dept. Navy, 1967-74; ptnr. Sidley & Austin, Washington; prof. Govt. Contracts, Fed. publs. George Washington U. Contbr. articles to profl. jours. Mem. ABA, D.C. Bar Assn., Pi Gamma Mu. Office: Sidley & Austin 1722 I St NW Washington DC 20006-3705*

RISHEL, JAMES BURTON, manufacturing executive; b. Omaha, Apr. 27, 1920; s. James Blaine and Elizabeth Helen (Kerr) R.; m. Alice Jane Snyder, June 30, 1945; children: James Richard, Sara Jane Rishel Fields. BSME, U. Nebr., 1946. Profl. engr., Ohio. Pres. Corp. Equipment Co., Cin., 1962-82; chmn. bd. Systecon Inc., Cin., 1982—. Author: The Water Management Manual, HVAC Pump Handbook, 1996; patentee hydraulic systems; contbr. numerous articles to profl. jours. Capt. USAF, 1942-46, 51-52. Fellow ASHRAE; mem. Am. Water Works Assn., Water Environment Fedn. Avocations: philanthropy, golf, walking. Home: 7570 Thumbelina Ln Cincinnati OH 45242-4937 Office: Systecon Inc 9750 Crescent Park Dr West Chester OH 45069

RISHEL, KENN CHARLES, school superintendent; b. Utica, N.Y., Nov. 19, 1946; s. Lester and Lois (Keehle) R.; m. Leslie Ann Syposs, Dec. 30, 1967; children: Samantha D., Andrea L. BS, SUNY, Oneonta, 1968; MS in Edn., SUNY, Cortland, 1973, Cert. Advanced Study/Adminstrn., 1985. Elem. tchr. Holland Patent (N.Y.) Ctrl. Sch., 1968-81, math coord., 1977-81; cons. CIMS program Oneida/Madison BOCES, New Hartford, N.Y., 1977-81; asst. supt. for bus. Carthage (N.Y.) Ctrl. Sch., 1981-87, supt., 1987-96; supervising adminstrn., CEO Carthage Area Hosp., 1994—; excelsior examiner N.Y. State Award for Quality, Albany, 1992-94; adj. prof. SUNY-Oswego, Watertown, 1994; notary pub., N.Y. State, 1984—. Mem. N.Y. Coun. Sch. Supts. (mem. ethics com. 1991-95, Pathways to Supt.-Gender Equity coord. 1994), Balck River Coun. Sch. Supts. (treas. 1987—), Am. Assn. Sch. Adminstrs., Assn. U.S. Army, Rotary (v.p., pres. 1981-86), Lions, Elks. Home: 33A Bridge St Carthage NY 13619-1352 Office: Carthage Central School 36500 NYS Rt 26 Carthage NY 13619

RISHEL, RICHARD CLINTON, banker; b. Oreland, Pa., June 7, 1943; S. Herbert Beale and Evelyn (Lauer) R.; m. Carol Staub, Apr. 3, 1965; children: Christian Daniel, Peter James. B.A., Pa. State U., 1965; postgrad., Drexel Inst. Tech., 1965-66. Credit analyst 1st Pa. Banking & Trust Co., Phila., 1965-69; comml. lending officer Nat. Bank of Chester County, West Chester, Pa., 1969; asst. v.p. Continental Bank of Norristown, Pa., 1969-70;

sec. Continental Bank of Norristown, 1970-71, v.p., 1971-73, sr. v.p., chief fin. officer, 1973-75, exec. v.p., chief fin. officer, 1975-81, vice chmn., 1981-83, pres., chief adminstrv. officer, 1984-89, also dir.; pres., chief exec. officer Continental Bank, Continental Bancorp, 1990-92; vice chmn. bd. Continental Bank, 1981-84; pres. parent co. Continental Bancorp., 1981-92; dir. Barnett Inst. U. North Fla., 1993-94; sec. of banking Commonwealth of Pa., 1995—. Office: 4567 Saint Johns Bluff Rd S Jacksonville FL 32224-2646

RISHER, JAMES A., electronics executive; b. 1943. MS in Econs. and Stats., U. Tex., 1943. With IBM Corps., 1969-80; v.p. Wang Labs., 1980-84; sr. v.p. Motorola Computer Systems, Inc., 1984-86; pres., CEO Exide Electronics Group, Inc., Raleigh, N.C., 1986—, now pres., CEO, 1986—; with Exide Electronics Corp. Office: Exide Electronics Corp 8521 Six Forks Rd Raleigh NC 27615-2993*

RISHER, JOHN ROBERT, JR., lawyer; b. Washington, Sept. 23, 1938; s. John Robert and Yvonne Gwendolyn (Jones) R.; m. Carol Adrienne Seeger, June 9, 1974; children—John David, Michael Temple, Mark Eliot, Conrad Zachary. B.A., Morgan Coll., 1960; LL.B., U. So. Calif., 1963; postgrad., John F. Kennedy Sch., Harvard U., 1977. Bar: Calif. 1963, D.C. 1967, U.S. Supreme Ct. 1975. Mem. staff Pres.'s Com. on EEO, Washington, 1965; atty. criminal fraud sect. Dept. Justice, Washington, 1965-68; assoc. Arent, Fox, Kintner, Plotkin & Kahn, Washington, 1968-75; ptnr. Arent, Fox, Kintner, Plotkin & Kahn, 1975-76; corp. counsel D.C., 1976-78; ptnr. Arent, Fox, Kintner, Plotkin & Kahn, Washington, 1978—; chmn. D.C. Criminal Justice Coord. Bd., 1976-78, D.C. Bar spl. com. on federal judiciary, 1985-87; trustee, 2d exec. com. Supreme Ct. Hist. Soc., 1990—; fellow Am. Bar Found., 1994—. Chmn. budget com. Jewish Social Svc. Agy., 1980-85; chmn. D.C. Commn. on Licensure to Practice Healing Arts, 1976-78; chmn. nominating com. D.C. Bd. Elections and Ethics, 1974-76; bd. dirs. D.C. Pub. Defender Svc., 1974-76; chmn. Montgomery County Civil Liberties Union, 1970-71; mem. exec. com. Nat. Capital Area Civil Liberties Union, 1969-71; pres. D.C. Jewish Cmty. Ctr., 1985-87, bd. dirs., 1985—; trustee, bd. dirs. capital camps United Jewish Appeal Fedn., 1987-93; bd. dirs. Washington Symphony Orch., 1990—. Mem. ABA, Bar Assn. D.C., Calif. Bar Assn., Fed. Bar Assn., Washington Bar Assn., DePriest 15. Democrat. Jewish. Home: 3311 Cleveland Ave NW Washington DC 20008-3456 Office: Arent Fox Kintner Plotkin Kahn 1050 Connecticut Ave NW 6th Floor Washington DC 20036-5339

RISI, LOUIS J., JR., business executive; b. Highland Park, Ill., July 2, 1936; s. Louis J. and Ann E. R.; m. Mary Jean Anson, Jan. 15, 1957; children: Steven, Janet, Andrew. B.S., Bradley U., 1958; MBA, U. Chgo. In mgmt. Arthur Young & Co., 1968-69; pres., bd. dirs., mem. exec. com. Norin Corp., Miami, Fla., 1969-81; exec. com. dir. Maple Leaf Mills Ltd., Toronto, Can., 1970-81; Corp. Foods, Inc., 1970-81; chmn. bd. dirs. Louis Sherry, Inc., 1976-81; chmn. bd., chief exec. officer Nat. Investors Fire & Casualty Co., 1975-77; exec. com. dir. Investors Equity Life Ins. Co. of Hawaii, 1970-75; pres., dir. The Abbey, Lake Geneva, 1970-75; exec. comm., dir. Upper Lakes Shipping, Ltd., Toronto, Can., 1970-76; pres., dir. The Pioneer Resort, Lake Oshkosh, 1971-76; exec. comm., dir. Port Weller and St. Lawrence Dry Dock, Ltd., St. Catharines, Can., 1971-76; pres., dir. Homosassa Springs Resort, Fla., 1971-78; exec. v.p., dir. Ivan Tors Films Inc., Culver City, Calif., 1972-76, Ivan Tors Studios Inc., Miami, Fla., 1976-80; exec. com. dir. Midland Nat. Bank, 1976-80; pres., dir. Norris Grain Co., 1980-82; chmn. bd., chief exec. officer CTC Corp., 1981-83; chmn. bd. dirs., CEO Red Wing Co., Oklawaha Farms, Inc., Assured Security Co.; dir. Breckinridge Resorts Group; exec. v.p., bd. dirs. Detroit Red Wings Hockey Club, Inc., 1978-82; bd. govs. Nat. Hockey League, 1978-82; bd. dirs. Chgo. Rock Island and Pacific R.R., dir. exec. com., Bankmgrs. Corp.; lt. comdr. U.S.N.R., 1959-67; U.S. rep. Grain negotiations with USSR; U.S. rep. Feedstuffs negotiations with China; mem. adv. coun. Am. Stock Exch.; mem. Agrl. Processors Liaison com. FTC; mem. adv. bd. Nat. Millers Assn.; exec. v.p., bd. dirs. Adirondack Red Wings Hockey Club, Inc., 1978-82, Ft. Worth Red Wings Hockey Club, Inc., 1975-78; bd. govs. Internat. Hockey League, 1978-82. Trustee Fairchild Tropical Garden, Miami, Fla. Mem. Ocean Reef Yacht Club (Key Largo, Fla.), Santa Rosa (Calif.) Country Club, Riviera Country Club (Coral Gables, Fla.), Anabelle's Club (London), St. James Club (London). Home: 10915 SW 53rd Ave Miami FL 33156-4209 Office: 200 NE 2nd Dr Homestead FL 33030-6119

RISINGER, C. FREDERICK, social studies educator; b. Paducah, Ky., July 15, 1939; s. Charles Morris and Mary Neal (Barfield) R.; m. Margaret M. Marker, July 4, 1994; children: Donna Lyne, Alyson, Laura, John. BS in Edn., So. Ill. U., 1961; MA in History, No. Ill. U., 1968. Newscaster, disc jockey WMOK Radio, Metropolis, Ill., 1955-61; tchr., adminstr., coach Lake Park H.S., Roselle, Ill., 1962-73; coord. sch. social studies Ind. U., Bloomington, 1973-86, assoc. dir. social studies devel. ctr., 1986-90, dir. nat. clearinghouse for U.S.-Japan studies, 1990-95, assoc. dir. tchr. edn., 1995—; mem. adv. bd. Learning Mag., Boston, 1988—; pres. Nat. Coun. for the Social Studies, 1990-91. Co-author: America! America!, 1974, America's Past and Promise, 1995; editor jour. News and Notes on the Social Sciences, 1973-86. Pres. Social Studies Suprs. Assn., Washington, 1985-86; exec. dir. Ind. Coun. for Social Studies, Bloomington, 1975-87. Recipient numerous pub. and pvt. ednl. grants; named Tchr. of Yr. DuPage County Edn. Assn., 1973. Mem. ASCD, Nat. Coun. for Social Studies, Ind. Assn. Historians, Phi Delta Kappa. Democrat. Home: 7039 E State Rd 45 # E Bloomington IN 47408-9580

RISINGER, PAUL N., electronics executive; b. 1933. V. chmn. Symmetricom, Inc., San Jose. Office: Symmetricom Inc 85 W Tasman Dr San Jose CA 95134-1703*

RISK, JOHN FRED, banker, investment banker; b. Ft. Wayne, Ind., Dec. 1, 1928; s. Clifford and Estella (Kline) R.; m. Viola Jean Tompt, July 12, 1953; children: Nancy Jean, John Thomas. B.S. cum laude, Ind. U., 1949, LL.B., J.D., 1951; postgrad., Nortwestern U.; LL.D., Ind. State U. With Harris Trust & Savs. Bank, Chgo., 1951-54, W.T. Grimm & Co., 1954-56; with Ind. Nat. Bank of Indpls., 1956-76, exec. v.p. dir., 1965-68, pres., 1968-76, chmn., 1971-76; chmn. Forum Group, Inc., 1976-91, Sovereign Group Inc., 1980—, Sargent & Greenleaf Inc., 1993—; bd. dirs. Steak 'n Shake, Inc., Standard Locknut, Inc., Somerset Corp., Nat. Homes Corp., Amli Realty Co., Security Group, Inc., Keystone Distbn., Inc. Lacy Diversified Industries, Inc., Excepticon, Inc., L. R. Nelson Corp., Breckenridge Corp., Canterbury Corp., Cygnet Enterprises, Inc., Franklin Corp., Haag Drug Co., Inland Container Corp., Ind. Bell Tel. Co., Ransburg Corp., Hook Drug Co., Northwestern Mut. Life Ins. Co., Consolidated Products Inc., Safemasters Co., Inc., Howard Sams Co. Bd. dirs. Hanover Coll., 1966-72, Ind. U. Found., 1968—, United Student Aid Fund; chmn. Indpls. Ctr. for Advanced Rsch., Ind. State Scholarship Com., 1968-72. Capt. inf. U.S. Army, 1950-51. Mem. Am. Bankers Assn., Ind. Bankers Assn., Res. City Bankers Assn., Ind. Bar Assn., Indpls. Bar Assn., Meridian Hills Country Club (Indpls.), Royal Poinciana Golf Club (Naples, Fla.), Quail Creek Country Club (Naples), Naples Sailing and Yacht Club. Methodist. Clubs: Meridian Hills Country (Indpls.); Royal Poinciana Golf (Naples, Fla.); Quail Creek Country (Naples). Office: Sovereign Group Inc 8900 Keystone Xing Ste 1150 Indianapolis IN 46240-2135

RISK, RICHARD ROBERT, health care executive; b. Chgo., Sept. 15, 1946; s. Clement Albert and Mary Catherine (Clarke) R.; m. Rebecca Ann Sandquist, Jan. 11, 1969 (div. Sept. 1984); children: Michael, Daniel, Laura; m. Louise L. Lawson, Dec. 1, 1984; stepchildren: Carrie Lawson, Valerie Lawson. BS in Econs., U. Ill., 1968; MBA in Health Adminstrn., U. Chgo., 1971. Asst. adminstr. U. Ill. Hosp., Chgo., 1969-72, Ctrl. DuPage Hosp., Winfield, Ill., 1972-74; mgmt. cons., v.p. Tribrook Group, Inc., Oak Brook, Ill., 1974-81; v.p. cons. svcs. Parkside Med. Svcs., Park Ridge, Ill., 1981-83; prin. health and med. divsn. Booz, Allen, & Hamilton, Inc., Chgo., 1983-84; exec. v.p. EHS Health Care, Oak Brook, 1984-92, pres., CEO, 1992-95; pres., CEO Advocate Health Care, Oak Brook, 1995—; mem. faculty Healthcare Fin. Mgmt. Assn., 1978-86, Am. Assn. Hosps. Cons., 1978-84; lectr. grad. program social scis. No. Ill. U., 1982-88; lectr., adv. bd. multi-hosp. system study Kellogg Sch. Health Mgmt. Program Northwestern U., 1985—; lectr. Grad. Program in Health Adminstrn. U. Chgo., 1982-94. Mem. access com. Gov.'s Task Force on Health Reform, 1992-94; mem. chancellor's adv. bd. U. Ill. at Chgo.; mem. dean's adv. bd. coll. of commerce DePaul U. Sgt. USAR, 1968-74. Fellow Am. Assn. Hosp. Cons. (bd. dirs., treas., chmn. govt. rels. com., chmn. membership task force, liaison Nat. Coun. Cmty. Hosps.); mem. Am. Healthcare Systems (bd. dirs., ad hoc ins. com., fin. com.), Am. Hosp. Assn. (del. healthcare systems sect.), Ill. Hosp. Assn. (chmn. coun. on health fin., mem. strategic plan com., bd. dirs.), U. Chgo. Hosp. Adminstrn. Alumni Assn. (pres. exec. com. alumni coun., chmn. 50th ann. com.), Chgo. Health Policy Rsch. Coun. Home: 801 Clinton Pl River Forest IL 60305-1501 Office: EHS Health Care 2025 Windsor Dr Oak Brook IL 60521-1586

RISKAS, HARRY JAMES, construction company executive; b. Shelton, Wis., Mar. 27, 1920; s. James and Anna (Pappeoanou) R.; student St. Mary's Naval Coll., 1941-43; m. Joan Evelyn Clark, Aug. 1, 1964; children—Lawrence, Douglas, Kimberly. Pres., Pacific Western Contractors, Inc., Millbrae, Cal., from 1951; pres., dir. Riskas Baker Riskas Devel. Corp., San Luis Properties, Inc.; pres., chmn. bd. Pacific Western Contractors, Inc., Sanfo-Bay Corp., H.J.R. Developers, Inc., Windrock Corp. Dir., Am. Properties, & Investment Fund, 1970. Lt. comdr. USNR, 1942-46. Mem. Young Pres.'s Orgn., Bankers Club, K.C. (San Francisco). Home: 241 Mainsail Ct Foster City CA 94404-3203 Office: 1650 S Amphlett Blvd Ste 226 San Mateo CA 94402-2515

RISKE, WILLIAM KENNETH, producer, cultural services consultant; b. Lamont, Alta., Can., May 9, 1949; s. Norman Elmer and Clara Jeanette (Krause) R.; m. Barbara Elizabeth Malcolm, Apr. 28, 1973; children: Elizabeth Nicola, William Norman Malcolm. BFA, U. Alta., 1969. Stage mgr. Royal Winnipeg Ballet, Man., Can., 1971-73; prodn. stage mgr. Royal Winnipeg Ballet, 1973-76, prodn. mgr., 1976-77, assoc. gen. mgr., 1978-79, gen. mgr., 1979-92, cultural svcs. cons., 1992—; assoc. prodr., gen. mgr. Cirque Du Soleil-Mystère, 1994—. Mem. Assn. Cultural Execs., Can. Assn. Profl. Dance Orgns. (pres. 1985-88), Dancevision (pres. 1990). Home: 227 Deer Crossing Way Henderson NV 89012

RISLEY, LARRY L., air transportation executive. CEO, chmn. bd. dirs. Mesa Air Corp. Office: Mesa Airlines 2325 E 30th St Farmington NM 87401-8900*

RISLEY, ROD ALAN, education association executive; b. Hutchinson, Kans., Oct. 17, 1954; s. Ralph Edward and Patricia Ann (Gaulding) R.; m. Lynn René Plimpton, Mar. 13, 1963. AA, San Jacinto Coll., 1975; BBA, Sam Houston State U., 1982; AA (hon.), Austin (Tex.) Community Coll., 1991; MBA, Millsap Coll., 1995; PhD (hon.), Highpoint U., 1996, Mt. Ida Coll., 1996. Dir. alumni affairs Phi Theta Kappa, 1976-82; assoc. dir. Phi Theta Kappa Internat. Hdqrs., Jackson, Miss., 1982-85, exec. dir., 1985—. Mem. Millsaps Coll. Second Century Planning Com.; judge Truman Scholarship Found., 1993, 94. Named one of Outstanding Young Men Am., 1982, 83, 84, 85, 86, 87, 88, 89, Top Bus. Leaders Miss., 1994. Mem. Am. Soc. Assn. Execs., Jackson C. of C. (edn. com.), Am. Assn. of Cmty. Colls. (disting. alumnus award 1996), Phi Theta Kappa (sec., pub. jour.). Episcopalian. Office: Phi Theta Kappa Soc PO Box 13729 Jackson MS 39236-3729

RISLEY, TODD ROBERT, psychologist, educator; b. Palmer, Alaska, Sept. 8, 1937; s. Robert and Eva Lou (Todd) R.; 1 child, Todd Michael. A.B. with distinction in Psychology, San Diego State Coll., 1960; M.S., U. Wash., 1963, Ph.D., 1966. Asst. prof. psychology Fla. State U., Tallahassee, 1964-65; research assoc. Bur. Child Research, U. Kans., Lawrence, 1965-77, sr. scientist, 1977—, asst. prof. dept. human devel., 1967-69, assoc. prof., 1969-73, prof., 1973-84; prof. psychology U. Alaska, Anchorage, 1982—; pres. Ctr. for Applied Behavior Analysis, 1970-82; dir. Johnny Cake Child Study Ctr., Mansfield, Ark., 1973-74; vis. prof. U. Auckland (N.Z.), 1978; acting dir. Western Carolina Ctr., Morgantown, N.C., 1981; dir. Alaska Div. Mental Health and Devel. Disabilities, 1988-91; cons. in field to numerous orgns. and instns. Co-author: The Infant Center, 1977, Shopping with Children: Advice for parents, 1978, The Toddler Center, 1979, Meaningful Differences, 1995; editor: Jour. Applied Behavior Analysis, 1971-74; mng. editor: Behavior Therapy, The Behavior Therapist, Behavioral Asessment, 1977-80; mem. editl. bds. of numerous profl. jours.; contbr. revs. and numerous articles. Co-chmn. Fla. task force on use of behavioral procedures in state programs for retarded, 1974—; mem. resident abuse investigating com. div. retardation Fla. Dept. Health and Rehab. Services, 1972—; mem. adv. com. Social Research Inst., U. Utah, 1977—; mem. Alaska Gov.'s Council on Handicapped and Gifted, 1983-88, NIH Mental Retardation Research Com., 1987-88, Alaska Mental Health Bd., 1988. Grantee NIMH, 1971-72, 72-73; research grantee Nat. Ctr. Health Services, 1976-79; grantee Nat. Inst. Edn., 1973, NIH, 1967—. Fellow Am. Psychol. Assn. (coun. of reps. 1982-85, pres. div. 25, 1989); mem. AAAS, Am. Psychol. Soc., Am. Assn. Mental Deficiency, Assn. Advancement of Behavior Therapy (dir. 1975-80, pres. 1976-77, chmn. profl. rev. com. 1977—, series editor Readings in Behavior Therapy 1977—), Soc. Behavioral Medicine, Assn. Behavior Analysis, Sigma Xi. Office: U Alaska-Anchorage Dept Psychology 3211 Providence Dr Anchorage AK 99508-4614

RISMAN, MICHAEL, lawyer, business executive, securities company executive; b. Everett, Mass., Apr. 2, 1938; s. Morris Charles and Doris (Rosenbaum) R.; m. Rebecca R. Fuchs, Mar. 23, 1974; 1 stepchild, Ian Carlton Murray; children: Matthew Craig, Deborah Gayle, Jared Evan. BA, U. Mich., 1960; LLB, Georgetown U., 1964. Bar: D.C. 1964. Staff mem. Democratic Nat. Com., Washington, 1964; atty. U.S. Fgn. Claims Settlement Commn., Washington, 1964-66, SEC, Washington, 1966-67; counsel Seaboard Planning Corp., Beverly Hills, Calif., 1967-72, pres., 1970-72; v.p. Seaboard Corp., Beverly Hills, Calif., 1970-72; sec. B.C. Morton Realty Trust, 1967-71; with Arlington Investments Corp., Santa Monica, Calif., 1979-86; founder The Quincey Group, 1986; owner, pres. Armstrong Kitchens, San Francisco, 1988-90; sr. v.p. AFC Am. Housing Corp., L.A., Calif., 1991—; bd. dir. Competitive Capital Fund, Income Fund Boston, Inc., Admiralty Fund. Home: 1133 Centinela Ave Santa Monica CA 90403-2316

RISOM, JENS, furniture designer, manufacturing executive; b. Copenhagen, May 8, 1916; came to U.S., 1939; naturalized, 1944; s. Sven J. and Inger Risom; m. Iben Haderup, Dec. 12, 1939 (dec. Jan. 1977); children: Helen Ann, Peggy Ann, Thomas Christian, Sven Christian; m. Henny Panduro, May 12, 1979. Student, Krebs, Denmark, 1922-27, St. Anne, 1927-32, Niels Brock Bus. Coll., 1932-34, Sch. for Fine Arts and Indust., Denmark, 1935-38. Freelance furniture designer, 1939-43; founder, pres. Jens Risom Design Inc., 1946-71; pres. Jens Risom Design, Inc. (became subs. Dictaphone Corp. 1971), N.Y.C., 1946-73; v.p. Dictaphone Corp., 1971-73; pres. Design Control, New Canaan, Conn., 1973—; cons. design, mktg., space planning. Trustee RISD, New Canaan Libr., Indsl. Design Soc. Am. Recipient awards Archtl. League, Am. Inst. Internat. Design, Lifetime Achievement award Bklyn. Mus. Art, 1994, numerous Danish and Am. design awards. Mem. Indsl. Designers Soc. Am. Home and Office: 103 Chichester Rd New Canaan CT 06840-3913 also: PO Box 596 Block Island RI 02807-0596

RISOM, OLE CHRISTIAN, publishing company executive; b. Copenhagen, Denmark, Oct. 3, 1919; came to U.S., 1941, naturalized, 1942; s. Sven and Inger (Henriques) R.; m. Agnes Grafin von Rechberg u Rothenloewen, May, 1947; children: Christopher, Camilla, Charles Nicholas. Art dir. Interior Design Mag., N.Y.C., 1948-50; assoc. art dir. McCall, Better Living Mag., N.Y.C., 1950-52; v.p., art dir. Golden Press Western Pub., N.Y.C., 1952-72; v.p., assoc. pub. juvenile div. Random House, N.Y.C., 1972-90. Author: I Am a Bunny, 1963 Little Bunny Follows its Nose, 1971, Max the Nosey Bear, 1972, Do You Know Colors, 1979, others. Served to sgt. U.S. Army, 1942-46, ETO. Decorated Bronze Star. Mem. Nat. Arts Club, Soc. Illustrators, Racquet and Tennis Club, Seawanhaka Corinthian Yacht Club, Royal Danish Yacht Club. Lutheran. Home: 160 Harbor Ln Roslyn NY 11576-1119

RISON, ANDRE, football player; b. Flint, Mich., Mar. 18, 1967. Student, Mich. State U. With Indpls. Colts, 1989, Atlanta Falcons, 1990-95, Cleve. Browns, 1995—. Named to Pro-Bowl, 1990, 91, Sporting News All-Pro team, 1990. Office: Cleveland Browns 80 First Ave Berea OH 44017-0679

RISS, ERIC, psychologist; b. Vienna, Austria, Oct. 10, 1929; s. David S. and Rebecca (Schneider) R.; came to U.S., 1940, naturalized, 1945; B.A., Bklyn. Coll., 1950; Ph.D., NYU, 1958; diplomate Am. Bd. Psychotherapy; m. Miriam Barbara Schoen, July 22, 1956; children: Arthur, Suzanne, Wendy. Pvt. practice psychotherapy, family therapy, marriage counseling, N.Y.C., 1952—; sr. psychologist N.Y.C. Diagnostic Center, 1954-57; with Marriage and Family Life Inst., N.Y.C., 1956-92; cons., 1956-58, dir. pub. edn., 1960-73, chmn. bd. dirs., 1961-73, dir., 1973-92; mem. attending staff, supr. psychotherapy and family therapy Payne Whitney Psychiat. Clinic, N.Y. Hosp., N.Y.C., 1971-78; clin. instr. psychology and psychiatry Cornell U. Med. Coll., 1971-72, clin. asst. prof., 1973-78; dir. Inst. for Exploration of Marriage, 1976-84; chief psychologist Artists, Writers and Performers Psychotherapy Center, 1978-92; lectr. Bklyn. Coll., 1955-62; cons. Fordham Hosp., 1956-68; psychotherapist N.Y. Neuropsychiat. Center, 1958-60; psychotherapist Community Guidance Service, N.Y.C., 1958-61. Mem. Am. Acad. Psychotherapy, N.Y. State Marriage, Family and Child Counseling Assn. (pres. 1971-72), Nat. Registry of Health Providers in Psychology, Acad. Family Psychology, Am., N.Y. State psychol. assns. Contbr. numerous articles to profl. jours. Office: 174 E 73rd St New York NY 10021-4352

RISS, MURRAY, photographer, educator; b. Stryj, Poland, Feb. 6, 1940; came to U.S., 1951, naturalized, 1958; s. Elias and Dora (Feit) R.; m. Karen Mason; children: Shanna, Adya. Student, CCNY, 1958-63; B.A., Cooper Union, 1966; M.F.A., R.I. Sch. Design, 1968. Prof., chmn. dept photography Memphis Acad. Arts, 1969—; lectr. film and photography Southwestern U., Memphis, 1972—; artist-in-residence U. Syracuse, N.Y., 1980, U. Haifa, Israel, 1976. One man shows include Art Inst., Chgo, 1971, Mpls. Inst. Fine Arts, 1971, U. Rochester, N.Y., 1975, Photographers Gallery, London, 1977, Afterimage Gallery, Dallas, 1979, Visual Studies Workshop, Rochester, 1980, Hampshire (Mass.) Coll., 1981, Loomis Inst., Conn., 1984; group shows include Mus. Modern Art, N.Y.C., 1970, 71, New Orleans Mus. Art, 1975, Nexus Gallery, Atlanta, 1981, Askew Nixon Gallery; touring show So. Arts Fedn., 1985-86; conceived, organized, dir. Southern Eye, Southern Mind, A Photographic Inquiry, Memphis, 1981; illustrator: History of Memphis Architecture until 1900, 1983, Guide to Mud Island, 1989; curator, dir. Emerging Southern Photographers, Memphis Coll. Art Gallery, 1992, Memphis Brooks Mus. Art, 1994. Nat. Endowment for Arts fellow, 1979. Mem. Soc. Photographic Edn. Home: 1306 Harbert Ave Memphis TN 38104-4514 Office: Murray Riss Photography 516 S Main St Memphis TN 38103-4443 *Had I designed the events and outcomes of my life I would not have done as well as my fate has done for me.*

RISS, ROBERT BAILEY, real estate broker; b. Salida, Colo., May 27, 1927; s. Richard Roland and Louise (Roberts) R.; married; children: Edward Stayton, G. Leslie, Laura Bailey, Juliana Warren. BSBA, U. Kans., 1949. Pres. Riss Internat. Corp., Kansas City, Mo., 1950-80, chmn. bd., 1964-86; founder, chmn. bd., pres. Republic Industries, Inc., Kansas City, Mo., 1969-86; chmn. bd. Grandview Bank and Trust Co., 1969-86, Commonwealth Gen. Ins. Co., 1986-93; Chmn. bd. dirs., exec. com. Heart of Am. Fire and Casualty Co.; chmn. bd. dirs. Comml. Equipment Co. Vice chmn. bd. trustees Kansas U. Endowment Assn., 1980-89. Recipient Silver Beaver award Kansas City Area coun. Boy Scouts Am., 1972; Disting. Svc. citation U. Kans., 1976; Fred Ellsworth medal U. Kans., 1979; named Most Outstanding Young Man in Mo. U.S. Jr. C. of C., 1956. Mem. Kans. U. Alumni Assn. (nat. pres. 1969-70), Sigma Nu. Episcopalian.

RISSANEN, JORMA JOHANNES, scientist; b. Pielisjarvi, Finland, Oct. 20, 1932; arrived in U.S. 1964; m. Riitta T. Åberg, Nov. 6, 1956; children—Juhani, Natasha. Ph.D., Finland Inst. Tech., 1960. Mem. research staff IBM, San Jose, Calif., 1960—. Contbr. articles to profl. jours. Patentee in field. Assoc. editor jour. of Control and Info. Recipient Outstanding Innovation award, IBM Research div., 1980, Best paper award Automatica, 1982. Home: 140 Teresita Way Los Gatos CA 95032-6040

RISSE, GUENTER BERNHARD, physician, historian, educator; b. Buenos Aires, Argentina, Apr. 28, 1932; s. Francisco B. and Kaete A. R.; m. Alexandra G. Paradzinski, Oct. 14, 1961; children—Heidi, Monica, Alisa. MD, U. Buenos Aires, 1958; PhD, U. Chgo., 1971. Intern Mercy Hosp., Buffalo, 1958-59; resident in medicine Henry Ford Hosp., Detroit, 1960-61, Mt. Carmel Hosp., Columbus, Ohio, 1962-63; asst. dept. medicine U. Chgo., 1963-67; asst. prof. dept. history of medicine U. Minn., 1969-71; asso. prof. dept. history of medicine and dept. history of sci. U. Wis., Madison, 1971-76; prof. U. Wis., 1976-85, chmn. dept. history of medicine, 1971-77; prof., chmn. dept. history health scis. U. Calif., San Francisco, 1985—; Mem. project com. Ctr. for Photog. Images in Medicine and Health Care. Author: Paleopathology of Ancient Egypt, 1964, Hospital Life in Enlgihtenment Scotland, 1986; editor: Modern China and Traditional Chinese Medicine, 1973, History of Physiology, 1973, Medicine Without Doctors, 1977, AIDS and the Historian, 1991; mem. editl. bd. Jour. History of Medicine, 1971-74, 90-93, Clio Medica, 1973-88, Bull. History of Medicine, 1980-94, Medizinhistorisches jour., 1981—, Med. History, 1989-95, Asclepio, 1995—. Served with Argentine Armed Forces, 1955. NIH grantee, 1971-73, 82-83, WHO grantee, 1979.. Mem. Am. Assn. History of Medicine (pres. 1988-90, William H. Welch medal 1988), History Sci. Soc., Internat. Acad. History Medicine, Deutsche Gesellschaft fur Geschichte der Medizin, European Assn. History of Medicine and Health, Mex. Soc. History and Philosophy of Medicine, Internat. Network for History of Pub. Health, Brit. Soc. for Social History of Medicine, Argentine Ateneo de Historia de la Medicina, AIDS History Group (co-chair 1988-94), Internat. Network for History of Hosps. (convenor 1995—), Bay Area Med. Hist. Club (pres. 1994—). Home: 600 Noriega St San Francisco CA 94122-4616 Office: Univ of Calif Dept History Health Scis 513 Parnassus Ave San Francisco CA 94143-0726

RISSER, ARTHUR CRANE, JR., zoo administrator; b. Blackwell, Okla., July 8, 1938; s. Arthur Crane and Mary Winn (Stevenson) R.; children: Michelle W., Stephen C., Michael R. BA, Grinnell Coll., Iowa, 1960; MA, U. Ariz., Tucson, 1963; PhD, U. Calif., Davis, 1970. Mus. technician, Smithsonian Instn., Washington, 1963-64; research assoc. Sch. Medicine U. Md., Balt., 1964-65; grad. teaching asst. U. Calif., Davis, 1965-70; asst. prof. biology U. Nev.-Reno, 1970-74; asst. curator birds Zool. Soc. San Diego, 1974-76, curator birds, 1976-81, gen. curator birds, 1981-86; gen. mgr. San Diego Zoo, 1986—; co-chmn. Calif. Condor Working Group on Captive Breeding and Reintroduction, 1983-85; mem. Calif. Condor Recovery Team, 1984-86. Treas., Planned Parenthood, Reno, 1972; bd. dirs. Internat. Found. Conservation Birds, 1979-88, Conservation Rsch. Found. of Papua New Guinea, 1991—. Fellow Am. Assn. Zool. Parks and Aquariums. Office: San Diego Zoo PO Box 551 San Diego CA 92112-0551

RISSER, JAMES VAULX, JR., journalist, educator; b. Lincoln, Nebr., May 8, 1938; s. James Vaulx and Ella Caroline (Schacht) R.; m. Sandra Elizabeth Laaker, June 10, 1961; children: David James, John Daniel. BA, U. Nebr., 1959, cert. in journalism, 1964; JD, U. San Francisco, 1962. Bar: Nebr. 1962. Pvt. practice law Lincoln, 1962-64; reporter Des Moines Register and Tribune, 1964-85, Washington corr., 1969-85, bur. chief, 1976-85; dir. John S. Knight fellowships for profl. journalists, prof. communication Stanford U., 1985—; lectr. Wells Coll., 1981; mem. com. on agrl. edn. in secondary schs. Nat. Acad. Scis., 1985-88. Trustee Reuter Found., 1989—; mem. Pulitzer Prize Bd., 1990—. Profl. Journalism fellow Stanford U., 1973-74; recipient award for disting. reporting public affairs Am. Polit. Sci. Assn., 1969; Thomas L. Stokes award for environ. reporting Washington Journalism Center, 1971, 79; Pulitzer prize for nat. reporting, 1976, 79; Worth Bingham Found. prize for investigative reporting, 1976; Raymond Clapper Meml. Assn. award for Washington reporting, 1976, 78; Edward J. Meeman award for Conservation Reporting, 1985. Mem. Nebr. Bar Assn., Soc. Environ. Journalists, Soc. Profl. Journalists (Disting. Svc. award 1976), Investigative Reporters and Editors Assn. Club: Gridiron. Home: 394 Diamond St San Francisco CA 94114 Office: Stanford U Communication Dept Stanford CA 94305-2050

RISSETTO, HARRY A., lawyer; b. Dec. 1, 1943. AB, Fairfield U., 1965; JD, Georgetown U., 1968. Bar: N.Y. 1969, D.C. 1970. Law clk. to Hon. John J. Sirica U.S. Dist. Ct. D.C., 1968-69; law clk. to Chief Justice Warren E. Burger U.S. Supreme Ct., 1969-70; ptnr. Morgan, Lewis & Bockius, Washington; adj. prof. law Georgetown U. Law Ctr., 1986-89. Mem. ABA (co-chmn. railway labor act com. sect. of labor and employment law 1987-

89). Office: Morgan Lewis & Bockius 1800 M St NW Washington DC 20036-5869

RISSING, DANIEL JOSEPH, hospital administrator; b. Fort Wayne, Ind., Mar. 25, 1944; married. BA, Ind. U., 1966; MA, Xavier U., 1968. Adm. res. Parkview Meml. Hosp., Fort Wayne, Ind., 1967-68, adminstrv. asst., 1968-69; adminstr. PHS Indian Hosp., Tuba City, Ariz., 1969-71; extern William N. Wishard Meml. Hosp., Indpls., Ind., 1971-73; adminstr. Dearborn County Hosp., Lawrenceburg, Ind., 1974-78; pres. Good Samaritan Med. Ctr., Zanesville, Ohio, 1978-88, Hosp. St. Raphael, New Haven, Conn., 1988-91, Toledo (Ohio) Hosp., 1991—; adj. educator in field. Lt. Comdr. U.S. Army, 1969-71. Mem. NEHA, Conn. Hosp. Assn. (community svc.), Ohio Hosp. Assn. (bd. dirs.), Ind. Hosp. Assn. (bd. dirs.), various healthcare orgns. Home: 4529 Woodhill Rd Toledo OH 43615-2200 Office: The Toledo Hosp 2142 N Cove Blvd Toledo OH 43606-3895*

RISSMAN, BURTON RICHARD, lawyer; b. Chgo., Nov. 13, 1927; s. Louis and Eva (Lyons) R.; m. Francine Greenberg, June 15, 1952; children: Lawrence E., Thomas W., Michael P. BS, U. Ill., 1947, JD, 1951; LLM, NYU, 1952. Bar: Ill. 1951, U.S. Dist. Ct. (no. dist.) Ill. 1954, U.S. Ct. Appeals (7th cir.) 1978, U.S. Supreme Ct. 1982. Assoc. Schiff, Hardin & Waite, Chgo., 1953-59, ptnr., 1959—, mem. mgmt. com., 1984-92, chmn. mgmt. com., 1986-90; mem. faculty Practicing Law Inst. Bd. editor U. Ill. Law Forum, 1949-51; contbr. articles to profl. jours. Trustee Crow Canyon Archaeol. Ctr. 1st lt. JAGC, USAF, 1952-54. Food Law fellow, 1951. Mem. ABA, Ill. State Bar Assn., Chgo. Bar Assn., Chgo. Coun. Lawyers, Am. Judicature Soc., Met. Club, Carlton Club. Office: Schiff Hardin & Waite 233 S Wacker Dr Chicago IL 60606-6306

RIST, ROBERT G., religious publishing executive. Pres. Warner Press Inc. Office: Warner Press Inc PO Box 2499 Anderson IN 46018-2499

RISTAU, KENNETH EUGENE, JR., lawyer; b. Knoxville, Tenn., Feb. 14, 1939; s. Kenneth E. and Frances (Besch) R.; m. Mary Emily George, Nov. 27, 1967 (div. Apr. 1985); children: Heidi, Mary Robin, Kenny, Michael, Robert; m. Emily Pettis, Mar. 31, 1990; 1 child, James Patrick. BA, Colgate U., 1961; JD, NYU, 1964. Bar: U.S. Ct. Appeals (9th cir.) 1968, U.S. Ct. Appeals (D.C. cir.) 1974, U.S. Supreme Ct. 1974, U.S. Dist. Ct., Southern Dist. of Calif., 1993. Assoc. Gibson, Dunn & Crutcher, L.A., 1964-69; ptnr. Gibson, Dunn & Crutcher, Newport Beach, Calif., 1969—. Mem. Employers Group (adv. bd.), Orange County Indsl. Rels. Rsch. Assn. (pres. 1992-93), Big Canyon Country Club, Rancho Las Palmas Country Club, Newport Beach Tennis Club, Santa Fe Hunt Club (pres., bd. dirs.). Office: Gibson Dunn & Crutcher Jamboree Ctr 4 Park Plz Irvine CA 92714

RISTINE, JEFFREY ALAN, reporter; b. Ann Arbor, Mich., Apr. 21, 1955; s. Harold G. and Amelita (Schmidt) R. BA, U. Mich., 1977. Reporter The Midland (Mich) Times, 1978-79, Johnstown (Pa.) Tribune-Dem., 1979-80, San Diego Tribune, 1980-92, San Diego Union-Tribune, 1992—. Recipient Appreciation award Am. Planning Assn., San Diego sect., 1988; named Best polit./govt. reporter San Diego Press Club, 1986. Avocations: puzzle-solving, bicycling, cat photography. Office: San Diego Union-Tribune 350 Camino De La Reina San Diego CA 92108-3003

RISTOW, GEORGE EDWARD, neurologist, educator; b. Albion, Mich., Dec. 15, 1943; s. George Julius and Margaret (Beattie) R.; 1 child, George Andrew Martin. BA, Albion Coll., 1965; DO, Coll. Osteo. Medicine and Surgery, Des Moines, 1969. Diplomate Am. Bd. Psychiatry and Neurology. Intern, Garden City Hosp., 1969-70; resident Wayne State U., 1970-74; fellow U. Newcastle Upon Tyne, 1974-75; asst. prof. dept. neurology Wayne State U., Detroit, 1975-77; assoc. prof. Mich. State U., East Lansing, Mich., 1977-83, prof., 1983-84, 95—, prof., chmn., 1984-95. Fellow Am. Acad. Neurology, Royal Soc. Medicine; mem. AMA, Am. Osteo. Assn., Pan Am. Med. Assn., Am. Coll. Neuropsychiatrists (sr.). Home: 2070 Riverwood Dr Okemos MI 48864-2814 Office: Mich State U Dept Internal Medicine 305 E Fee Hall East Lansing MI 48824-1316

RITCH, HERALD LAVERN, finance company executive; b. Los Angeles, Feb. 13, 1951; s. Herald Lester and Caroline (Lillevold) R.; m. Linda Suzanne Lundberg, June 11, 1972; children: Eleanor Loring, Seth Alden. BA in Econs., Stanford U., 1973; MBA, U. Pa., 1975. Assoc. Dean Witter Reynolds, Inc., N.Y.C., 1975-79, v.p., 1979-82, mng. dir., mgr. merger and acquisition dept., 1982-83; v.p. Kidder, Peabody & Co, Inc., N.Y.C., 1983-86, mng. dir., 1987-88; gen. ptnr. Freeman Spogli & Co., N.Y.C., 1988-90; managing dir. Donaldson Lufkin & Jenrette, N.Y.C., 1991-94, mng. dir. and dir. mergers and acquisitions, 1994—. Contbr. articles to profl. jours. Dir. Greenwich Assn. Retarded Citizens; elder 1st Presbyn. Ch., Greenwich. Mem. Stanwich Club, Met. Club. Avocations: tennis, skiing, reading. Office: Donaldson Lufkin & Jenrette 140 Broadway New York NY 10005-1101

RITCH, KATHLEEN, diversified company executive; Harbor Beach, Mich., Jan. 23, 1943; d. Eunice (Spry) R.; B.A., Mich. State U., 1965: student Katharine Gibbs Sch., 1965-66. Exec. sec., adminstrv. asst. to pres. Katy Industries, Inc., N.Y.C., 1969-70; exec. sec., adminstrv. asst. to chmn. Kobrand Corp., N.Y.C., 1970-72; adminstrv. asst. to chmn. and pres. Ogden Corp., N.Y.C., 1972-74; asst. sec., adminstr. office services, asst. to chmn. Ogden Corp., N.Y.C., 1974-81, corporate sec., adminstr. office services, 1981-84, v.p., corporate sec., adminstr. office services, 1984-92, v.p. corp. sec., 1992—; part-owner Unell Mfg. Co., Port Hope, Mich., 1966-87. Bd. dir. Young Concert Artists, Inc., 1991—. Mem. Am. Soc. Corporate Secs. Home: 500 E 77th St New York NY 10162-0025 Office: Ogden Corp Two Pennsylvania Pla New York NY 10121

RITCHESON, CHARLES RAY, university administrator, history educator; b. Maysville, Okla., Feb. 26, 1925; s. Charles Frederick and Jewell (Vaughn) R.; m. Shirley Marie Spackman, June 13, 1953 (div. July 1964); children: Charles Brendan, Mark Frederick; m. Alice Luethi, Oct. 11, 1965; children: Philip Luethi, Steven Whitefield, Andrew Shepherd, Peter Lorentz. B.A., Okla. U., 1946; postgrad., Zurich U., Switzerland, 1946-47, Harvard U., 1947-48; Ph.D. (Fulbright fellow), Oxford U., Eng., 1951; D.Litt. (hon.), Leicester U., Eng. Asst. prof. history Okla. Coll. for Women, 1951-52, asso. prof., 1952-53; assoc. prof. Kenyon Coll., Gambier, Ohio, 1953-60; prof. Kenyon Coll., 1960-64, chmn. dept. history, 1964; chmn., dir. grad. studies in history So. Meth. U., 1965-70; dir. Center Ibero-Am. Civilization, 1967-68; dir. with rank of dean Library Advancement, 1970-71; Colin Rhys Lovell Prof. Brit. history U. So. Calif., 1971-74, Lovell Disting. prof., 1977-84, The Univ. Prof., Univ. libr., dean, vice provost, spl. asst. to pres., 1984-90, The Univ. Prof. emeritus, Univ. libr. emeritus, 1990—; cultural attaché Am. Embassy, 1974-77; pres. So. Conf. on Brit. Studies, 1967-70, Pacific Coast br. Conf. on Brit. Studies, 1971-73; exec. sec. Nat. Conf. Brit. Studies, 1973-74; presdl. appointee Nat. Council on Humanities, 1982-86, Bd. of Fgn. Scholarships, 1986-88, Nat. Council on Humanities, 1988-90; Fulbright prof. Edinburgh U., Cambridge U., 1963-64. Author: British Politics and the American Revolution, 1954, Era of the American Revolution, 1968, British Policy Toward the U.S, 1783-1795, 1968; Contbr. articles to learned jours. Chmn. U.S.-U.K. Ednl. Commn., 1974-77; ofcl. observer Brit. Bicentennial Liaison Com., 1974-76; mem. internat. adv. coun. U. Buckingham, Eng.; v.p. Am. Friends of Covent Garden, 1982-85, Fund for Arts and Culture in Ea. Europe, 1992-96, exec. v.p.; mem. adv. coun. Ditchley Found.; chmn. Brit. Inst. U.S., 1978-81. Lt. (j.g.) USNR, 1942-45. Univ. award for creative scholarship, 1980; Social Sci. Research Council Faculty fellow, 1956-59; Eli Lilly-Clements Library fellow, 1960; Am. Council Learned Socs. fellow, 1963-64. Fellow Royal Hist. Soc.; mem. Tex. Inst. Letters, Soc. Francaise d'Archeologie, Phi Beta Kappa. Clubs: Brooks, Beefsteak (London), Cosmos (Washington).

RITCHEY, HAROLD W., retired chemical engineer; b. Kokomo, Ind., Oct. 5, 1912; s. Glen Robert and Mabel Ann (Wilson) R.; m. Helen Hively, Aug. 29, 1941; children: Stephen, David. BSChemE, Purdue U., 1934, MS in Chemistry, 1936, PhD in Chemistry, 1938; MSChemE, Cornell U., 1945. Rsch. chemist Union Oil Corp., Calif., 1938-41, 46-47; nuclear reactor engr. GE Co., Richland, Wash., 1947-49; tech. dir. rocket divsn. Thiokol Corp., Huntsville, Ala., 1949-50; v.p. rocket divsn. Thiokol Corp., Ogden, Utah, 1960-64; pres. Thiokol Corp., Bristol, Pa., 1964-70; CEO, chmn. bd. dir. Thiokol Corp., Newtown, Pa., 1970-77. Mem. Rotary Club, Ogden, 1974—. Lt. comdr. USN, 1941-46. Named Outstanding Chem. Engr., Purdue U., 1994. Mem. AIAA, ADPA, AUSA, AIA, AFA, Purdue Rsch. Found., Am. Rocket Soc. (bd. dirs. 1956-60, v.p. 1960, pres. 1961, C.N. Hickman award 1954), Sigma Xi, Phi Lambda Upsilon. Patentee in rocketry, astronautics, and petroleum and nuclear energy fields. Home: 1756 Doxey St Ogden UT 84403-0524

RITCHEY, JAMES SALEM, office furniture manufacturing company executive; b. Birmingham, Ala., June 15, 1950; s. Salem E. and Edna (George) R.; m. Rhonda Waddell, Jan. 20, 1989; children: Barry, John. BS in Acctg., U. Ala., 1972, MBA, 1981. CPA, Ala. Staff acct. Ernst & Young, Birmingham, 1971-74; asst. contr. United Chair Co., Inc., Leeds, Ala., 1974-81, contr., 1981-83; v.p. fin. Office Group Am. (United Chair Co., and Anderson Hickey Co.), Leeds, 1983-89, exec. v.p., 1989-91; pres. Office Group Am. (United Chair Co. and Anderson Hickey Co.), Leeds, 1991—; CPA. Named Acctg. Alumni of Yr., U. Ala., Birmingham, 1987. Mem. AICPA, Ala. Soc. CPA's, Nat. Assn. Accts. (past chpt. pres., Branhart-Strawn award 1982), Alpha Beta Psi. Avocations: golf, tennis, chess. Office: Office Group Am 114 Churchill Ave NW Leeds AL 35094-1458*

RITCHEY, PATRICK WILLIAM, lawyer; b. Pitts., July 9, 1949; s. Joseph Frank and Patricia Ann (Giovengo) R. BA, Haverford Coll., 1971; JD, Yale U., 1974. Bar: U.S. Dist. Ct. (we. dist.) Pa. 1974, U.S. Ct. Appeals (3d. cir.) 1976, U.S. Supreme Ct. 1980, U.S. Ct. Appeals (4th cir.) 1981, U.S. Ct. Appeals (6th cir.) 1982, U.S. Dist. Ct. (ea. dist.) Wis. 1987, U.S. Ct. Appeals (7th cir.) 1991, U.S. Ct. Appeals (D.C. cir.) 1993, U.S. Ct. Appeals (8th cir.) 1993. Assoc. Reed Smith Shaw & McClay, Pitts., 1974-82, ptnr., 1982—; mem. Pitts. Personnel Assn., Pitts., 1982—, U.S. Dist. Ct. Rules Task Force, Pitts., 1988. Mem. ABA (labor law sect.), Allegheny County Bar Assn. (labor law and fed. ct. sects.), Harvard-Yale-Princeton Club, Duquesne Club. Office: Reed Smith Shaw & McClay James H Reed Bldg 435 6th Ave Pittsburgh PA 15219-1809

RITCHEY, WILLIAM MICHAEL, chemistry educator; b. Mt. Vernon, Ohio, June 2, 1925; s. Joseph David nd Minnie (Tanury) R.; m. Minetta Hoover, July 27, 1947 (dec. Aug. 1992); children: Stephen, Joseph, Mark; m. Mary E. Golambush, Aug. 28, 1993. With Standard Oil of Ohio Research Ctr., Clev., 1955-68; prof. chemistry and macromolecular sci. Case Western Res. U., Cleve., 1968—; researcher nuclear magnetic resonance; cons. Co-editor: Atlas of Spectral Data and Physical Constants for Organic Compounds, 1978. Asst. scoutmaster Troop 424, Greater Clev. Council; active Lyndhurst Baptist Ch., (Ohio). Served with U.S. Army, 1943-46. Mem. Am. Chem. Soc., Soc. Applied Spectroscopy, Sigma Xi. Home: 851 Haywood Dr South Euclid OH 44121-3403 Office: Millis Sci Center Adelbert Rd Cleveland OH 44106-7078

RITCHIE, ALBERT, lawyer; b. Charlottesville, Va., Sept. 29, 1939; s. John and Sarah Dunlop (Wallace) R.; m. Jennie Wayland, Apr. 29, 1967; children: John, Mary. BA, Yale U., 1961; LLB, U. Va., 1964. Bar: Ill. 1964. Assoc. Sidley & Austin, Chgo., 1964-71, ptnr., 1972—. Bd. dirs. Erie Neighborhood House, Chgo., 1978-88; bd. dirs. United Charities of Chgo., 1979-90. Capt. U.S. Army, 1965-67. Mem. ABA, Am. Coll. Real Estate Lawyers, Chgo. Legal Aid Soc., Legal Club Chgo. (pres. 1986-87), U. Va. Law Sch. Alumni Assn. (v.p. 1989-93, pres. 1993-95), LaSalle Club, Indian Hill Club. Episcopalian. Office: Sidley & Austin 1 First Nat Plz Chicago IL 60603

RITCHIE, CEDRIC ELMER, banker; b. Upper Kent, N.B., Can., Aug. 22, 1927; s. E. Thomas and Marion (Henderson) R.; m. Barbara Binnington, Apr. 20, 1956. Student pub. schs., Bath, N.B. With The Bank of N.S., Bath, 1945—; chief gen. mgr. The Bank of N.S., Toronto, Ont., Can., 1970-72, pres., 1972-93, chief exec. officer, 1972-93, chmn. bd. dirs., 1974-95; dir. The Bank N.S.; mem. adv. coun. for Can. Exec. Svc. Orgn.; dir. Can. Life Assurance Co., Can. Nat. Rlwys., Ingersoll-Rand Co., J. Ray McDermott, S.A., Mercedes-Benz Can., Inc., Minorco, Moore Corp., Ltd. NOVA Corp., Alta, Pacific Basin Econ. Coun. Can. Com., The Japan Soc., McMaillan Bloedel Ltd. Mem. hon. com. Can. Orgn. for Devel. Through Edn.; internat. adv. coun. Ctr. for Inter-Am. Rels.; chmns. coun. Ams. Soc.; dir.-at-large Jr. Achievement Can.; gov. Asian Inst. Mgmt.; chmn. Can.-Philippines Coun., Can. Bus. Com. on Jamaica; mem. adv. coun. Can. Exec. Svc. Orgn.; hon. dir. Save Our N.W. Atlantic Resources. Decorated Officer Order of Can., 1981; recipient Sikatuna award Can. Fedn. for Humanities, 1993; named Bus. Man of Yr., Harvard Bus. Sch. Club, 1993, Bus. Leader of Yr., Western Bus. Sch. Club Toronto, 1993. Mem. Am. Soc. Edn. (mem. hon. com.), Spencer Hall Found. (pres., trustee). Clubs: Canadian, Donalda, Mt. Royal, Mid Ocean, National, Toronto, York, Lyford Cay. Office: Scotia Plz 44 King Street W, Toronto, ON Canada M5H 1H1

RITCHIE, DANIEL LEE, academic administrator; b. Springfield, Ill., Sept. 19, 1931; s. Daniel Felix and Jessie Dee (Binney) R. B.A., Harvard U., 1954, M.B.A., 1956. Exec. v.p. MCA, Inc., Los Angeles, 1967-70; pres. Archon Pure Products Co., Los Angeles, 1970-73; exec. v.p. Westinghouse Electric Corp., Pitts., 1975-78; pres. corp. staff and strategic planning Westinghouse Broadcasting Co., 1978-79, pres., chief exec. officer, 1979-81, chmn., chief exec. officer; chmn., chief exec. officer Westinghouse Broadcasting & Cable, Inc., 1981-87; owner Grand River Ranch, Kremmling, Colo., 1977—, Rancho Cielo, Montecito, Calif., 1977—; chancellor U. Denver, 1989—. With U.S. Army, 1956-58. Office: U Denver Office of the Chancellor University Park Denver CO 80208

RITCHIE, J. MURDOCH, pharmacologist, educator; b. Aberdeen, Scotland, June 10, 1925; came to U.S. 1956; s. Alexander Farquharson and Agnes Jane (Bremner) R.; m. Brenda Rachel Bigland; children: Alasdair J., A. Jocelyn. BSc, Aberdeen (Scotland) U., 1944, U. Coll. London, 1949; PhD, U. Coll. London, 1952, DSc, 1960; MA, Yale U., 1968; DSc, Aberdeen U., 1987. Lectr. physiology U. Coll. London, 1949-51; sci. staff Nat. Inst. Med. Rsch., London, 1951-55; asst. prof. to prof. Albert Einstein Coll. Medicine, N.Y.C., 1954-63, prof. pharmacology, 1963-68; prof. and chmn. pharmacology Yale U., New Haven, 1968-74, dir. biol. scis., 1975-78, prof. pharmacology, 1968—. Contbr. articles to profl. jours.; editor sci. books and jours. Fellow Royal Soc., Univ. Coll. London. Home: 47 Deepwood Dr Hamden CT 06517-3414 Office: Yale Univ Sch Medicine 333 Cedar St New Haven CT 06510-3206

RITCHIE, JAMES E., hotel executive; b. 1936. Exec. v.p. corp. mgt. Mirage Resorts Inc., Las Vegas; principle Paragon Gaming, Las Vegas. Office: Paragon Gaming 600 E Charleston Las Vegas NV 89109*

RITCHIE, MICHAEL BRUNSWICK, film director and producer; b. Waukesha, Wis., Nov. 28, 1938; s. Benbow Ferguson and Patricia (Graney) R.; m. Jimmie Bly, Oct. 1982; children from previous marriage: Lauren, Steven, Jessica; stepchildren: Lillian, Miriam, Nelly, Billy. A.B., Harvard U., 1960. Television dir., 1963-68, now dir. films. Dir.: Downhill Racer, 1969, Prime Cut, 1972, The Candidate, 1972, Smile, 1975, Bad News Bears, 1976, Semi Tough, 1977, The Island, 1980, Bette Midler's Divine Madness, 1980, The Survivors, 1983, Fletch, 1985, Wildcats, 1986, The Golden Child, 1986, The Couch Trip, 1987, Fletch Lives, 1989, Diggstown, 1989, Cops and Robbersons, 1994, The Scout, 1994; dir., writer: The Bad News Bears Go to Japan, 1978, An Almost Perfect Affair, 1979; (TV series) Profiles in Courage (also prod.), Man from U.N.C.L.E., Run for Your Life, Dr. Kildare, The Big Valley, others; TV films include The Positively True Adventures of the Alleged Texas Cheerleader-Murdering Mom, 1993; films invited to Venice Film Festival and U.S. Film Festival. Mem. Dirs. Guild Am. Office: care Marvin Freedman Freedman Kinzelberg & Broder 2121 Avenue Of The Stars Los Angeles CA 90067-5010 also: ICM 8942 Wilshire Blvd Beverly Hills CA 90211-1934

RITCHIE, RICHARD LEE, communications company executive, former railroad and forest products company executive; b. Grand Rapids, Mich., July 20, 1946; s. Robert George and Gertrude (Dryer) R.; m. Marlene Barton, Nov. 16, 1969; children: Gabrielle Gay, Steven Barton. B.A., Mich. State U., 1968, M.B.A., 1972; P.M.D., Harvard U., 1982. C.P.A., Mich. Sr. acct. Peat, Marwick, Mitchell & Co., Detroit, 1968-69, 72-74; mgr. corp. acctg. Grand Trunk Western R.R., Detroit, 1974-76; treas. Grand Trunk Western R.R., 1976-79, asst. v.p., treas., 1980-83; v.p., treas. James River Corp., Richmond, Va., 1984-86; sr. v.p. fin., chief fin. officer Harte Hanks Communications, San Antonio, 1987—; prof. Oakland Community Coll., Farmington, Mich. Served with AUS, 1969-71. Mem. AICPA, Mich. Assn. CPAs, Am. Acctg. Assn., Beta Alpha Psi, Beta Gamma Sigma. Jewish. Office: Harte Hanks Comm 200 Concord Plaza Dr Ste 800 San Antonio TX 78216-6942

RITCHIE, ROBERT FIELD, lawyer; b. Dallas, July 9, 1917; s. Robert Allan and Sallie Bowen (Field) R.; m. Catherine Canfield, Sept. 14, 1949; children—Allan, Lee, Ann, Kate, Sara, Beth. B.S., So. Meth. U., 1939, LL.B., 1941; LL.M., U. Mich., 1942, S.J.D., 1953. Bar: Tex. 1941. Ptnr. Ritchie Ritchie & Crosland, Dallas, 1946-66; ptnr. Ritchie Crosland & Egan, Dallas, 1966-82, Andrews & Kurth, Dallas, 1982—. Author: Integration of Public Utility Holding Companies, 1954. Elder Presbyn. Ch., Dallas, 1976—. Recipient Silver Beaver award Boy Scouts Am., 1970, Disting. Eagle Scout award, 1975, Order of San Jacinto, Sons Republic of Tex., 1979. Mem. ABA, Dallas Bar Assn., Tex. Bar Found., Crescent Club, Dallas Country Club, Tower Club, Kappa Alpha (Court of Honor 1974). Avocation: photography. Home: 3939 Marquette St Dallas TX 75225-5432 Office: Andrews & Kurth 4400 Thanksgiving Tower Dallas TX 75201

RITCHIE, ROBERT OLIVER, materials science educator; b. Plymouth, Devon, U.K., Jan. 2, 1948; came to U.S., 1974; s. Kenneth Ian and Kathleen Joyce (Sims) R.; m. Connie Olesen (div. 1978); 1 child, James Oliver; m. HaiYing Song, 1991. BA with honors, U. Cambridge, Eng., 1969, MA, PhD, 1973, ScD, 1990. Cert. engr., U.K. Goldsmith's rsch. fellow Churchill Coll. U. Cambridge, 1972-74; Miller fellow in basic rsch. sci. U. Calif., Berkeley, 1974-76; assoc. prof. mech. engring. MIT, Cambridge, 1977-81; prof. U. Calif., Berkeley, 1981—; dep. dir. Materials Scis. Divsn. Lawrence Berkeley Nat. Lab., Cambridge, 1990-94, dir. Ctr. for Advanced Materials, 1987-95, head Structural Materials, Materials Scis. Divsn., 1987-95; head Structural Materials Dept., Materials Scis. Divsn. Lawrence Berkeley Nat. Lab., 1995—; cons. Alcan, Allison, Boeing, Chevron, Exxon, GE, Grumman, Instron, Northrop, Rockwell, Westinghouse, Baxter, Carbomedics, Med. Inc., Shiley, St. Jude Med. Editor 8 books; contbr. over 275 articles to profl. jours. Recipient Curtis W. McGraw Rsch. award Am. Soc. Engring. Educators, 1987, Mathewson Gold medal Minerals, Materials, Metals, Soc., 1985, Rosenhain medal Inst. Materials London, 1992; named one of Top 100 Scientists, Sci. Digest mag., 1984. Fellow Inst. Materials (London), Am. Soc. Metals Internat., Internat. Congress on Fracture (hon., v.p.); mem. Am. Orchid Soc., Am. Soc. Materials, Materials Rsch. Soc., Minerals, Materials and Metals Soc. Avocations: skiing, antiques, orchids, tennis. Home: 590 Grizzly Peak Blvd Berkeley CA 94708-1238 Office: U Calif Dept Materials Sci & Mineral Engring Berkeley CA 94720

RITCHIE, STAFFORD DUFF, II, lawyer; b. Buffalo, June 13, 1948; s. Stafford Duff Ritchie and A. Elizabeth Smith Cavage; m. Rebecca P. Thompson, June 27, 1975; children: Stafford D. III, Thompson C., Glynis A. Student, Rensselaer Poly. Inst., Troy, N.Y., 1966-68; BS in Econs., U. Pa., 1970, JD, 1974. Bar: N.Y. 1975. Atty./advisor, asst. gen. counsel, spl. asst. gen. counsel Adminstrv. Office of U.S. Cts., Washington, 1974-82, assoc. gen. counsel, to 1982; gen. counsel Cavages, Inc., Buffalo, 1982-94; pvt. practice Buffalo, 1994—; counsel Coms. of Jud. Conf. of U.S., Jud. Conf. Com., Jud. Conf. of 9th Cir. of U.S.; spl. counsel for major procurement Supreme Ct. of U.S. Trustee Calasanctius Sch., Buffalo, 1990-92. Sgt. USMCR, 1970-76. Mem. ABA, Fed. Bar Assn., N.Y. State Bar Assn. Avocation: computers. Office: Law Office S D Ritchie II 200 Olympic Towers 300 Pearl St Buffalo NY 14202

RITCHIE, WALLACE PARKS, JR., surgeon, educator; b. St. Paul, Nov. 4, 1935; s. Wallace Parks and Alice Ransome (Otis) R.; m. Barbara Carey Jewell, Aug. 10, 1960; children: Stephanie, David, Jessica. BA, Yale U., 1957; MD, Johns Hopkins U., 1961; PhD, U. Minn., 1971. Diplomate Am. Bd. Surgery. Intern, resident in surgery Yale U., New Haven, 1961-63; resident in surgery U. Minn. Hosps., Mpls., 1963-69, instr. in surgery, 1969-70; from asst. prof. to prof. surgery U. Va. Sch. Medicine, Charlottesville, 1973-83; prof., chmn. dept. surgery Temple U. Sch. Medicine, Phila., 1983-93; exec. dir. Am. Bd. Surgery, Phila., 1994—. Editor textbook: Essentials of Surgery, 1994; contbr. over 125 sci. articles to profl. jours. Lt. col. Med. Corps U.S. Army, 1970-73. USPHS grantee, 1974-85. Office: Am Bd Surgery Inc 1617 John F Kennedy Blvd Philadelphia PA 19103

RITCHIE, WILLIAM PAUL, lawyer; b. Columbus, Ohio, June 3, 1946; s. Austin Everett and Helen (Drake) R.; m. Diane Smith, Aug. 2, 1969; 1 child, Elizabeth Drake. BS in Bus. Adminstrn., Ohio State U., 1968, JD, U. Va., 1971. Bar: Ohio 1971, Calif. 1973, Ill. 1987. Assoc. Jones, Day, Reavis & Pogue, Cleve., 1971-77, ptnr., 1977—, ptnr.-in-charge, Chgo., 1987—. Served to lt. USAR, 1972. Mem. ABA, Ohio Bar Assn., Calif. Bar Assn., Chgo. Bar Assn., Mayfield Country Club (Cleve.), Chgo. Club. Republican. Home: 55 W Goethe St # 1252 Chicago IL 60610-2276 Office: Jones Day Reavis & Pogue 77 W Wacker Dr Chicago IL 60601-1692*

RITER, STEPHEN, university administrator, electrical engineer; b. Providence, Mar. 7, 1940; s. Max and Jeannette (Finn) R.; m. Eve R. Hirsch, Aug. 11, 1963; children—Heidi L., Theodore H. B.A., Rice U., Houston, 1961, B.S. in Elec. Engring, 1962; M.S., U. Houston, 1967, Ph.D., 1968. Registered profl. engr., Tex. Dir. Center Urban Programs, Tex. A&M U., 1974-76, mem. univ. faculty, 1968-80, prof. elec. engring., 1976-80; dir. Tex. Energy Extension Service, 1976-79; prof. elec. engring., chmn. dept. elec. engring. and computer sci. U. Tex., El Paso, 1980-89, dean engring., 1989-95, dir. Ctr. for Environ. Resource Mgmt., 1989-95; interim v.p. acad. affairs U Tex, El Paso, 1995—; Active El Paso Utility Regulatory Bd., 1982-89; cons. in field. Author papers in field.; Editor: Trans. Geosci. Electronics, 1972-76. Mem. policy adv. com. Tex. Dept. Community Affairs, 1979-81; Tex. Border Health and Environ. Issues Task Force, 1990—. Served with U.S. Army, 1962-64. Mem. IEEE, Am. Soc. Engring. Edn. Home: 836 Cherry Hill Ln El Paso TX 79912-3325 Office: Univ Tex Office of VP Acad Affairs El Paso TX 79968

RITSCH, FREDERICK FIELD, academic administrator, historian; b. Covington, Va., Nov. 25, 1935; s. Frederick Field and Harriet Curtis (Miller) R.; m. Jeannette McClung, June 14, 1957 (dec.); children: Frederick Field III, Lise Catherina; m. Debra Ronning, Dec. 21, 1991; 1 child, Anne Ronning. BA, U. Va., 1956, MA, 1959, PhD, 1962; student, Univ. de Strasbourg, France, 1957-58. Instr. Randolph-Macon Women's Coll., Lynchburg, Va., 1959; vis. lectr. Sweet Briar (Va.) Coll., 1959-60; from asst. prof. to prof. Dana history and humanities Converse Coll., Spartanburg, S.C., 1960-83, dir. ctr. for humanities, head div. humanities; dean of faculty Elizabethtown (Pa.) Coll., 1984-85, provost, 1986—; cons. Ednl. Services, Inc., Washington, 1975-77; vice chmn. Communication Services, Inc., Spartanburg, 1978-82; dir. Ctr. for Study Contemporary Humanities, Spartanburg, 1972-81. Author: French Left and European Idea, 1967; author, editor: Issues and Commitment, 1976; editor: (with M. Goldberg) Probes and Projections, 1974; contbr. articles to profl. jours. and collections. Elder Donegal Presbyn. Ch., Mt. Joy, Pa. Fulbright fellow, 1957-58; NEH grantee, 1969; recipient Cert. Merit, Inst. Internat. Edn., 1978. Mem. Am. Hist. Assn., Pa. Acad. Deans Conf. (program chmn. 1984), So. Humanities Conf. (editor jour. Humanities in the South 1971-83, chmn. 1984), Phi Beta Kappa. Home: 600 S Spruce St Elizabethtown PA 17022-2552 Office: Elizabethtown Coll 1 Alpha Dr Elizabethtown PA 17022-2298

RITT, PAUL EDWARD, communications and electronics company executive; b. Balt., Mar. 3, 1928; s. Paul Edward and Mary (Knight) R.; m. Dorothy Ann Wintz, Dec. 30, 1950; children: Paul Edward, Peter M., John W., James T., Mary Carol, Matthew J. B.S. in Chemistry, Loyola U., Balt., 1950, M.S. in Chemistry, 1952; Ph.D. in Chemistry, Georgetown U., 1954. Research asso. Harris Research Lab., Washington, 1950-52; aerospace research chemist Melpar, Inc., Falls Church, Va., 1952-60; research dir. Melpar, Inc., 1960-62, v.p. research, 1962-65, v.p. research and engring., 1965-67; v.p., gen. mgr. Tng. Corp. Am., 1965-67; pres. applied sci. div., applied tech. div. Litton Industries, 1967-68; v.p., dir. research GTE Labs., Waltham, Mass., 1968-86; dir. acad. affairs Babson Coll., Wellesley, Mass., 1986—; bd. dirs. Abex Inc., N.Y.C. subs. IC Industries, 1983-89; bd. dirs. Pneumo/Abex Inc., Boston, 1986-89. Contbr. articles to profl. jours. Mem. dean's adv. coun. U. Mass. Sch. Engring.; mgmt. bd. advs. Worcester Poly. Inst.; adv. coun. Stanford U.; mem. Mass. High Tech. Coun.; trustee

Waltham-Weston Hosp., 1983—, New Eng. Coll. Fund., 1980-86. Fellow Am. Inst. Chemists, AAAS; mem. Am. Phys. Soc., Royal Soc. Chemistry, IEEE, Am. Inst. Physics, Electrochem. Soc., Am. Vacuum Soc., Am. Ceramic Soc., Am. Chem. Soc., Washington Acad. Sci., N.Y. Acad. Sci., Tech. Transfer Soc., Sigma Xi. Patentee in field. Home: 36 Sylvan Ln Weston MA 02193-1028 Office: Babson Coll Wellesley MA 02154

RITT, ROGER MERRILL, lawyer; b. N.Y.C., Mar. 26, 1950; m. Mimi Santini, Aug. 25, 1974; children: Evan Samuel, David Martin. BA, U. Pa., 1972; JD, Boston U., 1975, LLM, 1976. Bar: Mass. 1977, Pa. 1975, U.S. Tax Ct. Sr. ptnr. Hale and Dorr, Boston; adj. prof. grad. tax program Boston U., 1979-92; panelist Am. Law Inst., Mass. Continuing Legal Edn., World Trade Inst., NYU Inst. on Fed. Taxation; mem. exec. com. Fed. Tax Inst. New Eng. Editor tax highlights Boston Bar jour. Treas. Found. for Tax Edn. Mem. ABA (tax sect.), Boston Bar Assn. Office: Hale and Dorr 60 State St Boston MA 02109-1803

RITTBERG, ERIC DONDURO, political consultant; b. Queens, N.Y., Nov. 21, 1962; s. Samuel Herman and Ida Gerri (Turk) R.; m. Barbara Jean Carpenter, Jan. 28, 1982. BA in Polit. Sci., Fla. State U., 1990. Mem. rep. Fla. C. of C., Tallahassee, 1991-93; advance man/travel aide Ron Paul for Pres., Houston, 1987-88; condr. campaign Ron Paul for Congress, Tallahassee; exec. dir. Republican Liberty Caucus, Tallahassee, 1993—. Author: Activism for Liberty, 1995. Nat. committeeman Libertarian Party, 1986-87; precinct committeeman Leon County Rep. Party, Tallahassee, 1992—; chmn. County Conservation Dist. Bd. of Suprs., 1995—. With USN, 1981-85. Decorated Expiditiary medal USN, 1984. Mem. Vols. for Am. (pres. 1995—), Jews for the Preservation of Firearms Ownership, Young Reps. Republican. Jewish. Avocations: books, traveling. Home: 1549 A Willow Bend Way Tallahassee FL 32301 Office: Rep Libery Caucus # 434 1717 Apalachee Pkwy Tallahassee FL 32301

RITTER, ALFRED, aerospace consultant; b. Bklyn., Mar. 15, 1923; s. Max and Anna Ritter; m. Joyce Rimer, June 15, 1947; children: Michael Glenn, Erica Anne, Theodore William. BS in Aerospace Engring., Ga. Inst. Tech., 1943, MS in Aerospace Engring., 1947; PhD, Cornell U., 1951. Rsch. engr. Office of Naval Rsch., Washington, 1951-54; supr. aerophysics Rsch. Inst. Ill. Inst. Tech., Chgo., 1954-58, instr. calculus and fluid mechanics, 1956-58; pres. Therm Advanced Rsch., Inc., Ithaca, N.Y., 1958-68; asst. head applied mechanics dept. Calspan Corp. (formerly Cornell Aero. Lab.), Buffalo, 1968-70, asst. head aerodynamic rsch. dept., 1970-78, head aerodynamic rsch. dept., 1978-80; dir. tech. Arnold Engring. Devel. Ctr. div. Calspan Corp. (formerly Cornell Aero. Lab.), Tullahoma, Tenn., 1980-86; sr. assoc. Booz Allen & Hamilton, Huntsville, Ala., 1986-88; pres. A. Ritter, Inc., Huntsville, 1988—; vis. lectr. Cornell U., 1965; instr. aerospace U. Ala., Huntsville, 1985, 87, 88, adj. prof. aerospace engring., 1988—; exec. dir. Calspan Ctr. for Aerospace Rsch., U. Tenn., 1984-86, chmn. nat. adv. bd. Space Inst., 1987—; mem. gov.'s task force So. Mid. Tenn. High Tech. Initiative, 1985-86; reviewer Applied Mechanics Revs., 1955-84; presenter seminars many ednl. instns. Contbr. articles to profl. publs. Mem. Ithaca (N.Y.) Bd. Edn., 1967. 2nd lt. U.S. Army AC, 1943-46. Named Ga. Inst. Tech. Coll. of Engring. Hall of Fame, 1995. Fellow AIAA (nat. v.p. tech. activities 1981-85, bd. dirs. 1981-85, mem. various coms., participant confs.); mem. AAAS (rep. to atmospheric and hydrospheric scis. sect. 1978-80), U.S. Air Force Assn. (pres. Gen. H.H. Arnold chpt. 1985-86, medal of merit 1986), Internat. Coun. Aero. Scis., Nat. Rsch. Coun. (mem. earthquake engring. com. 1984, mem. assessment of nat. aero. wind tunnel facilities com. 1987-88), Strategic Def. Initiative Orgn. (blue ribbon panel to review missile programs 1989, 92), N.Y. Acad. Scis., Rotary, Sigma Xi. Avocations: reading, music, sports, swimming, cross-country skiing. Home: 10044 Meredith Ln Huntsville AL 35803-2632

RITTER, ALFRED FRANCIS, JR., communications executive; b. Norfolk, Va., Dec. 31, 1946; s. Alfred Francis Ritter and Lucile Grey (Thomas) Woodward; m. Caroline Buchanan O'Keefe, Aug. 10, 1968; children: Alfred F. III, Caroline O'Donnell. BA, Coll. of William and Mary, 1968. CPA, Va. Staff acct. Goodman & Co. CPAs, Norfolk, Va., 1971-76; corp. controller Landmark Communications, Norfolk, 1976-78, v.p., controller, 1978, v.p. fin., 1978; v.p. fin. TeleCable Corp., Norfolk, 1983-89, exec. v.p., 1989-96; exec. v.p. Landmark Comms., Inc., Norfolk, 1996—. Trustee Norfolk Acad., 1991—. Lt. USN, 1968-71. Mem. AICPAs, Va. Soc. CPAs. Episcopalian. Avocations: fishing, golf. Home: 1133 S Bay Shore Dr Virginia Bch VA 23451-3807 Office: Landmark Comms Inc 150 West Brambleton Ave Norfolk VA 23510

RITTER, ANN L., lawyer; b. N.Y.C., May 20, 1933; d. Joseph and Grace (Goodman) R. B.A., Hunter Coll., 1954; J.D., N.Y. Law Sch., 1970; postgrad. Law Sch., NYU, 1971-72. Bar: N.Y. 1971, U.S. Ct. Appeals (2d cir.) 1975, U.S. Supreme Ct. 1975. Writer, 1954-70; editor, 1955-66; tchr., 1966-70; atty. Am. Soc. Composers, Authors and Pubs., N.Y.C., 1971-72, Greater N.Y. Ins. Co., N.Y.C., 1973-74; sr. ptnr. Brenhouse & Ritter, N.Y.C., 1974-78; sole practice, N.Y.C., 1978—. Editor N.Y. Immigration News, 1975-76. Mem. ABA, Am. Immigration Lawyers Assn. (treas. 1983-84, sec. 1984-85, vice chair 1985-86, chair 1986-87, chair program com. 1989-90, chair speakers bur. 1989-90, chair media liaison 1989-90), N.Y. State Bar Assn., N.Y. County Lawyers Assn., Assn. Trial Lawyers Am., N.Y. State Trial Lawyers Assn., N.Y.C. Bar Assn., Watergate East Assn. (v.p., asst. treas. 1990—). Democrat. Jewish. Home: 47 E 87th St New York NY 10128-1005 Office: 420 Madison Ave New York NY 10017-1107

RITTER, BRUCE, commodities company executive. Exec. v.p. Louis Dreyfus Corp., Wilton, Conn., 1973—. Office: Louis Dreyfus Corp 10 Westport Rd Wilton CT 06897-4522*

RITTER, CHRISTOPHER LOUIS, marketing professional, management executive; b. Oneida, N.Y., Oct. 4, 1950; s. Richard Louis and Katherine (Cronin) R.; m. Mary Elizabeth, May 3, 1975 (dec. Dec. 1991). BA, St. Lawrence U. Sales rep. Oneida (N.Y.) Daily Dispatch, 1973-76; copywriter Oneida Silversmiths, 1976-80; copywriter Eric Mower & Assoc., Syracuse, N.Y., 1980-82, account exec., 1982-84, account supr., 1984-87, mgmt. supr., 1987-89; v.p., mgmt. supr. Eric Mower & Assoc., Syracuse, 1989-93, ptnr., 1993—. Bd. dirs. Elmcrest Children's Ctr. Mem. Nat. Agr. Mktg. Assn., Sales Mktg. Exec. Cen., Upstate N.Y. Direct Mktg. Assn., Syracuse Advt. Club. Office: Eric Mower & Assocs 500 Plum St Syracuse NY 13204-1401

RITTER, DALE FRANKLIN, geologist, research association administrator; b. Allentown, Pa., Nov. 13, 1932; s. C. Century and Elizabeth (Bowden) R.; m. Jacqueline Leh, Aug. 15, 1953 (dec. Jan. 1961); children: Duane, Darryl, Glen; m. Esta Virginia Lewis, Nov. 23, 1962; 1 child, Lisa Diane. BA in Edn., Franklin and Marshall Coll., 1955, BS in Geology, 1959; MS in Geology, Princeton U., 1963, PhD in Geology, 1964. From asst. to assoc. prof. geology Franklin and Marshall Coll., Lancaster, Pa., 1964-72; prof. geology So. Ill. U., Carbondale, 1972-90; exec. dir. Quaternary Sci. Ctr. Desert Rsch. Inst., Reno, Nev., 1990—. Author: Process Geomorphology, 2d edit., 1986. Fellow NSF, 1968-69; recipient Lindback award Disting. Teaching, Lindback Found., 1970, Outstanding Teaching award Amoco Found., 1979. Fellow Geol. Soc. Am. (chmn. quaternary geol./geomorphology divsn. 1988-89); mem. Am. Quaternary Assn., Assn. Am. Geographers, Yellowstone-Big Horn Rsch. Assn. (pres. 1983-85). Office: Quaternary Sci Ctr Desert Rsch Inst 7010 Dandini Blvd Reno NV 89512-3901

RITTER, DALE WILLIAM, obstetrician, gynecologist; b. Jersey Shore, Pa., June 17, 1919; s. Lyman W. and Weltha B. (Packard) Ritter; m. Winnie Mae Bryant, Nov. 13, 1976; children: Eric, Lyman, Michael, Gwendolyn, Daniel. AB, UCLA, 1942; MD, U. So. Calif., 1946. Diplomate Am. Bd. Obstetrics and Gynecology. Intern Los Angeles County Hosp., L.A., 1945-46, resident, 1948-52, admitting room resident, 1948-52; pvt. practice medicine specializing in obstetrics and gynecology, Chico, Calif., 1952—; founder, mem. staff, past chmn. bd. dirs. Chico Cmty. Meml. Hosp.; guest lectr. Chico State Coll., 1956—; mem. staffs Enole Hosp., Chico, 1952—, Glenn Gen. Hosp., Willows, Calif., 1953—, Gridley Meml. Hosp., Calif., 1953-80; spl. cons. obstetrics Calif. Dept. Pub. Health, No. Calif., 1958-70. Contbr. articles to med. and archeol. jours. Bd. dirs. No. dist. Children's Home Soc., Chico, 1954-70. Served with AUS, 1943-45, with M.C., AUS, 1946-48. Recipient Pro-Life award Calif. KC; Paul Harris fellow Rotary Internat. 1989. Fellow ACS, Am. Coll. Obstetrics and Gynecology; mem. AMA, SAR, Calif. Med. Assn., Internat. Soc. Hypnosis, Am. Soc. Clin. Hypnosis, Am. Fertility Soc., Pacific Coast Fertility Soc., Assn. Am. Physicians and Surgeons, Pvt. Drs. of Am., Butte-Glenn County Med. Soc. (past pres.), Am. Cancer Soc. (former bd. dirs. Butte County), AAAS, Christian Med. Soc., Am. Assn. Pro-Life Obstetricians and Gynecologists, Butte-Glenn County Tumor Bd., Anthrop. Assn. Am., Archaeol. Inst. Am., Soc. Calif. Archaeology, Oreg. Archaeology Soc., Archeol. Survey Assn., Southwestern Anthrop. Soc., Am. Rock Art Rsch. Assn.(Pioneer award), Australian Rock Art Rsch. Assn., Internat. Assn. for Study of Prehistoric and Ethnologic Religions, Fretted Instrument Guild Am. (dir. Banjo Kats 'n Jammers), North Valley Banjo Band, Am. Philatelic Soc., Am. Horse CouncilPeruvian Paso Horse Registry of N.Am.,, Assn. Owners Breeders Peruvian Paso Horses, Phi Chi, Lambda Sigma, Zeta Beta Sigma. Republican. Lodge: Rotary. Office: 572 Rio Lindo Ave Chico CA 95926-1851

RITTER, DANIEL BENJAMIN, lawyer; b. Wilmington, Del., Apr. 6, 1937; s. David Moore and Bernice Elizabeth (Carlson) R.; m. Shirley F. Sether, Jan. 29, 1971; 1 child, Roxane Elise. AB with honors, U. Chgo., 1957; LLB, U. Wash., 1963. Bar: Wash. 1963, U.S. Dist. Ct. (we. dist.) Wash. 1963, U.S. Tax Ct. 1965, U.S. Ct. Appeals (9th cir.) 1963. Assoc. Davis, Wright Tremaine (formerly Davis, Wright and Jones), 1963-69, ptnr., 1969—; lectr. Bar Rev. Assocs. Wash., Seattle, 1964-86; chmn. internat. dept. Davis, Wright and Jones, Seattle, 1984-85, chmn. banking dept., 1986-89. Casenote editor U. Wash. Law Rev., 1962-63; contbg. author: Washington Commercial Law Desk Book, 1982, rev. edit., 1987, Washington Community Property Desk Book, 1977. Trustee Cathedral Assoc., Seattle, 1980-86; legal counsel Wash. State Reps., Bellevue, 1983-92; bd. dirs. U. Chgo. Club Puget Sound, Seattle, 1982—, pres., 1984-86; bd. dirs. Am. Lung Assn. Wash., Seattle, 1983-92; mem. vis. com. U. Wash. Law Sch., 1984-88; trustee U. Wash. Law Sch. Found., 1989-92; chmn. alumni rels. coun. U. Chgo., 1986-88; mem. statute law com. State of Wash., 1978-87; bd. dirs. Seattle Camerata, 1991-93; bd. dirs. Early Music Guild, Seattle, 1993—. Mem. ABA (bus. law sect.), Wash. State Bar Assn. (chmn. bus. law sect. 1988-89, uniform comml. code com. 1980—, chmn. 1980-86, chmn. internat. law com. 1979-81, judicial recommendations com. 1991-93), Seattle-King County Bar Assn. (chmn. internat. and comparative law sect. 1980-82), Rainier Club, Order of Coif. Republican. Lutheran. Avocation: reading, theater, early music. Home: 1204 22nd Ave E Seattle WA 98112-3535 Office: Davis Wright Tremaine 2600 Century Sq 1501 4th Ave Seattle WA 98101-1662

RITTER, DAVID ALLEN, computer science consultant; b. West Reading, Pa., Oct. 14, 1954; s. David Franklin and Marjorie A. (Long) R. BS, No. Ill. U., 1976. Programmer, analyst Continental Ill. Nat. Bank, Chgo., 1976-79; sr. cons. SRZ Services, Chgo., 1979; sr. systems analyst United Airlines, Elk Grove Village, Ill., 1979-81; pres. Progressive Mgmt. Info. Systems, Schaumburg, Ill., 1981-82; sr. planner United Airlines, Elk Grove Village, 1982-86, computer systems engr., 1986-87; computer systems engr. Covia Corp., Rosemont, Ill., 1988-90; sr. cons. Computer and Engring. Cons., Ltd., Southfield, Mich., 1990-92; dir. consulting KnowledgeWare, Rosemont, Ill., 1992-94; dir. Proforma, Hoffman Estates, Ill., 1994—. Author: Preparing for AD/Cycle, 1990, Information Engineering and Strategic Planning, 1991; coauthor: Systems Prototyping, 1986, Developer Workstation, 1988. Fellow Pi Mu Epsilon; mem. Chgo. Area Devel. Ctr. Round Table (founder, coord. 1984-89), GUIDE User Group (project mgr. 1986-88), Internat. CASE User Group (conf. chmn. 1990, v.p. 1991). Office: 2500 W Higgins Rd Ste 530 Hoffman Estates IL 60195

RITTER, DEBORAH ELIZABETH, anesthesiologist, educator; b. Phila., May 16, 1947; d. Charles William and Elizabeth Angeline (Coffman) R. BA, Susquehanna U., 1968; MS, U. Pa., 1969; MD, Med. Coll. Pa., 1973. Diplomate Am. Bd. Anesthesiology (assoc. examiner oral bds. 1990, 92). Intern Thomas Jefferson Univ. Hosp., Phila., 1973-74, resident in anesthesia, 1974-76, clin. fellow in anesthesiology, 1976-77; affiliate resident in anesthesia Children's Hosp. Pa., Phila., 1975; assoc. in anesthesiology Frankford Hosp., Phila., 1977-78; clin. instr. anesthesiology Med. Coll. Pa., Phila., 1977-78; clin. instr. anesthesiology Thomas Jefferson U., 1978-80, clin. asst. prof., 1980-86, clin. assoc. prof., 1986—, vice chmn. dept. anesthesiology, 1985—. Contbr. articles to profl. jours. Named Top Doc, Phila. Mag., 1994. Mem. AMA, Am. Women's Med. Assn., Am. Soc. Anesthesiologists, Internat. Anesthesia Rsch. Soc., Soc. Edn. Anesthesia, Assn. Anesthesia Clin. Dirs. Lutheran. Avocations: gardening, music, history, wilderness preservation, American Indian culture. Office: Thomas Jefferson U Dept Anesthesiology 111 S 11th St Ste 6460G Philadelphia PA 19107-4824

RITTER, DONALD LAWRENCE, environmental policy institute executive; b. N.Y.C., Oct. 21, 1940; s. Frank and Ruth R.; m. Edith Duerksen; children: Jason, Kristina. B.S. in Metall. Engring., Lehigh U., 1961; M.S. in Phys. Metallurgy, MIT, 1963, Sc.D., 1966. Mem. faculty Calif. State Poly. U., also contract cons. Gen. Dynamics Co., 1968-69; mem. faculty dept. metallurgy and materials scis., asst. to v.p. for research Lehigh U., 1969-76; mgr. research program devel., 1976-79, mem. 96th-102d congresses from 15th Pa dist., 1979-93; scientist, chmn., pres. Nat. Environ. Policy Inst., Washington, 1994—; mem. energy and commerce com. and subcoms. telecommunications and fin.; ranking minority mem. transp. and hazardous materials; mem. sci., space and tech. com. and subcoms. environment and tech. and competitiveness; chmn. house Rep. task force on tech. and policy; co-chair Cngl. High Tech. Caucus; ranking minority mem. house Commn. on Security and Cooperation in Europe (Helsinki Commn.), mem. 1980-93; cochmn. ad hoc com. on Baltic sttes and Ukraine; treas. Congl. steel caudus; mem. Congl. textile and apparel caucus; mem. environ. and energy study conf.; sci. echange fellow U.S. Nat. Acad. Scis.-Soviet Acad. Sci., Baikov Inst., Moscow, 1966-67. Contbr. articles to environmental sci., engring. and quality jours. Recipient award for disting. pub. svc. IEEE, 1990. Fellow Am. Inst. Chemists (honor scroll award); mem. NSPE, Am. Soc. for Metals (disting. life), Sigma Xi, Tau Beta Pi, Pi Mu Epsilon. Unitarian. Home: 2746 Forest Dr Coopersburg PA 18036-9253 Office: Nat Environ Policy Inst Ste 330 1100 17th St NW Washington DC 20036

RITTER, FRANK NICHOLAS, otolaryngologist, educator; b. New Albany, Ind., July 30, 1928; s. Carl Joseph and Kathleen Mary (Wolfe) R.; m. Gertrude Erlacher; children: Raymond, Kathleen, Lawrence, Mary Elizabeth, Teresa, Joseph, Sharon, Michael. BS, Notre Dame U., 1949; MD, St. Louis U., 1953; MS, U. Mich., 1959. Diplomate Am. Bd. Otolaryngology (pres. 1990-93). Intern Mercy Hosp., Ohio, 1953-54; resident in otorhinolaryngology U. Mich. Hosp., 1954-60; asst. prof. otolaryngology U. Mich., Ann Arbor, 1960-65, assoc. prof., 1966-70, clin. prof., 1971—. Author: The Surgical Anatomy and Technique of Surgery on the Paranasal Sinuses, 1978, 3d edit. 1992; contbr. articles to profl. jours. Capt. USAF, 1955-57. Recipient Sr. award Med. Sch., U. Mich., 1965, Shovel award U. Mich. Med. Students, 1967. Mem. Am. Laryngol. Assn., Am. Otological Soc., Am. Acad. Otolaryngology, Head and Neck Surgery, Am. Bronchoesophagological Assn. (pres. 1985), Mich. Otolaryn. Soc. (pres. 1968), Soc. Univ. of Otolaryngologists, Triological Soc. (exec. sec. 1985-89, pres. 1993), Centurian (pres. 1984), Walter Wark Soc. (pres. 1986). Roman Catholic. Avocations: golf, fishing. Office: Reichert Health Bldg 5333 Mcauley Dr Rm 4016R Ypsilanti MI 48197-1001

RITTER, FREDERICK EDMOND, plastic surgeon, educator; b. Cin., Aug. 21, 1959; s. Edmond J. and Alexandra (Engel) R.; m. Christina Weltz, Aug. 2, 1993. BS, U. Cin., 1980; MD, Washington U., St. Louis, 1984. Intern, resident U. Medicine and Dentistry N.J., 1984-90; resident in plastic and reconstructive surgery U. Calif., San Francisco, 1990-92; asst. prof. surgery Duke U., Durham, N.C., 1992—. Contbr. chpts. in books and articles to profl. jours. Republican. Achievements include reducing thrombogenicity biomaterials in contact with blood, innovations in reconstructive microsurgery, tissue bioengineering. Office: Duke Univ Med Ctr Rm 132 Baker House Durham NC 27710

RITTER, HAL, newspaper editor. Mng. editor money sect. USA Today, Arlington, Va., now mng. editor news, 1995—. Office: USA Today 1000 Wilson Blvd Arlington VA 22209-3901

RITTER, JAMES WILLIAM, architect, educator; b. Richmond, Va., June 14, 1942; s. James William and Catherine (Luck) R.; m. Betty Ann Mauck, June 19, 1965; 1 child, Mark Channing. BArch., Va. Poly. Inst. and State U., 1965. Registered architect Va., Md., D.C., Del., Ky., W.Va., N.C., Pa. Assoc. Wilkes and Faulker, Architects, Washington, 1967-70, Winesett/Duke,Architects, Springfield, Va., 1970-74; prin. James William Ritter Architect, Alexandria, Va., 1974—; adj. prof. architecture Va. Poly. Inst. and State U., 1981—. 1st lt. U.S. Army, 1965-67. Recipient Design award Masonry Inst., 1987, 1st Pl. Residential award Va. Masonry Coun., 1989, Grand award for nat. housing innovations, 1984; included in Am. Architects, 1989. Fellow AIA (bd. dirs. No. Va. chpt. 1976-78, 83-85, pres. 1988-89, bd. dirs., 1st v.p. Va. Soc. 1990-91, pres. 1993, various awards 1977—); mem. Am. Arbitration Assn. (mediator 1984—), Alexandria C. of C., Mensa. Avocation: leader Buck Creek Jazz Band. Office: 705 King St Alexandria VA 22314-3014

RITTER, JOHN(ATHAN) (SOUTHWORTH), actor; b. Burbank, Calif., Sept. 17, 1948; s. Tex and Dorothy Fay (Southworth) R. BFA, U. So. Calif., 1971. Actor: (films) The Barefoot Executive, 1970, The Other, 1972, Nickelodeon, 1976, Americathon, 1979, Wholly Moses, 1980, Hero at Large, 1980, They All Laughed, 1981, Real Men, 1987, Skin Deep, 1989, Problem Child, 1990, Noises Off, 1992, Stay Tuned, 1992, North, 1994; (plays) Feiffer's People, Butterflies Are Free, The Glass Menagerie, The Tempest, As You Like It, The Unvarnished Truth, Love Letters, (TV shows) Who's Happy Now, Theatre in America, The Lie, Playhouse 90, (TV spl.) John Ritter: Being of Sound Mind and Body, 1980; (TV movies) Leave Yesterday Behind, The Comeback Kid, In Love With An Older Woman, Pray TV, Sunset Limousine, Love Thy Neighbor, Letting Go, Unnatural Causes, The Last Fling, A Prison for Children, My Brother's Wife, The Dreamer of Oz: The L. Frank Baum Story, 1990, The Summer My Father Grew Up, 1991, It, 1991, Danielle Steele's Heartbeat, 1993, The Only Way Out, 1993, Gramps, 1995, The Colony, 1995, Unforgivable, 1996; star (TV series) Three's Company, 1977-84 (Emmy award for best actor, Golden Globe award for best actor), Three's A Crowd, 1984-85, Hooperman, 1987-89 (Emmy nomination Best Actor, People's Choice award), Hearts Afire, 1992-95; prodr.: (series) Have Faith, 1989, Anything But Love, 1989-92. Host United Cerebral Palsy Assn. telethons. Mem. Screen Actors Guild, AFTRA, Actor's Equity. Office: care Robert Myman 11777 San Vicente Blvd Los Angeles CA 90049-5011

RITTER, ROBERT FORCIER, lawyer; b. St. Louis, Apr. 7, 1943; s. Tom Marshall and Jane Elizabeth (Forcier) R.; m. Karen Gray, Dec. 28, 1966; children: Allison Gray, Laura Thompson, Elisabeth Forcier. BA, U. Kans., 1965; JD, St. Louis U., 1968. Bar: Mo. 1968, U.S. Dist. Ct. (ea. and we. dists.) Mo. 1968, U.S. Ct. Mil. Appeals 1972, U.S. Supreme Ct. 1972, U.S. Ct. Appeals (8th cir.) 1980, U.S. Dist. Ct. (so. dist.) Ill. 1982. Assoc. Gray & Sommers, St. Louis, 1968-71; ptnr. Gray & Ritter, 1974—; bd. dirs. United Mo. Bank of St. Louis; adv. com. 22d cir. Supreme Ct., 1985-92; mem. Supreme Ct. com. on civil jury instrns., U.S. Dist. Ct. adv. com., 1993-95; lectr., author in field. Bd. dirs., Cystic Fibrosis Found., Gateway chpt. (pres. 1991). Served to capt. USAR, 1968-74. Recipient Law Week award Bur. Nat. Affairs, 1968. Fellow Internat. Soc. Barristers (bd. govs. 1994—), Am. Coll. Trial Lawyers, Internat. Acad. Trial Lawyers; mem. Bar Assn. Met. St. Louis (chmn. trial sect., 1978-79, exec. com. 1980-82, award of merit 1976, award of achievement 1982, chmn. bench bar conf. 1983), Mo. Bar Assn. (coun. practice and procedure com. 1972—, coun. tort law com. 1982—, bd. govs. 1984-91, fin. com. 1984-91), Mo. Bar Found. (outstanding trial lawyer award, 1978), ABA, Lawyers Assn. St. Louis (exec. com. 1976-81, pres. 1977-78), Mo. Assn. Trial Attys. (bd. govs. 1984—), Am. Judicature Soc., Assn. Trial Lawyers Am., Am. Bd. of Trial Advocates (advocate, award of merit Nat. Conf. Met. Cts. 1995), Noonday Club, Old Warson Country Club, Bellerive Country Club, John's Island Club, Racquet Club (bd. govs. 1988-93, pres. 1991-92). Presbyterian (elder 1992—). Contbr. articles to law jours. Office: Gray & Ritter PC 701 Market St Fl 8 Saint Louis MO 63101-1850

RITTER, ROBERT JOSEPH, lawyer; b. N.Y.C., Aug. 11, 1925; s. Robert Reinhart and Mary (Mandracchia) R.; m. Barbara Willis Foust, Oct. 1, 1955 (div. May 1977); children: Robert Thornton, Jan Willis Ritter Kelly, Nancy Carol Ritter dePoortere. Student, Bklyn. Poly. Inst., 1943; BA cum laude, Queens Coll., 1949; JD, NYU, 1953, LLM in Internat. Law, 1955. Bar: N.Y. 1953. Acct. UN Secretariat, N.Y.C., 1949-54; asst. counsel RCA Corp., N.Y.C., 1955-58; atty. CIBA-GEIGY Corp., Ardsley, N.Y., 1958-60, AT&T Bell Tel. Labs., Inc., Murray Hill, N.J., 1960-70; tax atty. AT&T Techs., Inc., N.Y.C., 1970-85; mgr. fin. AT&T Corp. Hdqrs., Parsippany, N.J., 1985-87; asst. sec. 14 subs. telephone cos. AT&T, 1985-87; v.p. CPPS Tax Cons., N.Y.C., 1987—. Contbr. articles to legal jours. Pres. Harry B. Thayer chpt. Tel. Pioneers Am., N.Y.C., 1983-84; trustee, sec. United Way Ctrl. N.J., Milltown, 1989—, chmn. cmty. divsn. govt. rels. allocations coms., 1990—; corp. program dir. Vol. Action Ctr. of Middlesex County, N.J., 1988; mem. adv. bd. Dept. Human Svcs., State of N.J., 1991—; mem. adv. coun. Project Resources, State of N.J., 1987—; bd. dirs. Somerset Hills YMCA, Bernardsville, N.J., 1971-73; bd. dirs., mem. Greater Raritan Pvt. Industry Coun./Workforce Investment Bd., New Brunswick, N.J., 1989—; Dem. candidate N.Y. State Assembly, Westchester County, N.Y., 1965; chmn. fund dr. Am. Cancer Soc., Bronxville, N.Y., 1964. With USAAF, 1943-46. Recipient Crusade award Am. Cancer Soc., 1965, Masonic Svc. award, 1947, Am. Legion Citizenship award, 1943, Vol. of Yr. award United Way, 1991. Mem. ABA (sr. lawyers divsn. 1990—), Nat. Tax Assn.-Tax Inst. Am. (chmn., advisor state sales and use taxation com. 1984-88, chmn. prodn. exemption subcom. 1978-84), Am. Soc. Internat. Law, Nat. Eagle Scout Assn., Assn. of Bar of City of N.Y., Internat. Platform Assn., Legal Aid Soc., NYU Law Alumni Assn., Rossmoor Old Guard (pres. 1994-95), Perth Amboy (N.J.) C. of C. (exec. dir. 1988-89), Rossmoor Tennis Club (pres. 1987-88), Church Club of N.Y., Kiwanis (1st v.p. 1970-71), Sigma Alpha. Democrat. Episcopalian. Home: 3-N Village Mall Jamesburg NJ 08831-1534 Office: CPPS Tax Cons Yorkville Sta PO Box 7022 New York NY 10128-0010

RITTER-CLOUGH, ELISE DAWN, consultant, former publishing company executive; b. Balt., Aug. 14, 1952; d. Nelson Fred and Marjorie Jean (Corke) Ritter; m. Philip Anthony Gibson, Apr. 7, 1979 (div. Feb. 1990); 1 child, Christopher Ritter Gibson; m. Victor Wayne Clough, Jr., Mar. 3, 1990; stepchildren: Wesley T., Lindsay, Sharon. Student, Austro-Am. Inst., Vienna, Austria, 1973; BS, U. Kans., 1974. Researcher, Impeachment Inquiry Staff U.S. Ho. of Reps., Washington, 1974; researcher APA, Washington, 1975; editor prodn. The New Republic Mag., Washington, 1976-77; copy editor Time-Life Books, Alexandria, Va., 1977-79, assoc. editor, 1979-83, series adminstr., 1983-87, asst. dir. editorial resources, 1988-90; dir. editorial resources Time Warner, Time-Life Books, Alexandria, 1990-94. Bd. dirs. Arlingtonians Ministering to Emergency Needs (AMEN), 1995—; chairperson outreach commn. Mt. Olivet Meth. Ch., Arlington, 1994—.

RITTERHOFF, C(HARLES) WILLIAM, retired steel company executive; b. Balt., Nov. 1, 1921; s. Ernest F. and Anna M. (Luerssen) R.; m. Margery A. McKenney, June 24, 1944 (dec. May 1987); children: Leslie, William, James; m. Marita C. Halsey, Feb. 20. 1988. B.S. in Mech. Engring, Mass. Inst. Tech., 1947; grad., Advanced Mgmt. Program, Harvard, 1973. Asst. engr. mech. dept., then various supervisory positions Bethlehem Steel Co., Sparrows Point, Md., 1948-57; asst. supt. Sparrows Point plate mills, 1957-60, asst. chief engr. plant engring. dept., 1960-63; asst. chief engr. Burns Harbor project, 1963, asst. gen. mgr., 1963-67; gen. mgr. Burns Harbor plant, 1967-70; v.p. manufactured products and West Coast steel plants, 1970-71, v.p. steel operations-prodn., 1971-74, dir., 1974-82, exec. v.p., 1974-77, vice chmn., 1977-80, exec. v.p. steel ops., 1980-82. Served to 1st lt. U.S. Army, 1943-46. Mem. NAM (past bd. dirs.), Am. Iron and Steel Inst., Assn. Iron and Steel Engrs., Hwy. Users Fedn. (past bd. dirs.), Moorings Club, Bridgehampton Club (N.Y.). Home: 150 Anchor Dr Vero Beach FL 32963-2957

RITTERHOUSE, KATHY LEE, librarian; b. Hutchinson, Kans., May 24, 1952; d. Fayne Lee and Elizabeth Rose (Tener) R.; m. Michael Raymond Demmitt, July 8, 1972 (div. Apr. 1990). BA in English, Kans. State U., 1974; MLS, U. Okla., 1979. Circulation libr. Grand Prairie (Tex.) Meml. Libr., 1979-80, libr. dir., 1980—. Bd. dirs. Grand Prairie Arts Coun., 1980-95, pres., 1989. Named Pub. Svc. Employee of Yr. Grand Prairie C. of C., 1989. Mem. ALA, Tex. Libr. Assn. (Tex./SIRS Intellectual Freedom award 1993), Metro Rotary Club (bd. dirs. 1992-95), Beta Phi Mu. Office: Grand Prairie Meml Libr 901 Conover Dr Grand Prairie TX 75051-1521

RITTERSKAMP, DOUGLAS DOLVIN, lawyer; b. St. Louis, July 7, 1948; s. James Johnstone Jr. and Linn M. (Dolvin) R.; m. Linda S. Vansant, Mar. 23, 1974; 1 child, Tammy. AB, Washington U., 1970, JD, 1973; LLM in Taxation, NYU, 1978. Bar: N.Y. 1974, Mo. 1979. Assoc. Patterson, Belknap, Webb & Tyler, N.Y.C., 1974-78; jr. ptnr. Bryan Cave LLP (and predecessors), St. Louis, 1978-82; ptnr. Bryan Cave, St. Louis, 1983—. Capt. USAR, 1970-79, active duty tng., 1973. Mem. ABA (employee benefits com. sect. taxation 1987-91), Bar Assn. Met. St. Louis (steering com. employee benefits 1989—), Masons (32d degree, knight comdr. ct. of honor), Shriners. Methodist. Home: 5223 Sutherland Ave Saint Louis MO 63109-2338

RITTINGER, CAROLYNE JUNE, newspaper editor; b. Swift Current, Sask., July 19, 1942; d. George Kelly Gaetz and Eva Evelyn (Hiebert) Olson; m. Robert Edward Rittinger, Aug. 16, 1958; children: Robert Wade, Angela Alison, Lisa Michelle. Women's editor Swift Current Sun, 1967-68; city editor Medicine Hat (Alta.) News, 1969-70; reporter Kitchener-Waterloo Record, Kitchener, Ont., 1972-75, copy editor, 1976, women's editor, then dist. editor, entertainment editor, wire editor, 1976-85, city editor, 1985-86, asst. mng. editor, 1986-89, mng. editor, 1989-92, editor, 1992—. Recipient News Story of Yr. award Calgary Women's Press Club, 1969, Best Feature Story on Fine Art award, 1970, Honorable Mention for A.R. McKenzie award for Info. Story, 1970; named Oktoberfest Woman of Yr., 1992. Avocations: downhill skiing, travel, live theatre. Office: Kitchener-Waterloo Record, 225 Fairway Rd, Kitchener, ON Canada N2G 4E5

RITTMER, SHELDON, senator, farmer; b. DeWitt, Iowa, Sept. 5, 1928; s. Elmer and Lois (Hass) R.; m. Elaine Heneke, June 11, 1950; children: Kenneth S., Lynnette Rittmer Jones, Robyn Jon (dec.), infant son (dec.). County supr. Clinton (Iowa) Conty Bd. Suprs., 1978-90; chmn. Clinton County Title III Com., 1987-90; v.p. Iowa Assn. County Suprs., Des Moines, 1989-90; senator dist. 19 State of Iowa, 1990—; mem. local govt. com., state govt. com., human svcs. appropriations subcom., 1990—; ranking mem. transp. com., 1994—, Dept. Elder Affairs Commn., 1990-94; adminstrv. rules rev. com. Iowa Legis., 1992—; mem. Iowa Coun. Human Investment, 1994—, Iowa Adv. Com. on Intergovtl. Rels., 1994—, Iowa Pub. Employees Retirement Sytem Bd., 1994—. Chmn. 1st Luth. Ch., Maquoketa, Iowa, 1964-68; active Clinton County Hist. Soc., 1980—. Recipient Spl. Recognition award Nat. Fedn. Ind. Bus., 1991-92, Spl. Recognition Iowa Soil Conservation award, 1994. Mem. Izaak Walton League Iowa, DeWitt Lions, Ducks Unlimited U.S.A, Clinton County Pork Prodr's. Assn., Clinton County Cattlemen's Assn., Pheasants Forever, City of Clinton C. of C., DeWitt C. of C., Bettendorf C. of C. Republican. Avocations: public speaking, governmental research, reading, agriculture. Home: 3539 230th St De Witt IA 52742-9208 Office: State Senate of Iowa State Capital Des Moines IA 50319

RITTNER, CARL FREDERICK, educational administrator; b. Boston, Feb. 28, 1914; s. Philip and Augusta (Beich) R.; m. Eunice Carin, 1940; 1 child, Stephen. BS in Edn., Boston U., 1936, EdM, 1937. Ednl. cons. Boston, 1940's; founder, dir. Rittners Floral Sch., Boston, 1947—. Coauthor: Flowers for the Modern Bride, 1965, Arrangements for All Occasions, 1966, Flowers for the Modern Bride (In Living Color), 1968, Rittner's Silver Anniversary Book, 1972, Dried Arrangements, 1978, Rittners Guide to Permanent Flower Arranging, 1978, Vase Arrangements for the Professional Florist, 1979, Christmas Designs, 1979, Flowers for Funerals, 1980, Manual of Wedding Design Styles, 1980, Contemporary Floral Designs, 1983, Floral Designs for That Special Occasion, 1985, Inexpensive Bread & Butter Designs, 1986. Mem. Soc. Am. Florists, Florist Transworld Delivery Svc., Phi Delta Kappa. Office: 345 Marlborough St Boston MA 02115-1799

RITTNER, EDMUND SIDNEY, physicist; b. Boston, May 29, 1919; s. Philip and Augusta (Beich) R.; m. Marcella Weiner, Oct. 6, 1942; 1 child, Leona. B.S., MIT, 1939, Ph.D., 1941. Research assoc. MIT, Cambridge, 1942-45; sect. chief Philips Labs., Briarcliff Manor, N.Y., 1946-62; dir. Dept. Physics, 1962-67, dir. exploratory research, 1967-69; exec. dir. phys. scis. COMSAT Labs., Clarksburg, Md., 1969-84; A.D. Little postdoctoral fellow MIT, 1941-42. Contbr. articles to profl. jours. Fellow Am. Phys. Soc., IEEE (Photovoltaic Founders award, 1985). Home: 700 New Hampshire Ave NW 116-S Washington DC 20037

RITVO, EDWARD ROSS, psychiatrist; b. Boston, June 1, 1930; s. Max Ritvo; m. Riva Golan, Sept. 11, 1989; children: Deborah, Eva, Anne, Matthew, Victoria, Skylre, Max. BA, Harvard U., 1951; MD, Boston U. Sch. Medicine, 1955. Diplomate Am. Bd. Psychiatry and Neurology, Am. Bd. Child Psychiatry. Prof. UCLA Sch. Medicine, 1963—. Author 4 books; contbr. over 150 articles to profl. jours. Capt. U.S. Army, 1959-61. Recipient Blanche F. Ittleson award Am. Psychiat. Assn., 1990. Mem. Nat. Soc. for Autistic Children, Profl. Adv. Bd. (chmn.). Office: UCLA Sch Medicine Dept Psychiatry 760 Westwood Plz Los Angeles CA 90024-8300

RITVO, ROGER ALAN, university dean, health management-policy educator; b. Cambridge, Mass., Aug. 12, 1944; s. Meyer and Miriam R.S. (Meyers) R.; m. Lynn Lieberman; children: Roberta, Eric. BA, Western Res. U., 1967; MBA, George Washington U., 1970; PhD, Case Western Res. U., 1976. Asst. adminstr. N.Y. Mental Health System, 1968-70; asst. prof., asst. dean Sch. Applied Social Scis. Case Western Res. U., Cleve., 1976-79, assoc. prof., 1981-84; assoc. prof., founding dir. Grad. Program in Health Adminstrn. Cleve. State U., 1984-87; prof. health mgmt. and policy, dean Sch. Health and Human Svcs. U. N.H., Durham, 1987—; sr. health policy analyst to sec. DHHS, Washington, 1980-81; vis. rsch. scholar WHO, Copenhagen, 1978; vis. prof. Am. U., Washington, 1980-81, U. W.I., 1993; vis. scholar U. Sheffield, Eng., 1985; cons. to numerous orgns. on profit and non-profit strategic planning. Editor, author 5 books; contbr. articles to profl. jours. Trustee Hosp. Sisters of Charity, Cleve., 1980-85, Greater Seacoast United Way, 1991-93; chmn. health care adv. com. Ohio Senate, 1983-85; bd. mem. Fairmount Temple, Beachwood, Ohio, 1980-85; trsutee Leadership Seacoast, 1991-93, bd. dirs., 1992-95; bd. dirs. N.H. chpt. United Way, 1992-95. Recipient Outstanding Adminstr. award, 1982, Cert. of Merit U. N.H. Pres.'s Commn. on Women, 1994; Govt. fellow Am. Coun. Edn., 1980-81. Mem. Nat. Tng. Labs. Inst. (bd. dirs. 1981-85, 92-96), Cert. Cons. Internat., Jewish Philatelic, Hist. Soc. N.Y.C. Avocations: collecting flat irons, philatelist, white water rafting. Office: U NH Sch Health and Human Svcs Durham NH 03824

RITZ, ESTHER LEAH, civic worker, volunteer, investor; b. Buhl, Minn., May 16, 1918; d. Matthew Abram and Jeanette Florence (Lewis) Medalie; m. Maurice Ritz, Apr. 8, 1945 (dec. 1977); children—David Lewis, Peter Bruce. B.A. summa cum laude, U. Minn, 1940, postgrad., 1940-41; postgrad., Duke U., 1941-42. Adminstrv. analyst, economist Office of Price Adminstrn., N.Y., Washington and Chgo., 1942-46. Pres., Nat. Jewish Welfare Bd., 1982-86; v.p. Council of Jewish Fedns., 1981-84; pres. World Conf. Jewish Community Ctrs., 1981-86; bd. dirs. Am. Jewish Joint Distbn. Com., 1977-93, bd. dirs. (hon. life mem.) Joint Distbn. Com., 1994; trustee United Jewish Appeal, 1982-87; vice-chmn. bd. dirs. Jerusalem Ctr. Pub. Affairs, 1984—; bd. dirs. Wurzweiler Sch. Social Work Yeshiva U., 1984-89, HIAS, 1983-86; mem. Jewish Agy. Com. on Jewish Edn., 1984-90, bd. govs., 1988-92; bd. dirs. Legal Aid Soc., Milw. County, 1983-85; mem. Community Issues Forum, Milw.; vice chmn. bd. United Way Greater Milw., 1977-81; pres. Florence G. Heller Jewish Welfare Bd. Research Ctr., 1979-83; pres. Mental Health Planning Council of Milw. County, 1976-79; vice chmn Large City Budgeting Conf., 1976-82; pres. Jewish Community Ctr. Milw., 1966-71; pres. Milw. Jewish Fedn., 1978-81; bd. dirs. Shalom Hartman Inst., 1989—; bd. dirs.; mem. exec. com., policy com. Nat. Jewish Dem. Coun., 1991—, vice-chmn. bd. dirs., 1994—; bd. dirs. Nat. Jewish Ctr. for Learning and Leadership, 1988-92, Ams. Peace Now, 1989—, vice-chmn. bd. dirs., 1995—, Coun. Initiatives Jewish Edn., 1990—, Friends of Labor Israel (steering com. 1988—, chair 1988-90); bd. vis. Ctr. for Jewish Studies U. Wis., Madison, 1994—. Named to Women's Hall of Fame YWCA, 1979; recipient Cmty. Svc. award Wis. Region NCCJ, 1977, William C. Frye award Milw. Found., 1984, Telesis award Alverno Coll., Milw., 1984, Hannah G. Solomon award Nat. Coun. Jewish Women, ProUrbe award Mt. Mary Coll., Evan P. Helfer award Milw. chpt. Nat. Soc. of Fund Raising Execs., 1994, Margaret Miller award Planned Parenthood of Wis., 1994. Mem. LWV, NAACP, NOW, Hadassah, Na'amat, Common Cause, Nat. Women's Polit. Caucus, Nat. Coun. Jewish Women, Planned Parenthood. Democrat. Avocations: golf, music, bridge, art collecting. Home: 626 E Kilbourn Ave Milwaukee WI 53202-3235

RITZ, LORRAINE ISAACS, nursing administrator; b. Wheeling, W.Va.; d. John and Anna (Julian) Isaacs; m. Robert H. Ritz, Apr. 24, 1953; children: Chris Casuccio, Bonnie, Amy. Diploma nursing, Wheeling Hosp.; BS in Nursing, W. Liberty State Coll.; MS in Nursing, W.Va. U. Staff nurse Wheeling Hosp., supr.; DON Wheeling (W.Va.) Hosp., 1980-88, asst. adminstr. nursing, 1988-96; mem. adv. bd. West Liberty State Coll., 1984-96, W.Va. No. C.C., 1981-96; pres. W.Va. Bd. Examiners, 1993, 94; bd. dirs. Wheeling Health Right, sec., 1992, 93, 95-96. Bd. dirs. Florence Crittenton, 1984-91, sec., 1990-91. Mem. ANA, Nat. League Nurses, W.Va. Orgn. Nurse Execs. (v.p. 1988-89, pres., 1991, 92, 93, W.Va. Exec. of Yr. 1991), Am. Orgn. Nurse Execs. Office: Wheeling Hosp Inc Med Park Wheeling WV 26003

RITZ, RICHARD ELLISON, architect, architectural historian, writer; b. Colfax, Wash., Dec. 8, 1919; s. Henry Clay and Katharine Fredericka (Failing) R.; m. Evelyn R. Robinson, Sept. 21, 1940; children: Margaret Karen Ritz Barss, Susan Elizabeth Ritz Williams. Student, Whitman Coll., 1936-37. Registered architect, Oreg. Draftsman, job capt. Pietro Belluschi, Architect, Portland, Oreg., 1946-51; project mgr., chief prodn. Belluschi and Skidmore, Owings & Merrill, Portland, 1951-56; project mgr., then gen. mgr. Skidmore, Owings & Merrill, Portland, 1956-82; pvt. practice architecture Portland, 1982—; founder Greenhills Press, 1991. Author: A History of the Reed College Campus, 1990, An Architect Looks at Downtown Portland, 1991; editor: A Guide to Portland Architecture, 1968; contbr. articles to profl. jours. Bd. dirs. Architecture Found., Portland, 1982-85; mem. Portland Hist. Landmarks Commn., 1987—. Sgt. USAF, 1942-45. Fellow AIA (bd. dirs. Portland chpt. 1975-79, pres. 1978, mem. handbook com. Fin. Mgmt. for Architects 1980); mem. Soc. Archtl. Historians, Oreg. Coun. Architects (del. 1975-79), Portland Art Mus., Oreg. Hist. Soc., Lang Syne Soc., City Club Portland, Univ. Club (Portland), Multnomah Athletic Club. Republican. Presbyterian. Home and Office: 4550 SW Greenhills Way Portland OR 97221-3214

RITZ, STEPHEN MARK, financial planner, lawyer; b. Midland, Mich., Aug. 23, 1962; s. Alvin H. and Patricia M. (Padway) R. BA, Northwestern U., 1985; JD, Ind. U., 1989. Bar: Ill. 1990, U.S. Dist. Ct. (no. dist.) Ill. 1990. Atty. Chapman & Cutler, Chgo., 1990-93; pres., CEO S.M. Ritz and Co., Inc., Indpls., 1994—; dir. Indsl. Logistics, Inc., Indpls., 1994—. Mem. ABA, Inst. CFPs, Registry CFPs, Internat. Assn. Fin. Planners. Office: SM Ritz and Co Inc 9465 Counselors Row Ste 108 Indianapolis IN 46240

RITZER, KAREN RAE, executive secretary, office administrator; b. Sioux City, Iowa, Nov. 26, 1946; d. Robert Leland and Wanda Lily (Kirby) Taylor; m. Thomas Arthur Ritzer, Nov. 23, 1963; children: Robert Arthur, Kristina Marie, Teresa Lynn Ritzer Jones, Carl Robert White. Grad., Arnolds Park (Iowa) High Sch., 1968. Office mgr., sec. Tom's Plumbing and Heating, Arnolds Park, 1964—; sec./treas., bd. dirs. Ritz Closet Seat Corp., Arnolds Park, 1985—. Sec./treas. Concerned Citizens Com., Arnolds Park, 1985, 86, 87; chairperson Centennial Bd. for Arnolds Park 100th Birthday Celebration. Mem. Nat. Trust for Hist. Preservation, The Smithsonian Assn., Am. Mus. Natural History (assoc.), United We Stand Am. (founding), Friends of Iowa Pub. TV, Ladies Aux. VFW. Avocations: writing poetry, oil painting, reading, outdoor activities. Address: PO Box 496 Arnolds Park IA 51331-0496

RITZHEIMER, ROBERT ALAN, educational publishing executive; b. Trenton, Ill., Dec. 29, 1931; s. Leslie H. and Hilda M. (Fochtmann) R.; m. Shirley Ann Wharrie, Sept. 11, 1954; children: Kim E. Ritzheimer Chase, Gina C. Ritzheimer Hartle, Scott D., Susan L. Ritzheimer Kelly. BS in Edn., Ill. State Normal U., 1953, MS in Edn., 1960; postgrad., Columbia U., 1955. Cert. tchr., supr., k-12, Ill. Tchr. Bloomington (Ill.) Pub. Schs., 1955-57; prin., elem. and jr. high sch. Wesclin Community Unit #3, New Baden, Ill., 1957-62; ednl. sales rep. Scott Foresman Co., Bradford Woods, Pa., 1962-81; field sales mgr. Scott Foresman Co., Sunnyvale, Calif., 1981-91; mgr. sales support Scott Foresman Co., Sunnyvale, 1992-93; ret., 1993; cons., pub. Calif. State Bd. Edn., Sacramento, 1981-93; guest lectr. Stanford U., Palo Alto, Calif., 1983, Santa Clara (Calif.) U., 1992. Treas. Little League, New Baden, Ill., 1958-62; pres. Ill. Edn. Assn., Kaskaskia Div., E. St. Louis, 1961. With U.S. Army, 1953-55. Mem. ASCD, NEA (life), Calif.Sci. Teachers Assn. Republican. Avocations: travel, swimming, plate collecting. Home: 1566 Deerfield Dr San Jose CA 95129-4707

RIVA, J. MICHAEL, art director, production designer. Prodn. designer: (films) I Never Promised You a Rose Garden, 1977, Bare Knuckles, 1978, Fast Charlie...the Moonbeam Rider, 1979, Halloween II, 1981, The Hand, 1981, Bad Boys, 1983, The Adventures of Buckaroo Banzai: Across the 8th Dimension, 1983, The Goonies, 1985, The Slugger's Wife, 1985, The Color Purple, 1985 (Academy award nomination best art direction 1985), The Golden Child, 1986, Lethal Weapon, 1987, Scrooged, 1988, Lethal Weapon 2, 1989, Tango & Cash, 1989, Radio Flyer, 1992, Dave, 1992, A Few Good Men, 1992, (TV movies) Callie & Son, 1981; art dir.: (films) Ordinary People, 1980, Brubaker, 1980; visual cons.: (films) Stranger's Kiss, 1984. Office: Innovative Artists Ste 2850 1999 Avenue Of The Stars Los Angeles CA 90067-6082

RIVARD, GILLES, government official, lawyer; b. Quebec City, Feb. 14, 1931; m. Lucie Rondeau; 5 children. Law degree, Laval U., 1958. Called to Bar of Que. 1958. Pvt. law practice; sr. ptnr. Rivard, Rivard; mem. Nat. Postal Mus. Adv. Com., 1987, Com. Inquiry on Soc. Alcools du Que., 1987-92; dir. Que. Indsl. Loan Office, 1987-92; chmn. Nat. Transp. Act Rev. Commn., Ottawa-Hull, Can., 1992; chmn., CEO Nat. Transp. Agy. Can., 1993—; pres. Hydro-Pontiac Inc.; bd. dirs. Coun. of Can. Adminstrv. Tribunals; pres. Que. Jr. Bar Assn.; mem. gen coun., exec. com. Que. Provincial Bar Assn., 1966-68, 74-76; batonnier Que. Bar, 1975-76. Founder, pres. Pavillion of Prevention of Heart Diseases. Named to Queen's Counsel, 1973. Mem. Can. Bar Assn., C. of C., Que. Garrison Club, Que. Rotary Club (pres. 1973-74), Ducks Unltd. (bd. dirs. 1980). Home: 2310 Rodrigue-Masson St, Sillery, PQ Canada G1T 1M8 Office: Nat Transp Agy Can, Office of Chmn, Ottawa, ON Canada K1A 0N9

RIVARD, WILLIAM CHARLES, mechanical engineering educator; b. Detroit, Sept. 2, 1942; s. William John and Ruby Marie (Theel) R.; m. Betty L. Slocum, Nov. 21, 1964; children: Michele, Traci. BS, U. Detroit, 1965, MS, 1966; PhD, Ill. Inst. Tech., 1968. Staff mem. explosive systems div. Los Alamos (N.Mex.) Nat. Lab., 1968-71, assoc. group leader theoretical div., 1971-80; v.p., co-owner Flow Sci., Inc., Los Alamos, 1980-87; Arthur O. Willey prof. mech. engring. U. Maine, Orono, 1987—; pres. Fluid Systems, Inc., East Holden, Maine, 1988—; cons. Exxon Rsch. Ctr., Florham Park, N.J., 1989—, McDonnell Douglas Space Systems, Huntington Beach, Calif., 1987—, Aerospatiale, Les Mereaux, France, 1989—, Technischer Uberwachungs-Verein, Hanover, Fed. Republic of Germany, 1985-88. Contbr. articles to profl. jours. Grad. fellow NSF, 1967, NASA, 1968. Office: U Maine Mech Engring Dept Orono ME 04469

RIVAS-VAZQUEZ, ANA VICTORIA, federal official; b. Miami, Fla., Aug. 25, 1963; d. Rafael A. and Ana (Albarran) R. BA in Govt., Georgetown U., 1985, MA in Latin Am. Studies, 1987. Staffer Times of the Americas, Washington, 1987-88; press aide Dukakis-Bentsen Campaign Hdqrs., Boston, 1988; assignment editor Univision, Miami, 1989; news prodr. Sta. WLTV-Channel 23, Miami, 1990-92; elections prodr. Univision News, Miami, 1992; asst. press sec. White House Press Office, Washington, 1993—. Avocations: tennis, photography, movies, travel. Office: White House Press Office 1600 Pennsylvania Ave NW Washington DC 20500

RIVENBARK, JAN MEREDITH, corporate executive; b. Spartanburg, S.C., Feb. 22, 1950; s. George Meredith and Audrey Isabel (Frady) R.; m. Barbara N. Newton, Sept. 25, 1976; children: Abigail, Justin, Patrick. BS in Math., Duke U., 1972; postgrad., Ga. State U., 1980. Mgmt. trainee Citizens & So. Nat. Bank, Atlanta, 1972, br. mgr., 1974, employee relations mgr., 1975-77, v.p. compensation, benefits, payroll and data mgmt., 1977-80; mgr. personnel First Tenn. Bank, Memphis, 1980-81; dir. compensation and benefits Hanes Group, Consol. Foods Corp. (now Sara Lee Corp.), Winston-Salem, N.C., 1981-83, exec. dir. compensation and benefits, Chgo., 1983-84; exec. dir. internat. staff Sara Lee Corp., 1985, exec. dir. corp. planning, 1985-87; sr. v.p., PYA/Monarch div. Sara Lee Corp., Greenville, S.C., 1987-89; pres., chief oper. officer JP Foodservice, Hanover, Md., 1989-92; CEO, PCA Internat., Inc., Charlotte, N.C., 1992—. Mem. Alpha Tau Omega (chpt. pres. 1971-72). Republican. Home: 2500 Greenbrook Pky Matthews NC 28105-7790 Office: PCA International Inc 815 Matthews Mint Hill Rd Matthews NC 28105-1705

RIVERA, ANGEL (ANDY) MANUEL, retired career officer, city official; b. Arecibo, P.R., Dec. 24, 1942; s. Ramon and Domitila (Viruet) R.; m. Rose Marie Wuchina; children: Tina Nikkole, Marc Anthony. BBA, U. P.R., Rio Pedras, 1960; MBA, Inter-Am. U. P.R., San German, 1969. Commd. 2d lt. USAF, 1965, advanced through grades to col., 1987; various positions SAC, Tng. Command Airlift Command, 13th Air Force, Vietnam and U.S., 1965-77; wing exec. 1605th Air Base Wing Lajes Field, Azores, Portugal, 1978; instr., liaison officer U.S. Army Sch. Ams., Ft. Gulick, Panama, 1978-79; sec. joint staff U.S. So. Command, Quarry Heights, Panama, 1979-80; ops. officer U.S./Panama NG Combined Bd. U.S. So. Command, Quarry Heights, Republic of Panama, 1980-82; chief pers. divsn. 42d Combat Support Group, Loring AFB, Maine, 1982-84; asst., dep. chief staff for pers. 8th Air Force, Barksdale AFB, La., 1984-87; comdr. 7th Combat Support Group, Carswell AFB, Tex., 1987-89; comdr., prof. aerospace studies Tex. Christian U., Ft. Worth, 1989-91; ret., 1991; exec. asst. to chancellor U. North Texas, Denton, 1991-92; dir. airport sys. City of Ft. Worth, 1992—; adj. faculty La. Tech. U., Barksdale AFB, 1986-87, U. Md. Lajes Field Azores, 1976-78, Ctrl. Tex. Coll., Lajes Field, 1976-78, Park Coll., Lajes Field, 1975-76, Big Bend C.C., Scott AFB, 1974-75; mem. civilian adv. coun. No. Maine Vocat. Tech. Inst., Presque Isle, 1983-84; instr. mgmt. and logistics U.S. Army Sch. Ams., 1978-79. Mem. Ft. Worth Airshow Com., Airport Minority Adv. Coun., Vets. Adv. Com., 12th Congl. Dist., Def./Mil. Adv. Com., 6th Congl. Dist. Adv. Com., Ft. Worth Lulac Coun. 601, Image of Ft. Worth, Am. G.I. Forum of Tarrant County, Forum Ft. Worth, Hispanics Friends of U. North Tex.; v.p. North Tex. Cemetary Commn., past mem. Metroplex Fed. Exec. Bd., Ft. Worth Crimestoppers Com., Star-Telegram Citizens Adv. Bd., Pres.'s Coun. U. North Tex.; past athletic trustee U. North Tex.; past exec. bd. dirs. Longhorn coun. Boy Scouts Am., past chmn. Silver Star dist.; past bd. dirs. Frontiers of Flight Mus., Love Fields, Dallas; past chmn. subcom. Ft. Worth chpt. Rev Com.; assoc. Greater Ft. Worth Civil Leaders Assn., United Hispanic Coun. Ft. Worth; past mem. exec. com. Sunshine dist. Girl Scouts Am., Panama Canal Zone; mem. Big Bros. and Big Sisters of Tarrant County, Ft. Worth Citizens Organized Against Crime, Alzheimers Assn. Tarrant County, Multiple Sclerosis Assn. Tarrant County. Decorated Legion of Merit with oak leaf cluster, Bronze Star, Def. M.S.M., A.F. M.S.M. with 3 oak leaf clusters, A.F.C.M. with oak leaf cluster, Armed Forces Honor medal 1st class, Air Svc. medal honor class, Gallentry Cross with palm (Vietnam), Air Force Achievement medal. Mem. Tex. Assn. Airport Execs., Am. Assn. Airport Execs., Air Force Assn. (life), Navy League, Ft. Worth Airpower Coun., Ft. Worth Hispanic C. of C., Ft. Worth C. of C., Forum Ft. Worth (chmn.), U. North Tex. Parents Assn., Rotary, Phi Beta Delta. Republican. Avocations: golf, sports. Office: Ft Worth Dept Aviation Ste 200 4201 N Main St Fort Worth TX 76106-2736

RIVERA, ANGEL LUIS, chemical engineer; b. Bayamon, P.R., Oct. 7, 1950; s. Luis and Felicita (Lopez) R.; m. Marta V. Rivera, Mar. 21, 1975; children: Luis E., Mayra Lynn, Carlos A. BAChemE, U. P.R., Mayaquez, 1974, MS in Nuclear Engring., 1976; PhD in Environ. Engring., Northwestern U., Evanston, Il., 1981; MBA, U. Tenn., 1986. Devel. engr. Oak Ridge (Tenn.) Nat. Lab., 1980-84, group leader, 1984-86, project mgr., 1986-89, program mgr., 1990—. Contbr. articles to profl. jours. and publs. Mem. Am. Chem. Soc., Am. Inst. Chem. Engrs., Am. Assn. Cost Engrs., Am. Mgmt. Assn., IEEE Computer Soc., Tau Beta Pi. Home: 107 Garnet Ln Oak Ridge TN 37830-5601 Office: Oak Ridge Nat Lab PO Box 2003 Oak Ridge TN 37831-2003

RIVERA, CHITA (CONCHITA DEL RIVERO), actress, singer, dancer; b. Washington, Jan. 23, 1933; d. Pedro Julio Figuerva del Rivero; m. Anthony Mordente. Student, Am. Sch. Ballet, N.Y.C. Broadway debut: Call Me Madam, 1952; appeared on stage in: Guys and Dolls, Can-Can, Seventh Heaven, Mister Wonderful, West Side Story, Father's Day, Bye Bye Birdie, Three Penny Opera, Flower Drum Song, Zorba, Sweet Charity, Born Yesterday, Jacques Brel is Alive and Well and Living in Paris, Sondheim-A Musical Tribute, Kiss Me Kate, Ivanhoe, Chicago, Bring Back Birdie, Merlin, Jerry's Girls, 1985, The Rink, 1984 (Tony award 1984), Can-Can, 1988, Kiss of the Spider Woman (Tony award, Best Actress in a musical), 1993; performs in cabarets and nightclubs around world; starred in: film Sweet Charity, 1969; numerous TV appearances include Kojak and the Marcus Nelson Murders, 1973, The New Dick Van Dyke Show, 1973-74, Kennedy Ctr. Tonight-Broadway to Washington!, Pippin, 1982, The Mayflower Madam, 1987, Sammy Davis Jr.'s 60th Birthday Celebration, 1990. Mem. AFTRA, SAG, Actors Equity Assn. Office: William Morris Agy care Gayle Nachlis 1325 Ave Americas New York NY 10019*

RIVERA, GERALDO, television personality, journalist; b. N.Y.C., July 4, 1943; s. Cruz Allen and Lillian (Friedman) R.; m. Sheri Rivera (div. 1984); m. C.C. Dyer, 1987; children: Gabriel Miguel, Isabella, Simone. BS, U. Ariz., 1965; JD, Bklyn. Law Sch., 1969; postgrad., U. Pa., 1969, Sch. Journalism, Columbia U., 1970. Bar: N.Y. 1970. Mem. anti-poverty neighborhood law firms Harlem Assertion of Rights and Community Action for Legal Svcs., N.Y.C., 1968-70; with Eyewitness News, WABC-TV, N.Y.C., 1970-75; reporter Good Morning America program ABC-TV, 1973-76, corr., host Good Night America program, 1975-77, corr., sr. producer 20/20 Newsmag., 1978-85; host syndicated talk show Geraldo, N.Y.C., 1987—; host investigative show Rivera Live, N.Y.C., 1994—. Author: Willowbrook, 1972, Island of Contrasts, 1974, Miguel, 1972, A Special Kind of Courage, 1976, Exposing Myself, 1991; host numerous syndicated TV spls.; film appearances: The Bonfire of the Vanities, 1990; television movie: Perry Mason: The Case of the Reckless Romeo. Recipient 7 Emmy awards, Peabody award, Kennedy Journalism award, 1973, 75, numerous others; named Broadcaster of Yr. N.Y. State AP, 1971, 72, 74; Smith fellow U. Pa., 1969. Jewish. Office: Geraldo Investigative News Group 555 W 57th St New York NY 10019-2925

RIVERA, JANE MARKEY, special education educator; b. Frederick, Md., Feb. 26, 1954; d. Willard Hanshew and Mary Leone (Palmer) Markey; m. Edric Rafael Rivera, Mar. 7, 1981; children: Edric Rafael Jr., Julian Rafael, Marisa Leona. BA, Wittenberg U., 1976; M in Spl. Edn., Antioch U., 1980. Remedial reading tchr. Cen. Bucks Sch. Dist., Doylestown, Pa., 1976-78; chpt. 1 reading tchr. Pennridge Sch. Dist., Perkasie, Pa., 1978-93, spl. edn. tchr., 1993—; student assistance team mem. Pennridge Sch. Dist., Perkasie, 1992—; youth aid panel Hilltown (Pa.) Police Dept., 1986—. Bd. mem. Deep Run. Valley Sports Assn., Hilltown, 1993—. Mem. St. Andrew's Ch. Handbell Choir. Avocations: gardening, reading, traveling, piano. Home: 310 S Perkasie Rd Perkasie PA 18944-2454 Office: Pennridge Cen Jr High Sch 1500 N 5th St Perkasie PA 18944-2207

RIVERA, RICHARD E., food products executive; b. Jan. 6, 1947; m. Leslie Suzanne Pliner, Nov. 18, 1984. BA, Washington & Lee U., 1968. Credit analyst Nat. Bank Commerce, Dallas, 1970-71; from mgmt. trainee to exec. v.p., dir. Steak Ale Restaurants of Am., Dallas, 1971-80; pres. restaurant div. El Chico Corp., 1980-82; exec. v.p., chief operating officer T.J. Applebee's and Taco Villa Mexican Restaurant, Dallas, 1982-87; exec. v.p. ops. TGI Friday's Inc., Dallas, 1987-88, pres., chief exec. officer, 1988—; now pres. Longhorn Steaks, Atlanta. Office: Longhorn Steaks 8215 Roswell Rd Bldg 200 Atlanta GA 30350*

RIVERA-MARTINEZ, SOCORRO, retired educator, assistant principal; b. Mayagüez, P.R., Apr. 19, 1942; d. Sotero R. and Rafaela Martinez; m. Carmelo Torres, Dec. 26, 1965; 1 child, Yolivette. AEd., Catholic U., 1963, BA in Elem. Edn., 1980. Cert. tchr., mentor tchr. Tchr. 1-6 grades P.R. Dept. Edn., Mayagüez, 1962-93; auxilliary adminstr. Colegio San Agustin, Cabo Rojo, P.R., 1993-94, asst. principal, 1994-95; tchr. in charge Rio Hondo Sch. Mayagüez, 1964-70, 73-93, gifted children club, 1990-91, dir.'s resource for tng., 1985-93; math and sci. counselor Rio Hondo, Sch., Castillo Sch., 1971-93. Co-leader troop 384 Girl Scouts Am., Rio Hondo Sch., Mayagüez, P.R., 1975-79; vol. leader Catholic Ch. Summer camp, Cabo

Rojo, P.R., 1990-92. Recipient Presidential award Excellence in Sci. and Math. Tchg. The White House, 1993, State award Excellence in Math. Nat. Coun. Math. Tchrs., 1993, Excellence in Math. award Dept. Edn., 1993; named Tchr. of the Year Dept. Edn., 1975, 82. Mem. Educadores Puertorriqueños en Acción, Coun. Elem. Sci. Internat., Coun. Presidential Awardees. Roman Catholic. Avocations: reading, poetry, writing, wire craft, gardening. Home: Calle 3 L 22 Borinquen Cabo Rojo PR 00623 Office: Colegio San Agustin Cabo Rojo PR 00623

RIVERA-RAMIREZ, ANA ROSA, secondary school educator; b. Bronx, Sept. 5, 1950; d. Marcelino and Ana Maria (Reyes) Rivera; m. Jose Antonio Ramirez, July 11, 1986; 1 child, Marisol Helena Feijoo. Bachelors, Hunter Coll., 1973, Masters, 1986; postgrad., NYU, 1990—. Cert. ESL tchr., N.Y. Tchr. bilingual Bethel Bapt. Day Care Ctr., Bklyn., 1974-75, Pequeños Souls Day Care Ctr., N.Y.C., 1975-76; tchr. Sacred Heart Sch., Carvin Sch., Santurce, P.R., 1977-79; tchr. adult edn. Mobicentrics Bus. Inst., Bronx, 1979-85; tchr. spl. edn. CJ High Sch. 145, Bronx, 1986-88, tchr. English, 1988—; tchr. ESL Clinton High Sch., Bronx, 1989-90; con. ESL curriculum Clinton High Sch., Bronx, 1988-89, cons., writer ESL curriculum Mobicentrics Bus. Inst., Bronx, 1984-85. Participant Constitution Works Program, N.Y.C., 1992. Recipient Bronx Rookie Tchr. award Bd. Edn., 1987. Mem. ASCD, AAUW, Phi Delta Kappa (NYU chpt.). Avocations: writing poetry, reading.

RIVERS, JOAN, entertainer; b. N.Y.C., June 8, 1937; d. Meyer C. Molinsky; m. Edgar Rosenberg (dec.), July 15, 1965; 1 child, Melissa. BA, Barnard Coll., 1958. Formerly fashion coordinator Bond Clothing Stores. Debut entertaining, 1960; mem. From Second City, 1961-62; TV debut Tonight Show, 1965; Las Vegas debut, 1969; nat. syndicated columnist Chgo. Tribune, 1973-76; creator: CBS TV series Husbands and Wives, 1976-77; host: Emmy Awards, 1983; guest hostess: Tonight Show, 1983-86; hostess The Late Show Starring Joan Rivers, 1986-87, Hollywood Squares, 1987—, (morning talk show) Joan Rivers (Daytime Emmy award 1990), 1989—, Can We Shop? Home Shopping Netwrok, 1994—; originator, screenwriter TV movie The Girl Most Likely To, ABC, 1973; other TV movies include: How to Murder A Millionaire, 1990, Tears and Laughter: The Joan and Melissa Rivers Story, 1994; cable TV spl. Joan Rivers and Friends Salute Heidi Abromowitz, 1985; film appearances include The Swimmer, 1968, Uncle Sam, The Muppets Take Manhattan, 1984; co-author, dir.: (films) Rabbit Test, 1978 (also acted), Spaceballs, 1987; actress: theatre prodn. Broadway Bound, 1988, Sally Marr...and her escorts, 1994; recs. include: comedy album What Becomes a Semi-Legend Most, 1983; author: Having a Baby Can be a Scream, 1974, The Life and Hard Times of Heidi Abromowitz, 1984, (autobiography with Richard Meryman) Enter Talking, 1986, (with Richard Meryman) Still Talking, 1991; debuted on Broadway (play) Broadway Bound, 1988, creator Seminar You Deserve To Be happy, 1995. Nat. chmn. Cystic Fibrosis, 1982—, benefit performer for AIDS, 1984. Recipient Cleo awards for commls., 1976, 82, Jimmy award for best comedian, 1981; named Hadassah Woman of Yr., 1983, Harvard Hasty Pudding Soc. Woman of Yr., 1984. Mem. Phi Beta Kappa.

RIVERS, JOHN MINOTT, JR., real estate developer; b. Charleston, S.C., May 28, 1945; m. Kathleen Hudson, Nov. 10, 1979. AB in Polit. Sci., U. N.C., Chapel Hill, 1967. Pres. Rivers Enterprises, Inc., Riverwood Devel. Corp., Chattooga Devel. Corp.; mem. adv. com. urban studies Coll. Charleston, 1975, exec. com. Miss. U.S.A./Universe, 1978, sustaining mem. Trident 2000; chmn. CBS TV Network Affiliates, 1982-83, govt. rels. com., 1980-87; organizer Bank of S.C., 1987; bd. dirs. Regional Devel. Alliance, chmn. mktg. com., 1994—. Explorer, mem. adv. bd. Charleston Coun. Boy Scouts Am., 1973-74; mem. com. Roper Hosp. Fund Drive, 1973-74; divsn. pres. United Way, 1974, vice chmn. budget bd., 1974, chmn., 1975, pacesetter divsn., 1976, mem. exec. com., 1975; fund raiser Spoleto U.S.A., 1978; bd. dirs. YMCA Mil. Svcs. Ctr., 1972-78, chmn. publicity com., 1977; treas. Charleston Travel Industry Devel. Coun., 1976, bd. dirs., 1977-78; mem. City Charleston All-Am. com., 1977-78, chmn., 1978; co-chmn. Charleston Area Campaign United Negro Coll. Fun, 1977-78; mem. City Charleston Clean Cmty. Sys. Com., 1977-79, chmn. subcom., 1978-79; mem. Charleston Area Cmty. Rels. com., 1977-78, vice chmn., 1979-82; mem. bd. trustees Ashley Hall, 1983-92, fund raising com. 1983—; mem. adv. bd. The Citizens and So. Nat. Bank S.C., 1974-86; bd. dirs. The Citizens & So. Nat. Bank S.C. Trust, 1981-86; mem. Gibbes Mus. Art, S.C. Hist. Soc., St. Cecilia Soc., St. Philips Episcopal Ch.; pres. adv. coun. Med. U. of S.C., 1994-95; cons. Trident Econ. Devel. Authority, 1994; chancellor's club U. N.C. Chapel Hill, 1987—, nat. devel. coun. 1989—, Wilson libr. fellows mem., 1993—; bd. trustees Choate Sch., 1990-94, exec. com., 1991-92, chmn. of compensation com., 1991-92; commn. mem. S.C. Edns. TV, 1983—, chmn. of new bldg. com., 1989—; exec. com., dir. Cheeha-Combahee Plantation, 1991—; mem. Charleston Mus.; sponsor Charleston Symphony Orch., Nat. Wild Turkey Fedn. Mem. S.C. Broadcasters Assn. (bd. dirs. endl. found. 1982-83), Charleston Indsl. Assn. (sec. 1975-80, bd. dirs. 1975-86, v.p. 1981-86), S.C. State C. of C. (bd. dirs. 1978-81), U. N.C. Alumni Assn. (life, bd. visitors 1989-92), U.S. Naval Supply corps Alumni Assn., Nat. Audubon Soc., Carolina Yacht Club, Yeaman's Hall Club, Wade Hampton Golf Club, High Hampton Golf and Country Club, Chatooga Club, U.S. Croquet Assn. (chmn. internat. rels. com. 1993—), Ducks Unltd., Everglades Club, Piedmont Driving Club. Office: PO Box 21050 Charleston SC 29413-1050

RIVERS, KENNETH JAY, judicial administrator, consultant; b. N.Y.C., Feb. 13, 1938; s. Alexander Maximillian and Albertina Ray (Gay) R.; m. Leah B. Files, Sept. 21, 1957 (div.); children: Londa Denise, Nancy Laura, Terrie Ruth, Kenneth J. Jr. AAS in Criminal Justice, St. Francis Coll., Bklyn., 1978, BS in Criminal Justice, 1978; MPA, L.I. Univ., 1981. Correction officer N.Y.C. Dept. Correction, 1965-69; ct. officer N.Y. State Unified Ct. System, N.Y.C., 1969-71, asst. ct. clk., 1971-73, sr. ct. clk., 1973-85, assoc. ct. clk., 1985-88, prin. ct. clk., 1988-90, dep. chief clk., 1991-93; ret., 1993; tng. instr. N.Y. State Unified Ct. System, N.Y.C., 1985—, pers. assessor, 1985—; lectr. John Jay Coll. NYU, N.Y.C., 1987. Author: Juvenile Crime Survey, 1982, New York State Jury Selection, 1984. Bd. dirs. Parkway Consumers Med. Coun., Bklyn., 1983—, Cen. Bklyn. Tenant's Rights, 1988—. Recipient Leadership award Tribune Soc., N.Y. State Cts., 1987, Svc. award, 1988, Cert. of Merit award Fedn. Afro-Am. Civil Svc. Orgns., 1987. Mem. ASPA, Internat. Pers. Mgmt. Assn., Acad. Polit. Sci., Conf. Minority Pub. Adminstrs., Masons. Democrat. Methodist. Avocation: jazz musician.

RIVERS, LARRY, artist; b. N.Y.C., 1923; m. Augusta Berger, 1945 (div.); 2 sons; m. Clarice Price, 1961; 2 children. Grad., N.Y. U.; student painting with Hans Hofmann. Exhibited one-man shows including: N.Y.C. galleries, 1949—, Kestner Gesellschaf, 1980-81, Staatliche Kunsthalle, Berlin, 1981, 82, Galerie Biederman, Munich, 1981, Hirshhorn Mus. and Sculpture Garden, Washington, 1981, Marlborough Gallery, N.Y.C., 1982, Gloria Loria Gallery, Bay Harbor, Islands, Fla., 1982, Lowe Art Mus., U. Miami, 1983, Guild Hall Mus., East Hampton, N.Y., 1983, Jewish Mus., N.Y.C., 1984, Hooks-Epstein Galleries, Houston, 1984; exhibited group shows: Vanguard Gallery, Paris, France, 1953, Am. Fedn. Arts traveling exhbn., 1954-55, Mus. Modern Art, N.Y.C., 1956, Museum de Arte Moderne, São Paulo, Brazil, 1957, Art Inst. Chgo., Mpls. Inst. Arts, La Jolla Mus. Art, 1980, Bklyn. Mus., 1980, 81, N.Y.U., 1981, Allen Mus., Berlin, 1981, Marquette U., Milw., 1981, Whitney Mus. Am. Art, 1981, 82, Los Angeles County Mus. Art, 1982, Nat. Gallery of Victoria, B.C., 1982, spl. exhbn. sponsored, Mus. Modern Art, Japan, Mus. Mexico City, Hirshhorn Gallery, Washington, Los Angeles County Mus., Mus. Caracas, Venezuela, 1979-80, Hanover (Ger.) Mus., 1980, permanent works in collections, William Rockhill Nelson Gallery Art, Kansas City, Mpls. Inst. Arts, State U. Coll. Edn., New Paltz, N.Y., Bklyn. Mus. Art, Met. Mus. Art, Mus. Modern Art, Whitney Mus. Am. Art, N.Y.C., R.I. Sch. Design, Providence, N.C. Mus. Art, Raleigh, Corcoran Gallery Art, Washington, also pvt. collections; stage designer: play The Toilet; appearance: film Pull My Daisy; executed mural History of the Russian Revolution.; Author: Drawings and Digressions, 1979, (with Arnold Weinstein) What Did I Do?, 1993. Recipient spl. awards Corcoran Gallery Art, 1954, spl. awards Arts Festival, Spoleto, Italy, also; Newport, R.I., 1958. Mem. NAD (assoc.). Address: Marlborough Gallery 40 W 57th St New York NY 10019-4001

RIVERS, LYNN N., congresswoman; b. Augres, Mich., Dec. 19, 1956. BA, U. Mich., 1987; JD, Wayne State U., 1992. Mem. sch. bd. City of Ann Arbor, Mich., 1984-92; mem. Mich. House of Reps., 1992-94. married; 2 children. Office: US House Reps 1116 Longworth House Office Bldg Washington DC 20515-0513*

RIVERS, MARIE BIE, broadcasting executive; b. Tampa, Fla., July 12, 1928; d. Norman Albion and Rita Marie (Monrose) Bie; m. Eurith Dickinson Rivers, May 3, 1952; children—Eurith Dickinson, III, Rex B., M. Kells, Lucy L., Georgia. Student, George Washington U., 1946. Engaged in real estate bus., 1944-51, radio broadcasting, 1951—; pres., CEO, part owner Sta. WGUN, Atlanta, 1951—, Stas. KWAM and KJMS, Memphis, Sta. WEAS-AM-FM, Savannah, Ga., Stas. WGOV and WAAC, Valdosta, Ga., Sta. WSWN and Sta. WBGF, Belle Glade, Fla.; owner, chairperson, pres., CEO Sta. WCTH, Islamorada, Fla.; pres., CEO The Gram Corp., real estate com. Creative Christian Concepts Corp., 1985, pres., CEO Ocala, 1986; owner Suncoast Broadcasting Inc. Author: A Woman Alone, 1986; contbr. articles to profl. jours. Mem. Fla. Assn. Broadcasters (bd. dirs.), Ga. Assn. Broadcasters (bd. dirs., William J. Brooks award for exceptional svc. to radio broadcasting 1995), Coral Reef Yacht Club (Coconut Grove, Fla.), Palm Beach Polo and Country Club, Kappa Delta. Roman Catholic. Avocations: travel, music, writing, canines, horses. Office: 11924 Forest Hill Blvd Ste 1 West Palm Beach FL 33414-6257 *It is my hope in life that no one will ever be worse off for having known me.*

RIVERS, RICHARD ROBINSON, lawyer; b. Dallas, June 9, 1942; s. Stewart Robinson and Madge (Fiske) R.; divorced; children: Laura Ellen, Jonathan Stewart. BA, Tulane U., 1964; JD, Cath. U. of Am., 1974. Bar: D.C. 1974. Writer Bauerlein, Inc., New Orleans, 1965-68; staff asst. Office of House Majority Whip, Washington, 1968-70, Office of House Majority Leader, Washington, 1971-73; internat. trade counsel Com. on Fin. U.S. Senate, Washington, 1973-77; gen. counsel Office Spl. Trade Rep., Washington, 1977-79; ptnr. Akin, Gump, Strauss, Hauer & Feld, Washington, 1979—; instr. Dalian (Peoples Republic of China) Inst. Tech., Aug. 1986. Mem. ABA, D.C. Bar Assn., Coun. Fgn. Rels. Democrat. Episcopalian. Home: 1600 Avon Pl NW Washington DC 20007-2910 Office: Akin Gump Strauss Hauer & Feld Ste 400 1333 New Hampshire Ave NW Washington DC 20036-1511

RIVERS, WILGA MARIE, foreign language educator; b. Melbourne, Australia, Apr. 13, 1919; came to U.S., 1970; d. Harry and Nina Diamond (Burston) R. Diploma in edn, U. Melbourne, 1940, BA with honours, 1939, MA, 1948; License es L., U. Montpellier, France, 1952; PhD, U. Ill., 1962; MA (hon.), Harvard U., 1974; D Langs. (hon.), Middlebury Coll., 1989. High sch. tchr. Victoria, Australia, 1940-48; asst. in English lang. France, 1949-52; tchr. prep. schs., 1953-58; asst. prof. French No. Ill. U., DeKalb, 1963-64; assoc. prof. Monash U., Australia, 1964-69; vis. prof. Columbia U., 1970-71; prof. French U. Ill., Urbana-Champaign, 1971-74; prof. Romance langs. and lit., coord. lang. instrn. Harvard U., 1974-89, prof. emerita, 1989—; cons. NEH, Ford Found., Rockefeller Found., others; lectr 41 countries and throughout U.S.; adv. coun. Modern Lang. Ctr., Ont. Inst. for Studies in Edn., Nat. Fgn. Lang. Ctr., Lang. Acquire Rsch. Ctr., San Diego. Author: The Psychologist and the Foreign-Language Teacher, 1964, Teaching Foreign-Language Skills, 1968, 2d edit., 1981, A Practical Guide to the Teaching of French, 1975, 2d edit., 1988; co-author: A Practical Guide to the Teaching of German, 1975, 2d edit., 1988, A Practical Guide to the Teaching of Spanish, 1976, 2d edit., 1988, A Practical Guide to the Teaching of English as a Second or Foreign Language, 1978, Speaking in Many Tongues, 1972, 3d edit., 1983, Communicating Naturally in a Second Language, 1983, Teaching Hebrew: A Practical Guide, 1989, Opportunities for Careers in Foreign Languages, 1993, others; editor, contbr. Interactive Language Teaching, 1978, Teaching Languages in College: Curriculum and Content, 1992; writing translated into 10 langs.; edtl. bd. Studies in Second Language Acquisition, Applied Linguistics, Language Learning, Mosaic, System; adv. com. Can. Modern Lang. Rev.; contbr. articles to profl. jours. Recipient Nat. Disting. Fgn. Lang. Leadership award N.Y. State Assn. Fgn. Lang. Tchrs., 1974. Decorated Chevalier des Palmes Académiques, 1995. Mem. MLA, Am. Assn. Applied Linguistics (charter pres.), Am. Coun. on Teaching Fgn. Langs. (Florence Steiner award 1977, Anthony Papalia award 1988), Mass. Fgn. Lang. Assn. (Disting. Svc. award 1983), Tchrs. of English to Speakers of other Langs., Am. Assn. Tchrs. French, Linguistic Soc. Am., Am. Assn. Univ. Suprs. and Coords. Fgn. Lang. Programs Northeast Conf. (Nelson Brooks award 1983), Internat. Assn. Applied Psycholinguistics (v.p. 1983-89), Japan Assn. Coll. English Tchrs. (hon.), Am. Assn. Tchrs. German (hon.), Internat. Assn. Lang. Labs. (hon.). Episcopalian. Home and Office: 84 Garfield St Watertown MA 02172-4916

RIVES, STANLEY GENE, university president emeritus; b. Decatur, Ill., Sept. 27, 1930; s. James A. and Frances (Bunker) R.; m. Sandra Lou Belt, Dec. 28, 1957; children: Jacqueline Ann, Joseph Alan. B.S., Ill. State U., 1952, M.S., 1955; Ph.D., Northwestern U., 1963. Instr. W. Va. U., 1955-56, Northwestern U., 1956-58; asst. prof. Ill. State U., Normal, 1958-63; assoc. prof. Ill. State U., 1963-67; prof. Ill. State U., Normal, 1967-80, asst. dean Coll. Arts and Scis., 1968-69, Am. Council on Edn. Fellows Program, 1969-70, assoc. dean faculties, 1970-72, dean undergrad. instrn., 1972-80, dir. W.K. Kellogg Faculty and Instructional Devel. Program, 1977-80, assoc. provost, 1976-80, acting provost, 1979-80; provost, v.p. acad. affairs, prof. Eastern Ill. U., Charleston, 1981-83, pres., 1983-92, pres. emeritus, 1992—; vis. prof. U. Hawaii, 1963-64. Author: (with Donald Klopf) Individual Speaking Contests: Preparation for Participation, 1967, (with Gene Budig) Academic Quicksand. Trends and Issues in Higher Education, 1973, (with others) Academic Innovation: Faculty and Instructional Development at Illinois State University, 1979, The Fundamentals of Oral Interpretation, 1981; contbr. articles to profl. jours. Bd. dirs. Ill. State Univs. Retirement System, 1992—, treas., 1995—, Ea. Ill. Univ. Found., 1993—, East Crtl. Ill. Devel. Corp., 1983-92, Charleston Area Econ. Devel. Found., 1986-92, Coles Together, 1988-92; mem. pres. commn. NCAA, 1986-91; trustee Nat. Debate Tournament, 1967-75. With U.S. Army, 1952-54. Mem. Am. Assn. State Colls. and Univs., Ill. State C. of C. (bd. dirs. 1990-92), Charleston C. of C. (bd. dirs. 1985-88), Rotary, Theta Alpha Phi, Phi Kappa Delta, Pu Gamma Mu. Home: 2231 Andover Pl Charleston IL 61920-3807

RIVEST, ANNE-MARIE THERESE, post-anesthesia nurse; b. Springfield, Mass., Dec. 25, 1959; d. Robert Frances and Marguerite Marie (Dupuis) R. BSN, Fitchburg State Coll., 1982. Cert. post anesthesia nurse; cert. in pediat. advanced life support. Staff nurse med./surg. fl. Baystate Med. Ctr., Springfield, Mass., 1982-86, staff nurse post anesthesia care unit, 1986—; annual conf. program dir. post anesthesia care unit Baystate Med. Ctr., Springfield, 1989-93, co-unit educator, 1992—; rep., sec. Intensive Peer Rev. Bd., 1992-95. Solicitor local United Way, Baystate Med. Ctr., 1986—; mem. Nat. Wildlife Fedn., Washington, 1994—, Nat. Arbor Day Found., Nebraska City, 1994—. Mem. Am. Soc. Post Anesthesia Nurses, Mass. Soc. Post Anesthesia Nurses. Roman Catholic. Avocations: camping, baking, crafts. Home: 166 Line St Easthampton MA 01027-2620 Office: Baystate Med Ctr 759 Chestnut St Springfield MA 01199-1001

RIVET, DIANA WITTMER, lawyer, developer; b. Auburn, N.Y., Apr. 28, 1931; d. George Wittmer and Anne (Jenkins) Wittmer Hauswirth; m. Paul Henry Rivet, Oct. 24, 1952; children: Gail, Robin, Leslie, Heather, Clayton, Eric. BA, Keuka Coll., 1951; JD, Bklyn. Law Sch., 1956. Bar: N.Y. 1956, U.S. Dist. Ct. (ea. and so. dists.) N.Y. 1975. Sole practice, Orangeburg, N.Y., 1957—; county atty. Rockland County (N.Y.), 1974-77; asst. to legis. chmn. Rockland County, 1978-79; counsel, adminstr. Indsl. Devel. Agy., Rockland County, 1980-91, Rockland Econ. Devel. Corp., 1981-90; counsel, exec. dir. Pvt. Industry Coun. Rockland County, 1980-90; pres., CEO Environ. Mgmt. Ltd., Orangeburg, 1980—; mem. air mgmt. adv. com. N.Y. State Dept. Environ. Conservation 1984-92, Orangetown Planning Bd., 1993—; pres. Indoor Enviroment Ltd. Pres. Rockland County coun. Girl Scouts U.S., 1981-84; chmn. Rockland County United Way campaign, 1983-84, 88-89, 93—, bd. dirs. 1988-94, 95—; bd. dirs. Rockland Bus. Assn., West Nyack, 1981—, Leadership Rockland, 1991-94. Recipient Cmty. Svc. award Keuka Coll., 1965, Disting. Svc. award Town of Orangetown, 1970, Disting. Svc. award Rockland County, 1989, Econ. Devel. award Rockland Econ. Devel. Corp., 1990; named Businessperson of Yr., Jour. News, Rockland County, 1982. Mem. ABA, N.Y. State Bar Assn. (mcpl. law sect. exec. com. 1976-83, environ. law sect. exec. com. 1974-86), Rockland County Bar Assn. (chair environ. law com. 1994—). Democrat. Mem. Religious Soc. of Friends. Home: 1 Lester Dr Orangeburg NY 10962-2316

RIVETTE, GERARD BERTRAM, manufacturing company executive; b. Syracuse, N.Y., May 18, 1932; s. George Francis and Helen (McCarthy) R.; m. Patricia Anne Yates, June 20, 1953; children: Kevin Gerard, Brian Yates. A.B., Syracuse U., 1954; postgrad., U. Buffalo, 1957-59, Rutgers U., 1962-65. Owner-mgr. Rivette Sales and Svc., Syracuse, 1950-54; sales rep. Sperry-Rand, Inc., Elmira, N.Y., 1954-55; with Hewitt-Robins Inc., Buffalo, 1955-62; mgr. conveyor equipment sales Hewitt-Robins Inc., Passaic, N.J., 1962-65; pres. Hewitt-Robins (Can.) Ltd., Montreal, 1965-69, also dir.; Can. regional mgr. Hewitt-Robins Inc., 1965-69; pres. Conergics Corp., Kansas City, Kans., 1970-86, Mid-West Conveyer Co., 1970-86, Alpine Metals Co., Salt Lake City, Con Cal Corp., Orange, Calif.; chmn. bd. Versa Corp., Mt. Sterling, Ohio, 1972-86, Baker Erection Co., Kansas City, Mo., 1971-86, Arrowhead Conveyer Corp., Oshkosh, Wis., 1979-86, Conveyer Sales and Mfg., Seattle, 1983-86; chmn. bd., pres. Conveyer Corp. Am., Ft. Worth, 1978-86, Mayfran Internat. Inc., Cleve., 1984-86, Mayfran Limburg B.V., The Netherlands, 1984-86, Guardian Devel. Corp., Palo Alto, Calif., 1982—; chmn. bd. Jeffrey Chain Co., Morristown, Tenn., 1985-96, Whitney Chain Corp., Morristown, 1985—; chmn. bd., pres. Guardian Resources Ltd., Redwood City, 1966-91, Jeffrey Chain Can. Inc., Toronto, 1987—; chmn. bd. Intelligent Software Internat. Inc., Redwood City, 1985—, Tsubakimoto Mayfran, Osaka, Japan, 1984-86, Greaves Midwest Engring. Ltd., Bangalore, India, 1977-86; bd. dirs. Jeffrey Chain Can., Toronto. Trustee U. Kansas City, 1983—, Midwest Rsch., Inst., 1984—; bd. dirs. Monterey Inst. International. Studies, 1989—. Mem. AIME. Office: PO Box 205 Pebble Beach CA 93953

RIVKIND, PERRY ABBOT, federal railroad agency administrator; b. Boston, Jan. 22, 1930; s. Samuel Alexander and Mae Edna (Polisnor) R.; m. Dolores Russo; children: Robert Douglas, Valerie Jean; m. Kathleen Marie Lysher, Aug. 14, 1989. AA, Miami (Fla.) Community Coll., 1963; BA, Fla. State U., 1965; MA, Fla. Atlantic U., 1966; postgrad., Nat. War Coll., Washington, 1981. Comml. charter pilot, 1956-58; police officer Met. Police Dept., Miami, 1958-61; chief investigator Dade County State Atty. Office, Miami, 1961-67; prof., dir. dept. Cen. Piedmont Coll., Charlotte, N.C., 1967-68; asst. dir. Fed. Bur. Narcotics, Washington, 1968-74; asst. adminstr. Law Enforcement Assistance Adminstrn., Washington, 1974-81; assoc. commr. U.S. Immigration and Naturalization Svc., Washington, 1981-84; dist. dir. U.S. Immigration and Naturalization Svc., Miami, 1984-88; safety mgr. Miami Herald Pub. Co., 1988-89; dep. adminstr. Fed. R.R. Adminstrn., Washington, 1989—; chmn. com. on tng. Pres.'s Coun. on Drug Abuse, Washington, 1971-74, chmn. com. on rsch. Working Group on Terrorism Nat. Security Coun., Washington, 1978-81. With U.S. Army, 1951-53. Perry A. Rivkind Day established in his honor City of Miami/Dade County/City of Miami Beach, 1985-89. Republican. Avocations: boating, hunting, fishing, motorcycling, camping.

RIVLIN, ALICE MITCHELL, economist; b. Phila., Mar. 4, 1931; d. Allan C. G. and Georgianna (Fales) Mitchell; m. Lewis Allen Rivlin, 1955 (div. 1977); children: Catherine Amy, Allan Mitchell, Douglas Gray; m. Sidney Graham Winter, 1989. B.A., Bryn Mawr Coll., 1952; Ph.D., Radcliffe Coll., 1958. Mem. staff Brookings Instn., Washington, 1957-66, 69-75, 83-93; dir. econ. studies Brookings Inst., 1983-87; dir. Congl. Budget Office, 1975-83; prof. pub. policy George Mason U., 1992; dep. dir. U.S. Office Mgmt. and Budget, 1993-94, dir., 1994—; dep. asst. sec. program coordination HEW, Washington, 1966-68, asst. sec. planning and evaluation, 1968-69; mem. Staff Adv. Commn. on Intergovtl. Rels., 1961-62. Author: The Role of the Federal Governemnt in Financing Higher Education, 1961, (with others) Microanalysis of Socioeconomic Systems, 1961, Systematic Thinking for Social Action, 1971, (with others) Economic Choices 1987, 1986, (with others The Swedish Economy, 1987, (with others) Caring for the Disabled Elderly: Who Will Pay?, 1988, Reviving the American Dream, 1992. MacArthur fellow, 1983-88. Mem. Am. Econ. Assn. (nat. pres. 1986). Office: U S Office Mgmt and Budget Office of the Director Old Exec Office Bldg Washington DC 20503*

RIVLIN, BENJAMIN, political science educator; b. Bklyn., July 10, 1921; s. Moses and Esther (Ribnick) R.; m. Leanne Green, July 9, 1957; 1 child, Marc Alexander. BA, Bklyn. Coll., 1942; MA, Harvard U., 1947, PhD, 1949. With OSS, 1943-45; teaching fellow Harvard U., 1948; mem. trusteeship dept. UN Secretariat, 1948, 50, 52; research assoc. Hoover Commn., 1948; mem. faculty Bklyn. Coll. of CUNY, 1949-75, prof. polit. sci., 1962-70, chmn. dept., 1966-70; mem. Grad. Sch. faculty CUNY, 1970-85, exec. officer Ph.D. program, 1970-75, dean research and univ. programs Grad. Sch. and Univ. Center, 1975-78, dir. Ralph Bunche Inst. on UN; vis. lectr. Johns Hopkins Sch. Advanced Internat. Studies, 1956; vis. prof. African and Middle East Insts., Columbia U., 1963-68. Author: The United Nations and The Italian Colonies, 1950, Self-Determination and Dependent Areas, 1955, (with J.S. Szyliowicz) The Contemporary Middle East: Tradition and Innovation, 1965, Ralph Bunche: The Man and His Times, 1990, (with Leon Gordenker) The Challenging Role of the UN Secretary-General, 1993; also articles. Served with AUS, 1942-45. Grantee Social Sci. Research Council, 1951, 54, 64; Fulbright scholar France and N. Africa, 1956-57. Fellow African Studies Assn., Middle East Studies Assn.; mem. Internat. Studies Assn. (pres. Middle Atlantic region 1978-80), Am. Polit. Sci. Assn., Acad. Coun. on UN System (vice chair 1990-91, dir. N.Y. liaison office). Office: CUNY 33 W 42nd St New York NY 10036-8003

RIVLIN, LEWIS ALLEN, lawyer, entrepreneur; b. N.Y.C., Oct. 15, 1929; s. Benjamin and Lena (Levy) R.; m. Alice Mitchell Rivlin, June 28, 1955 (div. Sept. 1977); children: Catherine Amy, Allan Mitchell, Douglas Gray; m. Dianne M. Farrington, Oct. 7, 1977; children: Benjamin, Leigh. BA, Swarthmore Coll., 1951; JD, Harvard Law Sch., 1957. Bar: D.C. 1957, U.S. Ct. Appeals (D.C. cir.) 1957, U.S. Supreme Ct. 1960. From ensign to commdr. U.S. Naval Reserve, 1951-71; atty. patent sect., civil divsn. U.S. Dept. Justice, Washington, D.C., 1957-59, sr. trial atty. gen. litigation sect., antitrust divsn., 1959-64; advanceman Hubert H. Humphrey For V.P. Campaign, 1964; ptnr. O'Connor, Green, Thomas, Walters & Kelly, Washington, D.C., 1965-68; del. coord. Hubert H. Humphrey For Pres. Campaign, Washington, D.C., 1968; Humphrey-Muskie campaign coord. Pa. Dem. Nat. Com., Harrisburg, Pa., 1968; founding ptnr. Peabody, Rivlin, Lambert & Meyers, Washington, D.C., 1969-81; chmn. & CEO New Venture Capital Corp., Rockville, Md., 1981—; founding ptnr. Johnston, Rivlin & Foley LLP, Washington, D.C., 1995—; chmn. bd. dirs., CEO Tribal Funding Devel. and Mgmt. Corp., Rockville, Md., 1984—; pres. Gen. Internat. Fin. Corp., Rockville, 1985—; dir. Asian Internat. Energy Corp., Bahrain, 1995—, dir., exec. v.p., gen. counsel China Petroleum Supply Corp., 1993—; dir., exec. v.p., gen. counsel Hainan Zhonge Refinery, People's Rep. China, 1996—;. Co-author: (book) Report of the D.C. Circuit Judicial Conference Committee on ABA Standards for the Administration of Criminal Justice, 1973. Mem. ABA, Fed. Comms. Bar Assn., Fed. Bar Assn. Avocations: tennis, classical music, travel, sailing. Office: Johnston Rivlin & Foley LLP Ste 200 1025 Connecticut Ave NW Washington DC 20036

RIVLIN, RICHARD SAUL, physician, educator; b. Forest Hills, N.Y., May 15, 1934; s. Harry Nathaniel and Eugenie (Graciany) R.; m. Barbara Melinda Pogul, Aug. 28, 1960 (div.); children: Kenneth Stewart, Claire Phyllis; m. Rita Klausner, Feb. 29, 1976; children: Michelle Elizabeth, Daniel Elliott. A.B. cum laude in Biochem. Scis., Harvard U., 1955; M.D. cum laude in Biochem. Scis., 1959. Diplomate Am. Bd. Internat Medicine. Intern Bellevue Hosp., N.Y.C., 1959-60; asst. resident in medicine Johns Hopkins U. Hosp., Balt., 1960-61; asst. resident Johns Hopkins U. Hosp., 1963-64; clin. assoc. endocrinology br. Nat. Cancer Inst., NIH, Bethesda, Md., 1961-63; fellow dept. physiol. chemistry, medicine Johns Hopkins U. Sch. Medicine, Balt., 1964-66; lectr. clin. medicine Johns Hopkins U. Sch. Medicine, 1965-66; attending physician med. service Balt. City Hosps., 1964-66; assoc. in medicine Columbia U. Coll. Physicians and Surgeons, N.Y.C., 1966-67; asst. prof. medicine Columbia U. Coll. Physicians and Surgeons, 1967-71, assoc. prof. medicine, 1971-79; mem. Inst. Human Nutrition, 1972-79; chief endocrinology, asst. physician Francis Delafield Hosp., N.Y.C., 1966-75; asst. physician Presbyterian Hosp., N.Y.C., 1966-73; assoc. attending physician Presbyterian Hosp., 1973-79; chief nutrition service Meml. Sloan-Kettering Cancer Ctr., N.Y.C., 1979-90; prof. medicine Cornell U. Med. Coll., 1979—; chief div. nutrition dept. medicine N.Y. Hosp. -Cornell Med. Center, 1979—; NSF grant reviewer, 1970—; vis. prof. Creighton U., 1974, U. Guadalajara (Mexico), 1974; vis. prof. N.J. Coll. Medicine and East Orange VA Hosp., Newark Med. Sch., N.J., 1974, 1976, 1983; Upjohn vis. prof. in nutrition Med. Coll. Ga., 1976; vis. prof. Syracuse U., 1980; Nat.

Dairy Council vis. prof. in nutrition U. Mich., Ann Arbor, 1982; vis. prof. Washington U.-Jewish Hosp., St. Louis, 1983; external examiner in physiology Calcutta U., India; vis. physician Rockefeller U., N.Y.C., 1979—; prin. investigator clin. nutrition rsch. unit Meml. Sloan-Kettering Cancer Ctr., N.Y.C., 1980—; rsch. program oversight com. Am. Inst. Cancer Rsch., 1995—; Sypen Stricker lectr. Med. Coll. Ga., 1989. Editor: Riboflavin, 1975; referee numerous profl. jours.; contbr. articles to profl. jours. Served with USPHS, 1961-63. Recipient Grace A. Goldsmith Lectre award Am. Coll. Nutrition, 1981. Fellow ACP; mem. Am. Soc. Clin. Nutrition (v.p. 1992-93, pres. 1993-94), Am. Fedn. Clin. Rsch., Endocrine Soc., AAAS, Harvey Soc., Am. Thyroid Assn., Am. Physiol. Soc., Am. Soc. Clin. Investigation, Am. Inst. Nutrition, Soc. Exptl. Biology & Medicine. Home: 30 Farragut Rd Scarsdale NY 10583-7206

RIVLIN, RONALD SAMUEL, mathematics educator emeritus; b. London, May 6, 1915; came to U.S., 1952, naturalized, 1955; s. Raoul and Bertha (Aronsohn) R.; m. Violet Larusso, June 16, 1948; 1 son, John Michael. BA, St. John's Coll., Cambridge U., 1937, MA, 1939, ScD, 1952; D.Sc. h.c., Nat. U. Ireland, 1980, Nottingham U., 1980, Tulane U., 1982; Dr. h.c., Sch. Tech. U. Thessaloniki, 1984. Rsch. physicist GE, Eng., 1937-42; sci. officer Telecom. Rsch. Establishment, Ministry Aircraft Prodn., Eng., 1942-44; rsch. physicist, head phys. rsch., supt. rsch. Brit. Rubber Prodrs. Rsch. Assn., 1944-52; head rsch. group Davy-Faraday Lab., Royal Instn., London, 1948-52; cons. Naval Rsch. Lab., Washington, 1952-53; prof. applied math. Brown U., 1953-63, L. Herbert Ballou U. prof., 1963-67, prof. applied math. and engring sci., 1963-67, chmn. divsn. applied math., 1958-63; professeur associé U. Paris, 1966-67; Centennial Univ. prof., dir. Ctr. for Application of Math. Lehigh U., Bethlehem, Pa., 1967-80; prof. emeritus Lehigh U., Bethlehem, 1980—, adj. Univ. prof., 1980-88; co-chmn. Internat. Congress Rheology, 1963; Russell Severance Springer vis. prof. U. Calif.-Berkeley, 1977; fellow Inst. Advanced Study, Berlin, 1984-85; Disting. vis. prof. U. Del., 1985-86. Contbr. articles profl. jours.; mem. editorial com. Jour. Rational Mechanics and Analysis, 1952-57, Archive for Rational Mechanics and Analysis, 1957-72, Jour. Math. Physics, 1960, Jour. Applied Physics, 1960-63, Acta Rheologica, 1963—, Internat. Jour. Biorheology, 1972-74, Mechanics Research Communications, 1974—, Jour. Non-Newtonian Fluid Mechanics, 1975—, Meccanica, 1975-94, Internat. Jour. Solids and Structures, 1990—, Zietschrift für Angewandte Mathematik und Mechanik, 1992—. Recipient Panetti prize, 1975, von Humboldt Sr. award, 1981, Charles Goodyear medal Am. Chem. Soc., 1992, von Karman medal ASCE, 1993; Guggenheim fellow, 1961-62. Fellow ASME (mem. exec. com. applied mechanics divsn. 1975-80, vice-chmn. and sec. 1978-79, chmn. 1979-80, Timoshenko Medal 1987), Acad. Mechanics, Am. Phys. Soc.; mem. NAE, Soc. Natural Philosophy (chmn. 1963-64), Am. Acad. Arts and Scis., Inst. Physics (gov. 1974-76), Soc. Rheology (exec. com. 1957-59, 71-77, Bingham medal 1958, v.p. 1971-73, pres. 1973-75, nat. com. theoretical and applied mechanics 1973-82, chmn. 1976-78, vice chmn. 1978-80), Internat. Union Theoretical and Applied Mechanics (gen. assembly 1975-82, chmn. U.S. del. 1978), Coun. Sci. Pres. (sec.-treas. 1975, exec. bd. 1975-77), Mex. Soc. Rheology (hon.), Accademia Nazionale dei Lincei (fgn.), Royal Irish Acad. (hon.). Home: 1604 Merryweather Dr Bethlehem PA 18015-5249

RIVNER, MICHAEL HARVEY, neurologist; b. Bklyn., Sept. 26, 1950; s. Norman and Carol (Simson) R.; m. Roberta Fran Gottlieb, Aug. 13, 1978; children: Asher, Joshua, Peter, Harold. BA, Duke U., 1972; MD, Emory U., 1978. Diplomate Am. Bd. Psychiatry & Neurology, added qualifications in clin. neurophysiology. Intern, resident in neurology Med. Coll. Ga., Augusta, 1978-82; from fellow to assoc. prof. neurology Med. Coll. Ga., 1982—; cons. neurology Eisenhower Med. Hosp., Ft. Gordon, Ga., 1982—, VA Med. Ctr., Augusta, 1982—. V.p., campaign chmn. Augusta Jewish Found., 1994, treas., 1991-95, pres., 1995-96; treas. CRSE Swim League, Augusta, 1993—. Fellow Am. Acad. Neurology; mem. Am. Assn. Electrodiagnostic Medicine (equipment com. 1984-87, tng. program com. 1989-92, edn. com. 1992—, chmn. edn. com. 1994-96). Avocations: computer programming, bicycling. Office: Med Coll Ga EMGLAB Augusta GA 30912

RIZK, MOHAMMED M., import/export executive. Pres. Rizkozaan, Inc., N.Y.C., 1987. Office: Rizkozaan Inc 211 E 43rd St Rm 1002 New York NY 10017-4707*

RIZZI, DEBORAH L., public relations professional; b. Jersey City, N.J., Feb. 26, 1955; d. Edwin Joseph and Beulah Marie (Ardoin) R. BA, Rutgers U., 1977. Program dir. Am. Cancer Soc., Jersey City, 1977-79; internat. program asst. Stevens Inst. Tech., Hoboken, N.J., 1980; dir. pub. rels. United Hosps. Med. Ctr., Newark, 1981-90; dir. practice devel. Stryker Tams & Dill, Newark, 1990-92; comm. mgr. United Water, Harrington Park, N.J., 1992—; adv. bd. Nat. Boxing Safety Ctr., Newark, 1984-88; sr. producer Children's Miracle Network Telethon, N.J., 1985-90. Contbg. author: (book) Children With HIV Source Book, 1990, (booklet) Guide for Victims of Sexual Assault, 1985, Child With AIDS . . . Guide for the Family, 1986; co-producer: (video) Diagnosing Sexual Assault in Children, 1990. Recipient Mercury award Internat. Acad. Comm. Arts and Scis., 1993, 94, 95, Galaxy award, 1993, 94, 95, ARC award, 1994, 95, Jaspar award Jersey Shore Pub. Rels. and Advt. Assn., 1994, 95. Mem. Internat. Assn. Bus. Communicators (Ace award N.Y. chpt. 1993, 94, 95, EPIC award Phila. chpt. 1994, Silver Quill award U.S. Dist. I 1994, 95, Iris award N.J. chpt. 1994, 95), Am. Hosp. Assn. (Nat. Touch Stone award 1987), Pub. Rels. Soc. Am., Nat. Assn. Law Firm Marketers, N.J. Hosp. Assn. (Percy award 1986, 88, 90). Avocation: bicycling. Office: United Water 200 Old Hook Rd Harrington Park NJ 07640

RIZZO, FRANCIS, arts administrator, writer, stage director; b. N.Y.C., Nov. 8, 1936; s. Patrick Charles and Mary Katherine (McTigue) R. AB, Hamilton Coll., 1958; student, Yale Sch. Drama, 1958-60. Gen. dir. (U.S.) Festival of Two Worlds, Spoleto, Italy, 1968-71; artistic adminstr. Wolf Trap Farm Park for the Performing Arts, Vienna, Va., 1972-78, artistic cons., 1985-94; artistic dir. The Washington Opera, 1977-87; free-lance stage dir. various U.S. cos. including N.Y.C. Opera, Houston Grand Opera, Santa Fe Opera, Opera Theater of St. Louis, others; cons. NEA, Washington, 1974—. Contbr. articles to Opera News, 1968—; translator supertitles, various U.S. opera cos., 1984—. Mem. Am. Guild Mus. Artists. Home: 590 W End Ave New York NY 10024-1722

RIZZO, JOANNE T., family nurse practitioner; b. Boston, Feb. 20, 1950; d. Anthony M. and Barbara A. Rizzo. BS, Northeastern U., 1972; MS, U. Colo., Denver, 1976. ACLS; cert. family nurse practitioner. RN pediatrics Mass. Gen. Hosp., Boston, 1972-75; family nurse practitioner Frontier Nursing Svc., Hyden, Ky., 1976-78; nurse practitioner migrant health program U. Colo., Alamosa, 1978-79; family nurse practitioner, clinic mgr. Plan de Salud del Valle, Ft. Lupton, Colo., 1979-82; family nurse practitioner Family Health Svc., Worcester, Mass., 1982-89; fgn. svc. nurse practitioner State Dept., Washington, 1989—; fgn. svc. nurse practitioner Am. Embassy, Bucharest, Romania, 1989-91, Lima, Peru, 1991—; nurse practitioner preceptor Robert Wood Johnson plan de salud del valle, Platteville, Colo., 1980-81, U. Lowell, Worcester, 1984-88, U. Wash., 1995. Recipient Cert. of Appreciation, Agy. Internat. Devel., Romania, 1990, Meritorious Honor award & Group Valor award, Romania, 1990, Dept. of State Health Practitioner of Yr. award, 1995. Mem. Sigma Theta Tau. Avocations: reading, scuba diving, traveling, photography. Home: Am Embassy Lima Unit 3755 APO AA 34031-3750

RIZZO, RICHARD C., lawyer; b. Phila., 1944. BA summa cum laude, LaSalle Coll., 1966; JD magna cum laude, U. Pa., 1969. Bar: Pa. 1970. Law clerk 3d cir. U.S. Ct. Appeals, 1969-70; ptnr. Dechert Price & Rhoads, Phila. Comment editor U. Pa. Law review, 1968-69. Mem. Order of Coif. Office: Dechert Price & Rhoads 4000 Bell Atlantic Tower 1717 Arch St Philadelphia PA 19103-2793*

RIZZO, RONALD STEPHEN, lawyer; b. Kenosha, Wis., July 15, 1941; s. Frank Emmanuel and Rosalie (Lo Cicero); children: Ronald Stephen Jr., Michael Robert. BA, St. Norbert Coll., 1963; JD, Georgetown U., 1965, LLM in Taxation, 1966. Bar: Wis. 1965, Calif. 1967. Assoc. Kindel & Anderson, L.A., 1966-71, ptnr., 1971-86; ptnr. Jones, Day, Reavis & Pogue, L.A., 1986-93, Chgo., 1993—; bd. dirs. Guy LoCicero & Son Inc., Kenosha, Wis. Contbg. editor: ERISA Litigation Reporter. Schulte zur Hausen fellow Inst. Internat. and Fgn. Trade Law, Washington, 1966. Fellow Am. Coll. Tax Counsel; mem. ABA (chmn. com. on employee benefits sect. on taxation 1988-89, vice chair com. on govt. submissions 1995—), Los Angeles County Bar Assn. (chmn. com. on employee benefits sect. on taxation 1977-79, exec. com. 1977-78, 90-92), State Bar Calif. (co-chmn. com. on employee benefits sect. on taxation 1980), Nat. Ctr. Employee Ownership, West Pension Conf. (steering com. L.A. chpt. 1980-83). Avocations: reading, golf, travel. Home: # 19C 1040 N Lakeshore Dr Chicago IL 60611 Office: Jones Day Reavis & Pogue 77 W Wacker Dr Chicago IL 60601-1629

RIZZO, WILLIAM OBER, lawyer; b. Boston, Aug. 19, 1948; s. Nicholas Daniel and Edith Katherine (Kepler) R.; m. Susan J. Parker, May 17, 1984; 1 child, Aura E.P. AB, Lawrence U., 1970; JD, Columbia U., 1973. Bar: Mass. 1974, U.S. Dist. Ct. (fed. dist.) Mass. 1975. Law clk. to Hon. Irving R. Kaufman U.S. Ct. Appeals (2d crct.) N.Y., 1973; assoc. Ropes & Gray, Boston, 1974-81; ptnr. McDermott & Rizzo, Boston, 1981-90, Kirkpatrick & Lockhart, Boston, 1990—. Bd. dirs. Lawrence U. Alumni Assn., 1980-86, Beacon Hill Civic Assn., 1977-91, chmn. zoning and licensing com., 1977-84, pres., 1984-86, chmn. bd. dirs., 1986-88; trustee Thompson Island Edn. Ctr., 1981—; chmn. Boston Groundwater Trust, 1986-91; mem. Beacon Hill Archtl. Commn., 1991-93. Avocations: reading, Italian opera, collecting prints and antiques, tennis. Office: Kirkpatrick & Lockhart One Internat Pl 13th fl Boston MA 02110

RIZZOLO, LOUIS B. M., artist, educator; b. Ferndale, Mich., Oct. 8, 1933; s. Louis and Bella Lonita (Bronson) R.; m. Patricia Ann, June 30, 1956 (div. 1982); children: Connie Lucille, Louis Matthew, Marc Angelo; m. Linda Talbot, Dec. 3, 1982; stepchildren: Heather MacIntyre, Cameron Smith, Jennifer Talbot, Meghan Smith. BS in Art, Western Mich. U., 1956; MA in Fine Art, U. Iowa, 1960; postgrad., U. Ga., 1969. Tchr. art Petoskey (Mich.) Pub. Schs., 1956-64; tchr. history, art studio North Ctrl. Mich. Coll., Petoskey, 1959-64; grad. teaching asst. U. Iowa, Iowa City, 1958-60; tchr. painting Kalamazoo Inst. Art, 1970-85; prof. art Western Mich. U., Kalamazoo, 1964—; tchr. painting, drawing, interdisciplinary/multi-media, installation/performance/exhbn., lectr. and tchr. internat. workshops, Switzerland, Austria, Can., France, Scotland, Hawaii, 1989—; artistic and gen. dir. Rizzolo and Assocs.: Inflatable Light Workshop, Kalamazoo, 1980-92; co-dir. rsch. Creative Learning Program, Kalamazoo, 1986-92; R.W.S. London Watercolor del. Rep. of China. Contbr.: Best of Watercolor Book, 1995. Capt. AUS, 1958-68. Grantee Ford Found., Dow Corning, Du Pont, UpJohn, Mich. Coun. Arts, Mich. Found. Arts, Edn. for the Arts, W.K. Kellogg, Kalamazoo Arts Coun., Nat. Exhbn./Collections: Western Mmich. U. fellow. Mem. Internat. Soc. Art & Tech., Mich. Watercolor Soc., World Forum of Acoustic Ecology, Laser Inst. Am. Independent. Home: PO Box 62 Glenn MI 49416-0062

RIZZUTO, PHILIP FRANCIS (SCOOTER), sports broadcaster, former professional baseball player; b. Brooklyn, N.Y., 1917; s. Fiore Francesco Rizzuto and Rose. m. Cora, 4 children, 2 grandchildren. Shortstop N.Y. Yankees, N.Y.C., 1941-43, 46-56; radio and TV broadcaster, 1956-94. USN, Pacific theatre, 1943-45. MVP 1950; Baseball Hall of Fame, 1994. Office: c/o NY Yankees Yankee Stadium E 161 St & River Ave Bronx NY 10451

RO, JAE YUN, pathologist; b. Seoul, Korea, Oct. 7, 1945; s. Kyeung-Yong and Soon Ie (Ha) R.; m. Jung-sil Cho, Oct. 23, 1972; 1 child, Bobby W. MD, Yonsei U. Sch. of Medicine, Seoul, Korea, 1969, MS, 1971, PhD, 1974. Diplomate Am. Bd. Pathology in Anatomic and Clin. Pathology; Korean Bd. Pathology in Anatomic Pathology; MD, Ohio, Tex., Ind. Resident dept. pathology Yonsei U., Seoul, Korea, 1969-73; chief dept. pathology Korean Army Hosp., Seoul, Korea, 1973-76; instr. dept. pathology Yonsei U., Seoul, 1976-78, asst. prof. dept. pathology, 1978-80; resident in anat. and clin. pathology Inst. Pathology Case Western Res. U., Cleve., 1980-84; fellow in pathology U. Tex./M.D. Anderson Cancer Ctr., Houston, 1984-85, asst. prof., 1987-89, assoc. prof., 1989-92, prof., 1992—. Mem. editorial bd. Internat. Jour. Surg. Pathology, 1993—, Advances in Anatomic Pathology, 1994—; guest editor Seminars in Diagnostic Pathology, 1988; contbr. over 250 articles to profl. jours., numerous abstracts to profl. publs., and numerous chpts. to books. Bd. dirs. Youth Meml. Mission Fund, Houston, 1990—. Maj. Korean Army, 1973-76. Named Top Honor Student, Yonsei U., 1969, Tchr. of Yr. M.D. Anderson Cancer Ctr., 1992, 94, 95; grantee NIH, 1988-92, 91-95, 93-96. Mem. AMA, Am. Soc. Clin. Pathologists (chmn. short courses 1993—), Ohio Med. Assn., Coll. Am. Pathologists, Houston Soc. Pathologists (co-chmn. spring seminar 1991), Cleve. Soc. Pathologists, Internat. Acad. Pathology, Korean Soc. Pathology (chmn. short course 1994), Arthur Purdy Stout Soc. Surg. Pathologists. Baptist. Avocations: reading, golf. Office: The Univ of Tex MD Anderson Cancer Ctr 1515 Holcombe Blvd Houston TX 77030

ROACH, ARVID EDWARD, II, lawyer; b. Detroit, Sept. 6, 1951; s. Arvid Edward and Alda Elizabeth (Buckley) R. BA summa cum laude, Yale U., 1972; JD cum laude, Harvard U., 1977. Bar: D.C. 1978, N.Y. 1978, U.S. dist. ct. D.C. 1978, U.S. dist. ct. (so. dist.) N.Y. 1978, U.S. Ct. Appeals (10th cir.) 1980, U.S. Ct. Appeals (2d cir.) 1981, U.S. Ct. Appeals (D.C. cir.) 1981, U.S. Ct. Appeals (7th and 9th cirs.) 1982, U.S. Supreme Ct. 1983, U.S. Dist. Ct. Md., 1985, U.S. Ct. Appeals (3d, 4th, 5th, 6th, 8th, 11th cirs.) 1988, U.S. Ct. Appeals (1st cir.) 1992. Law clk. to judge U.S. Dist. Ct., 1977-78; assoc. Covington & Burling, Washington, 1978-85, ptnr., 1985—. Mem. ABA, Am. Law Inst. Contbr. articles to legal jours. Office: Covington & Burling PO Box 7566 Washington DC 20044-7566

ROACH, EDGAR MAYO, JR., lawyer; b. Pinehurst, N.C., June 2, 1948; s. Edgar Mayo Sr. and Rhuamer (Richardson) R.; m. Deborah Day, Oct. 10, 1970; children: Edgar Mayo III, John Clifton. BA, Wake Forest U., 1969; JD with honors, U. N.C., 1974. Bar: N.C. 1974, Va. 1976, U.S. Ct. Appeals (4th cir.) 1976. Law clk. to judge U.S. Ct. Appeals (4th cir.), Abingdon, Va., 1974-75; assoc. Hunton & Williams, Richmond, Va., 1975-80; ptnr. Hunton & Williams, Raleigh, N.C., 1981-94; sr. v.p. Va. Power, Richmond, 1994—. Home: 3142 Monument Ave Richmond VA 23221-1457 Office: Va Power 1 James River Plz Richmond VA 23219-3229

ROACH, JAMES CLARK, government official; b. Charleston, W. Va., Sept. 29, 1943; m. Susan Roelke Roach, June 27, 1970; children: Edward J., Andrew A. BA in Social Studies and History, W. Va. Wesleyan Coll., 1965; MA in Am. History, W. Va. U. Historian Harpers Ferry (W. Va.) Nat. Hist. Pk., 1967-68, 70-72; chief interpretation resource mgmt. Ft. Frederica Nat. Monument, St. Simons Island, Ga., 1972-74; asst. chief interpretation visitor svcs. Colonial Nat. Hist. Pk., Yorktown, Va.; asst. chief interpretation, visitor svc. Colonial Nat. Hist. Pk., Jamestown, Va.; chief interpretation visitor svcs. Eisenhower Nat. Hist. Site, 1981-94, site mgr., 1995—. Sec. Gettysburg Peace Celebration Commn. Inc. (former bd. dirs.). With U.S. Army, 1968-70, Vietnam. Recipient Freeman Tilden award Mid-Atlantic Region Interpreter of Yr., 1984, Ea. Superior Performance award Nat. Park and Monument Assn., 1985, Spl. Events award GETT Travel Coun. award, 1986, 87. Mem. Assn. Nat. Park Rangers, Lincoln Fellowship Pa. (past pres.), Adams County Torch Club (pres.), Rotary. Lutheran. Avocations: gardening, reading, fishing, stamp collecting. Home: 84 Knoxlyn-Orrtanna Rd Gettysburg PA 17325 Office: Eisenhower Nat Hist Site 97 Taneytown Rd Gettysburg PA 17325

ROACH, JAMES R., university president; married. BS in Edn. cum laude, Boston Coll., 1957; postgrad., St. John's Coll., Brighton, Mass., 1963; certificat d'etude, U. Geneva, Switzerland, 1969; PhD in World Religions, Boston U., 1972; postgrad., Harvard U. Inst. Ednl. Mgmt., summer 1978. Tchr. Annotto Bay Coll., Jamaica, West Indies, 1957-58, Coll. Ctr., Salem State Coll., 1965-69; tchr. grad. sch. St. John's and Boston Univs., 1970-72; tchr. divsn. grad. studies Salem State Coll., 1972-73; tchr. divsn. grad. studies North Adams State Coll., 1974-75, tchr. dept. philosophy, 1973-76, dir. acad. counseling svcs., 1973-76, acad. dean, 1976-78, v.p. acad. affairs, 1978-86, acting pres., 1984; interim vice chancellor acad. affairs Mass. Bd. Regents, 1980-81; pres. U.Maine, Presque Isle, 1986-92, Western Conn. State U., Danbury, 1992—; bd. dirs. Savs. Bank Danbury; state rep. Am. Assn. State Colls. and Univs., chair com. acad. affairs, 1991-92, mem. task force on bldg. polit. support, 1991-92; chmn. reaccreditation vis. com. Castleton (Vt.) State Coll., 1991; mem Trustee Task Force on Rsch. and Grad. Edn.; mem. State of Maine Legislature's Spl. Commn. to Study and Evaluate the Status of Edn. Reform in Maine, 1990; mem. Univ. Sys./State Govt. Partnership Policy Group, 1989—, Mass.Bd. Regents Design Team for Collective Bargaining, 1983, Gov.'s Edn. Task Force, 1982-86, Mass. Bd. Regents Adv. Task Force on Program Rev., 1982-86; mem. Mass. State Coll. Sys. Task Force for Devel. Skills, 1977, Task Force for Profl. Devel., 1978, Pers. Mgmt. Adv. Com., 1979; dir. Maine Devel. Found., 1989-92; pres. Maine Higher Edn.Coun., 1989-92; chmn. bd. dirs. Maine Rsch. and Productivity Ctr., 1988-92; coord.-tchr. Monroe Ednl. Release Program, 1973-77; chmn. Mass. State Coll. Ad Hoc Com., 1979; corporator North Adams State Coll. Found., 1981-86; dir. acad. program evaluation project North Adams State Coll., 1977-82; cons. Wang Inst. Grad. Studies, 1983; state rep. Am. Assn. State Colls. and Univs. Acad. Affairs Resource Ctr. Assocs., 1982-86; presenter papers, spkr. various orgns. and confs. Bd. trustees United Way of No. Fairfield County, Inc.; mem. exec. bd. dirs. No. Maine Regional Planning Commn./Econ. Devel. Dist., 1987—; bd. dirs. Maine/Loring Assn., 1986—; bd. dirs. Croissant Club No. Berkshire County, 1984-86. With USN. Mem. Danbury C. of C. (bd. dirs.), Am. Acad. Religion, Am. Assn. Higher Edn.,Am. Assn. Colls. Tchr. Edn., Assn. Am. Colls., Internat. Assn. Univ. Pres., Pi Lamba Theta. Home: 177 Lake Pl S Danbury CT 06811

ROACH, JAMES RICHARD, academic administrator. V.p. acad. affairs North Adams State Coll., Mass., until 1986; pres. U. Maine, Presque Isle, 1986-92, Western Conn. State U., Danbury, 1992—. Office: Western Conn State Univ 181 White St Danbury CT 06810-6845

ROACH, JAMES ROBERT, retired political science educator; b. Rock Rapids, Iowa, Aug. 25, 1922; s. Paul Ramsey and Doris (Kline) R. BA, U. Iowa, 1943; AM, Harvard U., 1948, PhD, 1950. Mem. faculty, adminstrn. U. Tex., Austin, 1949—, prof. govt., 1965-95, prof. emeritus, 1995—, dir. spl. programs, 1965-69, vice provost, dean interdisciplinary programs, 1971-72, dean divsn. gen. and comparative studies, 1972-74; counselor for cultural affairs Am. embassy, New Delhi, 1974-78; Fulbright vis. lectr. polit. sci. Rajasthan U., India, 1961-62; mem. Bd. Fgn. Scholarships, 1965-74, chmn., 1969-71; mem. U.S. Commn. for UNESCO, 1966-69. With USNR, 1943-46. Fulbright rsch. grantee, Australia, 1951-52, Ford Found. fgn. fellow, India, 1956-57. Mem. Assn. Asian Studies, Phi Beta Kappa, Kappa Tau Alpha, Sigma Delta Chi, Phi Kappa Psi. Democrat. Conglist. Home: 8604 Dorotha Ct Austin TX 78759-8113 Office: U Tex Dept Of Govt Austin TX 78712-1087

ROACH, SISTER JEANNE, nun, hospital administrator; b. Denver, Aug. 25, 1934. R.N., Regina Sch. Nursing, 1956; BS, Coll. Mt. St. Joseph, 1964; MS, Trinity U., 1973. Joined Sisters of Charity, Roman Catholic Ch., 1951; med. supr. St. Mary-Corwin Hosp., Pueblo, Colo., 1956-58; operating room supr. San Antonio Hosp., Kenton, Ohio, 1958-61; dir. nursing service Mt. San Rafael Hosp., Trinidad, Colo., 1961-67; speciality supr. Penrose Hosp., Colorado Springs, Colo., 1967-69, dir. nursing service, 1969-70, asst. adminstr., 1970-71, asst. adminstr. profl. services, 1973-75; assoc. adminstr. and coordinator St. Joseph Hosp., Mt. Clemens, Mich., 1975-78; v.p. Good Samaritan Hosp., Cin., 1978-82; adminstr. Our Lady of the Way Hosp., Martin, Ky., 1982-85, Mother Margaret Hall Nursing Home, 1990—, Bayley Place Nursing Home, 1995—; CEO St. Joseph Hosp., Huntingburg, Ind., 1985-89. Trustee, treas. Ohio Valley Renal Disease Network, Inc., Louisville, 1981-83; bd. dirs. Mud Creek Clinic, Grethel, Ky., 1982-85, St. Mary-Corwin, Pueblo, Colo., Sunny Acres, Denver, St. Joseph's Home, Cin. Fellow Am. Coll. Health Care Adminstrs.; mem. Am. Mgmt. Assn., Am. Hosp. Assn., Cath. Health Assn., Ky. Hosp. Assn., Nat. League for Nursing. Office: Mother Margaret Hall 5900 Delhi Rd Mount Saint Joseph OH 45051-1500

ROACH, JOHN D. C., manufacturing company executive; b. West Palm Beach, Fla., Dec. 3, 1943; s. Benjamin Browning and Margaret (York) R.; m. Pam Flebbe, Dec. 29, 1967 (div. Aug. 1981); children: Vanessa, Alexandra; m. Elizabeth Louise Phillips, Aug. 28, 1982; children: Bruce Phillips, Bryce Phillips, Brian Phillips. BS in Indsl. Mgmt., MIT, 1965; MBA, Stanford U., 1967. Dir. mgmt. acctg. and info. systems Ventura div. Northrop Corp., Thousand Oaks, Calif., 1967-70; co-founder, mgr. Northrop Venture Capital, Century City, Calif., 1970-71; v.p., dir. Boston Consulting Group, Boston and Menlo Park, Calif., 1971-80; v.p., world-wide strategic mgmt. practice mng. officer Booz, Allen, Hamilton, San Francisco, 1980-82; Houston, 1982-83; vice chmn., mng. dir. Braxton Assocs., Houston, 1983-87; sr. v.p., chief fin. officer Manville Corp., Denver, 1987-88, exec. v.p. ops., 1988-91; pres. Manville Sales Corp., Denver, 1988-90, Manville Mining and Minerals Group, Denver, 1990-91, Celite Corp., Denver, 1990-91; chmn., pres., chief exec. officer Fibreboard Corp., Dallas, Calif., 1991-92; bd. dirs. Magma Power Corp., 1995—. Author: Strategic Management Handbook, 1983; contbr. articles to profl. jours. Bd. dirs. Cystic Fibrosis, Houston, 1986-87, Am. Leukemia Soc., Houston, 1986, Opera Colo., Denver, 1987-91, Bay Area Coun., San Francisco; bd. trustees Alta Bates Med. Ctr.; mem. exec. com. San Francisco Opera Assn. Mem. N.Am. Soc. Strategy Planners, Greater Denver C. of C. (bd. dirs.), Geol. Energy and Minerals Assn. (bd. dirs.), Colo. Forum, Soc. Corp. Planners (charter), Fin. Execs. Inst., Stanford Grad. Sch. Bus. Club, MIT Alumni Club, Met. Racquet Club (Houston), Denver Athletic Club, Cherry Hills Country Club (Englewood, Colo.), Contra Costa Country Club, Claremont Country Club. Avocations: running, bicycling, golf, snow skiing, hunting. Home: 4278 Bordeaux Dallas TX 75205

ROACH, JOHN HENDEE, JR., bank executive, investment banker, financial service executive; b. N.Y.C., Oct. 24, 1941; s. John Hendee and Julia (Casey) R.; m. Joan Hayden Muchmore, Sept. 23, 1972; children: Hayden, Cameron, John, Lauriston, Schuyler. BA, Washington & Jefferson Coll.; postgrad., Aspen Inst., 1987, Harvard U., 1989. With Chem. Bank, N.Y.C., 1968-71, sr. v.p. corp. bank, 1972-87, mng. dir. corp. fin., 1987-92; ret., 1992; sr. mng. dir., vice chmn. The Geneva Cos., N.Y.C., 1992-94; sr. mng. dir., client mgmt. and mktg. Am. Internat. Group, N.Y.C., 1994—. Capt. U.S. Army, 1964-66. Mem. Field Club (Greenwich, Conn.), Racquet and Tennis Club, Onwentsia (Lake Forest, Ill.), Chgo. Club, Round Hill Club. Republican. Roman Catholic. Home: 513 Lake Ave Greenwich CT 06830-3831 Office: American Internat Group 70 Pine St New York NY 10270

ROACH, JOHN ROBERT, retired archbishop; b. Prior Lake, Minn., July 31, 1921; s. Simon J. and Mary (Regan) R. B.A., St. Paul Sem., 1946; M.A., U. Minn., 1957; L.H.D. (hon.), Gustavus Adolphus Coll., St. Mary's Coll., St. Xavier U., Villanova U., U. St. Thomas, Coll. of St. Catherine. Ordained priest Roman Catholic Ch., 1946; instr. St. Thomas Acad., 1946-50, headmaster, 1951-68; named domestic prelate, 1966; rector St. John Vianney Sem., 1968-71; aux. bishop St. Paul and Mpls., 1971; consecrated bishop, 1971; pastor St. Charles Borromeo Ch., Mpls., 1971-73, St. Cecilia Ch., St. Paul, 1973-75; archbishop of St. Paul, 1975-95; appointed vicar for parishes, 1971, vicar for clergy, 1972—; Episc. moderator Nat. Apostolate for Mentally Retarded, 1974; Mem. Priests Senate, 1968-72; pres. Priests Senate and Presbytery, 1970; chmn. Com. on Accreditation Pvt. Schs. in Minn., 1952-57; mem. adv. com. Coll. Entrance Exam. Bd., 1964; Episc. mem. Bishops and Pres.'s Com.; chmn. Bishops Com. to Oversee Implementation of the Call to Action Program, 1979-80; chmn. priestly formation com.; mem. Cath. Charity Bd. Trustee St. Paul Sem. Sch. Div., 1971—, now chmn.; trustee Cath. U. Am., 1978-81, Coll. St. Catherine, 1975-95; chmn. bd. trustees St. Thomas Acad., U. St. Thomas, St. John Vianney Sem.; v.p. Nat. Conf. Cath. Bishops, 1977-80, pres., 1980-83, chmn. ad hoc com. on call to action, 1977; chair internat. policy com. U.S. Catholic Conf., 1990-93. Mem. Am. Coun. Edn. (del. 1963-65), Minn. Cath. Edn. Assn. (past pres.), Assn. Mil. Colls. and Schs. U.S. (past pres.), North Cen. Assn. Colls. and Secondary Schs., Nat. Conf. Cath. Bishops (adminstrv. com., priestly formation com., chmn. vocations com., priorities and plans com., com. on sexual abuse), U.S. Cath. Conf. (com. on social devel. and world peace 1990-93, priorities and plans com.), Nat. Cath. Edn. Assn. (chmn. bd. dirs.), Nat. Cath. Rural Life Conf. (past chmn. task force on food and agr. 1987-89). Address: Chancery Office 226 Summit Ave Saint Paul MN 55102-2121

ROACH, JOHN VINSON, II, retail company executive; b. Stamford, Tex., Nov. 22, 1938; s. John V. and Agnes M. (Hanson) R.; m. Barbara Jean Wiggin, Mar. 31, 1960; children: Amy, Lori. BA in Physics and Math., Tex. Christian U., 1961, MBA, 1965. V.p. Radio Shack, 1972-75, Radio Shack Mfg., 1975-78; exec. v.p. Radio Shack, 1978-80; gen. mgr. data processing Tandy Corp., Ft. Worth, 1967-73, pres., 1980—, chief exec. officer, 1981—, chmn., 1982—, also bd. dirs.; bd. dirs. Justin Industries. Bd. dirs. Van Cliburn Found.; chmn. bd. Tex. Christian U. Mem. Ft. Worth Club, City Club, Colonial Country Club, Rotary. Office: Tandy Corp 1800 1 Tandy Ctr Fort Worth TX 76102*

ROACH, MARGOT RUTH, biophysicist, educator; b. Moncton, N.B., Can., Dec. 24, 1934; d. Robert Dickson and Katherine (McMillan) R.; m. Franklyn St. Aubyn House, Dec. 20, 1994. B.Sc. in Math. and Physics with honors, U. N.B., Fredericton, Can., 1955; M.D., C.M. cum laude, McGill U., Montreal, Can., 1959; Ph.D. in Biophysics, U. Western Ont., Can., 1963; D.Sc. (hon.), U. N.B., St. John, Can., 1981. Jr. intern Victoria Hosp., London, Ont., Can., 1959-60, fellow in cardiology, 1962-63, asst. resident in medicine, 1963-64; asst. resident in medicine Toronto Gen. Hosp., 1964-65; mem. faculty, dept. biophysics U. Western Ont., London, Ont., Can., 1965—, head dept. biophysics, 1970-78, prof., 1971—, asst. prof. medicine, 1965-72, assoc. prof., 1972-78, prof., 1978—; mem. staff dept. medicine Victoria Hosp., 1967-72, U. Hosp., London, 1972—; Commonwealth vis. sci., dept. applied math. theoretical physics Cambridge U., 1975; vis. sci. Bioengring. Inst., Chonqing U., People's Republic of China, 1991; mem. bioengring. grants com. Med. Rsch. Coun. Can., 1993—; cons. and lectr. in field. Active civic orgns. and coms. including Univ. Rsch. Coun., 1976-79; mem. interview bd. London Conf. of United Ch., 1967-90; steward United Ch. Can., 1967-73, elder, 1973—; chmn. stewardship devel. com. Colborne St. United Ch., 1990-93. Recipient A. Wilmer Duff prize in physics U. N.B., 1955, Cushing prize in pediatrics, 1959, Ciba Found. award for research in aging, 1959, Teaching award Faculty of Medicine U. Western Ont., 1990; Med. Research Council fellow U. Western Ont., 1960-62; numerous other fellowships and grants in medicine. Fellow Royal Coll. Physicians (Can.), Am. Coll. Cardiology (Young Investigator's award 1963); mem. Can. Physiol. Soc., Can. Cardiovascular Soc. (off council), Can. Clin. Investigation Soc. (council 1980-84), Can. Biophys. Soc., Can. Soc. Internal Medicine. Home: 223 University Crescent, London, ON Canada N6A 2L7

ROACH, MAXWELL LEMUEL, musician; b. Elizabeth City, N.C., Jan. 10, 1924; s. Alphonzo and Cressie (Saunders) R.; m. Mildred Wilkinson, Jan. 14, 1949 (div.); children: Daryl, Maxine; m. Abbey Lincoln, Mar. 3, 1962 (div.). Student, Manhattan Sch. Music, N.Y.C.; Mus.D. (hon.), New Eng. Conservatory Music, 1982. Prof. music U. Mass., from 1973. Adapted use of tympani in jazz; musician specializing percussion instruments; with Charlie Parker, 1946-48, later appeared with Thelonious Monk, Bud Powell, Dizzy Gillespie; co-leader Max Roach-Clifford Brown Quintet; with Sonny Rollins, Harold Land, 1954-56, later with Booker Little, Ray Bryant, Eric Dolphy; appearances at Paris Jazz Festival, 1949, Newport Jazz Festival, 1972; composer: integration of jazz and dance Freedom Now suite; albums include: Percussion Bitter Sweet, It's Time, Drums Unlimited, Speak Brother Speak, The Loadstar, Conversations, Long as You're Living, Survivors, The Long March, Jazz in 3/4 Time, Scott Free, To the Max!, 1991, (with Dizzy Gillespie) Max and Dizzy: Paris 1989; producer, dir. and choreographer. Recipient Best Record of Year award Down Beat mag. 1956; winner Down Beat poll 1955, 57, 58, 59, 60, 84, metronome poll 1951-54. Mem. Jazz Artists Guild Inc. (organizer), Am. Acad. and Inst. of Arts and Letters (Hon.), 1992.

ROACH, NANCY KATHRYN, health facility administrator; b. Lexington, N.C., Feb. 25, 1954; d. Henry Herman Jr. and Evelyn Frances (Cline) R. BA in Speech Comm. Edn., U. N.C., 1977; postgrad., Ea. Ill. U., 1982-83. cert. dir. vol. svcs., N.C. Soc. Dirs. Vol. Svcs. Form art resource tchr. to learning lab coord. Davidson County Schs., Lexington, N.C., 1977-79; dir. Arts Coun. for Davidson County, Lexington, N.C., 1979-82; grad. asst. Ea. Ill. U., Charleston, 1982-83; asst. mgr. Gingerbread House Toy Store, Lexington, 1983-86; dir. vol. svcs. Lexington Meml. Hosp., 1986-89, Wesley Long Community Hosp., Greensboro, N.C., 1989-93, Cape Fear Valley Med. Ctr., Fayetteville, N.C., 1993—. Charter bd. dirs. Lexington Friends the Theater, 1980-82, Actor's Chairty Theatre, Lexington, 1984-89; loaned exec. United Way Guilford County, Greensboro, 1990-91. Mem. Am. Soc. Dir. Vol. Svcs. (state membership rep. 1991-92, affiliate group leader 1992-93), N.C. Soc. Dirs. Vol. Svcs. (bylaws chair 1988-89, pub. rels. chair 1989-90, recording sec. 1990-91, pres.-elect 1991-92, pres., bd. dirs. 1992-93, bd. dirs. certification chair 1995—, workshop leader 1993), Phi Alpha Theta. Methodist. Avocations: acting, antique doll collecting, art. Office: Cape Fear Valley Med Ctr 1638 Owen Dr Fayetteville NC 28304-3424

ROACH, ROBERT MICHAEL, JR., lawyer; b. Bronxville, N.Y., May 27, 1955; s. Robert M. and Mary Dee (Doolan) R.; m. Marcia E. Backus, June 14, 1986. BA, Georgetown U., 1977; JD, U. Tex., 1981. Bar: Tex. 1981, U.S. Dist. Ct. (so. dist.) Tex. 1982, U.S. Ct. Appeals (5th cir.) 1982, U.S. Dist. Ct. (we. dist.) Tex. 1984, U.S. Supreme Ct. 1986, U.S. Dist. Ct. (ea. dist.) 1986, U.S. Dist. Ct. (no. dist.) Tex. 1988. Assoc. Vinson & Elkins, Houston, 1981-83, Ryan & Marshall, Houston, 1983, Mayor, Day & Caldwell, Houston, 1983-88; ptnr. Mayor, Day, Caldwell & Keeton, Houston, 1989-93; founding ptnr. Cook & Roach LLP, Houston, 1993—; dir. appellate advocacy U. Houston Law Ctr., 1994—; adj. prof. law U. Houston, 1990-94; lectr. continuing legal edn. U. Houston Law Ctr., 1989—; lectr. continuing legal edn. State Bar Tex., U. Tex., South Tex. Coll. Law, So. Meth. U.; rschr., editor U.S. Senate Com. on Nutrition, 1975, 76, 77; rschr. U.S Supreme Ct., Washington, 1977; mem. Tex. Law Rev., 1979-81. Editor Def. Counsel Jour., 1990-93. Active U.S. Supreme Ct. Hist. Soc. Mem. Internat. Assn. Def. Counsel, Fedn. Ins. and Corp. Counsel, Def. Rsch. Inst. (grievance com.), Tex. State Bar Assn. (appellate subcom. 1989—), Houston Bar Assn. (appellate sect.), State Bar Tex., Houston Club, Houston Met. Racquet Club, Houston Ctr. Club. Avocations: music, travel, oenology, tennis. Office: Cook & Roach LLP Texaco Heritage Plz 1111 Bagby St Ste 2650 Houston TX 77002-2546

ROACH, THOMAS ADAIR, lawyer; b. Akron, Ohio, May 1, 1929; s. Edward Thomas and Mayme Bernice (Turner) R.; m. Sally Jane Bennett, July 11, 1953; children: Thomas, David, James, Dorothy, Steven, Patrick. AB, U. Mich., 1951, JD with distinction, 1953. Bar: Mich. 1953. Assoc. McClintock, Fulton, Donovan & Waterman (and successor firms), Detroit, 1956-62, ptnr., 1962-87; counsel Bodman, Longley & Dahling, Detroit and Ann Arbor, Mich., 1988-90; ptnr. Bodman, Longley & Dahling, Detroit and Ann Arbor, Mich., 1990—; bd. dirs. Ferndale Labs. Inc., Acme Abrasive Co. Contbr. articles to profl. jours. Vice chmn. 14th Congl. Dist. Democratic Orgn., 1971-75; chmn. platform and resolution com. Mich. Dem. Party, 1971-74, treas., 1975-87; permanent chmn. Dem. State Conv., 1976; mem. platform com. and drafting subcom. Dem. Nat. Conv., 1972, mem. rules com., 1980, alt. del., 1984; Bd. regents U. Mich., 1975-90; bd. dirs. Mich. Tech. Coun., 1983-92, vice chmn. 1984-86, south-ctrl. region 1992-95; pres. 9th Dist. Res. Policy Bd. 1976-77; nat. chmn. Ann. Giving, U., Mich., 1987—; mem. Mich. Higher Edn. Assistance Authority, Mich. Higher Edn. Student Loan Authority, 1990-94, Great Saulk Trail Coun., 1993—; bd. dirs. Wolverine Coun. Boy Scouts Am., 1991-93; officer Compensation Commn. Pittsfield Twp., 1991-93. Served to capt. USCGR, 1953-56; res. group comdr., 1974-77. Mem. ABA, Fed. Bar Assn., Mich. Bar Assn. (chmn. constrn. law com. 1983-85), Detroit Bar Assn., Washtenaw County Bar Assn., Res. Officers Assn., Order of Coif, Thomas M. Cooley Club, U. Mich. Club (gov. 1970-74), U. Mich. Alumni Assn. (bd. dirs. 1991-94, pres. 1995-97),Rotary Club (bd. dirs. Ann Arbor chpt. 1991-96, pres. 1994-95). Anglican. Home: 11825 Durston St Pinckney MI 48169-9502 Office: Bodman Longley & Dahling 110 Miller Ave Ste 300 Ann Arbor MI 48104-1339

ROACH, WAYNE E., retail automotive executive; b. 1946. Pres., COO Fred Jones Co., Inc., Oklahoma City, 1991—. Office: Fred Jones Cos Inc 123 S Hudson Ave Oklahoma City OK 73102-5020*

ROACH, WESLEY LINVILLE, lawyer, insurance executive; b. Norlina, N.C., Oct. 8, 1931; s. Joseph Franklin and Florence G. (Sink) R.; m. Mary Jon Gerald, Aug. 13, 1955; children: Gerald, Mary Virginia. B.S., Wake Forest U., 1953, J.D., 1955. Bar: N.C. 1955. With Pilot Life Ins. Co., Greensboro, N.C., 1958-86, also bd. dirs.; sr. v.p., gen. counsel Jefferson-Pilot Life Ins. Co., Greensboro, 1986-88; sec. Great Ea. Lif. Ins. Co., 1975-85; of counsel Smith, Anderson, Blount, Dorsett, Mitchell & Jernigan, Attys. at Law, Raleigh, N.C., 1988—; former chmn. bd. dirs. N.C. Life and Accident and Health Ins. Guaranty Assn., Va. Life, Accident and Health Guaranty Assn., S.C. Life, Accident and Health Guaranty Assn.; sec. JP Investment Mgmt. Co., Jefferson-Pilot Equity Sales, Inc., Spl. Services Agy., Inc., 1974-84; mem. exec. com., bd. dirs. N.C. Ins. Edn. Found., 1978—. Mem. fin. com. Greensboro United Fund, 1964-65; mem. fin. com. Greensboro 1st Bapt. Ch., 1963-66, 83-86, chmn., 1983-85, chmn. bd. deacons, 1974-76, 80-81; nat. chmn. alumni coun. coll. fund Wake Forest U., 1971-76, pres. nat. alumni coun., 1975-76, trustee univ., 1978-82; trustee So. Bapt. Theol. Sem., Louisville, 1973-84; trustee Bapt. Retirement Homes N.C., Inc., 1992—, chmn., 1993-94 With USNR, 1955-58. Mem. ABA, N.C. Bar Assn., Raleigh Bar Assn., Assn. Life Ins. Counsel (bd. govs. 1984-88), Greensboro C. of C. (chmn. nat. legis. com. 1973—), Nat. Orgn. Life Guaranty Assn. (bd. dirs. 1982-87). Democrat. Home: PO Box 1490 601 Selma Rd Wendell NC 27591-8648 Office: 2500 First Union Capitol Ctr PO Box 2611 Raleigh NC 27602-2611

ROACH, WILLIAM RUSSELL, training and education executive; b. Bedford, Ind., Jan. 1940; s. George H. and Beatrice M. (Schoenlaub) R.; m. Margaret R. Balogh, 1961 (div. 1994); children: Kathleen L., Keith W. BS in Fin. and Acctg., UCLA, 1961. CPA, Calif. Internal auditor Hughes Aircraft Co., L.A., 1961-62, Lockheed Aircraft Corp., L.A., 1962; sr. acct. Haskins & Sells, L.A., 1962-66; asst. to group v.p., asst. corp. contr. Lear Siegler, Inc., Santa Monica, Calif., 1966-71; exec. v.p., corp. sec., dir. Optimum Systems Inc., Santa Clara, Calif., 1972-79; pres., dir. Banking Systems Inc., subs. Optimum Systems Inc., Dallas, 1976-79, BancSystems, Inc., Santa Clara, 1976-79, DMA/Optimum, Honolulu, 1978-79; v.p. URS Corp., San Mateo, Calif., 1979-81; pres. URS Internat., Inc., 1980-81; pres., CEO, dir. Advanced Systems, Inc., from 1981, Applied Learning Internat., Inc. (formed from merger of Advanced Systems, Inc. and Deltak Training Corp.), Naperville, Ill., 1981-88; sr. v.p., bd. dirs. Nat. Edn. Corp. (parent co. Applied Learning Internat.), Irvine, Calif., 1988; chmn. bd., pres., chief exec. officer TRO Learning Inc., (acquisition tng. and edn. group Control Data Corp.), Hoffman Estates, Ill., 1989—; bd. dirs. Mil. Profl. Resources, Inc.; guest speaker numerous industry related funtions including Rep. Platform Com., 1988. Mem. AICPA, Calif. Soc. CPAs, Theta Delta Chi, Commonwealth Club (San Francisco); The Meadow Club (Chgo.). Office: TRO Learning Inc Poplar Creek Office Plz 1721 Moon Lk Blvd Ste 555 Hoffman Estates IL 60194

ROACHE, EDWARD FRANCIS, retired manufacturing company executive; b. Morristown, N.J., May 2, 1923; s. Vincent D. and Cecelia R. (Kennedy) R.; m. Beth Davidson, Aug. 8, 1948; children: Marc E., Steven P., Kevin J. B.S. in Economics, Fordham U., 1947; postgrad., Sienna Coll., 1953. With Gen. Electric Co., 1947—; mem. fin. mgmt. program, corporate audit staff, mgr. fin. various depts., gen. mgmt. assignments in electronics, computers, aircraft engine and intern Gen. Electric Co., Syracuse, N.Y., Phoenix, Lynn, Mass., Fairfield, Conn., 1978-83; v.p., gen. mgr. internat. constrn. bus. div. Gen. Electric Co., 1978-83, ret., 1983; dir. Gen. Electric Co., Italy, Australia, S. Korea, U.K. Served with USMC, 1943-46. Mem. Fin. Execs. Inst. Clubs: Pinnacle; Landmark (Stamford, Conn.). Home: 1161 Mill Hill Rd Southport CT 06490-1041

ROADEN, ARLISS LLOYD, retired higher education executive director, former university president; b. Bark Camp, Ky., Sept. 27, 1930; s. Johnie Samuel and Ethel Nora (Killian) R.; m. Mary Etta Mitchell, Sept. 1, 1951; children: Janice Arletta Roaden Skelton, Sharon Kay Roaden Hagen. Grad., Cumberland Coll., 1949; AB, Carson Newman Coll., 1951; MS, U. Tenn., 1958, EdD, 1961; PhD (hon.), Cumberland Coll., 1986; DLitt (hon.), Tusculum Coll., 1992. With Oak Ridge Inst. Nuclear Studies, 1957-59, Auburn U., 1961-62; mem. faculty Ohio State U., 1962-74, prof. edn., 1967-74, acting dean Coll. Edn., 1968-70, vice provost for research, dean Grad. Sch., 1970-74; pres. Tenn. Tech. U., 1974-85, pres. emeritus, 1985—; dir. Tenn. Higher Edn. Commn., Nashville, 1985-95, exec. dir. emeritus, 1995—; summer vis. prof. Marshall U., 1961, U. So. Calif., 1964, Ind. U., 1967; cons. ednl. instns., 1961—; pres. Tenn. Coll. Assn., 1978; chmn. sci. and tech. com. Am. Assn. State Colls. and Univs., 1980; chmn. task force on program and instl. assessment State Higher Edn. Exec. Officers', 1987, pres. 1993-94, chmn. coun. postsecondary accreditation liaison com., 1986-88, exec. com., 1988-95, pres. elect 1992-93; mem. exec. bd. trustees Southern Assn. Colls. and Schs., 1986—, chair communications com., 1990—, mem. task force, 1990—; mem. Southern Regional Edn. Bd., 1985—, chmn. procedures com. for reviewing bylaw changes and revisions, 1988-89; mem. exec. com., state rep., treas., chair Internal Audit Com., 1990-91, Edn. Commn. States, 1987-90; mem. Tenn. Econ. Cabinet Coun., 1988—, chmn.m 1988-91, bd. dirs. 1988—Fgn. Lang. Inst.; treas., chair Internal Audit Com., 1990-91; mem. Performance Standards in Vocat.-Tech. Edn. Working Group, U.S. Dept. Edn., 1990. Co-author: The Research Assistantship: Recommendations for Colleges and Universities, 1975; editor: Problems of School Men in Depressed Urban Areas, 1967; contbr. articles to profl. jours. State chmn. Tenn. Cancer Soc. Crusade, 1986-88, bd. dirs., 1987—; mem. exec. bd., commr. Mid. Tenn. coun. Boy Scouts Am., 1987-88, mem. nat. coun., 1988—, chmn. scouts membership rels. com.; mem. Phi Delta Kappa Found., 1965—, past chmn. bd. govs., mem. futures and diamond jubilee coms., 1989—; chmn. Blue Ribbon Com. To Respond to Edn. Goals, 1990; bd. dirs. Nat. Project 714, 1986—, pres.-elect, 1987-88, chmn., 1988-89; pres. alumni assn. bd. Cumberland Coll., 1987-88, chmn. devel. bd., 1994—; adult Sunday sch. tchr. Woodmont Bapt. Ch., chmn. pers. com. , 1989—. With U.S. Army, 1951-53. Research grantee Phi Delta Kappa Internat., 1968; named Distinguished Alumnus Cumberland Coll., 1970; recipient Distinguished Alumni and Faculty Centennial medallion Coll. Edn., 1970, Distinguished Service award Council Grad. Students, 1974; both Ohio State U.; recipient Silver Beaver award Boy Scouts Am., Rotarian of Yr., 1984; Eagle Scout honoree Middle Tenn. Coun. Boy Scouts Am., 1989, others. Fellow Oxford Soc. Scholars; mem. AAAS, Am. Assn. Higher Edn., Acad. Polit. and Social Scis., Am. Ednl. Rsch. Assn. (chmn. publs. com. 1979-80), Nat. Soc. Study Edn., Nat. Assn. State Colls. and Land Grant Univs.,, Lions (bd. dirs. Nashville 1988-90, pres. 1991-92, zone chmn. 1992-93, vice dist. gov. 1995), Rotary (bd. dirs.), Order of Lion and Eagle, Phi Kappa Phi, Phi Delta Kappa (Disting. Svc. award Ohio State U. chpt. 1974), Kappa Phi Kappa, Kappa Delta Pi. Baptist.

ROAF, WILLIAM LAYTON, professional football player; b. Pine Bluff, Ark., Apr. 18, 1970; s. Clifton George and Andree Yvonne (Layton) R. Left offensive tackle New Orleans Saints, 1993—. Named All-American, Sports Writers, 1993, finalist Outland Trophy, Sports Writers, 1993; named to All-Rookie Team, Football News, 1994, Pro-Bowl Alt., 1994. Episcopal. Dr. Z's All-Pro team, 1994. Office: New Orleans Saints 6928 Saints Dr Metairie LA 70003-5151

ROAN, JAMES CORTLAND, JR., air force officer; b. St. Louis, Apr. 10, 1937; s. James Cortland and Marguerite L. (Johnson) R.; m. Connie R. Brown, Nov. 10, 1962; children: James Bradley, Brian Edward. BSBA, JD, Washington U., St. Louis, 1960. Bar: Mo. 1960. Commd. 1st lt. USAF, 1960, advanced through grades to brig. gen., 1990; staff judge adv. Air Force Aero. Systems Div., Dayton, Ohio, 1982-85, Hdqrs. Air Force Logistics Command, Dayton, 1991-92, Hdqrs. Air Force Systems Command, Washington, 1985-87, 1990-91; staff judge adv. Air Force Electronic Systems Div., Boston, 1987-90; comdr. Hdqrs. Air Force Contract Law Ctr., Dayton, 1991-92; staff judge adv. Hdqrs. Air Force Materiel Command, Dayton, 1992-95; ret., 1995. Recipient Stuart R. Reichart award as outstanding sr. atty. in USAF, Air Force Assn., 1989. Mem. Fed. Bar Assn. (pres. Beverly Hills chpt. 1980-81). Avocation: woodworking. Home: 267 Smith Creek Rd Warrenton MO 63383

ROARK, CHARLES ELVIS, healthcare executive; b. Port Arthur, Tex., Feb. 11, 1946; s. Chris C. and Alene (Adams) R.; m. Marlene Jones, Jan. 18, 1969; children: Cari Joann, Carolyn Dianne, Charles Eric. BBA, Lamar U., Beaumont, Tex., 1969; MS, Trinity U., San Antonio, 1971; EdD, Tex. Tech U., 1994. Asst. adminstr. Hotel Dieu Hosp., El Paso, 1969-76; dir. planning Tex. Hosp. Assn., Austin, 1976-79; adminstr. Gulf Coast Hosp., Wharton, Tex., 1979-81; pres. Charles E. Roark & Assocs., El Paso, 1980—; exec. dir. Hospice of El Paso Inc., 1990—; bd. dirs. El Paso Ind. Sch. Dist. Pres. N.E. Civic Leaders Coun., Inc., 1986-90; mem. adv. bd. Anytown USA, 1987-88; mem. City of El Paso Sanitation Adv. Bd., 1987-88; bd. dirs. Keep El Paso Beautiful, 1986-88. Fellow Am. Coll. Healthcare Execs. (cert.); Mem. Rotary Club of El Paso, N.E. Civitan (pres. 1975-76, dist. gov. 1988-89), S.W. Healthcare Execs. (pres. 1991-92). Baptist. Avocations: sports, hunting, fishing. Office: Hospice of El Paso Inc 3901 N Mesa St Ste 400 El Paso TX 79902-1540

ROARK, TERRY PAUL, university president; b. Okeene, Okla., June 11, 1938; s. Paul J. and Erma K. (Morrison) R.; m. Beverly Brown, Sept. 7, 1963; 1 child, David. C. BA in Physics, Oklahoma City U., 1960; MS in Astronomy, Rensselaer Poly. Inst., 1962, PhD in Astronomy, 1966. Asst. provost for curricula Ohio State U., Columbus, 1977-79, assoc. provost for instrn., 1979-83; prof. physics Kent (Ohio) State U., 1983-87, v.p. acad. and student affairs, 1983-87, provost, 1985-87; pres. U. Wyo., Laramie, 1987—; bd. dirs. Rocky Mountain Fed. Savs. Bank, chmn. audit com., 1989-93; commr. Western Interstate Commn. for Higher Edn., 1987—, chmn., 1991; bd. dirs. Associated Western Univs., 1987-94, chmn., 1991, bd. trustees, 1994—; mem. adv. bd. Wyo. Geol. Survey, 1987—; mem. Warren AFB Civilian Adv. Coun., 1987—; bd. dirs. First Interstate Bank of Wyo. Mem., treas. Ctr. for Pub. Edn., Columbus, 1980-83; mem. fin. adv. com. LWV, Kent, 1986; mem. long range planning com. Cleve. Urban League, 1985-86; mem. adv. com. Battelle youth sci. program Columbus and Ohio Pub. Schs., 1982; bd. dirs. Ivinson Hosp. Found., 1987—. Mem. AAUP, Am. Astron. Soc., Astron. Soc. Pacific, Internat. Astron. Union, Nat. Assn. State Univs. and Land Grant Colls. (bd. dirs. 1994—, chair commn. on intenat. affairs 1995), Am. Assn. for Higher Edn., Sigma Xi, Phi Kappa Phi, Omicron Delta Kappa. Avocations: photography, music, hiking. Home: 1752 Edward Dr Laramie WY 82070-2331 Office: U Wyo Office of Pres PO Box 3434 Laramie WY 82071-3434

ROATH, KENNETH B., investment company executive. Pres., chmn. bd., CEO Health Care Property Investors, L.A., 1978—. Office: Health Care Property Investors 10990 Wilshire Blvd Los Angeles CA 90024-3913*

ROATH-ALGERA, KATHLEEN MARIE, massage therapist; b. Binghamton, N.Y., Feb. 7, 1952; d. Stephen James and Virginia Mary (Purdy) Roath; m. Parker Newcomb Wheeler Jr., Sept. 18, 1971 (div. June 1976); 1 child, Colleen Marie Wheeler; m. John M. Algera, Feb. 14, 1981. AS in Phys. Edn., Dean Jr. Coll., Franklin, Mass., 1971; BS in Edn., Boston U., 1977; postgrad., U. Ctrl. Fla., Orlando, 1981-82; grad., Reese Inst. Massage Therapy, Oviedo, Fla., 1988. Lic. massage therapist; master practitioner in myofascial release. Counselor Dept. Def., Orlando, 1979-84; tchr. Divine Mercy Cath. Sch., Merritt Island, Fla., 1984-85; courier Emery Worldwide, Orlando, 1985-89; massage therapist, dir., owner Massage Therapy Clinic of Titusville, Fla., 1989—; instr., supr. clin. internship Reese Inst., 1992-95; assoc. Todd Jaffe, M.D., 1995. Mem. Am. Massage Therapy Assn., Fla. State Massage Therapy Assn. (pres. Brevard County 1992—, Therapist of Yr. 1991-92), Nat. Cert. Bd. Therapeutic Massage and Bodywork (recert. chair 1994—). Home: 1660 Saratoga Dr Titusville FL 32796-4206 Office: Massage Therapy Clinic Titusville 3410 S Park Ave Titusville FL 32780-5139

ROBAK, KIM M., state official; b. Columbus, Nebr., Oct. 4, 1955; m. William J. Mueller; children: Katherine, Claire. BA with distinction, U. Nebr., 1977, JD with high distinction, 1985. Tchr. Lincoln (Nebr.) Pub. Schs., 1978-82; clerk Cline Williams Wright Johnson & Oldfather, Lincoln, 1983; summer assoc. Cooley Godward Castro Huddleson & Tatum, San Francisco, 1984, Steptoe & Johnson, Washington, 1985; ptnr. Rembolt Ludtke Parker & Berger, Lincoln, 1985-91; legal counsel Gov. E. Benjamin Nelson/State of Nebr., Lincoln, 1991-92, chief of staff, 1992-93; lt. gov. State of Nebr., Lincoln, 1993—; chair Prairie Fire Internat. Symposium on Edn., 1986. Fellow Leadership Lincoln, 1986-87, program com., 1987-90; chair program com. Leadership Lincoln Alumni Assn., 1987, selection com., 1990; chair Landfill Alternatives and Ops. Task Force, 1986-87; chair Gladys Forsyth award subcom. YWCA Tribute! to Women, 1987, chair nominations, 1991; mem. adv. com. U.S. Constn. Bicentennial Competition, 1987; gen. Dem. counsel, Nebr., 1985-92; mem. bd. women's ministries First Plymouth Congl. Ch., 1988-91, trustee, 1991-94; mem. Toll Fellowship Program, 1995; chair Nat. Conf. Lt. Govs., 1996; hon. chair Daffodil Day campaign Am. Cancer Soc.; hon. chair Walktoberfest, Am. Diabetes Assn.; hon. chair Nebr.'s campaign Prevent Blindness; hon. mem. Red Ribbon campaign Mothers Against Drunk Driving, 1994-95. Mem. Nat. Conf. Lt. Govs. (fed. practice com. 1986-92), Nat. Inst. Trial Advocacy, Nebr State Bar Assn. (ethics com. 1987-92, vice chair com. on pub. rels. 1988-92, chair com. on yellow pages advt. 1988, ho. of dels. 1989-92), Lincoln Bar Assn., U. Nebr. Coll. Alumni Assn. (bd. dirs. 1986-89), Updowntowners, Order of Coif. Office: Lt Gov's Office PO Box 94863 Rm 2315 State Capitol Bldg Lincoln NE 68509-4863

ROBAK, ROSTYSLAW WSEWOLOD, psychologist, educator; b. Passau, Germany, Nov. 15, 1948; s. Bohdan and Maria R.; m. Loretta J. Tallon; children: Marika, Boyan. BA, Seton Hall U., 1970; MA, Fairleigh Dickinson U., 1973; PhD, Hofstra U., 1976. Lic. psychologist N.Y., Pa., Mass. Prof. Pace U., Pleasantville, N.Y., 1988—; dir. M.S. program in substance abuse counseling Pace U., 1992—; adj. prof. Orange County Community Coll., Middletown, N.Y. 1985-88; founding faculty advisor Pace U. chpt. Psi Chi Nat. Honor Soc., 1991—. Author: A Primer for Today's Substance Abuse Counselor, 1991. Mem. APA, Am. Orthopsychiat. Assn., Nat. Register Health Svc. Providers in Psychology, Assn. Death Edn. and Counseling. Office: Pace Univ Dir Substance Abuse Counseling Prog Pleasantville NY 10570 *If I have learned one thing from my patients it is this: integrity is found in the struggle.*

ROBARDS, JASON NELSON, JR., actor; b. Chgo., July 26, 1922; s. Jason Nelson and Hope (Glanville) R.; m. Eleanore Pitman, May 7, 1948; children: Jason III, Sarah Louise, David; m. Lauren Bacall, July 4, 1961 (div.); 1 son, Sam; m. Lois O'Connor; children: Shannon, Jake. Student, Am. Acad. Dramatic Arts, 1946; D.H.L., Fairfield U., 1982; D.F.A., Williams Coll., 1983. Bd. dirs. Am. Acad. Dramatic Arts, 1957—. Broadway plays include Stalag 17, 1951-53, The Chase, 1952, The Iceman Cometh, 1956, Long Day's Journey Into Night, 1956-58, 76, 88, The Disenchanted, 1958, 1958-59, Toys in the Attic, 1960, Big Fish, Little Fish, 1961, A Thousand Clowns, 1962, After the Fall, 1964, But for Whom, Charlie, 1964, Hughie, 1964, The Devils, 1965, We Bombed in New Haven, 1968, The Country Girl, 1972, A Moon for the Misbegotten, 1973, A Touch of the Poet, 1977-78, A Month of Sundays, 1987, No Man's Land, 1993; other plays include Henry IV, Part I, Stratford (Ont., Can.), 1958, Macbeth, Stratford, Conn., You Can't Take It With You, 1983, Love Letters, 1989, Park Your Car in Harvard Yard, 1991; motion picture appearances include The Journey, 1959, By Love Possessed, 1961, Long Day's Journey into Night (Cannes Internat. Film Festival, Best Actor Award, 1962), A Thousand Clowns, Big Hand for the Little Lady, 1966, Any Wednesday, 1966, St. Valentine's Day Massacre, 1967, Night They Raided Minsky's, 1968, Hour of the Gun, 1967, Loves of Isadora, 1969, Once Upon a Time in the West, 1969, Ballad of Cable Hogue, 1970, Johnny Got His Gun, 1971, Murders in the Rue Morgue, 1971, The War Between Men and Women, 1972, Pat Garrett and Billy the Kid, 1973, All the President's Men, 1976, Julia, 1977, Comes a Horseman, 1978, Hurricane, 1979, Melvin and Howard, 1979, Something Wicked This Way Comes, 1983, Max Dugan Returns, 1983, Square Dance, 1987, The Good Mother, 1988, Parenthood, 1989, Quick Change, 1990, Storyville, 1992, The Trial, 1993, The Adventures of Huck Finn, 1993, Philadelphia, 1993, Little Big League, 1994, The Paper, 1994, Crimson Tide, 1995; TV appearance in For Whom the Bell Tolls, CBS, 1959; starred in TV films including: The Iceman Cometh, 1961, One Day in the Life of Ivan Denisovitch, 1963, Washington Behind Closed Doors, 1977, F.D.R.: The Last Year, 1980, The Day After, 1983, Sakharov, 1984, Johnny Bull, 1986, Inherit the Wind, 1988 (Emmy award, 1988), The Christmas Wife, 1988, Chernobyl: The Final Warning, 1991; appeared in TV miniseries Haywire, 1980, The Atlanta Child Murders, 1985. Served with USN, 1939-46. Recipient ANTA award for outstanding contbn. to living theater, 1959, Antoinette Perry award as best actor, 1959, Obie award, 1956, Tony award for best dramatic actor, 1959, Acad. awards for best supporting actor, 1976, 77, N.Y. Film Critics Circle award for best supporting actor, 1976, Presdl. citation. Club: Players (N.Y.C.). Address: C/O Paradigm Talent Agy 25th FL 10100 Santa Monica Blvd Los Angeles CA 90067*

ROBB, BRUCE, former insurance company executive; b. Norman, Okla., July 28, 1919; m. Betty Jane Sharrar, May 6, 1950; children: Elizabeth (dec.), Bruce. B.S., U.S. Naval Acad., 1941; M.B.A., Columbia U., 1949. Security analyst Clark, Dodge & Co., Inc., N.Y.C., 1948-52, 53-62; asst. treas. SAFECO Corp., Seattle, 1962-66; v.p., treas. SAFECO Corp., 1966-72, sr. v.p., treas., 1972-84. Mem. Wash. State Fin. Adv. Com., 1970-80; mem.

investment com. Diocese of Olympia, 1964-94. Mem. Sand Point Country Club, Beta Gamma Sigma. Home: 6307 NE 57th St Seattle WA 98105-2011

ROBB, CHARLES SPITTAL, senator, lawyer; b. Phoenix, AZ, June 26, 1939; s. James Spittal and Francis Howard (Woolley) R.; m. Lynda Bird Johnson, Dec. 9, 1967; children: Lucinda Desha, Catherine Lewis, Jennifer Wickliffe. Student, Cornell U., 1957-58; B.B.A., U. Wis., 1961; J.D., U. Va., 1973. Bar: Va. 1973, U.S. Supreme Ct. 1976. Law clk. to presiding justice U.S. Ct. Appeals, 1973-74; atty. Williams Connolly & Califano, 1974-77; lt. gov. Va., 1978-82, gov., 1982-86; ptnr. Hunton & Williams, Richmond, Norfolk, and Fairfax, Va., Washington; U.S. Senator from Va., 1989—; chmn. Nat. Conf. Lt. Govs., 1979-80, Am. Coun. Young Polit. Leaders Dels. to Peoples Republif of China, 1979, edn. Commn. of the States, 1985; vis. prof. pub. affairs George Mason U., spring 1987. Chmn. Jobs for Am.'s Grads. Inc., 1985-90, Dem. Leadership Coun., 1986-88; gov. Atlantic Inst. for Internat. Affairs, 1987. With USMC 1961-70. Decorated Bronze Star, Vietnam Service medal with 4 Stars; Vietnamese Cross of Gallantry with Silver Star; recipient Raven award, 1973, Seven Soc. award U. Va. Mem. ABA, Va. Bar Assn., So. Govs. Assn. (chmn.), Dem. Govs. Assn. (chmn.), Coalition for Dem. Majority, Res. Officers Assn., USMC Res. Officers Assn., U.Fa. La. Alumni Assn. (bd. dirs. 1974-85), Am. Legion, Raven Soc., Navy League U.S., Coun. on Fgn. Rels., Omicron Delta Kappa. Episcopalian. Office: US Senate 154 Russell Senate Office Bldg Washington DC 20510-4603*

ROBB, DAVID BUZBY, JR., financial services company executive, lawyer; b. Phila., Nov. 30, 1935; s. David Buzby and Sarah Whelan (Carson) R.; m. Patricia Ann Irons, Sept. 14, 1979; children: Steven C., David S.; step-children: Donald Irons, Steven Irons. B.A., Princeton U., 1958; J.D., U. Va., 1963; A.M.P., Harvard Bus. Sch., 1978. Bar: Pa., 1963. Assoc. firm Ballard, Spahr, Andrews, Ingersoll, Phila., 1963-69; sr. v.p., chief operating officer trust div. Provident Nat. Bank, Phila., 1976-82, sr. v.p., gen. counsel Provident Nat. Corp., Phila., 1970-76; dir., vice chmn. Provident Instl. Mgmt. Corp., 1977-82; dir., chmn., chief exec. officer Provident Capital Mgmt., 1978-82; exec. v.p. SEI Corp., Wayne, Pa., 1982-89; pres., chief exec. officer Trust Funds Group, 1982-89; dir., pres., chief exec. officer Premier Systems, Inc., Wayne, Pa., 1989-91; dir., pres., CEO J.P. Morgan Fla., 1991—. Bd. dirs. Landmark Soc., Phila. City Inst., Friends Hosp., Pa. Acad. Fine Arts, ARC S.E. Pa., 1981-93, Econ. Coun. Palm Beach County, Intracoastal Health Systems, Inc., Civic Assn. Palm Beach, Preservation Found. Served to lt. USN, 1958-60. Mem. ABA, Pa. Bar Assn., Phila. Bar Assn., Sunnybrook G.C., P.G.A. Nat. G.C., City Club. Breakers Club, Club Colette. Republican. Episcopalian. Office: JP Morgan Florida FSB 109 Royal Palm Way Palm Beach FL 33480-4249

ROBB, DAVID METHENY, JR., art historian; b. Mpls., Apr. 12, 1937; s. David Metheny and Jane (Howard) R.; m. Frances Louise Osborn, Feb. 12, 1965; children: Andrew Osborn, Matthew Howard. BA, Princeton U., 1959; MA, Yale U., 1967; mus. mgmt. inst., U. Calif., Berkeley, 1983. Research asst. Soc. for Preservation of New Eng. Antiquities, Boston, 1959, Nat. Gallery Art, Washington, 1963; curator Paul Mellon Collection, Upperville, Va., 1963-65; curatorial fellow Walker Art Ctr., Mpls., 1967-69; research curator Kimbell Art Mus., Ft. Worth, 1969-74, chief curator, 1974-83, acting dir., 1979-80; dir. Telfair Acad. Art & Scis., Savannah, Ga., 1983-85; dir. Huntsville (Ala.) Mus. Art, 1985-94, dir. emeritus, 1995; mus. cons., 1992—. Co-author: Star-Spangled History—Joseph Boggs Beale, 1975; editor: Kimbell Art Museum: Catalogue of the Collection, 1972, Kimbell Art Museum: Handbook of the Collection, 1981; author: catalogue Louis J. Kahn: Sketches for the Kimbell Art Museum, 1978, preface Elisabeth Louise Vigée Le Brun, Ft. Worth, 1982. Mem. adv. com. S.E. Inst. for Edn. in Visual Arts, Chattanooga, 1987-92, Leadership 2000 Program, Huntsville, 1989-90. Comdr. USNR, 1960-63. Heritage Found. fellow, 1958, Ford Found. fellow, 1967-69. Mem. Am. Assn. Mus. Coll. Art Assn., Ala. Mus. Assn. (chmn. long-range plans com. 1989), Tallulah Bankhead Soc. (treas. 1991—), Huntsville Club, Rotary, Princeton Alumni Schods Com. Home: 506 Lanier Rd SW Huntsville AL 35801-3214

ROBB, FELIX COMPTON, association executive, consultant; b. Birmingham, Ala., Dec. 26, 1914; s. Felix Compton and Ruth (Nicholson) R.; m. Virginia Lytle Threlkeld. A.B. summa cum laude, Birmingham-So. Coll., 1936; M.A., Vanderbilt U., 1939; postgrad., George Peabody Coll., 1939-40; Ed.D., Harvard U., 1952; D.Ped., W.Va. Wesleyan Coll., 1968; LL.D., Mercer U., 1968, U. S.C., 1978; D.H.L., U. Ala. System, 1975, Jacksonville U., 1981; H.H.D., Birmingham So. Coll., 1979. Tchr. jr. high sch. Irondale, Ala., 1936-37; tchr. Ensley High Sch., Birmingham, 1937-38; instr. English Birmingham-So. Coll., 1940-42, successively alumni sec., registrar, 1946; asst. to pres. Peabody Coll., 1947-51, acting dir. Libr. Sch., 1947-48, acting dean of coll. Libr. Sch., 1948-49, assoc. prof. higher edn. Libr. Sch., 1950-53, prof. Libr. Sch., 1953-66, acting dir. surveys and field svcs. Libr. Sch., 1951, dean instrn. Libr. Sch., 1951-61, coll. pres. Libr. Sch., 1961-66; dir. So. Assn. Colls. and Schs., Atlanta, 1966-79; exec. dir. So. Assn. Colls. and Schs., 1979-82, exec. dir. emeritus, 1982—; pres. Ginge, Inc., 1982-94; interim pres. Tallulah Falls Sch., 1988-89; sec., treas. So. Edn. Exec. Search Assocs., 1989-92; coord. edn. project, Republic of Korea, 1956-58; bd. dirs. Carnegie fellowships in tchg., 1950-60, Peabody Bldg. Fund Campaign, 1958; chief of staff The Study of Coll. and Univ. Presidency, 1958-60; mem. Tenn. Adv. Coun. on Tchr. Edn. and Cert., 1954-58; case writer Inst. for Coll. and Univ. Adminstrs., Harvard, 1955; nat. selection com. Fulbright awards, 1955-57; bd. dirs. workshops in TV, ednl. TV program series, Nashville; chmn. gov.'s conf. Edn. Beyond H.S., 1958; mem. com. specialized pers. Dept. Labor; mem. Tenn. Commn. Human Rels., 1964-66; exec. com. Met. Action Commn., 1965-66; chmn. S.E. Manpower Adv. Com., 1965-68; mem. bd. So. Edn. Reporting Svc., 1961-69; mem. nat. adv. com. Acad. of Sr. Profls. at Eckerd Coll., 1974-76; cons. Profl. Assn. Ga. Educators. Author: America's Urgent Agenda, 1990. Trustee, chmn. scholarship com. Presser Found.; trustee, chmn. fin. com. United Meth. Children's Home, 1985-88; trustee Longview Found., Reinhardt Coll.; mem. Cleve. Conf.; mem. devel. coun. Birmingham-So. Coll., adv. bd. Southall Trust; trustee, chmn. adminstrv. bd. Meth. ch., 1974. Mem. So. Coun. Tchr. Edn. (pres. 1956-57), Am. Soc. Assn. Execs., Loulie Compton Sem. Alumni Assn. (pres.), Phi Beta Kappa, Omicron Delta Kappa, Phi Delta Kappa, Kappa Phi Kappa, Pi Gamma Mu, Kappa Alpha Order, Kappa Delta Pi (Laureate mem., mem. ednl. found.), Rotary. Home: 377 Camden Rd NE Atlanta GA 30309-1513

ROBB, JAMES ALEXANDER, lawyer; b. Huntingdon, Que., Can., May 3, 1930; s. Alexander George and Irma Mary (Martin) R.; m. Katherine Ann Teare, June 26, 1960; children: Laura, John, Andrew. B.A., McGill U., 1951, B.C.L., 1954; postgrad., U. Montreal, 1961-63. Bar: Que. 1955, queen's counsel 1970. Lectr. comml. law and taxation Sir George Williams U., 1958-60; ptnr. Stikeman, Elliott and predecessor firm Stikeman, Elliott, Tamaki, Mercier & Robb, Montreal, 1967—; bd. dirs. Robapharm (Can.), Ltd., Itochu Can. Ltd., Majorich Investments Inc., YKK Can. Inc,. Hitachi (HSC) Can. Inc., NGK Spark Plugs Can. Ltd., Hitachi Credit (Can.) Inc., Descente Can. Inc., Klockner Stadler Hurter, Ltd., Bilwyn Franchise Concepts Inc.; pres. Que-Japan Bus. Forum, 1993-95. Mem. Protestant Sch. Bd. Greater Montreal, mem. ctrl. parents com.; chmn. bd. trustees Martlet Found., 1967-69; v.p. Que. Liberal Party, 1976-79; mem. adv. com. McGill Ctr. for Study of Regulated Industries; bd. dirs. Montreal Mus. Fine Arts, 1987-90; bd. govs. McGill U., 1991-95. Mem. Bar Que., Consumers Assn. Can. (pst chmn. regulated industries program), McGill Alumni Assn. (pres. 1996—), Can. Club Montreal (bd. dirs. 1988, pres. 1990-91), Univ. Club, Kanawaki Gold Club (Que.), Royal Montreal Curling Club, Hillside Tennis Club. Home: 9 Renfrew Ave, Westmount, PQ Canada H3Y 2X3 Office: 1155 René Lèvesque, Blvd W Ste 4000, Montreal, PQ Canada H3B 3V2

ROBB, JAMES WILLIS, Romance languages educator; b. Jamaica, N.Y., June 27, 1918; s. Stewart Everts and Clara Johanna (Mohrman) R.; m. Cecilia Uribe-Noguera, 1972. Student, Inst. de Touraine, Sorbonne, 1937-38; B.A. cum laude, Colgate U., 1939; postgrad., U. Nacional de Mex., 1948; M.A., Middlebury Coll., 1950; Ph.D., Catholic U. Am., 1958. Instr. Romance langs. Norwich U., 1946-50; asst. prof. Romance langs. George Washington U., Washington, 1950-58, assoc. prof., 1958-66, prof., 1966-88, prof. emeritus, 1988—. Author: El Estilo de Alfonso Reyes, 1965, 78, Repertorio Bibliográfico de Alfonso Reyes, 1974, Prosa y Poesia de Alfonso Reyes, 1975, 84, Estudios sobre Alf onso Reyes, 1976, Pro los Caminos de Alfonso Reyes, 1981, Imágenes de América en Alfonso Reyes y en Germán Arciniegas, 1990; contbr. articles to profl. jours. With USN, 1942-44, Brazil; with USNR, 1944-46, PTO. Recipient Alfonso Reyes Internat. Lit. prize, 1978; Lit. Diploma of Merit, State of Nuevo León and City of Monterrey, Mex., 1979; OAS grantee, 1964; Am. Philos. Soc. grantee, 1977. Mem. MLA, Internat. Assn. Ibero-Am. Lit., Am. Assn. Tchrs. Spanish and Portuguese, N.Am. Assn. Colombianistas, Phi Beta Kappa. Office: George Washington U Romance Langs Dept Washington DC 20052

ROBB, JOHN WESLEY, religion educator; b. Los Angeles, Dec. 1, 1919; s. Edgar Milton and Alta (Boger) R.; m. Ethel Edna Tosh, June 13, 1942; children: Lydia Joan Robb Durbin, Judith Nadine Robb Eggerman. A.B., Greenville Coll., 1941; Th.M., U. So. Calif., 1945, Ph.D., 1952; L.H.D., Hebrew Union Coll.-Jewish Inst. Religion, 1977. Asst. prof. philosophy and religion Dickinson Coll., Pa., 1948-51; fellow Fund for Advancement Edn., 1951-52; asso. prof. U. So. Calif., L.A., 1954-62, chmn. dept. religion, 1954-67, assoc. dean humanities Coll. Letters, Arts and Scis.,, 1963-68, Leonard K. Firestone prof., 1974-75, prof., 1962-87, prof. emeritus, 1987—; prof. Sch. Medicine U. So. Calif., 1981-87; coun. mem. Inst. of Lab. Animal Resources Nat. Acad. Scis. Nat. Rsch. Coun., 1986-93; prof. emeritus U. So. Calif., 1991—; vis. disting. prof. USAF Med. Ctr., Wilford Hall, Tex., 1985; mem. rev. com. NIH Guide for the Care and Use of Lab. Animals, NRC, NAS, 1993-96; advisor/tutor med. disciplinary bd. Dept. Health, State of Wash., 1994—; adj. prof. bioethics Sch. Medicine, U. So. Calif., 1989-91, prof. emeritus, 1991—. Author: Inquiry Into Faith, 1960; co-editor: Readings in Religious Philosophy; The Reverent Skeptic, 1979. Served as lt. (j.g.) USNR, 1945-47; to lt. 1952-54. Recipient award for excellence in tchg. U. So. Calif., 1960, 74, Dart award for acad. innovation, 1970, Raubenheimer Disting. Faculty award divsn. humanities, 1980, Outstanding Faculty award Student Senate, 1981, Disting. Emeritus award, 1995; Robert Fenton Craig award Blue Key, 1980. Fellow Soc. for Values in Higher Edn.; mem. Am. Acad. Religion (v.p. 1966, pres. 1967), Am. Philos. Assn., AAUP (v.p. Calif. Conf. 1977, pres. 1978-79), Phi Beta Kappa (hon.), Phi Kappa Phi, Phi Chi Phi. United Methodist. Home: 8001 Sand Point Way NE Apt C35 Seattle WA 98115-6356

ROBB, LYNDA JOHNSON, writer; b. Washington, Mar. 19, 1944; d. Lyndon Baines and Claudia Alta (Taylor) Johnson; m. Charles Spittal Robb, Dec. 9, 1967; children: Lucinda Desha, Catherine Lewis, Jennifer Wickliffe. BA with honors, U. Tex., 1966. Writer, McCall's mag., 1966-68; contbg. editor Ladies Home Jour., 1968-80; lectr. bd. dirs. Reading Is Fundamental, 1968—, Lyndon B. Johnson Family Found., 1969—. Mem. Va. State Coun. on Infant Mortality, Va. Maternal & Child Health Coun., Nat. Commn. to Prevent Infant Mortality, 1987-93; chmn. Pres.'s Adv. Com. for Women, 1979-81; bd. dirs. Nat. Home Libr. Found., Ford Theatre; chmn. Va. Women's Cultural History Project, 1982-85; mem. adv. bd. Commn. Presdl. Debates. Mem. Nat. Wildflower Rsch. Ctr., Zeta Tau Alpha. Democrat. Episcopalian.

ROBB, NATHANIEL HEYWARD, JR., national guard officer, real estate executive; b. Columbia, S.C., Sept. 10, 1942; s. Nathaniel Heyward Robb and Dorothy Claiborne (Cabell) Dortch; m. Louise Taber Rivers, Sept. 26, 1964; children: Elizabeth T., Nathaniel Heyward III, Catherine Pease. BSBA, The Citadel, 1964; grad. Realtors Inst., U. N.C., 1972; grad., Command and Gen. Staff Coll. Pres. Robb Realty, Raleigh, N.C., 1972-95; adj. gen. of N.C., 1989-93; dep. commdr. in chief U.S. Atlantic Command, 1993—; exec. sec. Gov.'s Adv. Commn. Mil. Affairs, 1985-89; mem. Raleigh Bd. Realtors, 1975-85; dir. state property office N.C. Dept. Adminstrn., 1975-77; pres., founding mem. Raleigh Comml. Listing Svc., 1975-85; asst. sec. N.C. Dept. Crime Crontrol and Safety, Raleigh, 1985-89; bd. dirs. Aerial Images, Inc., Raleigh. Dir. Mordecai Sq. Hist. Soc.; mem. Raleigh Hist. Dists. Commn., 1973-78; dir., v.p. Raleigh Hist. Properties Commn., 1973-78; mem. Gov.'s Mgmt. Coun., Raleigh, 1985-89, Gov.'s Waste Mgmt. Bd., 1985-89; mem. Gov.'s Drug Cabinet, 1988-89; mem. Nat. Rep. Com., 1970—. Maj. gen. inf., U.S. Army N.G., 1964-70, Vietnam; N.C. N.G., 1970—. Decorated D.S.M., N.C. D.S.M. with one device, Legion of Merit, Bronze Star with v device and one oak leaf cluster, Meritorious Svc. medal; Nat. Def. medal with star, USAR Components Achievement medal with four oak leaf clusters; Republic Vietnam Cross of Gallantry with bronze and silver stars and palm, other mil. awards; recipient Disting. Milit. Grad. award The Citadel, Humanitarian Svc. medal, Legion de Lafayette of Hist. Socs. of Militia and N.G. Mem. N.G. Assn. U.S., N.C. N.G. Assn., 2500 Club. Episcopalian. Avocations: skiing, pistol shooting. Home: 2115 Banbury Rd Raleigh NC 27608-1123 Office: USACOM J5V Ste 200 1562 Mitscher Ave Norfolk VA 23551-2488

ROBB, WALTER LEE, retired electric company executive, management company executive; b. Harrisburg, Pa., Apr. 25, 1928; s. George A. and Ruth (Scantlin) R.; m. Anne Gruver, Feb. 27, 1954; children: Richard, Steven, Lindsey. BS, Pa. State U., 1948; MS, U. Ill., 1950, PhD, 1951; DEng (hon.), Milw. Sch. Engring., 1994; Worcester Poly. Inst., 1988. With GE, 1951-93; mgr. R & D dept. silicone products GE, Waterford, N.Y., 1966-68; venture mgr. med. devel. ops. GE, Schenectady, N.Y., 1968-71; sr. v.p., group exec. med. sys. group GE, Milw., 1973-86; sr. v.p. corp. R & D GE, Schenectady, 1986-93; cons., pres. Vantage Mgmt., Schenectady, N.Y., 1993—; bd. dirs. Celgene Corp., Marquette Electronics, Inc., Cree Rsch., Inc.; chmn. Neopath, Inc. Recipient Nat. Tech. medal, 1993, IRI medal Indsl. Rsch. Inst., 1994. Mem. NAE. Achievements include patentee in field of membranes and gas separation; rsch. in permeable membranes, diagnostic imaging equipment. Home: 1358 Ruffner Rd Niskayuna NY 12309-2500 Office: Vantage Mgmt 3000 Troy-Schenectady Rd Schenectady NY 12309

ROBBEN, MARY MARGARET, portrait artist; b. Bethesda, Md., Oct. 30, 1948; d. John Otto and Mary Margaret (McConnaughy) R. Student, Ohio U., 1967-71; B.Visual Art, Ga. State U., 1984. Visual merchandising staff Macy's Dept. Store, Union City, Ga., 1985-86; embroidery designer So. Promotions, Peachtree City, Ga., 1987-90; portrait artist Personal Touch Portraits, Peachtree City, Ga., 1991-95, Margy's Portraiture, Peachtree City, 1996—. Mortar Bd. scholar, 1984. Fellow Internat. Biographical Ctr. (life); mem. AAUW, Ga. State U. Alumni Assn., Golden Key, Am. Bus. Women's Assn., Nat. Mus. of Women in the Arts. Avocations: cooking, gardening, reading. Home and Office: 207 Battery Way Peachtree City GA 30269-2126

ROBBIE, TIMOTHY JOHN, professional football team executive; b. Minneapolis, MN, Aug. 24, 1955; s. Joseph and Elizabeth Ann (Lyle) R.; m. Ann Marie Franklin, July 15, 1989. BA, Tulane U., 1977. Dir. pub. rels. Ft. Lauderdale (Fla.) Strikers Profl. Soccer Team, 1978, asst. gen. mgr., 1978, gen. mgr., 1980-83; gen. mgr. Minn. Strikers Profl. Soccer Team, Mpls., 1984-87; v.p. pub. affairs Miami (Fla.) Dolphins, 1987-89; pres. Miami Dolphins Ltd., 1990—; chmn. bd. Robbie Stadium Corp., Miami, 1990—. Trustee Fla. Internat. U., Miami, 1990—. Democrat. Roman Catholic. Avocations: reading, traveling, golf. Office: care Miami Dolphins Joe Robbie Stadium 2269 NE 199th St Miami FL 33180*

ROBBINS, ALLEN BISHOP, physics educator; b. New Brunswick, N.J., Mar. 31, 1930; s. William Rei and Helen Grace (Bishop) R.; m. Shirley Mae Gernert, June 14, 1952 (div. 1978); children: Catherine Jean, Marilyn Elizabeth, Carol Ann, Melanie Barbara; m. Alice Harriet Ayars, Jan. 1, 1979. Student, Oberlin Coll., 1948-49; B.S., Rutgers U., 1952; M.S., Yale U., 1953, Ph.D., 1956. Research fellow U. Birmingham (Eng.), 1957-58, lectr., 1960-61; instr. physics Rutgers U., New Brunswick, N.J., 1956-57; asst. prof. physics Rutgers U., 1957-60, assoc. prof., 1960-68, prof., 1968—, chmn. dept. physics and astronomy, 1979-95. Contbr. articles on nuclear physics to profl. jours. Recipient Lindbach Christian and Mary F. Lindbach Found., Rutgers U., 1975. Fellow Am. Phys. Soc.; mem. Am. Assn. Physics Tchrs., AAAS, Phi Beta Kappa, Sigma Xi. Office: Rutgers U Dept Physics & Astronomy PO Box 849 Piscataway NJ 08855-0849

ROBBINS, ANNE FRANCIS See REAGAN, NANCY DAVIS

ROBBINS, BRENDA SUE, early childhood educator; b. Langdale, Ala., June 28, 1950; d. Richard Cecil and Audrey Millicent (Smallwood) R. Student, Mich. State U., 1968-72; BS in Edn., Auburn U., 1974, MS in Edn., 1977. Title 1 reading, math tchr. Muscogee Co. Sch. Dist., Columbus, Ga., 1977-78, fed. preschool tchr., 1978-80, tchr. grade 1, 1980-81, 1984-85, tchr. kindergarten, 1981-84, 1985—; staff devel. instr. Muscogee County Sch. Dist., Columbus, Ga., 1994; presenter in field. Mem. Georgia Assn. Educators, Nat. Edn. Assn. Avocations: snorkeling, whitewater rafting, traveling, reading. Office: St Mary's Elem Sch 4408 St Mary's Rd Columbus GA 31907

ROBBINS, CHANDLER S(EYMOUR), research biologist; b. Belmont, Mass., July 17, 1918; s. Samuel Dowse and Rosa Margaret (Seymour) R.; AB, Harvard U., 1940; MS, George Washington U., 1950, ScD (hon.), U. Md., 1995; m. Eleanor Graham Cooley, Apr. 16, 1948; children: Jane S., Stuart B., George C., Nancy E. Wildlife rsch. biologist U.S. Fish and Wildlife Svc., Nat. Biol. Svc., Patuxent Wildlife Rsch. Ctr., Laurel, Md., 1945—; bd. dirs. Hawk Mountain Sanctuary Assn. Recipient Arthur A. Allen award Cornell Lab. Ornithology, 1979; Paul Bartsch award Audubon Naturalist Soc., 1979; Disting. Service award U.S. Dept. Interior, 1979, 87; Ludlow Griscom award Am. Birding Assn., 1984; Eugene Eisenmann medal Linnaean Soc. N.Y., 1987, Chuck Yeager award Nat. Fish and Wildlife Found., 1990. Fellow Am. Ornithologists' Union; mem. Am. Meteorol. Soc., Internat. Ornithol. Congress, Wilson Ornithol. Soc., Cooper Ornithol. Soc., Eastern Bird Banding Assn., Western Bird Banding Assn., Brit. Trust for Ornithology, Nature Conservancy, Mass. Audubon Soc. Democrat. Author: Birds of North America, 1966; co-author: Birds of Maryland and the District of Columbia, 1958. Editor: Maryland Birdlife, 1947—; tech. editor Audubon Field Notes/American Birds, 1954-89. Home: 7900 Brooklyn Bridge Rd Laurel MD 20707-2822 Office: Patuxent Wildlife Research Ctr Laurel MD 20708

ROBBINS, CONRAD W., naval architect; b. N.Y.C., Oct. 11, 1921; s. Girard David and Ethyl Rae (Bergman) R.; m. Danae Gray McCartney, Jan. 8, 1923 (dec. Jan. 1971); children: Lorraine, Linton, Jennifer; m. Melissa Jahn, Apr. 15, 1971 (dec. Mar. 1992). BSE, U. Mich., 1942. Estimator Pacific Electric Co., Seattle, 1946-47; pres. Straus-Duparquet, Lyons-Alpha, Albert Pick, N.Y.C. and Chgo., 1947-67, C.W. Robbins, Inc., Carefree, Ariz., 1967—; cons. in field. Capt. floating drydock USN, 1942-46. Avocations: travel, gardening, gourmet cooking. Home: 4401 E Mountainview Rd Phoenix AZ 85028 Office: CW Robbins Inc 7500 Stevens Rd Carefree AZ 85377

ROBBINS, CORNELIUS (VAN VORSE), education administration educator; b. Wilmington, Del., Nov. 2, 1931; s. Cornelius V. and Irene (Tatman) R.; m. Janet Porter, Aug. 1953; children: Eva Robbins Burke, Susan Robbins, Laurel Robbins Truax, Melissa Robbins Beegle. B.A. in Polit. Sci, U. Del., 1953, M.Ed. in Social Scis, 1961; Ed.D. in Ednl. Adminstrn, U. Pa., 1964. Mem. faculty U. Del., 1957-58; tchr. Marshallton (Del.) Sch. Dist., 1958-60, Mt. Pleasant (Del.) Sch. Dist., 1960-62; asst. to dir. sch. study councils U. Pa., 1962-64; dean instrn. Ocean County Coll., 1965-67; dean of coll. Community Coll. of Delaware County, Pa., 1967-69; sr. assoc., coll. div. dir. McManis Assocs., Washington, 1969-70; pres. Genesee Community Coll., 1970-75; assoc. chancellor for community colls. SUNY, 1975-85; acting pres. Potsdam State Coll. (N.Y.), 1982-83; pres. Cobleskill (N.Y.) Coll. Agr. & Tech., 1985-92; prof. edn. adminstrn. SUNY, Albany, N.Y., 1992—; cons. Middle States Assn. Colls.; area liaison officer U.S. Mil. Acad., 1972; chmn. SUNY West Pres.'s Council and mem. Chancellor's Council, 1973, 85, 91. Contbr. articles to profl. publs. Served with U.S. Army, 1954-56. Recipient Outstanding Educator's award N.Y. State Assn. Jr. Colls., 1975, Disting. Svc. award Faculty Coun. Community Colls., 1988. Mem. Am. Assn. Higher Edn., State Dirs. of Community Colls. Assn., Phi Delta Kappa. Office: SUNY Albany ED329 Albany NY 12222

ROBBINS, DONALD KENNETH, real estate investment advisor, consultant; b. Portland, Oreg., Sept. 21, 1928; s. Joseph and Anna Mae (Dexter) R.; m. Helen Virginia Holder (div. 1974); children: Beverly, Roland, Sandra, Debra, Roxanne; m. Barbara Ann Rabel, Mar. 10, 1976; children: Gia, Lisa. BS in Engring., U.S. Naval Acad., 1950; AA in Real Estate, Mt. Hood C.C., Gresham, Oreg., 1968. Cert. real estate cons., review appraiser, mortgage underwriter. Enlisted USN, 1945, commn. ensign, 1950, advanced through grades to lt. (j.g.), 1953, resigned, 1955; founder Realty Exch., Portland, 1955—; real estate broker Realty Exch., Portland, 1970-86; registered rep. Omega Securities, Portland, 1973; registered prin. Real Estate Securities Exch. Co., Portland, 1983; exec. dir. Better Housing Trustcorp, Portland, 1988-93; cons. in field; bd. dirs. Realty Factors, Inc., REO Properties, Ltd., Estate Liquidators, Inc., Realty Remodeling Contractors Inc., Realty Trustcorp, USA Bldg. Maintenance Systems Corp., Project 2000, Eagles Net. Com., 1995—, Genesis Group, LLC, 1993—; exec. mgr. Eagles' Investment Club, LLC, Portland, 1994—; State of Oreg. System of Higher Edn. accredited instr. U. Oreg., Eugene. Author, editor (newsletter) Investors' Clinic, 1970—; author DPP Study Outline (NASD), 1980; editor (newsletter) Eagles' Edge, 1995—; editor, pub. (electronic mag.) Eagles Network, 1995—; contbr. articles to Update newsletter, 1980-82. Mem. legis. coun. Oreg. Assn. Realtors, Salem, 1982-85; bd. dirs. Oreg. Housing Now!, Portland, 1990-92, Third Sector, Portland, 1991-92; regional v.p. for 5 Western states Real Estate Securities and Syndication Inst. of the Nat. Assn. Realtors, Chgo., 1981. Mem. Nat. Assn. Securities Dealers, Oreg. Mortgage Brokers Assn., Royal Rosarians of Portland, Oreg., Eagles' Network. Home and Office: 10285 NW Flotoma Dr Portland OR 97229-6218

ROBBINS, FRANK EDWARD, lawyer; b. Hamilton, Ont., Can., Nov. 25, 1924; came to U.S., 1938; s. Frank E. and Mary Swann (Boyd) R.; m. Beatrice Noback, Dec. 20, 1944; children: R. Bruce (dec.) Mary E. Robbins Collina, B. Joanne Robbins Hicken, Frank E. Jr., Jacqueline, John C., George R. B Chem. Engring., Rensselaer Poly. Inst., 1944; JD, George Washington U., 1953. Bar: D.C. 1953, U.S. Ct. Appeals (fed. cir.) 1954, N.Y. 1958, Ill. 1968. Ptnr. Beale & Jones, Washington, 1953-56; pvt. practice, Rochester, N.Y., 1956-60; gen. counsel Photostat div. Itek Corp., Rochester, 1960-63; dir. patents and licensing Kennecott Corp., N.Y.C., 1963-66; patent and trademark counsel CPC Internat., Inc., N.Y.C., 1966-76; assoc. Irons & Sears, Washington, 1976-79, ptnr., 1979-81; sr. ptnr. Robbins & Laramie, Washington, 1981-90; ptnr. Venable, Baetjer, Howard & Civiletti, Washington, 1990-94; sr. of counsel Roylance, Abrams, Berdo & Goodman, Washington, 1994—. Author: The Defense of Prior Invention, 1977; author, editor: Candor in Prosecution, 1985. Treas. Quaint Acres Civic Assn., Silver Spring, Md., 1984-89. Lt. (j.g.) USNR, 1944-47. Mem. ABA, Assn. Corp. Patent Counsel, Am. Intellectual Property Law Assn., Md. Patent Law Assn. (past pres., bd. govs. 1985—), D.C. Bar Assn., Assn. Bar D.C. Democrat. Unitarian. Avocation: gardening. Office: Roylance Abrams Berdo & Goodman 1225 Connecticut Ave NW Washington DC 20036-2680

ROBBINS, FRANK ERNEST, linguistics educator, administrator; b. Elmira, N.Y., May 12, 1926; s. David Earl and Anna Evelyn (Dunning) R.; m. Ethel Louise Anderson, Aug. 23, 1947; children: Sara, Larry, Anna Jo, David. BA in Greek and Latin, Houghton Coll., 1949, LittD (hon.), 1991; MA in Linguistics, Cornell U., 1960, PhD in Linguistics, 1965. Br. dir. Summer Inst. Linguistics, Mexico City, 1965-72; v.p. acad. affairs Summer Inst. Linguistics, Internat., 1972-75, exec. v.p., 1976-84; area dir. for Africa, rsch. supr. Summer Inst. Linguistics, Nairobi, Kenya, 1984-89; pres., bd. dirs. Summer Inst. Linguistics, Dallas, 1990—; dir. Okla. Summer Inst. Linguistics Sch. U. Okla., Norman, 1972-73; dir. Tex. Summer Inst. Linguistics Sch. U. Tex., Arlington, 1971-73; adj. prof. U. Tex., Arlington, 1990—; cons. in field; bd. dirs Ctr. for Applied Linguistics, 1976-84, vice chmn., 1983-84; mem. literacy adv. bd. Summer Inst. Linguistics, 1991—. Author: Quiotepec Chinantec Grammar; Training in Linguistics, SIL, Its Works and Contributions, 1977; contbr. articles to profl. jours. NDFL fellow, 1962-64. Mem. Linguistic Soc. Am., West African Linguistic Soc. Presbyterian. Office: Summer Inst Linguistics 7500 W Camp Wisdom Rd Dallas TX 75236-5628

ROBBINS, FREDERICK CHAPMAN, physician, medical school dean emeritus; b. Auburn, Ala., Aug. 25, 1916; s. William J. and Christine (Chapman) R.; m. Alice Havemeyer Northrop, June 19, 1948; children: Alice, Louise. AB, U. Mo., 1936, BS, 1938; MD, Harvard U., 1940; DSc (hon.), John Carroll U., 1955, U. Mo., 1958, U. N.C., 1979, Tufts U., 1983, Med. Coll. Ohio, 1983; LLD, U. N.Mex., 1968. Diplomate Am. Bd. Pediatrics. Intern Children's Hosp., Boston, 1941-42, resident, 1940-41, resident pediatrican, 1946-48; sr. fellow virus disease Nat. Rsch. Coun., 1948-50; staff rsch. div. infectious diseases Children's Hosp., Boston, 1948-50, assoc. physician, assoc. dir. isolation svc., asso. rsch. div. infectious diseases, 1950-

52; instr., assoc. in pediatrics Harvard Med. Sch., 1950-52; dir. dept. pediatrics and contagious diseases Cleve. Met. Gen. Hosp., 1952-66; prof. pediatrics Case Western Res. U., 1950-80, dean Sch. Medicine, 1966-80, univ. prof., dean emeritus, 1980—, univ. prof. emeritus, 1987—; pres. Inst. Medicine, NAS, 1980-85; vis. scientist Donner Lab., U. Calif., 1963-64. Served as maj. AUS, 1942-46; chief virus and rickettsial disease sect. 15th Med. Gen. Lab. investigations infectious hepatitis, typhus fever and Q fever. Decorated Bronze Star, 1945; recipient 1st Mead Johnson prize application tissue culture methods to study of viral infections, 1953; co-recipient Nobel prize in physiology and medicine, 1954; Med. Mut. Honor Award for, 1969; Ohio Gov.'s award, 1971. Mem. Assn. Am. Med. Colls. (Abraham Flexner award 1987), Nat. Acad. Scis., Am. Acad. Arts and Scis., Am. Soc. Clin. Investigation (emeritus mem.), Am. Acad. Pediatrics, Soc. Pediatric Research (pres. 1961-62, emeritus mem.), Am. Pediatric Soc., Am. Philos. Soc., Phi Beta Kappa, Sigma Xi, Phi Gamma Delta. Office: Case Western Res U Sch Med 10900 Euclid Ave Cleveland OH 44106-1712*

ROBBINS, HAROLD, author; b. N.Y.C., May 21, 1916; m. Lillian Machnivitz (div.); m. Grace Palermo (div.); children: Caryn, Adreana; m. Jann Stapp. Student pub. schs., N.Y.C. In food factoring bus., until 1940; shipping clk. Universal Pictures, N.Y.C., 1940-46. Author: Never Love a Stranger, 1948, The Dream Merchants, 1949, A Stone for Danny Fisher, 1951, Never Leave Me, 1953, 79 Park Avenue, 1955, Stiletto, 1953, The Carpetbaggers, 1961, Where Love Has Gone, 1962, The Adventurers, 1966, The Inheritors, 1969, The Betsy, 1971, The Pirate, 1974, Lonely Lady, 1976, Dreams Die First, 1977, Memories of Another Day, 1979, Goodbye, Janette, 1981, Spellbinder, 1982, Descent for Xanadu, 1984, The Storyteller, 1985, The Piranhas, 1991, The Raiders, 1994, The Stallion, 1996. Office: McIntosh & Otis 310 Madison Ave New York NY 10017 also: care Simon & Schuster 1230 6th Ave New York NY 10020-1513

ROBBINS, HARVEY ARNOLD, textile company executive; b. N.Y.C., Apr. 29, 1922; s. Ira B. and Mildred (Lowy) R.; student U. Mich., 1940-42, Cornell U., 1943, Columbia U., 1945; m. Carolyn Edith Goldsmith, June 8, 1947; children—Margaret Ann (Mrs. Jay Jacobson), James Andrew. Vice pres. Silberstein-Goldsmith, N.Y.C., 1946-50, North Advt., Chgo., 1950-59; v.p. M. Lowenstein & Sons, Inc., N.Y.C., also pres. Wamsutta/Pacific Domestic div., 1959-69; pres. Burlington Domestics div. Burlington Industries, N.Y.C., 1969-73; v.p. United Mchts. & Mfrs., N.Y.C., 1973-78; v.p. PRF Corp., 1978-80; exec. v.p. Whisper Soft Mills, N.Y.C., 1980-84; dir. product devel. Springs Industries, N.Y.C., 1984-85, textile cons., 1985—. Bd. dirs. Fedn. for Handicapped, Ednl. Found. for Fashion Industries; corp. mem. Lesley Coll., Cambridge, Mass. Served with U.S. Army, 1942-45. Decorated Purple Heart, Combat Inf. badge. Mem. Am. Mgmt. Assn., Am. Arbitration Assn., Nat. Bath, Bed and Linen Assn. (dir., treas.), Textile Distbrs. Assn. Clubs: Woodmere Bay Yacht (trustee); U. Mich. Alumni. Home and Office: 35 Brook Rd Valley Stream NY 11581-2401

ROBBINS, HENRY ZANE, public relations and marketing executive; b. Winston-Salem, N.C., Jan. 17, 1930; s. Romulus Mayfield and Vera Ethel (Daniel) R.; m. Barbara Anne Brown, Jan. 19, 1955; children: Zane Scott, Jill Stewart, Gail Ruth. AB, U. N.C., 1952; student, Emory U., 1952. Reporter Atlanta Constn., 1952; exhibit specialist Gen. Electric Co., Schenectady, 1952; employee relations specialist Gen. Electric Co., Cin., 1955; editor Gen. Electric Co., Schenectady, 1955; account supr. Gen. Electric Co., Winston-Salem, 1956-58; group supr. Gen. Electric Co., Schenectady, 1958-60; v.p., gen. mgr. Burson-Marsteller, Pitts. and Chgo., 1960-70, sr. v.p., 1970; pres., chief exec. officer SL&H-Robbins Inc., Chgo., 1970-72; also dir.; pres., chief exec. officer Beveridge Kraus Robbins & Manning, Chgo., 1973-75; also dir.; pres., dir., chief exec. officer Beveridge and Robbins Inc., Chgo., 1975-77; pres., chief exec. officer Financial Advt. of Ill., Inc., Chgo.; mng. dir. Sports Mgmt. Group, Chgo., 1975-77; dir. communications Arthur Andersen & Co., Chgo. and Geneva, Switzerland, 1977-81; dir. mktg. support services Arthur Andersen & Co., Chgo. and Geneva, 1981-89, dir. mktg. and comms., 1989-91; mem. Worldwide Alpha Group, 1991-96, exec. dir. global 1000 program, 1995—; prin. Arthur Andersen & Co., 1980—; exec. dir. Global 1000 Program, 1995—; mem. journalism adv. com. Harper Coll.; pub. relations com. Chgo. Met. Crusade Mercy; mem. Nat. Task Force on Environment; cons. sec. Dept. Health, Edn. and Welfare, 1970; chmn. pub. relations com. Honor Am. Day Com., 1970. Author: Vision of Grandeur, 1988; contbr. articles to profl. jours. Counselor Council of Mojave, 1972-74; gen. chmn. Chgo. Children's Classic Golf Tournament, 1974-77; chmn. Chgo. fin. com. Am.'s Freedom Train, 1976; chmn. fund devel. com. Presbytery of Chgo., 1977-83, maj. mission fund, 1977-79; dist. commr. Boy Scouts Am., 1976-79, chmn. Wildcat dist., 1980-83; mem. exec. bd. N.E. Ill. council, 1980-85; mem. Republican Citizens Com. Ill., 1960-61, Allegheny County (Pa.) Rep. Com., 1962-65; Trustee Roycemore Sch., Evanston, 1971-74; trustee, v.p. devel. Child and Family Services Chgo.; bd. dirs. Fellowship of Christian Athletes, U. N.C. Alumni Ill., Stockbrokers Assn. Chgo. Served to 1st lt. AUS, 1952-54. Elected to N.C. Pub. Rels. Hall of Fame, 1994. Mem. Pub. Relations Soc. Am., Nat. Investor Relations Inst., Midwest Travel Writers Assn., Chgo. Ednl. TV Assn., Pub. Relations Counselors Roundtable, Am. Mgmt. Assn., Environ. Writers Assn. Am., Chgo. Assn. Commerce and Industry, Art Inst. Chgo., Univ. Club, Sunset Ridge Country Club, Chi Psi. Republican. Presbyterian. Home: 2759 Broadway Ave Evanston IL 60201-1556 Office: 69 W Washington St Chicago IL 60602-3004

ROBBINS, HULDA DORNBLATT, artist, printmaker; b. Atlanta, Oct. 19, 1910; d. Adolph Benno and Lina (Rosenthal) Dornblatt. Student, Phila. Mus's. Sch. Indsl. Art, 1928-29, Prussian Acad., Berlin, 1929-31, Barnes Found., Merion, Pa., 1939. Poster designer and maker ITE Circuit Breaker Co. Inc., Phila., 1944; instr. serigraphy Nat. Serigraph Soc. Sch., N.Y.C., 1953-60; instr. creative painting Atlantic County Jewish Community Centers, Margate and Atlantic City, N.J., 1960-67; represented by WIlliam P. Carl, Fine Prints, Boston, The Picture Store, Boston. One-man shows, Lehigh U. Art Galleries, 1933, ACA Galleries, Phila., 1939, 8th St. Gallery, N.Y.C., 1941, Serigraph Gallery, N.Y.C., 1947, Atlantic City Art Center, 1961, 71, numerous group shows, 2d Nat. Print ann. Bklyn. Mus., Carnegie Inst., Library of Congress, LaNapoule Art Found., Am. Graphic Contemporary Art; represented in permanent collections, including, Met. Mus. Art, N.Y.C., Mus. Modern Art, N.Y.C., Bibliotheque Nationale, Smithsonian Instn., Art Mus. Ont., Can., Victoria and Albert Mus., London, U.S. embassies abroad, Lehigh U., Princeton (N.J.) Print Club. Recipient Purchase prize Prints for Children, Mus. Modern Art, N.Y.C., 1941; prize 2d Portrait of Am. Competition, 1945; 2d prize Paintings by Printmakers, 1948. Mem. Am. Color Print Soc., Print Club, Graphics Soc., Serigraph Soc. (mem. founding group, charter sec., Ninth Ann. prize 1948, 49). Home and Office: 16 S Buffalo Ave Ventnor City NJ 08406-2635 *To cherish and express living through devotion to art.*

ROBBINS, JANE BORSCH, library science educator, information science educator; b. Chgo., Sept. 13, 1939; d. Reuben August and Pearl Irene (Houk) Borsch; married; 1 child, Molly Warren. B.A., Wells Coll., 1961; M.L.S., Western Mich. U., 1966; Ph.D., U. Md., 1972. Asst. prof. library and info. sci. U. Pitts., 1972-73; asso. prof. Emory U., Atlanta, 1973-74; cons. to the bd. Wyo. State Library, 1974-77; asso. prof. La. State U., Baton Rouge, 1977-79; dean La. State U. (Sch. Library and Info. Sci.), 1979-81; prof., dir. Sch. Library and Info. Studies U. Wis., Madison, 1981-94; dean, prof. Sch. Libr. and Info. Studies Fla. State U., Tallahassee, 1994—. Author: Public Library Policy and Citizen Participation, 1975, Public Librarianship: A Reader, 1982, Are We There Yet?, 1988, Libraries: Partners in Adult Literacy, 1990, Keeping the Books: Public Library Financial Practices, 1992, Balancing the Books: Financing American Public Library Services, 1993, Evaluating Library Programs and Services: A Manual and Sourcebook, 1994; editor Libr. and Info. Sci. Rsch., 1982-92; contbr. articles to profl. jours. Mem. ALA (councilor 1976-80, 91-95), Am. Soc. Info. Sci., Assn. for Libr. and Info. Sci. Edn. (dir. 1979-81, pres. 1984), Wis. Libr. Assn. (pres. 1986), Fla. Libr. Assn. Democrat. Episcopalian. Office: Fla State U Sch Libr and Info Studies Louis Shores Bldg Tallahassee FL 32306

ROBBINS, JEFFREY HOWARD, media consultant, research writer, educator; b. N.Y.C., Mar. 29, 1941; s. Stanley Samuel and Miriam (Cooper) R.; m. Marsha Sue Rimler, Nov. 3, 1984; 1 child, Nina Camille. BSME, Carnegie Mellon U., 1962; MS in Physics, U. N.Mex., 1966, ABD in Physics, 1967; postgrad., U. Calif., Berkeley and L.A., 1963-64. Summer rsch. assoc. Linde Co., Tonawanda, N.Y., 1961; rsch. engr. N.Am. Aviation (Rockwell), Downey, Calif., 1962-64; summer rsch. assoc. Los Alamos (N.Mex.) Nat. Lab., 1965; sr. engr. Radio Engring. Labs., L.I., N.Y., 1968-70; engring. cons. PRD Electronics, Syosset, N.Y., 1972-73; sr. cons. Bendix Corp., Teterboro, N.J., 1974-76; sr. engr. Giordano Assocs., Franklin Lakes, N.J., 1977-81; sr. applications engr. Racal-Redak, Mahwah, N.J., 1981-83; tech. media cons. Allied Signal Corp., Teterboro, 1983-92, U.S. Army, Picatinny Arsenal, N.J., 1992, Ford Motor Co., Lansdale, Pa., 1992—; cons., rsch. writer media literacy programs Packer Collegiate Inst., Bklyn., N.Y.C., 1992-93, On TV, Inc., N.Y.C., 1992—; initiator, moderator Media Literacy Forum, 1995; evening sch. instr. New Sch. for Social Rsch., N.Y.C., 1979-85; presenter in field. Author: On Balance and Higher Education, 1970; contbr. articles to profl. jours. Organizer, co-moderator Future Impact of Artificial Intelligence, Robotics Forum, 1984. Recipient 1st prize for essay The World and I Mag., 1990; nominee Grawemeyer award in Edn., 1988; NDEA fellow, 1966-67, others; feature essay premier issue Plain mag., 1994. Mem. IEEE (presenter Internat. Symposium in Tech. and Soc. 1993, 96, Internat. Soc. Sys. Scis. Conf. 1993, 95, initiator, moderator, media literacy forum Packer Collegiate Inst. 1995), N.Y. Acad. Scis., Sigma Xi, Phi Kappa Phi, Pi Tau Sigma. Home: 133 E Penn St Long Beach NY 11561 Office: Cassiopeia Cons Inc PO Box 335 Long Beach NY 11561-0335

ROBBINS, JEROME, choreographer, director; b. N.Y.C., Oct. 11, 1918; s. Harry and Lena (Rips) R. Student, NYU, 1935-36, hon. degree, 1985; D.F.A. (hon.), Ohio U., 1975; studied ballet, modern, Spanish and Oriental dance.; hon. degree, CUNY, 1980. Mem. panel N.Y. Council on Arts, 1973-77, Nat. Council on Arts, Nat. Endowment for Arts, 1974-80; Ballet Theatre (N.Y.C.), 1940-44, soloist, 1941-44; choreographer N.Y.C. Ballet, 1944—, assoc. artistic dir., 1949-59, ballet master, 1969-83, co-ballet master-in-chief, 1983-89; dir., Ballet U.S.A., 1958-61, Jerome Robbins Chamber Dance Co., tour Peoples' Republic of China (sponsored by U.S. Internat. Communications Agency), 1981; ballets also in repertories of Am. Ballet Theatre, Joffrey Ballet, Royal Swedish Ballet, Batsheva Ballet, Royal Danish Ballet, Boston Ballet, Nat. Ballet of Canada, Harkness Ballet, Royal Winnipeg Ballet, London Ballet, Australian Ballet, San Francisco Ballet, Pennsylvania Ballet, Dance Theatre of Harlem, Paris Opera Ballet, Bayerischen Staatsoper (Munich), La Scala, Opernhaus (Surich), Finnish Ballet, Star Dancers Kinov Foundation. Debut as dancer Sandor-Sorel Dance Center, 1937; dancer Broadway musicals Great Lady, 1939, Straw Hat Review, 1939, Keep Off the Grass, 1940; dancer ballets Helen of Troy, 1942, Petrouchka, 1944, Three Virgins and a Devil, 1944, Romeo and Juliet, 1944, Concert Varieties, 1945, Summer Day, 1947, Facsimile, 1947, Bouree Fantasique, 1949, The Prodigal Son, 1950, The Age of Anxiety, 1950, The Pied Piper, 1951, Circus Polka, 1971, George Abbott...A Celebration, 1976; tours include Gypsy, 1959, 81, Fiddler on the Roof, 1964, 80, Peter Pan, 1981, Jerome Robbins Chamber Dance Company, 1981; ballets choreographed include Fancy Free, 1944, Interplay, 1945, Afterthought, 1946, Facsimile, 1946, Summer Day, 1947, Pas de Trois, 1948, The Guests, 1949, (with Balanchine) Jones Beach, 1950, Age of Anxiety, 1950, Pied Piper, 1951, The Cage, 1951, Ballade, 1952, Fanfare, 1953, Afternoon of a Faun, 1953, Wonderful Town, 1953, The Tender Land, 1954, Quartet, 1954, The Concert, 1956, N.Y. Export: Opus Jazz, 1958, Moves, 1959, Les Noces, 1965 (City of Paris award, Internat. Dance Festival 1971), 3X3, 1961, Events, 1961, (with Balanchine) Firebird, 1970, Dances at a Gathering, 1969, In the Night, 1970, The Goldberg Variations, 1971, Requiem Canticles, 1972, (with Balanchine) Dumbarton Oaks, 1972, (with Balanchine) Pulcinella, 1972, Watermill, 1972, Scherzo Fantastique, 1972, Circus Polka, 1972, Interplay, 1972, An Evening's Waltzes, 1973, Celebration: The Art of the Pas de Deux, 1973, Beethoven Pas de Deaux, 1973, Dybbuk Variations, 1974, Introduction & Allegro for Harp, 1975, Une Barque Sur L'Ocean, 1975, Concerto in G (later in G Major), 1975, Ma mere l'oye, 1975, Chansons Madecasses, 1975, Concert for the Royal Ballet, 1975, Introduction, 1975, Allegro For Harp, 1975, Mother Goose, 1975, Other Dances, 1976, A Sketchbook, 1978, (with Peter Martins and Jean-Pierre Bonnefous) Tricolore, 1978, The Dreamer, 1979, Le Bourgeois Gentilhomme, 1979, The Four Seasons, 1979, Opus 19: The Dreamer, 1979, Suite of Dances, 1980, Rondo, 1981, Andantino, 1981, Piano Pieces, 1981, (with Pulchinella 1972 and Firebird 1970) Allegro con Grazia, 1981, The Gershwin Concerto, 1982, Four Chamber Works, 1982, Glass Pieces, 1983, I'm Old Fashioned, 1983, Antique Epigraphs, 1984, (with Twyla Tharp) Brahms/Handel, 1984, Eight Lines, 1985, In Memory Of..., 1985, Quiet City, 1986, Piccolo Balletto, 1986, Ives, Songs, 1988, N.Y.C. Retrospective of Jerome Robbins' Ballets, 1989, (with Mikhail Baryshnikov) A Suite of Dances, 1994, 2+3 Part Inventions, 1994; choreographer of Broadway musicals Billion Dollar Baby (Donaldson award 1946), 1946, High Button Shoes (Tony award best choreographer 1948, New York Drama Critics' award 1948), 1947, Miss Liberty, 1949, The King and I, 1951 (Donaldson award 1951), Two's Company (Donaldson award 1952), 1952; dir. and choreographer stage musicals Look Ma, I'm Dancin', 1948, Call Me Madam, 1950, Peter Pan, 1954, Bells Are Ringing, 1956 (Tony award nomination best choreographer 1957), West Side Story, 1957 (Tony award best choreographer 1958, London Evening Standard Drama award 1958), Gypsy (Tony award nomination best director of musical 1960), 1959, Fiddler on the Roof (Drama Critics' Circle award best musical 1965, Tony award best choreographer 1965, Tony award best director of musical 1965), 1964, Jerome Robbins' Broadway (Tony award best director of musical 1989), 1989-90; dir. plays that include That's the Ticket, 1948, The Pajama Game (Donaldson award 1954), 1954, Oh Dad, Poor Dad, Mama's Hung You in the Closet and I'm Feelin So Sad, 1962; choreographer and creator On the Town, 1944; creator of The Small House of Uncle Thomas, 1951; dir. and producer (with Cheryl Crawford) Mother Courage and Her Children (Tony award nomination best play 1963, Tony award nomination best producer 1963), 1963; choreographer motion pictures The King and I (Box Office Blue Ribbon award 1956), 1956, West Side Story, 1960 (SBI Gold Owl award 1961, Outstanding Directorial Achievement award for feature films Directors Guild of Am. 1961, Academy award best director 1961, Laurel award Writer's Guild of Am. West 1961); TV credits include Ford 50th Anniversary Show (Sylvania award 1953), 1953, Peter Pan (Emmy award best choreographer 1955), 1955, 56, 60, Two Duets, 1980, Live from Studio 8H: An Evening of Jerome Robbins' Ballets, 1980. Decorated chevalier Order of Arts and Letters (France), comdr., 1964; chevalier Legion of Honor (France); Dance Magazine award for outstanding achievement 1950, 57, City of New York Citation, 1959, Hon. Award for Brilliant Achievements in the Art of Choreography on Film, Acad. Motion Picture Arts and Scis., 1961, Capezio Dance award, 1976, recipient Handel medallion N.Y.C., 1976, American-Israel Arts, Sciences, and Humanities award, 1979, Kennedy Ctr. honors, 1981, Brandeis U. Creative Arts award, 1984, Astaire Lifetime Achievement award, 1985, Nat. medal of Arts, 1988, H.C. Andersen Ballet Prize, Royal Danish Theatre, 1988, Drama Desk award, 1989, Commonwealth award of distinguished svc. in the dramatic arts, Bank of Delaware, 1990; named best choreographer Theatre des Nations, 1959. Mem. Am. Acad. and Inst. Arts and Letters (hon., Commonwealth award 1990, Commandeur de l'Ordre des Arts et des Lettres 1990), French Legion of Honor, 1993. Office: care NYC Ballet NY State Theater Lincoln Ctr Plz New York NY 10023

ROBBINS, JERRY HAL, educational administration educator; b. DeQueen, Ark., Feb. 28, 1939; s. James Hal and Barbara I. (Rogers) R. B.A. in Math, Hendrix Coll., 1960; M.Ed., U. Ark., 1963, Ed.D., 1966. Tchr. math. and music Clinton (Ark.) pub. schs., 1960-61; prin. Adrian (Mo.) High Sch., 1961-63; exec. sec. Ark. Sch. Study Council, Fayetteville, 1963-65; mem. faculty U. Miss., University, 1965-74; prof. ednl. adminstrn. U. Miss., 1970-74, chmn. dept. ednl. adminstrn., 1970-74; dean Coll. Edn., U. Ark., Little Rock, 1974-79; asso. v.p. for acad. affairs Ga. State U., Atlanta, 1979-84, dean Coll. Edn., 1984-90, prof. ednl. adminstrn., 1990-91; dean. Coll. Edn. Ea. Mich. U., Ann Arbor, 1991—. Co-author: (with S. B. Williams Jr.) Student Activities in the Innovative School, 1969, School Custodian's Handbook, 1970, Administrator's Manual of School Plant Administration, 1970. Mem. NEA, Am. Assn. Sch. Adminstrs., Am. Assn. Colls. Tchr. Edn. (dir. 1979-82), Nat. Assn. Secondary Sch. Prins., So. Regional Council Ednl. Adminstrn. (pres. 1970-71), Phi Delta Kappa, Kappa Delta Pi (v.p. chpt. devel. 1978-80, pres. elect 1980-82, pres. 1982-84, past pres. 1984-86). Mem. United Meth. Ch. Home and Office: 3323 Breckland Ct Ann Arbor MI 48108 Office: Ea Mich U Boone Hall Ypsilanti MI 48197

ROBBINS, JESSIE EARL, metallurgist; b. York, Ala., Feb. 17, 1944; s. Elbert Jessie and Ella Lee (Hurst) R.; m. Dolly Marie Welch, Apr. 7, 1977; children: Angela Michelle, Amanda Leigh. BS in Engring., U. Ala., 1974. Registered profl. engr. Tex. Welding engr. Chicago Bridge & Iron Co., Brimingham, Ala., 1974-77; metallurgist AMF Tuboscope, Houston, 1977-78; plant metallurgist Tubular Finishing Works, Navasota, Tex., 1978-80; welding engr. Daniel Inds., Houston, 1980-82; welding engr., metallurgist TRW-Mission, Houston, 1982-85; quality assurance engr. Vincotte USA, Houston, 1986-87; welding engr. LTV Missiles & Electronics, Camden, Ark., 1987-90; mgr. tech. svcs. Mavrick Tube Corp., Conroe, Tex., 1990—. With USN, 1961-65. Mem. Am. Petroleum Inst. (com. mem. 1992), Am. Soc. Testing and Materials (com. mem. 1992), Nat. Assn. Corrosion Engrs. (com. mem. 1992), Soc. Petroleum Engring., Grangerland Lions Club (charter). Independent.

ROBBINS, JOHN B., medical researcher; b. Bklyn., Dec. 1, 1932. BA, NYU, 1956, MD, 1959; MD (hon.), U. Goteborg, Sweden, 1976. Intern, resident Children's Med. Svc. Mass. Gen. Hosp., Boston, 1959-60; rsch. fellow dept. pediatrics U. Fla., 1961-64; guest scientist dept. chem. immunology Weizmann Inst. Sci., Rehovot, Israel, 1965-66; asst. prof. pediatrics and microbiology U. Fla., Gainesville, 1964-67; from asst. prof. to assoc. prof. pediatrics Albert Einstein Coll. Medicine, 1967-70; clin. dir. Nat. Inst. Child Health and Human Devel. NIH, 1970-72; chief devel. immunology br. NIH, 1971-74; dir. divsn. bacterial products FDA, 1974-83; chief lab. devel. and molecular immunity Nat. Inst. Child Health and Human Devel. NIH, 1983—; Henry Bale Meml. lectr. Nat. Inst. Biol. Stds. and Control, 1979, Erwin Neter Meml. lectr. U. Buffalo, 1984, Henry L. Barnett lectr. Albert Einstein Coll. Medicine, 1985, Maxwell Finland lectr. Infectious Disease Soc. Am., 1989, Louis Weinstein lectr. Tufts U., 1989. Recipient E. Mead Johnson award Am. Acad. Pediatrics, 1975. Fellow Am. Acad. Microbiology; mem. Inst. Med.-Nat. Acad. Sci., Soc. Pediatric Rsch., Soc. Infectious Disease, Am. Soc. Clin. Investigation, Assn. Am. Physicians, Am. Assn. Immunologists. Office: Nat Inst of Child Hlth & Hum Dev Developmental/Molecular Imm Lab 9000 Rockville Pike Bldg 6 Bethesda MD 20892-0001*

ROBBINS, JOHN CLAPP, management consultant; b. Cleveland, Jan. 22, 1921; s. John Clapp and Esther Turner (Holland) R.; m. Louise Severance Nash, Jan. 10, 1951 (div. Oct. 1974); children: Anne Millikin, Julia Severance, John Nash; m. Beatrice Blair, Aug. 2, 1975 (dec. July 1994). A.B., Harvard U., 1942. Copy boy, reporter, writer, promotion editor Cleve. Press, 1946-57; exec. internat. div. Mobil Oil Corp., N.Y.C., Istanbul, 1957-70; chief exec. officer Planned Parenthood/World Population, N.Y.C., 1970-75; prin. mgmt. cons. Stanford Research Inst., 1976-83; v.p. GPA Inc., N.Y.C., 1983—; pres. John Robbins Assocs. Author: Too Many Asians, 1959. Bd. dirs., pres. Am. Hosp.. Istanbul; treas. Sex Info. and Edn. Coun. U.S., Harvard Libr. in N.Y.C. Capt. AUS, 1942-45. Decorated Bronze Star, Purple Heart; Reid fellow, 1953. Mem. Internat. Planned Parenthood Fedn. London, N.Y. State Republican Family Com. Unitarian. Home: 115 E 9th St New York NY 10003-5414 Office: 98 Riverside Dr New York NY 10024-5323

ROBBINS, LANNY ARNOLD, chemical engineer; b. Wahoo, Nebr., Apr. 3, 1940; s. Earl Willard and Mildred Irene (Hanson) R.; m. Connie Lou Polich, Feb. 24, 1962; children: James Alan, Debra Renea. BS, Iowa State U., 1961, MS, 1963, PhD, 1966. Rsch. engr., project leader Dow Chem. Co., Midland, Mich., 1966-73, rsch. specialist, 1973-76, assoc. scientist, 1976-83, rsch. scientist, 1983-88, sr. rsch. scientist, 1988—; adj. prof. Va. Poly. Inst., Blacksburg, 1973-76, Mich. State U., Lansing, 1983; mem. indsl. adv. bd. Iowa State U., Ames, 1994—. Author (chpt.) Schweitzer's Handbook of Separation Techniques, 1979, Perry's Chemical Engineer's Handbook, 1984. Recipient H.H. Dow medal, 1993. Mem. AIChE. Republican. American Baptist. Achievements include patents for AquaDetox Aqueous Purification stripping devices and process, Sorbathene pressure swing adsorption vent emission control processes, liquid distributors for packed distillation. Avocations: genealogy rsch., maple syrup by mech. vapor recompression evaporation. Home: 4101 Old Pine Tr Midland MI 48642-8892 Office: Dow Chem Co 1319 Bldg Midland MI 48667

ROBBINS, LAWRENCE HARRY, anthropologist; b. Washington, Nov. 22, 1938; s. Maurice and Edith R.; m. Martha Ann Edwards, Dec. 16, 1967; children: Daniel, Brian, Michael, Mark. A.B., U. Mich., 1961, A.M., 1962; Ph.D., U. Calif., Berkeley, 1968. Asst. prof. U. Utah, 1967; mem. faculty Mich. State U., East Lansing, 1968—; prof. anthropology and African studies Mich. State U., 1977—, chairperson ANP dept., 1992-95; vis. research asso. U. Nairobi, Kenya, 1969-70, Nat. Mus. Kenya, 1975-76; Fulbright vis. prof. U. Botswana, 1982-83; vis. archaeologist Nat. Mus. and Art Gallery, Botswana, 1982-83. Author: Stones, Bones and Ancient Cities, 1990; contbr. articles to profl. jours. Grantee NSF, 1965-66, 69-70, 75-77, 91—, Nat. Geographic Soc., 1987, 89. Fellow Am. Anthropol. Assn.; mem. Soc. Africanist Archeologists in Am., So. African Archeol. Soc., Botswana Soc. Office: Dept Anthropology Mich State U East Lansing MI 48824

ROBBINS, MARION LE RON, agricultural research executive; b. Inman, S.C., Aug. 18, 1941; s. Jack Dennis and Christina (Champion) R.; m. Margaret Elanor Wilson, Sept. 25, 1965 (wid. Feb. 1995); children: Jack, Rona, Jeff, Kyle. BS, Clemson U., 1964; MS, La. State U., 1966; PhD, U. Md., 1968. Asst. prof. Iowa State U., Ames, 1968-72; rsch. scientist Clemson U., Charleston, S.C., 1972-83; resident dir. Sweet Potato Rsch. Sta., Chase, La., 1984-88, Calhoun (La.) Rsch. Sta., 1988—; advisor Farm Bur., Monroe, La., 1988-90, Agribus. Coun., Monroe, 1988—. Editor Jour. Vegetable Crop Prodn., 1992—; assoc. editor Crop Prodn. jour., 1972-90; contbr. more than 200 articles, abstracts, rsch. papers and revs. to profl. and trade jours. Delegation leader People to People Internat., Spokane, Wash., 1985—. Mem. Am. Soc. for Hort. Sci. (dir., pres. so. region 1982-83), Rsch. Ctr. Adminstrs. Soc. (dir. 1985), Calhoun Civic Club (pres. 1994-95) Rotary Club (pres. 1987-88), Exch. Club (pres. 1976-77). Presbyterian. Achievements include development of 22 varieties and genetic lines of crop plants, including 2 All-American winners and an All-Am. designate. Office: Calhoun Rsch Sta 321 Highway 80 E Calhoun LA 71225-9703

ROBBINS, MARJORIE JEAN GILMARTIN, elementary education educator; b. Newton, Mass., Sept. 19, 1940; d. John and Helen (Arbuckle) Gilmartin; m. Maurice Edward Robbins, Aug. 1, 1962; children: John Scott, Gregory Dale, Kris Eric. BS in Edn., Gordon Coll., 1962; postgrad., U. Maine, Augusta, 1976, U. Maine, Orono, 1986, U. Maine, Portland, 1987. Cert. tchr. Tchr. Ctr. St. Sch., Hampton, N.H., 1962-64, Claflin Sch., Newton, 1965-66, Israel Loring Sch., Sudbury, Mass., 1966-67, Cheney Sch., Orange, Mass., 1967-69, Palermo (Maine) Consolidated Sch., 1975—; founder, tchr. Primary Edn. Program, Palmero, 1990—; dir., author Child Sexual Abuse Program, Palmero, 1994—; mem. Title I Com., 1995—, Health Curriculum Com., 1995—. Mem. bd. Christian edn. Winter St. Bapt. Ch., Gardiner, Maine, 1993—, mem. bd. missions, 1993-94; bd. dirs. Hillside Christian Nursery Sch., 1994—; coord. student assistance team Maine Sch. Union #51, 1993—, bd. dirs. United Team, 1993—, mem. publicity com., 1991-92, health curriculum com., 1995—, Title I com., 1995—; coord. Nursing Home Ministry, Gardiner. Mem. NEA, Maine Tchrs. Assn., Palermo Tchrs. Assn. (pres. 1984-86), Maine Educators of the Gifted and Talented, Maine Sch. Union 51 (sec. certification steerin g com. 1990—, rep. gifted-talented com. 1976—), Palermo Sch. Club (exec. bd. 19 85-88. Avocations: travel, swimming, camping, basketball. Home: 204 Dresden Ave Gardiner ME 04345-2618 Office: Palermo Consolidated Sch RR 3 Palermo ME 04354

ROBBINS, NANCY LOUISE See MANN, NANCY LOUISE

ROBBINS, OREM OLFORD, insurance company executive; b. Mpls., Feb. 5, 1915; s. Douglas Ford and Grace (Rorem) R.; m. Annette Strand Scherer, May 17, 1992; children: Ford M., Ross S., Gail R. Tomei, Cynthia R. Rothbard. BBA with distinction, U. Minn., 1936; BS in Law, William Mitchell Coll. Law, 1946, JD, 1948. Comml. rep. NW Bell Telephone Co., Mpls., 1936-48; dep. dir. U.S. Treas. Dept., Mpls., 1948-49; sales rep. Conn. Gen. Life Ins. Co., Mpls., 1949-56; founder, chmn. Security Life Ins. Co. Am., Mpls., 1956—. Bd. dirs., past pres. Family and Children's Svcs., Mpls., 1968—; bd. govs., past chmn. Meth. Hosp., Mpls., 1960—; past treas., bd. dirs. Goodwill/Easter Seals, St. Paul, 1958-68, 75-88; life trustee Hamline U., St. Paul, 1979—, chmn. bd. trustees, 1990-91. Col. U.S. Army, 1941-46. Decorated Legion of Merit. Fellow Life Mgmt. Assn.; mem. Am. Soc. CLU (pres. Mpls. chpt. 1959), Health Underwriters Assn., Chartered Fin. Cons., Am. Legion, Skylight Club (Mpls.), Mpls. Minikahda, Hole in the Wall Golf Club, Naples Yacht Club, Masons. Republican. Methodist.

Office: Security Life Ins Co Am 10901 Red Circle Dr Minnetonka MN 55343-9304

ROBBINS, RAY CHARLES, manufacturing company executive; b. Syracuse, N.Y., Sept. 15, 1920; s. Frederick and Mary Elizabeth (Field) R.; children: Sandra Robbins Jannetta, Ray Charles Jr., Eric L. With Lennox Internat. Inc. (formerly Lennox Furnace Co.), 1940-48; asst sales mgr. Lennox Industries Inc. (formerly Lennox Furnace Co.), Syracuse, 1948-52; gen. mgr. new factory and sales office, Lennox Industries, Inc. (formerly Lennox Furnace Co.), Toronto, Ont., Can., 1952-67; dir. Lennox Can. and Timeplan Fin. Co. Ltd., 1953-65; pres. Lennox Can., 1965-69; exec. v.p. Lennox-Worldwide, 1969-70, pres., CEO, 1970-77; chmn. bd. Lennox Can., 1976-92; chmn. bd., chief exec. officer Lennox Industries Inc., 1977-80, chmn. bd., 1980-91, chmn. emeritus, 1991—; bd. dirs. Lennox Internat., First Interstate of Iowa, Inc., Hawkeye Security Ins. Co., Des Moines, Fin. Security Group, Inc., Des Moines, Q-Dot, Garland, Tex.; pres., founder, bd. dirs. Exec. Inst., Inc., Dallas, 1983—; bd. advisor Internat. Exec. Svc. Corp., 1993—. Bd. dirs. Metro Toronto Big Bros., 1964-69, Queensway Gen. Hosp., 1957-69, Texx Found., 1979-81, Bus. Industry Polit. Action Com.; bd. govs., mem. exec. com. Iowa Coll. Found., 1975-78; v.p., mem. exec. bd. Mid-Iowa County Boy Scouts Am., 1972-78; mem. Pres.' Phys. Fitness Council, from 1979; exec. bd. Circle 10 council Boy Scouts Am., from 1979; mem. Dallas Citizens Council; bd. of govs. Nat. Women's Econ. Alliance Found.; bd. dirs. North Tex. Commn. Served with AUS, 1942-45, PTO. Mem. ASHRAE (life), Am. Refrigeration Inst. (bd. dirs. 1973-74, 78, life from 1979, v.p. 1975-76, chmn. 1977), NAM (bd. dirs. 1974-76, dir. at large 1976, dir. State of Iowa 1977-78, dir. State of Tex. 1979-92), Nat. Mgmt. Assn. (exec. adv. com. 1979-92), Gas Appliance Mfrs. Assn. (past bd. dirs.), Can. Gas Assn. (pres.), Can. Mfg. Assn. (chmn. Toronto dist.), U.S. C. of C. (Can.-U.S. sect.), Bus.-Industry Polit. Action Com. (bd. dirs. 1991), Internat. Exec. Svc. Corps (bd. advs. 1993). Clubs: Park Cen., Landmark Athletic, Aerobics Activity Ctr. (Dallas); Canyon Creek Country (Richardson, Tex.). Office: Lennox Internat Inc PO Box 799900 Dallas TX 75379

ROBBINS, RICHARD, composer. Film scores include The Europeans, 1979, Jane Austen in Manhattan, 1980, Quartet, 1981, Heat and Dust, 1983, The Bostonians, 1984, A Room with a View, 1986, My Little Girl, 1986, Sweet Lorraine, 1987, Maurice, 1987, The Perfect Murder, 1988, Slaves of New York, 1989, Bail Jumper, 1990, Mr. and Mrs. Bridge, 1990, The Ballad of the Sad Cafe, 1991, Howards End, 1992 (Academy award nomination best original score 1993), The Remains of the Day, 1993 (Academy award nomination best original score 1993), Jefferson in Paris, 1995. Office: Creative Artists Agency 9830 Wilshire Blvd Beverly Hills CA 90212-1804

ROBBINS, ROBERT B., lawyer; b. Canton, Ohio, Aug. 31, 1951; s. Nathan H. and Evelyn (Cohen) R.; m. Melinda Abbot Street, Oct. 18, 1981; children: Julia Bates, Katherine Melinda, Caroline Rachel, Eli Street. AB, Cornell U., 1972; JD, Harvard U., 1975. Bar: D.C. 1975. Ptnr. Shaw, Pittman, Potts & Trowbridge, Washington, 1976—, also vice chmn. corp. group; chmn. D.C. Bar Commn. on Broker-Dealer Regulation, 1985-90; trustee, mem. exec. bd. Greater Washington Rsch. Ctr., 1993—; co-chmn. Ann. Course Study on Pvt. Placements, Am. Law Inst.-ABA, 1992—. Mem. D.C. Bar (steering com., sect. corp., fin. and securities law 1991-94, chmn. 1993-94). Office: Shaw Pittman Potts & Trowbridge 2300 N St NW Washington DC 20037-1122

ROBBINS, STEPHEN J. M., lawyer; b. Seattle, Apr. 13, 1942; s. Robert Mads and Aneita Elberta (West) R.; children: Sarah E.T., Alicia S.T. AB, UCLA, 1964; JD, Yale U., 1971. Bar: D.C. 1973, U.S. Dist. Ct. D.C. 1973, U.S. Ct. Appeals (D.C. cir.) 1973, U.S. Ct. Appeals (3d cir.) 1973, U.S. Dist. Ct. (ea. and no. dists.) Calif. 1982, U.S. Dist. Ct. (cen. dist.) Calif. 1983, Supreme Ct. of Republic of Palau, 1994. Pres. U.S. Nat. Student Assn., Washington, 1964-65; assoc. Steptoe & Johnson, Washington, 1972-75; chief counsel spl. inquiry on food prices, com. on nutrition and human needs U.S. Senate, Washington, 1975; v.p., gen. counsel Straight Arrow Pubs., San Francisco, 1975-77; dep. dist. atty. City and County of San Francisco, 1977-78; regional counsel U.S. SBA, San Francisco, 1978-80; spl. counsel Warner-Amex Cable Communications, Sacramento, 1981-82; ptnr. McDonough, Holland and Allen, Sacramento, 1982-84; v.p. Straight Arrow Pubs., N.Y.C., 1984-86; gen. legal counsel Govt. State of Koror, Rep. of Palau, Western Caroline Islands, 1994-95; ptnr. Robbins & Livingston, Sacramento, 1986—. Staff sgt. U.S. Army, 1966-68. Mem. ABA (sect. urban, state and local govt. law-land use, planning and zoning com., sect. real property, probate and trust law, sect. natural resources energy, environ. law, forum com. on affordable housing and cmty. devel.), Internat. Mcpl. Lawyers Assn., D.C. Bar, State Bar of Calif., Urban Land Inst. (assoc.), Am. Planning Assn. (planning and law divsn., internat. divsn.), Internat. Urban Devel. Assn., Law Assn. for Asia and the Pacific, LawAsia. Unitarian. Avocations: theatre, art, hiking. Office: Robbins & Livingston 3300 Douglas Blvd Ste 365 Roseville CA 95661-3829

ROBBINS, TIM(OTHY FRANCIS), actor; b. N.Y.C., Oct. 16, 1958. BA, UCLA, 1981. Founder, artistic dir. The Actor's Gang, 1981—. Actor: (films) No Small Affairs, 1984, Toy Soldiers, 1984, Fraternity Vacation, 1985, The Sure Thing, 1985, Howard the Duck, 1986, Top Gun, 1986, Five Corners, 1987, Bill Durham, 1988, Tapeheads, 1989, Eric The Viking, 1989, Twister, 1989, Miss Firecracker, 1989, Cadillac Man, 1990, Jacob's Ladder, 1990, Jungle Fever, 1991, The Player, 1992 (Best Actor award Cannes Film Festival 1992), Short Cuts, 1993, The Hudsucker Proxy, 1994, The Shawshank Redemption, 1994, Ready to Wear (Prêt-à-Porter), 1994, I.Q., 1994; dir., writer, actor: Bob Roberts, 1992; dir., writer: Dead Man Walking, 1995 (Golden Globe award nominee for best dir. of film 1996, Acad. award nominee for best dir. 1996); (TV movies) Quarterback Princess, 1983, Malice in Wonderland, 1985; dir., actor: (play) Ubu Roi (L.A. Weekly Dir. award); dir. (plays) A Midsummer's Night Dream, Methusalem, the Eternal Bourgeois, The Good Woman of Setzuan (L.A. Drama Critics Circle nominee); co-writer: Alagazam, After the Dog Wars, Violence: The Misadventures of Spike Spangle, Farmer, Carnage, A Comedy. Office: Care ICM 8942 Wilshire Blvd Beverly Hills CA 90211-1934

ROBBINS, TOM, author; b. Blowing Rock, N.C., 1936; m. Terrie Hemingway (div.); 1 child, Fleetwood Starr. Student, Washington and Lee U., 1954-56, U. Wash., 1963; degree in social sci., Va. Commonwealth U., 1959. Former copy editor Richmond (Va.) Times-Dispatch, Seattle Post-Intelligencer; art critic Seattle Times. Author: (biography) Guy Anderson, 1965, (fiction) Another Roadside Attraction, 1971, Even Cowgirls Get the Blues, 1976, Still Life with Woodpecker, 1980, Jitterbug Perfume, 1984, Skinny Legs and All, 1990, Half Asleep in Frog Pajamas, 1994. With USAF. Office: PO Box 338 La Conner WA 98257-0338

ROBBINS, VERNON EARL, lawyer, accountant; b. Balt., Aug. 16, 1921; s. Alexander Goldborough and Anne Jeanette (Bubb) R.; m. Ruth Adele Holland, Oct. 21, 1941; m. 2d, Alice Sherman Meredith, Feb. 17, 1961; 1 dau., Sharon R. Fick; 1 stepdau., Susan V. Henry. A.B.A., Md. Sch. Acctg., 1941; J.D., U. Balt., 1952. Bar: Md. 1952. Internal revenue agt. IRS, Balt., 1945-52; ptnr. Robbins, Adam & Co., C.P.A. firm, Cambridge, Md., 1952—; sole practice law, Cambridge, 1952—; bd. dirs. Bank of Eastern Shore. Served with U.S. Maritime Service, 1941-45. Named Boss of Yr., Tidewater chpt. Nat. Secs. Assn., 1978. Mem. ABA, Md. bar Assn., Am. Inst. C.P.A.s, Md. Assn. C.P.A.s, Am. Assn. Atty.-C.P.A.s, Am. Judicature Soc., Navy League, Dorchester County Hist. Soc., Dorchester Art Center. Democrat. Methodist. Club: Cambridge Yacht. Lodges: Elks, Masons, Shriners. Office: PO Box 236 126 Market Square Cambridge MD 21613

ROBBINS-WILF, MARCIA, educational consultant; b. Newark, Mar. 22, 1949; d. Saul and Ruth (Fern) Robbins; 1 child, Orin. Student, Emerson Coll., 1967-69, Seton Hall U., 1969, Fairleigh Dickinson U., 1970; BA, George Washington U., 1971; MA, NYU, 1975; postgrad., St. Peter's Coll., Jersey City, 1979, Fordham U., 1980; MS, Yeshiva U., 1981, EdD, 1986; postgrad., Monmouth Coll., 1986. Cert. elem. tchr., N.Y., N.J., reading specialist, N.J., prin., supr., N.J., adminstr., supr., N.Y. Tchr. Sleepy Hollow Elem. Sch., Falls Church, Va., 1971-72, Yeshiva Konvitz, N.Y.C., 1972-73; intern Wee Folk Nursery Sch., Short Hills, N.J., 1978-81, dir. day camp, 1980-81, tchr., dir., owner, 1980-81; adj. prof. reading Seton Hall U., South Orange, N.J., 1987, Middlesex County Coll., Edison, N.J., 1987-88; asst. adj. prof. L.I. U., Bklyn., 1988, Pace U., N.Y.C., 1988—; ednl. cons. Cranford High Sch., 1988; presenter numerous workshops; founding bd. dirs. Stern Coll. Women Yeshiva U., N.Y.C., 1987; adj. vis. lectr. Rutgers U., New Brunswick, N.J., 1988. Chairperson Jewish Book Festival, YM-YWHA, West Orange, N.J., 1986-87, mem. early childhood com., 1986—, bd. dirs., 1986—; vice chairperson dinner com. Nat. Leadership Conf. Christians and Jews, 1986; mem. Hadassah, Valerie Children's Fund, Women's League Conservative Judaism, City of Hope; assoc. bd. bus. and women's profl. divsn. United Jewish Appeal, 1979; vol. reader Goddard Riverside Day Care Ctr., N.Y.C., 1973; friend N.Y.C. Pub. Libr., 1980—; life friend Millburn (N.J.) Pub. Libr.; pres. Seton-Essex Reading Coun., 1991-94. Co-recipient Am. Heritage award, Essex County, 1985; recipient Award Appreciation City of Hope, 1984, Profl. Improvement awards Seton-Essex Reading Council, 1984-86, Cert. Attendance award Seton-Essex Reading Counci, 1987. Mem. N.Y. Acad. Scis. (life), N.J. Council Tchrs. English, Nat. Council Tchrs. English, Am. Ednl. Research Assn., Coll. Reading Assn. (life), Assn. Supervision and Curriculun Devel., N.Y. State Reading Assn. (council Manhattan), N.J. Reading Assn. (council Seton-Essex), Internat. Reading Assn., Nat. Assn. for Edn. of Young Children (life N.J. chpt., Kenyon group), Nat. Council Jewish Women (vice chairperson membership com. evening br. N.Y. sect. 1974-75), George Washington U. Alumni Club, Emerson Coll. Alumni Club, NYU Alumni Club, Phi Delta Kappa (life), Kappa Gamma Chi (historian). Club: Greenbrook Country (Caldwell, N.J.); George Washington Univ. Avocations: reading, theatre. Home: 242 Hartshorn Dr Short Hills NJ 07078-1914 also: 820 Morris Tpke Short Hills NJ 07078-2619

ROBE, LUCY BARRY, editor, educator; b. Boston, Jan. 15, 1934; d. Herbert Jr. and Lucy (Brown) Barry; m. Robert S. Robe Jr., Feb. 6, 1971; 1 child, Parrish C. BA, Harvard U., 1955; MA in Med. Writing, Pacific Western U., 1992. Writer Alcoholism Update Biomed. Info. Corp., N.Y.C., 1979-85; editor newsletter Am. Soc. of Addiction Medicine News, Washington, 1985-95; conf. mgr. Fla. Soc. of Addiction Medicine News; v.p. L.I. Coun. on Alcoholism, Mineola, N.Y., 1978-92. Author: Just So It's Healthy, 1978, Haunted Inheritance, 1982, Co-Starring: Famous Women & Alcohol, 1986; editor numerous books. Mem. Authors Guild of Am., Am. Med. Writer's Assn. Office: 509-D1 Sea Oats Dr Juno Beach FL 33408

ROBE, THURLOW RICHARD, engineering educator, university dean; b. Petersburg, Ohio, Jan. 25, 1934; s. Thrulow Scott and Mary Alice (McKibben) R.; m. Eleanora C. Komyati, Aug. 27, 1955; children: Julia, Kevin, Stephen, Edward. B.S.C.E., Ohio U., 1955, M.S. in Mech. Engring., 1962; Ph.D. in Applied Mechanics, Stanford U., 1966. Engr. Gen. Electric Co., Niles, Ohio, Cleve., Erie, Pa., Evendale,Ohio, 1954-60; instr. Ohio U., Athens, 1960-63; asst. prof to prof., assoc. dean U. Ky., Lexington, 1965-80; dean Ohio U., Athens, 1980-96, Cruse W. Moss prof. Engring. Edn., 1992-96; dir. Innovation Ctr. Authority Ohio U., 1983-96; dean emeritus Russ Coll. Engring. and Tech., U. Ohio, Athens, 1996—; pres., chmn. bd. Q.E.D. Assocs., Inc., Lexington, 1975-83; dir. Databeam Corp., Lexington; bd. dirs. Assn. Ohio Commodores; trustee Engring. Found. Ohio, 1988-94; bd. govs. Edison Materials Tech. Ctr., 1987—. Contbr. articles to profl. jours.; patentee trailer hitch. Bd. dirs. Athens County Community Redevel. Corp., 1980-86; treas. South Lexington Little League, 1976-80; vice chmn. Thoroughbred dist., Boy Scouts Am., 1975-77; pres. Tates Creek High Sch. PTA, Lexington, 1975-76; bd. dirs. U. Ky. Athletics Assn., 1975-80. Served to maj. USAF Res. (ret.). Recipient Alumni medal of merit Ohio U., 1993; named Am. Coun. on Edn. Adminstrn. fellow, 1970-71, Ohio U. Alumnus of Yr., 1996. Mem. ASME, NSPE (Profl. Engring. in Edn. exec. bd., ctrl. region vice-chmn. 1987-89), Am. Soc. Engring. Edn. (Outstanding Contbn. in Rsch. award 1966), Athens Country Club, Athens Reading Club, Athens Symposiarchs, Assn. of Ohio Commodores, Rotary, Sigma Xi, Tau Beta Pi Omicron Delta Kappa, Alpha Lambda Delta. Office: Russ Coll Engring & Tech Ohio U Athens OH 45701

ROBECK, MILDRED COEN, education educator; b. Walum, N.D., July 29, 1915; d. Archie Blane and Mary Henrietta (Hoffman) Coen; m. Martin Julius Robeck, Jr., June 2, 1936; children: Martin Jay Robeck, Donna Jayne Robeck Thompson, Bruce Wayne Robeck. BS, U. Wash., 1950, MEd, 1954, PhD, 1958. Ordnance foreman Sherman Williams, U.S. Navy, Bremerton, Wash., 1942-45; demonstration tchr. Seattle Pub. Schs., 1946-57; reading clinic dir. U. Calif., Santa Barbara, 1957-64; vis. prof. Victoria Coll., B.C., Can., summer 1958, Dalhousie U., Halifax, summer 1964; rsch. cons. State Dept. Edn., Sacramento, Calif., 1964-67; prof., head early childhood edn. U. Oreg., Eugene, Oreg., 1967-86; vis. scholar West Australia Inst. Tech., Perth, 1985; exec. faculty U. Santa Barbara, Calif., 1987-92, 1992-95; trainer evaluator U.S. Office of Edn. Head Start, Follow Thru, 1967-72; cons., evaluator Native Am. Edn. Programs, Sioux, Navajo, 1967-81; cons. on gifted Oreg. Task Force on Talented and Gifted, Salem, 1974-76; evaluator Early Childhood Edn., Bi-Ling. program, Petroleum and Minerology, Dhahran, Saudi Arabia, 1985. Author: Materials KELP: Kgn. Evaluation Learning Pot, 1967, Infants and Children, 1978, Psychology of Reading, 1990; contbr. articles to profl. jours. Evaluation cons. Rosenburg Found. Project, Santa Barbara, 1966-67; faculty advisor Pi Lambda Theta, Eugene, Oreg, 1969-74; guest columnist Oreg. Assn. Gifted and Talented, Salem, Oreg., 1979-81; editorial review bd. ERQ, U.S. Calif., L.A., 1981-91. Recipient Nat. Dairy award 4-H Clubs, Wis., 1934, scholarships NYA and U. Wis., Madison, 1934-35, faculty rsch. grants U. Calif., Santa barbara, 1958-64, NDEA Fellowship Retraining U.S. Office Edn., U. Oreg., 1967-70. Mem. APA, Am. Ednl. Rsch. Assn., Internat. Reading Assn., Phi Beta Kappa, Pi Lambda Theta. Democrat. Avocations: dyslexia research, historical research, duplicate bridge. Home: 95999 Hwy 101 S Yachats OR 97498

ROBEK, MARY FRANCES, business education educator; b. Superior, Wis., Jan. 30, 1927; d. Stephen and Mary (Hervert) R. BE, U. Wis., 1948; MA, Northwestern U., 1951; MBA, U. Mich., 1962, PhD, 1967. Tchr. Bergland (Mich.) High Sch., 1948, Tony (Wis.) High Sch., 1948-50, Sch. Vocat. and Adult Edn., Superior, 1950-58; prof. bus. edn. and office tech. Ea. Mich. U., Ypsilanti, 1958-93; instr. Jazyckova Gymnasium, Banská, Štiavnicá, Slovakia, 1994. Author: Information and Records Management, 1995. Assn. of Records Mgrs. and Adminstrs. fellow, 1992. Mem. Assn. Records Mgrs. and Adminstrs. (life), Inst. Cert. Mgrs. (pres. 1980-81), Cath. Daus. Am., Delta Pi Epsilon, Delta Kappa Gamma, Pi Lambda Theta. Republican. Roman Catholic. Home: 10844 S Nakota Rd Solon Springs WI 54873 *Opportunity to do creative and innovative things without infringing on the rights of others is limited only by priorities set considering people and technology.*

ROBENALT, JOHN ALTON, lawyer; b. Ottawa, Ohio, May 2, 1922; s. Alton Ray and Kathryn (Straman) R.; m. Margaret Morgan Durbin, Aug. 25, 1951 (dec. July 1990); children: John F., William A., James D., Robert M., Mary K., Margaret E., Thomas D.; m. Nancy Leech Kidder, Sept. 21, 1991. B.A., Miami U., 1943; LL.B., Ohio State U., 1948, J.D., 1948. Bar: Ohio 1948. Asst. atty. gen. Ohio, 1949-51; practice in Lima, Ohio, 1951-59; acting municipal judge Lima Municipal Ct., 1955-59; partner Robenalt, Daley, Balyeat & Balyeat, 1959-82; ptnr. Robenalt, Kendall & Robenalt, 1983-85, Robenalt, Kendall, Rodabaugh & Staley, 1985-92, Robenalt & Robenalt, 1993—. Chmn. Lima March of Dimes, 1957-58; Bd. dirs. Lima Civic Center, pres., 1971-72; bd. dirs. Lima Rotating Fund; trustee Allen County Regional Transit Authority, Lima, pres., 1975—. Served with AUS, 1943-45. Mem. ABA, Ohio Bar Assn., Allen County Bar Assn. (pres. 1969-70), Am. Legion, Lima Automobile Club (bd. dirs., pres. 1975-82), Shawnee Country Club (pres. 1968-70), Ohio Automobile Club (trustee 1982—, chmn. 1995—), Elks (bd. trustees 1991—), Rotary, Delta Tau Delta, Phi Delta Phi. Home: 1755 Shawnee Rd Lima OH 45805-3857 Office: 211215 N Elizabeth St Lima OH 45801-4300

ROBERGE, FERNAND ADRIEN, biomedical researcher; b. Thetford Mines, Que., Can., June 11, 1935. BAS, Engr., Poly. Sch. Montreal, Can., 1959, MScA, 1960; PhD in Control Engring., Biomedical Engring., McGill U., 1964. Devel. engr. numerical control Sperry Gyroscope Co., Montreal, 1960-61; from asst. prof. to prof. physiology faculty medicine U. Montreal, 1965-78, prof. biomedical engring., 1978—, dir. biomedical engring. inst. ecole poly., 1978-88, dir. rsch. group biomedical modeling, 1988—; mem. rsch. group neurol. sci. Med. Rsch. Coun. Can. U. Montreal, 1967-75, mem. grant com. biomedical engring., 1971-76; mem. Sci. Coun. Can., 1971-74; mem. sci. com. Can. Heart Found., 1974-77; mem. Killiam Program Can. Coun., 1974-77; mem. elec. engring. com. Nat. Sci. Engring. Rsch. Coun. Can., 1981-83, chmn., 1985-88. Recipient D. W. Ambridge award, 1964, Rousseau award Assn. Can.-France Advancement Sci., 1986, Leon Lortie award, 1987. Fellow IEEE, Can. Med. and Biol. Engring. Soc., Royal Soc. Can.; mem. AAAS, Internat. Fedn. Med. Electronics and Biol. Engring., Can. Physiol. Soc., Biomed. Engring. Soc. Achievements include research in membrane biophysics, cardiovascular regulation and control, cardiac arrhythmias; assessment of medical technologies.

ROBERSON, BRUCE H., lawyer; b. Wilmington, Del., Mar. 7, 1941; s. A. L. and Virginia Amelia (Heerdt) R.; m. Mary E. Abrams; children: Cheryl Anne, David B., Douglas M. B.S. cum laude, Washington and Lee U., 1963; J.D., U. Va., 1966. Bar: Va. 1966, Del. 1966, Fla. 1969. Mem. Morris, Nichols, Arsht & Tunnell, Wilmington, 1966-67; with Holland & Knight, Tampa, Fla., 1969—, ptnr., 1975—. Contbg. editor Warren, Gorham and Lamont Banking and Lending Institution Forms, 1992-96. Served to capt. U.S. Army, 1967-69. Decorated Bronze Star. Fellow Am. Bar Found., Fla. Bar Found. (corp. banking and bus. law sect. exec. coun. 1978-86, chmn. banking law com. 1982-84); mem. ABA (bus. law sect. com. on consumer fin. svcs. 1976—, banking law com. 1980—, savs. instns. com. 1989—), Am. Judicature Soc., Fla. Bar, Del. Bar Assn., Va. Bar Assn., Hillsborough County Bar Assn., Univ. Club, Tampa Yacht and Country Club, Lambda Chi Alpha. Republican. Methodist. Office: Holland & Knight 400 N Ashley Dr Ste 2300 PO Box 1288 Tampa FL 33601-1288

ROBERSON, DEBORAH KAY, secondary school educator; b. Crane, Tex., Jan. 15, 1955; d. David B. and Virginia L. (King) Cole; m. Larry M. Roberson; children: Justin, Jenai, Julie. BS in Secondary Edn., Coll. S.W., 1981; MA in Sch. Adminstrn., Sul Ross State U., 1991. Cert. biology and history tchr., mid-mgmt. cert., supt. cert., Tex., biology and history tchr., Okla. Sci. and social studies tchr. Andrews (Tex.) Ind. Sch. Dist., 1987-95; forum tchr.- gifted social studies program, social studies dept. chair Ctrl. Mid. Sch. Broken Arrow (Okla.) Pub. Schs., 1995—; mem. 7th grade history curriculum com., Andrews Ind. Sch. Dist., 1988, mem. outdoor classroom com., 1989-90, chair sci. curriculum com., 1989-90, chair health curriculum com., 1990-91, mem. Tex. pub. schs. open house com., 1989-90, 92-93, mem. dist. textbook com., 1990-91; secondary edn. rep. Ptnrs. in Parliament, Berlin, 1993; site-based com. Broken Arrow Pub. Schs., 1995—, B.A.S.I.S. com., 1995—, mem. discipline com. 1996—, mem. remediation com., 1996—, others; active Ptnrs. in Edn. Program, Broken Arrow, Tools for Tomorrow 1996 Conf. com. Broken Arrow Pub. Schs. Livestock leader Andrews County 4-H Program, 1985-89; vol. Am. Heart Assn., Andrews, 1988; vol., team mother Little League, Andrews, 1990; vol., treas. Mustang Booster Club, Andrews, 1993-95. Recipient Appreciation awards Mustang Booster Club, 1993, 94, VFW Ladies Aux. Post 10887 award, Broken Arrow, 1996—. Mem. AAUW, Nat. Assn. Secondary Sch. Prins., Nat. Staff Devel. Coun., Assn. Tex. Profl. Educators (pres. local unit 1992-93, mem. resolutions com. 1994-95, appreciation award 1993, sec. region 1993-94, v.p. region 1994-95), ASCD, Tex. Assn. Supervision and Curriculum Devel., Tex. Network for Continuous Quality Improvement, Nat. Coun. Social Studies, Okla. Assn. Supervision and Curriculum Devel., Okla. Alliance Geographic Edn. Avocations: meeting people, travel, golf, rafting, hiking. Home: 708 N Sweet Gum Ave Broken Arrow OK 74012 Office: Broken Arrow Pub Schs Ctrl Mid Sch 210 N Main St Broken Arrow OK 74012

ROBERSON, JAMES O., foundation executive; m. JoAnn Roberson; children: Melanie Merrill, Sharyl Rituccì, James Jr., Trisha Summersheim, Joel. AB in Journalism, Baylor U., 1956; student Indsl. Devel. Inst., U. Okla.; student Inst. Orgnl. Mgmt., U. Houston. Cert. econ. developer. Dir. info. West Tex. C. of C., Abilene, 1956-59; area devel. mgr. Mo.-Kans.-Tex. R.R., 1959-63; exec. dir. Albuquerque Indsl. Devel. Svc., 1963-65; dir. N.Mex. Dept. Devel., Santa Fe, 1965-69; mgr. Forward Metro Denver, 1969-72; dir. R.I. Dept. Econ. Devel., Providence, 1972-77; v.p., dir. new bus. devel. Howard Rsch. and Devel. Corp. subs. Rouse Co., Columbia, Md., 1977-79; sec. Md. Dept. Econ. and Community Devel., Annapolis, 1979-83; pres. Louisville C. of C., 1983-88; pres., CEO Rsch. Triangle Found. N.C., 1988—; chmn. bd. dirs. Charlotte br. Fed. Res. Bank Richmond; cons., speaker in field. Editor West Tex. Today mag., 1956-59. Bd. dirs. N.C. Citizens for Bus. and Industry, N.C. Biotech. Ctr. Fellow Am. Econ. Devel. Coun. (past chmn.); mem. Indsl. Devel. Rsch. Coun., Nat. Assn. State Devel. Agys. (past pres.).

ROBERSON, LINDA, lawyer; b. Omaha, July 15, 1947; d. Harlan Oliver and Elizabeth Aileen (Good) R.; m. Gary M. Young, Aug. 20, 1970; children: Elizabeth, Katherine, Christopher. BA, Oberlin Coll., 1969; MS, U. Wis., 1970, JD, 1974. Bar: Wis. 1974, U.S. Dist. Ct. (we. dist.) Wis. 1974. Legis. atty. Wis. Legis. Reference Bur., Madison, 1974-76, sr. legis. atty., 1976-78; assoc. Rikkers, Koritzinsky & Rikkers, Madison, 1978-79; ptnr. Koritzinsky, Neider, Langer & Roberson, Madison, 1979-85, Stolper, Koritzinsky, Brewster & Neider, Madison, 1985-93, Balisle & Roberson, Madison, 1993—; lectr. U. Wis. Law Sch., Madison, 1978—. Co-author: Real Women, Real Lives, 1981, Wisconsin's Marital Property Reform Act, 1984, Understanding Wisconsin's Marital Property Law, 1985, A Guide to Property Classification Under Wisconsin's Marital Property Act, 1986, 2d edit. 1996, Workbook for Wisconsin Estate Planners, 2d edit., 1993, Look Before You Leap, 1996, Family Estate Planning in Wis., 1992, rev. edit. 1996. Fellow Am. Acad. Matrimonial Lawyers; mem. ABA, Wis. Bar Assn., Dane County Bar Assn., Legal Assn. Women, Nat. Assn. Elder Law Attys. Office: Balisle and Roberson 217 S Hamilton # 302 PO Box 870 Madison WI 53701-0870

ROBERSON, MARK ALLEN, physicist, educator; b. Lufkin, Tex., Nov. 12, 1961; s. Roy and Thelma (Weist) R. AAS, Angelina County Jr. Coll., 1982; BSEE, Tex. A&M U., 1984; MS, Stephen F. Austin State U., 1989; PhD, Tex. Tech. U., 1994. From rsch. asst. to instr. Tex. Tech. U., Lubbock, 1990-95; instr. Vernon (Tex.) Regional Jr. Coll., 1995—. Robert A. Welch Found. fellow, 1991-94. Mem. AAAS, Am. Phys. Soc., Materials Rsch. Soc., Sigma Pi Sigma. Avocation: books. Office: Vernon Regional Jr Coll Vernon TX 76384-4092

ROBERSON, NATHAN RUSSELL, physicist, educator; b. Robersonville, N.C., Dec. 13, 1930; s. Nathan Russell and Myrtle (Taylor) R.; m. Ruth Haislip, June 19, 1954; children: David Wintner, Michael Taylor, Mary Russell. BS, U. N.C., 1954, MS, 1955; PhD, Johns Hopkins U., 1960. Jr. instr. Johns Hopkins U., Balt., 1955-60; research assoc. Princeton (N.J.) U., 1960-63; asst. prof. physics Duke U., Durhan, N.C., 1963-68, assoc. prof., 1968-74, prof., 1974-77; bd. dirs. Triangle Univs. Computation Ctr., 1975-81; mem. instrumentation subcom. Nuclear Sci. Adv. Com., 1982-85; mem. energy sci. network steering com. Dept. Energy, 1987-90, nuclear physics panel on computer networks, 1988-90, dep. dir. Triangle U. Nuclear Lab., 1990-92; dir. Triangle Univs. Nuclear Lab., 1992—. Contbr. articles on physics to profl. jours. Treas. N.C. Council Chs., 1974-79. Fellow Am. Phys. Soc.; mem. IEEE, Am. Assn. Physics Tchrs., Phi Beta Kappa. Presbyterian. Home: 3406 Ogburn Ct Durham NC 27705-5427 Office: Dept Physics Duke U Durham NC 27708

ROBERSON, PATT FOSTER, mass communications educator; b. Middletown, N.Y., Dec. 3, 1934; d. Gilbert Charles and Mildred Elizabeth (O'Neal) Foster; m. Murray Ralph Roberson Jr., May 10, 1963 (dec. 1968). AA, Canal Zone Jr. Coll., 1954; BA in Journalism, La. State U., 1957, MA in Journalism, 1973; MA in Media, So. U., Baton Rouge, 1981; PhD in Mass Communication, U. So. Miss., 1985. Exec. sec. Lionel H. Abshire and Assocs., AIA, Architects, Baton Rouge, 1958-60, Murrell and Callari, AIA, Architects, Baton Rouge, 1960-63; bus. mgr. So. Rev. La. State U., Baton Rouge, 1963-69; free-lance researcher, ind. contractor Baton Rouge, 1969-74; rep. dept. info. State of La., Baton Rouge, 1974-75; asst. prof. mass. comm. So. U., 1976-86, assoc. prof. mass comm., 1986-93, prof. mass comm., 1993—; reviewer Random House Pubs., N.Y.C., 1981; profl. devel. intern Baton Rouge Morning Advocate, 1991, Baker Observer, 1991-92; cons. advt. Baton Rouge Little Theater, 1971—; reporter-photographer Canal Record, Seminole, Fla., 1967—; biographer of Edward Livermore Burlingame, John H. Johnson, Daniel Kimball Whitaker, (book) American mag. journalists series, Dictionary Literary Biography, Detroit, 1986-87; tutor Operation Upgrade, 1978-82. Co-editor: La. State U. cookbook Tiger Bait, 1976; biographer Frank E. Gannett in Biographical Dictionary of American Journalism, 1987; freelance writer/editl. cons.; editl. bd. Am. Journalism, 1986-87; reviewer Longman Publs. 1991-92; contbr. articles to profl. jours. Mem. poll commn. East Baton Rouge Parish Govt., 1978—; pres. Our Lady Lake Regional Med. Ctr., 1971-72; bd. dirs. Dist. Atty.'s Rape Crisis Commn., 1976-79, Plan Govt. Study Commn., 1973-76, Selective Svc. System Bd. 8, Baton Rouge, 1986—; docent Greater Baton Rouge Zoo, 1974-77; vol. ARC, 1989—; mem. East Baton Rouge Parish Commn. on Govtl. Ethics, 1992-93; mayoral appointee Baker Mobile Home Rev. Bd., 1990—; v.p. Baker Hist. and Cultural Found., 1990-93; mem. Baker Inter-club Coun., 1990-91; organizer human-animal therapy svc. Baker Manor Nursing Home, 1994; mem. 1st class Citizens Basic Police Tng. Acad., Baton Rouge Police Dept., 1994. Mem. AAUP (sec.-treas. La. conf. 1988-89, sec. 1992-93, chmn. pub. rels. 1994-95), Assn. Edn. Journalism and Mass Comm., Am. Newspapers Pubs. Assn. (nat. coop. com. on edn. in journalism 1989-92), Women in Comm. (pres. Baton Rouge chpt. 1982, nat. judge Clarion awards 1987), Pub. Rels. Assn. La., La. State U. Journalism Alumni Assn. (pres. 1977), Soc. Profl. Journalists (pres. S.E. La. chpt. 1982), Am. Journalism Historians Assn., La. State U. Alumni Assn. (pres. East Baton Rouge Parish chpt. 1978-80), Popular Culture Assn., Investigative Reporters and Editors Assn., Baker C. of C., Toastmasters (adminstrv. v.p. Baton Rouge 1977), Pilot Club. Home: 2801 Allen Ct Baker LA 70714-2253

ROBERSON, ROBERT S., investment company executive; b. Mt. Kisco, N.Y., Nov. 30, 1942; s. Robert and Mercedes (Stack) R.; m. Barbara Drane, Oct. 21, 1967; children: Elizabeth de V., Merritt B., Barbara D. BS, NYU, 1964; MBA, Coll. William and Mary, 1973. Various positions in fin. and bldg. industries, 1964-67; mem. N.Y. Produce Exchange, 1965-66; with Weaver Bros., Inc., Newport News, 1967—, now pres., dir.; bd. dirs. First Peninsula Bank & Trust Co., Hampton, Va., 1977-78. Active Newport News Rep. City Com.; past dir. Peninsula Unit Am. Cancer Soc., Newport News; past dir. Heritage Coun. Girl Scouts U.S.A., Hampton; former trustee Newport News Pub. Libr., Va. Living Mus., Am. Assn. Mus., Newport News; former trustee Hampton Roads Acad., Newport News; former mem. bd. visitors to George Washington's Mt. Vernon Nat. Shrine; hon. dep. chief N.Y.C. Fire Dept. Mem. S.R., Newcomen Soc. of the U.S., Hon. Fire Officers Assn., Gen. Soc. Colonial Wars, St. Nicholas Soc. of the City N.Y., Colonial Order Acorn, Sovereign Mil. Order of the Temple of Jerusalem, Mil. Order Fgn. Wars of U.S., Squadron A Assn., Pilgrims of the U.S., Blue Key, Union Club, Church Club (N.Y.C.), Fishers Island (N.Y.) Club, James River Country Club, Hampton Roads German Club, The Hundred Club (Newport News, Va.), N.Y. Yacht Club, Fishers Island Yacht Club, Rotary Internat. (Paul Harris fellow), Delta Sigma Pi. Episcopalian. Home: PO Box 66 Williamsburg VA 23187-0066

ROBERT, BRUCE G., manufacturing executive, light. Chmn. bd., CEO Siegel Robert, Inc., Saint Louis. Office: Siegel Robert Inc 8645 S Broadway Saint Louis MO 63111-3810*

ROBERT, LESLIE (LADISLAS), research center administrator, consultant; b. Budapest, Hungary, Oct. 24, 1924; s. Louis and Elizabeth (Bardos) R.; m. Barbara Klinger, Nov. 19, 1949 (dec.); children: Marianne, Catherine, Elisabeth; m. Jacqueline Labat, Dec. 20, 1976. Student, U. Szeged, Budapest, Hungary, 1944-48; MD, U. Paris, 1953; PhD, U. Lille, France, 1977; D (hon.), Med. U. Budapest, 1991. Diplomate Coll. of Physicians and Surgeons. Mem. med. faculty dept. biochemistry U. Paris, 1950-59; postdoctoral rsch. fellow dept. biochemistry Sch. Medicine U. Ill., 1959-60; postdoctoral rsch. assoc., spl. fellow Columbia U., N.Y.C., 1960-61, 67; dir. biochemistry lab. Inst. for Immunobiology INSERM/CNRS, Broussais Hosp., Paris, 1962-66; founder 1st rsch. ctr. on connective tissue biochemistry CNRS, U. Paris XII, Créteil, France, 1966-94; adminstr. Cell Biology Lab. U. Paris VII, 1995—; rsch. dir. French Nat. Rsch. Ctr., Paris, 1974-94, hon. rsch. dir., 1995—; founder rsch. ctr. for clin. and biol. rsch. on aging Charles Foix-Jean Rostand Hosp., Ivry, France, 1993—; cons. several pharm. firms; mem. Sci. Coun. Arteriosclerosis Rsch. Inst., U. Munster, Fed. Republic of Germany, 1970—. Author 5 books on biology of aging, monograph series: Frontiers of Matr's Biology, 11 vols.; mem. editorial bd. several sci. jours.; contbr. more than 850 articles on connective tissues, biochemistry and pathology and aging to sci. jours. Recipient Spl. Sci. prize Sci. Writer, 1966, Reiss prize in Opthalmology, 1970, Verzar medal for gerontol. rsch. U. Vienna, Austria, 1994. Mem. French Atherosclerosis Soc. (pres. 1993—), Hungarian Acad. Sci. (fgn.), Acad. Scis. Westphalie-Rhen, Germany (corr.). Home: 7 Rue Lully, 94440 Santeny France Office: Univ Paris Dept Cell Biology, 2 Pl Jussieu-Tour 23/33, 75005 Paris France

ROBERT, PATRICK, playwright; b. Kilgore, Tex., Sept. 27, 1937; s. Robert and Beulah (Goodson) O'Connor. Author numerous plays produced off-off Broadway, off-Broadway, Broadway, also abroad including Robert Patrick's Cheep Theatricks (23 plays), 1972, Simultaneous Transmissions, 1973, Play-By-Play, 1975, The Golden Circle, 1975, Kennedy's Children, 1975, Let Me Tell It To You, Dr. Paroo, 1976, One Man, One Woman (6 plays), 1978, T-Shirts, 1979, Mutual Benefit Life, 1980, Mercy Drop and Other Plays (5 plays), 1980, My Cup Ranneth, 1984, Big Sweet, 1985, Untold Decades (7 plays), 1988, Drowned Out, 1990, Connie, 1991, Michaelangelo's Models, 1994, Bread Alone, 1994, The Trial of Socrates, 1994, Evan on Earth, 1995, Pouf Positive (CD), 1996; author: (novels) Temple Slave, 1986, Echo, 1990; teleplays include: High Tide, 1994, Robin's Hoods, 1995; contbr. poems, articles, stories to profl. jours. Recipient Show Bus. Best Playwright award 1968-69, Glasgow Citizens' Theatre Best World Playwright award, 1974, Omni-Act One award, 1975, Robbie award, 1976, Founders award Internat. Thespians Soc., 1980, Blue is for Boys weekends in Manhattan, 1983, 86; Rockefeller grantee, 1974, N.Y. State CAPS grantee, 1975. Home: 1837 N Alexandria Ave Apt 211 Los Angeles CA 90027-4068 *No object or action has any meaning except that given to it by a writer. Writers create the consciousness of humanity, which in turn creates our world. Writers write the world.*

ROBERTI, MARIO ANDREW, lawyer, former energy company executive; b. Denver, May 12, 1935; s. Emil and Elvira (Ligrano) R.; m. Patricia Ann Ludwig, Apr. 27, 1963; children: Andrea Louise, Paul Richard, Robert Raymond. B.S., Loyola U. (now Loyola Marymount U.), Los Angeles, 1957, J.D., 1960. Bar: Calif. 1961, Hawaii 1977, D.C. 1985. Dep. atty. gen. State of Calif., 1961-69; atty. Pacific Lighting Corp., Los Angeles, 1969-71; asst. gen. counsel, asst. sec. McCulloch Oil Corp., Los Angeles, 1971-76; v.p., gen. counsel Pacific Resources, Inc., Honolulu, 1976-88, sr. v.p., gen. counsel, 1988-92; with Reinwald, O'Connor, Marrack, Hoskins & Playdon, Honolulu, 1993—; bd. dirs. St. Francis Med. Ctr., Honolulu. Trustee Hawaii Sch. Girls, 1979-87; regent Loyola Marymount U., Chaminade U. Of Honolulu, 1982-93, chmn. bd. regents, 1987-89; adv. bd. Internat. Oil and Gas Ednl. Ctr., Southwestern Legal Found. Mem. ABA, D.C. Bar Assn., Hawaii Bar Assn. (chmn. corp. counsel sect. 1979), Calif. Bar Assn., Outrigger Canoe Club, Oahu County Club, Pacific Coast Gas Assn. (life, chmn. legal adv. com. 1983-84), Phi Alpha Delta, Phi Kappa Theta. Office: 24th Fl 733 Bishop St Fl 24 Honolulu HI 96813-4022

ROBERTI, MARY TERESA, retired English language educator; b. St. Mary's, Pa., Oct. 21, 1933; d. Alfonso and Antonietta (Irace) R.; m. Milan Anton Bradac, Aug. 29, 1977 (dec. Sept. 25, 1991). BA magna cum laude, Marygrove Coll., Detroit, 1958; cert., U. Rome, 1961; MA, U. Mich., 1964, PhD, 1972. English tchr. Cantrick Jr. High Sch., Monroe, Mich., 1958-70, Monroe High Sch., 1970-88; humanities chair Monroe County Community Coll., 1988-92, English prof., 1992-95; Italian tchr. Italian/Am. Soc., Monroe. Mem. Internat. Platform Assn., St. Mary Acad. Alumnae, Marygrove Coll. Alumnae, U. Mich. Alumni. Republican. Roman Catholic. Home: 5710 W Dunbar Rd Monroe MI 48161-3786 also: 4555 E Rhonda Dr Phoenix AZ 85018

ROBERTI, WILLIAM VINCENT, retail executive; b. Bridgeport, Conn., Oct. 18, 1946; s. Armand E. and La Junta Juanita (Swindle) R.; m. Christina Gura, May 30, 1970; children—Jennifer A., Jessica M. BA, Sacred Heart U., Bridgeport, 1969; MBA, So. Meth. U., 1987. Buyer, D.M. Read's div. Allied Corp., Bridgeport, 1968-73; div. mdse. mgr. Robinson's Fla. div. Associated Dry Goods Co., St. Petersburg, 1973-77; exec. v.p. Maas Bros. div. Allied Corp., Tampa, Fla., 1977-83; v.p., gen. mdse. mgr. Mervyn's, Hayward, Calif., 1983-84; chmn., CEO Diversified Group Zale Corp., Dallas, 1984-87; pres., chief exec. Brooks Brothers, 1987-95, pres., CEO, 1995—. Trustee Sacred Heart U., 1989—; bd. dirs. Jr. Achievement, Tampa, 1982-83, E&B Marine Inc.; mem. Pinellas County Com. 100, St. Petersburg, 1982-83; bd. govs. N.Y. chpt. Assn. U.S. Army; mem. Dept. Def. Clothing and Textile Bd.; mem. Nat. Multiple Sclerosis Soc.; mem. Vet. Corp Arty., N.Y.C. Col. USAR, 1966—. Roman Catholic. Mem. West Point Soc. (N.Y. chpt.), Assn. U.S. Army. Union League Club (N.Y.C.), St. Petersburg Yacht Club (Fla.), Brooklawn C.C. Office: Plaid Clothing Group, Inc 730 Fifth Ave New York NY 10019

ROBERTS, ALBERT ROY, social work educator; b. Bronx, N.Y., May 22, 1944; s. Harry and Evelyn (Schwartz) R.; m. Beverly Jean Schenkman, July 5, 1971; 1 child, Herbert. BA in Sociology, L.I. U., 1966, MA in Sociology, 1967; D Social Welfare, U. Md., Balt., 1978. Lectr. Rider Coll., Lawrenceville, N.J., 1970-71; asst. prof., chmn. Coppin State Coll., Balt., 1971-74; project dir. Am. Correctional Assn., College Park, Md., 1975-76; asst. prof. N.Y. Inst. Tech., Old Westbury, N.Y., 1976-78, Bklyn. Coll., CUNY, 1978-79; assoc. prof. U. New Haven, West Haven, Conn., 1979-81, Seton Hall U., South Orange, N.J., 1981-83; assoc. prof., chmn. Ind. U. Sch. Social Work, Indpls., 1984-89; prof. social work, program dir. Rutgers U., New Brunswick, N.J., 1989—; manuscript reviewer Dorsey Press, Chgo., 1984-88, Hosp. and Cmty. Psychiatry, Washington, 1986-95, Longman Pubs., White Plains, N.Y., 1987-92; founding social work series editor Springer Pub. Co., N.Y.C., 1980—. Author: Sourcebook on Prison Education, 1971, Sheltering Battered Women, 1981, Battered Women and Their Families, 1984, Runaways and Non Runaways in an American Suburb, 1987, Helping Crime Victims, 1990; editor: Juvenile Justice: Policies, Programs and Services, 1989 (main selection Behavioral Sci. Book Club 1990), Crisis Intervention Handbook, 1990, Critical Issues in Crime and Justice, 1994, Crisis Intervention and Time-Limited Cognitive Therapy, 1995, Helping Battered Women, 1996, Visions for Change, 1996, Crisis Management and Brief Treatment, 1996; founding editor-in-chief Crisis Intervention and Time-Limited Treatment Jour., 1992—. Bd. dirs. Ind. chpt. Nat. Com. for Prevention Child Abuse, Indpls., 1986-89; mem. state adv. bd. for probation N.J. Supreme Ct., Trenton, 1991—; mem. N.J. Gov.'s Juvenile Justice and Delinquency Prevention Commn., 1991-95. Recipient award for outstanding article Correctional Edn. Assn., 1975. Fellow Am. Orthopsychiat. Assn.; mem. NASW, Acad. Criminal Justice Scis. (life), Am. Soc. Criminology, Nat. Coun. Juvenile and Family Ct. Judges (assoc.), Alpha Delta Mu. Avocations: hiking, bicycling, reading. Office: Rutgers U Sch Social Work 536 George St New Brunswick NJ 08901-1167 *The primary objective of a scholar and educator is to build the knowledge base in a selected area of expertise and to transmit it to one's students. My life has been devoted to setting important goals, overcoming adversity and persevering in order to achieve major accomplishments in both my personal and academic life.*

ROBERTS, ALFRED WHEELER, III, law firm executive; b. N.Y.C., Aug. 3, 1938; s. Alfred Wheeler and Florence Henley (Kirk) R.; m. Pamela Anne Stover, June 29, 1967; children: Ashley Anne, Alfred Kirk, Michael Tyler. BA, Dartmouth Coll., 1960, MBA, 1961. CPA, N.Y. With Arthur Young & Co., N.Y.C., 1961-89, ptnr., 1971-89, vice chmn., 1982-88; ptnr. RFE Investment Ptnrs., New Canaan, Conn., 1989-90; exec. dir. Winthrop, Stimson, Putnam & Roberts, N.Y.C., 1991—. Bd. dirs., treas. Legal Aid Soc. N.Y., 1981-88; bd. dirs. YMCA of Greater N.Y., 1983-89, vice chmn., 1987-89. Mem. AICPA, Univ. Club. Congregationalist.

ROBERTS, ALICE, reservations service executive. With Regent Ins. Adjustors, Wichita, Kans., 1962-63, Western Control, Wichita, 1963-65, McCormick, Mathers Pub., Wichita, 1965-66, Southwest Nat. Bank, Wichita, 1966-69, Kennedy & Coe, Wichita, 1969-73, Coors of Kans., Wichita, 1973-79, Terry Scanlon, Wichita, 1979-81, Profl. Agrl. Supply, Wichita, 1981-83; with Corp. Lodging Conss., Wichita, 1983—, chmn. bd. dirs.; now pres. railroad div. Corp. Lodging Conss., Witchita. Office: Corp Lodging Conss 8110 E 32 St N Wichita KS 67226*

ROBERTS, ALICE NOREEN, educational administrator; b. Los Lunas, N.Mex., July 1, 1947; d. Earnest Lee and Lora Mae (Leatherman) Mayo; m. David Ivan Roberts, Apr. 18, 1975; children: Debra, Danielle, David II, Diana, Earnest. BA, Brescia Coll., 1970; MA, U. N.Mex., 1974. Cert. elem. tchr., adminstr., Calif. 5th and 6th grade tchr. St. John's Parochial Sch., Plattsmouth, Nebr., 1970-71; 5th grade tchr. Sacred Heart Parochial Sch., Farmington, N.Mex., 1971-72; 4th-6th grade tchr. Our Lady of Assumption Sch., Albuquerque, 1972-75; correctional officer Calif. Dept. Corrections, San Quentin, 1975-82; adult edn. tchr. Calif. Dept. Corrections, Soledad, 1983-86, San Luis Obispo, 1984; supr. acad. instrn. Calif. Dept. Corrections, Norco, 1986-90; supr. correctional edn. programs Calif. Dept. Corrections, Corcoran, 1990—; 6th grade tchr. St. Catherine's Parochial Sch., Martinez, Calif., 1981-82; mem. curriculum adv. com. Calif. Dept. Corrections, Sacramento, 1984-86, mem. computer adv. com., 1984-88, mem. literacy adv. com., 1990-94. Candidate for King City (Calif.) Bd. Edn., 1985; vol. Youth for Understanding rep., Hanford, 1994—. Mem. ASCD, Am. Vocat. Assn., Correctional Edn. Assn., Calif. Literacy, Inc., Calif. Coun. for Adult Edn., Hanford Emblem Club (rec. sec. 1994—). Roman Catholic. Avocations: computers, pencil puzzles, video games, crocheting. Office: Calif State Prison Visions Adult Sch PO Box 8800 Corcoran CA 93212

ROBERTS, ALIDA JAYNE, elementary school educator; b. Bristol, Conn., Aug. 11, 1967; d. James and Barbara Mae (Carlson) R. BA in Elem. Edn., Anna Maria Coll., Paxton, Mass., 1990; MS in Reading and Lang. Arts, Calif. State U., Fullerton, 1992. Cert. tchr., Conn., Mass., Calif. Elem. tchr. Rowland Unified Sch. Dist., Rowland Heights, Calif., 1990-94, Edgewood Elem. Sch., Bristol, Conn., 1994-95, Clara T. O'Connell Elem. Sch., Bristol, Conn., 1995—; tchr. Gifted and Talented Edn. After Sch. Program, West Covina, Calif., 1993-94, Chpt. 1 After Sch. Program, West Covina, 1993-94; intramural coach After Sch. Program Edgewood Elem. Sch., Bristol, Conn., 1994-95. Tchr. advisor PTA, La Puente, 1992-92, Clara T. O'Connell PTA, 1995-96. Scholar Bristol Fedn. Tchrs., 1986; grantee Anna Maria Coll., 1986-90. Mem. NEA, ASCD, Internat. Reading Assn., Calif. Reading Assn., Calif. Tchrs. Assn., Orange County Reading Assn., Bristol Fedn. Tchrs. Avocations: reading, physical fitness. Home: 291 Morris Ave Bristol CT 06010-4418

ROBERTS, ANNA RUTH, financial consultant; b. Sweetwater, Tex., Apr. 10, 1942; d. Charles Heddington and Ethel Dorothy (Harris) Elliott; m. David Ira Roberts, Apr. 10, 1960; children: Craig Spencer, Edward Aaron. BA in Edn., Ariz. State U., 1976. CFP. Acct. Miller-Wagner & Co. Ltd., Phoenix, 1982-87; asst. v.p., sr. fin. cons. Merrill Lynch, Sun City, Ariz., 1987—; organizer, presenter seminars Pres.'s Club. Recipient Dist. Merit award Boy Scouts Am., Flagstaff, Ariz., 1975. Mem. Am. Bus. Women Assn., B'nai B'rith Women (Edith K. Baum chpt., Woman of Yr. 1976), Kiwanis (pres. 1987—, Disting. Svc. award 1991). Avocations: hiking, white-water rafting. Home: 6090 W Lone Cactus Dr Glendale AZ 85308-6280 Office: Merrill Lynch 9744 W Bell Rd Sun City AZ 85351-1343

ROBERTS, ANTONETTE, special education educator; b. San Francisco, Nov. 14, 1940; d. Anthony Francis and Lois Wilma (Litton) Jacklevich; m. Raymond Daly Roberts, Feb. 1, 1964; children: Shirley Lois Roberts Murphy, Alice Evelyn, Daniel Anthony. BA, U. Calif., Davis, 1962; MS, U. Nebr., 1971. Cert. elem. and spl. edn. tchr., Iowa. Elem. educator Esparto (Calif.) Unified Sch. Dist., 1962-66; itinerant resource educator Pottawattamie County Schs., Council Bluffs, Iowa, 1972-75; multi-categorical resource educator Lewis Cen. Community Sch. Dist., Council Bluffs, 1976—. mem. tchr. cadre U. No. Ioa, Cedar Falls and Lewis Ctrl. Cmty. Schs., Council Bluffs, 1990—; sponsor Lakeview Sch. Student Coun., Council Bluffs, 1990-92; mem. Lewis Ctrl. Instructional Coun., 1992—, Lakeview Sch. Bldg. Cadre, 1994-95. Mem. NEA, Iowa State Edn. Assn., Lewis Cen. Edn. Assn., Coun. for Exceptional Children, Iowa Coun. Tchrs. of English, Phi Delta Kappa. Avocations: reading, writing, swimming, sewing, gardening. Office: Lakeview Sch Piute and Wright Rds Council Bluffs IA 51501

ROBERTS, ARCHIBALD EDWARD, retired army officer, author; b. Cheboygan, Mich., Mar. 21, 1915; s. Archibald Lancaster and Madeline Ruth (Smith) R.; grad. Command and Gen. Staff Coll., 1952; student U.S. Armed Forces Inst., 1953, U. Md., 1958; m. Florence Snure, Sept. 25, 1940 (div. Feb. 1950); children—Michael James, John Douglas; m. 2d, Doris Elfriede White, June 23, 1951; children—Guy Archer, Charles Lancaster, Christopher Corwin. Enlisted U.S. Army, 1939, advanced through grades to lt. col., 1960; served in Far East Command, 1942, 1953-55, ETO, 1943-45, 57-60; tech. info. officer Office Surgeon Gen., Dept. Army, Washington, 1950, Ft. Campbell, Ky., 1952-53, info. officer, Camp Chicamauga, Japan, Ft. Bragg, N.C., Ft. Campbell, Ky., 1953-56, Ft. Campbell, 1956-57, Ft. Benning, Ga., Wurzburg, Germany, 1957-58, spl. projects officer Augsburg, Germany, 1959-60, U.S. Army Info. Office, N.Y.C., 1960-61; writer program precipitating Senate Armed Services Hearings, 1962; ret., 1965; mgr., salesman Nu-Enamel Stores, Ashville, N.C., 1937-38; co-owner, dir. Roberts & Roberts Advt. Agy., Denver, 1946-49; pres. Found. for Edn., Scholarship, Patriotism and Americanism, Inc.; founder, nat. bd. dirs. Com. to Restore Constn., Inc., 1965—. Recipient award of merit Am. Acad. Pub. Affairs, 1967; Good Citizenship medal SAR, 1968; Liberty award Congress of Freedom, 1969; Man of Yr. awards Women for Constl. Govt., 1970, Wis. Legislative and Research Com., 1971; medal of merit Am. Legion, 1972; Speaker of Year award We, The People, 1973; Col. Arch Roberts Week named for him City of Danville, Ill., 1974; recipient Spl. Tribute State of Mich., 1979. Mem. Res. Officers Assn., Airborne Assn., SAR, Sons Am. Colonists. Author: Rakkasan, 1955; Screaming Eagles, 1956; The Marne Division, 1957; Victory Denied, 1966; The Anatomy of a Revolution, 1968; Peace: By the Wonderful People Who Brought You Korea and Viet Nam, 1972; The Republic: Decline and Future Promise, 1975; The Crisis of Federal Regionalism: A Solution, 1976; Emerging Struggle for State Sovereignty, 1979; How to Organize for Survival, 1982; The Most Secret Science, 1984; also numerous pamphlets and articles. Home: 2218 W Prospect PO Box 986 Fort Collins CO 80522-0986

ROBERTS, BERT C., JR., telecommunications company executive; b. 1942; married. BS, Johns Hopkins U., 1965. Project dir., mgr. Westinghouse Electric Corp., 1960-69; dir. Leasco Response Inc., 1969-72; with MCI Communications Corp., Washington, 1972—, v.p., 1974-76, sr. v.p., 1976-83, pres., 1983-85; chief operating officer MCI Telecommunications Corp., Washington, 1985-91, chief exec. officer, 1991—, chmn., 1992—. Office: MCI Comm Corp 1801 Pennsylvania Ave NW Washington DC 20006-3606*

ROBERTS, BETTY JO, retired librarian, speech therapist; b. Ft. Worth, Tex., Nov. 11, 1927; d. Harry Pulliam and Mamie Josephine (Parker) Easton; m. Robert Lester Roberts, Jr.; children: Jo Lu, Lee Ann. Student, Tex. State Coll. Women, Denton, 1945-47, Tex. Wesleyan Coll.; BS, SW Tex. State U., 1952. Tchr. Milton H. Barry Sch. for Physical Rehab., Houston, United Cerebral Palsy Ctr., Ft. Worth, Tex., San Marcos Pub. Schs., Tex., 1952-53; supr. practice tchrs. S.W. Tex. State, 1952-53; tchr. Waco (Tex.) Ind. Schs., 1953-54; speech therapist Providence Crippled Children's Hosp., Waco; tchr. phonics, creative art Latin Am. Ctr., Waco, 1961-69; ch. librarian Trinity United Methodist Ch., Waco, 1979-88; ch. lib. Cen. United Methodist Ch., Waco, Tex., 1988-91. Compilor, Editor: Swedishes and More 1984. Democrat. Methodist. Home: 3248 Village Park Dr Waco TX 76708-1582

ROBERTS, BILL GLEN, retired fire chief, investor, consultant; b. Deport, Tex., June 2, 1938; s. Samuel Westbrook and Ann Lee (Rhodes) R.; m. Ramona Ryall, June 1, 1963 (dec. Nov. 1988); 1 child, Renee Ann. Student, So. Meth. U., 1968, North Tex. State U., 1974; grad. paramedic course, U. Tex. Southwestern Med. Sch., 1974; grad. Exec. Program for Fire Service, Tex. A&M U., 1978; AAS, El Centro Jr. Coll., Dallas, 1980; grad. exec. fire officer program, Nat. Fire Acad., 1989. With Dallas Fire Dept., 1958-82, lt., 1964-67, capt., 1967-71, div. fire chief, 1971-79, asst. fire chief, 1979-83; fire chief Austin (Tex.) Fire Dept., 1983-94; tech. bd. dirs. Found. Fire Safety, Washington, 1982-85; adj. faculty Nat. Fire Acad., 1981-86; aft. State Life of Indpls., Dallas, 1962; owner Personnel Testing Lab., Dallas, 1963; real estate salesman Dale Copus Realtor, Dallas, 1963-66; salesman intercommunications equipment Chandler Sound, Dallas, 1966-67; field engr. IBM Corp., Dallas, 1968; cons. U. Tenn., 1974, Ga. Inst. Tech., 1974, Tex. Dept. Health Resources, 1973-78, Rand Corp., Washington, Mission Rsch., Santa Barbara, Calif., Macro. Author: EMS Dallas, 1978; (with others) Anesthesia for Surgery Trauma, 1976, EMS Measures to Improve Care, 1980; contbr. articles to periodicals. Com. chmn. Dallas Jaycees, 1962-65; mem. task force Am. Heart Assn., Austin, 1973-83; bd. dirs. Brackenridge Hosp., 1989, Rehab. Hosp. Austin, 1992-94, Austin Police Pensions Bd., 1989, Capitol Area coun. Boy Scouts Am., 1989-92. Recipient John Stemmons Service award Dallas Fire Dept., 1979; Internat. Assn. Fire Chiefs scholar, 1967. Mem. Internat. Assn. Fire Chiefs, Nat. Fire Protection Assn., Nat. Critical Care Inst., Am. Heart Assn., Am. Trauma Soc. (founder), Am. Assn. Trauma Specialists, Nat. Assn. Emergency Med. Technicians, Tex. Assn. Emergency Med. Technicians, ACS, North Tex. Coun. of Govts. (regional emergency svc. adv. coun. 1973-79), Internat. Rescue and First Aid Assn., Found. Fire Safety (tech. bd. dirs. 1982-85), Tex. Assn. Realtors, Austin World Affairs Coun., People to People Internat., Rotary Internat. Methodist. Home: 3 Highlander Rd Asheville NC 28804-1112

ROBERTS, BRIAN LEON, communications executive; b. Phila., June 28, 1959; s. Ralph J. and Suzanne F. Roberts; m. Aileen Kennedy, Dec. 28, 1985; children: Sarah, Tucker, Amanda. Student, U. Pa., 1981. V.p. ops. Comcast Cable Communications, Inc., Phila., 1985-86; exec. v.p. Comcast Corp., 1986—, also bd. dirs., now pres.; bd. dirs. Turner Broadcasting System, QVC Network, Viewer's Choice, Calbe Labs. Vice chmn. The Walter Katz Found. Mem. Nat. Cable TV Assn. (bd. dirs., exec. com.). Office: Comcast Corp 1500 Market St Philadelphia PA 19102*

ROBERTS, BURTON BENNETT, administrative judge; b. N.Y.C., July 25, 1922; s. Alfred S. and Cecelia (Schanfein) R.; m. Gerhild Ukryn. B.A., NYU, 1943, LL.M., 1953; LL.B., Cornell U., 1949. Bar: N.Y. 1949. Asst. dist. atty. N.Y. County, 1949-66; chief asst. dist. atty. Bronx County, Bronx, N.Y., 1966-68; acting dist. atty. Bronx County, 1968-69, dist. atty., 1969-72; justice Supreme Ct. State N.Y., 1973—, adminstrv. judge criminal br. Bronx County 12th Jud. Dist., 1984—, adminstrv. judge civil br. Bronx County 12th Dist., 1988—. Pres. Bronx div. Hebrew Home for Aged, 1967-72. With U.S. Army, 1943-45. Decorated Purple Heart, Bronze Star with oak leaf cluster. Mem. Assn. Bar City N.Y., Am. Bar Assn., N.Y. Bar Assn., Bronx County Bar Assn., N.Y. State Dist. Attys. Assn. (pres. 1971-72). Jewish (exec. bd. temple). Home: 215 E 68th St Apt 19A New York NY 10021-5727 Office: Supreme Ct Bronx County 851 Grand Concourse Bronx NY 10451-2901

ROBERTS, C. FRANK, broadcast executive. Pres. The New York Times Broadcasting Group, Memphis, Tenn. Office: The New York Times Broadcasting 803 Channel 3 Dr Memphis TN 38103-4603

ROBERTS, CALVIN, materials engineer; b. Savannah, Ga., Oct. 28, 1945; s. Fred and Hattie (Leach) R. AAS, Norwalk (Conn.) State Coll., 1968; BS in Civil Engring., NYU, 1971; MS in Civil Engring., Pa. State U., 1973. Registered profl. engr. N.Y., Conn., Mich. Sr. project engr. Wilbur Smith & Assocs., New Haven, 1979-81; project mgr. URS Co. Inc., N.Y.C., 1981-83; v.p. Salmon Assocs., P.E., L.I., N.Y., 1983-85; traffic and safety engr. State of Mich. Dept. Transp., Lansing, 1985-92, exec. office mgmt. assessment, 1992-94, engr. materials and tech., 1994—; engr. Frederic R. Harris Inc., Stamford, Conn., 1973-79. Mem. fin. com. Mich. Capital coun. Girl Scouts U.S., Lansing, 1988—; chmn. com. on minority engring. activities Pa. State U. Coll. Engring., University Park, 1988—. Mem. Transp. Rsch. Bd., Inst. Transp. Engrs., Nat. Com. on Uniform Traffic Control Devices (sec. signs tech. com. 1986-93), Am. Assn. State Hwy. Ofcls. (standing com. on hwy. traffic safety). Avocations: photography, sports, classical music, art collector. Home: 1775 Nemoke Trl Apt 5 Haslett MI 48840-8636 Office: Mich Dept Transp 425 W Ottawa St # 30050 Lansing MI 48933-1532

ROBERTS, CARL GEOFFREY, lawyer; b. Boston, June 17, 1948; s. Simon Matthew and Ruth (Gorfinkle) R.; m. Sharon Ash, Mar. 24, 1979. BA, Harvard U., 1970; JD, U. Pa., 1974. Bar: Pa. 1974, U.S. Dist. Ct. (ea. dist.) Pa. 1974, U.S. Ct. Appeals (3d cir.) 1978, U.S. Supreme Ct. 1980, U.S. Ct. Claims 1980, U.S. Dist. Ct. (mid. dist.) Pa. 1986. Law clk. U.S. Dist. Ct. (ea. dist.) Pa., Phila., 1974-76; assoc. Dilworth, Paxson, Kalish & Kauffman, Phila., 1978-82, ptnr., 1982-92; ptnr. Ballard, Spahr, Andrews & Ingersoll, Phila., 1992—. Bd. dirs. Phila. Chamber Ensemble, sec., 1977-92, pres., 1992-95. Mem. ABA (law practice mgmt. sect., coun. computer divsn., vice chmn. techs. and facilities group). Office: Ballard Spahr Andrews & Ingersoll 1735 Market St Ste 51 Philadelphia PA 19103-7501

ROBERTS, CAROL ANTONIA, county commissioner, real estate associate; b. Miami, Fla., June 22, 1936; d. Milton R. and Betty Shirley (Pallot)

Klein; m. Aug. 9, 1953; children: David, Jonathan, Mark, Stephen, Scott, Pamela. Student, Tuft U., 1953-54, Palm Beach (Fla.) Jr. Coll., 1960-62, Palm Beach Atlantic Coll., 1971-72. Host radio program Sta. WPBR, Palm Beach, Fla., 1976-83; co-founder Denman Roberts & Ross, West Palm Beach, Fla., 1978-80; pres. Sunshine Acad. Press, Inc., West Palm Beach, 1978-82; pres., broker VIP Mgmt. and Realty, Inc., West Palm Beach, 1980—. Commr. City of West Palm Beach, Fla., 1975, 77, 82, 84, vice mayor, 1976-77, 84-85, mayor, 1985-86; chair Palm Beach County Bd. Commrs., 1987, 88; bd. dirs., chair women's div. Palm Beach County Comprehensive Community Mental Health Ctr. Bd., 1978-80, Jewish Fedn. Palm Beach County, 1978-80, Palm Beach Inst. Med. Rsch., Goodwill Industries, Cities in Schs., Anti-Defamation League, Adopt-A-Family; vice chair Tri-County Rail Authority, chmn. mktg. com.; vice chair Solid Waste Authority, 1977-78; chair Art in Pub. Places, Artificial Reef com., Intracoastal Waterway com.; co-chair Water Resources Mgmt. Adv. Bd.; vice chair Fla. League of Cities Intergovtl. Rels. com.; mem. Palm Beach Sports Authority, So. Fla. Mental Health Consortium, Treasure Coast Regional Planning Coun.; mem Fla. Crime Prevention Commn., 1985; founder Jewish Cmty.Day Sch.of the Palm Beaches. John and Mabel Ringling Mus. Art grantee, Norton Art Gallery grantee, U. Ga. grantee, U. Fla. grantee, Tufts U. grantee, Fla. A&M U. grantee; named Woman of the Yr., Bus. and Profl. Women Palm Beaches, 1985, Leading Lady in Mcpl. Govt., Network Connection, 1985; recipient Appreciation award Tri-County Nat. Bus. League, 1985, Woman of the Yr. award Temple Beth El Sisterhood, 1986, Disting. medal Palm Beach Atlantic Coll., 1986, Disting mem. of Pres. Coun. U. Fla.; inducted into Fla.'s Hall of Fame, 1986. Mem. Fla. League of Cities (vice chair intergovtl. rels. com.), Fla. Assn. Counties (social svcs. policy com., pres. 1996—), Fla. Assn. Counties Bd. Dirs., Nat. Assn. Counties (intergovtl. rels. com., vice chair transp. and telecomms. steering com.), South Fla. Mental Health Consortium. Democrat. Jewish. Home: 6708 Pamela Ln West Palm Beach FL 33405-4175 Office: Office Bd County Commrs PO Box 1989 301 N Olive Ave West Palm Beach FL 33402-1989

ROBERTS, CASSANDRA FENDLEY, investment company executive; b. Port St. Joe, Fla., Sept. 24, 1951; d. Pope and Sophie Virginia (McGee) Fendley; m. Charles Stanton Roberts, Aug. 7, 1971; 1 child, Davis McGee. BSBA, Edison State Coll., 1983. Sales assoc., v.p. Cooper Corp., Atlanta, 1979-85; sales assoc., broker WTM Investments, Atlanta, 1985-92, v.p., 1992—. Mem. Nat. Bd. Realtors, Ga. Bd. Realtors, Atlanta Bd. Realtors. Avocations: mathematics, reading. Office: WTM Investments Inc PO Box 13256 Atlanta GA 30324-0256

ROBERTS, CECIL KENNETH, lawyer; b. Tyler, Tex., Mar. 31, 1930; s. Cecil Kelly and Blanche Lulu (Cash) R.; m. Cary N. Thornton, Sept. 1, 1951; children: Kenneth Kelly, Cristina Cary. BBA, U. Tex., Austin, 1950, JD, 1951; LLM, U. Tex., 1953; AMP, Harvard U., 1971. Bar: Tex. 1952. Atty. Exxon Co., U.S.A., Houston, 1954-64, N.Y.C., 1964-65; chief atty. refining, environment and labor rels. law Houston, 1965-67, adminstrv. mgr. Baytown refinery, 1967-68, mgr. pub affairs dept., 1969-72; exec. asst. to pres. Exxon Corp., N.Y.C., 1972-73, dep. mgr. pub. affairs dept., 1973-74, assoc. gen. counsel, 1974-79; gen. counsel Exxon Co., U.S.A., Houston, 1979-92; v.p., gen. counsel Exxon Corp., Dallas, 1993-95; of counsel Fulbright & Jaworski, Houston, 1995—; bd. dirs. Nat. Ctr. for State Cts., 1986-89; mem. steering com. Com. for Jud. Merit Election. Trustee Southwestern Legal Found., 1993—, U. Tex. Law Found., 1992—; bd. dirs. Landmark Legal Found., Kansas City, Mo., 1980—, vice chmn., 1987-93; mem. bd. visitors U. Tex. Law Sch., Austin; mem. bd. visitors Stanford U. Law Sch., 1980-84, mem. law and econs. adv. com., 1983-87. Recipient Paul C. Reardon award Nat. Ctr. for State Cts., 1990; named Outstanding Alumni, U. Tex. Sch. Law, 1993. Fellow Am. Bar Found.; mem. ABA, Tex. Bar Assn., Houston Bar Assn., Am. Law Inst., Am. Petroleum Inst. (gen. com. on law), Assn. Gen. Counsel, Am. Arbitration Assn. (bd. dirs. 1993—), Petroleum Club (bd. dirs.), River Oaks Country Club, Las Colinas Country Club, Univ. Club (N.Y.C.), Monterey Peninsula Country Club. Office: Fulbright & Jaworski 1301 Mckinney St Ste 5100 Houston TX 77010

ROBERTS, CHALMERS MCGEAGH, reporter; b. Pitts., Nov. 18, 1910; s. Franklin B. and Lillian B. (McGeagh) R.; m. Lois Hall, Sept. 11, 1941; children: David H., Patricia E. Roberts Monahan, Christopher C. A.B., Amherst Coll., 1933, L.H.D., 1963. Reporter Washington Post, 1933-34, Asso. Press., Pitts. bur., 1934-35, Toledo News-Bee, 1936-38, Japan Times, Tokyo, 1938-39; asst. mng. editor Washington Daily News, 1939-41; Sunday editor Washington Times-Herald, 1941; staff OWI, London, Washington, 1941-43, Life mag., 1946-47, Washington Star, 1947-49; staff writer Washington Post, 1949-71, reporter local and nat. news, 1949-53, chief diplomatic corr., 1953-71, contbg. columnist, 1971—; contbg. columnist San Diego Union, 1971-86. Author: Washington Past and Present, 1950, Can We Meet the Russians Half Way?, 1958, The Nuclear Years: The Arms Race and Arms Control 1945-70, 1970, First Rough Draft: A Journalist's Journal of Our Times, 1973, The Washington Post: The First 100 Years, 1977, rev. In the Shadow of Power: The Story of the Washington Post, 1989, How Did I Get Here So Fast? Rhetorical Questions and Available Answers from a Long and Happy Life, 1991; contbr. articles to popular mags. Capt. USAAF, 1943-46. Decorated Order of Merit (Germany); recipient Sigma Delta Chi award, 1953, nat. news award Washington Newspaper Guild, 1954, 60; citation Overseas Press Club, 1955, front page grand prize Washington Newspaper Guild, 1957, 60, Raymond Clapper Meml. award, 1957, Edward Weintal prize for diplomatic reporting, 1975, Frank Luther Mott Rsch. award Kappa Tau Alpha, 1978; named to Washington Journalism Hall of Fame, Sigma Delta Chi, 1982. Mem. Am. Newspaper Guild, State Dept. Corrs. Assn. (pres. 1958-59), Coun. Fgn. Rels., Nat. Book Critics Cir. Home: 6699 MacArthur Blvd Bethesda MD 20816-2247

ROBERTS, CHARLES PATRICK, congressman; b. Topeka, Kans., Apr. 20, 1936; m. Franki Fann, 1970; children: David, Ashleigh, Anne-Wesley. B.A., Kans. State U., 1958. Pub. Litchfield Park, Ariz., 1962-67; adminstrv. asst. U.S. Senator Frank Carlson, 1967-68, U.S. Congressman Keith Sebelius, 1968-80; mem. 97th to 104th Congresses from 1st Kans. Dist., 1980—. Served with USMC, 1958-62. Office: 1126 Longworth HOB Washington DC 20515-1601

ROBERTS, CHARLES S., software engineer; b. Newark, Sept. 25, 1937; s. Ben and Sara (Fasten) R.; m. Wendy Shadlen, June 8, 1959; children: Lauren Roberts Gold, Tamara G. Roberts. BS in Chemistry, Carnegie-Mellon U., 1959; PhD in Physics, MIT, 1963. MTS, radiation physics rsch. AT&T Bell Labs., Murray Hill, N.J., 1963-68, head info. processing rsch., 1968-73, head interactive computer systems rsch., 1973-82; head, advanced systems dept. AT&T Bell Labs., Denver, 1982-87; head software architecture planning dept. AT&T Bell Labs., Holmdel, N.J., 1987-88; R&D mgr., system architecture lab. Hewlett-Packard Co., Cupertino, Calif., 1988-90, R&D mgr. univ. rsch. grants, 1990-92; prin. lab. scientist Hewlett-Packard Labs., Palo Alto, Calif., 1992—. Contbr. articles to profl. jours. Westinghouse scholar Carnegie Mellon U., 1955-59; NSF fellow MIT, 1959-63. Mem. IEEE, Assn. for Computing Machinery, Am. Phys. Soc., Sigma Xi, Tau Beta Pi, Phi Kappa Phi. Achievements include 2 patents on associative information retrieval and dithered display system; development of early UNIX operating system for 32-bit computers; research on theory to explain electron loss in Van Allen Belts, on superimposed code techniques for associative information retrieval. Home: 210 Manresa Ct Los Altos CA 94022-4646 Office: Hewlett-Packard Labs PO Box 10490 1501 Page Mill Rd Palo Alto CA 94303-0969

ROBERTS, CLYDE FRANCIS, business executive; b. Lawrence, Mass., Sept. 10, 1924; s. Clyde F. and Blanche (Fellows) R.; May 18, 1947; 1 dau., Michele. B.S.B.A., Boston U., 1947; postgrad., Am. U., Beirut, 1954. Commd. fgn. affairs officer Dept. State, 1948-57; v.p. NAM, Washington, 1957-75; pres. Indsl. Fasteners Inst., Cleve., 1975-82; founding ptnr. RBJ Technologies, 1982—; pres. Nat. Assets Mgmt. Enterprises, 1984—; mem. instl. rev. bd. Fairview Gen. Hosp., 1985—; mem. adv. bd. Tabac Assocs., 1986—, Phoenix Corp, 1989—. Served with U.S. Army, 1943-45, Africa, Sicily, Italy, Greece. Mem. Nat. Indsl. Coun., Coun. Small Enterprise. Roman Catholic. Office: 18827 Cliff Cir Cleveland OH 44126-1707

ROBERTS, CORINNE BOGGS (COKIE ROBERTS), correspondent, news analyst; b. New Orleans, Dec. 27, 1943; d. Thomas Hale and Corinne Morrison (Claiborne) Boggs; m. Steven V. Roberts, Sept, 10, 1966; children: Lee Harriss, Rebecca Boggs. BA in Polit. Sci., Wellesley Coll., 1964; hon. degrees, Amherst Coll., Columbia Coll., Loyola U. of the South, Manhattanville Coll., Gonzaga U., Boston Coll., Hood Coll., Chestnut Hill Coll. Assoc. prodr., host Altman Prodns., Washington, 1964-66; prodr. Altman Prodns., L.A., 1969-72; reporter, editor Cowles Communications, N.Y.C., 1967; prodr. Sta. WNEW-TV, N.Y.C., 1968, Sta. KNBC-TV, L.A., Greece, 1972-74; reporter CBS News, Athens, Greece, 1974-77; corr. Nat. Pub. Radio, Washington, 1977—, MacNeil/Lehrer Newshour, Washington, 1984-88; spl. Washington corr. ABC News, Washington, 1988—; interviewer, commentator This Week With David Brinkley, Washington, 1992—; lectr. in field. Co-host weekly pub. TV program on Congress, The Lawmakers, 1981-84; producer, host pub. affairs program Sta. WRC-TV, Washington; producer Sta. KNBC-TV Serendipity, L.A. (award for excellence in local programming, Emmy nomination for children's programming); contbr. articles to newspapers, mags. Bd. dirs. Dirksen Ctr., Pekin, Ill., 1988-95, Everett Dirksen awrd, 1987; bd. dirs. Fgn. Students Svc. Ctr., Washington, 1990—, Manhattanville Coll., Purchase, N.Y., 1991—, Children's Inn at NIH, Bethesda, Md., 1992—. Recipient Broadcast award Nat. Orgn. Working Women, 1984, Everett McKinley Dirksen disting. reporting of Congress, 1987, Weintal award Georgetown U., 1988, Corp. Pub. Broadcasting award, 1988, Edward R. Murrow award Corp. Pub. Broadcasting, 1990, Broadcast award Nat. Women's Polit. Caucus, 1990, David Brinkley Comm. award, 1992, Mother of Yr. award Nat. Mothers' Day Com., 1992, Emmy award news and documentary, 1992. Mem. Radio-TV Corrs. Assn. (pres. 1981-82, bd. dirs. 1980-94), U.S. Capitol Hist. Soc. Roman Catholic. Office: ABC News 1717 Desales St NW Washington DC 20036-4401 Office: Nat Pub Radio 635 Massachusetts Ave NW Washington DC 20001

ROBERTS, DAVID, wholesale distribution executive; b. 1942. With Standard Liquors, Inc., Peoria, Ill., 1964-70, Heublein, Inc., Boston, 1971-87; with United Liquors Ltd., West Bridgewater, Mass., 1987—, pres., COO. Office: United Liquors Ltd 1 United Dr West Bridgewater MA 02379-1097*

ROBERTS, DAVID AMBROSE, lawyer; b. Pascagoula, Miss., Apr. 27, 1962; s. James Elmer and Edna Louise (Scott) R.; m. Elizabeth Anne Knecht, June 29, 1990. BA, U. Miss., 1985, JD, 1988. Bar: Miss. 1988, Supreme Ct. 1988, U.S. Dist. Ct. (no. dist.) Miss. 1988, U.S. Ct. Appeals (5th cir.) 1991, U.S. Dist. Ct. (so. dist.) Miss. 1991. Asst. dist. atty. Office of Dist. Atty., State of Miss., Pascagoula, 1988-90; ptnr. Gordon, Myers, Frazier & Roberts, Pascagoula, 1991-94; pvt. practice Pascagoula, 1994—. Recipient Am. Jurisprudence award, 1988; named to Outstanding Young Men in Am. Mem. Miss. Bar Assn., Jackson County Bar Assn., 5th Cir. Bar Assn., Nat. Assn. Criminal Def. Lawyers, Rotary. Office: PO Box 2009 Pascagoula MS 39569-2009

ROBERTS, DAVID GLENDENNING, state supreme court justice; b. Fort Fairfield, Maine, July 17, 1928; s. Melvin Philip and Ethel (Chamberlain) R.; m. Rose Marie Downie, Feb. 9, 1952; children: Michael, Mary, Dorothy, Catherine, Sarah, Joseph, Susan. A.B., Bowdoin Coll., 1950; LL.B., Boston U., 1956. Bar: Maine 1956, U.S. Dist. Ct. Maine 1959, U.S. Ct. Appeals (1st cir.) 1964. Ptnr. Pendleton and Roberts, Caribou, Maine, 1956-61; asst. U.S. atty. U.S. Dept. Justice, Bangor, Maine, 1961-66; pvt. practice Bangor, 1966-67; justice Maine Superior Ct., Bangor, 1967-80; assoc. justice Supreme Jud. Ct., Portland, 1980—; mem. Maine Jud. Council, Augusta, 1969-77, 80-86. Served to lt. U.S. Army, 1951-53. Democrat. Roman Catholic. Office: ME Supreme Jud Ct PO Box 269 142 Federal St Portland ME 04112

ROBERTS, DAVID HARRILL, English language educator; b. St. Petersburg, Fla., June 4, 1944; s. Thomas Harrill and Daphne Virginia (Spear) R.; m. Madonna Jean Richards, Sept. 16, 1967; children: Michael Anthony, Mark David. BA in English, Lander Coll., 1970; MA in Linguistics, U. S.C., 1973; PhD in Rhetoric, Ind. U. of Pa., Indiana, Pa., 1982. Corp. prodn. planner Abney Mills, Greenwood, S.C., 1965-70; secondary sch. tchr. Sumter, S.C., 1970-71; systems analyst, computer programmer ICI Am., Inc., Hopewell, Va., 1972-73; founder, dir. Baptist Lang. Centre, Bapt. Mission Zambia, Luanshya, 1973-76; dir. pub. and alumni rels., instr. English Bluefield Coll., Bluefield, Va., 1976-78; dir. McDowell Country Ctr., Bluefield State Coll., 1978-83; asst. prof. English Bluefield State Coll., 1978-83; founder, dir. SPICE Ctr., Bluefield State Coll., 1978-83; assoc. prof. English U. So. Miss., Hattiesburg, 1983-88; prof. English Samford U., Birmingham, Ala., 1988—, dir. univ. writing programs, 1989-94; bd. dirs. Office Tech. Acad., Milw.; pres., owner Bus. and Edn. Computer Support, 1984-88; exec. bd. Miss. Writing/Thinking Inst., 1987-88; pres. Roberts & Richards, Inc. med. edn. cons., 1989—; writing adv. bd. Southeastern Ednl. Improvement Lab., Research Triangle Park, N.C., 1986-88. Mem. editorial bd. Focuses, 1986—, Writing Ctr. Jour., 1986-89; author: First Lessons in Bemba, 1974, First Lessons in Chichewa A Study Guide, 1975, A Guide to Computer Aided Writing Instruction, 1989, Writing: From Private to Public, 1993; co-author: The Ophthalmology Residency Tracker, 1992; editor: Tales from Tall Pines, Volume 3, 1988, Selected Papers fo the Southeastern Writing Center Association, 1984-85, 86, Tales from Tall Pines, vol. 1, 1986 Scribblings in the Pines, 1987, Impact '92: Anthology of Teachers' Writings, Bluefield Coll. Press, 1978, Rev. 1970; developer Borzoi Online Handbook for Writers, 1990, McGraw-Hill Online Handbook, 1991, The Online Handbook for College Writers, 1992, Grammar Online!, 1993; contbr. articles to profl. jours. Recipient Rsch. award Nat. U. Continuing Edn. Assn., 1985, Exemplary Media Use award Bluefield State Coll., 1982; First Bapt. Ch. scholar, Bluefield, 1981, Charles B. Keesee scholar, 1973, Julian A. Hodgens scholar, 1973; J. F. Thompkins grantee, 1973; named Honary Alumnus, The Bapt. Theol. Sem. at Richmond, 1992. Mem. Nat. Writing Ctr. Assn. (exec. com. 1986—), Nat. Coun. Tchrs. English, Conf. on Coll. Composition and Comm., Ala. Coun. Tchrs. English, Southeastern Writing Ctr. Assn. (exec. com. 1984-88, v.p. 1984-85, pres. 1985-87), Soc. Tech. Comm., Phi Kappa Phi (life), Phi Delta Kappa. Avocations: hiking, music. Office: Samford U Box 292207 Birmingham AL 35209-6717

ROBERTS, DENNIS WILLIAM, association executive; b. Chgo., Jan. 7, 1943; s. William Owen and Florence Harriet (Denman) R. BA in Journalism, U. N.Mex., 1968; MA in Legal Studies, Antioch U., 1982; MA, St. John's Coll., 1984. Cert. assn. exec. Gen. assignment reporter Albuquerque Pub. Co., 1964, sports writer, 1960-64, advt. and display salesman, 1967-68; dir. info. N.Mex. bldg. br. Assoc. Gen. Contractors Am., Albuquerque, 1968-79, asst. exec. dir., 1979-82, dir., 1982—. Active United Way, Albuquerque, 1969-78; chmn. Albuquerque Crime Prevention Council, 1982; bd. dir. ARC (Rio Grande chpt., 1992—). Recipient Pub. Relations Achievement award Assoc. Gen. Contractors Am., 1975, 78. Mem. N.Mex. Pub. Relations Conf. (chmn. 1975, 82-83), Pub. Relations Soc. Am. (accredited, pres. N.Mex. chpt. 1981, chmn. S.W. dist. 1984, chmn. sect. 1988), Am. Soc. Assn. Execs. (cert.), Contrn. Specifications Inst. (Outstanding Industry Mem. 1974, Outstanding Com. Chmn. 1978), Sigma Delta Chi (pres. N.Mex. chpt. 1969). Republican. Lutheran. Clubs: Toastmasters (dist. gov. 1977-78, Disting. Dist. award 1978, Toastmaster of Year 1979-80), Masons, Shriners, Elks. Home: 1709 Hiawatha St NE Albuquerque NM 87112-4519 Office: Assn Gen Contractors 1615 University Blvd NE Albuquerque NM 87102-1717 *Personal philosophy: Set your priorities in life, then your goals. In pursuing your goals, visualize their accomplishment. Be persistent, and you will accomplish what you set out to accomplish. Learn to be fair to others and empathetic.*

ROBERTS, DONALD ALBERT, advertising, public relations, marketing and media consultant; b. Boston, Dec. 17, 1935; s. Albert Arthur and Linette Violette (Ouelette) R.; m. Gabrielle Dorothy St. Laurent, Apr. 20, 1957; children: Lynne Dianne, Tammy Denise. Student, U. Maine, 1987-88, Liberty U., 1988-89. Program mgr., dir. sports Sta. WIMA-TV, Lima, Ohio, 1965-68; v.p., gen. mgr. Sta. WABK/WKME, Gardiner, Maine, 1968-74; pres., owner Sta. WRDO, Augusta, Maine, 1974-77; cons. group gen. mgr. Valley Communications, Bangor, Maine, 1977-78; pres., owner Roberts Advt. Agy., Augusta, 1977-78; v.p., gen. mgr. Sta. WLOB AM/FM, Portland, Maine, 1978-80, Sta. WKCG/WFAU, Augusta, 1980-83; pres., owner Roberts & Co., Augusta, 1983—; exec. v.p. mktg., programming and advt. sales State Cable TV Corp., Augusta, 1983-92; cons. gen. mgr. Capital Weekly Newspaper, Augusta, 1993—; cons. New Eng. Ziebart Dealers Assn., 1982—; cons. gen. mgr. Capital Weekly Newspaper, Augusta, Maine, 1994—. Contbr. articles to profl. jours. Pres. Auburn (Maine) City Coun., 1957-60; chmn. Jefferson-Jackson Dinner, Rockland, Maine, 1959, Preserve Augusta Neighborhood Assn., 1989—; del. Dem. State Conv., Bangor, 1980; city councilor-at-large of Augusta, 1990—. Named Maine Sportscaster of Yr. Nat. Sportscasters Assn., 1962, 63; recipient Tiger award Maine Broadcasting System, 1965. Mem. So. Kennebec Valley Realtors Assn., Cable Advt. Bur., Cable TV Adminstrs. and Marketers, Ohio Sportscasters Assn. (co-founder 1965), Maine Assn. Broadcasters (bd. dirs.), Kennebec Valley C. of C. (bd. dirs.). Avocations: politics, reading, golf. Home and Office: 44 Longwood Ave Augusta ME 04330-4131

ROBERTS, DONALD FRANK, JR., communications educator; b. Seattle, Mar. 30, 1939; s. Donald Frank Sr., and Ruth Amalia (Geiger) R.; m. Karlene Hahn, 1963 (div. 1981): 1 child, Donald Brett; m. Wendy G. Roberts, Aug. 26, 1983; stepchildren: Richard L., David L., Katherine M. AB, Columbia U., 1961; MA, U. Calif., Berkeley, 1963; PhD, Stanford U., 1968. Instr., dept. English U. Hawaii, Honolulu, 1963-64; asst. dir. ednl. svc. bur. The Wall Street Jour., Princeton, N.J., 1964-65; asst. prof., rsch. assoc. dept. Comm., Inst. Comm. Rsch. Stanford (Calif.) U., 1970-76, assoc. prof., 1976-84, prof. Comm., 1984—, dir. Inst. Comm. Rsch., 1985-90, chmn. dept. Comm., 1990—, Thomas More Storke Prof., 1991—; cons. NIMH, 1970-71, Rand Corp., 1972-74, Sta. KQED-TV, 1975-77, Far West Lab. Ednl. Rsch. and Devel., 1978-79, FTC, 1978-80, Westinghouse Broadcasting, 1983-86, Soc. Nutrition Edn., 1984-86, The Disney Channel, 1986-87, WHO, 1988-89, SRI Internat., 1988-89, Carnegie Coun. Adolescence, 1989-90, NBC, 1992, Ctr. Disease Control, 1992, Software Pubs. Assn., 1994, Nickelodeon, 1994; bd. advisors Media Scope, 1992-94; v.p. Recreational Software Adv. Coun., 1994—; proposal reviewer NIMH, NSF, U.S. Agy. Internat. Devel., Can. Coun., John and Mary R. Markle Found., W.T. Grant Found.; speaker numerous seminars, confs., symposia. Co-author: Process and Effects of Mass Communication, 1971, Television and Human Behavior, 1978; mem. editl. bd. Jour. Broadcasting, 1980-88, Pub. Opinion Quarterly, 1981-86, Communicare, 1986—; editl. reviewer Commn. Rsch., Comm. Monograph, Comm. Yearbook, Human Comm. Rsch., Jour. Comm., Jour. Quarterly, Child Devel., Jour. Applied Psychology, Jour. Ednl. Psychology, Psychology Bull., Jour. Adolescent Health; contbr. articles to profl. jours, also monographs and book chpts. Fellow Human Scis. Rsch. Coun., Pretoria, South Africa, 1985, 1987, Fullbright Teaching fellow Inst. for Unterrichtstechnologie Und Medienpadagogic, Austria, 1987. Mem. APA, Internat. Comm. Assn., Assn. Edn. in Journalism and Mass Comm., Soc. Rsch. Child Devel., Soc. Personality and Soc. Psychology. Office: Stanford U Dept Comm McClatchy Hall Stanford CA 94305-2050

ROBERTS, DONALD JOHN, economics and business educator, consultant; b. Winnipeg, Man., Can., Feb. 11, 1945; came to U.S., 1967; s. Donald Victor and Margaret Mabel (Riddell) R.; m. Kathleen Eleanor Taylor, Aug. 26, 1967. B.A. (honours), U. Man., 1967; Ph.D., U. Minn., 1972. Instr. dept. managerial econs. and decision scis. J.L. Kellogg Grad. Sch. Mgmt., Northwestern U., Evanston, Ill., 1971-72, asst. prof., 1972-74; assoc. prof. J. L. Kellogg Grad. Sch. Mgmt., Northwestern U., Evanston, Ill., 1974-77; prof. J.L. Kellogg Grad. Sch. Mgmt., Northwestern U., Evanston, Ill., 1977-80, Grad. Sch. Bus., Stanford U., Calif., 1980; Jonathan B. Lovelace prof. grad. sch. bus. Stanford U., 1980—, assoc. dean grad. sch. of bus., 1987-90; dir. exec. program in strategy and orgn., 1992—; dir. global mgmt. program Stanford U., 1994—; prof. (by courtesy) dept. econs. Stanford U., 1986—; vis. rsch. faculty U. Catholique de Louvain, Belgium, 1974-75; cons. bus., econs. and antitrust, 1976—; vis. fellow All Souls Coll., Oxford U., 1995. Assoc. editor: Jour. Econ. Theory, 1977-92, Econometrica, 1985-87, Games and Economics Behavior, 1988—; mem. editorial bd. Am. Econ. Rev., 1991-95, Jour. Econs. and Mgmt. Strategy, 1991—; co-author: Economics, Organization and Management, 1992; contbr. articles to profl. jours. NSF grantee, 1973-93; rsch. fellow Ctr. Ops. Rsch. and Econometrics, Heverlee, Belgium, 1974, fellow Ctr. for Advanced Study in the Behavioral Scis., 1991-92. Fellow Econometric Soc. (mem. coun. 1994—); mem. Am. Econ. Assn., Beta Gamma Sigma. Home: 835 Santa Fe Ave Palo Alto CA 94305-1022 Office: Stanford U Grad Sch Bus Stanford CA 94305

ROBERTS, DONALD MUNIER, retired banker, trust company executive; b. Paterson, N.J., Aug. 3, 1935; s. Edward and Dorothy (Munier) R.; m. Sally D. Ingram, Sept. 6, 1958 (dec. Feb. 1978); 1 dau., Sarah M.; m. Mary Ayer Gordon, June 23, 1978; children: Edward (dec.), John, Martha. B.S., Yale U., 1957; M.B.A., NYU, 1961. Exec. v.p., 1979-90; vice chmn., treas. U.S. Trust Co. N.Y., N.Y.C., 1990-95; retired, 1995; bd. dirs. York (Pa.) Internat. Corp., Burlington Resources, Inc. Trustee, pres. St. Bernards Sch. Mem. N.Y. Road Runners Club Inc. (chmn.), Tau Beta Pi. Republican. Club: Links (N.Y.C.). Home: 10 Gracie Sq New York NY 10028-8031 Office: 430 Park Ave Ste 600 New York NY 10022

ROBERTS, DORIS, actress; b. St. Louis, Nov. 4, 1930; d. Larry and Ann (Meltzer) R.; m. William Goyen, Nov. 10, 1963 (dec.); m. Michael E. Cannata, June 21, 1950; 1 child, Michael R. Student, NYU, 1950-51; studies with, Sanford Meisner, Neighborhood Playhouse, N.Y.C., 1952-53, Lee Strasberg, Actors' Studio, N.Y.C., 1956. Ind. stage, screen and TV actress, 1953—. Profl. stage debut, Ann Arbor, Mich., 1953; appeared in summer stock Chatham, Mass., 1955; Broadway debut in The Time of Your Life, 1955; other Broadway and off-Broadway appearances include The Desk Set, 1955, The American Dream, 1961, The Death of Bessie Smith, 1961, The Office, 1965, The Color of Darkness, 1963, Marathon 33, 1963, Secret Affair of Mildred Wilde, 1972, Last of the Red Hot Lovers, 1969-71, Bad Habits, 1973 (Outer Circle Critics award 1974), Cheaters, 1976, Fairie Tale Theatre, 1985, The Fig Tree, 1987, It's Only a Play, 1992; movie debut Something Wild, 1961, movies include Barefoot in the Park, 1968, No Way to Treat a Lady, 1973, A Lovely Way to Die, 1969, Honeymoon Killers, 1969, A New Leaf, 1970, Such Good Friends, 1971, Little Murders, 1971, Heartbreak Kid, 1972, Hester Street, 1975, The Taking of Pelham, One, Two, Three, 1974, The Rose, 1979, Good Luck, Miss Wyckoff, 1979, Rabbit Test, 1979, Ordinary Hero, 1986, #1 with a Bullet, 1987, For Better or for Worse-Street Law, 1988, National Lampoon's Xmas Vacation, 1989, Used People, 1992, The Night We Never Met, Momma Mia, 1994, Walking to Waldheim, 1995, The Grass Harp, 1995; TV debut on Studio One, 1958, Mary Hartman, Mary Hartman, 1975, Mary Tyler Moore Hour, 1976, Soap, 1978-79, Angie, 1979-80, Remington Steele, 1984-88, Lily Tomlin Comedy Hour, Barney Miller, Alice, Full House, Perfect Strangers, Sunday Dinner, A Family Man, The Fig Tree (Pub. Broadcasting System), 1987, (TV films) The Story Teller, 1979, Ruby and Oswald, 1978, It Happened One Christmas, 1978, Jennifer: A Woman's Story, 1979, The Diary of Anne Frank, 1980, A Letter to Three Wives, Blind Faith, 1989, The Sunset Gang, 1990, Crossroads, 1993, Dream On, 1993, The Boys, 1993, A Time To Heal, 1994, Murder She Wrote, Step By Step, Burk's Law Walker, Texas Ranger, 1994, Amazing Grace, 1995, High Society, 1996, Everybody Loves Raymond, 1996. Recipient Emmy award Nat. Acad. TV Arts and Scis., 1984, 85, Emmy nominations, 1986, 88, 91. Mem. Screen Actors Guild, AFTRA, Actors Equity Assn., Dirs. Guild Am.

ROBERTS, DORIS EMMA, epidemiologist, consultant; b. Toledo, Dec. 28, 1915; d. Frederic Constable and Emma Selina (Reader) R. Diploma, Peter Bent Brigham Sch. Nursing, Boston, 1938; BS, Geneva Coll., Beaver Falls, Pa., 1944; MPH, U. Minn., 1958; PhD, U. N.C., 1967. RN, Mass. Staff nurse Vis. Nurse Assn., New Haven, 1938-40; sr. nurse Neighborhood House, Millburn, N.J., 1942-45; supr. Tb Baltimore County Dept. Health, Towson, Md., 1945-46; Tb cons. Md. State Dept. Health, Balt., 1946-50; cons., chief nurse Tb program USPHS, Washington, 1950-57; cons. divsn. nursing USPHS, 1958-63; chief nursing practice br. Health Resources Adminstrn., HEW, Bethesda, Md., 1966-75; adj. prof. U. N.C. Sch. Pub. Health, 1975-92; cons. WHO, 1961-82. Contbr. articles to profl. jours. With USPHS, 1945-75. Recipient Disting. Alumna award Geneva Coll., 1971, Disting. Svc. award USPHS, 1971, Outstanding Achievement award U. Minn., 1983. Fellow APHA (v.p. 1978-79, Disting. Svc. award Pub. Health Nursing sect. 1975, Sedgwick Meml. medal 1979), Am. Acad. Nursing (hon. fellow); mem. Inst. Medicine of NAS, Common Cause, LWV, Delta Omega. Democrat. Episcopalian. Avocations: reading, needlepoint, gardening. Home: Apt 1112 9707 Old Georgetown Rd Bethesda MD 20814-1727

ROBERTS, DWIGHT LOREN, management engineering consultant, novelist; b. San Diego, June 3, 1949; s. James Albert and Cleva Lorraine (Conn) R.; B.A., U. San Diego, 1976, M.A., 1979; m. Phyllis Ann Adair, Mar. 29, 1969; children: Aimee Renee, Michael Loren, Daniel Alexandr. Engring. aide Benton Engring. Inc., San Diego, 1968-73; pres. Robert's Tech. Research Co., also subs. Marine Technique Ltd., San Diego, 1973-76; pres. Research

Technique Internat., 1978—; freelance writer, 1979—; owner Agrl. Analysis, 1985-88; constrn. mgr. Homestead Land Devel. Corp., 1988—; sr. engr. cons. Morrison Knudson, 1992—. Served with U.S. Army, 1969-71. Mem. ASTM, AAAS, Nat. Inst. Sci., N.Y. Acad. Scis., Nat. Inst. Cert. in Engring. Techs., Soil and Found. Engr. Assn., Phi Alpha Theta. Baptist. Author: Geological Exploration of Alaska, 1898-1924, Alfred Hulse Brooks, Alaskan Trailblazer, Papaveraceae of the World, Demarchism, Arid Regions Gardening, Visions of Dame Kind: Dreams, Imagination and Reality, Antal's Theory of the Solar System, Science Fair-A Teacher's Manual, Common Ground: Similarities of the World Religions, Black Sheep-Scientific Discoveries From the Fringe, After Manhattan, The Christofilos Effect; and others; contbr. articles to profl. jours. Office: 3111 E Victoria Dr Alpine CA 91901-3679 *Personal philosophy: Honesty and ethical behavior at all times. Trueness of being throughout my life. Love of my wife and children makes my life worth living and is always a light when there is darkness. God watches over my shoulder.*

ROBERTS, EDWARD BAER, technology management educator; b. Chelsea, Mass., Nov. 18, 1935; s. Nathan (dec.) and Edna (Podradchik) R.; m. Nancy Helen Rosenthal, June 14, 1959; children: Valerie Jo Roberts Friedman, Mitchell Jonathan, Andrea Lynne. BS and MS in Elec. Engring., MIT, 1958, MS in Mgmt., 1960, PhD in Econs., 1962. Founding mem. system dynamics program MIT, 1958-84, instr., 1959-61, asst. prof., 1961-65, assoc. prof., 1965-70, prof., 1970—, David Sarnoff prof. mgmt. of tech., 1974—, assoc. dir. research program on mgmt. of sci. and tech., 1963-73, chmn. tech. and health mgmt. group, 1973-88, chmn. mgmt. of tech. and innovation, 1988—, chmn. ctr. for entrepreneurship, 1992-94, co-dir. internat. ctr. rsch. mgmt. tech., 1993—, dir. mgmt. of tech. program, 1980-89, co-chmn., 1989—; co-founder, dir. Med. Info. Tech., Inc., Westwood, Mass., 1969—; dir. mgmt. of tech. program MIT, 1980-89, co-chmn., 1989—; co-founder, gen. ptnr. Zero State Capital Group, 1981—; bd. dirs. Advanced Magnetics, Inc., Cambridge, Digital Products, Inc., Waltham, Mass., Selfcare, Inc., Waltham, High Point Sys., Inc., Lexington. Author: The Dynamics of Research and Development, 1964, Systems Simulation for Regional Analysis, 1969, The Persistent Poppy, 1975, The Dynamics of Human Service Delivery, 1976, Entrepreneurs in High Technology, 1991; prin. author, editor: Managerial Applications of System Dynamics, 1978; editor (with others) Biomedical Innovation, 1981; editor: Generating Technological Innovation, 1987; mem. editorial bd. IEEE Trans. on Engring. Mgmt., Internat. Jour. Tech. Mgmt., Indsl. Mktg. Mgmt., Jour. Engring. and Tech. Mgmt., Jour. Product Innovation Mgmt., Tech. Forecasting and Social Change. Mem. IEEE, Inst. Mgmt. Sci., Sigma Xi, Tau Beta Pi, Eta Kappa Nu, Tau Kappa Alpha. Home: 300 Boylston St Apt 1102 Boston MA 02116-3923 Office: MIT 50 Memorial Dr Cambridge MA 02142-1347

ROBERTS, EDWARD GRAHAM, librarian; s. Samuel Noble and Frances Johnson (Boykin) R.; m. Anna Jean Walker, Nov. 12, 1949; children: Galer Walker, Edward Graham, John Boykin. B.A., U. South, 1943; B.A. in Library Sci., Emory U., 1948; Ph.D., U. Va., 1950. Curator manuscripts Duke U., Durham, N.C., 1948-52; dir. libraries (Drake U.), Des Moines, 1952-56; dir. Southeastern Interlibrary Research Facility, Atlanta, 1956-59; asst. prof. info. sci. Ga. Inst. Tech., Atlanta, 1963-66, assoc. prof., 1966-69, prof., 1969-73, assoc. dir. libraries, 1966-71, dir. libraries, 1971-84; dir. emeritus Ga. Inst. Tech., 1984—; chmn. info bank com. Ga. Tech. Service Program, Atlanta, 1965-67; mem. exec. bd. Southeastern Library Network, Atlanta, 1973-74; library cons. So. Regional Edn. Bd., Atlanta, 1958-59. Compiler, editor: Southeastern Supplement to the Union List of Serials, 1959; author: Literature of Science and Engineering, 1966, 2d edit.,1969. Served with U.S. Army, 1942-43. Mem. ALA, Southeastern Library Assn., Ga. Library Assn. Democrat. Episcopalian. Home: 1639 Adelia Pl NE Atlanta GA 30329-3807

ROBERTS, EDWIN ALBERT, JR., newspaper editor, journalist; b. Weehawken, N.J., Nov. 14, 1932; s. Edwin Albert and Agnes Rita (Seuferling) R.; m. Barbara Anne Collins, June 14, 1958; children: Elizabeth Adams, Leslie Carol, Amy Barbara, Jacqueline Harding. Student, Coll. William and Mary, 1952-53, NYU, evenings 1955-58; AA in Coll. & Cmty. Svc., St. Petersburg Jr. Coll., 1994. Reporter N.J. Courier, Toms River, 1953-54, Asbury Park (N.J.) Press, 1954-57; reporter Wall Street Jour., N.Y.C., 1957, editorial writer, 1957-63; news editor Nat. Observer, Silver Spring, Md., 1963-68, columnist, 1968-77; editorial writer, columnist Detroit News, 1977-78, editorial page editor, 1978-83; editor editorial page Tampa Tribune, 1983—. Author: Elections, 1964, 1964, Latin America, 1965, The Smut Rakers, 1966, Russia Today, 1967; Editor anthology: America Outdoors, 1965. Recipient Disting. Reporting Bus. award U. Mo., 1969; Pulitzer prize for distinguished commentary, 1974. Mem. Am. Soc. Newspaper Editors, Nat. Conf. Editorial Writers. Office: 202 S Parker St Tampa FL 33606-2308

ROBERTS, ELIZABETH MCCREERY, magazine editor; b. Jacksonville, Fla., Aug. 31, 1956; d. Edward McCreery and Joan Marie (Warthling) R. BA, Trinity Coll., Washington, 1977. Assoc. editor Pan Am Clipper mag., N.Y.C., 1977-84; copy editor Fortune mag., N.Y.C., 1984-86; editor-in-chief Facets mag., N.Y.C., 1987-89; editor Collier's Ency., N.Y.C., 1993-95; mng. editor Child mag., N.Y.C., 1995—. Democrat. Roman Catholic. Office: Child Mag 110 5th Ave New York NY 10011

ROBERTS, ELLIOTT C., SR., public health educator; b. Balt., Jan. 20, 1927; married. BA, Morgan State U.; MA, George Washington U. Bus. mgr. Provident Hosp., Balt., 1953-58, asst. adminstr., 1958-60; chief acct. Crownsville (Md.) Hosp. Ctr., 1960-62, asst. supr., 1962-65; exec. asst. Mercy-Douglass Hosp., Phila., 1965, exec. dir., 1965-69; exec. dir. Harlem Hosp. Ctr., N.Y.C., 1969-72; commr. hosps. Detroit Gen. Hosp., 1972-77; exec. dir., asst. sec. Charity Hosp. New Orleans, 1977-80; v.p., assoc. project dir. Hyatt Med. Mgmt. Svcs., Chgo., 1980-81; dir., CEO Cook County Hosp., Chgo., 1981-84; prof. dept. health systems mgmt. Tulane U., New Orleans, 1984-94; prof. Coll. St. Francis; CEO Med. Ctr. La., New Orleans; prof. dept. health sys. rsch. and pub. health La. State U., New Orleans, 1994—; active Pro Pac Commn., Washington, 1990—. Mem. Am. Coll. Healthcare Execs. (del.), Assn. Am. Med. Colls. (del., bd. dirs.), Am. Hosp. Assn. (life, trustee 1971-76, Honor award 1993, Life Membership award 1993), Ill. Hosp. Assn. (trustee 1982-84). Office: La State U 1600 Canal St New Orleans LA 70112

ROBERTS, ERIC, actor; b. Biloxi, Miss., Apr. 18, 1956. Ed., Royal Acad. Dramatic Art, London, 1973-74, Am. Acad. Dramatic Art, N.Y.C. Appeared in stage prodns. Rebel Women, Streetcar Named Desire, others; TV appearances include Another World; films include King of the Gypsies, 1978, Raggedy Man, 1981, Star 80, 1983, The Pope of Greenwich Village, 1984, The Coca-Cola Kid, 1985, Runaway Train, 1985, Nobody's Fool, 1986, Rude Awakening, 1989, Blood Red, 1989, The Best of the Best, 1989, Final Analysis, 1992, The Best of the Best 2, 1993, Babyfever, 1994, The Specialist, 1994; TV films include Paul's Case, Miss Lonelyhearts, A Time to Heal, 1988, Love, Honor & Obey: The Last Mafia Marriage, 1993, Love, Cheat and Steal, 1993, others; Broadway plays include Burn This, 1988 (Theatre World award 1988). Office: United Talent Agency (UTA) 9560 Wilshire Blvd 5th Fl Beverly Hills CA 90212*

ROBERTS, ERNST EDWARD, marketing consultant; b. Wheeling, W.Va., Dec. 19, 1926; s. Charles Emmitt and Virginia Mae (Stephenson) R.; m. Donna Clare Davis, Dec. 27, 1949; children: Ernst Edward II, Carol Lee Roberts Gaydac. BS, U.S. Mil. Acad., 1949; MBA, Xavier U., Cin., 1954; MS in Mech. Engring., U. So. Calif., 1957; grad. with distinction, Air War Coll., 1970. Commd. 2nd lt. U.S. Army, 1949, advanced through grades to brig. gen., 1971; served as officer in combat U.S. Army, Korea, 1950-52; prof. mil. sci. Xavier U., Cin., 1952-54; mgmt. asst. to asst. comdt. U.S. Army Air Def. Sch., Fort Bliss, Tex., 1957-60; admissions officer U.S. Mil. Acad., West Point, N.Y., 1961-62, asst. to supt. (pres.), 1962-64, dir. admissions, 1964-65; comdg. officer 3d Missile Battalion, 71st Arty., Fed. Republic of Germany, 1965-67; staff officer Gen. Staff U.S. Army, Washington, 1968-70; comdg. officer NATO Air Defense Arty. Group, Fed. Republic of Germany, 1970-71; comdg. gen. 38th Air Def. Arty. Bridgade, Korea, 1971-72; asst. comdt. U.S. Army Air Def. Sch. and Ctr., Fort Bliss, Tex., 1972-74; retired U.S. Army, 1974; v.p. bldg. and property mgr. El Paso (Tex.) Nat. Bank and Corp., 1974-79, sr. v.p., dir. personnel and tng., 1979-83, exec. v.p., dir. mktg., 1983-92; mktg. cons., 1992—; mem. exec. mgmt. com. Tex. Commerce Bank, El Paso, 1983-92; vis. lectr. mktg. Webster U. Mem. bd. advisors SBA; mem. mayor's Citizens Com. on Police Dept. Matters, El Paso; mem. Task Force to Evaluate Mgmt. of Sheriff's Dept.; head bond-issue campaign, El Paso.; adv. dir. Armed Services YMCA, past pres.; adv. dir. nat. bd. dirs. Armed Svcs. YMCA, El Paso Community Found.; past pres. U. Tex.-El Paso Eldorados; mem. bd., trustee Found. Lighthouse for Blind; chmn. adv. bd. dirs. El paso Bus. Com. for Arts; chmn. capital fund drive com. Rio Grande Girl Scouts Am., Plaza Theatre-Plaza Park Restoration bd.; past mem. campaign cabinet United Way El Paso County; chmn. Capital Fund Drive, Air Def. Artillery Mus., Ft. Bliss, Tex.,; bd. dirs. City of El Paso, mem. steering com. Safe 2000; bd. dirs. Crimestoppers of El Paso. Decorated D.S.M., Legion of Merit, Silver Star, Meritorious Svc. medal; recipient Pro Eclesio Et Pontifice, Vatican, 1971; Conquistador award City of El Paso, Liberty Bell award Legal Community El Paso, 1988. Mem. Am. Inst. Banking, Assn. U.S. Army (gen. army Omar N. Bradley chpt.), El Paso C. of C. (mem. armed forces com., chmn. spl. task force to evaluate chamber mgmt.), El Paso Club (past pres., bd. dirs.), Rotary (past pres.), U.S. Army Air Def. Artillery Assn. (pres.). Republican. Roman Catholic. Home: 8212 Antero Pl El Paso TX 79904-2401

ROBERTS, EUGENE LESLIE, JR., newspaper executive, editor; b. Goldsboro, N.C., June 15, 1932; s. Eugene Leslie and Margaret (Ham) R.; m. Susan Jane McLamb, Feb. 23, 1957; children: Leslie Jane, Margaret Page, Elizabeth Susan, Polly Ann. AA, Mars Hill Jr. Coll., 1950-52; BA, U. N.C., 1952-54; postgrad., Harvard U., 1961-62; LLD (hon.), Colby Coll., 1989. Local govt. reporter Goldsboro News Argus, N.C., 1956-58; maritime reporter Norfolk Virginian-Pilot, Va., 1958-59; state capitol corr. Raleigh (N.C.) News & Observer, 1959-61, Sunday editor, 1962-63; labor writer Detroit Free Press, 1963-64, city editor, 1964-65; chief So. corr. N.Y. Times, 1965-67; war corr. N.Y. Times, Vietnam, 1968-69; nat. editor N.Y. Times, 1969-72; exec. editor, v.p. Phila. Inquirer and Phila. Newspapers, Inc., 1972-80, exec. editor, sr. v.p., 1980-86, exec. editor, pres., 1986-90; mng. editor New York Times, 1994—; mem. Pulitzer Prize bd., Columbia U., 1982-91, chmn., 1989-90; chmn. Am. com. Internat. Press Inst., 1987-93, internat. bd., 1990—; chmn. nat. adv. bd. UPI, Washington, 1986-91; bd. visitors Sch. Journalism U. Md., 1983-91, Sch. Journalism Pa. State U., 1983-89; chmn. bd. visitors Sch. Journalism U. N.C., 1989-91; chmn. bd. dirs. Knight Ctr. for Specialized Journalism, U. Md., 1987-91; bd. visitors U. Mich. Journalist-in-Residence program; bd. govs. Columbia U. Seminars and News Media on Soc., Grad. Sch. Journalism; bd. advisors Ctr. for Fgn. Journalists, 1987—; bd. dirs. World Press Freedom Com., 1986-93; bd. dirs. Arthur Burns Fellowship, 1990—; chmn. Woods Hole sci. writing fellowship Marine Biol. Lab., 1993-95; bd. dirs. Universal Press Syndicate, 1992-94; vice-chmn. Com. to Protect Journalists, 1995—. Author (with Jack Nelson) The Censors and the Schools, 1963; editor (with David R. Jones) Assignment America, 1973. With the counter intelligence corps, U.S. Army, 1954-56. Recipient William Allen White award U. Kans., 1985, John Peter Zenger award for Freedom of Press, U. Ariz., 1987, Disting. Contbns. to Journalism award Nat. Press Found., 1989, Elijah Parish Lovejoy award for Freedom of the Press, 1989; Disting. Achievement in Journalism award U. So. Calif., 1989, Reuben award for Disting. Contbns. to Newspaper Features, 1991, Fourth Estate award Nat. Press Club, 1993, Columbia Journalism award Columbia U., 1996; Nieman fellow, 1961-62. Mem. Am. Soc. Newspaper Editors, Soc. Profl. Journalists, Cosmos Club, Am. Antiquarian Soc., North Caroliniana Soc. Home: 113 E 81st St New York NY 10028-1403 Office: NY Times 229 W 43rd St New York NY 10036-3913

ROBERTS, FRANCES CABANISS, history educator; b. Gainesville, Ala., Dec. 19, 1916; d. Richard H. and Mary (Watson) R. B.S., Livingston State U., 1937; M.A., U. Ala., 1940, Ph.D., 1956, LHD, 1993; postgrad., Vanderbilt U., 1949-50. Tchr. pub. schs. Huntsville, Ala., 1937-52; teaching fellow U. Ala., 1952-53; mem. faculty U. Ala. at Huntsville, 1953-80; prof. history U. Ala., 1961-80, prof. emeritus, 1980—, chmn. dept., 1966-70, dir. Acad. Advisement Center, 1972-80. Author: Shadows on the Wall, The Life and Works of Howard Weeden, 1962, Civics for Alabama Schools, 1968, rev., 1970, History of the Church of the Nativity, 1843-1993, 1992; editor Huntsville Historical Review, 1989—. Bd. mem. Huntsville Civic Symphony, 1958-85; Bd. mem. Twickenham Hist. Preservation Assn., pres., 1983-84; Ala. state dir. on exec. bd. So. Heritage Found., 1964-65; bd. dirs. Burritt Mus., Huntsville, 1958-80; mem. Huntsville Historic Preservation Commn., 1972—, Commn. Restoration Capitol Bldg., 1973, Ala. Com. on Humanities and Pub. Policy, 1972-79; chmn. bd. Constitution Hall Park, 1979-83, Cahaba Hist. Commn., 1980-90; chair edn. com. for Vision 2000, Huntsville, 1988-90; chair edn. Summit, Huntsville, 1991; chair adv. com. Coll. Liberal Arts U. Ala., Huntsville, 1988—. Recipient Livingston State U. Alumni award, 1964; Ala. Historic Commn. award, 1969, 78; N.Ala. Bar Assn. Liberty Bell award, 1970; Life Sharer's award Kiwanis, 1973; Service award U. Ala., Huntsville, 1975; award of merit Am. Assn. State and; Alumni Faculty Appreciation award, 1976, 80; Disting. Citizen award Huntsville C. of C., 1990; Favorite Tchr. award TV Channel 19, 1991; Chapel of the Four Chaplins Legion of Honor award, 1992. Mem. Ala. Ednl. Assn., Huntsville Hist. Soc. (exec. bd. 1950—, pres. 1987-89), Ala. Council Social Studies (pres. 1947-48), Am. Hist. Assn., Ala. Hist. Assn. (pres. 1968-69, exec. bd. 1951-79), So. Hist. Assn., N. Hist. Assn. (exec. bd. 1956-64), Golden Key, Kappa Delta Pi, Phi Alpha Theta (scholarship award 1973), Phi Kappa Phi. Home: 603 Randolph Ave SE Huntsville AL 35801-4159

ROBERTS, FRANCIS JOSEPH, retired army officer, retired educational administrator, global economic advisor; b. Holyoke, Mass., July 26, 1918; s. Francis Raymond and Mary (Curry) R.; m. Mary Murray Prickett, May 30, 1942; children: Murray Francine Roberts Mux, Laurel Virginia Roberts Manning, Randall Curry, Phillip Raymond. BS, U.S. Mil. Acad., 1942; postgrad., George Washington U., 1960, Harvard U., 1964. Commd. 2d lt. U.S. Army, 1942, advanced through grades to brig. gen., 1966; comdg. officer (B Battery, 358th F.A.), 1942-43; ops. and tgn. staff 358th F.A., 1943-45; ops. and tng. staff officer (Hdqrs. III Corps), 1946; instr. tactics (U.S. Mil. Acad.), 1946, instr. academics, 1950-53, grad. mgr. athletics, dir. athletics, 1956-59; intelligence staff officer, plans officer (Amphibious Force U.S. Atlantic Fleet), 1946-48; pers. staff officer (Hdqrs. 101st Airborne Div.), 1948; dep. chief of staff 101th Airborne Divsn., 1948-49; plans and ops. staff officer (Hdqs. I Corps), Korea, 1953-54; comdg. officer (159th F.A.), Korea, 1954; plans and policy staff officer (J-3, Hdqs. Far East Command), Japan, 1954-55; chief pers. services div. (Office Asst. Chief of Staff for Pers.), Washington, 1960-61; mil. asst. to dep. sec. def. Washington, 1961-64; comdg. officer (4th Inf. Div. Arty.), 1964-66; chief war plans (SHAPE), 1966, chief strategic plans br., 1966-68; chief of staff (Alaskan Command), 1968-69; comdg. gen. (II Field Force Arty. Vietnam), 1969-70; chief of staff (Hdqs. II Field Force), Vietnam, 1970-71; chief (Europe-Middle East-Africa Div. Orgn. Joint Chiefs Staff), 1971-72, ret., 1972; dean of cadets N.Y. Mil. Acad., 1972, supt., 1972-82. Bd. dirs. Global Econ. Action Inst., 1980-93, Am. Child Guidance Found.; v.p. AMP 45, Harvard; bd. dirs., mem. exec. com. U.S. Olympic Com.; mem. exec. com. Ea. Collegiate Athletic Conf.; mem. Western Alaska coun. Boy Scouts Am.; mem. nat. bd. trustees Boys and Girls Clubs Am.; mem. panel Golf Digest. Decorated D.S.M., D.F.C., Silver Star, Legion of Merit with 3 oak leaf clusters, 10 Air medals, Croix de Guerre avec Etoile de Argent, Legion of Honor, Army Disting. Order 1st Class medal Vietnam, Vietnam Gallantry Cross with Palm, Nat. Honor medal Vietnam, Royal Army Aiguillette Thailand, others; first inductee Nat. Alumni Hall of Fame, Boys and Girls Clubs Am. Mem. Assn. Grad. West Point, Harvard Alumni Assn., Grads. Nat. War Coll., U.S. Golf Assn. (sectional affairs com.), U.S. Srs. Golf Assn. (bd. govs., sec. internat. golf team), Internat. Srs. Amateur Golf Soc., Assn. U.S. Army (chpt. pres., chmn. nat. resolution com., bd. advisors), Ret. Officers Assn.(bd. dirs., exec. com.), So. Srs. Golf Assn., N.C. Srs. Golf Assn., Global Econ. Action Inst. (bd. dirs.). Clubs: Army-Navy Country (Washington); Pinehurst (N.C.) Country; Union League (N.Y.C.); Harvard-Radcliffe of Hudson Valley (pres. 1976-80), Touchdown of Am. (dir.), Bryce Mountain (Va.) Golf and Country, Ambs. Club-Duke U. Address: PO Box 2017 Pinehurst NC 28374-2017

ROBERTS, FRANCIS JOY, educational consultant; b. Marblehead, Mass., July 19, 1931; s. Roland Merritt and Carrie (Ramsdell) R.; m. Patricia Zanio, Dec. 25, 1953; children: Elizabeth, Katherine, Cynthia. BS, Mass. State Coll., 1953; MA, Wesleyan U., 1957; EdD, Harvard U., 1959. Cert. tchr., N.Y., Conn. Tchr. Middlefield (Conn.) Pub. Schs., 1952-53, 55-56; prof. Springfield (Mass.) Coll., 1957-60; prin. Cold Spring Harbor (N.Y.) High Sch., 1960-66; rsch. fellow Yale U., New Haven, 1973; supt. Stony Brook, N.Y., 1966-73; pres. Bank St. Coll., N.Y.C., 1973-79; asst. dir. NEH, Washington, 1980-83; supt. NEH, Cold Spring Harbor, 1983-95; cons. various ednl. orgns. Contbg. editor (columns and features) Parents mag., 1978—. Trustee Heckscher Mus. of Art, Huntington, N.Y., 1985—, vice chmn., 1990—. With U.S. Army, 1953-55. Recipient Golden Apple award, 1988. Mem. Am. Assn. Sch. Adminstrs., Nat. Soc. for Study Edn., Marblehead Arts Assn., Harvard Club (bd. dirs. Washington chpt. 1982-83). Democrat. Avocations: painting, travel, gardening, writing.

ROBERTS, FRANCIS STONE, advertising executive; b. Scranton, Pa., Aug. 15, 1944; s. Gordon Link and Eleanor Swartz (Stone) R.; m. Anne Carter Housh, Dec. 21, 1974; children: Francis Stone, Link McGregor. B.A., Grove City (Pa.) Coll., 1966; A.M.P., U. Chgo., 1984. With media dept., then account exec. Compton Advt. Inc., N.Y.C., 1966-69; account exec. Tatham-Laird & Kudner Advt., N.Y.C., 1969-70; account supr., v.p. SSC&B Advt. Inc., N.Y.C., 1970-78, sr. v.p., mgmt. supr., 1994; group exec. v.p. SSC&B: Lintas Advt. Worldwide, 1987-89; COO, pres. Lintas, N.Y., 1990-94; mem. policy and ops. coms., chmn. strategy rev. bd. Lintas N.Y.; also dir. Lintas N.Y. and U.S.A.; CEO, chmn. The CEO-Gotham Grp., N.Y.C., 1994-95; chmn., CEO Gotham Inc., N.Y.C., 1995—; mng. dir. Gotham Ltd., London, 1996—. Emergency rm. com. Lenox Hill Hosp. Mem. Am. Assn. Advt. Agys. (Large Agy. com.), William Penn Charter Alumni Assn. (pres. N.Y. chpt. 1984-88), Ad Club N.Y., New Canaan Country Club. Republican. Presbyterian. Club: New Canaan Field, New Canaan Winter, New Canaan Country. Home: 208 Canoe Hill Rd New Canaan CT 06840-3707 Office: Gotham Inc 260 Madison Ave New York NY 10016

ROBERTS, GEORGE BERNARD, JR., business and government affairs consultant, former state legislator; b. Andover, Mass., June 13, 1939; s. George Bernard and Helene F. (Eversen) R.; m. Margaret Fay Edmunds, Aug. 26, 1967; children: Abigail Emerson, Jessica Swift. B.S., U. N.H., 1964, M.P.A., 1967. Ptnr. Roberts Real Estate Assocs., Gilmanton, N.H., 1966—; mem. N.H. Ho. of Reps., from 1967, majority leader, 1971-74, speaker, 1975-76, 77-78, 79-80; pres. Policy Mgmt. Assocs., govt. rels. cons., Concord, Concord Coach Soc. Del. Nat. Rep. Conv., 1972-76; mem. N.H. Constl. Conv., 1974, 84, N.H. Rep. Party Fin. Com.; pres. Nat. Conf. State Legislatures, 1979-80; chmn. exec. com. 1st Congl. Soc. Gilmanton. Mem. Nat. Rep. Legislators Assn. (founding, past pres.), Masons, Sigma Alpha Epsilon. Republican. Office: 4 Park St Ste 100 Concord NH 03301-6313

ROBERTS, GEORGE R., venture capital company executive; married; 3 children. JD, U. Calif., San Francisco. With Bears, Stearns, New York, until 1976; now ptnr. Kohlberg, Kravis, Roberts, San Francisco; dir. Beatrice Co., Chgo., Houdaille Industries Inc., Northbrook, Ill., Malone and Hyde, Memphis, Union Tex. Petroleum Holdings Inc., Houston. Office: Kohlberg Kravis Roberts & Co 2800 Sand Hill Rd Ste 200 Menlo Park CA 94025-7022*

ROBERTS, GLYN CAERWYN, psychology educator; b. Chester, England, Jan. 13, 1940; came to U.S., 1965; s. Daniel and Myfanwy (Ingman) R.; m. Norma, Apr. 3, 1965 (div. Feb. 1993). MS, U. Mass., 1966; PhD, U. Ill., 1969. Asst. prof. Kent (Ohio) State U., 1969-73; from asst. prof. to prof. U. Ill., Champaign, 1973—. Author: Motivation in Sports Psychology and Exercise, 1992; editor The Sport Psychologist Jour., 1988-93. Kinesiology scholar U. Ctr. Ga., Atlanta, 1986. Fellow Assn. for Advancement of Sport Psychology; mem. N.Am. Soc. Sports Psychology (pres. 1981-82), Internat. Soc. Sports Psychology (sec. gen. 1985-93), Internat. Assn. Applied Psychology (pres. (divsn. sport psychology 1994—), Lions. Home: 7B Evergreen Cir Savoy IL 61874 Office: U Ill 906 S Goodwin Ave Urbana IL 61801

ROBERTS, HARRY HEIL, geological research administrator; b. Huntington, W.Va., Feb. 2, 1940; m. Mary S. Hamb, 1963; 1 child, Andrew. BS, Marshall U., 1962; MS, La. State U., 1966, PhD in Giology, 1969. Asst. prof. geol. rsch. Coastal Studies Inst./La. State U., Baton Rouge, 1969-74, assoc. prof., 1974-78, prof. marine sci., 1978—, dir., 1987—. Mem. Soc. Econ. Paleontologists and Mineralogists, Am. Assn. Petrol Geologists, Coastal Soc., Internat. Assn. Sedimentol. Office: Louisiana State Univ Coastal Studies Inst Howe Russell Geoscience Complex Baton Rouge LA 70803 Office: Coastal Studies Inst La State Univ Baton Rouge LA 70803*

ROBERTS, HARRY MORRIS, JR., lawyer; b. Dallas, June 10, 1938; s. Harry Morris and La Frances (Reilly) R.; m. Nancy Beth Johnson, Mar. 7, 1964; children: Richard Whitfield, Elizabeth Lee. BBA, So. Meth. U., 1960; LLB, Harvard U., 1963. Bar: Tex. 1963, U.S. Dist. Ct. (no. dist.) Tex. 1964, U.S. Ct. Appeals (5th cir.), 1972, U.S. Supreme Ct. 1971. Assoc. Thompson & Knight, Dallas, 1963-69, ptnr., 1970-75, sr. ptnr., 1975—; chmn. real estate, probate and trust law sect. State Bar Tex., 1984-85; vis. scholar U. Tex. Law Sch., 1986. Contbr. articles to legal jours. Trustee Shelter Ministries of Dallas, 1982— (chmn. bd. trustees 1992-95). Mem. ABA, Dallas Bar Assn. (chmn. real estate sect. 1981), Am. Bar Found., Tex. Bar Found., Dallas Bar Found., Am. Coll. Real Estate Lawyers, Tex. Coll. Real Estate Attys. (vice chair, bd. dirs. 1990-93). Episcopalian. Clubs: Salesmanship (Dallas), Dallas Country. Office: Thompson & Knight 1700 Pacific Ave Ste 3300 Dallas TX 75201-4656

ROBERTS, HARRY VIVIAN, statistics educator; b. Peoria, Ill., May 1, 1923; s. Harry V. and Mary (Pickels) R.; m. June H. Hoover, Nov. 19, 1943; children: Andrew H., Mary D. BA, U. Chgo., 1943, MBA, 1947, PhD, 1955. Market researcher McCann-Erickson, Inc., Chgo., 1946-49; mem. faculty Grad. Sch. Bus., U. Chgo., 1949—, prof. stats., 1959-88, Sigmund E. Edelstone prof. of stats. and quality mgmt., 1988-93, emeritus, 1993—; cons. in field, 1950—. Author: (with James Lorie) Basic Methods of Marketing Research, 1951, (with Allen Wallis) Statistics: A New Approach, 1956, Converstaional Statistics, 1974, Time Series Analysis and Forecasting with IDA, 1983, Data Analysis for Managers with Minitab, 2d edit., 1991 (with Bernard Sergesketter) Quality is Personal, 1993; editor: Academic Initiatives in Total Quality for Higher Education, 1995; contbr. articles to profl. publs. Mem. rezoning commn. Village of Homewood, Ill., 1956-60, 71-73, mem. zone bd. appeals, 1962-75, chmn. zone bd. appeals, 1973-75, mem. plan commn., 1970-73; mem. mfg. bd., mem. sci. bd. Dept. Def., 1988-90. With AUS, 1943-45. Fellow AAAS (stats. sect.), Am. Statis. Assn. (census adv. com. 1973-78, asso. editor Jour. 1977-82); mem. Royal Statis. Soc., Inst. Math. Stats., Am. Econ. Assn. Home: 1353 Burr Oak Rd Homewood IL 60430-1908 Office: Univ Chgo Grad Sch Bus Chicago IL 60637

ROBERTS, HENRY REGINALD, management consultant, former life insurance company executive; b. Toronto, Ont., Can., June 2, 1916; came to U.S., 1945, naturalized, 1954; s. Alfred Reginald and Mary Margaret (Creighton) R.; m. Margaret Elizabeth Fisher, May 23, 1940; children: Michael Alfred, Barbara Elizabeth, William Henry, Margaret Jane. B.A. in Math. and Physics, U. Toronto, 1937; L.H.D. (hon.), Clarkson Coll. Tech., 1965; LL.D., Trinity Coll., 1970, U. Hartford, 1971. With Mfrs. Life Ins. Co., Toronto, 1937-42; with Conn. Gen. Life Ins. Co., Hartford, 1945-81; 2d v.p. Conn. Gen. Life Ins. Co., 1958-60, exec. v.p., dir., 1960-61, pres., 1961-76; chmn. bd. Aetna Ins. Co., subs., 1966-76; pres., dir. Conn. Gen. Ins. Corp. parent co., 1967-76; chmn. bd. CGIC, 1976-81, presiding dir., 1981; pres. Henry R. Roberts Co., Hartford, 1981-89; chmn. bd. DNA Plant Tech. Corp., 1987-88. Corporator St. Francis Hsop., Hartford Hosp.; mem. coun. Internat. Execs. Svc. Corps. Fellow Soc. Actuaries. Office: 171 Bloomfield Ave Hartford CT 06105-1008

ROBERTS, HOWARD RICHARD, food scientist, association administrator; b. Eldred, Pa., July 6, 1932; s. Edward Euclid and Irene Victoria (Bills) R.; m. Marylyn Ann Morrissey, Dec. 28, 1957; children: Cynthia Anne, Mark Edward, Mary Beth, John Michael. BS, George Washington U., 1955, MS, 1957, PhD, 1962. Cert. quality engr., D.C. Instr. George Washington U., Washington, 1958-59; ops. analyst Johns Hopkins U., Bethesda, Md., 1958-59; rsch. dir. Booz, Allen & Hamilton, Washington, 1959-67; v.p. Booz, Allen & Hamilton, Kansas City, Mo., 1967-72; dir. bur. foods FDA, Washington, 1972-78; dir. sci. affairs Nat. Soft Drink Assn., Washington, 1978-85, sr. v.p., 1986—; cons. George Washington U. Med. Sch., Washington, 1958-59; adv. panel AMA, Chgo., 1974-80; food expert panel FDA, Washington, 1990-91. Author: Food Safety, 1981; co-author: Caffeine - Perspectives from Recent Research, 1984, Agricultural & Food

Chemistry, 1978, Mycotoxins in Human and Animal Health, 1977; contbr. articles to Food Tech. Jour., Food Drug Cosmetic Jour., Food and Chem. Toxicology. Coach, official Vienna (Va.) Youth Inc., 1971-74. With USNR, 1950-54. George Washington U. fellow, 1957; recipient FDA award of Merit, 1978. Fellow Am. Soc. Quality Control (chmn. 1968-70, Svc. award 1971); mem. AAAS, ASTM, Am. Coll. Toxicology (coun. 1985-87), Inst. Food Technologists (profl.), N.Y. Acad. Scis., Internat. Food and Beverage Techs., Internat. Soc. Regulatory Toxicology and Pharmacology, Assn. Food and Drug Officials, Internat. Ozone Assn., Sigma Xi, Omicron Delta Kappa. Republican. Achievements include rsch. in risk assessment, consumption estimation. Office: Nat Soft Drink Assn 1101 16th St NW Washington DC 20036-4803

ROBERTS, HUGH EVAN, business investment services company executive; b. Marion, Ind., Aug. 29, 1923; s. Arthur Edwin and Georgina (Fankboner) R.; m. Ellen Langtree Gordon, Sept. 16, 1950; children: Ellen Langtree, Daniel Evan, Robert Gordon. BSME, U. Cin., 1950. With Procter & Gamble Co., 1950-63, Monsanto Co., 1963-69; with Binkley Co., 1969-81, v.p., div. mgr., 1971-73, pres., 1973-79; chief exec. officer Binkley Co., Warrenton, Mo., 1971-81, chmn. bd., 1979-81; assoc. Capital Assocs. Fund, St. Louis, 1982-85; chmn. bd. Grant Cooper & Assocs., St. Louis, 1985-90; ptnr. Lockett, McNearney & Roberts Inc., St. Louis, 1990-94; retired. Mem. bd. St. Louis County Spl. Sch. Dist., 1973-79, pres., 1976-79. Served to 1st lt., pilot USAAF, World War II. Decorated D.F.C., Air medal with 4 oak leaf clusters. Republican. Episcopalian. Clubs: Mo. Quail and Gun; Univ. (St. Louis). Patentee chemistry, mech. devices. Home: 17 Frontenac Est Dr Saint Louis MO 63131-2613

ROBERTS, HYMAN JACOB, internist, researcher, author, historian, publisher; b. Boston, May 29, 1924; s. Benjamin and Eva (Sherman) R.; m. Carol Antonia Klein, Aug. 9, 1953; children: David, Jonathan, Mark, Stephen, Scott, Pamela. M.D. cum laude, Tufts U., 1947. Diplomate Am. Bd. Internal Medicine. Intern, resident Boston City Hosp., 1947-49; resident Mcpl. Hosp., Washington, 1949-50; rsch. fellow, instr. med. Tufts Med. Sch., Boston, 1948-49, Georgetown Med. Sch., Washington, 1949-50; fellow in medicine Lahey Clinic, Boston, 1950-51; mem. active staff Good Samaritan and St. Mary's Hosps., West Palm Beach, Fla., 1955—; dir. Palm Beach Inst. Med. Rsch., West Palm Beach, 1964—, pres., Sunshine Sentinel Press, Inc. lectr. two day seminar on The New Frontiers in Legal Medicine, Seminar on Defense Against Alzheimer's Disease. U.S. rep. Council of Europe for Driving Standards, 1972. Author: Difficult Diagnosis, Spanish and Italian edits, 1958; The Causes, Ecology and Prevention of Traffic Accidents, 1971, Is Vasectomy Safe?, 1979, Aspartame (NutraSweet): Is It Safe?, 1989, Sweet'ner Dearest, 1992, Is Vasectomy Worth the Risk?, 1993, Mega Vitamin E: Is It Safe?, 1994, The Spirit of Modern Taiwan, 1994, West Palm Beach: Centennial Reflections, 1994, A Guide to Personal Peace, 1994, Defense Against Alzheimers Disease, 1995, The CACOF Conspiracy, 1996, Health and Wealth, Palm Beach Style, 1996; (play) My Wife, The Politician; assoc. editor: Tufts Med. Alumni Bull, Boston, 1978-87, Nutrition Health Rev.; contbr. sci. and med. articles to profl. and theol. jours. Pres. Jewish Community Day Sch., West Palm Beach, Fla., 1975-76; disting. mem. pres. council U. Fla., Gainesville, 1974—; founder, dir. Jewish Fedn. Palm Beach County, West Palm Beach, 1960-72. Served to lt. USNR, 1951-54. Named Fla. Outstanding Young Man Jr. C. of C. Fla., 1958; hon. Ky. col.; recipient Gold Share cert. and silver certs. Inst. Agr. and Food Scis., U. Fla., 1974-78; Paul Harris fellow Rotary Found., 1980. Fellow ACP, Am. Coll. Chest Physicians, Am. Coll. Nutrition, Stroke Council; mem. AMA, Am. Acad. Neurology, Endocrine Soc., Am. Diabetes Assn., Am. Heart Assn., Am. Fedn. Clin. Research, Am. Coll. Angiology (gov. 1981), Am. Coll. Legal Medicine, Pan Am. Med. Assn. (chmn. endocrinology 1982), So. Med. Assn., N.Y. Acad. Scis., Am. Physicians Fellowship of Israel Med. Assn., Confrerie de la Chaine des Rotisseurs, Alpha Omega Alpha, Sigma Xi. Club: Governors of West Palm Beach (a founder), Executive (founder). Lodges: Rotary; B'nai B'rith, Order St. George (knight of magistral grace 1992). Research in med. diagnosis, diabetes, hypoglycemia, postvasectomy state, Vitamin E metabolism, pentachlorophenol, heavy metal toxicity, narcolepsy, traffic accidents, thrombophlebitis, aspartame, Alzheimer's disease, brain tumors, nutrition and bioethics. Home: 6708 Pamela Ln West Palm Beach FL 33405-4175 Office: Palm Beach Inst Med Rsch 300 27th St West Palm Beach FL 33407-5202 also: Sunshine Sentinel Press Inc PO Box 17799 West Palm Beach FL 33416

ROBERTS, J. WENDELL, federal judge; b. Somerset, Ky., May 1, 1943; s. Earl C. and Dorothy (Whitaker) R.; children: Stephen A., Shannon L. BA, Ea. Ky. U., 1964; JD, U. Ky., 1966. Bar: Ky. 1966, U.S. Dist. Ct. (we. dist.) Ky. 1978, U.S. Ct. Appeals (6th cir.) 1983. Atty. Ky. Dept. Revenue, Frankfort, 1966; law clk. Ky. Supreme Ct., Frankfort, 1966-67; atty. Charles A. Williams & Assoc., Paducah, Ky., 1967, Westberry & Roberts, Marion, Ky., 1968-87; city atty. City of Marion, 1968-84; judge U.S. Bankruptcy Ct. Western Dist. Ky., Louisville, 1987—, chief judge, 1988-95. Vice chmn. Pennyrile Area Devel. Dist., Hopkinsville, Ky., 1968-72. Mem. Ky. Bar Assn., Louisville Bar Assn., Nat. Conf. Bankruptcy Judges (bd. govs. 1991-94), Mcpl. Attys. Assn. Ky. (pres. 1983). Methodist. Avocations: travel, antiques. Office: US Bankruptcy Ct 528 US Courthouse 601 W Broadway St Louisville KY 40202-2264

ROBERTS, JACK EARLE, lawyer, ski resort operator, wood products company executive, real estate developer; b. L.A., Nov. 5, 1928; s. James Earle and Illa Ann (Morgan) R.; m. Marilyn Humphreys, Sept. 13, 1954; children: Ronda, Cyndi, Scott, Robynne, Craig. B.S. in Accounting and Bus. Adminstrn, Brigham Young U., 1952; J.D., George Washington U., 1955, LL.M. in Taxation (Teaching fellow), 1956. Bar: Calif. 1957; CPA, Ariz. Pvt. practice L.A.; atty. Office Chief Counsel, IRS, L.A., 1956-60; mem. firm Roberts, Carmack, Johnson, Poulson & Harmer, L.A., 1961-78; pres. Park West Ski Resort, Park City, Utah, 1975-88; pres., dir. Accudyne Corp., Los Angeles, 1972-89, Richmark Corp., Los Angeles, 1972-77; chmn., dir. Comml. Wood Products Co., Los Angeles, 1968—; pres., dir. Snyderville Devel. Co., Inc., Utah, 1978-94, Community Water Co., Salt Lake City, 1987—, Roberts Mgmt. Corp., Salt Lake City, 1988—, Ste. Vacations, Inc., Salt Lake City, 1989—. Contbr. articles on legal subjects to tech. jours. Pres. Westwood Rep. Club, 1968; mem. cen. coms. Calif. State, L.A. County Rep. Party, 1974-77; mem. Utah State Cen. and Exec. Coms., 1981—, Summit County Rep. cen. and exec. coms., 1978-84; state sec. Utah Rep. Party, 1985-88, chmn., 1989; mem. Rep. Nat. Com., 1988-96; chmn. Summit County Rep. Party, 1981-83. Mem. Calif. Bar Assn., D.C. Bar Assn. Office: 150 Virginia St Salt Lake City UT 84103-4315

ROBERTS, JAMES ALLEN, urologist; b. Beach, N.D., May 31, 1934; s. Earl Fernando and Maria Ellen R.; m. Hilda Peachy, Nov. 29, 1987; children from previous marriage: Jennifer Lou Roberts Walsh, Mary Ellen Roberts Wargo, Thomas J. M.D., U. Chgo., 1959. Diplomate: Am. Bd. Urology. Intern U. Chgo. Sch. Medicine, 1959-60, resident in urology, 1961-65; mem. faculty Tulane U. Med. Sch., New Orleans, 1971—; prof. urology Tulane U. Med. Sch., 1975—, assoc. chmn., 1986—; sr. research scientist, head dept. urology Tulane Regional Primate Research Center, Covington, 1972—. Mem. editorial bd. Am. Jour. Kidney Diseases and Urol. Rsch.; contbr. articles to profl. jours. Bd. dirs. Highland Park Hosp., 1985-87. Recipient grants NIH. Fellow ACS; mem. St. Tammany Parish Med. Soc. (pres. 1979), Soc. Rsch. on Calculous Kinetics, La. Urol. Soc., Am. Urol. Assn., Soc. Univ. Urologists, Nat. Kidney Found., Soc. Exptl. Biology and Medicine, Sigma Xi. Office: 1323 S Tyler St Covington LA 70433-2338

ROBERTS, JAMES DONZIL, lawyer; b. St. Louis, Mo., Apr. 4, 1957; s. Donzil D. and Barbara V. Malona; m. Jody A. Garcia, Dec. 7, 1985; children: James D. Jr., Jessica E. Student, Calif. State U., Northridge, 1976-79, Calif. State U., Dominguez Hills, 1981; JD, U. LaVerne, 1985. Bar: Calif. 1985, U.S. Dist. Ct. (ctrl. dist.) Calif. 1986. Staff and supr. atty. Bollington Stilz & Bloeser, Woodland Hills, Calif., 1985-90; mng. atty. Bollington and Roberts, Long Beach, Calif., 1990—; judge pro tem Long beach Mcpl. Ct., Long Beach, 1992—; lectr. extension program UCLA, 1994—. Trustee U. LaVerne San Fernando Valley Coll. Law, Encino, 1984-85; active West L.A. County Coun., Boy Scouts Am., West Hills, Calif., 1995. Mem. Assn. Calif. House Counsel (founding mem.); mem. L.A. County Bar Assn., Long Beach Bar Assn., Assn. So. Calif. Def. Counsel, Long Beach Barristers Assn., Am. Inn Ct. (Long Beach, barrister). Avocations: baseball/softball, bowling, golf. Office: Bollington & Roberts Ste 540 3780 Kilroy Airport Way Long Beach CA 90806

ROBERTS, JAMES G., foundation executive; b. Lincoln, Nebr., May 20, 1922; s. Ellsworth James and Anna (Gillette) R.; m. Eleanor Ramsey, July 28, 1945; children—Kenneth James, Ellen Margaret. Student, Nebr. Wesleyan U., 1939-41; B.A., Colo U., 1942. Mgr. Littlefield C. of C., Tex., 1948-50; mgr. indsl. div. Amarillo C. of C., Tex., 1950-51; mgr. Plainview C. of C., Tex., 1951-53; mgr. Tulsa dist. U.S. C. of C., 1953-54; mgr. Southwestern div. U.S. C. of C., Dallas, 1954-58; gen. mgr. Greater Boston C. of C., 1958-59, exec. v.p., 1959-64; v.p. pub. info. New Eng. Mut. Life Ins. Co., Boston, 1964-67; pres. Roberts Assocs., 1968-72; exec. v.p. Greater Pitts. C. of C., 1972-75; gen. mgr. N.H. Bus. and Industry Assn., 1975-77, exec. v.p., 1977-83; pres. Gordon Coll. Found., Wenham, Mass., 1983-87; adminstr. St. Andrews Estates South, Boca Raton, Fla., 1988-91; 1st pub. Boston mag., 1962; pres. Back Bay Planning & Devel. Corp., Boston, 1965-67; bd. dirs. Wellesley Nat. Bank. Mem. exec. com. Billy Graham Crusade, 1964; trustee Gordon Coll., Joslyn Diabetes Found., Historic Park Street Ch.; bd. dirs. Salvation Army; deacon Presby. Ch.; Pensacola Mayor's com. for Elderly Affairs. Served to 1st lt. USAAF, World War II. Mem. Soc. Advancement of Mgmt. (v.p. pub. rels.), Fla. Life Care Residents Assn. (bd. dirs., mem. exec. com. 1995—), Boston BBB (bd. dirs.), No. Shore C. of C. (bd. dirs., Wellesley Club, Algonquin Club, Greater Boston Execs. Club (pres.), Ea. Yacht Club, Duquesne Club.

ROBERTS, JAMES HAROLD, III, lawyer; b. Omaha, Aug. 11, 1949; s. James Harold Jr. and Evelyn Doris (Young) R.; m. Marilyn Novak, June 29, 1974; children: Jessica Noël, Meredith Caitlin. BA, U. Notre Dame, 1971; JD, St. Louis U., 1974. Bar: Iowa 1974, U.S. Ct. Mil. Appeals 1974, U.S. Supreme Ct. 1979, D.C. 1981. Govt. contract atty. U.S. Gen. Acctg. Office, Washington, 1978-83, U.S. Dept. Treasury, Washington, 1983-88; pvt. practice Manatt Phelps & Phillips, Washington, 1988—. Editor St. Louis U. law rev., 1973-74. Served to capt. JAGC, U.S. Army, 1974-78, lt. col. USAR/NG, 1978—. Mem. ABA (pub. contract law sect.), D.C. Bar Assn., Fed. Bar Assn. Roman Catholic. Home: 308 N Monroe St Arlington VA 22201-1736 Office: Manatt Phelps & Phillips 1501 M St NW Ste 700 Washington DC 20005-1700

ROBERTS, JAMES LEWIS, medical sciences educator; b. Lima, Peru, Oct. 23, 1951; U.S. citizen; s. David and Mary (Fuller) R.; m. Mariann Blum, Mar. 7, 1986. BS, Colo. State U., 1973; PhD, U. Oreg., 1977. Fellow U. Calif., San Francisco, 1977-79; asst. prof. Columbia U., N.Y.C., 1979-86, assoc. prof., 1986; dir., prof. Mt. Sinai Sch. Medicine, N.Y.C., 1986-90, prof., 1990—; cons. Calif. Biotech., Mountain View, Calif., 1986-88, NIH, Bethesda, Md., 1979—. Recipient Golden Lamport award, Excellence Basic Sci.; NIH rsch. grantee, 1979—, NSF rsch. grantee 1981-84, 95—, Mellon Found. rsch. grantee, 1980-84. Mem. AAAS, Soc. for Neurosci., Endocrine Soc., Internat. Endocrine Soc., N.Y. Acad. Scis., Am. Soc. Biochemists and Molecular Biologists. Achievements include research in biosynthesis and regulation of the ACTH endorphin and gonadotropin releasing hormone precursor, recombinant DNA cloning of pituitary and brain ACTH endorphin, glucocorticoid and thyroid hormone regulation of gene expression, gene structure. Office: Mt Sinai Sch Medicine 1 Gustave L Levy Pl New York NY 10029-6504

ROBERTS, JAMES MCGREGOR, retired professional association executive; b. Moncton, N.B., Can., Nov. 24, 1923; came to U.S., 1949, naturalized, 1956; s. Roland M. and Edith M. (Shields) R.; m. Thelma E. Williams, May 6, 1944; 1 dau., Jana M. B.Commerce, U. Toronto, Ont., Can., 1949. Auditor Citizens Bank, Los Angeles, 1949-54; auditor Acad. Motion Picture Arts and Scis., Hollywood, Calif., 1954—; controller Acad. Motion Picture Arts and Scis., 1956-71, exec. dir., 1971-89, exec. sec. acad. found., 1971-89; exec. cons. Acad. Motion Picture Arts and Scis., Hollywood, Calif., 1989-92; exec. cons., 1990-93, ret., 1994. Served as pilot Royal Can. Air Force, World War II. Home: 4968 Lerkas Way Oceanside CA 92056-7428

ROBERTS, JAMES MILNOR, JR., professional society administrator; b. Pitts., Sept. 16, 1918; s. James Milnor and Elizabeth (Bennett) R.; m. Virginia Lee Sykes, Mar. 15, 1947 (dec. Apr. 1995); children: James Milnor III, Mary Lee Roberts Newman, Deborah Lee Roberts Gillespie, Todd Osborn; m. Priscilla Bruce, Nov. 24, 1995. Student, Lehigh U., 1936-40, U.S. Army Command and Gen. Staff Coll., 1962, Nat. Def. U., 1963, Army War Coll., 1970. Commd. 2d lt. inf. U.S. Army, 1940, advanced through grades to maj., 1944, discharged, 1945; mem. U.S. Army (Res.), 1946-70; with 1st battle group U.S. Army Res. 314th Inf. Regt., Pitts., 1947-62; comdr. combat command sect. 79th Command Hdqrs., Pitts., 1962-64; with Office Chief Info., Dept. Army, Washington, 1964-67; comdr. 99th Army Res. Command, Pitts., 1967-70; promoted to maj. gen. 99th Army Res. Command, 1971; dep. chief U.S. Army Res., Washington, 1970-71; chief U.S. Army Res., 1971-75; exec. dir. Res. Officers Assn. U.S., Washington, 1975-84; pub. The Officer mag., 1975-84; pres. Nat. Intelligence Study Ctr.; pres. Ams. for High Frontier, Arlington, Va., 1987-95, dir., 1995—. Chmn. Young Reps., Allegheny County, Pa., 1952-54; exec. v.p. Wind Symphony Orch., Pitts., 1961-62; bd. dirs. Pitts. Civic Light Opera, 1958-70; chmn. Com. for Free Afghanistan, 1983-93; pres. Nat. Hist. Intelligence Mus. Decorated D.S.M., Legion of Merit, Bronze Star; Croix de Guerre with silver star France; Mil. Cross Czechoslovakia; recipient USN Disting. Pub. Svc. award, USCG Disting. Pub. Svc. award, USAF Exceptional Svc. award; named Significant Sig Sigma Chi, 1973. Mem. Res. Officers Assn. (past chpt. officer), Am. Security Council, Assn. U.S. Army, Mil. Order World Wars, Ret. Officers Assn., The Dwight D. Eisenhower Soc. (chair 1992—), Soc. of Cin., SAR, VFW, Am. Legion, Army-Navy Club (Washington), Ft. Myer (Va.) Officers Club, Capital Hill Club, Masons. Home: 11910 Parkside Dr Fairfax VA 22033-2648 Office: High Frontier 2800 Shirlington Rd Ste 404 Arlington VA 22206-3601

ROBERTS, JAMES OWEN, financial planning executive, consultant; b. Madison, Wis., Aug. 19, 1930; s. John William and Sada (Buckmaster) R.; m. Georgianna Timmons, Jan. 30, 1954; children: Stephen, Susan, Ellen, Timmons. BS, Ohio State U., 1952; MBA, Case Western Res. U., 1970. With Owens-Ill., Inc., Toledo, Ohio, 1952, 54-55, salesman, Atlanta, 1955-58, N.Y.C., 1958-62, food div. mgr., N.Y.C., 1963-66, br. mgr., Cleve., 1966-71; mgr. corp. fin. Stone & Webster Securities Corp., Cleve., 1971-74; regional dir. Mgmt. Planning, Inc., Cleve., 1976-80, v.p., 1980-86, sr. v.p., 1986, mgmt. planning pres., 1986-96, chmn., 1996—; lectr. valuation and bus. ownership succession in field. Contbr. articles to profl. jours. Trustee Soc. for the Blind, Cleve., 1983-86, Ohio Motorists Assn., 1985-94, chmn., 1990-92; pres. Children's Svcs., Inc., 1986-88; trustee Great Lakes Theater; elder Fairmount Presbyn. Ch. 1st Lt. USAF, 1952-54. Mem. Fin. Analysts Fedn., Cleve. Soc. Security Analysts, Cleve. Skating Club, Nassau Club, Huron Yacht Club, Chgo. Athletic Assn. Republican. Avocations: sailing, skiing, flying, hiking, photography. Home: 2323 Stillman Rd Cleveland OH 44118-3520 Office: Mgmt Planning Inc 545 Hanna Bldg Cleveland OH 44115 also: 101 Poor Farm Rd Princeton NJ 08540-1941

ROBERTS, JARED INGERSOLL, lawyer; b. Phila., Mar. 20, 1946; s. Brooke and Anna (Ingersoll) R.; m. Katherine Marx Sherwood, May 17, 1986. BA, Princeton U., 1968; JD, U. Va., 1974. Bar: Pa. 1974, U.S. Dist. Ct. (ea. dist.) Pa. 1975, U.S. Ct. Appeals (3d cir.) 1978, U.S. Supreme Ct. 1978, D.C. 1985. Assoc. Duane, Morris & Heckscher, Phila., 1974-82; spl. counsel U.S. Dept. Transp., Washington, 1982-84; assoc. gen. counsel Nat. R.R. Passenger Corp., Washington, 1984—. Served to lt (j.g.) USN, 1968-70. Mem. ABA, Pa. Bar Assn., D.C. Bar Assn. Republican. Episcopalian. Avocations: sailing, skating, railroads. Home: 3607 N Glebe Rd Arlington VA 22207-4316 Office: Amtrak Law Dept 60 Massachusetts Ave NE Washington DC 20002-4225

ROBERTS, JAY, pharmacologist, educator; b. N.Y.C., July 15, 1927; s. Harry and Evelyn R.; m. Marion Camenson, June 18, 1950; children—Hunt, Kathy. B.S., L.I. U., 1949; Ph.D., Cornell U., 1953. Asst. prof., then asso. prof. pharmacology Cornell U. Med. Coll., 1956-66; prof. pharmacology U. Pitts. Med. Sch., 1966-70; prof. pharmacology, chmn. dept. Med. Coll. Pa., 1970—; chmn. dept. Med. Coll. Pa.-Hahneman U. Sch. Medicine, 1994—; cons. to industry; mem. NIH Study Sect. Contbr. numerous articles to profl. jours.; reviewer for numerous sci. jours.; assoc. editor (Pharmacology) Jour. Gerentology; asst. editor Jour. Pharmcol. and Exptl. Therap.; editor Jour. Gerentology & Biol. Scis. Served with USNR, 1945-46. Postdoctoral fellow N.Y. Heart Assn., 1953-57; Postdoctoral fellow USPHS, 1953-55; recipient Lindback Disting. Teaching award Med. Coll. Pa., 1973. Fellow Am. Coll. Cardiology, Am. Coll. Clin. Pharmacology, Coll. Physicians Phila. (chmn. geriatric sect. 1986-88), Gerontol. Soc. Am. (chmn. biol. sect. 1984); mem. Internat. Study Group Research Cardiac Metabolism, Am. Fedn. Clin. Research, AAAS, Am. Soc. Pharmacology and Exptl. Therapeutics, Soc. Exptl. Biology and Medicine, Cardiac Muscle Soc., Am. Heart Assn., Southeastern Pa. Heart Assn. (peer reviewer grants 1973-94, Sr. Investigation Achievement award 1990), Harvey Soc., Assn. Med. Sch. Pharmacology, Am. Coll. Clin. Pharmacology (charter), AAUP, U.S. Pharmacopeial Conv. (chmn. geriatric adv. panel 1980-90), Mid-Atlantic Pharmacology Soc. (pres. 1990-92), Sigma Xi. Home: Benson House 930 Montgomery Ave Bryn Mawr PA 19010-3044 Office: Med Coll Pa 3200 Henry Ave Philadelphia PA 19129-1137

ROBERTS, JEANNE ADDISON, literature educator; b. Washington; d. John West and Sue Fisher (Nichols) Addison; m. Markley Roberts, Feb. 19, 1966; children: Addison Cary Steed Masengill, Ellen Carraway Masengill Coster. A.B., Agnes Scott Coll., 1946; M.A., U. Pa., 1947; Ph.D., U. Va., 1964. Instr. Mary Washington Coll., 1947-48; instr., chmn. English Fairfax Hall Jr. Coll., 1950-51; tchr. Am. U. Assn. Lang. Center, Bangkok, Thailand, 1952-56; instr. Beirut (Lebanon) Coll. for Women, 1956-57, asst. prof., 1957-60, chmn. English dept., 1957-60; instr. lit. Am. U., Washington, 1960-62; asst. prof. Am. U., 1962-65, asso. prof., 1965-68, prof., 1968-93; dean faculties Am. U., 1974; lectr. Howard U., 1971-72; seminar prof. Folger Shakespeare Libr. Inst. for Renaissance and 18th Century Studies, 1974; dir. NEH Summer Inst. for High Sch. Tchrs. on Teaching Shakespeare, Folger Shakespeare Libr., 1984, 85, 86; dir. NEH summer inst. Va. Commonwealth U. 1995, 96 Writings By and About Women in The English Renaissance. Author: Shakespeare's English Comedy: The Merry Wives of Windsor in Context, 1979, The Shakespearean Wild: Geography, Genus and Gender, 1991; editor: (with James G. McManaway) A Selective Bibliography of Shakespeare: Editions, Textual Studies, Commentary, 1975; (with Peggy O'Brien) Shakespeare Set Free, vol. 1, 1993, vol. 2, 1994, vol. 3, 1995; contbr. articles to scholarly jours. Danforth Tchr. grantee, 1962-63; Folger Sr. fellow, 1969-70, 88. Mem. MLA (chmn. Shakespeare div. 1981-82), Renaissance Soc. Am., Milton Soc., Shakespeare Assn. Am. (trustee 1978-81, 87-89, pres. 1986-87), AAUP (pres. Am. U. chpt. 1966-67), Southeastern Renaissance Conf. (pres. 1981-82), Phi Beta Kappa, Mortar Board, Phi Kappa Phi. Episcopalian. Home: 4931 Albemarle St NW Washington DC 20016-4359 Office: Am U Dept Lit Washington DC 20016

ROBERTS, JERRY, newspaper editor. Polit. editor city desk San Francisco Chronicle, editl. pg. editor, 1995—. Office: San Francisco Chronicle 901 Mission St San Francisco CA 94103-2905

ROBERTS, JO ANN WOODEN, school system administrator; b. Chgo., June 24, 1948; d. Tilmon and Annie Mae (Wardlaw) Wooden; m. Edward Allen Roberts Sr. (div.); children: Edward Allen Jr., Hillary Ann. BS, Wayne State U., 1970, MS, 1971; PhD, Northwestern U., 1977. Speech, lang. pathologist Chgo. Bd. Edn., 1971-78, adminstr., 1978-88; dir. spl. svcs. Rock Island (Ill.) Pub. Schs., 1988-90; supt. Muskegon Hts. (Mich.) Pub. Schs., 1990-93; deputy supr. Chgo. Pub. Schs., 1993-96; supt. of schs. Hazel Crest (Ill.) Sch. Dist. #152 1/2, 1996—; instr. Chgo City Community Coll., 1976-77; project dir. Ednl. Testing Svc., Evanston, Ill., 1976-77; exec. dir. Nat. Speech, Lang. and Hearing Assn., Chgo., 1984-86; hon. guest lectr. Govs. State U., University Park, Ill., 1983-86; cons. in field. Author: Learning to Talk, 1974. Trustee Muskegon County Libr. Bd., 1990, Mercy Hosp. Bd., Muskegon, 1990, St. Mark's Sch. Bd. Dirs., Southborough, Mass., 1989, United Way Bd., Muskegon, 1990; mem. Mich. State Bd. Edn. Systematic Initiative in Math and Sci., 1991, Gov. John Engler Mich. 2000 Task Force, 1991, Chpt. II Adv. Commn., 1991. Recipient Leadership award Boy Scouts Am., 1990; named finalist Outstanding Young Working Women, Glamour Mag., 1984, Outstanding Educator, Blacks in Govt., 1990. Mem. Am. Assn. Sch. Adminstrs., Nat. Alliance Black Sch. Educators, Mich. Assn. Sch. Adminstrs., Assn. Supervision & Curriculum Devel., Phi Delta Kappa. Avocations: creative writing, peotry, modern dance, theater, drawing. Office: Chgo Pub Schs 1819 W Pershing Rd Chicago IL 60609-2317

ROBERTS, JOAN I., social psychologist, educator. BA in English, U. Utah, Salt Lake City, 1957; MA in Social Psychology, Columbia U., 1960, EdD in Social Psychology, 1970. Teaching asst. in English U. Utah, Salt Lake City, 1956-57; cons. psychologist Herrold Assocs. Mgmt. Cons., N.Y.C., 1958-61; research staff mem. Makerere Coll., Kampala, East Africa, 1961-63; research assoc. Hunter Coll., N.Y.C., 1964-67; coordinator Tng. Project and Research in Intergroup Relations, Madison, Wis., 1970-73; asst. prof. dept. ednl. policy studies U. Wis., Madison, 1968-75; assoc. prof. social scis. Upstate Med. Ctr./SUNY, Syracuse, 1976-79; chairperson dept. child, family, and community studies Syracuse (N.Y.) U., 1978-80, assoc. prof. dept. child, family, and community studies, 1978-84, prof. dept. child, family, and community studies, 1985—, prof. emerita, 1994—; prof. internat. programs abroad Syracuse U., London, 1984-85, 1990; adj. prof. Syracuse U. Sch. Nursing, N.Y., 1976—; adj. assoc. prof. social scis. SUNY, 1979-83; project dir. model caregivers tng. project N.Y. State Dept. Social Services, 1981; lectr. and presenter of papers to various academic and profl. groups; coordinator, mem. Wis. Coordinating Council of Women in Higher Edn., 1971-74. Author: School Children in the Urban Slum: Readings in Social Science Reseach, 1966, 2d rev. edit., 1968, Group Behavior in Urban Classrooms, 1968, Scene of the Battle: Group Behavior in Urban Classrooms, 1970; Beyond Intellectual Sexism: A New Woman, A New Reality, 1976; author: (with Prof. Sherri Akinsanya) Educational Patterns and Cultural Configurations: The Anthropology of Education, Vol. I, 1976, Schooling in the Cultural Context: Anthropological Studies of Education, Vol. II, 1975, Feminism and Nursing: Historical Perspectives on the Status, Power, and Political Activism in Nursing Profession, 1995. Mem. APA, Am. Anthrop. Assn., Corinthian Club, Brit. U. Womens Club.

ROBERTS, JOHN BENJAMIN, II, public policy consultant, television producer, writer; b. Albrook AFB, C.Z., Oct. 10, 1955; s. Robert Benjamin and Mary Pauline (Porath) R.; 1 child, John Benjamin III. BA, U. Calif., Irvine, 1973; MA with honors, Oxford U., Eng., 1978. Assoc. editor Handgunner, Ltd., London, 1979—, British Rifleman, 1995—; press aide Reagan-Bush Campaign, Arlington, Va., 1980, sr. policy analyst, Washington, 1984; dep. dir. communications Rep. Nat. Com., Washington, 1981, Nat. Rep. Congl. Com., 1991; dir. editorial policy U.S. Dept. Edn., Washington, 1981-83; assoc. dir. office planning and evaluation White House, Washington, 1983-84, assoc. dir. office polit. and govtl. affairs, 1985-86; sr. v.p. Russo, Watts & Rollins Inc., Washington, 1986-88, pres. Roberts Communications, Inc., Washington, 1988—; sr. v.p. Robinson, Lake/Sawyer Miller, Washington, 1991-94; TV producer McLaughlin Group, One on One, CNBC, 1986-96, v.p. programming, 1996—. Author: Entitlement Spending, 1984, Sons of Cincinnatus, 1996. Contbr. articles to newspapers, mags. Bd. dirs. Inst. for Rsch. on Small Arms in Internat. Security, Washington, 1989. Internat. Exch. Coun. (bd. dirs.), Oxford U. Pistol Club (Half-Blue Varsity award 1978), U.K. Practical Shooting Assn. (founder, life mem.), Oxford Soc . Avocations: competitive marksmanship, backpacking, photography. Home: 8507 Conover Pl Alexandria VA 22308 Office: Oliver Prodns Inc 1211 Connecticut Ave NW Ste 810 Washington DC 20036

ROBERTS, JOHN D., retired chemist, educator; b. L.A., June 8, 1918; s. Allen Andrew and Flora (Dombrowski) R.; m. Edith Mary Johnson, July 11, 1942; children: Anne Christine, Donald William, John Paul, Allen Walter. AB, UCLA, 1941, PhD, 1944; D in Natural Scis. (hon.), U. Munich, 1962; D.Sc. (hon.), Temple U., 1964, Notre Dame U., 1993, U. Wales, 1993; student, Scripps Rsch. Inst., 1996. Instr. chemistry UCLA, 1944-45; NRC fellow chemistry Harvard U., 1945-46, instr. chemistry, 1946; instr. chemistry MIT, 1946, asst. prof., 1947-50, assoc. prof., 1950-52; vis. prof. Ohio State U., 1952, Stanford U., 1973-74; prof. organic chemistry Calif. Inst. Tech., 1953-72, inst. prof. chemistry, 1972-88, inst. prof. chemistry emeritus, lectr., 1988—, dean of faculty, v.p., provost, 1980-83, lectr., 1988—, chmn. divsn. chemistry and chem. engring., 1963-68, acting chmn., 1972-73; Foster lectr. U. Buffalo, 1956; Mack Meml. lectr. Ohio State U., 1957; Falk-Plaut lectr. Columbia U., 1957; Reynaud Found. lectr. Mich. State U., 1958; Bachmann Meml. lectr. U. Mich., 1958; J.D. Roberts Symp lectr. Harvard U., 1995; Rhodes-Rawlin lectr. U. Wyo., 1995; Bristol-Meyers Squibb lectr. Syracuse U., 1995;,vis. prof. Harvard, 1958-59, M. Tishler lectr., 1965; Reilly lectr. Notre Dame U., 1960; Am.-Swiss Found. lectr., 1960; O.M. Smith lectr. Okla. State U., 1962; M.S. Kharasch Meml. lectr. U. Chgo., 1962; K. Folkers lectr. U. Ill., 1962; Phillips lectr. Haverford Coll., 1963; vis. prof. U. Munich, 1962; Sloan lectr. U. Alaska, 1967; Disting. vis. prof. U. Iowa, 1967; Sprague lectr. U. Wis., 1967; Kilpatrick lectr. Ill. Inst. Tech., 1969; Pacific Northwest lectr., 1969; E.F. Smith lectr. U. Pa., 1970; vis. prof. chemistry Stanford U., 1973-74; S.C. Lind lectr. U. Tenn.; Arapahoe lectr. U. Colo., 1976; Mary E. Kapp lectr. Va. Commonwealth U., 1976; R.T. Major lectr. U. Conn., 1977; Nebr. lectr. Am. Chem. Soc., 1977; Leermakers lectr. Wesleyan U., 1980; Iddles Meml. lectr. U. N.H., 1981; Arapahoe lectr. Colo. State U., 1981; Winstein lectr. UCLA, 1981; Gilman lectr. Iowa State U., 1982; Marvel lectr. U. Ill., 1982; vis. lectr. Inst. Photog. Chemistry, Beijing, People's Republic of China, 1983, King lectr. Kans. State U., 1984, Lanzhou U., People's Republic of China, 1985, Davis lectr. U. New Orleans, 1986, Du Pont lectr. Harvey Mudd Coll., 1987, 3M vis. lectr. St. Olaf Coll., 1987, Swift lectr. Calif. Inst. Tech., 1987, Berliner lectr. Bryn Mawr Coll., 1988; Friend E. Clark lectr. W. Va. U., 1990; George H. Büchi lectr. MIT, 1991; Henry Kuivala lectr. SUNY Albany, 1991, Fuson lect. U. Nev., 1992; dir., cons. editor W.A. Benjamin, Inc., 1961-67; cons. E.I. du Pont Co., 1950—; mem. adv. panel chemistry NSF, 1958-60, chmn., 1959-60, chmn. divisional com. math., phys. engring. scis., 1962-64, mem. math. and phys. sci. div. com., 1964-66; chemistry adv. panel Air Force Office Sci. Research, 1959-61; chmn. chemistry sect. Nat. Acad. Scis., 1968-71; chmn. Nat. Acad. Scis. (Class I), 1976-78, councillor, 1980-83, nominating com., 1992; dir. Organic Syntheses, Inc. Author: Basic Organic Chemistry, Part I, 1955, Nuclear Magnetic Resonance, 1958, Spin-Spin Splitting in High-Resolution Nuclear Magnetic Resonance Spectra, 1961, Molecular Orbital Calculations, 1961, (with M.C. Caserio) Basic Principles of Organic Chemistry, 1964, 2d edit., 1977, Modern Organic Chemistry, 1967, (with R. Stewart and M.C. Caserio) Organic Chemistry-Methane To Macromolecules, 1971; (autobiography) At The Right Place at the Right Time, 1990; cons. editor: McGraw-Hill Series in Advanced Chemistry, 1957-60; editor in chief Organic Syntheses, vol. 41; mem. editorial bd. Spectroscopy, Organic Magnetic Resonance in Chemistry, Asymmetry, Tetrahedron Computer Methodology. Trustee L.S.B. Leakey Found., 1983-92; bd. dirs. Huntington Med. Rsch. Insts., Organic Syntheses Inc., Coleman Chamber Music Assn.; mem. Calif. Competitive Tech. adv. com., 1989—. Guggenheim fellow, 1952-53, 55-56; recipient Am. Chem. Soc. awrd pure chemistry, 1954, Harrison Howe award, 1957, Roger Adams award in organic chemistry, 1967, Alumni Profl. Achievement award UCLA, 1967, Nichols medal, 1972, Tolman medal, 1975, Michelson-Morley award, 1976, Norris award, 1978, Pauling award, 1980, Theodore Wm. Richards medal, 1982, Willard Gibbs Gold medal, 1983, Golden Plate award Am. Acad. Achievement, 1983, Priestley medal, 1987, Madison marshall award, 1989, (with W. V.E. Doering) Robert A. Welch award, 1990, Nat. Medal Sci. NSF, 1990, Glenn T. Seaborg medal, 1991, Award in nuclear magnetic resource, 1991, Svc. to Chemistry award, 1991, Arthur C. Cope award Am. Chem. Soc. 1994, Chem. Pioneer awad, 1994, History Maker award from Pasadena Hist. Soc., 1994; named hon. alumnus Calif. Inst. Tech., 1990, SURF dedicatee, 1992. Mem. NAS (mem. com. on sci. and engring. pub. policy 1983-87), AAAS (councillor 1992-95), Am. Chem. Soc. (chmn. organic chemistry divsn. 1956-57), Am. Philos. Soc. (mem. coun. 1983-86), Am. Acad. Arts and Scis., Sigma Xi, Phi Lambda Upsilon, Alpha Chi. Sigma. Office: Calif Inst Tech Div of Chem 164-30 CR Pasadena CA 91125

ROBERTS, JOHN DERHAM, lawyer; b. Orlando, Fla., Nov. 1, 1942; s. Junius P. and Mary E. (Limerick) R.; m. Malinda K. Swineford, June 11, 1965; 1 child, Kimberlyn Amanda. Cert., Richmond (Va.) Bus. Coll., 1960; BS, Hampden-Sydney (Va.) Coll., 1964; LLB, Washington & Lee U., 1968. Bar: Va. 1968, Fla. 1969, U.S. Supreme Ct. 1969, U.S. Ct. Customs and Patent Appeals 1970, U.S. Tax Ct. 1970, U.S. Ct. Appeals (5th cir.) 1970, U.S. Ct. Appeals (9th cir.) 1974, U.S. Supreme Ct. 1969. Law clk. U.S. Dist. Ct., Jacksonville, Fla., 1968-69; assoc. Phillips, Kendrick, Gearhart & Aylor, Arlington, Va., 1969-70; asst. U.S. Atty. mid. dist. Fla. U.S. Dept. Justice, Jacksonville, 1970-74; asst. U.S. Atty. Dist. of Alaska, Anchorage, 1974-77, U.S. magistrate judge, 1977—. Bd. dirs. Teen Challenge Alaska, Anchorage, 1984-93; chmn. Eagle Scout Rev. Bd., 1993—; bd. dirs. Alaska Youth for Christ. Recipient Citizenship award DAR, Anchorage, 1984, plaque, U.S. Navy, Citizen Day, Adak, Alaska, 1980. Mem. ABA, Nat. Conf. Spl. Ct. Judges (exec. bd. 1985-92), 9th Cir. Conf. Magistrates (exec. bd. 1982-85, chmn. 1984-85), Alaska Bar Assn., Anchorage Bar Assn., Chi Phi, Psi Chi, Phi Alpha Delta. Republican. Office: US Magistrate Judge 222 W 7th Ave #46 Anchorage AK 99513-7504

ROBERTS, JOHN GLOVER, JR., lawyer; b. Buffalo, Jan. 27, 1955; s. John Glover and Rosemary (Podrasky) R. A.B. summa cum laude, Harvard U., 1976, J.D. magna cum laude, 1979. Bar: D.C. 1981, U.S. Ct. Appeals (fed. cir.) 1982, U.S. Ct. Appeals (D.C., 5th, 9th cirs.) 1988, U.S. Ct. Claims (3d and 10th cirs.) 1996, U.S. Ct. Claims 1982, U.S. Supreme Ct. 1987. Law clk. U.S. Ct. Appeals 2d cir., N.Y.C., 1979-80; law clk. to Justice William H. Rehnquist U.S. Supreme Ct., Washington, 1980-81; spl. asst. to U.S. atty. gen. Dept. Justice, Washington, 1981-82; assoc. counsel to Pres. U.S., Washington, 1982-86; assoc. Hogan & Hartson, Washington, 1986-87, ptnr., 1988-89, 93—; dep. solicitor gen. U.S. Dept. Justice, Washington, 1989-93. Editor: Harvard Law Rev., 1977-79. Mem. Am. Law Inst., Phi Beta Kappa. Republican.

ROBERTS, JOHN J., accounting firm executive; b. 1945. With Coopers & Lybrand, 1967—, ptnr., 1974—, dep. chmn., 1991—, chief oper. officer, 1994—. Office: Coopers & Lybrand LLP 1251 Avenue Of The Americas New York NY 10020-1104

ROBERTS, JOHN KENNETH, JR., life insurance company executive; b. Omaha, Mar. 4, 1936; s. John Kenneth and Vera Blanche (Graham) R.; m. Carol Jean Baer, July 1, 1961; children: John Kenneth III, Susan Beth. Student, Cornell Coll., Mount Vernon, Iowa; B.A. in Actuarial Sci., U. Iowa. With Pan-Am. Life Ins. Co., 1959—; pres., chief exec. officer Pan-Am. Life Ins. Co., New Orleans, 1984—; dir. Whitney Nat. Bank of New Orleans, Whitney Holding Corp. Bd. dirs., past chmn. United Way Greater New Orleans Area, also past campaign chmn.; bd. dirs. Children's Hosp., New Orleans, YMCA, New Orleans. Fellow Soc. Actuaries; mem. Am. Acad. Actuaries, Life Office Mgmt. Assn. (bd. dirs., pres. bd. trustees, past chmn.), Health Ins. Assn. Am. (bd. dirs., chmn. pub. rels. policy com. 1993-94), Am. Coun. Life Ins. (bd. dirs. 1992), New Orleans Country Club. Lutheran. Home: 453 Fairfield Ave Gretna LA 70056-7033 Office: Pan-Am Life Ins Co 601 Poydras St New Orleans LA 70130-6029

ROBERTS, JOHN PETER LEE, cultural advisor, administrator, educator, writer; b. Sydney, Australia, Oct. 21, 1930; s. Noel Lee and Myrtle Winifred (Reid) R.; m. Christina Van Oordt, July 28, 1962; children—Noel, Christina, Olga. Student, State Conservatorium Music, New South Wales; MA, Carleton U., 1988; DFA (hon.), U. Victoria, 1992. With CBC Radio, Toronto, Can., 1955—; producer CBC Radio, 1955—, head music and variety, 1971—, spl. adv. music and arts, 1975; sr. advisor cultural devel., head office Ottawa, 1983-87; mem. exec. bd. Internat. Music Centre, Vienna, 1968-80, first chmn. radio and comml. rec. group, 1969-70, hon. mem., 1980; mem. exec. bd. Internat. Inst. Music Dance and Theatre, Vienna, 1969-75; bd. govs. Can. Conf. Arts, 1970-76; exec. bd. Internat. Music Coun., Paris, 1973-79; v.p. Internat. Music Council, 1975, pres., 1978-79; pres. Can. Music Centre, Toronto, 1971-77; dir. gen. Can. Music Centre, 1977-81; pres. Can. Music Council, 1968-71, 75-77; dir. Festival Singers of Can., 1965-78, Elmer Iseler Singers, 1979-81, Toronto Mendelssohn Choir, 1969-81, Nat. Youth Orch. Can., 1973-80; chmn. 1st World Music Week, 1975, Internat. Music Day, 1975-82; v.p. Internat. Inst. Audio-Visual Communication and Cultural Devel. (Mediacult), Vienna, 1976-87, pres., 1987-93; pres. Internat. Rsch. Inst. for Media, Communication, Cultural Devel., Vienna, 1993-95; v.p. Musicians Internat. Mus. Aid Fund., Geneva, 1978, 79; pres. Les Jeunesses Musicales du Can., 1979-83; chmn. Internat. Vocal Competition, Rio de Janeiro, 1979; spl. advisor to chmn. Can. Radio-TV and Telecomms. Commn., 1981-83; sr. advisor cultural devel. CBC, 1983-87; dean of faculty of fine arts U. Calgary, 1987-95; vis. fellow McGill Inst. for Study of Can. McGill U., Montreal, 1995-96; adj. prof. U. Calgary, 1995—; bd. dirs. Nickle Arts Mus., 1987-95, Calgary Philharm. Orch., 1988-94, Ester Honen's Internat. Piano Competition, 1994. Mem. editorial bd. Can. Music Book, 1970-77. Mem. exec. bd. dirs. Can. Nat. Commn. for UNESCO, 1976-80; founding pres. Glenn Gould Found., Toronto, 1983—. Decorated Order of Can. (mem., 1983, officer, 1996); Cross of Honour for Sci. and the Arts (Austria). Mem. Can. assn. Fine Arts Deans (chmn. 1989-93), Internat. Coun. Fine Arts Deans (bd. dirs. 1992-94). Office: U Calgary Faculty Fine Arts, 2500 University Dr NW, Calgary, AB Canada T2N 1N4

ROBERTS, KATHLEEN MARY, school system administrator; b. Syracuse, N.Y., Apr. 15, 1947; d. Casimer and Lorrayne Arletta (Molloy) Piegdon; m. James C. Roberts, June 29, 1968 (div. Sept. 1988). BA, Cen. State U., Edmond, Okla., 1968, MEd, 1971; PhD, U. Okla., 1977. Cert. tchr., prin., supt., Okla.; cert. supt., N.Y. Tchr. Putnam City Schs., Oklahoma City, 1960-72; reading specialist Moore (Okla.) Pub. Schs., 1973-74; reading specialist Crooked Oak Pub. Schs., Oklahoma City, 1974-77, supt., 1990-95; rsch. assoc. Oklahoma City Pub. Schs., 1977-80; supt. Okla. Dept. Corrections, Oklahoma City, 1980-86, Healdton (Okla.) Pub. Schs., 1986-90, Piedmont (Okla.) Pub. Schs., 1995—. Contbr. articles to profl. publs. Bd. dirs. United Meth. Prism Ministry, Oklahoma City, 1986—, Children's Shelter, Ardmore, Okla., 1989-90; mem. State Vocat. Edn. Coun., Oklahoma City, 1980-85. Recipient citation Okla. State Senate, 1986. Mem. ASCD, Internat. Reading Assn., Am. Assn. Sch. Adminstrs., Okla. Assn. Sch. Adminstrs., Phi Delta Kappa, Alpha Chi, Kappa Delta Phi. Democrat. Roman Catholic. Avocations: furniture refinishing, reading, gardening. Office: Piedmont Schs 713 Piedmont Rd N Piedmont OK 73078

ROBERTS, KEITH EDWARD, SR., lawyer; b. White Hall, Ill., Apr. 27, 1928; s. Victor Harold and Ruby Harriet (Kelsey) R.; m. Marthan Dusch, Sept. 4, 1954; 1 child, Keith Edward. Student, Western Ill. U., 1946-47, George Washington U., 1947-48; BS, U. Ill., 1951, JD, 1953. Bar: Ill. 1953, U.S. Dist. Ct. (no. dist.) Ill. 1957, U.S. Dist. Ct. (so. dist.) Ill. 1961, U.S. Dist. Ct. (no. dist.) Ohio 1960, U.S. Ct. Mil. Appeals 1954, U.S. Ct. Appeals (7th cir.) 1968. Assoc. J.D. Quarant, Elizabethtown, Ill., 1953-56; staff atty. Pa. R.R. Co., Chgo., 1957-60; assoc. Henslee, Monek & Henslee, Chgo., 1960-67; sole practice, Naperville, Ill., 1967-68; ptnr. Donovan, Atten, Mountcastle, Roberts & DaRosa, Wheaton, Ill., 1968-77; pres. Donovan & Roberts, P.C., Wheaton, 1977—. Served to capt. U.S. Army, 1954-57. Mem. ABA, Internat. Soc. Barristers, Assn. Trial Lawyers Am., Ill. Bar Assn., DuPage County Bar Assn. (gen. counsel 1976-86). Presbyterian. Office: Donovan & Roberts PC PO Box 417 Wheaton IL 60189-0417

ROBERTS, KENNETH LEWIS, investor, lawyer, foundation administrator; b. Dungannon, Va., Dec. 12, 1932; s. Clarence Eugene and Katherine (Osborne) R.; m. Anne Foster Cook, Sept. 10, 1955; children—Kenneth L., Patrick Hagan Foster. B.A., Vanderbilt U., 1954, LL.B., 1959. Bar: Tenn. Assoc. prof. law Vanderbilt U., 1959-60; assoc. Waller, Lansden & Dortch, Nashville, 1960-66; exec. v.p. Commerce Union Bank, Nashville, 1966-71; pres., chief exec. officer, dir. Cen. Nat. Bank, Richmond, Va., 1971-76; pres., chief exec. officer First Am. Nat. Bank, Nashville, 1976-90; dir. First Am. Corp., Nashville, 1976-90, vice chmn., 1976-77, pres., chief exec. officer, 1977-79, chmn., chief exec. officer, 1979-90; pres., exec. dir. HCA Found., Nashville, 1991—; past pres., dir. Cen. Nat. Corp. Trustee Vanderbilt U.; bd. dirs. Leadership Nashville, Montgomery Bell Acad. Lt. Chem. Corps, AUS, 1955-57. Mem. ABA, Tenn. Bar Assn., Nashville Bar Assn., Nashville C. of C., Cumberland Club, Belle Meade Country Club, Univ. Club, Ponte Vedra (Fla.) Inn & Club. Office: HCA Foundation 3319 W End Ave #900 Nashville TN 37203-1076

ROBERTS, KEVIN, recreational facility executive. Pres. American Golf Corp., Santa Monica, Calif. Office: Am Golf Corp 1633 26th St Santa Monica CA 90404-4023*

ROBERTS, LARRY SPURGEON, zoologist; b. Texon, Tex., June 30, 1935; s. E. Fowler and Frances Wray (Huggins) R.; m. Maria Elek, Feb. 7, 1962; children: Gregory Lorinc, Bruce Tibor, Teresa Margit, Eric Miklos. B.S., So. Meth. U., 1956; M.S. (NSF predoctoral fellow), U. Ill., 1958; D.Sc. (NIH predoctoral fellow), Johns Hopkins U., 1961. Cert. scuba instr. Nat. Assn. Underwater Instrs. Asst. prof. zoology U. Mass., Amherst, 1963-69, assoc. prof., 1969-75, prof., 1975-79; prof. biol. scis. Tex. Tech U., Lubbock, 1979-90; chmn. dept. Tex. Tech U., 1979-84; adj. prof. biol. scis. U. Miami, 1990—, Fla. Internat. U., 1990-93. Author: (with others) Foundations of Parasitology, 1977, 5th edit., 1996, Integrated Principles of Zoology, 1979, 9th edit., 1993, Biology of Animals, 1982, 6th edit., 1994, The Underwater World of Sport Diving, 1991, Animal Diversity, 1994. Mem. Amherst Dem. Town Com., 1968-79, vice chmn., 1972-76; mem. Amherst Town Meeting, 1966-76; mem. Amherst Zoning Bd. Appeals, 1972-75, vice chmn., 1972-75; recorder West Tex. Dems., 1985-86; mem. Dade County Dem. Exec. Com., 1991—. NIH postdoctoral trainee, 1961-63; NIH fellow, 1969-70; recipient Disting. Service cert. Mass. Tchrs. Assn., 1979. Mem. AAAS, ACLU (vice chmn. Hampshire County chpt. 1966-68, bd. dirs. Lubbock chpt. 1985-89, vice chmn. 1988-89, bd. dirs. Miami, Fla. chpt. 1991—, Fla. State bd. dirs.), Am. Soc. Parasitologists (Henry Baldwin Ward medal 1971, council mem. at large 1980-83, v.p. 1984-85), Am. Micros. Soc. (v.p. 1974-75, exec. com. 1978-81), Mass. Soc. Profs. (pres. 1977-78), Soc. Protozoologists, Am. Soc. Tropical Medicine and Hygiene, Wildlife Disease Assn., Southwestern Assn. Parasitologists (v.p. 1982, pres. 1983), Southeastern Soc. Parasitologists (pres. elect 1993, pres. 1994), Internat. Soc. Reef Studies, Crustacean Soc., Am. Acad. Underwater Scis., Sigma Xi. Home: 27700 SW 164th Ave Homestead FL 33031-2846

ROBERTS, LAUREL LEE, lawyer; b. Lowell, Mass., Oct. 31, 1944; d. Angus Henry and Lorraine (Thompson) R. BA in History and Sociology, U. Calif., Santa Barbara, 1966, MA in Counseling, 1969, BA in Film Studies, 1973; PhD, U. So. Calif., 1976; JD, U. West L.A., 1982. Bar: Calif. 1984, U.S. Ct. Appeals 1985, U.S. Dist. Ct. (ctrl. dist.) Calif. 1985, U.S. Ct. Appeals (9th cir.) 1985; cert. secondary educator, Calif.; credential in pupil personnel svcs., Calif. Dormitory head resident U. Calif., Santa Barbara, 1964-69; counselor Foothill Elem. Sch., Goleta, Calif., 1968; univ. counselor U. Calif., Santa Barbara, 1969-73; adj. lectr. Grad. Sch. of Edn. U. So. Calif., L.A., 1975; asst. dean academic affairs Office of the Chancellor Calif. State U., Long Beach, 1976-86; atty. Law Office of Laurel Roberts, Hermosa Beach, Calif., 1984—; cons. U. So. Calif./Ind. U. Consortium on Instrnl. Devel., L.A., 1975, Nat. Commn. on Indsl. Innovation, Pasadena, Calif., 1986; lectr. Assn. for Devel. of Computer-based Instructional Systems, 1978. Author: (slide-tape presentation) CSU Educational Policy, 1980. Home legal svc. for elderly and infirmed, 1984—; participant Lt. Gov. Mike Curb's USA-Mexico Exch. Program, Fullerton, Calif., 1984; legal aid vol. U. West L.A., Culver City, 180-84; mem. Supt. of Pub. Instrn. Assessment Adv. Com., Sacramento, 1985. Recipient Am. Jurisprudence award Lawyers Coop. Pub. Co., 1982. Mem. Irish-Am. Bar Assn., Women Lawyers Assn. of L.A., L.A. County Bar Assn., Fed. Bar Assn. Republican. Roman Catholic. Avocations: travel, tennis, film, the arts. Office: 239 Pier Ave PO Box 594 Hermosa Beach CA 90254

ROBERTS, LAWRENCE GILMAN, telecommunications company executive; b. Dec. 21, 1937; s. Elliott John and Elizabeth (Gilman) R.; m. June Ellen Stuller, 1959 (div. 1973); children: Paul, Kenny. BS, MIT, 1959, MS, 1960, PhD, 1963. Staff mem. Lincoln Lab. MIT, 1962-69; dir. info. proc. U.S. Dept. Defense, Arlington, Va., 1969-73; pres., CEO GTE Telenet Corp., Vienna, Va., 1973-82; pres. DHL, Redwood City, Calif., 1982-83; chmn., CEO NetExpress, Inc., Foster City, Calif., 1983-93; pres. ATM Systems, Foster City, Calif., 1993—. Recipient L.M. Ericsson award for comms. Mem. IEEE, IEEE Computer Soc., Am. Fedn. Info. Processing (Harry Goode award, W. Wallace McDowell award), Assn. Computing Machinery, Sigma Xi. Office: ATM Systems 989E W Hillsdale Blvd # 290 San Mateo CA 94403-3839

ROBERTS, LEIGH MILTON, psychiatrist; b. Jacksonville, Ill., June 9, 1925; s. Victor Harold and Ruby Harriet (Kelsey) R.; m. Marilyn Edith Kadow, Sept. 6, 1946; children: David, Carol Roberts Mayer, Paul, Nancy Mills. B.S., U. Ill., 1945, M.D., 1947. Diplomate: Am. Bd. Psychiatry and Neurology. Intern St. Francis Hosp., Peoria, Ill., 1947-48; gen. practice medicine Macomb, Ill., 1948-50; resident in psychiatry U. Wis. Hosps., Madison, 1953-56; staff psychiatrist Mendota (Wis.) State Hosp., 1956-58; mem. faculty U. Wis. Med. Sch., Madison, 1959-89; prof. psychiatry U. Wis. Med. Sch., 1971-89, acting chmn. dept., 1972-75; mem. spl. rev. bd. Wis. Parole Bd. Sex Crimes Law, 1962-88, forensic cons., 1988—; mem. Dane County Devel. Disabilities Bd., 1962-66, Wis. Planning Com. Mental Health, 1963-65, Wis. Planning Com. Health, 1969-71, Wis. Planning Com. Vocat. Rehab., 1966-68, Wis. Planning Com. Health Centers, 1967-71, Wis. Mental Health Adv. Com., 1973-78; bd. dirs. Methodist Hosp., Madison, Dane County Rehab. House, Dane County Assn. Mental Health; cons. in field. Editor: Community Psychiatry, 1966, Comprehensive Mental Health, 1968; contbr. articles profl. jours. Pres. Wis. Council Chs., 1976-78; bd. dirs. Madison Campus Ministry, St. Benedict Center; trustee N.Central Coll., Naperville, Ill. Served with USNR, 1943-45, 50-53. Decorated Bronze Star, Purple Heart. Fellow Am. Psychiat. Assn. (bd. trustees 1981-84), Wis. Psychiat. Assn. (pres. 1967). Methodist. Home and Office: 722A Sauk Ridge Trl Madison WI 53705-1155 *Life is a precious gift whose journey is molded and shaped by cumulative experiences and relationships. Religious belief and practice which provides future-oriented hope, disciplined accountability and living service are balanced by professional psychiatric vistas on the uniqueness and worth of each human person.*

ROBERTS, LEONARD H., retail executive; b. Chgo., Feb. 19, 1949; s. Jack and Goldie (Solomon) R.; m. Laurie Susan Osser, Aug. 20, 1967; children: Dawn, Adina, Melissa. BS in Chemistry and Mktg., U. Ill., 1971; JD, DePaul U., 1974. Food scientist Armour Foods, Chgo., 1968-71, Cen. Soya, Chgo., 1971-74; govt. lobbyist Ralston Purina Co., St. Louis, 1974-76, dir. mktg., 1976-78; mng. dir. Raltech Ralston Purina Co., Madison, Wis., 1978-81; v.p. food service ops. Ralston Purina Co., St. Louis, 1981-85; pres., chief exec. officer Arby's Inc., Atlanta, 1985-89; chmn. bd., chief exec. officer Shoney's Inc., 1989-93; pres. Radio Shack, Fort Worth, TX, 1993—, Tandy Corp., Fort Worth, 1996—; vice chmn. bd. dirs. DWG Corp., 1987-89; bd. dirs. AFC Corp. Holder numerous patents on Soya protein research. Active United Way Met. Tarrant County, 1994, Nat. Crime Prevention Coun., 1994, Clark U. Students in Free Enterprise, Girl Scouts U.S., Harris Meth. Bd.; mem. exec. com. Fort Worth Symphony. Recipient Pvt. Sector Initiative award Office Pres. of U.S., Washington, 1987, Disting. Achievement award B'nai B'rith, Restaurant Bus. Leadership award, 1991, Golden Plate award Nations Restaurant News, 1991, Wall St. Bronze Critics award, 1992. Mem. ABA, Ill. Bar Assn. Home: 3516 Briarhaven Rd Fort Worth TX 76109-3128 Office: Radio Shack 1800 One Tandy Ctr Fort Worth TX 76102

ROBERTS, LORIN WATSON, botanist, educator; b. Clarksdale, Mo., June 28, 1923; s. Lorin Cornelius and Irene (Watson) R.; m. Florence Ruth Greathouse, July 10, 1967; children: Michael Hamlin, Daniel Hamlin, Margaret Susan. BA, U. Mo., 1948, MA, 1950; PhD in Botany, U. Mo.-Columbia, 1952. Asst. prof., then assoc. prof. botany Agnes Scott Coll., Decaur, Ga., 1952-57; vis. asst. prof. Emory U., 1952-55; mem. faculty U. Idaho, 1957—, prof. botany, 1967-91, prof. botany emeritus, 1991—; Fulbright research prof. Kyoto (Japan) U., 1967-68; research fellow U. Bari, Italy, 1968; Cabot fellow Harvard, 1974; Fulbright teaching fellow North-Eastern Hill U., Shillong, Meghalaya, India, 1977; Fulbright sr. scholar and fellow Australian Nat. U., Canberra, 1980; sr. researcher U. London, 1984; pres. botany sect. 1st Internat. Congress Histochemistry and Cytochemistry, Paris, 1960; Alexander von Humboldt vis. fellow Australian Nat. U., 1992. Author: Cytodifferentiation in Plants, 1976 (with J.H. Dodds) Experiments in Plant Tissue Culture, 1982, 2d edit., 3d edit. 1995, 1985 (with P.B. Gahan and R. Aloni) Vascular Differentiation and Plant Growth Regulators, 1988; contbr. articles to profl. jours. Served with USAAF, 1943-46. Decorated chevalier de l'Ordre du Merit Agricole France, 1961; Alexander von Humboldt fellow, 1992. Fellow AAAS; mem. N.W. Sci. Assn. (pres. 1970-71), Bot. Soc. Am., Am. Soc. Plant Physiologists, Internat. Assn. Plant Tissue Culture, Am. Inst. Biol. Scis., Idaho Acad. Scis., Sigma Xi, Phi Kappa Phi, Phi Sigma. Home: 920 Mabelle St Moscow ID 83843-3834

ROBERTS, LOUIS DOUGLAS, physics educator, researcher; b. Charleston, S.C., Jan. 27, 1918; s. Louis Wigfall and Evelyn (Douglas) R.; m. Marjorie Violette Staveley-Lawson, Aug. 29, 1942; 1 child, Joyce Carol. AB with honors, Howard Coll., 1938; postgrad., John Hopkins U., 1938-39; PhD, Columbia U., 1941. Rockefeller Found. fellow Cornell U., Ithaca, N.Y., 1941-42; rsch. physicist GE, Schenectady, N.Y., 1942-46, U. Calif. at Berkeley, 1944-45; prin. physicist Oak Ridge (Tenn.) Nat. Lab., 1946-68; Ford Found. prof. U. Tenn., Knoxville, 1963-68; prof. physics U. N.C., Chapel Hill, 1968—, Alumni Disting. prof., 1980—. Contbr. articles on physics to profl. jours.; holder numerous patents in semiconductor devices, magnetron design, nuclear power, metals and alloys, etc. Recipient Tanner teaching award U. N.C., 1977; Fulbright fellow Oxford U., 1958-59, Guggenheim Found. fellow, 1958-59. Fellow Am. Phys. Soc. (mem. Southeastern sect., 1948—, vice chmn. 1954-55, chmn. 1955-56). Republican. Avocations: reading, music, travel, garden, photography. Home: 1116 Sourwood Cir Chapel Hill NC 27514-4912 Office: Univ NC Dept Physics and Astronomy Chapel Hill NC 27599-3255

ROBERTS, LOUISE NISBET, philosopher; b. Lexington, Ky., Apr. 21, 1919; d. Benjamin and Helen L. Nisbet; m. Warren Roberts, June 14, 1952; children: Helen Ward Roberts Hill, Valeria Lamar Roberts Emmett. AB, U. Ky., 1942, MA, 1944; PhD, Columbia U., 1952. Instr. philosophy Fairfax Hall, Waynesboro, Va., 1943-44, Fairmount Casements, Ormond Beach, Fla., 1944-45; mem. faculty Newcomb Coll., Tulane U., 1948—, prof. philosophy, 1969-85, dept. head, prof. emeritus, 1985—. Chmn. Episc. Diocese HIV/AIDS Commn., 1993-96. Contbr. articles to profl. jours. Univ. scholar, 1945-46. Mem. AAUW (fellow 1947-48, pres. New Orleans chpt. 1986-88), DAR (vice regent New Orleans chpt. 1987-90), So. Soc. Philosophy and Psychology, Phi Beta Kappa (chpt. pres. 1956-57), Delta Delta Delta (fellow 1946-47). Democrat. Episcopalian. Office: Tulane U Dept Of Philosophy New Orleans LA 70118

ROBERTS, LYNN ERNEST, theoretical physicist, educator; b. N.Y.C., Aug. 10, 1948; s. Lynn Ernest Roberts and Dorothy Elizabeth (Mobile) Woods; m. Brenda Joyce James, Aug. 1985; children: Natasha, Timothy, Lynn, Brendan, Ashleigh. BS in Physics, SUNY, Stony Brook, 1972; MS in Physics, Adelphi U., 1976, PhD in High Energy Theory, 1981. Teaching asst. Adelphi U., Garden City, N.Y., 1973-77, rsch. fellow, 1977-79; rsch. fellow Ford Found., Atlanta, 1977-79; rsch. collaborator Brookhaven Nat. Lab., Upton, N.Y., 1979-81, rsch. assoc., 1981-83, physicist, 1983-85; assoc. prof. physics Lincoln U., Lincoln University, Pa., 1985-90, prof., 1991—, acting chair, 1992-94; chair, 1995—; vis. rsch. scientist Argonne (Ill.) Nat. Lab., 1986-88; rschr. NSF, Washington, 1989-92, proposal reviewer, 1990, 93. Contbr. articles to sci. jurs. Mem. Rotary (pres. Oxford, Pa. 1990), Inst. Advanced Sci. Studies (founding mem. and prin. officer). Home: 2501 Baynard Blvd Wilmington DE 19802-2961 Office: Lincoln U Dept Physics Wright Hall Lincoln University PA 19352

ROBERTS, LYNNE JEANINE, physician; b. St. Louis, Apr. 19, 1952; d. H. Clarke and Dorothy June (Cockrum) R.; m. Richard Allen Beadle Jr., July 18, 1981; children: Richard Andrew, Erica Roberts. BA with distinction, Ind. U., 1974, MD, 1978. Diplomate Am. Bd. Dermatology, Am. Bd. Pediatrics, Am. Bd. Laser Surgery. Intern in pediats. Children's Med. Ctr., Dallas, 1978-79, resident in pediats., 1979-80; resident in dermatology U. Tex. Southwestern Med. Ctr., Dallas, 1980-83, chief resident in dermatology, 1982-83, asst. instr. dermatology and pediatrics, 1983-84, asst. prof., 1984-90, assoc. prof., 1990—; physician Cons. Dermatol. Specialists, Dallas, 1990-93; pres. Lynne J. Roberts, MD, PA, Dallas, 1993—; dir. dermatology Children's Med. Ctr., Dallas, 1986—; dermatology sect. chief Med. City Dallas Hosp., 1994-95, 95—. Contbr. articles to profl. jours., chpts. to books. Recipient Scholastic Achievement Citation Am. Med. Women's Assn., 1978. Fellow Am. Acad. Dermatology, Am. Acad. Pediatrics, Am. Soc. Laser Medicine and Surgery (bd. dirs. 1994—); mem. Soc. Pediatric Dermatology, Am. Soc. Dermatologic Surgery, Tex. Med. Assn., Dallas Zool. Soc., Dallas Arboretum, Kappa Alpha Theta, Alpha Omega Alpha. Avocations: horseback riding, reading, fishing, swimming, camping. Office: 7777 Forest Ln Ste B314 Dallas TX 75230-2518

ROBERTS, MARGARET HAROLD, editor, publisher; b. Aug. 18, 1928. A.B., U. Chattanooga, 1950. Editor, pub. series Award Winning Art, 1960-70, New Woman mag., Palm Beach, Fla., 1971-84; editor, pub. Going Bonkers mag., 1992—. Author: juvenile book series Daddy is a Doctor, 1965. Office: PO Box 189 Palm Beach FL 33480-0189

ROBERTS, MARGOT MARKELS, business executive; b. Springfield, Mass., Jan. 20, 1945; d. Reuben and Marion (Markels) R.; children: Lauren B. Phillips, Debrah C. Herman. B.A., Boston U. Interior designer Louis

Legum Furniture Co., Norfolk, Va., 1965-70; buyer, mgr. Danker Furniture, Rockville, Md., 1970-72; buyer W & J Sloane, Washington, 1972-74; pres. Bus. & Fin. Cons., Palm Beach, Fla., 1976-80, Margot M. Roberts & Assocs., Inc., Palm Beach, 1976—; dealer 20th century Am. art and wholesale antiques Margot M. Roberts, Inc., Palm Beach, 1989—; v.p., dir. So. Textile Svcs. Inc., Palm Beach. Pres. Brittany Condominium Assn., Palm Beach, 1983-87; v.p. South Palm Beach Civic Assn., 1983-88, South Palm Beach Pres.'s Assn., 1984-88; vice chmn. South Palm Beach Planning Bd., 1983-88, 90-91; elected town commr. Town South Palm Beach, Fla., 1991-92, elected vice mayor, 1992-93, elected mayor, 1993—; apptd. Commn. on Status of Women of Palm Beach County, 1992-95; voting mem. Palm Beach County Mcpl. League, 1992—; vice chair Commn. Status of Women of Palm Beach County, 1994-95. Mem. Nat. Assn. Women in Bus., Palm Beach C. of C. Republican. Office: Town Hall South Palm Beach 3577 S Ocean Blvd Palm Beach FL 33480-5706

ROBERTS, MARIE DYER, computer systems specialist; b. Statesboro, Ga., Feb. 19, 1943; d. Byron and Martha (Evans) Dyer; BS, U. Ga., 1966; student Am. U., 1972; cert. systems profl., cert. in data processing; m. Hugh V. Roberts, Jr., Oct. 6, 1973. Mathematician, computer specialist U.S. Naval Oceanographic Office, Washington, 1966-73; systems analyst, programmer Sperry Microwave Electronics, Clearwater, Fla., 1973-75; data processing mgr., asst. bus. mgr. Trenam, Simmons, Kemker et al, Tampa, Fla., 1975-77; mathematician, computer specialist U.S. Army C.E., Savannah, Ga., 1977-81, 83-85, Frankfurt, W. Ger., 1981-83; ops. rsch. analyst U.S. Army Contrn. Rsch. Lab., Champaign, Ill., 1985-87; data base adminstr., computer systems programmer, chief info. integration and implementation div. U.S. Army Corps of Engrs., South Pacific div., San Francisco, 1987-93; computer specialist, IDEF repository coord., Functional Process Improvement Expertise, Defense Info. Systems Agy., Arlington, Va., 1993-95; computer specialist Ctr. Integration Def. Info. Systems Agy., MacDill AFB, Fla., 1995—. instr. computer scis. City Coll. of Chgo. in Franfurt, 1982-83. Recipient Sustained Superior Performance award Dept. Army, 1983, Nat. Performance Review Hammer award V.P. Gore, 1996. Mem. Am. Soc. Hist. Preservation, Data Processing Mgmt. Assn., Assn. of Inst. for Cert. Computer Profls., Assn. Women in Computing, Assn. Women in Sci., NAFE, Am. Film Inst., U. Ga. Alumni Assn., Sigma Kappa, Soc. Am. Mil. Engrs. Author: Harris Computer Users Manual, 1983. *Best is the eye of the beholder. I have learned that the perspective or view point of the customer is critical to providing acceptable service to that customer. Beware of being called an expert as you may eventually believe you are. Arrogence is a barrier to providing good customer service.*

ROBERTS, MARKLEY, economist, educator; b. Shanghai, China, Sept. 3, 1930; s. Donald and Frances Charlotte (Markley) R.; m. Jeanne Addison, Feb. 19, 1966; children: Addison, Ellen. A.B., Princeton U., 1951; M.A., Am. U., 1960, Ph.D., 1970. Reporter Washington Star newspaper, 1952-57; legis. asst. Office of Senator Hubert Humphrey of Minn., Washington, 1957-62; legis. asst., economist AFL-CIO, Washington, 1962—, asst. dir. econ. rsch. dept., 1989—; bd. dir., vice chmn. Econ. Edn. Found. for Clergy, 1972-80; chmn. labor research adv. council Bur. Labor Stats.-Dept. Labor, 1972—; adj. prof. econs. U. Md., 1966—, George Washington U., 1972—. Contbr. numerous articles on labor and econ. affairs, tech., productivity to various publs.; author monographs in field. Mem. D.C. Democratic Central Com., 1964-68; ward III coordinator Washington Mayor Walter Washington, 1974-78; bd. dirs. Laymen's Nat. Bible Com. Inc., N.Y.C., 1972-82. Mem. Am. Econ. Assn., Indsl. Rels. Rsch. Assn. (exec. bd. 1975-77), Am. Polit. Sci. Assn., Nat. Acad. Social Ins., Assn. Evolutionary Econs., Am. Statis. Assn., Nat. Consumers League (bd. dirs. 1991—), Newspaper Guild, Ams. for Dem. Action (exec. bd. 1992—), Social Democrats USA. Democrat. Episcopalian. Home: 4931 Albemarle St NW Washington DC 20016-4359 Office: AFL-CIO 815 16th St NW Washington DC 20006-4104

ROBERTS, MAURA M., secondary school educator; b. Washington, Mar. 2, 1944; d. John E. and Mary M. (McCann) Martin; m. Charles D. Roberts, Aug. 15, 1987; 1 child, Caragh M. McLaughlin. AB, U. Mass. at Lowell, 1965; MAT, Salem State Coll., 1973. Cert. tchr. English, Mass., S.C. Tchr. English Hilton Head (S.C.) Prep Sch.; with Concord (Mass.)-Carlisle Sch. Dist.; tchr. English Concord-Carlisle Sch. Dist. Mem. edn. adv. bd. Orchard House Mus., Concord, 1994—. Mem. ASCD, Nat. Coun. Tchrs. of English, Concord Carlisle Tchrs. Assn., Mass. Tchrs. Assn.

ROBERTS, MELVILLE PARKER, JR., neurosurgeon, educator; b. Phila., Oct. 15, 1931; s. Melville Parker and Marguerite Louise (Reimann) R.; m. Sigrid Marianne Magnusson, Mar. 27, 1954; children: Melville Parker III, Julia Pell, Erik Emerson. BS, Washington and Lee U., 1953; MD, Yale U., 1957. Diplomate: Am. Bd. Neurol. Surgery. Intern Yale Med. Ctr., 1957, neurosurg. resident, 1958-60, 62-64, Am. Cancer Soc. fellow in neurosurgery, 1962-64, instr., 1964; asst. prof. surgery Sch. Medicine U. Va., Charlottesville, 1965-69; practice medicine specializing in neurol. surgery Hartford, Conn., 1970—; mem. sr. staff Hartford Hosp., John Dempsey Hosp.; asst. prof. surgery Sch. Medicine U. Conn., Farmington, 1970-71; assoc. prof. U. Conn., 1972-75, assoc. prof. neurology, 1974-77, chmn. divsn. neurosurgery, 1971-84, prof. surgery, 1975—, acting chmn. dept. neurology, 1973-77, acting chmn. dept. surgery, 1974-77, William Beecher Scoville prof. neurosurgery, 1976—; James Hudson Brown rsch. fellow Yale U., 1957. Author: Atlas of the Human Brain in Section, 1970, 2d edition, 1987; mem. editorial bd.: Conn. Medicine, 1973—; contbr. articles to profl. jours. Capt. M.C., U.S. Army, 1960-61. Fellow ACS, Royal Soc. Medicine (London); mem. AAUP, Am. Assn. Neurol. Surgeons, Soc. Neurol. Surgeons, Congress Neurol. Surgeons (bd. dirs. joint spinal sect. with Am. Assn. Neurol. Surgeons, chmn. ann. meeting 1987, sci. program chmn. ann. meeting 1988), Assn. for Rsch. in Nervous and Mental Diseases, New Eng. Neurosurg. Soc. (bd. dirs. 1976-79, pres. 1989-91), Soc. Brit. Neurol. Surgeons, Rsch. Soc. Neurol. Surgeons, Soc. Rsch. into Hydrocephalus and Spina Bifida, Conn. Acad. Arts and Sci., Vereingung Schweizer Neurochirugen, Mory's Asns., Graduate Club, Beaumont Med. Club (pres. 1988), Sloane Club, Naval Club, La Grande Mare Golf Club. Episcopalian. Office: 85 Seymour St Ste 707 Hartford CT 06106-5526

ROBERTS, MERRILL JOSEPH, economist, educator; b. Glendive, Mont., Aug. 10, 1915; s. Merrill Joseph and Inez (Ludgate) R.; m. Janet Hunter Dion, Aug. 31, 1941; children: David, Michael, James, Patricia. B.A., U. Minn., 1938; M.B.A., U. Chgo., 1939, Ph.D., 1952. Transp. economist OPA, Washington, 1941, USDA, Washington, 1942-46, TVA, 1946-48; asst. prof. transp. and econs., then assoc. prof. U. Fla., Gainesville, 1948-54, prof., 1955-58; assoc. prof. transp. UCLA, 1954-55; vis. prof. econs. Mich. State U., 1956-57; prof. transp. and pub. utilities Grad. Sch. Bus., U. Pitts., 1958-72, head dept. transp. and pub. utilities, 1958-61, prof. econs., 1960-72, chmn. faculty, 1960-63; dir. Bur. Bus. Research, 1963-66; v.p., dir. econs. div. Wilbur Smith and Assocs., 1972-75; prof., chmn. transp., bus. and pub. policy U. Md., 1975-79, prof., 1979-82, prof. emeritus, 1983—; research cons. Nat. Transp. Policy Study Commn., 1977-79; cons. ICC, 1979-84, Dept. Transp., Washington, 1982-84, Md. Dept. Transp., 1987-88; Disting. Research lectr., Iowa State U., 1986; econ. adv. Estudio Integral de Transport de Bolivia, 1979; mem. adv. panel, R.R. merger project Rail Services Planning Office, ICC; dir. study Penn Central R.R. bankruptcy U.S. Senate, 1971-72; Econ. cons. numerous fgn. govts. including, New Zealand, Thailand, Singapore, Hong Kong, Korea, Spain, Nicaragua, Algeria; cons. transp. to bus. and govt. agys.; research staff Commn. Money and Credit, 1959-60; mem. Venezuelan Commn. Economica Ferroviaria Nacional, 1959-60; participant transp. study conf. Nat. Acad. Sci.-NRC, 1960; research staff Nat. Planning Assn. study, 1962-63; participant Am. Assembly Conf. on the Future of Am. Transp., 1971; mem. research com. Transp. Assn. Am., 1965-72; v.p. Am. Transp. Research Forum, 1960-63; mem. legis. com. Allegheny Regional Adv. Bd., 1959-72; mem. com. applications of econs. Transp. Research Bd., Nat. Acad. Scis., 1973-80. Author: (with T.C. Bigham) Citrus Fruit Rates, 1950, Transportation, 1952, Taxation of Railroads and Other State-Assessed Companies in Florida, 1957, Evaluation of Rate Regulation, 1959, Transportation in Region in Transition, 1962, Freight Transport Coordination, 1966, The Penn Central and Other Railroads, 1973; contbr. numerous articles to profl. jours. Bd. dirs. Port Authority Allegheny County, 1962-69; Bd. visitors Amy Transp. Sch., 1959-60. Served to lt. (s.g.) USNR, 1942-46. Recipient Johnson award for outstanding research, Transp. Research Bd., Nat. Acad. Scis., 1986. Mem. Am. Econs. Assn. (sec.-treas. transp. and pub. utilities group 1957-61, chmn. 1963), Am. Soc. Traffic and Transp. (founder mem.), Nat. Def. Transp. Assn. (life), Delta Nu Alpha, Phi Delta Theta, Beta Gamma Sigma. Presbyterian. Club: Cosmos (Washington). Home: #113 3749 Sarasota Square Blvd Sarasota FL 34238

ROBERTS, MICHAEL JAMES, lawyer; b. Salisbury, Md., Nov. 2, 1936; s. Wilmer C. Roberts and Augusta (Dayton) Doukas; m. Jean Murray, June 7, 1958; children: Mark William, Lisa Marie. BA, Duke U., 1958; JD, Am. U., 1965. Bar: D.C. 1966, Md. 1966, U.S. Dist. Ct. D.C., U.S. Ct. Appeals D.C. cir., U.S. Supreme Ct. Mem. staff U.S. congressman Carlton R. Sickles (Md.), Washington, 1963-64; assoc. Verner, Liipfert, Bernhard & McPherson, Washington, 1965-70; ptnr., mem. Verner, Liipfert, Bernhard, McPherson & Hand, Washington, 1970—, pres., mng. atty., 1987—. Vestry Christ Episcopal Ch., Stevensville, Md., 1984-86. Lt. USN, 1958-62, PTO. Democrat. Avocation: boating. Home: 300 Roberts Ln Stevensville MD 21666-2860 Office: Verner Liipfert Bernhard McPherson & Hand 901 15th St NW Washington DC 20005-2327

ROBERTS, MORTON SPITZ, astronomer; b. N.Y.C., Nov. 5, 1926; m. Josephine Taylor, Aug. 2, 1951; 1 dau., Elizabeth Mason. B.A., Pomona Coll., 1948; Sc.D. (hon.), 1979; M.Sc., Calif. Inst. Tech., 1950; Ph.D. (Lick Obs. fellow), U. Calif., Berkeley, 1958. Asst. prof. physics Occidental Coll., 1949-52; lectr. astronomy dept. U. Calif., Berkeley, 1959-60; lectr., research asso. Harvard Coll. Obs., Harvard U., 1960-64; scientist Nat. Radio Astronomy Obs., Charlottesville, Va., 1964-78; dir. Nat. Radio Astronomy Obs., 1978-84, sr. scientist, 1978—; Sigma Xi nat. lectr., 1970-71; vis. educator SUNY, Stony Brook, 1968, Cambridge U., 1972, 86-87, U. Groningen, 1972. Bd. editors: Astronomy and Astrophysics, 1971-80; asso. editor: Astron. Jour, 1977-79. NSF postdoctoral fellow, 1958-59. Fellow AAAS; mem. NAS, Am. Astron. Soc. (vis. prof. program 1965-73, v.p. 1971-72, mem. coun. 1983-86, publs. bd. 1979-80), Internat. Astron. Union (v.p. 1988-94, treas. 1993—), Internat. Sci. Radio Union. Home: 1826 Wayside Pl Charlottesville VA 22903-1631 Office: Nat Radio Astronomy Obs Edgemont Rd Charlottesville VA 22903

ROBERTS, NANCY, computer educator; b. Boston, Jan. 25, 1938; d. Harold and Annette (Zion) Rosenthal; m. Edward B. Roberts, June 14, 1959; children: Valerie Friedman, Mitchell, Andrea. AB, Boston U., 1959, MEd, 1961, EdD, 1975. Elem. tchr. Sharon (Mass.) Pub. Schs., 1959-63; asst. prof. Lesley Coll., Cambridge, Mass., 1975-79, assoc. prof., 1980-83; prof., 1983—; dir. grad. programs in tech. in edn. Lesley Coll., Cambridge, Mass., 1980—, dir. Project Bridge,, 1987-92; dir. Ctr. for Math., Sci. and Tech. in Edn., Cambridge, Mass., 1990-91; rsch. assoc. MIT, Cambridge, 1976-79;mem. nat. steering com. Nat. Edn. Computing Conf., Eugene, Oreg., 1979—, co-chmn. nat. conf., 1989, vice chmn. steering com., 1991-95. Author: Dynamics of Human Service Delivery, 1976, Practical Guide to Computers in Education, 1982, Computers in Teaching Mathematics, 1983, Introduction to Computer Simulation, 1983 (J.W. Forrester award 1983), Integrating Computers into the Elementary and Middle School, 1987, Computers and the Social Studies, 1988, Integrating Telecommunications into Education, 1990; mem. editorial bd. Jour. Ednl. Computing, 1983—, Jour. Rsch. in Sci. Teaching; editor Computers in Edn. book series, 1984-89. Mem. Computer Policy Com., Boston, 1982-84, mem. adv. bd. Electronic Learning, 1989-91; bd. dirs. Computers for kids, Cambridge, 1983-85; mem. State Ednl. Tech. Adv. Coun., 1990—. NSF grantee, 1985—. Mem. System Dynamics Soc. (bd. dirs. policy com. 1987-89). Republican. Jewish. Home: 300 Boylston St Apt 1102 Boston MA 02116-3923 Office: Lesley Coll 29 Everett St Cambridge MA 02138-2702

ROBERTS, NEIL FLETCHER, management consulting company executive; b. Salem, Oreg., Feb. 4, 1914; s. Harold D. and Rhoda (Haynes) R.; m. Lee (Roberts) R., June 23, 1937; children—Stephen L., Susan A. (Mrs. J.B. Persson). A.B., Dartmouth Coll., 1935; M.B.A., Harvard U., 1937. With United Bank Denver N.A. (formerly U.S. Nat. Bank, merger with Denver Nat. Bank 1959, became Denver U.S. Nat. Bank), 1937—, v.p., 1948-54, exec. v.p., 1954-62, pres., 1962-69, vice chmn., 1971—, chief exec. officer, 1969-71; v.p. United Banks Colo., Inc. (formerly Denver U.S. Bancorp., Inc.), 1964-70, exec. v.p., 1971-72, pres., 1972-77, chief exec. officer, 1974-79, chmn. bd., 1977-79; chmn. United Mortgage Co., 1971-74, dir., 1968-71, 74-77; chmn. United Banks Service Co., 1971-75, dir., 1975-77. Trustee Mile Migh United Way, 1971-79, chmn., pres., 1969-71. Served as lt. (j.g.) USNR, 1944-46. Mem. Phi Kappa Sigma. Episcopalian. Home: 3165 S Hills Ct Denver CO 80210-6829

ROBERTS, (GRANVILLE) ORAL, clergyman; b. nr. Ada, Okla., Jan. 24, 1918; s. Ellis Melvin and Claudius Priscilla (Irwin) R.; m. Evelyn Lutman, Dec. 25, 1938; children: Rebecca Ann (dec.), Ronald David (dec.), Richard Lee, Roberta Jean. Student, Okla. Bapt. U., 1942-44, Phillips U., 1947; LLD (hon.), Centenary Coll., 1975. Ordained to ministry Pentecostal Holiness Ch., 1936, United Meth. Ch., 1968. Evangelist, 1936-41; pastor Fuquay Springs, N.C., 1941, Shawnee, Okla., 1942-45, Toccoa, Ga., 1946, Enid, Okla., 1947; began worldwide evangelistic ministry thru crusades, radio, TV, printed page, 1947; founder Oral Roberts Evangelistic Assn., Inc., Tulsa, 1948, Univ. Village Retirement Center, 1970, City of Faith Med./Research Ctr., 1981, Healing Outreach Ctr., 1986; founder, pub. Abundant Life mag., Daily Blessing (quar. mag.); founder, chancellor Oral Roberts U., Tulsa, 1963—; founding chmn. Internat. Charismatic Bible Ministries. Author: over 50 books including: If You Need Healing, Do These Things, 1947, God is a Good God, 1960, If I Were You, 1967, Miracle of Seed-Faith, 1970, autobiography The Call, 1971, The Miracle Book, 1972, A Daily Guide to Miracles, 1975, Better Health and Miracle Living, 1976, How to Get Through Your Struggles, 1977, Receiving Your Miracle, 1978, Don't Give Up, 1980, Your Road to Recovery, 1986, Attack Your Lack, 1985, How I Learned Jesus Was Not Poor, 1989, How to Resist the Devil, 1989, Fear Not!, 1989, A Prayer Cover Over Your Life, 1990, Is God Your Source?, 1992, 11 Major Prophecies For You in 1992, 1992, Unleashing the Power of Praying in the Spirit, 1993; also numerous tracts and brochures, Bible commentaries. Recipient Indian of Yr. award Am. Broadcasters Assn., 1963; Okla. Hall of Fame, 1973; Oklahoman of Yr., 1974. Club: Rotary. Office: Oral Roberts U 7777 S Lewis Ave Tulsa OK 74171-0003

ROBERTS, PAUL CRAIG, III, economics educator, author, consultant; b. Atlanta, Apr. 3, 1939; s. Paul Craig and Ellen Lamar (Dryman) R.; m. Linda Jane Fisher, July 3, 1969; children: Pendaran Struan Sherman, Becky Ellen, Stephanie Bradford. BS, Ga. Inst. Tech., 1961; postgrad., U. Calif., Berkeley, 1962-63, Merton Coll., Oxford (Eng.) U., 1964-65; PhD (Earhart fellow), U. Va., 1967. Asst. prof. econs. Va. Poly. Inst., 1965-69; assoc. prof. U. N.Mex., 1969-71; rsch. fellow Hoover Instn., Stanford U., 1971-77, sr. rsch. fellow, 1978—; mem. U.S. Congl. Staff, 1975-78; asst. sec. of treasury for econ. policy Dept. Treasury, Washington, 1981-82; William E. Simon prof. polit. economy Georgetown U. Ctr. for Strategic and Internat. Studies, Washington, 1982-93; chmn. Inst. for Polit. Economy, 1985—, John M. Olin fellow, 1994—; disting. adj. scholar Ctr. Strategic and Internat. Studies Georgetown U., Washington, 1993—; adj. scholar Cato Inst., 1987-93, disting. fellow, 1993—; assoc. editor, columnist Wall St. Jour., N.Y.C., 1978-80; columnist Bus. Week, 1983—, Fin. Post, Can., 1988-89, Liberation, Paris, 1988-89, Erfolg, Fed. Rep. of Germany, 1988, Washington Times, 1988—, San Diego Union, 1988-92, Le Figaro, Paris, 1992—; nationally syndicated columnist Scripps Howard News Svc., 1989—; contbr. editor: Nat. Rev., 1993—, Reason Mag., 1993-95—; mem. Pres.-elect Reagan's Task Force on Tax Policy, 1980; dir. Value Line Investment Funds, N.Y.C., A. Schulman, Akron, Ohio; cons. Morgan Guaranty Trust Co., Lazard Freres Asset Mgmt.; pres. Econ. & Communication Svcs. Inc.; cons. Dept. Commerce, 1983, Dept. Def., 1983-84; mem. adv. bd. Marvin and Palmer; mem. Wright Investors' Svc. Internat. Bd. Econ. and Invesmtent Advisors; bd. dirs. Com. on Present Danger; trustee Intercollegiate Studies Inst., Com. on Developing Am. Capitalism; mem. selection com. Frank E. Seidman disting. award in Polit. Economy. Author: Alienation and the Soviet Economy, 1971, new edit., 1990, Marx's Theory of Exchange, 1973, new edit., 1983, The Supply-Side Revolution: An Insider's Account of Policymaking in Washington, 1984, The Cost of Corporate Capital in the U.S. and Japan, 1985, Meltdown: Inside the Soviet Economy, 1990, The New Color Line: How Quotas and Privilege Destroy Democracy, 1995; The Capitalist Revolution in Latin America, Oxford U. Press, 1996—; mem. editl. bd. Modern Age, Intercollegiate Rev.; contbg. editor Harper's Mag. Drafted original Kemp-Roth Bill, 1976. Recipient Meritorious Svc. award Dept. Treasury, 1982, Pub. Svc. award GSA, 1991, Warren Brookes award for Excellence in Journalism, 1992; Am. Philos. Soc. grantee, 1968; named to Chevalier de la Légion d'Honneur, 1987; Nat. Chamber Found. fellow, 1984-85. Mem. Mont Pelerin Soc., Beethoven Soc., Am. Soc. French Legion of Honor, U.S. C. of C. (taxation com.), Internat. Club Washington. Office: Cato Inst 1000 Massachusetts Ave NW Washington DC 20001-5400

ROBERTS, PETER A., banker; b. N.Y.C., Apr. 11, 1951; s. Louis Aaron and Ida Ann (Sterman) Rottenberg. B.A., Colgate U., 1973; M.B.A., Stanford U., 1976. Vol. VISTA, Louisville, 1973-74; v.p., investment banker Morgan Stanley & Co., N.Y.C., 1976-82; investment banker Lazard Freres, N.Y.C., 1982-86, gen. ptnr., 1985-86; chmn., CEO College Savs. Bank, Princeton, N.J., 1987—. Mem. N.Y. Athletic Club, Metedeconk Nat. Golf Club (Jackson, N.J.), Omicron Delta Epsilon. Office: College Savs Bank 5 Vaughn Dr Princeton NJ 08540-6313

ROBERTS, PETER ALLEN, physical education educator; b. Buffalo, Feb. 20, 1943; s. Hobart Vosburgh and Bertha Jane (Ash) R.; m. Sherri Ann Olson, Sept. 12, 1986; 1 child, Sarah Jane. BS, Mich. State U., 1966, MA, 1970. Cert. tchr., Mich.; cert. water safety instr. trainer, lifeguard instr. trainer, CPR instr. trainer, standard first aid instr.-trainer. Educator Alpena (Mich.) Pub. Sch., 1966-69; prof. Wayne State U., Detroit, 1970—; head coach swimming Wayne State U., Detroit, 1969-84; cons. in field. Bd. dirs. ARC, Detroit, chair aquatic com., 1972—, mem. aquatic enhancement adv. com., 1993; staff mem. Mich. Aquatic Sch., 1968—. Recipient Outstanding Svc. medal ARC, 1981, Fifteen Yrs. Outstanding Svc. award, 1985, Joan B. Warren award ARC, 1986, 30 Yr. Svc. Pin, ARC, 1992. Mem. AAHPERD, Mich. AHPERD, Coll. Swimming Coaches Assn., Phi Epsilon Kappa. Democrat. Methodist. Avocations: golf, swimming, racquetball, boating. Home: 23055 Beck Rd Novi MI 48374-3622 Office: Wayne State U 264 Matthaei Bldg Detroit MI 48202

ROBERTS, PRISCILLA WARREN, artist; b. Montclair, N.J., June 13, 1916; d. Charles Asaph and Florence (Berry) R. Student, Art Students League, 1937-39, Nat. Acad., 1939-43. Represented in permanent collections Met. Mus., Cin. Art Mus., Canton Art Inst., Westmoreland County Mus. Art, Pa., IBM, Dallaas Mus., Walker Art Ctr., Mpls., Butler Inst., Youngstown, Ohio, Nat. Mus. Am. Art, Washington. Recipient Proctor prize, 1947, popular prize Corcoran Biennial, 1947, prize Westmoreland County Mus., 3d prize Carnegie Internat., Pitts., 1950, Nat. Mus. Women in Arts, Washington, Snite Mus., U. Notre Dame, Ind. Mem. NAD (Hallgarten prize 1945), Allied Artists Am. (Zabriskie prize 1944, 46), Catherine Lorillard Wolfe Assn. (hon.). Address: PO Box 716 Georgetown CT 06829-0716

ROBERTS, RALPH JOEL, cable television, telephone communications and background music company executive; b. N.Y.C., Mar. 13, 1920; s. Robert and Sara (Wahl) Roberts; m. Suzanne Fleisher, Aug. 23, 1942; children: Catherine, Lisa, Ralph Jr., Brian, Douglas. BS in Econs., U. Pa., 1941. Account exec. Aitken Kynett Advt., Phila., 1946-48; v.p. Muzak Corp., N.Y.C., 1948-50; pres., chief exec. officer Pioneer Industries, Inc., Darby, Pa., 1950-61; pres. Internat. Equity Corp., Bala Cynwyd, Pa., 1961-83; chmn. bd., Comcast Corp., Phila., 1969—; chmn., chief exec. officer Sural Corp. (merger with Internat. Equity Corp. 1983); trustee, chmn. conflict interest com. Albert Einstein Med. Ctr. Bd. dirs. regional NCCJ; trustee Brandywine Mus. and Conservancy, charter mem. World Bus. Coun.; past mem. mentor program and Benjamin Franklin assocs. U. Pa.; bd. dirs. Phila. Orch., 1993; past v.p. Family Svc. Phila.; past bd. dirs., mem. budget and fees com. State Coll. and Univ. Dirs.; mem. re-regulation and legis. affairs coms. Nat. Cable TV Assn.; past mem. Gov.'s Rev. of Govt. Mgmt., Inc. Lt. USNR, 1942-45. Reipient americanism award Anti-Defamation League of B'nai B'rith, Brotherhood award NCCJ, 1989, award for outstanding svc. to cable TV industry Walter Kaitz Found., 1990, Acres of Diamonds Entrepreneurial Excellence award Entrepreneurial Inst. Temple U., 1991, Disting. Vanguard award for leadership Nat. Cable TV Assn., 1993; named to Broadcasting and Cable Hall of Fame, 1993. Avocations: tennis, travel. Home: Sural Farm 1375 Fairview Rd Coatesville PA 19320-4431 Office: Comcast Corp 480 E Swedesford Rd # 1 Wayne PA 19087-1822*

ROBERTS, RALPH S., restaurant chain executive; b. 1942. Co-founder, pres. Rusty Scupper Restaurant, San Francisco, 1969-76; pres. Stouffer Hospitality divsn. Nestlé, 1976-80; dep. group exec. ops. W.R. Grace Restaurant Group, Irvine, Calif., 1980-86; with American Restaurant Group, Newport Beach, Calif., 1986—; pres., COO various subs., Newport Beach, Calif.; now pres. American Restaurant Group Inc., Newport Beach, Calif. Office: Am Restaurant Group Inc 450 Newport Center Dr 6th fl Newport Beach CA 92660-7610*

ROBERTS, RANDOLPH WILSON, health and science educator; b. Scranton, Pa., Oct. 8, 1946; s. S. Tracy and Alecia Francis (Sullivan) R.; m. Martha Jeanne Burnite, July 12, 1969 (div. Dec. 1985); children: Gwendolyn Suzanne, Ryan Weylin; m. Ava Elaine Brown, June 17, 1989. AB in Biology, Franklin & Marshall Coll., 1968, MA in Geoscis., 1974; MS in Sci. Teaching, Am. U., 1977; MS in Counseling, Western Md. Coll., 1990; CHES, Towson State U., 1993; postgrad., U. Md., Johns Hopkins U., Loyola Coll., Md. Cert. tchr., counselor, health educator, health edn. specialist (CHES), tax cons. Tchr. sci. Woodlawn Jr. High Sch., Balt., 1968-73, Deer Park Jr. High/Mid. Sch., Randallstown, Md., 1973-87, Franklin Mid. Sch., Reisterstown, Md., 1987-89; counselor and chmn. health/sci. dept. Balt. County Home & Hosp. Ctr., 1989—; math and sci. tchr. Loyola H.S., Towson, Md., 1981-86, Talmudical Acad., Pikesville, Md., 1983-86; health educator Loyola Coll., Md., 1994—; ednl. cons. Scott & Fetzer co., Chgo., 1981-86; founder, pres. Tax Assistance, Ltd., Owings Mills, Md., 1981—; curriculum cons. Balt. County Bd. Edn., Towson, 1977-78, 93, 95-96. Author: Earth Sciences Workbook, 1979. Mem. Glyndon (Md.) Meth. Ch., 1993—, scholarship com. chmn., handbell choir mem., Christian edn. com., liturgist, Sunday sch. coord., adminstrv. coun. mem.-at-large; treas. Boy Scouts Am. Pack 315, Reis, Md., 1986-90, Webelos Den leader, 1987-90, advancement chmn., com. mem. Troop 315, 1990-93; fin. ptnr./treas. Bare Hills Investment Group. Mem. NEA, ACA, Am. Assn. Health Edn., Balt. Rd. Runners, Nature Conservancy, Chesapeake Bay Found., Phi Delta Kappa, Mu Upsilon Sigma, Eta Sigma Gamma. Avocations: traveling, gardening, running, bowling, investing. Home: 9 Indian Pony Ct Owings Mills MD 21117-1210 Office: Home and Hosp Ctr 6229 Falls Rd Baltimore MD 21209-2120

ROBERTS, RICHARD, mechanical engineering educator; b. Atlantic City, N.J., Feb. 16, 1938; s. Harold and Marion (Hofman) R.; m. Rochelle S. Perelman, Oct. 2, 1960; children: Lori, Lisa, Scott. BSME, Drexel U., 1961; MSME, Lehigh U., 1962, PhD in Mech. Engring., 1964. Asst. prof. mech. engring. Lehigh U., Bethlehem, Pa., 1964-68, assoc. prof., 1968-75, prof., 1975—. Editor: Proceedings of the Thirteenth Nat. Symposium on Fracture Mechanics, 1980, ASME PVP Division's Design Handbook, Materials and Fabrication, Vol. III. Recipient W. Sparagen award Am. Welding Soc., 1972, Adams Meml. award, 1981. Home: 317 Bierys Bridge Rd Bethlehem PA 18017-1142 Office: Lehigh Univ MSE/200 W Packer Bethlehem PA 18015

ROBERTS, RICHARD D., cable station executive; b. 1934. BS, U.S. Naval Acad.; MBA, Harvard U. With Landmark Comm. Inc., Norfolk, Va., 1967-73; with Telecable Corp., Norfolk, 1968—, pres., 1977-84, CEO, 1984—. Mem. Nat. Cable TV Assn. (bd. dirs. 1987, chair high definition TV com.). Office: Telecable Corp 999 Waterside Dr Ste 900 Norfolk VA 23510-3300

ROBERTS, RICHARD JOHN, molecular biologist, consultant, research director; b. Derby, Eng., Sept. 6, 1943; came to U.S., 1969; s. John Walter and Edna Wilhelmina (Allsop) R.; m. Elizabeth Dyson, Aug. 21, 1965 (dec.); children: Alison, Andrew; m. Jean E. Tagliabue, Feb. 14, 1986; children: Christopher, Amanda. BS, Sheffield (Eng.) U., 1965, PhD, 1968. Rsch. fellow Harvard U., Cambridge, Mass., 1969-70, rsch. assoc., 1971-72; sr. staff investigator Cold Spring Harbor Lab., N.Y., 1972-87, asst. dir., 1987-92; rsch. dir. New England Biolabs, 1992—, cons. New Eng. Biolabs, Beverly, Mass., 1974-92; sci. adv. bd. Genex, Rockville, Md., 1977-85, Molecular Tool, Balt., 1994—. Contbr. articles to profl. jours. Recipient Nobel prize in Physiology and Medicine, Nobel Foundation, 1993. John Simon Guggenheim Found. fellow, 1979. Fellow Royal Soc.; mem. Am. Soc. Microbiology, Am. Soc. Biol. Chemists. Office: New Eng Biolabs 32 Tozer Rd Beverly MA 01915-5510

ROBERTS, RICHARD N., psychologist. AB in Govt., Columbia U., 1968; MSW, U. Hawaii, 1974, PhD in Psychology, 1977. Asst. prof. dept. psychology U. N.C., Greensboro, 1978-82; dir. pre-kindergarten ednl. program Ctr. Devel. Early Edn. Kamehameha Schs., Honolulu, 1983-89; assoc. prof. dept. psychology Utah State U., Logan, 1989—, co-dir. Early Intervention Rsch. Inst., 1989—, dir. rsch. and evaluation Ctr. for Persons with Disabilities, 1989—; cons. to Hawaii State Hosp., 1977, Hawaii Job Corps, 1977, USAF, 1976, others. Editor: Coming home to preschool: The sociocultural context of early education, 1993; author monograph and workbook; contbr. chpts. to books, articles to profl. jours.; presenter in field. Served as lt. USN, 1968-72. Recipient numerous grants. Mem. APA, APHA, Utah Pub. Health Assn., Assn. Maternal and Child Health Programs, Soc. for Rsch. in Child Devel., Coun. for Exceptional Children. Office: Utah State U Early Intervention Rsch Inst Logan UT 84322-6580

ROBERTS, RICHARD STEWART, lawyer; b. Columbus, Ohio, May 18, 1945; s. Kibler Richard and Mary Christene (Wolf) R.; m. Carol Ann Redrow, June 13, 1970; children: Charles Kibler, Eric Wesley. BA cum laude, Ohio Wesleyan U., 1967; JD, U. Mich., 1969. Bar: Ohio 1970, U.S. Dist. Ct. (so. dist.) Ohio 1970, U.S. Ct. Mil. Appeals 1971, U.S. Supreme Ct. 1980. Assoc. Taft, Stettinius & Hollister, Cin., 1970, 74-80, ptnr., 1980—. Trustee Community Improvement Corp. of Greater Cin., 1982—; active mem. Anderson Hills United Meth. Ch., Cin., 1984—. Capt. JAGC, USAF, 1970-74. Mem. Masons, Phi Beta Kappa, Omicron Delta Kappa, Delta Tau Delta. Republican. Avocation: photography. Home: 835 Shawneetrace Ct Cincinnati OH 45255 Office: 1800 Star Bank Ct 425 Walnut St Cincinnati OH 45202-3904

ROBERTS, ROBERT WINSTON, social work educator, dean; b. Balt., July 23, 1932; s. Kelmer Swan Roberts and Lettie Mae (Collins) Johnston; m. Helen Elizabeth Perpich, Mar. 4, 1964. BA with high honors, San Francisco State U., 1957; MSW, U. Calif., Berkeley, 1959; D in Social Welfare, Columbia U., 1970. Caseworker Edgewood Protestant Orphanage, San Francisco, 1959-62, Jewish Family Service, San Francisco, 1962-63; research assoc. U. Calif., Berkeley, 1963-65; research analyst Family Service Assn. Am., N.Y.C., 1965-69; asst. prof. U. Chgo., 1967-70; prof. U. So. Calif., Los Angeles, 1970-90, dean sch. social work, 1980-88, dean emeritus, prof. emeritus, 1990—; vis. prof. Western Australia Inst. Tech., Perth, 1976-77, Chinese U. Hong Kong and U. Hong Kong, 1980; cons. Crittenton Services, Los Angeles, 1970-72, James Weldon Johnson Community Ctr., N.Y., 1966-67; bd. dirs. El Centro, Los Angeles. Editor: The Unwed Mother, 1966; co-editor: Theories of Social Casework, 1970, Child Caring: Social Policy and the Institution, 1973, Theories of Social Work with Groups, 1976, Theory and Practice of Community Social Work, 1980; editorial bd. Social Work Jour.; contbr. articles to profl. jours. Staff sgt. USAF, 1950-54; sgt. 1st class USAR, 1956-59. Fellow NIMH, 1957-58, 65-67, Crown Zellerbach Found., 1958-59; recipient Outstanding Educator award Los Amigos de la Humanidad, 1979; named Disting. Assoc., Nat. Acad. Practice in Social Work, 1985. Mem. Nat. Assn. Social Workers (chmn. social action com. 1960-61), Council on Social Work Edn. (bd. dirs. 1970-73, del. to assembly 1971-72, commn. minority groups 1972-73). Avocations: reading, travel, photography. Office: Univ So Calif Sch Social Work Rm 214 Montgomery Ross Fisher Bldg Los Angeles CA 90089-0411

ROBERTS, ROBIN, sportscaster; b. Nov. 23, 1960. BA in Comms. cum laude, Southeastern La. U., 1983. Sports dir. WHMD/WFPR Radio, Hammond, La., 1980-83; spl. assignment sports reporter KSLU-FM, 1982; sports anchor, reporter WDAM-TV, Hattiesburg, Miss., 1983-84, WLOX-TV, Biloxi, Miss., 1984-86, WSMV-TV, Nashville, 1986-88, WAGA-TV, Atlanta, 1988-89; with WVEE-FM, Atlanta; host. Sunday SportsDay, contbr. NFL Prime Time, reporter, interviewer ESPN, Bristol, Conn., 1990-95, host, anchor SportsCenter, host In the SportsLight, 1995—; host Wide World of Sports ABC, 1995—. Apptd. adv. bd. Women's Sports Found., 1991; spkr. charity, civic functions. Recipient DAR T.V. Award of Merit, 1990, Women at Work Broadcast Journalism award, 1992, Excellence in Sports Journalism award Broadcast Media Northeastern U. Ctr. Study of Sport in Society and Sch. Journalism, 1993; inducted to Hall of Fame Women's Inst. Sport and Edn. Found., 1994. Office: ESPN Inc Comms Dept ESPN Plz Bristol CT 06010*

ROBERTS, RUBY ALTIZER, poet, author, fiction; b. Floyd Co., Vt., Apr. 22, 1907; d. Waddy William and Dana Adeline (Cummings) Altizer; m. Laurence Luther Roberts, July 23, 1927; 1 child, Heidi. Grad., Christianburg (Va.) High Sch.; nursing course, Norfolk (Va.) Protestant Hosp.; DHL, Coll. William and Mary, 1961. Freelance writer, 1939—, newspaper corr.; rep. of Spirit of Va., 1993. Author: (with Rosa Altizer Bray) Emera Altizer and His Descendants, 1937, 2 vols. poetry, Forever is Too Long, Command the Stars, (biography) The Way It Was, 1979, The Way It Is, 1992, Look Down at the Stars, 1994; editor juvenile verse dept. Embers Mag., Batavia, N.Y., 1944—; owner, editor, pub. The Lyric Mag.; poetry columnist Va. newspaper; contbr. over 120 poems to anthologies, newspapes, mags., numerous articles to profl. jours. Recipient First Poetry prize Sanctuary Mag., Ballaman award Disting. Svc. to Poetry, 1956, citation Disting. Svc. Poetry Khalsa Coll.; named poet laureate Va. Gen. Assembly, 1950, poet laureate Va. emeritus Gen. Assembly Va., 1992. 1st Woman to be named Poet Laureate of state. Home: 301 Roanoke St Christiansburg VA 24073-3150

ROBERTS, SAMUEL ALDEN, secondary school educator; b. Kansas City, Kans., Oct. 30, 1930; s. Elester and Sadie Lillian (Lewis) R.; m. Sallie Senora, Aug. 26, 1962; children: Sadie, Alden, Samuel Jr., William, Tyrone;. AB, Knoxville Coll., 1954; MDiv, Interdenominational Theol. Ctr, 1960; MS, Ind. State U., 1974; DMin, Chgo. Theol. Sem., 1981; EdS, Ind. State U., 1986. Cert. secondary English tchr., secondary prin. Supt. Lott Carey Bapt. Mission Sch., Haiti, 1964-68, Hardy Jr. High Sch., Chattanooga; tchr. Wirt High Sch., Gary, Ind.; asst. prin. Elston Jr. High Sch., Michigan City, Ind., athletic dir., 1976-80; tchr. Rogers High Sch., Michigan City. Mem. ASCD, Internat. Reading Assn., Nat. Coun. Tchrs. English, Michigan City Area Coun. (past pres.), Fedn. Block Units of Urban League N.W. Ind. (pres.), Ind. State Reading Assn. (secondary curriculum com.), Fedn. Block Clubs, Phi Delta Kappa (v.p., U. Chgo./DePaul U. chpt.). Home: 2300 Adams St Gary IN 46407-3042

ROBERTS, SAMUEL SMITH, television news executive; b. Port Chester, N.Y., Feb. 8, 1936; s. Robert M. and Lillian (Smith) R.; children by previous marriage: Nancy, Pamela; m. Harriet Rubin, July 27, 1975; children: Rachel, David. BS, Northwestern U., 1957. UPI, N.Y.C., 1961, Capital Cities Broadcasting, Providence, 1962; With CBS News, 1962-95; sr. prodr. CBS Evening News, N.Y.C., 1978-81; nat. editor, 1982-84; fgn. editor CBS News, 1984-87; exec. prodr. CBS News Prodns., 1992-95, 20th Century with Mike Wallace, 1994-95; pres. Roberts Media Internat., N.Y.C., 1995—. Served to lt. USN, 1957-61. Office: 575 Madison Ave New York NY 10022

ROBERTS, SANDRA, editor; b. Humboldt, Tenn., July 22, 1951; d. Harold and Margaret (Headrick) R.; m. Parker W. Duncan Jr., Aug. 11, 1990. Student, Tex. Christian U., 1969-70; BS, U. Tenn., 1972; MLS, Peabody Coll. Libr. The Tennessean, Nashville, 1975-82, editorial writer, 1982-87, editorial editor, 1987—. Pres. Women's Polit. Caucus, Nashville, 1982. Recipient John Hancock award John Hancock Co., 1983, Freedom award Tenn. Trial Laywers Assn., 1988. Mem. Am. Soc. Newspaper Editors, Nat. Conf. Editorial Writers, Sigma Delta Chi (Nat. Headliner award 1982). Mem. Christian Ch. Office: The Tennessean 1100 Broadway Nashville TN 37203-3116

ROBERTS, SEYMOUR M. (SKIP ROBERTS), advertising agency executive; b. Detroit, Aug. 11, 1934; s. Jacob and Florence Rabinowitz; m. Carol Knight, Dec. 16, 1956; children: Bradley Alan, Tracey Knight, Kristen Sophia. B.S. in Advt., Mich. State U., 1955; M.A. in Journalism, Wayne State U., Detroit, 1956. With W.B. Doner & Co., Southfield, Mich., 1956-91; exec. v.p. W.B. Doner & Co., Southfield, 1973-84, exec. v.p., gen. mgr., 1984-91; dir. strategic planning N.W. Ayer, Detroit, 1992—, sr. v.p., sr. ptnr., 1995—. Chmn. Vis. Nurse Assn. of Southeastern Mich. With AUS, 1957-59. Mem. NATAS, Am. Assn. Advt. Agys. (past chmn. Mich. coun.), Adcraft Club Detroit (pres.), Franklin Hills Country Club. Office: NW Ayer 2000 W Fisher Bldg Detroit MI 48202-1287

ROBERTS, SIDNEY, biological chemist; b. Boston, Mar. 11, 1918; s. Samuel Richard and Elizabeth (Gilbert) R.; m. Clara Marian Szego, Sept. 14, 1943. B.S., Mass. Inst. Tech., 1939; postgrad., Harvard U., 1939-41; M.S., U. Minn., 1942, Ph.D., 1943. Instr. physiology U. Minn. Med. Sch., 1943-44, George Washington U. Med. Sch., 1944-45; rsch. assoc. Worcester Found. Exptl. Biology, Shrewsbury, Mass., 1945-47; asst. prof. physiol. chemistry Yale U. Med. Sch., 1947-48; mem. faculty U. Calif. Med. Sch., Los Angeles, 1948—; prof. biol. chemistry U. Calif. Med. Sch., 1957—; chmn. acad. senate UCLA, 1989-90; mem. adv. panel regulatory biology NSF, 1955-57, adv. panel metabolic biology, 1957-59; mem. metabolism study sect. NIH, 1960-63; basic sci. study sect. Los Angeles County Heart Assn., 1958-63; cons. VA Hosp., Long Beach, Calif., 1951-55, Los Angeles, 1958-62; air conservation tech. adv. com. Los Angeles County Lung Assn., 1972-76. Author articles, revs.; editor med. jours. Served to 2d lt. AUS, 1944-48. Guggenheim fellow, 1957-58. Fellow AAAS; mem. Am. Physiol. Soc., Endocrine Soc. (v.p. 1968-69, Ciba award 1953), Brit. Biochem. Soc., Soc. Neurosci., Am. Chem. Soc. (exec. com. div. biol. chemistry 1956-59), Am. Soc. Biol. Chemists, Am. Soc. Neurochemistry, Internat. Soc. Neurochemistry, Sigma Xi (pres. UCLA chpt. 1959-60). Home: 1371 Marinette Rd Pacific Palisades CA 90272-2627 Office: UCLA Sch Med Dept Biol Chemistry 10833 Le Conte Ave Los Angeles CA 90024

ROBERTS, SIDNEY I., lawyer; b. Bklyn., Nov. 29, 1913; s. David I. and Ray (Bleicher) Robinovitz; m. Arlene Lee Aron, June 4, 1961; 1 son, Russell Lewis. B.B.A., CCNY, 1935; LL.B. magna cum laude, Harvard U., 1938. Bar: N.Y. 1938; C.P.A., N.Y. With Michael Schimmel & Co. (C.P.A.s), N.Y.C., 1938-39, S.D. Leidesdorf & Co. (C.P.A.s), N.Y.C., 1939-49; with firm Roosevelt, Freidin & Littauer, N.Y.C., 1950-56, Anderson & Roberts, N.Y.C., 1956-57, Roberts & Holland, N.Y.C., 1957-94; adj. prof. law Columbia U., 1971-78; mem. adv. council Internat. Bur. Fiscal Documentation. Author: (with William C. Warren) United States Tax Income Taxation of Foreign Corporations and Nonresident Aliens, 1966, (with others) Annotated Tax Forms: Practice and Procedure, 1970; editor: Legislative History of United States Tax Conventions, 16 vols., 1986—; contbr. articles to profl. jours. Mem. Internat. Bar Assn., ABA (sect. on taxation, council dir. 1970-73, chmn. com. on cooperation with state and local bar assns. 1968-70, chmn. com. on taxation of fgn. income 1963-64), N.Y. State Bar Assn. (tax sect. exec. com. 1967-87, chmn. com. on tax sect. planning 1968-70, chmn. com. on tax policy 1970-72), Assn. of Bar of City of N.Y., N.Y. State Soc. CPA's, Internat. Fiscal Assn. (mem. exec. com. 1972-77, pres. U.S.A. br. 1972-73). Jewish. Office: 145 Central Park W New York NY 10023-2004

ROBERTS, THEODORE HARRIS, banker; b. Gillett, Ark., May 14, 1929; s. D. Edward and Gertrude (Harris) R.; m. Elisabeth Law, July 17, 1953; children: Susan, William (dec.), Julia, John. BA in Govt., Northwestern State U., 1949; MA in Polit. Sci., Okla. State U., 1950; attended, U. Chgo. Grad. Sch. Bus., 1956. With Harris Trust and Savs. Bank, Chgo., 1953-82; exec. v.p., sec., treas. Harris Bank and Harris Bankcorp Inc., 1971-82, dir., exec. com., 1975-82; pres. Fed. Res. Bank St. Louis, 1983-85; chmn. bd., chief exec. officer Talman Home Fed. Savs. & Loan, Chgo., 1985-92; pres. LaSalle Nat. Corp., 1992-95 retired. Mem. Chgo. Club, Comml. Club Chgo., Econ. Club Chgo., Exmoor Country Club (Highland Park, Ill.). Office: 135 S La Salle St Ste 1162 Chicago IL 60603-4105

ROBERTS, THOMAS G., lawyer; b. Bakersfield, Calif., May 25, 1949. BA, U. So. Calif., 1971, JD, 1974. Bar: Calif. 1974. Ptnr. Baker & Hostetler, L.A. Mem. ABA, State Bar Calif., L.A. County Bar Assn. (chair real estate fin. sect.), Am. Coll. Real Estate Lawyers, Am. Coll. Mortgage Attys. Office: Baker & Hostetler 600 Wilshire Blvd Ste 1200 Los Angeles CA 90017-3212*

ROBERTS, THOMAS GEORGE, retired physicist; b. Ft. Smith, Ark., Apr. 27, 1929; s. Thomas Lawrence and Emma Lee (Stanley) R.; m. Alice Anne Harbin, Nov. 14, 1958 (dec. 1994); children: Lawrence Dewey, Regina Anne; foster child, Marcia Roberts Dale; m. Betty Howard McElyea, July 28, 1995. AA, Armstrong Coll., 1953; BS, U. Ga., 1956, MS, 1957; PhD, N.C. State U., 1967. Research physicist U.S. Army Missile Command, Huntsville, Ala., 1958-85; cons. industry and govt. agys., 1970—; owner Technoco, Huntsville. Contbr. articles to profl. jours. Patentee in field. Served to sgt. USAF, 1948-52. Fellow Am. Optical Soc.; mem. Am. Phys. Soc., IEEE, Huntsville Optical Soc. Am. (pres. 1980, 92). Episcopalian. Club: Toastmaster Internat. (pres. 1963). Current work: Laser physics, optics, particle beams and instrumentation; diagnostic devices and techniques development. Subspecialties: Laser physics; Plasma physics. Office: Technoco PO Box 4723 Huntsville AL 35815-4723

ROBERTS, THOMAS MORGAN, federal official; b. Memphis, Apr. 14, 1937; s. James T. and Emily K. (Allen) R.; m. Margaret Elizabeth Boyle, Jan. 14, 1967 (div. Aug. 1992); children: Andrè Lovell, Elizabeth Boyle, Elinor Edgeworth. B.S., Ga. Inst. Tech., 1959. Asst. v.p. So. Boiler & Tank Works, Inc., Memphis, 1962-68, v.p., 1968-69, chmn. bd., pres., 1969-78; treas. George Bush for Pres. campaign, Houston, 1979-80; pvt. investor Washington, 1980-81; mem. U.S. Nuclear Regulatory Commn., Washington, 1981-90; underwriting mem. Lloyd's of London, 1979-94. Pres. Memphis Orchestral Soc., 1975-76; trustee Washington Opera, 1982-95. Lt. (j.g.) USN, 1959-62. Mem. James Smithson Soc. (life). Republican. Presbyterian. Clubs: Memphis Country, Memphis Hunt and Polo; Chevy Chase; Met.

ROBERTS, TONY (DAVID ANTHONY ROBERTS), actor; b. N.Y.C., Oct. 22, 1939; s. Kenneth and Norma R.; 1 child, Nicole. B.S., Northwestern U., 1961. Movie debut in The Million Dollar Duck, 1971; other film appearances include Star Spangled Girl, 1971, Play It Again, Sam, 1972, Serpico, 1974, The Taking of Pelham, One Two Three, 1974, Annie Hall, 1977, Lovers Like Us, 1977, Just Tell Me What You Want, Stardust Memories, 1980, A Midsummer Nights Sex Comedy, 1982, Question of Honor, 1982, Packin' It In, 1983, Amityville IIID, 1983, Hannah and her Sisters, 1986, 18 Again!, 1988, Popcorn, 1990, Switch, 1991; TV movies The Lindbergh Kidnapping Case, 1976, Girls in the Office, 1979, If Things Were Different, 1980, A Question of Honor, 1982, Our Sons, 1992, Not in My Family, 1993; regular on TV series The Edge of Night, 1963-65, Rosetti and Ryan, 1977, The Four Seasons, 1986, The Lucy Arnaz Show, 1987, The Thorns, 1989; other TV appearances include The Way They Were, 1980; Broadway debut in Something about a Soldier, 1962; toured with nat. co. of Come Blow Your Horn, 1962; other Broadway stage appearances Take Her, She's Mine, 1964, Never Too Late, Barefoot in the Park, The Last Analysis, 1964, Don't Drink the Water, 1966, How Now, Dow Jones, 1967 (nominated for Tony award), Play It Again, Sam, 1969 (nominated for Tony award), Promises, Promises, 1971, Sugar, 1972, Absurd Person Singular, 1974, Murder at the Howard Johnson's, 1979, They're Playing Our Song, 1981, Doubles, 1985, Arsenic and Old Lace, 1986, Jerome Robbins Broadway, 1990, The Seagull, 1992; London debut in Promises, Promises, 1969 (London Critics Poll award as Best Actor in Musical), 1974; appeared in: Darkroom, Yale Repertory Theatre, New Haven, Hamlet, Otterbein Coll. (Ohio) Winter Drama Festival, 1975, Taming of the Shrew, Atlanta, 1978, Let 'Em Eat Cake, Berkshire Theatre Festival, Serenading Louis, Acad. Festival Theatre; The Seagull, Saratoga Performance Arts Festival, 1985, Who's Afraid of Virginia Woolf, 1986. Served in U.S. Army. Mem. SAG (bd. dirs. 1990—), Actors Equity Assn. (governing coun. 1968-74). Office: care Agy for Performing Arts 888 7th Ave New York NY 10106*

ROBERTS, TROY, CBS anchorperson. News anchor, corr. CBS, N.Y.C. Office: CBS News 524 W 57th St New York NY 10019-2902

ROBERTS, VIRGIL PATRICK, lawyer, business executive; b. Ventura, Calif., Jan. 4, 1947; s. Julius and Emma D. (Haley) R.; m. Eleanor Green, Aug. 28, 1973; m. Brenda Cecilia Banks, Nov. 10, 1979; children: Gisele Simone, Hayley Tasha. AA, Ventura Coll., 1966; BA, UCLA, 1968; JD, Harvard U., 1972. Bar: Calif. 1972. Assoc. Pacht, Ross, Warne Bernhardt & Sears, L.A., 1972-76; ptnr. Manning, Reynolds & Roberts, L.A., 1976-79, Manning & Roberts, 1980-81; exec. v.p., gen. counsel Solar Records, L.A., 1981—; pres. Dick Griffey Prodns., L.A., 1982—, Solar Records, 1988—; judge pro tem L.A., Beverly Hills Mcpl. Cts., 1975—. Past bd. dirs. L.A. Black Leadership Coalition, L.A. Mus. African Am. Art, Beverly Hills Bar Assn., L.A. Legal Aid Found.; bd. dirs. Coro Found., 1984—, Calif. Cmty. Found., 1991—, L.A. Ednl. Alliance for Restructuring Now, Cmty. Build; past pres. Beverly Hills Bar Scholarship Found.; commr. Calif. Commn. for Tchr. Credentialing, 1980-83; chmn. L.A. Ednl. Partnership, 1989—, v.p. 1983-89; vice-chmn. Nat. Pub. Edn. Fund Network; chmn. bd. dirs. L.A. Annenberg Metropolitan Project. Trustee, Comm. Econ. Devel., 1991—. Recipient NAACP Legal Def. Fund Equal Justice award, 1988. Mem. Recording Industry Assn. Am., Black Entertainment and Sports Lawyers (treas., bd. dirs. 1982—). Lead atty. for NAACP in Crawford vs. Bd. Edn. desegregation case, L.A., 1979-80. Address: 4820 Vista De Oro Ave Los Angeles CA 90043-1552 Office: Bobbitt & Roberts 1620 26th Ste 150 S Santa Monica CA 90404

ROBERTS, WALTER HERBERT BEATTY, anatomist; b. Field, B.C., Can., Jan. 24, 1915; came to U.S., 1956, naturalized, 1965; s. Walter McWilliam and Sarah Caroline (Orr) R.; m. Olive Louise O'Neal, Sept. 1, 1937; children: Gayle, Sharon, David. M.D., Coll. Med. Evangelists (later Loma Linda U.), 1939. Intern St. Paul's Hosp., Vancouver, B.C., 1938-40; med. dir. Rest Haven Hosp. Sanitarium and Hosp., Sidney, Vancouver Island, B.C., 1940-53; post doctoral trg. White Meml. Hosp., Los Angeles, 1946-47, hosp., Edinburgh, Scotland, 1953-55; instr. in anatomy Loma Linda U., 1955-58, asst. prof. anatomy, 1959-62, asso. prof., 1962-70, prof., 1971—, chmn. dept. anatomy, 1974-81; prof. emeritus. Mem. Am. Assn. Anatomists, Sigma Xi, Alpha Omega Alpha. Adventist. Home: 11366 Campus St Loma Linda CA 92354-3302 Office: Loma Linda Univ Dept Path & Human Anatomy Divsn Human Anatomy Loma Linda CA 92350

ROBERTS, WALTER RONALD, political science educator, former government official; b. Waltendorf, Austria, Aug. 26, 1916; came to U.S., 1939, naturalized, 1944; s. Ignatius and Elizabeth (Diamant) R.; m. Gisela K. Schmarak, Aug. 22, 1939; children: William M., Charles E., Lawrence H. M.Litt., Cambridge U. (Eng.), 1940, Ph.D., 1980. Research asst. Harvard U. Law Sch., 1940-42; writer, editor Voice of Am., 1942-49; press officer U.S. del. to Austrian Treaty talks, 1949, 55; fgn. affairs officer Dept. State, 1950-53; dep. asst. dir. USIA, 1954-60; counselor of embassy for pub. affairs Am. Embassy, Belgrade, Yugoslavia, 1960-66; diplomat-in-residence Brown U., Providence, 1966-67; counselor U.S. Mission to Internat. Orgns., Geneva, 1967-69; dep. assoc. dir. USIA, Washington, 1969-71, assoc. dir., 1971-74; dir. diplomatic studies Ctr. Strategic and Internat. Studies Georgetown U., Washington, 1974-75; exec. dir. Bd. Internat. Broadcasting, Washington, 1975-85; diplomat-in-residence George Washington U., Washington, 1986—. Author: Tito, Mihailovic and the Allies, 1941-45, 73, paperback, 1987, (with Terry L. Deibel) Culture and Information: Two Foreign Policy Functions, 1976; contbr. articles to profl. pubs. Apptd. mem. U.S. Adv. Commn. on Pub. Diplomacy, 1991—; bd. dirs. Salzburg Seminar, 1993—. Recipient Disting. Honor award USIA, 1974. Mem. Washington Inst. Fgn. Affairs, Coun. Fgn. Rels., Oxford-Cambridge Com., USIA Alumni Assn. (bd. dirs. 1995—), Met. Club. Home: 4449 Sedgwick St NW Washington DC 20016-2713 Office: George Washington U Elliott Sch Internat Affairs 2013 G St NW Washington DC 20052

ROBERTS, WARREN ERROL, history educator; b. Los Angeles, May 8, 1933; s. Hugh Cedric and Mildred (Howe) R.; m. Anne Findlay, July 22, 1957; children: Erin, James, Thomas, Peter. BS, U. So. Calif., 1954; BA, U. Calif., Berkeley, 1959, MA, 1960, PhD, 1966. Asst. prof. SUNY, Albany, 1963-71, assoc. prof., 1971-81, prof. history, 1981-83, Disting. Teaching prof., 1983—. Author: Morality and Social Class in 18th Century French Literature and Painting, 1974, Jane Austen and The French Revolution, 1979, Jacques-Louis David, Revolutionary Artist: Art, Politics and the French Revolution, 1989. Presbyterian. Avocations: running, tennis, squash. Home: 13 Norwood St Albany NY 12203-3410 Office: SUNY Dept of History 1400 Washington Ave Albany NY 12222-0100

ROBERTS, WESS, author; b. Cedar City, Utah, Oct. 8, 1946; s. Lester Wyatt and Lura Virginia (Russell) R.; m. Cheryl Louise Barron, Mar. 22, 1968; children: Justin, Jaime, Jeremy. BS in Psychology, So. Utah U., 1970; MS in Psychology, Utah State U., 1972, PhD in Psychology, 1974. Project dir. Courseware, Inc., San Diego, 1976-78; project engr., tng. sys. specialist Northrop Svcs., Inc., San Diego, 1978-79; dir. ops. tng. Am. Express, N.Y.C., 1979-81; v.p. human resources Am. Express, Ft. Lauderdale, Fla., 1981-82, Salt Lake City, 1982-85; v.p. human resources devel. Firemans Fund Ins. Cos., Novato, Calif., 1985-91; pvt. practice lectr. Sandy, Utah, 1991—; ad hoc prof. Utah State U., Logan, 1970-73, mem. dean's adv. coun., 1984-85; cons. Utah State U. Devel. Ctr., Logan, 1970-75, INSGROUP, Inc., Huntington Beach, Calif., 1979; mem. evaluation com. Project EVE, Columbus, Ga., 1975; adj. prof. Nova U., Ctr. for the Study of Adminstrn., Ft. Lauderdale, 1981-85; mem. adv. bd. Inst. for Human Resource Mgmt., U. Utah, Salt Lake City, 1983-85; bd. advisors Sch. Profl. Studies, Westminster Coll., Salt Lake City, 1983-85; presenter in field; others. Author: Leadership Secrets of Attila the Hun, 1989, Straight A's Never Made Anybody Rich, 1991, Victory Secrets of Attila the Hun, 1993, Make It So: Leadership Lessons For The Next Generation, 1995; editorial rev. bd.: The Pers. Adminstr., 1982-84; contbr. articles to profl. jours. Trustee The Discovery Ctr., Ft. Lauderdale, 1981-82, The Chord, Inc., Pompano Beach, Fla., 1981-83; mem., loaned exec. Nat. Alliance Bus., Western Region, 1983-85; mem. comm. com. Great Salt Lake United Way, 1984; bd. dirs. Health Plan of the Redwoods, Santa Rosa, Calif., 1987. Maj. U.S. Army, 1973-76. Recipient two Bronze medals Internat. Film and TV Festival of N.Y., 1982, Patriotic Svc. award U.S. Dept. Treasury, Washington, 1984, Silver medal and cert. of merit INTERCOM, Chgo. Internat. Film Festival, 1986, Cert. for Creative Excellence, U.S. Film and Video Festival, 1988, others; named to U.S. Army Field Artillery OCS Hall of Fame, 1995. Mem. APA.

ROBERTS, WILLIAM B., lawyer, business executive; b. Detroit, Aug. 23, 1939; s. Edwin Stuart and Marjorie Jean (Wardle) R.; m. Cathleen Anne Thompson, Sept. 1, 1962; children: Bradford William, Brent William, Katrina Marjorie. BA, Mich. State U., 1961; JD with distinction, U. Mich., 1963; China law diploma, U. East Asia, Macau, 1989. Bar: Mo. 1964, Fla. 1983. Mem. firm Thompson & Mitchell, St. Louis, 1963-67; atty. Monsanto Co., 1967-70; sr. exec. v.p. adminstrn., sec., gen. counsel Chromalloy Am. Corp. (successor Segua Corp. N.Y.), St. Louis, 1970-78; exec. v.p.-adminstrn., gen. counsel, sec. Chromalloy Am. Corp. (successor Segua Corp. N.Y.), Clayton, Mo., 1978-82; pvt. practice law, 1983-87; mng. ptnr. Roberts and Nordahl, St. Louis and Naples, Fla., 1988-89, Law Offices of William B. Roberts, St. Louis and Naples, 1989-90, Darrow & Roberts, P.A., Naples, 1992-93; pres., mng. dir. Law Offices of William B. Roberts, Naples, 1994—; pres., mng. dir. The Fairborne Group, Ltd., St. Louis and Naples, 1988-91, William B. Roberts & Assocs. Co., Merger and Acquisitions Specialists, 1982—; mem. exam. com. of policyowners Northwestern Mut. Life Ins. Co., Milw., 1978; del. to U.S.-China Joint Session on Trade Investment and Econ. Law, Beijing, 1987; sports rep. Steve Carlton, St. Louis Cardinals, Phila. Phillies baseball clubs, 1987-89; pres., CEO Tropical Tracks, Inc., Naples, 1994—. Mem. ABA, Mo. Bar Assn., St. Louis Bar Assn. (chmn. antitrust sect. 1973), Fla. Bar Assn., Collier County Bar Assn., Delta Theta Phi. Methodist. Home: 2294 Royal Ln Naples FL 33962-5323 Office: 4532 Tamiami Trl E Naples FL 33962-6783

ROBERTS, WILLIAM EVERETT, lawyer; b. Pierre, S.D., May 12, 1926; s. Everett David and Bonnie (Martin) R.; m. Cynthia Cline, July 18, 1953; children: Catherine C. Roberts-Martin, Laura M., Nancy F. Weinreich, David H. BS, U. Minn., 1947; LLB, Yale U., 1950. Bar: Ind. 1950, U.S. Supreme Ct. 1964. Employee, ptnr. Duck and Neighbours, Indpls., 1950-58; ptnr. Cadick, Burns, Duck & Neighbours, Indpls., 1958-60, Roberts, Ryder, Rogers & Scism, Indpls., 1960-85; ptnr. Barnes & Thornburg, Indpls., 1986-93, of counsel, 1994—. Pres., bd. dirs. Park-Tudor Sch., Indpls., 1982-83; elder Second Presbyn. Ch., Indpls., 1962—; trustee Indpls. Mus. Art, 1978—; pres. New Hope of Ind., Indpls., 1986-87. Fellow Am. Bar Found.; mem. ABA, Ind. Bar Assn., Indpls. Bar Assn., Rotary, Meridian Hills Country Club (pres. 1983-84), Skyline Club. Republican. Home: 10466 Spring Highland Dr Indianapolis IN 46290 Office: Barnes & Thornburg 1313 Mchts Bank Bldg 11 S Meridian St Indianapolis IN 46204-3506

ROBERTS, WILLIAM HUGH, III, library director, consultant; b. Ridley Park, Pa., Oct. 21, 1936; s. William Hugh Jr. and Alison (Rush) R.; m. Barbara Lee Howard, Aug. 29, 1959; children: Cynthia Hope, Gloria Faith, Laura Susan, William Hugh IV. Student, Princeton U., 1954-55; AB, Earlham Coll., 1958; postgrad., U. Pa., 1958-61; MLS, Drexel Inst., 1963. Law clk. Duane, Morris and Heckscher, Phila., 1959-61; librarian Free Library of Phila., 1961-65; library dir. Clinton (Iowa) Pub. Library, 1965-67,

Roanoke (Va.) County Pub. Library, 1967-71, Forsyth County Pub. Library, Winston-Salem, N.C., 1971—; pres. W.H. Roberts & Assocs., libr. cons. co., Winston-Salem, 1975—; pres. Forsyth County Employees Credit Union, Winston-Salem, 1977—. Author New Orleans Branch Library Action Plan: To the Year 2000, 1991, various libr. action plans. Trustee Nature Sci. Ctr., Winston-Salem, 1972-78; regional fundraiser Princeton U., 1980—; bd. dirs. Winston-Salem Arts Coun., 1972—; pres. Forsyth County 4-H Found., Winston-Salem, 1983—. Mem. ALA (coun. 1990—), N.C. Libr. Assn. (sec. 1974-78, Libr. Dir. of Yr. award 1988), Southeastern Libr. Assn. (treas. 1978-80), N.C. Pub. Libr. Dirs. Assn. (pres. 1986), Kiwanis (club pres. 1982, lt. gov. Carolinas dist. 1986, gov. 1990, internat. trustee 1992—), Elks. Avocations: golf, tennis, genealogy. Home: 3116 Burkeshore Rd Winston Salem NC 27106-5532 Office: Forsyth County Pub Libr 660 W 5th St Winston Salem NC 27101-2705

ROBERTS, WILLIAM M., publishing executive. Pres. Brooks/Cole Publishing Co., Pacific Grove, Calif. Office: Brooks Cole Pub Co 511 Forest Lodge Rd Pacific Grove CA 93950-5040

ROBERTS, WILLIAM WOODRUFF, JR., applied mathematics educator, researcher; b. Huntington, W.Va., Oct. 8, 1942; s. William Woodruff Sr. and Sarah Louise (Huddleston) R.; m. Linda Louise Nelson, June 17, 1967; children: William Woodruff III, David Christopher. SB, MIT, 1964, PhD, 1969. Asst. prof. Sch. Engring. and Applied Sci. U. Va., Charlottesville, 1969-74, assoc. prof. Sch. Engring. and Applied Sci., 1974-82, prof. Sch. Engring. and Applied Sci., 1982-92, dir. math.-computational modeling lab., 1990—, Commonwealth prof. engring. and applied sci., 1992—; vis. scientist Kapteyn Astron. Inst., U. Groningen, The Netherlands, 1974; NORDITA guest prof. Stockholms Observatorium, Saltsjabaden, Sweden, 1974-75; pres. Computational Modeling Technologies, Inc., 1991—. Contbr. over 100 papers to profl. jours.; author 5 books. Mem. AAAS, AIAA, Am. Astron. Soc., Am. Men and Women of Sci. (div. dynamical astronomy), Am. Inst. Physics, Fiber Soc., Internat. Astron. Union, Soc. for Indsl. and Applied Math., Va. Acad. Scis., Sigma Xi. Office: U Va-Thornton Hall Inst Applied Math Dept Mech Aerospace & Nuclear Engring Charlottesville VA 22903

ROBERTS HARVEY, BONITA, secondary school educator; b. Detroit, June 24, 1947; d. Walter James and Mattie Louise (Pacely) Hall; stepfather, Dolphus Hall Sr.; m. Paul Randall Harvey, June 13, 1970 (div. Aug. 1980); 1 child, Paula Renee. BA, Grand Valley State U., 1974; Cert. in Continuing Edn., Western Mich. U. Art specialist Jenison (Mich.) Pub. Schs., 1974—; visual/performing artist Summer at Arts Place-Grand Rapids C.C., 1980-92; cons. art edn. Detroit Inst. Art, 1988. Bd. dirs., performing artist Robeson Players, Grand Rapids, Mich., 1973—, Cmty. Cir. Theatre, Grand Rapids, 1981-84, Coun. Performing Arts for Children, Grand Rapids, 1981-88; active First Cmty. African Meth. Episc. Ch., NAACP. Mem. ASCD, Nat. Art Edn. Assn., Mich. Art Edn. Assn., Mich. Edn. Assn. (tri-county pub. rels. 1994—), Mich. Alliance Arts Edn., Nat. Mus. Women in Arts, Jenison Edn. Assn. (pub. rels. 1993—), Delta Sigma Theta. Avocation: performing/visual arts advocate. Office: Jenison Pub Schs 8375 20th Jenison MI 49428

ROBERTSHAW, JAMES, lawyer, pilot; b. Greenville, Miss., May 19, 1916; s. Frank Newell and Hannah Mary (Aldridge) R.; m. Sylvia Schively, Apr. 26, 1956; children: Mary Nicholson, Sylvia Yale, Frank Paxton. SB, Miss. State U., 1937; JD, Harvard U., 1940, Vet.'s Cert., Harvard Bus. Sch., 1946; postgrad. Command and Gen. Staff Sch., 1943. Bar: Miss. 1940, U.S. Dist. Ct. (no. dist.) Miss. 1951, U.S. Ct. Appeals (5th cir.) 1954, U.S. Tax Ct. 1958, U.S. Supreme Ct. 1967, U.S. Dist. Ct. (so. dist.) Miss. 1984. Sole practice, Greenville, Miss., 1940, 46-62; ptnr. Robertshaw & Merideth, 1962-84; ptnr. Robertshaw, Terney & Noble, Greenville, 1984-95; of counsel, 1995. Chmn. Community and County Devel. Com., Miss. Econ. Council, 1968-70; mem. Miss. Ho. of Reps., 1953-56; chmn. Greenville Airport Commn., 1967-73, Indsl. Found., 1974; mem. com. tech. in the cts., mem. complaint tribunal Miss. Supreme Ct., 1987-93. Served to col. U.S. Army, 1941-46. Decorated Legion of Merit, Croix de Guerre (France). Mem. Am. Judicature Soc., Miss. Bar Found., Univ. Club, Greenville Golf and Country Club, Sigma Alpha Epsilon. Episcopalian. Home: PO Box 99 Greenville MS 38702-0099 Office: Robertshaw Terney & Noble 128 S Poplar St Greenville MS 38701-4025

ROBERTSON, A. HAEWORTH, actuary, benefit consultant, foundation executive; b. Oklahoma City, May 10, 1930; s. Albert Haeworth and Bonnie Twyman (Duckett) R.; m. Mary Adeline Kissee, Feb. 3, 1952 (div. July 1979); children—Valerie Lynn, Alan Haeworth, Mary Kathryn. B.A. in Math., U. Okla., 1951; M.A. in Actuarial Sci., U. Mich., 1953. Actuary Wyatt Co., Washington and Dallas, 1955-58; actuary Bowles, Andrews & Towne, Dallas, 1958-60; v.p., actuary W. Alfred Hayes & Co., St. Louis, 1960-63; pres. First Am. Security Life Ins. Co. Mo., St. Louis, 1964-68; pvt. practice internat. cons. actuary Barbados and Ghana, 1969-72; sr. actuary ILO, Geneva, Switzerland, 1973-75; chief actuary U.S. Social Security Adminstrn., Balt., 1975-78; mng. dir. William M. Mercer, Inc., Washington, 1978-88; pvt. practice, internat. cons., actuary Washington, Kuwait, Turkey, Guyana, Zimbabwe, China, The Philippines, 1988—; chmn. Retirement Bd. Actuaries, Dept. Def., 1984-95; mem. Edn. Benefits Bd. Actuaries, 1985-95; pres., founder Retirement Policy Inst. Inc., 1986—. Author: The Coming Revolution in Social Security, 1981, Social Security: What Every Taxpayer Should Know, 1992. Served to 2d lt. USAF, 1953-55. Recipient Commrs. Citation, Social Security Adminstrn., Washington, 1976, Arthur J. Altmeyer award HEW, Washington, 1978. Fellow Soc. Actuaries (bd. govs. 1979-81, v.p. 1985-87), Conf. Cons. Actuaries; mem. Am. Acad. Actuaries, Internat. Actuarial Assn., Internat. Assn. Cons. Actuaries, U.K. Inst. Actuaries (assoc.), Cosmos Club, Phi Beta Kappa, Phi Eta Sigma, Phi Kappa Sigma. Republican. Methodist.

ROBERTSON, ABEL L., JR., pathologist; b. St. Andrews, Argentina, July 21, 1926; came to U.S., 1952, naturalized, 1957; s. Abel Alfred Lazzarini and Margaret Theresa (Anderson) R.; m. Irene Kirmayr Mauch, Dec. 26, 1958; children: Margaret Anne, Abel Martin, Andrew Duncan, Malcolm Alexander. BS, Coll. D.F. Sarmiento, Buenos Aires, Argentina, 1946; MD suma cum laude, U. Buenos Aires, 1951; PhD, Cornell U., 1959. Fellow tissue culture div. Inst. Histoloty and Embryology, Sch. Medicine Inst. Histology and Embryology, 1947-49; surg. intern Hosp. Ramos Mejia, Buenos Aires, 1948-50; fellow in tissue culture research Ministry of Health, Buenos Aires, 1950-51; resident Hosp. Nacional de Clinicas, Buenos Aires, 1950-51; head blood vessel bank and organ transplants Research Ctr. Ministry of Health, Buenos Aires, 1951-53; fellow dept. surgery and pathology Sch. Medicine Cornell U., N.Y.C., 1953-55; asst. vis. surgery U. Hosp. N.Y., N.Y.C., 1955-60; asst. prof. research surgery Postgrad. Med. Sch. NYU, N.Y.C., 1955-56; asst. vis. surgeon Bellevue Hosp., N.Y.C., 1955-60; assoc. prof. research surgery NYU, 1956-60, assoc. prof. pathology Sch. Medicine and Postgrad Med. Sch., 1960-63; staff mem. div. research Cleve. Clinic Found., 1963-73, prof. research, 1972-73; assoc. clin. prof. pathology Case Western Res. U. Sch. Medicine, Cleve., 1968-72, prof. pathology, 1973-82, dir. interdisciplinary cardiovascular research, 1975-82; exec. head dept. pathology Coll. Medicine, U. Ill., Chgo., 1982-88; prof. pathology Coll. Medicine U. Ill., 1982-93, prof. emeritus, 1993-95; vis. prof. emeritus in cardiovascular medicine Stanford U. Coll. Medicine, 1995—; vis. prof. emeritus Stanford U. Coll. Medicine, 1995—; rsch. fellow N.Y. Soc. Cardiovasc. Surgery, 1957-58; mem. rsch. study subcom. of heart com. N.E. Ohio Regional Med. Program, 1969—. Mem. internat. editorial bd.: Atherosclerosis, Jour. Exptl. and Molecular Pathology, 1964—, Lab. Investigation, 1989—, Acta Pathologica Japonica, 1991—; contbr. articles to profl. jours. Recipient Research Devel. award NIH, 1961-63. Fellow Am. Coll. Cardiology, Am. Coll. Clin. Pharmacology, Am. Heart Assn. (established investigator 1956-61, nominating com. council on arteriosclerosis 1972), Royal Microscopical Soc., Royal Soc. Promotion Health (Gt. Britain), Am. Geriatrics Soc., N.Y. Acad. Scis., Cleve. Med. Library Assn.; mem. AMA, AAAS, AAUP, Am. Soc. for Investigative Pathology, Am. Inst. Biol. Scis., Am. Judicature Soc., Am. Soc. Cell Biology, Am. Soc. Pathologists, Am. Soc. Nephrology, Assn. Am. Physicians and Surgeons, Assn. Computing Machinery, Electron Microscopy Soc. Am., Assn. Pathology Chmn., Internat. Acad. Pathology, Soc. Cardiovascular Pathology, Internat. Cardiovascular Soc., Internat. Soc. Cardiology (sci. council on arteriosclerosis and ischemic heart disease), Internat. Fed. on Genetic Engring. and Biotechnology, Internat. Soc. for Heart Rsch., Internat. Soc. Nephrology, Internat. Soc. Stereology, Pan Am. Med. Assn. (life, councillor in angiology 1966), Ill. Registry Anatomical Pathology (treas. 1985-87), Chgo. Pathology Soc., Reticuloendothelial Soc. Leucocyte Biology, Soc. Cryobiology, Tissue Culture Assn., Ohio Soc. Pathologists, Electron Microscopy Soc. Northeastern Ohio (pres., trustee 1966-68), Heart Assn. Northeastern Ohio, N.Y. Soc. Cardiovascular Surgery, N.Y. Soc. Electron Microscopists, Cuyahoga County Med. Soc., Cleve. Soc. Pathologists, The Oxygen Soc., Sigma Xi. Home: 415 Lee Ave Half Moon Bay CA 94019-1367

ROBERTSON, ALVIN CYRRALE, professional basketball player; b. Barberton, Ohio, July 22, 1962; m. Jackie Robertson; 1 child, Alvin Jr. Student, Crowder Jr. Coll., Mo., U Ark., 1981-84. With San Antonio Spurs, 1984-89; player Milw. Bucks, 1989-93, Detriot Pistons, 1993, Denver Nuggets, 1993—; mem. NBA All-Star team, 1986-88, 91. Recipient Gold medal Olympics, L.A., 1984; ranked 1st in NBA for steals, 1985-87, 91; named NBA Defensive Player of Yr., 1986, Most Improved Player, 1986; named to NBA All-Defense First Team, 1987, 91. Office: Detroit Pistons Palace Alburn Hills Two Championship Dr Auburn Hills MI 48326*

ROBERTSON, ARMAND JAMES, II, judge; b. San Diego, Sept. 23, 1937; s. Armand James and Muriel H. R.; m. Marion Sperry, Aug. 11, 1962; children: Armand James, Laura Marie. A.M. in Econs, Stanford U., 1960; LL.B., Harvard U., 1965. Bar: Calif. 1966. Law clk. to Charles M. Merrill, U.S. Ct. Appeals (9th cir.), 1965-66; assoc. firm Howard, Prim, Rice, Nemerovski, Canady & Pollak, San Francisco, 1966-71; ptnr. Howard, Prim, Rice, Nemerovski, Canady & Pollak, 1971-77; dir. Howard, Rice, Nemerovski, Canady, Robertson & Falk (P.C.), San Francisco, 1977-95; judge of the Superior Ct. City and County of San Francisco, 1995—. Served to lt. (j.g.) USN, 1960-62. Mem. Am. Law Inst., ABA (antitrust sect.), Ct. for Pub. Resources, Phi Beta Kappa. Home: 178 Edgewood Ave San Francisco CA 94117-3713 Office: San Francisco Superior Ct Dept 5 633 Folsom St San Francisco CA 94107

ROBERTSON, BEVERLY CARRUTH, steel company executive; b. Texarkana, Ark., May 16, 1922; s. Glenn C. Robertson (dec.); m. Ruth Mulcare, Oct. 31, 1945 (dec. Oct. 1993); children: Glenn J., Beverly R. Dodds, Rebecca A. Robertson Deans; m. Charlotte Doty Lawler, June 2, 1995. In sales Nat. Supply Co., Laurel, Miss., 1941-51; purchasing agt. Kirby Petroleum co., Houston, 1951-54; exec. v.p. mktg. Lone Star Steel Co., Dallas, 1954-85; exec. v.p. Lone Star Steel Co., 1985-86; pres., dir., chief exec. officer LSSCO Trading Corp., 1985-86; owner BSEER Enterprises, Dallas, 1986—; ptnr. Clayton Equipment Co., Dallas, 1992—; chmn. Sir Alec Inc., 1985-94; cons. Pipeco, Inc., Houston, 1986-88; exec. v.p. mktg. and procurement Nat. Pipe and Tube Co., Houston, 1988-89; pres., CEO Tex. Am. Pipe & Supply Co., Inc., Dallas, 1989—; cons. Ipsco Steel, Inc., Camanche, Iowa, 1991-92. Served to capt. USAF, 1943-46, ETO. Named Supplier of Yr. Petroleum Industry Buyers group Nat. Assn. Purchasing Mgmt., 1982. Mem. Dallas Country Club, Dallas Petroleum Club. Republican. Episcopalian. Home: PO Box 12688 Dallas TX 75225-0688

ROBERTSON, C. R., insurance company executive; b. 1930; married. BBA, U. Tex., 1952. Mgr. audit staff Ernst & Ernst, 1955-65; staff asst. Am. Nat. Ins. Co., Galveston, Tex., 1965-67, asst. sec., 1967-69, controller, asst. sec., 1969-70, v.p., controller, 1970-74, sr. v.p., controller, 1974-77, exec. v.p. adminstrn., 1977-86, sr. exec. v.p. home office adminstrn., 1986—. Office: Am Nat Ins Co 1 Moody Plz Galveston TX 77550-7948

ROBERTSON, CLIFF, actor, writer, director; b. La Jolla, Calif., Sept. 9, 1925; s. Clifford Parker and Audrey (Willingham) R.; m. Dina Merrill, Dec. 21, 1966 (div.); children: Heather, Stephanie. DFA (hon.), Bradford Coll., 1981, MacMurray Coll., 1986, Susquehanna U., 1988. Contbr. articles to various publs.; stage appearances include Late Love, Wisteria Trees, Orpheus Descending; films include Picnic, 1956, Autumn Leaves, 1956, The Naked and the Dead, 1958, The Girl Most Likely, 1958, Gidget, 1959, All in a Nights Work, 1961, The Big Show, 1961, Under-World, U.S.A., 1961, As the Sea Rages, 1961, The Interns, 1962, PT 109, 1963, Sunday in New York, 1964, The Best Man, 1964, 633 Squadron, 1964, Love Has Many Faces, 1965, Masquerade, 1965, Up From the Beach, 1965, The Honey Pot, 1967, The Devil's Brigade, 1968, Charly, 1968, (Academy award for Best Actor 1969), The Great Northfield Minnesota Raid, 1972, Ace Eli and Rodger of the Skies, 1973, Too Late the Hero, 1970, Man on a Swing, 1974, 3 Days of the Condor, 1975, Out of Season, Obsession, 1976, Shoot, 1976, Star 80, 1983, Brainstorm, 1983, Malone, 1987, Wild Hearts Can't Be Broken, 1991, Wind, 1992, The Sunset Boys, 1995, Escape from L.A., 1996; TV movies and miniseries appearances include The Days of Wine and Roses, 1958, The Sunshine Patriot, 1968, The Game, 1968 (Emmy award) The Man Without a Country, 1973, A Tree Grows in Brooklyn, 1974, My Father's House, 1975, Return to Earth, 1976, Washington: Behind Closed Doors, 1977, Overboard, 1978, Two of a Kind, 1982, The Key to Rebecca, 1985, Dreams of Gold, 1986, Ford: The Man and The Machine, 1987, Dead Reckoning, 1990, Dazzle, 1995, The Last Best Place; appeared in TV series Falcon Crest; writer, dir.: play The V.I.P.'s, 1981; J. W. Coop. Served to lt. (j.g.) USNR. Recipient Wallace award Am. Scottish Found., 1984, Sharples aviation award AOPA, 1983, Theatre World award, 1970, award Advt. Age, 1985. Mem. SAG (bd. dirs. N.Y. chpt. 1980—), Dirs. Guild, Writers Guild Am., Bath & Tennis Club Palm Beach, Maidstone Club (East Hampton), River Club (N.Y.C.), Brook Club (N.Y.C.), Players (N.Y.C.), River Club, Wings Club. Presbyterian. Avocations: flying, skiing, soaring, tennis.

ROBERTSON, DAVID, pharmacologist, educator; b. Sylvia, Tenn., May 23, 1947; s. David Herlie and Lucille Luther (Bowen) R.; m. Rose Marie Stevens, Oct. 30, 1976; 1 child, Rose. B.A., Vanderbilt U., 1969, M.D., 1973. Diplomate Am. Bd. Internal Medicine, Am. Bd. Clin. Pharmacology. Intern, Johns Hopkins U., Balt., 1973-74, asst. resident, 1974-75, asst. chief service in medicine, 1977-78; fellow in clin. pharmacology Vanderbilt U., Nashville, 1975-77, asst. prof. medicine and pharmacology, 1978-82, assoc. prof., 1982-86, prof., 1986—, prof. neurology, 1991—; dir. clin. research ctr., 1987—; dir. Ctr. for Space Physiology and Medicine, 1989—; dir. Med. Sci. Tng. Program, 1993—; pclin. rsch. specializing in gene therapy and disorders of blood pressure regulation, Nashville, 1978—; mem. staff Vanderbilt Hosp., Burroughs Wellcome scholar in clin. pharmacology, 1985-91. Author: (with B.M. Greene and G.J. Taylor) Problems in Internal Medicine, 1980, (with C.R. Smith) Manual of Clinical Pharmacology, 1981, (with Italo Biaggioni) Disorders of the Autonomic Nervous System, 1995, Primer on the Autonomic Nervous System, 1996; editor-in-chief Drug Therapy, 1991-94; editorial bds. Jour. Autonomic Nervous System, Clin. Pharm. and Therapeutics, Clin. Autonomic Rsch., Am. Jour. Med. Sci., Current Topics in Pharmacology. Recipient Research Career Devel. award NIH, 1981, Grant W. Liddle award for leadership in rsch., 1991; Adolph-Morsbach grantee Bonn, Germany, 1968; Logan Clendening fellow Reykjavik, Iceland, 1969. Fellow Am. Heart Assn. Council Hypertension and Circulation, ACP (teaching and research scholar 1978-81); mem. Am. Autonomic Soc. (pres. 1992-94), Am. Acad. Neurology, Soc. Neurosci., Am. Inst. Aeronautics and Astronautics, U.S. Pharmacopeial Conv., Nat. Bd. Med. Examiners, Aerospace Med. Assn. (space station sci. and applications com.), FDA Consortium Rare Disorders, Rare Disorder Network, Am. Fedn. for Clin. Research, Am. Soc. Clin. Investigation, Assn. Am. Physicians, So. Soc. for Clin. Investigation, Am. Soc. for Clin. Pharmacology and Therapeutics, Phi Beta Kappa, Alpha Omega Alpha (hon., bd. dirs. 1995—). Baptist. Home: 4003 Newman Pl Nashville TN 37204-4308 Office: Vanderbilt U Clin Rsch Ctr 21st Ave S Nashville TN 37232-2195

ROBERTSON, DAVID GOVAN, lawyer; b. Chgo., May 3, 1947. AB with great distinction, Stanford U., 1969; JD, Yale U., 1973. Bar: Calif. 1973, U.S. Dist. Ct. (no., cen., ea. and we. dists.) Calif. 1973, U.S. Supreme Ct. 1988. Law clk. to chief judge U.S. Dist. Ct., 1973-74; assoc. Morrison & Foerster, San Francisco, 1974-79, ptnr., 1979—; adj. prof. legal ethics U. San Francisco Law Sch., 1993-94; vis. prof. theology U. San Francisco, 1995—. Danforth Found. Grad. fellow Yale, 1970-73. Mem. Phi Beta Kappa. Office: Morrison & Foerster 345 California St San Francisco CA 94104-2675*

ROBERTSON, DOUGLAS STUART, lawyer; b. Portland, Oreg., Jan. 9, 1947; s. Stuart Neil and Mary Katherine (Gates) R.; m. Nan Reinhorn, Dec. 27, 1970; 1 child, Lauren Amanda. BS, Oreg. State U., 1969, MA in Bus. Adminstrn., 1970; JD U. Denver, 1973. Bar: Oreg. 1973, U.S. Dist. Ct. Oreg. 1974, U.S. Ct. Appeal (9th cir.) 1977, U.S. Supreme Ct. 1977. Staff atty. Multnomah County Bar Assn. Legal Aid, Portland, 1973-75; ptnr. Bouneff, Chally & Marshall, Portland, 1975-80; asst. gen. counsel Orbanco Fin. Services, Portland, 1980-83; gen. counsel Hyster Credit Corp., Portland, 1983-86; v.p., gen. counsel PacifiCorp Credit Inc., 1986-90; ptnr. Lane, Powell, Spears Lubersky, Portland, 1990-91; v.p., gen. counsel, sec., In Focus Systems, Inc., Wilsonville, Oreg., 1991—; chmn. bd., CEO Deschutes River Preserve, Inc., Portland, 1982—. Mem. editl. bd. Denver Jour. of Internat. Law and Policy, 1971. Served with U.S. Army 1968-70. Mem. ABA, Comml. Law League, Multnomah County Bar Assn., Am. Assn. of Equipment (lessor's law forum), Am. Corp. Counsel Assn. (bd. dirs., treas. N.W. chpt.). Republican. Club: Flyfisher's of Oreg., Oreg. Trout. Home: 29 Hillshire Dr Lake Oswego OR 97034-7375 Office: In Focus Systems Inc 27700 B SW Parkway Ave Wilsonville OR 97070-9215

ROBERTSON, EDWARD D., JR., state supreme court chief justice; b. Durham, N.C., May 1, 1952; m. Renee Ann Beal; two children. BA, U. Mo., 1974, JD, 1977. Asst. atty. gen. Mo., 1978-79; assoc. mcpl. judge City of Belton, Mo., 1980-81; dep. atty. gen. City of Belton, 1981-85; justice Mo. Supreme Ct., Kansas City, 1985—; former chief justice, now judge Mo. Supreme Ct. Office: Mo Supreme Ct PO Box 150 Jefferson City MO 65102-0150*

ROBERTSON, EDWIN DAVID, lawyer; b. Roanoke, Va., July 5, 1946; s. Edwin Traylor and Norma Burns (Bowles) R.; m. Anne Littelle Ferratt, Sept. 7, 1968, 1 child, Thomas Therit. BA with honors, U. Va., 1968, LLB, 1971. Bar: N.Y. 1972, U.S. Ct. Appeals (2d cir.) 1972, U.S. Dist. Ct. (ea. and so. dists.) N.Y. 1973, U.S. Supreme Ct. 1975, U.S. Dist. Ct. (ea. dist.) Mich. 1986. Assoc. Cadwalader, Wickersham & Taft, N.Y.C., 1972-80; ptnr. Cadwalader, Wickershaft & Taft, N.Y.C., 1980—. Bd. dirs. Early Music Found. N.Y.C., 1983—, chmn., 1993—; bd. dirs. Oratorio Soc. of N.Y.C., 1988—, sec., 1991—. 1st lt. USAF, 1971-72. Mem. ABA, Fed. Bar Coun., N.Y. County Lawyers Assn. (chmn. bankruptcy com. 1983-87, bd. dirs. 1985-88, 95—, investment com. 1992—), Assn. Bar City N.Y. (com. onstate cts. of superior jurisdiction 1987-90, fed. legis. com. 1990-93), Jefferson Soc., Order of Coif, Soc. Colonial Wars, Down Town Assn. (N.Y.C.), Phi Beta Kappa, Phi Kappa Psi. Republican. Episcopalian. Home: 315 E 72nd St New York NY 10021-4625 Office: Cadwalader Wickersham & Taft 100 Maiden Ln New York NY 10038-4818

ROBERTSON, GEORGE LEVEN, retired association executive; b. Alexandria, La., Feb. 7, 1921; s. Ernest E. and Cornelia (La Croix) R.; m. Florence Horne, Feb. 7, 1943; children—Dana Carleton, Linda, Malcolm Ernest, Judy Elaine. B.S., La. State U., 1941; M.S., A. and M. Coll. Tex., 1947; Ph.D. (Gen. Edn. Bd. fellow 1949-50), U. Wis., 1951. Grad. asst. animal husbandry A. and M. Coll. Tex., 1941-42, instr., then asst. prof., 1946-49, asso. prof., 1951-55; grad. asst. U. Wis., 1949-51; prof. animal sci., head dept. La. State U., 1955-77, chmn. grad. council, 1961; exec. dir. Honor Soc. of Phi Kappa Phi, 1977-92. Trustee Baton Rouge Gen. Hosp.; deacon, trustee First Bapt. Ch., Baton Rouge. Served to capt. AUS, 1942-46; col. Res. Named Outstanding Tchr. A. and M. Coll. Tex. Sch. Agr., 1948-49. Fellow AAAS; mem. Am. Soc. Animal Sci. (pres. So. sect. 1967-68), AAUP, Assn. Coll. Honor Socs. (v.p. 1987-89, pres. 1989-91), Sigma Xi, Alpha Zeta, Phi Kappa Phi (nat. pres.-elect 1974-77), Gamma Sigma Delta, Omicron Delta Kappa. Clubs: Masons, Kiwanis. Home: 7017 Perkins Rd Baton Rouge LA 70808-4320

ROBERTSON, GREGG WESTLAND, diversified company executive; b. Sydney, Australia, Jan. 16, 1934; s. Alexander and Lillian R.; BA in Econs., Fairleigh Dickinson U., 1964; postgrad. Harvard U., 1980; m. Elizabeth Stimper, Apr. 30, 1957; children—Gregg Westland, Lisa. Asst. v.p. Bankers Trust Co., N.Y.C., 1964-69; asst. treas. Dillingham Corp., Honolulu, 1970-73, treas., 1974-77, v.p. fin., treas., chief fin. officer, 1977-82, sr. v.p. strategic devel., 1982-83, pres., chief exec. officer, 1986—; pres., chief exec. officer Calif. Gas Corp. subs., Sacramento, 1983-84, exec. v.p. parent co., San Francisco, 1984-86; pres., CEO Robertson & Co., San Francisco, 1987-93, Honolulu, 1992-93; exec. v.p., COO Liberty Bank, Honolulu, 1990-92; v.p., Cadinha & Co., Honolulu, 1993—. Bd. dirs. Aloha United Way, 1980-82, Sacramento United Way, 1983-84, Child & Family Svc. Mem. Fin. Execs. Inst. Clubs: Olympic (San Francisco), Outrigger Canoe (Honolulu), Pacific. Home: 1862 Halekoa Dr Honolulu HI 96821-1029

ROBERTSON, HORACE BASCOMB, JR., law educator; b. Charlotte, N.C., Nov. 13, 1923; s. Horace Bascomb and Ruth (Montgomery) R.; m. Patricia Lavell, Aug. 11, 1947; children—Mark L., James D. B.S., U.S. Naval Acad., 1945; J.D., Georgetown U., 1953; M.S., George Washington U., 1968. Commd. ensign U.S. Navy, 1945, advanced through grades to rear adm., 1972; line officer, 1945-55, law specialist, 1955-68; spl. counsel to sec. Navy, Washington, 1964-67; judge adv. Navy, 1968-76; spl. counsel to chief naval ops. Washington, 1970-72; dep. judge adv. gen. Navy Dept., Washington, 1972-75; judge adv. gen. Navy Dept., 1975-76; prof. law Duke U., 1976-89, sr. assoc. dean, 1986-89, ret., 1990; Chas H. Stockton chair of internat. law Naval War Coll., Newport, R.I., 1991-92. Decorated D.S.M. Mem. ABA, Am. Soc. Internat. Law. Methodist. Home: 5 Stoneridge Cir Durham NC 27705-5510 Office: Duke U Sch Law Durham NC 27708

ROBERTSON, HUGH DUFF, lawyer; b. Grosse Pointe, Mich., Mar. 14, 1957; s. Hugh Robertson and Louise (Grey) Bollinger. BBA in Fin., U. Wis., Whitewater, 1978; JD, Whittier Coll., 1982. Bar: Calif. 1983, U.S. Tax Ct. 1984. Pres., CEO, A. Morgan Maree Jr. & Assocs., Inc., L.A., 1979—. Mem. ABA (forum com. on entertainment 1982—), State Calif., L.A. County Bar Assn., Beverly Hills Bar Assn., Acad. TV Arts and Scis., Am. Film Inst., Phi Alpha Delta. Republican. Episcopalian. Avocations: sports, swimming, reading. Office: A Morgan Maree Jr & Assocs 4727 Wilshire Blvd Ste 600 Los Angeles CA 90010-3875

ROBERTSON, JACK CLARK, accounting educator; b. Marlin, Tex., Apr. 27, 1943; s. Rupert Cook and Lois Lucille (Rose) R.; m. Caroline Susan Hughes, Oct. 23, 1965; children: Sarah Ellen, Elizabeth Hughes. Student, Rice U., 1961-63; B.B.A. with honors, U. Tex., Austin, 1965, M.in Profl. Acctg., 1967; Ph.D., U. N.C., 1970. C.P.A., Tex. Tax acct. Humble Oil and Refining Co., Houston, 1964-65; auditor Peat, Marwick, Mitchell & Co., Houston, 1965-66; acct. Wade, Barton, Marsh C.P.A.s, Austin, Tex., 1966-67; asst. prof. U. Tex., Austin, 1970-74; assoc. prof. U. Tex., 1974-79, Price Waterhouse auditing prof., 1979-84, C.T. Zlatkovich Centennial prof. acctg., 1984—; acad. assoc. Coopers & Lybrand, N.Y.C., 1975-76; acad. fellow U.S. Securities and Exchange Commn. Office of the Chief Acct., Washington, 1982-83; Erskine fellow U. Canterbury, Christchurch, New Zealand, 1988; lectr. in field. Contbr. articles to profl. jours. Lay reader St. Matthews Episcopal Ch., Austin, 1972-75, mem. vestry, 1973-75, 77-79, 84-86, treas., 1974-75, 77—, chmn. bldg. fund, 1976-87, chmn. everymen. canvass, 1980, sr. warden, 1986; del. Diocese of Tex. Coun., 1993-95. Mem. AICPA, Am. Acctg. Assn. (chmn. auditing sect. 1978-79, chmn. auditing stds. com. 1980-81, chmn. SEC liaison com. 1983-84), Tex. Soc. CPAs (vice chmn., profl. ethics com. 1986-94, 95—, Presdl. citation 1994), Assn. Cert. Fraud Examiners (regent emeritus, cert.), Phi Kappa Phi, Beta Gamma Sigma, Beta Alpha Psi. Office: CBA Univ of Tex Cba 4M 202 Dept Of Acc Austin TX 78712

ROBERTSON, JAMES, judge; b. Cleve., May 18, 1938; s. Frederick Irving and Doris Mary (Byars) R.; m. Berit Selma Persson, Sept. 19, 1959; children: Stephen Irving, Catherine Anne, Peter Arvid. AB, Princeton U., 1959; LLB, George Washington U., 1965. Bar: D.C. 1966, U.S. Supreme Ct. 1969. Assoc. Wilmer, Cutler & Pickering, Washington, 1965-69, ptnr., 1973-94; U.S. dist. judge D.C., 1994—; chief counsel Lawyers Com. for Civil Rights Under Law, Jackson, Miss., 1969-70; dir. Lawyers Com. for Civil Rights Under Law, Washington, 1970-72, co-chmn., 1985-87; co-chmn. D.C. Lawyers Com. for Civil Rights Under Law, Washington, 1982-84; mem. com. on grievances U.S. Dist. Ct., 1988-92, vice chmn., 1989-92; bd. dirs. South Africa Legal Svcs. and Edn. Project, Inc., 1987—, pres., 1989-94; bd. dirs. D.C. Prisoners Legal Svcs., Inc., 1992-94. Editor in chief George Washington Law Rev., 1964-65. Lt. USN, 1959-64. Fellow Am. Coll. Trial Lawyers, Am. Bar Found.; mem. ABA, D.C. Bar (bd. govs. 1986-93, pres.-elect 1990-92, pres. 1991-92). Home: 11300 Cushman Rd North Bethesda MD 20852-3606 Office: Rm 6315 US Courthouse Washington DC 20001

ROBERTSON, JAMES COLVERT, insurance company executive; b. Takoma Park, Md., Feb. 2, 1932; s. Charles Edwin and Mary Louise

(Colvert) R.; m. Grace A. Shuler, May 7, 1971. BS in Econs., U. Md., 1957; LLB, George Washington U., 1959. Bar: D.C. 1960, Pa. 1965. Atty./analyst SEC, Washington, 1959-64; atty. McNees, Wallace & Nurick, Harrisburg, Pa., 1964-67; gen. counsel Consumers Life, Camp Hill, Pa., 1967-68; pres., chmn. bd. Consumers Life & Consumers Fin. Corp., Camp Hill, 1968—; dir. Consumers Fin. Bd. dirs. Harrisburg Hosp., 1982-86, Elizabethtown Coll., 1982—, Keystone Sports Found., 1983-88; treas. Susquehanna Art Mus. 1988—. With U.S. Army, 1951-53. Mem. Pa. Bar Assn., Fed. Bar Assn. West Shore Country Club (bd. dirs.). Republican. Home: 86 Greenwood Cir Wormleysburg PA 17043-1140 Office: Consumers Life Ins Co PO Box 26 1200 Camp Hill By-Pass Camp Hill PA 17001-0026

ROBERTSON, JAMES IRVIN, JR., historian, educator; b. Danville, Va., July 18, 1930; s. James Irvin and Mae (Kympton) R.; m. Elizabeth Green, June 1, 1952; children—Mae Elizabeth, James Irvin III, Howard Wells. BA, Randolph-Macon Coll., 1955, LittD, 1980; MA, Emory U., 1956, PhD, 1959. Ordained deacon Anglican Cath. Ch. Editor Civil War History, U. Iowa, 1959-61; exec. dir. U.S. Civil War Centennial Commn., 1961-65; assoc. prof. history U. Mont., 1965-67; prof. Va. Poly. Inst. and State U., Blacksburg, 1967-76, chmn. dept. history, 1969-77, C.P. Miles prof. history, 1977-92, Alumni disting. prof., 1992—. Author: Civil War Sites in Virginia, 1982, General A.P. Hill, 1987, Soldiers Blue and Gray, 1988, Civil War Virginia, 1991, Civil War! America Becomes One Nation, 1992, Jackson & Lee: Legends in Gray, 1995; contbr. articles to profl. jours. Recipient Harry S. Truman Hist. award, Bruce Catton award, Nevins Freeman award. Outstanding Faculty award Va. State Coun. Higher Edn., 1991, others. Mem. So. Hist. Assn., Va. Hist. Soc. Home: 405 Stonegate Dr Blacksburg VA 24060-3243 Office: Va Poly Inst History Dept Blacksburg VA 24061

ROBERTSON, JAMES MAGRUDER, geological research administrator; b. Port Clinton, Ohio, Sept. 24, 1943; married. BA, Carleton Coll., 1965; MS, U. Mich., 1968, PhD in Econ. Geology, 1972. Asst. prof. geology Mich. Technol. U., 1972-74; mining geologist N.Mex. Bur. Mines and Mineral Resources, 1974-86, sr. econ. geologist, 1986-88, assoc. dir., 1988-92; geologist Wis. Geol. Survey, Madison, 1992—. Mem. Geochem. Soc., Geol. Soc. Am., Soc. Econ. Geology, Sigma Xi. Office: Univ Wisconsin Geol & Natural History Survey 3817 MineralPoint Rd Madison WI 53705 Office: Wis Geol Survey 3817 Mineral Point Rd Madison WI 53705*

ROBERTSON, JAMES WOOLSEY, lawyer; b. Ft. Sam Houston, Tex., Aug. 6, 1942; s. Robert Charles Lee and Marjorie Evelyn (Woolsey) R.; 1 child, William Angus; m. Laura Ann Koons, Apr. 24, 1993. BBA, U. Tex., 1966, JD, 1967. Bar: Tex.; cert. real estate law specialist. Ptnr. Liddell, Sapp, Zivley, Hill & Laboon, L.L.P., Houston, 1971—, chmn. fin. com., 1985-90, chmn. banking and real estate sect. and computer com., 1992—. Chancellor Episc. Ch. Holy Spirit, Houston, 1984-92, trustee, 1984-87. Lt. comdr. USCGR, 1968-71. Mem. State Bar Tex., Houston Bar Assn., Houston Real Estate Lawyers Coun. Republican. Avocations: golf, fly fishing, skiing, hunting. Office: Liddell Sapp Zivley Et Al 3400 Tex Commerce Tower 600 Travis St Houston TX 77002

ROBERTSON, JERALD LEE, physicist; b. Webbs Cross Roads, Ky., Oct. 4, 1935; s. Marvin Lee and Eva Lee (Wheat) R.; m. Carol Ann Sanderson, Aug. 29, 1963 (div. Jan. 1970). BS in Physics and Chemistry, Wilmington (Ohio) Coll., 1960; postgrad., Amherst (Mass.) Coll., 1961, U. Dayton, 1964-65. Cert. hazardous materials mgr. Trainee, indsl. mgr. Ralston Purina, Sharonville, Ohio, 1961-63; rsch. physicist Monsanto Rsch., Dayton, 1963-68; graphic arts engr. Formica Corp., Evendale, Ohio, 1968-70; tech. svcs. mgr. Color Pac Inc., Franklin, Ohio, 1970-73; tech. svcs. rep. GE, Coshocton, Ohio, 1972-77; tech. svcs. mgr. Cin. Milacron, 1978-82; mgr. R&D Kornylak Corp., Hamilton, Ohio, 1983-96; citizen adv. bd. Henkel Corp., Cin., 1994—; bd. dirs. Hamilton Safety Coun., Rivers Unltd.-MCRP, Cin. Author: (with others) Pulp and Paper, 1980; columnist (weekly article) Suburban Press, 1983-85; contbr. articles to profl. jours. Councilman Village of Elmwood Place, Ohio, 1992-96, candidate for mayor, 1983, 87, 93; chmn. Mill Creek Watershed Steering Com., Cin., 1994-95; chmn. Citizens for Sensible Waste Mgmt., Cin., 1990-93; chmn. cmty. panel Bicentennial Commn., Cin., 1987; mem. sr. olympics basketball, 1992, 93. Mem. Ohio Alliance for the Environ., Am. Assn. for Ind. Investors. Avocation: wine tasting. Home: 111 Township Ave Cincinnati OH 45216-2425 Office: Kornylak Corp 400 Heaton St Hamilton OH 45011-1872

ROBERTSON, JERRY D., lawyer; b. Port Clinton, Ohio, Dec. 16, 1948; s. Edgar N. and Delores E. (Brough) R.; m. Kathryn A. Behlmer, Aug. 1, 1970; children: Matthew, Adam. BS, Bowling Green State U., 1971; JD, U. Toledo, 1974. Bar: Ohio 1974, U.S. Ct. Mil. Appeals 1974, U.S. Dist. Ct. (no. dist.) Ohio 1977, U.S. Supreme Ct. 1980. Pvt. practice Oak Harbor, Ohio, 1977—; instr. real estate law Terra tech. Coll., Fremont, Ohio, 1978-82; asst. pros. atty. Ottawa County, Ohio, 1980-84; law dir. Village of Oak Harbor, Ohio, 1982—; bd. dirs. Luther Home of Mercy, Williston, Ohio. Capt. U.S. Army, 1974-77. Decorated Meritorious Svc. medal. Mem. ABA, Nat. Network of Estate Planning Attys., Nat. Acad. Elder Law Attys., Ohio Bar Assn., Toledo Estate Planning Coun., Am. Legion. Lutheran. Home: 520 E Water St Oak Harbor OH 43449-1535 Office: PO Box 26 132 W Water St Oak Harbor OH 43449

ROBERTSON, JERRY EARL, retired mining and manufacturing company executive; b. Detroit, Oct. 25, 1932; s. Earl Howard and Nellie (Wright) R.; m. Joanne Alice Wesner, Sept. 3, 1955; children: Scott Clark, Lisa Kay, Stuart Todd. B.S., Miami U., Oxford, Ohio, 1954; M.S., U. Mich., 1956, Ph.D., 1959. With Minn. Mining & Mfg. Co., St. Paul, 1963—, tech. dir. med. products div., 1973-74, dept. mgr. surg. products dept., 1974-75, gen. mgr. surg. products div., 1975-79, div. v.p. surg. products div., 1979-80, group v.p. health care products and services, 1980-84, exec. v.p. life scis. sector, 1984-86, exec. v.p. life scis. sector and corp. svcs., 1986-94; ret., 1994; bd. dirs. Cardinal Health Distbn., Inc., Haemonetics Corp., Braintree, Mass., Allianz Life Ins. Co. of N.Am.; trustee Minn. Med. Found., Mpls., 1981-87. Bd. reference MAP Internat., Brunswick, Ga., 1986-94; bd. dirs. Project HOPE, 1988—, Manor Care Inc., 1989—, Cardinal Distbn., Inc., 1991—, Medwave, Inc., 1995—. Mem. Pharm. Mfrs. Assn. (bd. dirs. 1984-89), Health Industry Mfrs. Assn. (bd. dirs. 1982-91, chmn. 1990-91). Unitarian. Office: Minn World Trade Ctr 30 Seventh St E Ste 3050 Saint Paul MN 55101-4901

ROBERTSON, JOHN ALDEN, agrologist, researcher; b. Minnedosa, Man., Can., Mar. 28, 1937; s. Lorne Edgar and Frances Mary (Jones) R.; m. Isobel Anne McDonald; children: David, Lesley, Trevor. BS in Agr., U. Man., Winnipeg, 1959, MSc, 1961; PhD, Massey U., Palmerston North, New Zealand, 1969. Lectr. U. Sask., Saskatoon, Can., 1964-65; rsch. scientist Agr. Can., Melfort, Sask., 1965-85; dir. Agr. Can., Kamloops, B.C., Can., 1985-91, Brandon, Man., 1991—. Office: Agr Can Rsch Sta, PO Box 1000A RR #3, Brandon, MB Canada R7A 5Y3

ROBERTSON, JOHN ARCHIBALD LAW, nuclear scientist; b. Dundee, Scotland, July 4, 1925; s. John Carr and Ellen (Law) R.; m. Betty-Jean Moffatt, June 26, 1954; children: Ean Stuart, Clare Deborah, Fiona Heather. B.A., Cambridge (Eng.) U., 1950, M.A., 1953. Sci. officer U.K. Atomic Energy Authority, Harwell, Eng., 1950-57; research officer Atomic Energy Can. Ltd., Chalk River, Ont., 1957-63; head reactor materials br. Atomic Energy Can. Ltd., 1963-70, dir. fuels and materials div., 1970-75, asst. to v.p., 1975-82; dir. program planning Atomic Energy Can. Ltd. (Research Co. Head Office), 1982-85; cons., 1985—; mem. Atomic Energy Control Bd.'s Adv. Com. on Nuclear Safety, 1988—. Author: Irradiation Effects in Nuclear Fuels, 1969; editor: Jour. Nuclear Materials, 1967-71. Served to capt., Royal Engrs. Brit. and Indian armies, 1943-47. Recipient W.B. Lewis medal Can. Nuclear Assn., 1987, W.J. Kroll Zirconium medal W.J. Kroll Inst. for Extractive Metallurgy, 1993. Fellow Royal Soc. Can.

ROBERTSON, JOSEPH EDMOND, grain processing company executive; b. Brownstown, Ind., Feb. 16, 1918; s. Roscoe Melvin and Edith Penina (Shields) R.; m. Virginia Faye Baxter, Nov. 23, 1941; 1 son, Joseph Edmond. BS, Kans. State U., 1940, postgrad., 1940. Cereal chemist Ewing Mill Co., 1940-43, flour milling engr., 1946-50, feed nutritionist, 1951-59; v.p., sec. Robertson Corp., Brownstown, Ind., 1960-80, pres., 1980—. Mem. Kans. State U. Varsity Basketball Team, 1937-40; pres. Jackson County (Ind.) Welfare Bd., 1948-52; mem. Ind. Port Commn., 1986-91; mem. Ind. Gov.'s Coun. of Sagamores of the Wabash. Forest products tech. writer Forest Prodn. Jour., 1973-78. Served with USAAF, 1943-45. Named to Hon. Order Ky. Cols. Mem. Hardwood Plywood Mfrs. Assn. (v.p. affiliate div. 1971-73, 87-88, internat. lectr. forest prodn. industry 1973-94), Am. Assn. Cereal Chemists, Assn. Operative Millers, Am. Legion, Brownstown C. of C. (dir. All Am. city program 1955), Kans. State U. Alumni Assn. (life), Blue Key, Phi Delta Theta, Phi Kappa Phi, Alpha Mu. Presbyterian. Clubs: Harrison Lakes Country Club, Internat. Travelers Century (Los Angeles), Circumnavigators Club (N.Y.C.). Lodge: Elks. Home: Lake and Forest Club 1268 E Lake Shore Dr PO Box A Brownstown IN 47220 Office: 200 N Front St Brownstown IN 47220-1040

ROBERTSON, JOSEPH W., JR., investment company executive; b. 1947. BA, Houston Bapt. U., 1971. With Weingarten Realty Investors, Houston, 1971—, sr. v.p. Office: Weingarten Realty Investors 2600 Citadel Plaza Dr Ste 300 Houston TX 77008-1315*

ROBERTSON, LEON H., management consultant, educator; b. Atlanta, Jan. 25, 1934; s. Grady Jospeh and Pearline (Chandler) R.; m. S. Ann Parker, Aug. 27, 1971; children: Sharon, Michael. B.S. in Indsl. Mgmt., Ga. Inst. Tech., 1957, M.S., 1959; postgrad., U. Okla.-Norman, 1958, U. Mich., 1961; Ph.D. in Bus. Adminstrn., Ga. State U., 1968. Mgr. mgmt. cons. div. Arthur Anderson & Co., Atlanta, 1960-65; prof. bus. adminstrn. Ga. State U., 1965-75; corp. v.p. Tex. Gas Corp., Owensboro, Ky., 1975-78, sr. v.p., 1982-83; chmn., chief exec. officer Am. Carriers, Inc., Overland Park, Kans., 1978-88; chmn. bd. dirs. Midwest Coast Transport, Overland Park, 1988-89; prof. mgmt., dir. div. bus. adminstrn. U. Mo., Kansas City, 1990-96, dir. Internat. Acad. Programs, 1996—. Office: Univ of Mo-Kansas City Henry W Bloch Sch Bus & Pub Admn 5110 Cherry St Kansas City MO 64110-2426

ROBERTSON, LESLIE EARL, structural engineer; b. Los Angeles, Feb. 12, 1928; s. Garnett Roy and Tina (Grantham) R.; m. Saw-Teen See, Aug. 11, 1982; children: Jeanne, Christopher Alan, Sharon Miyuki, Karla Mei. BS, U. Calif., Berkeley, 1952; D in Engring. (hon.), Rensselaer Polytech. Inst., 1986; DSc (hon.), U. Western Ont., Can., 1988; DEng (hon.), Lehigh U., 1991. Lic. arch., Japan. Structural engr. Kaiser Engrs., Oakland, Calif., 1952-54, John A. Blume, San Francisco, 1954-57, Raymond Internat. Co., N.Y.C., 1957-58; mng. ptnr. Skilling, Helle, Christiansen, Robertson, N.Y.C., Seattle and Anchorage, 1958-82; chmn. Robertson, Fowler & Assocs., P.C., N.Y.C., 1982-85, Leslie E. Robertson Assocs., structural engrs., 1986—; chmn. Coun. on Tall Bldgs. and Urban Habitat; mem. Com. on Natural Disasters; commr., mem. U.S. Nat. Com. for the Decade for Natural Disasters Reduction; dir. Wind Engring. Rsch. Coun.; lectr. Rensselaer Poly. Inst., 1984, Johns Hopkins U., 1985, Nat. Bur. Standards, 1986, Cornell U., Hong Kong U., 1986, Technischische U., Delft, Holland, 1991, 93, Waseda (Japan) U., Musashi Inst. Tech., 1993, others; James L. Sherard lectr. U. Calif., Berkeley, 1991. Author papers in field. Bd. dirs. Architects/Designers/Planners for Social Responsibility; mem. Japan Structural Cons. Assn.; mem. human rights of scientists com. N.Y. Acad. Scis.; mem. U.S. Nat. Com. for Decade for Nat. Disaster Reduction; mem. engring. coll. coun. Cornell U. Served with USNR, 1944-46. Recipient Inst. Honor award AIA, 1989, Mayor's award for excellence in sci. and tech. Mayor of City of N.Y./N.Y. Acad. Scis., 1993, John R. Parmer award, 1991, Disting. Engring. Alumnus award U. Calif., Berkeley, 1991, Prof. Gengo Matsui prize, Japan, 1993, World Trade Ctr. Individual Svc. medal, 1993, Citation of Excellence, ENR, 1993, named Constrn. Man of Yr., 1989. Fellow ASCE (Raymond C. Reese Rsch. prize 1974), Singapore Structural Steel Soc.; mem. Nat. Acad. Engring. Archtl. League of N.Y. (v.p.), N.Y. Acad. of Scis. (Mayor Award Excellence in Sci. and Tech. 1993, 95), Tokyo Soc. Architects (Disting. Hon. mem.). Home: 45 E 89th St Apt 25C New York NY 10128-1230 Office: 211 E 46th St New York NY 10017-2935

ROBERTSON, LINDA L., federal agency administrator. BS with honors, U. So. Ill., 1976; JD, U. Tulsa, 1979; LLM in Taxation, U. Georgetown, 1986. Bar: Okla. 1980, D.C. 1987. From staff counsel to tax counsel Rep. James Jones, 1976-87; ptnr. Powell, Goldstein, Frazer and Murphy, Washington, 1987-93; dep. asst. sec. legis. affairs Dept. of the Treasury, Washington, 1993—. Mem. ABA (taxation sect.). Office: Legis Affairs Treasury Department 15th & Pennsylvania Ave NW Washington DC 20220*

ROBERTSON, LINWOOD RIGHTER, electric utility executive; b. Reedville, Va., Feb. 10, 1940; s. Reginald Linwood and Alliene Dewer (Righter) R.; m. Mildred Swift, Apr. 10, 1965; 1 child, William S. B.S., Va. Commonwealth U., 1970. Comml. fisherman Smith Fisheries, Belford, N.Y., 1964; supr. Philip Morris Co., Richmond, Va., 1965-68; various positions to sr. v.p., chief fin. officer Dominion Resources, Inc. (formerly Va. Power), Richmond, 1969—. With USN, 1962-64. Mem. Hermitage Country Club. Methodist. Home: 11 Quail Run Dr Manakin Sabot VA 23103-2632

ROBERTSON, MARY LOUISE, archivist, historian; b. L.A., May 19, 1945; d. Snell and Dorothy (Tregoning) R. BA, UCLA, 1966, MA, 1968, PhD, 1975. Teaching asst. dept. history UCLA, 1967-70; acting instr. UCLA Extension, 1973-74; acting instr. dept. history Pepperdine U., L.A., 1970, Calif. State U., Northridge, 1972-73; asst. curator manuscripts Huntington Libr., San Marino, Calif., 1975, assoc. curator, 1977, chief curator, 1979—; adj. prof. English Claremont Grad. Sch., 1994. Author: Guide to British Historical Manuscripts in the Huntington Library, 1982; co-author, editor: Guide to American Historical Manuscripts in the Huntington Library, 1979; contbr. articles on Tudor history to profl. jours. Mabel Wilson Richards dissertation fellow, 1970-72. Mem. Am. Hist. Assn., Soc. Am. Archivists, Soc. Calif. Archivists, N.Am. Conf. on Brit. Studies, Pacific Coast Conf. on Brit. Studies (treas. 1986-88, pres. 1988-90), Phi Beta Kappa. Office: Huntington Libr 1151 Oxford Rd San Marino CA 91108-1218

ROBERTSON, MICHAEL SWING, religious association administrator; b. Boston, July 20, 1935; s. Charles Stuart and Elizabeth (Swing) R.; m. Margaret Filoon, Sept. 17, 1960; children: Michael Swing, Ashlee Whipple, Christopher Filoon, Andrew Stuart. A.B., Harvard U., 1957, grad. Advanced Mgmt. Program, 1979. With Robertson Factories, Inc., 1957-80, exec. v.p., 1968-73, pres., 1973-79, chmn. bd., 1979-80; dir. Robertson-Swing Co., 1980—; pres. The Berkley Co. Inc., 1981-90, Reactions Inc., 1985-90; treas. Falmouth Marine Inc., 1981-88; pres., treas. Orchard Computer Inc., 1984-91, chmn., treas., 1991-93; exec. sec. Nat. Assn. Congl. Christian Chs., Oak Creek, Wis., 1991—. v.p. adv. coun. Coll. of Bus. and Industry, Southeastern Mass. U., North Dartmouth, Mass., 1979-91; selectman, Town of Berkley, Mass., 1974-80, chmn. 1979-80; mem. Pres.'s Adv. Com. for Trade Negotiations, 1983-86; bd. dirs. Mass. Easter Seal Soc., 1977-91, pres. 1982-83; bd. dirs. Nat. Easter Seal Soc., 1985-91, Wis. Easter Seal Soc., 1994-95; chmn. Berkley Rep. Town com., 1977-91; mem. Pilgrim Congl. Ch., Taunton, North Shore Congrl Ch., Fox Point, Wis.; Rep. nominee U.S. Senate from Mass., 1976, nominee for Mass. state auditor, 1982; co-chmn. Mass. Reagan for Pres. Com., 1980; Bristol County coord. Reagan/Bush campaign; co-chmn. Mass. Dole for Pres. Commn., 1987; chmn. Southeastern Mass. campaign Harvard Coll., 1981; chmn. Friends of Harvard Track, 1986-91; trustee Barnstable County Hosp., 1985-90, chmn., 1988. Mem. Harvard Varsity Club, Harvard Bus. Sch. Alumni Club of Wis. Home: 500 W Bender Rd # 51 Milwaukee WI 53217 Office: Nat Assn Congl Christian Ch 8473 S Howell Ave Oak Creek WI 53154-2922 *Accept responsibility with enthusiasm and gratitude. Our individual freedom is unmatched in history, compelling us to remain true to our heritage and Our God.*

ROBERTSON, NAN, journalist, correspondent; b. Chgo., July 11, 1926; d. Frank and Eva (Morrish) R.; m. Allyn Baum, Feb. 24, 1950 (div. 1961); m. Stanley Levey, Aug. 27, 1961 (dec. 1971). B.S. in Journalism, Northwestern U., 1948. Spl. corr. Paris Herald Tribune, Paris, Berlin and London, 1948-55, Milw. Jour., Paris, Berlin and London, 1948-55, Stars and Stripes, Paris, Berlin and London, 1948-55, Am. Daily, Paris, Berlin and London, 1948-55; reporter, corr. N.Y. Times, N.Y.C., Washington and Paris, 1955-83; reporter culture N.Y. Times, N.Y.C., from 1983. Author: The Girls in the Balcony: Women, Men and The New York Times, 1992. Recipient Pulitzer prize for feature writing, 1983; recipient Page One award N.Y. Newspaper Guild, 1983, Front Page award N.Y. Newswomen's Club, 1961, 80, 82, N.Y. Press Club award, 1983; MacDowell Colony fellow, 1981, 83; Woodrow Wilson nat. fellow, 1983. Episcopalian. Address: care Kelly Susa Random House Inc 201 E 50th St New York NY 10022-7703

ROBERTSON, NAT CLIFTON, chemist; b. Atlanta, July 23, 1919; s. Henry Booker and Eura Allen (Williams) R.; m. Elizabeth Bates Peck, Nov. 29, 1946; children: Henry Bartlett, Mary Amanda, Paul Edward. A.B., Emory U., 1939, Sc.D., 1970; Ph.D., Princeton U., 1942. Research asso. OSRD, 1942-43; chemist Standard Oil Co., N.J., 1943-47; group leader Celanese Corp. Am., 1947-51; dir. petrochems. dept. Nat. Research Corp., 1951-55; v.p., dir. research Escambia Chem. Corp., 1955-58; v.p. Spencer Chem. div. Gulf Oil Corp. (formerly Spencer Chem. Co.), Kansas City, Mo., 1958-66, Air Products & Chems., Inc., Allentown, Pa., 1966-69; sr. v.p. Air Products & Chems., Inc., 1969-77, also bd. dirs.; dir. Marion Labs., 1963-89. Trustee Midwest Research Inst.; bd. dirs. Kans. Research Found., 1963-66, pres., 1963-64. Mem. Am. Chem. Soc., Dirs. Indsl. Research, Indsl. Research Inst., Phi Beta Kappa, Sigma Xi. Democrat. Presbyterian. Club: Princeton (N.Y.C.). Home: 156 Philip Dr Princeton NJ 08540-5423

ROBERTSON, OSCAR PALMER (BIG O ROBERTSON), former professional basketball player, chemical company executive; b. Charlotte, Tenn., Nov. 24, 1938. BBBA, U. Cin., 1960. Player U.S. Olympic Basketball Team, 1960; basketball player Cin. Royals, 1960-70, Milw. Bucks, 1970-74; founder, pres., CEO, Orchem, Inc., Cin., 1981—, Orpack-Stone Corp., Herrin, Ill., 1990—, Oscar Robertson Constrn., Indpls., 1975—; player NBA Championship Team, 1971. Named Sporting News Coll. Player of Yr., 1958, 59, 60, Sporting News All-Star Fitrst Team, 1958, 59, 60, NBA Rookie of Yr., 1961, All NBA First Team, 1961-69; player NBA All Star Games, 1961-72; named MVP, NBA, 1964, M VP in NBA All-Star Games, 1961, 64, 69; named to NBA 35th Anniversary All-Star Team, 1980; elected to Naismith Meml. Basketball Hall of Fame, 1979. Office: Orchem Inc 4293 Mulhauser Rd Fairfield OH 45014-5450*

ROBERTSON, PAT (MARION GORDON ROBERTSON), religious broadcasting executive; b. Lexington, Va., Mar. 22, 1930; s. A. Willis and Gladys (Churchill) R.; m. Adelia Elmer; children: Timothy, Elizabeth, Gordon, Ann. BA, Washington and Lee U., 1950; JD, Yale U., 1955; MDiv, N.Y. Theol. Sem., 1959; ThD (hon.), Oral Roberts U., 1983. Ordained minister So. Bapt. Conv., 1961-87. Founder, CEO Christian Broadcast Network, Virginia Beach, Va., 1960—; host 700 Club, 1968—; founder, chancellor Regent Univ. (formerly CBN Univ.), 1977—; founder, chmn. Operation Blessing Internat. Relief and Devel. Inc., 1978—, Internat. Family Entertainment, Inc., 1990—, Asia Pacific Media Corp., 1993—; chmn. Starguide Digital Networks, Inc., 1995—, Porchlight Entertainment, Inc., 1995—; founder, pres. The Christian Coalition, 1989—, The Am. Ctr. for Law and Justice, 1990—; bd. dirs. United Va. Bank, Norfolk; mem. Pres. Task Force on Victims of Crime, Washington, 1982. Author: (with Jamie Buckingham) Shout It From the Housetops: The Story of the Founder of the Christian Broadcasting Network, 1972, My Prayer for You, 1977, The Secret Kingdom, 1982, Answers to 200 of Life's Most Probing Questions, 1984, Beyond Reason, 1984, 85, America's Dates with Destiny, 1986, The Plan, 1989, The New Millennium, 1990, The New World Order, 1991, The End of the Age, 1995. Candidate for Rep. nomination for Pres. U.S., 1988. Recipient Disting. Merit citation NCCJ, Knesset medallion Israel Pilgrimage Com., Faith and Freedom award Religious Heritage Am., Bronze Halo award So. Calif. Motion Picture Council, Humanitarian award Food for the Hungry, 1982, George Washington Honor medal Freedoms Found. at Valley Forge, 1983; named Internat. Clergyman of Yr. Religion in Media, 1981, Man of Yr. Internat. Com. for Goodwill, 1981. Mem. Nat. Broadcasters (bd. dirs. 1973—), Kentucky Colonels. Office: The Christian Broadcasting Network CBN Ctr Virginia Beach VA 23463

ROBERTSON, PAUL JOSEPH, lawyer, educator; b. Chgo., Dec. 31, 1963; s. Byron and Mary Ellen (Statom) R. BSBA in Mktg., Georgetown U., Washington, 1985; BA in Sociology, St. Leo (Fla.) Coll., 1988; MBA, U. Ill., 1992, JD, 1992. Bar: Ill. 1992, U.S. Dist. Ct. (no. and ea. dist.) Ill. 1992, U.S. Ct. Appeals (7th cir.) 1992. Counsel Region V U.S. Dept. Health and Human Svcs., Chgo., 1992-93, staff atty. Social Security Adminstrn., 1993-94; atty. Office Gen. Counsel U.S. Dept. Health and Human Svcs., Bethesda, Md., 1994—; lectr. NIH, Found. for Advanced Edn. in Scis., Bethesda, 1995—; mem. black employees fed. adv. com. NIH, 1994—. Campaign aide FEC compliance com. to elect Carol Moseley-Braun for U.S. Senate, Chgo., 1992. 1st lt. USAF, 1985-88. Decorated Air Force Meritorious Medal; recipient Joseph W. Rickert Award for Cmty. Svc., Faculty of Law, U. Ill., 1992. Mem. ABA, Nat. Bar Assn., Chgo. Bar Assn., Am. Legion, Masons. AME Ch. Avocations: Lacrosse, basketball, travel, reading, wine tasting. Office: NIH Bldg 31 Rm 2B-50 Bethesda MD 20892-2111

ROBERTSON, PETER BARRIE, mayor; b. N.Y.C., Nov. 4, 1938; s. Robert Barrie and Rosemary (Mecca) R.; m. Jo-Anne Chalmers; children: Scott, Kirk, Jodi. B Phys. Edn., U. Toronto, Ont., Can., 1961, BA in Psychology, 1964; MEd, Ont. Inst. Studies in Edn., Toronto, 1967. Tchr., coach Etobicoke Bd. Edn., 1962-66; cons. Toronto Bd. Edn., 1967-71; prof. faculty of edn. U. Toronto, 1972-95; councillor City of Brampton, Ont., 1974-91, mayor, 1991—; chmn. Greater Toronto Area Mayor's Com. on Mcpl. Tax Reform, 1994-95; rschr. on assisting street children; spkr. and workshop leader in field. Co-author: Health for Life, 1984, (multimedia kit) Sexually Transmitted Diseases, 1979, (video and teaching kit) Taking Control Family Violence, 1986. Sch. trustee, councillor Castlemore and Toronto Gore, Peel County, 1968-74; mem. nat. edn. nucleus com. Can. Cancer Soc.; founder Castlemore Cmty. Sch., Peel Dist. Health Coun., Victim Svcs. in Peel, Peel Drinking and Driving Awareness Com.; nat. bd. dirs. Inst. Prevention Child Abuse. Recipient Ministry of Health recognition Peel Dist. Health Coun., 1977-84, Silver Pin for Vol. Svc., Can. Cancer Soc., 1979-85, Multi Cultural award North American Sikh League, 1990. Mem. Can. Assn. Phys. Health and Recreation (nat. membership chmn.), Can. Mental Health Assn. (nat. bd. dirs.). Home: 11570 McVean Dr RR 9, Brampton, ON Canada L6T 3Z8 Office: City of Brampton, 2 Wellington St W, Brampton, ON Canada L6Y 4R2

ROBERTSON, RALPH S., secondary school principal. Prin. Richmond Sr. High Sch., Rockingham, N.C. Recipient Rlue Ribbon Sch. award U.S. Dept. Edn., 1990-91, Nat. award Dale Parnell Tech. Prep Program of Excellence, 1991; named Prin. of Yr., N.C. Burger King/Nat. Assn. of Secondary Sch. Prin., 1987. Office: Richmond Sr High Sch PO Box 1748 US Hwy 1 North Rockingham NC 28379

ROBERTSON, RICHARD BLAKE, management consultant; b. Ahoskie, N.C., July 28, 1929; s. James Henry and Janie Bell (Baker) R.; m. Elizabeth Parker Gardner, Aug. 19, 1941. BSEE, N.C. State U., 1951; MBA, U. Md., 1956. Design engr. Westinghouse Electric Co., Friendship Airport, Md., 1951-54; product planner Gen. Electric Co., Lynchburg, Pa., 1956-59; dir. mktg. Gen. Motors Corp., Milw., 1959-60; pres. Robertson and Assocs., Pinetops, N.C., 1960—. Mem. Phi Kappa Phi, Tau Beta Pi, Phi Eta Sigma, Theta Tau, Eta Kappa Nu. Office: Robertson & Assocs Inc PO Drawer B Pinetops NC 27864

ROBERTSON, RICHARD EARL, physical chemist, educator; b. Long Beach, Calif., Nov. 12, 1933; s. Earl Austin and A. Isobel (Roberts) R.; m. Joyce W. Conger, Sept. 4, 1955 (div. 1972); children: Christopher, Jill; m. Patricia L. Richmond, Apr. 20, 1974. BA, Occidental Coll., L.A., 1955; student, UCLA, 1955-56; PhD, Calif. Inst. Tech., 1960. Phys. chemist rsch. lab. GE, Schenectady, N.Y., 1960-70; staff scientist Ford Motor Co., Dearborn, Mich., 1970-86; prof. materials sci. and engring. U. Mich., Ann Arbor, 1986—, dir. Macromolecular Sci. and Engring. Ctr., 1995—. Contbr. articles to profl. jours. Postdoctoral fellow Washington U., St. Louis, 1959-60. Fellow Am. Phys. Soc.; mem. Am. Chem. Soc., Sigma Xi. Office: U Mich Dept Materials Sci Eng Ann Arbor MI 48109

ROBERTSON, RICHARD STUART, insurance holding company executive; b. Spokane, Wash., June 14, 1942; s. Stuart A. and Marjory (Moch) R.; m. Trudy Ann Prendergast, July 31, 1976; children: Thomas Stuart, Richard Andrew. B.S., Calif. Inst. Tech., 1963. Chief reinsurance actuary Lincoln Nat. Life Ins. Co., Ft. Wayne, Ind., 1963-74; sr. v.p., chief fin. officer Lincoln Nat. Corp., Ft. Wayne, 1974-86, exec. v.p., CFO,, 1986-92, exec. v.p., corp. risk officer, 1992—; bd. dirs. 1st Penn-Pacific, Linsco Reins. Co. Fellow Soc. Actuaries (pres. 1985-86); mem. Am. Acad. Actuaries (v.p. 1980-81), Actuarial Stds. Bd. (chmn. 1996). Episcopalian. Home: 12618 Aboite Center Rd Fort Wayne IN 46804-9725

ROBERTSON, ROBBIE, musician, popular; b. Toronto, 1943. Guitarist Ronnie Hawkins and The Hawks, 1959-63, The Hawks, 1963-65, The Band (with Bob Dylan), 1965-68; guitarist, songwriter The Band, 1968-76; solo performer, 1976—. Albums: (with The Band) Music from Big Pink, 1968, The Band, 1969, Stage Fright, 1970, Cahoots, 1971, Rock of Ages, 1972, Moondog Matinee, 1973, Northern Lights—Southern Cross, 1975, The Best of The Band, 1976, Islands, 1977, The Last Waltz, 1978, Anthology, 1978, (with Bob Dylan) Planet Waves, 1974, Before the Flood, 1974, The Basement Tapes, 1975, (solo) Robbie Robertson, 1987, Storyville, 1991; record prodr. for artists including: Neil Diamond, Jesse Winchester, Hirth Martinez; film composer: Raging Bull, 1980, The King of Comedy, 1983, The Color of Money, 1986; appearances in films: The Last Waltz, 1978, Carny, 1980. Group The Band inducted into Rock & Roll Hall of Fame, 1994. Office: Geffen Records 9130 W Sunset Blvd Los Angeles CA 90069-3110

ROBERTSON, ROBERT GORDON, retired Canadian government official; b. Davidson, Sask., Can., May 19, 1917; s. John Gordon and Lydia Adelia (Paulson) R.; m. Beatrice Muriel Lawson, Aug. 14, 1943; children: John Lawson, Karen Martha. B.A., U. Sask., 1938; B.A. Juris, Oxford U., 1940, D.C.L., 1983; M.A., U. Toronto, 1941; L.L.D., U. Sask., 1959, McGill U., 1963, U. Toronto, 1973, U. Dalhousie, 1977; Di de l'univ., U. Laval, 1975, Ottawa U., 1982, Carleton U., 1990. Mem. staff Dept. External Affairs, Govt. of Can., 1941-45; sec. to Office of Prime Minister, 1945-49; mem. staff Privy Council Office, 1949-53; dep. minister of No. Affairs and Nat. Resources; commr. Northwestern Territories, 1953-63; clk. Privy Council, sec. to cabinet, 1963-75, sec. to cabinet for fed.-provincial relations, 1975-79; chancellor Carleton U., 1980-90; ret., 1990; mem. Queen's Privy Coun. for Can., 1982. Decorated Companion of Order of Can. Fellow Royal Soc. Can. Mem. United Ch. of Can. Home: 20 Westward Way, Ottawa, ON Canada K1L 5A7

ROBERTSON, SAMUEL LUTHER, JR., special education educator, therapist; b. Houston, Apr. 28, 1940; s. Sam L. and Portia Louise (Burns) R.; children: Samuel Luther IV, Sean Lee (dec.), Ryan William, Susan Elizabeth (dec.), Henry Philmore. BS, McMurry U., 1969; MA, Hardin-Simmons U., 1973; PhD, U. Tex., 1993. Cert. tchr., adminstr., counselor, Tex.; lic. chem. dependency counselor, lic. clin. mental health counselor, alcoholism and drug counselor, Tex. Instr., coach, athletic dir. Tex. and La. schs., 1969-94; social worker, supr. Children's Protective Svcs., Abilene, Tex., 1978-79; instr., adminstr. Harlandale Sch. Dist., San Antonio, 1980-84, 87-90; adminstr. night sch. Harlandale Ind. Sch. Dist., San Antonio, 1988-89; instr. Edgewood Ind. Sch. Dist., San Antonio, 1985-87; developer, instr., integrated unit program San Antonio, 1990—; CEO The Educative Inst., San Antonio, 1992—; CEO Educative Therapeutic Processes, San Antonio, 1972—. Author: (play) The Challenged, 1965: (poem) Trains in the Night, 1969. State co-chmn. Youth for Kennedy-Johnson, Tex., 1960; mem. W. Tex. Dem. Steering Com., Abilene, 1962-63; founding dir. Way Off Broadway Community Theater, Eagle Pass, Tex., 1971-72; founding bd. dirs. Battered Women's Shelter, Abilene, 1978-79; v.p. bd. dirs. Mental Health Assn., San Antonio, 1980-83, bd. dirs Palmer Drug Abuse Program, San Antonio, 1985-87; pres., bd. dir. Alcoholic Rehab. Ctr., 1985-86, 1987-92; mem., vice chmn. Civilian and Mil. Addictive Programs, San Antonio, 1991-92; author, implementer Community Vitalization Program, 1994—. Named Tchr. of Yr. Southside Ind. Sch. Dist., San Antonio, 1970-71, Harlandale Alternative Ctr., San Antonio, 1987-88; Vol. of Yr., Mental Health Assn., San Antonio, 1982, Alcoholic Rehab. Ctr., San Antonio, 1992-93. Mem. ACA, NEA, Tex. State Tchrs. Assn., Am. Ednl. Rsch. Assn., Am. Assn. Sch. Adminstrs., Tex. Assn. Alcoholism and Drug Abuse Counselors, Nat. Alcoholism and Drug Abuse Counselors, N.Mex. Mental Health Counselors Assn., Phi Kappa Phi, Kappa Delta Pi. Methodist. Avocations: reading, writing, travel, theater, sports. Home: 14015 Big Tree San Antonio TX 78247 Office: Educative Therapeutic Processes 339 E Hildebrand Ave San Antonio TX 78212-2412 *I have participated in my life, my family's life, and my community's life in a responsible fashion through the Grace of God.*

ROBERTSON, STEWART, conductor; b. Glasgow, Scotland; m. Meryl Owen; children: Keren, Niel. Music dir. Glimmerglass Summer Opera Festival, 1988; past music dir., prin. condr. Santa Fe (N.Mex.) Symphony; music dir. Inland Empire Symphony Orchestra, San Bernardino, Calif.; guest condr. BBC Scottish Symphony, Ukraine State Philharmonic, Buenos Aires Philharmonic, Lille Festival, Fla. Philharmonic, Louisville Orchestra, Chgo. Lyric, N.Y.C. Opera, Cologne, Zurich, Scottish Opera, recordings Verdi-EMI. Office: 81 Poppy Rd Carmel Valley CA 93924

ROBERTSON, SUSAN JOYCE COE, counselor for emotionally disturbed, consultant; b. Pinedale, Wyo., May 22, 1954; d. Cecil James and Geraldine Ada (Greene) Coe; children: Jamie Michelle, Mark David. BS in Edn., Chadron (Nebr.) State Coll., 1976, MS in Counseling and Guidance, 1977; specialist in emotionally disturbed, U. No. Colo., 1982. Cert. crisis prevention intervention master trainer, peer mediation facilitator. Elem. tchr. pub. schs., Alliance, Nebr., 1976-77; social worker Community Action, Cheyenne, Wyo., 1978-79; Chpt. 1 tchr. Laramie County Sch. Dist. 1, Cheyenne, 1979-81, elem. tchr., 1981-84, tchr. severely emotionally disturbed, 1984-89, cons., specialist for severely emotionally disturbed, 1989-92, behavior intervention team specialist, 1992—; mem. Dist. Placement Com., 1981-92. Mem. Community Commn., Cheyenne, 1981-92; basketball coach YMCA, 1994. Mem. NEA, Am. Guidance and Counseling Assn., Coun. for Exceptional Children (faculty adviser 1991), Wyo. Edn. Assn., Cheyenne Tchr. Edn. Assn., Trailblazer Parent Assn., PEO. Presbyterian. Avocations: reading, swimming, racquetball, music. Home: 5425 Gateway Dr Cheyenne WY 82009-4035 Office: Laramie County Sch Dist 1 2810 House Ave Cheyenne WY 82001-2860

ROBERTSON, SUZANNE MARIE, primary education educator; b. Canton, Ohio, Nov. 21, 1944; d. Jules Michael and Emma Louise (Olmar) Franzen; m. William K. Robertson, June 30, 1973 (dec. 1979). BS in Early Childhood Edn., Kent State U., 1966; M in Early Childhood Edn., Southern Conn. U., 1976; postgrad., Fairfield U. and U. Bridgeport, 1981-82. Kindergarten tchr. Ridgefield (Conn.) Bd. Edn., 1966—, Internat. Sch. Basel, Switzerland, 1993-94; children's gymnastics instr. Ridgefield (Conn.) YMCA, 1982-83, Sherman Parks and Recreation, Conn., 1983-85; mem. com., facilitator Young Writer's Conf., Ridgefield, Conn., 1996. Toy designer; mem. nat. adv. bd. Learning Mag. Campaign vol. Cancer Fund of Am., Sherman, 1980-81. Awarded Honorable Mention Learning Mag., 1989; recipient Profl. Best Teaching awards. Mem. NEA, Tchrs. Assn. Supporting Children (chmn. 1986-89, Fairfield County pub. rels. com. 1986-89), Conn. Edn. Assn., Internat. Platform Assn., Sherman Hist. Soc., Phi Delta Kappa (historian 1989-90, rsch. rep. 1990-91). Avocations: collector children's books, water color painting, photography, winter skiing. Office: Farmingville Elem Sch 324 Farmingville Rd Ridgefield CT 06877-4241

ROBERTSON, SYLVIA DOUGLAS, middle school educator; b. Lynchburg, Va., June 25, 1952; d. Alfred Lynch and Rena (Irvin) Douglas; m. Lawrence Edward Robertson, Apr. 26, 1975 (div. May 1985); 1 child, Lawrence Edward Jr. BA, Cedar Crest Coll., 1974; MEd, Lynchburg Coll., 1990. Cert. tchr., Va. Tchr. 7th grade Big Island (Va.) Elem. Sch., 1974-89; tchr., team leader 7th grade Bedford (Va.) Mid. Sch., 1989—, tchr., grade level chairperson 7th grade, 1993-94. Facilitator Police, Pub. Educators and Peer Counselors Utilizing the Leadership of Students at Risk, Bedford, Va., 1991-92; vol. Free Clinic Ctrl. Va., Inc., Lynchburg, Va., 1993. Mem. Nat. Coun. Tchrs. Math., Nat. Sci. Tchrs. Assn., Nat. Energy Edn. Devel. Project, Bedford County Edn. Assn., Va. State Reading Assn., Va. Mid. Sch. Assn., Piedmont Area Reading Coun., Kappa Delta Pi, Phi Delta Kappa, Alpha Delta Kappa (corr. sec. 1993—), Alpha Kappa Alpha. Avocations: reading, drawing, walking. Home: Rte 7 Box 122 Arbor Ct Madison Heights VA 24572 Office: Bedford Mid Sch 503 Longwood Ave Bedford VA 24523-3401

ROBERTSON, TED ZANDERSON, judge; b. San Antonio, Sept. 28, 1921; s. Irion Randolf and Aurelia (Zanderson) R.; m. Margie Gardner. Student, Tex. A&I, 1940-42; LL.B., St. Mary's U., San Antonio, 1949. Bar: Tex. 1949. Chief civil dept. Dist. Atty.'s Office, Dallas County, Tex., 1960-65; judge Probate Ct. 2, Dallas County, 1965-69, Juvenile Ct. 2, Dallas County, 1969-75, 95th Dist. Ct., Dallas County, 1975-76, Ct. Civil Appeals, 5th Supreme Jud. Dist., Dallas, 1976-82, Supreme Ct. Tex., Austin, 1982; of counsel Frank Branson P.C., Dallas, 1989—; guest lectr. So. Meth. U., Dallas, Dallas County Juvenile Bd., Tex. Coll. of the Judiciary, 1970-82. Active Dallas Assn. for Retarded Children; active Dallas County Commn. on Alcoholism, Dallas County Mental Health Assn. Served as yeoman USCG, 1942-46. Recipient Golden Gavel St. Mary's U., San Antonio, 1979; named Outstanding Alumnus St. Mary's U., 1981. Mem. Am. Judicature Soc., Tex. Bar Assn., Dallas Bar Assn., Dallas County Juvenile Bd. Democrat. Methodist. Lodges: Masons; Lions. Home: 6233 Highgate Ln Dallas TX 75214-2157 Office: Frank Branson 4514 Cole Ave Ste 1800 Dallas TX 75205-5412

ROBERTSON, THOMAS L., health facility administrator; b. June 23, 1943. AA, Nat. Bus. Coll., 1965; postgrad., St. Louis U., 1971-74. CPA Anderson and Reed, Roanoke, Va.; with Carilion Health System, 1969—; pres., ceo Carilion Health System, Roanoke, VA, 1986—; also bd. dirs. Carilion Health System; chmn. bd. dirs. SunHealth Corp.; bd. dirs. Roanoke Electric Steel, Roanoke Gas Co., Shenandoah Life Ins. Co., 1st Union Corp. Va., Roanoke Valley Devel. Corp., Ctr. In The Sq. Chmn. Roanoke Valley Bus. Coun., Renew Roanoke; co-chmn. The New Century Coun.; bd. dirs. Va. Found. Ind. Colls., Roanoke Coll. Mem. Am. Hosp. Assn. (mem. ho. dels., mem. regional policy bd.), Va. Hosp. Assn. (bd. dirs., past chmn.), Roanoke Area Hosp. Coun. (past pres.), Hosp. Fin. Mgmt. Assn. (past pres. Va. chpt.), Roanoke Valley C. of C. (former pres.), Jaycees (past pres.), Roanoke Country Club (former pres.). Office: Carilion Health System PO Box 13727 Roanoke VA 24036-3727*

ROBERTSON, TIMOTHY B., cable television executive; b. 1955. With Christian Broadcasting Network, Inc., Virginia Beach, Va.; with Internat. Family Entertainment, Inc., Virginia Beach, 1989—, pres., CEO. Office: Internat Family Entertainment 2877 Guardian Ln Virginia Beach VA 23452

ROBERTSON, TIMOTHY JOEL, statistician, educator; b. Denver, Oct. 4, 1937; s. Flavel P. and Helen C. (Oliver) Girdner; m. Joan K. Slater, Aug. 18, 1959; children—Kelly, Jana, Doug, Mike. B.A. in Math., U. Mo., 1959, M.S. in Math., 1961, Ph.D. in Stats., 1966. Asst. prof. Cornell Coll., Mt. Vernon, Iowa, 1961-63; prof. stats. U. Iowa, Iowa City, 1965—; vis. prof. U. N.C., Chapel Hill, 1974-75, U. Calif.-Davis, 1983-84; Eugene Lukacs Disting. vis. prof. Bowling Green State U., 1991-92; vis. lectr. Com. Pres. Statis. Soc., 1971-74. Author: (with F.T. Wright and R.L. Dykstra) Order Restricted Statistical Inference; assoc. editor Am. Math. Monthly, 1977-81; mem. editl. bd. Comms. in Stats., 1981-92; assoc. editor Jour. Am. Statis. Assn., 1990-96; contbr. numerous articles to profl. jours. Recipient Collegiate Teaching award U. Iowa, 1990. Fellow Am. Statis. Assn. (council 1974-75), Inst. Math. Stats., Internat. Statis. Inst.; mem. Math. Assn. Am., Sigma Xi, Sierra Club. Democrat. Avocations: canoeing, camping, bicycling, walking. Home: 1811 Kathlin Dr Iowa City IA 52246-4617 Office: University of Iowa Dept Stats/Actuarial Sci Iowa City IA 52242

ROBERTSON, WILLIAM FRANKLIN, publishing executive; b. Richmond, Va., Sept. 1, 1917; s. Joseph William and Nancy Lucretia (Brooks) R.; m. Avis Dorothy Stillman, Aug. 7, 1943; children: Lynne Brooks, William Elden. BS, U. Richmond, 1938. Mgr. office Richmond Newspapers, Inc., 1941-46, credit mgr., contr., 1946-66, asst. treas., 1966-68, treas., asst. sec., 1968-87, cons., 1987-94; v.p., treas., asst. sec. Media Gen., Inc., 1977-87; cons. 1987-94. Trustee Va. Bapt. Homes; trustee, treas. Bapt. Mins. Relief Fund Va.; endowment fund trustee Richmond Bapt. Assn. Mem. Inst. Newspaper Contrs. and Fin. Officers (past dir.), Adminstrv. Mgmt. Soc. (pres. Richmond chpt. 1964-65), Fin. Execs. Inst., Phi Delta Theta. Avocation: private pilot. Home: 4 Ralston Rd Richmond VA 23229-8022 Office: 333 E Grace St Richmond VA 23293-1000

ROBERTSON, WILLIAM RICHARD, banker, holding company executive; b. Schenectady, N.Y., July 26, 1941; s. Bruce Manson and Mary Jo (Gillam) R.; m. Sarah Reed Parker, June 20, 1964; children: Deborah Graham, John William, Julie Elizabeth. AB, Colgate U., 1964; MBA, Case Western Res. U., 1967. Nat. City Bank/Nat. City Corp., 1964—; Exec. v.p., chief fin. officer Nat. City Corp., Cleve., 1982-89, dep. chmn. bd. dirs., 1986-95; pres., 1995—; bd. dirs. Nat. City Corp., Capitol Am. Fin. Corp., Kirtland Capital Corp. Trustee Coll. of Wooster, Ohio, 1982-91, Fairmount Presbyn. Ch., Cleve., 1983-86, St. Luke's Hosp., Cleve., 1984—, Cleve. Ballet, 1985-89, United Way, 1986-97, Karamu House, 1988—, Western Res. Hist. Soc., 1990—, Cleve. Mus. Art, 1991—, Salvation Army, 1985—, chmn. adv. bd., 1991-93; pres., trustee Big Bros. and Big Sisters, Cleve., 1973-80; chmn., bd. trustees United Way of Cleve., 1995—, trustee Musical Arts Assn., 1994—, chmn. vis. com. of Case Western Res. U. Weatherhead Sch. Mgmt., 1995—. Mem. Fin. Execs. Inst., Bankers Roundtable, Am. Bankers Assn., Cleve. Skating Club (pres. 1980-82), Union Club, Country Club, Pepper Pike Club, Ottawa Club, Desert Mountain Club. Republican. Avocations: travel, skiing, shooting, golf, history. Home: 2700 Chesterton Rd Shaker Hts OH 44122-1805 Office: Nat City Corp Nat City Ctr 1900 E 9th St Cleveland OH 44114-3401

ROBERTSON, WILLIAM WITHERS, lawyer; b. Morristown, N.J., Nov. 3, 1941; s. Thomas Withers and Jessie (Swain) R.; children: Barbara Ellen, William Withers, Jessie Swain. B.A., Rutgers U., 1964, LL.B., 1967. Bar: N.J. 1968. Law sec. to judge Superior Ct. N.J., 1967-68; asst. U.S. atty., 1972-76, 1st asst. U.S. atty., 1978-80; U.S. atty. Dist. N.J., 1980-81; chief Newark Organized Crime Strike Force, 1976-78; ptnr. firm Hannoch Weisman, Roseland, N.J., 1981—. Mng. editor Rutgers Law Rev., 1966-67. Trustee Rutgers U., 1984-88. Served to capt. JAGC USAR, 1968-72. Mem. Nat. Assn. Former U.S. Attys. (bd. dirs. 1990-93), Rutgers U. Law Sch. Alumni Assn. (pres. 1990-91), Rutgers U. Alumni Fedn. (pres. 1981-83). Office: Hannoch Weisman PO Box 1040 Newark NJ 07101-1040

ROBERTSON, WILLIAM WRIGHT, JR., orthopedic surgeon educator; b. Mayfield, Ky., Dec. 26, 1946; s. William Wright and Dorothy Frances (Beadles) R.; m. Karel Virginia Dierks, Jan. 26, 1974; children: Anna Elizabeth, Claire Alexandra. BA, Rhodes Coll., 1968; MD, Vanderbilt U., 1972. Intern U. Calif., San Diego, 1972-73, resident, 1975-76; resident Vanderbilt U., Nashville, 1976-79; asst. prof. orthopedics Tex. Tech U., Lubbock, 1979-86; assoc. prof. U. Pa., Phila., 1986-90; prof. orthopedic surgery George Washington U., Washington, 1990—; chair pediatric orthopedics Children's Nat. Med. Ctr., Washington, 1990—. Lt. USN, 1973-75. Fellow AMA, Am. Acad. Orthopedic Surgeons, Am. Acad. Cerebralpalsy Devel. Medicine, Am. Acad. Pediatrics, Am. Orthopedic Assn., Pediatric Orthopedic Soc. (bd. dirs. 1993—). Avocations: gardening, music. Office: Childrens Nat Med Ctr 111 Michigan Ave NW Washington DC 20010-2970

ROBERTSON-THORN, KAREN, middle school educator; b. Morgantown, W.Va., Nov. 18, 1954; d. Frederick Grey and Deloris Jean (Burnside) Robertson; m. Martin Albert Thorn, Apr. 15, 1978. BA in Psychology, W.Va. U., 1976, MA in Spl. Edn., 1981, postgrad., 1994. Learning disabilities tchr. Morgantown (W.Va.) H.S., 1981-86, Cheat Lake Jr. H.S., Morgantown, 1986-90; educator dual diagnosis unit Chestnut Ridge Psychiat. Hosp., Morgantown, 1990; reading educator Cheat Lake Jr. H.S., Suncrest Jr. H.S., Morgantown, 1990-92; learning disabilities tchr. Univ. H.S., Morgantown, 1992; reading educator South Jr. H.S., Morgantown, 1992—; mem. local sch. improvement coun. South Jr. H.S., Morgantown, 1994—, sch. based assistance team, 1994, v.p. faculty senate, 1994-95, curriculum com., 1994-95. Aerobics instr. Monongalia County Cmty. Schs., Cheat Lake Sch., 1989-92; mem. United We Stand Am., Morgantown, 1992—. Named Monongalia County Tchr. of Yr., Morgantown, 1985-86. Mem. W.Va. State Reading Coun., Internat. Reading Assn., Psi Chi, Alpha Delta Kappa (Julia Kovach Meml. scholar 1985), Phi Delta Kappa (Monongalia County Tchr. of Month 1995). Avocations: aerobics, basketball, showing Persian cats. Office: South Jr HS 500 E Parkway Dr Morgantown WV 26505-6839

ROBEY, KATHLEEN MORAN (MRS. RALPH WEST ROBEY), civic worker; b. Boston, Aug. 9, 1909; d. John Joseph and Katherine (Berrigan) Moran; B.A., Trinity Coll., Washington, 1933; m. Ralph West Robey, Jan. 28, 1941. Actress appearing in Pride and Prejudice, Broadway, 1935, Tomorrow is a Holiday, road co., 1935, Death Takes a Holiday, road co., 1936, Left Turn, Broadway, 1936, Come Home to Roost, Boston, 1936; pub. relations N.Y. Fashion Industry, N.Y.C., 1938-43. Mem. Florence Crittenton Home and Hosp., Women's Aux. Salvation Army, Gray Lady, ARC; mem. Seton Guild St. Ann's Infant Home. Mem. Christ Child Soc., Fedn. Republican Women of D.C. English-Speaking Union. Republican. Roman Catholic. Clubs: City Tavern, Cosmos (Washington), Nat. Woman's Republican. Home: 4000 Cathedral Ave NW Washington DC 20016-5249

ROBFOGEL, SUSAN SALITAN, lawyer; b. Rochester, N.Y., Apr. 4, 1943; d. Victor and Janet (Rosenthal) Salitan; m. Nathan Joshua Robfogel, July 12, 1965; children: Jacob Morris, Samuel Salitan. BA cum laude, Smith Coll., 1964; JD, Cornell U., 1967. Bar: N.Y.1967, U.S. Dist. Ct. (we. dist.) 1968, U.S. Ct. Appeals (2d cir.) 1971, U.S. Supreme Ct. 1971, U.S. Dist. Ct. (no. dist.) 1974, D.C. 1982. Asst. corp. counsel, then sr. asst. corp. counsel City of Rochester, N.Y., 1967-70; assoc. Harris, Beach & Wilcox, Rochester, 1970-75; ptnr. Harris, Beach, Wilcox, Rubin & Levey, Rochester, 1975-85; ptnr., chair health svcs. practice Nixon, Hargrave, Devans & Doyle, Rochester, 1985—; panel mem., Fed. Svc. Impasses Panel, Washington, 1983-94; mem., past chair Data Protection Rev. Bd., Albany, N.Y., 1984—. Mem. trustees vis. com. U. Rochester Med. Sch., 1990; mem. mgmt. adv. panel SUNY, 1990. Recipient Brockport Coll. Found. Community award, 1989. Fellow Am. Bar Found., N.Y. State Bar Found.; mem. ABA, N.Y. State Bar Assn., Washington D.C. Bar Assn., Monroe County Bar Assn. (Rodenbeck award 1988). Home: 1090 Park Ave Rochester NY 14610-1728 Office: Nixon Hargrave Devans & Doyle Clinton Sq PO Box 1051 Rochester NY 14603-1051 also: 437 Madison Ave New York NY 10022

ROBICHAUD, LOUIS JOSEPH, Canadian senator; b. St. Anthony, N.B., Oct. 21, 1925; s. Amedee and Annie (Richard) R.; m. Lorraine Savoie, Aug. 9, 1951; children: Jean Claude (dec.), Paul, Louis-Rene, Monique. B.A., Sacred Heart U., 1947, Dr. Polit. Sci., 1960; postgrad., Laval U., 1947-49; LL.D., U. N.B., 1960, St. Joseph's U., 1961, U. Montreal, 1961, U. Ottawa, 1962, St. Dunstan's U., 1964, U. St. Thomas, 1965, McGill U., 1967, Dalhousie U., 1969; D.C.L., Mt. Allison U., 1961, Moncton U., 1973. Bar: N.B. bar, Queen's counsel 1960. Practiced in Richibucto, N.B., 1952-60; mem. N.B. Legislature, 1952-71, financial critic, 1957-58, leader of opposition, 1958-60, 70-71, premier, 1960-70, atty. gen. N.B., 1960-65; minister of youth, 1968-70; mem. Privy Council, 1967—; chmn. Canadian sect. Internat. Joint Commn., 1971-73; summoned to Senate of Can., 1973—; leader Liberal Party of N.B., 1958-71. Past pres. Ottawa Valley chpt. Kidney Found. Can., bd. dirs. found. Decorated companion Order of Canada; recipient gold medal Laval U. Alumni Assn., 1963. Mem. N.B. Barristers Soc. Mem. Liberal Party. Roman Catholic. Home: 7 Pineland Ave, Nepean, ON Canada K2G 0E5 Office: Senate of Ont, 266 East Block, Ottawa, ON Canada K1A 0A4

ROBEY, SHERIE GAY SOUTHALL GORDON, secondary education educator, consultant; b. Washington, July 7, 1954; d. James Edward and Gene Elizabeth (Gray) Southall; children: m. Robert Jean Claude Robey; children: Michael Aaron Gordon, Robert Eugene Robey, Jamie Lea Robey. BS, U. Md., 1976; MA in Edn. and Human Devel., George Washington U., 1988. Tchr. Esperanza Mid. Sch., Hollywood, Md., 1980-84, Chopticon High Sch., Morganza, Md., 1984—; coach Odyssey of the Mind, 1985-95; sponsor Future Tchrs. Am., Morganza, 1990—, S.H.O.P/S.A.D.D., Morganza, 1990—; cons. Ednl. Cosn., Waldorf, 1980—; pres. BNA Swim Team, 1992—. Mem. Ednl. Rep. Assn. St. Mary's County, Lighthouse Hist. Soc. Methodist. Avocations: swimming, writing, visiting lighthouses, collection miniature lighthouses. Home and Office: 11181 Carroll Dr Waldorf MD 20601-2656

ROBILLARD, LUCIENNE, federal official; b. Montreal, Canada. BA, Coll. Bassile-Moreau, 1965; MA in Social Work, U. Montreal, 1967; Diploma in Adminstrn., École des hautes études commerciales, Montreal, 1983, MBA, 1986. Social worker, clin. practitioner Maisonneuve-Rosemont Hosp.; sr. adminstr. Centre de svcs. sociaux Richelieu; youth leader in a kibutz Israel, 1969-72; apptd. pub. curator City of Quebec, Canada, 1986-89; elected mem. Quebec Nat. Assembly for Chambly, 1989; apptd. min. cultural affairs, 1989-90, apptd. min. higher edn. and science, 1990-92, apptd. min. of edn., 1992-93, min. edn. and science, 1993-94, min. health and social svcs., 1994-95; elected mem. parliament Saint-Henri-Westmount, 1995—; min. citizenship and immigration, 1996—; mem. Corp. professionelle des travailleurs sociaux de Québec, 1967—; mem. editl. com. (book) Le travail social et la santé au Québec, 1984-86; pres. Commn. adminstrv. des svcs. de santé mentale of the Conseil régional de la Montérégie, 1983-86; cons. mental health dossier Rochon Commn., 1986. Office: 365 Laurier Ave W 21st Flr, Ottawa, ON Canada KIA ILI

ROBIN, CLARA NELL (CLAIRE ROBIN), English language educator; b. Harrisonburg, Va., Feb. 19, 1945; d. Robert Franklin and Marguerite Ausherman (Long) Wampler; m. Phil Camden Branner, June 10, 1967 (div. May 1984); m. John Charles Robin, Nov. 22, 1984 (div. Dec. 1990). BA in English, Mary Washington Coll., 1967; MA in English, James Madison U., 1974; postgrad., Jesus Coll., Cambridge, Eng., 1982, Princeton U., 1985-86; Auburn U., 1988, U. No. Tex., 1990-91. Cert. tchr. English, French, master cert., Tex. Tchr. 7th grade John C. Myers Intermediate Sch., Broadway, Va., 1967-68; tchr. 10th grade Waynesville (Mo.) H.S., 1968-70; tchr. 6th, 7th, 8th grades Mary Mount Jr. Sch., Santa Barbara, Calif., 1970-72; tchr. 9th grade Forest Meadow Jr. H.S. Richardson (Tex.) Ind. Sch. Dist., 1972-78, tchr. 10th grade Lake Highlands H.S., 1972-84; tchr. 11th, 12th grades Burleson (Tex.) H.S. Burleson Ind. Sch. Dist., 1986—; instr. composition Hill Coll., 1992-94. Contbg. author: (book revs.) English Journal, 1989-94, (lit. criticism) Eric, 1993. Vol. Dallas Theater Ctr., 1990—; mem. Kimbell Art Mus., Ft. Worth, 1990—, Modern Art Mus., Ft. Worth, 1992—, KERA Pub. TV, Dallas, 1990—. Fellow NEH, 1988, 89, 92, 95, Fulbright-Hays Summer Seminar, 1991; ind. study grantee Coun. Basic Edn., 1990; recipient Honorable Mention Tex. Outstanding Tchg. of the Humanities award, 1995. Mem. ASCD, NEA, Nat. Coun. Tchrs. English, Tex. State Tchrs. Assn., Epsilon Nu of Delta Kappa Gamma (1st v.p. 1988-94, v.p. 1992-94). Avocations: bicycling, traveling, reading, writing, theater. Home: 4009 W 6th St Fort Worth TX 76107-1619 Office: Burleson High Sch 517 SW Johnson Ave Burleson TX 76028-5312

ROBIN, RICHARD SHALE, philosophy educator; b. Stamford, Conn., Apr. 18, 1926; s. Edwin Joseph and Eva (Effron) R.; m. Joann Wilma Cohan, Jan. 29, 1961; children: David Seth, Deborah Elizabeth. B.A., Harvard U., 1948, Ph.D., 1958. Instr. philosophy U. Conn., Storrs, 1958-62; asst. prof. Mt. Holyoke Coll., South Hadley, Mass., 1962-66; assoc. prof. Mt. Holyoke Coll., 1966-71, prof., 1971—, chmn. dept., 1968-83; mem. grad. faculty U. Mass. at Amherst, 1963—. Co-editor, co-author: Studies in the Philosophy of Charles Sanders Peirce, 1963, From Time and Chance to Consciousness, 1994; editor: Annotated Catalogue of the Papers of Charles S. Peirce, 1967; editor trans.: Charles S. Peirce Soc., bd. advs.; Peirce edit. project; bd. cons. Arisbe Papers; mem. editorial bd. Jour. Speculative Philosophy; adv. bd. The Peirce Seminar Papers. Grantee Harvard, 1960-61, Henry P. Kendall Found., 1962, Mt. Holyoke Coll., 1969-70, 75-76; Danforth assoc., 1967—; John Dewey sr. research scholar, 1983-84; Fulbright sr. lectr. Tohoku U., 1984-85; lectr. Kyoto Am. Studies Seminar, 1984, Charles Warren Ctr., Harvard U., 1991. Mem. Charles S. Peirce Soc. (pres. 1965-67), Charles S. Peirce Found., Am. Philos. Assn., AAUP, Soc. Advancement Am. Philosophy (exec. circle). Home: 78 Woodbridge St South Hadley MA 01075-1129

ROBIN, THEODORE TYDINGS, JR., lawyer, engineer, consultant; b. New Orleans, Aug. 29, 1939; s. Theodore Tydings and Hazel (Corbin) R.; m. Helen Jones, June 8, 1963; children: Corbin, Curry, Ted, Phil. BME, Ga. Inst. Tech., 1961, MS in N.E., 1963, PhD, 1967; LLB, Blackstone Sch. Law, 1979. Bar: Calif 1980, U.S. Patent and Trademark Office 1982; registered profl. engr., Ala., Calif. Rsch. engr. Oak Ridge Nat. Lab., 1967; asst. prof. radiology and physics Emory U., 1968-69; project engr. Atomic Internat. div. N.Am. Rockwell, Canoga Park, Calif., 1970-72; engr. mgmt. engring. div. So. Co. Svcs., Birmingham, Ala., 1972-83, mgr. nuclear support and quality assurance, 1989-90, mgr. quality assurance and resources, 1991-92; mgr. Hatch Design Configuration, 1993-94; program mgr. pooled inventory mgmt. program So. Electric Internat., Birmingham, 1984-88; bd. dirs. polit. action com., 1985-87, patent atty. and cons., 1994—. Mem. ABA, ASME (mem. nuc. quality assurance subcom. on standards coordinating 1991-96), Am. Nuc. Soc. (chmn. Birmingham sect. 1987-88, nuclear power plant standards com. 1989-94). Presbyterian. Lodge: Rotary (pres. Shades Valley club 1987-88, chmn. dist. 6860 internat. youth exchange com. 1989-90, R.I. dist. gov. 6860, 1994-95). Research on power plant performance and reliability and effect of coal quality, space radiation effects on human cells, boiling heat transfer, nuclear reactor safety, multi-utility contracting, reliability economics, benchmarking and total quality management; patent law. Home and Office: 4524 Pine Mountain Rd Birmingham AL 35213-1828

ROBINER, DONALD MAXWELL, federal official, lawyer; b. Detroit, Feb. 4, 1935; s. Max and Lucia (Chassman) R.; divorced; children: Steven Ralph, Lawrence Alan. BA, U. Mich., 1957; postgrad., Wayne State U., 1957-58; JD, Case Western Res. U., 1961. Bar: Ohio 1961, U.S. Supreme Ct. 1964, U.S. Ct. Appeals (6th cir.) 1965; bd. cert. civil trial adv. emeritus Nat. Bd. Trial Advocacy. Assoc. Metzenbaum, Gaines, Schwartz, Krupansky & Stern, Cleve., 1961-67; ptnr. Metzenbaum, Gaines, Krupansky, Finley & Stern, Cleve., 1967-72; v.p. Metzenbaum, Gaines, Finley & Stern Co., L.P.A., Cleve., 1972-77, Gaines, Stern, Schwarzwald & Robiner Co., Cleve., 1977-81; exec. v.p., sec. Schwarzwald, Robiner & Rock, Cleve., 1981-90; prin. Buckingham, Doolittle & Burroughs, Cleve., 1991-94; U.S. trustee Ohio and Mich. region 9 U.S. Dept. of Justice, 1994—; v.p., sec. Richard L. Bowen & Assocs., Inc., Cleve., 1969-94; acting judge Shaker Heights Mcpl. Ct., 1973; mem. Bd. Bar Examiners, State of Ohio, Columbus, 1974-79; life mem. 6th Cir. Jud. Conf.; mediator alt. dispute resolution panel U.S. Dist. Ct. (no. dist.) Ohio, 1993—. Sec. Friends of Beachwood (Ohio) Libr., Inc., 1981-88, trustee, 1981—. Recipient Cert. of Appreciation Ohio Supreme Ct., 1974-79, Appreciation award Am. Soc. of Appraisers 1975. Mem. ABA (forum com. on the constrn. industry 1980-94), Cleve. Bar Assn., Cuyahoga County Bar Assn. (Cert. of Appreciation 1986-87), Ohio State Bar Assn. (coun. dels. 1987—, legis. screening com. 1987-89, 91, sch. law com. 1981-94, legal edn. com. 1987-92), Am. Arbitration Assn. (Svc. award 1975), Cuyahoga County Law Dirs. Assn., Ohio Coun. Sch. Bd. Attys. (exec. com. 1990-94), Jud. Conf. 8th Appellate Dist. Ohio (charter, life), KP. Home: 23512 E Silsby Rd Beachwood OH 44122-1266 Office: US Dept Justice Office of US Trustee BP America Bldg 200 Public Sq Ste 20-3300 Cleveland OH 44114-2301

ROBINETT, BETTY WALLACE, linguist; b. Detroit, June 23, 1919; d. Henry Guy and Beulah (Reid) Wallace; m. Ralph F. Robinett, Apr. 10, 1952 (dec. div. 1960); 1 child, Richard Wallace. BA, Wayne State U., 1940; MA, U. Mich., 1941, PhD, 1951. Instr., adminstrv. asst. English Lang. Inst., U. Mich., Ann Arbor, 1945-50; cons. Dept. Edn., San Juan, P.R., 1950-51, 52-57; lectr. English, U. Mich., 1951-52, 55-56; asso. prof. English InterAm. U., San German, P.R., 1957-59; asst. prof. English and linguistics Ball State U., Muncie, Ind., 1959-63; assoc. prof. English and linguistics English and linguistics Ball State U., 1963-67, prof., 1967-68; prof. dept. linguistics U. Minn., Mpls., 1968-88, dir. program in English as a second lang., 1968-80, acting asst. v.p. acad. affairs, 1979-80, asst. v.p. acad. affairs, 1980-84, assoc. v.p. acad. affairs, 1984-88, prof. emeritus, 1988; chmn. Univ. Senate Consultative Com., 1977-78; vis. prof. Pa. State U., 1994-95; chmn. adv. panel on English tchg. USIA, 1988-93. Author: (with C.H. Prator) Manual of American English Pronunciation, 1972, 4th edit., 1985, Teaching English to Speakers of Other Languages, Substance and Technique, 1978, (with J. Schachter) Second Language Learning: Contrastive Analysis, Error Analysis and Related Aspects, 1983; editor Tesol Quar., 1967-72. Internat. Programs travel grantee, 1972, 77; recipient Morse-Amoco award for Excellence in Teaching, 1977. Mem. Tchrs. English to Speakers of Other Langs. (pres. 1974, James Alatis Svc. award 1990), Assn. Tchrs. ESL (chmn. 1976-77), Am. Assn. Applied Linguistics (v.p., pres. 1980-82), Linguistic Soc. Am. Home: 1936 Park Forest Ave State College PA 16803-1329

ROBINETT, RUSH DALETH, III, research engineer; b. Albuquerque, July 14, 1960; s. Rush Daleth Jr. and Dorothy (Sohl) R.; m. Laurie Ellen Bowman, Dec. 28, 1993; 1 child Rush Daleth IV. Student, U. Notre Dame, 1978-80; BS magna cum laude, Tex. A&M U., 1982, PhD, 1987; MS, U. Tex., 1984. Teaching asst. U. Notre Dame, South Bend, Ind., 1979-80; rsch. asst. Tex. A&M U., College Station, 1981-82, U. Tex., Austin, 1983-84; rsch. assoc. Ctr. for Strategic Tech., College Station, 1984-87; rsch. engr., disting. mem. of tech. staff Sandia Nat. Lab., Albuquerque, 1988—; student intern NASA Hdqs. Washington, 1981; rsch. engr. Northrop Aircraft Divsn., Hawthorne, Calif., summer, 1983; adj. prof. U. N.Mex., Albuquerque, 1994—; cons. Corning, Elmira, N.Y., 1993—, Albuquerque Pub. Schs. Budget Rev. Bd., 1990; sci. advisor Albuquerque Pub. Schs., 1990-94, sci. instr., summer, 1988-90; presenter, cons. Explora, Albuquerque, 1992. Inventor: two axis hydraulic joint, sway suppressed crane control moving mass spacecraft attitude control system; contbr. articles to profl. jours. Mentor Valley Acad., Albuquerque, 1989-92. Mem. AIAA (sr., tech. com. 1991-93, student v.p. 1981-82, Best Presentation award 1992), N.Y. Acad. Scis., Am. Helicopter Soc., Phi Kappa Phi, Sigma Gamma Tau. Avocations: softball, volleyball, ice hockey, fishing, hunting. Home: PO Box 1661 Tijeras NM 87059-1661 Office: Sandia Nat Lab MS 1003 PO Box 5800 Albuquerque NM 87185

ROBINETTE, GARY E., lumber executive, wholesale distribution executive, retail executive; b. 1948. Grad., Xavier U., 1972. With Procter & Gamble, Cin., 1972-75, Avon Products, Cin., 1975-80, Mutual Mfg. & Supply, Cin., 1980-88; v.p. Carolina Builders Corp., Raleigh, N.C., 1988-93; pres. ERB Lumber Inc., Birmingham, Mich., 1993—. Office: ERB Lumber Inc 375 S Eton St Birmingham MI 48009-6569*

ROBINOWITZ, STUART, lawyer; b. Port Chester, N.Y., Apr. 6, 1929; s. Sam and Rose (Goldstein) R.; m. Anne, July 15, 1952; children: Cathy, Susan, Richard, Robert, Jane. B.A., Williams Coll.; LL.B., Yale U. Bar: N.Y. 1953. Ptnr. Rosenman, Colin, Kaye, Petschek & Freund, N.Y.C., 1961-70, Paul Weiss, Rifkind, Wharton & Garrison, N.Y.C., 1970—; vis. lectr. Yale U. Law Sch., 1981-83, 90-92, NYU Law Sch., 1996. Mem. ABA, N.Y. State Bar Assn., N.Y. County Lawyers Assn., Assn. of Bar of City of N.Y., Phi Beta Kappa. Office: Paul Weiss Rifkind Wharton & Garrison 1285 Avenue Of The Americas New York NY 10019-6028

ROBINS, H(ENRY) IAN, medical oncologist; b. N.Y.C., Feb. 17, 1945; s. Edwin and Matilda (Morgenstern) R. AB in Biology, Boston U., 1966, AM in Biochemistry, 1968, PhD in Molecular Biology, 1971, MD, 1976. Diplomate Am. Bd. Internal Medicine, Am. Bd. Med. Oncology, Am. Bd. Forensic Medicine, Am. Bd. Forensic Examiners. Intern in internal medicine Univ. Hosps., Madison, Wis., 1976-77, resident in internal medicine, 1977-79; fellow in clin. oncology Wis. Clin. Cancer Ctr., Madison, 1979-81, fellow in rsch. oncology, 1981-82; instr. dept. human oncology, dept. medicine Dept. Human Oncology, Dept. Medicine U. Wis. Sch. Medicine, Madison, 1982-83, asst. prof., 1983-86, assoc. prof., 1986—; chief sect. med. oncology, dir. U. Wis. Sch. Medicine, Madison, 1990-95, prof. dept. human oncology, medicine and neurology, 1992—. Contbr. numerous articles to profl. jours.; reviewer numerous sci. jours. including Biochem. Pharmacology, Internat. Jour. Radiation Biology, Jour. Clin. Oncology, New Eng. Jour. Medicine, others. Mem. N.Y. Acad. Scis., AAAS, ACP, Internat. Clin. Hyperthermia Soc., Radiation Rsch. Soc., N.am. Hyperthermia Group, Oncology Group, Am. Fedn. clin. Rsch., Ea. Coop. Oncology Group, European Soc. Hyperthermic Oncology, Vet. Cancer Soc., Transplantation Soc., Collaborative Ocular Melanoma Study Group, Am. Soc. Clin. Hypnosis, Minn. Soc. Clin. Hypnosis, Sigma Xi. Office: Clin Sci Ctr K4/662 600 Highland Ave Madison WI 53792-0001

ROBINS, JAMES DOW, counselor; b. Athens, Ga., Oct. 17, 1952; s. Gerald Burns and Fay Ann (Kennan) R.; m. Sharon Eileen Parker, Apr. 12, 1974 (div. 1976). BA in Psychology, SUNY, Albany, 1981; BA in Comm. cum laude, Tex. A&M U., 1981, MA in Secondary Edn., 1982; ABA, cert. legal asst., Southwestern Paralegal Inst., 1984; MS in Guidance and Counseling, Tex. A&M U., 1993. Bar: Tex., 1985; cert. counselor, psychologist, English and speech tchr., legal asst., Tex. Program dir. University City, Inc., Athens, 1971-73; sta. mgr. Bethany Broadcasting, Houston, 1973-76; program coord. for radio and TV, Tex. A&I U., Kingsville, 1977-82; dir. pub. rels. Kleberg Meml. Hosp., Kingsville, 1983-84; legal asst., cons. Kleberg, Dyer, Redford & Weil, Corpus Christi, Tex., 1984-86; tchr. English lit. Brownsville (Tex.) Ind. Sch. Dist., 1986-90; dir. testing and assessment, dir. suicide intervention Kingsville Ind. Sch. Dist., Kingsville, 1993—; counselor Kingsville Ind. Sch. Dist., 1993—; cons. Conner Mus., Kingsville, 1981-82. Author: The School Counselor: A Profession in Transition, 1993; contbr. articles to various publs. Recipient Disting. Svc. award for Excellence in Broadcasting, Tex. A&M, 1980-81. Mem. ACA (profl.), Tex. Counseling Assn., Mensa, The Blues Found. (internat. voting mem.), State Bar of Tex. (legal asst. div. 1985), Am. Counseling Assn., Tex. Counselors Assn., Tex. Sch. Counselors Assn., Tex. Assn. for Humanistic Edn. and Devel., Tex. Assn. for Multi-Cultural Counseling and Devel., Am. Assn. Assessment in Counseling, World Wildlife Fedn., Gulf Coast Counseling Assn., Gulf Coast Assn. for Counseling and Devel., The Blues Found., Phi Delta Kappa , Alpha Chi. Methodist. Avocations: writing, guitar, computers. Home: 515 University Blvd Kingsville TX 78363-4242 Office: 515 University Blvd Kingsville TX 78363

ROBINS, LEE NELKEN, medical educator; b. New Orleans, Aug. 29, 1922; d. Abe and Leona (Reiman) Nelken; m. Eli Robins, Feb. 22, 1946 (dec. Dec. 1994); children: Paul, James, Thomas, Nicholas. Student, Newcomb Coll., 1938-40; BA, Radcliffe Coll., 1942, MA, 1943; PhD, Harvard U., 1951. Mem. faculty Washington U., St. Louis, 1954—, prof. sociology in psychiatry, 1968-91, prof. sociology, 1969-91, univ. prof. social sci., prof. social sci. in psychiatry, 1991—; past mem. Nat. Adv. Coun. on Drug Abuse; past mem. task panels Pres.'s Commn. on Mental Health; mem. expert adv. panel on mental health WHO; Salmon lectr. N.Y. Acad. Medicine, 1983. Author: Deviant Children Grown Up, 1966; editor 11 books; N.Am. Assoc. editor Internat. Jour. Methods in Psychiat. Rsch.; mem. editl. bd. Psychol. Medicine, Jour. Child Psychology and Psychiatry, Devel. and Psychopathology, Jour. Studies on Alcohol, Epidemiol. e Psychiat. Sociale, Criminal Behavior and Mental Health; contbr. articles to profl. jours. Recipient Rsch. Scientist award USPHS, 1970-90, Pacesetter Rsch. award Nat. Inst. Drug Abuse, 1978, Radcliffe Coll. Grad. Soc. medal, 1979, Sutherland award Soc. Criminology, 1991, Nathan B. Eddy award Com. on Problems of Drug Dependence, 1993; rsch. grantee NIMH, Nat. Inst. on Drug Abuse, Nat. Inst. on Alcohol Abuse and Alcoholism. Fellow Am. Coll. Epidemiology, Royal Coll. Psychiatrists (hon.); mem. APHA (Rema Lapouse award 1979, Lifetime Achievement award sect. on alcohol and drug abuse 1994), World Psychiat. Assn. (sect. com. on epidemiology and cmty. psychiatry, treas.), Soc. Life History Rsch. in Psychopathology, Am. Coll. Neuropsychopharmacology, Am. Sociol. Assn., Internat. Sociol. Assn., Inst. Medicine, Internat. Epidemiol. Assn., Am. Psychopath. Assn. (pres. 1987-88, Paul Hoch award 1978). Office: Washington U Dept Psychiatry Med Sch Saint Louis MO 63110

ROBINS, MARJORIE KAPLAN, newspaper editor. Entertainment editor Saturday edit., travel editor Sunday edit. Newsday, Melville, N.Y. Office: Newsday Inc 235 Pinelawn Rd Melville NY 11747-4226

ROBINS, NORMAN ALAN, strategic planning consultant, former steel company executive; b. Chgo., Nov. 19, 1934; s. Irving and Sylvia (Robbin) Robins; m. Sandra Ross, June 10, 1956; children: Lawrence Richard, Sherry Lynn. BS in Chem. Engring., MIT, 1955, MS in Chem. Engring., 1956; PhD in Math., Ill. Inst. Tech., 1972. Asst. mgr. process systems and controls Inland Steel Co., East Chicago, Ind., 1962-67, assoc. mgr. process systems and controls, 1967-72, dir. process research, 1972-77, v.p. research, 1977-84, v.p. technol. assessment, 1984-86, v.p. strategic planning, 1986-91, ret., 1991; ind. cons. in strategic planning, 1991—. Mem. bd. edn. Homewood-Flossmoor High Sch., Ill., 1974-77. Mem. AIME (Nat. Open Hearth Conf. award 1972), AIChE, Midwest Soc. Profl. Cons., Strategic Leadership Forum.

ROBINS, RICHARD DENNIS, health science facility administrator; b. Cleve., Oct. 29, 1950; s. Syd and Lucyle Angelina (Palladino) R.; m. Marlene Eva Feit, June 23, 1970 (div. Feb. 1981); 1 child, Lauren Joann; m. Vickie Glyn Mothershed, Aug. 30, 1981. BSBA in Bus. and Acctg., U. Fla., 1973; M in Health Adminstrn., U. Colo., 1994. V.p. Winston Park Homeowners Assn., Miami, Fla., 1976-78, pres., 1978-80; pres. Promed Users Group, Birmingham, 1985-88; pres., CEO Med. Bus. Mgmt. Svcs. Group, Inc., Covington, La., 1992—. Mem. Am. Coun. Drug Edn., Nat. Assn. Accts., Assn. Mental Health Adminstrs. (v.p., pres. elect. ala. chpt. 1991—), Med. Group Mgmt. Assn., Employee Assistance Profl. Assn., Assembly for Mental Health Practice Adminstrs. (nat. pres., 1994—), Healthcare Fin. Mgrs. Assn., Birmingham C. of C., Jacksonville C. of C., Kiwanis Club Mandarin, Birmingham Jaycees. Democrat.

ROBINS, ROBERT SIDWAR, political science educator, administrator; b. Spangler, Pa., Apr. 20, 1938; s. Sydney and Katherine (Sidwar) R.; m. Marjorie McGann, Nov. 25, 1959; children: Anthony P., Nicholas A. BA, U. Pitts., 1959; MA, Duke U., 1961, PhD, 1963. Prof. polit. sci. Tulane U., New Orleans, 1965—, chmn. dept. polit. sci., 1979-90, dep. provost, 1991—; acad. visitor Inst. Commonwealth Studies, U. London, 1969-70, 78-79, mem. 1987-88; sr. assoc. mem. St. Antony's Coll., Oxford, Eng., 1972-73; vis. scholar Hastings Ctr., 1982; vis. scientist Tavistock Clinic, London, 1987-88. Author: Political Institutionalization and the Integration of Elites, 1976 (Carnegie Commn. report) Legislative Attitudes Toward Higher Education in Louisiana, 1968, Psychopathology and Political Leadership, 1977, Disease and Political Leadership, 1990; co-author: When Illness Strikes the Leader; contbr. articles to profl. publs. Vice chmn. Elections Integrity Commn., State of La., 1981-82. Recipient Excellence in Teaching award Tulane U., 1978; Fulbright scholar, 1961-62. Mem. Am. Polit. Sci. Assn., Internat. Soc. Polit. Psychology, New Orleans Fgn. Relations Assn. (bd. dirs.). Avocations: carpentry; gardening. Home: 727 Pine St New Orleans LA 70118-5118 Office: Tulane U Gibson Hall Office of The Provost New Orleans LA 70118

ROBINS, WILLIAM LEWIS, medical physicist; b. N.Y.C., July 2, 1953; s. Bertram Julius and Charlotte (Cohen) R.; m. Peggy Benison, Mar. 8, 1981; 1 child, Ilana Brooke. BS, Manhattan Coll., 1984; MS, Rutgers U., 1990. Cert. Am. Bd. Radiology, Therapeutic Radiol. Physics. Med. dosimetrist Mt. Sinai Med. Ctr., N.Y.C., 1982-88; med. physicist, cons. G. Zacharopoulos Inc., N.Y.C., 1988-93; med. physicist Meml. Regional Cancer Ctr., Hollywood, Fla., 1993—. Mem. Am. Assn. Physicists in Medicine, Am. Assn. Med. Dosimetrists, Am. Soc. Therapeutic Radiology and Oncology, Am. Coll. Radiology. Home: 500 Cambridge Dr Fort Lauderdale FL 33326-3561 Office: Meml Regional Cancer Ctr 3501 Johnson St Hollywood FL 33021-5421

ROBINSON, ADELBERT CARL, lawyer, judge; b. Shawnee, Okla., Dec. 13, 1926; s. William H. and Mayme (Forston) R.; m. Paula Kay Settles, Apr. 16, 1988; children from previous marriage: William, James, Schuyler, Donald, David, Nancy, Lauri. Student Okla. Baptist U., 1944-47; JD, Okla. U., 1950. Bar: Okla. 1950. Pvt. practice, Muskogee, Okla., 1956—; with legal dept. Phillips Petroleum Co., 1950-51; adjuster U.S. Fidelity & Guaranty Co., 1951-54, atty., adjuster-in-charge, 1954-56; ptnr. Fite & Robinson, 1956-62, Fite, Robinson & Summers, 1963-70, Robinson & Summers, 1970-72, Robinson, Summers & Locke, 1972-76, Robinson, Locke & Gage, 1976-80, Robinson, Locke, Gage & Fite, 1980-83, Robinson, Locke, Gage, Fite & Williams, Muskogee, 1983-95, Robinson, Gage, Fite & Williams, 1995—; police judge, 1964-68; mcpl. judge, 1964-70; prin. justice Temp. Div. 36 Okla. Ct. Appeals, 1981—; pres., dir. Wall St. Bldg Corp., 1969-78, Three Forks Devel. Corp., 1968-77, Rolo Leasing, Inc., 1971—, Suroya II, Inc., 1977—; sec. Muskogee Tom's Inc., Blue Ridge Corp., Harborcliff Corp.; bd. dirs. First Bancshares of Muskogee, Inc., First of Muskogee Corp., First City Bank, Tulsa; adv. dir. First Nat. Bank & Trust Co. of Muskogee; mng. ptnr. RLG Ritz, 1980—; ptnr. First City Real Estate Partnership, 1985-94. Del. to U.S./China Joint Session on Trade, Investment and Econ. Law, Beijing, 1987; chmn. Muskogee County (Okla.) Law Day, 1963; chmn. Muskogee Area Redevel. Authority, 1963; chmn. Muskogee County chpt. Am. Cancer Soc., 1956; pres. bd. dirs. Muskogee Cmty. Coun.; bd. dirs. United Way of Muskogee, Inc., 1980-88, v.p., 1982, pres. 1983; bd. dirs. Muskogee Cmty. Concert Assn., Muskogee Tourist Info. Bur., 1964-68; bd. dirs., gen. counsel United Cerebral Palsy Eastern Okla., 1964-68; trustee Connors Devel. Found., Connors Coll., 1981—, chmn., 1987-89; active Muskogee Housing Authority, 1992-95. With if. AUS, 1945-46. Mem. ABA, Okla. Bar Assn. (chmn. uniform laws com. 1970-72, chmn. profl. coop. com. 1965-69, past regional chmn. grievance com.), Muskogee County Bar Assn. (pres. 1971, mem. exec. coun. 1971-74), Okla. Assn. Def. Counsel (dir.), Okla. Assn. Mcpl. Judges (dir.), Muskogee C. of C., Delta Theta Phi. Methodist. Club: Rotary (pres. 1971-72). Home: 2408 St Andrews Ct Muskogee OK 74403-1657 Office: 530 Court St # 87 Muskogee OK 74401-6033

ROBINSON, ALEXANDER JACOB, clinical psychologist; b. St. John, Kans., Nov. 7, 1920; s. Oscar Frank and Lydia May (Beitler) R.; m. Elsie Louise Riggs, July 29, 1942; children: Madelyn K., Alicia A., David J., Charles A., Paul S., Marietta J., Stephen N. BA in Psychology, Ft. Hays (Kans.) State U., 1942, MS in Clin. Psychology, 1942; postgrad., U. Ill., 1942-44. Cert. psychologist, sch. psychologist. Chief psychologist Larned (Kans.) State Hosp., 1948-53, with employee selection, outpatient services, 1953-55; sch. psychologist County Schs., Modesto, Calif., 1955-61, Pratt (Kans.) Jr. Coll., 1961-66; fed. grantee, writer assoc. dir. Exemplary Federally Funded Program for Spl. Edn., Pratt, 1966-70; dir. spl. edn., researcher Stafford County Schs., St. John, 1970-81, ret., 1981; supr. testing and data Incidence of Exceptional Children in Kansas, Kans. State U., Ft. Hays, 1946; writer, asst. dir. Best Exemplary Federally Funded Program on Spl. Edn., Pratt, 1966-70; fed. grantee, researcher, writer, study dir. Edn. for the High-Performance Child, St. John, 1970—, Psychogenesis of the Sociopathic Personality, a longitudinal study. Minister, The Ch. of Jesus Christ. Served to 2d lt. U.S. Army, 1944-46, PTO. Mem. N.Y. Acad. Scis. Lodge: Lions (program chmn. St. John 1974-76). Avocations: history, ethnology, cultural anthropology, music, literature. Home and Office: RR 1 Box 121A Saint John KS 67576-9801

ROBINSON, ARTHUR HOWARD, geography educator; b. Montreal, Que., Can., Jan. 5, 1915; s. James Howard and Elizabeth (Peavey) R.; m. Mary Elizabeth Coffin, Dec. 23, 1938 (dec. Jan. 1992); children: Stephen Michael, Patricia Anne; m. Martha Elizabeth Rodabaugh Phillips, Feb. 6, 1993. BA, Miami U., Oxford, Ohio, 1936, LittD, 1966; MA, U. Wis., 1938; PhD in Geography, Ohio State U., 1947, DSc (hon.), 1984. Sec. to mem. Ohio Bd. Liquor Control, 1936; asst. geography U. Wis., 1936-38, Ohio State U., 1938-41; chief map div. OSS, 1941-46; mem. faculty U. Wis., 1945—, prof. geography, 1951-80, prof. emeritus, 1980—, chmn. dept., 1954-58, 66-68, Lawrence Martin prof. cartography, 1967—; dir. Univ. Cartographic Lab., 1966-73; hon. cons. cartography Library of Congress, 1974-80; Chief map officer U.S. Delegation Quebec and Cairo confs., World War II; pres. Internat. Cartographic Assn., 1972-76. Author: Look of Maps, 1952, Early Thematic Mapping in the History of Cartography, 1982; co-author: Elements of Geography, 4th edit., 1957, Elements of Cartography, 6th edit., 1995, Fundamentals of Physical Geography, 3rd edit., 1977, The Nature of Maps, 1976; co-editor: Cartographical Innovations, 1987; editor Am. Cartographer, 1974-76; also articles; designer Robinson map projection, 1963. Served to maj. AUS, 1944-45. Decorated Legion of Merit; recipient Carl Mannerfelt medal Internat. Cartographic Assn., 1981, Helen Culver Gold Medal Geog. Soc. Chgo., 1983, John Oliver LaGorce medal Nat. Geog. Soc., 1988, Silver medal Brit. Cartographic Soc., 1991; Guggenheim rsch. fellow, 1964, 78. Mem. Assn. Am. Geographers (council 1960-65, pres. 1963), Am. Congress Surveying and Mapping (hon.; chmn. cartography div. 1971). Home: 7438 Cedar Creek Trl Madison WI 53717-1504

ROBINSON, AUBREY EUGENE, JR., federal judge; b. Madison, N.J., Mar. 30, 1922; s. Aubrey Eugene and Mabel (Jackson) R.; m. Sara E. Payne, Dec. 31, 1946 (dec.); children: Paula Elaine Robinson Collins, Sheryl Louise; m. Doris A. Washington, Mar. 17, 1973. B.A., Cornell U., 1943, LL.B., 1947. Bar: N.Y. and D.C. 1948. Practice with law firms Washington, 1948-65; assoc. judge Juvenile Ct. D.C., 1965-66; assoc. judge U.S. Dist. Ct. D.C., 1966—, chief judge, 1982-92; gen. counsel Am. Council Human Rights, 1953-55, dir., 1955; mem. D.C. Commrs.'s Com. Child Placement Regulations, 1954-62; adj. prof. Am. U., 1975-84. Mem. D.C. Pub. Welfare Adv. Council, 1963-65; mem. Washington Urban League Adoption Project, 1959; mem. membership steering com. Health and Welfare Council D.C., 1961-66, Jud. Council of USA, 1982-92; mem. budget steering com. Health and Welfare Council Nat. Capital Area, 1963-66; mem. exec. com. Interreligious Com. Race Relations, 1966-67; exec. com., bd. dirs. D.C. Citizens for Better Pub. Edn., 1964-66; trustee United Planning Orgn. D.C., 1963-66, Washington Ctr. Met. Studies, 1967-74, Cornell U., 1982—; bd. dirs. Family and Child Services Washington, 1954-63, v.p., 1958-61; bd. dirs. Family Service Assn. Am., 1958-68, Washington Action for Youth, 1962-64, Barney Neighborhood Settlement House, 1962-64, Eugene and Agnes E. Meyer Found., 1969-85, Consortium Univs. Washington Met. Area, 1969-74, Fed. Jud. Ctr., 1978-82; mem. adv. council Cornell Law Sch., 1974-80. Served with AUS, 1943-46. Mem. ABA (mem. cts. and community 1972—, mem. adv. com. judges function 1970-72), Nat. Conf. Fed. Trial Judges (chmn. 1973). Office: US Dist Ct US Courthouse 3rd & Constitution Ave NW Washington DC 20001

ROBINSON, BARBARA PAUL, lawyer; b. Oct. 19, 1941; d. Leo and Pauline G. Paul; m. Charles Raskob Robinson, June 11, 1965; children: Charles Paul, Torrance Webster. AB magna cum laude, Bryn Mawr Coll., 1962; LLB, Yale U., 1965. Bar: N.Y. 1966, U.S. Dist. Ct. (so. and ea. dists.) N.Y. 1975, U.S. Tax Ct. 1972, U.S. Ct. Appeals (2d cir.) 1974. Assoc. Debevoise & Plimpton (formerly Debevoise, Plimpton, Lyons & Gates), N.Y.C., 1966-75, ptnr., 1976—; mem. adv. bd., lectr. Practicing Law Inst.; arbitrator Am. Arbitration Assn., 1987—, bd. dirs. Contbr. articles to profl. jours. Mem. adv. coun., bd. visitors CUNY Law Sch., Queens, 1984-90; trustee Trinity Sch., 1982-86, pres., 1986-88; bd. dirs. Found. for Child Devel., 1989—, chmn., 1991—; mem. Coun. on Fgn. Rels.; bd. dirs. Catalyst, 1993—, Am. Judicature Soc., Fund Modern Cts., 1990—, Wave Hill, 1994—, Garden Conservancy, 1996—; trustee The William Nelson Cromwell Found., 1993—. Fellow Am. Coll. Trust and Estate Counsel, Am. Bar Found., N.Y. Bar Found.; mem. ABA, N.Y. State Bar Assn. (vice chmn. com. on trust adminstrn., trusts and estates law sect. 1977-81, ho. of dels. 1984-87, 90-92, mem. com. ann. award 1993-94), Assn. of Bar of City of N.Y. (chmn. com. on trusts, estates and surrogates cts. 1981-84, judiciary com. 1981-84, coun. on jud. adminstrn. 1982-84, chair nominating com. 1984-85, mem. exec. com. 1986-91, chair 1989-90, v.p. 1990-91, pres. 1994-96, chair com. on honors 1993-94, mem. com on long-range planning 1991-94), Assn. of Bar of City of N.Y. Fund Inc. (bd. dirs., pres.), Women's Forum, Yale Coun., Yale Law Sch. Assn. N.Y. (mem. devel. bd., exec. com. 1981-85, pres. 1988-93), Yale Club, Washington Club. Office: Debevoise & Plimpton 875 3rd Ave New York NY 10022-6225

ROBINSON, BARRY R., lawyer; b. Dover, Ohio, Dec. 8, 1946. AB, Princeton U., 1969; JD cum laude, Ohio State U., 1972. Bar: Ohio 1972. Ptnr. Baker & Hostetler, Columbus, Ohio. Fellow Am. Coll. Trust and Estate Counsel; mem. ABA, Ohio State Bar Assn., Columbus Bar Assn. Office: Baker & Hostetler Capital Sq 65 E State St Ste 2100 Columbus OH 43215-4213

ROBINSON, BERNARD LEO, retired lawyer; b. Kalamazoo, Feb. 13, 1924; s. Louis Harvey and Sue Mary (Starr) R.; m. Betsy Nadell, May 30, 1947; children: Robert Bruce, Patricia Anne, Jean Carol. BS, U. Ill., 1947, MS, 1958, postgrad. in structural dynamics, 1959; JD, U. N.Mex., 1973. Rsch. engr. Assn. Am. Railroads, 1947-49; instr. architecture Rensselaer Poly. Inst., 1949-51; commd. 2d lt. Corps Engrs., U.S. Army, 1945, advanced through grades to lt. col., 1965, ret., 1968; engr. Nuclear Def. Rsch. Corp., Albuquerque, 1968-71; admitted to N.Mex. bar, 1973, U.S. Supreme Ct. bar, 1976; practiced in Albuquerque, 1973-85, Silver City, N.Mex., 1985-89, Green Valley, Ariz., 1989-90, Sierra Vista, Ariz., 1990-91; pres. Robinson Fin. Svcs., 1993-95. Dist. commr. Boy Scouts Am., 1960-62; vice chmn. Rep. Dist. Com., 1968-70. Decorated Air medal, Combat Infantry badge. Mem. ASCE, ABA, Ret. Officers Assn., DAV, Assn. U.S. Army, VFW. Home: 1037 W Eagle Look Ln Tucson AZ 85737-6986

ROBINSON, BINA AITCHISON, publisher, newsletter editor; b. Schenectady, N.Y., Aug. 31, 1923; d. Thomas Cant and Winifred Maud (Binless) Aitchison; m. David Dunlop Robinson, May 14, 1944; children: Challice Binless, Jean Aitchison, Andrew McLeod, Janet Davison. BA with honors, U. Rochester, 1944. Tchr. Phila. Pub. Schs., 1944-45, Brockport (N.Y.) Cen. Sch., 1946-47, Harley Sch., Rochester, N.Y., 1947-52; engring. asst. GE, Pittsfield, Mass., 1945-46; entrepreneur, developer, mgr. Swain (N.Y.) Ski Ctr., 1947-77; founder, coord., editor, prin. writer Coalition to Protect Animals in Parks & Refuges, Swain, 1985—; editor, prin. writer The Civil Abolitionist, 1985—; Am. cons. Drs. and Lawyers for Responsible Medicine; vis. lectr. schs. and colls. Contbr. articles to publs. Past pres. Allegany County Soc. Prevention Cruelty Animals, Wellsville, N.Y., 1978—. Mem. Am. Anti-Vivisection Soc., Nat. Resources Def. Coun., Internat. Primate Protection League, Nat. Alliance for Animals, N.Y. State Coalition for Animals, Action on Smoking and Health, Union Concerned Scientists, Civis/Civitas (exec. dir. 1983-91). Avocations: skiing, mountain hiking, swimming, canoeing, gardening. Home and Office: 1 Main St Swain NY 14884-0026

ROBINSON, BOB LEO, international investment services executive; b. Franklin, Tenn., Sept. 9, 1933; s. W.A. and Cornelia Irene (Lampley) R.; m. Carolyn Overton, Dec. 18, 1955; children: Richard Glenn, Leigh Ann, Elizabeth Lynne. BS in Indsl. Mgmt, Tenn. Tech. U., 1955. Cert. property mgr. Quality control engr. Gates Rubber Co., Nashville, 1960; tech. rep.

Home Ins. Co., 1961-65; civilian staff adminstrv. asst. Dept. Army, Nashville, 1965; exec. asst. to pres. Sullivan's Dept. Stores, Nashville, 1966-69; dir. engring. and devel. Venture Out in Am., Knoxville, Tenn., 1969; v.p., then exec. v.p. Hosp. Corp. Am., Nashville, 1970-79; pres., chief exec. officer Real Estate Group Inc., Nashville, 1974—, Fidelity Title Co., Nashville, 1974-83; pres. Internat. Bus. and Investment Services, Orlando, 1978—; gen. partner Union Sq. Ltd., Jacksonville, Fla., 1973-79; dir. Am. Travel Service, World Health Cons.; chmn. bd. emeritus Arnold Palmer Devel. Co., Orlando, Fla., 1988—; past vice chmn. bd. dirs., chief exec. officer Clin. Diagnostic Systems, Inc., Orlando, 1988-89; past vice chmn. Space Rail Corp., Orlando, 1991; speaker in field. Mem. Mayor Nashville Blue Ribbon Com., 1975-77; commr. City of Brentwood, Tenn., 1969-71, vice mayor, 1969-71, mayor, 1971, mem. planning commn., 1970-71; bd. dirs. Goodwill Industries Ctrl. Fla., exec. com., chmn. ops. com.; chmn. bldg. fund St. Cecilia Acad., Nashville, 1978; vice chmn. Audubon council Boy Scouts Am., 1968; founder Tenn. Tech. ROTC Gen.'s Cup Scholarship Found., 1986; aide U.S. Com. for Normandy Meml. Mus., Caen, France, 1987—; parachutist Israeli Def. Forces, 1989, Royal Thai Spl. Warfare Command, 1990; campaign dir. Drage for County Chmn., Orange County, Fla., 1990. Served as officer, master army aviator, parachutist, U.S. Army, 1955-60, USAR, 1960-83; maj. gen. (brevet) USAR, 1990. Decorated Army Commendation medal, Meritorious Service medal; recipient numerous public service awards; named to Tenn. Tech. ROTC Hall of Fame, 1988. Mem. Internat. Inst. Hosp. Cons., Inst. Real Estate Mgmt., Army Aviation Assn. Am., Res. Officers Assn., Internat. Assn. Airborne Vets., 82d Airborne Divsn. Assn. Republican. Baptist (past v.p. bd. trustees). Clubs: Arnold Palmer's Bay Hill (Orlando); Shriners.

ROBINSON, BRUCE BUTLER, physicist; b. Chester, Pa., Oct. 13, 1933; s. George Senior and Dorothy Conerly (Butler) R.; m. Dorothy Ross, June 4, 1960; children: Douglas Ross, Christopher Scott. BS in Physics, Drexel U., 1956; PhD in Physics, Princeton U., 1961; MBA, Rider U., 1977. Rsch. assoc. U. Calif., San Diego, 1961-63; rsch. scientist RCA David Sarnoff Lab., RCA, Princeton, N.J., 1963-73; exec. dir., mem. commerce tech. adv. bd. U.S. Dept. Commerce, Washington, 1973-75; dir. policy integration, dir. coal and synfuels policy U.S. Dept. Energy, Washington, 1975-81; sr. science advisor to v.p. rsch. Exxon Rsch. and Engring. Co., Linden, N.J., 1981-84; dep. dir. Office Naval Rsch., Arlington, 1984-87, dir. rsch., 1987-94, dep. dir. sci. and tech., 1994—; prin. author nat. energy policy plan U.S. Dept. Energy, 1981; U.S. rep. to internat. energy agy., govt. expert group on tech., Paris, 1979-81; mem. internat. team to rev. R&D programs Dutch Ministry Econs. and Fin., The Hague, The Netherlands, 1979; presenter sci. lectures. Contbr. articles to sci. jours. NSF fellow Princeton U., 1956-58, NSF internat. summer fellow, Varenna, Italy, 1962; recipient Meritorious Presdl. Rank award Pres. of U.S., 1989. Mem. IEEE, Am. Phys. Soc., The Oceanography Soc. (founding).

ROBINSON, CHARLES DAVID, financial services executive; b. Warren, Ohio, Sept. 26, 1944; s. Lee Elmo and Dora Mae (Wheeler) R.; m. Sharon Lynn Pemberton, Apr. 8, 1966 (div. July 1979); 1 child, Heather Lynn; m. Sharon Ann Dillon, June 20, 1980. Student, Ventura (Calif.) Jr. Coll., 1962, Harvard U., 1964; BA, Am. U., 1966; MA, Ohio State U., 1979. CFP. Mershon fellow Ohio State U., Columbus, 1966-72; dir. tng. NATPAC-SOUTH Inc., Washington, 1973-74; field underwriter N.Y. Life, Bailey's Cross-Roads, Va., 1974-75; dir. debate W.T. Woodson High Sch., Fairfax, Va., 1975-80; exec. account rep. VALIC, Fairfax, 1980-89, unit mgr., 1981-86; dist. mgr. VALIC, Phoenix, 1990-91, regional mgr., 1991-95; regional v.p. VAMCO, Phoenix, 1991-95; v.p. nat. markets VALIC, Houston, 1995—. Editor, author: (booklet) Mutual Fund Sales Kit, 1992, (brochures) New Mexico Alternative Retirement Plan, 1991, Arizona Optional Retirement Plan, 1991; co-developer: Portfolio Optimizer Asset Allocation Software, 1994. Asst. to chmn. conv. coms. Bush Campaign Republican Nat. Conv., New Orleans, 1988; chmn. Fairfax County Tchrs. for Vivian Watts, Va., 1979. Mem. Inst. Cert. Fin. Planners, Phi Alpha Theta, Alpha Tau Omega. Avocations: golf, tennis, skiing. Office: VALIC 2929 Allen Pkwy Houston TX 77019

ROBINSON, CHARLES E., building materials executive; b. 1941. BA, Northwestern U., Evanston, Ill., 1963; JD, U. Mich., 1966. V.p., gen. coun. Jim Walter Corp., Tampa, Fla., 1990. Office: Jim Walter Corp 4010 W Boy Scout Blvd Tampa FL 33607-5727

ROBINSON, CHARLES EMANUEL, systems engineer, consultant; b. Hayes, Clarendon, Jamaica, Jan. 14, 1946; came to U.S., 1986; s. Charles E. and Ethlyn C. (Singh) R.; m. Joy B. Cassanova, July 31, 1971; children: Sonya, Monique, Nicole, Kimberley. Student, Nat. Tech. Schs., L.A., 1966. Radio technician Chin's Radio & TV, Kingston, Jamaica, 1964-66; solid state technician Wonards Radio Engring., Kingston, 1966-68; instrument technician Ewarton Plant, Aluminum Co. Can., Jamaica, 1968-69; sr. field tech. engr. Ruel Samuels Ltd., Kingston, 1969-77; mng. dir. MSS Ltd., Kingston, 1977-80, Robinson Assocs., Mandeville, Jamaica, 1980-86; design engr. Seaboard Electronics, New Rochelle, N.Y., 1985-95, mgr. tech. svc., 1988-95; sys. engr. MobileComm, Ridgeland, Miss., 1995—. Mem. IEEE, Am. Mgmt. Assn. Avocations: photography, reading, electronic circuit design and simulation, writing computer programs in C++. Home: 875 William Blvd Apt 1102 Ridgeland MS 39157 Office: MobileComm 1800 E County Line Rd Ridgeland MS 39157

ROBINSON, CHARLES PAUL, nuclear physicist, diplomat, business executive; b. Detroit, Oct. 9, 1941; s. Edward Leonard and Mary Opal (Edmondson) R.; m. Barbara Thomas Woodard; children by previous marriage: Paula S., Colin C. BS in Physics, Christian Bros. U., 1963; PhD in Physics, Fla. State U., 1967. Mem. nuclear test staff Los Alamos (N.Mex.) Nat. Lab., 1967-69, chief test operator, 1969-70, mem. advanced concepts staff, 1971-72, assoc. div. leader, lasers, 1972-76, div. leader, 1976-79, assoc. dir., 1980-85; sr. v.p., bd. dirs. Ebasco Services Inc. subs. Enserch Corp., N.Y.C., 1985-88; ambass. to nuclear testing talks U.S. Dept. State, Geneva, 1988-90; v.p. Sandia Nat. Labs., Albuquerque, 1990-95, pres., 1995—; mem. sci. adv. group Def. Nuclear Agy., Washington, 1981-86; mem. nat. security bd. Los Alamos Nat. Lab., 1985-88; chmn. Presdl. Tech. Adv. Bd., 1991; mem. U.S. Strategic Command Adv. Bd. Pres. Student Concerts Inc., Los Alamos, 1972-74; instr. U. N.Mex., Los Alamos, 1974-76; exec. bd. Boy Scouts of N.Mex. Recipient Outstanding Pub. Svc. medal Joint Chiefs of Staff, 1996. Mem. Am. Phys. Soc., Am. Nuclear Soc., Rotary Internat. Avocation: choral singing. Office: Sandia Nat Labs Albuquerque NM 87185-0101

ROBINSON, CHARLES WESLEY, energy company executive; b. Long Beach, Calif., Sept. 7, 1919; s. Franklin Willard and Anna Hope (Gould) R.; m. Tamara Lindovna, Mar. 8, 1957; children: Heather Lynne, Lisa Anne, Wendy Paige. AB cum laude in Econs., U. Calif., Berkeley, 1941; MBA, Stanford U., 1947. Asst. mgr. mfg. Golden State Dairy Products Co., San Francisco, 1947-49; v.p., then pres. Marcona Corp., San Francisco, 1952-74; undersec. of state for econ. affairs Dept. State, Washington, 1974-75, dep. sec. of state, 1976-77; sr. mng. partner Kuhn Loeb & Co., N.Y.C., 1977-78; vice chmn. Blyth Eastman Dillon & Co., N.Y.C., 1978-79; chmn. Energy Transition Corp., Santa Fe and Washington, 1979-82; pres. Robinson & Assocs., Inc., Santa Fe, 1982—; pres. Dyna-Yacht, Inc., San Diego, 1982—; bd. dirs. The Allen Group, NIKE, Inc. Patentee slurry transport.. Brookings Instn., Washington, 1977—. Served to lt. USN, 1941-46. Recipient Disting. Honor award Dept. State, 1977. Republican. Methodist. Office: Robinson & Assocs Inc PO Box 2224 Santa Fe NM 87504-2224

ROBINSON, CHARLOTTE HILL, artist; b. San Antonio, Nov. 28, 1924; d. Lucius Davis and Charlotte (Moore) Hill; m. Floyd I. Robinson, Mar. 1943; children: Floyd I. Jr., Lawrence H., Elizabeth H. Student, Incarnate Word Coll., 1943, 44, 45, NYU, 1947, 48, Corcoran Sch. Art, 1951-52. Painting instr. Art League No. Va., Alexandria, 1967-75; Condr. Art World Seminar Washington Women's Art Ctr., 1975-80, drawing workshop Smithsonian Instn. Resident Assocs. Program, Washington, 1977; program dir. Nat. Women's Caucus for Art, 1979; project coord., exhbn. curator The Artist and the Quilt, nat. mus. traveling exhbn., 1983-86; vis. artist S.W. Craft Ctr., San Antonio, 1983-85; lectr. WFUV 90 FM, Fordham U., N.Y.C., 1990, San Antonio Art Inst., 1991, Nat. Mus. for Women in Arts, Washington, 1991, Iowa State U., Ames, 1991. Editor: The Artist & The Quilt, 1983; one-person shows include Thames Sic. Ctr., New London, Conn., 1991, Brunner Gallery & Mus., Iowa State U., 1991, 92, San Antonio Art. Inst., 1991, de Andino Fine Arts, Washington, 1992, Masur Mus. Art, Monroe, La., 1993, 96, Lee Hansley Art Gallery, Raleigh, N.C., 1993, 96, Sol Del Rio, San Antonio, 1995, 1812 Artic Gallery, Virginia Beach, Va., 1995; exhibited in group shows at Franklin Square and Watkins Gallery, Washington, 1992, Rutgers U., New Brunswick, N.J., 1992, 96, Brody's Gallery, Washington, 1992, Lee Hansley Art Gallery, Raleigh, 1993, 96, Emerson Gallery, McLean, 1993, 95, No. Va. C.C., 1994, Harvard U., 1996. Trustee Bronx (N.Y.) Mus., 1977; bd. dirs. Washington Women's Art Ctr., 1977; nat. bd. dirs. Women's Caucus for Art, 1983-84; bd. dirs. New Art Examiner, 1985-86. Recipient Concourse award Corcoran Sch. Art, 1952, Scholarship award Telfair Acad. Art, Savannah, Ga., 1959; Nat. Endowment for Arts grantee, 1977, 78-81; fellow Va. Ctr. for Creative Arts, Sweet Briar, Va., 1985.

ROBINSON, CHESTER HERSEY, retired dean; b. Yonkers, N.Y., Nov. 8, 1918; s. Sherman Alexander and Alice (Hersey) R.; m. Marguerite Davis, Dec. 14, 1945 (div. Oct. 1976); children—Barry, Roslyn; m. Heidemarie Höfler, Dec. 30, 1976. A.B., Union Coll., Schenectady, 1940; Ph.D., Stanford U., 1950. Asst. registrar Stanford U., 1949-50; dir. div. extension and summer session Miami U., Oxford, Ohio, 1950-54; assoc. dir. Sch. Gen. Studies, Hunter Coll., 1954-60; dir. Sch. Gen. Studies, Bronx campus, 1960-66, dean, 1966-68; dean Sch. Gen. Studies, Herbert H. Lehman Coll. CUNY, 1968-82, dean Continuing Edn., 1982-86; prof. emeritus, 1986—. Served to lt. USNR, 1942-46. Mem. NEA, Beta Theta Pi, Phi Delta Kappa. Presbyterian. Lodge: Elks. Home: PO Box 248 87 Roses Grove Rd Southampton NY 11969

ROBINSON, CHRISTOPHER THOMAS, artist; b. Cold Spring Harbor, N.Y., Mar. 18, 1951; s. Fred Marlin and Gladys (Langford) R.; m. Janet Thompson, Jan. 17, 1972; children: Justin Christopher, Sarah Williams. BFA, Fla. State U., 1973; MFA, U. Mass., 1975. Teaching assoc. U. Mass., Amherst, 1973-75; assoc. prof. U. S.C., Columbia, 1975—, dir. grad. studies; vis. artist U. Ala., Huntsville, 1977—, U. Cen. Ark., Conway, 1986—, McDowell Tech., Marion, N.C., 1986—, Coll. of Charleston, S.C., 1987—, U. N.C., 1987, Clemson U., 1989; ops. leader Operation Raleigh, Chile, 1985; expdn. leader U.S. Sci. Expdn., London, 1987-88, Global Patriots climb of Orizaba, Mex., 1990, Global Patriots climb of Aconcagua, Argentina, 1992; cons. S.C. State Mus., Columbia, 1986—; seminar speaker Internat. Leadership Seminar; guest artist Meadow Creek Project, Honors Program, Conway, 1987. Solo exhbns. include U. Mass., Amherst, 1974, 75, Heath Gallery, Atlanta, 1977, Greenville County Mus. Art, 1978, U. S.C. Museums, 1978, U. of the South, Sewanee, Tenn., 1980, Atlanta Art Workers Coalition Gallery, 1980, Columbia Coll., 1983, Coll. Charleston, S.C., 1987, U. N.C., Chapel Hill, 1987, S.C. State Mus., Columbia, 1989, Carolighting State House, Columbia, N.C., 1991, Fayetteville St. Mall, Raleigh, N.C., 1991, So. Bell Regional Hdqrs., Charlotte, N.C., 1991; exhibited in group shows at Seven Hills Gallery, Tallahassee, Fla., 1973, Fla. State U., 1973, Archives of Am. Art, 1975, Columbia Mus. of Art, 1976-77, 9th Nat. and Internat. Sculpture Conf., 1976, Southeastern Coll. Art, 1976, New Orleans Mus. Art, 1977, Nat. Sculpture Conf., Jonesboro, 1977, Arcosanti Festival, Cordes Junction, Ariz., 1978, 19th Nat. Art Roundup Las Vegas Mus. Art, 1979, Coll. Art Assn. Ann. Meeting, 1980, Appalachian State U., 1981, Eastern Ill. U., 1981, Southeastern Ctr. Contemporary Art, Winston-Salem, N.C., 1981, Netherlands/American Contemporary Print Exchange Exhibition, 1982, S.C. Arts Commn. Ann. Exhbn., 1976, 81, 83 (Purchase award-State Collection), Friends of Arts First Regional Juried Exhbn., Spartanburg, S.C., 1983, U.S. Nat. Fine Arts Competition, Tallahassee, Fla., 1984, Southeastern Ctr. Contemporary Art, Winston-Salem, N.C., 1984, Portrait of the South, Rome Exhibition, Palazzo Venezia, Rome Italy, 1984, Fact, Fiction and Fantasy: Recent Narrative Art in the S.E., Ewing Art Gallery, U. Tenn., 1987, Art in Transit, Arts Festival of Atlanta, 1989, Austin Peay State U., Clarksville, Tenn., 1993, Anderson County Arts Ctr., 1993 (Merit award 1993), S.C. State Mus., Columbia, 1994, Arts Festival Atlanta, 1994, Emblems, Yale U. Art Gallery. Bd. dirs. Lexington County Sch. Dist. 5, Ballentine, S.C., 1986—; vice chmn. sch. bd., Sch. Dist. 5, Lexington and Richland counties, chmn. bd. trusteees, 1993—; mem. boardmanship tng. cadre S.C. Sch. Bds. Assn., 1990; seminar speaker Hugh O'Brian Youth Found., Denver, 1987; treas. exec. bd. S.C. Sch. Bds. Assn., 1993—. Lt. candidate, USN, 1978. Artist grant S.C. Arts Com., 1976; grantee Southern Regional Edn. Bd., Atlanta, 1985-86; Faculty Devel. grantee U. S.C., 1986-87; recipient Merit award 18th Ann. Juried Show Anderson County Arts Ctr.; Venture Fund grantee U. S.C. Mem. Southern Assn. Sculptors, Nat. Sculpture Exhbn., World Coun., Sci. Exploration Soc. (hon. 1987-89). Youth Svc. Internat. (bd. dirs. 1991—). Avocations: flying, mountaineering. Leader Global Patriots Clime of south ridge St. Elias, 1993. Home: 300 Lost Creek Dr Columbia SC 29212-2487 Office: U SC Dept Art Columbia SC 29208

ROBINSON, CLARENCE AUBREY, JR., journalist; b. Mobile, Ala., June 30, 1933; s. Clarence Aubrey Sr. and Hariett Mervin (Webster) R.; m. Shriley Faye Crews (div. Dec. 1970); children: Michael Anthony, James Mitchell; m. Doris Jean Perry, Mar. 30, 1971; 1 child, William Perry. BA in Mil. History, U.S. Armed Forces Inst., 1960; student, Nat. Louis U., 1990; postgrad., Harvard U., Can. Nat. Def. U. Commd. 2d lt. USMC, 1961, advanced through grades to lt. col.; pub. info. officer Marine Corps Air Sta. USMC, Cherry Point, N.C., 1962-64; intelligence/photographic/civil affairs/ info. officer USMC, DaNang, Vietnam, 1964-65, asst. intelligence/ photographic/civil affairs officer, 1965; media officer USMC, Kansas City, Mo., 1965-68; rifle co. comdr. USMC, Dong Ha, Vietnam, 1968-69; officer-in-charge western region Fare East Network USMC, Japan, 1969-71; joint informational svcs. officer Ea. Area 2d Aircraft Wing USMC, 1971-72, resigned, 1972; sr. editor Aviation Week & Space Tech., 1972-84; pres. Robinson Comms. Ltd., 1984-89; pres., CEO Leading Techs., Inc., 1984-89; editor-in-chief SIGNAL Mag., 1989—; former adj. prof. Georgetown U. Grad. Sch.; cons. NBC TV News; advisor 60 Minutes, CBS; lectr. Tufts U. Contbr. syndicated columns through L.A. Times, articles to Time Mag., Ency. Britannica, Collier's Ency.; pub. mags. The Northern Marine and The Fighting Third, 1968-69. Mem. Westwood Country Club. Republican. Presbyterian. Avocations: golf, sailing, power boating, aerobics. Office: Signal Mag 4400 Fair Lakes Ct Fairfax VA 22033

ROBINSON, CUMMIE ADAMS, librarian; b. Mansfield, La., Sept. 27, 1945; d. Roosevelt and Annie B. Adams; m. Johnnie Robinson Jr.; children: Jared, Cynara, Cynecia. BS, So. U., Baton Rouge, 1967; MSLS, U. So. Calif., 1972; PhD, Walden U., 1992. Cert. tchr., La. Tchr. Compton (Calif.) Unified Schs., 1970-73; libr. Xavier U., New Orleans, 1973-75, Nicholls H.S., New Orleans, 1989—; tchr. Delgado C.C., 1992; adj. faculty So. U., New Orleans, 1994—. Block coord. Nat. Leukemia Soc., New Orleans, 1992—, March of Dimes, New Orleans, 1992—, Muscular Dystrophy Assn., New Orleans, 1988—. Mem. Nat. Coun. Negro Women, Delta Sigma Theta. United Methodist. Avocations: exercising, collecting crystal glasses and mugs, reading. Home: 5800 Kensington Blvd New Orleans LA 70127-2809 Office: 3820 Saint Claude Ave New Orleans LA 70117-5736

ROBINSON, D. THEODORE, insurance company executive. Chmn. bd. dirs., CEO N.Y. Ctrl. Mutual Fire Ins., Edmeston, N.Y., 1960—; bd. dirs. Ctrl. Nat. Bank, Canajoharie, N.Y. Office: NY Central Mutual Fire Ins 1899 Central Plz E Edmeston NY 13335-1890*

ROBINSON, DANIEL BARUCH, banker; b. Hamilton, Ont., Can., Dec. 4, 1937; s. David A. and Zelda (Frank) R.; m. Marta A. Calero, May 7, 1960; children—Allegra, Robert. B.Commerce, McMaster U., Hamilton, Ont., 1960; postgrad., U. Mich., 1969, Harvard U., 1971, Pontif Universidade Católica do Rio de Janeiro, 1979, Georgetown U., 1994, 96. Chartered acct. Vice pres. fin. Comsur, La Paz, Bolivia, 1971-72; fin. dir. Light Servicos, Rio De Janeiro, Brazil, 1972-78; sr. fin. analyst The World Bank, Washington, 1978-79; v.p. fin. Jari Florestal, Rio De Janeiro, 1979-80, Manalta Coal, Calgary, Alta, Can, 1981-82; exec.v.p. Atomic Energy Can. Ltd., Mississauga, Ont., 1983-85; rep. Interam. Devel. Bank, Barbados, 1985-89, Washington, 1989—. Pres. Canadian Club, Rio de Janeiro, 1974-75. Recipient Highest Standing prize Chartered Accts. Assn., 1961; Price, Waterhouse and Co. scholar, 1959. Mem. Inst. Chartered Accts. Ont., Canadian Inst. Chartered Accts., Fin. Execs. Inst. Clubs: Rio de Janeiro Yacht, Jockey Club do Rio de Janeiro, Itanhangá Golf (Rio de Janeiro), Sandy Ln. Property Owners Assn. (Barbados). Avocations: reading; translating from Spanish and Portuguese to English. Home: 12 4th St NE Washington DC 20002-5930 Office: Interam Devel Bank Washington DC 20577

ROBINSON, DANIEL N., psychology educator; b. N.Y., Mar. 9, 1937; s. Henry S. and Margaret R.; children from a previous marriage: Tracey, Kimberly; m. Francine Malasko, 1967. BA, Colgate U., 1958; MA, Hofstra U., 1960; PhD, CUNY, 1965. Rsch. psychologist, electronics rsch. labs. Columbia U., 1960-65, asst. dir. sci. honors program electronics rsch. labs., 1964-68, sr. rsch. psychologist, electronics rsch. labs., 1965-68, asst. dir. of life scis. electronics rsch. labs., 1967-68; asst. prof. dept. psychology Amherst Coll., 1968-70, assoc. prof., 1970-71; dir. grad. program dept. psychology Georgetown Univ., 1981-83, chmn. dept. psychology, 1973-76, 1985—, assoc. prof., 1971-74, prof., 1974—; adj. prof. philosophy Georgetown Univ., Washington, 1996—; vis. lectr. in Psychol. Princeton U., 1965-68; vis. prof. Folger Shakespeare Inst., 1977; vis. sr. mem. Linacre Coll., U. Oxford, 1991—; cons. NIH, 1967-70, NSF, 1965-75, PBS, 1978-84, 1985-88, MacArthur Found., 1985, Atty. Gen's. Task Force on Crime, 1980, Dept. Health and Human Svcs., NIH, 1988. Author: Psychology: A Study of Its Origins and Principles, 1972, The Enlightened Machine: An Anlytical Introduction to Neuropsychology, 1973, 80, Psychology: Traditions and Perspectives, 1976, An Intellectual History of Psychology, 1976, The Mind Unfolded: Essay's on Psychology's Historic Texts, 1978, Systems of Modern Psychology: A Critical Sketch, 1979, Psychology and Law: Can Justice Survive the Social Sciences?, 1980, An Intellectual History of Psychology-Revised Edition, 1981, 3rd edit., 1995, Toward A Science of Human Nature: Essays on the Psychologies of Hegel, Mill, Wundt, and James, 1982, Philosophy of Psychology, 1985, Aristotle's Psychology, 1989, (with William R. Uttal) Foundations of Psychobiology, 1983, (with Sir John Eccles) The Wonder of Being Human: Our Mind and Our Brain, 1984; editor Heredity and Achievement, 1970, Readings in the Origins and Principles of Psychology, 1972, Significant Contributions to the History of Psychology, 1977-78, Annals of Theoretical Psychology, 1990, Social Discourse and Moral Judgment, 1992, Wild Beasts and Idle Humours: Legal Insanity from Antiquity to the Present, 1996; contbr. chpts. to books, reference books, articles to profl. jours. Recipient Inst. for Advanced Study in the Humanities fellow, U. Edinburgh, 1986-87; Pres's. medal Colgate U., 1986, Pub. Svc. award Gen. Svcs. Adminstrn., 1986. Fellow Am. Psychol. Assn. (divsns. 3, 24, 26), British Psychol. Soc.; mem. Sigma Xi, Psi Chi. Home: 300 E Main St Middletown MD 21769-7927 Office: Georgetown U Dept Psychology Washington DC 20057

ROBINSON, DANIEL THOMAS, brokerage company executive; b. Los Angeles, June 17, 1925; s. George Thomas and Helen Theresa (Walsh) R.; m. Diane W. Robinson; children—Marc David, Matthew Curtis. B.S., U. So. Calif., 1948, M.B.A., 1950. Pres. Horton & Converse Inc., 1961—; v.p. Dart Industries, Inc., Los Angeles, 1962-63; sr. v.p. Bergen Brunswig Corp., Los Angeles, 1972-80; dir. bus. devel. Merrill Lynch, Los Angeles, 1981-82; with Internat. Network Brokerage, 1983—; bd. dirs. K.D.L. Corp., Home Interstate Bank Fin. Svcs., Healthbank Corp. Author: Medical Marketing of Seventies, 1968, Marketing Challenges of Biomedical Industry, 1969, Biomedical Marketing, 1975, Biomedical Representation, 1976, Real Estate Funding Principles, 1988, Desert Properties for a Future, 1988, Sea and Desert Investments, 1989, Principles of Network Brokerage Marketing, 1991, Medical Products Brokerage Avocation, 1993. Past pres., bd. dirs. Trojan Club, U. So. Calif.; past pres. Cardinal and Gold; past pres. U. So. Calif., bd. councillors. Mem. Am. Coll. Pharmacists (dir., past pres.), Am., Man. surg. trade assns., Health Industries Assn. Office: 32081 Via Flores San Juan Capistrano CA 92675-3867

ROBINSON, DAVID ADAIR, neurophysiologist; b. Boston, Dec. 9, 1925; s. Edwin Whitmore and Gladys (Mansley) Colby; m. Ellen Marie Rogus, June 13, 1980. B.A., Brown U., 1947; M.S., Johns Hopkins U., 1956, Dr.Engring., 1958. Project engr., dir. engring., v.p. charge research Airpax Electronics Inc., Ft. Lauderdale, Fla., 1951-61; mem. faculty Johns Hopkins U. Med. Sch., 1961—, prof. ophthalmology depts. ophthalmology and biomed. engring., 1975-93, prof. emeritus, 1993—; mem. vis. sci. study sect. div. research grants NIH, 1966-70, engring. in biology and med. tng. com., 1971-73; mem. communicative sci. cluster President's Biomed. Research Panel, 1975; mem. planning com. sensori-motor disorders vision Nat. Eye Inst., NIH, 1976, 81; cons. in field. Editorial bd.: Investigative Ophthalmology, Exptl. Brain Research, Vision Research, Jour. Neurophysiology. Served to ensign USN, 1947-49. Rsch. grantee Nat. Eye Inst., 1969—, Rsch. to Prevent Blindness, 1975-77. Mem. Am. Inst. Med. Biol. Engring., Assn. Research Vision and Ophthalmology, Soc. Neurosci., Bárány Soc. Democrat. Research and publs. on neurophysiology oculomotor system.

ROBINSON, DAVID BRADFORD, poet, scientific writer; b. Richmond, Va., Apr. 14, 1937; s. Albert Lewis and Martha Ellen (Lovern) R. BS, U. Miami, 1959, MS, 1961; AA, Miami-Dade Community Coll., 1970; DSc, Northwestern Coll., 1978, PhD, 1979. Author: Characteristics of Cesium, 1978, Collected Poems, 1987. Founder Ronald Reagan Rep. Ctr., Washington; exhibitor Statue of Liberty, Port of N.Y., 1986; mem. Heritage Found., 1989; sustaining sponsor Ronald Reagan Presdl. Found., 1987; charter mem. Ronald Reagan Trust; charter mem. Honor Roll Rep. Presdl. Task Force, 1990, life mem., 1989, Commemorative Honor Roll, 1991; mem. Nat. Rep. Senatorial Com. with Presdl. Commn., 1992; founding sponsor, founding mem. Space Life Sta., 1990. Recipient 2d Pl. Amateur Trophy, Capablanca Chess Club, 1964, Presdl. Sports award bicycling, 1976, Presdl. Achievement award Rep. Nat. Com., 1982, Cert. Good Standing Rep. Presdl. Task Force, 1982-85, Presdl. Merit medal, 1982, Appreciation cert. Sen. Paula Hawkins, 1986, Golden Poet Trophy award World of Poetry, 1987, Silver Anniversary Album, Nat. Geog. Soc., 1987, Pres. Ronald Reagan Appreciation cert., 1988, Pres. Bush Congl. Victory Squadron Recognition cert., 1989, Bush Inaugural/Freedom medal, 1989, World Time-capsule cert., 1990, Am. in Space medal, 1990, Pegasus Time Capsule plaque, 1991, Congl. Merit cert. Nat. Rep. Congl. Com., 1992, Battle of Normandy Found. Appreciation award, 1993, Presdl. Legion of Merit medal, 1993, Congl. Order of Liberty award, 1993, Appreciation cert. Sen. Kay Bailey Hutchinson, 1993, Rep. Presdl. award, 1994, Albert Einstein medal Brit. Bur. Degree Promotion, 1994, Cert. of Appreciation, The Golden Hart Club, Mil. Order of Purple Heart Svc. Found., Congl. Order of Freedom, 1995, numerous other awards Rep. Nat. Com., polit. orgns. Mem. Am. Air Mus. (Brit., founder 1991), Battle of Normandy Meml. Mus. (charter 1988), Sigma Xi, Russian Club, Phi Theta Kappa. Avocation: chess. Home: 715 NE 92nd St Apt 1A Miami FL 33138

ROBINSON, DAVID BROOKS, retired naval officer; b. Alexandria, La., Oct. 26, 1939; s. Donald and Marion (Holloman) R.; m. Gene Kirkpatrick, Aug. 1, 1964; children: Kirk, David. Student, Tex. A&M U., 1958-59; BS, U.S. Naval Acad., 1963; MS in Physics, Naval Postgrad. Sch., Monterey, Calif., 1969. Commd. ensign USN, 1963, advanced through grades to vice admiral, 1993; comdg. officer USS Canon and USS Ready, Guam, 1969-71; adminstrv. aide to Chmn. Joint Chiefs Staff, Washington, 1971-74; comdg. officer USS Luce, Mayport, Fla., 1976-78; surface comdr. assignment officer. and dir. fiscal mgt. and procedural control divsn. Naval Mil. Pers. Cmd., 1979-81; mem. Fgn. Service Inst. Exec. Seminar, Washington, 1982; comdg. officer USS Richmond K. Turner, Charleston, S.C., 1983-84; chief of staff, comdr. Naval Surface Force, Atlantic Fleet, Norfolk, Va., 1984; exec. asst. and sr. aide to vice chief Naval Ops., Washington, 1985, dir. Manpower and Tng. div., 1986, dir. Surface Warfare div., 1987-88; cmdr. cruiser destroyer group 8, 1988-89; vice dir. and subsequently dir. operational plans and interoperability directorate Joint Staff, Washington, 1989-91; dep., chief of staff to comdr. U.S. Pacific Fleet, 1991-93, comdr. naval surface force, 1993-96; ret. USN, 1996. Decorated Navy Cross, Def. D.S.M., D.S.M., Legion of Merit with 4 gold stars, Bronze Star, Purple Heart. Mem. Optimists (pres. Oakton, Va. 1986-87). Methodist. Avocations: golf, cycling, stamp collecting, reading. Office: COMNAVSURFPAC 2841 Rendova Rd San Diego CA 92155-5407

ROBINSON, DAVID CLINTON, reporter; b. Goffstown, N.H., Nov. 5, 1963; s. Clinton and Barbara Lee (Ploss) R.; m. Karen Ruth Eckhardt, July 3, 1992; children: Laura Lee, Lindsay Lee. AB, Syracuse U., 1985. Reporter The Buffalo News, 1985—. Mem. Buffalo Newspaper Guild (exec. com. 1989-95, vice chmn. 1991-92). Office: The Buffalo News 1 News Plz Buffalo NY 14203-2930

ROBINSON, DAVID G., management consultant. Pres., CEO CSC Index, Cambridge, Mass., 1981—. Office: CSC Index Inc 5 Cambridge Ctr 12th Fl Cambridge MA 02142-1493*

ROBINSON, DAVID MASON, cell physiologist; b. Barton, Eng., July 7, 1932; came to U.S., 1969, naturalized, 1979; s. Thomas Leon Mason and Mabel (Orr) R.; B.Sc. with 1st class honours, U. Durham, 1955, Ph.D. (Philip Buckle Meml. scholar), 1958; m. Jean Marcia Smith, Sept. 10, 1965; children—Jane Leonie Mason, Simon Henry Mason. Mem. sci. staff Namulonge Research Sta., Kampala, Uganda, 1959-61; research officer, tutor Hope Dept. Zoology, Oxford (Eng.) U., 1961-63; mem. sci. staff, biophysics group Med. Research Council, Radiobiol. Research Unit, Harwell, Eng., 1963-66; prin. sci. officer, head cell biology Microbiol. Research Establishment, Porton, Eng., 1966-69; asst. research dir., head cell biology ARC Blood Research Lab., Bethesda, Md., 1969-73; prof. biology, assoc. mem. Vincent Lombardi Cancer Research Ctr., Georgetown U., Washington, 1974-80, adj. prof. anatomy and cell biology, Sch. of Medicine, 1982-90; professorial lectr. in liberal studies Georgetown U., 1980—; assoc. dir. for sci. programs, div. heart and vascular disease Nat. Heart, Lung and Blood Inst., NIH, Bethesda, Md., 1980-94, acting dir., 1993, dir. vascular rsch. program, 1994—; mem. faculty biology and genetics NIH Grad. Sch., 1981-86; mem. faculty Brookings Inst., 1994—. Capt. 1st Royal Green Jackets, 43d and 52d, Brit. Ter. Army, 1962-65. Empire Cotton Growing Corp. postgrad. scholar, 1957. Recipient Vicennial medal Georgetown U., 1992. Mem. Biophys. Soc., Soc. Complex Carbohydrates, Soc. Cryobiology (sec. 1975), Am. Soc. Cell Biology, Sigma Xi (pres. Georgetown chpt. 1978), Alpha Sigma Nu (hon.). Democrat. Episcopalian. Club: Royal Green Jackets Officers. Author: (with G.A. Jamieson) Mammalian Cell Membranes, 5 vols., 1973-76; contbr. articles to profl. jours. Home: Stoneleigh Cottage PO Box 2164 Shepherdstown WV 25443-2164 Office: NIH Two Rockledge Ctr Ste 10193 Bethesda MD 20892-7956

ROBINSON, DAVID MAURICE, professional basketball player; b. Key West, Fla., Aug. 6, 1965. Grad., U.S. Naval Acad., 1987. Commd. ensign USN, 1987; with San Antonio Spurs, 1989—; mem. U.S. Olympic Basketball Team, 1988, 92. Recipient Naismith award, 1987, Wooden award, 1987, IBM award, 1990, 91, 94, Schick Pivotal Player award, 1990, 91; named to Sporting News All-Am. First Team, 1986, 87, Sporting News Coll. Player of Yr., 1987, NBA Rookie of Yr., 1990, All-NBA First Team, 1991, 92, All-Star team, 1990-94; named NBA Defensive Player of Yr., 1992, MVP, 1994-95, season MVP, 1995. Holder NCAA Divsn. 1 single season record most block shots per game (5.91), most blocked shots in 1 game (14), 1986, NBA career record most blocked shots per game (3.65). Office: care San Antonio Spurs 100 Montanta St San Antonio TX 78203-1031*

ROBINSON, DAVID WEAVER, surgeon, educator; b. Kansas City, Mo., Nov. 15, 1914; s. David Beach and Aileen (Weaver) R.; m. Margaret Sherwood, June 20, 1940 (dec. Feb. 1986); children: David S., Nancy K., Peter B., Mary A.; m. Alma L. Dallas Horner, Aug. 26, 1987 (dec. 1991). A.B., U. Kans., 1935, M.S., 1948; M.D., U. Pa., 1938. Diplomate: Am. Bd. Surgery, Am. Bd. Plastic Surgery. Intern Phila. Gen. Hosp., 1938-40; surg. trainee U. Kans. Med. Ctr., Kansas City, 1940-43, instr., 1941-43, asst. prof., 1948-50, assoc. prof., 1951-54, prof. surgery, 1954-85, Regents prof., 1973-85; disting. prof. emeritus U. Kans. Med. Ctr., 1985—, chmn. sect. plastic surgery, 1947-72, dir. U. Kans. Burn Ctr., 1972-83, vice chancellor clin. affairs, 1974-80, acting vice chancellor, 1975-76; mem. surg. study sect. NIH Research Council, 1962-65. Contbr. articles to med. jours. Trustee Kansas City Philharm. Assn., Kans., 1963—. Served to capt. M.C. AUS, 1943-45. Decorated Croix de Guerre France; recipient disting. alumni citation U. Kans., 1969. Mem. Am. Assn. Plastic Surgeons (honoree of yr. award 1982), Am. Assn. for Surgery Trauma, ACS (gov. 1973-79 honoree of yr. award), Am. Soc. Plastic and Reconstructive Surgery (pres. 1966), Am. Trauma Soc. (founding mem.), Am. Surg. Assn. (2d v.p. 1965), Central Surg. Assn., Western Surg. Assn., AMA, Assn. for Cleft Palate Rehab., Kans. Med. Soc. Plastic Surgery Research Council, Rocky Mountain Traumatological Soc., Soc. for Surgery Head and Neck, Soc. Univ. Surgeons, Am. Bd. Plastic Surgery (chmn. examining bd. 1966—), Societe Internationale de Chirurgie, Sigma Xi, Nu Sigma Nu, Alpha Omega Alpha, Beta Theta Pi. Republican. Presbyterian (ruling elder 1953—). Home: 7930 Bristol Ct Shawnee Mission KS 66208-5220 Office: U Kans Med Ctr Kansas City KS 66103

ROBINSON, DAVID ZAV, foundation administrator; b. Montreal, Que., Can., Sept. 29, 1927; s. Benjamin and Antonia (Seiden) R.; m. Nan Senior, Sept. 6, 1954; children: Marc, Eric. AB, Harvard U., 1946, AM, 1947, PhD, 1950. Asst. dir. rsch. Baird-Atomic Inc., Cambridge, Mass., 1949-59, 60-61; sci. liaison officer Office Naval Rsch., London, 1959-60; sci. advisor staff Office of Pres., Washington, 1961-67; v.p. acad. affairs NYU, 1967-70; v.p. Carnegie Corp. N.Y., N.Y.C., 1970-80, exec. v.p., 1981-85, exec. v.p., treas., 1986-88; exec. dir. Carnegie Commn. on Sci Tech. and Govt., 1988—; dir. Urban Research Corp., Chgo., 1968-75; cons. Congressional Office of Tech. Assessment, 1975-78; mem. coms. women in sci. NRC, 1975-82; mem. vis. com. dept. chemistry Harvard U., 1977-83; physics dept. Princeton U., 1970-76. Mem. N.Y. Energy Rsch. and Devel. Authority, 1971-77; trustee CUNY, 1976-81, Amideast, 1983-88, Citizen Union Found., 1985—, Inst. Schs. of the Future, 1986—, N.C. Sch. Sci. and Math., 1989—, Santa Fe Inst., 1987—, Prep for Prep, 1989—. Mem. AAAS, Optical Soc. Am., Coun. on Fgn. Rels., Am. Contract Bridge League, Harvard Club (N.Y.C.), Century Assn. (N.Y.C.). Office: 437 Madison Ave New York NY 10022-7001

ROBINSON, DAVIS ROWLAND, lawyer; b. N.Y.C., July 11, 1940; s. Thomas Porter and Cynthia (Davis) R.; m. Suzanne Walker, June 11, 1966; children: Christopher Champlin II, Gracyn Walker. B.A. magna cum laude, Yale U., 1961; LL.B. cum laude, Harvard U., 1967. Bar: N.Y. 1968, D.C. 1971, U.S. Supreme Ct. 1972. Fgn. svc. officer Dept. State, Washington, 1961-69; assoc. Sullivan & Cromwell, N.Y.C., 1969-71; assoc., ptnr. Leva, Hawes, Symington, Martin and Oppenheimer, Washington, 1971-81; the legal advisor Dept. State, Washington, 1981-85; ptnr. Pillsbury, Madison & Sutro, Washington, 1985-88, Le Boeuf, Lamb, Greene & MacRae, Washington, 1988—; adj. prof. Georgetown Univ. Law Ctr. Pres. Harvard Legal Aid Bur., 1966-67. Mem. ABA, Assn. Bar City N.Y., Am. Law Inst. (adviser fgn. rels. law of U.S.), Am. Soc. Internat. Law, Coun. on Fgn. Rels., Phi Beta Kappa. Office: Le Boeuf Lamb Greene & MacRae 1875 Connecticut Ave NW Washington DC 20009-5728

ROBINSON, DERRICK JEFFREY, lawyer; b. New Haven, Sept. 5, 1951; s. William Aron Robinson and Jean Eunice Monroe Johnson; m. Pamela Celestine Allen, Dec. 20, 1975; children: Naima, Marcus. BA, Howard U., Washington, 1974; JD, Antioch Sch. Law, Washington, 1978. Bar: N.Y. 1982, U.S. Dist. Ct. (ea. dist.) N.Y. 1984, U.S. Ct. Appeals (2nd cir.) 1991. Asst. county atty. Suffolk County Atty.'s Office, Hauppauge, N.Y., 1982-84, sr. asst., 1984-85, prin. asst. county atty., 1985—; counsel to health and safety bd. Suffolk County Govt., Hauppauge, 1988-90, Freedom of Information Law appeals officer, 1994—. Author newsletter of Suffolk County Anti-Bias Task Force, 1995. Pres. Martin Luther King Commn., Suffolk County, 1993-94, bd. dirs., 1989-95; counsel North Amityville (N.Y.) Cmty. Econ. Coun., 1989—. Recipient Vol. Recognition Program award Newsday, L.I., 1993, Pres.'s award Suffolk County Martin Luther King Commn., 1993. Avocations: racquetball, golf, community theatre production. Home: PO Box 148 Amityville NY 11701 Office: Suffolk County Attorneys Of Bldg 158 North Complex Veterans Memorial Hwy Hauppauge NY 11788

ROBINSON, DONALD LEONARD, social scientist, educator; b. Buffalo, Dec. 28, 1936; s. Sidney Smith and Marion Esther (Hershiser) R.; m. Molly McCaslin Jahnige, Jan. 1, 1983; children: John Samuel, David Wynn; stepchildren: Katherine Jahnige, Paul Jahnige. BA, Yale U., 1958; MDiv, Union Theol. Sem., 1962; PhD, Cornell U., 1966. Instr. govt. Cornell U., Ithaca, N.Y., 1965-66; asst. prof. Smith Coll., Northampton, Mass., 1966-71, assoc. prof., 1971-78, prof., 1978—, Sylvia Dlugasch Bauman chair Am. studies, 1990-93, dir. Am. studies, 1979-85; cons. Ford Found., 1986-88, 91-92, Media and Society, 1986-87, Comm. on Operation of U.S. Senate, 1976; dir. Project '87, 1977-78; vis. prof. Doshisha U., Kyoto, Japan, 1989. Author: Slavery in the Structure of American Politics, 1765-1820, 1971, To the Best of My Ability: The Presidency and the Constitution, 1987, Government for the Third American Century, 1989; mem. editorial bd. Presdl. Studies Quar., 1987—; editor: Reforming American Government: The Bicentennial Papers of the Committee on the Constitutional System, 1985. Adminstr. New Eng. Regional Commn., 1973; chmn. Dem. City Com., 1978-80, Northampton Planning Bd., 1980-82; warden St. John's Episcopal Ch., 1981-85; trustee Diocese of Western Mass., 1988—; bd. selectmen, Ashfield, Mass., 1992—. Rockefeller Bros. fellow, 1958-59; Kent fellow, 1962-66; Project '87 fellow, 1980; fellow Ctr. for Study Democratic Insts., 1971; Phi Beta Kappa vis. scholar, 1988-89; recipient Anisfield-Wolf award, 1971. Mem. Am. Polit. Sci. Assn., Cosmos Club, Phi Beta Kappa. Home: Norton Hill Rd Ashfield MA 01330 Office: Smith Coll Dept Govt Northampton MA 01063

ROBINSON, DONALD WALTER, university dean; b. Rockford, Ill.; s. Walter John and Viola (Anderson) R.; m. Betty Jane Zink, May 30, 1948; children: Deborah Beth, Galen Don, Darci Lynn, Gregory John. A.B., Carthage Coll., 1950; M.A., Bradley U., 1951, Ph.D., 1957. Various positions coll. and pub. sch. adminstrn., 1952-58; specialist in coll. adminstrn. U.S. Office of Edn., Washington, 1959-62; dir. mental retardation research centers program Nat. Inst. Child Health and Human Devel., Bethesda, Md., 1962-65; asst. dean, prof. higher edn. So. Ill. U., Carbondale, 1965-70; dean, prof. Coll. Edn. Youngstown (Ohio) State U., 1970-72; dean Coll. Edn., prof. psychology and higher edn. Okla. State U., Stillwater, 1972-88, dean, prof. emeritus, 1988; dean, prof. Sch. Edn. U. Mo., St. Louis, 1988-92, dean emeritus, 1967-93; cons. examiner North Ctrl. Assn. Schs. and Colls., 1967-93; bd. examiners Nat. Coun. Accreditation/Tchr. Edn., 1990-93; cons. New Eng. Assn. Schs. and Colls., USPHS, U.S. Office Edn., World Bank; bd. dirs. Holmes Group, 1987-88. Bd. dirs. Marymount U., Arlington, Va., 1962-66, St. Louis Sci. Ctr., 1989-92, Tenn Challenge Ark., St. Louis Regional Edn. Partnership, 1989-92; pres. bd. dirs. Cmty. Counseling Found., Hot Springs, Ark.; ruling elder John Calvin Presbyn. Ch., Bridgeton, Mo., Kirk in Pines, Hot Springs Village, Ark. With USAAF, 1944-46. Mem. Am. Assn. Colls. Tchr. Edn. (govt. rels. com. 1977-79, 88-91, bd. dirs. 1988-90), North Ctrl. Assn. Colls. and Schs. (dir. 1975-79, chmn. coun. rsch. and svc. 1977-79), Am. Psychol. Assn., Am. Edni. Rsch. Assn., Am. Assn. Higher Edn., Assn. Colls. and Schs. Edn. in State Univs., Land Grant Colls. and Affiliated Pvt. Univs. (sec. 1985-86, pres. elect 1987-88, pres. 1988-90, past pres., bd. dirs. 1990-92), Kiwanis. Home: 2 Caribe Ln Hot Springs Village AR 71909

ROBINSON, DOUGLAS GEORGE, lawyer; b. Hamilton, Mont., Feb. 24, 1943; s. Clarence Elijah and Frances Carolina (Alonzo) R.; m. Julia Elizabeth Sullivan, 1995; children by previous marriage: Stephen Douglas, Katherine Marielle. B.A. in Econs, U. Wash., 1965; J.D., George Washington U., 1969. Bar: D.C. Legis. asst. Wash. State Legis. Council, Olympia, 1965-66; assoc. firm Arnold & Porter, Washington, 1969-74; dep. gen. counsel Fed. Energy Adminstrn., Washington, 1974-76; mem. issues staff Carter-Mondale Presdl. Campaign, Atlanta, 1976; mem. Carter-Mondale Transition Group, Washington, 1976-77; spl. asst. to adminstr. for maj. energy projects Fed. Energy Adminstrn., Washington, 1977; asst. adminstr. for regulations and emergency planning Econ. Regulatory Adminstrn., U.S. Dept. Energy, Washington, 1977-78; dep. adminstr. for policy Econ. Regulatory Adminstrn., U.S. Dept. Energy, 1978-80, spl. asst. to sec., dep. sec., 1980-81; ptnr. Skadden, Arps, Slate, Meagher & Flom, Washington, 1981—. Editor-in-chief: George Washington Law Rev, 1968-69. Recipient John B. Larner medal George Washington U. Law Sch., 1969; cert. of superior service Fed. Energy Adminstrn., 1974; Outstanding Service medal Dept. Energy, 1979; Disting. Service medal Sec. of Energy, 1981. Mem. ABA (Nat. Pro Bono Publico award 1994), D.C. Bar Assn., Fed. Energy Bar Assn. Office: Skadden Arps Slate Meagher & Flom 1440 New York Ave NW Washington DC 20005-2111

ROBINSON, (DAVID) DUNCAN, museum administrator, art historian; b. Kidsgrove, Staffordshire, Eng., June 27, 1943; came to U.S., 1981; s. Tom and Ann Elizabeth (Clarke) R.; m. Elizabeth Anne Sutton, Jan. 7, 1967; children: Amanda Jane, Thomas Edward, Charlotte Elizabeth. B.A., Clare Coll., U. Cambridge, Eng., 1965; M.A., Clare Coll., U. Cambridge, 1969, Yale U., 1967. Asst. keeper paintings and drawings Fitzwilliam Mus., Cambridge, 1970-76, keeper paintings and drawings, 1976-80; dir. Fitzwilliam Mus. U. Cambridge, 1995—; prof. fellow Clare Coll., 1975-81, 95—; chief exec. officer Paul Mellon Ctr. for Studies in Brit. Art, London, 1981-95; dir. Yale Ctr. for Brit. Art, New Haven, 1981-95; adj. prof. Yale U., 1981-95; vis. com. dept. painting restoration Met. Mus. Art; mem. coun. mgmt. William Blake Trust, 1983—; bd. govs. Yale U. Press, 1987-95; mem. arts and artifacts indemnity adv. panel to Fed. Coun. on Arts and Humanities, 1991-94, chmn., 1992-94. Author: A Companion Volume to the Kelmscott Chaucer, 1975, Stanley Spencer, 1979, Morris & Co. in Cambridge, 1980, Town, Country, Shore and Sea: British Watercolors from VanDyck to Nash, 1982, Stanley Spencer, 1990. Mem. adv. panel Arts Coun. Gt. Britain, 1978-81, vice chmn. art adv. panel, 1981, coun. mem., 1981. Mellon fellow, 1965. Fellow Royal Soc. Arts; mem. Walpole Soc. (coun. 1986-89, 95—), Conn. Acad. Arts and Scis., New Haven Colony Hist. Soc. (bd. dirs. 1991-94), Athenaeum Club (London), Knickerbocker Club (N.Y.C.). Office: Fitzwilliam Museum New Haven CT 06510

ROBINSON, DWIGHT P., federal agency administrator; m. Linda; 1 child, Noah. BS in Urban Planning and Cmty. Devel., Mich. State U., 1975; postgrad., Ctrl. Mich. U. Various positions City of Flint, City of Ann Arbor, Mich.; with Mich. State Housing Devel. Authority, 1976—, dep. dir., chief mortgage underwriter, 1986-90; dir. single family affordable housing initiatives dept. Fed. Home Loan Mortgage Corp., 1990-93; pres. govt. nat. mortgage assn. U.S. Dept. Housing and Urban Devel., 1993—. Office: Dept Housing & Urban Devel Govt Nat Mortgage Assn 451 7th St SW Washington DC 20410-0001

ROBINSON, E. B., JR., bank executive; b. Centreville, Miss., Sept. 14, 1941; s. Emerson B. and Dolly (McGehee) R.; m. Judy M. Treppendahl, Sept. 7, 1963; children: E.B. III, John Green. BS, Davidson Coll., 1963; MBA, Harvard U., 1967. Mgmt. trainee Deposit Guaranty Nat. Bank, Jackson, Miss., 1967-69, investment officer, 1969-71, asst. v.p., 1971-73, v.p., 1973-75, exec. v.p., 1976-79, pres., chief ops. officer, 1979-84; pres., chief ops. officer Deposit Guaranty Corp., Jackson, 1982-84; chmn. and chief exec. officer Deposit Guaranty Nat. Bank and Deposit Guaranty Corp., Jackson, 1984—; bd. dirs. Fed. Res. Bank of Atlanta. Chmn. fin. com. Millsaps Coll., Jackson; treas. Council for Support of Pub. Higher Edn., Jackson; bd. dirs. Columbia Sem., Atlanta. Served with U.S. Army, 1963-65. J. Spencer Love fellow Harvard U., 1963. Mem. Young Pres.'s Orgn., Assn. of Res. City Bankers (govt. relations com.), Dealer Bank Assn. (Glass-Stegall com.), Jackson C. of C. (pres. 1987), Phi Beta Kappa. Presbyterian. Clubs: Country of Jackson; Harvard (N.Y.C.). Avocation: running. Office: Deposit Guaranty Corp PO Box 1200 Jackson MS 39215-1200*

ROBINSON, EDDIE GAY, college football coach; m. Doris Robinson; children: Lillian Rose, Eddie Jr. BA, Leland Coll., 1940; MS, U. Iowa; LLD (hon.), La. Tech. Coach football Grambling U., La., 1941—, v.p. athletics; head coach East-West Shrine Game, 1977. Recipient Horatio Alger award, Nat. Football Found. award, NAACP award, VFW award, Bear Bryant award, Liberty Bowl award, others, Spl. Commendations from Pres. Ronald Reagan, Nat. Collegiate Athletic Assn., U.S. Congress, State of La., B'nai B'rith; holds record of most college football victories. Mem. Nat. Assn. Sports & Phys. Edn., Nat. Assn. Intercollegiate Athletics, Southwestern Athletic Conf., La. Sports Hall of Fame, Pop Warner, Sugar Bowl, Black Coll. Winner 10 nat. Black coll. football championships. Office: Grambling State Univ Athletic Dept Grambling LA 71245*

ROBINSON, EDGAR ALLEN, oil company executive; b. Boston, Dec. 12, 1933; s. Herbert and Ruth (Solomon) R.; m. Ruth Enid Schwartz, July 24, 1956; children: Jeffrey Michael, Laurie Karen. AB, Brown U., 1955; MBA, Harvard U., 1960. Fin. analyst Exxon Corp., N.Y.C., 1960-66, asst. treas., 1966-70; corp. planning mgr. Esso Europe Inc., London, 1970-72; pres. Esso Africa Inc., London, 1972-75; dep. contr. Exxon Corp., N.Y.C., 1975-79; sr. v.p. Exxon Co. U.S.A., Houston, 1979-83; v.p., treas. Exxon Corp., Irving, Tex., 1983—. Bd. dirs. bus. Arts Fund, Houston, 1980-83, chmn., 1983; trustee Houston Ballet Found., 1980-83, Brown U., Providence, 1982-88; mem. Dean's adv. com. U. Chgo. Bus. Sch., 1984—, chmn., 1990-94; bd. dirs. Dallas Zoo, 1992—; bd. govs. Dallas Symphony, 1993—. Office: Exxon Corp 5959 Las Colinas Blvd Irving TX 75039

ROBINSON, EDWARD JOSEPH, cosmetics company executive; b. White Plains, N.Y., May 12, 1940; s. Edward D.J. and Christine (Walsh) R.; m. Gail Lee Robinson, June 15, 1963; 1 son, Michael. B.B.A., Iona Coll., 1962. CPA, N.Y. Supr. Peat, Marwick, Mitchell, N.Y.C., 1963-70; exec. v.p. fin., chief fin. officer RJR Nabisco, Inc., Atlanta, 1987-89; exec. v.p. fin., chief fin. officer Avon Products, N.Y.C., 1989-93, vice chmn., chief fin. and adminstrv. officer, 1993—, now pres. COO. Trustee Iona Coll. Recipient Loftus award for Disting. Achievement Iona Coll., 1976. Mem. Am. Inst. CPA's, N.Y. Soc. CPA's, Winged Foot Country Club (Mamaroneck, N.Y.), Met. Club (N.Y.C.), N.Y. Athletic Club (N.Y.C.). Republican. *

ROBINSON, EDWARD LEE, retired physics educator, consultant; b. Clanton, Ala., Nov. 6, 1933; s. Alonzo Lee and Ollie Sarah (Mims) R.; m. Shirley Anne Burnett (div. Sept. 1972); children: Edward Lee Jr., James Allan, Paul David; m. Linda G. Moon, 1990. AB with honors, Samford U., 1954; MS, Purdue U., 1958, PhD, 1962. Asst. prof. physics, chmn. dept. Samford U., Birmingham, Ala., 1961-62, assoc. prof., chmn. dept., 1962-66, prof., chmn. dept., 1966-67; assoc. prof. U. Ala., Birmingham, 1967-77, co-radiation safety officer, 1967-85, acting chmn. dept., 1973-74, prof. physics, 1977-91, adj. prof. forensic sci., 1983-91; cons. in applied physics and accident reconstrn., 1991—; cons. Hayes Internat. Corp., Birmingham, 1963-68, So. Research Inst., Birmingham, 1968-69; researcher Oak Ridge (Tenn.) Nat. Lab., 1968, 74-75, 82, U. Md., College Park, 1966, 67. Active Birmingham YMCA. Mem. Am. Phys. Soc., Soc. Automotive Engrs., AAAS, Ala. Acad. Sci. (v.p. 1964-65), N.Y. Acad. Sci. Baptist. Achievements include discovery, co-discovery of six radioisotopes. Avocations: handball, scuba diving. Home: 1692 Monteagle Dr Birmingham AL 35244-6735

ROBINSON, ENDERS ANTHONY, geophysics educator, writer; b. Boston, Mar. 18, 1930; s. Edward Arthur and Doris Gertrude (Goodale) R.; m. Eva Arborelius, Sept. 9, 1962 (div. 1973); children: Anna, Erik Arthur, Karin; m. Joyce McPeake, Aug. 8, 1992. BS in Math., MIT, 1950, MS in Econs., 1952, PhD in Geophysics, 1954. Dir. geophys. analysis group MIT, Cambridge, Mass., 1952-54; geophysicist Gulf Oil Corp., Pitts., 1954-55; instr. math. MIT, Cambridge, Mass., 1955-56; petroleum economist Standard Oil Co. N.J., N.Y.C., 1956-57; asst. prof. stats. Mich. State U., East Lansing, 1958; asst. prof. math. U. Wis., Madison, 1958-61, assoc. prof. math. (with tenure), 1961-62; dep. prof. stats. Uppsala (Sweden) U., 1960-64; v.p., dir. Digicon, Inc., Houston, 1965-70; pres. Robinson Rsch. Inc., Houston, 1970-82; vis. prof. theoretical and applied mechanics Cornell U., Ithaca, N.Y., 1981-82; McMan prof. geophysics U. Tulsa, 1983-93; Maurice Ewing and J.L. Worzel prof. geophysics Columbia U., N.Y.C., 1993—. Author 25 books on sci. and tech, including Einstein's Relativity in Metaphor and Mathematics, 1990; editor: Internat. Jour. of Imaging Systems & Tech., 1988—; assoc. editor: Jour. of Time Series Analysis, 1984—; editorial bd. Multidimensional Systems and Signal Processing, An Internat. Jour., 1990—. 2d lt. U.S. Army, 1950-51. Recipient Conrad Schlumberger award European Assn. of Exploration Geophysicists, 1969, Donald G. Fink Prize award IEEE, 1984. Mem. NAE, Nat. Rsch. Coun. (com. on undiscovered oil and gas resources), Soc. Exploration Geophysicists (hon., Best Paper award, 1964, medal 1969). Home: 560 Riverside Dr Apt 20J New York NY 10027-3236 Office: Columbia U Krumb Sch Mines New York NY 10027

ROBINSON, ESTHER MARTIN, secondary school educator; b. Buffalo, N.Y., Sept. 19, 1956; d. Douglas Charles and Esther (Hagen) Martin; m. Stephen Mark Robinson, May 6, 1978; children: Rachel Anne, Sarah Elizabeth. BA, Oral Roberts U., 1978; MA, U. Tulsa, 1983. Tchr. secondary sch. history Tulsa Pub. Schs., 1978-80; tchr. secondary sch. history Jenks (Okla.) High Sch., 1980-92, chair dept. social studies, 1990-92; tchr. world history, advanced placement U.S. history Langham Creek High Sch., Houston, 1992—; presenter in field. Mem. Nat. Coun. Social Studies, Tex. Coun. Social Studies, Cypress Fairbanks Coun. for Social Studies, Tex. Assn. Gifted and Talented. Home: 8022 Null Ct Spring TX 77379-6141 Office: Langham Creek High Sch 17610 FM 529 Houston TX 77095

ROBINSON, FARREL RICHARD, pathologist, toxicologist; b. Wellington, Kans., Mar. 23, 1927; s. Farrel Otis and Norine (Sloan) R.; m. Mimi Agatha Hathaway, June 5, 1949; children—Farrel Richard, Kelly S., E. Scott, Brian A. B.S., Kans. State U., 1950, D.V.M., M.S., 1958; Ph.D., Tex. A&M U., 1965. Diplomate: Am. Coll. Vet. Pathologists, Am. Bd. Vet. Toxicology (v.p. 1971-74, pres. 1976-79). Served with USN, 1945-46; commd. 2d lt. USAF, 1951, advanced through grades to lt. col., 1971; vet. pathologist Aerospace Med. Research Labs., Wright-Patterson AFB, Ohio, 1958-68; chief Vet. Pathology div. Armed Forces Inst. Pathology, Washington, 1968-74; ret., 1974; scientist assoc. Univs. Associated for Research and Edn. in Pathology, Inc., 1972-74; asst. clin. prof. pathology George Washington U. Sch. Medicine, 1972-74; instr. NIH Grad. Program, 1973-74; prof. toxicology-pathology Sch. Vet. Medicine, Purdue U., 1974-93; dir. Animal Disease Diagnostic Lab., 1978-85, head dept. vet. sci., 1978-85, head dept. vet. microbiology, pathology and pub. health, 1986-88, chief toxicology service, 1984-93; emeritus, 1993; cons. vet. pathology USAF surg. gen. and asst. surg. gen. for vet. services, 1970-74. Mem. editorial bd. Human and Vet. Toxicology, 1976—. Contbr. sci. articles to profl. jours. Decorated USAF Commendation medal, Meritorious Service medal; recipient Aerospace Med. Research Labs. Scientist of Year award, 1967. Mem. AVMA, Am. Bd. Vet. Toxicology, Am. Coll. Vet. Pathology, Am. Assn. Vet. Lab. Diagnosticians (bd. govs.1980-85, v.p. 1986, pres. 1987), Wildlife Disease Assn., Conf. Rsch. Workers in Animal Disease, Soc. Toxicology, U.S. Animal Health Assn., Sigma Xi, Phi Kappa Phi, Alpha Zeta, Phi Zeta. Democrat. Methodist. Home: 201 W 600 N West Lafayette IN 47906-9727 Office: Purdue U Animal Disease Diagnostic Lab West Lafayette IN 47907

ROBINSON, FLORINE SAMANTHA, marketing executive; b. Massies Mill, Va., Feb. 4, 1935; d. John Daniel and Fannie Belle (Smith) Jackson; m. Frederick Robinson (div. 1973); children: Katherine, Theresa, Freda. BS, Morgan State U., 1976; postgrad., U. Balt., 1977-81, Liberty U., 1987. Writer, reporter Phila. Independent News, 1961-63; freelance writer, editor Balt., 1963-71; asst. mng. editor Williams & Wilkins Pubs. Inc., Balt., 1971-76; mktg. rep., then mktg. mgr. NCR Corp., Balt., 1977-93; assoc. minister, trustee Christian Unity Temple, Balt., 1976—; pres. ABCOM, Inc., Balt., 1993—; bd. dirs. Armstrong & Bratcher, Inc., Balt. Editor: Stedman's Medical Dictionary, 1972; contbr. articles to profl. jours. Active PTA, Balt., 1963-65; bd. dirs. Howard Pk. Civic Assn., Balt., 1967—, pres. 1991—; leader, cons. Girl Scouts USA, 1970-73. Recipient Excellence in Rsch. award Psi Chi, 1976, Citizen citation Mayor of Balt. Mem. NAFE, Mid-Atlantic Food Dealers Assn., Am. Soc. Notaries, Internat. Platform Assn., Edelweiss Club, Order of Eastern Star. Democrat. Avocation: piano. Home: 3126 Howard Park Ave Baltimore MD 21207-6715

ROBINSON, FRANK, professional baseball team executive, former coach, former player; b. Beaumont, Tex., Aug. 31, 1935; s. Frank and Ruth (Shaw) R.; m. Barbara Ann Cole, Oct. 28, 1961; children: Frank Kevin, Nichelle. Student, Xavier U., Cin. Baseball player Cin. Reds, 1956-65, Balt. Orioles, 1966-71, L.A., 1972, Calif. Angels, 1973-74; baseball player Cleve. Indians, 1974-76, mgr., 1975-77; coach Calif. Angels, 1977; coach Balt. Orioles, 1978-80, 85-87, mgr., 1988-91, asst. to gen. mgr., 1991—; mgr. San Francisco Giants, 1981-84; batting coach Milw. Brewers, 1984. Author: (with Al Silverman) My Life is Baseball, 1967, (with Barry Steinbach) Extra Innings, 1989, Frank the First Year, 1976. Named Rookie of Yr. Nat. League, 1956, Most Valuable Player, 1961, Am. League, 1966, Am. League Mgr. of Yr., 1982, 89; mem. World Series Championship Team, 1966, 70, Nat. League All-Star Team, 1956-57, 59, 61.62, 65, Am. League All-Star Team, 1966-67, 69-71, 74; inducted into Baseball Hall of Fame, 1982. Office: care Balt Orioles 333 W Camden St Baltimore MD 21201-2435

ROBINSON, FRANKLIN WESTCOTT, museum director, art historian; b. Providence, R.I., May 21, 1939; s. Charles Alexander Robinson Jr. and Celia (Sachs) Stillwell; m. Margaret Dredge, Aug. 14, 1967; 1 child, John Alexander. BA, Harvard U., 1961, MA, 1964, PhD, 1970. Instr. Wellesley Coll., 1968-69; asst. prof. Dartmouth Coll., 1969-75; assoc. prof. Williams Coll., 1975-79; dir. Williams Coll. Mus., 1976-79, Mus. of Art, R.I. Sch. Design, Providence, 1979-92, Herbert F. Johnson Mus. Art, Cornell U., Ithaca, N.Y., 1992—. Author: Gabriel Metsu, 1975, Seventeenth Century Dutch Drawings from American Collections, 1977, Dutch and Flemish

Paintings from the Ringling Mus, 1980. Fulbright fellow, 1961-62; recipient Clairborne Pell award R.I. State Coun. Arts, 1992. Mem. Assn. Art Mus. Dirs., Coll. Art Assn. Clubs: Century, Hope. Office: Herbert F Johnson Mus Art Cornell University Ithaca NY 14853-4001

ROBINSON, FRED COLSON, English language educator; b. Birmingham, Ala., Sept. 23, 1930; s. Emmett Colson and Morwenna Hope (Bennett) R.; m. Helen Caroline Wild, June 21, 1959; children: Lisa Karen, Eric Wild. BA, Birmingham So. Coll., 1953; MA, U. N.C., 1954, PhD, 1961; DLitt (hon.), Williams Coll., 1985; MA (hon.), Yale U., 1989. Instr. Stanford (Calif.) U., 1960-61, asst. prof., 1961-65, assoc. prof., 1967-71, prof. English philology, 1971-72; asst. prof. Cornell U., Ithaca, N.Y., 1965-66, assoc. prof., 1966-67; prof. Yale U., New Haven, 1972-83, Douglas Tracy Smith prof., 1983—, chmn. medieval studies, 1975-78, 80; vis. prof. Harvard U., Cambridge, Mass., 1983; mem. pub. com. Medieval Acad. Monographs, Cambridge, 1987-90. Author: Old English Literature: Select Bibliography, 1970, Beowulf and the Appositive Style, 1985, The Tomb of Beowulf, 1993, The Editing of Old English, 1994; co-author: A Bibliography...on Old English Literature, 1980, Old English Verse Texts from Many Sources: A Comprehensive Collection, 1991, A Guide to Old English, 5th edit., 1992; editor Old English Newsletter, 1966-73, Early English MSS in Facsimile, 1971—, Anglo-Saxon England, 1972—, Anglistica, 1981—; contbr. over 70 articles to scholarly jours. Trustee Yale Univ. Library Assocs., New Haven, 1986-89, 91-95. With U.S. Army, 1954-56. Fellow Guggenheim Found., 1974-75, Am. Coun. Learned Socs., 1968-69, Inst. Social and Econs. Rsch., Rhodes U., 1978, Japan Soc. for Promotion Sci., 1989; grantee NEH, 1976, 79, 81, 85, Am. Philos. Soc., 1973, 85. Fellow AAAS, Medieval Acad. Am. (pres. 1983-84, Haskins medal 1984), Brit. Acad. (corr.), Meddeleeue-vereinigung van Suidelike Afrika (corr.); mem. New Eng. Medieval Conf. (pres. 1982-83), Conn. Acad. Arts and Scis. (pres. 1980-85), Elizabethan Club (bd. govs. 1986—, v.p. 1989-90, pres. 1990-92), Manuscript Club (v.p. New Haven chpt. 1990-92), Phi Beta Kappa. Episcopalian. Office: Yale Univ Dept of English New Haven CT 06520

ROBINSON, FREDERIC MURRY, agricultural products company executive; b. 1934. With Hanes Corp., Winston-Salem, N.C., 1967-69, Pfizer Genetics, Olivia, Minn., 1969-77, Anderson Clayton Seed Co., Belmont, Iowa, 1977-79, Agrigenetics Corp., Wickliffe, Ohio, 1979-88; pres. Delta and Pine Land Co., Scott, Miss., 1988—. Office: Delta & Pine Land Co 1 Cotton Row Scott MS 38772*

ROBINSON, G. WILSE, molecular physicist, educator; b. Kansas City, Mo., July 27, 1924; s. George Wilse, Jr. R. and Elizabeth (Millett) Ivison; m. Ellen Elizabeth Johnson, June 5, 1950. B.S. in Chemistry, Ga. Inst. Tech., 1947, M.S. in Chemistry, 1949; Ph.D. in Chemistry, U. Iowa, Iowa City, 1952. Research asst. phys. chemistry U. Iowa, 1950-52; research fellow in chemistry U. Rochester, N.Y., 1952-54; asst. prof. chemistry Johns Hopkins U., Balt., 1954-59; assoc. prof. phys. chemistry Calif. Inst. Tech., Pasadena, 1959-61; prof. Calif. Inst. Tech., 1961-75; prof. phys. chemistry, dept. chmn. U. Melbourne, Australia, 1975-76; Robert A. Welch prof. chemistry, prof. physics Tex. Tech U., Lubbock, 1976—; FMC lectr. Princeton U., 1964; Bourke lectr., 1967, A.D. Little lectr., 1967; adv. to U.S. Army Research Office, Durham, 1969-72; Erskine fellow U. Canterbury, 1971; Guggenheim fellow, 1971-72. Author: (with S.-B. Zhu, S. Singh, M.W. Evans) Water in Biology, Chemistry and Physics. Experimental Overviews and Computational Methodologies, 1996; editor Chem. Physics, 1972-75; assoc. editor Jour. Chem. Physics, 1963-65; editl. adv. bd. Chem. Physics Letters, 1966-84, Jour. Molecular Spectroscopy, 1967-71, Photochemistry and Photobiology, 1971-75, Chem. Physics, 1975—, Jour. Phys. Chemistry, 1988-94; mem. editl. com. Ann. Rev. Phys. Chemistry, 1966-71; contbr. 280 sci. articles to profl. jours. Served with USN, 1944-46. Recipient Alexander von Humboldt prize, 1984. Fellow Am. Phys. Soc. Home: 4810 1st Pl Lubbock TX 79416-3150 Office: Tex Tech U Dept Chemistry PO Box 41061 Lubbock TX 79409-1061 *Many scientists are pioneers. A few are explorers. I like to think of myself as being in the latter category. It greatly increases the fun of doing science, but diminishes somewhat the recognition. Scientific developments are easy to remember. Not many persons remember the footprints.*

ROBINSON, GAIL PATRICIA, mental health counselor; b. Medford, Oreg., Dec. 31, 1936; d. Ivan T. and Evelyn H. (Hamilton) Skyrman; m. Douglas L. Smith; children: Shauna J., James D. BS in Edn., Oreg. State U., 1958, PhD in Counseling, 1978; MS in Counseling, Western Oreg. State Coll., 1974. Lic. profl. counselor, Oreg. Tchr. Monterey (Calif.) Pub. Schs., 1958-59; tchr. Corvallis (Oreg.) Pub. Schs., 1959-62, 69-75, counselor, 1977-81; pvt. practice Corvallis, 1977-95; vol. therapist Children's Svcs. divsn., Linn and Benton Counties, 1982-83; asst. prof. Western Oreg. State coll., 1977, counselor, 1982-83; mem. grad. faculty Oreg. State U., Corvallis, 1978-95; presenter workshops, lectr. in field. Contbr. articles to profl. jours. Mem. Benton County Mental Helath Citizens Adv. Bd., 1979-85, chair, 1982-83; trustee WCTU Children's Farm Home, 1978-84, chair child welfare com., 1982-83, pres., 1984; mem. Old Mill Sch. Adv. Bd., 1979-85, chair, 1979-81; bd. dirs. Cmty. Outreach, 1979-83; mem. Benton Com. for Prevention of Child Abuse, 1979-85, v.p., 1982; mem. Oreg. Bd. Lic. Profl. Counselors and Therapists, 1989-95, chair, 1989-90. Mem. ACA (govt. rels. com. 1988-91, professionalization com. 1988-92, pres. 1996-97), Am. Mental Health Counselors Assn. (chair consumer and pub. rels. com. 1988-91, bd. dirs. Western region 1989-91, chair strategic planning com. 1994-95, pres. 1992-93), Oreg. Counseling Assn. (chair licensure liaison com. 1985-91, exec. bd. 1985-88, steering com. 1986-87, register editorial com. 1985-86, Disting. Svc. award 1985, 87, Leona Tyler award 1989), Oreg. Mental Health Counselors Assn., Assn. Religion and Values in Counseling, Phi Delta Kappa (chpt. pres. 1979-80).

ROBINSON, GARY DALE, aerospace company executive; b. Colcord, W.Va., Sept. 9, 1938; s. Samuel Claytor and Madge (Fraley) R. Jr.; m. Lorelei Mary Christl, June 25, 1967; children: John Claytor, Kirk Dean. BA in Latin Am. Econ. History, So. Ill. U., 1964; PhD in Orgn. Behavior, Case Western Res. U., 1977. Program tng. chief The Peace Corps, Washington, 1969-71; cons. self-employed Ohio, 1971-76; health planning advisor USAID, San Salvador, El Salvador, 1976; project dir. Cen. Am. Inst. for Pub. Adminstrn. and Ministry of Health, San Jose, Costa Rica, 1977-78; mgmt. advisor Agy. for Internat. Devel., Santo Domingo, Dominican Republic, 1978-79; indsl. rels. mgr. Boeing Comml. Airplane Co., Everett, Wash., 1979-83; human resource mgr. Boeing Marine Systems, Renton, Wash., 1983-85; indsl. rels. mgr. The Boeing Co., Seattle, 1985-86, internal audit mgr., asst. to v.p. controller, 1986-90, 90—; cons. in field; adj. prof. Cen. Wash. U., Ellensburg, 1984—; mem. adv. bd. Drake, Beam & Moran, Seattle, 1991—; mem. adv. bd. and faculty Sch. of Advanced Studies in Orgnl. Cons., Santiago, chile, 1992—. Contbg. author: International Organizational Behavior, 1986. chmn. Metrocenter YMCA, Seattle, 1990-91; mem. Peace Corps Nat. Adv. Coun., Wash., 1988-89; founding mem. Pacific N.W. Orgn. Devel. Network, Seattle, 1982-86; bd. advisors Nat. Found. for Study Religion & Edn., Greensboro, N.C., 1984-87; mem. edn. com. World Affairs Coun., Seattle, 1987-88; sec., treas. The Edmonds Inst., Lynnwood, Wash., 1989-90; mem. Internat. Rels. Com. Named Paul Harris fellow Rotary Internat., 1989. Mem. The Wash. Ctr. for Mgmt. and Leadership (founder, bd. dirs.), Inst. for Internal Auditors (co-editor Pistas newsletter 1991—), Nat. Orgnl. Devel. Network, Acad. of Mgmt., Earth Svcs. Corps (adv. bd.). Avocations: running, walking, reading.

ROBINSON, GLEN O., law educator; b. Salt Lake City, June 6, 1936; s. Burgham H. and Fern (Osmond) R.; m. Kay Costley, Dec. 20, 1960; children: Dean, Jennifer. BA, Harvard U., 1958; JD, Stanford U., 1961. Bar: D.C. 1961. Assoc. Covington & Bowling, Washington, 1961-67; from asst. prof. to prof. law U. Minn., Mpls., 1967-74; commr. FCC, Washington, 1974-76; from prof. law to John C. Skinner prof. law U. Va., Charlottesville, 1976—; now David A. Harrison prof. law U Va., Charlottesville; U.S. rep. world adminstrn. radion conf. Dept State, 1978-79; vis. prof. Boston U., 1983-84. Author: The Forest Service, 1975, American Bureaucracy, 1991; co-author: The Administrative Process, 1986. With U.S. Army, 1962-64. Mem. Order of Coif. Office: U Va Sch Law Charlottesville VA 22901*

ROBINSON, HERBERT HENRY, III, educator, psychotherapist; b. Leavenworth, Wash., Mar. 31, 1933; s. Herbert Henry II and Alberta (Sperber) R.; m. Georgia Murial Jones, Nov. 24, 1954 (div. 1974); children: Cheri Dean Asbury, David Keith, Peri Elizabeth Layton, Tanda Rene Graff, Gaila Daire. Grad. of Theology, Bapt. Bible Coll., 1959; BA in Philosophy/Greek, Whitworth Coll., 1968; MA in Coll. Teaching, Ea. Wash. U., 1976; postgrad., Gonzaga U., 1980—. Cert. psychotherapist, perpetrator treatment program supervision. Choir dir. Twin City Bapt. Temple, Mishawaka, Ind., 1959-61; min. Inland Empire Bapt. Ch., Spokane, 1961-73; tchr. philosophy Spokane (Wash.) C.C., 1969-72; dir. Alternatives to Violence, Women in Crisis, Fairbanks, Alaska, 1985-87; tchr. pub. rels. U. Alaska, Fairbanks, 1986-87; dir. Alternatives to Violence Men Inc., Juneau, 1988-89; tchr. leadership mgmt. U. Alaska S.E., Juneau, 1988-89; min. Sci. of Mind Ctr., Sandpoint, Idaho, 1989-92; dir., therapist Tapio Counseling Ctr., Spokane, 1991—; cert. psychotherapist, supr. perpetrator treatment program Wash.; cons. Lilac Blind/Alpha Inc./Marshall Coll., Spokane, 1975-85, Alaska Placer Mining Co., Fairbanks, 1987; tchr. Spokane Falls C.C., Spokane, 1979-85; seminar, presenter Human Resource Devel., Spokane and Seattle, Wash., Pa., 1980; guest trainer United Way/Kellogg Found. Inst. for Volunteerism, Spokane, 1983. 1st trombone San Diego Marine Band, 1953-56, Spokane Symphony, 1961; bd. dirs. Tanani Learning Ctr., Fairbanks, 1987; mem. consensus bldg. team Sci. of Mind Ctr., Sandpoint, 1989-92. Cpl. USMC, 1953-56. Mem. ACA, Assn. for Humanistic Edn. and Devel., Assn. for Religious Values in Counseling, Internat. Assn. Addictions and Offender Counselors, Internat. Assn. Marriage and Family Counselors, Am. Assn. Profl. Hypnotherapists, Masterson Inst. Home: 11611 E Maxwell Ave Spokane WA 99206-4867 Office: Tapio Counseling Svcs Red Flag Bldg # 101A 104 S Freya Tapio Ctr Spokane WA 99202

ROBINSON, HOBART KRUM, management consulting company executive; b. Quincy, Mass., Oct. 8, 1937; s. Hobart Krum and Charlotte Elizabeth (Hall) R.; m. Gerd Ingela Janhede, Oct. 17, 1964; children: Steven Whitney, Karina Jill, Peter Danforth. BA, Williams Coll., 1959; MBA, Columbia U., 1964. Market analyst Mobil Chem. Co., Richmond, Va., 1964-67; mgr. program analysis and control Polaroid Corp., Cambridge, Mass., 1967-69; exec. v.p., dir. Simplex Wire and Cable, Inc., North Berwick, Maine, 1969-73; sr. engagement mgr. McKinsey and Co., Inc., N.Y.C., 1973-76; prin. McKinsey and Co., Inc., Copenhagen, 1977-81, N.Y.C., 1985-89; prin. McKinsey and Co., Inc., Stockholm, 1989-95, dir. adminstrn. Eastern Europe, 1993-95; dir. adminstrn. McKinsey and Co., Inc., N.Y.C., 1995—; pres. and chief exec. officer Brink's Inc., Darien, Conn., 1981-84; dir. Burlington No. Air Freight, Inc., Newport Beach, Calif., 1982-84. Pres. Am. Club in Copenhagen, 1980-81; dir. Fulbright Commn., Copenhagen, 1980-81. Served as lt. USNR, 1959-62. Republican. Episcopalian. Clubs: Innis Arden Golf (Old Greenwich, Conn.) (gov. 1982-87, pres. 1986-87); Tournament Players (Ponte Vedra, Fla.); Ullna Golf (Akersberga, Sweden). Home: 14 Old Farm Ln Old Greenwich CT 06870 Office: McKinsey & Co Inc 55 E 52d St New York NY 10055

ROBINSON, HUGH GRANVILLE, consulting management company executive; b. Washington, Aug. 4, 1932; s. James Hill and Wilhelmina (Thomas) R.; m. Matilda Turner; 1 stepdau., Mia; children by previous marriage—Hugh Granville, Susan K. Student, Williams Coll., 1949-50; B.S., U.S. Mil. Acad., 1954; M.S., MIT, 1959; LL.D., Williams Coll., 1983. Commd. 2d lt. U.S. Army, 1954, advanced through grades to maj. gen., 1983; platoon leader, co. comdr. Co. B, 185th Engrs. Bn., Korea, 1955; platoon leader, ops. officer 74th Engr. Co., Korea, 1955-56; br. chief Engr. Supply Control Office, St. Louis, 1956-58; chief Catalog and Authorization div. Engr. Supply Control Agy., Orleans, France, 1960-62; co. comdr. 553d Engr. Bn., Orleans, 1962-63; chief combat br. War Plans div. Engr. Strategic Studies Group, Washington, 1963-65; Army asst. to armed forces aide to Pres. Washington, 1965-69; comdr. 39th Engr. Bn., Vietnam, 1969-70; br. chief war plans div. Office Dep. Chief Staff for Ops., Washington, 1970-71; assigned Nat. War Coll., 1972; comdr. 3d regt. U.S. Corps Cadets, West Point, N.Y., 1973-74, U.S. Army Engr. Sch. Brigade, Fort Belvoir, Va., 1974-76; dist. engr. U.S. Army Engr. Dist., Los Angeles, 1976-78; dep. dir. civil works office Chief of Engrs., Washington, 1978-80; comdr. Southwestern Div., U.S. Army C.E., 1980-83; ret., 1983; v.p. Southland Corp., Dallas, 1983-88; pres. Cityplace Devel. Corp.; sr. v.p. Grigsby Brandford Powell, Inc., 1988—; now chmn., chief executive officer The Tetra Group, Inc., Dallas, 1989—; mem. Mississippi River Commn., 1980-83, bd. engrs. for rivers and harbors, 1980-83, Coastal Engring. Rsch. Bd., 1980-83; bd. dirs. Belo Corp., TU-Electric, Smith Environ. Tech., Inc., Columbus Realty Trust, Circuit City Stores, Inc., Guaranty Fed.; chmn. Dallas Fed. Res. Bd., 1991. Mem. nat. bd. dirs. Keep Am. Beautiful, 1981-85; bd. dirs. Dallas Symphony, 1981-85, Dallas United Way, 1984-92, Baylor U. Med. Ctr. Found., 1983-91, Dallas Opera, 1983-90, Dallas Citizens Coun., 1987-91, Greater Dallas C. of C., 1986-91, Vietnam Vets Meml. Fund Tex.; chmn. African Am. Mus., Dallas Youth Svcs. Corp.; trustee Dallas Mus. Fine Arts, 1988-93. Mem. Am. Soc. Mil. Engrs. (past sec. Orleans chpt., regional v.p. Tex.), Assn. U.S. Army, Dallas Black C. of C., ASCE. Methodist. Office: The Tetra Group Inc Ste 550 8150 N Central Expwy Dallas TX 75206

ROBINSON, HUGH R., retired marketing executive; b. Syracuse, N.Y., Sept. 18, 1922; s. Frank J. and Gladys (Hunt) R.; m. Evelyn De Mattia, Nov. 24, 1949; children: Susan, Hugh R., Patrice. BS, Syracuse U., 1949. Dist. mgr. Syracuse China, 1949-59; with Royal Worcester Porcelain Co., N.Y.C., 1959-77; v.p. sales Royal Worcester Porcelain Co., 1971-75, pres., 1975-76; pres. Royal Worcester Spode, Inc., 1977, Lance Internat., N.Y.C., 1977-84; v.p., dir. Caithness Glass Inc., N.Y.C., 1980-84; v.p. sales amnd mktg. Weil Ceramics & Glass Inc., 1985-86, CEO, exec. v.p., 1986-88; CEO LLadro U.S.A. Inc., 1988-91; v.p. Lladro Realty, Inc., 1988-94, Lladro Galleries, Inc., 1988-94; retired, 1994; advisor Lladro Group, Valencia, Spain, 1991—. Served with USAAF, 1942-46. Mem. Alumni Assn. Syracuse U., Lladro Collectors Soc. (dir.). Home: 6101 34th St W Bradenton FL 34210

ROBINSON, IRWIN JAY, lawyer; b. Bay City, Mich., Oct. 8, 1928; s. Robert R. and Anne (Kaplan) R.; m. Janet Binder, July 7, 1957; children: Elizabeth Binder Schubiner, Jonathan Meyer, Eve Kimberly Wiener. AB, U. Mich., 1950; JD, Columbia U., 1953. Bar: N.Y. 1956. Assoc. Breed Abbott & Morgan, N.Y.C., 1955-58; asst. to ptnrs. Dreyfus & Co., N.Y.C., 1958-59; assoc. Greenbaum Wolff & Ernst, N.Y.C., 1959-65; ptnr. Greenbaum Wolff & Ernst, 1966-76; sr. ptnr. Rosenman & Colin, N.Y.C., 1976-90; of counsel Pryor, Cashman, Sherman & Flynn, 1990-92; sr. ptnr. Phillips, Nizer, Benjamin, Krim & Ballon, N.Y.C., 1992—; treas. Saarsteel, Inc., Whitestone, N.Y., 1970—. Bd. dirs. Henry St. Settlement, N.Y.C., 1960-85, Jewish Cmty. Ctr. Assn. N.Am., N.Y.C., 1967-94; bd. dirs. Heart Rsch. Found., 1989-94, pres., 1991-93. Mem. ABA, N.Y. State Bar Assn., Assn. Bar City of N.Y., Internat. Bar Assn., Philippine-Am. C. of C. (founder, bd. dirs. 1992-95, pres. 1992-95), Vietnam-Am. C. of C. (founder, bd. dirs. 1992-95, pres. 1992-95), Sunningdale Country Club (Scarsdale, N.Y.). Jewish. Home: 4622 Grosvenor Ave Bronx NY 10471-3305 Office: Phillips Nizer Benjamin Krim & Ballon 666 Fifth Ave New York NY 10103-0084

ROBINSON, JACK ALBERT, retail drug stores executive; b. Detroit, Feb. 26, 1930; s. Julius and Fannie (Aizkowitz) R.; m. Aviva Freedman, Dec. 21, 1952; children: Shelby, Beth, Abigail. B in Pharmacy, Wayne State U., 1952. Founder, chief exec. officer, chmn. bd. Perry Drug Stores, Inc., Pontiac, Mich., 1957-95; founder, chmn., pres. JAR Group LLC, Bloomfield, Mich., 1996. Chmn. Wayne State U. Fund, Detroit, 1986, Concerned Citizens for the Arts in Mich., 1990, 91—; chmn. ann. fund Detroit Symphony Orch.; bd. dirs. United Way of Pontiac, Mich., 1986, United Found. of Detroit, 1986, Pontiac Area Urban League, Cmty. Found., S.E. Mich., Detroit Svc. Group, Save Orch. Hall, Inc., Cranbrook Inst. Sci., Jewish Fedn. Apts., Wetzman Inst. Sci., Holocaust Meml. Ctr., Harper-Grace Hosp., Detroit; past dir. Pontiac Symphony Boys Club, Detroit Osteo. Hosp.; pres. United Jewish Found. Met. Detroit, 1992, Greater Detroit Interfaith Round Table NCCJ, 1994-95, co-chmn., 1992; pres. Jewish Fedn. Met. Detroit, 1992-94. Recipient Disting. Alumni award Wayne State U. Coll. Pharmacy, 1975, Eleanor Roosevelt Humanities award from State of Israel, 1978, B'nai B'rith Youth Svcs. Am. Tradition award, 1982, Wayne State U. Disting. Alumni award, 1985, Tree of Life award Jewish Nat. Fund, 1985, Disting. Citizen award Pontiac Boy Scouts Am., 1985, Corp. Leadership award Wayne State U., 1985, Booker T. Washington Bus. Assn. Brotherhood award, 1986, Humanitarian award March of Dimes, 1987, award Weizmann Rsch. Inst., 1987, Humanitarian award Variety Club, 1988, Fred M. Butzel award Jewish Fedn. Met. Detroit, 1991, B'nai B'rith Great Am. Traditions award, 1991, Cmty. Svc. award Am. Arabic and Jewish Friends, 1995; named Entrepreneur of Yr. Harvard U. Bus. Sch., Detroit, 1982. Mem. Nat. Assn. Chain Drug Stores (chmn. 1987, Lifetime Achievement award 1995, Robert B. Begley award 1995), Am. Pharm. Assn., Am. Found. for Pharm. Edn. (bd. dirs.), Econ. Club (bd. dirs. Detroit chpt.). Avocations: skiing, jogging, photography, classical music, glass collecting. Office: JAR Group LLC 500 North Woodward Ste 220 Bloomfield Hills MI 48304

ROBINSON, JAMES ARTHUR, university president emeritus, political scientist; b. Blackwell, Okla., June 9, 1932; s. William L. and Ethel Bell (Hicks) R.; children: Adelaide Ethel, William Luke Walton. AB, George Washington U., 1954, DPS (hon.), 1977; MA, U. Okla., 1955; PhD, Northwestern U., 1957; LLD (hon.), Kyungpook (Korea) Nat. U., 1979; cert. Inst. for Ednl. Mgmt., Harvard U., 1986. Instr. polit. sci. Northwestern U., 1958-59, asst. prof., 1959-62, assoc. prof., 1962-64; prof. polit. sci. Ohio State U., Columbus, 1964-71; dir. Mershon Center, 1967-70, v.p. acad. affairs, provost, 1969-71; pres., prof. polit. sci. Macalester Coll., St. Paul, 1971-74; pres. U. West Fla., Pensacola, 1974-88, pres. emeritus, 1988—, Regents prof. polit. sci., mgmt., ednl. leadership, 1988—. Author: (with R. C. Snyder) National and International Decision Making, 1961, Congress and Foreign Policy Making, rev. edit, 1967, House Rules Committee, 1964. Recipient Manning Dauer award Fla. Polit. Sci. Assn., 1992; Congl. fellow Am. Polit. Sci. Assn., 1957-58. Club: Cosmos (Washington).

ROBINSON, JAMES DIXON, III, corporate executive; b. Atlanta, Nov. 19, 1935; s. James Dixon Jr. and Josephine (Crawford) R.; m. Bettye Bradley (div.); children: Emily E. Robinson-Cook, James Dixon IV; m. Linda Gosden, July 27, 1984. BS, Ga. Inst. Tech., 1957; MBA, Harvard U., 1961; LHD (hon.), Spelman Coll., 1982; LLD (hon.), Adelphi U., 1982. Officer various depts. Morgan Guaranty Trust Co. of N.Y., N.Y.C., 1961-66, asst. v.p., staff asst. to chmn. bd. and pres., 1967-68; gen. partner corp. fin. dept. White, Weld & Co., 1968-70; exec. v.p. Am. Express Co., N.Y.C., 1970-75, pres., 1975-77, chmn. bd. dirs., CEO, 1977-93; pres. J.D. Robinson, Inc., N.Y.C., 1993—; pres., chief exec. officer Am. Express Internat. Banking Corp., 1971-73; bd. dirs. Bristol-Myers Squibb Co., Coca Cola Co., Union Pacific Corp.; former chmn., mem. Adv. Com. Trade Policy and Negotiations; bd. dirs. N.Y.C. Partnership. Chmn. bd. mgrs., chmn. bd. overseers Meml. Sloan-Kettering Cancer Ctr.; mem. Brookings Instn. Lt. USNR, 1957-59. Mem. Bus. Roundtable (former co-chmn.), N.Y.C. C. of C. and Industry (bd. dirs.), Brookings Inst., Japan Soc. (bd. dirs.), Coun. on Competitiveness, Econ. Club (N.Y.C.), Pilgrims of U.S. Club. Office: J D Robinson Inc 126 E 56th St 22nd fl New York NY 10022*

ROBINSON, JAMES G., film production executive; five children. Former owner automobile distributorship; businessman Balt.; founder, now chmn., chief exec. officer Morgan Creek Prodns. Co-exec. producer films Young Guns, 1988, Skin Deep, 1989, Enemies A Love Story, 1989, Renegades, 1989, Major League, 1989, Coupe de Ville, 1990, Nightbreed, 1990, Young Guns II, 1990, Pacific Heights, 1990, The Exorcist III, 1990, Robin Hood: Prince of Thieves, 1991, Freejack, 1992, White Sands, 1992, Stay Tuned, 1992, The Crush, 1993, True Romance, 1993, Ace Ventura: Pet Detective, 1994, Major League II, 1994, Trial By Jury, 1994, Silent Fall, 1994. Office: Morgan Creek Prodns 4000 Warner Blvd Bldg 76 Burbank CA 91522-0001

ROBINSON, JAMES KENNETH, lawyer, educator; b. Grand Rapids, Mich., Nov. 27, 1943; s. Kenneth and Marguerite (Anderson) R.; m. Marietta Sebree; children: Steven James, Renee Elizabeth. BA with honors, Mich. State U., 1965; JD magna cum laude, Wayne State U., 1968. Bar: Mich. 1968, U.S. Dist. Ct. (ea. and we. dists) Mich. 1969, U.S. Ct. Appeals (6th cir.) 1969, U.S. Supreme Ct. 1977. Law clk. to judge U.S. Ct. Appeals (6th cir.), 1968-69; assoc. Miller, Canfield, Paddock & Stone, Detroit, 1969-71; assoc., then ptnr. Honigman Miller Schwartz and Cohn, Detroit, 1972-77, ptnr., 1981-93, chmn. litigation dept.; U.S. atty. Ea. Dist. Mich., 1977-80; prof., dean Law Sch. Wayne State U., Detroit, 1993—; adj. prof. Detroit Coll. Law, 1970-73, Wayne State U. Law Sch., 1973-84; mem. evidence test drafting com.-multistate bar exam Nat. Conf. Bar Examiners, 1975—; mem. adv. com. on evidence rules Jud. Conf. U.S., 1993—; chmn. com. on rules of evidence Mich. Supreme Ct., 1975-78; lectr. Mich. Jud. Inst., 1977—, Mich. Inst. Continuing Legal Edn. Author: (with others) Introducing Evidence-A Practical Guide for Michigan Lawyers, 1988; (with others) Scope of Discovery, 1986; contbg. author Evidence in America - The Federal Rules in the States, 1987; also articles; editor in chief Wayne Law Rev., 1967-68. Chmn. Gov.'s Commn. on Future Higher Edn. in Mich., 1983-84; pres. State Bar of Mich., 1990-91, commr. 1980-81, 83-91. Recipient Disting. Alumni award Wayne State U. Law Sch., 1979, 1986. Fellow Am. Bar Found., Mich. Bar Found., Am. Coll. Trial Lawyers, Internat. Soc. Barristers, am. Acad. of Appellate Lawyers; mem. ABA (litigation and criminal justice sects., lectr.), Fed. Bar Assn. (dir. 1975-81), Detroit Bar Assn. (bd. dirs. 1975-81), Nat. Assn. Former U.S. Attys. (pres. 1984-85), Am. Law Inst., 6th Cir. Jud. Conf., Wayne U. Law Alumni Assn. (pres. 1975-76), Detroit Club, Detroit Yacht Club. Office: Wayne State U Law Sch Detroit MI 48202

ROBINSON, JAMES WILLIAM, retired management consultant; b. Bklyn., Feb. 22, 1919; s. Charles Edward and Adelaide (Reimer) R.; m. Dorothy L. Luckow, July 5, 1946; 1 child, Joan Barbara. AB, Cornell U., 1940, LLB, 1942. Bar: N.Y. 1942. Assoc. atty. Whitman, Ransom & Coulson, 1946-57; with Westvaco Corp., N.Y.C., 1957-69, sec., 1966-69; prin., mng. dir. Georgeson & Co. Inc., N.Y.C., 1969-82; mng. dir. Morrow & Co., N.Y.C., 1982-90; pres. J.W. Robinson Assocs., Inc., Gig Harbor, Wash., 1990—; mem. adv. com. shareholder comms. SEC; com. on shareowner comms. N.Y. Stock Exch., 1986-92. Editor: Tender Offers Handbook, Proxy Rules Handbook. Capt. AUS, 1942-46. Decorated Bronze (V) Star medal. Mem. ABA, N.Y. State Bar Assn., Assn. Bar City N.Y., Am. Soc. Corp. Secs., Canterwood Country Club, Phi Delta Phi, Lambda Chi Alpha. Home and Office: 4820 Old Stump Dr NW Gig Harbor WA 98332-8899

ROBINSON, JAY (THURSTON), artist; b. Detroit, Aug. 1, 1915; s. Carter Boston and Marie Rose (Steger) R.; m. Dorothy June Whipple, Sept. 15, 1937 (dec. 1968); children: Theodore Carter, Thomas Whipple, James Jay; m. Anne Frances Helen Posch, Nov. 5, 1970. BA, Yale U., 1937; MFA, Cranbrook Acad. Art, 1943. Illustrator: (books) Seventeenth Summer (Maureen Daly), 1948, The New York Guide Book, 1964; contbr. illustrations to others; one-man shows include, Guggenheim Mus. Non-Objective Painting, N.Y.C., 1947, Milch Galleries, N.Y.C., 1948, 51, 53, 54, 55, 56, J.B. Speed Art Mus., Louisville, 1953, Dayton Art Inst., 1953, Phila. Art Alliance, 1957, Monede Gallery, N.Y.C., 1961, 62, Raymond Burr Galleries, Beverly Hills, Calif., 1963, xxth Century West Gallery, N.Y.C., 1968, E. Kuhlik Gallery, N.Y.C., 1971, New Canaan Soc. for Arts, 1983, Broome St. Gallery, N.Y.C., 1994, group shows include, Guggenheim Mus., 1947, 49, Carnegie Inst., Pitts., 1949, Des Moines Art Center, 1950, Butler Inst., Youngstown, Ohio, 1953, also Audubon Artists, N.Y.C., Corcoran Gallery, Washington, Mich. Artists, Detroit, NAD, N.Y.C., Pa. Acad., Phila., Provincetown (Mass.) Annual, Va. Biennial, Richmond; represented in permanent collections, including, Detroit Inst. Art, Houston Mus. Fine Art, Witte Meml. Mus., San Antonio, Philbrook Art Center, Tulsa; Berea Coll., Goucher Coll., Fisk U.; represented in also corp. collections, including, IBM; Republic Steel Co., Prentice-Hall Pub., portrait painter, designer china and textiles. Served with OSS, 1943; Served with USN, 1943-46. Louis Comfort Tiffany Found. award, 1950; various purchase awards Am. Acad. Arts and Letters, 1951-64; Outstanding Alumnus award Detroit Country Day Sch., 1966. Mem. Artist Equity Assn. N.Y. Home and Studio: 305 East Landing Williamsburg VA 23185-8254 *I have always been drawn to the theme of Man in His Environment. By extension to our own, I love jazz music, many of whose players I have painted; classic cars; Japanese gardens; good company and active social life. Travel enables me to see what others have done and are doing, all of us alike in trying to cope as best we can. In painting, I can not only portray but participate in what goes on on our planet.*

ROBINSON, JERRY H., lawyer; b. Mason City, Iowa, Dec. 4, 1932; s. Moe Lester and Annette (Kropman) R.; m. Leona Esther Ohsman, Aug. 26, 1956 (dec.); children: Vicki Lynn, Brenda Jo, Andrew Franklin. B.S.c., U. Iowa, 1954; J.D., Stanford U., 1960. Bar: Calif. 1960; cert. tax specialist. Ptnr. Heller, Ehrman, White & McAuliffe, San Francisco, 1960—. Author, editor: Attorney's Guide to Pension & Profit Sharing Plans, 1973, 2d edit. 1978. Contbr. articles to profl. jours. Mem. exec. com. atty. sect. Jewish Community Fedn., San Francisco. Served to lt. U.S. Army, 1954-56; Germany. Fellow Am. Coll. Tax Counsel; mem. State Bar Tax Sect. (chmn. 1979, Jud Klein award 1984), ABA (tax sect.), Calif. State Bar Assn., San Francisco Bar Assn. (cmn. tax sect. 1970), Commonwealth Club of Calif.

Democrat. Jewish. Avocations: photography, traveling, gardening, woodworking, piano. Home: 28 Roselyn Ter San Francisco CA 94118-4321*

ROBINSON, JOHN ALAN, logic and computer science educator; b. Halifax, Eng., Mar. 9, 1930; came to U.S., 1952; naturalized citizen, 1990.; s. Harry and Clara (Pilkington) R.; m. Gwen Groves, Dec. 18, 1954; children: Alan Groves, Hugh Parke Custis, Gwen Owen. B.A. in Classics with honours, Corpus Christi Coll., Cambridge (Eng.) U., 1952; M.A., 1955; M.A. in Philosophy, U. Ore., 1953; M.A., Princeton, 1955, Ph.D., 1956; D in Applied Sci. honoris causa, Leuven, 1988; D in Philosophy honoris causa, Uppsala, 1994. Operations research analyst E.I. du Pont de Nemours & Co., Inc., 1956-60; post-doctoral research fellow U. Pitts., 1960-61; mem. faculty Rice U., 1961-67, prof. philosophy, 1964-65, prof. computer sci. and philosophy, 1965-66, prof. computer sci., 1966-67; disting. prof. logic and computer sci. Syracuse U., 1967-84, Univ. prof., 1984-92, univ. prof. emeritus, 1993—; cons. in applied math. divsn. Argonne Nat. Lab., 1961-67, Stanford Linear Acceleration Ctr., 1966-68; vis. rsch. fellow Australian Nat. U., 1989; Fujitsu vis. prof. U. Tokyo, 1991-92. Author: Logic: Form and Function, 1979; founder, editor-in-chief Jour. Logic Programming, 1984-86; contbr. articles to profl. jours. Served with RAF, 1948-49. Recipient Sr. U.S. Scientists prize Humboldt Found., 1995; Guggenheim Found. fellow, 1967-68; hon. rsch. fellow U. Edinburgh, 1967—. Fellow Am. Assn. for Artificial Intelligence; mem. Kokusai Bunka Kaikan (Tokyo). Office: 96 Highland Ave Greenfield MA 01301-3606

ROBINSON, JOHN BECKWITH, development management consultant; b. Portland, Oreg., May 23, 1922; s. Jewell King and Arvilla Agnes (Beckwith) R.; m. Dilys Walters, Sept. 8, 1945; children—John Gwilym, David Gwyn. B.A., U. Oreg., 1944; postgrad., U. Shrivenham, Eng., 1945, U. Oxford, Eng., 1946, Am. U., 1947. Staff Bur. Budget, 1948, 51-52; sr. program and budget officer UNESCO, 1948-51; chief personnel policy Mut. Security Agy., Washington, 1952-54; program officer Mut. Security Agy., Guatemala, 1954-59; planning officer, later acting asst. dep. dir. for program and planning Mut. Security Agy., Washington, 1959-61; dep. U.S. rep. devel. assistance com. OECD, 1961-64; asst. dir. devel. policy Pakistan, 1964-68; dep. dir. North Coast Affairs, AID, State Dept., Washington, 1969-71; dep. mission dir. U.S. Econ. Aid Program, Colombia, 1971-73; mission dir. U.S. Econ. Aid Program, Dominican Republic, 1973-76, Honduras, 1976-79; privatization adviser Gov. of Costa Rica, 1986-88; prin. assoc. J.B. Robinson & Assocs. (devel. mgmt. cons.), 1979—; mem. faculty, fellow Harvard U., 1968-69; cons. NATO, 1951, UN, 1959. Served to 1st lt., inf. AUS, 1943-46, ETO. Mem. Oriental Club (London), DACOR BACON House (Washington), Minchinhampton Golf Club, Minchinhampton Probus Club (pres. 1983-84). Episcopalian. Address: Anglezarke, The Hithe, Rodborough Common, Stroud GL5 5BN Gloucestershire, England also: 7130 SW Gable Pky Portland OR 97225-2620 *Always do more than what is asked for the task at hand. The extra effort always leads to unexpected opportunities for career advancement. Helping others to realize their potential has its own rewards and their success helps to realize your own hopes and aspirations, improve your own quality of life and satisfaction in a life well-spent. Never underestimate the contribtion of your wife and family.*

ROBINSON, JOHN BOWERS, JR., bank holding company executive; b. Laconia, N.H., Oct. 9, 1946; s. John Bowers and Lee (Osborn) R.; m. Jane Frances Moore, Aug. 31, 1968; children: John Paul, Claire Frances, David Moore, Leanne Elizabeth, Gregory Joseph, Peter August. BA, Fairfield U., 1968; MBA, Adelphi U., 1977. V.p., asst. to pres. Hempstead Bank, N.Y., 1977-79, exec. v.p., 1979-81, pres., 1981-82; v.p. planning Norstar Bancorp, Inc., Albany, N.Y., 1982-84, exec. v.p., 1984-87, pres., 1987-88; mng. dir. govt. banking Fleet Fin. Group, Albany, 1988—; bd. dirs. Fleet Securities, Inc.; mem. N.Y. State Banking Bd., 1990—, N.Y. State Bus. Coun., 1990—, Albany Med. Ctr., 1989—, Siena Coll., Loudonville, N.Y., 1989—. Mem. Ft. Orange Club, Schuyler Meadows Club. Home: 81 Old Niskayuna Rd Loudonville NY 12211-1349 Office: Fleet Fin Group Peter D Kiernan Plz Albany NY 12207

ROBINSON, JOHN C., manufacturing executive, light; b. 1943. Pres., coo King Bearing Inc., Cleve., 1992—. Office: Bearings Inc 3600 Euclid Ave Cleveland OH 44115-2515*

ROBINSON, JOHN DAVID, retired army officer; b. Concord, Mass., June 9, 1937; m. Roberta Jean Small; children: Mark D., Karen L. BA, U. Maine, 1961; MBA, U. Ala., 1972. Commd. 2d lt. U.S. Army, 1961, advanced through grades to maj. gen., 1990; student Naval War Coll., Newport, R.I., 1979-80; asst. tng. and doctrine, command systems mgr. U.S. Army Aviation Ctr., Ft. Rucker, Ala., 1980; dir. army model improvement program U.S. Army Combined Arms Ctr., Ft. Leavenworth, Kans., 1980-83; comdr. 9th Cav. Brigade, 9th Inf. Div., Ft. Lewis, Wash., 1983-85; dep. asst. comdt. U.S. Army Aviation Ctr., Ft. Rucker, 1985-86; comdg. gen. Tng. and Doctrine Analysis Command, Ft. Leavenworth, 1986-88; dep. dir. for force structure, resource and assessment Joint Staff, Washington, 1988-89, dir., 1989-91; comdg. gen. U.S. Army Aviation Ctr., Ft. Rucker, 1991-94; v.p. ops. Raytheon Aerospace, Madison, Miss., 1994—. Decorated Def. D.S.M., Army D.S.M., Legion of Merit (2), Air medal with V device, Bronze Star with oak leaf. Mem. Assn. U.S. Army (sr. v.p.), Army Aviation Assn. Am. (nat. exec. bd.). Home: 109 Clairemont Dr Ridgeland MS 39157 Office: Raytheon Aerospace 555 Industrial Dr S Madison MS 39110-9073

ROBINSON, JOHN GWILYM, conservationist; b. Paris, Nov. 22, 1949; s. John Beckwith and Dilys (Walters) R.; m. Linda Cox, June 8, 1974; children: David Andrew Cox, Amandia Siân Cox. BA in Zoology with honors, Swarthmore Coll., 1971; PhD in Zoology, U. N.C., 1977. Postdoctoral fellow dept. zool. rsch. Nat. Zool. Park, Smithsonian Instn., Washington, 1977-80, zoologist, 1980-83; affiliate assoc. curator Fla. Mus. Natural History, Gainesville, 1983—; affiliate assoc. prof. dept. wildlife and range scis. U. Fla., 1983-85, assoc. prof., 1985-90, courtesy prof., 1990—, dir. program for studies in tropical conservation, 1980-90; dir. wildlife conservation internat. Wildlife Conservation Soc. (former N.Y. Zool. Soc.), Bronx, N.Y., 1990-93, v.p. internat. conservation, 1993—; program dir. integrated approaches to tng. in conservation and sustainable devel. Pew Charitable Trusts, Phila., 1988-93; chmn. adv. group Sustainable Use Initiative, World Conservation Union, 1995—, mem. steering com. Species Survival Commn., 1991-93, regional mem. N.Am. and Caribbean, 1991-93, primate specialist Species Survival Commn., 1985—, sustainablue use specialist group, 1992—. Mem. editl. bd. Primates, 1991—; bd. editors Conservation Biology, 1993—; sci. com. Conservation and Mgmt., 1993—; editor: (with L.D. Navarro) Diversidad Biologica en La Reserva de la Biosphera de Sian Ka'an, 1990; (with K. H. Redford) Neotropical Wildlife Use and Conservation, 1991; contbr. articles to profl. jours., chpts. to books. Mem. tech. adv. bd. Fundaçao Biodiversitas, Brazil, 1989—; mem. coun. advisors Branger Found., Venezuela; bd. dirs. Wild Things Inc., 1992—, Global Coral Reef Alliance, 1992—, Greentree Group, Inc., 1993—, Sociedade Civil Mamirauá, Brazil, Sócio Efetivo, 1993—; bd. dirs. World Parks Endowment, Inc., 1994—. Mem. AAAS, Am. Soc. Primatologists (conservation com. 1984-88), Internat. Primatological Soc. (election com. 1990—, Martha T. Galante endowment overview com. 1989—, conservation com. 1986-92), Assn. Tropical Biology, Fauna and Flora Preservation Soc. Office: Wildlife Conservation Soc 185th St and Southern Blvd Bronx NY 10460

ROBINSON, JOHN LEWIS, geography educator; b. Leamington, Ont., Can., July 9, 1918; s. William John and Emily Laverne (Dunphy) R.; m. Josephine Rowan, Oct. 14, 1944; children: David, Jo-Anne, Patricia. B.A., Western Ont. U., 1940; M.A., Syracuse U., 1942; Ph.D., Clark U., 1946; LLD (hon.), Western Ont. U., 1984; DSc (hon.), U. B.C., 1994. Geographer N.W.T. Adminstrn., Ottawa, Ont., 1943-46; prof., head dept. geography U. B.C., Vancouver, 1946-68, prof. geography, 1968-85, prof. emeritus, 1985—. Author 14 books on aspects of regional geography of Can., including British Columbia: 100 Years of Geographical Change, 1973, Themes in the Regional Geography of Canada, 1983, 2d edit., 1989; contbr. articles to profl. jours. Recipient citation of merit Assn. Am. Geographers, 1966; Massey medal Canadian Geog. Soc., 1971. Mem. Canadian Assn. Geographers (pres. 1956, citation for service to profession 1976). Office: U BC, Dept Geography, Vancouver, BC Canada V6T 1Z2

ROBINSON, JOHN MINOR, lawyer, retired business executive; b. Uniontown, Pa., Mar. 18, 1910; s. John M. and Martha (Downs) R. A.B., Harvard U., 1932, LL.B, 1935. Bar: Calif. 1936. Assoc. firm Macdonald & Pettit, 1935-41; partner firm Musick, Peeler & Garrett, 1947-77; v.p., sec. Consol. Western Steel div. U.S. Steel Corp. (and predecessors), 1941-57. Clubs: Calif. (past pres. L.A.), Pacific Union (San Francisco); Cypress Point (Pebble Beach, Calif.); The Old Capital (Monterey, Calif.); Royal and Ancient Golf of St. Andrews (Fife, Scotland). Office: 9500 Center St Carmel CA 93923

ROBINSON, JOHN PETER, film composer, keyboardist; b. Fulmer, Eng., Sept. 16, 1945; s. John Lacey and Winifred Gertrude (Hayes) R.; m. Cecilia Karin Angela Gardtman, Nov. 4, 1983 (div. Jan. 1988); 1 child, Aimee-Jane Dadswell. Diploma, Royal Acad. Music, London, 1967. Founding mem., keyboardist Quatermass, 1969-71; keyboardist Stanley Clarke's School Days Band, 1977-78, Al Stewart, 1978-79; keyboardist Shawn Phillips, 1971-76, Stomu Yamashta, 1976-77, Al Jarreau, 1980-81, Eric Clapton, 1984, Phil Collins/Brand X, 1978-85. Composer for films The Believers, 1986, Cocktail, 1988 (Box Office award ASCAP 1988), Cadillac Man, 1990, Wayne's World, 1992 (Box Office award ASCAP 1992), Highlander 3, 1995. Recipient Best Music award nomination Acad. Sci. Fiction Fantasy/Horror Films, 1988. Home: care FMA 4146 Lankershim Blvd # 400 North Hollywood CA 91602

ROBINSON, JOSEPH EDWARD, geology educator, consulting petroleum geologist; b. Regina, Sask., Can., June 25, 1925; came to U.S., 1976; s. Webb Gabriel Wilton and Blanche Marion (Schiefner) R.; m. Mary Corrine Maclaughlin, Nov. 1, 1952 (div. 1977); children: Joseph Christopher, John Edward, Timothy Webb. B.Eng., McGill U., 1950, M.Sc., 1951; Ph.D., U. Alta., 1968. Registered profl. engr., Que., Can. Geophysicist Imperial Oil Ltd., Can., 1951-68; sr. geologist Union Oil Co. Can., Calgary, Alta., Can., 1968-76; cons. geologist J.E. Robinson & Assocs., Syracuse, N.Y., 1976—; prof. geology Syracuse U., 1976-91, prof. emeritus, 1991—. Author: Computer Applications in Petroleum Geology, 1982. Served with Can. Navy, 1943-46, ETO. Mem. Am. Assn. Petroleum Geologists, Soc. Exploration Geologists, Soc. Ind. Profl. Earth Scientists, Can. Assn. Petroleum Geologists, Internat. Assn. Math. Geology (assoc. editor 1976-78). Home: 837 Ackerman Ave Syracuse NY 13210-2906 Office: Syracuse U Dept Geology Syracuse NY 13244

ROBINSON, JULIAN B., church administrator. Dir. of bus. and records Ch. of God. Office: PO Box 2430 Cleveland TN 37320-2430

ROBINSON, JUNE KERSWELL, dermatologist, educator; b. Phila., Jan. 26, 1950; d. George and Helen S. (Kerswell) R.; m. William T. Barker, Jan. 31, 1981. BA cum laude, U. Pa., 1970; MD, U. Md., 1974. Diplomate Am. Bd. Dermatology, Nat. Bd. Med. Examiners, Am. Bd. Mohs Micrographic Surgery and Cutaneous Oncology. Intern Greater Balt. Med. Ctr., Hanover, N.H., 1974; resident in medicine Greater Balt. Med. Ctr., 1974-75; resident in dermatology Dartmouth-Hitchcock Med. Ctr., Hanover, N.H., 1975-78, chief resident, clin. instr., 1977-78; instr. in dermatology Dartmouth-Hitchcock Med. Ctr., Hanover, 1978; fellow Mohs; chemosurgery and dermatologic surgery NYU Skin and Cancer Clinic, N.Y.C., 1978-79; instr. in dermatology NYU, N.Y.C., 1979; asst. prof. dermatology Northwestern U. Med. Sch., Chgo., 1979, asst. prof. surgery, 1980-85, assoc. prof. dermatology and surgery, 1985-91, prof. dermatology and surgery, 1991—; mem. consensus devel. conf. NIH, 1992; lectr. in field. Author: Fundamentals of Skin Biopsy, 1985, also audiovisual materials; editor: (textbooks) Atlas of Cutaneous Surgery, 1996, Cutaneous Medicine and Surgery: An Integrated Program in Dermatology, 1996; mem. editl. bd. Archives of Dermatology, 1988—; sect. editor The Cutting Edge: Challenges in Med. and Surg. Therapeutics, 1989—; contbg. editor Jour. Dermatol. Surgery and Oncology, 1985-88; mem. editl. com. 18th World Congress of Dermatology, 1982; contbr. numerous articles, abstracts to profl. publs., chpts. to books. Bd. dirs. Northwestern Med. Faculty Found., 1982-84, chmn. com. on benefits and leaves, 1984, nominating com. 1988. Grantee Nat. Cancer Inst., 1985-91, Am. Cancer Soc., 1986-89, Skin Cancer Found., 1984-85, Dermatology Found., 1981-83, Northwestern U. Biomed. Rsch., 1981, Syntex, 1984. Fellow Am. Coll. Chemosurgery (chmn. sci. program ann. meeting 1983, chmn. publs. com. 1986-87, chmn. task force on ednl. needs 1989-90, co-editor bull. 1984-87); mem. AMA, Am. Dermatol. Assn., Am. Acad. Dermatology (dist. sec. treas. 1985, Stephen Rothman Lectr. award 1992, Presdl. citation 1992), Dermatology Found. (trustee 1995—), Internat. Soc. Dermatol. Surgery, Am. Soc. Dermatol. Surgery (pres. 1994-95), Soc. Investigative Dermatology, Women's Dermatol. Soc. (pres. 1990-92), Chgo. Dermatol. Soc. Home: 910 N Lake Shore Dr Apt 1419 Chicago IL 60611-1533

ROBINSON, KAREN ANN, special education educator; b. N.Y.C., May 30, 1959; d. Olen Wesley and Barbara Ann (Simmons) R. BS, Syracuse U., 1981; MA, George Washington U., 1984. Cert. advanced profl. in spl. edn., Md. Tchr. Shield of David, Bronx, N.Y., 1981, Cerebral Palsy Sch., Syracuse, N.Y., 1982, United Cerebral Palsy, Bronx, 1982-83, Low Meml. Day Care, Bklyn., 1983; program support tchr. specialist Montgomery County Pub. Schs., Rockville, Md., 1994—, insvc. tchr., 1986-89; instr. Johns Hopkins U. Continuing Studies, 1994—; com. mem. Supts. Com. on Evaluation, Rockville, 1988-89; guest lectr. Bowie (Md.) State U., 1990-91. Mem. NEA, Md. Tchrs. Assn. (del. 1985—, del. leadership conf. 1989), Montgomery County Edn. Assn. (organizer, assoc. rep. 1985—), Montgomery County Assn. Black Sch. Educators (newsletter editor), Nat. Assn. Black Sch. Educators. Avocations: dancing, exercise.

ROBINSON, KENNETH LEONARD, JR., trade association executive; b. Lynn, Mass., Feb. 14, 1929; s. Kenneth Leonard Sr. and Frances Ruth (Leighton) R.; m. Marie Louise Cormier, Sept. 1, 1951; children: Edward K., Elaine F., Ruth M., Doris A., Gordon M. BA, Boston Coll., 1950; MS, George Washington U., 1969. Advanced through grades to maj. gen. USMC, 1979; commdg. gen. Marine Corp. Base USMC, Camp Butler, Okinawa, 1977-79; commdg. gen. 3d Marine div. USMC, Okinawa, 1980; commdg. gen. Marine Corp. Base USMC, Camp Pendleton, Calif., 1980-83; ret. USMC, 1983; pres., chief exec. officer Nat. Assn. Fed. Credit Unions, Washington, 1984—; bd. dirs. San Diego (Calif.) Navy Fed. Credit Union, San Diego, Calif., 1981-83, Washington, 1975-77. Columnist on fin. topics for trade mags.; contbr. articles to trade publs. Mem. Far East Coun. Boy Scouts Am., Okinawa, 1977-80, San Diego Coun., 1980-83. Recipient Golden Eagle award Far East Coun. Boy Scouts Am., 1980, Silver Beaver award San Diego Coun., 1982. Mem. Am. Soc. Assn. Execs., Greater Washington Soc. Assn. Execs., USMC Hist. Soc. (bd. dirs. 1987—, chmn. audit com. 1987—), Army-Navy Club, Exchequer Club (Washington). Republican. Roman Catholic. Avocations: tennis, golf, bowling, chess. Home: 2538 N Vermont St Arlington VA 22207-4126 Office: Nat Assn Fed Credit Unions PO Box 3769 Washington DC 20007*

ROBINSON, LARRY CLARK, professional hockey coach; b. Winchester, Ont., Can., June 2, 1951. Head coach L.A. Kings, 1995—. Office: LA Kings Great Western Forum 3900 W Manchester Blvd Inglewood CA 90305

ROBINSON, LARRY ROBERT, insurance company executive; b. Indpls., Feb. 7, 1936; s. Manuel H. Robinson and Barbara Dawson Robinson Trees; m. Sharon Moore, Aug. 3, 1957; children: Christopher, Lizbeth, Lara, Jeremy. BA, DePauw U., Greencastle, Ind., 1957. Actuarial trainee State Life Ins. Co., Indpls., 1957-63, asst. actuary, 1963-66, actuary, 1966-67, asst. v.p., actuary, 1967-70, v.p., actuary, 1970-80, sr. v.p., actuary, 1980-83, exec. v.p., 1983—, also bd. dirs.; chmn. cost disclosure com. Am. Coun. Life Ins., Washington, 1985-87, chmn. actuarial com., 1990-91. Bd. dirs. Marion County Assn. Retarded Citizens, Indpls., 1980-86. With U.S. Army, 1961-62. Fellow Soc. Actuaries; mem. Am. Acad. Actuaries, Indpls. Actuarial Club (past pres.), Actuarial Club Ind., Ky. and Ohio (past pres.), Phi Beta Kappa. Office: State Life Ins Co 141 E Washington St Indianapolis IN 46204-3614

ROBINSON, LAURIE OVERBY, assistant attorney general; b. Washington, July 7, 1946; d. Kermit and Ethel Esther (Schlasinger) Overby; m. Craig Baab, Oct. 22, 1977; (div. 1991); 1 child, Teddy Baab; m. Sheldon Krantz, Dec. 8, 1991. BA in Polit. Sci. magna cum laude, Brown U., 1968. Desk editor Cmty. News Svc., N.Y.C., 1968-71; asst. staff dir. sect. criminal justice ABA, Washington, 1972-74, dir. sect. criminal justice, 1979-93; assoc. dep. atty. gen. U.S. Dept. Justice, Washington, 1993-94, asst. atty. gen. Office Justice Programs, 1994—; mem. ex-officio, bd. regents Nat. Coll. Dist. Attys., Houston, 1979-93; mem. adv. bd. Fed. Sentencing Reporter, N.Y.C., 1990—; chair Nat. Forum on Criminal Justice, Washington, 1991-93. Active Clinton Campaign Criminal Justice Com., 1992, Clinton Transition Com. Dept. Justice, 1992. Mem. ABA, Phi Beta Kappa. Democrat. Office: US Dept Justice 633 Indiana Ave NW Washington DC 20531

ROBINSON, LAWRENCE DEWITT, lawyer; b. Saginaw, Mich., Sept. 15, 1943; m. Lynne Howe; children: Tiffany, Julia. BS, Cen. Mich. U., 1965; JD, U. Mich., 1968. Bar: Mo. 1968, Tex. 1983. Atty. Stinson, May & Fizzell, Kansas City, Mo., 1968-89; ptnr. Bracewell & Patterson, Dallas, 1991-1996; general counsel FelCor, Irving, TX. Tchr. navigational class. Mem. ABA, Dallas Bar Assn. Office: FelCor 5215 N O'Connor Ste 330 Irving TX 75039*

ROBINSON, LAWRENCE PHILLIP, television engineer, inventor, consultant; b. Detroit, Feb. 10, 1933; s. Leroy Percival and Vida Irene (Thompson) R. Grad., DeVry Inst. Tech., Chgo., 1955-57; AS, Delta Coll., University Center, Mich., 1968; DD, Modern Apostles Sch., North Miami Beach, Fla., 1982; BS, Mich. State U., 1984. TV engr. Sta. WNEM-TV, Bay City, Mich., 1953-56, Sta. WKNX-TV, Saginaw, Mich., 1956-62, Sta. WUCM-TV, University Center, 1966-68, Sta. WEYI-TV, Flint, Mich., 1969-73; electronics tech. Am. Machine & Foundry, Saginaw, 1962-64; radio technician Sta. WBCM, Bay City, 1964-66; radio engr. Sta. WSGW, Saginaw, 1968, Sta. WKMF, Flint, 1968-69; TV engr. Sta. WKAR-TV, Mich. State U., East Lansing, 1973—. Author: The Stress-Strain Connection, 1981, Thoughts on the Nature of Matter, 1982, 3d rev. edit., 1988. With USNR, 1950-53. Recipient new product award Inventors Clubs Am., 1989, 90. Mem. AAAS, N.Y. Acad. Scis., Mich. State U. Alumni Assn. (life), Mensa (life), Camelo Pards, Am. Legion (life), Masons, Order of the Iron Test Pattern. Orthodox. Achievements include patents for shortened vertical antenna and the disk antenna for UHF-VHF. Home: AP 3 2756 E Grand River Ave East Lansing MI 48823 Office: Mich State U Sta WKAR-TV Comm Arts Bldg East Lansing MI 48824

ROBINSON, LAWRENCE WAYNE, protective services official; b. Dallas, Jan. 9, 1947; s. Henry Sherrod and Mary Ellen (Bannon) R.; m. Virginia Morgan, Aug. 9, 1980; children: Matthew Sherrod, Meghan Michelle, Joshua Morgan; 1 child from a previous marriage, Lawrence Wayne, Jr. BS in Psychology, No. Tex. State U., 1974; MS in Interdisciplinary Studies, U. Tex., Tyler, 1985. Cert. instr., firearms instr. Police officer Dallas Police Dept., 1966-68; salesman Nat. Cash Register, Dallas, 1968-69; police officer Denton (Tex.) Police Dept., 1969-71; adminstrv. asst. to chief No. Tex. State U., Denton, 1971-75, chief of police, 1976-83; coord. basic police training No. Ctrl. Tex. Regional Acad., Arlington, 1975-76; chief police Tyler (Tex.) Police Dept., 1983-94; chief of police McKinney (Tex.) Police Dept., 1994—; chmn. Gang Task Force, Tyler; founder S.T.A.R. elementary sch. program, Tyler, 1990—; co-founder Mayor's Anti-Crime Task Force, Greater Tyler Drug-Free Bus.; speaker in field. Leader Boy Scouts Am., Tyler, 1993-94; coach Tyler Soccer Assn., 1993-94, Rose Capital East Little League, Tyler, 1993-94; deacon First Bapt. Ch., 1993-94. With Tex. N.G., 1965-71. Recipient Outstanding Leadership and Founder award Drug Free Youth in Tex. Assn., 1993, Dir.'s Community Leadership award FBI, 1994. Republican. Avocations: running, back packing, camping, cycling. Office: McKinney Police Dept Office Police Chief Mc Kinney TX 75069

ROBINSON, LEE HARRIS, lawyer; b. N.Y.C., Aug. 2, 1939; s. Bernard and Bess (Polotnick) R.; children: Shari, Brett; m. Susan Stroble, June 22, 1985; stepchildren: Michael, Jonathan. BA, Cornell U., 1961; LLB cum laude, Columbia U., 1964. Bar: N.Y. 1965, U.S. Dist. Ct. (so. dist.) N.Y. 1968, U.S. Ct. Appeals (2d cir.) 1968. Ptnr. Rosenman & Colin, L.L.P., N.Y.C., 1964—. Contbr. articles to profl. jours. Mem. exec. com. young men's divsn. Albert Einstein Coll. Medicine, N.Y.C., 1979—; mem. Cornell Assn. Class Officers, 1981—. Mem. ABA (mem. benefits subcom. sect. on taxation, mem. exec. compensation com. sect. on real property, probate and trust law, chmn. subcom. on probated transactions 1994-95), N.Y. State Bar Assn. (mem. spl. com. on pension simplification, 1992-95, mem. com. on exec. compensation), Old Oaks Country Club (Purchase, N.Y.). Republican. Jewish. Avocation: golf. Home: 437 Orienta Ave Mamaroneck NY 10543-3939 Office: Rosenman & Colin LLP 575 Madison Ave New York NY 10022-2511

ROBINSON, LEONARD HARRISON, JR., international government consultant, business executive; b. Winston-Salem, N.C., Apr. 21, 1943; s. Leonard Harrison and Winnie Cornelia (Thomas) R.; children: Kimberly Michelle, Rani Craft. NSF cert., Bennett Coll., Greensboro, N.C., 1959; BA, Ohio State U., 1964; postgrad., SUNY, Binghamton, 1966-67, Am. U., 1982-89, Harvard U., 1991; LLD (hon.), Shaw U., Raleigh, N.C., 1983; LHD (hon.), Huston-Tillotson Coll., 1991. Vol. Peace Corps., Bihar, India, 1964-66; assoc. dir. for India Peace Corps, Madras, 1967-70; dir. recruitment Peace Corps., Washington, 1970-71; dir. inner-city programs EPA, Washington, 1971-72; dir. mgmt. Family Planning Internat. Assistance, N.Y.C., 1972-74; Africa dir. Family Planning Internat. Assistance, Accra, Ghana and Nairobi, Kenya, 1974-77; task force dir. U.S. Ho. Reps., Washington, 1977-78; dir. population Africa AID, Washington, 1978-79; dir. Internat. Devel. Ctr. Battelle Inst., Washington, 1979-83; dep. asst. sec., sr. exec. svc. Dept. State, Washington, 1983-85; pres. African Devel. Found., Washington, 1985-90; dep. asst. sec. state, sr. exec. svc. Dept. State, Washington, 1990-93; vice chmn., COO Washington Strategic Consulting Group, Inc., Washington, 1993—; cons. area studies U. Mo. Peace Corps, summer 1966; mgmt. analyst ATAC, Washington, 1971; mem. U.S. presdl. del. to Dakar, Senegal, 1987, to Malawi, Mozambique, and Uganda, Sept. 1988, to Mali, Uganda, and Kenya, Dec. 1988, v.p.'s visit to Africa, 1991; hon. consul Govt. Sao Tome and Principe, 1996—. Author: monographs Assessment and Analysis of Population Attitudes in Tanzania, 1981, Analyze African Official Attitudes Concerning U.S. Population Assistance in Lesotho, Tanzania, Senegal and Togo, 1981. Adviser Population Resource Ctr., N.Y.C., 1978-82; adviser internat. program for health and tng., U. N.C., Chapel Hill, 1980-84; vice-chmn. New Directions Task Force Rep. Party, Montgomery County (Md.), 1982-83; adv. coun. Nat. Coun. Returned Peace Corps Vols., 1987—; bd. dirs. Washington Ballet, 1982-85, 86-91, v.p. bd. dirs. 1988-90; bd. dirs. Friends of Smithsonian Mus. African Art, Washington, 1982-84, Coalition for Equitable Representation in Govt., Montgomery County, Montgomery County Bd. Soc. Svcs., 1986-89, Joint Agrl. Consultative Corp., 1985-86, Alan Gutmacher Inst., 1992—, Friends of the U. of Natal, South Africa, 1995—. Decorated commandeur de l'Ordre National du Niger, 1989; recipient Africare Disting. Svc. award, 1990, Key to the City of Greensboro, N.C., 1991, Christian D. Maxwell Disting. Svc. award Liberian Com. for Relief, Resettlement and Reconstruction, 1993. Mem. Soc. Internat. Devel. (dir. 1982), Am. Pub. Health Assn. (sec. population sect. 1979-81), Coun. on Fgn. Rels., C. of C. of D.C. (dir. 1979-82), Metro Club Washington, Kappa Alpha Psi, Sigma Pi Phi. Office: Washington Strategic Consulting Group 10th Fl 805 15th St NW Fl 10 Washington DC 20005-2207 *Human life is precious and extraordinary. I have strived to live to the fullest, by being productive, impact-oriented, and successful in contributng to the improvement of people's lives. This quest has brought me happiness and fulfillment.*

ROBINSON, LINDA GOSDEN, communications executive; b. L.A., Jan. 10, 1953; d. Freeman Fisher and Jane Elizabeth (Stoneham) Gosden; m. Stephen M. Dart (div. June 1977); m. James Dixon Robinson III. Student, UCLA, 1970-72; BA summa cum laude in Psychology, U. So. Calif., 1978. Dep. press sec. Reagan Presdl. Campaign, L.A., 1979; press sec., dir. pub. relations Rep. Nat. Com., Washington, 1979-80; dir. pub. affairs U.S. Dept. Transp., Washington, 1981-83; ptnr. pub. and govt. affairs Heron, Burchette, Ruckert & Rothwell, Washington, 1983; dep. to spl. envoy Office of the Pres., N.Y.C., 1985; sr. v.p. corp. affairs Warner Amex Cable Communications, N.Y.C., 1983-86; chmn., CEO Robinson, Lerer, Sawyer, Miller, N.Y.C., 1986—; bd. dirs. Revlon Group, Inc., N.Y.C., Lab. Cor. Am. Holdings, Burlington, N.C., Bozell, Jacobs, Kenyon & Eckhardt, N.Y.C., VIMRx Pharms. Inc., Stamford, Conn. Trustee NYU Med. Ctr., N.Y.C.; del. Rep. Nat. Conv., 1985. Mem. Nat. Women's Econ. Coun., Phi Beta Kappa. Avocations: horse showing, tennis, golf.

ROBINSON, MALCOLM, gastroenterologist; b. Amarillo, Tex., July 25, 1942; s. H. Malcolm and Frances Pauline (Kohn) R.; m. Susan Laird Robinson, June 22, 1969. BS with honors, Tulane U., 1964; MD, Okla. U.,

1968. Diplomate Am. Bd. Internal Medicine, Internal Medicine and Gastroenterology. Intern Cleve. Clinic, 1968-69; sr. resident, internal medicine U. Okla., Okla. City, 1974-75; GI fellow Duke U., Durham, N.C., 1969-71; sr. resident internal medicine U. Okla., Oklahoma City, 1974-75, asst. prof., 1975-76; chief GI Oklahoma City Clinic, 1976-89, Columbia Presbyn. Hosp., Okla. City, 1976—; pres., dir. Okla. Found. for Digestive Rsch., Oklahoma City, 1989-96; chief GI Presbyn. Hosp.; clin. assoc. prof. U. Okla., Oklahoma City, 1976-92, clin. prof., 1992—; mem. adv. bd. Glaxo, Inc., Solvay, Inc., Procter and Gamble, Inc., Merck-J&J, TAP Pharm., Inc., Eisai Inc.; mem. internat. editl. bd. Alimentary Pharmacology and Therapeutics; reviewer Am. Jour. Gastroenterology, Gastroenterology, Digestive Diseases and Sci., Gastrointestinal Endoscopy. Maj. M.C., U.S. Army, 1971-74. Benefactor 1 million dollar chair in Gastroenterology, U. Okla. Coll. of Medicine, 1996. Fellow ACP, Am. Coll. Gastroenterology; mem. Am. Soc. Gastrointestinal Endoscopy, Am. Gastroent. Assn. (Janssen award for outstanding achievement in clin. gastroenterology 1995). Office: Okla Found Digestive Rsch Ste 501 711 Stanton L Young Blvd Oklahoma City OK 73104 Office: Okla Found Digestive Rsch Ste 501 711 Stanton L Young Blvd Oklahoma City OK 73104-5022

ROBINSON, MARGUERITE STERN, anthropologist, educator, consultant; b. N.Y.C., Oct. 11, 1935; d. Philip Van Doren and Lillian (Diamond) Stern; m. Allan Richard Robinson, June 12, 1955; children: Sarah Penelope, Perrine, Laura Ondine. BA, Radcliffe Coll., 1956; PhD, Harvard U., 1965. Assoc. scholar Inst. for Ind. Study (now Bunting Inst.) Radcliffe U., Cambridge, Mass., 1964-65; asst. prof. anthology Brandeis U., 1965-72, assoc. prof., 1972-78, prof., 1978-85, dean Coll. Arts and Scis., 1973-75; assoc. fellow Inst. Internat. Devel. Harvard U., Cambridge, 1978-80, fellow Inst. Internat. Devel., 1980-85, inst. fellow Inst. Internat. Devel., 1985—; dir. Cultural Survival Inc., 1981—; dir. Am. Inst. Indian Studies, Chgo., 1977—, chmn., 1983-84; cons. Ministry of Fin., Govt. of Indonesia, Jakarta, 1979-92, USAID, 1992-95, Banco Solidario, Bolivia, 1993-95, Bank Rakyat Indonesia, 1994-96, World Bank, 1994-95, Bank Danamon Indonesia, 1995-96. Author: Political Structure in a Changing Sinhalese Village, 1974, Local Politics: The Law of the Fishes, 1988, Pembiayaan Pertanian Pedesaan, 1993; contbg. author: Cambridge Papers in Social Anthropology 3, 1962, Cambridge Papers in Social Anthropology 5, 1968, Enterprises for the Recycling and Composting of Municipal Solid Waste, 1993, The New World of Microenterprise Finance, 1994, New Perspectives on Financing Small Business in Developing Countries, 1995; contbr. articles to profl. jours. Mem. internat. coun. advisors Calmeadow Found.; pres. The Greatest Gift Corp. Fellow NIH, 1964-65; grantee NSF, 1966-70, Ford Found., 1972-74, 79, Calmeadow Found., 1994; fellow Indo-Am. Fellowship Program-Indo-U.S. Subcommn. on Edn. and Culture, 1976-77, Am. Inst. Indian Studies, 1976-77; grantee Calmeadow Found., 1994. Fellow Am. Anthrop. Assn., Soc. Bunting Inst. Fellows; mem. Assn. Asian Studies, India Internat. Centre. Office: Harvard U Inst Internat Devel One Eliot St Cambridge MA 02138

ROBINSON, MARSHALL ALAN, economics educator, foundation executive; b. Berkeley, Calif., Feb. 16, 1922; s. Webster Richard and Evelyn (Casey) R.; m. Ynid Douglas Rankin, June 5, 1944 (div. 1973); children: Joan Douglas, Margaret Elaine, Richard Webster; m. Flavia Derossi, Oct. 1974. A.B., U. Calif.-Berkeley, 1943; M.A., Ohio State U., 1948, Ph.D., 1950. Instr. econs. Ohio State U., 1948-50; asst. prof. econs. Tulane U., 1951-53; research asso. Nat. Bur. Econ. Research, 1951-52; asst. prof. econs. Dartmouth Coll., 1953-55; sr. staff mem., asst. to pres. Brookings Instn., 1955-60; prof. econs., dean Grad. Sch. Bus., U. Pitts., 1960-63; dir. econ. devel. and adminstrn. program Ford Found., 1964-67, program officer in charge higher edn. and research, 1967-71, dep. v.p. edn. and research, 1971-73, v.p. resources and environ., 1973-79; pres. Russell Sage Found., N.Y.C., 1979-86; vis. prof. Grad. Sch. CUNY, 1986-89; fellow Inst. Social and Policy Studies Yale U., 1989-91; v.p. Daniele Agostino Found., 1992—. Author: An Introduction to Economic Reasoning, 1956, 5th edit., 1981, The National Debt Ceiling, 1959. Bd. dirs. Belgium-Am. Ednl. Found., 1981-96; trustee Antioch U., 1987-90. Served to 1st lt. USMCR, 1943-45, PTO. Decorated Royal Order of Leopold, Belgium. Mem. Am. Econs. Assn., N.Y. Sci. Policy Assn., Coun. on Fgn. Rels., Century Assn., Alpha Delta Phi.

ROBINSON, MARTHA STEWART, retired legal educator; b. Topeka, Mar. 2, 1914; d. Robert Bigger and Lenora (Stubbs) Stewart; m. Albrecht Marburg Yerkes, July 3, 1940 (dec. 1963); children: Robert Stewart, William Marburg; m. Stephan B. Robinson, Jr., July 17, 1971. A.B. cum laude, Washburn U., 1934, LL.B., 1940; LL.M., Stanford U., 1953. Bar: Kans. 1940, Calif. 1945. Individual practice law Los Angeles, 1946-55; instr. law Southwestern U. Sch. Law, Los Angeles, 1946-55; cons. Los Angeles Superior Ct. Com. on Standard Jury Instrns., 1957-64; prof. law Loyola U. Sch. Law, Los Angeles, 1965-84, prof. emeritus, 1984—; judge pro tempore Los Angeles County Superior Ct., 1963. Mem. Am. Law Inst., Calif. Bar Assn., L.A. County Bar Assn. (trustee 1976-78), Women Lawyers Assn. L.A. (past pres.). Home: 625 Old Mill Rd Pasadena CA 91108-1737 Office: Loyola U Law Sch 1441 W Olympic Blvd Los Angeles CA 90015-3903

ROBINSON, MARTIN F., lawyer; b. Trenton, N.J., July 5, 1939. AB, Rutgers U., 1961; LLB, U. Pa., 1964. Bar: N.J. 1965, Ill. 1967. Law clk. to Hon. Joseph Halpern N.J. Superior Ct., 1964-65; atty. Office Gen. Coun. NLRB, 1965-66; ptnr. Sidley & Austin, Chgo.; instr. Chgo. Kent Coll. Law, 1975-79; mem. nat. adv. com. State of Ill., 1988-90. Mem. Nat. Assn. Bond Lawyers. Office: Sidley & Austin 1 First Nat Plz Chicago IL 60603*

ROBINSON, MARY JO, pathologist; b. Spokane, Wash., May 26, 1954; d. Jerry Lee and Mary Ann (Brodie) R. BS in Biology, Gonzaga U., 1976; DO, Coll. Osteo. Medicine and Surgery, U. Med. Health Scis., 1987. Diplomate Nat. Bd. Osteo. Med. Examiners, Am. Osteo. Bd. Pathology. Med. technologist Whitman Comty. Hosp., Colfax, Wash., 1977-81, Madigan Army Med. Ctr., Ft. Lewis, Wash., 1981-83; intern Des Moines Gen. Hosp., 1987-88; resident in pathology Kennedy Meml. Hosp., Stratford, N.J., 1988-92; asst. prof. pathology Sch. Medicine U. Medicine and Dentistry of N.J., Stratford, 1995—; staff pathologist Kennedy Meml. Hosp., Cherry Hill, N.J., 1995—; fellow in dermatopathology Jefferson Med. Coll., Phila., 1994. Fellow Coll. Am. Pathologists; mem. AMA, Am. Osteo. Coll. Pathologists (1st prize resident paper 1992), Am. Osteo. Assn., Am. Soc. Clin. Pathologists, N.J. Assn. Osteo. Physicians and Surgeons. Avocations: astronomy, antiques, science fiction. Office: Kennedy Meml Hosp U Med Ctr 2201 Chapel Ave W Cherry Hill NJ 08002-2048

ROBINSON, MARY KATHERINE, school system administrator; b. Asheville, N.C., Sept. 11, 1943; d. William Robert Jr. and Iris Myrtle (Holden) Sherrill; m. Marcus William Sumner, Oct. 26, 1962 (div. June 1973); 1 child, Marcus Kevin; m. Frank Pearson Robinson, Jr., Oct. 26, 1974 (div. 1996). BS in Edn., Western Carolina U., Cullowhee, N.C., 1968, MA in Edn., 1983. Cert. tchr., N.C. Tchr. reading Jackson County Bd. Edn., Sylva, N.C., 1968-69, elem. tchr., 1970-76; instr. reading Western Carolina U., 1968, instr. remedial reading, 1972; Reading Program developer Haywood County Bd. Edn., Waynesville, N.C., 1976-82, Resource and Program developer, 1982—; cons. divsn. health, safety and phys. edn. N.C. Dept. Pub. Instrn., Raleigh, 1974-75; mem. adv. bd. Haywood Tech. Inst., Clyde, N.C., 1978-79; mem. N.C. Textbook Commn., Raleigh, 1989-93; mem. curriculum rev. com. in mktg. edn., bus. edn. N.C. Dept. Pub. Instrn., 1992, health edn., 1993. Compiler: Robert Lee Holden Family, 1993; contbr. to periodical; creator vocabulary game Jaw Breakers, 1977. Vol. Reading Is Fundamental project Haywood County Libr., 1978-79; treas. PTO, 1971-72; active Haywood County Found. Bd., 1995—. Recipient Gold Key award N.C. State Supt., 1991. Mem. NEA, ASCD, N.C. Assn. Educators (sec. 1977, v.p./pres. elect 1994-95, pres. 1995-96), Internat. Reading Assn. (v.p. 1978-79, pres. 1979-80), Bus. and Profl. Women's Orgn., Friends of Haywood County Libr., Delta Kappa Gamma (corr. sec. 1988-90, v.p. 1990-92, pres. 1992-94), Phi Delta Kappa, Kappa Delta Pi. Democrat. Avocations: genealogy, travel. Home: PO Box 1017 Lake Junaluska NC 28745

ROBINSON, MARY LOU, federal judge; b. Dodge City, Kans., Aug. 25, 1926; d. Gerald J. and Frances Strueber; m. A.J. Robinson, Aug. 28, 1949; children: Rebecca Aynn Gruhlkey, Diana Ceil, Matthew Douglas. B.A., U. Tex., 1948, LL.B., 1950. Bar: Tex. 1949. Ptnr. Robinson & Robinson, Amarillo, 1950-55; judge County Ct. at Law, Potter County, Tex., 1955-59, (108th Dist. Ct.), Amarillo, 1961-73; assoc. justice Ct. of Civil Appeals for 7th Supreme Jud. Dist. of Tex., Amarillo, 1973-77; chief justice Ct. of Civil Appeals for 7th Supreme Jud. Dist. of Tex., 1977-79; U.S. dist. judge No. Dist. Tex., Amarillo, 1979—. Named Woman of Year Tex. Fedn. Bus. and Profl. Women, 1973. Mem. Nat. Assn. Women Lawyers, ABA, Tex. Bar Assn., Amarillo Bar Assn., Delta Kappa Gamma. Presbyterian. Office: US Dist Ct Rm 226 205 E 5th Ave # F13248 Amarillo TX 79101-1563

ROBINSON, MICHAEL ALLEN, lawyer; b. N.Y.C., Oct. 5, 1947. BA cum laude, Albany State Coll., 1972; JD, U. Denver, 1989. Bar: Colo. 1989, U.S. Ct. Appeals (10th cir.) 1993, U.S. Dist. Ct. Colo. 1990. Ptnr. Gubbels & Robinson, Castle Rock, Colo., 1991—. Bd. dirs. Cantril House Assistance, 1994; active Castle Rock Budget Commn., 1994—; chmn. Castle Rock Bd. Adjustment, 1994-96. With USN, 1966-70. Mem. Colo. Bar Assn., Douglas Bar Assn. (v.p., Atty. of Yr. 1992), Castle Rock C. of C. (bd. dirs. 1995—), VFW (post comdr. Castle Rock 1991-92). Democrat. Home: 596 W Prestwick Way Castle Rock CO 80104 Office: Gubbels & Robinson 210 5th St Castle Rock CO 80104

ROBINSON, MICHAEL HILL, zoological park director, biologist; b. Preston, Eng., Jan. 7, 1929; came to U.S. 1984; s. Samuel and Ethel (Hill) R.; m. Barbara Cragg Robinson, May 19, 1955 (divorced). B.S., U. Wales, U.K., 1963; D.Phil., U. Oxford, Eng., 1966. Tchr. sci. U.K. Secondary Schs., 1953-60; sr. sci. master Camborne Grammar Sch., 1958-60; biologist Smith. Tropical Research Inst., Panama, 1966-71; vis. lectr. U. Pa., Phila., 1969; reader in biology New U. Ulster, No. Ireland, 1971; biologist Smithsonian Tropical Research Inst., Panama, 1971-84; asst. dir. Smithsonian Tropical Research Inst., 1980, acting dir., 1980-81, dep. dir., 1981-84; adj. prof. U. Miami, Coral Gables, Fla., 1981—; dir. Nat. Zool. Park, Washington, 1984—. Contbr. articles to profl. jours. Sci. fellow Zool. Soc. London, 1956. Fellow Linnean Soc., Royal Entomol. Soc., Inst. Biology; mem. Brit. Arachnological Soc., Soc. for Study of Animal Behavior. Home: 2729 Ordway St NW Apt 5 Washington DC 20008-5052 Office: Nat Zool Pk 3000 Connecticut Ave NW Washington DC 20008

ROBINSON, MICHAEL R., aeronautical engineer. Dir. new product devel. Rockwell Internat. Corp., Seal Beach, Calif.; co-originator and first program manager of the X-31 enhanced maneuverability fighter demonstrator and originator of the international team to conduct the program. Recipient DGLR Team award in recognition of exceptional achievements in the field of Aeronautics, 1996. Fellow Am. Inst. Aeronautics & Astronautics (aircraft design award 1994). Office: Rockwell Internat Corp 2201 Seal Beach Blvd PO Box 3644 Seal Beach CA 90740-7644

ROBINSON, NAN SENIOR, not-for-profit organization consultant; b. Salt Lake City, Jan. 11, 1932; d. Clair Marcil Senior and Lillian (Worlton) Senior Davis; m. David Zav Robinson; Sept. 6, 1954; children: Marc S. Robinson, Eric S. Robinson. BA with hons., Mills Coll., 1952; MA, Harvard U., 1953. Spl. asst. to undersec. Dept. Housing and Urban Devel., Washington, 1966-69; asst. to the pres. U. Mass. Statewide System, Boston, 1970-73, v.p. for planning, 1973-78; dep. commr. Conn. Bd. Higher Edn., Hartford, 1978-81; v.p. adminstrn. The Rockefeller Found., N.Y.C., 1981-90; mem. governing coun. Rockefeller Archive Ctr., Pocantico Hills, N.Y., 1986-89; com. mem. Coun. on Founds. N.Y. Regional Assn. Grantmakers, 1985-89; mem. nat. advisory panel on governance Carnegie Found. for the Advancement of Teaching, Princeton, N.J., 1980-82. Trustee, chmn. fin. com. Inst. for Current World Affairs, Hanover, N.H., 1987-90; trustee Calif. Sch. Profl. Psychology, San Francisco, 1985—. Recipient Centennial award Am. Assn. U. Women Hartford Br., 1981; named Woman of Yr. Hartford YWCA, 1980; named to Centennial Honor List of 100 Women Barnard Coll., 1989. Mem. Soc. for Coll. and U. Planning (com. chmn. 1985-86, nominating com. 1980-85, regional rep. 1975-77), Phi Beta Kappa. Home: 622 Greenwich St Apt 5B New York NY 10014-3305

ROBINSON, NATHANIEL DAVID, physician; b. Providence, May 21, 1904; m. Dorothy Mae McLaughlin, Mar. 27, 1940; children: Nathaniel David Jr., Judith A. (Mrs. Joseph F. Baugher), Nancy L. (Mrs. Robert W. VanTuyle). BS, Tufts U., 1928, MD, 1931; postgrad. ophthalmology, N.Y.U., 1945-46. Diplomate Am. Bd. Ophthalmology. Intern Gallinger Mcpl. Hosp., Washington, 1931-32; physician gen. medicine Marine Hosp., Balt., 1935-36; gen. practice medicine Providence, 1936-40; resident ophthalmology Bellevue Hosp., N.Y.C., 1946-49; asst. to prof. ophtalmology N.Y.U., N.Y.C., 1949; practice medicine specilizing in ophthalmology Providence, 1949—; cons. staff R.I., Miriam, VA, Roger Williams, Chapin Hosps., Providence, Meml. Hosp., Pawtucket, R.I.; ophthalmologist Sr. Friendship Ctr., Naples, Fla. Served with USN, 1940-45, PTO, ret. capt. USNR, 1964. N.Y. Kiwanis Club grantee for ophthalmology. Mem. R.I., Providence, Collier County med. socs., R.I., New Eng., Pan Am. Ophthal. socs., AMA, Am. Acad. Ophthalmology, Pan. Am. Med. Assn., Soc. Eye Surgeons, R.I. Hist. Soc., English Speaking Union, Audobon Soc., Narragansett Bay Power Squadron, Ret. Officers Assn., Mil. Order Fgn. Wars, Navy League of the U.S. Unitarian. Clubs: University, Moorings Country. Home: 2880 Gulf Shore Blvd N Apt 308 Naples FL 33940-4326

ROBINSON, NEIL CIBLEY, JR., lawyer; b. Columbia, S.C., Oct. 25, 1942; s. Neil C. and Ernestine (Carns) R.; m. Judith Ann Hunter, Sept. 4, 1971 (div. Nov. 1979); 1 child, Hunter Leigh; m. Vicki Elizabeth Kornahrens, Mar. 2, 1985; children: Neil C. III, Taylor Elizabeth. BS in Indsl. Mgmt., Clemson U., 1966; JD, U. S.C., 1973. Bar: S.C. 1974, U.S. Ct. Appeals (4th cir.) 1974, U.S. Dist. Ct. S.C. 1976. Asst. to dean U. S.C. Law Sch., Columbia, 1973-74; law clk. to judge Charles E. Jr. Simons Jr. U.S. Dist. Ct. S.C., Aiken, 1974-76; assoc. Grimball & Cabaniss, Charleston, S.C., 1976-78; ptnr. Grimball, Cabaniss, Vaughan & Robinson, Charleston, 1978-84; ptnr., pres. Robinson, Wall & Hastie, P.A., Charleston, 1984-91; ptnr., mem. exec. com. Nexsen, Pruet, Jacobs, Pollard & Robinson, Charleston, 1991—; permanent mem. 4th Cir. Jud. Conf., 1982—; pres. Coastal Properties Inst., Charleston, 1981—. Bd. dirs. Southeastern Wildlife Exposition, Charleston, 1987—, pres. 1994—, Charleston Maritime Festival, 1993—, pres. 1994—, Parklands Found. of Charleston County; pres. S.C. Tourism Coun., Columbia, 1991—. Cpl. USMCR, 1960-66. Mem. ABA, Urban Land Inst., Am. Residential and Resort Devel. Assn., Recreational Devel. Coun., S.C. Bar Assn., Fed. Bar Assn., S.C. Def. Trial Lawyers Assn., Hibernian Soc. (mem. mgmt. com. 1984—), Kiawah Club, Haig Point Club, Country Club of Charleston, Phi Delta Phi. Presbyterian. Avocations: golf, hunting. Home: PO Box 121 Charleston SC 29402-0121 Office: Nexsen Pruet Jacobs Pollard & Robinson 200 Meeting St Ste 301 Charleston SC 29401-3156

ROBINSON, NELL BRYANT, nutrition educator; b. Kopperl, Tex., Oct. 15, 1925; d. Basil Howell and Lelia Abiah (Duke) Bryant; m. Frank Edward Robinson, July 14, 1945 (dec.); 1 child, John Howell Robinson. B.S., N. Tex. State U., 1945; M.S., Tex. Woman's U., 1958, Ph.D., 1967. Registered dietitian, Tex. Tchr. Comanche High Sch., Tex., 1945-46, Kopperl High Sch., Tex., 1946-48; county extension agt. Agrl. Extension Service, Tex., 1948-56; prof. nutrition Tex. Christian U., Fort Worth, 1957-92, chmn. dept. nutrition and dietetics, 1985-91, ret., 1992. Pres., bd. dirs. Sr. Citizens Svcs. of Greater Tarrant County, 1990-91. Contbr. chpt. to book. Named Top Prof., Tex. Christian U. Mortar Bd., 1978. Mem. Am. Dietetic Assn. (del. 1983-88, ethics com. 1985-88, coun. edn. 1988-90, chmn. coun. on edn. divsn. edn. accreditation/approval 1989-90, medallion award 1990), Am. Assn. Family and Consumer Scis., Tex. Dietetic Assn. (pres., 1972-73, Disting. Dietitian 1981), Tex. Assn. Family and Consumer Scis. (pres. 1978-80, Home Economist of Yr. 1975). Club: Fort Worth Women's. Lodge: Order Eastern Star. Home: 5729 Wimbleton Way Fort Worth TX 76133-3651

ROBINSON, NICHOLAS ADAMS, lawyer, law educator; b. N.Y.C., Jan. 20, 1945; s. Albert Lewis and Agnes Claflin (Adams) R.; m. Shelley Miner, Jan. 5, 1969; children: Cynthia M., Lucy A. BA cum laude, Brown U., 1967; JD cum laude, Columbia U., 1970. Bar: N.Y. 1971, U.S. Dist. Ct. (so. and ea. dists.) N.Y. 1972, U.S. Supreme Ct. 1974, U.S. Ct. Appeals (2d and 7th cirs.) 1972. Law clk. to U.S. dist. judge, so. dist. N.Y., 1970-72; assoc. Marshall, Bratter, Greene, Allison & Tucker, N.Y.C., 1972-78, counsel, 1978-82; assoc. prof. law Pace U. Sch. Law, White Plains, N.Y., 1978-81, prof., 1981—, dir. Ctr. for Environ. Legal Studies, 1982—; counsel Winer, Neuburger & Sive, N.Y.C., 1982-83; dep. commr., gen. counsel N.Y. State Dept. Environ. Conservation, Albany, 1983-85; counsel Sive, Paget & Reisel, 1985-92, Sidley & Austin, N.Y., London, 1992-96; del. U.S.A. environ. law meetings with USSR, 1974-92; chmn. Environ. Adv. Bd. to Gov. Mario Cuomo, 1985-94; dep. chair Commn. on Environ. Law Internat. Union for Conservation of Nature & Natural Resources, 1990—. Consulting editor Environ Law, 1996—; contbr. articles to profl. jours. Nat. bd. dirs. UN Assn. of U.S.A., 1966-76, 79-84, U.S. Com. for UNICEF, 1970-80, World Environment Ctr., 1981—, chmn., 1993—; bd. dirs. Westchester County Soil and Water Conservation Dist., 1976-83; chmn. N.Y. State Freshwater Wetlands Appeals Bd., 1976-83; mem. bd. edn. Union Free Sch. Dist. of Tarrytown, 1981-83, 85. Recipient N.Y. State Gov.'s Citation for Hist. Preservation, 1983, Eliz Haub prize in Environ. Law Free U. Brussels, 1992. Fellow Am. Bar Found.; mem. Internat. Council Environ. Law (gov. 1993—), Am. Soc. Internat. Law, ABA, ALI, N.Y. State Bar Assn. (chmn. environ. law sect. 1979-80, environ. law award 1981), Assn. Bar City N.Y. (chmn. environ. law com. 1977-78, mem. internat. law com. 1985-88, internat. environ. law com. 1990—, russian law com. 1992—), Westchester County Bar Assn., Sierra Club (nat. bd. dirs. 1979-83), Phi Beta Kappa. Democrat. Unitarian. Home: 258 Kelbourne Ave Tarrytown NY 10591-1322 Office: Pace U Sch Law 78 N Broadway White Plains NY 10603-3710

ROBINSON, PAMELA, dancer. Attended, Ctrl. Pa. Youth Ballet, Cin. Conservatory of Music, Lexington Ballet, Nat. Acad. Arts, Chempaign, Ill. Dancer Cleve. Ballet, Ala. Ballet, 1982-85; dancer Ballet West, Salt Lake City, 1985-88, prin. dancer, 1988—. Dance performances include Anna Karenina, Rosalinda, Lady of the Camellias, The Nutcracker, Sleeping Beauty, Swan Lake, Giselle, Carmina Burana (John Butler). Office: Ballet West 50 W 200 S Salt Lake City UT 84101-1642

ROBINSON, PATRICIA ELAINE, women's health nurse practitioner; b. St. Louis, June 30, 1955; d. Harold Winford and Robbie LaVeal (Ferguson) Hammett; m. Kenneth M. Robinson, Nov. 18, 1978 (div.); children: Barry Christopher, Emily Vanessa; m. C. gilbert, Nov. 20, 1990. ADN, St. Louis Community Coll., 1987; student, Webster U., 1990—; cert. in forensic pathology, St. Louis U., 1975; cert. in pharmacology, St. Louis Coll. Health, 1984; womens health nurse practioner, U. Mo., 1995. Per diem float nurse St. Louis U. Hosp.; coord. ob-gyn. unit Group Health Plan, St. Louis; staff nurse Barnes Hosp., St. Louis; staff nurse dept. ob-gyn. Washington U. Sch. Medicine, St. Louis, 1990-93; chief exec. study coord. women's health rsch. Obstetric & Gynecologic Diagnosis & Consultation, Florissant, Mo., 1992—; acting dir. Nurses for Reproductive Health Svcs., St. Louis, 1990-93. Mem. NAFE, Nurse Assn. Am. Coll. Obstetrics and Gynecologists, Med. Group Mgmt. Assn., Nat. Assn. Nurse Practitioners Reproductive Health, Phi Theta Kappa. Office: OBG Diagnosis & Consultation 1150 Graham Rd Ste 105 Florissant MO 63031-8013

ROBINSON, PAUL ARNOLD, historian, educator, author; b. San Diego, Oct. 1, 1940; s. Joseph Cook and Beryl Marie (Lippincott) R.; m. Ute Brosche, Aug. 3, 1964 (div. Aug. 1967); 1 child, Susan Marie. B.A., Yale U., 1962; postgrad., Free U. Berlin, 1962-63; PhD, Harvard U., 1968. Asst. prof. history Stanford U. (Calif.), 1967-73, assoc. prof., 1973-80, prof. history, 1980—, Richard W. Lyman prof. in the humanities, 1994—. Author: The Freudian Left, 1969, The Modernization of Sex, 1976, Opera and Ideas: From Mozart to Strauss, 1985, Freud and His Critics, 1993; editor: Social Thought in America and Europe, 1970; contbg. editor The New Republic, 1979-85. Guggenheim fellow, 1970-71, Stanford Humanities Ctr. fellow, 1984-85, Inst. for Advanced Study fellow, 1990-91. Fellow Am. Acad. Arts and Scis.; mem. Am. Hist. Assn. Home: 671 Santa Ynez St Palo Alto CA 94305-8542 Office: Stanford Univ Dept History Stanford CA 94305

ROBINSON, PETER, paleontology educator, consultant; b. N.Y.C., N.Y., July 19, 1932; s. Edward and Carol Nye (Rhoades) R.; m. Patricia Ellen Fisher, Sept. 11, 1954 (div. Mar. 1980); children: Diane Elizabeth, Nathan; m. Paola D'Amelio Villa, Dec. 8, 1984. BS, Yale U., 1954, MS, 1958, PhD, 1960. Instr. Harpur Coll. SUNY, Binghamton, 1955-57; rsch. assoc. Yale Peabody Mus., New Haven, 1960-61; curator geology U. Colo. Mus., Boulder, 1961—, asst. prof. natural history, 1961-67, assoc. prof., 1967-71, prof., 1971—, dir. mus., 1971-82, prof. geol. sci., 1971—; geologist Colo. Nubian Expdn., Sudan, 1962-66; chief Colo. Paleontol. Expdn., Tunisia, 1967—; mem. geol. adv. group Colo. Bur. Land Mgmt., Denver, 1983—. Mem. AAAS, Soc. Vertebrate Paleontology (pres. 1977-78), Australian Mammal Soc., Soc. Española Paleontologia, Sigma Xi. Democrat. Home: 5110 Williams Fork Trl Apt 204 Boulder CO 80301-3408 Office: Campus Box 315 Mus U Colo Boulder CO 80309

ROBINSON, PETER CLARK, general management executive; b. Brighton, Mass., Nov. 16, 1938; s. Richard and Mary Elizabeth (Cooper) R.; m. Sylvia Phyllis Petschek, Aug. 26, 1961 (div. 1973); children: Marc Louis, Nicholas Daniel, Andrea Suzanne; m. Sarah Lingham, Jan. 1, 1984. B.S. in Fgn. Service, Georgetown U., 1961; M.B.A., Babson Inst., 1963; AMP, Harvard U., 1986. Asst. supt. prodn. Mass. Broken Stone Co., Weston, 1961-62; night shift supt. Mass. Broken Stone Co., 1962-65, v.p. ops., 1968, v.p., 1969-75, 85-94, sr. v.p., 1995—, also dir.; gen. supt. Berlin Stone Co., 1965-67, v.p. ops., 1968; v.p. Holden Trap Rock Co., to 1975, also dir., v.p., 1985-94, sr. v.p., 1995—; pres. Blount Materials Inc., Saginaw, Mich., 1975-81; v.p. corp. mktg. Blount, Inc., Montgomery, 1978-79, v.p. corp. planning and mktg., 1979-92, v.p. corp. planning and devel., 1992-94; group exec., pres. Blount Agri/Indsl. Corp., 1984-90; pres. P.C. Robinson & Co., Montgomery, 1994—; mem. The Planning Forum; bd. dirs. Mass. Broken Stone Co. Mem. Nat. Stone Assn. (dir., exec. com., chmn. govt. affairs com., chmn. bd.), Am. Mgmt. Assn., Am. Soc. Agrl. Engrs., Newcomen Soc., Engring. Soc. Detroit, Pres. Assn., SME-AIME. Clubs: Montgomery Country, Capital City (Montgomery), Harvard (Boston). Home: 1822 Galena Ave Montgomery AL 36106-1910 Office: Robinson & Co 1067 Woodley Rd Ste C Montgomery AL 36106-2414

ROBINSON, PHIL ALDEN, director; b. Long Beach, Mar. 1, 1950; s. S. Jesse and Jessie Francis (Roth) Robinson. BA, Union Coll., 1971. Newscaster Stas. WGY/WRGB-TV, Schenectady, 1969-71; freelance filmmaker Los Angeles, 1974—. Screenwriter All of Me, 1984, (with others) Rhinestone, 1984, (TV) 2 episodes Trapper John, M.D., 1981-82; writer, dir. In the Mood, 1987; dir. (TV) 2 episodes George Burns Comedy Week, 1986; screenwriter, dir. Field of Dreams (nomination Writers Guild, Dirs. Guild, Best Picture and Best Screenplay Adaption Acad. award nominations); co-screenwriter, dir. Sneakers. Served to 1st lt. USAF, 1971-74. Named Screenwriter of Yr. Nat. Assn. Theatre Owners, 1990. Mem. Acad. Motion Picture Arts and Scis., Writers Guild Am. West, Dirs. Guild Am., ASCAP.

ROBINSON, PHILLIP DEAN, hospital executive; b. Houston, Aug. 30, 1956; s. Juan Dean and Beverly Ann (Moore) R. BA in Biology, Tex. A&M U., 1978; M of Health Adminstrn., Washington U., St. Louis, 1980. Adminstrv. resident The Meth. Hosp., Houston, 1980-81, adminstrv. asst., 1981-82, asst. v.p. diagnostic and therapeutic services, 1982-84, v.p. patient services, 1984-89; sr. v.p. The Meth. Hosps., Houston, 1989-93; exec. v.p., hosp. dir. Alton Ochsner Med. Found., New Orleans, 1994—; student sponsor U. Houston at Clear Lake, 1986-89; bd. dirs. Lifegift Organ Donor Ctr., Houston, 1987-93, vice chmn. bd., 1992-93, chmn. bd., 1993; adminstrv. dir. Cancer Control Rsch. Ctr., Baylor Coll. Medicine/The Meth. Hosp., Houston., bd. dirs. Vol. Ctr., 1989—, La. Organ Procurement Agy. Contbr. articles to profl. jours. Adminstrv. bd. St. Luke's United Meth. Ch., Houston, 1991—; bd. dirs. Juvenile Diabetes Found., New Orleans, Epilepsy Assn. Houston/Gulf Coast; mem. Leadership Houston, Class VI, 1987-88. Recipient Modern Healthcare's Up and Comers award 3M and Modern Healthcare, 1992. Fellow Am. Coll. Healthcare Execs.; mem. La. Hosp. Assn., Internat. Conf. on Health Effects of Low Dose Radiation (host com.), Internat. Leadership Assembly, New Orleans Met. Hosp. Coun., Assn. Former Students Tex. A&M U., Dietary Mgrs.' Assn. (mem. adv. coun. of healthcare adminstrs.). Avocations: travel, sailing, gardening, cycling. Home: 925 Jefferson Ave New Orleans LA 70115-3026 Office: Ochsner Found Hosp 1516 Jefferson Hwy New Orleans LA 70121-2429

ROBINSON, PREZELL RUSSELL, academic administrator; b. Batesburg, S.C., Aug. 25, 1922; s. Clarence and Annie (Folks) R.; m. Lulu Harris, Apr. 9, 1950; 1 dau. A.B. in Econs. and Social Sci., St. Augustine's Coll., 1946; M.A. in Sociology and Econs., Cornell U., 1951, Ed.D. in Sociology-Ednl. Adminstrn., 1956; D.C.L. (hon.), U. of the South, 1970; L.H.D., Cuttington U. Coll., Monrovia, Liberia, Voorhees Coll., 1981, Episcopal Theol. Sem., 1982; LL.D. (hon.), Bishop Coll., 1979; D.C.L., Columbia U., 1980; DHL (hon.), Kenyon Coll., 1988. Tchr. social sci., French Bettis Jr. Coll.,

Trenton, S.C., 1946-48; sucessively registrar, tchr., acting prin. high sch., acting dean jr. coll., instr., dir. adult edn. Voorhees Jr. Coll., Denmark, S.C., 1948-56; prof. sociology, dean coll. St. Augustine's Coll., Raleigh, N.C., 1956-64, exec. dean, 1964-66, acting pres., 1966-67, pres., 1967—; pres. United Negro Coll. Fund, Inc., 1978-81, Nat. Assn. Equal Opportunity Higher Edn., 1981-84, N.C. Assn. Coll. & U., Cooperating Raleigh Colls., 1981, 86—; bd. dirs. Learning Inst. N.C.; scholar-in-residence Nairobi (Kenya) U., 1973; vis. lectr. Dept. State del. to African nations, 1971, 73, 78; Dir. Wachovia Bank & Trust Co. Contbr. articles to profl. publs. Mem. exec. com. N.C. Edn. Com. on Tchr. Edn.; mem. N.C. Bd. Edn.; chmn. bd. Assn. Episcopal Colls.; mem. Mayor's Community Relations Com.; vice chmn. Wake County div. Occoneechee coun. Boy Scouts Am., 1959-67; chmn. Wake Occoneechee coun., 1963-66, mem. exec. com., from 1965; vice chmn. Wake County chpt. ARC; chmn. edn. div. United Fund of Raleigh, mem. budget com., 1965—; mem. exec. com. Wake County Libraries.; trustee Voorhees Coll. Fulbright fellow to India, summer 1965; former U.S. Pres. George Bush appointee U.S. Rep. or Public Member Amb. U.N., N.Y., 1992. Served with AUS, 1942. Recipient Distinguished Alumni award Voorhees Coll., 1967, Silver Anniversary award N.C. Community System, 1989; decorated Star of Africia Liberia; recipient numerous service awards and citations; named one of the most effective coll. pres.s in U.S. Coun. for Advancement and Support of Edn., Washington, 1986; Univ. fellow Cornell U., 1954, rsch. fellow, 1955, 56; Fulbright fellow, 1965. Mem. AAAS, Nat. Assn. Collegiate Deans and Registrars, Am. Acad. Polit. and Social Sci., Am. Sociol. Soc., N.C. Sociol. Soc. (exec. com.), Ctrl. Intercollegiate Athletic Assn. (exec. com.), N.C. Assn. Ind. Colls. and Univs. (dir.), Raleigh C. of C. (A.E. Finley Disting. Svc. award 1989), So. Sociol. Assn., Am. Acad. Polit. Sci., N.C. Lit. and Hist. Soc., N.C. Hist. Soc., Delta Mu Delta, Phi Delta Kappa, Phi Kappa Phi, Alpha Kappa Mu, Phi Beta Lambda. Protestant Episcopalian (lay reader). Home: 821 Glascock St Raleigh NC 27604 Office: St Augustine's Coll 1315 Oakwood Ave Raleigh NC 27610-2247

ROBINSON, R. CLARK, mathematician, educator; b. Seattle, Dec. 29, 1943; s. Rex J. and Ruth C. (Clark) R.; m. Peggie Crose, Aug. 20, 1966. From asst. prof. to assoc. prof. Northwestern U., Evanston, Ill., 1969-78, prof., 1978—. Author: Dynamical Systems: Stability Symnolic Dynamics, and Chaos, 1995; contbr. numerous articles to profl. jours. Mem. Am. Math. Soc., Math. Assn. Am., Soc. Indsl. and Applied Math. Presbyterian. Office: Math Dept Northwestern U 2033 Sheridan Rd Evanston IL 60208-0830

ROBINSON, RANDALL, think-tank executive. Exec. dir. Trans Africa Form, Wash., D.C.; now pres. Trans Africa Form, Wash, D.C. Office: TransAfrica 1744 R St NW Washington DC 20009-2410*

ROBINSON, RAY CHARLES See CHARLES, RAY

ROBINSON, RAYMOND EDWIN, musician, music educator, writer; b. San Jose, Calif., Dec. 26, 1932; s. Elam Edwin and Zula Mai (Hatley) R.; m. Ruth Aleen Chamberlain, Mar. 12, 1954; children: Cynthia Rae, Greg Edwin, David L., Brent Steven, Jeffrey Vernon. BA, San Jose State U., 1956; MMus, Ind. U., 1958, D in Mus. Edn., 1969; LHD, Westminster Choir Coll., 1987; postdoctoral study, Cambridge U., England, 1987-89, Jagiellonian U., Poland, 1995. Instr. music Ind. U., Bloomington, 1958-59; music critic Portland Reporter, 1962-63, Balt. Evening Sun, 1964-68; founder, tchr. seminar for music adminstrs., 1972—; chmn. divsn. fine arts Cascade Coll., Portland, Oreg., 1959-63; dean Peabody Inst., Balt., 1963-69; pres. Westminster Choir Coll., Princeton, N.J., 1969-87; vis. fellow Wolfson Coll. U. Cambridge, Eng., 1987-89; disting. prof. choral studies, choral condr. Palm Beach Atlantic U., West Palm Beach, Fla., 1989—; pres. Prestige Publs. Inc., 1978—;, 1992-95; music critic Palm Beach (Fla.) Post, 1991—; prof. Sch. Ch. Music Knox Theol. Sem., Ft. Lauderdale, Fla., 1989—; choral condr. Palm Beach C.C., Lake Worth, Fla., 1992-93; condr.-in-residence, dir. music First Presbyn. Ch., West Palm Beach, 1989—; spl. guest choral condr. Palm Beach Opera, 1990—; interim condr. Choral Soc. Palm Beaches, 1992; condr. Ray Robinson Chorale, 1994—. Author: The Choral Experience, 1976, Choral Music, 1978; Krzysztof Penderecki, A Guide to His Works, 1983, A Study of the Penderecki St. Luke Passion, 1983, John Finley Williamson: A Centennial Appreciation, 1987; co-author: German Diction for the Choral Singer, 1992, A Bach Tribute: Bach Essays in Honor of William H. Scheide, 1993; editor The Choral Tradition Series, Hinshaw Music Inc., 1978—, Studies in Penderecki, 1994—. Bd. dirs. Balt. Symphony Orch., 1967-69, Am. Boy Choir Sch., 1970-73, N.Y. Choral Soc., 1972—, Palm Beach Atlantic U. choral series Hinshaw Music Inc., 1990—; bd. dirs. Palm Beach County Coun. Arts, chmn. profl. artists com., mem. task force for master plan, 1990-92; mem. cultural plan com. Palm Beach County Cultural Coun., 1992—; mem. task force for edn. Fla. Philharm. Orch., 1994—. Recipient Disting. Alumni Merit award Ind. U., 1975, Disting. Alumni award Sch. Music, 1973, Disting. Alumni award San Jose State U., 1990. Mem. Coll. Music Soc. (life), Am. Choral Dirs. Assn. (life, chmn. rsch. and publs. com. 1986—), Internat. Heinrich Schütz Soc. (chmn. Am. sect. 1984-87), Univ. Club N.Y., Nassau Club Princeton, Govs. Club West Palm Beach. Presbyterian. Home: 2413 Medina Way West Palm Beach FL 33401-8019

ROBINSON, RICHARD FRANCIS, writer, author; b. Passaic, N.J., June 13, 1941; s. Francis Ward and Evelyn (Burnett) R.; m. Brenda Kay Moore, Feb. 6, 1970; 1 child, Kelly. Student, Coll. of William & Mary, 1959-60; BA in Journalism, Mich. State U., 1964. Reporter, columnist North Jersey Herald News, Passaic, 1964-67; med. writer, reporter The Oakland Press, Pontiac, Mich., 1967-75; staff reporter Nat. Enquirer, Lantana, Fla., 1975-79; staff writer Hank Meyer Assocs., Miami, Fla., 1987-88; pres. Dick Robinson Co., Delray Beach, Fla., 1979—; bd. dirs. Krynova Enterprises, Inc., St. Petersburg, Fla. Editor: Foot & Leg Function, 1988-90; contbr. numerous articles to publs. Delegate Mich. State Rep. Conv., Detroit, 1970; mem. exec. bd. Mich. Fedn. Young Reps., 1970. Recipient First Pl. award AP, 1973. Mem. Am. Med. Writers Assn. (bd. dirs. 1984-85, chmn. trade book awards com. 1986, founding pres. Fla. chpt. 1983-84, pres. 1986-88), Nat. Assn. Sci. Writers, Fla. Freelance Writers Assn., Athletic Club Boca Raton, Delray Beach Tennis Ctr. Avocations: tennis, computers, photography. Home and Office: 250 S Ocean Blvd Apt 252 Delray Beach FL 33483-6752 *To succeed at anything in life, honestly believe you can do it well-and you will.*

ROBINSON, ROBERT ARMSTRONG, pension fund executive; b. Waterbury, Conn., Sept. 11, 1925; s. Robert and Ethel (Armstrong) R.; m. D. Ann Harding, June 7, 1947; 1 child, Gayllis Robinson Ward. A.B. magna cum laude, Brown U., 1950, M.A., 1952; postgrad., U. Ill., 1954-55; Litt. D., Episcopal Theol. Sem. Ky., 1971; D.C.L., U. South, 1972; LL.D., Nashotah House, Oconomowoc, Wis. Instr. English Brown U., 1950-53; instr. English, asst. prof. rhetoric U. Ill., 1953-56; trust officer Colonial Bank & Trust Co., Waterbury, 1956-63; v.p., trust officer Colonial Bank & Trust Co., 1963-65, sr. trust officer, 1965-66; v.p., sec. Ch. Pension Fund and Affiliates, Ch. Life Ins. Corp., Ch. Ins. Co., Ch. Agy. Corp., Ch. Hymnal Corp., 1966-67, exec. v.p., 1967-68, pres., dir., 1968-91; pres. emeritus Ch. Pension Fund and Affiliates, Ch. Life Ins. Corp., et al., 1991—; mgr. East Side House Settlement; bd. dirs. Seabury Press, Inc., Mariners Instl. Funds, Inc., Mariner Tax Free Instl. Fund, UST Master Funds, Morehouse Pub. Co., Inc., Mariner Funds Trust, Mariner Equity Trust, Pigmy Corp., U.S.T. Master Tax Free Funds, U.S.T. Master Variable Series, Inc., Rosiclare Lead and Fluorspar Mining Co., Infinity Funds, Inc., others; cons. to exec. dir. Pension Benefit Guaranty Corp.; dir. Infinity Mutual Funds. Trustee Hillspeak, Eureka Springs, Ark., Canterbury Cathedral Trust in Am., Hoosac Sch. Washington Nat. Cathedral, Nashotah Theol. Sem., Wis., H.B. and F.K. Bugher Found., Living Ch. Found.; mem. exec. com. N.Y. couns. Boy Scouts Am., Ch. Pensions Conf.; mem. econ. adv. bd. Columbia U. Grad. Sch. Bus. Adminstrn, mem. John Carter Brown Libr. Assoc. With inf. AUS, 1943-46. Decorated Bronze Star, Purple Heart with oak leaf cluster, Mil. Order of the Purple Heart, Knights of Malta, Order St. John. Mem. Am. Numis. Soc. (councillor), Conn. Bankers Assn. (v.p., head trust divsn.), Am. Numis. Assn., Newsomen Soc., St. Andrew's Soc. (N.Y.C.), Brown Club (N.Y.C.), Union League Club (N.Y.C.), Church Club (N.Y.C.) (pres. 1991—), Country Club of New Canaan, Athenaeum Club (London), Pilgrims, Union, Met. Clubs (Washington), Yeaman's Hall Club (Charleston, S.C.), Phi Beta Kappa. Republican. Episcopalian (vestryman). Clubs: St. Andrew's Soc. (N.Y.C.), Brown (N.Y.C.), Union League (N.Y.C.), Church (N.Y.C.), Country of New Canaan, Athenaeum (London), Pilgrims, Union, Met. (Washington), Yeaman's Hall (Charleston, S.C.). Home: 2 Hathaway Common New Canaan CT 06840-5737 Office: 800 2nd Ave New York NY 10017-4709

ROBINSON, ROBERT BLACQUE, foundation administrator; b. Long Beach, Calif., Apr. 24, 1927; s. Joseph LeRoi and Frances Hansel R.; m. Susan Amelia Thomas, Jan. 21, 1960; children: Victoria, Shelly, Blake, Sarah. Student, Oreg. State Coll., 1946; BA, UCLA, 1950; student, U. Hawaii. Partner, Pritchard Assocs. (Mgmt. Cons.), Honolulu, 1956-58; asst. dir. Econ. Planning and Coordination Authority, Hawaii, 1959; dep. dir. dept. econ. devel. State of Hawaii, 1960-63; asst. mgr. Pacific Concrete and Rock Co., Ltd., Honolulu, 1963-66, exec. v.p. and gen. mgr., 1966-68, pres. and gen. mgr., 1968-75; chmn. Pacific Concrete and Rock Co., Ltd., 1976-77; pres. C. of C. of Hawaii, Honolulu, 1977—. Bd. govs. Hawaii Employers Coun., 1969-74, mem. exec. com., 1969-74; vice chmn., 1973-74; bd. dirs. Pacific Aerospace Mus., 1982-86; mem. Hawaii Tourism Conf., 1977, chmn., 1981-82; bd. dirs. Aloha United Fund, 1970-76, sec., 1972, v.p., 1973-76; bd. dirs. Oahu Devel. Conf., 1970-75; treas., bd. dirs. Crime Stoppers Hawaii, 1981—; mem. Hawaii Joint Coun. on Econ. Edn., 1985—; bd. dirs. Jr. Achievement Hawaii, 1967-73, pres., 1969; bd. dirs. Hawaii Ednl. Coun., 1974-75, Health and Community Services Coun. Hawaii, 1982-84; mem. exec. com. Hawaii Conv. Ctr. Coun., 1984—, Interagency Energy Conservation Coun., State of Hawaii, 1978—; trustee Cen. Union Ch., 1983-86; bd. dirs. Waikiki Improvement Assn. Inc., 1986—; mem. Ctr. for Tropical and Subtropical Aquaculture industry Adv. Coun., 1987—; chmn. Mayor's Adv. Com. on Pacific Nations Ctr., 1988-89. Lt. comdr. USNR, 1945-46, ret. Mem. Japan-Am. Conf. of Mayors and C. of C. Pres. (mem. Am. exec. com. 1974—), Am. Soc. Assn. Execs. (past dir. Hawaii chpt.), Hawaii Execs. Coun. (found. , Young Pres. Assn. (past mem.), Aloha Soc. Assn. Execs., C. of C. Hawaii (dir. 1972-75, chmn. 1975), Coun. of Profit Sharing Industries (past dir. Hawaii sect.), Cement and Concrete Products Industry of Hawaii (pres. 1968), Hawaii Mfrs. Assn. (past dir.), Navy League of U.S. (Hawaii council), Engring. Assn. Hawaii, Pacific Club, Rotary, Sigma Chi. Home: 1437 Kalaepohaku St Honolulu HI 96816-1804 Office: C of C Hawaii 735 Bishop St Ste 220 Honolulu HI 96813-4816

ROBINSON, ROBERT GEORGE, psychiatry educator; b. Pitts., May 22, 1945; s. Robert Campbell and Rosetta M. (Martindale) R.; m. Gretchen Priscilla Smith, Jan. 5, 1974; children: Christopher, Jonathan. BS in Engring. Physics, Cornell U., 1967, MD, 1971. Intern Montefiore Hosp. and Albert Einstein Med. Ctr., 1971-72; resident Cornell U., White Plains, 1972-73; rsch. assoc. NIMH, Washington, 1973-75; resident Johns Hopkins U., 1975-77, asst. prof. to assoc. prof., 1977-90, prof., 1990-91; prof., head of dept. U. Iowa Coll. Medicine, Iowa City, 1991—; mem. editorial bds. Jour. Neuropsychiatry & Clinical Neurosciences, Int. Jour. Psychiatry in Medicine, Psychiatry. Editor: Depression and Coexisting Disease, 1989; contbr. 159 articles and chpts. to pubs. Mullen Engring. scholar Cornell U., 1967; recipient Sandra Lee Shaw award for rsch. in neurology and pharmacology, Cornell U., 1969, Research Scientist award, NIMH, 1989; Mellon fellow Johns Hopkins U., 1977. Fellow APA; mem. Soc. for Neuroscience, Royal Coll. of Psychiatrist, AAAS, Soc. of Biological Psychiatry. Office: U Iowa Coll Med 500 Newton Rd Iowa City IA 52246

ROBINSON, ROBERT L., financial service company executive, lawyer; b. Ridgeway, Va., Feb. 22, 1936; s. Gerald L. and Annie (McBride) R.; m. Audrey M. Allen, July 30, 1960; children: Robert, Diane, Kelly. B.A., Va. State Coll., 1957; LL.B., Harvard U., 1960; M.B.A., U. Conn., 1976. Bar: N.Y. 1961, Pa. 1978. Atty. N.Y. Central Ry. Co., N.Y.C., 1960-63; asst. gen. counsel Crane Co., N.Y.C., 1963-71; counsel Xerox Corp., Stamford, Conn., 1971-77; v.p., asst. gen. counsel and sec. INA Corp., Phila., 1977-82; sr. v.p., gen. counsel investment group CIGNA Corp., Bloomfield, Conn., 1982-84, sr. v.p., asst. gen. counsel, corp. sec., 1984-87; sr. v.p., gen. counsel property & casualty group CIGNA Corp., Phila., 1987-88, sr. v.p., chief counsel litigation, 1988—. Dir. Com. of Seventy. Served to lt. U.S. Army, 1957. Mem. ABA, Pa. Bar Assn., Westchester-Fairfield Corp. Counsel Assn. (founder, bd. dirs. pres. 1976-77), Great Oak Yacht Cub, Harvard Club (N.Y.C.), Merion Cricket Club, Phila. Club. Republican. Office: CIGNA Corp 1601 Chestnut St Philadelphia PA 19192-0003

ROBINSON, RONALD ALAN, oil company executive, manufacturing executive; b. Louisville, Mar. 23, 1952; s. J. Kenneth and Juanita M. (Crosier) R.; m. Joan Parker, 1986; children: Rex., Jay. BS, Ga. Inst. Tech., 1974; MBA, Harvard U., 1978. Staff engr., asst. to exec. v.p. ops. Dual Drilling Co., Wichita Falls, Tex., 1978-80; v.p. Dreco, Inc., Houston, 1980-84, pres., dir. subs. Triflo Industries Internat. Inc.; pres., COO Ramteck Systems, Inc., 1984-87; chm. and CEO Denver Techs. Inc., 1988-95; pres. Suedale Industries, Inc., 1996—. Recipient Optimist Internat. Citizenship award, 1970; Gardiner Symonds fellow, 1977. Mem. Harvard Alumni Assn. Home: 4815 Newstead Pl Colorado Springs CO 80906-5935 Office: Denver Equipment Co 621 S Sierra Madre St Colorado Springs CO 80903-4021

ROBINSON, RONALD MICHAEL, health care financial executive, financial consultant; b. N.Y.C., May 1, 1942; s. Arthur John and Matilda (Siegel) R.; m. Mary Jane Reemelin, Feb. 25, 1972; children: Scott Edward, Elizabeth Drew. BS, Ohio State U., 1964; MBA, U. Pa., 1966. CPA, Pa. Fin. mgr. Am. Airlines, Inc., N.Y.C., 1969-72; mgmt. cons. Coopers & Lybrand, Phila., 1973-75; pres. Robinson Assocs., Inc., Paoli, Pa., 1975-81; dir. fin. and adminstr., chief fin. officer Decision Scis. Corp., Jenkintown, Pa., 1981-82; sr. v.p. fin., chief fin. officer Presbyn. Homes, Inc., Camp Hill, Pa., 1982—. Bd. dirs. Healthamerica. Mem. Carlisle (Pa.) Borough Council, 1988-92. Mem. AICPA, Pa. Inst. CPAs, Health Care Fin. Mgmt. Assn., Fin. Execs. Inst., Pa. Assn. Non-Profit Homes for Aging, Masons, Rotary. Home: PO Box 908 Carlisle PA 17013-5908 Office: Presbyn Homes Inc 1217 Slate Hill Rd Camp Hill PA 17011-8012

ROBINSON, ROSCOE ROSS, nephrologist, educator; b. Oklahoma City, Aug. 21, 1929; s. Roscoe and Tennie (Ross) R.; m. Ann Allen, Aug. 24, 1952; children: Susan, Brooke. BS, U. Ctrl. Okla., 1949; MD, U. Okla., 1954, LHD, 1994. Diplomate: Nat. Bd. Med. Examiners, Am. Bd. Internal Medicine (asso. mem. bd. govs. 1975-78, mem. 1979-82, chmn. test com. on nephrology 1979-82). Intern in medicine Duke U. Med. Ctr., Durham, N.C., 1954-55, jr. asst. resident in medicine, 1955-56, chief resident, instr. medicine, 1957-58, assoc. in medicine, 1960-62, asst. prof. medicine, dir. div. nephrology, 1962-65, assoc. prof. medicine, dir. div. nephrology, 1965-69, prof. medicine, dir. div. nephrology, 1969-78, Florence McAlister prof. medicine, dir. div. nephrology, 1978-81, asso. v.p., 1976-81; chief exec. officer Duke U. Hosp., 1976-81; prof. medicine, vice chancellor health affairs Vanderbilt U. Med. Ctr., Nashville, 1981—; Am. Heart Assn. rsch. fellow, vis. fellow dept. medicine Columbia-Presbyn. Med. Ctr., N.Y.C., 1956-57; clin. investigator Durham VA Hosp., 1960-62, attending physician, 1962-81; cons. nephrology Fayetteville and Asheville, N.C.; cons. nephrology Research Triangle (N.C.) Inst., 1964-81; nat. cons. to surgeon gen. USAF, 1970-89; chmn. N.C. Kidney Coun. Region 21, Dept. HEW, 1977-81; bd. dirs. Research!America, 1993—. Mem. editorial bd. Archives Internal Medicine, 1970-80, Seminars in Nephrology, 1972-93, Mineral and Electrolyte Metabolism, 1977—; mem. editorial com. Fogerty internat. com. Monograph on Prevention of Kidney and Urinary Tract Disease; cons. editor renal diseases: Cecil Textbook of Medicine, 15th edit., 16th edit.; contbr. articles to profl. jours. Bd. dirs. SunHealth Corp., 1986-92, 1st Am. Corp., Tenn., 1992—; trustee Montgomery Bell Acad., Nashville, 1983—, Duke U., 1994—. Fellow ACP; mem. Am. Clin. and Climatol. Assn., Am. Fedn. Clin. Rsch. (councillor So. sect. 1968-71), Assn. Am. Physicians, European Dialysis and Transplant Assn., Am. Heart Assn., N.C. Heart Assn. (sr. investigator 1962-74, exec. com., bd. dirs. 1971-72), Am. Soc. Clin. Investigation, So. Soc. Clin. Investigation (councillor 1977-80), Am. Physiol. Soc., Am. Soc. Artificial Internal Organs (councillor 1968-71), Internat. Soc. Nephrology (editor Kidney Internat. jour. 1971-84, exec. com. 1972-95, v.p. 1984-87, pres.-elect 1987-90, pres. 1990-93), Am. Soc. Nephrology (councillor 1977-80, pres.-elect 1980-81, pres. 1981-82), Nat. Kidney Found. (sci. adv. bd. 1970-75), Kidney Found. N.C., Assn. Acad. Health Ctrs. (bd. dirs. 1985-91, chmn. 1989-90), Soc. Med. Adminstrs. (pres.-elect 1989-91, pres. 1991-93), Nat. Inst. Diabetes, Digestive and Kidney Diseases (nat. adv. coun. 1987-90), Alpha Omega Alpha. Home: 501 Jackson Blvd Nashville TN 37205-3427 Office: Vanderbilt U Med Center Nashville TN 37232

ROBINSON, SALLY WINSTON, artist; b. Detroit, Nov. 2, 1924; d. Harry Lewis and Lydia (Kahn) Winston; m. Eliot F. Robinson, June 28, 1949; children: Peter Eliot, Lydia Winston, Sarah Mitchell, Suzanne Finley. BA, Bennington Coll., 1947; postgrad. Cranbrook Acad. Art, 1949; grad. Sch. Social Work, Wayne U., 1948, MA, 1972; MFA, Wayne State U., 1973. Psychol. tester Detroit Bd. Edn., 1944; pyschol. counselor and tester YMCA, N.Y.C., 1946; social caseworker Family Service, Pontiac, Mich., 1947; instr. printmaking Wayne State U., Detroit, 1973—. One person shows U. Mich., 1973, Wayne State U., 1974, Klein-Vogol Gallery, 1974, Rina Gallery, 1976, Park McCullough House, Vt., 1976, Williams Coll., 1976, Arnold Klein Gallery, 1977; exhibited group shows Bennington Coll., Cranbrook Mus., Detroit Inst. Art, Detroit Artists Market, Soc. Women Painters, Soc. Arts and Crafts, Bloomfield Art Assn., Flint Left Bank Gallery, Balough Gallery, Detroit Soc. Women Painters, U. Mich., U. Ind., U. Wis., U. Pittsburg, Toledo Mus., Krannert Mus.; represented in permanent collections, Detroit, N.Y.C., Birmingham, Bloomfield Hills; tchr. children's art Detroit Inst. Art, 1949-50, now artistic advisor, bd. dirs. drawing and print orgn. Bd. dirs. Planned Parenthood, 1951—, mem. exec. bd., 1963—; bd. dirs. PTA, 1956-60, Roeper City and Country Sch., U. Mich. Mus. Art, 1978; trustee Putnam Hosp. Med. Research Inst., 1978; mem. Gov.'s Commn. Art in State Bldgs., 1978-79; mem. art and devel. coms. So. Vt. Art Ctr., 1987-88; mem. vol. com. Marie Selby Gardens. Mem. Detroit Artists Market (dir. 1956—), Bennington Coll. Alumnae Assn. (regional co-chmn. 1954), Detroit Soc. Women Painters, Birmingham Soc. Women Painters (pres. 1974-76), Bloomfield Art Assn. (program co-chmn. 1956), Founders Soc. Detroit Inst. Art., Village Women's Club (Birmingham, Mich.), Women's City Club (co-ordinator art shows Detroit 1950), Garden Club, Am. Club (Bennington, Vt., Sarasota, Fla.), Cosmopolitan (N.Y.C.). Unitarian. Home: 7 Monument Cir Bennington VT 05201-2134 also: 840 N Casey Key Rd Osprey FL 34229-9779 also: 200 E 69th St Apt 7B New York NY 10021

ROBINSON, SHARON PATTYSON, English educator; b. Rockville Center, N.Y., Mar. 15, 1947; d. Jack Ward and Mary Margaret (Coogan) Pattyson; m. W. Bruce Robinson, July 18, 1971; 1 child, Margaret L. AB, Vassar Coll., 1969; MA, Johns Hopkins U., 1970; PhD, U. Toledo, 1976. Lectr. English dept. U. Conn., Stamford, 1975-77; vis. asst. prof. U. Minn., Mpls., 1977-78; assoc. prof., chair English dept. Russell Sage Coll., Troy, N.Y., 1978—. Contbr. articles to profl. jours. Pres. N.Y. State Theatre Inst. Citizens Bd., Albany, N.Y., 1989—. Vis. humanities scholar NYU/Mellon Found., 1990. Mem. MLA, AAUP (sec. 1989-90). Democrat. Office: Russell Sage Coll 45 Ferry St Troy NY 12180-4115

ROBINSON, SHARON PORTER, federal official; b. Louisville. B in Edn., English and Psychology, U. Ky., 1966, M in Edn., Curriculum and Instrn., 1976, D in Ednl. Adminstrn. and Supervision, 1979. Tchr. Lexington, Ky., U.S. AFB, Bitburg, Germany; assoc. dir. Jefferson County Edn. Consortium, Ky., late 1970's; dir. instrn. and profl. devel. NEA, 1980-89, dir. R & D arm Nat. Ctr. Innovation, 1989-93; asst. sec. ednl. rsch. and improvement U.S. Dept. Edn., 1993—; cons. Nat. Bd. Profl. Teaching Standards; head tchr. edn. initiative Nat. Ctr. Innovation. Office: Dept of Education Educational Rsch & Improvement 555 New Jersey Ave NW Ste 600 Washington DC 20208-5530*

ROBINSON, SMOKEY, singer, composer; b. Detroit; m. Claudette Rogers (div.); children: Berry William, Tamla Claudette. V.p. Motown Record Corp. Formed group, Smokey Robinson and the Miracles, with Miracles, 1957-72, performed Detroit nightclubs, co-founder, Tamla record label, 1959; numerous singles and album recs. including: Sweet Harmony, 1973, Virgin Man, 1974, Agony and the Ecstasy, 1975, Quiet Storm, 1976, Open, 1976, There will Come a Day (I'm Gonna Happen to You), 1977; appearances at clubs, colls., also network TV shows including Shindig; star own TV spl., 1971; solo albums include Smokey, 1973, A Quiet Storm, Smokey's Family Robinson, Deep in My Soul, Smokin', Warm Thoughts, Being with You, 1989, Smokey's World, Shop Around, One Heartbeat, 1987, Love Smokey, 1990, Blame It on Love & All the Great Hits, 1990, Double Good Everything, 1992; appeared on Broadway in An Evening with Smokey Robinson, 1985; author: (autobiography with David Ritz) Smokey: Inside My Life, 1989. Inducted Rock 'n Roll Hall of Fame, 1986, Songwriters Hall of Fame, 1986; recipient Grammy award for best male rhythm & blues vocal perfomance, 1987, Founders award ASCAP, 1988. Office: care Michael Roshkind 6255 W Sunset Blvd Fl 18 Los Angeles CA 90028-7403

ROBINSON, SPENCER, JR., retired service club executive, accountant; b. Bridgeport, Conn., Apr. 16, 1942; s. Spencer Robinson and Helen (Diesinger) McNeill; m. Sally Emptage, June 21, 1963; children: David Spencer, Todd Wallace, John Marshall, Sarah Ann. BSIM, Ga. Tech. U., 1963; BS in Acctg., Jacksonville U., 1969; MSHA, U. Ala., Birmingham, 1989. Mng. ptnr. Deloitte Haskins & Sells, N.Y.C., 1963-85; exec. v.p., chief operating officer U. Ala. Health Svcs. Found., Birmingham, 1985-90; gen. sec., chief adminstrv. officer Rotary Internat., Evanston, Ill., 1990-94; adj. prof. Montreat Coll. Sch. Profl. and Adult Studies, 1995-96. Contbr. articles to profl. jours. Gen. sec. Rotary Found., Evanston, 1990-94; mem. Gov.'s Com. of 100, La., 1985; trustee Nat. Multiple Sclerosis Soc., La., 1984; sec., treas. Crimestoppers, Inc., New Orleans, 1983. Recipient Razzberry award Birmingham Press Club, 1989, Disting. Alumni award Jacksonville U., 1993. Republican. Presbyterian. Home: PO Box 280 Montreat NC 28757-0280

ROBINSON, SPENCER T. (HERK ROBINSON), professional baseball team executive; b. June 25, 1940; m. Kathy Robinson; children: Ashley, Amanda. Student, U. Miami, Washington U., St. Louis. With Cin. Reds., 1962-67; asst. Baltimore Orioles, 1968; asst. scouting dir. Kansas City Royals, 1969-72, dir. stadium ops., 1973-74, v.p., 1975-85, exec. v.p. adminstrn., 1985-90, v.p., 1975-85, exec. v.p., gen. mgr., 1990—, former mem. bd. dirs. Office: Kans City Royals PO Box 419969 Kansas City MO 64141-6969

ROBINSON, STEPHEN MICHAEL, applied mathematician, educator; b. Columbus, Ohio, Apr. 12, 1942; s. Arthur Howard and Mary Elizabeth (Coffin) R.; m. Chong-Suk Han, May 10, 1968; children: Diana Marie, James Andrew. BA, U. Wis., 1962, PhD, 1971; MS, NYU, 1963; Doctor honoris causa, Univ. Zürich, 1996. Adminstr. U. Wis., Madison, 1969-72, asst. prof., 1972-75, assoc. prof., 1975-79, prof. indsl. engring. and computer scis., 1979—, chmn. dept. indsl. engring., 1981-84; cons. to various agys. Dept. Def., 1971—. Editor: Math. of Ops. Rsch., 1981-86, assoc. editor, 1975-80, Jour. Ops. Rsch., 1974-86, Math. Programming, 1986-91; mem. bd. editors Annals Ops. Rsch., 1984—, Set-Valued Analysis, 1992—, Jour. Convex Analysis, 1994—; adv. editor Math. of Ops. Rsch., 1987—; contbr. numerous articles to profl. jours. Trustee Village of Shorewood Hills, Wis., 1974-76, mem. fin. com. , 1973-87; bd. overseers Simon's Rock Coll., Great Barrington, Mass., 1991—. Served to capt. U.S. Army, 1963-69, Korea, Vietnam. Decorated Legion of Merit, Bronze star, Air medal, Army Commendation medal with 2 oak leaf clusters. Mem. Inst. for Ops. Rsch. and Mgmt. Scis. (mem. Ops. Rsch. Soc. Am. coun. 1991-94), Inst. Indsl. Engrs., Soc. Indsl. and Applied Math., Math. Programming Soc. (mem.-at-large of coun. 1991-94), Madison Club. Home: 1014 University Bay Dr Madison WI 53705-2251 Office: U Wis Dept Indsl Engring 1513 University Ave Madison WI 53706-1572

ROBINSON, SUE L(EWIS), federal judge; b. 1952. BA with highest honors, U. Del., 1974; JD, U. Pa., 1978. Assoc. Potter, Anderson & Corron, Wilmington, Del., 1978-83; asst. U.S. atty. U.S. Attys. Office, 1983-88; U.S. magistrate judge U.S. Dist. Ct. (Del. dist.), 1988-91, dist. judge, 1991—. Mem. Del. State Bar Assn. (sec. 1986-87). Office: US Dist Ct J Caleb Boggs Fed Bldg 844 N King St Lockbox 31 Wilmington DE 19801-3519*

ROBINSON, SUMNER MARTIN, college administrator; b. Boston, Dec. 7, 1928; s. Eli and Fannie (Solov) R.; m. Leanore Reiss, Dec. 20, 1953; children: Andrew, Eric, Evan. A.B., U. Maine, 1949; B.S., Mass. Coll. Pharmacy, 1954, M.S., 1956, Ph.D., 1961. Asst. prof. pharmacology Mass. Coll. Pharmacy, Boston, 1961-65; research biologist-pharmacologist U.S. Army Research Inst. Environ. Medicine, Natick, Mass., 1965-76, cons., 1976—; dean Mass. Coll. Pharmacy, Boston, 1976-83; pres. St. Louis Coll. Pharmacy, 1983-93, Mass. Coll. Pharmacy & Applied Health Sci., Boston, 1993—. Recipient Coll. medal Mass. Coll. Pharmacy, 1983. Mem. Am. Assn. Colls. Pharmacy, Am. Pharm. Assn., Nat. Assn. Retail Druggists.

Democrat. Home: 59 Whitewood Rd Westwood MA 02090-2146 Office: Mass Coll Pharmacy & Allied Health Sci 179 Longwood Ave Boston MA 02115-5804

ROBINSON, SUSAN MITTLEMAN, data processing executive; b. Bklyn., Nov. 18, 1941; d. Samuel and Ida (Priest) Mittleman; m. Sheldon N. Robinson, June 5, 1962; children: Edward Bruce, Nancy Michelle, Jonathan Scott, Karen Barbara, Judith Lynn. AAS in Computer Sci., BCC, Lincroft, N.J., 1981; BBA, CUNY, 1962; MS in Computer Sci., Fairleigh Dickinson U., 1983; postgrad., Seton Hall U., 1983-85. Engr. asst. United Technologies, East Hartford, Conn., 1962-64; programmer, systems analyst Litton Industries (Sweda), Pine Brook, N.J., 1981-83; asst. prof. data processing Mercer Coll., West Windsor, N.J., 1983-85; adj. instr. data processing Brookdale Community Coll., Lincroft, N.J., 1983—; coord. MIS N.J. Dept. Health, Trenton, 1985—; Novell Lan administr. N.J. Dept. Health, Trenton, N.J., 1994—; world wide web webmaster N.J. Dept. Health, Trenton; med. data set liaison N.J. Dept. Health and HCFA, 1996—; outsource cons. Medicare/Medicaid, Trenton, 1989—; cons. Health Care Fin. Authority, Balt., 1995—. Author (reference material) Info-Henco, 1987, Automated Survey Processing Environment Users Training Manual, 1993; developer computerized sys. to help patients and their family select a nursing home. Exec. bd. Temple Beth Am, Parsippany, N.J., 1972-80. Mem. SAS Users Group, N.J. DOH Prime Users Group. Avocations: knitting, puzzle-solving, travel. Office: NJ Dept Health CN 367 Trenton NJ 08625

ROBINSON, SYLVIA EVANS, educational administrator; b. Boston, Mar. 16, 1948; d. Warren Douglas and Sylvia Lucille (Johnson) Evans; m. John M. Robinson; children: Kamilah, Nailah, Earl, Matthew. BA, Sanford U., 1970; MA, Occidental Coll., L.A., 1972. Cert. tchr. K-12, Mass., Calif. Dean Wellesley (Mass.) Coll., 1977-86; spl. asst. to commr. R.I. Office Higher Edn., Providence, 1986-91; exec. dir. R.I. Children's Crusade for Higher Edn., Providence, 1991—. Bd. dirs. Leadership R.I., Providence, 1988—, Pub. Edn. Fund, Providence, 1987-94, R.I. Anti-Drug Coalition, Providence, 1992-94; bd. trustees Johnson and Wales U., Providence, 1993—; adv. com. Children's Initiative Task Force, United Way of S.E. New Eng., Providence, 1992-94. Recipient Disting. Cmty. Leadership award Nat. Assn. for Cmty. Leadership, 1993, David Sweet Leadership award Leadership R.I., 1992. Mem. Am. Assn. Higher Edn., Am. Coun. of Edn. Episcopalian. Avocations: tennis, biking. Home: 12721 Franklin Farm Rd Herndon VA 22071-1914 Office: RI Childrens Crusade 301 Promenade St Providence RI 02908-5720

ROBINSON, THEODORE CURTIS, JR., lawyer; b. Chgo., Jan. 22, 1916; s. Theodore Curtis and Edna Alice (Willard) R.; m. Marynel Werner, Dec. 28, 1940; children: Theodore Curtis III, Peter S. BA, Western Res. U., 1938, LLB, 1940. Bar: Ohio 1940, U.S. Dist. Ct. (no. dist.) Ohio 1946, U.S. Ct. Appeals (8th cir.) 1948, U.S. Dist. Ct. (we. dist.) Wis. 1950, U.S. Dist. Ct. (we. dist.) N.Y. 1950, U.S. Ct. Appeals (6th cir.) 1950, Ill. 1957, U.S. Dist. Ct. (no. dist.) Ill. 1957, U.S. Ct. Appeals (7th cir.) 1964, U.S. Supreme Ct. 1972. Assoc. Davis & Young, Cleve., 1940; law clk. no. dist. ea. div. U.S. Dist. Ct., Cleve., 1940-42; assoc. Leckie, McCreary, et al, Cleve., 1945-52; ptnr. McCreary, Hinslea & Ray, Cleve., 1953-57, McCreary, Hinslea, Ray & Robinson, Chgo., 1957-90; counsel Ray, Robinson, Hannin & Carle, Chgo., 1990-91, Ray, Robinson, Carle, Davies & Snyder, Chgo., 1991—; mem. exec. com. Maritime Law Assn. of U.S., N.Y.C., 1981-83; pres. Propellor Club of U.S., Chgo., 1966-67; sec., treas. Internat. Shipmasters Assn., Chgo., 1958-91. Lt. USCG, 1943-45. Fellow Am. Coll. Trial Lawyers; mem. ABA, Chgo. Bar Assn. (com. chmn. 1973), Internat. Assn. Def. Counsel, Order of Coif, Traffic Club Chgo. (dir. 1986, 87), Whitehall Club (N.Y.), Nat. Eagle Scout Assn. Republican. Avocations: gardening, golf, reading. Office: Ray Robinson Carle Davies & Snyder 850 W Jackson Blvd Chicago IL 60607-3025

ROBINSON, THOMAS BULLENE, retired civil engineer; b. Kansas City, Mo., Feb. 28, 1917; s. David Beach and Aileen March (Weaver) R.; m. Suzanne Callaway, May 24, 1941; children: Suzanne, Thomas Bullene, Alice Robinson Levy. B.S., Kans. U., 1939; M.S., Columbia U., 1940. Diplomate: Am. Acad. Environ. Engrs. Asst. engr. Black & Veatch (cons. engr.), Kansas City, 1940-43; prin. asst. engr., prin. engr. Black & Veatch (cons. engr.), 1946-56, partner, 1956-65, asst. mng. partner, 1965-72, mng. partner, 1973-82; chmn. bd. Black & Veatch Internat., 1973-82; cons., 1982—. Past pres. Heart of Am. United Campaign; trustee Kansas City U., U. Kans. Endowment Assn., Midwest Research Inst. Served to lt. Civil Engr. Corps, USNR, 1943-46. Recipient Honor award for disting. service in engring. U. Mo., 1971; Disting. Service citation U. Kans., 1975; Disting. Engring. Service award U. Kans., 1982. Fellow ASCE (hon. mem.), Am. Cons. Engrs. Council (pres. 1970-71); mem. Nat. Acad. Engring., Nat. Soc. Profl. Engrs., Am. Water Works Assn. (hon.), Sigma Xi, Tau Beta Pi, Sigma Tau, Beta Theta Pi. Club: Kansas City Country (Kansas City). Home: 6401 Norwood St Shawnee Mission KS 66208-1826

ROBINSON, THOMAS CHRISTOPHER, academic administrator, educator; b. Buffalo, Oct. 16, 1944; s. Christopher Sidney and Eleanor Florence (Martin) R.; m. Helen Dare Tew, June 21, 1986; children: Diane Dunn, Kristen Elizabeth, Molly Lindsay, Norman Ashley. BA, SUNY, Buffalo, 1966, EdM, 1968, PhD, 1971; grad. mgmt. devel. program, Harvard U., 1989. N.Y. State sec. sch. cert in social studies. Admissions officer, office of admissions of record SUNY, Buffalo, 1966-72, assoc. dean Sch. Health Related Professions, 1975-78; asst. dir. Erie County Lab., Buffalo, 1972-75; assoc. dean Coll. Health Professions, U. Ky., Lexington, 1978-84, dean, 1984—; cons. MDS Labs., Hamilton, Ont., Can., 1973-75, Joint U.S.-Arabian Commn. on Econ. Cooperation, 1986-87, West Sussex Inst. Higher Edn., Bogner Regis, U.K., 1987, U. Wis. Sys. Ctrs. of Excellence Program, 1988, Pub. Health Svc. Health Resources Adminstrn., 1983, 90-91; mem. exec. com. Nat. Practitioner Data Bank, 1992-94, cons. 1994-95; hon. mem. faculty Khabarovsk (Russia) Med. Inst., 1996; mem. bd. dirs. Ky. Healthcare Access Found., 1996—. Contbr. articles to profl. jours. Mem. Health Sys. Agy. Coun., Buffalo, 1977-78, Western N.Y. Hemophilia Soc. Bd. Buffalo, 1977-78, Lexington-Fayette County Bd. Health, Lexington, 1987-91, program excellence project Ohio Bd. Regents, United Way of Bluegrass Healthcare Devel. Bd., 1991; mem. La. Bd. Regents, 1995, Univ. Wolverhampton, U.K. With N.Y. Army N.G., 1968-74. Recipient Svc. award Jour. Allied Health, 1986. Mem. Assn. Schs. Allied Health Professions (bd. dirs. 1985-87, Svc. award 1987, Fellow award 1988, pres. 1991-94, past pres. 1994-95, Outstanding Member award 1995), Ky. Allied Health Consortium (bd. dirs. 1985-93, chair 1995-96), So. Assn. Allied Health Deans (sec. 1986-88, chmn. 1988-90), Assn. Schs. Allied Health Professions (pres. 1991-94), Ky. Hosp. Assn., Ky. Assn. of Healthcare Facilities, Ky. Primary Assn., Lexington C. of C., Civil War Round Table, Sigma Phi Epsilon. Avocations: golf, travel, geneology, gardening. Home: 620 Centennial Ln Lexington KY 40502-2770 Office: U Ky Coll Allied Health Professions Bldg Office of the Dean Rm 220 121 Washington Ave Lexington KY 40536

ROBINSON, THOMAS NATHANIEL, pediatrician, educator, researcher; b. Detroit, May 11, 1960; s. Kenneth J. and Judith R. (Rattner) R. BS in Biol. Scis., Stanford U., 1983, MD with rsch. honors, 1988; MPH in Maternal and Child Health, U. Calif., Berkeley, 1987. Diplomate Nat. Bd. Med. Examiners, Am. Bd. Pediatrics. Intern dept. medicine Children's Hosp. and Harvard Med. Sch., Boston, 1988-89, jr. asst. resident, 1989-90, sr. asst. resident, 1990-91; clin. fellow in pediatric medicine Harvard Med. Sch., Boston, 1988-91; Robert Wood Johnson clin. scholar Sch. Medicine Stanford U., Palo Alto, 1991-93, clin. instr. divsn. gen. pediatrics dept. pediatrics, acting dir. youth studies Ctr. for Rsch. in Disease Prevention Sch. Medicine, 1992-93, acting. asst. prof. divsn. gen. pediatrics dept. pediatrics, co-dir. youth studies Ctr. for Rsch. in Disease Prevention, 1993—; attending physician divsn. gen. pediatrics dept. pediatrics Stanford U. Hosp., Palo Alto, 1992—, Lucile Salter Packard Children's Hosp., Palo Alto, 1992—; clinician scientist Am. Heart Assn., 1993—; presenter in field. Contbr. articles to med. and sci. jours. Alumni Med. scholar Stanford U., 1985; grantee Met. Life Found., 1985-87. Fellow Am. Acad. Pediatrics (sch. health com. No. Calif. dist. 1992—, chair 1993—), Am. Heart Assn. (grantee 1993—, phys. activity subcom. 1993—). Office: Stanford U Sch Med Ctr for Rsch Disease Prevention 1000 Welch Rd Palo Alto CA 94304-1811

See ROBINSON, JAY (THURSTON)

ROBINSON, TONI, lawyer, educator; b. New Rochelle, N.Y.; d. Benjamin Mag and Eugenie (Lee) R.; m. Michael P. Plouf, Feb. 3, 1968. BA, Sarah Lawrence Coll., 1972; JD, Columbia U., 1976; LLM in Taxation, NYU, 1985. Bar: N.Y. 1977, U.S. Dist. Ct. (so. dist.) N.Y. 1977, U.S. Tax Ct. 1987. Assoc. Roberts & Holland, N.Y.C., 1976-79, Battle, Fowler, Jaffin & Kheel, N.Y.C., 1979-82; asst. prof. law U. Bridgeport, Conn., 1982-85, assoc. prof., 1985-88, prof., 1988-95, dir. tax clinic, 1987—; prof. law Quinnipiac Coll., Hamden, Conn., 1993—; tax adviser Conn. Small Bus. Adv. Svc., Bridgeport, 1987-92; asst. sec. UN Expert Group on Tax Treaties, N.Y.C., 1978-79, dep. sec., 1979-82; legal adviser Internat. Percy Grainger Soc., White Plains, N.Y., 1985-91; presenter, author study materials continuing legal edn. programs; vis. prof. law Coll. of William and Mary, Williamsburg, Va., 1989-90. Contbr. articles on taxes to profl. publs. Mem. ABA (tax sect.), N.Y. State Bar Assn. (tax sect.), Assn. of Bar of City of N.Y., Conn. Women's Bar Assn., Phi Delta Phi. Democrat. Mem. Soc. of Friends. Avocations: sailing, horses. Office: Quinnipiac Coll Sch Law 275 Mt Carmel Ave Hamden CT 06518-1947

ROBINSON, VAN NESS D., insurance company executive; b. 1935. Exec. v.p., sec., vice chmn. N.Y. Ctrl. Mut. Fire Ins., Edmeston, N.Y., 1957—. Office: NY Ctrl Mut Fire Ins 1899 Central Plz E Edmeston NY 13335*

ROBINSON, WALTER, newspaper editor. Asst. mng. editor local news, Metro Desk Boston Globe. Office: Boston Globe 135 Morrissey Boston MA 02107

ROBINSON, WALTER GEORGE, arts management and funding consultant; b. London, June 18, 1911; s. Walter and Annie (Ledger) R.; m. Ruth V. Holden, Sept. 14, 1941 (dec. Mar. 1987); stepchildren: Malcolm D. Whitman III, Gail W. Hughes; m. Vesta H. Bogle, May 31, 1990. Student, NYU, 1943; D.F.A. (hon.), Mpls. Coll. Art and Design, 1975. Engaged in investment bus. N.Y.C., 1928-33; with Bass River Savs. Bank, South Yarmouth, Mass., 1934-60, pres., 1952-60; dir. Cape & Vineyard Electric Co., 1958-60, Hyannis Trust Co., until 1960; pres. Mpls. Soc. Fine Arts, governing and supporting orgn. for Mpls. Inst. Arts, Mpls. Coll. Art and Design, Children's Theatre Co., 1960-72, vice chmn., treas., sec., 1972-75; acting dir. Mpls. Sch. Art, 1962-63; acting pres. Mpls. Coll. Art and Design, 1974-75; dir. resource devel. Mus. Fine Arts, Boston, 1975-77; arts mgmt. and funding cons., 1977—; pres. Am. Art Advocates, Inc., 1984-87; trustee Farmers & Mechanics Savs. Bank. Vice pres. Cape Cod Hosp., 1955-60; chmn. Mpls. Com. for Urban Environment, 1968-70, 72-74; mem. Minn. State Arts Council, 1967-73, Minn. Heritage Preservation Commn., 1972-75; chmn. Mpls. Bicentennial Commn., 1974-75; mem. Minn. Com. on Esthetic Environment, 1973-75; founding dir. E.B. Kelley Found., Hyannis, Mass., 1954-87, v.p., 1985-87; bd. dirs. Tyrone Guthrie Theatre Found., Mpls., 1960-70; trustee Northwestern Hosp., 1967-74, Am. Assn. Museums, 1973-75. Clubs: Skylight, Minneapolis, Minnesota (Mpls.). Home: PO Box 490 Damariscotta ME 04543-0490

ROBINSON, WALTER STITT, JR., historian; b. Matthews, N.C., Aug. 28, 1917; s. Walter Stitt and Mary Irene (Jamison) S.; m. Constance Lee Mock, Mar. 18, 1944; children—Ethel Barry, Walter Lee. B.A. summa cum laude, Davidson (N.C.) Coll., 1939; M.A., U. Va., 1941, Ph.D., 1950. Asst. prof., then assoc. prof. history Florence (Ala.) State Coll., 1946-48; mem. faculty U. Kans., Lawrence, 1950—; prof. history U. Kans., 1959-88, prof. emeritus, 1988—, chmn. dept., 1968-73; mem. Nat. Civil War Centennial Commn., 1961-65, Kans. Com. Humanities, 1971-78, chmn., 1976-77. Author: Land Grants in Virginia, 1607-1699, 1957, The Southern Colonial Frontier, 1607-1763, 1979, James Glen: From Scottish Provost to Royal Governor of South Carolina, 1996; editor: Indian Treaties of Colonial Virginia, 2 vols., 1983, Indian Treaties of Colonial Maryland, 1987; mem. editl. bd. 18th century bibliography in Philos. Quar., 1975-78; contbr. articles to profl. jours. Mem. adminstrv. bd. First United Methodist Ch., Lawrence, 1952—; exec. com., bd. dirs. Kans. Sch. Religion, pres., 1983-86. Served to capt. AUS, 1941-45. Decorated Bronze Star; recipient Disting. Scholarship award U. Kans., 1976; grantee Social Sci. Rsch. Coun., 1959-60, Am. Philos. Soc., 1967, 83, NEH, 1994. Mem. Orgn. Am. Historians (chmn. program com. 1959), So. Hist. Assn., Kans. Hist. Soc. (bd. dirs., exec. com. 1989—, v.p. 1996), Douglas County Hist. Soc. (pres. 1979-81, pres. 1995-96, bd. dirs.), Raven Soc., Phi Beta Kappa, Phi Alpha Theta (internat. coun. 1978-80, adv. bd. 1980-81, 86-87, pres. 1984-85). Home: 801 Broadview Dr Lawrence KS 66044-2490 Office: Dept History U Kans Lawrence KS 66045

ROBINSON, WILKES COLEMAN, federal judge; b. Anniston, Ala., Sept. 30, 1925; s. Walter Wade and Catherine Elizabeth (Coleman) R.; m. Julia Von Poellnitz Rowan, June 24, 1955; children: Randolph C., Peyton H., Thomas Wilkes Coleman. AB, U. Ala., 1948; JD, U. Va., 1951. Bar: Ala. 1951, Va. 1962, Mo. 1966, Kans. 1983. Assoc. Bibb & Hemphill, Anniston, Ala., 1951-54; city recorder City of Anniston, 1953-55; judge Juvenile and Domestic Relations Ct. of Calhoun County, Ala., 1954-56; atty. legal dept. GM&O R.R., Mobile, Ala., 1956-58; commerce counsel, asst. gen. atty. Seaboard Air Line R.R., Richmond, Va., 1958-66; commerce counsel Monsanto Co., St. Louis, 1966-70; gen. counsel, v.p. Marion Labs., Inc., Kansas City, Mo., 1970-79; pres. Gulf and Gt. Plains Legal Found., Kansas City, Mo., 1980-85; atty. Howard, Needles, Tammen & Bergendoff, Kansas City, 1985-86, also bd. dirs.; v.p. S.R. Fin. Group, Inc., Overland Park, Kans., 1986-87; judge U.S. Ct. Fed. Claims, Washington, 1987—. Bd. govs. Kansas City Philharmonic Orch., 1975-77. Served with USNR, 1943-44. Mem. Army Navy Country Club, Skyline Club, Univ. Club, Mason, Scottish Rite, Phi Beta Kappa (past treas. Kansas City, Mo. chpt.), Phi Eta Sigma, Phi Alpha Theta, Kappa Alpha. Episcopalian. Home: 2353 S Queen St Arlington VA 22202-1550 Office: US Ct Fed Claims 717 Madison Pl NW Washington DC 20005-1011

ROBINSON, WILLIAM ANDREW, health service executive, physician; b. Phila., Jan. 31, 1943; s. Colonial Washington and Lillian Dorothy (Ivey) R.; m. Jacqueline Ellen Garcia, Mar. 28, 1980; 1 child, David Alan; 1 child by previous marriage, William Andrew Jr. BA, Hampton U., 1964; MD, Meharry Med. Coll., 1971; MPH, Johns Hopkins U., 1973. Diplomate Nat. Bd. Med. Examiners; lic. physician, Md. Rotating intern George W. Hubbard Hosp., Nashville, 1971-72, emergency rm. physician, 1972; med. officer gastrointestinal drug sect., bur. drugs FDA USPHS, Dept. Health, Edn. and Welfare, Rockville, Md., 1973-75; dep. dir. office health resources opportunity USPHS, Dept. Health and Human Svcs., Rockville, 1975-80, dep. dir. bur. health professions health resources adminstn., 1980-87, chief med. officer health resources and svcs. adminstn., 1987-89; dep. asst. sec. minority health, dir. office minority health USPHS, Dept. Health and Human Svcs., Washington, 1989-91; acting adminstr. health resources and svcs. adminstn. USPHS, Dept. Health and Human Svcs., Rockville, 1993-94, chief med. officer health resources and svcs. adminstrn., 1991—; chmn. sr. execs. performance rev. bd. Office of Asst. Sec. for Health, 1990-91; pub. health svc. rep. 2d Internat. Conf. on Health Promotion, Adelaide, South Australia; health cons. com. on interior and insular affairs U.S. Ho. of Reps., Washington, 1982-83; appointed field faculty dept. family and comty. health Meharry Med. Coll., 1979; U.S. rep. to WHO Primary Health Care Conf., Alma Ata, Kazahkstan. Mem. nat. editl. bd. Jour. Health Care for the Poor and Underserved, 1991; contbr. articles to profl. jours. Capt. U.S. Army, 1964-67. Recipient Nat. Urban Coalition Comty. Health Svc. award, 1972, Letter of Appreciation, Chmn. Congl. Black Caucus Health Braintrust, U.S. Ho. of Reps., 1988. Mem. AMA, APHA, Am. Acad. Family Physicians, Blacks in Govt., Fed. Physicians Assn., Nat. Med. Assn., Sr. Execs. Assn., Delta Omega (Alpha chpt.). Office: 5600 Fishers Ln Rm 14-39 Rockville MD 20857-0001

ROBINSON, WILLIAM FRANKLIN, retired legal consultant; b. Hammond, Ind., Feb. 10, 1916; s. William P. and Pauline M. (Hopkins) R.; m. Betty Jo Powell, Sept. 15, 1946; children: William Franklin, Stephen Powell, Michael Paul. BA with high honors, Ind. U., 1942, JD, 1944. Bar: Ind. 1944, Mich. 1946, Calif. 1957. Spl. atty. Office Chief Counsel IRS, Washington, Detroit, 1944-46; pvt. practice Detroit, 1946-51; asst. gen. counsel, asst. sec. Montgomery Ward & Co. Inc., Chgo., 1951-56; v.p., gen. counsel, sec., dir. Transam. Fin. Corp., L.A., 1956-82, ret., 1982; legal cons., 1982-83; spl. instr. Wayne State U. Law Sch., U. Detroit, 1947-51. Contbr. articles to profl. jours., chpts. to textbooks. Mem. sch. bd., Calumet City, Ill., 1954-55; apptd. to Gov.'s Credit Retail Adv. Com., 1981; mem., bd. dirs., past pres. Ocean Hills Country Club Homeowners' Assn. Mem. Calif. Loan and Fin. Assn. (chmn. laws and regulations com.), Nat. Consumer Fin. Assn., Conf. Personal Fin. Law, Am., L.A. County bar assns., Acacia, Phi Beta Kappa, Phi Delta Phi. Home: 4136 Andros Way Oceanside CA 92056-7401

ROBINSON, WILLIAM J., health facility adminstrator; b. 1951. Controller Meml. Hosp., Worcester, Mass., 1972-82, Leonard Morse Hosp., Methuen, Mass., 1982-85, Valley Regional Health Sys., Inc., Methuen, Mass., 1985-88; treas. New England Daconess Hosp., Boston, 1988—. Office: New England Daconess Hosp 375 Longwood Ave Boston MA 02215-5324

ROBINSON, WILLIAM M., lawyer; b. Pitts., June 30, 1941. AB, Princeton U., 1963; LLB, U. Pa., 1966. Bar: Pa. 1967. Ptnr. Reed Smith Shaw & McClay, Pitts. Office: Reed Smith Shaw & McClay 435 6th Ave Pittsburgh PA 15219-1809*

ROBINSON, WILLIAM P., academic administrator, consultant, speaker; b. Elmhurst, Ill., Sept. 30, 1949; s. Paul Frederick and Lillian (Horton) R.; m. Bonnie Van Laan, Aug. 10, 1974; children: Brenna Kay, Benjamin Paul, Bailley Kay. Student, Moody Bible Inst., Chgo., 1967-70; AB, U. No. Iowa, 1972; postgrad., Princeton (N.J.) Theol. Sem., 1972-73; MA, Wheaton Coll., 1975; PhD, U. Pitts., 1979. Assoc. minister First Presbyn. Ch., Pitts., 1975-77; instr. U. Pitts., 1977-79; asst. prof. sch. continuing studies Nat. Coll. Edn., Evanston, Ill., 1979-80, dean sch. continuing studies, 1980-84, sr. v.p., 1984-86; pres. Manchester Coll., North Manchester, Ind., 1986-93, Whitworth Coll., Spokane, Wash., 1993; bd. dirs. Coun. Indep. Colls., Ind. Colls. Wash., Whitworth Coll.; cons., speaker for U.S. corps. and svc. orgns. Bd. dirs. Wash. Friends of Higher Edn., Spokane Symphony; vol. various orgns., especially prion work and hunger projects. Recipient various acad. awards. Mem. Nat. Assn. Ind. Colls. and Univs., Coun. Ind. Colls., Spokane Country Club, Spokane Club. Presyterian. Avocation: sports. Home: 215 Hawthorne Rd Spokane WA 99218 Office: Whitworth Coll Spokane WA 99251

ROBINSON, WILLIAM PHILIP, III, lawyer; b. Providence, Jan. 30, 1940; s. William Philip and Dorothy Frances (Hayes) R.; m. Marlene H. Zieky, Sept. 1, 1974; children: Jeffrey, Kevin, Courtney. BA, U. de Louvain, Belgium, 1962; MA, U. R.I., 1966; PhD, U. Conn., 1971; JD, Boston Coll., 1975. Bar: R.I. 1975, Mass. 1985, U.S. Ct. Appeals (1st cir.) 1977, U.S. Supreme Ct. 1989. Instr. U. Conn., Storrs, 1967-71; law clk. U.S. Ct. Appeals, Boston, 1975-77; assoc. Edwards & Angell, Providence, 1977-81, ptnr., 1981—; bd. trustees Providence Country Day Sch., East Providence, 1991—. Mem. East Greenwich Sch. Com., 1988—, vice chmn., 1990-94; mem. exec. com. R.I. Assn. of Sch. Coms.; mem. East Greenwich Dem. Town Com., 1988—; mem. Fed. Bd. Bar Examiners, R.I., 1994—; mem. R.I. Jud. Performance Evaluation Com., 1993—. Mem. Boston Coll. Law Sch. Alumni Assn. (v.p. R.I. chpt. 1990-93, pres. 1993—), Order of Coif, Phi Beta Kappa. Democrat. Roman Catholic. Avocations: reading, skiing, golf. Office: Edwards & Angell 2700 Hospital Trust Tower Providence RI 02903

ROBINSON, WILLIAM WHEELER, editor; b. Elizabeth, N.J., Oct. 4, 1918; s. Henry Pearson and Clare Stearns (Wheeler) R.; m. Jane Dimock, Feb. 27, 1942; children: William Wheeler Jr., Martha Robinson Bliss, Alice. B.A., Princeton U., 1939. Traffic rep., traffic dept. Eastern Airlines, N.Y.C., 1939-41; mgr. pub. relations Elco Yacht Div., Bayonne, N.J., 1945-47; sportswriter Newark Evening News, 1947-55; sportswriter, syndicated columnist Newark Star-Ledger, 1955-57; assoc. editor Yachting Mag., N.Y.C., 1957-67; editor, exec. v.p. Yachting Mag., 1967-78, editor-at-large, 1979-86; editor-at-large Cruising World Mag., 1987—; mem. exec. bd. Sea Ventures, Ft. Hancock, N.J., 1974-77; writer radio, TV shows on boating; freelance writer. Author: The Science of Sailing, 1960, New Boat, 1961, A Berth to Bermuda, 1961, Where the Trade Winds Blow, 1963, Expert Sailing, 1965, Over the Horizon, 1966, The World of Yachting, 1966, Better Sailing for Boys and Girls, 1968, (with H.L. Stone) The America's Cup Races, 1970, Legendary Yachts, 1971, rev., 1978, The Sailing Life, 1974, Right Boat For You, 1974, Great American Yacht Designers, 1974, America's Sailing Book, 1976, A Sailor's Tales, 1978, Cruising, the Boats and the Places, 1981, South to the Caribbean, 1981, Where to Cruise, 1984, Islands, 1985, Caribbean Cruising Handbook, 1986, 80 Years of Yachting, 1987, Cruising the Easy Way, 1990, Best Sailing Spots Worldwide, 1991, Destruction at Noonday, 1992, The Sailing Mystique, 1994, A Winter in the Sun, 1995; contbr. numerous articles to profl. jours. Vice pres. Rumson (N.J.) Community Appeal, 1952; mem. Rumson-Fair Haven (N.J.) Regional Bd. Edn., 1955-60, Rumson Environ. Commn., 1973-77. Served with USNR, 1941-45. Decorated Bronze Star with gold star. Mem. Met. Squash Racquets Assn. (v.p. 1973-75), Cruising Club Am. (historian 1972-77), Corinthians (master afterguard 1951-52). Clubs: Princeton of N.Y. (pres. 1984-87), N.Y. Yacht, Royal Bermuda Yacht, Seabright Beach. Avocation: squash. Home: 14 Oyster Bay Dr Rumson NJ 07760-1822 *The key to a "good life" is to enjoy going to work each morning and to enjoy coming home in the evening. Combining vacation and avocation is extremely rewarding, and there is great satisfaction in the list of books that resulted.*

ROBINSON-PETERSEN, CAROLE ANN, insurance executive, retired; b. Omaha, Dec. 21, 1935; d. Harry B. and Mildred (Daley) Baker; widowed Mar. 1989; 1 child, Pamela Fleming. Clk. Blue Cross/Blue Shield Colo., Denver, 1969-70; mgr. Blue Cross/Blue Shield Colo., 1970-72, asst. to treas., 1972-74, dir., 1974-79, treas., 1980-86, sr. v.p., treas., 1986-90; v.p., treas., chief investment officer Rocky Mountain Health Care (Holding Co.), Denver, 1991-93, sr. v.p., chief investment officer, CFO, 1986-93; ret., 1993; bd. dirs. Denver, Colo. Compensation Ins. Authority, Denver, Combined Health Appeal, Denver. Mem. investment com. City and County of Denver, 1988. Mem. Colo. Cash. Mgmt. Assn., Nat. Cash Mgmt. Assn., Life Office Mgmt. Assn. (treasury ops. com. 1985-93). Republican. Avocations: cooking, entertaining, gardening, reading. Office: Rocky Mountain Health Care 700 Broadway Ste 990 Denver CO 80203-3421

ROBISON, ANDREW CLIFFE, JR., museum curator; b. Memphis, May 23, 1940; s. Andrew Cliffe and Elfrieda (Barnes) R.; 1 child, Claire Catherine. A.B., Princeton U., 1962, Ph.D., 1974; B.A. (Marshall scholar), Oxford U., 1965, M.A., 1968. Instr. philosophy U. Ill., 1970-73, asst. prof. philosophy, 1973-75; curator, head dept. prints and drawings Nat. Gallery Art, Washington, 1974—, sr. curator, 1983-91, Andrew W. Mellon sr. curator, 1991—; Fulbright research scholar, India, 1965-66. Author: Giovanni Battista Piranesi: Prolegomena to the Princeton Collections, 1970, Paper in Prints, 1977, Master Drawings, 1978, Giovanni Battista Piranesi: The Early Architectural Fantasies, 1978, The Museum Curator and Fine Prints: Past, Present and Future, 1984, German Expressionist Prints from the Collection of Ruth and Jacob Kainen, 1985, Piranesi: Early Architectural Fantasies: A Catalogue Raisonné of the Etchings, 1986, Dürer to Diebenkorn, 1992, The Glory of Venice, 1994; contbr. articles and revs. to lit. Danforth fellow, 1966-70. Mem. Print Council Am. (pres. 1975-81), Master Drawings Assn. (internat. editorial adv. bd. 1981—), Drawing Soc. (bd. dirs. 1984—), Internat. Adv. Com. of Keepers of Pub. Collections of Graphic Art (pres. 1984-88), Ateneo Veneto, Phi Beta Kappa. Club: Grolier. Office: Nat Gallery of Art Washington DC 20565

ROBISON, BARBARA ANN, retired newspaper editor; b. Portland, Oreg., July 15, 1933; d. Louis Keith and Marjorie (Work) R.; 1 child, Nancy. Student, Coll. Idaho, 1951-54, U. Utah, 1968-70. Reporter Caldwell (Idaho) News Tribune, 1951-54; sports editor LaGrande (Oreg.) Evening-Observer, 1954-55; reporter Idaho Daily Statesman, Boise, 1955-57; asst. women's editor Tacoma (Wash.) News Tribune, 1958-59; lifestyle editor Salt Lake Tribune, 1967-93. Episcopalian. Avocations: reading, walking, animals. Home: 4210 Caroleen Way Salt Lake City UT 84124-2507

ROBISON, CLARENCE, JR., surgeon; b. Tecumseh, Okla., Dec. 9, 1924; s. Clarence Sr. and Margaret Irene (Buzzard) R.; m. Patricia Antoinette Hagee, May 27, 1951; children: Timothy D., Paul D., John D., Rebecca A. AS, Stanford U., 1943; MD, U. Okla., 1948. Intern Good Samaritan Hosp., Portland, Oreg., 1948-49; fellow pathology and oncology U. Okla., 1949-51; pathologist USAF Hosp., Cheyenne, Wyo., 1951-53; resident in surgery Okla. U. Health Scis.-Va. Svc., Oklahoma City, 1953-56; mem. faculty surgery dept. Okla. U. Health Scis., Oklahoma City, 1956-57, clin. prof. surgery, 1957—; mem. bd. advisors Mercy Health Ctr., Oklahoma City, 1974-81, sec. of staff, 1974-84, chief surgery, 1992-95; bd. dirs. Okla. Found.

for Peer Rev., Oklahoma City. Mem. Commn. on Mission Indian Nations Presbytery, 1980-91; bd. dirs. Found. Sr. Citizens, 1964—; elder Presbyn. Ch.; presdl. elector Dem. Party, 1960. Capt. USAF, 1951-53. Fellow ACS, Am. Cancer Soc (past pres. Okla. divsn., exec. com., bd. dirs., nat. del. dir.); mem. AMA (del. hosp. med. staff Mercy Health Ctr. 1989—), Okla. State Med. Assn. (alt. del. to AMA 1991-93, 96—), SAR, Oklahoma County State Med. Soc. (bd. dirs. Oklahoma County chpt. 1989-93), Okla. State Med. Assn. (alt. trustee Okla. 1989-92, trustee 1993-96), Okla. Surg. Assn. (sec., treas. 1966-68), Okla. City Surg. Soc. (pres. 1967-69), Petroleum Club, Oak Trees, Men's Dinner Club, Masons (32 degree Scottish Rite, commandery York Rite), Kiwanis, Shriners. Office: 4200 W Memorial Rd Oklahoma City OK 73120-8305

ROBISON, JAMES EVERETT, management consulting company executive; b. Alfred, N.D., Nov. 22, 1915; s. John J. and Myrtle (Klundt) R.; m. Jeanette Hoffman, June 6, 1942 (dec.); 1 child, Martha Ann Davies. A.B., U. Minn., 1938; M.B.A., Harvard U., 1940; Sc. D. (hon.), Suffolk U., 1968. Salesman Nashua Mfg. Co., N.Y.C., 1940-41, Textron, Inc., N.Y.C., 1947-53; chief textile br. OPS, Washington, 1951; pres., chief exec. officer, dir. Indian Head, Inc., N.Y.C., 1953-67; chmn. bd., chief exec. officer Indian Head, Inc., 1967-72, chmn. fin. com., 1971-75; pres. Lonsdale Enterprises, Inc., 1975—. Mem. com. univ. resources Harvard U., 1966-69, mem. vis. com. Grad. Sch. Bus. Adminstrn., 1966-72, 73-79; chmn. bd. Assocs. Harvard Bus. Sch., 1968-70, bd. dirs., 1988-92; trustee Air Force Aid Soc., 1968-94, mem. fin. com., 1969-94; bd. dirs. Bus. Com. for Arts, 1973-80; trustee Com. Econ. Devel., 1965-74, Calif. Inst. Tech., 1970—; vice chmn. president's coun. U. Vt. Sch. Bus., 1982-89. Maj. USAAF, 1942-46. Decorated D.F.C., Air Medal with three oak leaf clusters; recipient Distinguished Service award Harvard Bus. Sch. Assn., 1969; Outstanding Alumni award U. Minn., 1974. Mem. Conf. Bd., Am. Textile Mfrs. Inst. (bd. dirs. 1961-64), Harvard Bus. Sch. Assn., Soaring Soc. Am., U. S. C. of C., Air Force Res. Assn., Harvard Club, Harvard Bus. Sch. Club Greater N.Y. (past bd. dirs., pres. 1967-68), Stanwich Club (Greenwich, Conn.), Bedford Golf and Tennis Club (N.Y.), Lyford Cay Club (Bahamas), Phi Delta Theta. Avocations: golf, skiing, soaring.

ROBISON, OLIN CLYDE, political science educator, former college president; b. Anacoco, La., May 12, 1936; s. Audrey Clyde and Ruby (Cantrell) R.; m. Sylvia Margaret Potter, Apr. 10, 1959; children: Gordon Reece, Blake Elliott, Mark Edward. BA, Baylor U., 1958, LLD, 1979; D.Phil., Oxford (Eng.) U., 1963; LHD (hon.), Ehrenburger-Johannes Gutenberb U., Mainz, Fed. Republic Germany, 1977, Monterey Inst. Internat. Studies, 1982, Hofstra U, 1988; LLD (hon.), U. Vt., 1989. Dean students San Marcos (Tex.) Acad., 1963-64; regional officer Peace Corps, Washington, 1964-65; dir. univ. affairs Peace Corps, 1965-66; spl. asst. dep. under-sec. for polit. affairs Dept. State, Washington, 1966-68; asso. provost for social scis. Wesleyan U., Middletown, Conn., 1968-70; provost, dean faculty, sr. lectr. govt. and legal studies Bowdoin Coll., Brunswick, Maine, 1970-75; prof. polit. sci. Middlebury (Vt.) Coll., 1975-95, pres., 1975-90, pres. emeritus, 1990—; pres. Salzburg Seminar, 1991—; chmn. Am. Collegiate Consortium, 1987-94; cons. State Dept., 1968-72, 77-88; bd. dirs. Investment Co. Am., Am. Mut. Fund, TDX Corp., Bank of Vt., 1989-92, The Noel Group, N.Y.C, 1989-91; cons. Paine Webber Mitchell Hutchins Inc., Am. Coun. Life Ins., 1968-81, Washington Forum, Met. Life Ins. Co. Bd. dirs. Atlantic Info. Center for Tchrs., London, 1970-77, Am. Com. on U.S.-Soviet Rels., Washington; chmn. Vt. com. Rhodes Scholarship Trust, 1976-77; bd. dirs. Am. Coun. Young Polit. Leaders, 1968-78, 81-90, Inst. East-West Security Studies, N.Y.C., Nat. Spinal Cord Injury Assn., Washington, Atlantic Coun. U.S., 1973-78, 81-91, U.S. Commn. for United World Coll. Schs.; mem. U.S. Adv. Commn. on Public Diplomacy, 1978-83, chmn., 1978-81, visiting comm. Harvard Div. Sch., Cambridge, Mass., 1980-86, adv. comm. Harvard U., Ctr for Middle Ea. Studies, Cambridge, 1992—; adviser U.S. del. Conf. on Security and Coop. in Europe, Belgrade, 1977-78; U.S. del. Conf. on Security and Coop. in Madrid, 1980, in Vienna, 1986-87; mem. Royal United Svcs. Inst. Def. Studies, London; bd. dirs. Nat. Endowment for Democracy, 1984-92; bd. dirs., chmn. Chatham House Found., 1985-93. Named Ehrenburger Johannes Gutenberg Universitat, Mainz, Fed. Republic Germany, 1977; Rockefeller Found./Aspen Inst. fellow, 1978-79; Presdl. fellow Aspen Inst. Humanistic Studies, 1979-80, Harry Luce fellow Aspen Inst., 1982-83. Fellow Royal Inst. Internat. Affairs (London); mem. Internat. Inst. Strategic Studies (London), Soc. Values in Higher Edn., Council Fgn. Relations, UN Assn. U.S. (panel on approaches to collective security), Atlantic Treaty Assn. (Atlantic edn. com. 1972-1976). Baptist. Clubs: Federal City (Washington); Century (N.Y.C.); United Oxford and Cambridge (London). Office: Salzburg Seminar The Marble Works PO Box 886 Middlebury VT 05753

ROBISON, PAULA JUDITH, flutist; b. Nashville, June 8, 1941; d. David Victor and Naomi Florence R.; m. Scott Nickrenz; Dec. 29, 1971; 1 child, Elizabeth Hadley Amadea Nickrenz. Student, U. So. Calif., 1958-60; B.S., Juilliard Sch. Music, 1963. Founding artist, player Chamber Music Soc., N.Y.C., 1970-90, NY ChôroBand, 1994; co-dir. chamber music Spoleto Festival, Charleston, S.C., 1978-88; Filene artist-in-residence Skidmore Coll., Saratoga Springs, N.Y., 1988-89; mem. faculty New Eng. Conservatory Music, 1991—; co-dir. (with Leon Kirchner) Gardner Chamber Orch., Boston, 1995—. Soloist with various major orchs., including N.Y. Philharm., London Symphony Orch.; player, presenter Concerti di Mezzogiorno, Spoleto (Italy) Festival, 1970—; commd. flute concertos by Leon Kirchner, Toru Takemitsu, Oliver Knussen, Robert Beaser, Kenneth Frazelle; author: The Paula Robison Flute Warmups Book, 1989, The Andersen Collection, 1994, Paula Robison Masterclass: Paul Hindemith, 1995; recos. on CBS Masterworks, Music Masters, Vanguard Classics, New World Records, Omega, Arabesque, Sony Classical, King Recs., Mode Recs. Recipient First prize Geneva Internat. Competition, 1966, Adelaide Ristori prize, 1987; named Musician of Month, Musical Am., 1979, House Musician for Isamu Noguchi Garden Mus., N.Y.C., 1988; Martha Baird Rockefeller grantee, 1966; Nat. Endowment for Arts grantee, 1978, 86; Fromm Found. grantee, 1980; Housewright Eminent scholar Fla. State U., 1990-91. Mem. Sigma Alpha Iota (hon.). Office: by arrangement with Matthew Sprizzo 477 Durant Ave Staten Island NY 10308

ROBITAILLE, ALBERT LEO, lawyer, chemist; b. Pawtucket, R.I., May 21, 1958; s. Albert Henri Jr. and Jeannette Noella (Emery) R.; m. Catherine Patricia Kulis, June 20, 1981. BS in Chemistry, U. Conn., 1980, MS in Polymer Sci., MBA in Mgmt., 1984; JD, U. Conn., Hartford, 1991. Teaching asst. U. Conn., Storrs, 1980-84; mgmt. trainee Laticrete Internat., Bethany, Conn., 1984-85; project chemist Springborn Internat., Enfield, Conn., 1986; polymer chemist Tectonic Industries, Berlin, Conn., 1986-88; quality assurance profl. Spalding Sports Worldwide, Chicopee, Mass., 1988-89; patent solicitor United Techs. Corp., Hartford, 1989-90, patent atty., 1991—. Leader local unit Boy Scouts Am., R.I. and Conn., 1976—; dir. Northbrook Ct. Condo Assn., East Hartford, Conn., 1986-87. State of R.I. scholar, 1976-80; PPG Industries fellow, 1981. Mem. ABA, Soc. Plastics Engrs., Am. Inst. Chemists, Conn. Bar Assn., Phi Lambda Upsilon, Phi Delta Phi. Republican. Roman Catholic. Home: 210 Pine St Apt 307 Manchester CT 06040

ROBITAILLE, LUC, professional hockey player; b. Montreal, P.Q., Can., Feb. 17, 1966. With Hull Olympiques Major Jr. Hockey League, Que., 1983-84, L.A. Kings, 1984-94, Pitts. Penguins, 1994—; scored winning goal for nat. team of Can. at 1994 World Hockey Championship. Recipient Guy LaFleur trophy, 1985-86, Can. Hockey Player of Yr. award, 1985-86, Calder Meml. trophy, NHL Rookie of Yr., 1986-87; named to NHL All-Star team, 1987, 88, 90-91, 92-93. Office: Pitts Penguins Gate No 9 Pittsburgh PA 15219*

ROBLE, CAROLE MARCIA, accountant; b. Bklyn., Aug. 22, 1938; d. Carl and Edith (Brown) Dusowitz; m. Richard F. Roble, Nov. 30, 1969. MBA with distinction, N.Y. Inst. Tech., 1984. CPA, Calif., N.Y. Compt. various orgns. various orgns., 1956-66; staff acct. ZTBG CPA'S, L.A., 1966-67; sr. acct. J.H. Cohn & Co., Newark, 1967-71; prin. Carole M. Roble, CPA, South Hempstead, N.Y., 1971-90; ptnr. Roble & Libman, CPAs, Baldwin, N.Y., 1990-93; prin. Carole M. Roble, CPA, Baldwin, N.Y., 1993—; speaker, moderator Found. for Acctg. Edn., N.Y., 1971—; lectr. acctg. various schs. including New Sch., Queens Coll., Empire State Coll., Touro Coll., N.Y. Inst. Tech., N.Y.C., Parsons Sch., 1971—. Guest various N.Y. radio and TV stas. Treas. Builders Devel. Corp. of L.I., Westbury, N.Y., 1985; dir. Women Econ. Devels. of L.I., 1985-87. Recipient Sisterhood citation Nat. Orgn. Women, 1984, 85, cert. of Appreciation Women Life Underwriters, 1988, Women in Sales, 1982, 84; named top Tax Practitioner Money Mag., 1987. Mem. AICPA, Am. Acct. Assn. (auditing sect.), Am. Soc. Women Accts. (pres. N.Y. chpt. 1980-81), Am. Woman's Soc. CPAs, Nat. Conf. CPA Practitioners (trustee L.I. chpt. 1981-82, sec. 1982-83, treas. 1983-84, v.p. 1984-85, 1st v.p. 1985-86, pres. 1986-87, nat. nominating com. 1983-84, 88-89, nat. continuing profl. edn. chmn. 1988-90, nat. treas. 1991-94, nat. v.p. 1994—), Calif. Soc. CPAs, N.Y. State Soc. CPAs (bd. dirs. Nassau chpt. 1981-86, 91-93, bd. dirs. profl. devel., 1982-86, sec., mem. fin. acctg. standards com. 1990—), Kiwanis (program chmn. County Seat chpt. 1989-90, sec. 1990-91, pres. 1991-92), Baldwin C. of C. (treas. 1990-93). Avocations: golf, gourmet cuisine, water skiing, music. Home: 626 Willis St Hempstead NY 11550-8000

ROBLIN, DUFF, Canadian senator; b. Winnipeg, Man., Can., June 17, 1917; s. C.D. and Sophia May (Murdoch) R.; m. Mary Linda MacKay, Aug. 30, 1958; children—Andrew, Jennifer. Student, St. John's Coll. Sch., U. Chgo.; LL.D., McGill U., Man. U., Winnipeg U. Mem. Man. Legislature, Can., 1949-68, premier, 1958-67, sworn to privy council, 1967; appointed companion Order of Can., 1970; senator Can. Parliament, 1978-82, dep. leader opposition, 1980-84, leader of Govt. in Senate, 1984-86; pres. Canadian Pacific Investments Ltd., 1970-75. Progressive Conservative. Anglican. Office: 977 Century St, Winnipeg, MB Canada R3H 0W4

ROBOCK, STEFAN HYMAN, economics educator emeritus; b. Redgranite, Wis., July 31, 1915; s. Samuel and Elizabeth (Kushner) R.; m. Shirley Bernstein, June 17, 1946 (div. Mar. 1980); children: Alan David, Jerry, Lisa (Mrs. Stephen Shaffer). B.A., U. Wis., 1938; M.A. (Adminstrn. fellow), Harvard U., 1941, Ph.D., 1948; Prof. Honoris Causa, U. Recife, Brazil, 1956; M. Honoris Causa, E.S.T.E., San Sebastian, Spain, 1974. Economist Nat. Resources Planning Bd., Washington, 1940-41; antitrust div. U.S. Dept. Justice, Washington, 1941-42, Boston, 1948-49; chief economist TVA, Knoxville, 1949-54; devel. adviser UN, Brazil, 1954-56; tech. asst. missions UN, Chile, 1955; Colombia, 1956; with Midwest Rsch. Inst., 1956-58; mem. Com. Econ. Devel., 1958-60; prof. internat. bus. Ind. U., Bloomington, 1960-67; R.D. Calkins prof. internat. bus. Columbia U., N.Y.C., 1967-84, prof. emeritus, 1984—; internat. economist Dept. Commerce, 1975-76; trustee Inst. Current World Affairs, 1981-86; cons. fgn. countries, 1959—; bd. dirs. Econs. Inst., Boulder, Colo., 1984-89; adv. bd. World Trade Inst., 1974-95; mem. bd. sci. and tech. NAS, 1969-72; vis. prof. Beijing Mgmt. Inst., 1985, U. Internat. Bus. and Econ., Beijing, 1989, Internat. Mgmt. Ctr., Budapest, Hungary, 1992. Author: Brazil's Developing Northeast, 1963, Brazil: A Study in Development Progress, 1975, International Business and Multinational Enterprises, 4th edit., 1989; Editorial bd.: Columbia Jour. World Bus, 1975-85. Served with USNR, 1942-46. Mem. Soc. Internat. Devel. (mem. council 1966-69), Am. Econ. Assn., Acad. Internat. Bus. (v.p. 1983-85), Latin Am. Studies Assn., Phi Kappa Phi, Beta Gamma Sigma, Phi Eta Sigma. Club: Columbia Tennis. Home: 560 Riverside Dr Apt 21J New York NY 10027-3237

ROBOL, RICHARD THOMAS, lawyer; b. Norfolk, Va., Feb. 8, 1952; s. Harry James and Lucy Henley (Johnson) R.; m. Melissa Janet Sengstack, June 3, 1978; children: Thomas Coke, Robert Talbot, Charles Taliaferro. BA, U. Va., 1974; JD, Harvard U., 1978. Bar: Va. 1979, U.S. Dist. Ct. (ea. dist.) Va. 1979, U.S. Ct. Appeals (4th cir.) 1979, U.S. Dist. Ct. (we. dist.) Va. 1981, U.S. Supreme Ct. 1982, D.C. 1991, U.S. Ct. Appeals (6th and 9th cirs.) 1995. Law clk. to presiding justice U.S. Dist. Ct. (ea. dist.) Va., 1978-79; ptnr. Seawell, Dalton, Hughes & Timms, Norfolk, 1979-87, Hunton and Williams, Norfolk, 1987-92; exec. v.p., gen. counsel Columbus Am. Discovery Group, Inc., 1992—; pro bono counsel Nat. Commn. for Prevention Child Abuse, Norfolk, 1983, Tidewater Profl. Assn. on Child Abuse, 1983, Parents United Va., 1981-82, Sexual Abuse Help Line, 1983-86; mem. Boyd-Graves Conf. on Civil Procedure in Va., 1981-87. Contbr. articles to law revs.; contbg. editor: International Law for General Practitioners, 1981. Bd. dirs. Va. Opera Assn. Guild, Norfolk, 1983-87, Tidewater br. NCCJ, 1991-92; deacon Ctrl. Bapt. Ch., Norfolk, 1980-83. 1st lt. USAR, 1992—. Fulbright scholar, 1974. Mem. Va. State Bar Assn. (bd. dirs. internat. law sect. 1984-87, chmn. 1982-83), Va. Young Lawyers Assn. (cir. rep. 1984-88), Va. Assn. Def. Attys., Maritime Law Assn., Norfolk-Portsmouth Bar assn. (chmn. speakers bur. 1987-88), Assn. Def. Trial Attys. (chmn. Va. 1987), Def. Rsch. Inst., 1982-88. Avocations: camping, rowing, scuba diving. Home: 60 Kenyon Brook Dr Worthington OH 43085 Office: Columbus Am Discovery Group 433 W 6th Ave Columbus OH 43201-3136

ROBOLD, ALICE ILENE, mathematician, educator; b. Delaware County, Ind., Feb. 7, 1928; d. Earl G. and Margaret Rebecca (Summers) Hensley; m. Virgil G. Robold, Aug. 21, 1955; 1 son, Edward Lynn. B.S., Ball State U., 1955, M.A., 1960, Ed.D., 1965. Substitute elem. tchr. Am. Elem. Sch., Augsburg, Germany, 1955-56; instr. Ball State U., Muncie, Ind., 1960-61; teaching fellow Ball State U., 1961-64, asst. prof. math. scis., 1964-69, assoc. prof., 1969-76, prof., 1976—. Mem. Nat. Coun. Tchrs. Math., Ind. Coun. Tchrs. Math., Sch. Sci. and Math. Assn., Pi Lambda Theta. Mem. Ch. of God. Office: Ball State U Dept Math Scis Muncie IN 47306

ROBRENO, EDUARDO C., federal judge; b. 1945. BA, Westfield State Coll., 1967; MA, U. Mass., 1969; JD, Rutgers U., 1978. With antitrust divsn. U.S. Dept Justice, Phila., 1978-81; ptnr. Meltzer & Schiffrin, Phila., 1981-86, Fox, Rothschild, O'Brien & Frankel, Phila., 1987-92; judge U.S. Dist. Ct. for Ea. Dist. Pa., Phila., 1992—; mem. Jud. Conf. Com. on Bankruptcy Rules. Fellow Am. Bar Found., Am. Law Inst. Office: US Courthouse Rm 3810 Philadelphia PA 19106

ROBSMAN, MARY LOUISE, education educator; b. Galena, Ill., June 19, 1943; d. Wilbur Henry and Stella Loretta (Bussan) Timpe; m. Igor Victor Robsman, Dec. 29, 1987. BS in Edn. and Math., No. Ill. U., 1964; MA in Edn. and Gifted Edn., U. Cen. Fla., 1981, EdD in Curriculum Instr. and Psychology, 1991. Cert. tchr. K-9. Tchr. math grades 7-8, grade 5 Dist. 300, Dundee, Ill., 1964-67; tchr. grade 5 Dept. Def. Overseas Schs., Frankfurt, Germany, 1967-69, Dist. 120, Galena, Ill., 1969-70; tchr. grades 5-6 Franklin-McKinley Dist., San Jose, Calif., 1970-72; tchr. math. grades 7-8 Dept. Def. Overseas Schs., Spangdahlem, Germany, 1972-74, tchr. grades 5-6, 1975; tchr. grades 5-6 Dubuque (Iowa) Comty. Schs., 1976-80, tchr. learning resource K-6, 1981-87; instr. edn. dept. U. Cen. Fla., Orlando, 1988-91, Rollins Coll., Cocoa, Fla., 1991-93; prof. Rollins Coll., Melbourne, Fla., 1993—. Recipient Recognition of Svc. award Omicron Lambda, 1992, Appreciation award Kappa Delta Pi, 1994; Critchfield rsch. study grantee, 1994. Mem. ASCD, Nat. Coun. Tchrs. of Math., Omicron Lambda-Kappa Delta Pi. Republican. Roman Catholic. Avocations: international travel, creative writing. Home: 1578 Omega St NE Palm Bay FL 32907-2305 Office: Rollins Coll 475 S John Rodes Blvd West Melbourne FL 32904-1009

ROBSON, CHARLES BASKERVILL, JR., lawyer, international projects developer; b. Durham, N.C., Oct. 24, 1938; s. Charles Baskervill and Harriet Eleanor (Hardison) R.; m. Lucie Lea White, Sept. 20, 1969; children: Charles B. III, Patrick Lea. Student, Freie U. of Berlin, 1958-59; BA, Yale U., 1961; JD with honors, U. N.C., Chapel Hill, 1966. Bar: N.C. 1966, U.S. Dist. Ct. (mid. and ea. dists.) N.C. 1967, U.S. Ct. Appeals (4th cir.) 1967, U.S. Tax Ct. 1968, Ga. 1972, Mich. 1974. Assoc. McLendon, Brim, Holderness & Brocks, Greensboro, N.C., 1966-71; mem. law faculty U. Ga., Athens, 1971-75; mgr. legal affairs Carolina Power and Light, Raleigh, N.C., 1975-80; v.p., gen. counsel Hosp. Affiliates Internat., Nashville, 1980-81; ptnr. Foster, Conner & Robson, Raleigh, 1983-88, Patton, Boggs & Blow, Raleigh, 1988-93; chmn. Baskervil & Co., LLC, Raleigh, 1994—. Contbr. to profl. publs. Mem. Order of Coif. Republican. Episcopalian. Office: Baskervill & Co LLC PO Box 40855 4020-90 Capital Blvd Raleigh NC 27629

ROBSON, DONALD, physics educator; b. Leeds, Eng., Mar. 19, 1937; came to U.S., 1963; s. Albert and Rose Hannah (Parbutt) R.; m. Joy Olivia Burkitt Findlay, Aug. 1960 (div. May 1971); children: Donald Peter, David Ian, Karen Joy; m. Martha Breitenlohner, Aug. 26, 1971. BSc, U. Melbourne, Australia, 1959, MSc, 1961, PhD, 1963. Rsch. assoc. Fla. State U., Tallahassee, 1963-64, asst. prof. physics, 1964-65, assoc. prof., 1965-67, prof., 1967—, chmn. dept. physics, 1985-91, Disting. prof., 1990—. Editor: (with J.D. Fox) Isobaric Spin in Nuclear Physics, 1966, Nuclear Analogue States, 1976; assoc. editor Nuclear Physics A., 1972-96; contbr. more than 100 articles to profl. jours. Chmn. bd. trustees Southeastern Univ. Rsch. Assn., 1996—. Fulbright scholar, 1963-64; A.P. Sloan fellow, 1966-67; Alexander Von Humboldt sr. scientist, 1976-77. Fellow Am. Phys. Soc. (co-recipient Tom W. Bonner prize 1972). Avocations: chess, golf, running. Office: Fla State U Dept Physics Tallahassee FL 32306

ROBSON, GEORGE T., SR., computer company executive; b. 1947. BS Wharton Sch. of Bus., U. Pa., 1969; MS, SUNY, 1969. Various mgmt. positions IBM, 1969-82; mgmt. Burroughs Corp., 1982-86; v.p., corp. contr. Unisys Corp., Blue Bell, Pa., 1986-1995; sr. v.p. CFO Unisys Corp., 1995-96.

ROBSON, JOHN MERRITT, library and media administrator; b. Gordon, Nebr., Sept. 22, 1930; s. John Wesley Robson and Martha Mildred (Shook) Belknap; m. Kathryn Mae Baker, Aug. 26, 1951; children: Deborah Dawn, Diana Lynn, Denise Anne. BS in Edn., U. Nebr., 1953; MA in Librarianship, Denver U., 1959. Ordained deacon Episc. Ch., 1991. Ref. asst. Lincoln (Nebr.) City Librs., 1957-58; ref. and inter libr. loan Denver U. Libr., 1958-59; cataloger humanities USAF Acad. Libr., Colo., 1959-61; cataloger St. Cloud (Minn.) U., 1961-63, acquisitions libr., 1963-66; libr. dir. Southwest State U., Marshall, Minn., 1966-71, dir. media svcs., 1971-81; head libr., prof. libr. and instructional tech. Nebr. Wesleyan U., Lincoln, 1981-91, dir. media svcs., 1991-95; ret., 1995; mem. S.E. Nebr. Regional Libr. Bd., Lincoln, 1983-84; steward teamsters Faculty /Adminstrv. Bargaining Unit, Marshall, 1977-78. Author: Index to Publications of the Hakluyt Society, 1963; contbr. articles to profl. jours. Mem. gov's. task force on librs. State of Minn., St. Paul, 1973. Mem. Nebr. Libr. Assn. (Mentor of Yr. 1989), Nebr. Edtl. Media Assn. (conv. planning com. 1984—), Nebr. Assn. for Ednl. Data Processing. Avocations: stained glass, wood working, photography. Home: 1620 Atlas Ave Lincoln NE 68521-1654 Office: Nebr Wesleyan U 5000 St Paul Ave Lincoln NE 68504-2760

ROBSON, MARIAN LORRAINE, Canadian federal official. BA in English, U. Saskatchewan, Can., 1964; postgrad. in Polit. Sci., U. B.C., Can., 1965-67, U. Saskatchewan, 1965-67. Spl. asst. to Hon. Otto Lang Transport Can., 1970's; corp. sec. B.C. Railway, 1977-80; chmn. Vancouver Port Corp., 1983-84; dir. Can. Ports Corp., 1983-84; trans. and econ. devel. cons., 1984-89; mgr. pub. affairs CN Rail B.C., 1990-93; dir. Cascadia Inst., 1993-94; v.p. Hill and Knowlton, 1994-95; mem. Nat. Transp. Agy., Vancouver, B.C., Can., 1995—. Office: Nat Transp Agy, 250-1095 W Pender St, Vancouver, BC Canada V6E 2M6

ROBSON, MARTIN CECIL, surgery educator, plastic surgeon; b. Lancaster, Ohio, Mar. 8, 1939; children: Karen Iredell, Douglas Spears, Martin Cecil III. Student, Northwestern U., 1957-59; B.A., Johns Hopkins U., 1961, M.D., 1964. Diplomate Am. Bd. Surgery, Am. Bd. Plastic Surgery. Intern U. Chgo. Hosps. and Clinics, 1964-65; resident in surgery Balt. City Hosp., 1965-67, Brooke Gen. Hosp., Ft. Sam Houston, Tex., 1967-69; resident in plastic surgery Yale-New Haven Hosp., 1971-73; instr. dept. surgery Yale U. Sch. Medicine, New Haven, 1973-74, asst. prof. plastic surgery, 1973-74, assoc. prof., 1974; assoc. prof., chief plastic surgery U. Chgo., 1974-77, assoc. prof. and chief plastic surgery, 1977-83, dir. Burn Center, 1976-83; prof., chmn. divsn. plastic and reconstructive surgery Wayne State U., Detroit, 1983-88; dir. Detroit Med. Ctr. Burn Ctr., 1983-88; Truman Blocker Disting. prof., chief divsn. plastic surgery U. Tex. Med. Br., 1988-93; dir. surg. svcs. Shriners' Burn Inst., Galveston, Tex., 1988-93; prof. surgery, chair divsn. surg. rsch. U. South Fla., Tampa, 1993—; chair surg. svc. Bay Pines (Fla.) VA Med. Ctr., 1993—. Mem. editl. bd. Jour. Burn Care and Rehab.; editl. cons. bd.: Jour. Trauma. Served to maj. M.C. U.S. Army, 1967-71; col. USAR Med. Corps, 1991—. Recipient Writing award Am. Med. Technologists, 1979, 80, 81, 82; recipient Lancer Authors' award, 1981, 82, Fisher award, 1982. Fellow ACS, Royal Australian Coll. Surgeons (hon.); mem. Plastic Surgery Rsch. Coun. (chmn. 1983-84), Am. Burn Assn. (pres. 1985-86, Disting. Svc. award), Am. Surg. Assn., Am. Assn. Plastic Surgery, Am. Soc. Plastic and Reconstructive Surgeons, Nu Sigma Nu, Phi Delta Theta, Alpha Omega Alpha. Office: Bay Pines VA Med Ctr Bay Pines FL 33504

ROBY, JASPER, bishop. Sr. bishop, exec. head Apostolic Overcoming Holy Ch. of God, Inc., Birmingham, Ala. Office: Apostolic Overcoming Holy Church God Inc 1120 N 24th St Birmingham AL 35234-3194

ROBY, REGINALD HENRY, professional football player; b. Waterloo, Iowa, June 30, 1961. Student, U. Iowa. With Miami (Fla.) Dolphins, 1983-92, Washington Redskins, 1993-94; punter Tampa Bay (Fla.) Buccaneers, 1995—. Named to The Sporting News NFL All- Pro Team, 1984, 94; selected to Pro Bowl, 1984, 89, 94. Achievements include leading NFL in net punting average, 1984, 86. Office: Tampa Bay Buccaneers One Buccaneer Pl Tampa FL 33607

ROCCO, DOMENIC PATRICK, JR., trust company executive, retired army officer; b. Bakerton, Pa., Mar. 17, 1937; s. Domenic Joseph and Nancy Marie (Gemus) R.; divorced; children: David M., Domenic Rocci III (dec.). Commd. 2d. lt. U.S. Army, 1963, advanced through grades to brig. gen., 1987; asst. divsn. comdr. 1st Armoured Divsn. and Cmty. Comdr. U.S. Army, Bamberg, Germany; dep. comdg. gen. U.S. Army Tng. Ctr. U.S. Army, Ft. Dix, N.J.; command dir. N.Am. Aerospace Def. Command U.S. Army, Colorado Springs, Colo.; inspector gen. 7th Army U.S. Army, Heidelberg, Germany; exec. officer to Comdr. in Chief UN Command U.S. Army; dep. dir. Combined Mil. Interrogation Ctr. U.S. Army, Vietnam; ret. U.S. Army, 1990; pres., CEO First Commonwealth Trust Co., Indiana, Pa., 1990—. Commr. Southwestern Pa. Heritage Preservation Commn.; bd. dirs., mem. exec. com., chmn. strategic planning com. Found. of Indiana U. of Pa.; vol. cons. Jr. Achievement S.W. Pa., chmn. fund dr., 1985-86; mem. adv. bd. Indiana chpt. ARC; mem. com. Indiana County Heritage Preservation Com.; bd. dirs. Indiana Hosp., Indiana County Devel. Corp.; mem. Greater Indiana Strategic Planning Study Commn.; mem. Senator Rich Santorum of Pa. Vet.'s Adv. Bd. Decorated Legion of Merit with 3 oak leaf clusters, Bronze Star, Purple Heart. Mem. Indiana C. of C. (v.p. bd. dirs.), Indiana Country Club (sec.-treas. bd. govs.). Home: 163 Wren St Indiana PA 15701 Office: 614 Philadelphia St Indiana PA 15701-3904

ROCCO, RON, artist; b. Ft. Hood, Tex., Nov. 21, 1953; s. Raymond Anthony and Dorothy Ann (D'Angelo) R. Student, Fordham U., 1972; BFA, SUNY, Purchase, 1976; MS in Visual Arts, MIT Ctr. for Advanced Visual Studies, 1983. Artist-in-residence Exptl. TV Ctr., Owego, N.Y., 1982-87; guest lectr., artist-in-residence The Banff (Alta., Can.) Ctr., 1987; artist-in-residence Kunstlerhaus Bethanian, Berlin, 1991; artist-in-residence inter. studio program Kunst and Complex, Rotterdam, Netherlands, 1993; guest lectr. various univs., 1977-90; mem. UN Internat. Conf. on Communication Tech. and Traditional Cultures, N.Y.C., 1983, Art Corp. Am., N.Y.C., 1979-81. Performance at The Solomon R. Guggenheim Mus., N.Y.C., 1983; works exhibited UN: Comm. Ctr. of Population Inst., N.Y.C., 1983, The Asia Soc., N.Y.C., 1985, Internat. Exhibit of Computer Art Forms, Kortijk, Belgium, 1986, Inst. for Art and Urban Resources, N.Y.C., 1987, Found. Artgarden, Amsterdam, The Netherlands, 1989, The Katonah (N.Y.) Mus. Art, 1990, The Bklyn. Mus., 1990, Fundacao Rocha, Fortalesca, Brazil, 1991, Kunstlerhaus Bethanien, Berlin, 1991, Amerika Haus, Berlin, 1992; artistic dir. Laser Sculpture/Dance, 1981; producer, dir. Zaroff's Tale, 1983 (N.Y. State Coun. on Arts grantee); co-dir., collaborator Buddah Meets Einstein at the Great Wall, 1985 (Nat. Endowment Arts award); collaborator, sculptor Light and Sound Sphere Study, 1986 (N.Y. State Coun. on Arts grantee). Founder, dir. Ithaca Artists Coop., 1977-80. Creative and Performing Arts Coun. grantee Cornell U., Ithaca, N.Y., 1977, expansion arts program grantee Nat. Endowment Arts, 1977-79; recipient Netherland-Am. Found. award, 1989, Art Matters award, 1989, N.Y. Found. for the Arts award, 1989, The Found. for Contemporary Performance Arts award, 1989. Mem. ACLU. Buddhist. Studio: 59 Harrison Ave Brooklyn NY 11211-8115

ROCCOBERTON, BART P., performance artist, puppetier, educator. BA in Speech and Theatre, Montclair State Coll., 1973; MFA in Puppet Arts, U. Conn., 1990. Owner, dir., designer, lead puppeteer, builder, musician Pandemonium Puppet Co., 1976—; founder, dir. The Eugene O'Neill Theater Ctrs. Inst. Profl. Puppetry Arts, 1984-90; asst. prof. dept. dramatic arts U. Conn., 1990—; panelist various festivals and confs. including Nat. Festival Puppeteers of Am., Tahlequah, Okla., 1991, Puppetry Futurism Conf. III,

San Luis Obispo, Calif., 1992, N.E./Mid-Atlantic Regional Festival of Puppeteers of Am., Bryn Mawr, Pa., 1992, Puppetry '93 Nat. Festival Puppeteers of Am., San Francisco, 1993, In Pursuit of Excellence, Nat. Festival Puppeteers of Am., Bryn Mawr, 1995. Puppet designer, dir., builder various prodns. including Beauty and the Beast, W.Va. U., 1989, Invitations to Heaven, Sandglass Theatre, 1990, Birds End, Cricket Theater, Mpls., 1990, A Christmas Carol., U. Conn., Storrs, 1992, Into the Woods, Conn. Repertory Theatre, U. Conn., Storrs, 1993, Peter and the Wolf, Ea. Conn. Symphony Orch., New London, 1994, Beyond the Box, Digital Equipment Co., N.Y.C., 1994, Destination: Digital, Digital Equipment Co., Las Vegas, 1994, Fiddler on the Roof, Conn. Repertory Theatre, U. Conn., Storrs, 1994, many others; contbr. articles to profl. jours. Mem. Union Internat. de la Marionnette (bd. dirs. U.S.A. 1992—, del. internat. plenary Ljubljana, Slovenia, coun. internat. profl. tng. commn., liaison to 1994 Henson Internat. Puppetry Festival, del. 1996 internat. plenary Budapest). Office: Sch Fine Arts Dept Dramatic Arts Box U-127 Rm 242 802 Bolton Storrs CT 06269-1127

ROCEK, JAN, chemist, educator; b. Prague, Czechoslovakia, Mar. 24, 1924; came to U.S., 1960, naturalized, 1966; s. Hugo and Frida (Loebl) Robitschek; m. Eva Trojan, June 26, 1947; children: Martin, Thomas. M.S., Tech. U., Prague, 1949, Ph.D., 1953. Scientist Czechoslovak Acad. Sci., Prague, 1953-57; sr. scientist Czechoslovak Acad. Sci., 1957-60; vis. scientist U. Coll., London, 1958; research fellow Harvard U., 1960-62; asso. prof., then prof. Cath. U. Am., 1962-66; prof. chemistry U. Ill., Chgo., 1966-95; acting head dept. U. Ill., 1980-81, head dept., 1981-93; vice chancellor rsch., dean grad. coll. U. Ill., Chgo., 1993-95; acting dean Grad. Coll. U. Ill., 1969-70, dean Grad. Coll., 1970-79, asso. mem. Ctr. for Advanced Studies, 1968-69; ret., 1995; vis. scholar Stanford U., 1979-80, Cambridge U., 1980. Contbr. articles to profl. jours. Mem. Am. Chem. Soc., AAAS, Czechoslovak Soc. Arts and Scis. in Am., AAUP, Sigma Xi (pres. chpt. 1976-77, 85-86), Phi Kappa Phi. Home: 2636 Laurel Ln Wilmette IL 60091-2202

ROCHA, ARMANDINO CORDEIRO DOS SANTOS, accountant, educator, auditor; b. Porto, Portugal, Oct. 19, 1934; s. Mario dos Santos and Maria de Conceicão (Cordeiro) R.; m. Maria Laura Oliveira Silva, Sept. 1, 1957 (div. 1976); children: Isabel Maria, Mario Rui; m. Ana Rosalina Sa Ribeiro, July 2, 1977; 1 child, Ana Sofia. B in Acctg., Inst. Comercial, Porto, 1962; B in Social Polit., Inst. Estudos Socials, Lisbon, Portugal, 1969; B in Sociology, Inst. Superior Ciencias, 1982; BBA, Inst. superior C. Trab. Empresas, 1975; PhD in Bus. and Econs. Scis., U. Minho-Braga, 1991. Fin. dir. Fabrica Fiacão E Tecidos Da Portela, Delães, Portugal, 1960-72, Tinturaria Vaz Ferreira, S. Mamede De Infesta, Portugal, 1962-73; regional dir. Companhia Seguros Bonanca, Porto, 1973-87; auditor Emaco, Sa, Lisboa, Porto, 1979-85, Imobur S.A. and Riguadiana S.A., Porto, 1979-85, Estaleiros Navais De Viana, Porto, 1979-82; auditor Efi-Ed Ferreirinha and Irmao S.A., Porto, 1984-88, Feruni-Sicicdade de Fundicão S.A., Trofa, Portugal, 1984-93, Portocork, Internat., S.A., Feira, Portugal, 1987-91, Copo Antlantica, Industria De Poliurentano S.A., Santo Tirso, Portugal, 1987—, Vasconcelos Lyncke, LDA, Feira, Portugal, 1989—, CYC, S.A.-Vilamoura, Portugal, 1989-92, Ferreirinhas Maquinas, S.A., Trofa, Portugal, 1989, Textil Artificial de Porto, 1989-90, Arnaldo Trindade, 1989; prof. acctg. U. Do Minho, Braga, Portugal, 1980—. Author: Principios Do Seguro, 1982; contbr. articles to profl. jours. Mem. Assn. Para O Desenvolvimento Economico E Social, Portugal Economists Assn., Portugal Mgmt. Assn., Inst. Dos Actuários Portugueses. Clubs: Vigorosa Sport, Fenianos. Avocations: chess, music, reading, traveling. Home: 2 Quinta Da Boavista, Villa D'Uryais C 4, 4710 Braga Portugal Office: Universidade Do Minho, Gualtar, P-4119 Braga Portugal

ROCHA, GUY LOUIS, archivist, historian; b. Long Beach, Calif., Sept. 23, 1951; s. Ernest Louis and Charlotte (Sobus) R. BA in Social Studies and Edn., Syracuse U., 1973; MA in Am. Studies, San Diego State U., 1975; postgrad., U. Nev., 1975—. Cert. archivist Am. Acad. Cert. Archivists. Tchr., Washoe County Sch. Dist., Reno, Nev., 1975-76; history instr. Western Nev. C.C., Carson City, 1976; curator manuscripts Nev. Hist. Soc., Reno, 1976-81, interim asst. dir., 1980, interim dir., 1980-81; state adminstr. archives and records Nev. State Libr. and Archives, Carson City, 1981—; hist. cons. Janus Assocs., Tempe, Ariz., 1980, Rainshadow Assocs., Carson City, 1983—; mem. State Bd. Geographic Names. Co-author The Ignoble Conspiracy: Radicalism on Trial in Nevada, 1986, The Earp's Last Frontier: Wyatt and Virgil Earp in Nevada 1902-1905, 1988; contbr. to book and govt. study; host weekly radio talk show Sta. KPTL, Carson City, 1988—. Ex-officio mem. Nev. Commn. Bicentennial U.S. Constitution, 1986-91. Mem. Washoe Heritage Council, Reno, 1983-85; editorial bd. Nev. Hist. Soc., Reno, 1983—; mem. Washoe County Democratic Central Com., Reno, 1984-87. Mem. Conf. Intermountain Archivists (Council mem 1979-87, v.p. 1984-85, pres. 1985-86), No. Nev. Pub. Adminstrs. Group (pres. 1986-87), S.W. Labor Studies Assn., State Hist. Records Adv. Bd. (dep. coordinator 1984-86, coordinator 1986—), Westerners Internat. Nev. Corral (dep. sheriff 1980-81, sheriff 1984-85, mem. state coordinators steering com. 1985-87, vice chmn. 1986-87), Soc. Am. Archivists, Western History Assn., Nat. Assn. Govt. Archives and Records Adminstrs., Orgn. Am. Historians. Democrat. Home: 1824 Pyrenees St Carson City NV 89703-2331 Office: Nev State Libr & Archives 100 Stewart St Carson City NV 89710

ROCHA, OSBELIA MARIA JUAREZ, librarian; b. Odessa, Tex., Aug. 3, 1950; d. Tomas R. and Maria Socorro (Garcia) Juarez; m. Ricardo Rocha, July 8, 1972; children: Nidia Selina, René Ricardo. AA, Odessa Coll., 1970; BA, Sul Ross State U., 1972; MA, Tex. A & I U., 1977; MLS, Tex. Woman's U., 1991. Cert. tchr., reading specialist, Tex. Math. tchr. Del Rio (Tex.) Jr. High Sch., 1972-78; reading tchr. Del Rio High Sch., 1978-79; math. tchr. Ector High Sch., Odessa, 1979-81, Permian High Sch., Odessa, 1981-88; libr. Blackshear Elem. Magnet Sch., Odessa, 1988-93, Bowie Jr. H.S., Odessa, 1993-95, Ector Jr. H.S., Odessa, 1995—. Reviewer of children's and adolescents' books for MultiCultural Review; author articles. Mem. NEA, Internat. Reading Assn., Nat. Coun. Tchrs. Math., Tex. State Tchrs. Assn., Tex. Reading Assn., Tex. Libr. Assn., Tex. Coun. Tchrs. Math., West Tex. Assn. Bilingual Edn., Permian Basin Reading Assn., Beta Phi Mu. Roman Catholic. Avocations: reading, needlework, camping, photography, baking. Home: 1717 W 24th St Odessa TX 79763-2309 Office: Ector Jr HS 900 W Clements Odessa TX 79763

ROCHA, PEDRO, JR., academic administrator; b. Indé, México, Dec. 25, 1939; came to U.S., 1955; s. Pedro Sr. and Maria (Hernández) R.; m. Maria-Cruz Molina, Dec. 6, 1969; children: Diana-Marie, Delma-Irene, Pedro-Hugo. BA in History, U. Tex., El Paso, 1967, MA in Spanish, 1969; PhD in Edn. Adminstrn., U. Tex., 1981. Cert. secondary tchr., supr., adminstr., supt., Tex. Textbook adminstr. Ysleta Jr. High Sch., El Paso, 1976; secondary tchr. Ysleta Ind. Sch. Dist., El Paso, 1969-77; grad. student asst. U. Tex., El Paso, 1976-77; rsch. assoc. U. Tex., Austin, 1979-80; adminstrv. intern Austin (Tex.) C.C., 1978, substitute assoc. dean, 1981-83; rsch. intern S.W. Ednl. Devel. Lab., Austin, 1980-81; tax examiner div. clk. IRS, Austin, 1982; dir., coord. Cook Community Sch., Austin, 1982-85; from ESL instr. to dir., coord. Brooke Community Sch., Austin, 1985-86; dean Mesabi C.C., Virginia, Minn., 1987-92; v.p. for instrn. Trinidad (Colo.) State Jr. Coll., 1992—; Spanish instr. Vermilion C.C., Ely, Minn., 1990; cons.-evaluator for Commn. on Instns. of Higher Edn. of North Ctrl. Assn. Colls. and Schs.; cons. Raton (N.Mex.) Arts and Humanities Coun., 1993, U. Tex., Austin, 1982-86, Tex. Assn. Chicanos in Higher Edn., Denton, 1982, Mexican Am. Legal Def. & Edn. Fund, San Antonio, 1982, Intercultural Rsch., Inc., El Paso, 1981. Author: Staff Orientation Program: Welcoming the Employee to Our Team, (calendar) Historic Trinidad 1996: Hispanic Contributions to Las Animas County. Active mem., bd. dirs. So. Colo. Coal Miners Meml. and Scholarship Fund, 1994; pres. Marquette Sch. Bd., Virginia, 1991-92; active San Juan Coun. Cmty. Agencies, Farmington, 1986-87; leader Quarterly Dates Group, Farmington, 1986-87; adv. bd. Austin Cmty. Gardens, 1985-86. With USAF, 1961-65. Richardson fellow U. Tex., 1977-79; nominated and selected for Nat. Cmty. Coll. Hispanic Coun. Leadership Tng. Program for Hispanic C.C. Adminstrs., 1994. Mem. Am. Assn. for Higher Edn., Am. Assn. Cmty./Jr. Coll., Minn. Chief Acad. Adminstrs., Colo. Coun. Acad. Deans and Vice Pres., Colo. Ednl. Svcs. Coun., Kiwanis Club (first v.p. Trinidad 1995), Hispanic C. of C. (bd. dirs. Trinidad-Las Animas County Hispanic C. of C., pres. 1995-96), K.C. (mem. coun. 1072, 1995—), Kappa Delta Pi, Sigma Delta Pi. Democrat. Roman Catholic. Avocations: bowling, basketball, walking, travel. Home: 112 Benedicta Ave Trinidad CO 81082-2002 Office: Trinidad State Jr Coll 600 Prospect St Trinidad CO 81082-2356

ROCHBERG, GEORGE, composer, educator; b. Paterson, N.J., July 5, 1918; s. Morris and Anna (Hoffman) R.; m. Gene Rosenfeld, Aug. 18, 1941; children—Paul Bernard (dec.), Frances Ruth. B.A., Montclair State Tchrs. Coll., 1939, L.H.D., 1962; B.Mus., Curtis Inst. Music, 1948; M.A., U. Pa., 1949, Mus.D. (hon.), 1988; Mus.D. (hon.), Phila. Mus. Acad., 1964, Curtis Inst. Music, 1988. Mem. faculty Curtis Inst. Music, 1948-54; Fulbright fellow Am. Acad., Rome, 1950-51; editor, dir. publs. Theo. Presser Co., Bryn Mawr, Pa., 1951-60; chmn. Music dept. U. Pa., 1960-68; ret., 1983; Annenberg prof. humanities U. Pa., 1979. Commd. to compose ballet music for Anna Sokolov, Lincoln Center Fund, 1965; recordings include numerous others; (recipient Gershwin Meml. award 1952, Soc. for Publ. Am. Music award 1956, Koussevitzky commn. 1957, Naumberg Rec. award 1961); Composer: Symphony No. 1, 1948-49, Night Music, 1949, String Quartet No. 1, 1952, Serenata d Estate, 1955, Symphony No. 2, 1956, La Bocca della Verita, 1958, String Quartet No. 2, 1959-61, Blake Songs, 1961, Time-Span (II), 1962, Trio for Violin, Cello and Piano, 1963, Zodiac, 1964, Black Sounds, 1965, Contra Mortem et Tempus, 1965, Music for the Magic Theater, 1965, Symphony No. 3, 1969, Tableaux for chamber ensemble, 1968, String Quartet No. 3, 1972, Violin Concerto premiered by Isaac Stern, 1975, Piano Quintet (Nat. Endowment for Arts commn.), 1975, Symphony No. 4, 1976; monodrama Phaedra, 1976, String Quartet No. 4, 1979 (1st place Kennedy Center Friedheim award), The Confidence Man, an Opera, 1981, Piano Trio No. 2 (for Beaux Arts Trio), 1983, Symphony No. 5, Chgo. Symphony, 1986, Symphony No. 6, Pitts. Symphony, 1987, Muse of Fire for flute and guitar, 1989, Piano Trio No. 3 (for Beaux Arts Trio), 1991, Sonata for Violin and Piano, 1988, Sonata-aria for Cello and Piano, 1992, Concerto for Clarinet and Orchestra, 1994-95, others. Served to 2d lt., inf. AUS, 1942-45, ETO. Decorated Purple Heart with cluster; gold medal in music Brandeis Creative Arts award, 1985; Nat. Inst. Arts and Letters grant, 1962; Fromm Found. commn., 1965; Guggenheim fellow, 1957, 1966-67; Nat. Endowment for Arts grantee, 1972-73. Mem. Am. Acad. Arts and Scis., Am. Musicological Soc., ASCAP, Internat. Webern Soc. (v.p.), Am. Acad. Arts and Letters. *I have always clung fast to these fundamentals: that music was given man so he could express the best he was capable of; that the best he was capable of had to do with his deepest feelings; that his deepest feelings are rooted in what I believe to be a moral order in the universe which underlies all real existence.*

ROCHE, BURKE BERNARD, manufacturing company executive; b. Billings, Mont., Oct. 26, 1913; s. John Francis and Bertha (Buchanan) R.; m. Mary Constance Kayser, Aug. 5, 1950. Ph.B., Loyola U., 1936; postgrad. law, Northwestern U., 1937; LL.B., DePaul U., 1939, LL.D., 1973. Bar: Ill. 1940. With Binks Mfg. Co., Chgo., 1946-47, v.p., 1948-49, pres., 1949—, chief exec. officer, 1973—; also dir., chmn. bd., pres. Binks Mfg. Co., Franklin Pk., Ill.; pres., chmn. bd. Binks Internat., Brussels, Belgium, Binks Italia, Zingonia, Italy, Binks Deutschland GmbH, Mulheim, Fed. Republic Germany, Binks Can. Ltd., Toronto, Can., Binks Japan, Ltd., Tokyo, Binks Research and Devel. Corp, Boulder, Colo., Sames S.A., Grenoble, France; dir. Binks Bullows, Eng., Australia, Sweden, Binks de Mex., Mexico City; now pres, ceo Binks Mfg., Franklin Park, IL. Served to lt. USN, 1943-46, PTO. Mem. Ill. State Bar Assn., Am. Mgmt. Assn., Soc. Plastics Industry. Republican. Clubs: Chgo. Athletic, Econ., Loyola U. Pres.'s, Carlton. Office: Binks Mfg Co 9201 W Belmont Ave Franklin Park IL 60131-2807*

ROCHE, DANIEL F., retail executive; b. 1928. Chmn.bd. dirs. Roche Bros. Supermarkets, Inc., Wellesley, Mass., 1952—; now co-chmn. Roche Bros. Supermarkets, Inc., Wellesley. With USMC, 1948-50. Office: Roche Bros Supermarkets Inc 70 Hastings St Wellesley Hills MA 02181*

ROCHE, DOUGLAS DAVID, lawyer, bar examiner; b. Detroit, Oct. 29, 1936; s. James Michael and Louise Carolyn (McMillan) R.; widowed; children: Douglas Jr., Michael, Daniel, Thomas, Robert, Barbara. AB with honors, Holy Cross Coll., Worcester, Mass., 1958; JD, Harvard U., 1963. Bar: Mich. 1963, U.S. Supreme Ct., 1978. Ptnr. Dickinson, Wright, Moon, Van Dusen & Freeman, Detroit, 1963—. Lt. (j.g.) USNR, 1958-60. Mem. ABA, Can. Bar Assn., Fed. Bar Assn. (chmn. Detroit chpt. bankruptcy sect. 1991-92), Mich. Bar Assn., Detroit Bar Assn., Nat. Conf. Bar Examiners (chmn. 1987-88, bd. mgrs. 1981-89, chmn. multistate bar examination policy com. 1988-94), Mich. Bd. Law Examiners (pres. 1975-77), Orchard Lake (Mich.) Country Club, Detroit Athletic Club. Republican. Office: Dickinson Wright 500 Woodward Ave Ste 4000 Detroit MI 48226

ROCHE, GEORGE CHARLES, III, college administrator; b. Denver, May 16, 1935; s. George Charles, Jr. and Margaret (Stewart) R.; m. June Bernard, Feb. 11, 1955; children: George Charles, IV, Muriel Eileen, Margaret Clare, Jacob Stewart. B.S., Regis Coll., Denver, 1956; M.A., U. Colo., 1961, Ph.D., 1965. Tchr. jr. and sr. high schs. Salida, Colo., 1958-60; mem. faculty U. Colo., 1963-64, Colo. Sch. Mines, 1964-66; pres. Hillsdale (Mich.) Coll., 1971—; dir. seminars Found. Econ. Edn., N.Y.C., 1966-71, trustee, 1971-90. Author: Power, 1967, American Federalism, 1967, Education in America, 1969, Legacy of Freedom, 1969, Frederic Bastiat: A Man Alone, 1971, The Bewildered Society, 1972, The Balancing Act: Quota Hiring in Higher Education, 1974, America by the Throat: The Stranglehold of Federal Bureaucracy, 1983, Going Home, 1986, A World Without Heroes, 1987, A Reason for Living, 1989, One By One, 1990, The Fall of the Ivory Tower: Government Funding, Corruption, and the Bankrupting of American Higher Education, 1994; also articles, newspaper column. Chmn. acad. adv. council Charles Edison Meml. Youth Bd., Nat. Council Ednl. Research, 1982-85. Served to 1st lt. USMCR, 1956-58. Recipient Freedom Leadership award Freedoms Found., 1972. Mem. Am. Hist. Assn., Am. Acad. Polit. and Social Sci., Am. Assn. Pres.'s Ind. Colls. and Univs., Mt. Pelerin Soc., Phila. Soc. Office: Hillsdale Coll 33 E College St Hillsdale MI 49242-1205

ROCHE, GERARD RAYMOND, management consultant; b. Scranton, Pa., July 27, 1931; s. Joseph Arthur and Amelia Jane (Garcia) R.; m. Marie Terotta, Apr. 27, 1957; children: Mary Margaret, Anne Elizabeth, Paul Joseph. B.S. in Acctg., U. Scranton, 1953; M.B.A., NYU, 1958. Mgmt. trainee AT&T, Phila., 1955-56; account exec. ABC-TV, N.Y.C., 1956-58; sales and mktg. positions Kordite Corp. subs. Mobil Oil Co., Macedon, N.Y., 1959-63; assoc. Heidrick & Struggles, Inc., N.Y.C., 1964-68, ptnr., 1968—, mgr. N.Y., 1968-73, mgr. East, 1973-77; pres., chief exec. officer Heidrick & Struggles, Inc., N.Y.C., 1978-81; chmn. Heidrick & Struggles, Inc., N.Y.C., 1981—; bd. dirs. Gulfstream Aerospace Corp. Trustee Cath. U. Am., U. Scranton; bd. dirs. Covenant House, N.Y.C. Served to lt. USN, 1953-55. Mem. Univ. Club, Sky Club, Yale Club, Sleepy Hollow Country Club (bd. govs.), Blind Brook Club, Loxahatchee Club, Loblolly Pines C. C., Knights of Malta, Alpha Sigma Nu (past treas.). Roman Catholic. Home: 111 Paulding Dr Chappaqua NY 10514-2817 Office: Heidrick & Struggles Inc 245 Park Ave New York NY 10167-0002

ROCHE, JAMES MCMILLAN, lawyer; b. Detroit, Apr. 16, 1934; s. James Michael and Louise Cullen (McMillan) R.; m. Laura Jane McMillion, Oct. 27, 1962; children: James, Laura, David, Elizabeth. AB, Holy Cross Coll., 1956; LLB, Harvard U., 1959; LLM, Georgetown U., 1962. Bar: Mich. 1959, Ill. 1962. Ptnr., mem. mgmt. com. McDermott, Will & Emery, Chgo., 1962—; bd. dirs. Time Med Labeling, Inc., Burr Ridge, Ill. Contbr. articles to profl. jours. Chmn. Chgo. Econ. Devel. Corp., 1979-81; pres. Village of Kenilworth, Ill., 1982-85; bd. dirs. St. Francis Hosp., Evanston, 1987—. Served to capt. USAF, 1959-62. Mem. ABA, Ill. Bar Assn., Chgo. Bar Assn., Mich. Bar Assn., Glen View (Ill.) Golf Club, Monroe Club (Chgo.), The Boulders Club (Ariz.). Roman Catholic. Avocations: golf, Indian art, wine. Office: McDermott Will & Emery 227 W Monroe St Chicago IL 60606-5016

ROCHE, JAMES RICHARD, pediatric dentist, university dean; b. Fortville, Ind., July 17, 1924; s. George Joseph and Nelle (Kinnaman) R.; m. Viola Marie Morris, May 15, 1949; 1 child, Ann Marie Roche Potter. DDS, Ind. U., 1947, MS in Dentistry, 1983. Diplomate Am. Bd. Pediat. Dentistry (exec. sec.-treas. 1982—). Prof. emeritus Ind. U. Sch. Dentistry, Indpls., 1968—, chmn. divsn. grad. pediat. dentistry, 1969-76, asst. dean faculty devel., 1976-80, assoc. dean faculty devel., 1980-87, assoc. dean for acad. affairs, 1987-88; cons. Coun. Dental Edn., Hosp. Dental Svc. and Commn. Accreditation, Chgo., 1977-83. Capt. U.S. Army, 1952-54. Recipient Distinguished Teaching Recognition award Ind. U., 1976. Fellow Internat. Coll. Dentists, Am. Coll. Dentists, Am. Acad. Pediat. Dentistry (bd. dirs. 1967-70), Pierre Fauchard Acad.; mem. ADA (cons. Bur. Dental Health Edn. 1977), Am. Soc. Dentistry for Children (award of excellence 1993), Ind. Dental Assn. (v.p. 1973-74, chmn. legis. com. 1968-77, lobbyist 1970-77), Indpls. Dist. Dental Assn. (pres. 1967-68), Ind. U.-Purdue U. Indpls. Sr. Acad. (charter), Masons, Omicron Kappa Upsilon. Home and Office: 1193 Woodgate Dr Carmel IN 46033-9232

ROCHE, JOHN EDWARD, human resources management consultant, educator; b. St. Albans, N.Y., Nov. 11, 1946; s. John F. and Carolyn C. (Miller) R.; m. Valerie Vastola; children: Christopher B., Danielle, Ryan J., Jennifer M. BA, Marist Coll., 1968, MBA, 1975; MS in Edn., SUNY, New Paltz, 1974. Tchr. Kingston (N.Y.) City Schs., 1968-76; employment supr. ACLI Internat. Inc., N.Y.C., 1976-78; dir. pers. Balfour MacLaine Internat., N.Y.C., 1978-80; mgr. employee rels. Harcourt Brace Jovanovich, N.Y.C., 1980-82; nat. dir. pers. Hayt, Hayt & Landau, Great Neck, N.Y., 1982-86; pres. Pers. Mgmt. Svcs., Great Neck, N.Y., 1983-86, Martin-Roche Assocs., Inc., Levittown, N.Y., 1986-92; prof. edn. N.Y. Inst. Tech., Old Westbury, 1989—; pres. Human Resources Dept. Inc., Garden City, N.Y., 1994—, L.I. Bus. Network, Inc., 1995—; pres. Martin-Roche Internat. Ltd., Plainview, N.Y., 1992-94. Exec. dir. Jr. Achievement, Kingston, 1972-76, coach Syosset Basseball Assn., CYO Basketball Assn. Mem. ASTD, Am. Compensation Assn. (cert. compensation profl.), Soc. for Human Resource Mgmt. (cert. sr. profl. in human resources), KC (grand knight 1967-68). Republican. Roman Catholic. Avocations: astronomy, photography. Home: 17 Meadow Ln Syosset NY 11791-4126 Office: Human Resources Dept Inc 747 Zeckendorf Blvd Garden City NY 11530-2110 also: NY Inst Tech Dept Edn Old Westbury NY 11568-8000

ROCHE, JOHN J., banking company executive, corporate lawyer. BS, Manhattan Coll., 1957; LLB, Harvard U., 1963. Assoc., then ptnr. Shearman & Sterling, 1963-89; exec. v.p. Citicorp/Citibank, N.A., N.Y.C., 1989—. Office: Citicorp/Citibank NA 153 E 53d St 23d fl New York NY 10043*

ROCHE, JOHN JEFFERSON, lawyer; b. N.Y.C., Apr. 12, 1934; s. William and Florence E. (Garvey) R.; m. Judith J. Stackpole, Sept. 4, 1980; 1 child from previous marriage, Forrest B. A.B., Brown U., 1957; LL.B., Boston U., 1964. Bar: Mass. 1964, U.S. Tax Ct. 1976. Asst. atty. gen. Dept. Atty. Gen., Boston, 1964-67; ptnr. Hale and Dorr, Boston, 1967-90; pvt. practice Cambridge, Mass., 1991—. Trustee The Hotchkiss Sch., 1986-91; bd. dirs. Indian Soc. Served with U.S. Army, 1959-62. Fellow Am. Coll. Probate Counsel, Internat. Acad. Estate and Trust Law; mem. ABA, Mass. Bar Assn., Boston Bar Assn. Republican. Congregationalist. Club: Wig and Penn (London); Winchester Country. Lodge: Masons. Office: John J Roche & Assocs Ste 405 One Cambridge Ctr Cambridge MA 02142

ROCHE, (EAMONN) KEVIN, architect; b. Dublin, Ireland, June 14, 1922; came to U.S., 1948, naturalized, 1964; s. Eamon and Alice (Harding) R.; m. Jane Tuohy, June 10, 1963; children: Eamon, Paud, Denis, Anne, Alice. B.Arch., Nat. U. Ireland, 1945; D.Sc. (hon.), Nat. U. Ireland, 1977; postgrad., Ill. Inst. Tech., 1948; D.F.A. (hon.), Wesleyan U., 1981, Yale U., 1995. With Eero Saarinen and Assocs., Hamden, Conn., 1950-66; partner Kevin Roche John Dinkeloo and Assocs., Hamden, from 1966. Prin. works include Ford Found. Hdqs., 1967, Oakland (Calif.) Mus, 1968, Met. Mus. Art, N.Y.C., Creative Arts Ctr., Wesleyan U., Middletown, Conn., 1971, Fine Arts Ctr., U. Mass., 1971, Union Carbide Corp. World Hdqs., Conn., Gen. Foods Corp. Hdqs., Rye, N.Y., 1977, 1978, Conoco Inc. Hdqs., Houston, 1979, Central Pk. Zoo, N.Y.C., 1980, DeWitt Wallace Mus. Fine Arts, Williamsburg, Va., 1980, Bouygues World Hdqs., Paris, 1983, J.P. Morgan and Co. Hdqs., N.Y.C., 1983, UNICEF Hdqrs., N.Y.C., 1984, Leo Burnett Co. Hdqs., Chgo., 1985, Corning (N.Y.) Inc. Hdqs., 1986, Merck & Co. Inc. Corp. Office Facility, N.J., 1987, Dai Ichi Hdqs./Norinchukin Bank Hdqrs., Tokyo, 1989, Nations Bank Hdqs., Atlanta, 1989, N.Y.C. Exchs. Hdqs., 1989, Pontiac Marina Pvt. Ltd., Singapore, 1990, Metropolitano, Madrid, 1990, Borland Internat., Inc., Scotts Valley, Calif., 1990, Internat. Trade Ctr., Dusseldorf, Germany, 1991, Eczacibasi Group Hdqs., Istanbul, 1991, Hdqs. Tanjong & Binariang/Ampang Tower, Kuala Lumpur, Malaysia, 1993, Mus. of Jewish Heritage Holocaust Meml., N.Y.C., 1993, Tata Cummins Pvt. Ltd., Jamshedpur, India, 1994, Vis. Ctr., Columbus, Ind., 1994, Cummins Engine Co. APEX Mfg. Facility, 1994, DBS Devel., Beijing, China, 1994, Hyundai Kangnam Office Bldg., Seoul, Korea, 1995, Lucent Techs. Hdqs., Murray Hill, N.J., 1996. Mem. Fine Arts Commn., Washington; trustee Am. Acad. in Rome, 1968-71, Woodrow Wilson Center for Scholars in Smithsonian Instn. Recipient Creative Arts award Brandeis U., 1967; A.S. Bard award City Club N.Y., 1968, 77, 79; award Gov. of Calif., 1968; N.Y. State award Citizens Union N.Y., 1968; total design award Am. Soc. Interior Design; Pritzker Archtl. prize, 1982; Albert S. Bard award, 1990. Fellow AIA (medal of honor N.Y. chpt. 1968, Gold Medal award 1993), AAAS; mem. NAD (academician), AAAL (pres. 1994-97), Am. Acad. and Inst. Arts and Letters (Brunner award 1965, Gold medal 1990), Académie d'Architecture (Grand Gold medal 1977), Mcpl. Art Soc. N.Y. (Brendan Gill prize 1989), Acad. di San Luca. Office: Kevin Roche John Dinkeloo & Assoc PO Box 6127 20 Davis St Hamden CT 06517-0127

ROCHE, KEVIN JOSEPH, finance executive; b. Newburyport, Mass., Mar. 31, 1935; s. Francis A. and Johanna (Murphy) R.; m. Arleen Ann Tangney, Oct. 16, 1965; children: Elizabeth, Edward. BBA, Merrimack Coll., 1962. Various positions Dow Jones & Co., Inc., N.Y.C., 1977-87; comptroller Dow Jones & Co., Inc., Princeton, N.J., 1987—; v.p. fin., chief fin. officer Dow Jones & Co., Inc., 1987—. Contbr. articles to profl. jours. Served to sgt. USAF, 1954-58. Mem. Fin. Exec. Inst., Internat. Newspaper Fin. Execs. Office: Dow Jones & Co Inc 200 Liberty St New York NY 10281-1003*

ROCHE, MARK WILLIAM, German language educator; b. Weymouth, Mass., Aug. 29, 1956; s. Jason Bernard and Joan (Murphy) R.; m. Barbara Hampshire, June 13, 1981. BA, Williams Coll., 1978; MA, U. Tübingen, Germany, 1980, Princeton (N.J.) U., 1982; PhD, Princeton (N.J.) U., 1984. Asst. prof. German Ohio State U., Columbus, 1984-90, assoc. prof., 1990-96, chair dept. German, 1991-96; Joyce prof. German lang. and lit. and chmn. dept. German/Russian U. Notre Dame, South Bend, Ind., 1996—. Author: Dynamic Stillness, 1987, Gottfried Benn's Static Poetry, 1991. Fulbright fellow Germany, 1978-80, Whiting fellow, 1983-84, ACLS fellow, 1985; NEH Summer Stipend grantee, 1991, DAAD Study Visit Rsch. grantee, 1991. Mem. Soc. for Philosophic Study of contemporary Visual Arts (vice pres. 1990-92). Home: 2019 Surrey Dr Blacklick OH 43004-9758 Office: Ohio State U 312 Cunz Hall Columbus OH 43210

ROCHELEAU, JAMES ROMIG, academic administrator; b. Anchorage, Mar. 21, 1940; s. James Albert and Sophia (Rivord) R.; m. Margaret Anne Sheehan, Nov. 28, 1981; children from previous marriage: Renee, Tanya, Andrea. BA, U. Idaho, 1968, MA, 1969; PhD, Wash. State U., Pullman, 1975. Account exec. Spokesman Rev., Spokane, Wash., 1963; sales rep. RJR Nabisco, Inc., Spokane, 1963-66; grad. asst. U. Idaho, Moscow and Wash. State U., Pullman, 1967-70; instr. history Wash. State U., 1970-71; asst. prof. history Buena Vista Coll., Storm Lake, Iowa, 1971-76, dir., 1976-81, dean continuing edn., 1981-84; pres. Upper Iowa U., Fayette, 1984-94, pres. emeritus, 1994—; cons. North Cen. Assn., Chgo., 1981—, Kellogg Found., 1994—. Active N.E.-Midwest Leadership Coun. Served with U.S. Army, 1958-61. Mem. Nat. Assn. Ind. Colls. and Univs., Iowa Assn. Ind. Colls. Univs., Coun. Ind. Colls., Iowa Coordinating Coun. for Post-High Sch. Edn., C. of C. Home: 14455 90th Ave Seminole FL 34646-1925 Office: PO Box 373 Indian Rocks Beach FL 34635-0373

ROCHEN, DONALD MICHAEL, osteopathic physician; b. Buffalo, Apr. 15, 1943; s. Leo Kant and Phoebe (Elkan) R.; m. Phyllis Helene Been, Aug. 15, 1971; children: Steven, Douglas, Deborah, Andrew. B.A., Northwestern U., 1964; D.O., Coll. Osteo. Medicine and Surgery, Des Moines, 1968. Intern, Detroit Osteo./Bi County Cmty. Hosps., 1968-69, resident in otorhinolaryngology, 1969-73; practice otorhinolaryngology oto-laryngic allergy oro-facial plastic surgery, Madison Heights, Warren, Farmington Hills and Mt. Clemens, Mich., 1973—; program dir. residency and chmn. dept. otolaryngology and orofacial plastic surgery Bi County Cmty. Hosp., Warren, Mich.; past chmn. dept. otolaryngology Mt. Clemens Gen. Hosp.;

mem. staff Mt. Clemens Gen. Hosp. (Mich.), Oakland Gen. Hosp., Botsford Gen. Hosp., Bi County Community Hosp.; assoc. prof. Mich. State U. Coll. Osteo. Medicine and Surgery, 1975—; adj. prof. Coll. Osteo. Medicine and Surgery, Des Moines, 1981—. Fellow Osteo. Coll. Ophthalmology and Otorhinolaryngology (diplomate), Am. Acad. Otolaryngology, Head and Neck Surgery, Am. Acad. Otolaryngic Allergy; mem. Am. Osteo. Assn., Mich. Assn. Osteo. Physicians and Surgeons, Am. Acad. Otolaryngic Allergy, N.Y. Acad. Scis., Mich. Otolaryngol. Soc., Oakland County Osteo. Assn., Macomb County Osteo. Assn. Home: 4808 Tyndale Ct West Bloomfield MI 48323-3351 Office: 27483 Dequindre Rd Madison Heights MI 48071-3491

ROCHER, LUDO, humanities educator; b. Hemiksem, Belgium, Apr. 25, 1926; s. Jules and Anna Van Den (Bogaert) R.; m. Rosane Debels, Apr. 1, 1961. B.A., U. Ghent, Belgium, 1946, M.A., 1948, LL.D., 1950, Ph.D., 1952. Agrege U. Ghent, 1958-59; prof. Sanskrit and comparative philology U. Brussels, 1959-67; prof. Sanskrit U. Pa., Phila., 1966—, W. Norman Brown prof. South Asian studies, 1981—; chmn. dept. Oriental studies U. Pa., 1967-75, 88-94, chmn. dept. South Asia regional studies, 1975-78; dir. Center for Study of South and S.E. Asia, U. Brussels, 1961-67. Author: A Hindu Legal Digest, 1956, Manual of Modern Hindi, 1958, Bibliography of Hindu Law, 1963, Smrticintamani, 1976, Paulinus a S. Bartholomaeo on the Sanskrit Language, 1977, Ezourvedam, 1984, The Puranas, 1985; contbr. articles to profl. jours. Served with Belgian Army, 1950-52. Research fellow Nat. Found. for Sci. Research, Belgium, 1952-58. Fellow Royal Acad. for Overseas Scis. Belgium, Asiatic Soc. Calcutta; mem. Am. Philos. Soc., Am. Oriental Soc. (pres. 1985-86), Assn. for Asian Studies, Royal Asiatic Soc. (Eng.). Home: 226 W Rittenhouse Sq Apt 1506 Philadelphia PA 19103-5747

ROCHESTER, MICHAEL GRANT, geophysics educator; b. Toronto, Ont., Can., Nov. 22, 1932; s. Reginald Baillie Rochester and Ruth Ellen (Bonwick) Rochester Konrad; m. Elizabeth Manser, May 9, 1958; children—Susan, Fiona, John. BA with honors, U. Toronto, 1954, MA, 1956; PhD, U. Utah, 1959. Aerodynamicist A. V. Roe Can. Ltd., Malton, Ont., 1954-55; lectr. geophysics U. Toronto, 1959-60, asst. prof., 1960-61; asst. prof. U. Waterloo, Ont., 1961-65; assoc. prof. U. Waterloo, 1965-67, Meml. U. Nfld., St. John's, Can., 1967-70; prof. Meml. U. Nfld., 1970—, univ. research prof., 1986—. Mem., officer Nat. Spiritual Assembly of Baha'is of Can., 1963-92. Grantee NRC, Natural Scis. and Engring. Research Council Can. Fellow Royal Soc. Can.; mem. Internat. Union Geodesy and Geophysics (Can. nat. com. 1971-75, 84-88), AAAS, Am. Geophys. Union, Can. Assn. Physicists, Can. Geophys. Union (Tuzo Wilson medal, 1986), Internat. Astron. Union (commn. rotation of the Earth 1973—), Royal Astron. Soc. London, Sigma Xi. Avocations: hiking, swimming, history. Office: Meml Univ Nfld, Dept Earth Scis, Saint John's, NF Canada A1B 3X5

ROCHETTE, EDWARD CHARLES, retired association executive; b. Worcester, Mass., Feb. 17, 1927; s. Edward Charles and Lilia (Viau) R.; m. Mary Ann Ruland, July 29, 1978; children by previous marriage—Edward Charles, Paul, Philip. Student, Washington U., St. Louis, Clark U. Exec. editor Krause Publs., Iola, Wis., 1960-66; acting exec. dir. Am. Numismatic Assn., Colorado Springs, Colo., 1967-68, exec. v.p., 1972-87, ret., 1987; editor jour. The Numismatist, Colorado Springs, Colo., 1968-72. Bd. overseers Inst. Philatelic and Numismatic Studies, Adelphi U., Garden City, N.Y., 1979-81; chmn. medals com. Colo. Centennial Bicentennial Commn., 1976; mem. adv. panel Carson City Silver Dollar program Gen. Services Adminstrn., 1979-80; mem. U.S. Assay Commn., 1965. Served with USN, 1944-46. Recipient Gold medal for syndicated column Numismatic Lit. Guild, 1980, 86-88. Mem. Am. Numis. Assn. (life, medal of merit 1972), Am. Soc. Assn. Execs., Colo. Soc. Assn. Execs. (pres. 1988-89). Democrat. Roman Catholic. Lodge: Pikes Peak Kiwanis (pres. 1987-88). Office: Am Numis Assn PO Box 7083 Colorado Springs CO 80933-7083

ROCHETTE, LOUIS, retired shipowner and shipbuilder; b. Quebec City, Que., Can., Feb. 19, 1923; s. Evariste and Blanche (Gaudry) R.; m. Nicole Barbeau, Oct. 12, 1968; children: Louise, Ann, Guy. M. Commerce, Laval U., Que., 1948. Chartered Accountant, Que. Chief auditor retail sales tax Govt. Que. Quebec City, 1953-55; treas. Davie Shipbldg., Ltd., Lauzon, Que., 1955-65; exec. v.p. Marine Industries, Ltd., Montreal, Que., 1965-76; chmn., CEO Davie Shipbldg. Ltd., Lauzon, Que., 1976-82; pres., CEO Soconav Inc., Quebec, 1982-86; pres. Gesconav Inc., 1986—; bd. dirs. Hawker Siddeley Can. Inc., Leader Industries, Inc; past chmn. Lloyd's Com. for Can. Author: Le Reve Separatiste, 1969. Bd. dirs. Gov. Coun. for Can. Unity; gov. Laval U. Found, Quebec Opera Found. Pilot RCAF, 1943-45, ETO. Named Hon. Col., Royal Can. Artillery. Fellow Inst. Chartered Accts. Can., Que. C. of C., Can. Inst. of Mgmt. Accts. Home and Office: 1155 Turnbull St #1002, Quebec, PQ Canada G1R 5G3 *Whatever success I have met with throughout my career was mainly achieved through perseverance in the face of what often looked like insurmountable obstacles.*

ROCHLIS, JAMES JOSEPH, manufacturing company executive; b. Phila., Apr. 12, 1916; s. Aaron and Gussie (Pearlene) R.; m. Riva Singer, Mar. 21, 1943; children: Jeffrey A., Susan J. Ed. pub. schs. Salesman Mid-City Tire Co., Phila., 1945-46, gen. mgr., 1946-49; pres. Ram Rubber Co., Phila., 1948-49; rep. Blair & Co., Phila., 1949-61, bus. analyst, 1955-61; pres., chief exec. officer Baldwin-Montrose Chem. Co., Inc., N.Y.C., 1961-68; v.p. Chris-Craft Industries, Inc., N.Y.C., 1968-69; pres. Chris-Craft Corp., Pompano Beach, Fla., 1969-71; exec. v.p. Chris-Craft Industries, Inc., N.Y.C., 1969-87, also bd. dirs.; pres. Baldwin-NAFI Industries div. Chris-Craft Industries, 1968—, Chris-Craft Internat., 1977-87; pres. Chris-Craft Indsl. Products, Inc., Pompano Beach, 1981-86, chmn., bd. dirs., cons., 1986—; bd. dirs. Montrose Chem. Co. Calif., Torrance and Mex., So. Mass. Cablevision Corp., N.Y.C., Piper Aircraft Corp., Lock Haven, Pa., Chris-Craft Pacific, Inc., Calif. Mem. AIAA, Fin. Analysts Soc. Phila., Soc. Naval Architects and Marine Engrs., Antique and Classic Boat Soc. Club: Lotus (N.Y.C.). Home: 150 E 69th St New York NY 10021-5704 also: 10601 Wilshire Blvd Los Angeles CA 90024-4518 Office: Chris-Craft Industries Inc 767 Fifth Ave New York NY 10153

ROCHON, JOHN PHILIP, cosmetics company executive; b. Sept. 20, 1951; s. Philip Benjamin and Helena Sylvia (McCullough) R.; m. Donna J. Hewitt, Dec. 15, 1972; children: Heidi C., William J., Lauren. BS, U. Toronto, Ont., 1973, MBA, 1976. Plant mgr. Econs. Lab. Ltd., Toronto, 1976-80; dir. mfg. Mary Kay Cosmetics, Ltd., Toronto, 1980-82; contr. mfg. group Mary Kay Cosmetics, Inc., Dallas, 1982-84, corp. contr., 1984, v.p. fin., chief fin. officer, 1984-85, exec. v.p., chief fin. officer, 1986-87, vice chmn. bd., 1987-93; pres., CEO Mary Kay Cosmetics Corp., Dallas, 1993—; also bd. dirs. Mary Kay Cosmetics, Ltd., Dallas; bd. dirs. Mary Kay Holding Corp., Dallas, Strategic Assessment, Inc.; mem. fin. com. U. Tex., Dallas, 1985—. Mem. Cosmetic, Toiletry and Fragrance Assn., Direct Selling Assn., Verandah Club. Republican. Home: 4315 Firebrick Ln Dallas TX 75287-5138*

ROCHOWICZ, JOHN ANTHONY, JR., mathematics and physics educator; b. Reading, Pa., Mar. 20, 1950; s. John Anthony and Sara Jane (Binckley) R. BS in Math., Albright Coll., 1972; MS in Math., Lehigh U., 1974; secondary edn. cert. math., Albright Coll., 1975; EdD in Ednl. Tech., Lehigh U., 1993. Cert. secondary teaching, Pa. Math. tchr. Bethlehem (Pa.) Cath. High Sch., 1980-81; instr. math. Pa. State U.-Berks, Reading, 1982-84, Kutztown (Pa.) U., 1983-84, Lehigh County C.C., Schnecksville, Pa., 1984, Alvernia Coll., Reading, 1984, Reading (Pa.) Area C.C., 1984-86; prof. math. Alvernia Coll., 1985—. Recipient Alumni Educator award Albright Coll., Reading, 1987. Mem. AAUP, Math. Assn. Am., Assn. for the Advancement Computing in Edn., Assn. for Ednl. Communications and Tech., Nat. Coun. Tchrs. Math.; contbr. articles to scientific jours. Democrat. Roman Catholic. Avocations: collecting music, computers, calculators, billiards, swimming. Home: 41 Columbia Ave SCM Reading PA 19606-1316 Office: Alvernia College 400 Saint Bernardine St Reading PA 19607-1756

ROCHWARGER, LEONARD, former ambassador; b. Buffalo, Aug. 3, 1925; s. Max and Sarah (Wallace) R.; m. Arlene Bassuk, June 19, 1949; children: Jeffrey Alan, Michelle. BS, U. Buffalo, 1949; PhD (hon.), Canisius Coll. Chief auditor Western N.Y. State, Buffalo, 1949-61; sr. ptnr. S. L. Horowitz & Co., Buffalo, 1961-65; chmn., chief exec. officer Rockmont Corp., Buffalo, 1965-87, 90—; U.S. amb. to Fiji Republic of Kiribati, Kingdom of Tonga and Tuvalu, 1987-89; chmn. bd. Indpls. Morris Plan Corp., Firstmark Fin. Corp., 1972-87; chmn. bd. Israel Am. Leasing Ltd., 1971-87; dir. Marine Midland Bank-Western, Nat. Fuel Gas Co.; adj. prof. SUNY, Buffalo; bd. chmn. Menorah Campus, 1993—. Past gen. chmn. United Way Buffalo and Erie Co., 1973; past trustee, past chmn. bd. regents Canisius Coll.; past chmn. United Jewish Appeal, Buffalo, 1969; past. pres., life dir. Buffalo Jewish Ctr.; past mem. nat. bd. dirs. NCCJ; past bd. dirs., hon. life pres. Nat. Jewish Welfare Bd.; life mem., past pres. Jewish Fedn. Greater Buffalo; past bd. dirs. Coun. Jewish Fedns.; mem. adv. coun. Johns Hopkins U. Sch. Adv. Internat. Studies, Washington, 1986-88, 90—; past pres. Found. Jewish Philanthropies, Buffalo; trustee U. Buffalo Found., Inc. With AUS, 1943-46. Decorated Bronze Star, Conspicous Svc. Cross, Combat/Infantryman's Badge. Jewish. Home: 81 Nottingham Ter Buffalo NY 14216-3620

ROCK, ALLAN MÍCHAEL, Canadian government official; b. Ottawa, Ont., Can., Aug. 30, 1947; s. James Thomas and Anne (Dane) R.; m. Deborah Kathleen, June 24, 1983; children: Jason, Lauren, Andrew, Stephen. BA, U. Ottawa, 1968, LLB, 1971. Certified specialist in civil litigation. Sr. ptnr. Fasken Campbell Godfrey and Fasken Martineau; min. of justice, atty. gen. Govt. of Can., 1993—; treas. Law Soc. U.C., 1992—; bencher Law Soc., 1983, 87, 91; former chmn. discipline and legal edn. coms.; chmn. litigation dept. Fasken Campbel Godfrey. Fellow Am. Coll. Trial Lawyers. Office: Justice Canada, Justice Bldg 239 Wellington St, Ottawa, ON Canada K1A 0H8

ROCK, ANGELA, volleyball player; b. Carlsbad, Calif., Oct. 15, 1963. BA in Psychology, San Diego State U., 1994. Fire-fighter San Diego; profl. volleyball tour player; mem. U.S.A. Nat. Team, 1987-90. Winner bronze medal Pan Am. Games, 1987; named USVBA Most Valuable Player, 1987, WPVA Best Hitter, 1991, Winner of the Miller Lite Ice Cup. Mem. Assn. Volleyball Profls., Women's Profl. Volleyball Assn. Competed Goodwill Games, 1987, Olympic, Seoul, 1988; compiled 18 WPVA Open Wins; won AVP Women's Tour Event with Linda Hanley, Ocean City, 1993, 1st ever with Holly McPeak, Phoenix, Miller Lite Opens, (receipient Miller Lite Ice Cup), Grand Haven and Nestea Opens, Atlanta, Dallas with Nancy Reno, Phoenix, 1994. Office: care Assn Volleyball Profls 15260 Ventura Blvd Ste 2250 Sherman Oaks CA 91403-5352*

ROCK, ARTHUR, venture capitalist; b. Rochester, N.Y., Aug. 19, 1926; s. Hyman A. and Reva (Cohen) R.; m. Toni Rembe, July 19, 1975. BS, Syracuse U., 1948; MBA, Harvard U., 1951. Gen. ptnr. Davis & Rock, San Francisco, 1961-68, Arthur Rock & Assocs., San Francisco, 1969-80; bd. dirs. Argonaut Group, Inc., L.A., Echelon, Palo Alto, Calif., AirTouch Comm., San Francisco; mem. exec. com. Teledyne, Inc., L.A., 1961-94; founder, chmn. exec. com., bd. dirs., past chmn. bd. dirs. Intel Corp., Santa Clara, Calif. Trustee Calif. Inst. Tech.; bd. dirs. San Francisco Opera Assn., 1970-92, San Francisco Mus. Modern Art; mem. vis. com. Harvard U. Bus. Sch., 1982-88. Recipient Medal of Achievement Am. Electronics Assn., 1987, Am. Acad. Achievement, 1989; named to Jr. Achievement Hall of Fame, 1990, Calif. Bus. Hall of Fame, 1990, Bay Area Bus. Coun. Hall of Fame, 1995. Office: 1 Maritime Plz Ste 1220 San Francisco CA 94111-3502

ROCK, DOUGLAS LAWRENCE, manufacturing executive; b. Glen Cove, N.Y., Jan. 25, 1947; s. Herb and Beatrice (Vyse) R.; m. Cindy Pegoraro, May 11, 1967 (div. Apr. 1973); 1 child, Jason; m. Mary Sue Bell, Mar. 23, 1991. BS in Psychology and Chemistry, Pa. State U., 1968; postgrad., U. Chgo., 1971-73. Rsch. chemist FMC Corp., Princeton, N.J., 1968-69; mfg. system project leader A.O. Smith Corp., Erie, Pa., 1969-71; dir. materials and info. systems Joy Mfg., Michigan City, Ind., 1971-74; dir. info. systems Smith Tool div. Smith Internat. Inc., Irvine, Calif., 1974-75, dir. materials, 1975-77, v.p. mfg., 1977-80, sr. v.p. ops., 1980-82, pres., 1985-87; pres. Drilco div. Smith Internat. Inc., Houston, 1982-85; pres., chief exec. officer Smith Internat. Inc., Houston, 1987—, chmn. bd., 1991—. Named Golden Knight, Nat. Mgmt. Assn., 1983. Mem. Internat. Assn. Drilling Contractors, Am. Petroleum Inst., Petroleum Equipment Suppliers Assn. (bd. dirs. Houston chpt. 1987—), Nat. Offshore Industries Assn. (fin. com. 1988—, audit com. 1989), Kingwood Country Club, Greenspoint Club . Avocations: golf, racquetball, reading. Office: Smith Internat PO Box 60068 16740 Hardy Rd Houston TX 77205-0068

ROCK, HAROLD L., lawyer; b. Sioux City, Iowa, Mar. 13, 1932; s. Harold L. and Helen J. (Gormally) R.; m. Marilyn Beth Rock, Dec. 28, 1954; children: Michael, Susan, John, Patrick, Michele, Thomas. BS, Creighton U., 1954, JD, 1959. Bar: Nebr., N.Y., Minn., Mont., Wyo. Law clk. to judge U.S. Ct. Appeals 8th Circuit, Omaha, 1959-60, Fitzgerald Hamer Brown & Leahy, Omaha, 1960-65; ptnr. Kutak Rock, Omaha, 1965—; chmn. Nebr. Bd. Bar Examiners, 1989—; bd. dirs. Mid City Bank, Omaha. Bd. dirs. Douglas County Hist. Soc., 1992—. Served to 1st lt. U.S. Army, 1954-56. Mem. ABA (ho. of dels. 1990—, bd. govs. 1992-95), Nebr. Bar Assn. (ho. of dels., bd. dirs. 1985—, pres. 1988, Nebr. Bar found. bd. dirs., 1982—), Omaha Bar Assn. (pres. 1972-73), Omaha Legal Aid Soc. (pres. 1969-72), Nebr. State Bd. Pub. Accts. (bd. dirs. 1981-85). Roman Catholic. Office: Kutak Rock The Omaha Bldg 1650 Farnam St Omaha NE 68102

ROCK, JOHN AUBREY, gynecologist and obstetrician, educator; b. Corpus Christi, Tex., Oct. 21, 1946; s. William A. and Burta (Wheeler) R.; m. Barbara McAlpine, Oct. 8, 1976; children: John Aubrey Jr., Deborah Ellen, Daniel Authur. BS in Zoology, La. State U., Baton Rouge, 1968; MD, La. State U., New Orleans, 1972. Asst. prof. Johns Hopkins U. Sch. Medicine, Balt., 1978-80, assoc. prof., 1980-87, prof. ob-gyn, 1987-92, prof. pediatrics, 1988-92, dir. reproductive endocrinology, 1979-91, dep. dir. med. sch., 1985-88; chmn. Union Meml. Hosp., Balt., 1991-92; James Robert McCord prof., chmn. dept. ob-gyn. Emory U. Sch. Medicine, Atlanta, 1992—; cons. Dept. Army, Washington, 1982-93, NASA, Houston, 1988—; chmn. ad hoc com. on in vitro fertilization State of Md., 1985. Author: Reparative and Constructive Surgery of the Female Generative Tract, 1983, Endometriosis, 1988, TeLinde's Operative Gynecology, 1991, 95; mem. editl. bd. Fertility and Sterility jour., 1986-94, Gynecology Surgery, 1989—. Fellow ACOG; mem. Am. Gynecol. and Obstet. Soc., Soc. Gynecol. Surgeons, Am. Fertility Soc. (bd. dirs. 1989-92), Soc. Gynecologic Investigation, Soc. Reproductive Surgeons (pres. 1986), Am. Soc. for Reproductive Medicine (pres. 1996—), Rotary Club, Phi Kappa Phi. Methodist. Office: Emory U Sch Medicine Atlanta GA 30303-9999

ROCK, KENNETH WILLETT, history educator; b. Abilene, Kans., Dec. 12, 1938; s. Kenneth Melvin and Marjorie (Taylor) R.; m. Mercedes Alice de Sola, Aug. 22, 1964; children: Kenneth Teodoro, Laurel Elizabeth. BA, U. Kans., 1960; MA, Stanford U., 1962, PhD, 1969. Instr. history Colo. State U., Ft. Collins, 1965-68, asst. prof., 1968-72, advisor Fulbright, Marshall, Rhodes scholarships, 1968-80, assoc. prof., 1972-83, prof., 1983—, acting dir. Office Internat. Edn., 1984-85; vis. scholar Tech. U., Budapest, Hungary, 1993. Author (booklet) German Footprints in Colorado, 1983; contbr. articles to profl. jours.; chpts. to books. Fulbright scholar Inst. Internat. Edn., Vienna, Austria, 1964-65; fellow NEH, Vienna, 1972-73, NEH, U. Va., 1978; assoc. Danforth Found., 1978-84. Mem. Am. Assn. Advancement Slavic Studies, Conf. Group Cen. European History, Am. Hist. Assn., Am. Hist. Soc. Germans from Russia, Rocky Mountain Slavic Studies Assn., Phi Beta Kappa, Phi Alpha Theta. Democrat. Avocations: reading, historical miniatures, travelling, photography, painting. Home: 3212 Shore Rd Fort Collins CO 80524-1688 Office: Colo State U Dept History Fort Collins CO 80523

ROCK, MILTON LEE, publisher; b. Phila., Feb. 25, 1921; s. Maurice and Mary (Lee) R.; m. Shirley Cylinder, Aug. 3, 1943; children: Susan Rock, Robert Henry. BA, Temple U., 1946, MS, 1947; Ph.D., U. Rochester, 1949. Mng. ptnr. Hay Group, Phila., 1949-85; chmn. MLR Enterprises, Inc., Phila., 1985—; pres. Assn. Mgmt. Cons. Firms, N.Y.C., 1972-73. Coauthor: The Executive Perceptanalytic Scale, 1963, The Development of Bank Management Personnel, 1969; editor: Handbook of Wage and Salary Administration, 1972, 2d edit., 1983, Compensation Handbook, 1990, The Mergers and Acquisitions Handbook, 1987, 2d edit., 1994, Corporate Restructuring, 1989. Chmn. Mid. Atlantic Regional Manpower Adv. Com., Labor Dept., 1972-73; mem. Pres.'s Nat. Commn. for Manpower Policy, 1974-77; bd. govs. Temple U. Hosp., 1975—, chmn., 1985-92, trustee Univ., 1979—; bd. dirs. Phila. Orch., 1981-87, 89-94, Curtis Inst. Music, Phila., 1983—, chmn., 1989—; bd. dirs. Pa. Ballet, 1983—, chmn., 1994; bd. dirs. Phila. Mus. Art, 1986—, Fgn. Policy Rsch. Inst., 1987-90; mem. adv. coun. J.L. Kellogg Grad. Sch. Mgmt., Northwestern U., 1981—. Fellow Am. Psychol. Assn.; mem. Inst. Mgmt. Cons. (dir., founding). Home: Pocono Pines PA 18350 Office: MLR Enterprises Inc 229 S 18th St Philadelphia PA 19103-6144

ROCK, RICHARD RAND, lawyer, former state senator; b. Wichita Falls, Tex., Sept. 27, 1924; s. Parker Francis and Ruth Ann (Phillips) R.; m. Rosalee Deardorff, Aug. 23, 1947; children: Richard R. II, Darci Lee, Devon Ray, Robert Regan. BA, Washburn U., 1948, LLB, 1950, JD, 1970. Bar: Kans., U.S. Dist. Ct. Kans., U.S. Ct. Appeals (4th and 10th cirs.). Dir. indsl. rels. Maurer-Neuer Packers, Arkansas City, Kans., 1950-52, plant supt., 1952-54; atty. Rock, Smith & Mason, Arkansas City, Kans., 1955-95; pres., owner Shreveport (La.) Packing Co., 1972-83, Amarillo (Tex.) Beef Processors, 1977-82, Lubbock (Tex.) Beef Processors, 1978-81, Montgomery (Ala.) Food Processors, 1978-91, Humboldt (Iowa) Sausage Co., 1985-92, Great Bend (Kans.) Packing Co., 1984-95; state senator, asst. minority leader State of Kans., 1988—; chmn. bd. dirs. Rockgate Mgmt. Co., Overland Park, Kans. Judge Cowley County, Kans., 1952-56; state rep. State of Kans., 1957-61; authority mem. Kans. Turnpike Authority, 1980-83, chmn., 1993—; commr. Children with Spl. Health Care Needs, Kans., 1993-95. Served USN Air Corps, 1943-45. Mem. Kans. Bar Assn., Nat. Counsel State Legislatures, Kans. C. of C., VFW. Democrat. Mem. Disciples of Christ. Avocations: golf, yard work.

ROCKART, JOHN FRALICK, information systems reseacher; b. N.Y.C., June 20, 1931; s. John Rachac and Janet (Ross) R.; m. Elise Jean Feldmann, Sept. 16, 1961; children: Elise B. Liesl, Scott F. AB, Princeton U., 1953; MBA, Harvard U., 1958; PhD, MIT, 1968. Sales rep. IBM, 1958-61, dist. med. rep., 1961-62, fellow in Africa, 1962-64; instr. MIT, Cambridge, Mass., 1966-67; asst. prof. IBM, Cambridge, Mass., 1967-70, assoc. prof., 1970-74, sr. lectr., 1974—; dir. MIT, Cambridge, 1976—; bd. dirs. Keane, Inc., Boston, Comshare, Inc., Ann Arbor, Mich., Transition Systems, Inc., Boston, Multiplex, St. Louis, Renaissance Solutions, Lincoln, Mass., Synon, Inc., Larkspur, Calif. Co-author: Computers & Learning Process, 1974, Rise of Managerial Computing, 1986, Executive Support Systems, 1988 (Computer Press Assn. 1989); contbr. articles to profl. jours. Trustee New Eng. Med. Ctr., Boston; mem. Mass. Gov. Adv. Coun. on Info. Tech., Boston. Lt. USN, 1953-56. Mem. Assn. for Computing Machinery, Inst. for Mgmt. Sci., Ops. Rsch. Soc. Am., Soc. for Info. Mgmt. (bd. dirs. mem. at large 1989-94), New Eng. Med. Ctr. Audit Com., Weston (Mass.) Golf Club, Lake Sunapee Country Club (New London, N.H.). Republican. Unitarian. Home: 150 Cherry Brook Rd Weston MA 02193-1308 Office: CISR MIT Sloan Sch Mgmt E40-187 77 Massachusetts Ave # E40-187 Cambridge MA 02139-4301

ROCKBURNE, DOROTHEA GRACE, artist; b. Montreal, Que., Can, Oct. 18, 1934. Student, Black Mountain Coll. Milton and Sally Avery Disting. prof. Bard Coll., 1986; trustee Ind. Curators Inc., N.Y., Art in Gen.; artist in residence Am. Acad. in Rome, 1991; vis. artist Skowhegan Sch. Printing and Sculpture, 1984. One-person shows include Sonnabend Gallery, Paris, 1971, New Gallery, Cleve., 1972, Bykert Gallery, N.Y.C., 1970, 72, 73, Galleria Toselli, Milan, Italy, 1972, 73, 74, Galleria D'Arte, Bari, Italy, 1972, Lisson Gallery, London, 1973, Daniel Weinberg Gallery, San Francisco, 1973, Galerie Charles Kriwin, Brussels, 1975, Galleria Schema, Florence, Italy, 1973, 75, 92, John Weber Gallery, N.Y.C., 1976, 78, Galleria la Polena, Geona, Italy, 1977, Tex. Gallery, Houston, 1979, 80, 81, Xavier Fourcade Gallery, N.Y.C., 1980, 82, 83, 85, 86, David Bellman, Toronto, 1980, 81, Margo Leavin, Calif., 1982, Arts Club of Chgo., 1987, André Emmerich Gallery, N.Y.C., 1988, 89, 91, 92, 94, 95, 10 yr. retrospective Rose Art Mus., 1989, P. Fong & Spratt Galleries, San Jose, Calif., 1991, Sony Music Hdqs., N.Y.C., 1993, Frederick Spratt Gallery, San Jose, 1994; group shows include Whitney Mus. Am. Art, 1970, 73, 77, 79, 82, Mus. Modern Art; N.Y.C., 71, 73, 84, 86, 93, 94 ;Buenos Aires, 1971, Kolner Kunst Market, Cologne, Germany, 1971, Stedelijk Mus., Holland, 1971, Spoleto (Italy) Festival, 1972, Palazzo Taverna, Rome, 1973, Nat. Gallery Victoria, Melbourne, Australia, 1973, Art Gallery NSW, Sydney, 1973, Auckland (New Zealand) City Art Gallery, 1973, Inst. Contemporary Art, London, 1974, Mus. d'Arte de la Ville, Paris, 1975, Galerie Aronowitsch, Stockholm, 1975, Stadtiches Mus., Manchengladbach, Germany, 1975, Galleria D'Arte Moderna, Bologna, Italy, 1975, Art Gallery Ont., Toronto, Can., 1975, Mus. Fine Art, Houston, 1975, Contemporary Arts Ctr., Cin., 1973, 75, 81, Mus. Contemporary Art, Chgo., 1971, 77, 86, Corcoran Gallery of Art, Washington, 1975, 87, Städtisches Mus., Leverkusen, Germany, 1975, Cannaviella Studio d'Arte Rome, 1976, Phila. Coll. Art, 1976, 83, Balt. Mus. Art, 1976, New Mus., N.Y.C., 1977, 80, 84, 83, Renaissance Soc. of U. Chgo., 1976, Lowe Art Mus., U. Miami, Fla., 1976, Inst. Contemporary Art, Boston, 1976, Seibu Mus. Art, Tokyo, 1976, N.Y. State Mus., Albany, 1977, Drawing Ctr., 1977, Kansas City (Mo.) Art Inst., 1977, Smithsonian Inst., Washington, 1977, Kassel, Fed. Republic Germany, 1972, 77, Ackland Art Ctr., Chapel Hill, N.C., 1979, 84, Milw. Art Ctr., 1978, 81, Biblioteca Nacional, Madrid, 1980, Gulbenkian Mus., Lisbon, Portugal, 1980, Bklyn. Mus., 1981, 89, Guggenheim Mus., 1982, 88, 89, Albright Knox Art Gallery, Buffalo, 1979, 80, 88, 89, Kuustforeningen Mus., Copenhagen, 1980, Venice Biennale, 1980, Cranbrook (Mich.) Acad. Art, 1981, Mus. Fine Arts, Boston, 1983, Contemporary Arts Mus., Houston, 1983, Norman Mackenzie Art Gallery, U. Regina, Sask., Can., 1983, Galleriet, Sweden, 1983-84, Seattle Art Mus., 1979-84, Nat. Mus. Art., Osaka, Japan, 1984, Fogg Art Mus., Cambridge, Mass., 1984, Am. Acad. and Inst. Arts and Letters, N.Y.C., 1984, 87, L.A. County Mus. Art, 1984, 86, Wadsworth Atheneum, Hartford, Conn., 1981, 84, Evehart Mus., Pa., 1984, Grey Art Gallery, NYU, 1977, 84, 87, Avery Ctr. Arts, Bard Coll., N.Y., 1985, 87-88, Stamford (Conn.) Mus., 1985, Aldrich Mus., Conn., 1979, 82, Bronx Mus. Arts, N.Y.C., 1985, High Mus., Atlanta, 1975, 81, Phila. Mus. Art, 1986, Nat. Gallery Art, Washington, 1984, Mus. Art, Ft. Lauderdale, Fla., 1986, Nat. Mus. Women in Art, Washington, 1987, Xavier Fourcade Gallery, 1983, 87, L.A. County Mus. Modern Art, 1986-87, The Hague, The Netherlands, 1986, Carnegie-Mellon Art Gallery, Pitts., 1979, 87, Balt. Mus. Art, 1975, 76, 88, Ctr. for Fine Arts, Miami, 1989, Milw. Art Mus., 1989, Cin. Art Mus., 1989, New Orleans Mus., 1989, Denver Art Mus., 1989, Parrish Art Mus., South Hampton, N.Y., 1990, 91, Margo Leavin Gallery, L.A., 1991, Mus. of Modern Art, N.Y.C,, 1991, Guild Hall Mus., East Hampton, N.Y., 1991, Am. Acad., Rome, 1991, Mus. Contemporary Art, L.A., 1991, Hunter Coll., N.Y., 1991, Centro Cultural/Arte Contemporanea, Mexico City, 1991, Hilton, San Jose, Calif., 1992, Hillwood Art Mus., L.I., N.Y., 1992, Am. Acad. and Inst. Arts and Letters, 1992, Neuberger Mus., 1992, Statue of Liberty Group, 1993, Foster Harmans Galliers of Am. Art, Sarasota, Fla., 1993, Kohn-Abrams Gallerie, L.A., 1993, The Gallery at Bristol Myers Squibb, N.J., 1993, Friends of Art and Preservation in Embassies, N.Y.C., 1993, Just Art, N.Y.C., 1993, Mus. Modern Art, N.Y.C., 1994, TZ Art and Co., N.Y.C., Andre Emmerich Gallery, N.Y.C., 1993, Nat. Gallery of Art, Washington, 1994, Fred Spratt Gallery, San José, Calif., 1994, RAAB Galarie, Berlin, 1994, Gallary at Bristol Myer Squibb, N.J., 1994, Moma, N.Y.C., 1994, N.Y. Studio Sch., N.Y.C., 1995, Aldrich Mus., Conn., 1995; represented in permanent collections Milw. Art Ctr., Mus. Modern Art N.Y.C., Fogg Mus., Cambridge, Mass., Phila. Mus. Art, High Mus. Art, Atlanta, Houston Mus. Fine Arts, Corcoran Gallery, Washington, Mpls. Art Inst., Mpls. Art Mus., Met. Mus. Art, N.Y.C., Guggenheim Mus., N.Y.C., Ludwig Mus., Aachen, Fed. Republic Germany, Holladay, Washington, Saatchi, London, Bard, Albright-Knox Art Gallery, Buffalo, Whitney Mus. Am. Art, N.Y.C., U. Mich., Ann Arbor, Ohio State U., Columbus, Gilman Paper Co., N.Y., Auckland (New Zealand) City Art Mus., Portland (Oreg.) Art Mus., Aaken Art Mus., Oberlin, Ohio, Highhold Internat., S. Africa, U. Ohio Art Gallery, Columbus, HHK Charitable Found., Milw., Art Gallery Ont., Toronto, Can., Nat. Mus. Women in Art, Washington, Chase Manhattan Bank, N.Y.C., Hilton Hotel, San Jose, Calif., Sony Music Hdqs. Mem. artists adv. bd. New Mus. of Contemporary Art, N.Y.C.; trustee Ind. Curators, N.Y.C. Recipient Witowsky prize 72d Am. Exhbn., Art Inst., Chgo., 1976, Creative Arts award Brandeis U., 1985, Bard Coll., 1986; Guggenheim fellow, 1972; Nat. Endowment Arts grantee, 1974, Am. Acad., Rome, 1991.

ROCKE, DAVID MORTON, statistician, educator; b. Chgo., June 4, 1946; s. Sol J. and Verva (Coleman) R.; m. Carrie Clausen, Dec. 30, 1971; children: Emily Carolyn, Miriam Ruth. AB, Shimer Coll., 1966; PhD, U. Ill., Chgo., 1972, postdoctoral, 1977-79. Vis. lectr. math. dept. U. Ill., Chgo., 1972-74; prof. Govs. State U., Park Forest South, Ill., 1974-80; assoc. prof. grad. sch. mgmt. U. Calif., Davis, 1980-86, prof., 1986—, dir., Ctr. for Stats. in Sci. and

Tech., 1995—; cons. Calif. State Water Bd., Sacramento, 1987—, Calif. Air Resources Bd., Sacramento, 1988—, U.S. Bur. Reclamation, Sacramento, 1986, Sherwin-Williams Rsch. Ctr., Chgo., 1980. Contbr. articles to profl. jours. Recipient Youden prize for articles Technometrics, 1983. Fellow Am. Statis. Assn. (Interlab. Testing award 1985); mem. AAAS, Inst. Math. Stats., Royal Statis. Soc., Am. Soc. for Quality Control (Shewell award 1987), Biometric Soc., Bernoulli Soc., Am. Math. Soc., Soc. for Indsl. and Applied Math., Math. Assn. Am. Office: U Calif Sch Mgmt Davis CA 95616

ROCKEFELLER, DAVID, banker; b. N.Y.C., June 12, 1915; s. John Davison Jr. and Abby Greene (Aldrich) R.; m. Margaret McGrath, Sept. 7, 1940; children: David, Abby A., Neva, Margaret D., Richard G., Eileen M. BS, Harvard Coll., 1936; student, London Sch. Econs.; LLD (hon.), Harvard U., 1969; PhD, U. Chgo., 1940; LLD (hon.), Columbia U., 1954, Bowdoin Coll., 1958, Jewish Theol. Sem., 1958, Williams Coll., 1966, Wagner Coll., 1967, Rockefeller U., 1980, Pace Coll., 1970, St. John's U., 1971, Middlebury, 1974, U. Liberia, 1979, Am. U., 1987, U. Miami, 1988; DEng (hon.), Colo. Sch. Mines, 1974, U. Notre Dame, 1987. Sec. to Mayor Fiorello H. La Guardia, 1940-41; asst. regional dir. Office Def., Health and Welfare Services, 1941-42; asst. mgr. for. dept. Chase Nat. Bank, N.Y.C., 1946-47, asst. cashier, 1947-48, 2d v.p., 1948-49; v.p. Chase Nat. Bank, 1949-51, sr. v.p., 1951-55; exec. v.p. Chase Manhattan Bank (Chase Nat. Bank merged with Bank of Manhattan), 1955-57; vice chmn. bd. Chase Manhattan Bank, 1957-61, pres., chmn. exec. com., 1961-69, chmn., 1969-81, CEO, 1969-80; chmn. bd. dirs. Chase Internat. Investment Corp., 1961-81, Chase Internat. Adv. Com., 1980—, Rockefeller Group, Inc., 1981-94, Rockefeller Ctr. Properties, Inc., 1986-92, N.Y. Clearing House, 1971-78, Ctr. for Intern-Am. Rels., 1966-70, Overseas Devel. Coun., U.S.-USSR Trade and Econ. Coun. Inc.; chmn. Internat. Exec. Svc. Corps., 1964-68. Author: Unused Resources and Economic Waste, 1940, Creative Management in Banking, 1964. Active Urban Devel. Corp., N.Y. State Bus. Adv. Coun., 1968-72, U.S. Adv. Com. on Reform on Internat. Monetary System, 1973-77, U.S. exec. com. Dartmouth Conf. Bd. Inst. Internat. Econs., Am. Friends of LSE, U.S. Hon. Fellows LSE, Bus. Com. for Arts; founding mem. Commn. on White House Fellows, hon. mem., 1964-65; exec. com., chmn. Downtown Lower Manhattan Assn., 1958-75; trustee Rockefeller U., 1940-95, Carnegie Endowment Internat. Peace, Hist. Hudson Valley, 1981—; chmn. Rockefeller Bros. Fund, 1981-87, vice-chmn., 1968-80; hon. trustee Rockefeller Family Fund; life trustee U. Chgo.; trustee, chmn. bd., exec. com. Mus. Modern Art, 1962-72, 87-93; bd. overseers Harvard Coll., 1954-60, 62-68; co-founder Trilateral Commn., 1973-91, N.Am. chmn. 1981-92, hon. chmn., 1992; hon. chmn. Internat. House, 1940—, dir., 1940-63; pres. Morningside Heights, Inc., 1947-57, chmn., 1957-65; chmn. Am. Soc., 1981-92, hon. chmn., 1992—, N.Y.C. Partnership, 1979-88. Capt. AUS, 1942-46, NATOUSA, ETO. Decorated Legion of Honor France; Order of Merit, Italy, Order of Southern Cross, Brazil, Order of the White Elephant and Order of Crown, Thailand, Order of the Cedar, Lebanon, Order of the Sun, Peru, Order of the Humane African Redemption, Liberia, Order of the Crown, Belgium, Nat. Order of Ivory Coast, Grand Cordon Order of Sacred Treasure, Japan, Order Bernardo O'Higgins, Chile; recipient Merit award N.Y. chpt. AIA, 1965, Gold medal Nat. Inst. Social Scis., 1967, AIA medal of Honor for City Planning N.Y.C., 1968, Charles Evans Hughes award NCCJ, 1974, World Brotherhood award Jewish Theol. Sem, 1953, C. Walter Nichols award NYU, 1970, Regional Planning Assn. award, 1971; Hadrian award, World Monuments Fund, 1994. Mem. Internat. Exec. Service Corps (dir., chmn. 1964-68), Center Inter-Am. Relations (dir., hon. chmn.), Council Fgn. Relations (dir. 1949-51 , v.p. 1951-70, chmn. 1970-85), Century Club, Harvard, River Club, Univ. Club. Links Club, Knickerbocker Club, N.Y. Yacht Club. Avocation: sailing. Address: 30 Rockefeller Plz New York NY 10112

ROCKEFELLER, EDWIN SHAFFER, lawyer; b. Harrisburg, Pa., Sept. 10, 1927; s. Edwin S. and Nancy Rhea (McCullough) R.; m. Marilie Gould Wallace, Dec. 22, 1952; children: Ben Wallace, Edwin Palmer. AB, Yale U., 1948, LLB, 1951, M in Internat. Pub. Policy, Johns Hopkins U., 1989. Bar: Conn. 1951, D.C. 1956, U.S. Supreme Ct. 1957. Atty., FTC, 1956-61, asst. to gen. counsel, 1958-59, exec. asst. to chmn., 1960-61; pvt. practice, Washington, 1961—; ptnr. Schiff Hardin & Waite, Washington, 1981-93, of counsel, 1994—; mem. USIA Inspection Team, Pakistan, 1971; adj. prof. Georgetown U. Law Ctr., Washington, 1985-87. 1st lt. JAGC, U.S. Army, 1953-56. Mem. ABA (chmn. sect. antitrust law 1976-77, ho. of dels. 1979-82), Chevy Chase Club, Met. Club (Washington), Yale Club (N.Y.C.). Author: Antitrust Questions & Answers, 1974; Desk Book of FTC Practice & Procedure, 3d edit., 1979; Antitrust Counseling for the 1980s, 1983. Office: Schiff Hardin & Waite 1101 Connecticut Ave NW Ste 600 Washington DC 20036-4303

ROCKEFELLER, JOHN DAVISON, IV (JAY ROCKEFELLER), senator, former governor; b. N.Y.C., NY, June 18, 1937; s. John Davison III and Blanchette Ferry (Hooker) R.; m. Sharon Percy, Apr. 1, 1967; children: John, Valerie, Charles, Justin. B.A., Harvard U., 1961; student, Japanese lang. Internat. Christian U., Tokyo, 1957-60; postgrad. in Chinese, Yale U. Inst. Far Eastern Langs., 1961-62. Apptd. mem. nat. adv. council Peace Corps, 1961, spl. asst. to dir. corps, 1962, ops. officer in charge work in Philippines, until 1963; desk officer for Indonesian affairs Bur. Far Eastern Affairs, U.S. State Dept., 1963; later asst. to asst. sec. state for Far Eastern affairs; cons. Pres.'s Commn. on Juvenile Delinquency and Youth Crime, 1964; field worker Action for Appalachian Youth program, from 1964; mem. W.Va. Ho. of Dels., 1966-68; sec. of state W.Va., 1968-72; pres. W.Va. Wesleyan Coll., Buckhannon, 1973-75; gov. State of W.Va., 1976-84; U.S. senator from W.Va., 1985—, mem. vets. affairs com., fin. com., commerce, sci. and transp. com., chmn. Sen. steel caucus, Bipartisan Com. on Comprehensive Health Care; chmn. Nat. Commn. on Children, natural resources and environ. com. Nat. Govs. Assn., 1981-84. Contbr. articles to mags. including N.Y. Times Sunday mag. Trustee U. Chgo., 1967—; chmn. White House Conf. Balanced Nat. Growth and Econ. Devel., 1978, Pres.'s Commn. on Coal, 1978-80, White House Adv. Com. on Coal., 1980; active Commerce, Sci., and Transp. Com., Fin. Com.; chmn. Vet. Affairs Com. Office: US Senate 109 Hart Senate Bldg Washington DC 20510

ROCKEFELLER, LAURANCE S., business executive, conservationist; b. N.Y.C., May 26, 1910; s. John Davison, Jr. and Abby Greene (Aldrich) R.; m. Mary French, Aug. 15, 1934; children—Laura Rockefeller Chasin, Marion French Rockefeller Weber, Lucy Rockefeller Waletzky, Laurance. BA, Princeton U., 1932; LLD (hon.), SUNY Sch. Forestry at Syracuse U., 1961, U. Vt., 1968; D.Pub. Svc. (hon.), George Washington U., 1964; LHD (hon.), Tex. Tech. Coll., 1966, Duke U., 1981, Marymount Coll., 1983; HHD (hon.), Princeton U., 1987. Chmn. Rockefeller Center, Inc., 1953-56, 58-66, dir., 1936-78; founding trustee, pres., chmn. Rockefeller Bros. Fund, 1958-80, vice chmn., 1980-82, adv. trustee, 1982-85; dir. Ea. Airlines, 1938-60, 77-81, adv. dir., 1981-87; chmn. Woodstock Resort Corp.; bd. dirs. Readers Digest Assn., 1973-93. Mem. Nat. Cancer Adv. Bd., 1972-79; hon. chmn. N.Y. Zoological Soc.,1975; Meml. Sloan-Kettering Cancer Ctr., 1947-60, chmn. 1960-82, hon. chmn. 1982—; chmn. Citizens Adv. Com. on Environ. Quality, 1969-73, Jackson Hole Preserve, Inc., 1940—; pres. Palisades Interstate Pk. Commn., 1970-77, commr. emeritus, 1978—; chmn. Outdoor Recreation Resources Rev. Commn., 1958-65, White House Conf. on Natural Beauty, 1965; life mem. corp. MIT; trustee emeritus Princeton U.; hon. trustee Nat. Geog. Soc.; trustee Alfred P. Sloan Found., 1950-82, Greenacre Found., Nat. Pk. Found., 1968-76, Sleepy Hollow Restorations, 1975-87, Hist. Hudson Valley, 1987—; chmn. Woodstock Found., 1968—; hon. dir. Nat. Wildflower Ctr., 1988—. Decorated commandeur de Ordre Royal du Lion, Belgium, 1950; comdr. most excellent Order Brit. Empire, 1971; recipient Conservation Service award U.S. Dept. Interior, 1956, 62, Horace Marden Albright Scenic Preservation medal, 1957, Disting. Service medal Theodore Roosevelt Assn., 1963, Audubon medal, 1964, Nat. Inst. Social Scis. award, 1959, 67, Alfred P. Sloan, Jr. Meml. award Am. Cancer Soc., 1969, Medal of Freedom, 1969, Cert. of Award, Am. Assn. for Cancer Research, 1980, James Ewing Layman's award Soc. Surg. Oncology, 1980, Congl. gold medal, 1990, McAneny Hist. Pres. medal, 1993, Chmn.'s award Nat. Geograph. Soc., 1995, Theodore Roosevelt Nat. Park medal of honor, 1995. Mem. Am. Conservation Assn. (pres. 1958-80, chmn. 1980-85, hon. chmn. 1985—), N.Y. Zool. Soc. (hon. chmn. 1975). Clubs: River, Princeton, University, Brook, Capitol Hill, Links, Boone and Crockett, Knickerbocker, Lotos (N.Y.C.), Sleepy Hollow (Tarrytown). Office: Rm 5600 30 Rockefeller Plz New York NY 10112

ROCKEFELLER, MARGARETTA FITLER MURPHY (HAPPY ROCKEFELLER), widow of former vice president of U.S.; m. Nelson Aldrich Rockefeller (dec.); children: James B. Murphy, Margaretta H. Bickford, Carol Murphy Lyden, Malinda Murphy Menotti, Nelson A. Rockefeller, Jr., Mark F. Rockefeller. Dir. Archer-Daniels-Midland Co.., Decatur, Ill.; alt. rep. of U.S. to 46th Session of UN Gen. Assembly, 1991, 47th Session, 1992. *

ROCKEFELLER, SHARON PERCY, broadcast executive; b. Oakland, Calif., Dec. 10, 1944; d. Charles H. and Jeanne Dickerson Percy; m. John D. Rockefeller IV; children: John, Valerie, Charles, Justin. BA cum laude, Stanford U.; LLD (hon.), U. Charleston, 1977, Beloit Coll., 1978; LHD (hon.), West Liberty State Coll., 1980, Hamilton Coll., 1982, Wheeling Coll., 1984. Founder, chmn. Mountain Artisans, 1968-78; chmn. Corp. Pub. Broadcasting, Washington, 1981-84; bd. dirs. Stas. WETA-TV-FM, Washington, 1987-89, pres., 1989—; bd. dirs. State. WETA-TV-FM, Washington, 1987-89, pres., 1989—; bd. dirs. Pub. Broadcasting Svc., W.Va. Edn. Broadcasting Authority. Mem.-at-large Dem. Nat. Conv., del., 1976, 80, 84; bd. dirs. Rockefeller Bros. Fund. Office: Sta WETA-FM 3700 S Four Mile Run Dr Arlington VA 22206-2304

ROCKELMAN, GEORGIA F(OWLER) BENZ, retail furniture executive; b. Jefferson City, Mo., June 7, 1920; d. Charles Herman and Marinda Julia (Fowler) Benz; m. Elvin John Henry Rockelman, Nov. 9, 1940; 1 child, Barbara Jean. BBA, Lincoln U., 1964, MBA, 1977. Sec./acct. Harry Benz Enterprises, Jefferson City, 1932-52; ptnr. Benz Furniture Co., Jefferson City, 1952-59, Benz-Rockelman Furniture Co., Jefferson City, 1961-82; v.p., sec. Benz-Rockelman Ltd., Jefferson City, 1982-93, pres., sec., 1993-94. Pres. Trinity-Luth. PTA, Jefferson City, 1952-54; pres. Jefferson City Council Nat. Congress PTA, 1954-56; mem. City Water Flouridation com., 1956; candidate Jefferson City Council, 1983; bd. dirs. Southside Bus. League, Jefferson City, 1981-82, v.p., 1983-84; Rep. com. women Cole County, 1984, 86. Mem. AAUW (sec. 1990-94), DAR, Am. Legion, Cole County Hist. Soc., Hist. City of Jefferson City, Cole County Rep. Women's Club. Lutheran. Home: 216 W Ashley St Jefferson City MO 65101-1606 Office: 121 and 129 W Dunklin St Jefferson City MO 65101

ROCKENSIES, JOHN WILLIAM, mechanical engineer; b. N.Y.C., May 30, 1932; s. John William and Wilma (Mercz) R.; m. Marion Pauline Peachman, Sept. 16, 1956; children: Kenneth John, Karen Martha Rockensies Steinbeck. B of Mech. Engring., CCNY, 1954, M of Mech. Engring., 1960; postgrad., Bklyn. Polytechnic Inst., 1955, Columbia U., 1956. Registered prof. engr., N.Y. Jet engine performance and compressor devel. Curtiss Wright Corp., Woodridge, N.J., 1954-56; product devel. engr. Sperry Gyroscope Corp., Lake Success, N.Y., 1956-60; sr. exptl. test engr. Pratt & Whitney Corp., East Hartford, Conn., 1960-62; project engr. Stratos Corp., Bayshore, N.Y., 1962; prin. propulsion engr. Republic Aviation Corp., Farmingdale, N.Y., 1963-64; power plant design engr., group and project leader, project engr., engr. specialist and mgr. Grumman Aerospace Corp., Bethpage, N.Y., 1964-95; retired, 1995; contract staff engr. Northrup-Grumman Corp., Bethpage, N.Y., 1996; mem. SAE E-32 Engine Condition Monitoring com., 1983; instr. navigation Smithtown Bay Power Squadron. Author tech. papers in field. Deacon, trustee, elder First Presbyn Ch. of Smithtown. Recipient Apollo Achievement award NASA, Washington, 1970. Assoc. fellow AIAA; mem. NSPE, ASME, U.S. Power Squadrons (sr.). Avocations: sailing/boating, jogging, tennis, camping, model aircraft, travel. Home: 65 Parnell Dr Smithtown NY 11787-2428 Office: Grumman Aircraft Systems MS B69-001 Bethpage NY 11713-5820

ROCKENSIES, KENNETH JULES, physicist, educator; b. N.Y.C., June 10, 1938; s. John William and Wilma (Mercz) R.; m. Eileen Regina Dros, June 6, 1970; children: Kevin John, Patricia Ann, Regina Marie. BS in Physics, Polytech. U. Bklyn., 1960, MS in Physics, 1962; postgrad., NYU, 1965-67, Adelphi U., 1969-75, Nova U., 1992—. Physicist We. Union Telegraph, N.Y.C., 1962-63; prof. CUNY, Bklyn., 1963-93, Coll. Misericordia, Dallas, Pa., 1993—. Mem. NSTA, Am. Assn. Physics Tchrs., Soc. Coll. Sci. Tchrs., Optical Soc. Am. Achievements include rsch. in interferometry, relativistic optics, electrostatic data storage, electrosensitive recording papers and statis. studies in edn. Office: Coll Misericordia 301 Lake St Dallas PA 18612-1008

ROCKENSTEIN, WALTER HARRISON, II, lawyer; s. Walter Harrison and Martha Lee (Morris) R.; m. Jodell Lynn Steinke, July 29, 1972; children: Martha Liv, Andrew Harrison. BA cum laude, Coll. of Wooster, 1965; LLB, Yale U., 1968. Bar: Minn. 1968, U.S. Dist. Ct. Minn. 1968, U.S. Ct. Appeals (8th crct.) 1977. Spl. asst. atty. gen., chief antitrust divsn. Office of Minn. Atty. Gen., 1970-72; assoc. Head & Truhn, 1972-73; alderman 11th ward Mpls. City Coun., 1974-83; assoc. Faegre & Benson, Mpls., 1984-85, ptnr., 1986—; mem. Capital Long-Range Improvements Com., 1974-82, Gov.'s Econ. Roundtable, 1980-82, Hennepin County Waste Disposal & Energy Recovery Adv. Com., 1976-77; chmn. devel. strategies com. League of Minn. Cities, 1979-80, bd. dirs., 1980-83; Mpls. del. Metro. Aircraft Sound Abatement Coun., 1977-90, chmn., 1982-90; mem. aviation subcom. of transp. tech. adv. com. Metro. Coun., 1977-83; mem. airport noise adv. bd. Minn. Pollution Control Agy., bd. dirs. noise com., 1982-85, mem. tech. adv. com., 1990; adv. com. Nat. League of Cities, steering com. Environmental Quality, 1975-79, vice chmn., 1976, chmn., 1978, steering com. Energy, Environment and Natural Resources, 1980-83, Energy Task Force, 1977-79, Nat. Urban Policy Com., 1978; mem. Noise Task Force, Nat. League of Cities/Nat. Assn. of Counties, 1977-80; regional dir. Nat. Org. to Insure a Sound-Controlled Environment, 1976-90, v.p. legal affairs, 1983-90; cons. group nuclear waste mgt., U.S. Dept. Energy, 1978. Elder Westminster Presbyn. Ch., 1975-80, 95—, trustee, 1982-87, chair stewardship com., 1989, chair pastor nominating com., 1992-94; bd. dirs. Loring Nicollet-Bethlehem Cmty. Ctrs., Inc., 1984—, pres., 1988-92; bd. dirs. U. Minn. Underground Space Ctr. Adv. Bd., 1985-95, chair, 1988-95; bd. dirs. Minn. Ctr. for Book Arts, 1988-93; com. mem. Cub Scout pact 196, Diamond Lake Luth Ch., 1988-91, com. chair, 1990-91; alumni trustee, alumni bd. dirs. The Coll. of Wooster, 1990—; com. mem. Boy Scout Troop 187. Recipient Cert. of Appreciation, Upper Midwest chpt. Acoustical Soc. Am., 1977, Resolution of Appreciation, City of Mpls., 1983, Citation of Honor, Hennepin County, 1983, Cert. of Recognition, League of Minn. Cities, 1983, Hope of Rotary award City of Lakes Rotary Club, 1989, WCCO Good Neighbor award, 1992. Mem. Minn. State Bar Assn., Hennepin County Bar Assn., Delta Sigma Rho-Tau Kappa Alpha, Phi Sigma Alpha. Republican. Presbyterian. Avocations: reading, backpacking, cross-country skiing, woodworking. Office: Faegre & Benson 2200 Norwest Ctr 90 S 7th St Minneapolis MN 55402-3901

ROCKETT-BOLDUC, AGNES MARY, nurse; b. Medford, Mass., Jan. 19, 1930; d. John Francis and Agnes Mary (Connor) R.; m. Richard Joseph Bolduc, Mar. 23, 1928. Diploma, Lawrence Meml. Hosp., 1951; BSN, Boston Coll., 1958; MEd, Tufts U., 1962. RN; cert. nurse oper. rm. Staff nurse Mass. Gen. Hosp., Boston, 1951-56; instr. nursing Lawrence Meml. Hosp., Medford, Mass., 1958-61; asst. dir. Boston Lying-In Hosp., 1962-67; asst. dean admissions Tufts Med. Sch., Boston, 1967-71; chmn. dept. oper. rm. nursing svcs. Mass. Gen. Hosp., 1971-86; nurse mgr. oper. rm. Portsmouth (N.H.) Regional Hosp., 1987-92; pres. Rover Sky Corp., Hampton, N.H., 1992—; part-time staff nurse Phillips Exeter (N.H.) Acad., 1992—. Author: The Roving Reporter, 1969; mem. editorial bd. Today's Oper. Rm. Nurse, 1978-86. Trustee St. Elizabeth's Hosp., Boston, 1969-72, St. Margaret's Hosp., Boston, 1972-74; bd. dirs. Lifewise, N.H., 1992—; vol. Spl. Olympics, N.H., 1991-92, Hampton C. of C., 1993; chmn. Seacoast Heart Assn., 1989-90; mem. State N.H. Health Ins. Adv. Com., 1981-88. Mem. Am. Assn. Oper. Rm. Nurses, Sigma Theta Tau. Roman Catholic. Avocations: quilting, cycling, cross-country skiing, gardening, theatre. Home and Office: 15 Penniman Ln Hampton NH 03842-2714

ROCKEY, JAY, public relations company executive. Chmn. Rockey Co., Inc., Seattle. Office: Rockey Co Inc 2121 5th Ave Seattle WA 98121-2510*

ROCKEY, PAUL HENRY, physician, medical educator, university official; b. Idaho Falls, Idaho, Apr. 3, 1944; m. Linda Marie Miller, Dec. 27, 1964; 3 children. MD with honors, U. Chgo., 1970; BS in Biochemistry with high honors, Mich. State U., 1966; MPH, U. Wash., 1978. Diplomate Am. Bd. Internal Medicine, Nat. Bd. Med. Examiners, Am. Bd. Med. Mgmt. Rotating intern Harborview Med. Ctr., Seattle, 1970-71; dir. Indian Health Ctr., Rocky Boy Reservation, Box Elder, Mont., 1971-73; resident, chief resident in medicine, 1973-76; Robert Wood Johnson clin. scholar, acting instr. U. Wash. Sch. Medicine, Seattle, 1976-78, instr., asst. prof., assoc. prof., 1978-88, asst. dean, 1983-87; adj. asst. prof., adj. assoc. prof. dept. health svcs. U. Wash. Sch. Pub. Health and Cmty. Medicine, 1980-88; chief resident USPHS Hosp. (name now Pacific Med. Ctr.), Seattle, 1975-76, asst. chief medicine, residency coord., 1978-80, med. dir., 1980-86; assoc. prof., assoc. dean U. Mass. Med. Sch., Worcester, 1988-90; prof. depts. medicine and med. humanities So. Ill. U. Sch. Medicine, Springfield, 1991—, assoc. dean for clin. affairs, 1991—, acting chmn. dept. family practice, 1991-93; mem. med. staff No. Mont. Hosp., Havre, 1971-73, v.p. med. staff, 1973; mem. med. staff Pacific Med. Ctr., Seattle, 1976-88, U. Wash. Hosp., Seattle, 1978-87, Providence Med. Ctr., Seattle, 1987-88, Madigan Army Med. Ctr., Ft. Lewis, Wash., 1986-88, Meml. Med. Ctr., Springfield, 1991—, St. John's Hosp., Springfield, 1991—; sr. v.p. for med. affairs St. Vincent Healthcare Sys., Inc. and St. Vincent Hosp., Worcester, 1988-90; coord. rev. Joint Commn. on Accreditation Hosps., 1980-83, 88-90; mem. exec. com. of med. staff St. Vincent Hosp., 1988-90; pres. Pacific Health Assocs. of Seattle, 1981-87; dir., vice chmn., bd. dirs. Pacific Health Plans, HMO, 1985-87; mem. Group Health Plan Credentialing Com. for Ctrl. Ill., 1994—; cons. in quality assurance and utilization mgmt. Westminster Hosp., London, 1988; mem. mgmt. adv. team to U. del Norte and Hosp. Infantal San Francisco de Paula, Barranquilla, Colombia, 1989-90; presenter in field. Contbr. articles and abstracts to med. jours., chpts. to books. Pres., bd. dirs. N.W. GIRLCHOIR, 1982-85, mem., 1985-88; mem. steering com. Seattle Area Program for Affordable Health Care, 1983; mem. Alpental Doctor Patrol, 1975-86, Ski Acres Doctor Patrol, Snoqualmie Pass, Wash., 1982-86; trustee Ill. Cancer Coun., 1991-92; bd. dirs. Ancilla Sys., Hobart, Ind., 1993—, mem. compensation com., 1995—; vol. physician Health First Clinic, 1994—; mem. Golden Rule Aard Panel Springfield, 1994; participant med. edn. subcom. Ill. Gov.'s Medicaid Adv. Com., 1994-95; chmn. bd. dirs. Ancilla Med. Found., 1995—; regional interviewer student selection com. U. Chgo. Pritzker Sch. Medicine, 1978-88. With USPHS, 1971-81; maj. Wash. Army N.G., 1986-88; lt. col. Mass. Army N.G., 1988-96; lt. col. Ill. Army N.G., 1996—. Alumni disting. scholar Mich. State U., 1962-66, scholar U. Chgo., 1966-70. Fellow ACP, Am. Coll. Physician Execs.; mem. AMA, Soc. Gen. Internal Medicine, Ill. Med. Soc., Sangamon County Med. Soc., Alpha Omega Alpha, Phi Kappa Phi. Home: 1433 Williams Blvd Springfield IL 62704-2344 Office: So Ill U Sch Medicine PO Box 19230 Springfield IL 62794-9230

ROCKHILL, JACK KERRIGAN, collections company executive; b. Alliance, Ohio, Sept. 10, 1930; s. Carl Columbus and Lovell Fanny (Brown) R.; m. Karen Sue Rocki, Aug. 30, 1969; children: Michele, Martin. Student, Canton Actual Bus. Coll., Ohio, 1955, Internat. Corr. Schs., 1960, Kent State U., Canton, Ohio, 1962-65. Lic. pvt. investigator, 1960. Player Washington Senators, 1948-49; collection unit mgr. Nationwide Audit & Investigations, Canton, Ohio, 1960-66; pres. Fidelity Collections & Investigations, Alliance, 1966—; cons. Fidelity Properties, Inc., Alliance, 1980—, pres., 1984—. With USMC, 1950-58. Republican. Methodist. Avocations: golfing, yachting, scuba diving. Home: 1487 Glenking Ln Alliance OH 44601-3666 Office: Fidelity Collections PO Box 2055 Alliance OH 44601-0055

ROCKLAGE, SISTER MARY ROCH, health system executive; b. St. Louis, Mar. 5, 1935; d. Henry B. and Catherine (Lohman) R. RN, St. John's Sch. Nursing, St. Louis, 1959; BS in Nursing, St. Xavier Coll., Chgo., 1961; MHA, St. Louis U., 1963; LLD (hon.), Maryville Coll., 1983. Supr. Mercy Villa, Springfield, Mo.; tng. coord. St. John's Hosp., St. Louis; dir. cen. dispatch St. John's Mercy Hosp., St. Louis, 1962-65, supr. intensive care unit, 1965-67; dir. nursing svc. St. John's Mercy Hosp., 1967-69; adminstr., pres. ST. John's Mercy Med. Ctr., St. Louis, 1969-79; provincial adminstr. Sisters of Mercy, St. Louis, 1979-85; chief exec. officer, pres. Sisters of Mercy Health System, St. Louis, 1985—; vice chairperson bd. dirs. Holy Cross Health System, South Bend, Ind.; asst. prof. health care adminstn. Washington U., St. Louis, 1970-79; preceptor Washington U., St. Louis, 1970-79, St. Louis U., 1970-79, U. Mo., Columbia, 1976-79; bd. dirs. Health Care for the Homeless, St. Louis, 1984—; mem. health commn., govt. comm. Sisters of Mercy, Province St. Louis, local coord. St. Joseph's Convent of Mercy, St. Louis, 1969-76, 77-79, province personnel bd. 1973-75, health adv. bd., 1973—. Bd. trustees Maryville Coll, St. Louis, 1972-75, Mercy Hosp., Mercy Hosp., New Orleans, 1974-75; governing bd. St. John's Med. Ctr., Joplin, Mo., 1973-77, Mo. Hosp. Assn., Jefferson City, 1974-78, St. Edward Mercy Med. Ctr., Ft. Smith, Ark., 1975-80, Mercy Health Ctr., Oklahoma City, 1975-80, McAuley Hall, St. Louis, 1977-83, Mercy Hosp., Laredo, Tex., 1978-80, St. Anthony's Hosp., Alton, Ill., 1985—; pres. Greater St. Louis Health System Agy., 1976-77, bd. dirs. 1978-79. Named Woman of Achievement, St. Louis Globe-Democrat, 1974, to Nat. Register Prominent Citizens, 1975; recipient A.C.H.E. Kenrick award. Mem. Am. Nurses' Assn., Am. Coll. Hosp. Adminstrs., Catholic Health Assn. (bd. trustees 1980—, chairperson 1984-85, sec. 1981-84, bylaws, fin. and mission svcs. coms.), Catholic Hosp. Assn. (coun. on hosp. orgn. and adminstrn.),. Home: Sisters of Mercy Health System-St Louis 2039 N Geyer Rd Saint Louis MO 63131-3332*

ROCKLEN, KATHY HELLENBRAND, lawyer, banker; b. N.Y.C., June 30, 1951. BA, Barnard Coll., 1973; JD magna cum laude, New England Sch. Law, 1977. Bar: N.Y. 1978, U.S. Dist. Ct. (so. and ea. dists.) N.Y. 1982, U.S. Dist. Ct. (no. dist.) Calif. 1985. Interpretive counsel N.Y. Stock Exchange, N.Y.C.; 1st v.p. E.F. Hutton & Co. Inc., N.Y.C.; v.p., gen. counsel and sec. S.G Warburg (U.S.A.) Inc., N.Y.C.; counsel Rogers & Wells, N.Y.C; pvt. practice N.Y.C. Office mgr. Com. to elect Charles D. Breitel Chief Judge, N.Y. Named one of Outstanding Young Women in Am. Mem. ABA, N.Y. State Bar Assn., N.Y. Women's Bar Assn., Assn. Bar of City of N.Y. (sec. 2d century com., sex and law com., young lawyers'com., corp. law com., chair spl. com. drugs and law, chair fed. legis. com., securities law com.). Avocation: running. Office: Law Office 515 Madison Ave New York NY 10022-5403

ROCKLER, WALTER JAMES, lawyer; b. Nov. 25, 1920; s. Nathan Rockler and Evelyn (Terfansky) Norian; m. Elsie Spira, June 14, 1942 (div. 1946); m. Aino Allekand, Aug. 16, 1949; children—Elliot, James, Nicolas, Julia. B.A., U. Chgo., 1940; J.D., Harvard U., 1943. Bar: Ill. 1947, N.Y. 1950, D.C. 1953. Pros. atty. Nuremberg (Germany) War Crimes Trials, 1947-49; assoc. Chapman, Bryson, et al., N.Y.C., 1949-51, Paul, Weiss, et al., N.Y.C. and Washington, 1951-53; ptnr. Lederer, Livingston, et al., Chgo., 1954-60, Pennish, Steele & Rockler, Chgo., 1961-63, Cotton, Watt, Rockler & Jones, Chgo., 1964-66, Arnold & Porter, Washington, 1966—; dir. Office of Spl. Investigations U.S. Dept. Justice, Washington, 1979-80. Contbr. articles to profl. jours. Served to 1st lt. USMC, 1943-46. Decorated Bronze Star. Mem. Chgo. Bar Assn. (chmn. tax com. 1958-59), ABA (mem. tax com. 1964—), Phi Beta Kappa. Democrat. Jewish. Avocations: tennis; bridge; piano. Home: 11129 Stephalee Ln Rockville MD 20852-3655 Office: Arnold & Porter 555 12th St NW Washington DC 20004-1202

ROCKOFF, MARK ALAN, pediatric anesthesiologist; b. Jersey City, Apr. 13, 1948; s. Aaron and Rose (Drescher) R.; m. Elizabeth Sceery, Aug. 6, 1978; children: Benjamin, Jillian, Michael. BS, MIT, 1969; MD, Johns Hopkins U., 1973. Diplomate Am. Bd. Pediatrics, Am. Bd. Critical Care Pediatrics, Am. Bd. Anesthesiology. Pediatric intern and resident Mass. Gen. Hosp., Boston, 1973-75, anesthesia resident, 1975-77, assoc. dir. pediatric ICU, 1979-81; neuroanesthesia fellow U. Calif., San Diego, 1978-79; assoc. dir. ICU Children's Hosp., Boston, 1981-89, assoc. anesthesiologist-in-chief, 1988—; med. dir. operating rm., 1992—; assoc. prof. anesthesia/pediatrics Harvard Med. Sch., Boston, 1987—. Editor jours. Survey of Anesthesiology, 1984-94, Jour. Neurosurg. Anesthesiology, 1994—. Fellow Am. Soc. Anesthesiologists, Am. Acad. Pediats., Soc. Critical Care Medicine; mem. Soc. Pediat. Anesthesia (pres. 1996—). Office: Children's Hosp 300 Longwood Ave Boston MA 02115

ROCKOFF, S. DAVID, radiologist, physician, educator; b. Utica, N.Y., July 21, 1931; s. Samuel and Sarah (Rattinger) R.; m. Jacqueline Garsh; children—Lisa E., Todd E., Kevin D. A.B., Syracuse U., 1951; M.D., Albany Med. Coll., 1955; M.Sc. in Medicine, U. Pa., 1961. Diplomate: Am. Bd. Radiology. Intern U.S. Naval Hosp., Bethesda, Md., 1955-56; resident and fellow in radiology, USPHS trainee dept. radiology p. of U. Pa., Phila., 1958-61; staff radiologist NIH, Bethesda, Md., 1961-65; asst. prof. radiology Yale U. Sch. Medicine, New Haven, 1965-68; assoc. prof. Yale U. Sch. Medicine, 1968; asst. attending radiologist Yale-New Haven Med. Center, 1965-68; assoc. prof. radiology Washington U. Sch. Medicine, St. Louis, 1968-71; asst. radiologist Barnes and Allied Hosps., St. Louis, 1969-71; cons. radiologist VA Hosp., St. Louis, 1969-71, Homer G. Phillips Hosp., St. Louis, 1968-71; prof. radiology George Washington U. Sch. Medicine, Washington, 1971—; chmn. dept. radiology George Washington U. Sch. Medicine, 1971-77, head pulmonary radiology, 1978—, interim chmn. dept. radiology, 1989-90, prof. emeritus radiology, 1993—; cons. NIH, 1972—; vis. prof. Hadassah U., Beersheba U., Rambam Hosp., Israel, 1977; cons. in radiology VA Hosp., Washington, 1972-77, U.S. Naval Med. Center, Bethesda, 1973-77; mem. diagnostic radiology adv. com. NIH, 1973-76; mem. Cancer Research Manpower Rev. Com., NIH, 1978. Editor-in-chief: Investigative Radiology, 1965-76; editor-in-chief emeritus, 1976—; editor Jour. Thoracic Imaging, 1985; Contbr. numerous articles to med. jours. Served with USN, 1955-58; Served with USPHS, 1961-63. Recipient numerous USPHS grants. Fellow Am. Coll. Radiology (pres.-elect D.C. chpt. 1976), Am. Coll. Chest Physicians; mem. Am. Fedn. Clin. Research, D.C. Med. Soc. (mem. med.-legal com. 1975-78), AMA, Radiol. Soc. N.Am., Assn. Univ. Radiologists, Soc. Thoracic Radiology (pres. 1983-84, exec. dir. 1984-87). Home: PO Box 675650 Rancho Santa Fe CA 92067-5650

ROCKOFF, SHEILA G., nursing and health facility administrator, educator, college administrator; b. Chgo., Mar. 15, 1945; d. Herbert Irwin and Marilyn (Victor) R.; divorced. ADN, Long Beach City Coll., 1966; BSN, San Francisco State U., 1970; MSN, Calif. State U.-L.A., 1976; EDD , South Ea. Nova U., 1993. RN, pub. health nurse, nursing instr., prof., health facility supr., Calif. Staff nurse Meml. Hosp., Long Beach, Calif., 1966-67, Mt. Zion Med. Ctr., San Francisco, 1967-69; instr. nursing Hollywood Presbyn. Med. Ctr., L.A., 1970-74; nursing supr. Orthopedic Hosp., L.A., 1974-76; instr. nursing Ariz. State U., Tempe, 1976-78; nurse supr. Hoag Meml. Hosp., Newport Beach, Calif., 1977-78; nurse educator U. Calif.-Irvine and Orange, Calif., 1978-80, Rancho Santiago Coll. (Calif.), 1980-89, dir. health svcs., 1989-95; dir., chair Health Occupations, 1995—; nursing prof. Rancho Santiago C.C., Santa Ana Campus; nurse cons. Home Health Care Agy., Irvine, 1983; educator, cons. Parenting Resources, Tustin, Calif., 1985-89. Contbr. articles to profl. jours. Mem. Nat. Assn. Student Personal Adminstrs., Am. Coll. Health Assn., Calif. Nurses Assn. (chmn. com. 1970-73), Assoc. of Calif. C.C. Administr., Calif C.C. Health Occpl. Educators, Assn. (bd. dirs.), Pacific Coast Coll. Health Assn., Phi Kappa Phi. Democrat. Jewish. Office: Rancho Santiago CC 1530 W 17th St Santa Ana CA 92706-3315

ROCKRISE, GEORGE THOMAS, architect; b. N.Y.C., Nov. 25, 1916; s. Thomas S. and Agnes M. (Asbury) R.; m. Margaret Lund Paulson, June 12, 1948 (dec. Aug. 1957); children: Christina, Peter; m. Sally S. Griffin, Dec. 1959 (div.); 1 child, Celia; m. Anneliese Warner, Nov. 27, 1985. B.Arch., Syracuse U., 1938; M.S. in Architecture, Columbia U., 1941. Fellow architecture Columbia U., 1940-41; architect Army and Navy, Panama, 1941-45; designer Edward D. Stone, N.Y.C., 1945-46, UN Hdqrs. Planning Commn., 1946-47; archtl. assoc. Thomas D. Church, San Francisco, 1948-49; pvt. practice architecture San Francisco, 1949-86, Glen Ellen, Calif., 1986-87; chmn. bd. Rockrise, Odermatt, Mountjoy Assocs. (architects and planners); lectr. Sch. Architecture, U. Calif., 1949-53; adviser to faculty com. Sch. Architecture, U. Venezuela, Caracas, 1954; mem. San Francisco Art Commn., 1952-56; cons. architect U.S. Dept. State, Japan, 1957-58, Fed. Republic Germany, Venezuela, Brazil, 1978-80, Bahrain, Brazil, Venezuela, Fed. Republic of Germany, 1981; architect U.S. embassy, Bahrain; vis. lectr. Cornell U., Clemson Coll., 1961, Syracuse U., U. Utah, Stanford U., 1962-65, Nat. U. Mex.; lectr. urban design Spanish Ministry Housing and Devel., Madrid, 1978; mem. San Francisco Planning Commn., 1961-62; adviser to Sec. for design HUD, 1966-67; participant State Dept. AID Urban Seminars Latin Am., 1971; mem. U.S. del. Pan Am. Congress Architects, Caracas, 1980; vis. prof. Universidad Central, Mex., 1985. Mem. pres.'s adv. com. U. Mass., 1971; mem. adv. council San Francisco Planning Urban Renewal Assn.; bd. dirs. Telegraph Hill Dwellers Assn., 1985-86, v.p.; pres. Archtl. Found. No. Calif., 1986; apptd. San Francisco Art Commn., 1986-87. Recipient AIA nat. award for residential work, 1953, 59, prog. architecture award citation, 1956, award of honor and award of merit AIA Homes for Better Living Program, 1956, regional awards for residential architecture AIA, 1957, others; Fulbright fellow in urban design U. Rome, 1978-79. Fellow AIA (pres. No. Calif. chpt. 1961, nat. v.p. from 1969, mem. nat honor awards jury, mem. nat. commn. urban design and planning 1978); mem. Am. Soc. Planning and Housing Ofcls., Am. Inst. Cert. Planners, Am. Soc. Landscape Architects, Nat. Assn. Housing and Redevel. Ofcls., Delta Kappa Epsilon, Tau Sigma Delta, Lambda Alpha. Home and Studio: 1280 Hill Rd Glen Ellen CA 95442-9658 *My adult life as architect and planner has been devoted to the construction and improvement of the man-made environment. I have come to believe through this endeavor, that it is the concern and responsibility of all thinking persons, whether professional or lay person to comprehend the forces for change in the environment and to work for the protection and enhancement of our cities and the natural environment.*

ROCKRISE, SALLY SCOTT, real estate broker; b. Mpls., Oct. 28, 1929; d. Harold Francis Scott and Mabel Vivien (Verdolyack) Alexander; m. George T. Rockrise, Dec. 18, 1959 (div. Jan. 1965); 1 child, Celia Rockrise Clarke. BS, Francis Shimer Coll., 1950. Pres./CEO Verdolyack Paper Specialties, 1952-57; mgr. ROMA, Inc., San Francisco, 1959-65; real estate agt. various cos., Palm Beach, Fla., 1965-82; mgr. Cutler Gardens, Inc., Miami, Fla., 1989-91; pres. S.E. Savs. Realty, Inc., West Palm Beach, 1982—; cons., paralegal to homeowner assns., 1991—. Mem. Community Assn. Inst., Million Dollar Club. Office: SE Savs Realty Inc 707 S Chillingworth Dr West Palm Beach FL 33409-4124

ROCKSTEIN, MORRIS, science writer, editor, consultant; b. Toronto, Ont., Can., Jan. 8, 1916; came to U.S., 1923; s. David and Mina (Segal) R.; children: Susan M. Bumgarner, Madelaine Jo Schitle. AB magna cum laude, Bklyn. Coll., 1938; MA, Columbia U., 1941; PhD, U. Minn., 1948; cert., Oak Ridge (Tenn.) Inst. Nuclear Studies, 1950. Research asst. entomology U. Minn., St. Paul, 1941-42; asst. prof., assoc. prof. zoophysiology Wash. State U., Pullman, 1948-53; asst. prof., then assoc. prof. physiology NYU Sch. Medicine, N.Y.C., 1953-61; prof. physiology U. Miami Sch. Medicine, 1961-81, chmn. dept., 1967-71; pres. Cortisol Med. Research, Inc., 1983-85; chmn. sci. adv. bd. Anorexia Nervosa Inst., Melbourne, Fla., 1983-85, Fla. Med. Ctr., Lauderdale Lakes, 1971-78; cons. entomology APHA, 1961-78; del. White House Conf. on Aging, Washington, 1961, 71; cons. insect physiology Sect. Tropical Medicine and Parasitology NIH, Washington, 1962-66, NASA, 1980-92, BIOS, 1983-85; mem. corp. Marine Biol. Lab., 1961—, trustee, 1961-93, life mem., trustee emeritus, 1993—; vis. lectr. Minority Insts. FASEB MARCPROG, 1983-88. Sr. author: Biology of Human Aging, 1978; editor: (with G.T. Baker) Molecular Genetic Mechanisms in Development and Aging, 1972, Development and Aging in the Nervous System, 1973, Physiology of Insecta, 6 vols., 1973-74, Theoretical Aspects of Aging, 1977; (with R.T. Goldman) Physiology and Pathology of Human Aging, 1978, Biochemistry of Insects, 1978; editor Miscellaneous Publs. and Thos Say Found. Monographs, 1983-92; contbr. articles to profl. jours. Mem. resource and mgmt. com. Area Agy. on Aging, 1988-90. Served with USAAF, 1942-46, as Scientist, USPHS, 1951-81. NRC fellow in natural scis. U. Minn., 1946-48; recipient Disting. Alumnus award Bklyn. Coll., 1959, Outstanding Alumnus Achievement award U. Minn., 1977; named knight comdr. of merit Knights of Malta, 1982. Fellow AAAS (life, mem. coun. 1962-64), Gerontol. Soc. (pres. 1965-66), Entomol. Soc. Am. (life mem.); mem. Internat. Assn. Gerontology (mem. exec. coun. 1963-66), Internat. Assn. Prolongation of Human Life Span (v.p. 1974-92), Am. Physiol. Soc., Am. Soc. Zoologists, Soc. Gen. Physiologists, Sunflower Soc. Miami (v.p. 1986-88), People to People Fla., Army-Navy Club, Miami Internat. Press Club, Coral Gables Country Club (bd. dirs. Fleet 1994-96), PHi Beta Kappa, Sigma Xi.

ROCKWELL, ALVIN JOHN, lawyer; b. Kalamazoo, Dec. 29, 1908; s. John S. and L. B. (DeVall) R.; m. Anne Hayward, Aug. 24, 1933; 1 son, John Sargent. A.B., DePauw U., 1929, LLD (hon.), 1991; postgrad., London Sch. Econs., 1929-30; J.D., Harvard U., 1933. Bar: Mass. 1933, Calif. 1948. Spl. asst. to U.S. atty. gen., 1940-43; gen. counsel NLRB, 1944-45; legal adviser to U.S. Mil. Govt., Germany, 1946-48; partner firm Brobeck, Phleger & Harrison, San Francisco, 1948-79; of counsel Brobeck, Phleger & Harrison, 1979—. Trustee De Pauw U., 1958-80, life trustee, 1980—; trustee San Francisco Law Library, 1975-81; trustee, later pres. San Francisco Bar Assn. Found., 1976-80; mem. Commn. on Uniform State Laws, 1962-69. Fellow Am. Bar Found.; mem. Am. Law Inst, Harvard Law Sch. Assn. No. Calif. (past pres.), World Affairs Council No. Calif. (past pres.), Phi Beta Kappa. Clubs: Commonwealth (San Francisco), Pacific-Union (San Francisco), Bohemian (San Francisco); Cosmos (Washington). Home: 1400 Geary Blvd Apt 2403 San Francisco CA 94109-6574 Office: Spear St Tower 29th Floor One Market Plaza San Francisco CA 94105

ROCKWELL, BRUCE MCKEE, retired banker, retired foundation executive; b. Denver, Dec. 18, 1922; s. Robert B. and Florence (McKee) R.; m. Virginia Packard, Apr. 22, 1950; children—David, Jane, Sarah. BA, Yale U., 1945. Exec. sec. to mayor City of Denver, 1947-51; pub. rels. and advt. account exec. William Kostka & Assocs., 1952-53; with Colo. Nat. Bank, Denver, 1953-85; pres. Colo. Nat. Bank, 1970-75, chmn., CEO, 1975-85, also dir.; pres. Colo. Trust, Denver, 1985-91; sr. cons. BBC, Inc., Denver, 1991. Chmn., bd. dirs. The Denver Partnership, Inc., Kaiser Permanente, 1980-92; bd. dirs. Am. Pub. Welfare Assn., 1989-91; chmn. Denver Urban Renewal Authority, 1958-68; nat. coun. Salk Inst., 1978-84; trustee C.C. Denver, Com. Econ. Devel., 1979-85, Denver Symphony Orch., 1974-77, Denver Art Mus., 1965-72, 82-86, Denver Health & Hosp., 1995—. Ensign USNR, 1945-46. Named Colo. Bus. Man of Yr., Colo. Bus. Mag., 1976. Mem. Assn. Res. City Bankers (dir. 1975-85), Denver C. of C. Clubs: University, Tennis (Denver). Home: 815 Vine St Denver CO 80206-3741

ROCKWELL, DON ARTHUR, psychiatrist; b. Wheatland, Wyo., Apr. 24, 1938; s. Orson Arthur and Kathleen Emily (Richards) R.; m. Frances Pepitone-Arreola, Dec. 23, 1965; children: Grant, Chad. BA, Wash. U., 1959; MD, U. Okla., 1963; MA in Sociology, U. Calif., Berkeley, 1967. Diplomate Am. Bd. Psychiatry and Neurology. Intern in surgery San Francisco Gen. Hosp., 1963-64; resident in psychiatry Langley-Porter Neuropsychiatric Inst. U. Calif. Med. Ctr., San Francisco, 1964-67; instr. dept. psychiatry U. Calif. Sch. Medicine, Davis, 1969-70, asst. prof., 1970-74, assoc. prof., 1974-80, acting. assoc., dean curricular affiars, 1979-80, acting assoc. dean student affairs, 1980, assoc. dean student affairs, 1980-82, prof., 1980-84; career tchr. NIMH, 1970-72; assoc. psychiatrist Sacramento Med. Ctr.; med. dir. U. Calif. Med. Ctr., Davis, 1982-84; prof., vice chmn. dept. psychiatry and biobehavioral scis. UCLA, 1984-96; dir. of profl. svcs., 1996—; chief profl. staff Neuropsychiat. Inst., UCLA, 1984-85, also dir. outpatient svcs.; chmn. U. Calif. Hosp. Dirs. Council, 1988-89; cons. Nat. Commn. on Marijuana, Washington, 1971-73. Co-author: Psychiatric Disorders, 1982; contbr. chpts. to books; articles to profl. jours. Bd. dirs. Bereavement Outreach, Sacramento, 1974-84, Suicide Prevention, Yolo County, 1969-84; bd. visitors U. Okla. Sch. Medicine; chmn. hosp. dirs. coun. U. Calif. Hosp.; governing coun. AHA Psychiat. Hosp. Fellow Am. Psychiat. Assn., Am. Coll. Psychiatrists, Am. Coll. Mental Health Adminstrs.; mem. AMA (gov. coun. psych. hosp.), Am. Sociologic Assn., Cen. Calif. Psychiat. Assn. (sec.-pres. 1977-78), U. Okla. Alumni Assn. (trustee 1981-86), Alpha Omega Alpha. Home: 1816 E Las Tunas Rd Santa Barbara CA 93103-1744

ROCKWELL, ELIZABETH DENNIS, retirement specialist, financial planner; b. Houston; d. Robert Richard and Nezzell Alderton (Christie) Dennis. Student Rice U., 1939-40, U. Houston, 1938-39, 40-42. Purchasing agt. Standard Oil Co., Houston, 1942-66; v.p. mktg. Heights Savs. Assn., Houston, 1967-82; sr. fin. planner Oppenheimer & Co., Inc., Houston, 1982—; 2d v.p. Desk and Derrick Club Am., 1960-61. Contbr. articles on retirement planning, tax planning and tax options, monthly article 50 Plus sect. for Houston Chronicle newspaper. Bd. dirs. ARC, 1985-91, Houston Heights Assn., 1973-77; named sr. v.p. Oppenheimer, 1986—; mem. Coll. Bus. U. found. bd. Houston, 1990, mem. million dollar roundtable, 1991—, mem. ct. of the table, 1991—, mem. sys. planned giving coun., 1992—, mem. coll. bus. adv. bd., 1992—, mem. alumni bd., 1987-95; appointed trustee U. Houston Sys. Found., Inc., 1992. Named Disting. Alumnae Coll. Bus. Alumn. Assn. U. Houston, 1992; named YWCA Outstanding Woman of Yr., 1978. Mem. Am. Savs. and Loan League (state dir. 1973-76, chpt. pres. 1971-72; pres. S.W. regional conf. 1972-73; Leaders award 1972), Savs. Inst. Mktg. Soc. Am. (Key Person award 1974), Inst. Fin. Edn., Fin. Mgrs., Soc. Savs. Instns., U.S. Savs. and Loan League (com. on deposit acquisitions and adminstrn.), Houston Heights Assn. (charter, dir. 1973-77), Friends of Bayou Bend, Harris County Heritage Soc., U. Houston Alumni Orgn. (life), Rice U. Bus. and Profl. Women, River Oaks Bus. Womens Exchange Club, U. Houston Bus. Womens Assn. (pres. 1985), Forum Club, Greater Houston Women's Found. (charter). Office: Oppenheimer & Co Inc 1600 Smith St Ste 3100 Houston TX 77002-4103

ROCKWELL, ELIZABETH GOODE, dance company director, consultant, educator; b. Portland, Oreg., Sept. 10, 1920; d. Henry Walton and Elizabeth (Harmon) Goode; m. William Hearne Rockwell, Feb. 3, 1948; children: Enid, Karen, William. BA, Mills Coll., 1941; MA, NYU, 1946. Instr. dance Monticello Jr. Coll., Alton, Ill., 1941-42; dir. masters program in dance Smith Coll., Northampton, Mass., 1946-48; 1st dir. dance dept. High Sch. of Performing Arts, N.Y.C., 1948-51, 53-54; dir. Elizabeth Rockwell Sch. Dance, Bedford, N.Y., 1956-86, Rondo Dance Theater, Bedford, 1971-93; tchr. continuing dance classes CCAE, 1994—; mem. adv. ednl. com. Calif. Ctr. for Arts, Escondido, Calif., 1993-95, dir. dance workshops, 1994—. Choreographer (suite of dances) Jazz Suite, 1966, (50-minute dances) Catch the Wind, 1969, Genesis, 1972, (narrative modern ballet) The Executioner, 1974, Decathalon, 1982; dir. (subscription series) Dance-Art-Poetry-Jazz, 1978-79, (dance/music 1600-1900) Stages in Ages, 1981, (Am. dance revivals) Masterpieces of American Dance, 1982-84, Dances of the Decades, 1985-90, (revival & new choreography) Dances of Our Times, 1991; dir. dance workshops for Calif. Ctr. Arts, 1994, 95, 96; creator performing group of older dancers Golden Connections, CCAE, 1996. Bd. dirs. Coun. for Arts in Westchester, White Plains, N.Y., 1978-79, affiliate, 1978—. Recipient Medal for Performance, Israeli Army, 1966, Award for Excellence in Arts Edn. Alumnae of High Sch. of Performing Arts, 1990, various grants N.Y. State Coun. on Arts, 1971-93, Coun. Arts in Westchester, 1973-92, dance touring program grant Nat. Endowment for Arts, 1975-79. Mem. Am. Dance Guild, Westchester Dance Coun. (program dir. 1965-69), Assn. Am. Dance Cos., San Diego Area Dance Alliance (bd. dirs. 1995—). Avocations: writing, swimming, touring, reading. Home: 205 Tampico Gln Escondido CA 92025-7359

ROCKWELL, GEORGE BARCUS, financial consultant; b. Chgo., Jan. 5, 1926; s. Thomas S. and Irene G. (Barcus) R.; m. Lois Ladd, Sept. 30, 1950; children: Susan, Cynthia. A.B. in Econs, Harvard U., 1949, grad. Advanced Mgmt. Program, 1967. Salesman IBM, 1949, products mgr., 1956; asst. mgr. IBM, Boston, 1958; mgr. IBM, Albany, N.Y., 1960; v.p., dir. head computer services State St. Bank & Trust Co., Boston, 1963; v.p., head mut. funds div. State St. Bank & Trust Co., 1966, sr. v.p., 1968, bank sales coordinator, 1968, exec. v.p., 1968, pres., 1970-75; vice chmn. bd. State St. Boston Fin. Corp., 1975-76; also industry dir.; v.p., mng. dir. fin. industries Arthur D. Little, Inc., Cambridge, Mass., 1976-89; v.p., dir. Webster-Atlas Bldg. Corp., Keane-Assocs., Inc., 1970-75; pres., dir. State St. Bank Boston Internat., State St. Boston Securities Svcs. Corp., State St. Boston Credit Co., Inc., SSB Investments, Inc.; dir., exec. com. Nat. BankAmericard Inc., 1970-75, Royal Bus. Group, Inc., 1980-84, Computer Ptnrs., 1983-86; bd. dirs. Sandwich Coop. Bank. Bd. overseers Boys' Clubs Boston, 1969-75; trustee coun. Boston U. Med. Ctr., 1969-74, trustee Lahey Clinic, 1973-95, Lahey Hitchcock Clinic, 1995—. Served to 1st lt., inf. AUS, 1944-46. Mem. Greater Boston C. of C. (bd. dirs. 1969-76), Harvard Bus. Sch. Assn. Boston (bd. govs. 1969-72). Clubs: Wellesley Country, Rio Verde Country Club, Rotary. Home: 376 Glen Rd Weston MA 02193-1403

ROCKWELL, HAYS HAMILTON, bishop; b. Detroit, Aug. 17, 1936; s. Walter Francis and Kathryn (McElroy) R.; m. Linda Hullinger, Sept. 7, 1957; children: Keith, Stephen, Sarah, Martha. AB, Brown U., 1958; BD, Episcopal Theol. Sch., Cambridge, Mass., 1961; DD (hon.), Episcopal Theol. Seminary SW, Austin, Tex., 1984; BD, Kenyon Coll., 1974; HHD, St. Louis U., 1994. Ordained to ministry Episcopal Ch. as deacon, 1961, as priest, 1962; ordained bishop, 1991. Chaplain St. George's Sch., Newport, R.I., 1961-69, Univ. of Rochester, N.Y., 1969-71; dean Bexley Hall, Rochester, 1971-76; rector St. James' Ch., N.Y.C., 1976-91; bishop coadjutor Diocese of Mo., St. Louis, 1991-93, bishop, 1993—; dir. Union Theol. Seminary, N.Y.C., 1976, 87, 91. Author: Steal Away, Steal Away Home, 1985. Mem. Coun. on Fgn. Rels., N.Y.C., 1988; former trustee U. Rochester, N.Y.C.; trustee Mo. Bot. Garden, St. Luke's Hosp., Mo. Mem. Century Assn. (N.Y.C.). Office: Diocese of Missouri 1210 Locust St Saint Louis MO 63103-2322

ROCKWELL, JOHN SARGENT, arts administrator, music critic, writer; b. Washington, Sept. 16, 1940; s. Alvin John and Anne Sargent (Hayward) R.; m. Linda Mevorach; 1 child, Sasha Eve. B.A., Harvard U., 1962; postgrad., U. Munich, 1962-63; M.A., U. Calif., Berkeley, 1964, Ph.D., 1972. Music and dance critic Oakland (Calif.) Tribune, 1969; asst. music and dance critic Los Angeles Times, 1970-72; freelance music critic N.Y. Times, 1972-74, staff music critic, 1974-91; European cultural corr. and prin. classical recordings critic N.Y. Times, Paris, 1992-94; dir., Lincoln Ctr. Festival Lincoln Ctr. for the Performing Arts, N.Y.C., 1994—; lectr. in field. Author: All American Music: Composition in the Late 20th Century, 1983, Sinatra: An American Classic, 1984. Harvard-German Govt. fellow, 1962-63; Woodrow Wilson fellow, 1963-64. Mem. Music Critics Assn., Century Assn., Phi Beta Kappa. Office: Lincoln Ctr Performing Arts 70 Lincoln Ctr Plaza New York NY 10023

ROCKWELL, KAY ANNE, elementary education educator; b. Brighton, Mich., Feb. 12, 1952; d. Philip Oscar and Patricia Irene (Bennett) Newton; m. Lawrence Edward Rockwell, Aug. 23, 1975. BA in Social Sci. & Elem. Edn. cum laude, Spring Arbor Coll., 1974; MA in Early Childhood Edn., Ea. Mich. U., 1981. Dir. child care St. Luke's Luth. Day Care Ctr., Ann Arbor, Mich., 1980-82; tchr. 3d grade Colo. Christian Sch., Denver, 1982-94; tchr. 1st grade Front Range Christian Sch., Littleton, Colo., 1994—; chmn. Nat. Children's Book Week Colo. Christian Sch., 1993-94, chmn. ACSI spelling bee, 1991-94, chmn. ACSI speech meet, 1985-86. Spring Arbor Coll. scholar, 1972-74. Office: Front Range Christian Sch 4001 S Wadsworth Blvd Littleton CO 80123-1358

ROCKWELL, R(ONALD) JAMES, JR., laser and electro-optics consultant; b. Cin., May 7, 1937; s. Ronald James and Mary Cornelius (Thornton) R.; m. Diane Lundin, Feb. 3, 1968; children: James Gregory, Christopher Derrick. BS, U. Cin., 1960, MS, 1964. Directing physicist, assoc. prof. laser scis., laser research labs. Med. Center, U. Cin., 1963-76; dir. continuing edn. services Electro-Optical Systems Design Jour., Cin., 1976-77; v.p. laser/electro-optics Control Dynamics, Inc., Cin., 1977-79; pres. Rockwell Assocs., Inc. (cons. lasers, optics and electro-optics), Cin., 1979-89; pres., chief exec. officer Rockwell Laser Industries (cons. lasers, optics and electro-optics), Cin., 1989—; exec. com. sate use lasers com. Am. Nat. Standards Inst., 1971—; exec. sec. Laser Inst. Am., 1976-77, dir., 1972-92, pres., 1974; mem. adv. com. Laser History Project, 1983-89; dir. Laserworks, Inc., Rockwell Devel. Co.; cons. WHO, Internat. Electrotechnical Commn., founder Consortium of Laser and Tech. Cons., 1988; mem. tech. com. Laser Fire Protection of the Nat. Fire Protection Assn., 1991—. Co-author: Lasers in Medicine, 1971; author: Laser Safety Training Manual, 1982, Laser Safety in Surgery and Medicine, 1985, Laser Safety: Concepts, Analysis and Controls, 1992, Laser Safety: Modularized Training Package, 1994; created software program: Laser Hazard Analysis, 1987, LAZAN for Windows, 1995; co-developer: LAZERNET page on the World-Wide Web (Internet), 1966; contbr. chpts. to books and articles to profl. jours.; editor jours. in field; mem. editl. bd. Jour. Laser Applications, 1994—. Co-chmn. Internat. Laser Safety Conf., 1990, 92. Recipient Pres.' award Laser Inst. Am., 1985. Mem. IEEE, N.Y. Acad. Scis., Am. Soc. Laser Medicine and Surgery, Midwest Bio-Laser Inst., Internat. Laser Display Assn., Newcomen Soc., Sigma Xi (nat. lectr. 1971-75), Delta Tau Delta (D.S.C. award 1985, dir. acad. affairs, nat. bd. dirs. 1975-83). Methodist. Designer, builder portable laser entertainment system in laser light artistic shows; patentee in field. Home: 6282 Coachlite Way Cincinnati OH 45243 Office: PO Box 43010 7754 Camargo Rd Cincinnati OH 45243

ROCKWELL, THEODORE, nuclear engineer; b. Chgo., June 26, 1922; s. Theodore G. and Paisley (Shane) R.; m. Mary Juanita Compton, Jan. 25, 1947; children—Robert C., William T., Lawrence E., Juanita C. B.S. in Engring, Princeton U., 1943, Chem.E. (M.S.), 1945; grad. courses, Oak Ridge, 1944-49; D.Sc. (hon.), Tri-State U., 1960. Registered profl. engr., D.C. Process improvement engr. Manhattan Project, Oak Ridge, 1944-45; head shield engring. group Oak Ridge Nat. Lab., 1945-49; nuclear engr., naval reactors br. AEC, also nuclear propulsion divs. Navy Bur. Ships, 1949-55, tech. dir., 1955-64; founding officer, dir. MPR Assos., Inc., Washington, 1964-87; sole practice, 1988—; research asso. Johns Hopkins U. Center Fgn. Policy Research, 1965-66; Chmn. Atomic Indsl. Forum Reactor Safety Task Force, 1966-72; mem. adv. group artificial heart program NIH, 1966; cons. to Joint Congl. Com. on Atomic Energy, 1967. Author: The Rickover Effect: How One Man Made a Difference, 1992; co-author: Shippingport Pressurized Water Reactor, 1958, Arms Control Agreements/Designs Verification, 1968; co-founder Princeton Engr.; editor: Reactor Shield Design Manual, 1956; contbg. editor New Realities, 1988-92; contbr. sci. articles to profl. publs., non-tech. articles nat. mags.; holder patents, patent applications for neutron-absorbing cermets, process for leaching uranium from slags, process for prodn. boron-containing plastic sheet, others. Mem. adv. council dept. chem. engring. Princeton U., 1966-72. Recipient Disting. Civilian Svc. medal USN, 1960, Disting. Svc. medal AEC, 1960, Lifetime Contbn. award Am. Nuclear Soc. (1st, now known as Rockwell award), 1986. Fellow Am. Soc. Psychical Rsch. (life); mem. AAAS (rep. of Parapsychol. Assn. to AAAS 1975-87), Soc. for Sci. Exploration, U.S. Psychotronic Assn. (dir. 1988-91), Authors Guild, Writers Ctr., Washington Ind. Writers, Cosmos Club (Washington), Nat. Press Club. Presbyterian (elder). Address: 3403 Woolsey Dr Chevy Chase MD 20815-3924

ROCKWELL, WINTHROP ADAMS, lawyer; b. Pittsfield, Mass., May 7, 1948; s. Landon Gale Rockwell and Ruth (Adams) Lonsdale; m. Barbara Washburn Wood, June 20, 1970; children: Samuel Adams, Madeleine McCord. AB, Dartmouth Coll., 1970; JD, NYU, 1975. Bar: Minn. 1975, U.S. Dist. Ct. Minn. 1975. Asst. newsman fgn. desk N.Y. Times, N.Y.C., 1970-71; asst. to pres. Dartmouth Coll., Hanover, N.H., 1971-72; assoc. Faegre & Benson, Mpls., 1975-79; assoc. chief counsel Pres.'s Commn. on Accident at Three Mile Island, Washington, 1979; assoc. Faegre & Benson, Mpls., 1979-82, ptnr., 1983—, chmn. diversity com., 1990-95, head gen. litigation group, 1995—. Bd. dirs., v.p. Children's Theatre, Mpls., 1982-83; bd. dirs. Actors Theatre St. Paul, 1975-79, Trinity Films, Mpls., 1978-82, Minn. Ctr. for Book Arts, 1996—. With U.S. N.G., 1970-76. Brit.-Am. Project fellow, 1987. Mem. ABA, Minn. Bar Assn., Hennepin County Bar Assn., Am. Agrl. Law Assn., Adirondack 46ers, Adirondack Mountain Club. Avocations: writing, tennis, mountaineering, gardening. Home: 1901 Knox Ave S Minneapolis MN 55403-2840 Office: Faegre & Benson 2200 Norwest Ctr 90 S 7th St Minneapolis MN 55402-3903

ROCKWOOD, RUTH H., former library science educator; b. Chgo., Oct. 15, 1906; d. Charles Edward and Myrtle Isabelle (Wheeler) Humiston; m. George Herbert Rockwood, Apr. 14, 1928 (dec.); children: Charles Edward, Nancy Hoyt Rockwood Haigh, Alice Frances Rockwood Bethke. A.B., Wellesley Coll., 1927; M.S., U. Ill., 1949; Ed.D., Ind. U., 1960. Adminstrv. asst., instr. U. Ill. Library Sch., 1949-52; Fulbright lectr. Chulalongkorn U., Bangkok, Thailand, 1952-53; vis. asst. prof. Ind. U. Library Sch., 1958-59; prof. library sci. Fla. State U., 1953-79, prof. emeritus, 1979—. Mem. Fla. Trail Assn., Sierra Club, Beta Phi Mu. Club: Pilot (Tallahassee). Home: 4449 Meandering Way #PC408 Tallahassee FL 32308-5740 Office: Sch Library Sci Fla State U Tallahassee FL 32306

ROCO, MIHAIL CONSTANTIN, mechanical engineer, educator; b. Bucharest, Romania, Nov. 2, 1947; came to U.S., 1980; s. Constantin M. and Armande Ch.-Ad. (Cantacuzino) R.; m. Ecaterina (Cathy) Roco, July 24, 1986; children: Constance-Armanda M., Charles Michael. PhD, Polytechnic Inst., Bucharest, 1976; diploma strat. planning/exec. leadership, U.S. OPM, Washington, 1992; diploma leadership program, U. Md., 1994. Prof. U. Ky., Lexington, 1981—; program dir. engring. NSF, Arlington, Va., 1990—, coord. "Grant Opportunities for Acad. Liaison with Industry", 1994; part-time prof. Johns Hopkins U., Balt., 1993; vis. prof. U. Paderborn, Fed. Republic of Germany, 1979, U. Sask., Can., 1990, Tohoku U., Sendai, Japan, 1988-89, Calif. Inst. Tech., Pasadena, 1988-89; cons. to industry in U.S.,

Can., Europe and Australia, 1981-92; cons. to U.S. govt. agys., 1983-89; lectr. postgrad. engring. Japan, Chile, Ga., Fla., 1982-91. Author: (with others) Principles and Practice of Slurry Flow, 1991, Particulate Two-Phase Flow, 1993; assoc. tech. editor Jour. Fluids Engring., 1985-89; contbr. over 100 articles to sci. and engring. jours and several articles symbolist poetry in literary jours. Recipient Carl Duisberg Soc. award, Fed. Republic Germany, 1979, Outstanding Rsch. Professorship award U. Ky., 1986-87, Outstanding Performance award NSF, 1994; grantee NSF, Rsch. Founds. USA, Can., Fed. Republic Germany, OAS, 1979-91. Fellow ASME (editor internat. symposium series 1984-94, chmn. multiphase flow com. 1992-94), Particle Tech. Forum (vice chmn. 1994-96, chmn. 1996—); mem. AIChE, AIAA, Soc. Rheology, Acad. Mechanics, N.Y. Acad. Scis. Achievements include formulation of innovative numerical methods for fluid and particulate flows (finite volume, probabilistic, marching), computer-aided-engineering for centrifugal slurry pumps, hydrotransport of solids through pipelines, and electro-imaging (fast laser printers); 13 inventions of fluid machineries, wear resistant equipment, methods to increase pipe transport capacity, viscosimeter; research on multiphase flow modeling, laser Doppler anemometry, flow visualization, power stations, pumps, and wear mechanisms. Office: NSF 4201 Wilson Blvd Rm 525 Arlington VA 22230-0001

ROCQUE, VINCENT JOSEPH, lawyer; b. Franklin, N.H., Nov. 27, 1945; s. Francis Albert and Mary Helen (O'Grady) R.; m. Emily Adams Arnold, May 31, 1969; children: Amanda Adams, Peter O'Connor, Caroline Quin. AB magna cum laude, Georgetown U., 1967; JD, Columbia U., N.Y.C., 1970. Bar: D.C. 1971, U.S. Supreme Ct., 1973. Assoc. Hogan & Hartson, Washington, 1970-73; counsel, spl. asst. to commr. Barbara Franklin U.S. Consumer Product Safety Commn., Washington, 1973-77; asst. dir. bur. trade regulation U.S. Dept. Commerce, Washington, 1977-80; ptnr. Sullivan & Worcester, Washington, 1980-90; pvt. practice law Washington, 1990—. V.p., co-pres. Janney Pub. Elem. Sch. PTA, Washington, 1982-84; vol. coord. homeless shelters Cath. Charities, Washington and Silver Spring, Md., 1984-90. Staff sgt. USAR, 1969-75. Mem. ABA (adminstrv. law and regulatory practice sect., internat. law and practice sect.), Fed. Bar Assn. (adminstrv. law and internat. law sects.), Mid-Atlantic Literary Edification Soc., Nat. Capital YMCA, Phi Beta Kappa. Catholic. Avocations: reading, travel, American Civil War history, basketball. Office: 1155 Connecticut Ave NW Ste 400 Washington DC 20036-4306

RODALE, ARDATH, publishing executive. Chmn. Prevention Mag. Office: Rodale Press Inc 33 E Minor St Emmaus PA 18049-4113*

RODBELL, CLYDE ARMAND, distribution executive; b. Atlanta, Aug. 16, 1927; s. Joseph Hirsch and Fannie (Turetzky) R.; m. Cecile Rosenson, Mar. 27, 1949 (div.); children: Marsha, Jeffrey, Keith, Kim; m. Robin Graham McKenzie Rodbell, Dec. 15, 1974; 1 child, Lindsey. BBA, Emory U., 1949. Pres. Apex Supply Co. Inc., Atlanta, 1949—. Co-chmn. George Bush Presdl. Fund Raising, Ga., 1988-89; mem. State of Ga. Electoral Coll., 1989, exec. commr. Am. Bicentenial Pres. Inaugural Bus. Adv., 1989, Pres' Commn. on White House Fellowships, 1989-92. With U.S. Army, 1945. Mem. Wholesale Assn. Ga., Southern Wholesalers Assn., Am. Supply Assn., Standard Club, Rotary Club. Republican. Jewish. Avocations: reading, gardening, antiquing, politics, fund raising.

RODBELL, MARTIN, biochemist; b. Balt., Dec. 1, 1925; s. Milton William and Shirley Helen (Abrams) R.; m. Barbara Charlotte Ledermann, Sept. 10, 1950; children: Paul, Suzanne, Andrew, Phillip. BA, Johns Hopkins U., 1949; PhD, U. Wash., 1954; DSc (hon.), U. Montpelier, 1992, U. Wash., U. Geneva. Nutrition and endocrinology chemist NIH, Bethesda, Md., 1956—; chief lab. nutrition and endocrinology NIAMD, Bethesda, Md., 1972-84; sci. dir. Nat. Inst. Environ. Health Scis., Rsch. Triangle Park, N.C., 1985-89, chief sect. signal transduction, 1989-94; scientist emeritus Nat. Inst. Environ. Health Scis., Rsch. Triangle Park, 1994—. Recipient Supr. Svc. award HHS, 1974, Gairdner Found. award, 1984, Jacobeus award, 1973, Nobel Prize for Physiology or Medicine, 1994. Mem. NAS (Richard Lounsbery award 1987), Am. Soc. Biol. Chemists., Am. Acad. Arts and Scis. Office: NIH Environmental Health Scis Research Triangle Park NC 27709

RODDIS, RICHARD STILES LAW, insurance company executive, consultant, legal educator; b. Washington, Mar. 18, 1930; s. Louis Harry and Winifred Emily (Stiles) R.; m. Joanne Margreta Hagen, Aug. 16, 1953; children: Kathryn Hazel Roddis Meyer, Linda Marie Roddis McGinley, Victoria Anne Roddis Hoefer, Margaret Mae Roddis Rumpeltes, Richard Louis Martin. A.B., San Diego (Calif.) State Coll., 1951; J.D., U. Calif.-Berkeley, 1954. Bar: Calif. 1955, Wash. 1981, U.S. Supreme Ct. 1959. Dep. atty. gen. Calif. San Francisco, 1954-58; dep. atty. gen., chief sect. bus. law and investment frauds unit Los Angeles, 1961-63; practiced law San Diego, 1958-61; chief dep. ins. commr. Calif. Los Angeles, 1963-65; ins. commr., 1966-68; prof. law U. Wash., Seattle, 1968-95; prof. emeritus U. wash., Seattle, 1995—; dean U. Wash. (Sch. Law), 1970-78; chmn., chief exec. officer Unigard Security Ins. Co., Seattle, 1984-88; dir. Stewart Econs., Inc., 1988—; adviser U.S. Dept. Transp., 1968-70, Nat. Conf. Commrs. on Uniform State Laws, 1971-72; chmn. Gov. Wash. Task Force on Catastrophic Health Care Costs, 1973-74; mem. steering com. Med. Injury Compensation Study, Inst. Medicine NAS, 1976. Bd. dirs. Saul Haas Found.; bd. dirs. Crista Ministries, 1986-91. Mem. ABA (com. to improve liability ins. system 1988), State Bar Calif., State Bar Wash., Nat. Assn. Ins. Commrs. (chmn. blanks com., chmn. laws and legis. com., vice chmn. exec. com. 1966-68). Republican. Lutheran. Home: 15524 SE 53rd Pl Bellevue WA 98006-5102

RODE, HELEN JANE, special education educator; b. N.Y.C., Apr. 25, 1949; d. David Edward and Celia Zelda (Sandek) Gould; m. Robert Rode, Aug. 13, 1972; children: Rachel Beth, Jason Scott. BA in Psychology, Hofstra U., Hempstead, N.Y., 1972, MS in Elem./Spl. Edn., 1976. Cert. tchr. elem. edn. K-6, spl. edn. N-12, edn. of orthopedically impaired and learning disabled, N.Y. Learning disabilities cons. Hauppauge (N.Y.) Sch. Dist., 1977-78; tchr. Middle Country Sch. Dist., Centereach, N.Y., 1979; tchr./chair Island Trees Mid. Sch., Levittown, N.Y., 1979—, team leader grade 7, 1993-94, tchr. mem. com. on spl. edn., 1992—. Mem. Suburban Temple, Wantagh, N.Y., 1990-94. Mem. ASCD, United Tchrs. Island Trees, Nassau Reading Coun., PTA, Island Trees Spl. Edn. PTA. Avocations: piano playing, reading, travel. Office: Island Trees Middle School 45 Wantagh Ave S Levittown NY 11554

RODE, LEIF, real estate personal computer consultant; b. Copenhagen, Aug. 24, 1926; came to U.S., 1948, naturalized, 1960; s. Stig and Kirsten (Bay) R.; m. Elsa B. Ringressy, Feb. 14, 1992; children from previous marriage: Christian, Lise. BS magna cum laude, Columbia U., 1959. ChFC; CLU; cert. internal auditor; lic. realtor assoc. GRI. Mgr. East Asiatic Co., N.Y.C., 1952-54; various auditing positions N.Y. Life Ins. Co., N.Y.C., 1954-70, asst. gen. auditor, 1970-71, gen. auditor, 1971-82, sr. v.p., gen. auditor, 1982-87, cons., 1987-89; real estate agt., Weichert Realtors, Holmdel, N.J., 1989-90, Fraybern Realtors, Holmdel, 1990-92, Colts Neck Realty, Colts Neck, 1992—. Bd. dirs. Sports Found., Inc., Colts Neck, N.J., 1973-75, pres., 1975-77; mem. Bd. Edn., Colts Neck, 1975-76, v.p., 1976-78; trustee Bayshore Community Hosp., Holmdel, N.J., 1986-87; mcpl. liaison to Colts Neck Twp. for N.J. Assn. Realtors, 1989-94, real estate personal computer cons., 1995—. Served with Royal Danish Navy, 1946-47. Recipient award of honor N.Y. State Soc. CPA's, 1960; Merle M. Hoover scholar, 1960. Mem. Inst. Internal Auditors, Am. Soc. of CLU and Chartered Fin. Cons., Monmouth County Bd. Realtors (constn. and by-laws com. 1989-92, co-chair 1991-92, strategic planning com. 1992-93), N.J. Assn. Realtors (bd. dirs. 1993, legis. com. 1990-93, vice-chair 1992, chmn. 1993, new products and tech. com. 1990-92), Nat. Assn. Realtors. Republican. Lutheran. Home: 47 Blackbriar Dr Colts Neck NJ 07722-1203 Office: Colts Neck Realty PO Box 128 Colts Neck NJ 07722-0128

RODEFFER, STEPHANIE LYNN HOLSCHLAG, archaeologist, government official; b. Newark, Ohio, Oct. 5, 1947; d. Jerry Bernard and Joan Elizabeth (Dasher) Holschlag; m. Michael Joe Rodeffer, Sept. 11, 1971. BA, U. Ky., 1969; PhD, Wash. State U., 1975. Instr., then asst. prof. anthropology Lander Coll., Greenwood, S.C., 1974-77; archaeologist interagy. archaeol. svcs. Nat. Park Svc./Heritage Conservation and Recreation Svc., Atlanta, 1977-80; archaeologist divsn. cultural programs Heritage Conservation and Recreation Svc./Nat. Park Svc., Albuquerque, 1980-81; archaeologist div. cultural programs Nat. Park Svc., Santa Fe, N.Mex., 1981-82; archaeologist, acting chief preservation planning br. Nat. Park Svc., Phila., 1982-86; chief interagy. archaeol. svcs. br. div. nat. register programs Nat. Park Svc., San Francisco, 1986-90; chief mus. collections repository Western Archaeol. and Conservation Ctr. Nat. Park Svc., Tucson, 1990—. Muster Chmn. Star Ft. Hist. Com., Ninety Six, S.C., 1975. Recipient spl. achievement award Nat. Park Svc., 1980, 82, mgmt. award So. Ariz. Fed. Execs. Assn., 1992; Woodrow Wilson fellow, 1969. Mem. Soc. for Hist. Archeology (membership chmn. 1976-78, sec.-treas. 1978—, Carol Ruppé Disting. Svc. award 1994), Soc. for Am. Archaeology, Soc. Profl. Archaeologists, Phi Beta Kappa. Roman Catholic. Avocations: genealogical research, quilting. Office: Nat Park Svc Western-Archaeol Cons Ctr 1415 N 6th Ave Tucson AZ 85705-6643

RODEMEYER, MICHAEL LEONARD, JR., lawyer; b. Balt., May 25, 1950; s. Michael Leonard and Claire Isabel (Gunther) R.; m. Dorrit Carolyn Green, June 7, 1975; children: Justin, Christopher. AB, Princeton U., 1972; JD, Harvard U., 1975. Bar: Md. 1977, D.C. 1980, U.S. Ct. Appeals (10th cir.) 1980. Atty. Fed. Trade Commn., Washington, 1976-81, atty. advisor, 1981-84; counsel Subcom. on Natural Resources, Agr. Rsch. & Environ., Washington, 1984-88; staff dir., counsel U.S. Ho. of Reps., Washington, 1988-90, house com. on sci., chief dem. counsel, 1990—. Bd. dirs. Glen Echo (Md.) Park Found., 1991. Democrat. Avocations: computing, bicycling. Home: 6000 Harvard Ave Glen Echo MD 20812-1114 Office: Com on Sci 822 O'Neill HOB Washington DC 20515

RODEN, DAN MARK, cardiologist, medical educator; b. Montreal, Can., Apr. 15, 1950; came to U.S., 1978; s. Rudolph George and Eva (Vonchovsky) R.; m. Rosemary Wetherill, Dec. 29, 1972; children: Mark McKenzie, Paul Joseph, Rosemary Claire. BSc, McGill U., 1970, MD, 1974. Diplomate Am. Bd. Internal Medicine, Am. Bd. Cardiovascular Disease, Am. Bd. Clinical Cardiac Electrophysiology, Am. Bd. Clinical Pharmacology; Lic. physician, Quebec, Canada and Tenn.; Cert. Med. Coun. of Canada, Nat. Bd. Med. Examiners. Intern Royal Victoria Hosp., Montreal, Can., 1974-75, resident, 1975-76, 77-78; pvt. practice Montreal, Can., 1976-77; rsch. fellow clin. pharmacology Vanderbilt U., Nashville, 1978-81, fellow cardiol., 1980-81, asst. prof., 1981-85, assoc. prof., 1985-89, prof. Med. and Pharmacology, 1989—, also dir. divsn. clin. pharmacology, 1992—; del. 4th U.S.-USSR Symposium on Sudden Death, Birmingham, Ala., 1985; mem. Nat. VA Merit Review Cardiovasc. Disease com., 1986-88, chmn. 1988-89; ad hoc reviewer, Pharmacology Study and Cardiovasc. and Pulmonary Study sects., NIH, mem. Cardiovasc. and Pulmonary Study sect., 1991-94, chmn. 1994-96; adv. panel cardiovasc. and renal drugs, U.S. Phamacopeial Conv., 1990-95; mem. external adv. com., Pharmacological Scis. Tng. Grant, Columbia U., 1992—; mem. Clin. Cardiac Electrophysiology Test Writing com., Am. Bd. Internal Medicine, 1992—; mem. adv. com., Vanderbilt Clin Rsch. Ctr., 1989-91, chmn. 91-92, faculty appointments and promotions, Vanderbilt U. Dept. Med., 1992-95; mem. instl. review bd., Vanderbilt U. Dept. Health Scis., 1991-93, chmn. 1993-94. Author 27 book chpts., over 150 abstracts and 130 articles to profl. jours.; mem. editl. bd. Jour. Cardiovasc. Electrophys., 1990—; mem. adv. bd. The Med. Letter (newsletter), 1991—. Fellow Am. Coll. Physicians, Am. Coll. Cardiology (annual scientific session program com. 1992-93), Royal Coll. Physicians of Can.; mem. Am. Fedn. Clin. Rsch., Am. Soc. Clin. Pharmacology Therapeutics (bd. dirs. 1994—, chmn. cardiovasc. and pulmonary sect., 1995—), North Am. Soc. Pacing and Electrophysiol., Cardiac Electrophysiol. Soc., Biophysical Soc., Am. Soc. Pharmacol. and Experimental Therapeutics, So. Soc. Clin. Investigation, Am. Soc. Clin. Investigation, Am. Heart Assn. (clinician-sci.t award, 1981-86, long-range planning com. 1995—, basic sci. coun. exec. com. 1995—). Office: Vanderbilt U 532B Medical Rsch Bldg I Nashville TN 37232-6602

RODENBACH, EDWARD FRANCIS, lawyer; b. Phillipsburg, N.J., Apr. 16, 1951; s. L. Ernst and Harriett T. (Reinbold) R.; m. Joanne B. Pursell, Aug. 18, 1973; children: Megan, Kyle. AB, Lafayette Co., Easton, Pa., 1973; JD, Cornell U., 1976. Bar: Conn. 1976, U.S. Dist. Ct. Conn. 1976, U.S. Tax Ct. 1976. Assoc. Cummings & Lockwood, Stamford, Conn., 1976-84, ptnr., 1984-87; ptnr. in charge fiduciary acctg. group, 1984-90; ptnr. Cummings & Lockwood, Greenwich, Conn., 1987—, mng. ptnr. Greenwich office, 1988—; v.p., mem. exec. com. Cummings & Lockwood, 1988—, mem. fin. com., 1993—. Mem. stewardship com. 1st Congl. Ch., Ridgefield, Conn., 1987-90, chmn. 1988-90; mem. endowment com. YMCA of Ridgefield, 1986-90. Mem. ABA (estates and real property sect.), Conn. Bar Assn. (estates and probate sect.), Estate Planning Coun. Lower Fairfield County (exec. com. 1985-89, pres. 1988-89). Republican. Avocation: skiing. Home: 44 Golf Ln Ridgefield CT 06877-4819 Office: Cummings & Lockwood 2 Greenwich Plz Greenwich CT 06830-6353

RODENBERGER, CHARLES ALVARD, aerospace engineer, consultant; b. Muskogee, Okla., Sept. 11, 1926; s. Darcy Owen and Kathryn Martha (Percival) R.; m. Molcie Lou Halsell, Sept. 3, 1949; children: Kathryn Sue Wilcox, Charles Mark. Student, U. Ark., 1944-45; B.S. in Gen. Engring., Okla. State U., 1948; M.S.M.E., So. Meth. U., 1959; Ph.D. in Aero. Engring., U. Tex.-Austin, 1968. Registered profl. engr., Tex. Petroleum engr. Amoco Oil Co., Levelland, Tex., 1948-51; chief engr. McGregor Bros., Odessa, Tex., 1953; petroleum engr. Gen. Crude Oil Co., Hamlin, Tex., 1954; sr. design engr. Gen. Dynamics, Ft. Worth, 1954-60; aerospace engr. NASA, Houston, summer 1962; prof. aerospace engring. Tex. A&M U., College Station, 1960-82, prof. emeritus, 1982—; chmn. bd. Meiller Research, Inc., College Station, 1967-82; pres. JETS, Inc., N.Y.C., 1977-79; cons. Southwest Research Inst., Gen. Motors Corp., Gen. Dynamics. Patentee hypervelocity gun and orthotic device. Served with USAAF, 1945; served with USAF, 1951-53. NSF fellow, 1964-65; recipient Disting. Teaching award Tex. A&M U., 1962. Fellow AIAA (assoc.); mem. Nat. Soc. Profl. Engrs. (v.p. 1980-81), Tex. Soc. Profl. Engrs., ASME, Am. Soc. for Engring. Edn., Sigma Xi. Methodist. Home: HC 85 Box 60 Baird TX 79504-9603

RODENKIRK, ROBERT FRANCIS, JR., journalist; b. Evanston, Ill., Apr. 28, 1952; s. Robert Francis and Joan Marie (Wolter) R. BA in History and Journalism, Ind. U., 1974; postgrad., Northwestern U., 1976. Program dir., pub. affairs dir. WIUS Radio, Bloomington, Ind., 1972-74; reporter City News Bur. of Chgo., 1974-77; news dir. WNUR Radio, Evanston, Ill., 1977; announcer WDHF Radio, Chgo., 1977; news dir. WMET Radio, Chgo., 1977-78; Chgo. corr. AP Radio Network, 1978-79; reporter, anchor WINS Radio, N.Y.C., 1984-88, WMAQ Radio, Chgo., 1979-84, 88—. Recipient Nat. Broadcast awards UPI, 1979, 81, 83, 90, Nat. award Sigma Delta Chi, 1996, others. Mem. Ill. News Broadcasters Assn. (bd. dirs. 1988—, v.p. 1994-96, pres. 1996—), Soc. Profl. Journalists, Radio-TV News Dirs. Assn., Chgo. Headline Club (bd. dirs. 1993—, pres.-elect 1995-96, pres. 1996—, Peter Lisagor award 1988, 96), Branford Electric Ry. Assn., Ill. Ry. Mus., Fox River Trolley Mus. (publicity dir.). Roman Catholic. Avocations: railroading, bicycling. Office: WMAQ Radio News 455 N Cityfront Plaza Dr Chicago IL 60611-5503

RODER, RONALD ERNEST, accountant; b. Milw., Nov. 8, 1948; m. Marilyn L. Frederick, June 13, 1970; children: Lori A., Ronald J. BBA, U. Wis., 1970. CPA, Wis. Fin. svcs. officer U. Wis., Milw., 1970-73; asst. v.p. 1st Wis. Corp., Milw., 1973-79; sr. v.p., contr. 1st Wis. Nat. Bank, Madison, 1979-87; 1st v.p. mergers and acquisitions 1st Wis. Corp., Milw., 1987-88; sr. v.p. info. svcs. 1st Wis. Nat. Bank, Milw., 1988-89; pres. Firstar Info. Svcs. Corp., Milw., 1990—. Mem. Wis. Inst. CPAs. Office: Firstar Info Svcs Corp 16900 W Capitol Dr Brookfield WI 53005-2188

RODERICK, RICHARD MICHAEL, petroleum distribution and real estate company financial executive; b. Buffalo, Oct. 18, 1948; m. Patricia Suzanne Rosick, Oct. 2, 1971; children: Kristina, Thomas, Carolyn. BBA in Acctg., U. Notre Dame, 1970; MS in Computer Systems Mgmt., U.S. Naval Postgrad. Sch., 1971; postgrad., Harvard U., 1984; MBA, U. Maine, 1985. CPA, Maine. Acct. Arthur Young & Co., Portland, Maine, 1976-79; corp. contr. Dead River Co., Bangor, Maine, 1979-87, v.p., contr., 1987-90, v.p., CFO, treas., 1990-94, v.p., CFO, v.p. real estate, 1994—. Bd. dirs., exec. com. United Way of Penobscot Valley, 1990-94, pres. 1992-94. Lt. USN, 1970-76. Mem. Greater Bangor C. of C. (bd. dirs. 1989-94, treas. 1991-92), Diocese of Portland Fin. Com. Roman Catholic. Office: Dead River Co 55 Broadway Bangor ME 04401-5201

RODERICK, ROBERT LEE, aerospace executive; b. Chgo., Oct. 19, 1925; s. Albert Lee and Betha Manilla (Powers) R.; m. Lisa Wolf, Dec. 28, 1950; children: Diane Gale, Robert Kirk. Student, Iowa State U., 1943; BSEE, Ill. Inst. Tech., 1948; PhD, Brown U., 1951. V.p. Litton Industries, Beverly Hills, Calif., 1968-73; group v.p. Hughes Aircraft Co., Canoga Park, Calif., 1973-87; v.p. corp. tech. ctrs. Hughes Aircraft Co., L.A., 1987-90. Patentee instanteous vertical speed indicator. With USN, 1943-46. Recipient Spl. Recognition award Ill. Inst. Tech., 1967, named to Hall of Fame, 1983; recipient Pub. Svc. award NASA, 1967, Am. Machinist's award Am. Machinists Assn., 1970. Mem. Assn. U.S. Army, Am. Def. Preparedness Assn., Sigma Xi, Tau Beta Phi, Eta Kappa Nu. Avocations: tennis, personal computing. Home: 3426 Alginet Dr Encino CA 91436-4124

RODERICK, WILLIAM RODNEY, academic administrator; b. Chgo., Aug. 6, 1933; s. William Forrest and June Hazel (Kurtz) R.; m. Dorothy Jean Paetel, Oct. 21, 1965. BS in Chemistry, Northwestern U., 1954; SM in Chemistry, U. Chgo., 1955, PhD in Chemistry, 1957. Prof. chemistry U. Fla., Gainesville, 1958-62; rsch. chemist Abbott Labs., North Chicago, Ill., 1962-71; prof. chemistry Roosevelt U., Chgo., 1972—; assoc. dean acad. affairs Roosevelt U., Arlington Heights, Ill., 1993—. Mem. AAAS, Am. Chem. Soc. (Tour Speaker of Yr. award 1969, 71), Sigma Xi, Phi Beta Kappa. Home: 15193 W Redwood Ln Libertyville IL 60048-1447 Office: Roosevelt U 1651 McConnor Pkwy Schaumburg IL 60173-4344

RODGERS, AGGIE GUERARD, costume designer; m. Peter Laxton; children: James, Thomas. Grad., Fresno State Coll., 1967; MA in Theatre Arts, Calif. State U., Long Beach. Former wardrobe supr. Am. Conservatory Theatre, San Francisco. Costume designer: (films) American Graffiti, 1973, The Conversation, 1974, One Flew Over the Cuckoo's Nest, 1975, Corvette Summer, 1978, More American Graffiti, 1979, Return of the Jedi, 1983, The Adventures of Buckaroo Banzai: Across the 8th Dimension, 1983, Pee Wee's Big Adventure, 1985, Warning Sign, 1985, Cocoon, 1985, The Color Purple, 1985 (Acad. Award nomination best costume design 1985), Fatal Beauty, 1987, Leonard Part VI, 1987, The Witches of Eastwick, 1987, *batteries not included, 1987, My Stepmother is an Alien, 1988, Beetlejuice, 1988, I Love You to Death, 1989, In Country, 1989, Forever Young, 1992, Grand Canyon, 1992, Benny and Joon, 1993, The Fugitive, 1993. Office: care Lawrence Mirisch The Mirisch Agency 10100 Santa Monica Blvd Los Angeles CA 90067-4011*

RODGERS, BERNARD F., JR., academic administrator, dean; b. Hazleton, Pa., Mar. 21, 1947; s. Bernard F. and Anna V. (Gulla) R.; m. Patricia Hick, Dec. 6, 1969 (div. June, 1982); m. Jane Powell, Oct. 27, 1984. BS in English and Edn., Mt. St. Mary's Coll., 1969; MA in English, U. Bridgeport, 1972; PhD in English with honors, U. Chgo., 1975. Tchr. Eng., dir. drama Somers Ctrl. High Sch., Lincolndale, N.Y., 1969-72; seminar coord. Shakespeare Inst. U. Bridgeport, 1972; lectr. Am. Lit. U. Chgo. Extension, 1975; instr., asst. prof. lit. and humanities City Colls. Chgo., 1975-82, spl. asst. to chancellor, 1984-85; faculty Eng. Simon's Rock Coll. of Bard, Great Barrington, Mass., 1985—, dean acad. affairs, 1985-87, v.p., dean, 1987—; chair lit. and humanities sect. coll. accreditation program Chgo. City-Wide Coll., 1977-78, chair coll. acceleration program, 1977-78, mem. adminstrv. coun., 1980-81; bd. overseers Simon's Rock Coll. of Bard, 1987—; evaluator NEH Summer Insts. H.S. English Tchrs., 1985, 86; proposal evaluator Fund for Empowerment Postsecondary Edn., 1984; mem. planning com. humanists Write On, Chgo., 1982-83; mem. nom. com. Eisenhower Fellowship, Am. Embassy, Warsaw, Poland, 1980; mem. writing panel artists-in-residence program Chgo. Coun. Fine Arts, 1978. Author: Philip Roth: A Bibliography, 1974, 2d edit., 1984, Philip Roth, 1978, Contemporary American Fiction 1944-79: A Chronology, 1980; essayist, reviewer in field; contbr. essays, reviews Art in Review, 1980-85; assoc. prodr. TV talk show U. Chgo., 1974-75, prodr., 1975-76; prodr., host interview program City Colls. Chgo., 1981-82; spkr. in field. Bd. dirs. Fairview Hosp., Great Barrington, Mass. Found. for Humanities, chair, 1992-94, vice chair, 1991-92, chair program com., 1990-92, Friends of Chgo. Pub. Libr., 1982; mem. South County cabinet Berkshires United Way, 1988, mem. planning com. humanists Read Ill., 1984-85, ad hoc com. excellence Ill. C.C. Trustees Assn., 1984-85. U. Chgo. fellow, 1973, Ford Found. fellow, 1974-75, Fulbright-Hays sr. lectr. to Poland, 1979-80, Chgo. Pub. Libr. assoc. scholar, 1976-78. Mem. So. Berkshire C. of C. (bd. dirs. 1987-90), New Eng. Assn. Schs. and Colls. (evaluation team chair commn. instns. higher edn. 1986—), North Ctrl. Assn. Colls. and Schs. (asst. dir. commn. instns. higher edn 1982-84), Soc. Midland Authors (chair fiction award com. 1985), Lambda Iota Tau, Pi Delta Epsilon, Delta Epsilon Sigma. Home: PO Box 778 Great Barrington MA 01230-0778 Office: Simon's Rock Coll of Bard 84 Alford Rd Great Barrington MA 01230-1559

RODGERS, BILLY RUSSELL, chemical engineer, research scientist; b. Fitzgerald, Ga., Sept. 5, 1936; s. Jimmie R. and Ruby Doris (Morris) R.; divorced; children: Cheryl, Donna, Angie, Rusty. AA, U. Fla., 1956, BSChemE with high honors, 1966, MS in Engring., 1967; PhD, U. Tenn., 1980. Project leader Shell Devel. Co., 1968-72; group leader Keene Corp. Fluid Handling, Cookeville, Tenn., 1972-74, Oak Ridge (Tenn.) Nat. Lab., 1974-92; sr. engr. Walk Haydel & Assocs., New Orleans, 1992-94; pres. Rodgers USA Enterprises, Orange Park, Fla., 1992—, Intelligent Cons., Orange Park, 1993—. Author 3 books in field; contbr. articles to profl. publs. Fellow AIChE (bd. dirs. 1993-97, chmn. fuels and petrochem. divsn. 1992-95, chmn. program com. fuels and petrochem. divsn. 1990-92). Republican. Achievements include 1 patent in field. Avocation: computers. Office: Rodgers USA Enterprises 794 Foxridge Center Dr Orange Park FL 32065

RODGERS, DANIEL TRACY, history educator; b. Darby, Pa., Sept. 29, 1942; s. Oliver Eliot and Dorothy (Welch) R.; m. Irene Wylie, 1971; children: Peter Samuel, Dwight Oliver. AB, BS in Engring., Brown U., 1965; PhD in History, Yale U., 1973. Instr. history U. Wis., Madison, 1971-73, asst. prof., 1973-78, assoc. prof., 1978-80; assoc. prof. history Princeton (N.J.) U., 1980-86, prof., 1986—, chair, 1988-95; Fulbright lectr., Frankfurt, Fed. Republic Germany, 1983-84. Author: The Work Ethic in Industrial America, 1860-1920 (Frederick Jackson Turner award 1978), 1978, Contested Truths: Keywords in American Politics since Independence, 1987. Recipient Chancellor's award U. Wis., Madison, 1978; Am. Coun. Learned Socs. fellow, 1976, NEH fellow, 1987-88, Ctr. for Advanced Study in Behavioral Scis. fellow, 1991-92. Office: Princeton U Dept History Princeton NJ 08544

RODGERS, EUGENE, writer; b. Bklyn., July 22, 1939; s. Thomas Aquinas and Catherine (Slattery) R.; m. Carol Diane Huber, 1977; children: Eric Eugene, Catherine Huber. BS, Villanova U., 1961; postgrad., U. Wis., 1961-63; MS, Va. Commonwealth U., 1991. Research asst. sci. writing U. Wis., Madison, 1961-63; pub. info. officer U.S. Antarctic Research Program, 1963-65; freelance writer Washington, 1965-67; mgr. sci. pub. relations Westinghouse Electric Corp., Pitts., 1967-75; editor Atomic Indsl. Forum Inc., Washington, 1975-76; speechwriter ERDA, Washington, 1976, IBM, Armonk, N.Y., 1977-79, United Techs. Corp., Hartford, Conn., 1979-82; free-lance writer, 1982-84; sr. writer Virginia Power, Richmond, VA, 1984-87; editor, pub. Electric RD&D Newsletter, Midlothian, Va., 1987-88; freelance writer Midlothian, 1988—; adj. instr. Va. Commonwealth U., Richmond, 1991-92. Author: Beyond the Barrier: The Story of Byrd's First Expedition to Antarctica, 1990. Home: 2621 Ellesmere Dr Midlothian VA 23113-3939

RODGERS, FRAN SUSSNER, human services administrator, entrepreneur; b. N.Y.C., Dec. 14, 1946; m. Charles Rodgers, May 2, 1971. BA, Barnard Coll., 1967; MA, Tufts U., 1971; cert., Mass. Gen. Hosp., 1971. Cons. Edn. Devel. Ctr., Newton, Mass.; tng. specialist U.S. Dept. Health and Human Svcs.; fed. adminstr. N.J. and N.Y. Child Care and Community programs; CEO Work/Family Directions, Inc., Boston; mem. Mass. Children's Lobby. Contbr. articles to profl. jours. Bd. dirs. Child Action Campaign; mem. bd. of overseers Stone Ctr. at Wellesley Coll.; mem. Horizons Initiative; entrepreneurial adv. bd. Babson Coll.; mem. com. of 200; mem. Internat. Women's Forum;. Recipient Bus. of the Yr. award Am. Soc. on Aging, 1995; named Socially Responsible Entrepreneur of the Yr. Inc. Mag., 1994. Fellow Nat. Acad. of Human Resources.

RODGERS, FRANK, librarian; b. Darlington, Eng., July 28, 1927; came to U.S., 1956; s. Charles Bede and Frances (Page) R.; m. Sarah Louise Edelson, Dec. 18, 1971; children: Hilda Marie, Norah Frances. BA with honors, King's Coll., U. Durham, 1947; diploma librarianship, London U., 1952. Libr. Poplar Tech. Coll., London, 1951-53, St. Martin's Sch. Art, 1953-56; sr. libr. adult svcs. divsn. Akron (Ohio) Pub. Libr., 1956-59; asst. reference libr. U. Ill., 1959-64; chief reference libr., then asst. dir. pub. svcs. Pa. State U. Librs., 1965-69; dir. Portland (Oreg.) State U. Libr., 1969-79; dir. librs. U. Miami, Fla., 1979—; mem. Oreg. adv. coun. librs., 1973-74 ; bd. dirs. Pacific N.W. Bibliog. Ctr., 1973-77; tech. adv. com. librs. Columbia Regional Assn. Govts., 1976-79; vis. fellow U. Southampton, Eng., 1975-76; pres. Oreg. Libr. Assn., 1974-75; mem. nominating com. Southeastern Libr. Network, 1984-85; bd. dirs. S.E. Fla. Libr. Info. Network, 1984—, pres. 1991-92; mem. exec. coun. Assn. Caribbean U. Rsch. and Instl. Librs., 1985-88; chmn. local organizing com. for 1981 and 1987 confs. in Miami; mem. Fla. Libr. Network Coun., 1985—, NEH challenge grant rev. panel, 1987, Howard U. ann. inspection team, 1989, Reaffirmation com., Tex. Christian U., 1993. Author, editor various libr. publs., guides. Sr. fellow Grad. Sch. Libr. and Info. Sci. UCLA, 1983; grantee Coun. Libr. Resources, 1975-76. Fellow Libr. Assn. U.K.; mem. ALA, Assn. Rsch. Librs. (office mgmt. studies adv. com. 1981-83, stats. and measurements com. 1993—), Assn. Specialized and Coop. Libr. Agys. (membership promotion com. 1994—, chair 1990 program com.), Assn. Southeastern Rsch. Librs. (chmn. membership com. 1982—). Home: 5630 Twin Lakes Dr Miami FL 33143-2038 Office: U Miami Library Coral Gables FL 33124

RODGERS, FREDERIC BARKER, judge; b. Albany, N.Y., Sept. 29, 1940; s. Prentice Johnson and Jane (Weed) R.; m. Valerie McNaughton, Oct. 8, 1988; 1 child: Gabriel Moore. AB, Amherst Coll., 1963; JD, Union U., 1966. Bar: N.Y. 1966, U.S. Ct. Mil. Appeals 1968, Colo. 1972, U.S. Supreme Ct. 1974, U.S. Ct. Appeals (10th cir.) 1981. Chief dep. dist. atty., Denver, 1972-73; commr. Denver Juvenile Ct., 1973-79; mem. Mulligan Reeves Teasley & Joyce, P.C., Denver, 1979-80; pres. Frederic B. Rodgers, P.C., Breckenridge, Colo., 1980-89; ptnr. McNaughton & Rodgers, Central City, Colo., 1989-91; county ct. judge County of Gilpin, 1987—; presiding mcpl. judge cities of Breckenridge, Blue River, Black Hawk, Central City, Edgewater, Empire, Idaho Springs and Westminster, Colo., 1978-95; chmn. com. on mcpl. ct. rules of procedure Colo. Supreme Ct., 1984—; mem. gen. faculty Nat. Jud. Coll. U. Nev., Reno, 1990—, elected to faculty coun., 1994—. Author: (with Dilweg, Fretz, Murphy and Wicker) Modern Judicial Ethics, 1992; contbr. articles to profl. jours. Mem. Colo. Commn. on Children, 1982-85, Colo. Youth Devel. Coun., 1989—, Colo. Family Peace Task Force, 1994—. Served with JAGC, U.S. Army, 1967-72; to maj. USAR, 1972-88. Decorated Bronze Star with oak leaf cluster, Air medal. Recipient Outstanding County Judge award Colo. 17th Judicial Dist. Victim Adv. Coalition, 1991; Spl. Community Service award Colo. Am. Legion, 1979. Mem. ABA (jud. adminstrn. div. exec. coun. 1989—, ho. dels. 1993—), Colo. Bar Assn. (bd. govs. 1986-88, 90-92, 93—), Continental Divide Bar Assn., Denver Bar Assn. (bd. trustees 1979-82), First Jud. Dist. Bar Assn., Nat. Conf. Spl. Ct. Judges (chmn. 1989-90), Colo. County Judges Assn. (pres. 1995—), Colo. Mcpl. Judges Assn. (pres. 1986-87), Colo. Trial Judges Coun. (v.p. 1995—), Denver Law Club (pres. 1981-82), Colo. Women's Bar Assn., Am. Judicature Soc., Nat. Coun. Juvenile and Family Ct. Judges, Univ. Club (Denver), Arlberg Club (Winter Park), Marines Meml. Club (San Francisco), Westminster Rotary Club. Episcopalian. Office: Gilpin County Justice Ctr 2960 Dory Hill Rd Golden CO 80403

RODGERS, JAMES FOSTER, association executive, economist; b. Columbus, Ga., Jan. 15, 1951; s. Laban Jackson and Martha (Jackson) R.; m. Cynthia Lynne Bathurst, Aug. 20, 1975. B.A., U. Ala., Tuscaloosa, 1973; Ph.D., U. Iowa, 1980. Fed. intern Office Rsch. and Stats., Social Security Adminstrn., Washington, 1976-77; rsch. assoc. Ctr. Health Policy Rsch., AMA, Chgo., 1979-80, rsch. dir., 1980-82, asst. to dep. exec. v.p. AMA, 1982-85; dir. AMA Ctr. Health Policy Rsch., Chgo., 1985—. Contbr. articles on health econs. to profl. jours. Pharm. Mfrs. Assn. grantee, 1978; NSF grantee, 1978; Hohenberg fellow, 1969-70. Mem. Am. Econ. Assn., Am. Soc. Assn. Exec., Am. Statis. Assn., So. Econ. Assn., Western Econ. Assn. Home: 2233 N Orchard St Chicago IL 60614-3713 Office: AMA Ctr for Health Policy Rsch 515 N State St Chicago IL 60610-4320

RODGERS, JOHN, geologist, educator; b. Albany, N.Y., July 11, 1914; s. Henry D. and Louise W. (Allen) R. B.A., Cornell U., 1936, M.S., 1937; Ph.D., Yale U., 1944. Geologist, U.S. Geol. Survey, 1938-46, intermittently, 1946-95; sci. cons. U.S. Army Engrs., 1944-46; instr. geology Yale U., New Haven, 1946-47; asst. prof. Yale U., 1947-52, asso. prof., 1952-59, prof., 1959-62, Silliman prof., 1962-85, Silliman prof. emeritus, 1985—; vis. lectr. Coll. de France, Paris, 1960; sec.-gen. commn. on stratigraphy Internat. Geol. Congress, 1952-60; commr. Conn. Geol. and Natural History Survey, 1960-71. Author: (with C.O. Dunbar) Principles of Stratigraphy, 1957, The Tectonics of the Appalachians, 1970; also articles in field.; editor Symposium on the Cambrian System, 3 vols., 1956, 61; recording artist: (with W. Ruff) The Harmony of the World, 1979; asst. editor Am. Jour. Sci., 1948-54, editor, 1954—. NSF Sr. postdoctoral fellow France, 1959-60; exchange visitor Geol. Inst., Acad. Scis. USSR, 1967; Guggenheim fellow Australia, 1973-74; recipient Medal of Freedom U.S. Army, 1947, James Hall medal N.Y. State Geol. Survey, 1986; exchange scholar Inst. of Geology Academia Sinica (Beijing) 1986; recipient Médaille Paul Fourmarier Académie Royale des Sciences, Lettres et Beaux-Arts de Belgique, 1987, William Clyde DeVane medal Phi Beta Kappa, 1990. Fellow AAAS, Geol. Soc. Am. (councillor 1962-65, pres. 1970, Penrose medal 1981), Am. Geophys. Union; mem. NAS, Am. Acad. Arts and Scis., Am. Assn. Petroleum Geologists, Conn. Acad. Sci. and Engring. (charter), Conn. Acad. Arts and Scis. (pres. 1969), Geol. Soc. London (hon.), Société géologique de France (assoc. mem., v.p. 1960, Prix Gaudry 1987), Am. Philos. Soc., Russian Acad. Scis. (hon. fgn. mem.), Academia Real de Ciencias y Artes Barcelona (fgn. corr. mem.), Sigma Xi, Phi Beta Kappa. Club: Elizabethan (New Haven). Office: Dept Geology Yale U P O Box 208109 New Haven CT 06520-8109

RODGERS, JOHN JOSEPH, III, school administrator; b. Jamaica, N.Y., Oct. 13, 1941; s. John Joseph Jr. and Edith (McInerney) R.; children: Janet, John Joseph IV. BS, Fordham U., 1962; Profl. diploma, St. Johns U., 1970, EdD, 1979; postgrad., CUNY, Flushing. Asst. prin. N.Y.C. Bd. Edn., 1972-82; prin. Howard T. Herber Sch., Malverne, N.Y., 1982-85, Norman Thomas High Sch., N.Y.C., 1988—. Mem. ASCD, Nat. Assn. Secondary Sch. Prins. Home: PO Box 1491 New York NY 10156-1491 Office: 111 E 33 St New York NY 10016

RODGERS, LAWRENCE RODNEY, physician, educator; b. Clovis, N.Mex., Mar. 9, 1920; s. Samuel Frank and Lillian (O'Connor) R.; m. Ivy Lorna Piper, Aug. 6, 1943; children: Lawrence Rodney (dec.), Ivy Elizabeth, George Piper. B.S., West Tex. State U., 1940; M.D., U. Tex., 1943. Diplomate Am. Bd. Internal Medicine. Intern Phila. Gen. Hosp., 1943-44, resident in medicine, 1946-49; assoc. internist Tumor Inst., U. Tex. M.D. Anderson Hosp., Houston, 1949—; chmn. dept. medicine Hermann Hosp., Houston, 1966-71; assoc. prof. clin. medicine Baylor U., 1949—; prof. clin. medicine U. Tex., 1972—. Editor: Harris County Physician, 1976-80. Bd. dirs. Tex. Med. Found.; trustee Houston Mus. Med. Sci., 1981. Served to maj. M.C. AUS, 1944-46. Decorated Bronze Star with two oak leaf clusters; recipient Ashbel Smith Disting. Alumnus award U. Tex. Med. Br.-Galveston, 1993, Mastership award Am. Coll. Physicians, 1996. Fellow ACP (gov. for Tex. 1979-83, Laureate Internist Tex. award 1994); mem. AMA (del.), Harris County Med. Soc. (exec. bd. 1978-82, v.p. 1984), Am. Heart Assn., Houston Soc. Internal Medicine (pres. 1974), Houston Acad. Medicine (pres. 1981), Houston Philos. Soc. (pres. 1993-94), Doctor's Club Houston (bd. govs. 1984-88, pres. 1986).

RODGERS, MARY COLUMBRO, academic administrator, English educator, author; b. Aurora, Ohio, Apr. 17, 1925; d. Nicola and Nancy (DeNicola) Columbro; m. Daniel Richard Rodgers, July 24, 1965; children: Robert, Patricia, Kristine. AB, Notre Dame Coll., 1957; MA, Western Res. U., 1962; PhD, Ohio State U., 1964; postgrad., U. Rome, 1964-65; EdD, Calif. Nat. Open U., 1975, DLitt, 1978. Tchr. English Cleve. elem. schs., 1945-52, Cleve. secondary schs., 1952-62; supr. English student tchrs. Ohio State U., 1962-64; asst. prof. English U. Md., 1965-66; assoc. prof. Trinity Coll., 1967-68; prof. English D.C. Tchrs. Coll., 1968—; pres. Md. Nat. U., 1972—; chancellor Am. Open U., 1965—; dean Am. Open U. Acad. Author numerous books and monographs, latest works include: A Short Course in English Composition, 1976, Chapbook of Children's Literature, 1977, Comprehensive Catalogue: The Open University of America System, 1978-80, Open University of America System Source Book, V, VI, VII, 1978, Essays and Poems on Life and Literature, 1979, Modes and Models: Four Lessons for Young Writers, 1981, Open University Structures and Adult Learning, 1982, Papers in Applied English Linguistics, 1982, Twelve Lectures on the American Open University, 1982, English Pedagogy in the American Open University, 1983, Design for Personalized English Graduate Degrees in the Urban University, 1984, Open University English Teaching, 1945-85: Conceptual History and Rationale, 1985, Claims and Counterclaims Regarding Instruction Given in Personalized Degree Residency Programs Completed by Graduates of California National Open University, 1986, The American Open University, 1965 t0 1985: History and Sourcebook, 1986, New Design II: English Pedagogy in the American Open University, 1987, The American Open University, 1965 to 1985: A Research Report, 1987, The American Open University and Other Open Universities: A Comparative Study Report, 1988, Poet and Pedagogue in Moscow and Leningrad: A Travel Report, 1989, Foundations of English Scholarship in the American Open University, 1989, Twelve Lectures in Literary Analysis, 1990, Ten Lectures in Literary Production, 1990, Analyzing Fact and Fiction, 1991, Analyzing Poetry and Drama, 1991, Some Successful Literary Research Papers: An Inventory of Titles and Theses, 1991, A Chapbook of Poetry and Drama Analysis, 1992, Convent Poems, 1943-61, 93, Fables for Fiction Analysis, 3d edit., 1993, First Access List to the Open University Literary Trust, 1993, Catholic Marriage Poems, 1962-79, 1993, New Design Responses 1945-1993, 10 vols., 1993, Catholic Widow with Children Poems, 1979-93, 1994, Journals: Reflections and Resolves, 1984-1995, 16 vols., 1995, Biographical Sourcebook: Mary Columbro Rodgers, 1969-1995, 1995, Catholic Teacher Poems, 1945-1995, 1995, Second Access List to the Mary Columbor Rodgers Literary Trust, 1995. Fulbright scholar U. Rome, 1964-65. Fellow Cath. Scholars; mem. Poetry Soc. Am., Nat. Coun. Tchrs. English, Am. Ednl. Rsch. Assn., Am. Acad. Poets, Ohioana Libr. Assn., Friends John Henry Newman Assn., Writer's Ctr. Md., Pi Lambda Theta. Home and Office: Coll Heights Estates 3916 Commander Dr Hyattsville MD 20782-1027 *My life as a Catholic scholar has focused on the literate and humane. Both as a student and as a scholar I have made my work a disciplined commitment to English literature, English language, and English pedagogy. My life's goal has been the effective, everyday transmission of humane values defined in my Catholic heritage to younger generations through my teaching, research and writing. My epitaph should read: She saw with the writer's eye and worked with the scholar's tools before she spoke with the teacher's tongue.*

RODGERS, NANCY LUCILLE, corporate executive; b. Denver, Aug. 22, 1934; d. Francis Randolph and Irma Lucille (Budy) Baker; student public schs.; m. George J. Rodgers, Feb. 18, 1968; children by previous marriage: Kellie Rae, Joy Lynn, Timothy Francis, Thomas Francis. Mgr., Western Telearm, Inc., San Diego, 1973-93; pres. Rodgers Police Patrol, Inc., San Diego, 1973-80; br. mgr. Honeywell Inc., Protection Services div., San Diego, 1977-80; pres. Image, Inc., Image Travel Agy., Cairo, Egypt, 1981-83, Western Solar Specialties, 1979-80; founder, pres. Internat. Metaphysicians Associated for Growth through Edn., San Diego, 1979; founder, dir. Point Loma Sanctuary, 1983-86; co-founder, producer Zerciee Prodns. Unltd., 1986—, co-founder, producer, dir. mktg., 1986—; co-founder Philoe West, Breeder of Am. Bashkir Curleys. Bd. dirs. Cen. City Assn. Named Woman of Achievement Cen. City Assn., 1979. Mem. Nat. Assn. for Holistic Health, Am. Bus. Women's Assn. (Woman of Yr. 1980), Am. Union Metaphysicians, Inst. Noetic Scis., Am. Bashkir Curly Assn. Republican.

RODGERS, PAUL, lawyer, government official; b. St. Augustine, Fla., Aug. 9, 1933; m. Barbara Broadrick, July 1, 1955; 3 children. A.B., Mercer U., 1955, J.D., 1957. Bar: Ga. 1956, U.S. Supreme Ct. 1961, U.S. Ct. Appeals (5th cir.) 1964, D.C. 1968, U.S. Ct. Appeals (D.C. cir.) 1968, U.S. Ct. Appeals (4th cir.) 1970, U.S. Ct. Appeals (9th cir.) 1973, U.S. Ct. Appeals (10th cir.) 1984. Atty. Atlanta Gas Light Co., 1957-60; asst. atty. gen. State of Ga., 1960-65; adminstrv. dir., gen. counsel Nat. Assn. Regulatory Utility Commrs., Washington, 1965—. Served to 2d lt. Inf. U.S. Army, capt. Res. Mem. ABA, D.C. Bar Assn., Ga. Bar Assn., Fed. Communications Bar Assn., Fed. Power Bar Assn. Office: Nat Assn Regulatory Utility Commrs Ste 1102 1201 Constitution Ave NW Washington DC 20044-0684

RODGERS, RICHARD MALCOLM, management accountant; b. Montgomery, Ala., June 23, 1949; s. Charles Malcolm and Betty Jean (Gilbert) R.; m. Linda Joyce Meeks, Dec. 9, 1966 (div. Mar. 1970); 1 child, Angela Christina Rodgers Bolin; m. Sharon Lynn Thomas, May 10, 1992. Student, Emory U., 1967-69; BBA magna cum laude, Ga. State U., 1988. Cert. mgmt. acct. Staff acct. Charter Enterprises, Inc., College Park, Ga., 1971-72; contr. Royal Arts & Crafts, Inc., Atlanta, 1972-73; justice of peace Justice's Ct. Dist. 531, Decatur, Ga., 1973-76; chief cost acct. Gen. Assembly Mission Bd., Presbyn. Ch. U.S., Atlanta, 1974-80; internal audit mgr. Waffle House, Inc., Norcross, Ga., 1980-87; acctg. mgr. W.L. Thompson Cons. Engrs., Inc., Atlanta, 1988-90; contr. Hudson Everett Simonson Mullis & Assocs., Inc., Atlanta, 1990—; free-lance cons. and writer, 1995—. Poet, contbg. editor Archon mag., 1968-70 (Anthology award 1970); composer, lyricist: (musical play) Many a Glorious Morning, 1971; playwright, composer, lyricist: (musical play) Take the Money and Run!, 1979, 91. Exec. com. mem. DeKalb County Rep. Party, Decatur, 1969-76; v.p. Ga. Assn. Justices of the Peace and Constables, Warner Robbins, Ga., 1973-74; treas., founding dir. Ga. Bus. Com. for Arts, Inc., Atlanta, 1981-86; sec. Ga. State Poetry Soc., Inc., Atlanta, 1986 (Judge for Chapbook award 1991). Stipe scholar Emory U., 1968. Mem. AAAS, Inst. Mgmt. Accts., N.Y. Acad. Scis., Idealists Internat. (charter), The Dramatists Guild, Golden Key Nat. Honor Soc. (charter), Beta Gamma Sigma, Phi Kappa Phi. Democrat. Episcopalian. Avocations: field archeology, geophysical rsch., acting, bridge, playing jazz on trumpet. Home: 1111 Clairmont Rd # K-2 Decatur GA 30030 Office: Hudson Everett Simonson Mullis & Assocs Inc 530 Means St NW Ste One Atlanta GA 30318-5793

RODGERS, ROBERT AUBREY, physicist; b. Huntsville, Ala., May 10, 1967; s. Aubrey and Peggy Joyce (Hairald) R. BS, U. Ala., Huntsville, 1990, MS, 1992; MSHP, Ga. Inst. Tech., 1993. Grad. student physics rschr. Polarization and Lens Design Lab., U. Ala., Huntsville, 1991-92; grad. student med. physics rschr. Emory U.-Ga. Inst. Tech., Atlanta, 1992—. U. Ala.-Huntsville Honor scholar, 1988-89, scholar, 1986-87. Mem. Am. Assn. Physicists in Medicine, Biomed. Optics Soc., Internat. Soc. for Optical Engrs., Health Physics Soc. (med. sect.). Baptist. Achievements include research on development of scattering polarimeter and measurement/analysis of diffraction grating polarization and efficiency properties, validation of compton scatter and attenuation correction methods for cardiac SPECT imaging. Home: 216 Creek Trl Madison AL 35758-8586

RODGERS, STEVEN EDWARD, tax practitioner, educator; b. Pierre, S.D., Feb. 8, 1947; s. Thomas Edward and Dorothy Zoe (Barker) R.; m. Donna Lynn Joyner, June 10, 1984; 1 child, Michelle Ann. Student, State U. S.D., 1964-65, U. Calif., Berkeley, 1968-72; cert., Coll. for Fin. Planning, 1986-87; fellow, Nat. Tax Practice Inst., 1988-89. CFP, Enrolled Agent. Collection mgr. Cenval Leasing-Ctrl. Bank, Long Beach, Calif., 1972-77; tax preparer Rodgers Tax Svc., Las Vegas, 1977-78; CEO Rainbow Tax Svc. Inc., Las Vegas, 1978—; pres. Rainbow Tax Svc., Inc., Las Vegas, 1978-90. Author: Marketing To Build Your Tax Practice, 1994. Active Amnesty Internat., Mensa; chmn. Best in the West Edn. Found., Las Vegas, 1994—, Nat. Assn. Enrolled Agents Edn. Found., 1995-96. With U.S. Army, 1965-68, Vietnam. Mem. Nat. Assn. Enrolled Agts. (nat. sec. 1989-90, nat. treas. 1990-91, nat. edn. chair 1994-95, named Tax Educator of the Yr., 1995), Nat. Assn. Enrolled Agents Edn. Found. (chair 1995-96), Nev. Soc. Enrolled Agts. (charter pres. 1985-86, fellow edn. found.), So. Nev. Assn. Tax Cons. (pres. 1981-82), Nat. Soc. Pub. Accts., Vietnam Vets. Am. Home: 1101 Cahill Ave Las Vegas NV 89128-3335 Office: Rainbow Tax Svc Inc 6129 Clarice Ave Las Vegas NV 89107

RODGMAN, ALAN, chemist, consultant; b. Aberdare, Wales, Feb. 7, 1924; came to U.S., 1954, naturalized, 1961; s. Arch and Margaret (Llewellyn) R.; m. Doris Curley, June 7, 1947; children: Eric, Paul, Mark. B.A. in Chemistry, U. Toronto, 1949, M.A. in Organic Chemistry, 1951, Ph.D. in Organic Chemistry, 1953. Rsch. asst. med. rsch. dept. U. Toronto, 1947-51, rsch. assoc., 1951-54; tchr., courses in organic chemistry, phys. chemistry, math. Chem. Inst. Can., 1951-54; sr. rsch. chemist R.J. Reynolds Tobacco Co., Winston-Salem, N.C., 1954-65; head smoke rsch. sect. R.J. Reynolds Tobacco Co., 1965-75, mgr. analytical rsch., 1975-76, dir. rsch., 1976-80, dir. fundamental rsch. and devel., 1980-87; cons. in field, 1987—. Mem. editorial bd. Tobacco Sci., 1963-67 (Vol. 31 Tobacco Sci. dedicated in his name 1987), Beitrage zur Tabakforschung Internat., 1978-87. Mem. Tobacco Working Group, Nat. Cancer Inst., 1976-77, Tech. Study Group on Cigarette and Little Cigar Fire Safety, 1984-87, Sci. Commn. Cooperation Ctr. for Sci. Rsch. Relative to Tobacco, 1982-84. With Can. Navy, 1942-45. Mem. Chem. Inst. Can., Am. Chem. Soc., N.Y. Acad. Scis., N.C. Acad. Sci., Sigma Xi. Episcopalian. Club: Winston-Salem Sertoma (award 1972). Home: 2828 Birchwood Dr Winston Salem NC 27103-3410

RODIBAUGH, ROBERT KURTZ, judge; b. Elkhart County, Ind., July 2, 1916; s. Ralph Leedy and Rose (Kurtz) R.; m. Doris Ann Siekemeyer, Jan. 1, 1942 (dec.); children—David L., Bob K. m. 2d, Eunice Margaret Room, Nov. 25, 1972. B.S.C., U. Notre Dame, 1940, J.D., 1941. Bar: Ind. 1941, U.S. Dist. Ct. (no. dist.) Ind. 1946, U.S. Ct. Appeals (7th cir.) 1972, U.S. Supreme Ct. 1965. Dep. pros. atty. Ind. 60th Jud. Cir., St. Joseph County, 1948-50, 53-57; judge U.S. Bankruptcy Ct., No. Dist. Ind., South Bend, 1960—; lectr. in law U. Notre Dame, 1973; atty. St. Joseph County Bd. Zoning Appeals, 1958-60. V.p. No. Ind. council Boy Scouts Am., 1967-77; bd. dirs. St. Joseph County chpt. ARC, 1970-77. Capt. U.S. Army, 1941-46; PTO. Recipient Silver Beaver award Boy Scouts Am., 1969. Mem. ABA, Seventh Fed. Cir. Bar Assn., Ind. Bar Assn., St. Joseph County Bar Assn. (gov. 1953-56), Am. Judicature Soc., Comml. Law League, Nat. Conf. Bankruptcy Judges (dir. 1977-79), Exchange Club, Masons, DeMolay Club (Legion of Honor), Shriners. Office: US Bankruptcy Ct 204 S Main St Rm 201 South Bend IN 46601-2122

RODIMER, FRANK JOSEPH, bishop; b. Rockaway, N.J., Oct. 25, 1927; s. Frank Grant and Susan Elizabeth (Hiler) R. Student, St. Charles Coll., Catonsville, Md., 1944-45; B.A., St. Mary's Coll.-Sem., Balt., 1947; postgrad., Immaculate Conception Sem., Darlington, N.J., 1947-50; S.T.L., Cath. U. Am., 1951, J.C.D., 1954. Ordained priest Roman Catholic Ch., 1951; asst. chancellor, 1954-64, chancellor, 1964-77, apptd. papal chaplain, 1963; apptd. 6th Bishop of Paterson, N.J., 1977; consecrated 6th Bishop of Paterson, 1978, ordained, 1978—. Office: 178 Derrom Ave Clifton NJ 07540*

RODIN, ALVIN ELI, retired pathologist, medical educator, author; b. Winnipeg, Man., Can., Mar. 25, 1926; came to U.S., 1963; s. Paul and Bessie (Oretsky) R.; m. Bernice Block, Dec. 15, 1951 (div. Dec. 1973); children: Beverly, Paula, Mindy, Lisa; m. Jean Colladay, Feb. 10, 1974. MD, U. Man., Winnipeg, 1950, MSc in Medicine, 1960. Diplomate Am. Bd. Pathology, Am. Bd. Clin. Pathology. Sr. intern Shaughnessy Hosp., Vancouver, B.C., Can.; asst. resident in pathology, demonstrator in parasitology Deer Lodge Hosp., U. Man., Winnipeg, 1955-56, resident in clin. pathology, demonstrator in parasitology, 1957-58, rsch. assoc., 1958-59; resident in pathology, teaching fellow in pathology Queen's U., 1956-57; pvt. practice medicine Minitonas, Man., 1951-54; asst. pathologist Royal Alexander Hosp., Edmonton, Alta., Can., 1959-60; dir. labs. Misericordia Hosp., Edmonton, 1960-63; prof. pathology, dir. pathology edn. U. Tex. Med. Br., Galveston, 1963-75; prof. pathology, chmn. dept. postgrad. edn. Sch. Medicine, Wright State U., Dayton, Ohio, 1975-88, chmn. dept. pathology, 1976-77; dir. med. edn. Green Meml. Hosp., Xenia, Ohio, 1976-92; mem. Miami Valley Health Improvement Coun., Dayton, 1986—. Author: 11 books; contbr. numerous articles to profl. jours. Recipient Golden Apple award Student Am. Med. Assn., 1969, 73-74, Tchr. of Month award Rotary, Galveston, 1974, Outstanding Community Svc. award United Health Svcs., Dayton, 1980. Fellow Royal Soc. Medicine; mem. Am. Osler Soc. (pres. 1992), Soc. for Health and Human Values, Group for Rsch. in Pathology Edn. (pres. 1971-73), Internat. Acad. Medicine, Toastmasters (pres. Galveston club 1968-70). Home and Office: 3041 Maginn Dr Beavercreek OH 45434-5833

RODIN, JUDITH SEITZ, academic administrator, psychology educator; b. Phila., Sept. 9, 1944; d. Morris and Sally R. (Winson) Seitz. AB, U. Pa., 1966; PhD, U. Columbia, 1970. Asst. prof. psychology NYU, 1970-72; assoc. prof. Yale U., 1975-79, prof., dir. grad. studies, 1982-89, Philip R. Allen prof. psychology, medicine and psychiatry, 1984-94, chmn. dept. psychology, 1989-91, dean Grad. Sch., 1991-92, provost, 1992-94; pres. U. Pa., Phila., 1994—, prof. psychology, medicine and psychiatry, 1994—; chmn. John D. and Catherine T. MacArthur Found. Rsch. Network on Determinants and Consequences of Health-Promoting and Health-Damaging Behavior, 1983-93. Author: (with S. Schachter) Obese Humans and Rats, 1978, Exploding the Weight Myths, 1982, Body Traps, 1992; chief editor Appetite Jour., 1979-92; contbr. articles to profl. jours. Mem. Pa. Task Force on Higher Edn. Funding, 1994. Fellow Woodrow Wilson Found., 1966-67, John Simon Guggenheim Found., 1986-87; grantee NSF, 1973-82, NIH, 1981—. Fellow AAAS, Am. Acad. Arts and Scis., Am. Psychol. Assn. (bd. sci. affairs 1979-82), Soc. Behavioral Medicine; mem. Inst. Medicine of NAS, Acad. Behavioral Medicine Rsch., Ea. Psychol. Assn. (exec. bd. 1980-82, pres. divsn. 38 health psychology 1982-83, Outstanding Contbn. award 1980, Disting. Sci. award 1977), Phi Beta Kappa, Sigma Xi (pres. Yale chpt. 1986-87). Office: U Pa 121 College Hall Philadelphia PA 19104-6380

RODITE, ROBERT R.R., engineering scientist; b. Easton, Pa., Oct. 17, 1942; s. Victor James and Alice Cecilia (Zatovich) R.; m. Patricia Ann Sule, Apr. 8, 1967; children: Colleen P., Robert J. BSEE, Lafayette Coll., 1964; MSEE, Caif. Inst. Tech., 1965. Rsch. engr., mgr. mfg. rsch. lab. IBM, Endicott, N.Y., 1965-70, mfg. engring. mgr. electronic packaging mfg., 1970-72, devel. engring. mgr. electronic packaging engring., 1972-77; program dir. corp. engring., programming & tech. staff IBM, Armonk, N.Y., 1977-79; product engring. mgr., sr. engr. multichip module devel. IBM, East Fishkill, N.Y., 1979-81; system mgr., sr. tech. staff mem. fin. industry devel. IBM, Charlotte, N.C., 1981-92; sr. tech. staff mem. corp. tech. strategy devel. staff IBM, Armonk, 1992-93; pres. Rodite Assocs., Inc., Charlotte, N.C., 1993—; workgroup mem. Am. Nat. Standards Inst. Com. X9B Stds. Com., 1991—; chmn. IBM Image Processing and Visualization Interdivisional Tech. Liaison Com., 1992-93. Contbr. articles to profl. jours.; patentee in field. Asst. scoutmaster Boy Scouts Am., Charlotte, 1991, 92; mid. sch. basketball coach, Charlotte, 1991, 92, 93, 94; com. mem. Town County Consolidation Com., Endicott, 1970s; Cath. sch. bd. mem. Diocese of Charlotte, 1988-90. Tau Beta Pi fellow Calif. Inst. Tech., 1964. Mem. IEEE (sr.), Assn. for Info. and Image Mgmt. Internat., Phi Beta Kappa, Tau Beta Pi, Eta Kappa Nu. Avocations: personal computers, camping. Home: 10022 Thomas Payne Cir Charlotte NC 28277-8872

RODMAN, ALPINE CLARENCE, arts and crafts company executive; b. Roswell, N.Mex., June 23, 1952; s. Robert Elsworth and Verna Mae (Means) R.; m. Sue Arlene Lawson, Dec. 13, 1970; 1 child, Connie Lynn. Student, Colo. State U., 1970-71, U. No. Colo. Ptnr. Pinel Silver Shop, Loveland, Colo., 1965-68, salesman, 1968-71; real estate salesman Loveland, 1971-73; mgr. Traveling Traders, Phoenix, 1974-75; co-owner Deer Track Traders, Loveland, 1975-85; pres. Deer Track Traders, Ltd., 1985—. Author: The Vanishing Indian: Fact or Fiction?, 1985. Mem. Civil Air Patrol, 1965-72, 87-92, dep. comdr. for cadets, 1988-90; cadet comdr. Ft. Collins, Colo., 1968, 70, Colo. rep. to youth tng. program, 1969, U.S. youth rep. to Japan, 1970. Mem. Bur. Wholesale Sales Reps., Western and English Salesmen's Assn. (bd. dirs. 1990), Internat. Platform Assn., Indian Arts and Crafts Assn. (bd. dirs. 1988-94, exec. com. 1989-92, v.p. 1990, pres. 1991, market chmn. 1992), Crazy Horse Grass Roots Club. Republican. Office: Deer Track Traders Ltd PO Box 448 Loveland CO 80539-0448 *Personal philosophy: I believe that most good and bad in the world comes out of respect or lack of respect for one's self, fellow man, environment and creator.*

RODMAN, DENNIS KEITH, basketball player; b. Trenton, May 13, 1961. Student, Cooke County Jr. Coll., Gainesville, Tex., 1982-83, Southeastern Okla. State U., 1983-86. With Detroit Pistons, 1986-93; forward San Antonio Spurs, 1993-95, Chicago Bulls, 1995—. Author: (with Tim Keown) Bad As I Wanna Be, 1996. Named NBA Defensive Player of Yr., 1990, 91, NBA All-Defensive First Team, 1989, 90, 91, 92, 93, All-Star team, 1990, 92, NBA All-Defense Second Team, 1994; mem. NBA chmpionship team, 1989-90, 96. Office: Chgo Bulls United Ctr 1901 W Madison St Chicago IL 60612*

RODMAN, HARRY EUGENE, architect, educator, acoustical and illumination consultant; b. Plainfield, Iowa, Sept. 29, 1913; s. Harry Irwin and Iva (Reade) R.; m. Marion G. Rooney, Feb. 14, 1942; children—Harry Eugene, Bruce Ervin, Gerald Reade, Blair Douglas. B. Archtl. Engring., Iowa State U., 1936; M.Arch., Harvard, 1937. Instr. Wash. State U., 1937-41; designer Austin Co., Cleve., 1941-45; asso. architect U. Ill. at Urbana, 1945-46; mem. faculty Rensselaer Poly. Inst., 1946-78, prof. architecture, 1955-78; vis. prof. Sch. Architecture and Environ. Design, Calif. Poly. State U., 1979-82; profl. practice Troy, N.Y., 1946-78; cons. in field, 1946—; Chmn. N.Y. State Bd. Examiners Architects, 1962-64; bd. dirs. Nat. Council Archtl. Registration Bds., 1964-71, sec., 1967-71, chmn. com. exams., 1965-70; sec. Nat. Archtl. Accrediting Bd., 1969-70; mem. tech. adv. com. Illuminating Engring. Research Inst., 1972-78; mem. U.S. nat. com. Internat. Commn. on Illumination. Contbr. to profl. jours. Mem. exec. bd. Uncle Sam council Boy Scouts Am., 1956-70. Recipient Profl. Achievement citation Iowa State U., 1980. Fellow AIA (pres. Eastern N.Y. chpt. 1952, bd. dirs. 1953), Illuminating Engring. Soc.; mem. N.Y. State Assn. Architects (bd. dirs. 1954); asso. Acoustical Soc. Am.; mem. Allied Arts Com., Illuminating Engring. Soc. (vice chmn. Mohawk-Hudson sect. 1956, bd. mgrs. 1971-74), Am. Arbitration Assn. (panel constrn. arbitrators), Tau Beta Pi, Tau Sigma Delta, Scarab. Home: 196 Luneta Dr San Luis Obispo CA 93405-1552

RODMAN, JAMES PURCELL, astrophysicist, educator; b. Alliance, Ohio, Nov. 11, 1926; s. Clarence James and Hazel (Purcell) R.; m. Margaret Jane Kinsey, Aug. 14, 1950; children: William James, Jeffrey Kinsey, David Lawrence, Gretchen. B.S. in Physics, Chemistry and Math, Mt. Union Coll., 1949; M.A. in Nuclear Physics, Washington U., St. Louis, 1951; Ph.D. in Astrophysics, Yale U., 1963. Sec. Alliance Ware, Inc., 1954-55, Alliance Machine Co., 1959-69; v.p., treas. Alliance Tool Co., 1951-54, pres., 1954-59; instr. dept. physics and math. Mt. Union Coll., Alliance, 1951-59; assoc. prof. physics Mt. Union Coll., 1962-66, prof., 1966-92, head dept. physics, 1963-65, head dept. physics and astronomy, 1965-74, 77-85, staff astronomer, 1992—; dir. Clarke Obs., 1953-94, Computer Center, 1967-74, 77; coll. marshal, 1990-92, prof. emeritus, 1993; rsch. assoc. astronomy Yale U., 1963-68, rsch. fellow, 1982; cons. astrophys. engr. astron. instrumentation, 1962—; chief engr., owner Rodman Rsch., 1988—; v.p. and chmn. bd. Westmont Inc., 1984—; bd. dirs. United Nat. Bank & Trust Co., Canton, Ohio, 1964—, United Nat. Bank Corp., 1984—. Author books; also contbr. articles to profl. jours.; leader JR4 Musical Combo, 1962—. Mem. Alliance Bd. Edn., 1957-59, pres., 1959; exec. com. Buckeye coun. Boy Scouts Am., 1963-77, mem. nat. scouting com., 1973-77; dept. sheriff Stark County, 1972-73; spl. police officer Alliance Police Dept., 1974-90, tech. insp., 1976-90; exec. com. Stark County Disaster Svcs., 1976-78, chmn., 1979; trustee Western Res. Acad., 1969-92, Alliance Comty. Hosp., Inc., 1980-87, pres., 1986; mem. Cape May Cottagers Assn. Inc., 1967—; grand marshal Carnation City Parade, 1986. With USNR, 1944-45. Recipient Gt. Tchr. award, 1976, Alliance Mayor's Award as outstanding citizen, 1978. Fellow AAAS, Royal Astron. Soc.; mem. Am. Phys. Soc., Am. Astron. Soc., Astron. Soc. Pacific, Am. Assn. Physics tchrs., Optical Soc. Am., Nantucket Maria Mitchell Assn. (pres. 1974), Masons (32 degree), Shriners, Corinthian Yacht Club, Beach Cape May Club, Alliance Country Club, Wranglers Club (pres. 1986—), Sigma Xi. Home: 1125 Fernwood Blvd Alliance OH 44601-3764 Also: 1613 Beach Dr Cape May NJ 08204-3608

RODMAN, LEIBA, mathematics educator; b. Riga, Latvia, June 9, 1949; came to U.S., 1985; s. Zalman and Haya Rodman; m. Ella Levitan, Feb. 2, 1983; children: Daniel, Ruth, Benjamin, Naomi. Diploma in maths., Latvian State U., 1971; MA in Statis., Tel Aviv (Israel) U., 1976, PhD in Maths., 1978. Instr. Tel Aviv U., 1976-78, sr. lectr., 1981-83, assoc. prof., 1983-85; postdoctoral fellow U. Calgary, Can., 1978-80; from assoc. to full prof. Ariz. State U., Tempe, 1985-87; prof. math. Coll. William and Mary, Williamsburg, Va., 1987—. Author: Introduction to Operator Polynomials, 1989, (with others) Matrix Polynomials, 1982, Matrices and Indefinite Scalar Products, 1983, Invariant Subspaces of Matrices with Applications, 1986, Interpolation of Rational Matrix Functions, 1990, Algebraic Riccati Equations, 1995; co-editor: Contributions to Operator Theory and Its Applications, 1988. Mem. IEEE, Am. Math. Soc., Math. Assn. Am., Internat. Linear-Algebra Soc., Soc. Indsl. and Applied Maths. Office: Coll of William & Mary Dept Of Math Williamsburg VA 23187

RODMAN, LEROY ELI, lawyer; b. N.Y.C., Feb. 22, 1914; s. Morris and Sadie (Specter) R.; m. Toby Chertcoff, Mar. 14, 1943; children: John Stephen, Lawrence Bernard. AB, CCNY, 1933; J.D. (James Kent scholar), Columbia, 1936. Bar: N.Y. 1937. Practiced in N.Y.C., 1937-43, 46—; law sec. to U.S. dist. judge Bklyn., 1936; law asst. Am. Law Inst., N.Y.C., 1937; chief food enforcement unit N.Y. Regional Office, OPA, 1942-43; mem. firm Lawrence R. Condon, N.Y.C., 1937-42; ptnr. Joseph & Rodman, N.Y.C., 1946-53; sr. ptnr. Rodman, Maurer & Dansker, N.Y.C., 1964-73, Carro, Spanbock, Londin, Rodman & Fass, N.Y.C., 1973-78, Rodman & Rodman, N.Y.C., 1978-89, Teitelbaum, Hiller, Rodman, Paden & Hibsher, P.C., N.Y.C., 1990—; tchr. fed. taxation Pace Coll., N.Y.C., 1953-55; bd. dirs., v.p., sec. Francosteel Corp., N.Y.C.; sec. Ameribrom, Inc. Editorial bd.: Columbia Law Rev, 1934-36; Contbr. articles to legal jours. Bd. dirs. Manhattan coun. Boy Scouts Am., 1960—, v.p., 1961-68, pres., 1972-75; exec. bd. Greater N.Y. coun., 1972—. Capt. JAGD AUS, 1943-46. Recipient Certs. Svc., Silver Beaver award Boy Scouts Am., 1962. Fellow Am. Coll. Trust and Estate Counsel; mem. ABA, N.Y. County Lawyers Assn., Assn. of Bar of City of N.Y., Judge Adv. Assn., Phi Beta Kappa. Jewish (trustee, v.p. synagogue, pres. brotherhood 1958-60). Clubs: Univ. (N.Y.C.); Metropolis Country (White Plains, N.Y.) (sec. 1976-77, 80-82, v.p. 1977-78, bd. govs. 1976-82). Home: 535 E 86th St New York NY 10028-7533 Office: 260 Madison Ave New York NY 10016-2401

RODMAN, OLIVER, newspaper publishing executive. V.p. advt. Globe Newspaper Co., Boston. Office: Globe Newspaper Co 135 Morrissey Blvd Boston MA 02107

RODMAN, PETER WARREN, foreign policy specialist; b. Boston, Nov. 24, 1943; s. Sumner and Helen Rhoda (Morris) R.; m. F. Veronique Boulad, Apr. 13, 1980; children: Theodora, Nicholas. BA summa cum laude, Harvard U., 1964, JD, 1969; BA, MA, Oxford (Eng.) U., 1966. Staff mem. NSC, Washington, 1969-77; fellow in diplomatic studies Ctr. for Strategic and Internat. Studies, Washington, 1977-83; dir. rsch. Kissinger Assocs., Washington, 1982-83; mem. policy planning council Dept. of State, Washington, 1983-84, dir. policy planning staff, 1984-86; dep. asst. to pres. for nat. security affairs (fgn. policy) NSC, Washington, 1986-87, counselor, spl. asst. to pres. for nat. security affairs, 1987-90; fellow Johns Hopkins Fgn. Policy Inst., Washington, 1990-93; dir. Middle East and Eurasian studies Ctr. for Strategic and Internat. Studies, Washington, 1994-95; dir. nat. security programs Nixon Ctr. for Peace and Freedom, Washington, 1995—; sr. advisor on fgn. policy Rep. Platform Com., 1992. Author: More Precious Than Peace: The Cold War and the Struggle for the Third World, 1994; sr. editor Nat. Rev., 1991—; contbr. articles to profl. jours. V.p. World Affairs Coun., Washington, 1996—. Mem. Coun. on Fgn. Rels., Internat. Inst. for Strategic Studies, Atlantic Coun. U.S., Cosmos Club. Office: Nixon Ctr for Peace and Freedom 1620 I St NW Ste 900 Washington DC 20006

RODMAN, SUE ARLENE, wholesale Indian crafts company executive, artist; b. Fort Collins, Colo., Oct. 1, 1951; d. Marvin F. and Barbara I. (Miller) Lawson; m. Alpine C. Rodman, Dec. 13, 1970; 1 child, Connie Lynn. Student Colo. State U., 1970-73. Silversmith Pinel Silver Shop, Loveland, Colo., 1970-71; asst. mgr. Traveling Traders, Phoenix, 1974-75; co-owner, co-mgr. Deer Track Traders, Ltd., Loveland, 1975-85, v.p., 1985—. Author: The Book of Contemporary Indian Arts and Crafts, 1985. Mem. U.S. Senatorial Club, 1982-87, Rep. Presdl. Task Force, 1984-90; mem. Civil Air Patrol, 1969-73, 87-90, pers. officer, 1988-90. Mem. Internat. Platform Assn., Indian Arts and Crafts Assn., Western and English Sales Assn., Crazy Horse Grass Roots Club. Mem. Am. Baptist Ch. Avocations: museums, piano, recreation research, fashion design, reading. Office: Deer Track Traders Ltd PO Box 448 Loveland CO 80539-0448

RODMAN, SUMNER, insurance executive; b. Malden, Mass., Aug. 5, 1915; s. Nathan Markel and Sara Ruth (Slater) R.; m. Helen Rhoda Morris, July 2, 1942; children: Peter Warren, John Slater. A.B. cum laude, Harvard, 1935. C.L.U. Agt. Aetna Life Ins. and Annuity Co., Boston, 1935—; with Rodman Ins. Agy., Inc., Newton Ctr., Mass.; life ins. adviser, 1953—; Pres. Boston Life Ins. and Trust Council, 1958-59. Bd. dirs. Jewish Family and Children's Service, Boston, 1953-85, Boston Estate Planning Council, 1960-85, Youth Tennis Found. New Eng., 1963-85, Simons-Gutman Found., 1965—, Alzheimers Assn. Ea. Mass., 1990—; hon. trustee Combined Jewish Philanthropies of Greater Boston, 1967—; mem. Am. Jewish Com., Anti.-Defamation League of B'nai Brith; mem. World Affairs Coun. Boston; hon. trustee Temple Israel, Boston.. Served to capt. AUS, 1941-46, ETO. C.L.U. Inst. fellow, 1952, 61; named to New Eng. Tennis Assn. Hall of Fame, 1992. Mem. The Am. Coll. (trustee 1971-74), Boston Life Underwriters Assn. (pres. 1965-66), Am. Soc. CLUs (pres. 1972-73), Million Dollar Round Table (life), New Eng. Lawn Tennis Assn. (bd. dirs. 1966-68), Golden Key Soc. Jewish (trustee temple). Clubs: Harvard (Boston), Harvard Varsity (Boston); Newton (Mass.) Squash and Tennis; Wightman Tennis Center (Weston, Mass.). Lodge: Masons. Home: 94 Vine St Chestnut Hill MA 02167-3050 Office: 75 Wells Ave Newton MA 02159-3214

RODNEY, JOEL MORRIS, dean; b. Bklyn., Nov. 9, 1937; s. Samuel Seymour and Jane (Loorya) R.; m. Judith DeStefano, July 22, 1994; children from previous marriage: Jonathan, Adam, Benjamin. BA cum laude, Brandeis U., 1959; PhD, Cornell U., 1965; attended, Inst. Ednl. Mgmt. Harvard U., 1976. From instr. to assoc. prof. Wash. State U., Pullman, 1963-70; chmn. div. social scis., assoc. prof. history Elmira (N.Y.) Coll., 1970-72, coordinator flood relief and community planning, 1973; dean arts and sci., prof. history Widener Coll., Chester, Pa., 1973-76, acting chief acad. officer, dean, 1976-77, chief acad. officer, dean, 1977-81, dir. univ. grad. programs, 1979-81; v.p. acad. affairs Salisbury (Md.) State Coll., 1981-86; provost Rockford (Ill.) Coll., 1986-90; dean U. Wis. Ctr.-Washington County, West Bend, 1990—. Editor Albion, 1967-78; contbr. articles to profl. jours. Vice chmn. Md. Gov.'s Com. on Employment of Handicapped, 1985-86, chmn. and mem. Lower Shore divsn., 1983-86; chmn. adv. bd., mem. Crozer-Chester Med. Health Ctr., Chester, 1974-77; project evaluator NEH, 1986, RSA, 1993; mem., sec. Delaware County Mental Health/Mental Retardation Bd., 1975-81; adv. bd. Rehab. Inst. of Chgo., 1988-94; mem. coun. Ct. of Gov.'s Regents Coll., London, 1986-90, Rock Valley Coll. Indsl. Coun., Rockford, 1989-90; bd. dirs. Moraine Symphony Orch., 1990-93, Welcome Holme, Inc., 1990, pres., 1992; citizens adv. bd. West Bend Bank One, 1991, Washington County Vol. Ctr., 1991-92; bd. dirs. The Threshold, 1992; apptd. to State Wis. Coun. Phys. Disabilities, 1994, vice chmn., 1995; exec. com. Moraine area Tech. Prep. Coun., 1994; mem. Wis. Gov.'s Com. on Persons with Disabilities, 1994; mem. adv. bd. S.E. Wis. Area Health Edn. Coun., 1995; mem. West Bend C. of C. Ambs., 1995. Recipient Disting. Service award Widener Meml. Sch., 1978, Award of merit Md. Gov.'s Com. on Employment of Handicapped, 1984; named to Legion of Honor, Chapel of Four Chaplains, 1978; honoree West Phila. Vets. and Handicapped Employment Com., 1977. Mem. Am. Assn. Acad. Deans, Conf. on Brit. Studies, Am. Assn. Univ. Adminstrs., Nat. Spinal Cord Injury Assn. (bd. dirs. Ill. chpt. 1988-90), Rotary, Phi Alpha Theta. Republican. Home: 229 Bittersweet Dr West Bend WI 53095-4907 Office: U Wis Ctr Washington County 400 S University Dr West Bend WI 53095-3619

RODNICK, ELIOT HERMAN, psychologist, educator; b. New Haven, Nov. 27, 1911; s. Louis D. and Bertha (Caplan) R.; m. Helen Percival Hollander, Nov. 20, 1940; children: Jonathan Eliot, Marion Percival Rodnick Bell. AB with high oration, Yale U., 1933, PhD, 1936. Asst. research Yale U., 1934-36; research psychologist, research service Worcester (Mass.) State Hosp., 1936-46, dir. psychol. research, chief psychologist, 1946-49; acting dir. Worcester Child Guidance Clinic, 1946-47; instr. Mt. Holyoke Coll., 1939; asst. prof. psychology Clark U., 1942-46, assoc. prof., 1946-49; vis. lectr. summer session U. Wis., 1949, Harvard U., 1952, U. Colo., 1958; prof. psychology, dir. clin. tng. psychology Duke U., 1949-61, chmn. dept. psychology, 1951-61; prof. psychology, dir. clin. tng. psychology U. Calif. at Los Angeles, 1961-79, prof. emeritus, 1979—; cons. psychologist VA, 1949-79, mem. central office adv. com. to chief, dept. psychiatry and neurology, 1957-61; mem. mental health study sect. NIH, 1954-57, behavorial sci. study sect., 1957, mental health projects rev. commn., 1957-60, chmn. spl. mental health grants rev. com., 1960-62; bd. dirs. Los Angeles Psychiat. Service, 1961-66, Didi Hirsch Mental Health Center, 1973-82, Calif. Sch. Profl. Psychology, 1981-83; cons. Calif. Dept. Mental Hygiene; mem. com. on research tng. in biol. scis. Nat. Inst. Mental Health, 1962-66, chmn., 1965-66; mem. mental health council Western Commn. Higher Edn., 1961-66; adv. com. abuse of stimulant and depressant drugs FDA, 1966-68; sci. adv. com. on drug abuse U.S. Dept. Justice, 1968-75; Cons. Narcotics Control Commn. N.Y., 1969-75; cons. Calif. Sch. Profl. Psychology. Editorial bd.: Am. Jour. Orthopsychiatry, 1954-57, Jour. Personality, 1955-60, Jour. Abnormal and Social Psychology, 1957-62, Am. Jour. Community Psychology, 1972-77, Family Process, 1977-81. Trustee Calif. Sch. Profl. Psychology, 1981-83. Commd. officer USPHS Res. Recipient Stanley Dean prize for outstanding research in schizophrenia, 1967; Wilbur Lucius Cross medal for outstanding profl. performance Yale Grad. Sch. Assn., 1975. Fellow AAAS, APA (bd. dirs. 1962-65, Disting. Contbn. to Clin. Psychology award 1976), Western Psychol. Assn. (pres. 1966-67), Am. Psychol. Soc. (James McKeen Cattell fellow award), Calif. Psychol. Assn. (Disting. Sci. Contbns. in Psychology award 1975), Los Angeles County Psychol. Assn., N.C. Psychol. Assn. (past pres.), Am. Orthopsychiat. Assn. (bd. dirs. 1966-69, pres. 1967-68); mem. Cosmos Club (Washington), Phi Beta Kappa, Sigma Xi. Home: 7577 Oak Leaf Dr Santa Rosa CA 95409-6254 Office: Dept Psychology U Cal 405 Hilgard Ave Los Angeles CA 90024-1301

RODNUNSKY, SIDNEY, lawyer, educator; b. Edmonton, Alta., Can., Feb. 3, 1946; s. H. and I. Rodnunsky; m. Teresita Asuncion; children: Naomi, Shawna, Rachel, Tevie, Claire, Donna, Sidney Jr. BEd, U. Alberta, 1966, LLB, 1973; MEd, U. Calgary, 1969, grad. diploma, 1990; BS, U. of State of N.Y., 1988; MBA, Greenwich U., 1990. Served as regional counsel to Her Majesty the Queen in Right of the Dominion of Can.; former gov. Grande Prairie Regional Coll.; now asst. prin. legal counsel Can.; Alta. coord. for gifted children Mensa Can.; past pres. Grande Prairie and Dist. Bar Assn. Author: Breathalyzer Casebook; editor: The Children Speak. Decorated Knight Grand Cross Sovereign and Royal Order of Piast, Knight Grand Cross Order of St. John the Baptist; knight Hospitaller Order St. John of Jerusalem; named to Honorable Order of Ky. Colonels; named adm. State of Tex.; recipient Presidential Legion of Merit. Mem. Law Soc. Alta., Law Soc. Sask., Can. Bar Assn., Inst. Can. Mgmt., Phi Delta Kappa. Home: 3 Grandview Garden Ct, 4802-46A Ave, Athabasca, AB Canada T9S 1H9

RODOWSKY, LAWRENCE FRANCIS, state judge; b. Balt., Nov. 10, 1930; s. Lawrence Anthony and Frances (Gardner) R.; m. Colby Fossett, Aug. 7, 1954; children: Laura Rodowsky Ramos, Alice Rodowsky-Seegers, Emily Rodowsky Savopoulos, Sarah Jones Rodowsky, Gregory, Katherine, Ann O'Connor. A.B., Loyola Coll., Balt., 1952; LL.B., U. Md., 1956. Bar: Md. 1956. Ct. crier, law clk. U.S. Dist. Ct. Md., 1954-56; asst. atty. gen. State of Md., 1960-61; assoc., ptnr. firm Frank, Bernstein, Conaway & Goldman, Balt., 1956-79; assoc. judge Ct. Appeals Md., Annapolis, 1980—; mem. rules com. Ct. Appeals Md., 1969-80; lectr., asst. instr. U. Md. Law Sch., 1958-68, 87-91; reporter jud. dept. Md. Constl. Conv. Commn., 1966-67. Chmn. Gov. Md. Commn. Racing Reform, 1979. Fellow Am. Coll. Trial Lawyers; mem. Md. Bar Assn., Balt. Bar Assn. Roman Catholic. Home: 4306 Norwood Rd Baltimore MD 21218-1118 Office: Ct Appeals Md 620 C M Mitchell Jr CTHS Baltimore MD 21202

RODRICKS, DANIEL JOHN, columnist, television commentator; b. Brockton, Mass., Mar. 8, 1954; s. Joseph Allen and Rose Mary (Popolo) R.; m. Lillian M. Donnard, Sept. 6, 1980. B.A., U. Bridgeport, 1976. Reporter The Patriot Ledger, Quincy, Mass., 1973-75; wire editor Middletown Times Record, N.Y., 1975; reporter Balt. Evening Sun, 1976-79, columnist, 1979—; reporter, commentator Sta. WBAL-TV, Balt., 1980—. Recipient Heywood Broun award Newspaper Guild, 1983, Front Page award, 1983; awards from Sigma Delta Chi, Md.-Del.-D.C. Press Assn., Firefighters Internat., also others. Mem. Sigma Delta Chi. Democrat. Roman Catholic. Avocations: cooking, fishing, theater, operetta. Office: Baltimore Sun 501 N Calvert St Baltimore MD 21202-3604

RODRIGUE, CHRISTINE M(ARY), geography educator, business consultant; b. L.A., Oct. 27, 1952; d. John-Paul and Josephine Genevieve (Gorsky) R. AA in French, German, L.A. Pierce Coll., 1972; BA in Geography summa cum laude, Calif. State U., Northridge, 1973, MA in Geography, 1976; PhD in Geography, Clark U., 1987. Computer analyst Jet Propulsion Labs., Pasadena, Calif., 1977; teaching asst. Clark U., Worcester, Mass., 1976-79, rsch. asst., 1977-78; instr. geography L.A. Pierce Coll., Woodland Hills, Calif., 1981—; cons. Area Location Systems, Northridge, 1984—, tech. writer, 1990—; asst. prof. urban studies and geography Calif. State U., Northridge, 1980-89; asst. prof. geography and planning Calif. State U., Chico, 1989-94, assoc. prof., 1994—; co-dir. Ctr. for Hazards Rsch., 1994—; faculty senator Calif. State U., Chico, 1990-92, grad. geog. adviser, 1992-93; owner Nomad Arabians. Contbr. numerous articles to refereed profl. publs. Recipient Meritorious Performance and Profl. Promise award Calif. State U., 1987, 88, 89, Calif. State U. summer scholar grant, 1990, 92, 94. Mem. AAAS, NOW, Assn. Am. Geographers (chmn. splty. group 1983-84, councillor splty. group 1994—), Capitalism Nature Socialism (mem. editl. bd. 1991—), L.A. Geog. Soc. (v.p. 1987, pres. 1988, editor 1981-84), Union Concerned Scientists, Planetary Soc., Sierra Club, Internat. Arabian Horse Assn., Arabian Horse Registry. Democrat. Avocations: Arabian horses, sci. fiction, hiking, camping, baroque music. Office: Calif State U Dept Geography & Planning Chico CA 95929-0425

RODRIGUE, GEORGE PIERRE, electrical engineering educator, consultant; b. Paincourtville, La., June 19, 1931; s. George Pierre and Catherine (Barstow) R.; m. Mary Merritt, June 25, 1955; children: George Pierre III, Edward, Catherine, Frances, Jane, Dorothy. B.S., La. State U., 1952, M.S., 1954; Ph.D., Harvard U., 1958. Grad. asst. La. State U., 1952-54, Harvard U., 1955-56; sr. staff engr. Sperry-Rand, Clearwater, Fla., 1958-61, research engr., 1961-68; prof. elec. engring. Ga. Inst. Tech., Atlanta, 1968-77, Regents prof., 1977—; dir., cons. Electromagnetic Scis. Inc., Atlanta; cons. Litton Industries, Los Alamos Nat. Lab. Patentee Microwave devices and materials. Named Outstanding Tchr. Ga. Inst. Tech., 1971, 72, 79, 95. Fellow IEEE (dir., v.p. publs. 1982-83, Centennial medal 1984, Outstanding Engring. Educator award Region III 1984); mem. IEEE Microwave Theory and Techniques Soc. (pres. 1976, Outstanding Service award 1985, Disting. Educator award 1995). Roman Catholic. Home: 1090 Kingston Dr Atlanta GA 30342 Office: Sch Elec Engring Ga Inst Tech Atlanta GA 30332

RODRIGUES, ALFRED BENJAMIN KAMEEIAMOKU, marketing consultant: b. Honolulu, Jan. 23, 1947; s. Alfred Benjamin Kameeiamoku and Ruth Shiegeko (Kameda) R. BA, U. San Francisco, 1969; postgrad. U. Wis., 1977. Pub. info. mgr. Hawaiian Tel.-GTE, Honolulu, 1979-80, pub. affairs program mgr., 1980-84, dir. pub. affairs, 1984-85, dir. mktg. communications, 1986-87, dir. mktg. communications and svcs., 1987-89 sr. v.p., Milici, Valenti and Gabriel Advt., Inc., 1989-91, exec. v.p., 1991-92; pres. Al Rodrigues & Assocs., 1992—. Bd. dirs., pub. rels. chmn. Am. Lung Assn., 1981-88; trustee, v.p. Hawaii Army Mus. Soc., 1982—; bd. dirs. ARC Hawaii, 1983-85; budget com. Aloha United Way. Maj. USAR, 1969-89. Decorated Bronze Star with three oak leaf clusters, Meritorious Svc. medal with oak leaf cluster, Army Commendation medal with 2 oak leaf clusters, Purple Heart with oak leaf cluster, Air medal with oak leaf cluster. Mem. Am. Mktg. Assn. (bd. dirs. Hawaii chpt.), Am. Advt. Fedn., Hawaii Advt. Fedn. (bd. dirs., pres., Advt. Man of Yr., 1989), Pub. Rels. Soc. Am. (pres. Hawaii), Res. Officers Assn., Hawaii C. of C., Rotary. Republican. Roman Catholic.

RODRIGUES, JOSEPH E., grain company executive; b. 1936. Tchr. Helderberg Coll., Sommerset, West Africa, 1960-67; with Ford Motor Co., Port Elizabeth, South Africa, 1967-69; CFO Arbor Acres, South Africa, 1969-74; with Seaboard Flour Corp., Iran, 1974-80; CFO, CEO Seaboard Corp., 1980—; vice pres Seaboard Corp., KS. Office: Seaboard Corp PO Box 2972 Shawnee Mission KS 66201*

RODRIGUEZ, ADOLFO, library director, historian; b. Piedras Negras, Coahuila, Mex., Mar. 28, 1942; s. José Valentín Rodríguez González and Guadalupe Gallardo de Rodríguez; m. María Mercedes del Carmen Villatoro A.; children: Ernesto Rodríguez Villatoro, Diego Rodríguez Villatoro. M History, El Colegio de México, México City, 1964; MLS, U. Texas, 1970. Info. coord. Armo Industry, Mexico City, 1970-73; subdir. Sec. de Edn. Pub. Nat. Sch. Libr. Scis., Mexico City, 1971; dir. Sec. de Edn. Pub. Nac. Sch. Libr. Scis., Mexico City, 1972-76, 1977; dir. Univ. Nac. Autonoma de Mex. Gen. Dir. of Librs., Mexico City, 1973-77, acad. coord., 1977-81, libr. assessor faculty Philosophy and Letters, 1979-81, dir. Centro Universitario de Investigaciones Bibliotecológicas, 1982-84, dir., 1985—. Author: Las bibliotecas en los informes presidenciales, 1990, Historia de la legislacion bibliotercaria de la UNAM, 1994, El regazo en las bibliotecas, 1996; co-author Bibliografía comentada sobre educacion bibliotecologica en Mexico, 1987; contbr. articles to profl. jours. Named 1st level Nat. Investigator Nat. System Investigators, México, 1991, named 2d level, 1994. Mem. Internat. Fedn. Documentation (rep. 1973), Am. Libr. Assn., Internat. Fedn. Assns. Librs. (Comité para Am. Latina com. 1987-92), Nat. Assn. Librs. (pres. 1981-83). Home: Cerrada de Iliada # 24, Col Axomiatla, DF 01820, Mexico Office: Dir Gen de Bibliotecas, Ciudad Universitaria, 04510 Mexico City Mexico

RODRIGUEZ, ANTONIO JOSE, lawyer; b. New Orleans, Dec. 7, 1944; s. Anthony Joseph and Josephine Olga (Cox) R.; m. Virginia Anne Soignet, Aug. 23, 1969; children: Henry Jacob, Stephen Anthony. BS, U.S. Naval Acad., 1966; JD cum laude, Loyola U. of the South, New Orleans, 1973. Bar: La. 1973, U.S. Dist. Ct. (ea. dist.) La. 1973, U.S. Ct. Appeals (5th cir.) 1973, U.S. Dist. Ct. (mid. dist.) La. 1975, U.S. Dist. Ct. (we. dist.) La. 1977, U.S. Ct. Appeals (11th cir.) 1981, U.S. Supreme Ct. 1987, U.S. Dist. Ct. (so. dist.) Miss. 1991, U.S. Ct. Appeals (4th cir.) 1991, U.S. Ct. Internat. Trade, 1991. Assoc. Phelps, Dunbar, Marks, Claverie & Sims, New Orleans, 1973-77; ptnr. Phelps Dunbar, New Orleans, 1977-92, Rice Fowler, New Orleans, 1992—; prof. law Tulane U., New Orleans, 1981—; mem. nat. rules of the road adv. coun. U.S. Dept. Transp., Washington, 1987-90, chmn. nat. navigation safety adv. coun., 1990-94; spkr. on admiralty and environ. Co-author: Admiralty-Limitation of Liability, 1981, Admiralty-Law of Collision, 1990; author: (chpt.) Benedict on Admiralty, 1995; assoc. editor Loyola Law Rev., 1971-73; contbr. articles to profl. maritime and environ. jours. Bd. dirs. Greater New Orleans Coun. Navy League, 1988—. Lt. USN, 1966-70; capt. USNR, 1970-94. Decorated Navy Commendation medal; recipient Disting. Pub. Svc. award U.S. Dept. Transp., 1993. Fellow La. Bar Found.; mem. ABA, La. Bar Assn., La. State Law Inst., Maritime Law Assn. U.S. (proctor 1975—), New Orleans Bar Assn., Southeastern Admiralty Law Inst., Assn. Average Adjusters U.S., Assn. Average Adjusters U.K., Naval Res. Assn. (chpt. pres. 1982-84), U.S. Naval Acad. Alumni Assn. (chpt. pres. 1981-83), Bienville club, Phi Alpha Delta, Alpha Sigma Nu. Republican. Roman Catholic. Home: 4029 Mouton St Metairie LA 70002-1303 Office: Rice Fowler 201 St Charles Ave 36th Fl New Orleans LA 70170

RODRIGUEZ, ARTURO SALVADOR, labor union official; b. San Antonio, June 23, 1949; s. Arthur Salvador and Felice (Quintero) R.; m. Linda Fabela Chavez, Mar. 30, 1974; children: Olivia, Julie, Arthur. BA in Sociology, St. Mary's U., 1971; MSW, U. Mich., 1973. Various positions United Farm Workers of Am., Keene, Calif., 1973-90, v.p., 1981-93, organizer, 1990-92; pres. United Farm Workers Am. AFL-CIO, Keene, 1993—. Chief instr. UFW Sch., Keene, 1978-79; coord. Edward Kennedy Presdl. Dr., San Antonio, 1980. Office: United Farm Workers Am AFL-CIO PO Box 62-La Paz 29700 Woodford Tehachapi Rd Keene CA 93531*

RODRIGUEZ, BEATRIZ, ballerina; b. Ponce, P.R.. Attended, Newark Acad. Ballet, N.J. Sch. of Ballet; scholarship student, Joffrey Ballet Sch. Former dancer N.J. Ballet; dancer Richard Englund's Dance Repertory Co., 1970; mem. Joffrey II Dancers, 1971-72; mem., sr. dancer Joffrey Ballet, N.Y.C., 1972—. Repertory includes: Cakewalk, Dream Dances, Illuminations, Love Songs, Offenbach in the Underworld, Petrouchka, Return to the Strange Land, Rodeo, and The Green Table, Moves, Interplay, Deuce Coupe, As Time Goes By, Billy the Kid, The Dream, Taming of the Shrew, Wedding Bouquet, Force Field, Concerto Grosso, Valentine, Trinty, Kettentans, Fanfarita, The Rite of Spring, Cotillion, Romeo and Juliet, Forgotten Land, Le Sacre du Printemps, The Green Table. Recipient Dance Mag. award, 1993. Office: The Joffrey Ballet 130 W 56th St New York NY 10019-3818

RODRIGUEZ, CARLOS AUGUSTO, lawyer; b. Havana, Cuba, Sept. 1, 1954; came to U.S., 1960; s. Urbano and Estela (Cardenas) R.; m. Valerie Carr, May 27, 1989. BA magna cum laude, Furman U., 1977; JD, U. Fla., 1980. Bar: Fla. 1980, U.S. Ct. Appeals (5th cir.) 1981, U.S. Dist. Ct. (so. dist. and trial bar) Fla. 1984, U.S. Ct. Appeals (11th cir.) 1995; bd. cert. civil trial atty. Asst. pub. defender Broward County Pub. Defender's Office, Ft. Lauderdale, Fla., 1980-83, chief asst. pub. defender, 1983-85; assoc. Fazio, Dawson & DiSalvo, Ft. Lauderdale, Fla., 1985-87; sole practice Ft. Lauderdale, Fla., 1987—; assoc. prof. U. Miami Sch. Law, Miami, 1983-85; lectr. criminal procedure Nova Law Cen., Ft. Lauderdale, 1983-85, lectr. on law Broward Community Coll., Ft. Lauderdale, 1983-87; mem. Nuisance Abatement Bd., 1989—; vice chmn. Marine ADv. Bd., 1990. Mem. Marine Adv. Bd., Broward, Fla., 1986—; rep. Primary Rep. Port Everglades Commn., Broward, 1984. Mem. ABA, Assn. Trial Lawyers Am., Acad. Fla. Trial Lawyers, Broward County Bar Assn., Phi Beta Kappa. Republican. Roman Catholic. Avocations: scuba diving, fishing, water and snow skiing. Home: 2424 SE 13th Ct Pompano Beach FL 33062-7211 Office: 633 S Andrews Ave Ste 300 Fort Lauderdale FL 33301-2849

RODRIGUEZ, CARMEN VILA, artist, art educator, art historian; b. N.Y.C., July 16, 1927; d. Manuel and Julia (Lopez) Vila; m. Sabino Rodriquez Jr., Aug. 22, 1948; children: Sabino III, Manuel. BA in Art, Hunter Coll., 1948; studied with muralist Raul Anguiano, U. Mexico, 1966; student in advanced Ceramics and Jewelry, Calif. Coll. Arts and Crafts, 1966; student, U. Madrid, Spain, 1968; MA in Art and Art History, Columbia U., 1969, EdD in Art and Art Edn., 1977, DLitt, 1977; postgrad., Fairfield U., 1982-93. Cert. in adminstrn. and supervision, Conn., art tchr., Conn., N.Y. Art tchr. Yorkville Vocat. H.S., N.Y.C., 1951-52; art history lectr. Instituto de Bellas Artes, Caracas, Venezuela, 1953-55; art tchr., dept. chmn. Eastchester (N.Y.) Sch. Dist. 1, 1958-92; cons., pres. Visual Instrnl. Libr. Art, Inc., 1981—; art edn. leader, lectr. art history Discovery Mus., Bridgeport, Conn., 1992—; co-chair ednl. programs Lockwood-Mathews Manor Mus., Norwalk, Conn., 1992-94; adj. faculty Daytona Beach C.C., 1993—; presenter Rockefeller Fleishman Commn., 1972; art instr. Norwalk (Conn.) Sr. Citizen Ctr., 1992-95, New Canaan (Conn.) Sr. Ctr., 1993—, Girl Scouts USA, Norwalk, 1990-93. Author: Tracy Loves Picasso, 1993; one-woman shows include Picture This Gallery, Westport, Conn., 1995, 1st Fidelity Bank, Norwalk, 1995, Sun Trust Bank, Daytona Beach, Fla.; group shows include Rowayton (Conn.) Arts Ctr., 1994 (ribbon 1994), Bonnie Blair Country Club, Scarsdale, N.Y., 1962, N.Y. Gallery, 1970, Scarsdale Pub. Libr., 1975, Portland Gallery, Norwalk, Conn., 1996, Sun Trust Bank, 1996; editor J. Walter Thompson Advt., N.Y.C., 1970; editor, head stylist Trimble Studios, N.Y.C., 1949-53; contbr. articles to profl. jours. Art instr. Norwalk (N.Y.) Sr. Citizen Ctr., 1992—, Girl Scouts USA, Norwalk, Conn., 1990-93. Recipient Painting ward Eastchester Womens Club, 1964, Premio Major de Arte U. Mex., 1961. Mem. NEA, AAUW, NOW, Nat. Art Edn. Assn., Rowayton Art Assn., Art League Daytona Beach, Port Orange Art Assn. Avocations: painting, travel, sculpture, writing, art history. Home: Vantage Point 2947 S Atlantic Ave Daytona Beach Shores FL 32118 Office: VILA Inc PO Box 466 466 E Norwall Norwalk CT 06855

RODRIGUEZ, CESAR, librarian; b. Callao, Peru, Oct. 23, 1945; came to U.S., 1957; s. Jose Rodriguez and Angela (Seminario) Tabarne; m. Daisy Rodriguez, June 21, 1969. AA, Concordia Coll., 1965; BA, Queens Coll., 1970, MLS, 1975; M in Internat. Affairs, Columbia U., 1983. Libr. acquisitions asst. McKinsey & Co., Inc., N.Y.C., 1971-73; acquisitions libr. Info. for Bus., Inc., N.Y.C., 1973-76; acquisitions libr. Yale U. Libr., New Haven, Conn., 1976-86, curator L.Am. Collection, 1986—; mem. exec. bd. Casa Cultural Julia De Burgos, New Haven, 1993—. Contbr. to books. Corp. U.S. Marines, 1965-68, Vietnam. Mem. ALA, L.Am. Studies Assn., Seminar of L.Am. Libr. Materials (exec. bd. 1993—, chair coms. 1979—). Episcopalian. Office: Yale U L Am Collection Box 208240 130 Wall St New Haven CT 06520

RODRIGUEZ, CHI CHI (JUAN RODRIGUEZ), professional golfer; b. Bayamon, P.R., Oct. 13, 1935. Profl. golfer, 1960—. Contbg. columnist golf. mags. Winner PGA Tour Denver, 1963, Lucky Internat., 1964, Western Tour, 1964, Tex. Tour, 1967, Sahara Tour, 1968, Byron Nelson Tour, 1973, Greater Greensboro, 1973, KO Olina Invitational, 1992; named to Ryder Cup Team, 1973.Inducted into the World Sports Humanitarian Hall of Fame, 1994. Leading money winner on sr. tour, 1987; represented P.R. in 12 world cups; ranked # 5 on PGA sr. tour, 1992; ranked # 4 among scoring leaders PGA sr. tour, 1992. Office: PGAA 100 Avenue Of Champions Palm Beach Gardens FL 33418-3653*

RODRIGUEZ, DAVID G., JR., art and religion educator, priest; b. San Antonio, Tex., June 9, 1947; s. David Campos and Maria Beatrice (Gonzalez) R. BFA, Coll. St Francis, 1979; M in pastoral studies, Loyola U., 1984; M in divinity, Cath. Theo. Union, 1988; M in arts inter-discipline, Columbia Coll., 1993; MFA, Md. Inst. Coll. Art, 1995. Cert. elem. tchr., art tchr., Ill. Clerical U.S. Air Force, 1968-72; tchr. St. Ann's Cath. Sch., Great Falls, Mont., 1969-72; sales & design General Men's Wear, San Antonio, 1972-73; tchr. art & religon St. Jude's Cath. Sch., New Lenox, Ill., 1974-79; tchr. cont. edn. Joliet Jr. Coll., New Lenox, Ill., 1976-77; tchr., chair fine arts Providence H.S., New Lenox, Ill., 1979-84; tchr., chair arts & religion Hales Francisan H.S., Chgo., 1984—; priest Chgo. & Joliet Dioc., Chgo., 1989—; chaplain Cruise Lines, Fla., 1989—; art teach core mem. Chgo. Cath. H.S., 1989—; art dept. evaluator Ill. North Cen., Chgo., 1990—; curriculum staff and evaluator Hales Franciscan H.S., 1990—; adj. faculty art edn. dept. The Sch. of Art Inst. Chgo., 1994—. Juror fine arts Art Reach, Chgo., 1990—; mem. Arts Basics, Art. Inst. Chgo., 1990—; mem. Gt. Falls Symphony Chorus. With USAF, 1968-72. Coca-Cola fellow Md. Inst. Coll. Art, 1991-95. Mem. Nat. Cath. Edn. Assn., Nat. Art Edn. Assn., Cath. Edn. Archdiocese of Chgo., Facets Cinema, Art Inst. Chgo., Mex. Fine Arts Mus. Roman Catholic. Avocations: dance, remodeling design, floral design, cooking, choreography, painting. Home: 4930 S Cottage Grove Ave Chicago IL 60615-2616 Office: Hales Franciscan HS Province 4930 S Cottage Grove Ave Chicago IL 60615-2616

RODRIGUEZ, ELENA GARCIA, retired pension fund administrator; b. Havana, Cuba, Mar. 21, 1944; came to U.S., 1959; d. Eliseo and Elena (Suarez) Garcia; divorced; children: Victor, Yvonne, Daniel. B in Profl. Studies, Barry U., 1983; MS in Mgmt., St. Thomas U., 1985; postgrad., U. Phila., 1989, UCLA, 1990. With City of Miami, Fla., 1969-95, pension adminstr., 1978—, ret., 1995. Author: General and Sanitation Pension Benefit Booklet, 1982, Fire and Police Pension Benefit Booklet, 1982, Retirement Planning Booklet, 1985; author numerous programs dealing with pension and acctg. for pension assets. Mem. Leadership Miami, 1985—. Mem. NASD (arbitrator), Internat. Found. Employee Benefit Plans, Internat. Pers. Mgmt. Assn., Inst. Fiduciary Edn., Fla. Assn. City Clks., New York Stock Exch. (arbitrator), Am. Stock Exch. (arbitrator), Am. Arbitration Assn., Better Bus. Bur. (arbitrator). Republican. Roman Catholic. Avocations: growing orchids, stained glass, tile mosaics, painting.

RODRIGUEZ, ELIAS C., judge; b. Dallas, Sept. 7, 1919; s. Elias S. and Anna (Fernandez) R.; m. Alberta Lenore Durbin, Jan. 1, 1949; children—Michael, Robert, Richard. B.A., So. Meth. U., 1941; J.D., Georgetown Law Sch., 1948, LL.M., 1953. Bar: Tex. 1948, D.C. 1948. Atty. IMF, Washington, 1948-51; fgn. service officer Dept. State, Washington, 1952-69; 1st sec. Am. Embassy Rome, Italy, 1960-65; atty. CAB, Washington, 1971-78, adminstrv. law judge, 1977-84; chief adminstrv. law judge, CAB, 1982-84; chief adminstrv. law judge Dept. Transp., Washington, 1984-87. Served to lt. col. U.S. Army, 1942-46, ETO.

RODRÍGUEZ, FERDINAND, chemical engineer, educator; b. Cleve., July 8, 1928; s. José and Concha (Luís) R.; m. Ethel V. Koster, July 28, 1951; children: Holly Edith, Lida Concha. B.S., Case Western Res. U., 1950, M.S., 1954; Ph.D., Cornell U., 1958. Devel. engr. Ferro Corp., Bedford, Ohio, 1950-54; asst. prof. chem. engring. Cornell U., 1958-61, asso. prof., 1961-71, prof., 1971—; on sabbatic leave at Union Carbide Corp., 1964-65, Imperial Chem. Industries, Ltd., 1971, Eastman Kodak Co., 1978-79; cons. to industry. Author: Principles of Polymer Systems, 4th edit., 1996; contbr. numerous articles to profl. jours.; songwriter. Served with U.S. Army, 1954-56. Recipient Excellence in Teaching award Cornell Soc. Engrs., 1966, Edn. Achievement award Hispanic Engr. Mag., 1991. Fellow Am. Inst. Chem. Engrs.; mem. Am. Chem. Soc., Soc. Hispanic Profl. Engrs., Soc. Plastics Engrs. Lutheran. Home: 107 Randolph Rd Ithaca NY 14850-1720 Office: 230 Olin Hall Cornell U Ithaca NY 14853

RODRIGUEZ, GENO (EUGENE RODRIGUEZ), artist, arts administrator; b. N.Y.C., June 2, 1940; s. Eugenio and Juana (Lopez) R.; m. Janice Rooney, Oct., 1966; 1 dau., Samantha Marisol. Student, Internat. Peoples Coll., Elsinor, Denmark, 1961-62; nat. diploma in art, Hammersmith Coll. Art, London, 1966. Founder, pres., exec. dir. Alternative Center for Internat. Arts Alternative Museum, N.Y.C., 1975—; instr. photography Sch. Visual Arts, N.Y.C., 1978-82, Rutgers U., 1977-79; mem. Artists Cert. Appeals Bd., N.Y.C., 1979, spl. artist task force N.Y. State Council on Arts, 1981; panelist, cons. NEA, Dept. Cultural Affairs N.Y.C.; lectr. in field. Exhibited in one-man shows Il Diaframa Gallery, Milan, Italy, 1979, Mus. Contemporary Arts, Caracas, Venezuela, 1979, Real Art Ways Gallery, Hartford, Conn., 1980, Cayman Gallery, N.Y.C., 1980, CEPA Gallery, Buffalo, 1987, Sheldon Meml. Art Gallery U. Nebr., Lincoln, 1989; group shows include Autoren Gallery, Munich, 1980, Miss. Mus. Art, Jackson, 1981, Palacio de Minerias, Mexico City, 1981, J.A.M. Gallery, N.Y.C., 1981, Chrysler Mus., Norfolk, Va., 1981, Am. Indian Gallery, 1982, Roger Litz Gallery, N.Y., 1982, Tweed Gallery, N.J., 1983, Baumgartner Gallery, Washington, 1983, Municipality of Genoa, Italy, 1984, Phila. Arts Alliance, 1985, Jayne H. Baum Gallery, N.Y.C., 1985-86, Gerald Melberg Gallery, Charlotte, N.C., 1985, Eupherat Gallerty, Calif., 1986, N.Y. State Mus., Albany, 1986, Hillwood Art Gallery, N.Y., 1986, Stux Gallery, Boston, 1986, San Diego Mus. Art, 1987, Alternative Mus., N.Y.C., 1987, Graham Modern, N.Y.C., 1987, Internat. Ctr. Photography, N.Y.C., 1987, Haggerty Mus. Art Marquette U., Milw., 1988, Herter Art Gallery U. Mass., 1989, Nat. Mus. Am. Art Smithsonian Instn., 1989; represented in permanent collections Internat. Ctr. Photography, N.Y.C., Mus. City of N.Y., Met. Mus. Art, N.Y.C., Everson Mus. Art, Syracuse, N.Y., Am. Mus. Natural History, N.Y.C., Mus. Contemporary Art, Caracas, Venezula; author: The Islands: Worlds of the Puerto Ricans, 1974, Mira, Mira, Mira Puerto Rican New Yorkers, 1975. Active Clinton/Gore Presdl. Transition Team for Arts and Humanites, 1992. Served with USN, 1959-63. Recipient Phelps-Stokes Fund award, 1977; Ludwig Vogelstien Found. award, 1981; Nat. Endowment for Arts fellow, 1979. Mem. Am. Assn. Mus. (exec. mem. curators com. 1985). Office: Alternative Museum 594 Broadway Rm 402 New York NY 10012-3234

RODRIGUEZ, IVAN, professional baseball player; b. Vaga Baja, P.R., Nov. 30, 1971. With Tex. Rangers, 1988—; mem. Am. League All-Star Team, 1992-96, Am. League Silver Slugger Team The Sporting News, 1994. Recipient Gold Glove award, 1992-95. Office: Tex Rangers 1000 Ballpark Way Arlington TX 76011-5168*

RODRIGUEZ, JOSEPH H., federal judge; b. 1930; m. Barbara Marriner. AB, La Salle Coll., 1955; JD, Rutgers U., 1958. Assoc. Brown, Connery et al, Camden, N.J., 1959-82; pub. advocate, pub. defender State of N.J., 1982-85; judge U.S. Dist. Ct. N.J., Camden, 1985—; instr. law Rutgers U., N.J., 1972-82, 93—; chmn. State Commn. Investigation, N.J., 1974-79. Chmn. State Bd. of Higher Edn., N.J., 1971-73. Mem. N.J. State Bar Assn. (pres. 1978-79). Office: US Dist Ct Rm 6060 US Courthouse One John F Gerry Plz Camden NJ 08101*

RODRIGUEZ, JUAN ALFONSO, technology corporation executive; b. Santiago, Cuba, Feb. 10, 1941; came to U.S., 1953; s. Alfonso and Marie Madeleine (Hourcadette) R. BEE, CCNY, 1962; MEE, NYU, 1963. Engr. IBM, Poughkeepsie, N.Y. and Boulder, Colo., 1963-68; engring. mgr. IBM, 1968-69; dir. tech. Storage Tech. Corp., Louisville, Colo., 1969-74, v.p. engring., 1974-77, v.p., gen. mgr. disk, 1977-79; v.p., gen. mgr. optical disk Storage Tech. Corp., Longmont, Colo., 1979-85; pres., CEO Exabyte Corp., Boulder, 1985-87, CEO, 1987-90; chmn., 1987-92; pres. Sweetwater Corp., 1992-93, chmn., 1992-95, also bd. dirs.; prof. elec. and computer engring. and engring. mgmt. U. Colo., 1992—; chmn. Datasonix, 1992-96, Vixel, 1995—; mem. devel. coun. Coll. Engring. U. Colo., 1990-92; Kapre Corp.; mem. engring. adv. bd. CCNY, bd. dirs. Colo. Advanced Tech. Enterprise, 1994—, co-exec. dir. Joint Ctr. for Entre Preneurship, U. Colo., 1994—; Robert J. Appel Disting. lectr. law and tech. Law Sch. U. Denver, 1990. Patentee in field. Bd. dirs. Boulder YMCA, 1982-87, U. Colo. Artist Series, 1988—; mem. bd. govs. Boulder County United Way, 1989-93, chairperson campaign, 1992; commr. Colo. Advance Tech. Inst., 1988-92. Recipient Ind. Quality award Rocky Mountain sect. Am. Soc. Quality Control, 1990, Gen. Palmer award for Outstanding Engr. in Industry The Am. Cons. Engrs. Coun. of Colo., 1995; named Boulder Spirit Entrepreneur of Yr., 1989, Entrepreneur of the Decade Boulder C. of C., 1994; finalist Entrepreneur of Yr., Arthur Young & Inc Mag., 1989. Fellow IEEE; mem. Computer Soc. of IEEE (mem. steering com. on mass storage 1981-93), Soc. Photo-Optical Instrumentation Engrs., Boulder C. of C. (chmn. entrepreneurs support program 1989), Greater Denver C. of C. (bd. dirs. 1990-91). Office: Univ Colo PO Box 425 Boulder CO 80309-0425

RODRIGUEZ, JUAN GUADALUPE, entomologist; b. Espanola, N.Mex., Dec. 23, 1920; s. Manuel D. and Lugardita (Salazar) R.; m. Lorraine Ditzler, Apr. 17, 1948; children: Carmen, Teresa, Carla, Rosa. BS, N.Mex. State U., 1943; MS, Ohio State U., 1946, PhD, 1949. Asst. entomologist U. Ky., Lexington, 1949-55, assoc. entomologist, 1955-61, prof. entomology, 1961—; adv. entomology U. de San Carlos, Guatemala, 1961; vis. scientist Warsaw U., 1961; sec. V Internat. Congress Acarology, 1978; del. internat. confs. Vienna, Moscow, San Jose, Costa Rica, Nottingham, Eng., Prague, Saalfelden, Austria, Kyoto, Japan, Edinburgh, Scotland, Hamburg, Fed. Republic Germany; bd. dirs. Ky. Sci. & Tech. Coun., 1990—; cons. to food industry, 1989—. Ky. steering com. Eisenhower Math/Sci. Consortium Appalachia Ednl. Lab., 1992—. Bd. dirs. Lexington chpt. NCCJ, Ky. Sci. & Tech. Coun., 1989—, Ky. steering com. of Appalachia Edn. Lab., 1993—. Served with inf., AUS, World War II; ex POW. Recipient Disting. Research award U. Ky. Alumni Assn., 1963; Thomas Poe Cooper award U. Ky. Coll. Agr., 1972, Outstanding Acarologist award Am. Registry Profl. Entomologists, 1984. Fellow AAAS, Royal Entomol. Soc. London; mem. Nat. Assn. Acads. Sci. (pres.-elect, 1996), Am. Inst. Biol. Scis., Acarol. Soc. Am. (governing bd.), Ky. Acad. Sci. (pres. 1982-83; pres. Found. 1982—, Disting. Scientist award 1985, exec. sec. 1988—), Can. Entomol. Soc., Ont. Entomol. Soc., Entomol. Soc. Am. (br. sec.-treas. 1963-65, br. com. man at large 1968-71, br. pres. 1982-83, North Cen. States br. rep. to governing bd. 1984-87, chmn. centennial com. 1987-89, hon. mem. 1989), Order Ky. Cols., Ky. Dept. Am. ex-POWs (comdr. 1992-94), Sigma Xi (pres. U. Ky. chpt. 1977), Gamma Alpha, Gamma Sigma Delta. Roman Catholic. Editor: Insect and Mite Nutrition, 1972, Recent Advances in Acarology, vols. I and II, 1979; co-editor: Current Trends in Insect Endocrinology and Nutrition, 1981, Leafhoppers and Planthoppers, 1985, Nutritional Ecology of Insects, Mites and Spiders, 1987; mem. editorial bd. Internat. Jour. Acarology; contbr. articles to profl. jours. Home: 1550 Beacon Hill Rd Lexington KY 40504-2304

RODRIGUEZ, LINDA TAKAHASHI, secondary school educator; b. L.A., June 22, 1941; d. Edward S. and Mary Takahashi; divorced; children: Regina Marie, Marla Sari. AA, Trinidad (Colo.) Jr. Coll., 1961; BA, We. State Coll., Gunnison, Colo., 1963; MA, U. Colo., Denver, 1991. Cert. tchr., adminstr., Colo. Tchr. Stratton (Colo.) Jr./Sr. High Sch., 1964-65, Pikes Peak Elem. Sch., Colorado Springs, 1966-68, Prince Sch., Tucson, 1968-70, Ipava (Ill.) Grade Sch., 1970-72, Macomb (Ill.) Schs., 1972-74, Colchester (Ill.) Jr./Sr. High Schs., 1979-83, Hazel Park (Mich.) Alternative Sch., 1984-85; tchr. 8th grade lang. arts and social studies Denver Pub. Schs., 1986-95, chair lang. dept., 1987-95, tchr. reading resource, 1987-92; creator, dir. Reading Summer Sch., 1987-95; presenter insvcs. Denver Pub. Schs., 1987-94; mentor Alternative Tchr. Cert. Program; mem. bd. dirs. Asian Cultural Ctr. Advisor Asian Edn. Adv. Bd., Denver, 1989-95; bd. dirs. Colo. Youth-at-Risk, Denver, 1992-93. Mem. Landmark Edn. Forum, Highland Park Optimists, Delta Kappa Gamma. Avocations: reading, skiing, personal growth, swimming, socializing. Home: 1617 Daphne St Broomfield CO 80020-1155

RODRIGUEZ, LOUIS JOSEPH, university president, educator; b. Newark, Mar. 13, 1933; m. Ramona Dougherty, May 31, 1969; children: Susan, Michael, Scott. BA, Rutgers U., 1955; MA, La. State U., 1957, PhD, 1963. Dean, Coll. Bus. Adminstrn., Alcee Fortier Disting. prof. Nichols State U., Thibodaux, La., 1958-71; dean Coll. Bus. U. Tex.-San Antonio, 1971-72, v.p. acad. affairs, dean faculty, 1972-73; dean Sch. Profl. Studies U. Houston-Clear Lake City, 1973-75, vice-chancellor, provost, 1975-80; pres. Midwestern State U., Wichita Falls, Tex., 1981—, Hardin Found. prof., 1994—; vice chmn. Coun. Tex. Pub. Univ. Pres. and Chancellors, 1992-93; mem. formula and health professions edn. adv. coms. Tex. Higher Edn. Coordinating Bd. Author 4 books; contbr. over 50 articles to profl. jours. Chmn. bd. Tex. Council on Econ. Edn., Houston, 1981-83; bd. dirs. Joint Council on Econ. Edn., N.Y.C., 1981-83, Goodwill Industries Am., Washington, 1976-82, Robert Priddy Found., 1993-96; pres. Wichita Falls Bd. Commerce and Industry, 1988-89, Clear Lake City Devel. Found., Houston, 1976-77, Goals for Wichita Falls, Inc., 1983; mem. internat. adv. com. Tex. Higher Edn. Coordinating Bd. Recipient Tchr. Edn. Supportive Pres. award Am. Assn. Colls. Tchr. Edn., 1991; named Wichitan of the Yr., 1987; Ford Found. grantee, 1964; Fulbright fellow, 1976. Mem. Am. Assn. State Colls. and Univs. (bd. dirs.), So. Assn. Colls. and Schs. (Commn. on Colls.), Assn. Tex. Colls. and Univs. (pres. 1988-89), Rotary (pres. Downtown Wichita Falls club 1990-91). Mem. Ch. of Christ. Home: 2405 Midwestern Pky Wichita Falls TX 76308-2911 Office: Midwestern State U 3410 Taft Blvd Wichita Falls TX 76308-2095

RODRIGUEZ, MARIA, social worker, counselor; b. Mayaquez, P.R., Jan. 2, 1953; d. Pablo Velez and Genara Valle; m. Carlos A. Rodriguez (div. 1990); children: Carlos A. Jr., Leslie A. Student, Passaic C.C., Patterson, N.J. Cert. HIV specialist. Case mgr. Mayaquez (P.R.) Med. Ctr., 1970-71, Hispanic Multi-Purpose Ctr., Patterson, N.J., 1989-90, Cure AIDS Now, Miami, Fla., 1991-93; adminstrv. asst. Carles Imports & Exports, Patterson, 1975-80; tchg. asst. St. John's Sch., Patterson, 1981-87; counselor Passaic (N.J.) City Hall, 1987-89; hot line counselor Health Crisis Network, Miami, 1990-91; job placement coord. Alternatives Svcs., Hialeah, Fla., 1993-94; social worker Beckham Hall for Homeless, Miami, 1994, Metro Dade Human Resouces, Miami, 1994—. Dep. registrar Metro Dade Elections Dept., Miami, 1991; chairperson L.Am. Com., North Miami Beach, Fla., 1993; advocate people with disabilities Archdiocese of Miami, 1994; active Voters Coun. North Miami Beach, 1993; active LWV of Dade County, Policemen's Benevolent Assn. Recipient Appreciation cert. Coalition of Homeless, 1993, City Hall of North Miami Beach for svcs. in cmty., 1993, State of Fla., 1993. Mem. NAFE. Democrat. Roman Catholic. Avocations: reading, writing, social events. Home: 1301 NE 181st St North Miami Beach FL 33162-1327

RODRIGUEZ, MATT L., protective services professional. AA in Bus. Adminstrn. with high honors, Wright Coll., 1972; B in Pub. Adminstrn. with honors, Roosevelt U., 1975, MPA with honors, 1976; postgrad., Northwestern U., 1976-77. Joined Chgo. Police Dept., 1959, advanced through grades to capt., 1988, patrolman, 1959-60, investigator Organized Crime sect., 1960-70, patrol sgt., 1970-71, investigative sgt. Criminal Investigation div., 1971-73, watch comdr., coord. gambling unit Vice Control div., 1973-76, 77-78, field lt. Patrol div., 1979, commanding officer area 6 youth div. Bur. Investigative Svcs., 1979, commanding officer gambling sect. Vice Control div., 1979-80, adminstrv. asst. to supt., 1980, dep. supt. Bur. Tech. Svcs., 1980-92, supt., 1992—; adj. prof. criminal justive dept. U. Ill., Chgo., 1979—, mem. adv. com. office internat. criminal justice; mayoral appointee Chgo. Emergency Telephone Systems Bd.; chmn. bd. Hispanic Inst. Law Enforcement; mem. adv. coun. Atty. Gen./State of Ill. Victim Assistance Program; lectr. Pub. Svcs. U., Beijing, 1984, Acad. Criminal Justive Scis., Orlando, Fla., 1984, Bramhill Police Coll., Hampshire, Eng., 1986, Am. Soc. Criminology ann. conf., Chgo., 1988, numerous others; keynote speaker IRS, Chgo., 1987, Northwestern U. Traffic Inst., 1989; panelist Nat. Conf. Criminal Justice Info. Law and Policy, CHgo., 1984, U.S. Dept. Justice Community Rels. Svcs.; participant numerous seminars and internat. confs. Contbr. articles to profl. jours. Bd. advisors Cath. Charities, Archdiocese of Chgo.; bd. dirs. Chgo. chpt. March of Dimes Birth Defects Found., Mental Health Assn. Greater Chgo., Law Found. Ill.; mem. community adv. com. Sta. WYCC-TV; mem. adv. bd. Malcom X Coll. Recipient Man or Yr. award Puerto Rican Congess Law and Order, 1983, Man of Yr. award Mex. Am. Legal Def. Ednl. Fund, 1987, Outstanding Achievement award Puerto Rican Congress Mut. Aid, Inc., 1987, Outstanding Support award Mex. Civic Soc. Ill., Inc., 1987, Cert. Appreciation Near North Kiwanis Chgo., 1988, Man of Yr. award Polonia Cares Found., 1989, Outstanding Alumnus award Wright Coll., 1989, Alumni award Holy Trinity High Sch., 1989, Citation of Honor Jewish Nat. Fund, 1991, Cert. Appreciation Drug Enforcement Adminstrn., 1991. Mem. Hispanic Am. Police Command Officers Assn. (1st v.p.), Internat. Assn. Chiefs of Police (com. on civil rights, Cert. Appreciation for Outstanding Contbns. Towards Professionalization Law Enforcement 1990), Latin Am. Police Assn. (bd. dirs., Man of Yr. award 1984). Office: Chgo Police Dept Office of Supt 1121 S State St Rm 400 Chicago IL 60605-2304*

RODRIGUEZ, PLACIDO, bishop; b. Celaya, Mex., Oct. 11, 1940; came to U.S., 1953; s. Eutimio and Maria Concepcion (Rosiles) R. STB, STL, Cath. U., Washington, 1968; MA, Loyola U., 1971. Ordained priest Roman Cath. Ch., 1968, ordained to bishop, 1983. Pastor Our Lady Guadalupe Ch., Chgo., 1972-75, Our Lady of Fatima Ch., Perth Amboy, N.J., 1981-83; vocat. dir. Claretians, Chgo., 1975-81; bishop aux. Archdiocese of Chgo., 1983-94; bishop Diocese of Lubbock, Tex., 1994—. Office: The Catholic Ctr PO Box 98700 Lubbock TX 79499-8700*

RODRIGUEZ, RITA MARIA, bank executive; b. La Havana, Cuba, Sept. 6, 1944; came to U.S., 1960; Tomas and Adela (Mederos) R.; m. E. Eugene Carter, Jan. 7, 1972; 1 child, Adela-Marie R. Carter. BBA, U. Puerto Rico, 1964; MBA, NYU, 1968, PhD, 1969. Bus. adminstrn. asst. prof., then assoc. prof. Harvard Bus. Sch., Cambridge, Mass., 1969-74, 74-78; fin. prof. U. Ill., Chgo., 1978-82; dir. (apptd. by U.S. Pres. & confirmed by U.S. Senate) Export-Import Bank of U.S., Washington, 1982—; cons. Polaroid Corp. and Indsl. Devel. Bank in Ecuador (Corporacion Financiera Nacional), 1978-82, U.S. IRS, 1982; bd. dirs. Acad. Ednl. Devel., Washington, 1989-93; bd. advisors Pew Econ. Freedom Fellows, Washington, 1991—. Author: (with E. Eugene Carter) International Financial Management, 1976, 2d edit., 1979, 3rd edit., 1984, (with Heinz Riehl) Foreign Exchange Markets: A Guide to Foreign Currency Operations, 1977, Foreign Exchange Management in U.S. Multinationals, 1980 (with Heinz Riehl) Foreign Exchange and Money Markets, 1983, Japanese, Spanish, Portuguese translations, The Export-Import Bank at Fifty, 1987; contbr. numerous fin. articles to profl. publs. Recipient Outstanding Achievement award, Nat. Coun. of Hispanic Women, 1986; Outstanding Hispanic Achievement award, Hispanic Corp. Achievers, 1988; National Leadership award-Government, The Nat. Network of Hispanic Women, 1989. Mem. Coun. Foreign Rels., Am. Econ. Assn. Roman Catholic. Avocations: gardening, music. Home: 3075 Ordway St NW Washington DC 20008-3255 Office: Export-Import Bank of U.S. 811 Vermont Ave NW Washington DC 20571-0001

RODRIGUEZ, TERESA IDA, elementary education educator, educational consultant; b. Levittown, N.Y., Oct. 10, 1951; d. George Arthur and Frieda (Diaz) R. BA in Secondary Edn., Hofstra U., 1973, MA in Bilingual Edn., 1978; profl. diploma in multicultural leadership, L.I. U., 1990. Cert. permanent nursery, kindergarten, elem. Spanish, bilingual K-6, ESL tchr., sch. dist. adminstr., sch. adminstr., supr., N.Y. Bilingual elem. tchr. Long Beach (N.Y.) Pub. Schs., 1973-76, Hempstead (N.Y.) Pub. Schs., 1976-79; account exec. Adelante Advt., N.Y.C., 1979-81; adminstrv. asst. Assocs. and Nadel, N.Y.C., 1981-84; freelance outside prop and set decorator for TV commls. N.Y.C., 1984-88; tchr. ESL Central Islip (N.Y.) Pub. Schs., 1988-92, bilingual tchr., 1992-95; bilingual tchr. Central Islip (N.Y.) Pub. Schs., Princeton, N.J., 1995—; cons. on tchr. tng. Staff Devel. Ctr. Islips, Central Islip, 1989—; cons. on staff devel. Nassau Bd. Coop. Ednl. Svcs., Westbury, N.Y., 1990—, edn. instrn. specialist IBM, 1991; presenter confs., workshops, seminars; cons. and grant writer, N.Y.C. and suburbs. Grantee N.Y. State Div. Bilingual Edn., 1988-90, Staff Devel. Ctr. Islips, 1988, Suffolk Bd. Coop. Ednl. Svcs., 1989; WLIW Pub. TV mini grantee; Pres.'s fellow L.I.U., 1989-90. Mem. ASCD, Nat. Assn. Bilingual Educators, State Assn. Bilingual Educators, Internat. Reading Assn. (presenter nat. conf. 1992, 93), N.Y. State ASCD, Suffolk Reading Coun., Smithtown Township Arts Coun. Avocations: tennis, interior design, historical archaeology, bicycling, swimming. Home: 30 Wheelwright Ln Levittown NY 11756-5233 Office: 1 Broadway Central Islip NY 11722

RODRIGUEZ, VINCENT ANGEL, lawyer; b. Cayey, P.R., 1921; s. Vicente and Maria (Antongiorgi) R. B.S., Harvard U., 1941; LL.B., Yale U., 1944. Bar: N.Y. 1947. Assoc. Sullivan & Cromwell, N.Y.C., 1944-56, ptnr., 1956—; dir. Deltec Internat. Ltd., Eng., Am. Investors, Inc., Bermuda. Mem. Council Fgn. Relations, ABA, Assn. Bar City N.Y., Am. Soc. Internat. Law. Club: River (N.Y.C.). Home: 4521 Fisher Island Dr Fisher Island FL 33109-0156 Office: Sullivan & Cromwell 125 Broad St New York NY 10004-2400

RODRIGUEZ, WILLIAM JULIO, physician; b. Ponce, P.R., June 18, 1941. BS, MD, Georgetown U., Washington, 1967; PhD, Georgetown U., 1975. Intern and resident Univ. Hosp., San Juan, P.R., 1967-72; fellow Children's Hosp., Washington, 1972-75; attending in infectious disease Children's Hosp. Nat. Med. Ctr., Washington, 1975—; assoc. chief infectious disease and microbiology rsch. Children's Hosp. Med. Ctr., 1979-80, chief infectious disease and microbiology, 1980-83, chmn. infectious disease dept., 1983—; cons. staff Hosp. for Sick Children, Washington, 1985—; cons. staff Shady Grove Adventist Hosp., Rockville, Md., 1988—, Holy Cross Hosp., Silver Spring, Md., 1988—, Columbia Hosp. for Women, 1990—. contbr. articles to profl. jours. MARC fellow, XIII, 1973-76. Fellow Infectious Disease Soc.; mem. AAAS, Am. Fedn. Clin. Rsch., Am. Soc. Microbiology, Assn. of Puerto Ricans in Sci. & Engring. Office: Childrens Nat Med Ctr 111 Michigan Ave NW Washington DC 20010-2970

RODRIGUEZ-ACEVEDO, FELIX MANUEL, secondary school educator; b. Guaynabo, P.R., Mar. 16, 1958; s. Felix and Dolores (Acevedo) Rodriguez. BA in Secondary Edn., U. P.R., Rio Piedras, 1981; cert. in philosophy, St. Alphonsus Coll., Suffield, Conn., 1982; MS in Adminstrn./Supervision, Ctrl. Conn. State U., 1988; MA in Theology, Holy Apostles Coll., Cromwell, Conn., 1992; PhD in Curriculum and Instrn., U. Conn., 1992. Tchr. sci. Dept. Edn., San Juan, P.R., 1980-81; religious edn. tchr. Sagrados Corzaones Cath. Sch., Guaynabo, 1984-85; tchr. math. Hartford (Conn.) Bd. Edn., 1985-94, tchr. Spanish lang. arts, 1985-90, tchr. sci., 1994—; cons. U.S. Dept. Edn., Washington, 1993; vis. instr. Spanish Holy Apostles Coll., 1991-92; guest spkr. U. Hartford, 1992-94; panel moderator U. Conn., Hartford, 1989-93. Cultural advisor Am. Sch. for the Deaf, West Hartford, Conn., 1994; guest spkr. outreach New England Assn. Supts., Middletown, Conn., 1993. Mem. Am. Ednl. Rsch. Assn., Nat. Assn. Bilingual Edn., Conn. Assn. Bilingual-Bicultural Edn. Roman Catholic. Avocations: dancing, roller skating, travel, reading. Home: 285 Elm St Apt A6 Windsor Locks CT 06096-2228 Office: Hartford Pub HS 55 Forest St Hartford CT 06105

RODRÍGUEZ-ARIAS, JORGE HERMINIO, retired agricultural engineering educator; b. Ponce, P.R., Apr. 24, 1915; s. Herminio Rodriguez Colón and Rosa Maria Arias Ríos; m. Carmen Teresa Quiñones Sepúlveda, May 9, 1948; children: Jorge H., Jaime Osvaldo, Nelson Rafael. BS in Agriculture, U. P.R., Mayaguez, 1936; BS in Agrl. Engring., Tex. A&M U., 1945; MS in Agrl. Engring., Kans. State U., 1947; PhD in Agrl. Engring., Mich. State U., 1956; D (hon.), U. P.R., Mayaguez, 1986. Instr. vocat. agriculture P.R. Reconstruction Adminstrn., Aibonito, 1936-37; instr. horticulture U. P.R., Mayaguez, 1937-43, from asst. to assoc. to prof. agrl. engring., 1947-77, dir. agrl. engring. dept., 1948-77; panelist UN Program for Devel., Lima, Peru, 1959. With USN, 1945-46. Fellow Am. Soc. Agrl. Engrs. (life), Instn. of Agrl. Engrs.; mem. Am. Soc. for Engring. Edn. (life), Inst. of Food Technologists (profl.). Home and Office: U PR PO Box 5158 College Station Faculty Residences # 3-B Mayaguez PR 00681

RODRIGUEZ-CAMILLONI, HUMBERTO LEONARDO, architect, historian, educator; b. Lima, Peru, May 30, 1945; came to U.S., 1963; s. Alfonso and Elda (Camilloni) R.; m. Mary Ann Alexanderson, July 1, 1972; children: Elizabeth Marie, William Howard. BA magna cum laude, Yale U., 1967, MArch, 1971, MPhil, 1973, PhD, 1981. Rsch. asst. Sch. Architecture Yale U., 1964-70, teaching fellow dept. history art, 1971-72, 74-75; chmn. research dept. Centro de Investigacion y Restauracion de Bienes Monumentales Instituto Nacional de Cultura, Lima, 1973; restoration architect OAS, Washington, 1976—; asst. prof. Sch. Architecture Tulane U., New Orleans, 1975-82; assoc. prof., dir. Henry H. Wiss Ctr. Theory and History of Art and Architecture, Coll. Architecture and Urban Studies Va. Poly. Inst. and State U., Blacksburg, 1983—, dir. Ctr. for Preservation and Rehab. Tech., Coll. Architecture, 1986—; vis. prof. U. Ill., Chgo., 1982-83; reviewer, cons. Choice, 1975—; mem. interim bd. dirs. Ctr. Planning Handbook Latin-Am. Art, 1978—; cons., adviser Internat. Exhbn. and Symposium Latin-Am. Baroque Art and Architecture, 1980; mem. adv. bd. Mountain Lake Symposium on Art and Architecture Criticism, 1985—, Internat. Symposium Luis Barragan, 1990; coord., advisor exhbn. Tradition and Innovation: Painting, Architecture and Music in Brazil, Mex. and Venezuela between 1950-80, 1991, Internat. Art History Colloquium, 1993, 48th Internat. Congress of Americanists, 1994; coord., adv. exhbn. Frank Lloyd Wright: An Architect in America, 1995. Author: (with Walter D. Harris) The Growth of Latin American Cities, 1971; (with Charles Seymour, Jr.) Italian Primitives, The Case History of a Collection and its Conservation, 1972, Religious Architecture in Lima of the Seventeenth and Eighteenth Centuries: The Monastic Complex of San Francisco el Grande, 1984; contbg. editor Handbook of Latin American Studies, 1987—, The Dictionary of Art, 1991—. Named Ellen Battell Eldridge fellow, 1970-72, Robert C. Bates Jr. fellow Jonathan Edwards Coll., Yale U., 1970-71, Social Sci. Rsch. Coun. fellow, 1972-74, Yale Concilium Internat. Studies fellow, 1972-73, Giles Whiting fellow, 1974-75, NEH fellow Columbia U., 1983, Hobart and William Smith Colls. fellow, 1987, U. Ill. fellow, 1990, Edilia De Montequin fellow, 1991, NEH fellow U. N.Mex., 1992. Mem. Soc. Archtl. Historians (bd. dir. 1977-80, past. pres., past sec. South Gulf chpt.) SE sect. Soc. Archtl. Historians, Coll. Art Assn. Am., SE Coll. Art Conf., Latin Am. Studies Assn., Assn. Latin Am. Art, Assn. Preservation Va. Antiquities, New River Valley Preservation League (bd. dir. 1987—), Nat. Trust Historic Preservation, Save our Cemeteries (past dir.), Preservation Resource Ctr. (past bd. dir.), Assn. for Preservation Tech., Blacksburg Regional Art Assn. (bd. dir), Inter-Am. Inst. Advanced Studies in Cultural History (bd. dirs. 1996—). Roman Catholic. Office: Va Poly Inst and State U Coll Architecture & Urban Studies Blacksburg VA 24061-0205 *As an educator across the years, I have come to realize that the true art of teaching consists of reaching both the human mind and the human heart.*

RODRIGUEZ-DEL VALLE, NURI, microbiology educator; b. San Juan, P.R., May 25, 1945; d. Paulino and Lucila (del Valle) Rodriguez-Rolan; m. Juan C. Perez-Otero, June 1, 1968; children: Juan Carlos, Claudia Rosalia. BS, U. P.R., 1967, MS, 1970, PhD, 1978. Rsch. asst. Coll. Pharmacy U. P.R., Rio Piedras, 1966-67, instr. biochemistry Med. Sch., 1970-78, asst. prof. microbiology, 1978-82, assoc. prof., 1982-92, prof., 1992—, ad honorem asst. prof. biology, 1984—; prin. investigator MBRS-NIH Grant, 1981—. Tchr. adult chatechism, 1992. Named Disting. Scientist Mobil Oil Co., San Juan, 1981, Disting. Prof. Student Rsch. Forum, San Juan, 1989. Mem. AAAS (coun. mem. Caribbean div. 1990-92, pres.-elect 1993, pres. 1994), Am. Soc. Microbiology (coun. mem. 1981-89, sec., pres. elect, pres. P.R. br. 1982-89, Dr. Arturo Carrion lectr. 1983), Soc. Exptl. Biology and Medicine, N.Y. Acad. Medicine, Sigma Xi. Roman Catholic. Office: U PR Dept Microbiology PO Box 365067 San Juan PR 00936-5067

RODRIGUEZ-ERDMANN, FRANZ, physician; b. Mexico City, Feb. 2, 1935; came to U.S., 1961; m. Irma Villarreal; 1 child, Foro. M.B., U. Heidelberg, Germany, 1958, M.D., 1960. Diplomate: Am. Bd. Internal Medicine. Intern Univ. Hosps., Heidelberg, 1958-61, Mercy Hosp., Detroit, 1962-63; research assoc. Wayne State U. Med. Sch., Detroit, 1961-62; jr. asst. resident in medicine Tufts U. New Eng. Med. Center, Boston, 1964-65; research fellow hematology Tufts U. New Eng. Med. Center, 1964, clin. fellow cardiology, 1965-66; resident in medicine Boston City Hosp., 1966-67; sr. resident in medicine Georgetown U., Washington, 1967-68; fellow in hematology Peter Bent Brigham Hosp., Boston, 1968-69; assoc. in medicine Peter Bent Brigham Hosp., 1969-71; practice medicine specializing in internal medicine and hematology; attending physician Boston City Hosp.; instr., then asst. prof. Harvard U. Med. Sch., 1969-71; prof. medicine U. Ill. Med. Sch., 1971—; chief hematology sect. and hemostasis unit Edgewater Hosp., Chgo., 1979-82. Contbr. numerous articles to profl. jours. Fellow A.C.P.; mem. Internat. Soc. Hematology, Am. Fedn. Clin. Research, Am. Soc. Hematology, Internat. Soc. Hemostasis and Thrombosis, Council on Thrombosis, World Fedn. Hemophilia, Brazilian Coll. Hematology, Mex. Nat. Acad. Medicine, Bolivian Soc. Internal Medicine, Colombian Soc. Hematology, Alpha Omega Alpha. Home: 3255 Brookdale Rd Northbrook IL 60062-7501 Address: 5015 N Paulina St Chicago IL 60640-2717

RODRIGUEZ-MOJICA, WILMA, radiologist, educator; b. Mayaguez, P.R., Mar. 23, 1946; d. Manuel and Rosa (Mojica) Rodriguez; divorced; 1 child, Rebecca Rodriguez-Rodriguez. BS, U. P.R., Mayaguez, 1966; MD, U. P.R., San Juan, 1970. Diplomate Am. Bd. Radiology. Intern U. P.R. Dist. Hosp., 1970-71, resident in diagnostic radiology, 1971-75; radiologist Auxilio Mutuo Hosp., Rio Piedras, P.R., 1976-79; radiologist ptnr. Advanced Radiology Group, Hato Rey, P.R., 1979—; assoc. prof. radiology dept. radiol. scis. U. P.R. Sch. Medicine, Rio Piedras, 1986—; dir. ultrasound Univ. Hosp. Med. Scis. Campus U. P.R., 1980—, proctor radiology electives for med. students, 1975—. Recipient Disting. Citizen award Jaycees Club, 1979, Lions Club, 1987, Mcp. Assembly Women's Week, 1993. Mem. Am. Coll. Radiology (P.R. chpt., treas. 1982-84, counselor 1992, 94), Radiol. Soc. N.Am., Am. Inst. Ultrasound in Medicine, Am. Assn. Women Radiologists, Soc. Radiologists in Ultrasound. Democrat. Roman Catholic. Avocations: reading, drawing. Home: Parque de las Fuentes Apt 2403 Hato Rey PR 00918

RODRIGUEZ-ORELLANA, MANUEL, law educator; b. Rio Piedras, P.R., Mar. 7, 1948; s. Manuel Rodriguez-Ramos and Elena (Orellana-Ramos) Rodriguez; m. Maria Dolores Pizarro-Figueroa, Jan. 30, 1984; 1 child, Laura Elena Rodriguez-Pizarro. BA, Johns Hopkins U., 1970; MA, Brown U., 1972; JD, Boston Coll., 1975; LLM, Harvard U., 1983. Bar: P.R. 1975, U.S. Dist. Ct. P.R. 1976. Staff atty. P.R. Legal Svcs., Inc., San Juan, P.R., 1975-77, dir. consumer law div., 1977-79; dean students Inter-Am. U. Sch. Law, San Juan, P.R., 1979-80, asst. prof. law, 1980-83; assoc. prof. law Northeastern U. Sch. Law, Boston, 1983-89, prof. law, 1989-93; cons. Office Ind. Counsel-Prosecutor of Commonwealth P.R., San Juan, 1985, Office Minority Leader of P.R. Ind. Party, Senate P.R., San Juan, 1985—; vis. scholar Harvard Law Sch., Cambridge, Mass., 1988; electoral commr. Commonwealth P.R., 1989-95; pvt. practice in civil litigation, 1995—; vis. prof. Eugenio M. de Hostas Sch. Law, Mayaguez, P.R., 1995-96. Author: Después de Todo: Poemas de Noche y Circunstancia, 1982. Mem. ABA, Colegio de Abogados de P.R. (bd. govs. 1977-78).

RODWELL, JOHN DENNIS, biochemist; b. Boston, Oct. 9, 1946; s. William Joseph and Lillian Catherine (Cunningham) R.; m. Ellen M. McCaffrey, Dec. 18, 1971; children: Elizabeth Ann, Sarah Catherine. BA in Chemistry, U. Mass., 1968; MS in Organic Chemistry, Lowell Technol. Inst., 1971; PhD in Biochemistry, UCLA, 1976. Postdoctoral fellow Sch. Medicine U. Pa., Phila., 1976-80; rsch. asst. prof. U. Pa. Sch. Medicine, 1980-81; with Cytogen Corp., Princeton, N.J., 1981—; v.p. discovery rsch. Cytogen Corp., 1987-88, v.p. R & D, 1989—; adj. asst. prof., then adj. assoc. prof. Sch. Medicine, U. Pa., 1981—; series editor, Marcel Dekker, Inc., N.Y.C., 1988—. Patentee, antibody conjugates for compound delivery, antibody metal ion complexes; editor: Antibody Mediated Delivery Systems, 1988; coeditor: Covalently Modified Antigens and Antibodies in Diagnosis and Therapy, 1989. Recipient Nat. Rsch. Svc. award NIH, 1978-80, Thomas Alva Edison Patent award, 1993. Mem. AAAS, Am. Assn. Immunologists, Am. Chem. Soc. (assoc. editor 1989-93), N.Y. Acad. Scis., Soc. Nuclear Medicine. Democrat. Avocations: boating, flying. Home: 1340 Eagle Rd New Hope PA 18938-9222 Office: Cytogen Corp 201 College Rd E Princeton NJ 08540-6603

RODZIANKO, PAUL, energy and environmental company executive; b. Washington, Oct. 22, 1945; s. Paul and Aimee Rodzianko; m. Chauncie McKeever, May 1988; children: Marina, Alexander. BA, Princeton U., 1967; MA, Inst. Critical Langs., 1967. With GE Co., 1967-76; pres. U.S. Geothermal Corp., N.Y.C., 1976-77, Geothermal Energy Corp., N.Y.C., 1977-83, Geothermal Food Processors, Inc., Fernley, Nev., 1979-82; exec. v.p. Grace Geothermal Corp., 1981-83, bd. dirs., 1981-83; pres. Bay Capital Corp., Oyster Bay, N.Y., 1983-85, Data Port Co., 1985-86; v.p. spl. projects Kvaerner Energy Devel., Inc., Dover, N.J., 1992-95; pres., CEO Tuxedo Venture Mgmt. Group Inc., 1995—; bd. dirs. McGill Environ. Sys., Inc., Fresh Creek Technologies, Inc.; chmn. bd. dirs. Mt. Hope Hydro, Inc., 1986-92, Halecon, Inc., 1986-92, Kvaerner Venture Inc., 1992-95; v.p. Little Horn Energy Who., 1993. Vice chmn. Russian Orthodox Theol. Fund, 1978—; chmn., CEO Mt. Hope Waterpower Project, 1989-92; mem. Town Coun., Tuxedo, N.Y., 1992—, co-chmn. revitalization com., mem. Rockaway Twp. Econ. Devel. Com., 1995. Fellow Royal Geog. Soc., Explorers Club, New Eng. Soc.; mem. Geothermal Resources Coun. (bd. dirs., chmn. audit com. 1980-82), Nat. Inst. Social Scis., Rockaway Area C. of C. (bd. dirs. 1988-92), Camp Fire Club, Tuxedo Club, Rotary (hon., Paul Harris fellow 1988-92), Lions (mem.-at-large). Office: 627 Mount Hope Ave Wharton NJ 07885-2811

ROE, BENSON BERTHEAU, surgeon, educator; b. L.A., July 7, 1918; s. Hall and Helene Louise (Bertheau) R.; m. Jane Faulkner St. John, Jan. 20, 1945; children: David B., Virginia St. John. AB, U. Calif., Berkeley, 1939; MD cum laude, Harvard U., 1943. Diplomate Am. Bd. Surgery, Am. Bd. Thoracic Surgery (dir. 1971-83, chmn. bd. 1981-83, chmn. exam. com. 1978, chmn. long-range planning com. 1980, chmn. program com. 1977). Intern Mass. Gen. Hosp., Boston, 1943-44, resident, 1946-50; nat. rsch. fellow dept. physiology Med. Sch., Harvard U., Boston, Mass., 1947, instr. surgery, 1950; Moseley Traveling fellow Harvard. U. at U. Edinburgh, Scotland, 1951; asst. clin. prof. surgery U. Calif., San Francisco, 1951-58, chief cardiothoracic surgery, 1958-76, prof. surgery, 1966-89, emeritus prof., 1989—; pvt. practice medicine specializing in cardiothoracic surgery San Francisco, 1952-85; cons. thoracic surgery VA Hosp., San Francisco Gen. Hosp., Letterman Army Hosp., St. Lukes Hosp., Blue Shield of Calif., Baxter Labs., Ethicon, Inc.; bd. dirs. Control Laser Corp.; vis. prof. U. Utah, U. Ky., U. Gdansk, Poland, Nat. Heart Hosp., London, U. Ibadan, Nigeria, Sanger Clinic, Charlotte, Rush-Presbyn. Hosp., Chgo., Penrose Hosp., Colorado Springs; bd. dirs. Internat. Bioethics Inst. Mem. editl. bd. Annals of Thoracic Surgery, 1969-82, Pharos; editor 2 med. texts; author 21 textbook chpts.; contbr. 174 articles to profl. jours. Bd. dirs. United Bay Area Crusade, 1958-70, mem. exec. com., 1964-65; bd. dirs. chmn. exec. com. San Francisco chpt. Am. Cancer Soc., 1955-57; bd. dirs. San Francisco Heart Assn., 1964-72, pres., 1964-65, chmn. rsch. com., 1966-71; mem. various coms. Am. Heart Assn., 1967-70; pres. Miranda Lux Found., 1982-94; trustee Avery Fuller Found.; bd. dirs. Internat. Bioethics Inst., Point Reyes Bird Observatory. Served with Med. Svc. Corps, USNR, 1944-46. Fellow Am. Coll. Cardiology, ACS (chmn. adv. coun. thoracic surgery, program chmn. thoracic surgery, cardiovascular com.), Polish Surg. Assn. (hon.); mem. Am. Assn. Thoracic Surgery (chmn. membership com. 1974-75), AMA (residency rev. com. for thoracic surgery), Am. Surg. Assn., Pacific Coast Surg. Assn., Calif. Acad. Medicine (pres. 1974), Calif. Med. Assn., Soc. Univ. Surgeons, Soc. Throacic Surgerons (pres. 1972, chmn. standards and ethics com.), Soc. Vascular Surgery (v.p.). Clubs: Cruising of Am, Pacific Union, St. Francis Yacht, Calif. Tennis. Office: U Calif Div Cardiothoracic Surgery U Calif M593 San Francisco CA 94143-0118

ROE, BYRON PAUL, physics educator; b. St. Louis, Apr. 4, 1934; s. Sam S. and Gertrude Harriet (Claris) R.; m. Alice Susan Krauss, Aug. 27, 1961; children: Kenneth David, Diana Carol. B.A., Washington U., St. Louis, 1954; Ph.D., Cornell U., 1959. Instr. physics U. Mich., Ann Arbor, 1959-61, asst. prof., 1961-64, assoc. prof., 1964-69, prof., 1969—; guest physicist SSC Lab., 1991. Author: Probability and Statistics in Experimental Physics, 1992, Particle Physics at the New Millennium, 1996 (Libr. Sci. Book Club selection). CERN vis. scientist Geneva, 1967, 89; Brit. Sci. Rsch. Coun. fellow, Oxford, 1979; recipient inventor's prize CDC Worldtech, Edina, Minn., 1982, 83. Fellow Am. Phys. Soc. Home: 3610 Charter Pl Ann Arbor MI 48105-2825 Office: U Mich Physics Dept 500 E University Ave Ann Arbor MI 48109-1120

ROE, DAVID HARTLEY, insurance company executive, retired air force officer; b. Denver, Dec. 11, 1940; s. Jo Dick and Helen Lucille (Hill) R.; m. Ada Clason, Dec. 21, 1963; children: David Arne, Christie, Stephanie. BS, USAF Acad., 1962; 1st BM exam., Oxford (Eng.) U., 1964; MS, U. Ill., 1969, PhD, 1970. CPCU; CLU, ChFC; registered series 7, 24 and 63, Nat. Assn. Securities Dealers. Commd. 2d lt. USAF, 1962, advanced through grades to brig. gen., 1985; prin. dir. NATO policy Office Asst. Sec. Def. for Internat. Security Policy, Washington, 1985-86; ret., 1986; exec. v.p., chief of staff, then pres. fin. svcs. div. USAA, San Antonio, 1986-89, pres. property and casualty ins., 1989-90, exec. v.p., CFO, 1990-91; pres. United Svcs. Life Ins. Co., Arlington, Va., 1991-95, chmn., CEO, 1992-95; pres., COO, US-LICO Corp., Arlington, 1992-95; sr. v.p. Reliaster, 1995—; CEO United Svcs. Life & Bankers Security Life, 1995—; chmn., CEO Bankers Security Life, Arlington, 1992-95. Mem., past chmn. adv. coun. U. Tex. Coll. Bus., San Antonio, 1986-91; trustee, mem. exec. com. San Antonio Med. Found., 1989-91; trustee Falcon Found., 1986—, White House Fellows Found., 1991—; bd. dirs. Army Retirement Residence Found., 1992—, USO Met. Wash., 1993—. Rhodes scholar, 1962-64; White House fellow, 1975-76. Mem. Assn. Grads. USAF Acad. (past pres.), Assn. Am. Rhodes Scholars, White House Fellows Assn., Nat. War Coll. Alumni Assn., Air Force Assn., Sigma Xi. Republican. Mem. Christian Ch. (Disciples of Christ). Avocations: running, golf, soccer, reading. Home: 6105 Still Water Way McLean VA 22101 Office: United Svcs Life Ins Co 4601 Fairfax Dr Arlington VA 22203-1500

ROE, JOHN H., manufacturing company executive; b. 1939. BA, Williams Coll., 1962; MBA, Harvard U., 1964. With Bemis Co. Inc., Mpls., 1964—, plant supt., 1964-67, sales rep., 1967-68, sales mgr., 1968-70, plant mgr., 1970-73, gen. mgr. film div., 1973-76, exec. v.p. ops., 1976-87, pres., chief oper. officer, from 1987, chief exec. officer, 1990—, also bd. dirs., chmn. Office: Bemis Co Inc 222 S 9th St Minneapolis MN 55402-3389*

ROE, MARK J., law educator; b. N.Y.C., Aug. 8, 1951; m. Helen Hsu, Aug. 12, 1974; children: Andrea Hsu, Jessica Hsu. BA, Columbia U., 1972; JD, Harvard U., 1975. Bar: N.Y. 1976. Atty. Fed. Res. Bank, N.Y.C., 1975-77; assoc. Cahill Gordon & Reindel, N.Y.C., 1977-80; prof. Rutgers U. Law Sch., Newark, 1980-86, prof. U. Pa. Law Sch., 1986-88; prof. Sch. Law Columbia U., N.Y.C., 1988—. Author: Strong Managers, Weak Owners: The Political Roots of American Corporate Finance, 1994. Office: Columbia U Sch Law 435 W 116th St New York NY 10027-7201

ROE, MICHAEL FLINN, lawyer; b. Washington, Oct. 28, 1959; s. Jerrold M. Roe and Marilyn Theresa (Matacia) Benstead; m. Patricia Eileen Barrett, Aug. 23, 1987; children: Brendan, Caitrin. BA, U. Notre Dame, 1981; JD, U. San Diego, 1985. Bar: Calif. 1985, Ill. 1992. Asst. counsel, dir. GSI, Inc., Chgo., 1984-88; dep. prosecutor criminal divsn. San Diego, 1988-90; trial atty. Corboy & Demetrio, P.C., Chgo., 1991—; guest lectr. trial techniques John Marshall Law Sch., Chgo., 1994; instr. Near North Metro High Sch., Chgo., 1994. Mem. ATLA, Ill. Trial Lawyers Assn. (product liability com. 1994-95), Ill. State Bar Assn., Amnesty Internat., Ireland C. of C., Ireland Soc. Democrat. Roman Catholic. Avocations: coaching, golf, tennis, horsemanship. Office: Corboy & Demetrio 33 N Dearborn St Chicago IL 60602-3102

ROE, RICHARD C., industry consultant, former home furnishings manufacturing executive; b. Des Moines, Jan. 4, 1930; s. Lloyd E. and Mary E. (Nuzum) R.; m. Sally McGlothlen, Dec. 27, 1952; children: Stephen James, Julie Ann. B.S. in Gen. Engring, Iowa State U., 1952. Registered profl. engr., Iowa, Ind., Ill. Indsl. engr. Maytag Co., Newton, Iowa, 1952-56; gen. mgr. mfg. Schnadig Corp., Chgo., 1956-66; v.p. mfg. Sealy Inc., Chgo., 1966-76, group v.p., 1976-86; pres. Sealy Inc., 1987-89; cons. to industry, 1989—; bd. dirs. Schnadig Corp., Chgo., Serta, Inc., Chgo. Former chmn. adv. com. dept. mgmt. Iowa State U., mem. adv. council coll. bus. Recipient profl. achievement citation in engring. Iowa State U., 1989. Mem. NSPE, Am. Inst. Indsl. Engrs., Internat. Sleep Products Assn. (Exceptional Svc. award 1989). Republican. Clubs: Merchants and Mfrs. (Chgo.); Elks. Patentee in field. Home: 2435 Hamilton Dr Ames IA 50014-8203 Office: 225 S Rohlwing Rd Apt 101 Palatine IL 60067-6468

ROE, ROGER ROLLAND, lawyer; b. Mpls., Dec. 31, 1947; s. Roger Rolland Roe; m. Paula Speltz, 1974; children: Elena, Madeline. BA, Grinnell Coll., 1970; JD, U. Minn., 1973. Bar: Minn. 1973, U.S. Dist. Ct. Minn. 1974, U.S. Ct. Appeals (8th cir.) 1977, U.S. Supreme Ct. 1978, Wis. 1988, U.S. Dist. Ct. Nebr. 1995, U.S. Dist. Ct. (ea. and we. dists.) Wis. Law clk. to Hon. Judge Amdahl Hennepin County Dist. Ct., Mpls., 1973-74; from assoc. to ptnr. Rider, Bennett, Egan & Arundel, Mpls., 1974-91; mng. ptnr. Yaeger, Jungbauer, Barczak & Roe, Ltd., Mpls., 1992—; mem. nat. panel arbitrators Am. Arbitration Assn.; judge trial practice class and moot ct. competitions law sch. U. Minn.; guest lectr. Minn. Continuing Legal Edn. courses. Fellow Internat. Soc. Barristers; mem. ATLA (guest lectr.), Am. Bd. Trial Advs. (diplomat, Mass. chpt. pres. 1996-97), Minn. Trial Lawyers Assn., Million Dollar Round Table. Avocations: golfing, downhill skiing. Office: Yaeger Jungbauer Barczak & Roe Ltd 701 4th Ave S Ste 1400 Minneapolis MN 55415

ROE, THOMAS ANDERSON, building supply company executive; b. Greenville, S.C., May 29, 1927; s. Thomas Anderson and Leila (Cunningham) R.; m. Shirley Marie Waddell, Aug. 2, 1980; children: Elizabeth Overton Roe Mason, Thomas Anderson, Philip Stradley, John Verner; 1 stepchild, Amy Elizabeth Waddell Willcox. BS, Furman U., 1948, LLD, 1980; diploma in bus. mgmt., LaSalle Extension U., 1956. Cancer rsch. asst. Furman U., 1947-48; with Builder Marts of Am., Inc., Greenville, S.C., 1948-87, pres., 1961-69, chmn., 1969-87, CEO, 1969-78; chmn. First Piedmont Corp., 1967-74, First Piedmont Bank & Trust Co., 1967-74; bd. dirs. Swiss Tex. Mem. Greenville County Redevel. Authority, 1971-75; vice chmn. S.C. Republican Com., 1963-64, fin. chmn. 1986—; mem. Nat. Rep. Fin. Com., 1963-64; hon. asst. sgt.-at-arms Rep. Nat. Conv., Chgo., 1960; past bd. dirs. Nat. Found. Ileitis and Colitis, Greenville United Cerebral Palsy, Greenville chpt. ARC; past chmn. adv. council Furman U.; pres. S.C. Policy Council, Columbia, 1986-90, now founding chmn., bd. dirs.; bd. govs. Council for Nat. Policy, 1984-94; past trustee Greenville Symphony, 1985-93, Inst. Rsch. on Econs. of Taxation, 1983-90; trustee Christ Ch. Episc. Sch., 1970-72, Coker Coll., 1975-81, Intercollegiate Studies Inst., 1983—, Heritage Found., 1985—, Free Congress Rsch. and Edn. Found., Washington, 1987—; mem. bd. govs. Found. Francisco Marroquin, Guatemala, Internat. Policy Forum, Washington, 1984-90; bd. dirs., mem. exec. com. Peace Ctr. for Performing Arts, Greenville; founding chmn., bd. dirs. State Policy Network, Ft. Wayne, Ind.; pres. Charity Ball Bd., Rose Ball, Greenville, S.C. Named builder of yr. Greenville Home Builders Assn., 1962. Mem. Nat. Assn. Home Builders (internat. housing com.), Greenville Home Builders Assn. (v.p. 1962-63), Nat. Lumber Bldg. Material Dealers Assn., Carolina Bldg. Material Dealers Assn. (pres. 1965-66), Greenville Bldg. Materials Assn. (pres.), Mont. Pelerin Soc., Greenville C. of C. (dir. 1967-70, pres. 1970), Players Club (pres. 1951), Sertoma Club (pres. local club 1960-61, disting. svc. award 1959, superior leaderhsip award 1961), World Trade Ctr. Club, Poinsett Club. Home and Office: 712 Crescent Ave Greenville SC 29601-4350

ROE, THOMAS COOMBE, former utility company executive; b. Dover, Del., Sept. 22, 1914; s. John Moore and Elizabeth Lindale (Cooper) R.; m. Emma Lillian Scotton, Oct. 16, 1937; children: Thomas C., Margaret Ruth (dec.). B.S. in Elec. Engring, U. Del., 1935; DHL (hon.), Wesley Coll., 1987. With Eastern Shore Public Service, 1936-43; with Delmarva Power & Light Co., 1943—; pres. subs. Delmara Power & Light Co., 1971-76, chmn. bd., 1976-79, dir., 1971-80, ret., 1980. Hon. trustee Peninsula Gen. Hosp. Med. Center, Salisbury, Md.; trustee Wesley Coll., Dover, Del.; former chmn. Wesley Coll.; former trustee Wesley Theol. Sem., Washington. Served with AUS, 1941-45. Republican. Methodist. Club: Rotary (past pres.).

ROE, THOMAS LEROY WILLIS, pediatrician; b. Bend, Oreg., Sept. 1, 1936. MD, U. Oregon Health Scis. U., Portland, 1961. Diplomate Am. Bd. Pediatrics. Intern U. Calif., San Francisco, 1961-62, resident, 1962-64; physician Sacred Heart Med. Ctr., Eugene, Oreg.; pvt. practice Peace Health Med. Group, Eugene, 1985—; clin prof. pediatrics U. Oregon, Eugene, 1985—. Fellow Am. Acad. Pediatricians; mem. AMA, North Pacific Pediatrics Soc. Office: Eugene Clin 1162 Williamette St Eugene OR 97401

ROECK, THOMAS J., JR., airline financial executive; b. Berwyn, Ill., June 21, 1944; s. Thomas Joseph and Ruth R. (Lovings) R.; m. Carol A. Hansen, Sept. 29, 1973. B.S. in Acctg., U. So. Calif., 1971. With Global Marine Inc., L.A., 1966-84, asst. treas., 1973-78, treas., 1978-80, v.p., treas., 1980-84; sr. v.p., chief fin. officer Western Air Lines, Inc., L.A., 1984-87; v.p. fin. adminstrn. Delta Air Lines Inc., Atlanta, 1987-88, sr. v.p. fin., chief fin. officer, 1988—. Served as sgt. U.S. Army, 1968-70, Korea. Office: Delta Air Lines Inc Hartsfield Atlanta Internat Airport Atlanta GA 30320

ROEDDER, EDWIN WOODS, geologist; b. Monsey, N.Y., July 30, 1919; s. Hans and Edna (Woods) R.; m. Kathleen Rea; children: Spencer, Lucy. BA, Lehigh U., 1941; MA, Columbia U., 1947, PhD, 1950; DSc (hon.), Lehigh U., 1976. Rsch. engr. Bethlehem Steel Corp., Bethlehem, Pa., 1941-46; predoctoral fellow Geophys. Lab., Carnegie Inst., Washington, 1946-47; asst. in geology Columbia U., N.Y.C., 1946-49; asst. prof., assoc. prof. U. Utah, Salt Lake City, 1950-55; chief solid state group U.S. Geol. Survey, Washington, 1955-60, staff geologist, 1960-62, geologist, 1962-73, rsch. geologist, 1974-87; assoc. Harvard U., 1987—; scientist emeritus U.S. Geol. Survey, Washington, 1987—; mem. or cons. various adv. bds, vis. coms., panels for U.S. govt. and several universities. Author: Composition of Fluid Inclusions, 1972, Fluid Inclusions, 1984; editor: Research on Mineral Forming Solutions, 1965, Fluid Inclusion Research (ann. book), 1968—; patentee in field. Recipient Exceptional Sci. Achievement medal NASA, 1973, Disting. Svc. medal U.S. Dept. Interior, 1978, Abraham Gottlob-Werner medaille Deutschen Min. Gesellschaft, 1985, Cyril Purkyne medal Czech Geol. Survey, 1991; first H.C. Sorby medal, 1993; grantee NSF, others. Fellow AAAS, Am. Geophys. Union (pres. V.G. and P. sect. 1978-80), Mineral Soc. Am. (v.p. 1981-82, pres. 1982-83, Washington A. Roebling medal 1986); mem. NAS, Geochem. Soc. (sec. 1967-70, v.p. 1975-76, pres. 1976-77), Soc. Econ. Geologists (R.A.F. Penrose medal 1988). Avocations: music, travel, stamp collecting. Office: Harvard U Dept Earth & Planetary Scis Cambridge MA 02138

ROEDEL, PAUL ROBERT, steel company executive; b. Millville, N.J., June 15, 1927; s. Charles Howard and Irene (Voorhees) R.; m. June Gilbert Adams, June 25, 1951; children—Beth Anne, Meg Adams. B.S. in Accounting, Rider Coll., 1949. With Carpenter Tech. Corp., Reading, Pa., 1949—; asst. controller Carpenter Tech. Corp., 1957-65, controller, 1965-72, treas., 1972-73, v.p. fin., treas., 1973-75, exec. v.p., 1975-79, pres., 1979—, chief operating officer, 1979-81, chief exec. officer, 1981-92, dir., 1973—, chmn., CEO, 1987-92; dir. Meridian Bancorp Inc., 1974—, Gen. Public Utilities Corp., 1979—, P.H. Glatfelter Co., 1992—. Bd. dirs. Hawk Mountain coun. Boy Scouts Am., Pa. 2000 Edn. Coalition; trustee Gettysburg Coll.; pres. Wyomissing Found. With USNR, 1945-46. Home: 416 Wheatland Ave Reading PA 19607-1326 Office: Carpenter Tech Corp 101 Bern St Reading PA 19601-1203

ROEDER, DOUGLAS N., sales executive; b. Newark, Apr. 17, 1950; s. Jesse N. And Elizabeth R.; m. Debra O. Roeder, Apr. 6, 1974; children: Courtney Beth, Kelly Christine, Kyle Robert. BA, Muhlenberg Coll., 1972. Account exec. Nat. Lampoon, N.Y.C., 1974-76; assoc. pub. Profl. Golf Assn. Tour Mag., N.Y.C., 1976-77; mgr. travel/liquor Saturday Rev., N.Y.C., 1977-79; mgr. liquor/tobacco New West, N.Y.C., 1979-80, Tex. Monthly/Calif. Mag., N.Y.C., 1980—; v.p., nat. sales mgr. Mediatex Nat. Sales, N.Y.C., 1980-88; dir. advt. Bon Appétit, 1988—. Mem. N.Y. Advt. Club, Princeton Club, Rockland Country Club.

ROEDER, GLORIA JEAN, civil rights specialist, private investigator; b. Des Moines, Iowa, Dec. 4, 1945; d. Gerald Arthur and Dorothy Jean (Pardekooper) R. BA, Simpson Coll., 1970; postgrad., Iowa State U., 1991. Examiner disability determination divsn. Disability Determination Div. State of Iowa, Des Moines, 1970-75; owner, pres. Aaron Investigations, Des Moines, 1975—; pvt. investigator Des Moines; cons. All Area Detective Agy., Des Moines, 1965-78. Civil rights specialist Iowa Civil Rights Commn., Des Moines, 1978—, local liaison; mem. ctrl. com. Iowa Dem. Com. Polk, Des Moines, 1991—; vol. Luth. Social Svcs., 1988—; mem. Christ the King Cath. Ch., mem. social concerns com., 1995-96, chair mem., 1995-96, eucharistic min., 1996. Mem. Nat. Assn. Human Rights Workers, Nat. Assn. Prevention Child Abuse (bd. dirs. 1988-91), Iowa Assn. Pvt. Investigators (chair constn. com. 1994-95, sec. bd. dirs. 1996). Democrat. Avocations: poetry, drawing, painting, swimming, reading. Office: Iowa Civil Rights Commn 211 Maple St Des Moines IA 50309-1858

ROEDER, REBECCA EMILY, software engineer; b. Findlay, Ohio, Nov. 2, 1959; d. Brian Eldon and Barbara Lee (Melton) R.; m. Stephen William Bigley, May 28, 1983. BS in Edn. and Computer Sci., Bowling Green State U., 1983, MS in Computer Sci., 1993. Systems analyst NCR Corp., Dayton, Ohio, 1983-84; sr. systems analyst Unisys (Burroughs) Corp., Detroit, 1984-88; asst. dir. St. Vincent Med. Ctr., Toledo, 1988-95; sr. cons. Advanced Programming Resources, Inc., Columbus, Ohio, 1996—. Active Sta. WGTE/WGLE Pub. Radio, Toledo, 1984-96, Sta. WOSU Pub. Radio, Columbus, 1996—, Sta. WCBE Pub. Radio, Columbus, 1996—, Toledo Mus. Art, 1988-96, Toledo Zoo, 1993-96; presenter Women in Sci. Career Day, Lourde's Coll., 1992. Marathon scholar Marathon Oil Co., Findlay, 1978, Hancock scholar Findlay Area C. of C., 1978. Mem. AAUW, Assn. for Computing Machinery, Columbus Computer Soc. Republican. Episcopalian. Avocations: instrumental and choral music, drum and bugle corps, reading. Home: 4964 Vicksburg Ln Hilliard OH 43026 Office: Advanced Programming Resources Inc 2929 Kenny Rd Columbus OH 43221

ROEDER, RICHARD KENNETH, business owner, lawyer; b. Phila., Oct. 11, 1948; s. Walter August and Gloria (Miller) R.; m. Frederika Anne Beesemyer, June 25, 1983; 1 child, William Frederick. AB, Amherst Coll., 1970; JD, U. Calif., Berkeley, 1973, Cambridge U., 1973-74. Assoc. Paul, Hastings, Janofky & Walker, L.A., 1974-81, ptnr., 1981-90; ptnr. Aurora Capital Ptnrs., L.A., 1990—. Office: Aurora Capital Ptnrs 1800 Century Park E Ste 1000 Los Angeles CA 90067-1513

ROEDER, ROBERT GAYLE, biochemist, educator; b. Boonville, Ind., June 3, 1942; s. Frederick John and Helene (Bredenkamp) R.; m. Suzanne Himsel, July 11, 1964 (div. 1981); children: Kimberly, Michael; m. Cun Jing Hong, June 2, 1990. BA summa cum laude (Gilbert scholar), Wabash Coll., 1964, DSc (hon.), 1990; MS, U. Ill., 1965; PhD (USPHS fellow), U. Wash., 1969. Am. Cancer Soc. fellow dept. embryology Carnegie Instn. Washington, Balt., 1969-71; asst. prof. biol. chemistry Washington U., St. Louis, 1971-75; assoc. prof. Washington U., 1975-76, prof., 1976-82, prof. genetics, 1978-82, James S. McDonnell prof. biochem. genetics, 1979-82; prof. lab. biochemistry and molecular biology Rockefeller U., N.Y.C., 1982—; Arnold O. and Mabel S. Beckmann prof. molecular biology and biochemistry Rockefeller U., 1985—; cons. USPHS, 1975-79, Am. Cancer Soc., 1983-86. Recipient Dreyfus Tchr.-Scholar award Dreyfus Found., 1976, molecular biology award NAS-U.S. Steel Found., 1986, outstanding investigator award Nat. Cancer Inst., 1986—, Rosenstiel award for disting. work in basic med. scis. Brandeis U., 1995, Passano award Passano Found., Inc., 1995; grantee NIH, 1972—, NSF, 1975-79, Am. Cancer Soc., 1979-85. Fellow AAAS, Am. Acad. Arts & Scis., Am. Acad. Microbiology, N.Y. Acad. Scis.; mem. NAS, Am. Chem. Soc. (Eli Lilly award 1977), Am. Soc. Biol. Chemists, Am. Soc. Microbiologists, Harvey Soc. (pres. 1994), Phi Beta Kappa. Home: 504 E 63rd St Apt 36P New York NY 10021-7929 Office: Rockefeller University 1230 York Ave New York NY 10021-6307

ROEDER, STEPHEN BERNHARD WALTER, chemistry and physics educator; b. Dover, N.J., Aug. 26, 1939; s. Walter Martin and Katherine E.R. (Holz) R.; m. Phoebe E. Barber, June 28, 1969; children: Adrienne H.K., Roland K.W. B.A., Dartmouth Coll., 1961; Ph.D., U. Wis., 1965. Postdoctoral fellow Bell Telephone Labs., Murray Hill, N.J., 1965-66; lectr. physics U. Oreg., Eugene, 1966-68; asst. prof. chemistry and physics San Diego State U., 1968-72, assoc. prof., 1972-75, prof., 1975—, chmn. dept. physics, 1975-78, chmn. dept. chemistry, 1979-86, acting dir. Master of Liberal Arts Program, 1987, 89, chmn. dept. physics, 1991-94, chmn. dept. of chemistry, 1995—; vis. staff mem. Los Alamos Nat. Labs., 1974-92; vis. assoc. prof. chemistry U. B.C., Vancouver, Can., 1974-75; vis. prof. physics Tex. A&M U., College Station, 1982; cons. Lovelace Med. Found., 1985-90. Author: (with others) Experimental Pulse NMR, 1981. Recipient Outstanding Teaching award San Diego State U., 1971, Outstanding Prof. award San Diego State U., 1992; grantee Rsch. Corp., 1968, 71, 72. Mem. AAAS, Am. Chem. Soc., Am. Phys. Soc., Sigma Xi. Republican. Home: 6789 Alamo Way La Mesa CA 91941-5807 Office: San Diego State U Dept of Chem San Diego CA 92182-1030

ROEDERER, JUAN GUALTERIO, physics educator; b. Trieste, Italy, Sept. 2, 1929; came to U.S., 1967, naturalized, 1972; s. Ludwig Alexander and Anna Rafaela (Lohr) R.; m. Beatriz Susana Cougnet, Dec. 20, 1952; children: Ernesto, Irene, Silvia, Mario. Ph.D., U. Buenos Aires, 1952. Research scientist Max Planck Inst., Gottingen, W.Ger., 1952-55; group leader Argentine Atomic Energy Commn., Buenos Aires, 1953-59; prof. physics U. Buenos Aires, 1959-66, U. Denver, 1967-77; prof. physics U. Alaska, Fairbanks, 1977-93, prof. emeritus, 1993—, dir. Geophys. Inst., 1977-86, dean Coll. Environ. Scis., 1978-82; vis. staff Los Alamos Nat. Lab., 1969-81; chmn. U.S. Arctic Research Com., 1987-91. Author: Dynamics of Geomagnetically Trapped Radiation, 1970, Physics and Psychophysics of Music, 1973, 3d edit., 1995; contbr. articles to profl. jours. Nat. Acad. Sci. NASA sr. research fellow, 1964-66. Fellow AAAS, Am. Geophys. Union; mem. Assn. Argentina de Geodestas y Geofisicos, Nat. Acad. Sci. Argentina (corr.), Nat. Acad. Sci. Austria (corr.), Third World Acad. Scis. (assoc.). Lutheran. Research on plasma and energetic particles in earth's magnetosphere, policy issues for Arctic, perception of music. Home: 105 Concordia Dr Fairbanks AK 99709-3029 Office: Geophys Inst U Alaska Fairbanks AK 99775-7320

ROEDIGER, JANICE ANNE, artist, educator; b. Trenton, N.J.; d. John and Anne Balint; m. Paul Margerum Roediger; children: Pamela Anne, Matthew Paul, Joan Margaret. Student, Beaver Coll., 1975-78; grad. cert., Pa. Acad. Fine Arts, 1988. Instr. multi-media Jane Law Long Beach Island Gallery, Surf City, N.J., 1992-94, 94-96; instr. drawing Long Beach Island Found., Loveladies, N.J., 1994; docent Mus. Am. Art, Pa. Acad. Fine Arts, Phila., 1992-94. Exhibited in group shows at Rittenhouse Galleries, Phila., 1988-94, Phila. Mus. Art, ASR Gallery, 1992-96, Schaff Gallery, Cin., 1995-96. Mem. vestry, rector's warden St. Anne's Episcopal Ch., Abington, Pa., 1970-73; chair med. staff aux. Abington Meml. Hosp., 1973-7, chair scholarship com., 1974; coord. student com. Pa. Acad. Fine Arts, Phila., 1986-88; active Phila. Mus. Art, 1972—. Recipient Rohm & Haas Outstanding Achievement award Pa. Acad. Fine Arts, 1987, Pearl Van Sciver award Woodmere Mus., 1991, Blumenthal award Cheltenham Ctr. for Arts, 1991, Lance Lauffler award for visionary painting Pa. Acad. Fine Arts, 1988. Mem. Nat. Mus. Women in Arts, Phila. Art Alliance, Artists Cultural Exch. (bd. dirs. 1989—). Episcopalian. Avocations: writing, collecting, golf, walking, travel. Home: 1244 Rydal Rd Rydal PA 19046-1415 Studio: 1010 Arch St Philadelphia PA 19107-3003

ROEG, NICOLAS JACK, film director; b. London, Aug. 15, 1928; s. Jack Nicolas and Mabel Getrude (Silk) R.; m. Susan Rennie Stephen, May 12, 1957; children: Joscelin Nicolas, Nicolas Jack, Lucien John, Sholto Jules; m. Theresa Russell, 1985; children: Maximilian Nicolas Sextus, Statten Jack. Student Brit. schs.; LittD, Hull (Eng.) U., 1995. Cinematographer films The Caretaker, 1963, Masque of Red Death, 1964, Fahrenheit 451, 1966, A Funny Thing Happened on the Way to the Forum, 1966, Far from the Madding Crowd, 1967, Petulia, 1968; co-dir. film Performance, 1970; dir. films Walkabout, 1970, Don't Look Now, 1973, Glastonbury Fayre, 1973, The Man Who Fell to Earth, 1976, Bad Timing, 1980, Eureka, 1982, Insignificance, 1985, Castaway, 1986, 89, Track 29, 1987, Aria, 1987, The Witches, 1988-89, Cold Heaven, 1990, Heart of Darkness, 1994, Two Deaths, 1994, Hotel Paradise, 1995, Full Body Massage, 1995, Samson & Delilah, 1996; dir. TV films: Sweet Bird of Youth, 1989, Heart of Darkness, 1994; exec. producer Without You I'm Nothing, 1989, Young Indy, 1991. Fellow Brit. Film Inst.; mem. Dirs. Guild Am., Dir. Guild Gt. Britain, Acad. Motion Picture Arts and Scis., Assn. Cinematograph, TV and Allied Technicians. Office: care Robert Littman Beverly Hills CA 90210

ROEGNER, GEORGE PETER, industrial designer; b. Flushing, N.Y., Sept. 3, 1932; s. George Elmer and Margaret (Hanna) R.; B.F.A., Pratt Inst., 1954; m. Jane R. Kramer, Aug. 29, 1959; children—George Curtis, John Hanson, Nicholas Meade. Staff designer Gen. Motors Corp., 1954-55, Raymond Loewy Assocs., N.Y.C., Westinghouse Corp., Metuchen, N.J., 1960-66; product design mgr. RCA, Indpls., 1966-70; dir. design Lenox Inc., Trenton, 1972-74; pres. Curtis Hanson Meade Inc., Far Hills, N.J., 1974—; ptnr. Furniture Concepts Internat. Ltd.; dir. Cove House Corp. Bd. dirs. Clarence Dillon Library; vice chmn. Far Hills Bd. Adjustment; councilman Borough of Far Hills, 1982—, police chmn., 1984—. Served with U.S. Army, 1956-58. Recipient design awards ID Mag., Nat. Paper Box, Consumer Electronics Show, Printing Industries, Print Mag., Wescon. Mem. Indsl. Designers Soc. Am. (past nat. com. chmn.), Somerset Hills Assn., Raritan Valley Watershed Assn. Republican. Clubs: Eastward Ho Country, Stage Harbor Yacht. Designs shown at Mus. Modern Art, Smithsonian Instn., N.Y. World's Fair, Brussels, Zagreb Fairs, Indpls. Art Mus.

ROEHL, JERRALD J(OSEPH), lawyer; b. Austin, Tex., Dec. 6, 1945; s. Joseph E. and Jeanne Foster (Scott) R.; m. Nancy J. Meyers, Jan. 15, 1977; children: Daniel J., Katherine C., J. Ryan, J. Taylor. BA, U. N.Mex., 1968; JD, Washington and Lee U., 1971. Bar: N.Mex. 1972, U.S. Ct. Appeals (10th cir.) 1972, U.S. Supreme Ct. 1977. Practice of Law, Albuquerque, 1972—; pres. Roehl Law Firm P.C. and predecessors, Albuquerque, 1976—; lectr. to profl. groups; real estate developer, Albuquerque. Bd. dirs. Rehab. Ctr. of Albuquerque, 1974-78; mem. assocs. Presbyn. Hosp. Ctr., Albuquerque, 1974-82; incorporator, then treas. exec. com. Ctr. City Coun., 1991—. Recipient award of recognition State Bar N.Mex., 1975, 76, 77. Mem. ABA (award of achievement Young Lawyers div. 1975, council econs. of law practice sect. 1978-80, exec. council Young Lawyers div. 1979-81, fellow div. 1984—, council tort and ins. practice sect. 1981-83), N.Mex. Bar Assn. (pres. young lawyers sect. 1975-76), Albuquerque Bar Assn. (bd. dirs. 1976-79), N.Mex. Def. Lawyers Assn. (pres. 1983-84), Sigma Alpha Epsilon, Sigma Delta Chi, Phi Delta Phi. Roman Catholic. Clubs: Albuquerque Country, Albuquerque Petroleum. Bd. advs. ABA Jour., 1981-83; bd. editors Washington and Lee Law Rev., 1970-71. Home: 4411 Constitution Ave NE Albuquerque NM 87110-5721 Office: Roehl Law Firm PC 300 Central Ave SW Albuquerque NM 87102-3249

ROEHL, JOSEPH E., lawyer; b. Albuquerque, Feb. 17, 1913; s. H.C. and Elizabeth J. (Walsh) R.; m. Jeanne F. Scott, Nov. 1, 1938. BA, U. N.Mex., 1936; LLB; LL.B., U. Tex., 1946. Bar: Tex. 1946, N.Mex. 1946, U.S. Ct. Appeals (10th cir.). Asst. adminstr. OPA, 1942-44; librarian Supreme Ct. Tex., Austin, 1945-46; practice in Albuquerque, 1946—; law clk. U.S. Circuit Judge Sam G. Bratton, Albuquerque, 1946-47; assoc. Simms & Modrall, 1947-53; mng. partner Modrall, Seymour, Sperling, Roehl & Harris, 1954-74; sr. dir. Modrall, Sperling, Roehl, Harris & Sisk, 1953—; chmn. com. uniform jury instrns. Supreme Ct. N.M., 1962-83; bd. dirs. Mountain States Mut. Casualty Ins. Co., 1977-93; Pres. Rio Grande Lumber Co., 1959-68; pres. Rico, Inc. Co-author, editor: New Mexico Civil Jury Instruction, 1966, 2d edit., 1981; Contbr. articles on law office econs. and mgmt. profl. jours.; speaker before profl. groups. Recipient First Nat. award for state bar activities, 1962. Fellow Am. Bar Found.; mem. ABA, Tex. Bar Assn., N.Mex. Bar Assn. Office: Sun West Bank Tower 500 4th St NW PO Box 2168 Albuquerque NM 87103

ROEHL, KATHLEEN ANN, financial executive; b. Chgo., June 1, 1948; d. Walter Steven and Catherine (Puss) Kalchbrenner; m. Eric C. Roehl, June 28, 1969; children: Aaron C., Marc E. BA with honors, U. Ill., 1969. Registered investment advisor. Tchr. Ft. Huachuca (Ariz.) Accomodation Schs., 1969-70; interior designer Key Kitchens, Dearborn Heights, Mich., 1979-80; stockbroker, fin. cons. Merrill Lynch, Dearborn, Mich., 1980-81; v.p., registered investment advisor Merrill Lynch, Northbrook, Ill., 1982—; bd. dirs ATA Info. Systems. Mem. Ill. Govt. Fin. Officers Assn., Internat. Assn. for Fin. Planning (bd. dirs. 1987-88), Northbrook C. of C. (bd. dirs. 1991-93), Northbrook Early Risers Rotary (charter mem.). Avocations: horticulture, architecture. Office: Merrill Lynch 400 Skokie Blvd Northbrook IL 60062-2816

ROEHLING, CARL DAVID, architect; b. Detroit, June 25, 1951; m. Barbara K. Jeffries; children: Carl Robert, Kristin Virginia. BS in Architecture, U. Mich., 1973, MArch, 1975. Registered arch., Mich.; cert. Nat. Coun. Archtl. Registration Bd. Architect Minoru Yamasaki and Assocs., Inc., Troy, Mich., 1976-77; TMP Assocs., 1977-81; architect Harley Ellington Pierce Yee Assocs., Inc., Southfield, Mich., 1981-83, Giffels/Hoyem Basso Assocs., Troy, 1983-87, Smith, Hinchman & Grylls Assocs., Inc., Detroit, 1987—; with Chrysler World Hdqs., 1994. Prin. works include CBS/Fox Video Hdqrs., Livonia, Mich. (Honor award Mich. Masonry Inst., 1985), First Ctr. Office Bldg., Southfield, Mich. (Honor award AIA Mich., 1988), Ind. U. Chemistry Bldg., Bloomington (Honor award AIA Detroit, 1990, AIA Mich., 1990), U. Mich. Aerospace Lab. Bldg., Ann Arbor, 1993, Los Alamos (N.Mex.) Materials Sci. Lab., 1993, others. George Booth travelling fellow U. Mich., 1976; Albert Kahn grad. scholar U. Mich., 1974-75. Mem. AIA (Mich. chpg. pres. bd. dirs. 1989, mem. nat. com. on environ. 1991, Detroit chpt. pres. 1994, initiated Place mag., Young Arch. of Yr., AIA Detroit, 1986, AIA Mich., 1991, regional dir. 1996—, nat. bd. dirs.), Mich. Archtl. Found. (chmn. pres. scholarship program 1990). Office: Smith Hinchman & Grylls 150 W Jefferson Ave Ste 100 Detroit MI 48226-4415

ROEHM, MACDONELL, JR., retail executive; b. Semerang, Indonesia, July 6, 1939; s. MacDonell and Mary Bennett (Cobb) R.; m. Nedra Ann Zeth, May 11, 1974. B.A., Colgate U., 1961; M.B.A., Harvard U., 1966. Fin. analyst Exxon Corp., 1966-68; asso. Lazard Freres, N.Y.C., 1968-71; gen. partner J. Bush & Co., N.Y.C., 1971-73; v.p. planning and devel. Cerro Corp., N.Y.C., 1973-75; v.p., treas. N L Industries, Inc., N.Y.C., 1976-79; sr. v.p. ops., devel. and planning N L Petroleum Services/N L Industries, Inc., Houston, 1979-80; pres. N.L. Shaffer/NL Industries, Inc., 1980-82; exec. v.p. NL Industries, Inc., 1982-85; ptnr. AEA Investors, Inc., 1985-95; chmn., pres., CEO Bill's Dollar Stores, Inc., 1995—. Served with USN 1961-64. Decorated Silver Star, Bronze star, Purple Heart. Office: Bills Dollar Stores Inc 3800 I-55 North Jackson MS 39211

ROEHRIG, C(HARLES) BURNS, internist, health policy consultant, editor; b. Brookline, Mass., Jan. 21, 1923; s. Gilbert Haven and Helen (Burns) R.; m. Patricia Joan Orme, July 22, 1952; children—Joan Russell Roehrig Vater, Jennifer Orme Roehrig Munn, Charles Burns, Jr. Student, Amherst Coll., 1941-43, Vanderbilt U., 1943-44; M.D., U. Md., 1949; cert. in internal medicine, U. Pa. Grad. Sch. Medicine, Phila., 1953. Diplomate Am. Bd. Internal Medicine. Intern Boston City Hosp., 1949-50; resident in internal medicine and diabetes Joslin Clinic, New Eng. Deaconess Hosp., Boston, 1952-54; practice medicine specializing in internal medicine and diabetes Boston, 1954—; chief of staff, pres. med. adminstrv. bd. New Eng. Deaconess Hosp., Boston, 1972-75; dir., mem. exec. com. Blue Shield of Mass., Inc., Boston, 1977-88, dir., 1989—; mem. exec. com. Met. Boston Hosp. Coun., 1982-86; mem. physician adv. council Mass. Hosp. Assn., Burlington, 1982-86. Editor: The Internist: Health Policy in Practice, Washington, 1987—; contbr. med. articles to profl. jours. Bd. dirs. Camping Svcs. Bd., Greater Boston YMCA, 1966—; mem. physician adv. group Health Care Financing Adminstrn., Washington, 1983-88; mem. adv. panel on physician payment and med. tech. Office of Tech. Assessment, U.S. Congress, Washington, 1984-85; chmn. Federated Coun. for Internal Medicine, Washington, 1985-86; trustee New Eng. Deaconess Hosp. Capt. (flight surgeon) USAF, 1949-52. Fellow ACP; mem. AMA (chmn. coun. on long range planning and devel., Chgo.), New Eng. Diabetes Assn. (pres. 1963-64), Mass. Soc. Internal Medicine (pres. 1971-72), Am. Soc. Internal Medicine (pres. 1984-85). Republican. Episcopalian. Club: Wellesley Country (Mass.). Office: PO Box 812900 Wellesley MA 02181-0026

ROEHRKASSE, PAULINE CATHERINE HOLTORF, retired secondary education educator; b. Malmo, Nebr., Sept. 14, 1909; d. Jurgen Heinrich and Wiebke (Knuth) Holtorf; m. Raymond Roehrkasse, June 11, 1935; children: Paula Joan Knepper, Claire Rae Eason, Kathryn Grace Trebelhorn. Grad. in Music, Luther Jr. Coll., Wahoo, Nebr., 1929; BS in Edn., U. Nebr., 1967; postgrad., Kearney State U., Nebr., 1970. Tchr. Grand Island (Nebr.) pub. schs., 1951-72; pipe organist Trinity Luth. Ch., 1938-53. Author: A Flowering: A Festival, 1984. V.p. Ctrl. States Coalition on Aging, 1989-90; elected U.S. Silver Haired Senator from Nebr., 1988-97; sec. steering com. Nat. Silver Haired Congress, 1988-95; publicity chmn. Nat. Coun. Silver Haired Legislators, 1985-93; organizer Internat. Luth. Women's Missionary League, Chgo., 1942, corr. sec., 1942-52, pres. Nebr. South dist., 1948-52. Mem. AAUW (legis. chmn., program chmn.), Am. Assn. Ret. Persons (program chmn. 1983-85, legis. chmn. 1985-92), Ret. Tchrs. Assn., Alpha Delta Kappa (pres. Epsilon chpt.). Democrat. Lutheran. Home: 503 S Broadwell Ave Grand Island NE 68803-5951

ROEL, RON, newspaper editor. Dep. bus. editor Newsday, Inc., Melville, N.Y., now dep. nat. editor, 1995—. Office: Newsday Inc 235 Pinelawn Rd Melville NY 11747-4226

ROELLIG, LEONARD OSCAR, physics educator; b. Detroit, May 17, 1927; s. Oscar Otto and Laura K. (Rutz) R.; m. B. Pauline Cowdin, June 20, 1952; children: Thomas Leonard, Mark Douglas, Paul David. A.B., U. Mich., 1950, M.S., 1956, Ph.D., 1959. From asst. prof. to prof. physics Wayne State U., Detroit, 1958-78; dean Wayne State U., 1971-72, asso. provost, 1972-76; pres. Central Solar Energy Research Corp., Detroit, 1977; prof. physics CCNY, 1978—; vice chancellor acad. affairs CUNY, 1978-83; vis. prof. Univ. Coll., London, 1968-69, Tata Inst. Fundamental Rsch., Bombay, India, 1973, Paul Scherrer Inst., Villigen, Switzerland, 1991-92; chmn. bd. advisers Midwest Regional Solar Energy Planning Venture, 1977. Co-author: Positron Annihilation, 1967; contbr. articles to profl. jours. Bd. dirs. Luth. Publicity Bur., 1981-91, v.p., 1984-85, pres., 1985-89; v.p. Grosse Pointe (Mich.) Human Rels. Coun., 1969-70. With USN, 1945-46, U.S. Army, 1950-52. Recipient Wayne State U. Fund Research Recognition award, 1963, Probus Club award for acad. achievement, 1968, Probus Club award for acad. leadership, 1977. Mem. Am. Phys. Soc., N.Y. Acad. Sci. Home: 167 E 67th St New York NY 10021-5914 Office: Dept Physics CCNY 138th St And Convent Ave New York NY 10031

ROELOFS, WENDELL LEE, biochemistry educator, consultant; b. Orange City, Iowa, July 26, 1938; s. Edward and Edith (Beyers) R.; m. Donna R. Gray, Dec. 23, 1989; children by previous marriage: Brenda Jo, Caryn Jean, Jeffrey Lee, Kevin Jon. BA, Central Coll., Pella, Iowa, 1960, DSc (hon.), 1985; PhD, Ind. U., 1964, DSc (hon.), 1986; DSc (hon.), Hobart and William Smith Colls., 1988, U. of Lund, Sweden, 1989, Free U. Brussels, 1989. Asst. prof. Cornell U., Geneva, N.Y., 1965-69, assoc. prof., 1969-76, prof., 1976—, Liberty Hyde Bailey prof. insect biochemistry, 1978—, chmn. dept., 1991—. Contbr. over 300 articles to sci. jours. Recipient Alexander von Humboldt award in Agr., 1977, Outstanding Alumni award Central Coll., 1978, Wolf prize for agr., 1982, Disting. Alumnus award Ind. U., 1983, Nat. Medal of Sci., 1983, Disting. Svc. award USDA, 1986, Silver medal Internat. Soc. Chem. Ecology, 1990; postdoctoral fellow MIT, 1965. Fellow AAAS, Entomol. Soc. Am. (J. Everett Bussart Meml. award 1973, Founder's Meml. award 1980, Disting. Achievement award Ea. br. 1983); mem. NAS, Am. Chem. Soc. (Sterling B. Hendricks award 1994), Am. Acad. Arts and Sci., Sigma Xi. Republican. Presbyterian. Patentee in field (10). Home: 4 Crescence Dr Geneva NY 14456-1302 Office: Cornell Univ Insect Biochemistry Geneva NY 14456

ROELS, OSWALD ALBERT, oceanographer, educator, business executive; b. Temse, Belgium, Sept. 16, 1921; came to U.S., 1958, naturalized, 1965; s. Ghisleen and Elvire (Heirwegh) R.; m. Dorothy Mary Broadhurst, Sept. 16, 1950; 1 dau., Margaret Ann Roels Talarico. B.S., U. Louvain, Belgium, 1940, M.S., 1942; Ph.D., 1944. Prof. Columbia U., N.Y.C., 1960-75, CCNY, 1969-76; prof., dir. dept. marine sci. U. Tex., Austin, 1976-80; chmn. Maritek Corp., Corpus Christi, Tex., 1980-92; pres. Bradley Barges Inc.; adj. prof. Rockefeller U., N.Y.C., 1969-80; vis. research prof. Laval U., Que., Can., 1972-80; dir. mariculture research Port Aransas (Tex.) Marine Lab., U. Tex. Marine Sci. Inst., 1976-80. Author numerous articles in field.; assoc. editor: Nutrition Revs., 1961-68. Served with Belgian Army, 1940. Recipient Postdoctoral award U. Brussels, 1945, Postdoctoral award U. Liverpool, Eng., 1946, Postdoctoral award Sorbonne, 1957; Research Career Devel. award NIH, 1962-65; WHO fellow, 1957; Hoffman-LaRoche vis. lectr., 1974. Mem. AAAS, Am. Chem. Soc., Am. Inst. Nutrition, Am. Soc. Biol. Chemists, Am. Soc. Limnology and Oceanography, Chemici Lovanienses, Inst. Environ. Scis., Inst. Food Tech., Internat. Conf. Biochem. Lipids, Marine Tech. Soc., N.Y. Acad. Scis., N.Y. Lipid Club, Photoelectric Spectrometry Group Gt. Britain, World Mariculture Soc. Home: 28 Hewit Dr Corpus Christi TX 78404-1663

ROELS, PHILIP, insurance company executive. V.p. Dorinco Reinsurance Co., Midland, Mich., 1977—. Office: Dorinco Reinsurance Co 1320 Waldo Ave Ste 200 Midland MI 48642-5850*

ROEMER, EDWARD PIER, neurologist; b. Milw., Feb. 10, 1908; s. John Henry and Caroline Hamilton (Pier) R.; m. Helen Ann Fraser, Mar. 28, 1935 (dec.); children: Kate Pier, Caroline Pier; m. Marion Clare Zimmer, May 24, 1980. BA, U. Wis., 1930; MD, Cornell U., 1934. Diplomate Am. Bd. Neurology. Intern Yale-New Haven Hosp., 1934-36; resident internal medicine N.Y. Hosp., 1936; resident neurology Bellevue Hosp., N.Y.C., 1936-38; instr. Med. Sch. Yale U., New Haven, 1935-36; asst. prof. neurology Cornell U., N.Y.C., 1936-41; prof. neurology U. Wis., Madison, 1946-64; chief of neurology Huntington Meml. Hosp., Pasadena, Calif., 1964-78; pvt. practice Capistrano Beach, Calif., 1978—; founder, dir. Wis. Neurol. Found., Madison, 1946-64; dir. Wis. Multiple Sclerosis Clinic, Madison, 1946-64; adv. bd. Inst. Antiquities and Christianity, Claremont Grad. Sch., 1970—; dir. found. Univ Good Hope, S.Africa. Contbr. rsch. articles on multiple sclerosis, neuropathies to profl. jours. Lt. col. med. corps U.S. Army, 1941-46, ETO. Fellow ACP, Royal Coll. Medicine, L.S.B. Leakey Found.; mem. Rotary Internat., Annandale Golf Club, El Niguel Country Club, Nu Sigma Nu, Phi Delta Theta. Republican. Achievements include significant findings in field of anthropology and archaeology in Egypt and southwest U. S. relative to prehistory and PreColumbian European influences. Home: 35651 Beach Rd Capistrano Beach CA 92624

ROEMER, ELAINE SLOANE, real estate broker; b. N.Y.C., Apr. 23, 1938; d. David and Marion (Frauenthal) Sloane; m. David Frank Roemer, June 21, 1959; children: Michelle Sloane Wolf, Alan Sloane. BBA, U. Fla., 1959; MEd, U. Miami, 1963. CFP; cert. tchr. Tchr. math. and bus. Dade County Pub. Schs., Miami, 1959-80, Miami Dade Community Coll., 1968-80; tchr. edn. Fla. Internat. U., Miami, 1977-80; real estate broker Miami, 1978—; tchr. math. St. Leo's Coll., Miami, 1991-92; mortgage broker, Miami, 1986—; speaker in field. Contbr. articles to profl. jours. Mem. Kendall-Perrine Assn. Realtors (sec., treas. 1992-93, bd. dirs. 1991-92, grievance com. 1990, arbitration com. 1991, pres.-elect 1994, pres. 1995), Fla. Assn. Realtors (rep. dist. 4 1992-95, honor soc. 1995), Nat. Assn. Realtors, NEA, Fla. Edn. Commn., Classroom Tchrs. Assn., Dade County Edn. Assn., Fla. Coun. Tchrs. Math., Fla. Bus. Edn. Assn., Assn. Classroom Educators, Dade County Assn. Ednl. Adminstrs., ASCD, Alpha Delta Kappa. Home: 7705 SW 138th Ter Miami FL 33158-1120 Office: 9036 SW 152nd St Miami FL 33157-1928

ROEMER, ELIZABETH, astronomer, educator; b. Oakland, Calif., Sept. 4, 1929; d. Richard Quirin and Elsie (Barlow) R. BA with honors, U. Calif., Berkeley, 1950, PhD (Lick Obs. fellow), 1955. Tchr. adult class Oakland pub. schs., 1950-52; lab technician U. Calif. at Mt. Hamilton, 1954-55; grad. research astronomer U. Calif. at Berkeley, 1955-56; research asso. Yerkes Obs. U. Chgo., 1956; astronomer U.S. Naval Obs., Flagstaff, Ariz., 1957-66; asso. prof. dept. astronomy, also in lunar and planetary lab. U. Ariz., Tucson, 1966-69; prof. U. Ariz., 1969—; astronomer Steward Obs., 1980—; Chmn. working group on orbits and ephemerides of comets commn. 20 Internat. Astron. Union, 1964-79, 85-88, v.p. comm. 20, 1979-82, pres., 1982-85, v.p. commn. 6, 1973-76, 85-88, pres., 1976-79, 88-91; mem. adv. panels Office Naval Research, Nat. Acad. Scis.-NRC, NASA; researcher and author numerous publs. on astrometry and astrophysics of comets and minor planets including 79 recoveries of returning periodic comets, visual and spectroscopic binary stars, computation of orbits of comets and minor planets. Recipient Dorothea Klumpke Roberts prize U. Calif. at Berkeley, 1950, Mademoiselle Merit award, 1959; asteroid (1657) named Roemera, 1965; Benjamin Apthorp Gould prize Nat. Acad. Scis., 1971; NASA Spl. award, 1986. Fellow AAAS (council 1966-69, 72-73), Royal Astron. Soc. (London); mem. Am. Astron. Soc. (program vis. profs. astronomy 1960-75, council 1967-70, chmn. div. dynamical astronomy 1974), Astron. Soc. Pacific (publs. com. 1962-73, Comet medal com. 1968-74, Donohoe lectr. 1962), Internat. Astron. Union, Am. Geophys. Union, Brit. Astron. Assn., Phi Beta Kappa, Sigma Xi. Office: U Ariz Lunar and Planetary Lab Tucson AZ 85721-0092

ROEMER, MILTON IRWIN, physician, educator; b. Paterson, N.J., Mar. 24, 1916; s. Jacob and Mary (Rabinowitz) R.; m. Ruth Rosenbaum., Sept. 1. 1939; children: John, Beth. B.A., Cornell U., 1936, M.A., 1939; M.D., NYU, 1940; M.P.H., U. Mich., 1943. Diplomate: Am. Bd. Preventive Medicine. Intern Barnert Meml. Hosp., Paterson, 1940-41; with N.J. Health Dept., Trenton, 1941-42, USPHS, Washington, 1943-48; mem. faculty Yale U. Med. Sch., 1949-51; with WHO. Geneva, 1951-53, Sask. (Can.) Health Dept., 1953-56; mem. faculty Cornell U., 1957-61; prof. health adminstrn. U. Calif. Sch. Pub. Health, Los Angeles, 1962—; cons. in field. Author: numerous books, including Health Care Systems in World Perspective, 1976, Comparative National Policies on Health Care, 1977, Ambulatory Health Services in America, 1981, National Health Systems of the World: Vol. 1: The Countries, 1991, Vol. 2: The Issues, 1993. Mem. Inst. Medicine, Am. Pub. Health Assn. (award for excellence in internat. health 1977, Sedgwick medal 1983), Am. Coll. Preventive Medicine, Internat. Epidemiol. Assn., Physicians Forum, Group Health Assn. Am., Phi Beta Kappa, Sigma Xi, Alpha Omega Alpha, Phi Kappa Phi, Delta Omega. Home: 365 S Westgate Ave Los Angeles CA 90049-4207 Office: Univ Calif Sch Pub Health Los Angeles CA 90024

ROEMER, TIMOTHY J., congressman; b. South Bend, Ind., Oct. 30, 1956; m. Sarah Lee Johnston, 1989. BA in pol. sci, U. Calif., San Diego, 1979; MA, PhD in internat. rels., U. Notre Dame, 1986. Staff asst. to congressman John Brademas U.S. Congress; def., trade and fgn. policy advisor to senator Dennis DeConcini; mem. prof. 102nd-103rd Congresses from 3rd Ind. dist., 1991—; mem. economic and ednl. opportunity com., mem. sci. com.; adj. prof. Am. U. Office: 407 Cannon House Office Bu Washington DC 20515 also: 217 N Main St South Bend IN 46601-1216*

ROEMER, WILLIAM FREDERICK, banker; b. Youngstown, Ohio, Sept. 21, 1933; s. James Alexander and Helen France (James) R.; m. Linda Jo Cooper, June 30, 1956; children: Karen Roemer Seese, James Cooper, Gail Irwin, Sarah. B.A., Princeton U., 1955. Various positions Mellon Bank, Pitts., 1959-69; pres. Bradford (Pa.) Nat. Bank, 1970-72, First Laurel Bank, St. Marys, Pa., 1972-75; pres. Pennbank, Titusville, Pa., 1975-82, chmn., 1982-85; pres., chief exec. officer Pennbancorp, 1980-88; pres., chief exec. officer Integra Fin. Corp., Pitts., 1989-90, chmn., chief exec. officer, 1991-96; chmn. National City Bank of PA.(merged with Integra Fin. Corp.), Pitts., 1996-; bd. dirs. Pitts. br. of Fed. Res. Bank Cleve., 1990-92. Bd. dirs. Titusville Hosp., 1977-86, pres., 1979-81; sr. warden, lay reader St. James Episcopal Ch., Titusville, 1980-88; various coms. Episcopal Diocese Northwestern Pa., 1979-88, diocesan coun., 1982-88, campaign chmn. for venture in mission capital fund drive, 1981; vestryman St. Stephens Episcopal Ch., Sewickley, 1990—; mem. standing com. Episcopal Diocese Pitts., 1992—; bd. dirs. Pitts. Symphony Orch., 1990—, United Way Southwestern Pa., 1990—, campaign chmn. 1993, Greater Pitts. Coun. Boys Scouts Am., 1990—, Allegheny Conf. Community Devel., 1991—, Penn's S.W., 1990—. Lt. USN, 1955-58. Mem. Am. Bankers Assn. (govt. rels. coun. 1982-85, bank polit. action com. 1989-90), Bankers Roundtable, Pa. Bankers Assn. (dir. pub. affairs com. 1977-88, govt. rels. policy com. 1987-90, exec. com. 1989-90), Duquesne Club (bd. dirs. 1992-94), Allegheny Country Club, Laurel Valley Golf Club. Republican. Home: Little Sewickley Creek Rd Sewickley PA 15143*

ROEMING, ROBERT FREDERICK, foreign language educator; b. Milw., Dec. 12, 1911; s. Ferdinand August and Wanda E. (Radtke) R.; m. Alice Mae Voss, Aug. 30, 1941; 1 child, Pamela Alice. BA in Econs./Acctg., U. Wis., 1934, MA in Italian, 1936, PhD in French, 1941. Mem. faculty U. Wis.-Milw., 1937—, prof. French and Italian, 1956—, assoc. dean Coll. Letters and Sci., asst. to provost for devel. of spl. programs, 1957-62, sole dir. dept. lang. labs., 1964-70, dir. English as 2d lang., 1967-70, founder and dir. Ctr. Twentieth Century Studies, 1970-74, prof. emeritus, 1980—; founder, chief investigator Camus Bibliography Research Collection, Golda Meir Library, 1985; rep. D.C. Heath Co., 1943-46; cons., 1946-50; cons. computer systems Harnischfeger Corp., Milw., 1953-57; chmn. tech. sect. Internat. Congress on Fgn. Lang. Tchg., Pädagogisches Zentrum, Berlin, summer 1964; guest InterAm. Congress of Linguists, Montevideo, Uruguay, 1966; ofcl. guest Romanian govt. 10th Internat. Congress Linguists, summer 1967; dir. Insts. in Adult Basic Edn., 1969, U.S. Office Edn.; pres., treas. Electronic Rsch. Instruments Co., Inc., Nashotah, Wis., 1969-93. Author: (with C.E. Young) Introduction to French, 1951, Camus, A Bibliography, 1969, rev. and augmented computer-microfiche 11th edit., 1993, Little Magazine Catalog (NEH grantee), 1976-77; editor Modern Lang. Jour., 1963-70; contbr. numerous monographs and articles to profl. jours., 72 taped radio programs on French Black lit. Chmn. bldg. commn. Village of Chenequa, Wis., 1972-88; trustee, chmn. Midwest chpt. Jose Greco Found. for Hispanic Dance, Inc., 1970-76; mem. Wis. Bd. Nursing, 1977-79, chmn., 1979; mem. numerous nat. conservation orgns. and local civic groups. Decorated chevalier, officier, commandeur Ordre Palmes Académiques (France); recipient Travel award Italian Govt., 1934. Mem. MLA (life, index com. 1970-79), Nat. Fedn. Modern Lang. Tchrs. Assn. (exec. com. 1963-70), Verband Deutscher Schriftsteller, Wis. News Photographers Assn. (hon. life, Pres.'s award 1972), Soc. des Etudes Camusiennes, Am. Assn. of French Acad. Palms, Wis. Assn. for the Blind and Physically Handicapped, Chenequa Country Club, Lake Country Racquet and Athletic Club, Phi Eta Sigma, Phi Kappa Phi, Tau Kappa Epsilon. Research in application of the computer to humanities, applied linguistics and contemporary French and Italian Lit. Home: 6078 N Oakland Hills Rd Nashotah WI 53058 Office: U Wis-Milw Golda Meir Libr W240 2311 E Hartford Ave Milwaukee WI 53211-3175

ROEMMELE, BRIAN KARL, electronics, publishing, financial and real estate executive; b. Newark, Oct. 4, 1961; s. Bernard Joseph and Paula M. Roemmele. Grad. high sch., Flemington, N.J. Registered profl. engr., N.J. Design engr. BKR Techs., Flemington, N.J., 1980-81; acoustical engr. Open Reel Studios, Flemington, 1980-82; pres. Ariel Corp., Flemington, 1983-84, Ariel Computer Corp., Flemington, 1984-89; pres., chief exec. officer Ariel Fin. Devel. Corp., N.Y.C., 1987-91; pres., CEO Avalon Am. Corp., Temecula, Calif., 1990—; CEO United Credit Card Acceptance Corp., Beverly Hills, 1992—, United ATM Card Acceptance Corp., Beverly Hills, 1992—; pres. Multiplex Media Corp., Beverly Hills, 1993—; pres., CEO Coupon Book Ltd., 1987-89, Value Hunter Mags., Ltd., AEON Cons. Group, Beverly Hills; bd. dirs. Waterman Internat., Whitehouse Station, N.J.; electronic design and software cons., L.A., 1980—. Pub., editor-in-chief: Computer Importer News, 1987—. Organizer Internat. Space Week or Day, 1978-83, Internet Engrs. Soc., 1993, Internet Soc., Geneva, 1993—; lectr. Trenton (N.J.) State Mus., 1983; chmn. Internet tech. com. Safe Water Internat., Paris; assoc. dir. World Payment Assn., Geneva. Mem. AAAS, AIAA, ABA, IEEE, World Wide Web Assn. (founder), Am. Bankers Assn., Bankcard Svcs. Assn., Boston Computer Soc., Ford/Hall Forum, Am. Soc. Notaries, Planetary Soc. Avocations: musician, surfing, cycling, reading, numismatics. Office: Avalon Am Corp PO Box 1615 Temecula CA 92593-1615

ROEN, PHILIP RUBEN, urologist, surgeon, medical educator; b. N.Y.C., Aug. 5, 1914; s. Nathaniel and Ida (Brickman) R.; m. Florence Sonia Gluck, Dec. 23, 1944; children: Janet Leslie. BA, Columbia Coll., 1934, MD, 1938. Diplomate Am. Bd. Urology. Fellow Cleve. Clinic; resident in urology N.Y. Hosp.; dir. urology St. Clare's Hosp., N.Y.C., 1959—; attending urologist Roosevelt Hosp., N.Y.C., 1980—; prof. clin. urology N.Y. Med. Coll., Valhalla, 1980—. Author: Atlas of Genitourinary Surgery, 1951, Atlas of Urologic Surgery, 1967, Male Sexual Health, 1974; contbr. articles to profl. jours. Chmn. profl. rels. Blue Shield, N.Y.C., 1978-80. Mem. ACS, Am. Urol. Assn., N.Y. Urol. Assn., Princeton Club N.Y.C. Office: 220 Madison Ave New York NY 10016-3422

ROEN, SHELDON R., publisher, psychologist; b. N.Y.C.; s. Morris Rosenthal and Gussie (Weininger) R.; m. Selma Lois Pollets, Feb. 21, 1954; children—Randa M., Marjorie A., Harris L. B.S., City U. N.Y., 1950, M.A., 1951; Ph.D., Columbia U., 1955; postgrad., New Sch. Social Research, 1951-53, Harvard Sch. Pub. Health, 1961-62. Diplomate: Am. Bd. Examiners in Profl. Psychology. Tchr. pub. schs. N.Y.C., 1950-53; chief Clin. Psychology Svc., Ft. Sill, Okla., 1955-58; instr. Cameron Coll., Okla. A. and M. U., 1956-58; asst. prof. U. N.H., 1958-60; asst. chief psychol. services Mass. Mental Health Center, Boston, 1960-63; instr. Harvard, 1961-63; rsch. assoc. Med. Sch., 1960-63; dir. rsch. S. Shore Mental Health Center, Quincy, Mass., 1962-66; assoc. prof. dept. psychology Tchrs. Coll., Columbia, N.Y.C., 1966-72; dir. Psychol. Consultation Center, 1966-72; chmn. bd., pres., psychologist Human Scis. Press, N.Y.C., 1972—; Lectr. L.I. U., summer 1958, Tufts U., 1961-62; mem. N.H. Gov.'s Com. on Spl. Edn., also Study Com. on Mental Health Reorgn., 1961-62; cons. VISTA program OEO, 1966-67; mem. juvenile problems research rev. com. NIMH, 1968-69; mem. research rev. com. Title III Elementary and Secondary Edn. Act project application Ohio Dept. Edn., 1969-72; mem. mental health coordinating com. local sch. dist. 5, N.Y.C., 1969-72; mem., research dir. work incentive program for welfare recipients Wharton Sch. Pa., U.S. Dept. Labor, 1969-72; mem. mental health and community control com. N.Y. Psychologists for Social Action, 1969-72. Authors, editor books.; Editor: Mass. Psychol. Assn. Newsletter, 1963-65, Community Mental Health Jour; contbr. articles to profl. jours. and chpts. to books. Chmn. bd. trustees Bristol Acres Sch., Taunton, Mass., 1965-67. Fellow Am. Psychol. Assn. (mem. com. pre-coll. behavioral scis. 1968-71, founder div. 27 community psychology div. 1969, chmn. subcom. pre-high sch. behavioral sci. 1969-72), Am. Pub. Health Assn., Am. Orthopsychiat. Assn. (com. on research edn. 1965-67), Am. Sociol. Assn.; mem. New Eng. Psychol. Assn. (steering com. 1965-68), N.H. Psychol. Assn. (legis. chmn. 1961-62). Office: 3205 Beacon St Pompano Beach FL 33062-1207

ROENICK, JEREMY, professional hockey player; b. Boston, Jan. 17, 1970. Center Chgo. Blackhawks, 1988—. Named The Sporting News NHL Rookie of the Yr., 1989-90. Played in NHL All-Star Games, 1991-94. Office: Chgo Blackhawks 1901 W Madison St Chicago IL 60612-2620*

ROEPER, RICHARD, columnist; b. Chgo., Oct. 17, 1959; s. Robert and Margaret R. BA, Ill. State U., 1982. Freelance writer, 1982-87; columnist Chgo.-Sun Times, 1987—; talk show host Sta. WLS-FM, Chgo.; commentator Fox Thing in the Morning, Sta. WFLD-TV, Fox TV, Chgo. Recipient Outstanding Columnist Ill. Press Assn., 1992, Nat. Headliner award for top columnist Atlantic City Press Club, 1992, Emmy award, 1994. Mem. Am. Fedn. TV & Radio Artists, Chgo. Newspaper Guild. Office: Chgo Sun-Times 401 N Wabash Ave Chicago IL 60611-3532

ROESCH, CLARENCE HENRY, banker; b. Egg Harbor City, N.J., Aug. 22, 1925; s. Joseph Aloysius and Bertha (Heumann) R.; m. Helen Regina Owens, Sept. 25, 1954; children: Kathleen Marie, Helena Patricia, Maryanne Cornelia. BBA, Rutgers U., 1949, postgrad., 1961; certificate, Am. Inst. Banking, 1961; grad., Trust Sch., Bucknell U., 1971. Cert. internal auditor, data processing auditor. Bookkeeper, teller, head teller, asst. sec., trust officer, auditor Egg Harbor Bank & Trust Co., 1949-61; bank examiner Phila. Fed. Res. Bank, 1962-65; chief auditor Am. Bank & Trust Co. of Pa. (name changed to Meridian Bancorp Inc. 1985), Reading, 1966—, v.p. audit dept., 1968-88; ret. officer Am. Bank & Trust Co. of Pa. (name changed to Meridian Bancorp Inc. 1985), 1988; parish sec. St. Benedict Ch., Plowville, 1989—; sr. staff auditor Nat. Penn Bank, Boyertown, 1990—; mem. faculty Berks County chpt. Am. Inst. Banking, 1966-68; instr. bank auditing Bank Adminstrn. Inst., U. Richmond, 1968; pres., past mems. chpt. Am. Banking Inst., Atlantic County, N.J., 1958-59. Budget com. Berks County chpt. United Way, 1967-73; bd. dirs. Berks Reading Coun. Camp Fire, 1966-93, chmn. fin. com., 1973, 75, treas., 1974-84; instr. 55 Alive Program AARP, 1989-93. Recipient John Johnston award as outstanding banker N.J., 1955; award U.S. Savs. Bond Com., 1961; Luther Halsey Gulick award for vol. services Camp Fire, 1975; John C. Collier award for outstanding bus. and fin. services, 1981, Blue Ribbon award for vol. services Camp Fire, 1984, award for corp. vol. of yr. Meridian Bancorp Inc., 1984, 85, Outstanding Svc. in Fin. Mgmt. award Camp Fire, 1988. Mem. Inst. Internal Auditors (dir. ctrl. Pa. chpt.), Berks County Bankers Assn., Travelers Protective Assn., Berks Reading C. of C., Bank Administration Inst. (past pres., dir. Penn-Jersey chpt.), Spring Lawn Optimist Club (bd. dirs. 1992, Key Mem. award 1992, chmn. fin. and budget com. 1992-94). Home: 24 Medinah Dr Flying Hills Reading PA 19607

ROESELER, WOLFGANG GUENTHER JOACHIM, city planner; b. Berlin, Mar. 30, 1925; s. Karl Ludwig and Therese (Guenther) Ph.D., Philipps State U. of Hesse, Marburg, W.Ger., 1946-49; LL.B., Blackstone Sch. Law, Chgo., 1958; m. Eva Maria Jante, Mar. 12, 1947; children—Marion, Joanie, Karl. Asso. planner Kansas City (Mo.) Planning Commn., 1950-52; city planning dir. City of Palm Springs, Calif., 1952-54; sr. city planner Kansas City, 1954-56; prin. assoc. Ladislas Segoe & Assos., Cin., 1956-64; dir. urban and regional planning Howard, Needles, Tammen & Bergendoff, cons. Kansas City, N.Y.C., 1964-68; owner W.G. Roeseler, Cons. City Planner and Transp. Specialist, Bryan, Tex., 1969—; head dept. urban and regional planning Tex. A&M U., 1975-81, 85-88, prof., 1975-90, dir. Tex. A&M Ctr. Urban Affairs, 1984-88, exec. officer for edn. College of Architecture, 1987-88, prof. emeritus, 1990—. Fellow Inst. Transport Engrs.; mem. Am. Inst. Cert. Planners (life mem.), Am. Planning Assn., Transport Planners Coun., Urban Land Inst. Author: Successful American Urban Plans, 1982. Contbr. articles to profl. jours. Home: 2508 Broadmoor PO Box 4007 Bryan TX 77805-4007 Office: Tex A&M U PO Box 4007 College Station TX 77844-4007

ROESER, ROSS JOSEPH, audiologist, educator; b. Louisville, Nov. 14, 1942; s. Carl Henry and Yvonne Marie (Phillips) R.; m. Sharon Lynn Hill, June 9, 1962; children: Wendy Ann, Elizabeth Marie, Jennifer Yvonne. BS, Western Ill. U., 1966; MA, No. Ill. U., 1967; PhD, Fla. State U., 1972. Audiologist Anna (Ill.) State Hosp., 1967-69; chief of audiology Callier Ctr., Dallas, 1972-88, dir., 1988—; prof. audiology U. Tex., Dallas, 1975—; clin. prof. dept. otolaryngology U. Tex. Southwestern Med. Ctr., 1975—. Author: Auditory Disorders, 1982; founder Ear and Hearing jour., 1979. Recipient Alumni Achievement award Western Ill. U., 1978, Fla. State U., 1990. Mem. Tex. Speech-Lang.-Hearing Assn. (Jack L. Bangs award 1994), Acad. Dispensing Audiologists (Joel Wernick award 1990). Home: 1921 Marydale Rd Dallas TX 75208-3034 Office: Callier Ctr 1966 Inwood Rd Dallas TX 75235-7205

ROESLER, JOHN BRUCE, lawyer; b. Portland, Oreg., Oct. 9, 1943; s. Bruce Emil Roesler and Charlotte Amanda (Naess) Ledger; m. Kathryne Elise Nilsen, Aug. 14, 1965 (dec. July 1974); children: Paul, Mark; m. Gloria Ruiz, Oct. 15, 1988; children: Joaquin, Nico. BA, U. Kans., 1966, JD, 1971. Bar: Mo. 1971, N.Mex. 1979, U.S. Dist. Ct. (we. dist.) Mo. 1971, U.S. Dist. Ct. N.Mex. 1979, U.S. Ct. Appeals (10th cir.) 1979, U.S. Ct. Appeals (5th cir.) 1988, U.S. Ct. Appeals (4th cir.) 1992, U.S. Supreme Ct. 1987. Assoc. Gage & Tucker, Kansas City, Mo., 1971-74; civil rights advocate State of N.Mex. Human Rights, Santa Fe, 1977-78; law clk. Hon. Edwin L. Felter N.Mex. Supreme Ct., Santa Fe, 1978-79; asst. dist. atty. Taos (N.Mex.) Dist. Atty.'s Office, 1979-80; asst. spl. pros. Santa Fe Dist. Atty.'s Office, 1980-82; pvt. practice, 1982—; instr. John Marshall Law Sch., Chgo., summer 1974; spkr. civil rights and children's rights issues U. Miami Sch. Law, 1991, U. Miami Sch. Medicine, 1991. Author: (books) How To Find the Best Lawyers, In Harm's Way: Is Your Child Safe in School; mem. law rev. com. U. Kans. Sch. Law, 1970-71; contbr. articles to profl. jours. and treatise. Speaker convention Nat. Com. for the Prevention of Child Abuse, 1988, 89, 90. Mem. N.Mex. Bar Assn., N.Mex. Trial Lawyers Assn. Democrat. Roman Catholic. Avocation: skiing. Home: 1384 Santa Rosa Dr Santa Fe NM 87505 Office: 347 E Palace Ave Santa Fe NM 87501

ROESLER, KARL, electronics executive; b. 1941. Grad., U. Notre Dame, 1962. With GE, Fairfield, Conn., 1963-90; v.p. fin. Therm-O-Disc Inc., Mansfield, Ohio, 1990—. Office: Therm-O-Disc Inc 1320 S Main St Mansfield OH 44907-2516*

ROESLER, ROBERT HARRY, city official; b. Hammond, La., Oct. 5, 1927; s. Albert N. and Hilda (Schwartz) R.; m. Cloe Alferez, May 7, 1955; children: Kim, Bob, Toby. Student, Tulane U. Mem. sports staff Times Picayune, New Orleans, 1949-94, sports editor, 1964-80; exec. sports editor Times Picayune and States-Item, 1980-94; sports coord. New Orleans Met. Conv. and Visitors Bur., 1994—; CEO Roesler Media Cons. Vice chmn. Navy Recruiting Dist.; mem. assistance coun., New Orleans, 1992—. Served with USNR, World War II; Served with USNR, Korean conflict. Mem. Profl. Football Writers Assn. Am. (pres. 1976-77), Nat. Turf Writers Assn., Football Writers Assn. Am., Am. Legion, Navy League U.S., New Orleans Press Club (pres. 1959-60, sports writing awards). Home: 6958 Colbert St New Orleans LA 70124-2334 Office: 1520 Sugar Bowl Dr New Orleans LA 70112-1255

ROESNER, LARRY AUGUST, civil engineer; b. Denver, Mar. 14, 1941; s. Walter George and Sarah Jane (Merrick) R.; m. Kathleen Ann Fahrenbruch, Dec. 13, 1964; children: David John, Kevin Walter, Nathan August, Melissa Jane. B.S., Valparaiso (Ind.) U., 1963; M.S., Colo. State U., 1965; Ph.D., U. Wash., Seattle, 1969. Registered profl. engr., Calif., Mich., Va., Md., Fla., Ohio. Part-time grad. research asst. Colo. State U., 1963-65, U. Wash., 1965-68; assoc. engr., then prin. engr. Water Resources Engrs., Inc., Walnut Creek, Calif., 1968-77; assoc., then v.p. Camp Dresser & McKee Inc., Annandale, Va., 1977-85; sr. v.p. and dir. water resources Camp, Dresser & McKee Inc., Maitland, Fla., 1985-92; chief tech. officer Camp Dreser & McKee Inc., Maitland, Fla., 1992—; chmn. Engr. Found. Conf. on Current Practice and Design Criteria Urban Runoff Quality Controls, 1988; guest lectr., cons. urban hydrology and surface water quality; invited lectr. NATO Adv. Rsch. Conf. on Urban Runoff Pollution, 1985; invited participant ASCE Rsch. Conf. Engring. in 21st Century, 1987; NRC exec. com. Wastewater Mgmt. in Urban Coastal Areas, 1992; chmn. task force com. on urban runoff quality mgmt. Water Environ. Fedn. Author rsch. reports, tech. revs., contbg. author on urban hydrology in several books. Fellow ASCE (control mem. rsch. and edn. com. water resources div., nat. chmn. 1995 water resources planning and mgmt. div. splty. conf., nat. Walter L. Huber civil engring. rsch. prize 1975); mem. NAE, Am. Acad. Environ. Engrs. (diplomate), Am. Water Resources Assn., Am. Cons. Engrs. Assn., Water Environ. Fedn. (chmn. nonpoint sources of pollution com., urban runoff task force), Tau Beta Pi (eminent engr.). Republican. Lutheran. Achievements include development of several widely used mathematical models for U.S. government agencies including QUAL-II stream quality model for the EPA; STORM, an urban stormwater management model for the U.S. Army CE; SWMM-EXTRAN, a dynamic hydraulics model for storm drainage and sewer systems for the EPA. Home: 205 Wild Creek Ct Longwood FL 32779-3351 Office: Camp Dresser & McKee Inc 1950 Summit Park Dr Ste 300 Orlando FL 32810-5931 *An environmental engineer is a caretaker in God's garden, the earth. The challenge for the environmental engineer is to maintain a balance between the needs of man and those of nature so that man may both use and enjoy the garden. It is the responsibility of the environmental engineer to leave the garden a little nicer than he found it.*

ROESNER, PETER LOWELL, manufacturing company executive; b. Winchester, Ind., July 3, 1937; s. Lowell LeClair and Martha Christine (Overmyer) R.; children: Peter Lowell II, David Brandon, John Franklin. Student, Durham (Eng.) U., 1957-58; B.A., DePauw U., 1959; J.D., U. Mich., 1962; M.B.A., Harvard U., 1964. Bar: Ind. 1962, N.J. 1992. Asst. to pres. Overmyer Corp., Muncie, Ind., 1964-65, corp. sec., 1965-69, pres., 1969-84, also dir.; pres. Clinitemp Inc., Indpls., 1985-88; pres., owner Middletown (N.J.) Interiors Inc., 1993—; dir. Mchts. Nat. Bank, 1974-84. Trustee Purdue U., 1978. Mem. Ind. Mfrs. Assn. (dir. 1970-82, pres. 1975, chmn. Phoenix Award com. 1974), Glass Packaging Inst. (trustee 1981-84), ABA. Episcopalian. Office: Middletown Interiors 1270 Highway 35 Middletown NJ 07748-2014

ROESS, ROGER PETER, engineering educator; b. Flushing, N.Y., Dec. 12, 1947; s. Charles Gordon and Theresa (Welchner) R.; m. Janet Elaine Mitchell, July 4, 1970; children: Roger Michael, Christopher John. BCE, Poly. Inst. N.Y., Bklyn., 1968, MS in Transp. Planning, 1969, PhD in Transp. Planning, 1972. Instr. Poly. Inst. N.Y., 1969-72, asst. prof., 1972-77, assoc., 1977-83, prof., 1983-86; prof. Poly. U., Bklyn., 1986—, dean engring., 1984-95, assoc. provost acad. affairs, 1990-93; v.p. for academic affairs Poly U., Bklyn., 1993-95. Contbr. articles to profl. jours. Vice pres. Garden City South Little League, N.Y., 1981-87; trustee Franklin Sq. Bd. Edn., N.Y., 1984-90, 94—. Recipient D. Grant Mickle award Transp. Research Bd., 1979. Mem. Transp. Rsch. Bd (hwy. capacity and quality service com. 1985-96), Inst. Transp. Engrs. (assoc.),Sigma Xi, Chi Epsilon, Tau Beta Pi. Office: Poly U Dept Civil-Environ Engring Brooklyn NY 11201-2907

ROESSER, JEAN WOLBERG, state legislator; b. Washington, May 8, 1930; d. Solomon Harry Wolberg and Mary Frances Brown; m. Eugene Francis Roesser, Aug. 3, 1957; children: Eugene Francis, Jr., Mary Roesser Calderon, Anne. BA, Trinity Coll., Washington, 1951; postgrad. in econs., Cath. U. of Am., 1951-53. Congl. relations asst. U.S. Info. Agy., Washington, 1954-58; news reporter for Montgomery County Council Suburban Record, 1983-86; del. Md. Gen. Assembly, Annapolis, 1986-94; mem. State Senate, Md. Gen. Assembly, Annapolis, 1994—, mem. fin. com., ethics com., 1994—. Former mem. Md. Gov.'s Task Force on Energy; former pres. Montgomery County Fedn. Rep. Women, Potomac Women's Rep. Club; former 3d v.p. Md. Fedn. Rep. Women; founding mem. Montgomery

County Arts Coun.; alt. del. Rep. Nat. Conv., 1992, del., 1996. Recipient Cmty. Achievement awrd Washington Psychiat. Soc., 1994, Trinity Coll. Leadership award, 1994, Common Cause Md. award, 1993, Md. Underage Drinking Preventio Coalition award, 1994. Mem. Women Legislators Md., also area citizens assns. and chambers commerce. Republican. Roman Catholic. Home: 10830 Fox Hunt Ln Potomac MD 20854-1553 Office: James Senate Office Bldg 110 College Ave Annapolis MD 21401-1991

ROESSLER, RONALD JAMES, lawyer; b. Kansas City, Mo., Aug. 10, 1939; s. Robert Louis and Eleanor Florence (Ramsdell) R.; m. Sally Jo Canfield, Aug. 18, 1962; children: Martha Lee, Elizabeth Ramsdell. BA in Govt., Miami U., 1961; postgrad. Law Sch., Duke U., 1961-62; JD, Wis. Law Sch., 1964; LLM, George Washington U., 1968. Bar: Wis. 1964, D.C. 1970, W.Va. 1971, Md. 1972, N.Y. 1985. Atty. Dept. Agr., Washington, 1964-66, Office Gen. Counsel, CIA, Washington, 1966, 68-69, C & P Tel. Co., Washington, 1969-72; sr. v.p., gen. counsel Alexander & Alexander Services Inc., N.Y.C., 1972-81, Alexander & Alexander Svcs. Inc., N.Y.C., 1972-94; sr. counsel Rollins Hudig Hall, N.Y.C., 1995—; adj. prof. bus. law Towson State U., 1981-82. Trustee Bryn Mawr Sch., Balt., 1980-83. Served with USAF, 1966-68. Mem. ABA, Wis. Bar Assn., D.C. Bar Assn., W. Va. Bar Assn., Md. Bar Assn., Assn. of Bar of City of N.Y. Home: 15 Ferncliff Rd Cos Cob CT 06807-1206 Office: Rollins Hudig Hall Two World Trade Ctr New York NY 10048

ROESSNER, BARBARA, journalist; b. Elizabeth, N.J., Sept. 16, 1953; d. Gilbert George and Dorothy Anne (Hector) R.; m. Craig William Baggott, Jan. 20, 1982; children: Craig, Taylor, Liam, Katherine, Elizabeth. BA, Wesleyan U., 1975. Reporter, editor Meriden (Conn.) Record-Jour., 1975-78; reporter The Hartford (Conn.) Courant, 1978-81, chief polit. writer, 1981-86, columnist, 1986—; column distributed worldwide by L.A. Times-Washington Post News Svc. Recipient Best Mag. Column award Soc. Profl. Journalists, 1993, Best Mag. Feature award, 1993. Home: 22 Vanderbilt Rd West Hartford CT 06119-1341 Office: Hartford Courant Co 285 Broad St Hartford CT 06115-2500

ROESSNER, ROLAND GOMMEL, architect, educator; b. Terre Haute, Ind., Nov. 19, 1911; s. Elmer George and Florence Carol. Roessner; m. Virginia Gail Humberger, Nov. 17, 1943 (dec. Oct. 1955); 1 son., Roland Gommel. BArch, Miami U., Oxford, Ohio, 19356; MArch, U. Cin., 1942. Registered architect Ohio, Fla., Tex., interior designer, Tex. Assoc. Grunkeymeyer & Sullivan & Assocs., Cin., 1935-42; designing architect; pvt. practice architecture schs., pvt. residences St. Petersburg, Fla., 1945-47, Austin, Tex., 1947—; prof. Sch. Architecture U. Tex., Austin, 1947-82, chmn. design dept., 1954-67, mem. grad. faculty, 1958-82, acting dir., 1966, founder, dir. profl. residency program, 1971-82, prof. emeritus, 1982; assoc. Creer & Roessner, Austin, 1958-63; prin. R. Gommel Roessner, 1977—; design cons. O'Connell, Probst, Grobe, Inc. Architects/Engrs., Austin, 1979—; cons. community standards com. Dept. Commerce; mem. rsch. unit Naval Res.; adviser design State Bd. Archtl. Registration, Tex., 1960-68. Contbr. articles to profl. jours. Lt. comdr. USNR, 1942-45. Recipient numerous awards, citations in Am., fgn. publs. for architecture. Fellow AIA (mem. design com.); mem. Am. Concrete Inst., Am. Mil. Inst., Tex., Ohio, Fla. archtl. assns., Nat. Coun. Archtl. Registration Bds., Univ. Coop. Soc. (chmn. bd. dirs.), Am. Legion, VFW A'telier, Optimist Club, Westwood Country Club, U. Tex. Faculty Club, Headliners, Tarryhouse, Delta Phi Delta, Alpha Rho Chi, Delta Upsilon. Roland G. Roessner Professorship established Sch. Architecture U. Tex. Home: 3416 Pecos St Apt A Austin TX 78703-1012

ROETHEL, DAVID ALBERT HILL, consultant; b. Milw., Feb. 17, 1926; s. Albert John and Elsie Margaret (Hill) R.; children: Elizabeth Jane, Susan Margaret. BS, Marquette U., 1950, MS, 1952; cert., Oak Ridge Sch. Reactor Tech., 1953. Chem. engr. naval reactors br. AEC, Washington, 1952-57; mgr. profl. relations, asst. to exec. sec. Am. Chem. Soc., Washington, 1957-72; exec. dir. Nat. Registry in Clin. Chemistry, Washington, 1967-72, Am. Assn. Clin. Chemists, Washington, 1968-70, Am. Orthotic and Prosthetic Assn., 1973-76, Am. Acad. Orthotists and Prosthetists, Am. Bd. Cert. in Orthotics and Prosthetics, 1973-76; exec. dir., fellow Am. Inst. Chemists, Washington, 1977-90; bd. dirs., exec. com. Am. Inst. Chemists, 1981-90, exec. dir. Nat. Certification Commn. in Chemistry and Chem. Engring., 1977-90, exec. dir., trustee Am. Inst. Chemists Found., 1982-90, sec., 1990; pres. Peachtree Promotions, 1991—; dir. Chemical Heritage Found., 1992—; treas. Cons. Consortium, 1994—; sec., vice chmn., then chmn. Intersoc. Com. on Health Lab. Svcs., 1966-72; v.p. Pensions for Profls., Inc., Washington, 1970-72; vice chmn., then chmn. Engrs. and Scientists Joint Commn. on Pensions, 1978-80, vice chmn., 1985-87, chmn., 1988-90, 94-95, sec., 1996—; mem. Commn. Profls. in Sci. and Tech., 1978—, sec.-treas., 1979-82, bd. dirs., 1989—, v.p., 1990-91, exec. com., 1990-93, 95; sec. gen. 7th Internat. Congress in Orthotics and Prosthetics, 1975-76, 2d World Congress in Prosthetics and Orthotics, 1975-77; chmn. U.S. arrangements Can.-Am. Chem. Congress, 1982-84; bd. dirs. China-U.S. Sci. Exchanges, 1985-89. Editor: Almanac, 1973-76, Chemist, 1977-90. Mem. Md. Gov.'s Com. on Sci. Devel., 1969; bd. dirs. Episcopal Ctr. for Children, 1991—, sec., 1992-93, pres., 1993-95. Served with U.S. Army, 1944-46, CBI. Recipient Outstanding Svc. award Intersoc. Com. on Health Lab. Svcs., 1972, Appreciation award Nat. Reg. in Clin. Chemistry, 1972. Mem. Am. Chem. Soc. (dir. fed. credit union 1967-70, pres. 1968-70), Coun. Engring. and Sci. Soc. Execs. (bd. dirs. 1983-86), Am. Inst. Chemists, D.C. Inst. Chemists (sec. 1992-94, pres.-elect 1995—), Sports Car Am. Club (bd. dirs. 1964-67, 75-77, vice chmn., sec. 1967, 75-76, local officer 1960-74, historian 1989—), Alpha Chi Sigma (pres. Washington profl. chpt. 1963-64, 89-90, 95—, bd. dirs. 1991—, Profl. Achievement award 1986, bd. mgrs. 1986-90, dist. counselor 1964-68, nat. profl. rep. 1986-92, grand prof. alchemist 1992-94), Sigma Gamma Chi, Pi Mu Epsilon.

ROETHENMUND, OTTO EMIL, financial and banking executive; b. Thun, Switzerland, Sept. 1, 1928; came to U.S., 1951, naturalized, 1957; s. Franz and Berta (Dallenbach) R.; m. Ermina Grassi, May 7, 1955; children—Robert, Denise. M.A., U. Neuchatel, 1948. Mgmt. trainee Kantonalbank, Bern, 1948-51; exec. trainee J. Henry Schroeder Banking and Trust Corp., N.Y.C., 1951-56; with Deak-Perera Group, N.Y.C., 1956—; vice chmn., group partner Deak-Perera Group, 1962—; v.p., then sr. v.p. Deak & Co. (holding co.), 1962-74, exec. v.p., 1974-80, pres., chief exec. officer, 1980-86; pres., dir. Inter-Nation Capital Mgmt. Corp., 1986—; lectr. internat. monetary and investment seminars. Served to lt. Swiss Army, 1948-51. Decorated knight Mil. Order Ss. Salvador and Brigitta (Sweden). Mem. Explorers Club, Met. Club (N.Y.C.), Westchester Country Club. Home: 2 Shore Rd Rye NY 10580-1031 Office: Inter-Nation Capital Mgmt Corp 230 Park Ave Rm 650 New York NY 10169-0699

ROETMAN, ORVIL M., retired airplane company executive; b. Slayton, Minn., Aug. 28, 1925; s. Ernest Gilbert and Olava (Christianson) R.; m. Lavera Jones, Mar. 14, 1948; 1 child, Debra Roetman Caldwell. BA, U. Minn., 1950; BS in Aerospace Engring., U.S. Naval Post Grad. Sch., 1955; JD, George Washington U., 1965; postgrad. Naval War Coll., 1961. Bar: D.C., 1966. Commd. ensign U.S. Navy, 1945, advanced through grades to comdr., 1962, ret., 1965; sole practice law, Washington, 1965-66; in legal services Boeing Co., Seattle, 1966-67, dir. contract adminstrn., 1968, dir. internat. sales, 1971-79, v.p. internat. sales, 1979-83, v.p. contracts, 1983-87, corp. v.p. govt. and internat. affairs, 1988-90, ret., 1990. Mem. bd. regents, pres. adv. bd. Concordia Theol. Sem., Fort Wayne, Ind., 1979—. Mem. Navy League (life). Republican. Lutheran.

ROETT, RIORDAN, political science educator, consultant; b. N.Y.C., Sept. 10, 1938; s. Riordan Jr. and Marion (Underwood) R. BA, Columbia U., 1959, MIA, 1962, PhD, 1968. Postdoctoral fellow Ctr. for Internat. Studies, MIT, Cambridge, Mass., 1966-67; asst. prof., assoc. prof. polit. sci. Vanderbilt U., Nashville, 1967-73; prof. polit. sci. Sch. Advanced Internat. Studies, Johns Hopkins U., Washington, 1973—; sr. polit. analyst internat. capital markets Chase Manhattan Bank, N.Y.C., 1983-95; sr. advisor World Econ. Forum, Geneva; bd. dirs. Global Ptnrs. Income Fund, Emerging Markets Income Fund I & II, Salomon Bros. Worldwide Income Fund, Emerging Markets Floating Rate Fund, Salomon Bros. 2008 Worldwide Dollar Govt. Term Trut. Editor, co-author: Latin America, Western Europe, and the U.S.: Reevaluating the Atlantic Triangle, 1985, Mexico and the U.S.: Managing the Relationship, 1988, Paraguay: The Legacy of Personalist Politics, 1990, Mexico's External Relations in the 1990's, 1991, Political and Economic Liberalization in Mexico, 1993, The Challenge of Institutional Reform in Mexico, 1995. Fulbright fellow, 1962. Mem. Latin Am. Studies Assn. (v.p. 1977, pres. 1978), Coun. on Fgn. Rels., Cosmos Club. Democrat. Roman Catholic. Home: 2301 Connecticut Ave NW Apt 1B Washington DC 20008-1730 Office: Johns Hopkins U SAIS 1740 Massachusetts Ave NW Washington DC 20036-1984

ROETTGER, NORMAN CHARLES, JR., federal judge; b. Lucasville, Ohio, Nov. 3, 1930; s. Norman Charles and Emma Eleanora R.; children: Virginia, Peggy. BA, Ohio State U., 1952; LLB magna cum laude, Washington and Lee U., 1958. Bar: Ohio 1958, Fla. 1958. Assoc. Frost & Jacobs, Cin., 1958-59; asso. firm Fleming, O'Bryan & Fleming, Ft. Lauderdale, Fla., 1959-63, partner, 1963-69, 71-72; dep. gen. counsel HUD, Washington, 1969-71; judge U.S. Dist. Ct. (so. dist.) Fla., Ft. Lauderdale, 1972—. Lt. (j.g.) USN, 1952-55; to capt. Res. 1972. Mem. ABA, Fed. Bar Assn., Fla. Bar Assn., Broward County Bar Assn., Am. Judicature Soc., Order of Coif, Masons, Coral Ridge Yacht Club, Omicron Delta Kappa, Kappa Delta Rho. Presbyterian. Clubs: Masons; Coral Ridge Yacht (Ft. Lauderdale). Office: US Dist Ct 299 E Broward BlvdRm 205 F Fort Lauderdale FL 33301-1944*

ROETZEL, DANNY NILE, lawyer; b. Hancock, Mich., July 6, 1952; s. J.D. and Deva Dale (Butler) R.; m. Zenobia Ann Kennedy, Sept. 30, 1973. BS, SUNY, 1980; MA, Cen. Mich. U., 1987; JD cum laude, St. Louis U., 1987, MA, 1989. Bar: Mo. 1987. Youth counselor Mo. div. of Youth Svcs., Jefferson City, 1973-77; juvenile parole officer Mo. div. of Youth Svcs., Kansas City, 1977-79; facility mgr. II Mo. div. of Youth Svcs., Jefferson City, 1979-84; spl. cons. to dean Sch. Bus. and Adminstrn. St. Louis U., 1984-87; law clk. to chief magistrate U.S. Dist. Ct. (ea. dist.) Mo., St. Louis, 1987-89; staff atty. 8th Cir. Ct. Appeals, St. Louis, 1989-90; trial atty. criminal enforcement sect. Tax div. U.S. Dept. Justice, Washington, 1990; spl. asst. U.S. atty. Eastern Dist. Va., 1990-91; trial atty. criminal enforcement sect. Tax div. U.S. Dept. Justice, Washington, 1991-96; spl. asst. U.S. Atty. So. Dist. Calif., 1992—. Active White County Young Dems., Searcy, Ark., 1970-71, Harding U. Young Dems., 1970-71; exec. officer North St. Louis County Young Dems., 1985-87. Mem. Mo. Bar Assn., Sigma Iota Epsilon, Phi Alpha Delta. Avocations: reading history, travel. Home: 6107 Havener House Way Centreville VA 22020-3270 Office: US Dept Justice Tax Div Crim Enforcement Sect 10th Constitution Ave NE Washington DC 20530-0001

ROFF, ALAN LEE, lawyer, consultant; b. Winfield, Kans., July 2, 1936; s. Roy Darlis and Mildred Marie (Goodaile) R.; m. Sonyia Ruth Anderson, Feb. 8, 1954; 1 child, Cynthia Lee Roff Edwards; m. Molly Gek Neo Tan, July 21, 1980. BA with honors and distinction, U. Kans., 1964, JD with distinction, 1966. Bar: Okla. 1967. Staff atty. Phillips Petroleum Co., Bartlesville, Okla., 1966-75, sr. atty., 1976-85, sr. counsel, 1986-94; cons. in Asia, 1995—. Editorial bd. Kans. Law Rev., 1965-66. Precinct com. man Rep. Party, Lawrence, Kans., 1963-64; assoc. justice Kans. U. Chancery Club; mem. Kans. U. Young Reps. Elizabeth Reeder scholar U. Kans., 1965-66, Eldon Wallingford award, 1964-66. Mem. ABA, Okla. Bar Assn., Washington County Bar Assn., Phoenix Club (Bartlesville) (bd. dirs. 1985-86, gen. counsel 1986-91), Order of the Coif, Masons, Phi Alpha Delta, Pi Sigma Alpha. Mem. First Christian Ch. Avocation: travel.

ROFF, J(OHN) HUGH, JR., energy company executive; b. Wewoka, Okla., Oct. 27, 1931; s. Hugh and Louise Roff; m. Ann Green, Dec. 23, 1956; children—John, Charles, Andrew, Elizabeth, Jennifer. A.B., U. Okla., 1954, LL.B., 1955. Bar: Okla., Mo., N.Y. Law clk. to presiding justice U.S. Ct. Appeals (10th cir.), 1958; atty. Southwestern Bell Telephone Co., St. Louis, 1959-63, AT&T, N.Y.C., 1964-68; v.p., gen. atty. Long Lines, N.Y.C., 1969-73, gen. atty., 1973-74; chmn., pres., chief exec. officer United Energy Resources, Houston, 1974-86; chmn. PetroUnited Terminals Inc., Houston, 1986—. Past chmn. Cen. Houston Inc.; mem. adv. bd. Ctr. for Strategic and Internat. Studies, Washington; mem. coun. overseers Jones Sch. Bus. Adminstrn., Rice U.; trustee Baylor Coll. Medicine; chmn. adv. bd. The Salvation Army, Houston. 1st lt. JACG, U.S. Army, 1955-58. Mem. Order of Coif, Phi Beta Kappa, Beta Theta Pi. Clubs: Houston Country, Coronado, Houstonian. Office: 333 Clay St Ste 4300 Houston TX 77002-4103

ROFF, WILLIAM ROBERT, history educator, writer; b. Glasgow, Scotland, May 2, 1929; came to U.S., 1969; s. Robert Henry William and Isabella (Anderson) R.; m. Susanne Rabbitt, Aug. 2, 1978; children: Sarah, Emily. B.A., U. New Zealand, 1957, M.A., 1959; Ph.D., Australian Nat. U., 1965. Lectr. history Monash U., Australia, 1963-66; lectr., sr. lectr. U. Malaya, Malaysia, 1966-69; assoc. prof. Columbia U., N.Y.C., 1969-73, prof., 1973-90, prof. emeritus, 1990—; vis. prof. Yale U., 1971, L'Ecole des Hautes Etudes en Sciences Sociales, Paris, 1985; vis. fellow Australian Nat. U., 1974, Trinity Coll., Oxford U., Eng., 1981; hon. fellow Edinburgh U., Scotland, 1992—. Author: The Origins of Malay Nationalism, 1967, (with others) In Search of Southeast Asia, 1971, Bibliography of Malay and Arabic Periodicals, 1972; author, editor: Kelantan: Religion, Society and Politics, 1973; editor: Islam and the Political Economy of Meaning, 1987. Guggenheim Found. fellow 1973; Rockefeller Found. fellow, 1982. Mem. Royal Asiatic Soc. (life), Assn. for Asian Studies, Asian Studies Assn. Australia, Brit. Soc. for Middle East Studies, Middle East Studies Assn. Avocation: parenting. Home: 29 Shore St, Cellardyke Fife, Scotland

ROFFE-STEINROTTER, DIANN, Olympic athlete. Silver medalist, Giant Slalom Albertville Olympic Games, 1992. Silver medalist Giant Slalom, Albertville Olympic Games, 1992, Gold medalist Super-G, Lillehammar Olympic Games, 1994. Address: PO Box 611 Potsdam NY 13676-0611*

ROFFMAN, HOWARD, motion picture company executive; b. Phila.. Student, U. Pa.; JD, U. Fla. Assoc. Morgan, Lewis & Bockius, Washington; from legal counsel to gen. counsel Lucasfilm, Ltd., San Rafael, Calif., 1980-84, acting chief operating officer, 1984-85, v.p. licensing, 1986-93, v.p. licensing, thx, 1993—. Author: Presumed Guilty, 1974, Understanding the Cold War, 1976. Mem. Calif. Bar Assn., Washington Bar Assn., Licensing Industry Merchandising Assn. Office: Lucasfilm Ltd PO Box 2009 San Rafael CA 94912-2009

ROGAL, PHILIP JAMES, physician; b. N.Y.C., Dec. 23, 1939; s. Abraham and Cecilia (Sandor) R.; m. Susan Regan, June 17, 1967; Michael James, Elizabeth. BA, Princeton (N.J.) U., 1960; MD, Columbia U., 1964. Diplomate Am. Bd. Internal Medicine, Am. Bd. Cardiology. Intern Yale-New Haven Hosp., 1964-65; resident Bellevue Hosp., N.Y.C., 1965-67, Presbyn. Hosp., N.Y.C., 1967-68; fellow Bronx Mcpl. Hosp., 1970-71; pvt. practice internist, cardiologist N.Y.C., 1971-88, Tampa, Fla., 1988—; admissions com. Albert Einstein Coll. of Medicine, N.Y.C., 1983-88; chief of medicine Meml. Hosp., Tampa, 1995—. Capt. USAF, 1968-70. Fellow Am. Coll. Cardiology; mem. ACP, Alpha Omega Alpha. Avocations: squash racquets, tennis, travel, music. Office: Palma Ceia Med Group Ste 106 2919 Swann Ave Tampa FL 33609

ROGALLO, FRANCIS MELVIN, mechanical, aeronautical engineer; b. Sanger, Calif., Jan. 27, 1912; s. Mathieu and Marie Rogallo; m. Gertrude Sugden, Sept. 14, 1939; children: Marie, Robert, Carol, Frances. Degree in Mech. and Aero. Engring., Stanford U., 1935. With NACA (name changed to NASA), Hampton, Va., 1936-70, Kitty Hawk Kites, Nags Head, N.C.; lectr. on high lift devices, lateral control, flexible wings and flow systems. Contbr. articles to profl. jours. Active Rogallo Found. Recipient NASA award, 1963, Nat. Air and Space Mus. trophy, Lifetime Achievement award Smithsonian Instn., 1992; named to N.C. Sports Hall of Fame, 1987. Mem. Am. Kite Assn., U.S. Hang Gliding Assn. Episcopalian. Achievements include patents for Flexible Wing, Corner Kite, others; research in aerodynamics, wind tunnels. Home: 91 Osprey Ln Kitty Hawk NC 27949-3839 Office: Kitty Hawk Kites PO Box 1839 Nags Head NC 27959-1839

ROGALSKI, CAROL JEAN, clinical psychologist, educator; b. Chgo., Sept. 25, 1937; d. Casimir Joseph and Lillian Valentine Rogalski. BS, Loyola U., Chgo., 1961; PhD, NYU, 1968; cert. in psychoanalysis, Postgrad. Ctr. Mental Health, 1973. Lic. clin. psychologist, N.Y., Ill. Rsch. assoc. William Alanson White Inst., N.Y.C., 1961-66; rsch. asst., intern Hillside Hosp., Glen Oaks, N.Y., 1966-68; cons. Mt. Sinai Hosp., N.Y.C., 1968-73; staff psychologist Westside VA Hosp., Chgo., 1974—; asst. clin. prof. U. Ill. Med. Sch., 1996—; assoc. clin. prof. dept. psychiatry Med. Sch. U. Ill., 1996—. Mem. editorial bd. Internat. Jour. Addictions, 1994—; contbr. articles to profl. publs. Mem. APA, Communal Studies Assn., Chgo. Soc. for Psychotherapy Rsch. (chair 1988-91). Avocation: watercolors. Office: Westside VA Hosp 820 S Damen Ave Chicago IL 60612-3728

ROGALSKI, EDWARD J., university administrator; b. Manville, N.J., Feb. 16, 1942; s. Joseph Stanley and Wladyslawa (Kraszewski) R.; m. Barbara Ann Bogk, June 01, 1968; children: Edward, James, Daniel, David, Christopher. BA, Parsons Coll., 1965; MA, U. Iowa, 1968, PhD, 1985; LittD (hon.), Loras Coll., 1990. Dean of men, asst. dean of students Parsons Coll., Fairfield, Iowa, 1965-67; dean of students St. Ambrose Coll., Davenport, Iowa, 1968-74, v.p. adminstrn., 1974-80, sr. v.p., 1980-86, exec. v.p., 1986-87; pres. St. Ambrose U., Davenport, 1987—; bd. dirs., corp. sec. Genesis Med. Ctr., 1994—; bd. dirs. Firstar Bank Davenport N.A.; cons. ednl. div. Marriott Corp., 1988—. Vice chairperson Civil Rights Commn., Davenport, 1975; bd. dirs. Handicapped Devel. Ctr., Davenport, 1987, Jr. Achievement, 1988, Big Brothers-Big Sisters, 1988, Iowa Coll. Found., 1992—. Grantee Kettering Found., 1968. Mem. Iowa Assn. Ind. Colls. and Univs. (exec. com., treas. 1992—), Am. Assn. Higher Edn., Davenport C. of C. (bd. dirs. 1992), Rotary, Phi Delta Kappa. Roman Catholic. Home: 806 W Rusholme St Davenport IA 52804-1928 Office: St Ambrose U 518 W Locust St Davenport IA 52803-2829

ROGALSKI, LOIS ANN, speech and language pathologist; b. Bklyn.; d. Louis J. and Filomena Evelyn (Maro) Giordano; m. Stephen James Rogalski, Jun e 27, 1970; children: Keri Anne, Stefan Louis, Christopher James, Rebecca Blair, Gregory Alexander. BA, Bklyn. Coll., 1968; MA, U. Mass., 1969; PhD., NYU, 1975. Lic. speech and lang. pathologist, N.Y. Speech, lang. and voice pathologist Rehab. Ctr. of So. Fairfield County, Stamford, Conn., 1969, Sch. Health Program-P.A. 481, Stamford, 1969-72; pvt. practice speech, lang. and voice pathology Sch. Health Program-P.A. 481, Scarsdale, N.Y., 1972—; cons. Bd. Coop. Ednl. Svcs., 1976-79, Handicapped Program for Preschoolers for Alcott Montessori Sch., Ardsley, N.Y., 1978—; rsch. methodologist Burke Rehab. Ctr., 1977. Mem. profl. adv. bd. Found. for Children with Learning Disabilities, 1978—; bd. dirs. United Way of Scarsdale-Edgemont, 1988-89; instr. religious instr. CCD Immaculate Heart of Mary Ch., Scarsdale, 1991—. Fellow Rehab. Svcs. Adminstrn., 1968-69; N.Y. Med. Coll., 1972-75. Mem. N.Y. Speech & Hearing Assn., Westchester Speech & Hearing Assn., Am. Speech, Hearing & Lang. Assn. (cert. clin. competence), Coun. for Exceptional Children, Assn. on Mental Deficiency, Am. Acad. Pvt. Practice in Speech Pathology & Audiology (bd. dirs., treas. 1983-87, pres. 1987-89), Internat. Assn. Logopedics & Phoniatrics, Sigma Alpha Eta. Office: PO Box 1242 Scarsdale NY 10583-9242

ROGAN, ELEANOR GROENIGER, cancer researcher, educator; b. Cin., Nov. 25, 1942; d. Louis Martin and Esther (Levinson) G.; m. William John Robert Rogan, June 12, 1965 (div. 1970); 1 child, Elizabeth Rebecca. AB, Mt. Holyoke Coll., 1963; PhD, Johns Hopkins, 1968. Lectr. Goucher Coll., Towson, Md., 1968-69; rsch. assoc. U. Tenn., Knoxville, 1969-73; rsch. assoc. U. Nebr. Med. Ctr., Omaha, 1973-76, asst. prof., 1976-80, assoc. prof. Eppley Inst., dept. pharm. scis. and dept. biochemistry and molecular biology scis., U. Nebr., 1980-90, prof., 1990—. Contbr. articles to profl. jours. Predoctoral fellow USPHS, Johns Hopkins U., 1965-68. Mem. AAAS, AAUP, Am. Assn. Cancer Rsch., Am. Soc. Biochem. Molecular Biology. Democrat. Roman Catholic. Home: 8210 Bowie Dr Omaha NE 68114-1526 Office: U Nebr Med Ctr Eppley Inst 600 S 42nd St Omaha NE 68198-6805

ROGATZ, PETER, physician; b. N.Y.C., Aug. 5, 1926; s. Julian and Sally (Levy) R.; m. Marjorie Plaut, June 10, 1949; children—Peggy Joy, William Peter. B.A., Columbia Coll., 1945; M.D., Cornell U., 1949; M.P.H., Columbia U., 1956. Intern Lenox Hill Hosp., N.Y.C., 1949-50; resident Lenox Hill Hosp., 1950-51, VA Hosp., Bronx, N.Y., 1951-52, N.Y. Hosp., N.Y.C., 1952-53; dep. dir. Montefiore Hosp., N.Y.C., 1960-63; dir. L.I. Jewish Med. Center, 1964-68, Univ. Hosp., SUNY, Stony Brook, 1968-71; sr. v.p. Blue Cross/Blue Shield of Greater N.Y., 1971-76; prin., founding ptnr. RMR Health and Hosp. Mgmt. Cons., Inc., Roslyn Heights, N.Y., 1976-84; v.p. med. affairs Vis. Nurse Service, N.Y., 1984-91; med. dir. Staff Builders, Inc., 1992—; prof. cmty. medicine SUNY, Stony Brook, 1968—; mem. N.Y.C. Mayor's Commn. on Delivery of Health Svcs., 1967; v.p. Health and Welfare Coun. of Nassau County, 1968-72; bd. dirs. Cmty. Coun. Greater N.Y., 1974-77; mem. Task Force on N.Y.C. Crisis, 1976-81; chmn. bd. dirs. Cmty. Health Program (affiliated with L.I. Jewish Med. Ctr.), 1989-94; chmn. bd. dirs. Managed Health Inc., 1990-94. Author: Organized Home Medical Care in New York City, 1956, (with Eli Ginzberg) Planning for Better Hospital Care, 1961; mem. editorial bd.: Preventive Medicine, 1975-81; contbr. articles to profl. jours. Bd. dirs. Choice in Dying, 1994—. Commonwealth Fund fellow, 1955; recipient Dean Conley award Am. Coll. Hosp. Adminstrs., 1975. Fellow ACP, N.Y. Acad. Medicine, Am. Public Health Assn., Am. Coll. Preventive Medicine; mem. Am. Hosp. Assn., N.Y. Public Health Assn., AMA, N.Y. State Med. Soc., N.Y. County Med. Soc. Home and Office: 76 Oakdale Ln Roslyn Heights NY 11577-1535

ROGENESS, MARY SPEER, state legislator; b. Kansas City, Kans., May 18, 1941; d. Frederic A. and Jeannette (Hybskmann) Speer; m. Dean Rogeness, Aug. 31, 1964; children: Emily, James, Paul. BA, Carleton Coll., 1963. Computer analyst Dept. Def., Ft. Meade, Md., 1963-66; freelance writer, editor Longmeadow, Mass., 1982-91; mem. Mass. Ho. of Reps., Boston, 1991—. Editor: Reflections of Longmeadow, 1983. Mem. Longmeadow Rep. Town Com., 1983—; Mass. alt. del. Rep. Nat. Conv., Houston, 1992. Mem. Am. Legis. Exch. Coun., World Affairs Coun. of Western Mass. (bd. dirs. 1990—). Office: Mass House of Reps State House Boston MA 02133

ROGER, JERRY LEE, school system administrator; b. Chase, Kans., Mar. 11, 1945; s. LeRoy J. and Lottie E. (Maphet) R.; m. Tucky Saint Smith, 1995. BS, U. Tulsa, 1966, MA, 1969, EdD, 1975. Cert. tchr., supt., Okla. Math. tchr. Kansas City (Mo.) Pub. Schs., 1966-67, Shawnee Mission (Kans.) Pub. Schs., 1967-71; rsch. asst. Tulsa Pub. Schs., 1972-73, rsch. coord., 1973-81, adminstrv. asst., 1981-90, rsch. dir., 1990-95, dir. planning and assessment, 1995—; adj. instr. Tulsa Jr. Coll., 1975-88; adj. asst. prof. U. Tulsa, 1980-85. Contbr. book revs. to Tulsa Sunday World, 1990-92. Paul Harris fellow; Rotary benefactor. Mem. NEA, Nat. Book Critics Ctr., Nature Conservancy, The Nat. Conf., Phi Delta Kappa. Home: 3538 S Winston Ave Tulsa OK 74135 Office: Tulsa Pub Schs 3027 S New Haven Ave Tulsa OK 74114-6131

ROGER, JOHN W., parks and recreation director. Pres. Chgo. Park Dist. Office: Chicago Park Dist 425 E McFetridge Dr Chicago IL 60605-2801*

ROGERS, A. KAY, construction company executive; b. Phoenix, June 11, 1935; s. Arthur W. Rogers and Irene Higbee; m. Sandra M. Magleby, Oct. 15, 1957; children: Kaylene Willis, Kathlene, Kristine. BS in Civil Engring., Ariz. State U., 1962. Registered profl. engr.; registered land surveyor. Estimator Tanner Bros. Constrn., Phoenix, 1962-65; gen. constrn. supt. The Tanner Cos., Phoenix, 1965-74, pres., 1974-83; owner, pres. A.K. Rogers Co., Phoenix, 1983—. Bishop LDS Ch. Mem. AGC (bd. dirs. Ariz. chpt. 1974-81, pres. 1982). Office: A K Rogers Co 1122 E Campbell Ave Phoenix AZ 85014-3913*

ROGERS, ALAN VICTOR, former career officer; b. Hannibal, Mo., Nov. 13, 1942; s. Julian Alan and Gladys Cuneo R.; m. Linda Rae Peterson, May 8, 1966; children: Kimberly Rae, Krista Anne, Peter Alan. BS in Mil. Sci., USAF Acad., 1964; MBA with distinction, Harvard Bus. Sch., 1972; grad. with distinction, Air War Coll., 1980. Commd. 2d lt. USAF, 1964, advanced through grades to maj. gen., 1989, ret., 1993; combat fighter pilot 355th Tactical Fighter Wing, Takhli, Thailand, 1966-67; jet pilot instr. Flying Tng. Wing, Williams AFB, Ariz., 1967-69; student Harvard Bus. Sch., Cambridge, Mass., 1970-72; pers. officer Cols. Group USAF Pentagon, Washington, 1972-75; student Air War Coll., Maxwell AFB, Ariz., 1980; wing comdr. 5th Bomb Wing, Minot AFB, N.D., 1982-84, 96th Bomb Wing (1st B-1B Wing), Dyess AFB, Tex., 1984-86; dir. ops. SAC, Offutt AFB, Nebr., 1986-89; asst. chief of staff ops. Supreme HQ Allied Powers Europe, Mons, Belgium, 1989-91; dir. J-7 Joint Staff, Washington, 1991-93; assoc. Burdeshaw Assocs., Ltd., Bethesda, Md., 1993-94; prin. Gemini Consulting, Morristown, N.J.,

1994—. Mem., mil. adviser C. of C., Minot, N.D., 1982-84, Abilene, Tex. 1984-86. Decorated D.S.M., Legion of Merit, D.F.C. with two oak leaf clusters, Purple Heart. Mem. Air Force Assn., Red River Valley Fighter Pilots Assn., Nat. Eagle Scout Assn., Daedalians (chpt. pres. 1986). Republican. Roman Catholic. Avocations: skiing, travel, antiques, Porsche-356B. Home: 2405 Lexington Rd Falls Church VA 22043-3222 Office: Gemini Consulting 25 Airport Rd Morristown NJ 07960

ROGERS, ARTHUR HAMILTON, III, lawyer; b. Florence, S.C., Apr. 19, 1945; s. Arthur Hamilton Jr. and Suzanne (Wilson) R.; m. Karen Lyn Hess, June 22, 1968; children: Sarah Elizabeth, Thomas Hess. BA, Rice U., 1967; JD, Harvard U., 1970. Bar: Tex. 1970. Assoc. Fulbright & Jaworski LLP, Houston, 1970-74; participating assoc. Fulbright & Jaworski L.L.P., Houston, 1974-77; ptnr. Fulbright & Jaworski, L.L.P., Houston, 1977—; gen. counsel Lifemark Corp., Houston, 1981-82; sec. Mosher, Inc., Houston, 1984—. Dir. Alley Theatre, Houston, 1990—, Autry House, 1994—; mem. exec. com. Rice U. Fund Coun., Houston, 1993—, vice-chair, 1996—. Mem. ABA, State Bar Tex., Assn. of Rice Alumni (treas. 1995—), Ramada-Tejas Club. Episcopalian. Home: 5309 Bordley Dr Houston TX 77056-2323 Office: Fulbright & Jaworski LLP 1301 Mckinney St Fl 51 Houston TX 77010

ROGERS, BERNARD WILLIAM, military officer; b. Fairview, Kans., July 16, 1921; s. William Henry and Lora (Haynes) R.; m. Ann Ellen Jones, Dec. 28, 1944; children: Michael W., Diane E., Susan A. Student, Kans. State Coll., 1939-40; BS, U.S. Mil. Acad., 1943; BA (Rhodes scholar), Oxford (Eng.) U., 1950, MA, 1954, DCL (hon.), 1983; grad., Command and Gen. Staff Coll., 1954-55, Army War Coll., 1959-60; LLD, Akron U., 1978, Boston U., 1981. Commd. lt. U.S. Army, 1943, advanced through grades to gen., 1974; aide to supt. U.S. Mil. Acad., 1945-46, comdt. cadets, 1967-69; aide to high commr. Austria Gen. Mark W. Clark, 1946-47; bn. comdr. Korea, 1952; exec. to comdr.-in-chief Far East Command, 1953-54; mil. asst. to Chief Staff U.S. Army, 1956-59; exec. to chmn. (Joint Chiefs of Staff), 1962-66; asst. div. comdr. (1st Inf. Div.), Vietnam, 1966-67; comdg. gen. (5th Inf. Div.), Ft. Carson, Colo., 1969-70; chief legis. liaison Dept. Army, 1971-72, dep. chief of staff for personnel, 1972-74; comdg. gen. U.S. Army Forces Command, 1974-76; chief of staff U.S. Army, 1976-79; supreme allied comdr. Europe; comdr. in chief (U.S. European Command), 1979-87; ret. U.S. Army, 1987; former bd. dirs. Atlantic Coun. U.S., George C. Marshall Found., Gen. Dynamics Co., Kemper Nat. Ins. Co., Thomas Industries; former sr. cons. The Coca-Cola Co.; chmn. USO World Bd. of Govs., 1988-94. Decorated DSC, Def. DSM, DSM of Army, Navy and Air Force, Silver Star, Legion of Merit with 3 oak leaf clusters, D.F.C. with 2 oak leaf clusters, Bronze Star medal with V device; hon. fellow Univ. Coll., Oxford U.; recipient Disting. Svc. Citation U. Kans., 1984, Disting. Grad. award U.S. Mil. Acad., 1995. Mem. VFW, Assn. U.S. Army (bd. dirs.), Assn. Am. Rhodes Scholars, Soc. 1st Inf. Divsn., Am. Soc. French Legion of Honor, Ret. Officers Assn., Mil. Order of World Wars, The Pilgrims, Army-Navy Country Club, Army and Navy Club, Alfalfa, Phi Delta Theta.

ROGERS, BRIAN DEANE, librarian; b. New London, Conn., June 26, 1937; s. Albert Nash and Janette (Loofboro) R.; m. Carol Priscilla Mallett, May 18, 1962; children: Alison, Paul, Amy. BA, Alfred U., 1959; MLS, Rutgers U., 1967. Asst. registrar Salem (W. Va.) Coll., 1964-66; reference librarian Wesleyan U., Middletown, Conn., 1967-69, head pub. services, 1969-75; librarian Conn. Coll., New London, 1975-93, spl. collections libr., 1993—; Mem. State Adv. Council on Libraries, Hartford, 1976, chair 1977; mem. library bd. Mystic Seaport Maritime Mus., Mystic, Conn., 1987—. Mem. accreditation teams New England Assn. Sch. & Colls., 1985-90. Served with U.S. Army, 1961-64. Mem. ALA, Assn. Coll. and Research Libraries (com. on coll. library standards 1982-86), Conn. Acad. Arts & Scis., Beta Phi Mu. Clubs: Columbiad (Meriden, Conn.); Acorn (Hartford, Conn.). Home: 114 Library St Mystic CT 06355-2420 Office: Conn Coll Library 270 Mohegan Ave New London CT 06320-4196

ROGERS, BRYAN LEIGH, artist, art educator; b. Amarillo, Tex., Jan. 7, 1941; s. Bryan Austin and Virginia Leigh (Bull) R.; m. Cynthia Louise Rice; 1 child, Kyle Austin Rogers. BE, Yale U., 1963; MS, U. Calif., Berkeley, 1966, MA, 1969, PhD, 1971. Design engr. Monsanto Co., Texas City, Tex., 1962; research engr. Rocketdyne, Canoga Park, Calif., 1963-64; research scientist Lawrence Livermore (Calif.) Lab., 1966; lectr. U. Calif., Berkeley, 1972-73; fellow Akademie der Bildenden Künste, Munich, 1974-75; prof. art San Francisco State U., 1975-88; dept. head., prof. art. Carnegie Mellon U., Pitts., 1988—, dir. Studio for Creative Inquiry, 1989—; fellow Ctr. Advanced Visual Studies MIT, Cambridge, Mass, 1981. Editor Leonardo Jour., San Francisco, 1982-85. One-man shows include: Laguna Beach (Calif.) Mus. Art, 1974, DeSaisset Art Gallery U. Santa Clara, Calif., 1974, San Francisco Mus. Modern Art, 1974, Baxter Art Gallery Calif. Inst. Tech., Pasadena, 1979, Contemporary Crafts gallery, Portland, Oreg., 1987; group exhbns. include: Berkeley (Calif.) Art Ctr., 1969, Hansen-Fuller Gallery, San Francisco, 1970, San Francisco Arts Commn. Gallery, 1984, Clocktower Gallery, N.Y.C., 1984, Otis-Parsons Gallery, Los Angeles, 1985, P.P.O.W. Gallery, N.Y.C., 1985, 18th Internat. Bienal, São Paulo, Brazil, 1985, MIT, Cambridge, 1990, Objects Gallery, Chgo., 1992, ARTEC 93 Internat Biennale, Nagoya, Japan, 1993, Chgo. Cultural Ctr., 1993, Am. Iron and Steel Expo., Pitts., 1993, Pitts. Ctr. for Arts, 1994. Fellow NEA, Washington, 1981, 82, Deutscher Akademischer Austauschdienst, Fed. Republic of Germany, 1974, NSF, Washington, 1965-69; recipient SECA award San Francisco Mus. Modern Art, 1974. Office: Carnegie Mellon U Art Dept Pittsburgh PA 15213

ROGERS, C. B., lawyer; b. Birmingham, Ala., July 10, 1930; s. Claude B. Rogers and Doris (Hinkley) Rogers Lockerman; m. Patricia Maxwell DeVoe, Dec. 22, 1962; children: Bruce Lockerman, Evelyn Best, Brian DeVoe. A.B., Emory U., 1951, LL.B., 1953. Bar: Ga. 1953. Adj. prof. litigation Emory U., 1968-70; assoc., then partner firm Powell, Goldstein, Frazer & Murphy, 1954-76; partner firm Rogers & Hardin, Atlanta, 1976—. Fellow Am. Coll. Trial Lawyers; mem. Am. Law Inst., Capital City Club (Atlanta). Democrat. Episcopalian. Home: 1829 W Wesley Rd NW Atlanta GA 30327-2019 also: Brandon Mill Rd Lakemont GA 30335 also: 1160 Swallow Pointe Big Canoe GA 30143 Office: Rogers & Hardin 2700 Cain Tower 229 Peachtree St NE Atlanta GA 30303

ROGERS, CHARLES EDWIN, physical chemistry educator; b. Rochester, N.Y., Dec. 29, 1929; s. Charles Harold and Maybelle (Johnson) R.; m. Barbara June Depuy, June 12, 1954; children: Gregory Newton, Linda Frances, Diana Suzanne. BS in Chemistry, Syracuse U., 1954; PhD in Phys. Chemistry, SUNY at Syracuse U., 1957. Rsch. assoc. dept. chemistry Princeton U., 1957-59, Goodyear fellow, 1957-59; mem. tech. staff Bell Telephone Labs., Murray Hill, N.J., 1959-65; assoc. prof. macromolecular sci. Case Western Res. U., Cleve., 1965-74, prof., 1974—; sr. vis. fellow Imperial Coll., U. London, 1971; assoc. dir. Ctr. for Adhesives Sealants Coatings, Case Western Res. U., 1984-88, dir., 1988-91; co-dir. Edison Polymer Innovation Corp., Ctr. for Adhesives, Sealants and Coatings, 1991—; cons. to polymer and chem. industries; devel. overseas ednl. instns. Editor: Permselective Membranes, 1971, Structure and Properties of Block Copolymers, 1977; contbr. numerous articles to profl. jours.; patentee in field. Served with U.S. Army, 1946-49. Mem. Am. Chem. Soc., Am. Phys. Soc., N.Am. Membrane Soc., Cleve. Coatings Soc., The Adhesion Soc. Home: 8400 Rockspring Dr Chagrin Falls OH 44023-4645 Office: Case Western Reserve U Dept Macromolecular Sc Cleveland OH 44106-7202

ROGERS, CHARLES FORD, II, architect; b. Middlebury, Vt., May 22, 1937; s. Benjamin Earle and Elsie (Jenney) R.; m. Marga Rapuano, 1960 (div. 1992); children: Mara, Charles III; m. Alice B. Hyde, Aug. 30, 1992. BArch, Cornell U., 1960, MArch, 1962. Registered architect, 1971. Archtl. designer Freeman, French & Freeman, Burlington, Vt., 1957-58; architect, designer Office Dan Kiley, Charlotte, Vt., 1959-60, Office Werner Seligman, Cortland, N.Y., 1961-62, Aebli & Hoesli, Zurich, Switzerland, 1963-65, Office Karl Fleigh, Zurich, 1963-65, Perry, Dean, Hepburn & Stewart, Boston, 1965-71; prin. Perry, Dean, Ptnrs., Boston, 1971-84; pres. Perry, Dean, Rogers & Ptnrs., Boston, 1984-93, chmn. bd., 1993—; archtl. draftsperson Cornell-Harvard Archaeol. Expedition, Sardis, Turkey, 1959-60; assoc. prof. coll. architecture Cornell U., Ithaca, N.Y., 1962-63; asst. prof. Swiss Fed. Inst. Tech., Zurich, 1963-65; design critic in architecture Harvard U., 1980. Prin. works include Wellesley Coll. Sci. Ctr., 1976, Hall Mercer Children's Ctr., 1980, Seeley Mudd Chemistry Bldg., 1985, Roe Visual Arts Bldg., 1985, Wesleyan Olin Libr., 1986, Amherst Campus Ctr., 1987, William M. Bristol Jr. Pool, 1988, Catoctin Broodmare Barns, 1989, Kreitzberg Libr. Norwich U., 1992, U.S. Embassy, Amman, Jordan, 1992, Bienecke Student Village Hamilton Coll., 1994, Richard Riley Hall Furman U., 1994. Trustee New Eng. Bapt. Hosp., Boston, 1977-92, William M. Bristol Jr. Swimming Pool, 1988. Biddle Found. scholar, 1959. Mem. AIA. Episcopalian. Club: Union (Boston).

ROGERS, CHARLES RAY, minister, religious organization administrator; b. Grapevine, Tex., Nov. 26, 1935; s. Arlin Avery and Bessie Lorene (Deaton) R.; m. Oma Fay Hines, Aug. 21, 1954; children: Sheree Gay Rogers Saberjissa, Charles Denne Ray, Robin Celeste Rogers Eddins. MS in Christian Edn., Faith Bible Coll., 1980, DD in Humanities (hon.), 1981; D of Ministry in Humanities (hon.), Sem. of Theol. Missions, Escuintla, Guatemala, 1992. Pastor various Bapt. chs., Athens, Dallas, Ft. Worth, 1960-64, various interdenominational chs., Houston, Longview, 1965-69; pres. Evangelism in Action, Ft. Worth, 1969—; bd. dirs. World Ministry Fellowship, Plano, Tex., dir. world missions, 1970—; leader Over 100 Mission, humanitarian trips Evangelism in Action, Ft. Worth, 1976—. Author: Joy, 1979, Handbook for Victorious Living, 1980, How to Develop Christian Love, 1981; vocalist (rec.) Charlie, 1981. Republican. Avocations: golf, tennis, swimming, running, computers. Home: 6417 Rogers Dr Fort Worth TX 76180-4807 Office: Evangelism in Action PO Box 820724 Fort Worth TX 76182-0724

ROGERS, CHARLIE ELLIC, entomologist; b. Booneville, Ark., Aug. 13, 1938; s. Robert Wesley and Parthenia Fern (Mahoney) R.; m. Donna Carol Ray, Jan. 29, 1971; children: Christian Edward, Cheryl Elaine. BS, Northern Ariz. U., 1964; MS, U. Ky., 1967; PhD in Entomology, Okla. State U., 1970. Cert. entomologist. Tchr. biology, social studies Dysart Pub. Sch., Glendale, Ariz., 1964-65; grad. rsch. asst. U. Ky., Lexington, 1965-67; grad. rsch. asst. Okla. State U., Stillwater, 1967-70, postdoctoral rsch. assoc., 1970-71; asst. prof. agrl. experimental station Tex. A&M U., College Station, 1971-75; rsch. entomologist SW Gt. Plains Rsch. Ctr., USDA Agrl. Rsch. Svc., Bushland, Tex., 1975-80; supervisory rsch. entomologist, rsch. leader Conservation & Prodn. Rsch. Ctr., USDA, Bushland, Tex., 1980-83; dir. Insect Biology and Population Mgmt. Rsch. Lab. Agrl. Rsch. Svc.-USDA, Tifton, Ga., 1983—; editor Biol. Control Acad. Press, San Diego, 1990—; rsch. com. Sunflower Assn. Am., Fargo, N.D., 1981-83; dir. elect Bd. Cert. Entomologist Entomol. Soc. Am., Lantham, Md., 1992. Author: Sunflower Species of the United States, 1982; co-editor: The Entomology of Indigenous and Naturalized Systems in Agriculture, 1988; editor: Biological Control, 1990—; contbr. articles to profl. publs. Sch. bd. mem. Bushland Ind. Sch. Dist., 1981-83; tchr. First Bapt. Ch., Tifton, 1986-91; mem. Rotary Club, Vernon, Tex., 1974-76. With U.S. Army, 1958-61. Recipient Profl. Excellence award Am. Agrl. Econ. Assn., 1979, Leadership award USDA, 1987, Profl. Svc. award Am. Registered Profl. Entomologists, 1987, Outstanding Performance award USDA, 1991, 95, Disting. Alumni award 1992. Mem. Entomol. Soc. Am. (bd. cert. entomologist), Ga. Entomol. Soc., Entomol. Soc. S.C, Sigma Xi, Tifton Club (pres. 1992-93). Republican. Baptist. Achievements include study of biology, ecology, and control of sheep nose bot, oestrus ovis; biology and augmentation of Propylea 14-punctata against the green bug; control of guar midge Conterina texana; control of insect pests of sunflowers; biology, taxonomy and pathogenicity of the nematode Noctuidonema. Home: 1711 Sarah Dr Tifton GA 31794-4287 Office: USDA/ARS Insect Biology & Population Mgmt Rsch Lab PO Box 748 Tifton GA 31793

ROGERS, CURTIS L., JR., wholesale distribution executive. Chmn. bd. Rogers Am. Co. Inc., Charlotte, N.C. Office: Rogers Am Co Inc 7315 Pineville Matthews Rd Charlotte NC 28226-8192*

ROGERS, DAVID, apparel executive. With Pickwick Internat., Mpls.; pres. Wilson's House of Suede, Mpls., 1979—. Office: Rosedale Wilsons Inc 400 Highway 169 S Ste 600 Minneapolis MN 55426-1114*

ROGERS, DAVID, playwright, novelist, actor; b. N.Y.C.; s. George and Deborah (Samuels) Rosenberg; m. June Lois Walker, Oct. 14, 1962; children—Dulcy Dru, Amanda Brooke. Student, Am. Theatre Wing Sch., 1948, 49. N.Y.C. prodns. include Ziegfld Follies, 1957, Vintage '60, 1960, New Faces of 1962, Fun City, 1967, Charlie and Algernon, 1980 (Tony award nomination); London prodns. include Jubilee Girl, 1956, Young at Heart, 1961, Flowers for Algernon, 1979, Killing Jessica, 1986; pub. plays include Tom Jones, 1964, Flowers for Algernon, 1969, Brave New World, 1970, F.L.I.P.P.E.D, 1971, Here and Now, 1973, Soft Soap, 1982, Rehearsal for Murder, 1983; pub. musicals include Best of Broadway, 1961, Cheaper by the Dozen, 1969, The Hobbit, 1972, The Truth About Cinderella, 1974, The Dream on Royal Street, 1981; TV The Hero; opera, 1966 (winner Prix d'Italia Concorso Internat. Per Opere Radiofoniche e Televisive), Carol Burnett show, 1970; novels Oh Eden, 1974, The Bedroom Set, 1976, Somewhere There's Music, 1977, The Great American Alimony Escape, 1979, The In-Laws, 1979; actor Broadway prodns. Doubles, 1985, George Abbott's Broadway, 1987, internat. tour Grand Hotel, 1991; regional theatre appearances include Players Theatre, Columbus, 1992, Birmingham (Mich.) Theatre, Jupiter (Fla.) Theatre, 1993, Great Lakes Theatre Festival, Cleve., 1994, Phoenix Theatre, Purchase, N.Y., 1995, Denver Ctr. Theatre Co., 1996. Served with U.S. Army, 1951-52, Korea. Mem. Dramatists Guild, Writers Guild Am. East, AFTRA, Broadcast Music Inc., Actors Equity. Club: Theatre Artists Workshop (Westport, Conn.) (bd. dirs. 1985).

ROGERS, DAVID HUGHES, finance executive; b. Chgo., May 21, 1947; s. Joseph Gordon and Viola Winifred (Hughes) R.; 1 child, Kirsten Morgan. BA, U. Mich., 1968; PhD, Columbia U., 1975. Economist Fed. Res. Bank of Cleve., 1974-75; asst. treas. B.F. Goodrich Co., Akron, Ohio, 1975-82; exec. v.p., chief fin. officer First Tex. Savs. Assn., Dallas, 1982-83; sr. exec. v.p., chief operating officer PriMerit Bank, Las Vegas, 1984-87, pres., dir., 1987-91; vice chmn., 1991-92; chief oper. officer The Baird Cos., Las Vegas, Nev., 1992—. Author: Consumer Banking in New York, 1975; also articles. Mem. exec. bd. Boulder Dam Area coun. Boy Scouts Am., 1986—; bd. dirs. Nev. Sch. Arts, 1988—, Temple Beth Am, 1994—, Las Vegas Bus. Bank, 1995—. Office: The Baird Cos 3753 Howard Hughes Pky Las Vegas NV 89109-0938

ROGERS, DESIREE GLAPION, state official; b. New Orleans, June 16, 1959; d. Roy and Joyce Glapion; m. John Rogers, Jr.; 1 child, Victoria. B in Polit. Sci., Wellesley Coll., 1981; MBA, Harvard U., 1985. Customer svc. mktg. mgr. AT&T, N.J., 1985-87; dir. devel. Levy Orgn., Chgo., 1987-89; founder, pres. Mus. Ops. Consulting Assocs., Chgo., 1989-91; dir. Ill. State Lottery, Chgo., 1991—. Pres. The Chgo. Children's Mus.; bd. dirs. Mus. Sci. and Industry, Frances Xavier Warde Sch., WTTW/Ch. 11; bd. trustees Harvard Bus. Sch. Club Chgo.; mem. women's bd. Mus. Contemporary Art; sec. Marwen Found. Mem. The Econ. Club, Harvard Bus. Sch. Club, Wellesley Club. Office: Ill State Lottery Ste 2040 676 N Saint Clair St Chicago IL 60611

ROGERS, DONALD ONIS, language educator; b. Springfield, Mo., Oct. 9, 1938; s. Onis Lee and Wilma (Gideon) R.; m. Mora Jeannine, Aug. 19, 1961; children—Donald Scott, Anne Margaret. B.S., SW Mo. State U., 1961; M.A., La. State U., 1968; Ph.D., Southwestern La. U., 1978. Lang. coordinator Ralls County Pub. Schs., Mo., 1961-66; grad. teaching asst. La. State U., Baton Rouge, 1966-68; asst. prof. La. State U., Eunice, 1968-74, assoc. prof., 1974-79, head div. liberal arts, dir. acad. affairs, 1973-78, prof. English, dean acad. affairs and services, 1979-91, prof. English, vice chancellor for acad. affairs, 1991—. Bd. dirs. Bayouland Library System, 1974-78. Served with USNR, 1957-59. Mem. Ralls County Tchrs. Assn. (pres. 1965-66), Coll. English Assn., La. Council Tchrs. English, S.W. Regional Conf. English in 2-Yr. Colls., MLA, South Central MLA. Democrat. Home: PO Box 301 Cheneyville LA 71325-0301 Office: PO Box 1129 Eunice LA 70535-1129

ROGERS, DONALD PATRICK, business administration educator; b. Tucson, Aug. 28, 1947; s. Patrick Joseph and Pearl Anna (Howarter) R.; m. Fran Carlin, Aug. 3, 1974; children: Tracy Lynn, Anne Marie. BS, U. Ariz., 1969; MBA, Ohio U., 1971, PhD, 1973. Sales rep. TMC, Tucson, 1966-68; asst. prof. SUNY, Buffalo, 1972-78; assoc. prof. SUNY, Genesseo, 1978-87; prof. bus. adminstrn. Rollins Coll., Winter Park, Fla., 1987—; dir. Survey Info. Rsch. Ctr., Geneseo, N.Y., 1978-87, dir. masters in human resources Rollins Coll., Winter Park, 1993—; rsch. cons. various cos., Winter Park, 1976—. Co-author: Auditing Organizational Communications, 1978; editor: Fundamental Concepts of Business, 1984, Contemporary Issues in Human Resource Management, 1994, Cases in Human Resource Management, 1995; co-editor: Integrated Business Analysis, 1985; contbr. articles to profl. publs. Mem. Acad. Mgmt. (divsn. chmn. 1982-83, svc. award 1993), Soc. Human Resource Mgmt., Am. Compensation Assn. Democrat. Office: Rollins Coll Holt Ave Winter Park FL 32789

ROGERS, EARL LESLIE, artist, educator; b. Oakland, Calif., July 8, 1918; s. Robert Ray and Addie Myrtle (Dice) R.; m. Eileen Estelle MacKenzie, Apr. 9, 1945; children: Leslie Eileen, Brian Donald (dec.). Student, L.A. Valley Coll., 1949-52, Northridge State U., 1958-59, UCLA Extension, 1967, Sergei Bongart Sch. Art, 1967-68; AA, Pierce Coll., 1958. Cert. tchr., Calif. Various positions City of L.A., Van Nuys, Calif., 1948-55, Reseda, Calif., 1955-68; pvt. practice Canoga Park, Calif., 1948-68; art tchr. Mariposa (Calif.) County High Sch., 1969-70; art instr. Merced (Calif.) County Coll., 1970—; instr. Earl Rogers Studio Workshop, Mariposa, Calif., 1969—; art dir. Yosemite Nat. Park, Calif., 1973; instr. art Asilomar Conf. Grounds, Pacific Grove, Calif., 1980; juror various art orgns., 1971-95; demonstrator Clovis (Calif.) Art Guild, 1971, 89, Sierra Artists, Mariposa, 1972, 81, 82, 84, 91, Merced Art League, 1976, Yosemite Western Artists, Oakhurst, Calif., 1973, Madera (Calif.) Art Assn., 1978, Chowchilla (Calif.) Art Guild, 1983, 86, 87, 89, 91, Soc. Western Artists, 1981, 89, 93. One-man shows include L.A. City Hall, 1968, Merced Coll., 1969, 95, Mariposa Title Co. Bldg., 1969, Coffee's Gallery, 1970, others; exhibited in group shows including West Valley Artists Assn., 1966-68, L.A. City Hall, 1967, Yosemite Nat. Park, 1973, Soc. Western Artists, 1977-78, Cannon Bldg. Rotunda, Washington, 1982, Mother Lode Gallery, Columbia, Calif., 1977, 78, Arbor Gallery, Merced, 1988, Gold Country Gallery, 1990, 91, Merced Coll., 1969-92, others; represented in permanent collections including John C. Freemont Hosp., Mariposa, Mariposa County Arts Coun., Mariposa Mus. and History Ctr. Asst. scout master Boy Scouts of Am., Canoga Park, Calif., 1956-58; art instr. L.A. Recreation Corps, L.A. Parks and Recreation Dept., 1967. Mem. Soc. Western Artists (Neva Rall Meml. award 1978), Mariposa Mus. and Hist. Ctr. (life), Pastel Soc. West Coast, Oil Painters of Am. Avocations: piano and books. Home and Office: 5323 State Highway 49 N Mariposa CA 95338-9503

ROGERS, EDDY J., lawyer; b. Belleville, Ill., Nov. 29, 1940. AB, Harvard U., 1962, LLB, 1965. Bar: Tex. 1965, U.S. Dist. Ct. (so. dist.) Tex. 1975. Ptnr. Mayer Brown & Platt, Houston, Mayor, Day & Caldwell, Houston. Contbr. articles to profl. jours. Mem. ABA, State Bar Tex., Houston Bar. Assn., Phi Beta Kappa. Office: Mayor, Day & Caldwell 700 Louisiana St Ste 1900 Houston TX 77002*

ROGERS, EDWARD SAMUEL, communications company executive; b. Toronto, May 27, 1933; s. Edward Samuel and Velma Melissa (Taylor) R.; m. Loretta Anne Robinson, Sept. 25, 1963; children: Lisa Anne, Edward Samuel, Melinda Mary, Martha Loretta. BA, Trinity Coll., U. Toronto, 1956; LLB, Osgoode Hall Law Sch., 1961; DSc (hon.), Clarkson U., 1989; LLD (hon.), U. Victoria, 1990; LLD, York U., 1994. Bar: Ont., 1962. Founder, prin. Rogers Telecomm. Ltd., Toronto, 1960—; pres., CEO Rogers Comm. Inc., 1978—; vice-chmn. Rogers Cablesystems Ltd., Rogers Broadcasting Ltd.; bd. dirs. The Hull Group, The Toronto Dominion Bank, Can. Pub. Corp., Mercedes-Benz Can., Inc., Rogers Cable TV Ltd., Rogers Cablesystems Ltd., Rogers Broadcasting Ltd. Bd. dirs. Jr. Achievement Can. Mem. Royal Can. Yacht Club, Albany Club, Granite Club, York Club, Muskoka Golf & Country Club, Rideau Club Ottawa, Lyford Cay Club (gov.), Balboa Bay Club, Sigma Chi (Beta Omega chpt.). Progressive Conservative. Mem. Anglican Ch. Office: Rogers Comms Inc PO Box 1007, 40 King St W Ste 6400 Scotia Plz, Toronto, ON Canada M5H 3Y2

ROGERS, EDWIN EARL, newspaper editor; b. Carbondale, Pa., Sept. 7, 1929; s. William Earl and Jessie (Pethick) R.; m. Eleanor Louise Hopkins, Feb. 28, 1959; children: Karen, Kevin, Kyle, Kathryn. Sports editor News-Leader, Carbondale, Pa., 1944-46; bur. reporter, photographer The Scranton (Pa.) Tribune, 1946-51; bur. reporter, photographer The Scranton Times, 1953-54, reporter, 1954-66, state editor, 1966-73, city editor, 1973-80, mng. editor, 1980-95, editor Good Times for Srs., 1995—. Trustee Steamtown Found., Scranton, 1984; bd. dirs. Lackawanna County R.R. Authority, Scranton, 1984. Cpl. U.S. Army, 1951-53. Mem. Soc. Newspaper Design, Pa. Assn. Press Mng. Editors (pres. 1985). Republican. Methodist. Avocations: railroading, travel. Office: The Scranton Times PO Box 3311 149 Penn Ave Scranton PA 18503

ROGERS, ELIZABETH BARLOW, urban planner, municipal park administrator; b. San Antonio, Feb. 6, 1936; d. Caleb Leonidas and Elizabeth (Ewing) Browning; m. Edward Lee Barlow, July 6, 1957 (div. 1979); children: Elizabeth Ewing, David Browning; m. Theodore Courtney Rogers, June 28, 1984. BA in Art History, Wellesley Coll., 1957; MA in City Planning, Yale U., 1964. Open space cons. Parks Council N.Y., 1965-69; legis. asst. N.Y. State Senate, 1967-68; freelance journalist, author, 1969-74; screenwriter Time-Life Film Series, N.Y.C., 1974-75; exec. dir. Central Park Task Force, N.Y.C., 1975-79; adminstr. N.Y.C. Dept. Parks and Recreation, 1979-95; founder, pres. Cen. Park Conservancy, 1980-95; pres. Cityscape Inst., 1996—. Author: The Forests and Wetlands of New York City, 1971, Frederick Law Olmsted's New York, 1972; co-author: East Hampton, A History and Guide, 1976, The Central Park Book, 1978, Rebuilding Central Park, A Management and Restoration Plan, 1985, others. Ptnr. N.Y.C. Partnership. Recipient John Burroughs medal, 1971, Honor award AIA, 1985, Urban Beautification award Am. Hort. Soc., 1987, Disting. Alumnae Achievement award Wellesley Coll., 1989, Hist. Preservation award and medal Garden Club Am., 1992, Citizen Leadership medal Nat. Park Found., 1994. Mem. Century Assn., Cosmopolitan Club, Georgica Assn. Home: 211 Central Park W New York NY 10024 Office: 121 Avenue of the Americas New York NY 10013

ROGERS, ERNEST MABRY, lawyer; b. Demopolis, Ala., Sept. 22, 1947; s. James B. and Ernestine B. (Brewer) R.; m. Jeanne Edwards, Dec. 15, 1979; children—Gilbert B., Katherine B., Mary C. B.A., Yale U., 1969; J.D., Harvard U., 1974. Bar: Ala. 1974, U.S. Dist. Ct. (no. dist.) Ala. 1975, U.S. Ct. Appeals (5th cir.) 1976, U.S. Ct. Appeals (11th cir.) 1981, U.S. Supreme Ct. 1981, U.S. Ct. Claims 1983, U.S. Ct. Appeals (6th cir.) 1987. Law clk. to judge U.S. Dist. Ct. (no. dist.) Ala., 1974-75; ptnr. Bradley, Arant, Rose & White, Birmingham, Ala., 1981—. Contbr. articles to profl. jours. Fellow, Am. Coll. of Constrn. Lawyers. Episcopalian. Lodge: Kiwanis. Office: Bradley Arant Rose & White PO Box 830709 Birmingham AL 35283

ROGERS, EUGENE CHARLES, investment firm executive; b. Bklyn., Sept. 29, 1932; s. Eugene Aloysius and Agnes Hilda (Scharbach) R.; m. Anita Therese Tobin, May 13, 1961; 1 son, Eugene Charles. B.B.A., St. John's U., Bklyn., 1954; M.B.A., N.Y. U., 1960. C.P.A., N.Y. Staff accountant Haskins & Sells (C.P.A.s), N.Y.C., 1954-60, Bache & Co., N.Y.C., 1960-62; controller, then chief fin. officer Reynolds Securities Inc., N.Y.C., 1962-72; v.p., treas. Reynolds Securities Inc., 1972—; 1st v.p., treas. Dean Witter Reynolds Inc., 1978-81, sr. v.p., treas., 1981—; guest lectr., panelist in field. Bd. advisors Coll. Bus. Adminstrn., St. John's U. Served with U.S. Army, 1954-56. Mem. N.Y. State Soc. C.P.A.'s, Fin. Execs. Inst., Fin. Club of N.Y. U. Grad. Sch. Bus., Securities Industry Assn. (past pres. fin. mgmt. div.), Sun and Surf Beach Club, World Trade Ctr. Club, Hempstead Golf and Country Club. Roman Catholic. Home: 15 Whitby Ct Rockville Centre NY 11570-1641 Office: Dean Witter Reynolds Inc 2 World Trade Ctr New York NY 10048-0203

ROGERS, EUGENE JACK, medical educator; b. Vienna, Austria, June 13, 1921; came to U.S., 1937; s. Louis and Malvina (Haller) R.; m. Joyce M. Lighter, Feb. 9, 1952; children: Jay A., Robert J. B.S., CCNY; M.B., Chgo. Med. Sch., 1946, M.D., 1947. Diplomate Am. Bd. Phys. Medicine and Rehab. Intern Misericordia and Cabrini Meml. Hosps., N.Y.C., 1946-48; resident Madigan Hosp., Tacoma, 1951, Mayo Clinic, Rochester, Minn., 1951, N.Y. Med. Coll. Met. Med. Ctr., 1953-55; USPHS fellow, 1955-56; ship's surgeon U.S. Lines, Grace Lines, N.Y.C., 1948-49; indsl. physician Abraham & Strauss Stores, Bklyn., 1949-51; practice medicine specializing in phys. medicine and rehab. Bklyn., 1956-73; dir. rehab. service, attending physician N.Y. City Hosp. Dept., 1955-73; prof. and chmn. dept. rehab. medicine Chgo. Med. Sch., North Chicago, Ill., 1973—; cons. N.Y.C. Mayor's Adv. Com. for Aged, 1957; asst. prof. SUNY Downstate Med. Sch., Bklyn., 1958-73; med. dir. Schwab Rehab. Hosp., Chgo., 1973-75; acting chief rehab. service VA Center, North Chicgo, 1975-77; chmn. Ill. Phys. Therapy Exam. Com., 1977-78; examiner Am. Bd. Phys. Medicine and Rehab., 1983; sec., dir. Microtherapeutics, Inc., 1972. Editor: Total Cancer Care, 1975; contbr. articles to med. jours.; contbg. editor Ill. Med. Jour., 1983-89. Served to capt. U.S. Army, 1951-53. Recipient Bronze medal Am. Congress Rehab. Medicine, 1974. Fellow ACP, Am. Acad. Phys. Medicine and Rehab.; mem. Ill. Med. Soc. (chmn. workmen's compensation com. 1980-83), Ill. Soc. Phys. Medicine and Rehab. (pres. 193-84), Chgo. Med. Sch. Faculty Assembly (spkr. 1980), Chgo. Med. Sch. Alumni Assn. (exec. com., asst. treas. 1983-93, treas. 1993—, sec. 1995—, Presdl. plaque Greater N.Y. chpt., Disting. Alumnus award 1980), Odd Fellows (pres. 1961-62), Alpha Omega Alpha, Phi Lambda Kappa (trustee 1980). Home: 1110 N Lake Shore Dr Chicago IL 60611-1054 Office: Finch U Health Scis Chgo Med Sch 3333 Green Bay Rd North Chicago IL 60064-3037 *To render good medical care: Prevent disease, evaluate the patient, treat the condition, educate patient and family, restore function.*

ROGERS, FRANCES NICHOLS, assistant principal; b. Fontana Dam, N.C., July 25, 1944; d. Fred Edward and Violet Bernice (Slagle) Nichols; m. Terry William Rogers, July 3, 1970. BA in English, Berea Coll., 1966; MA in Elem. Edn., U. Ky., 1968; postgrad., U. N.C., 1992. Tchr. intern Breathitt County Schs., Jackson, Ky., 1966-68; tchr. elem. sch. Haywood County Schs., Waynesville, N.C., 1968-72, resource program developer, 1972-75, 77-83, asst. prin., 1983-89, 92—, prin., 1989-92; pres. Haywood County Chpt. N.C. Edn. Assn., 1969-70. Author: Mount Zion United Methodist Church: A History 1850-1982, 1982; author of poems; contbr. articles to profl. jours. Mem. Friends of Libr., Waynesville, 1980—, Haywood Animal Welfare Assn., Waynesville, 1980—, Youth for Christ, Waynesville, 1980—. Named Outstanding Young Educator Waynesville Jaycees, 1968-69, Leader of Am. Elem. Edn., 1971. Mem. ASCD, Tarheel Assn. Prins. and Adminstrs., Haywood County Prins. Assn., Internat. Reading Assn. (sec. local chpt. 1973-74). Methodist. Avocations: travel, reading, gardening. Home: RR 1 Box 296 Clyde NC 28721-9751

ROGERS, FRED BAKER, medical educator; b. Trenton, N.J., Aug. 25, 1926; s. Lawrence H. and Eliza C. (Thropp) R. A.A., Princeton U., 1947; M.D., Temple U., 1948; M.S. in Medicine, U. Pa., 1954; M.P.H., Columbia U., 1957; spl. student, Johns Hopkins U., 1962. Diplomate: Am. Bd. Preventive Medicine. Intern Temple U. Hosp., Phila., 1948-49; chief resident physician Temple U. Hosp., 1953-54; USPHS fellow Temple U. Sch. Medicine, 1954-55, asst. prof. preventive medicine, 1956-58, assoc. prof., 1958-60, prof., 1960-90, prof. emeritus, 1991—, chmn. dept., 1970-77; lectr. epidemiology Columbia U. Sch. Pub. Health, 1957-68, Sch. Nursing, U. Pa., 1964-67; cons. USN Hosp., Phila., 1964-73. Author: A Syllabus of Medical History, 1958, Help-Bringers: Versatile Physicians of N.J, 1960, Epidemiology and Communicable Disease Control, 1963, Studies in Epidemiology, 1965, (with A.R. Sayre) The Healing Art, 1966, (with M.E. Cashel) Your Body is Wonderfully Made, 1974; mem. editorial bd. Am. Jour. Pub. Health, 1967-73; contbr. articles to profl. jours. Served with M.C. USNR, 1950-53, Korea. Recipient Chapel of Four Chaplains award, 1982. Fellow ACP; mem. AMA (past chmn. sect. preventive medicine), Am. Pub. Health Assn., Royal Soc. Medicine of London (hon.), Sigma Xi, Alpha Omega Alpha, Phi Rho Sigma. Clubs: Campus (Princeton); Franklin Inn (Phila.); Charaka (N.Y.C.); Osler (London). Home: 333 W State St Trenton NJ 08618-5722 Office: Temple U Sch Medicine Philadelphia PA 19140

ROGERS, FRED MCFEELY, television producer and host; b. Latrobe, Pa., Mar. 20, 1928; s. James Hillis and Nancy (McFeely) Flagg; m. Sara Joanne Byrd, July 9, 1952; children: James Byrd, John Frederick. MusB, Rollins Coll., 1951; MDiv, Pitts. Theol. Sem., 1962; DHL (hon.), Thiel Coll., 1969; HHD (hon.), Eastern Mich. U., 1973; LittD (hon.), St. Vincent Coll., 1973; DD (hon.), Christian Theol. Sem., 1973, Washington and Jefferson Coll., 1984, Westminster Coll., 1987; LHD (hon.), Yale U., 1974, Lafayette Coll., 1977, Washington and Jefferson Coll., 1984, Linfield Coll., 1982, Duquesne U., 1982, Slippery Rock Coll., 1982, U. S.C., 1985, MacMurray Coll., 1986, Drury Coll., 1986, Bowling Green State U., 1987; DFA (hon.), Carnegie-Mellon U., 1976; MusD (hon.), Waynesburg Coll., 1978, U. Ind., 1988; LLD (hon.), Hobart and William Smith Colls., 1985, U. Conn., 1991, Ind. U., Pa., 1992, Boston U., 1992, Moravian Coll., 1992; hon. degree, Goucher Coll., 1993, U. Pitts., 1993; DHL(hon.), U. W.Va., 1995. Adj. prof. U. Pitts., 1976; pres. Family Communications, Inc., Pitts.; asst. producer NBC, N.Y.C., 1951-53; exec. producer Sta. WQED, Pitts., 1953-62; producer, host CBC, Toronto, Ont., 1962-64; exec. producer, host Mister Rogers' Neighborhood (PBS), Pitts., 1965—; prodr., host Old Friends, New Friends PBS interview series, 1979-81; host Fred Rogers' Heros PBS, 1994. Author: Mister Rogers Talks with Parents, 1983, Mister Rogers' First Experiences Books, 1985, Mister Rogers' Playbook, 1986, Mr. Rogers Talks About Divorce, 1987, Mister Rogers-How Families Grow, 1988, You are Special, 1994; producer five audio cassettes of original songs-Many Ways to Say I Love You, audio cassettes Bedtime, 1992, Growing, 1992; composer: Mr. Rogers' Songbook; host, writer, producer five one hour videocassettes home videos CBS, 1987-88. Chmn. child devel. and mass media forum White House Conf. on Children; mem. Esther Island Preserve Assn.; bd. dirs. McFeely Rogers Found.; hon. chmn. Nat. PTA, 1992-94. Recipient Peabody award for finest children's TV program; award for excellence in children's programming Nat. Ednl. TV; Emmy award, 1980; Ohio State award, 1983, ACT award, 1984, The Christopher award, 1984, Ga. Assn. Broadcasters award, 1984; Lamplighter award Ednl. Press. Assn. Am., 1985; Disting. Service award Spina Bifida Assn. Am., 1985; Children's Book Council award, 1985, Emmy award for outstanding writing in children's series, 1985, Assn. Childhood Edn. award, 1986; Director's award-Ohio State award, 1986; Gold medal Internat. Film and TV Festival, 1986, award Nat. Assn. State Dirs. Migrant Edn., 1987, Ollie award Am. Children's TV Festival, 1987, Immaculata (Pa.) Coll. medal, 1988, Bronze medal Internat. Film and TV Festival, 1988, Outstanding Pa. Author award, 1988, Parent's Choice award, 1987, 88, Spl. Recognition award Nat. Assn. Music Mchts., 1989, PBS award in recognition of 35 yrs. in pub. TV, 1989, Hall of Fame award Action for Children's TV, 1988, Man. of Yr. award Pitts. Vectors, 1990, Peabody award, 1993, Disting Svc. medal, Colgate Rochester Divinity Sch., 1994, Eleanor Roosevelt Val-Kill medal, 1994, Joseph F. Mulach, Jr. award, 1995. Mem. Luxor Ministerial Assn. Presbyterian. Office: 4802 5th Ave Pittsburgh PA 15213-2957 *Every person in this life is so much more than meets the eye or ear. I'm continually surprised at the complexity of all those whom I'm fortunate enough really to get to know.*

ROGERS, GARTH WINFIELD, lawyer; b. Fort Collins, Colo., Nov. 4, 1938; s. Harlan Winfield and Helen Marie (Orr) R.; m. Joanne Kathleen Rapp, June 16, 1962; children: Todd Winfield, Christopher Jay, Gregory Lynn, Clay Charles. BS, U. Colo., 1958, LLB, 1962. Bar: Colo. 1962; U.S. Dist. Ct. Colo. 1962. Law clk. to presiding justice U.S. Dist. Ct., Denver, 1962-63; assoc. Allen, Stover & Mitchell, Ft. Collins, 1963-68; ptnr. Allen, Rogers Metcalf & Vahrenwald, Ft. Collins, 1968—. Articles editor Rocky Mountain Law Rev., 1961-62. Bd. advs. Salvation Army, Ft. Collins; past bd. dirs. United Way of Ft. Collins, Trinity Luth. Ch., Ft. Collins, others. Mem. Ft. Collins C. of C. (past bd. dirs.), ABA, Colo. Bar Assn., Larimer County Bar Assn. Avocations: Nicaragua projects, participative sports, amateur writing, reading. Office: Allen Rogers Metcalf & Varenwald 125 S Howes St Fort Collins CO 80521-2737

ROGERS, GERALD D., electronics executive. Pres., CEO Cyrix Corp., Richardson, Tex. Office: Cyrix Corp 2703 N Central Expy Richardson TX 75080-2010*

ROGERS, HAROLD DALLAS (HAL ROGERS), congressman; b. Barrier, KY, Dec. 31, 1937; m. Shirley McDowell, 1957; children: Anthony, Allison, John Marshall. BA, U. Ky., 1962, LLB, 1964. Bar: Ky. 1964. Pvt. practice Somerset, Ky., 1967-69; Commonwealth atty. Pulaski and Rockcastle counties, Ky., 1969-80; mem. 97th-104th Congresses from 5th Dist. Ky., 1981—; mem. appropriations com., subcom. commerce and justice, energy and water. Mem. appropriations coms. Ky. N.G., 1957-64. Republican. Office: US Ho of Reps 2468 Rayburn Bldg Washington DC 20515-0005*

ROGERS, HARRY, school system administrator. Supt. Valdez (Alaska) City Sch. Dist. State finalist Nat. Supt. Yr. award, 1993. Office: Valdez City Sch Dist PO Box 398 1112 W Klutina St Valdez AK 99686-0398

ROGERS, HERBERT F., manufacturing company executive; b. 1925; married. BS, Purdue U., 1949, D Engring. (hon.), 1979. With Gen. Dynamics Corp., 1949-91; v.p. mktg. Gen. Dynamics Corp., Ft. Worth, 1974-76, v.p. F-16 program, 1976-81, v.p., gen. mgr., 1981-87, exec. v.p. aerospace, 1987-88, pres., COO, 1988-90, vice chmn., 1990, ret., 1991.

ROGERS, HOWARD H., chemist; b. N.Y.C., Dec. 26, 1926; s. Julian Herbert and Minnie (Jaffa) R.; m. Barbara Kniaz, Mar. 27, 1954 (div. 1978); children: Lynne, Mark David, Susan; m. Maureen Dohn, Dec. 28, 1978. BS in Chemistry, U. Ill., 1949; PhD in Inorganic Chemistry, MIT, 1953. Research group leader Allis-Chalmers Mfg. Co., West Allis, Wis., 1952-61; sr. tech. specialist Rocketdyne div., Rockwell, Canoga Park, Calif., 1961-70; chief research scientist Martek Instruments, Newport Beach, Calif., 1970-73; sr. scientist, engr. Hughes Electronics Co., Torrance, Calif., 1973—. Developer nickel-hydrogen battery; patentee; contbr. sci. papers to profl. publs. in field. Served with USN, 1944-46. Recipient Lawrence A. Hyland Patent award Hughes Aircraft Co., 1987. Mem. Electrochem. Soc. (chmn. So. Calif./Nev. sect. 1976-78), Am. Chem. Soc., Sigma Xi. Home: 18361 Van Ness Ave Torrance CA 90504-5309 Office: Hughes Electronics Co B231/1720 PO Box 2999 Torrance CA 90509-2999 *In my 70 years of living experience I have found that these two items are vital: focus on what you intend to do, not what you have already done; complete honesty to yourself and to others in interpreting and reporting results is mandatory.*

ROGERS, IRENE, retired librarian; b. Yonkers, N.Y., Oct. 12, 1932; d. Franklyn Harold and Mary Margaret (Nealy) R.; BS in Edn., New Paltz State Tchrs. Coll., 1954; MLS (N.Y. State Tng. grantee), Columbia U., 1959. Tchr., West Babylon (N.Y.) Sch. System, 1954-57, Yonkers Sch. System, 1957-58; reference librarian Yonkers Pub. Library, 1959-67, adult services coordinator, 1967-73, asst. library dir., 1973-92, ret., 1993. Mem. Mayor's Adv. Com. Consumer Edn., Yonkers, 1970—; active United Way of Yonkers; mem. curriculum adv. com., report card revision com. Office Supt. Schs., 1982; mem. Yonkers unit Am. Cancer Soc. West Library System grantee, 1966. Mem. ALA, Westchester, N.Y. library assns., Soroptimists (pres. 1978-79, 80-81, sec. dist. I North Atlantic region), Bus. and Profl. Women's Club (pres. Yonkers chpt. 1989-90). Home: 41 Amackassin Ter Yonkers NY 10703-2213

ROGERS, ISABEL WOOD, religious studies educator; b. Tallahassee, Aug. 26, 1924; d. William Hudson and Mary Thornton (Wood) R. BA, Fla. State U., 1945; MA, U. Va., 1947; MRE, Presbyn. Sch. Christian Edn., 1949; PhD, Duke U., 1961; DD (hon.), Austin Coll., 1986; LLD (hon.), Westminster Coll., 1988; LHD, Centre Coll., 1989. Campus min. 1st Presbyn. Ch., Milledgeville, Ga., 1949-52; campus chaplain Ga. Coll., Milledgville, 1952-61; prof. of applied Christianity Presbyn. Sch. Christian Edn., Richmond, Va., 1961—; elder Ginter Pk. Presbyn. Ch., Richmond, 1976-79, 89—; moderator of Gen. Assembly, Presbyn. Ch. U.S.A., 1987-88; lectr. Presbyn. chs. Author: The Christian and World Affairs, 1965, In Response to God, 1969, Our Shared Earth, 1980, Sing A New Song, 1981. Vol. Richmond Community Action Program, 1968-75, YWCA, Women's Advocacy Program, 1982—; bd. dirs. Presbyn. Outlook Found., Richmond, 1987—. Du Pont fellow U. Va., 1946. 47, Kearns fellow Duke U. Mem. Soc. Christian Ethics, Phi Kappa Phi, Phi Beta Kappa. Democrat. Avocations: hiking, jogging, tennis, gardening, stamp collecting. Home and Office: Presbyn Sch Christian Edn 1205 Palmyra Ave Richmond VA 23227-4417

ROGERS, JACK DAVID, plant pathologist, educator; b. Point Pleasant, W.Va., Sept. 3, 1937; s. Jack and Thelma Grace (Coon) R.; m. Belle C. Spencer, June 7, 1958. BS in Biology, Davis and Elkins Coll., 1960; MF, Duke U., 1960; PhD, U. Wis., 1963. From asst. prof. to prof. Wash. State U., Pullman, 1963-72, chmn. dept. plant pathology, 1986—. Contbr. articles to profl. jours. Recipient William H. Weston Teaching Excellence award Mycological Soc. Am., 1992. mem. Mycological Soc. of Am. (pres., 1977-78), Am. Phytopathol. Soc., Botanical Soc. Am., British Mycological Soc.

ROGERS, JAMES ALBERT, lawyer; b. Chgo., May 15, 1944; s. Albert Lee and Edith Jane (Magee) R.; m. Jane Austin Pughe, May 14, 1967 (div. 1980); m. Ellen Sheriff, Sept. 26, 1987; children: Alison Sheriff, Emily Sheriff. B.A., Carleton Coll., 1966; J.D., U. Mich., 1969. Bar: Minn. 1969, Wis. 1971, D.C. 1975. Law clk. Justice C. Donald Peterson, Supreme Ct. of Minn., 1969-70; asst. atty. gen. State of Wis., 1971-73; assoc. gen. counsel water and solid waste U.S. EPA, 1977-80; ptnr., head environment dept. Skadden, Arps, Slate, Meagher & Flom, Washington, 1981-91; ptnr., head environment group Wilmer, Cutler & Pickering, Washington, 1991—. Contbr. articles to profl. jours. Recipient Presidential award for meritorious sr. exec. service Pres. Carter, 1980. Mem. D.C. Bar Assn., Minn. Bar Assn., Wis. Bar Assn., Environ. Law Inst. (bd. dirs. 1982—, chmn. bd. 1987-90), Am. Law Inst. Democrat. Office: Wilmer Cutler & Pickering 2445 M St NW Washington DC 20037-1435

ROGERS, JAMES DEVITT, judge; b. Mpls., May 5, 1929; s. Harold Neil and Dorothy (Devitt) R.; m. Leanna Morrison, Oct. 19, 1968. AB, Dartmouth Coll., 1951; JD, U. Minn., 1954. Bar: Minn. 1954, U.S. Supreme Ct. 1983. Assoc. Johnson & Sands, Mpls., 1956-60; sole practice Mpls., 1960-62; judge Mpls. Municipal and Dist. Ct., 1959-91; mem. faculty Nat. Judicial Coll. Bd. dirs. Mpls. chpt. Am. Red Cross, chmn. service to mil. families and vets. com.; bd. dirs. Minn. Safety Council, St. Paul, 1988-91. Served to sgt. U.S. Army, 1954-56. Mem. ABA (chmn. nat. conf. spl. ct. judge, spl. com. housing and urban devel. law, traffic ct. program com., chmn. criminal justice sect., jud. adminstrn. div.), Nat. Jud. Coll. (bd. dirs.), Nat. Christmas Tree Grower's Assn. (pres. 1976-78), Mpls. Athletic Club. Congregational. Office: 14110 Prince Pl Minnetonka MN 55345-3027

ROGERS, JAMES EDWARD, paper company executive; b. Richmond, Va., Aug. 13, 1945; s. Olin Adair and Marjorie (Aiken) R.; children: James Edward Jr., Catherine, Margaret. BS in Physics, Va. Mil. Inst., 1967; MS in Nuclear Engring., U. Va., 1969; postgrad., Harvard U., 1987. Licensing engr. Va. Electric and Power Co., Richmond, 1969-71; sales engr., sales mgr., v.p. sales and mktg. James River Paper Co., Richmond, 1971-77, 79-82, sr. v.p., gen. mgr., 1977-82; v.p. corp. devel., 1982-87; sr. v.p., group exec., specialty paper bus. James River Corp., Richmond, 1987-92; pres., CEO Specialty Coatings Intl., Richmond, 1992-93; mng. dir. SCI Investors Inc., Richmond, 1993—; chmn., bd. dirs. Custom Papers Group Inc., Richmond; bd. dirs. Owens and Minor, Inc., Richmond, Wellman, Inc., Shrewsbury, N.J., Caraustar Industries, Inc., Austell, Ga., Marine Devel. Corp., Richmond. Bd. dirs. Richmond Childrens Mus., Maymont Found., Richmond, 1987; mem. adv. coun. Va. Home, Richmond, Commonwealth Girl Scouts. Mem. Pub. Affairs Group, Storm Try Sail Club. Republican. Clubs: Commonwealth (Richmond); Fishing Bay Yacht (Deltaville, Va.) (commodore 1980); N.Y. Yacht (N.Y.C.). Office: SCI Investors Inc 823 E Main St Ste 1200 Richmond VA 23219-3309

ROGERS, JAMES EUGENE, electric and gas utility executive; b. Birmingham, Ala., Sept. 20, 1947; s. James E. and Margaret (Whatley) R.; m. Robyn McGill (div.); children: Chrissi, Kara, Ben; m. Mary Anne Boldrick, Oct. 28, 1977. BBA, U. Ky., 1970, JD, 1974. Asst. atty. gen. Commonwealth Ky., Louisville; asst. chief trial atty. Fed. Energy Regulation Commn., Washington, dep. gen. counsel litigation and enforcement; law clk. to presiding justice Supreme Ct Ky., Louisville; ptnr. Akin, Gump, Strauss, Hauer & Feld, Dallas, Akin Gump Strauss Hauer & Feld, Houston, 1985-86; formerly pres. Transwestern Pipeline, Houston; now with CINergy Corp. (formerly PSI Resources, Inc.), Cin.; bd. dirs. CINergy Corp., A O Irkutsk Energo, Fifth Third Bank, Bankers Life Holding, Inc., Edison Electric Inst., Duke Realty Investments, Inc. Trustee Nat. Symphony Orch.; bd. dirs. Cin. Mus. Assn., The Nature Conservancy-Ind. chpt., Butler U., Indpls., U. Ky. Bus. Partnership Found. Mem. FBA, Young Pres.' Orgn., Ky. Bar Assn., D.C. Bar Assn., Skyline Club, Meridian Hills Country Club, Crooked Stick Golf Club, Queen City Club, Bankers Club, Met. Club. Baptist. Avocations: tennis, biking, skiing, golf. Office: CINergy Corp PO Box 960 Cincinnati OH 45201

ROGERS, JAMES FREDERICK, banker, management consultant; b. Centerville, Iowa, June 27, 1935; s. John W. and Mildred Holly (Morris) R.; m. Janet L. Marsden, June 27, 1957; children: Jennifer Burke, John William. AB, U. Mo., 1957; postgrad., Rutgers U. Grad. Sch. Banking, 1970-72. With Am. Security and Trust Co., Washington, 1959-85; exec. v.p. Am. Security and Trust Co., 1980-83; bd. dirs., pres. Am. Security Corp., 1983-85; cons. B.E.I.-Golembe Assoc., 1985-93; chmn. Nat. Bank of No. Va., 1988-89. Commr. Arlington County Planning Commn., 1979-80; asst. treas. Kennedy Ctr. Performing Arts; pres., trustee Leonard Wood Found.; trustee Friends of Nat. Zoo, Greater Washington Rsch. Ctr., Washington Dulles Task Force, Arena Stage, Sch. Commerce U. Va. Officer AUS, 1958-59. Mem. D.C. Bankers Assn. (pres. 1984-85), Davenport Soc., U. Mo., Met. Club (Washington), Chevy Chase. Presbyterian. Home: 4201 38th Rd N Arlington VA 22207-4554

ROGERS, JAMES THOMAS, lawyer; b. Denver, Oct. 3, 1941; s. John Thomas and Elizabeth (Milligan) R. JD, U. Wis., 1966. Bar: Wis. 1966, U.S. Tax Ct. 1976, U.S. Ct. Claims, 1975, U.S. Ct. Customs and Patent Appeals, 1975, U.S. Supreme Ct. 1973. Chmn., Madison (Wis.) Legal Aid Soc., 1965-66; dist. atty. Lincoln County (Wis.), 1967, 69-73; spl. dist. atty. pro tem Oneida County (Wis.), 1972, Price County (Wis.), 1972-76, Lincoln County (Wis.), 1976-84; spl. city atty. City of Wausau (Wis.), 1973, 74, 77; ptnr. Rogers & Bremer, Merrill, Wis., 1973-89; prin. Rogers Criminal Law Offices, Merrill, 1989—. bd. dirs. Merrill Fed. Savings & Loan Assn., 1990—. Chmn. Judiciary Com., N.E. Crime Control Commn., 1971-72. Chmn., Lincoln County Republican Com., 1971-73; pub. defender bd. State of Wis., 1988—, 2d vice chmn., 1989-93, 1st vice chmn., 1993—. Bd. dirs. Wis. Judicare, 1990-92. Mem. State Bar Wis. (spl. com. on prosecutorial improvements 1983-89, spl. com. to rev. criminal sanctions 1987-88, conv. and entertainment com. 1989-93), Lincoln County Bar Assn. (pres. 1969-70), Wis. Dist. Attys. Assn. (life), ABA (liaison drunk driving com. of criminal justice sect., vice chmn. asset and investment mgmt. com. sec. econs. of law practice, marriage and cohabitation com. family law sect., def. svcs. commn. criminal law sect., liaison criminal justice sect.), Nat. Assn. Criminal Def. Lawyers (state and local def. bar liaison com., ad hoc subcom. on property of DNA evidence), Assn. Trial Lawyers Am. (constl. challenge com. 1988-92), Wis. Acad. Trial Lawyers (chmn. constl. challenge com. 1988-91), bd. dirs. 1985-91), Tex. Trial Lawyers Assn., N.Y. State Trial Lawyers Assn., Wis. Assn. Criminal Def. Lawyers (sec. 1986-87, pres.-elect 1987-88, pres. 1988-89, bd. dirs. 1986—, liaison to ABA criminal justice sect., State Wis. Pub. Defender Bd. 1988—, vice-chmn. 1993—), Wausau Club. Home: PO Box 438 1408 E 8th St Merrill WI 54452-0438 Office: Rogers Criminal Law Offices 301 Grand Ave PO Box 1085 Wausau WI 54402-1085

ROGERS, JAMES WILSON, church official; b. Vancouver, BC, Canada, Feb. 18, 1943; m. Carol Haney; children: Amy, Darren. Student, L.I.F.E. Bible Coll. With real estate profession, 1963-69; br. mgr. Wall & Redekop Realty, 1969-74, v.p., gen. mgr., 1974-90; exec. asst. to pres. Internat. Ch. of Foursquare Gospel, 1990—; dir. bus. devel. Realty World Can.; con. to numerous offices, Western Can.; Western regional dir. Comml. Divsn. Coun. mem. Kingsway Foursquare Ch., Vancouver, B.C.; bd. dirs. Youth for Christ Greater Vancouver; mem. pres.'s adv. com. Trinity Western U.; bd. dirs., bd. regents L.I.F.E. Bible Coll. Can.; founding dir., officer Foursquare Ch. Can., nat. bd. dirs., 1979-90. Office: Internat Ch Foursquare Gospel 1910 W Sunset Blvd Ste 200 Los Angeles CA 90026-3247

ROGERS, JEAN GREGORY, lawyer; b. Panama City, Fla., Dec. 15, 1934; d. William Green and Jean (Balkom) Gregory. BA in English, Agnes Scott Coll., Decatur, Ga., 1956; LLB, U. Md., Balt., 1962. Bar: Md. Ct. Appeals, 1963, U.S. Supreme Ct., 1968, U.S. Dist. Ct., Md., 1968, U.S. Ct. Appeals (4th cir.), 1969, U.S. Ct. Appeals (5th cir.), 1985, U.S. Ct. Appeals (10th cir.), 1988. Asst. county solicitor Office of County Solicitor Balt. County, Towson, Md., 1963-68; sole practitioner pvt. practice, Towson, Md., 1963-68; asst. U.S. atty. Office of U.S. Atty. Dept. Justice, Balt., 1968-73; asst. regional counsel Fed. Hwy. Adminstrn., Balt., 1973-75; regional counsel Fed. Hwy. Adminstrn., Fort Worth, Tex., 1975-96; mem., project com. SP20-6, Nat. Coop. Hwy. Rsch. Program Nat. Rsch. Coun., Transp. Rsch. Bd., Washington, 1986—; mem., Group Coun. on Legal Resources, Transp. Rsch. Bd., Washington, 1979-82. Recipient Superior Achievement award for superior handling of complex litigation, Fed. Hwy. Adminstr., 1980. Mem. ABA, Md. State Bar Assn. Presbyterian. Home: 2709 Whispering Trail Pantego TX 76013

ROGERS, JEANNE VALERIE, art educator, artist; b. Islip, N.Y., Dec. 1, 1935; d. Joseph Oliver and Louise Valerie (Bayer) Fields; m. James Aubrey Rogers, Jan. 1, 1956; children: Bradley, Tyler, Lisa, Todd. BFA in Ceramics Design, Alfred U., 1957; MS in Art Edn., SUNY, New Paltz, 1962; postgrad., L.I. U., 1986-90, Parsons Sch. Design, 1988-90. Cert. art edn. tchr. K-12, elem. tchr., N.Y. Elem. art tchr. Sayville (N.Y.) Sch. Dist., 1957-61, high sch. art tchr., 1987-90; art tchr. Bayport (N.Y.)/Bluepoint Sch. Dist., 1980; art dir., art tchr. The Hewlett Sch., East Islip, N.Y., 1984-87; field supr. of student tchrs. Dowling Coll., Oakdale, N.Y., 1990—; high sch. art tchr. Torah Acad., Commack, N.Y., 1991—; instr. watercolor painting Staff Devel. Ctr. of The Islips, East Islip 45, N.Y.C., N.Y., 1996—; instr. oil painting adult edn. East Islip High Sch., 1961-62; dir. children's art Summer Outdoor Art Workshops, East Islip, 1967-78; adj. prof. Dowling Coll., 1991-92, art cons., 1990—; instr. watercolor painting for tchrs. Staff Devel. Ctr. of the Islips, East Islip H.S., N.Y., 1996—. Co-author/illustrator: Suffolk Scribes Galligraphic Poetry, 1980 (Libr. award East Islip, 1980); exhibited juried show at Babylon (N.Y.) Citizens Coun. Arts, 1994 (Best in Show award), Invitational Exhibit of Women Artists, Patchogue, N.Y., 1995; reader children's poetry Women in the Arts cable TV show, 1974; contbr. painting as cover design Suffolk Woman Watch Newspaper (premier issues), 1994. Instr. life saving and water safety ARC, Islip, 1955-61; tchr. Sunday sch. Presbyn. Ch., Islip, 1957-63; instr., dir. lifesaving and water safety Shoreham Beach Club, Sayville, 1965-70; instr. preschool, youth and adult swimming Bayshore YMCA, Lasalle Acad., Oakdale, 1971-88, instr., swim dir., 1983-88; art judge C. of C. Summerfest, Sayville, 1990. Recipient award of merit in painting, Nat. League Am. PEN Women, Vanderbilt Mus., Centerport, N.Y., 1993, 94, Chem. Bank award for painting Arts Coun., 1992, East Islip Pub. Libr., 1992, hon. mention Huntington Township Art LEague, Northeast Sopke Gallery N.Y., 1991, HTAL winners show Hutchins Gallery, CW Post Campus/L.I. U., 1991, others. Mem. AAUW (implementation chair soc.'s reflection in arts study 1972-74, legis. chair Islip area br. 1972-74, cultural interests chaor 1973-75), summer socials chmn. General and Ednl. grants Fundraising, 1995-97, Suffolk Scribes (charter mem., corr. sec. 1988-89), Nat. League Am. PEN WOmen (corr. sec. 1996-97), South Shore Watervolor Soc., South Bay Art Assn., N.Y. State Tchrs. Assn., L.I. Art Tchrs. Assn. Republican. Presbyterian. Avocations: tennis, swimming, ballroom dancing, reading, travel. Home: 274 Marilynn Ct East Islip NY 11730-3315

ROGERS, JEFFREY, dancer. Attended, Sch. Am. Ballet. Dancer Ballet West, Salt Lake City, 1984-89; soloist Ballet West, 1989-91, prin. artist, 1991—; instr., guest artist Ballet West Conservatory. Dance performances include The Dream, Abdallah, Romeo & Juliet, Giselle, Sleeping Beauty, The Age of Anxiety (John Neumeier). Recipient Princess Grace Found. award, 1984. Office: Ballet West 50 W 200 S Salt Lake City UT 84101-1642

ROGERS, JERRY, principal. Prin. Westwood Elem. Sch., Springdale, Ark. Recipient DOE Elem. Sch. Recognition award, 1989-90. Office: Westwood Elem Sch 1800 Mcray Ave Springdale AR 72762-4024

ROGERS, JERRY L., federal agency administrator; b. Tex., Dec. 22, 1938; s. Ancell Robert and Grace Evalena (Coin) R.; m. Peggy Floretta Sifford, Apr. 6, 1963; children: Tiana Lynne Conklin, Elvin Houston, Jeffrey Martin. BA in History, Tex. Tech, 1962, MA, 1965. Historian Nat. Park Svc., Ft. Davis, Tex., 1965-66; historian Nat. Register Nat. Park Svc., Washington, 1967-69, chief registration, 1972-73, chief grants divsn., 1973-75, chief archeology and hist. preservation, 1975-79, assoc. dir. cultural programs, 1981-83, assoc. dir. cultural resources, 1983-94; regional dir. S.W. region, 1994-95, supt. S.W. office, 1995—; dir. Ranching Heritage Ctr. Tex. Tech Mus., Lubbock, 1969-72; dep. assoc. dir. Heritage Conservation Svc., Washington, 1979-81; internat. cons. in hist. preservation to Italy, Russia, Spain, China, India, Egypt. Contbr. articles to prof. jours. Mem. adv. com. on cemeteries and memls. VA, Washington, 1987-94. Recipient Meritorious

Svc. award Dept. Interior, 1992. Mem. AIA (mem. com. hist. resources, ex-officio mem. 1979-94), Nat. Trust Hist. Preservation (trustee 1981-94), Civil War Trust. Avocations: geneology, classic automobiles. Home: 27 Bosque Loop Santa Fe NM 87505-2231 Office: Nat Park Svc 1100 Old Santa Fe Trail PO Box 728 Santa Fe NM 87504

ROGERS, JOEL EDWARD, law, sociology and political science educator; b. Long Ranch, N.J., Mar. 19, 1952; s. Edward Franklin and Ann (Flemming) R.; m. Sarah Siskind, Dec. 2, 1980; children: Helen, Sophia. BA, Yale U., 1972, JD, 1976; MA, Princeton U., 1978, PhD, 1984. Bar: N.Y., U.S. Ct. Appeals (7th and 8th cirs.). Assoc. prof. law U. Miami, 1986-87; asst. prof. law and sociology U. Wis., Madison, 1987-88, assoc. prof. law and sociology, 1988-90, prof. law and sociology, 1990—; affiliate Inst. for Rsch. on Poverty, Madison, 1988—; assoc. dir. A. Eugene Havens Ctr., Madison, 1988—; co-dir. Disputes Processing Rsch. Program, Madison, 1988—; dir. Ctr. on Wis. Strategy, Madison, 1993—; prof. law, polit. sci. and sociology U. Wis., Madison, 1991—. Co-author: (book) Right Turn: The Decline of the Democrats and the Future of American Politics, 1986, On Democracy, 1983; co-editor: (book) Works Councils: Consultation, Representation, and Cooperation in Industrial Relations, 1995. Exec. com. chair New Party, N.Y.C., 1992—; bd. chair Ctr. for a New Democracy, Washington, 1992—; exec. com. chair Sustainable America, Madison, 1994—. Office: U Wis Law Sch 975 Bascom Mall Madison WI 53706*

ROGERS, JOHN JAMES WILLIAM, geology educator; b. Chgo., June 27, 1930; s. Edward James and Josephine (Dickey) R.; m. Barbara Bongard, Nov. 30, 1956; children: Peter, Timothy. BS, Calif. Inst. Tech., 1952, PhD, 1955; MS, U. Minn., 1952. Lic. geologist, N.C. From instr. to prof. Rice U., Houston, 1954-75, master Brown Coll., 1966-71, chmn. geol. dept., 1971-74; W.R. Kenan Jr. prof. geology U. N.C., Chapel Hill, 1975—. Author: A History of the Earth, 1993; co-author: Fundamentals of Geology, 1966, Precambrian Geology of India, 1987; co-editor: Holocene Geology of Galveston Bay, 1969, Precambrian of South India, 1983, Basalts, 1984, African Rifting, 1989; regional editor Jour. African Earth Scis., 1982-93; contbr. articles to profl. jours. Fellow Geol. Soc. Am., Geol. Soc. India, Geol. Soc. Africa (hon.); mem. Mineral. Soc. Am., Am. Assn. Petroleum Geologists, Soc. Econ. Paleontologists and Mineralogists. Home: 1816 Rolling Rd Chapel Hill NC 27514-7502 Office: U of NC Dept Geology CB #3315 Chapel Hill NC 27599-3315

ROGERS, JOHN M., food Products executive. Pres., CEO B.C. Rogers Processors Inc., Morton, Miss. Office: B C Rogers Prcessors Inc 4688 Old Highway 80 E Morton MS 39117-9770*

ROGERS, JOHN S., union official; b. Scranton, Pa., Nov. 19, 1930. Student, U. Wis., 1959-61, U. Mich., 1963; student spl. studies, Am. U., 1965-66, Harvard U. Bus. Sch., 1967. Internat. rep. United Brotherhood of Carpenters and Joiners of Am., Washington, 1958-65, asst. to gen. pres., 1966-74, dir. edn., 1971-82, mem. gen. exec. bd., 1974-78, gen. sec., 1978-91; sec.-treas. Suffolk County (N.Y.) Dist. Coun. Carpenters, 1957-58; v.p. N.Y. State Bldg. and Constrn. Trades Council, 1974-78, N.Y. State Fedn. Labor, 1974-78; pres. N.Y. State Coun. Carpenters, 1974-78; vice chmn. N.Y. State Commn. Jobs and Energy; mem. Suffolk County Pub. Employment Rels.s Bd.; vis. lectr. George Meany Ctr. Labor Studies. Author numerous trade union leadership mans. and instructional materials, 1966-79. Bd. dirs. L.I. action com. Assn. Help for Retarded Children, 1956-60; labor co-chmn United Cerebral Palsy, N.Y.C., 1977-78; v.p. Leukemia Soc. Mem. Harvard Trade Union Alumnae Assn. Home: 7026 Darby Towne Ct Alexandria VA 22315-4752

ROGERS, JOHN WASHINGTON, JR., investment management company executive; s. John W. Sr. and Jewel (Mankarious) R.; m. Desiree Glapion. BS in Econs., Princeon U. Broker William Blair & Co.; now pres. Ariel Capital Mgmt., Inc., Ariel Mut. Funds, Chgo. Bd. dirs. Chgo. Urban League, Chgo. Park Dist., Chgo. Symphony Orch., Rush Presbyn. St. Luke's Hosp., Nat. Assn. Securities Dealers, Aon Corp., Morrison Knudsen Inc., Am. Nat. Bank. Office: Ariel Capital Mgmt Ariel Mut Funds 307 N Michigan Ave Ste 500 Chicago IL 60601-5305*

ROGERS, JUDITH W., federal circuit judge; b. 1939. AB cum laude, Radcliffe Coll., 1961; LLB, Harvard U., 1964; LLM, U. Va., 1988; LLD (hon.), D.C. Sch. Law, 1992. Bar: D.C. 1965. Law clk. Juvenile Ct. D.C., 1964-65; asst. U.S. atty. D.C., 1965-68; trial atty. San Francisco Neighborhood Legal Assistance Found., 1968-69; atty. assoc. atty. gen.'s office U.S. Dept. Justice, 1969-71, atty. criminal divsn., 1969-71; gen. counsel Congl. Commn. on Organization of D.C. Govt., 1971-72; coordinator legis. program Office of Dep. Mayor D.C., 1972-74, spl. asst. to mayor for legis., 1974-79, corp. counsel, 1979-83; assoc. judge D.C. Ct. Appeals, 1983-88, chief judge, 1988-94; cir. judge U.S. Ct. Appeals-D.C. Cir., 1994—; mem. D.C. Law Revision Commn., 1979-83; mem. grievance com. U.S. Dist. Ct. D.C., 1982-83; mem. exec. com. Conf. Chief Justices, 1993-94. Bd. dirs. Wider Opportunities for Women, 1972-74; mem. vis. com. Harvard U. Sch. Law, 1984-90; trustee Radcliffe Coll., 1982-88. Recipient citation for work on D.C. Self-Govt. Act, 1973, Disting. Pub. Svc. award D.C. Govt., 1983, award Nat. Bar Assn., 1989; named Woman Lawyer of Yr., Women's Bar Assn. D.C., 1990. Fellow ABA; mem. D.C. Bar, Nat. Assn. Women Judges, Conf. Chief Justices (bd. dirs. 1988-94), Am. Law Inst., Phi Beta Kappa. Office: US Ct Appeals 333 Constitution Ave NW Washington DC 20001-2802*

ROGERS, JUSTIN TOWNER, JR., retired utility company executive; b. Sandusky, Ohio, Aug. 4, 1929; s. Justin Towner and Barbara Eloise (Larkin) R. AB cum laude, Princeton U., 1951; JD, U. Mich., 1954. Bar: Ohio 1954. Assoc. Wright, Harlor, Purpus, Morris & Arnold, Columbus, 1956-58; with Ohio Edison Co., Akron, 1958-93, v.p., then exec. v.p., 1970-79, pres., 1980-91, chmn. bd., 1991-93; ret., 1993; bd. dirs. 1st Nat. Bank Ohio, 1st Merit Corp; past mem. coal adv. bd. Internat. Energy Agy. Past pres., trustee Akron Cmty. Trusts, Akron Child Guidance Ctr.; past chmn. Akron Assoc. Health Agys., U. Akron Assocs.; past chmn., trustee, mem. exec. com. trustees Akron Gen. Med. Ctr., Health Network Ohio; trustee Sisler McFawn Found., VNS-Hospice Found.; mem. Gt. Trail Coun. Boys Scouts Am. Mem. Portage Country Club, Mayflower Club, Rockwell Springs Trout Club (Castalia, Ohio), Princeton Club (N.Y.C.), Phi Delta Phi, Beta Gamma Sigma.

ROGERS, KATE ELLEN, interior design educator; b. Nashville, Dec. 13, 1920; d. Raymond Lewis and Louise (Gruver) R.; diploma Ward-Belmont Jr. Coll., 1940; BA in Fine Arts, George Peabody Coll., 1946, MA in Fine Arts, 1947; EdD in Fine Arts and Fine Arts Edn., Columbia U., 1956. Instr., Tex. Tech. Coll., Lubbock, 1947-53; co-owner, v.p. Design Today, Inc., Lubbock, 1951-54; student asst. Am. House, N.Y.C., 1953-54; asst. prof. housing and interior design U. Mo., Columbia, 1954-56, assoc. prof., 1956-66, prof., 1966-85, emeritus, 1985—, chmn. dept. housing and interior design, 1973-85; mem. accreditation com. Found. for Interior Design Edn. Rsch., 1975-76, chmn. stds. com., 1976-82, chmn. rsch., 1982-85. Mem. 1st Bapt. Ch., Columbia, Mo.; bd. dirs. Meals on Wheels, 1989-91. Nat. Endowment for Arts rsch. grantee, 1981-82. Fellow Interior Design Educators Coun. (pres. 1971-73, chmn. bd. 1974-76, chmn. rsch. com. 1977-78); mem. Am. Soc. Interior Designers, (hon., medal of honor 1975), Am. Home Econs. Assn., Columbia Art League (adv. bd. 1988-93), Pi Lambda Theta, Kappa Delta Pi, Phi Kappa Phi (hon.), Gamma Sigma Delta, Delta Delta Delta (Phi Eta chpt.), Phi Upsilon Omicron, Omicron Nu (hon.). Democrat. Author: The Modern House, USA, 1962; editor Jour. Interior Design Edn. and Research, 1975-78.

ROGERS, KENNETH RAY, entertainer, recording artist; b. Houston, Aug. 21, 1938; s. Edward Floyd and Lucille (Hester) R.; 1 child by 1st marriage, Carol; 1 child by 2d marriage, Kenneth; m. Marianne Gordon; 1 child, Christopher Cody. Student, U. Houston. Appeared on American Bandstand, 1958; mem. Bobby Doyle Trio, 1959-66, Christy Minstrels, 1966-67, The First Edition, 1967-69, Kenny Rogers and The First Edition, 1969-75, pursued solo career, 1975—; performed numerous concerts in U.S., Can., Eng., Scotland, New Zealand, Australia, Japan; hosted TV spls. Kenny Rogers Classic Weekend, 1988, 89, 90, Kenny, Dolly & Willie, 1989, Kenny Rogers in Concert, 1989, Goodwill Games, 1990; starred in TV series Rollin' with The First Edition, 1972; appeared in movies Six Pack, 1982, Wild Horses, 1985; appearances Tonight Show; appeared in TV movies: Kenny Rogers as the Gambler, 1980, Coward of the County, 1981, Gambler, Part II, 1983, Gambler III: The Adventure Continues, 1987, Christmas in America, 1989, The Gambler Returns, The Luck of the Draw (Gambler IV), 1991; appeared in TV spl. Very Special Arts; (TV series): MacShayne, 1994—; rec. artist with Liberty Records, 1976-82, RCA Records, 1983—; toured Kenny & Dolly, Dollywood, 1990, British Isles, 1990; recs. include That Crazy Feeling (Gold single), I Don't Need You (Brit. Country Music Assn. award, Acad. Country Music award), Love is What We Make It, 1985, The Heart of the Matter, 1985, They Don't Make Them Like They Used To, What About Me, I Prefer the Moonlight, 1987, When You Put Your Heart in It, 1988 (ofcl. theme song U.S. Gymnastics Fedn.), Christmas in America, 1989, Love Is Strange, 1990, Greatest Country Hits, 1990, If Only My Heart Had a Voice, 1993, Greatest Hits, 1994; number #1 albums include Kenny Rogers-Lucille, 1976, Love or Something Like It, 1978, The Gambler, 1978, Kenny, 1979, Gideon, 1980, Share Your Love, 1981, Eyes That See in the Dark, 1983, Something Inside So Strong, 1989; author photographic works Kenny Roger's America, 1986, Your Friends and Mine, 1987; rec. artist Warner/Reprice, 1988—; TV host A&E The Real West, 1993. Hon. capt. 1988 U.S. Gymnastics Team. Named Cross-Over Artist of Year Billboard mag., 1977, named Top Male vocalist People mag., 1979, 80; recipient Country Music Assn. award, 1978, 79, Am. Music award, Best Male Vocalist, Best Album, 1984, Am. Music award, Best Male Country Vocalist, Best Album, 1985, Country Music Found. Roy Acuff award, 1985, UN Peace award, 1984, Rec. Industry Assn. Am. Most Awarded Artist award, 1984 (11 platinum, 18 gold albums), Grammy award for best male country vocal, 1977, 79, co-recipient (with Ronnie Milsap) for best country vocal duet, 1987, 1st Harry Chapin award for humanitarianism ASCAP, 1988, Horation Alger award, 1990; numerous other music awards. Address: care Kragen & Co 1112 N Sherbourne Dr Los Angeles CA 90069-2202

ROGERS, KENNETH SCOTT, professional baseball player; b. Savannah, Ga., Nov. 10, 1964. Ed., Plant City, Fla. Pitcher Tex. Rangers, 1989—. Named to Am. League All-Star Team, 1995; pitched perfect game against Calif. Angels, 1994.

ROGERS, LAWRENCE H., II, retired television executive, investor, writer; b. Trenton, N.J., Sept. 6, 1921; s. Norman Tallman and Nancy (Titus) R.; m. Suzanne Long; children: Hallie, Suzanne, Lawrence H. III, Campbell, Natalie, Christian. Grad., Lawrenceville Sch., 1939; BA with honors in history, Princeton U., 1943; student, Harvard U., 1963. A pioneer broadcast editorials; built sta. WSAZ-TV Inc.; with Taft Broadcasting Co., Cin., 1960-76; pres. Taft Broadcasting Co., 1963-76; pres., CEO Omega Comms., Inc., Orlando, Fla., 1977-92; chmn. bd. dirs. Cin. br. Fed. Res. Bank of Cleve., 1975-82; bd. dirs. Cin. Fin. Corp., Cardinal Group of Funds, Columbus, Ohio; past mem. TV Code Rev. Bd.; treas. TV Bur. Advt., then chmn. bd. dirs.; vice chmn. bd. Sta. NBC-TV Affiliates; v.p., dir. Assn. Maximum Svc. Telecaster, Washington; mem. info. com. Nat. Assn. Broadcasters, then editl. com.; mem. TV Code Rev. Bd.; cons. to USIA, Africa, 1967, USSR and Ea. Europe, 1971; mem. summit trip and SALT signing with Pres. Richard Nixon, 1972. Author: Business of Broadcasting, 1963, Orlando Shoot-Out, 1990. Vice chmn. trustees distbn. com. Greater Cin. Found.; Former Gov. W.Va. Econ. Devel. Agy.; Bd. dirs. Theatre Devel. Fund; gen. chmn. Greater Cin. Fine Arts Fund. Served to capt. F.A. AUS, World War II, ETO. Recipient Distinguished Service award U.S. Jr. C. of C., 1956. Mem. Internat. Radio TV Exec. Soc., Newcomen Soc. Clubs: Queen City (Cin.); Camargo, N.Y. Yacht, Brook (N.Y.C.); Rolling Rock (Ligonier, Pa.); Commonwealth (Cin.). Home and Office: 4600 Drake Rd Cincinnati OH 45243-4118

ROGERS, LEE FRANK, radiologist; b. Colchester, Vt., Sept. 24, 1934; s. Watson Frank and Marguerite Mortimer (Cole) R.; m. Donna Mae Brinker, June 20, 1956; children: Michelle, Cynthia, Christopher, Matthew. BS, Northwestern U., 1956, MD, 1959. Commd. 2d lt. U.S. Army, 1959, advanced through grades to maj., 1967; rotating intern Walter Reed Gen. Hosp., 1959-60; resident radiology Fitzsimons Gen. Hosp., 1960-63; ret., 1967; radiologist Baptist Meml. Hosp., San Antonio, 1967-68, U. Tex. Med. Sch., San Antonio, 1968-71; dir. residency tng., radiologist U. Tex. Med. Sch., Houston, 1972-74; prof., chmn. dept. radiology Northwestern U. Med. Sch., Chgo., 1974-95; editor-in-chief Am. Jour. Roentgenology, Winston-Salem, N.C., 1995—; prof. radiology Bowman Gray Sch. Medicine Wake Forest Univ. Fellow Am. Coll. Radiology (past pres.), Am. Roentgen Ray Soc. (past pres.); mem. Assn. U. Radiologists (past pres.), Radiol. Soc. N.Am., Am. Bd. Radiology (past pres.), Alpha Omega Alpha. Episcopalian. Office: Am Jour Roentgenology 101 S Stratford Rd #303 Winston Salem NC 27104 *The source of most problems is previous solutions.*

ROGERS, LEE JASPER, lawyer; b. Fort Monmouth, N.J., May 6, 1955; s. Peter and Ethel Mae (Williams) R.; m. Vanessa Walisha Yarbrough, Apr. 18, 1981 (div. Oct. 1988); 1 child, Stephanie Alexandria. Student, Drew U., 1975, Monmouth Coll., 1975; BA in History, Hampton Inst., 1977; JD, Howard U., 1980. Pvt. practice Red Bank, N.J., 1981-91, 95—; asst. dep. pub. defender Ocean County region, Toms River, N.J., 1991-92; mortgage loan officer Allied Fin. Svcs., Neptune, N.J., 1992-93, Mortgage Money Mart, Edison, N.J., 1993-94, Residential First, Inc., Shrewsbury, N.J., 1994-95, Fairmont Funding, Lakewood, N.J., 1995—; vol. counsel Pro Bono Legal Svcs., Red Bank, N.J., 1982-91; pres., chmn. bd. Jay-Mar Entertainment Enterprises, Inc., 1986—. Author numerous poems; vocal singing group Pizazz, 1991-94, Nu Eara, 1992. Pres., bd. dirs. Ct. Basie Learning Ctr., Red Bank, N.J.; chmn. Red Bank Republican Club. Mem. ABA, NAACP (exec. com. Red Bank chpt. 1983-88), Assn. Trial Lawyers Am., Elks (sec. ho. com. Bates lodge #220 1988-90, loyal knight 1990-91, esteemed loyal knight 1993-94, chmn. by-laws com. 1993-94). Baptist. Home: 298 Shrewsbury Ave Apt 3 Red Bank NJ 07701-1319 *Mastery is achieved through the development of the spirit, and the resulting obtainment of bliss. We should all seek to be at one within ourselves and with the world around us. To do this, we must walk with God. Only then can we find true happiness!.*

ROGERS, LON B(ROWN), retired lawyer; b. Pikeville, Ky., Sept. 5, 1905; s. Fon and Ida (Brown) R.; BS, U. Ky., 1928, LLB, 1932; LHD (hon.), Pikeville Coll., 1979, LHD (hon.) Centre Coll. of Ky., 1992; m. Mary Evelyn Walton, Dec. 17, 1938; children: Marylon Walton, Martha Brown, Fon II. Bar: Ky. 1932. Practiced law in Lexington, 1932-38, Pikeville, 1939-80. Dir. East Ky. Beverage Co., Pikeville, 1940-90, Pikeville Nat. Bank & Trust Co. Elder, 1st Presbyterian Ch, Pikeville, Ky., 1947-75; mem. Pikeville City Council, 1951; mem. local bd. SSS, 1958-69; mem. Breaks Interstate Park Commn., Ky.-Va., 1960-68, chmn., 1960-62, 64-66, vice chmn., 1966-68; chmn. Community Services Commn., Pikeville Model Cities, 1969-71; mem. Ky. Arts Commn., 1965-72, Ky. Travel Council, 1967-70, 73-75; pres. Ky. Mountain Laurel Festival Assn., 1971-72. Chmn. bd. trustees Presbytery Ebenezer, U.S.A., 1950-71; trustee Pikeville Coll., 1951-72, 73-79, trustee emeritus, 1979—; trustee Presbytery of Transylvania, 1971-83; mem. bd. nat. missions United Presbyn. Ch. USA, 1954-66; trustee Appalachian Regional Hosps., Inc., 1963-67, Ky. Ind. Coll. Found., 1973-82; bd. dirs. Meth. Hosp. of Ky., 1966-82; mem., Presbyn. Ch., Lexington, 1982—, trustee, 1989-91; am. mem., trustee 2nd Presbyterian Ch.. Mem. Ky. C. of C. (regional v.p. 1962-64, 69-74), Ky. Hist. Soc., S.A.R., Civil War Round Table, Blue Grass Kiwanis (past lt. gov.), Filson Club, Blue Grass Automobile (pres. 1971-74, dir.), Sigma Alpha Epsilon, Phi Delta Phi. Republican. Home: 505 E Main St Lexington KY 40508-2309 Office: 300 E Main St Ste 403 Lexington KY 40507-1539

ROGERS, LORENE LANE, university president emeritus; b. Prosper, Tex., Apr. 3, 1914; d. Mort M. and Jessie L. (Luster) Lane; m. Burl Gordon Rogers, Aug. 23, 1935 (dec. June, 1941). B.A., N. Tex. State Coll., 1934; M.A. (Parke, Davis fellow), U. Tex., 1946, Ph.D., 1948; D.Sc. (hon.), Oakland U., 1972; LL.D. (hon.), Austin Coll., 1977. Prof. chemistry Sam Houston State Coll., Huntsville, Tex., 1947-49; research scientist Clayton Found. Biochem. Inst. U. Tex., Austin, 1950-64, asst. dir., 1957-64, prof. nutrition, 1962-80, assoc. dean Grad. Sch., 1964-71, v.p. univ., 1971-74, pres., 1974-79, mem. exec. com. African grad. fellowship program, 1966-71; research cons. Clayton Found. for Research, Houston, 1979-81; Vis. scientist, lectr., cons. NSF, 1959-62; cons. S.W. Research Inst., San Antonio, 1959-62; mem. Grad. Record Exams Bd., 1972-76, chmn., 1974-75; adv. com. ITT Internat. Fellowship, 1973-83; dir. Texaco, Inc., Gulf States Utilities, Republic Bank, Austin. Bd. dirs. Tex. Opera Theatre, Austin Lyric Opera; chmn. bd. trustees Texaco Philanthropic Found.; chmn. council of presidents Nat. Assn. State Univs. and Land-Grant Colls., 1976-77, mem. exec. com., 1976-79; mem. com. on identification of profl. women Am. Council on Edn., 1975-79, mem. com. on govt. relations, 1978-79; mem. target 2000 project com. Tex. A&M U. System; mem. ednl. adv. bd. John E. Gray Inst., Lamar U., Beaumont, Tex. Eli Lilly fellow, 1949-50; Recipient U. Tex. Students Assn. Teaching Excellence award, 1963; Disting. Alumnus award N. Tex. State U., 1972; Outstanding Woman of Austin award, 1950, 60, 71, 80; Disting. Alumnus award U. Tex., 1976; Honor Scroll award Tex. Inst. Chemists, 1980. Fellow Am. Inst. Chemists; mem. AAAS, Am. Chem. Soc. (sec. 1954-56), Am. Inst. Nutrition, Am. Soc. Human Genetics, Nat. Soc. Arts and Letters, Assn. Grad. Schs. (internat. edn. com. 1967-71), Sigma Xi, Phi Kappa Phi, Iota Sigma Pi, Omicron Delta Kappa. Research in hydantoin synthesis, intermediatry metabolism, biochem. nutritional aspects of alcoholism, mental retardation, congenital malformations. Home: 4 Nob Hill Cir Austin TX 78746-3650

ROGERS, MALCOLM AUSTIN, museum director, art historian; b. Scarborough, Yorkshire, Eng., Oct. 3, 1948; s. James Eric and Frances Anne (Elsey) R. M.A., Magdalen Coll., U. Oxford , Eng., 1973; D. Phil., Christ Ch., U. Oxford, 1976. Asst. keeper Nat. Portrait Gallery, London, 1974-83, dep. dir., 1983-94; dir. Mus. Fine Arts, Boston, 1994—. Author: Blue Guide: Museums and Galleries of London, 1983; also articles. Fellow Soc. Antiquaries. Avocations: wine and food; travel; opera. Home: 20 Charles River Sq Boston MA 02114 Office: Mus Fine Arts 465 Huntington Ave Boston MA 02115-5523

ROGERS, MARK CHARLES, physician, educator; b. N.Y.C., Oct. 25, 1942; s. Gerald and Inez (Kaufman) R.; m. Elizabeth Ann London, Dec. 30, 1972; children: Bradley, Meredith. BA, Columbia U., 1964; MD, SUNY, Syracuse, 1969; MBA, U. Pa., 1991; PhD (hon.), U. Ljubljana Slovenia, 1995. Diplomate Am. Bd. Anesthesiology (examiner 1982—), Am. Bd. Pediatrics. Intern Mass. Gen. Hosp., Boston, 1969-70, resident, 1973-75; resident Boston Children's Hosp., 1970-71; fellow Duke U. Med. Ctr., Durham, N.C., 1971-73; asst. prof. dept. anesthesiology and critical care medicine Johns Hopkins U., Balt., 1977-79, assoc. prof., 1979-80, prof., chmn. dept., 1980-93, assoc. dean Sch. Medicine, 1990-93, dir. pediatric ICU, 1977-93; CEO Duke Hosp. and Health Network, 1993—; pres. Critical Care Found., Balt., 1981—; cons. WHO, Bangkok, 1982-83. Editor in chief: Yearbook of Critical Care, 1983—, Textbook of Pediatric Intensive Care, 1987, 91, 96, Principles and Practices of Anesthesiology, 1990; editor: Perioperative Management, 1989, dep. editor in chief Critical Care Medicine Jour., 1990—. Maj. U.S. Army, 1975-77. Recipient Club of Mainz award, Mainz, Fed. Republic of Germany, 1981, award Assn. Univ. Anesthetists, 1980; Fulbright scholar, Ljubljana, Yugoslavia, 1990. Mem. Inst. Medicine. Home: 4406 W Cornwallis Rd Durham NC 27705-8126 Office: Duke U Med Ctr PO Box 3708 Durham NC 27710

ROGERS, MARY MARTIN, publishing company executive; b. Nov. 22, 1945; married; 3 children. BA in English, U. Hawaii, 1967. Prodn. editor Academic Press, N.Y.C., 1968-70; asst. prodn. mgr. U. Miami Press, Coral Gables, Fla., 1970-75; mng. editor Am. Statis. Assn., Washington, 1976-78; prodn. mgr. Am. Anthropological Assn., Washington, 1978-79; prodn. editor, books Raven Press, Ltd., N.Y.C., 1981-84, book prodn. mgr., 1984-85, acquisitions editor, 1985-87, exec. editor acquisitions, 1986-87, v.p., editor-in-chief, acquisitions, 1987-91, pres., 1991-95; pres., CEO Lippincott-Raven Publ., Phila., 1995—; comms. specialist So. Fla. Regional Planning Coun., Miami, 1970-75. Office: Lippincott Raven Publ 227 E Washington Sq Philadelphia PA 19106-3713

ROGERS, MICHAEL ALAN, writer; b. Santa Monica, Calif., Nov. 29, 1950; s. Don Easterday and Mary Othilda (Gilbertson) R.; m. Suzanne Elaine Lavoie, May 21, 1995. BA in Creative Writing, Stanford U., 1972. Assoc. editor Rolling Stone Mag., San Francisco, 1972-76; editor-at-large Outside mag., San Francisco, 1976-78; sr. writer Newsweek mag., San Francisco, 1983—; mng. editor Newsweek InterActive, San Francisco, 1993—; exec. prodr. broadband divsn. The Wash. Post Co., 1995-96; v.p. Post-Newsweek New Media, 1996—; vis. lectr. fiction U. Calif., Davis, 1980. Author: Mindfogger, 1973, Biohazard, 1977, Do Not Worry About The Bear, 1979, Silicon Valley, 1982, Forbidden Sequence, 1988; contbr. articles to mags., newspapers. Recipient Disting. Sci. Writing award AAAS, 1976, Best Feature Articles award Computer Press Assn., 1987. Mem. Author Guild, Sierra Club. Avocations: backpacking, horses. Office: Wash Post Broadband Divsn 655 Montgomery St Ste 1010 San Francisco CA 94111

ROGERS, MILLARD FOSTER, JR., retired art museum director; b. Texarkana, Tex., Aug. 27, 1932; s. Millard Foster and Jessie Bell (Hubbell) R.; m. Nina Olds, Aug. 3, 1963; 1 son, Seth Olds. BA with honors, Mich. State U., 1954; MA, U. Mich., 1958; studied with, John Pope-Hennessy; LHD, Xavier U., 1987. Gosline fellow Victoria and Albert Mus., London, Eng., 1959; curator Am. art Toledo Mus. Art, 1959-67; coord. Ford Found. intern program; dir. Elvehjem Art Ctr., prof. art history U. Wis.-Madison, 1967-74; dir. Cin. Art Mus., 1974-94, dir. emeritus, 1994—; vis. scholar Principia Coll., Elsah, Ill., 1982, 94; pres. Mariemont Preservation Found., Ohio, 1982-91, 95—; adj. prof. U. Cin., 1987-91. Author: Randolph Rogers, American Sculptor in Rome, 1971, Spanish Paintings in the Cincinnati Art Museum, 1978, Favorite Paintings from The Cincinnati Art Museum, 1980, Sketches and Bozzetti by American Sculptors, 1800-1950, 1988. Served with AUS, 1954-56. Named Outstanding Citizen of Mariemont, 1991. Mem. Assn. Art Mus. Dirs. (hon.), Am. Assn. Mus., Ohio Mus. Assn., Phi Beta Kappa. Office: Cin Art Mus Eden Park Cincinnati OH 45202-1596

ROGERS, NATHANIEL SIMS, banker; b. New Albany, Miss., Nov. 17, 1919; s. Arthur L. and Elizabeth (Bouton) R.; m. Helen Elizabeth Ricks, July 3, 1942; children—Alice, John, Lewis. AB, Millsaps Coll., 1941; MBA, Harvard U., 1947. With Deposit Guaranty Bank and Trust Co., Jackson, Miss., 1947-69, 1st v.p., 1957-58, pres., dir., 1958-69; pres., dir. 1st City Nat. Bank Houston, 1969-81, chmn., 1982-84; pres. 1st City Bancorp. of Tex., Houston, 1970-83, chmn., 1983-85, also bd. dirs. Chmn. Jackson United Givers Fund, 1957, pres., 1959, bd. dirs., 1958-61; pres. Andrew Jackson area coun. Boy Scouts Am., 1962; trustee Miss. Found. Ind. Colls., 1959-69; past pres., trustee Millsaps Coll.; trustee Methodist Hosp., Houston; chmn. ofcl. bd. Meth. ch. Lt. (s.g.) USNR, 1942-46. Named Outstanding Young Man of Year Jackson Jr. C. of C., 1955. Mem. Am. Bankers Assn. (pres. 1969-70), Miss. Bankers Assn. (pres. jr. banker sect. 1952-53, pres. 1964-65), Robert Morris Assocs. (pres. S.E. chpt. 1954-55, nat. dir. 1959-62), Assn. Res. City Bankers (bd. dirs. 1980-83), Jackson C. of C. (pres. 1962), Houston C. of C. (chmn. 1979-80), Young Pres.'s Orgn., Millsaps Coll. Alumni Assn. (pres. 1955-56), Newcomen Soc., Phi Beta Kappa, Omicron Delta Kappa, Kappa Alpha. Methodist.

ROGERS, OSCAR ALLAN, JR., college president; b. Natchez, Miss., Sept. 10, 1928; s. Oscar Allan and Maria Pinkie (Jackson) R.; m. Ethel Lee Lewis, Dec. 20, 1950; children—Christopher, Christian, Christoff. A.B., Tougaloo Coll., 1950; S.T.B., Harvard U., 1953, M.A.T., 1954; Ed.D., U. Ark., 1960; postgrad. U. Wash., 1968-69; LHD (hon.), Oklahoma City U., 1992,. Ordained to ministry Congl. Ch., 1953, Baptist Ch., 1955, Methodist Ch., 1962. Asst. pastor St. Mark Congl. Ch., Roxbury, Mass., 1951-54; dean-registrar Natchez Jr. Coll., Miss., 1954-56; pres. Ark. Bapt. Coll., Little Rock, 1956-59; dean students prof. social sci. and edn. Jackson State U., Miss., 1960-68, dean Grad. Sch., 1969-84; pres. Claflin Coll., 1984-94, pres. emeritus, 1994—; postdoctoral fellow U. Wash., Seattle, 1968-69; pastor Asbury-Kingsley Charge, Bolton and Edwards (Miss.) United Meth. Ch., 1962-84, Merton (Miss) Cir. United Meth. Chs., 1994-96. Served with USN, 1946-47. Recipient Order of the Palmetto Gov. Campbell (S.C.), 1994. Mem. Conf. Deans of Black Grad. Schs. (pres. 1975-76, treas. 1979-84), AAUP, NAACP, Phi Delta Kappa, Kappa Delta Pi, Alpha Phi Alpha. Democrat. Author: My Mother Cooked My Way Through Harvard with These Creole Recipes, 1973; Mississippi: The View from Tougaloo, 1979. Home and Office: 5932 Holbrook Dr Jackson MS 39206-2003

ROGERS, PAUL GRANT, lawyer, former congressman; b. Ocilla, Ga., June 4, 1921; s. Dwight L. and Florence (Roberts) R.; m. Rebecca Bell, Dec. 15, 1962; 1 child, Rebecca Laing. BA, U. Fla., 1942, JD, 1948, LLD; LLD (hon.), Fla. Atlantic U., U. Md., Duke U., L.I. U.; DSc (hon.), George Washington U., U. Miami, Albany Med. Coll. of Union U.; D.Sc. (hon.),

Commonwealth U. Va.; H.H.D. (hon.), Nova U.; L.H.D. (hon.), N.Y. Med. Coll., N.Y. Coll. Podiatric Medicine, Hahnemann Med. Coll.; D.Med. Sci. (hon.), Med. U. S.C. Bar: Fla. 1948. Partner Burns, Middleton, Rogers, Farrell & Faust, 1952-69; mem. 84th-95th congresses from 11th Dist. Fla., 1955-79; chmn. house subcom. on health and environ. Hogan & Hartson, Washington, 1979—, ptnr., 1979—. Trustee Cleve. Clinic Found., The Scripps Rsch. Inst.; bd. dirs. Am. Cancer Soc.; co-chmn. nat. Leadership Coalition on Health Care Reform; chmn. bd. dirs. Nat. Coun. Patient Info. and Edn., Found. for Biomed. Rsch.; chmn. Nat. Osteoporosis Found., Friends of Nat. Libr. Medicine; mem. health scis. coun. Sch. Medicine, U. Va.; mem. nat. coun. Washington U. Sch. Medicine; mem. coun. for the div. biol. scis. U. Chgo.; mem. dean's coun. Harvard Sch. Pub. Health. Recipient Pub. Welfare medal Nat. Acad. Scis., 1982, Sea Grant award, 1985, Yr. 2000 award Nat. Cancer Inst., 1987, Albert Lasker award for pub. svc., 1993, Hugo Schaefer award APHA, 1994, NOF Leadership award, 1995, Maxwell Finland award, 1996. Mem. ABA, Fla. Bar Assn. (gov. jr. sect. 1952-53), Palm Beach County Bar Assn., D.C. Bar Assn., Inst. Medicine of NAS, Phi Delta Phi, Phi Delta Theta. Methodist (steward). Office: Hogan & Hartson 555 13th St NW Ste 1200 Washington DC 20004-1109

ROGERS, PETER PHILIPS, environmental engineering educator, city planner; b. Liverpool., England, Apr. 30, 1937; came to U.S., 1960, naturalized, 1977; s. Edward Joseph and Ellen (Duggan) R.; m. Rosemarie Rogers, July 11, 1964; children: Christopher, Justin. B in Engring., Liverpool U., 1958; MS, Northwestern U., 1961; PhD, Harvard U., 1966. Asst. engr. Sir Alfred McAlpine & Sons Ltd., Cheshire, Eng., 1958-60; mem. faculty Harvard U., 1966—, Gordon McKay prof. environ. engring., 1974—, prof. city planning, 1974—; mem. Center Population Studies, Harvard U. Sch. Pub. Health, 1974—; cons. World Bank, UN, U.S. Agy. for Internat. Devel., Govt. India, Govt. Pakistan, Govt. Bangladesh, Govt. Nepal, Govt. Italy, Govt. Costa Rica, Commonwealth P.R. Co-author: Urbanization and Change, 1970, Land Use and The Pipe: Planning for Sewerage, 1975, Resource Inventory and Baseline Study Methods for Developing Countries, 1983, Systems Analysis for River Basin Management, 1985, Evaluacion de Projectos de Desarrollo, 1990, America's Waters, 1993, Water in the Arab World, 1994. Gordon McKay tchg. fellow 1961; Radley rsch. student, 1962-64; doctoral dissertation fellow Resources for Future 1964-65; recipient Clemens Herschel prize Harvard U., 1964; Guggenheim fellow, 1973, 20th Century Found. fellowship, 1989. Mem. Third World Acad. Scis. (corr.), Indian Inst. Agrl. Engring. (life), Cosmos Club (Washington), Sigma Xi. Home: 20 Berkeley St Cambridge MA 02138-3410 Office: Harvard U 116 Pierce Hall Cambridge MA 02138

ROGERS, RALPH B., industrial business executive; b. Boston, 1909; married. Ed., Northeastern U. With Cummins Diesel Engine Corp., Edwards Co., Hill Diesel Engine Co., Ideal Power Lawnmower Co., Indian Motocycle Co., Rogers Diesel & Aircraft Corp., Rogers Internat. Corp., Armstrong Rubber Export Corp.; with Tex. Industries Inc., Dallas, 1950—, chmn. bd., pres., CEO, 1951-75, chmn. bd., 1975—; dir. numerous subsidiaries. Chmn. bd. dirs. Tex. Industries Found.; chmn. emeritus Pub. Communication Found. North Tex., Pub. Broadcasting Svc., Univ. Med. Ctr., Inc.; past bd. dirs. Nat. Captioning Inst.; trustee Northeastern U.; trustee, chmn. emeritus St. Mark's Sch. of Tex.; former chmn. bd. mgrs. Dallas County Hosp. Dist.; founding chmn., chmn. emeritus Dallas Arboretum and Bot. Soc.; pres. Dallas Found. for Health, Edn. and Rsch.; co-founder Children's TV Workshop; founder, chmn. Zale Lipshy Univ. Hosp. Mem. Masons. Office: Tex Industries Inc 1341 W Mockingbird Ln Ste 700W Dallas TX 75247-6905

ROGERS, RAYMOND JESSE, federal railroad associate administrator; b. Eugene, Oreg., Mar. 1, 1941; s. Raymond Everett and Virginia Elaine (Simpkins) R.; m. Joan Katherine Peterson, June 6, 1964 (div. Aug. 1974); 1 child, Virginia Arlene; m. Kim Lien Nguyen, Dec. 26, 1974; children: Kim Lan, Vincent Minh. Student, Santa Rosa (Calif.) Jr. Coll., 1960-61, U.S. Army Non-commd. Officer Acad., Anchorage, Alaska, 1963, U. Md., 1967-74, Fed. Exec. Inst., Charlottsville, Va., 1981. Lic. real estate agt., Va. Sr. asst. mgr. Household Fin. Corp., Md., 1964-67; contract specialist Dept. Navy, Washington, 1967-71; contract svcs. officer AID, Saigon, Vietnam, 1971-76; contracting officer Dept. Transp., Fed. R.R. Adminstrn., Washington, 1976-80, dir. fin. svcs., 1980-84, assoc. adminstr. for adminstrn., 1984—. Leader local group Boy Scouts Am., Vienna, Va., 1987-92, Izaac Walton League of Am., Am. Legion, Am. Assn. of Retired Persons. Sgt. U.S. Army, 1961-64. Decorated Vietnam Civilian Svc. medal. Mem. U.S. Sr. Exec. Svc., Fed. Exec. Inst. Alumni Assn. Avocations: fishing, hiking, camping, waterskiing. Home: 102 Yeonas Dr SW Vienna VA 22180-6557 Office: Dept Transp Fed RR Adminstrn 400 7th St SW Washington DC 20590-0001

ROGERS, RICHARD DEAN, federal judge; b. Oberlin, Kans., Dec. 29, 1921; s. William Clark and Evelyn May (Christian) R.; m. Helen Elizabeth Stewart, June 6, 1947; children—Letitia Ann, Cappi Christian, Richard Kurt. B.S., Kans. State U., 1943; J.D., Kans. U., 1947. Bar: Kans. 1947. Ptnr. firm Springer and Rogers (Attys.), Manhattan, Kans., 1947-58; instr. bus. law Kans. State U., 1948-52; partner firm Rogers, Stites & Hill, Manhattan, 1959-75; gen. counsel Kans. Farm Bur. & Service Cos., Manhattan, 1960-75; judge U.S. Dist. Ct., Topeka, Kans., 1975—. City commr., Manhattan, 1950-52, 60-64, mayor, 1952, 64, county atty., Riley County, Kans., 1954-58, state rep., 1964-68, state senator, 1968-75; pres. Kans. Senate, 1975. Served with USAAF, 1943-45. Decorated Air medal, Dfc. Mem. Kans., Am. bar assns., Beta Theta Pi. Republican. Presbyterian. Club: Masons. Office: US Dist Ct 444 SE Quincy St Topeka KS 66683

ROGERS, RICHARD F., construction company executive, architect, engineer; b. Chgo., July 25, 1942; s. Frank S. and Emily H. (Novak) R.; m. Christina L. Rogers, June 30, 1963; children: Mitchell, Cynthia. B in Architectural Engineering, U. Ill., Chgo., 1964. Registered architect, Ill., Wis., Mich., profl. engr., Ill. Architect Einstein Assocs. Inc., Skokie, Ill., 1963-69; v.p. Land Am. Corp., Chgo., 1969-70; project architect M.A. Lombard Constrn. Co., Alsip, Ill., 1970-73; sr. project mgr. W.E. O'Neil Constrn. Co., Chgo., 1973-78; pres. A.C.M. Assocs. Inc., Mt. Prospect, Ill., 1978—. Mem. AIA, Builders Assn. Chgo. Office: ACM Assocs Inc 322 N Wolf Rd Mount Prospect IL 60056-2724

ROGERS, RICHARD HILTON, hotel company executive; b. Florence, S.C., May 26, 1935; s. Leslie Lawton and Bessie (Holloway) R.; m. Evelyn Pascuito; children: Richard Shannon, Leslie Anne. Student, U. N.C., 1953-55; BA in Bus. Adminstrn. cum laude, Bryant Coll., 1962; postgrad., Memphis State U., 1964. Innkeeper Helmsley Spear, N.Y.C., 1961-62; v.p. Holiday Inns of Am., Memphis, 1962-73; exec. v.p. First Hospitality Corp., Hackensack, N.J., 1974-77; v.p., chief oper. officer Cindy's Inc., Atlanta, 1978-81; v.p. 1982 World's Fair, Knoxville, Tenn.; pres., chief exec. officer Hospitality Internat., Atlanta, 1982-92; dir. franchise devel. Budgetel Inns, Norcross, Ga., 1992—; developer, operator The Warehouse Rest., Oxford, Miss., 1973-75, Beauregard's Rest., Hattiesburg, Miss., 1975-78, Walter Mitty's Rest., Auburn, Ala., 1980-83. Contbr. to profl. jours. Mem. adv. bd. Bethune-Cookman Coll. With USN, 1954-58, Korea. Mem. Am. Hotel/Motel Assn. (mktg. com. 1986-92, adv. coun. 1987-92, industry adv. bd.), Economy Lodging Coun. Avocations: sailing, photography. Home: 245 Rhine Dr Alpharetta GA 30202-5455 Office: Budgetel Inns 6855 Jimmy Carter Blvd Ste 2150 Norcross GA 30084*

ROGERS, RICHARD HUNTER, lawyer, business executive; b. Flushing, N.Y., Sept. 11, 1939; s. Royden Harrison and Frances Wilma (Hunter) R.; children: Gregory P., Lynne A., Reade H. B.S. in Bus. Adminstrn, Miami U., 1961; J.D., Duke, 1964. Bar: Ill. 1964, Ohio 1973. Atty. Continental Ill. Nat. Bank, Chgo., 1964-65; sr. atty. Brunswick Corp., Chgo., 1965-70; corporate counsel The A. Epstein Cos., Inc. (real estate developers), Chgo., 1970-73; v.p., gen. counsel, sec. Price Bros. Co., Dayton, Ohio, 1973-82; v.p., div. mgr. Water Systems Tech. div. Price Bros. Co., Dayton, Ohio, 1982-85; v.p., div. mgr. Internat. div. Price Bros. Co., Dayton, Ohio, 1986-88; chmn. Rogers Internat. Inc., 1988—; pvt. practice law Dayton, 1988—. Pres. adv. coun. Miami U. Bus. Sch.; bd. dirs. Red and White Club, Miami U.; mem. Washington Twp. Task Force on Future Govt.; trustee Woodhaven, Inc.; mem., vice chmn. Washington Twp. Zoning Commn. Mem. ABA (forum com. on constrn.), Ill. Bar Assn., Ohio Bar Assn., Dayton Bar Assn. (chmn. corp. law dept. com. 1983-84, exec. com. 1986-87, editor Bar Briefs 1990-91), Miami U. Alumni Assn. (pres.), Miami U. Pres.'s Club., Sycamore Creek Country Club. Office: 7333 Paragon Rd Ste 200 Dayton OH 45459-4157 Adddress: PO Box 509 Dayton OH 45409

ROGERS, ROBERT BURNETT, naval officer; b. Plainfield, N.J., May 25, 1931; s. Jack Willoughby and Margaret (Snyder) R.; m. Jeanne Weaver, Mr. 15, 1956 (dec. Sept. 1978); children: Robert Burnett, Steven Michael, John Weaver, Kathryn Patricia; m. Marolyn Maybelline Templeton, May 25, 1981. B.S., U.S. Naval Acad., 1954; M.S., George Washington U., 1968. Commd. ensign U.S. Navy, 1954, advanced through grades to rear adm., 1981; comdg. officer U.S.S. Austin, Norfolk, Va., 1977-78; asst. chief of staff Naval Surface Force Atlantic, Atlantic Fleet, Norfolk, 1978-80; dep. comdr. Naval Surface Force Atlantic, Norfolk, 1982-83; comdr. Destroyer Squardron Eight, Mayport, Fla., 1980-81; dep. chief of staff Supreme Allied Command Atlantic, Norfolk, 1981-82; comdr. Amphibious Group Two, Norfolk, 1983-86; dir. logistics Atlantic Fleet, Norfolk, 1986, ret., 1986. City Commr. Fernandina Beach, 1994. Decorated Legion of Merit with 4 gold stars; recipient William S. Sims award Navy League U.S. Mem. U.S. Naval Inst., Marine Corps. Assn. Roman Catholic. Home: 2056 Oak Marsh Dr Fernandina Beach FL 32034-2407

ROGERS, ROBERT ERNEST, medical educator; b. West Palm Beach, Fla., Nov. 16, 1928; s. Jessie H. and Willie L. (Bahr) R.; m. Barbara Ann Hill, May 16, 1950; children: Robert E. Jr., Stephanie Ann Thompson, Cheri Lee Heck. BS, John B. Stetson U., 1949; MD, U. Miami, 1957. Diplomate Am. Bd. Ob-Gyn. Commd. 1st lt. M.C., U.S. Army, 1952, advanced through grades to col., 1971; intern Brooke Gen. Hosp., San Antonio, 1957-58, chief resident ob-gyn, 1960-61; resident in ob-gyn Jackson Meml. Hosp., Miami, Fla., 1958-60; fellow gynecology M.D. Anderson Hosp., Houston, 1965-66; asst. chief ob-gyn Tripler Army Med. Ctr., Honolulu, 1966-69; chmn. ob-gyn Walter Reed Med. Ctr., Washington, 1969-70, Madigan Army Med. Ctr., Tacoma, Wash., 1970-74; ret. U.S. Army, 1974; prof. Ind. U. Sch. Medicine, Indpls., 1974—, also chief gynecol. div., 1974—; chief ob-gyn svd. Wishard Meml. Hosp., Indpls., 1983-87. Contbr. articles on ob-gyn to profl. jours. Mem. AMA, Am. Coll. Ob-Gyn (chmn. gynecol. practice com., commr. practice), Soc. Gynecol. Surgeons (pres. 1983-84), Soc. Gynecol. Oncologists. Office: Ind U Sch Medicine 550 University Blvd Indianapolis IN 46202-5274

ROGERS, ROBERT MARK, physician; b. Upper Darby, Pa., June 9, 1933; s. John Francis and Clara (Baumann) R.; m. Sandra Betz, Feb. 14, 1968; children: Janet Marie, Robert Mark, Linda, William Bradford, David Philip. BA cum laude, LaSalle Coll., Phila., 1956; MD, U. Pa., 1960. Intern Hosp. of U. Pa., 1960-61, chief emergency svcs., 1968-69, founder, dir. respiratory ICU, 1968-72, dir. pulmonary disease sect. tng. program, 1970-72; resident Case Western Res. U. Hosps., Cleve., 1961-63; fellow in pulmonary disease VA Hosp., Cleve., 1963-64; fellow in pulmonary disease U. Pa., 1964-65, postdoctoral trainee in physiology, 1966-68, asst. prof. medicine and assoc. in physiology, 1968-72; prof.medicine, assoc. prof. physiology Okla. Health Scis. Ctr. Coll. Medicine, 1972-80, also chief pulmonary disease sect., dept. medicine, dir. clin. pulmonary physiology lab. hosp. and clinics; prof. medicine, chief pulmonary, allergy & critical care medicine U. Pitts. Med. Sch., 1980—, dir. Comprehensive Lung Ctr., 1990—. Editor: Respiratory Intensive Care, 1977; mem. editl. bd. Current Opinion in Pulmonary Medicine and Critical Care; contbr. rsch. articles to profl. publs. Mem. ACP (U.S. rep. to Chinese Med. Assn. 1979, founding editor-in-chief audio cassettes program 1978-80), Am. Thoracic Soc. (founding dir. Learning Resources Ctr. 1971-77, Presdl. commendation 1977), Am. Fedn. Clin. Rsch., Am. Coll. Chest Physicians, Am. Physiol. Soc., Soc. Critical Care Medicine, Am. Heart Assn., Ctrl. Soc. Clin. Rsch., So. Soc. Clin. Rsch., Pa. Thoracic Soc. (pres. 1985-88), Coll. Physicians Phila. Home: 4116 Bigelow Blvd Pittsburgh PA 15213-1408 Office: U Pitts Sch Medicine 440 Scaife Hall Pittsburgh PA 15261-2004

ROGERS, RODNEY ALBERT, biologist, educator; b. Lucas, Iowa, Aug. 24, 1926; s. Harold A. and Ardis (Allen) R.; m. Frances A. Ritchey, July 1, 1956; children—Robert, William. B.A., Drake U., 1949, M.A., 1951; Ph.D., U. Iowa, 1955. Asst. prof. biology Drake U., Des Moines, 1955-60; asso. prof. Drake U., 1961-64, prof., 1965—, chmn. biology dept., 1966-92; asso. program dir. NSF, 1967-68. Served with AUS, 1944-46, PTO. Mem. A.A.A.S., Am. Inst. Biol. Sci., Am. Soc. Parasitologists, Soc. Am. Microbiologists, Am. Soc. Zoologists, Am. Assn. U. Profs., Am. Soc. Tropical Medicine and Hygiene, Sigma Xi, Omicron Delta Kappa. Home: 4203 40th St Des Moines IA 50310-3702

ROGERS, ROSEMARY, author; b. Panadura, Ceylon, Dec. 7, 1932; came to U.S., 1962; naturalized citizen.; d. Cyril Allan and Barbara (Jansze); m. Summa Navaratnam (div.); children: Rosanne, Sharon; m. Leroy Rogers (div.); children: Michael, Adam; m. Christopher Kadison (div.). B.A., U. Ceylon. Writer features and pub. affairs info. Associated Newspapers Ceylon, Colombo, 1959-62; sec. billeting office Travis AFB, Calif., 1964-69; sec. Solano County (Calif.) Parks Dept., Fairfield, 1969-74; part-time reporter Fairfield Daily Republic. Author: (novels) Sweet Savage Love, 1974, The Wildest Heart, 1974, Dark Fires, 1975, Wicked Loving Lies, 1976, The Crowd Pleasers, 1978, The Insiders, 1979, Lost Love, Last Love, 1980, Love Play, 1981, Surrender to Love, 1982, The Wanton, 1985, Bound by Desire, 1988, The Tea Planter's Bride, 1995. Mem. Authors Guild of Authors League Am., Writers Guild Am.

ROGERS, ROY (LEONARD FRANKLIN SLYE), country musician, actor; b. Cin., Nov. 5, 1911; s. Andrew E. and Mattie Martha (Womach) Slye; m. Arlene Wilkins, 1936 (dec. Nov. 1946); children: Cheryl Darlene, Linda Lou, Roy Jr., Marion, Scottish Ward; m. Dale Evans; children: Robin (dec.), John (dec.), Mary Little Doe, Deborah (dec.). pres. Roy Rogers Enterprises; past owner Roy Rogers Apple Valley Inn; owner Roy Rogers Western World and Mus., Victorville, Calif.; franchised Roy Rogers Family Restaurants. Organized western group Sons of the Pioneers; appeared in numerous films including Under Western Stars, 1938, The Old Corral, Frontier Pony Express, Silver Spurs, My Pal Trigger, Son of Paleface, Mackintosh & T.J.; former radio singer; TV series, spls.; actor, prodr. TV films; host TV show The Great Movie Cowboys, 1975; many personal appearances rodeos, fairs; rec. artist Capitol Records, 20th Century Records, RCA Records; albums include, Best Of, 1990, Tribute, 1991; author: (with Dale Evans) Happy Trails: Our Life Story, 1994. Mem. AFTRA, SAG, Am. Guild Variety Artists, Musicians Union, Masons. Address: RCA/BMG Music 1 Music Cir N Nashville TN 37203-4310

ROGERS, RUTHERFORD DAVID, librarian; b. Jesup, Iowa, June 22, 1915; s. David Earl and Carrie Zoe (Beckel) R.; m. E. Margaret Stoddard, June 4, 1937; 1 child, Jane Shelley. B.A., U. No. Iowa, 1936, Litt.D., 1977; M.A., Columbia, 1937, B.S. (Lydia Roberts fellow), 1938; D.Library Adminstrn. (hon.), U. Dayton, 1971. Asst. N.Y. Pub. Library, 1937-38; reference librarian Columbia Coll. Library, Columbia U., 1938- 41, acting librarian, 1941-42, librarian, 1942-45; research analyst Smith, Barney & Co., N.Y.C., 1946-48; dir. Grosvenor Library, Buffalo, 1948-52, Rochester Pub. Library, 1952-54; chief personnel office N.Y. Library, 1954-55; chief reference dept., 1955-57; chief asst. librarian of Congress, Washington, 1957-62; dep. librarian of Congress, 1962-64; dir. univ. libraries Stanford U., 1964-69; univ. librarian Yale U., 1969-85, univ. librarian emeritus, 1985—; dir. H.W. Wilson Co., 1969—; founder, chmn. bd. dirs. Rsch. Librs. Group, Inc.; mem. Exam. Com. for Pub. Librarians' Certs., N.Y. State, 1951-54; mem. U.S. Adv. Coun. Coll. Libr. Resources; bd. govs. Yale U. Press; bd. dirs., v.p. H.W. Wilson Found., 1995—; chmn. program mgmt. com. Internat. Fedn. Libr. Assns. Author: Columbia Coll. Library Handbook, 1941, (with David C. Weber) University Library Administration, 1971; also articles in profl. jours. Served from pvt. to 1st sgt. Air Transp. Command USAAF, 1942-43; from 2d lt. to capt., planning officer, chief, spl. Planning Div., Office Asst. Chief Staff, Plans, Air Transport Command 1943-46. Decorated officier de L'Ordre de la Couronne Belge; recipient U. No. Iowa Alumni Achievement award, 1958, Disting. Alumni award Columbia U. Sch. Libr. Svc., 1992. Fellow Am. Acad. Arts and Scis.; mem. A.L.A. (chmn. com. Intellectual Freedom 1950-51), (1950-60), (2d v.p. 1965-66), (mem. exec. bd. 1961-66), (trustee endowment fund), Assn. Research Libraries (dir., pres. 1967-68), N.Y. Library Assn., AAUP, Bibliog. Soc. Am., Assn. Coll. and Reference Libraries, Blue Key, Kappa Delta Pi, Sigma Tau Delta, Theta Alpha Phi. Clubs: Grolier; N.Y. Library (N.Y.C.), Columbia U. (N.Y.C.), Yale (N.Y.C.); Cosmos (Washington), Kenwood Country (Washington); Roxburghe (San Francisco); Book of Calif. Home: 1111 S Lakemont Ave Apt 605 Winter Park FL 32792-5474

ROGERS, SAMUEL SHEPARD See SHEPARD, SAM

ROGERS, SHARON J., university administrator; b. Grantsburg, Wis., Sept. 24, 1941; d. Clifford M. and Dorothy L. (Beckman) Dickau; m. Evan D. Rogers, June 15, 1962 (div. Dec. 1980). BA summa cum laude, Bethel Coll., St. Paul, 1963; MA in Libr. Sci., U. Minn., 1967; PhD in Sociology, Wash. State U., Pullman, 1976. Lectr., instr. Alfred (N.Y.) U., 1972-76; assoc. prof. U. Toledo, 1977-80; assoc. dean Bowling Green (Ohio) State U. Librs., 1980-84; univ. libr. George Washington U., Washington, 1984-92, asst. v.p. acad. affairs, 1989-92, assoc. v.p. acad. affairs, 1992—, co-dir. Univ. Teaching Ctr., 1990—; mem. Online Computer Libr.Ctr. Users Coun., 1985-92, pres., 1989-90, mem. rsch. adv. com., 1990-92, trustee, 1992—. Contbr. articles to profl. jours. Bd. dirs. ACLU, Toledo, 1978-84, CapAccess, 1993-95, treas., 1993—. Jackson fellow U. Minn., 1964-65; NSF trainee Wash. State U., 1969-72. Mem. ALA (exec. coun. 1987-91, pub. com. 1989-93, chair 1990-93), Assn. Coll. and Rsch. Librs. (pres. 1984-85), Am. Sociol. Assn., Washington Rsch. Libr. Consortium (bd. dirs 1987-90), Universal Serials and Book Exch. (bd. dirs., treas. 1987). Office: George Washington Univ 2121 I St NW Washington DC 20037-2353

ROGERS, STEPHEN, newspaper publisher; b. Lansing, Mich., Feb. 24, 1912; s. Anthony and Anna (Kruszewska) R.; m. Athenia A. Andros, Oct. 19, 1935; children: Stephen A., Christopher A., Elizabeth A. A.B., Mich. State Coll., 1933; LLD (hon.), Syracuse U., 1988. Writer Detroit Times, 1934-35; copy editor N.Y. Herald-Tribune (European edit.), Paris, France, 1936-37; spl. writer Newark Ledger, 1937-38; editorial writer, city editor Long Island Daily Press, 1938-41; editor Long Island Star-Jour., 1941-55; pub. Post Standard, Syracuse, N.Y., 1955-58, Herald-Journal, Herald-Am., Syracuse; and pres. The Herald Co., 1958—; dir. N.Y. Dental Service Corp., N.Y.C., Mchts. Nat. Bank; pres. Met. Devel. Assn., 1980—. Bd. dirs. Crouse-Irving Hosp., Syracuse. Mem. N.Y. State Pubs. Assn. (pres. 1963), Am. Newspaper Pubs. Assn. Roman Catholic. Office: Syracuse Newspapers Ltd Clinton Sq PO Box 4915 Syracuse NY 13221-4915

ROGERS, STEPHEN HITCHCOCK, former ambassador; b. Flushing, N.Y., June 21, 1930; s. Francis Walker and Julia (Wheeler) R.; m. Kent Brain, June 23, 1956; children: Kryston R. Fischer, F. Halsey, Julia L., John H. BA, Princeton U., 1952; MA, Columbia U., 1956; MPA, Harvard U., 1962. Fgn. svc. officer Dept. of State, 1956-93; econ. counselor Am. Embassy, London, 1970-72; counselor U.S. Mission to OECD, Paris, 1972-75; office dir. Bur. Inter.-Am. Affairs Dept. of State, Washington, 1975-78; econ. counselor Am. Embassy, Mexico City, 1978-82; prof. Nat. Def. U., Washington, 1982-85; econ. counselor Am. Embassy, Pretoria, South Africa, 1986-90; amb. Am. Embassy, Mbabane, Swaziland, 1990-93. Lt. (jg) USN, 1952-55. Mem. United Ch. of Christ. Home: 3803 Ivydale Dr Annandale VA 22003-2006

ROGERS, STEVEN RAY, physicist; b. Tachikawa, Honshu, Japan, Dec. 6, 1952; came to U.S., 1953; s. Culis Doyle Martin and Mary Lu (Bowles) Rogers; m. Robina Rae Behel, Dec. 27, 1975; children: Miranda Rae, Kellina Gail. BA in Math./Physics magna cum laude, U. No. Colo., 1975; MS in Physics, Kans. State U., 1977. Rschr., instr. Kans. State U., Manhattan, 1975-79; tech. staff ElectroMagnetic Applications, Lakewood, Colo., 1979-82; lead engr. MITRE Corp., Colorado Springs, Colo., 1982—; cons., advisor on system survivability and hardening North Am. Aerospace Def. Command * U.S. Space Command, Colorado Springs, 1982—; adj. prof. Webster U., Colorado Springs, 1994. Contbr. articles to Jour. Physics: Atomic & Molecular, IEEE Transactions on Nuclear Sci. and other profl. jours. Mentor for gifted students Colorado Springs Schs. #20, 1992-93; host family for cadet USAF Acad., Colorado Springs, 1994—. Recipient Program Recognition award MITRE Corp., 1988, 1996. Mem. IEEE (sr., chmn. Pikes Peak sect. 1993-94), Sigma Pi Sigma, Lambda Sigma Tau. Achievements include co-invention of global situation awareness information distribution system (patent pending); co-founder of programs that sustain the survivability of NORAD and U.S. Space Command systems; evaluation and integration of NORAD systems. Home: 5510 Broadmoor Bluffs Dr Colorado Springs CO 80906-7971 Office: MITRE Corp 1150 Academy Park Loop Ste 212 Colorado Springs CO 80910-3716

ROGERS, THEODORE COURTNEY, investment company executive; b. Lorain, Ohio, Aug. 25, 1934; s. William Theodore and Leona Ruth (Gerhart) R.; m. Elizabeth B. Barlow, June 28, 1984; children by previous marriage: Pamela Anne Rogers Harmon, Theodore Courtney Jr. BS in Social Sci., Miami U., Oxford, Ohio, 1956; postgrad. Johns Hopkins U., 1957; MBA summa cum laude, Marquette U., 1968. With Armco Inc., 1958-80; pres. Olympic Fastening Systems, 1970-74, with Bathey Mfg. Co. subs., 1970, group v.p. indsl. products, 1971-74, exec. v.p. Nat. Supply Co. subs., Houston, 1974-76, pres., 1976-80, v.p. parent co., 1976-79, group v.p. parent co., 1979-80; pres., COO NL Industries, Inc., N.Y.C., 1980-82, pres., CEO, 1982-83, chmn., pres., CEO, 1983-87; ptnr. Am. Indsl. Ptnrs., N.Y., 1987—; bd. dirs. Sweetheart Cup, Smith Steelite, Inc., Day Internat., Derby Internat., Nottingham, Eng.; chmn. bd. Sunshine Materials, Easco Aluminum, RBX Corp. Bd. dirs. United Cerebral Palsy Rsch. and Ednl. Found., Inc., Lincoln Ctr. for Performing Arts, Poets & Writers, Am. Alliance for Rights and Responsibilities, Nat. Ocean Industries Assn.; chmn. bd. Theatre for New Audience; former chmn. N.Y.C. Ballet. Lt. USN, 1956-58. Mem. Petroleum Equipment Suppliers Assn. (bd. dirs.), N.Y. Soc. Libr. (trustee), World Pres. Orgn., Century Assn. (N.Y.), Bus. Roundtable, Poets and Writers (bd. dirs.), Achilles Track Club (founder, bd. dirs.), Ramada Club, Houston Country Club, Links Club, Sky Club, Econ. Club (N.Y.), Met. Club (Washington), The Union Club (Cleve.), Century Assn., Beta Gamma Sigma (bd. dirs.), Kappa Phi Kappa, Sigma Chi. Office: Am Indsl Ptnr 551 5th Ave Ste 3800 New York NY 10176

ROGERS, THOMAS FRANCIS, foundation administrator; b. Providence, Aug. 11, 1923; s. Thomas Francis and H. Ann (Flaharty) R.; m. Estelle E. Hunt, July 6, 1946; children: Clare, Judith Reynolds, Hope Grove. BS cum laude, Providence Coll., 1945; MA, Boston U., 1949. Rsch. assoc. Radio Rsch. Lab. Harvard U., Cambridge, Mass., 1944-45; TV engr. Bell and Howell Co., Chgo., 1945-46; electronics scientist AF Cambridge Rsch. Ctr., Cambridge, Mass., 1946-54; assoc. group leader MIT Lincoln Lab., Cambridge, 1951-53; lab. head AF Cambridge Rsch. Ctr., Bedford, Mass., 1954-59; div. head and steering com. mem. MIT Lincoln Lab., Bedford, 1959-64; asst. dir. def. rsch. and engring. Office of Sec. Def., Washington, 1964-65, dep. dir. def. rsch. and engring., 1965-67; dir. rsch. and tech. Office of Sec. HUD, Washington, 1967-69; v.p. The Mitre Corp., Washington, Bedford, 1969-72; pres. The Sophron Found., McLean, Va., 1980—; dir. U.S. Congress Office of Tech. Assessment Study on Civilian Space Stas. and U.S. Future in Space, Washington, 1982-84; pres. The Space Transp. Assn., Arlington, 1992—; founding chmn. bd. dirs. External Tanks Corp., Boulder, Colo.; bd. dirs. Internat. Radio Satellite Corp., Washington, Space Destinations Svcs., Inc., 1994—; chmn. bd. dirs. Luna Corp., Great Falls, Va., 1991—; chmn. POLARIS Command-Comm. Co., USN, 1960-64; mem. Satellite Comm. Panel, Pres.'s Sci. Adv. Com., 1961-63; mem. Dept. Def. NASA Satellite Comm. Com., 1961-64; U.S.A. del. UN Conf. on Applications of Sci. and Tech. by Lesser Developed Nations, Geneva, 1963; mem. Fed. Aeronautics and Astronautics Coordinating Bd., 1965-67, Fed. Coun. on Sci. and Tech., 1967-69; mem. Space Program Adv. Coun., NASA, 1971-73, chmn. applications com., 1972-73; mem. NAS com. on regional emergency med. comm. systems, 1976-78, space applications bd. com. on NASA space comms. 1986-87, com. on antenna, satellite broadcasting and emergency preparedness for Voice of Am., 1986-88, adv. com. study space transp. U.S. Congrl. Office Tech. Assessment, 1994-95. Contbr. articles to jours., chpts. to books. Trustee X-Prize Found., 1995—. Recipient Outstanding Performance award CSC, 1957, cert. commendation Sec. Navy, 1961, Meritorious Civilian Svc. award and medal, Sec. Def., Constrn.'s Man of Yr. award Engring. News Record, 1969, Space Pioneer award Nat. Space Soc., 1988. Fellow IEEE (past chmn. aerospace R&D policy com. 1991-95, Profl. Achievement award 1995); mem. Cosmos Club (Washington). Home and Office: 7404 Colshire Dr Mc Lean VA 22102-7404

ROGERS, VANCE DONALD, former university president; b. Frontenac, Minn., May 16, 1917; s. Azzy Floyd and Mary C. (Martinson) R.; m.

Barbara Marie Yarwood, June 22, 1940; children: Nancy Ann Rogers Steele, Mary Lou Rogers Frederickson. Student, Gustavus Adolphus Coll., St. Peter, Minn., 1934-36; A.B., Hamline U., 1938, LL.D., 1976; postgrad., Northwestern U., 1940-41; M.Div., Garrett Bibl. Inst., 1941; D.D., Nebr. Wesleyan U., 1955; LL.D., Mt. Union Coll., 1958; L.H.D., Morningside Coll., 1960; Litt.D., Lane Coll., 1966; L.H.D., U. Nebr., 1968; S.T.D., Oklahoma City U., 1984. Ordained to ministry Methodist Ch., 1941; minister Meth. Ch., Dundee, Ill., 1941-43, Brookfield, Ill., 1946-53; minister Trinity Meth. Ch., Lincoln, Nebr., 1953-57; pres. Nebr. Wesleyan U., Lincoln, 1957-77; chmn. bd. Pure Water, Inc., 1978-80; ret., 1981; staff cons. Lincoln Found., Inc. (Nebr.), 1981-86; sr. assoc., v.p. Larry Price & Assocs., Lincoln, 1986-87; adv. dir. Nat. Bank Commerce, Lincoln, 1986-94. Served as lt. comdr. Chaplains Corps, USNR, 1943-46. Mem. Neb. Acad. Scis., Newcomen Soc. N.Am., Am. Legion, Blue Key, C. of C., Phi Kappa Phi, Phi Eta Sigma, Pi Kappa Delta. Clubs: Mason (Lincoln) (Shriner, K.T.), Univ. (Lincoln), Lincoln Country (Lincoln), Rotary (Lincoln). Home: 3731 Faulkner Dr Apt 310 Lincoln NE 68516-4746 *A successful life is one that is: disciplined (body, mind, and spirit); adventuresome (seeking new ideas, innovative approaches to problem solving, and new areas of exploration); dedicated (to personal standards that call for mature responses-to ideal patterns of behavior-to moral and spiritual ideals rooted in the Judeo-Christian tradition).*

ROGERS, WARREN JOSEPH, JR., journalist; b. New Orleans, May 6, 1922; s. Warren Joseph and Rose Agatha (Tennyson) R.; m. Hilda Kenny, Dec. 23, 1943 (dec.); children: Patricia Ann, Sean; m. Alla Bilajiw, Dec. 26, 1973; 1 son, Michael (dec.). Student, Tulane U., 1940-41, La. State U., 1951. Copy boy, cub reporter New Orleans Tribune, 1939-41; copyreader, columnist New Orleans Item, 1945-47; reporter A.P., Baton Rouge, 1947-51; reporter A.P., Washington, 1951-53, diplomatic corr., 1953-59; mil., fgn. affairs corr. assignments abroad Wash. Bur. N.Y. Herald Tribune, 1959-63; chief Washington corr. Hearst Newspapers, assignments abroad, 1963-66; Washington editor LOOK mag., 1966-69, chief, 1969-70; mil., fgn. affairs corr. Washington bur. Los Angeles Times, 1970-71; Washington columnist Chgo. Tribune-N.Y. News syndicate, 1971-73; v.p. pub. affairs Nat. Forest Products Assn., Washington, 1973-76; editorial dir. Plus Publs., Washington, 1977-78; v.p., editor-in-chief Plus Publs., 1978-79; free-lance, 1979—; Washington bur. chief The Trib of N.Y., 1977-78; editor White House Weekly, 1981-89; exec. editor Associated Features, Inc., Washington editor, 1992—; editor This Week in the White House, 1989-90, Georgetown Courier, 1991-92; bd. dirs. Nat. Press Found.; founder Robert F. Kennedy Journalism awards; lectr. presdl. politics, mil. and fgn. affairs. Author: The Floating Revolution, 1962, Outpost of Freedom, 1965, (with others) An Honorable Profession: A Tribute to Robert F. Kennedy, 1968, (with Paul Watson) Sea Shepherd, 1982, When I think of Bobby: A Personal Memoir of the Kennedy Years, 1993. Served with USMCR, 1941-45. Recipient citation Overseas Press Club N.Y., 1963, Disting. Svc. award Nat. Press Found., 1991. Clubs: Nat. Press (pres. 1972), Federal City Club, Gridiron Club, Washington Ind. Writers. Home: 1622 30th St NW Washington DC 20007-2903 *In more than 50 years of reporting, I have learned that people yearn for the truth, as long as it is about somebody else. But they go to almost any length to conceal it or put a spin on it when it is about themselves. Yet, telling the truth is what a reporter must do. No wonder we rank behind Congress in the popularity polls.*

ROGERS, WERNER, state superintendent schools. State supt. schs. Ga. Dept. Edn., Atlanta; exec. dir. Georgia Public Broadcasting, 1995—. Office: Georgia Public Broadcasting 1540 Stewart Ave SW Atlanta GA 30310*

ROGERS, WILLIAM, psychologist, consultant, writer, lecturer, journalist. BA in Broadcast Journalism, L.A. Inst. Arts, 1970; BA in Psychology, We. Ill. U., Macomb, 1979; MS in Counseling Psychology, Our Lady of the Lake U., San Antonio, 1989; PhD in Psychology, Columbia Pacific U., San Rafael, Calif., 1993; postgrad., Rollo May Ctr. Social Rsch. Saybrook Inst., San Francisco, 1994. Fgn. and domestic correspondent ABC News, NBC News, UPI Internat., KTRH Radio News, WOAI Radio News, 1970-85. Author: The Technology of Behavior, 1993, The Behavior Management Handbook, 1994, Creating Positive Behavior, 1995, Recovered Memory and Other Assaults Upon the Mysteries of Consciousness, 1995; feature stories include Cmty. Responsibility, Behavior and Consequences, 1974, Missing Children, 1984; contbr. articles to profl. jours., TV and radio shows. Recipient George Foster Peabody Nomination Tex. Med. Assn., Wendall mays Pub. Svc. award Tex. Bar Assn., Gov.'s award AP, Tex. Assn. Broadcasters, Radio-T.V. News Dirs. Assn., Tex. Legislature Commendation, League of United Lat. Am. Citizens award Tex. State Network News, Coastal Bend Planning Commn. Spl. Svc. award, Headliner's News award; citation ABA, U.S. Senate, Spl. Citation City of Corpus Christi, Tex., Spl. Resoultion of Commendation Tex.Ho. Reps., Exceptional Recognition Entered Into Perpetuity State of Tex. Archives. Office: Behavior Mgmt Broadway Profl Bldg Ste 228 7201 Broadway San Antonio TX 78209

ROGERS, WILLIAM BROOKINS, financial consultant; b. Atlanta, Mar. 31, 1938; s. William Brookins and Mildred (LaHatte) R.; m. Carolyn Ansley Duren, May 28, 1966; children: W. Brandon, Alicia Deanne. BBA in Acctg., Ga. State U., 1965, MBA in Fin., 1968, PhD student in fin., 1968-70. CPA Ga., cert. mediator, arbitrator; state registered nutral mediator and arbitrator. Sr. acct. A.M. Pullen & Co. CPA's, Atlanta, 1964-69; pres., chmn. Ponderosa Internat., Inc., Atlanta, 1970-76; exec. v.p., chief op. ofcr. GRC/Tidewater Group, Atlanta, 1976-79; pres., CEO Atlanta Bil, Inc., 1979-86, Brookins Mgmt. Co., Inc., Atlanta, 1979—, Hilton Enterprises, Inc., Atlanta, 1981-96; bd. dirs. Ranick Ltd., Athens, Ga., 1981-96; lectr. Am. Mgmt. Assn., Atlanta, 1969-75, Bus. Grad. Sch. U. Ala., Tuscaloosa, 1970, Bus. Sch. Augusta State Coll., 1971, Western and Gwinnette Jud. Cirs.; panel of mediators Justice Ctr. of Atlanta; mem. nat. panel of arbitrators Am. Arbitration Assn. With U.S. Army, 1959-61. Fellow AICPA; m. Am. Arbitration Assn. (arbitrator nat. panel), Soc. Profls. in Dispute Resolution (assoc.), Beta Gamma Sigma, Omicron Delta Kappa, Beta Alpha Psi. Republican. Episcopalian. Avocations: family, business. Home: 4355 Candacraig Alpharetta GA 30202-5164 Office: Brooking Mgmt Co Inc PO Box 920158 Norcross GA 30092-0158

ROGERS, WILLIAM CECIL, political science educator; b. Manhattan, Kans., 1919; s. Charles Elkins and Sadie (Burns) R.; m. Mary Jane Anderson, Aug. 31, 1941; children: Shelley, Faith, Mary Sarah. B.A., U. Chgo., 1940, M.A., 1941, Ph.D., 1943. Asst. to dir. Pub. Adminstrn. Clearing House, Chgo., 1943-47; lectr. internat. relations U. Chgo., 1945-47; asst. prof. U. Va., 1947-48; asso. prof. polit. sci. Western Res. U., 1948-49; dir. World Affairs Center, U. Minn., Mpls., 1949-84; cons. Minn. Internat. Ctr., 1984—; dir. Program Info. on World Affairs, Mpls. Star and Tribune, 1951-73. Author: Community Education in World Affairs, 1956, A Guide to Understanding World Affairs, 1966, Global Dimensions in U.S. Education: The Community, 1972; co-author: The Winter City Book, 1980. Pres. Minn. Jazz Sponsors, 1966-67; chmn. Mpls. Com. on Urban Environ., 1976-80. Mem. Nat. Univ. Extension Assn. (past sec.-treas.), Winter Cities Assn. (co-founder 1982). Home: 3510 Mckinley St NE Minneapolis MN 55418-1511 Office: 711 E River Rd Minneapolis MN 55455-0369

ROGERS, WILLIAM DILL, lawyer; b. Wilmington, Del., May 12, 1927; m. Suzanne Rochford, Sept. 7, 1926; children: William Rogers, Daniel. B.A., Princeton U., 1948; LL.B., Yale U., 1951. Bar: D.C. 1952, U.S. Supreme Ct. 1954. Ptnr. Arnold & Porter, Washington, intermittently 1953—; dep. U.S. coordinator Alliance for Progress, AID, 1962-65; pres. N.Y. Ctr. Inter.-Am. Relations, 1965-72; asst. sec. of state inter-Am. relations Dept. State, 1974-76, undersec. of state for econ. affairs, 1976-77; mem. law faculty Cambridge U., Eng., 1982-83; sr. counselor Bipartisan Commn. on Central Am., 1983-84; vice chmn. Kissinger Assocs. Inc. Author: The Twilight Struggle: The Alliance for Progress and U.S.-Latin-American Relations, 1967. Co-chmn. U.S.-Mexico Binat. Commn.; bd. dirs. Coun. Fgn. Rels., 1981-90. Mem. Am. Soc. Internat. Law (pres. 1971-73), ABA. Office: Arnold & Porter 1200 New Hampshire Ave NW Washington DC 20036-6802

ROGERS, WILLIAM RAYMOND, college president, psychology educator; b. Oswego, N.Y., June 20, 1932; s. William Raymond and A. Elizabeth (Hollis) R.; m. Beverley Claire Partington, Aug. 14, 1954; children: John Partington, Susan Elizabeth Howell, Nancy Claire Glassman. BA magna cum laude, Kalamazoo Coll., 1954; BD, U. Chgo. and Chgo. Theol. Sem., 1958; PhD, U. Chgo., 1965; MA (hon.), Harvard U., 1970. Cons., staff counselor Counseling and Psychotherapy Rsch. Ctr., U. Chgo., 1960-62; teaching fellow, counselor to students Chgo. Theol. Sem., 1961-62; asst. prof. psychology and religion, dir. student counseling Earlham Coll., Richmond, Ind., 1962-68; assoc. prof. psychology and religion, assoc. dean of Coll. Earlham Coll., 1968-70; vis. lectr. pastoral counseling Div. Sch. Harvard U., Cambridge, Mass., 1969-70, prof. religion and psychology Div. and Edn. Schs., 1970-80, faculty chmn. clin. psychology and pub. practice, 1970-72, chmn. counseling and cons. psychology, 1979-80; prof. psychology and religious studies Guilford Coll., Greensboro, N.C., 1980—;, 1980-96; bd. dirs. Br. Bank and Trust. Author: The Alienated Student, 1969, Project Listening, 1974, Nourishing the Humanistic in Medicine, 1979; Contbr. articles to profl. jours. Bd. dirs. Greensboro Symphony Soc., Greensboro Day Sch., Moses Cone Hosp., Canterbury Sch., mary Reynolds Babcock Found., Cemala Found. Danforth Found. fellow, Blatchford Traveling fellow U. Chgo. and Chgo. Theol. Sem., 1958. Mem. Soc. Values in Higher Edn., Friends Assn. Higher Edn., Nat. Assn. Ind. Colls. and Univs., N.C. Assn. Ind. Colls. and Univs., So. Assn. Colls. and Schs., Rotary (club pres.). Mem. Soc. of Friends. Home: 5400 Westfield Dr Greensboro NC 27410-9223

ROGERS, WILMER ALEXANDER, biologist; b. Mt. Dora, Fla., Aug. 17, 1933; married, 1961; 4 children. BS, U. So. Miss., 1958; MS, Auburn U., 1960, PhD in Fish Mgmt., 1967. Biologist aide Miss. Game & Fish Commn., 1957-58; fishery biologist Ala. Dept. Conservation, 1960-62, U.S. Fish & Wildlife Svc., 1962-64; from instr. to assoc. prof. Auburn (Ala.) U., 1964-77, prof. fisheries, 1977—; leader Southeastern Coop. Fish Disease Project, 1968—. Editor: Southeastern Game and Fish Procs., 1974-77, Jour. Aquatic Animal Health, 1988—. Mem. Am. Fisheries Soc. (pres. So. divsn. 1977-78, fish health sect. 1986-87), Am. Soc. Parasitology, Wildlife Disease Assn., Am. Micros. Soc. Achievements include research in general parasites and diseases of fish, especially taxonomy of monogenea; intensive culture of fish; fish immunology. Office: U Auburn Dept Fish & Allied Aquaculture Auburn AL 36849-5419*

ROGGE, RICHARD DANIEL, former government executive, security consultant, investigator; b. N.Y.C., July 5, 1926; s. Daniel Richard and Bertha (Sarner) R.; m. Josephine Mary Kowalewska, June 6, 1948 (dec. June 1995); children: Veronica Leigh Rogge-Erbeznik, Richard Daniel, Christopher Ames, Meredith Ann Rogge-Pierce. BS in Bus. Adminstrn., NYU, 1952. Cert. profl. investigator. Clerical worker FBI, N.Y.C., 1947-52, spl. agt., Phila., 1952-54, Washington, 1954-58, supr., 1958-65, asst. spl. agt. in charge, Richmond, Va., 1965-66, Phila., 1966-67, L.A., 1967-69, inspector, 1969, spl. agt. in charge, Honolulu, 1969-72, Richmond, 1972-74, Buffalo, 1974-77, now security cons., investigator, Calif.; police tng. instr.; writer, lectr. in field. With USMC, 1944-46; PTO. Recipient Order of Arrow award Boy Scouts Am., 1943, Svc. to Law Enforcement awards Va. Assn. Chiefs Police, 1975, N.Y. State Assn. Chiefs Police, 1977, others. Mem. Am. Soc. Indsl. Security, Calif. Assn. Lic. Investigators, Calif. Peace Officers Assn. of Los Angeles County, World Assn. Detectives, Inc., Soc. Former Agts. FBI, Inc., FBI Agents Assn., Am. Legion, K.C., Elks. Republican. Roman Catholic. Home and Office: 32010 Watergate Ct Westlake Village CA 91361-4022

ROGGER, HANS JACK, history educator; b. Herford, Germany, Sept. 9, 1923; s. Max and Berni (Heilbronn) R.; m. Claire Ryan, Jan. 2, 1955; 1 son, Alexander. B.A., Sarah Lawrence Coll., 1948; Ph.D., Harvard U., 1956. Asst. prof. Sarah Lawrence Coll., Bronxville, N.Y., 1953-58; asso. prof. Sarah Lawrence Coll., 1958-61; asso. prof. UCLA, 1961-66, prof. history, 1966-92, chmn. dept., 1978-83, dir. Russian and East European Studies Center, 1962-66, prof. emeritus, 1992—; fellow Russian Rsch. Ctr., Harvard U., 1962; sr. mem. St. Antony's Coll., Oxford U., 1972; vis. scholar George Kennan Ctr. Advanced Russian Studies, 1975, mem. acad. coun., 1984-88; sr. assoc. fellow Oxford Ctr. Postgrad. Hebrew Studies, 1984—; co-dir. Rand/UCLA Ctr. Soviet Studies, 1989-93. Author: (with E. Weber) The European Right, 1965, 66, 74, (with H. Hyman) Heard Round the World, 1969, National Consciousness in 18th Century Russia, 1960, 70, Russia in Modernization and Revolution, 1881-1917, 1983, Jewish Policies and Right-Wing Politics in Imperial Russia, 1985; contbr. chpts. to book: Shared Destiny: Fifty Years of Soviet-American Relations, 1985, Pogroms: Anti-Jewish Violence in Modern Russia History, 1991, Hostages of Modernization, 1993, Guerre et Culture, 1994; mem. editl. bd.: Am. Hist. Rev., 1982-85, Slavic Rev., 1985-91, Contention, 1992—, also assoc. editor, 1993—. Served with USN, 1943-46. Recipient Guggenheim fellowship, 1964-65; Am. Council Learned Socs. fellow, 1962; Nat. Endowment Humanities fellow, 1975-76. Mem. AAUP, Am. Assn. Advancement Slavic Studies (bd. dirs. 1982-85), Am. Hist. Assn. Office: Dept History UCLA Los Angeles CA 90024

ROGGEVEEN, RICHARD, operation services executive, executive recruiter; b. 1942. Pres. Horsemans Guarantee Corp. Am., Palatine, Ill., Am. Data Ctr. Inc., Palatine, Ill. Office: Horsemans Guarantee Corp AM 25 W Palatine Rd Palatine IL 60067-5101 Also: Am Data Centre Inc 25 W Palatine Rd Palatine IL 60067-5199*

ROGIN, GILBERT LESLIE, editor, author; b. N.Y.C., Nov. 14, 1929; s. Robert I. and Lillian Carol (Ruderman) R. Student, State U. Iowa, 1947-49; A.B., Columbia, 1951. Editor-at-large Time Inc. Ventures, N.Y.C., 1955—. Author: The Fencing Master, 1965, What Happens Next?, 1971, Preparations for the Ascent, 1980. Served with AUS, 1952-54. Recipient award for creative work in lit. Am. Acad. Inst. Arts and Letters 1972. Home: 43 W 10th St New York NY 10011-8701 Office: Time Pub Ventures Time & Life Bldg New York NY 10020

ROGLIANO, ALDO THOMAS, publishing executive; b. Tuckahoe, N.Y., Mar. 7, 1925; s. Alfred and Nancy (Morrone) R.; m. Bettie Eleanor Fehrs, June 13, 1948; children: Susan Rogliano Shortley, Betsy Rogliano Dyer, Guy, Barbara Rogliano Tracy, Robert. Student, Syracuse U., 1946-49. Newsstand promotion mgr. Fawcett Publs. Inc., Greenwich, Conn., 1949-54; promotion mgr. Fawcett Publs. Inc., 1957-68, MacFadden Pub. Co., N.Y.C., 1954-57; account exec., promotion mgr. Dell Pub. Co., 1968-71; v.p., dir. pub. relations MacFadden-Bartell Corp., N.Y.C., 1971-74; promotion dir. Internat. Circulation Distbrs., N.Y.C., 1974-77, Kable News Co., 1977-78; v.p., dir. promotion and publicity Publishers Distbg. Corp. (a Filmways co.), N.Y.C., 1978-80; advt. and promotion dir. Flynt Distbg. Co., Los Angeles, 1980-83. Served with USMCR, 1943-45. Decorated Purple Heart; recipient Pub. Relations Gold Key award, 1971. Home: 4417 San Lucian Ln Fort Myers FL 33903-1360

ROGLIERI, JOHN LOUIS, health facility administrator; b. Plainfield, N.J., June 24, 1939; s. Vito and Grace Mary (DeCristofaro) R.; m. Geraldine Ann Piller, June 15, 1963; children: Maria Roglieri Friedman, Anna, John. BSChemE, Lehigh U., 1960, AB in Applied Scis., 1960; MD, Harvard U., 1966; MS in Bus., Columbia U., 1978. Diplomate Nat. Bd. Med. Examiners. Intern Bellevue Hosp., Columbia Svc., 1966-67; resident Presbyn. Hosp., N.Y.C., 1969-71, dir. divsn. ambulatory medicine, 1973-75, v.p. ambulatory svcs., 1975-82, dir. employee health svc., 1988-92; fellow Harvard Med. Sch., Boston, 1971-73; asst. dir. Lab. Computer Sci. Mass. Gen. Hosp., 1972-73, dir. Ambulatory Screening Clinic, 1972-73; med. dir. N.Y. Health Plan, Inc., N.Y.C., 1988-92; corp. med. dir. Sanus Corp. Health Sys., Ft. Lee, N.J., 1992-95, NYL Care Health Plans Inc., N.Y.C., 1996—; cons. Nat. Ctr. Health Svc. Rsch. and Devel., 1973-75; dir. clin. scholar program Columbia U., 1975-77, asst. prof. clin. medicine Coll. Physicians and Surgeons, 1973—; health edn. cons. Basic Internat. Investments, 1975-76; v.p., bd. dirs. AMARCO Internat., N.Y.C., 1975-85; mem. adv. bd. Western and Upper Manhattan Regional Perinatal Network, Coll. Physicians and Surgeons, N.Y.C., 1975-80; appeared in various TV and radio programs. Author: Odds on Your Life, 1980; mem. editorial bd. Managed Care, 1992—, Jour. Applied Rsch. in Health Adminstrn., 1979-81; book rev. cons. Acad. Press, Inc., N.Y.C.; contbr. articles to profl. publs.;. Capt. USPHS, 1967-69. Mem. APHA, Am. Fedn. Clin. Rsch., Am. Soc. Internal Medicine, N.Y. State Soc. Internal Medicine, Soc. for Rsch. and Edn. in Primary Care Internal Medicine, Nat. Assn. Managed Care Physicians. Roman Catholic. Avocations: surfcasting, woodworking. Office: NYL Care Health Plan 1 Liberty Plz New York NY 10006

ROGNE, CAROL JEAN, school psychologist, therapist, educator; b. Mankato, Minn., Feb. 10, 1941; d. James Arnold and Evelyn Francis (Nelson) Gisvold; m. Duane John Rogne, May 11, 1960 (div. Apr. 1991); children: Jay Louis, Dustin Boe. BA in Psychology, Moorhead State U., 1978-80, MS in Sch. Psychology Level II, 1980-82; postgrad., Clayton U., 1989-90. Lic. psychologist, N.D., Minn.; diplomate Nat. Bd. Cert. Counselors. Supr. sch. psychology grad. students Moorhead State U., Fargo, N.D., 1981; dir. ednl. counseling ctr. Concordia (Minn.) Coll., 1982-84; founder and dir. Discovery Counseling and Ednl. Ctr., Fargo, 1984—; sch. psychologist, 1981—; supr./liaison practicum placements and instr. Moorhead State U.; instr. grad. counseling program N.D. State U., 1988-94; supr. counseling grad. studies, 1991—; instr. Moorhead Tech. Coll., 1988—; co-founder, dir. Discovery Ednl. Workshops, 1991—; mem. grant task force Dilworth-Glyndon-Felton Cmty. Sch., Dilworth, Minn., 1993—; spkr. in field, 1984—. Author: Understanding and Enhancing Self-Esteem, 1992, Dealing With Guilt, Control and Power in Relationships, 1992. Active Stop the Violence, Moorhead, Dilworth, 1993—, Rape and Abuse Crisis Ctr., Fargo. Recipient Women of Distinction award Soroptomist Club, 1994. Mem. Am. Counseling and Devel. Assn. Democrat. Lutheran. Avocations: tennis, real estate mgmt., creation of non-violence learning ctr. Office: Discovery Counseling and Ednl Ctr 115 N University Dr Fargo ND 58102-4667

ROGO, KATHLEEN, safety engineer; b. Carrollton, Ohio, Sept. 28, 1952; d. Silvio and Mary (Siragusano) R. Grad. high sch., Carrollton; PhD in Med. Sci. (hon.), Ohio Valley Pathologists, Inc., 1992. Cert. histotechnologist, emergency med. technologist, safety engr. Rsch. pathology trainee Aultman Hosp., Canton, Ohio, 1970-75, supr. anatomic pathology, 1974-75; lab. mgr. W. Morgan Lab., Canton, 1973-74; supr. anatomic pathology Dr.'s Hosp., Massillon, Ohio, 1975-78; emergency med. technician Canton Fire Dept., 1976-81; safety engr. Ashland Oil Co., Canton, 1980-82; rsch. pathologist assoc., med. cons, v.p. Ohio Valley Pathologists, Inc., Wheeling, W.Va., 1990—. Mem. Am. Soc. Clin. Pathology (cert. histotechnician), Am. Soc. Safety Engrs. (cert.), Am. Soc. Emergency Med. Technicians (cert.), Ohio State Med. Soc., Internat. Platform Assn. Democrat. Roman Catholic. Avocations: professional model, dancer and musician.

ROGOFF, JEROME HOWARD, psychiatrist, psychoanalyst, forensic expert; b. Detroit, Dec. 21, 1938; s. Abraham Solomon and Sarah Riva (Epstein) R.; (div. 1983); m. Erika Kathleen Keller, Sept. 25, 1983. BA, Harvard Coll., 1960; MD, Case Western Reserve U., 1965. Diplomate Am. Bd. Psychiatry and Neurology. Physician Peace Corps USPHS, Kathmandu, Nepal, 1966-68; clin. fellow psychiatry Harvard Med. Sch., Boston, 1975-79; staff psychiatrist Westwood (Mass.) Lodge Hosp., 1972-74; assoc. clin. prof. psych. Tufts Med. Sch., Boston, 1977-86; assoc. chief, psychiatry and dir., inpatient Psychiatry, day hosp. Faulkner Hosp., Boston, 1975-94; cons. psychiatrist Mass. Parole Bd. Probate Ct. Plymouth County, Mass., LEAA, Washington, 1971-78; med. psychiat. dir. ct. diversion program Boston TASC-A, 1974-75; treas., bd. dirs. Guild for Continuing Edn., Boston, 1981-95; founding dir. Law and Psychiatry Resource Ctr., Boston, 1983—; adj. prof. Simmons Sch. Social Work, Boston, 1981-85; lectr. on psychiatry Harvard Med. Sch., Boston, 1980-81, 84-94. Chmn. psychiatry team Combined Jewish Philanthropies, Boston, 1978-83, assoc. chmn. med. team, 1984-87, mem. social planning and allocations com., 1991—; bd. dirs. Jewish Vocat. Svc., Boston, 1987-91. Fellow Am. Psychiat. Assn. (pub. affairs rep. 1988-92, 93-94); mem. Mass. Psychiat. Soc. (councillor 1988-94, chair pub. affairs com. 1988-92, 93-94, chair nominating com. 1990), Am. Psychoanalytic Assn., Boston Psychoanalytic Soc., Am. Acad. Psychiatry and Law. Democrat. Avocations: cabinetry, carpentry, cooking, classical music, squash, languages. Home and Office: 659 Chestnut St Newton MA 02168-2035 *Two guiding principles, both from my father: "When in doubt, do the right thing." Sounds trite and naive, but turns out in the event to be profound; one almost always knows deep down what the right thing is. "When you are born, you cry, andeveryone around you laughs. So live your life that when you come to leave it, you laugh, and everyone around you cries. On my profession of psychiatry and psychoanalysis: psychotherapy adds insight to injury.*

ROGOFF, KENNETH S., economics educator; b. Rochester, N.Y., Mar. 22, 1953; s. Stanley Miron and June Beatrice (Goldman) R.; m. Evelyn Jane Brody, Aug. 18, 1979 (div. 1989); m. Natasha Lance, June 25, 1995. BA/MA in Econs., Yale U., 1975; PhD in Econs., MIT, 1980. Economist Internat. Monetary Fund, Washington, 1983; economist, sect. chief Internat. Fin. div., Bd. Govs. of the Fed. Res. Sys., Washington, 1979-84; assoc. prof. econs. U. Wis., Madison, 1985-89; prof. econs. U. Calif., Berkeley, 1989-92; prof. econs. and internat. affairs Princeton (N.J.) U., 1992—; Charles and Marie Robertson prof. of internat. affairs Princeton U., 1995—; vis. scholar San Francisco Fed. Res., 1990-92, World Bank, Washington, 1989, IMF, Washington, 1988-94. Author books and contbr. articles to profl. jours. Alfred P. Sloan Rsch. fellow, 1986-87, Hoover Instn. Nat. fellow, 1986-87, NSF fellow, 1985—. Fellow Econometric Soc.; mem. Am. Econ. Assn., World Chess Fedn., Grandmasters Assn. Office: Princeton U Woodrow Wilson Sch Princeton NJ 08544-1013

ROGOLS, SAUL, food scientist; b. Cambridge, Mass., July 27, 1933; s. Barney Barkan and Dora (Cohen) R.; m. Donna Janelle, May 25, 1985. BSc in Biology and Chemistry, Antioch Coll., 1955; MSc in Bacteriology and Biochemistry, Ohio State U., 1958, postgrad., 1959-60; postgrad., Ohio State U., 1961-62; MBA, Ohio U., Lancaster, 1982. Cert. med. technician; cert. instr. ARC. Tech. dir. quality control/quality assurance A. E. Staley Mfg. Co., 1961-79; med. technologist Children's Hosp., Columbus, Ohio, 1961-75; materials control mgr. Essex Group div. United Technologies, 1979-80; dir. quality assurance Hexcel Corp., 1980-82; sr. scientist Amstar Corp., 1982-84; sr. food scientist Grain Processing Corp., 1986-91; dir. tech. svcs. Penwest Foods Co., Englewood, Colo., 1991—. Mem. adv. bd. Chem. Week Mag.; contbr. articles to profl. jours.; patentee in field. Fellow Am. Inst. Chemists; mem. TAPPI, Am. Assn. Cereal Chemists (charter mem. carbohydrate div.), Am. Chem. Soc. (biol. chemistry div.), Inst. Food Technologists (carbohydrate exec. com.), Am. Assn. Candy Technologists, N.Y. Acad. Sci., Sigma Xi. Avocation: model ship building. Home: 23573 Pondview Pl Golden CO 80401-5761 Office: Penwest Foods Co 11011 E Peakview Ave Englewood CO 80111-6808

ROGOSHESKE, WALTER FREDERICK, lawyer, former state justice; b. Sauk Rapids, Minn., July 12, 1914; m. Dorothy Heywood, Sept. 29, 1940; children: James, Thomas (dec.), Mark, Paul, Mary Alice. BA, U. Minn., 1937, LLB, 1939; LLD, William Mitchell Coll. Law. Bar: Minn. 1940. Gen. practice Sauk Rapids, 1940-50; dist. judge 7th Jud. Dist., 1950-62; assoc. justice Supreme Ct. Minn., 1962-80; lectr. law U. Minn. Law Sch., 1951-74, adj. prof., 1980-84; cons. arbitration and mediation proceedings, 1980-95. Chmn. Mpls.-St. Paul Met. Airports Commn., 1949-50; Mem. Minn. Ho. of Reps., 1943-49; Bd. dirs. Amicus, Inc.; past pres. Big Bros., St. Paul. Served with AUS, 1944-45. Fellow Am. Bar Found.; mem. ABA (chmn. adv. com. prosecution and def. function, criminal law project 1968-71, mem. council sect. criminal justice 1970-74), Minn. Bar Assn., 7th Dist. Bar Assn., Am. Judicature Soc., Inst. Jud. Adminstrn., U. Minn. Law Alumni Assn. (dir.). Lutheran. Home and Office: 138 Canabury Ct Saint Paul MN 55117-1503

ROGOSKI, PATRICIA DIANA, financial executive; b. Chgo., Dec. 29, 1939; d. Raymond Michael and Bernice Rose (Konkol) R. BS in Acctg. and Econs., Marquette U., 1961, postgrad., 1965-66; postgrad., NYU, 1966-68, St. John's U., 1975-76; cert. mgmt. acct., 1979. Sr. fin. analyst Blackhawk Mfg. Co., Milw., 1961-66; mgr., sr. analyst Shell Oil Co., N.Y.C., 1966-71; mgr. data processing Bradford Nat./Penn Bradford, Pitts., 1971-75; asst. mgr. fin. controls ITT, N.Y.C., 1975-79; v.p., comptr. ITT Consumer Fin. Corp., Mpls., 1979-80; sr. v.p. fin. ITT Fin. Corp., St. Louis, 1980-84; v.p., exec. asst., group exec. ITT Coins, Secaucus, N.J., 1984-85; pres. Patron S., Ltd., Wilmington, Del., 1986—; CFO, sr. v.p. Guardsmark, Inc., Memphis, 1989-94; sr. v.p. Peoplemark, Inc., Memphis, 1989-94. Bd. dirs. St. Louis Repertory Theater, 1983-84. Named to Acad. Women Achievers, YWCA, N.Y.C., 1980. Mem. Fin. Execs. Inst., Inst. Mgmt. Acctg., Econ. Club. Avocation: duplicate bridge. Office: Patron S Ltd NE Hercules Plz 1313 N Market St Ste 3410 Wilmington DE 19801-1151

ROGOVIN, JOHN ANDREW, lawyer; b. Washington, July 10, 1961; s. Mitchell and Sheila Ann (Ender) R. AB, Columbia U., 1983; JD, U. Va., 1987. Bar: N.Y. 1989, D.C. 1990. Law clk. hon. Laurence Silberman U.S.

Ct. Appeals (D.C. Cir.), Washington, 1987-88; assoc. Kramer, Levin et al, N.Y.C., 1988-89, O'Melveny & Myers, Washington, 1990-92; dep. transition counsel Presdl. Transition, Little Rock, 1992-93; asst. to atty. gen. U.S. Dept. Justice, Washington, 1993, dep. asst. atty. gen. Civil Divsn., 1993-96. Mem. ABA, D.C. Bar Assn. Office: US Dept Justice Rm 3143 10th St & Constitution Ave Washington DC 20530

ROGOVIN, MILTON, documentary photographer, retired optometrist; b. N.Y.C., Dec. 30, 1909; s. Jacob and Dora (Shainhouse) R.; m. Anne Setters, Apr. 7, 1942; children—Ellen, Mark, Paula. B.S. in Optics and Optometry, Columbia U., 1931; M.A. in American Studies, SUNY-Buffalo, 1972; DFA (hon.), U. Buffalo, 1994, Buffalo State Coll., 1994, Dyouville Coll., 1994. Optometrist, Buffalo, 1931-75; freelance documentary photographer, 1958—. Author: Milton Rogovin: The Forgotten Ones, 1985, Portraits in Steel, 1993, Triptychs Buffalo's Lower West Side Revisited, 1993. Served with U.S. Army, 1942-45. Recipient W. Eugene Smith Meml. Fund award, 1983. Home: 90 Chatham Ave Buffalo NY 14216-3109

ROGOW, BRUCE JOEL, information technology consultant; b. Phila., Aug. 22, 1945; s. Abraham I. and Eunice (Friedman) R.; m. Lois Lee Kutun, Aug. 20, 1967 (div. Mar. 1973); children: Mark Alan, Michelle Renee; m. Winnie Ruth Teitelbaum, Mar. 7, 1980; 1 child, Geoffrey Evan. BCE, U. Fla., 1967. Systems engr. IBM, Gainesville, Fla., 1968-69, mktg. rep., 1969-72; staff instr. IBM, Poughkeepsie, N.Y., 1973-77; cons. Nolan, Norton & Co., Lexington, Mass., 1977-79, prin., 1979-82; sr. mng. prin. Nolan, Norton & Co./Peat Marwick & Co., Lexington, 1982-87; v.p. cons. Gartner Group, Inc., Stamford, Conn., 1987-88, exec. v.p. analytic resources, 1988-90, exec. v.p. cons. svcs., 1991-92, fellow, 1992—; pvt. cons. firm Marblehead, Mass., 1992—; speaker info. tech. industry. Republican. Jewish. Avocations: reading, skiing, family. Home and Office: 220 Ocean Ave Marblehead MA 01945-3629

ROGOWSKY, ROBERT ARTHUR, trade commission director; b. Vancouver, B.C., Can., Mar. 12, 1951; s. Michael Randall and Ruth Ann (Wellman) R.; m. Linda Sue George, June 17, 1972; children: Vanessa, Heather, Tara, Nichole, Alexis. BA in Econs., Boston U., 1973; MA in Econs., U. Va., 1975, PhD in Econs., 1982. Asst. prof. dept. econs. George Mason U., Fairfax, Va., 1977-78; rsch. economist Bur. Econs. FTC, Washington, 1979-83; econ. advisor to commrs. Consumer Product Safety Commn., Washington, 1983-84, acting exec. dir., asst. to dir., 1984; pres. Econ. Edn. for Clergy, Inc., Bethesda, Md., 1985-86; exec. asst. to chmn. Internat. Trade Commn., Washington, 1986-87; dep. dir. Bur. Consumer Protection FTC, Washington, 1987-89; dir. office of industries U.S. Internat. Trade Commn., Washington, 1989-92, dir. ops., 1992—; instr. U. Va., 1976-77; econ. rschr. Am. Enterprise Inst., 1976; econ. rsch. analyst Econ. Policy Office, U.S. Dept. Justice, 1974-75; presenter in field. Contbr. articles to profl. jours. Mem. Am. Mgmt. Assn., Am. Econs. Assn., Assn. Christian Economists. Lutheran. Home: 729 Forest Park Rd Great Falls VA 22066-2907 Office: US International Trade Comm Operations 500 E St NW Washington DC 20436-0003

ROGULA, JAMES LEROY, consumer products company executive; b. Rock Island, Ill., Nov. 8, 1933; s. Andrew and Nellie Pearl (Cook) R.; m. Adelaide F. Dittbrenner, May 29, 1960; children: James Lyle, Adelaide Ann, John Andrew. BA, Knox Coll., 1955; MBA, NYU, 1964. Group product mgr. Am. Chicle Co., Long Island City, N.Y., 1958-66; v.p. new product devel. Carter Wallace, Inc., N.Y.C., 1966-72; v.p. new products J.B. Williams Co., N.Y.C., 1972-74; sr. v.p. E.J. Brach & Sons, Chgo., 1974-77; v.p., gen. mgr. A.E. Staley Mfg. Co., Oak Brook, Ill., 1977-80; exec. v.p. Booth Fisheries Corp., Chgo., 1980-82; v.p., gen. mgr. Arm & Hammer div. Church & Dwight, Inc., Princeton, NJ, 1982-90; pres. Am. Candy Co., Richmond, Va., 1990-94; sr. v.p. consumer bus. group Scotts Co., Marysville, Ohio, 1994—. With U.S. Army, 1956-58. Mem. Sunset Ridge Country Club, Econ. Club Chgo., Commonwealth Club Richmond. Home: 10527 Cardigan Ridge Pl Powell OH 43065 Office: Scotts Co 14111 Scottslawn Rd Marysville OH 43041

ROHAN, BRIAN PATRICK, lawyer; b. Bklyn., July 1, 1964; s. John Eamon and Janet Dee (Trebian) R.; m. Lori Lanahan, Aug. 18, 1990; 1 child, Connor James. BS, SUNY, Plattsburgh, 1986; MBA, Union Coll., 1990; JD, Union U., 1990. Bar: N.Y. 1991, Mass. 1991, U.S. Dist. Ct. (no. dist.) N.Y. 1991. Atty. Waite & Assocs., P.C., Albany, N.Y., 1990—. Bd. dirs. Catholic Family & Cmty. Svcs., Albany, 1991-94. Mem. ABA, N.Y. State Bar Assn. Office: Waite & Assocs 90 N Pearl St Albany NY 12207

ROHATYN, FELIX GEORGE, investment company executive; b. Vienna, Austria, May 29, 1928; came to U.S., 1942, naturalized, 1950; s. Alexander and Edith (Knoll) R.; m. Jeannette Streit, June 9, 1956; children: Pierre, Nicolas, Michael; m. Elizabeth Fly, May 31, 1979. BS, Middlebury (Vt.) Coll., 1948; LLD (hon.), Adelphi U., Bard Coll., Hofstra U., 1981, L.I. U., 1981, Middlebury Coll., 1982, Fordham U., 1983; LLB (hon.), NYU, 1979, Brandeis U., 1987. With Lazard Freres & Co., LLC, N.Y.C., 1948—, mng. dir., 1960—; bd. dirs. Pfizer Co., Gen. Instrument. Served with AUS, 1951-53, Korea. Office: Lazard Freres & Co 30 Rockefeller Plz New York NY 10020

ROHDE, RICHARD A., plant pathologist educator; b. Peekskill, N.Y., Sept. 28, 1929; s. Frederick Allen and Ruth Winifred (Gallaher) R.; m. Suzanne Eloise Walker, Oct. 11, 1956; children: Melissa, Leigh, Katherine, David. AB, Drew U., 1951; MS, U. Md., 1956, PhD, 1958. Asst. prof. U. Mass., Amherst, Mass., 1959-65, assoc. prof., 1965-68, prof., head dept plant pathology, 1968-81; assoc. dean, assoc. dir. Mass. Agrl. Exptl. Sta., U. Mass., Amherst, Mass., 1981—, prof. emeritus, 1994; vis. scientist Rothamsted Exp. Sta., Harpenden, 1967, U. Ariz., Tucson, 1974, USDA-CSRS, Washington, D.C., 1981. Editor: Plant-Parasitic Nematodes, 3 Vols., 1971-81; contbr. articles to profl. jours. Cpl. U.S. Army, 1952-54. Recipient Alumni Achievement award Drew U., 1970. Mem. Am. Phytopathological Soc. (councilor, pres.), Soc. Nematologists. Lutheran. Home: 18 Butterhill Rd Pelham MA 01002-9737 Office: University of Massachusetts Agricultural Experiment Sta 217 Stockbridge Hall Amherst MA 01003

ROHE, WILLIAM MICHAEL, urban planning educator; b. N.Y.C., Apr. 23, 1950; s. Victor Joseph and Grace (White) R.; m. Jamie Stone, June 10, 1989. AAS, SUNY, Farmingdale, 1970; BS, SUNY, Buffalo, 1972; M Regional Planning, Pa. State U., 1975, PhD in Man Environ. Rels., 1978. Asst. prof. Pa. State U., University Park, 1977-78; asst. prof. city, regional planning U. N.C., Chapel Hill, 1978-85, assoc. prof., 1985-92; prof., 1992-94, Dean E. Smith prof., 1994—; dir. Ctr. for Urban and Regional Studies U. N.C., Chapel Hill, 1994—; cons. Rsch. Triangle Inst., Rsch. Triangle Park, N.C., 1979—; cons. Urban Systems Rsch. and Engring., Cambridge, Mass., 1985-87; HUD vis. scholar, Washington, 1984-85. Author: Planning with Neighborhoods, 1985; contbr. articles to profl. jours. Mem. Chapel Hill Planning Commn., 1980-86; Chapel Hill Small Area Planning Com., 1990—; mem. N.C. Gov.'s Crime Commn., 1995. Grantee Nat. Inst. Justice, 1982, HUD, 1987, 95, rsch. grantee Ford Found., 1988, 91. Mem. AAUP (pres.-elect U. N.C. chpt. 1990-91, pres. 1991-93), Am. Planning Assn. (Best Paper award 1992, 95), Fed. Nat. Mortgage Assn. Avocation: basketball. Office: U N C CB # 3140 Dept City Regional Planning Chapel Hill NC 25799

ROHLF, F. JAMES, biometrician, educator; b. Blythe, Calif., Oct. 24, 1936. BS, San Diego State Coll., 1958; PhD in Entomology, U. Kans., 1962. Asst. prof. biology U. Calif., Santa Barbara, 1962-65; assoc. prof. statis. biology U. Kans., 1965-69; assoc. prof. biology SUNY, Stony Brook, 1969-72, prof., 1972—, chmn. dept. ecology and evolution, 1975-80, 90-91; statis. cons. N.Y. Pub. Svc. Commn., 1975-78, IBM, 1977-81, U.S. EPA, 1978-80; vis. scientist IBM, Yorktown Heights, N.Y., 1976-77, 80-81. Mem. Biometric Soc., Assn. Computing Machinery, Soc. Systematic Biology, Classification Soc. Achievements include research and development of software for applications of multivariate analysis, cluster and factor analysis to morphometrics, systematics, and population biology. Office: SUNY at Stony Brook Dept Ecology and Evolution Stony Brook NY 11794-5245

ROHLFF, DONNA L., geriatrics nurse; b. Passaic, N.J., Dec. 28, 1959; d. Richard and Harriet C. (Norris) Trenschel; m. Kenneth W. Rohlff, Feb. 14, 1988; 1 child, Catherine M.; stepchildren: Kenneth E., Carol A. BSN, Bloomfield (N.J.) Coll., 1984. RN, N.J. Staff nurse ICU-CCU, Chilton Meml. Hosp., Pompton Plains, N.J.; night supr. Troy Hills Ctr., Parsippany, N.J., DON; asst. dir. nursing Hartwyck at Cedar Grove, N.J.

ROHLFING, FREDERICK WILLIAM, lawyer, judge; b. Honolulu, Nov. 2, 1928; s. Romayne Raymond and Kathryn (Coe) R.; m. Joan Halford, July 15, 1952 (div. Sept. 1982); children: Frederick W., Karl A., Brad (dec.); m. Patricia Ann Santos, Aug. 23, 1983. BA, Yale U., 1950; JD, George Washington U., 1955. Bar: Hawaii 1955, Am. Samoa 1978. Assoc. Moore, Torkildson & Rice, Honolulu, 1955-60; ptnr. Rohlfing, Nakamura & Low, Honolulu, 1963-68, Hughes, Steiner & Rohlfing, Honolulu, 1968-71, Rohlfing, Smith & Coates, Honolulu, 1981-84; sole practice Honolulu, 1960-63, 71-81, Maui County, 1988—; dep. corp. counsel County of Maui, Wailuku, Hawaii, 1984-87, corp. counsel, 1987-88; land and legal counsel Maui Open Space Trust, 1992—; prin. Frederick W. Rohlfing III, Honolulu; magistrate judge U.S. Dist. Ct. Hawaii, 1991-96. Mem. Hawaii Ho. Reps., 1959-65, 80-84; Hawaii State Senate, 1966-75; U.S. alt. rep. So. Pacific Commn., Noumea, New Caledonia, 1975-77, 1982-84. Capt. USNR, 1951-87. Mem. Hawaii Bar Assn., Fed. Magistrate Judges Assn. Avocation: ocean swimming. Home and Office: RR #1 Box 398 Kekaulike Ave Kula HI 96790

ROHLFING, JOAN BELEN, federal agency administrator. BA, U. Ill., 1984; MPA, U. Md., 1986; postgrad., Stanford U., 1987-88. Cons. Rand Corp., Santa Monica, Calif.; presdl. mgmt. intern Office of Sec. of Defense, Washington, 1987-89, asst. to dir. for strategic forces policy, 1989-91; staff Ho. of Reps. Armed Svcs. Com., Washington, 1991-94; special asst. to dep. sec. of energy for defense issues U.S. Dept. Energy, Washington, 1994-95, dir. office of nonproliferation and nat. security, 1995—. Office: US Dept Energy Nonprolif & Nat Security 1000 Independence Ave SW Washington DC 20585

ROHLIN, DIANE ELIZABETH, financial public relations executive; b. N.Y.C., June 18, 1958; d. Edward F. and Elaine (Wittenstein) R. BA, Mich. State U., 1979. Account exec. Prudential Bache, Chgo., 1980, A.G. Becker, Chgo., 1981-82; sr. ptnr. Fin. Rels. Bd., Chgo., 1983—. Republican. Avocations: reading, golfing, horseback riding. Office: Fin Rels Bd 875 N Michigan Ave Chicago IL 60611-1803*

ROHLOFF, LORI LUANNE, special education educator; b. Calgary, Alberta, Can., June 23, 1961; came to U.S., 1977; d. Robert John and Catherine Anne (Sled) R.; m. Leon A. Peek, 1993. BS in Psychology, U. N. Tex., 1984; BA in Edn., Tex. Women's U., 1991. Cert. tchr. spl. edn., Tex. Mental health counselor Brookaven Psychiat. Pavilion, Farmer's Br., Tex., 1984-86; spl. edn. art educator Jane Marshall Elem., Middle Sch., Denton, Tex., 199-91; spl. edn. educator high sch. Sanger (Tex.) Ind. Sch. Dist., 1991—; tchr. secondary art Sanger High Sch., 1994—. One-woman shows include Connectivity, 1992; exhibited in group shows at North Tex. Area Arts League, 1993 (Best of Show). Mem. NEA, Tex. State Tchrs. Assn., Coun. for Exceptional Childen, Nat. Mus. for Women in the Arts, Nat. Art Edn. Assn., Mortarboard. Democrat. Episccopalian. Avocations: photography, jogging, gardening. Office: Sanger High Sch 105 Berry St Sanger TX 76266-9365

ROHM, CHARLES EDWARD, insurance company executive; b. Detroit, Oct. 8, 1935; s. John T. and Bernice L. (Shook) R.; m. Joy T. Gwinn, Sept. 8, 1956; 1 child, Barbara. BA, Wabash Coll., 1957; MA, U. Mich., 1958. CLU. Actuarial asst. Prin. Fin. Group, Des Moines, 1963-68, asst. actuary, 1968-70, actuary, 1970-72, 2d v.p., actuary, 1972-74, v.p., 1974-79, v.p., chief actuary, 1979-84, sr. v.p., 1984-92, exec. v.p., 1992—; chmn., pres., bd. dirs. Prin. Mut. Life. Chmn., bd. trustees Simpson Coll., Indianola, Iowa; past chmn. United Way of Cen. Iowa, Des Moines. Mem. Am. Acad. Actuaries, Am. Soc. CLUs, Soc. of Actuaries, Life Ins. Mktg. Rsch. Assn. (bd. dirs.). Office: The Prin Fin Group 711 High St Des Moines IA 50392-0001*

ROHM, ROBERT HERMANN, sculptor, educator; b. Cin., Feb. 6, 1934; s. Hermann George and Anna Katherine (Sager) R.; m. Patricia Jean Cutlip, Dec. 6, 1959 (div. 1978); children: Hans Tobin, Kyle Curtis. B in Indsl. Design, Pratt Inst., 1956; MFA in Sculpture, Cranbrook Acad. Art, 1960. Instr. Columbus (Ohio) Coll. Art and Design, 1956-59, Pratt Inst., Bklyn., 1960-65; prof. art U. R.I., Kingston, 1965-95; pres. emeritus U. R.I., Kingston, N.Y., 1996—. One-man shows: O.K. Harris Gallery, N.Y.C., 1970, 72, 73, 75, 77, 80, 83, 84, 86, 89, 92, 94, Parker St. 470 Gallery, Boston, 1970, 72, Univ. Rochester, N.Y., 1971, N.S. Coll. Art, Halifax, 1970, Worcester Art Mus. (Mass.), 1978, Univ. R.I., 1981, 88, 94, Nielsen Gallery, Boston, 1985, 86, 92, La Jolla Mus. Contemporary Art, Calif., 1985, Lenore Gray Gallery, Providence, 1990, 93, 95; group shows include Boston Mus., 1974, Whitney Mus., N.Y.C., 1962, 64, 69, 70, 73, 83, Va. Mus., Richmond, 1970, Fogg Mus., Cambridge, Mass., 1971, Seattle Art Mus., 1969, Vancouver Art Mus., B.C., Can., 1970, N.J. State Mus., Trenton, 1969, R.I. State Coun. on Arts, 1973, 82, Vassar Coll., 1971, Inst. Contemporary Art, Boston, 1975, Miss. Mus. Art, Jackson, 1979-80, Grey Art Gallery, NYU, 1980, Montclair (N.J.) Art Mus., 1978, Aldrich Mus. Contemporary Art, Ridgefield, Conn., 1981, 82, SUNY-Plattsburgh, 1981, Zone Gallery, Springfield, Mass., 1982, Cumberland Gallery, Nashville, 1986, 93, Allan Frumkin Gallery, N.Y.C., 1985, Beitzel Fine Arts Inc., N.Y.C., Addison Gallery Am. Art, Andover, Mass., 1989, Nielsen Gallery, Boston, 1990-91, Soma Gallery, San Diego, 1993, Palo Alto (Calif.) Cultural Ctr., Centre Coll., Danville, Ky.; represented in permanent collections Columbus Gallery Fine Art, Finch Coll., N.Y.C., Pa. State U., Kunsthalle, Zurich, Va. Mus. Fine Arts, Mus. Modern Art, N.Y.C., U. N.Mex., Albuquerque, Albright-Knox Gallery, Buffalo, Whitney Mus. Am. Art, N.Y.C., Met. Mus. Art, N.Y.C., Rose Art Mus., Brandeis U., Waltham Mass., Mus. Fine Art, Boston, Mus. of Contemporary Art, Chgo., Newport (R.I.) Art Mus. Grantee Guggenheim Found., 1964, R.I. State Council on Arts, 1973, 82, 93, NEA, 1974, 86; recipient Cassandra Found. award, 1967, award Boston 200 Bicentennial Commn., 1975. Subject of numerous articles in jours. and catalogues. Office: U RI Art Dept Fine Arts Ctr Kingston RI 02881

ROHN, REUBEN DAVID, pediatric educator and administrator; b. Israel, Apr. 12, 1945; came to U.S., 1954; s. Aryeh and Rachel (Brenner) R.; m. Judith Semel, Sept. 6, 1971; 1 child, Karen. BA cum laude, Bklyn. Coll., 1967; MD, N.Y. Med. Coll., 1971. Diplomate Am. Bd. Pediat., Am. Bd. Pediatric Endocrinology, Am. Bd. Pediatrics-Adolescent Medicine. Intern in pediatrics Montefiore Hosp., Bronx, N.Y., 1971-72, resident in pediatrics, 1972-74; fellow in adolescent medicine U. Md. Hosp., Balt., 1974-76; preceptor in pediatrics Johns Hopkins U. Sch. Health Svcs., Balt., 1975-76; asst. prof. dept. pediatrics Ea. Va. Med. Sch., Norfolk, 1976-82; coord. pediatric clerkship Ea. Va. Med. Sch., Children's Hosp. of King's Daughters, Norfolk, 1977-90; prof. dept. pediatrics Ea. Va. Med. Sch., Norfolk, 1989—; adj. prof. chemistry Old Dominion U., Norfolk, 1984—; dir. adolescent medicine/endocrinology Children's Hosp. of King's Daughters, Norfolk, 1976—; mem. curriculum com. Ea. Va. Med. Sch., 1977-79, clerkship coords. com. 1977-90, genetics com., 1978-80, evaluation com. 1979-91, chmn. selectives com., 1981-82, ad hoc com. on consultation, 1982-83, student progress com., 1983-85, student health com., 1985-87, LCME com. on curriculum, 1990-92; mem. child abuse com. Children's Hosp. of King 's Daus., 1976-80, chmn. adolescent adv. com., 1976-80, patient care com. 1980-94, nutrition com. 1980-94, utilization rev. com., 1980-82, med. records com., 1987-89, gen. med./surg. task force com., 1987-88; bd. dirs. Pediat. Fac. Assocs., 1994—; speaker in field. Reviewer Jour. Adolescent Health Care, 1986—, mem. editorial bd., 1989-92; contbr. articles to profl. jours. Mem. Norfolk Sch. Health Coun., 1977—, mem. ad hoc com. infant screening program for hypothroidism Commonwealth of Va., 1977-79, cons., 1979—; mem. cmty. adv. bd. Norfolk Adolescent Pregnancy Prevention Svc. Project, 1981-83; bd. dirs. Elizabeth River chpt. Am. Diabetes Assn., 1982-85, South Hampton Roads chpt. 1985-93; mem. adv. com. Norfolk-Virginia Beach Jr. League, 1987-88; judge ann. Health Edn. Fair, Norfolk Pub. schs., 1980-94. Recipient grant Bressler Rsch. Fund, 1975-76, Biomed. Rsch. Devel. grant Ea. Va. Med. Sch., 1978, 78-79, 79-80, 81-82, 83-84, Children's Health Found. grant, 1988-89. Fellow Am. Acad. Pediatrics (youth and adolescence com. Va. chpt. 1978—); mem. Soc. Adolescent Medicine (abstract reviewer 1984-91), Lawson Wilkins Pediatric Endocrine Soc., Sigma Xi. Avocations: photography, folk dancing. Home: 4653 Larkwood Dr Virginia Beach VA 23464-5815 Office: Childrens Hosp Kings Daus 601 Childrens Ln Norfolk VA 23507-1910

ROHNER, RALPH JOHN, lawyer, educator, university dean; b. East Orange, N.J., Aug. 10, 1938. A.B., Cath. U. Am., 1960, J.D., 1963. Bar: Md. 1964. Teaching fellow Stanford (Calif.) U., 1963-64; atty. pub. health div. HEW, 1964-65; prof. law Cath. U. Am. Sch. Law, Washington, 1965—, acting dean, 1968-69, assoc. dean, 1969-71, dean, 1987-95; staff counsel consumer affairs subcom. U.S. Senate Banking Com., 1975-76; cons. Fed. Res. Bd., 1976-83, chmn. consumer adv. council, 1981; cons. FDIC, 1978-80; spl. counsel Consumer Bankers Assn., 1984—; cons. U.S. Regulatory Coun., 1979-80; bd. dirs. Hanover Funds, Inc., N.Y.C. Co-author: Consumer Law: Cases and Materials, 1979, 2d edit., 1991; co-author, editor The Law of Truth in Lending, 1984. Bd. dirs. Migrant Legal Action Program, Inc., Washington, Automobile Owners Action Coun., Washington, Credit Rsch. Ctr., Purdue U. Mem. ABA, Am. Law Inst., Coll. of Consumer Fin. Svcs. Lawyers. Home: 10909 Forestgate Pl Glenn Dale MD 20769-2047 Office: Cath U Sch Law 620 Michigan Ave NE Washington DC 20064-0001 *We learn from those we teach, we are inspired to write by those who read, and we should serve as examples to those who aspire.*

ROHNER, THOMAS JOHN, JR., urologist; b. Trenton, N.J., Jan. 1, 1936; s. Thomas J. and Julia (Kanyo) R.; m. Jessie Rohner; children: Christopher, James. BA, Yale U., 1957; MD, U. Pa., 1961. Diplomate Am. Bd. Urology. Intern Hosp. U. Pa., Phila., 1961-62, resident in gen. surgery, 1962-64, resident in urology, 1964-67; asst. prof. surgery M.S. Hersey Med. Ctr., Pa. State U., Hershey, 1970-71, assoc. prof., 1971-75, prof., 1975—, chief urol. divsn., assoc. dean for clin. affairs, 1970-96; urologic cons. VA Hosp., Lebanon, Pa., 1970—; assoc. dean for clin. affairs M.S. Hersey Med. Ctr., Pa. State U., Hershey, 1996—; corp. mem. Pa. Blue Shield, 1991—, bd. dirs., 1993—. Contbr. articles to profl. jours. Served to maj. M.C., U.S. Army, 1967-69. USPHS fellow, 1969-70; grantee HEW, 1971-76, USPHS, 1971-76. Fellow ACS (pres. cen. Pa. chpt. 1983-84, bd. govs. 1991—); mem. AMA, Am. Urol. Assn. (pres. mid-Atlantic sect. 1986-87), Urol. Assn. Pa., Phila. Urol. Soc. (pres. 1980-81), Assn. Acad. Surgeons, Am. Bd. Urology (trustee 1995—), Pa. Med. Soc., Dauphin County Med. Soc., Soc. Pediat. Urology, Soc. Univ. Urologists (pres. 1990-91), Nat. Urol. Forum, Societe Internationale d'Urologie, Transamerican Urol. Rschrs., Internat. Continence Soc., Coll. Physicians of Phila. Home: 2907 Mt Gretna Rd Elizabethtown PA 17022-9689 Office: Milton S Hershey Med Ctr Pa State Univ PO Box 850 Hershey PA 17033-0850

ROHR, BRENDA ANN, band and vocal director; b. Hays, Kans., Dec. 10, 1962; d. Gilbert Julius and Edna Marie (Wasinger) R. B of Music Edn., Fort Hays State U., 1986. Cert. music educator, Kans. Band dir. Lincoln (Kans.) Unified Sch. Dist. 298, 1986-88; band dir., vocal tchr. Claflin (Kans.) Unified Sch. Dist. 354, 1988-91, Atwood (Kans.) Unified Sch. Dist. 318, 1991-92, Macksville (Kans.) Unified Sch. Dist. 351, 1992—; tenor sax player Jay Bennet Band, Great Bend, Kans., 1988; bass clarinet, clarinet player Kans. Winds, Hutchinson, 1988—; lead tenor sax player Pawnee County Big Band, Larned, Kans. Mem. Kans. Bandmasters Assn. (sec. 1990-92), Kans. Music Educators Assn., Kans. Nat. Educators Assn., Phi Beta Mu. Republican. Roman Catholic. Avocations: photography, bowling, golf, bicycle riding, collecting pig figurines. Home: 226 N Colyer Box 336 Macksville KS 67557 Office: Macksville High Sch 417 N Gilmore Box 307 Macksville KS 67557

ROHR, DAVID BAKER, federal agency commissioner; b. Hartford, Conn., Apr. 18, 1933; s. Charles James and Margaret Elizabeth (Getzendanner) R.; m. Loretta Avonne French, Apr. 25, 1959 (dec. Sept. 1991); children: Sharon Elizabeth, Derek Robert; m. Pamela P. Quinn, Nov. 18, 1995. BS, Colo. State U., 1958, MS in Econs., 1963. Master scheduler Stanley Aviation Corp., Denver, 1959-60; internat. economist U.S. Dept. Commerce, Washington, 1961-70; pub. affairs fellow Stanford U., Palo Alto, Calif., 1967-68; dir. trade negotiations and agreements U.S. Dept. Commerce, Washington, 1970-74; profl. staff mem. Com. on Ways and Means U.S. Ho. of Reps., Washington, 1974-80, staff dir. subcom. on trade, 1980-84; commr. U.S. Internat. Trade Commn., Washington, 1984—. Bd. dirs. West Laurel (Md.) Civic Assn., 1970-80. With U.S. Army, 1953-55. Democrat. Episcopalian. Avocations: skiing, fishing, swimming. Office: US Internat Trade Commn 500 E St SW Washington DC 20436-0003

ROHR, DAVIS CHARLES, aerospace consultant, business executive, retired air force officer; b. Burlington, Wis., Oct. 29, 1929; s. Charles Davis Rohr and Dorothy Elizabeth (Hahn) Rohr Larson; m. Gayle Lynn White, Aug. 22, 1959; children—Ellen Louise, Jean Elizabeth. Student, Northwestern U., 1947-48; B.Sc., U.S. Mil. Acad., 1952; M.A., U. Wash., 1960. Commd. 2d lt. USAF, 1952, advanced through grades to maj. gen, 1980; fighter pilot USAF, Ohio, Korea, Japan, 1954-58; asst. prof. history USAF Acad., Colo., 1960-64; fighter pilot, squadron ops. officer Idaho and, Fed. Republic Germany, 1965-69; fighter squadron comdr. Vietnam, 1969-70; country dir. S.Am. Office of Sec. of Def., Washington, 1970-73; exec. officer, dep. dir. maintenance Hdqrs. Tactical Air Command, 1973-75; tactical fighter wing comdr. Tex., Utah, 1976-79; chief Office of Mil. Coop., Cairo, 1979-81; dir. plans and policy U.S. European Command, Stuttgart, Fed. Republic Germany, 1981-84; dep. comdr. in chief U.S. Cen. Command, MacDill AFB, Fla., 1984-87, ret.; aerospace cons., 1988—; prof. history U.S. Air Force Acad. Decorated Def. D.S.M., 2 Def. Superior Service medals, Legion of Merit with cluster, D.F.C., Meritorious Service medal, Air medal with 14 clusters, Air Force Commendation medal, Purple Heart.

ROHR, DONALD GERARD, history educator; b. Toledo, Oct. 10, 1920; s. Lewis Walter and Marie (Pilliod) R.; m. Joan Willis Michener, Sept. 14, 1948; children: Karen, Kristin. B.A., U. Toronto, Ont., Can., 1943, M.A., 1949; Ph.D., Harvard U., 1958. Instr., then asst. prof. Williams Coll., 1953-59; mem. faculty Brown U., 1959—, prof. history, 1963-86, emeritus, 1986—, chmn. dept., 1960-65, 66-69, 72-74, sec. faculty, 1969-72, assoc. dean faculty and acad. affairs, 1976-81; adminstv. dir. Howard Fedn., 1989-92. Author: The Origins of Social Liberalism in Germany, 1963, (with Robert Ergang) Europe Since Waterloo, 1967. Served with AUS, 1943-46, ETO. Mem. Am. Hist. Assn., Conf. Group Ctrl. European History, Providence Com. Fgn. Rels. (sec. 1968-81, chmn. 1981-92), Thomas Becket Fedn. (v.p. 1983-84, pres. 1984-86), English Speaking Union (pres. Providence br. 1986-88), U. Club, Faculty Club (Providence, pres. 1981-83). Democrat. Roman Catholic. Home: 71 Grotto Ave Providence RI 02906-5609

ROHR, JAMES EDWARD, banker; b. Cleve., Oct. 18, 1948; s. Charles E. and Loretta (Kramer) R.; m. Sharon Lynn Chambers, Dec. 29, 1970; children—Julie, James, Kristen. B.A., Notre Dame U., 1970; M.B.A., Ohio State U., 1972. Comml. banking officer Pitts. Nat. Bank, 1974-76, asst. v.p., 1976-77, v.p., 1977-83, sr. v.p., 1983-85, exec. v.p., 1985-88, pres., 1988-89, chmn., chief exec. officer, 1989-93, pres., CEO, 1993—; vice chmn. PNC Bank Corp., 1989-92, pres., 1992—; bd. dirs. Shadyside Hosp., Pitts., Allegheny Ludlum Corp., Pvt. Export Funding Corp., Student Loan Mktg. Assn., United Way, Greater Pitts. Coun. Boy Scouts Am., Cultural Trust, Carnegie-Mellon U. Mem. adv. bd. Salvation Army, Pitts., 1983—; chair Civic Light Opera, Nat. Flag Found. Mem. Am. Bankers Assn., Bankers Roundtable, Allegheny Conf., Young Pres.' Orgn., Pa. Bus. Roundtable (vice chmn.), Duquesne Club (dir.). Roman Catholic. Office: PNC Bank Corp 249 Fifth Ave Pittsburgh PA 15222-2707

ROHRABACHER, DANA, congressman; b. June 21, 1947; s. Donald and Doris Rohrabacher. Student, L.A. Harbor Coll., 1965-67; BA in History, Long Beach State Coll., 1969; MA in Am. Studies, U. So. Calif., 1976. Reporter City News Svc./Radio West, L.A., 4 yrs.; editorial writer Orange County Register, 1979-80; asst. press. sec. Reagan for Pres. Campaign, 1976, 80; speechwriter, spl. asst. to Pres. Reagan White House, Washington, 1981-88; mem. 101st-103rd Congresses from 45th Calif. dist., 1989-92, 103d Congress from 45th dist. Calif., 1993—; U.S. del. Young Polit. Leaders Conf., USSR; disting. lectr. Internat. Terrorism Conf., Paris, 1985; mem. Internat. Rels. com.; chmn. Sci. subcom. on energy and environ. Recipient Disting. Alumnus award L.A. Harbor Coll., 1987. Avocations: surfing, skiing, white water rafting. Office: US House of Reps Rayburn Bldg 2338 Washington DC 20515-0545*

ROHRBACH, ROGER PHILLIP, agricultural engineer, educator; b. Canton, Ohio, Oct. 12, 1942; s. Clarence A. and Beatrice E. (Burens) R.; m. M. Jeanette Weishner, June 12, 1965; children: Sharon E., Gregory A., Sara L. BS in Agrl. Engring., Ohio State U., 1965, PhD, 1968. From asst. prof.

to assoc. prof. N.C. State U., Raleigh, 1968-78, prof., 1978—. Author: Design in Agricultural Engineering, 1986, Engineering Principles of Agriculture Machines, 1993. Fellow Am. Soc. Agrl. Engrs. (Young Designer award 1981). Office: NC State U Biol and Agrl Engring Dept PO Box 7625 Raleigh NC 27695-7625

ROHRBOUGH, ELSA CLAIRE HARTMAN, artist; b. Shreveport, La., Sept. 26, 1915; d. Adolph Emil and Camille Claire (Francis) Hartman; m. Leonard M. Rohrbough, June 19, 1937 (dec. Jan. 1977); children: Stephen, Frank, Leonard. Juried exhbns. (painting) Massur Mus. Art, Monroe, La., Mobile (Ala.) Art Gallery, Gulf Coast Juried Exhibit, Mobile, Juried Arts Nat., Tyler, Tex., Greater New Orleans Nat., La. Watercolor Soc. Nat., Ky. Watermedia Nat., So. Watercolor Ann., La. Women Artist, many others. One-woman shows include Le Petit Theatre du Vieux Carre, New Orleans World Trade Ctr.'s Internat. House, Singing River Art Assn., Pascagoula, Miss., La. Font Inn, Pascagoula, Mandeville (La.) City Hall, St. Tammany Art Assn., Covington, La., others; exhibited in groups shows at 1st Guaranty Bank, Hammond, La., St. Tammany Art Assn., Ft. Isabel Gallery, Covington, S.E. La. State U. Mem. Nat. League Am. Pen Women (v.p. S.E. La. br. 1986-87, pres. 1987-92, 94-98), St. Tammany Art Assn. (bd. dirs. 1985-86, 87, instr. 1977-78, classes chmn. 1986-88). Republican. Roman Catholic. Avocations: sewing, flower arranging, gardening, ethnic cooking, American antiques. Home: 2525 Lakeshore Dr Mandeville LA 70448-5627

ROHREN, BRENDA MARIE ANDERSON, therapist, educator; b. Kansas City, Mo., Apr. 18, 1959; d. Wilbur Dean and Katheryn Elizabeth (Albright) Anderson; m. Lathan Edward Rohren, May 10, 1985; 1 child, Amanda Jessica. BS in Psychology, Colo. State U., 1983; MA in Psychology, Cath. U. Am., 1986. Lic. mental health practitioner. Mental health therapist, sr. case mgr. Rappahannock Area Community Svcs. Bd., Fredericksburg, Va., 1986-88; mental health therapist, case mgmt. supr. Rappahannock Area Community Svcs. Bd., 1988; rsch. assoc. Inst. Medicine, NAS, Washington, 1988-89; supr. adult psychiat. program Lincoln (Nebr.) Gen. Hosp., 1989, program supr. mental health svcs., 1989-91; adj. instr. S.E. Community Coll., Lincoln, 1990—; assessment & referral specialist Rivendell Psychiat. Ctr., Seward, Nebr., 1993-95; therapist Lincoln Day Treatment Ctr., Lincoln, Nebr., 1993-95; adj. inst. Coll. of St. Mary, 1994—; therapist Rape/Spouse Abuse Crisis Ctr., Lincoln, 1996—; computer cons. Syscon Corp., Washington, 1983-84. Author: (report) Bottom Line Benefits: Building Economic Success Through Stronger Families; editor: (newsletter) Alliance for Mentally Ill, Lincoln. Active Lincoln Alliance for the Mentally Ill, Nebr. Domestic Violence/Sexual Assault Coalition. Mem. NOW, APA (assoc.), Nat. Alliance for Mentally Ill, Nebr. Psychol. Assn. (assoc.). Democrat. Roman Catholic. Avocations: interior decorating, reading, landscaping, camping. Home: 3821 S 33rd St Lincoln NE 68506-3806 Office: SE Community Coll 8800 O St Lincoln NE 68520-1227 also: Coll of St Mary 4600 Valley Rd Rm 403 Lincoln NE 68510

ROHRER, GEORGE JOHN, retired lawyer; b. Elmira, N.Y., Oct. 24, 1931; s. George J. and Lois (Hess) R.; m. Martha M. Jacobs, Jan. 6, 1952; children: Jacquelyn D. Berbusse, Michael A., John S. JD with distinction, Pacific Coast U., 1967. Bar: Calif. 1969, U.S. Dist. Ct. (ctrl. dist.) 1969. Incentive dir. Blue Chip Stamp Co., L.A., 1963-69; gen. ptnr. Songer, Leavell Rohrer, Bellflower, Calif., 1969-80; sr. ptnr. Rohrer & Holtz, Anaheim, Calif., 1980-94; ret., 1994; panel atty. Calif. Assn. of Realtors/State, Hotline, Calif. 1977—; Founder/Dir. Midcities Nat. Bank, Bellflower, 1981-90; trustee S.E. area Bar Assn., Norwalk, Calif., 1974-75. Pres. Bellflower Kiwanis Club, 1972-73; dir. Los Cerritos Y.M.C.A., Bellflower, 1977-78; vol. counsel Am. Radio Relay League, 1987-92. Mem. Orange County Bar Assn., Los Angeles County Bar Assn., Orange County Amicus (pro bono), Bellflower C. of C. (pres. 1975-76), Masons, Shriners. Republican. Avocations: amature radio, fishing, travel.

ROHRER, HEINRICH, physicist; b. Buchs, Switzerland, June 6, 1933. Diploma in Physics, Swiss Inst. Tech., Zurich, 1955, PhD in Physics, 1960; D. Sci. (hon.), Rutgers U., 1987, Marseille U., 1988, Madrid U., 1988, Tsukuba U., 1994. Rsch. asst. Swiss Inst. Tech., Zurich, 1960-61; post-doc. Rutgers U., New Brunswick, N.J., 1961-63; with IBM Rsch. Lab., Zurich, 1963—; vis. scholar U. Calif., Santa Barbara, 1974-75; bd. dirs. Swiss Fed. Insts. Tech., 1993. Co-recipient King Faisal Internat. prize for sci., 1984, Hewlett Packard Europhysics prize, 1984, Nobel prize for Physics, 1986, Cresson medal Franklin Inst., Phila., 1987; Magnun Seal, U. Bologna, Italy, 1988; IBM fellow, 1986; named to Nat. Inventors Hall of Fame, 1994. Fellow Royal Microscopical Soc. (hon. 1988); mem. NAS (fgn. assoc.), Swiss Acad. Tech. Scis., Swiss Phys. Soc. (hon. 1990), Swiss Assn. Engring. and Architecture (hon. 1991), Zurich Phys. Soc. (hon. 1992). Office: IBM Rsch Divsn Zurich Rsch Lab, Saeumerstrasse 4, CH-8803 Rueschlikon Switzerland

ROHRER, MAURICE PIERRE, journalist; b. Geneva, July 8, 1931; s. Henri Louis Rohrer and Germaine Marie-Josephine Rohrer-Joguin. Lic. in Econ. Geography, Geneva U., 1954, PhD in Econs., 1959. Tchr. Ecole Supérieure de Commerce Genève/Coll. Genève, Geneva, 1954-92; asst. dept. geography U. Geneva, 1959-62; dep. Gen. Dept. Secondary Edn., Geneva, 1965-93; freelance journalist numerous publs., Switzerland, France, Germany, 1975—; subs. prof. U. Geneva, 1962, Centre d'Etudes Industrielles, Geneva, 1962; expert economist commn. urbanization, Geneva, 1962-65; methodol. cons. pedagogical studies secondary education, Geneva, 1965-81; expert geographer fed. consultative commn. Schweizer Weltatlas, 1978-93. Author: Placez Mieux Votre Argent, 1966, L'Epargne-Investissement, 1969; editor econs. and fin. Jour. de Genève, 1960-72, L'Illustré, 1962-75; contbr. articles to profl. jours. Roman Catholic. Avocations: fine arts, painting. Home: Rue d'Ermenonville 7, CH-1203 Geneva Switzerland

ROHRER, SAMUEL EDWARD, state legislator; b. Dover, Ohio, Aug. 11, 1955; s. David A. and Edith A. (Paulus) R.; m. Ruth Ann Hastie, Aug. 13, 1977; children: Nathan, David, Jason, Julia. BS in Mgmt., Bob Jones U., Greenville, S.C., 1977. Gen. mgr. KCCV Radio, Independence, Mo., 1977-79; prodn. scheduler Graco Children's Products Inc., Elverson, Pa., 1979-81, dir. mkgt., 1981-92; mem. Pa. Gen. Assembly, Harrisburg, 1992—. Patentee in field. Mem. Am. Legis. Exch. Coun., Washington, 1992—. Mem. Berks C. of C. Republican. Office: PO Box 100 Reading PA 19607-0100

ROHSENOW, WARREN MAX, retired mechanical engineer, educator; b. Chgo., Feb. 12, 1921; s. Fred and Selma (Gorss) R.; m. Katharine Towneley Smith, Sept. 20, 1946; children—John, Brian, Damaris, Sandra, Anne. B.S., Northwestern U., 1941; M.Eng., Yale, 1943, D.Eng., 1944. Teaching asst., instr. mech. engring. Yale, 1941-44; mem. faculty Mass. Inst. Tech., 1946-85, prof. mech. engring., 1955-85, dir. heat transfer lab., 1954-85, prof. emeritus, 1985; bd. dirs. Dynatech Corp., Thermal Process System. Author: (with Choi) Heat Mass and Momentum Transfer, 1961; Editor: Developments in Heat Transfer, 1964, (with Hartnett) Handbook of Heat Transfer, 1973, 2d edit., 1985. Served as lt. (j.g.) USNR, 1944-46; mech. engr. gas turbine div. Engring. Expt. Sta. Annapolis, Md. Recipient Pi Tau Sigma gold medal Am. Soc. M.E., 1951; award for advancement sci. Yale Engring. Assn., 1952; merit award Northwestern Alumni, 1955. Fellow Am. Acad. Arts and Scis., Nat. Acad. Engring., Am. Soc. M.E. (hon. mem., Heat Transfer Meml. award 1967, Max Jakob Meml. award 1970); mem. Sigma Xi, Tau Beta Pi, Pi Tau Sigma. Home: 32 Carroll St Falmouth ME 04105-1908 Office: MIT Cambridge MA 02139

ROHWER, WILLIAM D., JR., university dean; b. Denver, Oct. 2, 1937. AB, Harvard U., 1959; PhD, U. Calif., Berkeley, 1964. Asst. prof. education U. Calif., Berkeley, 1964-68, assoc. prof., 1968-70, prof., 1970-95, acting assoc. dean grad. div., 1969-70, assoc. dean, 1970, acting dir. Inst. Human Learning, 1971, chmn. div. ednl. psychology, vice-chmn. dept. edn., 1982, assoc. dean edn., 1983-86, acting dean, 1989-90, dean, 1990-95, prof. emeritus, dean emeritus, 1996—; vis. lectr. psychology U. Wis., Madison, 1967; rsch. psychologist U.S. Naval Pers. Rsch. Activity, San Diego, 1964. Contbr. articles to profl. jours.; ad hoc reviewer Child Develop., Devel. Psychology, Jour. Ednl. Psychology, Jour. Exptl. Child Psychology, Psychol. Rev., Sci. Recipient Palmer O. Johnson Meml. award Am. Ednl. Rsch. Assn., 1972; fellow Van Leer Jerusalem Found., 1974-75, Ctr. Advanced Study Behavioral Scis. Stanford U., 1979-80; scientific adviser Bernard Van Leer Found., 1974-75; grantee U.S. Office Edn., OEO, NSF, Nat. Inst. Child Health and Human Devel. Office: U Calif Office Dean Edn 1501 Tolman Berkeley CA 94720

ROIGNANT, SARA ALICE, secondary school educator, small business owner; b. Joliet, Ill., Aug. 3, 1939; d. Ernest Richard and Mary Claire (Steffen) Blondis; m. Germain Herve Roignant, Nov. 27, 1965; children: Marie Claire Louise, Jane Noelle, Jeremiah John. BA, Barat Coll., 1961; postgrad., Alliance Francaise,, Paris, 1963; postgrad. studies French, U. Calif., San Francisco, 1968-70; contg. edn. in edn., De Paul, Loyola Univs., Chgo., 1970—. Cert. tchr., Ill., Calif. Tchr. Wilshire Sch., Fullerton, Calif., 1961-63, Berlitz Sch., Paris, 1963; Berlitz Sch., N.Y.C., 1964; tchr. San Francisco City Schs., 1965-70; tchr., tutor, substitute tchr. St. Sebastian's Elem. Sch., Chgo., 1975-79; tchr. Films, TV, Commercials, Chgo., 1979—; restaurateur La Creperie, Chgo., 1972—. Producer, writer, dir.: several plays including Savon at La Creperies Cafe Theatre, 1972-82. Bd. dirs. Our Lady of Mt. Carmel Sch., 1987-90. Mem. Lakeview E. C. of C. (bd. dirs. 1990—, sec. 1992-93). Roman Catholic. Avocations: theater, choir, film-writing, aerobics. Home: 2845 1/2 N Clark St Chicago IL 60657-5207 Office: 2845 N Clark St Chicago IL 60657-5207

ROIN, HOWARD JAMES, lawyer; b. Chgo., Aug. 28, 1953; s. Dan Ronald and Maureen Elizabeth (Mintz) R.; m. Judith Carol Seidel, Dec. 18, 1976; children: Benjamin N., Andrew C., Katharine A. BA, Amherst Coll., 1975; JD, U. Chgo., 1978. Bar: Ill. 1978, U.S. Ct. Appeals (D.C. cir.) 1979, U.S. Ct. Appeals (7th cir.) 1982, U.S. Dist. Ct. (no. dist.) Ill. 1981. Law clk. to Judge George MacKinnon U.S. Ct. Appeals (D.C. cir.), Washington, 1978-79; spl. asst. to Judge William Webster, dir. FBI, Washington, 1979-81; assoc. Mayer, Brown & Platt, Chgo., 1981-84, ptnr., 1985-93. Trustee Village of Glencoe, Ill., 1985-93. Mem. Chgo. Council Lawyers. Democrat. Office: Mayer Brown & Platt 190 S La Salle St Chicago IL 60603-3410

ROISEN, FRED JERROLD, neurobiologist, educator, researcher, anatomy educator; b. N.Y.C., Sept. 12, 1941; s. Israel Jacob and Louise M. (Friedman) R.; m. Maxine G. Gerson, Mar. 28, 1965; children: Kim Felice, Alexandra Suzanne. PhD, Princeton U., 1966, 69. Asst. prof. Rutgers U., New Brunswick, N.J., 1969-72; asst. prof. Med. Sch. Rutgers U., Piscataway, N.J., 1972-75, assoc. prof. Med. Sch., 1975-80; prof. Med. Sch. U. Medicine & Dentistry of N.J., Piscataway, 1980-83, acting dept. chair, prof. Med. Sch., 1983-86; chmn., prof. Sch. of Medicine U. Louisville, 1986—; chair ad hoc com. shared instrumentation NIH, Bethesda, Md., 1987-90. Author: Histology Review, 1980; contbr. over 100 articles to profl. jours. Pres., chair AAUP, Piscataway, 1977-80. Recipient numerous grants. Jewish. Home: 5800 River Knolls Dr Louisville KY 40222-5863 Office: U Louisville Sch Medicine Dept Anat Sci Neurobio Louisville KY 40292

ROITER, ERIC D., lawyer; b. Newton, Mass., Nov. 18, 1948; s. Irving J. and Hilda (Cohen) R.; m. Teddy Joan Roiter, July 8, 1973; children: Rebekah, Jonathan, David. BA, U. Rhode Island, 1970; JD, Georgetown U., 1973, MA, 1981. Bar: D.C. 1973, N.Y. 1984. Assoc. Williams & Jensen, Washington, 1973-76; atty., spl. counsel, asst. gen. counsel SEC, Washington, 1976-81; assoc. Debevoise & Plimpton, Washington, 1981-84, ptnr., 1985—. Contbr. articles to profl. jours. Mem. ABA (chmn. sect. adminstrv. law, com. securities, commodities and exchs. 1988-89). Democrat. Jewish. Avocations: running, tennis. Office: Debevoise & Plimpton 555 13th St NW Ste 1100E Washington DC 20004-1109*

ROITMAN, JUDITH, mathematician; b. N.Y.C., Nov. 12, 1945; d. Leo and Ethel (Gottesman) R.; m. Stanley Lombardo, Sept. 26, 1978; 1 child, Ben Lombardo. BA in English, Sarah Lawrence Coll., 1966; MA in Math., U. Calif., Berkeley, 1971, PhD in Math., 1974. Asst. prof. math. Wellesley (Mass.) Coll., 1974-77; from asst. prof. to prof. math. U. Kans., Lawrence, 1977—. Author: Introduction to Modern Set Theory, 1990; contbr. articles to profl. jours. Grantee NSF, 1975-87, 92-95. Mem. Assn. Symbolic Logic, Am. Math. Soc., Assn. Women in Math. (pres. 1979-81, Louise Hay award 1996), Kans. Assn. Tchrs. Math., Nat. Assn. Tchrs. Math. Avocation: poetry.

ROIZMAN, BERNARD, virologist, educator; b. Chisinau, Rumania, Apr. 17, 1929; came to U.S., 1947, naturalized, 1954; s. Abram and Liudmilla (Seinberg) R.; m. Betty Cohen, Aug. 26, 1950; children: Arthur, Niels. B.A., Temple U., 1952, M.S., 1954; Sc.D. in Microbiology, Johns Hopkins, 1956; D.H.L. (hon.), Gov.'s State U., 1984; MD (hon.), U. Ferrara (Italy), 1991. From instr. microbiology to asst. prof. Johns Hopkins Med. Sch., 1956-65; mem. faculty div. biol. scis. U. Chgo., 1965—, prof. microbiology, 1969-84, prof. biophysics, 1970—, chmn. com. virology, 1969-85, 88—, Joseph Regenstein prof., 1981-83, Joseph Regenstein Disting. Svc. prof., 1984—, chmn. dept. molecular genetics and cell biology, 1985-88; convener herpes virus workshop, Cold Spring Harbor, N.Y., 1972; lectr. Am. Found. for Microbiology, 1974-75; mem. spl. virus cancer program, devel. rsch. working group Nat. Cancer Inst., 1967-71, cons. inst., 1967-73; mem. steering com. human cell biology program NSF, 1971-74, cons. found., 1972-74; mem. adv. com. cell biology and virology Am. Cancer Soc., 1970-74; chmn. herpes virus study group Internat. Commn. Taxonomy of Viruses, 1971-93; mem. Internat. Microbiol. Genetics Commn. Internat. Assn. Microbiol. Scis., 1974-81; mem. sci. adv. coun. N.Y. Cancer Inst., 1971-88; med. adv. bd. Leukemia Rsch. Found., 1972-77; mem. herpes-virus working team WHO/FAO, 1978-81; mem. bd. sci. cons. Sloan Kettering Inst., N.Y.C., 1975-81; mem. study sect. exptl. virology NIH, 1976-80; mem. task force on virology Nat. Inst. Allergy and Infectious Disease, 1976-77; mem. external adv. com. Emory U. Cancer Ctr., 1973-81, Northwestern U. Cancer Ctr., 1979-89; cons. Inst. Merieux, Lyon, France, 1979-91; mem. com. to establish vaccine priorities Nat. Inst. Medicine, 1983-85; chmn. sci. adv. bd. Teiky-Showa Univs. Ctr., Tampa Bay Rsch. Inst., 1983—, chmn. bd. trustees, 1991—. Author sci. papers, chpts. in books; editor: Herpes Viruses, Vol. 1, 1982, Vol. 2, 1983, Vols. 3 and 4, 1985, The Human Herpesviruses, 1993, Infectious Diseases in an Age of Change, 1995; adv. editor Progress in Surface Membrane Science, 1972; editor-in-chief Jour. Infectious Agts. and and Disease, 1992—; mem. editl. bd. Jour. Hygiene, 1985-61, Infectious Diseases, 1965-69, Jour. Virology, 1970—, Jour. Intervirology, 1972-85, Archives of Virology, 1975-81, Virology, 1976-78, 83—, Microbiologica, 1978—, Cell, 1979-80, Gene Therapy, 1994. Trustee Goodwin Inst. for Cancer Rsch., 1977—. Recipient Lederle Med. Faculty award, 1960-61, Career Devel. award USPHS, 1963-65, Pasteur award Ill. Soc. Microbiology, 1972, Esther Langer award for achievement in cancer research, 1974, Outstanding Alumnus in Pub. Health award Johns Hopkins U., 1984; named hon. prof. Shandong Acad. Med. Scis., People's Republic of China, 1985; Am. Cancer Soc. scholar cancer research at Pasteur Inst. Paris, 1961-62; ICN Internat. prize in virology, 1988; faculty research assoc., 1966-71; traveling fellow Internat. Agy. Research Against Cancer, Karolinska Inst., Stockholm, Sweden, 1970; grantee USPHS/NIH, 1958—, Am. Cancer Soc., 1962-90, NSF, 1962-79, Whitehall Found., 1966-74. Fellow Japanese Soc. for Promotion of Sci., Pan Am. Cancer Soc. (hon.); mem. Nat. Acad. Scis., Hungarian Acad. of Scis. (hon.), Am. Acad. Arts and Scis., Am. Acad. Microbiology, Am. Assn. Immunologists, Am. Soc. Microbiology, Am. Soc. Virology, Am. Soc. Biol. Chemists, Brit. Soc. Gen. Microbiology, Johns Hopkins U. Soc. Scholars, Quadrangle Club (Chgo.). Home: 5555 S Everett Ave Chicago IL 60637-1968 Office: U Chgo MB Kouler Viral Oncology Labs 910 E 58th St Chicago IL 60637-1432

ROIZMAN, OWEN, cinematographer; b. Brooklyn, N.Y., Sept. 22, 1936; s. Sol R.; m. Mona Lindholm, Dec. 6, 1964; 1 child, Eric. BA, Gettysburg Coll., 1958. Cinematographer: (films) The French Connection, 1971 (Academy award nomination best cinematography 1971), The Gang That Couldn't Shoot Straight, 1971, The Heartbreak Kid, 1972, Play It Again, Sam, 1972, (with Billy Williams) The Exorcist, 1973 (Academy award nomination best cinematography 1973), The Taking of Pelham One, Two, Three, 1974, The Stepford Wives, 1975, Three Days of the Condor, 1975, Independence, 1976, Network, 1976 (Academy award nomination best cinematography 1976), The Return of a Man Called Horse, 1976, Sergeant Pepper's Lonely Hearts Club Band, 1978, Straight Time, 1978, The Electric Horseman, 1979, The Black Marble, 1980, Absence of Malice, 1981, True Confessions, 1981, Taps, 1981, Tootsie, 1982 (Academy award nomination best cinematography 1982), Vision Quest, 1985, I Love You to Death, 1990, Havana, 1990, Grand Canyon, 1991, The Addams Family, 1991, Wyatt Earp, 1994 (Academy award nomination best cinematography 1994), French Kiss, 1995, (TV spls.) Singer Presents Liza with a "Z", 1972 (Emmy award nomination best cinematography 1972). Office: c/o Perry & Neidorf PO Box 1166 9720 Wilshire Blvd 3d floor Beverly Hills CA 90212

ROJ, WILLIAM HENRY, lawyer; b. Phila., Mar. 29, 1949; s. Joseph S. and Mary B. (Schmidt) R.; m. Mary Lynn Durham, Dec. 20, 1969; children: Wesley Durham, Douglas Durham. BA, Western Md. Coll., 1970; MA in Econs., Duke U., 1971; JD, U. Va., 1975. Bar: Ohio 1975. Assoc. Jones, Day, Reavis & Pogue, Cleve., 1975-82, ptnr., 1983—; pres Erico Intnl, Cleveland, OH, 1995; sec., bd. dirs. Austin Powder Corp., Cleve., 1984—, DM&M Corp., Coeburn, Va., 1985—; bd. dirs. Erico Investment Corp., Schuylkill Holdings, Inc., Sinter Metals, Inc. Trustee Austin Powder Found., Cleve., 1984—, Am. Contemporary Music Devel. Corp.; sec. Rock and Roll Hall of Fame and Mus., Inc. 1st lt. U.S. Army, 1970-71. Nat. Def. Fellow Duke U., 1970. Office: Erico International 3000 Aurora Rd Cleveland OH 44139*

ROJAS, CARLOS, Spanish literature educator; b. Barcelona, Spain, Aug. 12, 1928; s. Carlos and Luisa (Vila) R.; m. Eunice Anne Mitcham, Mar. 19, 1966; children: Carlos, Eunice Anne. MA, U. Barcelona, 1951; PhD, U. Cen., Madrid, 1955; PhD (hon.), U. Simón Bólivar, Barranquilla, Colombia, 1985. Teaching asst. U. Barcelona, 1951-52; fgn. asst. U. Glasgow, Scotland, 1952-54; asst. prof. Rollins Coll., Winter Park, Fla., 1957-60; asst. prof. Emory U., Atlanta, 1960-63, assoc. prof., 1963-68, prof., 1968-80, Charles Howard Candler prof. Spanish lit., 1980-96. Author: Auto de fe, 1968 (Premio Nacional de Literatura 1968), Azana, 1973 (Planeta award 1973), El Igenioso Hidalgo y Poeta F.G. asciende a los infiernos, 1980 (Nadal award 1980), El Sueno de Sarajevo, 1982, El Jardin de las Hespèrides, 1988, El Jardin de Atocha, 1990, Yo, Goya, 1990, Proceso A Godoy, 1992, Salvador Dali, or the Art of Spitting on Your Mother's Portrait, 1993, Alfonso de Borbón Habla Con El Demonio, 1995, !Muera La Inteligencia! !Viva La Muerte! Salamanca, 1995. Recipient Premio Espejo de España award, Madrid, 1984, Encomienda al Mérito Civil, King of Spain, 1986, Univ. Scholar/Tchr. award Emory U., 1987; honoree of yr. Philol. Assn. of Carolinas, 1987. Mem. MLA, Am. Assn. Tchrs. Spanish and Portuguese, Assn. Doctores y Licenciados Españoles en los Estados Unidos (bd. dirs.), South Atlantic MLA. Avocation: painting. Home: 1378 Harvard Rd NE Atlanta GA 30306-2413 Office: Emory U Dept Spanish Atlanta GA 30322

ROJAS GUTIERREZ, CARLOS, Mexican government official. Degree in engring., Nat. U. Mex. With Nat. Indiginist Inst., 1978-82; dir. marginalized zones program Secretariat of Programmation and Budget, 1982-87; coord. for undersec. regional devel., coord. fed. decentralized program; coord. spl. events Office of Presdl. Candidate Salinas de Gortari; gen. coord. Nat. Program Solidarity; sec. social devel. Govt. of Mex., Mexico City, 1993—. Office: Avda Constituyentes 947 Edif B, Colonia Belen de las Flores, 01110 Mexico City Mexico*

ROJEK, KENNETH J., health facility administrator, hospital; m. Carol Rojek; 2 children. BS, U. Ill.; MBA with honors, Roosevelt U. Diplomate, cert. healthcare exec. Am. Coll. Healthcare Execs. Lab. mgr., tech. dir. Rush-Presbyn.-St. Lukes Med. Ctr., Chgo.; adminstr. Wyler Children's Hosp., dept. pediatrics U. Chgo.; v.p., exec. dir. Luth. Gen. Med. Group, S.C., Chgo.; CEO Luth. Gen. Hosp., Park Ridge, Ill.; adj. faculty U. Minn., St. Francis Coll., Joliet, Ill. Active numerous cmty. and civic orgns., cmty. devel. couns. Fellow Am. Coll. Med. Practice Execs. Med. Group Mgmt. Assn. Office: Luth Gen Hosp 1775 Dempster St Park Ridge IL 60068-1174

ROJHANTALAB, HOSSEIN MOHAMMAD, chemical engineer, researcher; b. Tehran, Iran, Sept. 26, 1944; came to U.S., 1984; s. Mohammad Rojhantalab and Sakineh (Fakhri) Nasser-Ghandi; 1 child, Ayda. MS, Calif. State U., Hayward, 1972; PhD, Oreg. State U., 1976. Asst. prof. Ahwaz (Iran) U., 1976-77, Shiraz (Iran) U., 1977-82; cons., chemist Water-Con Co., Tehran, 1982-84; rsch. assoc. U. Oreg., Eugene, 1985-88; lithography engr. Intel Corp., Hillsboro, Oreg., 1988-91; thin film CVO, Aloha, Oreg., 1991-93; Tungsten polish team leader Intel Corp., Alpha, Oreg., 1993—; transl. Popular Sci. Pub. Co., Tehran, 1980-83, UNESCO workshop, 1984; editor, CEO, DNA Pub. Co., Tehran, 1982-84; vis. prof. chemistry Ore. State U., 1985. Editor, translator 4 books on genetic code, controlled nuclear fusion to Farsi, 1981-84; contbr. articles to sci. jours. Scholar Calif. State U., 1971-72; grantee Oreg. State U., 1975-76, CENTO, 1978-79. Mem. Electrochem. Soc. Am. Achievements include patent on single pass graded NSG/BPSG glass for deep trench fill; development of thin BPSG film for defect detection of O.2 - 10 microns. Home: PO Box 6652 Aloha OR 97007-0652

ROKER, AL, broadcast journalist; m. Deborah Roberts. Grad., SUNY, Oswego. Weathercaster, graphic artist WTVH-TV, Syracuse, N.Y., 1974-76; weathercaster WTTG-TV, Washington, 1976-78, WKYC-TV, Cleve., 1978-83, WNBC-TV, N.Y.C., 1983—; weatherman NBC News Today Show, N.Y.C., 1995—. Named Best Weatherman, N.Y. mag., 1985. Mem. Am. Meteorol. Soc. (recipient Seal of Approval). Office: NBC News 30 Rockefeller Plz Rm 1420 New York NY 10012

ROKKE, ERVIN JEROME, air force officer, university president; b. Warren, Minn., Dec. 12, 1939; s. Edwin K. and Joan (Ivery) R.; m. Pamela Mae Patterson, June 6, 1962; children: Lisa Mae, Eric Scott. Student, St. Olaf Coll., 1957-58; BS, USAF Acad., 1962; MPA, Harvard U., 1964, PhD in Polit. Sci., 1970. Commd. 2d lt. USAF, 1962, advanced through grades to lt. gen., 1994; intelligence officer Pacific Air Forces, Hawaii, Japan, 1965-68; assoc. prof. dept. polit. sci. USAF Acad., Colorado Springs, Colo., 1968-73, permanent prof., 1976-80, dean of faculty, 1982-86; plans officer NATO Hdqrs., Brussels, 1973-76; air attache Am. Embassy, London, 1980-82; def. attache Am. Embassy, Moscow, 1987-89; sr. staff Nat. Security Agy., Ft. Meade, Md., 1989-91; dir. intelligence Hdqrs. European Command, Stuttgart, Fed. Republic Germany, 1991-93; assigned to Hdqs. USAF, Washington, 1993-94; pres. Nat. Def. U., Ft. Lesley J. McNair, DC, 1994—; cons. Dept. State, 1969. Editor: American Defense Policy, 1973. Decorated Def. Disting. Svc. medal, Disting. Svc. medal, Def. Superior Svc. medal, Legion of Merit. Mem. Coun. on Fgn. Rels., Am. Polit. Sci. Assn. (assoc.). Lutheran. Avocations: reading, skiing, squash. Home: Qtrs 12 Ft Lesley J McNair Washington DC 20024 Office: Nat Def U 300 5th Ave Ft Lesley J McNair Washington DC 20319-6000

ROLAND, ANNE, registrar Supreme Court of Canada; b. Neuilly-sur-Seine, France, Feb. 27, 1947; d. Pierre Philippe Roland and Geneviève Lehman; m. Alphonse Morisette, Dec. 3, 1975; 1 child, Julien. BA Philosophy, Caen, France, 1965; diploma, Inst. Supérieur d'interprétation et de traduction, 1969; lic. in law, Paris, 1969; LLB, U. Ottawa, 1979. Bar: Quebec 1980. Legal trans., revisor Paris, 1971-75; chief trans. svcs. customs and excise Sec. of State, Can., 1975-76; spl. asst. to chief justice Can., 1976-81; chief law editor Supreme Ct. Can., 1981-88, dep. registrar, 1988-90, registrar, 1990. Mem. Can. Bar Assn., Assn. Can. Ct. Adminstrs., Assn. Francophone Jurists, Can. Inst. Adminstrn. Justice, Assn. Reporters Jud. Decisions. Office: Supreme Ct of Can Office Reg, Wellington St., Ottawa, ON Canada K1A 0J1

ROLAND, BILLY RAY, electronics company executive; b. Grandview, Tex., June 12, 1926; s. Marvin Wesley and Minnie Mae (Martin) R.; m. Ruth Ranell Sheets, Mar. 9, 1950 (div. 1982); children: Carl Ray and Darla Kay (twins); m. Linda Sue Leslie, Feb. 21, 1986 (div. Nov. 1991); m. Martha Kay Redford, May 17, 1993. B.S., Tex. Christian U., 1954. C.P.A., Tex. Ticket and baggage agt. Southwestern Greyhound Co., Ft. Worth, 1943-44, 46-51; supr. acctg. dept. Tandy Leather Co., 1954-60; controller, asst. sec., treas. Tandy Corp., 1960-75, Tandy crafts, Inc., 1975-78; v.p. Tandy Corp., 1978-85, ret. V.p., treas. David L. Tandy Found., 1966—; mng. trustee James L. and Eunice West Charitable Trust, 1980-91; treas. Benjamin F. Johnston Found., 1984—. Served with inf. U.S. Army, 1944-46. Mem. Am. Inst. C.P.A.s, Tex. Soc. C.P.A.s, Ft. Worth Soc. C.P.A.s, Ft. Worth C. of C. Democrat. Methodist. Clubs: Colonial Country, Petroleum, Lake Country Golf and Country. Home: 8937 Random Rd Fort Worth TX 76179-2739

ROLAND, CHARLES GORDON, physician, medical historian, educator; b. Winnipeg, Man., Can., Jan. 25, 1933; s. John Sanford and Leona (McLaughlin) R.; m. Marjorie Ethel Kyles, 1953 (div. 1973); children: John Kenneth, Christopher Franklin, David Charles, Kathleen Siobhan; m.

Connie Rankin, 1979. Student, U. Toronto, Ont., Can., 1952-54; MD, U. Man., 1958, BSc, 1958. Intern St. Boniface Hosp., Man., 1958-59; pvt. practice medicine specializing in family medicine Tillsonburg, Ont., 1959-60, Grimsby, Ont., 1960-64; sr. editor Jour. Am. Med. Assn., Chgo., 1964-69; head sect. publs. Mayo Clinic, 1969-70, chmn. dept. biomed. communications, 1970-77; prof. history medicine, prof. biomed. communications, coordinator family practice track, chmn. adminstrv. com. dept. family medicine Mayo Med. Sch., 1971-77; mem. admissions, edn. and curriculum coordinators coms., hon. mem. med. staff West Lincoln Meml. Hosp., Grimsby; mem. grants com. Hannah Inst. History of Medicine, Toronto, 1974-77, 87-91, mem. publs. com., 1991-95; Jason A. Hannah prof. history of medicine McMaster U., Hamilton, Ont., Can., 1977—; assoc. mem. dept. history. McMaster U.; chmn. archives com. Faculty of Health Scis. McMaster U., Hamilton, Ont., Can., 1983—; chmn. spl. grants com. Hannah Inst. for History of Medicine, 1981-85; Sid W. Richardson vis. prof. Inst. Med. Humanities U. Tex. Med. Br., Galveston, 1984. Author: (with L.S. King) Scientific Writing, 1968, (with J.P. McGovern) William Osler, The Continuing Education, 1969, Good Scientific Writing, 1971, William Osler's The Master Word in Medicine: A Study in Rhetoric, 1972, (with L.S. Baker) You and Leukemia: A Day at a Time, 1976, (with P. Potter) An Annotated Bibliography of Canadian Medical Periodicals, 1826-1975, 1979, Clarence Meredith Hincks 1885-1964: Mental Health Crusader, 1990, Courage Under Seige:: Starvation, Disease and Death in the Warsaw Ghetto, 1992, Harold Nathan Segall: Pioneer Canadian Cardiologist, 1995; editor: (E.P. Scarlett) In Sickness and In Health, 1972; co-editor: An Annotated Checklist of Osleriana, 1976, Sir William Osler 1849-1919: A Selection for Medical Students, 1982, Health Disease and Medicine: Essays in Canadian History, 1984, Bibliography of Secondary Sources in Canadian Medical History, 1985, (with J.P. McGovern) The Collected Essays of Sir William Osler (3 vols.), 1985; editor, author introduction: Medical Topography of Upper Canada, 1985; (with Richard Golden) Sir William Osler: An Annotated Bibiography with Illustrations, 1987; co-editor: The Persisting Osler, 1984, The Persisting Osler II, 1994; editor in chief Can. Bulletin of Med. History, 1987-90; mem. editorial adv. bd. Canadian Family Physician, 1964-72, Chest, 1966—, Med. Communications, 1971-75, Postgrad. Med. Jour., London, 1967-72, Mayo Clinic Procs., 1969-77, Bioscis. Communications, 1975-80, Ont. Med. Rev., 1979-84, HSTC Jour., 1980-87, Can. Bull. Med. History, 1983-90, Med. History (London), 1982-87, Jour. History of Medicine and Allied Scis., 1991-94, 96—. Mem. bd. curators Osler Library, McGill U., Montreal, 1981—. Recipient Jason A. Hannah medal Royal Soc. Can., 1994. Fellow AAAS (council 1969-74), Am. Med. Writers Assn. (pres. 1969-70); mem. Can. Med. Assn., Am. Assn. History Medicine (sec.-treas. 1976-80, publs. com. 1979-85), Acad. Medicine Toronto (Grogan lecture com. 1978-83), Am. Mil. Inst., Internat. Inst. Prisoners of War, Soc. Internat. d'Histoire de la Medicine (internat. del. for Can. 1983-86), Can. Soc. for History of Medicine (v.p. 1982-87, pres. 1993-95), Soc. Med. History Chgo. (sec.-treas. 1966-69), Can. Ctr. for Studies in Hist. Horticulture (exec. com. 1982-89), Council Biology Editors, Med. Hist. Club Toronto (pres. 1977-78), Ont. Hist. Soc., Can. Hist. Assn., Bibliog. Soc. Can., Am. Osler Soc. (sec.-treas. 1975-85, v.p. 1985-86, pres. 1986-87), Japan Osler Soc. (hon.), Royal Soc. Medicine (London), Royal Can. Mil. Inst., Champlain Soc. (Toronto), History of Second World War (Can. com.), Soc. Army Hist. Reh, Sigma Xi. Clubs: Univ. (Rochester); Osler (London); Alpine of Can.; Literary (Chgo.). Office: McMaster U, 3N10-HSC Med Ctr 1200 Main St W, Hamilton, ON Canada L8N 3Z5

ROLAND, CRAIG WILLIAMSON, architect; b. Lincoln, Nebr., Feb. 20, 1935; s. Harold Eugene and Nell (Williamson) R.; m. Edith Shearman Shaw, July 30, 1960; 1 child, Leah. B.Arch., U. Wash. Pres. Roland/Miller/Assocs., Santa Rosa, Calif., 1966-93; vis. instr. U. Calif.-Berkeley, 1983-84. Mem., chmn. design rev. bd. City of Santa Rosa, 1973-76, mem. planning commn., 1976-78; pres. bd. Sonoma County YMCA, Santa Rosa, 1979—. Served with U.S. Army, 1957-58. Recipient numerous local, state and nat. archtl. design awards. Home: 5441 Buttercup Dr Santa Rosa CA 95404-9628 Office: Craig W Roland Arch 5441 Buttercup Dr Santa Rosa CA 95404-9628

ROLAND, DONALD EDWARD, printing company executive; b. Dalhart, Tex., Nov. 14, 1942; s. Vernon O. Roland and Doris M. (Cox) Roland Hutson; m. Kathleen Marie Bennett, Feb. 1, 1964; children—Aileen, Donald E., Jenny. B.S., Calif. State U.-Los Angeles, 1964; M.A., U. Calif.-Riverside, 1967; exec. mgmt. cert. UCLA, 1979, Claremont Grad. Sch., 1974. Dir. computer graphics Times Mirror Press, Los Angeles, 1966-78, plant mgr., 1978-81, v.p. prodn., 1981-83; group v.p. ops. Treasure Chest Advt., Glendora, Calif., 1983-84, sr. v.p. ops., 1984-93, exec. v.p. 1993-94, pres., CEO, 1995—. Republican. Home: 4 Norwood Rd Annapolis MD 21401 Office: Treasure Chest Advt 250 W Pratt St Baltimore MD 21201

ROLAND, FRANK H., textile products executive, chemicals executive; b. 1935. BS, U. Ala., 1957. CPA. With AMCA Internat. Corp., Hanover, N.H., 1967-86, H.H. Robertson Co., Pitts., 1986-88; with Halstead Industries Inc., Greensboro, N.C., 1988—, pres.; pres. Rubber Textile Corp., Roanoke, VA. Office: Rubber Textile Corp 5221 Valley Park Dr Roanoke VA 24019*

ROLAND, JOHN, newscaster; b. Pitts., Nov. 25, 1941; s. John Roland and Marion (Costlow) Gingher. BA in English., U. Calif., Long Beach, 1963. Rschr. NBC News, L.A., 1966-69; reporter KTTV, L.A., 1969; anchorman Fox News, N.Y.C., 1970—. Recipient Emmy award, 1978, 83, Pub. Svc. award Am. Fed. Govt. Employees Assn., 1974, Cert. of Appreciation, Goldwater Hosp., N.Y., 1975, N.Y. City Patrolman's Benevolent Assn. Journalism award, 1982, Good Samaritan award Bronx C. of C., 1983, Excelsior award N.Y.C. Coun., 1983, Man of the Yr. award N.Y.'s Finest Found., 1989; named Crimefighter of the Week, N.Y. Daily News, 1983. Mem. N.Y.C. Police Dept. Detective Endowment Assn. (hon.), Sigma Alpha Epsilon. Avocations: boating, tennis, golf. Office: Fox TV News 205 E 67th St New York NY 10021

ROLAND, RAYMOND WILLIAM, lawyer; b. Ocala, Fla., Jan. 3, 1947; s. Raymond W. and Hazel (Dunn) R.; m. Jane Allen, Dec. 28, 1968; children: John Allen, Jason William. BA, Fla. State U., 1969, JD, 1972. Bar: Fla. 1972, U.S. Dist. Ct. (no. dist.) Fla. 1973, U.S. Dist. Ct. (mid. dist.) Fla. 1985, U.S. Ct. Appeals (5th cir.) 1974, U.S. Ct. Appeals (11th cir.) 1983, U.S. Supreme Ct. 1985; cert. civil trial lawyer; cert. cir. ct. mediator. Assoc. Keen, O'Kelley & Spitz, Tallahassee, 1972-74, ptnr., 1974-77; ptnr., v.p. McConnaughhay, Roland, Maida & Cherr, P.A., Tallahassee, 1978—; mem. exec. bd. NW Fla. chpt. March of Dimes. Bd. dirs. So. Scholarship Found., Tallahassee, 1985-89, v.p. 1989. Mem. Internat. Assn. Def. Coun., Assn. Internat. Droit Assurance, Internat. Soc. Ins. Law (U.S. chpt.), Def. Rsch. Inst., Fla. Bar (mem. Judicial Adminstrn., Selection and Tenure com.), Fla. Def. Lawyers Assn., Tallahassee Bar Assn. (treas. 1979), Kiwanis (life, lt. gov. 1984-85), Capital City Kiwanis Club (Kiwanian of Yr. 1978, pres. 1979), Fla. Kiwanis Found. (life fellow). Republican. Baptist. Avocations: reading, hiking, camping, golf. Home: 1179 Ox Bottom Rd Tallahassee FL 32312-3519

ROLANDI, GIANNA, coloratura soprano; b. N.Y.C., Aug. 16, 1952; d. Enrico G. and Jane E. (Frazier); m. Andrew Davis, 1 child, Edward. Mus.B., artist diploma, opera cert., Curtis Inst. Music, 1975. Made operatic debut at, N.Y.C. Opera, 1975; numerous appearances N.Y.C. Opera, made Met. Opera debut, 1979, numerous appearances Met. Opera, 1979—; star roles in: Tales of Hoffman, Ariadne auf Naxos, Rigoletto, The Barber of Seville, Daughter of the Regiment, Giulio Cesare, The Cunning Little Vixen, Marriage of FigAro, Lucia di Lammermoor, others; appeared with major opera cos. and symphonies throughout U.S., Eng., France, Italy, Switzerland; (rec.) Marriage of Figaro-Mozart; (video) Arabella; numerous appearances on Live from Lincoln Ctr., PBS, Including Lucia di Lammermoor, Cunning Little Vixen. Winner Met. Opera Audition; Rockefeller grantee; Nat. Opera Inst. grantee.

ROLETT, ELLIS LAWRENCE, medical educator, cardiologist; b. N.Y.C., July 10, 1930; s. Daniel Meyer and Mary Elaine (Warshaw) R.; m. Virginia Ann Vladimir, Mar. 25, 1956; children: Roderic Lawrence, Barry Vladimir, Daniel Alfred. B.S., Yale U., 1952; M.D. cum laude, Harvard U., 1955. Diplomate: Am. Bd. Internal Medicine, Am. Bd. Cardiovascular Disease. Intern, resident in medicine Mass. Gen. Hosp., Boston, 1955-56, 59-61; asst. resident N.Y. Hosp.-Cornell U. Med. Ctr., N.Y.C., 1956-57; Am. Heart Assn. research fellow Peter Bent Brigham Hosp., Boston, 1961-63; mem. faculty U. N.C., Chapel Hill, 1963-74, then prof., 1971-74; prof. UCLA, 1974-77; chief cardiology VA Wadsworth Hosp., Los Angeles, 1974-77; prof. Dartmouth Med. Sch., Hanover, N.H., 1977—; chief cardiology Dartmouth-Hitchcock Med. Ctr., Hanover, N.H., 1977-87; vis. scientist August Krogh Inst., Copenhagen, 1984; mem. merit rev. bd. Cardiovascular studies VA, 1976-79, chmn., 1978-79; mem. regional rsch. rev. com. New Eng. Am. Heart Assn., 1978-83; mem. sci. bd. Stanley J. Sarnoff Endowment for Cardiovascular Sci., 1992—, chmn., 1994-95; literature section review com. Nat. Library Medicine, 1995—; dir. Vt.-Karelia (Russia) Med. Project, 1992—. Bd. dirs. N.H. affiliate Am. Heart Assn., 1978-85; pres. N.H. affiliate Am. Heart Assn., 1983-85. Served to capt. M.C. USAF, 1957-59. Recipient Lederle Med. Faculty award, 1965-68, USPHS Career Devel. award, 1967-72; grantee USPHS/NIH, 1964-76, VA Merit Rev. Rsch. Program, 1975-77, Mathers Found., 1984-86, 93—, Am. Heart Assn., 1989-91. Mem. AAAS, Am. Coll. Cardiology, Am. Fedn. Clin. Research, Am. Heart Assn., Am. Physiol. Soc., Internat. Soc. Heart Research, Phi Beta Kappa, Alpha Omega Alpha. Home: 4 Balch Hill Ln Hanover NH 03755-1622 Office: Dartmouth-Hitchcock Med Ctr Dept Cardiology Lebanon NH 03756

ROLEY, JERRY, bank executive; b. 1946. With Avco Corp., Silver Spring, Md., 1969-72, U.S. Ho. Rep. Credit Union, Washington, 1972-90; pres. U.S. Senate Credit Union, Washington, 1990—. With USAF, 1966-70. Office: US Senate FCU PO Box 77920 Washington DC 20013-8920

ROLF, TOM, film editor. Editor: (films) Lucky Lady, 1975, French Connection II, 1975, (with Marcia Lucas and Melvin Shapiro) Taxi Driver, 1976, Black Sunday, 1976, (with Marica Lucas) New York, New York, 1977, Blue Collar, 1978, Prophecy, 1979, Hard Core, 1979, (with Lisa Fruchtman, Jerry Greenberg, and William Reynolds) Heaven's Gate, 1980, Ghost Story, 1981, (with Glenn Farr, Fruchtman, Stephan A. Rotter, and Douglas Stewart) The Right Stuff, 1983 (Acad. award best film editing 1983), Wargames, 1983, Thief of Hearts, 1984, 9 1/s Weeks, 1986, Quicksilver, 1986, Outrageous Fortune, 1987, (with Michael Ripps) Stakeout, 1987 (with Seth Flaum and William Gordean) The Great Outdoors, 1988, Black Rain, 1989, Jacob's Ladder, 1990, Sneakers, 1992, (with Trudy Ship) The Pelican Brief, 1993, Mr. Jones, 1993, Dangerous Minds, 1994 (with Dov Hoenig, Pat Bulba, Bill Goldenberg) Heat, 1995. Mem. Am. Cinema Editors (pres.). Home: 12417 Mulholland Dr Beverly Hills CA 90210-1336 Office: Broder Kurland Webb Uffner Agency 9242 Beverly Blvd Ste 200 Beverly Hills CA 90210-3710

ROLFE, JOHN L., lawyer; b. Washington, Jan. 30, 1944. BS in Econs., U. Pa., 1966, JD, 1969; LLM in Taxation, Temple U., 1984. Bar: Pa. 1970, U.S. Dist. Ct. (ea. dist.) Pa. 1970, U.S. Ct. Appeals (4th cir.) 1970, U.S. Ct. Appeals (3d cir.) 1976, N.Y. 1977, U.S. Dist. Ct. (no. dist.) N.Y. 1977, U.S. Supreme Ct. 1977, U.S. Tax Ct. 1984, U.S. Claims Ct. 1984. Law clk. U.S. Ct. Appeals for 4th Cir., Richmond, Va., 1969-71; asst. defender Phila. Pub. Defender's Office, Phila., 1971-72; asst. atty. gen. Pa. Crime Commn., St. Davids, 1972-74; pvt. practice, Devon, Pa., 1974-92; shareholder, seminar presenter Rolfe & Rosenbaum, P.C., Devon, Pa., 1992—. Author: Affirmations Book for Sharing, 1990. Sec. St. Lawrence County Environ. Mgmt. Coun., Canton, N.Y., 1979-80. Avocations: badminton, karate, writing movie scripts. Office: 222 Lancaster Ave Ste 349 Devon PA 19333

ROLFE, MICHAEL N., management consulting firm executive; b. Chgo., Sept. 9, 1937; s. Mark Alexander and Antoinette (Wittgenstein) R.; m. Judith Mary Lewis, June 16, 1959; children—Andrew, Lisa, James. A.B. in Econs., U. Mich., 1959; MBA, U. Chgo., 1996. Sales staff Lewis Co., Northbrook, Ill., 1961-62; systems mgmt. staff Brunswick Corp., Chgo., 1962-68; v.p. Kearney Mgmt. Cons., Chgo., 1968-81; ptnr. KPMG/Peat Marwick, Chgo., 1981-92; dir. Keystone Group, Evanston, Ill., 1992—. Author: AMA Management Handbook, 1969. Bd. dirs. Common, Chgo., 1972-75, U. Chgo. Cancer Rsch., 1985-88, Am. Cancer Soc., Chgo., 1985—; trustee Michael Reese Med. Ctr., 1986-91; pres. Sch. Bd. Dist. 113, Highland Park, Ill., 1977-83, Sch.Dist. 113 Found., 1993—; mem. Am. Jewish Com., 1996—. Lt. (j.g.) USNR, 1959-61. Clubs: Northmoor Country (Highland Park); Standard (Chgo.). Home: 800 Deerfield Rd Apt 109 Highland Park IL 60035-3531 Office: Keystone Group 1560 Sherman Ave Evanston IL 60201-3624

ROLFE, ROBERT MARTIN, lawyer; b. Richmond, Va., May 16, 1951; s. Norman and Bertha (Cohen) R.; m. Catherine Dennis Stone, July 14, 1973; children: P. Alexander, Asher B., Joel A., Zachary A. BA, U. Va., 1973, JD, 1976. Bar: Va. 1976, N.Y. 1985, U.S. Dist. Ct. (ea. and we. dists.) Va. 1976, U.S. Supreme Ct. 1979, U.S. Ct. Appeals (4th cir.) 1976, U.S. Ct. Appeals (2d cir.) 1979, U.S. Dist. Ct. (ea. dist.) Mich. 1985, U.S. Ct. Appeals (D.C. cir.) 1985, U.S. Dist. Ct. (so. dist. and ea. dist.) N.Y. 1985; U.S. Ct. Appeals (7th cir.) 1995. Assoc. Hunton & Williams, Richmond, 1976-83, ptnr., 1983—. Contbr. articles to profl. jours. Bd. dirs. Jewish Family Svcs., Richmond, pres., 1993-95; bd. mgrs., 2d v.p. Congregation Beth Ahabah, 1995—. Mem. ABA (litigation sect., natural resources, energy and environ. law sect.), Va. Bar Assn., Va. State Bar, Richmond Bar Assn., Am. Arbitration Assn. (comml. arbitrators panel), Order of Coif (Alumni award for acad. excellence U. Va. 1976). Home: 18 Greenway Ln Richmond VA 23226-1630 Office: Hunton & Williams Riverfront Plz East Tower 951 E Byrd St Richmond VA 23219-4040 Also: 200 Park Ave New York NY 10166-0005

ROLFE, ROBIN ANN, trade association executive, lawyer; b. Mineola, N.Y., July 10, 1949; d. Justin B. and Joan (Sussman) R.; m. Edward F. Simpson, Aug. 22, 1971 (div. Oct. 1976); m. Arnold L. Saltzman, May 12, 1985. BA, Pa. State U., 1971; JD cum laude, Seton Hall U., 1977. Bar: N.J. 1977. Paralegal Jackson and Nash, N.Y.C., 1971-73; paralegal Lowenstein, Sandler, Kohl, Fisher and Boylan, Roseland, N.J., 1973-77, assoc., 1977-80; trademark atty. Chesebrough-Pond's Inc., Greenwich, Conn., 1980-81; exec. dir. Internat. Trademark Assn. (formerly U.S. Trademark Assn.), N.Y.C., 1981—; pres. Brand Names Edn. Found., N.Y.C., 1988—. mem. adv. bd. Ctr. for Legal Studies Montclair State Coll., 1983—; regional coord. alumni admissions program Pa. State U., No. N.J., 1986-95. Mem. ABA, N.J. Bar Assn., Am. Soc. Assn. Execs. Home: 300 Gorge Rd Cliffside Park NJ 07010-2759 Office: Internat Trademark Assn 1133 Avenue Of The Americas New York NY 10036-6710

ROLFE, RONALD STUART, lawyer; b. N.Y.C., Sept. 5, 1945; s. Nat and Florence I. (Roth) R.; m. Yvonne Susan Quinn, Sept. 1, 1979; 1 child, Andrew Quinn. AB, Harvard U., 1966; JD, Columbia U., 1969. Bar: N.Y. 1969, U.S. Ct. Appeals (2d cir.) 1970, U.S. Dist. Ct. (so. and ea. dists.) N.Y. 1971, U.S. Supreme Ct. 1973, U.S. Ct. Appeals (9th cir.) 1977, U.S. Dist. Ct. (no. dist.) Calif. 1982, U.S. Ct. Appeals (5th cir.) 1982, U.S. Ct. Appeals (6th cir.) 1984, U.S. Dist. Ct. (ea. dist.) Ky. 1984, U.S Ct. Appeals (fed. cir.). Law clk. to judge U.S. Dist. Ct. (so. dist.) N.Y., 1969-70; assoc. Cravath, Swaine & Moore, 1970-77, ptnr., 1977—. Sec. bd. trustees Allen-Stevenson Sch., 1981-91, pres., 1992—; trustee Lawrenceville Sch., 1987—; v.p., trustee Prep for Prep. Kent and Stone scholar, 1969; mem. bd. visitors Columbia Law Sch. Fellow Am. Bar Found.; mem. ABA, N.Y. State Bar Assn., Assn. of Bar of City of N.Y., Fed. Bar Coun. (trustee 1989-94), Am. Law Inst., Harvard Club, Univ. Club, Stanwich Club (Greenwich, Conn.), Turf and Field Club (N.Y.C.), Royal Automobile Club (London). Office: Cravath Swaine & Moore Worldwide Plz 825 8th Ave New York NY 10019-7475

ROLFE, STANLEY THEODORE, civil engineer, educator; b. Chgo., July 7, 1934; s. Stanley T. and Eunice (Fike) R.; m. Phyllis Williams, Aug. 11, 1956; children: David Stanley, Pamela Kay, Kathleen Ann. B.S., U. Ill., 1956, M.S., 1958, Ph.D., 1962. Registered profl. engr., Pa., Kans. Supr. structural-evaluation sect. ordnance products div. U.S. Steel Corp., 1962-69, div. chief mech. behavior of metals div., 1969; A.P. Learned prof. civil engring. U. Kans., 1969—, chmn. civil engring. dept., 1975—; Chmn. metall. studies panel ship research com. Nat. Acad. Scis., 1967-70. Co-author: Fracture and Fatigue Control in Structures—Applications of Fracture Mechanics; co-author: textbook Strength of Materials; Contbr.: numerous articles to profl. jours. T.R. Higgins lectr., 1980; Recipient Sam Tour award Am. Soc. Testing Materials, 1971, H.E. Gould Distinguished Teaching award U. Kans., 1972, 75, AWS Adams Meml. Educator award, 1974; U. Ill. Civil Engring. Disting. Service award, 1985, U. Ill. Coll. Engring. Alumni Honor award Disting. Service in Engring., 1987; U. Kans. Irvin E. Youngberg research award, 1985. Mem. Nat. Acad. Engring., ASCE (chmn. task force on fracture, State of Art award 1983), Am. Soc. Testing Materials, ASME, Soc. Exptl. Stress Analysis, Am. Soc. Engring. Edn., Chi Psi. Presbyterian. Home: 821 Sunset Dr Lawrence KS 66044-2433

ROLL, DAVID LEE, lawyer; b. Pontiac, Mich., May 1, 1940; s. Everett Edgar and Garnette (Houts) R.; m. Nancy E. Roll, Aug. 17, 1963; children: Richard, Molly. BA cum laude, Amherst Coll., 1962; JD, U. Mich., 1964. Bar: Mich. 1965, U.S. Dist. Ct. (ea. dist.) Mich. 1965, U.S. Ct. Appeals (6th cir.) 1969, D.C. 1974, U.S. Dist. Ct. D.C. 1975, U.S. Supreme Ct. 1975, U.S. Ct. Appeals (4th cir.) 1976, U.S. Ct. Appeals (D.C. cir.) 1983, U.S. Ct. Appeals (3rd and 11th cirs.) 1985, U.S. Ct. Appeals (9th cir.) 1992, U.S. Ct. Appeals (fed. cir.) 1993. Assoc. Hill, Lewis, Detroit, 1965-70, ptnr., 1970-72; asst. dir. gen. litigation Bur. of Competition Fed. Trade Commn., Washington, 1972-75; ptnr. Steptoe & Johnson, Washington, 1975-93, chmn., 1993—. Mem. ABA (chair Robinson Patman Act com., antitrust sect. 1984-86, Clayton Act com., antitrust sect. 1986-88, Energy Litigation com., litigation sect. 1992—, mem. task force on indsl. competitiveness 1987, coun., antitrust sect. 1988-91, author, editor antitrust sect.). Office: 1330 Connecticut Ave NW Washington DC 20036-1704

ROLL, IRWIN CLIFFORD (WIN ROLL), advertising, marketing and publishing executive; b. N.Y.C., Aug. 21, 1925; s. Arnold and Bertha (Vogel) R.; m. Marilyn Witlin, Apr. 10, 1949; children: Richard J., Douglas W. B.B.A. magna cum laude, CCNY, 1948; postgrad., Columbia U., 1952. Asst. advt. mgr. Standard Motor Products, Inc., Long Island City, N.Y., 1948-50; advt. and sales promotion exec. RCA, Harrison, N.J., 1950-54; account exec. Fuller & Smith & Ross, Inc., N.Y.C., 1954-59; group v.p. Fuller & Smith & Ross, Inc., 1959-66; pres., dir. Henderson & Roll, Inc., advt. and pub. relations agy., 1966-77; pres., dir., chief exec. officer Henderson, Roll & Friedlich, Inc., 1977-79; chmn. bd., treas., chief exec. officer, dir. Listfax Corp., nat. computerized info. services co., 1966-79; pres., CEO Win Roll and Co., Inc., N.Y.C., 1979-89; chmn. bd. Roll-Bender Research, 1980-82, Devonshire Communications, Ltd., 1980-83; sr. v.p. Tradewell Industries, Inc., 1983-87; exec. v.p. Internat. Mktg. Sys. Inc., 1988-90; pres. Concord Cons. Group, 1990—; corp. devel. dir. Ind. Media Svcs., Inc., 1990-92; pres., chief ops. officer, bd. dirs. Megaworld, Inc., 1993—. Mem. mktg. com. Nat. Multiple Sclerosis Soc.; bd. dirs. Westchester County chpt. Multiple Sclerosis Soc., 1983-89; pres. Rosedale Residential Assn., 1983-85, bd. dirs., 1980—. With U.S. Army, 1943-46, ETO. Mem. Ad-Net Nat. Advt. Orgn. (bd. dirs. 1983-90, pres. 1986-88), Adv. Club of N.Y., Beta Gamma Sigma (bd. dirs., v.p. N.Y. Alumni chpt. 1986-89, pres. 1989-91, adv. bd. 1991—), Alpha Delta Sigma. Home: 11 Cedarwood Rd White Plains NY 10605-5331

ROLL, JOHN MCCARTHY, judge; b. Pitts., Feb. 8, 1947; s. Paul Herbert and Esther Marie (McCarthy) R.; m. Maureen O'Connor, Jan. 24, 1970; children: Robert McCarthy, Patrick Michael, Christopher John. B.A., U. Ariz., 1969, J.D., 1972, LLM U. Va., 1990. Bar: Ariz. 1972, U.S. Dist. Ct. Ariz. 1974, U.S. Ct. Appeals (9th cir.) 1980, U.S. Supreme Ct. 1977. Asst. pros. atty. City of Tucson, 1973; dep. county atty. Pima County (Ariz.), 1973-80; asst. U.S. atty. U.S. Atty.'s Office, Tucson, 1980-87; judge Ariz. Ct. Appeals, 1987-91, U.S. Dist. Ct. Ariz., 1991—; lectr. Nat. Coll. Dist. Attys. U. Houston, 1976-87; mem. criminal justice mental health standards project ABA, 1980-83. Contbr. to Trial Techniques Compendium, 1978, 82, 84, Merit Selection: The Arizona Experience, Arizona State Law Journal, 1991, The Rules Have Changed: Amendments to the Rules of Civil Procedure, Defense Law Journal, 1994. Coach, Frontier Baseball Little League, Tucson, 1979-84; mem. parish coun. Sts. Peter and Paul Roman Catholic Ch., Tucson, 1983-91, chmn., 1986-91; mem. Roman Cath. Diocese of Tucson Sch. Bd., 1986-90. Recipient Disting. Faculty award Nat. Coll. Dist. Attys., U. Houston, 1979, Outstanding Alumnus award U. Ariz. Coll. Law, 1992. Mem. Am. Judicature Soc., Fed. Judges Assn., Pima County Bar Assn. Republican. Lodge: K.C. (adv. coun. 10441). Office: US Dist Ct 55 E Broadway Blvd Tucson AZ 85701-1719

ROLL, TERESA J., restaurant chain executive; b. 1952. JD, U. Kans., 1982. Lawyer Wichita, Kans., 1982-86; with Lake Mich. Mgmt. Co., Milw., 1986—, pres., treas., 1989—. Office: Lake MI Mgmt Co 3333 N Mayfair Rd Ste 214 Milwaukee WI 53222-3219*

ROLLAND, DONALD F., printing company executive. CEO Big Flower Press, Glendora, Calif. Office: Big Flower Press 511 W Citrus Edge Glendora CA 91740

ROLLAND, IAN MCKENZIE, insurance executive; b. Fort Wayne, Ind., June 3, 1933; s. David and Florence (Hunte) R.; m. Miriam V. Flickinger, July 3, 1955; children: Cheri L., Lawrence D., Robert A., Carol Ann, Sara K. B.A., DePauw U., 1955; M.A. in Actuarial Sci., U. Mich., 1956. With Lincoln Nat. Life Ins. Co., Ft. Wayne, 1956—, sr. v.p., 1973-75, pres., 1977-81, chief exec. officer, 1977-91, chmn., pres., 1981-92, chmn., chief exec. officer, 1992—; pres. Lincoln Nat. Corp., 1975-91, CEO, 1977-91, chmn., CEO, 1992—; bd. dirs. K&K Ins. Cos., No. Ind. Pub. Svc., Lincoln Fin. Corp., GTE North, Inc., Tokheim Corp., Am. States Ins. Cos., 1st Penn-Pacific Ins. Co., The Richard Leahy Corp., Vantage Global Advisors, Inc.; past chmn. Am. Coun. Life Ins.; mem. exec. com. Assn. Ind. Life Ins. Cos. Mem. adv. bd. Ind. U.-Purdue U., 1977, Fort Wayne Leadership, Fort Wayne Community Found., Corp. Innovation Devel. Ventures; bd. dirs. Associated Colls. Ind., Corp. Innovation Devel.; chmn. Ind. Fiscal Policy Com.; trustee Hudson Inst.; mem. Indiana Acad. Mem. Soc. Actuaries, Acad. Actuaries, Health Ins. Assn. Am., Am. Council Life Ins. (past chmn. bd. dirs.), Assoc. Ind. Life Ins. Cos. (exec. com.), Ind. Ins. Soc. (bd. dirs.), Internat. Ins. Soc. (bd. dirs.), Ind. C. of C. (mem. exec. com.). Office: Lincoln Nat Corp 200 E Berry St Fort Wayne IN 46802-2706

ROLLAND, LUCIEN G., paper company executive; b. St. Jerome, Que., Can., Dec. 21, 1916; s. Olivier and Aline (Dorion) R.; m. Marie de Lorimier, May 30, 1942; children: Nicolas, Natalie, Stanislas, Dominique, Christine, Etienne, David. Student, Coll. Jean de Brebeuf, Montreal; Profl. Engr., Loyola Coll., U. Montreal, B.A., B.A.Sc., C.E., also D.C.Sc. (hon.), 1960. Registered profl. engr. With Rolland Paper Co. Ltd. (name changed to Rolland inc. 1979), 1942—, v.p., gen. mgr., 1952, pres., gen. mgr., 1952-78, pres., CEO, 1978—, chmn., pres., CEO, 1984, chmn., CEO, 1985, chmn., 1991; cons. in field, 1995; pres. Tarascon Holdings, Inc. Bd. govs. Notre-Dame Hosp., Montreal Children's Hosp., Montreal Gen. Hosp., Hôpital Marie Enfant. Decorated Knight Comdr. Order St. Gregory, officer Order of Can. Mem. Can. Pulp and Paper Assn. (hon.), Corp. Profl. Engrs., Montreal Bd. Trade, Province of Que., C of C, Montreal C. of C., Engring. Inst. Can. Home: Apt B-60, 1321 Sherbrooke St W, Montreal, PQ Canada H3G 1J4 Office: Rolland Inc, 2 Rolland Ave, Saint Jerome, PQ Canada J7Z 5S1 Office: Tarascon Inc, 1200 McGill College #1100, Montreal, PQ Canada H3B 4G7

ROLLANS, JAMES O., service company executive; b. Glendale, Calif., July 7, 1942; s. Henry Leo and Geraldine Ada (Berg) R.; children: Jodie Helene, Thomas James, Daniel Joseph. BS, Calif. State U., Northridge, 1967. Vice pres., dir. Chase Manhattan Bank, 1976-78; v.p. corp. communications Dart Industries, Los Angeles, 1978-80; v.p. bus. analysis and investor relations Dart & Kraft, Chgo., 1980-82; sr. v.p., chief adminstrv. officer Fluor Corp., Irvine, Calif., 1982—; bd. dirs. Plaza Comm., Lafayette Pharms. Corp., Irvine Med. Ctr. Mem. BW/IP, Inc. Episcopalian. Avocations: boating; skiing; fishing; hunting. Office: Fluor Corp 3333 Michelson Dr Irvine CA 92730

ROLLE, ANDREW F., historian, educator, author; b. Providence, Apr. 12, 1922; m. Frances Squires, Dec. 1945 (div.); children: John Warren, Alexander Frederick, Julia Elisabeth.; m. Myra Moss, Nov. 1983. B.A., Occidental Coll., 1943; M.A., UCLA, 1949, Ph.D., 1953; grad., So. Calif. Psychoanalytic Inst., 1976. Am. vice consul Genoa, Italy, 1945-48; editorial asso. Pacific Hist. Rev., 1952-53; from asst. prof. to Cleland prof. history Occidental Coll., 1953-88; rsch. scholar Huntington Libr., San Marino, Calif., 1988—. Author: Riviera Path, 1946, An American in California, 1956, reprinted, 1982, The Road to Virginia City, 1960, reprinted, 1989, Lincoln: A Contemporary Portrait, 1961, (with Allan Nevins, Irving Stone) California: A History, 1963, rev. edits., 1969, 78, 87, Occidental College: The First Seventy-Five Years, 1963, The Lost Cause: Confederate Exiles in Mexico, 1965, 1992, The Golden State, 1967, rev. edit., 1978, 1989,

California, A Student Guide, 1965, Los Angeles, A Student Guide, 1965; Editor: A Century of Dishonor (Helen Hunt Jackson), 1964, Life in California (Alfred Robinson), 1971; The Immigrant Upraised, 1968, The American Italians: Their History and Culture, 1972, Gli Emigrati Vittoriosi, 1973; (with George Knoles others) Essays and Assays, 1973, (with others) Studies in Italian American Social History, 1975, (with others) Los Angeles: The Biography of a City, 1976, 2d edit., 1991, (with Allan Weinstein and others) Crisis in America, 1977, The Italian Americans: Troubled Roots, 1980, 2d edit. 1985, Los Angeles: From Pueblo to Tomorrow's City, 1981, 2nd edit., 1995, Occidental College: A Centennial History, 1986, John Charles Frémont: Character as Destiny, 1991, Henry Mayo Newhall and His Times, 1992. Served to 1st lt. M.I. AUS, 1943-45, 51-52. Decorated Cavaliere Ordine Merito Italy; recipient silver medal Italian Ministry Fgn. Affairs; Commonwealth award for non-fiction; Huntington Library-Rockefeller Found. fellow; resident scholar Rockefeller Found. Center, Bellagio, Italy. Fellow Calif. Hist. Soc.; mem. Phi Beta Kappa. Office: Huntington Libr Rsch Div San Marino CA 91108

ROLLE, CHRISTOPHER DAVIES, lawyer; b. Tokyo, Dec. 25, 1951; s. Norman Benjamin and Mavis Cameron (Williams) R.; children: Christopher Davies Jr., Zachery B. BA, Ark. State U., 1974; JD, Stetson U., 1977. Bar: Fla. 1978, U.S. Dist. Ct. (mid. dist.) Fla. 1979, U.S. Dist. Ct. (no. and so. dists.) Fla. 1980, U.S. Ct. Appeals (5th cir.) 1979, U.S. Ct. Appeals (11th cir.) 1981, U.S. Supreme Ct. 1981. Asst. state's atty. 20th Jud. Cir., Ft. Myers, Fla., 1978; atty. securities fraud unit and office compt. State of Fla., Tampa, 1978-79; asst. atty. gen. adminstrv. law sect. State of Fla., Tallahassee, 1979-83; ea. regional counsel Nat. Med. Enterprises, Inc., Tampa, 1983-84; gen. counsel, v.p. Retirement Corp. Am., Bradenton, Fla., 1984-85; with Holland & Knight, Bradenton and Orlando, Fla., 1985-88; assoc. Baker & Hostetler, Orlando, Fla., 1988-90; ptnr. Foley & Lardner, Orlando, 1990—; mem. health com. Orlando Naval Tng. Ctr. Reuse Commn. Editorial bd. Physician's Mktg. and Mgmt. Chmn. Jim Smith's gubernatorial campaign, Bradenton, 1986; bd. dirs. Retirement Housing Coun., 1985-87, v.p., 1986-87, Health Care Ctr. for Homeless, Inc.; chmn. bd. dirs. Children's Wish Found., Orlando, 1988—; grad. Leadership Orlando, 1990-91. Named one of Outstanding Young Men Am., 1988. Mem. ABA (forum on health law), Fla. Bar Assn. (vice chmn. commn. on elderly 1990-91, pub. rels. com. 1988-92, vice chmn. health law com. 1987-88, adminstrv. law sect. exec. coun., founding mem., exec. coun. health law sect. 1988-91, chmn. 1989-90), Manatee County Bar Assn. (treas. 1987-88), Orange County Bar Assn., Fla. Hosp. Assn., Fla. Acad. Healthcare Attys. (bd. dirs.), Am. Hosp. Assn., Am. Acad. Healthcare Attys., Nat. Health Lawyers Assn., Greater Orlando C. of C., Lambda Chi Alpha. Office: Foley & Lardner 111 N Orange Ave Ste 1800 Orlando FL 32801-2387

ROLLE, ESTHER, actress; b. Pompano Beach, Fla., Nov. 8; d. Jonathan Rolle. Student, Spellman Coll., Hunter Coll., New Sch. for Social Research. Dancer, Shogola Obola Dance Co., then mem., Negro Ensemble Co.; off-Broadway debut: The Blacks, 1962; London stage debut: God is a (Guess What?), 1969; numerous stage appearances include Macbeth, Amen Corner, Blues for Mister Charlie, Don't Play Us Cheap; toured Scandinavia in stage prdn. The Skin of Our Teeth; toured Australia, New Zealand in stage prdns. Black Nativity; other stage prdns. The Member of the Wedding, 1988, Nothing But a Man, 1964, Cleopatra Jones, 1973, Don't Play Us Cheap, 1973, P.K. and the Kid, 1982, Driving Miss Daisy, 1989, The Mighty Quinn, 1989, Color Adjustment, 1991, House of Cards, 1993, Nobody's Girls, 1994; TV series include Maude, 1972-74, One Life to Live, 1972-74, Good Times, 1974-77, 78-79, Singer and Sons, 1990; TV appearances include Summer of My German Soldier, 1979 (Emmy award 1979), I Know Why the Caged Bird Sings, 1979, Age Old Friends, 1989, The Kid Who Loved Christmas, 1990, Dinah's Place, N.Y.P.D., Like It Is, East Side, West Side, To Dance with a White Dog, 1993, Message From Nam, 1993, Scarlet, 1994. Hon. chmn. Pres.'s Com. on Employment of Handicapped.; Grand Marshall Cherry Blossom Festival, Washington, 1975. Named Woman of Yr. 3d World Sisterhood, 1976; recipient Image awards, NAACP, 1973, 74, 79, Leadership award, 1990, Hall of Fame, 1987; guest Bahamian gov. dedication Nat. Bank, 1993. Office: William Morris Agy 152 S El Camino Dr Beverly Hills CA 90212-2705*

RÖLLER, HERBERT ALFRED, biology and medical scientist, educator; b. Magdeburg, Germany, Aug. 2, 1927; came to U.S., 1962; s. Alfred H. and Elfriede (Wartner) R.; m. Manuela R. Buresch, Dec. 20, 1957. Abiturium, Christian Thomasius Schule, Halle/Saale, 1946; Dr.rer.nat., Georg August U., Goettingen, 1962. Project assoc. zoology U. Wis., Madison, 1962-65; asst. prof. pharmacology U. Wis., 1965-66, research assoc. zoology, 1966-67, assoc. prof. zoology, 1967-68; prof. biology Tex. A&M U., 1968-83, prof. biochemistry and biophysics, 1974-83, dir. Inst. Devel. Biology, 1973-83, Disting. prof., 1977—, Alumni prof., 1980-85; v.p. research Zoecon Corp., Palo Alto, Calif., 1968-72, sci. adv., 1972-85, chief scientist, Zoecon Research Inst., Palo Alto, 1985-88; sci. adv. European Community, 1988—; sci. adv. Affymax Rsch. Inst., Palo Alto, 1989—; adv. panel regulatory biology, div. biol. and med. scis. NSF, 1969-72; mem. Internat. Centre Insect Physiology and Ecology, Nairobi, Kenya, 1970—, dir. research, 1970-75. Editorial bd.: Jour. Chem. Ecology, 1974—; Contbr. articles to profl. publs. Recipient Disting. Achievement award for research Tex. A&M U., 1976. Fellow Tex. Acad. Sci.; mem. Deutsche Akademie Naturforscher Leopoldina, AAAS, Am. Soc. Zoologists, Entomol. Soc. Am., Am. Soc. Devel. Biology, Sigma Xi. Home: 824 N Rosemary Dr Bryan TX 77802-4309

ROLLER, ROBERT DOUGLAS, III, psychiatrist; b. Charleston, W.Va., Nov. 17, 1928; s. Francis Oliver and Mary Elizabeth (Rice) R.; m. Anthonia Ijsselstein, Mar. 7, 1970; children: Robert Douglas IV, Katherine Willis, David Nelson, Anthonia Elizabeth, Alexander Robert, John Richard. BA, U. Va., 1950, MD, 1960; postgrad. in philosophy, U. Pa., 1953-56. Tchr. Chestnut Hill Acad. Phila./Raven Soc., U. Va., 1953-56; intern U. N.C. Hosp., Chapel Hill, 1960-61, resident, 1961-62; resident Med. Coll. of Va., Richmond, 1963; NIMH research and teaching fellow U. Calif. Med. Ctr., San Francisco, 1963-66; pvt. practice Berkeley, 1966—; assoc. psychiatrist, rsch. psychiatrist U. Calif., Berkeley, 1965-71; clin. asst. prof. U. Calif. Med. Sch., San Francisco, 1970—; clin. instr. Stanford U. Med. Sch., Palo Alto, Calif., 1969-78, C.G. Jung Analytic Inst., 1964-72; mem. staff Alta Bates Hosp., 1971—, Lodi (Calif.) Meml. Hosp., 1971—, Cmty. Hosp., 1971-88; chief psychiatrist Clear Water Ranch for Children, Santa Rosa, Calif., 1964-71. Mem. Episcopal and Presbyn. Ch. With USNR, 1950-51. Mem. Farmington Country Club (Charlottesville, Va.), U. Calif. Faculty Club, St. Anthony Club of N.Y., St. Elmo Club (Va.), Sleepy Hollow Tennis Club, Bankers Club of San Francisco, Phila. Cricket Club. Home: 757 San Diego Rd Berkeley CA 94707-2025 Office: 2999 Regent St Ste 422 Berkeley CA 94705-2119

ROLLER, THOMAS BENJAMIN, manufacturing company executive; b. Phila., Mar. 4, 1950; s. Clarence Thomas and Anne Dolores (Marrese) R.; m. Christine Louise Rebman, Oct. 14, 1978; children: Thomas Nathaniel, Laura Anne, Elizabeth Anne. BA, Clemson U., 1972; MBA, Duke U., 1974. Fin. analyst E.I. duPont de Nemours & Co., Wilmington, Del., 1974-75; sr. fin. analyst Rockwell Internat. Corp., Pitts., 1975-77; mgr. acquisitions Rockwell Internat. Corp., Troy, Mich., 1978, mgr. bus. planning, 1979; dir. worldwide bus. devel. Rockwell Internat. Corp., London, 1979-81; v.p. mktg. automotive div. United Techs., Lausanne, Switzerland, 1981-83; v.p. corp. planning carrier United Techs., Syracuse, N.Y., 1984-85, v.p., gen. mgr. replacement components div., 1985-87, pres. residential products div., 1988-90; pres., CEO Plywood Panels, Inc., New Orleans, 1990-92; CEO Fruehauf Trailer Corp., Indpls., 1992—. Com. mem. U.S. Dept. Commerce Indsl. Sector Adv. Com. Capital Goods, Washington, 1986-89; pres. adv. Clemson U., 1990—; bd. dirs. alumni coun. Fuqua Sch. Bus. Duke U., Durham, N.C., 1985-87. Republican. Avocations: fishing, N.Am. archaeology.

ROLLHAUS, PHILIP EDWARD, JR., diversified manufacturing corporation executive; b. Phila., Sept. 29, 1934; s. Philip Edward and Elizabeth Snow (Bedford) R.; m. Jacqueline Merrill, Feb. 13, 1965 (div. 1975); children: Natalie, Philip Edward III; m. Barbara Lynn Walker, Oct. 8, 1983. BA in English Lit., Wesleyan U., 1956. Dir. gen. Société Rollhaus, Paris, 1960-64; regional mgr. Bus. Internat., Chgo., 1964-67; mgr. pvt. placements Woolard & Co., Chgo., 1967-69; founder, chmn., CEO Quixote Corp., Chgo., 1969—, pres., 1969-95; bd. dirs. Chgo. Capital Fund., 1986-91, DeVry, Inc., 1987-90, Keller Grad . Sch. Mgmt., Chgo., 1974-87, Alliance Francaise de Chicago, 1993—; mem. Am. Bus. Conf., Washington, 1987—; chmn. Starlight Found., Chgo., 1986-88, Gastro-Intestinal Rsch. Found., Chgo., 1984-90; trustee Inst. Psychoanalysis, Chgo., 1983-89, Nat. Symphony Orch., Washington, 1989-92; bd. assocs. Gallaudet U., Washington, 1993—; mem. adv. bd. Inst. Internat. Edn., 1995—; active Wilson coun. Woodrow Wilson Internat. Ctr. for Scholars, Washington, 1995—. Served to lt. (j.g.) USN, 1956-60. Mem. Econ. Club of Chgo., Soc. Mayflower Descs., Chicago Club, Racquet Club, Tavern Club, Bath and Tennis Club (Palm Beach, Fla.), Palm Beach Yacht Club, Shelter Island (N.Y.) Yacht Club, Bohemian Club (San Francisco), Metro. Club (Washington). Home: 1500 N Lake Shore Dr Chicago IL 60610-1624 Office: Quixote Corp 1 E Wacker Dr Fl 30 Chicago IL 60601

ROLLIN, BERNARD ELLIOT, philosophy educator, consultant on animal ethics; b. N.Y.C., Feb. 18, 1943; s. Phillip and Yetta Ethel (Bookchin) R.; m. Linda Mae Schieber, Aug. 30, 1964; 1 child, Michael David Hume. BA, CCNY, 1964; PhD, Columbia U., 1972. Preceptor Columbia U., N.Y.C., 1968-69; asst. prof. philosophy Colo. State U., Ft. Collins, 1969-73, assoc. prof., 1973-78, prof., 1978—, prof. physiology and biophysics, 1980—, dir. bioethical planning, 1981—; cons. Can., Australian, South African, The Netherlands, and U.S. govts., various univs. and agys. including U. Calif., Berkeley, Wash. State U., U. Fla., USDA, NIH, 1980—, United Airlines, Denver, 1985—; lectr. on animal ethics, 1978—. Author: Natural and Conventional Meaning, 1976, Animal Rights and Human Morality, 1981, 2d edit., 1992 (Outstanding Acad. Book award Choice Mag. Am. Assn. U. Librs., 1982, Gustavus Meyers Ctr. award for study of human rights 1993), The Unheeded Cry, 1989, The Experimental Animal in Biomedical Research, 1990, vol. 2, 1995, The Frankenstein Syndrome: Ethical and Social Issues in the Genetic Engineering of Animals, 1995, Farm Animal Welfare, 1995; mem. editl. bd. Jour. AVMA, Between the Species, Agrl. Ethics, Acta Semiotica et Linguistica, Studies in Animal Welfare Sci., numerous others; contbr. articles to profl. jours. Recipient Harris T. Guard award Colo. State U., 1981, honors prof., 1983; Waco F. Childers award Am. Humane Assn., 1982, svc. award Colo. Vet. Med. Assn., 1983, Disting. Faculty award Colo. State U. Coll. Vet. Med., 1993, Gustavus Myers Human Rights award 1994, Brownlee award Animal Welfare Found. Can., 1994. Jewish. Avocations: weightlifting, horseback riding, motorcycles. Office: Colo State U Dept Philosophy Fort Collins CO 80523-1781

ROLLIN, BETTY, author, television journalist; b. N.Y.C., Jan. 3, 1936; d. Leon and Ida R.; m. Harold M. Edwards, Jan. 21, 1979. BA, Sarah Lawrence Coll., 1957. Assoc. features editor Vogue mag., 1964; sr. editor Look mag., 1965-71; network corr. NBC News, N.Y.C., 1971-80, contbg. corr., 1985—; network corr. ABC News Nightline, 1982-84; lectr. in field. Profl. actress on stage and television, 1958-64; Author: I Thee Wed, 1958, Mothers Are Funnier Than Children, 1964, The Non-Drinkers' Drink Book, 1966, First, You Cry, 1976, reissue, 1993, Am I Getting Paid for This?, 1982, Last Wish, 1985; columnist Hers, N.Y. Times; Contbr. articles to popular mags. Office: care NS Bienstock Inc 1740 Broadway New York NY 10019-4315

ROLLINGS, MARTHA ANDERSON, school system administrator; b. Andersonville, Va., Sept. 3, 1929; d. Herbert Greenway and Alma Virginia (Abernathy) Anderson; m. Norman Gregory Rollings, Aug. 11, 1951 (dec. Feb. 1969); 1 child,Alma Faye Rollings-Carter. BA with honors, Longwood Coll., 1948; MEd, Coll. William and Mary, 1967. Cert. postgrad. profl. Tchr. English/Spanish Culpeper (Va.) County H.S., 1948-49, Surry (Va.) County H.S., 1949-53, Wakefield (Va.) H.S., 1959-64, Waverly (Va.) H.S., 1964-70; tchr., counselor, headmistress Surry (Va.) County Acad., 1970-75; tchr. English/Spanish Surry County H.S., Dendron, Va., 1975-78, asst. prin., assoc. prin., 1978-89; dir. instrn. Surry County Schs., 1989-91, asst. supt., 1991—. Sec. bd. dirs. Am. Heart Assn., Surry, 1993-94; treas. Dendron United Meth. Ch., 1968-94. Named Adminstr. of Yr. SCAEOP, Surry, 1992, 94; recipient Alumni Achievement award Longwood Coll., Farmville, Va., 1994. Mem. ASCD, Va. ASCD, AASA, Surry C. of C., Delta Kappa Gamma (sec. 1986-88, 2nd v.p. 1988-90, 1st v.p. 1990-92, pres. 1992-94). Avocations: reading, travel, working crossword puzzles. Office: Surry County Pub Schs School St Govt Ctr Surry VA 23883

ROLLINS, ALDEN MILTON, documents librarian; b. Billerica, Mass., July 31, 1946; s. Alden Milton and Agnes Morgan (Simpson) R. BA, Am. U., 1968; MLS, U. R.I., 1973. Cert. geneal. record specialist, Bd. for Certification of Genealogists., Va., N.H. Documents libr. U. Alaska Libr., Anchorage, 1973—. Author: The Fall of Rome: A Reference Guide, 1983, Rome in the Fourth Century A.D., 1991, Vermont Warnings Out, 1995. With U.S. Army, 1969-71. Mem. Nat. Geneal. Soc., Geneal. Soc. Vt., N.H. Geneal. Soc., New Eng. Hist. Geneal. Soc., N.H. Hist. Soc., Vt. Hist. Soc. (life), Piscataqua Pioneers (life). Avocation: genealogy. Home: 221 E 7th Ave Apt 114 Anchorage AK 99501-3639 Office: U Alaska Libr Govt Documents 3211 Providence Dr Anchorage AK 99508-4614

ROLLINS, ALFRED BROOKS, JR., historian, educator; b. Presque Isle, Maine, May 28, 1921; s. Alfred Brooks and Clarissa (Jack) R.; m. Ernestine Emma McMullin, Nov. 6, 1942 (dec. Aug. 28, 1972); children: John Douglas, Nancy Jane, James Scott; m. Faith Kenyon, June 16, 1973 (dec. Mar. 1979); m. Helen Anrod Jones, Feb. 28, 1981. BA, Wesleyan U., Middletown, Conn., 1942, MA, 1946; PhD, Harvard U., 1953. From instr. to prof. history State U., N.Y. at New Paltz, 1948-63; prof., chmn. dept. history State U. N.Y. at Binghamton, 1964-67; dean U. Vt., Burlington, 1967-70; v.p. acad. affairs U. Vt., 1970-76; pres. Old Dominion U., Norfolk, Va., 1976-85; prof. history Old Dominion U., Norfolk, 1976-91, pres. emeritus, prof. emeritus, 1991—; Cons. oral history project John F. Kennedy Library, 1965. Author: Roosevelt and Howe, 1962; Editor narrative: Franklin D. Roosevelt and the Age of Action, 1960, Woodrow Wilson and the New America, 1965; Contbr. articles to profl. jours. Served to 1st lt. USAAF, 1943-46. Decorated D.F.C., Air medal with four clusters. Mem. Am. Hist. Assn., Orgn. Am. Historians, Phi Beta Kappa, Chi Psi.

ROLLINS, EDWARD TYLER, JR., newspaper executive; b. Durham, N.C., May 23, 1922; s. Edward Tyler and Bessie (Steed) R.; m. Frances Louise Page, Oct. 5, 1963; children: Edward Tyler III, William Lawson. AB, U. N.C., 1947. V.p., asst. sec. Durham (N.C.) Herald Co., 1949-69, v.p., sec.-treas., 1969-81, pres., pub., 1982-88, chmn., bd. dirs., 1985—; pres. Durham Radio Corp. Stas. WDNC-AM, WDCG-FM, 1982-88. Bd. dirs. Chowan Coll. Graphic Arts Found., 1986—; bd. dirs. Sch. of Journalism Found. of N.C., 1982-88; mem. Friends of Duke Art Mus., mem. adv. bd. N.C. Nat. Bank, 1979-89; mem. Gov.'s Bus. Coun. on Arts and Humanities, 1989-90; mem. Duke Pres.'s Art Mus. com., 1994—; trustee Meredith Coll., Raleigh, N.C., 1966-69, Durham Pub. Libr., 1961-81; former bd. dirs. Durham Salvation Army; pres. Durham YMCA, 1952; former bd. dirs. Family Svc. Assn.; supporter N.C. Symphony. With U.S. Army, 1943-46. Mem. Newspaper Assn. Am., N.C. Press Assn., So. Newspaper Pubs. Assn., The English Speaking Union, Durham C. of C. (bd. dirs. 1969), Kiwanis, Hope Valley Country Club, Treyburn Country Club, Univ. Club, Carolina Club. Presbyterian. Office: Durham Herald Co Inc 2828 Pickett Rd Durham NC 27705-5613

ROLLINS, GARY WAYNE, service company executive; b. Chattanooga, Aug. 30, 1944; s. Orville Wayne and Grace (Crum) R.; m. Ruth Magness; children: Glen William, Ruth Ellen, Nancy Louise, Orville Wayne. BSBA, U. Tenn., 1967. Sales mgmt. Orkin Exterminating Co., Atlanta, 1967-72, v.p. ops., 1975-78, pres., 1978—; v.p., gen. mgr. Dwoskin, Atlanta, 1972-75; with Rollins, Inc., Atlanta, 1959—, v.p., 1972-84, pres., COO, 1984—, also bd. dirs.; pres. Rollins Supply, Inc., Atlanta; v.p. LOR, Inc., Atlanta, 1978—; bd. dirs. Rollins Leasing Co., Wilmington, Del., Rollins Energy Services, Atlanta, RPC Energy Svcs., Inc. Mem. Atlanta Symphony, 1970—, Atlanta Humane Soc., 1970—, Atlanta High Mus. Art, 1970—, Ga. Structural Pest Control Commn., 1967; founding dir. Tuxedo Park Civic Assn., Atlanta, 1984—. Recipient de Tocqueville Soc. award United Way, 1987. Mem. PADI Open Water Diving, Piedmont Driving Club. Methodist. Club: Cherokee (Atlanta). Avocations: hunting, camping, scuba diving, family activities. Office: Rollins Inc 2170 Piedmont Rd NE Atlanta GA 30324-4135*

ROLLINS, HENRY, musician, author, publisher; b. Feb. 13, 1961. Prin., pub. 2.13.61, L.A.; prin. Human Pitbull Music Pub. Formerly with Black Flag; now songwriter, lead singer Rollins Band; albums with Rollins Band include Hot Animal Machine, 1987, Drive By Shooting, 1987, Life Time, 1988, Do It, 1989, Hard Volume, 1989, Turned On, 1990, The End of Silence, 1992, Electro Convulsive Therapy, 1993, Weight, 1994; albums with Black Flag include My War, 1983, Family Man, 1984, Slip It In, 1984, Live '84, 1984, Loose Nut, 1985, The Process of Weeding Out, 1985, In My Head, 1985, Who's Got the 10, 1986; spoken word releases include Short Walk on a Long Pier, Big Ugly Mouth, Sweatbox, Live at McCabe's, Human Butt, The Boxed Life; video Talking From the Box; author: High Adventure in the Great Outdoors, 1984, Hallucinations of Grandeur, 1986, You Can't Run from God, 1986, Pissing in the Gene Pool, 1987, Works, 1988, Art to Choke Hearts, 1989, Bang!, 1990, One From None, 1991, Black Coffee Blues, 1992, See a Grown Man Cry, 1992, Now Watch Him Die, 1993; contbr. Details mag., Village Voice, Spin, Sounds, Melody Maker, The Face, various anthologies; film appearances include: The Chase, 1994, Johnny Mnemonic, 1995; spoken word performer, 1983—. Grammy nomination, Best Metal Performance for "Liar", 1995. Office: 2 13 61 PO Box 1910 Los Angeles CA 90078 also: care Imago Recording Co 152 W 57th St New York NY 10019-3310

ROLLINS, JACK, motion picture producer; b. 1914. Co-founder talent mgmt. firm Rollins, Joffe, Morra, Brezner Prodns., N.Y.C . Producer films: (with Charles Joffe) Take The Money and Run, 1969, Bananas, 1971, Everything You Always Wanted to Know...But Were Afraid To Ask, 1972, Sleeper, 1973, Love and Death, 1975, The Front, 1976, Annie Hall, 1977, Interiors, 1978, Manhattan, 1979, Stardust Memories, 1980, Zelig, 1983; producer, actor films: The Purple Rose of Cairo, 1985, Hannah and Her Sisters, 1986, Radio Days, 1986, September, 1987, Another Woman, 1988, New York Stories (Oedipus Wrecks), 1989, Crimes and Misdemeanors, 1989, Shadows and Fog, 1992, Husbands and Wives, 1992, Manhattan Murder Mystery, 1993; TV producer Dick Cavett Show, Late Night with David Letterman; mgmt. firm handles careers of Woody Allen, Mike Nichols, Elaine May, Robin Williams, Robert Klein, Dick Cavett, Billy Crystal. Office: Rollins Joffe Morra Brezner Productions 130 W 57th St New York NY 10019

ROLLINS, JAMES GREGORY, air force officer; b. Vandenberg AFB, Calif., Apr. 6, 1963; s. Clarence Leslie and Mary Ethel (Brooks) R. BS in Bus. Adminstrn., San Jose State U., 1985; MSA in Gen. Adminstrn., Ctrl. Mich. U., 1992; MBA in Aviation Mgmt., Embry-Riddle Aero. U., 1992. Commd. 2d lt. USAF, 1985, advanced through grades to capt., 1989; minuteman intercontinental ballistic missile dep. crew comdr. USAF, Grand Forks AFB, N.D., 1985-86, minuteman intercontinental ballistic missile instr. dep. crew comdr., 1986-87, minuteman intercontinental ballistic missile evaluator dep. crew comdr., 1987-88, strategic air command missile combat competition instr., 1987-88, intercontinental ballistic missile crew comdr., 1988-89, scheduling br. chief ops., 1989-90, order tng. officer emergecy war, 1990-91, intercontinental ballistic missile ops. plans officer, 1991-92; acquisition info. mgr. USAF, L.A. AFB, 1992-93, dep. dir. program control divsn., 1993-94, chief plans and analysis divsn., 1994-96; dep. chief Peace Shield Deployment USAF, Hanscom AFB, Mass., 1996—. Editor (newsletters) Families First, 1991, Vol. Network, 1990-91. Asst. project officer Project Sandbox fundraiser, 1986; founder Above and Beyond Vol. Tutoring, 1988, cons., 1988—; vol. staff Youth Ctr., Grand Forks AFB, 1988-91, Rebuild L.A. Edn. and Job Tng. Task Force; base project officer Rob's Coats for Kids, 1990, 91; vol. Grand Forks United Way Cmty. Svcs., 1990-91; mem. Points of Light Found., 1991—, Minn. Office Vol. Svcs., 1991-95, Commdrs. Cmty. Ptnrs. Program, 1994-96; project coord. L.A. Works, 1995-96; Vol. Habitat for Humanity, 1995—; vol. People Making a Difference, 1996—; vol. Boston Cares, 1996—. Decorated Air Force Achievement medal, 1990, Air Force Commendation medal, 1992; named Vol. of Yr., 321st Strategic Missile Wing, 42d Air Divsn., 8th Air Force, Strategic Air Command, 1990; recipient Presdl. award for volunteerism, 1991. Mem. Air Force Assn., Air Force Cadet Officer Mentor Action Program, Performance Mgmt. Assn., Soc. Cost Estimating & Analysis, Tuskegee Airmen, Inc., Assn. of Air Force Missileers, Points of Light Found., Ctr. Corp. Cmty. Rels., Nat. Assn. Ptnrs. in Edn. Home: 176 East St # 202 Methuen MA 01844 Office: USAF ESC/ISD SMC/CW Hanscom AFB MA 01731-1644

ROLLINS, JIMMY DON, school system administrator. Supt. Springdale (Ark.) Sch. Dist. State finalist Nat. Supt. Yr. award, 1992. Office: Springdale Sch Dist 202 W Emma Ave Springdale AR 72764-4307

ROLLINS, JOHN W., JR., transportation executive, environmental services administrator; b. 1942. BBA, So. Meth. U., 1942; MBA, Northwestern U., 1965. With Rollins Truck Leasing Corp., Wilmington, Del., 1965—, sr. v.p., 1973, exec. v.p., 1975, pres., COO, 1975; with Rollins Eviron. Svcs. Inc., Wilmington, 1982—, chmn. bd. dirs., 1982, vice chmn., 1983, sr. vice chmn., 1988; with Matlack Systems Inc., Wilmington, 1988—, chmn. bd. dirs. Office: Matlack Systems Inc PO Box 1791 1 Rollins Plz Wilmington DE 19899*

ROLLINS, LANIER, recording company executive; b. New Orleans, Mar. 12, 1937; s. John and Iola Rollins. BA in Music, Chgo. Conservatory Music, 1962; AA in Bus., L.A. Trade Tech. Coll., 1976. Cert. employee plans specialist IRS. Clk., tech. U.S. Postal Svc., Chgo. and L.A., 1959-72; contact rep. Social Security Adminstrn., L.A., 1974-77; employee plans specialist IRS, L.A., 1977-90; pres., prodr. BFN Records, Inc., L.A., 1966-84, Lanier Equity Records, Inc., Atlanta, 1984—; mgmt. analyst VAF Edwards Group, Alta Loma, Calif., 1989—; pub. Ethnicity Connection, Alta Loma, 1989—; Author: The Human Race is a Gang, 1964; pub. (mag.) Ethnicity Connection, 1994. Recipient Music Mony awards ASCAP, N.Y.C., 1976, 81. Mem. Black Entrepreneur Bus. Club (chmn. 1993-94), Rancho Cucamonga (Calif.) C. of C. Avocations: musician, singer, writer, composer. Home: 10801 Lemon Ave Ste 1321 Alta Loma CA 91737

ROLLINS, R. RANDALL, diversified services company executive. Sr. vice chmn. Rollins, Inc., Atlanta. Office: RPC Energy Svcs Inc 2170 Piedmont Rd NE Atlanta GA 30324-4135*

ROLLINS, ROYCE L., public relations executive. Exec. v.p., sr. ptnr., CFO Fleishman Hillard, Inc., St. Louis. Office: Fleishman Hillard Inc 200 N Broadway Saint Louis MO 63102-2730*

ROLLINS, SANDRA L., academic administrator; b. Phila., May 16, 1952; d. Joseph and Leola Schuriq; divorced; 1 child, Gregory Clay Rollins. BA in Edn., LaSalle U., 1975; postgrad., Rider U., 1990—. Counselor fin. aid Jefferson Med. Coll., Thomas Jefferson U., Phila., 1975-77, asst. to dean of admissions, 1977-81; coord. admissions and fin. aid Coll. Grad. Studies, Thomas Jefferson U., 1984-90; asoc. dir. fin. aid U. Medicine and Dentistry N.J., Stratford, 1990—. Mem. AAUW, N.J. Assn. Student Fin. Aid Adminstrs. (tng. chair 1992-94, grad. and prof. concerns com. 1994-95), Nat. Assn. Student Fin. Aid Adminstrs., Middestates Assn. Coll. Registrars and Officers of Admission, com. chair conf. 1987-90). Home: 2 Cobblestone Ln Shamong NJ 08088-8404 Office: U Medicine & Dentistry NJ 40 Laurel Rd E Stratford NJ 08084-1350

ROLLINS, SHERRIE SANDY, television executive; b. Roanoke, Va., June 11, 1958; d. William Gresham and Charlotte (Weeks) Sandy; m. Edward John Rollins, Jr., May 2, 1987. BA, U. Va., 1980. Sr. v.p. ABC TV Network, N.Y.C., 1994—; advt. dir. Georgetown mag., Alexandria, Va., 1980-81; exec. dir. Bus. and Profl. Assn. Georgetown, Washington, 1981-84; v.p. communications The Oliver Carr Co., Washington, 1985-89; asst. sec. for pub. affairs HUD, Washington, 1989-90; dir. news info. ABC News, N.Y.C., 1990-92; asst. to Pres. of U.S. for pub. liason and intergovtl. affairs The White House, Washington, 1992; sr. v.p. U.S. News and World Report, Washington, 1992-94; sr. v.p. Network Comms. ABC TV Network, N.Y.C., 1994-96, exec. v.p. network comm., 1996—; bd. dirs. Am. Coun. Young Pol. Leaders, Cities in Schs. Mem. U. Va. Alumni Assn. (bd. mgrs.). Home: 107 Dellwood Rd Bronxville NY 10708 Office: Capital Cities/ABC 77 W 66th St New York NY 10023-6201

ROLLINS, (THEODORE) SONNY, composer, musician; b. N.Y.C., Sept. 7, 1930; s. Walter and Valborg (Solomon) R.; m. Dawn Finney, 1956 (div.); m. Lucille Pearson, Sept. 7, 1959. Ed. high sch., N.Y.C.; ArtsD, Bard Coll., 1992. Condr. Sonny Rollins & Co. Orch., concert tours in Europe, Far East,

1973—; composed, scored and played music for motion picture Alfie; recs. for Milestone, Fantasy-Prestige compositions include Way Out West, also others. Recipient numerous awards Guggenheim fellow, 1972. Home: RR 9 # G Germantown NY 12526

ROLLMAN, STEVEN ALLAN, communication educator; b. N.Y.C., Aug. 3, 1947; s. Leo and Margot (Seelenberger) R.; m. Nancy Sue Toberen, June 15, 1973; 1 child, Benjamin Allan. BA, C.W. Post Coll., 1970; MA, Ohio U., 1972; PhD, Pa. State U., 1977. Instr. Pa. State U., University Park, 1976; asst. prof. James Madison U., Harrisonburg, Va., 1977-83, assoc. prof., 1983-95, coord. interpersonal communication, 1986-90, prof., 1995—; cons. various sch. dists., Va., 1978—, Swissair, Zurich, 1971-72; book reviewer Choice, 1982—. Contbr. articles to profl. jours.; editor: Virginia Journal of Communication, 1980-81. Mem. Speech Comm. Assn., So. States Comm. Assn., Va. Speech Comm. Assn., Internat. Listening Assn. Avocations: computers, music, film, automobiles, tennis. Home: 608 Wynhdam Woods Cir Harrisonburg VA 22801-1668 Office: James Madison U Sch Speech Comm Harrisonburg VA 22807

ROLLO, F. DAVID, hospital management company executive, radiology educator; b. Endicott, N.Y., Apr. 15, 1939; s. Frank C. and Augustine L. (Dumont) R.; m. Linda Wood, June 1, 1991; children : Mindee, Alex. BA, Harpur Coll., 1959; MS, U. Miami, 1965; PhD, Johns Hopkins U., 1968; MD, Upstate Med. Ctr., Syracuse, N.Y., 1972. Diplomate Am. Bd. Nuclear Medicine. Asst. chief nuclear medicine services VA Hosp., San Francisco, 1974-77; chief nuclear medicine VA Hosp., Nashville, 1977-79; sr. v.p. med. affairs Humana Inc., Louisville, 1980-92; dir. nuclear medicine div. Vanderbilt U. Med. Ctr., Nashville, 1977-81; prof. radiology Vanderbilt U., Nashville, 1979—; pres., CEO Metricor Inc., Louisville, 1992-95; sr. v.p. med. affairs HCIA, Louisville, 1995—; mem. med. adv. com. IBT, Washington, 1984—; mem. pvt. sector liaison panel Inst. of Medicine, Washington, 1983—; bd. dirs. ADAC Labs., KBL Healthcare, Positron Corp., Inc., Raytel Med. Corp., Cambridge Heart. Editor: Nuclear Medicine Physics, Instruments and Agents, 1977; co-editor: Physical Basis of Medical Imaging, 1980, Digital Radiology: Focus on Clinical Utility, 1982, Nuclear Medicine Resonance Imaging, 1983; mem. editorial adv. bd. ECRI, 1981—. Pres. bd. dirs. Youth Performing Arts Coun., Louisville, 1984-85; bd. dirs. Louisville-Jefferson County Youth Orch., 1983-85; sr. v.p., exec. com. USA Internat. Harp Competition, 1992-94, chmn., 1994—. Fellow Am. Coll. Nuclear Physicians (profl. com. 1982-84, chmn. 1984); mem. AMA, Soc. Nuclear Medicine (trustee 1979-83, 84—, Cassen Meml. lectr. western region 1980, 84), Radiol. Soc. N.Am., Am. Coll. Radiology, Ky. Sci. Tech. Coun. (exec. bd. 1987—), Advancement Med. Instrumentation (bd. dirs. 1986—), Louisville C. of C. (chmn. MIC com. 1987—). Avocations: racquetball, squash. Home: 5646 Bailey Grant Rd Jeffersonville IN 47130-8607 Office: 462 S 4th Ave Ste 405 Louisville KY 40202

ROLLO, MARY-JO VIVIAN, special education educator; b. Port Chester, N.Y., Aug. 16, 1938; d. Salvatore James and Vivian (Cusamano) R.; children: Vivian, Phyllis, Cynthia, Mary-Jo, Salvatore, Joseph. BA, Pace U., 1968; MA, Western Conn. U., 1973; MS, Nova U., 1992, postgrad. Cert. tchr., N.Y., Fla. Tchr. Mahopac (N.Y.) Mid. Schs., 1968-71; tchr., spl. edn. specialist Karafin Schs., Mt. Kisco, N.Y., 1971-76; remedial reading specialist Lincoln Hall, Lincolndale, N.Y., 1976-78; tchr., specialist in emotionally handicapped students Orange County Schs., Orlando, Fla., 1978-93; owner, dir. SAT Prep. Ctr., Maitland, Fla., 1993—. Contbr. articles to profl. publs. De. Seminole Dem. Com., Seminole County, Fla., 1988. Mem. NEA (sec.), Fla. Tchrs Profession (sec. 1984-86), Classroom Tchrs. Assn. (sec. 1984-86, coord. coun. 1984-86), Coun. Exceptional Children, Nat. Coun. Tchrs. English. Roman Catholic. Avocations: reading, fishing, sports, cooking, travel.

ROLNIK, ZACHARY JACOB, senior editor, publisher; b. Bayonne, N.J., Oct. 2, 1961; s. Joseph and Katie (Simon) R. BA, U. Rochester, 1982; M. in Pub. Policy, Harvard U., 1984. Ops. analyst, presdl. mgmt. intern U.S. Dept. Treasury, Washington, 1984-85; sr. editor, pub. Kluwer Acad. Pubs., Norwell, Mass., 1985—. Home: 146 Pleasant St Hanover MA 02339-1844 Office: Kluwer Acad Pubs 101 Philip Dr Norwell MA 02061-1615

ROLPHE, BEN RICHARD, JR., publishing company executive; b. L.A., June 19, 1932; s. Ben R. and Ruth LaVern (Bronson) R.; m. Shirley G. Foote, Mar. 21, 1951 (wid. Aug. 1976); children: Hope Anderson, B. Randy, Pennie Sanders; m. Anna Marie Swan, Feb. 14, 1980. Student, U. Santa Clara, 1953-59. Owner Calif. Meter Svc., San Jose, 1955-62, Western Svc. Systems, Portland, Oreg., 1962-71; pub. Glacier Herald Newspaper, Kalispell, Mont., 1971-76; pres., CEO Century Pub. Co., Coeur d'Alene, Idaho, 1976-93, chmn. of bd., 1993—; instr. Oreg. Real Estate Commn., Salem, 1978-82; cons. Mini-Maid Systems, Inc., Salem, 1971-80, Wishing Star Found., Coeur d'Alene, 1985-89; del. U.S.-China Joint Session on Ind., Beijing, 1988. Author: How to Make Advertising Pay, 1980. Bd. dirs. Pan Am. Hwy. Commn., Yakima, Wash., 1968-69, Youth Help Line, 1991, Pacific Travel Assn., Bend, Oreg., 1970-71, Boy Scouts Am., Panhandle Coun., 1992, North Idaho Coll. Found., 1992-93. Lt. USAF, 1949-53. Named Best Original Editorial, Nat. Assn. Pub., 1976; recipient Employer of Yr. Am. Legion, 1989, Vets. of Fgn. Wars, 1990. Mem. Am. Pres. Assn., Masons, Shriners, Coeur d'Alene C. of C. (bd. dirs. 1990-93), Coeur d'Alene C. of C. Commodores. Republican. Baptist. Avocations: flyfishing, aviation. Home: 12582 Strahorn Rd Hayden ID 83835-9303 Office: Century Pub Co PO Box 730 Coeur D Alene ID 83816-0730

ROLSTON, HOLMES, III, theologian, educator, philosopher; b. Staunton, Va., Nov. 19, 1932; s. Holmes and Mary Winifred (Long) R.; m. Jane Irving Wilson, June 1, 1956; children: Shonny Hunter, Giles Campbell. BS, Davidson Coll., 1953; BD, Union Theol. Sem., Richmond, Va., 1956; MA in Philosophy of Sci., U. Pitts., 1968; PhD in Theology, U. Edinburgh, Scotland, 1958. Ordained to ministry Presbyn. Ch. (USA), 1956. Asst. prof. philosophy Colo. State U., Ft. Collins, 1968-71, assoc. prof., 1971-76, prof., 1976—; vis. scholar Ctr. Study of World Religions, Harvard U., 1974-75; lectr. Yale U., Vanderbilt U., others; official observer UNCED, Rio de Janiero, 1992. Author: Religious Inquiry: Participation and Detachment, 1985, Philosophy Gone Wild, 1986, Science and Religion: A Critical Survey, 1987, Environmental Ethics, 1988, Conserving Natural Value, 1994; assoc. editor Environ. Ethics, 1979—; mem. editorial bd. Oxford Series in Environ. Philosophy and Pub. Policy, Zygon: Jour. of Religion and Sci.; contbr. chpts. to books, articles to profl. jours. Recipient Oliver P. Penock Disting. Svc. award Colo. State U., 1983, Coll. Award for Excellence, 1991., Univ. Disting. Prof., 1992; Disting. Russell fellow Grad. Theol. Union, 1991, Disting. Lectr. Chinese Acad. of Social Scis., 1991, Disting. Lectr. Nobel Conf. XXVII. Mem. AAAS, Am. Acad. Religion, Soc. Bibl. Lit. (pres. Rocky Mountain-Gt. Plains region), Am. Philos. Assn., Internat. Soc. for Environ. Ethics (pres. 1989-94), Phi Beta Kappa. Avocation: bryology. Home: 1712 Concord Dr Fort Collins CO 80526-1602 Office: Colo State U Dept Philosophy Fort Collins CO 80523

ROM, (MELVIN) MARTIN, securities executive; b. Detroit, Mar. 2, 1946; s. Jack and Thelma (Meyer) R.; m. Barbara Miller, July 12, 1970. BA magna cum laude, U. Mich., 1967. Founder MultiVest, Inc., Southfield, Mich., 1969; pres. MultiVest, Inc., Southfield, 1969-73; chmn. bd., chief exec. officer MultiVest, Inc., 1973-75; pres. Real Estate Securities and Syndication Inst., Nat. Assn. Realtors, Washington, 1975—; dir., bd. govs. Real Estate Securities and Syndication Inst., Nat. Assn. Realtors, 1972—; pres. Martin Rom Co., Inc., 1976—; vice chmn. Sports Illus. Ct. Clubs, Inc., 1977-79; bd. dirs. Mocatta Corp., Med. Informatics Corp.; mem. joint com. Nat. Assn. Securities Dealers-Nat. Assn. Realtors, 1975-76; mem. adv. com. on market instruments Commodity Futures Trading Commn. Author: Nothing Can Replace the U.S. Dollar . . . and It Almost Has, 1975; Adv. bd.: Housing and Devel. Reporter, Washington. Trustee U. Chgo. Found. Mem. Nat. Assn. Securities Dealers, Com. on Gold Regulations, Phi Beta Kappa. Home and Office: 60 Quarton Ln Bloomfield Hills MI 48304-3456

ROM, WILLIAM NICHOLAS, physician; b. San Francisco, July 6, 1945; s. William N. and Barbara J. (Berlin) R.; m. Holly Wight Meeker, Oct. 7, 1973; children: Nicole, Meredith. BA, U. Colo., 1967; MD, U. Minn., 1971; MPH, Harvard U., 1973. Diplomate Am. Bd. Internatl Medicine, Am. Bd. Pulmonary Disease, Am. Bd. Preventive Medicine, Occupational Medicine. Internship U. Calif.-Davis, 1971-72; residency, 1973-75; from asst. to assoc. prof. U. Utah, Salt Lake City, 1977-83; sr. investigator NIH, Bethesda, Md., 1983-89; chief Divsn. Pulmonary/Critical Care Medicine NYU Med. Ctr., 1989—. Author: Canoe Country Wilderness, 1987; editor: Environmental and Occupational Medicine, 1992. Capt. USAFR, 1972-77. Recipient Harriet Hardy award New Eng. Occupational Med. Assn., 1993. Fellow Explorer's Club, Pulmonary and Occupational Medicine, Mt. Sinai, N.Y., 1975-77. Democrat. Avocations: skiing, mountain climbing, canoeing, cabin building, travel. Home: 4 Stanley Keyes Ct Rye NY 10580-3259 Office: NYU Med Ctr 550 1st Ave New York NY 10016-6481

ROMAGOSA, ELMO LAWRENCE, clergyman, retired editor; b. Thibodaux, La., Jan. 11, 1924; s. Lawrence Gabriel and Lydie (Achee) R. Ed., St. Joseph Sem., Notre Dame Sem., New Orleans, 1947. Ordained priest Roman Cath. Ch., 1947. Asst. pastor Cut Off, La., 1947-50, New Orleans, 1950-58; chaplain Ursuline Convent and Nat. Shrine Our Lady of Prompt Succor, 1958-63; pastor St. John's Ch., New Orleans, 1963-70; asst. dir. Soc. for Propagation of Faith, 1950-60, dir., 1962; communications dir. Archdiocese New Orleans, 1962; founding editor Clarion Herald newspaper, 1963-74; priest in residence Sts. Peter and Paul Ch., New Orleans, 1970-72; pastor Holy Trinity Ch., New Orleans, 1972-74, St. Rose of Lima Ch., New Orleans, 1974-76, St. Clement of Rome Ch., Metairie, La., 1976-84; chaplain Port of New Orleans, 1984-88; pastor Ch. of Infant Jesus, Harvey, La., 1988—; nat. sec. Cath. Broadcasters Assn., 1963-65; mem. U.S. Cath. bishops subcoms. on Cath.-Jewish relations, 1965; named prelate of honor, 1980. Editor Airtime, 1963-64. Dir. Stella Maris Maritime Ctr., 1984-88; chaplain Harbor Police, Port of New Orleans, 1984-88; mem. Nat. Conf. Seafarers, 1984, pres., 1986—, mem. legal adv. com. Ctr. for Seafarers Rights, 1986; mem. Nat. Cath. Conf. for Seafarers, 1984, pres., 1986-88. Recipient First Place award for best editorial and best feature photo Press Club New Orleans, 1965, First Place award for best column Press Club New Orleans, 1972; named Prelate of Honor, Pope John II, 1980. Mem. Cath. Press Assn. (1st Place awards for gen. excellence 1963-65), Sociedad Espanola New Orleans (founding sec.-treas.), Equestrian Order of Holy Sepulchre of Jerusalem (knight 1978, knight comdr. 1983, master of ceremonies 1986, Gold Palms of Jerusalem medallion 1993). Republican. Home and Office: Ch of the Infant Jesus 700 Maple Ave Harvey LA 70058-4008

ROMAGUERA, MARIANO ANTONIO, consulting engineer; b. Mayaguez, P.R., May 4, 1928; s. Jose Mariano and Aminta (Martinez) R.; BS, MIT, 1950; MS, U. P.R., 1975; m. Virginia Casablanca, July 3, 1952; children: Jose Mariano, Jorge Enrique, Alberto, Ana Maria. Asst. engr. Arturo Romaguera, Cons. Engr., Colombia, 1950-51; asst. engr. Ingenio Providencia, Palmira, Colombia, 1951; shift engr. Central Igualdad and Western Sugar Refinery, Mayaguez, 1954; erection engr., asst. project mgr., Pradera Valle, Colombia, 1954-55, plant supt., chief engr., 1955-57; project engr. Ingenior Providencia, Palmira, Colombia, 1957, chief engr. ops. and maintenance, 1958-64; exec. v.p. Romaguera & Vendrell Devel. Corp., Mayaguez, P.R., 1964-68; pres. RomaVel, Inc., Mayaguez, 1965-68, Yagueka Equipment, Inc., 1968-78, Mariano A. Romaguera and Assocs., Engrs., Appraisers and Cons., Mayaguez, 1974—; sr. ptnr. Camino, Romaguera & Assocs., 1976—; sr. ptnr. M/E Appraisers, 1976—; cons. engr. Sugar Corp. P.R., Commonwealth of P.R., Biomass Steam Generation Rsch.; bd. regents Cath. U. P.R. Pres., Yagueka dist. P.R. coun. Boy Scouts Am., 1965-69, mem. exec. bd. P.R. coun.; chmn. ARC, 1966; bd. dirs. Mayaguez YMCA; mem. MIT Edn!. Coun.; mem. bd. regents Catholic U. of P.R. With Army, 1952-54, Korea. Recipient Silver Beaver award P.R. coun.l Boy Scouts Am., 1969. Mem. NSPE, ASME (pres. S.W. P.R. group), Am. Soc. Appraisers, Instituto de Evaluadores de P.R., Colegio Ingenieros y Agrimensores de P.R. (past pres. Mayaguez dist.), Instituto de Ingenieros Mecanicos de P.R., P.R. Soc. Profl. Engrs., Assn. Engring. Socs., Am. Right of Way Assn., Internat. Soc. Sugar Cane Technologists, P.R. Assn. Real Estate Bds., Mayaguez Bd. Realtors, M.I.T. Alumni Assn., Nu Sigma Beta, Alpha Phi Omega. Roman Catholic. Lodge: Rotary. Home: 16 Calle Peral N Mayaguez PR 00680-4855 Office: PO Box 1340 Mayaguez PR 00681-1340

ROMAIN, BELLA MARY, graphic designer; b. Oakland, Calif., June 16, 1949; d. John Thomas Kondrup and Anna (Rabinowitz) Friedman; m. Stewart Jay Romain, Mar. 19, 1972. Student, SUNY, Stony Brook, 1967-68, Sch. Visual Arts, 1973-75; BFA magna cum laude, West Ga. Coll., 1989. Asst. to editor Dell Pub. Co., N.Y.C., 1968-72; reporter, proofreader Local News, Long Island, N.Y., 1973-76; graphic designer, editor Yellow Book Corp., N.Y.C., 1976-78; freelance graphic designer, editor N.Y.C., 1978-82; owner, graphic designer, editor designplus, Carrollton, Ga., 1982—; publs. cons. West Ga. Coll., Carrollton, 1985—. Paintings exhibited in numerous juried shows, including Alexandria Mus. Art, 1992. Speaker to civic groups, Carrollton, 1993; vol. Amateur Radio Emergency Svcs., Carrollton, 1985—; vol. designer Carroll County Humane Soc., Carrollton, 1993—. Recipient Fine Arts Achievement award Binney & Smith, 1989. Mem. Nat. Mus. Women in Arts, Lions Internat., Am. Bus. Women's Assn., Toastmasters (chair membership local chpt. 1993), Carroll County C. of C., Phi Kappa Phi. Avocations: amateur radio, painting. Home and Office: 285 Timber Ridge Trl Carrollton GA 30117-8884

ROMAINE, HENRY SIMMONS, investment consultant; b. N.Y.C., May 30, 1933; s. Theodore Cole and Cornelia (Simmons) R.; m. Susan Donaldson; children: Henry, Hilary, Kathryn. BA, Harvard U., 1954. Asst. security analyst Mutual Life Ins. Co., N.Y.C., 1958-60, investment analyst, 1960-61, investment specialist, 1961-64, asst. dir. investments, 1964, dir. investments, 1964-66, asst. v.p. for securities investment, 1966-68, 2d v.p. for securities investment, 1969-71, v.p. for securities investment, 1971-72, sr. v.p., 1972-78, sr. v.p., chief investment officer, 1976-78, exec. v.p., 1978-81, pres., 1981-86; vice chmn., chief investment officer Am. Gen. Corp., Houston, 1986-93; dir. MONY Life Ins. Co. of Can.; chmn. bd. MONY Real Estate Investors, 1978-86; mem. adv. bd. Chem. Bank, 1974-93. Served with USN, 1954-57. Mem. Links Club, Harvard Club. Home: 7 Conquest Ave Sullivans Island SC 29482-9779

ROMAN, CECELIA FLORENCE, cardiologist; b. Phila., June 12, 1956; d. Stanley Jeremiah and Doris (Manus) Romanowski. BA magna cum laude, Boston U., 1977; DO, Phila. Coll. Osteo. Medicine, 1981. Intern, internal medicine resident Del. Valley Med. Ctr., Langhorne, Pa., 1981-84; cardiology fellow Deborah Heart and Lung Ctr., Browns Mills, N.J., 1984-86, cardiology attending dir. med. intensive care unit, 1986-90; clin. instr. dept. medicine Robert Wood Johnson Med. Sch., U. Medicine, Dentistry N.J.; cardiology attending physician Clin. Cardiology Group, Langhorne, Pa., 1990-93; pvt. practice Clin. Cardiology Group, Bristol, Pa., 1993—; staff cardiologist Albert Einstein Med. Ctr., Med. Coll. Pa., Del. Valley Med. Ctr., Lower Bucks Hosp., St. Mary's Hosp. Author med. videos; lectr. in field; contbr. articles to profl. jours. Recipient Physicians Recognition award, 1987—. Fellow Am. Coll. Angiology, Am. Coll. Osteo. Internists; mem. Am. Osteo. Assn., Pa. Osteo. Med. Assn., Am. Coll. Osteo. Internists-cardiology and geriatric divs. Avocations: sailing, flying, hot air ballooning, travel. Home: 12 Duffield Dr Trenton NJ 08628

ROMAN, KENNETH, JR., corporate communications executive; b. Boston, Sept. 6, 1930; s. Kenneth J. and Bernice (Freedman) R.; m. Ellen L. Fischer, Mar. 27, 1953. B.A., Dartmouth Coll., 1952. Asst. advt. promotion mgr. Interchem Crp., N.Y.C., 1952-55; mgr. advt. sales promotion Raymond Rosen Co., Phila., 1955-56; advt. mgr. Allied Chem. Corp., 1956-63; account mgr. Ogilvy & Mather, N.Y.C., 1963-79; pres. Ogilvy & Mather, U.S., 1979-85, Ogilvy and Mather Worldwide, 1985-89; chmn., chief exec. The Ogilvy Group, 1988-89; exec. v.p. RCA Distbr., N.Y.C., 1989-91; bd. dirs. Brunswick Corp., Compaq Computer Corp., IBJ Schroder Bank & Trust Co., Penncorp Fin. Group. Co-author: The New How to Advertise, 1992, Writing That Works, 1992. Bd. dirs. N.Y. Bot. Garden, Meml. Sloan-Kettering Cancer Ctr. Mem. Univ. Club (N.Y.C.), The Century Assn. Home: 7 Gracie Sq New York NY 10028-8030 Office: 866 3rd Ave Fl 26 New York NY 10022-6221

ROMAN, STANFORD AUGUSTUS, JR., medical educator, dean; b. N.Y.C.; s. Stanford Augustas and Ivy L. (White) R.; children: Mawiyah Lythcott, Jane E. Roman-Brown. AB, Dartmouth Coll., 1964; MD, Columbia U., 1968; MPH, U. Mich., 1975. Diplomate Nat. Bd. of Med. Examiners. Intern in medicine Columbia U.-Harlem Hosp. Ctr., 1966-69, resident in medicine, 1969-71, chief resident in medicine, 1971-73; assoc. dir. ambulatory care Columbia U. Harlem Hosp., N.Y.C., 1972-73; instr. in medicine Columbia U., N.Y.C., 1972-73; asst. physician Presbyn. Hosp., 1972-73; clin. dir. Healthco, Inc., Soul City, N.C., 1973-74; dir. ambulatory care, asst. prof. medicine/sociomed. scis. Boston City Hosp., 1974-78; asst. prof. medicine U. N.C., Chapel Hill, 1973-74; asst. dean Boston U. Sch. Medicine, 1974-78; med. dir. D.C. Gen. Hosp., Washington, 1978-81; assoc. dean acad. affairs Dartmouth Med. Sch., Hanover, N.H., 1981-86, assoc. prof., 1981-87, dep. dean, 1986-87; dean, v.p., prof. medicine Morehouse Sch. Med., Atlanta, 1987-89; sr. v.p., med. and profl. affairs Health and Hosps. Corp., N.Y.C., 1989-90; dean med. sch., prof. community health and social medicine CUNY, 1990—; dir. Boston Comprehensive Sickle Cell Ctr., 1975-78; bd. dirs. Nat. Bd. Med. Examiners, Phila., 1988-92, Winifred Masterson Burke Rehab. Hosp., White Plains, N.Y.; mem. Dartmouth Hitchcock Med. Ctr. Bd. of Medicine, N.Y.; trustee Dartmouth Coll., Hanover, N.H. Contbr. to book chpts. and profl. jours. and editls. Fellow N.Y. Acad. Medicine; mem. AMA, APHA, Nat. Med. Assn., N.Y. State Coun. Grad. Med. Edn., N.Y. State Dept. Edn. Bd. Medicine. Democrat. Episcopalian. Avocations: photography, travel, music. Office: CUNY Med Sch J 909 Convent Ave and 138th St New York NY 10031

ROMAN-BARBER, HELEN, corporate executive. LLB, U. Paris, 1971, M of Internat. Law, 1972. Chmn., chief exec. officer Roman Corp. Ltd., Toronto, Ont., Can. Office: Roman Corp Ltd, 200 King St W Box 82, Toronto, ON Canada M5H 3T4

ROMANEK, MARK, video director. Recipient Best Music Video-Short Form Grammy award, 1996. Office: Propaganda Films 940 N Mansfield Ave Hollywood CA 90038*

ROMANELLI, G. JACK, journalist; b. San Benedetto Del Tronto, Ascoli Piceno, Italy, Oct. 16, 1959; arrived in Can., 1965; s. Martino and Ida (Michetti) R.; m. Lily Bramante, Aug. 30, 1985; children: Alexa, Julian. BA in Journalism, Loyalist Coll., 1983. Reporter Alliston (Ont.) Herald, Can., 1983; reporter, columnist Burlington (Ont.) Gazette, 1983-84; copy editor Montreal (Que.) Gazette, Can., 1984-88, asst. sports editor, 1988-91; exec. sports editor Montreal (Que.) Gazette, 1991-95, asst. mng. editor sports and projects, 1995—; chmn. sports editors' com. Southam Newspaper Group, 1993-95; chmn. Can. region AP Sports Editors, 1994—. Avocations: reading, golf, racquetball, baseball stats. analysis. Home: 1538 Baxter St, LaSalle, PQ Canada H8N 2T5 Office: The Montreal Gazette, 250 St Antoine St W, Montreal, PQ Canada H2Y 3R7

ROMANI, JOHN HENRY, health administration educator; b. Milan, Italy, Mar. 6, 1925; s. Henry Arthur and Hazel (Pettengill) R.; m. Barbara A. Anderson; children: David John, Paul Nichols, Theresa A. Anderson. BA, U. N.H., 1949, MA, 1949; PhD, U. Mich., 1955. Instr. U. N.H., 1950-51; instr. U. Mich., Ann Arbor, 1954-55, assoc. prof., asst. to assoc. dean Sch. Pub. Health, 1961-69, assoc. v.p., 1971-75, chmn. health planning and adminstrn., 1975-80, prof., 1971-93, prof. emeritus pub. health adminstrn., 1993—; interim chair Pub. Health Policy and Adminstrn., 1991-92; asst. prof. Western Mich. U., 1956-57; assoc. dir. Cleve. Met. Svcs. Commn., 1957-59; assoc. prof. U. Pitts., 1959-61; vice chancellor, prof. U. Wis.-Milw., 1969-71; rsch. fellow Brookings Instn., 1955-56; mem. task force Nat. Commn. on Orgn. Cmty. Health Svcs., 1963-66; dir. staff Sec.'s Com. on Orgn. Health Activities, HEW, 1965-66; dir. Govtl. Affairs Inst., 1969-75, chmn., 1970-72; trustee Pub. Adminstrn. Svc., 1969-75, chmn., 1973-75; bd. dirs. Delta Dental Plan Mich., 1972-78, chmn. consumers' adv. coun., 1975-77; bd. dirs. Ctr. for Population Activities, 1975-81, chmn., 1975-81; lifetime vis. prof. Capital U. Economics and Bus., Beijing, 1996—. Author: The Philippine Presidency, 1956; editor: Changing Dimensions in Public Administration, 1962; contbr. articles to profl. jours. Mem. Citizens League, Cleve., 1957-59; mem. Ann Arbor Citizens Coun., 1965-69; bd. dirs. Southeastern Mich. Family Planning Project, 1975-77; trustee Congregational Summer Assembly, 1982-85; commr. Accrediting Commn. no Edn. for Health Svcs. Adminstrn., 1989-95. Served with AUS, 1943-46, ETO. Fellow Am. Pub. Health Assn. (chmn. program devel. bd. 1975-77, mem. exec. bd. 1975-80, mem. governing coun. 1975—, pres. 1979, chmn. publs. bd. 1984-88), Royal Soc. Health (hon.), Am. Polit. Sci. Assn. (life); mem. Am. Soc. Pub. Adminstrn. (past mem. coun.), Phi Kappa Phi, Pi Sigma Alpha, Pi Gamma Mu, Delta Omega. Home: 2670 Bedford Rd Ann Arbor MI 48104-4010 Office: PO Box 7903 Ann Arbor MI 48107-7903

ROMANKIW, LUBOMYR TARAS, materials engineer; b. Zhowkwa, Ukraine, Apr. 17, 1931. BSc, U. Alta., 1955; MSc and PhD in Metallurgy, MIT, 1962. Mem. rsch. staff materials and processes, Thomas J. Watson Rsch. Ctr. IBM Corp, Yorktown Heights, N.Y., 1962-63, mgr. magnetic components divsn., 1965-68, mgr. magnetic material and devices, 1968-78, mgr. material and process studies, 1981-91, dep. mgr.; fellow IBM Corp, 1986; head Ctr. for Electrochem. Tech. and Microfabrication IBM Corp, Yorktown Heights, N.Y., 1991—; instr. MIT, 1959-61; cons. East Fishkill Devel. Lab. & Mfg. IBM Corp, 1978-80, San Jose Devel. Lab. anf Mfg. Recipient Perkin medal Am. Chem. Soc., 1993; IBM fellow, 1986, ECS fellow, 1990, IBM Acad. Tech. fellow, 1987. Mem. IEEE (Morris Liebman award 1994), Electrochem. Soc. (sec.-treas. 1979-80, Vittorio de Nora medal and award 1994), Am. Electroplaters Soc. award, Acad. Engring. Sci. of Ukraine, Sigma Xi. Achievements include research in magnetic thin films, deposition of thin films, ray lithography mask devel. dielectrics, magnetic device design, material selection and fabrication, electrodeposition, magnetic materials, electronic and magnetic device fabrication, chemical engineering, and metallurgy. Office: IBM-Thomas J Watson Research Ctr PO Box 218 Yorktown Heights NY 10598-0218

ROMANO, ANTONIO, microbiologist; b. Penns Grove, N.J., Mar. 6, 1929; s. Antonio and Maria R.; m. Marjorie J. Backus, 1953; children: Stephen, James, Charles. BSc in Biology, Rutgers U., 1949, PhD, 1952. Assoc. microbiologist Ortho Rsch. Found., Raritan, N.J., 1952-54; instr. microbial biochemistry Waksman Inst. Microbiology, Rutgers U., 1954-56; sr. asst. scientist to sr. scientist R.A. Taft San. Engring. Ctr., USPHS, Cin., 1956-59; from assoc. prof. to prof. bacteriology U. Cin., 1959-71, head dept. biol. scis., 1964-66; prof. biology U. Conn., Storrs, 1971—, head microbiology sect., 1974-85, dean Coll. Liberal Arts and Scis., 1992-96; sr. vis. fellow dept. biochemistry U. Leicester, Eng., 1967-68; vis. fellow in biochemistry Clare Hall, U. Cambridge, Eng., 1979; program dir. for cell biology NSF, Washington, 1984-85; vis. scholar dept. biology U. Calif. San Diego, La Jolla, 1989; U.S. rep. NATO Adv. Panel on Collaborative Rsch. Grants, 1990-92. Author/co-author books and monographs; mem. editorial bd. Jour. Bacteriology, 1971-80, Applied and Environ. Microbiology, 1973-76; contbr. chpts. to books, numerous articles to profl. jours. N.J. State scholar, 1945-49, Rutgers Rsch. and Endowment Found. fellow, 1949-51; NSF sr. postdoctoral fellow, 1967-78. Mem. AAAS, Am. Soc. for Microbiology, Sigma Xi. Office: U Conn Wood Hall Box U-125 Storrs CT 06269-3125

ROMANO, DOMINICK V., food products executive; b. 1934. V.p. Ronetco Supermarkets, Inc. subs. Shoprite Supermarkets, Inc., Succasunna, N.J., 1953—; treas., bd. dirs., chmn. bd. Shoprite Supermarkets, Inc., Edison, N.J., 1985—. Office: Shoprite Supermarkets Inc 130 Campus Plz Edison NJ 08837-3936*

ROMANO, DONNA MARIE, secondary school educator; b. Boston, Dec. 17, 1941; d. Adolph F. and Edna M. (Brill) DeSalvo; m. Nunzio Romano, June 24, 1961; children: Salvatore, William A. A Bus. Sci., Cardinal Cushing Coll., Brookline, Mass., 1961; BA in Social Studies, South Mass. U., 1974; MEd in Computer in Edn., Leslie Coll., 1991. Cert. English, bus., social studies, computer tchr., Mass. Tchr. bus. edn. New Bedford (Mass.) H.S., 1974—, tchr. tech. preparation program, 1991, tchr. computer workshop, 1992; mem. adv. bd. for occupl. Edn., New Bedford, 1990. Author, editor: Word Perfect 5.1 for the Classroom, 1992. Mem. ASCD, NEA, AAUW, Mass. Tchrs. Assn., Mass. Bus. Edn. Assn., New Bedford Educators Assn. (sec. 1989-90), Bristol County Edn. Assn. Avocations: travel, gourmet cooking, collecting pairpoint glass. Home: 749 Pine Hill Dr New Bedford MA 02745-1932 Office: New Bedford HS 230 Hathaway Blvd New Bedford MA 02740-2818

ROMANO, JOSEPH ANTHONY, marketing and public relations executive; b. Bklyn., Sept. 5, 1946; s. Anthony Wilbur and Anne (Fusco) R.; m. Linda Rose Giacalone, Sept. 23, 1972; children: Nicholas Joseph, Christine Dianne. Student, Villanova U., 1964-66; BS in Pharm. Sci., Columbia U.,

1970, D Pharmacy, 1972. Clin. resident Lenox Hill Hosp., N.Y.C., 1970-72; BS in Pharm. Sci. Columbia U., N.Y.C., 1972-76; PharmD SUNY, Buffalo, 1976-78; assoc. dean, assoc. prof. U. Wash., Seattle, 1978-83; assoc. dir. medicine Pfizer Labs., N.Y.C., 1983-85, product mgr., 1985, asst. to exec. v.p., 1985-87; sr. v.p., group dir. Hill & Knowlton, Inc., N.Y.C., 1987-88; exec. dir. external affairs Sandoz Pharm. Corp., N.Y.C., 1988-89; pres. Audio Visual Med. Mktg., N.Y.C., 1989-92; vice chair Nelson Communications, Inc., N.Y.C., 1992—; mem. U.S. Nat. Adv. Com. Health Profls., Washington, 1980-85. Co-author: Clinical Pharmacology, 1980, Pharmacy State Board Reviews, 1976, 78, 85, The Vitamin Book, 1985; cons. editor Med. Intercom, N.Y.C., 1986-89; contbr. articles to profl. jours. Fellow Royal Soc. Health London; mem. Am. Pharm. Assn., Am. Soc. Healthcare Pharmacists, Am. Assoc. Study Headaches, Nat. Headache Found., Am. Assn. Colls. Pharmacy, U.S. Golf Assn., Rho Chi. Avocations: photography, philately, golf, music. Office: Nelson Communications Inc 41 Madison Ave New York NY 10010-2202

ROMANO, LOUIS, JR., industrial gas company executive; b. Bridgeport, Conn., July 3, 1945; s. Louis and Santa (Cutuli) R.; m. J. Johnson (div. June 1986), children: Marjorie S., Angela J.; m. Ann Elizabeth Fox Berk, Aug. 27, 1988. BS in Engring., U.S. Naval Acad., 1967; postgrad., Manhattan Coll., 1975, George Washington U., 1991. Sales engr. Union Carbide Corp., Chgo., 1974-77; asst. sales mgr. Union Carbide Corp., Houston, 1977-81; divsn. sales mgr. Union Carbide Indsl. Svcs. Co., Houston, 1981-83; product mgr. Linde div. Union Carbide, Danbury, Conn., 1983-87; worldwide market mgr. Union Carbide Indsl. Gases Inc., Danbury, 1987-92; worldwide market mgr. Praxair Inc., Danbury, 1992, dir. merchant sales ctrl. region, 1992—. Contbr. articles to profl. jours. Vol. Spl. Olympics, Conn., 1988—; bd. dirs. Kleinwood Mcpl. Utility Dist., Spring, Tex., 1981-83; mentor Whisonier Middle Sch., Brookfield, Conn. With USN, 1967-74, lt. comdr. USNR, 1974-88. Mem. AICE, Am. Chem. Soc., U.S. Naval Acad. Alumni Assn. Republican. Avocations: tennis, bridge, scuba diving. Office: Praxair Inc 2 Summit Park Dr Cleveland OH 44131-2553

ROMANO, ROBERTA, law educator; b. Bklyn., Jan. 27, 1952. AB with highest honors, U. Rochester, 1973; MA, U. Chgo., 1975; JD, Yale U., 1980. Law clk. U.S. Ct. Appeals (2d cir.), Hartford, Conn., 1980-81; asst. prof. Stanford (Calif.) U., 1981-84, assoc. prof., 1984-85; prof. of law Yale U., New Haven, Conn., 1985—, Allen Duffy prof. of law, 1991—. Co-editor Jour. Law, Econs., and Orgn., 1988—. Mem. Assn. Am. Law Schs. (exec. coun., bus. assns. sect. 1987-90, chmn. 1990), Phi Beta Kappa. Office: Yale Law Sch 127 Wall St Drawer 401A Yale Sta New Haven CT 06520

ROMANOFF, MILFORD MARTIN, building contractor, architectural designer; b. Cleve., Aug. 21, 1921; s. Barney Sanford and Edythe Stolpher (Bort) R.; student Coll. Arch., U. Mich., 1939-42; B.B.A., U. Toledo, 1943; m. Marjorie Reinwald, Nov. 6, 1945; children—Bennett S., Lawrence M., Janet Beth (dec.). Pres., Glass City Constrn. Co., Toledo, 1951-55, Milford Romanoff Inc., Toledo, 1956—. Co-founder, Neighborhood Improvement Found. Toledo, 1960; mem. Lucas County Econ. Devel. Com., 1979—; mem. citizens adv. bd. Recreation Commn. Toledo, 1973-86; mem. campus adv. com. Med. Coll. Ohio, 1980—; trustee Cummings Treatment Center for Adolescents, 1981—; mem. Children's Services Bd. Lucas County, 1981—; pres. Ohio B'nai Brith, 1959-60, Toledo Lodge, 1958-59; bd. dirs. Anti-Defamation League, 1955-60, Ohio Hillel Orgns., Lucas County Dept. Human Svcs., Arthritis Assn., 1995—; chmn. Toledo Amateur Baseball and Softball Com., 1979-81; mem. Democratic Precinct Com., 1975-78, Arthritis Bd. Dirs.; trustee Temple Brotherhood, 1956-58, bd. dirs., 1981—; pres. Cherry Hill Nursing Home, 1964-85; cons. U.S. Care Corp., 1985—; mem. Crosby Gardens Bd. Advisors, 1983—; bd. govs. Toledo Housing for Elderly, 1982-84, sec., 1989, pres. bd. govs., 1990—, pres, 1991—; bd. advisors Ret. Sr. Vol. Program, 1987-89, chmn. 1988-90, 93—, sec. adv. bd., 1990—; mem. adv. bd. Salvation Army (vice chmn. 1986-87, chmn. 1988-90, ct. apptd. spl. advocate adv., bd. treas. 1988—), chmn. Mental Health Adv. Bd., 1983-84, sec., 1989; bd. dirs. Kidney Found. Northwestern Ohio, 1986—, sec., 1989; bd. dirs. Toledo Urban Forestry Commn., 1991—, pres., 1993, 95, Lucas County Dept. Human Svcs. Bd.; bd. dirs. Arthritis Assn. Lt. (j.g.) USN, 1943-46. Mem. U. Toledo Alumni Assn., Toledo Mus. Art (asso.), Econ. Opportunity Planning Assn. Greater Toledo (adv. bd.), U. Mich. Alumni Assn., Toledo Zool. Soc., Zeta Beta Tau. Clubs: Masons; B'nai B'rith (pres. Toledo lodge 1958-59, statewide pres. 1959-60), Hadassah (assoc. Toledo chpt.). Home and Office: Milford Romanoff Inc 2514 Bexford Pl Toledo OH 43606-2414

ROMANO-MAGNER, PATRICIA RENÉE, educator; b. N.Y.C., Mar. 22, 1928; d. Alfonso and Nicole (Siriani) Romano; m. Ralph Marvin Magner, Dec. 26, 1954. BA, Calif. State U., L.A., 1952, MA, 1953; postgrad., Stanford U., 1960, U. Chgo., 1958. Cert. elem. edn. tchr. Asst. prof. Calif. State U., L.A., 1959; master tchr. Stanford U., Palo Alto, Calif., 1960. Docent Felicita Found. for the Arts, Escondido, Calif., 1991. Mem. AAUP, Stanford U. Club. Avocations: music, art, writing, sports, books. Address: 1037 4th St San Diego CA 92101-4802

ROMANOS, NABIL ELIAS, business development manager; b. Roumie, Metn, Lebanon, June 3, 1965; came to U.S., 1982; s. Elias Rachid and Kamale (Salame) R. BA in Econs. and History magna cum laude, Georgetown U., 1986; postgrad., Hautes Etudes Commerciales, France, 1989; MBA, U. Calif., Berkeley, 1989. Rsch. assoc. Am. Fin. Svcs. Assn., Washington, 1986-87; fin. analyst Varian Assocs., Palo Alto, Calif., 1988, sr. fin. analyst, 1989-91; mgr. fin. mkt. analysis Varian Oncology Systems, Palo Alto, 1991-92; mgr. bus. devel. Varian Health Care Systems, Palo Alto, 1992-94, Zug, Switzerland, 1994-95, São Paulo, 1996—. Author: Finance Facts Yearbook, 1987. Vol. tutor for refugees Community Action Coalition, Washington, 1985-86; vol. interpreter emergency room Georgetown U., Washington, 1984-86; internat. vol. Internat. House U. Calif., Berkeley, 1987-89. Scholar Georgetown U., 1985-86, U. Calif., Berkeley, 1987-89. Mem. Phi Alpha Theta. Maronite Catholic.

ROMANOW, ROY JOHN, provincial government official, barrister, solicitor; b. 1939; s. Michael and Tekla R.; m. Eleanore Boykowich, 1967. Arts and Laws degrees, U. Sask. Mem. Sask. Legislative Assembly, 1967-82, 1986—, provincial sec., 1971-72, atty. gen. of province, 1971-82, minister of intergovernmental affairs, 1979-82, leader, Sask. New Dem. Party, 1987—, leader of the opposition, 1987-91, leader of the majority, 1991—, premier, 1991—; opposition house leader for New Dem. Party Caucus, 1986. Co-author: Canada Notwithstanding, 1984. Office: Legislative Assembly, 2405 Legislative Dr, Regina, SK Canada S4S 0B3

ROMANOWITZ, BYRON FOSTER, architect, engineer; b. Covington, Ky., Nov. 14, 1929; s. Harry Alex and Mildred (Foster) R.; m. Mildred Elaine Gize, June 15, 1957; children: Laura Ann, Mark Walter, Cynthia Ellen. B.S. in Civil Engring, U. Ky., 1951; M.F.A. in Architecture, Princeton, 1953. Instr. sch. architecture Princeton U., 1954; architect Brock & Johnson, Lexington, 1958-59, Johnson & Romanowitz, Architects, Lexington and Louisville, 1960—; pres. Ky. Bd. examiners and Registration of Archs., 1975-91; instr. U. Ky. Sch. Architecture, 1996. Prin. works include U. Ky. campus bldgs., 1959-91, Ea. Ky. U. campus bldgs., 1959-77, Centre Coll., Danville, Ky., campus bldgs., 1967-89, Georgetown (Ky.) Coll. campus bldgs., 1964-84, Asbury Coll., Wilmore, Ky., 1972-78, Asbury Theol. Sem., 1978-93, Berea Coll. bldgs., 1978-91, Transylvania U. bldgs., 1974-90, U. Louisville, 1990, 11 downtown Lexington office bldgs. Mem. Lexington Urban Renewal Commn., 1963-69; chmn. adv. bd. Salvation Army, 1971-72; trustee Midway (Ky.) Coll., 1986-95. With USNR, 1955-58; lt. comdr. Res. Recipient award of merit nat. archtl. competition AIA/Ednl. Facilities Lab., 1966. Fellow AIA (1st honor awards Ky. archtl. competition 1959, 61, 68, 70, 73, 78, 80, 81, pres. East Ky. chpt. 1965); mem. Ky. Soc. Architects (pres. 1966), Masons, Rotary, Lexington Club, Cotillion Club, Tau Beta Pi, Phi Mu Alpha, Phi Sigma Kappa. Home: 2057 Lakeside Dr Lexington KY 40502-3016 Office: Johnson Romanowitz/ Arch & Assoc 300 E Main St Ste 301 Lexington KY 40507-1538

ROMANOWSKI, THOMAS ANDREW, physics educator; b. Warsaw, Poland, Apr. 17, 1925; came to U.S., 1946, naturalized, 1949; s. Bohdan and Alina (Sumowski) R.; m. Carmen des Rochers, Nov. 15, 1952; children—Alina, Dominique. B.S., Mass. Inst. Tech., 1952; M.S., Case Inst. Tech., 1956, Ph.D., 1957. Rsch. assoc. physics Carnegie Inst. Tech., 1956-60; asst. physicist high energy physics Argonne Nat. Lab., Ill., 1960-63; assoc. physicist Argonne Nat. Lab., 1963-72, physicist, 1972-78; prof. physics Ohio State U., Columbus, 1964-92, prof. emeritus, 1992—; sr. scientist Argonne Nat. Lab., 1992. Contbr. articles to profl. jours. and, papers to sci. meetings, seminars and workshops. Served with C.E. AUS, 1946-47. Fellow Am. Phys. Soc., AAAS; mem. Lambda Chi Alpha. Achievements include research in nuclear and high energy physics. Home: 4408 Morgal St Rockville MD 20853-2162 Office: Dept Energy Div High Energy Physic Washington DC 20585

ROMANS, DONALD BISHOP, corporate executive; b. Louisville, Apr. 22, 1931; s. Albert D. and Moneta (Bishop) R.; m. Marilyn Yvonne Neff, June 13, 1953; children: Rebecca Ann, Jennifer. BS, U. Louisville, 1953; MBA, Harvard U., 1958. Mgr. internal auditing and data processing, mem. contr. staff Container Corp. Am., Chgo., 1958-62; successively asst. to pres., asst. treas., treas., v.p. fin., sr. v.p. fin., exec. v.p. Trans Union Corp., Chgo., 1962-81; exec. v.p., chief fin. officer Sunbeam Corp., Chgo., 1981-82, Bally Mfg. Corp., Chgo., 1982-87; fin. cons. Chgo., 1987; pres. Romans and Co., Chgo., 1987-93; chmn. Merlin Corp., Geneva, Ill., 1990; bd. dirs. Burnham Fund Inc., N.Y.C.; trustee Zweig Series Trust, N.Y.C.; life trustee St. Mary of Nazareth Hosp. Capt. USMCR, 1953-56. Mem. Econ. Club. Republican. Avocations: tennis, boating.

ROMANS, JOHN NIEBRUGGE, lawyer; b. Bklyn., May 23, 1942; s. John McDowell and Helen Pond (Niebrugge) R.; m. Caroline Ward; children: John A., Andrew C. BA, Williams Coll., 1964; LLB, Columbia U., 1967. Bar: N.Y. 1967, U.S. Dist. Ct. (so. and ea. dist.) N.Y. 1971, U.S. Ct. Appeals (2d cir.) 1971, U.S. Ct. Appeals (3rd cir.) 1976, U.S. Ct. Appeals (4th and 7th cirs.) 1987, U.S. Ct. Appeals (9th cir.) 1992, U.S. Supreme Ct. 1971. Ptnr. Curtis, Mallet-Prevost, Colt & Mosle, N.Y.C., 1982-90, Katten Muchin & Zavis, N.Y.C., 1990—; lectr. on air law topics at various seminars. Contbr. articles to profl. jours. Trustee Summit (N.J.) Unitarian-Universalist Ch., 1978; bd. dirs. Robert Sterling Clark Found., 1989—; bd. trustees Mamaroneck Pub. Libr. Dist., 1990—. Lt. USNR, 1968-71. Mem. Internat. Assn. Def. Counsel, Assn. of Bar of City of N.Y. (mem. aero. com. 1983-85, chmn. 1986-89, 92—, products liability com. 1989-91), Larchmont (N.Y.) Yacht Club. Avocations: sailing, tennis. Office: Katten Muchin & Zavis 40 Broad St New York NY 10004-2315

ROMANSKY, MICHAEL A., lawyer; b. Washington, Apr. 26, 1952. BSS, Northwestern U., 1974; JD with honors, George Washington U., 1977. Bar: D.C. 1977. Ptnr. McDermott Will & Emery, Washington. Mem. D.C. Bar Assn., Phi Eta Sigma. Office: McDermott Will & Emery 1850 K St NW Washington DC 20006-2213*

ROMANSKY, MONROE JAMES, physician, educator; b. Hartford, Conn., Mar. 16, 1911; s. Benjamin and Henrietta (Levine) R.; m. Evelyn Muriel Lackman, Jan. 10, 1943; children: Stephen, Gerald, Michael, Richard. A.B., U. Maine, 1933; M.D., U. Rochester, 1937. Diplomate: Am. Bd. Internal Medicine. Intern Strong Meml. Hosp.-U. Rochester, N.Y., 1937-38; asst. resident Strong Meml. Hosp.-U. Rochester, 1938-39, James Gleason Research fellow studies on relationship of kidneys to hypertension, 1939-40, chief resident, 1940-41, instr. in medicine, 1941-42; investigator Office Sci. Research and Devel., Surgeon Gen. U.S., 1941-42; chief biochemistry and antibiotic research Walter Reed Army Hosp., 1942-46; asso. prof. Sch. Medicine, George Washington U., Washington, 1946—; prof. medicine Sch. Medicine, George Washington U., 1957—; dir. George Washington U. med. div. D.C. Gen. Hosp., 1950-69; dir. infectious diseases research lab. and infectious diseases div. D.C. Gen. Hosp., 1950-69; cons. internal medicine antibiotics Walter Reed Army Hosp., Washington, 1946—; Cons. internal medicine antibiotics VA Hosp., Washington, 1952—, NIH, Bethesda, Md., 1953—, Surgeon Gen. USAF, 1966—; mem. Asian influenza adv. com. D.C., 1956-61; mem. ad hoc adv. com. Bur. Medicine FDA, 1966-67; examiner Am. Bd. Internal Medicine, 1965, 67, 69. Editorial bd.: Antimicrobial Agts. and Chemotherapy, 1961-72; Contbr. to profl. jours. Trustees council U. Rochester, 1965—. Served with M.C., AUS, 1942-46. Decorated Legion of Merit; recipient Founders award Tau Epsilon Phi, Disting. Career award U. Maine. Fellow ACP (adv. bd. to gov. D.C. 1969—); mem. Am. Soc. Internal Medicine, Am. Fedn. Clin. Research, Soc. Exptl. Biology and Medicine, Am. Soc. Microbiology, Infectious Diseases Soc. (founding council 1963-66), Soc. Med. Cons. to Armed Forces, Sigma Xi, Alpha Omega Alpha. Club: Woodmont Country. Pioneer work in prolonging action of penicillin, requiring only single daily injection, Romansky Formula, 1944; nutritional studies in obesity as related to weight reduction. Home: 5600 Wisconsin Ave Chevy Chase MD 20815-4408

ROMBOUT, LUKE, museum designer, administrator; b. Amsterdam, Netherlands, May 4, 1933; emigrated to Can., 1954, naturalized, 1959; s. Louis and Aleida (VanBuren) R. B.F.A., Mt. Alison U., Sackville, N.B., 1967. Acting curator Owens Art Gallery/Mt. Allison U., 1965-67, dir., 1968-71; chmn., asst. prof. visual arts program York U., Toronto, Ont., 1972-74; mem. arts adv. panel Can. Council, Ottawa, Ont., 1969-70; dir. art bank Can. Council, 1972-74, head visual arts film sect., 1974-75; dir. Vancouver Art Gallery (B.C., Can.), 1975-84; lectr. Can. Art History/Mt. Allison U., 1968-71; lectr. art history N.S. Coll. Art Design (Can.), 1970-72; lectr. U. Ottawa, 1974-75; mem. adv. com. art Can. Dept. Pub. Works, 1973; mem. design adv. com. Can. Post., 1973; mem. fine arts com. Can. Dept. External Affairs, 1973-75; bd. dirs. Anna Wyman Dance Theatre, 1976-85; dir. McCord Mus. Can. History, Montreal, Can., 1990-94; dean, faculty of creative work George Brown Coll., Toronto, Can., 1994—. Prin. works include Owens Art Gallery, Mt. Allison Univ., Sackville, N.B., 1970, Art Bank Repository, Can. Coun., Ottawa, Ont., 1972, Vancouver (B.C.) Art Gallery, 1983, Palais de la Civilisation Ville de Montréal, 1985, Expo'86 Contemporary Art Mus. Roundhouse Renovation, Vancouver, 1986, Expo'86 Ramses II Pavilion, Vancouver, 1986, McCord Mus. Can. History, Montréal, 1992. Fellow Royal Soc. Arts; mem. Order of Can., Assn. Internat. Critiques d'Art. Home and Office: 214 Blvd St Joseph E, Montreal, PQ Canada H2T 1H6

ROME, DONALD LEE, lawyer; b. West Hartford, Conn., May 17, 1929; s. Herman Isaac and Juliette (Stern) R.; m. Sheila Ward, Apr. 20, 1958; children: Adam Ward, Lisa, Ethan Stern. SB, Trinity Coll., 1951; LLB, Harvard U., 1954. Bar: Conn. 1954, U.S. Dist. Ct. 1955, U.S. Cir. Ct. Appeals 1965, U.S. Supreme Ct. 1965. Assoc. Ribicoff and Kotkin, Hartford, Conn., 1954-58, ptnr., 1958-67; ptnr. Rosenberg, Rome, Barnett, Sattin & Santos and predecessor, Hartford, 1967-83; now ptnr. Robinson & Cole, Hartford, 1983—; mem. Conn. Gov.'s Study Commn. on Uniform Consumer Credit Code, 1969-70; chmn. Conn. bar adv. com. of attys. to make recommendations to U.S. Dist. Ct. for proposed changed of bankruptcy rules in dist. Conn., 1975-77; mem. Bankruptcy Merit Screening Com. for Dist. Ct., 1980-81; mem. adv. com. Conn. Law Revision commn. on article 2A for Uniform Comml. Code, 1987-89; mem. CPR Inst. for Dispute Resolution Panel of Disting. Neutrals and CPR Fin. Svcs. Panel of Disting. Neutrals; mem. panel of mediators for U.S. Dist. Ct. and U.S. Bankruptcy Ct., Hartford; lectr. law U. Conn., 1965-74, 81-83; mem. faculty Sch. Banking of South, La. State U., 1982-84; lectr. continuing legal edn. on secured creditors' rights, comml. fin., bankruptcy and uniform comml. code, 1958—. Prin. author, editor: Business Workouts Manual, 1985, 1992; co-author: A Comparative Analysis and Study of the Uniform Consumer Credit Code in Relation to the Existing Consumer Credit Law in Connecticut, 1970; contbg. author: Connecticut Practice Book, 1978, Collier Bankruptcy Practice Guide, 1981, Asset-Based Financing: A Transactional Guide, 1984, Controllers Business Advisor, 1994; mem. bd. editors Jour. Bankruptcy Practice, 1991—; contbr. articles to profl. jours. Past mem. bd. dirs. New Eng. region Am. Jewish Com., also Hartford chpt., Hebrew Home for Aged, Hartford; past mem. bd. trustees Temple Beth Israel, West Hartford. Mem. ABA (bus. bankruptcy com. and comml. fin. svcs. com., sect. on bus. law, mediation com., sect. on dispute resolution), Fed. Bar Assn. (bankruptcy law com.), Conn. Bar Assn. (chmn. sect. comml. law and bankruptcy 1977-80, exec. com. banking law sect. 1984-95, chmn. spl. com. scope and correlation 1983-84, dispute resolution sect.), Hartford County Bar Assn., Conn. Bar Found., Assn. Comml. Fin. Attys. (pres. 1978-80), Am. Arbitration Assn. (nat. panel comml. arbitrators, mediator), Am. Law Inst., Am. Coll. Comml. Fin. Lawyers (chmn. alternate dispute resolution com., bd. regents), Am. Bankruptcy Inst., Turnaround Mgmt. Assn., Harvard Law Sch. Assn. Conn. (pres. 1970-71), Hartford Club, Harvard of N.Y.C. Club, Masons (32 deg., trial commn. Conn. grand lodge 1970-82). Home: 46 Belknap Rd West Hartford CT 06117-2819 Office: Robinson & Cole 1 Commercial Plz Hartford CT 06103-3597 *We are told by Kipling that success and failure are "imposters." I have found this fundamental teaching to be most helpful in the practice of law and in life generally. Concentration on long-term relationships and basic values is so much more important than ephemeral successes and failures.*

ROME, JOHN L., restaurant chain executive; b. Alliance, Ohio, 1954. Pres. internat. div. Wendy's Internat. Inc.; CEO Total Quality Inc., Dublin, Ohio, 1994—. Office: Total Quality Inc. 1084 Limberlost Ct Dublin OH 43017*

ROMEO, CHRISTINA IOANNIDES, speech language pathologist; b. Livingston, N.J., Oct. 19, 1968; d. Paul M. and Carol J. (Mancuso) Ioannides; m. Michael J. Romeo, Mar. 26, 1994. BS, Trenton State Coll., 1990; MA, Kean Coll. N.J., 1992. Grad. asst., asst. tchr. comm. handicapped class Kean Coll. N.J., Union, 1990-92; speech lang. specialist Old Bridge (N.J.) Twp. Bd. Edn., 1992—. Fundraiser Am. Cancer Soc., Edison, N.J., The Valerie Fund, Maplewood, N.J.; cmty. svc. vol. Local Vets. Orgn., Iselin, N.J. Mem. NEA, N.J. Edn. Assn., Old Bridge Edn. Assn., Am. Speech Lang. Hearing Assn. (cert. clin. competence), N.J. Speech Lang. Hearing Assn., Jonas Salk Middle Sch. PTA, Walter Schirra Sch. PTA, Shore Athletic Club. Avocation: race walking. Home: 357 Bordentown Ave South Amboy NJ 08879-1808 Office: Old Bridge Twp Bd Edn Jonas Salk Middle Sch 370 W Greystone Rd Old Bridge NJ 08857

ROMEO, LUIGI, linguist, educator; b. Tropea, Italy, Sept. 20, 1926; came to U.S., 1953; s. Pasquale and Beatrice (Lo Torto) R.; m. Elenore Ruth Andersen, Aug. 10, 1983. B.A. in Fgn. Langs., Wash. State U., 1957; M.A. in Romance Langs., U. Wash., 1959, Ph.D., 1960. Instr. Romance langs. U. Wash., Seattle, 1959-60, acting asst. prof. Romance langs., 1960-61; asst. prof. Italian U. Toronto, 1961-65; assoc. prof. Italian U. Colo., Boulder, 1965-68, prof. linguistics, 1968-84, prof. linguistics emeritus, 1984—.

ROMEO, PETER JOHN, lawyer; b. Darby, Pa., Aug. 1, 1942; s. Joseph Paul and Rose Marie (Beckett) R.; m. Nancy Virginia Schmidt, July 15, 1972; children: Christopher, Jeffrey, Michael. BSBA, Georgetown U., 1964; JD, George Washington U., 1967, LLM, 1969. Bar; Va. 1968, U.S. Dist. Ct. D.C. 1969, U.S. Supreme Ct. 1972; CPA, D.C. Acct. Schumaker & Yates, Washington, 1964-69; atty. U.S. Securities and Exchange Com., Washington, 1969-72, spl. counsel, 1972-79, chief counsel div. corp. finance, 1980-84; ptnr. Hogan & Hartson LLP, Washington, 1984—. Author: Comprehensive Section 16 Outline, 1984 (updated annually), The Registration Process, 1985 (updated annually); co-author: Section 16 Reporting Guide, 1989, Section 16 Forms and Filing Handbook, 1991 (updated 1993), Section 16 Treatise and Reporting Guide, 1994; contbr. articles to profl. jours. Mem. ABA (mem. fed. regulation securities com., chmn. task force on sect. 16 devels.), D.C. Bar Assn., Va. State Bar. Roman Catholic. Office: Hogan & Hartson 555 13th St NW Washington DC 20004-1109

ROMER, PAUL MICHAEL, economics educator; b. Denver, Nov. 7, 1955; s. Roy R. and Beatrice A. (Miller) R.; m. Virginia K. Langmuir, Feb. 28, 1980; children: Geoffrey M., Amy J. BA in Math., U. Chgo., 1977, PhD in Econs., 1983. Asst. prof. dept. econs. U. Rochester (N.Y.), 1982-88; prof. dept. econs. U. Chgo., 1988-90; fellow Ctr. for Advanced Study in Behavioral Scis., Stanford, Calif., 1989-90; prof. econs. U. Calif., Berkeley, 1990—; prof. Stanford U. Grad. Sch. Bus., 1996—. Fellow Econometric Soc.; mem. Am. Econs. Assn., Nat. Bur. Econ. Rsch. Office: Hoover Instn Stanford University Stanford CA 94305

ROMER, ROY R., governor; b. Garden City, Kans., Oct. 31, 1928; s. Irving Rudolph and Margaret Elizabeth (Snyder) R.; m. Beatrice Miller, June 10, 1952; children: Paul, Mark, Mary, Christopher, Timothy, Thomas, Elizabeth. B.S. in Agrl. Econs., Colo. State U., 1950; LL.B., U. Colo., 1952; postgrad., Yale U. Bar: Colo. 1952. Engaged in farming in Colo., 1942-52; ind. practice law Denver, 1955-66; mem. Colo. Ho. of Reps., 1958-62, Colo. Senate, 1962-66; owner, operator Arapahoe Aviation Co., Colo. Flying Acad., Geneva Basin Ski Area; engaged in home site devel.; owner chain farm implement and indsl. equipment stores Colo.; commr. agr. State of Colo., 1975, chief staff, exec. asst. to gov., 1975-77, 83-84, state treas., 1977-86, gov., 1987—; chmn. Gov. Colo. Blue Ribbon Panel, Gov. Colo. Small Bus. Council; mem. agrl. adv. com. Colo. Bd. Agr. Bd. editors Colo. U. Law Rev., 1960-62. Past trustee Iliff Sch. Theology, Denver; mem., past chmn. Nat. Edn. Goals Panel; co-chmn. Nat. Coun. on Standards and Testing. With USAF, 1952-53. Mem. Dem. Gov.'s Assn. (chmn.), Nat. Gov.'s Assn. (former chmn.), Colo. Bar Assn., Order of the Coif. Democrat. Presbyterian. Office: Office of Gov State Capitol Denver CO 80203*

ROMERO, ELIZABETH RIVERA, public health nurse; b. Manila, Jan. 10, 1958; d. Vivencio Delapaz and Erlinda (Magalona) Rivera; m. Oscar Dedios Romero; 1 child, Sherilynn R. BS in Nursing cum laude, San Francisco State U., 1980. R.N., Calif.; cert. profl. utilization review. Staff nurse St. Lukes Hosp., San Francisco, 1980-85; pub. health nurse St. Mary's Hosp., San Francisco, 1984-85, Kimberly Home Patient Care, Pinole, Calif., 1984-87, utilization rev. case mgr. Brookside Hosp., San Pablo, Calif, 1987-90; head nurse, utilization mgmt. case mgr. San Francisco General Hosp., 1990—; Mem. ANA, Calif. Nurses Assn., Golden Gate Nurses Assn., Am. Heart Assn. (Contra Costa chpt.), Calif. Scholarship Fedn., Interqual ISD Registry. Roman Catholic. Avocations: dancing; travel; camping; photography.

ROMERO, GEORGE A., film director; b. N.Y.C., Feb. 4, 1940. Dir.: (films) Night of the Living Dead, 1968, There's Always Vanilla, 1972, The Crazies, 1972, Hungry Wives, 1973, Martin, 1978, Dawn of the Dead, 1979, Creepshow, 1982, Day of the Dead, 1985, Monkey Shines: An Experiment in Terror, 1988, Two Evil Eyes, 1990, The Dark Half, 1993; dir., screenwriter Knightriders, 1981; exec. producer, scriptwriter Tales from the Dark Side:The Movie, 1990, Night of the Living Dead, 1990; Television: (exec. prodr., screenwriter) Tales From the Darkside. Office: care The Gersh Agy 232 N Canon Dr Beverly Hills CA 90210-5302

ROMERO-BARCELÓ, CARLOS ANTONIO, former political party executive, former governor of Puerto Rico; b. San Juan, P.R., Sept. 4, 1932; s. Antonio S. Romero and Josefina Barceló; m. Kathleen Donnelly, Jan. 2, 1966; children: Juan Carlos, Melinda Kathleen; children by previous marriage: Carlos, Andrés. BA, Yale U., 1953; LLB, U. P.R., 1956; LLD (hon.), U. Bridgeport, 1977. Bar: P.R. 1956. Mem. Herrero-Frank & Romero-Barceló, 1956-58; ptnr. Rivera-Zayas, Rivera-Cestero & Rúa, San Juan, 1958-63, Segurola, Romero & Toledo, 1963-68; pres. Citizens for State 51, 1965-67; mayor, San Juan, 1969-77; gov. P.R., 1977-85, 92—; pres. New Progressive Party, 1974-85, 89-91; resident commr., 1991—. Recipient Hoey award for Interracial Justice, Cath. Interracial Council of N.Y., 1977, Spl. Gold Medal award Spanish Inst., N.Y., 1979, U.S. Atty.-Gen.'s medal, 1981. Mem. Nat. Govs. Assn., So. Govs. Assn. (chmn. 1980-81), Conf., Nat. League Cities (pres. 1975), U.S. Conf. Mayors (bd. dir.). Roman Catholic. Author: Statehood is for the Poor; contbr. articles to profl. jours. Office: 428 Cannon House Office Bldg Washington DC 20515*

ROMEY, WILLIAM DOWDEN, geologist, educator; b. Richmond, Ind., Oct. 26, 1930; s. William Minter and Grace Warring (Dowden) R.; m. Lucretia Alice Leonard, July 16, 1955; children—Catherine Louise, Gretchen Elizabeth, William Leonard. A.B. with highest honors, Ind. U., 1952; student, U. Paris, 1950-51, 52-53; Ph.D., U. Calif. at Berkeley, 1962. Asst. prof. geology and sci. edn. Syracuse U., 1962-66, assoc. prof., 1966-69; exec. dir. earth sci. ednl. program Am. Geol. Inst., 1969-72; prof., chmn. dept. geology St. Lawrence U., Canton, N.Y., 1971-76; prof. St. Lawrence U., 1976—, prof., chmn. dept. geography, 1983-93; prof. emeritus, 1993—; ednl. cons., 1962—; NAS visitor USSR Acad. Sci., 1967; vis. geoscientist Am. Geol. Inst., 1964-66, 71; earth sci. cons. Compton's Ency., 1970-71; adj. prof. Union Grad. Sch., 1974—; mem. bd. rsch. advisers and readers Walden U., 1981—; prof. Grad. Sch. Am., 1993—; travel writer and cruise ship lectr., 1990—. Author: (with others) Investigating the Earth, 1967, (with J. Kramer, E. Muller, J. Lewis) Investigations in Geology, 1967, Inquiry Techniques for Teaching Science, 1968, Risk-Trust-Love, 1972, Consciousness and Creativity, 1975, Confluent Education in Science, 1976; co-editor: Geochemical Prospecting for Petroleum, 1959; assoc. editor: Jour. Coll. Sci. Teaching, 1972-74, Geol. Soc. Am. Bull, 1979-84, Jour. Geol. Edn, 1980—; editor-in-chief: Ash Lad Press, 1975—; contbr. articles on geology, geography and edn. to profl. publs. Bd. dirs. Onondaga Nature Centers, Inc., 1966-69. Served to lt. USNR, 1953-57; lt. comdr. Res. Woodrow Wilson Found. fellow, 1959-60, 61-62; NSF sci. faculty fellow U. Oslo, 1967-68. Fellow Geol. Soc. Am., AAAS; mem. Nat. Assn. Geology Tchrs. (v.p. 1971-72), N.Y. Acad. Scis., Nat. Assn. Geology Tchrs. (pres. 1972-73), Assn. Am. Geographers, Am. Geophys. Union, Geol. Soc. Norway, Assn. Educating Tchrs. of Sci., Can. Assn. Geographers, Assn. for Can. Studies in U.S., Phi Beta Kappa, Sigma Xi, Phi Delta Kappa. Home: PO Box 294 East Orleans MA 02643-0294 Office: St Lawrence U Dept Geography Canton NY 13617

ROMINE, THOMAS BEESON, JR., consulting engineering executive; b. Billings, Mont., Nov. 16, 1925; s. Thomas Beeson and Elizabeth Marjorie (Tschudy) R.; m. Rosemary Pearl Melancon, Aug. 14, 1948; children—Thomas Beeson III, Richard Alexander, Robert Harold. Student, Rice Inst., 1943-44; B.S. in Mech. Engring, U. Tex., Austin, 1948. Registered profl. engr., Tex., Okla., La., Ga. Jr. engr. Gen. Engring. Co., Ft. Worth, 1948-50; design engr. Wyatt C. Hedrick (architect/engr.), Ft. Worth, 1950-54; chief mech. engr. Wyatt C. Hedrick (architect/engr.), 1954-56; chmn., chief mech. engr. Thomas B. Romine, Jr. (now Romine Romine & Burgess, Inc. cons. engrs.), Ft. Worth, 1956—; mem. heating, ventilating, and air conditioning controls com. NRC, 1986-88. Author numerous computer programs in energy analysis and heating and air conditioning field; contbr. articles to profl. jours. Mem. Plan Commn., City of Ft. Worth, 1958-62; mem. Supervisory Bd. Plumbers, City Ft. Worth, 1963-71, chmn., 1970-71; chmn. Plumbing Code Rev. Com., 1968-69; mem. Mech. Bd., City Ft. Worth, 1974-82, chmn., 1976-82; chmn. plumbing code bd. North Central Tex. Council Govts., Ft. Worth, 1971-75; Bd. mgrs. Tex. Christian U.-South Side YMCA, 1969-74; trustee Ft. Worth Symphony Orch., 1968—, Orch. Hall, 1975—. Served with USNR, 1943-45. Disting. fellow ASHRAE (pres. Ft. Worth chpt. 1958, nat. committeeman 1974—); fellow Am. Cons. Engrs. Coun., Automated Procedures for Engring. Cons. (trustee 1970-71, 75, 1st v.p. 1972-73, internat. pres. 1974); mem. NSPE, Tex. Soc. Profl. Engrs. (bd. dirs. 1956, treas. 1967), Cons. Engrs. Coun. Tex. (pres. North Tex. chpt., also v.p. state orgn. 1965, dir. state orgn. 1967), Starfish Class Assn. (nat. pres. 1970-73, nat. champion 1976), Delta Tau Delta (v.p. West div. 1980-90), Pi Tau Sigma. Episcopalian (vestryman). Clubs: Colonial Country, Rotary. Home: 3232 Preston Hollow Rd Fort Worth TX 76109-2051 Office: Romine Romine & Burgess 300 Greenleaf St Fort Worth TX 76107-2316 *It has long been my belief that, in this technological age, the general public can do little more than accept on faith the propriety of mechanical and electrical systems provided for use in their homes and businesses, and that without an understanding and knowledgeable agent to guide them this faith is often misplaced. It is thus incumbent upon the Professional Engineer to use his expertise in this field to insure competency and safety in those projects under his control, and to assist wherever possible in guiding and influencing appropriate legislation in this regard along sound engineering pathways.*

ROMINGER, RICHARD, federal agency administrator; b. Woodland, Calif., July 1, 1927; M. Evelyne Rowe; children: Richard S., Charles A., Ruth E., Bruce J. BS in Plant Sci., U. Calif., Davis, 1949. Farmer Calif.; dir. Dept. Food and Agriculture, Calif., 1977-82; dep. sec. USDA, 1993—. Recipient Disting. Svc. award Calif. Farm Bur. Fedn., 1991; named Agriculturalist of Yr. Calif. State Fair, 1992; numerous others. Office: US Dept of Agriculture Office of the Deputy Secy 14th & Independence Ave SW Washington DC 20250-0002

ROMNEY, CARL F., seismologist; b. Salt Lake City, June 5, 1924; m. Barbara Doughty; children: Carolyn Ann, Kim. B.S. in Meteorology, Calif. Inst. Tech., 1945; Ph.D., U. Calif., Berkeley, 1956. Seismologist U.S. Dept. Air Force, 1955-58; asst. tech. dir. Air Force Tech. Applications Center, 1958-73; dep. dir. Nuclear Monitoring Research Office, Def. Advanced Research Projects Agy., 1973-75, dir., 1975-79; dep. dir. Def. Advanced Research Projects Agy., 1979-83; dir. Ctr. Seismic Studies, 1983-91; v.p. Sci. Applications Internat. Corp., 1987—; tech. adviser U.S. reps. in negotiations Test Ban Treaty; mem. U.S. del. Geneva Conf. Experts, 1958, Conf. on Discontinuance Nuclear Weapons Tests, 1959, 60; negotiations on threshold Test Ban Treaty, Moscow, 1974; mem. U.S. del. Peaceful Nuclear Explosions Treaty, Moscow, 1974-75. Contbr. articles to tech. jours. Recipient Exceptional Civilian Service awards Air Force, 1959, Exceptional Civilian Service awards Dept. Def., 1964, 79; Pres.'s award for Distinguished Fed. Civilian Service, for outstanding contbns. to devel. of control system for underground nuclear tests, 1967; Presdl. Rank of Meritorious Exec., 1980. Research on earthquake mechanism, seismic noise; generation, propagation, detection seismic waves from underground explosions. Home: 4105 Sulgrave Dr Alexandria VA 22309-2629 Office: Ste 1450 1300 N 17th St Arlington VA 22209-3801

ROMNEY, RICHARD BRUCE, lawyer; b. Kingston, Jamaica, Dec. 29, 1942; came to U.S., 1945, naturalized, 1956; s. Frank Oswald and Mary Ellen (Burton) R.; m. Beverly Cochran, Sept. 11, 1965 (dec. 1984); children: Richard Bruce, Jr., Stephanie Cochran; m. Lynthia H. Walker, Aug. 14, 1988; children: Alisa Dawn, Kristen Elizabeth. BA, U. Pa., 1964; JD, U. Va., 1972. Bar: N.Y. 1973, U.S. Ct. Appeals (2d cir.) 1975. Assoc. Dewey, Ballantine, Bushby Palmer & Wood, N.Y.C., 1972-80, ptnr., 1981—. Mem. editorial bd. U. Va. Law Rev., 1970-72. Served to lt. USN, 1964-68. Mem. ABA, N.Y. State Bar Assn., Assn. Bar City N.Y., Order of Coif. Republican. Home: 35 Deerfield Rd Chappaqua NY 10514-1604 Office: Dewey Ballantine 1301 Avenue Of The Americas New York NY 10019-6022

ROMNEY, SEYMOUR LEONARD, physician, educator; b. N.Y.C., June 8, 1917; s. Benjamin and Anne (Senter) R.; m. Shirley Gordon, Nov. 4, 1945; children: Benjamin, Mary Clark, Tim Hayes, Anne. A.B., Johns Hopkins, 1938; M.D., N.Y. U., 1942. Intern Beth Israel Hosp., Boston, 1942-43; resident Boston Lying-in Hosp., Free Hosp. for Women, Boston, 1946-51; fellow, instr. Harvard Med. Sch., 1947-51, asst. prof. obstetrics and gynecology, 1951-57; prof., chmn. dept. gynecology and obstetrics Albert Einstein Coll. Medicine, N.Y.C., 1957-72; prof. Albert Einstein Coll. Medicine, 1972-89, prof. emeritus, 1989—, dir. research gynecol. oncology, 1972—; dir. obstetrics and gynecology Bronx Mcpl. Hosp. Ctr., N.Y.C., 1957-72; cons. WHO. Chair Soc. of Physicians for Reproductive Choice and Health; mem. med. adv. com. Maternity Ctr. Assn.; bd. dirs. Planned Parenthood, N.Y.C. Served to lt. comdr. M.C. USNR, 1943-45. Mem. ACOG, AAAS, Am. Assn. Med. Colls. (life), Am. Gynecol. and Obstet. Soc., Soc. Gynecologic Investigation, Am. Assn. Cancer Rsch., Maternity Ctr. Assn., Population Assn. Am., N.Y. Obstet. Soc., N.Y. Acad. Medicine, N.Y. Acad. Sci. Home: 1300 Morris Park Ave Bronx NY 10605-5008 Office: Einstein Coll Morris Park Ave East Bronx NY 10461

ROMNEY, W. MITT, investment company executive; b. Detroit, Mar. 12, 1947; s. George W. and Lenore (Lafount) R.; m. Ann D., Mar. 21, 1969; children: Taggart, Matthew, Joshua, Benjamin, Craig. BA, Brigham Young U., 1971; JD, Harvard U., 1975, MBA, 1975. Cons. Boston Consulting Group, 1975-77; cons. Bain & Co., Boston, 1977-78, v.p., 1978-84, chmn., CEO, 1991—; mng. ptnr., CEO Bain Capital, Inc., Boston, 1984—; bd. dirs. Marriott Corp., Bethesda, Md., Staples Inc., Framingham, Mass., Babbages Inc., Dallas, Tex., Damon Corp., Needham, Mass. Pres. Boston Stake LDS Ch., 1986—; adv. bd. Brigham Young U. Sch. Bus., Provo, Utah, 1990—; vis. com. Harvard Bus. Sch., Cambridge, Mass; mem. nat. exec. bd. Boy Scouts Am.; trustee Belmont (Mass.) Hill Sch., 1989—. Baker scholar Harvard Bus. Sch., Cambridge, Mass., 1975. Mem. Belmont Hill CLub. Office: Bain Capital 2 Copley Pl Boston MA 02116-6502*

ROMOFF, JEFFREY ALAN, university officer, health care executive; b. N.Y.C., Nov. 30, 1945; s. Richard Warren and Evelyn (Alter) R.; m. Vivian Irene Goodman, Aug. 25, 1966 (dec. June 1983); children: Jennifer Ann, Rebecca Lynn; m. Maxine Ketterer, July 28, 1984. B.S. magna cum laude in Social Scis., CCNY, 1967; M.Phil. in Polit. Scis., Yale U., 1971. Teaching fellow Yale U., 1969-70, teaching assoc., 1970-71; exec. dir. Central Naugatuck Valley Mental Health Council, Waterbury, Conn., 1971-73; regional programing dir. Western Psychiat. Inst. and Clinic (U. Pitts.), 1973-74, assoc. dir. div. edn. and research, 1974-75; assoc. dir. Western Psychiat. Inst. and Clinic, 1975—; adj. asst. prof. pub. health U. Pitts., 1981—, instr. psychiatry, 1982—, assoc. v.p. health scis., 1984-86, vice chancellor health scis., 1986-92; exec. v.p. U. Pitts. Med. Ctr., 1986-92; sr. vice chancellor for Health Adminstrn. U. Pitts., 1992—; pres. U. Pitts. Med. Ctr., 1992—. N.Y.C. Regents scholar CCNY, 1963-67. Mem. Am. Hosp. Assn. (governing coun. sect. for mental health and psychiat. scvs. 1986-89), Am. Psychiat. Assn. (chmn. joint com. with Am. Hosp. Assn. 1983-84), Hosp. Assn. Pa., Coun. Psychiat. Svc. Providers (exec. com. 1981-84). Jewish. Home: 447 Dover Dr Pittsburgh PA 15238 Office: U of Pitts Medical Ctr 3811 Ohara St Pittsburgh PA 15213-2593

ROMOND, JAMES, principal. Prin. La Salle Inst., Troy, N.Y. Recipient Blue Ribbon Sch. award U.S. Dept. Edn., 1990-91. Office: La Salle Inst 174 Williams Rd Troy NY 12180-7723

ROMOSER, GEORGE KENNETH, political science educator; b. Kingston, N.Y., Sept. 14, 1929; s. Carl August and Alva (Becker) R.; m. Mechthild von Tresckow, Apr. 30, 1967; children: Alexandra Ada, Valerie Anna. A.B., Rutgers U., 1951; A.M., U. Chgo., 1954, Ph.D., 1958. Research asst. Nat. Opinion Research Center, 1953; asst. Freiburg (Germany) U., 1955-56; instr. Ohio State U., 1957-61; asso. prof. Conn. Coll., 1963-67; asst. prof., asso. prof., prof. polit. sci. U. N.H., Durham, 1961-62, 67—, chmn. dept., 1968-71, prof. Internat. Affairs, 1986-93, course dir. Internat. Perspective Ctr., 1986-88, dir. program on tech., society and values, 1995—; Fulbright prof. Faculty of Law, Mainz U., Fed. Republic Germany, 1962-63; dir. Emigre Meml. German Internship Programs, 1965—; vis. prof. Free U., Berlin, 1964, Mannheim U., 1968, 82-83, Johns Hopkins, Bologna, Italy, 1969, Munich U., 1973-74, U. Pa., 1986, Kobe U., Japan, 1988-89, Bowdoin Coll., 1990, Freiburg U., Germany, 1993-94, Fulbright Sr. Prof., 1993-94; adj. prof. Mannheim U., Fed. Republic Germany, 1983—; Fulbright sr. rsch. fellow, 1974; Rockefeller fellow Aspen Inst. for Humanistic Studies, 1978-79; cons. Com. on Internat. Exchange of Persons, 1965-66; NEH fellow Yale U., 1993; co-founder Conf. Group on German Politics, 1968—, chmn., 1968-84, regional dir., 1984-87; founder, dir. New Eng. Workshops on German Affairs, 1980—; co-founder Pacific Coast Workshops on German Affairs, 1983-93; commuting fellow Ctr. European Studies Harvard U., 1983—; founder The Japanese Circle, 1989—. Co-author: West German Politics in the Mid-Eighties, 1985, Germany's New Politics, 1995; contbr. articles to profl. jours., books. Chmn. com. on govtl. reorgn. Democratic party N.H., 1962. Decorated Civilian Knight's Cross Fed. Republic of Germany). Mem. Am. Coun. on Germany, Phi Delta Theta, Pi Sigma Alpha, Delta Phi Alpha, Phi Alpha Theta. Home: Worster Rd Eliot ME 03903 Office: U NH Durham NH 03824

ROMSDAHL, MARVIN MAGNUS, surgeon, educator; b. Hayti, S.D., Apr. 2, 1930; s. Conrad Magnus and Hilda Johanna (Shelsta) R.; m. Virginia McElvany; children: Christine Ann, Laura Marie. AB, U. S.D., 1952, BS, 1954; MD, U. Ill., Chgo., 1956; PhD, U. Tex., Houston, 1968. Diplomate Am. Bd. Surgery. Clin. assoc. NIH, NCI, Bethesda, Md., 1958-60; instr. surgery U. Ill., Chgo., 1963-64; asst. surgeon, asst. prof. surgery U. Tex./M.D. Anderson Cancer Ctr., Houston, 1967-69; assoc. grad. faculty mem. Grad. Sch. Biomed. Sci., U. Tex., Houston, 1969-72; assoc. surgeon/asso. prof. surgery U. Tex./M.D. Anderson Cancer Ctr., Houston, 1969-75; dep. dept. head U. Tex./M.D. Anderson Cancer Ctr., 1979-85; grad. faculty mem. U. Tex. Health Sci. Ctr., Houston, 1972—; prof. surgery U. Tex. Med. Sch., Houston, 1975—; surgeon, prof. surgery U. Tex./M.D. Anderson Cancer Ctr., Houston, 1975—; lectr. in field. Contbr. articles to profl. jours. Pfizer scholar, 1953; recipient Sr. Clin. Traineeship award, USPHS, 1963, Spl. Fellowship award, 1964; ACS Mead Johnson award, 1965, Ann. Outstanding Tchr. award, Dept. Gen. Surgery, U. Tex. M.D. Anderson Cancer Ctr., 1988. Mem. ACS, AMA, Am. Assn. Cancer Rsch., Am. Radium Soc., Assn. for Acad. Surgery, Collegium Internationale Chirugiae Digestivae, Harris County Med. Soc., Houston Acad. Medicine, Houston Philos. Soc., Soc. for Surgery of Alimentary Tract, Soc. of Surg. Oncology, S.W. Sci. Forum, Tex. Med. Assn., Tex. Surg. Soc., Houston Surg. Soc., W.H. Cole Soc., Western Surg. Assn., Sigma Xi. Republican. Home: 4530 Verone St Bellaire TX 77401-5514 Office: UT M D Anderson Cancer Ctr 1515 Holcombe Blvd Houston TX 77030-4009

RONALD, ALLAN ROSS, internal medicine and medical microbiology educator, researcher; b. Portage, Man., Can., Aug. 24, 1938; s. David E. and Muriel M. (MacFarlane) R.; m. Myrna Jean Marchyshyn, Oct. 19, 1962; children: Wendy, Sandra, Vickie. BSc in Medicine, U. Man., Winnipeg, 1961, MD with honors, 1961. Resident in internal medicine U. Md., 1962-64; fellow in infectious disease and microbiology U. Wash., 1964-68; asst. prof. U. Man., 1968-72, assoc. prof., 1972-77, prof., head med. microbiology, 1976-85, Disting. prof., head dept. internal medicine, physician-in-chief Health Scis. Ctr., 1985-90; head infectious diseases St. Boniface Gen. Hosp., Winnipeg, 1991-94; assoc. dean rsch. faculty of medicine U. Manitoba, Winnipeg, 1993—; vis. prof., researcher AIDS epidemiology U. Nairobi, Kenya, 1980—; Malcolm Brown Meml. lectr. Can. Soc. Clin. Investigation, 1985; mem. Med. Rsch. Coun. Can., 1987-93. Contbr. articles to profl. jours. Decorated Officer of Order of Can., 1994; recipient Jubilee award U. Man. Alumni Assn., 1990, Thomas Parran award Am. Venereal Disease Assn., 1991, Ortho award Can. Infectious Disease Soc., 1991. Fellow ACP (gov. 1995); mem. Infectious Disease Soc. Am. (councillor 1990-93), Internat. Soc. Infectious Diseases (pres.-elect 1994), Am. Soc. Clin. Investigation, Assn. Am. Physicians, Can. Inst. Acad. Medicine. Home: 3232 Assiniboine, Winnipeg, MN Canada R3K 0B1 Office: Saint Boniface Gen Hosp, 400 Tache ave, Winnipeg, MB Canada R2H 2A6

RONALD, PAULINE CAROL, school system administrator; b. York, Yorkshire, Eng., Feb. 28, 1945; came to U.S., 1966; d. Peter Vincent Leonard and Doris Annie (Clark) Hume-Shotton; m. James Douglas Ronald, July 16, 1966 (div. 1986); 1 child, Alexia Denise; m. James Donald Wadsworth, Feb. 15, 1991 (div. July 1994). Diploma, Harrogate Sch. Art, Yorkshire, 1965, U. New Castle, Upon Tyne, 1966; MA, Ball State U., 1977. Cert. art tchr., Ind. Art tchr. Knightstown (Ind.) Schs., 1966-67, Dunkirk (Ind.) Schs., 1967-68, Richmond (Ind.) High Sch., 1968—; part time tchr. Ind. U., Earlham Coll., Richmond 1974-84; set painter Richmond Civic Theatre. Exhibited in numerous group shows; illustrator History of Wayne County, History of Centerville. Coach State Acad. Fine Arts State Team Champions, 1988, 96, 2d Pl. for the state, 1989, 95; bd. dirs., mem. permanent collection com. Richmond Art Mus. Recipient Best Set Painting awards, also numerous awards for drawing and painting. Mem. NEA, Ind. State Tchrs. Assn., Art Assn. Richmond., Indpls. Art Mus. Avocations: painting, gardening, cooking, reading, travel. Home: 417 S 20th St Richmond IN 47374-5729

RONALD, PETER, utility executive; b. Duluth, Minn., Aug. 26, 1926; s. George W. and Florence (Jones) R.; m. Mary Locke Boyd, Nov. 25, 1950; children: Peter Webb, Pauline Morton, Samuel Herschel. B.A., U. Va., 1950. With Louisville Gas & Electric Co., 1950-88, treas., 1962—, v.p., 1969-82, sr. v.p., 1982-88, dir., 1979-89. Bd. dirs., mem. exec. com. Bus. Devel. Corp. Ky., 1967-75, pres., 1971-72; bd. dirs. Louisville Community Chest, 1967-72, v.p., 1969-72; bd. dirs., v.p. Louisville Rehab. Ctr., 1964-82, pres., 1970-71; bd. overseers Louisville Country Day Sch., 1967-70; trustee Children's Hosp. Found., 1978-81, sec.-treas., 1978-81; bd. govs. Captiva (Fla.) Civic Assn., 1990-94, v.p., 1992. With USNR, 1945-46. Mem. Louisville Country Club, Pendennis Club, Captiva Yacht Club, Zeta Psi. Home: Mockingbird Valley Rd Louisville KY 40207 Home: 1112 Schefflera Ct PO Box 893 Captiva FL 33924-0893

RONALD, THOMAS IAIN, financial services executive; b. Glasgow, Scotland, Feb. 16, 1933; s. Newton Armitage and Elizabeth (Crawford) R.; m. Cristina de Yturralde, Aug. 30, 1962; children: Christopher, Isobel. B in Law, Glasgow U., 1956; MBA, Harvard U., 1963. Chartered acct. Pres., CEO Zellers, Inc., Winnipeg, Man., Can., 1982-85; exec. v.p., dir. Hudson's Bay Co., Winnipeg, Man., Can., 1985-87; pres. Mgmt. Svcs. Group CIBC, Montreal, 1987-88, Adminstrv. Bank CIBC, 1988-92; vice chmn. Adminstrv. Bank CIBC, Toronto, 1992-95 (ret.); dir. CIBC; adv. bd. dirs. Amdahl Can. Ltd., The North West Co. Inc., Loblaw Co. Ltd., Wittington Investments Ltd., Leon's Furniture Ltd., Mobil Oil Can. Ltd.; chmn. Commcorp Fin. Svcs. Inc., Can. Life Assurance Co., T.A.L. Investment Counsel Ltd. Bd. dirs. Toronto Symphony Orch. Served as lt. Royal Navy, 1956-58. Fellow Inst. Chartered Accts. Ont.; mem. Inst. Chartered Accts. Scotland. Presbyterian. Club: Granite (Toronto). Avocations: music, squash, tennis. Office: Can Imperial Bank of Commerce, Commerce Court, Toronto, ON Canada M5L 1A2*

RONALD, WILLIAM, artist; b. Stratford, Ont., Can., Aug. 13, 1926; came to U.S., 1954, naturalized, 1964; s. William Stanley and Lillian M. (Plant) R.; m. Helen Marie Higgins, Sept. 6, 1952 (div. 1988); children: Suzanne Marie, Dianna Louise, ; m. Alana Michelle Harris, 1989 (div. 1994). Grad. with honors, Ont. Coll. Art, Toronto, 1952; pupil, Jock Macdonald. founding mem. Painters Eleven Group, Toronto, 1952; radio and TV broadcaster, from 1966; newspaper columnist, book reviewer. One man shows include Hart House, U. Toronto, 1954, Greenwich Gallery, Toronto, 1957, Laing Galleries, Toronto, 1960, Douglass Coll., New Brunswick, N.J., Kootz Gallery, N.Y.C., 1957-60, 62, 63, Princeton Mus., 1963, Issacs Gallery, Toronto, 1963, David Mirvish Gallery, Toronto, 1965, Dunkelman Gallery, Toronto, 1970, Tom Thompson Meml. Gallery, Owen Sound, Ont., 1971, Brandon (Man.) U., 1972, Morris Gallery, Toronto, 1975, Gustafssen Gallery, Brampton, Ont., Brampton Pub. Libr. and Art Gallery, Bramlea, Ont., 1976; retrospective exhbn. Ronald-25 Yrs. at Robert McLaughlin Gallery, Oshawa, Ont., 1975, Musee d'Art Contemporain, Montreal, Que., Can., Rodman Hall Arts Centre, St. Catherines Art Gallery and Mus., Charlottetown, P.E.I., Edmonton (Alta.) Art Gallery, Burnaby (B.C.) Art Gallery, 1976, Art Gallery of Windsor, Ont., Morris Gallery, Toronto, 1977, 78, 79, 80, Wells Gallery, Ottawa, Ont., 1982, Quan-King Gallery, Toronto, ,Moore Gallery, Hamilton, Ont., 1990; exhbns. of work The Prime Ministers (of Can.) Art Gallery of Ont., 1984, Art Gallery of Windsor, 1984, Manulife Pl., Edmonton, 1984, The N.B. Mus., St. John, 1985, Art Gallery N.S., 1985, Can., Montreal Gallery of Contemporay Art, 1986, The Jolliette (Que.) Mus., 1988; group exhbns. include Trinity Coll., Toronto, 1951, Eglinton Gallery, Toronto, 1953, Biennial exhbns. Nat. Gallery Can., 1955, 57-58, Smithsonian Travelling Exhbn., 1956, Riverside Mus., N.Y.C., Contemporary Can. Painters, 1957, Carnegie Internat., 1957, Brussels World Fair and Travelling Show, Sao Paulo Biennale, 1959, Whitney Mus. Ann., Corcoran Biennial, 1962-63, Toysby Contemporary Artists, 1966, Artists on Campus, York U., Toronto, 1970, Toronto Painting, 1972, Robert McLaughlin Gallery, Oshawa, 1978; represented in permanent collections Art Gallery Ont., Bklyn. Mus., Carnegie Inst., Guggenheim Mus., Mus. Modern Art, Nat. Gallery Can., R.I. Sch. Design, Albright Knox Gallery, Buffalo, Aldrich Mus., Ridgefield, Conn., U. B.C., Art Inst. Chgo., Internat. Minerals and Chems. Corp., Skokie, Ill., James A. Michener Found., Allentown, Pa., Montreal Mus. Fine Arts, York U., David Rockefeller Collection, Nelson A. Rockefeller Collection, U. N.C., Phoenix Art Mus., Balt. Mus., Walker Art Ctr., Mpls., Williams Coll., Princeton Mus., Queens U., Kingston, Ont., Brandeis U., Wadsworth Atheneum, Hartford, Conn., Whitney Mus. Am. Art, Washington Gallery Modern Art, Newark Mus., N.J. State Mus., Trenton, U. Tex., Can. Coun. Collection, Can. Art Bank, Windsor Art Mus., Hudson River Mus., Pasadena (Calif.) Mus. Modern Art, Peel County Mus. Brampton, Wellington County Mus., Kitchener Waterloo Art Mus., Masters Sch. and Mercy Coll., Dobbs Ferry, N.Y., Toronto Dominion Bank, Notre Dame U., U. Okla. Art Mus., Norman, numerous others; commd. artist prime mins. Can. Recipient Hallmark Art award for watercolor, 1952, Guggenheim Mus. award Can. painting, 1956, Sr. Arts award Can. Coun., 1977; Ind. Order Daus. Empire scholar, Can., 1951, Can. Amateur Hockey Assn. scholar Can. Found., 1956. Mem. Royal Can. Acad. Home: 206 Robert St, Toronto, ON Canada M5S 2K7

RONAN, WILLIAM JOHN, management consultant; b. Buffalo, Nov. 8, 1912; s. William and Charlotte (Ramp) R.; m. Elena Vinadé, May 29, 1939; children: Monica, Diana Quasha. A.B., Syracuse U., 1934; Ph.D., N.Y. U., 1940, LL.D., 1969; certificate, Geneva Sch. Internat. Studies, 1933. Mus. asst. Buffalo Mus. Sci., 1928-30; with Niagara-Hudson Power Co., 1931; transfer dept. N.Y.C.R.R., 1932; Penfield fellow internat. law, diplomacy and belles lettres, 1935, Univ. fellow, 1936; editor Fed. Bank Service, Prentice-Hall, Inc., 1937; instr. govt. N.Y. U., 1938, exec. sec. grad. div. for tng. in pub. services, 1938, asst. dir., 1940, asst. prof. govt., dir. grad. div. for tng. pub. service, 1940, assoc. prof. govt., 1946-47, prof., 1947, dean, grad. sch. pub. adminstrn. and social service, 1953-58; Cons. N.Y.C. Civil Service Commn., 1938; prin. rev. officer, negotiations officer U.S. Civil Service Commn., 1942; prin. div. asst. U.S. Dept. State, 1943; cons. Dept. State, 1948, Dept. Def., 1954; dir. studies N.Y. State Coordination Commn., 1951-58; project mgr. N.Y. U.-U. Ankara project, 1954-59; cons. ICA, 1955, N.Y. State Welfare Conf.; adminstrv. co-dir. Albany Grad. Program in Pub. Adminstrn.; 1st dep. city adminstr. N.Y.C., 1956-57; exec. dir. N.Y. State Temporary Commn. Constl. Conv., 1956-58; sec. to Gov. N.Y., 1959-66; chmn. interdept. com. traffic safety, commr. Port Authority N.Y. and N.J., 1967-90, vice chmn., 1972-74, chmn., 1974-77; with UTDC Corp., West Palm Beach, Fla.; trustee Crosslands Savs. Bank; chmn. bd. L.I. R.R., 1966-74; chmn. Tri-State Transp. Com., N.Y., N.J., Conn., 1961-67; chmn. interstate com. New Haven R.R., 1960-63; chmn. N.Y. Com. on L.I. R.R., 1964-65; mem. N.Y. State Commn. Internstate Coop., 1961, N.Y. State Com. Fgn. Ofcl. Visitors, 1961, N.Y. State Coordination Commn., 1960; mem. N.Y. Civil Svc. Commn., Temporary State Commn. on Constl. Conv., 1966-67; chmn. N.Y. State Met. Commuter Transp. Authority, 1965-68, Met. Transp. Authority, 1968-74, Tri-Borough Bridge and Tunnel Authority, 1968-74, N.Y.C. Transit Authority, 1968-74, Manhattan and Bronx Surface Transit Operating Authority, 1968-74; chmn. bd., pres. 3d Century Corp., 1974-94; mem. Commn. Critical Choices for Am., 1973—, acting chmn., 1975—; mem. urban transp. adv. com. U.S. Dept. Transp.; sr. adviser Rockefeller family, 1974-80; pres. Nelson Rockefeller Collection, Inc., 1977-80; trustee Power Authority of State of N.Y., 1974-77; cons. to trustees Penn Ctrl. Transp. Co.; vice chmn. bd. CCX, Inc.; sec.-treas. Sarabam Corp. N.V.; chmn., dir. UTDC (U.S.A.) Inc., 1987-88; chmn. UTDC Corp., 1989-94, Transit Svcs. Corp., 1989-94; cons. Herzog Transit Svcs., 1995—, Dime Savs. Bank, Metal Powder Products Inc., Prometech, Inc., Internat. Mining and Metals Inc., Quadrant Mgmt. Inc., 1990—, Ohio Highspeed Rail Authority, 1991-93; chmn. N.Y. and N.J. Inland Rail Rate Com.; dir. Nat. Mgmt. Coun., 1951. Author: Money Power of States in International Law, 1940, The Board of Regents and the Commissioner, 1948, Our War Economy, 1943, (with others), articles in profl. jours.; adviser: Jour. Inst. Socio-Econ. Studies. Mem. U.S. FOA, Am. Public Health Assn.; staff relations officer N.Y.C. Bd. Edn.; Mem. Nat. Conf. Social Work, Nat. Conf. on Met. Areas, Citizens Com. on Corrections, Council on Social Work Edn.; bd. dirs. World Trade Club; adv. bd. World Trade Inst.; mem. 42d St. Redevel. Corp., chmn., 1980-94; mem. Assn. for a Better N.Y.; bd. advisers Inst. for Socioecon. Studies, 1977—; dir. Nat. Health Council, 1980-86; dep. dir. policy Nelson Rockefeller campaign for Republican presdl. nomination, 1964; mem. N.Y. State Gov.'s Com. on Shoreham Nuclear Plant, 1983-85, Nassau County Indsl. Devel. Authority, 1982-90, U.S. Dept. Transp. Com. on Washington and Capital Dist. Airports, 1985-86; bd. dirs. Ctr. Study Presidency, 1986-90, Alcoholism Council of N.Y., 1986—; trustee N.Y. Coll. Osteopathic Medicine, 1986-91. Served as lt. USNR, 1943-46. Mem. NEA, Am. Polit. Sci. Assn., Acad. Pub. Adminstrn., Am. Soc. Pub. Adminstrn., Civil Svc. Assembly of U.S. and Can., Internat. Assn. Met. Rsch. and Devel., Nat. Mcpl. League, Mcpl. Pers. Soc., Citizens Union of N.Y., Nat. Civil Svc. League, Am. Acad. Polit. and Social Sci., L.I. Assn. Commerce and Industry (dir.), Internat. Inst. Adminstrv. Scis., Am. Fgn. Law Assn., Internat. Union Pub. Transport (mgmt. com., v.p.), Am. Pub. Transit Assn. (chmn. 1974-76), Nat. Def. Transp. Assn. (v.p. for Mass transit), Met. Opera Club, Maidstone Club, Devon Yacht Club, Knickerbocker Club, Hemisphere Club, Harvard Club, Creek Club, Wings Club, Traffic Club, Univ. Club, Am. Club Riviera, Beach Club (Palm Beach), Everglades Club. Home: 525 S Flagler Dr West Palm Beach FL 33401-5922 Home: Villa La Pointe Du Cap, Ave de La Corniche, 06230 Saint Jean Cap Ferrat France

RONAYNE, MICHAEL RICHARD, JR., academic dean; b. Boston, Apr. 29, 1937; s. Michael Richard and Margaret (Fahey) R.; m. Joanne Maria, Aug. 7, 1971; 1 child, Michelle Eileen. BS, Boston Coll., 1958; PhD, U. Notre Dame, 1962. Instr. chemistry Providence Coll., 1962-63, asst. prof. chemistry, 1963-64; rsch. chemist Panametrics, Inc., Waltham, Mass., 1964-66; asst. prof. chemistry Suffolk U., Boston, 1966-67, assoc. prof., 1967-70, prof., chmn. dept. chemistry, 1970-72, dean Coll. Liberal Arts and Sci., 1972—; reaccreditation vis. team mem. New Eng. Assn. Schs. and Colls., Winchester, Mass., 1974-80, Mass. Dept. Edn., Boston, 1975; mem. acad. adv. com. Mass. Bd. Higher Edn., Boston, 1977. Contbr. articles to sci. jours., profl. publs. Mem. Winchester Sch. Com., 1983-92, chmn., 1984-85, 86-87; mem. Winchester Town Meeting, 1983—, mem. town capital planning com., 1983-84, town coun. on youth, 1987-88, 89-90; mem. exec. com., bd. dirs. Mass. Bay Marine Studies Consortium, 1985-87; project dir. U.S. Dept.

of Edn. Title III Grants. Shell Oil Corp. fellow, 1958-59, AEC fellow 1959-62; recipient Contbns. in Sci. and Edn. citation New Eng. Sch. Art and Design, Boston, 1991. Mem. AAAS, Am. Chem. Soc., Am. Conf. Acad. Deans, Coun. for Liberal Learning, Am. Assn. for Higher Edn., Sigma Xi, Phi Alpha Theta, Phi Gamma Mu, Sigma Tau Delta, Omicron Delta Epsilon, Sigma Zeta. Office: Suffolk U Beacon Hill Boston MA 02114

RONDEAU, CHARLES REINHARDT, lawyer; b. Jefferson, La., Oct. 14, 1966; s. Clement Robert and Irmtraut Juliana Rondeau. BA, Columbia U., 1988; JD, Southwestern U., L.A., 1992; diploma in Advanced Internat. Legal Stud, McGeorge Sch. Law, 1993. Bar: Calif. 1993, N.Y., N.J., U.S. Dist. Ct. N.J., U.S. Dist. Ct. (so. and ea. dists.) N.Y., U.S. Dist. Ct. (cent. dist.) Calif., U.S. Ct. Appeals (3rd cir.), U.S. Tax Ct. 1994. Visiting jurist Cabinet Berlioz et Cie, Paris, 1992-93; assoc. Stanley A. Teitler, P.C., N.Y.C., 1993-95; ptnr. Rondeau & Homampour, Beverly Hills, Calif., 1995—. Editor: Southwestern U. Law Rev., 1989-92. Mem. ABA, L.A. County Bar Assn., Beverly Hills Bar Assn. Avocations: jazz, skiing, sailing. Office: Rondeau & Homampour PC 8383 Wilshire Blvd Ste 830 Beverly Hills CA 90211

RONDEAU, DORIS JEAN, entrepreneur, consultant; b. Winston-Salem, N.C., Nov. 25, 1941; d. John Delbert and Eldora Virginia (Klutz) Robinson; m. Robert Breen Corrente, Sept. 4, 1965 (div. 1970); m. Wilfrid Dolor Rondeau, June 3, 1972. Student Syracuse U., 1959-62, Fullerton Jr. Coll., 1974-75; BA in Philosophy, Calif. State U.-Fullerton, 1976, postgrad., 1976-80. Ordained to ministry The Spirit of Divine Love, 1974. Trust real estate clk. Security First Nat. Bank, Riverside, Calif., 1965-68; entertainer Talent, Inc., Hollywood, Calif., 1969-72; co-founder, dir. Spirit of Divine Love, Huntington Beach, Calif., 1974—; pub., co-founder Passing Through, Inc., Huntington Beach, 1983—; instr. Learning Activity, Anaheim, Calif., 1984—; chmn. bd., prin. D.J. Rondeau, Entrepreneur, Inc., Huntington Beach, 1984—; co-founder, dir. Spiritual Positive Attitude, Inc., Moon In Pisces, Inc., Vibrations By Rondeau, Inc., Divine Consciousness, Expressed, Inc., Huntington Beach, Doris Wilfrid Rondeau, Inc., Huntington Beach, Calif. Author, editor: A Short Introduction To The Spirit of Divine Love, 1984; writer, producer, dir. performer spiritual vignettes for NBS Radio Network, KWVE-FM, 1982-84; author: Spiritual Meditations to Uplift the Soul, 1988. Served with USAF, 1963-65. Recipient Pop Vocalist First Place award USAF Talent Show, 1964, Sigma chpt. Epsilon Delta Chi, 1985, others. Mem. Hamel Bus. Grads., Smithsonian Assocs., Am. Mgmt. Assn., Nat. Assn. Female Execs. Avocations: long-distance running, body fitness, arts and crafts, snorkeling, musical composition.

RONDEPIERRE, EDMOND FRANCOIS, insurance company executive; b. N.Y.C., Jan. 15, 1930; s. Jules Gilbert and Margaret Murray (Moore) R.; m. M. Anne Lerch, July 5, 1952; children: Aimee S., Stephen C., Peter E., Anne W. BS, U.S. Mcht. Marine Acad., 1952; JD, Temple U., 1959. Bar: D.C. 1959, Conn. 1988, U.S. Supreme Ct. 1992. Third mate Nat. Bulk Carriers, 1952-53; field rep. Ins. Co. N.Am., 1955-59, br. mgr., 1959-61; asst. sec. underwriting Ins. Co. N.Am., Phila., 1965-67, asst. gen. counsel, 1967-70, sr. v.p., gen. counsel, 1970-76; v.p., dep. chief legal affairs INA Corp., Phila., 1976-77; v.p., gen. counsel Gen. Reins. Corp., Stamford, Conn., 1977-79, sr. v.p., corp. sec., gen. counsel, 1979-94, sr. v.p., 1994-95; pres. ARIAS-US, 1994—; bd. dirs. Gen. Reins. Ltd. (UK), Tempest Re Ltd, Herbert Clough, Inc. Lt. USN, 1953-55. Lt. USN, 1953-55. Mem. ABA, Conn. Bar Assn., D.C. Bar Assn., Inter-Am. Bar Assn., Soc. CPCU, Internat. Assn. Def. Counsel (past bd. dirs.), AIDA Reins. and Ins. Arbitration Soc. (dir., pres.), Stamford Yacht Club. Roman Catholic.

RONDILEAU, ADRIAN, college president; b. N.Y.C., May 8, 1912; s. Leon J. and Bessie (Caspere) R.; m. Martha L. Denison, Aug. 15, 1936 (dec. 1983); m. Mary Masterson Hamblen, June 1, 1985. A.B., CCNY, 1932; M.A., Columbia U., 1934, Ph.D., 1942; L.H.D., Yankton Coll., 1982; D. Pub. Admstrn., Mass. Maritime Acad., 1986; D. Pub. Svc., Bridgewater State Coll., 1989. Instr. Central Mich. Coll., 1935-37; adminstr. speech research, adult edn. and curriculum Mich. Dept. Pub. Instrn., 1937-41; dir. vocat. guidance and in-service tng. War Manpower Commn., 1941-43; spl. cons., lectr. Brazilian Ministry Edn. and coordinator inter-Am. affairs Rio de Janeiro and Sao Paulo, 1943-46; dean bus. adminstrn., chmn. dept. econs. Associated Colls. Upper N.Y., 1946-49; dean liberal arts Pace Coll., 1950-54; pres. Yankton (S.D.) Coll., 1954-62, Bridgewater (Mass.) State Coll., 1962-86, 88-89; chmn. coll. and univ. com. YMCA 6-State N. Central Area; dir. North Central Area YMCA; adv. bd. Upper Midwest Research and Devel. Council; pres. S.D. Found. Pvt. Colls.; v.p. S.D. Assn. Colls. and Univs.; mem. Lady Doak Coll. Funds Corp.; trustee Mass. State Colls. Adv. Commn. Author: (with Donald Hayworth) Research Studies in the Teaching of College Public Speaking, 1939; author: Education for Installment Buying, 1943, People and Scenes of Brazil, 1945, Public Higher Education in the City of New York: The Master Plan Study Report (with D.P. Cottrell), 1950, The Capital Plant Needs of American Higher Education, 1951, Reminiscences: Bridgewater State College (1960-89), Adventure in Excellence, 1991; also articles. Rackham fellow, 1935-36; Stevens scholar, 1934-35; Hoe scholar, 1933-34. Mem. Mass. State Coll. Council of Pres. (pres. 1976-78), N. Central Assn. Colls. and Secondary Schs., New Eng. Assn. Colls. and Secondary Schs., Mass. Council of Pub. Coll. Pres. and Chancellors, Southeastern Mass. Consortium Pub. and Pvt. Colls. (pres. 1976-77, 1984-85), S.D. Ednl. Assn., Am. Econ. Assn., Am. Coll. Pub. Relations Assn., Brazil-Am. Cultural Soc., NEA, C. of C., Phi Delta Kappa, Pi Kappa Delta. Congregationalist. Lodges: Masons, Shriners, Elks, Rotary (dir.). Home: 150 Lakeside Dr Bridgewater MA 02324-1018 Office: Bridgewater State College Office of Pres Emeritus Bridgewater MA 02324

RONDINELLI, DENNIS A(UGUST), business administration educator, research center director; b. Trenton, N.J., Mar. 30, 1943; s. August P. and Vincentia (Madalena) R.; m. Soonyoung Chang, Dec. 19, 1976; children: Linda, Lisa. BA, Rutgers U., 1965; PhD, Cornell U., 1969. Asst. prof. urban affairs U. Wis., Milw., 1971-73; assoc. prof. grad. sch. of mgmt. Vanderbilt U., Nashville, 1973-76; assoc. prof. planning Maxwell Sch. of Citizenship and Pub. Affairs Syracuse U., N.Y., 1976-79, prof. social scis., 1979-86; prin. scientist and sr. policy analyst Office for Internat. Programs, Research Triangle Inst., Research Triangle Park, N.C., 1986-90; Glaxo Disting. Internat. Prof. Mgmt. Kenan-Flagler Bus. Sch.; dir. Ctr. Global Bus. Rsch., Kenan Inst. Pvt. Enterprise U. N.C., Chapel Hill, N.C., 1990—; cons. World Bank, U.S. Dept. State, UN Devel. Program, Govts. of Colombia, South Korea, Can., Indonesia, Philippines, China, India. Author: Decentralization and Development: Policy Implementation in Developing Countries, 1983, Applied Methods of Regional Analysis: The Spatial Dimensions of Development Policy, 1985, Development Administration and U.S. Foreign Aid Policy, 1987, Urban Services in Developing Countries: Public and Private Roles in Urban Development, 1988, Planning Education Reforms in Developing Countries, 1990, Development Projects as Policy Experiments, 1993, Privatization and Economic Reform in Central Europe, 1994, Expanding Sino-American Business and Trade: China's Economic Transition, 1994, Great Policies: Strategic Innovations in Asia and the Pacific, 1995, Policies and Institutions for Managing Privatization, 1996. Adv. Bd. Inst. Regional Devel. Studies, Kanpur, India, 1984—; editorial adv. bd. Bangladesh Jour. of Pub. Adminstrn., Dhaka, 1986—. Captain U.S. Army, 1965-72. Decorated Julio Lieras Order of Merit (Colombia); recipient Rural Devel. medal Republic of Vietnam, 1971, Ethnic Minorities Devel. medal, 1971; East-West Ctr. sr. fellow, 1975-76, Pacific Basin Rsch. Ctr./Soka U. of Am./Harvard U. rsch. fellow, 1991-92. Avocations: gardening, writing nonfiction. Office: Kenan Inst Pvt Enterprise CB#3440 The Kenan Ctr U NC Chapel Hill NC 27599-3149

RONE, WILLIAM EUGENE, JR., newspaper editor; b. Atlanta, Nov. 7, 1926; s. William Eugene and Marguerite (Kellett) R.; m. Margaret Louise Banks, July 17, 1953; 1 child, James Kellett. AB, Wofford Coll., 1949; LLB, U. S.C., 1951; grad., U.S. Army Command and Gen. Staff Coll., 1974. With The State (newspaper), Columbia, S.C., 1950—, city editor, 1962-65, asso. editor, 1966-69, editorial page editor, 1969-90, sr. editor, 1990-93; consulting editor, 1993—; S.C. corr. So. Edn. Reporting Service, Nashville, 1962-68; columnist Raleigh (N.C.) News & Observer, 1968-83, Atlanta Jour.-Constn., 1973-84. Author: Biography of Max Hirsch, 1956. Chmn. S.C. Athletic Hall of Fame, 1957-61. Served with USNR, 1945-46. Recipient S.C. AP award for reporting in depth, 1962. Mem. Am. Soc. Newspaper Editors, Nat. Conf. Editorial Writers, S.C. Bar, Phi Beta Kappa, Kappa Sigma, Phi Delta Phi. Episcopalian. Home: 726 Fairway Ln Columbia SC 29210-5715 Office: care State-Record Co Shop Rd PO Box 1333 Columbia SC 29202

RONEN, CAROL, state legislator. BS, Bradley U.; MA, Roosevelt U. Dir. legis. and cmty. affairs Chgo. Dept. Human Svcs., 1985-89; exec. dir. Chgo. Commn. on Women, 1989-90; dir. planning and rsch. Chgo.-Cook County Criminal Justice Commn.; asst. commn. Chgo. Dept. Planning, 1991, Chgo. Dept. Housing; mem. Ill. Ho. of Reps., 1993—. Former pres. Ill. Task Force on Child Support; bd. dirs. Cook County Dem. Women, St. Martin De Porres Shelter for Women and Children. Democrat. Home: 6033 N Sheridan Rd Chicago IL 60660-3003 Office: Ill Ho of Reps State Capitol Springfield IL 62706*

RONEY, JOHN HARVEY, lawyer, consultant; b. L.A., June 12, 1932; s. Harvey and Mildred Puckett (Cargill) R.; m. Joan Ruth Allen, Dec. 27, 1954; children: Pam Peterson, J. Harvey, Karen Louise Hanke, Cynthia Allen Harmon. Student, Pomona Coll., 1950-51; B.A., Occidental Coll., 1954; LL.B., UCLA, 1959. Bar: Calif. 1960, D.C. 1976. Assoc. O'Melveny & Myers, L.A., 1959-67, ptnr., 1967-94, of counsel, 1994—; gen. counsel Pa. Co., 1970-78, Baldwin United Corp., 1983-84; dir. Coldwell Banker & Co., 1969-81, Brentwood Savs. & Loan Assn., 1968-80; spl. advisor to dep. Rehab. of Mut. Benefit Life Ins. Co., 1991-94; cons., advisor to Rehab. of Confederation Life Ins. Co., 1994-95; mem. policy adv. bd. Calif. Ins. Commn., 1991-95. Served to 1st lt. USMCR, 1954-56. Mem. ABA, Calif. Bar Assn. (ins. law com. 1991-95, chmn. 1993-94), Los Angeles County Bar Assn., D.C. Bar Assn., N.Y. Coun. Fgn. Rels., Pacific Coun. on Internat. Policy, Conf. Ins. Counsel, Calif. Club, Sky Club (N.Y.). Republican. Home: The Strand Hermosa Beach CA 90254 Office: 400 S Hope St Ste 1600 Los Angeles CA 90071-2899

RONEY, PAUL H(ITCH), federal judge; b. Olney, Ill., Sept. 5, 1921; m. Sarah E. Eustis; children: Susan M., Paul Hitch Jr., Timothy Eustis. Student, St. Petersburg Jr. Coll., 1938-40; B.S. in Econs, U. Pa., 1942; LL.B., Harvard U., 1948; LL.D., Stetson U., 1977; LL.M., U. Va., 1984. Bar: N.Y. 1949, Fla. 1950. Assoc. Root, Ballantine, Harlan, Bushby & Palmer, N.Y.C., 1948-50; ptnr. Mann, Harrison, Roney, Mann & Masterson (and predecessors), St. Petersburg, Fla., 1950-57; pvt. practice law, 1957-63; ptnr. Roney & Beach, St. Petersburg, 1963-69, Roney, Ulmer, Woodworth & Jacobs, St. Petersburg, 1969-70; judge U.S. Ct. Appeals (5th cir.), St. Petersburg, 1970-81; judge U.S. Ct. Appeals (11th cir.), St. Petersburg, 1981-86, chief judge, 1986-89, sr. cir. judge, 1989—; mem. adv. com. on adminstrv. law judges U.S. CSC, 1976-77; pres. judge U.S. Fgn. Intelligence Surveillance Ct. of Rev., 1994—. With U.S. Army, 1942-46. Fellow Am. Bar Found.; mem. ABA (chmn. legal adv. com. Fair Trial-Free Press 1973-76, mem. task force on cts. and public 1973-76, jud. adminstrn. div., chmn. appellate judges conf. 1978-79, mem. Gavel Awards com. 1980-83), Am. Judicature Soc. (dir. 1972-76), Am. Law Inst., Fla. Bar, St. Petersburg Bar Assn. (pres. 1964-65), Nat. Jud. Coll. (faculty 1974, 75), Jud. Conf. U.S. (subcom. on jud. improvements 1978-84, exec com. 1986-89, com. to review circuit coun. conduct and disability orders 1991-93). Home: Bayfront Tower 1 Beach Dr SE Saint Petersburg FL 33701-3924 Office: US Ct Appeals 11th Circuit 601 Federal Bldg 144 1st Ave S Saint Petersburg FL 33701-4397

RONEY, ROBERT KENNETH, retired aerospace company executive; b. Newton, Iowa, Aug. 5, 1922; s. Louie Earl and Hazel Iona (Cure) R.; m. Alice Lorraine Mann, Oct. 6, 1951; children: Stephen P., Karen Margaret Dahl. BSEE, U. Mo., 1944; MSEE, Calif. Inst. Tech., 1947, PhD, 1950. Engr. rsch. Jet Propulsion Lab. Calif. Inst. Tech., Pasadena, 1948-50; engr. rsch. Hughes Aircraft Co., Culver City, Calif., 1950-54, mgr. sys. analysis, 1955-59, dir. tech. R&D, 1960, assoc. mgr. space sys. divsn., 1961-68, mgr. space sys. divsn., 1968-70, v.p. asst. group exec., 1970-85, sr. v.p. corp. tech., 1986-88, ret., 1988. Mem. adv. bd. Dept. Transp. Comml. Space Transp., 1984-87, Engring. Sch. U. Kans., 1988-91. Lt. (j.g.) USNR, 1944-46, PTO. Recipient Honor award for Disting. Svc. in Engring. U. Mo.-Columbia, 1979. Fellow IEEE; mem. NAE, Caltech Assocs. Home: 1105 Georgina Ave Santa Monica CA 90402-2027

RONEY, SHIRLEY FLETCHER, retail company executive; b. Atlanta, Dec. 3, 1935; d. Grady Franklin and Grace Ilene (Camp) Fletcher; student public schs., Atlanta; m. Sept. 19, 1953 (div.); 1 son, Joseph Clay. Collection corr. GMAC, Atlanta, 1953-64; sales rep. Washburn Realty, Atlanta, 1964-67; sec.-treas. Frank Jackson Lincoln Mercury, Inc., Sandy Springs, Ga., 1967-79, sec. treas., 1971—, comptroller, 1979—, pres., gen. mgr., 1983—; v.p., dir. J&J Investment Corp., 1975—; v.p., dir. Rivergate Corp., 1979-86, pres. 1986—; sec. treas., dir. Ajax Rent a Car, Sandy Springs Toyota. Div. vice chmn. United Way, 1979; treas. Martins Landing Found., 1994—; bd. dirs. Ga. Spl. Olympics. Mem. Am. Bus. Womens Assn., Am. Contract Bridge League. Office: 7555 Roswell Rd Atlanta GA 30350-4838

RONEY, WALLACE, musician; b. Phila., May 25, 1960. Studied with Sigmund Haring, Howard U.; student, Berklee Coll. Trumpeter Art Blakey's Jazz Messengers, Tony Williams Quintet. Recorded 8 albums under own name, Verses, 1987, Intuition, 1989, Obsession, 1991, Seth Air, 1992, Misterios, 1994; other recs. include Story of Neptune (with Tony Williams), Seth Air Tribute to Miles Davis (with Herbie Hancock, Wayne Sholter, Ron Carter and Tony Williams), Live at Montreux (with Miles Davis), Killer Joe (with Art Blakey). Nominee for Grammy award, 1994. Office: care Blue Horn Prodns PO Box 1546 New York NY 10011-1546

RONSMAN, WAYNE JOHN, insurance company executive; b. Milw., Jan. 21, 1938; s. Harry Martin and Martha Elizabeth (Popp) R.; m. Joan P. Murphy-Mays, Nov. 30, 1974; children: Allison, Alanna; children by previous marriage: Rosemary, Harry, Martha. Student Marquette U., 1955-58, U. San Francisco, 1960-66. CLU, chartered fin. cons.; cert. fin. planner; registered fin. planner. Acct. Otis McAllister & Co., 1960-62; acct., salesman of data processing Statis. Tabulation Corp., San Francisco, 1962-66; chief acct., gen. mgr. Dillingham Bros. Ltd., Honolulu, 1966-67; ins. salesman Mut. Benefit Life Ins. Co., 1968-91, mgr. Met Life Honolulu, 1991—, gen. agt., Hawaii and Alaska, 1991; v.p. Brenno Assos., Honolulu, 1972-80; prin. Ronsman-Brenno, Anchorage, Alaska, 1980-90; owner Ronsman, Hammond & Assocs., 1991—; bd. dirs. Aloha Nat. Bank, Kihei, Maui, 1989-90; guest lectr. Chaminade U. Law Sch., Honolulu. Mem. Gov's Task Force to Program Correctional Facilities Land, 1970-72; mem. State Bd. Paroles and Pardons, 1972-75; treas. Spl. Edn. Center of Oahu, 1969-78; pres. Ballet Alaska, 1986-87, Maui Ballet Co. Ltd., 1992-93; v.p. devel. Make A Wish Hawaii, 1992—. Served with USMCR, 1958-60. Mem. Inst. Mgmt. Acct. (pres. Anchorage chpt. 1989-90), Am. Soc. CLUs, Hawaii Estate Planning Coun. (dir. 1994), Honolulu Assn. Life Underwriters (million dollar round table 1973—), Inst. Mgmt. Accts. (pres. Honolulu 1994-95, 95-96), Hawaii (state editor 1970-71, nat. dir. 1972-73), Kailua (pres. 1968-69) Jaycees, Hawaii C. of C., Nat. Assn. Securities Dealers, Kailua C. of C. (pres. 1977-78). Roman Catholic. Home: Ronsman-Hammond & Assocs 1099 Alakea St Ste # 1500 Honolulu HI 96813 Office: PO Box 336 Honolulu HI 96809-0336

RONSTADT, LINDA MARIE, singer; b. Tucson, July 15, 1946; d. Gilbert and Ruthmary (Copeman) R. Rec. artist numerous albums including Evergreen 1967, Evergreen Vol. 2, 1967, Linda Ronstadt, The Stone Poneys and Friends, Vol. 3, 1968, Hand Sown, Home Grown, 1969, Silk Purse, 1970, Linda Ronstadt, 1972, Don't Cry Now, 1973, Heart Like a Wheel, 1974, Different Drum, 1974, Prisoner In Disguise, 1975, Hasten Down the Wind, 1976, Greatest Hits, 1976, Simple Dreams, Blue Bayou, 1977, Living in the U.S.A., 1978, Mad Love, Greatest Hits Vol. II, 1980, Get Closer, 1982, What's New, 1983, Lush Life, 1984, For Sentimental Reasons, 1986, Trio (with Dolly Parton, Emmylou Harris), 1986, 'Round Midnight, 1987, Canciones de Mi Padre, 1987, Cry Like a Rainstorm-Howl Like the Wind, 1989, Mas Canciones, 1991, Frenesi, 1992, Winter Light, 1993, Feels Like Home, 1995; starred in Broadway prodn. of Pirates of Penzance, 1981, also in film, 1983, off Broadway as Mimi in La Boheme, 1984. Recipient Am. Music awards, 1978, 79, Grammy awards, 1975, 76, 87 (with Emmylou Harris and Dolly Parton), 1988, 89 (with Aaron Neville), 1990 (with Aaron Neville), 1992 (2), Acad. Country Music award, 1987, 88. Office: care Peter Asher Mgmt Inc 644 N Doheny Dr West Hollywood CA 90069-5526

ROOB, RICHARD, manufacturing executive; b. 1932. Degree, Hamilton Coll., 1953; JD, Columbia U., 1956. Assoc. Gifford, Woody, Palmer & Serles, N.Y.C., 1956-77; with Benjamin Moore & Co., Montvale, N.J., 1977—, vice chmn. bd., 1982-84, CEO, chmn. bd. dirs., 1984—. Office: Benjamin Moore & Co 51 Chestnut Ridge Rd Montvale NJ 07645*

ROOBOL, NORMAN RICHARD, industrial painting consultant, educator; b. Grand Rapids, Mich., Aug. 19, 1934; s. Pleune and Henrietta (Sietsema) R.; m. Joan Lois Ezinga, Aug. 15, 1957; children—Kerri Linda, Michael Eric, Victoria May, Sara Elizabeth Angelique. B.S., Calvin Coll., 1958; Ph.D. in Organic Chemistry, Mich. State U., 1962. Rsch. chemist Shell Oil Co., Emeryville, Calif., 1962-65; asst. prof. chemistry GMI Engring. Inst., Flint, Mich., 1965-68, assoc. prof., asst. head dept. math., sci., 1968-72, prof., 1972-89; pres. NR Painting Cons. Co., Peachtree City, Ga., 1989—; Rhodes prof. Russelsheim, Fed. Republic of Germany, 1980-81; tchr. short course on paint; cons. on coatings application processes; frequent spkr. on indsl. painting methods to paint soc. meetings; painting advisor, instr. Bombardier of Can., 1988—, Compaq-Asia, Singapore, 1991—, Harley-Davidson, 1992—, Outboard Marine Corp., 1986—; adj. prof. Kent (Ohio) State U., 1986—, Okla. State U., 1994—. Author: Painting Problems Solved, 1987, Industrial Painting Principles and Practices, 1991; monthly columnist, tech. editor Industrial Finishing jour.; contbr. numerous articles to profl. jours.; patentee in field. Sr. adviser Flint Sci. Fair. Served with Signal Corps, U.S. Army, 1954-56. Johnson fellow, 1957-58; NSF fellow, 1960-62; Dow fellow, 1961-62. Fellow Am. Inst. Chemists; mem. AAUP, Am. Sci. Affiliation, Soc. Mfg. Engrs. (bd. dirs.), Assn. Finishings Proc. (v.p. profl. devel. council), Sigma XI, Alpha Tau Omega, Pi Tau Sigma (chpt. sr. adviser 1979-86). Home and Office: NR Painting Cons Co 507 Haddington Ln Peachtree City GA 30269-3340

ROOD, DAVID S., linguistics educator; b. Albany, N.Y., Sept. 14, 1940; s. J. Henry and Pearl B. (Stanley) R.; m. Juliette A. Victor; 1 child, Jennifer. AB, Cornell U., 1963; MA, U. Calif., Berkeley, 1965; PhD, U. Calif., 1969. Instr. U. Colo., Boulder, 1967-69, asst. prof., 1969-77, assoc. prof., 1977-82, prof., 1982—. Author: Wichita Grammar, 1975, Siouan Languages Archive, 1982; (with others) Beginning Lakhota, 1976; editor Internat. Jour. of Am. Linguistics, 1981—; contbr. articles to profl. jours. NSF grantee, 1972—, NEH grantee, 1972—. Mem. Linguistic Soc. Am., Soc. for Study Indigenous Langs. Am., Soc. for Linguistic Anthropology, Tchrs. of English to Speakers Other Langs. Office: U of Colo Dept of Linguistics Campus Box 295 Boulder CO 80309-0295

ROOF, ROBERT L., broadcast executive, sales executive; b. Circleville, Ohio, Apr. 15, 1946; s. Roger A. and Doris (Kraft) R.; m. Linda Anderson, Nov. 28, 1969; children: Jennifer, Leslie. BA, Franklin U. Sales, disc jockey Sta. WPKO Radio, Waverly, Ohio, 1969-72, Sta. WSCR Radio, Scranton, Pa., 1972-75; sales Sta. WSPD Radio, Toledo, Ohio, 1975-78; sales Sta. WTVN Radio, Columbus, Ohio, 1978-81, local sales mgr., 1981-83, gen. sales mgr., 1984-87; v.p., gen. mgr. Sta. WDVE Radio, Pitts., 1987-93, pres., gen. mgr., 1993—. Bd. dirs. Southwest PA Jr. Achievement, Pitts., 1994—. Recipient Bronze Leadership award Jr. Achievement, Pitts., 1994. Mem. Columbus Sales Club (pres. 1982), Pitts. Sales Club (pres. 1989), Pitts. Radio Orgn. (pres. 1994). Methodist. Avocations: golf, hunting, Am. history. Home: 916 Summit Dr Wexford PA 15090-7580 Office: Sta WDVE-FM 200 Fleet St Pittsburgh PA 15220-2908

ROOK, JUDITH RAWIE, producer, writer; b. Long Beach, Calif., Jan. 25, 1942; d. Wilmer Ernest and Margaret Jane (Towle) Rawie; children: Daryn Kirsten, Dawn Malia; m. Timothy Daniel Rook. BBA, Loyola-Marymount Coll., 1964; BA in Visual Arts and Communications, U. Calif., San Diego, 1978. Producer/writer PBS series Achieving (Emmy award 1982, ACE nominee), assoc. dir. rsch. and video/producer IABC, San Francisco, 1982; dir. programming Group W Cable, Westinghouse Co., 1983-85; devel. Nelson/Embassy Home Entertainment, 1986-87; ptnr. Real Magic, 1988-89; ind. prodr.- screenwriter R2 Prodns., 1989—. Mem. adv. bd. U. Calif.-Irvine Screenwriting/Film Prodn., 1996—; active Found. U. Art Mus., 1996—; co-pres. Contemporary Coun., U. Art Mus., 1996—. Mem. Am. Film Inst., Women in Film, Ind. Features Assn., Found. Long Beach Mus. Art, Democrat. Episcopalian.

ROOKE, DAVID LEE, retired chemical company executive; b. San Antonio, Tex., May 2, 1923; s. Henry Levi, Jr. and Annie (Davidson) R.; m. Esthermae Litherland, June 2, 1945; children—Eugene, Mark, Paul, Bruce. B.S. in Chem. Engring, Rice Inst., Houston, 1944; postgrad., U. Houston. With Dow Chem., Midland, Mich., 1946-88, v.p. ops., 1977-78; pres. Dow U.S.A., 1978-82; v.p. Dow Chem. Corp., 1978-82, exec. v.p., 1982-83, sr. v.p., 1983-86, sr. cons., 1986-88, ret., 1988, also bd. dirs.; bd. dirs. Dow Corning Corp. nat. exec. bd. Boy Scouts Am., 1979-86; bd. dirs. Meth. Mission Home, San Antonio. Served with USNR, 1944-46. Mem. AICE, United Meth. Reporter Found. (Dallas). Methodist.

ROOKLIDGE, WILLIAM CHARLES, lawyer; b. Portland, Oreg., Aug. 10, 1957; s. Chester Herbert and Barbara Kathryn (Dodson) R.; m. Kathryn Elaine Roosa, Aug. 20, 1983; children: Elizabeth Jill, Matthew Joseph. BS, U. Portland, 1979; JD, Lewis & Clark, 1984; LLM, George Washington U., 1985. Bar: Oreg. 1985, U.S. Patent Office 1985, U.S. Ct. Appeals (fed. cir.) 1985, Calif. 1988, U.S. Dist. Ct. (cen. dist.) Calif. 1988, U.S. Ct. Appeals (9th cir.) 1988, U.S. Supreme Ct. 1993, U.S. Dist. Ct. (so. dist.) Calif. 1992, U.S. Dist. Ct. (so. dist.) Calif. 1989. Engr. Tube Forgings Am., Inc., Portland, 1978-82; jud. clk. U.S. Ct. Appeals (fed. cir.), Washington, 1985-87; assoc. Knobbe, Martens, Olson & Bear, Newport Beach, Calif., 1987-89, ptnr., 1990-94; dir. Howard, Rice, Nemerovski, Canady, Falk & Rabkin, Newport Beach, Calif., 1995—. Contbr. articles to profl. jours. Recipient Joseph Rossman Meml. award Patent & Trademark Office Soc., 1988, Gerald Rose Meml. award John Marshall Law Sch., 1993. Mem. ABA (sect. intellectual property law, com. chair 1992—), Am. Intellectual Property Law Assn. (com. chair 1988-93, dir. 1995—, Robert C. Watson award 1987), Orange County Patent Law Assn. (bd. dirs. 1990-93, pres. 1994). Republican. Presbyterian. Office: Howard Rice Nemerovski Canady et al 610 Newport Ctr Dr Ste 450 Newport Beach CA 92660-6420

ROOKS, CHARLES SHELBY, minister; b. Beaufort, N.C., Oct. 19, 1924; s. Shelby A. and Maggie (Hawkins) R.; m. Adrienne Martinez, Aug. 7, 1946; children: Laurence Gaylord, Carol Ann. AB, Va. State U., 1949; MDiv, Union Theol. Sem., 1953; LHD (hon.), Howard U., 1981, Va. State U., 1984, Talladega Coll., 1989; DD (hon.), Coll. Wooster, 1968, Interdenominational Theol. Ctr., 1979, Va. Union U., 1980; LLD (hon.), Dillard U., 1986, Heidelberg Coll., 1990; LittD (hon.), Huston-Tillotson Coll., 1989. Ordained to ministry United Ch. of Christ, 1953. Pastor Shanks Village Ch., Orangeburg, N.Y., 1951-53; pastor Lincoln Meml. Congl. Temple, Washington, 1953-60; assoc. dir. Fund for Theol. Edn., Princeton, N.J., 1960-67, exec. dir., 1967-74; pres. Chgo. Theol. Sem., 1974-84; exec. v.p. United Ch. Bd. for Homeland Ministries, N.Y.C., 1984-92, ret., 1992; mem. exec. bd. dept. ministry Nat. Coun. Chs., 1962-70; chmn. bd. United Ch. of Christ Office of Comm., 1964-81, chmn. com. structure Ctrl. Atlantic Conf., 1962-64; mem. Union Theol Sem. Alumni Coun., 1966-70, Theol. Perspectives Commn. on Nat. Com. Black Churchmen, 1968-74; vis. fellow Episc. Theol. Sem. S.W., Austin, Tex., 1966; lectr. in field., 1960-94. Author: Rainbows and Reality, 1984, The Hopeful Spirit, 1987, Revolution in Zion, 1990; editor: Toward a Better Ministry, 1965; mem. editorial bd. Theology Today, 1966, New Conversations, 1977; contbr. articles to religious jours. Chmn. planning com. Nat. Consultation Negro in Christian Ministry, 1965; trustee Bexley Hall Theol. Sem., Colgate-Rochester Div. Sch., 1968-73, Lancaster Theol. Sem., Pa., 1969-74, Eastern Career Testing Ctr., Lancaster, 1969-74; mem. Princeton Regional Sch. Bd., 1969-70, exec. bd. Nat. Com. Religion and Labor, 1987-91; bd. dirs. The Africa Fund, 1987-91, Wash. Urban League, 1955-60, chmn. housing com., 1956-60; chmn. ednl. adv. com. Chgo. Urban League, 1978-84; pres. Communications Improvement, 1971-81; vice chair Nat. Com. for Full Employment, 1987-91. Served with AUS, 1943-46, PTO. Recipient Elizabeth Taylor Byrd Fund Outstanding Community Service award, 1969. Mem. Va. State U. Nat. Alumni Assn. (pres. 1966-67), Soc. for Study Black Religion (pres. 1970-74, 80-84), Assn. Theol. Schs. (cons. Black ch. studies 1970-71, mem. commn. on accrediting 1976-82, chmn. 1980-82, exec. com. 1982-84, Disting. Svc. medal 1992).

ROOKS, JUDITH PENCE, family planning, maternal health care, midwifery consultant; b. Spokane, Wash., Aug. 18, 1941; d. Lawrence Cyrus and Christine Atrice (Snow) Pence; m. Peter Geoffrey Bourne, Mar. 1972 (div.); m. Charles Stanley Rooks, Sept. 21, 1975; 1 child, Christopher Robert. BS, U. Wash., 1963; MS, Cath. U. Am., 1967; MPH, Johns Hopkins U., 1974. Cert. edpidemiology, nursing, nurse-midwife, mediator. Staff nurse The Clin. Ctr., NIH, Bethesda, Md., 1965; asst. prof. nursing dept. San Jose (Calif.) State Coll., 1967-69; epidemiologist Ctrs. for Disease Control, Atlanta, 1970-72, 74-78; asst. prof. dept. ob-gyn. Oreg. Health Sci. U., Portland, 1978-79; expert Office of the Surgeon Gen., Dept. HHS, Washington, 1979-80; project officer U.S. AID, Washington, 1980-82; prin. investigator Columbia U. Sch. Pub. Health, N.Y.C., 1988-89; cons. Portland, 1982—; mem. tech. adv. com. Family Health Internat., Research Triangle Park, N.C., 1986—; mem. editorial adv. com. population info. program Johns Hopkins U., Balt., 1984—; mem. com. Inst. of Medicine NAS, Washington, 1983-85; academic faculty cmty.-base nurse-midwifery edn. program Frontier Sch. Midwifery and Family Nursing, Hyden, Ky., 1993-95. Co-author: Nurse-Midwifery in America, 1986, Reproductive Risk in Maternity Care and Family Planning Services, 1992; contbr. articles to profl. jours. Bd. advisors World Affairs Coun. Oreg., Portland, 1987—; bd. dirs. Planned Parenthood of the Columbia/Willamette, Portland, 1987-90; chm. Ga. Citizens for Hosp. Abortion, Atlanta, 1969-70. Mem. APHA (chair com. on women's rights 1982-83, governing coun. 1976-77, 79-82, Martha May Eliot award for svc. to mothers and children 1993), Am. Coll. Nurse0Midwives (life, pres. 1983-85). Avocations: gardening, running, reading, traveling, cooking. Home and Office: 2706 SW English Ct Portland OR 97201-1622

ROOMANN, HUGO, architect; b. Tallinn, Estonia, Mar. 25, 1923; came to U.S., 1951, naturalized, 1957; s. Eduard August and Annette (Kask) R.; m. Raja R. Suursoho, Sept. 15, 1945; children—Katrin-Kaja, Linda-Anu. B.S., Inst. Tech. Carolo Wilhelmina, Braunschweig, W. Ger., 1950; M.F.A. in Arch. (scholar 1956-57), Princeton U., 1957. Archtl. engr. Austin Co., Roselle, N.J., 1951-54; archtl. designer Epple & Seaman, Newark, 1954-55, 57-61; propr. Hugo Roomann, Cranford and Elizabeth, N.J., 1961-66; partner A.M. Kinney Assocs. (Architects and Engrs.), Cin., N.Y.C. and Chgo., 1966-89; dir. architecture, v.p. corp. ops. A.M. Kinney, Inc., Cin., 1967, 77, 89; dir. Walter Kidde Constructors, Inc., 1973, A.M. Kinney, Inc., A.M. Kinney Assocs. Inc., Chgo.; pres. Design Art Corp., 1986. Prin. works include Grad. Rsch. Ctr. for Biol. Scis., Ohio State U., 1970, Lloyd Libr., Cin., 1968, offices, labs. and mfg. facilities, Miles Labs., West Haven, Conn., 1969, Am. Mus. Atomic Energy, Oak Ridge, 1975, Renton K. Brodie Sci. Ctr., U. Cin., 1970, EPA Nat. Labs., Cin., 1975, NALCO Tech. Ctr., Naperville, Ill., 1979, Brown & Williamson Corp. Hdqrs., Louisville, 1983, U. Cin. Kettering Lab., 1989. Pres. Citizens League, Elizabeth, N.J., 1966, Estonian Heritage Assn. Cin., 1991-94; bd. dirs., pres. Inter-Ethnic Coun. of Greater Cin., 1992-95. Recipient Top Ten Plant award Factory mag., 1967, Top Ten Plant award Modern Mfg. mag., 1970. Mem. AIA (Ohio chpt. award for Renton K. Brodie Sci. Ctr. 1971, for NALCO Ctr. 1980), Soc. Archtl. Historians, Princeton Club. Lutheran. Office: 2856 Observatory Ave Cincinnati OH 45208-2340

ROOMBERG, LILA GOLDSTEIN, lawyer; b. Bklyn., Oct. 21, 1929; d. William H. and Mary (Abramowitz) Goldstein; m. Lawrence A. Simon (div. 1965); 1 child, Virginia Simon Feil; m. Gerald Armon Roomberg (dec. 1995). BA, NYU, 1949, JD, 1951. Bar: N.Y. 1952, Pa. 1963. Assoc. Ballard, Spahr, Andrews & Ingersoll, Phila., 1959-71, ptnr., 1971-91, of counsel, 1992—. Mem. ABA, Pa. Bar Assn., Phila. Bar Assn., Phila. Bar Found. (sec. 1984-87, trustee 1981-87). Home: 120 Spruce St Philadelphia PA 19106-4315 Office: Ballard Spahr Andrews & Ingersoll 1735 Market St Philadelphia PA 19103-7501

ROONEY, ANDREW AITKEN, writer, columnist; b. Albany, N.Y., Jan. 14, 1919; s. Walter S. and Ellinor (Reynolds) R.; m. Marguerite Howard, Mar. 21, 1942; children: Ellen, Martha, Emily, Brian. Student, Colgate U., 1942. Writer-producer CBS-TV News, 1959—; newspaper columnist Tribune Co. Syndicate, 1979—. Author: (with O.C. Hutton) Air Gunner, 1944, The Story of Stars and Stripes, 1946, Conquerors' Peace, 1947, The Fortunes of War, 1962, A Few Minutes with Andy Rooney, 1981, And More By Andy Rooney, 1982, Pieces of My Mind, 1984, Word for Word, 1986, Not That You Asked, 1989, Sweet and Sour, 1992, My War, 1995; TV programs include An Essay on War, Mr. Rooney Goes to Washington, Mr. Rooney Goes to Dinner; regular commentator-essayist: 60 Minutes, 1978—. Served with AUS, 1941-45. Decorated Air medal, Bronze Star.; recipient awards for best written TV documentary Writers Guild Am., 1966, 68, 71, 75, 76, Emmy awards, 1968, 78, 81, 82. Office: CBS News/60 Minutes 524 W 57th St New York NY 10019-2902

ROONEY, DANIEL M., professional football team executive; b. 1932; s. Arthur Joseph and Kathleen (McNulty) R. Former salesman advt., editor Pitts. Steelers Program; now pres. Pitts. Steelers; mem. exec. coms. NFL. Office: Three Rivers Stadium 300 Stadium Cir Pittsburgh PA 15212-5729*

ROONEY, FRANCIS CHARLES, JR., corporate executive; b. North Brookfield, Mass., Nov. 24, 1921; s. Francis Charles and Evelyn Fullerbrown (Murray) R.; m. Frances Elizabeth Heffernan, June 10, 1950; children: Peter, Michael, Stephen, Jean, William, Carol, Frances, Clare. BS in Econs., U. Pa., 1943; D of Comml. Sci. (hon.), Suffolk U., 1968, St. John's U., 1973; PhD (hon.), Boston Coll., 1986. Mem. sales staff John Foote Shoe Co., Brockton, Mass., 1946-48; mem. sales staff Florsheim Shoe Co., Chgo., 1948-53; various positions Melville Shoe Co., N.Y.C., 1953—; pres. Thom McAn div. Melville Shoe Corp., N.Y.C., 1961-64; pres., chief exec. officer Melville Corp., Harrison, N.Y. and N.Y.C., 1964-77; chmn., pres., chief exec. officer Melville Corp., Harrison, 1977-80, chmn., chief exec. officer, 1980-86, former chmn. exec. com.; chmn. bd., CEO H.H. Brown Shoe Co., Inc., Greenwich, Conn.; dir. Bankers Trust Co., N.Y.C., Crystal Brands Inc., Southport, Conn., N.Y.C., The Neiman Marcus Group, Chestnut Hill, Mass. Bd. dirs. United Cerebral Palsy, N.Y.C., 1960, Smithsonian Assocs., 1975; overseers Wharton Sch. U. Pa.; trustee N.Y. Med. Coll. Lt. (j.g.) USN, 1943-46. Republican. Roman Catholic. Clubs: Round Hill (Greenwich); Links (N.Y.C.); Winged Foot (Mamaroneck, N.Y.). Office: H H Brown Shoe Co Inc 124 W Putnam Ave Greenwich CT 06830-5317*

ROONEY, GAIL SCHIELDS, college administrator; b. St. Francis, Kans., Feb. 15, 1947; d. Fred Harlan and Darlene Mary (Saint) Schields; m. Thomas Michael Rooney, June 27, 1970; children: Shane Michael, Shauna Meghan. BA, U. Colo., 1969; MS, George Williams Coll., 1974; PhD, U. Ill., 1982. Asst. dir. Spl. Svcs. Program Cleve. State U., 1970-71; admissions counselor George Williams Coll., Downers Grove, Ill., 1972-73; coord. of career exploration ctr. Women's Programs Cuyahoga Community Coll., Cleve., 1973-76; vis. asst. prof. Sch. Clin. Medicine U. Ill., Champaign, 1981-82; counselor, instr. Cuyahoga Community Coll., Cleve., 1982-84, dir. counseling, career and psychol. svcs., 1984-85; dir. career, counseling and health svcs. Briar Cliff Coll., Sioux City, Iowa, 1985-88, v.p. for student devel., 1988-95, ednl. cons. and adj. faculty, 1996—; mem. faculty psychology Mesa (Ariz.) C.C., 1995; adj. instr. counselor edn. Wayne (Nebr.) State Coll., 1988; program presenter Myers Briggs Type Indicator, Sioux City, 1986—. Bd. dirs. Gordon Chem. Dependency Ctr., Sioux City, 1986-89, St. Luke's Gordon Recovery Ctr., Sioux City, 1991-95. Mem. ACA, Am. Coll. Pers. Assn., Nat. Assn. Student Pers. Adminstrs. Home: 52 Red Bridge Dr Sioux City IA 51104

ROONEY, J. PATRICK, insurance company executive; b. Lawrenceville, Ill., Dec. 13, 1927; s. Michael Andrew and Mary Francis (Loftus) R.; married; children: Therese, Andrew, Cathleen, Christine. BA in Econs., St. John's U., 1948. CLU. With Golden Rule Ins. Co. (formerly Golden Rule Life Ins. Co.), Lawrenceville, Ill., 1946—, pres., 1955-59, chmn. bd., chief exec. officer, 1974—, chmn. bd. Golden Rule Fin. Corp., 1972—. Republican. Roman Catholic.*

ROONEY, JOHN EDWARD, communications company executive; b. Evergreen Park, Ill., Apr. 24, 1942; s. John Edward and Margaret Wilma (Stolte) R.; m. Germaine Rose Dettloff, June 26, 1965; children: Kathleen, John, Colleen. BS, John Carroll U., 1964; MBA, Loyola U., 1969. Credit analyst Fed. Res. Bank, Chgo., 1964-69, adminstrv. asst., 1969-70; asst. treas. Pullman Inc., 1970-73, asst. contr., 1973-78; v.p. fin. Pullman Standard, 1978-79; sr. v.p. fin. Trailmobile, Chgo., 1979-81; treas. Firestone Tire & Rubber Co., Akron, Ohio, 1981-87, v.p. retail fin. services, 1987-88, sr. v.p. MasterCare Svc. Ctrs., 1988-90; v.p., treas. Ameritech, Chgo., 1990-92; pres. Ameritech Cellular Svcs., Chgo., 1992—; instr. fin. Ill. Benedictine Coll., 1975-80. Mem. Ohio Mfrs. Assn. (trustee 1983-87), Ohio Pub. Expenditure Coun. (trustee 1986-87), Glen Oak Country Club (Glen Ellyn, Ill.), Boulders Club (Carefree, Ariz.), The Tavern Club (Chgo.). Home: 2S 311 Davis Ct Wheaton IL 60187 Office: Ameritech # 3H 70 2000 W Ameritech Center Dr Hoffman Estates IL 60195-5000

ROONEY, JOHN PHILIP, law educator; b. Evanston, Ill., May 1, 1932; s. John McCaffery and Bernadette Marie (O'Brien) R.; m. Jean Marie Kliss, Feb. 16, 1974 (div. Oct. 1988); 1 child, Caitlin Mairin. BA, U. Ill, 1953; JD, Harvard U., 1958. Bar: Ill. 1958, Calif. 1961, Mich. 1975, U.S. Tax Ct. 1973. Assoc. lawyer Chapman & Cutler, Chgo., 1958-60, Wilson, Morton, San Mateo, Calif., 1961-63; pvt. practice San Francisco, 1963-74; prof. law Cooley Law Sch., Lansing, Mich., 1975—. Author: Selected Cases (Property), 1985; contbr. articles to profl. jours. Pres. San Francisco coun. Dem. Clubs, 1970. 1st lt. U.S. Army, 1953-55. Recipient Beattie Teaching award Cooley Law Sch. Grads., 1979, 90, 92. Mem. ABA (real estate fed. tax problems com. 1986—, title ins. com.), Mich. Bar Title Stds. Com., Ingham County Bar Assn., Univ. Club. Democrat. Unitarian. Office: Cooley Law Sch 217 S Capitol Ave Lansing MI 48933-1503

ROONEY, KEVIN DAVITT, lawyer; b. Springfield, Mass., June 23, 1944; s. Davitt Michael and Elizabeth Isabel (Wlodyka) R.; m. Annette Eloise Benevento, Nov. 11, 1972; children: Kathryn Denise, Mary Elizabeth. B.A., St. Marys Coll., 1966; J.D., George Washington U., 1975. Bar: Va. 1975, D.C. 1977. Computer systems analyst VA, Washington, 1967-68, 70-73; chief legal programs and budget Dept. Justice, Washington, 1973-77, exec. asst. to assoc. atty. gen., 1977, asst. atty. gen. for adminstrn., 1977-84; prin. Rooney & Assocs, Washington, 1984-87, 90-94, Rooney & Barry, Washington, 1987-89; assoc. dir. Exec. Office for Immigration Rev., U.S. Dept. Justice, Falls Church, Va., 1995—; bd. dirs., v.p. Joint Action in Cmty. Svcs., Inc., Washington, 1988-94. Served with U.S. Army, 1968-70. Mem. ASPA, Fed. Bar Assn., Va. Bar Assn., D.C. Bar Assn. Office: US Dept Justice Office Immigration Review 5107 Leesburg Pike Ste 2400 Falls Church VA 22041-3234

ROONEY, MATTHEW A., lawyer; b. Jersey City, May 19, 1949; s. Charles John and Eileen (Dunphy) R.; m. Jean M. Alletag, June 20, 1973 (div. Dec. 1979); 1 child, Jessica Margaret; m. Diane S. Kaplan, July 6, 1981; children: Kathryn Olivia, S. Benjamin. AB magna cum laude, Georgetown U., 1971; JD with honors, U. Chgo., 1974. Bar: Ill. 1975, U.S. Dist. Ct. (no. dist.) Ill. 1975, U.S. Ct. Appeals (7th cir.). 1990. Law clk. to cir. judge U.S. Ct. Appeals (7th cir.), Chgo., 1974-75; assoc. Mayer, Brown & Platt, Chgo., 1975-80, ptnr., 1981—. Assoc. editor U. Chgo. Law Rev., 1973. Mem. ABA, 7th Cir. Bar Assn., Order of Coif, Phi Beta Kappa. Democrat. Roman Catholic. Avocations: jogging, golfing. Home: 2718 Sheridan Rd Evanston IL 60201-1754 Office: Mayer Brown & Platt 190 S La Salle St Chicago IL 60603-3410

ROONEY, MICHAEL FRANCIS, publisher; b. Bronxville, N.Y., July 4, 1953; s. Francis Charles and Frances (Heffernan) R.; m. Joann Paulsen, Apr. 30, 1977; children: Leigh Ann, Hank. BS in Mktg., Boston Coll., 1976. V.p. Paulsen Pub. Inc., N.Y.C., 1979-85; regional sales mgr. Field & Stream Mag., N.Y.C., 1985-87, pub.; pub. Men's Health Mag., 1987-91, Discover Mag., 1991-94, Field and Stream Mag., Outdoor Life, 1994—; prof., grad. pub. program Pace U. Mem. adv. bd. Outward Bound U.S.A. Mem. Mag. Pubs. Am. (mktg. com.), Larchmont Yacht Club, Winged Foot Golf Club. Roman Catholic. Avocations: running, golf, fishing. Office: Times Mirror Mags Inc Two Park Ave New York NY 10016-5695

ROONEY, MICKEY (JOE YULE, JR.), actor; b. Bklyn., Sept. 23, 1920; s. Joe and Nell (Carter) Yule; m. Ava Gardner, Jan. 10, 1942 (div. May 1943); m. Betty Jane Rase, Sept. 30, 1944 (div. 1949); children: Mickey Jr., Timothy; m. Martha Vickers, June 3, 1949 (div.); m. Elaine Mahnken (div. 1958); m. Barbara Thomason, Dec. 1958; children: Kerry, Kyle, Kelly Ann, Kimmy Sue; m. Margie Lang, Sept. 1966 (div. 1967); m. Carolyn Hockett, (div.); 1 adopted child, Jimmy, 1 child, Jonell; m. Jan Chamberlin, July 28, 1978; stepchildren: Chris Aber, Mark Aber. Ed. in, Dayton Heights and Vine Street grammar sch., Pacific Mil. Acad., under tutors. First appeared in vaudeville with parents; then appeared with Sid Gould, numerous TV programs; appeared in motion pictures Judge Hardy's Children, Hold That Kiss, Lord Jeff, Love Finds Andy Hardy, Boys Town, Stablemates, Out West With the Hardys, Huckleberry Finn, Andy Hardy Gets Spring Fever, Babes in Arms, Young Tom Edison, Judge Hardy and Son, Andy Hardy Meets Debutante, Strike Up the Band, Andy Hardy's Private Secretary, Men of Boystown, Life Begins for Andy Hardy, Babes on Broadway, A Yank at Eton, The Human Comedy, Andy Hardy's Blonde Trouble, Girl Crazy, Thousands Cheer, National Velvet, Ziegfeld Follies, The Strip, Sound Off, Off Limits, All Ashore, Light Case of Larceny, Drive A Crooked Road, Bridges at Toko-Ri, The Bold and Brave, Eddie, Private Lives of Adam and Eve, Comedian, The Grabbers, St. Joseph Plays the Horses, Breakfast at Tiffany's, Somebody's Waiting, Requiem For A Heavyweight, Richard, Pulp, It's a Mad, Mad, Mad, Mad World, Everything's Ducky, The Secret Invasion, The Extraordinary Seaman, The Comic, The Cockeyed Cowboys of Calico County, Skidoo, B.J. Presents, That's Entertainment, The Domino Principle, Pete's Dragon, The Magic of Lassie, Black Stallion, Arabian Adventure, Erik the Viking, My Heroes Have Always Been Cowboys, 1991, (voice) Little Nimo: Adventures in Slumberland, 1992; starred in TV prodns. Pinocchio, 1957, Leave 'Em Laughing, 1981, Bill, 1981 (Emmy, Golden Globe), Senior Trip!, 1981, Bill on His Own, 1983, Little Spies (Acad. Hon. award 1982), It Came upon the Midnight Clear, 1984, Bluegrass, 1988, Legend of Wolf Mountain, 1992, That's Entertainment! III, 1994, Revente of the Red Baron, 1994, Radio Star-die AFN-Story, 1994, The Legend of O.B. Taggart, 1995; appeared on stage in Sugar Babies, 1979, The Will Rogers Follies, 1993; appeared in TV series A Year at the Top, The Mickey Rooney Show; author: I.E. An Autobiography, 1965, Life Is Too Short, 1991, Search for Sonny Skies, 1994; fgn. films: Midsummer Nights Dream, 1937, Words and Music, 1946, Rachels, 1973, To Hong Kong with Love, 1975, Oddessy of the Pacific, 1979. With AUS, WWII. Recipient Spl. Acad. Award, 1940, Tony award for best mus. actor, 1980; named One of Top 10 Money-Making Stars, Herald-Fame Poll, 1938-43. Office: PO Box 3186 Thousand Oaks CA 91359-0186*

ROONEY, PAUL C., JR., lawyer; b. Winnetka, Ill., Oct. 23, 1943; s. Paul C. and Mary K. (Brennan) R.; m. Maria Elena Del Canto, Sept. 6, 1980. BA, Harvard U., 1963, LLB, 1966. Bar: Mass. 1968, N.Y. 1972, Fla. 1980, Tex. 1980, U.S. Dist. Ct. (ea. and so. dists.) N.Y., U.S. Ct. Appeals (2d cir.). Ptnr. White & Case, N.Y.C., 1983—. Served to lt. USNR, 1966-69. Mem. ABA, N.Y. State Bar Assn., Fla. Bar Assn., Tex. Bar Assn., Dallas Bar Assn., Univ. Club (N.Y.C.), Harvard Club (N.Y.C.), Mashomack Preserve, Sharon (N.Y.) Country Club. Home: 417 Park Ave New York NY 10022-4401 also: 11 Lake Ln Sharon CT 06069 Office: White & Case 1155 Ave Of The Americas New York NY 10036-2711

ROONEY, PAUL GEORGE, mathematics educator; b. N.Y.C., July 14, 1925; s. Geoffrey Daniel and Doris Elizabeth (Babcock) R.; m. Mary Elizabeth Carlisle, June 20, 1950; children: Francis Timothy, Elizabeth Anne, Kathleen Doris, John Edward, James Carlisle. B.Sc., U. Alta., 1949; Ph.D., Calif. Inst. Tech., 1952. Asst. prof. math. U. Alta., 1952-55; asst. prof. U. Toronto, 1955-60, assoc. prof., 1960-62, prof., 1962-91, prof. emeritus, 1991—; dir. Commonwealth Petroleum Co., Calgary, 1946-59. Editor in chief Can. Jour. Math. 1971-75; contbr. articles to profl. jours. Bd. dirs. Francis F. Reeve Found., 1954-85. Served with Can. Army, 1943-45. Fellow Royal Soc. Can.; Mem. Can. Math. Soc. (councillor 1960-64, 66-70, 76-78, v.p. 1979-81, pres. 1981-83), Am. Math. Soc., Math. Assn. Am. Office: U Toronto, Dept Math, Toronto, ON Canada M5S 1A1

ROONEY, PAUL MONROE, former library administrator; b. Buffalo, Apr. 16, 1918; s. John Francis and Marguerite (Cass) R.; m. Elizabeth Dorsey, Jan. 22, 1955; children: James, Thomas. B.S., State Tchrs. Coll., Buffalo, 1938; B.S. in L.S, U. Buffalo, 1940. Br. librarian Buffalo Pub. Library, 1940-42; head reference dept. Grosvenor Library, 1945-59; head tech. dept. Buffalo and Erie County Pub. Library, 1959-61, asst. dep. dir., 1961-63, dep. dir., 1963-75, dir., 1975-83; chmn. N.Y. State Pub. Librarians Certification Com., 1959-60; trustee Western N.Y. Library Resources Council, 1966-83, pres., 1969-70. Served with USAF, 1942-45. Mem. ALA, N.Y. Libr. Assn. Roman Catholic. Home: 522 Ashland Ave Buffalo NY 14222-1307

ROONEY, TERENCE, public relations executive; b. 1951. V.p. Morgen-Walke Assocs., 1983-87, sr. v.p., 1987-89, ptnr./dir. press rels. group, 1989—. Office: Morgen-Walke Assocs Inc 380 Lexington Ave New York NY 10168-0002*

ROONEY, WILLIAM RICHARD, magazine editor; b. New Brunswick, N.J., Mar. 12, 1938; s. William Richard and Bernadette (Huether) R.; m. Rita Ann Scherer, July 20, 1963; children—Karen, Kevin, Brian, Kristin. B.S. in English, St. Peter's Coll., Jersey City, 1959. Asst., then asso. editor Marine Engring./Log mag., N.Y.C., 1960-64; asso. editor Outdoor Life mag., N.Y.C., 1964-72; mng. editor Outdoor Life mag., 1972-76, sr. editor, 1976-77; editor Am. Forests mag., Washington, 1977-95, v.p. for publs., 1991—; editor articles Sports Afield ann. outdoor mags., 1983-90. Contbr. to: Complete Outdoors Ency, 1972; others. Served with AUS, 1959-60. Mem. Outdoor Writers Assn. Am. Roman Catholic. Home: 7916 Carrie Ln Manassas VA 22111-2548 Office: 1516 P St NW Washington DC 20005-1932

ROOP, EUGENE FREDERIC, religion educator; b. South Bend, Ind., May 11, 1942; s. G. Frederic and Lois Elizabeth (Berkebile) R.; m. Delora Ann Mishler, Aug. 24, 1963; children: Tanya Marie, Frederic John. BS, Manchester (Ind.) Coll., 1964; MDiv, Bethany Theol. Seminary, Oakbrook, Ill., 1967; PhD, Claremont (Calif.) Grad. Sch., 1972. Asst. prof. Earlham Sch. Religion, Richmond, Ind., 1970-74, assoc. prof., 1975-77; assoc. prof. Bethany Theol. Seminary, 1977-78, prof. Bibl. studies, 1978-86, Wieand prof. Bibl. studies, 1987—; pres. Bethany Theol. Sem., 1992—; dir. Ch. of Brethren Outdoor Ministries Assn., Elgin, Ill., 1982-88; bd. dirs. Ecumenical Ctr. for Stewardship Studies, N.Y.C., 1979—. Author: Coming Kingdom Teacher's Guide, 1982, Living the Biblical Story, 1979, Commentary on Genesis, 1987, Heard in our Hand, 1990, Let the Rivers Run, 1991. Active sch. bd. adv. com., Villa Park, Ill., 1981-85. So. Ohio Seminary Consortium summer fellow, 1975, Assn. Theol. Schs. summer fellow, 1974, Sea-Atlantic Fund rsch. fellow, 1978-79. Mem. Soc. Bibl. Lit., Chgo. Soc. Bibl. Rsch., Assn. Case Tchrs. Avocations: photography, travel, tennis. Office: Bethany Theol Seminary 615 Natl Road West Richmond IN 47374

ROOP, JAMES JOHN, public relations executive; b. Parkersburg, W.Va., Oct. 29, 1949; s. J. Vaun and Mary Louise (McGinnis) R.; m. Margaret Mary Kuneck (div. 1982); m. Susan Lynn Hoell (div. 1989); m. Daisy P. Billue, 1990. BS in Journalism, W. Va. U., 1971. Various account mgmt. postions Ketchum Pub. Rels., Pitts., 1972-77, v.p., 1977-79; v.p. Burson-Marsteller, Chgo., 1979-81; sr. v.p. Hesselbart & Mitten/Watt, Cleve., 1981-84, exec. v.p., 1984-86, pres., 1986-87; pres. Watt, Roop & Co. (formerly Hesselbart & Mitten/Watt), Cleve., 1987—. Contbr. articles to profl. jours. Bd. dirs. Ctr. for Families and Children. Fellow Pub. Rels. Soc. Am. (chmn. investor rels. sect. 1984-85, chmn. honors and awards com. 1995); mem. Nat. Investor Rels. Inst. (charter pres. Cleve./Akron chpt., sr. investor rels. roundtable), Boys Hope, Police Athletic League, Econs. Am., Leadership Cleve., Cleve. Skating Club, Mayfield Country Club. Republican. Home: 2574 Fairmount Blvd Cleveland Hts OH 44106-3241 Office: Watt Roop & Co 1100 Superior Ave E Ste 1350 Cleveland OH 44114-2518

ROORDA, JOHN FRANCIS, JR., business consultant; b. Evanston, Ill., Jan. 16, 1923; s. John Francis and Sadie M. (Daley) R.; m. Elizabeth Mulcahy, July 2, 1949; children: Elizabeth Roorda Barker, John F., Ann Roorda Hollis. B.S. in Chem. Engring, Purdue U., 1943, Ph.D., 1949. With Shell Oil Co., 1949-83; gen. mgr. combined oil products/chem. econs. dept., 1973-74, v.p. planning and econs., 1974-77; v.p. Shell Devel. Co., Houston, 1977-78; v.p. corp. planning Shell Oil Co., 1978-83; pres. John Roorda, 1983—; coordinator Exec. Service Corps, Houston, 1985—. Served to lt. (j.g.) USNR, 1943-46. Recipient Disting. Engring. Alumnus award Purdue U., 1976, Outstanding Chem. Engr. award Purdue U., 1993. Mem. Sigma Xi. Roman Catholic. Office: 2401 Fountainview Suite 910 Houston TX 77057

ROOS, CASPER, actor; b. N.Y.C., Mar. 21, 1925; s. Jacob and Sabina (Uhlenbusch) R.; m. Shirley Anne Nicholson, June 27, 1953; 1 child, Pieter Nicholson. Student, N.Y. Coll. Music. treas. Actors Equity Found., N.Y.C., 1982-88; co-chmn. research subcom. Nat. Theater Com., N.Y.C., 1983—. Prin. actor Shenandoah, N.Y.C., 1975-78, Brigadoon, N.Y.C., 1979-80, My One and Only, N.Y.C., 1982-85, Into the Light, 1986, Man of La Mancha, Zurich, 1988, (Broadway prodn.) Shenandoah Revival, 1989; numerous regional theater prodns. Served with U.S. Mcht. Marines, 1943-46. Mem. Actors Equity (treas. 1982-88, councilor 1964-79, 88-93). Home: PO Box 11 Gilbertsville NY 13776-0011 *Don Quixote wanted to 'add a little grace to the world.' I, too, would like to add a 'little' to this world, whether it be grace or laughter or tears to an audience or service to my colleagues. If, like Don Quixote, I look a little foolish, so be it. I prefer a life of striving for the ultimate to the easier smug acceptance of the status quo.*

ROOS, DANIEL, civil engineering educator; b. Bklyn., Apr. 12, 1939; s. Sigmund and Anita (Sperling) R.; m. Eva Bonis, June 1, 1969; children—Richard Joseph, Linda Suzanne. B.S. in Civil Engring, M.I.T., 1961, M.S., 1963, Ph.D., 1966. Mem. faculty MIT, Cambridge, 1963—, assoc. prof. civil engring., 1970-76, prof., 1976—, head transp. systems div., 1977-78, dir. Ctr. for Transp. Studies, 1978-85, dir. Ctr. Tech., Policy and Indsl. Devel., 1985—, Japan Steel Industry prof., 1985—; mem. Commn. on Indsl. Productivity MIT, 1987-89; founder, dir. Multisystems Inc., Cambridge, 1965-85; chmn. com. to assess advanced vehicle and hwy. techs., NRC, 1990-91; mem. com. on fuel economy NRC, 1991-92; dir. Internat. Motor Vehicle Program, 1980—; co-dir. Lean Aircraft Initiative, 1992—. Author: ICES System Design, 1964; The Future of the Automobile, 1984, Auto Futures, 1990; co-author: Made in America, 1989, The Machine That Changed the World, 1990; contbr. articles to profl. jours. Mem. U.S. Task Force on Transp., 1969. Recipient Shingo Prize for Excellence in Mfg. Rsch., 1994. Mem. ASCE (Frank M. Masters Transp. Engring. award 1989), Assn. Computing Machinery, Ops. Research Soc. (treas. transp. sci. sect. 1970-71), Transp. Research Bd. (chmn. para-transit com. 1974-80, group coun. 1980-84), Coun. Univ. Transp. Ctrs. (pres. 1983). Developer Dial-A-Ride transp. concept, 1965; dir. Internat. Motor Vehicle. Home: 28 Baskin Rd Lexington MA 02173-6929 Office: MIT Ctr Tech Policy & Indsl Devel 77 Massachusetts Ave Cambridge MA 02139-4301

ROOS, ERIC EUGENE, plant physiologist; b. Charleroi, Pa., May 23, 1941; s. Carl F. and Isabelle (McPherson) R.; m. Lois Bonita Bruno, Aug. 24, 1964; children: Michael, Erin. BS, Waynesburg Coll., 1963; PhD, W.Va. U., 1967. Supr. plant physiologist, rsch. leader Nat. Seed Storage Lab, Agrl. Research Service of USDA, Ft. Collins, Colo., 1967—. Fellow Am. Soc. Agronomy, Am. Soc. Hort. Sci., Crop Sci. Soc. Am.; mem. Sigma Xi, Gamma Sigma Delta. Office: USDA Agrl Research Service 1111 S Mason St Fort Collins CO 80521-4500

ROOS, FREDERICK RIED, film producer; b. Santa Monica, Calif., May 22, 1934; s. Victor Otto and Florence Mary (Stout) R. BA, UCLA, 1956. Producer Zoetrope Studios, San Francisco. Casting dir., story editor various cos., 1960-70, film producer, 1964—; producer: Back Door to Hell, 1964-65, Flight to Fury, 1964-65, The Conversation (Acad. award nomination), Godfather Part II, 1973-79 (Acad. award Best Picture), Apocalypse Now, 1979, The Black Stallion, Hammett, 1982, The Escape Artist, The Outsiders, 1983, Rumble Fish, One From the Heart, Cotton Club, 1984, One Magic Christmas, Seven Minutes in Heaven, 1986, Gardens of Stone, 1987, Barfly, 1986, Tucker: The Man and His Dream, 1988, New York Stories, 1989, Wait Until Spring Bandini, 1990, The Godfather Part III, 1990, Hearts of Darkness: A Filmaker's Apocalypse, 1991, The Secret Garden, 1993; assoc. producer: Drive He Said, 1970. Served with AUS, 1957-59. Office: 2980 N Beverly Glen Cir Los Angeles CA 90077-1726

ROOS, JOSEPH CHARLES, III, publisher, pastor; b. Kansas City, Mo., July 19, 1946; s. Joseph Charles and Juanita (Ladage) R. BS in Physics, U. Mo., Kansas City, 1968; MS in Atmospheric Sci., U. Mo., Columbia, 1970. Pub. Sojourners Mag., Washington, 1971—; bd. dirs. Assoc. Ch. Press, Phoenix, 1989—, pres., 1995—. Field organizer McGovern forPres., Chgo., 1992; bd. dirs. Evangs. for Social Action, Phila., 1983-86, vice-chmn., 1985-

86. Avocations: astronomy, meteorology. Home: 1208 Fairmont St NW Washington DC 20009 Office: Sojourners 2401 15th St NW Washington DC 20009

ROOS, THOMAS BLOOM, biological scientist, educator; b. Peoria, Ill., Mar. 19, 1930; s. Seymour G. and Clara Gertrude (Bloom) R.; m. Marilyn A. Siker, June 14, 1953; children: David S., Sara D. AB, Harvard U., 1951; MS, U. Wis., 1953, PhD, 1960; MA (hon.), Dartmouth Coll., 1971. Instr. U. Wis., Madison, 1959-60; instr. Dartmouth Coll., Hanover, N.H., 1960-61, asst. prof., 1961-66, assoc. prof., 1966-71, prof., 1971—; vis. prof. St. George's Med. Sch., London, 1973-75; Fulbright lectr. U. Delhi, U. Calcutta, Bhabha Atomic Rsch. Centre, Coun. Indsl. and Sci. Rsch. Labs., Calcutta, Hyderabad; vis. scientist Harvard Med. Sch., 1988; cons. Commn. on Undergrad. Edn. in Biol. Scis., Washington, 1967-71, St. George's Med. Sch., 1974—, CSP, Inc., Billerica, Mass., 1986—. Inventor Master Scan Image Analyzing Computer. Mem. Dem. Town Com., Hanover, N.H., 1961-68. With U.S. Army, 1954-56. Spl. postdoctoral fellow NIH, Leyden, Netherlands, 1965-66; hon. fellow Univ. Coll., London, 1972-73. Mem. AAAS, Am. Soc. Zoologists. Club: Faculty (Hanover, N.H.) (pres. 1981-85). Avocations: music, computer programming, poetry. Home: 19 Rayton Rd Hanover NH 03755-2211 Office: Dartmouth Coll Dept Of Biology Hanover NH 03755

ROOSEVELT, EDITH KERMIT, journalist; b. N.Y.C., Dec. 19, 1927; d. Archibald Bulloch and Grace Stackpole (Lockwood) R. Grad., Barnard Coll., 1948. Reporter UPI, San Francisco, L.A., 1951-53, Siskiyou Daily News, 1953, UPI, Washington, 1953-55; writer McCann Erickson Co., N.Y.C., 1956-57; assoc. editor Spadea Syndicate, N.Y.C., 1957-59; reporter, feature writer Newark Star Ledger, 1959-63; syndicated columnist numerous newspapers, 1963-80; Washington editor, corr. Nutrition & Health Review, 1980—; lectr. in field. Contbr. numerous articles to profl. jours. Recipient J.C. Meriam, Ervin S. Cobb & Rupert Hughes award of merit Am. Acad. Pub. Affairs. Address: 1661 Crescent Pl NW Washington DC 20009-4048

ROOSEVELT, THEODORE, IV, investment banker; b. Jacksonville, Fla., Nov. 27, 1942; s. Theodore III and Anne Mason (Babcock) R.; m. Constance Lane Rogers, Aug. 1, 1970; 1 child, Theodore Roosevelt V. AB, Harvard U., 1965, MBA, 1972. Assoc. Lehman Bros., N.Y.C., 1972-76; corp. v.p. Lehman Bros. Kuhn Loeb, N.Y.C., 1976-82; sr. v.p. Lehman Comml. Paper Inc., N.Y.C., 1982-85; mng. dir. Lehman Brothers (formerly Shearson Lehman Bros., Inc.), N.Y.C., 1985—; bd. dirs. Lehman Bros. Fin. Products, Inc.; publ. bd. World Policy Jour. Bd. dirs. Trout Unltd., League of Conservation Voters; trustee of the Reservations, Mass.; mem. chmn.'s coun. Nat. Resource Def. Counsel, N.Y.C.; mem. N.Y. State Park Recreation and Hist. Preservation Commn. for City of N.Y.; trustee Am. Mus. Natural History. Mem. Coun. Fgn. Rels., Fgn. Policy Assn. (gov.), The Links (N.Y.C.), The Heights Casino Club (Bklyn.), Explorers Club, Harvard Club (N.Y.C.). Republican. Home: 1 Pierrepont St Brooklyn NY 11201-3361 Office: Lehman Brothers 3 World Fin Ctr New York NY 10285-1000

ROOT, ALAN CHARLES, diversified manufacturing company executive; b. Essex, Eng., Apr. 11, 1925; came to U.S., 1951, naturalized, 1959; s. Charles Stanley and Lillian (Collins) R. B.A., Oxford U., 1943; M.A., Cambridge U., 1951; M.B.A., Stanford U., 1953. Rsch. analyst Dow Chem. Co., Midland, Mich., 1954-55; mgr. mktg. rsch. Gen. Electric Co., 1955-61; v.p. bus. planning Mosler Safe Co., Hamilton, Ohio, 1961-70; v.p. corp. planning Am. Standard Inc., N.Y.C., 1970-76, sr. v.p. ops. svcs., 1976-86, sr. v.p., 1986-88, sr. advisor, 1989; trustee 1995 Trust Fund; sr. advisor Unit Ice, 1995—; bd. dirs. Am.-Standard Energy Inc., Amstan Trucking Inc., 1976-86. Bd. dirs., pres. Brit. Schs. and Univs. Found., admission to Order of St. John of Jerusalem sanctioned by H.M. Elizabeth II, 1986; trustee, treas. N.J. Chamber Music Soc., 1988-95. Served to capt. AUS, 1944-48. Admission to Order of St. John of Jerusalem sanctioned by Her Majesty Queen Elizabeth II, 1986 and decorated comdr. Order of St. John of Jerusalem. Mem. AIChE (assoc. producer TV series Midland sect. 1955), Pilgrims U.S., NEwcomen Soc. N.Am., Univ. Club (N.Y.C.), Order of St. John of Jerusalem (comdr. 1994). Home: 4934 Mt Pleasant Ln Las Vegas NV 89113-0114 *Good luck meant that my industrial career drew on the education I enjoyed as a young man. Professional advancement came by building on prior experience at each step and through long-term, managerial continuity.*

ROOT, ALLEN WILLIAM, pediatrician, educator; b. Phila., Sept. 24, 1933; s. Morris Jacob and Priscilla R.; m. Janet Greenberg, June 15, 1958; children: Jonathan, Jennifer, Michael. AB, Dartmouth Coll., 1955, postgrad. Med. Sch., 1954-56; MD, Harvard U., 1958. Diplomate Am. Bd. Pediatrics (mem. bd. 1986—), Am. Pediatric Endocrinology (mem. bd. 1985-90, chmn. 1990). Intern Strong Meml. Hosp., Rochester, N.Y., 1958-60; resident in pediatrics Hosp. U. Pa., Phila., 1960-62; fellow in pediatric endocrinology Children's Hosp. of Phila., 1962-65; assoc. physician in pediatrics U. Pa. Sch. Medicine, 1964-66, asst. prof. pediatrics, 1966-69; assoc. prof. pediatrics Temple U. Sch. Medicine, Phila., 1969-73; prof. Temple U. Sch. Medicine, 1973; asst. physician in endocrinology Children's Hosp. Phila., 1965-69; chmn. divsn. pediatrics Albert Einstein Med. Center., Phila., 1969-73; prof. pediatrics U. South Fla. Coll. Medicine, Tampa, 1973—, prof. biochemistry, 1987—, assoc. chmn. dept. pediatrics, 1974—, dir. sect. pediatric endocrinology, 1973—; dir. univ. tchg. svcs. All Children's Hosp., St. Petersburg, 1973-89; mem. Fla. Infant Screening Adv. Coun., 1979—, chmn., 1994—; mem. Hillsborough County Thyroid Adv. Com., 1980; mem. med. adv. com. Nat. Pituitary Agy., 1974-78, mem. growth hormone subcom., 1972-79, 81-85. Author: Human Pituitary Growth Hormone, 1972; editor: (with C. La Cauza) Problems in Pediatric Endocrinology, 1980; mem. editl. bd. Jour. Pediats., 1973-81, Jour. Adolescent Health Care, 1979-95, Jour. Pediat. Endocrinology and Metabolism, 1985—, Jour. Clin. Endocrinology and Metabolism, 1993—, Growth, Genetics and Hormones, 1993—, Pediats. in Rev., 1995—; assoc. editor Adolescent and Pediat. Gynecology, 1992—. USPHS grantee; Birth Defects Found. grantee. Mem. AAAS, Am. Pediatric Soc., Soc. Pediatric Rsch., Lawson Wilkins Pediatric Endocrine Soc. (treas. 1979-88, pres. 1988-89), Endocrine Soc., Am. Acad. Pediatrics, Am. Fedn. Clin. Rsch., Soc. Exptl. Biology and Medicine, Soc. Nuclear Medicine, N.Y. Acad. Scis., Phila. Coll. Physicians, Phila. Endocrine Soc. (bd. dirs. 1971-72, treas. 1973), Dartmouth Coll. Alumni Coun., Dartmouth Club. Office: 801 6th St S Saint Petersburg FL 33701-4816

ROOT, DORIS SMILEY, portrait artist; b. Ann Arbor, Mich., June 28, 1924; d. George O. and Hazel (Smith) Smiley. Student, Art Inst. of Chgo., 1943-45, N.Y. Sch. Design, 1976-77, Calif. Art Inst., 1984-85. Creative dir. All May Co.'s, L.A., 1962-63; advt. sales pro. dir. Seibu, L.A., 1963-64; v.p. Walgers & Assocs., L.A., 1964-70; owner, designer At The Root of Things, L.A., 1970-73; adv. sales pro. dir. Hs. of Nine, L.A., 1973-74; asst. designer MGM Grand, Reno, Nev., 1974-76; designer, office mgr. Von Hausen Studio, L.A., 1976-82; ABC libr. ABC/Cap Cities, L.A., 1982-89; portrait artist (also known as Dorian), AKA Dorian, art studio, L.A., 1982—. One-man shows include Cookeville, Tenn., 1989, Beverly Hills, Calif., 1991; artist in residence, Cookeville, 1989-90. Republican. Presbyterian. Avocations: painting, golf. *I'm one of the luckiest women alive. I love fun and found a little of it the best space to create in, in my career and in my personal life. People feel free to try things in a fun place to work. And I must admit, I'm still having fun with painting people's portraits!.*

ROOT, EDWARD LAKIN, education educator, university administrator; b. Cumberland, Md., Dec. 5, 1940; s. Lakin and Edna Grace (Adams) R. BS, Frostburg (Md.) State Coll., 1962, MEd, 1966; EdD, U. Md., 1970. Cert. tchr., Md. Tchr. Allegany County Bd. of Edn., Cumberland, 1962-66; grad. fellow U. Md., College Park, 1966-67, fellow, 1967-69; with Frostburg State U., 1969—, prof., head edn. dept., 1980-87, dean, 1987-95, prof., head MEd. adminstrn., 1995—; mem. Profl. Standards Bd. Md., Balt., 1980-87, 95—, Cert. Rev. Bd. Md., Balt., 1987-90, Md. Task Force Adminstrn., Balt., 1985-88, Md. Task Force: Essentials in Tchr. Edn., 1995, Md. Task Force: Prisoners of Time and Response; task force tchr. assessment, 1995—. Mem. Allegany County (Md.) Planning and Zoning Bd. Appeals, 1995—. Mem. Nat. Assn. Secondary Sch. Prins., Nat. Soc. for the Study of Edn., Mensa, Elks, Shriners, Masons, Phi Delta Kappa. Democrat. Methodist. Avocation: photography. Home: 100 Pennsylvania Ave Cumberland MD 21502-4236 Office: Frostburg State U College Ave Frostburg MD 21532-1724

ROOT, FRANKLIN RUSSELL, business educator; b. Hartford, Conn., Jan. 30, 1923; s. Albert Edward and Marie Rose (Benard) R.; m. Liliane Anny Weissbrod, Feb. 2, 1951 (dec. 1975); children: Michele, Peter, Valerie, Allan, Jonathan; m. Joyce Elinor Halfen, Aug. 1, 1976. BS, Trinity Coll., 1947; MBA, Wharton Sch., 1948; PhD, U. Pa., 1951. Instr. Wharton Sch. U. Pa., Phila., 1948-50; from assoc. to full prof. bus. Wharton Sch. U. Pa., 1956-93; asst. prof. U. md., College Park, 1951-55; rsch. economist UN, N.Y.C., summer 1949, 50; Fulbright prof. Copenhagen Sch. Econs. and Bus. Adminstrn., Denmark, 1963-64; prof. Naval War Coll., Newport, R.I., 1967-68; regional adv. UN, Santiago, Chile, 1970. Author: Strategic Planning for Export Marketing, 1964, International Trade and Investment, 1959, rev. edit., 1994, Entry Strategies for International Markets, 1982, rev. edit., 1994, International Strategic Management, 1992; contbr. articles to profl. jours. Cpl. AUS, 1943-46. Fellow Acad. Internat. Bus. (pres. 1981-83); mem. Am. Econ. Assn., Acad. Mgmt., Internat. Trade and Fin. Assn. (pres. 1991), Phi Beta Kappa. Independent. Unitarian. Avocations: carpentry, swimming. Office: U Pa Wharton Sch Philadelphia PA 19104

ROOT, JAMES BENJAMIN, landscape architect; b. Detroit, Jan. 26, 1934; s. William Jehial and Helen Elizabeth (English) R. BBA, Memphis State U., 1960; B in Landscape Architecture, U. Ga., 1966. Registered landscape architect; lic. real estate agt., Va. Asst. prof. W.Va. U., Morgantown, 1973-75, 93; pvt. practice Charlottesville, Va., 1976-85, 91—; site planner LBA, PH&R, Charles P. Johnson & Assocs., Fairfax, Va., 1986-90; pvt. practice as golf course architect, Charlottesville, 1976—; instr. Parkersburg C.C., 1975, Piedmont Va. C.C., 1981. Author: Fundamentals of Landscaping and Site Planning, 1985; contbr. articles to profl. jours. Mem. Planning Commn., Marietta, Ohio, 1972. Mem. Nat. Golf Found., Elks, Va. Writers Club. Avocation: playing piano. Office: PO Box 7017 Charlottesville VA 22906-7017

ROOT, LYNAL A., fast food company executive; b. Eagle Grove, Iowa, July 23, 1930; s. Arthur Wellington and Ruth Mary (Grandgeorge) R.; m. Betty McNaughton, Aug. 7, 1948 (div. 1972); children: Connie, Kathy, Diane, Randall; m. Deborah Kay Armstrong, Jan. 22, 1984; children: Christine Armstrong, Jennifer. Grad., Ea. Waterloo High Sch., 1948; student, Miltonvale Wesleyan Coll. Mgr. Rath Packing Co., Waterloo, Iowa, 1949-66; chmn. purchasing divsn. McDonald's Corp., Oak Brook, Ill., 1966—. Republican. Home: 1215 Hawthorn Ln Hinsdale IL 60521-2908 Office: McDonald's Corp 1 Mcdonalds Plz Oak Brook IL 60521

ROOT, M. BELINDA, chemist; b. Port Arthur, Tex., May 2, 1957; d. Robert A. and Charlene (Whitehead) Lee; m. Miles J. Root, Nov. 8, 1980; children: Jason Matthew, Ashley Erin. BS in Biology, Lamar U., 1979; MBA, U. Houston, 1994. Asst. chemist Merichem Co., Houston, 1979-81, project chemist, 1982-84, instrument chemist, 1984-85, quality assurance coord., 1986-89, product lab. supr., 1989-91; quality control supr. mfg. Welchem Inc. subs. Amoco, 1991—; mgr. Quality Control Petrolite Corp., 1993; mgr. quality control Akzo-Nobel Chems., Pasadena, Tex., 1994—. Editor (newsletter) Merichemer, 1989-91. Mem. MADD, 1989—, PTA, 1988—. Recipient Gulf Shore Regional award Cat Fanciers Assn., 1981, Disting. Merit award, 1990. Mem. NAFE, Am. Soc. Quality Control (cert. quality auditor, quality engr.), Am. Chem. Soc., United Silver Fancier (sec. 1980-82), Lamar U. Alumni Assn., Beta Beta Beta (sec. 1978-79), Beta Gamma Sigma. Avocations: camping, gardening. Office: Akzo-Nobel Chem Inc 13000 Bay Park Dr Pasadena TX 77507

ROOT, NILE, photographer, educator; b. Denver, Dec. 11, 1926; s. Victor Nile and Ella May (Holaway) R.; student U. Denver, 1968; MS in Instructional Tech., Rochester Inst. Tech., 1978; m. Abigail Barton Brown, Feb. 5, 1960; 1 child, James Michael. Microphotographer, U.S. Dept. Commerce, Field Info. Agy. Tech., Fed. Republic Germany, 1946-48; free-lance photographer, 1949-51; pres. Photography Workshop, Inc., Denver, 1952-60; dir. dept. biophotography and med. illustration Rose Meml. Med. Ctr., Denver, 1960-70; dir. med. illustration dept. Children's Hosp., Denver, 1970-71; dir. Photography for Sci., Denver, 1971-72; prof. biomed. photog. communications Rochester Inst. Tech. (N.Y.), 1972-86 , chmn. dept., 1974-86, prof. emeritus Coll. Imaging Arts and Scis., 1986—; travel writer, photographer, Japan, China, S.E. Asia, 1986-89; writer, photographer, Tucson, 1989—. dir. HEW project for devel. of field, 1974-77. Served with USN, 1945-46. Recipient numerous awards for sci. photographs; Eisenhart Outstanding Tchr. award Rochester Inst. Tech., 1986; 1st Ann. Faculty fellow Sch. Photog. Arts and Scis., Rochester Inst. Tech., 1979. Fellow Biol. Photog. Assn. (registered, emeritus, bd. govs. 1977-79, Louis Schmidt award 1986); mem. Ctr. Creative Photography, Friends of Photography, Internat. Mus. Photography. Democrat. Contbr. illustrations to med. textbooks; represented in numerous mus. photog. exhibits and numerous pvt. collections. Home and Office: 314 N Banff Ave Tucson AZ 85748-3311

ROOT, NINA J., librarian; b. N.Y.C., Dec. 22; d. Jacob J. and Fannie (Slivinsky) Root; BA, Hunter Coll.; MSLS, Pratt Inst.; postgrad. U.S. Dept. Agr. Grad. Sch., 1964-65, City U. N.Y., 1970-75. Reference and serials libr. Albert Einstein Coll. Medicine Libr., Bronx, N.Y., 1958-59; asst. chief libr. Am. Cancer Soc., N.Y.C., 1959-62; chief libr. Am. Inst. Aeros. and Astronautics, N.Y.C., 1962-64; head ref. and libr. svcs. sci. and tech. div. Libr. Congress, Washington, 1964-66; mgmt. cons. Nelson Assocs., Inc., N.Y.C., 1966-70; dir. libr. svcs. Am. Mus. Natural History, N.Y.C., 1970—; freelance mgmt. cons. and libr. planning, 1970—. Trustee Barnard Found., 1984-91; mem. libr. adv. coun. N.Y. State Bd. Regents, 1984-89, trustee Metro, 1987-92; bd. dirs. Hampden/Booth Libr., Players, 1990—; trustee Mercantile Libr. N.Y., 1993-95. Recipient Meritorious Svc. award Libr. of Congress, 1965. Mem. ALA (preservation com. 1977-79, chmn. libr./binders com. 1978-80, chmn. preservation sect. 1980-81, mem. coun. 1983-86), Spl. Librs. Assn. (sec. documentation group N.Y. chpt. 1972-73, 2d v.p. N.Y. 1975-76, treas. sci. and tech. group N.Y. 1975-76, mus. arts and humanities div. program planning chairperson-conf. 1977), Archons of Colophon (convener 1978-79), Soc. Natural History (N.Am. rep. 1977-85), N.Y. Acad. Scis. (mem. publs. com. 1975-80, 89-91, archives com. 1976-78, search com. 1976). Home: 400 E 59th St New York NY 10022-2342

ROOT, STANLEY WILLIAM, JR., lawyer; b. Honolulu, Mar. 2, 1923; s. Stanley William and Henrietta E. (Brown) R.; m. Joan Louise Schimpf, Sept. 3, 1949; children: Henry, Louise. AB, Princeton U., 1947; LLB, U. Pa., 1950. Bar: Pa. 1950, U.S. Ct. Mil. Appeals 1951, U.S. Supreme Ct. 1971. Ptnr. Foley, Schimpf & Steeley, Phila., 1952-69; ptnr. Ballard, Spahr, Andrews & Ingersoll, Phila., 1970-91, of counsel, 1992—; lectr. Pa. Bar Assn., 1970-80; bd. dirs. Boardman-Hamilton Co., sec. 1980—. Exec. v.p. Chestnut Hill Cmty. Assn., Phila., 1978; with Whitpain Farm Assn., Blue Bell, Pa., 1987, 90, pres., 1992-94; with St. Paul's Ch. Vestry, Phila., 1969-75; bd. dirs. Lansdale (Pa.) Med. Group, 1972—, E.B. Spaeth Found. Wills Hosp., Phila., 1975-88, Chevalier Jackson Clinic, Phila., 1965-88; trustee Civil War Libr. and Mus., 1985-93, v.p., 1989, sec., 1992-93, mem. adv. bd., 1993-95; trustee Soc. Protestant Episc. Ch., Pa. Diocese, 1955-95. Lt. col. U.S. Army, 1942-45, ETO, 1950-52, Korea. Decorated Bronze Star; recipient Pa. Commendation medal State of Pa., 1962; named Comdr., Mil. Order Fgn. Wars, 1972. Mem. Union League (pres. 1983-85), Phila. Cricket Club, Sunnybrook Golf Club, Royal Poinciana Golf Club, Brit. Officers Club, Mil. Order Loyal Legion. Republican. Episcopalian. Avocations: golf, tennis, fishing. Home: 16 Hounds Run Ln Blue Bell PA 19422-2456 Office: Ballard Spahr Andrews & Ingersoll 51st Fl 1735 Market St Fl 51 Philadelphia PA 19103-7501

ROOT, STUART DOWLING, lawyer, former banker and government official; b. Chagrin Falls, Ohio, Oct. 14, 1932; s. Elton Albert and Virginia Saxton (Dowling) R.; m. Jean D. Youse, Dec. 28, 1957 (div. Jan. 1972); children: Bryan, Kathleen, Timothy, Todd; m. Patricia Stoneman Graff, Apr. 24, 1976. BA, Ohio Wesleyan U., 1955; JD, Columbia U., 1960. Bar: N.Y. 1960. Assoc. Cadwalader Wickersham and Taft, N.Y.C., 1960-68, ptnr., 1969-81, 84-87; pres. Bowery Savs. Bank, N.Y.C., 1981-82, vice chmn., 1982-83; exec. dir. Office Fed Savs. and Loan Ins. Corp., Washington, 1988-89; chmn. bd. Fin. Instn. Svcs. Corp., Washington, 1989; lectr. ABA, Practicing Law Inst., Infocast, Am. Law Inst.; bd. dirs Bowest Corp., 1969-81. Contbr. articles to profl. jours. Chmn. bd. dirs. Harlem Sch. Arts, N.Y.C., 1974-83, Open Space Inst., 1976-80, 84-87, 89—, Nat. Choral Soc. N.Y.C., 1981-86; trustee emeritus Harlem Sch. Arts, 1984—; trustee N.Y. Geneal. and Biographical Soc., 1981-85; pub. interest dir. Fed. Home Loan Bank N.Y., N.Y.C., 1985-87. With U.S. Army, 1955-57. Mem. Down Town Assn. (N.Y.C.), Century Assn. (N.Y.C.). Republican. Episcopalian. Avocations: liturgical music, fly fishing, golf. Home: 18 Alden Pl Bronxville NY 10708-4813

ROOT, WILLIAM ALDEN, export control consultant; b. Boston, Sept. 20, 1923; s. John Alden and Louise Joy (Eppich) R.; m. Constance Hilda Young, Dec. 14, 1945; children: Carl David, Margaret Anne Root Bruck, John Alden, Christine Eppich Root Wiley. B.A., Colo. Coll., 1943; M. Internat. Affairs, Columbia, 1948; certificate, Russian Inst., 1948. Budget examiner Bur. Budget, Washington, 1948-50; mgmt. and budget officer Dept. State, Washington, 1950-52, Bonn, Germany, 1952-55; budget officer for Europe Dept. State, 1955-59; economist Am. embassy, Copenhagen, Denmark, 1959-63; dep. dir. Office East-West Trade, Dept. State, 1964-69; econ. officer Am. embassy, Vietnam, 1969-71; econ. counselor U.S. Mission, Berlin, 1971-74; dir. Office Soviet and Eastern European Sci. and Tech. Affairs Dept. State, 1974-76, dir. Office East West Trade, 1976-83; export control cons., 1983—; mem. Tech. Adv. Com., 1989—. Author: United States Export Controls, Aspen Law and Business. Served to lt. (j.g.) USNR, 1943-46. Mem. Phi Beta Kappa. Address: 4024 Franklin St Kensington MD 20895-3826

ROOT, WILLIAM LUCAS, electrical engineering educator; b. Des Moines, Oct. 6, 1919; s. Frank Stephenson and Helen (Lucas) R.; m. Harriett Jean Johnson, Dec. 10, 1918; children: William Lucas Jr., Wendy Elizabeth Root Cate. BEE, Iowa State U., 1940; MEE, MIT, 1943, PhD in Math., 1952. Staff mem. MIT Lincoln Lab., Lexington, Mass., 1952-61, group leader, 1959-61; lectr. Harvard U., Cambridge, Mass., 1958-59; visitor U. Wis., Madison, 1963-64; vis. prof. Mich. State U., East Lansing, 1966, 68, U. Calif., Berkeley, 1966-67; prof. aerospace engring. U. Mich., Ann Arbor, 1961-87, prof. emeritus, 1988—; vis. fellow U. Cambridge (Eng.), 1970; mem. U.S. Army Sci. Bd., 1979-82. Co-author: Random Signals and Noise, 1958 (Russian and Japanese transls.); assoc. editor: (IEEE) Information Theory Transactions, 1977-79; Soc. Indsl. and Applied Math. Jour. Applied Mathematics, 1962-72; contbr. 65 articles to profl. jours., book chpts. and conf. procs. Served to lt. USMCR, 1943-45. NSF Sr. postdoctoral fellow, 1970, vis. fellow Cambridge Clare Hall, 1970; recipient Claude E. Shannon award IEEE Info. Theory Soc., 1986, Career Achievement award ComCon Conf. Bd., 1987. Life fellow IEEE (vice chmn. adminstrv. com. info. theory group 1965-66); mem. Am. Math. Soc. Home: PO Box 3785 Ann Arbor MI 48106-3785 Office: U Mich Dept Aerospace Engring Ann Arbor MI 48109

ROOT, WILLIAM PITT, poet, educator; b. Austin, Minn., Dec. 28, 1941; s. William Pitt and Bonita Joy (Hilbert) R.; m. Judith Carol Bechtold, 1965 (div. 1970); 1 dau., Jennifer Lorca; m. Pamela Uschuk, 1987. B.A., U. Wash., 1964; M.F.A., U. N.C. at Greensboro, 1967; postgrad. (Wallace Stegner Writing fellow), Stanford, 1968-69. Asst. prof. Mich. State U., 1967-68; tchr. writing Mid-peninsula Free U., 1969; writer-in-residence Amherst Coll., U. Southwestern La., 1976, U. Mont., 1978, 80, 83-84; with poet-in-schs. program state art councils Oreg., Miss., Idaho, Ariz., Vt., Mont., Wyo., Wash., Tex., 1971—; Distinguished writer-in-residence Wichita State U., 1976; vis. writer in residence U. Mont., 1978, 80, 83-86, Hunter Coll., N.Y.C., 1986—; vis. writer NYU, 1986; vis. writer Westside Young Men's Hebrew Assn., N.Y.C., 1988, Pacific Lutheran U., 1990. Author: The Storm and Other Poems, 1969, Striking the Dark Air for Music, 1973, The Port of Galveston, 1974, Coot and Other Characters, 1977, 7 Mendocino Songs, 1977, A Journey South, 1977, Fireclock, 1981, Reasons for Going It on Foot, 1981, In the World's Common Grasses, 1981, The Unbroken Diamond: Nightletter to the Mujahideen, 1983, Invisible Guests, 1984, Faultdancing, 1986; transl. Trace Elements from a Recurring Kingdom, 1994; collaborated (with filmmaker Ray Rice) on poetry films Song of the Woman and the Butterflyman (Orpheus award 1st Internat. Poetry Film Festival 1975), 7 For a Magician, 1976, Faces, 1981. Rockefeller Found. grantee, 1969-70; Guggenheim Found. grantee, 1970-71; Nat. Endowment for Arts grantee, 1973-74; U.S./U.K. Bicentennial Exchange Artist, 1978-79, Wallace Stegner creative writing fellow Stanford U., 1968-69; recipient 1st prize univ. poetry contest Acad. Am. Poets, 1966, Atlantic Young Poet award, 1967, Stanley Kunitz Poetry award, 1981, Guy Owen Poetry Prize, 1982, Pushcart Prize (Poetry), 1977, 1980, 1985. Address: CUNY Hunter Coll Dept Eng 695 Park Ave New York NY 10021-5024 *With Rilke I believe the measure of one's life consists in a growing capacity to change life even as one is changed by it, to engage ever more fully in that dance between what we call will and what we call fate until the result is a contagion of vitality powerful enough to dissipate the spell of habits and to recreate in oneself that first spirit which is intuitive, sympathetic, and clear. Poems simply record the complex effort.*

ROOT-BERNSTEIN, ROBERT SCOTT, biologist, educator; b. Washington, Aug. 7, 1953; s. Morton Ira and Maurine (Berkstresser) Bernstein; m. Michèle Marie Root-Bernstein, Sept. 2, 1978; children: Meredith Marie, Brian Robert. AB, Princeton U., 1975, PhD, 1980. Postdoctoral fellow Salk Inst. for Biol. Studies, La Jolla, Calif., 1981-82, rsch. assoc., 1983-84; asst. prof. Mich. State U., East Lansing, 1987-89, assoc. prof., 1989—; cons. Biolark, Inc., San Diego, 1988-89, Parke-Davis Pharm. Rsch. Divsn., Ann Arbor, 1990-96, Chiron Corp., 1992-96; mem. adv. bd. Soc. for Advancement Gifted Edn., Chgo., 1987-92; Sigma Xi nat. lectr., 1994-96. Author: Discovering, 1989, Rethinking AIDS, 1993; columnist The Scis. mag., 1989-92; contbr. numerous articles to profl. jours. MacArthur Found. fellow, 1981-86; recipient D.J. Ingle Meml. Writing prize, 1988. Mem. Phi Beta Kappa (hon.). Avocations: drawing, painting, photography, cello. Office: Mich State U Dept Physiology Giltner Hall East Lansing MI 48824

ROOTMAN, JACK, ophthalmologist, surgeon, pathologist, oncologist, artist; b. Calgary, Alta., Can., June 22, 1944; s. Abraham S. and Lillian (Walman) R.; m. Jenny Puterman, June 20, 1965; children: Russel Mark, Kathryn Anne, Daniel Benson. MD, U. Alta., 1968. Res. ophthalmology U. Alta., Edmonton, 1973, clin. asst. prof. ophthalmology and pathology, 1973-75; from asst. prof. to assoc. prof. ophthalmology & pathology U. B.C., Vancouver, 1976-84, prof. ophthalmology & pathology, 1985—, chmn. ophthalmology, 1990—; cons. pathologist Vancouver Gen. Hosp., 1989; pathology cons. Can. Reference Ctr. Cancer Pathology, Ottawa, Ont., 1989; mem. adv. com. Internat. Congress Ophthalmology, 1990—; reviewer Med. Rsch. Coun. Can., 1981, 83-84, 89—; chmn. ocular & orb tumor group B.C. Cancer Agy., 1980—. Author: Diseases of the Orbit: A Multidisciplinary Approach, 1988; contbr. chpts. to books, numerous articles to profl. jours.; inventor Rootman Orbital Surgery Set, numerous orbital surgical procedures; reviewer Can. Jour. Ophthalmology, 1981—, Survey Ophthalmology, 1990—, Am. Jour. Ophthalmology, 1992, Cancer, 1992, others in field; paintings exhibited in group shows Vancouver Gen. Hosp. Gallery, 1988, Zack Gallery, Vancouver, 1989, N.W. Watercolor Soc. Nat. Exhibition, 1994; one-man shows include Taylor Gallery, Mayne Island, B.C., 1989, U. B.C. Faculty Club, 1990, C.J. Herman Galleries, Vancouver, 1991, 92, 93. Chmn. Vancouver Talmud Torah, 1982-84; bd. dirs. Contemporary Art Gallery, Vancouver, 1991. Recipient 1st Prize (tied) Can. Fed. Artists 50th Anniversary Show, 1991; Can. Cancer Soc. fellow, 1i74, Med. Rsch. Coun. fellow, 1977-78, E.A. Baker Found. fellow, 1978, 82, 91; Vancouver Found. grantee, 1978, B.C. Cancer Found. grantee, 1978, McLean Fund grantee, 1979, B.C. Health Care Rsch. Found. grantee 1979-81, 83-85, 87-89, 92, B.C. Med. Svcs. Found. grantee 1982-83, Med. Rsch. Coun. grantee, 1982-88, others. Fellow Royal College Surgeons; mem. Royal Coll. Pathologists (cert.), Am. Acad. Ophthalmology (cert.), Royal Coll. Physicians and Surgeons (specialty com. ophthalmology, accrediation surveys), B.C. Soc. Eye Physicians and Surgeons, Can. Med. Assn., Can. Ocular Pathology Study Group, Can. Oculoplastic Study Group, Can. Ophthalmol. Soc., Hogan Soc., Internat. Orbit Soc., Internat. Soc. Eye Rsch., N.Am. Skull Base Soc. (charter), Am. Assn. Ophthalmic Pathologists. Office: Univ BC Dept Ophthalmology, 2550 Willow St, Vancouver, BC Canada V5Z 3N9

ROOTS, ERNEST FREDERICK, scientific advisor emeritus; b. Salmon Arm, B.C., Can., July 5, 1923; s. Ernest and Margaret Frances (Sharpe) R.; m. June Christine Blomfield, Jan. 15, 1955; children: Charles, Frances, Hannah, Jane, Robin. BASc, U. B.C., Vancouver, 1946, MASc, 1947; PhD, Princeton U., 1949; DSc (hon.), U. Victoria, B.C., 1986. Asst. meteorologist Can. Meteorol. Br., Banff, Alta., 1938-40; topog. surveyor Nat. Parks Svc., various locations, B.C., various locations, Alta., 1940-41; student asst. Geol. Survey Can., Ottawa, Ont., 1942-46, geologist, 1947-49, 53-58; geologist Norwegian, Brit. and Swedish Antarctic Expdn., 1949-52; asst. prof. geology

Princeton (N.J.) U., 1952-54; coord. polar continental shelf project Can. Dept. Energy, Mines and Resources, Ottawa, 1958-73; sci. advisor Dept. Environ. Can., Ottawa, 1973-90, spl. advisor, 1990—; chmn. Can. Environ. Assessment Rsch. Coun., Ottawa, 1986-91; co-chmn. environ. sci. rev. group Nuclear Waste Environ. Assessment Rev. Panel, Ottawa, 1990—; pres. Internat. Arctic Sci. Com., 1990-93; chmn. Man and Biosphere No. Sci. Network, UNESCO, Paris, 1992—. Contbr. over 130 articles to sci. jours., chpts. to books. Decorated officer Order of Can.; recipient Patron's medal Royal Geog. Soc., London, 1960, Polar medals, Norway, 1952, USSR, 1960, U.K., 1984, U.S., 1986. Fellow Royal Soc. Can. Home: RR 3, Wakefield, PQ Canada J0X 3G0

ROPER, BERYL CAIN, writer, publisher, retired library director; b. Long Beach, Calif., Mar. 1, 1931; d. Albert Verne and Ollie Fern (Collins) Cain; m. Max H. Young, Aug. 22, 1947 (div. 1958); children: Howard, Wade, Debra, Kevin, John R., Christopher; m. George Albert Roper, Mar. 24, 1962 (dec. July 1978); children: Ellen, Georgianne; m. Jack T. Hughes, Sept. 21, 1993. BA, West Tex. State U., 1986; MA, Tex. Womans U., 1989. Libr. clk. Cornette Libr., West Tex. State U., Canyon, 1981-87; dir. Clarendon (Tex.) Coll. Libr., 1988-96; lectr. in history and archaeology; co-owner Aquamarine Publs. Editor, pub.: In the Light of Past Experience, 1989, Transactions of the Southwest Federation of Archaeological Societies, 1993, Greenbelt Site, 1996; author, pub.: Trementina, 1990, Trementina Revisited, 1994; author articles on women and history. Mem. Clarendon Archaeol. Soc. (charter, v.p. 1990-91), Tex. Libr. Assn., Tex. Jr. Coll. Tchrs. Assn., Tex. Intertribal Indian Orgn. (charter), Pi Gamma Mu, Beta Phi Mu, Alpha Chi, Phi Alpha Theta. Republican. Mem. LDS Ch. Avocations: teacher Sunday sch., music, gardening, decorating, remodeling old houses. Office: Aquamarine Publs 1903 3d Ave Canyon TX 79015

ROPER, BIRDIE ALEXANDER, social sciences educator; b. New Orleans; d. Earl and Ethel (Charmer) Alexander; m. Morris F. Roper; 1 child, Andree Marie Driskell. BS, U. Dayton, 1949; MA, Azusa Pacific U., 1971, Claremont Grad. Sch., 1978; PhD, Claremont Grad. Sch., 1980. DON Flint Goodridge Hosp., New Orleans, 1954, 55; sch. nurse, health educator, classroom tchr. L.A. Unified Sch. Dist., 1963-91; extended day prof. social scis. dept. Pasadena City Coll., 1972—; clin. instr. dept. nursing Calif. State U., San Bernardino, 1993—; researcher, author, cons. in gerontology. Editor: (newsletter Calif. Nurses Assn.) Vital Signs. Mem. ANA, Am. Soc. Univ. Profs., Am. Soc. on Aging, Inst. for Rsch. on Aging, Nat. Coun. on Aging, Nat. Gerontol. Nursing Assn., Nat. Assn. Profl. Geriatric Care Mgrs., Phi Delta Kappa (bd. mem. San Antonio chpt. 1981-92), Alpha Kappa Alpha. Home and Office: 1657 W Sunnyview Dr Rialto CA 92376-1572

ROPER, BURNS WORTHINGTON, retired opinion research company executive; b. Creston, Iowa, Feb. 26, 1925; s. Elmo Burns and Dorothy Camille (Shaw) R.; m. Elizabeth Kellock, Feb. 7, 1945 (div.); children: Bruce, David, Douglas; m. Helen Gillette Lanagan, Dec. 26, 1958 (dec. Apr. 1990); 1 child, Candace Gillette; m. Helen Grinnell Page, Sept. 19, 1991. Hon. doctorate, Colgate U., 1996. Rsch. asst. Elmo Roper, N.Y.C., 1946-48, project dir., 1948-55; ptnr. Elmo Roper & Assocs., N.Y.C., 1955-66; pres., chmn. bd. Roper Rsch. Assocs., N.Y.C., 1967-70, The Roper Orgn., Inc., N.Y.C., 1970-93; exec. v.p. Roper Starch Worldwide, Mamaroneck, N.Y., 1981-94; chmn. bd. The Roper Pub. Opinion Rsch. Ctr., Storrs, Conn., 1970-94, trustee 1947—. Contbr. numerous articles on polls to profl. jours., book chpts. Trustee Nat. Urban League, N.Y.C., 1955-64, UN Assn. Am., N.Y.C., 1964—, Freedom House, N.Y.C., 1970—. 1st lt. USAAF, 1943-45, ETO. Decorated DFC, Air medal with five oak leaf clusters. Mem. Am. Assn. Pub. Opinion Rsch. (nat. pres. 1982-83, award 1988), Nat. Coun. on Pub. Polls (bd. dirs. 1969—, chmn. bd. trustees 1980-93), Market Rsch. Coun. (pres. 1967-68, inducted into Hall of Fame 1990), Wings Club. Democrat. Home: 70 Old Dam Rd Bourne MA 02532 *When public opinion differs from my opinion, the first thing I do is reassess my opinion. The public can be wrong but its track record is awfully good. Those you buy from should be treated in the same manner as those you sell to; those who work for you should be treated as those you work for.*

ROPER, EDDIE JOE, energy company executive; b. Wichita Falls, Sept. 11, 1950; s. Johnnie Fletcher and Lera Fay (Horn) R.; m. Patsy Ann Wester, Dec. 3, 1977; children: Amber Michelle, Aaron Joseph. BS, Tex. Tech. U., 1973. Driller Tom Brown, Inc., Midland, Tex., 1974-76, tool pusher, 1976-78, drilling supt., 1978-81; pres. Roper Energy Co., Midland, Tex., 1981—; bd. dirs. Internat. Assn. Drilling Contractors, Washington. Mem. chorale Midland-Odessa Sumphony &Chorale, Midland, 1991, 92, 93. Republican. Baptist. Avocation: music. Office: Roper Energy Co PO Box 8005 Midland TX 79708-8005

ROPER, JOHN LONSDALE, III, shipyard executive; b. Norfolk, Va., Jan. 19, 1927; s. John Lonsdale II and Sarah (Dryfoos) R.; m. Jane Preston Harman, Sept. 29, 1951; children: Susan Roper, John Lonsdale IV, Sarah Preston Roper Massey, Jane Harman Roper Van Sciver, Katherine Hayward Roper Stout. BSME, U. Va., Charlottesville, 1949; BS in Naval Architecture and Marine Engring., MIT, 1951. CEO, pres. Norfolk Shipbuilding & Drydock Corp., 1985-91, pres., CEO, 1991—, also bd. dirs.; dir. John L. Roper Corp., Cruise Internat., Inc., The Flagship Group Ltd.; pres., dir. Lonsdale Bldg. Corp. Marepcon Corp.-Internat. With USCG, 1945-46. Mem. Shipbuilders Coun. Am. (bd. dirs.). Episcopalian.

ROPER, JOHN MARLIN, federal magistrate judge; b. Greenville, Ala., Dec. 11, 1942; s. Marlin Ross and Ruby Lois (Martin) R.; m. Virginia Gene Kerth, Apr. 2, 1966; 1 son, John Marlin. B.S. Auburn U., 1964; J.D., Tulane U., 1968. Bar: Ala. 1968, Miss. 1974. Counselor/program dir. Juvenile Delinquency Instn., New Orleans, 1966-69; sr. law clk. to judge U.S. Dist. Ct. (so. dist.) Miss., 1969-75, magistrate, 1975—. Mem. Fed. Magistrate Judges Assn. (dir. 5th cir. 1976-82, nat. officer 1982-86, nat. pres. 1986-87, security com. jud. conf. 1987-89, budget com. 1989—). Methodist. Office: US District Court 725 Washington Loop Biloxi MS 39530-1164

ROPER, KATHERINE RUTH ARCHER, retired occupational health nurse; b. Cantonment, Okla., Sept. 28, 1925; d. James Henderson and Martha Katherine (Osborn) Archer; m. Ozon Albert Colwell (dec.); 1 child, Kenneth Gerald; m. Clay Mitchell Roper, Sept. 6, 1956; children: Norman Frank, Martha Grace, Fred Dwight. Diploma in nursing, U. Okla., Oklahoma City, 1948; student, U. Okla., Norman, 1969-70, Rockhurst Coll., 1978. RN, Okla. Staff nurse Presbyn. Hosp., Oklahoma City, 1968-77; nurse Medox, Oklahoma City, 1977-79; occupational health nurse U.S. Postal Svc., Oklahoma City, 1979-89; ret., 1989. Recipient numerous awards of appreciation. Mem. Am. Assn. Occupational Health Nurses, Nat. Postal Profl. Nurses Assn. (nat. v.p. 1983-89), Okla. Hist. Soc., Okla. Geneal. Soc., Spencer Hist. Soc., Nat. Assn. Ret. Fed. Employees (pres. 1993-94), Archer Reunion Assn. (pres.). Home: 8309 NE 28th St Spencer OK 73084-3617

ROPER, WILLIAM LEE, physician, government executive; b. Birmingham, Ala., July 6, 1948; s. Richard Barnard and Jean (Fyfe) R.; m. Maryann Roper, Jan. 14, 1978. A.A., Fla. Coll., 1968; B.S., U. Ala, 1970, M.D., 1974, M.P.H., 1981. Diplomate Am. Bd. Pediatrics, Am. Bd. Preventive Medicine. Intern, resident in pediatrics U. Colo. Med. Ctr., Denver, 1974-77; health officer Jefferson County Dept. Health, Birmingham, 1977-82, 83; White House fellow Washington, 1982-83, spl. asst. to Pres. for health policy, 1983-86; adminstr., Health Care Finance Adminstrn. HHS, Washington, 1986-89; dep. asst. to pres. for domestic policy The White House, Washington, 1989-90; adminstr. Agy. for Toxic Substances and Disease Registry and dir. Ctrs. for Disease Control, Atlanta, 1990—. Mem. Phi Beta Kappa, Alpha Omega Alpha. Republican. Home: 2401 Haven Ridge Dr NW Atlanta GA 30305-4016 Office: Centers For Disease Control 1600 Clifton Rd NE Atlanta GA 30329-4018

ROPP, ANN L., nursing consultant; b. Cin., June 24, 1939; d. William Howard and C. Louise (Kloecker) R. Diploma in nursing, Good Samaritan Hosp. Sch. Nursing, Cin., 1960; BA, U. Minn., 1970; MS, Coll. St. Francis, Joliet, Ill., 1985. RN, Minn.; cert. in maternal-child nursing. Clin. nurse specialist Fairview Southdale Hosp., Edina, Minn., 1986-87; dir. nursing St. Mary's Hosp., Mpls., 1987; nursing cons. Mpls., 1986—; dir. maternal-child nursing svcs. Fairview Riverside Med. Ctr., Mpls., 1987-95; dir. perinatal svcs. Fairview Ridges Hosp., Burnsville, Minn., 1995; svc. line mgr. svcs. for women and children St. Luke's Heath Sys., Kansas City, Mo., 1995—. Author: Guidelines for Education and Practice for Intrapartum Nurses, Quality Assurance for OGN Nurses. Mem. Assn. for Women's Health Obstetrics, Neonatal Nursing (pres. 1991), Am. Coll. Healthcare Execs., Sigma Theta Tau. Office: St Luke's Health Sys Svc Line Mgr Svcs for Women & Children Kansas City MO 64112

ROPSKI, GARY MELCHIOR, lawyer; b. Erie, Pa., Apr. 19, 1952; s. Joseph Albert and Irene Stefania (Mszanowski) R.; m. Barbara Mary Schleck, May 15, 1982. BS in Physics, Carnegie-Mellon U., 1972; JD cum laude, Northwestern U. Sch. Law, 1976. Bar: Ill. 1976, U.S. Patent and Trademark Office 1976, U.S. Dist. Ct. (no. dist.) Ill. 1976, U.S. Ct. Appeals (7th cir.) 1977, U.S. Dist. Ct. (ea. dist.) Wis. 1977, U.S. Ct. Appeals (3d cir.) 1981, U.S. Ct. Claims 1982, Pa. 1982, U.S. Ct. Appeals (Fed. cir.) 1982, U.S. Supreme Ct. 1982, U.S. Dist. Ct. (ea. dist.) Mich. 1984, U.S. Dist. Ct. (no. dist.) Calif. 1986. Assoc. Brinks Hofer Gilson & Lione, Chgo., 1976-81, shareholder, 1981—; adj. prof. patents and copyrights Northwestern U. Sch. Law, Chgo., 1982—. Contbr. numerous articles to profl. jours. Mem. ABA, Am. Intellectual Property Law Assn., Patent Law Assn. Chgo., Chgo. Bar Assn. Roman Catholic. Clubs: University, Chgo. Yacht. Home: 1416 S Plymouth Ct Chicago IL 60605-2729 Office: Hofer Gilson & Lione NBC Tower Ste 3600 455 N Cityfront Plaza Dr Chicago IL 60611-5503

ROQUE, MARGARITA, government administrator; b. El Paso; d. Jose Matias and Dolores (Rincon) R.; children: Daniel, Joseph, Elena, Williams. BA, Hood Coll., Frederick, Md., 1984. Fiscal asst. sec. Dept. of Commerce, NOAA, Rockville, Md., 1977-81; comms. specialist Hood Coll., 1981-84; staff asst. Chs. Com. for Voter Registration, Washington, 1984; program coord. Women's Vote Project, Washington, 1984; site supr., info. analyst The Maxima Corp., Washington, 1984-86; legis. dir. Congl. Hispanic Caucus, Washington, 1987-89, exec. dir., 1989-92; with pers. office Clinton/Gore Transition Office, Washington, 1992-93; spl. asst. to sec. Dept. Edn., Washington, 1992; dir., exec. secretariat Dept. Transp., Washington, 1992—. Mem. Fed. Women's Program Adv. Com.; mem. Campaign 88-Women of Color Access Project; mem. Hispanic adv. com. A Woman's Place; mem. Up-County Citizens Adv. Com.; mem. Planning Adv. Bd., Damascus, Md.; bd. dirs. D.C. Latino Civil Rights Task Force. Mem. Mexican Am. Women's Nat. Assn., League of United Latin Am. Citizens, Women of Color Leadership Coun. Office: Dept of Transportation Rm 10205 400 7th St SW Washington DC 20590-0001

ROREM, NED, composer, author; b. Richmond, Ind., Oct. 23, 1923; s. Clarence Rufus and Gladys (Miller) R. Student, Northwestern U., 1940-42, Curtis Inst., Phila., 1943; B.A., Juilliard Sch. Music, 1946, M.A., 1948; D.F.A. (hon.), Northwestern U., 1977. Slee prof., composer-in-residence Buffalo U., 1959-61; prof. composition U. Utah, 1965-67, Curtis Inst., 1980-94. Composer: symphonies No. 1, premiere Vienna, Austria, 1951, No. 2, premiere La Jolla, Calif., 1956, No. 3, premiere with Leonard Bernstein and N.Y. Philharmonic, 1959, Three Piano Sonatas, 1949, 50, 54, Lento for Strings, 1950, Design for Orch., 1954, Pilgrims for Strings, 1958, Eagles for Orch., 1958, Lions, 1964, Ideas for Easy Orch, 1961, Piano Concerto No. 2, 1951, 3d Piano Concerto, 1970, Eleven Studies, 1959, Water Music, 1966, Sun; for voice and orch., commd. by N.Y. Philharmonic, 1966, Air Music for Orch, 1974 (Pulitzer prize 1976), Assembly and Fall, 1975, Sunday Morning for Orch., 1977, Remembering Tommy, 1981; numerous chorus works, latest being Letters from Paris, 1965; for chorus and orch., commd. by Koussevitzky Found. in Library of Congress, Little Prayers, 1972, Whitman Cantata, 1982, An American Oratorio, 1983, Homer, 1986, Seven Motets, 1986, Te Deum, 1986, What is Pink?, 1987, The Death of Moses, 1987, Goodbye My Fancy, 1988; operas A Childhood Miracle, 1952, Three Sisters Who Are Not Sisters, 1969, Fables, 1970, Bertha, 1968, Miss Julie, 1964 (Ford Found. grantee), Hearing, 1976, Cycles: War Scenes, 1969, Six Songs for High Voice and Orchestra, 1954, Six Irish Poems, 1951, Poems of Love and the Rain, 1964, Ariel for Voice, clarinet and piano, 1971, Last Poems of Wallace Stevens for voice, cello and piano, 1971, Serenade for voice, violin, viola and piano, Women's Voices, 1975, The Nantucket Songs, 1979, Three Calamus Poems, 1982, The Schuyler Songs, 1987, Day Music and Night Music for Violin, 1972-73, Etudes for Piano, 1975, Book of Hours for flute and harp, A Quaker Reader for Organ, 1976, The Santa Fe Songs, 1980, Remembering Tommy, 1980, Views From the Oldest House for organ, 1981, Winter Pages, 1981, Picnic on the Marne, 1982, Dances for Cello, 1983, Violin Concerto, 1984, Organ Concerto, 1985, String Symphony, 1985, Septet: Scenes from Childhood, 1985, Trio: End of Summer, 1985, Quintet: Bright Music, 1988, Diversions for Brass Quintet, 1989, Trio (Spring Music), 1990, Three Organbooks; The Auden Poems, Trio for Violin, Cello, Piano, 1990, Swords and Plowshares (for 4 solo voices and orch.), 1991, Third Quartet, 1991, Fourth Concerto for Piano (left hand) and Orch., 1991, Present Laughter for mixed chorus, piano and brass, 1993, Songs of Sadness for quartet of baritone, guitar, clarinet and cello, 1994; commns. for U.S. Bicentennial include compositions for, Cin. Symphony, N.C. Symphony, Nat. Endowment of the Arts, Am. Harp Soc.; Author: The Paris Diary of Ned Rorem, 1966, Music from Inside Out, 1967, The New York Diary, 1967, Music and People, 1968, Critical Affairs, 1970, Pure Contraption, 1973, The Later Diaries, 1974, An Absolute Gift, 1978, Setting the Tone, 1983, Paul's Blues, 1985, The Nantucket Diary, 1987, Settling the Score, 1988, Knowing When To Stop, 1994, also articles newspapers, mags., Recs. for, Columbia, Decca, Odyssey, Desto, Phillips, Premier, C.R.I., Westminster, Orion, New World Records. Recipient Music Libraries Assn. award for song Lordly Hudson 1948, Gershwin Meml. award 1949, Lili Boulanger award 1950, Nat. Inst. Arts and Letters award 1968, Pulitzer prize in music 1976, Grammy award for Best Orchestral Rec., 1989; Fulbright fellow Paris, 1951-52; Guggenheim fellow, 1957-58, 77-78. Mem. PEN, ASCAP, Am. Acad. and Inst. Arts and Letters. Mem. Soc. of Friends. Address: PO Box 764 Nantucket MA 02554-0764

RORER, LEONARD GEORGE, psychologist, writer; b. Dixon, Ill., Dec. 24, 1932; s. Leonard Gleason and Marion Emma (Geyer) R.; m. Gail Evans, Apr. 30, 1958 (div. May 11, 1964); children: Liat, Eric Evans; m. Nancy McKimens, Jan. 9, 1969 (div. Jan. 19, 1976); 1 child, Mya Noelani. BA, Swarthmore Coll., 1954; PhD, U. Minn., 1963 . Rsch. assoc., then assoc. dir. Oreg. Rsch. Inst., Eugene, 1963-75; prof. psychology Miami U., Oxford, Ohio, 1975-93, dir. clin. psychology tng. program, 1976-86; pres. Oreg. Psychol. Assn., 1973-75. NIMH spl. rsch. fellow, 1967-68; fellow Netherlands Inst. Advanced Study, 1971-72; postdoctoral fellow Inst. for Rational-Emotive Therapy, 1982-83. Fellow APA (coun. reps. 1968-72), Am. Psychol. Soc. (charter), We. Psychol. Assn.; mem. Midwestern Psychol. Assn., Assn. Advancement Behavior Therapy, Soc. Multivariate Exptl. Psychology. Author articles in field, mem. editorial bds. profl. jours. Home: 116 Adobe St Santa Cruz CA 95060-3721

RORICK, WILLIAM CALVIN, librarian, educator, portrait artist; b. Elyria, Ohio, June 23, 1941; s. Harold R. and Edythe E. (Harris) R.; m. Anne L. Sherbondy, Aug. 21, 1971. BA in Econs. and Bus. Adminstrn., Ohio Wesleyan U., 1963; MusB in Music History and Lit., U. Utah, 1968; MusM in Music History and Lit., Northwestern U., 1970; MLS, Pratt Inst., 1974; MA in Musicology, NYU, 1982; trainee in portraiture, various art schs., workshops, 1990—. Curator orchl.-choral libr., reference asst., office mgr. Manhattan Sch. Music Libr., N.Y.C., 1970-74; music reference libr. CUNY Queens Coll. Music Libr., Flushing, 1974-96, instr., 1974-79, asst. prof., 1979-96, mem. senate nominating com., del.-at-large arts div., 1984-86. Contbr. articles and revs. to profl. jours. Grantee Rsch. Found. CUNY, 1981-84; recipient art awards including Best in Show Conn. Classic Arts Assn., 1996. Mem. Am. Musicological Soc., Am. Printing History Assn., Assn. for Recorded Sound Collections, Internat. Assn. Music Librs., Libr. Assn. CUNY (chmn. grants com. 1978-80, mem. publs. com. 1979-81, editor Directory 1980-81, del. 1983-85), Music Libr. Assn. (program chmn. Greater N.Y. chpt. 1977-79, sec.-treas. 1979-81, chpt. chmn. 1983-85, mem. nat. subcom. on basic music collection 1977-79, chmn. nat. membership com. 1979-82, mem. Music Pubs. Assn. joint com. 1986-88), Am. Soc. Portrait Artists, Sonneck Soc., Beta Phi Mu.*. Home and Studio: 63 Beacon Hill Dr Southbury CT 06488-1914

RORIE, CONRAD JONATHAN, naval officer, scientist; b. Henning, Tenn., Oct. 28, 1930; s. Elvy and Lena (Jenkins) R.; m. Patricia Paris Cunliffe, Feb. 7, 1952; children: Michael Stephen, Catherine Jean, Patrick Jonathan. BS, Union U., Jackson, Tenn., 1952; MSEE, U.S. Naval Postgrad. Sch., 1961; PhD in EE, Vanderbilt U., 1970. Enlisted USN, 1952, advanced through grades to rear adm., 1971; comdg. officer various ships, 1957-72; comdr. U.S. Naval Surface Weapons Ctr., Dahlgren, Va., 1974-77; dep. comdr. for surface combatants and weapons systems engr. Naval Sea Systems Command, Washington, 1977-81; comdr. Naval Surface Forces Middle Pacific & Naval Base Pearl Harbr, Hawaii, 1981—; planning dir. Johns Hopkins U., Applied Physics Lab., 1984—; mem. numerous naval bd. for officer career devel., chmn. Weapons Systems Mgr./Ordnance Adv. Bd. to Naval Postgrad. Sch. President Hawaii Navy Relief Soc. and Red Cross, 1980; chmn. Combined Fed. Campaign Charity Dr., 1981; bd. dirs. Govs. for Navy Charity Retail Store, 1981; commissioning chmn. USS Antietam, 1987, USS Raleigh Burke, 1991; mem. panel Navy/Civilian U. Lab., 1988; mem. curricula rev. com. Naval Postgrad. Sch., 1977-81. Decorated Legion of Merit (4), Meritorious Svc. medal with gold star; recipient Ann. Disting. Alumnus award Union U., 1975, Am. Spirit of Honor medal. Mem. Naval Inst., Am. Soc. Naval Engrs., Nat. Security Indsl. Assn., AIAA, Am. Astronaut. Soc., U.S. Navy League, Armed Forces Communications and Electronics Assn., Mil. Order of Carabao, Masons, Bapt. Club, Sigma Xi, Eta Kappa Nu, Alpha Tau Omega. Home: 12412 Hooper Ct Fulton MD 20759-9645 Office: Johns Hopkins U Applied Physics Lab Johns Hopkins Rd Laurel MD 20707

RORIE, NANCY KATHERYN, elementary and secondary school educator; b. Union County, N.C., May 31, 1940; d. Carl Van and Mary Mildred (Pressley) R. BA, Woman's Coll. U. N.C., 1962; MEd, U. N.C., 1967; EdD, Duke U., 1977. Cert. curriculum and instrnl. specialist, social studies tchr. for middle and secondary levels, English tchr., N.C. Social studies and English tchr. Guilford County Schs., Greensboro, N.C., 1962-67; social studies instr. Lees-McRae Coll., Banner Elk, N.C., 1967-76; social studies tchr. Monroe (N.C.) City Schs., 1977-93; curriculum instrnl. specialist, social studies tchr. Union County Schs., Monroe, N.C., 1993—. Named Woman of Yr., ABI, 1995. Mem. Prof. Educators N.C., Phi Alpha Theta, Kappa Delta Pi. Democrat. Baptist. Home: 2401 Old Pageland Rd Monroe NC 28112-8163

RORIG, KURT JOACHIM, chemist, research director; b. Bremerhaven, Germany, Dec. 1, 1920; came to U.S., 1924, naturalized, 1929; s. Robert Herman and Martha (Grundke) R.; m. Helen Yonan, Mar. 20, 1949; children: James, Elizabeth, Miriam. BS, U. Chgo., 1942; MA, Carleton Coll., 1944; PhD, U. Wis., 1947. Lectr. Loyola U., Chgo., 1950-62; chemist to dir. Chem. Research G.D. Searle & Co., Chgo., 1947-87; pres. Chemo-Delphic Cons. Ltd., Chgo., 1987—; adj. prof. chemistry U. Ill., Chgo., 1989—. Patentee in field. Mem. Sch. Bd., Wilmette, Ill., 1969-71. Mem. Am. Chem. Soc. (dir. Chgo. sect.), Am. Soc. Pharm. and Exptl. Therapeutics, N.Y. Acad. Scis., AAAS, Chgo. Chemists Club (past pres.). Presbyterian. Home and Office: 337 Hager Ln Glenview IL 60025-3329

RORIMER, LOUIS, lawyer; b. N.Y.C., Feb. 17, 1947; s. James J. and Katherine (Serrell) R.; m. H. Savery Fitz-Gerald, July 1, 1978; children: Sarah, James. Student, Phillips Acad., 1965; BA, Harvard U., 1969; JD, Case Western Res. U., 1975. Bar: Ohio 1975. Assoc. Jones, Day, Reavis & Pogue, Cleve., 1975-83, ptnr., 1984—. Served to lt. (j.g.) USNR, 1969-71, PTO. Mem. ABA. Home: 17900 S Park Blvd Shaker Hts OH 44120-1717 Office: Jones Day Reavis & Pogue North Point 901 Lakeside Ave Cleveland OH 44114-1116*

RORKE, LUCY BALIAN, neuropathologist; b. St. Paul, June 22, 1929; d. Aram Haji and Karzouhy (Ousdigian) Balian; m. Robert Radcliffe Rorke, June 4, 1960. A.B., U. Minn., 1951, M.A., 1952, B.S., 1955, M.D., 1957. Diplomate Am. Bd. Pathology. Intern Phila. Gen. Hosp., 1957-58, resident anat. pathology and neuropathology, 1958-62, asst. neuropathologist, 1963-67, chief pediatric pathologist, 1967-68, chief neuropathologist, 1968-69, chmn. dept. anat. pathology and chief neuropathologist, 1969-73, chmn. dept. pathology, 1973-77, pres. med. staff, 1973-75; practice medicine specializing in neuropathology Phila., 1962—; neuropathologist Children's Hosp., Phila., 1965—, pres. med. staff, 1986-88, acting pathologist-in-chief, 1995—; cons. neuropathologist Wyeth Rsch. Labs., Radnor, Pa., 1961-87, Wistar Inst. Anatomy and Biology, Phila., 1967-93; assoc. prof. pathology U. Pa. Sch. Medicine, Phila., 1970-73, prof., 1973—, clin. prof. neurology, 1979—; forensic neuropathologist Office of Med. Examiner, Phila., 1977—. Author: Myelinization of the Brain in the Newborn, 1969, Pathology of Perinatal Brain Injury, 1982; mem. editl. bd. Jours. Neuropathology Exptl. Neurology, 1980-85, 93—, Pediatric neurosurgery, 1984—, Child's Nervous System, 1984-88, Brain pathology, 1990-95; contbr. articles to profl. jours. NIH fellow in neuropathology, 1961-62; NIH grantee for study of neonatal brain, 1963-68. Fellow Coll. Am. Pathologists; mem. Phila. Gen. Hosp. Med. Staff (pres. 1973-75), Phila. Neurol. Soc. (v.p. 1971-72, editor Transactions 1973, pres. 1975-76), Am. Assn. Neuropathologists (exec. council 1976-85, v.p. 1979-80, pres. 1981-82), Am. Neurol. Assn., AMA, Burlington County Med. Soc., Phila. Coll. Physicians. Home: 120 Chestnut St Moorestown NJ 08057-2937 Office: Children's Hosp of Philadelphia 324 S 34th St Philadelphia PA 19104-4301

RORQUIST, IVOR CARL, mechanical engineer; b. Wadena, Sask., Can., Nov. 19, 1920; s. John Theodore and Alma (Samuleson) R.; m. Hazel Irene Bonney, June 9, 1947 (wid. May 1978); children: John Alan, Karen Janice; m. Gladys Kildoo, Nov. 12, 1983. B Engring., U. Saskatchewan, 1951. Project engr. Steel Co. of Can., Hamilton, Ont., Can., 1951-58; projects mgr. Aetna Std. Engring., Ellwood City, Pa., 1958-83; chief engr., cons. engr. Fabrimac, Inc., Ellwood City, Pa., 1983-88, Thimons, Inc., Ellwood City, Pa., 1988-91; cons. engr. ADS Machy, Thimons & others, Ellwood City, 1991—. Founding mem. Oakes/Adult Day Care Ctr., Ellwood, 1992-95. LAC RCAF, 1942-45. Mem. Rotary (treas. 1992—). Home: 111 2nd St Ellwood City PA 16117-2109

RORSCHACH, RICHARD GORDON, lawyer; b. Tulsa, Aug. 9, 1928; s. Harold Emil and Margaret (Hermes) R.; m. Martha Kay King, Dec. 23, 1979; children by previous marriage: Richard Helm, Reagan Cartwright, Andrew Maxwell. BS, MIT, 1950; MS, U. Okla., 1952; JD, U. Houston, 1961. Bar: Tex. 1961. Cons. civil engr. Freese & Nichols, Ft. Worth, 1955; cons. engr. Freese, Nichols & Turner, Houston, 1955-56; petroleum engr. Marathon Oil Co., Bay City, Tex., 1956-57, Houston, 1957-61; atty. Marathon Oil Co., 1961-64; ptnr. Broady, Kells & Rorschsch, Houston, 1964-68; ptnr. Ragan, Russell & Rorschach, Houston, 1968-80, Kilgore, Tex., 1980—; mem. exec. com. Colonial Royalties Co., Tulsa, 1970-77; officer Little River Oil &Gas Co., 1980-88; mng. ptnr. Pentagon Oil Co., 1988—; pres. Nat. Assn. Royalty Owners-Tex., 1993—; mem. exec. com. Nat. Assn. Royalty Owners, Inc.; owner, breeder, exhibitor Arabian Horses Shadowbrook Farm, Kilgore, Tex., 1980—. Served to 1st lt. C.E., AUS, 1952-54, Korea. Mem. ASME, ASCE, Tex. Bar Assn., Rotary Club (pres. Kilgore chpt. 1984-85), Sigma Xi, Sigma Alpha Epsilon. Republican. Presbyterian. Home: RR 4 Box 210 Kilgore TX 75662-9023 Office: 1100 Stone Rd PO Box 1934 Kilgore TX 75663-1934

RORTY, RICHARD MCKAY, philosophy educator; b. N.Y.C., Oct. 4, 1931; s. James Hancock and Winifred (Raushenbush) R.; m. Amelie Sarah Oksenberg, June 15, 1954 (div. 1972); 1 son, Jay; m. Mary R. Varney, Nov. 4, 1972; children: Patricia, Kevin. BA, U. Chgo., 1949, MA, 1952; PhD, Yale U., 1956; DHL, Northwestern U., 1992, Fla. Internat. Univ., 1994. Instr. philosophy Yale U., 1955-57; instr. Wellesley Coll., 1958-60, asst. prof., 1960-61; mem. faculty Princeton U., 1961-82, prof. philosophy, 1970-81, Stuart prof. philosophy, 1981-82; Univ. prof. humanities U. Va., 1982—. Author: Philosophy and the Mirror of Nature, 1979, Consequences of Pragmatism, 1982, Contingency, Irony and Solidarity, 1989, Objectivity, Relativism and Truth, 1991, Essays on Heidegger and Others, 1991. Served with AUS, 1957-58. Guggenheim fellow, 1973-74; MacArthur fellow, 1981-86. Mem. Am. Philos. Assn. (pres. Eastern div. 1979), Am. Acad. Arts and Scis. Home: 402 Peacock Dr Charlottesville VA 22903-9725 Office: 412 Cabell Hall Charlottesville VA 22903

ROSA, EDWARD A., principal. Prin. Mansfield (Mass.) High Sch. Recipient Blue Ribbon School award U.S. Dept. Edn., 1990-91. Office: Mansfield High Sch 250 East St Mansfield MA 02048-2526

ROSA, RAYMOND ULRIC, retired banker; b. New Britain, Conn., Jan. 30, 1927; s. Kenneth E. and Regina (Chenette) R.; m. Irene M. Asselin, Feb. 5, 1949; children: R. James, David M., Cathryn P., Michael F., Nancy A.,

Kenneth E. AS, Hillyer Coll., 1949. CPA, Conn. Pvt. practice pub. accounting Manchester, Conn., 1949-52; auditor Auditors of Pub. Accounts, State of Conn., Hartford, 1952-65; dir. Fed.-State Relations Dept. Finance and Control, Conn., 1965-69; dep. commr. Finance and Control, Conn., 1969-71; sr. v.p., auditor Soc. Savings, Hartford, 1971-90, ret., 1990; mem. Windsor Locks (Conn.) Bd. Fin., 1973-81; pres. Savs. Bank Forum, 1981-82; trustee Mease Manor, Inc., Dunedin, Fla., 1995—. Treas. Mental Health Assn. Conn., 1974-77, v.p., 1977-80, pres., 1980-83; bd. dirs. Nat. Assn. Mental Health, 1977-85, v.p. region 1, 1982-83; bd. dirs. Combined Health Appeal of Greater Hartford, 1982-90. Served with USNR, 1944-46. Mem. AICPA, Conn. Soc. CPAs, Conn. Soc. Govtl. Accts., KC, Dunedin Country Club, Suffield Country Club (bd. govs. 1984-91). Home: 2060 Golf View Dr Dunedin FL 34698-2330

ROSADO-MAY, FRANCISCO JAVIER, agricultural studies educator, researcher; b. Felipe Carrillo Puerto, Mex., Apr. 26, 1955; s. Alfredo Rosado Esquivel and Lilia May Tiran; m. Silvia Cuellar; 1 child, Silvia R. Rosado Cuellar; m. Patricia Salvidar Garcia, Aug. 2, 1989; 1 child, Francisco A. Rosado-May. BA in Tropical Agriculture, Colegio Superior de Agricultura Tropical, Cardenas, Tabasco, Mex., 1979, MSc in Tropical Ecology, 1980; PhD in Biology, U. Calif., Santa Cruz, 1991. Rsch. asst. Nat. Inst. Agrl. Rsch., Oaxaca, Mex., 1977; prof., rschr. dept. crop prodn. Colegio Superior de Agricultura Tropical, H. Cardenas, Tabasco, Mex., 1981-85, coord. agrl. prodn. courses, 1982-83, coord. extension program, 1984-85; founder U. Quintana Roo, 1991; rschr. Centro de Investigaciones de Quintana Roo, Chetumal, Quintana Roo, Mex., 1991-93, chair terrestial ecology dept., 1991-93; prof., acad. coord., rschr. Universidad de Quintana Roo, Chetumal, 1993—, gen. sec., 1993, acad. sec., 1993-94, dir. scis. and engring. divsn., 1994—; mem. coun. teaching and rsch. Colegio Superior de Agricultura Tropical, H. Cardenas, Tabasco, 1980, undergrad. seminars coord. dept. crop prodn., 1981, 82, 83, asst. to rsch. subdir., 1983-84, mem. editl. com., 1983-85; founder U. Quintana, Roo, Mex. Contbr. articles to profl. jours. Nat. Coun. Sci. and Tech. fellow, 1979-81, 85-89, 92-96, U. Calif.-Mexus Consotrium fellow, 1989, Secretaria de Educacion Publica fellow, 1992, 94, 95, 96. Mem. Ecol. Soc. Am., Botanical Soc. Am., Econ. Botany Soc. Am., Sigma Xi. Avocations: dancing, music, racket ball. Home: Ave Benito Juarez # 775, 77200 Felipe Carrillo Puerto Mexico Office: U de Quintana Roo, Boulevard Bahia & I Comonfort, Chetumal Mexico

ROSALDO, RENATO IGNACIO, JR., cultural anthropology educator; b. Champaign, Ill., Apr. 15, 1941; s. Renato Ignacio and Mary Elizabeth (Potter) R.; m. Michelle Sharon Zimbalist, June 12, 1966 (dec. Oct. 1981); children: Samuel Mario, Manuel Zimbalist; m. Mary Louise Pratt, Nov. 26, 1983; 1 child, Olivia Emilia Rosaldo-Pratt. AB, Harvard U., 1963, PhD, 1971. Asst. prof. cultural anthropology Stanford (Calif.) U., 1970-76, assoc. prof., 1976-85, prof., 1985—, Mellon prof. interdisciplinary studies, 1987-90, dir. Ctr. for Chicano Rsch., 1985-90; chair anthropology, 1994—, Lucie Stern prof. social scis., 1993—. Author: Ilongot Headhunting 1883-1974, 1980, Culture and Truth, 1989. Recipient Harry Benda prize Assn. for Asian Studies, 1983; Guggenheim fellow, 1993. Avocations: swimming, drawing, dancing. Home: 2520 Cowper St Palo Alto CA 94301-4218 Office: Stanford U Dept Anthropology Stanford CA 94305-2145

ROSALES, SUZANNE MARIE, hospital coordinator; b. Merced, Calif., July 23, 1946; d. Walter Marshall and Ellen Marie (Earl) Potter; children: Anita Carol, Michelle Suzanne. AA, City Coll., San Francisco, 1966. Diplomate Am. Coll. Utilization Review Physicians. Utilization review coord. San Francisco Gen. Hosp., 1967-74; mgr. utilization review/discharge planning UCLA Hosp. and Clinics, 1974-79; nurse III Hawaii State Hosp., Kaneohe, 1979-80; review coord. Pacific Profl. Std. Review Orgn., Honolulu, 1980-81; coord. admission and utilization reviewq The Rehab. Hosp. of the Pacific, Honolulu, 1981-85; coord. Pacific Med. Referral Project, Honolulu, 1985-87; dir. profl. svcs. The Queen's Healthcare Plan, Honolulu, 1987-88; utilization mgmt. coord. Vista Psychiat. Physician Assocs., San Diego, 1989; admission coord. utilization review San Francisco Gen. Hosp., 1989-91, quality improvement coordinator, 1991—; cons. Am. Med. Records Assn. Contbr. articles to profl. jours. Mem. Nat. Assn. Utilization Review Profls. Home: 505 Hanover St Daly City CA 94014-1351 Office: San Francisco Gen Hosp 1001 Potrero Ave San Francisco CA 94110-3518

ROSAN, RICHARD MARSHALL, real estate executive, architect; b. Bronxville, N.Y., Jan. 15, 1942; s. Richard A. and Helen (Marshall) R.; m. Nancy Davis, Apr. 12, 1969; children—Elizabeth, Christina, Peter. B.A., Williams Coll., 1964; M.Arch., U. Pa., 1967. Registered architect, N.Y. Chmn., dir. Office of Downtown Bklyn. Devel., N.Y.C., 1972-75; dir. office of Devel., City of N.Y., 1975-80; pres. Real Estate Bd. N.Y., N.Y.C., 1980-86; sr. v.p. Silverstein Properties, 1986—; trustee Lincoln Savs. Bank, Turner Equity Investors. Pres. bd. trustees Berkeley-Carroll Street Sch., Bklyn., 1977—; bd. dirs. Bklyn. Acad. Music, 1980—; pres. bd. Park Slope Neighborhood Family Care Ctr., Bklyn., 1982—. Mem. AIA. Democrat. Congregationalist. Home: 2950 Davenport St NW Washington DC 20008-2165 Office: Silverstein Properties 521 5th Ave New York NY 10175

ROSAND, DAVID, art history educator; b. Bklyn., Sept. 6, 1938; s. Johan Herbert and Frieda (Grotenstein) R.; m. Ellen Fineman, June 18, 1961; children: Jonathan, Eric. AB, Columbia Coll., 1959; MA, Columbia U., 1962, PhD, 1965. Instr. art history Columbia U., N.Y.C., 1964-67, asst. prof., 1967-69, assoc. prof., 1969-73, prof., 1973-95, chmn. Soc. of Fellows in the Humanities, 1979-83, Meyer Schapiro prof. art history, 1995—. Author: (with Michelangelo Muraro) Titian and the Venetian Woodcut, 1976, Titian, 1978, Painting in Cinquecento Venice: Titian, Veronese, Tintoretto, 1982, The Meaning of the Mark: Leonardo and Titian, 1988, (with Robert Cafritz and Lawrence Gowing) Places of Delight: The Pastoral Landscape, 1988; editor: (with Robert W. Hanning) Castiglione: The Ideal and the Real in Renaissance Culture, 1983, Titian: His World and His Legacy, 1982; editorial bd. Arion, Imago Musicae, Venezia Cinquecento. Mem. bd. advisors CASVA Nat. Gallery Art., 1990-94. Fulbright Commn. fellow, 1962-63; NEH fellow, 1971-72, 85-86, 91-92; John S. Guggenheim Meml. Found. fellow, 1974-75. Mem. Coll. Art Assn. Am., Renaissance Soc. Am. (mem. exec. bd. 1981—), Save Venice, Inc. (mem. gen com. 1992—), Ateneo Veneto (fgn.). Home: 560 Riverside Dr New York NY 10027-3202 Office: Columbia U Dept Art History and Archaeology 826 Schermerhorn Hall New York NY 10027

ROSAR, VIRGINIA WILEY, librarian; b. Cleve., Nov. 22, 1926; d. John Egbert and Kathryn Coe (Snyder) Wiley; m. Michael Thorpe Rosar, April 8, 1950 (div. Feb. 1968); children: Bruce Wiley, Keith Michael, James Wilfred. Attended, Oberlin Coll., 1944-46; BA, U. Puget Sound, 1948; MS, C.W. Post Coll., L.I.U., Greenvale, N.Y., 1971. Cert. elem. and music tchr., N.Y.; cert. sch. library media specialist, N.Y. Music programmer Station WFAS, White Plains, N.Y., 1948; prodn. asst. NBC-TV, N.Y.C., 1948-50; tchr. Portledge Sch., Locust Valley, N.Y., 1967-70; librarian Syosset (N.Y.) Schs., 1970-71, Smithtown (N.Y.) Schs., 1971-92; ret., 1992; pres. World of Realia, Woodbury, N.Y., 1969-86; founder Cygnus Pub., Woodbury, 1985-87. Active local chpt. ARC, 1960-63, Community Concert Assn., 1960-66, Leukemia Soc. Am., 1978—. Mem. AAAS, N.Y. Acad. Scis., L.I. Alumnae Club of Pi Beta Phi (pres. 1964-66). Republican. Presbyterian. Avocations: music, sewing, gardening, writing. Home: 10 Warrenton Ct Huntington NY 11743-3750

ROSATI, MARIO, mathematician, educator; b. Rome, Jan. 5, 1928; s. Aristide and Maria (Gabrielli) R.; m. Maria Luisa Marziale, Aug. 3, 1968; children: Francesca, Nicoletta, Giulio. Laurea in Math., U. Rome, 1950. Asst. prof. U. Rome, 1952-66; prof. math. U. Padua, Italy, 1966—; dir. Applied Math. Inst., Padua U., 1978-86, Dept. Pure Applied Math., 1987-92, Seminario Matematico, 1994—. Co-editor: (with G. Tedone) Collana di Informazione Scientifica, 1965-78; contbr. books and articles in field. Fellow U. Goettingen 1955. Mem. Italian Math. Union, Am. Math. Soc., Nat. Rsch. Ctr. Roman Catholic. Home: 43 G Leopardi, 35126 Padua Italy Office: Dept Pure Applied Math, 7 GB Belzoni, 35131 Padua Italy

ROSATO, FRANCIS ERNEST, surgeon; b. Phila., June 2, 1934; s. Ernest Lancelot and Mary Rita (Huggard) R.; m. Gertrude Blount Doman, Oct. 27, 1962; children—Ernest, Ann, Gertrude, Frank, Aimee. Student, St. Joseph's Coll., Phila., 1952-55; M.D., Hahnemann Med. Coll., Phila., 1959. Diplomate: Nat. Bd. Med. Examiners. Resident in surgery U. Pa.; mem. faculty to prof. surgery, 1965-74; prof. surgery, chmn. dept. Eastern Va. Med. Sch., Norfolk, 1974-78; prof., chmn. dept. surgery Jefferson Med. Coll. of Thomas Jefferson U., Phila., 1978—; Advanced clin. fellow Am. Cancer Soc. Author: Surgery of the Breast, 1986, Atlas of Surgical Technique, 1992; contbg. author: Cameron's Current Surgical Therapy, Ana Sabiston's Text of Surgery; contbr. articles to med. jours. Fellow ACS; mem. Soc. Univ. Surgeons, Am. Surg. Assn., So. Surg. Assn., Halstead Soc., Phila. Country Club, Merion Cricket Club, Union League, Friendly Sons. of St. Patrick. Roman Catholic. Home: 900 Merion Square Rd Gladwyne PA 19035-1510 Office: Jefferson Med Coll 1025 Walnut St Philadelphia PA 19107-5001

ROSBERG, CARL GUSTAF, political science educator; b. Oakland, Calif., Feb. 28, 1923; s. Carl Gustaf and Ethel (Moore) R.; m. Elizabeth Joanna Wilson, Oct. 23, 1954; children—James Howard, David Nils. B.S., Georgetown U., 1948, M.S., 1950; D.Phil., Oxford (Eng.) U., 1954. Asst. prof., research asso. African studies program Boston U., 1955-58; vis. asst. prof. U. Calif., Berkeley, 1958-59, asst. prof. dept. polit. sci., 1959-63, asso. prof., 1963-67, prof., 1967-91, prof. emeritus, 1991—, chmn. dept. polit. sci., 1969-74, dir. Inst. Internat. Studies, 1973-89. Author: (with John Nottingham) The Myth of Mau Mau: Nationalism in Kenya, 1966, (with George Bennett) The Kenyatta Election: Kenya, 1960-61, 1961, (with Robert Jackson) Personal Rule in Black Africa: Prince, Autocrat, Prophet, Tyrant, 1982; editor: (with James S. Coleman) Political Parties and National Integration in Tropical Africa, 1964, (with William H. Friedland) African Socialism, 1964, (with Thomas Callaghy) Socialism in Sub-Saharan Africa, 1979, (with Robert M. Price) The Apartheid Regime: Political Power and Racial Domination, 1980, (with David E. Apter) Political Development and the New Realism in Sub-Saharan Africa, 1994. Served with USAAF, 1943-45. Decorated Purple Heart, Air medal, Prisoner of War medal; Ford Found. fellow, 1954-55. Mem. Coun. Fgn. Rels., African Studies Assn. (past pres.). Home: 1515 Oxford St Apt 2C Berkeley CA 94709 Office: Dept Polit Sci U Calif Berkeley CA 94720

ROSBERG, DAVID WILLIAM, plant sciences educator; b. Superior, Wis., Jan. 3, 1919; s. Albert and Hulda (Sundin) R.; m. Helen Dana McDonald, Nov. 8, 1941; children—David William, Dana Karin. B.A., St. Olaf Coll., 1940; postgrad., Tex. A&M Coll., 1940-41; M.S., Ohio State U., 1947, Ph.D., 1949. Grad. asst. biology dept. Tex. A&M U., College Station, 1940-42, lab asst. Tex. Agrl. Exptl. Sta., 1942, asst. prof. plant physiology and pathology dept., 1949-54, asso. prof., 1954-58, prof., 1958-60, prof., head dept. plant scis., from 1960, prof. emeritus, 1981—; insp. R.R. Perishable Inspection Agy., N.Y.C., 1941; grad. asst. dept. botany Ohio State U., 1946-48, research asst.; Research Found., 1948-49; lab. asst. Battelle Meml. Inst., Columbus, O., 1948. Named Disting. Alumnus Ohio State U., 1972. Mem. AAAS, Am. Phytopath. Soc., Tex. Acad. Sci., Sigma Xi, Phi Kappa Phi, Gamma Sigma Delta. Home: 11630 Sh # 30 College Station TX 77845 Office: Dept Plant Scis Tex A&M U College Station TX 77843

ROSBERG, MERILEE ANN, education educator; b. Oak Park, Ill., June 1, 1942; d. Andrew Clark and Martha (Kester) Adamson; m. William H. Rosberg, Aug. 17, 1963; children: Peter E., Trent W. AB, Augustana Coll., 1963; MA, U. Iowa, 1971, PhD, 1985. Tchr. Cedar Rapids (Iowa) Pub. Schs., 1963-65, Internat. Sch. Kuwait, 1965-67, N. Winnishoik Cmty. Schs., Decorah, Iowa, 1967-69, St. Mark's Luth. Ch. Presch., Cedar Rapids, 1969-71; staff tng. specialist Linn County Day Care Svcs., Cedar Rapids, 1971-76; dir. early childhood program Jane Boyd Comty. House, Cedar Rapids, 1976-86; prof., divsn. chair Mt. Mercy Coll., Cedar Rapids, 1986—; vis. prof. U. Sts. Cyril & Methodius, Veliko Turnovo, Bulgaria, 1992, Czech Tech. U., Prague, Czech Rep., 1990. Fulbright scholar U. Brunei Darusalam, 1994-95. Mem. Nat. Assn. Early Childhood Edn., Nat. Coun. Tchrs. English, Internat. Readign Assn., Orgn. Mondiale Pour L'Education Prescolaire (U.S. nat. com.). Avocations: reading, travel. Home: 1900 Bever Ave SE Cedar Rapids IA 52403-2715 Office: Mt Mercy Coll 1330 Elmhurst Dr NE Cedar Rapids IA 52402

ROSBOTTOM, RONALD CARLISLE, French, arts and humanities educator; b. New Orleans, July 15, 1942; s. Albert Carlisle and Marjorie Catherine (Chavez) R.; m. Betty Elane Griffin, Sept. 5, 1964; 1 child, Michael K. B.A., Tulane U., 1964; M.A., Princeton U., 1966, Ph.D., 1969; MA (hon.), Amherst Coll., 1990. Instr. U. Pa., Phila., 1967-69, asst. prof., 1969-73; assoc. prof. Ohio State U., Columbus, 1973-78, prof. French lit., 1978-89, chmn. Romance langs., 1982-88; dean of faculty Amherst (Mass.) Coll., 1989-95, prof. French lit. and European studies, 1989—, Robert and Winifred Arms prof. arts and humanities, 1996—. Author: Marivaux's Novels, 1974, Choderlos de Laclos, 1979 (Havens prize 1980); editor: Studies in 18th Century Culture, 1975, 76, Essays in the French Enlightenment, 1991; mem. editorial bds. Eighteenth Century: Theory & Interpretation, Romance Quarterly. Decorated Ordre des Palmes Académiques; Woodrow Wilson Found. fellow, 1964-65, 66-67; Am. Council Learned Socs. summer fellow, 1970. Mem. MLA, Internat. Soc. 18th Century Studies (exec. com. 1978-83), Am. Soc. 18th Century Studies (exec. sec. 1978-83, 2d v.p. 1992-93, 1st v.p. 1993-94, pres. 1994-95), Am. Assn. Tchrs. French, Phi Beta Kappa. Democrat. Home: 326 Shays St Amherst MA 01002-2943 Office: Amherst Coll Box 2255 Amherst MA 01002-5000

ROSCH, JOHN THOMAS, lawyer; b. Council Bluffs, Iowa, Oct. 4, 1939; s. H.P. and Phebe Florence (Jamison) R.; m. Carolyn Lee, Aug. 18, 1961; children: Thomas Lee, Laura Lee. BA, Harvard U., 1961, LLB, 1965. Bar: Calif. 1966, U.S. Dist. Ct. (no. dist.) Calif. 1966, U.S. Dist. Ct. (ea. dist.) Calif. 1967, U.S. Ct. Appeals (9th cir.) 1966. Assoc. McCutchen, Doyle, Brown & Enersen, San Francisco, 1965-72, ptnr., 1972-73, 75-93; ptnr. Latham & Watkins, San Francisco, 1994—; dir. Bur. Consumer Protection, FTC, Washington, 1973-75. Contbr. articles profl. jours. Fellow Am. Bar Found., Am. Coll. Trial Lawyers; mem. ABA (past chmn. antitrust sect.), State Bar Calif., San Francisco Bar Assn., Calif. State and Antitrust and Trade Regulation Sect. (sect. chair law sect.). Republican. Episcopalian. Office: Latham & Watkins 505 Montgomery St San Francisco CA 94111

ROSCH, PAUL JOHN, physician, educator; b. Yonkers, N.Y., June 30, 1927; s. Samuel Joseph and Mary (Gang) R.; m. Lorraine Marie Hunt, June 27, 1951; children: David Carl, Jonathan Hunt, Jane Ellen, Michael Edward, Richard Joseph, Donna Marie; m. Marguerite Delamater, Sept. 12, 1972. AB, Brown U., NYU, 1948; MA, NYU, 1950; MD, Albany Med. Coll., 1954. Diplomate Am. Bd. Internal Medicine. Fellow Inst. Exptl. Medicine and Surgery, U. Montreal, Que., Can., 1951-52; intern, asst. resident in medicine Johns Hopkins Hosp., 1954-56; resident in medicine, then chief dept. metabolism Walter Reed Med. Ctr., 1956-58; physician-in-charge nuclear medicine St. John's Riverside Hosp., Yonkers, 1959-67, dir. endocrine clinic, sr. attending physician, 1959-96, vice chief of staff, 1977; chief endocrine clinic St. Joseph's Hosp., 1959, sr. cons. in medicine, 1980—; pres. Am. Inst. Stress, Yonkers, 1978—, sr. cons. in medicine, 1980—; clin. prof. medicine and psychiatry N.Y. Med. Coll., 1980—; asst. clin. prof. medicine Mt. Sinai Hosp. Sch. Medicine, 1963-67; former adj. prof. medicine in psychiatry U. Md. Sch. Medicine. From asst. to assoc. editor Health Comm. and Informatics; editor-in-chief Stress Medicine, 1990—; mem. editorial bd. AMA Archives Internal Medicine, Folia Clinica Internat, Jour. Human Stress, Internat. Jour. Psychosomatics, Am. Jour. Health Promotion, Cardiovascular Revs. & Reports, Internat. Jour. Stress Mgmt., Comprehensive Therapy, Jour. Human Behavior; contbg. editor Creative Living; contbr. articles to profl. jours. Bd. govs. Jewish Community Ctr.; bd. dirs. Family Svc. Soc., Mensana Clinic, 1980—; chmn. bd. Internat. Found. Biosocial Devel. and Human Health, 1980—; mem. adv. bd. Image Inst., 1980—. Capt. AUS, 1956-58. Fellow ACP, Internat. Stress Mgmt. Assn. (hon. v.p. 1991—), Am. Coll. Cardiology, Internat. Acad. Medicine, Am. Coll. Angiology, N.Y. Diabetes Assn.; mem. Westchester Diabetes Assn. (pres. 1968), Internat. Law Enforcement Stress Assn. (adv. bd. 1980—), Yonkers Acad. Medicine (bd. govs., pres. 1971), N.Y. Cardiology Soc., Acad. Psychosomatic Medicine, Soc. Behavioral Medicine, N.Y. Acad. Scis., Endocrine Soc., Am. Diabetes Assn., Westchester Soc. Internat. Medicine (past pres.), Stress Mgmt. Assn. (hon. v.p.), N.Y. State Soc. Internal Medicine (pres. 1974), Soc. Nuclear Medicine (bd. dirs.), Am. Fedn. Clin. Rsch., Am. Soc. Internal Medicine, Am. Geriatrics Soc., Elmwood Country Club, Atlantis Golf Club, Breakers Golf Club, St. Andrews Golf Club, La Coquille Club (Palm Beach, Fla.). Home: 10 Old Jackson Ave Hastings On Hudson NY 10706 also: 221 N Country Club Dr Atlantis FL 33462-1113

ROSCHE, LORETTA G., medical, surgical nurse; b. New Philadelphia, Ohio, Sept. 16, 1934; d. Seldon E. and Margaret (Murphy) Donohue; m. Thomas R. Rosche, Sept. 6, 1954; children: Melanie Rosche Smith, Cynthia Rosche Geeker, Lori Rosche Davis, Julia Rosche Sivyer. Diploma, Lafayette Sch. Nursing, 1984; cert., Jewish Hosp., 1985; student, Am. Healthcare Inst. RN, Va. Office mgr., nurse, surg. asst. to pvt. physician Williamsburg, Va., 1979—; advanced tng. in laparoscopic surgery Abbott Northwestern Hosp., Mpls., 1990; surg. nurse vol. surg. team Esperanza, Amazon region of Brazil, 1988, 91; lectr. various groups including Med. Soc., Rotary, Hand Soc. Named Speaker of Yr. Psi Beta, 1990. Mem. Assn. Hand Care Profls. (co-founder, treas.), Am. Assn. Med. Assts. (cert.), Soc. Laparoendoscopic Surgeons. Home: 128 Country Club Dr Williamsburg VA 23188-1516

ROSCOE, STANLEY NELSON, psychologist, aeronautical engineer; b. Eureka, Calif., Nov. 4, 1920; s. Stanley Boughton and Martha Emma (Beer) R.; m. Margaret Hazel Brookins, Dec. 21, 1948 (dec.); children: Lee Marin Roscoe Bragg, Jack; m. Elizabeth Frances Lage, Mar. 12, 1977 (dec.); 1 child, Catherine Marie; m. Gayle Buchanan Karshner, Mar. 15, 1990. AB in Speech and English, Humboldt State U., 1943; postgrad., U. Calif., Berkeley, 1942, 46; MA in Psychology, U. Ill., 1947, PhD in Psychology, 1950. Cert. psychologist, Calif. Research asst. U. Ill., Champaign, 1946-50, research assoc., 1950-51, asst. prof., 1951-52; assoc. dir. Inst. Aviation, head aviation research lab., Champaign, 1969-75, prof. psychology and aero. and astronautical engring., 1969-79, prof. emeritus, 1979—; prof. N.Mex. State U., Las Cruces, 1979-86, prof. emeritus, 1986—; with Hughes Aircraft Co., Culver City, Calif., 1952-69, 75-77, dept. mgr., 1962-69, sr. scientist, 1975-77; tech. adviser, cons. in field; pres. Illiana Aviation Scis. Ltd., Las Cruces, N.Mex., 1976—. Author: Aviation Psychology, 1980, Flightdeck Performance: The Human Factor, 1990; editor: Aviation Research Monographs, 1971-72, Heydays in Humboldt, 1991, From Humboldt to Kodiak, 1992; assoc. editor: Human Factors Jour., 1982—; cons. editor Internat. Jour. Aviation Psychology, 1991—; contbr. numerous articles to profl. jours. 1st lt. AC, U.S. Army, 1943-46. Fellow APA (Franklin V. Taylor award 1976), Human Factors Soc. (pres. 1960-61, Jerome H. Ely award 1968, 73, 89, 91, Alexander C. Williams award 1973, Paul M. Fitts award 1974, Pres.'s award 1990), Soc. Engring. Psychologists, Royal Aero Soc. (Eng.); mem. IEEE, AIAA, Inst. Navigation, Assn. Aviation Psychologists (ann. career award 1978), Aerospace Human Factors Assn. (Paul T. Hansen award 1994), Sigma Xi, Phi Kappa Phi, Phi Sigma, Chi Sigma Epsilon. Patentee, inventor in field. Home: 2750 Sunnygrove Ave McKinleyville CA 95519 Office: PO Box 4498 Las Cruces NM 88003-4498

ROSCOPF, CHARLES BUFORD, lawyer; b. Marvell, Ark., Apr. 21, 1928; s. Emmett Lee and Sally Virginia (King) R.; m. Mary Anne Maddox, Aug. 22, 1954; children—Charles David; Ann Karen. Student, Hendrix Coll., 1948-50; J.D., U. Ark., 1954. Bar: Ark. bar 1954, U.S. Dist. Cts 1955, 64, U.S. Supreme Ct. bar 1965. Pvt. practice Helena, Ark., 1954—; assoc. firm Burke, Moore & Burke, 1954-58; ptnr. firm Burke & Roscopf, 1958-64; sr. ptnr. Roscopf and Roscopf, P.A., 1964—; mem. Ark. Ho. of Reps., 1953-58; del. Ark. Constl. Conv., 1968; mem. Ark. Probate Drafting Com.; mem. Ark. State Bd. Law Examiners, 1973-79; spl. justice Ark. Supreme Ct. Served with USN, 1946-48; served with USAFR, 1962-68. Fellow Ark. Bar Found. (pres. 1995-96); mem. ABA, ATLA, Ark. Bar Assn. (pres. 1990-91), Am. Law Inst., Rotary (Paul Harris fellow), Masons, Shriners, Kappa Sigma. Methodist. Home: 117 Avalon Pl Helena AR 72342-1722 Office: Nat Bank Bldg 408 Helena PO Box # 610 Helena AR 72342

ROSDEITCHER, SIDNEY SAMUEL, lawyer; b. Bayonne, N.J., June 2, 1936; s. Morris and Lee (Rosenbluth) R.; m. Linda Latter, Aug. 28, 1960; children: Elizabeth, David, Emily. AB, Columbia U., 1958; LLB magna cum laude, Harvard U., 1961. Bar: N.Y., D.C., U.S. Dist. Ct. (so. and ea. dists.) N.Y., U.S. Claims Ct., U.S. Tax Ct., U.S. Ct. Appeals (1st, 2d, 3d, 4th, 5th, 8th, 9th, 10th, 11th, D.C. and fed. cirs.), U.S. Supreme Ct. Atty. office of legal counsel U.S. Dept. Justice, Washington, 1961-62; advisor to commr. FTC, Washington, 1965-66; assoc. Paul, Weiss, Rifkind, Wharton & Garrison, N.Y.C., 1962-65, 66-72, ptnr., 1972—; adj. prof. civil liberties Bklyn. Law Sch., 1974-75; lectr. profl. responsibility Columbia Law Sch., 1990-93. Article editor Harvard U. Law Rev., 1960-61; contbr. articles to legal jours. Trustee Lawyers Com. for Civil Rights Under Law, 1992—; bd. dirs. NAPIL Fellows, 1992—. Mem. D.C. Bar Assn. (model rules spl. com. 1982-85), Assn. of Bar of City of N.Y. (chmn. profl. and jud. ethics com. 1979-82, fed. cts. com. 1982-85, chmn. com. on internat. human rights 1991-94, chmn. coun. on internat. affairs 1995—, civil rights com. 1994—). Home: 90 Riverside Dr New York NY 10024-5306 Office: Paul Weiss Rifkind Wharton & Garrison 1285 Avenue Of The Americas New York NY 10019-6064

ROSE, ADAM ZACHARY, economist, educator; b. Bergen-Belsen, Germany, Jan. 5, 1948; s. Isaac and Gusta Eugenia (Kaiser) R.; m. Anne Lynn Carver, Oct. 15, 1972; children: Eleanor, Jonathan. BA, U. Utah, 1970; MA, Cornell U., 1972, PhD, 1974. Sr. economist N.Y. Council Econ. Advisers, N.Y.C., 1974-75; asst. prof. U. Calif., Riverside, 1975-81; assoc. prof. W.Va. U., Morgantown, 1981-84; faculty assoc. Regional Research Inst., Morgantown, 1981-88; vis. assoc. EQL, Calif. Inst. Tech., Pasadena, 1986; prof. mineral econs. W.Va. U., 1984-88, chmn. dept., 1981-83, 86-88; prof. mineral econs., head dept. energy, environ. & mineral econs. Pa. State U., University Park, 1988—, faculty assoc. Earth System Sci. Ctr., 1993—, faculty assoc. Environ. Pollution Control Program, 1995—; cons. Mayor's Office, City of L.A., 1980, NSF, Washington, 1980, U.S. Forest Svc., 1982-83, So. Calif. Gas Co., 1983, 85, U.S. Corps of Engrs., 1984, 92-93, San Francisco City Atty's Office, 1986, Nat. Coal Assn., 1990, U.S. Dept. Energy, 1990, EUREMCO, 1991-92, UNCTAD, 1991-92, Foster Wheeler, Inc., 1992, Air Products & Chemicals Inc., 1992-93, Ctr. Energy and Econ. Devel., 1994-95, EQE Internat., 1996; expert witness U.S. Senate, Washington, 1985, W.Va. Pub. Svc. Commn., 1991, Pa. Pub. Utility Commn., 1992. Sr. author: Forecasting Gas Demand, 1987, Natural Resource Policy and Income Distribution, 1988, Combating Global Warming: A Global System of Tradeable Carbon Emission Entitlements, 1992; editor, author: Geothermal Energy and Regional Development, 1979, Frontiers of Input-Output Analysis, 1989; author (monograph): Dynamic Interindustry Model of Pollution Abatement, 1976; guest editor: Jour. Policy Modeling, 1989; Resource and Energy Economics, 1993, Energy Policy, 1996; assoc. editor: Jour. Regional Sci., 1985—; editorial bd. mem. Resources Policy, 1989—, Resource and Energy Economics, 1993—, Pacific & Asian Jour. Energy, 1996. Recipient Outstanding Planning Program Honor award Am. Planning Assn., 1983; Woodrow Wilson Found. fellow, Cornell U., 1970-71; grantee U.S. Dept. Energy, 1983-84, 92-95, grantee NSF, Washington, 1987-88, 90-91, 93—; grantee Nat. Ctr. Earthquake Engring. Rsch., 1992-96; grantee Argonne Nat. Lab., 1992-94. Mem. Am. Econ. Assn. (rep. to AAAS 1986-92), AAAS (mem. sect. K exec. com.), Regional Sci. Assn., Internat. Assn. Energy Economists, Assn. Resource & Environ. Economists, Mineral Econs. and Mgmt. Soc. Democrat. Jewish. Home: 1702 Princeton Dr State College PA 16803-3259 Office: Pa State U 222 Walker Bldg University Park PA 16802

ROSE, ALAN DOUGLAS, lawyer; b. Flushing, N.Y., Dec. 22, 1945; s. William Allen and Josephine (Grohe) R.; m. Janet Louise Clift, Aug. 20, 1966; children: Alan Douglas Jr., Windsor, Ainsley, Vanessa, Hillary, Lacey. BA, Harvard U., 1967; MSc, London Sch. Econs., 1969; JD, U. Va., 1972. Bar: Mass. 1974, U.S. Dist. Ct. Mass. 1975, U.S. Ct. Claims 1983, U.S. Ct. Appeals (1st cir.) 1976, U.S. Ct. Appeals (fed. cir.) 1986, U.S. Supreme Ct. 1991. Law clk. to judge U.S. Dist. Ct. Mass., Boston, 1972-73; assoc. Choate Hall & Stewart, Boston, 1973-75; asst. U.S. Atty. Dept. Justice, Boston, 1975-80; ptnr. Nutter McClennen & Fish, Boston, 1980-95; mgr. litigation dept., 1991-93; ptnr. Rose & Assocs., Boston, 1995—; lectr. Law Sch. Harvard U., Cambridge, Mass., 1981-82; spl. asst. atty. gen. Commonwealth Mass., 1991-92; mem. U.S. Dist. Ct. Civil Justice Adv. Bd., 1995—. Mem. ABA, Boston Bar Assn. (vice chair joint bar com. on jud. appointments 1991-92), City Mission Soc. (chmn., bd. dirs.). Democrat. Mem. United Ch. Christ. Home: 50 Bristol Rd Wellesley MA 02181-2728 Office: Rose & Assocs One Boston Pl Boston MA 02108-4400

ROSE, BEATRICE SCHROEDER (MRS. WILLIAM H. ROSE), harpist, educator; b. Ridgewood, N.J., Nov. 15, 1922; d. Henry William and Ida (LeHovey) Schroeder; m. William Harrison Rose, Apr. 10, 1954; 1 child,

Daniel. Student, Inst. Musical Art, 1940-41, Mannes Coll. Music, 1942-44; studies with, Lucile Lawrence and Carlos Salzedo. Concert and radio debut N.Y. World's Fair, 1939; soloist Damrosch Music Appreciation Hour broadcast, 1940, Duke of Windsor's Save the Children Fund, Nassau, The Bahamas, 1941; assoc. harpist Radio City Music Hall Orch., N.Y.C., 1944-50; various radio and solo performances N.Y. area, 1944-51; concert artist Italy, U.S. and Can., 1952; prin. harpist Houston Symphony, 1953-84; instr. harp U. Houston, 1953—; soloist Contemporary Music Soc., 1959, 60, Houston Chamber Orch., 1969; dir. Christmas Festival of Harps, Houston Harp Ensemble, PBS, 1978, Harps of Gold, 1983; instr. Shepherd Sch. Music, Rice U., 1977-93. Author: Troubadour Harp: A Guide for Teachers and Students, 1976, rev. edits., 1982, 92; co-author; Outline of Six-Year Harp Course for Elementary, Junior and Senior High School, 1966; composer works include Enchanted Harp, rev. edit., 1975; recs. for Houston Symphony, Stokowski, Everest, Capitol, Comissiona, Vanguard Records. Recipient 1st prize Federated Music Clubs Contest, 1936; N.Y. Hour of Music award, 1945. Mem. Am. Harp Soc., Tex. Music Educators Assn. (adjudicator All-State competitions), Nat. Fedn. Music Clubs (harp adviser 1991—), Phi Beta. Home: 1315 Friarcreek Ln Houston TX 77055-6714 Office: U Houston Sch Music Houston TX 77004

ROSE, BEVERLY ANNE, pharmacist; b. Lewiston, Idaho, June 11, 1950; d. Burton Roswell and Nell Dora (Greenburg) Stein; m. Fred Joseph Rose, July 21, 1973 (div. Aug. 1980). BS in Pharmacy, Ohio No. U., 1973; MBA, Cleve. State U., 1987. Registered pharmacist, Ohio, N.Y. Staff pharmacist Lorain (Ohio) Community Hosp., 1973-79, dir. pharmacy, 1979-91; dir. dept. pharmacy svcs. The House of the Good Samaritan Health Care Complex, Watertown, N.Y., 1991-93; adj. faculty, clin. tng. specialist U. Toledo Coll. Pharmacy, 1980-91; computer cons. Hosp. Pharmacy Network; mem. State Bd. Legis. Rule Rev., Ohio State Bd. Pharmacy, 1987, 88; mem. pres. adv. bd. Ohio No. U., Ada, 1990—. Mem. editl. bd. Aspen Publs., 1992—. Mem. Am. Soc. Health Sys. Pharmacists (apptd. coun. legal and pub. affairs 1988-89, 89-90, state del. ho. of dels. Ohio 1984, 85, 86, 87, 88, 89, mem. psychotherapeutics-spl. practice group 1990—), Adminstrs. Practice Mgmt. Group, Am. Pharm. Assn., Ohio Soc. Hosp. Pharmacists (pres. 1985-89, Squibb Leadership award 1988, Ciba-Geigy Svc. award 1988, Evlyn Gray Scott award 1987), N.Y. State Coun. Hosp. Pharmacists, Am. Soc. Parenteral and Enteral Nutrition, Fedn. Internat. Pharmaceutique, N.Y. Chpt. Am. Coll. Clin. Pharmacy, others. Avocations: computers, photography, classical music, singing. Home: 20 Cambridge Dr Apt 4 Georgetown OH 45121-9746

ROSE, C. KIMBALL, retired judge. Formerly presiding judge Ariz. Superior Ct., Phoenix. Office: Superior Ct 201 W Jefferson St Phoenix AZ 85003-2205

ROSE, CAROL DENISE, orthopedic unit nurse administrator, educator; b. Las Vegas, Nev., July 31, 1960; d. Howard Elden and Sarah (Haley) Heckethorn; m. Michael Shaun Rose, June 19, 1982; 1 child, Carissa Denise. ADN, U. Nev., Las Vegas, 1981, BSN, 1985. Staff nurse orthopedic unit Univ. Med. Ctr. So. Nev., Las Vegas, 1981-84, acting head nurse, then head nurse orthopedic unit, 1984-88, asst. mgr. orthopedic unit, 1988, orthopedic unit mgr., 1988—; adj. faculty health scis. dept. Clark County C.C., North Las Vegas, Nev.; speaker at profl. confs. Mem. ANA, Nat. Assn. Orthopaedic Nurses (pres. So. Nev. chpt.), Sigma Theta Tau, Phi Kappa Phi. Democrat. Roman Catholic. Avocations: sewing, embroidery, skiing, boating, reading. Office: Univ Med Ctr So Nev 1800 W Charleston Blvd Las Vegas NV 89102-2329

ROSE, CAROL MARGUERITE, law educator; b. Washington, Apr. 12, 1940; d. J. Hugh and Marie (Meenehan) R. BA, Antioch Coll., 1962; MA, U. Chgo., 1963, JD, 1977; PhD, Cornell U., 1970. Bar: Ill. 1977, Calif. 1978, D.C. 1978. Instr. history Ohio St. U., Columbus, 1969-73; assoc. dir. So. Govtl. Monitor Project, Atlanta, 1975-76; law clk. to judge U.S. Ct. Appeals (5th cir.), Austin, Tex., 1977-78; asst. prof. law Stanford (Calif.) U., 1978-80; acting prof. law U. Calif., Berkeley, 1980-82; prof. law Northwestern U., Chgo., 1982-88, Yale U., 1988—; bd. editors Found. Press, Mineola, N.Y., 1986—. Mem. Am. Assn. Law Schs., Am. Acad. Arts and Scis., Order of Coif.

ROSE, CHARLES, television journalist. B in History, Duke U., JD; post-grad., NYU. Interviewer Sta. WPIX-TV, N.Y.C., 1972; mng. editor Bill Moyers Internat. Report, from 1974; exec. producer Bill Moyers Jour., from 1975; corr. U.S.A.: People in Politics, PBS, 1976; polit. corr. NBC News, 1976-77; co-host A.M. Chgo., 1978; host The Charlie Rose Show Sta. KXAS-TV, Dallas, Ft. Worth, 1979-81; host nationally syndicated The Charlie Rose Show Sta. WRC-TV, Washington, 1981-83; former host, interviewer CBS News Nightwatch, Washington, from 1984; now host "Charlie Rose" Rose Comms., Inc for PBS, N.Y.C., 1994—. Producer: (TV program) A Conversation with Jimmy Carter (Peabody award). Recipient News and Documentary Emmy award for Conversation with Roger Payne, 1992, 14th Annual Cable ACE award, 1992. Office: 499 Park Ave Fl 15 New York NY 10022-1240

ROSE, CHARLES DAVID, consulting company executive; b. Corpus Christi, Dec. 28, 1939; s. Robert Chester and Gladys (Blackmon) R.; m. Mary Ann McKinney, Apr. 23, 1965; children: David, Elizabeth, Katherine. BS in Physics magna cum laude, La. Tech. U., 1964; postgrad., Iowa State U. From engr. to dist. level supr. staff ops. South Ctrl. Bell Telephone Co., 1964-70; mgr. sales and engring. Hycaloader Co., 1970-74; owner Charles Rose Cons., Monroe, La., 1974—. Contbr. numerous articles to profl. jours. Mem. ASTM (various coms.), Am. Statis. Assn., Am. Soc. for Quality Control. Achievements include devel. of fractal variogram model for use in geostatistics; designated U.S. expert for ISO on coal sampling. Home: 3370 Deborah Dr Monroe LA 71201-2151 Office: Charles Rose Cons PO Box 4344 808 N 31st St Monroe LA 71211-4344

ROSE, CHARLES GRANDISON, III (CHARLIE ROSE), congressman; b. Fayetteville, N.C., Aug. 10, 1939; s. Charles Grandison Jr. and Anna Frances (Duckworth) R.; m. Stacye Hefner; children: Charles Grandison IV, Sara Louise, Kelly Josephine. AB, Davidson Coll., 1961; LLB, U. N.C., 1964. Bar: N.C. 1964. Chief prosecutor Dist. Ct., 12th Jud. Dist., 1967-70; mem. 93nd-104th Congresses from 7th N.C. dist., Washington, 1972—; mem. agrl. com., subcom. Specialty Crops and Natural Resources, Gen. Farm Commodities 93nd-104th Congresses from 7th N.C. dist.; co-founder Congl. Rural Caucus; founder Congl. Clearing House on the Future. Pres. N.C. Young Democrats, 1968. Presbyterian. Office: US Ho of Reps 242 Cannon Bldg Washington DC 20515-0003*

ROSE, DANIEL, real estate company executive, consultant; b. N.Y.C., Oct. 31, 1929; s. Samuel B. and Belle (Bernstein) R.; m. Joanna Semel, Sept. 16, 1956; children: David Semel, Joseph Benedict, Emily, Gideon Gregory. Student, Yale U., 1947-50; cert. of proficiency in Russian lang., U.S. Air Force Program, 1951; B.A., Syracuse U., 1952; postgrad., U. Paris. With Dwelling Mgrs., Inc., N.Y.C., 1954—; pres. Dwelling Mgrs., Inc., 1960—, vice chmn., sec.-treas. Baltic-Am. Enterprise Fund, 1994—; dir. Dreyfus Tax Exempt Bond Fund Inc., 1976-82, Dreyfus Money Market Fund, Inc., 1980-82; pres., CEO Rose Assocs., Inc., N.Y.C., 1980—; 22 Dreyfus Funds, 1992—; assoc. fellow Pierson Coll. Yale U., 1974—; bd. govs., hon. life mem. Technion-Israel Inst. Tech.; bd. dirs., mem. grants com. Realty Found. N.Y.; vice chmn. Lionel Trilling seminars Columbia U., 1977—; bd. dirs. Nat. Humanities Ctr., Ventures in Edn.; trustee, mem. exec. and compensation and benefits coms. U.S. Trust Co. of N.Y., 1982-92; trustee, vice chmn. mixed use devel. coun. Urban Land Inst., 1986-93; trustee, mem. investment and compensation coms. Corp. Property Investors; mem. exec. com. Urban Land Found., 1989—, gov., 1993—; designated Cert. Property Mgr. Inst. for Real Estate Mgmt. Expert adv. to sec. HUD, 1972; expert/cons. to commr. edn. HEW, 1974; cons. HUD panel on urban devel., 1984-86; dir. N.Y. Coun. Humanities, 1980-86, N.Y. Conv. Ctr. Devel. Corp., 1980-90, Get Ahead Found., 1989—, Fifth Ave. Assn., 1989—; mem. Governor's Task Force on Housing, 1975, Task Force on Taxation, Mcpl. Assistance Corp., 1976-77, Planning Commn. Theatre Adv. Group, coun. of fellows, vis. com. to grad. faculty, bd. overseers Ctr. for Study of N.Y.C. affairs New Sch. for Social Rsch.; overseers com. to visit Ctr. Internat. Affairs Harvard U., 1992—; mem. adv. bd. CUNY-TV channel A, 1986—, Mcpl. Broadcasting System, 1977-78, MIT Ctr. for Real Estate Devel.; donor Daniel Rose chair urban econs., trustee NYU N.Y. Inst. for Humanistic Studies, Mus. of City of N.Y., 1984-90, Jewish Publ. Soc., Com. for Econ. Devel., N.Y.C. Rand Inst.; chmn. bd. trustees, Horace Mann-Barnard Sch., 1971-74, trustee, 1962-89, hon. trustee, 1989— ; v.p., assoc. treas., bd. dirs. Police Athletic League of N.Y., vice chmn. Cen. Harlem Facility; pres. Harlem Ednl. Activities Fund Inc., YM & YWHA of the Bronx, 1963-67; v.p. N.Y. Landmarks Conservancy, bd. dirs. 1977-90; bd. dirs. Jewish Cmty. Ctrs. Assn., 1970—, pres. 1974-78, hon. pres. 1978—; v.p. World Confedn. of Jewish Cmty. Ctrs., 1977-83; former trustee and exec. com. mem. Fedn. of Jewish Philanthropies of N.Y., chmn. standing functional com. on cmty. ctrs., 1969-73; ptnr. N.Y.C. Partnership, 1990—; treas., bd. dirs. Citizens Housing and Planning Coun. of N.Y., 1972-90; chmn. Dem. platform adv. com., 1984 Nat. Conv.; bd. advisors Dem. Leadership Coun., 1992—, Progressive Policy Inst.; trustee Dem. Nat. Com., 1988; chmn. Del. Svcs. Host Com., N.Y.C. Served with USAF, 1951-54. Mem. Internat. Inst. Strategic Studies (dir. Am. com. for IISS 1987—), Coun. on Fgn. Rels., Fgn. Policy Assn. (bd. dirs. 1971—, chmn. fgn. policy assocs. 1972-75), Inst. for East-West Security Studies (bd. dirs. 1982—, treas. 1988—, co-chmn. fin. com. 1990—), Am. Soc. Real Estate Counselors (mem. publs.-rsch. com.), Real Estate Bd. of N.Y. Inc. (chmn. housing com. 1975—, mem. bd. govs. 1977-80, 90—, mem. REBNY Found.), Assn. of Yale Alumni (del.-at-large 1978-81, class of 1951 del. 1986-89), Coffee House, Yale Union League Club, Cosmos (Washington), Racquet and Tennis, Quaker Ridge Country Club, Noyac Country Club, Econ. Club N.Y. Home: 895 Park Ave New York NY 10021-0327 Office: Rose Associates Inc 380 Madison Ave New York NY 10017-2593

ROSE, DAVID ALLAN, investment manager; b. N.Y.C., Feb. 15, 1937; s. Edward William and Marion (Nadelstein) R.; m. Frances Helaine Dushman, Aug. 16, 1959; children: Evan Denali, Mitchell Franklin. BS in Acctg., Queens Coll., 1958; MBA, Syracuse U., 1968. Fin. mgr. U.S. Army, Fort Richardson, Alaska, 1961-75; comptroller U.S. Army, Fort Richardson, 1975; exec. dir. Alaska Mcpl. Bond Bank Authority, Anchorage, 1975-82, Alaska Indsl. Devel. Authority, Anchorage, 1980; co-owner Downtown Investment Co., Anchorage, 1980—, Downtown Delicatessen, Inc., Anchorage, 1976—; CEO, Alaska Permanent Fund Corp., Juneau, 1982-92; chmn., CEO, Alaska Permanent Capital Mgmt. Co., Inc., Anchorage, 1992—; ptnr. Russian Alaska Export/Import Co., Anchorage, 1993—; fin. advisor Fin. Green Lake Dam, Sitka, Alaska, 1977, Fin. Dutch Harbor Port, Unalaska, Alaska, 1979-80, Fin. Kenai-Anchorage Pipeline, Anchorage, 1979-80, Fin. Pulp Mill Pollution Control, Ketchikan, Alaska, 1979-80, Govt. of Republic of Sakha, Russia, 1994—. Mem. City Coun., Anchorage, 1971-75, Borough Assembly, Anchorage, 1971-75, Mcpl. Assembly, Anchorage, 1975-80; pres. Alaska Mcpl. League, 1975, Mcpl. Assembly, Anchorage, 1975-77; vice chmn. endowment fund Alaska Pacific U., 1994—. Recipient Golden Man award Boys Club Alaska, Anchorage, 1974, Decoration for Meritorious Civilian Service, U.S. Army, 1975, Pub. Service award City and Borough, Juneau, 1986, Lions Internat. awards; named Pub. Adminstr. Yr., Am. Soc. Pub. Adminstrn., Alaska chpt., 1986. Mem. Rotary (awards). Republican. Jewish. Avocations: boating, raising ducks and geese, gardening. Office: Alaska Permanent Capital 900 W 5th Ave Ste 601 Anchorage AK 99501-2029

ROSE, DAVID CAMERON, company executive; b. Vance County, N.C., Nov. 10, 1942; s. Thomas Benton, Jr. and Kathryn (Hunt) R.; m. Margaret Diane Oakley, June 26, 1965; children: David Cameron, Thomas Benjamin. B.B.A., Wake Forest U., Winston-Salem, N.C., 1965; M.B.A., Wharton Sch., U. Pa., 1967. C.P.A., N.C. Staff accountant Haskins & Sells (C.P.A.s), Greensboro, N.C., 1967-69; with Rose's Stores, Inc., Henderson, N.C., 1969-91; controller Rose's Stores, Inc., 1971-72, treas., 1972-89, v.p. fin., 1975-86; sr. v.p. fin. and adminstrn. Rose's Stores, Inc., Henderson, N.C., 1986-91; also dir. Rose's Stores, Inc.; bus. and fin. cons., 1991-94; CFO Bioxy Inc., Raleigh, N.C., 1994-95, pres., CEO, 1995—; dir. Ctrl. Carolina Bank, Durham, N.C. Chmn. Henderson/Vance County Parks and Recreation Commn., 1979-92; pres. Vance Acad., Inc., Henderson, 1982-84; trustee Maria Parham Hosp., 1985-92. Mem. Am. Inst. C.P.A.s, N.C. Assn. C.P.A.s, Fin. Execs. Inst. Methodist. Home: 3205 Cameron Dr Henderson NC 27536-3816 Office: Bioxy Inc 3733 National Dr Ste 120 Raleigh NC 27612

ROSE, DAVID L., lawyer; b. Ft. Monmouth, N.J., Feb. 18, 1955; s. Llewellyn Paterson and Bebe (Faulk) R.; m. Laura Marie Jarvis, Sept. 3, 1989; children: Allison Michelle, Jessica Morgan, Ashley Elizabeth. BA in Comm., U. Colo., 1980; JD, Ariz. State U., 1991. Bar: Ariz.; U.S. Dist. Ct. Ariz.; U.S. Ct. Appeals (9th cir.). Law clk. Bonn & Anderson, Phoenix, 1988-91, Maricopa County Superior Ct., Phoenix, 1990-91; lawyer Anderson, Brody, Levinson, Weiser & Horwitz, Phoenix, 1991-92, Brandes, Lane & Joffe, Phoenix, 1992-93; pvt. practice Phoenix, 1993—; gen. counsel Counsel for Children's Rights, Ariz. Editor: Missive, 1992. Bd. dirs. Maricopa County Family Support Adv. Com., Phoenix; adv. coun. Washington Sch. Dist., Phoenix; mem. Ariz. State Legis., Domestic Rels. Reform Com., Phoenix. Mem. Maricopa County Bar Assn. (adv. family law com.), ABA (adv. family law sect.), Nat. Congress for Men (pres.), Father's for Equal Rights of Colo. (pres.). Avocations: aviation, computer systems. Office: Ste 101 1221 E Osborn Rd Phoenix AZ 85014

ROSE, DONALD JAMES, computer science educator; b. Santa Ana, Calif., May 25, 1944; 1 child, Tamar Rose. BA, U. Calif., Berkeley, 1966; AM, Harvard U., 1967, PhD, 1970. Instr. applied math. Harvard U., Cambridge, Mass., 1970; asst. prof. math. U. Denver, 1970-72; asst. prof. applied math. Harvard U., 1972-74, assoc. prof., 1974-77; prof., chmn. dept. computer sci. Vanderbilt U., Nashville, 1977-78; researcher Bell Labs., Murray Hill, N.J., 1978-84; prof., chmn. dept. computer Sci. Duke U., Durham, N.C., 1984-91, prof., 1991—; cons. MCNC, Research Triangle Park, 1984-89, Bell Labs, Murray Hill, 1984—, Tanner Rsch. Pasadena, Calif., 1993-94. Co-editor: Sparse Matrices and Their Applications, 1972, Sparse Matrix Computations, 1976; contbr. more than 50 articles to profl. jours. Mem. IEEE, Am. Math. Soc., Math. Assn. Am., Assn. Computing Machinery, Soc. Indsl. Applied Math. Office: Duke U Dept Computer Sci D112A LSRC Box 90129 Durham NC 27708-0129

ROSE, DONALD MCGREGOR, lawyer; b. Cin., Feb. 6, 1933; s. John Kreimer and Helen (Morris) R.; m. Constance Ruth Lanner, Nov. 29, 1958; children: Barbara Rose Mead, Ann Rose Weston. AB in Econs., U. Cin., 1955; JD, Harvard U., 1958. Bar: Ohio 1958, U.S. Supreme Ct. 1962. Asst. legal officer USNR, Subic Bay, The Philippines, 1959-62; with Office of JAG USNR, The Pentagon, Va., 1962-63; assoc. Frost & Jacobs, Cin., 1963-70, ptnr., 1970-93; sr. ptnr., 1993—; co-chmn. 6th Cir. Appellate Practice Inst., Cin., 1983, 90, mem. 6th Cir. adv. com., chmn. subcom. on rules, 1990-94, chmn., 1994—. Trustee, chmn. Friends of Cin. Pks., Inc., 1986-89, pres. 1980-86; trustee Am. Music Scholarship Assn., Cin., 1985-88; pres. Social Health Assn. Greater Cin. Area Inc., 1969-72; co-chmn. Harvard Law Sch. Fund for So. Ohio, Cin., 1985-87; pres. Meth. Union, Cin., 1983-85; chmn. trustees Hyde Pk. Cmty. United Meth. Ch., Cin., 1974-76, chmn. coun. on ministries, 1979-81, chmn. adminstrv. bd., 1982-84, chmn. mem. canvass, 1985, chmn. staff parish rels. com., 1988-90, chmn. commn. missions, 1993-95; trustee Meth. Theol. Sch. Ohio, vice chmn. devel. com., 1990-94, sec. 1992-94, chmn. devel. com., 1994—. Lt. USNR, 1959-63. Mem. ABA (co-chmn. advocacy tng. subcom., appellate practice com., litigation sect. 1988—), Ohio Bar Assn., Cin. Bar Assn., U. Club (Cin.), Cin. Country Club. Republican. Avocations: sailing, golf. Home: 8 Walsh Ln Cincinnati OH 45208-3423 Office: Frost & Jacobs 2500 PNC Ctr 201 E 5th St Cincinnati OH 45202-4117

ROSE, EDWARD W. (RUSTY ROSE), professional sports team executive. Gen. partner Texas Rangers, Arlington, TX. Office: care Texas Rangers 1000 Ballpark Way Arlington TX 76011-5168*

ROSE, ELIHU, real estate executive; b. N.Y.C., Mar. 30, 1933; s. Samuel B. and Belle (Bernstein) R.; m. Susan Wechsler, Feb. 6, 1965; children: Amy, Isabel, Abigail. BS, Yale U., 1954; MA, NYU, 1969, PhD, 1978. Ptnr. Rose Assocs., N.Y.C., 1956—; trustee Tchrs. Coll., Columbia U. Contbr. articles to profl. mil. jours. Trustee Jewish Mus. of N.Y., 1992—, Internat. Ctr. Photography; bd. visitors Boston U. Med. Sch., 1978—, past chmn.; bd. dirs. Sta. WNET (PBS), Lincoln Ctr. Theater, 1992—. Mem. Internat. Inst. Strategic Studies, Council Fgn. Relations, Century Assn. Jewish. Clubs: Yale of N.Y.; Army and Navy (Washington). Office: Rose Assocs 200 Madison Ave New York NY 10016-3998

ROSE, ELIZABETH, author, satirist, poet, publisher, environmental poisoning expert; b. N.Y.C., Sept. 18, 1941; children: Kimberly, Dana. Nurse, Lenox Hill Hosp. Sch. Nursing, 1962; BA summa cum laude, U. Redlands, 1976. Asst. head nurse emergency room N.Y.C., 1963-66; head nurse San Pedro (Calif.) Hosp., 1968-69; pub. Butterfly Pub. Co., Santa Monica, 1985; radio and TV personality L.A., 1985—; founder Candida Anonymous, Santa Monica, 1985; cons. health profls. Author: Lady of Gray: Healing Candida-The Nightmare Chemical Epidemic, 1985, 2d edit. 1987, 3d edit. 1989, Sainthood and Single Motherhood, 1990. Recipient Internat. World Leader award, Cambridge, Eng., 1989; N.Y. State Regents scholar, 1959. Mem. UCLA Alumni Assn. (life), Cousteau Soc., Tesla Soc., L.A. Blue Book Club. Avocations: plays and movies, ice skating, crossword puzzles, dancing, reading.

ROSE, ERNST, dentist; b. Oldenburg, Germany, July 22, 1932; s. William and Elsie (Lowenbach) R.; came to U.S., 1940, naturalized, 1946; m. Shirley Mae Glassman, Dec. 24, 1960; children: Ruth Ellen, Michele Ann, Daniel Scot, Seth Joseph. BS, Georgetown U., 1955; DDS, Western Res. U., 1963. Intern, Waterbury (Conn.) Hosp., 1964; pvt. practice dentistry, Hubbard, Ohio, 1964—; pres., treas. Dr. Ernst Rose, Inc. Lab. instr. Ohio State U., Columbus, 1956-57; dental adviser Assoc. Neighborhood Ctr. Mem. Liberty Twp. Zoning Commn., 1967-74, 1988-92, vice chmn.; chmn., 1970-74, chmn., 1990; chmn. Hubbard (Ohio) Urban Renewal Com., 1968-74. Mem. brotherhood bd., 1967—, treas. 1971-73, 88-90, pres. 1975-77, 90-92, temple bd. dirs. 1975-84, 89-95. Served with AUS, 1957-59. Mem. ADA, Ohio Dental Assn., Corydon Palmer Dental Soc. (mem. coun. 1983-87), Warren Dental Soc., Hubbard C. of C. (bd. dirs. 1967—, v.p. 1995—), Jewish Chatauqua Soc. (life), Alpha Omega (council mem. 1968—, sec. 1970-71, v.p. 1971-72, pres. 1972-73, pres. 1989-90). Lodges: B'nai B'rith (pres. 1970-71, trustee 1971—), Rotary (vice chmn. Kashrut com. 1983-85, chmn. Kashrut com. 1985—, vice chmn. Mikvah com. 1983-93). Home: 418 Arbor Cir Youngstown OH 44505-1916 Office: 30 N Main St Hubbard OH 44425-1653

ROSE, EVANS, JR., lawyer; b. Sewickley, Pa., Mar. 10, 1932; s. Evans and Jane Eline (Murphy) R.; m. Patricia Stallings, July 16, 1983; children: Virginia, Susan, Henry, Hilary, Jennifer. A.B., Yale U., 1954; J.D., U. Pitts., 1959. Bar: Pa. 1960. Assoc. firm Rose, Schmidt, Hasley & DiSalle, Pitts., Washington and Harrisburg, 1960-64; ptnr. Rose, Schmidt, Hasley & DiSalle, 1964-90, sr. ptnr., 1970-90, co-mng. ptnr., 1985-86, mng. ptnr., 1986-89, chmn., 1989-90; dir. Cohen & Grigsby, P.C., 1990—, exec. com., 1992—; bd. dirs. Dietrich Industries, Inc., The Stackpole Corp., Integra Trust Co.; chmn. Pa. Client Security Fund, 1994—; pres. coun. Borough of Sewickley Heights; sec. Fed. Ct. Nominating Commn. of Pa., 1977-81; chmn. Appellate Ct. Nominating Commn. of Pa., 1979-81. Article editor: U. Pitts. Law Rev, 1958-59. Trustee West Penn Hosp., Pitts., Carnegie Hero Fund Commn., U. Pitts.; chmn. Pa. Republican Fin. Com., 1979; del. Rep. Nat. Conv., 1976, 80; chmn. fin. com. Rep. Gov.'s Assn., 1985. Served with U.S. Army, 1954-56. Mem. Am. Law Inst., Law Allegheny County (Pa.) Bar Assn., ABA, Pa. Bar Assn. Republican. Presbyterian. Clubs: Duquesne, Rolling Rock, Allegheny Country. Home: Scaife Rd Sewickley PA 15143 Office: 2900 Cng Towers Pittsburgh PA 15222

ROSE, FREDERICK PHINEAS, builder and real estate executive; b. N.Y.C., Nov. 16, 1923; s. Samuel and Belle (Bernstein) R.; m. Sandra Priest, June 28, 1948; children: Deborah, Jonathan Frederick Phineas, Samuel Priest, Adam Raphael. B.C.E., Yale U., 1944. V.p. Rose Assocs., Inc., N.Y.C., 1946-60, pres., 1960-80, chmn., 1980—; vice chmn. N.Y. State Facilities Devel. Corp., 1970-75, Phoenix Home Life Mut. Ins. Co., 1972-93; mem. publs. com. Commentary Mag., 1964—, chmn. publs. com., 1979-84; trustee United Mut. Savs. Bank, 1977-82, Consol. Edison Co. N.Y., 1977-79; gov. N.Y. Real Estate Bd., 1972-75, 86-89, 94—; mem. Coun. Fgn. Rels.; U.S. del. to UN Conf. on Housing, Planning, and Bldg. Rsch., 1962-63, 67; bd. dirs. Olympia & York Co. Pres. Fedn. Jewish Philanthropies of N.Y., 1974-77, chmn. bd. dirs., 1981-83, hon. chmn., 1983—; vice chmn. Greater N.Y. Fund, 1974-76; bd. dirs. Henry Kaufmann Campgrounds, 1950-66, pres., 1962-66; trustee Lexington Sch. for Deaf, 1954-70, Mills Coll. Edn., 1960-68, Children's Aid Soc., 1964-75; trustee Scarsdale (N.Y.) Bd. Edn., 1966-71, pres., 1969-70; trustee Mt. Sinai Sch. Medicine, Hosp. and Med. Ctr., 1966-73, Rockefeller U., 1984—, Citizens Budget Commn., N.Y.C., 1969-94, Energy Fund, 1970-75, Inst. Pub. Adminstrn., 1970-81, Asia Soc., 1976-82, 94—, Philharm. Symphony Soc. N.Y., Inc., 1979—, Aspen Inst. Humanistic Studies, 1979-91, Met. Mus. Art, 1981—, Manhattan Inst., 1987—, Yale U., 1989-94, Am. Mus. Natural History, 1991—; trustee, treas. Jewish Communal Fund, 1982-85; trustee Inst. Internat. Edn., 1984-89; chmn. bd. govs. Assn. Yale Alumni, 1972-75; bd. dirs. N.Y.C. Partnership, Inc., 1982-90, Lincoln Ctr. for the Performing Arts, Inc., 1984—, vice chmn., 1991—; mem. Univ. Council Yale U., 1976-81; trustee Rye Hist. Soc., 1992-94. Served to lt. (j.g.) USNR, World War II. Recipient Yale medal, 1976, Urban Leadership award N.Y. U., 1978, Patron of Art award Yale Sci. and Engring. Soc., 1991; Jonathan Edwards Coll. fellow. Mem. Union League Club N.Y. Clubs: Century Assn., Beach Point Yacht, Century Country; Yale (N.Y.C.). Home: 8 S Manursing Is Rye NY 10580-4310 Office: Rose Assocs Inc 200 Madison Ave New York NY 10016-3998

ROSE, GREGORY MANCEL, neurobiologist; b. Eugene, Oreg., Feb. 3, 1953; s. Mancel Lee and Ilione (Schenk) R.; m. Kathleen Ann Frye, June 30, 1979; 1 child, Julian Mancel. BS cum laude, U. Calif., Irvine, 1975, PhD, 1980. Research fellow M.P.I. for Psychiatry, Munich, 1976; rsch. assoc. Miescher Labor, M.P.I., Tuebingen, Republic of Germany, 1980-81; regular fellow dept. pharmacology U. Colo. Health Sci. Ctr., Denver, 1981-84, asst. prof., 1984-89, assoc. prof., 1989—; rsch. biologist VA Med. Ctr., Denver, 1981—, co-dir. neurosci. tng. program, 1986-89, assoc. rsch. career scientist, 1989—. Achievements include discovery of importance of stimulus patterning for induction of hippocampal synaptic plasticity. Bd. dirs. Greater Park Hill Community, 1987-90. VA Rsch. Svc. grantee, 1984, 86, 89, 93, NSF grantee, 1988, 90, NIMH grantee, 1989, 94, NIA grantee, 1991. Mem. AAAS, Am. Aging Assn., Soc. Neurosci., Internat. Brain Rsch. Orgn., N.Y. Acad. Sci. Democrat. Episcopalian. Avocations: fine woodworking, fly fishing. Office: VA Med Ctr Med Rsch 151 1055 Clermont St Denver CO 80220-3308

ROSE, HENRY, lawyer; b. Olean, N.Y., Mar. 28, 1927; s. Irving and Sarah (Cohen) R.; m. Norma Lefcowitz, Feb. 16, 1957 (div. 1981); children: Benjamin, Andra, Jonathan. BA cum laude, U. Buffalo, 1950, LLB cum laude, 1951. Bar: N.Y. 1951, D.C. 1953, U.S. Ct. Appeals (D.C., 2nd, 3d, 4th, 5th, 6th, 9th, 10th cirs.), U.S. Dist. Ct. (we. and so. dists.) N.Y., U.S. Dist. Ct. (so. dist.) Tenn., U.S. Supreme Ct. 1956. Sterling fellow Yale U., New Haven, 1956-57; atty. NLRB, 1952-53; pvt. practice Buffalo, 1953-56; assoc. prof. U. Toledo, Ohio, 1957-58, Rutgers U., Camden and Newark, N.J., 1958-62; from spl. asst. to solicitor, dep. assoc. solicitor for legislation and legal counsel U.S. Dept. Labor, Washington, 1962-70, assoc. solicitor, 1970-74; gen. counsel Pension Benefit Guaranty Corp., Washington, 1974-84; ptnr., chmn. employee benefits dept. Epstein Becker & Green, P.C., Washington, 1985-92, of counsel, 1993-95; pvt. practice, Washington, 1995—; teaching assoc. Northwestern U., 1951-52; part-time lectr. U. Buffalo, 1954-56, U. Va., 1968; guest lectr. Harvard U., Am. U., Cath. U., Georgetown U., George Washington U.; acad. visitor London Sch. Econs., 1971-72; speaker in field. Contbr. articles to profl. jours. Asst. spl. counsel emergency crime com. Chgo. City Coun., 1952. Rsch. grantee Ford Found., 1959. Mem. ABA (chmn. joint com. on employee benefits 1995-96), D.C. Bar Assn. Home: 700 New Hampshire Ave NW Washington DC 20037-2406

ROSE, HUGH, management consultant; b. Evanston, Ill., Sept. 10, 1926; s. Howard Gray and Catherine (Wilcox) R.; m. Mary Moore Austin, Oct. 25, 1952; children: Susan, Nancy, Gregory, Matthew, Mary. BS in Physics, U. Mich., 1951, MS in Geophysics, 1952; MBA with highest distinction, Pepperdine U., 1982. Mgr. Caterpillar, Inc., Peoria, Ill., 1952-66; v.p., mktg. mgr. Cummins Engine Co., Columbus, Ind., 1966-69; pres., CEO Cummins Northeastern, Inc., Boston, 1969-77; pres. Power Systems Assocs., L.A., 1980-83, C.D. High Tech., Inc., Austin, Tex., 1984-87; mgmt. cons. Rose and Assocs., Tucson, 1984, 87—. Contbr. paleontol. articles to various publs. Bd. dirs. Raymond Alf Mus., Claremont, Calif., 1975—, Comstock Found., Tucson, 1988, Environ. Edn. Exch., 1991, Heart Ctr. U. Ariz.,

Tucson, 1992. With USAAF, WWII. Fellow AAAS; mem. Acacia, Soc. Vertebrate Paleontology, Beacon Soc. Boston (pres. 1979-80), Algonquin Club Boston (v.p., bd. dirs. 1974-80), Duxbury Yacht Club, Longwood Cricket Club, Phi Beta Kappa, Delta Mu Delta, Sigma Gamma Epsilon, Beta Beta Beta. Republican. Presbyterian. Office: Rose & Assocs 5320 N Camino Sumo Tucson AZ 85718-5132

ROSE, HUGH, retired economics educator; b. London, July 20, 1920; came to U.S., 1960, naturalized, 1977; s. William and Ann (Ogus) R. Student, Oxford (England) U., England, 1939-40, 45-47, Nuffield Coll., England, 1950-52. Lectr. in econs. Rhodes U., South Africa, 1947-50, lectr., 1952-53; lectr. in econs. Exeter U., England, 1954-60; assoc. prof. econs. U. Rochester, N.Y., 1961-63, prof., 1965-70; assoc. prof. econs. U. Toronto, Can., 1963-65; hon. rsch. assoc. Harvard U., Cambridge, Mass., 1969-70; prof. econs. Johns Hopkins U., Balt., 1970-91. Author: Macroeconomic Dynamics, 1991; contbr.a rticles to profl. jours. With British Army, 1940-45. Home: 112 Cross Keys Rd Apt D Baltimore MD 21210-1536 Office: Johns Hopkins U Dept Econs 3400 N Charles St Baltimore MD 21218-2608

ROSE, ISRAEL HAROLD, mathematics educator; b. New Britain, Conn., May 17, 1917; s. Abraham and Dora (Dubrow) R.; m. Pearl Nitzberg, Jan. 24, 1942 (div. Feb. 1956); 1 son, Steven Philip; m. Susan Ann Lazarus, Mar. 26, 1961; children: Dora, Eric. Student, CCNY, 1934-36; A.B., Bklyn. Coll., 1938, A.M., 1941; Ph.D., Harvard, 1951. Tutor, instr. Bklyn. Coll., 1938-41; instr. Pa. State Coll., 1942-46; asst. prof. U. Mass., 1948-54, assoc. prof., 1954-60; faculty Hunter Coll., 1960-68, prof. math., 1965-68, chmn. dept., 1966-68; prof. math. Lehman Coll., CUNY, 1968-82, prof. emeritus, 1983—, chmn. dept., 1968-72, 80-82, resident prof., 1983—; Vis. asst. prof. Mt. Holyoke Coll., 1951-52, vis. assoc. prof., 1954-55, 58-59; sci. cons. AID, India, summer 1965. Author: A Modern Introduction to College Mathematics, 1959, Algebra: An Introduction to Finite Mathematics, 1963, Vectors and Analytic Geometry, 1968, Elementary Functions: A Precalculus Primer, 1973, (with Esther R. Phillips) Elementary Functions, 1978. NRC predoctoral fellow Harvard, 1946-48; fellow Fund Advancement Edn., 1952-53. Mem. Am. Math. Soc., Math. Assn. Am. (chmn. Met. N.Y. sect. 1973-75), Nat. Council Tchrs. Math., Assn. Tchrs. Math. New Eng. (pres. Conn. Valley sect. 1956-57), Sigma Xi (pres. Hunter Coll. chpt. 1966-67). Home: 18 Floral Dr Hastings Hdsn NY 10706-1202 Office: Lehman Coll Bedford Park Blvd W Bronx NY 10468

ROSE, JALEN, professional basketball player; b. Detroit, Jan. 30, 1970; s. Jeanne R. Student, U. Mich. Guard Denver Nuggets, 1994—. Named Honorable Mention All-Am., AP, 1991; set Michigan freshman scoring record, 1991; selected as All-Am., Parade Magazine, Third-Team All-Am., USA Today; set Nuggets' rookie record for assists, 1994-95 season; named to All-Rookie Second Team, NBA, 1995;. Office: Denver Nuggets 1635 Clay St Denver CO 80204*

ROSE, JAMES MCKINLEY, JR., lawyer, government official; b. N.Y.C., Aug. 8, 1927; m. Anne Louise Bourne, Aug. 19, 1960; children: Anne Clark, Louise Barnes. Grad., Phillips Exeter Acad., 1946; B.A., Princeton U., 1951; J.D., Harvard U., 1954. Bar: N.Y. 1955, D.C. 1977. With firm Dewey, Ballantine, Bushby, Palmer & Wood, N.Y.C., 1954-57; asst. U.S. atty. So. Dist. N.Y., 1957-61; legal asst. to pres. Atlantic Mut. Ins. Co., 1961-65, sec., counsel, 1965-71; asst. fed. ins. adminstr. U.S. Dept. Housing and Urban Devel., Washington, 1971-81; exec. asst. to adminstr. Fed. Ins. Adminstrn., Fed. Emergency Mgmt. Agy., Washington, 1981-93. Mem. men's com. Am. Mus. Natural History, 1968-71. Served with AUS, 1946-47. Mem. D.C. Bar Assn., Bar Assn. City of N.Y., St. Nicholas Soc., Prouts Neck Assn. (pres. 1979-85). Republican. Episcopalian (sr. warden) Clubs: Prouts Neck (Maine) Country; Chevy Chase (Washington). Home: 4913 Rodman St NW Washington DC 20016-3238

ROSE, JAMES TURNER, aerospace consultant; b. Louisburg, N.C., Sept. 21, 1935; s. Frank Rogers and Mary Burt (Turner) R.; m. Daniele Raymond, Sept. 15, 1984; children by previous marriage—James Turner, Katharine S. B.S. with high honors, N.C. State U., 1957. Aero. research engr. NASA, Langley Field, Va., 1957-59; project engr. NASA (Mercury and Gemini), Langley Field, Va. and Houston, 1959-64; program systems mgr. McDonnell Douglas Astronautics Co (MDAC), St. Louis, 1964-69; mgr. shuttle ops. and implementation (MDAC) McDonnell Douglas Astronautics Co., St. Louis, 1969-72; mgr. shuttle support (MDAC) St. Louis, 1972-74; dir. space shuttle engring. NASA, Washington, 1974-76; mgr. space processing programs McDonnell Douglas Astronautics Co., St. Louis, 1976-83; dir. electrophoresis ops. in space McDonnell Douglas Astronautics Co (MDAC), St. Louis, 1983-86; asst. adminstr. comml. programs NASA, Washington, 1987-91; aerospace cons., 1992—. Recipient Lindberg award for mgmt. leadership AIAA, 1983, Presdl. Meritorious Rank award, 1989, NASA Exceptional Svc. medal, 1990, Laurels award Aviation Week, 1990, Aerospace Contribution to Soc. award AIAA, 1993. Mem. Phi Kappa Phi. Episcopalian.

ROSE, JEFFREY RAYMOND, economist, educator, negotiator; b. Toronto, Ont., Can., Sept. 23, 1946; s. Albert and Thelma (Harris) R.; m. Sandra Black; 1 child, Adam. B.A. with honors, U. Toronto, 1968, M.Indsl. Relations, 1983; postgrad., London Sch. Econs., 1968-69. Planner planning dept. City of Toronto, 1976-80; pres. local 79 Can. Union Pub. Employees, Toronto, 1980-83; nat. pres. Can. Union Pub. Employees, Ottawa, Ont., 1983-91; dep. min. intergovtl. affairs Govt. of Ont., Toronto, 1991-95; sr. fellow Harrowston program in conflict mgmt.-negotiation U. Toronto, 1995—; gen. v.p. Can. Labour Congress, 1983-91. Exec. mem. Ont. New Dem. Party, 1982-91; bd. dirs. Inst. for Rsch. on Pub. Policy, 1988-91; mem. fed. coun. New Dem. Party, 1988-91; co-chmn. Ont.-Que. Commn. for Cooperation, 1991-95. Home: 55 Sunnydene Crescent, Toronto, ON Canada M4N 3J5 Office: U Toronto Faculty Law, Rm 3029 Laskin Libr, Toronto, ON Canada M5S 2C5

ROSE, JOEL ALAN, legal consultant; b. Bklyn., Dec. 26, 1936; s. Edward Isadore and Adele R.; BS in Econs., N.Y.U., 1958; MBA, Wharton Grad. Sch., U. Pa., 1960; m. Isadora Fenig, Apr. 12, 1964; children: Susan, Terri. Asst. purchasing agt. Maidenform, Inc., N.Y.C., 1960-62; personnel dir. E.J. Korvette, Inc., N.Y.C., 1962-66; mgmt. cons. Daniel J. Cantor & Co., Inc., Phila., 1966—, sr. v.p., 1987—; prin. Joel Alan Rose & Assocs. Inc., Cherry Hill, N.J., 1987—; mgmt. cons. to legal profession; coordinator Ann. Conf. on Law Firm Mgmt. and Econs. Served with U.S. Army, 1960, Res. 1960-66. Fellow Coll. of Law Practice Mgmt.; mem. Inst. Mgmt. Cons., Am. Arbitration Assn. (nat. panel), ABA (chmn. acquisition and mergers com., practice mgmt. sect., large law firm interest group), Adminstrv. Mgmt. Soc. (past chpt. pres.), Am. Mgmt. Assn., Assn. Legal Adminstrs. Author: Managing the Law Office; mem. adv. bd. Law Office Economics and Management; contbg. columnist N.Y. Law Jour. Nat. Law Jour.; also articles; bd. editors Acctg. For Law Firms; edit. adv. bd. Corp. Counsel's Guide to Law Dept. Mgmt. Office: Joel A Rose & Assoc Inc 1766 Rolling Ln PO Box 162 Cherry Hill NJ 08003-0162

ROSE, JOHN CHARLES, physician, educator; b. N.Y.C., Dec. 13, 1924; s. Hugh Stanley and Marie-Louise (Delury) R.; m. Dorothy Anne Donnelly, June 26, 1948; children—Nancy, Ellen, John Charles, Richard, Christopher. B.S., Fordham U., 1946; M.D. magna cum laude, Georgetown U., 1950, D.Sc. (hon.), 1973; LL.D. (hon.), Mt. St. Mary's Coll., 1973. Diplomate: Am. Bd. Internal Medicine, Am. Bd. Family Practice. Intern Walter Reed Army Hosp., 1950-51; resident, research fellow Georgetown U., VA hosps., Washington, 1950-54; established investigator Am. Heart Assn., 1954-57; instr., asst. prof. medicine Georgetown U., 1954-57, coord. med. edn., 1957-58, assoc. prof. physiology and biophysics, 1958-60, prof., 1960-91, chmn. dept. physiology and biophysics, 1958-63, dean Sch. Medicine, 1963-73, 78-79, prof. medicine, 1973-91, prof. emeritus, 1991—, vice chancellor Med. Ctr., 1984-87. Assoc. editor Am. Family Physician, 1955-62, chief med. editor, 1962-88; assoc. editor Acad. Medicine, 1992-95; contbr. articles to sci. pubs. Bd. dirs. Charles E. Culpeper Found. Served to 2d lt. USAAF, 1943-45. Decorated Air medal. Fellow A.C.P.; mem. Am. Physiol. Soc., Biophys. Soc. (charter), Soc. Exptl. Biology and Medicine (nat. councillor 1962-63), Am. Heart Assn. (fellow sect. circulation). Club: Cosmos (Washington). Home: 5710 Surrey St Chevy Chase MD 20815-5520

ROSE, JOHN THOMAS, finance educator; b. Ft. Worth, Aug. 20, 1943; s. Paul Pittman and Francis Nan (White) R.; m. Sandra Kaye Rolen, Sept. 5, 1969; children: Melanie Ann, Leah Nan, Lynnelle Renee. BA with honors, Tex. A&M U., 1965; MA, Washington U., St. Louis, 1968, PhD, 1976. Economist Bd. Govs. of Fed. Reserve System, Washington, 1972-82, sr. economist, 1982-84; Harriette L. and Walter G. Lacy, Jr. prof. of banking Baylor U., Waco., Tex., 1984—. Contbr. articles to profl. jours. Bd. visitors Abilene (Tex.) Christian U., 1989-92. Capt. U.S. Army, 1969-71. Decorated Bronze Star U.S. Army; recipient Disting. Bus. Prof. award, 1988, Hankamer Sch. Bus. Baylor U., 1988; Econ. Devel. Adminstrn. U.S. Dept. of Commerce fellow, 1968-69; Ernst & Young Found. Rsch. grantee, 1991. Mem. Am. Fin. Assn., So. Fin. Assn., Southwestern Fin. Assn., Fin. Mgmt. Assn., Omicron Delta Epsilon, Beta Gamma Sigma. Mem. Ch. of Christ. Office: Baylor U Hankamer Sch of Bus Dept Fin Ins and Real Estate PO Box 98004 Waco TX 76798-8004

ROSE, JONATHAN CHAPMAN, lawyer; b. Cleve., June 8, 1941; s. Horace Chapman and Katherine Virginia (Cast) R.; m. Susan Anne Porter, Jan. 26, 1980; 1 son, Benjamin Chapman. A.B., Yale U., 1963; LL.B. cum laude, Harvard U., 1967. Bar: Mass. 1968, D.C. 1972, U.S. Supreme Ct. 1976, Circuit Ct. Appeals 1977, Ohio 1978. Law clk. Justice R. Ammi Cutter, Mass. Supreme Jud. Ct., 1967-68; spl. asst. to U.S. pres., 1971-73; gen. counsel Council on Internat. Econ. Policy, 1973-74; assoc. dept. atty. gen. U.S. Dept. Justice, 1974-75; dept. asst. atty. gen. U.S. Dept. Justice (Antitrust Div.), 1975-77; asst. atty. gen. Office of Legal Policy, 1981-84; ptnr. firm Jones, Day, Reavis & Pogue, Washington, 1977-81, 84—. Prin. Ctr. for Excellence in Govt.; pres. Yale Daily News Found. 1st lt. U.S. Army, 1969-71. Mem. ABA, D.C. Bar Assn., Mass. Bar Assn., Ohio Bar Assn., Fed. Bar Assn., Am. Law Inst. Republican. Episcopalian. Clubs: Met, Chevy Chase, Union, Yale, Harvard. Office: Jones Day Reavis & Pogue 1450 G St NW Ste 600 Washington DC 20005-2001

ROSE, JOSEPH HUGH, clergyman; b. Jewett, Ohio, Nov. 21, 1934; s. Joseph Harper and Lottie Louella (VanAllen) R.; m. Nila Jayne Habig, Feb. 14, 1958; children: J. Hugh II, Stephanie Jayne, David William, Dawnella Jayne. ThB, Apostolic Bible Inst., St. Paul, 1955, DD, 1990. Ordained United Pentecostal Ch. Assoc. min. Calvary Tabernacle, Indpls., 1956-73; Ind. youth sec. United Pentecostal Ch., 1958-60, Ind. youth pres., 1960-72; bd. edn. United Pentecostal Ch., Hazelwood, Mo., 1974—; presbyter Ohio dist. United Pentecostal Ch., 1975—; pastor Harrison Hills Ch., Jewett, Ohio, 1973—. Editor, Ind. Dist. News, 1959-70; narrator radio svc. Harvestime, 1961—. Republican. Avocations: travel, classical music. Office: United Pentecostal Ch 8855 Dunn Rd Hazelwood MO 63042-2212

ROSE, LARRY LEE, newspaper executive; b. Holcomb, Mo., Aug. 17, 1943; s. Harry Rose and Elizabeth Elaine (Kephart) LaFemina; m. Lucinda Patricia Blumenfeld, Dec. 1969 (div. May 1980); 1 child, Kirsten Marie; m. Lauraine Francine Miller, Feb. 6, 1981. BS, Kent State U., 1971. Sect. editor Sun-Sentinel, Ft. Lauderdale, Fla., 1964-66, Miami (Fla.) Herald, 1971-79; news editor Washington Star, 1979-81; asst. mng. editor Dallas Morning News, 1981-87; exec. editor Corpus Christi (Tex.) Caller-Times, 1987-94, exec. v.p., gen. mgr., 1994—; adj. prof. Tex. A&M U., Kingsville, 1989—. With U.S. Army, 1966-69, Vietnam. Recipient Best Daily Newspaper award Press Club Dalla, 1989, 90, 91, 93, 94, 95, 1st Amendment award Scripps Howard Found., 1991, Freedom of Info. award Tex. Associated Press, 1991. Fellow Amundsen Inst.; mem. Am. Soc. Newspaper Editors, Newspaper Assn. Am., Soc. Profl. Journalists, Corpus Christi Country Club, Corpus Christi Town Club. Avocations: photography, painting, travel. Office: Corpus Christi Caller-Times 820 N Lower Broadway St Corpus Christi TX 78401-2025

ROSE, LAURA RAUCH, lawyer; b. Rivera, Calif., Mar. 25, 1958; d. Roscoe Roland and Lola Jane (Swihart) Rauch; m. Gary G. Rose, Feb. 14, 1994. BS in Polit. Sci., Shepherd Coll., 1981; JD, W.Va., 1984. Bar: W.Va 1984; bd. cert. in civil trial advocacy. Assoc. Lewis, Ciccarello, Masinter & Friedberg, Charleston, W.Va., 1984-85, Martin and Seibert, Martinsburg, W.Va., 1985-86, Askin, Pill, Scales and Burke, L.C., 1986-88; ptnr. Greenberg and Coltelli, Martinsburg, 1988-92, Law Offices of Laura Rose and Assocs., Martinsburg, 1992—. Legal editor mag. W.Va. Women, 1985; host Sta. WRNR radio show Legally Speaking. Bd. dirs. Legal Svcs. Plan W.Va., 1988-90; mem. adv. bd. Salvation Army, Martinsburg, Berkeley County Dep. Sheriff Civil Svc. Bd., 1991-92. Named one of Top 10 Women on the Move Tri-State Area, 1993, Ofcl. Belle Boyd B.C. Hist. Soc., 1995-96. Mem. NAFE, Assn. Trial Lawyers Am. (vice chairperson Aquatic Injury Safety Group), W.Va. Bar Assn. (com. mem., bd. dirs. young lawyers div.), W.Va. Trial Lawyers Assn. (bd. govs. 1988—, exec. com. 1990-92, pres. elect 1996), Berkeley County Bar Assn. (pres. 1990-91), Nat. Bd. Trial Advocacy (bd. dirs.), Order of Barristers, Martinsburg/Berkeley County C. of C. Democrat. Office: Law Offices Laura Rose Asso 210 W Burke St Martinsburg WV 25401-3322

ROSE, LEATRICE, artist, educator; b. N.Y.C., June 22, 1924; d. Louis Rose and Edna Ades; m. Sol Greenberg (div.); children: Damon, Ethan; m. Joseph Stefanelli, Oct. 10, 1975. Student, Cooper Union, 1941-45, Arts Students League, 1946, Hans Hoffman Sch., 1947. Solo exhbns. include Hansa Gallery, N.Y.C., 1954, Zabriskie Gallery, N.Y.C., 1965, Landmark Gallery, N.Y.C., 1974, Tibor de Nagy Gallery, N.Y.C., 1975, 78, 81, 82, Elaine Benson Gallery, Bridgehampton, N.Y., 1980, Armstrong Gallery, N.Y.C., 1985, Benton Gallery, Southampton, N.Y., 1987, Cyrus Gallery, N.Y.C., 1989; group exhbns. include Sam Kootz Gallery, N.Y.C., 1950, Peridot Gallery, N.Y.C., 1952, Poindexter Gallery, N.Y.C., 1959, Tanager Gallery, N.Y.C., 1960, 62, Riverside Mus., N.Y.C., 1964, Frumkin Gallery, N.Y.C., 1964, Pa. Acad. Fine Arts, Phila., 1966, N.Y. Cultural Ctr., 1973, The Queens (N.Y.) Mus., 1974, 83, Nat. Acad. Design, N.Y.C., 1974, 75, 76, 92, 93, Weatherspoon Art Gallery, Greensboro, N.C., 78, 81, Whitney Mus. Am. Art, N.Y.C., 1978, Albright-Knox Gallery, Buffalo, 1978, 81, Met. Mus. Art, 1979, Vanderwoude Tananbaum Gallery, N.Y.C., 1982, Benton Gallery, 1986, 87.; public collections include Albrect Gallery, St. Joseph, Mo., Guild Hall Mus., East Hampton, N.Y., Tibor de Nagy, Met. Mus. Art. Grantee N.Y. State Coun. Arts, 1974, The Ingram Merrill Found., 1974, AAUW, 1975, NEA, 1977, Esther and Aldolph Gottlieb Found., 1980, 88; recipient Altman prize NAD, 1974, Phillips prize NAD, 1992, award AAAL, 1992, Am. Inst. Art award. Mem. NAD. Avocations: reading, walking. Office: Apt A924 463 West St New York NY 10014

ROSE, LLOYD, theatre critic. Office: The Washington Post 1150 15th St NW Washington DC 20071-0001

ROSE, MARGARETE ERIKA, pathologist; b. Esslingen, Germany, Feb. 12, 1945; came to U.S., 1967; d. Wilhelm Ernst and Lina (Schurr) Pfisterer; m. Arthur Caughey Rose, Feb. 3, 1967; children: Victoria Anne, Alexandra Julia, Frederica Isabella. MD, U. So. Calif., L.A., 1972. Diplomate Am. Bd. Anatomic and Clin. Pathology. Pathologist St. Joseph Med. Ctr., Burbank, Calif., 1977-78, Glenview Pathology Med. Ctr., Culver City, Calif., 1979—; dir. anatomic pathology Glenview Meml. Pathology, Culver City, 1988—; dir. Life Chem. Lab., Woodland Hills, Calif.; co-dir., lab. Holy Cross Med. Ctr., Mission Hills, Calif., 1994-95. Mem. Because I Love You, L.A., 1994. Fellow Am. Soc. Pathology, Coll. Am. Pathology. Avocations: cross-stitching, gardening, traveling. Office: Brotman Med Ctr Dept Pathology 3828 Hughes Ave Culver City CA 90232-2716

ROSE, MARIAN HENRIETTA, physics researcher; b. Brussels, Belgium; (parents Am. citizens); m. Simon Rose, Oct. 20, 1948 (dec. Jan. 1981); children: Ann, James, David, Simon. BA, Barnard Coll., 1942; MA, Columbia U., 1944; PhD, Harvard U., 1947. Teaching fellow Harvard U., Cambridge, Mass., 1945-46; adj. asst. prof. Courant Inst., N.Y.C., 1947-48, rsch. assoc., 1951-65, sr. rsch. scientist, 1965-75; vis. fellow Yale U., New Haven, Conn., 1981-93; bd. dirs. Minna-James-Heineman Stiftung, Essen, Fed. Republic of Germany. Contbr. articles to profl. jours. Bd. dirs. Jay Heritage Ctr., Rye, N.Y.; mem. Wetlands Control Commn., Bedford, N.Y., 1992—, Conservation Bd., Bedford, 1989-93. Mem. Sierra Club (conservatin chair Atlantic chpt. 1992-95, chair N.E. regional conservation com. 1995—, del. at large to Westchester County Environ. Mgmt. Coun. 1994—), Phi Beta Kappa, Sigma Xi. Avocations: skiing, hiking.

ROSE, MARK ALLEN, humanities educator; b. N.Y.C., Aug. 4, 1939; s. Sydney Aaron and Rose (Shapiro) R.; divorced; 1 son, Edward Gordon. A.B. summa cum laude, Princeton, 1961; B.Litt., Merton Coll., Oxford (Eng.) U., 1963; Ph.D., Harvard, 1967. From instr. to assoc. prof. English Yale, 1967-74; prof. English U. Ill., Urbana, 1974-77; prof. English U. Calif., Santa Barbara, 1977—, chmn. English dept., 1987-89; dir. U. Calif. Humanities Rsch. Inst., 1989-94. Author: Heroic Love, 1968, (fiction) Golding's Tale, 1972, Shakespearean Design, 1972, Spenser's Art, 1975, Alien Encounters, 1981, Authors and Owners, 1993; editor: Twentieth Century Views of Science Fiction, 1976, Twentieth Century Interpretations of Antony and Cleopatra, 1977, (with Slusser and Guffey) Bridges to Science Fiction, 1980, Shakespeare's Early Tragedies, 1994. Woodrow Wilson fellow, 1961, Henry fellow, 1961-62, Dexter fellow, 1966, Morse fellow, 1970-71, NEH fellow, 1979-80, 90-91. Mem. MLA, Renaissance Soc. Am., Shakespeare Soc. Am., Phi Beta Kappa. Home: 1135 Oriole Rd Montecito CA 93108-2438

ROSE, MASON H., IV, psychoanalyst; b. Charlevoix, Mich., July 4, 1915; s. Mason III and Catharine (Diebel) R.; m. Marlene Alexander, 1990. Student, Philips Exeter, 1932, U. Fla., 1933, Duke U., 1934, U. So. Calif., 1935; B.A., Inst. Religious Sci., 1939; MS, Calif. Inst. Advanced Studies, 1943, PhD, 1946; LL.D. (hon.), Asso. Univs., Hong Kong, 1959. Tennis profl. The Inn, Charlevoix, 1932-35; lectr. Inst. Religious Sci., 1937-43; pvt. practice psychoanalysis Los Angeles, 1941-81; exec. dir. Nat. Found. Psychol. Research, 1940-60; feature writer L.A. Herald Express, 1945-55; psychol. cons. Med. Found. Am., 1948-62; leader Humanist Ch. of Religious Sci., 1957—; v.p., dean undergrad. sch. Calif. Inst. Advanced Study, 1959-65; chancellor Pacific Inst. Advanced Studies, 1965—; pres. Mason Rose & Assocs.; chmn. Gt. Books of Modern World, 1959—; exec dir. Olympic League Am., 1967—; bd. dirs. Ctr. Organic Ecology, 1968—, Everywoman's Village, 1960-70, Disease Prevention and Life Extension Ctr.; cons. World Ecology Corp., 1969—, World Environ. Systems, 1970—. Author: You and Your Personality, 1944, Community Plan for the Returning Serviceman, 1945, Sex Education from Birth to Maturity, 1948, Creative Education, 1953, Humanism as Religion, 1959, The Nutra-Bio-Zyme Soil Management System, 1969, The Nutra-Bio-Zyme Manutrol system, 1970, Bio-N-Gest Sewage Treatment and Water Reclamation System, 1970, Bio-N-Gest Waste Recycling System, 1970, Bio-Dynamics, 1970, The Island Tribe, 1971, New Hopes for the Emotionally Disturbed Child, 2nd 1974, Humanics Health System, 1975, Medical Survey of Nutrition for Pregnancy and Lactation, 1976, How to Provide Optimum Nutrition for You and Your Child, 1978, Suntanning, The World's Most Dangerous Sport, 1979, How to Scare Your Teenager Straight, 1980, Radiant Living, 1986, Multimodal System for the Management of Pain and Stress, 1987, Glasscrete System of Construction, 1987, Macho Manifesto, How to Avoid Rape, 1991, Glamorous Hollywood-Fabulous Hollywood, 1994; syndicated newspaper column You and Your Child, 1950-54; TV programs, 1951-52. Mem. AAAS, NAACP, ACLU, Fedn. Am. Scientists, Soc. Social Responsibility in Sci., Aircraft Owners and Pilots Assn., Helms Athletic Found. (life), So. Calif. Olympic Games Com., Philips Exeter Acad. Alumni Assn., PEN, So. Calif. Publicists, Trojan Football Alumni, Athletic Club (L.A.), Press Club (L.A., adv. bd. 1952-75). *During forty years of clinical psychoanalysis my constant preoccupation has been to develop a wholistic treatment individualized to the human person. This has resulted in the concept of human ecology which utilizes biopsyen, i.e. biological-psychological-environmental therapy.*

ROSE, MERRILL, public relations counselor; b. Beaufort, N.C., Apr. 20, 1955; d. Robert Lloyd Rose and Betty Lou (Merrill) Ellis. Student, U. N.C., 1977. Reporter, editor Consumer News, Washington, 1978-79; v.p. Fraser/Assocs., Washington, 1979-82; sr. assoc. Porter/Novelli, Washington, 1982-85, v.p., 1985-87; sr. v.p., food practice leader Porter/Novelli, N.Y.C., 1989-91, exec. v.p., 1990—; gen. mgr. Chgo. Porter/Novelli, 1991—. Bd. dirs. CARE, 1991—; bd. visitors U. N.C. Sch. Journalism, Chapel Hill, 1992—; bd. dirs. Friends of Prentice affiliate Northwestern Meml. Hosp., 1993—; mem. accrediting com. Accrediting Coun. for Edn. in Journalism and Comm., 1994—. Mem. Am. Inst. of Wine and Food, Pub. Rels. Soc. Am. Office: Porter/Novelli 303 E Wacker Dr Ste 12 Chicago IL 60601-5212

ROSE, MICHAEL DEAN, lawyer, educator; b. Johnstown, Pa., Oct. 22, 1937; s. Theodore Earl and Geraldine Ethel (Boyer) R.; m. Veda Sue Garber, June 27, 1959; children: Christopher John, Susan Elizabeth. BA, Ohio Wesleyan U., 1959; JD, Case Western Res. U., 1963; LLM, Columbia U., 1967. Bar: Ohio 1963. Assoc. firm Porter, Stanley, Treffinger & Platt, Columbus, Ohio, 1963-66; asst. prof. law Ohio State U., Columbus, 1967-69, assoc. prof., 1969-72, prof., 1972—, Lawrence D. Stanley prof. law, 1987—; staff asst. to chief counsel IRS, Washington, 1970-71. Author: (with Leo J. Raskind) Advanced Federal Income Taxation: Corporate Transactions, 1978, (with Joseph S. Platt) A Federal Taxation Primer, 1973, Hornbook on Federal Income Taxation, 3d edit., 1988; editor Selected Federal Taxation Statutes and Regulations, 1973—, Ohio Will Manual, 1986—. Fellow Am. Coll. Trust and Estate Counsel; mem. Am. Law Inst. Home: 1327 Friar Ln Columbus OH 43221-1527 Office: Ohio State U 55 W 12th Ave Columbus OH 43210-1391

ROSE, MICHAEL THOMAS, state legislator, lawyer; b. Charleston, S.C., Oct. 13, 1947; s. Artman Alvin Rose and Lynnette Marguerite (Davis) Pullen; m. Vivian Osborn, May 25, 1985. BS, USAF Acad., 1969; JD, NYU, 1973; MBA, Harvard U., 1981. Bar: Pa., 1973, Calif. 1975, Minn., 1978, Colo. 1981, S.C. 1983, U.S. Dist. Cts., U.S. Ct. Claims, U.S. Ct. Mil. Appeals, U.S. Supreme Ct. Atty. Robins, Davis & Lyons, St. Paul, 1977-79; exec. dir. Farmers Assistance Relief Mission Inc., Summerville, S.C., 1986-94; mem. S.C. Senate, 1988—; vice chmn. Rep. Forum, 1989-91; S.C. chmn. Am. Legis. Exch. Coun., 1990-91. Editor NYU Law Rev., 1971-73; contbr. articles to profl. jours. Founder Save the Yorktown, Inc.; founder, dir. Adopt-A-Cow Program; chmn. Dorchester County Legis. Delegation, 1989-90, 94-95; active Bethany United Meth. Ch.; project dir. Entrepreneurship Ctr. U. Charleston, 1994-95. Capt. USAF, 1969-74. Decorated Order of Palmetto, Gov. S.C.; named Outstanding State Legislator, Am. Legis. Exchange Coun., 1990. Mem. Summerville Noon Lions Club, Goose Creek Rotary Club, Summerville Lodge, Elks. Avocations: travel, sports, genealogy. Home: 409 Central Ave Summerville SC 29483-5903 Office: Mortimer Leiendecker & Rose 1410 Trolley Rd Summerville SC 29485-8293

ROSE, MICHEL, construction materials company executive. Pres., CEO Lafarge Corp., Reston, Va., 1992—. Office: Lafarge Corp 11130 Sunrise Valley Dr Ste 300 Reston VA 22091-4329*

ROSE, MILTON CURTISS, lawyer; b. Cleve., June 5, 1904; s. Benjamin Holly and Evelyn (Curtiss) R.; m. Emily White Mason, Sept. 6, 1930; children: Stephen Curtiss, Mason Curtiss, Jonathan Holly. Grad., Phillips Exeter Acad., 1923; A.B., Williams Coll., 1927; LL.B., Harvard, 1930. Bar: N.Y. bar 1932. Asso. Baldwin, Hutchins & Todd, N.Y.C., 1930-38; partner firm Mudge, Rose, Guthrie Alexander & Ferdon (and predecessor firms), N.Y.C., 1938—. Bd. dirs. Royal Soc. Medicine Found., Gustavus and Louise Pfeiffer Research Found.; life trustee Pfeiffer Coll.; trustee Shaker Community, Inc.; bd. overseers emeritus Simon's Rock; bd. dirs., v.p., sec. Mario Negri Inst. Found. Mem. ABA, N.Y. State Bar Assn., Assn. of Bar of City of N.Y., N.Y. County Lawyers Assn., Century Assn. (N.Y.C.), Grolier Club (N.Y.C.), University Club (N.Y.C.). Presbyterian. Home: PO Box 427 Great Barrington MA 01230-0427

ROSE, NOEL RICHARD, immunologist, microbiologist, educator; b. Stamford, Conn., Dec. 3, 1927; s. Samuel Allison and Helen (Richard) R.; m. Deborah S. Harber, June 14, 1951; children: Alison, David, Bethany, Jonathan. BS, Yale U., 1948; MA, U. Pa., 1949, PhD, 1951; MD, SUNY, Buffalo, 1964; MD (hon.), U. Cagliari, Italy, 1990; ScD (hon.), U. Sassari, Italy, 1992. From instr. to prof. microbiology SUNY Sch. Medicine, Buffalo, 1951-73; dir. Center for Immunology SUNY Sch. Medicine, 1970-73, dir. Erie County Labs., 1964-70; dir. WHO Collaborating Center for Autoimmune Disorders, 1968—; prof. immunology and microbiology, chmn. dept. immunology and microbiology Wayne State U. Sch. Medicine, 1973—82; prof., chmn. dept. immunology and infectious diseases Johns Hopkins U. Sch. Hygiene and Pub. Health, Balt., 1082-93, prof. medicine and environ. health scis., 1982—, prof. molecular microbiology and immunology, 1993—; prof. pathology, dir. immunology Johns Hopkins U. Sch. Medicine, 1994—; cons. in field. Editor: (with others) International Convocation on Immunology, 1969, Methods in Immunodiagnosis, 1973, 3d rev. edit., 1986, The Autoimmune Diseases, 1986, 2d edit., 1992, Microbiology, Basic Principles and Clinical Applications, 1983 Principles of Immunology,

1973, 2d rev. edit., 1979, Specific Receptors of Antibodies, Antigens and Cells, 1973, Manual of Clinical Laboratory Immunology, 1976, 2d rev. edit., 1980, 4d edit. 1992, Genetic Control of Autoimmune Disease, 1978, Recent Advances in Clinical Immunology, 1983, Clinical Immunotoxicology, 1992; editor in chief Clin. Immunology and Immunopathology, 1988—; contbr. articles to profl. jours. Recipient award Sigma Xi, 1952, award Alpha Omega Alpha, 1976, Lamp award, 1975, Faculty Recognition award Wayne State U. Bd. Govs., 1979, Pres.'s award for excellence in teaching, 1979, Disting. Service award Wayne State U. Sch. Medicine, 1982, U. Pisa medal, 1986; named to Acad. Scholars Wayne State U., 1981; Josiah Macy fellow, 1979. Fellow APHA, Am. Acad. Allergy and Immunology, Am. Acad. Microbiology; mem. AAAS, Acad. Clin. Lab. Physicians and Scientists, Am. Assn. Immunologists, Am. Soc. Investigative Pathology, Am. Soc. Clin. Pathologists, Am. Soc. Microbiology (Abbott Lab. Clin. and Diagnostic Immunology award 1993), Brit. Soc. Immunology, Coll. Am. Pathologists, Sociètè Française d'Immunologie, Can. Soc. Immunology, Soc. Exptl. Biology and Medicine Coun., Clin. Immunology Soc. (sec., treas., pres. 1993), Austrian Immunology Soc. (hon. mem.), Sigma Xi (pres. Johns Hopkins U. chpt. 1988), Alpha Omega Alpha, Delta Omega. Office: Johns Hopkins U Sch Hygiene & Pub Health Dept Molecular Microbiology & Immunology 615 N Wolfe St Baltimore MD 21205-2103

ROSE, PAUL EDWARD, publishing company executive; b. Spokane, Wash., Apr. 27, 1947; s. Albert Edward and Karen (Murray) R.; m. Karen Pearl Rose, Aug. 23, 1971; children: Marcus, David, Julianne. BS, Brigham Young U., 1970, M in Acctg., 1971. CPA, N.Y., Ill. Auditor Ernst & Whinney, N.Y.C., 1971-75; budget mgr. Dun & Bradstreet, N.Y.C., 1975-77; contr., dir. circulation sales Offcl. Airline Guides, Oak Brook, Ill., 1977-82; fin. contr. John Morrell & Co., Northfield, Ill., 1982-83; v.p. fin. Standard Rate and Data Svc., Wilmette, Ill., 1983-85; sr. v.p. Macmillan Directory Div., Wilmette, 1985-87, exec. v.p., 1987-89, pres. Nat. Register Pub. Co., 1989-91; exec. v.p., Directory Div. Reed Reference Pub., Wilmette, 1991; v.p. Landmark Communications, Inc., Norfolk, Va., 1992—; pres. Promotion Info. Mgmt., Chgo., 1992—. Recipient Outstanding Pianist award Wash. State Music Tchrs. Assn., 1968. Mem. AICPA. Office: Landmark Communications Inc 150 W Brambleton Ave Norfolk VA 23510-2018*

ROSE, PETER EDWARD, former professional baseball player and manager; b. Cin., Apr. 14, 1941; s. Harry Rose; m. Karolyn Ann Englehardt (div.); children: Fawn, Peter; m. Carol Woliung, Apr. 1984; children: Cara, Tyler. Player Cin. Reds, 1963-78, player mgr., 1984-87, mgr., 1987-89; player Phila. Phillies, 1979-83, Montreal Expos, 1984; host weekly radio show Pete Rose on Baseball Sta. WCKY, Cin., 1992; now host syndicated show Talk Sports with Pete Rose Sta. WGTO-AM, Orlando, Fla. Author: (with Bob Hertzel) Charlie Hustle, 1975, Winning Baseball, 1976, (with Peter Golenback) Pete Rose on Hitting, 1985, (with Roger Kahn) Pete Rose: My Story, 1989. Named Nat. League Rookie of Yr., 1963, Most Valuable Player, 1973, Most Valuable Player World Series, 1975, Nat. League Player of Yr. The Sporting News, 1968, Ball Player of Decade, 1979; named to Nat. League All-Star Team, 1965, 67-71, 73-79, 80-81. Second player in baseball history to exceed 4000 hits, all time leader in hits. Office: Sta WGTO-AM 821 Marshall Farms Rd Ocoee FL 34761-3316 also: care Sta KCKY-AM 219 Mcfarland St Cincinnati OH 45202-2614

ROSE, PETER ISAAC, sociologist, writer; b. Rochester, N.Y., Sept. 5, 1933; s. Aaron E. and Lillian (Feld) R.; m. Hedwig Hella Cohen, Mar. 25, 1956; children: Elisabeth Anne, Daniel Eric. AB, Syracuse U., 1954; MA, Cornell U., 1957, PhD, 1959. Instr. Goucher Coll., 1958-60; mem. faculty Smith Coll., Northampton, Mass., 1960—; prof., 1967—; chmn. dept. sociology and anthropology Smith Coll., 1967-74, 79-80, Sophia Smith prof., 1973—; dir. Am. Studies Diploma program, 1975—; mem. grad. faculty U. Mass., 1961—; Fulbright prof. U. Leicester, Eng., 1964-65, Kyoto (Japan) Am. Studies Inst., Flinders U., Australia, 1970; vis. prof. Wesleyan U., Middletown, Conn., 1966-67, U. Colo., 1968, Yale U., 1970, Clark U., 1970-71; vis. scholar Harvard U., 1983, 84-85, vis. prof., spring 1984; vis. scholar Chinese Acad. Social Sci., Beijing, 1986; resident scholar Rockefeller Study Ctr., Bellagio, Italy, summer 1987; vis. fellow St. Catherine's Coll., Oxford, spring, 1995, Hoover Instn., Stanford U., 1996. Author: They and We, 1964, 5th edit., 1997, The Subject is Race, 1968, Strangers in Their Midst, 1977, Mainstream and Margins, 1983; co-author: Sociology, 1977, 2d edit., 1982, Understanding Society, 1978, 3d edit., 1968; editor: The Study of Society, 1967, 4th edit., 1977, The Ghetto and Beyond, 1969, Americans From Africa, 1970, Nation of Nations, 1972, reissued, 1981, Seeing Ourselves, 1972, rev. edit., 1975, Socialization and the Life Cycle, 1979, Working With Refugees, 1986, Interminority Relations in the U.S., 1993; co-editor: Through Different Eyes, 1973. Mem. Am. Sociol. Assn. (mem. coun. 1974-77), Mass. Sociol. Assn. (pres. 1967-68), Soc. Study of Social Problems (v.p. 1968-69), Ea. Sociol. Soc. (v.p. 1970-71, pres. 1991-92). Home: 66 Paradise Rd Northampton MA 01060-2907

ROSE, PHYLLIS, English language professional, author; b. N.Y.C., Oct. 26, 1942; d. Eli and Minnie Davidoff; m. Mark Rose, (div. 1975); 1 son, Ted.; m. Laurent de Brunhoff, 1990. BA summa cum laude, Radcliffe Coll., 1964; M.A., Yale U., 1965; Ph.D., Harvard U., 1970. Teaching fellow Harvard U., Cambridge, Mass., 1966-67; acting instr. Yale U., New Haven, 1969; asst. prof. Wesleyan U., Middletown, Conn., 1969-76, assoc. prof., 1976-81, prof. English, 1981—; vis. prof. U. Calif., Berkeley, 1981-82; chmn. fiction jury Nat. Book Awards, 1993; bd. dirs. Wesleyan Writers Conf. Key West Literary Seminar. Author: Woman of Letters: A Life of Virginia Woolf, 1978, Parallel Lives: Five Victorian Marriages, 1983, Writing of Women, 1985, Jazz Cleopatra: Josephine Baker in Her Time, 1989, Never Say Goodbye: Essays, 1991; editor: The Norton Book of Women's Lives, 1993; book reviewer N.Y. Times Book Rev., The Atlantic; essayist; contbr. editor Civilization mag. Nat. Endowment for Humanities fellow, 1973-74; Rockefeller Found. fellow, 1984-85; Guggenheim fellow, 1985. Mem. PEN, Nat. Book Critics Circle, Authors Guild. Home: 122 E 82 2D New York NY 10001 Office: Wesleyan U Dept English Middletown CT 06457

ROSE, REGINALD, television writer, producer; b. N.Y.C., Dec. 10, 1920; s. William and Alice (Obendorfer) R.; children: Jonathan, Richard, Andrew and Steven (twins); m. Ellen McLaughlin, July 6, 1963; children—Thomas, Christopher. Student, Coll. City N.Y., 1937-38. pres. Defender Prodn., Inc., 1961—. Author TV plays, 1951—, including: Twelve Angry Men, 1954, The Sacco Vanzetti Story, 1959, The Defenders, 1961-65, Escape From Sobibor, 1987; film scripts include: Crime in the Streets, 1956, Twelve Angry Men, 1957, Baxter!, 1973, Somebody Killed Her Husband, 1978, The Wild Geese, 1978, The Sea Wolves, 1980, Whose Life Is It Anyway?, 1981; plays include Black Monday, 1962, Twelve Angry Men, 1958, The Porcelain Year, 1965, Principals Only, 1995; books include Six TV Plays, 1956, The Thomas Book, 1972. Pres. Reginald Rose Found., 1963—. Served to 1st lt. AUS, 1942-46. Recipient Emmy awards, 1954, 62, 63; numerous others including Laurel award Writers Guild Am., 1987. Address: 20 Wedgewood Rd Westport CT 06880-2735

ROSE, RICHARD LOOMIS, lawyer; b. Long Branch, N.J., Oct. 21, 1936; s. Charles Frederick Perrott and Jane Mary (Crotta) R.; m. Marian Frances Irons, Apr. 1, 1960; children: Linda, Cynthia, Bonnie. BA, Cornell U., 1958; JD, Washington and Lee U., 1963. Bar: N.Y. 1963, Conn. 1965, U.S. Dist. Ct. (so. dist.) N.Y. 1964, U.S. Dist. Ct. Conn. 1965, U.S. Ct. Appeals (2d cir.) 1965, U.S. Supreme Ct. 1970. Assoc. Cummings & Lockwood, Stamford, Conn., 1965-71; ptnr. Cummings & Lockwood, Stamford, 1971-91, Kleban & Samor, P.C., Southport, 1991-93; of counsel Whitman Breed Abbott & Morgan, Greenwich, Conn., 1993-95; prin. Roberts, Gaillard & Kambas, P.C., Stamford, Conn., 1995—; bd. dirs. and sec. Index Corp., Laing Constrn. Svcs.; bd. dirs. TUV Rhineland N.Am. Inc.; v.p., bd. dirs. OCE Credit Corp.; mem. adv. com. Conn. Banking Commr. on Conn. Securities Laws, 1982—; dir. Conn. World Trade Assn. Editor: Washington and Lee Law Rev. Chmn. Fgn. Trade Zone Com. to Mayor of City of Bridgeport, Conn., 1988-90; mem. fgn. trade awareness com. S.W. Area Industry and Commerce Assn., Task Force, 1987-88. 1st lt. U.S. Army, 1958-60, Korea. Mem. ABA, Conn. Bar Assn. (exec. com. banking sect.), Internat. Bar Assn., New Canaan Country Club, Campfire Club Am. (bd. govs.), Phi Delta Phi, Omicron Delta Kappa, Phi Delta Theta. Republican. Office: Roberts Gaillard & Kambas PO Box 15630 1055 Washington Blvd Stamford CT 06901

ROSE, ROBERT CARLISLE, banker; b. Gutheria, Okla., Aug. 14, 1917; s. Warren Glenn and Elizabeth Aileen (Landenberger) R.; m. Maejeanne Harker, June 17, 1939; children—Sharon Sue, Barbara Ann. Student public schs.; diploma, Sch. Banking, U. Wis., 1962. With Am. Nat. Bank, Vincennes, Ind., 1935—; chmn. bd. dirs. Am. Nat. Bank, 1975—, also dir. Bd. dirs. Vincennes Community Sch. Corp.; sec. Harmony Soc., Vincennes. Served with USNR, World War II. Mem. Ind. Bankers Assn., Independent Bankers Assn. (dir.), Am. Legion, Vincennes C. of C. (dir.). Democrat. Baptist. Club: Elks. Office: Am Nat Bank 302 Main St Vincennes IN 47591

ROSE, ROBERT E(DGAR), state supreme court justice; b. Orange, N.J., Oct. 7, 1939. B.A., Juniata Coll., Huntingdon, Pa., 1961; LL.B., NYU, 1964. Bar: Nev. 1965. Dist. atty. Washoe County, 1971-75; lt. gov. State of Nev., 1975-79; judge Nev. Dist. Ct., 8th Jud. Dist., Las Vegas, 1986-88; justice Nev. Supreme Ct., Carson City, 1989—, chief justice, 1993-94. Office: Nev Supreme Ct 201 S Carson St Carson City NV 89701

ROSE, ROBERT GORDON, lawyer; b. Newark, June 25, 1943; s. Harry and Ann Shirley (Gordon) R.; m. Ellen Nadley Berkowitz, July 2, 1966; children: Lisa Pauline, Michael Allan. BA, SUNY, Buffalo, 1965; MA, Columbia U., 1969; JD, Seton Hall U., 1974. Bar: N.J. 1974, U.S. Dist. Ct. N.J. 1974, U.S. Ct. Appeals (3rd cir.) 1974, U.S. Ct. Appeals (2nd cir.) 1975. Law clk. to Hon. John J. Gibbons U.S. Ct. Appeals (3rd cir.), Newark, 1974-75; assoc. Pitney, Hardin, Kipp & Szuch, Morristown, N.J., 1975-80, ptnr., 1980—. Contbr. articles to profl. jours. Mem. ABA, N.J. Bar Assn., Morris County Bar Assn. (trustee 1989-90). Avocations: travel, philately. Office: Pitney Hardin Kipp & Szuch Pk Ave at Morris County PO Box 1945 Morristown NJ 07962-1945

ROSE, ROBERT HENRY, arts education administrator; b. Butler, Pa., Sept. 10, 1948; s. Robert C. and Olga (Matzko) R.; m. Melanie Sue McKamish, Sept. 12, 1987; children: Aaron, Joseph, Julie. BS, Geneva Coll., Beaver Falls, Pa., 1991; MEd, Pa. State U., 1993. Cert. in environ. protection CDC; cert. in human resource devel. With Armco Steel Corp., Butler, Pa., 1978-83; commd. U.S. Army, 1983, advanced through grades to master sgt., 1992; ret., 1995; dir. Oakbridge Acad. Arts, 1995—. Decorated Purple Heart; Vets. grantee PHEAA, 1990. Mem. Masons, Elks (lecturing knight 1983-84), Strategic Planning Com. Plum Boro Sch. Dist., Pi Lambda Theta. Avocations: running, writing, golf, tennis. Home: 155 Shearer Rd New Kensington PA 15068-9320 Office: 1309 Greesburg Rd Lower Burrell PA 15068

ROSE, ROBERT JOHN, bishop; b. Grand Rapids, Mich., Feb. 28, 1930; s. Urban H. and Maida A. (Glerum) R. Student, St. Joseph Sem., 1944-50; B.A., Seminaire de Philosophie, Montreal, Que., Can., 1952; S.T.L., Pontifical Urban U., Rome, 1956; M.A., U. Mich., 1962. Ordained priest Roman Catholic Ch., 1955; dean St. Joseph Sem., Grand Rapids, 1966-69; dir. Christopher House, Grand Rapids, 1969-71; rector St. John's Sem., Plymouth, Mich., 1971-77; pastor Sacred Heart Parish, Muskegon Heights, Mich., 1977-81; bishop Diocese of Gaylord, Mich., 1981-89, Diocese of Grand Rapids, Mich., 1989—. Mem. Nat. Conf. Cath. Bishops. *

ROSE, ROBERT LAWRENCE, financial services company executive; b. N.Y.C., Mar. 10, 1945; s. Martin and Helen (Diamond) R.; m. Andrea Joan Hoffman, Dec. 27, 1964 (div. June 1972); 1 child, Dawn; m. Julia Frances Knipl, Jan. 2, 1974 (div. Mar. 1991); children—Justin, Adam, Andrew. BS, Mich. State U., 1966; JD, U. Mich., 1969; LLM in Taxation, NYU, 1978. Bar: N.Y., Conn., Calif. Assoc. Kindel & Anderson, 1969-72; owner, mgr. Carol's Restaurant, N.Y.C., 1972-74; assoc. gen. counsel Equitable Life Ins. Co., N.Y.C., 1974-77; tax counsel Conn. Gen. Life Ins. Co., Bloomfield, 1977-80, assoc. gen. counsel, 1980-82; chief counsel employee benefits and fin. services CIGNA Corp., Bloomfield, 1982-84, sr. v.p., chief counsel investment group, 1984-89; v.p. corp. acctg. and planning CIGNA Corp., Phila., 1989-95, v.p. strategic growth and devel., 1995—. Author: Group Insurance Tax, 1980, Annual Meeting-Annuity Taxation, 1983, Tax Shelters, 1984; editor U. Mich. Law Rev., 1968-69, Duke U. Law Jour., 1978. Mem. Leadership Greater Hartford, 1984, Am. Leadership Forum, 1986. Mem. Am. Council Life Ins. (fin. regulatory policy subcom.), U. Conn. Sch. of Law Ins. Inst. (chmn.), Assn. Life Ins. Counsel, Calif. Bar Assn., Conn. Bar Assn., N.Y. Bar Assn. Avocations: skiing, tennis, travel. Office: CIGNA Corp 1 Liberty Pl PO Box 7716 1650 Market St Philadelphia PA 19192-1520

ROSE, ROBERT MICHAEL, materials science and engineering educator; b. N.Y.C., Apr. 15, 1937; s. Lawrence Lapidus and Lillian (Rosen) R.; m. Martha Gibbs, Oct. 15, 1961; children: Cynthia J., James L., Joshua S. S.B., MIT, 1958, Sc.D., 1961. Registered profl. engr., Mass. Asst. prof. materials sci. and engring MIT, Cambridge, 1961-66, assoc. prof., 1966-72, prof., 1972—; dir. MIT Concourse program, 1988—; prof. health scis. and tech. Harvard Med. Sch.- MIT, 1978-90; dir. Cryoelectro Assocs., Wenham, Mass., 1978-90; mem. Mass. Bd. Registration of Profl. Engrs. and Land Surveyors, 1991-93; bd. dirs. Data Tech., Woburn, Mass.; adj. prof. Tufts U. Sch. Vet. Medicine. Author: Structure and Properties of Materials, 1964, Practical Biomechanics for the Orthopedic Surgeon, 1979, 92, The Chicken From Minsk, 1995. Recipient Kappa Delta prize Am. Acad. Orthopedic Surgeons, 1973. Mem. Am. Soc. Metals (vice chmn. 1971-72, Bradley Stoughton prize, chmn. 1972-73), Metal Soc. AIME, Dolphin Yacht Club (Marblehead, Mass.), Boston Yacht Club. Jewish. Home: 18 Morgan St Wenham MA 01984-1114 Office: Room 4-132 MIT 77 Massachusetts Ave Cambridge MA 02139-4301 *I would share my thoughts with you if I were satisfied with what I am. But I submit to you that anyone who is truly satisfied with his personal success doesn't understand the nature of his own achievement. Distrust all advice (including this!).*

ROSE, ROBERT NEAL, brokerage house executive; b. Chgo., Feb. 27, 1951; s. James Allan Rose and Hazel (Gordon) Kaufman; m. Anna Yvette Trujillo, Aug. 23, 1981; children: David James, Michelle Elizabeth, Daniel Jonathan. BS, Georgetown U., 1973; MPA, Harvard U., 1995. Trader Salomon Bros., N.Y.C., 1974-75; regional coord. Latin Am. Merrill Lynch Govt. Securities, N.Y.C., 1975-76; dir. fed. govt. affairs Pub. Service of N.Mex., Albuquerque, 1977-78; exec. dir. Gov. Jerry Apodaca, Washington, 1979-80; expert cons. U.S. Dept. Commerce, Washington, 1980-81; asst. treas. Am. Express Internat. Bank, N.Y.C., 1981-82; sr. v.p. Refco, Inc., N.Y.C., 1982-84; v.p., mgr. Thomson McKinnon Securities, N.Y.C., 1984-88; sr. v.p. Lehman Bros., N.Y.C., 1988-92; mng. dir. Credit Agricole Futures Inc., N.Y.C., 1992-95, Bear Stearns, N.Y.C., 1995—; cons. BDM Corp., McLean, Va., 1981-88, 1988—; Presdl. appointee J. William Fulbright Fgn. Scholarship Bd., 1993-96. Mng. trustee Dem. Nat. Com., 1989-94, mem. conv. site selection com., 1989-90; mem. arrangements com. Dem. Conv., San Francisco, 1984; mem. governing com. Levitt Pavilion for the Performing Arts, Westport, Conn., 1989-90; mem. Dem. Town Com., Westport, 1990-96; fin. chmn. Conn. Dem. State Ctrl. Com., 1993—; mem. exec. com. Am. Israel Pub. Affairs Com., 1993—; event chmn. N.Y. Presdl. Gala, N.Y.C., 1993; chmn. Dem. Gov.'s Assn. Presdl. Dinner, 1994. Wexner Heritage Found. fellow, 1992-94. Jewish. Avocation: skiing. Office: Bear Stearns 275 Park Ave New York NY 10167

ROSE, ROBERT R., JR., lawyer; b. Evanston, Ill., Nov. 1, 1915; s. Robert R. and Eleanor B. R.; m. Kathryn Lorraine Warner, June 14, 1948; children: Robert R. III, Cynthia Ann. JD, U. Wyo., 1941. Bar: Wyo. bar 1941. Atty. Dept. Justice, 1941; with UNRRA, China; asst. sec. Dept. Interior, 1951-52; sr. partner firm Rose, Spence, Dobos and Duncan, Casper, Wyo., 1968-75; justice Wyo. Supreme Ct., 1975-85, chief justice, 1981-82; assoc. Spence, Moriarity and Schuster, Cheyenne, Wyo., 1985-95; ptnr. Rose, Rose & O'Donnell, L.L.C., 1995—; organizer, past pres., chmn. bd. Title Guaranty Co. Wyo.; faculty Nat. Coll. Criminal Def., 1977-90; founder, instr. Western Trial Advocacy Inst., 1977-93; founder Western Trial Advocacy Inst., 1977—; vis. prof. trial practice U. Wyo. Coll. Law, 1985-86; Milward Simpson chair in polit. sci. U. Wyo., 1985-86; Gerry Spence faculty, corp. officer Trial Lawyer's Coll., 1994, 95. Author legal articles. Past chmn. fund drive Casper Community Chest, Am. Cancer Soc.; mem. Wyo. Ho. of Reps., 1949-51; mayor of, Casper, 1950-51; past trustee Casper Coll. Served with USAAF, World War II. Recipient Jud. Achievement award Nat. Assn. Criminal Def. Lawyers, 1983. Mem. Am. Law Inst., Order of Coif (hon.), Trial Lawyers Coll. (founder, treas. bd. dirs. 1994—), Land and Water L. Rev. (bd. advs.). Episcopalian. Address: PO Box 1006 Cheyenne WY 82003-1006

ROSE, ROSLYN, artist; b. Irvington, N.J., May 28, 1929; d. Mark and Anne Sarah (Green) R.; m. Franklin Blou, Nov. 26, 1950; 1 child, Mark Gordon Blue (dec.). Student, Rutgers U., 1949-51, Pratt Ctr. for Contemporary, Printmaking, N.Y.C., 1967; BS, Skidmore Coll., 1976. Artist. One-person shows include Midday Gallery, Caldwell, N.J., 1972, Caldwell Coll., 1972, Kean Coll., Union, N.J., 1973, Art Corner Gallery, Millburn, N.J., 1974, Brandeis U., Mass., 1974, Newark (N.j.) Mus., 1974, George Frederick Gallery, Rochester, N.Y., 1981, Robbins Gallery, Washington, 1981, Signatures Gallery, Washington, 1981, Arnot Art Mus., Elmira, N.Y., 1982, Douglas Coll. Rutgers U., New Brunswick, 1987, Nathans Gallery, West Paterson, N.J., 1984, 86, 89, 96; exhibited in group shows at Seattle Art Mus., Portland (oreg.) Mus., NYU U. Small Works Show, Montclair Art Mus., N.J., Middlesex County Mus., Piscataway, N.J., and others; permanent collections include N.J. State Mus., Trenton, Citibank of N.Y., Russia, N.J. State Libr., Trenton, Roddenbery Meml. Libr., Cairo, Ga., Rosenberg Libr., Galveston, Tex., Newark Mus., Newark Pub. Libr., AT&T, BASF Wyandotte Corp., Canon Calculator Systems, N.Y.C., First Fed. Bank, Rochester, Gulf & Western Industries, Irving Trust Co., N.Y., Kidder, Peabody & Co., N.Y., McAllen Internat. Mus., Tex., Nabisco Brands Corp., East Hanover, N.J., N.J. Bell, Readers Digest Collection, Voorhees-Zimmerli Mus., Rutgers U., New Brunswick, N.J., others; creator UNCIF cards, 1979-80. Recipient graphic award Westechester (N.Y.) Art Soc., 1973, Best-in-Show award Livingston (N.J.) Art Assn., 1971, Best-in-Show award N.J. Ctr. for Visual Arts, Summit, 1969, Mixed Media Merit award Salmagundi Club, N.Y.C., 1995; numerous others. Mem. Nat. Assn. Women Artists (Innovative Painting award 1990), N.Y. Artists Equity, Pen and Brush Club (N.Y.C. Stauffer Mixed Media award 1996). Avocation: tennis. Office: Atelier Rose PO Box 5095 Hoboken NJ 07030-5095

ROSE, RUBYE BLEVINS (PATSY MONTANA), singer; b. Hot Springs, Ark., Oct. 30; d. Augustus Marion and Victoria Amanda (Meeks) Blevins; m. Paul Edward Rose, July 3, 1934; children: Beverly Losey, Judy (dec.). Student public schs., Hope, Ark. Country and Western singer with appearances in 49 states, also U.K., The Netherlands, toured Eng. and Europe, 1972, 75, 76, 77, 78; concerts in Paris, Berlin, 1986; composer over 200 pub. songs including I Want to be a Cowboy's Sweetheart; rec. for over 200 pub. songs including Columbia, Decca, RCA, Birch, Look Records, Huddersfield, Eng., 1975, Munich Records, Holland, 1978, Cattle Records, W. Ger., 1981, Flying Fish Records, Chgo.; including million seller I Want to be a Cowboy's Sweetheart; performer: Wake Up and Smile, ABC, 1944 (Recipient Pioneer award Acad. Country and Western Music 1970, awards from Pres. Roosevelt 1937, Gov. Love of Colo. 1973, various from VFW), Library of Congress, Washington, 1987; guest on David Letterman show, NBC. Named Queen of Country and Western Music, 1973; named Ky. col., 1978, Ark. Hall of Fame, 1985, Nat. Cowgirl Hall of Fame, Hereford, Tex., 1987. Mem. VFW Aux., Screen Actor's Guild, AFTRA, ASCAP, Country Music Assn., Acad. Country and, Western Music. Republican. First country and western female singer to have a million selling record. Avocations: swimming, music, meeting people. *Talent is God given, be humble. Fame is man given, be grateful. Conceit is self given, be careful.*

ROSE, SELWYN H., chemical company executive; b. N.Y.C., May 1, 1933; s. Rubin and Ruth Rosenthal; BS, CCNY, 1954; MS, Ohio State U., 1958, PhD, 1961; MBA with honors, U. Chgo., 1979; m. Helen Diana De Mov, July 25, 1957; children: Michelle, Wendy, Suzanne. CFP. Sr. rsch. chemist Pennwalt Corp., King of Prussia, Pa., 1961-65; dept. mgr. Horizons Inc., Beachwood, Ohio, 1965-72, dir. rsch., 1972-74; mgr. long range rsch. De Soto Inc., Des Plaines, Ill., 1974-79; dir. rsch., cen. rsch. lab. Borg-Warner Chems., Des Plaines, 1979-85; v.p. tech. Parker Chem. Co., Madison Heights, Mich., 1985-88; gen. mgr. rsch. and devel. Himont Inc., Wilmington, Del., 1988-91, v.p. product devel., 1991-93; pres. SHR Fin. Advisors, Wilmington, 1993—. Served as 1st lt. U.S. Army, 1954-56. Recipient IR 100 award Indsl. Rsch. mag., 1971; award Roon Found., 1979. Mem. Am. Chem. Soc., Internat. Assn. Fin. Planners, Inst. Cert. Fin. Planners. Contbr. articles to profl. jours.; patentee in field. Achievements include development of polyphosphazene polymers. Home: 1704 N Park Dr Wilmington DE 19806-2144

ROSE, SHARON MARIE, critical care nurse; b. Big Spring, Tex., Feb. 16, 1958; d. William Coleman Smith and Grace Marie (Arnett) Karns; m. Christopher Robin Rose, Jan. 21, 984; 1 child, Crystal Alyss. AAS, Odessa Coll., 1981; BS in Occupational Edn., Wayland Bapt., 1987. Critical care RN Univ. Med. Ctr., Lubbock, Tex., 1981-88; med-surg. instr. Lubbock (Tex.) Gen. Hosp., 1988-89; dialysis RN St. Mary of the Plains Hosp., 1989-91; asst. CCU mgr. St. Mary of the Plains Hosp., Lubbock, 1990-91; health occupations instr. Lubbock Ind. Sch. Dist., 1991-94; in-svc. coord. Dialysis Ctr. Lubbock, Tex., 1994—; tchr. summer session Asst. for Med. Terminology course, 1993; mem. Health Occupations Adv. Com., Lubbock, 1988. Mem. Nat. Kidney Found. Mem. Tex. Health Occupations Assn. (v.p. 1993-94), Health Occupation Students Am. (advisor 1991-94), Tex. Tech. Med. Alliance, Nat. Kidney Found. (coun. nephrology nurses and technicians). Baptist. Avocations: jigsaw puzzles, reading, family, skiing. Home: 2802 N Quaker Ave Spc 57 Lubbock TX 79415-2707 Office: Dialysis Ctr Lubbock 4110 22nd Pl Lubbock TX 79410

ROSE, SUSAN CAROL, restaurant executive, chef, consultant; b. Rochester, N.Y., Jan. 29, 1942; d. Frederick Raymond Smith and Grace Eunice (Read) Smith Drum; m. Larry Anthony Rose, Jan. 5, 1963 (div. Jan. 1976); children: John David, Karen Michelle Haines, Patricia Anne. Student, Monroe Community Coll., Rochester, 1959-60; cert. exec. steward, Innisbrook Resort, 1976; student, St. Petersburg Jr. Coll., Tarpon Springs, Fla., 1978-80, Pinellas Voc. Tech., 1987—. With Blue Cross-Blue Shield, Rochester, 1959-67; from coffee service mgr. to exec. steward Innisbrook Resort, Tarpon Springs, 1974-84; catering team supr. Bon Appetit Restaurant, Dunedin, Fla., 1984, Bounty Caterers, Dunedin, 1984; asst. mgr. trainee Wendy's Internat., Largo, Fla., 1984; store mgr. Long John Silver's, Largo, 1984-85; exec. steward, banquet chef, room service mgr., cons. Sandestin Beach Hilton, Destin, Fla., 1985; day mgr. Shells Restaurant, Clearwater, Fla., 1986-87; sous chef, kitchen mgr. Saltwaters Seafood Grille, Palm Harbor, Fla., 1987; exec. steward Adam's Mark Caribbean Gulf Resort, Clearwater Beach, 1987—; chef/kitchen mgr. Seafood Broiler, 1990-91; chef Hwy. Ribbery Restaurant, 1991, Boomerangs Cafe, 1992; galley supr., cook Empress Cruise Lines, 1992-94; chef Wards Seafood, 1994—; garde manger 94th Aero Squadron Restaurant, Las Fontanas Restaurant; cons. restaurant mgmt. Mem. Nat. Assn. Female Execs., Hospitality Industry Assn., Smithsonian Inst. Assocs., Holiday Inn Priority Club, Internat. Travel Club, Encore Travel Club, Clearwater Jaycees. Democrat. Roman Catholic. Avocations: school, music, reading, bowling. Home: 1162 Jackson Rd Clearwater FL 34615-4605 Office: Adam's Mark Caribbean Gulf Resort Gulfview Blvd Clearwater FL 34616

ROSE, SUSAN PORTER, federal commissioner; b. Cin., Sept. 20, 1941; d. Elmer Johnson and Dorothy (Wurst) Porter; m. Jonathan Chapman Rose, Jan. 26, 1980; 1 child, Benjamin Chapman. BA, Earlham Coll., 1963; MS, Ind. State U., Terre Haute, 1970. Staff asst. Congressman Richard L. Roudebush, Washington, 1963-64; asst. dean George Sch., Bucks County, Pa., 1964-66; asst. dir. admissions Mt. Holyoke Coll., South Hadley, Mass., 1966-71; asst. dir. correspondence First Lady (Mrs. Nixon) The White House, 1971-72, appointments sec. to First Lady (Mrs. Nixon), 1972-74, to First Lady (Mrs. Ford), 1974-77; spl. asst. to asst. atty. gen. Office Improvements in Adminstrn. Justice, Washington, 1977-79, Justice Mgmt. div. U.S. Dept. Justice, 1979-81; chief of staff to Mrs. Bush, asst. to v.p. Office of V.P. of U.S. Washington, 1981-89; dep. asst. to Pres. of U.S., chief of staff to First Lady (Mrs. Bush) The White House, 1989-93; commr. U.S. Commn. Fine Arts, 1993—. Bd. dirs. Barbara Bush Found. for Family Literacy; bd. trustees Bush Presdl. Libr. and Ctr. Recipient Dist. Alumni award Earlham Coll., 1992, Ind. State U., 1991. Mem. Ind. Acad. Home: 501 Slaters Ln Apt 1001 Alexandria VA 22314-1118

ROSE, T. T., bishop. Bishop of Cen. Ill., Ch. of God in Christ, Springfield.

ROSE, THOMAS ALBERT, artist, art educator; b. Washington, Oct. 15, 1942; s. Francis John and Ann Elizabeth (Voelkel) R.; m. Mary Melinda Moyer, Aug. 21, 1965; children: Sarah, Jessica. Student, U. Wis., 1960-62; BFA, U. Ill., 1965; MA, U. Calif., Berkeley, 1967; postgrad., Lund (Sweden) U., 1967-68. Instr. U. Calif., Berkeley, 1968-69, N.Mex. State U., Las

Cruces, 1969-72; faculty mem. U. Minn., Mpls., 1972—, prof. art, 1983—. Author: Winter Book; one-man shows include Clock Tower, N.Y.C., 1977, Truman Gallery, N.Y.C., 1977-78, Rosa Esman Gallery, N.Y.C., 1979, 81, 82, Marianne Deson Gallery, Chgo., 1984-86, Robert Thomson Gallery, Mpls., 1986, 91, 92, 95, Deson Saunders Gallery, Chgo., 1989, Mpls. Inst. Art, 1992, Weisman Art Mus., Mpls., 1994, Tweed Mus., Duluth, Minn., 1995, Steinbaum/Krauss Gallery, N.Y., 1996; exhibited in group shows at Walker Art Ctr., Mpls., 1974, 76, 77, Whitney Mus. Downtown, N.Y.C., P.S. #1, N.Y.C., 1978, Wave Hill, Bronx, N.Y., 1981, Hirshhorne Mus., Washington, 1981, Am. Ctr. in Paris, 1982, Harvard U. Sch. Architecture, 1983, Cultural Ctr., Chgo., 1983, Hal Bromm Gallery, N.Y.C., Sheldon Mus., Lincoln, Nebr., 1989, Tampa (Fla.) Mus., 1988, MCAD, Mpls., 1996, Minn. Mus. Art, 1996; represented in permanent collections Walker Art Ctr., Joslyn Mus., Omaha, Park St. Lofts, Springfield, Mass., U. Minn., Mpls., Am. Lung Assn. Target Ctr., Mpls., St. Lukes Episcopal Ch., Mpls.; set designer: Fool for Love, Cricket Theater, Mpls., 1985, Circus, Theater de Jeune Lune, 1986; project dir. Works of Art in Pub. Places for Humphrey Inst. Pub. Affairs, Mpls., 1988. Fellow Nat. Endowment for Arts, 1977, 81, Bush Found., 1979, Minn. State Arts Bd., 1979, 84, McKnight Found., 1981, McKnight Found. Rsch., 1993-96; McKnight Artist fellow, 1995, travel fellow Dayton-Hudson/Jerome, 1990, 95, Jerome Found. Arts, 1993-94, Mellon Found., 1993; grantee Arts Bd. Opportunities, 1993; Rockefeller resident Bellagio, Italy, 1993. Home: 91 Nicollet St Minneapolis MN 55401-1513 Office: Univ Minn 208 Studio Arts 23d Ave SE Minneapolis MN 55455

ROSE, VICTORIA LASDON, magazine publisher. Pub. YM/Young & Modern mag., N.Y.C. Office: YM/Young & Modern 685 Third Ave New York NY 10017*

ROSE, W. AXL (WILLIAM BRUCE BAILEY), singer; b. Lafayette, Ind., Feb. 6, 1962; s. L. Stephen (stepfather) and Sharon Bailey; m. Erin Everly, 1991 (div. 1992). Lead singer (band) Guns N' Roses; albums include Live Like A Suicide, 1986, Appetite For Destruction, 1987, GN'R Lies, 1988, Use Your Illusion I, 1991, Use Your Illusion II, 1991, The Spaghetti Incident?, 1993. Office: care of David Geffen Co 9130 W Sunset Blvd West Hollywood CA 90069-3110

ROSE, WIL, foundation executive; b. Townsend, Ohio, Sept. 13, 1931; s. William Marion and Dorothy Louise (Arnold) R.; m. Anna Marie Thielmann, Mar. 4, 1952 (div. 1976); children: Sharon, Dan; m. Princess Pale Moon, Oct. 7, 1977; children: Michael, Robert, John Mark. AA in Comml. Photography, Santa Monica City Coll., 1956; LitD, Ashland U., 1982. With motion picture prodn. dept. Moody Inst. Sci., Santa Monica, Calif., 1955-57; pres., founder DATA Internat., Palo Alto, Calif., 1958-66, PlanAm. Consulting, Falls Church, Va., 1981—; pres. People to People, Inc., Kansas City, 1966-67; CEO Am. Indian Heritage Found., Falls Church, 1973—. Charitable devel. officer Nat. Heritage Found. Inc., Falls Church, Va., 1968—; pres., founder Nat. Found. Philanthropy, Mpls., 1978-80; bd. devel. officer Congrl. Awards for Youth, Fairfax, Va., 1978—; mem. presdl. task force Reagan Adminstrn., Washington, 1984. Staff sgt. USMC, 1950-54, Korea. Decorated Purple Heart; recipient Nat. Achievement award SERTOMA Internat., 1964; named Outstanding Young Man, Calif. Jaycees, 1962, Outstanding Young Man in U.S., U.S. Jaycees, 1966. Mem. Rotary Club (various com. chmn.). Avocations: writing, speaking. Office: Am Indian Heritage Foundation 6051 Arlington Blvd Falls Church VA 22044-2721

ROSE, WILLIAM ALLEN, JR., architect; b. Flushing, N.Y., Nov. 26, 1938; s. William Allen and Josephine (Grohe) R.; m. Sandra L. Latham, June 24, 1961; children: Lindsay E., Lesley A. AB cum laude, Harvard U., 1960; MArch, Columbia U., 1964. Architect Rose Beaton Corsbie Dearden & Crowe, N.Y.C. and White Plains, N.Y., 1964-69; ptnr. Rose Beaton & Rose, White Plains, 1969-92; prin. Einhorn Yaffee Prescott, White Plains, 1993—. Chmn. White Plains Citizens Adv. Com., 1970-73; pres. Hillair Circle Civic Assn., White Plains, 1972-76, Am. Inst. Architects Rsch. Corp., 1980-81; mem. White Plains City Coun., 1974-78, pres., 1976-78; mem. White Plains Urban Renewal Agy., 1988—, White Plains Comprehensive Plan Management Group, 1994-95; bd. dirs. White Plains YMCA, 1970-73, chmn. bd. trustees, 1981-83; bd. govs. YMCA Cen. and No. Westchester, 1983—, vice-chmn., 1983-85, chmn., 1985-87; chmn. bd. mgrs. McBurney Sch., N.Y.C., 1973-76, trustee, 1981-85; trustee Rye Country Day Sch., N.Y., 1981-87; trustee Baldwin League of Ind. Schs., 1986-88; trustee Mercy Coll., 1980-91, vice-chmn., 1982-88, chmn. 1988-91; bd. dirs. Burke Rehab. Inst., 1979-84, v.p., 1981-84; chmn. Commn. Fed. Procurement of Archtl. and Engring. Svcs., 1983-84. Recipient Robert Ross McBurney medal McBurney Sch., 1956, Design award Bell Sys., 1971, 76, Honor award for Archtl. Excellence L.I. Assn., 1971, 76, award Westchester Easter Seals, 1976, Outstanding Citizenship award United Way White Plains, 1980, World Fellowship award YMCA, 1988. Fellow AIA (pres. chpt. 1975-76, regional dir. 1978-81, nat. v.p. 1982, Upjohn fellow, 1991, trustee polit. action com. 1981-82, bursar Coll. of Fellows 1986-88, vice chancellor 1989, chancellor 1990, gold medal Westchester chpt. 1983); mem. N.Y. State Assn. Architects (pres. 1977-78, trustee polit. action com. 1981-84, Del Gaudio award 1982, James W. Kideney award 1988), Columbia Archtl. Alumi Assn. (v.p. 1969), Am. Archtl. Found. (regent 1990), St. Andrew's Soc. N.Y., Rotary, N.Y. Athletic Club (N.Y.C.), Harvard of Westchester Club, Sunningdale Golf Club (U.K.), Royal & Ancient Golf Club (St. Andrews, Scotland), John's Island Club, Winged Foot Golf Club. Republican. Congregationalist. Office: Einhorn Yaffee Prescott 81 Main St White Plains NY 10601-1711

ROSE, WILLIAM SHEPARD, JR., lawyer; b. Columbia, S.C., Mar. 9, 1948; s. William Shepard and Meta Cantey (Boykin) R.; m. Frances John Hobbs, Aug. 11, 1973; children: Katherine Cummings, William Shepard, III, Whitaker Boykin. BA in English, U. South, 1970; JD, U. S.C., 1973; LLM in Taxation, Georgetown U., 1976. Bar: S.C. 1973, Ohio 1977, D.C. 1974, U.S. Dist. Ct. D.C. 1976, U.S. Tax Ct. 1976, U.S. Supreme Ct. 1976, U.S. Claims Ct. 1978, U.S. Ct. Appeals (10th cir., 5th cir., 4th cir.) 1987, U.S. Ct. Appeals (3d, 6th, 7th, 8th, 9th and 11th cirs.) 1988. Trial atty. Office of Chief Counsel IRS, Washington, 1973-77; assoc. Frost & Jacobs, Cin., 1977-80, McNair Law Firm, PA, Hilton Head Island, S.C., and Washington, 1980-83, ptnr., 1983-87, 89—; asst. atty. gen., tax div. U.S. Dept. of Justice, Washington, 1987-89; chmn. and dir. Sea Pines Montessori Sch., 1983-86, Hilton Head Broadcasting, 1983-87, Hilton Head Planned Parenthood, 1985-87, MBR Corp., Adwell Corp., Links Group Inc., Hilton Head Prep. Sch., 1986-87, 89-93, dir. Boys & Girls Club of Hilton Head Island, 1992—, Hilton Head Humane Soc., 1985. Contbr. articles to profl. jours. Asst. to chmn. of bus. fund raising Beaufort County United Way, Hilton Head Island, 1984; vice-chmn. Beaufort County Rep. Party, 1991-92, 93, chmn. 1992-93, vice chmn. 1993-95; mem. Beaufort County Transportation Com., 1994-95; commr. Sea Pines Pub. Svc. Dist. Mem. ABA (past co-chmn. subcom. tax sect.), Ohio Bar Assn., D.C. Bar Assn., S.C. Bar Assn., Beaufort County Bar Assn., Hilton Head Bar Assn. Republican. Episcopalian. Clubs: S.C. Yacht Club (bd. govs. 1989-94, exec. com. 1993-94, rear commodore 1993-94), Hilton Head Cotillion, Ducks Unltd., Caroliniana Ball. Home: 11 Jessimine Pl Hilton Head Island SC 29928-4255 Office: Palmeto Bay Office 31 C Bow Circle PO Drawer 7787 Hilton Head Island SC 29938

ROSE, ZELDON E., public relations consultant; b. N.Y.C., Mar. 22, 1932; s. Abraham and Mildred (Amada) R.; m. Sally Ann Grossman, Dec. 20, 1953; children—Nancy S., Peter S., Linda J. BS, NYU, 1953. Wire editor Suffolk News Herald, Va., 1953; reporter, editor Asbury Park Press, N.J., 1953-58; unit publicist, asst. mag. editor ABC-TV, N.Y.C., 1958-64; account exec., v.p. Harshe-Rotman and Druck, N.Y.C., 1964-70; sr. v.p. John DiNigris Assocs., Inc., N.Y.C., 1970-71; pres. Porter, LeVay and Rose, Inc., N.Y.C., 1971-95. Pres. Congregation B'nai Sholom, West End, N.J. 1981-83. Mem. Breakwater Beach Club (N.J.), New Shrewsbury Racquet Club (Tinton Falls, N.J.). Avocations: tennis; reading. Home: 27 Hilltop Rd West Long Branch NJ 07764-1813 Also: Sapphire Village Saint Thomas VI 00802 Office: Porter LeVay & Rose Inc 7 Penn Plz New York NY 10001-3900

ROSE-ACKERMAN, SUSAN, law and political economy educator; b. Mineola, N.Y., Apr. 23, 1942; d. R. William and Rosalie (Gould) Rose; m. Bruce A. Ackerman, May 29, 1967; children: Sybil, John. B.A., Wellesley Coll, 1964; Ph.D., Yale U., 1970. Asst. prof. U. Pa., Phila, 1970-74; lectr. Yale U., New Haven, Conn., 1974-75, asst. prof., 1975-78, assoc. prof., 1978-82; prof. law and polit. economy Columbia U., N.Y.C., 1982-87, dir. Ctr. for Law and Econ. Studies, 1983-87; Ely prof. of law and polit. econ. Yale U., New Haven, 1987-92, Luce prof. jurisprudence (law and polit. sci.), 1992—; rev. panelist Program on Regulation and Policy Analysis, NSF, Washington, 1982-84, Am. studies program Am. Coun. Learned Socs., 1987-90; review panelist, faculty Fulbright Commn., 1993-96; vis. rsch. fellow World Bank, 1995-96. Author: (with Ackerman, Sawyer and Henderson) Uncertain Search for Environmental Quality, 1974 (Henderson prize 1982); Corruption: A Study in Political Economy, 1978; (with E. James) The Nonprofit Enterprise in Market Economies, 1986; editor: The Economics of Nonprofit Institutions, 1986; (with J. Coffee and L. Lowenstein) Knights, Raiders, and Targets: The Impact of the Hostile Takeover, 1988, Rethinking the Progressive Agenda: The Reform of the American Regulatory State, 1992, Controlling Environmental Policy: The Limits of Public Law in Germany and the United States, 1995; contbr. articles to profl. jours.; bd. editors: Jour. Law, Econs. and Orgn., 1984—, Internat. Rev. Law and Econs., 1986—, Jour. Policy Analysis and Mgmt., 1989—, Polit. Sci. Quar., 1988—. Guggenheim fellow 1991-92, Fulbright fellow, Free U. Berlin, 1991-92. Mem. Am. Law and Econs. Assn. (bd. dirs. 1993—), Am. Econ. Assn. (mem. exec. com. 1990-93), Am. Polit. Sci. Assn., Assn. Am. Law Schs., Assn. Pub. Policy and Mgmt. (mem. policy coun. 1984-88). Democrat. Office: Yale U Law Sch PO Box 208215 New Haven CT 06520-8215

ROSEANNE, actress, comedienne, producer, writer; b. Salt Lake City, Nov. 3, 1952; d. Jerry and Helen Barr; m. Bill Pentland, 1974 (div. 1989); children: Jessica, Jennifer, Brandi, Buck, Jake; m. Tom Arnold, 1990 (div. 1994); m. Ben Thomas, 1994. Former window dresser, cocktail waitress; prin. Full Moon & High Tide Prodns., Inc. As comic, worked in bars, church coffeehouse, Denver; produced showcase for women performers Take Back the Mike, U. Boulder (Colo.); performer The Comedy Store, L.A.; showcased on TV special Funny, 1986, also The Tonight Show; featured in HBO-TV spl. On Location: The Roseanne Barr Show, 1987 (Am. comedy award Funniest female performer in TV spl., 1987, Ace award funniest female in comedy, 1987, Ace award Best Comedy Spl. 1987); star of TV series Roseanne ABC, 1988— (U.S. Mag. 2d Ann. Readers Poll Best Actress Comedy series, 1989, Golden Globe nomination Outstanding lead actress comedy series 1988, Emmy award Outstanding Lead Actress in a Comedy Series, 1993); actress: (motion picture) She-Devil, 1989, Look Who's Talking Too (voice), 1990, Freddy's Dead, 1991, Even Cowgirls Get the Blues, 1994, Blue in the Face, 1995; TV movies: Backfield in Motion, The Woman Who Loved Elvis, 1993; appeared in TV spl. Sinatra: 80 Years My Way, 1995; author: Roseanne: My Life as a Woman, 1989, My Lives, 1994. Active various child advocate orgns. Recipient Peabody award, People's Choice award (4), Golden Globe award (2), Am. Comedy award, Humanitas award. Office: Full Moon & High Tide Prodns 4024 Radford Ave # 916 917 Studio City CA 91604-2101*

ROSEBERG, CARL ANDERSSON, sculptor, educator; b. Vinton, Iowa, Sept. 26, 1916; s. Swan Bernard and Selma (Olson) R.; m. Virginia M. Gorman, Aug. 23, 1942. B.F.A., U. Iowa, 1939, postgrad., 1939-41, M.F.A., 1947; postgrad., Cranbrook Acad. Art, summers 1947-48, U. Hawaii, 1950-51, U. Va., summer 1964, Mysore (India) U., summer 1965, Tyler Sch. Art, Temple U., summer 1967. Faculty Coll. William and Mary, Williamsburg, Va., 1947—; prof. fine arts Coll. William and Mary, 1966-82, prof. emeritus, 1982—, William and Mary Heritage fellow, 1968-82; founding bd. mem. 20th Century Gallery, Williamsburg.; active judge various art groups. Exhibited one man shows at Radford Coll., 1962, Roanoke Fine Art Gallery, 1962-63, Norfolk Mus., 1963, Asheville (N.C.) Gallery Art, 1963, Longwood Coll., 1966, Phi Beta Kappa Hall, William and Mary Coll., 1970; 35 yr. retrospective William and Mary Coll., 1982; retrospective Twentieth Century Gallery, 1983; exhibited in numerous group shows; represented in permanent collections at U. Iowa, Springfield (Mo.) Mus., Va. Mus. Fine Arts, Colonial Williamsburg, Chrysler Mus. Norfolk, Rockingham County Citizens Com., Longwood Coll., Farmville, Va., Thalhimer Bros., Inc., Swem Libr., Coll. William and Mary, others; designer, creator bronze meml. plaque honoring Donald W. Davis for, Millington Hall, Coll. William and Mary, 1970, bronze plaque honoring William G. Guy, Rogers Hall, 1975; I.L. Jones, Jr., Bruton Parish Ch., 1985. designer: James City County Bicentennial Medallion, 1976; designer, creator Carter O. Lowance Bronze Medallion Marshall-Wythe Sch. Law Coll. William and Mary, 1989, Bronze Medallion honoring 300th Ann. Coll. William and Mary, 1991, Bronze Medallion honoring L. I'Anson Marshall-Wythe Sch. Law, 1991. Served to comdr. USNR, 1941-45, 50-52; ret. Res. Recipient Thomas Jefferson award, 1971, numerous art awards, Cheek award William & Mary, 1993. Fellow Internat. Inst. Arts and Letters; mem. Am. Audubon Artists, Fulbright Assn., Res. Officers Assn. Am., Va. Watercolor Soc., Navy League U.S., Williamsburg German Club, Mid. Plantation Club, Masons, Lambda Chi Alpha. Presbyterian. Home: 4998 Hickory Sign Post Rd Williamsburg VA 23185-2464

ROSEBERRY, DONALD G., chief administrator. Chief adminstr. So. Prairie Area Edn. Agency 15, Ottumwa, Iowa. Recipient State Finalist for Nat. Supt. of Yr. award, 1993. Office: So Prarie Area Edn Agy 15 900 Terminal Ave Ottumwa IA 52501-9413

ROSEBERRY, EDWIN SOUTHALL, state agency administrator; b. Roanoke, Va., July 4, 1925; s. Edwin Alexander and Gladys Edmonia (Southall) R.; m. Mary Louise Sprengel, Sept. 2, 1949 (dec. 1978); children: Edwin Jr., David, Kevin; m. Alice Proffit Boger, Dec. 27, 1980; 1 stepdaughter, Elizabeth Leigh Boger. BS in Commerce, U. Va., 1949. Registered sanitarian, Hawaii, Va. Store mgr. Allied Arts, Charlottesville, Va., 1949-51; retail credit sales mgr. B.F. Goodrich Co., Charlottesville, 1951-53; environ. health specialist Dept. of Health, Charlottesville, 1953-84, Dept. of Labor, Honolulu, 1987—; self-employed photographer, Charlottesville, 1949-85, Honolulu, 1985—. Contbr. photographs: The Inward Eye, 1986. Election ofcl. State of Hawaii, Honolulu, 1988—. With USN, 1944-46. Recipient numerous nat. awards Eastman Kodak Co., nat. newspapers, and photography mags., 1951-69. Mem. VFW (life), Am. Indsl. Hygiene Assn., Austrian Hawaiian Club (v.p., bd. dirs. 1985), Antique Auto Assn. (pres. Piedmont region 1964), Hawaii Photo Soc. (v.p. 1989), Elks (tiler and inner guard 1985), Am. Legion, Masonic Lodge, Pi Delta Epsilon. Episcopalian. Avocations: photography, stamp collecting, antique automobiles, figure skating. Home: 1101E Kumukumu St Honolulu HI 96825-2602 Office: State of Hawaii DLIR/DOSH 830 Punchbowl St Honolulu HI 96813-5045

ROSEBERY, RICHARD JAY, manufacturing company executive; b. Gary, Ind., May 5, 1935; s. William J. and Vivian Ethel (Schnell) R.; m. Charleen Annette Bennett, July 30, 1966; children: Susan Dare, Richard J., Jr. BS in Elec. Engring., Purdue U., 1957. Program mgr. Emerson Electric, St. Louis, 1957-62; v.p. elec. engring. and contracting group Dynalectron Corp., McClean, Va., 1962-72; v.p. corp. affairs Arthur Corp., Phoenix, 1972-74; v.p., treas., chief fin. officer Elcor Corp., Dallas, 1975-93, exec. v.p., chief fin. and adminstrv. officer, 1993—; exec. v.p. Elcor Svc. Corp.; v.p. bd. dirs. Chromium Corp.; v.p. Elk Corp. Am.; bd. dirs. Ortloff Corp., Ortloff Internat. Corp., Ortloff Engrs., Ltd., Elk Corp. of Ala., Elk Corp. of Ark., Elk Corp. of Tex., Elk Corp. of Dallas; chmn. bd. dirs., pres. G.A. Industries Corp., M. Machinery Co., M. Svc. Co. Mem. fin. United Way, Midland, Tex., 1985-87, v.p., Dallas chpt., 1995—. Mem. Fin. Execs. Inst., Conf. Bd., Am. Mgmt. Assn., Nat. Assn. of Mfrs., U.S. C. of C., Tex. C. of C., Dallas C. of C. Home: 5703 Club Oaks Dr Dallas TX 75248-1119

ROSEBUSH, JAMES SCOTT, international management and public affairs consultant, former government official; b. Flint, Mich., June 1, 1949; s. Kenneth F. and Jacqueline (Porter) R.; m. Nancy Paull, May 18, 1974; children: Claire Haisley, Lauren Culver. BA, The Principia, Elsah, Ill., 1971; MA, Boston U., 1973. Cons. Boston, 1972-76; v.p. Nat. Chamber Found., Washington, 1976-79; assoc. dir. corp. contbn. Standard Oil Co., Cleve., 1979-81; dir. Office Bus. Liaison, U.S. Dept. Commerce, Washington, 1981, spl. asst. to pres. for pvt. sector initiatives, Washington, 1981-82; dept. asst. to pres., chief staff for First Lady The White House, Washington, 1982-86; pres. James Rosebush & Co., 1986—; lectr. Georgetown U., Washington, 1977-79, George Washington U., Washington, 1977-79; presdl. appointee Nat. Mus. Svcs. Bd. Author: First Lady, Public Wife, 1987; contbr. articles to profl. jours. Mem. rev. com. United Way, Cleve., 1979; mem. community relations com. Cleve. Orch., 1979; bd. mem. Concord Art Assn., 1972. Recipient Internat. award Rotary Internat., 1970. Republican. Avocations: tennis, skiing, reading, travelling. Office: 1250 24th St NW Ste 300 Washington DC 20037-1124

ROSEGGER, GERHARD, economist, educator; b. Bruck/Mur, Austria, July 28, 1930; came to U.S., 1954, naturalized, 1961; s. Walter and Irmgard Elsa (Stark) R.; m. Clara Louise Tretter, July 17, 1954; children: Karin Andrea, Michael Lorenz, Nora Lynn, Thomas Martin. Dr.iur., U Graz, Austria, 1953; MBA, U. Pa., 1954. From instr. to asst. prof. Rutgers U. Coll. of S. Jersey, Camden, N.J., 1956-61; asst. prof. Case Inst. Tech., Cleve., 1962-65; assoc. prof. Case Western Res. U., 1965-75, prof. econs., 1975—, Frank Tracy Carlton prof. econs., 1978—; Fulbright vis. prof. U. Innsbruck, Austria, 1983-84, 91; vis. prof. U. Cin., 1988, U. Kassel, Germany, Helsinki (Finland) Sch. Econs., 1991, Vienna Tech. U., 1995; vis. rsch. scholar U. Waikato, Hamilton, N.Z. Author: The Economics of Production and Innovation, 1980, 2d edit., 1986, 3d edit., 1995, (with others) Evaluating Technological Innovations, 1980, Technological Progress and Industrial Leadership, 1984; contbr. chpts. to books, numerous articles to profl. jours. Fulbright scholar, 1950-51; recipient research and travel grants. Mem. Am. Econ. Assn., Inst. Mgmt. Scis., Sigma Xi. Mem. Christian Ch. (Disciples of Christ). Home: 15719 Chadbourne Rd Cleveland OH 44120-3333 Office: Case Western Reserve Univ Economics Dept Cleveland OH 44106

ROSEHART, ROBERT GEORGE, university president, chemical engineer; b. Owen Sound, Ont., Can., July 29, 1943; s. Clarence Daniel and Evaline (Sutton) R.; m. Rita June Purvis, Aug. 26, 1967; children—Robert George, William, Karen Ann. Ch.E., B.A.Sc., U. Waterloo, 1967, M.A.Sc., 1968, Ph.D., 1970. Registered chem. engr. Assoc. prof. chem. engring Lakehead U., Thunder Bay, Ont., Can., 1970-77, dean univ. schs., 1977-84, pres., 1984—; sci. counsellor Porter Royal Commn. on Electric Power Planning, 1975-77; mem. Thunder Bay waferboard study Govt. of Ont., 1986-87; chmn. Ont. Forest Resources Inventory Com.; govt. reviewer No. Labour Mgmt. Issues; bd. dirs. Ont. Energy Corp. Contbr. articles to profl. jours. Chmn. com. on resource coms., 1985, Premiers Coun. Sci. and Tech. Grantee in field. Mem. Can. Pulp and Paper Assn., Assn. Profl. Engrs. Ont. Roman Catholic. Avocations: curling, skiing, boating. Home: 588 Riverview Dr, Thunder Bay, ON Canada P7C 1R7 Office: Lakehead U, Off of Pres, Thunder Bay, ON Canada P7B 5E1

ROSEIG, ESTHER MARIAN, veterinary researcher; b. Bklyn., July 23, 1917; d. Chone and Rebecca (Kaplan) Fogel; m. Seymour Roseig, Jan. 21, 1967. Cert., Med. Assts. Sch., N.Y.C., 1967; student, Orange County Community Coll., Middletown, N.Y., 1967-68. Cert. clin. lab. technician, N.Y. Gen. lab. technician Arden Hill Hosp., Goshen, N.Y., 1967-68; tech. rsch. asst. Lamont-Doherty Geol. Obs., 1968-70. Democrat. Achievements include research on the organism saccharomyces cerevisiae in its inactive dry state as brewers yeast or bakers yeast, and its ability to repel the parasites, fleas and ticks from domestic pets through a biochemical process of metabolism in conjunction with meat protein: the end product as CO(NH2)2" in solution in sweat; a coincidental process of coat pigment losses in both dogs and cats fed the initial Yeast was resolved by adjusting the B, A, D Vitamins and Calcium.

ROSEL, CAROL ANN, artist; b. Dodge City, Kans., June 12, 1944; d. John Elbert and Mary Claire (Wetmore) Frazier; m. Herbert Carey Zortman, Aug. 21, 1960 (div. Jan. 1989); children: Elaine Marie, Anita Louise, Stanley Dale; m. George D. Rosel, Sept. 22, 1990 (dec. June 1995). Student, Ctrl. Coll., McPherson, Kans., 1961; BFA cum laude, Ft. Hays State U., 1994. Cert. machine embroidery instr. Dress designer Ms. Cosmo Ltd., Wichita, Kans., 1975-76; designer artistic embroidery garments, 1977-80; owner Carol Ann's Gallery, Liberal, Kans.; part-time art tchr. C.C.s, Baker Art Ctr., Seward County C.C., schs. in Liberal. One-woman show Ft. Hays Libr., 1993. Mem. Baker Art Ctr., Liberal, 1989—, Hays (Kans.) Arts Coun., 1993; tchr. Sunday sch.; counselor girls ch. camp; solo pianist ch. weddings and comty. functions. Recipient All Am. Scholar Collegiate award, 1994, Grand Champion award State Fair, 1989, 90, 95, Purple Champion award, 1990, others; named Woman of World, 1995-96. Mem. Mid. Am. Arts and Crafts Assn., Pinnacle Honor Soc., Art Club. Republican. Avocations: piano, singing, dramatics. Home and Office: 406 Harvard Ave Liberal KS 67901-3024

ROSELLA, JOHN DANIEL, clinical psychologist, educator; b. Phila., Sept. 12, 1938; s. Orazio and Angela Theresa (Cardone) R.; B.S. in Psychology, Villanova U., 1961; cert. in Edn., St. Joseph's U., 1963; M.Ed., Temple U., 1966, postgrad., 1969-72; Ph.D., Walden U., 1981; Diplomate Am. Bd. Forensic Examiners; cert. hynotherapist; m. Rose Mary Theresa Malloy, Nov. 14, 1964; children—Anne-Marie, John Daniel Jr. Tchr., counselor Father Judge High Sch., Phila., 1962-67; counselor Bristol Twp. Sch. Dist., Bucks County, Pa., 1967-69; prof. Bucks County Community Coll. Divsn. Social & Behavioral Scis., 1994, subject area coord., 1995, Newtown, Pa., 1968—, founder coll. reading and study skills program, 1968-70, founding chmn. dept. basic studies, 1970-76; dir. psychol. services Fairless Hills (Pa.) Med. Center, 1978-89, dir. clin. svcs., 1989—; asst. clin. prof. Widener U., 1990; cons. Office of Vocat. Rehab., 1977—; psychol. cons. Eugenia Hosp., 1980—, Bur. Disability Determination, 1982—, Human Growth Center, Inc., 1987—, Crestview North Nursing Home and Rehab. Ctr., 1990—, cons. staff psychologist, Attleboro Nursing Home and Rehabilitation Ctr., 1993, cons. staff psychologist; clin. assoc. prof. Dept. Mental Health Scis. Hahnemann U., 1982-94; cons. Bucks County (Pa.) Family Ct., 1985—; grad. clin. supr. Trenton State Coll., 1985-86; grad. counseling intern supr. Rider Coll., 1988-95; participant 1st Internat. Colloquium on Family Health, Sri Lanka, 1983, Australia, 1988, ednl. profl. travel, Italy and Switzerland, 1991; Bd. dirs. Valley Day Sch., 1978-81, Bucks County Community Centers, 1980-85; co-founder Newtown Twp. Dem. Party, 1978, 1st vice chmn., 1979-80, Dem. committeeman, 1989-92; active Right to Read Task Force, 1972-73; mem. 8th Congressional Dist. Adv. Council on Health Care, 1981-83; project dir. Fairless Hills Psychiat. Hosp. bldg. program, 1982-83; pres. bd. trustees Friends of the Library Found., Bucks County Community Coll., 1984—. Recipient Man of Yr. award Assn. to Advance Ethical Hypnosis, 1976, Disting. Teaching recognition Phi Theta Kappa, 1981, 83, Faculty Svc. award, 1989, Profl. Achievement award Bucks County Community Coll. Alumni Assn., 1991. Lic. psychologist, Pa. Fellow Internat. Council for Sex Edn. and Parenthood of Am. U., Pa. Psychol. Assn.; mem. Am. Psychol. Assn., Am. Assn. Marriage and Family Therapy (clin.), Pa. Assn. Marriage and Family Therapy, Am. Legion. Roman Catholic, Profl. Acad. Custody Evaluators (registered custody evaluator 1993), . Clubs: KC, Sons of Italy. Author: Reading and Study Skills: A Counseling Approach, 1970; Effects of the Basic Studies Program on the Academic Achievement of High Risk Students, 1973-74; The Professor and the Law, 1975; Research in Hypnosis for Students, 1976; Marriage and Family Therapy: Its Evolution from Revolution, 1980; others; (audio-tapes) Developing Successful Study Skills, Guided Imagery Exercises; also articles. Office: Offices at Oxford Crossing 333 S Oxford Valley Rd Ste 202 Fairless Hills PA 19030-2627

ROSELLE, CATHY COLMAN, kindergarten education, educational consultant; b. Riverside, Calif., Dec. 2, 1946; d. Carl Eugene and Elma (Skinner) Colman; m. Charles Perry Roselle, Sept. 1, 1968; children: Robert Andrew, Charles Eugene, Scott Perry. BSEE, N.Mex. State U., Las Cruces, 1977; MA, Hood Coll, 1990. Cert. tchr., reading specialist, Ariz. Bilingual kindergarten tchr. P.T. Coe Sch., Phoenix, 1977-80; bilingual 1st grade tchr. Alta Loma Sch., Phoenix, 1981-83; Chpt. I reading tchr. Carpenter Mid. Sch., Nogales, Ariz., 1990; Chpt. I bilingual kindergarten tchr. A.J. Mitchell, Nogales, 1991—; ednl. specialist S.W. Internat. Tech., Rio Rico, Ariz., 1994—; team leader Ariz. Student Assessment Profile, Nogales, 1992; mem. curriculum com. Project Wellhead, 1993-95. Co-author: Chapter I Handbook for Nogales School District, 1990. Campaign mgr. Sch. Bd Election Charles P. Roselle, Rio Rico, 1994. Mem. NEA, Ariz. Edn. Assn., Ariz. Assn. for Edn. of Young Children. Avocations: reading, Scrabble, hiking, computer techonology in education. Office: Nogales Pub Schs 855 Juan Bautista Nogales AZ 85621

ROSELLE, DAVID PAUL, university president, mathematics educator; b. Vandergrift, Pa., May 30, 1939; s. William John and Esther Suzanne (Clever) R.; m. Louise Helen Dowling, June 19, 1967; children—Arthur Charles, Cynthia Dowling. BS, West Chester State Coll., 1961; PhD, Duke U., 1965; LLD, West Chester U., 1994. Asst. prof. math. U. Md., College Park, 1965-68; assoc. prof. math. La. State U., Baton Rouge, 1968-73, prof., 1973-74;

prof. Va. Poly. Inst. and State U., Blacksburg, 1974-87, dean grad. sch., 1979-81, dean research and grad. studies, 1981-83, provost, 1983-87, chmn. Commn. on Rsch., 1981-83, chmn. Commn. on Grad. Studies, 1983-87; prof. U. Ky., 1987-90, pres., 1987-90; prof. math., pres. U. Del., 1990—; pres. COMAP, Inc., Lexington, Mass., 1986-95; bd. dirs. Bell Atlantic Del., Wilmington Trust Corp., VTLS, Inc. Editor: Proc. of the First Louisiana Conf. on Combinatorics, Graph Theory and Computing, 1970, Proc. of the Second Louisiana Conf. on Combinatorics, Graph Theory and Computing, 1971; mem. editorial bd. The Bicentennial Tribute to American Mathematics, 1977; contbr. numerous research articles to profl. jours. Mem. Del. Roundtable, 1990—, Bus.and Pub. Edn. Coun., 1990—; trustee Winterthur Mus., 1991—; bd. dirs. Del. Acad. Medicine, 1991—, Med. Ctr. Del., 1991—. Named Outstanding Alumnus West Chester State Coll., 1979; Westinghouse Coop. scholar, 1957; NSF grantee, 1965-75; Teaching Excellence Cert., 1978; Digital Equipment grant, 1984; Nat. Coun. Tchrs. Math. Cert. of Appreciation, 1984; founding fellow of Inst. for Combinatorics and Its Applications, 1990; numerous invited addresses at univs. and profl. soc. meetings. Mem. Am. Math. Soc., Math. Assn. Am. (sec., fin. com., exec. com., com. on publs. 1975-84; com. on spl. funds 1985—; chmn. com. on accreditation 1985; numerous other coms.). Home: 47 Kent Way Newark DE 19711-5201 Office: U Del Hullihen Hall Newark DE 19716

ROSELLE, WILLIAM CHARLES, librarian; b. Vandergrift, Pa., June 30, 1936; s. William John and Suzanne Esther (Clever) R.; m. Marsha Louise Lucas, Aug. 2, 1959; 1 child, Paul Lucas. BA, Thiel Coll., 1958; MLS, U. Pitts., 1963. Lic. profl. guide State of Mont., 1978. Mem. faculty Milton Hershey (Pa.) Sch., 1960-62; trainee Pa. State Library, 1962-63; asst. catalog librarian Pa. State U., 1963-65; engring., math. librarian U. Iowa, 1965-66, library adminstrv. asst., 1966-69, asst. dir. libraries, 1969-71; prof., dir. library U. Wis.-Milw., 1971-89; dir. univ. library system U. Pitts., 1989-90; pvt. cons. Thiensville, Wis., 1991—; chmn. Morris Fromkin Meml. Lectr. Com., 1972-89; chmn. planning task force on computing U. Wis. System, 1973-74, mem. library planning study com., 1978-79, co-chmn. library automation task force, 1983-85; chmn. computing mgmt. rev. team U. Wis.-Stout, 1976; chmn. Council for U. Wis. Libraries, 1981-82; library cons. Grambling (La.) State U., Viterbo Coll., LaCrosse, Wis., N.C. A&T U., Greensboro, Mt. Mary Coll., Milw., U. Ill. at Chgo., Milw. Sch. Engring., Bklyn. Coll., U. South Ala., Concordia Coll., Milw., Metrics Rsch. Corp., Cardinal Stritch Coll., Milw., N.Y. Inst. Tech., Indiana U. of Pa., Med. Coll. Wis., Wis. Luth. Coll., Milw.; participant Library Adminstrs. Devel. Program, U. Md., 1973, micrographics seminar Nat. Microfilm Assn., 1973, Mgmt. Skills Inst., Assn. Rsch. Libraries, Kansas City, Mo., 1977, Meadowbrook Symposium Midwest Library Network, 1976; mem. sect. geography and map libraries Internat. Fedn. Library Assns. and Instns., 1978-83; mem. bldg. com. Ctr. for Rsch. Libraries, 1980-82. Editorial cons. The Quest for Social Justice, 1983, Current Geographical Publications, 1978-89; contbr. articles to profl. jours. Pres. Thiensville (Wis.) Village Bd., 1987; bd. dirs. Charles Allis Art Mus., 1979-84. Served with AUS, 1958-60. Named Disting. Alumnus, Thiel Coll., 1985. Hon. fellow Am. Geog. Soc.; mem. Spl. Libraries Assn. (spl. citation 1979), ALA (life), Iowa Library Assn. (chmn. audit com. 1968-70, chmn. intellectual freedom com. 1969-70), Wis. Library Assn., Midwest Acad. Librarians Conf. (chmn. 1969-71), AAUP (treas. U. Iowa chpt. 1969-70), Coun. Wis. Libraries (chmn. 1973-74), Soc. Tympanuchus Cupido Pinnatus, Milw. Civil War Round Table, Beta Beta Beta, Beta Phi Mu, Phi Alpha Theta, Phi Kappa Phi, Phi Delta Kappa. Lutheran. Home: 324 Sunny Ln Thiensville WI 53092-1334

ROSELLI, RICHARD JOSEPH, lawyer; b. Chgo., Mar. 2, 1954; s. H. Joseph and Dolores Roselli; m. Lisa McNelis; children: Nicholas Joseph, Christiana Elise, Alexandra Grace, Michaela Luciana. BA, Tulane U., 1976, JD, 1980. Bar: Fla. 1981, U.S. Dist. Ct. (so. dist.) Fla. 1981, U.S. Ct. Appeals (5th and 11th cirs.); bd. cert. civil trial lawyer. Assoc. Krupnick & Campbell, Ft. Lauderdale, Fla., 1981-84; ptnr. Krupnick, Campbell, Malone Roselli, Ft. Lauderdale, 1984-91, Krupnick Campbell Malone Roselli Buser Slama & Hancock P.A., Ft. Lauderdale, 1991—. Trustee Fla. Democrat. Party. Mem. ATLA, Am. Bd. Trial Advocates, Am. Soc. Law and Medicine, So. Trial Lawyers Assn., Acad. Fla. Trial Lawyers (bd. dirs. 1987—, exec. com. 1990—, sec. 1993, treas. 1994, pres. 1996—, chmn. Fla. lawyers action group-PAC 1996, Golden Eagle award, 1989, Silver Eagle award, 1990), Trial Lawyers for Pub. Justice, Lawyer Pilots Bar Assn., St. Jude Catholic Ch. (mem. edn. and adv. coun.). Office: Krupnick Campbell Malone Roselli Buser Slama & Hancock 700 SE 3rd Ave Fort Lauderdale FL 33316-1154

ROSEMAN, JACK, computer services company executive; b. Lynn, Mass., June 13, 1931; s. Abraham and Bessie (Guz) R.; m. Judith Ann Rosenthal, Feb. 21, 1960; children: Laura, Alan, Shari. BA, Boston U., 1954; MS, U. Mass., 1955. Instr. U. Mass., 1958-60; dir. info. processing CEIR, Inc., Washington, 1960-66; v.p. KMS Tech. Ctr., Washington, 1966-70; pres. On-Line Systems, Inc., Pitts., from 1970-79 also bd. dirs.; pres., chmn. United Computing Internat. subs. of United Telecommunications, 1992—; pvt. investor, ptnr. J.R. Assocs., Pitts, 1988—; Donald H. Jones Disting. adj. prof. in entrepreneurship, Carnegie Mellon U., 1985—; assoc. dir. Donald H. Jones Ctr. Entrepreneurship, 1992—; dir. emeritus Pitts. High Tech. Coun.; cons. North Side Civic Devel. Coun., Inc., Pitts., 1987—; rsch. staff mem. whilwind project computation ctr. MIT; chmn. bd. dirs. Omega Systems, Inc., 1994—. Recipient Judges' award for Entrepreneurship Ernst & Young, and Merill Lynch Inc. mags. Mem. AAUP, Am. Assn. Advancement Sci., Assn. Computing Machinery.

ROSEMAN, SAUL, biochemist, educator; b. Bklyn., Mar. 9, 1921; s. Emil and Rose (Markowitz) R.; m. Martha Ozrowitz, Sept. 9, 1941; children: Mark Alan, Dorinda Ann, Cynthia Bernice. B.S., CCNY, 1941; M.S., U. Wis., 1944, Ph.D., 1947; (hon.) M.D., U. Lund, Sweden, 1984. From instr. to asst. prof. U. Chgo., 1948-53; from asst. prof. to prof. biol. chemistry, also Rackham Arthritis Research Unit, U. Mich., 1953-65; Ralph S. O'Connor prof. biology Johns Hopkins U., Balt., 1965—, chmn. dept., 1969-73; dir. McCollum-Pratt Inst., 1969-73, chmn. dept. biology , dir., 1988-90; cons. NIH, NSF, Am. Cancer Soc., Hosp. for Sick Children, Toronto; sci. counselor Nat. Cancer Inst.; Lynch lectr. U. Notre Dame, 1989; Van Niel lectr. Stanford U., 1992. Author articles on metabolism of complex molecules containing carbohydrates and on solute transport.; former mem. editorial bd.: Biochemistry, Jour. Biol. Chemistry. Served with AUS, 1944-46. Recipient Sesquicentennial award U. Mich., 1967, T. Duckett Jones Meml. award Helen Hay Whitney Found., 1973, Rosenstiehl award Brandeis U., 1974, Internat. award Gairdner Found. award, 1981, Townsend Harris award CUNY, 1987, Spl. award 11th Internat. Symposium on Glycoconjugates, 1991, Karl Meyer award Soc. Glycobiology, 1993. Fellow Am. Acad. Microbiology; mem. Am. Soc. Biol. Chemists, Am. Soc. Cell Biology, Am. Acad. Arts and Scis., Nat. Acad. Scis., Am. Chem. Soc., Am. Soc. Microbiologists, Biochem. Soc. Japan (hon.). Office: Johns Hopkins U 34th Charles St Baltimore MD 21218

ROSEMARIN, CAREY STEPHEN, lawyer; b. Englewood, N.J., Aug. 19, 1950; s. Jack L. and Muriel Ruth (Gordon) R.; m. Joan Maxine Lafer, June 17, 1973; children: Benjamin Joseph, Meryl Ruth. BS, U. Mich., 1972; MS, Pa. State U., 1974; JD, U. Tenn., 1978. Bar: Tenn. 1978, Ill. 1982, U.S. Dist. Ct. (ea. dist.) Tenn. 1978, U.S. Dist. Ct. (no. dist.) Ill. 1982. Rsch. assoc. Union Carbide Corp., Oak Ridge Nat. Lab., 1974-80; asst. regional counsel U.S. EPA, Chgo., 1980-86; ptnr. Katten, Muchin, & Zavis, Chgo., 1986-90, Jenner & Block, Chgo., 1990—. Mem. ABA, Tenn. Bar Assn., Chgo. Bar Assn. (chmn. environ. law com. 1985-86), Environ. Law Inst. (assoc.). Jewish. Avocations: licensed glider pilot, bicycling. Office: Jenner & Block 1 E Ibm Plz Chicago IL 60611

ROSEMBERG, EUGENIA, physician, scientist, educator, medical research administrator; b. Buenos Aires, Argentina, Apr. 25, 1918; came to U.S., 1948, naturalized, 1956; d. Pedro and Fanny (Hestrin) R. BS, Liceo Nacional de Senoritas, Buenos Aires, 1936; MD, U. Buenos Aires, 1944. Intern Hosp. Pirovano, Buenos Aires, 1940-41; resident Hosp. Nacional de Clinicas, U. Hosp., U. Buenos Aires, 1941-44, assoc. in pediatrics, 1943-48; instr. in anatomy Hosp. Nacional de Clinicas, U. Hosp., U. Buenos Aires (Med. Sch.), 1940-46, instr. pediatrics, 1946-48; practice medicine specializing in pediatrics, 1946-48; research in endocrinology Balt., 1948-51, Worcester, Mass., 1955—; Mead Johnson fellow dept. endocrinology Johns Hopkins Med. Sch., Balt., 1948-49; vis. scientist Med. Sch., U. Montevideo, Uruguay, 1950; research fellow NIH, Bethesda, Md., 1951-53, Nat. Inst. Arthritis and Metabolic Diseases, 1951-53, Med. Research Inst. and Hosp., Oklahoma City, 1953; mem. staff Worcester Found. Exptl. Biology, Shrewsbury, Mass., 1953-62; research dir. Med. Research Inst. of Worcester, Inc., 1962—; cons. Center for Population Research, Nat. Inst. Child Health and Human Devel., NIH, 1969-70, chief contraceptive devel. br., 1970-71; prof. pediatrics U. Md. Hosp., Balt., 1970-73; prof. medicine U. Mass. Med. Sch., Worcester, 1972—; mem. staff Worcester City Hosp., 1955-85, sec. human experimentation com., 1965-83, chmn., 1984-85, dir. clin. research, 1972-85; Sec. subcom. on gonadotropins Nat. Hormone and Pituitary Program, Nat. Inst. Arthritis, Diabetes, Digestive and Kidney Diseases, 1965-69, chmn., 1969-85, mem. med. adv. bd., 1969-72, 73-85, sec. subcom. on standards endocrinology study sect., 1968. Author: Gonadotropins, 1968, (with C.A. Paulsen) The Human Testis, 1970, Gonadotropin Therapy in Female Infertility, 1973, (with C. Gual) Hypothalamic Hypophysiotropic Hormones—Physiological and Clinical Studies, 1973; Mem. editorial bd.: Giner, 1970—, Procs. 1st Ann. Meeting Am. Soc. Andrology, supplement, Vol. 8, 1976, Andrologia, 1978—, Jour. Andrology, 1979-82, Internat. Jour. Andrology, 1978—; assoc. editor: Reproduccion, 1970—, Andrologia jour, 1974-77; Contbr. articles and book chpts. on research in endocrinology to med. texts and jours.; Translator: from Spanish Diagnosis and Treatment of Endocrine Disorders in Childhood and Adolescence (L. Wilkins). Patentee in field, U.S., Can., Europe. Fellow AAAS; mem. Am. Med. Women's Assn., Endocrine Soc. U.S. (mem. com. pub. affairs 1971, v.p. 1975-76), Soc. for Research in Biology of Reproduction, Soc. for Study of Reproduction, Am. Fertility Soc., Peru Fertility Soc. (fgn. corr.), N.Y. Acad. Scis., New Eng. Cardiovascular Soc., Am., Mass. heart assns., Argentine Endocrine Soc., Argentine Pediatric Soc., Sociedad Argentine Para El Estudio de la Esterilidad., Pan Am. Med. Women's Alliance, Am. Soc. Andrology (program chmn. 1975-76, exec. council 1976-78, chmn. publ. com. 1975-80, Disting. Andrologist award 1982), Internat. Com. for Study Andrology (exec. council 1976-79).

ROSEMONT, NORMAN, television and feature producer; b. N.Y.C., Dec. 12, 1924. Prodns. include A Tale of Two Cities, Brigadoon, Carousel, Kiss Me Kate, Kismet, Stiletto, The Man Without a Country, Miracle on 34th Street, A Tree Grows in Brooklyn, The Red Badge of Courage, The Count of Monte Cristo, The Man in the Iron Mask, The Mad Mad Mad Mad World of the Super Bowl, Captains Courageous, The Court Martial of George Armstrong Custer, Four Feathers, Les Miserables, All Quiet on the Western Front, Pleasure Palace, Little Lord Fauntleroy; TV miniseries: Master of the Game, 1984, Camille, 1985, The Secret Garden, 1987, The Tenth Man, 1988, Ironclads, 1991, Long Road Home, 1991, Shadow of a Doubt, 1991, Fergie and Andrew, 1992, Harmful Intent, 1993.

ROSEN, ARTHUR MARVIN, advertising executive; b. N.Y.C., Dec. 28, 1930; s. Joseph and Cornelia (Grob) R.; m. Maureen Elizabeth Reilly; children: Ellen Jessica, Deborah Lynn, Daniel Joshua. BA, Cuny, 1952; MA, Yale U., 1953; postgrad., Columbia U., 1955-57. Analyst research Dancer-Fitzgerald-Sample, N.Y.C., 1955-56; supr. research Benton and Bowles, N.Y.C., 1956-61; account exec. Young and Rubicam, N.Y.C., 1961-66; v.p. account supr. Grey Advt., N.Y.C., 1966-69; pres. Met. Diagnostic, N.Y.C., 1969-73; v.p. group mgmt. Grey Advt., N.Y.C., 1973-81; exec. v.p. Sudler and Hennessey, N.Y.C., 1981-94; mktg. cons. Himmel Nutrition, Inc., 1994-95, Martin Himmel, Inc., 1994-95; spkr. in field. Contbr. articles to profl. jours. Pres. Temple Beth Or, Washington Twp., N.J., 1973-74; chmn. Soc. Families, Colgate U., 1983-84; served as cpl. U.S. Army, 1953-55. Republican. Jewish.

ROSEN, BENJAMIN MAURICE, venture capitalist, computer company executive; b. New Orleans, Mar. 11, 1933; s. Isidore J. and Anna Vera (Leibof) R.; m. Alexandra Ebere, Sept. 29, 1967; children—Jeffrey Mark, Eric Andrew. B.S., Calif. Inst. Tech., 1954; M.S., Stanford U., 1955; M.B.A., Columbia U., 1961. Engr. Raytheon Corp., Oxnard, Calif., 1955-56; engr. Sperry Corp., Great Neck, N.Y., 1957-59; v.p. Quantum Sci. Corp., N.Y.C., 1961-65; ptnr. Coleman & Co., N.Y.C., 1965-75; v.p. Morgan Stanley & Co. Inc., N.Y.C., 1975-80; pres. Rosen Research Inc., N.Y.C., 1980-83; ptnr. Sevin Rosen Mgmt. Co., N.Y.C., 1981—, chmn. bd., 1982—; also chmn. Compaq Computer Corp, Houston, TX; former founder dir. Lotus Devel. Corp.; mem. bd. overseers and mgrs. Meml. Sloan Kettering Cancer Ctr., N.Y.C.; mem. bd. overseers Columbia U. Grad. Sch. Bus., N.Y.C. Trustee Calif. Inst. Tech., Pasadena. Office: Sevin Rosen Mgmt Co 200 Park Ave New York NY 10166-0005 also: Compaq Computer Corp PO Box 692000 B Houston TX 77269-2000

ROSEN, BENSON, business administration educator; b. Detroit, Oct. 9, 1942; s. David and Laura R.; m. Brenda M. Leibroder, Dec. 17, 1966; children: Gregory Scott, David Loren. BS, Wayne State U., 1964, MA, 1968, PhD, 1969. Asst. prof. U. N.C., Chapel Hill, 1969-74, assoc. prof., 1974-80, prof. bus. adminstrn., 1980—, Hanes prof., 1992, sr. assoc. dean acad. affairs, 1995—; vis. prof. U. Minn., 1981; cons. to bus., industry, govt.; cons. EEOC. Author: Becoming Aware, 1976; Older Employees: New Roles for Valued Resources, 1985; mem. editorial rev. bd. Acad. Mgmt. Jour., 1978-84; contbr. articles to profl. jours. Bd. dirs. SHRM Found., 1994—. Recipient Young Scholars award Spencer Found., 1976, 78, Disting. Rsch. award, 1993, PhD Teaching award, 1994; NSF grantee, 1973-75; Adminstrn. on Aging grantee, 1978-80. Fellow APA; mem. Acad. Mgmt., Soc. Human Resource Mgmt. Office: Kenan Flagler Bus Sch U NC Chapel Hill NC 27599-3490

ROSEN, BERNARD H., chemical engineer; b. N.Y.C., Sept. 29, 1922; s. Max and Dorothy (Hildebr) R.; m. Anita Ruth Greenberg, Aug. 26, 1947; children: Jeffrey Paul, Seth Gordon, Lise Ann. B.S. in Chem. Engring., CCNY, 1943; M.S., NYU, 1947; postgrad., Harvard U., 1943-44, Okla. A&M U., 1949, Ill. Inst. Tech., 1949-50, Columbia U., 1955-56. Grad. asst. NYU, 1946-47; with Cities Service Research and Devel. Co., 1947-82; successively research chem. engr. Cities Service Research and Devel. Co., Tallant, Okla.; asso. chemist Cities Service Research and Devel. Co., East Chicago, Ind.; chem. engr. Cities Service Research and Devel. Co., Camden, N.J.; asst. v.p. Cities Service Research and Devel. Co., N.Y.C., 1947-57; mgr. products devel. Cities Service Research and Devel. Co., Cranbury, N.J., 1957-58; mgr. Cranbury Lab., 1958-65; dir. product and process research Cities Service Oil Co., 1965-71; mgr. research and planning, chems. and metals group Cities Service Co., N.Y.C., 1971-72; dir. research Cities Service Co., 1972-76; pres. Cities Service Research & Devel. Co., Cranbury, 1972-76; gen. mgr. tech. systems div. Cities Service Research & Devel. Co., Tulsa, 1976-78; gen. mgr. metal fabrication Cities Service Research & Devel. Co., Chester, N.Y., 1978-80; cons. Cities Service Research & Devel. Co., 1980-81; gen. engr. U.S. Army, Ft. Monmouth, N.J., 1982-91; cons., 1992—. Contbr. articles to profl. jours. Served as 1st lt. AUS, 1943-46; capt. Res. Mem. Sigma Xi. Patentee in field. Home: 13 Buena Vista Ave Rumson NJ 07760-1109

ROSEN, CAROL MENDES, artist; b. N.Y.C., Jan. 15, 1933; d. Bram de Sola and Mildred (Bertuch) Mendes; m. Elliot A. Rosen, June 30, 1957. BA, Hunter Coll., 1954; MA, CUNY, 1962. Tchr. art West Orange (N.J.) Pub. Schs., 1959-85; co-curator exhibit Printmaking Coun. N.J., Sommerville, 1981; exhibit curator 14 Sculptors Gallery, N.Y.C, 1988, Collection: Nat. Collection of Fine Arts, Smithsonian Instn., Newark Mus., N.J. State Mus., Bristol-Myers Squibb, AT&T, Noyes Mus. Contbr. articles to arts mags. Fellow N.J. State Coun. on Arts, 1980, 83; recipient Hudson River Mus. award, Yonkers, 1983. Jewish. Avocations: gardening, reading. Home: 10 Beavers Rd Califon NJ 07830-3433

ROSEN, CHARLES, production designer. Prodn. designer: (films) Charly, 1968, A Separate Peace, 1972, Heroes, 1977, Empire of the Ants, 1977, Big Wednesday, 1978, Invasion of the Body Snatchers, 1978, Last Embrace, 1979, The Main Event, 1979, Inside Moves, 1980, My Favorite Year, 1982, The Entity, 1983, Flashdance, 1983, The Whoopee Boys, 1986, Broadcast News, 1987, Touch & Go, 1987, My Stepmother Is an Alien, 1988, My Blue Heaven, 1990, Downtown, 1990, The Butcher's Wife, 1991, Stop! or My Mon Will Shoot, 1992, Free Willy, 1993, My Girl 2, 1993, (TV movies) City in Fear, 1981. Office: care Lawrence Mirisch The Mirisch Agency 2705 Outpost Dr Los Angeles CA 90069

ROSEN, CHARLES, pianist, music educator; b. N.Y.C., May 5, 1927; s. Irwin and Anita (Gerber) R. B.A. summa cum laude, Princeton, 1947, M.A., 1949, Ph.D., 1951; Dr. Music honoris causa, Trinity Coll., Dublin, 1976, U. Leeds, 1976, U. Durham, Eng., 1980, U. Cambridge, Eng., 1992, U. Bristol, 1994. Asst. prof. modern langs. MIT, 1953-55; prof. music SUNY-Stony Brook, 1971-90; Ernest Bloch prof. U. Calif., Berkeley, 1977; Norton prof. poetry Harvard U., 1980-81; George Eastman prof. Balliol Coll., Oxford U., Eng., 1987-88; prof. music and social thought U. Chgo., 1988-96; Messenger lectr. Cornell U., 1975. Author: The Classical Style: Haydn, Mozart, Beethoven, 1971, Schoenberg, 1975, Sonata Forms, 1980, (with Henri Zerner) Romanticism and Realism, 1984, The Musical Languages of Elliott Carter, 1985, Frontiers of Meaning, 1994, The Romantic Generation, 1995; New York debut at Town Hall, 1951; first rec. Debussy Etudes, 1951; recs. include Elliott Carter's Double Concerto, 16 Beethoven Sonatas; concertized throughout Europe and Am. Recipient Nat. Book award, 1972; Edison prize, 1974; Deems Taylor award ASCAP, 1972, 76, 81; Fulbright fellow, 1951-53; Guggenheim fellow, 1973-74. Mem. Nat. Acad. Arts and Scis.

ROSEN, CHARLES, II, lawyer; b. New Orleans, Jan. 29, 1925; s. Louis Leucht and Nita (Silverstein) R.; m. Mary Alice Waldauer (div. 1976); children: Charles III, Virginia, Jane, James Louis; m. Sandra Reed (div. 1995); m. Emily Hart, 1995. BA, Tulane U., 1948, LLB, 1951. Bar: La. 1951. Assoc. Rosen, Kammer, Wolff, Hopkins & Burke, New Orleans, 1951-55; assoc. Jones, Walker, Waechter, Poitevent, Carrere & Denegre, New Orleans, 1955-58, ptnr., 1958-90; spl. counsel Locke, Purnell, Rain, Harrell, New Orleans, 1990—; mem. exec. com., past chmn. Golf & Sports Attractions, Inc. Past trustee Touro Synagogue; hon. trustee Touro Infirmary; chmn. lawyers div. Jewish Fedn. Greater New Orleans, 1969; past chmn. lawyers div. United Fund. 1st lt. U.S. Army, 1944-46, PTO. Mem. ABA, La. Bar Assn., New Orleans Bar Assn., Am. Coll. Real Estate Attys., Anglo Am. Real Property Inst., So. Golf Assn. (past bd. dirs.), New Orleans Golf Assn. (past pres., past bd. dirs.), Tulane Green Wave Club (past bd. dirs.), Lakewood Country Club (past pres., bd. dirs.). Republican. Avocation: golf. Home: 410 Northline Metairie LA 70005 Office: Locke Purnell Rain Harrell 601 Poydras St Ste 2400 New Orleans LA 70130-6029

ROSEN, COREY M., professional association executive; b. Denver, Nov. 26, 1948; s. Abraham and Dorothy Lillian (Bernstein) R.; m. Karen Young, Aug. 4, 1979; 1 child, Jessica. BA, Wesleyan U., 1970; MA, Cornell U., 1972, PhD, 1973. Asst. prof. govt. Ripon (Wis.) Coll., 1973-75; congressional fellow U.S. Senate, Washington, 1975-76; staff profl. Sen. James Abourezk, Washington, 1976-78; com. staff Senate Sm. Bus. Com., Washington, 1978-81; exec. dir. Nat. Ctr. for Employer Ownership, Oakland, Calif., 1981—. Author: Employee Ownership in America, 1986, Employee Ownership at Work, 1986, Understanding Employee Ownership, 1991. Democrat. Jewish. Avocations: running, bicycling, racquetball, reading. Office: Nat Ctr Employee Ownership 1201 Martin Luther King Hwy Oakland CA 94612

ROSEN, DAVID PAUL, book editor; b. Buffalo, May 23, 1959; s. Paul Maurice and Ethel A. (Witt) R. BA summa cum laude, Elmira Coll., 1981; MA, Temple U., 1984. Mktg. assoc. Temple U. Press, Phila., 1982-85; editor The Advocate, L.A., 1985-87, Ziff-Davis, N.Y.C., 1987-89; sr. editor Book-of-the-Month Club/Time Warner, N.Y.C., 1989-95; exec. editor Book-of-the-Month Club, N.Y.C., 1995-96, editl. dir. Quality Paperback Book Club, 1996—; lectr. pub. course NYU, 1994-96. Editor (book series) Triangle Classics, 1993—. Recipient Robertson prize Temple U., 1984, GLAAD award, 1994. Mem. Pub. Triangle, Wallace Stevens Soc., Phi Beta Kappa. Office: BOMC QPB 1271 Ave of Americas 3d Fl New York NY 10020

ROSEN, ELLEN FREDA, psychologist, educator; b. Chgo., Jan. 28, 1941; d. Samuel Aaron and Clara Laura (Pauker) R. BA, Carleton Coll., 1962; MA, U. Ill., 1965, PhD, 1968. Instr. psychology U. Ill., Urbana, 1966-67; prof., dir. grad. studies in psychology Coll. William and Mary, Williamsburg, Va., 1967-93; cons. Ctr. for Teaching Excellence Hampton (Va.) U., 1988-94. Author: Ednl. Computer Software, (with E. Rae Harcum) The Gatekeepers of Psychology, 1993; contbr. articles to profl. jours. Mem. Soc. for Computers in Psychology, Psychonomic Soc., Va. Psychol. Assn., Eastern Psychol. Assn., C.G. Jung Soc. of Tidewater, Am. Psychol. Soc., Assn. for Anorexia and Bulimia of Va. Office: Coll of William and Mary Dept of Psychology Williamsburg VA 23187

ROSEN, FRED SAUL, pediatrics educator; b. Newark, May 26, 1930; s. Philip and Amelia (Feld) R. AB, Lafayette Coll., 1951; MD, Western Res. U., 1955; MA (hon.), Harvard U., 1970; DSc (hon.), Lafayette Coll., 1978. From asst. to assoc. prof. pediatrics Harvard Med. Sch., Boston, 1966-72, James L. Gamble prof. pediatrics, 1972—; chief. div. immunology Children's Hosp., Boston, 1968-85, program dir. Gen. Clin. Rsch. Ctr., 1977-91; pres. Ctr. for Blood Rsch., Boston, 1987—; chmn. sci. com. on immunodeficiencies WHO, Boston, 1988—. Author: Dictionary of Immunology, 1989. Pres. Am. Friends of Jenner Appeal, Boston, 1985—; Sr. asst. surgeon USPHS, 1957-59. Recipient E. Mead Johnson award for pediatric rsch. Am. Acad. Pediatrics, 1970, Gen. Clin. Rsch. Ctrs. Program 4th Ann. award NIH, 1992; John Simon Guggenheim Meml. Found. fellow, 1974. Mem. Am. Assn. Immunology, Am. Soc. Clin. Investigation, Am. Pediatric Soc., Assn. Am. Physicians, NAS Inst. Medicine, St. Botolph Club, Harvard Club, Somerset Club. Home: 101 Chestnut St Boston MA 02108 Office: The Ctr for Blood Rsch 800 Huntington Ave Boston MA 02115-6303*

ROSEN, GEORGE, economist, educator; b. St. Petersburg, Russia, Feb. 7, 1920; s. Leon and Rebecca (Rosenoer) R.; m. Sylvia Vatuk; 1 son, Mark. B.A., Bklyn. Coll., 1940; M.A., Princeton U., 1942, Ph.D., 1949. Prof. econs. Bard Coll., Annandale-on-Hudson, N.Y., 1946-50; economist Dept. State, Washington, 1951-54, Council Econ. Indsl. Research, Washington, 1954-55, MIT, Cambridge, 1955-59, UN, N.Y.C., 1959-60, Ford Found., N.Y.C., India, 1960-62, Rand Corp., Santa Monica, Calif., 1962-67; chief economist Asian Devel. Bank, Manila, Philippines, 1967-71; prof. econs. U. Ill.-Chgo., 1972-85, prof. econs. emeritus, 1985—, head dept., 1972-77; fellow Woodrow Wilson Internat. Ctr., Washington, 1989-90; adj. prof. Johns Hopkins U.-Nanjing U. Ctr. Chinese-Am. Studies, 1986-87; cons USAID, Egypt, 1994; book rev. editor Econ. Devel. and Cultural Change, 1988—; treas. Am. Com. for Asian Econ. Studies, 1990-95. Author: Industrial Change in India, 1958, Some Aspects of Industrial Finance in India, 1962, Democracy and Economic Change in India, 1966, 67, Peasant Society in a Changing Economy, 1975, Decision-Making Chicago-Style, 1980, Western Economists and Eastern Societies, 1985, Industrial Change in India 1970-2000, 1988, Contrasting Styles of Industrial Reform: China and India in the 1980s, 1992, Economic Development in Asia, 1996. Ford Found. fellow NYU, 1971-72; grantee U. Ill., 1977-78, Social Sci. Research Council and Am. Inst. Indian Studies, 1980-81, Am. Inst. Indian Studies, 1983-84, 87-88, Rockefeller Found. Bellagio Study Ctr., 1984. Office: U Ill Dept Econs M/C 144 601 S Morgan St Chicago IL 60607-7100

ROSEN, GERALD ELLIS, federal judge; b. Chandler, Ariz., Oct. 26, 1951; s. Stanley Rosen and Marjorie (Sherman) Cahn; m. Laurie DeMond. BA, Kalamazoo Coll., 1973; JD, George Washington U., 1979. Researchist Swedish Inst., Stockholm, 1973; legis. asst. U.S. Senator Robert P. Griffin, Washington, 1974-79; law clk. Seyfarth, Shaw, Fairweather & Gerardson, Wash., 1979; from assoc. to sr. ptnr. Miller, Canfield, Paddock and Stone, Detroit, 1979-90; judge U.S. Dist Ct. (ea. dist.) Mich., Detroit, 1990—; mem. Jud. Evaluation Com. (co-chmn. 1983-88), Detroit; adj. prof. law Wayne State U., 1992, 93, U. Detroit Law Sch., 1994—; mem. U.S. Jud. Conf. Com. on Criminal Law; lectr. CLE confs., others. Contbr. articles to profl. jours. Rep. candidate for U.S. Congress, Mich., 1982; chmn. 17th Congl. Dist. REp. Com., 1983-85; mem. Mich. Criminal Justice Commn., 1985-87; mem. Jewish Cmty. Ctr. Fellow Kalamazoo Coll. (sr. 1972). Jewish. Office: US Courthouse Rm 802 231 W Lafayette Blvd Detroit MI 48226-2799

ROSEN, GERALD HARRIS, physicist, consultant, educator; b. Mount Vernon, N.Y., Aug. 10, 1933; s. David A. and Shirley (Schapiro) R.; m. Sarah Louise Sweet, June 8, 1963; children: Lawrence Alexander, Karlyn Penelope. B.S.E. (Guggenheim Jet Propulsion scholar, Whiton Engring.-Physics scholar), Princeton U., 1955, M.A. (NSF predoctoral fellow), 1956, Ph.D., 1958. NSF predoctoral fellow Inst. Theoretical Physics, Utrecht, Netherlands, 1957-58; research asso. dept. aero. engring. Princeton, 1958-59; NSF postdoctoral fellow Inst. Theoretical Physics, Stockholm, 1959-60; tech. cons. weapon systems evaluation div. The Pentagon, 1960; prin. scientist

Martin-Marietta Aerospace div., Balt., 1960-63; cons. to a tech. v.p. Southwest Research Inst., 1963-66; prof. physics Drexel U., Phila., 1966-73; M.R. Wehr prof. physics Drexel U., 1973—; cons. fin., indsl. and govt. agys., 1966—. Author: Formulations of Classical and Quantum Dynamical Theory, 1969, A New Science of Stock Market Investing, 1990; assoc. editor Bull. Math. Biology, 1982—; contbr. revs., articles to Math. Revs., Am. Phys. Soc., other profl. jours. Sponsor San Antonio Chamber Music Soc., 1963-66; mem. Franklin Inst., 1967—; mem. publ. bd. Soc. Math. Biol., 1983—. Fellow Am. Phys. Soc., AAAS; mem. Am. Math. Soc. Patentee in field. Home: 415 Charles Ln Wynnewood PA 19096-1604 Office: Drexel U Dept Physics Philadelphia PA 19104 *The meaning of life has transcended human understanding up to the present time, but there are reasons to believe that future discoveries in science will illuminate the significance of life in nature. We must break completely free of non-rational dogma and illusion, and attempt to solve this mystery with factual clues revealed by scientific progress.*

ROSEN, GERALD ROBERT, editor; b. N.Y.C., Nov. 17, 1930; s. Sol and Essie (Shapiro) R.; m. Lois Lehrman, May 9, 1958; 1 son, Evan Mark. BS, Ind. U., 1951, MA, 1953. Intelligence analyst Dept. Def., N.Y.C., 1955-58; assoc. editor Challenge: The Mag. of Econ. Affairs, N.Y.C., 1959-61; mng. editor Challenge: The Mag. of Econ. Affairs, 1961-64, 65-66; sr. editor Dun's Rev., N.Y.C., 1964-65, nat. affairs editor, 1967—; exec. editor Dun's Rev. (now Bus. Month), 1978-90; editor IMF survey Washington, 1990-93; mng. dir. Global Insights Svcs., Washington, 1993—; fin. corr. Westinghouse Broadcasting Co. Served with CIC U.S. Army, 1953-55. Mem. Soc. Am. Bus. and Econ. Writers, N.Y. Fin. Writers Assn., White House Corrs. Assn. Club: Nat. Press. Home: 3210 Grace St NW Washington DC 20007-3628 Office: 1700 K St NW Washington DC 20006-3817

ROSEN, HOWARD ROBERT, lawyer; b. Montreal, Que., Can., Apr. 15, 1960; came to U.S. 1967; s. Kelvin and Binnie Lynn (Michaels) R. ; m. Adrienne Joy Unger, Apr. 11, 1987. BA, Emory U., 1982; JD, U. Miami, Coral Gables, Fla., 1985. Bar: Fla. 1985. Asst. state atty. Dade County State Atty. Office, Miami, Fla., 1985—. Avocations: travel, sports. Home: 17931 NW 9th Ct Pembroke Pines FL 33029 Office: Dade County State Atty 1350 NW 12th Ave Miami FL 33136-2102

ROSEN, JAMES MAHLON, artist, art historian, educator; b. Detroit, Dec. 3, 1933; s. Joseph and Lillian Rosen; children: Shira Del, Phyllis Dresser, Jeremy-Joseph. Student, Cooper Union, 1956; BS, Wayne State U., 1957; MFA, Cranbrook Acad. Art, 1958. Mem. faculty dept. art Wayne State U., 1961-63, U. Hawaii, 1965-67; mem. faculty Santa Rosa (Calif.) Jr. Coll., 1967-84, U. Calif., 1987-88; Wm. Morris Eminent scholar in art Augusta Coll., 1989—; artist-in-residence, guest lectr. Deep Springs Coll., R.I. Sch. Design, Montclair State Coll., San Bernardino State Coll., Pa. Acad. Fine Arts; artist-in-residence Ferrara, Italy. Author: Notes From a Painter's Journal, 1960, An American Homage to Piero della Francesca, In the Realm of Light, William Bartram Sketches: The Field and the Image, Qualities of Camouflaging, 1970, On the Sheer Nonsense of Liking Anything, 1979; exhbns. include Betty Parsons Gallery, N.Y.C., Donald Morris Gallery, Detroit, Gallery Paule Anglim, San Francisco, Mus. Modern Art Penthouse Show, Eva Gelfman Gallery, Thomas Babeor Gallery, La Jolla, Calif., La Jolla Mus. Contemporary Art; dir., curator William Bartram Art Exhbn.; reprsenteted in permanent collections in Mus. Modern Art, N.Y.C., Whitney Mus. Am. Art, Ga. Mus. Art, Syracuse U., Ashmolean Mus., U. Calif. Berkeley Mus., San Francisco Mus. Modern Art, Met. Mus. of Art, Cranbrook Mus. Art, Victoria and Albert Mus., London; bd. dirs. Arts Meridian-A Cultural Jour. Ams.; commissions include Sheraton Hotel, Venice, Ascott Residencies, London, Occidental Grand Hotel, Atlanta, Fairmont Hotel, Chgo. Served with M.C. U.S. Army, 1953-55. Grantee Huntington Hartford Found., Yaddo, MacDowell Found., NEH, Djerassi Found. Arts, Ga. Coun. on Arts. Mem. Am. Soc. Art, Religion and Culture (bd. dirs.), Soc. So. Painters (pres.), Soc. of Art, Religion and Contemporary Culture (bd. dirs.). Home: 824 Johns Rd Augusta GA 30904-6116

ROSEN, JON HOWARD, lawyer; b. Bklyn., May 20, 1943; s. Eli and Vera (Horowitz) R.; m. Georgeanne Evans, 1993; children of a previous marriage: Jason Marc, Hope Terry. BA, Hobart Coll., 1965; JD, St. John's U., 1968; postgrad. Bernard Baruch Sch. Bus., CCNY, 1969-71. Bar: N.Y. 1969, Calif. 1975, Wash. 1977. Atty. FAA, N.Y.C., 1968-71; regional atty., contract adminstr. Air Line Pilots Assn., N.Y.C., Chgo., L.A., San Francisco, 1971-77; pvt. practice Seattle, 1977-80; ptnr. Frank and Rosen, Seattle, 1981—; instr. labor studies Shoreline Community Coll., 1978-90. Mem. ABA (union co-chmn. com. on Employee Rights and Responsibilities, regional EEOC liaison), Seattle-King County Bar Assn. (past chmn. aviation and space law sect., past chmn. Pacific Coast Labor Law Conf., past chmn. labor law sect.), Nat. Employment Lawyers Assn. (state steering com.). Home: 335 Ward St Seattle WA 98109-3738 Office: Frank & Rosen 705 2nd Ave Ste 1200 Seattle WA 98104-1711

ROSEN, JUDAH BEN, computer scientist; b. Phila., May 5, 1922; s. Benjamin and Susan (Hurwich) R.; children—Susan Beth, Lynn Ruth. BSEE, Johns Hopkins U., 1943; PhD in Applied Math., Columbia U., 1952. Rsch. assoc. Princeton (N.J.) U., 1952-54; head applied math. dept. Shell Devel. Co., 1954-62; vis. prof. computer sci. dept. Stanford (Calif.) U., 1962-64; prof. dept. computer sci. and math. rsch. ctr. U. Wis., Madison, 1964-71; prof., head dept. computer sci. U. Minn., Mpls., 1971—; fellow Supercomputer Inst. U. Minn., 1985—; sr. fellow Supercomputer Ctr., San Diego, 1993—; adj. rsch. prof. dept. computer sci. and engrin. U. Calif. San Diego, La Jolla, 1992—; Fulbright prof. Technion, Israel, 1968-69, Davis vis. prof. 1980; invited lectr. Chinese Acad. Sci., Peking, 1980; lectr., cons. Argonne (Ill.) Nat. Lab.; mem. Nat. Computer Sci. Bd. Author: Topics in Parallel Computing, 1992; editor: Nonlinear Programming, 1970, Supercomputers and Large-Scale Optimization, 1988; assoc. editor Global Optimization, 1990—, Annals of Ops. Rsch., 1984—; contbr. articles to profl. jours. and procs. Grantee NSF, 1995—, ARPA/NIST, 1994—. Mem. Assn. Computing Machinery, Soc. Indsl. and Applied Math., Math. Programming Soc. Research interests: supercomputers and parallel algorithms for optimization, computation of molecular structure by energy minimization, algorithms for structured approximation in signal processing. Home: 10305 28th Ave N Plymouth MN 55441-3219 also: 322 Prospect St La Jolla CA 92037 Office: EE/CSci Bldg U Minn Minneapolis MN 55455-0100 also: Univ Calif-San Diego Dept Computer Sci Engring 9500 Gilman Dr La Jolla CA 92093-0114

ROSEN, KAY, painter. BA, Tulane U.; MA, Northwestern U. adv. bd. Visual Arts Panel Ind. Arts Commn., 1986, Arts Midwest Focus Groups, 1988; curator, vis. artist Sch. Art Inst. Chgo., 1988, U. Chgo., 1990; lectr. Columbia Coll., 1989, Ind. U. N.W., Gary, 1992; panelist Midwest Coll. Art Assn. Conf., Cin., 1989, Mass. Artists Fellowship Program Painting Panel, 1990; graduate critique panelist, Sch. Art Inst. Chgo., 1989; rev. panelist, Arts Midwest New Partnership Grants Visual Artists, 1990; spkr., panelist, Mountain Cake Symposium, Va., 1990; grad. faculty advisor Sch. Art Inst. Chgo., 1992; spkr. Ind. State U., Terre Haute, 1993. Editor Spunky Internat., 1992; exhibited at Whitney Mus. Art, 1991, Mus. Contemporary Art, Chgo., Shoshana Wayne Gallery, Santa Monica, Calif., Forefront Gallery Indpls. Mus. Art, Victoria Miro Gallery, London, Galeria Massimo de Carlo, Milan, 1994, Galerie Erika & Otto Friedrich, Berne, Switzerland, 1995. Recipient Visual Arts award Hirshhorn Mus., Albequerque Mus., Toledo Mus. Art, 1991, Mus. Modern Art, Melbourne, Australia, various others. Address: 6925 Indian Boundary Gary IN 46403*

ROSEN, LAWRENCE, anthropology educator; b. Cin., Dec. 9, 1941; s. George and Hannah (Persky) R. B.A., Brandeis U., 1963; M.A., U. Chgo., 1965, Ph.D., 1968, J.D., 1974. Bar: N.C. 1975, U.S. Supreme Ct. 1979. Asst. prof. anthropology U. Ill., Urbana, 1968-70; mem. Inst. for Advanced Study, Princeton, N.J., 1970-71; assoc. prof. anthropology Duke U., Durham, N.C., 1974-77; prof. anthropology Princeton U., 1977—; adj. prof. Columbia U. Law Sch., 1979—; vis. prof. Northwestern U. Law Sch., Chgo., 1985-87, U. Pa. Law Sch., Phila., 1985-86, Georgetown Law Ctr., 1994; Lewis H. Morgan lectr. U. Rochester, 1985. Co-author: Meaning and Order in Moroccan Society, 1978, Bargaining for Reality, 1984, The Anthropology of Justice, 1989; editor: The American Indian and the Law, 1974, Other Intentions, 1995. Legal asst. Native Am. Rights Fund., Boulder, Colo., 1973. Woodrow Wilson fellow, 1964, Guggenheim fellow, 1981, John & Catherine MacArthur Found. fellow, 1981, Fulbright fellow, 1991; recipient Princeton U. Women's Orgn. award, 1994. Fellow Am. Anthrop. Assn.

ROSEN, LEE SPENCER, lawyer; b. Miami, Fla., May 23, 1961; s. Maurice and Virginia Lee (Philpot) R.; m. Lisa C., June 23, 1990. BA, U. N.C., 1983; JD, Wake Forest U., 1986. Bar: N.C. 1987, U.S. Dist. Ct. (ea. dist.) N.C. 1987, U.S. Ct. Appeals (4th cir.) 1987. Atty. Crisp, Davis et al, Raleigh, N.C., 1987-89; ptnr. Rosen & Robbins, P.A., Raleigh, 1989-92, The Rosen Law Firm, Cary, N.C., 1992—. Contbr. articles to profl. jours. Mem. ABA (chairperson 1989-92), N.C. Bar Assn. (coun. mem. 1989-92). Office: 4101 Lake Boone Trl Ste 105 Raleigh NC 27607-7506

ROSEN, LOUIS, physicist; b. N.Y.C., June 10, 1918; s. Jacob and Rose (Lipionski) R.; m. Mary Terry, Sept. 4, 1941; 1 son, Terry Leon. BA, U. Ala., 1939, MS, 1941; PhD, Pa. State U., 1944; DSc (hon.), U. N.Mex., 1979, U. Colo., 1987. Instr. physics U. Ala., 1940-41, Pa. State U., 1943-44; mem. staff Los Alamos Sci. Lab., 1944-90, group leader nuclear plate lab., 1949-65, alt. div. leader exptl. physics div., 1962-65, dir. meson physics facility, 1965-85, div. leader medium energy physics div., 1965-86, sr. lab. fellow, 1985-90, sr. fellow emeritus, 1990—; Sesquicentennial hon. prof. U. Ala., 1981; mem. panel on future of nuclear sci., chmn. subpanel on accelerators NRC of NAS, 1976, mem. panel on instnl. arrangements for orbiting space telescope, 1976; mem. U.S.A.-USSR Coordinating Com. on Fundamental Properties of Matter, 1971-90. Author papers in nuclear sci. and applications of particle accelerators.; bd. editors: Applications of Nuclear Physics; co-editor Climate Change and Energy Policy, 1992. Mem. Los Alamos Town Planning Bd., 1962-64; mem. Gov.'s Com. on Tech. Excellence in N.Mex.; mem. N.Mex. Cancer Control Bd., 1976-80, v.p., 1979-81; co-chmn. Los Alamos Vols. for Stevenson, 1956; Dem. candidate for county commr., 1962; bd. dirs. Los Alamos Med. Ctr., 1977-83, chmn., 1983; bd. govs. Tel Aviv U., 1986. Recipient E.O. Lawrence award AEC, 1963, Golden Plate award Am. Acad. Achievement, 1964, N.Mex. Disting. Pub. Svc. award, 1978; named Citizen of Yr., N.Mex. Realtors Assn., 1973; Guggenheim fellow, 1959-60; alumni fellow Pa. State U., 1978; Louis Rosen prize established in his honor by bd. dirs. Meson Facility Users Group, 1984; Louis Rosen Auditorium dedicated, 1995. Fellow AAAS (coun. 1989), Am. Phys. Soc. (coun. 1975-78, chmn. panel on pub. affairs 1980, div. nuclear physics 1985, mem. subcom. on internat. sci. affairs 1988). Home: 1170 41st St Los Alamos NM 87544-1913 Office: Los Alamos Sci Lab PO Box 1663 Los Alamos NM 87544-0600 *I have come to believe that only after one has learned to manage and set worthy goals for himself should he attempt to do so for others.*

ROSEN, MATTHEW STEPHEN, botanist, consultant; b. N.Y.C., Oct. 7, 1943; s. Norman and Lucille (Cass) R.; m. Deborah Louise Mackay, June 16, 1974 (div. Feb. 1983); children: Gabriel Mackay, Rebecca Mackay; m. Kay Eloise Williams, July 11, 1987. MFSc, Yale U., 1972; BS, Cornell U., 1967. Instr. ornamental horticulture SUNY-Farmingdale, 1968-69; landscape designer Manhattan Gardener, N.Y.C., 1969-70; instr. ornamental horticulture McHenry County Coll., Crystal Lake, Ill., 1972-74; coord. agrl. studies, asst. prof. biology, chemistry Mercer County Community Coll., West Windsor, N.J., 1974-79; adminstr. Des Moines Botanical Ctr., 1979-96, horticulture divsn. mgr., 1996—; consulting dir. West Mich. Horticultural Soc., 1993; cons. in field. Contbr. articles to profl. jours. Com. chmn. United Way Cen. Iowa, 1982, div. chmn. 1983-86, 88-89, 91, group chmn. 1987, chmn. arts adv. com. 1985-86, pres. 1986, bd. dirs. Arts and Recreation Council, 1985-86, com. chmn., 1992; mem. career vocat. com. Des Moines Indsl. Sch. Dist., 1986, co-chmn., 1987, mem. Ptnrs. for Progress com., 1988-90, mem. sci. monitoring program, 1991, 92; chmn. Two Rivers Festival, 1987-88; active Des Moines Sister City Program, Kofu, Japan, 1984, delegation, 1989, Naucalpan, Mexico, 1986, 87, Shijiazhuang, China, 1986, 90, 92; mem. edn. com. Am. Assn. Botanical Gardens & Arboretum, mem. membership com., mem. conservation com. Mem. Am. Assn. Botanical Gardens and Arboreta (edn. com.), Greater Des Moines C. of C. (team leader 1984—, chmn. new mem. sales, chmn. 8 O'clock new, Pres. Cabinet award 1983, 84, 85, Achievement award C. of C. Fedn. 1986, mem. exec. com. 1995, 96), East Des Moines C. of C. (bd. dirs. 1992—, v.p., sec. 1993—, pres.- elect 1994, pres. 1995, 96, sister cities commn. 1994, china chair 1995, 96, treas. 1995, 96), Greater Des Moines Conv. and Visitors Bur. (chmn. new mem. sales com. 1988-89), Iowa Advt. Rev. Coun., Affiliate Pres.'s Coun. of Chambers (chair 1995), bd. of dirs. DM Gen. Hosp., 1994-95, 96, Rotary, Phi Kappa Phi, Pi Alpha Xi. Democrat. Jewish. Avocations: photography, reading, model trains, collecting old books, writing. Home: 1042 22nd St West Des Moines IA 50265-2219 Office: Des Moines Botanical Ctr 909 E River Dr Des Moines IA 50316-2854

ROSEN, MEYER ROBERT, chemical engineer; b. Bklyn., Mar. 9, 1943; s. Philip and Jeanne (Rosenzweig) R.; children: Carrie, David; m. Selma Mirman. BS, Poly. Inst. Bklyn., 1964, MS, 1966. Diplomate Am. Bd. Forensic Examiners; bd. cert. forensic examiner, profl. chemist, profl. chem. engr.; chartered chemist. Rsch. engr. Union Carbide Corp., Tonawanda, N.Y., 1966-73, project scientist, 1973-79; devel. scientist Union Carbide Corp., Tarrytown and Boundbrook, N.J., 1979-92; dir. chemistry and chem. engring. Inter-City Testing and Cons. Corp., Mineola, N.Y., 1993—; cons. Brookfield Engring. Labs., Stoughton, Mass., 1979-81; course dir. Ctr. for Profl. Advancement, East Brunswick, N.J., 1994; adj. prof. chemistry Westchester C.C., 1970-84; spkr. in field of chem. engring. and energy medicine. Contbr. articles to profl. publs., including Polymer Plast. Tech. Engr., Jour. Coatings Tech., Jour. Coll. Interface Sci., Am. Jour. Acupuncture, Union Carbide World Mag.; author 2 books on Hyperacusis ear disorder. Fellow Am. Inst. Chemists, Royal Soc. Chemistry London; mem. ASTM, Am. Chem. Soc. (divsn. colloid and surface chemistry), Am. Indsl. Hygiene Assn., Am. Soc. Safety Engrs., Assn. of Cons. Chemists and Chem. Engrs., Nat. Fire Protection Assn., Nat. Assn. Tchrs. of Acupuncture and Oriental Medicine, Am. Assn. Acupuncture and Oriental Medicine, Acupuncture Soc. Pa., Nat. Dental Acupuncture Soc. (mem. exec. bd.), Acupuncture Soc. N.Y., Nat. Alliance of Acupuncture and Oriental Medicine (bd. cert. in pain mgmt.). Achievements include patents for process for fire fighting foams, antifoams, for flocculation of phosphatic slimes, high molecular weight water soluble polymers and flocculating method, process for producing polymer water-in-oil emulsion, process for agglomerating ore concentrate utilizing clay and dispersions of polymer binders or dry powder binders, removal of residual ethylene oxide from poly(ethylene oxide), development of treatment of previously incurable ear disorder, seminar leader in Reflex-Correspondence Training. Publications include Polyox Water Soluble Resin Worldwide Technical Literature; Rheology of Non-Newtonian Fluids; Energy Medicine; Auriculotherapy; Korean Hand Therapy. Office: Inter-City Testing & Cons 167 Willis Ave Mineola NY 11501

ROSEN, MOISHE, religious organization administrator; b. Kansas City, Mo., Apr. 12, 1932; s. Ben and Rose (Baker) R.; m. Ceil Starr, Aug. 18, 1950; children: Lyn Rosen Bond, Ruth. Diploma, Northeastern Bible Coll., 1957; DD, Western Conservative Bapt. Sem., 1986. Ordained to ministry Bapt. Ch., 1957. Missionary Am. Bd. Missions to the Jews, N.Y.C., 1956; minister in charge Beth Sar Shalom Am. Bd. Missions to the Jews, Los Angeles, 1957-67; dir. recruiting and tng. Am. Bd. Missions to the Jews, N.Y.C., 1967-70; leader Jews for Jesus Movement, San Francisco, 1970-73, exec. dir., 1973—, founder, chmn., 1973—; speaker in field. Author: Saying of Chairman Moishe, 1972, Jews for Jesus, 1974, Share the New Life with a Jew, 1976, Christ in the Passover, 1977, Y'shua, The Jewish Way to Say Jesus, 1982, Overture to Armageddon, 1991, The Universe is Broken: Who on Earth Can Fix It?, 1991, Demystifying Personal Evangelism, 1992. Trustee Western Conservative Bapt. Sem., Portland, Oreg., 1979-85, 86-91, Bibl. Internat. Coun. on Bibl. Inerrancy, Oakland, Calif., 1979-89; bd. dirs. Christian Advs. Serving Evangelism, 1987-91. Office: Jews for Jesus 60 Haight St San Francisco CA 94102-5802

ROSEN, MYOR, harpist, educator; b. N.Y.C., May 28, 1917; s. Caesar and Rose (Seidenberg) R.; m. Esther Rosen, May 25, 1941; children: Linda, David. Diploma, Juilliard Sch. Music, 1940. Faculty Juilliard Sch. Music, 1947-69. Prin. harpist, Mexico Symphony Orch., 1941-42, Indpls. Symphony Orch., 1941-42, Mpls. Symphony Orch., 1943-44, staff harpist, CBS, Columbia Records and free lanced, 1945-60, prin. harpist, N.Y. Philharm., 1960-87; Composer incidental music for; NBC series Arts and the Gods, 1946, CBS Camera Three, 1947, Solomon, The King, 1948. Served with U.S. Army, 1945. Mem. Am. Fedn. Musicians, Bohemians. *Having been the fortunate recipient of a 7-year scholarship through the New York Philharmonic Symphony Society and the Juilliard School of Music when I began my career as a harpist, I can think of no greater honor than my privilege in having been accepted as principal harpist with the same organization which trained me. I now bend my efforts to train future harpists to excel in like manner. In my opinion, the most important function of a teacher is to teach his students how to teach themselves; self-development.*

ROSEN, NATHANIEL KENT, cellist; b. Altadena, Calif., June 9, 1948; s. David Leon and Frances Jean (Kaufman) R.; m. Jennifer Langham, Aug. 27, 1976 (div. 1986); m. Margo Shohl, May 21, 1989; children: Samuel Gregory, Stella Rosalie. Student, Pasadena (Calif.) City Coll., 1965-67; Mus.B., U. So. Calif., 1971. Teaching asst. U. So. Calif., 1968-75, mem. faculty 7th ann. Gregor Piatigorsky Seminar Sch. Music, 1984; asst. prof. Calif. State U. at Northridge, 1970-76; mem. faculty Manhattan Sch. Music, N.Y.C., 1982-88, 94—; now mem. faculty U. Ill., Urbana, 1988-94. Prin. cellist, Los Angeles Chamber Orch., 1970-76, Pitts. Symphony, 1977-79, concert cellist worldwide; recordings include Orientale: Romantic Music for the Cello. Recipient 1st prize Naumburg Competition, 1977, 1st prize Moscow Tchaikovsky Competition, 1978; Ford Found. grantee, 1970-71; Rockefeller Found. grantee, 1973-74. Mem. Violoncello Soc. N.Y., Century Assn. N.Y. Office: Shaw Concerts 1900 Broadway New York NY 10023-7004 also: North Star Recordings 95 Hathaway St Providence RI 02907

ROSEN, NORMAN EDWARD, lawyer; b. Providence, July 2, 1938; s. Albert and Lillian R.; m. Estelle Cutler, Sept. 5, 1966; children: James, Vanessa. AB, Harvard U., 1959; LLB, Columbia U., 1962; MA, George Washington U., 1965. Bar: N.Y. 1962, D.C. 1963, U.S. Supreme Ct. 1966. Trial atty. FTC, Washington, 1962-67; assoc. Paskus, Gordon & Hyman, N.Y.C., 1967-69; ptnr. Levin, Kreis, Ruskin & Gyory, N.Y.C., 1970-72; staff v.p., sr. counsel trade regulation and licensing RCA, N.Y.C., 1972-82, Princeton, N.J., 1982-86; sr. v.p., gen. counsel Gen. Electric and RCA Licensing Mgmt. Operation, Inc., Princeton, 1986—, GE Trading Co., N.Y.C., 1989—. Contbr. articles to profl. jours. Mem. ABA (chmn. patent trademark and know-how com. antitrust sect. 1983-86, mem. coun. antitrust sect. 1986-89, mem. task forces on Dept. Justice antitrust guidelines and mergers and know-how in European econ. community, spl. com. on internat. antitrust, vice chmn. antitrust sect. 1991-92), Am. Intellectual Property Law Assn., Harvard Club, Surf Club. Office: GE 2 Independence Way Princeton NJ 08540-6620

ROSEN, PETER, health facility administrator, emergency physician, educator; b. Bklyn., Aug. 3, 1935; s. Isadore Theodore and Jessie Olga (Solomon) R.; m. Ann Helen Rosen, May 16, 1959; children: Henry, Monte, Curt, Ted. BA, U. Chgo., 1955; MD, Washington U., St. Louis, 1960. Diplomate Am. Bd. Surgery, Nat. Bd. Med. Examiners, Am. Bd. Emergency Medicine; cert. Advanced Cardiac Life Support Instr., Advanced Trauma Life Support Provider. Intern U. Chgo. Hosps. & Clinics, 1960-61; resident Highland County Hosp., Oakland, Calif., 1961-65; assoc. prof. divsn. emergency medicine U. Chgo. Hosps. & Clinics, 1971-73, prof. divsn. emergency medicine, 1973-77; dir. divsn. emergency medicine Denver City Health & Hosps., 1977-86, 87-89; asst. dir. dept. emergency medicine U. Calif., San Diego Med. Ctr., 1989—, dir. edn. dept. emergency medicine, 1989—, dir. emergency medicine residency program, 1991—; attending physician Hot Springs Meml. Hosp., Thermopolis, Wyo., Worland (Wyo.) County Hosp., Basin-Graybull Hosp., Basin, Wyo., 1968-71, U. Chgo. Hosps. & Clinics, 1971-77; dir. emergency medicine residency program, divsn. emergency medicine U. Chgo. Hosps. & Clinics, 1971-77; emergency medicine med. advisor State of Colo., 1977-85; dir. emergency medicine residency program Denver Gen. Hosp., St. Anthony Hosp. Systems, St. Joseph Hosp., 1977-88; clin. prof. divsn. emergency medicine Oreg. Health Scis. U., Portland, 1978-89; prof. sect. emergency medicine, dept. surgery U. Colo. Health Scis. Ctr., 1984-89; dep. mgr. med. affairs Denver Dept. Health & Hosps., 1986-87; med. dir. life flight air med. svc. U. Calif., San Diego Med. Ctr., 1989-91; mem. hosp. staff U. Calif., San Diego Med. Ctr., Tri-City Med. Ctr., Oceanside, Calif., 1989—; base hosp. physician, adj. prof. medicine & surgery U. Calif., San Diego Med. Ctr., 1989—; chair med. ethics com., mem. ethics consult team U. Calif., San Diego Med. Ctr., 1990—, mem. recruitment and admissions com., 1992—; lectr. in field; cons. in field. Author: (with others) Case Reports in Emergency Medicine: 1974-76, 1977, Encyclopedia Brittannica, 1978, 85, Principles and Practice of Emergency Medicine, 1978, 86, Protocols for Prehospital Emergency Care, 1980, 84, Cardiopulmonary Resuscitation, 1982, An Atlas of Emergency Medicine Procedures, 1984, Critical Decisions in Trauma, 1984, Emergency Pediatrics, 1984, 86, 90, Controversies in Trauma Management, 1985, Standardized Nursing Care Plans for Emergency Department, 1986, Emergency Medicine: Concepts and Clinical Practice, 1988, 92, The Clinical Practice of Emergency Medicine, 1991, Essentials of Emergency Medicine, 1991, Current Practice of Emergency Medicine, 1991, Care of the Surgical Patient, 1991, Diagnostic Radiology in Emergency Medicine, 1992, Pediatric Emergency Care Systems: Planning and Management, 1992, The Airway: Emergency Management, 1992; contbg. editor, editor abstracts sect. Jour. Am. Coll. Emergency Physicians, Annals of Emergency Medicine, 1976-83; mem. editorial bd. Topics in Emergency Medicine, 1979-82, ER Reports, 1981-83; consulting editor Emergindex Microindex, 1980—; editor in chief Jour. Emergency Medicine, 1983—; contbr. articles to profl. jours. Capt. USMC, 1965-68, lt. col. Res. inactive. Recipient AMA award, 1970, Am. Hosp. Assn. award, 1973. Fellow Am. Coll. Surgeons, Am. Burn Assn., Am. Coll. Emergency Physicians (chmn. edn. com. 1977-79, bd. dirs. Colo. chpt. 1977-80, pres. Colo. chpt. 1981-82, N.C. chpt. award 1976, Outstanding Contbns. and Leadership in Emergency Medicine award 1977, Silver Tongue Debater award 1980, John. D. Mills Outstanding Contbn. to Emergency Medicine award 1984); mem. Am. Trauma Soc. (founding), Soc. Acad. Emergency Medicine (Leadership award 1990), Alpha Omega Alpha Honor Med. Soc. (grad.), Coun. Emergency Medicine Dirs. Office: U of California-San Diego 200 W Arbor Dr San Diego CA 92103-1911

ROSEN, RAYMOND, health facility executive; b. Louisville, Feb. 5, 1950; s. Sam and Olga Rosen; m. Deborah Joy Rubinow, June 25, 1972; children: Lisa, Jessica. BS, Pa. State U., 1972; MA, George Washington U., 1974. Adminstrv. resident York (Pa.) Hosp., 1973-74, asst. to pres., 1974-75, asst. adminstr.-adminstrn., 1975-77, asst. adminstr.-med. affairs, 1977-79, adminstr.-med. affairs, 1979-87, v.p. opers., 1987—. Pres. Young Adminstrs. Group Ctrl. Pa., 1980-82; pres. Community Transit, Inc., 1992—, vice chmn., 1989-92, chmn., 1992—; bd. dirs. Fedn. South Ctrl. Pa. Emergency Health Svcs., 1978-92, mem. adv. com., 1992-93, York County Emergency Health Svcs. Coun., 1978-92, Jewish Community Ctr., 1986-91; divsn. chmn. United Way York County, 1988, York County Transp. Auth., 1995—. Fellow Am. Coll. Healthcare Execs. (regent south ctrl. Pa. 1991-95), mem. Am. Hosp. Assn., Hosp. Assn. Pa. (planning com. 1992—). Office: York Health Sys 1001 S George St York PA 17403-3676

ROSEN, RICHARD GARY, newspaper editor; b. Bronx, N.Y., May 21, 1951; s. Louis and Esther (Schiffman) R.; m. Jane Ruth Calem, May 14, 1983; children: Joanna, Sarah, Elizabeth. B Journalism, U. Mo., 1972. Reporter Paterson (N.J.) News, 1972-74; reporter, asst. city editor The Star-Ledger, Newark, 1974-80; reporter, dep. city editor The Daily News, N.Y.C., 1980-87, city editor, Sunday editor, 1988-93, dep. mng. editor, 1993—; editor The N.Y. Times, N.Y.C., 1987-88; adj. instr. grad. sch. Columbia U., N.Y.C., 1986. Avocations: running, swimming, reading. Office: The Daily News 450 W 33d St New York NY 10001-2603

ROSEN, RICHARD LEWIS, lawyer, real estate developer; b. N.Y.C., Mar. 6, 1943; s. Morris and Lorraine (Levy) R.; m. Doris Ellen Bloom, Aug. 28, 1983. BA, Cornell U., 1965; JD, N.Y. Law Sch., 1968; cert. N.Y.U. Real Estate Inst., 1980. Bar: N.Y. 1968, U.S. Dist. Ct. (so. and ea. dists.) N.Y. 1972; lic. real estate broker. Sole practice, N.Y.C., 1971-73; ptnr. Rosen, Wise, Felzen & Salomon, N.Y.C., 1973-79; ptnr. Rosen & Felzen, N.Y.C., 1979-84, Rosen, Rudd, Kera, Graubard & Hollender, 1985-88, Bell, Kalnick, Klee and Green, N.Y.C., 1989-90, Rosen, Einbinder & Dunn, P.C., N.Y.C., 1990—. Mem. ABA (mem. franchising com. anti-trust div.), Am. Assn. Franchisees and Dealers (mem. legal steering com., fair franchising standards com.), N.Y. State Bar Assn. (mem. franchise law com.), Assn. Bar City N.Y. (panel mem. com. on franchising), Red Key Hon. Soc., Cornell U., Sphinx Head Hon. Soc., Cornell U., Spiked Shoe Soc., Cornell U., Ea. Intercollegiate Athletic Assn. (named Lightweight Football All Ea. Selection, 1963,

64). Named Ea. States Lightweight Weightlifting Champion, 1968; N.Y. State Regents scholar. Avocations: tennis, skiing, phys. fitness, guitar, reading. Home: 1 Old Jericho Tpke Jericho NY 11753-1205 Also: Lamb Ave Quogue NY 11959 Office: Rosen Einbinder & Dunn PC 641 Lexington Ave New York NY 10022-4503 *While the shortest distance between two points is, invariably, a straight line, it is helpful if one has a good compass to guide one along the way. Further, detours are frequently necessary, even if only to view the scenery, while traveling towards our chosen destination.*

ROSEN, ROBERT CHARLES, lawyer; b. Valley Forge, Pa., Oct. 4, 1945; s. Morris and Fanella Rosen; m. Theresa J. Rosen, Mar. 19, 1972; children: Diane, Joanne, Marlene, Edgar, Lesa, Mitchell, Patty, Charlene. BS, U. Minn., 1967; JD, Duquesne U., 1970; LLM, Harvard U., 1979. Bar: Calif., D.C., Pa., U.S. Dist. Cts., U.S. Ct. Appeals. Legal intern Law Offices of Goldring and Nernberg, 1968-69; rsch. fellow Fletcher Sch. Law and Diplomacy, Tufts U., Boston, 1971-72; asst. atty. gen. Bur. Consumer Protection, Dept. Justice, Pa., 1972-73; atty., trial atty.-fin., legal asst. to commr., sr. counsel U.S. SEC, Washington, 1973-85; ptnr. Lewis, D'Amato, Brisbois & Bisgaard, L.A., 1985-94; atty. pvt. practice, L.A., 1994—; program chmn. Glendon Tremain Symposium, L.A., 1991, Internat. Securities, Regulations Trading and Transactions Symposium, L.A., 1991, Recent Devels. in Securities and Comml. Arbitration, L.A., 1989, Recent Devels. in Securities Class Actions, L.A., 1988; co-chmn. seminar Regulation of Internat. Securities Transactions, N.Y.C., 1989. Gen. editor: International Securities Regulation, 6 vols.; author: Commercial Business and Trade Laws: India, 1982; contbr. articles to profl. jours. Mem. ABA (internat. law sect., banking and bus. law sect., spl. task force on securities arbitration), Internat. Bar Assn. (com. on issues and trading in securities bus. law sect.), Inter-Am. Bar Assn., L.A. County Bar Assn. (internat. law sect., bus. and corps. law sect., exec. com. 1986—, chmn. 1993-94, chmn. securities law enforcement subcom.). Office: 633 W Fifth St 58th Fl Los Angeles CA 90071

ROSEN, ROBERT THOMAS, analytical and food chemist; b. Concord, N.H., Nov. 5, 1941; s. Maurice J. and Miriam M. (Miller) R.; m. Sharon Lynne Beres, Apr. 23, 1972. BA (cum laude), Nasson Coll.; PhD, Rutgers U. Sr. rsch. scientist Chem. Rsch. and Devel. Ctr., FMC Corp., Princeton, N.J., 1966-84; program dir. analytical support facilities, 1984—; assoc. dir. Ctr. for Advanced Food Technology, Rutgers U., New Brunswick, N.J., 1993—; chmn. North Jersey ACS Mass Spectrometry Topical Group, 1987-88. Assoc. editor The Mass Spec Source, 1988-90; contbr. articles and book reviews to profl. jours. Fellow Am. Inst. Chemists; mem. Am. Soc. for Mass Spectrometry, Am. Chem. Soc. N.Y. Acad. Scis., N.Am. Native Fishes Assn., Inst. Food Technologists, Phi Lambda Upsilon (hon.). Achievements include research in gas and liquid chromatography, free and glycosidically bound organic compounds in fruits and vegetables, determination of nonvolatile and thermally labile pesticides and phytochemicals in food, natural products and the environment by liquid chromatography and mass spectrometry. Home: Keats Rd Apt 293 Pottersville NJ 07979 Office: Rutgers U Cook Coll Ctr for Advanced Food Tech New Brunswick NJ 08903

ROSEN, ROBERTA, philosophy educator; b. Madawaska, Maine, Aug. 9, 1935; d. Bernard and Dolores (Bourgoin) Dionee; m. Frank Rosen, June 8, 1963; children: Ruth, Rachael, David, Sarah. BA, Gov. State U., University Park, Ill., 1975, MA, 1976; PhD, Walden U., 1977; postdoctoral, K.A.M.I.I. Temple. Free-lance writer Chgo.; dir. religious edn. ASFU, Chgo.; minister All Souls 1st Universalist Soc., Chgo.; prof. philosophy Prairie State Coll., Chicago Heights, Ill.; leader seminars on prevention of child abuse. Author: (novel) Call Her Dolores, (children's) Johnny Linny's Nightmare; contbr. articles to religious jours. Bd. trustees Gov. State U., Unitarian-Universalist Women's Fedn. Recipient Humanitarian award, Humane Soc. award; named Best Tchr. Mem. Unitarian-Universalist Women's Assn. (life). Address: 10 Strauss Ln Olympia Fields IL 60461-1622

ROSEN, SAM, economics educator emeritus; b. Balt., Apr. 1, 1920; s. Louis and Belle (Kurtz) R.; m. Mary Berman, Mar. 5, 1943; children—Michael David, Laura Elizabeth, Jonathan Donald. A.B., U. Wis., 1942; M.A., Harvard U., 1948, Ph.D., 1952. Asst. prof. econs. U. Wyo., Laramie, 1949-51, U. Del., Newark, 1952-57; assoc. prof. U. N.H., Durham, 1957-63; prof. U. N.H., 1963-74, Nashua Corp. prof. econs., 1974-85, emeritus prof. econs., 1985—; vis. prof. Inst. Social Studies, Holland, 1969, People's Republic China, 1987; vis. Fulbright prof., Malta, 1975. Author: National Income, 1963, National Income and Other Social Accounts, 1972; Contbr. articles to profl. jours. Served to lt. USN, 1942-45. Mem. AAUP (pres. U. N.H. chpt. 1962-63, 72-73), Am. Econ. Assn., Internat. Assn. Rsch. in Income and Wealth, Am. Fin. Assn., Ret. Faculty Assn. (chmn., bd. dirs.), N.H. Assn. for the Elderly, Seacoast Jazz Soc. (bd. dirs.). Office: Whittemore Sch Bus-Econs Mcconnell Hall Durham NH 03824

ROSEN, SAUL WOOLF, research scientist, health facility administrator; b. Boston, July 29, 1928; s. David Tsvi and Ida (Hannah) Sadwin; m. Mary Jean Westfall, June 14, 1959 (div. 1986); children: Craig, Laura, David; m. Deborah Susan Kieffer, Nov. 3, 1989. BA cum laude, Harvard U., 1947, MD, 1956; PhD, Northwestern U., 1955. Intern U. Calif. Med. Ctr., San Francisco, 1956-57, resident, 1957-58, sr. res., 1960-61; clin. assoc. Nat. Inst. Arthritis and Metabolic Diseases, Bethesda, Md., 1958-60; sr. investigator NIH Nat. Inst. Arthritis and Metabolism Disease, Bethesda, Md., 1961-84; dept. dir. Clin. Ctr. NIH, Bethesda, Md., 1984-90; acting dir. NIH, Bethesda, 1990-94; vis. scientist Nat. Inst. Med. Rsch., London, Eng., 1975-76. Contbr. articles to profl. jours. U.S. Rubber Co. fellow, Northwestern U., 1950. Fellow ACP; mem. Assn. Am. Physicians, Endocrine Soc. Avocations: opera, lexicography, philately, weightlifting. Home: 7401 Westlake Ter Apt 1104 Bethesda MD 20817-6531

ROSEN, SHERWIN, economist, educator; b. Chgo., Sept. 29, 1938; s. Joe W. and Nell (Rudy) R.; m. Sharon Ginsberg, June 11, 1961; children: Jennifer, Adria. BS, Purdue U., 1960; M.A., U. Chgo., 1962, Ph.D., 1966. Mem. faculty dept. econs. U. Rochester, N.Y., 1964-75, Kenan prof. econs., 1975-77; prof. econs. U. Chgo., 1977-83, Bergman prof. econs., 1984—, chmn. econ. dept., 1988-94; sr. rsch. fellow Hoover Instn.; vis. prof. U. Buffalo, 1970, Harvard U., 1971-72, Columbia U., 1973, Stanford U., 1976; bd. trustees Joint Coun. on Econ. Edn., 1990—. Editor: Jour. of Polit. Economy, 1986—; contbr. articles to profl. jours. Fellow Econometric Soc., Am.. Acad. Arts and Scis.; mem. Am. Econ. Assn. (exec. com. 1985--88, v.p. 1994). Home: 5714 S Kimbark Ave Chicago IL 60637-1615 Office: U Chgo Dept Econs 1126 E 59th St Chicago IL 60637-1580

ROSEN, STANLEY HOWARD, humanities educator; b. Warren, Ohio, July 29, 1929; s. Nathan A. and Celia (Narotsky) R.; m. Francoise Harlepp, Sept. 5, 1955; children: Nicholas David, Paul Mark, Valerie. B.A., U. Chgo., 1949, Ph.D., 1955; student, Am. Sch. Classical Studies, Athens, Greece, 1955-56. Mem. faculty Pa. State U., 1956-94, prof. philosophy, 1966-94; Fulbright research prof. U. Paris, 1960-61; research fellow Humanities Research Inst., U. Wis., 1963-64; Inst. Arts and Humanities research sr. fellow Pa. State U., 1972—, Evan Pugh prof. philosophy, 1985-94; Bowne prof. philosophy Boston U., 1994—; vis. prof. U. Calif., San Diego, 1978, U. Nice, 1981; cos. lectr. U. Barcelona, Spain, 1992. Author: Plato's Symposium, 1968, Nihilism, 1969, G.W.F. Hegel, 1974, The Limits of Analysis, 1980, Plato's Sophist: The Drama of Original and Image, 1983, Hermeneutics as Politics, 1987, The Quarrel Between Philosophy and Poetry, 1988, The Ancients and the Moderns, 1989, The Question of Being, 1993, Plato's Statesman: The Web of Politics, 1995, The Mask of Enlightenment, 1995. Research grantee Am. Philos. Soc., 1961; Research grantee Earhart Found., 1971, 73, 81. Mem. Metaphys. Soc. Am (pres. 1990-91). Home: 117 Brook St Wellesley MA 02181-6632 Office: 745 Commonwealth Ave Boston MA 02215-1401

ROSEN, STEPHEN LESLIE, lawyer; b. St. Paul, Minn., Nov. 20, 1948. BA, Hamline U., 1970; JD, So. Tex. U., 1974. Bar: Fla. 1974, U.S. Dist. Ct. Fla. 1975, U.S. Supreme Ct. 1980. Atty. Marlow, Mitzel, Ortmayer, Tampa, Fla., 1974-76, Wagner, Cunningham, Tampa, 1976-79, Morris and Rosen, Tampa, 1980-92, Rosen and Osborne, PA, Tampa, 1992—. Author: Worker's Compensation, Florida Bar, 1975, Longshore and Harborworkers Law, Florida Bar, 1978. Mem. Fla. Bar Assn. (chmn. worker's compensation bd. cert. com. 1988-90, chmn. statewide judicial nominating com., 1990-93, chmn. worker's compensation sect. 1992, Bud Adams award 1991). Office: Rosen and Osborne PA 4016 Henderson Blvd Tampa FL 33629

ROSEN, STEVEN TERRY, oncologist, hematologist; b. Bklyn., Feb. 18, 1952; married, 1976; 4 children. MB, Northwestern U., 1972, MD, 1976. Genevieve Teuton prof., med. sch. Northwestern U., 1989—, dir. cancer ctr., 1989—; dir. clin. programs Northwestern Meml. Hosp., 1989—. Editor-in-Chief Jour. Northwestern U. Cancer Center, 1989—, Contemporary Oncology, 1990-95. Mem. AAAS, ACP, AMA, Am. Soc. Hematology, Am. Soc. Clin. Oncology, Ctrl. Soc. Clin. Rsch. Achievements include research in cutaneous T-cell lymphomas, biology of lung cancer, biologic therapies, and hormone receptors. Office: Northwestern U Robert H. Lurie Cancer Ctr Olson Pavilion Rm 8250 303 E Chicago Ave Chicago IL 60611-3008

ROSEN, THOMAS J., food and agricultural products executive. CEO Rosen's Diversified, Fairmont, Minn. Office: Rosen's Diversified 1120 Lake Ave Fairmont MN 56031

ROSEN, WILLIAM, English language educator; b. Boston, July 1, 1926; s. Louis H. and Alice (Goldstein) R.; m. Barbara Cooper, Aug. 13, 1960; children: Judith Anne, Susan Eleanor. AB, Harvard U., 1948, AM, 1949, PhD, 1958. Instr. U. Wis., Madison, 1956-60; asst. prof. U. Conn., Storrs, 1960-63, assoc. prof., 1963-65, prof. English, 1965-92; prof. emeritus, 1992—; coordinator English grad. studies U. Conn., Storrs, 1979-80, 81-84, head English dept., 1987-92; Old Dominion prof. humanities Hampton Inst., Va., 1969-70; vis. fellow Clare Hall, Cambridge U., Eng., 1980-81, 88-89. Author: Shakespeare and the Craft of Tragedy, 1960; co-editor: Julius Caesar, 1963; contbr. articles to profl. jours. Vol. long term care adv., ombudsman program State of Conn., 1994—; mem. Town of Mansfield Commn. on Aging, 1995—. Pvt. U.S. Army, 1953-55. Mem. Am. Assn. Univ. Profs. (v.p. 1974-75, pres. 1975-76, chief negotiator U. Conn. chpt. 1976-77), Shakespeare Assn., MLA, Renaissance Soc. Am. Democrat. Jewish. Avocations: reading, gardening. Home: 233 Hanks Hill Rd Storrs Mansfield CT 06268-2333 Office: U Conn Dept English Storrs CT 06268

ROSEN, WILLIAM WARREN, lawyer; b. New Orleans, July 22, 1936; s. Warren Leucht and Erma (Stich) R.; m. Eddy Kahn, Nov. 26, 1965; children: Elizabeth K., Victoria A. BA, Tulane U., 1958, JD, 1964. Bar: La. 1964, U.S. Dist. Ct. (ea. dist.) La. 1965, U.S. Ct. Appeals (5th cir.) 1965, U.S. Supreme Ct. 1984, U.S. Dist. Ct. (mid. dist.) La. 1985, Colo. 1989. Assoc. Dodge & Friend, New Orleans, 1965-68, Law Office of J.R. Martzell, New Orleans, 1968-70; pvt. practice New Orleans, 1970-79, 89-90; ptnr. Lucas & Rosen (and predecessor firms), New Orleans, 1979-87, Herman, Herman, Katz & Cotlar, New Orleans, 1987-88, Rosen and Samuel, New Orleans, 1990-95; of counsel Rittenberg & Samuel, New Orleans, 1996; founder, dir. Litigation Consultation Svcs., 1996—; adj. prof. trial advocacy Law Sch. Tulane U., 1988—, mem. adv. com. paralegal studies program, 1977-86, instr. bus. orgns., 1978, instr. legal interviewing, 1980-81; mem. adv. com. Paralegal Inst. U. New Orleans, 1990—, instr. legal interviewing and investigations, 1986-87; lectr. legal and paralegal fields; lectr. real and demonstrative evidence Nat. Edn. Network, 1993. Author: (with others) Trial Techniques publ. La. Trial Lawyers Assn., 1981; columnist Briefly Speaking publ. New Orleans Bar Assn., 1993—. Mem. budget and planning com. Jewish Welfare Fedn., 1970-73; mem. adv. coun. on drug edn. La. Dept. Edn., 1973; mem. profl. adv. com. Jewish Endowment Found., 1982—; mem. exec. com. U.S. Olympic Com., La., 1982-84; bd. dirs. Planned Parenthood La., 1994—; pres. Dad's Club, Isidore Newman Sch., 1984-85, Uptown Flood Assn., 1982-85; bd. dirs. Jewish Children's Home Svc., 1973-76, Met. Crime Commn. New Orleans, 1976-82; spl. agt. Office Spl. Investigations USAF, 1958-61. Fellow, Inst. of Politics. Loyola U. Mem. ABA (vice chmn. pub. rels. com. 1970-73, 88-89, past chmn. state youth drug abuse edn. program, vol. lawyers for arts 1986—, chmn. sr. counsel com. 1995-96), New Orleans Bar Assn. (continuing legal edn. com. 1990-91, chmn. 1991-92), Am. Inns of Ct. (master 1992—, mem. ADR com. 1996—), Assn. Trial Lawyers Am. (keyperson com. 1986-89, paralegal mem. com., vice chmn. 1989-91, family law adv. com. 1989-90, legal edn. lectr. 1990-92, 94, contbr. Trial mag. 1994), La. Trial Lawyers Assn. (life, bd. govs. 1982-85, pres.'s adv. coun. 1980-82, 85-88, legal edn. lectr. 1979, 81, 83-84, 86, 88), Am. Arbitration Assn., Nat. Fedn. Paralegal Assn. (adv. coun. 1989ú), Assn. atty. Mediators (pres. La. chpt. 1995), Nat. Choice in Dying (legal adv. com. 1992—), Nat. Edn. Network (legal edn. lectr. 1993). Avocation: photography (included in Louisiana Photographers publ. Contemporary Arts Ctr. 1988). Office: Litigation Consultation Svc Ste 200 715 Girod St New Orleans LA 70130-3505

ROSENAU, JAMES NATHAN, political scientist, author; b. Philadelphia, Nov. 25, 1924; s. Walter Nathan and Fanny Fox (Baum) R.; m. Norah McCarthy, Aug. 5, 1955 (dec. July 1974); 1 child, Heidi Margaret; m. Pauline Vaillancourt, June 14, 1987 (div. 1993); m. Hongying Wang, Dec. 11, 1993. A.B., Bard Coll., 1948; A.M., Johns Hopkins U., 1949; Ph.D., Princeton U., 1957. Instr. Rutgers U., New Brunswick, N.J., 1949-54; asst. prof. Rutgers U., New Brunswick, 1954-60, assoc. prof., 1960-62, prof., 1962-70; prof. Ohio State U., Columbus, 1970-73; prof. polit. sci. U. So. Calif., Los Angeles, 1973-92; univ. prof. of internat. affairs George Washington U., 1992—; research asst. Inst. Advanced Study, Princeton, N.J., 1953-54; research assoc. Princeton U., N.J., 1960-70; dir. Sch. Internat. Relations U. So. Calif., Los Angeles, 1976-79; dir. Inst. for Transnat. Studies, U. Southern Calif., Los Angeles, 1973-92. Author: Public Opinion and Foreign Policy, 1961, National Leadership and Foreign Policy, 1963, The Dramas of Politics, 1973, Citizenship between Elections, 1974, The Scientific Study of Foreign Policy, 1980, Turbulence in World Politics, 1990, The United Nations in a Turbulent World, 1992, (play) Kwangju: An Escalatory Spree, 1991; co-author: American Leadership in World Affairs, 1984, Global Voices, 1993, Thinking Theory Thoroughly, 1995, International Political Economy, 1995; co-editor: Journeys through World Politics, 1989, Global Changes and Theoretical Challenges, 1989, Governance without Government, 1992. Trustee Bard Coll., Annandale-on-Hudson, 1968-70, Odyssey Theater Ensemble, Los Angeles, 1987-88. Served with U.S. Army, 1942-46. Fellow Ford. Found., 1958-59, Guggenheim fellow, 1987-88; rsch. grantee NSF, 1970, 73, 78, 79, 83, 88, 92, 96, grantee NEH, 1976. Mem. Internat. Studies Assn. (pres. 1984-85), Am. Polit. Sci. Assn. (mem. exec. council 1975-77). Democrat. Office: 2110 G St NW Washington DC 20037-2741

ROSENBAUM, ALLEN, art museum administrator; b. N.Y.C., Jan. 28, 1937. B.A., Queens Coll., 1958; M.A., NYU, 1962. Instr. Sch. Gen. Studies, Queens Coll., N.Y.C., 1961; lectr. Metropolitan Mus. Art, N.Y.C., 1964-69, sr. lectr., 1970-72; instr. Sch. Fine Arts, U. Calif.-Irvine, 1972; asst. dir. Schickman gallery, N.Y.C., 1972-73; asst. dir. Art Mus. Princeton U., N.J., 1974, dir. Art Mus., 1980—; bd. dirs. Ternbach-Godwin Mus. Queens Coll., 1982—; mem. com. on art Port Authority of N.Y. and N.J. Contbr. articles on art to profl. jours.; author exhbn. catalogue, Nat. Gallery Art, 1979. Inst. Fine Arts scholar, 1960-62; grantee Inst. Fine Arts, 1961, Met. Mus. Art, 1966, 68, 70; Fulbright fellow, 1962-63. Mem. Assn. of Art Mus. Dirs., The Century Assn. Office: The Art Mus Princeton University Princeton NJ 08544

ROSENBAUM, ARTHUR ELIHU, radiologist, educator; b. Cleve., June 30, 1935; s. Lionel Clarence and Dora Beatrice (Heldman) R.; m. Rona C. Rosenbaum, Dec. 25, 1981; children: Jeffrey, Lisa. L. Anne. Student, Case-Western Res. U., 1953-54, AB, 1958; student, U. Mex., 1954-56; MD, U. Miami, 1962. Diplomate Am. Bd. Radiology. Med. intern Jefferson Davis-Ben Taub Hosps., Houston, 1962-63; asst. resident, resident, then chief resident Montefiore Hosp. and Med. Center, N.Y.C., 1963-66; instr. in radiology Albert Einstein Coll. Medicine, N.Y.C., 1966-67; asst. vis. physician Bronx Mcpl. Hosp. Center, 1966-67; cons. in neuroradiology Bronx-Lebanon Hosps., 1966-67; radiologist-in-chief USPHS Hosp., S.I., N.Y., 1968-69; clin. instr. radiology Sch. Medicine, U. Calif., San Francisco, N.Y., 1969; asst. clin. prof. radiology Sch. Medicine U. Calif., San Francisco, 1969; vis. asst. prof. radiology Harvard Med. Sch., Boston, 1970, asst. to assoc. prof. radiology, 1970-75; chief neuroradiology sect. Peter Bent Brigham Hosp., Boston, 1970-75; lectr. radiology Tufts U. Sch. Medicine, Boston, 1974-75; chief neuroradiology sect. Beth Israel Hosp., Boston, 1971-75; prof. radiology U. Pitts. Sch. Medicine, 1975; chief neuroradiology div. Children's Hosp. of Pitts., 1977, dir. pediatric neuroradiology, from 1979; neuroradiologist-in-chief U. Pitts. Sch. Medicine and Affiliated Hosps. of U. Health Center, 1978-80; prof. radiology Johns Hopkins U. Sch. Medicine and Med. Instns., Balt., 1980-87; chmn. div. radiology Cleve. Clinic Found., 1988; prof. radiology, dir. neuroradiology rsch. SUNY-Health Sc. Ctr., Syracuse, N.Y., 1989—; dir. neuroradiology div. SUNY Health Sci., Syracuse, 1992—; cons. Luth. Med. Ctr., Cleve., 1988-89, Cleve. Spine and Arthritis Inst.; spl. cons. to editor Neuroradiology, 1990—. Mem. editorial bd. Neuroradiology, 1974-82, Stroke, 1986-90; adv. editorial bd. Am. Jour. Neuroradiology, 1979-86; contbr. articles to profl. jours., presenter papers profl. confs. U.S., France, Mex., Uruguay, Can., Norway, Bermuda, Chile, lectr. in field, author (sci. exhibits profl. convs.), designer (radiologic equipment), developer (radiologic equipment). Trustee, mem. edn., benefits and devel. coms. Syracuse Symphony Orch., 1990-92, chmn. young orch. com., 1992—, chiar youth orch., 1993-94, artistic divsn., 1993—,mktg. divsn., 1996—; sec. Performing Arts Medicine of Ctrl. N.Y., 1990-91, mem. exec. com., 1990-94. With USPHS Res., 1967-69. Fellow Am. Coll. Radiology (diplomate); mem. AAAS, Am. Soc. Neuroradiology (nat. sec. 1974-77, pres. 1982-83), Radiol. Soc. N.Am. (chair neuroradiology program com. 1978-81), Assn. Univ. Radiologists, Soc. Photo-Optical Instrumentation Egnrs., Am. Soc. Stereotactic and Functional Neurosurgery, World Soc. Sterotactic and Functional Neurosurgery, Itnernat. Med. Soc. for Advancement of Sci., Phi Sigma, Alpha Omega Alpha. Fellow Am. Coll. Radiology (diplomate); mem. AAAS, Am. Soc. Neuroradiology (nat. sec. 1974-77, pres. elect 1981, pres. 1982-83), Radiol. Soc. N.Am., Assn. Univ. Radiologists, Soc. Photo-Optical Instrumentation Engrs., Am. Soc. for Stereotactic and Functional Neurosurgery, Internat. Med. Soc. for Advancement of Sci., Phi Sigma, Alpha Omega Alpha. Office: SUNY Health Sci Ctr 750 E Adams St Syracuse NY 13210-2306

ROSENBAUM, IRVING M., retail store executive; b. Dresden, Germany, Apr. 20, 1921; came to U.S., 1938, naturalized, 1943; s. Max and Clara (Koerner) R.; m. Hanni Schein, Oct. 15, 1953; children: Eli M., Daniel S., Michael J. B.A. in Econs., New Sch. Social Research, 1953; M.A. in Econs., NYU, 1956. Stockman, S.E. Nichols Inc., N.Y.C., 1938-40; asst. store mgr. S.E. Nichols Inc., 1940-43, store mgr., 1946-48, buyer, 1949-56, mdse. mgr., 1957-60, pres., 1960-72, chmn. bd., 1972-83, vice-chmn. bd., 1983-85, also bd. dirs.; v.p. Venture Israel Ltd., Balt., 1985—, Israel Pharms., Balt., 1976-83; chmn. bd. F.R. Schreiber Co., Lititz, Pa., 1975-82; adv. com. mem. AMIFID Ptnrs. L.P., N.Y.C. Bd. dirs., chmn. bd. overseers Solomon Schechter Day Sch., Nassau and Suffolk Counties, 1985-90; bd. dirs. United Jewish Appeal, Fedn. Jewish Philanthropies, Israel Bond Orgn. Greater N.Y.; nat. chmn. Friends of the Open U. Israel, 1989—. With U.S. Army, 1943-45. Recipient Prime Minister's medal Israel, 1976, 88. Mem. Nat. Mass Retailing Inst., U.S. C. of C. (govt. and regulatory affairs com. 1977-79, adminstrv. law coun. 1980-85). Club: Lake Mohawk Country (Sparta, N.J.). *Only a person who appreciates his own background, traditions and values is able to appreciate those of others.*

ROSENBAUM, JACOB I., lawyer; b. Cleve., Oct. 4, 1927; s. Lionel C. and Dora (Heldman) R.; m. Marjorie Jean Arnold, Apr. 20, 1952; children: Laura Rosenbaum, Alexander, Judith Bartell. JD, U. N.Mex., 1951. Bar: N.Mex. 1951, Ohio 1952. Pres. Ohio Savs. Assn., Cleve., 1955-60, sr. v.p., 1960-92, also dir.; ptnr. Burke, Haber & Berick, Cleve., 1955-79; chmn. bd. Mercury Holdings, Inc., Richmond Heights, Ohio, 1967—; ptnr. Arter & Hadden, Cleve., 1979—. Pres. Temple Emanu El, University Heights, Ohio, 1965-67; active Judson Retirement Cmty., Cleveland Heights, Ohio, 1990—, trustee, 1981-94, pres., 1990-92; trustee Cleve. Zool. Soc., 1983—; pres. adv. bd. Cleve. Women's Orch., 1983—; trustee Cleve. Nat. Air Show, 1981—, pres., 1987-90, 94—. Mem. Lawyer-Pilots Bar Assn. (pres. 1981-82, editor jour. 1982—), Ohio Bar Assn. (chmn. aviation law com. 1981-84), Greater Cleve. Bar Assn., Nat. Transp. Safety Bd. Bar Assn., Cleve. Execs. Assn. (pres. 1989, chmn. 1990), Kiwanis (pres. 1970-71). Democrat. Jewish. Avocation: flying. Home: 28050 N Woodland Rd Cleveland OH 44124-4521 Office: Arter & Hadden 1100 Huntington Bldg 925 Euclid Ave Cleveland OH 44115

ROSENBAUM, JAMES EDWARD, psychologist, educator; b. Plainfield, N.J., Dec. 11, 1943; s. Irving and Dorothy Louise (Berger) R.; m. Virginia Ruth Warcholik, Aug. 4, 1974; 1 child, Janet. BA, Yale Coll., 1966; PhD, Harvard U., 1973. Asst. prof. Yale U., New Haven, Conn., 1973-79; prof. Northwestern U., Evanston, Ill., 1979—; advisor commn. on youth and Am's. future, commn. on workforce quality U.S. Dept. Labor, Washington, 1988—, U.S. GAO, Washington, 1988—, U.S. Dept. HHD, Washington, 1990; cons. Leadership Coun., Chgo., 1982—. Author: Making Inequality, 1976, Careers in Corporations, 1984, Blacks in White Suburbs, 1990, Transition from High School to Work, 1990, Youth Apprenticeship in America, 1993. Grantee Spencer Found., 1982, Mott Found., 1989, Ford Found., 1989, U.S. Dept. Labor, 1977, Joyce Found., 1985. Mem. Am. Sociol. Assn., Am. Psychol. Assn. Office: Northwestern U Soc Dept 2040 Sheridan Rd Evanston IL 60208-0001

ROSENBAUM, JAMES MICHAEL, judge; b. Fort Snelling, Minn., Oct. 12, 1944; s. Sam. H. and Ilene D. (Bernstein) R.; m. Marilyn Brown, July 30, 1972; children: Alexandra, Victoria and Catherine (twins). BA, U. Minn., 1966, JD, 1969. Bar: Minn. 1969, Ill. 1970, U.S. Supreme Ct. 1979. VISTA staff atty. Leadership Council for Met. Open Communities, Chgo., 1969-72; assoc. Katz, Taube, Lange & Frommelt, Mpls., 1972-77; ptnr. Rosenbaum & Rosenbaum, Mpls., 1977-79, Gainsley, Squier & Korsh, Mpls., 1979-81; U.S. dist. atty. U.S. Dept. Justice, Mpls., 1981-85; judge U.S. Dist. Ct., Minn., 1985—. Author booklet: Guide to Practice Civil Rights Housing, 1972; co-author: U.S. Courts Design Guide, 1991-96. Campaign chmn. People for Boschwitz, Minn., 1978, bd. vis. U. Minn. Law Sch. (pres.-elect 1995—). Mem. Fed. Bar Assn. (bd. dirs., pres. 1992-93). Republican. Jewish. Office: US Dist Ct 669 US Courthouse 110 S 4th St Minneapolis MN 55401-2221

ROSENBAUM, JOAN HANNAH, museum director; b. Hartford, Conn., Nov. 24, 1942; d. Charles Leon and Lillian (Sharasheff) Grossman; m. Peter S. Rosenbaum, July 1962 (div. 1970). AA, Hartford Coll. for Women, 1962; BA, Boston U., 1964; student, Hunter Coll. Grad Sch., 1970-73; cert., Columbia U. Bus. Sch. Inst. Non Profit Mgmt., 1978; DHL (hon.), Jewish Theol. Sem., 1993. Curatorial asst. Mus. Modern Art, N.Y.C., 1966-72; dir. mus. program N.Y. Council on Arts, N.Y.C., 1972-79; cons. Michal Washburn & Assocs., N.Y.C., 1979-80; dir. Jewish Mus., N.Y.C., 1980—; mem. adv. bd. Pub. Ctr., N.Y.C. Bd. dirs. Artists Space, 1980—; officer Council Am. Jewish Mus., 1981—; mem. policy panel Nat. Endowment Arts, 1982-83. Created knight (Denmark); recipient Disting. Alumni award Boston U. Coll. Libera Arts, 1994; European travel grantee Internat. Coun. Mus., 1972. Mem. Am. Assn. Mus. (cons. 1979—), Assn. Art Mus. Dirs., N.Y. State Assn. Mus. (mem. coun. 1981-90). Office: Jewish Mus 1109 5th Ave New York NY 10128-0118

ROSENBAUM, KENNETH E., journalist, editor; b. N.Y.C., Aug. 30, 1942; s. Abraham Rosenbaum and Lena (Sentner) Schroeder; m. Mary Hercelia Zeller, Aug. 30, 1964 (div. 1972); children: Sandra, Steven; m. Karen Marie Tiefenbach, June 14, 1980; stepchildren: Stephanie Kay Burket and Stacey Jo Burket. BA, Ohio State U., 1965. Editor Ohio Jewish Chronicle, Columbus, 1963-64; mng. editor Medina (Ohio) County Gazette, 1965-68; copy editor, reporter Akron (Ohio) Beacon Jour., 1968; news editor Cleve. Press, 1968-82; slotman, asst. news editor St. Louis Globe-Dem., 1982-84; systems editor Toledo Blade, 1984-87, asst. mng. editor, graphics, 1987-89, dir. photography, 1989-93, dir. news systems, 1993—; photography judge Medina County Fair, 1977-82; instr. journalism Cuyahoga Community Coll., Cleve., 1982, Bowling Green State U., 1989, 91. Democrat. Jewish. Lodges: Lions (bd. dirs. Medina chpt. 1970-71), Masons (steward 1986-87), Shriner. Avocations: photography, golf, motorcycling, rotisserie baseball. Home: 7045 Leicester Rd Toledo OH 43617-1310

ROSENBAUM, LOIS OMENN, lawyer; b. Newark, Apr. 10, 1950; d. Edward and Ruth (Peretz) Omenn; m. Richard B. Rosenbaum, Apr. 4, 1971; children: Steven, Laura. AB, Wellesley Coll., 1971; JD, Stanford U., 1974. Bar: Calif. 1974, Oreg. 1977, D.C. 1974, U.S. Supreme Ct. 1990. Assoc., Fried, Frank, Harris, Shriver & Kampelman, Washington, 1974-75, Orrick, Herrington, Rowley & Sutcliffe, San Francisco, 1975-77, Stoel Rives LLP (formerly Stoel, Rives, Boley, Jones & Grey), Portland, Oreg., 1977-81, ptnr., 1981—; mem. U.S. Dist. Ct. Mediation Panel. Bd. dirs. Providence Med. Found., Robison Jewish Home; past mem. Nat. Legal Com. Am. Jewish Com. Wellesley Coll. scholar, 1971. Mem. ABA, Multnomah County Bar

Assn. (arbitration panel), Am. Arbitration Assn (panel mem.). Clubs: Multnomah Athletic, Wellesley (Oregon) (pres. 1987-88). Office: Stoel Rives LLP 900 SW 5th Ave Ste 2300 Portland OR 97204-1232

ROSENBAUM, MICHAEL A., investor relations consultant; b. Chgo., May 13, 1953; s. Robert and Muriel (Caplan) R.; m. Jill Ann Rubenstein, Oct. 12, 1975; children: Susan Brooke, Stephanie Ilyse. BS in Communications, U. Ill., 1974; MBA, Roosevelt U., 1979. Reporter Peoria (Ill.) Jour. Star, 1974, Compass Newspaper, Hammond, Ind., 1974-75; corr. UPI, Chgo., 1975-78; mng. editor Purchasing World Mag., Barrington, Ill., 1978-79; chief Midwest bur. The Jour. of Commerce, Chgo., 1979-83; sr. assoc. The Fin. Rels. Bd., Inc., Chgo., 1983-85, ptnr., 1985-88, sr. ptnr., 1988-90, dep. mng. ptnr., chief oper. officer, 1990—. Author: Selling Your Story to Wall Street: The Art and Science of Investor Relations, 1994; contbr. articles to profl. jours. Chmn. capital campaign Congregation Beth Judea, Long Grove, Ill., 1984-87, v.p. programming & membership, 1993-94; mem. capital campaign com. Infant Welfare Soc., Chgo., 1990-92, dir., 1993—, v.p., 1994—. Recipient Ann. Report Excellence award Fin. World Mag., 1988-95, Nat. Assn. of Investment Clubs, 1986, 88-95, Assn. of Publicly Traded Cos., 1988-95, Publicity Club of Chgo., 1989, 96. Mem. Nat. Investor Rels. Inst., Nat. Assn. Corp. Dirs.. Jewish. Office: Financial Relations Bd John Hancock Ctr 875 N Michigan Ave Chicago IL 60611-1803

ROSENBAUM, PATRICIA JEANNE, nurse, educator; b. Mobile, Ala., May 7, 1943; d. Alvin Monroe Pitt and Betty Jeanne (Brown) Russell; m. James Steven, May, 1961 (div. 1963); 1 child, James Randall Rosenbaum. BS, Okla. Bapt. U., 1983; MEd, U. Ctrl. Okla., 1993; postgrad., U. Okla. Registered critical care nurse, registered med. surg. clinician. Staff nurse oper. rm. Bapt. Meml. Hosp., Oklahoma City, 1966-67; perfusionist Drs. Greer, Carey, Zuhdi, Hawley, Hartsuck, Inc., Oklahoma City, 1967-78; med.-surg. charge nurse Shawnee (Okla.) Med. Ctr., 1979-81; asst. head nurse Presbyn. Hosp., Oklahoma City, 1981-89; staff nurse coronary care Bapt. Med. Ctr., Oklahoma City, 1989-90, critical care instr., 1990-93; comty. nurse educator S.W. Med. Ctr., Oklahoma City, 1993, dir. emergency svcs., 1993—; guest lectr. So. Nazarene U., Bethany, Okla., 1993—; guest lectr. cardiac related topics various civic, comty. and religious orgns., Oklahoma City, 1993—; adj. faculty critical care Okla. State U., Oklahoma City, 1989-90. Contbr. Okla. Polit. Action Com., Oklahoma City, 1993—; vol. nurse Good Shepherd Clinic, Oklahoma City, 1992—, various city sponsored runs, walks, bikathons for Am. Heart Assn., March of Dimes, Oklahoma City, 1986—. Fellow Am. Soc. Extracorporeal Circulation; mem. AACN (chair recognition com. 1987-89), Okla. Orgn. Nurse Execs., Sigma Theta Tau. Democrat. Evangelical. Avocations: jogging, tennis, reading, music, skiing. Home: 6601 Edgewater Dr Oklahoma City OK 73116-1822 Office: S W Med Ctr 4401 S Western Ave Oklahoma City OK 73109-3413

ROSENBAUM, ROBERT ABRAHAM, mathematics educator; b. New Haven, Nov. 14, 1915; s. Joseph and Goldey (Rostow) R.; m. L. Louise Johnson, Aug. 1, 1942; children: Robert J., Joseph, David; m. Marjorie Rice Daltry, Aug. 26, 1980. A.B., Yale U., 1936, Ph.D., 1947; L.H.D. (hon.), St. Joseph Coll., 1970, Wesleyan U., Middletown, Conn., 1981; DSc (hon.), Conn. State U., 1993. Henry Fund fellow St. John's Coll., Cambridge (Eng.) U., 1936-37; Gen. Edn. Bd. fellow Reed Coll., 1939-40, from instr. to prof. math., 1940-53; prof. math. Wesleyan U., 1953-85, chmn. dept. math., 1953-63, dean sci., 1963-65, provost, 1965-69, v.p. for acad. affairs, 1967-69, chancellor, 1970-73, univ. prof., 1977-85, prof. emeritus, 1985—; vis. prof. Swarthmore Coll., 1950-51, U. Mass., 1973, Coll. of St. Thomas, 1983; dir. Project to Increase Mastery Math. and Sci., 1979-95, chmn., 1995—; mem. exec. com. Hartford Alliance for Edn. in Math., Sci. and Tech., 1988-92, mem. coordinating com. Project CONNSTRUCT, 1991—; bd. dirs. Conn. Acad. for Edn. in Math., Sci. and Tech., 1991—, pres., 1992-96. Served with USNR, 1942-45. Named hon. alumnus Reed Coll.; recipient Baldwin medal Wesleyan U., 1985, Transylvania medal, 1992. Fellow AAAS, Soc. for Values in Higher Edn.; mem. AAUP (chpt. pres. 1959-61, coun. 1981-84), Math. Assn. Am. (2d v.p. 1961-62, editor 1966-68, Christie lectr. 1994), Am. Math. Soc., Conn. Acad. Sci. and Engring. (charter mem., treas., chair edn. com.), Phi Beta Kappa, Sigma Xi. Office: Wesleyan U Middletown CT 06459

ROSENBAUM, STEVEN IRA, public relations and publishing executive, photographer; b. N.Y.C., Feb. 8, 1946; s. Samuel Meyer and Mary (Slobodow) R.; m. Janet Marilyn Hart, July 12, 1970; children—Elizabeth Jean, Mark Edward. B.S., Rochester Inst. Tech., 1967. Tech. rep. E.I. DuPont de Nemours and Co., Inc., Wilmington, Del., 1967-72; pres. Photog. Pleasures, Inc., Great Neck, N.Y., 1972-75; East coast editor Photog. mag. Petersen Pub. Co., Los Angeles, Calif., 1975-77; account supr. Bozell & Jacobs Advt. Agy., N.Y.C., 1977-80; v.p., assoc. pub. Modern Photography mag. ABC Pub. Co., N.Y.C., 1980-81, v.p., pub. High Fidelity mag., Schwann Record and tape Guides, Mus. Am. Internat. Directory of Performing Arts, 1981-86, v.p. circulation, 1986, v.p., pub., editorial dir. Modern Photography mag., 1986-89; v.p., mgmt. supr. Bozell Inc. Pub. Rels., N.Y.C., 1990—, sr. v.p., 1992—; faculty Winona Sch. Profl. Photography, Winona Lake, Ind., 1972-75. Contbr. articles to profl. jours. Mem. Northport Bay Estates Civic Assn., N.Y., 1971—. Mem. Profl. Photographers Am., Soc. for Imaging Sci. and Tech., Am. Photog. Hist. Soc. (life), Mag. Pubs. Assn., Bay Boat Club. Avocations: photography; reading; music; walking; cooking. Home: 21 Hawkins Dr Northport NY 11768-1527 Office: Bozell Pub Rels Inc 75 Rockefeller Plz New York NY 10019-6908*

ROSENBERG, ALAN DAVID, accountant; b. Mt. Vernon, N.Y., Apr. 11, 1946; s. Benjamin Bernard and Miriam Mickey (Nierenberg) R.; m. Wendy Patricia Cutler, May 25, 1975; children: Kerri L., Joshua Z., Brian S. BS in Acctg., NYU, 1967; MBA in Taxation, Baruch Coll., 1970. CPA, N.Y. Sr. acct. Ernst & Ernst, N.Y.C., 1967-70; dir. acctg., CFO various firms, N.Y.C., 1970-75; pres. Alan D. Rosenberg, CPA, P.C., N.Y.C., New Rochelle, N.Y., 1975—. Mem. AICPA (mem. tax practice mgmt. com. 1992—), N.Y. State Soc. CPAs, Inst. Mgmt. Accts., Nat. Conf. CPA Practitioners, Alliance of Practicing CPAs, Estate Planning Coun. Westchester County, Tax Soc. NYU. Jewish. Avocations: sports, reading, family activities. Office: 2 W 45th St Ste 1208 New York NY 10036-4212

ROSENBERG, ALAN GENE, newspaper editor; b. Chgo., Sept. 14, 1957; s. Earl David and Lorraine Faith (Blum) R.; m. Avis Beth Gunther-Rosenberg, Apr. 8, 1984; children: Ethan Elijah, Rebecca Greer. BS in Journalism, Northwestern U., 1978. From state staff reporter to asst. features editor Providence (R.I.) Jour.-Bulletin, 1978—. Mem. Am. Assn. Sunday and Feature Editors. Office: Providence Jour-Bulletin 75 Fountain St Providence RI 02902

ROSENBERG, ALAN STEWART, lawyer; b. N.Y.C., Mar. 29, 1930; s. Louis and Sadye (Knobler) R.; m. Ilse Rosenberg/Klein, Aug. 15, 1963; children: Gary, Robert. BA, Stanford U., 1949; LLB, Columbia U., 1952; LLM, NYU, 1960. Bar: N.Y. 1955. Assoc. Wolf Haldenstein Adler & Freeman, N.Y.C., 1955-56; ptnr., chmn. tax dept. Proskauer Rose Goetz & Mendelsohn, N.Y.C., 1957-94; bd. dirs. PEC Israel Econ. Corp. Contbr. articles to profl. jours. Mem. exec. com., bd. visitors Stanford (Calif.) U. Law Sch., 1982-85, advisor Humanities Ctr., 1985—, Jewish studies program, 1986—; chmn. bd. N.Y. Alliance for the Pub. Sch., 1988-91; mem. adv. com. on pub. issues Advt. Coun., 1991-94; bd. dirs., sec. Univ.-Urban Schs. Nat. Task Force Inc., 1981—; mem. bd. visitors Columbua U. Law Sch., 1991-96; mem. bd. advisors Ctr. Ednl. Innovation, 1994—; bd. dirs., treas. Justice Resource Ctr., 1994—. Lt. (j.g.) USN, 1952-55. Avocations: amateur opera singer; tennis. Home: 115 Central Park W New York NY 10023-4153

ROSENBERG, ALEX, mathematician, educator; b. Berlin, Germany, Dec. 5, 1926; came to U.S., 1949, naturalized, 1959; s. Theodore and Rela (Banet) R.; m. Beatrice Gershenson, Aug. 24, 1952 (div. Apr. 1985); children: Theodore Joseph, David Michael, Daniel Alex; m. Brunhilde Angun, June 14, 1985. B.A., U. Toronto, 1948, M.A., 1949; Ph.D., U. Chgo., 1951. From instr. to assoc. prof. math. Northwestern U., 1952-61; prof. math. Cornell U., Ithaca, N.Y., 1961-88; chmn. dept. Cornell U., 1966-69; prof., chmn. dept. U. Calif., Santa Barbara, 1986-87, prof., 1986—, prof. emeritus, 1994—; mem. com. undergrad. program math. Math Assn. Am., 1966-76; mem. Inst. Advanced Study, 1955-57; vis. prof. U. Calif., Berkely, 1961, 1979, U. Calif., Los Angeles, 1969-70, 82, U. London, Queen Mary Coll., 1963-64, U. Munich, 1975-76, E.T.H Zurich, 1976, U. Dortmund, 1984-85; trustee Am. Math Soc., 1973-83. Editor: Proc. Am. Math. Soc., 1960-66, Am. Math. Monthly, 1974-77; Contbr. articles to profl. jours. Recipient Humboldt Stiftung Sr. U.S. Scientist award U. Munich, 1975-76, U. Dortmund, 1981. Home: 1225 Plaza Del Monte Santa Barbara CA 93101-4819

ROSENBERG, ALEX JACOB, art dealer, curator, fine arts appraiser, educator; b. N.Y.C., May 25, 1919; s. Israel and Lena (Zar) R. Student, Albright Coll., 1935-37, Sch. Phila. Mus. Art, 1937-40; BS, Phila. Coll. Textiles and Sci., 1948; DHL (hon.), Hofstra U., 1989, postgrad., 1992—. Pres., Anserphone, 1959-66; sec., dir. Gen. Cablevision Tex., 1968-72; v.p., dir. Communicable, Inc., Fla., 1967-71, Five Beaches C.A.T.V. Corp., Fla., 1967-71; Gen. Cablevision Palatka, Fla., 1967-71, Beacon Cable Corp., 1966-71; pres., dir. Modern Cable Corp., 1966-71, B.F.C.-C.A.T.V. Corp., 1966-71; v.p., dir. Starfax Corp. Real Estate, 1968-70; gen. ptnr. Lakewood Plaza Assocs., N.J., 1973-92, Rostin Assocs., Austin, Tex., 1970-83; pres. Transworld Art Inc., Alex Rosenberg Gallery and Alba Edits., N.Y.C., 1968-89, Rostin Mgmt. Corp., 1986-89, The Abbot Group, 1987-89, Ardmore Affiliates Ltd., Alex Rosenberg Fine Art, 1985—, Neikrug-Rosenberg Assocs., 1989—; lectr. Parsons Sch. Design, N.Y.C., 1979-88; instr. appraising modern art NYU, 1992—, adj. prof. appraising NYU, 1995—; vis. prof. fine art Advanced Inst. Arts, Havana, Cuba, 1993—; organizer Henry Moore exhibition Mus. Budapest, Bratislava and Prague, 1993. Contbr. articles to profl. jours.; co-curator Romare Bearden as Printmaker 1992—; assoc. editor exhbn. catalogue; curator An American Portrait Mus. Fine Art, Havana, Cuba, 1992-93; co-curator Henry Moore Mother and Child Exhbn., 1987-88; trustee Alice Baber Art Fund, 1991-93, Phila. Coll. Textiles and Sci., 1992-95. Bd. dirs. Artists' Rights Today, 1974-80; mem. adv. com. Inst. Study for Older Adults, 1983-86; mem. mus. adv. bd. Hofstra Mus., Hempstead, N.Y., 1987-92; mem. collection and exhbn. com. Parrish Art Mus., Southhampton, N.Y., 1989—; trustee Guttman Inst., 1979-92; mem. exec. bd. Nat. Emergency Civil Liberties Com., 1970—, treas., 1981—; trustee Nat. Emergency Civil Liberties Found., 1984—, chmn., 1990—; nat. bd. dirs. and bd. dirs. local coun. SANE, 1974-83; trustee, treas. New Lincoln Sch., 1968-71; trustee Givat Haviva Ednl. Found., N.Y.C., 1969—, chmn. exec. com., 1992—; trustee Givat Haviva Inst., Hadera, Israel, 1993—, Stephen Wise Free Synagogue, 1967-70, 73-76, Mus. Borough Bklyn., 1986-89; del. 28th World Zionist Congress, Jerusalem, 1972; mem. Community Planning Bd. # 7, 1965-67, 70-72; mem. Lower West Side Anti-Poverty Bd., 1965-66, Lincoln Ctr. Community Coun., 1968-74, Com. for Ind. Civilian Police Rev. Bd., 1967; mem. steering com. Com. Pub. Edn. and Religious Liberty; chmn. Am. Israel Civil Liberties Coalition, 1988-89; Dem. dist. leader, 1964-74, state committeeman, 1970-73, mem. county exec. com., 1964-74; del. Dem. Nat. Conv., 1968, 72; former treas., bd. dirs. Raoul Wallenberg Commn. of U.S., 1986—, chmn., 1990-92; mem. print and drawing coun. Israel Mus., 1980-85; assoc. dir. Snug Harbor Cultural Ctr, S.I., 1982-88. 2d lt. USAAF, 1943-45. Recipient Spl. prize Grenschen Triennial, Switzerland, 1976, Israel prize, 1974, Cuban Order of Culture, 1995. Mem. Am. Soc. Appraisers (sr., bd. examiners 1988—, presonal property com. 1988-90), Appraisers Assn. Am. (cert. mem., bd. dirs. 1990—, v.p. 1992-94, 1st v.p. 1994, pres. 1994—), Fine Art Pubs. Assn. (v.p., bd. dir. 1981-83, pres. 1983-86, treas. 1986-89), Nat. Arts Club.

ROSENBERG, ALISON P., public policy official; b. Miami, Fla., Sept. 5, 1945; d. Mortimer I. and Gail (Sklar) Podell; m. Jeffrey Alan Rosenberg, May 4, 1969; 1 child, Robert Aaron. BS in Econs., Smith Coll., 1967. Mng. officer Citibank, N.Y.C., 1967-69; legis. aide Senator Charles Percy, Washington, 1969-80; profl. staff mem. Senate Fgn. Rels. Com., Washington, 1981-85; assoc. asst. adminstr. Agy. for Internat. Devel., Washington, 1985-87; dir. African affairs Nat. Security Coun., Washington, 1987-88; dep. asst. sec. for Africa State Dept., Washington, 1988-92; asst. adminstr. for Africa Agy. for Internat. Devel., Washington, 1992-93; co-financing advisor to the v.p. for Africa The World Bank, Washington, 1993—.

ROSENBERG, ARTHUR JAMES, company executive; b. Boston, Dec. 8, 1926; s. Benjamin R. and Lillian (Wolfson) R.; m. Naomi C. Solomon, Oct. 16, 1949; children: Deborah L., Janis E., Mia B. B.S. magna cum laude, Tufts U., 1948; M.A., Harvard U., 1951, Ph.D., 1952. Research scientist Merck & Co., Inc., 1951-54; mem. tech. staff Lincoln Lab., MIT, Cambridge, 1954-60; pres. Tyco Labs., Inc., Waltham, Mass., 1960-70, Epidyne, Inc., Hawthorne, Calif., 1972-79, Panatech Research and Devel. Corp., Los Angeles, 1980—. Office: Panatech Rsch & Devel Corp PO Box 23160 Albuquerque NM 87192-1160

ROSENBERG, BARR MARVIN, investment advisor, economist; b. Berkeley, Calif., Nov. 13, 1942; s. Marvin and Dorothy Fraser R.; m. June Diane Weinstock, Sept. 8, 1966. B.A., U. Calif., Berkeley, 1963; M.S. in Econs, London Sch. Econs., 1965; Ph.D., Harvard U., 1968. Asst. prof. Univ. Calif., Berkeley, 1968-74; assoc. prof. Univ. Calif., 1974-77, prof. bus. adminstrn., 1978-83, dir. Berkeley Program in Fin., 1979-81; prin. Barr Rosenberg Assos., Berkeley, Calif., 1975-81; mng. partner Barr Rosenberg Assos., 1981-83, cons., 1983-86; mng. ptnr. Rosenberg Instnl. Equity Mgmt., Orinda, Calif., 1985—. Marshall scholar, U.K., 1963-65. Mem. Am. Econ. Soc., Econometric Soc., Am. Statis. Assn., Am. Fin. Assn., Western Fin. Assn. Office: Rosenberg Instnl Equity Mgmt 4 Orinda Way Bldg E Orinda CA 94563-2515

ROSENBERG, BRUCE ALAN, English language educator, author; b. N.Y.C., July 27, 1934; s. Howard Alyne and Audrey (Olenick) R.; m. Ann Harleman, June, 1981; children: Eric Peter, Seth Allan, Bradley Michael, Sarah Stewart. Student, Alfred U., 1952-54; B.A., Hofstra U., 1955; M.A., Pa. State U., 1962; Ph.D., Ohio State U., 1965. Mem. faculty U. Calif., Santa Barbara, 1965-67, U. Va., Charlottesville, 1967-69, Pa. State U., State College, 1969-77; prof. English lit. and Am. civilization Brown U., 1977—; Fulbright lectr., Warsaw, Poland, 1981. Author: The Art of the American Folk Preacher, 1970, Custer and the Epic of Defeat, 1976, The Code of the West, 1981, The Spy Story, 1987, Can These Bones Live?, 1988, Ian Fleming, 1989, Folklore and Literature, 1991, The Neutral Ground, 1994; asst. editor Chaucer Rev., 1967-69, Jour. Am. Folklore, 1970-79; contbg. editor Oral Tradition, 1985—. Served with U.S. Army, 1955-57. Recipient James Russell Lowell prize, 1970; Chgo. Folklore prize, 1970, 76; Am. Council Learned Socs. fellow, 1967; Nat. Endowment Humanities fellow, 1976-77; Guggenheim fellow, 1982-83. Mem. MLA, Folklore Fellows Internat., Am. Folklore Soc. Jewish. Home: 55 Summit Ave Providence RI 02906-2709 Office: Brown U 82 Waterman St Brown Sta Providence RI 02912-0001

ROSENBERG, BURTON M., apparel company executive. Chief fin. officer Style Undies, N.Y.C., 1960-69; pres. Henry I. Siegel Co., Inc., N.Y.C., 1969—. Office: Chic By HIS Inc 1372 Broadway Fl 12 New York NY 10018-6106*

ROSENBERG, CHARLES ERNEST, historian, educator; b. N.Y.C., Nov. 11, 1936; s. Bernard and Marion (Roberts) R.; m. Carroll Ann Smith, June 22, 1961 (div. 1977); 1 child, Leah; m. Drew Gilpin Faust, June 7, 1980; 1 child, Jessica. B.A., U. Wis., 1956; M.A., Columbia U., 1957, Ph.D., 1961. Fellow Johns Hopkins U., Balt., 1960-61; asst. prof. U. Wis., 1961-63; assoc. prof. U. Pa., Phila., 1965-68; prof. history U. Pa., 1968—, chmn. dept., 1974-75, 79-83; Bd. dirs. Mental Health Assn. Southeastern Pa., 1973-76, Library Co. of Phila., 1980—. Author: The Cholera Years: The United States in 1832, 1849 and 1866, 1962, The Trial of the Assassin Guiteau: Psychiatry and Law in the Gilded Age, 1968, No Other Gods: On Science and Social Thought in America, 1976, The Care of Strangers: The Rise of America's Hospital System, 1987, Explaining Epidemics and Other Studies in the History of Medicine, 1992; editor Isis, 1986-89. Nat. Inst. Health Research grantee, 1964-70; Guggenheim Found. fellow, 1965-66, 89-90; Nat. Endowment Humanities fellow, 1972-73; Rockefeller Found. humanities fellow, 1975-76; fellow Inst. Advanced Study, 1979-80, Ctr. Advanced Study in Behavioral Scis., 1982-83. Fellow Am. Acad. Arts and Scis.; mem. Inst. Medicine of NAS, Am. Assn. History of Medicine (William H. Welch medal 1969, coun. 1974-76, pres. 1992-94), History of Sci. Soc. (George Sarton medal 1995, coun. 1972-75), Soc. Social History of Medicine (pres. 1981), Orgn. Am. Historians (exec. bd. 1985-88). Home: 746 Beacom Ln Merion Station PA 19066-1604 Office: U Pa Dept History & Sociology Philadelphia PA 19104-6310

ROSENBERG, CHARLES HARVEY, otorhinolaryngologist; b. N.Y.C., June 10, 1919; s. Morris and Bessie (Greditor) R.; m. Florence Rich, Dec. 27, 1942; children: Kenneth, Ina Garten. BA cum laude, Alfred U., 1941; MD, U. Buffalo, 1944. Intern Jewish Hosp. Bklyn., 1944-45; resident otolaryngology Mt. Sinai Hosp., N.Y.C., 1945-46, 48-50; teaching faculty, sr. clin. asst. Mt. Sinai Hosp. and Med. Sch., N.Y.C., 1950-72; attending surgeon Stamford (Conn.) Hosp., St. Joseph's Hosp., 1953—; dir. dept. otolaryngology Stamford Hosp. and St. Joseph's Hosp., 1973-79. Campaign chmn. United Jewish Fedn., Stamford, 1978-81, pres., 1981-83, exec. com., 1978—; mem. pres.'s coun. Alfred (N.Y.) U., 1990—. Capt. U.S. Army, 1945-46. Fellow ACS; mem. AMA, Stamford Med. Soc., Fairfield Med. Soc., Conn. State Med. Soc., Am. Bd. Otolaryngology, Am. Acad. Ophthalmology and Otolaryngology. Democrat. Jewish. Home: 304 Erskine Rd Stamford CT 06903-1001 Office: 810 Bedford St Stamford CT 06901-1115

ROSENBERG, CHARLES MICHAEL, art historian, educator; b. Chgo., Aug. 3, 1945; s. Sandor and Laura (Fried) R.; m. Carol Ann Weiss, June 25, 1967; children: Jessica Rachel, Jasper Matthew. BA, Swarthmore Coll., 1967; MA, U. Mich., 1969, PhD, 1974. Asst. prof. SUNY, Brockport, 1973-80; assoc. prof. U. Notre Dame, Ind., 1980-96, prof., 1996—. Author: 15th Century North Italian Painting and Drawing: Bibliography, 1986, Art and Politics in Late Medieval and Early Renaissance Italy, 1990; contbr. articles to Art Bull., Renaissance Quar., others. Kress Found. fellow Kunsthistorsches Inst., Florence, Italy, 1971-73, Am. Coun. Learned Socs. fellow, 1977-78, NEH fellow, Brown U., 1979-80, Villa i Tatti, Florence, 1985-86. Mem. Coll. Art Assn., Renaissance Soc. Am., Centro di Studi Europa Della Corti. Office: Notre Dame U Dept Art Art History & Design Notre Dame IN 46556

ROSENBERG, CLAUDE NEWMAN, JR., investment adviser; b. San Francisco, Apr. 10, 1928; s. Claude Newman and Elza (Wolff) R.; m. Louise Jankelson, Dec. 19, 1968; children: Linda Kay, Douglas Claude. BA, Stanford U., 1950, MBA, 1952. Research analyst J. Barth & Co., San Francisco, 1955-62; partner charge research J. Barth & Co., 1962-70; investment adviser, pres. Rosenberg Capital Mgmt., San Francisco, 1970—; lectr. and mem. adv. council Grad. Sch. Bus., Stanford. Author: Stock Market Primer, 1962, rev., 1970, 76, 81, 87, The Common Sense Way to Stock Market Profit, 1968, rev., 1978, Psycho-Cybernetics and the Stock Market, 1970, Investing with the Best, 1986, rev., 1993, Wealthy and Wise, 1994. Bd. dirs. Jewish Welfare Fedn., Presbyn. Children's Cancer Research Center, Internat. Hospitality Center, Jewish Community Center; trustee San Francisco Ballet Assn., Univ. High Sch., San Francisco.; chmn. adv. council Stanford U. Sch. Bus. Served with USNR, 1951-53. Recipient Arbuckle award Stanford U. Grad. Sch. Bus., 1984, Daniel I. Forrestal Leadership award, AIMR, 1992, Lilywhite award Employee Benefit Rsch. Inst., 1994, Bus. Statesman award Harvard Bus. Sch. Assn. of No. Calif., 1995. Mem. Financial Analysts San Francisco, Alumni Assn. Stanford U. Grad. Sch. Bus. (pres.). Republican. Jewish religion. Clubs: Family (San Francisco), Concordia-Argonaut (San Francisco), Calif. Tennis (San Francisco), Family (San Francisco). Home: 2465 Pacific Ave San Francisco CA 94115-1237 Office: Four Embarcadero Center 29th Floor San Francisco CA 94111

ROSENBERG, DAN YALE, retired plant pathologist; b. Stockton, Calif., Jan. 8, 1922; s. Meyer and Bertha (Naliboff) R.; AA, Stockton Jr. Coll., 1942; AB, Coll. Pacific, 1949; MS, U. Calif. at Davis, 1952; m. Marilyn Kohn, Dec. 5, 1954; 1 son, Morton Karl. Jr. plant pathologist Calif. Dept. Agr., Riverside, 1952-55, asst. plant pathologist, 1955-59, assoc. plant pathologist, 1959-60, pathologist IV, 1960-63, program supr., 1963-71, chief exclusion and detection, div. plant industry, 1971-76, chief nursery and seed svcs. div. plant industry, 1976-82, spl. asst. div. plant industry, 1982-87; pres. Health, Inc., 1972-73; agrl. cons., 1988—; mem. Citrus Rsch. Adv. com. U. Calif., Riverside, 1992—; mem. Gov.'s Interagy. Task Force on Biotech., 1986—; bd. dirs. Health Inc., Sacramento, 1967, pres., 1971-72, 79-81, 81-83. Served with AUS, 1942-46; ETO. Mem. Am. Phytopath. Soc. (fgn. and regulatory com. 1975—, grape diseases sect. 1977-79, grape pests sect. 1979—), Calif. State Employees Assn. (pres. 1967-69). Contbr. articles to profl. jours. Home and Office: 2328 Swarthmore Dr Sacramento CA 95825-6867

ROSENBERG, DAVID, lawyer; b. N.Y.C., May 6, 1946; s. Marvin and Helene (Feller) R.; m. Bernice Leber, June 25, 1989. BA, U. Chgo., 1968; JD, N.Y.U., 1971. Bar: N.Y. 1972, U.S. Dist. Ct. (so. dist.) N.Y. 1975, U.S. Dist. Ct. (ea. dist.) N.Y. 1975, U.S. Supreme Ct. 1980, U.S. Ct. Appeals (2nd. cir.) 1981. Atty. N.Y.C. Housing & devel. Adminstrn., 1971-72; law clk. N.Y. Supreme Ct., 1972-80; assoc., ptnr. Feldesman & D'Atri, N.Y.C., 1980-81; assoc. Summit Rovins & Feldesman, N.Y.C., 1981-82, ptnr., 1983-89, Marcus Borg Rosenberg & Diamond, 1989—; mem. Com. Character & Fitness 1st Jud. Dept., N.Y.C., 1984—; asst. counsel N.Y. Com. Jud. Nomination, 1982-89; mem. Adv. Council N.Y.C. Civil Ct., 1982—, chmn. 1986—. Mem. N.Y. Bar Assn. (real property law sect. exec. com. 1979—, landlord & tenant com. chmn. 1977-88), ABA (real property litigation, corp. sects. 1971—), N.Y.C. Bar Assn. (civil ct. com. 1981-84, judiciary com. 1985-88, chair common state cts. superior jurisdiction 1989-93). Home: 20 W 86th St New York NY 10024-3604 Office: Marcus Borg Rosenberg & Diamond 488 Madison Ave New York NY 10022-5702

ROSENBERG, DAVID ALAN, military historian, educator; b. N.Y.C., Aug. 30, 1948; s. Sidney and Fay (Breitman) R.; m. Deborah Lee Haines, July 1, 1973; 1 child, Rebecca Haines. BA in History, Am. U., 1970; MA in History, U. Chgo., 1971, PhD in History, 1983. Asst. historian, cons. Lulejian & Assocs., Inc., Falls Church, VA., 1974-75; instr. history U. Wis., Milw., 1976-78; pvt. practice cons., researcher Chgo., Washington, 1978-82; asst. prof. history U. Houston, University Park, 1982-83; sr. fellow Strategic Concepts Devel. Ctr., Nat. Def. U., Washington, 1983-85; prof. strategy and ops. U.S. Naval War Coll., Newport, R.I., 1985-90; assoc. prof. history Temple U., Phila., 1990—; Admiral Henry W. Hill prof. of maritime strategy Nat. War Coll., Washington, D.C., 1996—; mem. U.S. exec. com. four Nation Nuclear History Program, project dir. Berlin Crisis, 1989-95; cons. Office of Chief of Sec. Def., 1990-93; mem., chair Sec. Navy's Adv. Subcom. of Naval History, 1995—. Co-editor: (15 vol. book set) U.S. Plans for War, 1945-1950, 1990; contbr. articles to Jour. Am. History (2 awards nat. hist. assns. 1980), 22 others, also 15 book chpts. With USNR, 1982—. Advanced rsch. scholar U.S. Naval War Coll., 1974-79; Ford Found grantee, 1985-86, MacArthur rsch. grantee 1987-88; MacArthur fellow 1988-93. Mem. Orgn. Am. Historians (Binkley-Stephenson article prize), Soc. for Historians of Am. Fgn. Rels. (Bernath article prize), Soc. for Mil. History, U.S. Naval Inst., Internat. Inst. for Strategic Studies. Jewish.

ROSENBERG, DOUGLAS OWEN, healthcare management executive; b. Chgo., July 13, 1941; s. Owen Carl and Doris Raven (Ambrose) R.; m. Deloris Anne Wimmer, Aug. 19, 1967; children: Kevin Douglas, Jeffrey Kendall. BS in Biology, U. Chgo., 1963, MBA in Hosp. Adminstrn., 1969. Adminstrv. asst., asst. adminstr., assoc. adminstr. Ohio State U. Hosps., Columbus, 1969-74; v.p. adminstrn. Ravenswood Hosp., Chgo., 1974-76; v.p. clin. svc., exec. v.p. ops., pres. Glenbrook Hosp., 1976-92; pres., CEO Howard Young Health Care, Woodruff, Wis., 1994—; grad. student preceptor various univs., 1980-92. Pres. Glenview (Ill.) Safety Com., 1979-83; v.p. Glenview chpt. Am. Cancer Soc., 1979-86; budget chmn. United Way, Northbrook, Ill., 1986-94. Capt. U.S. Army, 1964-67, Vietnam. Decorated Bronze Star; Inst. Medicine fellow, 1977-92. Mem. Wis. Hosp. Assn. Methodist. Avocations: history, numismatics, canoeing, tennis. Home: 7066 Hwy J Saint Germain WI 54558 Office: Howard Young Health Care PO Box 470 Woodruff WI 54568

ROSENBERG, GARY ARON, construction executive, lawyer; b. Green Bay, Wis., June 18, 1940; s. Ben J. and Joyce Sarah (Nemzin) R.; m. Gloria Davis, Nov. 1967 (div. 1975); children: Myra, Meredith; m. Bridgit A. Maile, Apr. 9, 1983. BS, Northwestern U., 1962, MBA, 1963; JD, U. Wis., 1966. Bar: Wis. 1966, Ill. 1967. Atty. U.S. SEC, Washington, 1966-67; pvt. practice Chgo., 1967-74; founder, chmn. bd., CEO UDC Homes, Inc. (formerly UDC-Universal Devel., L.P.), Chgo., 1968-1995; mem. adv. bd. Kellogg Grad. Sch. Mgmt. Northwestern U., Evanston, Ill., 1985—, founder, chmn. adv. bd. Real Estate Rsch. Ctr., 1986—, adj. prof., 1982—; founder Shadow Hill Entertainment Corp., Beverly Hills, Calif., 1990. Recipient Arts Edn. Svc. award Ill. Alliance for Arts Edn., Chgo., 1988, Kellogg Schaffner Disting. Alumni award Kellogg Grad. Sch. Mgmt., 1993. Mem. Nat. Assn. Home Builders (coun. 1989-90), John Evans Club. Avocations: skiing, hiking, climbing, tennis, golf, reading. Office: UDC Homes Inc Camter Development 1 E Superior Ste 401 Chicago IL 60611-4501 also: UDC Homes Inc 4812 S Mill Ave Tempe AZ 85282-6730*

ROSENBERG, HENRY A., JR., petroleum executive; b. Pitts., Nov. 7, 1929; s. Henry A. and Ruth (Blaustein) R.; children: Henry A. III, Edward Lee, Frank Blaustein; m. Dorothy Lucibello, June 30, 1984. B.A. in Econs., Hobart Coll., 1952. With Crown Cen. Petroleum Corp., Balt., 1952—, pres., 1966-75, chmn. exec. com., 1966—, chmn. bd., 1975—, also chief exec. officer; dir. Am. Trading & Prodn. Corp., USF&G Corp., Signet Banking Corp. Bd. dirs. Johns Hopkins Hosp., Goucher Coll., McDonogh Sch., Nat. Flag Day Found., YMCA Greater Balt., United Way Ctrl. Med., Crohn's and Colitis Found. Md., Nat. Aquarium Balt.; mem. nat. exec. bd., mem. N.E. regional bd., v.p. program group nat. coun., past pres., exec. bd., adv. coun. Balt. Area coun. Boy Scouts Am.; past chmn., mem. adv. bd. William Donald Schaefer Ctr. for Pub. Policy; past chmn. bd. dirs. Balt. Area Conv. and Visitors Assn.; trustee Hobart and William Smith Colls. and Loyola Coll. Md. Mem. Nat. Petroleum Refiners Assn. (chmn., bd. dirs., exec. com.), Nat. Petroleum Coun., 25 Yr. Club Petroleum Industry. Office: Crown Cen Petroleum Corp 1 N Charles St PO Box 1168 Baltimore MD 21203

ROSENBERG, HOWARD ANTHONY, journalist; b. Kansas City, Mo., June 10, 1942; s. Sherman Rosenberg and Claire (Kanchuk) Rosenberg Magady; m. Carol Finkel; 1 child, Kirsten. Journalist Los Angeles Times, now TV critic, columnist. Recipient Editorial award Los Angeles Times, 1981; Headliner award Atlantic City Press Club, 1984; Pulitzer prize Columbia U., 1985. Office: Los Angeles Times Times Mirror Sq Los Angeles CA 90012

ROSENBERG, IRWIN HAROLD, physician, educator; b. Madison, Wis., Jan. 6, 1935; s. Abraham Joseph and Celia (Mazursky) R.; m. Civia Muffs, May 24, 1964; 1 child, Ilana. BS, U. Wis., 1956; MD, Harvard U., 1959. Diplomate Am. Bd. Internal Medicine. Intern Mass. Gen. Hosp., Boston, 1959-60, resident, 1960-61; instr. medicine Harvard Med. Sch., Boston, 1965-66, assoc. in medicine, 1966-68, asst. prof., 1968-70; assoc. prof. medicine U. Chgo., 1970-75, prof., 1975-86, Sarah and Harold Lincoln Thomson prof. medicine, 1983-86; prof., dir. USDA Human Nutrition Rsch. Ctr. on Aging Tufts U., Boston, 1986—, Jean Mayer prof., 1993; mem. food and nutrition bd. Nat. Acad. of Scis., 1971-83, chmn., 1981-83; W.O. Atwater lectr. USDA, 1993. Co-chair local br. Med. Com. on Human Rights, Boston, 1967; mem. adv. bd. Hebrew Coll., Boston, 1987, 91; chmn. bd. dirs. Hillel Found., U. Chgo. With USPHS, 1961-64. Recipient Josiah Macy Faculty award Macy Found., 1974, Goldsmith award Am. Coll. Nutrition, 1984. Fellow AAAS; mem. Am. Soc. for Clin. Nutrition (pres. 1983-84, Herman award 1989), Internat. Life Sci. Inst. (editor nutrition revs. 1989—), Inst. of Medicine, Nat. Acad. Scis. Jewish. Avocations: sports, music, Judaica. Office: Tufts U USDA Human Nutrition Rsch Ctr 711 Washington St Boston MA 02111-1524

ROSENBERG, JAMES WILLIAM, marketing executive; b. Boston, Nov. 23, 1958; s. Sumner Harold and Ruth (Sheff) R.; m. Donna Gail Siskind, Oct. 23, 1982; children: Randall Alexandra, Bari Elizabeth. BBA, U. Mass., Amherst, Mass., 1980; MBA, Bentley Coll., Waltham, Mass., 1985. Fin. analyst Raytheon/Telex Data Systems, Norwood, Mass., 1980-85; direct mktg. dir. ISM, Strategic Mktg., Inc., Boston, 1985-92; exec. v.p. mktg. Berenson, Isham & Ptnrs., Boston, 1992-96; v.p. mktg. dir. IQ & J Group 121, Boston, 1996—; bd. dirs. Leveathal-Siddman Jewish Cmty. Ctr., Newton, Mass., 1991—; mem. judging com. Direct Mktg. Assn., N.Y.C., 1989-91; guest speaker Fla. Direct Mktg. Assn., Ft. Lauderdale, 1990; instr. continuing profl. studies Bentley Coll. Contbr. articles to profl. jours.; speaker Integrated Direct Mktg. Am. Mktg. Assn., 1989. Mktg. chmn. Leventhal-Siddman Jewish Community Ctr., Newton, Mass., 1989-92. Recipient ECHO award Direct Mktg. Assn. N.Y., 1989-90; NEDMA award New Eng. Direct Mktg. Assn., Boston, 1989-94. Mem. Direct Mktg. Assn., New England Direct Mktg. Assn. Avocations: swimming, woodworking, restorations, automobiles.

ROSENBERG, JEROME DAVID, physicist; b. N.Y.C., June 15, 1920; s. Hyman D. and Hilda (Cantor) R.; m. Shirley Sirota, 1947; children: Jonathan, Hindy. BS in Physics, CCNY, 1948; postgrad., Nat. Bur. Standards Grad. Sch., 1949-52, George Washington U., 1952, U. Md., 1951-53, Cath. U. Am., 1953-54. Engr. officer USCG Acad., 1944-45; project mgr., adminstr. test nuclear reactor Harry Diamond Labs., Washington, 1950-62; ops. mgr. tech. utilization NASA, Washington, 1962-64, program and project mgr. space applications program, 1964-69, dep. dir. comm. program, 1969-74, dir. tech. applications divsn., 1974-77, dir. office energy programs divsn. bus. mgmt., 1977-78; spl. assignment to solar applications & conservation, barriers and incentive br. Dept. Energy, 1978-79; leader solar energy group Mitre Corp., McLean, Va., 1979-81; prin. energy and environ. divsn. Booz, Allen & Hamilton, Washington, 1980-82; sr. staff officer Bd. Telecomm. and Computer Applications, NRC-NAS, Washington, 1982-85; exec. dir. NASA Alumni League, Washington, 1986—; mem. Outlook for Space Study Group, NASA planning group to develop U.S. space programs, 1975. Recipient NASA Exceptional Svc. medal, 1973. Mem. Fed. Exec. Inst., Sigma Pi Sigma. Office: NASA Alumni League 750 First Ave NE Washington DC 20002

ROSENBERG, JEROME I., lawyer; b. Passaic, N.J., June 9, 1931; s. Emanuel and Sylvia S. (Schwartz) R.; m. Dorothy Elaine Teninbaum, Aug. 21, 1955; children—Peter, Michael. B.A., NYU, 1953; LL.B., Harvard U., 1956. Bar: N.Y. 1966, D.C. 1957, U.S. Supreme Ct. Tax law specialist IRS, Washington, 1960-63; mem. firm Hughes Hubbard & Reed, N.Y.C., 1968—; dir. 1016 Properties, Inc., N.Y.C.; lectr. NYU Tax Inst. Contbr. articles to Jour. of Taxation. Served as lt. USAF, 1957-60. Mem. N.Y. State Bar Assn., Assn. of Bar of City N.Y., D.C. Bar Assn., Phi Beta Kappa. Office: Hughes Hubbard & Reed One Battery Park Plz New York NY 10004-1466

ROSENBERG, JEROME LAIB, chemist, educator; b. Harrisburg, Pa., June 20, 1921; s. Robert and Mary (Katzman) R.; m. Shoshana Gabriel, Sept. 15, 1946; children—Jonathan, Judith. AB, Dickinson Coll., 1941; MA, Columbia U., 1944, PhD, 1948. Rsch. chemist S.A.M. Labs., 1944-46; Instr. chemistry Columbia U., 1946-48; rsch. assoc. (asst. prof.) inst. Radiobiology and Biophysics, U. Chgo., 1950-53; mem. faculty U. Pitts., 1953-91, chmn. dept. biophysics and microbiology, 1969-71, prof. biol. scis., 1976-91, dean faculty arts and scis., 1970-86, vice provost, 1978-89, chmn. biol. scis., 1989-90, interim chmn. communication, 1991, assoc. dean faculty arts and scis., 1991-92, rsch. integrity officer, 1992—, prof. emeritus biol. scis., 1991—, dir. Jewish studies program, 1991—. Author: Photosynthesis, 1965; editor, reviser: Outline Theory and Problems of College Chemistry (Schaum), 1949, 58, 66, 80, 90; contbr. articles to profl. jours. NSF sr. fellow Technion Israel Inst. Tech., 1962-63, AEC fellow U. Chgo., 1948-50; recipient Pitts. award Am. Chem. Soc., 1987. Mem. AAUP (nat. coun. 1968-69, pres. Pa. div. 1968-69). Home: 1029 S Negley Ave Pittsburgh PA 15217-1045

ROSENBERG, JERRY MARTIN, business administration educator; b. N.Y.C., Feb. 5, 1935; s. Frank and Esther (Gardner) R.; m. Ellen Young, Sept. 11, 1960; children: Lauren, Elizabeth. B.S., Coll. City N.Y., 1956; M.A., Ohio State U., 1957; certificate, Sorbonne, 1958; Ph.D., N.Y.U., 1963. Asst. prof. Cornell U. Sch. Indsl. and Labor Relations, 1961-64; asst. prof. Columbia U., 1964-68; pvt. practice cons. N.Y.C., 1968-71; assoc. prof. CUNY, 1971-74; prof. mgmt., chmn. dept. Poly. Inst. N.Y., N.Y.C., 1974-77; prof. mgmt. Lehman Coll., CUNY; prof. bus. adminstrn. and mgmt., chmn. dept. bus. adminstrn. Rutgers U., Newark, 1977-88, prof. grad. sch. mgmt., chmn. dept. internat. bus., 1988—; testified before U.S. Senate on privacy; dir. Ctr. for Middle East-N. Africa Bus. Studies, 1996—. Author: Automation Manpower and Education, 1966, The Computer Prophets, 1969, The Death of Privacy, 1969, Dictionary of Business and Management, 1978, Dictionary of Banking and Financial Services, , 1982, Inside the Wall Street Journal, 1982, Dictionary of Computers, Data Processing and Telecommunications, 1983, Investor's Dictionary, 1986, Dictionary of Artificial Intelligence and Robotics, 1986, The New Europe, 1991, Dictionary of Business Acronyms, Abbreviations and Initials, 1992, Dictionary of Wall Street Acronyms, Abbreviations and Initials, 1992, Dictionary of Information Technology and Computer Acronyms, Abbreviations and Initials, 1992, The New American Community, 1992, Dictionary of International Trade, 1994, Encyclopedia of NAFTA, The New American Community and Latin-American Trade, 1994, Dictionary of Marketing and Advertising, 1995, Dictionary of Retailing and Merchandising, 1995, The Peace Dividend: Creating a Middle East/N. Africa Community, 1996. Recipient Fulbright and French Govt. awards, 1957. Known as Am.'s foremost bus. and tech. lexicographer. Home: 515 Tulfan Ter Bronx NY 10463-1705 Office: Rutgers U Mgmt Edn Ctr Newark NJ 07102

ROSENBERG, JILL, realtor, civic leader; b. Shreveport, La., Feb. 17, 1940; d. Morris H. and Sallye (Abramson) Schuster; m. Lewis Rosenberg, Dec. 23, 1962; children: Craig, Paige. BA in Philosophy, Tulane U., 1961, MSW, 1965; grad., Realtor Inst., 1994. Cert. residential specialist Residential Sales Coun.; grad. Realtor Inst. Social worker La. Dept. Pub. Welfare, 1961-62, 63-64; genetics counselor Sinai Hosp., Balt., 1967-69; ptnr. Parties Extraordinaire, cons., 1973-77; realtor assoc. Robert Weil Assocs., Long Beach, Calif., 1982—. Pres. western region Brandeis U. Nat. Women's Com., 1972-73; bd. dirs. Long Beach Symphony Assn., 1984-85; v.p. Jewish Cmty. Fedn. Long Beach and West Orange County, 1983-86, bd. dirs., 1982-86; pres. Long Beach Cancer League, 1987-88, exec. bd. dirs., 1984—; pres. Long Beach Jewish Cmty. Sr. Housing Corp., 1989-91; v.p. fundraising S.E. unit Long Beach Harbor chpt. Am. Cancer Soc., 1989-90; bd. dirs. Westerly Sch. Assoc., 1991—; bd. trustees St. Mary Med. Ctr. Found., 1991—; fund chair St. Mary Med. Ctr., 1992-94; pres. nat. conf. NCCJ, 1994-96; pres. Leadership Long Beach, 1994-95; Phoenix Long Beach Mus. Art, 1995—, numerous others. Recipient Young Leadership award Jewish Community Fedn. Long Beach and West Orange County, 1981, Jerusalem award State of Israel, 1989, Hannah G. Solomon award Nat. Coun. Jewish Women, 1992, Alumnus of Yr. award Leadership Long Beach, 1995; scholar La. Dept. Pub. Welfare, 1962, NIMH, 1964. Office: Robert Weil Assocs 5220 E Los Altos Plz Long Beach CA 90815-4251

ROSENBERG, JOHN DAVID, English educator, literary critic; b. N.Y.C., Apr. 17, 1929; s. David and Dorothy Lilian (Shatz) R.; m. Barbara E. Hatch, 1952 (div. 1969); m. Maurine Ann Hellner, June 11, 1972; 1 child, Matthew John. BA, Columbia U., 1950, MA, 1951, PhD, 1960; BA, Clare Coll., Cambridge U., 1953, MA, 1958. Editor-in-chief Columbia Rev., 1949-50; lectr. English Columbia U., N.Y.C., 1953-54, asst. prof., 1962-65, assoc. prof., 1966-67, prof. English, 1967—, William Peterfield Trent prof., 1994—; instr. CCNY, 1954-62; chmn. Columbia Coll. humanities program, 1970-73, dir. grad. studies in English, 1986-89; vis. prof. English, Harvard U., summer 1968, U. B.C., Summer 1970, Princeton U., 1978; vis. fellow Clare Hall, Cambridge (Eng.) U., 1969; guest lectr. U.S. Mil. Acad., Cambridge U., Queens U. Author: The Darkening Glass: A Portrait of Ruskin's Genius, 1961, The Fall of Camelot: A Study of Tennyson's Idylls of the King, 1973, Carlyle and the Burden of History, 1985; editor: The Genius of John Ruskin, 1963, Mayhew, 1968, Swinburne: Selected Poetry and Prose, 1968, The Poems of Alfred, Lord Tennyson, 1975; contbr. essays and reviews on English lit. to N.Y. Times Book Rev., Harper's mag., Hudson Rev. and profl. jours. Recipient Clarke F. Ansley award Columbia U., 1960; Coun. for Rsch. in Humanities grant-in-aid, 1965; Euretta J. Kellett fellow Cambridge U., 1951-53, Edward Coe fellow, 1956-57, Samuel S. Fels fellow, 1959-60, Am. Coun. Learned Soc. fellow, 1965-66, 70, Lawrence H. Chamberlain fellow, 1965-66, Guggenheim fellow, 1968-69, NEH fellow, 1982-83. Mem. MLA (chmn. exec. com. Victorian divsn. 1970, exec. com. 1979-83), Tennyson Soc., Ruskin Assn., Camp Rising Sun Alumni Assn., Columbia Coll. Alumni Assn. (dir. 1980-82, Alexander Hamilton medal 1994), Phi Beta Kappa. Office: Columbia U Dept English New York NY 10027

ROSENBERG, JOHN K., lawyer; b. N.Y.C., May 13, 1945; s. Robert and Joyce (Kane) R.; m. Fern Kaufman; children: Joyce, Amie. BA, Pa. State U., 1967; JD, Columbia U., 1970. Bar: N.Y. 1971, Kans. 1980, U.S. Dist. Ct. (no. dist.) N.Y. 1971, U.S. Dist. Ct. Kans. 1980, U.S. Ct. Appeals (10th cir.) 1982, U.S. Ct. Appeals (5th cir.) 1986, U.S. Supreme Ct. 1990. Staff counsel N.Y. Pub. Svc. Commn., Albany, 1970-74; prin. atty. N.Y. Consumer Protection Bd., Albany, 1974-78; asst. gen. counsel The Kans. Power & Light Co., Topeka, 1979-87, v.p. gen. counsel, 1987-89, exec. v.p., gen. counsel, sec., 1989-92; exec. v.p., gen. counsel Western Resources, Inc., Topeka, 1992—; mem. legal com. Edison Elec. Inst., 1987—. Bd. dirs. Friends of the Topeka 20, 1983-89, 94—, pres., 1988; mem. Mayor's Commn. on Literacy, 1990-93; bd. dirs., sec. Concerned Citizens of Topeka, 1995—. Mem. Am. Gas. Assn. (legal mng. com. 1986—). Avocations: golf, flyfishing, hiking. Office: Western Resources Inc 818 S Kansas Ave Topeka KS 66612-1203

ROSENBERG, JUDITH LYNNE, middle school educator; b. Bklyn., Nov. 1, 1944; d. Benjamin and Rose (Delbaum) Jackler; m. Joel Barry Rosenberg, Aug. 26, 1965; children: Jeffrey Alan, Marc David. BA in Edn., Queens Coll., Flushing, N.Y., 1966, MS in Edn., 1972. Lic. advanced profl. elem. and mid. sch. math., Md., elem. edn., N.Y. Elem. tchr. N.Y.C. and Cranston, R.I., 1966-68; tchr. math. Earl B. Wood Mid. Sch., Rockville, Md., 1981-82, Walt Whitman High Sch., Bethesda, Md., 1982-83, Robert Frost Mid. Sch., Rockville, Md., 1983-89; math. and interdisciplinary resource Julius West Mid. Sch., Rockville, 1989—. Mem. NEA, Nat. Coun. Tchrs. Math., Md. State Tchrs. Assn. Home: 16 Flameleaf Ct Gaithersburg MD 20878-5216 Office: Julius West Mid Sch Great Falls Rd Rockville MD 20850

ROSENBERG, JUDITH META, brokerage executive; b. N.Y.C., Sept. 17, 1964. BS in Fin., Lehigh U., 1986. With Morgan Stanley, N.Y.C., 1986; broker Bear Stearns & Co., N.Y.C., 1987, v.p., 1988, assoc. dir., 1989; mng. dir., 1990. Bd. dirs. Henry Kaufmann Campgrounds. Mem. N.Y. Jr. League, Lehigh Alumni Assn., Women's Nat. Rep. Club. Republican. Office: 245 Park Ave Fl 9 New York NY 10167-0002

ROSENBERG, LEON EMANUEL, medical educator, geneticist, university dean; b. Madison, Wis., Mar. 3, 1933; s. Abraham Joseph and Celia (Mazursky) R.; m. Elaine Lewis, Aug. 29, 1954 (div. Nov. 1971); children—Robert, Diana, David; m. Diane Drobnis, July 4, 1979; 1 child, Alexa. BA, U.Wis., Madison, 1954, MD, 1957, Dsc (hon.), 1989. Diplomate Am. Bd. Internal Medicine. Intern Columbia Presbyn. Med. Ctr., N.Y., 1957-58, resident, 1958-59; resident Yale U.- New Haven Hosp., 1962-63; fellow metabolism Nat. Inst. Health, Bethesda, Md., 1959-62; Asst. prof. medicine Yale Sch. Medicine, New Haven, 1965-68, assoc. prof. pediatrics and medicine, 1968-72, prof. human genetics, medicine and pediatrics chmn. dept. human genetics, 1972-84, dean Sch. Medicine, 1984—, C.N.H. Long prof., 1980—; now rsch. scientist Bristol-Myers Squibb Pharmacology Rsch. Inst., Princeton, N.J.; mem. adv. council NIADDK, 1980-83; mem. com. on infant health Robert Wood Johnson Found., 1982-90; mem. panel Inst. Medicine, NIH, 1983-84; chmn. adv. com. scholars program Hartford Found., N.Y.C., 1984-85. Author: Amino Acid Metabolism and Its Disorders, 1974; editor: Metabolic Control and Disease, 1981. Served to sr. surgeon USPHS, 1959-65. Recipient Disting. Alumnus citation U. Wis.-Madison, 1982. Fellow NAS, Inst. Medicine of NAS, AAAS, Am. Acad. Arts and Scis.; mem. Am. Soc. Clin. Investigation (v.p. 1978-79), Am. Soc. Human Genetics (pres. 1980-81), Assn. Am. Physicians (councillor 1986—), Am. Pediatric Soc., Am. Soc. Biol. Chemists, Assn. Am. Med. Colls. (coun. deans, chair elect 1990-91, chair 1991—). Democrat. Jewish. Avocations: tennis; skiing; jogging. Office: Bristol-Myers Squibb Pharmacology Rsch Inst PO Box 4000 Princeton NJ 08543-4000*

ROSENBERG, LEON JOSEPH, marketing educator; b. Atlanta, Oct. 9, 1918; s. Harry Manville and Gertrude Dora (Hassenbusch) R.; m. Phylis Jane Israel, Feb. 6, 1943 (dec. Mar. 1976); children: Joanne Rosenberg Larson, Paul Harvey; m. Louise Marjorie Nachman, Oct. 15, 1977. B.S. in Indsl. Mgmt, Ga. Inst. Tech., 1939; M.S. (Univ. scholar), Columbia U., 1940; Ph.D., N.Y. U., 1967. Mem. staff Nat. Retail Mchts. Assn., N.Y.C., 1947-49; sr. research analyst Federated Dept. Stores, Inc., Cin., 1949-52; research dir. Sanger Harris Dept. Store, Dallas, 1952-56; gen. supt. Sanger Harris Dept. Store, 1956-67; assoc. prof. Coll. Bus. Adminstrn., U. Ark., Fayetteville, 1967-74; prof., mktg. and transp. Coll. Bus. Adminstrn., U. Ark., 1975-89, dept. head, 1986-88; prof. emeritus U. Ark., 1989—; mktg. cons. Lindsey & Assocs. Inc., Fayetteville, 1990—; real estate cons., 1968—; disting. vis. prof. Calif. State U., San Bernardino, 1990. Contbr. articles to profl. jours. Pres. Jewish Family Svc., Dallas, 1960-62, Temple Shalom, Fayetteville, 1992—; mem. exec. com. Dallas Jewish Fedn., 1963-67; bd. dirs. New Orleans Jewish Children's Regional Svc., 1962-73, 75—, Jewish Fedn. Ark., 1992—; pres. N.W. Ark. unit B'nai B'rith, 1992—; bd. dirs. Washington County (Ark.) chpt. Am. Cancer Soc., 1979-86, pres., 1982-83. Capt. USAAF, 1940-46. Mem. Acad. Mktg. Sci., Am. Mktg. Assn., So. Mktg. Assn., S.W. Mktg. Assn., S.W. Small Bus. Inst. Assn., Econs. and Bus. History Soc. (trustee 1986-89), Masons, Alpha Phi Omega (svc. award 1971), Beta Gamma Sigma, Delta Nu Alpha. Home: 1125 Lakefront Dr Fayetteville AR 72703 Office: Lindsey & Assocs Inc PO Box 1174 Fayetteville AR 72702-1174

ROSENBERG, LEONARD See **RANDALL, TONY**

ROSENBERG, MANUEL, retail company executive; b. Boston, Apr. 26, 1930; s. Israel and Lillian (Wirin) R.; m. Audray Merle Gold, Aug. 28, 1955; children: Peter Neal, Beth Susan. A.B., Harvard U., 1951, M.B.A., 1953. V.P. Filene's, Boston, 1967-73; pres., chief exec. officer Gimbel's, Phila., 1973-75, chmn. bd., chief exec. officer, 1975-77; exec. v.p. Garfinckel, Brooks Bros., Miller & Rhoads, Inc., Washington, 1977-79, pres., 1979-82, also dir.; chmn. bd., chief exec. officer Morse Shoe, Inc., Canton, Mass., 1982-92. Trustee Beth Israel Hosp., Boston, Mass. Eye and Ear Infirmary, Boston. Lt. USN, 1953-56. Mem. Univ. Club, Harvard Club. Home: 370 Beacon St Boston MA 02116-1002

ROSENBERG, MARILYN ROSENTHAL, artist, visual poet; b. Phila., Oct. 11, 1934; m. Robert Rosenberg, June 12, 1955; 2 children. B in Profl. Studies in Studio Arts, SUNY, Empire State Coll., 1978; MA in Liberal Studies, NYU, 1993. Author, pub., creator unique edit. poetry/painting books; solo exhbns. include Irvine Gallery, State U. Calif., Irvine, 1981, The Sandor Tezsler Libr. Gallery, Spartanburg, S.C., 1983, U. Wis., River Falls, 1984, 361 Degrees Gallery, Greenfield, Mass., 1987; two-person exhbns. include SUNY Purchase Libr., 1982, The Hudson River Mus., Yonkers, N.Y., 1984, Women's Studio Workshop Inskirts Gallery, Rosendale, N.Y., 1986, Brownson Art Gallery, Purchase, N.Y., 1988, (with collaborator) Westchester County Gallery, White Plains, N.Y., 1989, Marymount Coll., Tarrytown, N.Y., 1993; group exhbns. include Long Beach (Calif.) Mus. Art, 1977, Kathryn Markel Fine Arts Gallery, N.Y.C., 1978, Pratt Graphic Ctr. Gallery, N.Y.C., 1978, Polytechnic State U. Gallery, San Luis Obispo, Calif., 1979, Phila. Art Alliance, Glassboro State Coll., Pa., 1979, Ridotte del Treatro Comunale, Italy, 1980, SUNY Purchase Gallery, 1982, Galerie Caroline Corre, Paris, 1983, Thorpe Intermedia Gallery, Sparkhill, N.J., 1983, U. Rochester Gallery, Rochester, N.Y., 1984, 14 Sculptors Gallery, N.Y.C., 1984, Georgetown U., Washington, 1984, Franklin Furnace, N.Y.C., 1986, Douglas & Cook Colleges, New Brunswick, N.J., 1985, City Without Walls, Newark, 1986, Galleri T.V., Malmo, Sweden, Post Machina Group and Am. Consulate, Bologna, Italy, 1986, Technical U. of Nova Scotia, Halifax, 1986, Museu Municipal, Figuira Da Foz, Portugal, 1987, King Stephen Mus., Szekesfehrvar, Hungary, 1987, Allen Meml. Art Mus., Oberlin, Ohio, 1987, Cultural Centre of San Paulo, Brazil, 1988, Centro Cultural de la Caja de Ahorros de Valencia, Spain, 1988, Cooper Union Art, N.Y.C., 1989, San Francisco Craft and Folk Art Mus., 1990, Alternatives Gallery, San Luis Obispo, Calif., 1990-91, San Antonio Art Inst., 1991, Sazama Gallery, Chgo., 1992, SUNY Oneonta, 1992, Ralston Fine Arts, Johnson City, Tenn., 1993, Va. Ctr. for Craft Arts, 1993, Libr. Can., 1993, Muée de la Post, Paris, 1993, Pratt Inst., N.Y.C., 1993, Musée de la Poste, Paris, 1993-94, Papertrail, Ottawa, Can., 1993-94, Nexus Found. for Arts, Phila., 1994, Va. Ctr. for Craft Arts, Richmond, 1994, Ormond Meml. Art Mus., Fla., 1994, Libr. Nat. Mus. Women, Washington, 1994-95, Spirit Sq. Ctr. Arts, Charlotte, N.C., 1995, Ellipse Arts Ctr., Arlington, Va., 1995, Monterserrat Coll. Art Gallery, Beverly, Mass., 1995, Yale U. Art Gallery Sculpture Hall, New Haven, Conn., 1995, Harper Collins, N.Y.C., 1995, Brookfield Craft Ctr., Conn., 1995, Muscatine Art Ctr., Iowa, 1995, Sangre de Cristo Art Ctr., Pueblo, Colo., 1995, Lake George (N.Y.) Art Project, 1995, Mus. Nebr. Arts, U. Nebr., Kearney, 1995; public collections and archives include Art Gallery New South Wales, Sydney, Australia, Artpool Art Rsch. Ctr., Budapest, Hungary, Bibliotheque Nationale, Paris, Canadian Postal Mus. Archive, Ottawa, Electrografia Museo Internacional, La Mancha, Cuenca, Spain, Fogg Art Mus., Cambridge, Mass., Mus. of Modern Art Libr., N.Y.C., The Ruth and Marvin Sackner Archive, Miami Beach, Fla., Tate Gallery Libr., London, Yale U. Libr., New Haven, Ct., Canberra Sch. Art Gallery, Australia, Cleve. Inst. Art Libr., Harvard U. Fogg Mus. and Houghton Libr., Cambridge, Mass., Rochester (N.Y.) Inst. Tech., Sch. Art Inst. Chgo. Libr., Amherst (Mass.) Coll. Libr., Atlanta Coll. of Art Libr., Brown U. Libr., Cleve. Inst. of Art Libr., Dartmouth Coll., Sherman Art Libr., Georgetown U. Library, The N.Y. Pub. Libr., Rhode Island Sch. of Design, Stanford U. Libr., Temple U. Library, Phila., U. Calif. at Davis, Santa Barbara Librs., U. Chgo. Libr., U. Utah, Mariott Libr., U. Va. Libr., Va. Commonwealth U. Libr., Wellesley Coll. Libr., Libr. Mus. Fine Arts, Boston, Sch. Mus. of Fine Art Libr., Boston, Nat. Art Libr., Victoria and Albert Mus., London; works included in various publs. and periodicals. Studio: 67 Lakeview Ave West Peekskill NY 10566-6415

ROSENBERG, MARK B., think-tank executive; b. Athens, Ohio, Aug. 15, 1949; married; 2 children. BA, Miami U., Ohio; PhD in Polit. Sci., U. Pitts. Asst. prof. polit. sci. Fla. Internat. U., Miami, 1976—, chairperson Caribbean L.Am. studies coun., 1977-79, founding dir. L.Am. and Caribbean Ctr., 1979—, founding/acting dean Coll. Urban and Pub. Affairs, 1994—, vice provost for internat. studies; co-dir. Fla. Caribbean Inst., Fla. Mexico Inst. Author, editor, co-editor 6 books; contbr. articles to profl. jours. Mem. Greater Miami C. of C. (vice chairperson exec. com. for internat. econ. devel.). Office: Fla Internat Univ North Miami Campus ACI-200 Coll Urban and Pub Affairs Miami FL 33181

ROSENBERG, MARK L., health facility administrator; b. Newark, July 30, 1945; m. Jill Rosenberg; children: Julie, Ben. BA in Biology magna cum laude, Harvard Coll., 1967, MD cum laude, 1972, M of Pub. Policy, 1972. Diplomate Am. Bd. Internal Medicine, Am. Bd. Psychiatry and Neurology. Intern Mass. Gen. Hosp., Boston, 1972-73, resident in medicine, 1973-74; resident in preventive medicine Ctrs. for Disease Control, Atlanta, 1975-76; resident in psychiatry Beth Israel Hosp., Boston, 1980-83; clin. assoc. prof. dept. cmty. medicine & family practice Morehouse Sch. Medicine, Atlanta, 1984-93; clin. prof. psychiatry Emory U. Sch. Medicine, Atlanta, 1993—; dir. Nat. Ctr. for Injury Prevention and Control, Atlanta, 1994—, acting assoc. dir. for public health practice, 1992-93; dir. divsn. injury control Ctr. for Environ. Health and Injury Control, 1989-92; spl. asst. for behavioral sci. office of dep. dir. Ctrs. for Disease Control, Atlanta, 1989, advisor to dep. dir., 1988, asst. dir. for sci. divsn. injury epidemiology and control, 1986-88, liaison officer office program planning and evaluation, 1979-80; assoc. dir. office extramural health programs Harvard Sch. Pub. Health, Boston, 1979-80; clin. fellow in psychiatry Harvard Med. Sch., Boston, 1980-83; vis. prof. dept. cmty. health Emory U. Sch. Medicine, Atlanta, 1984-91, clin. asst. prof. psychiatry, 1985-87, clin. assoc. prof., 1988-93; adj. prof. Emory U. Sch. Public Health, Atlanta, 1991—; clin. prof. dept. cmty. health and preventive medicine Morehouse Sch. Medicine, Atlanta, 1993; staff physician Womens Med. Clinic, Atlanta, 1974-76, Harvard St. Neighborhood Health Ctr., Boston, 1976-77, Winchester (Mass.) Hosp., 1978-83; emergency rm. physician Burbank Hosp., Fitchburg, Mass., 1976-77, Harrington Hosp., Southbridge, Mass., 1976-77; vis. physician dept. psychiatry Grady Meml. Hosp., Atlanta, 1985—; lectr. and cons. in field. Mem. editl. bd. Violence and Victims, 1985-88, Violence, Aggression and Terrorism, 1986—; contbr. articles to profl. jours. Bd. dirs. southeastern divsn., sci. adv. coun. Am. Suicide Found., 1990—; active Calif. Wellness Found., 1993—. Mass. Gen. Hosp. fellow, 1977-78, Mead-Johnson fellow, 1982; John Harvard scholar, 1964; recipient Coulter Lecture award Am. Congress Rehab. Medicine, 1991, William S. Stone award Am. Trauma Soc., 1991, Outstanding Achievement award, 1994, World Health Day award Am. Assn. for World Health, 1993, Disting. Svc. award Ga. Assn. Family and Marital Therapists, 1994. Mem. Phi Beta Kappa, Alpha Omega Alpha. Avocation: photography. Home: 972 Oakdale Rd Atlanta GA 30307

ROSENBERG, MARK LOUIS, lawyer; b. Lexington, Ky., Sept. 21, 1947; s. Edward George and Shirley Lee (Berkin) R.; m. Betty Adler, May 16, 1982; stepchildren—Aaron and Sarah Claxton; children: Eli, Daniel. B.A., U. Mich., 1969; J.D., Harvard U., 1973, LL.M. in Raxation, Georgetown U., 1985. Bar: D.C. 1973, U.S. Dist. Ct. D.C. 1973, U.S. Ct. Appeals (D.C. cir.) 1973. Asst. to v.p. George Washington U., 1973-75; counsel U.S. Ho. of Reps., Washington, 1975-77; sr. atty. FTC, Washington, 1977-85; atty. Ross

& Duerk, Washington, 1985-89; pntr. Gordon, Feinblatt et al, Washington, 1989-91; prin. Law Offices of Mark L. Rosenberg, 1991-94; ptnr. The Jacobovitz Law Firm, 1994—. Mem. Fed. Bar Assn. (Disting. Service award 1982, 83, 87, dep. sect. coordinator), ABA (legis. monitor adminstrv. law sect.). Democrat. Jewish. Home: 6101 Shady Oak Ln Bethesda MD 20817-6027 Office: The Jacobovitz Law Firm 1914 Sunderland Pl NW Washington DC 20036

ROSENBERG, MICHAEL, lawyer; b. N.Y.C., Oct. 13, 1937; s. Walter and Eva (Bernstein) R.; m. Jacqueline Raymonde Combe, Apr. 29, 1966; children: Andrew James, Suzanne Jennifer. AB in Econs. with honors, Ind. U., 1959; LLB, Columbia U., 1962. Bar: N.Y. 1963, U.S. Dist. Ct. (so. and ea. dists.) N.Y. 1966, U.S. Ct. Appeals (2d cir.) 1975, U.S. Dist. Ct. (ea. dist. so. div.) Mich. 1989. From. dep. asst. atty. gen. to asst. atty. gen. N.Y. State Dept. Law, N.Y.C., 1963-66; assoc. Hellerstein, Rosier & Rembar, N.Y.C., 1966-73; assoc. gen. counsel Gen. Instrument Corp., N.Y.C., 1973-78; from assoc. gen. counsel to dep. gen. counsel U.S. Filter Corp., N.Y.C., 1978-82; v.p., gen. counsel, sec. Alfa-Laval Inc., Ft. Lee, N.J., 1982-88; counsel Becker Ross Stone De Stefano & Klein, N.Y.C., 1988-89; ptnr. Rosenberg & Rich, White Plains, N.Y., 1989-95, Quinn, Marantis & Rosenberg, LLP, White Plains, N.Y., 1995—. Mem. Zoning Bd. Appeals Town of North Castle, N.Y., 1995—. Mem. ABA, N.Y. State Bar Assn., Westchester County Bar Assn. Office: Quinn Marantis & Rosenberg LLP 3 Barker Ave White Plains NY 10601-1509

ROSENBERG, MICHAEL JOSEPH, financial executive; b. Passaic, N.J., Apr. 19, 1928; s. Emanuel and Sylvia Sarah (Schwartz) R.; m. Judith Ann Melnick, Dec. 6, 1964 (div. 1983); children: Ann Kirsten, Emily Jeanne; m. Kathleen Ann Jennings, Mar. 3, 1990. BS, Upsala Coll., 1951; MBA, NYU, 1955, postgrad., 1955-59. Asst. v.p. Meinhard & Co., N.Y.C., 1953-58, A.J. Armstrong Co., N.Y.C., 1958-59, Sterling Nat. Bank, N.Y.C., 1959-61; exec. v.p. Rosenthal & Rosenthal, Inc., N.Y.C., 1961—; bd. dirs. D.V.L., Inc., N.Y.C.; dir. Am. com. Shenkar U. Contbr. numerous articles on comml. fin. to newspapers and mags. Bd. dirs., treas. Town Hall Found., N.Y.C., 1982—; treas. Citizens for Clean Air, N.Y.C., 1984. Capt. U.S. Army, 1951-53, Korea. Decorated Silver Star, Bronze Star; recipient Meritorious Svc. award NYU, 1983; Albert Gallatin fellow, 1981. Mem. Albert Gallatin Assocs. (chmn. 1984-87), NYU Bus. Forum (pres. 1981-82), NYU Grad. Sch. Bus. Adminstrn. Alumni Assn. (pres. 1978-79), NYU Ptnrs. (co-chmn. 1987-89, chmn. 1990-93), NYU Club (pres. 1975-77, 82-85). Avocations: skiing, tennis, running, sailing. Office: Rosenthal & Rosenthal Inc 1370 Broadway New York NY 10018-7302

ROSENBERG, NATHAN, economics educator; b. Passaic, N.J., Nov. 22, 1927; s. Joseph and Mary (Kaplan) R.; m. Rina Gordon, Jan. 12, 1954; children: Karen, Gordon, Jonathan, David. B.A., Rutgers U., 1950; M.A., U. Wis., 1952, Ph.D., 1955. Lectr. Ind. U., Bloomington, 1955-57; asst. prof. U. Pa., Phila., 1957-61; assoc. prof. Purdue U., West Lafayette, 1961-64, prof., 1964-67; vis. prof. Harvard U., 1967-69; prof. U. Wis., Madison, 1969-74; prof. Economic History Cambridge U., U.K., 1989-90; prof. econs. Stanford U., Calif., 1974—. Author: Technology and American Economic Growth, 1972, Perspectives on Technology, 1976, Inside the Black Box, 1982, (with L.E. Birdzell) How the West Grew Rich, 1985, (with David C. Mowery) Technology and the Pursuit of Economic Growth, 1989, Exploring the Black Box, 1994, The Emergence of Economic Ideas (Essays in the History of Economics), 1994; editor: Jour. Econ. History. Served as sgt./C.E. U.S. Army, 1945-47, Korea. Fellow Am. Acad. Arts and Scis., Royal Swedish Acad. Engring. (fgn.); mem. Am. Econs. Assn., Econ. History Assn., Royal Econ. Soc. Jewish. Office: Stanford Univ Dept Econs Landau Bldg Stanford CA 94305

ROSENBERG, NORMAN, surgeon; b. N.Y.C., Apr. 25, 1916; s. Leo and Rose (Kamerman) R.; m. Ruth Harriet Feller, Nov. 30, 1940; children: Lois A. Rosenberg Ebin, Ralph. BA, U. Pa., 1934; MD, NYU, 1938. Diplomate Am. Bd. Surgery, Am. Bd. Gen. Vascular Surgery. Intern Mt. Sinai Hosp., N.Y.C., 1939-41; resident Mt. Sinai Hosp., 1942-43; practice medicine, specializing in vascular surgery New Brunswick, N.J., 1946-80; sr. attending surgeon St. Peters Med. Center, New Brunswick, from 1946, now emeritus sr. attending surgeon; chief staff Middlesex Gen. Hosp., New Brunswick, 1959-66, chief vascular surgery, 1960-86, dir. dept. surgery, 1975-81; cons. surgeon Roosevelt Hosp., Metuchen, N.J., 1956-87 , Raritan Valley Hosp., Greenbrook, N.J., 1970-81, Somerset Hosp., Somerville, N.J., 1952-88 , J.F. Kennedy Hosp., Edison, N.J., 1969-88 ; clin. prof. surgery Robert Wood Johnson Med. Sch., U. Medicine and Dentistry N.J., New Brunswick, 1972-81, chief vascular surgery sect., 1981-86, prof. surgery, 1981-91, prof. emeritus, 1991—; cons. Johnson & Johnson Research Center, New Brunswick, 1954-78. Author: Handbook of Carotid Artery Surgery Facts and Figures, 1989, 2d edit., 1994; contbr. articles to books and profl. jours.; co-inventor modified bovine arterial graft. Trustee Robert Wood Johnson Found., 1958—. Capt. M.C., AUS, 1943-46. Fellow A.C.S., Southeastern Surg. Congress; mem. Soc. Vascular Surgery, Internat. Soc. Cardiovascular Surgery, Soc. Surgeons N.J. Home: 48 North Dr East Brunswick NJ 08816-1122

ROSENBERG, NORMAN JACK, agricultural meteorologist, educator; b. Bklyn., Feb. 22, 1930; s. Jacob and Rae (Dombrowitz) R.; m. Sarah Zacher, Dec. 30, 1950; children: Daniel Jonathon, Alyssa Yael. BS, Mich. State U., 1951; MS, Okla. State U., 1958; PhD, Rutgers U., 1961. Soil scientist Israel Soil Conservation Service, Haifa, 1953-55, Israel Water Authority, Haifa, 1955-57; asst. prof. agrl. meteorology U. Nebr., Lincoln, 1961-64, assoc. prof., 1964-67, prof. agrl. meteorology, 1967—, prof. agrl. engring., 1975—, prof. agronomy, 1976—, George Holmes prof. agrl. meteorology, 1981-87, prof. emeritus, 1987—, leader sect. agrl. meteorology, 1975-79, acting asst. vice chancellor for research, 1983-85; sr. fellow, dir. climate resources program Resources for the Future, Washington, 1987-92; chief scientist integrated earth studies eenrgy sci. divsn. Battelle Pacific N.W. Nat. Lab., Washington, 1992—; cons. Dept. State AID, NOAA, Oak Ridge Assoc. Univs., 1986-87, Elec. Power Rsch. Inst. 1989-92, Sandia Nat. Labs., 1990; mem. numerous ad hoc coms. and mem. standing com. on atmospheric sci. Nat. Acad. Scis./NRC, 1975-78, mem. bd. on atmospheric sci. and climate, 1982-85, mem. U.S. com. Internat. Geosphere-Biosphere Program, 1984-86, mem. panel on policy implications of climate change, 1990-91; mem. bd. coun. Agrl. Sci. and Tech.; vis. prof. agrl. meteorology Israel Inst. Tech., Haifa, 1968; trustee Nat. Inst. Global Environ. Change, 1992, vice-chmn., 1992—. Author: Microclimate: The Biological Environment, 1974, 2d edit., 1983, Chinese transl., 1983, Malay transl., 1987; also numerous articles in profl. jours.; editor: North American Droughts, 1978, Drought in the Great Plains: Research on Impacts and Strategies, 1980, Greenhouse Warming: Abatement and Adaptation, 1989; editor: Toward an Integrated Impact Assessment of Climate Change: The MINK Study, 1993; tech. editor Agronomy Jour., 1974-79; cons. editor Agrl. and Forest Meteorology, Climatic Change. Mem. Intergovernmental Panel on Climate Change, 1993—. Recipient Centennial medal Nat. Weather Svc., 1970; sr. fellow in sci., NATO, 1968, rsch. fellow U. Nebr., 1968, Lady Davis fellow Hebrew U., Jerusalem, 1977, nat. resources fellow Resources for Future, 1986; grantee State of Nebr., 1970-73, NSF, 1971-87, U.S. Dept. Commerce, 1972-74, 80-82, 83-85, 88-89, NASA, 1972-73, 85-86, U.S. Dept. Interior, 1974-75, 77-79, 88—, USDA, 1979-82, 88-89, U. Nebr. Found., 1982, Nat. Ctr. Atmospheric Rsch., 1984-85, U.S. Dept. Energy, 1989-92, G. Gunnar Vetleson Found., 1987-92, UN Environ. Program, 1989, EPA, 1988-89, NASA, 1995—, NOAA, 1996. Fellow AAAS (com. climate 1984-89, com. global change 1992—, adv. panel Earth Explorer ency. 1992-95), Am. Soc. Agronomy, Am. Meteorol. Soc. (Outstanding Achievement in Bioclimatology award 1978, councillor 1981-84); mem. Am. Assn. State Climatologists (Nebr. rep. 1979-81), Arid Zone Soc. India, Sigma Xi, Alpha Zeta, Gamma Sigma Rho. Jewish. Club: Cosmos (Washington). Office: Battelle Pacific Northwest Nat Lab 901 D St SW Washington DC 20024-2169

ROSENBERG, PAUL, physicist, consultant; b. N.Y.C., Mar. 31, 1910; s. Samuel and Evelyn (Abbey) R.; m. Marjorie S. Hillson, June 12, 1943; 1 child, Gale B.E. AB, Columbia U., 1930, MA, 1933, PhD, 1941. Chemist Hawthorne Paint & Varnish Corp., N.J., 1930-33; grad. asst. physics Columbia U., 1934-39, lectr., 1939-41; instr. Hunter Coll., N.Y.C., 1939-41; rsch. assoc. elec. enging. MIT, Cambridge, 1941; mem. staff Radiation Lab., Nat. Def. Rsch. Com., 1941-45; pres. Paul Rosenberg Assocs. (cons. physicists), Larchmont, N.Y., 1945—, Inst. Nav., 1950-51; mem. war com. radio Am. Standards Assn., 1942-44; gen. chmn. joint meeting Radio Tech. Commn. for Aeros., Radio Tech. Commn. for Marine Services and Inst. of Nav., 1950; co-chmn. Nat. Tech. Devel. Com. for upper atmostphere and interplanetary nav., 1947-50; mem. maritime research adv. com. Nat. Acad. Scis.-NRC, 1959-60; chmn. cartography panel space programs Earth resources survey NRC, 1973-76; chmn. panel on nav. and traffic control space applications study Nat. Acad. Scis., 1968; bd. dirs. Ctr. for Environment and Man, 1976-85. Mem. editorial com. Jour. Aerospace Scis., 1952-60; contbr. chpts. to books, entries to encys., over 70 articles to sci. tech. publs.; patentee in field. Recipient James S. Cogswell award U.S. Dept. Def., 1986. Fellow AAAS (v.p. 1966-69, mem. coun. 1961-73), IEEE, AIAA (assoc.), Am. Inst. Chemists, Explorers Club; mem. Am. Phys. Soc., Am. Chem. Soc., Nat. Acad. Engring., Acoustical Soc. Am., Armed Forces Communication Assn., Optical Soc. Am., Am. Soc. Photogrammetry (Talbert Abrams Grand award 1955), Am. Assn. Physics Tchrs., N.Y. Acad. Scis., Inst. Navigation (hon., pres. 1950-51), Beach Point Yacht Club (Mamaroneck, N.Y.), Columbia U. Club, Sigma Xi, Zeta Beta Tau. Home: 53 Fernwood Rd Larchmont NY 10538-1705 Office: Paul Rosenberg Assocs PO Box 729 Larchmont NY 10538-0729

ROSENBERG, PHILIP, production designer. Prodn. designer: (films) The Anderson Tapes, 971, The Possession of Joel Delaney, 1972, Child's Play, 1972, From the Mixed-up Files of Mrs. Basil E. Frankweiler, 1973, The Gambler, 1974, Network, 1976, Next Stop, Greenwich Village, 1976, The Sentinel, 1977, (with Tony Walton) The Wiz, 1978 (Academy award nomination best art direction 1978), (with Tony Walton) All the Jazz, 1979 (Academy award best art direction 1979), Eyewitness, 1981, Soup for One, 1982, Lovesick, 1983, Daniel, 1983, Garbo Talks, 1984, The Manhattan Project, 1986, Moonstruck, 1987, Running on Empty, 1988, The January Man, 1989, Family Business, 1989, Q & A, 1990, Other People's Money, 1992, Beyond Innocence, 1993, Guilty as Sin, 1993, The Pelican Brief, 1993, Night Falls on Manhattan, 1995. Office: Smith/Gosnell/Nicholson & Assoc PO Box 1166 1515 Palisades Dr Pacific Palisades CA 90272

ROSENBERG, PIERRE MAX, museum director; b. Paris, Apr. 13, 1936; s. Charles and Gertrude (Nassauer) R.; m. Béatrice de Rothschild, July 29, 1981. Baccalauréat, Lycée Charlemagne, Paris; Licence, Law Faculty, Paris; Diplome, Louvre Sch., Paris. Chief curator dept. paintings Musée du Louvre, Paris, 1982-94, prés., dir., Musé du Louvre, 1994—. Author: Chardin, 1963; Peyron, 1983; (catalogue) La peinture française du XVIIe siècle dans les coll. américaines, 1981; (catalogue) Watteau, 1984, 96, Fragonard, 1987, Fréres Le Nain, 1993, Poussin, 1994. Mem. Société de l'Histoire de l'Art Français (prés. 1982-84), Comité Français d'Histoire de l'Art (pres. 1984). Home: 35 rue de Vaugirard, 75006 Paris France Office: Musée du Louvre, 34 quai du Louvre, 75058 Paris France

ROSENBERG, RALPH, former state senator, lawyer, consultant, educator; b. Chgo., Oct. 7, 1949; s. Nathan Benjamin and Rhea (Matlow) R.; m. Teresa Marie Sturm, July 11, 1989; children: Jacob Louis, Joel Patrick. BS in Commerce and Bus. Adminstrn., U. Ill., 1972; JD, Drake Law Sch., 1974. Bar: Iowa 1974. Sole practice Rosenberg Law Firm, Ames, Iowa, 1974—; mem. Iowa Ho. of Reps., Des Moines, 1981-90, Iowa Senate, Des Moines, 1990-94; adj. faculty Des. Moines Area C.C., 1980—, Drake Law Sch., 1992, Upper Iowa U., 1993, Iowa State U., 1994—; dir. Environ. Planning Rsch. Group, Ames, 1976-77; exec. dir. Story County Legal Aid Soc., Nevada, Iowa, 1977-78; asst. Story County atty. County Attys. Office, Nevada, 1979-81; exec. dir., mng. atty. Youth Law Ctr., Des Moines, 1989-92; coord. Leadership in Govt. Inst., 1994—; exec. dir. Coalition for Family and Childrens Svcs., 1995—. Author, editor: Public Interest Law, 1992; author: Family Theory, Law, Policy and Practice, 1994; editor: Descriptive Analysis of Iowa Environmental Agencies, 1977. Co-chair Midwest Leadership Inst. of Coun. of State Govt.; bd. dirs. Iowa Protection and Advocacy, regional adv. bd. Legal Svcs. Corp. Iowa, Child and Family Policy Ctr.; past bd. dirs. Co-op. Child Care Svcs., Ames Cmty. Action Rsch. Group, Rural Iowa. Recipient Outstanding Contbn. to Well-being of Children award Youth and Shelter Svcs., 1992, Excellence in Svc. award Legal Svcs. Group, 1993, Iowa LWV Cornerstone award, 1994, Iowa Farmers' Union Friend of the Farmer award, 1994, Iowa Consumer Action Network Citizen Svc. award, 1994; named LEgislator of Yr., Sierra Club, 1988, Isaak Walton League, 1993; named Legis. Conservationist of Yr., Wildlife Soc., 1988, Elected Ofcl. of Yr., Iowa Corrections Assn., 1984. Mem. Iowa State Bar Assn. (family law com. 1993—), Nat. Conf. State Legislators (criminal justice com. 1986-94). Home: 1202 Northwestern Ave Ames IA 50010-5256 Office: 111 Ninth Ste 200 Des Moines IA 50314

ROSENBERG, RICHARD M., lawyer; b. Chgo., May 14, 1934. BA, Harvard U., 1956, LLB, 1959. Bar: Ill. 1960. Ptnr. Mayer, Brown & Platt, Chgo.; adj. prof. Loyola Law Sch., 1983—. Contbr. articles to profl. jours. Mem. ABA, Chgo. Bar Assn., Chgo. Coun. Lawyers, Phi Beta Kappa. Office: Mayer Brown & Platt 190 S La Salle St Ste 3900 Chicago IL 60603-3410*

ROSENBERG, RICHARD MORRIS, banker; b. Fall River, Mass., Apr. 21, 1930; s. Charles and Betty (Peck) R.; m. Barbara K. Cohen, Oct. 21, 1956; children: Michael, Peter. BS, Suffolk U., 1952; MBA, Golden Gate U., 1962; LLB, Golden Gate Coll., 1966. Publicity asst. Crocker-Anglo Bank, San Francisco, 1959-62; banking services officer Wells Fargo Bank, N.A., San Francisco, 1962-65; asst. v.p. Wells Fargo Bank, N.A., 1965-68, v.p. mktg. dept., 1968, v.p., dir. mktg., 1969, sr. v.p. mktg. and advt. div., 1970-75, exec. v.p., from 1975, vice chmn., 1980-83; vice chmn. Crocker Nat. Corp., 1983-85; pres., chief operating officer Seafirst Corp., 1986-87, also dir.; pres., chief operating officer Seattle First Nat. Bank, 1985-87; vice chmn. bd. BankAm. Corp., San Francisco, 1987-90, chmn., CEO, 1990-96; dir. Airborne Express, Potlatch Corp., Northrop Cor., PacTel, Pacific Mut.; past chmn. Mastercard Internat. Bd. dirs. San Francisco Symphony, United Way; trustee Calif. Inst. Tech., U. So. Calif. Jewish. Office: BankAm Corp Dept 3001 PO Box 37000 San Francisco CA 94137-1501

ROSENBERG, ROBERT ALLEN, psychologist, educator, optometrist; b. Phila., July 31, 1935; s. Theodore Samuel and Dorothy (Bailes) R.; m. Geraldine Bella Tishler, Sept. 3, 1961; children: Lawrence David, Ronald Joseph. BA, Temple U., 1957, MA, 1964; BS, Pa. Coll. Optometry, 1960, OD, 1961. Lic. optometrist, psychologist, Pa. Instr. Pa. Coll. Optometry, Phila., 1962-65, asst. prof., 1965-67; asst. prof. psychology Community Coll. Phila., 1967-76, assoc. prof., 1976—; pvt. practice optometry, Roslyn, Pa., 1965-95; assoc. in practice optometry, Huntingdon Valley, Pa., 1995—. Contbr. articles to profl. jours. Named Humanitarian Chapel of Four Chaplains Bapt. Temple, 1980. Fellow Am. Acad. Optometry; mem. Am. Optometric Assn., Pa. Optometric Assn., Bucks-Montgomery Optometric Assn., Alumni Assn. Pa. Coll. Optometry (v.p. 1991—, sec. 1992—). Avocations: singing, acting, photography, writing, public speaking. Home: 970 Corn Crib Dr Huntingdon Valley PA 19006-3304 Office: Community Coll Phila 1700 Spring Garden St Philadelphia PA 19130-3936

ROSENBERG, ROBERT BRINKMANN, research organization executive; b. Chgo., Mar. 19, 1937; s. Sidney and Gertrude (Brinkmann) R.; m. Patricia Margaret Kane, Aug. 1, 1959 (dec. Feb. 1988); children: John Richard Debra Ann; m. Maryann Bartoli Manrot, June 25, 1989. B.S. in Chem. Engring. with distinction, Ill. Inst. Tech., 1958, M.S. in Gas Tech, 1961, Ph.D. in Gas Tech, 1964. Registered profl. engr., Ill. Adj. asst. prof. Ill. Inst. Tech., 1965-69; mem. staff Inst. Gas Tech., Chgo., 1962-77; v.p. engring. research Inst. Gas Tech., 1973-77; v.p. research and devel. Gas Research Inst., Chgo., 1977-78; exec. v.p. Gas Research Inst., 1978-84, v.p., 1984-96; pres. RBR Vision, 1996—; also bd. dirs. IEA Internat. Ctr. for Gas Tech. Info. Author. Mem. Hinsdale (Ill.) Home Rule Ad Hoc Com., 1975-77; bd. dirs. Hinsdale Arts Coun., 1977-85, dir. emeritus, 1985-95; pres. Triangle Frat. Edn. Found., 1974—; mem. vis. com. dept. chemistry U. Tex.; mem. adv. coun. U. Tex. Coll. Natural Scis. Found.,1990-95. Recipient Gas Industry Research award, 1985, Energy Exec. of Yr. award, 1987, Triangle Frat. Svc. Key and Outstanding Alumnus awards, 1987. Mem. AIChE, Am. Gas Assn. (operating sect. award of merit 1989), Inst. Gas Engrs., Combustion Inst. (past treas. bd. cen. states sect.), Atlantic Gas Rsch. Exch. (chmn. mng. bd. 1980-96), Internat. Gas Union (U.S. rep. subcom. F-2 1974-83), Gas Appliance Engrs. Soc. (past trustee), Air Pollution Control Assn. (past sect. com. residential pollution sources). Patentee in field. Home: 28 Lake Ridge Club Dr Hinsdale IL 60521-7937 Office: Gas Rsch Inst 8600 W Bryn Mawr Ave Chicago IL 60631-3505

ROSENBERG, ROBERT CHARLES, housing corporation executive; b. Bronx, N.Y., Oct. 21, 1934; s. Bernard L. and Flora (Popiel) R.; BS, NYU, 1955; LLB, Columbia U., 1958; JD (hon.), 1995; m. Diane Stricof, Jan. 28, 1962 (dec.); children: Andrew, Scott; m. Frances Kaufman, Sept. 11, 1976; stepchildren: Michael Kaufman, Benjamin Kaufman. Bar: N.Y. 1959. Adminstrv. asst. N.Y. State Dept. Law, N.Y.C., 1957-58; assoc. firm Barron Rice & Rochmore, N.Y.C., 1959-62, Carro Spanbock & Londin, N.Y.C., 1962-68; first dep. commr. for devel. dept., N.Y.C. Housing and Devel. Adminstrn., 1968-73; dir., 1st sr. v.p. Starrett Corp., N.Y.C., 1973—; gen. mgr. Starrett City; pres., chmn. bd. Grenadier Realty Corp., 1976—; lectr. Practicing Law Inst., Real Estate Bd. N.Y.C., others. Candidate for N.Y. State Assembly, 1958, 65; sec. N.Y. State Assn. Young Republican Clubs, 1959-61; bd. dirs., chmn. Bklyn. Philharmonic; corp. rep. Nat. Com. U.S.-China Rels.; mem. N.Y.C. Mayor's-Beijing (China) Sister City Com.; bd. dirs. Bklyn. Acad. Music; v.p. Citizen's Housing and Planning Council, exec. v.p. N.Y.C. Associated Builders and Owners; v.p., exec. commn. Nat. Housing Conf. Served with USAF, 1958. Mem. ABA, N.Y. State Bar Assn., N.Y. County Lawyers Assn., Nat. Assn. Housing and Renewal Ofcls., N.Y. State Assn. Housing and Renewal Ofcls., Urban Land Inst. Author N.Y. acts for residential constrn., rent. Home: 70 E 77th St New York NY 10021-1811 Office: 909 3rd Ave New York NY 10022-4731 also: 1230 Pennsylvania Ave Brooklyn NY 11239-1915

ROSENBERG, ROBERT M., food chain executive; b. 1938. Pres., CEO Baskin Robbins, Inc., Glendale, Calif., 1992—. Office: Baskin Robbins Inc 31 Baskin Robbins Pl Glendale CA 91201-2738*

ROSENBERG, ROBERT MICHAEL, restaurant franchise company executive; b. Boston, Mar. 4, 1938; s. William and Bertha (Greenberg) R.; children: James Lee, John Matthew, Jennifer Beth. BS in Hotel and Restaurant Adminstrn., Cornell U., 1959; MBA, Harvard U., 1963; DBA (hon.), Nathaniel Hawthorne Coll., Antrim, N.H., 1980; LLD (hon.), N.H. Coll., 1982; D in Food Svc. Mgmt. (hon.), Johnson and Wales U., 1990. Pres. Dunkin' Donuts Inc., Randolph, Mass., from 1963; now chmn.; CEO Allied Domecq Retailing, 1993—; bd. dirs. Allied Domecq, Allied Domecq Retailing, Ltd., Sonic Industries. Co-author: Profits from Franchising, 1969. Bd. dirs., trustee Dana Farber Cancer Found.; mem. bd. overseers Mus. Fine Arts, Boston; past dir. Am. Bus. Dir. Recipient Outstanding Man of Yr. award Jr. C. of Co., Boston, 1968, Bus. award Bryant and Stratton Coll., Boston, 1968, award of excellence Am. Acad. Achievement, 1968, Leadership award Restaurant Bus. Mag., 1987, Gold Plate Winner as Foodsvc. Op. of Yr. 1983 Internat. Food Svc. Mfrs. Assn. Mem. Nat. Restaurant Assn. (bd. dirs., Silver Plate award 1984, 86, 87), Internat. Franchise Assn. (past pres., bd. dirs.), Am. Bus. Conf., Harvard Bus. Sch. Assn. Office: Dunkin' Donuts Inc PO Box 3117 14 Pacella Park Dr Randolph MA 02368-1756*

ROSENBERG, ROGER NEWMAN, neurologist, educator; b. Milw., Mar. 3, 1939; s. Sol J. and Cora D. (Newman) R.; m. Adrienne Turick, June 24, 1962; children—Jennifer, Lara. Student, Tufts U., 1957-60; BS, Northwestern U., 1961, MD with distinction, 1964. Diplomate Am. Bd. Psychiatry and Neurology. Intern Harvard Med. Service, Beth Israel Hosp., Boston, 1964-65; resident in neurology Neurol. Inst., Columbia U., N.Y.C., 1965-67, instr. neurology, 1967-68; research assoc. Lab. of Biochem. Genetics, NIH, Bethesda, Md., 1968-70; clin. instr. Howard U. Med. Sch., Washington, 1969-70; asst. prof. neuroscis. Sch. Medicine, U. Calif.-San Diego, 1970-71; assoc. prof. neuroscis. and pediatrics, attending neurologist Univ. Hosp., U. Calif.-La Jolla, 1971-74; prof., chmn. dept. neurology U. Tex. Southwestern Med. Ctr., Dallas, 1973-91, prof. physiology, 1976—, Zale Disting. chair, prof. neurology, 1990—, dir. Alzheimer's Disease Rsch. Ctr., 1989—; attending neurologist Parkland Meml. Hosp. and Children's Med. Ctr., Dallas, 1974—, Zale Lipshy Univ. Hosp., 1990—; mem. staff Presbyn. Hosp., Dallas, 1974—, St. Paul's Hosp., Dallas, 1974—; cons. staff VA Hosp., Dallas, 1974—; mem. nat. med. adv. bd. Nat. Ataxia Found., Mpls., 1971—, Myasthenia Gravis Found., 1973; chmn. med. adv. bd., dir. med. sci. research Internat. Joseph Diseases Found., Livermore, Calif., 1977—; lectr. Japanese Soc. Neurology, 1987, 94, Chinese Neurol. Soc., 1987, Spanish Neurol. Soc., 1992; chmn. bd. sci. councilors NIH, 1984-86; pres. (hon.), Intl. French Soc. of Neurology Charcot Centenary Symposium, 1993. Editor Jour. Neurogenetics; mem. editorial bd. Neurology, 1977-82, 91—, Trends in Neurosci., 1980-86, Current Opinion in Neurology & Neurosurgery, 1990—; contbr. articles to med. jours. Bd. dirs. Winston Sch., Dallas, 1974-80. 1st Woody Guthrie scholar, 1971; USPHS grantee; recipient Disting. Alumnus award Neurol. Inst., N.Y., 1994. Fellow AAAS; mem. Am. Acad. Neurology (chmn. sci. program com. nat. meetings 1979-84, elected councillor exec. bd. 1984-89, pres. 1991-93), Am. Neurochem. Soc., Tissue Culture Soc., Soc. Neurosci., Am. Fedn. Clin. Rsch., Soc. Pediat. Rsch., Internat. Child Neurology Assn., Am. Neurol. Assn. (1st v.p. 1987), Ctrl. Soc. Neurol. Rsch., Can. Congress Neurol. Scis. (hon.), Spanish Neurol. Soc. (hon. 1994), Sigma Xi, Alpha Omega Alpha (Merit award Northwestern U. Alumni Assn. 1986). Home: 4425 Wildwood Rd Dallas TX 75209-2801 Office: U Tex Southwestern Med Ctr Dallas TX 75235

ROSENBERG, RUTH HELEN BORSUK, lawyer; b. Plainfield, N.J., Feb. 23, 1935; d. Irwin and Pauline (Rudich) Borsuk; children—Joshua Cohen, Sarah, Rebecca, Daniel, Miriam, Tziporah, Isaac. A.B., Douglass Coll., 1956; J.D., U. Pa., 1963. Bar: Pa. 1964, N.Y. 1967, D.C. 1986, Md. 1987, Va. 1994, Mass. 1995, U.S. Ct. Appeals (3d cir.) 1969, U.S. Supreme Ct. 1969, U.S. Ct. Appeals (4th cir.) 1994. Law clk. Ct. Common Pleas, Phila., 1963-64; assoc. Blank, Rudenko, Klaus & Rome, Phila., 1964-67; atty. Office Corp. Counsel, City of Rochester, 1967-68; assoc. Nixon, Hargrave, Devans & Doyle, Washington, 1968-74, ptnr., 1975—; vice chairperson character and fitness com. Appellate divsn. 4th dept. 7th Jud. Dist. N.Y. Supreme Ct., 1976-80, mem. grievance com., 1981-84. Bd. dirs. Soc. Prevention Cruelty to Children, 1976-77, N.Y. Civil Liberties Union, 1972-85, v.p. 1976-85; bd. dirs. Jewish Home and Infirmary, 1978-83, pres., 1980-83; v.p. Jewish Fedn. Rochester, 1983, Yachad, Inc., Jewish Cmty. Housing Devel. Corp., 1990-94; bd. dirs. Jewish Cmty. Coun., Greater Washington, 1989-93, Leadership Washington, 1990-91, Libr. Theatre, 1994—, Op. Understanding, D.C., 1994-95. Mem. ABA, D.C. Bar Assn., Md. Bar Assn., Va. Bar Assn., Phi Beta Kappa. Office: Nixon Hargrave Devans & Doyle 1 Thomas Cir NW Ste 700 Washington DC 20005-5802

ROSENBERG, SAMUEL NATHAN, French and Italian language educator; b. N.Y.C., Jan. 19, 1936; s. Israel and Etta (Friedland) R. AB, Columbia U., 1957; PhD, Johns Hopkins U., 1965. Instr. Columbia U., N.Y.C., 1960-61; lectr. Ind. U., Bloomington, Ind., 1962-65; asst. prof. Ind. U., Bloomington, 1965-69; assoc. prof. Ind. U., Bloomington, Ind., 1969-81; prof. dept. French and Italian Ind. U., Bloomington, 1981—, chmn. dept., 1977-84. Author: Modern French CE, 1970, (with others) Harper's Grammar of French, 1983, (with W. Apel) French Secular Compositions of the 14th Century, 3 vols., 1970-72, (with H. Tischler) Chanter m'estuet: Songs of the Trouveres, 1981; translator: (with S. Danon) Ami and Amile, 1981, Lyrics and Melodies of Gace Brulé, 1985, (with H. Tischler) The Monophonic Songs in the Roman de Fauvel, 1991, Lancelor-Grail Cycle, vol. 2, 1993, Chansons des trouvères, 1995. Pres. Mid-Am. Festival of the Arts, Inc., Bloomington, Ind., 1984-85. Woodrow Wilson Found. fellow, 1959-60; Fulbright fellow, 1960-61; Lilly Faculty fellow, 1986-87. Mem MLA, Am. Assn. Tchrs. French; mem. Medieval Acad. Am., Internat. Courtly Lit. Soc., Am. Literary Translators Assn., Phi Beta Kappa. Home: PO Box 1164 Bloomington IN 47402-1164 Office: Dept French and Italian Ind U Bloomington IN 47405

ROSENBERG, SARAH ZACHER, institute arts administration executive, humanities administration consultant; b. Kelem, Lithuania, Jan. 10, 1931; came to U.S., 1938; d. David Meir Zacher and Rachel Korbman; m. Norman J. Rosenberg, Dec. 30, 1950; children: Daniel, Alyssa. BA in History, U. Nebr., 1970, MA in Am. History, 1973. Rsch. historian U. Mid-Am., Lincoln, Nebr., 1974-78, program developer dept. humanities, 1978-79, asst. dir. div. acad. planning, 1980-81, dir. program devel., 1981-82; exec. dir. Nebr. Humanities Coun., Lincoln, 1982-87, Nebr. Found. for Humanities, Lincoln, 1984-87; exec. dir. Am. Inst. for Conservation Hist. and Artistic Works, Washington, 1987—, exec. dir. found., 1991—; program officer, spl. cons. mus. div. NEH, Washington, 1987, external reviewer, 1981, 89; lay participant long-range planning conf. Nebr. Bar Assn., Hastings, 1986. Co-editor: The Great Plains Experience: Readings in the History of a Region, 1978; contbr. articles to profl. jours. Action mem. Haddasah, Lincoln, 1961-87, Tifereth Israel Synagogue, 1961-87, Beth El Congregation, Bethesda, Md., 1988—; bd. dirs. Sta. KUCV, affiliate Nat. Pub. Radio, Lincoln, 1986-87, Lincoln Community Playhouse, 1986-87. NEH grantee, 1981, 86, merit awards, 1983, 87; Humanities Resource Ctr. grantee, Peter Kiewit Found., 1984. Mem. Am. Hist. Assn., Western Hist. Assn., Alpha Theta. Democrat. Home: 8102 Appalachian Ter Potomac MD 20854-4050 Office: Am Inst for Conservation 1717 K St NW Ste 301 Washington DC 20006-1501

ROSENBERG, SAUL ALLEN, oncologist, educator; b. Cleve., Aug. 2, 1927. BS, Western Res. U., 1948, MD, 1953. Diplomate Am. Bd. Internal Medicine, Am. Bd. Oncology. Intern Univ. Hosp., Cleve., 1953-54; resident in internal medicine Peter Bent Brigham Hosp., Boston, 1954-61; research asst. toxicology AEC Med. Research Project, Western Res. U., 1948-53; asst. prof. medicine and radiology Stanford (Calif.) U., 1961-65, assoc. prof., 1965-79, chief div. oncology, 1965-93, prof., 1970-95; prof. emeritus, 1995—; Am. Cancer Soc. prof. Stanford (Calif.) U., 1983-89, assoc. dean, 1989-92; chmn. bd. No. Calif. Cancer Program, 1974-80. Contbr. articles to profl. jours. Served to lt. M.C. USNR, 1954-56. Master ACP; mem. Am. Assn. Cancer Research, Inst. Medicine Nat. Acad. Sci., Am. Assn. Cancer Edn., Am. Fedn. Clin. Research, Am. Soc. Clin. Oncology (pres. 1982-83), Assn. Am. Physicians, Calif. Acad. Medicine, Radiation Research Soc., Western Soc. Clin. Research, Western Assn. Physicians. Office: Stanford U Sch Medicine Div Oncology M-211 Stanford CA 94305

ROSENBERG, SEYMOUR, psychologist, educator; b. Newark, Sept. 7, 1926; s. Morris and Celia (Weiss) R.; children: Harold Stanley, Michael Seth. B.S., The Citadel, 1948; M.A., Ind. U., 1951, Ph.D., 1952. Research psychologist USAF, San Antonio, 1952-58, U. Kans., Lawrence, 1958-59, Bell Telephone Labs., Murray Hill, N.J., 1959-65; vis. prof. psychology Columbia, N.Y.C., 1965-66; prof. psychology Rutgers U., New Brunswick, N.J., 1966—; chmn. dept. psychology Rutgers U., 1981-83, 94-95; adj. prof. Rutgers U. Med. Sch., 1974—; vis. scholar U. Leuven, Belgium, 1983, 92, Université de Provence, France, 1990; panel mem. NSF, 1970-72. Cons. editor Jours. Personality and Social Psychology, 1968-69; assoc. editor, 1970-73; contbr. articles to profl. jours. Served with USN, 1945-46. NSF grantee, 1965—; NIMH, 1966-68; NIMH research scientist grantee, 1968-73; Social Sci. Research Council fellow, 1973-74. Fellow Am. Psychol. Assn.; mem. Soc. Exptl. Social Psychology, Psychometric Soc., Classification Soc., N.Y. Acad. Sci., Eastern Psychol. Assn. Home: 689 Canal Rd Somerset NJ 08873-7327 Office: Rutgers U Dept Psychology ED Livingston Campus New Brunswick NJ 08903

ROSENBERG, STEVEN AARON, surgeon, medical researcher; b. N.Y.C., Aug. 2, 1940; s. Abraham and Harriet (Wendroff) R.; m. Alice Ruth O'Connell, Sept. 15, 1968; children—Beth, Rachel, Naomi. B.A., Johns Hopkins U., 1960, M.D., 1963; Ph.D., Harvard U., 1968. Resident in surgery Peter Bent Brigham Hosp., Boston, 1963-64, 68-69, 72-74; resident fellow in immunology Harvard U. Med. Sch., Boston, 1969-70; clin. assoc. immunology br. Nat. Cancer Inst., Bethesda, Md., 1970-72; chief surgery Nat. Cancer Inst., 1974—, assoc. editor Jour., 1974—; mem. U.S.-USSR Coop. Immunotherapy Program, 1974—, U.S.-Japan Coop. Immunotherapy Program, 1975—; clin. assoc. prof. surgery George Washington U. Med. Ctr., 1976—; prof. surgery Uniformed Services U. Health Scis. Contbr. articles to profl. jours. Author: The Transformed Cell: Unlocking the Mysteries of Cancer, 1992. Served with USPHS, 1970-72. Recipient Meritorious Service medal Pub. Health Service, 1981; co-recipient Armand Hammer Cancer prize, 1985; named 1990 Scientist of the Yr., R&D magazine. Mem. Soc. Univ. Surgeons, Am. Surg. Assn., Soc. Surg. Oncology, Surg. Biology Club II, Halsted Soc., Transplantation Soc., Am. Assn. Immunologists, Am. Assn. Cancer Research, Phi Beta Kappa, Alpha Omega Alpha. Office: Nat Cancer Inst 9000 Rockville Pike Bethesda MD 20892-0001*

ROSENBERG, STEVEN H., health facility administrator; b. 1953. BS, U. Conn., 1975; MBA, U New Haven, 1981. Sr. v.p., CFO St. Francis Hosp. Med. Ctr., Hartford, Conn., 1986—. Office: St Francis Hosp Med Ctr 114 Woodland St Hartford CT 06105-1200*

ROSENBERG, STUART, film director; b. Bklyn., Aug. 11, 1927; s. David and Sara (Kaminsky) R.; m. Margot Pohoryles, Aug. 4, 1950; 1 son, Benjamin. B.A., NYU, 1949. Editor, producer, dir. over 300 TV shows, 1950-65, in films, 1965—; films directed include Murder, Inc., 1962, Cool Hand Luke, 1967, April Fools, 1969, WUSA, 1970, Voyage of the Damned, 1977, Amityville Horror, 1979, Brubaker, 1980, The Pope of Greenwich Village, 1984; (Recipient Emmy award for dramatic directing 1962, Dir.'s Guild award nominee (4). Served with USNR, 1945-47.

ROSENBERG, SUSAN, lawyer; b. Bklyn., July 24, 1945; d. Harold and Kitty (Paris) Schildkraut; m. Neil David Rosenberg, June 10, 1967; children—Lonnie Stuart, Seth Ian. A.B., Washington U., 1967; J.D. cum laude, Marquette U., 1983. Bar: Wis. 1983. Tchr. history Balt. City Pub. Schs., 1967-70; assoc. Samster, Aiken, & Mawicke, S.C., Milw., 1983-88; ptnr. Aiken & Mawicke, S.C., Milw., 1988-90, Domnitz Mawicke Goisman & Rosenberg SC, 1990—; Bd. dirs. Women to Women, Inc., Milw., 1984-86, Ctr. Pub. Representation, 1992-95. Thomas More scholar, 1981-83; Adolph I. Mandelker scholar, 1982-83. Mem. Wis. Acad. Trial Lawyers (bd. dirs. 1989—), Assn. Women Lawyers (bd. dirs. 1994—). Jewish. Mem. Marquette U. Law Rev., 1981-83. Office: Domnitz Mawicke Golsman & Rosenberg S C 1509 N Prospect Ave Milwaukee WI 53202-2323

ROSENBERG, SYDNEY J., security company executive; b. San Francisco, Sept. 3, 1914; s. Morris and Gussie (Kaufman) R.; m. Joyce Wexler, Nov. 15, 1939 (div. Mar. 1968); children: Brad, Jill Rosenberg Hughes, Todd; m. 2d Jaclyn Barde, Mar. 22, 1968; stepchildren: Gregg Cobarr, Glenn Cobarr. B.A., Stanford U., 1936; M.B.A., Harvard U., 1938. Pres., chief exec. officer Am. Bldg. Maintenance Industries, Los Angeles, from 1938; now chmn. bd. Am. Bldg. Maintenance Industries, San Francisco; chmn. ABM Security Svcs.; bd. dirs. Craig Corp., AMPCO Parking Svcs., AMTECH Elevator Svcs., AMTECH Lighting Svcs., Comm. Air. Mech. Svcs., Easterday Supply Co., Rose Pest Control Co.; pres. OPTIC Fund. Bd. govs. Performing Arts Council; bd. govs. Los Angeles Music Ctr.; trustee Jewish Big Bros.; mem. dirs. council Children's Orthopaedic Hosp. Mem. Chief Execs. Orgn., Urban Land Inst., World Bus. Council. Republican. Jewish. Clubs: Hillcrest (Los Angeles); Big Canyon (Newport, Calif.). Office: American Building 9831 W Pico Blvd Los Angeles CA 90035*

ROSENBERG, THEODORE ROY, financial executive; b. Nyack, N.Y., Aug. 6, 1933; s. Rebecca Sheer R.; m. Eleanor Schmalsteig, Feb. 19, 1956 (div); children: Bradley Scott, Martha Ann; m. Mary Frances McVay, Sept. 21, 1991. BS, U. Conn., 1955; MBA, U. Pa., 1964. Commd. 2d lt. U.S. Army, 1955, advanced through grades to col., 1976, retired, 1982; portfolio mgr. The Burney Co., Falls Church, Va., 1979—, v.p. mktg., 1982-94, v.p., 1994—. Active exec. com. Our Daily Bread, Fairfax, Va., 1991—; bd. dirs. Army Transp. Mus., U. Conn. Found., 1995—. Decorated Legion of Merit, Bronze Star; recipient Vietnam Medal of Honor, Govt. of Vietnam, 1966; inducted into Alumni Hall of Fame, U. Conn. Sch. Bus. Adminstrn., 1994. Mem. U. Pa. Mid-Atlantic Regional Adv. Bd., Wharton Club of Washington (Man of Yr. 1995). Avocations: scuba diving, snorkeling. Office: The Burney Co 121 Rowell Ct Falls Church VA 22046-3126

ROSENBERGER, BRYAN DAVID, lawyer; b. Johnstown, Pa., Oct. 8, 1950; s. Clarence Haines and Ida Rae (Neiderheiser) R.; m. Barbara Leah Byer, July 4, 1977; children: Laura Michelle, Lisa Renee. BS, Juniata Coll., 1971; JD, Coll. of William and Mary, 1974. Bar: Pa. 1974. Assoc. Eckert Seamans Cherin & Mellott, Pitts., 1974-82, ptnr., 1983—, chmn. corp. and bus. dept., 1992—; mem. exec. com., 1994—. Active new leadership bd. Pitts. Symphony Soc., 1990—. Mem. ABA, Pa. Bar Assn., Allegheny County Bar Assn. Home: 1358 Oakledge Ct Upper Saint Clair PA 15241-3540 Office: Eckert Seamans Cherin & Mellott 600 Grant St Ste 42 Pittsburgh PA 15219-2703

ROSENBERGER, CAROL, concert pianist; b. Detroit, Nov. 1, 1935; d. Maurice Seiberling and Whilamet (Gibson) R. B.F.A., Carnegie-Mellon U., 1955; postgrad., Acad. Performing Arts, Vienna, 1956-59. Mem. artist faculty U. So. Calif.; vis. artist numerous colls. and univs. Internat. concert career, 1964—; New York debut, 1970; appeared several times at Carnegie Hall; soloist Am. Symphony, Nat. Symphony, Royal Philharmonic, San Diego Symphony, Detroit Symphony, Houston Symphony, St. Louis Symphony, Indpls. Symphony, Los Angeles Chamber Orch.; performed world premiere of Buenaventura; piano concerts with Philippine Philharmonic, 1977, Am. Symphony, 1977; recital series in Am., European, Asian music capitals; recordings include Hindemith's Four Temperaments with London Royal Philharm., Water Music of the Impressionists, works of Beethoven, Schubert, Szymanowski, Night Moods, 1989, Perchance To Dream, 1989, Reveries: Music of Chopin, others; contbr. articles to music publs. Recipient Steinway Centennial medal, 1954, Critics Choice award Gramaphone mag., 1980. Mem. Nat. Acad. Rec. Arts and Scis. Chosen to represent Am. women musicians by Nat. Commn. on Observance Internat. Womens Year, 1976. Office: care Dorothy Cone Artist Rep 60 E 86th St New York NY 10028-1009 also: Delos Internat Inc 1645 N Vine St Ste 340 Los Angeles CA 90028

ROSENBERGER, DAVID A., research scientist, cooperative extension specialist; b. Quakertown, Pa., Sept. 14, 1947; s. Henry and Ada C. (Geissinger) R.; m. Carol J. Freeman, July 28, 1973; children: Sara, Matthew, Nathan. BS in Biology, Goshen Coll., 1969; PhD in Plant Pathology, Mich. State U., 1977. Asst. prof. Hudson Valley lab. Cornell U., Highland, N.Y., 1977-84, assoc. prof., 1984—; supt. Hudson Valley Lab. Cornell U., Highland, 1990—. Mem. AAAS, Am. Phytopathological Soc., Coun. Agrl. Sci. and Tech. Avocations: church activities, gardening, hiking, jogging. Office: Cornell U Hudson Valley Lab PO Box 727 Highland NY 12528

ROSENBERGER, ERNST HEY, judge; b. Hamburg, Germany, Aug. 31, 1931; came to U.S., 1935, naturalized, 1943; s. Ferdinand and Edith (Heymann) R.; m. Judith Ann Brailey, June 10, 1978; children: John Brailey, Anne Elizabeth. BA, CCNY, 1955; JD, N.Y. Law Sch., 1958; cert. in criminal law and practice, Northwestern U., summer 1960; cert., Nat. Coll. State Judiciary, U. Nev., 1976; LLM, U. Va., 1996. Bar: N.Y. 1958, U.S. Dist. Ct. 1959, 61, U.S. Ct. Appeals 1962, U.S. Customs Ct 1962, U.S. Supreme Ct. 1970. Assoc. Kunstler & Kunstler, N.Y.C., 1958-59; pvt. practice N.Y.C., 1959-69; ptnr. Ordover, Rosenberger & Rosen, N.Y.C., 1970-72; judge Criminal Ct. City of N.Y., 1972-76; acting justice Supreme Ct. N.Y., 1973-76, justice, 1977—; presiding justice Extraordinary Spl. and Trial Term of Supreme Ct., 1978-85; justice Appellate divsn. Supreme Ct. N.Y., 1985—; instr. courses for N.Y. State Supreme Ct. Justices, N.Y. Civil and Criminal Ct.; mem. faculty Hastings Coll. Law, U. Calif., San Francisco, 1979; adj. prof. law N.Y. Law Sch., 1976—; guest lectr. Bklyn. Law Sch., St. John's Law Sch., John Jay Coll., New Sch., Pratt Inst., N.Y.C. Police Dept., NYU Postgrad. Med. Sch.; chmn. Criminal Trial Advocacy Course, Appellate divsn., 1st Jud. Dept.; tech. assistance and evaluations cons. to dir. legal svcs. OEO, Washington, 1970; U.S. rep. to study youth laws and cts., Germany, 1975. Editor in chief: N.Y. Law Rev. (Moot Ct. award); contbr. book reviews to profl. jours. Trustee N.Y. Law Sch., Tng. Inst. Mental Health Practitioners, Congregation Habonim; bd. dirs. Blue Card. With U.S. Army, 1949-51. N.Y. Law Sch. scholar, 1958, Northwestern U. scholar, summer 1960, U. Va. scholar, 1993-95. Mem. ABA, Am. Judicature Soc., Am. Soc. Legal History, N.Y. State Bar Assn. (mem. exec. com. criminal justice sect., award for work in Criminal Law Edn. 1980, award for Outstanding Jud. Contbn. to Criminal Justice 19890, Assn. Justices Supreme Ct. State of N.Y., NCYLA Am. Inn of Ct. (pres.), New York County Lawyers Assn. (guest lectr.), Assn. of Bar of City of N.Y., Scribes. Jewish. Home: 1165 Fifth Ave New York NY 10029 Office: Supreme Ct NY 27 Madison Ave New York NY 10010-2201

ROSENBERGER, FRANZ ERNST, physics educator; b. Salzburg, Austria, May 31, 1933; came to U.S., 1966; s. Franz and Hertha (Sompek) R.; m. Renate Hildegard Suessenbach; children: Uta, Bernd, Till. BS in Physics, U. Stuttgart, 1960, diploma in physics, 1964; PhD in Physics, U. Utah, 1970. Asst. prof. physics U. Utah, Salt Lake City, 1970-77, assoc. prof., 1977-81, prof., 1981-86; prof. physics U. Ala., Huntsville, 1986—, dir. Ctr for Microgravity and Materials Rsch., 1986—. Author: Fundamentals of Crystal Growth, 1979; editor Jour. Crystal Growth, 1981—; contbr. articles to profl. jours. Mem. Am. Phys. Soc., Am. Assn. for Crystal Growth. Avocations: windsurfing, skiing, photography, home improvements. Home: 171 Stoneway Trl Madison AL 35758-8543

ROSENBERGER, JAMES LANDIS, statistician, educator, consultant; b. Hatfield, Pa., Nov. 15, 1946; s. Raymond Henning and Sallie Moyer (Landis) R.; m. Gloria Horst, June 14, 1970; children: Grant Horst, Laura Horst, Kurt Horst. BA in Math., Ea. Mennonite U., 1968; MS in Math., Polytechnic U., Bklyn., 1972; PhD in Biometry, Cornell U., 1977. Programmer and statis. asst. NYU Med. Ctr., 1968-72; asst. prof. stats. Pa. State U., University Park, 1976-82, assoc. prof. stats., 1982-92, acting head stats. dept., 1990-91, head stats. dept., 1991—, prof. stats., 1992—; rsch. fellow in biostats. Harvard U. Sch. Pub. Health, Boston, 1980; vis. lectr. biometry U. Zimbabwe, Harare, 1984-86; statistician Strategic Hwy. Rsch. Program, Washington, 1986-92; cons. Minitab, Inc., State College, Pa., 1986-92, Pa. Dept. Revenue, Harrisburg, 1986-88. Editor newsletter Statis. Computing & Statis. Graphics, 1993-95; contbr. articles to profl. jours. Mem. citizen adv. com. State College Area Sch. Dist., 1989-90; bd. trustees Ea. Mennonite U., Harrisburg, 1989—, vice chair, 1995-96; treas. Boy Scout Troop 31, State College, 1992-95. Postdoctoral fellow Nat. Cancer Inst., 1980. Mem. Am. Statis. Assn., The Biometry Soc. (program chair 1996), Inst. Math. Stats., Bernoulli Soc., Internat. Statis. Inst. Democrat. Mennonite. Avocations: sailing, skiing, jogging, biking, reading. Office: Pa State U Dept Stats State College PA 16802-2111

ROSENBLATT, ALBERT MARTIN, judge; b. N.Y.C., Jan. 17, 1936; s. Isaac and Fannie (Dachs) R.; m. Julia Carlson, Aug. 23, 1970; 1 dau., Elizabeth. BA, U. Pa., 1957; LLB (JD), Harvard U., 1960. Bar: N.Y. 1961. Dist. atty. Dutchess County, N.Y., 1969-75, county judge, 1976-81; justice N.Y. State Supreme Ct., 1982-89, appellate div., 1989—; chief adminstrv. judge N.Y. State, 1987-89; vis. prof. Vassar Coll., 1993—; mem. N.Y. State Fair Trial Free Press Conf., 1973-75; creator Dutchess County 1st consumer protection bur., 1973; instr. newly elected state supreme ct. judges and county judges; chmn., curriculum head tng. programs state dist. attys., asst. dist. attys., 1974, 75; instr. N.Y. State Police Acad. law tng., 1981; lectr. Nat. Dist. Attys. Assn., 1968-74. Area fund raising rep. Harvard U. Law Sch., 1974; alumni fund raising chmn. U. Pa., 1965, 66; bd. dirs. United Way Community Chest, 1970; bd. dirs. Bardavon 1869 Opera House, Dutchess County Hist. Soc.; mem. adv. bd. Jewish Cmty. Ctr., 1987—. With USAR, 1960-66. Mem. N.Y. State Bar Assn. (named Outstanding Prosecutor 1974, Outstanding Jud. Svcs. award 1994), N.Y. State Dist. Attys. Assn. (pres. 1974, Frank S. Hogan award 1987, Jud. Svcs. award, 1994), Profl. Ski Instrs. Am. (cert. 1984—). Republican. Jewish. Club: Baker St. Irregulars (former assoc. editor Baker St. Jour.). Mem. bd. editors N.Y. State Bar Jour., 1992—; contbr. to N.Y. State Bench Book for Trial Judges, 1986-87; contbr. articles on law to profl. jours. and popular mags. Home: 300 Freedom Rd Pleasant Valley NY 12569-5437 Office: Supreme Ct Chambers 40 Garden St Poughkeepsie NY 12601-3106

ROSENBLATT, ARTHUR ISAAC, architect, former museum director; b. N.Y.C., Aug. 31, 1931; s. Harry and Helen (Satz) R.; m. Ruth Anne Turteltaub, Aug. 5, 1956; children: Paul Mark, Judith Alice. Diploma in architecture, Cooper Union, 1952; BArch, Carnegie-Mellon U., 1956. Registered architect, N.Y. Designer Katzman Assocs., N.Y.C., 1956-57, Isadore & Zachary Rosenfield, N.Y.C., 1957-60, Skidmore, Owings & Merrill-Harrison, Abramovitz, Pomerance and Breines, N.Y.C., 1960-61; chief designer Irwing S. Chanin, Architect, N.Y.C., 1961-65; first dep. commr. N.Y.C. Dept. Parks, Recreation and Cultural Affairs, 1966-68; v.p., vice dir. Met. Mus. Art, N.Y.C., 1968-86; dir. capital projects N.Y. Pub. Libr., N.Y.C., 1982-86; dir. U.S. Holocaust Meml. Mus., Washington, 1986-88; v.p. Grand Cen. Partnership, N.Y.C.; assoc. dir. Bryant Park Restoration Corp., 1989-95; v.p. 34th St. Partnership, 1991-95; faculty Sarah Lawrence Coll., Bronxville, N.Y., 1967-69; dir. capital projects N.Y. Pub. Libr., N.Y.C., 1982-86; cons. arch. Butler Mus. Am. Art, 1980, Whitney Mus. Am. Art, N.Y.C., 1981, Chrysler Mus. Art, Norfolk, Va., 1982, Internat. Ctr. Photography, N.Y.C., 1985-86, Mus. and Archive Acad. Hebrew Lang., Jerusalem, Newport Harbor Art Mus., 1990-91, J.B. Speed Art Mus., Louisville, 1992, Museo de Arte de Ponce, Ponce, P.R., 1995, P.R. Tourism Co., Commonwealth of P.R., 1995, Museo de Arte de P.R., 1996. Author: Temple of Dendur, 1978; co-author: Movie Song Catalog, 1993; contbr. articles to mags. and jours. Vice chmn. cmty. planning bd. # 8, N.Y.C., 1964-66; trustee The Cooper Union, 1983-86; commr. N.Y.C. Conn. Environment; v.p. Met. Hist. Structures Assn.; presl. appointee Nat. Mus. Svc. Bd., 1995. With U.S. Army, 1953-55. Nat. Endowment for the Arts grantee, 1981. Fellow AIA (pres. N.Y. chpt. 1982-83, spl. citation 1978), Nat. Inst. for Archtl. Edn. (bd. dirs. 1978); mem. Mcpl. Art Soc., Archtl. League N.Y. (pres. 1970-72). Home and Office: 1158 5th Ave New York NY 10029-6917

ROSENBLATT, GERD MATTHEW, chemist; b. Leipzig, Germany, July 6, 1933; came to U.S., 1935, naturalized, 1940; s. Edgar Fritz and Herta (Fisher) R.; m. Nancy Ann Kaltreider, June 29, 1957 (dec. Jan. 1982); children: Rachel, Paul; m. Susan Frances Barnett, Nov. 23, 1990. BA, Swarthmore Coll., 1955; PhD, Princeton U., 1960; Doctorate in Physics (hon.), Vrije Universiteit Brussel, 1989. Chemist Lawrence Radiation Lab., Univ. Calif., 1960-63, cons., guest scientist, 1968-84; from asst. to assoc. prof. chemistry Pa. State U., University Park, 1963-70, prof., 1970-81; assoc. div. leader Los Alamos (N.Mex.) Nat. Lab., 1981-82, chemistry div. leader, 1982-85; dep. dir. Lawrence Berkeley (Calif.) Lab., 1985-89, sr. chemist, 1985—; lectr. U. Calif., Berkeley, 1962-63; vis. prof. Vrije U. Brussels, 1973; vis. fellow Southampton U., 1980, King's Coll., Cambridge, 1980; adj. prof. chemistry U. N.Mex., 1981-85; cons. Aerospace Corp., 1979-85, Solar Energy Rsch. Inst., 1980-81, Xerox Corp., 1977-78, Hooker Chem. Co., 1976-78, Los Alamos Nat. Lab., 1978; mem. external adv. com. Ctr. for Materials Sci., 1985-93; mem. rev. com. chemistry divsn., 1985; mem. rev. com. for chem. engring. divsn. Arbonne Univ. Assn., 1974-80, chmn., 1977-78; mem. rev. com. for chem. sci. Lawrence Berkeley Lab., 1984; chmn. rev. com. for chem. and materials sci. Lawrence Livermore Nat. Lab., 1984-91; mem. bd. advs. Combustion Rsch. Facility, Sandia Nat. Lab., 1985-89; mem. bd. advs. R&D divsn. Lockheed Missiles & Space Co., 1985-87; chmn. chemistry III panel Nat. Com., Com. on Date for Sci. and Tech., 1986-92, Internat. Union of Pure and Applied Chemistry, 1986-92; mem. basic scis. lab. program panel energy, 1985-89; sec. IUPAC Commn. on High Temperature and Solid State Chemistry, 1992-95, chmn., 1996-97. Editor: (jour.) Progress in Solid State Chemistry, 1977—; mem. editorial bd. High Temperature Sci., 1979—; contbr. articles to profl. jours. Du Pont grad. fellow, Princeton U., 1957-58; fellow Solvay Inst., 1973, U.K. Rsch. Coun., 1980. Fellow AAAS; mem. Am. Chem. Soc., Am. Phys. Soc., Electrochem. Soc., Nat. Rsch. Coun. (chmn. high temperature sci. and tech. com. 1977-79, 84-85, panel on exploration of materials sci. and tech. for nat. welfare 1986-88, sci. and tech. info. bd. 1990-91, chmn. numerical data adv. bd. 1986-90, solid state scis. com. 1988-91, chmn. western regional materials sci. and engring. meeting 1990, panel on long-term retention of selected sci. and tech. records of fed. govt. 1993). Achievements include first use of imaging detectors to obtain Raman compositional profiles and two-dimensional maps of chemical compositions, of rotational Raman scattering as a temperature and state-population probe in high temperature and combustion systems; elucidation of role of crystal defects and molecular structure in the evaporation of solid materials; first experimental determination of how molecular polarizability anisotrophies change with internuclear distance; estimation of thermodynamic properties and molecular structures for gaseous molecules. Home: 1177 Miller Ave Berkeley CA 94708-1754 Office: Lawrence Berkely Nat Lab Berkeley CA 94720-0001

ROSENBLATT, JASON PHILIP, English language educator; b. Balt., July 3, 1941; s. Morris D. and Esther (Friedlander) R.; m. Zipporah Marton, June 2, 1964; children: Noah David, Raphael Mark. BA, Yeshiva U., 1963; MA, Brown U., 1966, PhD, 1969. Asst. prof. English U. Pa., Phila., 1968-74; asst. prof. English Georgetown U., Washington, 1974-76, assoc. prof., 1976-83, prof. English, 1983—; vis. lectr. English lit. Swarthmore (Pa.) Coll., 1972-73; cen. exec. com. Folger Inst./Folger Shakespeare Libr., Washington, 1976-88. Author: Torah and Law in "Paradise Lost", 1994; co-editor: Not in Heaven: Coherence and Complexity in Biblical Narrative, 1991; mem. editl. bd. Milton Studies, 1992—; contbr. articles to scholarly publs. Guggenheim Found. fellow, 1977-78; NEH fellow, 1990-91. Mem. MLA (del. assembly 1989-91, exec. com. div. religion and lit. 1982-86), Milton Soc. Am. (exec. com. 1977-80, James Holly Hanford award 1989), Milton Seminar, Phi Beta Kappa. Democrat. Jewish. Avocations: Talmud study, music, swimming. Office: Dept English Georgetown Univ 37th St at O St Washington DC 20057

ROSENBLATT, JOAN RAUP, mathematical statistician; b. N.Y.C., Apr. 15, 1926; d. Robert Bruce and Clara (Eliot) Raup; m. David Rosenblatt, June 10, 1950. AB, Barnard Coll., 1946; PhD, U. N.C., 1956. Intern Nat. Inst. Pub. Affairs, Washington, 1946-47; statis. analyst U.S. Bur. of Budget, 1947-48; rsch. asst. U. N.C., 1953-54; mathematician Nat. Inst. Standards and Tech. (formerly Nat. Bur. Standards), Washington, 1955—, asst. chief statis. engring., 1963-68, chief statis. engring. lab., 1969-78, dep. dir. Ctr. for Applied Math., 1978-88; dep. dir. Computing and Applied Math. Lab., Gaithersburg, 1988-93, dir., 1993-95; mem. com. on indsl. rels. Dept. Stats. Ohio State U.; mem. adv. com. in math. and stats. USDA Grad. Sch., 1971—; mem. Com. Applied and Theoretical Stats., Nat. Rsch. Coun., 1985-88. Mem. editorial bd. Communications in Stats., 1971-79, Jour. Soc. for Indsl. and Applied Math., 1965-75, Nat. Inst. Stds. and Tech. Jour. Rsch., 1991-93; contbr. articles to profl. jours. Chmn. Com. on Women in Sci., Joint Bd. on Sci. Edn., 1963-64. Rice fellow, 1946, Gen. Edn. Bd. fellow, 1948-50; recipient Fed. Woman's award, 1971, Gold medal Dept. Commerce, 1976, Presdl. Meritorious Exec. Rank award, 1982. Fellow AAAS (chmn. stats. sect. 1982, sec. 1987-91), Inst. Math. Stats. (coun. 1975-77), Am. Statis. Assn. (v.p. 1981-83, dir. 1979-80, Founders award 1991), Washington Acad. Scis. (achievement award math. 1965); mem. AAUW, IEEE Reliability Soc., Am. Math. Soc., Royal Statis. Soc. London, Philos. Soc. Washington, Internat. Statis. Inst., Bernoulli Soc. Probability and Math. Stats., Caucus Women Stats. (pres. 1976), Assn. Women Math., Exec. Women Govt., Phi Beta Kappa, Sigma Xi (treas. Nat. Bur. Standards chpt. 1982-84). Home: 2939 Van Ness St NW Apt 702 Washington DC 20008-4628 Office: Nat Inst Stds and Tech Rm 353 NIST North Gaithersburg MD 20899-0001

ROSENBLATT, JOSEPH, poet, editor; b. Toronto, Ont., Can., Dec. 26, 1933; s. Samuel and Bessie (Tee) R.; m. Faye Carole Smith, Oct. 13, 1969; 1 son, Eliot Howard. Grad. pub. schs. Writer-in-residence U. Western Ont., 1979-80, U. Victoria, 1980-81, U. Rome and U. Bologna, Italy, 1987. Author: Voyage of the Mood, 1963, The LSD Leacock, 1966, Winter of the Luna Moth, 1968, Dream Craters, 1974, Top Soil, 1976, Loosely Tied Hands, 1978, Tommy and the Ant Colony, 1979, Sleeping Lady, 1979, Brides of the Stream, 1983, Escape from the Glue Factory, 1985, The Kissing Goldfish of Siam, 1989, Beds and Consenting Dreamers, 1994, Madre Tentacolare, 1995, Tentacled Mother, 1995, Joe Rosenblatt Reader, 1995; author, illustrator: Greenbaum, 1971, The Bumblebee Dithyramb, 1972, The Blind Photographer, 1972, Virgins and Vampires, 1975; illustrator: Dr. Anaconda's Solar Fun Club, 1978, Snake Oil, 1978; editor: Jewish Dialogue, 1969—; poems included in Oxford Book of Canadian Verse, 1968, Poets of the Sixties, 1973, Poets of Canada, 1978, Gridi nel buio (Italian), 1990, other anthologies; exhibited ink drawings one-man show Gadatsy Gallery. Can. Coun. grantee, 1966, 68, 73, 80, 86, 92; B.C. Arts Coun. grantee, 1991; recipient Ont. Arts Coun. poetry award, 1970, Gov. Gen.'s award for poetry, 1976, B.C. Book prize, 1986. Mem. Writers Union of Can.

ROSENBLATT, LESTER, naval architect; b. N.Y.C., Apr. 13, 1920; s. Mandell and Rosa (Wolff) R. BS, CCNY; BS in Naval Architecture and Marine Engring., U. Mich., 1942; DSc (hon.), Webb Inst. Naval Architecture, 1993. Registered profl. engr., N.Y., Mass. Naval architect John H. Wells, Inc., 1942-47; naval acrhitect USN Pearl Harbor Navy Yard, 1944-46; co-founder, chmn., chief exec. officer, naval architect M. Rosenblatt & Son Inc., Naval Architects and Marine Engrs., N.Y.C. and throughout U.S., 1947—; designer maj. ships, U.S. and fgn. Contbr. numerous tech. papers. Trustee (hon.) Webb Inst. Naval Architecture; mem. United Jewish Appeal N.Y., Maritime Friends of Seamen's Ch. Inst. Recipient U. Mich. Sesquicentennial award in ship design, 1967, 1st RosenBlatt-Mich. award, U. Mich., 1992; Admiral's honoree SUNY Maritime Coll., 1992. Fellow Soc. Naval Architects and Engrs. (pres. 1978-80, nat. chmn. membership com.

1964-78, mem. coun. and exec. com., Land medalist, hon. mem., chmn. N.Y. sect. 1961-82); mem. Am. Bur. Shipping, Bur. Veritas, Am. Soc. Naval Engrs. (Harold Saunders award 1987), Marine Soc. N.Y. (hon.), Internat. Maritime Hall of Fame, Soc. Marine Cons., N.Y. Yacht Club, Tau Beta Pi. Home: 8 E 83rd St Apt 12B New York NY 10028-0418 Office: M Rosenblatt & Son Inc 350 Broadway New York NY 10013-3911

ROSENBLATT, MICHAEL, medical researcher, educator; b. Lund, Sweden, Nov. 27, 1947; s. Arthur Rosenblatt and Jean (Strosberg) Bialer; m. Patricia Ellen Regenbogen, Aug. 23, 1969; children: Anna Miriam, Adam Richard. AB summa cum laude, Columbia U., 1969; MD magna cum laude, Harvard U., 1973. Diplomate Am. Bd. Internal Medicine. Intern then resident Mass. Gen. Hosp., Boston, 1973-75, clin. rsch. fellow in endocrinology and metabolism, 1975-77, chief endocrine unit, 1981-84; instr. in medicine Harvard U., Boston, 1976-78, asst. prof. medicine, 1978-82, assoc. prof. medicine, 1982-85; v.p. for biol. rsch. Merck Sharp & Dohme Rsch. Labs., 1984-87, v.p. for biol. rsch. and molecular biology, 1987-89; sr. v.p. rsch. Merck Sharp & Dohme Rsch. Labs., West Point, Pa., 1989-92; Ebert prof. molecular medicine Harvard Med. Sch., Boston, 1992—; dir. div. health scis. and tech. Harvard-MIT, 1992—; chief div. bone and mineral metabolism Beth Israel Hosp., Boston, 1992-96; faculty dean acad. programs Beth Israel Hosp., Harvard Med., 1996; sr. v.p. acad. affairs Beth Israel Hosp., 1996; exec. dir. Harvard Med. Sch./Beth Israel Healthcare Found. for Rsch. and Edn., 1996. Editor: Atrial Natriuretic Factor Endocrinology and Metabolism Clinics of N.Am., 1987; contbr. numerous sci. articles on parathyroid hormone and calcium metabolism to leading sci. jours. Recipient Vincent du Vigneaud award Gordon Confs., Kingston, R.I., 1986, Fuller Albright award Am. Soc. for Bone and Mineral Rsch., 1986, citation Japan Endocrine Soc., Tokyo. Fellow AAAS; mem. The Endocrine Soc., Am. Soc. for Biochemistry and Molecular Biology, Am. Soc. for Clin. Investigation, Am. Soc. Bone and Mineral Rsch. (pres.-elect 1996), Assn. Am. Physicians, Inter-Urban Clin. Club. Home: 130 Lake Ave Newton MA 02159-2108 Office: Harvard Med Sch HST MEC 213 260 Longwood Ave Boston MA 02115-5701

ROSENBLATT, MURRAY, mathematics educator; b. N.Y.C., Sept. 7, 1926; s. Hyman and Esther R.; m. Adylin Lipson, 1949; children—Karin, Daniel. B.S., CCNY, 1946; M.S., Cornell U., 1947, Ph.D. in Math., 1949. Asst. prof. statistics U. Chgo., 1950-55; assoc. prof. math. Ind. U., 1956-59; prof. probability and statistics Brown U., 1959-64; prof. math. U. Calif., San Diego, 1964—; vis. fellow U. Stockholm, 1953; vis. asst. prof. Columbia U., 1955; guest scientist Brookhaven Nat. Lab., 1959; vis. fellow U. Coll., London, 1965-66, Imperial Coll. and Univ. Coll., London, 1972-73, Australian Nat. U., 1976, 79; overseas fellow Churchill Coll., Cambridge U., Eng., 1979; Wald lectr., 1970; vis. scholar Stanford U., 1982. Author: (with U. Grenander) Statistical Analysis of Stationary Time Series, 1957, Random Processes, 1962, (2d edit), 1974, Markov Processes, Structure and Asymptotic Behavior, 1971, Studies in Probability Theory, 1978, Stationary Sequences and Random Fields, 1985, Stochastic Curve Estimation, 1991; editor: The North Holland Series in Probability and Statistics, 1980; mem. editorial bd. Jour. Theoretical Probability. Recipient Bronze medal U. Helsinki, 1978; Guggenheim fellow, 1965-66, 71-72. Fellow Inst. Math Statistics, AAAS; mem. Internat. Statis. Inst., Nat. Acad. Scis. Office: U Calif Dept Math La Jolla CA 92093

ROSENBLATT, PAUL GERHARDT, federal judge. AB, U. Ariz., 1958, JD, 1963. Asst. atty. gen. State of Ariz., 1963-66; adminstrv. asst. to U.S. Rep., 1967-72; sole practice, Prescott, 1971-73; judge Yavapai County Superior Ct., Prescott, 1973-84; judge, U.S. Dist. Ct. Ariz., Phoenix, 1984—. Office: US Dist Ct US Courthouse & Fed Bldg 230 N 1st Ave Ste 7012 Phoenix AZ 85025-0007*

ROSENBLATT, PETER RONALD, lawyer, former ambassador; b. N.Y.C., Sept. 4, 1933; s. William and Therese Amalia (Steinhardt) R.; m. Naomi Henriette Harris, July 1, 1952; children: Therese Sarah Sonenshine, Daniel Harris, David Steinhardt. B.A., Yale U., 1954, LL.B., 1957; postgrad. fellow, Tel-Aviv U., 1971. Bar: N.Y. 1959, D.C. 1969. Teaching asst. history Yale U., New Haven, 1954-55; asst. dist. atty. N.Y. County, 1959-62; asso. Stroock & Stroock & Lavan, N.Y.C., 1962-66; dep. asst. gen. counsel AID, Washington, 1966; mem. White House staff, Washington, 1966-68; jud. officer, chmn. bd. contract appeals U.S. Post Office Dept., Washington, 1968-69; v.p., dir. EDP Technology, Inc., Washington, 1969-71; chmn. bd. Internat. Devel. Services, Washington, 1969-71; spl. cons. to Senator Edmund S. Muskie, 1970-72; practice law Washington, 1972-77, 81-91; ptnr. Heller & Rosenblatt, Washington, 1991—; personal rep. of Pres. with rank amb. to conduct negotiations on future polit. status of Trust Ter. of Pacific Islands, Washington, 1977-81; mem. Mid. East study group Dem. Adv. Coun. Elected Ofcls., 1974-76; bd. dirs. MediSense, Inc., 1983-96. Sec., chmn. exec. com. Coalition for a Dem. Majority, 1973-77, pres., 1983-93; bd. dirs. Com. on Present Danger, 1976-77, 82-93; mem. U.S. Nat. Com. Pacific Econ. Cooperation, 1986, sec., 1987—; bd. govs. Haifa (Israel) U., 1990-94; sec.-treas. Fund for Democracy and Devel., 1991-94, pres., 1994—. 2d lt. QMC, AUS, 1957-58. Mem. ABA, N.Y., D.C. Bar, Coun. Fgn. Rels. Jewish. Office: Heller & Rosenblatt 1501 M St NW Washington DC 20005-1700

ROSENBLATT, ROGER, writer; b. N.Y.C., Sept. 13, 1940; m. Virginia Rosenblatt; children: Carl, Amy, John. PhD in English and Am. Lit., Harvard U.; hon. doctorates, U. Md., Claremont Grad. Sch., U. Utah, Pace U. Tchr. lit. and creative writing Harvard U., 1968-73; dir. edn. NEH, 1973-75; lit. editor The New Republic, 1975-78; columnist Washington Post, mem. editorial bd., 1976-79; essayist, sr. writer Time, 1980-88; essayist MacNeil/Lehrer News Hour, PBS, 1983—; columnist, editor-at-large Life mag., 1989-92; contbg. editor N.Y. Times Mag., New Republic, Vanity Fair, also others. Author: Black Fiction, 1974, Children of War, 1983 (Robert F. Kennedy Book prize), Witness: The World Since Hiroshima, 1985, Life Itself: Abortion in the American Mind, 1992 (Melcher award), The Man in the Water, 1994, (plays) Free Speech in America, 1991, And, 1992, Bibliomania, 1993. Fulbright scholar, Dublin, Ireland, 1965; recipient numerous journalistic honors including two George Polk awards, George Foster Peabody award, Emmy award.

ROSENBLATT, ROGER ALAN, physician, educator; b. Denver, Aug. 8, 1945; s. Alfred Dreyfus and Judith Ann (Ginsburg) R.; m. Fernne Schnitzer, Sept. 23, 1942; children: Eli Samuel, Benjamin. BA magna cum laude, Harvard U., 1967, MD cum laude, M in Pub. Health, 1971. Diplomate Am. Bd. Family Practice, Nat. Bd. Med. Examiners. Intern internal medicine U. Wash., Seattle, 1971-72, resident in family medicine, 1974; regional med. cons. region X Pub. Health Service, Seattle, 1974-76, dir. Nat. Health Services Corps., 1976-77; asst. prof. dept. family medicine U. Wash., Seattle, 1977-81, assoc. prof. dept. family medicine, 1981-85, prof., vice chmn. dept. family medicine, 1985—; cons. U.S. Agy. for Internat. Devel., 1978, Western Interstate Commn. Higher Edn., 1981-82; vis. prof. medicine U. Auckland, New Zealand, 1983-84, Royal Australia Coll. Gen. Practitioners, Victoria, 1984, U. Calgary, 1988, U. Mo., 1988; vis. prof., Fogarty Ctr. Sr. Internat. fellow dept. ob-gyn. NIH, Coll. Medicine, U. Wales, Cardiff, 1992-93. Author: Rural Health Care, 1982; contbr. numerous articles on healthcare to profl. jours. Mem. Beyond War, Physicians for Social Responsiblity. Served with USPHS, 1974-77. Recipient Hanes Rsch. award North Am. Primary Care Rsch. Group, 1996. Mem. Am. Acad. Family Physicians (Hanes Rsch. award 1996), Am. Pub. Health Assn., Soc. Tchrs. Family Medicine (Hanes Rsch. award 1996), Nat. Rural Health Assn., Nat. Council Internat. Health, Nat. Acad. Sci. (elected inst. medicine 1987), Am. Rural Health Assn. (Research award 1985), Phi Beta Kappa. Office: U Wash Dept Family Medicine # Hq-30 Seattle WA 98195

ROSENBLATT, STEPHEN PAUL, marketing and sales promotion company executive; b. N.Y.C., Feb. 13, 1935; s. Jack Aaron and Ruth (Kloth) R.; m. Dorothy Freedman, Apr. 7, 1962; children: Gregg, Amy, Robert. BEd, NYU, 1957. Tchr. art N.Y.C. Schs., 1957-78; art dir. Morse Internat., N.Y.C., 1958-65; v.p. L.C. Gumbinner Advt., N.Y.C., 1966-71; group mktg. dir. Norcliff Thayer, Tarrytown, N.Y., 1971-75; pres. BMS Mktg. Services, Inc., N.Y.C., 1975-89, The Promotion Group Inc. subs. Doctus PLC, N.Y.C., 1989-91, SPQR Inc., Yorktown Heights, N.Y., 1991—. Home and Office: 1451 White Hill Rd Yorktown Heights NY 10598-3543

ROSENBLEETH, RICHARD MARVIN, lawyer; b. Phila., Mar. 20, 1932; s. Morris B. and Henrietta (Friedman) R.; m. Judith A. Alesker, June 20, 1954; children—Dori, Lyn. BS in Econs., U. Pa., 1954, JD, 1957. Bar: Pa. 1958, U.S. Supreme Ct. 1961. Asst. dist. atty. City of Phila., 1957-62; assoc. Richman, Price & Jamieson, 1962-65; ptnr. Blank, Rome, Comisky & McCauley, Phila., 1965—; mem. Civil Justice Reform Act Adv. Group, U.S. Dist. Ct. (ea. dist.) Pa., 1991—; co-chair Mayor Rendell's Transition Task Force on the Law Dept., 1991; judge pro tem Phila. Ct. Common Pleas, 1992—. Pres. Merion Park Civic Assn., Pa., 1967; mem. Citizens Crime Commn., Phila., 1979-87; commr. Youth Svcs. Coordinating Commn., Phila., 1979-85; Pa. state mem. chair U.S. Supreme Ct. Hist. Soc., 1994-95; bd. dirs. Corp. Alliance for Drug Edn., 1995—. Fellow Am. Coll. Trial Lawyers (chmn. Pa. state com. 1993-94), Internat. Acad. Trial Lawyers, Am. Bar Found.; mem. ABA, Pa. Bar Assn., Phila. Bar Assn., Phila. Bar Found. (pres. 1994). Avocations: golf; art collecting. Office: Blank Rome Comisky et al 1200 Four Penn Ctr Plz Philadelphia PA 19103

ROSENBLITH, WALTER ALTER, scientist, educator; b. Vienna, Austria, Sept. 21, 1913; came to U.S., 1939, naturalized, 1946; s. David A. and Gabriele (Roth) R.; m. Judy Olcott Francis, Sept. 27, 1941; children: Sandra Yvonne, Ronald Francis. Ingenieur Radiotelegraphiste, U. Bordeaux, 1936; Ing. Radioelectricien, Ecole Supérieure d'Electricité, Paris, 1937; ScD (hon.), U. Pa., 1976, S.D. Sch. Mines, 1980, Brandeis U., 1988, U. Miami, Fla., 1992; PhD (hon.), Fed. U. of Rio de Janeiro, 1976. Research engr. France, 1937-39; research asst. N.Y. U., 1939-40; grad. fellow, teaching fellow physics U. Calif. at Los Angeles, 1940-43; asst. prof., asso. prof., acting head dept. physics S.D. Sch. Mines and Tech., 1943-47; research fellow Psycho-Acoustic Lab., Harvard U., 1947-51; lectr. otology and laryngology Harvard Med. Sch., 1969—; assoc. prof. comm. biophysics MIT, Cambridge, Mass., 1951-57, prof., 1957-84, inst. prof., 1975-84; inst. prof. emeritus MIT, Cambridge, 1984—; staff Research Lab. Electronics, 1951-69, chmn. faculty, 1967-69, assoc. provost, 1969-71, provost, 1971-80; dir. Kaiser Industries, 1968-76; chmn. com. electronic computers in life scis. Nat. Acad. Scis.-NRC, 1960-64, mem. brain scis. com., 1965-68, chmn., 1966-67; mem. cen. coun. Internat. Brain Rsch. Orgn., 1960-68, mem. exec. com., 1960-68, hon. treas., 1962-67; cons. life scis. panel Pres.'s Sci. Adv. Com., 1961-66; mem. coun. Internat. Union Pure and Applied Biophysics, 1961-69; inaugural lectr. Tata Inst. Fundamental Rsch., Bombay, 1962; Weizmann lectr. Weizmann Inst. Sci., Rehovoth, Israel, 1962; U.S. Nat. Commn. on Pure and Applied Biophysics, 1964-69; mem. Pres.'s Com. Urban Housing, 1967-68; cons. communications scis. WHO, 1964-65; mem. bd. medicine NAS, 1967-70; charter mem. Inst. Medicine, 1970—, mem. coun., 1970-76; mem. adv. com. to dir. NIH, 1970-74; mem. governing bd. NRC, 1974-76; mem. adv. com. med. sci. AMA, 1972-74; mem. selection com. Tyler Prize for Environ. Achievement, 1973—; chmn. sci. adv. coun. Callier Ctr. for Communication Disorders, 1968-85; chmn. rsch. com of the Health Effects Inst., 1981-89, bd. dirs., 1989—; chmn. internat. adv. panel of Chinese U. Devel. Project, 1986-91; mem. gov. coun. Internat. Centre Insect Physiology and Ecology, Kenya, 1987-90; mem. Am. and internat. panels on UNESCO (UN Assn. U.S. Am.), 1988-89; mem. Com. on Scholarly Communication with People's Republic of China, 1977-86, Coun. on Fgn. Rels., 1983-92. Bd. Fgn. Scholarships, 1978-81, chmn., 1980-81; co-chmn. NRC-IOM com. for study of saccharin and food safety policy, 1978-79; cons. Carnegie Corp. N.Y., 1986—, Carnegie Commn. on Sci., Tech. and Govt., 1988—; hon. consulting prof. U. of Electronic Sci. and Tech. of China, 1988. Contbr. articles, chpts. to profl. publs. Bd. govs. Weizmann Inst. Sci., 1973-86; chmn. com. on rehab. of physically handicapped NRC, 1975-77; trustee Brandeis U., 1979—. Decorated croix du chevalier Legion d'Honneur (France); recipient Alexander von Humboldt medal, 1989; Rosenblith lectr. created in his honor NAS, 1992, Rosenblith chair of neuroscis. named in his honor MIT, 1995. Fellow Acoustical Soc. Am., World Acad. Art and Sci., Am. Acad. Arts and Scis. (exec. bd. 1970-77), AAAS, IEEE; mem. Internat. Council Sci. Unions (v.p. 1984-88), Biophys. Soc. (council 1957-61, 69-72, exec. bd. 1957-61), NAE, NAS (fgn. sec. 1982-86), Soc. Exptl. Psychologists, Engring. Acad. of Japan (fgn. assoc.). Office: MIT Cambridge MA 02139

ROSENBLOOM, ARLAN LEE, physician, educator; b. Milw., Apr. 15, 1934; s. Harris Phillip and Esther (Schneider) R.; m. Edith Kathleen Peterson, Sept. 14, 1958; children: Eric David, Maliah Jo, Disa Lynn, Harris Phillip. BA, U. Wis., 1955, MD, 1958. Diplomate Am. Bd. Pediatrics, Am. Bd. Pediatric Endocrinology, Am. Coll. Epidemiology. Intern Los Angeles County Gen. Hosp., 1958-59; resident in gen. practice Ventura County Hosp., Ventura, Calif., 1959-60; physician-in-chief Medico Hosp., Kratie, Cambodia, 1960-61; med. officer Pahang, Malaysia, 1961-62; resident in pediatrics U. Wis. Hosp., Madison, 1962-63, 64-65; fellow in pediatric endocrinology U. Wis. Hosp., 1963-64, 65-66; asst. prof. pediatrics U. Fla., Gainesville, 1968-71; asso. prof. U. Fla., 1971-74, prof., 1974-96; disting. svc. prof. U. Fla., Gainesville, 1996—; founder, chief div. endocrinology U. Fla., 1977-94; dir. Office for Internat. Health Programs, 1995—; mem. Ctr. for African Studies U. Fla., mem. Ctr. for Latin Am. Studies; assoc. dir. Clin. Research Center, 1969-74, dir., 1974-80; dir. Nat. Found. March of Dimes Birth Defects Center, 1969-73; med. dir. Gainesville Youth Clinic, 1972-74; mem. adv. com. Nat. Disease and Therapy Index; mem. Fla. Com. Children and Youth, 1972; data work group chmn. Nat. Diabetes Commn., 1975; mem. epidemiology and disease control study sect. NIH, 1978-82; vis. prof. McMaster U. Med. Centre, 1974-75; cons. epidemiologist Boston U. Health Policy Inst., West Africa, 1983-84; mem. affiliate faculty dept. clin. psychology U. Fla., 1984—; pres., dir. Fla. Camp for Children and Youth with Diabetes, 1970-90; dir. N. Fla. Regional Diabetes Program Children and Youth, 1974-88; dir. U. Fla. Diabetes Rsch. Edn. and Treatment Ctr., 1977-90; clin. and sci. adv. bd. Children's Diabetes Found., Denver, 1978-86; dir. N. Fla. Regional Diabetes and Endocrine Program for Children and Youth, 1988—; asst. med. dir. Children's Med. Svcs., Dist. 3, 1986—; mem. nat. diabetes adv. bd. NIH, 1990-94; internat. cons. Inst. for Endocrinology, Metabolism and Reproduction, Quito, Ecuador, 1990—. Editor Acta Paediactria Belgica, 1979-82, Today in Medicine (Diabetes), 1989—; mem. editl. bd. European Jour. Pediat., 1982—, Jour. Pediat. Endocrinology and Metabolism, 1983—, Clin. Pediat., 1989—, Diabetes Care, 1992-95, Jour. Clin. Endocrinology and Metabolism, 1995—, Clin. Diabetes, 1996—; contbr. numerous articles to profl. jours. Chief med. officer Hole in the Wall Gang Fund/South, 1990-95; bd. dirs. Chinn Med. Adv. Commn. Boggy Creek Gang Camp, 1995; epidemiologist smallpox eradication program USPHS, Yaounde, Cameroon, 1966-68, comdr. inactive Res., 1968-69, capt. Ready Res., 1987—. Recipient Best Drs. in Am., 1992-94, Faculty Rsch. prize U. Fla. Coll. Medicine, 1994, U. Wis. Med. Alumni Citation, 1995, U. Fla. Blue Key Disting. Faculty award, 1995. Mem. Am. Acad. Pediatrics, Am. Fedn. Clin. Rsch., Am. Diabetes Assn. (bd. dirs. 1986-90), Brit. Diabetic Assn., Fla. Diabetes Assn. (dir.), Alachua County Med. Soc., Internat. Soc. Pediatric Adolescent Diabetes, Endocrine Soc., Nat. Coun. for Internat. Health, Lawson Wilkins Pediatric Endocrine Soc., Am. Pediatric Soc., Internat. Diabetes Epidemiology Group, Soc. Pediatric Rsch. Home: 2902 SW 1st Ave Gainesville FL 32607-3002 Office: Children's Med Svcs Ctr 1701 SW 16th Ave Rm 2163 Gainesville FL 32608-1153

ROSENBLOOM, BERT, marketing educator, consultant, writer; b. Phila., Feb. 2, 1944; s. Max and Dora (Cohen) R.; m. Pearl Friedman, Aug. 18, 1968; children: Jack Alan, Robyn. B.S., Temple U., 1966, M.B.A., 1968, Ph.D., 1974. Instr. mktg. Rider Coll., Trenton, N.J., 1968-72, asst. prof., 1972-74; asst. prof. mktg. Baruch Coll. CUNY, 1974-76; assoc. prof. Drexel U., Phila., 1976-80, prof., 1980-85, G. Behrens Ulrich prof. mktg., 1985—, assoc. dean grad. programs, 1994—; cons. editor mktg. Random House, N.Y.C., 1977—; cons. in field; mem. bd. dirs. Reality Lnadscaping Corp., 1991—, McKee Real Estate Devel. Corp., 1991—. Author: Marketing Channels, 1978, 3d edit., 1987, Market Functions and the Wholesaler Distribution, 1987, Marketing Channels: A Management View, 4th edit., 1991, 5th edit., 1995; Retail Marketing, 1981, Direct Selling Channels, 1993; editor: Journal of Marketing Channels, 1989—, Jour. Consumer Mktg., Jour. Global Mktg., Jour. Acad. Mktg. Sci.; contbr. articles to profl. jours. Named dist. Erskine fellow U. Canterbury, New Zealand, 1986; recipient outstanding educator award Chapel of Four Chaplains, 1984, rsch. award Distbn. Rsch. and Edn. Found., 1986, rsch. award Direct Selling Found., 1986, 91; Nat. Assn. Wholesaler Distbrs. grantee, 1991; honored as disting. prof Retail Mktg. Inst. of Australia, 1985; Vis. scholar Ecole Superiore de Commerce de Paris, 1993. Fellow Acad. Mktg. Sci. (bd. govs. 1978-89); mem. Internat. Mgmt. Devel. Assn. (pres. 1992—), Am. Mktg. Assn. (v.p. Phila. chpt. 1978-79), Beta Gamma Sigma. Office: Drexel U Sch Bus 32d and Market Sts Philadelphia PA 19104

ROSENBLOOM, DANIEL, investment banker, lawyer; b. N.Y.C., Feb. 11, 1930; s. Sol and Florence (Vogel) R. BA, U. Va., 1951, JD, 1954; LLM, NYU, 1960. Bar: Va. 1954, N.Y. 1956. Atty. Paskus, Gordon & Hyman, N.Y.C., 1956-61; v.p., sec., gen. counsel Phila. & Reading Corp., N.Y.C., 1962-67; ptnr. First Manhattan Co., 1967—. Trustee Nat. Found. for Facial Reconstruction, NYU Med. Ctr., Univ. Va. Law Sch. Found. 1st lt. AUS, 1954-56. Mem. Sunningdale Country Club, Farmington Country Club, Harmonie Club, City Athletic Club, Atlantic Golf Club, Phi Alpha Delta, Phi Epsilon Pi. Jewish. Office: First Manhattan Co 437 Madison Ave New York NY 10022-7001

ROSENBLOOM, H. DAVID, lawyer; b. N.Y.C., May 26, 1941; s. Milton M. and Rose Gold R.; m. Carla L. Peterson, June 23, 1968; children: Sarah Alix, Julia Micol. A.B., Princeton U., 1962; postgrad. (Fulbright scholar), U. Florence, Italy, 1962-63; J.D., Harvard U., 1966. Bar: N.Y. 1967, D.C. 1968. Spl. asst. to Arthur J. Goldberg U.S. amb. to UN, 1966-67; law clk. to Abe Fortas U.S. Supreme Ct., 1967-68; assoc. Caplin & Drysdale, Washington, 1968-72, ptnr., 1972-77, 81—; spl. asst. to dep. asst. sec. for tax policy Dept. Treasury, Washington, 1977, internat. tax counsel, 1978-81; lectr. Harvard U. Law Sch., 1984-87, 90-93, 95-96, Stanford U. Law Sch., 1988, Columbia U. Law Sch., 1997—. Mem. D.C. Bar. Home: 2948 Garfield Ter NW Washington DC 20008-3507 Office: One Thomas Circle NW Washington DC 20005

ROSENBLOOM, JOEL, molecular biologist, educator; b. Denver, Co., July 18, 1935; s. Isadore and Ida (Berman) R.; m. Joan Caplan, June 8, 1958; children: Aaron, Eric. AB, Harvard U., 1957; MD, U. Pa., 1962, PhD, 1965. Asst. prof. med. sch. U. Pa., Phila., 1968-72, assoc. prof. dental sch., 1972-75, prof., 1978—. Contbr. articles to profl. jours. Recipient Flory award U. Adelaide, 1989. Mem. Am. Soc. Boilogy and Molecular Biology, Biophysical Soc. Home: 4620 Hazel Ave Philadelphia PA 19143-2104 Office: U Pa Rsch Ctr in Oral Biology 4010 Locust St Philadelphia PA 19104-4117

ROSENBLOOM, LEWIS STANLEY, lawyer; b. Fort Riley, Kans., Feb. 28, 1953; s. Donald and Sally Ann (Warsawsky) R.; m. Rochelle Leavitt, Dec. 16, 1973; children: Micah, Shaina. BA, Lake Forest Coll., 1974; JD with high honors, DePaul U., 1977. Bar: Ill. 1977, U.S. Dist. Ct. (no. dist.) Ill, 1977, U.S. Ct. Appeals (7th cir.) 1979, U.S. Ct. Appeals (9th cir.) 1987, U.S. Ct. Appeals (3d cir.) 1993, U.S. Supreme Ct. 1983. Sr. acct. Gale, Takahasi & Channon, Chgo., 1973-74; law clk. to Hon. Robert L. Eisen U.S. Dist. Ct. (no. dist.) Ill., Chgo., 1976; assoc. Nachman, Munitz & Sweig, Ltd., Chgo., 1976-82, prin., 1982-87; ptnr., co-chmn. involvency, bankruptcy & bus. reorgn. dept. Winston & Strawn, Chgo., 1987-93; ptnr., sr. bankruptcy reorgn. counsel McDermott, Will & Emery, Chgo., 1994—; co-chmn. distressed transactions SBU; mem. bd. advisors to bankruptcy, comml. law advisor Bus. Laws, Inc., 1988—; lectr. in field. Contbr. articles to profl. jours. Mem. adv. com. and fin. subcom. Ill. Bd. Higher Edn., Springfield; mem. state edn. and legal aid subcom. Ill. Coun. on Children and Youth Welfare, Chgo. Coll. scholar Lake Forest Coll., 1973-74. Fellow Am. Coll. Bankruptcy; mem. ABA (bus. bankruptcy com. 1982—, chmn. new and pending bankruptcy legis. subcom. 1982-85, chmn. transp. reorganizations subcom. 1985-88), Chgo. Bar Assn. (bankrupcy reorganization com., co-chmn. subcom. on retention and fees 1987-88). Office: McDermott Will & Emery 227 W Monroe St Chicago IL 60606-5016

ROSENBLOOM, SANFORD M., lawyer; b. Phila., Sept. 24, 1928; s. Fred L. and Pauline B. (Basen) R.; m. Irene Nelson, 1961 (div. 1974); m. Willa Glazer, Nov. 21, 1976. BS, U. Pa., 1951; JD, Rutgers U., 1955. Bar: Pa. 1956, U.S. Dist. Ct. (ea. dist.) Pa. 1956, U.S. Ct. Appeals (3d cir.) 1957. Ptnr. Schnader, Harrison, Segal & Lewis, Phila., 1955-93, ret., 1993. Mem. Phila. Bar Assn. (former chmn. com. real estate sect.), Pa. Bar Assn. (ho. of dels., chmn. real property, probate and trust law sect. 1991-92), Am. Coll. Real Estate Lawyers, Vesper Club, Bala Golf Club (Phila.). Republican. Jewish. Avocations: tennis, golf. Home: The Philadelphian 2401 Pennsylvania Ave Philadelphia PA 19130-3005 Office: Schnader Harrison Segal et al 1600 Market St Ste 3600 Philadelphia PA 19103-7240

ROSENBLOOM, STEVE, sportswriter. Sports columnist Chgo. Sun Times. Office: Chgo Sun-Times 401 N Wabash Ave Chicago IL 60611-3532

ROSENBLUM, CONSTANCE, newspaper editor. Arts and leisure sect. editor N.Y. Times, N.Y.C. Office: The NY Times 229 W 43rd St New York NY 10036-3913

ROSENBLUM, EDWARD G., lawyer; b. Union City, N.J., Aug. 2, 1944; s. Milton and Frances (Nardi) R.; m. Charis Ann Schlatter, Dec. 1, 1971; children: Deborah, Michelle. BA, Rutgers U., 1966, JD, 1969. Bar: N.J. 1969. Ptnr. Rosenblum & Rosenblum, P.A., Jersey City, 1971-79, Secaucus, N.J., 1979-93; Rosenblum Wolf & Lloyd, P.A., Secaucus, 1994—; lectr. in field. Author: N.J. Lawyer, 1980, N.J. Municipalities, 1987. Active Hudson County chpt. Am. Cancer Soc., Hoboken, N.J., 1987—. Mem. N.J. State Bar Assn. (vice chmn. tax ct. rules com. taxation sect. 1984—, chmn. real property tax com. 1984—, vice chmn. taxation sect. 1987—, chmn.-elect 1987, chmn. 1988-89, Supreme Ct. com. on tax ct. 1982-92). Office: One Harmon Plaza Secaucus NJ 07094

ROSENBLUM, HAROLD ARTHUR, grocery distribution executive; b. Sharon, Pa., Jan. 5, 1923; s. H. David and Carol (Thaler) R.; m. Irene F. Rosen, June 25, 1950; children—Julia M., Mark A., Lee S., Joel N., Ruth C. (dec.). Student, Western Res. U., 1939-40; A.B. cum laude, Harvard, 1943, J.D., 1949. Bar: Pa. 1949. With Sharon div. Peter J. Schmitt Co. (formerly Golden Dawn Foods, Inc.), Sharon, 1950-85; pres. Golden Dawn Foods, Inc., 1961-80, chmn. bd., 1980-83, treas., 1961-73; sec. H.M. Pollock Co., Kittanning, Pa., 1982-90. Mem. Mercer County Mental Health/Mental Retardation Bd., 1967-90, chmn., 1967-70, 80-81, sec., 1984-90; chmn. Community Council Com. Mental Health/Mental Retardation, 1965-67, Shenango Valley Jewish Fedn., 1964—; pres. Friends of Buhl Henderson Library, 1973-75; treas. Mercer County Mental Health Assn., 1964-66; bd. dirs. Mercer County Cmty. Mental Health & Counseling Ctr., 1959-82, sec., 1961-63, pres., 1963-65; v.p. Mercer County Drug and Alcohol Coun., Inc., 1973-74; mem. exec. bd. Shenango Valley Human Rels. Coun., 1960-68; mem. econ. devel. com. Multi-County Manpower Devel. Corp., 1972-73; mem. Sharon Human Relations Commn., 1969-88 , sec., 1984, chmn. 1985-86; sec. Mercer County Comprehensive Health Planning Bd., 1972-74, mem. adv. com., 1971-74; charter mem. Pa. Freedom of Choice in Family Planning; mem. Mercer County Commn. on Drug and Alcohol Abuse, 1973-78; mem. adv. bd. Shenango Valley Campus, Pa. State U., 1976; exec. com. Mercer County br. NAACP, 1964-71; pres. bd. dirs. Playhouse 600, 1973-76; bd. dirs. Sharon Regional Health System (formerly Sharon Gen. Hosp.), 1964—, sec., 1966-77, chmn., 1977—, home health adv. com., 1973—; mem. Mayor's Com. for Arts, 1973-75; trustee-at-large Pa. council Union Am. Hebrew Congregations, 1966-76, 85-90; bd. dirs. Shenango Valley Urban League, 1971-73, Pa. Mental Health Assn., 1968-72; bd. dirs. Mercer County Edn. and Rehab. Ctr. (formerly Mercer County Crippled Children's and Adults Soc.), 1981-94, exec. com., 1983-94, sec., 1986-92; bd. dirs. Family and Children's Svc. of Youngstown Area Jewish Fedn., 1981—, sec., 1986-87, v.p., 1987-89, pres. 1990-92; bd. dirs. Temple Beth Israel, Sharon, 1951-63, 82-89, v.p., 1956-58, pres., 1958-63, 84-87 ; bd. dirs. Cmty. Food Warehouse, 1983-88 , pres., 1985-86; Youngstown State U. Human Services Devel. Adv. Bd., 1986-92; adv. bd. Behavioral Health Ctr., 1988—. Served with AUS, 1943-46. Buhl Day honoree, 1985. Mem. Nat. Am. Wholesale Grocers Assn. (bd. govs. 1964-66), Shenango Valley C. of C. (bd. dirs. 1969-71, treas. 1970, Person of Yr. 1985). Clubs: Rotary (Sharon) (pres. 1978-79), Sharon Country (Sharon), University (Sharon) (fin. sec., pres. 1978-79); F.H. Buhl (dir. 1977-79). Home: 1700 Hannah Ct Sharon PA 16146-3818

ROSENBLUM, JOHN WILLIAM, dean; b. Houston, Jan. 1, 1944; s. H. William and Susan (Ullmann) R.; m. Carolyn Edith Jones, Sept. 12, 1964; children: J. Christopher, Kathryn, Nicholas. A.B., Brown U., 1965; M.B.A., Harvard U., 1967, D.B.A., 1972. Instr. Harvard U. Bus. Sch., Boston, 1969-72, asst. prof., 1972-75, assoc. prof., 1975-79; prof. Darden Grad. Sch. Bus. Adminstrn., U. Va., Charlottesville, 1979-80, assoc. dean, 1980-82, dean, 1982-93; Tayloe Murphy prof., 1993—; dean Jepson Sch. Leadership Studies, U. Richmond, Va., 1996—; bd. dirs. Chesapeake Corp., Cadmus Comms., Inc., T. Rowe Price Assocs., Comdial Corp., Cone Mills Corp., The Providence Jour. Co. Co-author: Strategy and Organization, 1973, (2d edit.),

1977, Cases in Political Economy-Japan, 1980. Mem. Phi Beta Kappa, Omicron Delta Kappa. Home: RR 3 Box 530 Crozet VA 22932-9319 Office: Jepson Sch Univ Richmond Richmond VA 23173

ROSENBLUM, M. EDGAR, theater director; b. Bklyn., Jan. 8, 1932; s. Jacob and Pauline (Feldman) R.; m. Cornelia Hartmann, May 1, 1960; 1 child, Jessica Alex. Student, Bard Coll., 1951-55. Prodr. Folk Rock Chamber Music Series, Woodstock, N.Y., 1956-72; dir. Polari Gallery, Woodstock, 1959-72; asst. to mgr. Nat. Music League, N.Y.C., 1958-59; stage mgr. Joffrey Ballet Nat. Tour, 1960; prodr. When I Was a Child, 41st St Theatre, N.Y.C., 1960-61, Woodstock Playhouse, 1960-73; stage mgr. Turn of the Screw Nat. Tour, 1961; exec. dir. Hudson Valley Repertory Theatre, Woodstock, 1964-67; exec. prodr. The Shadow Box, N.Y.C., 1977; exec. dir. Long Wharf Theatre, New Haven, 1970—; producer and owner, Woodstock (N.Y.) Playhouse, 1959-73; cons. Fedn. for Ext. and Devel. of Am. Profl. Theatre, N.Y.C., 1970, Arts Couns. of New Haven, R.I., Alaska, Conn., Ohio, 1970—; bd. trustees Am. Arts Alliance, chmn of bd. 1982-84; vis. lectr. Yale U., New Haven, 1985-91. With U.S. Army, 1953. Recipient award New Haven Arts Coun., 1994; Ezra Stiles Coll. fellow Yale U., 1973. Mem. Am. Arts Alliance (chmn. 1982-84), League of Resident Theatres (mem. exec., liaison and negotiating coms. 1974, v.p. 1993-96, pres. 1996—), Nat. Corp. Theatre Fund (founding pres. 1976), Conn. Advocates for the Arts (bd. dirs. 1978—), Greater New Haven C. of C. (bd. dirs.). Office: Long Wharf Theatre 222 Sargent Dr New Haven CT 06511-5919

ROSENBLUM, MARVIN, mathematics educator; b. Bklyn., June 30, 1926; s. Isidore and Celia (Mendelsohn) Rosenblum; m. Frances E. Parker, May 30, 1959; children: Isidore, Mendel, Jessie, Rebecca, Sarah. B.S., U. Calif.-Berkeley, 1949, M.A., 1951, Ph.D., 1955. Instr. math. U. Calif.-Berkeley, 1954-55; asst. prof. U. Va., Charlottesville, 1955-59, assoc. prof., 1960-65, prof., 1965—, now Commonwealth prof.; mem. Inst. Advanced Study, 1959-60. Served with USNR, 1944-46. Mem. Am. Math. Soc., Am. Math. Assn., Soc. Indsl. and Applied Math. Jewish. Office: U Va Dept Math Kerchof Hall Charlottesville VA 22903

ROSENBLUM, MICHAEL F., lawyer; b. N.Y.C., Sept. 23, 1940. BA, Harvard U., 1962; JD, Villanova U., 1968. Bar: D.C. 1968, Ill. 1971. Ptnr. Mayer, Brown & Platt, Chgo.; mem. Nat. Rels. Bd. appellate ct. divsn., 1968-71. Mem. ABA, Fed. Bar Assn., D.C. Bar. Office: Mayer Brown & Platt 190 S La Salle St Chicago IL 60603-3410*

ROSENBLUM, MYRON, chemist, educator; b. N.Y.C., Oct. 21, 1925; m. Rachel Susan Jacobson, June 22, 1958; children: Miriam, Jonathan, Leah. AB, Columbia U., 1949; AM, Harvard U., 1950, PhD, 1954. Postdoctoral fellow Columbia U., N.Y.C., 1953-55; asst. prof. chemistry Ill. Inst. Tech., Chgo., 1955-58; asst. prof. Brandeis U., Waltham, Mass., 1958-60, assoc. prof., 1960-66, prof., 1966—. Author: (monograph) The Iron Group Metallocenes, 1967. Sgt. inf. U.S. Army, 1943-46, ETO. Guggenheim fellow, 1965, Fulbright fellow. Mem. Am. Chem. Soc. Avocation: woodworking. Office: Brandeis U Dept of Chemistry Waltham MA 02254

ROSENBLUM, ROBERT, art historian, educator; b. N.Y.C., July 24, 1927; s. Abraham H. and Lily M. (Lipkin) R.; m. Jane Kaplowitz, June 23, 1977; children: Sophie Lila, Theodore Abraham. BA, Queens Coll., 1948; MA, Yale U., 1950; PhD, NYU, 1956; MA (hon.), Oxford U., 1972; ArtsD (hon.), Queens Coll., 1992. Mem. faculty U. Mich., Ann Arbor, 1955-56, Princeton (N.J.) U., 1956-66, Yale U., New Haven, 1966-67; mem. faculty NYU, N.Y.C., 1967—; prof. fine arts NYU, 1967—. Author: Cubism and Twentieth Century Art, 1960, Transformations in Late Eighteenth Century Art, 1967, Ingres, 1967, Frank Stella, 1971, Modern Painting and the Northern Romantic Tradition, 1975, The International Style of 1800, 1976, Andy Warhol: Portrait of the 70s, 1979, 19th Century Art, 1984, The Dog in Art From Rococo to Post-Modernism, 1988, The Romantic Child From Runge to Sendak, 1989, Paintings in the Musee d'Orsay, 1989, The Jeff Koons Handbook, 1992, Andy Warhol Portraits, 1993, Mel Ramos: Pop Images, 1994, The Paintings of August Strindberg, The Structure of Chaos, 1995. Served with U.S. Army, 1945-46. Recipient Frank Jewett Mather award for art criticism, 1981. Fellow Am. Acad. Arts and Scis.; mem. Coll. Art Assn. Am. Office: NYU Dept Fine Arts Washington Sq N New York NY 10003-6635

ROSENBLUM, SCOTT S., lawyer; b. N.Y.C., Oct. 4, 1949; s. Harold Lewis and Greta Blossom (Lesher) R.; m. Barbara Anne Campbell, Oct. 29, 1977; children: Harold, Emma, Casey. AB summa cum laude, Dartmouth Coll., 1971; JD, U. Pa., 1974. Bar. U.S. Dist. Ct. (so. dist.) N.Y. 1975. Assoc. Stroock & Stroock & Lavan, N.Y.C., 1974-82, ptnr., 1983-91; ptnr. Kramer, Levin, Naftalis, Nessen, Kamin & Frankel, N.Y.C., 1991-93, mng. ptnr., 1994—; N.Y. Adv. Bd. Mid. East Quarterly, Phila., 1994—; bd. dirs. Dovenmuehle Mortgage, Inc., Schaumburg, Ill, 1991—, Greg Manning Auctions, Inc., West Caldwell, N.J., 1993—. Co-author: Public Limited Partnerships and Roll-Ups, Securities Law Techniques, The Practitioner's Guide to Transactions and Litigation, 1995. Trustee Village of Saltaire, N.Y., 1993—. Mem. ABA (high tech. com. 1983-84), Assn. Bar City N.Y. (corps. com. 1991-94), Phi Beta Kappa. Avocation: sailing. Home: 19 Wildwood Cir Larchmont NY 10538 Office: Kramer Levin Naftalis Nessen Kamin & Frankel 919 3rd Ave New York NY 10022

ROSENBLUM, VICTOR GREGORY, political science and law educator; b. N.Y.C., June 2, 1925; s. George and Vera (Minster) R.; m. Louise Rann, Feb. 21, 1946; children: Susan, Ellen, Laura, Keith, Jonathan, Peter, Warren, Joshua. A.B., Columbia U., 1945, LL.B., 1948; Ph.D., U. Calif.-Berkeley, 1953; D.H.L., Hebrew Union Coll., 1970; D.L., Siena Heights Coll., 1982. Bar: Ill., N.Y., U.S. Supreme Ct. Lectr. polit. sci. U. Calif., Berkeley, 1949-52, asst. prof. polit. sci., 1953-57; assoc. prof. polit. sci. Northwestern U., 1958-63, prof. polit. sci. and law, 1963-68, 70-88, Nathaniel L. Nathanson prof., 1988—; pres. Reed Coll., Portland, Oreg., 1968-70; sr. legal cons. project on bankruptcy govtl. studies div. Brookings Instn., 1964-69; vis. Fulbright lectr. Sch. Law U. Louvain, Belgium, 1966-67, vis. prof., 1978-79, 91-92; mem. Adminstrv. Conf. U.S., 1982—. Editor in chief Adminstrv. Law Rev., 1958-62; author: Law As A Political Instrument, 1955, (with A.D. Castberg) Cases on Constitutional Law: Political Roles of the Supreme Court, 1973, (with Frances Zemans) The Making of a Public Profession, 1981; contbr. to law revs., also law and polit. sci. books. Staff assoc. Govtl. Affairs Inst., Washington, 1952-53; cons., assoc. counsel Subcom. on Exec. and Legis. Reorgn., Com. on Govt. Ops., U.S. Ho. of Reps., 1956-57; bd. dirs. Center for Adminstrv. Justice, 1972-78. Mem. ABA (council sect. adminstrv. law 1962-65, 72-75, chmn. 1977-78), Fed. Bar Assn., Am. Polit. Sci. Assn., Law and Soc. Assn. (pres. 1970-72), Am. Judicature Soc. (dir. 1982-90, chmn. bd. 1985-86), Assn. Am. Law Schs. (exec. com. 1984-88, pres. 1987), Consortium of Social Sci. Assns. (pres. 1987-88), Phi Beta Kappa, Pi Sigma Alpha. Democrat. Jewish. Home: 2030 Orrington Ave Evanston IL 60201-2912 Office: Northwestern U Sch Law 357 E Chicago Ave Chicago IL 60611-3008

ROSENBLUTH, LUCILLE MAXINE, health research facility administrator; b. N.Y.C., Sept. 18, 1931; d. David and Rhea (Farber) Moses; m. Sol Rosenbluth, June 8, 1952; children: Shelly Kratzer, Martin. BA in Polit. Sci., Bklyn. Coll., 1952; M in Pub. Adminstrn., NYU, 1953. Intern N.Y. State Adminstrn. Internship Program, 1953-54; rsch. aide N.Y. State Workmen's Compensation Bd., 1954-55; personnel asst. Dept. Personnel, N.Y.C., 1955-57; lectr. Bklyn. Coll., 1958, 59; rsch. asst. Temporary State Commn. on Operation N.Y.C. Govt., 1959-60; cons. Dept. Health, N.Y.C., 1960-61; rschr. study of profl., tech. and managerial manpower needs City of N.Y. Brookings Instn., 1961-63; cons. personnel utilization Dept. Health, N.Y.C., 1963-64; chief rschr. Med. and Health Rsch. Assn. N.Y.C., Inc., 1964-67, project coord., work com. chmn. systems study of sch. health records, 1967-70, project dir., policy com. chmn. N.Y.C. infant day care study, 1970-75, exec. v.p., 1975-86, pres., 1986—; cons. Commonwealth of Mass., 1982; mem. adj. faculty grad. sch. program in pub. health, dept. environ. and community medicine Rutger Med. Sch. U. Medicine and Dentistry N.J., 1984-86; mem. maternal and child health steering com. Sch. Pub. Health Columbia U., 1983—, lectr. pub. health, 1986—. Author: (with others) Caring Prescriptions: Comprehensive Health Care Strategies for Young Children in Poverty, 1993; contbr. articles to profl. jours. Fellow N.Y. Acad. Medicine (assoc., exec. com. on pub. health); mem. APHA (chair breastfeeding com. 1985, 86, 87), Family Planning Couns. Am. (chair grantee adv. com. Region II 1987, 88), N.Y. State Family Planning Advocates, N.Y. State Pub. Health Assn. (co-chmn. legis. com., bd. dirs. 1986—), Pub. Health Assn. N.Y.C., Soc. Rsch. Adminstrs., Health Care Execs. Forum (pres. 1988, 89), Hermann Biggs Soc., Women's City Club N.Y. (chair com. pub. health 1982-84). Office: Medical Health Rsch Assn of NYC 40 Worth St # 720 New York NY 10013-2904*

ROSENBLUTH, MARSHALL NICHOLAS, physicist, educator; b. Albany, N.Y., Feb. 5, 1927; s. Robert and Margaret (Sondheim) R.; m. Sara Unger, Feb. 6, 1979; children by previous marriage—Alan Edward, Robin Ann, Mary Louise, Jean Pamela. BA, Harvard, 1945; MS, U. Chgo., 1947, PhD, 1949. Inst. Stanford U., 1949-50; staff mem. Los Alamos Sci. Lab., 1950-56; sr. research adviser Gen. Atomic Corp., San Diego, 1956-67; prof. U. Calif., San Diego, 1960-67, Inst. for Advanced Study, Princeton U., N.J., 1967-80; dir. Inst. for Fusion Studies, U. Tex., 1980-87; prof. U. Calif., San Diego, 1987-92; chief U.S. scientist Internat. Thermonuclear Engring. Reactor, 1992—; lectr. with rank prof. in astrophys. scis. Princeton U.; also vis. sr. research physicist Princeton U. (Plasma Physics Lab.), 1967-80; Andrew D. White vis. prof. Cornell U., 1976; cons. AEC, NASA, Inst. Def. Analysis. Served with USNR, 1944-46. Recipient E.O. Lawrence award, 1964, Albert Einstein award, 1967, Maxwell prize, 1976, Enrico Fermi award Dept. Energy, 1985. Mem. Am. Phys. Soc., Nat. Acad. Sci., Am. Acad. Arts and Scis. Home: 2311 Via Siena La Jolla CA 92037-3933 Office: U Calif at San Diego Dept Physics 9500 Gilman Dr La Jolla CA 92093-5003

ROSENBLUTH, MORTON, periodontist, educator; b. N.Y.C., Sept. 28, 1924; s. Jacob and Eva (Bigeleissen) R.; m. Sylvia Fradin, July 2, 1946; children: Cheryl Bonnie, Hal Glen. BA, NYU, 1943, grad. program in periodontia, oral medicine, DDS, 1946. Diplomate Am. Bd. Periodontology. Intern Bellevue Hosp. N.Y.C., 1946-47, resident, 1947; individual practice dentistry, N.Y.C., 1947-59; individual practice periodontia, North Miami Beach, Fla., 1960—, individual practice periodontia, TMJ, implantology, Bar Harbor Islands, Fla., 1995—; periodontist Mt. Sinai Hosp., N.Y., Polyclinic Hosp. and Med. Sch. N.Y., Mt. Sinai Hosp., Miami Beach, Fla., Parkway Gen. Hosp.; chief dental dept. North Miami Gen. Hosp.; chmn. periodontia sect. Dade County Research Ctr.; clin. assoc. prof. div. oral and maxillofacial surgery U. Miami Sch. Medicine; assoc. clin. prof. Southeastern U. Health Scis.; lectr. throughout U.S.A., Israel, Mexico, Rome, Teheran, Bangkok, Hong Kong, Tokyo, Honolulu, Jamaica, Paris, London, Sicily, Budapest, Berlin, Luxembourg, South Africa, and others; vis. lectr. U. Tenn. Dental Coll., NYU Dental Coll.; cons. VA Hosp., Miami. Mem. adv. bd. U. Fla. Coll. Dentistry; mem. profl. adv. bd. North Dade Children's Center, Hope Sch. Mentally Retarded Children; mem. sci. adv. com. United Health Found.; chmn. Dental div. United Fund of Dade County, Combined Jewish Appeal; nat. chmn. Hebrew U. Sch. Dental Medicine; bd. dirs. Health Planning Council S. Fla. Contbr. articles to profl. jours. Pres. Condominium Assn.; bd. dirs. and bd. overseers Am. Friends of Hebrew U.; mem. med. adv. bd. Dade-Broward Lupus Found.; trustee Jewish Congregation, 1961-64. With AUS, 1943-44, as capt. USAF, 1951-52. Recipient Maimonides award State of Israel, 1979. Fellow Am. Coll. Dentists, Internat. Coll. Dentists; mem. ADA, Am. Acad. Periodontology, Am., Fla. socs. periodontists, Am. Assn. Hosp. Dental Chiefs, Am. Acad. Dental Medicine, Am. Soc. Advancement Gen. Anesthesia in Dentistry, Northeastern Soc. Periodontists, Fla. (chmn. council on legislation), Miami, Miami Beach, East Coast (sec.-treas. 1968, pres. 1971-72), North Dade (pres. 1963-64) dental socs., Fedn. Dentaire Internationale, Fla. Acad. Dental Practice Adminstrn., Alpha Omega (pres. 1967-68, internat. regent 1973-75, internat. editor 1975-77, internat. pres.-elect 1977-78, internat. pres. 1979, chmn. bd. Alpha Omega Found. 1985-90) Am. Dental Interfrat. Council (pres. 1981-82), Nocoma Club (pres. 1958-60), NYU Century Club (local chmn.), Jockey Club (bd. govs.), KP, Masons, Kiwanis (bd. dirs. 1965), Chaine Des Rotisseurs (Miami Beach charge de missions). Home: 11111 Biscayne Blvd Apt 857 Miami FL 33181-3404 Office: 1166 Kane Concourse Bal Harbour FL 33154-2021

ROSENDAHL, ROGER WAYNE, lawyer. B, U. So. Calif., 1965; JD, Georgetown U., 1969, LLM, 1971. Bar: Calif., N.Y. Mng. ptnr. Cadwalader, Wickersham & Taft, L.A.; lectr. law U. Frankfurt, Germany. Mng. editor Law and Policy in Internat. Bus. Mem. fgn. svc. adv. com. U.S. Trade Rep. Schulte zur Hausen fellow. Mem. ABA (past officer, coun.), Asia-Pacific Lawyers Assn. (founding coun. 1991-92), L.A. County Bar Assn. (bd. advisors, exec. com.), Am. Arbitration Assn. Office: Cadwalader Wickersham & Taft 660 S Figueroa St 23d Fl Los Angeles CA 90017

ROSENDHAL, JEFFREY DAVID, federal science agency administrator, astronomer; b. Bklyn., June 21, 1941; s. Louis and Beulah (Goldsmith) R.; m. Sharon E. Katzman, Dec. 27, 1964 (div. Jan. 25, 1989); children—Martin Andrew, Rachel Lynn; m. Ellen R. Anderson, Feb. 14, 1992. B.A., Williams Coll., 1962; M.S., U. Ill., 1963; Ph.D. (NASA fellow 1966-68), Yale U., 1968. Vis. asst. prof. astronomy U. Wash., Seattle, 1968-69; asst. prof. U. Wis., Madison, 1969-71, U. Ariz., Tucson, 1971-74; with NASA, Washington, 1974—; mgr. advanced programs and tech., astrophysics div. NASA, 1978-80; asst. assoc. adminstr. advanced planning Office Space Sci., 1980-81; asst. assoc. adminstr. for sci. Office Space Sci. and Applications, 1981-87, spl. asst. to assoc. adminstr. for space sci. and applications, 1987-89, 92-93; spl. asst. for policy Office of Exploration, 1989-90; asst. dir. for exploration (internat.) Office of Aeronautics, Exploration and Tech., 1990-91; asst. dir. strategic planning Astrophysics Divsn. Office of Space Sci., 1993-96, asst. assoc. adminstr. for edn. and outreach, 1996—; vis. prof. internat. rels. George Washington U., 1988-89; staff energy subcom. House Sci. Space and Tech. Com., 1992. Mem. editorial adv. bd. Jour. Brit. Interplanetary Soc., 1988—; contbr. articles to Astrophys. Jour., Astrophysics and Space Sci., Physics Today, Issues in Sci. and Tech., Acta Astronautica, other jours. and conf. procs. Recipient NASA Sr. Exec. Svc. Performance awards, 1980, 82-86, Outstanding Leadership medal, 1984, group achievement awards, 1986 (2), 95, European Space Agy. Team Achievement award, 1983, 85, 86, Presdl. award of Meritorious Exec. in Sr. Exec. Svc., 1987; NSF grantee, 1971, 72-73; hon. Woodrow Wilson fellow, 1962. Mem. AIAA, Astron. Soc. Pacific, Am. Astron. Soc., Royal Astron. Soc., Internat. Acad. Astronautics (corr.), Internat. Astron. Union, Phi Beta Kappa. Club: Cosmos (Washington). Achievements include discovery of the variability of the microturbulence in early-type high luminosity stars; direction of the selection of flight experiments for every major NASA scientific mission 1980-88; development of strategic and implementation plans for incorporating education and the public understanding of science into space science research programs and missions. Home: 11446 Links Dr Reston VA 22090-4813 Office: NASA Hdqrs Office Space Sci Code S Washington DC 20546

ROSENDIN, RAYMOND JOSEPH, electrical contracting company executive; b. San Jose, Calif., Feb. 14, 1929; s. Moses Louis and Bertha C. (Pinedo) R.; m. Jeanette Marie Bucher, June 30, 1951 (dec. Feb. 1967); children: Mark R., Patricia A., Debra M., Cynthia C., David R.; m. Nancy Ann Burke, July 6, 1984; children: Raymond M., Callie R., Blake W. Student engring., San Jose State U., 1947-48; B.S.E.E., Heald's Engring. Coll., San Francisco, 1950. V.p., CEO Rosendin Electric, Inc., San Jose, Calif., 1953-59, exec. v.p., CEO, 1969-75, pres., CEO, 1975-94, chmn., CEO, 1995—; former dir. Community Bank, San Jose. Bd. fellows U. Santa Clara, Calif., 1966-93, pres. bd., 1969-72, bd. regents, 1972-82; bd. dirs. United Way, Santa Clara, 1970-74; O'Connor's Hosp., San Jose, 1979-85, Community Hosp., Los Gatos, Calif., 1968-74. Recipient Man of Yr. award Santa Clara Valley Youth Village, 1963, Optimist of Yr. award Optimist Club, San Jose, 1970. Mem. C. of C. Greater San Jose (past dir.), Nat. Elec. Contractors Assn. (past pres., gov., dir.). Republican. Roman Catholic. Club: St. Claire (San Jose). Avocation: boating. Office: Rosendin Electric Inc 880 Mabury Rd San Jose CA 95133-1021

ROSENFELD, ARNOLD SOLOMON, newspaper editor; b. N.Y.C., Apr. 18, 1933; s. William and Sarah (Cohen) R.; m. Ruth Doris Lilly, Sept. 30, 1956; children—William Bennett, Jonathan Andrew, Lauren. Student, U. Houston, 1951; Profl. Journalism fellow, Stanford U., 1967. Mem. staff Houston Post, 1953-67; assoc. editor Detroit mag., Detroit Free Press, 1967; editor Detroit mag., 1968; mng. editor Dayton Daily News, Ohio, 1968-76; editor Dayton Daily News, 1976-80, Dayton Daily News and Jour. Herald, 1980-84, Austin Am.-Statesman, Tex., 1984-88, Atlanta Jour.-Constitution, 1988-89; editor-in-chief Cox Newspapers, Atlanta, 1989—; dir. The Temple, Atlanta, 1994—. Editor: A Thomason Sketchbook, 1969. Pres. Temple Israel Dayton, 1984; bd. dirs. Antioch U., 1978-84, Huston-Tillotson Coll., 1987-89. With AUS, 1951-53. Recipient Editorial Writing award A.P. Mng. Editors Assn. Tex., 1966; Tex. Theta Sigma Phi award, 1969, 72; Media award Nat. Assn. Mental Health, 1976. Mem. Am. Soc. Newspaper Editors Found. (bd. dirs., treas. 1992—). Home: 5875 Riverwood Dr NW Atlanta GA 30328-3728 Office: Cox Newspapers PO Box 105720 Atlanta GA 30348-5720

ROSENFELD, ARTHUR H., lawyer, publisher; b. Bklyn., May 24, 1930; s. Abraham and Sadie (Albert) R.; m. Lois E. Glantz, Apr. 15, 1956; children: Felicia Ann, Carolyn Jane, Sara Ellen. Student, St. Andrew's U., 1950-51; AB, Union Coll., Schenectady, 1952; JD, Harvard U., 1955; postgrad., CCNY, 1962-63. Bar: N.Y. 1955. Pres. Warren, Gorham & Lamont, Inc., N.Y.C., 1970-81, Internat. Thomson Profl. Pub., N.Y.C., 1981-84; chmn. bd. Rosenfeld, Emanuel Inc., Larchmont, N.Y., 1984-88; pres. Prentice Hall Tax & Profl. Ref., N.Y.C., 1988-89, Maxwell Macmillan Profl. and Bus. Reference Div., Englewood Cliffs, N.J., 1989-92, Arthur H. Rosenfeld Assocs., 1991—; Civic Rsch. Inst., Inc., 1992—; of counsel Am. Assn. Legal Publishers, 1995—; exec. dir. Fund for Pub. Access to the Law, 1995—. Vice chmn., bd. dirs. Coun. Econ. Priorities, 1990—. Mem. ABA, N.Y. State Bar Assn., Am. Assn. Pubs. (exec. coun. 1991). Democrat. Club: Harvard. Office: 330 W 72nd St New York NY 10023-2641

ROSENFELD, AZRIEL, computer science educator, consultant; b. N.Y.C., Feb. 19, 1931; s. Abraham Hirsh and Ida B. (Chadaby) R.; m. Eve Hertzberg, Mar. 1, 1959; children—Elie, David, Tova. B.A., Yeshiva U., 1950, M.H.L., 1953, M.S., 1954, D.H.L., 1955; M.A., Columbia U., 1951, Ph.D, 1957; D.Tech. (hon.), Linkoping U., Sweden, 1980; D of Tech. (hon.), Oulu U., Finland, 1994. Ordained rabbi, 1952. Physicist Fairchild Controls Corp., N.Y.C., 1954-56; engr. Ford Instrument Co., Long Island City, N.Y., 1956-59; mgr. research electronics div. Budd Co., Long Island City and McLean, Va., 1959-64; prof., dir. Ctr. for Automation Rsch. U. Md., College Park, 1964—, Disting. univ. prof., 1995—; vis. asst. prof. Yeshiva U., N.Y.C., 1957-63; pres. ImTech, Inc., Silver Spring, Md., 1975-92. Author, editor numerous books; editor numerous jours. Fellow IEEE (Emanuel R. Piore award 1985), IEEE Computer Soc. (Harry Goode Meml. award 1995), IEEE Sys., Man and Cybernetics Soc. (Norbert Wiener award 1995), Washington Acad. Scis. (Sci. Achievement award 1988), Am. Assn. for Artificial Intelligence (founding), Assn. Computing Machinery (founding); mem. Math. Assn. Am., Machine Vision Assn. (bd. dirs. 1984-88, Pres.'s award 1987), Internat. Assn. Pattern Recognition (pres. 1980-82, K.S. fu award 1988, founding fellow 1994), Assn. Orthodox Jewish Scientists (pres. 1963-65), Nat. Acad. Engring. of Mex. (corr.). Home: 847 Loxford Ter Silver Spring MD 20901-1132 Office: U Md Ctr Automation Rsch Computer Vision Lab College Park MD 20742-3275

ROSENFELD, HARRY MORRIS, editor; b. Berlin, 1929; s. Sam and Esther Laja (Sherman) R.; m. Anne Hahn, Feb. 28, 1953; children: Susan, Amy, Stefanie. BA, Syracuse U., 1952; postgrad., NYU, 1954, Columbia U., 1955-59. With N.Y. Herald Tribune, 1954-66, fgn. editor, 1962-66; mng. editor Herald Tribune News Svc., 1959-62; with Washington Post, 1966-78, fgn. editor, 1967-69; asst. mng. editor Met. News, 1970-74, Nat. News, 1974-76, Outlook/Book World, 1976-78; editor Times Union and Knickerbocker News, Albany, N.Y., 1978-88, L.A. Herald Examiner, 1985, The Times Union and Sunday Times Union, 1978—; dir. daily Watergate coverage for Washington Post (newspaper award Pulitzer Gold medal for pub. svc.); vice chmn. N.Y. Fair Trial Free Press Conf., 1985-96; co-chmn. N.Y. State, Reporters Com. for Freedom of Press; mem. adv. com. Harvard Journalism Fellowship for Advanced Studies in Pub. Health. Recipient Black United Front award, 1973, First Amendment award Anti-Defamation League-B'nai B'rith, L.A., Outstanding Alumni award, Syracuse U. Coll. of Arts and Scis., Media Responsibility award N.Y. State Martin Luther King Jr. Inst. for Non-Violence, 1993. Mem. Am. Soc. Newspaper Editors, N.Y. State AP Assn. (pres. 1983, 3d pl. column award 1983, 85, 1st pl. column award 1987), N.Y. State Soc. Newspaper Editors, Internat. Press Inst., UPI Fgn. News Com. (rep. for N.E., adv. com. on cameras in N.Y. Cts., Pulitzer Juror 1987-88, 96), Soc. Profl. Journalists (adv. bd. Albany chpt.), Cameras in the Cts. (adv. com.). Office: Times Union PO Box 15000 Albany NY 12212

ROSENFELD, JOEL, ophthalmologist, lawyer; b. Jan. 27, 1957; s. Jacques Maurice and Mazal (Attia) R.; m. Amy Beth Garon. BS with high honors, U. Mich., 1976, MD, 1980; JD cum laude, U. Detroit, 1993. Diplomate Nat. Bd. Med. Examiners, Am. Bd. Ophthalmology; bar: Mich. 1994. Intern Baylor Coll. Medicine, Houston, 1980-81; resident in ophthalmology Kresge Eye Inst./Wayne State U., Detroit, 1981-84; fellow in ultrasound U. Iowa, Iowa City, 1984; chief of ophthalmology Wheelock Hosp., Goodrich, Mich., 1984—, Huron Meml. Hosp., Bad Axe, Mich., 1988—; St. Joseph Mercy Hosp., Pontiac, Mich., 1989—; co-founder, pres., gen. counsel Mktg. Systems, Inc., 1994—. Author rsch. reports. Supporting mem. Boys and Girls Club Am., Pontiac, Mich., 1984—, Pontiac Rescue Mission, 1988—. Recipient Man of Yr. award Boys and Girls Clubs Am., 1988; named Hon. Citizen, Father Flanagan Boys Home, Boys Town, Nebr., 1991, Ptnr. of Conscience, Amnesty Internat., N.Y.C., 1991. Fellow AMA, Am. Acad. Ophthalmology, Am. Coll. Legal Medicine; mem. ABA, FBA, Am. Soc. Law, Medicine and Ethics, Mich. State Med. Soc., Nat. Health Lawyers Assn. Jewish. Avocations: internat. politics and fin., history, reading autobiographies, travel. Home: 4612 W Maple Rd Bloomfield Hills MI 48301-1415

ROSENFELD, MARK KENNETH, retail store executive; b. Jackson, Mich., Mar. 17, 1946; s. Nathan and Marjorie N. (Leopold) R.; children: Edward Robert, Zachary, Alix Caitlin. B.A., Amherst Coll., 1968; S.M., MIT, 1970. With Jacobson's, Jackson, 1972—, v.p., real estate group mgr., 1976-78, exec. v.p., 1978-82, pres, 1992-93; chmn. and CEO Jacobson's, Jackson, Mich., 1993—, chmn., CEO, 1993—; bd. dirs. Jacobson Stores, 275 N Woodward Co., Gt. Lakes Bancorp, TCF Fin. Corp. With U.S. Army, 1969-70. Jewish. Office: Jacobson Stores Inc 3333 Sargent Rd Jackson MI 49201-8847

ROSENFELD, MICHAEL G., medical educator. Prof. dept. medicine U. Calif. Med. Sch., La Jolla. Mem. NAS. Office: U Calif San Diego Sch Medicine M-013 Dept Medicine La Jolla CA 92093*

ROSENFELD, SARENA MARGARET, artist; b. Elmira, N.Y., Oct. 17, 1940; d. Thomas Edward and Rosalie Ereny (Fedor) Rooney; m. Robert Steven Bach, June 1958 (div. 1963); children: Robert Steven, Daniel Thomas; m. Samson Rosenfeld III, June 5, 1976. Student, Otis/Parson Art Inst., L.A., 1994—, Idyllwild Sch. Music and Arts, 1994—. One-woman shows and group exhbns. include Robert Dana Gallery, San Francisco, Gordon Gallery, Santa Monica, Calif., Hespe Gallery, San Francisco, Gallery 444, San Francisco, Art Expressions, San Diego, Ergane Gallery, N.Y.C., Nat. Mus. of Women in the Arts, Washington, also in L.A., La Jolla, Calif., Aspen, Colo., New Orleans, Soho, N.Y.C., Santa Barbara, Calif., Tanglewood, Mass., Honolulu, Johannesburg, South Africa, La Sierra U., Riverside, Calif. Mem., vol., animal handler Wildlife Waysta., Angeles Nat. Forest, Calif. Recipient Best of Show award Glendale Regional Arts Coun., 1984-85, 1st pl. awards Santa Monica Art Festival, 1982, 83, 84, 85, 86, Sweepstakes award and 1st pl., 1986, Purchase prize awards L.A. West C. of C., 1986-87, Tapestry in Talent Invitational San Jose Arts Coun., 1986, 1st pl. awards Studio City and Century City Arts Couns., 1976-84. Mem. Nat. Mus. of Women in the Arts. Republican. Home: 6570 Kelvin Ave Canoga Park CA 91306-4021

ROSENFELD, STEPHEN SAMUEL, newspaper editor; b. Pittsfield, Mass., July 26, 1932; s. Jay C. and Elizabeth R.; m. Barbara Bromson, Oct. 28, 1962; children: David, Rebecca, Emmet, James. B.A., Harvard U., 1953;; M.A., Columbia U., 1959. Reporter Berkshire Eagle, Pittsfield, 1955-57; successively reporter, fgn. corr., editorial writer, columnist, dep. editor editorial page Washington Post, 1959—. Co-author: (with Barbara Rosenfeld) Return from Red Square, 1967; author: The Time of Their Dying, 1977. Served to 1st lt. USMC, 1953-55. Mem. Coun. on Fgn. Rels., Alexandria Lit. Soc., Century Assn. Home: 202 S Saint Asaph St Alexandria VA 22314-3744 Office: Washington Post Co 1150 15th St NW Washington DC 20071-0001

ROSENFELD, STEVEN B., lawyer; b. N.Y.C., Apr. 12, 1943; s. Eugene David and Laura (Sipin) R.; m. Naomi Eve Winkler, Aug. 21, 1965; children: Kathryn Anne, Elizabeth Jane. BA, Columbia Coll., 1964; LLB, Columbia U., 1967. Bar: N.Y. 1967, D.C. 1984, U.S. Dist. Ct. (so. dist.) N.Y. 1969, U.S. Dist. Ct. (ea. dist.) N.Y. 1970, U.S. Ct. Appeals (2d cir.) 1971, U.S. Ct. Appeals (3d cir.) 1974, U.S. Ct. Appeals (Fed. cir.) 1978, D.C. 1979, U.S. Supreme Ct. 1979, U.S. Ct. Appeals (5th cir.) 1982, U.S. Ct. Appeals (6th and D.C. cirs.) 1984, U.S. Ct. Appeals (4th and 9th cirs.) 1987, U.S. Ct. Appeals (1st cir.) 1989, U.S. Ct. Appeals (10th cir.) 1991. Law clk. to Hon. Charles M. Metzner U.S. Dist. Ct. (so. dist.) N.Y., 1967-68; assoc. Rosenman & Colin, N.Y.C., 1968-71; dep. gen. counsel N.Y. State Commn. on Attica, N.Y.C., Batavia, N.Y., 1971-72; assoc. Paul, Weiss, Rifkind, Wharton & Garrison, N.Y.C., 1972-75, ptnr., 1976—; lectr. Columbia U. Sch. Law, 1995—. Contbr. articles to profl. jours. Bd. dirs. N.Y. Assn. New Ams., N.Y.C., 1973-95; trustee Dalton Sch., N.Y.C., 1988-94; trustee Putney Sch. Putney, Vt., 1995—. Mem. N.Y. State Bar Assn., Assn. of Bar of N.Y.C. (exec. com. 1992-96, past mem. various coms.), Legal Aid Soc. (pres. 1989-91, bd. dirs., exec. com. 1978-95). Democrat. Jewish. Avocations: opera and chamber music, theatre, tennis. Office: Paul Weiss Rifkind Wharton & Garrison 1285 Avenue Of The Americas New York NY 10019-6028

ROSENFELD, STEVEN IRA, artistic director, music publisher; b. Bklyn., May 24, 1949; s. Harry Allen and Rosina (DeStefano) R. BA, Southampton Coll., 1971; MFA, St. Francis Coll., Bklyn., 1975. V.p. mktg. JVC, Inc., Maspath, N.Y., 1972-74; dir. Yamaha Internat. Corp., Buena Park, Calif., 1974-75; v.p., gen. mgr. Audio Mktg. Cons., Yorktown, N.Y., 1976-88; pres. World Wide Mgmt., Yorktown, 1970—; dir. Parsec Electronics, Wilmington, Del., 1986-88; mng. dir. Westchester Shakespeare Festival, N.Y.C., 1987-90; dir. The Roger Hendricks Simon Studio, N.Y.C., 1987—; v.p. Barnett Labs., Houston, 1992-93; CEO Apple Pie Products, 1996—. Editor (newspaper) The Windmill, 1968-69. Mem. Internat. Platform Assn., Audio Engring. Soc. (cert.), Soc. Audio Cons. (cert.), Nat. Trust, Nat. Acad. Rec. Arts and Scis. Jewish. Address: PO Box 599 Yorktown Heights NY 10598-0599

ROSENFELD, STEVEN IRA, ophthalmologist; b. N.Y.C., Nov. 18, 1954; s. Frederick and Pearl (Stern) R.; m. Lisa Allyson Klar, June 24, 1978; children: Michael, Julie. BA, Johns Hopkins U., 1976; MD, Yale U., 1980. Diplomate Am. Bd. Ophthalmology, Nat. Bd. Med. Examiners. Intern Yale-New Haven Hosp., 1980-81; resident Barnes Hosp., St. Louis, 1981-84; fellow Bascom Palmer Eye Inst., Miami, Fla., 1984-85; ptnr. in pvt. practice Delray Eye Assocs., Delray Beach, Fla., 1985—; clin. instr. Bascom Palmer Eye Inst., 1985-90, asst. clin. prof., 1990—; assoc. examiner Am. Bd. Ophthalmology, Phila., 1993—. Author: Lens and Cataract: The Eye in Systemic Disease; contbr. articles to profl. jours. Recipient Harry Rosenbaum Rsch. award Washington U. Sch. Medicine, 1984; named one of Best Doctors in Am., 1996; Heed Ophthalmic Found. fellow, 1984. Fellow ACS, Am. Acad. Ophthalmology, Soc. Heed Fellows; mem. Castroviejo Corneal Soc., Eye Bank Assn. Am., Fla. Med. Assn., Fla. Soc. Ophthalmology, Assn. for Rsch. in Vision and Ophthalmology, Ocular Microbiology and Immunology Group, Phi Beta Kappa, Alpha Omega Alpha. Avocations: tennis, golf, fly fishing, lacrosse. Office: Delray Eye Assocs 16201 S Military Trl Delray Beach FL 33484-6503

ROSENFELD, WALTER DAVID, JR., architect, writer; b. N.Y.C., May 30, 1930; s. Walter David and Florence (Romann) R.; m. Marilyn Smith, Oct. 15, 1954; children: John W., Sarah E., Susannah, Elizabeth A. AB, U. Pa., 1952; postgrad. Ind. U., 1953-54, Yale U., 1954-55, 57-60. Registered architect, Mass., N.H., Pa.; cert. Nat. Coun. Archtl. Registration Bds.; cert. constrn. specifier. Draftsman, specifier Perry Dean Stewart, Boston, 1960-67; architect, specifier, v.p., prin. The Architects Collaborative, Cambridge, 1967-86, also dir., 1980-84, consulting architect Walter Rosenfeld, CSI, Newton, Mass., 1986—. Author: The Practical Specifier, 1985. Contbg. editor Progressive Architecture mag., 1980-94; contbr. articles to profl. jours. Pres. Friends of Newton Free Libr., Mass, 1970-72; chmn. Newton Ward 1 Dem. Com., 1974-80; vice chmn. designer selection com. City of Newton, 1976-86; bd. dirs. Mass. Audubon Soc., 1987—. With U.S. Army, 1955-57, Fed. Republic Germany. Mem. Constrn. Specifications Inst. (bd. dirs. Boston chpt. 1980-86, pres. Boston chpt. 1987-88), AIA, Boston Soc. Architects. Avocation: sailing. Office: Walter Rosenfeld CSI PO Box 380909 Cambridge MA 02238-0909

ROSENFELT, FRANK EDWARD, motion picture company executive; b. Peabody, Mass., Nov. 15, 1921; s. Samuel and Ethel (Litvack) R.; m. Judith Roman, Nov. 1, 1943; children: Fred, Peter, Karen. B.S., Cornell U., 1948, LL.B., 1950. Bar: N.Y. 1950, Mass. 1950, Calif. 1971. Atty. RKO Radio Pictures, 1950-55; with Metro-Goldwyn-Mayer, Inc., 1955—, pres., chief exec. officer, dir., 1973-90; chmn. bd., chief exec. officer Metro-Goldwyn-Mayer Film Co., 1980-83; vice chmn. bd. emeritus in charge European ops. Metro-Goldwyn-Mayer Film Co., London, 1983-85; vice chmn. bd. in charge European ops. MGM/UA Communications Co. (formerly MGM/UA Entertainment Co.), London, 1985-90; exec. cons. Metro-Goldwyn-Mayer Inc., Culver City, Calif., 1990—. Bd. editors: Cornell Law Quar, 1948-50. Served with inf. AUS, World War II. Decorated Purple Heart. Mem. Acad. Motion Picture Arts and Scis. (bd. govs. 1977-85), Order of Coif. Office: Metro-Goldwyn-Mayer Inc 10000 Washington Blvd Ste 3023 Culver City CA 90232-2706

ROSENFIELD, ALLAN, physician; b. Cambridge, Mass., Apr. 28, 1933; s. Harold Herman and Beatrice (Garber) R.; m. Clare Stein, July 31, 1966; children: Paul Allan, Jill Emilie. BA cum laude, Harvard U., 1955; MD, Columbia U., 1959. Diplomate Am. Bd. Ob-Gyn. Intern, surgical resident Beth Israel Hosp., Boston, 1959-61; resident in ob-gyn Boston Hosp. for Women (now Brigham and Woman's Hosp.), Boston, 1963-66; rep., med. advisor The Population Council and Ministry Pub. Health, Bangkok, 1967-73; asst. dir. tech. assistance div. The Population Council, N.Y.C., 1973-75; prof. ob-gyn Columbia U., N.Y.C., 1975-88, prof. pub. health, 1975-86, DeLamar Prof. pub. health, 1986—, dir. ctr. for population and family health, 1975-88, acting chmn. dept. ob-gyn., 1984-86, dean sch. pub. health, 1986—. Contbr. over 100 articles to profl. jours. Capt. USAF, 1961-63. Fellow Am. Coll. Obstetricians and Gynecologists; mem. Inst. Medicine of NAS (several coms. and bds.), Am. Pub. Health Assn. Jewish. Avocations: tennis, skiing, music. Home: 4 Crosshill Rd Hartsdale NY 10530-3014 Office: Columbia U Sch Pub Health 600 W 168th St New York NY 10032-3702

ROSENFIELD, BRUCE ALAN, lawyer; b. Mpls., Apr. 30, 1951; s. Arnold M. and Phyllis M. (Fruchtman) R.; m. Bonnie S. Brier, Aug. 15, 1976; children: Rebecca, Elizabeth, Benjamin. AB, Dartmouth Coll., 1973; JD, Stanford U., 1976. Bar: Pa. 1976, U.S. Dist. Ct. (ea. dist.) Pa. 1976. Law clk. to Hon. Raymond Broderick U.S. Dist. Ct. (ea. dist.) Pa., Phila., 1976-78; assoc. Schnader, Harrison, Segal & Lewis, Phila., 1978-85, ptnr., 1986—; cons. Pa. Joint State Govt. Adv. Com. on Decedent and Estate Laws, 1991—; bd. dirs. Rittenhouse Fin. Svcs. Fellow Am. Coll. Trust and Estate Coun.; mem. Pa. Bar Assn. (coun. real property and trust law sect. 1995—), Phila. Bar Assn. (chmn. probate sect. 1993). Home: 132 Fairview Rd Penn Valley PA 19072-1331 Office: Schnader Harrison Segal & Lewis 1600 Market St Ste 3600 Philadelphia PA 19103-7240

ROSENFIELD, JAMES HAROLD, communications executive; b. Boston, July 18, 1929; s. Harold and Beatrice (Garber) R.; m. Nancy Lee Stenbuck, Oct. 19, 1952; 2 children. BA, Dartmouth Coll., 1952; D of Comml. Sci. (hon.), St. John's U., 1981. TV network sales exec. NBC, N.Y.C., 1954-57; advt. mgr. Polaroid Corp., Boston, 1956-59; v.p. mktg. Airequipt, Inc., New Rochelle, N.Y., 1959-65; TV account exec. CBS, Inc., N.Y.C., 1965-67, dir. daytime sales, 1967-70, v.p. Ea. sales, 1970-75, v.p. network sales adminstrn., 1975-77, v.p., nat. sales mgr., 1977, pres. TV Network Div., 1977-81; exec. v.p. CBS/Broadcast Group, N.Y.C., 1981-83, sr. exec. v.p., 1983-86; chmn., CEO John Blair Communications, Inc., N.Y.C., 1987-93; pres. JHR Assocs., Consulting, N.Y.C., 1993; mng. dir. Veronis, Suhler & Assocs., N.Y.C., 1994—. Mem. nat. bd. dirs. Jr. Achievement Inc.; past alumni trustee Roxbury Latin Sch., Mass.; bd. dirs., former chmn. Advt. Coun. With Signal Corps, AUS, 1950-53. Mem. NATAS (bd. dirs. internat. coun.), Internat. Radio and TV Soc. (past pres.).

ROSENFIELD, JAY GARY, publisher; b. Roslyn, N.Y., June 25, 1948; s. Maurice Ullman and Harriet Jessica (Obstfield) R.; m. Lily Schwartzberg, Aug. 23, 1975; children—Adam, Amanda. B.A. in History, Ithaca Coll., 1970. Pres. Reese Communications, N.Y.C., 1970—, creator, founder, pub. Video mag., 1977—; pres. R.G.H. Pub. Inc., 1989—; pres., mem. bd. dirs. Art Levis Found. Bd. dirs. Denton Green Sr. Dwellings, Inc., New Hyde Park, N.Y., 1979—. Mem. ACLU, Whipporwill Assn. (bd. dirs. 1988—), Internat. Motoring Press Assn. Office: Video Mag Hachette Filipacchi Mags 1633 Broadway New York NY 10019

ROSENFIELD, JOHN MAX, art educator; b. Dallas, Oct. 9, 1924; s. John M. and Claire (Burger) R.; m. Ella Hopper, Jan. 2, 1948; children—Sarah, Paul Thomas. Student, U. Tex., 1941-43; BA, U. Calif., Berkeley, 1945; BFA, So. Meth. U., 1947; MFA, U. Iowa, 1949; PhD, Harvard U., 1959. Instr. art U. Iowa, 1949, 52-54; asst. prof. UCLA, 1957-60; rsch. fellow Harvard U., 1960-65, faculty, 1965-91, prof. art, 1968-91, Abby Aldrich Rockefeller prof. East Asian Art, 1974-91, chmn. dept. fine arts, 1971-76, curator Asian Art, 1976-91, acting dir. Art Mus., 1982-85, emeritus, 1991—. Author: Dynastic Arts of the Kushans, 1967; Japanese Art of the Heian Period, 1967; co-author: Traditions of Japanese Art, 1970, Courtly Tradition of Japanese Art and Literature, 1972, Journey of Three Jewels, 1979, Song of the Brush, 1979, Masters of Japanese Calligraphy, 1984; editor: Archives of Asian Art, 1973-84, Japanese Arts Library, 1977-80. Trustee Mus. Fine Arts, Boston, 1975-77. Served with AUS, 1943-46, 50-51. Mem. Assn. Asian Studies, Coll. Art Assn., Am. Acad. Benares, Am. Acad. Arts and Scis. Research history Buddhist art and Japanese art. Home: 75 Coolidge Rd Arlington MA 02174-7737 Office: Harvard U 32 Quincy St Cambridge MA 02138-3845*

ROSENFIELD, ROBERT LEE, pediatric endocrinologist, educator; b. Robinson, Ill., Dec. 16, 1934; s. Irving and Sadie (Osipe) R.; m. Sandra L. McVicker, Apr. 14, 1973. BS, Northwestern U., 1956, MD, 1960. Diplomate Am. Bd. Pediatric Endocrinology. Intern, Phila. Gen. Hosp. and Children's Hosp., Phila., 1960-63, 65-68; practice medicine specializing in pediatric endocrinology; prof. pediatrics, medicine U. Chgo., 1968—. Contbr. research articles to profl. jours. Served to capt. USMC, 1963-65. Fogarty Sr. Internat. fellow, USPHS, Weizmann Inst., Israel, 1977-78. Mem. Am. Bd. Pediatrics (sub.-bd. pediatric endocrinology 1983-86), Am. Pediatric Soc., Lawson Wilkins Pediatric Endocrinology Soc., Endocrine Soc., Soc. Gynecol. Investigation, Chgo. Pediatric Soc. (pres. 1981). Democrat. Jewish. Avocation: photography. Home: 5474 S Greenwood Ave Chicago IL 60615-5104 Office: U Chgo Med Ctr 5841 S Maryland Ave Chicago IL 60637-1463

ROSENGREN, WILLIAM R., lawyer, corporation executive; b. 1934; LL.B., U. Minn., 1959. Pvt. practice, 1959-67; instr. bus. law U. Minn., 1963-69; Asst. sec. and sr. atty. Internat. Multifoods Corp., to 1973; with Ecolab Inc., St. Paul, 1973—, v.p., gen. counsel, 1973, v.p., sec., gen. counsel, 1974-83, sr. v.p., gen. counsel, sec., 1983-92; sr. v.p. law, gen. counsel, 1992—. Office: Ecolab Inc Ecolab Ctr 370 Wabasha St N Saint Paul MN 55102-1306

ROSENHEIM, DANIEL EDWARD, journalist, newspaper editor; b. Chgo., Aug. 12, 1949; s. Edward W. and Margaret Morton (Keeney) R.; m. Christina J. Adachi, May 10, 1976 (div. 1979); m. Cindy Catherine Salans, June 20, 1980; children: Joseph Michael, James Salans, Nicholas Edward. BA, Wesleyan U., 1971. Factory worker Pitts. and Chgo., 1972-77; reporter Sun-Jour., Lansing, Ill., 1977; bus./labor editor Hammond (Ind.) Times, 1977-80; bus. writer Chgo. Sun Times, 1980-82, spl. writer, 1982-84; bus. writer Chgo. Tribune, 1984-85; econs. editor San Francisco Chronicle, 1985-87, city editor, 1987-95, mng. editor, 1995—. Mem. Am. Soc. Newspapers Editors, San Francisco Tennis Club. Avocations: tennis, golf, fly fishing. Office: San Francisco Chronicle 901 Mission St San Francisco CA 94103-2905

ROSENHEIM, DONALD EDWIN, electrical engineer; b. N.Y.C., Mar. 23, 1926; s. Seymour Lawrence and Leah Rebecca (Rosenberg) R.; m. Judith Comfort Hyman, June 22, 1958; children—Micah Robert, Jay Aaron. B.S. in Elec. Engring. magna cum laude, Poly. Inst. Bklyn., 1949; M.S., Columbia U., 1957. Devel. engr. Servo Corp. Am., 1949-51; mem. research staff IBM Corp., 1951—; dir. San Jose (Calif.) Rsch. Lab., 1973-83, dir. tech. coordination, 1983-84; asst. dir. Almaden Rsch. Ctr., San Jose, 1984-92. Fellow IEEE; mem. Sigma Xi, Tau Beta Pi, Eta Kappa Nu. Home: 128 Smith Creek Dr Los Gatos CA 95030-1634

ROSENHEIM, EDWARD WEIL, English educator; b. Chgo., May 15, 1918; s. Edward Weil and Fannie (Kohn) R.; m. Margaret Morton Keeney, June 20, 1947; children: Daniel Edward, James Morton, Andrew Keeney. B.A., U. Chgo., 1939, M.A., 1946, Ph.D., 1953. Publicity writer Pub. Relations Service, Chgo., 1939-40; instr. Gary (Ind.) Coll., 1946; faculty U. Chgo., 1947—, prof. English, 1962—, David B. and Clara E. Stern prof., 1980-88, prof. emeritus, 1988—, assoc. chmn. dept. English, 1967-75, dir. broadcasting for univ., 1954-57; dir. Nat. Humanities Inst., 1977-80; Disting. vis. prof. Pa. State U., 1961; Disting. lectr. Nat. Coun. Tchrs. English, 1967; mem. Ill. Humanities Coun., 1982—, pres., 1985-87. Author: What Happens in Literature, 1960, Swift and the Satirist's Art, 1963; editor: Selected Prose and Poetry of Jonathan Swift, 1958, Jour. Gen. Edn., 1954-56; co-editor: Modern Philology, 1968-88. Served to capt. inf. AUS, 1941-46. Recipient Alumni Svc. medal U. Chgo., 1990; Willet Faculty fellow, 1962, Guggenheim Meml. fellow, 1967. Mem. Am. Soc. 18th Century Studies, Johnson Soc. (pres. Central region 1971). Clubs: Quadrangle, Wayfarers, Caxton. Home: 5805 S Dorchester Ave Chicago IL 60637-1730 Office: 1050 E 59th St Chicago IL 60637-1512

ROSENHEIM, HOWARD HARRIS, management consultant; b. Williamson, W.Va., Oct. 1, 1915; s. William Spiller and Frances Minerva (Harris) R.; m. Marjorie Jane Griffin, June 30, 1945; children: Cathy (Mrs. Mark Bustamante), William Spiller. B.S., Northwestern U., 1936, M.B.A., 1954; grad., Advanced Mgmt. Program, Harvard U. Grad. Sch. Bus., 1956. Civilian dir. indsl. planning div. USAF, Dayton, Ohio, 1947; pres. Internat. Register Co., elec. mfg. co., Chgo., 1948-70; pres. home study sch. Internat. Accts. Soc., Chgo., 1971; pres. Denoyer-Geppert Co. ednl. pub. subs. Times Mirror Co., Chgo., 1972-79, Internat. Assocs., Ltd., cons., 1980—; chmn. Camelot Controls, Ltd. (Eng.), 1966-70; dir. Extel Corp., Chgo., Telecommunication Radio Inc., Chgo., Data One, Inc., Chgo.; Vis. prof. bus. Northwestern U., Evanston, Ill., 1956-71, trustee, 1968-70; cons. Presdl. Commn. Nat. Air Policy, 1947; adv. to ministry of edn. Kingdom of Saudi Arabia, 1976-79. Pub. over 800 titles of ednl. materials in Arabic for schs. in Saudi Arabia; author articles to profl. jours. Served to maj. USAF, 1942-46. Decorated Award of Merit; recipient Disting. Educator award Northwestern U., 1972. Mem. Am. Mktg. Assn., Northwestern U. Alumni Assn. (pres. 1966-67). Methodist (mem. ofcl. bd. 1965-70). Clubs: Union League (Chgo.); Park Ridge (Ill.) Country. Inventor various time switches. Home: 2411 Farrell Ave Park Ridge IL 60068-1167

ROSENHEIM, MARGARET KEENEY, social welfare policy educator; b. Grand Rapids, Mich., Sept. 5, 1926; d. Morton and Nancy (Billings) Keeney; m. Edward W. Rosenheim, June 20, 1947; children: Daniel, James, Andrew. Student, Wellesley Coll., 1943-45; J.D., U. Chgo., 1949. Bar: Ill. 1949. Mem. faculty Sch. Social Service Adminstrn., U. Chgo., 1950—, assoc. prof., 1961-66, prof., 1966—, Helen Ross prof. social welfare policy, 1975—, dean, 1978-83; lectr. in law U. Chgo., 1980—; vis. prof. U. Wsh., 1965, Duke U., 1984; acad. visitor London Sch. Econs., 1973; cons. Pres.'s Commn. Law Enforcement and Adminstrn. Justice, 1966-67, Nat. Advt. Commn. Criminal Justice Standards and Goals, 1972; mem. Juvenile Justice Standards Commn., 1973-76; trustee Carnegie Corp. N.Y., 1979-87, Children's Home and Aid Soc. of Ill., 1981—; dir. Nat. Inst. Dispute Resolution, 1981-89, Nuveen Bond Funds, 1982—; mem. Chgo. Network, 1983. Editor, contbr.: Justice for the Child, 1962, reprinted, 1977, Pursuing Justice for the Child, 1976, Early Parenthood and Coming of Age in the 1990s, 1992; contbr. articles and book revs. to profl. jours. Home: 5805 S Dorchester Ave Chicago IL 60637-1730 Office: 969 E 60th St Chicago IL 60637-2640

ROSENHOFFER, CHRIS, lawyer; b. Cin., Apr. 19, 1913; s. Joseph and Barbara (Stitzel) R.; m. Alberta Arlene Jarvis, Dec. 28, 1935 (div. Apr. 1992); children: Chris Jr., Dennis P., Gary A., John J., Nancy A., Todd D. BS Commerce, Salmon P. Chase Coll. Commerce, Cin., 1948; JD, Salmon P. Chase Coll. Law, Cin., 1951. Bar: Ohio, 1951, U.S. Dist. Ct. (so. dist.) Ohio 1952. Acct., log buyer Al J. Boehm Walnut Co., Kenova, W.Va., 1938-44; acct. The Green Embry Co., Cin., 1948-51; judge Clermont County Ct., Batavia, Ohio, 1958-62, 67-86; pvt. practice law Batavia, 1951—; spl. counsel Atty. Gen. of Ohio, Batavia, 1963-64. Treas. Clermont County Rep. Club, Batavia, 1957-58; team mem. Citizens Amb. Program, Seattle, 1988, 93; mem. sch. bd. West Clermont Local Sch. Dist., Amelia, Ohio, 1958-74. With U.S. Army, 1944-46. Mem. Ohio State Bar Assn., Ohio Acad. Trial Lawyers, Clermont County Bar Assn. (pres. 1962), Cin. Bar Assn., Am. Legion. Methodist. Avocations: fishing, hunting. Office: 97 Main St Batavia OH 45103

ROSENHOUSE, IRWIN J., artist, designer; b. Chgo.. B.F.A., Cooper Union, N.Y.C., 1950. Designer Mus. Modern Art, 1954-57, Harcourt, Brace & Co., 1957, Dell Books, 1963; tchr. art Mus. Modern Art, 1967-69, Pratt Graphic Center, N.Y.C., 1972, 85, Bklyn. Coll., 1972-73, Bklyn. Mus. Art Sch., 1974, Nassau C.C., 1972-96, N.Y. Tech. Coll., 1983-86; owner Rosenhouse Gallery, N.Y.C., 1963-72; lectr. art, book illustration, design; preparer graphics for Arab-Israeli peace confs.: The Road to Peace, Convocation for Peace, N.Y.C., 1989-90; dir. monthly ednl. lecture series N.Y. Artist Equity, 1989-91. One-man shows N.Y.C., Bklyn., Easthampton, N.Y., Dance Theater Workshop Gallery, N.Y.C., 1992, also various colls. and mus. in U.S.; exhibited in group shows numerous mus., painting socs. exhbns. throughout U.S.; represented in permanent collections Met. Mus., N.Y. Pub. Libr., Everhart Mus., Cooper Union Mus., Bklyn. Coll. Collection; illustrator: (juvenile) Have You Seen Trees?. Served with U.S. Mcht. Marine, 1944-51. Recipient Louis Comfort Tiffany Found. award, 2 Huntington Hartford Found. awards, Billboard Ann. award, Illustrators Club award, 1st prize Rome Collaborative; record cover designs included in Smithsonian ethnic music collection. Address: 256 Mott St New York NY 10012-3457 *Humanist imagery has been my main concern and the pursuit of a simple, direct image of nature.*

ROSENKER, MARK VICTOR, trade association executive; b. Balt., Dec. 8, 1946; s. Stanley and Irene (Moss) R.; m. Heather Beldon. BA in Communications, U. Md., 1969, postgrad., 1970-71; grad., USAF Air Command and Staff Coll., 1986, USAF Air War Coll., 1990. Asst. to events producer, relief engr. ABC-TV News, Washington, 1968-69; dep. dir. radio and TV Com. Reelect Pres., Washington, 1972; staff asst. to sec. U.S. Dept. Interior, Washington, 1972-73; account exec. Daniel Edelman Pub. Relations, Inc., Washington, 1973-75; dir. communications Motorized Bicycle Assn., Washington, 1975; dep. press sec. Pres. Ford Com., Washington, 1976; v.p. Electronic Industries Assn., Washington, 1977—; bd. of vis. Cmty. Coll. USAF, Maxwell, Ala., 1981-86; apptd. commr. Am. Battle Monument Commn., 1990-94. Active Campaign to Elect Reagan/Bush, Washington, 1980, 84, Campaign to Elect Bush/Quayle, 1988, 92—; cons. Bob Dole Presdl. campaign, 1995-96. 1st lt. USAF, 1969-72, col. USAFR, 1972—. Recipient Chuck Docekal Meml. award, 1987, Am. Battle Monuments Commn. Meritorious Svc. award, 1994. Mem. Am. Soc. Assn. Execs., Greater Washington Soc. Assn. Execs., Res. Officers Assn. Club, Capitol Hill Club, Army Navy Club. Avocations: sailing, tennis, skiing, golf. Home: 1626 Great Falls St Mc Lean VA 22101-5079 Office: Electronic Industries Assn 2500 Wilson Blvd Arlington VA 22201-3834

ROSENKOETTER, GERALD EDWIN, engineering and construction company executive; b. St. Louis, Mar. 16, 1927; s. Herbert Charles and Edna Mary (Englege) R.; m. Ruth June Beekman, Sept. 10, 1949; children: Claudia Ruth, Carole Lee. BSCE, Washington U., St. Louis, 1951; MSCE, Sever Inst. Tech., St. Louis, 1957. Registered profl. engr. Colo., Del., D.C., Fla., Ga., Idaho, Kans., Mass., Mich., Mo., N.C., N.J., Ohio, Pa., Tex., Utah, Wis. Sr. structural engr. Sverdrup & Parcel, Inc., St. Louis, 1951-56, project engr., 1956-60; engring. mgr. Sverdrup & Parcel, Inc., Denver, 1960-62; project mgr. Sverdrup & Parcel & Assocs., St. Louis, 1962-69, chief engr., 1969-74, v.p., 1974-80; pres. SPCM, Inc., St. Louis, 1980-85; exec. v.p. Sverdrup Corp., St. Louis, 1985-88, vice-chmn., 1988-93; pres. Sverdrup Hydro, Inc., 1988-93; engr. and fin. cons. Sarasota, 1993—; asst. prof. Washington U., 1955-60; ptnr. 3 Sverdrup Partnerships, 1977-93; expert witness Sverdrup & Parcel & Assocs., 1970-75; cons. engring. and constrn. projects, 1993—. Councilman City of Berkeley, Mo., 1956-58, councilman-at-large, 1958-60, chmn. city planning and zoning com., 1963-65; dir. Conservatory and Sch. Arts, St. Louis, 1989-92. Sgt. U.S. Army, 1945-46. Engrs. Club of St. Louis scholar, 1950. Mem. ASCE (chmn. continuing edn. 1965-66, named Outstanding Sr. Engring. Student 1951), Forest Hills Country Club (St. Louis), Bent Tree Country Club (Sarasota, Fla.). Lutheran. Avocations: golfing, sailing.

ROSENKRANTZ, DANIEL J., computer science educator; b. Bklyn., Mar. 5, 1943; s. Harry and Ruth (Sirota) R.; m. Carole Jaffee, Aug. 2, 1969; children: Holly, Sherry, Jody, Andrew. BS, Columbia U., 1963, MS, 1964, PhD, 1967. With Bell Telephone Labs., Murray Hill, N.J., 1966-67; info. scientist GE Co. R & D Ctr., Schenectady, N.Y., 1967-77; prof. dept. computer sci. U. Albany-SUNY, Albany, 1977—, dept. chair, 1993—; prin. computer scientist Phoenix Data Systems, Albany, 1983-85. Author: (with P.M. Lewis II and R.E. Stearns) Compiler Design Theory, 1976. Fellow ACM (editor-in-chief jour. 1986-91, area editor for formal langs. and models of computation 1981-86, mem. numerous conf. coms.); mem. IEEE Computer Soc., ACM Spl. Interest Group on Automata and Computability Theory (sec. 1977-79). Home: 1261 Cranbrook Ct Niskayuna NY 12309-1203 Office: SUNY Dept Computer Sci Albany NY 12222

ROSENKRANZ, HERBERT S., environmental toxicology educator, cancer researcher; b. Vienna, Sept. 27, 1933; came to U.S., 1948; s. Samuel and Lea Rose (Marilles) R.; m. Deanna Eloise Green, Jan. 27, 1959; children: Pnina Gail, Eli Joshua, Margalit E., Dara V., Jeremy Amiel, Sara C., Naomi, Tsilila. BS, CCNY, 1954; PhD, Cornell U., 1959. Postdoctoral fellow Sloan-Kettering Inst. for Cancer Rsch., 1959-60, U. Pa., Phila., 1960-61; asst. prof. microbiology Columbia U., N.Y.C., 1961-65, assoc. prof., 1965-69, prof., 1969-76; prof., chmn. microbiology dept. N.Y. Med. Coll., Valhalla, 1976-81; prof. Case Western Res. U., Cleve., 1981-90, dir. Ctr. Environ. Health Sci., 1981-84, chmn. dept. environ. health sci., 1985-90; prof., chmn. dept. environ. and occupational health U. Pitts., 1990—, dir. Ctr Environ. and Occupational Health and Toxicology. Lalor Found. awardee, 1963; Nat. Cancer Inst. Research Career Devel. awardee, 1965-75. Mem. AAAS, Am. Assn. Cancer Research, Am. Soc. Biol. Chemists, Environ. Mutagen Soc., Soc. Toxicology. Jewish. Office: U Pitts Grad Sch Pub Health Dept Environ and Occup Health 260 Kappa Dr Pittsburgh PA 15238-2818

ROSENKRANZ, ROBERT BERNARD, military officer; b. Paterson, N.J., Sept. 26, 1939; s. Irving Morton and Lucille (Kane) R.; m. Barbara Jean Larson, May 17, 1970; children: Stephen Robert, Deborah Anne, Diana Rebecca, Susan Leslie. BS, U.S. Mil. Acad., 1961; MA, U. Pa., 1969. Comd. 2d. lt. U.S. Army, 1961, advanced through grades to maj. gen., 1992; officer U.S. Army, Fed. Republic of Germany, 1962-65; battalion exec. officer U.S. Army, Korea, 1973-74; battery comdr. U.S. Army, Vietnam, 1966-67; battery and brigade comdr. U.S. Army, Fed. Republic of Germany, 1977-79, 83-85; assoc. prof. U.S. Mil. Acad., West Point, N.Y., 1969-72; dir. soviet studies U.S. Army War Coll., Carlisle, Pa., 1981-83; sr. mil. asst. under sec. of def. Pentagon, Washington, 1986-88; dep. dir. Army Ops., Readiness and Mobilization U.S. Army Pentagon, Washington, 1988-89, dir. force programs, 1989-92; comdr. U.S. Army Optec, Washington, 1992-95; v.p. test and evaluation/ranges Dyncorp, Reston, Va., 1995—. Decorated Bronze Star, Air medal; recipient Superior Svc. medal U.S. Dept. Def., 1988, D.S.M., 1992, 95. Mem. Internat. Inst. of Strategic Studies, Assn. of the U.S. Army, Internat. Test and Evaluation Assn. Republican. Jewish. Avocations: jogging, reading, woodworking, golf, racquetball. Home: 3222 Wynford Dr Fairfax VA 22031-2828

ROSENKRANZ, STANLEY WILLIAM, lawyer; b. N.Y.C., Aug. 20, 1933; s. Jacob and Adele R.; m. Judith Ossinsky, Aug. 14, 1960; children: Jack Michael, Andrew Lawrence. BS in Acctg, U. Fla., 1955, JD with honors, 1960; LLM (Kenneson fellow), NYU, 1961. Bar: Fla. 1960, Ga. 1970; cert. tax lawyer. Mem. firm Macfarlane, Ferguson, Allison & Kelly, Tampa, Fla., 1961-68, 71-79; with King & Spalding, Atlanta, 1969-71, Holland & Knight, Tampa, 1979-86, Shear, Newman, Hahn & Rosenkranz P.A., Tampa, 1986—; adj. prof. Grad. Sch. Law, U. Fla., 1975-79, Grad. Coll. Bus. Adminstrn., U. Tampa, 1989; dir. Life Savs. Bank, 1979-88. Pres. Congregation Schaarai Zedek, Tampa, 1981-83; bd. dirs. Union Am. Hebrew Congregations, 1990—, v.p. S.E. region, 1988-90, pres., 1992—. With U.S. Army, 1955-57. Named Young Man of Year Tampa Jaycees, Fla., 1967. Mem.

ABA, Am. Coll. Tax Counsel, Am. Law Inst., Fla. Bar Assn., Ga. Bar Assn., Greater Tampa C. of C. (bd. govs., chmn. anti-drug task force). Home: 1125 Shipwatch Cir Tampa FL 33602-5785 Office: 201 E Kennedy Blvd Tampa FL 33602

ROSENMAN, LEONARD, composer; b. Brooklyn, N.Y., Sept. 7, 1924. Condr. Rome, 1962-66; instr. U. So. Calif.; musical dir. New Muse Chamber Orch. Music dir., composer: (film scores) The Outsider, 1962, Barry Lyndon, 1975 (Academy award best adapted score 1975), Bound for Glory, 1976 (Academy award best adapted score 1976), The Lord of the Rings, 1978; music condr.: (TV movies) Sherlock Holmes in New York, 1976; composer: (film scores) The Cobweb, 1955, East of Eden, 1955, Rebel without a Cause, 1955, Bombers B-52, 1957, Edge of the City, 1957, The Young Stranger, 1957, Lafayette Escadrille, 1958, Pork Chop Hill, 1959, The Bramble Bush, 1960, The Crowded Sky, 1960, The Plunderers, 1960, The Rise and Fall of Legs Diamond, 1960, The Chapman Report, 1962, Convicts Four, 1962, Hell is for Heroes, 1962, A Covenant with Death, 1966, Fantastic Voyage, 1966, Countdown, 1968, The Savage Land, 1969, Beneath the Planet of the Apes, 1970, A Man Called Horse, 1970, The Todd Killings, 1971, Battle for the Planet of the Apes, 1973, Race with the Devil, 1975, Birch Interval, 1976, The Car, 1977, 9/30/55, 1977, An Enemy of the People, 1978, Promises in the Dark, 1979, Prophecy, 1979, Hide in Plain Sight, 1980, The Jazz Singer, 1980, Making Love, 1982, Cross Creek, 1983 (Academy award nomination best original score 1983), Heart of the Stag, 1984, Sylvia, 1985, Star Trek IV: The Voyage Home, 1986 (Academy award nomination best original score 1986), Robocop 2, 1990, Ambition, 1991, (TV movie scores) Banyon, 1971, In Broad Daylight, 1971, Vanished, 1971, The Bravos, 1972, The Cat Creature, 1973, Judge Dee and the Monastery Murders, 1974, Nakia, 1974, The Phantom of Hollywood, 1974, The First Thirty-Six Hours of Dr. Durant, 1975, Sky Heist, 1975, Kingston: The Power Play, 1976, Lanigan's Rabbi, 1976, Sybil, 1976 (Emmy award best music composition for dramatic underscore 1977), Mary White, 1977, The Possessed, 1977, The Other Side of Hell, 1978, Friendly Fire, 1979 (Emmy award best music composition for dramatic underscore 1979), Nero Wolfe, 1979, City in Fear, 1980, Murder in Texas, 1981, The Wall, 1982, Celebrity, 1984, Heartsounds, 1984, The Return of Marcus Welby, M.D., 1984, First Steps, 1985, Promised a Miracle, 1988, Where Pigeons Go to Die, 1990, Aftermath: A Test of Love, 1991, Keeper of the City, 1992, (TV series scores) Men from Shiloh, 1970, Primus, 1971, Nakia, 1974, Gibbsville, 1976, Holmes and Yoyo, 1976, Rafferty, 1977, Joshua's World, 1980, (musical works) Threnody on a Song of K.R., 1971, Chamber Music 5, 1979, Foci I, 1981.

ROSENN, HAROLD, lawyer; b. Plains, Pa., Nov. 4, 1917; s. Joseph and Jennie (Wohl) R.; m. Sallyanne Frank, Sept. 19, 1948; 1 child, Frank Scott. BA, U. Mich., 1939, JD, 1941; LLD (hon.), Coll. Misericordia, 1991. Bar: Pa. 1942, U.S. Supreme Ct. 1957. Ptnr. Rosenn & Rosenn, Wilkes Barre, Pa., 1948-54; ptnr. Rosenn, Jenkins & Greenwald, Wilkes Barre, 1954-87, of counsel, 1988—; mem. Pa. State Bd. Law Examiners, 1983-93, Pa. Gov.'s Justice Commn., 1968-73, Pa. Crime Commn., 1968-73, Fed. Jud. Nominating Com., Pa., 1977-79, Appellate Ct. Nominating Com., Pa., 1979-81; asst. dist. atty. Luzerne County, Pa., 1952-54. Chmn. ARC, Wilkes-Barre, 1958-60 (life mem. bd.); pres. Pa. Coun. on Crime and Delinquency, Harrisburg, 1969-71; bd. dirs. Coll. Misericordia, Dallas, Pa., 1976-86, emeritus, 1986—, Hoyt Libr., Kingston, Pa., 1971-78, Nat. Coun. on Crime and Delinquency, N.Y.C., 1969-71; chmn. United Way Campaign of Wyoming Valley, 1978-80; pres. Temple Israel of Wilkes Barre, 1972-74 (chmn. bd. 1974-84, life mem. bd.); comdr. post 395 Am. Legion, Kingston, 1948; mem. bd. dirs. Keystone State Games, 1982—. Capt. USAAF, 1942-45, ETO. Decorated presdl. citation with cluster; recipient Erasmus medal Dutch Govt., Disting. Svc. award in Trusteeship, Assn. Governing Bds. Univs. and Colls., 1990; Disting. Community Svc. award Greater Wilkes-Barre Soc. Fellows Anti-Defamation League, 1991, Clara Barton honor award Wyoming Valley chpt. ARC, 1992, Lifetime Achievement award United Way of Wyoming Valley, 1992; honoree Wyoming Valley Interfaith Coun., 1986; named Golden Key Vol. of Yr., United Way of Pa., 1989. Mem. ABA, Pa. Bar Assn., Am. Judicature Soc., The Pa. Soc. Republican. Jewish. Clubs: U. Mich. (N.E. Pa.) (pres. 1946-76), Westmoreland (Wilkes Barre). Lodge: B'nai Brith (pres. Wilkes Barre 1952-53, Community Service award 1976).

ROSENN, KEITH SAMUEL, lawyer, educator; b. Wilkes-Barre, Pa., Dec. 9, 1938; s. Max and Tillie R. (Hershkowitz) R.; m. Nan Raker, June 21, 1960; 1 child, Eva; m. Silvia R. Rudge, Mar. 21, 1968; children—Jonathan, Marcia. A.B., Amherst Coll., 1960; LL.B., Yale U., 1963. Bar: Pa. 1964, U.S. Ct. Appeals (3d cir.) 1979, Fla. 1981, U.S. Ct. Appeals (11th cir.) 1982. Law clk. to Judge Smith U.S. Ct. Appeals for 2d Circuit, 1963-64; asst. prof. law Ohio State U. Coll. Law, 1965-68, assoc. prof., 1968-70, prof., 1970-79; project assoc. Ford Found., Rio de Janeiro, 1966-68; assoc. Escritorio Augusto Nobre, Rio de Janeiro, 1979-80; prof. law U. Miami, Fla., 1979—; project coordinator Olin Fellowship Program Law and Econs. Ctr., U. Miami, Fla., 1980-81, assoc. dean Law Sch., 1982-83, dir. fgn. grad. law program, 1985—; cons. Hudson Inst., 1977, U.S. State Dept., 1981-82, World Bank, 1988-90; Fulbright lectr. Argentina, 1987, 88. Author: (with Karst) Law and Development in Latin America, 1975; Law and Inflation, 1982, Foreign Investment in Brazil, 1991; co-editor: A Panorama of Brazilian Law, 1992; advisor InterAm. Law Rev.; contbr. articles to law jours. Recipient Order of Democracy award Congress of Republic of Colombia, 1987, Lawyer of the Ams. award, 1989; grantee Social Sci. Rsch. Coun., 1970, Dana Found., 1982. Mem. ABA, Am. Law Inst., Inter-Am. Bar Assn., Fla. Bar, Am. Soc. Comparative Law (bd. dirs.). Jewish. Office: U Miami Law Sch PO Box 248087 Coral Gables FL 33124

ROSENN, MAX, federal judge; b. Plains, Pa., Feb. 4, 1910; s. Joseph and Jennie (Wohl) R.; m. Tillie R. Hershkowitz, Mar. 18, 1934; children: Keith S., Daniel Wohl. BA, Cornell U., 1929; LLB, U. Pa., 1932. Bar: Pa. 1932, U.S. Supreme Ct. 1955, Cts. of Philippines 1946. Gen. practice Wilkes-Barre, Pa., 1932-41; dir. Franklin Fed. Savs. & Loan, Wilkes-Barre, 1937-70; spl. counsel Pa. Dept. Justice, 1939; asst. dist. atty. Luzerne County, 1942-44; also solicitor various mcpl. boroughs, ptnr. firm Rosenn & Rosenn, 1947-54, Rosenn, Jenkins & Grenwald, Wilkes-Barre, 1954-66, 67-70; sec. pub. welfare Pa., 1966-67; judge U.S. Ct. Appeals (3d cir.), 1970-81, sr. judge, 1981—; former mem. criminal procedure rules com. Supreme Ct. Pa., 1958-85; mem. Pa. Commn. to Revise Pub. Employee Laws, 1968-69; Pa. chmn. White House Conf. on Children and Youth. Contbr. articles to legal pubs. Mem. Pa. Bd. Pub. Welfare, 1963-66; chmn. Pa. Gov.'s Hosp. Study Commn., Pa. Gov.'s Coun. for Human Svcs., 1966-67; mem. exec. bd. Commonwealth of Pa., 1966-67; chmn. Commn. Met. Govt., 1957-58; pres. Property Owners Assn. Luzerne County, 1955-57; chmn. Pa. Human Rels. Commn., 1969-70, Pa. Comm. Children and Youth, 1968-70, Legis. Task Force Structure for Human Svcs., 1970; alt. del. Rep. Nat. Conv., 1964; pres. Wyoming Valley Jewish Com., 1941-42; life trustee Wilkes-Barre Jewish Community Ctr.; chmn. Flood Recovery Task Force, 1972. Fellow Am. Coll. Trial Lawyers, Internat. Acad. Trial Lawyers; mem. ABA, Pa. Bar Assn., Luzerne County Bar Assn., Am. Law Inst., Am. Soc. Law and Medicine (charter mem., former assoc. editor jour.), Am. Judicature Soc., B'nai B'rith (pres. dist. grand lodge 1947-48, life bd. govs., former chmn. bd. dirs. Anti-Defamation League Pa., W.Va. and Del. 1955-58, nat. commr. 1964—), Westmoreland Club, Masons (33d degree), Alpha Epsilon Pi. Jewish. Office: US Ct Appeals 229 US Courthouse 197 Main St Wilkes Barre PA 18701-1500*

ROSENNE, MEIR, lawyer, government agency administrator; b. Iasi, Romania, Feb. 19, 1931; came to Israel, 1944; s. Jacob and Mina Rosenhaupt; m. Vera Ayal, June 9, 1959; children—Mihal, Dafna. M.A. in Polit. Sci., Inst. Polit. Sci., Paris, 1953; LL.B., Sorbonne, U. Paris, 1955, Ph.D. in Internat. Law with honors, 1957; grad., Inst. Internat. Studies, Paris, 1953. In govt. service Israel, 1953—; consul Israeli Consulate, N.Y.C., 1967-69; sr. lectr. in polit. sci. U. Haifa, Israel, 1969-71; coordinator Atomic Energy Commn. Israel, 1969-71; chief legal adviser Fgn. Office Israel, Jerusalem, 1971-79; Israeli amb. to France, Paris, 1979-83; Israeli amb. to U.S. Washington, 1983-87; pres. State of Israel Bonds, N.Y., 1989-93; ptnr. Balter, Guth, Aloni & Co., Jerusalem, 1994—. Contbr. articles to N.Y. Times, Washington Post, N.Y. Herald Tribune, also others. Chmn. internat. bd. govs. Share-Zedek Hosp., Jerusalem, 1989-94. Sgt. Israeli Air Force, 1948-50. Recipient Harold Weil medal NYU Sch. Law, Elie Wiesel award. Mem. Internat. Law Soc. (France), Soc. Internat. Law, Israeli Bar Assn., Am. Soc. Internat. Law, French Assn. Internat. Law. Jewish. Club: Internat. (Washington). Avocations: volleyball; swimming. Office: Balter Guth & Aloni, 23 Hillel St, Jerusalem Israel

ROSENOW, EDWARD CARL, III, medical educator; b. Columbus, Ohio, Nov. 2, 1934; s. Oscar Ferdinand and Mildred Irene (Eichelberger) R.; m. Constance Donna Grahame, Sept. 7, 1957; children: Sheryl Lynn, Scott Edward. BS, Ohio State U., 1955, MD, 1959; MS in Medicine, U. Minn., 1969. Diplomate Am. Bd. Internal Medicine (mem. pulmonary subbd. 1982-88); cert. in Subspecialty Pulmonary Diseases. Intern Riverside Meth. Hosp., Columbus, Ohio, 1959-60; resident in internal medicine Mayo Grad. Sch. Medicine, Rochester, Minn., 1960-65, clin. fellow in thoracic diseases, 1965-66; cons. in internal medicine (pulmonary diseases) Mayo Clinic, Rochester, 1966; instr. in medicine Mayo Grad. Sch. Medicine, Rochester, 1969-73; asst. prof. medicine Mayo Med. Sch., Rochester, 1973-77, assoc. prof. medicine, 1977-80, prof. medicine, 1980; chmn. divsn. pulmonary and critical care medicine, 1987-94; assoc. dir. internal medicine residency program Mayo Clinic, Rochester, 1977-79, program dir. internal medicine residency program, 1979-84, sec. Mayo staff, 1979; pres. Mayo staff, 1986; Arthur M. and Gladys D. Gray prof. medicine Mayo Clinic, Rochester, 1987—; cons. NASA, Houston. Capt. M.C., U.S. Army, 1962-64. Recipient Alumni Achievement award Coll. Medicine Ohio State U., 1989, Disting. Mayo Clinician award, 1994, Henry S. Plummer Disting. Internist award, 1994; Edward W. and Betty Knight Scripps Professorship named in his honor Mayo Med. Sch., 1994. Fellow ACP (gov. Minn. chpt. 1987-91, Ralph S. Claypoole Sr. award for Lifetime Dedication to Patient Care 1995, Minn. chpt. Laureate award 1994), Am. Coll. Chest Physicians (editl. bd. CHEST 1973-78, editor spl. case reports 1975-90, com. on postgrad. med. edn. 1978-84, sci. program com. 1982, com. on undergrad. med. edn. 1981-82, co-chmn. sci. program com. Internat. Coll. Chest Physicians meeting, Sydney, Australia, 1985, regent 1984-88, pres. elect 1988-89, pres. 1989-90); mem. AMA, So. Minn. Med. Assn., Minn. Thoracic Soc., Am. Thoracic Soc., Sigma Xi. Office: Mayo Clinic Div Pulmonary Diseases 200 1st St SW Rochester MN 55905-0001

ROSENOW, JOHN EDWARD, foundation executive; b. Lincoln, Nebr., Sept. 15, 1949; s. Lester Edward and Lucille Louise (Koehler) R.; m. Nancy Kay Hadley; children: Matthew, Stacy. BS in Agrl. Engring., U. Nebr., 1971. Dir. of tourism Nebr. Dept. Econ. Devel., Lincoln, 1971-79, interim dept. dir., 1985; founder Nat. Arbor Day Found., 1972; exec. dir. million-mem. Nat. Arbor Day Found., Lincoln and Nebraska City, 1979-94; pres. Nat. Arbor Day Found., 1994—. Co-author: (book) Tourism: the good, the bad, and the ugly, 1979. Democrat. Mem. United Ch. of Christ. Office: Nat Arbor Day Found 211 N 12th St Lincoln NE 68508-1422

ROSENOW, JOHN HENRY, surgeon, educator; b. Chgo., Sept. 16, 1913; s. Edward Carl and Lydia Barbara (Senty) R.; m. Jane Dexter, June 8, 1938; children: Joan (Mrs. Charles Jackson), Peter Dexter, Philip John, Charles Edward, Margaret (Mrs. Theodore Hope), Barbara (Mrs. Derek Von Schlegall). B.A., Carleton Coll., Northfield, Minn., 1934; M.D., Harvard U., 1938; M.S. in Surgery, Mayo Found., U. Minn., 1944. Diplomate: Am. Bd. Surgery. Intern Presbyn. Hosp., Chgo., 1939-40; fellow in surgery Mayo Clinic, 1941-43, 46-47; pvt. practice medicine specializing in gen. surgery Mpls., 1948-63; part-time editor Modern Medicine Publs., Inc., Mpls., 1955-63; sr. med. editor Modern Medicine Publs., Inc., 1963-75; clin. instr. surgery U. Minn. Med. Sch., 1955—; chief med. officer Mil. Entrance Processing Sta., Mpls., 1975-88; mem. staff Abbott-Northwestern Hosp., Fairview-Southdale hosps., Hennepin County Med. Center. Contbr. articles to med. jours. Mem. diocesan standing com. Episcopal Ch., 1961-64, 70-73. Served with M.C. USNR, 1943-46, PTO. Decorated Bronze Star. Fellow A.C.S.; mem. Am., Minn. med. assns., Hennepin County Med. Soc., Minn. Surg. Soc., Mpls. Acad. Medicine.

ROSENSAFT, MENACHEM ZWI, lawyer, author, community activist; b. Bergen-Belsen, Germany, May 1, 1948; came to U.S., 1958, naturalized, 1962; s. Josef and Hadassah (Bimko) R.; m. Jean Bloch, Jan. 13, 1974; 1 child, Joana Deborah. BA, MA, Johns Hopkins U., 1971; MA, Columbia U., 1975, JD, 1979. Bar: N.Y. 1980. Adj. lectr. dept. Jewish studies CCNY, 1972-74, professorial fellow, 1974-75; rsch. fellow Am. Law Inst., 1977-78; law clk. to judge U.S. Dist. Ct. (so. dist.) N.Y., N.Y.C., 1979-81; assoc. Proskauer, Rose, Goetz & Mendelsohn, N.Y.C., 1981-82, Kaye, Scholer, Fierman, Hays & Handler, N.Y.C., 1982-89; v.p., sr. assoc. counsel Chase Manhattan Bank, N.Y.C., 1989-93; spl. counsel Hahn & Hessen, N.Y.C., 1994-95; sr. internat. counsel Ronald S. Lauder Found., N.Y.C., 1995—. Author: Moshe Sharett, Statesman of Israel, 1966, Fragments, Past and Future (poetry), 1968, Not Backward to Belligerency, 1969; editor: Bergen Belsen Youth mag., 1965; book rev. editor Columbia Jour. Transnat. Law, 1978-79; co-editor (with Yehuda Bauer) Antisemitism: Threat to Western Civilization, 1988; contbg. editor: Reform Judaism, 1993—; contbr. to various publs. including N.Y. Times, Newsweek, N.Y. Post, L.A. Times, Phila. Inquirer, Miami Herald, Internat. Herald Tribune, Jerusalem Post, Liberation, Paris, Davar, Tel Aviv, El Diario, Santiago de Chile, Columbia Human Rights Law Rev., Jewish Social Studies, Leo Baeck Inst. Year Book XXI, Columbia Jour. Environ. Law, (with Michael I. Saltzman) Tax Planning Internat. Rev., Fellowship, Reform Judaism, United Synagogue Rev., Forward Midstream, N.Y. Jewish Week, Jewish Telegraphic Agy. Bull.; subject of profile "Survivor's Son" in Present Tense mag., 1990. Chmn. Internat. Network Children Jewish Holocaust Survivors, 1981-84, founding chmn., 1984—; nat. pres. Labor Zionist Alliance, 1988-91; chmn. commn. human rights World Jewish Congress, 1986-91, chmn. exec. com. Am. sect., 1986-90; mem. Gen. Coun. World Zionist Orgn., 1987-92; mem. U.S. Holocaust Meml. Coun., 1994—, chmn. content com., 1994—, chmn. collections and acquisitions com., 1996—; mem. N.Y.C. Holocaust Meml. Commn., 1982—, chmn. collections com., 1987-89; bd. dirs., exec. com. Nat. Com. for Labor Israel, 1988-91, 95—; mem. Am. Zionist Tribunal, 1988-90, chmn., 1990; sec. Am. Zionist Fedn., 1990-93; bd. dirs. Am. Jewish Joint Distbn. Com., 1988-91, Mercaz, 1991—; mem. nat. adv. bd. United Synagogue Conservative Judaism, 1995—, also chmn. United Synagogue delegation to Nat. Jewish Cmty. Rels. Adv. Coun., 1994—; mem. exec. com. Nat. Jewish Cmty. Rels. Adv. Coun., 1994—; mem. N.Y. County Dem. Com., 1981-85; organizer, leader demonstration against Pres. Reagan's visit to Bitburg Cemetery and Bergen-Belsen concentration camp, 1985; del. meeting on recognition of Israel between five Am. Jews and leaders of Palestine Liberation Orgn., Stockholm, 1988; mem. adv. coun. Park Ave. Synagogue, 1993-94, trustee, 1994—, chmn. Sherr Inst. Adult Jewish Studies, 1993—. Recipient Abraham Joshua Heschel Peace award, 1989, Parker Sch. recognition of achievement with honors in internat. and fgn. law, 1979; Harlan Fiske Stone scholar, 1977-79. Mem. ABA, Assn. of Bar of City of N.Y., Phi Beta Kappa. Home: 179 E 70th St New York NY 10021-5154 Office: Ronald S Lauder Found Ste 4200 767 Fifth Ave New York NY 10153

ROSENSHIELD, GARY, Russian literature educator; b. Bklyn., May 14, 1944; s. Wolf Samuel R. and Bertha (Davis) Weiss; m. Jill Kathleen Bast; children: Mark, Adam. BA, Bklyn. Coll., 1965; MA, U. Wis., 1968, PhD, 1972. Asst. prof. Slavic langs. U. Wis., Madison, 1970-76, assoc. prof. Slavic langs., 1976-93, prof. Slavic langs., 1993—. Contbr. articles to profl. jours. Mem. N.Am. Dostocusky Soc. Office: U Wis Slavic Langs Dept Madison WI 53706

ROSENSHINE, ALLEN GILBERT, advertising agency executive; b. N.Y.C., Mar. 14, 1939; s. Aaron and Anna (Zuckerman) R.; m. Suzan Weston-Webb, Aug. 31, 1979; children: Andrew, Jonathan. A.B., Columbia Coll., 1960. Copywriter J.B. Rundle (advt.), N.Y.C., 1962-65; copywriter Batten, Barton, Durstine & Osborn, N.Y.C., 1965, copy supr., 1967, v.p., 1968, asso. creative dir., 1970, sr. v.p., creative dir., 1975-77, exec. v.p., 1977-80, pres., 1980-82, chief exec. officer, 1981-86, chmn., 1983-86, also dir., mem. exec. com.; pres., chief exec. officer BBDO Internat., N.Y.C., 1984-86, also bd. dirs.; pres., chief exec. officer Omnicom Group, N.Y.C., 1986-88; chmn., chief exec. officer BBDO Worldwide, N.Y.C., 1988—; lectr. gen. studies Bklyn. Coll., 1961-65. Office: BBDO Worldwide Inc 1285 Avenue Of The Americas New York NY 10019-6028*

ROSENSTEEL, GEORGE T., physics educator, nuclear physicist; b. Balt., Sept. 30, 1947; s. Walter St. George and Marie Emily (White) R. BSc, U. Toronto, Ont., Can., 1973, PhD, 1975. Can. fellow NRC, 1976-78; prof. physics Tulane U., New Orleans, 1978—, chmn. dept., 1985-91; vis. fellow Brit. Sci. and Engring. Coun., U. Sussex, Eng., 1986; vis. prof. Nat. Inst. Nuclear Theory, U. Washington, 1992. Contbr. numerous articles to profl. jours. Delivered grad. sch. commencement address Tulane U., 1987; recipient 7 grants NSF, 1979—. Mem. Am. Phys. Soc., Am. Math. Soc., Sigma Xi (young scientist award 1987). Office: Tulane U Dept of Physics New Orleans LA 70118

ROSENSTEEL, JOHN WILLIAM, insurance company executive; b. Chgo., June 4, 1940; s. Harold Eugene and Alice (Shanahan) R.; m. Judith; children: Elizabeth, Margaret, Jill. BS in Econs., Holy Cross Coll., 1962. Chartered life underwriter. Home office rep. Aetna Life and Casualty, Chgo., 1967-72, regional dir., 1972-75; dir. Aetna Life and Casualty, Hartford, Conn., 1975-81; nat. dir. Aetna Life and Casualty, Hartford, 1981-83, v.p., 1983-86; sr. v.p. European region Aetna Internat., Inc., Hartford, 1986-90; sr. v.p. European region & United Kingdom Aetna Internat., Hartford, London & Madrid; now chief exec. officer Keyport Life Insurance Co., Boston, Mass., 1993—; bd. dirs. Aetna Internat. U.K., London, La Estrella de Seguros, Madrid, Keyport Life. Lt. USN, 1963-66, Vietnam. Mem. Nat. Assn. Life Underwriters. Republican. Roman Catholic. Avocations: golf, swimming, reading. Home: 13 Glen Oak Dr Wayland MA 01778-3921 Office: Keyport Life 125 High St Boston MA 02110-2704

ROSENSTEIN, ALLEN BERTRAM, electrical engineering educator; b. Balt., Aug. 25, 1920; s. Morton and Mary (Epstein) R.; m. Betty Lebell; children: Jerry Tyler, Lisa Nan, Adam Mark. B.S. with high distinction, U. Ariz., 1940; M.S., UCLA, 1950, Ph.D., 1958. Elec. engr. Consol. Vultee Aircraft, San Diego, 1940-41; sr. elec. engr. Lockheed Aircraft Corp., Burbank, Calif., 1941-42; chief plant engr. Utility Fan Corp., Los Angeles, 1942-44; prof. engring. UCLA, 1946—; founder, chmn. bd. Inet, Inc., 1947-53, cons. engr., 1954—; founder, chmn. bd. dirs. Pioneer Magnetics, Inc., Pioneer Research Inc., Anadex Instruments Inc.; dir. Internat. Transformer Co., Inc., Fgn. Resource Services; cons. ednl. planning UNESCO, Venezuela, 1974-76. Author: (with others) Engineering Communications, 1965, A Study of a Profession and Professional Education, 1968; contbr. articles to profl. jours.; patentee in field. Bd. dirs. Vista Hill Psychiat. Found. Served with USNR, 1944-46. Fellow IEEE (com. on competitiveness); mem. AAAS, NSPE (coun. on competitiveness), Am. Soc. Engring. Edn., N.Y. Acad. Scis., Am. Electronics Assn. (competitiveness steering com.), Sigma Xi, Phi Kappa Phi, Delta Phi Sigma, Tau Beta Pi. Home: 314 S Rockingham Ave Los Angeles CA 90049-3638

ROSENSTEIN, BERYL JOEL, physician; b. Boston, Jan. 5, 1937; s. Benjamin and Doris (Goldhagen) R.; m. Carolyn S., Aug. 31, 1958; children: Susan Eileen, Jonathan David. BA, Boston U., 1957; MD, Tufts U., 1961; M Adminstrv. Sci., Johns Hopkins U., 1987. Diplomate Am. Bd. Pediatrics. Intern in pediatrics Johns Hopkins Hosp., Balt., 1961-62, resident in pediatrics, 1962-64, dir. cystic fibrosis clinic, 1972—, v.p. med. affairs, 1994—; prof. pediatrics Johns Hopkins Sch. Med., Balt., 1989—; med. dir. Mt. Washington Pediatric Hosp., Balt., 1988-93; med. adv. coun. Cystic Fibrosis Found., Bethesda, Md., 1980-88, trustee, 1986—. Author: Pediatric Pearls: Handbook of Pediatrics, 1989, Primary Care of the Newborn, 1992; contbr. over 100 articles to profl. jours. and chpts. to books. Lt. comdr. USPHS, 1964-66. Fellow Am. Acad. Pediatrics, Ambulator Pediatric Assn.; mem. Am. Thoracic Soc., Am. Pediatric Soc., Alpha Omega Alpha. Avocations: tennis, bicycling, antique cars, travel, art. Office: Johns Hopkins Hosp Park 315 Baltimore MD 21287-2533

ROSENSTEIN, JAMES ALFRED, lawyer; b. Phila., Jan. 4, 1939; s. Louis Charles and Natalie Selma (Stern) R.; m. Linda Merle Lederman, Sept. 7, 1969; 1 child, Judith Esther. A.B., Harvard U., 1961, J.D., 1968. Bar: Pa. 1968. Assoc. Wolf, Block, Schorr and Solis-Cohen, Phila., 1968-76; ptnr. Wolf, Block, Schorr and Solis-Cohen, 1976—; mem. adv. com. task force on condominiums Joint State Govt Commn., Pa. Gen. Assembly, 1977-79; mem. condominium-coop. steering com. Phila. City Planning Commn., 1980-81. Contbr. articles to profl. jours. Trustee exec. com. Jewish Fedn. of Greater Phila., 1977—, chmn. com. on local svcs., 1986-89, sec., 1987-88, v.p., 1988-94, chmn. com. on allocations and planning, 1989-92; v.p. jewish Cmty. Rels. Coun., 1982-85, 89-90; trustee United Way of Greater Phila., 1979-84, bd. dirs., 1982-85, 91—. Lt. USN, 1961-64. Mem. ABA (chmn. devel. and financing of condominium projects 1993—), Pa. Bar Assn. (chmn. common interest ownership com. 1980-93, chmn. real property divsn. 1993-95, chmn. real property, probate and trust law sect. 1995-96), Phila. Bar Assn. (chmn. legis. rels. com. 1996—), Am. Coll. Real Estate Lawyers, Coll. Cmty. Assn. Lawyers, Coun. Jewish Fedns. (bd. dirs. 1986—, chmn. com. on svcs. to aging 1991-94, vice chair nat. funding coun. 1995—). Office: Wolf Block Schorr and Solis-Cohen Packard Bldg 12th Fl 111 S 15th St Philadelphia PA 19102

ROSENSTEIN, LEONARD, real estate company executive; b. Phila., Aug. 4, 1922; s. Benjamin and Esther (Zibulski) R.; m. Eleanor M. Peterson, Mar. 11, 1960; children: Elissa L., Risa B., Tedd B. BS in Pharmacy, Temple U., 1943; BS in Pharmacy (hon.), New Orleans. Lic. pharmacist, Pa., N.J. Pres. Lincoln Pharmacy, Atlantic City, N.J., 1947-69, Mercy Ambulance, Las Vegas, Nev., 1971-73, Nev. Devel. and Realty Co., Las Vegas, 1973—, am. Mgmt. Co., Las Vegas, 1973—; chmn. Players Express Travel, Las Vegas, 1990—. Editor: Temple University Apothecary, 1943. Chmn. Downtown Improvement Authority, Atlantic City, N.J., 1982-84; pres. N.J. Pharm. Assn., 1960; chmn., pres. Nat. Assn. Retail Druggists, Washington, 1969; commr. So. Nev. Regional Housing Bd., Las Vegas, 1993-94.; mem. Beth Sholem Congregation, 1971—. Cpl. U.S. Army, 1943-46, ETO. Recipient award Am. Legion, 1940, E.R. Squibb, 1960, Bowl of Hygea, A.H. Robbins, 1965; named Ky. Col., 1965—. Mem. Greater Las Vegas Realtor Assn., Inst. Real Estate Mgmt., Jewish War Vets, Am. Legion, Elks, Alpha Zeta Omega. Avocations: photography, reading. Home: 909 Cashman Dr Las Vegas NV 89107-4429 Office: Nev Devel & Realty Co 2980 Meade Ave Las Vegas NV 89102

ROSENSTEIN, MARVIN, public health administrator; b. Sept. 5, 1939. BSChemE, U. Md., 1961; MS in Environ. Engring., Rensselaer Poly. Inst., 1966; PhD in Nuclear Engring., U. Md., 1971. Rschr. U.S. Bur. Mines/College Park (Md.) Metall. Rsch. Sta., 1961; commd. ensign Commd. Corps Pub. Health Svc., 1962, advanced through grades to capt., 1983; with N.E. Radiological Health Lab., Winchester, Mass., 1962, program coord. analytical quality control svc. divsn. radiological health, 1962; with data collation and analysis sect. radiation surveillance ctr. Divsn. Radiological Health, Washington, 1966; chief radiation exposure intelligence sect. standards and intelligence br. Nat. Ctr. for Radiological Health, Rockville, Md., 1967; dep. chief radiation measurements and calibration br. divsn. electronic products Bur. Radiological Health, Rockville, 1971, spl. asst. to dir. divsn. electronic products, 1972, dep. dir. divsn. electonic products, 1973; dep. assoc. commr. for policy coordination office policy coordination FDA, Rockville, 1978; sr. sci. advisor, 1979; dir. office health physics Ctr. for Devices and Radiological Health, Rockville, 1982-95; sr. staff fellow Ctr. for Devices and Radiol. Health, Rockville, Md., 1995—; mem. USASI Standards Com. N101, 1968-69; guest worker Ctr. for Radiation Rsch., Nat. Bur. Standards, 1969-74; faculty rsch. assoc. lab. for polymer and radiation sci. dept. clin. engring. U. Md., 1971-74; asst. clin. prof. radiology sch. medicine and scis. George Washington U., 1977-90. Contbr. over 70 publs. to profl. and sci. jours. Recipient Fed. Engr. of Yr. award NSPE/Dept. Health and Human Svcs., 1987. Mem. Nat. Coun. on Radiation Protection and Measurements (coun. 1988—, sci. com. 44 1976—, sci. com. 62 1980-85, chmn. sci. com. 46-12 1992-96), Health Physics Soc. (publs. com. 1967-77, del. to 4th internat. congress Internat. Radiation Protection Assn. 1977, contbg. editor newsletter 19982—), Com. on Interagy. Radiation Rsch. and Policy Coord. (alt. HHS policy panel 1984-95, vice chmn. sci. panel 1985-94, exec. com. 1985-94, chmn. subpanel on use NAS com. on biol. effects of ionizing radiation report V and UN sci. com. on the effects of atomic radiation 1988, report in risk assessment 1989-92), Internat. Commn. on Radiol. Protection (com. 3 on radiol. protection in medicine 1985—, corr. mem. task group on rev. publ. 21 1979-88), Internat. Commn. on Radiation Units and Measurements (report com. on dosimetry in diagnostic radiology for the patient 1994—), Commd. Officers Assn., Sigma Xi. Achievements include patent for radiation dosimeter; research in absorbed dose from medical X rays, radiation risk estimates, dosimetry for epidemiological studies, absorbed dose to the public from radiation emergencies, electron depth-dose and dosimetry, radiochemistry and environmental health, radioactivity in food, general radiological health. Office: FDA Ctr Devices & Radiol Health 2094 Gaither Rd Rockville MD 20850-4011

ROSENSTEIN, ROBERT BRYCE, lawyer, financial advisor; b. Santa Monica, Calif., Feb. 26, 1954; s. Franklin Lee and Queen Esther (Shall) R.; m. Resa Shanee Brookler, Nov. 30, 1980; children: Shaun Franklin, Jessica Laney, Madeline Frances. BA, Calif. State U., Northridge, 1976; JD, Southwestern U., 1979. Bar: Calif. 1979, U.S. Dist. Ct. (cen. and no. dists.) Calif. 1980, U.S. Tax Ct. 1981; registered environ. assessor. Service rep. Social Security Adminstrn., Los Angeles, 1974-77; tax cons. Am. Tax Assocs., Los Angeles, 1970-78, ptnr., 1978; prin., pres. Robert B. Rosenstein, PC, Los Angeles, 1979-84; ptnr. Rosenstein and Werlin, Los Angeles, 1984-87; pres. Robert Bryce Rosenstein Ltd., Temelula, 1987—; chief fin. officer BSE Mgmt. Inc., Los Angeles, 1987-90, corp. counsel, 1987-92, sr. v.p. corp. devel., acquisitions, 1990-92; corp. counsel, 1995—; bd. dirs. BSE Mgmt. Inc, Sirius Computer Corp., Spartan Computer, Unicomp, Inc., Diagnostic Engring. Inc.; pres. Will Find Inc., 1986-87. Recipient Am. Jurisprudence award Bancroft Whitney; Order of Cheviler. Mem. ABA (taxation and environ. coms., vice chmn. gen. bus. sect.), Assn. Trial Lawyers Am., L.A. Bar Assn. Democrat. Jewish. Lodges: Masons, Ionic, Composite. Avocations: sports, reading, golf. Office: 27450 Ynez Ste 222 Temecula CA 92591

ROSENSTOCK, LINDA, medical educator; b. N.Y.C., Dec. 20, 1950. AB in Psychology, Brandeis U., 1971; student, U. B.C., Vancouver, Can., 1971-72; MD, Johns Hopkins U., 1977, MPH, 1977. Diplomate Am. Bd. Internal Medicine, Am. Bd. Preventive Medicine; lic. physician and surgeon, Wash. Med. resident then chief resident U. Wash., Seattle, 1977-80, resident in preventive medicine, instr. medicine, 1980-82, asst. prof., 1982-83, 83-87, lectr. environ. heatlh, 1982-83, adj. asst. prof., 1983-86, mem. grad. sch. faculty, 1985—, assoc. prof., 1987-93, prof. medicine and environ. health, 1993—, also dir. programs; dir. Harborview Med. Ctr., Seattle, 1981-87, acting sect. head, 1992-94; dir. Nat. Isnt. Occupational Safety and Health, Washington, 1994—. Assoc. editor Internat. Jour. Occupational Medicine and Toxicology, 1991—; mem. editorial bd. Am. Jour. Indsl. Medicine, 1985-94, Jour. Gen. Internal Medicine, 1987-90, Environ. Rsch., 1987—, Western Jour. Medicine, 1990—; contbr. numerous articles to profl. jours. Mem. exec. bd. Physicians for Human Rights, 1990—; mem. occupl. health adv. bd. United Auto Workers GM, 1990-94, chair, 1993-94; mem. task force on pneumoconioses Am. Coll. Radiology, 1991-94; mem. external adv. panel Agrl. Health and Safety Ctr., 1992-93; mem. adv. com. Ctrs. for Disease Control, 1992-94; mem. com. to survey health effects of mustard gas and lewisite Inst. Medicine, 1992, mem. bd. health promotion and disease prevention, 1993-94; mem. bd. sci. counselors HHS, 1993-94, mem. exec. com. nat. toxicology program, 1994—; mem. med. adv. bd. Teamsters Internat., 1993-94. Recipient Upjohn Achievement award Harborview Med. Ctr., 1978, Jean Spencer Felton MD award Western Occupational Med. Assn., 1988, Environ. and Occupational Medicine award Nat. Isnt. Environ. Health Scis., 1991-94; Robert Wood Johnson scholar, 1980-82, Henry j. Kaiser scholar, 1984-89. Fellow ACP (health promotion subcom. 1989-90, clin. practicie subcom. 1990-91), Collegium Ramazzini; mem. APHA (chair membership com. 1983-85, chairperson occupational helath and safety sect. 1985-86, gov. coun. 1986-88), Am. Coll. Occupational Medicine (mem. jud. com. 1989-94), Am. Thoracic Soc. (com. health care policy and clin. practice 1990-93), Internat. Commn. Occupational Health (sci. com. epidemiology in occupational health 1989—), Soc. Gen. Internal Medicine (program planning com. 1987, Glaser award com. 1993-94), Western Assn. Physicians, Pacific Interurban Clin. Club. Office: Nat Inst Occupational Safety & Health 200 Indpendence Ave SW Washington DC 20201

ROSENSTOCK, SUSAN LYNN, orchestra manager; b. Bklyn., Nov. 2, 1947. BS, SUNY, Cortland, 1969; MBA, So. Meth. U., 1977, MFA, 1978. Cert. fund raising exec. Asst. mgr. Columbus (Ohio) Symphony Orch., 1978-82; grants program dir., info. officer Greater Columbus Arts Coun., 1982-83, asst. dir. grants and adminstrn., 1983-84; dir. annual giving and spl. events Columbus Symphony Orch., 1984-86, dir. devel., 1986-90, orch. mgr., 1990—; panelist Ohio Arts Coun. Music Panel, 1986, 87, Challenge Grants Panel, 1991, J.C. Penney Gold Rule Award Judges Panel, 1993, 94. Mem. Am. Symphony Orch. League (devel. dirs. steering com. nat. conf. 1987, 88), Nat. Soc. Fund Raising Execs. (program com. Ctrl. Ohio chpt. 1988—, chmn. program com. 1993, 94, bd. dirs. 1993—, treas. 1995). Office: Columbus Symphony Orch 55 E State St Columbus OH 43215-4216

ROSENSWEIG, DAN, publishing executive. Pub. PC Mag. divsn. Ziff-Davis Pub. Co., N.Y.C. Office: PC Mag Ziff-Davis Pub Co 1 Park Ave New York NY 10016*

ROSENSWEIG, RONALD ELLIS, scientist consultant; b. Hamilton, Ohio, Nov. 8, 1932; s. Herman and Deana (Meisel) R.; m. Ruth Evelyn Cohen, Sept. 5, 1954; children—Scott Elliot, Beth Ellen, Perry Ethan. Chem. Engr., U. Cin., 1955; S.M., MIT, 1956, Sc.D., 1959. Asst. prof. dept. chem. engring. MIT, Cambridge, 1959-62; prin. scientist Avco Corp., Wilmington, Mass., 1962-69; pres., tech. dir., co-founder Ferrofluidics Corp., Burlington, Mass., 1969-73, also dir., 1969-85; rsch. assoc. Exxon Corp., Annandale, N.J., 1973-78, sr. rsch. assoc., 1978-85, sci. advisor, 1985-95; internat. rsch. chair Blaise Pascal, Paris, 1996—; vis. prof. U. Minn., Mpls., 1980, U. Chgo., 1990. Author: Ferrohydrodynamics, 1985; contbr. articles to profl. jours.; patentee in field. Fellow NSF, MIT, 1955-56; recipient IR-100 awards Indsl. Rsch. Pubs., 1968, 69, 71; named Young Engr. of Yr., Avco Corp., 1966, Disting. Engring. Alumnus U. Cin., 1986. Mem. Nat. Acad. Engring., Am. Inst. Chem. Engrs. (Alpha Chi Sigma award for rsch. 1985), Am. Phys. Soc., Magnetic Fluids Conf., Internat. Steering Com. (chmn. 1977-92). Jewish. Home: 34 Gloucester Rd Summit NJ 07901-3023

ROSENSWEIG, STANLEY HAROLD, retail executive; b. Phila., May 5, 1918; s. Emanuel Martin and Jennie (Hoffman) R.; m. Elaine Gordon Decker, Dec. 4, 1967; children by previous marriage—Susan, Ellen, Tod, Lisa. A.B. in Bus. Adminstrn., George Washington U., 1939. Chmn. bd. Electronics Wholesalers Co., Washington, 1947-68; chmn. bd. CWF Corp., Washington, 1963-73; pres. Sun Appliance Wholesalers, Washington, 1950-69; pres. Gem Internat. Inc., St. Louis, 1961-65, chmn. exec. com., 1963-66; bd. dirs. St. Louis Blues, 1966-74; chmn. bd. Lewis & Thomas Saltz Clothiers, Inc., Washington, 1977-84; dir. St. Louis Arena Inc., Action Leasing Inc. Trustee Boys Club, Greater Washington Jewish Community Found.; exec. bd. United Jewish Appeal, Washington; bd. dirs. Jewish Social Services Agy., Washington; bd. dirs. Nat. Symphony Orch., Child Guidance Clinic, Washington. Lt. U.S. Navy Res., 1941-45, PTO, 1944-45. Mem. Young Pres. Orgn. Clubs: Standard (Chgo.); Woodmont Country, Circus Saints and Sinners (Washington). Home: Fern Hill McClean VA 22101 Office: 3201 New Mexico Ave NW Washington DC 20016-2756

ROSENTHAL, AARON, management consultant; b. N.Y.C., July 12, 1914; s. Zelig and Sarah (Shapinsky) R.; m. Edna Blanche Finkel, Sept. 3, 1940; children—Stephen Mark, Marjorie Ann. B.A., Coll. City N.Y., 1934, M.S. in Edn, 1935; postgrad., Georgetown U. Law Sch., 1937-39, Am. U., 1950-53. Dir. Internal Audit Service, VA, Washington, 1953-58; controller VA, 1958-60; dir. financial mgmt. NASA, 1960-61; comptroller NSF, 1961-69, Nat. Acad. Scis., 1969-76; exec. cons. Coopers & Lybrand; fin. cons. to Ctr. for Devel. and Population Activities; fin. and mgmt. cons. to Joint Oceanographic Instns. Inc.; U.S. rep. supr. Radiation Effects Rsch. Found., Hiroshima, Japan; mem. nat. adv. coun. nat. Ctr. for Higher Edn. Mgmt. Systems; bd. dirs. TCOA, Inc., Manchester Center, Vt. Trustee Sci. Service Inc. Served with AUS, 1943-45. Recipient Exceptional Service award VA, 1960; Merit citation Nat. Civil Service League, 1957; Distinguished Service award NSF, 1969. Fellow AAAS; mem. Am. Soc. Pub. Adminstrn., Assn. Govt. Accts. Home: 3001 Veazey Ter NW Washington DC 20008-5454 Office: 2101 Constitution Ave NW Washington DC 20418-0007

ROSENTHAL, ALAN SAYRE, former government official; b. N.Y.C., Sept. 30, 1926; s. Morris S. and Elizabeth (Ralph) R.; m. Helen Miller, Sept. 8, 1951; children: Edward S., Susan L., Richard M., James M. A.B., U. Pa., 1948; LL.B., Yale U., 1951. Bar: N.Y. 1952. Asst. in instrn. Yale U. Law Sch., 1950-51; law clk. to U.S. Circuit Judge Henry W. Edgerton, Washington, 1951-52; atty. appellate sect., civil div. Justice Dept., 1952-72, asst. chief, 1958-72; admnstrv. judge atomic safety and licensing appeal panel AEC (now Nuclear Regulatory Commn.), Washington, 1972-91, chmn., 1972-88; adminstrv. judge pers. appeals bd. GAO, Washington, 1991-96, chmn., 1992-94; mem. ethics panel Montgomery County Bd. Edn., 1987-93; lectr. law U. Pa., 1981-83, Am. U., 1991-92. Pres. Kensington Elem. Sch. PTA, 1966-67; pres. North Chevy Chase Swimming Pool Assn., 1974-76; chmn. trustees Cedar Ln. Unitarian Ch., 1970-71; bd. dirs. Montgomery chpt. ACLU, 1967-69. Served with USAAF, 1944-46. Recipient John Marshall award Justice Dept., 1969, Disting. Svc. award Nuclear Regulatory Commn., 1988. Mem. Order of Coif, Phi Beta Kappa, Pi Gamma Mu, Delta Sigma Rho. Home: 3203 Kent St Kensington MD 20895-3210

ROSENTHAL, ALBERT JAY, advertising agency executive; b. Chgo., Sept. 30, 1928; s. Harry and Jennie (Comm) R.; m. Rhoda R. Rosenstein, June 18, 1950; children: Jayne, Michael, James, Nancy. BA, U. Ill., 1950. Reporter Transradio Press, Chgo., 1950-51; columnist Lerner Newspapers, Chgo., 1951-53; creative dir. Elliot, Jaynes & Baruch, Chgo., 1953-61; chmn. Albert Jay Rosenthal & Co., Chgo. and N.Y.C., 1961-85; chmn. Midwest div. HBM/Creamer-Albert Jay Rosenthal, Chgo., 1985-88, Della Femina, McNamee WCRS, Inc., Chgo., 1988-93; chmn. DFM/Tatham, Chgo., 1993; founder, pres. Franchising & Licensing World Ctr., Chgo., 1994—. Bd. dirs. Ill. Arts Alliance Found., Ill. Arts Alliance, Court Theatre U. Chgo.; mem. sustaining fund com. Ravinia Festival Assn.; mem. mktg. com. World Bus. Coun., Washington; vice chmn. Chgo. Internat. Film Festival; v.p. Gastro-Intestinal Rsch. Found. U. Chgo. Named one of Chgo. Ten Outstanding Young Men, Chgo. Jr. Assn. of Commerce, 1962, Advt. Man of Yr., Alpha Delta Sigma, 1978, Communicator of Yr., Jewish United Fund, 1988. Jewish. Home: 179 E Lake Shore Dr Chicago IL 60611-1351 Office: Franchising & Licensing World Ctr 239 The Merchandise Mart Chicago IL 60654

ROSENTHAL, ALBERT JOSEPH, university dean, law educator, lawyer; b. N.Y.C., Mar. 5, 1919; m. Barbara Snowden, June 30, 1953; children: Edward H., Thomas S., William I. B.A., U. Pa., 1938; LL.B., Harvard U., 1941. Bar: N.Y. 1942, U.S. Supreme Ct. 1947. Law clk. to judge U.S. Ct. Appeals 1st Circuit, Boston, 1941-42; spl. appellate atty. OPA, Washington, 1946-47; law clk. to Justice Frankfurter U.S. Supreme Ct., Washington, 1947-48; asst. loan officer IBRD, Washington, 1948-50; atty. Dept. Justice, Washington, 1950-52; gen. counsel Small Def. Plants Adminstrn., Washington, 1952-53; ptnr. Golden Wienshienk & Rosenthal, N.Y.C., 1953-64; prof. law Columbia U., N.Y.C., 1964-89, Maurice T. Moore prof., 1974-89, dean Sch. Law, 1979-84, prof. emeritus, dean emeritus, 1989—; hearing officer N.Y. State Dept. Environ. Conservation, 1975, 77; mem. N.Y. State Law Revision Commn., 1987—; vis. prof. law St. John's U., 1989-92, disting. prof. 1992—; spl. master U.S. Dist. Ct. N.Y., 1990—. Author: (with H. Korn and S. Lubman) Catastrophic Accidents in Government Programs, 1963, (with F. Grad and G. Rathjens) Environmental Control: Priorities, Policies and the Law, 1971, Federal Regulation of Campaign Finance, 1972, (with F. Grad and others) The Automobile and the Regulation of Its Impact on the Environment, 1975; editor: (with L. Henkin) Constitutionalism and Rights: The Influence of the U.S. Constitution Abroad, 1989; contbr. articles to law jours. Mem. Logan Airport Master Plan Study Team, 1975. Served to capt. U.S. Army Air Corps, 1942-45. Fellow Am. Acad. Arts and Scis., Am. law Inst. Home: 15 Oak Way Scarsdale NY 10583-1415 Office: Columbia U Law Sch 435 W 116th St New York NY 10027-7201

ROSENTHAL, AMNON, pediatric cardiologist; b. Gedera, Israel, July 14, 1934; came to U.S., 1949, naturalized, 1959; s. Joseph and Rivka Rosenthal; m. Prudence Lloyd, July 22, 1962; children: Jonathan, Eben, Nathaniel. M.D., Albany Med. Coll., 1959. Intern Buffalo Children's Hosp., 1959-60; resident in pediatrics Children's Hosp. Med. Center, Boston, 1960-62; resident in pediatric cardiology Children's Hosp. Med. Center, 1965-68; asso. prof. pediatrics Children's Hosp. Med. Center and Harvard U. Med. Sch., Boston, 1975-77; dir. pediatric cardiology, prof. pediatrics C.S. Mott Children's Hosp., U. Mich., Ann Arbor, 1977—, assoc. dir. dept. pediatrics, 1989-92. Served to capt. M.C. USAF, 1962-65. Amnon Rosenthal endowed professorship U. Mich., 1994. Mem. Am. Acad. Pediatrics, Soc. for Pediatric Rsch., Am. Pediatric Soc., Am. Heart Assn., Am. Coll. Cardiology, Am. Bd. Pediatrics, Am. Bd. Pediatric Cardiology (chmn. 1987-88). Office: CS Mott Children's Hosp Ann Arbor MI 48109-0204

ROSENTHAL, ANDREW, newspaper editor. Washington bur. editor N.Y. Times. Office: The NY Times Washington Bur 1627 I St NW Fl 7 Washington DC 20006-4007

ROSENTHAL, ARNOLD H., film director, producer, writer, graphic designer, calligrapher; b. Chgo., Jan. 31, 1933; s. Gus and Sara (Ariel) R.; children: Michel, Jason, Anthony. B.A., U. Ill., 1954. Graphic designer Whitaker-Guernsey Studios, Chgo., 1954-55; art dir. Edward H. Weiss Advt., Chgo., 1956-60; owner Arnold H. Rosenthal & Assos., Chgo., 1960-70; partner, creative dir., pres. Meyer & Rosenthal Inc. (mktg. communications), Chgo., 1970-75; sr. v.p., creative dir. Garfield-Linn & Co. (Advt.), Chgo., 1975-81; pres., exec. prodr./dir. Film Chgo., 1981—; TV comml. jury chmn. Chgo. Internat. Film Festival, 1977, 78, 79, 87, mem. governing bd., 1984—; represented at Moscow Film Fest, 1990; TV jury chmn. U.S. Festival, 1980; lectr. Columbia Coll., Purdue U., U. Ill., Ohio State U. Contbr. articles to profl. publs. Bd. dirs. Jewish United Fund. Served with AUS, 1955-56. Recipient creative awards Communication Clubs Chgo., N.Y.C., 1960—, Silver medal N.Y. Film Festival, 1986, Clio award, 1981. Mem. Soc. Typographic Arts (design awards 1958—, pres. 1971-72), Am. Inst. Graphic Arts (spl. award 1974), Dirs. Guild Am., Jazz Inst. Chgo. (charter, jazz drummer), Tau Epsilon Phi, Alpha Delta Sigma.

ROSENTHAL, ARTHUR JESSE, publisher; b. N.Y.C., Sept. 26, 1919; s. Arthur J. and Grace (Ellinger) R.; m. Margaret Ann Roth, Dec. 12, 1975; children: James, Kathryn, Paul. BA, Yale U., 1941; postgrad., Harvard U. Bus. Sch., 1942. Spl. asst. to U.S. ambassador to Israel, Jerusalem, 1948; pres., editor in chief Basic Books, Inc., N.Y.C., 1949-72; dir. Harvard U. Press, Cambridge, 1972-90; pub. Hill and Wang, N.Y.C., 1990—; founding trustee Bank St. Coll. Edn., 1952-68. Editorial bd.: Pub. Interest, Harvard Bus. Rev, Family Process, Yale U. Press. Trustee Austen Riggs Center, Stockbridge, Mass. Served to capt., M.I. U.S. Army, 1942-46. Clubs: Century Assn. (N.Y.C.); St. Botolph (Boston).

ROSENTHAL, BRIAN DAVID, lawyer; b. Glen Ridge, N.J., May 1, 1952; s. Charles and Dorothy H. (Stanger) R.; m. Joy N. Weisman, Aug. 11, 1974; children: Adam M., Elizabeth J., Alexander H. BA magna cum laude, U. Pa., Phila., 1974; JD, Georgetown U., Washington, 1977. Bar: Pa. 1977, U.S. Dist. Ct. (ea. dist.) Pa. 1983, U.S. Ct. Appeals (3rd cir.) 1984. Asst. dist. atty. Phila. Dist. Attys. Office, 1977-82; assoc. atty. Ominsky Joseph & Welsh PC, Phila., 1982-85; ptnr. Ominsky Welsh & Rosenthal PC, Phila., 1986-92; pres., founding ptnr. Rosenthal & Weisberg PC, Phila., 1992—; commr. Bd. Commrs., Lower Merion Township, Pa., 1994—; settlement master Phila. Ct. Common Pleas, 1993—. Author: Medical Malpractice in Pennsylvania, 1993, Insurance Litigation in Pennsylvania, 1993. Pres. Lower Merion Little League, 1991—; dir. baseball Kaiserman J.C.C., Penn Wynne, Pa., 1985; bd. dirs. Nat. Multiple Sclerosis Soc., PHila., 1979-84. Named Outstanding Vol. Kaiserman Jewish Cmty. Ctr., Penn Wynne, 1985, Outstanding Adult Vol. Lower Merion Little League, 1993. Mem. ABA (sects. on litigation, tort and ins. practice, criminal justice), Assn. Trial Lawyers Am., Pa. Trial Lawyers Assn., Pa Bar Assn., Phila. Bar Assn. (coms. medico legal com., state judiciary com. 1993—), Phi Beta Kappa. Avocations: baseball, reading, travel, coaching. Office: Rosenthal & Weisberg PC 2 Logan Sq Ste 1565 Philadelphia PA 19103-2707

ROSENTHAL, CHARLES MICHAEL, financial executive; b. Bklyn., Nov. 21, 1935; s. David B. and Edna (Lefcort) R.; m. Eva F. Sonnenberg, July 7, 1963; children: Andrea (dec.), Nicole. BA, Colgate U., 1957. Rsch. asst. Fed. Res. Bank N.Y., N.Y.C., 1960-62; v.p. L.M. Rosenthal & Co., Inc., 1962-74; ptnr. 1st Manhattan Co., N.Y.C., 1974—. Trustee Brown U., Providence, 1992—. Capt. USAF, 1957-60. Mem. Investment Assn. N.Y., Security Traders Assn. N.Y., Am. Coun. on Germany, East Hampton Tennis Club. Jewish. Home: 784 Park Ave New York NY 10021-3553 Office: 1st Manhattan Co 437 Madison Ave New York NY 10022-7001

ROSENTHAL, DAVID, physician; b. Phila., Sept. 30, 1929; m.; Suzanne Rosenthal; children: Michael, Samuel, Abrielle. Student, Julliard Sch. Music, 1948-49, George Washington U., 1953-54, Temple U., 1954-56; DO, Phila. Coll. Osteopathic Med., 1960. Diplomate Am. Bd. Osteopathic Rehabilitation Medicine. Internship Youngstown (Ohio) Osteopathic Hosp., 1960-61; resident VA Hosp. U. Pa., 1970-73; asst. medical dir. Moss Rehabilitation Hosp., Phila., 1974-77; gen. practice Phila., 1960-70; chmn. div. physical medicine & rehabilitation Suburban Gen. Hosp., Norristown, Pa., 1977—; medical dir. Medical Ctr. Performing Artists, Norristown, Pa., 1984—; medical dir. The Rehab Station, Norristown, Pa., 1988—, exec. dir., 1994—; asst. instr. in phys. medicine and rehab. U. Pa., 1972-73; asst. prof. Temple U., 1973-77, asst. clin. profl., 1977—; asst. clin. prof. Phila. Coll. Ostopathic Medicine, 1978-81; adj. clin. prof. N.Y. Coll., 1980-84; clin. assoc. prof. Phila. Coll., 1981—; hosp. affiliation Moss Rehab. Hosp., Grad. Hosp. City Ave. and Parkview Divsns., Albert Einstein Med. Ctr., Frankford Hosp., Suburban Gen. Hosp.; chmn. med. audit com. Moss Rehab. Hosp., 1974-77, chmn. med. records com., 1974-77; surveyor Commn. on Accreditation of Rehab. Facilities, 1994—. Contbr. articles to profl. jours. Profl. Standards Review Orgn. Health Systems of South Eastern Pa., 1977-82; cons. to com. Rehabilitation and Spl. Devices Food and Drug Adminstrn., 1979-84, panel mem. com., 1979-84. Mem. Am. Osteopathic Assn., Pa. Osteopathic Medical Assn., Dist. X Pa. Osteopathic Medical Assn., Am. Osteopathic Coll. Rehabilitation Medicine (trustee 1975-79, vice chmn., 1977-78, pres. 1979-80, past pres. 1980-81), Am. Congress Rehabilitation Medicine, Phila. Soc. Physical Medicine and Rehabilitation (sec.-treas. 1975-76, v.p. 1975-77, pres. 1977-78), Am. Geriatrics Soc., Pan-Am. Medical Assn., Am. Coll. Sports Medicine, Am. Osteopathic Acad. Sports Medicine, Am. Acad. Clinical Neurophysiology. Home: 210 W Rittenhouse Sq Apt 2506 Philadelphia PA 19103 Office: Physiatric Assn Ltd 2705 Dekalb Pike Norristown PA 19401-1852

ROSENTHAL, DONALD B., political scientist, educator; b. N.Y.C., July 14, 1937; s. Max and Bessie Dora (Silverman) R. AB, Bklyn. Coll., 1958; AM, U. Chgo., 1960, PhD, 1964. Asst. prof. polit. sci. SUNY, Buffalo, 1964-68, assoc. prof., 1968-72, prof., 1972—, chmn. dept., 1978-80, 86-91. Author: The Limited Elite, 1970, The Expansive Elite, 1977, (monograph) Sticking Points and Ploys in Federal-Local Relations, 1979; Urban Housing and Neighborhood Revitalization, 1988; co-author: The Politics of Community Conflict, 1969, (monograph) Local Power and Comparative Politics, 1974; editor: The City in Indian Politics, 1976, Urban Revitalization, 1980; contbr. articles to profl. jours. Fellow Am. Inst. Indian Studies, 1963-64, 70, Nat. Assn. Schs. Pub. Affairs and Adminstrn., 1977-78, Rockefeller Inst., 1983; NSF grantee, 1974-75. Mem. Am. Polit. Sci. Assn., Am. Soc. Pub. Adminstrn. Democrat. Jewish. Office: SUNY Buffalo Amherst Campus Dept of Polit Sci Buffalo NY 14260

ROSENTHAL, DOUGLAS EURICO, lawyer, author; b. N.Y.C., Feb. 12, 1940; s. Jacob and Edna Louise (Muir) R.; m. Erica Switzen Kremen, Nov. 12, 1967; children: Benjamin Muir, Rachel Elizabeth. BA summa cum laude, Yale U., 1961, LLB, 1966, PhD in Polit. Sci, 1970; postgrad., Oxford (Eng.) U., 1962; MA, Columbia U., 1963. Bar: N.Y. 1968, U.S. Supreme Ct. 1976, D.C. 1980. Project dir. Russell Sage Found., N.Y.C., 1968-70; assoc. Fried, Frank, Harris, Shriver & Jacobson, N.Y.C., 1970-74; asst. chief fgn. commerce sect., antitrust div. Dept. Justice, Washington, 1974-77, chief, 1977-80; ptnr. Sutherland, Asbill & Brennan, Washington, 1980-88, Coudert Bros., 1989-94, Sonnenschein, Nath & Rosenthal, Washington, 1994—; reporter Am. Law Inst.-Am. Bar Assn. Model Lawyer Peer Rev. System, 1980; adj. prof. Tokyo U. Law Sch., 1992; speaker USIA, Australia, Eng., Can., Germany, Japan; escrow agt. Boesky settlement funds paid to U.S. Govt. Author: (with D. Baker and others) Antitrust Guide for International Operations, 1977; author: Lawyer and Client: Who's in Charge?, 1972, 2d rev. edit., 1977 (with Knighton) National Law and International Commerce: The Problem of Extraterritoriality, 1982, A Competition Policy in Hufbauer, Europe, 1992: An American Perspective, 1990; co-editor (with Carl Green) Competition Regulation in the Pacific Rim, 1996; author (with others) Global Competition Policy, 1996; chmn. bd. advisor Euro Watch; mem. bd. advisors Antitrust and Trade Regulation Reporter, George Washington Jour. Law and Econs., Can. Competition Policy Record; contbr. articles to profl. publs. Committeeman Nassau County (N.Y.) Dem. Com., 1963-65; lifetime mem. corp. Culinary Inst. Am. Recipient Edward S. Corwin award Am. Polit. Sci. Assn., 1971; Henry fellow Balliol Coll., Oxford U., 1962, Nobel Internat. and Woodrow Wilson fellow Columbia U., 1963. Mem. ABA (internat. law, litigation and antitrust sect.), Coun. on Fgn. Rels., The European Inst., Am. Law Inst. (adv. com. law governing lawyers), Confrerie des Chevaliers du Tastevin, Mory's Assn., Phi Beta Kappa. Jewish. Office: 1301 K St NW Ste 600 Washington DC 20005-3317

ROSENTHAL, FRANZ, language educator; b. Berlin, Aug. 31, 1914; came to U.S., 1940, naturalized, 1943; s. Kurt W. and Elsa (Kirschstein) R. Ph.D., U. Berlin, 1935; DHL (hon.), Hebrew Union Coll.; PhD (hon.), Hebrew U., Tel Aviv U., U. Tübingen; Columbia U. Asst. prof. Semitic langs. Hebrew Union Coll., Cin., 1940-48; prof. Arabic, U. Pa., 1948-56; Louis M. Rabinowitz prof. Yale U., 1956-67, Sterling prof. Near Eastern langs., 1967-85, prof. emeritus, 1985—. Author: Aramaistische Forschung, 1939, Technique and Approach of Muslim Scholarship, 1947, Hist. of Muslim Historiography, 1952, Humor in Early Islam, 1956, Ibn Khaldun, The Muqaddimah, 1958, The Muslim Concept of Freedom, 1960, Fortleben der Antike im Islam, 1965, Knowledge Triumphant, 1970, The Herb: Hashish versus Medieval Muslim Society, 1971, Gambling in Islam, 1975, Sweeter than Hope, 1983, History of al-Tabari 38, 1985, 89, Muslim Intellectual and Social History: A Collection of Essays, 1990. Served with AUS, OSS, 1943-45. Fellow AAAS, Brit. Acad. (corr.); mem. Am. Philos. Soc., Am. Oriental Soc. (pres. 1964-65), Accademia Nazionale dei Lincei, Société Asiatique (hon.), Deutsche Morgenländische Ges (hon.). Home: 80 Heloise St Hamden CT 06517-3422

ROSENTHAL, HAROLD LESLIE, biochemistry educator; b. Elizabeth, N.J., Mar. 26, 1922; s. Isadore and Sophia (Shapiro) R.; m. Rose Schwartz, June 7, 1947; children: Jenifer Ann, Pamela Susan. B.Sc., U. N. Mex., 1944; Ph.D., Rutgers U., 1951. Rsch. asst. Rutgers U., New Brunswick, N.J., 1948-51; instr. Tulane U., New Orleans, 1951-53; chief biochemist Rochester Gen. Hosp., N.Y., 1953-58; prof. biomed. scis. Washington U., St. Louis, 1958-87, prof. emeritus, 1987—; vis. scientist Minerva Found., Finland, 1966, Nat. Acad. Sci., Hungary, 1974. Served with USN, 1943-46. Fellow AAAS; mem. Am. Chem. Soc. (emeritus), Am. Inst. Nutrition, Am. Soc. for Biochemistry and Molecular Biology, Sigma Xi. Avocations: gardening; oenology. Home: 7541 Teasdale Ave Saint Louis MO 63130-3923

ROSENTHAL, HELEN NAGELBERG, county official, advocate; b. N.Y.C., June 6, 1926; d. Alfred and Esther (Teichholz) Nagelberg; m. Albert S. Rosenthal, Apr. 10, 1949; children: Lisa Rosenthal Michaels, Apryl Meredith Rosenthal Stuppler. BS, CUNY, 1948; MA, NYU, 1950; postgrad., Adelphia U., L.I. U., Lehman Coll., 1975. Cert. early childhood and gifted edn. tchr., N.Y., N.J., elem. and secondary tchr., Fla. Tchr. gifted students N.Y. Bd Edn., Bklyn., 1949-77, 79-87, Baldwin (N.Y.) Pub. Schs., 1977-79; rep. community affairs County of Dade, Fla., 1988-92; ret., 1992. Author: Criteria for Selection and Curriculum for the Gifted, 1977, Science Experiments for Young Children, 1982, Music in the Air...and in Our Minds. Dir. Condominium, 1989-91. Recipient Departmental award, 1948. Mem. Concerned Citizens for Educating Gifted and Talented (officer N.Y.C. chpt.), Assn. Gifted and Talented Edn. (N.Y. chpt.), Am. Inst. Cancer Rsch., Bklyn. Coll. Alumni Assn. (pres. Broward-Dade chpt. 1995-96, v.p. membership 1996—).

ROSENTHAL, HOWARD LEWIS, political science educator; b. Wilkinsburg, Pa., Mar. 4, 1939; s. Arnold Sidney R. and Elinor (Kaufman) (Rosenthal) Lewis; m. Annie Regine Lunel, June 30, 1960 (div. Nov., 1967); children: Illia Rebecca, Jean Laurent; m. Margherita Guastoni Spampinato, Feb. 6, 1968; 1 son, Gil Guastoni. B.S., MIT, 1960, Ph.D., 1964. Asst. prof. polit. sci. U. Calif.-Irvine, 1965-66; asst. prof. and assoc. prof. polit. sci. Carnegie-Mellon U., Pitts., 1966-71, prof., 1971-93; Roger Williams Straus prof. social scis. Princeton U., N.J., 1993—; vis. prof. Hebrew U., Jerusalem, 1968-69, U. Calif., San Diego, 1976-77, MIT, Cambridge, 1989-90, U. Paris I, 1990; vis. grad. lectr. Fondation Nat. des Scis. Politiques, Paris, 1972-73. Author: Prediction Analysis of Cross Classifications, 1977, Analysis of Ordinal Data, 1977, Partisan Politics, Divided Government and the Economy, 1995; Congress: A Political-Economic History of Roll Call Voting, 1996; mem. editl. bd. Pub. Choice, Econs. and Politics. Fellow NSF, 1969-92; fellow Ford Found., 1972-73, Social Sci. Rsch. Coun., 1964-65; Nat. fellow Hoover Instn., Stanford U., 1979-80; Sherman Fairchild disting. scholar Calif. Inst. Tech., 1982-83; fellow Internat. Ctr. for Econ. Rsch.,

Turin, Italy, 1991-93, Ctr. for Advanced Study in the Behavioral Scis., 1991-92, ECARE U. Libre de Brussels (Belgium), 1995. Fellow Am. Acad. Arts and Scis.; mem. Pub. Choice Soc. (Duncan Black award 1979), Am. Polit. Sci. Assn. (CQ Press award 1985), French Polit. Sci. Assn. Office: Princeton Univ Politics Dept Princeton NJ 08544

ROSENTHAL, IMRE, financial company executive. Chmn. bd. Rosenthal Inc., N.Y.C., 1964—. Office: Rosenthal Inc 1370 Broadway New York NY 10018-7302*

ROSENTHAL, IRA MAURICE, pediatrician, educator; b. N.Y.C., June 11, 1920; s. Abraham Leon and Jean (Kalotkin) R.; m. Ethel Ginsburg, Oct. 17, 1943; children: Anne, Judith. Student, CCNY, 1936-38; A.B., Ind. U., 1940, M.D., 1943. Intern Lincoln Hosp., N.Y.C., 1943-44; resident in pathology Albert Einstein Hosp., Phila., 1947-48; resident in pediatrics Fordham Hosp., N.Y.C., 1948-49; practice medicine specializing in pediatrics Bklyn., 1950-52; instr. U. Ill. Coll. Medicine, Chgo., 1953; asst. prof. U. Ill. Coll. Medicine, 1953-55, assoc. prof., 1955-63, prof. pediatrics, 1963-90, prof. emeritus, 1990—, head dept., 1973-82; clin. prof. pediatrics Stritch Sch. Medicine Loyola U., Chgo., 1990-91, lectr., 1991-93; clin. assoc. in pediatrics U. Chgo., 1990-91, clin. prof. pediatrics, 1991—; mem. med. service adv. com. Nat. Found. March of Dimes, 1975-80. Served to capt. U.S. Army, 1944-46. Mem. Am. Pediatric Soc., Soc. Pediatric Research, Acad. Pediatrics, Lawson Wilkins Pediatric Endocrine Soc., Endocrine Soc. Home: 5490 S South Shore Dr Chicago IL 60615-5984 Office: U Chgo Dept Pediats MC 118 5841 S Maryland Ave Chicago IL 60615-5984

ROSENTHAL, JACOB (JACK ROSENTHAL), newspaper editor; b. Tel-Aviv, June 30, 1935; came to U.S., 1938, naturalized, 1943; s. Manfred and Rachel (Kaplan) R.; m. Holly Russell, Dec. 21, 1985; children by previous marriage: John, Ann; stepchildren: Christopher Russell, Andrew Russell. A.B., Harvard U., 1956. Reporter, editor Portland Oregonian, Reporter, 1950-61; asst. dir., dir. public info. U.S. Dept. Justice, Washington, 1961-66; exec. asst. to Undersec. of State, 1966-67; Kennedy fellow Harvard Inst. Politics, 1967-68; nat. urban corr. Life Mag., N.Y.C., 1968-69; urban corr. N.Y. Times, Washington, 1969-73; asst. Sun. editor, mag. editor N.Y. Times, N.Y.C., 1973-77, dep. editorial page editor, 1977-86, editorial page editor, 1986-93; mag. editor, 1993—. Prin. author: Kerner Commn. Report on Urban Riots, 1968. Mem. Harvard Crimson Grad. Bd. Recipient Best Editorial award Internat. Labor Press Assn., 1961, Loeb award, 1973, Pulitzer prize for editorials, 1982. Office: NY Times Co 229 W 43rd St New York NY 10036-3913

ROSENTHAL, JAMES D., retired federal official, former U.S. ambassador; b. San Francisco, Jan. 15, 1932. B.A., Stanford U., 1954; student Fgn. Service Inst., 1960-61, Nat War Coll., 1974-75. With U.S. Fgn. Service, 1956-90, adminstrv. officer, Port of Spain, Trinidad, 1958-60; polit officer, Saigon, Vietnam, 1961-65; faculty U.S. Mil. Acad., 1965-67; internat. relations officer Vietnam affairs Dept. State, 1967-70; mem. U.S. dele. to Vietnam Peace Talks, Paris, 1970-72; dep. chief of mission, Bangui, 1972-74; dir. Vietnam, Laos and Cambodia affairs Dept. State, 1975-77; dep. chief of mission Kuala Lumpur, Malaysia, 1977-79; dep chief mission, Manila, 1979-83; ambassador to Guinea, Conakry, 1983-86, dep. dir. mgmt. ops. Dept. State, Washington, 1986-90; exec. dir. Commonwealth Club of Calif., 1990-96.

ROSENTHAL, JULIAN BERNARD, lawyer, association executive; b. N.Y.C., July 4, 1908; s. Alex Sidney and Katherine (Goodman) R.; m. Frances Stone, Nov. 14, 1941; children—Brian, John L. Student, Columbia, 1925-26; LL.B., Fordham U., 1929. Bar: N.Y. 1931. Practiced in N.Y.C., 1931-72, Ga., 1972-78; mem. firm Javits & Javits, 1968-72, of counsel, 1972-74; mem. Air Force Assn., 1945—, life mem., 1946—, sec., 1946-59, chmn. bd. dirs., 1959-60, chmn. constn. com., 1946-71, chmn. resolutions com., 1946-61, permanent bd. dirs., 1960-84, dir. emeritus, 1984—; chmn. bd. dirs. Aerospace Edn. Council, N.Y.C., 1965-73; mem. Atlanta consumer adv. panel Gulf Oil Corp.; Govt. appeal agent SSS, 1943-44; chmn. steering com., Ga. joint legis. com. Am. Assn. Ret. Persons-Nat. Ret. Tchrs. Assn., 1975-78, mem. Ariz. joint state legis. com., 1978-81; mem. motion picture div. Dem. Nat. Com., 1940; past treas., dir. Lydia M. Morrison Found.; former sec. bd. dirs. Herbert I. and Shirley C. Rosenthal Found.; former v.p., treas., dir. Vanguard Found.; past trustee, sec. Aerospace Edn. Found.; mem. tech. adv. com. Health Planning Agy., Ga., 1987. Vol. legal aide North Cen. Legal Assistance Program, Durham, N.C., 1990—. Served with USAAF, 1944-45. Recipient Man of Yr. award Air Force Assn., 1953, Exceptional Svc. medal USAF, 1996. Mem. ABA, Am. Assn. Ret. Persons (mem. nat. legis. adv. com. 1977, capitol task force Ga. 1987-89). Address: 2701 Pickett Rd Apt 4014 Durham NC 27705-5652

ROSENTHAL, LAURENCE, composer; b. Detroit, Nov. 4, 1926. Numerous film scores include: A Raisin in the Sun, 1961, The Miracle Worker, 1962, Requiem for a Heavyweight, 1962, Becket, 1964, Man of La Mancha, 1972, Rooster Cogburn, 1975, The Return of a Man Called Horse, 1976, The Island of Dr. Moreau, 1977, Who'll Stop the Rain, 1978, Meteor, 1979, Clash of the Titans, 1981, Heart Like a Wheel, 1983, Easy Money, 1983; TV work includes: Fantasy Island, 1977, Peter the Great, 1986, The Bourne Identity, 1988, My Name Is Bill W., 1989, The Young Indiana Jones Chronicles, 1992 (Emmy award, Outstanding Achievement in Music Composition for a series 1995). Office: Gorfaine-Schwartz Agy Ste 201 3301 Burham Blvd Los Angeles CA 90068*

ROSENTHAL, LEE H., federal judge; b. Nov. 30, 1952; m. Gary L. Rosenthal; children: Rebecca, Hannah, Jessica, Rachel. BA in Philosophy with honors, U. Chgo., 1974, JD with honors, 1977. Bar: Tex. 1979. Law clk. to Hon. John R. Brown U.S. Ct. Appeals (5th cir.), 1977-78; assoc. Baker & Botts, 1978-86, ptnr., 1986-92; judge U.S. Dist. Ct. (so. dist.) Tex., 1992—. Editor topics and comments Law Rev. U. Chgo., 1977-78. Active vis. com. Law Sch. U. Chgo., 1983-86, 94—; mem. devel. coun. Tex. Children's Hosp., 1988-92; pres. Epilepsy Assn. Houston/Gulf Coast, 1989-91; trustee Briarwood Sch. Endowment Found., 1991-92; bd. dirs. Epilepsy Found. Am., 1993—. Fellow Tex. Bar Found.; mem. ABA, Am. Law Inst., Texas Bar Assn., Houston Bar Assn. Office: US Dist Ct US Courthouse Rm 8631 515 Rusk St Houston TX 77002

ROSENTHAL, LEIGHTON A., aviation company executive; b. Buffalo, Jan. 27, 1915; s. Samuel and Sadie (Dosberg) R.; m. Honey Rousuck, June 30, 1940; children: Cynthia, Jane. Student, Phila. Textile Sch.; grad. Wharton Sch., U. Pa.; hon. doctorate, Cleve. Coll. Jewish Studies, 1973. Pres. Cleve. Overall Co., 1956-61, Work Wear Corp., 1961-86, The Purity Uniform Service Inc., 1986-89, Lars Mgmt. div. Purity Uniform Service Inc., 1986-89, Lars Aviation Inc., 1990—; chmn. Architecture Commn., City of Palm Beach. Trustee Jewish Community Fedn. Cleve., Leighton A. Rosenthal Family Found., Samuel Rosenthal Found., Preservation Found. Palm Beach; bd. dirs. Ohio Motorists Assn. Fellow Am. Assn. Jewish Edn., Oakwood Club, Union Club, Poinciana Club, Marks Club, Annabels Club. Office: Lars Aviation Inc 1228 Euclid Ave Ste 310 The Halle Bldg Cleveland OH 44115

ROSENTHAL, LUCY GABRIELLE, writer, editor, educator; b. N.Y.C.; d. Henry Moses and Rachel (Tchernowitz) R. AB, U. Mich., 1954; MS in Journalism, Columbia U., 1955; MFA, Yale Sch. Drama, 1961; postgrad. Writers Workshop, U. Iowa, 1965-68. Asst. editor Radiology mag., Detroit, 1955-57; free-lance editorial cons. various pub. houses, lit. agts. N.Y.C., 1957-73; mem. admissions staff U. Iowa Writers Workshop, Iowa City, 1965-68; editor Book-of-the-Month Club, N.Y.C., 1973-74, mem. editorial bd. judges, 1974-79; sr. editorial advisor Book-of-the-Month Club, 1979-87; mem. biography jury Pulitzer Prize, 1980; mem. bd. Am. Book Awards, 1981-82; adj. prof. English, NYU, 1986—; mem. guest faculty in writing Sarah Lawrence Coll., 1988—; lectr. writing program Columbia U. Sch. Gen. Studies, 1990—, Humanities faculty, 92nd St. YM/YWCA, 1987; fiction workshop The Writer's Voice, West Side YMCA, summer 1991; adj. prof. NYU Sch. Continuing Edn., 1988; mem. faculty Sarah Lawrence Ctr. for Continuing Edn., 1989, 90; instr. fiction writing course Art Workshop Internat., Assisi, Italy, summer 1993. Plays produced at Eugene O'Neill Meml. Theater Ctr., 1966, 67; author: The Ticket Out, 1983; editor: Great American Love Stories, 1988, The World Treasury of Love Stores, 1995; contbr. articles and revs. to various mags. and periodicals including Washington Post and Chgo. Tribune Book World, Saturday Rev., Ms. mag., Mich. Quar. Rev., N.Y. Times Book Rev.; contbr. fiction to Global City Rev., 1995. Pulitzer fellow critical writing, 1968. Mem. Authors Guild, Authors League, Nat. Book Critics Circle, Women's Media Group (bd. mem. 1979-81), PEN, Associated Writing Programs, Eugene O'Neill Meml. Theater Ctr., Phi Beta Kappa, Phi Kappa Phi. Office: care of Wendy Weil Agy Inc 232 Madison Ave Ste 1300 New York NY 10016-2901

ROSENTHAL, LYOVA HASKELL See GRANT, LEE

ROSENTHAL, MACHA LOUIS, author, educator; b. Washington, Mar. 14, 1917; s. Jacob and Ethel (Brown) R.; m. Victoria Himmelstein, Jan. 7, 1939; children: David, Alan, Laura. B.A., U. Chgo., 1937, M.A., 1938; Ph.D., N.Y. U., 1949. Faculty Mich. State U., 1939-45; faculty NYU, N.Y.C., 1945—; prof. NYU, 1961-87, English prof. emeritus, 1987—; 1st Moss chair of excellence in English Memphis State U. (now Memphis U.), 1989; founder, dir. NYU Poetics Inst., 1977-79; poetry editor The Nation, 1956-61, Humanist, 1970-78, Present Tense, 1973-91; vis. specialist U.S. Cultural Exch. programs, Germany, 1961, Pakistan, 1965, Poland, Romania, Bulgaria, 1966, Italy and France, 1980, 88; lectr. New Zealand univs., 1989, Italian univs., 1995; vis. prof. U. Pa., 1974, U. Zurich, 1984, U. Bologna, 1995; vis. poet, Israel, 1974, Yugoslavia, 1980, World Poetry Festival, Can., 1993; Disting. Scholar Exch. Program, China, 1982, World Poetry Festival, Toronto, 1993; dir. summer seminar NEH, 1981, 93, dir. NEH Inst., 1985; mem. Bolligen award com., 1968-70; chmn. Delmore Schwartz Meml. award, 1970—; mem. creative arts awards lit. jury Brandeis U., 1976. Author: (with A.J.M. Smith) Exploring Poetry, 1955, 73, The Modern Poets: A Critical Introduction, 1960, A Primer of Ezra Pound, 1960, Blue Boy on Skates: Poems, 1964, The New Poets: American and British Poetry since World War II, 1967, Beyond Power: New Poems, 1969, The View from the Peacock's Tail: Poems, 1972, Randall Jarrell, 1972, Poetry and the Common Life, 1974, 83, She: A Sequence of Poems, 1977, Sailing into the Unknown: Yeats, Pound, and Eliot, 1978, Poems, 1964-80, 1981, (with Sally M. Gall) The Modern Poetic Sequence: The Genius of Modern Poetry, 1983, 86, The Poet's Art, 1987, As for Love: Poems and Translations, 1987, Our Life in Poetry: Selected Essays and Reviews, 1991, Running to Paradise: Yeats' Poetic Art, 1994, In the World Pub.: A Sequence or Opera Seria (in Exile, 1995); editor: The Macmillan Paperback Poets, 1957-62; Selected Poems and Two Plays of W.B. Yeats, 1962, 73, The William Carlos Williams Reader, 1966, The New Modern Poetry: An Anthology of American and British Poetry since World War II, 1967, 69, 100 Postwar Poems, British and American, 1968, Selected Poems and Three Plays of William Butler Yeats, 1986; co-editor: Chief Modern Poets of Britain and America, 1970; gen. editor Poetry in English: An Anthology, 1987; editor Persea Books Lamplighters Series, 1982-92, Works-in-Progress (issue Ploughshares mag.), 1991; translator: The Adventures of Pinocchio: Tale of a Puppet, 1983; poetry adviser Macmillan Co., 1957-62; contbr. articles and poems to profl. pubs. Recipient Explicator Found. award, 1984, 1st Yeats Soc. award for Disting. Contbns. to Yeats Scholarship, 1993; Fellow Am. Coun. Learned Socs., 1942, 50-51, Guggenheim Found., 1960-61, 64-65, Rockefeller Found. Rsch. Ctr., Bellagio, Italy, 1988. Mem. AAUP, MLA, PEN, Poetry Soc. Am. (v.p., bd. govs. 1989-92), Am. Lit. Assn., Yeats Soc., Phi Beta Kappa. Home: 17 Bayard Ln Suffern NY 10901 Office: NYU Dept English 19 University Pl New York NY 10003-4501

ROSENTHAL, MARK ELLIOTT, hospital administrator; b. Columbus, Ohio, May 30, 1952; s. Bert L. and Betty L. (Robbins) R.; m. Phyllis Bidnick, Aug. 3, 1975; children—Heather, Emily. B.A. in Pre-med. Sci., U. Mo., 1974, M.S. in Pub. Health-Health Services Mgmt., 1977. Adminstrv. staff asst. Meml. Med. Ctr., Springfield, Ill., 1977-79, adminstrv. dir. phys. medicine and rehab., 1979-81; adminstr. Rehab. Inst. Okla., Oklahoma City, 1981-83; assoc. adminstr. Dallas Rehab. Inst., 1983-86, COO, 1986-89; adminstr. Rehab. Hosp. Austin, 1989; adminstr., CEO CPC Capital Hosp., 1990-93; asst. adminstr. rehab. svcs. & adminstrn. Ctr. Rehab. Medicine Emory U., 1993—; regents adv. bd. ACHE, 1993—; bd dirs. GARF, 1993—, adminstrv. surveyor CARF, 1993—; sec. GAHE, 1995, v.p., 1996; mem. consumer cons. com. Tex. Rehab. Commn., 1983-85; mem. nat. adv. com. Commn. Accreditation of Rehab. Facilities; mem. Ill. Gov's. steering com. Internat. Yr. Disabled Persons, 1981, chmn. Springfield Mayor's Exec. Com., 1981.; mem. Plano Cable TV Adv. Bd., Tex., 1984-86. Named one of Outstanding Young Men of Am., 1982. Fellow Am. Coll. Healthcare Execs.; mem. Assn. Med. Rehab. Dirs. and Coordinators (Tex. Lone Star region rep. 1984), Am. Hosp. Assn., U. Mo. Grad. Studies Health Svcs. Mgmt. Alumni Assn. Jewish. Avocations: golf, water sports, photography, computers. Office: Emory Univ Hosp 1441 Clifton Rd NE Atlanta GA 30307-1055

ROSENTHAL, MICHAEL ROSS, academic administrator, dean; b. Youngstown, Ohio, Dec. 2, 1939; s. Samuel Herman and Frances Vance (Schlesinger) R.; m. Linda Gabler, Sept. 6, 1963; children: Heidi, Erika, Nicolas Gabler. AB, Case Western Res. U., 1961; MS, U. Ill., 1963, PhD, 1965. Asst. prof. chemistry Bard Coll., Annandale, N.Y., 1965-68, assoc. prof. chemistry, 1968-73, prof. chemistry, 1973-84, assoc. dean acad. affairs, 1980-84; v.p. acad. affairs St. Mary's Coll. of Md., St. Mary's City, 1984-89; provost, dean faculty, prof. chemistry Southwestern U., Georgetown, Tex., 1989-96; dep. sec. Md. Higher Edn. Commn., Annapolis, 1996—; acad. cons., ind. and as rep. of Assn. Am. Colls. Author or co-author of numerous articles in jours. of inorganic chemistry and chem. edn. Chmn. Environ. Mgmt. Coun., Dutchess County, N.Y., 1978-84; founding chmn. Heritage Task Force for Hudson River Valley, 1980-84; pres., bd. dirs. Hudson River Heritage, N.Y., 1978-84; bd. dirs. Hudson River Rsch. Coun., 1976-84; teaching assoc. Danforth Found., 1980. Recipient Outstanding Community Svc. award, Dutchess County (N.Y.) Legislature, 1980. Mem. Am. Chem. Soc., The Royal Society (Chemistry, London), Am. Conf. Acad. Deans, Hudson River Environ. Soc., Sigma Xi, Phi Beta Kappa, Phi Lambda Upsilon. Democrat. Office: Md Higher Edn Commn 16 Francis St Annapolis MD 21401-1781 *Those of us who spend our professional lives as educators are subject to many pressures and influences - financial influences, political influences, intellectual influences. I try to remember that in the usually chaotic world of education the only really important thing is the welfare of the student.*

ROSENTHAL, MILTON FREDERICK, minerals and chemical company executive; b. N.Y.C., Nov. 24, 1913; s. Jacob C. and Louise (Berger) R.; m. Frieda Bojar, Feb. 28, 1943; 1 child, Anne Rosenthal Mitro. BA, CCNY, 1932; LLB, Columbia U., 1935. Bar: N.Y. 1935. Rsch. asst. N.Y. State Law Revision Commn., 1935-37; law sec. Fed. Judge William Bondy, 1937-40; assoc. atty. Leve, Hecht & Hadfield, 1940-42; sec., treas. Hugo Stinnes Corp., 1946-48, exec. v.p., treas., 1948-49, pres., dir., chief exec. officer, 1949-64; pres., dir., chief exec. officer Minerals and Chems. Philipp Corp., N.Y.C., 1964-67; pres., dir., COO Engelhard Minerals & Chem. Corp., N.Y.C., 1967-71; chmn., pres., CEO, dir. Engelhard Minerals & Chems. Corp., N.Y.C., 1971-81; dir. emeritus Salomon, Inc., N.Y.C., Ferro Corp., Cleve. Trustee Mt. Sinai Med. Ctr. and Mt. Sinai Hosp.; bd. dirs. United Cerebral Palsy Rsch. and Ednl. Found., Inc.; ret. trustee Am. Fedn. Arts, Manhattanville Coll., Purchase Coll. Found. 1st lt. JAG dept. U.S. Army, 1942-45. Mem. Assn. of Bar of City of N.Y., Chgo. Bar Assn., Columbia Law Sch. Alumni Assn., Judge Adv. Assn., Phi Beta Kappa. Home: 450 Woodlands Rd Harrison NY 10528-1220 also:: PO Box 5192 Carefore AZ 85377 Office: 450 Park Ave Ste 2701 New York NY 10022-2605

ROSENTHAL, MURRAY WILFORD, chemical engineer, science administrator; b. Greenville, Miss., Feb. 25, 1926; s. Monnie and Esther (Bernstein) R.; m. Miriam Sylvia Teplit, Aug. 7, 1949; children: Elaine, Douglas I. BSChemE, La. State U., 1949; PhDChemE, MIT, 1953. Devel. engr. heat transfer rsch., reactor exptl. engring. div. Oak Ridge (Tenn.) Nat. Lab., 1953-55, group leader aqueous homogeneous reactor analysis, 1956-59, group leader analysis advanced reactors, reactor div., 1959-61, project engr., 1961-63, chief planning and analysis sect., 1963-65, dir. planning, 1965, dir. molten salt reactor program, 1966-73, acting dep. dir., 1973, assoc. dir. advanced energy systems, 1974-89, dep. dir., 1989-93, lectr. in reactor engring. sch. reactor tech., 1955; cons., 1994—; vis. prof. chem. engring. MIT, Boston, 1961; tech. asst. to asst. gen. mgr. AEC, Washington, 1966. Vice chmn. Oak Ridge Charter Commn., 1955-56, chmn., 1962-63; mem. Oak Ridge Human Rels. Adv. Bd., 1963-65, Adv. Task Force on Tenn. Energy Future, Oak Ridge, 1978. Lt. (j.g.) USN, 1943-46. Recipient Disting. Career award Fusion Power Assocs., 1993, Disting. Svc. award Nat. Mgmt. Assn., 1994; inducted into Engring. Hall of Distinction, La. State U., 1982; Humble fellow MIT, 1950, Std. Oil fellow, 1951, Pan Am. fellow, 1952. Fellow Am. Nuclear Soc. (bd. dirs. 1970-73, exec. com. 1971-73); mem. NAE, AAAS, Sigma Xi. Home and Office: 124 Carnegie Dr Oak Ridge TN 37830-7732

ROSENTHAL, MYER H., anesthesiologist; b. Boston, July 11, 1941. MD, U. Vt., 1967. Intern Naval Hosp. Bethesda, Md., 1967-68; resident Fell Critical Care Medicine Naval Hosp. San Diego, 1968-70; attending anesthesiologist Stanford (Calif.) Med. Ctr., 1975—; prof. Stanford U., 1975—. Office: Med Dir Intensive Care Stanford U Med Ctr 300 Pasteur Dr Palo Alto CA 94304-2203*

ROSENTHAL, MYRON MARTIN, retired electrical engineer, educator, author; b. Bklyn., Nov. 5, 1930; s. Murray Morris and Selma Locke (Belsky) R.; m. Charlene Powell, Sept. 16, 1989; children from previous marriage: Lynn, Debbie, Richard; stepchildren: Christi Ackerson, Michael Ackerson. BEE, CCNY, 1953; MS, Adelphi U., 1957. Registered profl. engr., N.J., Pa., N.J. Sr. engr. Republic Aviation Corp., Farmingdale, L.I., 1955-61; pres. Myron M. Rosenthal & Staff, Farmingdale, L.I., 1957-61; program mgr. Loral Electronics, Bronx, N.Y., 1962-64; engring. mgr. Singer-Kearfott div. The Singer Co., Wayne, N.J., 1964-87; prof. Poly. U., Bklyn., N.J., 1954-87; bd. dirs. Electronics and Aerospace Conv., 1971-82, treas., 1972-82, chmn. bd., 1974; bd. dirs. Nat. Aerospace and Electronics Conf., 1972-75; notary pub., N.J., N.Y., Fla. Patentee inflatable antenna, cylindrical flat plate 35 GHz antenna, rotating lens antenna seeker-head. Founder Randal Carter PTA cultural workshop, Wayne, 1965; lighting commr. Wayne, 1956. Recipient Picatinny Arsenal U.S. Army Engring. and Leadership commendations, 1969, 71, 73; Poly. U. N.Y. faculty award, 1975 Disting. Faculty award, 1982; Nat. Aerospace and Electronics Conf. award, 1968, 75, 76; Electronics and Aerospace Conv. award, 1974, 80, 82; Poly Service award, 1984. Mem. IEEE (sr. mem., award 1972, 74, Centennial medal 1984, life), NSPE, AIAA, ASME, ASCE, ASTM, Illuminating Engring. Soc., Am. Assn. Clin. Chemistry, Am. Inst. Indsl. Engrs., Audio Engring. Soc., Cincinatus Soc., Forest Products Rsch. Soc., Am. Inst. Chemists, Nat. Fire Protection Assn., Nat. Rehab. Assn., Assn. U.S. Army, Navy League, U.S. Naval Inst., Marine Corps Assn., Am. Def. Preparedness Assn., Air Force Assn., Aerospace Electronics and Systems Soc. (bd. govs. 1968-82, v.p. 1972, chmn. N.Y.-N.J. Met. chpt. 1972-82, Disting. Service award 1972, 74, 79, 82), Armed Forces Communications and Electronics Assn., AAUP, N.Y. Acad. Sci., Am. Soc. Indsl. Security, Am. Chem. Soc., Am. Assn. Physics Tchrs., Am. Physics Soc., Am. Soc. Safety Engrs. (profl. mem.), Am. Vocat. Assn. (life), Constrn. Specifications Inst., Am. Soc. Public Adminstrn., Am. Public Works Assn., Am. Assn. Cost Engrs., Am. Ceramic Soc., Nat. Mgmt. Assn. (certified), Nat. Council Tchrs. of Math., Nat. Council Tchrs. of English, Adult Edn. Assn., Inst. Cert. Profl. Mgrs. (cert.), Am. Radio Relay League, Nat. Assn. Accts., Nat. Soc. Public Accts., ALA, Soc. Automotive Engrs., Am. Craft Council, Nat. Soc. Architects, Am. Soc. Interior Design, Nat. Sci. Tchrs. Assn., Soc. Plastics Engrs., Audio Engring. Soc., Internat. Assn. Assessing Officers, Am. Hist. Assn., Am. Philos. Assn., MLA, Inst. of Nav. (program com. 1978), Am. Judicature Soc., Aircraft Owners and Pilots Assn., Refrigeration Service Engrs. Soc., AAAS, Boat Owners Assn., Am. Assn. Higher Edn., Nat. Aeros. Assn., Nat. Assn. Social Workers, Nat. Council Young Israel, Am. Rose Soc., Nat. Audubon Soc., Nat. Assn. of Deaf, Nat. Eye Research Found., Am. Council for Blind, Am. Diabetes Assn., Nat. Rehab. Assn., Am. Jewish Congress, Workmen's Circle, Am. Council Museums, Triple Nine Soc., Mensa, Intertel, Am. Nuclear Soc., Gold Coast Amateur Radio Club, United Otomy Assn., Sigma Xi, Eta Kappa Nu. Republican. Jewish. Clubs: B'nai B'rith (trustee 1976-77), Toastmasters (pres. 1969, area gov. 1970, best speaker of the year 1967, 68, 69, 75, 77). Avocation: amateur radio operator. Home: 6858 Giralda Cir Boca Raton FL 33433-7734

ROSENTHAL, NAN, curator, author; b. N.Y.C., Aug. 27, 1937; d. Alan Herman and Lenore (Fry) R.; m. Otto Piene (div.); m. Henry Benning Cortesi, Sept. 5, 1990. BA, Sarah Lawrence Coll., 1959; MA, Harvard U., 1970, PhD, 1976. Asst. prof. art history U. Calif., Santa Cruz, 1971-77, assoc. prof., 1977-84, prof., 1985-86, chair dept. art history, 1976-80; curator 20th-century art Nat. Gallery Art, Washington, 1985-92; cons. Dept. of 20th Century Art, Metro. Mus. of Art, N.Y.C., 1993—; Lila Acheson Wallace vis. prof. of Fine Arts Inst. of Fine Arts, NYU, 1996—; vis. prof. art history Fordham U., Lincoln Ctr., 1981, 85; vis. scholar N.Y. Inst. for Humanities, NYU, 1982-83; vis. lectr. visual arts Princeton U., 1985, 88, 92. Author: George Rickey, 1977; also exhbn. catalogues, catalogue essays and articles; art editor Show, 1963-64; assoc. editor, then editor at large and contbg. editor Art in Am., 1964-70. Radcliffe Inst. fellow, 1968-69, scholar, 1970-71; travelling fellow Harvard U., 1973-74, rsch. fellow U. Calif., 1978, Ailsa Mellon Bruce curatorial fellow Nat. Gallery of Art, 1988-89; rsch. and travel grantee U. Calif., Santa Cruz, 1974, 77-80, 82-85. Office: Met Mus of Art 20th Century Art 1000 Fifth Ave New York NY 10028-0113

ROSENTHAL, PAUL EDMOND, lawyer; b. Miami, May 1, 1951; s. David and Helen (Kaplan) R. BA, U. Fla., 1973, JD, 1976. Bar: Fla. 1977, U.S. Dist. Ct. (mid. dist.) Fla. 1977. Asst. city atty. City of Orlando (Fla.), 1977-79, asst. to mayor and council, 1979-80; assoc. Van den Berg, Gay & Burke, Orlando, 1980-81; ptnr. Van den Berg, Gay, Burke, Wilson & Arkin, Orlando, 1982-85, Foley & Lardner, Orlando, 1985—; mem., chmn. 9th Jud. Cir. Nominating Commn., Orlando, 1984-88; atty. City of Ocoee, Fla., 1988—. Mem. ABA, Orange County Bar Assn., Delta Upsilon (sec. alumni club). Democrat. Jewish. Office: Foley & Lardner 111 N Orange Ave Ste 1800 Orlando FL 32801-2387*

ROSENTHAL, PETER, public relations executive; b. N.Y.C., Nov. 1, 1946; s. Walter and Rita (Horn) R.; m. Terri Thompson; children: Daniel, Joel. BA, Lehman Coll., 1969; MA, Ball State U., 1972. Tchr., N.Y.C. Bd. Edn., 1969-71; reporter Bklyn. Today, 1972-73; asst. dir. pub. rels. St. Vincents Hosp., N.Y.C, 1973-76; account exec. Howard Rubenstein Assocs., N.Y.C., 1976-78, v.p., 1978-81, sr. v.p., 1981-84, exec. v.p., 1984-87, sr. exec. v.p., 1987—; mem. bd. gov's. science and endowment fund Bronx H.S. Mem. Internat. Assn. Bus. Communications, Nat. Assn. Real Estate Editors, Nat. Assn. Real Estate Investment Trust, Urban Land Inst. (assoc.) Jewish. Avocations: reading, theater, travel. Office: Howard J Rubenstein Assocs Inc 1345 Avenue Of The Americas New York NY 10105

ROSENTHAL, ROBERT, psychology educator; b. Giessen, Germany, Mar. 2, 1933; came to U.S., 1940, naturalized, 1946; s. Julius and Hermine (Kahn) R.; m. Mary Lu Clayton, Apr. 20, 1951; children: Roberta, David C., Virginia. A.B., UCLA, 1953, Ph.D., 1956. Diplomate: clin. psychology Am. Bd. Examiners Profl. Psychology. Clin. psychology trainee Los Angeles Area VA, 1954-57; lectr. U. So. Calif., 1956-57; acting instr. UCLA, 1957; from asst. to assoc. prof., coordinator clin. tng. U. N.D., 1957-62; vis. assoc. prof. Ohio State U., 1960-61; lectr. Boston U., 1965-66; lectr. clin. psychology Harvard U., Cambridge, Mass., 1962-67, prof. social psychology, 1967—, chmn. dept. psychology, 1992-95, Edgar Pierce prof. psychology, 1995—. Author: Experimenter Effects in Behavioral Research, 1966, enlarged edit., 1976; (with Lenore Jacobson) Pygmalion in the Classroom, expanded edit., 1992, Meta-analytic Procedures for Social Research, 1984, rev. edit., 1991, Judgement Studies, 1987; (with others) New Directions in Psychology 4, 1970, Sensitivity to Nonverbal Communication: The Pons Test, 1979; (with Ralph L. Rosnow) The Volunteer Subject, 1975, Primer of Methods for the Behavioral Sciences, 1975, Essentials of Behavioral Research, 1984, 2d edit., 1991, Understanding Behavioral Science, 1984, Contrast Analysis, 1985, Beginning Behavioral Research, 1993, 2d edit., 1996; (with Brian Mullen) BASIC Meta-analysis, 1985; editor: (with Ralph L. Rosnow) Artifact in Behavioral Research, 1969, Skill in Nonverbal Communication, 1979, Quantitative Assessment of Research Domains, 1980, (with Thomas A. Sebeok) The Clever Hans Phenomenon: Communication With Horses, Whales, Apes and People, 1981; (with Blanck and Buck) Nonverbal Communication in the Clinical Context, 1986; (with Gheorghiu, Netter and Eysenck) Suggestion and Suggestibility: Theory and Research, 1989. Recipient Donald Campbell award Soc. for Personality and Social Psychology, 1988, James McKeen Cattell Sabbatical award, 1995-96; Guggenheim fellow, 1973-74, fellow Ctr. for Advanced Study in Behavioral Scis., 1988-89; sr. Fulbright Scholar, 1972. Fellow AAAS (co-recipient Sociopsychol. prize 1960, co-recipient Behavioral Sci. Rsch. prize 1993), APA (co-recipient Cattell Fund award 1967), Am. Psychol. Soc.; mem. Soc. Exptl. Social Psychology (Disting. Scientist award 1996), Ea. Psychol. Assn. (Disting. lectr. 1989), Mid-western Psychol. Assn., Mass. Psychol. Assn. (Disting. Career Contbn. award 1979), Soc. Projective Techniques (past treas.), Phi Beta Kappa, Sigma Xi. Home: 12 Phinney Rd Lexington MA 02173-7717 Office: Harvard U 33 Kirkland St Cambridge MA 02138-2044

ROSENTHAL, ROBERT JON, newspaper editor, journalist; b. N.Y.C., Aug. 5, 1948; s. Irving and Ruth (Moss) R.; m. Inez Katherina von Sternenfels, Nov. 22, 1985; children: Adam, Benjamin, Ariella. BA, U. Vt., 1970. News asst. N.Y. Times, N.Y.C., 1970-73; reporter Boston Globe, 1974-79; reporter Phila. Inquirer, 1979-82, Africa corr., Nairobi, Kenya, 1982-86, fgn. editor, Phila., 1986-91, city editor, 1991-93, asst. mng. editor, daily, 1993-94; assoc. mng. editor, 1994-96, exec. editor, 1996—. Recipient Third World Reporting award Nat. Assn. Black Journalists, 1983, Mag. award Overseas Press Club, 1985, Disting. Fgn. Corr. award Sigma Delta Chi, 1985, Mag. Writing award World Population Inst., 1986. Avocations: sports, painting, fishing, cooking. Office: Phila Inquirer 400 N Broad St Philadelphia PA 19130-4015

ROSENTHAL, SOL, lawyer; b. Balt., Oct. 17, 1934; s. Louis and Hattie (Getz) R.; m. Diane Myra Sackler, June 11, 1961; children: Karen Abby, Pamela Margaret, Robert Joel. AB, Princeton U., 1956; JD, Harvard U., 1959. Bar: Md. 1959, Calif. 1961. Law clk. to chief judge U.S. Ct. Appeals, 4th cir., Balt., 1959-60; assoc. Kaplan, Livingston, Goodwin, Berkowitz & Selvin, Beverly Hills, Calif., 1960-66, ptnr., 1966-74; ptnr. Buchalter, Nemer, Fields & Younger, L.A., 1974-96; of counsel Blanc, Williams, Johnston & Kronstadt, L.A., 1996—; bd. dirs. Playboy Enterprises, Inc., Chgo.; arbitrator Dirs. Guild Am., L.A., 1976—, Writers Guild Am., L.A., 1976—, Am. Film Mktg. Assn., 1989—; negotiator Writers Guild-Assn. Talent Agts., L.A., 1978—. Founder Camp Ronald McDonald for Good Times, L.A., 1985; charter founder Mus. Contemporary Art, L.A., 1988. Mem. ABA, Calif. Bar Assn., L.A. County Bar Assn. (trustee 1981-82), L.A. Copyright Soc. (pres. 1973-74), Acad. TV Arts and Scis. (bd. govs. 1990-92), Beverly Hills Bar Assn. (pres. 1982-83), Phi Beta Kappa. Office: Buchalter Nemer et al Ste 2400 1801 Century Park E Los Angeles CA 90067-2326

ROSENTHAL, STANLEY LAWRENCE, meteorologist; b. Bklyn., Dec. 6, 1929; s. Louis and Fay (Pokorne) R.; m. Mildred Farlow, Aug. 8, 1953; children—Russell K., Sarah Lynn, David Scott. B.S., CCNY, 1951; M.S., Fla. State U., 1953, Ph.D., 1958. With NOAA, Dept. Commerce, 1960-93; chief theoretical studies group Nat. Hurricane Research Lab., Miami, Fla., 1960-75, chief modeling group, 1975-77, chief analytical and theoretical studies group, 1977-93, dir., 1980-93; dir. Nat. Hurricane and Exptl. Meterology Lab., 1977-80; dep. dir. Atlantic Oceanographic and Meteorol. Labs., 1981; sr. rsch. assoc. Coop. Inst. for Marine & Atmospheric Scis. U. Miami, 1993—; adj. prof. meteorology U. Miami, Coral Gables, Fla., 1964-84. Contbr. articles to profl. jours. Served with U.S. Army, 1953-55. Recipient Gold medal U.S. Dept. Commerce, 1970. Fellow Am. Meteorol. Soc. (council 1980-83), mem. com. on hurricanes and tropical meteorology 1981-85, past chmn. Greater Miami br.), AAAS (past officer sect. W). Home: 13301 SW 99th Pl Miami FL 33176-6163

ROSENTHAL, STEVEN SIEGMUND, lawyer; b. Cleve., May 22, 1949; s. Fred Siegel and Natalie Josephine Rosenthal; m. Ilene Edwina Goldstein, Oct. 1, 1983; 1 child, Alexandra M. AB, Dartmouth Coll., 1971; JD, Harvard U., 1974. Bar: Fla. 1974, D.C. 1975, U.S. Supreme Ct. 1978, Calif. 1983. Law clk. U.S. Ct. Appeals (D.C. cir.), 1974-75; assoc. Covington & Burling, Washington, 1975-80; assoc. Morrison & Foerster, Washington, 1980-81, ptnr., 1981—; lawyer rep. Jud. Conf. D.C. Cir., 1981-83. Pres. Family and Child Services Washington, 1986-88, trustee, 1978—. Mem. ABA, Am. Law Inst., Phi Beta Kappa. Republican. Office: Morrison & Foerster Ste 5500 2000 Pennsylvania Ave NW Washington DC 20006-1812

ROSENTHAL, TONY (BERNARD), sculptor; b. Highland Park, Ill., Aug. 9, 1914; s. Nathan H. and Bessie (Baumgarden) R.; m. Halina Kotlowicz, Apr. 2, 1946. AB, U. Mich., 1936; student, Art Inst. Chgo., Cranbrook Acad. Arts; hon. doctorate, Hofstra U., 1989. Exhbns. include Art Inst. Chgo., Met. Mus. Art, Mus. Modern Art, N.Y., Whitney Mus. Am. Art, N.Y.C., Pa. Acad. Fine Arts, Archtl. League, N.Y., Yale U., U. Ill., U. Nebr., 100 Biennale Exhbn., Sao Paulo, Brazil, Brussel's Fair, 1958, others; one man shows include San Francisco Mus, Western Mus. Assn. Travel Exhbn., Santa Barbara (Calif.) Mus., Long Beach (Calif.) Mus., Catherine Viviano Gallery N.Y., Kootz Gallery, N.Y.C., M. Knoedler & Co., Denise Rene Gallery, Paris, 1988, others; archtl. commn. include Temple Emanuel, Beverly Hills, Calif., 1955, IBM Bldg., 1958, Southland Ctr., Dallas, IBM Western Hdqrs., Los Angeles, Police Plaza, N.Y.C., Fullerton (Calif.) State Coll., Fin. Ctr. Pacific, Honolulu, Holocaust Meml., Buffalo, Metro-Rail Sta., Miami, S.E. Nat. Bank, Miami, Grove Isle, Miami, Met. Hosp., Phila., 1010 Lamar, Houston, Crantsrook Acad. Art, Bloomfield Hills, Mich., Steelpark, 400 E. 80th St, N.Y.C., Alamo, Astor Pl., N.Y.C., Rondo, 111 E. 59th St., N.Y.C., U. Ind., Hofstra U., N.Y., others; works in permanent collections Milw. Art Ctr., Ill. State U., Los Angeles County Mus., Long Beach, Lincoln (Mass.) Mus., Ariz. State Coll., Mus. Modern Art, Whitney Mus. Art, Albright Knox Art Gallery, Buffalo, U. Ill., NYU, Yale U., Middelheim Mus., Antwerp, Belgium, Guggenheim Mus., N.Y.C., Hofstra U. Fashion Inst. Art, N.Y.C., others; pvt. collections. Served with AUS, 1942-46. Recipient awards, prizes San Francisco Mus., 1950, Los Angeles City Exhbn., 1951, 52, Audubon Artists, N.Y., 1953, Pa. Acad. Fine Arts, 1953, Los Angeles County Mus., 1950, 57, Santa Barbara Mus. Art, 1959, Art in Steel award Iron and Steel Inst., 1974-75, Disting. Alumni award U. Mich., 1977, Sculpture award Inst. Arts and Letters, N.Y.C., 1985. Address: 173 E 73rd St New York NY 10021-3510

ROSENTHAL, WILLIAM FORSHAW, advertising executive; b. St. Louis, Apr. 11, 1933; s. William Arthur and Elizabeth (Forshaw) R.; m. Carol Gage Johnson, Aug. 23, 1975. AB, Washington U., St. Louis, 1955. With Proctor & Gamble Co., 1957-59, D'Arcy-MacManus & Masius, 1960-85; sr. v.p., gen. mgr. Twin Cities office, Mpls., 1978-79; pres. D'Arcy-MacManus & Masius, N.Y.C., 1980-82, also dir., mem. worldwide planning group.; exec. v.p. D'Arcy-MacManus & Masius, World-wide, 1982-85; exec. v.p. Einson-Freeman, Paramus, N.J., 1985-90, also bd. dirs.; dir. bus. devel. Einson-Freeman, Paramus, 1990—; sr. v.p. N.W. Ayer, N.Y.C., 1992—; exec. v.p. Dentsu divsn. Nova Promotion, 1993—, bd. dirs.; mem. compensation and long range planning coms. Einson-Freeman. Bd. dirs. Save African Endangered Wildlife. With AUS, 1955-57. Mem. Am. Assn. Advt. Agys. (mem. govt. affairs com., vice chmn. N.Y. council 1983, chmn. council 1984); Mem. Beta Theta Pi. Clubs: Tavern (Chgo.); Friars (N.Y.C.); Washington U. (St. Louis).

ROSENTHAL, WILLIAM J., lawyer; b. Balt., Nov. 4, 1920; s. Justin J. and Ray Marian (Stern) R.; m. Margaret Irwin Parker, July 4, 1956; children—Adriane Leigh, Jacqueline Rae, John Justin. A.B., Johns Hopkins U., 1941; LL.B., U. Balt., 1950. Bar: Md. 1950. Adminstrv. asst. Office Price Adminstrn., Washington, 1941-42; assoc. firm Earle K. Shawe (name changed to Shawe & Rosenthal 1967), Balt., 1951-67; ptnr. Shawe & Rosenthal, Balt., 1967—; lectr. U. Balt., 1952-56; mem. regional adv. council NLRB; vets. rep. Md. Constrn. Adv. Council, 1946-49; lectr. NYU Conf. Labor Relations, Boston U. Labor Law Seminar, 1985; expert witness on labor law, legis. and congl. coms. Contbg. author: The Developing Labor Law; contbr. articles to profl. jours. Served to lt. USNR, 1942-46, ETO. Mem. ABA, Md. Bar Assn., Balt. Bar Assn., Spiked Shoe Soc., Omicron Delta Kappa, Pi Delta Epsilon. Club: Suburban of Baltimore County (bd. govs., pres.). Home: 8207 Cranwood Ct Baltimore MD 21208-1823 Office: Shawe & Rosenthal Sun Life Bldg Charles Center Baltimore MD 21201

ROSENWALD, E. JOHN, JR., brokerage house executive, investment banker; b. 1930. AB, Dartmouth Coll., 1952, MBA, 1953. With Bear Stearns Cos. Inc., N.Y.C., 1953—, past pres., vice-chmn., sr. mng. dir. Office: 245 Park Ave New York NY 10167-0002*

ROSENWALD, WILLIAM, investment executive, philanthropist; b. Chgo., Aug. 19, 1903; s. Julius and Augusta (Nusbaum) R.; m. Ruth G. Israels, Dec. 1995. B.S., Mass. Inst. Tech., 1924; student, Harvard Coll., 1924-25, London (Eng.) Sch. Econs. and Polit. Sci., 1925-27; hon. Dr. Hebrew Letters, Hebrew Union Coll., 1944; LL.D., Tuskegee Inst., 1964. Dir. Sears, Roebuck & Co., 1934-38; established W.R. Enterprises, 1936. Hon. v.p. Am. Jewish Com., Am. Jewish Joint Distbn. Com., Inc.; hon. pres. United Jewish Appeal-Fedn. Jewish Philanthropies N.Y. Inc.; life trustee, hon. nat. chmn. United Jewish Appeal, Inc.; life mem. bd. dirs. Coun. Jewish Fedns.; hon. v.p. Am. Jewish Com.; life mem., v.p. Hebrew Immigrant Aid Soc.; hon. trustee Tuskegee U.; hon. life trustee Mus. Sci. and Industry, Chgo.; gen. chmn. nat. United Jewish Appeal, 1954, 55, 56 Campaigns. Mem. Harmonie Club (N.Y.C.). Office: 122 E 42nd St New York NY 10168-0002

ROSENWASSER, LARRY JEFFREY, allergist, immunologist; b. N.Y.C., Mar. 3, 1948. MD, NYU, 1972. Cert. in allergy and immunology; cert. in internal medicine. Intern U. Calif.-HC Moffitt Hosp., San Francisco, 1972-73; resident U. Calif. Affiliated Hosps., San Francisco, 1973-74. Mem. Alpha Omega Alpha, Sigma Xi. Office: Nat Jewish Ctr Im/Resp Med 1400 Jackson St San Francisco CA 80206-2761*

ROSENZWEIG, CHARLES LEONARD, lawyer; b. N.Y.C., Apr. 12, 1952; s. William and Frieda (Dechner) R.; m. Rya R. Mehler, June 14, 1975; children: Jessica Sara, Erica Danielle. AB cum laude, Princeton U., 1974; JD, NYU, 1977. Bar: N.Y. 1978, U.S. Dist. Ct. (ea. and so. dists.) N.Y. 1978, U.S. Ct. Appeals (7th cir.) 1980, U.S. Ct. Internat. Trade 1981, U.S. Ct. Appeals (2d cir.) 1985. Assoc. Graubard, Moskovitz et al, N.Y.C., 1977-85; ptnr. Rand, Rosenzweig, Smith, Radley, Gordon & Burstein LLP, N.Y.C., 1987—. Editor NYU Jour. Internat. Law. and Politics. Mem. ABA (internat. law sect.), N.Y. State Bar Assn. (co-chair internat. litigation com.), Am. Arbitration Assn., NYU Alumni Assn. (chmn. jour. internat. law and politics alumni 1985-87), Princeton Club. Avocations: skiing, cycling, tennis, scuba diving. Home: 37 Franklin Rd Scarsdale NY 10583-7563 Office: Rand Rosenzweig et al 605 3rd Ave New York NY 10158

ROSENZWEIG, HERBERT STEPHEN, stockbroker; b. Phila., Aug. 5, 1943; s. Morton and Helen (Katzen) R.; m. Myra Pauline Saltzburg, June 7, 1964; children: Helene, Michael, Elisa, Jeffrey. BS in Fin., Temple U., 1965. CFP. Stockbroker Walston & Co., Phila., 1967-73, Reynolds Securities, Phila., 1974, Merrill Lynch, Riverside, Calif., 1974—. Vol. Spl. Olympics, 1980—; chmn. Pomona Valley Coun. Chs. Hunger Walk; pres. Upland Youth Accountability Bd. Mem. Kiwanis (past pres., lt. gov. Divsn. 15 1992-93, Club Kiwanian of Yr., Divsn. Kiwanian of Yr. 1992). Republican. Jewish. Office: Merrill Lynch PO Box 472 Riverside CA 92502-0472

ROSENZWEIG, JANICE POPICK, lawyer; b. Balt., Apr. 23, 1950; d. Bernard and Harlee Sedell (Senzer) Popick; m. Richard Michael Pearlstein, Aug. 5, 1972 (div. July, 1977); 1 child, Rachel A.; m. Norman Rosenzweig, Sept. 25, 1983. BA in Psychology cum laude, Brandeis U., 1972; JD, U. Md., Balt., 1992. Bar: Md. 1992, U.S. Dist. Ct. Md. 1993. Program coord. N. Charles Found., Cambridge, Mass., 1976-78; tenant rels. coord. Equity Mgmt. Group, Boston, 1976-79; dir. planning, rsch., data processing The Parole Bd., State of Mass., Boston, 1978-80; program mgr. Chesapeak Physicians, P.A., Balt., 1980-81; regional sales mgr. Dart Med., Mason, Mich., 1982-83; profl. med. rep. Syntex Labs., Inc., Palo Alto, Calif., 1983-86; mktg. cons. Harford Physicians PPO and Healthfast, Inc., Balt., 1985-87; med. sales rep. G.D. Searle & Co., Chgo., 1987-89; lawyer, pvt. practice Brooklandville, Md., 1992—; sec., bd. dirs. State Med., Inc., Balt., 1990-94; bd. dirs. Leagl Aid Bur. Inc., 1995—. Co-editor (newspaper) The Raven, U. Md. Sch. of Law, 1989-91, editor, 1991-92 (2d pl. ABA Law Sch. Newspaper Contest non-polit. cartoon 1990); acting editor (newsletter) Mid-Atlantic Ethics Com., 1994-95; contbr. Bedford County Pa. Guide, 1987. Mem. Pleasant View Comty. Assn., Balt., 1984—; chair Brandeis U. area alumni admissions coun., Balt., 1986—. Mem. ABA, Balt. County Bar Assn., Balt. City Bar Assn. Office: Janice P Rosenzweig Atty PO Box 952 Brooklandville MD 21022-0952

ROSENZWEIG, MARK RICHARD, psychology educator; b. Rochester, N.Y., Sept. 12, 1922; s. Jacob and Pearl (Grossman) R.; m. Janine S.A. Chappat, Aug. 1, 1947; children: Anne Janine, Suzanne Jacqueline, Philip Mark. B.A., U. Rochester, 1943, M.A., 1944; Ph.D., Harvard U., 1949; hon. doctorate, U. René Descartes, Sorbonne, 1980. Postdoctoral research fellow Harvard U., 1949-51; asst. prof. U. Calif., Berkeley, 1951-56; assoc. prof. U. Calif., 1956-60, prof. psychology, 1960-91, assoc. research prof., 1958-59, research prof., 1965-66, prof. emeritus, 1991—; prof. grad. sch. U. Calif., Berkeley, 1994—; vis. prof. biology Sorbonne, Paris, 1973-74; mem. exec. com. Internat. Union Psychol. Sci., 1972—, v.p., 1980-84, pres., 1988-92, past pres. 1992-96; mem. U.S. Nat. Com. for Internat. Union Psychol. Sci., NRC Nat. Acad. Sci., 1984—, chmn., 1984-88. Author: Biologie de la Mèmoire, 1976, (with A.L. Leiman) Physiological Psychology, 1982, 2d edit., 1989, (with M.J. Renner) Enriched and Impoverished Environments: Effects on Brain and Behavior, 1987, (with D. Sinha) La Recherche en Psychologie Scientifique, 1988; editor: (with P. Mussen) Psychology: An Introduction, 1973, 2d edit., 1977, (with E.L. Bennett) Neural Mechanisms of Learning and Memory, 1976, International Psychological Science: Progress, Problems, and Prospects, 1992, (with A.L. Leiman and S.M. Breedlove) Biological Psychology, 1996; co-editor: (with L. Porter) Ann. Rev. of Psychology, 1968-94; contbr. articles to profl. jours. Served with USN, 1944-46. Recipient Disting. Alumnus award U. Rochester; Fulbright research fellow; faculty research fellow Social Sci. Research Council, 1960-61; research grantee NSF, USPHS, Easter Seal Found., Nat. Inst. Drug Abuse. Fellow AAAS, APA (Disting. Sci. Contbn. award 1982), Am. Psychol. Soc.; mem. NAS, NAACP (life), Am. Physiol. Soc., Am. Psychol. Soc., Internat. Brain Rsch. Orgn., Soc. Exptl. Psychologists, Soc. for Neurosci., Société Française de Psychologie, Sierra Club (life), Common Cause, Fulbright Assn. (life), Phi Beta Kappa, Sigma Xi. Office: U Calif Dept Psychology 3210 Tolman Hall Berkeley CA 94720-1650

ROSENZWEIG, NORMAN, psychiatry educator; b. N.Y.C., Feb. 28, 1924; s. Jacob Arthur and Edna (Braman) R.; m. Carol Treleaven, Sept. 20, 1945; 1 child, Elizabeth Ann. MB, Chgo. Med. Sch., 1947, MD, 1948; MS, U. Mich., 1954. Diplomate Am. Bd. Psychiatry and Neurology. Asst. prof. psychiatry U. Mich., Ann Arbor, 1957-61, asst. prof., 1963-67, assoc. prof., 1967-73; prof. Wayne State U., Detroit, 1973—; chmn. dept. psychiat. Sch. Med. Wayne State U., Detroit, 1987-90, Sinai Hosp., Detroit, 1961-90; spl. cons., profl. advisor Oakland County Community Mental Health Services Bd., 1964-65; mem. protem med. adv. panel Herman Kiefer Hosp., Detroit, 1970, psychiat. task force N.W. Quadrangle Hosps., Detroit, 1971-78, planning com. mental health adv. council Dept. Mental Health State of Mich., Lansing, 1984-90, tech. adv.rsch. com., 1978-82; psychiat. bed need task force Office Health and Med. Affairs State of Mich., 1980-84; bd. dirs. Alliance for Mental Health, Farmington Hills, Mich., 1986-94; speaker in field. Author: Community Mental Health Programs in England: An American View, 1975; co-editor: Psychopharmacology and Psychotherapy-Synthesis or Antithesis?, 1978, Sex Education for the Health Professional: A Curriculum Guide, 1978; contbr. articles to profl. jours. and chpts. to books. Mem. profl. adv. bd. The Orchards, Livonia, Mich., 1963. Served as capt. USAF, 1955-57. Recipient Appreciation and Merit cert. Mich. Soc. Psychiatry and Neurology, 1970-71, Career Svc. award Assn. Mental Health in Mich., 1994. Fellow Am. Coll. Mental Health Adminstrn., fellow emeritus Am. Coll. Psychiatrists (hon. membership com., com. on regional ednl. programs, liaison officer to The Royal Australian and New Zealand Coll. Psychiatrists 1984-88), Am. Psychiat. Assn. (life fellow, coun. on internat. affairs 1970-79, chmn. 1973-76, assembly liaison to coun. on internat. affairs 1979-80, 82-84, reference com. 1973-76, nominating com. 1978-79, internat. affairs survey team 1973-74, assoc. representing Am. Psychiat. Assn. to Inter-Am. Coun. Psychiat. Assns. 1973-75, treas. APA lifers 1991-94, v.p. 1994-95, pres. 1995—, com. on sr. psychiatrists 1993—, others, Rush Gold Medal award 1974, cert. Commendation, 1973-76, 78-80, Warren Williams award 1986); mem. AAUP, AMA (Physician's Recognition award 1971, 74, 77, 80-81, 84, 87, 90, 92), Am. Assn. Dirs. Psychiat. Residency Tng. (nominating com. 1972-74, task force on core curriculum 1972-74), Am. Assn. Gen. Hosp. Psychiatry, Puerto Rico Med. Assn. (hon., presdl. award 1981), Am. Hosp. Assn. (governing coun. psychiat. svcs. sect. 1977-79, ad hoc com. on uniform mental health definitions, chmn. task force on psychiat. coverage under Nat. Health Ins. 1977-79, others), Brit. Soc. Clin. Psychiatrists (task force on gen. hosp. psychiatry 1969-74), Can. Psychiat. Assn., Mich. Assn. Professions, Mich. Hosp. Assn. (psychiat. and mental health svcs. com. 1979-81), Mich. Psychiat. Soc. (com. on ins. 1965-69, chmn. com. on community mental health svcs. 1967-68, chmn. com. on nominations of fellows 1972-73, mem. com. on budget 1973-74, task force on pornography 1973-74, chmn. commn. on health professions and groups 1974-75, pres. elect 1974-75, pres. 1975-76, chmn. com. on liaison with hosp. assns. 1979-81, chmn. subcom. on liaison with Am. Hosp. Assn. 1979-81, numerous others, Past Pres. plaque, 1978, cert. Recognition, 1980, Disting. Service award 1986), Mich. State Med. Soc. (vice chmn. sect. psychiatry 1972-73, chmn. sect. psychiatry 1974-75, mem. com. to improve membership 1977-78, alt. del for Mich. Psychiat. Soc. to Ho. of Dels. 1978-79, del. from Wayne County Med. Soc. to Mich. Med. Soc. Ho. of Dels. 1982-88), N.Y. Acad. Scis., Pan Am. Med. Assn., Wayne County Med. Soc. (com. on hosp. and prof. rels., 1983-84, com. on child health advocacy 1983-87, med. edn. com. 1983-87, mental health com. 1983-87), Royal Australian and New Zealand Coll. Psychiatrists (hon.), Indian Psychiat. Soc. (hon. corr.), World Psychiat. Assn., Sect. GeHosp. Psychiat. Avocations: music, films, reading. Home: 1234 Cedarholm Ln Bloomfield Hills MI 48302-0902 Office: Ste 602 26211 Ctrl Park Blvd Southfield MI 48076-4107

ROSENZWEIG, RICHARD STUART, publishing company executive; b. Appleton, Wis., Aug. 8, 1935; s. Walter J. and Rose (Bahcall) R. B.S., Northwestern U., 1957; Advanced Mgmt. Program, Harvard U., 1975. Credit rep. Dun & Bradstreet, Inc., 1958; with Playboy Enterprises, Inc., 1958—, exec. asst. to pres., 1963-73, sr. v.p., dir., 1973—, dir. mktg., 1974—, exec. v.p. publs. group, 1975-77, exec. v.p., head West Coast ops., 1977-80; exec. v.p. corp. affairs Playboy Enterprises, Inc., Los Angeles, 1980-82; exec. v.p., chmn. emeritus Playboy Enterprises, Inc., 1982—; pres. Playboy Jazz Festivals, 1989—; dir. I. Bahcall Industries, Appleton. Trustee L.A. Film Expn.; mem. 2d decade coun. Am. Film Inst.; bd. dirs. Mus. Contemporary Art, Chgo., Periodical and Book Assn. Am., Internat. Inst. Kidney Diseases of UCLA, Children of Night, Maple Ctr. Beverly Hills; mem., chmn. bd. UCLA Legis. Network, Town Hall of Calif.; adv. bd. West Hollywood Mktg. Corp., 1985—; bd. dirs. So. Calif. ACLU, 1985—; mem. Los Angeles County Mus.; apptd. to blue ribbon com. project West Coast Gateway. With AUS, 1957. Recipient Do-ers award, 1988, Beverly Hills medal Beverly Hills City Coun., 1993. Mem. Am. Mktg. Aslsn., L.A. Pub. Affairs Officers Assn., UCLA Chancellor's Assocs., Pres.'s Cir., Beverly Hills C. of C. (bd. dirs., visitors' bur., v.p.), Beverly Hills Fine Art Commn. (chmn.), Beverly Hills Econ. Devel. Coun., Founders Circle of Music Ctr., Pub. Affairs Coun., Craft and Folk Art Mus., Pres.' Coun. and Contemporary ARts Coun. L.A. Mus. Contemporary Art, The Am. Cinematheque (groundbreaker), Variety Club So. Calif. (bd. dirs.). Office: Playboy Enterprises Inc 9242 Beverly Blvd Beverly Hills CA 90210

ROSENZWEIG, ROBERT MYRON, educational consultant; b. Detroit, Aug. 27, 1931; s. Louis and Gertrude (Lifsitz) R.; m. Adelle Ruth Rotman, Aug. 30, 1953; children—Kathryn Ann, David Michael. B.A., U. Mich., 1952, M.A., 1953; Ph.D., Yale U., 1956. Instr. polit. sci. Amherst Coll., 1955-57; with U.S. Office Edn., 1958-62, spl. asst. to commnr., 1961-62; assoc. dean Grad. Div., Stanford U., 1962-67, assoc. provost of univ., 1967-71, vice provost, adviser to pres., 1971-74, v.p. pub. affairs, 1974-83; pres. Assn. Am. Univs., Washington, 1983-93, pres. emeritus, 1993—; lectr. polit. sci. Grad. Div., Stanford U., 1963—; dir. Ctr. Rsch. Internat. Studies, 1967-68; chmn. steering com. Coalition for Advancement Fgn. Langs. and Internat. Studies, 1988-90. Author: (with H.D. Babbidge, Jr.) Federal Interest in Higher Education, 1962, The Research Universities and Their Patrons, 1982; also articles. Bd. dirs. CUNY Rsch. Found., 1986-92. Recipient Harvey Cushing Orator award Am. Assn. Neurol. Surgeons, 1984, Disting. Alumni award U. Mich., 1988. Mem. AAAS, Assn. Ind. Calif. Colls. and Univs. (v.p. 1978-80, pres. 1980-82), Am. Polit Sci. Assn. (coun. and adminstrv. com. 1987-89), Coun. Fgn. Rels., Am. Acad. Arts & Scis. Home and Office: 1462 Dana Ave Palo Alto CA 94301-3115

ROSENZWEIG, SAUL, psychologist, educator, administrator; b. Boston, Feb. 7, 1907; s. David and Etta (Tuttle) R.; m. Louise Ritterskamp, Mar. 21, 1941; children: Julia, Ann. A.B. summa cum laude, Harvard U., 1929, M.A., 1930, Ph.D., 1932. Research assoc. Harvard Psychol. Clinic, 1929-34, Worcester (Mass.) State Hosp., 1934-43; affiliate prof. Clark U., Worcester, 1938-43; chief psychologist Western State Psychiat. Ins. and Clinic, Pitts., 1943-48; lectr. psychology U. Pitts., 1943-48; assoc. prof. psychology and med. psychology Washington U., St. Louis, 1949-51; prof. Washington U., 1951-75, prof. emeritus, 1975—; chief psychologist Child Guidance Clinic, 1949-59; cons., mem. life scis. study sect. NIH, 1964-68; mng. dir. Found. for Idiodynamics and the Creative Process. Author: (with Kate L. Kogan) Psychodiagnosis, Grune and Stratton, 1949, Rosenzweig Picture-Frustration Study, 1948, Aggressive Behavior and the Rosenzweig Picture-Frustration Study, 1978, Freud and Experimental Psychology: The Emergence of Idiodynamics, 1986, Sally Beauchamp's Career, 1987, Freud, Jung, and Hall the King-Maker, 1992; assoc. editor: Jour. Abnormal and Social Psychology, 1950-56; cons. editor: Psychol. Monographs, 1948-57, Zeitschrift für Diagnostische Psychologie und Persönlichkeitsforschung, 1953-58, Diagnostica, 1959—; adv. editor: Jour. Cons. Psychology, 1959-64, Jour. Abnormal Psychology, 1965-67; mem. editorial bd. Aggressive Behavior, 1974—; contbr. articles to profl. jours. Fellow Am. Psychol. Assn. (rep. Internat. group for Coordination Psychiatry and Psychol. Methods 1955-61), Am. Psychopathol. Assn.; mem. Internat. Soc. for Research on Aggression (founding pres. 1972-73, archivist 1981-88), Soc. Prof. Emeriti Washington U. (founding pres. 1978), Sigma Xi, Phi Beta Kappa. Home: 8029 Washington Ave Saint Louis MO 63114-6333 Office: Washington U Box 1125 Saint Louis MO 63130

ROSES, ALLEN DAVID, neurologist, educator; b. Paterson, N.J., Feb. 21, 1943. BS in Chemistry summa cum laude, U. Pitts., 1963; MD, U. Pa., 1967. Diplomate Am. Bd. Psychiatry and Neurology. Intern Hosp. of the U. Pa., Phila., 1967-68; resident in neurology N.Y. Neurol. Inst., Columbia U., N.Y.C., 1968-70; chief resident divsn. neurology Duke U. Med. Ctr., 1970-71, assoc. in medicine divsn. neurology, 1970-73, asst. prof. medicine divsn. neurology, 1973-76, assoc. prof. medicine divsn. neurology, 1976-79, asst. prof. biochemistry, 1977-89, prof. neurology dept. medicine, 1979—, prof. neurobiology, 1989—, Jefferson-Pilot Corp. prof. neurobiology and neurology, 1990—, chief divsn. neurology dept. medicine, 1977—; fellow Nat. Multiple Sclerosis Soc., Lab. Neurochemistry, Divsn. Neurology, Duke U. Med. Ctr., Lab. Virology, Divsn. Pediat. Neurology, Duke U. Med. Ctr., 1971-73, dir. Duke Neuromuscular Rsch. Clinic, 1974—, dir. neurosciences study program Sch. Medicine, 1975-85, investigator Howard Hughes Med. Inst., 1977-81, dir. Duke Muscular Dystrophy Assn. Clinic, 1979—, Joseph and Kathleen Bryan Alzheimer's Disease Rsch. Ctr., 1985— ; cons. neurologist N.C. State Hosp. Sys., Cherry Hosp., Goldsboro, 1973-76, N.C. State Hosp. Sys., Lenox Baker Hosp., Durham, 1974—; chmn. internat. sci. adv. com. Australian Neuromusclar Rsch. Inst., 1989-92; sci. adv. Cyprus Isnt. Neurology and Genetics, 1990—; mem. external adv. com. Neonatal Neurology Ctr., SUNY, Stonybrook, Epidemiology of Dementia in an Urban Cmty. Program Project Renewal. Assoc. editor Molecular and Cellular Neuroscis., 1989-94; mem. editl. bd. Amyloidosis Jour., An Internat. Jour. Exptl. and Clin. Investigation, 1993—, Neurobiology of Disease, 1993—, Fondation Ipsen, Rsch. and Perspectives in Neuroscis., 1994—, Alzheimer's Rsch., 1995—, Contemporary Neurology, 1995—, Alezheimer's Disease Rev., 1995—; contbr. articles to profl. jours. Capt. USAFR, 1967-72. Recipient Rsch. Career Devel. award Nat. Inst. Neurol. and Communicative Disorders and Stroke, 1976, Best in the Triangle-Aerobics Instr. award Spectator Mag., 1986, Leadership in Excellence in Alzheimer's Disease award Nat. Inst. Aging, 1988, Met.-Life Found. prize for outstanding med. rsch., 1994, Potamkin prize for Alzheimer's Disease Rsch., 1994; Basil O'Connor Starter Rsch. grantee Nat. Found. March of Dimes. Fellow Am. Acad. Neurology; mem. Am. Soc. for Clin. Investigation, Am. Soc. for Clin. Rsch., Am. Neurol. Assn. (trustee 1982-84), Assn. Univ. Profs. Neurology, Assn. Brit. Neurologists (hon. fgn. mem.), Muscular Dystrophy Assn. (genetics task force and rev. com. 1989—, med. adv. com. 1990—, nat. v.p. nat. hdqrs. 1994—), Alzheimer's Assn. (med. sci. adv. com. 1989—, vice chair 1991—, Sigma Tau award 1990, Rita Hayward Gala award 1994), Phi Beta Kappa. Office: Duke Univ Med Ctr Durham NC 27710-7599 also: Divsn Neurology Box 2900 Durham NC 27710

ROSETT, ARTHUR IRWIN, lawyer, educator; b. N.Y.C., July 5, 1934; s. Milton B. and Bertha (Werner) R.; m. Rhonda K. Lawrence; children: David Benjamin, Martha Jean, Daniel Joseph. A.B., Columbia U., 1955, LL.B., 1959. Bar: Calif. 1968, N.Y. State 1960, U.S. Supreme Ct. 1963. Law clk. U.S. Supreme Ct., 1959-60; asst. U.S. atty. So. Dist. N.Y., 1960-63; practice law N.Y.C., 1963-65; assoc. dir. Pres.'s Commn. on Law Enforcement and Adminstrn. Justice, 1965-67; acting prof. law UCLA, 1967-70, prof., 1970—. Author: Contract Law and Its Application, 1971, 5th revised edit., 1994, (with D. Cressey) Justice by Consent, 1976, (with E. Dorff) A Living Tree,

1987. Served with USN, 1956-58. Mem. Am. Law Inst. Home: 641 S Saltair Ave Los Angeles CA 90049-4134 Office: UCLA Law Sch 405 Hilgard Ave Los Angeles CA 90095

ROSETT, RICHARD NATHANIEL, economist, educator; b. Balt., Feb. 29, 1928; s. Walter and Essie (Stofberg) R.; m. Madelon Louise George, June 24, 1951; children: Claudia Anne, Martha Victoria, Joshua George, Sarah Elizabeth, Charles Richard. B.A., Columbia U., 1953; M.A., Yale U., 1954, Ph.D., 1957. Instr. Yale U., 1956-58; mem. faculty U. Rochester, 1958-74, chmn. dept. econs., 1966-74, prof. econs., 1967-74, prof. preventive medicine and community health, 1969-74; prof. bus. econs. Grad. Sch. Bus., U. Chgo., 1974-84, dean, 1974-83; dean Faculty Arts and Scis. Washington U., 1984-87, prof. econs., 1984-90; dean Coll. Bus. Rochester (N.Y.) Inst. Tech., 1990-96, instr. tech., 1990-96, dir. quality cup programs, 1990—; pres. U.S. Bus. Sch. in Prague, Inc., 1990—; bd. dirs. Hutchinson Techs., Inc., Lumbermans Mut. Ins. Co., Nat. Bur. Econ. Rsch., chmn., 1986-89, ORMEC; trustee Keuka Coll., 1992—. Editor: The Role of Health Insurance in the Health Services Sector, 1976; Contbr. articles to profl. jours. Mem. Am. Econ. Assn., Mont Pelerin Soc., Chgo. Club, Phi Beta Kappa, Beta Gamma Sigma. Home: 26 Whitestone Ln Rochester NY 14618-4118 Office: Rochester Inst Tech Office of Dean 108 Lomb Meml Dr Rochester NY 14623-5608

ROSEWATER, ANN, federal official; b. Phila., July 30, 1945; d. Edward and Maxine (Friedmann) R. BA with distinction, Wellesley Coll., 1967; MA, Columbia U., 1969. Rsch. editl. asst. Tchrs. Coll. Columbia U., N.Y.C., 1969; rsch. asst. to pres., v.p. rsch. Met. Applied Rsch. Ctr., N.Y.C., 1969-70; asst. to v.p. Nat. Urban Coalition, Washington, 1970-73; nat. edn. staff Childrens Def. Fund, Washington, 1973-77; assoc. prodr. Smithsonian World Nat. Pub. TV Series, Washington, 1977-78; sr. legis. asst. U.S. Ho. of Reps., Washington, 1979-83, dep. staff to staff dir. com. on children, youth and families, 1983-90; sr. assoc. Chapin Hall Ctr. for Children/U. Chgo., 1990-93; dep. asst. sec. Dept. Health & Human Svcs., Washington, 1993—; pub. policy and found. cons. in field, 1977-79, 90-93; grad. instr. Harvard Sch. Pub. Health, Nova U., George Washington U., 1977-79; mem. Nat. Adv. Com. on Svcs. for Families with Infants and Toddlers, Washington, 1994, Nat. Adv. Com. for Campaign Against Domestic Violence, 1992-93. Contbr. articles to profl. jours. Bd. dirs. Family Resources Coalition, Chgo., 1990-93, Youth Law Ctr., San Francisco, 1990-93, Jewish Fund for Justice, N.Y.C., 1990-93, Georgians for Children, Atlanta, 1990-93. Recipient Leadership award Leadership Atlanta, 1992-93, Pres. cert. for outstanding svc. Am. Acad. Pediat., 1990, Leadership in Human Svc. award Am. Pub. Welfare Assn., 1989-90. Mem. D.C. Bar Assn. (mem. citizens adv. com. 1974-79, fee conciliation svc., panel bd. on profl. responsibility). Office: Admin for Children & Families 370 L'Enfant Plz Washington DC 20447-0001

ROSHEL, JOHN ALBERT, JR., orthodontist; b. Terre Haute, Ind., Apr. 7, 1941; s. John Albert and Mary M. (Griglione) R.; B.S., Ind. State U., 1963; D.D.S., Ind. U., 1966; M.S., U. Mich., 1968; m. Kathy Roshel; children—John Albert III, James Livingston, Angela Kay. Individual practice dentistry, specializing in orthodontics Terre Haute, 1968—. Mem. ADA, Am. Assn. Orthodontists, Terre Haute C. of C., Lambda Chi Alpha, Delta Sigma Delta, Omicron Kappa Upsilon. Clubs: Terre Haute Country, Lions, Elks, K.C. Roman Catholic. Home: 15 E Wedgeway Dr Terre Haute IN 47802-4983 Office: 4241 S 7th St Terre Haute IN 47802-4367

ROSHON, GEORGE KENNETH, manufacturing company executive, b. Pottstown, Pa., July 30, 1942; s. George Washington III and Ellen Eleanor (Knopf) R.; B.S. in Elec. Engring., Pa. State U., 1964; M.S., Drexel U., Phila., 1974, postgrad., 1974-75; m. Ella Maye Barndt, Nov. 21, 1964; 1 child, Kirsten Renee. Sr. engr. Am. Electronics Labs., Inc., Colmar, Pa., 1966-69; v.p. engring. Acrodyne Industries, Inc., Montgomeryville, Pa., 1969-74; mgr. electric design W-J div. Hayes-Albion Corp., Norristown, Pa., 1974-78; mgr. quality assurance PSMBD, Gen. Electric Co., Phila., after 1978, mem. exec. com. electronics test council after 1980, mgr. advanced systems engring., 1983-84, mgr. communications engring., Malvern, Pa., 1984-86; v.p. quality assurance Hercules Aerospace Display Systems, Inc., Hatfield, Pa., 1986-88, v.p. engring., 1988-90; mgr. Electronics Group Westcode, Inc., Malvern, Pa., 1991-92; v.p. manufacturing Epitaxx Inc., West Trenton, N.J., 1992—. Patentee in field. Served to lt. USNR, 1964-66. Registered profl. engr., Pa. Mem. Nat. Soc. Profl. Engrs., Am. Soc. Quality Control (cert. quality engr.), Pa. Soc. Profl. Engrs., Gen. Electric Mgmt. Assn., Elfun Soc., Drexel U. Alumni Assn., Pa. State U. Alumni Assn., Tri-County Arabian Horse Assn. Home: 454 Eagle Ln Lansdale PA 19446-1547 Office: 7 Graphics Dr Trenton NJ 08628

ROSICA, GABRIEL ADAM, corporate executive, engineer; b. N.Y.C., Jan. 9, 1940; s. Gabriel J. and Elma (P.) R.; m. Bettina R. Nardozzi, Sept. 8, 1962; children: Gregory A., Julie Ann, Mark A. BA in Math. and Physics, Columbia U., 1962, BSEE, 1963; MSEE, Rensselaer Poly. Inst., 1966; MBA, Boston U., 1971. Registered profl. engr., Mass. Rsch. engr. United Aircraft Research Labs., East Hartford, Conn., 1963-67; mgr. electronic devel. The Foxboro (Mass.) Co., 1967-75, gen. mgr. U.S. div., 1975-77, v.p., 1977-80; pres., chief operating officer Modular Computer Systems, Inc., Ft. Lauderdale, Fla., 1980-82, pres., chmn., chief exec. officer, 1982-88; pvt. practice bus. cons. Boca Raton, Fla., 1988-91; sr. v.p. Elsag Bailey Corp., Pepper Pike, Ohio, 1991-92; exec. v.p. Bailey Controls Co., Wickliffe, Ohio, 1993-94; COO Bailey Control Co., Wickliffe, Ohio, 1994-96; sr. v.p. Keithley Instruments, Solon, Ohio, 1996—; bd. dirs. Sturtevant Co., Dorchester, Mass., Keithley Instruments, Solon, Ohio; chmn. engring. adv. coun. U. Fla., Gainesville, 1987-90; chmn. hi tech adv. coun. Coll. Boca Raton, Fla., 1987-90. Mem. Pres.'s Coun. Fla. Atlantic U., Boca Raton, 1987-91; trustee Nova U., Ft. Lauderdale, Fla., 1987-94. Recipient Boston U. Chair, 1971, Outstanding Young Engr. of Year award Mass. Soc. Profl. Engrs., 1974. Mem. IEEE (sr. mem.), Am. Electronics Assn. (bd. dirs. 1987, chmn Fla. bd. dirs. 1987-88), Fla. High Tech. and Industry Coun. Home: 35640 Spicebush Ln Solon OH 44139-5063 Office: Keithley Instruments Inc 28775 Aurora Rd Solon OH 44139

ROSICH, RAYNER KARL, physicist; b. Joliet, Ill., Aug. 28, 1940; s. Joseph F. and Gretchen (Cox) R.; BS in Physics cum laude with spl. honors, U. Mich., 1962, MS in Physics, 1963; PhD, U. Colo., 1977; MBA, U. Denver, 1982; m. Judy Louise Jackson, Aug. 20, 1966; children: Heidi Ann, Kimberly Ann, Dawn Ann. Teaching fellow and rsch. asst. U. Mich., Ann Arbor, 1962-67; staff, Argonne (Ill.) Nat. Lab. Applied Math. Div., summers 1961-63; physicist, project leader Inst. for Telecommunication Sci., U.S. Dept. Commerce, Boulder, Colo., 1967-80; sr. scientist and program mgr. Electro Magnetic Applications, Inc., Denver, 1980-82; applications mgr. Energy Systems Tech., Inc., Denver, 1982-83, mgr. R&D, 1983; prin. scientist, program mgr. Contel Info. Systems, Inc., Denver, 1983-84, dir. tech. audits, 1985, dir. basic and applied R&D, 1986; lab. scientist for systems engring. lab. Hughes Aircraft Co., Denver, 1986, lab. scientist for data systems lab, 1986-90, lab. scientist for systems lab., 1990-92; prin. engr., Advanced System Techs., Inc., Denver, 1992-95; project mgr. Evolving Systems, Inc., 1995; network planning engr., project mgr. Apollo Travel Svcs., 1996—. instr. math. Arapahoe Cmty. Coll., 1987—. Vol. judo instr., county recreation dist., 1976-77. Recipient Spl. Achievement award U.S. Dept. Commerce, 1974, Outstanding Performance award, 1978, Sustained Superior Performance award, 1979; Libbey-Owens-Ford Glass Co./U. Mich. Phoenix Meml. fellow, 1964-66; NSF Summer fellow, 1965. Mem. Am. Phys. Soc., AAAS, IEEE, Assn. Computing Machinery, Applied Computational Electromagnetics Soc., Soc. Computer Stimulation, Sigma Xi, Phi Kappa Phi. Home: 7932 W Nichols Ave Littleton CO 80123-5558 Office: Apollo Travel Svcs 5347 S Valentia Way Englewood CO 80111

ROSIN, WALTER L., religious organization administrator. Sec. Luth. Ch.-Mo. Synod, St. Louis. Office: The Lutheran Ch-Missouri Synod 1333 S Kirkwood Rd Saint Louis MO 63122-7226

ROSINSKI, EDWIN FRANCIS, health sciences educator; b. Buffalo, June 25, 1928; s. Theodore Joseph and Josephine M. (Wolski) R.; m. Jeanne C. Hueniger, Oct. 27, 1951; children: John T., Mary E., Sarah J. BS, SUNY, Buffalo, 1950; EdM, U. Buffalo, 1957, EdD, 1959. Prof. health scis. Med. Coll. Va., Richmond, 1959-66; dep. asst. sec. HEW, Washington, 1966-68; exec. vice chancellor U. Calif., San Francisco, 1968-72, prof., 1972-94; prof. emeritus medicine & pharmacy, 1994—; adv. Rockefeller Found., N.Y.C., 1962-67, WHO, Geneva, 1962-78, Imperial Com. Health, Tehran, Iran, 1974-77; cons. Stanford Research Inst., Menlo Park, Calif., 1975-79. Author: The Assistant Medical Officer, 1965; contbr. over 100 articles to profl. jours. Served with USAF, 1950-54. Recipient spl. citation HEW, 1968, Merrell Flair award, 1991; named disting. prof. Australian Vice Chancellors Office, 1974, disting. vis. prof. Tulane U., New Orleans, 1983. Fellow AAAS; mem. Assn. Am. Med. Colls. (Merrel Flair award), Am. Ednl. Research Assn., Soc. Health and Human Values (founding mem.), Calif. Pharmacists Assn. (hon.), Phi Delta Kappa. Roman Catholic. Avocation: physical fitness. Home: 80 Sotelo Ave San Francisco CA 94116-1423

ROSKAM, JAN, aerospace engineer; b. The Hague, The Netherlands, Feb. 22, 1930; came to U.S., 1957, naturalized, 1962; s. Kommer Jan and Agatha (Bosman) R.; m. Janice Louise Thomas-Barron, Dec. 21, 1994. M.A. in Aerospace Engring, Tech. U. Delft, 1954; Ph.D. in Aeros. and Astronautics, U. Wash., 1965. Asst. chief designer Aviolanda Aircraft Co., Netherlands, 1954-57; sr. aerodynamics engr. Cessna Aircraft Co., Wichita, Kans., 1957-59; sr. group engr. Boeing Co., Wichita and Seattle, 1959-67; Ackers disting. prof. aerospace engring. U. Kans., Lawrence, 1967—; pres. Roskam Aviation and Engring. Corp., 1972—, Design, Analysis and Rsch. Corp., 1991—; cons. to govt. and industry. Author: Airplane Flight Dynamics and Automatic Flight Controls, 2 vols, 1979; co-author: Airplane Aerodynamics and Performance, 1981, Airplane Design, Parts I-VIII, 1986. Served to 1st lt. Royal Netherlands Air Force, 1954-56. Fellow AIAA, Soc. Automotive Engrs.; mem. Air Force Assn., Am. Def. Preparedness Assn., Aircraft Owners and Pilots Assn., Royal Aero. Soc., Koninklijk Instituut van Ingenieurs, U.S. Chess Fedn., Exptl. Aircraft Assn., Internat. Wildlife Assn., Sigma Xi, Tau Beta Pi, Sigma Gamma Tau, Omicron Delta Kappa. Office: U Kans 2004 Lea Hall Lawrence KS 66045

ROSKAM, PETER JAMES, state legislator, lawyer; b. Hinsdale, Ill., Sept. 13, 1961; s. Verlyn Ronald and Martha (Jacobsen) R.; m. Elizabeth Andrea Gracey, June 18, 1988; children: Gracey, James (dec.), Frances, Stephen. BA, U. Ill., 1983; JD, Ill. Inst. Tech., 1989. Bar: Ill. 1989. Tchr. All Saints Sch., St. Thomas, V.I., 1984-85; legis. asst. to Congressman Tom Delay U.S. Ho. of Reps., Washington, 1985-86, legal asst. to Congressman Henry Hyde, 1986-87; exec. dir. Ednl. Assistance Ltd., Glen Ellyn, Ill., 1987-93; ptnr. Salvi & Roskam, Wheaton, Ill., 1994—; mem. Ill. Gen. Assembly, Springfield, 1993—. Republican. Mem. Evangelical Covenant Ch. Office: Salvi & Roskam 1755 S Naperville Rd Wheaton IL 60187-8132

ROSKENS, RONALD WILLIAM, international business consultant; b. Spencer, Iowa, Dec. 11, 1932; s. William E. and Delores A.L. (Beving) R.; m. Lois Grace Lister, Aug. 22, 1954; children: Elizabeth, Barbara, Brenda, William. BA, U. No. Iowa, 1953, MA, 1955, LHD (hon.), 1985; PhD, State U. Iowa, 1958; LLD (hon.), Creighton U., 1978, Huston-Tillotson Coll., 1981, Midland Luth. Coll., 1984, Hastings Coll., 1981; LittD (hon.), Nebr. Wesleyan U., 1981; PhD (hon.), Ataturk U., Turkey, 1987; LHD (hon.), U. Akron, 1987; DSc (hon.), Jayewardenepura U., Sri Lanka, 1991; LHD (hon.), Am. Coll. of Greece, Athens, 1994. Lic. min. United Ch. of Christ (Congl. and E&R). Tchr. Minburn (Iowa) High Sch., 1954, Woodward (Iowa) State Hosp., summer 1954; asst. counselor to men State U. Iowa, 1956-59; dean of men, asst. prof. spl. edn. Kent (Ohio) State U., 1959-63, assoc. prof., then prof., 1963-72, asst. to pres., 1963-66, dean for adminstrn., 1968-71, exec. v.p., prof. ednl. adminstrn., 1971-72; chancellor, prof. ednl. adminstrn. U. Nebr., Omaha, 1972-76; pres. U. Nebr. System, 1977-89, pres. emeritus, 1989; hon. prof. East China Normal U., Shanghai, 1985; adminstr. USAID, Washington, 1990-92; pres. Action Internat., Inc., Omaha, 1993-96, Global Connections, Inc., Omaha, 1996—; bd. dirs. ConAgra Inc., 1992—, MFS Comms. Co. Inc., 1993—, Enron Corp., 1979-90, Art's Way Mfg. Co., 1981-90, Guarantee Mut. Life Ins. Co., 1979-90, Am. Charter Fed. Savs. and Loan Assn., 1986-90; mem. Bus.-Higher Edn. Forum, 1979-89, exec. com., 1984-87; mem. govtl. relations com. Am. Council Edn., 1979-83, bd. dirs., 1981-86, vice chair, 1983-84, chair, 1984-85; chmn. com. on financing higher edn. Nat. Assn. State Univs. and Land Grant Colls., 1978-83, vice chmn. com. on financing higher edn., 1983-84, chmn. com. on fed. student fin. assistance, 1981-87; mem. nat. adv. com. on accreditation and instl. eligibility U.S. Dept. Edn., 1983-86, chmn., bd. dirs., 1986; exec. bd. North Cen. Assn., 1979-84, chmn. exec. bd., 1982-84, pres., 1989-90; active Environ. Ams. Bd., 1991-92, Strategic Command Consultation Commn., 1993—, Nat. Exec. Res. Corps, Fed. Office Emergency Preparedness, 1968-88; chmn. Omaha/Douglas Pub. Bldg. Commn., 1996—. Co-editor: Paradox, Process and Progress, 1968; contbr. articles profl. jours. Mem. Kent City Planning Commn., 1962-66; bd. dirs. United Ch. of Christ Bd. Homeland Ministries, 1968-74, Met. YMCA, Omaha, 1973-77, Mid-Am. council Boy Scouts Am., 1973-77, Midlands United Community Services, 1972-77, NCCJ, 1974-77, Omaha Rotary Club, 1974-77, Found. Study Presdl. and Congl. Terms, 1977-89, First Plymouth Congl. Ch., 1989-90, Midland Luth. Coll., 1993—, Coun. Aid to Edn., 1985-89; trustee Huston Tillotson Coll., Austin, Tex., 1968-81, chmn., 1976-78, Joslyn Art Mus., 1973-77, Nebr. Meth. Hosp., 1974-77, 1st Ctrl. Congregational Ch., Brownell-Talbott Sch., 1974-77, Harry S. Truman Inst., 1977-89, Willa Cather Pioneer Meml. and Ednl. Found., 1979-87; pres. Kent Area C. of C., 1966; active Met. Commn. Coll. Found., 1993—. Decorated comdr.'s cross Order of Merit (Germany); recipient Disting. Svc. award for community svc., Kent, Ohio, 1967, Brotherhood award NCCJ, 1977, Americanism citation B'nai B'rith, 1978, Legion of Honor, Order of DeMolay, 1980, gold medal Nat. Interfrat. Coun., 1987, Agri award Triumph Agr. Expn., Omaha, 1989; named Nat. 4-H Alumnus, 1967, Outstanding Alumnus, U. No. Iowa, 1974, Midlander of Yr., Omaha World Herald, 1977, King Ak-Sar-Ben LXXXVI, 1980; named to DeMolay Hall of Fame, 1993. Mem. AAAS, APA, AAUP, Am. Coll. Pers. Assn., Assn. Urban Univs. (pres. 1976-77), Am. Ednl. Rsch. Assn., Coun. on Fgn. Rels., Chief Execs. Orgn., Young Pres. Orgn., Lincoln C. of C. (bd. dirs. 1989-90), Masons (33 deg.), Rotary (bd. dirs. Omaha 1974-77), Phi Delta Kappa, Phi Eta Sigma, Sigma Tau Gamma (pres. grand coun. 1968-70, Disting. Achievement award 1980, Disting. scholar 1981), Omicron Delta Kappa (nat. pres. 1986-90, Found. pres. 1986—). Home: 1311 N 97taha NE 68114-2101

ROSKIND, E. ROBERT, real estate company executive; b. N.Y.C., Mar. 18, 1945; s. Edward R. and Harriet (Weinberg) R.; m. Diane L. Albert, Aug. 4, 1966; children: Dina Lee Walsh, Scott. BA, U. Pa., 1966; JD, Columbia U., 1969. Mng. ptnr. The LCP Group, N.Y.C., 1974—; chmn. Lexington Corp. Prop., N.Y.C., 1993—; dir. Berkshire Realty, Boston, Krupp Govt. Income Trust, Krupp Govt. Income Trust II. Chmn. Babies Heart Fund, N.Y.C., 1984—; mem. health & scis. adv. com. Columbia Presbyn. Hosp., N.Y.C., 1990—. Office: The LCP Group 355 Lexington Ave New York NY 10017-6603

ROSKOSKI, ROBERT, JR., biochemist, educator, author; b. Elyria, Ohio, Dec. 10, 1939; s. Robert and Mary R.; m. Laura Martinsek, Aug. 27, 1974. B.S., Bowling Green State U., 1961; M.D., U. Chgo., 1964, Ph.D., 1968. Asst. prof. U. Iowa, Iowa City, 1972-75; assoc. prof. U. Iowa, 1975-79; prof., head dept. biochemistry and molecular biology Med. Center, La. State U., New Orleans, 1979—, Fred G. Brazda prof., 1991—; cons. biochemistry test com. Nat. Bd. Med. Examiners, merit rev. bd. for basic scis. Dept. Vet. Adminstrn. Affairs. Served with USAF, 1966-69. NIH postdoctoral fellow U. Chgo., 1964-66; NIH spl. fellow Rockefeller U., 1969-71. Mem. Am. Chem. Soc., Am. Soc. Neurochemistry, Soc. for Neurosci., Am. Soc. Biol. Chemists, Am. Soc. Pharmacology and Exptl. Therapeutics, Internat. Soc. Neurochemistry, Assn. Med. and Grad. Depts. Biochemistry (sec. 1994-96). Condr. research enzymology. Home: 1206 Aline St New Orleans LA 70115-2421 Office: 1100 Florida Ave New Orleans LA 70119-2714

ROSKY, BURTON SEYMOUR, lawyer; b. Chgo., May 28, 1927; s. David T. and Mary W. (Zelkin) R.; m. Leatrice J. Darrow, June 16, 1951; children: David Scott, Bruce Alan. Student, Ill. Inst. Tech., 1944-45; BS, UCLA, 1948; JD, Loyola U., L.A., 1953. Bar: Calif. 1954, U.S. Supreme Ct 1964, U.S. Tax Ct 1964; C.P.A., Calif. Auditor City of L.A., 1948- 51; with Beidner, Temkin & Ziskin (C.P.A.s), L.A., 1951-52; supervising auditor Army Audit Agy., 1952-53; practiced law L.A., Beverly Hills, 1954—; ptnr. Duskin & Rosky, 1972-82; s Rosky, Landau & Fox, 1982-93; ptnr. Rosky, Landau, Stahl & Sheehy, Beverly Hills, 1993-94; lectr. on tax and bus. problems; judge pro tem Beverly Hills Mcpl. Ct., L.A. Superior Ct.; mem. L.A. Mayor's Community Adv. Council. Contbr. profl. publs. Charter supporting mem. Los Angeles County Mus. Arts; contbg. mem. Assocs. of Smithsonian Instn.; charter mem. Air and Space Mus; mem. Am. Mus. Natural History, L.A. Zoo; supporting mem. L.A. Mus. Natural History; mem. exec. bd. So. Calif. coun. Nat. Fedn. Temple Brotherhoods, mem. nat. exec. bd. With USNR, 1945-46. Walter Henry Cook fellow Loyola Law Sch. Fellow Jewish Chautauqua Soc. (life mem.); mem. Am. Arbitration Assn. (nat. panel arbitrators), Am. Assn. Attys.-CPAs (charter mem. pres. 1968), Calif. Assn. Attys.-CPAs (charter mem., pres. 1963), Calif. Soc. CPAs, Calif., Beverly Hills, Century City, Los Angeles County bar assns., Am. Judicature Soc., Chancellors Assocs. UCLA, Tau Delta Phi, Phi Alpha Delta.; mem. B'nai B'rith. Jewish (mem. exec. bd., pres. temple, pres. brotherhood). Club: Mason. Office: Rosky Landau Stahl & Sheehy 8383 Wilshire Blvd Beverly Hills CA 90211-2410

ROSKY, THEODORE SAMUEL, insurance company executive; b. Chgo., Apr. 14, 1937; s. Theodore and Lora Marie (O'Connell) R.; m. Jacqueline Reed, Apr. 19, 1958; 1 child, Laura Marie. B.A., State U. Iowa, 1959. Various actuarial positions Conn. Gen. Life Ins. Co., Hartford, 1959-66; assoc. actuary Conn. Gen. Life Ins. Co., 1967-70, controller, 1970-73, 2d v.p., actuary, 1973, v.p., 1973-78; exec. v.p. Capital Holding Corp., 1978-84, exec. v.p., CFO, 1984-91, exec. v.p., 1991-92; bd. dirs. Legend Funds, 1993—, SBM Mut. Funds, 1995—, SBM Certificate Co., 1996—; instr. State U. Iowa, 1958-59, U. Hartford, 1964-66, U. Conn., 1967-68. Bd. dirs. Hartford Coll. for Women, 1974-78, Macauley Theater, 1983-85, Louisville Fund for the Arts, 1980—, Louisville Luth. Home, 1983—, Louisville Orch., 1982-88, 89-95, Ky. Opera, 1992—, Lincoln Found., 1992—, Actors Theatre of Louisville, 1995—; bd. dirs. Oak and Acorn, 1994—, mem. bd. pensions, 1996—; mem. bd. pensions Evangel. Luth. Ch. Am., 1974-82, 84-87, 89-95. Recipient award Soc. Actuaries, 1958. Fellow Soc. Actuaries; mem. Am. Acad. Actuaries, Southeastern Actuaries Club. Republican. Lutheran. Club: Pendennis. Home: 2304 Speed Ave Louisville KY 40205-1642

ROS-LEHTINEN, ILEANA, congresswoman; b. Havana, Cuba, July 15, 1952; d. Enrique Emilio and Amanda (Adato) Ros; m. Dexter Lehtinen. AA, Miami (Fla.)-Dade C.C., 1972; BA, Fla. Internat. U., 1975, MS, 1987. Prin. Ea. Acad., from 1978; mem. Fla. Ho. of Reps., Tallahassee, 1982-86, Fla. Senate, 1986-89, 101st-104th Congresses from 18th Fla. Dist., 1989—; mem. govt. ops. com., subcom. employment, housing, commerce, consumer monetary affairs., govt. info., justice agrl., fgn. affairs. com. Roman Catholic. Office: US Ho of Reps 2440 Rayburn Bldg Washington DC 20515-0918*

ROSNER, ANN See SEAMAN, BARBARA

ROSNER, FRED, physician, educator; b. Berlin, Oct. 3, 1935; came to U.S., 1949, naturalized, 1955; s. Sidney and Sara (Feingold) R.; m. Saranne Eskolsky, Feb. 24, 1959; children: Mitchel, Miriam, Aviva, Shalom. B.A. cum laude, Yeshiva Coll., 1955; M.D., Albert Einstein Coll., 1959. Diplomate: Am. Bd. Internal Medicine. Intern Maimonides Med. Center, Bklyn., 1959-60, resident in medicine, 1960-62, fellow in hematology, 1962-63, asst. dir. hematology, 1967-70; instr. SUNY Downstate Med. Center, Bklyn., 1968-70; asst. prof. medicine SUNY Downstate Med. Center, 1970; asso. prof. SUNY, Stony Brook, 1970-78, prof. medicine, 1978-89; asst. dean, prof. medicine Albert Einstein Coll. Medicine, 1989-93; prof. medicine Mt. Sinai Sch. Medicine, N.Y.C., 1993—; dir. hematology Queens Hosp. Center, Jamaica, N.Y., 1970-78; dir. medicine Queens Hosp. Center, 1978—. Author: Modern Medicine and Jewish Law, 1972, Medicine in the Bible and Talmud, 1977, 2d edit., 1995, Biblical and Talmudic Medicine, 1978, 2d edit., 1995, Jewish Bioethics, 1979, Modern Medicine and Jewish Ethics, 1986, 2d edit., 1991, Practical Medical Halachah, 1990, Medicine and Jewish Law vol. I, 1990, vol. II, 1993; translator, editor: several Moses Maimonides' works including Moses Maimonides' Treatise on Hemorrhoids and Responsa, 1969; Medical Aphorisms of Moses Maimonides, 1970, Sex Ethics in the Writings of Moses Maimonides, 1974, 94, Moses Maimonides' Introduction to the Mishnah, 1975, 95, Maimonides Glossary of Drug Names, 1979, Moses Maimonides' Commentary on Sanhedrim, 1981, Maimonides' Treatise on Resurrection, 1982, Medicine in the Mishneh Torah of Maimonides, 1984, Maimonides' Treatises on Poisons, Hemorrhoids and Cohabitation, 1984, Maimonides' Commentary on the Aphorisms of Hippocrates, 1987, Maimonides' Medical Aphorisms, 1990, The Existance and Unity of God: Three Treatises Attributed to Moses Maimonides, 1990, Moses Maimonides' Three Treatises on Health, 1990, Six Treatises Attributed to Maimonides, 1991, Maimonides: Physician, Philosopher and Scientist, 1993, Maimonides' Treatise on Asthma, 1994, Maimonides' Glossary of Drug Names, 1995; mem. editl. bd. Medica Judaica, 1970—, Cancer Invest, Mt. Sinai Jour. Medicine; contbr.: Ency. Boethics; contbr. articles to tech. lit. Served with USPHS, 1963-65. Recipient Maimonides award Michael Reese Hosp., Chgo., 1969, Bernard Revel Meml. award Yeshiva U., 1971; Maimonides award of Wis., 1977. Fellow A.C.P., N.Y. Acad. Medicine; mem. AMA, Am. Assn. History Medicine, N.Y. Soc. Study of Blood, Am., Internat. socs. hematology, Am. Fedn. Clin. Research. Home: 750 Elvira Ave Far Rockaway NY 11691-5405 Office: Queens Hosp Ctr 82-68 164th St Jamaica NY 11432-1140

ROSNER, JONATHAN LINCOLN, physicist, educator; b. N.Y.C., July 23, 1941; s. Albert Aaron and Elsie Augustine (Lincoln) R.; m. Joy Elaine Fox, June 13, 1965; children: Hannah, Benjamin. BA, Swarthmore Coll., 1962; MA, Princeton U., 1963, PhD, 1965. Research asst. prof. U. Wash., Seattle, 1965-67; vis. lectr. Tel Aviv U., Ramat Aviv, Israel, 1967-69; asst. prof. physics U. Minn., Mpls., 1969-71, assoc. prof., 1971-75, prof., 1975-82; prof. U. Chgo., 1982—. Contbr. numerous articles to profl. and scholarly jours. Alfred P. Sloan fellow, 1971-73. Fellow Am. Phys. Soc. Democrat. Jewish. Avocations: fishing, hiking, skiing, amateur radio. Office: U Chgo Enrico Fermi Inst 5640 S Ellis Ave Chicago IL 60637-1433

ROSNER, LEONARD ALLEN, lawyer; b. N.Y.C., Apr. 13, 1967; s. Arnold and Betty (Zimmerman) R.; m. Rachel Stein, Nov. 19, 1994. AB in Polit. Sci., Syracuse U., 1989, AB in Pub. Rels., 1989, JD cum laude, 1992. Bar: N.Y. 1993. Assoc. Law Office Stephen D. Rogoff Esq., Rochester, N.Y., 1992—. Fin. editor Syracuse Jour. Internat. Law and Commerce, 1991-92. Assigned coun. Monroe County Assigned Coun., Rochester, 1993-94. Mem. N.Y. Bar Assn., Monroe County Bar Assn. Avocations: golfing, reading, television sports, nautilus. Home: Apt # 5 128 Crittenden Way Rochester NY 14623 Office: 1551 Monroe Ave Rochester NY 14618-1412

ROSNER, M. NORTON, business systems and financial services company executive; b. Camden, N.J., Aug. 17, 1931; s. Adolph and Anne (Cotler) R.; m. M. Patricia Eskin, Oct. 18, 1953; children—Robert, Susan, Jan. B.S. in Econs., U. Pa., 1953; M.B.A., U. Mich., 1965. From acct. to mgr. overhead standards RCA Corp., Camden, N.J., 1953-62; supr. methods and programs, then internal cons. forward model planning Ford Motor Co., Dearborn, Mich., 1962-66; asst. controller, then v.p. planning Singer Co., N.Y.C., 1966-70; treas., then v.p. fin. Popular Services, Passaic, N.J., 1970-72; dir. fin. planning, then asst. controller, then gen. mgr. GSD, then v.p. RE/GSD Xerox Corp., Rochester, N.Y., 1972-90; retired, 1990; bd. dirs., treas. Parcel Post Assn., N.Y.C., 1970-71; dir. Harbinger, Stamford, Conn.; chmn. Xerox Realty Corp., Stamford. Vice chmn. Compeer, Inc., Rochester, N.Y., 1981-87, chmn., 1987-89; chmn. DP2, Rochester, 1985-87; bd. dirs., treas. Rochester Blue Cross-Blue Shield, 1987-89; dir. Palm Beach County Mental Health Assn., 1992, treas., 1993, v.p., 1994-95, pres., 1995-96; dir. JARC, 1992, v.p., 1993, pres., 1994-96. Recipient Nat. Vol. Action award Pres. U.S. Clubs: U. Mich.; U. Pa. Home: 17831 Heather Ridge Ln Boca Raton FL 33498-6423

ROSNER, ROBERT, astrophysicist; b. Garmisch-Partenkirchen, Bavaria, Germany, June 26, 1947; came to U.S., 1959; s. Heinz and Faina (Brodsky) R.; m. Marsha Ellen Rich, Nov. 8, 1950; children: Daniela Karin, Nicole Elise. BA, Brandeis U., 1969; PhD, Harvard U., 1975. Asst. prof. Harvard U., Cambridge, Mass., 1978-83, assoc. prof., 1983-86; astrophysicist Smithsonian Astrophys. Observatory, Cambridge, 1986-87; prof. U. Chgo., 1987—; trustee Adler Planetarium, Chgo., 1989—, chmn. dept. astronomy and astrophysics, 1991—. Contbr. more than 120 articles to profl. jours. Woodrow Wilson fellow, 1969. Fellow Am. Phys. Soc.; mem. Am. Astron. Soc., Soc. Indsl. and Applied Math. Home: 4950 S Greenwood Ave Chicago IL 60615-2816 Office: U Chicago Astrophysics 5640 S Ellis Ave Chicago IL 60637-1433

ROSOFF, BARBARA LEE, religious education administrator; b. Chgo., Apr. 14, 1936; d. Ben Zion and Ruth Gwendolyn (Daniels) Ginsburg; m. Jack Rosoff, June 18, 1957; children: Ranana, Aviva, Joshua. AB cum laude, Brandeis U., 1957; MA in Teaching summa cum laude, Monmouth Coll., 1977; EdD, Rutgers U., 1990. Lic. early childhood-nursery sch. tchr., elem. tchr., N.J.; lic. tchr. and rpin. Nat. Bd. Lic. of Jewish Edn. Svc. N.Am. Supr. Congregation B'nai Israel Religious Sch., Rumson, N.J., 1965-78, dir. edn., 1978—; condr. seminars and workshops in field; mem. Jewish Educators' Assembly, United Synagogue Commn. on Jewish Edn.; ednl cons. Behrman House Pub. Co., West Orange, N.J., 1985—; instr. religious edn. Monmouth Coll. Grad. Sch. Edn., West Long Branch, N.J., 1976-77; prin., tchr. trainer Solomon Schecter Sch., Marlboro, N.J., 1979-81; mem. part-time faculty Rutgers U., New Brunswick, N.J., 1986-92, Fairleigh Dickinson U., Teaneck, N.J., 1991; instr., lectr. United Synagogue Tchr. Tng., N.Y.C., 1991—. Editor Coalition for the Advancement of Jewsih Education jour., 1994—; contbr. articles to profl. publs. Guiding mem. Interfaith Cmty. Coun., Rumson, 1992—. Mem. Phi Delta Kappa, Kappa Delta Pi. Avocations: swimming, yoga. Home: 33 Majestic Ave Lincroft NJ 07738-1719 Office: Congregation B'nai Israel Rumson NJ 07760

ROSOFF, JEANNIE I., foundation administrator; b. Clamart, France, Nov. 8, 1924; came to U.S., 1948; d. Georges Auguste Marie and Suzenne (Philomene) Martin; m. Morton Rosoff, Dec. 8, 1945 (div. 1958); 1 child, Ann Susan. BA in Law cum laude, U. Paris, 1946. Cmty. organizer East Harlem Project, N.Y.C., 1953-56; assoc. dir. N.Y. Com. for Dem. Voters, N.Y.C., 1960-64; spl. projects coord. Planned Parenthood Fedn. Am., N.Y.C., 1964-74, assoc. dir., 1968-74, assoc. dir. Ctr. for Family Planning Program Devel., 1968-74; v.p. govt. affairs Planned Parenthood Fedn. Am., Washington, 1974-77, dir. Washington office, 1976-81; sr. v.p. Alan Guttmacher Inst., Washington, 1974-78, pres., 1978—; participant in UN Population Conf., Bucharest, 1974, UN Conf. on Internat. Women's Yr., Mexico City, 1975; ofcl. U.S. del. UN Conf. on Population and Devel., Cairo, 1994; del.-at-large Internat. Women's Yr. Conf., Houston, 1977. Author: Teenage Pregnancy in Industrialized Countries, 1986, Health Care Reform: A Unique Opportunity, 1993, (govt. publs.) Family Planning: An Analysis of Laws, 1974, Family Planning: Contraception, 1979. Recipient merit award Nat. Family Planning and Repro. Health Assn., 1980, Ten for Ten award Ctr. for Population Options, 1990. Mem. APHA (pres., chair population sect. 1976, Carl S. Schultz award 1980; maternal and child health sec. 1973-76), Nat. Health Lawyers Assn., Population Assn. Am., Nat. Inst. Child Health and Human Devel., Pathfinder Internat. (bd. dirs. 1993—). Office: Alan Guttmacher Inst 120 Wall St Fl 21 New York NY 10005-4001

ROSOFF, LEONARD, SR., retired surgeon, medical educator; b. Grand Forks, N.D., May 5, 1912; s. Albert and Sophie (Koblin) R.; m. Marie Louise Aronsfeld, June 1, 1935; 1 son, Leonard. BA, U. So. Calif., 1931; MD, U. Tex., 1935. Diplomate: Am. Bd. Surgery (dir. 1970-76). Intern, then resident gen. surgery Los Angeles County Hosp., 1935-40; from instr. to prof. surgery U. So. Calif. Sch. Medicine, 1946-80, emeritus, 1980—, chmn. dept., 1969-79; chief surg. services, dir. surgery Los Angeles County-U. So. Calif. Med. Center, 1955-77, sr. attending surgeon, 1977-80, ret., 1980; clin. prof. surgery U. Tex. Health Ctr., San Antonio, 1992—; hon. staff Hosp. Good Samaritan, Cedars-Sinai, Los Angeles Children's, Huntington Meml. hosps.; lectr. in field. Contbr. articles to med. jours., textbooks. Served with M.C., AUS, 1942-45. Recipient Outstanding Alumnus award U. Tex. Med. Br., 1971. Fellow ACS (bd. govs. 1975-81, 2d v.p. 1981), Tex. Surg. Soc. (hon.); mem. Am. Surg. Assn. (1st v.p. 1984), Western Surg. Assn. (2d v.p.), Pacific Coast Surg. Assn., L.A. Surg. Assn. (pres. 1970), Am. Assn. Endocrine Surgeons (bd. councilors 1980-87, pres. 1984), Am. Assn. Surgery Trauma, Soc. Surgery Alimentary Tract (pres. 1979-80), Internat. Soc. Surgery, L.A. Acad. Medicine, L.A. Athletic Club, Giraud Club (San Antonio). Research surgery parathyroids, thyroid gland and other endocrine systems, surgery peptic ulcer and other gastrointestinal diseases, studies in shock. Home: One Towers Park Ln # 1115 San Antonio TX 78209

ROSOFF, WILLIAM A., lawyer, executive; b. Phila., June 21, 1943; s. Herbert and Estelle (Finkel) R.; m. Beverly Rae Rifkin, Feb. 7, 1970; children: Catherine D., Andrew M. BS with honors, Temple U., 1964; LLB magna cum laude, U. Pa., 1967. Bar: Pa. 1968, U.S. Dist. Ct. (ea. dist.) Pa. 1968. Law clk. U.S. Ct. Appeals (3d cir.), 1967-68; instr. U. Pa. Law Sch., Phila., 1968-69; assoc. Wolf, Block, Schorr & Solis-Cohen, Phila., 1969-75, ptnr., 1975-96, chmn. exec. com., 1987-88; vice chmn. Advanta Corp., Horsham, Pa., 1996—; trustee RPS Realty Trust; guest lectr. confs. and seminars on tax law; mem. tax adv. bd. Commerce Clearing House, 1983-94; mem. legal activities policy bd. Tax Analysts, 1978—; mem. Little, Brown Tax Adv. Bd., 1994-96. Editor U. Pa. Law Rev., 1965-67; mem. bd. contbg. editors and advisors Jour. Partnership Taxation, 1983—; author reports and papers on tax law. Bd. dirs., mem. com. on law and social action Phila. coun. Am. Jewish Congress. Fellow Am. Coll. Tax Counsel; mem. Am. Law Inst. (cons. taxation of partnerships 1976-78, assoc. reporter taxation of partnerships, 1978-82, mem. adv. group on fed. income tax project 1982—), Locust Club (dir.), Order of Coif, Beta Gamma Sigma, Beta Alpha Psi. Office: Advanta Corp 300 Welsh Rd Horsham PA 19044

ROSOVSKY, HENRY, economist, educator; b. Danzig, Sept. 1, 1927; came to U.S., 1940, naturalized, 1949; s. Selig S. and Sophie (Rosovsky) R.; m. Nitza Brown, June 17, 1956; children—Leah, Judith, Michael. A.B., Coll. William and Mary, 1949, LL.D., 1976; A.M. (John E. Thayer scholar), Harvard U., 1953; Ph.D., 1959; L.H.D. (hon.), Yeshiva U., 1977, Hebrew Union Coll., 1978, Colgate U., 1979, Brandeis U., 1984; Ph.D. (hon.), Hebrew U. of Jerusalem, 1982; LL.D. (hon.), Queen's U., Ont., 1984, U. Hartford, 1984, CUNY, 1986, U. Mass., 1986; DHL (hon.), Hebrew Coll., Brookline, Mass., 1987, NYU, 1993; DL, St. Mary's Coll. Md., 1989. From asst. prof. to prof. econs. and history U. Calif.-Berkeley, 1958-65; chmn. Center Japanese and Korean Studies, 1962-65; prof. econs. Harvard U., 1965—, Walter S. Barker prof. econs., 1975-84, Geyser univ. prof., 1984—, chmn. dept., 1969-72, dean Faculty Arts and Scis., 1973-84; assoc. dir. East Asia Research Center, 1967-69; mem. Harvard U. Corp., 1985—; vis. prof. Hitotsubashi U., Tokyo, 1957, Tokyo U., 1962, Hebrew U., Jerusalem, 1965; bd. dirs. Corning, Inc., Paine Webber Group, Japan Fund. Author: Capital Formation in Japan, 1868-1940, 1961, Quantitative Japanese Economic History, 1961, (with K. Ohkawa) Japanese Economic Growth, 1973, The University: An Owner's Manual, 1990; editor: Explorations in Entrepreneurial History, 1954-56, Industrialization in Two Systems, 1966, Discord in the Pacific, 1972, (with H. Patrick) Asia's New Giant, 1976, (with P. Higonnet, D. Landes) Favorites of Fortune, 1991, (with S. Kumon) The Political Economy of Japan, Vol. 3: Cultural and Social Dynamics, 1992. Chmn. bd. trustees Am. Jewish Congress, 1975-88. Served to 1st lt. AUS, 1946-47, 50-52. Jr. fellow Soc. Fellows, 1954-57; recipient Schumpeter prize Harvard, 1963, Clark Kerr medal U. Calif., Berkeley, 1992. Fellow Am. Acad. Arts and Scis., Am. Philos. Soc.; mem. Am. Econ. Assn., Econ. History Assn., Assn. Asian Studies, Chevalier, Legion of Honor, Order of Sacred Treasure, Star (Japan). Home: 37 Beechcroft Rd Newton MA 02158-2403 Office: Harvard Univ 218 Littauer Ctr Cambridge MA 02138

ROSOW, JEROME MORRIS, institute executive; b. Chgo., Dec. 2, 1919; s. Morris and Mary (Cornick) R.; m. Rosalyn Levin, Sept. 28, 1941; children: Michael, Joel. BA cum laude, U. Chgo., 1942. Position classification analyst Dept. Army, Washington, 1942-43; orgn. and methods examiner, asst. mgr. wage and salary div. Dept. Army, 1948-51; dir. compensation War Assets Adminstrn., Washington, 1946-48; dir. policy, salary stblzn. bd. Econ. Stblzn. Agy., 1952-53; with Creole Petroleum Corp. subs. Standard Oil N.J., Caracas, Venezuela, 1953-55; various exec. positions including coordinator of compensation, indsl. relations research Standard Oil N.J., N.Y.C., 1955-66; mgr. employee relations dept. ESSO Europe, Inc., London, 1966-69; asst. sec. labor for policy, evaluation and research Dept. Labor, 1969-71; planning mgr. pub. affairs. dept. Exxon Corp., 1971-77; founder, pres. Work in Am. Inst., 1976—; cons. fed. pay plans U.S. Bur. Budget and U.S. CSC, 1964; mem. bus. adv. research com. Bur. Labor Stats., 1958-65; chmn. council of compensation Nat. Indsl. Conf. Bd., 1959-66; asso. seminar on labor, Columbia U., 1961—; dir. N.Y.C. Vocat. Adv. Service, 1961—, chmn. finance com., 1962-65; mem. White House Working Group on Welfare Reform, 1969-71; chmn. cabinet com. White House Conf. Children and Youth, 1970-71; chmn. subcabinet com. nat. growth policy; U.S. del OECD Ministers Conf., Paris, 1970, 74; vice-chmn. Nat. Productivity Commn., 1971; chmn. tech. experts multinat. indsl. relations OECD, Paris, 1972; chmn. subcom. manpower and social affairs; chmn. Pres.'s Adv. Com. Fed. Pay, 1971-82; adviser Pres. U.S.; chmn. Am. assembly The Changing World at Work. Editor: American Men in Government, 1949, The Worker and the Job: Coping with Change, 1974; Editor: (with Clark Kerr) Work in America: The Decade Ahead, 1979, Productivity: Prospects for Growth, 1981, Views from the Top, 1985, Teamwork: Joint Labor-Management Programs in America, 1986, Global Marketplace, 1988, Training-The Competitive Edge, 1988, Allies in Education Reform, 1988; contbr. articles on manpower, compensation, welfare reform, indsl. relations, orgn. transformation, labor mgmt. relations to profl. jours. Bd. dirs. Young Audiences; trustee Nat. Com. Employment of Youth; adviser Com. Econ. Devel., 1972—, Nat. Planning Assn., 1973—; mem. Nat. Commn. Productivity and Quality of Work, 1975; v.p. Population Edn. Inc., 1975—; mem. Study Group Work and Edn. in China, 1978; cons. comptroller gen. U.S., 1972—, Ford Found.; mem. Mayor's Commn. on Gainsharing, N.Y.C., 1993. With AUS, 1943-46. Recipient Comptroller Gen.'s Public Service award, 1980. Mem. Indsl. Relations Research Assn. (life, exec. bd., pres. 1979). Jewish. Home: 117 Fox Meadow Rd Scarsdale NY 10583-2301 Office: 700 White Plains Rd Scarsdale NY 10583-5013

ROSOW, STUART L., lawyer; b. N.Y.C., Mar. 28, 1950; s. Bernard and Lillian (Bonime) R.; m. Amy Berk Kuhn. AB cum laude, Yale U.; JD cum laude, Harvard U. Law clk. to presiding justice U.S. Ct. Appeals (7th cir.), Chgo., 1975-76; assoc. Paul, Weiss et al, N.Y.C., 1976-79; assoc. Kaye, Scholer, Fierman, Hays & Handler, N.Y.C., 1979-84, ptnr., 1984—. Mem. ABA, N.Y. State Bar Assn., Assn. of Bar of City of N.Y. Office: Kaye Scholer Fierman Hays & Handler 425 Park Ave New York NY 10022-3506

ROSOWSKI, ROBERT BERNARD, manufacturing company executive; b. Detroit, July 23, 1940; s. Bernard and Anna (Maciag) R.; m. Kathleen Patricia Bates, Aug. 26, 1961; children: John, Paul, Mary, Judith. BS, U. Detroit, 1962; MBA, Mich. State U., 1974. CPA, Mich. Auditor, staff supr. Coopers and Lybrand, Detroit, 1962-71; fin. analyst Masco Corp., Taylor, Mich., 1971-73, controller, 1973-85, v.p., controller, 1985—. Bd. dirs. Econ. Devel. Coun. City of Taylor, 1983—; chmn. bd. dirs. Acctg. Aid Soc. Met. Detroit, 1987—, Oakwood Hosp. Found., 1990—. Mem. Am. Inst. CPA's, Mich. Assn. CPA's. Avocations: golf, fishing, boating, photography. Office: Masco Corp 21001 Van Born Rd Taylor MI 48180-1340

ROSS, ADRIAN E., drilling manufacturing company executive; b. Clintonville, N.Y., Mar. 6, 1912; s. James A. and Bertha (Beardsley) R.; B.S. in Elec. Engring., M.I.T., 1934, M.S. in Elec. Engring., 1935; m. Ruth T. Hill, Mar. 2, 1934; children—James A., Daniel R. Materials engr. USN, 1935-37; devel. engr. Electrolux Corp., 1937-41; chief engr. and asst. to pres. Sprague & Henwood, Inc., Scranton, Pa., 1946-53, dir., 1951—, pres., 1953-74, chmn. bd., 1963—; pres., dir. Sprague & Henwood de Venezuela; dir. Hands Eng. Ltd., Scranton Lackawanna Indsl. Bldg. Co. (emeritus), N.E. Bank of Pa. (emeritus), profl. engrs. Past chmn. bd., dir. emeritus Keystone Jr. Coll.; pres., dir. Ross Family Found.; former chmn. bd., dir. emeritus Johnson Sch. Tech. Served from lt. to lt. col. Air Communication. USAAF, 1941-46. Registered profl. engr., Pa. Mem. Diamond Core Drill Mfrs. Assn. (past pres.), AIME, ASCE, Soc. Profl Engrs., U.S. Nat. Council Soil Mechanics, Indsl. Diamond Assn. Am. (past pres.), C. of C. Presbyn. Clubs: Mining (N.Y.C.); Scranton, M.I.T. (Scranton, Pa.). Contbr. articles to Mining Congress Jour., Mining Engring., Engring. and Mining Jour., Diamond Drill Handbook. Home: 5 Overlook Rd Clarks Summit PA 18411-1121

ROSS, ALBERTA BARKLEY, retired chemist; b. Moores Hill, Ind., July 26, 1928; d. Lawrence Houston and Stella Olcott (Wright) Barkley; m. Joseph Hansbro Ross, June 2, 1956; children: Mary Angela, Joseph Hansbro Jr., Robert Barkley, Kathleen. BS, Purdue U., 1948, Wash. U., 1951; PhD, U. Md., 1957. Tech. libr. Monsanto Chem. Co., St. Louis, 1948-53; rsch. assoc. U. Mich., Ann Arbor, 1957-58; supr. Radiation Chemistry Data Ctr. U. Notre Dame (Ind.), 1964-95; ret., 1995. Mem. Am. Chem. Soc. (chmn. St. Joseph Valley chpt. 1977-78), Sigma Xi (chpt. pres. 1980-81), Iota Sigma Pi.

ROSS, ALEXANDER DUNCAN, art librarian; b. N.Y.C., Aug. 3, 1941; s. Donald Duncan and Anita (Petersen) R.; m. Susan Dixon Getman, July 29, 1967 (div. 1977); m. Eleanore Saunders Stewart, June 22, 1985 (div. 1994). B.A., Columbia U., 1966, M.S., 1968, M.A., 1971. Asst. art librarian Columbia U., N.Y.C., 1968-71; assoc. librarian Cleve. Mus. Art, 1971-75; head art librarian Stanford U., Calif., 1975—. Contbr. articles to profl. jours. Mem. Art Libraries Soc. N. Am. Home: 4175 Wilkie Way Palo Alto CA 94306-4159 Office: Stanford U Art & Arch Libr 102 Cummings Art Bldg Stanford CA 94305

ROSS, ALLAN ANDERSON, music educator, university official; b. Amesbury, Mass., Jan. 16, 1939; s. Frank Albert and Ruth Ethel (Anderson) R.; m. Barbara Kay Bedford, Apr. 15, 1962; children: Karen Elizabeth, Judith Carol, Donna Susan, Linda Beth, Jason Andrew. A.B., U. Rochester, 1961; MusM, Ind. U., 1962, MusD, 1968. Asst. dir. music U. Rochester, N.Y., 1962-65; instr. music Ind. U., Bloomington, 1967-69, asst. prof. music, 1969-71, assoc. prof., dir. undergrad. studies, 1971-73, prof., 1977-79, asst. to dean, 1973-79; dean Shepherd Sch. Music, Rice U., Houston, 1979-81; prof. music U. Okla., Norman, 1981—, dir. music, 1981-92, devel. officer Coll. Fine Arts, 1992-93; condr. U. Okla. Symphony Orch., 1993—; dir. music Trinity Methodist Ch., Rochester, N.Y., 1963-65, First United Meth. Ch., Bloomington, Ind., 1969-79, 1st Christian Ch., Norman, Okla., 1981-91; bd. dirs. Riemenschneider Bach Inst.; bd. dirs., exec. bd. Okla. Summer Arts Inst. Guest condr. and adjudicator at music festivals throughout, U.S.; Author: Techniques for Beginning Conductors, 1976. Bd. dirs. United Way of Norman, Helpline of Norman, Okla. Arts Inst.; mem. gov.'s commn. for Okla. Symphony Orch. NDEA Title IV fellow, 1965. Mem. Music Educators Nat. Conf., Am. Choral Dirs. Assn., Coll. Music Soc., Nat. Assn. Schs. of Music (grad. commn., evaluator), Okla. Music Educators Assn., Phi Mu Alpha Sinfonia, Pi Kappa Lambda. Home: 1879 Rolling Hills St Norman OK 73072-6707 Office: U Okla Sch Music 560 Parrington Oval Norman OK 73019-3040

ROSS, ALLAN MICHAEL, physician, medical educator; b. N.Y.C., June 20, 1939; s. Irving and Rose (Jarin) R.; m. Loleta Saylors, Nov. 1, 1965; children—Jenifer, Aaron, Jed. B.A., Northwestern U., 1960; M.D., Chgo. Med. Sch., 1964. Diplomate Am. Bd. Internal Medicine. Fellow in cardiology Yale U., New Haven, 1971-72; instr. medicine Yale U., 1972-73, asst. prof. medicine, 1975-77, assoc. prof., 1977-78; dir. cardiol. cath. lab. West Haven VA Hosp., 1973-75; prof. medicine, dir. div. cardiology George Washington U., Washington, 1979-94; prof./assoc. chmn. dept. medicine, dir. cardiovascular rsch. George Washington U., 1994—. Inventor spl. function cardiac catheters; designer cardiologic diagnostic algorhythms. Served with M.C. U.S. Army, 1968-71. Am. Heart Lung and Blood Inst. prin. investigator, 1983. Fellow Am. Coll. Cardiology (bd. govs. D.C. sect. 1982-85); mem. Am. Heart Assn. (fellow coun. on clin. cardiology, D.C. counsellor 1983). Office: George Washington U 2150 Pennsylvania Ave NW Washington DC 20037-2396

ROSS, ALLYNE R., federal judge; b. 1946. BA, Wellesley Coll., 1967; JD cum laude, Harvard Law Sch., 1970. Assoc. Paul, Weiss, Rifkind, Wharton & Garrison, 1971-76; asst. U.S. atty. U.S. Dist. Ct. (N.Y. ea. dist.), 2nd circuit, Brooklyn, 1976-83, chief, appeals div., 1983-86, magistrate judge, 1986-94, dist. judge, 1994—. Mem. Federal Bar Coun., New York City Bar Assn. Office: US District Court 225 Cadman Plz E Rm 252 Brooklyn NY 11201-1818*

ROSS, ANN DUNBAR, secondary school educator; b. Longview, Tex., Jan. 21, 1945; d. Louie and Myra Lee (Fanning) Dunbar; m. John Reuben Ross, Sept. 9, 1967; children: Jennifer Ann, John Byron. BA in Math., U. Tex., 1968; M in Liberal Arts, So. Meth. U., 1974; Endorsement in Gifted Edn., U. North Tex., 1992. Tchr. math. Dallas, 1968-72, Duncanville (Tex.) High Sch., 1979-89; tchr. math., dept. chairperson Duncanville Ninth Grade Sch., 1989—; vertical team mem. Math. Dept. Duncanville High Sch., 1993—; site based mgmt. mem. Duncanville Ninth Grade Sch., 1993; presenter in field at math. conf. Mem. Nat. Coun. Tchrs. Math., Tex. Coun. Tchrs. Math., Tex. Fedn. Tchrs., Tex. Classroom Tchrs. Assn. (local rep.), ASCD. Avocation: ceramics.

ROSS, AUSTIN, health care executive; b. Milw., Aug. 12, 1929; s. Austin and Elizabeth (Greene) R.; m. Annette Wolff, Dec. 28, 1950; children: Carol, Randall, Becky, Austin. BSBA, U. Calif., Berkeley, 1951, MPH, 1955. Adminstrn. intern Cowell Meml. Hosp., Berkeley, 1953-55; adminstrn. resident Virginia Mason Hosp., Seattle, 1955-56, assoc. adminstr., 1966-68, adminstr., 1968-77, v.p., exec. adminstr., 1977-90; asst. adminstr. The Mason Clinic, Seattle, 1956-66; prof. U. Wash., 1991—, chmn. external adv. com., 1983—; chmn. bd. dirs. Blue Cross Plan of Wash./Alaska, 1980-82, exec. com. mem., 1973-83; bd. dirs. Wash./Alaska Regional Med. Program, 1970-76, vice chmn. bd. trustees, 1976; cons. W.K. Kellogg Found., 1979-88, project co-dir. Health Svcs. Consortium Project, 1973-77; mem. Accrediting Commn. on Edn. for Health Svcs. Adminstrn., 1978-81; active numerous other local and nat. profl. orgns. Author: (with others) Ambulatory Care Organization and Management, 1984, Cornerstones of Leadership, 1992; co-editor: Integration of Clinical and Financial Information Systems, 1986; mem. editorial bd. Hosp. Health Svcs. Adminstrn. Jour., 1976-85, Jour. Ambulatory Health Care Mgmt., 1978—; contbr. articles, reports, book revs. to profl. publs. Bd. dirs. Downtown Seattle Devel. Assn., 1980-85, Alki Found., 1981-90, Bellevue Pk.-Episcopal Retirement Home Project, 1983-87; chmn. hosp. divsn. United Way, 1979, Pers. Commn. Episcopal Diocese of Olympia, 1983-85; sr. warden St. Thomas Episcopal Ch., 1979, 82; pres. bd. trustees St. Thomas Day Sch., 1978; adv. bd. Pike Market Community Clinic, 1986—. Lt. U.S. Army, 1950-53. Recipient Edgar Hayhow Article of Yr. award Am. Coll. Hosp. Adminstrs., 1982, Exec. Adminstr. of Yr. award Am. Group Practice Assn., 1987. Mem. Am. Coll. Healthcare Execs. (chmn. 1984-85, bd. govs. 1979-83, regent Wash./Alaska 1972-76, Gold medal 1989), Am. Coll. Med. Group Adminstrs. (bd. mem. 1973-74, Harry J. Harwick Disting. Svc. award 1983, Article of Yr. award 1982, 85), Am. Hosp. Assn. (chmn. ad hoc com. on physician involment 1989, mem. structure com. 1986-87, chmn. R & D coun. 1982-83, mem. adv. panel Ctr. Ambulatory Care 1979-80, coun. on manpower and edn. 1976-79), Assn. Western Hosps. (bd. mem. 1971-81, pres. 1976-77, Alfred Mafley Adminstr. on Campus award 1981), Med. Group Mgmt. Assn. (chmn. joint rsch. com. 1982-83, joint edn. com. 1980-81, pres. 1976-77), Seattle Area Hosp. Coun. (pres. 1968-70), Wash. State Hosp. Assn. (pres. 1971-72), Rainier Club. Republican. Office: Virginia Mason Med Ctr 1100 9th Ave Seattle WA 98101-2756

ROSS, BEATRICE BROOK, artist; b. N.Y.C., Mar. 31, 1927; d. Alexander and Ray (Tennenbaum) Brook; m. Alexander Ross, Dec. 23, 1945; children: Robert Alan, Kenneth Jay, Stefani Lynn. Student, Hunter Coll., 1943, CCNY, 1944, Bklyn. Mus. Art Sch., 1959-60, 64-65; pupil of Ruben Tam, Wang Chi Yuan, Leo Manso; scholar, Sch. Chinese Brush Work, 1973. Owner, operator Jean Rosenthal Bea Ross Gallery, Jericho, 1961-64; represented by Gillary Gallery, Jericho, N.Y., Patrician Gallery, West Palm Beach, Fla.; founder Birchwood Art League, 1958-63; lectr. bd. edn., Ont., Can., 1972; mem. ad hoc com. with Lucy Lippard Women in Art, 1970-74. Exhbns. include Women in Art, Huntington, N.Y., 1972, C.W. Post Coll., 1972, 73-76, Guild Hall Mus., East Hampton, 1969-72, Lever House, Inc., 1969-72, J. Walter Thompson Loan Show, 1970, Whitehouse Gallery, 1970, Park Ave. Synagogue, 1970, Locust Valley Ann., 1970, Nat. Arts Club, 1970, Loeb Student Ctr., NYU, 1969, Suffolk Mus., Stony Brook, N.Y., 1969, Lynn U., Boca Raton, 1992, Suffolk Mus., Stony Brook, N.Y., 1971, NAD, 1968, Audubon Artists, 1968, 70, Silvermine Guild, 1968, 71, Port Washington (N.Y.) Library, 1968, 70, 76, Profl. Artists Guild L.I., 1968, Bklyn. Coll., 1968, Huntington Twp. Art League, Cold Spring Harbor, N.Y., 1967, Gillary Gallery, Jericho, N.Y., 1966, 68, 70, 72, 79, 83, Hecksher Mus., 1960, 63, 70, Ho. of Reps., 1965, Library of Congress, 1965, Merrick (N.Y.) Gallery, 1963, N. Shore Community Art Ctr. ann., Roslyn, N.Y., 1959, 62, Birchwood Art League, Jericho, N.Y., 1958, 61-62, Hofstra U., 1960, City Ctr., N.Y.C., 1960, Emily Lowe Gallery, 1960, Nassau Democratic County Com. ann., 1958, R.A.A. Gallery, N.Y.C., 1969-70, 77, Roosevelt Field Art Gallery, Garden City, N.Y., 1958, Boca Raton (Fla.) City Hall, 1991, Bryant Library, Roslyn, N.Y., 1973, Women's Interart Ctr., N.Y.C., 1974, Wantagh (N.Y.) Library, 1975, Port Washington Library, 1976, LIU, 1976, N.Y. Tech., 1974, C.W. Post Coll. Schwartz Library, 1976, St. Johns U., 1976, Union Carbide, N.Y.C., 1977, Harley U. Ctr. Gallery, Adelphi U., 1976, 82, Lincoln Ctr., N.Y.C., 1978, 82, Gallery 84, N.Y.C., 1981, Am. Properties Inc., Boca Raton, Fla., 1996; represented in pvt. collections, traveling shows in France, Italy and Japan; mus. curated show No. Trust Bank, Boca Mus., Fla., 1992, Nations Bank, Boca Raton Mus., Fla., 1995. Recipient 1st prize oil Birchwood Art League, 1958; certificate award outstanding contbn. Mid Island Plaza Art League, Hicksville, N.Y., 1961, 2d prize oil, 1962; hon. mention oil Operation Democracy, Inc. ann., Locust Valley, 1967, 1st prize oil, 1970; Benjamin Altman landscape prize N.A.D., 1968; 2d prize Heckscher Mus., Huntington, N.Y., 1970; hon. mention Port Washington Ann., 1971, Benjamin Altman Landscape prize, Nat. award Nat. Acad. Design, N.Y.C., 1969, RAA Gallery, 1967-78, Harbor Gallery, Glen Cove, N.Y., 1983-85, Gillary Gallery Jericho, N.Y., 1984, Judge's Recognition award Boca Raton Mus., 1989, 2d prize, 1990, others; named to Nat. Women's Hall of Fame; MacDowell fellow, 1975, 80. Mem. Profl. Artists Guild L.I. (v.p. admissions 1971-74, exec. v.p. 1975-77, Judge's Recognition award at Boca Raton Mus. 1989, 2d prize for group show 1990), Profl. Artists Guild Fla., Easthampton Guild-Women in Arts, N.Y. Artists Equity, Nat. Mus. Women in Arts (charter), Gallery 84 (N.Y. chpt. 1979-85). Home and Studio: 5253 Bolero Cir Delray Beach FL 33484

ROSS, BERNARD, engineering consultant. BME, Cornell U., 1957; MSc in Aero. Engring., Stanford U., 1959, PhD in Aero. and Aerospace Engring., 1965; Diploma, Ecole Nat. Superieure L'Aero., France, 1960; cert., U. Edinburgh, Scotland, 1961. Registered profl. engr., Calif. Structural test engr. Gen. Dynamics Corp., Montreal, Quebec, Can., 1956; servomechanism and control sys. design engr. Marquardt Corp., Van Nuys, Calif., 1957; stress analyst Douglas Aircraft Co., Santa Monica, Calif., 1959; vibration and dynamics engr. ONERA, Paris, 1960; rsch. asst. Stanford U., 1961-63, rsch. assoc., 1963-65; sr. rsch. engr., program mgr. Stanford Rsch. Inst., Menlo Park, Calif., 1965-70; cons. engr. Failure Analysis Assocs., San Francisco, 1967—; vis. prof. U. Santa Clara, Calif., 1970-79; adv. coun. Stanford U., 1991—, cons. prof., 1992—; mem. internat. adv. bd. structural failure, product liability and tech. ins. confs. U. Vienna, 1986—; speaker and lectr. in field. Contbr. articles to Exptl. Mechanics, AIAA Jour., Israel Jour. Tech., Profl. Safeyt, others. Cons. U.S. Consumer Product Safety Commn., Washington. NATO scholar, 1960. Mem. ASME, NSPE, AIAA, AAAS, Am. Soc. Safety Engrs., Am. Soc. Agrl. Engrs., Calif. Soc. Profl. Engrs., Soc. Automotive Engrs., Soc. Exptl. Mechanics. Achievements include research in analysis of structural collapse, mechanics of impact and penetration, sea ice-hydraulic structure collapse, mechanics of impact and penetration, sea ice-hydraulic structure interaction, mechanical failure of machine parts, high speed ground transportation system. Office: Failure Analysis Assocs PO Box 3015 149 Commonwealth Dr Menlo Park CA 94025

ROSS, BRIAN ELLIOTT, news correspondent; b. Chgo., Oct. 23, 1948; s. Kenneth Earl and Shirley Louise (Johnston) R. B.A., U. Iowa, 1971. Corr. KWWL-TV, Waterloo, Iowa, 1971, WCKT-TV, Miami, Fla., 1972-74; news corr. NBC News, Cleve. and N.Y.C., 1974—. Recipient Peabody award, 1974, 92, Columbia-DuPont award, 1975, 85, 86, Sigma Delta Chi award, 1976, Robert F. Kennedy award, 1979, Nat. Emmy award, 1980, 85, 88, 92, Nat. Headlines award, 1976, 77, 78, 87, Overseas Press Club award, 1988, 90, 92, George M. Polk award, 1989, 93, Sidney Hillman award, 1993.

ROSS, CHARLES, artist; b. Phila., Dec. 17, 1937; s. Fred H. and Gertrude (Hill) R.; m. Elizabeth Ginsberg, 1977. A.B. in Math, U. Calif., Berkeley, 1960, M.A. in Sculpture, 1962. Exhibited in one-man shows: Dilexi Gallery, San Francisco, 1961, 65, 66, 68, Dwan Gallery, N.Y.C., 1968, 69, 71, Daytons Gallery 12, Mpls., 1968, John Weber Gallery, N.Y.C., 1972, 77, 79, 81, The Clocktower, N.Y.C., 1974, Utah Mus. Fine Arts, Salt Lake City, 1975, Mus. Contemporary Art, La Jolla, Calif., 1976, Chgo., 1976, Inst. Contemporary Art, Phila., 1977, Susan Caldwell Gallery, N.Y.C., 1977, MIT, 1977, Portland Center for Visual Arts, 1981, Sena Gallery, Santa Fe, 1991, Johnson Gallery U. N.Mex., 1992, Humphrey Gallery, N.Y.C., 1995; exhibited in group shows: Archtl. League of, New York, 1967, Albright Knox Art Gallery, Buffalo, 1967, Finch Coll., N.Y.C., 1967, Aldrich Mus., Ridgefield, Conn., 1967, Nelson Atkins Mus., Kansas City, 1968, Milw. Art Center, 1968, Whitney Mus., N.Y.C., 1969, Art Inst. Chgo., 1969, Art Gallery of Ont., Toronto, 1969, Galeries-pilotes, Lausanne, Switzerland, 1970, Mus. Fine Arts, Boston, 1971, Indpls. Mus. Art, 1974, Neuberger Mus., SUNY, Purchase, 1975, Stadtisches Mus., Leverkusen, Germany,

1975, Phila. Coll. Art, 1977, Hirshhorn Mus., Washington, 1977, Old Customs House, N.Y.C., 1977, Mus. Natural History, N.Y.C., 1977, Leo Castelli Gallery, N.Y.C., 1978, Yale U. Art Gallery, 1978, Dartmouth Coll. Gallery, 1978, Aspen (Colo.) Center for Visual Arts, 1980, Centre Georges Pompidou, Paris, 1980, Renwick Gallery, Smithsonian Instn., Washington, 1980, Mus. Contemporary Art, Chgo., 1981, MIT, Cambridge, 1981, Bard Coll., 1984, Light Gallery, N.Y.C., 1985, Venice Biennale, 1986, Differentes Natures la Defense, Paris, 1992; commn. include: prism and/or solar spectrum skylight sculpture for Fed. Bldg, Lincoln, Nebr., 1976, U. Pa., 1977, Dietrich Found., Phila., 1979, Spectrum Bldg, Denver, 1980, Grand Rapids Art Mus., Mich., 1982, Towson State U., Md., 1983, Cumberland Rapid Transit Sta., Chgo., 1983, Linay Corp., Kansas City, Mo., 1985, Plaza of the Americas, Dallas, 1985, Wells Fargo Bldg., San Diego, 1986, San Francisco Internat. Airport, 1987, Anchorage Internat. Airport, 1987, Naugatuck Higher Edn. Ctr., Conn., 1990, Harvard Bus. Sc. Chapel, 1992, French Ministry of Culture Chateau d'Oiron, 1993; represented in permanent collections Nelson Atkins Mus., Whitney Mus. Am. Art, Berkeley Art Mus., Indpls. Mus. Art, Butler Inst. Am. Art, Herbert F. Johnson Mus. Art Cornell U., GSA Art and Architecture Program, U. Pa., Dietrich Found., Grand Rapids Art Mus., Gen. Elec. Corp., City Chgo., Towson State U., Becton Dickinson Corp., Security Pacific Bank, Found. Ctr., N.Y.C., Wynne Jackson Inc., Albuquerque Mus., Linclay Corp., Witco Chem. Corp., City of San Diego, Walker Art Ctr., City of San Francisco, State of Alaska, Koll Co., Los Angeles County Mus. Art; works in progress include: Star Axis, monumental sculpture/observatory atop a mesa in N.Mex. Author: Sunlight Convergence Solar Burn (Am. Inst. Graphic Arts award 1976); films Sunlight Dispersion, 1972, Solar Eclipse, 1972. Recipient Art and Architecture Collaborations award Boston Soc. Architects, 1993. Office: Richard Humphrey Gallery PO Box 1358 Canal St Sta New York NY 10013-0377 *As I work to focus light and energy into material form, my work has shown me that it is possible for us to gain an intimacy with the stars.*

ROSS, CHARLES ROBERT, lawyer, consultant; b. Middlebury, Vt., Feb. 24, 1920; s. Jacob Johnson and Hannah Elizabeth (Holmes) R.; m. Charlotte Sells Hoyt, Aug 28, 1948; children—Jacqueline Hoyt, Peter Holmes, Charles Robert. A.B., U. Mich., 1941, M.B.A., 1948, LL.B., 1948. Bar: Ky. 1949, Vt. 1954, U.S. Supreme Ct. 1968. Instr. Oreg. State Coll., 1948-49; practice law Louisville and Burlington, Vt., 1949-59; chmn. Vt. Pub. Service Commn., 1959-61; commr. FPC, 1961-68; mem. U.S. sect. Internat. Joint Commn., 1962-81; mem. Nat. Consumers Energy Com., 1973-74; pub. mem. Adminstrv. Conf. U.S., 1971-74; adj. prof. econs. U. Vt., 1969-74. Served to capt. USAAF, 1942-46. Home: 806 Wake Robin Dr Shelburne VT 05482

ROSS, CHARLES WORTHINGTON, IV, metals company executive; b. Frederick, Md., Jan. 27, 1933; s. Charles Worthington and Priscilla Avis (Wilson) R., 3d; student U. Md., 1951-54; m. Betty Lou Waldvogel, May 26, 1956; children: Holly Theresa Ross-Hartung, Kristna Lynn Ross-Serpico, Amy Louise Ross-Drummond, Carol Ann. BA in Polit. Sci., Syracuse U., 1963; MA in Occupational Safety and Health, NYU, 1976. Commd. 2d lt. U.S. Air Force, 1954, safety officer, 1966-68; ret., 1968; gen. mgr. Mgmt. Recruiters, Inc., Norfolk, Va., 1968-71; regional safety mgr. Mobil Oil Corp., Scarsdale, N.Y., 1971-75; corp. safety mgr. Schering-Plough Corp., Kenilworth, N.J., 1975-79; corp. mgr. safety and health Westvaco Corp., N.Y.C., 1979-81; v.p. mktg., safety and health cons., dir. IHI-KEMRON, Huntington, N.Y., 1981-83, WAPORA, Inc., 1983-86, Essex Chem. Corp., Clifton, N.J., 1986-89; mgr. safety and loss control Handy & Harman, Rye, N.Y., 1989—; instr. safety mgmt. Kean Coll., Union, N.J., 1978-79. Recipient 2d place award for tech. paper Am. Soc. Safety Engrs./Vets. Safety, 1980. Registered profl. engr., Calif.; cert. safety profl., hazard control mgr. (masters level). Mem. Am. Soc. Safety Engrs. (profl. mem.), System Safety Soc., Nat. Safety Mgmt. Soc., Am. Indsl. Hygiene Assn., Safety Execs. N.Y. (pres.). Democrat. Episcopalian. Author: Computer Systems for Safety and Health Management, 1984, 2d edit., 1991; contbr. articles to profl. jours. Home: 10 Ames Rd Morristown NJ 07960-2954 Office: 555 Theodore Fremd Ave Rye NY 10580-1437

ROSS, CHARLOTTE PACK, suicidologist; b. Oklahoma City, Oct. 21, 1932; d. Joseph and Rose P. (Traibich) Pack; m. Roland S. Ross, May 6, 1951 (div. July 1964); children: Beverly Jo, Sandra Gail; m. Stanley Fisher, Mar. 17, 1991. Student U. Okla., 1949-52, New Sch. Social Rsch., 1953. Cert. tchr. Exec. dir. Suicide Prevention and Crisis Ctr. San Mateo County, Burlingame, Calif., 1966-88; pres., exec. dir. Youth Suicide Nat. Ctr., Washington, 1985-93; exec. dir. Death with Dignity Edn. Ctr., San Mateo, Calif., 1994—; pres. Calif. Senate Adv. Com. Youth Suicide Prevention, 1982-84; speaker Menninger Found., 1983, 84; instr. San Francisco State U., 1981-83; conf. coord. U. Calif., San Francisco, 1971—; cons. univs. and health svcs. throughout world. Contbg. author: Group Counseling for Suicidal Adolescents, 1984, Teaching Children the Facts of Life and Death, 1985; mem. editorial bd. Suicide and Life Threatening Behavior, 1976-89. Mem. regional selection panel Pres.'s Commn. on White House Fellows, 1975-78; mem. CIRCLON Svc. Club, 1979—, Com. on Child Abuse, 1981-85; founding mem. Women for Responsible Govt., co-chmn., 1974-79. Recipient Outstanding Exec. award San Mateo County Coordinating Com., 1971, Koshland award San Francisco Found., 1984. Fellow Wash. Acad. Scis.; mem. Internat. Assn. Suicide Prevention (v.p. 1985—), Am. Assn. Suicidology (sec. 1972-74, svc. award 1990), bd. govs. 1976-78, accreditation com. 1975—, chair region IX, 1975-82), Assn. United Way Agy. Execs. (pres. 1974), Assn. County Contract Agys. (pres. 1982), Peninsula Press Club.

ROSS, CHESTER WHEELER, retired clergyman; b. Evansville, Ind., Nov. 3, 1922; s. Mylo Wheeler and Irma (Berning) R.; AB cum laude, Kans. Wesleyan U., 1952; MDiv, Garrett Theol. Sem., 1954; D Ministry, St. Paul Sch. Theology, 1979; postgrad. in Computers Kans. Vocat.-Tech, 1989.; m. Ruth Eulaine Briney, Aug. 30, 1949; children: James W., Deborah R., Judith R., Martha S., John W. Ordained to ministry United Meth. Ch., 1953; enlisted pvt. USAAF, 1942, advanced through grades to lt. col., 1968; chaplain, Africa, Europe, Alaska, Greenland, Taiwan; installation chaplain, Columbus AFB, Miss., 1972-75; ret., 1975; pastor Unity Parish, Iuka, Kans., 1975-80, Ness City (Kans.) United Meth. Ch., 1980-88. active ARC, Boy Scouts Am.; vol. parolee counselor; mem. USD 303 Sch. Bd. Paul Harris fellow Rotary Internat.; Decorated Air medal (2), Meritorious Svc. medal (2); recipient Silver Beaver award, Boy Scouts Am., 1975. Mem. PRIDE, Am. Police Assn., Rail to Trails, Ministers Assn., Mil. Chaplains Assn., Stephen Ministry, Rural Chaplins Assn., 301st Vets Assn., Acad. Parish Clergy, Ret. Officers Assn., Air Force Assn., Nat. Hist. Soc., Am. Assn. Christian Counselors, Cmty. Vol. Svcs., Air Force Gunners Assn., Appalachian Trail Conf., Menninger Found., Kans. Sheriffs Assn. Assn. Ret. Persons, Order Ky. Col., Am. Legion, VFW. Address: 1102 Arcade St Goodland KS 67735-3426

ROSS, CHRISTOPHER WADE STELYAN, diplomat; b. Quito, Ecuador, Mar. 3, 1943 (parents Am. citizens); s. Claude G. Anthony and Antigone Andrea (Peterson) R.; m. Carol Geraldine Canning, Nov. 30, 1968; 1 child, Anthony Gordon. AB summa cum laude, Princeton U., 1965; cert. Middle East Centre for Arab Studies, 1964; MA, Johns Hopkins U., 1967. Editorial asst. Middle East Jour., Washington, 1965-68; instr. Arabic lang. Columbia U., N.Y.C., 1966, Princeton U., 1967; pub. affairs trainee USIA, 1968-69; jr. officer trainee Am. Embassy, Tripoli, Libya, 1969-70; dir. Am. Cultural Ctr., Fez, Morocco, 1970-73; press attache Am. Embassy, Beirut, 1973-76; pub. affairs officer Am. Embassy, Algiers, Algeria, 1976-79, dep. chief mission and charge d'affaires, 1979-81; pub. affairs adviser Bur. Near Eastern and South Asian Affairs, Dept. State, Washington, 1981-82, spl. asst. to presdl. emissaries to Lebanon and Middle East, 1982-84, dir. regional affairs, 1984-85; exec. asst. to Under Sec. State for Polit. Affairs, Washington, 1985-88; amb. to Algeria, 1988-91; amb. to Syria, Damascus, 1991—; chmn. bd. trustees Am. Sch. Algiers, 1977-80; hon. chmn., bd. trustees Damascus Community Sch., 1991—. Contbr. articles to profl. jours. Recipient Superior Honor award U.S. Info. Agy., 1976, 83, Dept. State, 1988, Presdl. Meritorious Svc. award, 1983, 85, 89, 93. Mem. Coun. Fgn. Rels., Am. Fgn. Svc. Assn., Assn. for Diplomatic Studies, Middle East Inst., Middle East Studies Assn. of N.Am., Royal Soc. for Asian Affairs. Greek Orthodox. Club: Princeton (Washington). Avocations: classic cars; bicycling. Office: Damascus Dept State Washington DC 20521 also: Am Embassy, 2 al-Mansur St Abu Rumaneh, Damascus Syria

ROSS, COLEMAN DEVANE, accountant, insurance company consultant; b. Greensboro, N.C., Mar. 18, 1943; s. Guy Matthews and Nancy McConnell (Coleman) R.; m. Carol Louise Morde, Aug. 26 1965; children: Coleman, Jonathan, Andrew. BS in Bus. Adminstrn., U. N.C., 1965; postgrad. Grad. Sch. of Banking of South, 1982-84, U. N.C. Advanced Mgmt. Program, 1994. CPA, CLU, ChFC; cert. bank auditor. With Price Waterhouse, Tampa, 1965-76, Toronto, 1970, Hartford, Conn., 1976-93, N.Y.C., 1993—, ptnr., 1977—, mng. ptnr. Nat. Ins. Svcs. Group, 1988-94. Mem. bd. dirs. N.E. Region Boy Scouts Am., 1988—, v.p., 1993-96, pres. New Eng. area, 1988-91; mem. bd. dirs. Greater N.Y. Couns. Boy Scouts Am., 1994—; mem. exec. bd. Conn. Rivers coun. Boy Scouts Am., 1978—, pres. 1985-88, vice chmn., 1996—; corporator Inst. Living, 1992—, Vis. Nurses Assn. Health Care Greater Hartford, 1992—, Hartford Hosp., 1995—; div. campaign chmn. United Way of Capital Area, 1984; bd. dirs., treas. Family Svc. Soc. Greater Hartford, 1977-80; participant Leadership Greater Hartford, 1977. Recipient Silver Beaver award Boy Scouts Am., 1987, Silver Antelope award, 1991. Fellow Life Mgmt. Inst.; mem. AICPA (ins. cos. com. 1985-88, reins. auditing and acctg. task force 1979-85, rels. with actuaries com. 1982-85), N.Y. Soc. CPAs, N.C. Assn. CPAs, Conn. Soc. CPAs, Soc. Ins. Fin. Mgmt., Am. Soc. CLUs and ChFCs., N.Y.C. Soc. CLUs and ChFCs, Internat. Ins. Soc., Nat. Soc. Chartered Bank Auditors, Assn. Mut. Ins. Accts., Hartford Club (bd. govs. 1977-84). Home: 6 Wild Flower Ln West Simsbury CT 06092-2434 Office: Price Waterhouse 1177 Avenue Of The Americas New York NY 10036-2714

ROSS, DANIEL R., lawyer; b. Stamford, Conn., Oct. 20, 1941; s. Adrian E. and Ruth (Hill) R.; m. Faye Zerwekh, Aug. 15, 1965; children: Kevin S., Eric D., David W. SB, MIT, 1963; LLB, U. Pa., 1966. Atty. adviser to Hon. Theodore Tannenwald, Jr. U.S. Tax Ct., Washington, 1966-68; assoc. Drinker, Biddle & Reath, Phila., 1970-77, ptnr., 1977—. Presenter in field. Pres. bd. trustees First United Meth. Ch. Germantown, 1984—. Capt. U.S. Army, 1968-70, Vietnam. Mem. ABA (chair com. on income of estates and trusts 1985-87, com. on govt. subcoms. 1988-91, taxation sect.). Avocations: bicycling, skiing, tennis, computers. Office: Drinker Biddle & Reath 1100 PNB Bldg 1345 Chestnut St Philadelphia PA 19107-3426

ROSS, DAVID A., art museum director; b. Malverne, N.Y., Apr. 26, 1949; s. Joshua and Grayce R.; m. Margaret Gronner; children—Lindsay, Emily. B.A., Syracuse U.; postgrad. Grad. Sch. Fine Arts, Syracuse. Curator video art Everson Mus. Art, Syracuse, N.Y., 1971-74; dep. dir. program devel. and TV Long Beach Mus. Art, Calif., 1974-77; chief curator Univ. Art Mus., Berkeley, Calif., 1977-82; dir. Inst. of Contemporary Art, Boston, 1982-91; dir., CEO Whitney Mus. Am. Art., 1991—. Active Fed. Adv. Com. om Internat. Exbns., 1990—. Contbr. articles to profl. jours. Mem. Assn. Art Mus. Dirs. Office: Whitney Museum Am Art 945 Madison Ave New York NY 10021-2701

ROSS, DAVID EDMOND, church official; b. Lewiston, Maine, Oct. 1, 1950; s. Rev. and Mrs. Lorne Arla Collins R.; m. Shirley Evelyn Godin, Aug. 19, 1972. BA in Theology cum laude, Berkshire Coll., 1973; MPA, U. Maine, 1989. Ordained to ministry Advent Christian Ch., 1975. Pastor State Road Advent Christian Ch., Presque Isle, Maine, 1973-91; exec. dir. Advent Christian Ch. Gen. Conf., Charlotte, N.C., 1991—; v.p. Maine State Conf. Advent Christian Chs., 1975-76, pres., 1976-81, 86-91; mem. exec. coun. Advent Christian Ch., 1981-90, long range strategy com., 1986—; seminar leader Am. Festival of Evangelism, Kansas City, 1981; dir. Northern Lights Youth Choir, 1974-90. Office: Advent Christian Church PO Box 23152 Charlotte NC 28227-0272

ROSS, DAVID LEE, lawyer; b. Chgo., Dec. 12, 1948; s. Herman Milton and Minnie (Devinatz) R.; m. Abby Lynn Kolber, June 20, 1971; children: Natalie, Jason, Blake. BS in Polit. Sci., Northwestern U., 1970; JD with honors, U. Chgo., 1973. Bar: Ga. 1973, U.S. Dist. Ct. (no. dist.) Ga. 1974, U.S. Ct. Appeals (5th cir.) 1974, Fla. 1979, U.S. Dist. Ct. (so. dist.) Fla. 1979, U.S. Dist. Ct. (mid. dist.) Fla., U.S. Ct. Appeals (11th cir.), U.S. Ct. Appeals (9th cir.). Assoc. Haas, Holland, Levison & Gibert, Atlanta, 1973-77; ptnr. Haas, Holland, Levison & Gilbert, Atlanta, 1977-78; assoc. Greenberg, Traurig, Hoffman, Lipoff, Rosen & Quentel, P.A., Miami, Fla., 1978-80; shareholder Greenberg, Traurig, Hoffman, Lipoff, Rosen & Quentel, P.A., Miami, 1980—. Trustee Coconut Grove Playhouse, Miami, 1989-93. Mem. ABA (civil practice and procedure com. antitrust sect. 1991—), Fla. Bar (chmn. comml. litigation com. 1982-86, bus. law sect. 1987-88), Order of Coif. Office: Greenberg Traurig Hoffman Lipoff Rosen & Quentel PA 1221 Brickell Ave Miami FL 33131-3200

ROSS, DELMER GERRARD, historian, educator; b. Los Banos, Calif., Nov. 5, 1942; s. Elmer G. and Orva Beth (Dickinson) R.; m. Karen Ann Gibson, June 17, 1977; children: Michelle, Richard. BA, Pacific Union Coll., 1965; MA, U. Calif., Santa Barbara, 1967, PhD, 1970. Instr. Pacific Union Coll., Angwin, Calif., 1968-69; from asst. to assoc. prof. Oakwood Coll., Huntsville, Ala., 1970-76; from assoc. prof. to prof. history Loma Linda U., Riverside, Calif., 1976-91, chmn. dept. history and polit. sci., 1986-90; prof. history and polit. sci. La Sierra U., Riverside, 1991—. Author: Visionaries and Swindlers, 1975, Rails Across Costa Rica, 1976, Rails in Paradise, 1991, Gold Road to La Paz, 1992; chmn. editorial bd. Adventist Heritage mag., 1987-90. Bd. dirs. Inst. for Research in Latin Am., Mobile, Ala., 1968-82. Mem. Am. Hist. Assn., Conf. Latin Am. History (Caribe-Centroamerica regional com. chmn. 1973-75), Assn. 7th Day Adventist Historians (exec. sec. 1973-74, sec.-treas. 1974-75, pres. 1981-82), Assn. Western Adventist Historians, Nat. Railway Hist. Soc., Colo. Railroad Hist. Found., Railway and Locomotive Hist. Soc. Republican. Office: La Sierra U Dept of History Riverside CA 92515

ROSS, DIANA, singer, actress, entertainer, fashion designer; b. Detroit, Mar. 26, 1944; d. Fred and Ernestine R.; m. Robert Ellis Silberstein, Jan. 1971 (div. 1976); children: Rhonda, Tracee, Chudney; m. Arne Naess, Oct. 23, 1985; 1 son: Ross Arne. Grad. high sch. Pres. Diana Ross Enterprises, Inc., fashion and merchandising, Anaid Film Prodns., Inc., RTC Mgmt. Corp., artists mgmt., Chondee Inc., Rosstown, Rossville, music pub. Started in Detroit as mem. the Primettes; lead singer until 1969, Diana Ross and the Supremes; solo artist, 1969—; albums include Diana Ross, 1970, 76, Everything Is Everything, 1971, I'm Still Waiting, 1971, Lady Sings The Blues, 1972, Touch Me In The Morning, 1973, Original Soundtrack of Mahogany, 1975, Baby It's Me, 1977, The Wiz, 1978, Ross, 1978, 83, The Boss, 1979, Diana, 1981, To Love Again, 1981, Why Do Fools Fall In Love?, 1981, Silk Electric, 1982, Swept Away, 1984, Eaten Alive, 1985, Chain Reaction, 1986, Diana's Duets, 1987, Workin' Overtime, 1989, Red Hot Rhythm and Blues, 1987, Surrender, 1989, Ain't No Mountain High Enough, 1989, The Force Behind the Power, 1991, Stolen Moment: The Lady Sings... Jazz & Blues, 1993, Musical Memories Forever, 1993, The Remixes, 1994; films include Lady Sings the Blues, 1972, Mahogany, 1975, The Wiz, 1978; NBC-TV spl., An Evening With Diana Ross, 1977, Diana, 1981, numerous others; TV movie Out of Darkness, 1994; album Endless Love, 1982; author: Secrets of a Sparrow, 1993. Recipient citation Vice Pres. Humphrey for efforts on behalf Pres. Johnson's Youth Opportunity Program, citation Mrs. Martin Luther King and Rev. Abernathy for contbn. to SCLC cause, awards Billboard, Cash Box and Record World as worlds outstanding singer, Grammy award, 1970, Female Entertainer of Year NAACP, 1970, Cue award as Entertainer of year, 1972, Golden Apple award, 1972, Gold medal award Photoplay, 1972, Antoinette Perry award, 1977, nominee as best actress of year for Lady Sings the Blues Motion Picture Acad. Arts and Scis., 1972, Golden Globe award, 1972; named to Rock and Roll Hall of Fame, 1988. Office: RTC Mgmt PO Box 1683 New York NY 10185-1683 also: care Shelly Berger 6255 W Sunset Blvd Los Angeles CA 90028-7403

ROSS, DONALD, JR., English language educator, university administrator; b. N.Y.C., Oct. 18, 1941; s. Donald and Lea (Meyer) R.; m. Sylvia Berger (div.); 1 child, Jessica; m. 2d, Diane Redfern, Aug. 27, 1971; children—Owen, Gillian. B.A., Lehigh U., 1963, M.A., 1964; Ph.D., U. Mich., 1967. Asst. prof. English U. Pa., Phila., 1967-70; prof. English U. Minn., Mpls., 1970—, dir. composition program, 1982-86, dir. Univ. Coll., 1984-89; ret., 1989. Co-author: Word Processor and Writing Process, 1984, Revising Mythologies: The Composition of Thoreau's Major Works, 1988; contbr. articles to profl. jours. Grantee Am. Coun. Learned Socs., 1976, 90, NSF, 1974, Fund for Improvement of Postsecondary Edn., 1982-85; recipient Disting. Teaching award U. Minn., 1992. Mem. Assn. for Computers and Humanities (exec. sec. 1978-88), MLA, Assn. for Lit. and Linguistic Computing. Office: U Minn Composition Program 209 Church St SE Minneapolis MN 55455-0152

ROSS, DONALD EDWARD, university administrator; b. Mineola, N.Y., June 29, 1939; s. Alexander Walker and Florence M. (Carville) R.; m. Helen Landgren, June 23, 1966; children: Ellen Ross Sarafian, Kevin McAndrew. BFA, N.Y. Inst. Tech., 1962, LLD (hon.), 1978; MS, Hofstra U., 1970. Dean of students N.Y. Inst. Tech., Old Westbury, 1962-68; pres. Wilmington (Del.) Coll., 1968-77; pres., CEO Lynn U. (formerly Coll. of Boca Raton), Fla., 1971—; chmn. adv. com. U.S. Army Command and Gen. Staff Coll. Bd. dirs. Fla. Endowment Fund, 1989—; trustee Boca Raton Community Hosp., 1990—; mem. governing bd. Philharmonic Orch. Fla., 1990—; mem. U.S. Mil. Screening Com. Named Industrialist of Yr., Greater Boca Raton C. of C., 1992, Man of the Yr., City of Hope; recipient Boy Scouts Am. Leadership Svc. award, Boca Raton award, 1991. Mem. Assn. Univ. Pres., Econ. Coun. of Palm Beach County, Royal Palm Yacht and Country, Loggerhead Club, Adirondack League Club, Old Forge Club, City (Boca Raton). Avocations: snowskiing, tennis, reading, travel. Home: 212 Coconut Palm Rd Boca Raton FL 33432 Office: Lynn Univ 3601 N Military Trl Boca Raton FL 33431-5507

ROSS, DONALD EDWARD, engineering company executive; b. N.Y.C., May 2, 1930; m. Jeanne Ellen McKessy, Apr. 4, 1954; children: Susan, Christopher, Carolyn. BA, Columbia U., 1952, BS in Mech. Engring., 1953; MBA, NYU, 1960. Registered profl. engr., N.Y., 14 other states. Engr. Carrier Corp., N.Y.C., 1955-70; v.p. Dynadata, 1970-71; with Jaros, Baum & Bolles, N.Y.C., 1971—, ptnr., 1977—. Mem. adv. coun. Columbia U. Sch. Engring. and Applied Sci. Lt. (j.g.) USN, 1953-55. Fellow ASHRAE; mem. ASME, NSPE, Nat. Acad. Enrs. (mech. engring. peer com.), Am. Cons. Engrs. Coun., Nat. Bur. Engring. Registration, N.Y. Assn. Cons. Engrs. (pres. 1984-86), Coun. on Tall Bldgs. and Urban Habitat (vice chmn. N.Am., mem. steering group), Univ. Club (N.Y.C.), Nassau Country Club, Tau Beta Pi. Office: Jaros Baum & Bolles 345 Park Ave New York NY 10154-0004

ROSS, DONALD HUGH, fraternal organization executive; b. Delta, Ohio, Aug. 19, 1949; s. Hugh Archbald and Margaret Baker (Harlton) R.; m. Mary Lynn Feuerborn, Dec. 21, 1974; children: Jon, Michael. BS, Miami U., Oxford, Ohio, 1971. Auditor Moose Internat., Mooseheart, Ill., 1971-76, dep. supreme sec., 1976-78, asst. comptroller, 1978-83; supreme sec. Supreme Lodge, Mooseheart, Ill., 1983—; sec. Mooseheart Bd. Govs., Moosehaven Bd. Govs., 1983—. Mem. editorial bd. Moose Action publ.; contbr. articles to newspapers and profl. jours. Republican. Club: Interact (Delta) (pres. 1966-67). Lodge: Moose (past gov. 1976, Pilgrim Degree of Merit 1983). Avocations: golf, bowling. Home: 1119 Woodland Ave Batavia IL 60510-3049 Office: Supreme Lodge Moose Internat Mooseheart IL 60539

ROSS, DONALD KEITH, retired insurance company executive; b. Rochester, N.Y., July 1, 1925; s. Alexander L. and Althea G. (Granger) R.; m. Mary F. Fyffe, June 4, 1949; children: Catherine (Mrs. Charles P. Lesher), Susan (Mrs. William Gardner Morris, Jr.), Donald Keith, Deborah Anne (Mrs. Michael Holt). B.E., Yale U., 1946; M.B.A., Harvard U., 1948. With N.Y. Life Ins. Co., N.Y.C., 1948—, exec. v.p., 1974-79, vice chmn., 1979-80, pres., 1980-81, chmn. bd., CEO, 1981-90, chmn. exec. com., 1990-93, also bd. dirs.; ret., 1993; trustee Consol. Edison of N.Y. Office: NY Life Ins Co 51 Madison Ave New York NY 10010-1603

ROSS, DONALD KENNETH, consulting engineering executive; b. St. Louis, Apr. 15, 1925; s. Maurice James and Babe Cyril (Grodsky) R.; m. Peggy Grosberg, July 1, 1951; 1 dau., Pamela Toder. BSEE, U. Minn., 1946; MS, MIT, 1948; ScD, Washington U., St. Louis, 1960. Rsch., teaching asst. MIT, 1946-48; electronics engr. Mo. Rsch., Inc., 1949-51; prin. Donald Ross & Assocs., St. Louis, 1953-61; pres. Ross & Baruzzini, Inc., St. Louis, 1961-91, chmn., 1991—; pres. Hanlon & Assocs., Inc., St. Louis, 1976-85; profl. assoc. Bldg. Rsch. and Adv. Bd., Nat. Acad. Scis.; lectr. Washington U. Patentee to 3 U.S. Patents. With USNR, 1943-46, 1951-53 Korea. Recipient Outstanding Achievement award IEEE Industry Applications Soc., 1989, Engring. Alumni Achievement award Washington U., 1993. Fellow Am. Cons. Engrs. Council, IEEE; mem. Assn. Profl. Material Handling Cons. (pres. 1976-77), Mo. Assn. Cons. Engrs. (past pres.), Sigma Xi, Tau Beta Pi, Eta Kappa Nu. Office: 1300 Baur Blvd Saint Louis MO 63132-1903

ROSS, DONALD ROE, federal judge; b. Orleans, Nebr., June 8, 1922; s. Roe M. and Leila H. (Reed) R.; m. Janice S. Cook, Aug. 29, 1943; children: Susan Jane, Sharon Kay, Rebecca Lynn, Joan Christine, Donald Dean. JD, U. Nebr., 1948, LLD (hon.), 1990. Bar: Nebr. bar 1948. Practice law Lexington, Nebr., 1948-53; mayor City of Lexington, 1953; assoc. Swarr, May, Royce, Smith, Andersen & Ross, 1956-70; U.S. atty. Dist. Nebr., 1953-56; gen. counsel Rep. party, Nebr., 1956-58; mem. Rep. Exec. Com. for Nebr., 1952-53; nat. com. mem. Rep. Nat. Com., 1958-70, vice chmn., 1965-70; sr. judge U.S. Ct. Appeals 8th cir., 1971—.

ROSS, DONNA LEE, auditor; b. San Francisco, Dec. 1, 1956; d. Arthur J. and Myrtle Joan (Haynes) Lee; m. Eugene Ross Sr., Mar. 31, 1990. BS in Acctg., U. San Francisco, 1983. CPA, Calif. Sales supr. Macy's Calif., San Francisco, 1974-84; acctg. clk. 3/33 Ins. Co., San Francisco, 1979-80; advt. acct. San Francisco Newspaper Agy., 1980-83; supervising sr. auditor Arthur Young & Co., San Francisco, 1984-87; corp. auditor Hewlett-Packard Co., Palo Alto, Calif., 1987-90; ea. region audit mgr. Hewlett-Packard Co., Paramus, N.J., 1990-92, sr. internal auditor, 1992—. Author: (classroom tng. material) Understanding Basic Business Controls in a Changing Environment, 1992. Active Hist. Preservation Soc. Mem. Nat. Assn. Black Accts., State Soc. CPAs, Inst. Internal Auditors (mem. N.J. chpt.). Democrat. Roman Catholic. Avocation: restoration of historic house.

ROSS, DOUGLAS, lawyer, legal academic administrator; b. L.A., July 12, 1948; s. Mathew and Brenda Butler (Boynton) R.; m. Lynne Rose Maidman, June 14, 1970. AB cum laude, Tufts U., 1970; JD with honors, George Washington U., 1973. Bar: Ohio 1973, D.C. 1980, U.S. Supreme Ct. 1976. Asst. atty. gen., antitrust sect. Office of Ohio Atty. Gen., Columbus, 1973-74; spl. asst. U.S. atty. Ea. Dist. Va., Alexandria, 1977; trial atty. antitrust divsn. U.S. Dept. Justice, Washington, 1975-82; atty. advisor Office of Legis. Affairs, 1984-86, Office of Legal Policy, 1987-89, Office Policy Devel., 1989-92; Supreme Ct. counsel Nat. Assn. Attys. Gen., 1982-91; ran advocacy project for states to enhance their effectiveness before Supreme Ct., 1982-91, operated clearinghouse on state constl. law, 1987-91; civil divsn. Appellate Staff, 1992-94, Office of Consumer Litigation, 1994—. Recipient Meritorious award Dept. Justice, 1979, Spl. Achievement award, 1984. Mem. Supreme Ct. Hist. Soc., D.C. Bar Assn., Supreme Ct. Opinion Network (bd. dirs. 1989-91), Arlington County Sports Commn. (chair subcom. on swimming pools 1995—). Jewish. Home: 3153 19th St N Arlington VA 22201-5103 Office: US Dept Justice PO Box 386 Washington DC 20044-0386

ROSS, DOUGLAS TAYLOR, retired software company executive; b. Canton, Republic of China, Dec. 21, 1929; (parents Am. citizens); s. Robert Malcolm and Margaret (Taylor) R.; m. Patricia Mott, Jan. 24, 1951; children: Jane R. Yoos, Kathryn R. Chow, Margaret R. Thrasher. AB in Math. cum laude, Oberlin Coll., 1951; SM, MIT, 1954, postgrad. math., 1958. Head computer applications group elec. systems lab. MIT, Cambridge, 1952-69, lectr. dept. elec. engring. and computer sci., 1960-69, 83—, exec. com. MIT Enterprise Forum, 1984-89; pres. SofTech, Inc., Waltham, Mass., 1969-75, chmn. bd., 1975-89, 91-93, chmn. emeritus, 1989-91, 93-94, chmn. emeritus ret., 1994—. Mem. town meeting, Lexington, Mass., 1960-70; trustee, bd. dirs. Charles Babbage Inst., 1984—. Mem. United Ch. of Christ. Home and Office: 33 Dawes Rd Lexington MA 02173-5926

ROSS, EDWARD, cardiologist; b. Fairfield, Ala., Oct. 10, 1937; s. Horace and Carrie Lee (Griggs) R.; BS, Clark Coll., 1959; MD, Ind. U., 1963; m. Catherine I. Webster, Jan. 19, 1974; children: Edward, Ronald, Cheryl, Anthony. Intern, Marion County Gen. Hosp., Indpls., 1963; resident in internal medicine Ind. U., 1964-66, 68, cardiology rsch. fellowship, 1968-70, clin. asst. prof. medicine, 1970; cardiologist Capitol Med. Assn., Indpls., 1970-74; pvt. practice medicine, specializing in cardiology, Indpls., 1974—; staff cardiologist Winona Meml. Hosp., Indpls.; staff Meth. Hosp., Indpls., chmn. cardiovascular sect., 1989—; dir. cardiovascular ctr. Meth. Hosp.,

1990-92; bd. dirs. Meth. Hosp. Heart-Lung Ctr., 1990—, med. dir. cardiovascular svcs., 1991—. Mem. Cen. Ind. Health Planning Coun., 1972-73; bd. dir. Ind. chpt. Am. Heart Assn., 1973-74, multiphasic screening East Side Clinic, Flanner House of Indpls., 1968-71; med. dir. Nat. Ctr. for Health Service Rsch. and Devel., HEW, 1970; consumer rep. radiologic device panel health, FDA, 1988-92; dir. hyptertensive screening State of Ind., 1974; J.B. Johnson Cardiovascular lectr. Nat. Med. Assn., 1991. Assoc. editor Angiology, Jour. Vascular Disease. Capt., MC, USAF, 1966-68. Woodrow Wilson fellow, 1959; Nat. Found. Health scholar, 1955, Gorgas Found. scholar, 1955. Diplomate Am. Bd. Internal Medicine. Fellow Royal Soc. Promotion of Health (Eng.), Am. Coll. Angiology (v.p. fgn. affairs, sec. 1993—), Internat. Coll. of Angiology, Am. Coll. Cardiology, Assn. Black Cardiologists (mem. bd. dirs. 1990-94); mem. AMA, Am. Soc. Contemporary Medicine and Surgery, Nat. Med. Assn. (council sci. assembly 1985-89), Ind. Med. Soc., Marion County Med. Soc., Am. Soc. Internal Medicine, Am. Heart Assn., Ind. Soc. Internal Medicine (pres. 1987-89), Ind. State Med. Assn. (chmn. internal medicine sect. 1987-89), Aesculapean Med. Soc., Hoosier State Med. Assn. (pres. 1980-85, 90—), NAACP, Urban League, Ind. Med. Soc., Alpha Omega Alpha, Alpha Kappa Mu, Beta Kappa Chi, Omega Psi Phi. Baptist. Sr. editor Jour. Vascular Medicine, 1983—. Office: 3737 N Meridian St Ste 400 Indianapolis IN 46208-4348

ROSS, EDWARD JOSEPH, architect; b. Everett, Mass., Dec. 13, 1934; s. Miriam R.; m. Gail Tishler, Feb. 2, 1963; children: Linda Joy, Melissa Carol. Student Boston Archtl. Ctr., 1952-55, 61-62, USAF Surveying Sch., 1955-56, Boston Soc. Civil Engrs., 1956-57, Carl Bolivar Structural Engring., 1962-63. Registered architect, Mass., Calif., N.Y., Fla., N.H., Vt.; cert. Nat. Coun. Archtl. Registration Bds.; lic. constrn. supr., Mass.; expert witness. Draftsman, assoc. William W. Drummey, Architect, Boston, 1952-59; job capt., designer Drummey-Rosane-Anderson, Boston, 1959-64; projects architect Maginnis & Walsh & Kennedy, Boston, 1964-69; v.p. William Nelson Jacobs Assocs., Inc., Boston, 1969-73; staff architect, Robert Charles Assocs., Inc., Architects, Boston, 1973-74; office mgr. Charles F. Jacobs Assocs., Inc., Cambridge, Mass., 1974-76; cons. architect Linenthal, Eisenberg & Anderson, Boston, 1976-77; staff architect Eisenberg Haven Assocs., Inc., Boston, 1977-78; chief architect, chief inspector Boston Housing Authority, 1978-83; prin. Edward J. Ross, AIA/FARA, Randolph, Mass., 1983-84; architect, sr. assoc., dir. constrn. administrn., Stull and Lee, Inc., Boston, 1984-91; practice architecture, Randolph, 1963—. Mem. Ancient and Honorable Arty. Co. of Mass. Staff sgt. USAF; capt. Mass. Mil. Res. Fellow Soc. Am. Registered Architects; mem. Am. Arbitration Assn. (mem. nat. panel 1965—), AIA, Boston Soc. Architects (housing com. 1982-86), Mass. State Assn. Architects, Constrn. Specifications Inst., Air Force Assn. (pres. Boston chpt.), Mass. Air Nat. Guard Historical Assn., Ten of Us Club, Linderhof Golf Course Site One Assn. (pres. 1980-86), Elks, Knights of Pythias, Am. Legion. Home and Office: 10 Patricia Dr Stoughton MA 02072-1223

ROSS, EDWIN WILLIAM, rubber company executive; b. Phila., May 28, 1938; s. Edwin Morrison and Frances Louise (Ort) R.; m. Dorothy Anne Reilly, Sept. 24, 1966; children: E. William Jr., Catherine Anne, James David. BSBA, Lehigh U., 1960. Chmn. bd., CEO, Key Chems., Inc., Phila., 1965-87, Ross Enterprises, Inc., Villanova, Pa., 1987—; pres., CEO Pelmor Labs., Inc., Newtown, Pa., 1989—; mem. adv. bd. First Sterling Bank, Devon, Pa., 1995—. Deacon Bryn Mawr (Pa.) Presbyn. Ch., 1977-81, elder, 1985-91. Recipient Alumni award Lehigh U., 1985. Mem. MidAtlantic Employers Assn. (chmn. 1995—), Metal Finishing Suppliers Assn. (pres. 1986-88, 89-90, Munning award 1992), N.E. Phila. C. of C. (chmn. 1983), Exch. Club (pres. Frankford-Phila. 1972), Phila. Country Club (pres. 1986-89). Republican. Avocations: downhill skiing, hunting, travel, golf. Home: 1514 Willowbrook Ln Villanova PA 19085-1912 Office: Pelmor Labs Inc 401 Lafayette St Newtown PA 18940-2151

ROSS, ELINOR, soprano; b. Tampa, Fla., Aug. 1, 1932; d. Joe D. and Lillian Rosenthal; m. Aaron M. Diamond; 1 son, Ross. Student, Syracuse U. Debuts include: Turandot, Met. Opera, N.Y.C., Il Trovatore, Cin. Opera, Cavalleria Rusticana, La Scala, Milan, Tosca, Bolshoi, Moscow; leading soprano roles with, Met. Opera, LaScala, Bolshoi, Chgo. Lyric Opera, San Francisco Opera, Tulsa Opera, Cin. Opera, Staatsoper, Vienna, LaFenice, Venice, Teatro Colon, Buenos Aires, Argentina, Arena de Verona, Massimo de Palermo; inaugurated Rossini Festival in Pesaro; televised concert tour in Peoples Republic of China, Taiwan; appeared in concerts, opera, symphony in Hong Kong, Japan, Thailand, Korea; appeared with symphony orchs. throughout world. Recipient medal of honor Novosibiresk, Siberia. Jewish.

ROSS, EUNICE LATSHAW, judge; b. Bellevue, Pa., Oct. 13, 1923; d. Richard Kelly and Eunice (Weidner) Latshaw; m. John Anthony Ross, May 29, 1943 (dec. Jan. 1978); 1 child, Geraldine Ross Coleman. BS, U. Pitts., 1945, LLB, 1951. Bar: Pa. 1952. Atty., Pub. Health Law Research Project, Pitts., 1951-52; atty. jud. asst., law clk. Ct. Common Pleas, Pitts., 1952-70; adjunct law prof. U. Pitts., 1967-73; dir. family div. Ct. Common Pleas, Pitts., 1970-72; judge Ct. Common Pleas of Allegheny County, Pitts., 1972—; mem. Bd. Jud. Inquiry and Rev., Commonwealth of Pa., 1984-89, Gov's Justice Commn., 1972-78. Author: (with others) Survey of Pa. Public Health Laws, 1952. Author: Justice, 1995; co-author: Will Contests, 1992; contbr. articles to legal publs. Com. person for 14th ward, vice chmn. Democratic Com., Pitts., 1972; exec. com. bd. trustees U. Pitts., 1980-86, bd. visitors law sch., 1985—, bd. visitors sch. health, 1986—; adv. bd. Animal Friends, Pitts., 1973—; bd. mem. The Program, Pitts., 1983-87, Pitts. History and Landmarks FDTN., West Pa. Hist. Soc., West Pa. Conservancy. Recipient Disting. Amumna award U. Pitts., 1973, Medal of Recognition, 1987, Susan B. Anthony award Womens' Bar Assn. Western Pa., 1993, Probate and Trusts award, 1994; named Girl Scout Woman of Yr., Pitts. coun. Girl Scouts U.S., 1975; cert. of Achievement Pa. Fedn. Women's Clubs, 1975, 77. Mem. Scribes, Allegheny County Bar Assn. (vice chmn., exec. com. young lawyers sect. 1956-59), Pa. State Trial Judges Conf., Order of Coif. Home: 1204 Denniston Ave Pittsburgh PA 15217-1329 Office: Frick Bldg 3d Fl Pittsburgh PA 15219

ROSS, FRED MICHAEL, organic chemist; b. N.Y.C., Aug. 26, 1921; s. Albert N. and Shirley (Honig) R.; m. Nee Kilar Ross, May 9, 1954; children: Robin, Bonnie, Richard. BS, Mich. Tech. U., 1943. Sr. gas analyst Pure Oil Co., Chgo., 1943-44; chief chem. engr. Multiplate Glass Corp., Jamaica, N.Y., 1945-51; founder, CEO Diamond Dust Co., Inc., Mineola, N.Y., 1952-80; chmn. bd. dirs. Portfolio Mgmt., Inc., Rochester, N.Y., 1976-80; founder, pres. Gemery Corp., Mineola, 1974-80; CEO, chmn. Robonard, Inc., Boca Raton, Fla., 1980—. Contbr. over 40 articles to profl. publs. Campaign chmn. for R. Shaw for Ariz. Ho. of Reps, 1994. Officer USN, 1944-45. Recipient Silver medal for Outstanding Alumnus Mich. Tech. U., 1978. Fellow Am. Inst. Chemists. Achievements include development of process for manufacture of ovate diamonds for use in petroleum bits and geological core drills, process for reclamation and recovery of industrial diamond bearing waste materials. Home: 10325 Crosswind Rd Boca Raton FL 33498-4757 Office: Robonard Inc 10325 Crosswind Rd Boca Raton FL 33498-4757

ROSS, GEORGE MARTIN, investment banker; b. Phila., July 24, 1933; s. David L. and Beatrice (Rittenberg) Rosenkoff; m. Lyn Merry Goldberg, Nov. 26, 1959; children: Merry Beth, Michael John. BS, Drexel U., 1955. Mgmt. trainee Sears, Roebuck & Co., Phila., 1955-58; assoc. Goldman, Sachs & Co., Phila., 1959-68, v.p., 1968-70, gen. ptnr., 1971-90, ltd. ptnr., 1991—. Mem. Mayor's Cultural Adv. Coun., Phila., 1987-91, campaign steering com. Bus. Leadership Organized for Cath. Schs., 1983-89; campaign policy com. United Way Southeastern Pa., 1983-84, We the People 200 com., 1984-86, Gov.'s Pvt. Sector Initiatives Task Force, 1983-84, Gov.'s Commn. on Financing Higher Edn., 1983-84, Wills Eye Hosp. Adv. Coun., 1979-81, nat. bd. govs., exec. com., past pres., bd. dirs., past chmn. Phila chpt. Am. Jewish Com.; v.p., exec. com. Jewish Fedn. Greater Phila.; gov. Phila. Stock Exch., 1981-85; trustee Episcopal Acad., 1981-84; chmn. bd. trusts, mem. exec. com. Drexel U., Phila., 1981—; bd. dirs. Ave. of the Arts, 1994—, Phila. Orch. Assn. and Acad. Music Phila., 1985-91, Cystic Fibrosis Found., 1978-83, Nat. Found. Jewish Culture, 1986-91; mem. nat. bd., Phila. co-chmn. One to One; mem. investment com. U.S. Holocaust Mus.; mem. Gov. Sports & Exposition Facilities Task Force, 1996. Mem. Urban Affairs Partnership (bd. dirs. 1978-83), Greater Phila. C. of C. (mem. exec. com. 1989—), Bond Club Phila., Sunday Breakfast Club (Phila.), Locust Club, Phila. Club. Home: 1116 Barberry Rd Bryn Mawr PA 19010-1908 Office: Goldman Sachs & Co Mellon Bank Ctr Fl 26 Philadelphia PA 19103

ROSS, GEORGE WILLIAM, social scientist, educator; b. Cambridge, Mass., Aug. 18, 1940; s. Donald Reynolds and Mabel (Cumming) R.; m. Anne Gillain, Aug. 12, 1964 (div. 1967); m. Jane Jenson, Jan. 18, 1978; 1 child, Bridget Jenson. AB, Williams Coll., 1962; MSc in Econs., London Sch. Econs., 1964; PhD, Harvard U., 1972. Asst. prof. dept. sociology Brandeis U., Waltham, Mass., 1971-76, assoc. prof., 1976-82, prof. sociology, 1982—, Morris Hillquit prof. in labor and social thought, 1986—, chmn. dept. sociology, 1987-90; sr. assoc. Ctr. European Studies, Harvard U., Cambridge, 1983—. Author: Workers and Communists in France, 1982, (with others) Unions, Crisis and Change, 1982, The View from Inside, 1984; editor: The Mitterrand Experiment, 1987, Searching for the New France, 1991, Jacques Delors and European Integration, 1994; corp. editor Theory and Society, 1978—; co-editor French Politics and Society, 1982—. German Marshall Fund of U.S. fellow, 1978-79, 91-92, Fulbright fellow, 1984-85; Bellagio resident, Rockefeller Found., 1987. Mem. Am. Sociol. Assn., Am. Polit. Sci. Assn., Coun. European Studies (exec. com., chair coun.), Conf. Group French Politics and Soc. (exec. sec. 1985—). Avocations: music, hiking, skiing. Office: Brandeis Univ Dept Of Sociology Waltham MA 02154

ROSS, GERALD FRED, engineering executive, researcher; b. N.Y.C., Dec. 14, 1930; s. Samuel Henry and Jenny (Saltzman) Rozansky; m. Vivian Ida Turkish, Dec. 24, 1953; children: Jayne T. Ross Kaufman, Steven A., Helene B. Ross Joseph. BEE, CCNY, 1952; MEE, Poly. U., 1955, PhD, 1963. Registered profl. engr., N.Y., Mass. Rsch. asst. U. Mich., Ann Arbor, 1952-53; sr. engr. W.L. Maxson Corp., N.Y.C., 1954-58; rsch. sect. head Sperry Gyroscope Co., Great Neck, L.I., N.Y., 1958-65; dept. mgr. Sperry Rsch. Ctr., Sudbury, Mass., 1965-81; CEO, chmn. ANRO Engring., Inc., Sarasota, Fla., 1981—; pres., v.p., treas. Adams Pool Corp., Lexington, Mass., 1968-81. Capt. USAFR, 1953—. Contbg. author 3 books, 1986, 90, 93; contbr. numerous articles to profl. jours.; 56 patents in field. Fellow Polytechnic U. Fellow IEEE (life, K.C. Black Nerem Best paper award 1974), Nat. Acad. Engring. (life); mem. Electromagnetics Acad., Res. Officers Assn., Lexington Golf Club, Longboat Key Club, Sigma Xi (sr.), Tau Beta Pi, Eta Kappa Nu. Republican. Jewish. Avocations: golf, tennis. Office: ANRO Engring Inc 1800 2nd St Ste 878 Sarasota FL 34236-5907

ROSS, GLORIA FRANKENTHALER, tapestry artist, consultant; b. N.Y.C., Sept. 5, 1923; d. Alfred and Martha (Lowenstein) Frankenthaler; m. John J. Bookman; children: Alfred Frankenthaler Ross, Beverly Ross, Clifford Ross. BA, Mt. Holyoke Coll., 1943. Owner, operator Gloria F. Ross Tapestries, N.Y.C., 1963—; lectr. Internat. Tapestry Symposium, Australian Bicentennial, Fashion Inst. Tech., N.Y., Harvard Club, Shared Horizons, Santa Fe. Exhibited in group shows at Rutgers Barclay Gallery, Santa Fe, Feigen Gallery, Chgo., Washington and N.Y., Pace Gallery, N.Y.C., Pace Edits., N.Y., The Ringling Mus., Sarasota, Fla., Lausanne Biennale, Kauffman Gallery, Houston; represented in permanent collections at IBM, J.C. Penney Co., Tougaloo (Miss.) Coll. Art Mus., Kennedy Internat. Airport, N.Y., Bank of Tokyo, N.Y., Citibank, N.Y.; commd. tapestries replacement Westinghouse Broadcasting Co., Phila., Winters Bank, Dayton, Ohio, Fed. Courthouse, Portland, Oreg., Mazza Gallery Prudential Ins. Co., Washington, Congregation Emanu-El, N.Y.; collaborator tapestries with various artists, including Avery Bearden, Stuart Davis, Hofmann Motherwell, Youngerman. Chmn. Child Devel. Ctr., N.Y.C., 1960's; trustee Mt. Holyoke Coll., South Hadley, Mass., 1986—; active numerous civic groups, N.Y.C. Mem. Am. Craft Council, ArtTable, Cooper Hewitt, Met. Mus. Modern Art, Mus. Natural History, Textile Mus., Mt. Holyoke Coll. Art Mus. Avocation: sports.

ROSS, GLYNN, opera administrator; b. Omaha, Dec. 15, 1914; s. Herman and Ida (Carlson) R.; m. Angelamaria Solimene, Nov. 15, 1946; children: Stephanie, Claudia, Melanie, Anthony. Student, Leland Powers Sch. Theater, Boston, 1937-39. founder O.P.E.R.A. am.; bd. dirs. Nat. Opera Inst., Soc. for Germanic Music Culture; founder, dir. Pacific N.W. Festival, 1975—. Opera stage dir., U.S., Can., 1939-63, debut, San Francisco Opera, 1948, gen. dir., founder Seattle Opera Assn., Inc., 1963-83; dir. Ariz. Opera, 1983—; founder Pacific N.W. Ballet. Served to 1st lt. AUS, 1942-47. Office: Ariz Opera Assn 3501 N Mountain Ave Tucson AZ 85719-1925

ROSS, GUY MATTHEWS, JR., international leaf tobacco executive; b. Guilford County, N.C., May 5, 1933; s. Guy Matthews and Nancy McConnell (Coleman) R.; m. Patricia Jane Fields, Aug. 27, 1955; children: Charles Alan, Steven York. BSBA, U. N.C., Chapel Hill, 1955. With fin. mgmt. program, then supr. sales acctg. and billing, corp. audit staff, fin. analyst Gen. Electric Co., Ft. Wayne, Ind., Schenectady, Pittsfield, Mass., 1955-56, 58-66; chief acct., v.p. fin. and adminstrn. Imperial Group Ltd., Am. Leaf Orgn., Wilson, N.C., 1966-80; treas., sec. Std. Comml. Corp., Wilson, 1980-92, v.p., sec., 1992—; bd. dirs. Wachovia Bank and Trust Co., Wilson. Pres., heart fund chmn. Wilson div. N.C. Heart Assn., 1967-68; dir., exec. com. Wilson United Way; instl. rep. East Carolina council Boy Scouts Am., 1967-76, mem. adminstrv. bd. and fin. com., 1971-78; pres. Men's Fellowship Class, First United Methodist Ch., 1975-76. Served with U.S. Army, 1956-58. Mem. U. N.C. Alumni Assn. (life; mem. Ednl. Found.), Fin. Execs. Inst. (dir. N.C. chpt., pres. 1993-94), Nat. Investor Relations Inst., Kiwanis (life mem., disting. lt. gov. 1978-79). Home: 1804 Chelsea Dr NW Wilson NC 27896-1412 Office: Standard Comml Corp 2201 Miller Rd S Wilson NC 27893-6860

ROSS, HENRY RAYMOND, advertising executive and legal counsel; b. Toronto, Ont., Can., Nov. 9, 1919; S. Joseph and Mary (Rotenburg) R.; m. Ann Clarfield, Nov. 5, 1944; children: Ellen Louise, Janice Carol. Grad., Ont. Coll. Art, 1936. Pres. Ferris Theaters, Toronto, 1937-39, Ross Enterprises, Toronto, 1939-44; with F.H. Hayhurst Co. Ltd., Toronto, 1944—, sr. v.p., dir. creative svcs., 1957-73, sr. v.p., dir. industry, govt. and corp. affairs, 1973-79; dir., pres. Contemporary Paintings, Toronto, 1969—; sr. ptnr. H.M.S. Investments, Toronto, 1975—; pres. Henry R. Ross Cons. Inc., Toronto, 1979—; chmn. broadcast com. Assn. Can. Advertisers, Toronto, 1970—; chmn. talent negotiation com., bd. dirs. Can. Advt. Rsch. Found.; trustee Am. Fedn. Musicians; resource advisor Fed. and Provincial Govts. in devel. advt. bus. practices laws. Contbr. articles to jours. in field. Served with Can. Armed Forces, 1943-44. Fellow Inst. Can. Advt. (chmn. broadcast com. 1970—); mem. Art Dirs. Club Toronto, Broadcast Execs. Soc., Donalda Country Club. Home: 127 Munro Blvd, Willowdale, ON Canada M2P 1C7 Office: 55 Eglinton Ave E, Toronto, ON Canada M4P 1G9 *If only we would realize that we are indeed the masters of our own life's accomplishments. And so every deed and thought must be considered in that light, long before life passes us by.*

ROSS, HERBERT DAVID, film director; b. Bklyn., May 13, 1927; m. Nora Kaye, Aug. 21, 1959 (dec. 1987); m. Lee Radziwill, Sept., 1988. Dir. motion pictures Goodbye Mr. Chips, 1969, The Owl and The Pussycat, 1970, T. R. Baskin, 1971, Play It Again Sam, 1972, The Last of Sheila, 1973, Funny Lady, 1975, The Sunshine Boys, 1975, The Seven Percent Solution, 1976, The Goodbye Girl, 1977, The Turning Point, 1977, California Suite, 1978, Nijinsky, 1980, Pennies From Heaven, 1981, I Ought To Be in Pictures, 1982, Max Dugan Returns, 1983, Footloose, 1984, Protocol, 1984, The Secret of My Sucess, 1987, Dancers, 1987, Steel Magnolias, 1988, Undercover Blues, 1993; dir., producer: My Blue Heaven, 1989, True Colors, 1990, Boys On The Side, 1995; exec. prodr. Soapdish, 1991, choreographer: Spoleto (Italy) Festival, Berlin (Germany) Festival; active in numerous Broadway prodns., including Anyone Can Whistle; dir.: Broadway Chpt. Two, I Ought to Be in Pictures, 1980; opera dir. La Boheme, L.A. Music Ctr., 1993; recipient Golden Globe award 1978, award of distinction Dance mag. 1980. Office: care Rand Holsten CAA 9830 Wilshire Blvd Beverly Hills CA 90212-1804

ROSS, HUGH COURTNEY, electrical engineer; b. Dec. 31, 1923; s. Clare W. and Jeanne F. Ross; m. Sarah A. Gordon (dec.); m. Patricia A. Malloy; children: John C., James G., Robert W. Student, Calif. Inst. Tech., 1942, San Jose State U., 1946-47; BSEE, Stanford U., 1950, postgrad., 1954. Registered profl. elec. engr., Calif. Instr. San Benito (Calif.) High Sch. and Jr. Coll., 1950-51; chief engr. vacuum power switches Jennings Radio Mfg. Corp., San Jose, Calif., 1951-62; chief engr. ITT Jennings, San Jose, Calif., 1962-64; pres. Ross Engring. Corp., Campbell, Calif., 1964—. Contbr. articles to tech. jours.; patentee in field. Fellow IEEE (life) (chmn. Santa Clara Valley subsect. 1960-61); mem. Am. Vacuum Soc., Am. Soc. Metals. Avocations: electronics, electric autos, camping, ranching, solar power. Office: 540 Westchester Dr Campbell CA 95008-5012

ROSS, IAN MUNRO, electrical engineer; b. Southport, Eng., Aug. 15, 1927; came to U.S., 1952, naturalized, 1960; m. Christina Leinberg Ross, Aug. 24, 1955; children: Timothy Ian, Nancy Lynn, Stina Marguerite. BA, Gonville and Caius Coll., Cambridge U., 1948; MA in Elec. Engring, Cambridge U., 1952, PhD, 1952; DSc (hon.), N.J. Inst. Tech., 1983, Poly. U., 1988; D of Engring. (hon.), Stevens Inst. Tech., 1983; DSc (hon.), Polytech. U., 1988. With AT&T Bell Labs. (and affiliates), 1952-92, exec. dir. network planning div., 1971-73, v.p. network planning and customer svcs., 1973-76; exec. v.p. systems engring. and devel. AT&T Bell Labs. (and affiliates), Holmdel, N.J., 1976-79, pres., 1979-91; pres. emeritus AT&T Bell Labs. Inc., Holmdel, 1991—; dir. Thomas & Betts Corp., B.F. Goodrich Co.; chmn. Nat. Adv. Commn. on Semicondrs. Patentee in field. Recipient NASA Pub. Svc. award, 1969, 75, medal Ind. Rsch. Inst., 1987. Fellow IEEE (Founders' medal 1988, Am. Acad. Arts and Scis.; mem. NAS, NAE, Nat. Sci. Bd. Home: 5 Blackpoint Horseshoe Rumson NJ 07760-1500 Office: AT&T Bell Labs 101 Crawfords Corner Rd Holmdel NJ 07733-1900

ROSS, JAMES BARRETT, finance and insurance educator; b. Cleve., Apr. 25, 1930; s. James Barrett and Marjorie (Stutsman) R.; m. Ann Penney, July 1, 1950; children: James, Scott, Alison, Andrea, Alan, Dana, Ann Elizabeth, Brandon, Mary Ellen, Marjorie, Wendy. BA cum laude, Harvard Coll., 1951; MBA, U. R.I., 1988; PhD, U. Conn., 1992. CLU; CPCU; ChFC. With Conn. Gen. Life Ins. Co., 1951-62; pres., dir. Puritan Life Ins. Co., Providence, 1962-68; exec. v.p. mktg. Keystone Custodian Funds Inc., Boston, 1968-73; sr. v.p. Met. Life Ins. Co., N.Y.C., 1973-80; chmn., chief exec. officer INA Internat., 1980-83; sr. exec. v.p. Ins. Co. N.Am., 1980-83; pres. Continental Vision Fin. Svcs., 1983-86; vice chmn. Andersen & Walsh, 1986-91; assoc. prof. fin. and ins. Radford (Va.) U., 1992—. Fellow Soc. Actuaries, Life Mgmt. Inst.; mem. Am. Acad. Actuaries, Fin. Mgmt. Assn., Ea. Fin. Assn., Midwestern Fin. Assn., So. Fin. Assn., Southwestern Fin. Assn., Acad. Fin. Svcs., Am. Risk and Ins. Assn., So. Risk and Ins. Assn., Beta Gamma Sigma, Phi Kappa Phi. Congregationalist. Home: 1103 Scott Alan Cir Blacksburg VA 24060

ROSS, JAMES ELMER, economist, administrator; b. Danville, Ill., Jan. 15, 1931; s. Carl Henry and Lura Jane (Witherspoon) R.; m. Barbara Lou Becker, Dec. 24, 1958 (dec. Aug. 1982); 1 child, Candis Anne; m. Erin Elizabeth O'Shea, June 20, 1986. BS, U. Ill., 1953, MS, 1959, PhD, 1966. Agrl. counselor Am. Embassy, Caracas, Venezuela, 1976-78, Cairo, Egypt, 1978-81; asst. adminstr. Fgn. Agrl. Svc., Washington, 1981-83; mem. Sr. Exec. Seminar, Dept. State, 1983-84; alt. permanent rep. U.S. Mission to UN Agys., Rome, 1984-87; agrl. counselor U.S. Embassy, Seoul, Republic of Korea, 1987-88; dir. trade assistance and planning office Fgn. Agrl. Svc., Washington, 1988-92; adj. prof. U. Fla., 1992—; pres. J.E. Ross & Assocs., Inc., 1993—; cons. Govt. of Ecuador, 1971-72; mem. internat. programs U. Fla., Costa Rica, 1966-69, Ghana, 1969-70; assoc. dir., 1970-72; asst. dean Fla. Coop. Extension Svc., 1972-75; spl. asst. to undersecretary USDA, 1975-76. Author: Cooperative Rural Electrification, 1972; co-author: Rural Electrification and Development, 1978. Col. USAR, ret. Mem. Internat. Assn. Agrl. Economists, Am. Agrl. Econs. Assn., Assn. for Internat. Agriculture and Rural Devel., Assn. for the Study of the Cuban Economy, Internat. Agrl. Trade Rsch. Consortium, Internat. Agribus. Mgmt. Assn., Masons. Republican. Home: RR 1 Box 287-B18 Hawthorne FL 32640-8116

ROSS, JAMES FRANCIS, philosophy educator; b. Providence, Oct. 8, 1931; s. James Joseph and Teresa Marie (Sullivan) R.; m. Kathleen Marie Fallon, Dec. 1, 1956; children: Seamus, Ellen, Richard Fallon, Therese. A.B., Cath. U. Am., 1953, M.A. (Basselin Found. fellow), 1954; Ph.D., Brown U., 1958; J.D., U. Pa., 1974. Bar: Pa. bar 1975. Instr., then asst. prof. philosophy U. Mich., 1959-61; asst. prof. U. Pa., 1962-65, asso. prof., 1965-68, prof., 1968—, prof. philosophy and law, 1994—, chmn. philosophy dept. and grad. group in philosophy, 1966-70, 81-83; Rackham rsch. fellow U. Mich., 1960-61; NEH fellow, mem. Inst. Advanced Study, Princeton, 1975-76; vis. prof. Brown U., summer 1977; assoc. mem. Darwin Coll., Cambridge U. (Eng.), 1982-83. Author: Philosophical Theology, 1969, 2d edit., 1980, Introduction to Philosophy of Religion, 1970, Portraying Analogy, 1981; translator, editor: Suarez on Formal and Universal Unity, 1964; editor: Inquiries in Medieval Philosophy, 1971. Recipient Christian B. and Mary L. Linbach Found. award for Disting. Teaching, 1966; Disting. Scholarship award Cath. U. Am., 1971; Guggenheim fellow, 1982-83. Fellow Soc. Values in Higher Edn.; mem. Am. Philos. Assn., Am. Cath. Philos. Assn. (pres. 1987-89), Soc. for Medieval and Renaissance Philosophy, Am. Theol. Soc., Soc. Theol. Discussion. Roman Catholic. Home: Grange Ave Little Compton RI 02837 Office: U Pa 3440 Market St Ste 460 Philadelphia PA 19104-3337

ROSS, JAMES NEIL, JR., veterinary educator; b. Akron, Ohio, Dec. 18, 1940; s. James Neil and Ruth Evelyn (Gray) R.; m. Marcia Day Collins, June 27, 1964; children: Stephanie, Amy, Lisa. DVM, Ohio State U., 1965, MSc, 1967; PhD, Baylor Coll. Medicine, 1972. Diplomate in cardiology and internal medicine Am. Coll. Vet. Internal Medicine; diplomate Am. Coll. Vet. Emergency and Critical Care. Lectr., cardiologist Ohio State U. Vet. Sch., Columbus, 1965-67; asst. prof. surgery and physiology Baylor Coll. Medicine, Houston, 1967-74; assoc. prof. physiology Med. Coll. Ohio, Toledo, 1974-80; prof. and chmn. dept. medicine Tufts U. Sch. Vet. Medicine, North Grafton, Mass., 1981—; cons. Proctor & Gamble, Cin., 1976-84; mem. scientist rev. bds. of various jours. including Jour. of Investigative Surgery, Am. Jour. Vet. Rsch. 1983-86. Contbr. chpts. to books, articles to profl. jours. Named Veterninarian of the Yr. Animal Sci. Assn., 1972; grantee NIH, 1965-67; fellow NIH, 1969-71. Mem. AVMA (coun. on edn. 1989-95), Am. Bd. vet. spltys.), Am. Coll. Vet. Internat Medicine, Am. Heart Assn., Am. Animal Hosp. Assn., Vet. Emergency and Critical Care Soc. (pres. 1991-92), Phi Eta Sigma, Gamma Sigma Delta, Am. Coll. Vet. Emergency and Critical Care (treas. 1989—, recording sec. 1993—), Omega Tau Sigma, Phi Gamma Delta. Methodist. Achievements include research in cardiovascular disease in animals; assisted circulation. Office: Tufts U Sch Vet Medicine 200 Westboro Rd North Grafton MA 01536-1828

ROSS, JAMES ULRIC, lawyer, accountant, educator; b. Del Rio, Tex., Sept. 14, 1941; s. Stephen Mabrey and Beatrice Jessie (Hyslop) R.; m. Janet S. Calabro, Dec. 28, 1986; children: James Ulric Jr., Ashley Meredith. BA, U. Tex., 1963, JD, 1965. Bar: Tex. 1965, U.S. Tax Ct. 1969; CPA, Tex. Estate tax examiner IRS, Houston, 1965-66; tax acct. Holmes, Raquet, Harris & Shaw, San Antonio, 1966-67; pvt. practice law and acctg., Del Rio and San Antonio, 1968—; instr. St. Mary's U., San Antonio, 1973-75; assoc. prof. U. Tex., San Antonio, 1975—. Active Am. Cancer Soc., Residential Mgmt., Inc., Am. Heart Assn. Mem. ABA, Tex. Bar Assn., Tex. Soc. CPAs, San Antonio Bar Assn., San Antonio Estate Planners Coun. Contbr. articles on U.S. and Internat. Estate Planning and Taxation to legal and prof. jours. Home: 3047 Orchard Hl San Antonio TX 78230-3078 Office: 760 Tex Commerce Bank Bldg 7550 IH 10 W San Antonio TX 78229

ROSS, JEFFREY ALLAN, political scientist, organization executive, educator; b. N.Y.C., Dec. 24, 1947; s. Joseph and Pearl (Epstein) R.; B.A. in Polit. Sci. summa cum laude with high honors, SUNY, Binghamton, 1969; Ph.D. in Polit. Sci. (Ford Found. fellow, Ford Found. grantee), U. Minn., 1982; m. Marjorie Appelson, Aug. 30, 1970; children—Craig, Eric, Brian, Allison. N.Y. State Regents' fellow, teaching asst. U. Minn., Mpls., 1969-71, research asst., 1971-73, instr., 1973; instr. Kirkland Coll., Clinton, N.Y., 1973-78, Huber Found. faculty research grantee, 1973, 74, 77, Mellon Found. grantee, 1974, research prof., 1975-76; instr. govt. Hamilton Coll., Clinton, 1978-80, asst. prof., 1980-82; vis. prof. polit. sci. Syracuse U., 1984; adj. prof. polit. sci. Queens Coll., CUNY, 1987-88; dir. campus affairs dept. Anti-Defamation League of B'nai B'rith, 1984—; v.p., bd. dirs. Research Ctr. for Religion and Human Rights in Closed Socs.; exec. bd. Com. for Pub. Higher Edn.; chmn., mem. various profl. panels; Mpls. Found., Frances E. Andrews Fund All-Univ. research fellow, surveyor Soviet Jewish emigrants, Israel, 1972. Precinct rep. Democratic Farm Labor Party, Mpls., 1972-73. Mem. Am. Polit. Sci. Assn., N.E. Polit. Sci. Assn. (exec. council), Internat. Polit. Sci. Assn., Internat. Studies Assn., Mongolia Soc., Can.-Mongolia Soc., Comparative Interdisciplinary Studies Soc. (exec. coun.), N.Y. State

Polit. Sci. Assn. (v.p. 1982-83, pres. 1983-84), Sound Cyclists Bicycle Club (v.p. 1989-90, 94, pres. 1991-93), Norwalk Ski Club (v.p. 1992-93). Democrat. Author: (with Ann Cottrell) The Mobilization of Collective Indentity: Comparative Perspectives, 1980, Pamyat: Hatred Under Glasnost, 1989; contbr. articles to profl. jours.; mem. editorial bd. Teaching Polit. Sci., 1971-81; editor Hamilton Social Sci. Rev., 1977-79; reviewer manuscripts for profl. jours., book pubs. Home: 20 Soundview Loop South Salem NY 10590 Office: Anti-Defamation League 823 United Nations Plz New York NY 10017-3518 *A satisfying life must be multidimensional. One's community, family and recreation have a necessary place alongside one's career. A fully realized person becomes also a fully realized professional.*

ROSS, JIMMY DOUGLAS, army officer; b. Hosston, La., May 23, 1936; s. Horace Eugene and Lucile Marie (Pontious) R.; m. Patricia L. Cox., Dec. 18, 1955; children: Sabra, DiAnna, Tony. B.S., Henderson State U., 1958; M.A. in Bus. Mgmt., Central Mich. U., 1975. Commd. 2d lt. U.S. Army, 1958, advanced through grades to 4 Star Gen., 1994, served comdr. co., bn., brigade levels; comdg. gen. 2d Support Command (Corps) VII Corps U.S. Army, Nellingen, W. Ger., 1980-82; dir. transp., energy and troop support Office Dep. Chief of Staff for Logistics, U.S. Army, Washington, 1982-84; chief staff U.S. Army Materiel Command, Alexandria, Va., 1984-86; comdr. U.S. Army Depot System Command, Chambersburg, Pa., 1986-87; dep. chief of staff for logistics U.S. Army, Washington, 1987-92; commdg. gen. U.S. Army Materiel Command, Alexandria, Va., 1992-94; retired, 1994; bd. dirs. VSE Engring. Co.; chmn. Def. Industry Conf. Bd.; pres. bd. dirs. Indsl. Coll. of Armed Forces Assn. Dist. commr. Alpine dist. Boy Scouts Am., 1980-82; sr. v.p. Biomed. Svcs., ARC Nat. Hdqrs., 1994—. Decorated D.S.M. with oak leaf cluster, Legion of Merit, Bronze Star, Air medal. Fellow Assn. U.S. Army (sr.); mem. Am. Def. Preparedness Assn., Nat. Def. Transp. Assn., Armed Forces Benefit Assn. (bd. dirs.). Methodist. Home: 9208 Cross Oaks Ct Fairfax Station VA 22039-3337

ROSS, JOHN, physical chemist, educator; b. Vienna, Austria, Oct. 2, 1926; came to U.S., 1940; s. Mark and Anna (Krecmar) R.; m. Virginia Franklin (div.); children: Elizabeth A., Robert K.; m. Eva Madarasz. BS, Queens Coll., 1948; PhD, MIT, 1951; D (hon.), Weizmann Inst. Sci., Rehovot, Israel, 1984, Queens Coll., SUNY, 1987, U. Bordeaux, France, 1987. Prof. chemistry Brown U., Providence, 1953-66; prof. chemistry MIT, Cambridge, 1966-80, chmn. dept., 1966-71; chmn. faculty of Inst. MIT, 1975-77; prof. Stanford (Calif.) U., 1980—, chmn. dept., 1983-89; cons. to industries, 1979—; mem. bd. govs. Weizmann Inst., 1971—. Author: Physical Chemistry, 1980; editor Molecular Beams, 1966; contbr. articles to profl. jours. 2nd lt. U.S. Army, 1944-46. Recipient medal Coll. de France, Paris. Fellow AAAS, Am. Phys. Soc.; mem. NAS, Am. Acad. Arts and Scis., Am. Chem. Soc. (Irving Langmuir Chem. Physics prize 1992). Home: 738 Mayfield Ave Palo Alto CA 94305-1044 Office: Stanford U Dept Chemistry Stanford CA 94305-5080

ROSS, JOHN, cultural organization administrator; b. Tahlequah, Okla., Feb. 16, 1955; s. John and Nancy (Augerhole) R.; m. Anita Faye Franklin, Jan. 1, 1976; children: Anthony John, Adam John. Student, U. Ark., 1976; degree, Nutrition and Diatetics Tng. Ctr., 1981; AA Health in Phys. Edn. and Recreation, Rogers State Health, 1982; cert. in food svc. mgmt., St. Louis U., 1984; BA Social Sci., Northeastern State U., 1985. Cook Claremore Indian Hosp., Okla., 1979-86; asst. mgr. Horseshoe Bend Bingo, Sperry, Okla., 1986-87; owner/operator South Greasy Smokeshop, Stilwell, Okla., 1988; material handler Allied Signal, Tulsa, Okla., 1988-92; various elected and apptd. positions United Keetoowah Band of Cherokee Indians in Okla., 1985—, chief, 1992—. Office: United Keetoowah Cherokee Indians PO Box 746 Tahlequah OK 74465-0746

ROSS, JOHN MICHAEL, editor, magazine publisher; b. Bklyn., Oct. 17, 1919; s. Albert Henry and Dorothy Veronica (Murray) R.; m. Kathleen M. Courtney; children: Donna Patricia Ross Easterbrook, Maureen Courtney Ross Quick. Student pub. schs., N.Y.C. Sports writer Bklyn. Eagle, 1937-41, The Newspaper PM, 1946-47; editor Am. Law Tennis mag., 1947-50, Macfadden Publs., 1950-51, 60-61; contbg. editor Am. Weekly, 1952-60; editor-in-chief Golf mag., 1961-67, Golf Bus. mag., 1963-65, Golfdom mag., 1965-67; v.p. Universal Pub. and Distbn. Corp., 1965-67; pres. Golf Promotions, Inc., 1967-70; pub. Golf Bus. Almanac, also Golf TV Guide, 1969; pub. relations dir. Profl. Golfers Assn. Golf Tour, 1970-71; editor-in-chief Golf mag., 1972-79, assoc. pub., 1979-84; publishing dir., v.p. The Golf Link, 1985-87; editorial dir. Am. Golf mag., 1990-94; sr. ptnr. J.M. Ross Assocs., Westport, Conn., 1994—; bd. dirs. World Golf Hall of Fame, 1974-83, mem. adv. bd. 1993—; chmn. Women's Golf Scholarship Fund, 1976-82; exec. dir. World Cup Golf Internat. Golf Assn., 1977-84. Co-author: Nothing But The Truth, 1960; editor: Encyclopedia of Golf, 1977; contbr. numerous articles to nat. publs. including Reader's Digest, Life, Sports Illustrated. Justice of peace, Newtown, Conn., 1960-64. Served with AUS, 1942-46. Recipient Christopher award for best mag. story, 1957; recipient Lincoln Werden award for golf journalism, 1991. Mem. U.S. Golf Assn. (nat. com. 1977—), Lawn Tennis Writers Assn. (sec. 1949-50), Golf Writers Assn. Am. (gov. 1966-67), Met. Golf Writers Assn. (pres. 1975-76), Assn. of Golf Writers (Great Britain), Am. Soc. Mag. Editors, Overseas Press Club (N.Y.C.), Patterson Club (Fairfield, Conn.). Roman Catholic. Home: 19 Riverfield Dr Weston CT 06883-2908 Office: J M Ross Assocs PO Box 774 Westport CT 06881-0774

ROSS, JOSEPH COMER, physician, educator, academic administrator; b. Tompkinsville, Ky., June 16, 1927; s. Joseph M. and Annie (Pinckley) R.; m. Isabelle Nevins, June 15, 1952; children: Laura Ann, Sharon Lynn, Jennifer Jo, Mary Martha, Jefferson Arthur. BS, U. Ky., 1950; MD, Vanderbilt U., 1954. Diplomate Am. Bd. Internal Medicine (bd. govs. 1975-81), Am. Bd. Pulmonary Disease. Intern Vanderbilt U. Hosp., Nashville, 1954-55; resident Duke U. Hosp., Durham, N.C., 1955-57, rsch. fellow, 1957-58; instr. medicine Ind. U. Sch. Medicine, Indpls., 1958-60, asst. prof., 1960-62, assoc. prof., 1962-66, prof., 1966-70; prof., chmn. dept. medicine Med. U. of S.C., Charleston, 1970-80; vis. prof. Vanderbilt U. Sch. Medicine, Nashville, 1979-80, prof. medicine, 1981—, assoc. vice chancellor for health affairs, 1982—; mem. cardiovascular study sect. NIH, 1966-70, program project com., 1971-75; mem. adv. coun. Nat. Heart, Lung and Blood Inst., 1982-86; mem. ad hoc coms. NAS, 1966, 67; mem. Pres.'s Nat. Adv. Panel on Heart Disease, 1972; mem. merit rev. bd. in respiration VA Rsch. Svc., 1972-76, chmn., 1974-76. Mem. editorial bd. Jour. Lab. and Clin. Medicine, 1964-70, Chest, 1968-73, Jour. Applied Physiology,1968-73, Archives of Internal Medicine, 1976-82, Heart and Lung, 1977-86; contbr. articles to profl. jours. Bd. dirs., past pres. Nashville Ronald McDonald House; bd. dirs. Agape, Leadership Nashville; mem. adv. com. Davidson County Cmty. Health Agy.; active Tenn. Lung Assn. With U.S. Army, 1945-47. Fellow ACP, Am. Coll. Chest Physicians (gov. S.C. 1970-76, vice chmn. bd. govs. 1974-75, chmn. bd. govs. 1975-76, exec. council 1974-80, pres.-elect 1976-77, pres. 1978-79, chmn. sci. program com. 1973), Am. Coll. Cardiology; mem. AMA (sect. on med. schs.), Am. Fedn. Clin. Rsch. (chmn. Midwest sect.), Am. Physiol. Soc., Am. Soc. Clin. Investigation, Assn. Am. Physicians, Assn. Profs. Medicine, Cen. Soc. Clin. Rsch., S.C. Med. Soc., Am. Thoracic Soc. (nat. councillor 1972-76), So. Soc. Clin. Rsch., S.C. Lung Assn. (v.p. 1974-75), Am. Soc. Internal Medicine, Phi Beta Kappa, Alpha Omega Alpha. Mem. Ch. of Christ (elder). Office: Vanderbilt University D 3300 Medical Ctr N Nashville TN 37232

ROSS, JOSEPH FOSTER, physician, educator; b. Azusa, Calif., Oct. 11, 1910; s. Verne Ralph and Isabel Mills (Bumgarner) R.; m. Eileen Sullivan, Dec. 19, 1942; children: Louisa, Elisabeth, Joseph, Jeanne, Marianne. AB with great distinction, Leland Stanford Jr. U., 1933; MD cum laude with spl. honors in Physiology, Harvard U., 1936. Diplomate Am. Bd. Internal Medicine (mem. 1973-83), Am. Bd. Nuclear Medicine (founding, sec. 1971-72, 79, chmn. 1973-77, pres., chief exec. officer 1980—). Asst. topographical anatomy Harvard U. Sch. Medicine, 1934-37, research fellow biochemistry, 1943-46; med. house officer Harvard cancer commn. Huntington Meml. Hosp., 1934-35; Palmer Meml., New Eng. Deaconess hosps., 1935-36; resident pathology Mallory Inst. Pathology, 1936-37; intern Harvard Med. Svc. Boston City Hosp., 1937-39; asst. pathology U. Rochester Sch. Medicine, 1939-40; resident pathology Strong Meml. Hosp., Rochester, N.Y., 1939-40; physician, dir. hematology and radioisotope divs. Mass. Meml. Hosp., 1940-54; instr., asst. prof., assoc. prof. medicine Boston U., 1940-54; dir. radioisotope unit Cushing VA, Boston VA hosps., 1948-54; prof. medicine UCLA, 1954—, prof. radiobiology, 1954-59, assoc. dean, 1954-58, chmn. dept. nuclear med. and radiation biology, 1958-60, dir. Lab. Nuclear Med. and Radiation Biology, 1958-65, prof., chmn. dept. biophysics and nuclear medicine, 1960-65, chief div. hematology, 1969-76; chief staff U. Calif. Hosp., Los Angeles, 1954-58; attending physician U. Calif. Hosp., 1954—; U.S. del. Internat. Conf. Peaceful Uses Atomic Energy, Geneva, 1955; mem. U.S. Atoms for Peace mission to Latin Am., 1956, U.S. AEC Life Scis. Mission to, Greece, Turkey, 1961; mem. USA AEC sci. mission to USSR, 1966; mem. Calif. Adv. Council on Cancer, 1959-84, chmn., 1963-66, 74-77; mem. CENTO Sci. Mission Iran, Turkey, Pakistan, 1963; mem. nat. adv. cancer council Nat. Cancer Inst., 1956-60; Research preservation whole blood OSRD, World War II. Editorial bd.: Blood, Jour. Hematology, 1946-76, Annals Internal Medicine, 1960-70, Jour. Nuclear Medicine, 1968; med. book div., Little Brown Co., 1958-68, med. book series, U. Calif. Press, 1962-70; Contbr. articles to profl. jours. Recipient cert. of merit Pres. U.S., 1948, Van Meter award Am. Goiter Soc., 1953, Dorothy Kirsten French Meml. award for disting. contbn. to medicine French Found. for Alzheimer's Disease Rsch., 1994; Wilson medalist, lectr. Am. Clin. and Climatol. Assn., 1964; Disting. fellow Am. Coll. Nuclear Physicians, 1994. Fellow Am. Coll. Nuclear Medicine (Disting. fellow 1988); mem. ACP, AMA, Am. Soc. Exptl. Pathology, Am. Soc. Clin. Investigation, Assn. Am. Physicians, Am. Acad. Arts and Scis., Biophys. Soc., Radiation Research Soc. (council 1964-65), Internat. Soc. Hematology, Am. Soc. Hematology (pres. 1961-62), Western Assn. Physicians (pres. 1962-63), Am. Bd. Nuclear Medicine (co-founder 1972, sec. 1972-75, chmn., pres. 1975-78, exec. dir. 1978-79, pres. 1980—), Soc. Nuclear Med. (trustee 1962-72, pres. So. Calif. chpt. 1964-65, Nuclear Pioneer lectr. 1971, 77, Disting. Scientist award Western. sect. 1977, Disting. Svc. award 1984, Spl. Presdl. Recognition award 1991, Hevesy Nuc. Pioneer award and lectr., 1995), L.A. County Med. Assn. (dist. v.p. 1976-77, 78-79, del. to Calif. Med. Assn. 1978-79), Am. Bd. Med. Spltys. (exec. com. 1982-84), Council Med. Splty. Socs. (sec. 1981-82, dir. 1980-82), World Fedn. Nuclear Medicine and Biology (chmn. statutes com. 1980-84), Phi Beta Kappa, Sigma Xi, Alpha Omega Alpha, Theta Xi, Nu Sigma Nu. Presbyterian (exec. com. Westminster Found. So. Calif. 1962-72, pres. 1968). Clubs: Harvard (Boston); Cosmos (Washington). Home: 11246 Cashmere St Los Angeles CA 90049-3503 Office: Am Bd Nuclear Med 900 Veteran Ave Rm 12-200 Los Angeles CA 90024

ROSS, JOYCE ADAMS, gerontological clinical specialist; b. Phila., June 29, 1944; d. Thomas Grandville and Dorothy (Anglea) Adams; m. Jerome Samuel Ross, June 8, 1963; children: Mary Teresa, Dorothy, Jerome Jr., Michael, Erin. ADN, Gwynedd Mercy Coll., 1987, BSN cum laude, 1988, MSN, 1992. RN Pa.; cert. gerontol. nurse., nurse practitioner. Gerontol. nurse clinician Franklin Sq. Hosp. Ctr., Balt., 1988-89; instr. Fair Acres Geriatric Ctr., Lima, Pa., 1989; dir. staff devel., cert. gerontol. clin. specialist Dunwoody Village Continuing Care Retirement Cmty., Newtown Square, Pa., 1989—, mem. speakers bur., 1989—; nursing home adminstr., mem. speakers bur.; long term care consortium Main Line, Inc.; evaluator continuing care accreditation Am. Assn. Homes for the Aged, 1993—, nursing home adminstr., 1994—. Nurst of Hope Am. Cancer Soc., Media, Pa., 1981, mem. edn. com., 1990-92. Mem. Delaware Valley Geriatric Soc., Sigma Theta Tau (Iota Kappa chpt.). Roman Catholic. Home: 347 Sussex Blvd Broomall PA 19008-4153 Office: Hosp U Pa Maloney Bldg Philadelphia PA 19104

ROSS, JUNE ROSA PITT, biologist; b. Taree, New South Wales, Australia, May 2, 1931; came to U.S., 1957; d. Bernard and Adeline Phillips; m. Charles Alexander, June 27, 1959. BS with honors, U. Sydney, New S. Wales, Australia, 1953, PhD, 1959, DSc, 1974. Research assoc. Yale U., New Haven, 1959-60, U. Ill., Urbana, 1960-65; research assoc. Western Wash. U., Bellingham, 1965-67, assoc. prof., 1967-70, prof. biology, 1970—, chair dept. biology, 1989-90; pres. Western Wash. U. Faculty Senate, Bellingham, 1984-85; conf. host Internat. Bryozoology Assn., 1986. Author: (with others) A Textbook of Entomology, 1982, Geology of Coal, 1984; editor (assoc.) Palaios, 1985-89; contbr. articles to profl. jours. NSF grantee; recipient Award of Excellence Sydney U. Grads. Union of N.Am., 1995. Mem. Australian Marine Scis. Assn., The Paleontol. Soc. (councillor 1984-86, treas. 1987-93), U.K. Marine Biol. Assn. (life), Microscopy Soc. of Am., Internat. Bryozoology Assn. (pres. 1992-95). Avocations: hiking, classical music. Office: Western Wash U Dept Biology Bellingham WA 98225-9160

ROSS, KATHLEEN ANNE, college president; b. Palo Alto, Calif., July 1, 1941; d. William Andrew and Mary Alberta (Wilburn) R. BA, Ft. Wright Coll., 1964; MA, Georgetown U., 1971; PhD, Claremont Grad. Sch., 1979; LLD (hon.) Alverno Coll. Milw., 1990, Dartmouth Coll., 1991, Seattle U., 1992; LHD (hon.) Whitworth Coll., 1992, LLD (hon.) Pomona Coll., 1993. Cert. tchr., Wash. Secondary tchr. Holy Names Acad., Spokane, Wash., 1964-70; dir. rsch. and planning Province Holy Names, Wash. State, 1972-73; v.p. acads. Ft. Wright Coll., Spokane, 1973-81; rsch. asst. to dean Claremont Grad. Sch., Calif., 1977-78; assoc. faculty mem. Harvard U., Cambridge, Mass., 1981; pres. Heritage Coll., Toppenish, Wash., 1981—; cons. Wash. State Holy Names Schs., 1971-73; coll. accrediting assn. evaluator N.W. Assn. Schs. and Colls., Seattle, 1975—; dir. Holy Names Coll., Oakland, Calif., 1979—; cons. Yakama Indian Nation, Toppenish, 1975—; speaker, cons. in field. Author: (with others) Multicultural Pre-School Curriculum, 1977, A Crucial Agenda: Improving Minority Student Success, 1989; Cultural Factors in Success of American Indian Students in Higher Education, 1978. Chmn. Internat. 5-Yr. Convocation of Sisters of Holy Names, Montreal, Que., Can., 1981, 96; TV Talk show host Spokane Council of Chs., 1974-76. Recipient E.K. and Lillian F. Bishop Founds. Youth Leader of Yr. award, 1986, Disting. Citizenship Alumna award Claremont Grad. Sch., 1986, Golden Aztec award Washington Human Devel., 1989, Harold W. McGraw Edn. prize, 1989, John Carroll award Georgetown U., 1991, Holy Names medal Ft. Wright Coll., 1981, Pres. medal Eastern Washington U., 1994; named Yakima Herald Rep. Person of Yr. 1987, First Annual Leadership award Region VIII Coun. Advancement and Support Edn., 1993; Wash. State Medal of Merit, 1995; numerous grants for projects in multicultural higher edn., 1974—. Mem. Nat. Assn. Ind. Colls. and Univs., Am. Assn. Higher Edn., Soc. Intercultural Edn., Tng. and Rsch., Sisters of Holy Names of Jesus and Mary-SNJM. Roman Catholic. Office: Heritage Coll Office of Pres 3240 Fort Rd Toppenish WA 98948-9562

ROSS, LEONARD LESTER, anatomist; b. N.Y.C., Sept. 11, 1927; s. Aaron Theodore and Shirley (Smolen) R.; m. Marcella Gamel, June 23, 1951; children: Jane, Jill. A.B., NYU, 1946, Ph.D., 1954. Asst. prof. U. Ala. Med. Coll., 1954-57; assoc. prof. Cornell U. Med. Coll., 1957-69, prof., 1969-73; vis. prof. Cambridge U., 1967-68; prof., chmn. dept. anatomy Med. Coll. Pa., Phila., 1973-89; exec. v.p., Annenberg dean Med. Coll. Pa., 1989-93, pres. and Annenberg dean, 1993-94; provost Med. Coll. Pa., Hahnemann Univ., Phila., 1994—; exec. v.p. Allegheny Health, Edn. and Rsch. Found. Assoc. editor: Anat. Record, 1976. Served with M.C., U.S. Army, 1946-47. Recipient Lindback award for teaching, 1976; NIH sr. research fellow, 1967-68. Mem. Am. Assn. Anatomists (exec. com. 1984-88), Soc. Neurosci., Soc. Cell Biology, N.Y. Soc. Electron Microscopists (pres. 1975-76), Assn. Anatomy Chairmen (pres. 1983-84), AAUP (nat. council 1974-77), Sigma Xi. Office: Broad and Vine St Philadelphia PA 19102-5087

ROSS, MADELYN ANN, newspaper editor; b. Pitts., June 26, 1949; d. Mario Charles and Rose Marie (Mangieri) R. B.A., Indiana U. of Pa., 1971; M.A., SUNY-Albany, 1972. Reporter Pitts. Press, 1972-78, asst. city editor, 1978-82, spl. assignment editor, 1982-83, mng. editor, 1983-93; mng. editor Pitts. Post-Gazette, 1993—; bd. dirs. PG Pub. Co.; instr. Community Coll. Allegheny County, 1974-81; Pulitzer Prize juror, 1989, 90. Mem. Task Force Leadership Pitts., 1985-92; v.p. Old Newsboys Charity Fund; bd. dirs. Dapper Dan Charity. Mem. Am. Soc. Newspaper Editors, Women's Press Club. Democrat. Roman Catholic. Avocations: tennis; piano; organ. Office: Pitts Post-Gazette 34 Blvd Of The Allies Pittsburgh PA 15222-1204

ROSS, MALCOLM, mineralogist, crystallographer; b. Washington, Aug. 22, 1929; s. Clarence Samuel and Helen Hall (Frederick) R.; m. Daphne Dee Virginia Riska, Sept. 1, 1956; children: Christopher A., Alexander MacC. BS in Zoology, Utah State U., 1951; MS in Chemistry, U. Md., 1959; PhD in Geology, Harvard U., 1962. Rsch. mineralogist U.S. Geol. Survey, Washington, 1954-5, 61-74, Reston, Va., 1974—; prin. investigator lunar sci. program NASA, 1969-74. Author: Asbestos and Other Fibrous Minerals, 1988; contbr. numerous articles to profl. jours. First Lt. U.S. Army, 1952-54. Recipient Disting. Svc. award, U.S. Dept. Interior, 1986. Fellow Mineral. Soc. Am., Geol. Soc. Am., AAAS; mem. Am. Geophys. Union, Clay Minerals Soc., Mineral Soc. Am. (bd. dirs. treas. 1976-80, v.p. 1990, pres. 1991, Pub. Svc. award, 1990). Avocation: long distance bicycling. Home: 1608 44th St NW Washington DC 20007-2025 Office: US Geol Survey MS # 955 Reston VA 22092

ROSS, MARION, actress; b. Albert Lea, Minn.; children: Jim, Ellen. Grad., San Diego State U. Performed with Globe Theatre, San Diego, LaJolla Summer Theatre; Broadway debut in Edwin Booth; starred in touring prodns. of Never Too Late, Barefoot in the Park, The Glass Menagerie, Long Days Journey Into Night, Love Letter, Steel Magnolias, film debut in Forever Female, 1953; on woman show A Lovely Light, 1988—; TV series include Life with Father, 1953-55, Paradise Bay, 1965-66, Happy Days, 1974-84, Love Boat, 1985-86, Brooklyn Bridge, 1991-93 (Emmy nomination for lead actress in a comedy 1992, 93), Eight for 13, 1995, Evening Star, 1996. Office: Marion Ross Enterprises Inc 14159 Riverside Dr Apt 101 Sherman Oaks CA 91423-2346

ROSS, MARTIN HARRIS, advertising executive; b. Phila., Dec. 7, 1937; s. Simon Max and Sarah (Tofsky) R.; m. Lorraine Rosenthal, Mar. 11, 1962; children: Bradley Allen, Steven Andrew. BS, NYU, 1959. Copywriter William Douglas McAdams, Inc., N.Y.C., 1959-66; sr. copywriter Robert A. Becker, Inc., N.Y.C., 1966-68; copy chief Sudler & Hennessey, Inc., N.Y.C., 1968-73; founder, exec. v.p. Dugan/Farley Comm. (divsn. Bozell Jacobs Kenyon & Eckhardt), Upper Saddle River, N.J., 1973—. Mem. New Hyde Park Republican Club, 1983—. Served with U.S. Army, 1959. Mem. Healthcare Mktg. Coun. (mem. creative com. 1984—). Jewish. Avocations: tennis, golf, antique collecting. Home: 169 Lawrence St New Hyde Park NY 11040-2044 Office: Dugan Farley Comm Divsn Bozell Jacobs Kenyon & Eckhardt 600 E Crescent Ave Saddle River NJ 07458-1846

ROSS, MARY O., religious organization administrator. Pres. Women's Auxiliary Convention of the Nat. Baptist Ch. USA, Detroit. Office: Women's Auxiliary Conv 584 Arden Park Blvd Detroit MI 48202-1304

ROSS, MARY RIEPMA COWELL (MRS. JOHN O. ROSS), retired lawyer; b. Oklahoma City, Okla., Oct. 1, 1910; d. Sears F. and Elizabeth (Van Zwaluwenburg) Riepma; AB, Vassar Coll., 1932; LLB, Memphis State U., 1938; LLD, U. Nebr., 1973; m. Richard N. Cowell, Mar. 1, 1946 (dec. Jan. 1953); m. 2d, John O. Ross, Mar. 31, 1962 (dec. June 1966). Bar: Tenn. 1938, D.C. 1944, N.Y. 1947. Atty. U.S. Govt., Washington, 1940-44; pvt. practice Cromelin & Townsend, Washington, 1944-46. Royall, Koegel & Rogers and predecessors, N.Y.C., 1946-61; individual practice law, 1961-88; dir. 39 E. 79th St. Corp., 1966-73; dir. 795 Fifth Ave. Corp., 1977-90; mem. adv. com. N.Y. Commn. on Estates, 1965-67. Bd. dirs. Silver Cross Day Nursery, N.Y.C., 1963-70, Cunningham Dance Found., 1969-72, Central Park Community Fund, 1977-81, Mary Riepma Ross Film Theatre, 1988—; trustee U. Nebr. Found., 1966—, bd. dirs., 1974-79; hon. trustee Nebr. Art Assn. Mem. Am. Bar Assn., N.Y. Women's Bar Assn. (pres. 1955-57, dir. 1957-63, 74-80, adv. coun. 1963—), Bar Assn. City N.Y. (surrogate cts. com. 1961-65, library com. 1965-78, com. on profl. responsibility 1972-75), Nat. Assn. Women Lawyers (assembly del. 1962-64, 73-74, UN observer 1965-67, v.p. 1967, chmn. 1971 ann. conv., distinguished service award 1973), Vassar Coll. Alumnae Assn., Phi Alpha Delta, Delta Gamma, Dinner Dances, Inc. (bd. govs. 1979-93). Address: 2 E 61st St Apt 2404 New York NY 10021-8402

ROSS, MATTHEW, lawyer; b. N.Y.C., Dec. 28, 1953; s. Harvey and Cecile (Shelsky) R.; m. Susan Ruth Goldfarb, Apr. 20, 1986; children: Melissa Danielle, Henry Max, Thomas Frank. BS in Econs., U. Pa., 1975; JD, U. Va., 1978. Bar: N.Y. 1979, U.S. Dist. Ct. (so. dist.) N.Y. 1979. Assoc. Cravath, Swaine & Moore, N.Y.C., 1978-84; prin., assoc. gen. counsel KPMG Peat Marwick LLP, N.Y.C., 1984-90; prin., deputy gen. counsel Deloitte & Touche LLP, N.Y.C, 1990—. Mem. ABA (corp. law sect.), N.Y. State Bar Assn. (corp. banking and bus. law sect.), Assn. of Bar of City of N.Y. (corp. law com.), Beta Gamma Sigma. Avocations: basketball, tennis, skiing, travel. Home: 17 Carthage Ln Scarsdale NY 10583-7507 Office: Deloitte & Touche LLP 1633 Broadway New York NY 10019-6708

ROSS, MICHAEL AARON, lawyer; b. Newark, Sept. 15, 1941; s. Alexander Ash and Matilda (Blumenthal) R.; m. Leslie Gordon, June 26, 1976; children—Christopher Gordon, Alan Gordon. B.A., Franklin and Marshall Coll., 1963; J.D., Columbia U., 1966; M.S. in Econs., U. London, 1967. Bar: N.Y. 1968. Assoc., then ptnr. Shearman & Sterling, N.Y.C., 1967-93; sr. v.p. Legal Affairs Citicorp, N.Y.C., 1993—. Mem. ABA, Am. Law Inst., New York County Lawyers Assn., Assn. of Bar of City of N.Y., Conf. Bd., University Club. Office: Citicorp 399 Park Ave New York NY 10022-4614

ROSS, MONTE, electrical engineer; b. Chgo., May 26, 1932; s. Jacob Henry and Mildred Amelia (Feller) R.; m. Harriet Jean Katz, Feb. 10, 1957; children—Karyn, Dianne, Ethan. B.S. in Elec. Engring., U. Ill., 1953; M.S., Northwestern U., 1962. Devel. engr. Chance Vought, Dallas, 1953-54; sr. electronics engr. Motorola, Chgo., 1955-56; project engr. Motorola, 1957-59, assoc. dir. research, 1960-63; dir. research Hallicrafters Co., Chgo., 1964-65; mgr. laser tech. McDonnell Douglas Astronautics Co., St. Louis, 1966-70, dir. laser communications; program mgr. Laser Space Communications, 1971-87; pres. Ultradata Sys., Inc. (formerly Laser Data Tech.), St. Louis, 1987—; mem. alumni bd. dept. elec. and computer engring. U. Ill., 1985-90; guest lectr. various univs.; cons. NSF. Author: Laser Receivers, 1966; tech. editor Laser Applications Series, vol. 1, 1971, vol. 2, 1974, vol. 3, 1977, vol. 4, 1980; patentee in field. Recipient St. Louis High Tech. Entrepreneur of Yr. award, 1995; McDonnell Douglas Corp. fellow, 1985. Fellow IEEE; mem. Internat. Laser Communications Soc. (pres. 1988-89), Sigma Xi. Home: 19 Beaver Dr Saint Louis MO 63141-7901 Office: Ultradata Sys Inc 9375 Dielman Industrial Dr Saint Louis MO 63132-2212

ROSS, MURRAY GEORGE, social science educator, university president emeritus; b. Sydney, N.S., Can., Apr. 12, 1910; s. George Robert and Catherine (MacKay) R.; m. Janet Kennedy Lang, May 10, 1940; children—Susan Janet, Robert Bruce. B.A., Acadia U., 1936, D.C.L., 1960; M.A., U. Toronto, 1938, LL.D., 1970; Ed.D., Columbia, 1948; D.Litt., York U., 1970; D.Un., U. York, Eng., 1973; LL.D., Laurentian U., 1977. Prof. U. Toronto, 1950-55, v.p., 1955-60; pres. York U., Downsview, Ont., 1960-70, prof. social sci., 1970—, pres. emeritus, 1972—; former dir. Continental Can Co., Can., McGraw Hill Ryerson, Ltd., Time Can., Capital Growth Fund Ltd., Walwyn, Que. and Toronto; mem. N.Am. adv. bd. Volvo Co. Author: Religious Beliefs of Youth, 1950, The Y.M.C.A. in Canada, 1951, (with C.E. Hendry) New Understanding of Leadership; A Survey and Application of Research, 1957, Case Histories in Community Organization, 1958, The New University, 1961, New Universities in the Modern World, 1965, Community Organization: Theory and Principles; and fgn. edits., 1955, 2d edit., 1965, The University: The Anatomy of Academe, 1976, Canadian Corporate Directors on the Firing Line, 1980, The WayMust Be Tried, 1992; editor: Towards Professional Maturity, 1948; contbr. articles to profl. jours. Past chmn. bd. trustees Hist. Series; trustee Sunnybrooke Hosp. Decorated officer Order of Can., Order of Ont.; recipient Book award Am. Coun. on Edn., 1976, Centennial medal, 1967, Queen's Jubilee medal, 1978, Commemorative medal 125th Anniversary of Can. Confedn. Fellow Am. Sociol. Soc. Home: 75 Highland Crescent, Willowdale, ON Canada M2L 1G7 Office: Glendon Coll, 2775 Bayview Ave, Toronto, ON Canada M4N 3M6

ROSS, MURRAY LOUIS, lawyer, business executive; b. Rochester, N.Y., Apr. 26, 1947; s. Charles Allen and Florence L. (Falk) R.; m. Linda Marie Wabschall, Dec. 26, 1970. AB in History, Lycoming Coll., 1969; JD, U. Toledo, 1972. Bar: Pa. 1976. Asst. to exec. v.p. Falk Machinery Inc., Rochester, 1972-74; asst. v.p. Phila. (Pa.) Stock Exch., 1975-78, dir. securities dept., 1978-79, dir. market surveillance, 1979-82, v.p., corp. sec., 1982—; corp. sec. Phila. (Pa.) Bd. Trade Inc., 1984—, Phila. (Pa.) Depository Trust Co., 1987—, Stock Clearing Corp. Phila., 1986—. Mem. ABA, Phila. Bar Assn., Securities Assn. of Phila. Avocations: wine, golf, ice hockey. Home: 1126 Woodstock Ln West Chester PA 19382-7244 Office: Phila Stock Exchange Inc 1900 Market St Philadelphia PA 19103-3527

ROSS, NELL TRIPLETT, financial consultant, educator, corporate secretary; b. Winterville, Miss., Feb. 14, 1922; d. Ethel Earl and Myrtie (Harrison) Triplett; m. William Dee Ross, Jr., July 25, 1944; 1 child, William Dee III. BA, Millsaps Coll., 1942. Tchr., Consol. Sch. of Chatham (Miss.), 1942-43, Glen Allan (Miss.) Consol. Sch., 1943-46; sec. econs. dept. Duke U., Durham, N.C., 1946; tchr. Durham High Sch., 1947, E.K. Powe Sch., Durham, 1947-48, Lakewood Elem. Sch., Durham, 1948-49; with purchasing dept. La. State U., Baton Rouge, 1949-50; enrollment officer La. Hosp. Service, Inc., Baton Rouge, 1950-51; owner Mentone Plantation, Erwin and Chatham, Miss., 1961—; owner, dir., v.p., corp. sec. Fin. Cons. Svcs., Inc., 1970—. Methodist. Clubs: Baton Rouge Country, Camelot. Home: 2738 Mcconnell Dr Baton Rouge LA 70809-1113 also: 2763 E Bocage Ct Baton Rouge LA 70809-1143

ROSS, NORMAN ALAN, publisher; b. Bklyn., Nov. 1, 1942; s. Robert E. and Bertha (Cohen) R.; m. Leslie Ann Sandler, Oct. 10, 1969; children: Caroline Beth, Juliet Michelle. B.B.A., CCNY, 1964, postgrad., 1967-74. Prodn. mgr. Thomas Pub. Co., 1964-67; systems analyst Reuben H. Donnelley Corp., 1968-70; project mgr. Holt Rinehart & Winston, 1971-73; pres. Clearwater Pub. Co., Inc., N.Y.C., 1973-88, Video Strategies USA, Inc., N.Y.C., 1981-84, Broadside Ltd. pub. Broadside Mag., 1983-87, Norman Ross Pub. Inc., 1987—. Author: Index to the Decisions of the Indian Claims Commission, 1973, Index to the Expert Testimony Before the Indian Claims Commission, 1973, Guide to Architectural Trade Catalogs from the Avery Library, 1989, Guide to Yiddish Children's Books from the Yivo Inst., 1989. Mem. Assn. Info. Mgmt. Home: 392 Central Park W Apt 20-c New York NY 10025-5860 Office: Norman Ross Pub Inc 330 W 58th St New York NY 10019-1827

ROSS, NORMAN ALEXANDER, retired banker; b. Miami, Fla., Jan. 30, 1922; s. Norman DeMille and Beatrice (Dowsett) R.; children: Isabel, Diana. A.B., Stanford U., 1946; postgrad., Trinity Coll., Oxford U., Eng., 1953; D.H.L., Lincoln Coll., Ill., 1959, Fisk U., 1978, Roosevelt U., 1979; Litt.D., Lake Forest Coll., 1967. Airport mgr. Pan Am. Airways, 1943; asst. to producer Metro-Goldwyn-Mayer, 1943-44; ptnr. Norman Ross & Co., 1947-50; owner Norman Ross Record Club, 1951-52; v.p. pub. affairs First Nat. Bank Chgo., 1968-79, sr. v.p. communications dept., 1979-81, sr. v.p. community affairs, 1981-86; pres. Ross-McElroy Prodns., Inc., 1962-68; sr. affairs commentator Sta. WLS-TV, Chgo., 1989—; radio-TV commentator NBC, ABC, Chgo., 1953-64, ABC, Stas. WGN and WBKB, Chgo., 1964-68; former columnist Chgo. Daily News. Served with inf. AUS, World War II. Decorated cavaliere Dell Ordine Repubblica Italiana, Knight 1st Class Republic of Austria, 1989; U.S. Army Outstanding Civilian Service medal; officier and cross of chevalier Legion of Honor France; recipient Peabody award for TV program Off the Cuff 1964. Mem. Phi Gamma Delta. Clubs: Chgo., Racquet, Oxford, Econ. (Chgo.), Wayfarers, Casino. Home: 1200 N Lake Shore Dr Apt 801 Chicago IL 60610-2347 Office: Pilot Knob Bed & Breakfast Inn PO Box 1280 Pilot Mountain NC 27041-1280 *"Doing onto others as you would have them do unto you" is even more important today than it was 2000 years ago.*

ROSS, PATTI JAYNE, obstetrics and gynecology educator; b. Nov. 17, 1946; d. James J. and Mary N. Ross; B.S., DePauw U., 1968; M.D., Tulane, U., 1972; m. Allan Robert Katz, May 23, 1976. Asst. prof. U. Tex. Med. Sch., Houston, 1976-82, assoc. prof., 1982—, dir. adolescent ob-gyn., 1976—, also dir. phys. diagnosis, dir. devel. dept. ob-gyn.; speaker in field. Bd. dirs. Am. Diabetes Assn., 1982—; mem. Rape Coun. Diplomate Am. Bd. Ob-Gyn. Mem. Tex. Med. Assn., Harris County Med. Soc., Houston Ob-Gyn. Soc., Assn. Profs. Ob-Gyn., Soc. Adolescent Medicine, AAAS, Am. Women's Med. Assn., Orgn. Women in Sci., Sigma Xi. Roman Catholic. Clubs: River Oak Breakfast, Profl. Women Execs. Contbr. articles to profl. jours. Office: 6431 Fannin St Houston TX 77030-1501

ROSS, PERCY NATHAN, business executive, newspaper columnist; b. Laurium, Mich., Nov. 22, 1916; s. William and Ruth (Schuman) R.; m. Laurian Averbook, July 2, 1939; children—Steven, Larry. Grad., Calumet High Sch., Mich., 1934. Businessman, owner Ross Tire & Battery Service Laurium, Mich., 1933-36; with West End Iron and Metal Corp., 1936-41, Duluth Hide and Fur Co., 1936-41; owner United Hide and Fur Co., Alexandria, Minn., 1941-44; operator Percy's Fur House, Wadena, Minn., 1944-45; owner N.W. Fur Auction Co., Mpls., 1946-51, Ross & Ross Auctioneers, Inc., Mpls., 1951-58, Indian Head Plastics, Eau Claire, Wis., 1958-59, Poly-Tech Corp., Bloomington, Minn., 1959-69; investment entrepreneur, 1969—; chmn. B. F. Nelson Co., Edina, Minn.; numerous TV appearances including Cable Network News, CBS Morning News with Diane Sawyer, Late Night with David Letterman, profile on 20/20, Larry King Live, Joan Rivers, W-5, Can., Lifestyles of Rich and Famous, Gerardo. Author: Ask for the Moon and Get It, 1987; author nationally syndicated newspaper column Thanks a Million in over 600 newspapers, 1983—; host radio show Thanks a Million, 1990—. Recipient Mike Douglas Spl. People award, 1977, Swede of Yr. award Swedish Community Minn., 1978, Am. Hero award Big Bros./Big Sisters, 1991. Clubs: Decathalon, Oak Ridge Country (Mpls.). Lodge: Masons. Numerous philanthropic activities throughout U.S. and Can., Australia, India and the Orient, 1969—, including his now traditional silver dollar distribution to needy children. Home: 6566 France Ave S PH-04 Edina MN 55435 Office: Thanks A Million 5151 Edina Industrial Blvd Minneapolis MN 55439-3013

ROSS, PHILIP ROWLAND, library director; b. Indiana, Pa., Apr. 7, 1940; s. David Biddle and Miriam Elizabeth (Hill) R.; m. Elaine Lucille George, July 17, 1965; children: Mary Elizabeth, David Bruce. BA, Pa. State U., 1962; MSLS, U. Md., 1969. Postal fin. officer USAF, Tachikawa AFB Tokyo, 1963-65; chief data control and quality control Hdqrs. Air Force Systems Command, Andrews AFB, Md., 1965-68; asst. libr. acquisitions West Liberty (W.Va.) State Coll., 1969-86; dist. mgr. Wheeling (W.Va.) office First Investors Corp., 1986-89; divs. mgr. State of Ark. First Investors Corp., Little Rock, 1989-92; dir. Lonoke (Ark.) Prairie County Regional Libr. System, 1992—; founder, treas.-mgr. West Liberty (W.Va.) State Coll. Fed. Credit Union, 1977-82, chmn. bd., 1984-85; mem. Ark. On Line Network Adv. Com., Little Rock, 1993-96, Libr. Devel. Dist. State Coun., Little Rock, 1993-96, vice chmn., 1996. Maj. USAF, 1962-68; maj. Res., 1968-84, ret. Maj. USAF, 1962-68; maj. Res., 1968-84, ret. Decorated various USAF medals and decorations. Mem. Assn. Ark. Pub. Librs. (treas.-sec. 1993, 94, v.p. pres.-elect 1995, prse. 1996), Ark. Libr. Assn. (com. mem. 1994-95, conv. com. 1996), Lonoke, Ark. C. of C., Am. Legion, Lions. Republican. Methodist. Avocations: reading, gardening, refinishing antique furniture. Home: 691 Wayne Elmore Rd Lonoke AR 72086-9126 Office: Lonoke/Prairie County Regional Libr System 303 Court St Lonoke AR 72086-2858

ROSS, RHODA, artist; b. Boston, Dec. 24, 1941. Student, Skowhegan Sch. Painting; BFA, RISD, 1964; MFA, Yale U., 1966. tchr. NYU, 1994—, Chautaqua (N.Y.) Sch. Art, 1991; participant Art in Embassies Program Dept of State, Havana, Cuba, 1991-93. One-woman shows include Frick Gallery, Belfast, Maine, Yale U., New Haven, Convent of the Sacred Heart, Mcpl. Art Soc., L.I. U., Emma Willard Sch. Dietal Gallery, Marymount Manhattan Coll., N.Y.C., N.Y.C. Landmarks Preservation Commn. 25th Silver Ann., numerous others; groups shows include The Crane Collection, Boston, Michael Ingbar Gallery, N.Y., N.Y. Studio Sch., N.Y.C., Am. U., Washington, Springfield (Mo.) Art Mus., numerous others; permanent collections include The White House, Gracie Mansion, N.Y.C., The Juilliard Sch., N.Y.C., Bankers Trust, Mus. City of N.Y., Chem. Bank Nat. Hqrs., Lehman Coll., Waldorf Astoria Hotel, N.Y.C., Russian Tea Rm., Rose Assocs., Bklyn. Union Gas, numerous other pvt. and pub. collections; artwork appears on New Sch. Social Rsch. catalog cover, Gifts and Decorative Accessories Mag. cover, UNICEF greeting card. Treas. R.I. Sch. Design Alumni Exec. com., 1986-90. Fellow Va. Ctr. for Creative Arts. Mem. RISD Alumni Assn. (treas. 1986, mem. alumni exec. com.), Phi Tau Gamma. Home and Studio: 473 W End Ave New York NY 10024-4934

ROSS, RICHARD FRANCIS, veterinarian, microbiologist, educator; b. Washington, Iowa, Apr. 30, 1935; s. Milton Edward and Olive Marie (Berggren) R.; m. Karen Mae Paulsen, Sept. 1, 1957; children: Scott, Susan. D.V.M., Iowa State U., 1959, M.S., 1961, Ph.D., 1965. Rsch. assoc. Iowa State U., Ames, 1959-61, asst. prof., 1962-65, assoc. prof., 1966-72, prof., 1972—, assoc. dir., assoc. dean, 1990—, interim dean, 1992-93, dean, 1993—; oper. mgr. Vet. Lab. Inc., Remsen, Iowa, 1961-62; postdoctoral fellow Rocky Mountain Lab., NIAID, Hamilton, Mont., 1965-66; sr. U.S. scientist Alexander von Humboldt Found., Bonn, Fed. Republic Germany, 1975-76; chmn. Internat. Research Program on Comparative Mycoplasmology, 1982-86; pres. Iowa State U. Research Found., Ames, 1984-86; Howard Dunne meml. lectr. Am. Assn. Swine Practitioners, 1984. Contbr. numerous articles to profl. publs., 1963—. Named Disting. Prof., Iowa State U., 1982, Hon. Master Pork Producer, Iowa Pork Producers Assn., 1985; recipient faculty citation Iowa State U. Alumni Assn., 1984, Beecham award for rsch. excellence, 1985, Howard Dunne Meml. award Am. Assn. Swine Practitioners, 1988, Am. Feed Mfg. award for rsch., 1995, Sec. of Agr. award for personal and profl. accomplishment, 1996. Mem. Am. Coll. Vet. Microbiologists (diplomate, vice chmn. 1974-75, sec.-treas. 1977-83), Am. Soc. Microbiology (chmn. div. 1985-86), Internat. Orgn. Mycoplasmology (chair 1990-92), AVMA, AAAS, Osborn Research Club, Conf. Rsch. Workers in Animal Diseases (coun. mem., pres. 1992). Republican. Lutheran. Avocations: fishing, gardening, walking, reading. Home: 2003 Northwestern Ave Ames IA 50010-4522 Office: Iowa State U Coll Vet Medicine Ames IA 50011

ROSS, RICHARD S., cardiologist, dean, educator. Undergrad. diploma, Harvard U., MD cum laude. Intern, resident Osler Med. Svc. The Johns Hopkins Hosp., Balt., fellow in physiology, 1952-53, chief med. resident Osler Med. Svc., 1953-90, dean emeritus, 1990—, prof., 1965—; mem. nat. adv. bd. Nat. Heart Lung and Blood Inst., chair cardiovascular study sect., 1966-69. Contbr. over 150 articles to profl. jours. Capt. U.S. Army, 1949-51. Mem. Am. Heart Assn. (pres. 1973-74, Gold Heart award 1976, James B. Herrick award 1982). Office: Sch of Medicine Johns Hopkins Univ Baltimore MD 21218

ROSS, RICHARD STARR, medical school dean emeritus, cardiologist; b. Richmond, Ind., Jan. 18, 1924; s. Louis Francisco and Margaret (Starr) R.; m. Elizabeth McCracken, July 1, 1950; children: Deborah Starr, Margaret Casad, Richard McCracken. Student, Harvard U., 1942-44, M.D. cum laude, 1947; Sc.D. (hon.), Ind. U., 1981; LHD (hon.), Johns Hopkins U., 1994. Diplomate: Nat. Bd. Med. Examiners, Am. Bd. Internal Medicine. (subsplty. bd. cardiovascular disease). Successively intern, asst. resident, chief resident Osler Med. Service, Johns Hopkins Hosp., 1947-54; research fellow physiology Harvard Med. Sch., 1952-53; instr. medicine Johns Hopkins Med. Sch., 1954-56, asst. prof. medicine, 1956-59, assoc. prof., 1959-65, assoc. prof. radiology, 1960-71, prof. medicine, 1965—, Clayton prof. cardiovascular disease, 1969-75; dir. Wellcome Research Lab., Johns Hopkins; physician Johns Hopkins Hosp.; dir. cardiovascular div. dept. medicine, adult cardiac clinic Johns Hopkins Sch. Medicine and Hosp., dir. myocardial infarction research unit, 1967-75; dean med. faculty, v.p. medicine Johns Hopkins U., 1975-90, dean. emeritus, 1990—; Sir Thomas Lewis lectr. Brit. Cardiac Soc., 1969; John Kent Lewis lectr. Stanford U., 1972; bd. dirs. emeritus Johns Hopkins Hosp., Francis Scott Key Med. Ctr.; mem. cardiovascular study sect. Nat. Heart and Lung Inst., 1965-69, chmn. cardiovascular study sect., 1966-69, mem. tng. grant com., 1971-73, chmn. heart panel, 1972-73, adv. coun., 1974-78; mem. Inst. of Medicine, 1976—; chmn. vis. com. Harvard Med. and Dental Sch., 1979-86; bd. overseers Harvard U., 1980-86. Editor Modern Concepts Cardiovascular Disease, 1961-65, The Principles and Practice of Medicine, 17th-22nd edits., 1968-88; mem. editorial bd. Circulation, 1968-74; mem. editorial com. Jour. Clin. Investigation, 1969-73; contbr. numerous articles on cardiovascular disease and physiology to profl. jours. Served as capt. M.C. AUS, 1949-51. Flexner award, Assn Am. Med. Coll., 1994; hon. fellow UMDS, Guy's and St. Thomas' Hosps., London, 1996. Fellow Am. Coll. Cardiology; mem. ACP (master 1979), Boylston Med. Soc., Am. Fedn. Clin. Research, Am. Physiol. Soc., Assn. Am. Physicians, Am. Soc. Clin. Investigation (councillor 1967-69), Am. Clin. and Climatol. Assn. (pres. 1978-79, councillor 1979-83, Metzger lecture 1986), Assn. Univ. Cardiologists (councillor 1972-75), Am. Heart Assn. (chmn. sci. sessions program com. 1965-67, chmn. publs. com. 1970-73, pres. 1973-74, dir. 1974-77, Connor lectr. 1979, Gold Heart award 1976, James B. Herrick award 1982), Heart Assn. Md. (pres. 1967-68), Sigma Xi, Alpha Omega Alpha; corr. mem. Brit. Cardiac Soc., Sociedad Peruana de Cardiologie, Cardiac Soc. Australia and New Zealand. Clubs: Peripatetic, Interurban (pres. 1978), Elkridge, Blue Hill Country Club (Maine). Home: 901 Drohomer Pl Baltimore MD 21210 Office: Johns Hopkins U 1830 E Monument St Baltimore MD 21205-2100

ROSS, ROBERT, health agency administrator. Exec. dir. Muscular Dystrophy Assn., Tucson. Office: Muscular Dystrophy Assn 3300 E Sunrise Dr Tucson AZ 85718*

ROSS, ROBERT JOSEPH, head professional football coach; b. Richmond, Va., Dec. 23, 1936; s. Leonard Aloysius and Martha Isabelle (MMiller) R.; m. Alice Louise Bucker, June 13, 1959; children: Chris, Mary Catherine, Teresa, Kevin, Robbie. BA, Va. Mil. Inst., 1959. Tchr., head football coach Benedictine High Sch., Richmond, 1959-60; tchr., coach Colonial Heights (Va.) High Sch., 1962-65; asst. football coach Va. Mil. Inst., Lexington, 1965-67, Coll. William and Mary, Williamsburg, Va., 1967-71, Rice U., Houston, 1971-72, U. Md., College Park, 1972-73; head football coach The Citadel, Charleston, S.C., 1973-77; head coach U. Md., College Park, 1982-87; head football coach Ga. Inst. Tech., Atlanta, 1987-91; asst. coach Kansas City (Mo.) Chiefs, 1978-82; head coach San Diego Chargers, 1992—. 1st lt. U.S. Army, 1960-62. Named Coach of Yr., Washington Touchdown Club, 1982, Kodak Coach of Yr., 1990, Bobby Dodd Coach of Yr., 1990, Bear Bryant Coach of Yr., 1990, Scripps-Howard Coach of Yr., 1990, Nat. Coach of Yr., CBS Sports, 1990, Coach of Yr., Walter Camp Football Found., 1990, NFL Coach of Yr. UPI, 1992, Pro Football Weekly, 1992, Pro Football Writers' Assn., 1992, Football News, 1992, Football Digest, 1992, Maxwell Football Club, 1992, AFC Coach of Yr. Kansas City 101 Banquet. Mem. Am. Football Coaches Assn., Coll. Football Assn. (coaching com. 1988-92). Roman Catholic. *

ROSS, ROBERT THOMAS, neurologist, educator; b. Winnipeg, Man., Can., June 25, 1924; s. John L. and Alberta I. (Gray) R.; m. Margot Joan Ellacott, May 27, 1950; children: Gray T., John L., Mary E.; m. Angela Morrow Brady, Aug. 14, 1970; children: Diana Gray Salter, Drew Garland Salter. MD, U. Man., 1948. Intern Winnipeg Gen. Hosp., 1947-50; resident Nat. Hosp. Queen Sq., London, 1950-52; lectr. dept anatomy U. Man., Winnipeg, 1953-55, asst. prof. dept. medicine, 1955-59, assoc. prof., 1959-77, prof. medicine, 1977—, head sect. neurology, 1971-84. Editor., pub., founder: Can. Jour. Neurol. Scis., 1972-81; author: How to Examine the Nervous System, 1978, 2d edit., 1985; Syringobulbia-A Contribution to the Pathophysiology of the Brain Stem, 1986, Syncope, 1988. Trustee Man. Med. Svc., 1958-64; pres. United Health Found., Winnipeg, 1969-71; bd. dirs. Man. Med. Coll. Found., 1983-85; mem. senate U. Manitoba, 1988—. Recipient E.L. Drewry prize E.L. Drewry Found., 1948; recipient Can. Centennial Medal, 1967, Queen Elizabeth Jubilee Medal, 1977. Fellow Royal Coll. Physicians (Can. and London), Am. Acad. Neurology; mem. Can. Neurol. Soc. (pres. 1971), Coll. Physicians and Surgeons of Man (pres. 1971), Am. Neurol. Assn., Order of Can. Baptist. Home: 312 Park Blvd, Winnipeg, MB Canada R3P 0G7 Office: Univ Man Sect Neurology, PE126 820 Sherbrook St, Winnipeg, MB Canada R3A 1R9

ROSS, ROBINETTE DAVIS, publisher; b. London, May 16, 1952; d. Raymond Lawrence and Pearl A. (Robbinette) Davis; m. William Bradford Ross, III, Mar. 16, 1979; children: Nellie Tayloe, William Bradford IV; stechild, Aviza Tayloe. Student, Am. U., 1977-78. Asst. to editor The Chronicle of Higher Edn., Washington, 1978, advt. mgr., 1978-82, advt. dir., 1983-88, assoc. pub., 1988-94; assoc. pub. The Chronicle of Philanthropy, 1988-94; publ. The Chronicle of Higher Edn., Washington, 1994—; pub. The Chronicle of Philanthropy, Washington, 1994—. Mem. Nat. Press Club, Am. News Women's Club, City Tavern Club. Episcopalian. Home: 3908 Virgilia St Chevy Chase MD 20815-5026 Office: The Chronicle of Higher Edn 1255 23rd St NW Washington DC 20037-1125

ROSS, RODERIC HENRY, insurance company executive; b. Jamestown, N.Y., July 14, 1930; s. Edwin A. and Mary (Dornberger) R.; m. Patricia Johnson, Aug. 6, 1955; children: Timothy, Amy, Jane, Christopher. BA, Hobart Coll., 1952, LLD (hon.), 1979. CLU, ChFC. Gen. agt. Phila. Life Ins. Co., 1957-70, sr. v.p. mktg., 1972-73, pres., 1973-83, vice chmn., 1983-84; chmn., CEO Keystone State Life Ins. Co., Phila., 1985—; bd. dirs. PNC Bank Corp., Pitts., Hunt Mfg. Corp., Phila., Pa. Mfrs. Corp., Phila., Home Capital Group, Louisville, Ky., Home Mut. Life Ins. Group, Louisville; past chmn. Ins. Fedn. Pa. Rector's warden St. David's Ch., Radnor, Pa., 1989-90; trustee Hobart-William Smith Colls., Geneva, N.Y., 1972—, chmn. bd., 1983-88. Sgt. U.S. Army, 1952-54. Mem. Am. Soc. CLUs, Nat. Assn. Nat. Assn. Life Underwriters, Million Dollar Round Table (life), Union League (former dir.), Orpheus Club, St. David's Golf Club (Wayne, Pa.), Pine Valley Golf Club (Clementon, N.J.). Republican. Episcopalian. Avocations: golf, tennis. Home: 770 Pugh Rd Wayne PA 19087-2011 Office: Keystone State Life Ins Co 1401 Walnut St Philadelphia PA 19102-3128

ROSS, RUSSELL, pathologist, educator; b. St. Augustine, Fla., May 25, 1929; s. Samuel and Minnie (DuBoff) R.; m. Jean Long Teller, Feb. 22, 1956; children: Valerie Regina, Douglas Teller. A.B., Cornell U., 1951; D.D.S., Columbia U., 1955; Ph.D., U. Wash., 1962; DSc (hon.P, Med. Coll. of Pa., 1987. Intern Columbia-Presbyn. Med. Ctr., 1955-56, USPHS Hosp., Seattle, 1956-58; spl. research fellow pathology sch. medicine U. Wash., Seattle, 1958-62, asst. prof. pathology and oral biology sch. medicine and dentistry, 1962-65, assoc. prof. pathology Sch. Medicine, 1965-69, prof. Sch. Medicine, 1969—, adj. prof. biochemistry Sch. Medicine, 1978—, assoc. dean for sci. affairs sch. medicine, 1971-78, chmn. dept. pathology sch. medicine, 1982-94; dir. Ctr. for Vascular Biology, 1991—; vis. scientist Strangeways Rsch. Lab., Cambridge, Eng.; mem. rsch. com. Am. Heart Assn.; mem. adv. bd. Found. Cardiologique Princess Liliane, Brussels, Belgium; life fellow Clare Hall, Cambridge U.; mem. adv. coun. Nat. Heart, Lung and Blood Inst., NIH, 1978-81; vis. prof. Royal Soc. Medicine, U.K., 1987, 95. Editorial bd. Procs. Exptl. Biology and Medicine, 1971-86, Jours. Cell Biology, 1972-74, Exptl. Cell Rsch., 1982-92, Jour. Exptl. Medicine, Growth Factors, Am. Jours. Pathology, Internat. Cell Biology Jour., Circulation, Arteriosclerosis & Thrombosis, Growth Regulation; assoc. editor Arteriosclerosis, 1982-92, Jours. Cellular Physiology, Jours. Cellular Biochemistry; exec. editor Trends in Cariovascular Medicine; reviewing editorial bd. Sci. mag., 1987-90; contbr. articles to profl. jours. Trustee Seattle Symphony Orch. Recipient Birnberg Rsch. award Columbia U., 1975, Nat. Rsch. Achievement award Am. Heart Assn., 1990, Rous-Whiple award Am. Assn. Pathologists, 1992, Glorney-Raisbeck award N.Y. Acad. Medicine, 1995, Gordon Wilson medal Am. Clin. and Climatol. Assn., 1981; named to Inst. Medicine, Nat. Acad. Scis., Japan Soc. Promotion of Sci. fellow, 1985, Guggenheim fellow, 1966-67. Fellow AAAS, Am. Acad. Arts and Scis.; mem. Am. Soc. Cell Biology, Tissue Culture Assn., Am. Assn. Pathologists (Rous-Whipple award 1992), Internat. Soc. Cell Biology, Electron Microscope Soc. Am., Am. Soc. for Investigative Pathology (pres. 1994-95), Am. Heart Assn. (fellow Coun. on Arteriosclerosis, Nat. Rsch. Achievement award 1990), Royal Micros. Soc., Harvey Soc. (hon.), Am. Soc. Biochemistry and Molecular Biology, Romanian Acad. Med. Scis. (hon.), Royal Belgian Acad. Scis. (fgn. corr. mem.), Sigma Xi. Home: 3812 48th Ave NE Seattle WA 98105-5227 Office: U Wash Sch Medicine 1959 NE Pacific St Seattle WA 98195-0004

ROSS, RUSSELL MARION, political science educator; b. Washington, Iowa, June 2, 1921; s. Harold Ellis and Lucille Carrie (Dorris) R.; m. Jo Ellen Rude; children: Sheryl Ross, Julie. BA, U. Iowa, 1942; cert., Harvard U., 1945; MA, U. Iowa, 1946, PhD, 1948. Instr. dept. polit. sci. U. Iowa, Iowa City, 1946-48, asst. prof., 1948-52, assoc. prof., 1952-60, research prof., 1963-64, prof., 1965—, chmn. dept., 1970-91; prof. emeritus, 1991—; adminstrv. asst. to atty. gen., Iowa, 1960; exec. asst. to Gov. Iowa, 1961-62. Author: Iowa Government and Administration, 1958, State and Local Government and Administration, 1966, Gubernatorial Transitions, 1985, Political Science at the University of Iowa, 1990. Chmn. Regional Planning Commn., 1966-68; pres. Iowa City Community Sch. Bd., 1969-70; chmn. Iowa Campaign Finance Disclosure Commn., 1973-77; Mayor University Heights, 1954-60; Bd. dirs. Goodwill Industries S.E. Iowa. Served to lt. USNR, 1942-45. Mem. AAUP, Internat. City Mgrs. Assn. (hon.), Am. Pub. Adminstrn. Soc., Am. Polit. Sci. Assn., Mid-West Polit. Sci. Assn., Phi Beta Kappa, Phi Delta Kappa, Pi Sigma Alpha, Alpha Sigma Lambda. Club: Kiwanian. Home: 315 Highland Dr Iowa City IA 52246-1602

ROSS, SADYE LEE TATMAN, home health geriatrics nurse; b. Albuquerque, Dec. 5, 1937; d. Charles Robert Tatman and Cecilia Marie Zimmer; m. E. Ray Ross, Nov. 16, 1974. Diploma, Henry Ford Hosp., 1959. RN, Miss., Calif.; cert. gerontol. nurse. Head nurse Orange Meml. Hosp., Orlando, Fla., 1963-64; assoc. dir. Coll. of Calif. Med. Affiliates, San Francisco, 1964-65; ICU staff nurse So. Pacific Hosp., San Francisco, 1965-66; office mgr. Mortimer Weiss, M.D., San Francisco, 1966-70; staff nurse Kwajalein (Marshall Island) Missile Range Hosp., 1970-72, nursing supr., 1974-76; nursing svc. supr. St. Francis Hosp., San Francisco, 1972-74; staff nurse Lawrence County Nursing Ctr., Monticello, Miss., 1989-93, South Miss. Home Health, Prentiss, Miss., 1993—. Mem. Nat. Gerontol. Nurses Assn., Sorosis Club (pres. 1992-94). Avocations: quilting, needlepoint. Home: RR 2 Box 372 Silver Creek MS 39663-9504 Office: South Miss Home Health PO Box 663 Prentiss MS 39474-0663

ROSS, SALLY PRICE, artist, mural painter; b. Cleve., Oct. 25, 1949; d. Philip E. and Mimi (Einhorn) Price; m. Howard D. Ross, Mar. 3, 1979; children: Sasha, Emily. BFA, Kent State U., 1971; MA, U. Iowa, 1974, MFA, 1975; student, Art Students League, N.Y.C., 1976-78. art cons. Art Options, Cleve., 1990-96; 1st and only woman artist to paint murals in the U.S. Capitol/Ho. of Reps. corridors, 1978-79, Comm. to paint two Murals for Rainbow Babies Children's Hosp., (Univ. Hosp.), Cleve. Art exhbns. include Cain Park Art Gallery, Cleve., 1967, Jewish Cmty. Ctr. Cleve., 1967, 86, Canton (Ohio) Art Inst., 1969, Studio Theatre, Iowa City, 1973; designed and executed murals Montefiore Nursing Home, Cleve., 1995; commns. include Univ. Hosps., Cleve., 1996. Edwin Abbey scholar, 1975-77, Fresco scholar Skowhegan Sch. Painting and Sculpture, 1977. Home: 25 Millcreek Ln Chagrin Falls OH 44022-1265

ROSS, SAMUEL D., JR., insurance company executive; b. 1933. Pres., ceo Medical Servives Assn of Pa., Camp Hill, 1970—. Office: Medical Services Assn of PA 1800 Center St Camp Hill PA 17089-1702*

ROSS, SHELDON JULES, dentist; b. N.Y.C., June 17, 1924; s. Sam and Regina (Rosner) R.; 1 stepson, Nathan Sudnow; m. Carolyn L. M. Loesch, Apr. 26, 1946; children: Jane, Eric, Ellen, Lisa. D.D.S., NYU, 1949. Diplomate: Am. Bd. Periodontology, Am. Bd. Oral Medicine (examiner 1980-85). Pvt. practice periodontology N.Y.C., 1949—; prof. periodontics and oral medicine N.Y. U. Sch. Dentistry, 1949—; resident oral medicine Montefiore Hosp., N.Y.C., 1956-57; charge periodontics Montefiore Hosp., 1951-70, oral medicine, 1951-81, cons., 1981-95; attending charge oral medicine and periodontics Beth Abraham Hosp., Bronx, N.Y., 1961-81, cons., 1981-87; cons. in oral medicine Goldwater Meml. Hosp., N.Y.C., 1982—; former cons., lectr. periodontics and oral medicine Cabrini Hosp. and Med. Ctr., N.Y.C.; lectr. in field; honored lectr. Internat. Odontological Congress, Maringa, Brazil, 1972. Editor Jour. Oral Medicine, 1971-88, Annals of Dentistry, 1971-88; contbr. articles to dental jours., chpts. to textbooks. Served with AUS, 1942-43. Fellow Am. Coll. Dentists, N.Y. Acad. Dentistry (v.p. 1989-90, pres.-elect 1990-91, pres. 1991-92), Am. Acad. Oral Medicine (pres. 1980); mem. ADA, Am. Assn. Dental Editors, Am. Acad. Oral Medicine, Am. Acad. Oral Pathology, Am. Acad. Periodontology, N.E. Soc. Periodontists, Orgn. Tchrs. Oral Diagnosis, Am. Heart Assn., Omega Kappa Upsilon. Home and Office: 40 Twisting Ln Wantagh NY 11793-1947 *None admit to having any new ideals except loving redemption of some souls: Man expects rational and normal deliberation instead.*

ROSS, SHERMAN, psychologist, educator; b. N.Y.C., Jan. 1, 1919; s. Max R. and Rachel (Khoutman) R.; m. Jean Goodwin, Aug. 18, 1945; children: Norman Kimball, Claudia Lisbeth (Mrs. Overway), Michael Lachlan. B.S., CCNY, 1939; A.M., Columbia U., 1941, Ph.D., 1943. Asst. psychology, research psychologist Columbia U., 1941-44; asst., then assoc. prof. psychology Bucknell U., 1946-50; research fellow N.Y. Zool. Soc., 1948; guest investigator, sci. asso. Jackson Lab., 1947-77; assoc. prof., then prof. psychology U. Md., 1950-60; spl. cons. Psychopharmacology Svc. Ctr. NIMH, 1956-63; asst. chief NIMH, 1956-57; exec. sec. edn. and tng. bd., sci. affairs officer APA, 1960-68; prof. psychology Howard U., 1968-89, emeritus, 1989—; exec. sec., spl. asst., assembly of behavioral and social scis. Nat. Acad. Scis.-NRC, 1968-76; lectr. Himmelfarb Mobile U., 1994—; cons. VA, Human Ecology Fund, Stanford Research Inst., Office Naval Research,

U.S. Sci. Exhibit, Am. U., HRB-Singer, Inc.; bd. dirs. Interdisciplinary Communications Assocs., Washington; adv. council Woodrow Wilson Rehab. Center Found.; mem. Md. Bd. Examiners Psychology, 1957-58, 84-89; chmn. bd. dirs. Inst. for Research, State Coll., Pa.; mem. Montgomery County Health Planning Commn.; mem. Md. Statewide Health Coordinating Coun., Met. Washington Area Council of Health Planning Agys., Emergency Med. Svcs. Adv. Council; commr. health emeritus Montgomery County, Md. Trustee Carver Research Found., Tuskegee U. Served to lt. (j.g.) USNR, 1944-46; capt. USNR (ret.). Fellow APA, Am. Coll. Neuropsychopharmacology, Royal Soc. Health, Washington Acad. Scis.; mem. Aerospace Med. Assn., Am. Soc. Zoologists, Ecol. Soc., Ergonomics Rsch. Soc., Md. Psychol. Assn. (pres. 1973-74), D.C. Psychol. Assn. (pres. 1982), Cosmos Club (Washington), Sigma Xi (pres. U. Md. 1957-58, pres. Howard U. 1983-84), Phi Kappa Phi, Psi Chi (nat. pres. 1964-68). Home: 382 Russell Ave Gaithersburg MD 20877-2863 also: Glen Mary Rd Bar Harbor ME 04609-1301

ROSS, SHIRLEY S., retired English educator; b. Hardy, Ky., Feb. 15, 1936; d. Thomas Jefferson and Margaret (Stiltner) Stacy; m. Clarence Edwin Ross, Aug. 17, 1957; children: Cheryl Ann, Elizabeth Kay, Naomi Ruth. BA, Milligan (Tenn.) Coll., 1958. 7th grade English tchr. Galion (Ohio) city schs.; part-time staff Lifeline Christian Mission, Haiti; lectr. in field. Mem. NEA, Nat. Coun. Tchrs. English, Ohio Edn. Assn., Galion Edn. Assn., Order Ea. Star, Clan Ross Assn. Am. (dep. commr. of Ohio). Home: 235 S Jefferson St Galion OH 44833-2417

ROSS, STAN, accounting firm executive; b. 1939. With Kenneth Leventhal & Co., L.A., 1964—, now mng. ptnr. Office: Kenneth Leventhal & Co 2049 Century Park E Ste 1700 Los Angeles CA 90067-3101*

ROSS, STANFORD G., lawyer, former government official; b. St. Louis, Oct. 9, 1931; m. Dorothy Rabin, June 9, 1958; children: John, Ellen. AB with honors, Washington U., 1953; JD magna cum laude, Harvard U., 1956. Bar: D.C. 1969, Calif. 1956, N.Y. 1959. Assoc. firm Irell & Manella, Los Angeles, 1956-57; teaching fellow, research asst. Harvard Law Sch., 1957-58; assoc. firm Dewey, Ballantine, Bushby, Palmer & Wood, N.Y.C., 1958-61; asst. tax legis. counsel U.S. Dept. Treasury, 1961-63; prof. law N.Y. U., 1963-67; White House staff asst. to Pres. Johnson, 1967-68; gen. counsel U.S. Dept. Transp., 1968-69; ptnr. Caplin & Drysdale, Washington, 1969-78; commr. Social Security Adminstrn., Washington, 1978-79; ptnr. Califano, Ross & Heineman, Washington, 1980-82, Arnold & Porter, Washington, 1983—; pub. trustee Social Security Trust Funds, Washington, 1990-95. Editor: Harvard Law Rev, 1954-56. Mem. ABA, Fed. Bar Assn., Internat. Fiscal Assn., Nat. Acad. Social Ins. (bd. dirs.). Office: Arnold & Porter 555 Twelfth St NW Washington DC 20004-1202

ROSS, STANLEY RALPH, writer, publisher, producer, software manufacturing executive; b. N.Y.C., July 22, 1940; s. Morris Harvey and Blanche (Turer) R.; m. Neila Hyman, Dec. 14, 1957; children: Andrew Steven, Lisa Michelle Turer, Nancy Ellen. Student, Pratt Inst.; DD, Universal Life Ch., Modesto, Calif., 1973; PhD in Lit., L.A. U., 1976. Self-employed photographer N.Y.C., 1956; copywriter Fuller, Smith & Ross, Los Angeles, 1956-60, Universal Pictures, Los Angeles, 1960-61; advt. exec. Universal Studios, Universal City, Calif., 1960-62; program exec. ABC-TV, Los Angeles, 1961-63; creative dir. Cole, Fischer & Rogow, Beverly Hills, Calif., 1963-65, Becker Advt., Long Beach, Calif., 1964-65; pres., freelance film and TV writer Neila, Inc., Los Angeles, 1965—; assoc. prof. U. So. Calif.; guest lectr. Calif. Luth. Coll., L.A. Coll., Sherwood Oaks U., others; tchr. writing, assoc. prof. U. So. Calif.; cons. in field; exec. v.p., bd. dirs. Crime Books, Wilmette, Ill., 1983—; bd. dirs. The Writers Group, L.A.; pres., CEO Comedy Software, Ltd., Disktop Pub., Inc.; pres. Hollywood Showcase, Inc.; new products cons. RJR Nabisco. Author: Games for Planes, 1974, Speak When You Hear the Beep, 1975, Swan Song, Any Port in a Storm, The Motion Picture Guide; writer TV programs All in the Family, The Monkees, Batman, The Man from UNCLE; developer programs Wonder Woman, The Electric Company, That's My Mama, The Kallikaks, The Monster Squad, The Challenge of the Sexes; Scriptwriter Banacek, Colombo, Kids, Inc., Tales from the Crypt, TV film Coffee, Tea or Me?, Gold of the Amazon Women, Murder at the Mardi Gras, The Town That Went on a Diet, Three on a Date, Mrs. R., (films) The Answer, Tomorrow's News, Jojo, Rodeo Drive, Follow Me, Saturday Matinee; editor, author: (with Jay Robert Nash) The Motion Picture Guide, feature film ency., 24 vols.; actor appeared in (TV) Punky Brewster, The Facts of Life, Falcon Crest, Ellery Queen, Hart to Hart, Bill Cosby Show, Double Life of Henry Phyfe, Divorce Court, Superior Court, Family Medical Center, Superman, The Munsters Today (films) Sleeper, Romantic Comedy, John Goldfarb Please Come Home, Tony Rome, Sideout, numerous commls.; voice over cartoons, commls.; columnist Restaurant Row mag. Vol. The Thalians, Beverly Hills, 1972—, Nosotros, Los Angeles, 1985—, The Soc. of Singers. Recipient UNICEF award, 1974, West Los Angeles Coll. Presdl. citation, 1974, Carson (Calif.) citation, 1973, Cert. Appreciation Personal Freedom Alliance, 1974, Inkpot award San Diego Comicon, 1977, Emmy award nomination Nat. Acad. TV Arts and Scis., 1970, 71, 72, Golden Eagle awards, Nat. Assn. Theater Owners awards, 3 Emmy nominations Nat. Acad. TV Arts and Scis.; named to Bklyn. Hall of Fame Celebrity Path, 1992. Mem. Writers Guild Am. West (award 1971, 72, 74, Family Film award 1990), Producers Guild, Dirs. Guild, Dramatists Guild, Screen Actors Guild, AFTRA, ASCAP, Hon. Order Ky. Cols, TV Acad., Beverly Hills C. of C. Republican. Mem. Universal Life Ch. Club: Saints and Sinners (Los Angeles). Avocations: composing, writing lyrics, baseball, oil painting. Home: 451 S Beverwil Dr Beverly Hills CA 90212-4209 Office: Neila Inc PO Box 3605 Beverly Hills CA 90212-0605 *My goal in life has been to have a good time and do only what I care to. I feel that I cannot do something that is alien to my nature and have so refused over the years until I discovered that writing was my true vocation. In the past three decades, I have enjoyed myself and had more success than in all my former work years due to this independence. The only other principle I espouse is the law of Karma. For every effect, there is a cause; and every good thing one does is noted in a grand book and the rewards for doing good are reaped here on earth.*

ROSS, STUART B., corporate financial executive; b. N.Y.C., Apr. 16, 1937; s. Bernard Theodore and Ruth R.; m. Stephanie Banks, Dec. 15, 1962; children: Jessica, Benjamin. BS, NYU, 1958; MBA, CCNY, 1966. Pub. acct. Harris, Kerr, Forster, N.Y.C., 1958-63; fin. analyst MacMillan Co., N.Y.C., 1963-66; with Xerox Corp., Stamford, Conn., 1966—, CFO, 1985—, exec. v.p., 1990—, also mem. pvt. sector coun., conf. bd.; chmn., CEO, Xerox Fin. Svc., Stamford, 1990—; bd. dirs. ECKO Group, Inc. Mem. AICPA, Fin. Execs. Inst. Office: Xerox Corp PO Box 1600 800 Long Ridge Rd Stamford CT 06904*

ROSS, SUE, entrepreneur, author, fundraising executive; b. Chgo., Feb. 2, 1948; d. Irving and Rose (Stein) R. BA in Secondary Edn., Western Mich. U., 1971; postgrad., Northwestern U., Chgo. State U., U. Ill., 1971-75. Dir. youth employment Ill. Youth Svcs. Bur., Maywood, Ill., 1978-79; exec. dir. Edn. Resource Ctr., Chgo., 1979-82; asst. dir. devel. Art Inst. Chgo., 1982-83, mgr. govt. affairs, 1983-84, dir. govt. affairs, 1984-85; v.p. devel. Spertus Inst. of Judaica, Chgo., 1985-90; mgmt. and fundraising counsel Sue Ross Enterprises, Chgo. and San Francisco, 1990—; founder, pres. Kid Angels Internat., San Francisco, 1994—; lectr. Sch. Art Inst., Chgo., 1982-85, Episcopalian Archdiocese, Chgo., 1984, Nat. Soc. Fund Raising Execs. and Donor's Forum, Chgo., 1987; instr. DePaul U. Sch. for New Learning, 1987-88, Columbia Coll., Chgo., 1980-91. Resident counsel for devel. The Joffrey Ballet, 1990-91; adv. panelist Chgo. Office Fine Arts, 1981-82; v.p., bd. dirs. Lines Contemporary Ballet, 1995—; mem. adv. coun. Greater Chgo. Food Depository, 1984-85; exec. com. Chgo. Coalition Arts in Edn., 1981-82; mem. info. svcs. com. Donors' Forum Chgo., 1986-88, mem. internationally renowned Gospel Choir of Glide Meml., 1991-93, San Francisco City Chorus, 1994; mem. com. Congregation Sherith Israel, San Francisco Angel Club, 1994, Angel Collector's Club of Am., 1994—, Angels of World, 1994—; resident counsel for devel. The 1995 Children's World Peace Festival. Mem. Nat. Soc. Fund Raising Execs. (mem. svcs. com. Golden Gate chpt. 1993). Democrat. Jewish. Avocations: community service, singing. Home and Office: 1807 Octavia St San Francisco CA 94109-4328

ROSS, THOMAS BERNARD, communications company executive; b. N.Y.C., Sept. 2, 1929; s. Henry M. and Evelyn (Timothy) R.; m. Gunilla Ekstrand, Nov. 2, 1963; children: Maria, Anne, Kristina. BA, Yale, 1951. Reporter Internat. News Svc., 1955-58, UPI, 1958; mem. staff Chgo. Sun-Times, 1958-77, mem. staff Washington Bur., 1958-68; fgn. corr. Chgo. Sun-Times, Beirut and Paris, 1968-70; Washington bur. chief Chgo. Sun-Times, 1970-77; asst. sec. def. for pub. affairs, 1977-81; dir. corp. comm. Celanese Corp., 1981-82; sr. v.p. corp. affairs RCA Corp., 1982-86; sr. v.p. NBC News, 1986-90; sr. v.p., dir. media rels. worldwide Hill and Knowlton, N.Y.C., 1990-94; spl. asst. to pres., sr. dir. pub. affairs NSC, White House, Washington, 1994-95; v.p. comms. Globalstar, N.Y.C., 1995—. Author: (with David Wise) The U-2 Affair, 1962, The Invisible Government, 1964, The Espionage Establishment, 1967. Lt. (j.g.) USNR, 1951-54. Nieman fellow Harvard U., 1964; recipient Marshall Field award, 1961, 71; decorated Def. Disting. Pub. Svc. medal. Mem. Coun. on Fgn. Rels., Elizabethan Club (New Haven), Gridiron Club (Washington), Century Club (N.Y.C.). Home: 1148 5th Ave New York NY 10128-0807 Office: 600 Third Ave New York NY 10016

ROSS, THOMAS J., JR., personal finanical adviser; b. N.Y.C., Aug. 25, 1954; s. Thomas J. Sr. and Margaret (Byrne) R.; m. Elise Mary Bishop, Sept. 20, 1980; children: Kaitlyn Ann, John Patrick, Brendan Christopher. BA in English magna cum laude, Boston Coll., 1976; MBA in Fin., U. Pa., 1980. Cons. Wharton Applied Rsch. Ctr., Phila., 1978-80; part owner, v.p. Asset Mgmt. Group, Parsippany, N.J., 1980-86; dir. Coopers & Lybrand, Parsippany, 1986-89, ptnr., 1989-92, regional ptnr. personal fin. svcs. group, N.Y. Metro Area, 1992—; mem. adv. bd. Summit Bank, Chatham, N.J.; mem. nat. PFS steering com. Coopers & Lybrand, N.Y.C., 1987—, mem. investment policy com., 1996—. Editor newsletter Growing Your Wealth, 1992—; contbr. numerous tax and fin. articles to Chief Exec. Mag., Bottom Line Fin., N.J. Law Jour. Mem. Kickoff Classic Tix Com., Ind. Coll. Fund of N.J., Summit, 1990—; mem. Boston Coll. Alumni Admissions Coun., Chestnut Hill, Mass., 1976—; mem. No. West N.J. Estate Planning Coun., 1986—; soccer, baseball and lacrosse coach Mountain Lakes Youth Leagues, 1989—; mem. pre-cana team St. Catherine of Siena. Recipient scholarships Boston Coll., Imaculate Heart Guild, others, 1972-76; named Fin. Coun. of Yr., Asset Mgmt. Group, 1983-85. Mem. AICPAs, N.J. Soc. CPAs (com. mem. 1990-92), Wharton Bus. Club of N.Y., Fiddlers Elbow Club, Rockaway River C. of C. (house mem. 1991—), Park Ave. Club, Boston Coll. Clubs of N.J. and N.Y.C. Avocations: golf, racquetball, coaching, reading. Home: 140 Kenilworth Rd Mountain Lakes NJ 07046-1156 Office: Coopers & Lybrand One Sylvan Way Parsippany NJ 07054

ROSS, THOMAS MCCALLUM, professional society administrator; b. Hamilton, Ont., Can., May 5, 1931; s. Laverne Robinson and Della Louise (McCallum) R.; m. Marguerite Hilda Ross, Aug. 14, 1954; children: Thomas Wayne, Gregory (dec.), Karyn. Mgr. Sutherland Pharmacy, Hamilton, 1955-60; assoc. sec. Can. Pharm. Assn., Toronto, Ont., 1960-63; mem. research staff Royal Commn. Health Services Govt. Can., Ottawa, Ont., 1963-64; exec. dir. Can. Retail Hardware Assn., Toronto, 1964—. Bd. dirs. People for Sunday Assn., pres. 1987-88. Founding fellow Hardware Mgmt. Inst.; mem. Internat. Fedn. Ironmongers Assn. (coun. 1970—), Can. Soc. Assn. Execs. (chmn. edn. com. 1986-88, bd. dirs. 1990-92, Pinnacle award 1989), Am. Soc. Assn. Execs., Can. C. of C. Home: 59 Walby Dr, Oakville, ON Canada Office: Can Retail Hardward Assn, 6800 Campobello Rd, Mississauga, ON Canada

ROSS, VERNON, JR., software engineer; b. Utica, Miss., Mar. 18, 1960; s. Vernon and Lee Dellar (Marks) R. BS in Computer Sci. and Math., Jackson State U., 1982; MS in Computer Edn., Phila. Coll. Textiles & Sci., 1991. Assoc. programmer Burroughs Corp., Downingtown, Pa., 1982-86; software analyst GE Co., King of Prussia, Pa., 1986-89; sr. systems analyst Unisys Corp., Blue Bell, Pa., 1989-91; sr. tech. tng. specialist Martin Marietta Co., King of Prussia, 1991—. Sch. bd. dirs. Norristown (Pa.) Area Sch. Dist., 1994—; mem. com. Montgomery County Ctr. for Tech. Studies, Plymouth Meeting, Pa. Ednl. grantee Network of Vol. Assn., 1994. Mem. Am. Soc. for Tng. and Devel., Pa. Sch. Bd. Assn., Lions, Alpha Phi Alpha. Democrat. Methodist. Avocations: travel, skiing, singing. Home: 534 E Marshall St Norristown PA 19401

ROSS, VONIA PEARL, insurance agent, small business owner; b. Taylorville, Ill., Dec. 4, 1942; d. Alvin Clyde and Lois Eva (Weller) Brown; m. Wyatt Gene Ross, Nov. 11, 1962 (Div. Nov. 1986); children: Craig Allen Ross, Cayle Allen Ross. Student, So. Ill. U., 1962-64, Palomar Coll., 1986-88, San Diego State U., 1988-90. Real estate agt. Joe Foster Agy., Collinsville, Ill., 1964-69; ofice mgr. real estate Bank of St. Louis, 1969-73; real estate agt. Palmer-Stelman, San Diego, 1986-89; office mgr. real estate McMillin Realty, San Diego, 1989-90; mgr., ins. agt. Calif. Plus Ins., San Diego, 1990-93; prin. Vonia Ross Ins. Agy., 1993—, Bernardo Flooring, 1993—; mem. Calif. Assn. Real Estate, Sacramento, 1986—, San Diego Bd. Realtors, 1986—, Health Underwriters, 1991—. Mem. adv. com. Rancho Bernardo Libr. Campaign, 1994—; active NOW, San Diego, 1988; mem. activist Barbara Boxer Campaign, San Diego, 1992, Susan Golding Campaign, San Diego, 1992, Barbara Warden Campaign for San Diego City Councilwoman. Scholar Ill. Assembly, 1962. Mem. Rancho Bernardo C. of C. (v.p., bd. dirs. 1993—, pres.-elect 1996—), Soroptimists (pres. Rancho Bernardo 1993-94, 95-96). Avocations: walking, biking, mountain climbing, hiking, tennis, music, reading. Home: 18284 Fernando Way San Diego CA 92128-1213

ROSS, WALTER BEGHTOL, music educator, composer; b. Lincoln, Nebr., Oct. 3, 1936; s. Robert Thurber and Barbara Adeline (Ellis) R.; m. Marion Helen Wright, July 22, 1960; 1 child, Douglas Campbell. BA, U. Nebr., 1960, MusM, 1962; student, Inst. Torcuato Di Tella, Buenos Aires, 1965-66; D of Mus. Arts, Cornell U., 1966. Asst. prof. music CUNY, Cortland, 1966-67; prof. U. Va., Charlottesville, 1967—; mem. judging panel symphonic awards ASCAP, 1978, Internat. Biennial Composition Contest, P.R., 1981, Va. chpt. Coll. Band Dir.'s Nat. Assn. Nat. Band Composition Contest, 1982, 88; bass Blue Ridge Chamber Orch., Charlottesville, 1992—. Composer over 100 works, including compositions for symphony orch., symphonic band, brass, chamber music, piano, voice, opera, theatre, and film; recs. include Concerto for Piano and Orch., Wind Quintet, Nos. 2 and 3, Harlequinade for piano and wind quintet, Escher's Sketches, Concerto for Wind Quintet and String Orch., also others. Nominee Pulitzer Prize, 1973; recipient ASCAP award, 1974—, 1st prize Internat. Trombone Assn., 1982; grantee Am. Music Ctr., 1983; fellow Presser Found., 1958, 59, Orgn. Am. States, 1965, NEA, 1975. Democrat. Avocations: chess, cooking, amateur astronomy. Office: U Va Music Dept Charlottesville VA 22903

ROSS, WENDY CLUCAS, newspaper editor, journalist; b. Balt., Apr. 15, 1942; d. Charles Max and Jean (Talbot) Clucas; m. David N. Ross, Sept. 5, 1964 (div. 1979). BA, Bradley U., 1964. Women's editor DeKalb (Ill.) Daily Chronicle, 1968-69; reporter Chgo. Tribune, 1969-70; copy editor, mag. editor Mpls. Tribune, 1970-72; copy editor Peoria (Ill.) Jour. Star, 1973-75, Miami (Fla.) Herald, 1975-77; asst. news editor Washington Post, 1977-83, dep. news editor, 1983-87, news editor, 1987-93; asst. mng. editor news desk, 1993—. Recipient award of excellence Soc. Newspaper Design, 1985, 87-91, Disting. Alumnae award Bradley U. Centurion Soc., 1994; Nieman fellow Harvard U., 1983-84. Avocations: skiing, sailing, reading, travel. Office: The Washington Post 1150 15th St NW Washington DC 20071-0001

ROSS, WILLIAM JARBOE, lawyer; b. Oklahoma City, May 9, 1930; s. Walter John and Bertha (Jarboe) R.; m. Mary Lillian Ryan, May 19, 1962; children: Rebecca Anne Roten, Robert Joseph, Molly Kathleen. B.B.A., U. Okla., 1952, LL.B., 1954. Bar: Okla. 1954. Since practiced in Oklahoma City; asst. municipal counselor Oklahoma City, 1955-60; mem. firm Rainey, Ross, Rice & Binns, 1960—, partner, 1965—; mem. admissions and grievences com. U.S. Dist. Ct. (we. dist.) Okla.; bd. dirs. PetroUnited Terminals, Inc.; bd. dirs., mem. exec. com. Boatmen's First Nat. Bank of Okla. Past pres. bd. dirs. St. Anthony's Hosp. Found.; bd. dirs. Harn Homestead; trustee Ethics and Excellence in Journalism Found., Inasmuch Found. Mem. Okla. Bar Assn., Okla. Heritage Assn. (chmn. edn. com.), The Newcomen Soc., Phi Alpha Delta, Beta Theta Pi. Clubs: Oklahoma City Golf and Country, Econ. (Okla.). Lodges: Rotary, K.C. Home: 6923 Avondale Ct Oklahoma City OK 73116-5008

ROSS, WILLIAM WARFIELD, lawyer; b. Washington, Oct. 3, 1926; s. W. Warfield and Vera Elfleda (Payne) R.; m. Jennie Fitch, Jan. 30, 1963; children—James, Mary, Billy. A.B., St. John's Coll., Annapolis, Md., 1948; LL.B., Yale U., 1951. Bar: D.C. 1951. Legal asst. Exec. Office Pres. Harry S. Truman, 1952-53, Pres. Dwight D. Eisenhower, 1953; atty. appellate sect. civil div. Dept. Justice, Washington, 1954-57; asst. to solicitor FPC, Washington, 1957-59; ptnr. Wald, Harkrader & Ross, Washington, 1963-87, Pepper, Hamilton & Scheetz, Washington, 1987-91; adj. prof. Cornell U. Grad. Sch. Bus. and Pub. Adminstrn., 1977-80; chmn. D.C. Council Commn. on Bd. Appeals and Rev. of D.C. Govt., 1972. Chmn. Nat. Capital area ACLU, 1966-68; chmn. audit hearing panel Title I ESEA of 1965, 1976-80. Served with USN, 1945-46. Mem. ABA (chmn. sect. adminstrv. law 1978-79), Bar Assn. D.C. (chmn. adminstrv. law sect. 1968-69, gov. 1969-70), D.C. Bar, Fed. Bar Assn., Fed. Energy Bar Assn. (contbr. articles to jour.). Club: Metropolitan (Washington). Home: 4978 Sentinel Dr Apt 303 Bethesda MD 20816-3573

ROSSANO, AUGUST THOMAS, environmental engineering educator; b. N.Y.C., Feb. 1, 1916; s. August Thomas and Rosa (Cosenza) R.; m. Margie Chrisney, Dec. 6, 1944; children: August Thomas III, Marilyn, Pamela, Jeannine, Renee, Christopher, Stephen, Teresa. B.S., M.I.T., 1938; M.S., Harvard U., 1941, S.D., 1954. Diplomate Am. Acad. Environ. Engrs., Am. Bd. Indsl. Hygiene. Commd. lt. (j.g.) USPHS, 1941, advanced through grades to capt., 1955; assigned Hdqrs. USPHS, 1941, 48, Taft Engrng. Ctr., Cin., 1954-59; ret., 1963; prof. air resource engring. U. Wash., Seattle, 1963-81, prof. emeritus, 1981—; pres. Rossano Inc., 1981—; vis. prof. Calif. Inst. Tech., 1960-63; Mem. expert adv. panel on air pollution WHO, Geneva, 1960—, Pan Am. Health Orgn., 1975—; cons. European office WHO, 1960—, U.S. Dept. HEW, 1962—, U.S. Dept. State, 1962—, U.S. Dept. Commerce, 1962—, State of Wash., 1963—, Puget Sound Air Pollution Control Agy., 1967—; cons. govts. U.S., Can., Greece, Czechoslovakia, Republic of China, Peoples Republic of China, Belgium, Netherlands, Mexico, Syria, Iran, Egypt, Brazil, Peru, Chile, Barbados, P.R., Philippines, Venezuela, Curacao, also; Smithsonian Instn. and World Bank, various other nat. and multi-nat. corps.; mem. subcom. on hydrogen sulfide NRC; Bd. dirs. Environ. Resources Assos., Bellevue Montessori Sch., Environ. Sci. Service div. E.R.A., N.W. Environmental Scis. Ltd., Inst. Exec. Research, Nat. Air Conservation Commn.; lectr. applied physics and environment Bellevue Montessori Sch., WAsh., 1981—, Arbor Elem. Sch., Issaquah, Wash., 1993—; lectr. in field; co-founder Internat. Environ. Inst., 1988. Author: (with Hal Cooper) Source Testing for Air Pollution Control, 1971; Editor: Air Pollution Control, 1969; Contbr. 115 articles to tech. jours. Patentee pollution control device. Served with C.E. AUS. Recipient Spl. Svc. award USPHS, 1958, Disting. Achievement award Pacific NW-Internat. sect. Air Pollution Control Assn., Lyman A. Ripperton award Air and Waste Mgmt. Assn., 1993, Fulbright Travel Lectr. award to eight univs. and rsch. instns. Italy, 1987; HEW tng. grantee, 1964-70; EPA grantee, 1971—; cert. achievement for 45 Yrs. Continuous Svc., Am. Indsl. Hygiene Assn., 1995. Mem. Harvard Pub. Health Alumni Assn. (pres.), Sigma Xi, Delta Omega, Tau Beta Pi. Clubs: Bellevue Triangle Pool, Bellevue Athletic, Alderbrook (Wash.) Golf and Yacht, Wapato Point Resort, Elliott Bay Yacht, Columbia Towers. Home and Office: Emerald Heights 10901 176th Cir NW Apt 4702 Redmond WA 98052

ROSSANT, JAMES STEPHANE, architect, artist; b. N.Y.C., Aug. 17, 1928; s. Marcus and Anne (Orbach) R.; m. Colette Solange Palacci, Sept. 7, 1955; children—Marianne, Juliette, Cecile, Thomas. B.Arch., U. Fla., 1950; M.City and Regional Planning, Harvard U., 1953. Registered architect, N.Y., Calif., Fla. Architect Mayer & Whittlesey, N.Y.C., 1956-60; assoc. Whittlesey & Conklin, N.Y.C., 1961-65; ptnr. Whittlesey Conklin Rossant, N.Y.C., 1966-67, Conklin Rossant, N.Y.C., 1967-94; prin. James Rossant Architects, N.Y.C., 1994—; prof. Pratt Inst., Bklyn., 1958-61, Columbia U., N.Y.C., 1968, NYU, 1976-81, Harvard U., Cambridge, Mass., 1985-89; architect art commn. City of N.Y., 1979-83. Prin. works include design of Reston, Va., Dodoma, Tanzania, Butterfield House, Ramaz Sch. at N.Y.C.; one man shows include Gallery of Architecture, N.Y., 1976, John Nichols Gallery, 1990, Gallery Ueda, Tokyo, 1991, Galeria Pecanins, Mexico City, 1993, Galerie Mantoux-Gignac, Paris, 1995. Fellow AIA (medal of honor N.Y. chpt. 1977). Democrat. Office: 114 Sullivan St New York NY 10012-3604

ROSSBACHER, LISA ANN, dean, geology educator, writer; b. Fredericksburg, Va., Oct. 10, 1952; d. Richard Irwin and Jean Mary (Dearing) R.; m. Dallas D. Rhodes, Aug. 4, 1978. BS, Dickinson Coll., 1975; MA, SUNY, Binghamton, 1978, Princeton U., 1979; PhD, Princeton U., 1983. Cons. Republic Geothermal, Santa Fe Springs, Calif., 1979-81; asst. prof. geology Whittier (Calif.) Coll., 1982-84; asst. prof. geology Calif. State Poly. U., Pomona, 1984-86, assoc. prof. geol. sci., 1986-91, assoc. v.p. acad. affairs, 1987-93, prof. geol. sci., 1991-93; v.p. acad. affairs, dean faculty Whittier (Calif.) Coll., 1993-95; dean of coll., prof. geology Dickinson Coll., Carlisle, Pa., 1995—; vis. researcher U. Uppsala, Sweden, 1984. Author: Career Opportunities in Geology and the Earth Sciences, 1983, Recent Revolutions in Geology, 1986; (with Rex Buchanan) Geomedia, 1988; columnist Geotimes, 1988—; contbr. articles to profl. jours. Recipient scholarship Ministry Edn. of Finland, Helsinki, 1984; grantee NASA, 1983-94. Mem. AAAS (geol. nominating com. 1984-87), Geol. Soc. Am., Sigma Xi (grantee 1976). Office: Dickinson Coll Dean of the Coll Carlisle PA 17013

ROSSBERG, ROBERT HOWARD, psychology educator, former university dean; b. Bklyn., Mar. 9, 1926; s. Benjamin William and Mollie (Linn) R.; m. Mary Jo Kogan, June 22, 1947; 1 child, Susan Lea. Student, U. Mich., 1943-44; B.S., CCNY, 1949; M.A., Columbia U., 1951; Ph.D., N.Y. U., 1956. Counselor, Fedn. of, 1950-51; staff psychologist N.Y. U. Med. Center, 1951-53; asst. chief psychologist, 1953-56; asst. prof. edn. and psychology SUNY, Buffalo, 1956-59; assoc. prof. SUNY, 1959-64, prof., 1964—, dir. grad. programs in counseling and ednl. psychology, 1959-65, assoc. dean, 1965-67; dean Faculty Ednl. Studies, 1978-80, v.p. for acad. affairs, 1980-84, dean faculty of health related profession, 1987-88, chair dept. psychology, 1988—, disting. svc. prof., 1990; prof. emeritus SUNY, 1995—; cons. in field. Author: Youth: Myths and Realities, 1972; co-author: Counseling Psychology, Strategies and Services, 1989; co-author: Counseling: Theory and Practice, 1993; contbr. articles to profl. publs.; editorial assoc. Urban Edn., 1961-70. Served with USAAF, 1944-46. Rehab. Counseling grantee, 1956-60; NDEA grantee, 1959-60; Office Edn.; leadership tng. grantee, 1969-70. Mem. Am. Psychol. Assn., AAUP. Home: 105 Summerview Rd Buffalo NY 14221-1343 Office: SUNY Buffalo 562 Capen Blvd Amherst NY 14226-2822 *I am increasingly impressed by how much I owe to role models in my family, in schools, and in the work place. Values, ethics, and social priorities are learned through these important others.*

ROSS-BURNETT, CAROL, dean; b. San Antonio; d. Frank and Verdia Lee (Coleman) R.; m. Ronald Lee Burnett, June 21, 1980; 2 children. AB in Social Sci., U. Calif., Berkeley, 1972; MA in Counseling, San Francisco State U., 1974. Asst. to exec. dir. admissions & placement Loyola Law Sch., L.A., 1983-84, assoc. dir. career svcs. & adminstr., clin. programs, 1984-86, dir. career svcs., 1986-89, asst. dean career svcs., 1989—. Author: (with others) Interviewing Candidates from Under-Represented Groups, 1992, Your New Lawyer; co-author/editor: (brochure) Handling Discrimination Complaints, 1991; co-exec. producer (video) All Things Being Equal, 1990. Mem. ABA (commn. on minorities, co-editor newsletter 1992-95), Nat. Assn. Law Placement (bd. dirs. 1994-95, dir. com., chair, regional coord.), Calif. State Bar Assn. (adv. com. attys. with disabilities 1991-93), L.A. County Bar Assn. (joint minority bar diversity task force 1993—, co-vice chair com. on legal profls with disabilities 1995—), Law Sch. Career Advisors So. Calif. (founding mem.), Phi Beta Kappa, Pi Lambda Theta. Avocations: singing/songwriting, writing and producing music. Office: Loyola Law Sch 919 S Albany St Los Angeles CA 90015 also: CRB Cons PO Box 37186 Los Angeles CA 90037

ROSSE, JAMES N., newspaper publishing executive. CEO Freedom Comms., Irvine, Calif. Office: Freedom Comms PO Box 19549 Irvine CA 92713

ROSSE, THERESE MARIE, reading and special education educator, curriculum and instruction specialist; b. Orleans, Nebr., Dec. 23, 1936; d. Ford Huston and Bertha Therese (Flamming) McCoy; m. John A. Rosse, Apr. 19,

1958 (div. 1979); children: Michelle, John, Robert, David. BS, Coll. St. Mary, Omaha, 1972; MS, U. Nebr., Omaha, 1973; PhD, U. Nebr., Lincoln, 1994. Cert. tchr. reading, spo. edn., history, elem. Tchr., reading clinician Omaha Pub. and Parochial Schs., 1958-72; grad. asst. U. Nebr., Omaha, 1972-73; reading cons. Ralston (Nebr.) Pub. Schs., 1973-75; reading and spl. edn. cons. Area Edn. Agy. 13, Council Bluffs, Iowa, 1975—; adj. prof. Buena Vista Coll., Storm Lake, Iowa, 1976-79, U. Nebr. Omaha, 1978-79, Marycrest Coll., Danveport, Iowa, 1985—, N.W. Mo. State U., Maryville, 1985—, Met. Cmty. Coll., Omaha, 1990—; tester Ednl. Testing Svcs., Princeton, N.J., 1972-73; cons. Creative Cons., Muncie, Ind., 1973-75, Midlands Ednl. Cons., Omaha, 1974-75; rschr. Iowa Dept. Pub. Instrn., Dept. Edn., Des Moines, 1980-82, advisor, 1987-89; text reviewer Scott Foresman, Glenview, Ill., 1980-82; evaluation team North Ctrl. Accreditation Assn., 1980-82. Author: Viewing Reading Comprehension as a Problem Solving Skill: Approaches to Developing Comprehensive Strategies, 1982, Breaking the Language Barrier of Mathematical Thought Problems, 1982, A Grounded Theory of An Organizaed Learner; A Balanced Ecological System, 1994. Advisor Mayor's Commn. on Status of Women Edn. Divsn., Omaha, 1973-75. Mem. ASCD, Internat. Reading Assn. (state bd. sec. 1973-75, v.p. local chpt., state co-chairperson, reading chairperson), Am. Ednl. Rsch. Assn., Coun. Exceptional Children, Phi Delta Kappa, Phi Delta Gamma (pres. local chpt. 1979-80, mem. nat. bd. 1980-82), Phi Alpha Theta. Avocations: travel, reading, classical music and art, writing/research, tennis. Home: 817 N 131 Plz Omaha NE 68154

ROSSE, WENDELL FRANKLYN, immunology educator; b. Sidney, Nebr., June 5, 1933; m. Simonne Vernier, July, 1959; children: Christopher, Stephanie, Philippe. Student, U. Chgo., 1949-52, MD with honors, 1958; BA, U. Omaha, 1953; student, U. Nebr. Sch. Medicine, 1953-55; M.S. in Physiology, Grad. Sch., 1956. Intern., resident Duke Hosp., Durham, N.C., 1958-60; sr. investigator Nat. Cancer Inst. NIH, Bethesda, Md., 1964-66; asst. prof. medicine Duke U. Med. Center, 1966-68, assoc. prof. medicine, 1966-72, assoc. prof. immunology, 1970-76, prof. medicine, 1972—, prof. immunology, 1976—, Florence McAllister prof. medicine, 1981—, chief sect. immunohematology, 1971-86, co-dir. blood bank, 1971-87, dir. hematology and transfusion svc., 1987-92, chief hematology-oncology, 1976-89; chief med. service Durham VA Hosp., 1973-76; vis. research prof. Institut de Pathologie Cellulaire, Paris, 1974; investigator Howard Hughes Med. Inst., 1976-81; bd. govs. Am. Bd. Internal Medicine, 1988-93. Contbr. numerous articles to med. publs. Mem. regional adv. com. ARC; mem. N.C. Gov's Council on Sickle Cell Syndrome. Recipient Career Devel. award, 1968, Golden Apple Student Teaching award Duke U. Med. Center, 1968, Thomas Kinney Meml. prize for teaching, 1980, Alumni Disting. Teaching award, 1991; Josiah Macy, Jr., scholar, 1974. Mem. Am. Soc. Hematology (Stratton lectr. 1976, pres. 1986-87), Assn. Am. Physicians, Am. Soc. Clin. Investigation, Am. Fedn. Clin. Research, Nat. Blood Club (pres. 1975), Red Cell Club, N.C. Assn. Blood Banks, N.C. Heart Assn., Alpha Omega Alpha. Home: 4605 Timberly Dr Durham NC 27707-9538 Office: Duke U Medical Ctr PO Box 3934 Durham NC 27710

ROSSEELS, GUSTAVE ALOIS, music educator; b. Malines, Belgium, Jan. 19, 1911; came to U.S., 1946; s. Karel Hubert and Elisabeth (Rooms) R.; m. Jacqueline Crepin, Sept. 5, 1944; children: Marc, Elisabeth, Susanne. Grad. with highest distinction, Royal Conservatory Music, Brussels. Lectr. violin & chamber music U. Mich. Sch. Music, 1957, prof., 1962, prof. emeritus, 1978; instr. violin and chamber music Mills. Coll., Brigham Young U., Aspen (Colo.), Inst., All-State Program Nat. Music Camp, Interlochen, Mich., summers 1981, 82. Violinist, Pro Nova Quartet, Paganini Quartet, Stanley Quartet, Baroque Trio; condr. Jackson (Mich.) Symphony, 1960; author: (autobiography) A Remembering Journey, 1981. Avocations: swimming, golf, reading. Home: 3076 Bolgos Cir Ann Arbor MI 48105-1513

ROSSELL, CHRISTINE HAMILTON, political science educator; b. Bklyn., Jan. 22, 1945; d. Robert Hamilton and Ann (Bezold) R.; 1 child, Elise. AB, UCLA, 1967; MA, Calif. State U., Northridge, 1969; PhD, U. So. Calif., 1974. Asst. prof. Pitzer Coll., Claremont, Calif., 1973-74; rsch. assoc. U. Md., College Park, 1974-75; asst. prof. Boston U., 1975-82, assoc. prof., 1982-89, prof., 1989—, chair dept. polit. sci., 1992-95; vis. asst. prof. Duke U., Durham, N.C., 1977-78, U. Calif., Berkeley, 1981; vis. lectr. Canberra (Australia) Coll., 1985. Author: Strategies for Effective Desegregation (with others), 1983, Carrot or Stick for School Desegregation, 1990; co-editor: Consequences of School Desegregation, 1983. Mem. Citywide Coord. Coun., Boston, 1976-77. Home: 44 High St Brookline MA 02146-7707 Office: Boston U Dept Polit Sci 232 Bay State Rd Boston MA 02215-1403

ROSSELLINI, ISABELLA, actress, model; b. Rome, June 18, 1952; d. Roberto Rossellini and Ingrid Bergman; m. Martin Scorsese, Sept. 1979 (div. Nov. 1982); m. Jonathan Wiedemann (div.); 1 child, Elettra Ingrid. Student, Finch Coll., 1972, New Sch. for Social Research, N.Y.C. Became model for Lancôme, 1982. Appeared in films A Matter of Time, 1976, Il Pap'occhio, 1980, The Meadow, 1982, White Nights, 1985, Blue Velvet, 1986, Siesta, 1987, Red Riding Hood, 1987, Tough Guys Don't Dance, 1987, Zelly and Me, 1988, Cousins, 1989, Wild at Heart, 1990, Les Dames Galantes, 1990, Death Becomes Her, 1992, The Pickle, 1992, Fearless, 1993, Wyatt Earp, 1994, Immortal Beloved, 1994, The Innocent, 1995; TV films: The Last Elephant, 1990, Lies of the Twins, 1991. Office: United Talent Agency 9560 Wilshire Blvd Fl 5 Beverly Hills CA 90212-2401*

ROSSELLÓ, PEDRO, governor; b. San Juan, P.R., Apr. 5, 1944; m. Maga Nevares, Aug. 9, 1969; children: Juan Oscar, Luis, Ricardo. BS, U. Notre Dame, 1966; MD, Yale U., 1970; MPH, U. P.R., 1981; LLD (hon.), U. Notre Dame, 1995, U. Mass., 1995. Intern straight surgery Beth Israel Hosp., Boston, 1970-71, resident gen. surgery, 1971-74; resident cardiac and burns Mass. Gen. Hosp., Boston, 1972; resident trauma San Francisco Gen. Hosp., 1973; sr. resident pediat. surgery Children's Hosp., Boston, 1974-75, chief resident, pediat. surgery-urology, 1975-76; instr. surgery Harvard Med. Sch., 1975-76; pvt. practice San Juan, 1976-92; asst. prof. surgery U. P.R., 1978-82, assoc. prof. surgery, 1982-92; dir. Dept. Health City of San Juan, 1985-87; chief surgery San Jorge Hosp., San Juan, 1989-92, med. dir., 1990; gov. Puerto Rico, 1993—; lead gov. So. Regional Project Infant Mortality; chair So. States Energy Bd.; mem. intergovtl. policy adv. com. U.S. Trade Rep.; v.p. Coun. State Govts. Contbr. articles to profl. jours. Mem. P.R. Olympic Com., 1982-84, 87-88; v.p. New Progressive Party, 1988-91, pres., 1991—; mem. steering com. Edn. Commn. States; bd. visitors Georgetown U. Law Ctr., Washington. Capt. USNG, 1970-76. Mem. Nat. Govs. Assn. (host. 1996 ann. meeting), So. Govs. Assn. (vice chair), Dem. Govs. Assn. (mem. exec. com.), P.R. Tennis Assn. (pres. 1982-84), Caribbean Tennis Assn. (pres. 1983-84), Alpha Omega Alpha. Avocations: jogging, tennis, ocean kayaking.

ROSSEN, JORDAN, lawyer; b. Detroit, June 13, 1934; s. Nathan Paul and Rebecca (Rizy) R.; m. Susan Friebert, Mar. 24, 1963 (div. June 1972); 1 child, Rebecca; m. M. Elizabeth Bunn, Jan. 3, 1981; children—N. Paul, Jordan David. B.A., U. Mich., 1956; J.D., Harvard U., 1959. Bar: Mich. 1960, U.S. Dist. Ct. (ea. dist.) Mich. 1960, U.S. Ct. Appeals (6th cir.) 1966, U.S. Ct. Appeals (7th cir.) 1974, U.S. Supreme Ct. 1966. Assoc. Sullivan, Elmer, Eames & Moody, Detroit, 1960-62; assoc. Sugar & Schwartz, Detroit, 1962-64; asst. gen. counsel UAW, Detroit, 1964-74, assoc. gen. counsel, 1974-83, gen. counsel, 1983—; vice pres. N.P. Rossen Agy., Inc., Detroit, 1960-83; gen. counsel Mich. Health & Social Security Research Inst., Inc., Detroit, 1965-83; dir. UAW Job Devel. & Tng. Corp., Detroit, 1984-90. Editor: Mich. Bar Labor Section Publication, 1961-64. Contbr. articles to profl. jours. Pres. Young Democrats, Mich., 1963-65; chmn. Americans for Democratic Action, Mich., 1966-68; chmn. Voter Registration Dem. Party, Mich., 1967. Recipient Human Rights award City of Detroit, 1978. Mem. ABA, Mich. Bar Assn., Nat. Bar Assn., Fed. Bar Assn., Wolverine Bar Assn., Women Lawyers Assn., Lawyers Guild. Jewish. Office: UAW Legal Dept 8000 E Jefferson Ave Detroit MI 48214-2699

ROSSER, ANNETTA HAMILTON, composer; b. Jasper, Fla., Aug. 28, 1913; d. Carlos Calvin and Jermai Reuben (Gilbert) Hamilton; m. John Barkley Rosser, Sept. 7, 1935 (dec. Sept. 1989); children: Edwenna Merryday, John Barkley Jr. BM, Fla. State U., 1932. Cert. tchr., Fla. Tchr. music Kirby-Smith Jr. High Sch., Jacksonville, Fla., 1932-35; 1st violinist Santa Monica (Calif.) Symphony, 1949-50; concertmaster Ithaca (N.Y.) Chamber Orch., 1948-56; concertmaster Cornell Univ. Orch., Ithaca, 1948-56, soloist, 1957; 1st violinist Princeton (N.J.) Symphony, 1959-61; concertmaster Madison (Wis.) Symphony Orch., 1963-66, 1st violinist, 1967-82. Composer of over 100 vocal and instrumental compositions including Meditations on Cross, song cycle for 2 voices, flute and piano, 1976, An Offering of Song, book of 48 songs, 1977, Songs of a Nomad Flute, song cycle for soprano, flute and piano, 1978, Six Songs of the T'ang Dynasty for soprano and violin, 1983, Nocturne for violin and piano, 1989, Trio for flute, violin and piano, 1991, Scherzo for flute ensemble, 1991. Bd. dirs. Madison Opera Guild, 1972-86, Madison Civic Music Assn., 1983-85; past pres. Madison Symphony Orch. League, Ithaca Federated Music Club, Ithaca Composers Club; trustee Madison Art Ctr., 1979-83, Madison Civics Club, 1976-79, Madison Woman of Distinction, 1980. Recipient Sr. Svc. award Rotary Club, 1994. Mem. AAUW, Univ. League, Univ. League Bird Study Group, Madison Club, Madison Federated Music Club, PEO, Phi Kappa Phi, Pi Kappa Lambda, Sigma Alpha Iota. Republican. Presbyterian. Avocations: Chinese snuff bottles, English brass rubbings, birding. Home: 4209 Manitou Way Madison WI 53711-3703

ROSSER, EDWIN MICHAEL, mortgage company executive; b. Denver, Oct. 11, 1940; s. Edwin Michael and Anne (Ratliff) R.; m. Keren Call, July 17, 1969; children: Kevin, William. BS, Colo. State U., 1964; MA, U. No. Colo., 1974. Cert. mortgage banker. Mktg. officer United Bank Mortgage, Denver, 1968-74; dir. nat. accounts PMI Mortgage Ins. Co., Denver, 1974-85; v.p. Moore Mortgage Co., Denver, 1985-87, Pacific First Mortgage Corp., Englewood, Colo., 1987-89; 1st v.p. 1st Nat. Bank, San Francisco, 1990-93; bd. dirs. Rocky Mtn. Women's Inst. Photographer represented in Denver Art Mus., The Buffalo in Winter, (1st place award 1981). Steering com. Blueprint for Colo., Govs. Unified Housing Task Force; mem. Colo. Housing Coun. (chmn. 1986-87); bd. dirs. Colo. State Found. Mem. Mortgage Bankers Assn. Am. (bd. govs. 1986-90, state and local achievement award 1986, Ernest P. Schumacher award 1988), Colo. Mortgage Bankers Assn. (bd. dirs. 1979-88, pres. 1986, E.C. Spelman award 1978), Colo. Assn. Commerce and Industry, Denver Mus. Natural History, Denver C. of C., Colo. State U. Alumni Assn. (nat. pres. 1985, bd. dirs. 1979-87, mem. found. bd. 1987-91, 93—, Honor Alumnus 1984), City Club Denver, Commonwealth Club. Calif. Republican. Roman Catholic. Avocations: competitive swimming, photography. Home: 12478 E Amherst Cir Aurora CO 80014-3306 Office: United Residential Ins Co 6312 So Fiddlers Greencircle Englewood CO 80111

ROSSER, JAMES MILTON, academic administrator; b. East St. Louis, Ill., Apr. 16, 1939; s. William M. and Mary E. (Bass) R.; 1 child, Terrence. B.A., So. Ill. U., 1962, M.A., 1963, Ph.D., 1969. Diagnostic bacteriologist Holden Hosp., Carbondale, Ill., 1961-63; research bacteriologist Eli Lilly & Co., Indpls., 1963-66; coordinator Black Am. studies, instr. health edn. So. Ill. U., Carbondale, 1968-69; asst. prof. Black Am. studies dir. So. Ill. U., 1969-70, asst. to chancellor, 1970; asso. vice chancellor for acad. affairs U. Kans., Lawrence, 1970-74; assoc. prof. edn., pharmacology and toxicology U. Kans., 1971-74; vice chancellor dept. higher edn. State of N.J., Trenton, 1974-79; acting chancellor State of N.J., 1977; pres., prof. health care mgmt. Calif. State U., Los Angeles, 1979—; mem. tech. resource panel Ctr. for Research and Devel. in Higher Edn., U. Calif., Berkeley, 1974-76; mem. health maintenance orgn. com. Health Planning Coun., State of N.J., 1975-79; mem. standing com. on research and devel. bd. trustees Ednl. Testing Service, 1976-77; mem. steering com. and task force on retention of minorities in engring. Assembly of Engring. NRC, 1975-78; mem. Bd. Med. Examiners, State of N.J., 1978-79; vis. faculty mem. Inst. Mgmt. of Lifelong Edn., Grad. Sch. Edn., Harvard U., 1979; mem. Calif. State U. Trustees Spl. Long Range Fin. Planning Com., 1982-87; mem. Am. Coun. on Edn., 1979—, AFL/CIO Labor Higher Edn. Coun., 1983—, Nat. Commn. Higher Edn. Issues, 1981-82; mem. The Calif. Achievement Coun., 1983-89, strategic adv. counc. Coll. and Univs. Systems Exchange, 1988-91; bd. dirs. Am. Humanities Coun., So. Calif. Am. Humanics, Inc. Coun., Sanwa Bank Calif., 1993—, Edison, Fedco, Inc. Author: An Analysis of Health Care Delivery, 1977. Mem. exec. bd., chmn. varisty scouting program L.A. area coun. Boy Scouts Am., 1980—; bd. dirs. Hispanic Urban Ctr., L.A., 1979—, L.A. Urban League, 1982—, Cmty. TV of So. Calif., Sta. KCET, 1980-89, United Way, L.A., 1980-91, Orthopaedic Hosp., 1983-86; mem. Citizen's Adv. Coun. Congl. Caucus Sci. and Tech., 1983—; bd. dirs. L.A. Philharm. Assn., 1986—; mem. performing arts coun./edn. coun. Music Ctr., 1984—; mem. minority bus. task force Pacific Bell, 1985-86; mem. bd. govs. Nat. ARC, 1986-91, Mayor's Blue Ribbon Task Force on Drugs, City of L.A., 1988; Nat. Adv. Coun. on Aging, 1989-93; bd. dirs. Nat. Health Found., 1990—, Calif. C. of C., 1993—; bd. trustees Woodrow Wilson Nat. Fellowship Found., 1993—. NSF fellow, 1961; NDEA fellow, 1967-68; recipient award of recognition in Edn. Involvement for Young Achievers, 1981, Pioneer of Black Hist. Achievement award Brotherhood Crusade, 1981, Alumni Achievement award So. Ill. U., 1982, Friend of Youth award Am. Humanics, Inc., 1985, Leadership award Dept. Higher Edn. Ednl. Equal Opportunity Fund Program, 1989, Medal of Excellence Gold State Minority Found., 1990, Take Charge of Learning Success award Inst. for Redesign of Learning. Mem. Calif. C. of C. (bd. dirs. 1993—), Alhambra C. of C. (bd. dirs. 1979—), Los Angeles C. of C. (bd. dirs. 1985-90), Am. Assn. State Colls. and Univs., Kappa Delta Pi, Phi Kappa Phi. Roman Catholic. Office: Calif State Univ Office of the Pres 5151 State University Dr Los Angeles CA 90032-8500

ROSSER, RHONDA LANAE, psychotherapist; b. Champaign, Ill., Aug. 29, 1953; d. Neill Albert and Grace Lee (Byers) R.; (div. June 1, 1993); children: Anthony Neill Williams, Joseph Neill Jackson Hogan. BS in Psychology, Guilford Coll., 1975; MEd in Edn., U. N.C., Greensboro, 1979, PhD in Counseling, 1991. Joined 3rd Order of Secular Franciscans/Order of St. Francis. Instr. U. N.C., Greensboro, 1985-88; dir. Montagnard Program Luth. Family Svcs., Greensboro, 1985-88; psychotherapist pvt. practice, Greensboro, 1989—. Contbr. articles to profl. jours. Recipient Presdl. citation U.S. Govt., 1987. Mem. Am. Counseling Assn. (Outstanding Rsch. award 1991), Chi Sigma Iota. Democrat. Roman Catholic (3d order of Secular Franciscans/Order of St. Francis). Avocations: fox hunting, bird watching, snow skiing. Home and Office: 2318 W Cornwallis Dr Greensboro NC 27408-6802

ROSSER, RICHARD FRANKLIN, education consultant; b. Arcanum, Ohio, July 16, 1929; s. Harold Arm and Margaret (Whitacre) R.; m. Donna Eyssen., Mar. 21, 1951; children—Eric, Carl, Edward. B.A., Ohio Wesleyan U., 1951; M.P.A., Syracuse U., 1952, Ph.D., 1961. Joined U.S. Air Force 1952, advanced through grades to col., 1968; prof. polit. sci. U.S. Air Force Acad., Colorado Springs, Colo., 1959-73; head dept. U.S. Air Force Acad., 1967-73, ret., 1973; prof. polit. sci., dean Albion (Mich.) Coll., 1973-77; pres. DePauw U., Greencastle, Ind., 1977-86, chancellor, 1986; pres. Nat. Assn. Ind. Colls. and Univs., Washington, 1986-93; cons. in higher edn. pvt. practice, Traverse City, Mich., 1993—. Author: An Introduction to Soviet Foreign Policy, 1969; Contbr. articles to profl. jours. Mem. univ. senate United Meth. Ch., 1980-84; mem. spl. commn. of Chief of Staff on Honor Code U.S. Mil. Acad., 1989; bd. visitors Air U., 1991-94; bd. trustees Ohio Wesleyan U., 1991—; mem. nat. adv. com. Instnl. Quality and Integrity, 1994—. Decorated Legion of Merit with oak leaf cluster. Mem. Am. Polit. Sci. Assn., Phi Beta Kappa, Omicron Delta Kappa. Presbyterian. Home and Office: 2161 Harbor Reach Dr Traverse City MI 49686-9721

ROSSET, BARNET LEE, JR., publisher; b. Chgo., May 28, 1922; s. Barnet Lee and Mary (Tansey) R.; m. Joan Mitchell, 1950 (div. 1952); m. Hannelore Eckert, Aug. 1953 (div. 1957); 1 child, Peter; m. Cristine Agnini, Mar. 11, 1965 (div. 1979); children—Tansey, Beckett; m. Elisabeth Krug, 1980 (div. 1991; 1 child, Chantal. Ph.B., U. Chgo., 1947; B.A. New Sch. Social Research, N.Y.C., 1952. Pub., editor Grove Press, Inc., 1951-86, Evergreen Rev., Rosset and Co., Inc., 1957-73, Blue Moon Books, Inc., N.Y.C., 1987—. Served to 1st lt. Signal Corps AUS, 1942-46. Recipient Ninth Pub. citation PEN Am. Ctr., 1988. Mem. PEN Club.; mem. Overseas Press. Office: 61 4th Ave New York NY 10003-5202

ROSSET, LISA KRUG, editor; b. N.Y.C., Nov. 11, 1952; d. George William and Rita (Earle) Krug; m. Barney Rosset, Nov. 5, 1980 (div. Dec. 1990); 1 child, Chantal. B.A. magna cum laude, Smith Coll., 1974; M.A., Columbia U., 1976. Editor Latin Am. Series, N.Y.C., 1976-86; gen. editor Grove Press, N.Y.C., 1976-86; mng. editor Aperture, N.Y.C., 1987-90; pvt. practice N.Y.C., 1990—; cons. editor UNICEF, N.Y.C., 1995—. Author: James Baldwin, 1989, Thurgood Marshall, 1993, Outstanding Book For Teenagers, 1994. Mem. Phi Beta Kappa. Office: 106 Perry St New York NY 10014-3236

ROSSEY, PAUL WILLIAM, school superintendent, university president; b. Richmond, Ind., July 7, 1926; s. Chris C. and Lela (Longman) R.; m. Adelaide Elizabeth Finnegan; 1 dau., Joanne Rossey Sczubelek. B.S., Jersey City State Coll., 1952, Litt. D., 1971; M.A., NYU, 1953, Ed.D. (Kellogg Found. fellow 1955), 1958. Head jr. sch. Peddie Sch., Hightstown, N.J., 1952-53; cons., elem. sch. instr. West Hempstead, N.Y., 1953-55; prin. elem. sch. Dobbs Ferry, N.Y., 1955-58; supt. schs. Litchfield, Conn., 1958-60, Scotch Plains-Fanwood, N.J., 1960-67; dist. supt. schs. Nassau County, N.Y., 1967-69; pres. West Chester (Pa.) State U., 1969-74; supt. schs. Millburn-Short Hills, N.J., 1974-92; ret.; lectr. NYU, 1954-67. Contbr. articles to profl. jours. County dir. Boy Scouts Am.; v.p. YMCA; bd. dirs. Garbe Found., Community Fund; trustee NYU, 1970-74, The Peddie Sch., 1974-92; mem. exec. com. N.J. Coun. Edn., 1977-83. With USNR, 1944-46, USMCR, 1972-86; ret. Named Outstanding Alumnus, Jersey City State Coll., 1962; recipient NYU medallion, 1966, Ernest O. Melby award human relations, 1970. Mem. Am. Assn. Sch. Adminstrs. (chmn. N.J. 1965-67), Am. Council Edn., Aircraft Owners and Pilots Assn., N.J. Assn. Sch. Adminstrs. (exec. com. 1964-67, 81-85), Horace Mann League U.S. (nat. pres. 1977-78), Kappa Delta Pi, Phi Delta Kappa. Republican. Presbyn. Clubs: Exchange (dir.), N.J. Schoolmasters. Home: 219 Summit Ave Summit NJ 07901-2213

ROSS-FLANIGAN, NANCY, reporter. Sci. reporter The Detroit Free Press. Office: Detroit Free Press Inc 321 W Lafayette Blvd Detroit MI 48226-2705

ROSSI, ALICE S., sociology educator, author; b. N.Y.C., Sept. 24, 1922; d. William A. and Emma (Winkler) Schaerr; m. Max Kitt, Dec. 1941 (div. Sept. 1951); m. Peter H. Rossi, Sept. 29, 1951; children: Peter Eric, Kristin Alice, Nina Alexis. BA, Bklyn. Coll., 1947; PhD, Columbia U., 1957; 9 hon. degrees. Rsch. assoc. Cornell U., Ithaca, N.Y., 1951-52, Harvard U., Cambridge, Mass., 1952-55, U. Chgo., 1961-67, Johns Hopkins U., Balt., 1967-69; prof. sociology Goucher Coll., Balt., 1969-74; prof. sociology U. Mass., Amherst, 1974-91, prof. emerita, 1991—. Author/editor: 11 books; contbr. numerous articles to profl. jours. Founder, bd. mem. NOW, 1966-70; pres. Sociologists for Women in Soc., 1971-72. Career grantee NIMH, 1965-69, rsch. grantee Rockefeller Found., Ford Found., NIH, NSF, others; CommonWealth Disting. Scholarship award, 1988. Mem. Am. Sociol. Assn. (pres. 1983-84), Ea. Sociol. Soc. (pres. 1973-74). Avocations: design, sewing, gardening, creative writing. Home: 34 Stagecoach Rd Amherst MA 01002-3527

ROSSI, ANTHONY GERALD, lawyer; b. Warren, Ohio, July 20, 1935; s. Anthony Gerald and Lena (Guarnieri) R.; m. Marilyn J. Fuller, June 22, 1957; children: Diana L., Maribeth, Anthony Gerald III. BS, John Carroll U., 1957; JD, Cath. U. Am., 1961. Bar: Ohio 1961. Ptnr. Guarnieri & Secrest, Warren, 1961—; former acting judge Warren Municipal Ct. Mem. Mahoning-Shenango Estate Planning Coun., 1968—, past sec.; past pres. Warren Olympic Club; past bd. govs. Cath. U. Am. Law Sch. Coun.; past trustee Trumbull Art Guild, Warren Civic Music Assn. Capt. Transp. Corps, AUS, 1957-65. Mem. ABA, Ohio Bar Assn., Trumbull County Bar Assn. (exec. com. 1975—, pres. 1976-77), Am. Arbitration Assn., Ohio Motorist Assn. (corp. mem., trustee 1980-86, 92—), Wolf's Club, KC, Elks. Home: 2500 Hidden Lakes Dr NE Warren OH 44484-4159 Office: 151 E Market St Warren OH 44481-1102

ROSSI, ENNIO C., internist, educator; b. Madison, Wis., Apr. 3, 1931; s. Joseph and Esther (D'Amelio) R.; m. Anna Maria Bianchi, June 22, 1957; children: Roberta, Marco. BA, U. Wis., 1951, MD, 1954. Diplomate Am. Bd. Internal Medicine. Intern Ohio State U. Hosps., 1954-55; resident medicine U. Wis. Hosps., 1958-61, fellow, 1961-63; instr. medicine Marquette U., Milw., 1963-64, asst. prof. medicine, 1964-66; assoc. prof. medicine Northwestern U., Chgo., 1966-72, prof. medicine, 1972—, chief hematology, 1967-84, chief transfusion medicine, 1984—; v.p. med. affairs Life Source Blood Ctr., Glenview, Ill., 1988-93; vis. scientist Mario Negri Inst., Milan, 1977. Co-editor: Haemostasis and the Kidney, 1989; sr. editor: Principles of Transfusion Medicine, 1991, 2d edit., 1996. Capt. U.S. Army, 1956-58. Fulbright scholar, U.S. Dept. State, U. Rome, 1955; Nat. Heart, Lung Blood Inst. Transfusion Medicine Acad. awardee, 1983; WHO travelling fellow, 1985. Fellow ACP; mem. Am. Soc. Hematology, Am. Soc. Pharmacology and Exptl. Therapeutics, Am. Assn. Blood Banks (chmn. acad. transfusion medicine com. 1988-93), Internat. Soc. Blood Transfusion. Office: Northwestern U 303 E Chicago Ave Chicago IL 60611-3008

ROSSI, FAUST F., lawyer, educator; b. 1932. BA, U. Toronto, 1953; JD, Cornell U., 1960. Bar: N.Y. 1960. Tax trial atty., Dept. Justice, Washington, 1960-61; sole practice, Rochester, N.Y., 1961-66; assoc. prof. Cornell U., Ithaca, N.Y., 1966-69, prof. 1970—, assoc. dean, 1973-75, Samuel S. Leibowitz prof. trial techniques, 1982—; vis. fellow Wadham Coll., Oxford, 1987-88; vis. prof. Emory U., 1990; cons. report of fed. class actions Am. Coll. of Trial Lawyers, 1971-72; cons. com. on proposed fed. rules of evidence N.Y. Trial Lawyers Assn., 1970; cons., instr. annual seminar N.Y. State Trial Judges, 1970-78; cons., instr. Nat. Inst. for Trial Advocacy, 1974-75, 80-84, 88; cons. N.Y. Law Revision Commn. Project for N.Y. Code of Evidence, 1978-80. Lt. j.g. USN. Recipient Jacobsen prize for teaching trial advocacy, 1992. Mem. Order of Coif. Author: Study of the Proposed Federal Rules of Evidence, 1979, Report on Rule 23 Class Actions, 1972, The Federal Rules of Evidence, 1970, Expert Witnesses, 1991; contbr. articles to profl. jours. Office: Cornell U Law Sch Myron Taylor Hall Ithaca NY 14853

ROSSI, HARALD HERMANN, retired radiation biophysicist, educator, administrator; b. Vienna, Austria, Sept. 3, 1917; came to U.S., 1939; s. Oswald J. and Hedwig E. (Braun) R.; m. Ruth Gregg, June 22, 1946; children: Gerald, Gwendolyn Gladstone, Harriet Furey. Student, U. Vienna, 1935-39, U. Bristol, Eng., 1939; Ph.D., Johns Hopkins U., 1942. Cert. in radiol. physics Am. Bd. Radiology. Instr. Johns Hopkins U., Balt., 1940-45; research physicist Nat. Bur. Standards, Washington, 1945; physicist and radiation protection officer Presbyn. Hosp., N.Y.C., 1954-60; rsch. scientist radiol. rsch. lab. Columbia U., N.Y.C., 1946-60, asst. prof. radiology, 1949-53, assoc. prof., 1953-60, prof. radiology and physics, dir. radiol. rsch. lab., 1960-84, prof. radiation oncology, 1984-87, prof. emeritus, 1988—; cons., 1988—; cons. NIH, NRC, Dept. Energy, FAA; chmn. tech. com. Radiation to Health Commr. of N.Y.C., 1978-82; mem. Internat. Com. on Radiation Units and Measurements, Main Com., Washington, 1959—, Nat. Coun. on Radiation Protection, Main Coun., 1954-83, hon. mem., 1983—. Co-author: Advances in Biological and Medical Physics, 1967, Radiation Dosimetry, 1968, Cancer: A Comprehensive Treatise, 1982. Trustee, pres. Upper Nyack sch. Bd., N.Y., 1957-60; trustee Rockland County Day Sch., 1961-63. Recipient Shonka Meml. Found. award, 1972, Gray medal Internat. Commn. on Radiation Units and Measurements, 1985, Disting. Scientific Achievement award Health Physics Soc., 1987. Fellow Am. Coll. Radiology; mem. AAAS, Radiation Research Soc. (pres. 1974-75), Am. Coll. Radiology, Radiol. Soc. N.Am., Sigma Xi. Office: 105 Larchdale Ave Nyack NY 10960-1003

ROSSI, MARIO ALEXANDER, architect; b. Chgo., Apr. 9, 1931; s. Gastone J. and Irma (Giorgi) R.; m. Jo Ann Therese Kneip, Apr. 12, 1958; children: John Vincent, Lyn Ann, Paul Alexander, Mara Ann. BArch, Ill. Inst. Tech., 1955. Architect Omnimetrics, L.A., 1967-78; pvt. practice Seal Beach, Calif., 1975—. Prin. works include fin. models for Calif. Fed. Bank, L.A., First Nat. City Bank, N.Y.C., Glendale (Calif.) Fed. Bank, Wailea, Alexander and Baldwin, Hawaii. Lt. (j.g.) USN, 1955-58. Research computerized techniques in architecture and economic feasibility land development. Home and Office: 1721 Catalina Ave Seal Beach CA 90740-5710

ROSSI, PETER HENRY, sociology educator; b. N.Y.C., Dec. 27, 1921; s. Peter Maxim and Elizabeth (Porcelli) R.; m. Alice Schaerr, Sept. 29, 1951; children: Peter Eric, Kristin Alice, Nina Alexis. B.S., CCNY, 1943; Ph.D., Columbia, 1951. Research asso. Bur. Applied Social Research, Columbia U., 1947- 51; asst. prof. Harvard U., 1951-55; prof. dept. sociology U. Chgo.,

1955-67; dir. Nat. Opinion Research Center, 1960-67; prof. dept. social relations Johns Hopkins, 1967-74, chmn. dept., 1967-70; dir. research Center for Met. Planning and Research, 1972-74; prof. sociology, dir. Social and Demographic Research Inst., U. Mass., Amherst, 1974-92; Stuart A. Rice prof. sociology, dir. Social and Demographic Research Inst., U. Mass., 1984-92, prof. emeritus, 1992—; faculty assoc. Chapin Hall U. Chgo., 1994—. Author: Why Families Move, 1956, The Politics of Urban Renewal, 1962, The Education of Catholic Americans, 1966, New Media and Education, 1967, Ghetto Revolts, 1970, Cities Under Siege, 1971, Evaluating Social Programs, 1972, Roots of Urban Discontent, 1974, Reforming Public Welfare, 1976, Prison Reform and State Elites, 1977, Evaluation: A Systematic Approach, 1979, Money, Work & Crime, 1980, After the Clean-up, 1980, Social Science and Natural Hazards, 1981, Measuring Social Judgements, 1982, Natural Hazards and Public Choice, 1982, Under the Gun, 1983, Applied Sociology, 1983, Without Shelter, 1989, Down and Out in America, 1989, Of Human Bonding, 1990; editor: Am. Jour. Sociology, 1957-58; assoc. editor: Am. Sociol. Rev, 1957-60, Am. Sociologist, 1964-66; editor: Social Sci. Research, 1972-89; contbr. articles to profl. and popular jours. Served with AUS, 1942-45. Recipient Alvah and Gunnar Myrdal award for contbns. to evaluation research, 1981; Commonwealth award for contbns. to sociology, 1985; faculty research grantee Social Sci. Research Council, 1959; Carnegie sr. fellow, 1965. Fellow Am. Acad. Arts and Scis.; mem. Am. Sociol. Assn. (sec. 1968-72, pres.-elect 1979-80, pres. 1980-81), Am. Evaluation Assn.

ROSSI, STEVEN B., newspaper publishing executive. Grad., Ursinus Coll., 1971; MBA, U. Pa., 1974. With UI Internat. Corp., Phila., 1974-78, UGI Corp., Phila., 1978-87; with Phila. Newspapers, 1987—, exec. v.p., gen. mgr. Office: Phila Newspapers Inc 400 N Broad St Philadelphia PA 19130-4015

ROSSIDES, EUGENE TELEMACHUS, lawyer, writer; b. N.Y.C., Oct. 23, 1927; s. Telemachus and Anna (Maravel) R.; m. Elinor Burcham (div.); 1 child, Gale; m. Aphrodite Macotsin, Dec. 30, 1961; children: Michael, Alexander, Eleni. AB, Columbia U., 1949, JD, 1952. Criminal law investigator Office of Dist. Atty., N.Y.C., 1952; assoc. Rogers & Wells, N.Y.C., 1954-56, 61-66, ptnr., 1966-69, 73-92, sr. counsel, 1993—; asst. atty. gen. State of N.Y., N.Y.C., 1956-58; asst. to undersec. Dept. Treasury, Washington, 1958-61, asst. sec., 1969-73; bd. dirs. Sterling Nat. Bank, N.Y.C. Author: U.S. Import Trade Regulation, 2d edit., 1986, Foreign Unfair Competition, 3d edit., 1991, United States Import Trade Law, 1992, also articles; chief import editor Internat. Trade Reporter, Bur. Nat. Affairs, 1980—; editor: Doing Business in Greece, 1993. Mem. Grace Commn., Washington, 1981-82; chmn. nationalities div. Reagan Bush Com., Washington, 1980; campaign mgr. N.Y.C. Nixon for Pres. Com., 1968, Keating for Senator Com., N.Y. State, 1964; bd. dirs. Eisenhower World Affairs Inst., Washington, Am. Hellenic Inst. Inc. Capt. USAF, 1952-60. Recipient Medal for Excellence, Columbia U., 1972, Young Lawyer's award Columbia Law Sch. Alumni Assn., 1972, Silver Anniversary award NCAA, 1974, John Jay award Columbia Coll. Alumni Assn., 1994. Mem. ABA, N.Y. State Bar Assn., Fed. Bar Assn. Republican. Greek Orthodox. Avocations: tennis, photography. Home: 3666 Upton St NW Washington DC 20008-3125 Office: Rogers & Wells 607 14th St NW Washington DC 20005-2007

ROSSIE, CARLOS ENRIQUE, computer school administrator, consultant; b. Havana, Cuba, Oct. 7, 1948; s. Dionisio M. and Edelmira (Blanco) R.; came to U.S., 1966; m. Claudia V. Velilla, Mar. 24, 1972; children—Cynthia Patricia, Claudette Marie, Carlos Fernando. Assoc. in Sci., Miami Dade Jr. Coll., 1970; postgrad., Fla. Internat. U., 1978—; B in Computers, Internat. Coll. of Cayman Islands, 1988; MBA, Internat. Coll., 1990; EdD, Nova Southeastern U., 1994. Dir., owner Programar Computer Sch., Colombia, 1972-78; computer system and procedures analyst, dir. programmers and analysts tng. Burger King Corp., Miami, Fla., 1978-79; asst. v.p. computer dept. Flagler Fed. Savs. and Loans, Miami, 1979-81; dir., owner Fla. Programming Computer Sch., Miami, 1981—; pres. READ (Rossie Ednl. Advisors), Miami, 1994—; computer cons. for Cuban-Am. Orgn. program, Dade County (Fla.), 1981—; computer presentations Dade County High Schs. Author: Cobol Computer Language, 1974 (Best Cobol Book award Columbia, S.Am.), How to Design and Implement a Recruitment Program for International Students, 1994; 3 other computer books and intro. to data processing computer book. Cons. econ. com. Colombian Conservative Party. Roman Catholic. Office: 10415 SW 145th Ave Miami FL 33186-2918

ROSSING, CATHERINE BARRETT SCHWAB, dental hygienist; b. San Francisco, Apr. 8, 1932; d. Richard James and Mary Ann (McAuliff) and Richard Thomas Barrett; m. Donald Theodore Schwab, Aug. 8, 1954 (div. 1965); 1 child, Carla Diane; m. Alan Robert Rossing, Mar. 31, 1989. AA, U. Calif., Berkeley, 1952, BS, 1954; MPA, Calif. State U., 1983. Registered dental hygienist, Calif. Preventive specialist Dr. Thomas Evans Office, Anaheim, Calif., 1968-72, 90; mem. T.E.A.M. program U. So. Calif., L.A., 1972-73; staff hygienist Dr. Joseph Berger Dental Office, Fountain Valley, Calif., 1974-88; pub. Rossing Enterprises, Pebble Beach, Calif., 1991—; co-founder Preventive Dental Care, L.A., 1985-90; co-owner Schwab/Flora Meeting Organizers, Anaheim, 1981-90. Mem. Calif. Dental Hygienists' Assn. (editor jour. 1974-76, 81-84, 89-95, Golden Pen award 1976), Am. Dental Hygienists' Assn. (trustee 1977-81, Recognition award 1981). Avocations: Monterey Bay Aquarium, gardening. Home: 1060 Old Dr Pebble Beach CA 93953-2509

ROSSING, THOMAS D., physics educator; b. Madison, S.D., Mar. 27, 1929; s. Torstein H. and Luella E. Rossing; children: Karen, Barbara, Erik, Jane, Mary. BA, Luther Coll., 1950; MS, Iowa State U., 1952, PhD, 1954. Rsch. physicist Univac div. Sperry Rand, 1954-57; prof. physics St. Olaf Coll., 1957-71, chmn. physics dept., 1963-69; prof. physics No. Ill. U., DeKalb, 1971—, Disting. Rsch. prof., chmn. dept., 1971-73; rschr. Microwave Lab., Stanford (Calif.) U., 1961-62, Lincoln Lab., MIT, Cambridge, Mass., summer 1963, Clarendon Lab., Oxford (Eng.) U., 1966-67, physics dept. MIT, 1976-77; rsch. assoc. Argonne (Ill.) Nat Lab., 1974-76, scientist-in-residence, 1990—; vis. lectr. U. New Eng., Armidale, Australia, 1980-81; vis. exch. scholar People's Republic of China, 1988; guest rschr. Royal Inst. Tech., Stockholm, 1983, 84, 85, Inst. Perception Rsch., Eindhoven, The Netherlands, 1984, 85, Physikalisch-Technische Bundesanstalt, Braunschweig, Germany, 1988-89. Author 10 books in field; contbr. more than 250 articles to profl. publs. Fellow AAAS, Acoustical Soc. Am. (Silver medal in mus. acoustics 1992); mem. IEEE, Am. Phys. Soc., Am. Assn. Physics Tchrs. (pres. 1991), Catgut Acoustical Soc., Percussive Arts Soc., Guild Am. Luthiers, Sigma Xi (nat. lectr. 1984-87), Sigma Pi Sigma. Achievements include research in musical acoustics, psychoacoustics, speech and singing, vibration analysis, magnetic levitation, environmental noise conrol, surface effects in fusion reactors, spin waves in metals, physics education; 9 U.S. and 11 foreign patents in field. Office: No Ill U Physics Dept De Kalb IL 60115

ROSSINGTON, DAVID RALPH, physical chemistry educator; b. London, July 13, 1932; s. George Leonard and Clara Fanny (Simmons) R.; children: Andrew, Carolyn, Nicholas, Philip. BSc with honors, U. Bristol, Eng., 1953, PhD, 1956. Postdoctoral research fellow N.Y. State Coll. Ceramics at Alfred (N.Y.) U., 1956-58; tech. officer Imperial Chem. Industries Ltd., Eng., 1958-60; asst. prof. phys. chemistry Alfred U., 1960-63, assoc. prof., 1963-69, prof., 1969-95, head div. ceramic engring., 1976-79, 82-84, dean sch. engring., 1984-91. Editor: Advances in Materials Characterization, 1983; contbr. numerous articles to profl. jours. Town Justice, Alfred, 1976-86. Fulbright scholar, 1956, 58. Fellow Am. Ceramic Soc.; mem. Am. Chem. Soc., Ceramic Edn. Coun., Materials Rsch. Soc., Am. Soc. Engring. Edn., Tau Beta Pi, Phi Kappa Phi. Democrat. Episcopalian. Office: Alfred U Sch Of Engring Alfred NY 14802

ROSSINI, ALDO A., medical educator; b. Queens, N.Y., Mar. 9, 1942. BS, U. Dayton, 1963; MD, St. Louis U. Sch. Medicine, 1968. Intern in internal medicine St. Louis U. Group Hosps., 1968-69; resident in internal medicine, 1969-70; rsch. assoc. Dept. Medicine S.C. Sch. Med. Sch., North Columbia, 1971-72; rsch. fellow in Medicine Harvard Med. Sch. Peter Bent Brigham Hosp., Joslin Rsch. Lab., Boston, 1972-74; instr. in Medicine Harvard Med. Sch., 1974-75; jr. assoc. in medicine Joslin Rsch. Lab., 1974-75; asst. prof. Medicine, 1975-78; physician Joslin Clinic, Boston, 1976-78; assoc. prof. Medicine U. Mass. Med. Ctr., Worcester, 1978-82, prof. Medicine, dir. Divsn. Diabetes, 1982—, vice chmn. Dept. Medicine, 1990—; chmn. Juvenile Diabetes Found. Rsch. Review, 1987-89, Am. Diabetes Assn. Rsch. Com., 1992-93; Kroc lectr. U. Ala., Birmingham, 1987; Alexander Marble lectr., N.E. Deaconess Hosp. Lt. comdr. USN, 1970-72. Recipient Meritorious Svc. USN, Charleston, S.C., 1972, Marios Balodimos award, 1974, Capps fund award, Harvard Med. Sch., 1974-76, David Rumbough award, 1986, Donald M. Silver Excellence in Rsch. award, 1987, Golden Apple award, Basic Sci., 1994, 95, Clin. Sci., 1994. Mem. ACP, Am. Diabetes Assn., Boston Diabetes Club, Greater Boston Diabetes Soc., Inc., Am. Fedn. for Clin. Rsch., The Mass. Med. Soc., Mass. Med. Soc., Mass. Soc. Intrnal Medicine, The Endocrine Soc., ADA Rsch. Grant Review Panel (chair), Bd. Scientific Counselors. Office: Univ Massachusetts Med Ctr 55 Lake Ave N Worcester MA 01655*

ROSSINI, JOSEPH, contracting and development corporate executive; b. New Rochelle, N.Y., Nov. 25, 1939; m. Antonia Rossini; children: Katherine, Anthony, Andrew. Student, Fordham U., 1965-66, Iona Coll., 1972. Pres. Rossini Contracting Corp., New Rochelle, 1963—; prin. Rossini Devel. Co., Monticello, N.Y., 1965—; bd. dirs. Circuit Realty Corp., New Rochelle, 1970-71. Mem. planning bd. City of New Rochelle, 1986-92, mem. bldg. dept. adv. com., 1985; vol. instr. N.Y. State Dept. Environ. Conservation, Albany, 1968—; vice chmn. New Rochelle Conservative Party, 1984—; county committeeman Westchester County Conservative Party; v.p. bd. trustees Beechwoods Cemetery, New Rochelle; dir. New Rochelle Neighborhood Revitalization Corp. With USN, 1959-61. Mem. NRA, Gen. Contractors Assn. N.Y., Constrn. Industry Coun. Westchester and Hudson Valley, Bldg. Trades Employers Assn., Soc. Explosives Engrs., Deep Founds. Inst., Young Ams. for Freedom, Am. Lauretana Assn., Mensa, Assoc. Gen. Contractors Am. Roman Catholic. Office: Rossini Contracting Corp 113 Edison Ave Mount Vernon NY 10550-5005

ROSSITER, ALEXANDER, JR., news service executive, editor; b. Elmira, N.Y., Mar. 2, 1936; s. Alexander H. and Eleanor (Howell) R.; m. Sylvia Lee Vanlandingham, June 11, 1960; children: Alexander H. III, Jill Jarrell. BA, Rutgers U., 1958; postgrad., Emory U., 1959. With UPI, 1959-92; newsman Atlanta, 1959-61, Richmond, Va., 1961-63; bur. mgr. Cape Canaveral, Fla., 1963-73; sci. editor Washington, 1973-87, exec. editor, 1987-88, exec. editor, sr. v.p., 1988-91, editor, exec. v.p., 1991-92; asst. v.p., dir. news svc. Duke U., Durham, N.C., 1992—; mem. nat. adv. bd. Knight Ctr. for Specialized Journalism, Colleg Pk., Md., 1988-92. Recipient Grady-Stack medal Am. Chem. Soc., 1987, other journalism awards. Mem. Nat. Assn. Sci. Writers, Edn. Writers Assn. Office: Duke U 615 Chapel Dr Durham NC 27706-2500 *Enthusiasm is the key to success. Take on your education, your family responsibilities and your work with enthusiasm and good things will result.*

ROSSITER, BRYANT WILLIAM, chemistry consultant; b. Ogden, Utah, Mar. 10, 1931; s. Bryant B. and Christine (Peterson) R.; m. Betty Jean Anderson, Apr. 16, 1951; children: Bryant, Mark, Diane, Steven, Linda, Karen, Matthew, Gregory. BA, U. Utah, 1954, PhD, 1957. Researcher Eastman-Kodak Co., Rochester, N.Y., 1957-63, head color phys. chem. lab., 1963-70, dir. chemistry div., 1970-84, dir. sci., tech. devel., 1984-86; pres. Viratek Inc., Costa Mesa, Calif., 1986-89; sr. v.p. ICN Pharms., Costa Mesa, 1989-90; ret., 1990; pres., chief exec. officer Wrecon Corp., cons., Laguna Hills, Calif., 1991—; sr. editor John Wiley & Sons, N.Y.C., 1970—; chmn. bd. Nucleic Acid Rsch. Inst., Costa Mesa, 1987-88; trustee Eastman Dental Ctr., Rochester, 1973-93 (bd. pres. 1982-85); bd. dirs. Verax & Corp. Editor: (chem. treatises) Physical Methods of Chemistry (11 vols.), 1970-76, Physical Methods, (12 vols.), 1986—, Chemical Experimentation Under Extreme Conditions, 1979. Mem. rsch. adv. com. U.S. Agy. for Internat. Devel., Washington, chmn. rsch. adv. com., 1989-92; mem. panel on biosci. Pres.' Coun. Advisors on Sci. and Tech., 1991; mem. adv com. Cornell Internat. Inst. for Food, Agr. and Devel., 1991; presiding officer Ch. Jesus Christ Latter Day Saints, Ea. U.S. and Can., 1959-86. 1st lt. USAFR, 1951-58. Named Hon. Alumni Brigham Young U., Provo, Utah, 1982. Fellow AAAS, Am. Inst. Chemists (lectr., Fellows award 1988, Will Judy award Juanita Coll. 1978); mem. Internat. Union Pure and Applied Chemistry (chmn. U.S. nat. com., orignator, chmn. Chemical Rsch. Applied to World Needs com. 1975-87, chmn. Chemical Rsch. Applied to World Needs II The Internat. Conf. on Chemistry and World Food Supplies, 1982), Am. Chem. Soc. (chmn. internat. activities). Avocations: horseback riding, reading, fishing. Home and Office: 25662 Dillon Rd Laguna Hills CA 92653

ROSSITER, MARGARET WALSH, history of science educator; b. Malden, Mass., July 8, 1944; d. Charles Aston and Mary Julia (Madden) R. AB, Radcliffe Coll., 1966; MS, U. Wis., 1967; MPhil, Yale U., 1969, PhD, 1971. Acting asst. prof., lectr. dept. history U. Calif., Berkeley, 1973-74, 75-76, rsch. assoc. Office for History of Sci. and Tech., 1976-82; rsch. assoc. Am. Acad. Arts and Scis., Cambridge, Mass., 1977-86; program dir. history and philosophy of sci. program NSF, Washington, 1982-83; vis. lectr., vis. scholar dept. history of sci. Harvard U., Cambridge, Mass., 1983-86; NSF vis. prof. history sci., dept. history Cornell U., Ithaca, N.Y., 1986-88, prof. history sci., 1988-91, prof. dept. sci. and tech. studies, 1991—; mem. adv. com. NSF, 1981-82, 83-84; Kreeger-Wolf Disting. vis. prof. Northwestern U., 1985; Regents lectr. U. Calif., Riverside, 1986; A.H. Compton lectr. Washington U., St. Louis, 1996. Author: The Emergence of Agricultural Science: Justus Liebig and the Americans, 1975, Women Scientists in America: Struggles and Strategies to 1940, 1982, paperback, 1984, Women Scientists in America: Before Affirmative Action, 1940-1972, 1995; co-editor: (with Sally Gregory Kohlstedt) Historical Writing on American Science, 1986; compiler Bibliography of the History of the Agricultural Sciences, 1980; assoc. editor Am. Nat. Biography, 1989—; mem. editl. bd. Tech. and Culture, 1978-84, Osiris, 1983-90, Isis, 1989—; editor Osiris, 1993—; reviewer sci. books; contbr. articles to jours. Recipient Silver medal Justus-Liebig U., Giessen, Germany, 1979, Berkshire prize for best book in field of history by Am. woman, 1983, Wilbur Cross medal Yale U. Grad. Sch., 1984, Hoopes Teaching award Harvard U., 1984, Rsch. prize Justus-Liebig U., 1985; Rockefeller fellow; Guggheim fellow; MacArthur Found. fellow. Mem. AAUP (com. A. acad. freedom and tenure 1989-92), AAAS (Sarton lectr. 1990), History of Sci. Soc. (numerous coms.), Internat. Commn. on History of Women in Scis., Tech. and Medicine (pres. 1981-89), Forum for the History of Am. Sci. (coun. 1989-92, keynote speaker 1989), Agrl. History Soc. (exec. com. 1979-82), Soc. for History Tech. (numerous coms. 1979-84). Roman Catholic. Office: Cornell U Dept Sci and Tech Studies 726 University Ave # 201 Ithaca NY 14850-3914

ROSSITER, ROBERT E., diversified corporation executive; b. 1946. With Lear Siegler Inc., 1971-87, former pres. seating div.; pres., chief oper. officer Lear Seating Corp., Southfield, Mich., 1987—, also bd. dirs. Office: Lear Seating Corp 21557 Telegraph Rd Southfield MI 48034-4248*

ROSSLER, WILLIS KENNETH, JR., petroleum company executive; b. Houston, Nov. 17, 1946; s. Willis Kenneth and Fay Lee (Olle) R.; BS in Indsl. Engring., Tex. Tech. U., 1969; postgrad. in bus. Stanford U.; children: Nancy Kay, Deborah Anne, Ryan Konrad, Eric George. Dist. mgr. Tex.-La. ops. Continental Pipe Line Co., Lake Charles, La., 1974-75, mgr. engring., Houston, 1976-77; asst. mgr. corp. planning and devel. Conoco, Inc., Houston, 1977-78; v.p. project devel. PetroUnited, Inc., Houston, 1978-80, pres., 1981-86, also dir. Pres., Village Pl. Community Assn., Houston, 1978, also partnership com. Antwerp Gas Terminal, V.G.N., 1982-85, v.p., gen. mgr., Pilko and Assoc., Inc., Houston, 1986-90; pres., CEO Houston Fuel Oil Terminal Co., 1990—; bd. dirs. Pilko and Assocs., Naylor Industries, Inc., Clean Channel Assn., Greater Houston Port Bur., Grace Presbyn. Sch. Mem. Am. Inst. Indsl. Engrs., Am. Petroleum Inst., Houston Mgmt. Council, Intensive Mgmt. Devel. Inst. (adv. dir. 1983-84), Ind. Liquid Terminals Assn. (vice chmn. 1986, chmn.-elect 1987), Am. Mgmt. Assn., Planning Forum (pres. chpt. 1985), Petroleum Club of Houston, Lakeside Country Club. Office: Houston Fuel Oil Terminal Co 16642 Jacintoport Blvd Houston TX 77015-6541

ROSSMAN, JANET KAY, architectural interior designer; b. Lansing, Mich., Feb. 13, 1954; d. Elmer Chris and Jean Elizabeth (Schell) R.; m. Farzad Moazed; children: Alexander, Christina. BA with High Honors, Mich. State U., 1976. Designer Tilton & Lewis Assocs., Inc., Chgo., 1977-79, Swanke Hayden Connell & Ptnrs., N.Y.C., 1979-81, Bonsignore Brignati & Mazzotta Architects, N.Y.C., 1982-84; dir. design, assoc. SPGA Group, Inc., N.Y.C., 1984—; instr. Design Edn. Ctr., Lansing, 1975-76. Fellow Mus. Modern Art, N.Y.C., 1977—. Mem. Am. Soc. of Interior Designers (chair. 1973-76, editor Collage 1973-76), Inst. Bus. Designers, Nat. Assn. for Female Execs., Omicron Nu. Republican. Club: Atrium, Landmark. Avocations: photography, equestrian activities, travel. Home: 367 W Hill Rd Stamford CT 06902-1709

ROSSMAN, RICHARD ALAN, lawyer; b. Albany, N.Y., June 16, 1939; s. Kenneth Fisher and Edith Bell (Wheeler) R.; m. Patricia Margaret Booth, Jan. 2, 1965; children: Lisa, Jeffrey. AB, U. Mich., 1961, JD, 1964. Asst. pros. atty. Oakland County, Pontiac, Mich., 1965-67, 70-71; chief dep. fed. defender, Detroit, 1972-75, sole practice, 1975-77; chief asst. U.S. Atty. Ea. Dist. Mich., Detroit, 1977-80, U.S. atty., 1980-81; ptnr. Butzel, Long, Gust, Klein & Van Zile, Detroit, 1981-86, Pepper, Hamilton & Scheetz, Detroit, 1986—. Mem. ABA, Fed. Bar Assn. (pres. Detroit chpt. 1982-83), Mich. Bar Assn. (chair standing com. on U.S. cts. 1996—, rep. assembly 1980-82), Oakkland County Bar Assn., Detroit Bar Assn. (trustee found. 1984-86). Office: Pepper Hamilton & Scheetz 100 Renaissance Ctr Ste 3600 Detroit MI 48243-1101

ROSSMAN, ROBERT HARRIS, management consultant; b. Phila., Jan. 27, 1932; s. Benjamin Bernard and Vivian (Silnutzer) R.; m. Wanda Ward, Aug. 9, 1980; 1 child, Victoria Anne; children from previous marriage: Rodger Samuel, Robbi Jennifer, Ronni Esther. BS, U.S. Merchant Marine Acad., 1953; MSME with honors, U.S. Naval Postgrad. Sch., 1963; cert. advanced naval architecture, MIT, 1973. Cert. mgr. human resources; cert. value specialist. Commd. ensign USN, 1953, advanced through grades to comdr., 1967, shipboard engr., 1953-55, maintenance and repair officer Reserve Fleet, 1955-57; served as ship supt. Norfolk Naval Shipyard, Portsmouth, Va., 1957-60; maintenance and logistics planning officer Amphibious Squadron Twelve, Little Creek, Va., 1963-65; planning and estimating supt. U.S. Naval Ship Repair Facility, Yokosuka, Japan, 1965-67; design and planning advisor USN, Saigon, Republic Viet Nam, 1967-68; chief prodn. engring. Def. Contract Adminstrn. Svcs., Alexandria, Va., 1968-70; dir. cost reduction Naval Ship Systems Command, Washington, 1970-73; dep. program mgr. new ship class Naval Ship Engring. Ctr., Hyattsville, Md., 1973; ret. USN, 1973; ptnr. Kempter-Rossman Internat., Washington, 1974-91; owner Rossman Assocs. Internat., 1991—; cons. in cost and time reduction, mgmt. improvement, productivity and competition enhancement. Author: (textbook) Function Based Analysis, 1983, Total Cycle Time Reduction, 1992; editor mag. Performance, 1970-73; contbr. articles to profl. jours. Pres. PTA, Fairfax County, Va., 1969-70, Community Civic Assn., Fairfax County, 1970-71; chmn. Boy Scouts Am. and Weblos troops, 1969-71, del. at large 1st Congl. Dist. Rep. Com., N.C., 1989-90; chmn. Chowan County (N.C.) Rep. Com., 1990-92. Decorated USN Commendation medals, Honor medal-1st Class (Republic of Vietnam Armed Forces), Combat Action medal. Fellow Soc. Am. Value Engrs. (v.p. 1970-73, Disting. Svc. award 1976); mem. U.S. Merchant Marine Acad. Alumni Assn., Am. Legion, Sigma Xi. Jewish. Avocations: gardening, home remodeling, restoration, writing. Home: 110 Old Hertford Rd Edenton NC 27932-9602 Office: Rossman Assocs Internat Speight House 110 Old Hertford Rd Edenton NC 27932-9602

ROSSMAN, RUTH SCHARFF, artist, educator; b. Bklyn.; d. Joseph and Elsie (Frankel) Scharff; m. Phillip Rossman; 1 dau., Joanne. Grad., Cleve. Inst. Art, 1934; BS, Case Western Res. U., 1934; postgrad., Kahn Inst. Art, 1947-50, UCLA, 1960. Art instr. Canton (Ohio) public schs., 1934-39, Canton Art Inst., 1937-45, Rustic Canyon Art Center, Los Angeles, 1978-81. One-woman shows at Heritage Gallery, L.A., 1963, 66, Canton (Ohio) Community Ctr., 1967, Marymount Coll., U. Judaism, 1980, L.A. Fedn. Bldg., 1981, 89, Platt Gallery, 1986, 93, others; exhibited in group shows Mus. Modern Art, N.Y.C., Butler Mus., Washington and Jefferson Coll., Denver Mus., Space Mus., Mt. St. Mary's Coll., L.A., M.H. de Young Mus., San Francisco Mus. Art, Venice Art Walk, ann. 1981-94, Univ. Judaism, 1986, 93, Brand Art Gallery, 1987, others; represented in permanent collections Pa. Acad. Fine Arts, Phila., Brandeis-Bardin Inst., U. Redlands, Calif., Nat. Watercolor Soc., Ahmanson Collection, Rocky Mt. Nat., others; paintings included in book The California Romantics: Harbingers of Watercolor, 1987. Chair selection com. for Platt Gallery, U. Judaism, L.A., 1986—. Recipient purchase-cash awards Los Angeles All-City Art Exhbn. Mem. Nat. Watercolor Soc. (pres. 1974-75, juror 75th Ann. Exhbn. 1995).

ROSSMAN, STUART T., lawyer; b. Bklyn., Jan. 7, 1954; s. Marvin Warren and Phyllis (Berenbaum) R.; m. Rochelle S. Sorkin, May 18, 1975; children: Jessie Joanne, Rachel Joy. BA, U. Mich., 1975; JD, Harvard U., 1978. Bar: Mass. 1978, U.S. Dist. Ct. Mass. 1979, U.S. Ct. Appeals (1st cir.) 1979, U.S. Claims Ct. 1984, U.S. Supreme Ct. 1984. Assoc. Gaston & Snow, Boston, 1978-87, ptnr., 1987-91; asst. atty. gen. Mass., 1991; chief of trial divsn., 1992-95, chief bus. and labor protection bur., 1995—, exec. Editor: (handbook) Homeless Not Helpless, 1988, Social Change, 1986, Boston Bar Jour. Mem. United Jewish Appeal Young Leadership Cabinet, N.Y.C., 1983-92, nat. chmn., 1991-92, Coun. Jewish Fedns. Leadership Devel. Com., N.Y.C., 1986-92; mem. exec. bd. Combined Jewish Philanthropies, Boston, 1994—, chmn., 1994—; dir. Vol. Lawyers Project, Boston, 1983—; HRD CJP chmn., 1994—; bd. dirs. Bur. Jewish Edn., 1993—, v.p., 1994—; mem. Jewish Cmty. Rels. Coun., 1992—, v.p., 1994—. Recipient 10 Outstanding Young Leaders award Boston Jaycees, 1995; Wexner Heritage Found. fellow, 1991-93. Mem. Mass. Bar Assn., Boston Bar Assn. (chmn. young lawyers sect. 1983-86). Democrat.

ROSSMANN, JACK EUGENE, psychology educator; b. Walnut, Iowa, Dec. 4, 1936; s. Wilbert C. Rossmann and Claire L. (Mickel) Walter; m. Marilyn Martin, June 14, 1958; children: Ann, Charles, Sarah. BS, Iowa State U., 1958, MS, 1960; PhD, U. Minn., 1963. Lic. cons. psychologist, Minn. Asst. prof. Macalester Coll., St. Paul, 1964-68, assoc. prof., 1968-73, prof., 1973—, v.p. acad. affairs, 1978-86; chair dept. psychology Macalester Coll., 1990—; cons. Pers. Decisions Inc., Mpls., 1989—; cons.-evaluator North Ctrl. Assn., 1975—. Author: (with others) Open Admissions at CUNY, 1975; contbr. articles to profl. jours. Bd. dirs. Twin City Inst. for Talented Youth, St. Paul, 1978-91, United Theol. Sem., UTS bd., 1984-96—. New Brighton, Minn., 1984-96—. 2d lt. U.S. Army, 1959. Mem. APA, AAUP (pres. Minn. conf. 1993-95), Am. Psychol. Soc., Assn. for Instl. Rsch., Am. Assn. for Higher Edn. Home: 99 Cambridge St Saint Paul MN 55105-1947 Office: Macalester Coll 1600 Grand Ave Saint Paul MN 55105

ROSSMANN, MICHAEL GEORGE, biochemist, educator; b. Frankfurt, Germany, July 30, 1930; s. Alexander and Nelly (Schwabacher) R.; m. Audrey Pearson, July 24, 1954; children—Martin, Alice, Heather. B.Sc. with honors, Polytechnic, London, 1951, M.Sc. in Physics, 1953; Ph.D. in Chemistry, U. Glasgow, 1956. Fulbright scholar U. Minn., 1956-58; research scientist MRC Lab. Molecular Biology, Cambridge, Eng., 1958-64; asso. prof. biol. scis. Purdue U., West Lafayette, Ind., 1964-67; prof. Purdue U., 1967-78, Hanley Disting. prof. biol. scis., 1978—, prof. biochemistry, 1975—. Editor: The Molecular Replacement Method, 1972; mem. editl. bd. Jour. Biol. Chemistry, 1975-80; contbr. over 300 articles to profl. jours. Grantee NIH, NSF; recipient Fankuchen award Am. Crystallographc Assn., 1986, Horwitz prize Columbia U., 1990, Gregori Arminoff prize Royal Swedish Acad. Sci., 1994, Stein & Moore award Protein Soc., 1994, Ewald prize Internat. Union Crystallography. Mem. Am. Soc. Biol. Chemists, Am. Chem. Soc., Biophys. Soc., Am. Crystallographic Assn., Brit. Biophys. Soc., Inst. Physics., Chem. Soc. (U.K.), AAAS, NAS, Indian Nat. Sci. Acad., Royal Soc. Democrat. Club: Lafayette Sailing. Home: 1208 Wiley Dr West Lafayette IN 47906-2434 Office: Dept Biol Scis Purdue Univ West Lafayette IN 47907-1392

ROSSMILLER, GEORGE EDDIE, agricultural economist; b. Gt. Falls, Mont., June 8, 1935; s. Albert E. and Romaine (Hennford) R.; m. Betty Ann Rinio, Dec. 20, 1955 (dec. Mar. 1990); children: David W., Diane J. BS, Mont. State U., 1956, MS, 1962; PhD, Mich. State U., 1965. Rsch. assoc. Mich. State U., East Lansing, 1965-66, asst. prof., 1967-71, assoc. prof., 1972-76, prof. agrl. econs., 1977-80; agrl. attache to OECD, Fgn. Agrl. Service, USDA, Paris, 1978-79; asst. adminstr. internat. trade policy Fgn. Agrl. Svc., USDA, Washington, 1979-81, dir planing and analysis, 1981-85; sr. fellow and dir. Nat. Ctr. Food and Agr. Policy, Resources for the Future, 1986-92; also exec. dir. Internat. Policy Council on Agr. and Trade, 1988-92; chief situation and policy studies svc. Food and Agr. Orgn. of UN, Rome, 1992—. Author: The Grain-Livestock Economy of West Germany with Projections to 1970 and 1975, 1968, (with others) Korean Agricultural

Sector Analysis and Recommended Development Strategies, 1971-1985, 1972; editor: (with others) Agricultural Sector Planning: A General System Simulation Approach, 1978. Served with U.S. Army, 1956-59. Recipient service citation Korean Ministry of Agrl. and Fisheries, 1973, service citation Office of Prime Minister of Korea, 1977, Superior Service award U.S. Dept. Agr., 1983, Fgn. Agrl. Service merit award, 1984. Mem. Am. Agrl. Econs. Assn. (Disting. Policy Contbn. award 1992), Internat. Assn. Agrl. Economists. Presbyterian. Home: Interno 20, Via dell, Accademia Albertina 38, 00147 Rome Italy Office: Food and Agrl Orgn UN, viale delle Terme di Caracalla, 00100 Rome Italy

ROSSO, LOUIS T., scientific instrument manufacturing company executive; b. San Francisco, 1933; married. A.B., San Francisco State Coll., 1955; M.B.A., U. Santa Clara, 1967. Product specialist Spinco div. Beckman Instruments, Fullerton, Calif., 1959-63, mktg. mgr., 1963-69, mgr. Spinco div., 1969-70, mgr. clin. instruments div., 1970-74, corp. v.p., mgr. analytical instruments group, 1974-80, corp. sr. v.p., 1980-83, pres., 1983—, now also chmn., chief exec. officer; also bd. dirs. Beckman Instruments, Inc.; v.p. SmithKline Beckman Corp., Phila. Office: Beckman Instruments Inc 2500 N Harbor Blvd Fullerton CA 92634-2607*

ROSSO DE IRIZARRY, CARMEN (TUTTY ROSSO DE IRIZARRY), finance executive; b. Ponce, P.R., Feb. 9, 1947; d. Jorge Ignacio and Carmen Teresa (Descartes) Rosso Castain; m. Alfredo R. Irizarry Sile, Aug. 29, 1967. BBA, U. P.R., Rio Piedras. Vice pres. Alcay Inc., San Juan, P.R., 1972—, also bd. dirs.; v.p. J.I.C. Corp., M.I.C. Corp.; bd. dirs., now pres. bd. Construcciones Urbanas Inc., Internat. Fin. Corp. Troop leader Girl Scouts U.S.A., 1977-80; bd. dirs. PTA, San Juan, 1978-81, 86-88; activities coord. Colegio Puertorriqueño Niñas, San Juan, 1987-88; judge Miss P.R. Pageant, San Juan 1987-88, 94, Miss World P.R. Pageant, San Juan, 1987-88, Miss World of P.R., 1990; pres. fundacion dept. Oncologia Pediatrica Hosp. Universitario Dr. Antonio Ortiz, 1990; organizer Best of Saks Fifth Avenue Benefit, 1991, 92, 93, 94, pres. 1992, 94; com. mem. Make a Wish Found. Coleccion Alta Moda, 1994; mem. com. Muceo Ponce Gala, 1994; mem. com. Museo Ponce Coala, 1994; luminaria J.C. Penney, 1994; destellos de la Moda, 1994; pres. Best of Saks 5th Avenue Benefit, 1993, 94. Named to Ten Best Dressed List, San Juan Star, 1986-87, Hall of Fame of Ten Best Dressed, 1989; recipient luminaria J.C. Penney, 1994. Fellow Assn. Porcelanas; mem. Club de Leones (Garden Hills, P.R., Lady of Yr. award 1978), Caparra Country Club (pres. 1985-86), Club Civicos Damas (judge hat how 1989, in charge spl. events 1992), Mu Alpha Phi. Republican. Roman Catholic. Avocations: china painting, boating, water skiing. Office: Internat Fin Corp PO Box 8486 Santurce San Juan PR 00910-0486

ROSSOF, ARTHUR HAROLD, internal medicine educator; b. Chgo., Dec. 12, 1943; s. Jack and Libby (Gordon) R.; m. Rebecca Ann, Aug. 11, 1967 (div. 1983); children: Jacob Earl, Lizabeth Eva; m. Kristine Ann, Feb. 14, 1985. Student, Bradley U., 1961-64; MD, U. Ill., 1968. Diplomate Nat. Bd. Med. Examiners, Am. Bd. Internal Medicine, Am. Bd. Oncology, Am. Bd. Hematology. Fellow sect. neurobiology dept. neurology Presbyn.-St. Luke's Hosp., Chgo., 1965-68, intern straight medicine, 1968-69, resident dept. medicine, 1969-71, Eastern Coop. Oncology Group fellow sect. oncology, dept. medicine, 1971-72, asst. attending physician dept. internal medicine, 1976-80, assoc. attending physician, dept. internal medicine, 1980-82, sr. attending physician dept. internal medicine, 1982-90; med. dir. MacNeal Cancer Ctr., Berwyn, Ill., 1985—; asst. medicine U. Ill. Coll. Medicine, 1969-71; clin. asst. prof. medicine U. Tex. health Sci. Ctr., San Antonio, 1973-76; instr. medicine Rush Med. Coll., 1971-72, asst. prof. medicine, 1976-81, assoc. prof. medicine, 1981-90; assoc. prof. medicine Loyola U. Med. Ctr., Chgo., 1990-91, prof., 1991—; mem. resident selection com. Rush-Presbyn.-St. Luke's Med. Ctr., 1976-88, mem. ethics conf. planning group, 1981-90, tumor com., 1981-90, chmn. cancer edn. subcom., 1982-90; mem. pharmacy and therapeutics com., chmn. instnl. rev. bd., chmn. cancer com. MacNeal Hosp.; cons. Cancer Info. Svcv., Ill. Cancer Coun., mem. clin. trials com. 1978—, credentials rev. com.; mem. adv. com. Lincoln Park Zoo, 1978—. Author: Lithium Effects on Granulopoiesis and Immune Function, 1980; contbr. articles in field to profl. jours.; patentee in field. Maj. M.C., USAF, 1972-76. Fellow ACP; mem. Internat. Soc. Exptl. Hematology, Am. Soc. Clin. Oncology, Am. Fedn. Clin. Research, Am. Assn. Cancer Research, Am. Soc. Hematology, N.Y. Acad. Scis., Soc. Air Force Physicians, Cell Kinetic Soc., Internat. Assn. Study Lung Cancer, Soc. Med. History Chgo., Chgo. Soc. Internal Medicine, AAAS, Am. Assn. Cancer Edn., Assn. Community Cancer Ctrs., Sigma Xi, Phi Eta Sigma, Alpha Omega Alpha. Republican. Jewish. Avocation: tennis. Office: MacNeal Cancer Ctr 3340 Oak Park Ave Berwyn IL 60402-3420

ROSSOLIMO, ALEXANDER NICHOLAS, management consultant; b. Paris, June 8, 1939; came to U.S., 1952; s. Nicholas S. and Vera A. (Boudakovitch) R.; m. Meryl Louise Stowbridge, Sept. 10, 1977; children: Gregory, Katherine, Elizabeth. BEE, CCNY, 1962; MA in Applied Math., Harvard U., 1963, PhD in Applied Physics, 1973; MBA, MIT, 1973. Cert. in bus. French. Fin. analyst Péchiney, Paris, 1972; brand/advt. mgmt. The Clorox Co., Oakland, Calif., 1973-74; cons. The Boston Consulting Group, 1974-76; dir. planning and fin. analysis United Brands, Boston, 1977-80; sr. dir. Digital Equipment Corp., Maynard, Mass., 1980-92; pres. International Strategy Associates, Newton, Mass., 1992-94; pres., chief exec. officer Internat. Strategy Assocs., Newton, Mass., 1994—; vis. fellow Harvard U., Cambridge, Mass., 1991-93; bd. dirs. ACG Internat., Chgo., 1994—; bd. dirs. Ctr. for Security and Social Progress, Inc., 1995—; bd. dirs. Newton Consulting Group, 1995—. Contbr. numerous articles to bus. and internat. newspapers. Mem. search com. Ecole Bilingue, French-Am. Internat. Sch. of Boston, 1991-93; fund raiser Milton (Mass.) Acad., 1994—. Recipient award in elec. engring. Blonder-Tongue Found., N.Y.C., 1961, Belden medal in math. CCNY, 1960; NSF fellow, 1962. Mem. Nat. Assn. Corp. Dirs., Bus. Execs. for Nat. Security, Boston Security Analysts Soc., French Am. C. of C., Japan Soc. Boston, World Affairs Coun., Assn. for Corp. Growth Boston (chmn. 1995-96), Harvard Club Boston, Toastmasters (pres.), Tau Beta Pi, Eta Kappa Nu. Avocations: jogging, tennis, foreign languages, international organizations. Office: International Strategy Associates PO Box 207 Waban MA 02168

ROSSON, GLENN RICHARD, building products and furniture company executive; b. Galveston, Tex., Aug. 17, 1937; s. John Raymond and Elsie Lee (Reece) R.; m. Edwina Lucille Hart, June 2, 1956; children—Darrell Richard, Alex Mark. B.B.A., Tex. Tech U., 1959. C.P.A., Tex. Supr., accountant Axelson div. U.S. Industries Inc., Longview, Tex., 1960-67; controller U.S. Industries Inc., 1968; group financial v.p. U.S. Industries Inc., Dallas, 1969; group chmn. U.S. Industries Inc., 1969-72, v.p., 1973-74, sr. v.p., 1974, exec. v.p., 1974-80, also dir.; pres. Rosson Investment Co., 1980—; chmn. bd. Yorktowne Inc., 1988—. Mem. Am. Inst. C.P.A.s, Tex. Soc. C.P.A.s, Nat. Assn. Accts. (past nat. dir., past pres. E. Tex. chpt.), Assn. for Corp. Growth (past pres.). Club: Dallas Athletic, TBARM Raquet. Home: 11367 Drummond Dr Dallas TX 75228-1946 Office: 5910 N Central Expy Ste 1000 Dallas TX 75206-5142

ROSSOTTI, BARBARA JILL MARGULIES, lawyer; b. Englewood, N.J., Feb. 28, 1940; d. Albert and Loretta (Jill) Margulies; m. Charles Ossola Rossotti; children: Allegra Jill, Edward Charles. BA magna cum laude, Mount Holyoke Coll., 1961; LLB, Harvard U., 1964. Bar: D.C. 1966. Assoc. Nutter McClennen & Fish, Boston, 1964-65, Covington & Burling, Washington, 1965-72; assoc. Shaw, Pittman, Potts & Trowbridge, Washington, 1972-73, ptnr., 1973—. Trustee Mt. Holyoke Coll., South Hadley, Mass., 1984, vice chmn., 1989-94, chmn., 1994—; chmn. exec. com. Campaign for Mt. Holyoke Coll., 1986-91; trustee Legal Aid Soc., D.C., 1979-92, pres. 1985-89, mem. pres. coun., 1992—; trustee Choral Arts Soc., Washington, 1989—, chair, 1993-95; bd. dirs. Washington Home, 1989—. Fellow Am. Bar Found.; mem. ABA, Am. Soc. Internat. Law, Internat. Law Assn., D.C. Bar. Office: Shaw Pittman Potts & Trowbridge 2300 N St NW Washington DC 20037-1122

ROSSOTTI, CHARLES OSSOLA, computer consulting company executive; b. N.Y.C., Jan. 17, 1941; s. Charles C. and V. Elizabeth (Ossola) R.; m. Barbara Jill Margulies, June 9, 1963; children: Allegra Jill, Edward Charles. AB magna cum laude, Georgetown U., 1962; MBA with high distinction, Harvard U., 1974. Mgmt. cons. Boston Cons. Group, 1964-65; prin. dep. asst. sec. Office of Systems Analysis, Dept. Def., Washington, 1965-70; prin. dep. asst. sec. of Def. Office of Systems Analysis, Dept. Def., 1969-70; pres. Am. Mgmt. Systems, Inc., Arlington, Va., 1970—, chief exec. officer, 1981—, chmn. bd., 1989—; bd. dirs. Intersalv, Inc. Bd. dirs. Georgetown U., 1969-77, 92—; trustee Woodstock Theol. Ctr., 1990—; chmn. Corp. Against Drug Abuse, 1993—. Mem. Coun. Fgn. Rels. Office: Am Mgmt Systems Inc 4050 Legato Rd Fairfax VA 22033-4003

ROSS-RAY, FRANCES ANN, lawyer; b. Painesville, Ohio, June 17, 1959; d. Francis Kelly and Patsy Paige (Banks) Ross; m. Robert Joseph Ray, Aug. 13, 1983; children: Nicholas Ross, Robert Gordon, Francis Andrew. BS in Polit. Sci., U. Houston, 1986, JD, 1989. Bar: Pa. 1989, U.S. Dist. Ct. Pa. 1989. Atty. Buchanan Ingersoll, Pitts., 1989-92, Babst Calland Clements & Zomnir, Pitts., 1992—. Mem. ABA, Pa. Bar Assn. Alleghany County Bar Assn., Order of Coif. Home: 9570 Saratoga Dr Pittsburgh PA 15237 Office: Babst Calland Clements & Zomnir 2 Gateway Ctr Pittsburgh PA 15222

ROSSTON, EDWARD WILLIAM, lawyer; b. San Francisco, Nov. 14, 1918; s. Ernest William and Goldah Ray (Charmak) R.; m. Maxine Goldmark Aaron, June 28, 1947; children—Edward William, Richard Mark, Ellen Maxine Rosston Neft, Jean Frances. A.B., U. Calif.-Berkeley, 1939, JD, 1947; LL.M., Columbia U., 1948. Bar: Calif. 1947. Assoc. Heller Ehrman White & McAuliff, San Francisco, 1948-58; ptnr. Heller Ehrman White & McAuliff, 1958—; instr. Hastings Coll. Law, U. Calif., San Francisco, 1949-51; bd. dirs. Consumer Credit Counsellors, San Francisco, 1965-95; sec. MPC Ins. Ltd., 1986-93. Nat. trustee Lawyers Com. for Civil Rights, 1977—; co-chmn., mem. exec. com. San Francisco Lawyers Com. for Urban Affairs, 1972-83; trustee The Mechanics Inst. and Chessroom, 1991—, v.p., 1993-95. Lt. USNR, 1941-46, PTO. Mem. ABA, State Bar Calif., Bar Assn. San Francisco (bd. dirs., com. chmn. 1959-65), Am. Arbitration Assn. (arbitrator and mediator, adv. coun. North Calif. chpt. 1988—), Boalt Hall Alumni Assn. (trustee 1977-79). Democrat. Jewish. Club: Commonwealth (San Francisco). Office: Heller Ehrman White & McAuliffe 333 Bush St San Francisco CA 94104-2806

ROST, PETER, pharmaceutical company executive; b. Bollebygd, Sweden, May 31, 1959; came to U.S., 1987; s. Siegfrid and Kathie (Zerne) R.; m. Tina Forssten, Apr. 21, 1984. MD, U. Gothenburg, Sweden, 1984. Intern anesthesiology dept. Ea. Hosp., Gothenburg, 1984, practice medicine specializing in anesthesiology, 1984; pres., CEO Bus. Lit. Inc., Gothenburg, 1985-87; copywriter Ehrenstrahle & Co., Gothenburg, 1985, Ogilvy & Mather, Gothenburg, 1985; account supr., copywriter Grey Gothenburg, Gothenburg, 1985-87; med. dir., account supr. Maher Kaump & Clark, Inc., L.A., 1987-92; assoc. dir. med. edn. Lederle Labs. divsn. Am. Cyanamid Co., Wayne, N.J., 1992, dir. med. edn., 1993; product mgr. Lederle Labs. divsn. Am. Cyanimid Co., Wayne, N.J., 1993-94; mkt. planning mgr. Wyeth-Ayerst Internat., St. Davids, Pa., 1995, dir. mktg internal medicine products, 1995—; chmn., chief exec. officer W. Sweden Model Group, Gothenburg, 1985. Author: Emergency Surgery, 1985, The Art of Driving a Car Free, 1985. Mem. AMA, Am. Coll. Physician Execs., Pharm. Advt. Coun. Office: Wyeth-Ayerst Internat Inc PO Box 8616 Philadelphia PA 19101-8616 also: 150 Radnor-Chester Rd Saint Davids PA 19087

ROST, THOMAS LOWELL, plant biology educator; b. St. Paul, Dec. 28, 1941; s. Lowell Henry Rost and Agnes Marie (Wojtowicz) Jurek; m. Ann Marie Ruhland, Aug. 31, 1963; children: Christopher, Timothy, Jacquelyn. BS, St. John's U., Collegeville, Minn., 1963; MA, Mankato State U., 1965; PhD, Iowa State U., 1970. Postdoctoral fellow Brookhaven Nat. Lab., Upton, N.Y., 1970-72; prof., chmn. plant biology sect. U. Calif., Davis, 1972—, faculty asst. to chancellor, 1982-83; cons. faculty of agronomy U. Uruguay, 1979, 89; vis. fellow Rsch. Soc. Biol. Sci., Canberra, Australia, 1979-80; vis. prof. U. Wroclaw, Poland, 1987, U. Exeter, Eng., 1993. Coauthor: Botany: A Brief Introduction to Plant Biology, 1979, Botany: An Introduction on Plant Biology, 1982; co-editor: Mechanisms and Control of Cell Division, 1977; also numerous articles to profl. jours. Served to capt. U.S. Army, 1965-67. Fellow Japan Soc. Promotion of Sci.; mem. Bot. Soc. Am., Soc. Exptl. Biology, Am. Inst. Biol. Sci. Democrat. Roman Catholic. Avocations: horseback riding, community theatre, reading. Office: U Calif Sect Plant Biology Davis CA 95616-8537

ROST, WILLIAM JOSEPH, chemist; b. Fargo, N.D., Dec. 8, 1926; s. William Melvin and Christine Ruth (Hamerlik) R.; m. Rita Cincoski, Sept. 15, 1951; children—Kathryn, Patricia, Carol. B.S., U. Minn., 1948, Ph.D., 1952. From asst. prof. to prof. pharm. chemistry Sch. Pharmacy U. Kansas City, Mo., 1952-63; prof. pharm. chemistry Sch. Pharmacy U. Mo., Kansas City, 1963—. Co-author: Principles of Medicinal Chemistry, 1974, 3d rev. edit., 1988; contbr. articles profl. jours. Mem. Am. Pharm. Assn., Am. Chem. Soc., Sigma Xi, Kappa Psi, Rho Chi, Phi Lambda Upsilon. Home: 709 W 115th Ter Kansas City MO 64114-5597 Office: U Mo Sch of Pharmacy Kansas City MO 64110

ROSTAGNO, DERRICK, professional tennis player; b. Los Angeles, Calif., Oct. 25, 1965; s. Juan and Helga R. Student, Stanford U. Mem. U.S. Olympic Team, 1984; 6th in U.S. Tennis Assn. rankings, 13th in world ranking, 1991, ranked 14th in U.S. Tennis Assn., 1993.

ROSTEN, IRWIN, writer, producer, director. Mgr. news and pub. affairs Du Mont TV Network, N.Y.C., 1950-54; writer-producer news, pub. affairs Sta. KNXT-CBS, Los Angeles, 1954-60; dir. news, pub. affairs Sta. KTLA, Los Angeles, 1960-63; writer-producer, dir. Wolper Prodns., Inc., Los Angeles, 1963-67; chief documentary dept. MGM Studios, Culver City, Calif., 1967-72; pres. Ronox Prodns., Inc., Los Angeles, 1970-87. Writer-prodr.-dir. Nat. Geog. Soc. spls.: Splendid Stones, Elephant, Great Moments with National Geographic, The Thames, Mysteries of the Mind, Gold!, The Legacy of L.S.B. Leakey, The Volga, The Incredible Machine, Grizzly!, The Eerie World of Jacques-Yves Cousteau, National Parks: Playground or Paradise?, numerous other shows including Unsolved Mysteries, The Wolf Men, Ripley's Believe It or Not, Sports Illustrated, Trial by Wilderness, Hollywood: The Dream Factory, Kifaru: The Black Rhinoceros, Birds Do It, Bees Do It, Indestructible People, Journey Into Life, One Man's Noise: Stories of an Adventursome Oceanographer, Tiger: Lord of the Wild; video prodr. opening ceremonies 1984 Olympic Games, L.A., Interactive Multimedia: Columbus, Evolution/Revolution. Recipient Emmy award Acad. TV Arts and Scis.; recipient Writers Guild Am. award, Peabody award, Am. Med. Writers Assn. award, Christophers award, Ohio State U. award, Saturday Rev. award, CINE Golden Eagle award. Mem. Writers Guild Am., Dirs. Guild Am., Acad. TV Arts and Scis., Internat. Documentary Assn. Office: 2217 Chelan Dr Los Angeles CA 90068-2620

ROSTER, MICHAEL, lawyer; b. Chgo., May 7, 1945. AB, Stanford U., 1967, JD, 1973. Bar: Calif. 1973, D.C. 1980. Reporter UPI, Chgo., 1965; writer Time-Life, San Francisco, 1966-67; ptnr. McKenna, Conner & Cuneo, L.A. and Washington, 1973-87, Morrison & Foerster, L.A. and Washington, 1987-93; gen. counsel Stanford (Calif.) U., 1993—; bd. dirs. Silicon Valley Bancshares, vice chmn., 1995—. Contbr. articles to profl. jours. Chmn. Cityscape Panel of Strategic Planning Commn., Pasadena, Calif., 1985-86; bd. dirs. Pasadena Heritage, 1986-87. Lt. (j.g.) USN, 1969-71. Mem. ABA (chmn. com. on svas. insts. 1985-89, fin. svcs. com. 1981—, banking com. 1989—), Calif. Bar Assn. (chmn. banking com. 1978-79), Am. Corp. Counsl Assn., Stanford U. Alumni Assn. (chmn. 1992), Univ. Club (Washington), Univ. Club (Washington). Office: Stanford U Gen Counsel Box N Stanford CA 94309

ROSTKER, BERNARD, federal official; m. Louise Rostker; children: David, Michael. BS in Econs. and Edn., NYU, 1964; M in Econs., Syracuse U., PhD in Econs. Economist Manpower Requirements Directorate Office of the Asst. Sec. of Def. for Sys. Analysis, 1968-70; rsch. economist RAND Corp., 1970-72, program dir. manpower per. and tng. program, 1972-77; prin. dep. asst. sec. for manpower and res. affairs USN, 1977-79, dir. selective svc., 1979-81, dir. navy mgmt. program Ctr. for Naval Analyses, 1981-83; dir. sys. mgmt. divsn. Sys. Rsch. and Applications Corp., 1983-84; program dir. force devel. and employment program RAND Corp.-The Arroyo Ctr., 1984-90, assoc. dir., 1984-90; dir. Def. Manpower Rsch. Ctr. RAND Nat. Def. Rsch. Ctr., 1990-94; asst. sec. Navy for Manpower and Res. Affairs, 1994—. Office: Dept of the Navy Manpower & Reserve Affairs The Pentagon Washington DC 20350-1000

ROSTKY, GEORGE HAROLD, editor; b. N.Y.C., Feb. 28, 1926; s. Morris and Mary (Wyloge) R.; m. Rhoda Thelma Bornstein, June 29, 1950; children: Mark, Lisa. B.E.E., CCNY, 1957. Assoc. editor Electronic Design, N.Y.C., 1957-61; editor-in-chief Electronic Design, Rochelle Park, N.J., 1971-78; editorial dir./assoc. pub. Electronic Engring. Times, Manhasset, N.Y., 1978-85; cons., 1985—; founder George Rostky Assocs., Focus Rsch., Great Neck, N.Y.; securities analyst McDonnell & Co., N.Y.C., 1961-62; editorial dir. Mactier Pub. Co., N.Y.C., 1962-71; U.S. Dept. Commerce industry tech. rep. to U.S. Electronics Catalog Exhbn., India, 1980. Served with AUS, 1942-45. Recipient Indsl. Mktg. award for editorial excellence, 1964, Neal awards, 1967, 74, 75, 77. Home: 39 Cumberland Ave Great Neck NY 11020-1422 Office: 600 Community Dr Manhasset NY 11030-3847

ROSTOKER, GORDON, physicist, educator; b. Toronto, Ont., Can., July 15, 1940; s. Louis and Fanny (Silbert) R.; m. Gillian Patricia Farr, June 29, 1966; children: Gary David, Susan Birgitta, Daniel Mark. BSc in Physics, U. Toronto, 1962, MA in Physics, 1963; PhD in Geophysics, U. B.C., Can., 1966. Postdoctoral fellow Royal Inst. Tech., Stockholm, 1966-68; asst. prof. physics U. Alta., B.C., 1968-73, assoc. prof., 1973-79, prof., 1979—, McCalla Rsch. Prof., 1983-84, ann. Killam Prof., 1991-92, dir. Inst. Earth and Planetary Physics, 1985-91; assoc. chmn. dept. physics U. Alta., 1976-79, univ. rep. to bd. dirs. Can. Network for Space Rsch., 1992-94, mem. univ. rsch. policy com., 1987-91; cons. TRW Sys. Group, 1973, Dome Petroleum Ltd., 1981, U. Western Ont., 1983, York U., 1986; contract rschr. Energy, Mines and Resources, Can., Hydro-Québec; mem. assoc. com. space rsch. Nat. Rsch. Coun. Can., 1975-80, mem. com. on internat. sci. exchanges, 1977-79, others; mem. physics and astronomy com. Natural Scis. and Engring. Rsch. Coun., 1979-82, mem. spl. ad hoc com. on physics and astronomy, 1987-91, mem. grant selection com. for sci. publs., 1988-92; prin. investigator CA-NOPUS, 1989—; chmn. divsn. III Internat. Assn. Geomagnetism and Aeronomy, 1979-83; chmn. working group on data analysis phase of Internat. Magnetospheric Study Sci. Com. on Solar Terrestrial Physics of Internat. Coun. Sci. Unions, 1980-86, co-chmn. steering com. for Solar-Terrestrial Energy Program, 1987-89, chmn., 1989—. Editor Can. Jour. Physics, 1980-86, mem. editorial adv. bd., 1986—; contbr. over 250 articles to profl. publs. Mem. pub. adv. com. Govtl. Environ. Conservation Authority of Province of Alta., Edmonton, 1973-74. Recipient Steacie prize EWR Steacie Meml. Fund, 1979, Geophys. Centenary medal Acad. Scis. USSR, 1984. Fellow Royal Soc. Can.; mem. Am. Geophys. Union (assoc. editor Jour. Geophys. Rsch. 1976-79, 92-94, Jour. Geomagnetism and Geoelectricity 1993—), Can. Assn. Physicists (sec.-treas. Can. Geophys. Union 1973-74, chmn. divsn. aeronomy and space physics 1977-78, publs. com. 1980-86), Internat. Assn. Geomagnetism and Aeronomy (v.p. 1995—). Achievements include use of ground magnetometer arrays to discover stepwise evolution of electric current systems which flow in the ionosphere and magnetosphere during episodes of strong auroral disturbance. Office: U Alta, Dept Physics, Edmonton, AB Canada T6G 2J1

ROSTOKER, MICHAEL DAVID, micro-electronics company executive, lawyer; b. Quincy, Mass., Mar. 15, 1958; s. David and E. Louise (Berleue) R. Student, Carnegie-Mellon U., 1976-78; BS in Indsl. Engring., U. Pitts., 1980; JD, Franklin Pierce Law Ctr., 1984; PhD in Indsl. Engring., City U., L.A., 1992. Bar: U.S. Patent and Trademark Office 1983, N.H. 1984, U.S. Dist. Ct. N.H. 1984, Mass. 1985, Pa. 1985, U.S. Dist. Ct. D.C. 1985, U.S. Ct. Appeals (D.C. cir.) 1985. Lectr. in computer sci. Point Park Coll., Pitts., 1979-80; sys. analyst GE, Fitchburg, Mass., 1980-81; patent atty. Rines and Rines, Boston and Concord, N.H., 1983-85; patent counsel Schlumberger Well Svcs., Houston, 1985-87; sr. counsel intellectual property Intel Corp., Santa Clara, Calif., 1987-88; v.p. strategic alliances LSI Logic Corp., Milpitas, Calif., 1988—; cons. in field, Concord, 1981-85; mem. faculty computer sci. and math. Franklin Pierce Coll., Rindge, N.H., 1981-85; mem. adj. faculty law Franklin Pierce Law Ctr., 1983-85; edtl. bd. Software Protection Reporter, 1984-94; lectr. seminars in field. Author: Computer Jurisprudence: Legal Responses to the Information Revolution, 1985, Technology Management: Licensing and Protection for Computers in the World Market, 1993; contbr. articles to profl. jours.; patentee in field. Mem. ABA (patents, sci. and tech., litigation sects.), Am. Trial Lawyers Assn., Am. Intellectual Property Assn. Republican. Jewish. Avocations: volleyball, racquetball, weightlifting, theater, music. Home: 108 McPherson Ct Boulder Creek CA 95006-9203 Office: LSI Logic Corp 1525 Mccarthy Blvd Milpitas CA 95035-7424

ROSTON, ARNOLD, information specialist, educator, advertising executive, artist, editor; b. Racine, Wis., June 29, 1923; s. Felix and Hannah (Epstein) R.; m. Evelyn Eisen, June 16, 1944 (dec.); children: Karen Laurie, Susan Joyce. Student, CCNY, New Sch., 1942, Harvard Grad. Sch., 1975. Info. specialist Exec. Office of the Pres. Office of Emergency Mgmt., 1942, Joint (U.S.) Army Navy Intelligence Svc.-BSC, 1943; asst. to adminstrv. v.p., co-dir., advt. and promotion, creative dir. MBS-RKO, 1944-59; creative group head Grey Advt. Agy., 1959-60; dir. creative services Van Brunt & Co., 1961-64; pres. Roston & Co., 1965-76, chmn., 1979—; instr. secret U.S.A. Officer Tng. Sch. Marshall Field State, Oyster Bay, N.Y., 1942; exec. editor Budget Decorating Mag., 1973-76; dean Ctr. for Understanding Media of The New Sch., 1975; organizer, exec. sec. The Election Process and The New Media Workshop Conf., N.Y.C., 1975; dir. program devel. art therapy deg. program & accreditation Sch. Visual Arts, N.Y.C., 1976-77; cultural affairs corr. Broadcasting Co. of the Carolinas Inc., 1976-88; instr. Cooper Union, 1947-53, Bklyn. Mus. Art Sch., 1949-51, Pratt Inst. Grad. Seminar, 1954-55, CUNY, 1973; designer 29th Art Dirs. ann., 1949-50; instr. workshop in advt. design Am. Inst. Graphic Arts, 1951; chmn. Great Neck Com. Art and Design, N.Y., 1967-77; chmn. 36th Ann. Nat. Exhbn. Art and Design, 1956-57; founder, pres., dir. Art Dirs. Scholarship Fund, Inc., 1971-73, also mem. bd., chmn. coms.; mem. pres.'s adv. commn. N.Y. H.S. of Art and Design, 1974-94; organizer N.Y.C. Bd. Edn. "Expo '74" in Times Sq. and Radio City. Exhbns. include Met. Mus. Art, Mus. Modern Art, Pa. Acad. Fine Arts, N.Y. World"s Fair, Bklyn. Mus., Heckscher Mus., Montclair Art Mus., N.Y. Mcpl. Art Galleries, Lever House, Cooper Hewitt Mus., others; represented in permanent collections: Met. Mus. Art, Mus. Modern Art, Libr. of Congress, N.Y. Pub. Libr., Aldridge Mus., Ridgefield, Conn., The Vatican; mural Great Neck Pub. Libr.; contbr. articles on design, advt., scholarship to profl. jours. Trustee, sec. Sch. Art League Bd. Edn., N.Y.C., 1969-79; chmn. Landmarks Preservation Commn. Inc., Village of Great Neck, 1979-84; bd. dirs. Canterbury Crossing, 1984-85. George Foster Peabody-Yaddo Found. resident fellow; recipient awards including Suydam Silver medal NAD, Nat. Exhbn. Advt. and Editorial Art and Design awards, Certs. of Excellence and Gold medals Art Dirs. ann. nat. exhibits; Mus. Modern Art nat. hemispherical poster awards, 1940, 41, Certs. of Excellence Am. Inst. Graphic Arts, Ptnr. in Edn. award N.Y.C. Bd. Edn., 1979, Gt. Trademarks of World catalog, Milan, Italy, others. Mem. Princeton Club of N.Y., Art Dirs. Club. Studio: PO Box 717 Shrub Oak NY 10588-0717

ROSTON, DAVID C., lawyer; b. Evanston, Ill., Oct. 15, 1943. BA cum laude, Brandeis U., 1964; JD cum laude, Harvard U., 1967. Bar: Ill. 1967. Ptnr. Altheimer & Gray, Chgo. Mem. ABA, Ill. State Bar Assn., Chgo. Bar Assn., Chgo. Coun. Lawyers. Office: Altheimer & Gray 10 S Wacker Dr Ste 4000 Chicago IL 60606-7407*

ROSTOW, CHARLES NICHOLAS, lawyer, educator; b. Geneva, Switzerland, Mar. 3, 1950; s. Eugene Victor and Edna (Greenberg) R.; m. Heyden White, Oct. 31, 1987; children: Theodore Isaac, Celia A.M. BA, Yale U., 1972, PhD. 1979, JD, 1982. Assoc. Shearman & Sterling, N.Y.C., 1982-85; spl. asst. to legal adviser U.S. Dept. State, Washington, 1985-87; dep. legal adviser Nat. Security Coun., Washington, 1987, spl. asst. to Pres., legal adviser, 1987-93; Disting. rsch. prof. Coll. of Law, U. Tulsa, 1995—; exec. dir. Mass. Office Internat. Trade and Investment, 1995—. Author: Anglo-French Relations 1934-36, 1984; editor: Akten zur deutschen auswaertigen Politik: 1918-1945, vols. XIV-XXI, 1980-83; contbr. articles to profl. jours. Hon. dir. John Goodwin Tower Ctr. for Polit. Studies, So. Meth. U.; nat. adv. bd. Am. Jewish Com. Mem. Royal Inst. Internat. Affairs, Coun. Fgn. Rels., Assn. of Bar of City of N.Y., Phi Beta Kappa, Cosmos Club, Yale Club (N.Y.C.), Elizabethan Club (New Haven). Jewish. Office: c/o Internat Trade Ste 1302 100 Cambridge St Boston MA 02202

ROSTOW, ELSPETH DAVIES, political science educator; b. N.Y.C.; d. Milton Judson and Harriet Elspeth (Vaughan) Davies; m. Walt Whitman Rostow, June 26, 1947; children: Peter Vaughan, Ann Larner. AB, Barnard

Coll., 1938; AM, Radcliffe Coll., 1939; MA, Cambridge (Eng.) U., 1949; LHD (hon.), Lebanon Valley Coll.; LLD (hon.), Austin Coll., 1982, Southwestern U., 1988. Mem. faculty various instns. Barnard Coll., N.Y.C. and MIT, Boston, 1939-69; mem. faculty U. Tex., Austin, 1969—, dean div. gen. and comparative studies, 1975-77, prof. govt., 1976—, dean Lyndon B. Johnson Sch. Pub. Affairs, 1977-83, Stiles prof. Am. studies, 1985-88, Stiles prof. emerita, 1988—; mem. Pres.'s Adv. Com. for Trade Negotiations, 1978-82, Pres.'s Commn. for a Nat. Agenda for the Eighties, 1979-81; rsch. assoc. OSS, Washington, 1943-45; Geneva corr. London Economist, 1947-49; lectr. Air War Coll., 1963-81, Army War Coll., 1965, 68, 69, 78, 79, 81, Nat. War Coll., 1962, 68, 74, 75, Indsl. Coll. Armed Forces, 1961-65, Naval War Coll., 1971, Fgn. Svc. Inst., 1974-77, Dept. of State, Europe, 1973; bd. dirs. U.S. Inst. of Peace, vice chmn., 1991, chmn. 1991-92; co-founder The Austin Project, 1991; mem. Gov.'s Task Force on Revenue, Tex., 1991. Author: Europe's Economy After the War, 1948, (with others) American Now, 1968, The Coattailless Landslide, 1974; editor (with Barbara Jordan) The Great Society: A Twenty-Year Critique, 1986; columnist Austin Am. Statesman, 1985-92; contbr. articles to revs., poems to scholarly jours., newspapers, and mags. Trustee Sarah Lawrence Coll., 1952-59, Nat. Acad. Pub. Adminstrn., 1989-95, So. Ctr. for Internat. Studies, 1990—; bd. visitors and govs. St. John's Coll., 1986-89; bd. dirs. Barnard Coll., 1962-66, Lyndon Baines Johnson Found., 1977-83, Salzburg Seminar, 1981-89; vis. scholar Phi Beta Kappa, 1984-85; mem. bd. adv. to pres. Naval War Coll., Newport, R.I., 1995—. Recipient award Air U.,; Fulbright lectr., USIA participant, 1983-84, 90. Mem. Tex. Philos. Soc. (trustee 1989-95), Headliners Found. (vice-chmn. 1996—), Phi Beta Kappa, Phi Nu Epsilon (hon.), Mortar Bd. (hon.), Omicron Delta Kappa. Home: One Wild Wind Point Austin TX 78746 Office: U Tex Drawer Y Univ Station Austin TX 78713

ROSTOW, EUGENE VICTOR, lawyer, educator, economist; b. Bklyn., Aug. 25, 1913; s. Victor A. and Lillian (Helman) R.; m. Edna Berman Greenberg; children: Victor A. D., Jessica, Charles Nicholas. AB, Yale U., 1933, LLB, 1937, AM, 1944; postgrad., King's Coll., Cambridge (Eng.) U., 1933-34; M.A., Cambridge U., 1959, LL.D., 1962; LL.D., Boston U., 1976, U. New Haven, 1981, N.Y. Law Sch., 1984. Bar: N.Y. 1938. Practice in N.Y.C., 1937-38; mem. faculty Law Sch. Yale, 1938—, prof. law, 1944-84, prof. emeritus, sr. research scholar, 1984—, dean, 1955-65, Sterling prof. law and pub. affairs, 1964-84; master Trumbull Coll., 1966; dir. ACDA, 1981-83; Disting. vis. research prof. law and diplomacy Nat. Def. U., 1984-90, 92—; under-sec. state for polit. affairs, 1966-69; pres. Atlantic Treaty Assn., 1973-76; vis. prof. U. Chgo., 1941; Pitt prof. Am. history and instns., professorial fellow King's Coll., Cambridge U., 1959-60; William W. Cook lectr. Mich. U., 1958; John R. Coen lectr. U. Colo., 1961; Leary lectr. U. Utah, 1965; Brandeis lectr. Brandeis U., 1965; Rosenthal lectr. Northwestern U., 1965; George Eastman vis. prof., fellow Balliol Coll., Oxford (Eng.) U., 1970-71; Adviser Dept. State, 1942-44; asst. exec. sec. Econ. Commn. for Europe, UN, 1949-50; mem. Jud. Council of Conn., 1955-66, Atty. Gen.'s Nat. Com. Study Antitrust Laws, 1954-55; chmn. exec. com. Com. on the Present Danger, 1976-81, 86-92. Author: Planning for Freedom, 1959, The Sovereign Prerogative, 1962, Law, Power and the Pursuit of Peace, 1968, Peace in the Balance, 1972, The Ideal in Law, 1978, Toward Managed Peace, 1993, A Breakfast for Bonaparte, 1994; editor: Is Law Dead?, 1971. Decorated Chevalier Legion d'Honneur (France), Grand Cross Order of Crown (Belgium); recipient Disting. Civilian Svc. award U.S. Army, 1990; Guggenheim fellow, 1959-60, Randolph fellow U.S. Inst. Peace, 1990-92, hon. fellow Hebrew U. of Jerusalem, 1992—. Fellow Am. Acad. Arts and Scis.; mem. Am. Law Inst., Phi Beta Kappa, Alpha Delta Phi, Elizabethan Yale Club, Century Assn. N.Y.C. Club, Cosmos Club Washington. Democrat. Jewish. Home: 1315 4th St SW Washington DC 20024-2201 Office: Nat Def U Washington DC 20319-6000 also: Yale U Sch Law New Haven CT 06520

ROSTOW, WALT WHITMAN, economist, educator; b. N.Y.C., Oct. 7, 1916; s. Victor Aaron and Lillian (Helman) R.; m. Elspeth Vaughan Davies, June 26, 1947; children: Peter Vaughan, Ann Larner. BA, Yale U., 1936, PhD, 1940. Instr. econs. Columbia U., 1940-41; asst. chief German-Austrian econ. div. Dept. State, 1945-46; Harmsworth prof. Am. history Oxford (Eng.) U., 1946-47; asst. to exec. sec. Econ. Commn. for Europe, 1947-49; Pitt. prof. Am. history Cambridge (Eng.) U., 1949-50; prof. econ. history MIT, 1950-60; staff mem. Center Internat. Studies, 1951-60; dep. spl. asst. to Pres. for nat. security affairs, 1961; counselor, chmn. policy planning council Dept. State, 1961-66; spl. asst. to Pres., 1966-69; U.S. rep., ambassador Inter-Am. com. Alliance for Progress, 1964-66; now Rex G. Baker Jr. prof. polit. economy, depts. econs. and history U. Tex., Austin, prof. emeritus; mem. Bd. Fgn. Scholarships, 1969-72; chmn. bd., task force dir. Austin Project, 1982—. Author: The American Diplomatic Revolution, 1947, Essays on the British Economy of the Nineteenth Century, 1948, The Process of Economic Growth, 1953, 2d edit., 1960, (with A.D. Gayer, A.J. Schwartz) The Growth and Fluctuation of the British Economy, 1790-1850, 1953, 2d edit., 1975, (with A. Levin, others) The Dynamics of Soviet Society, 1953, (with others) The Prospects for Communist China, 1954, (with R.W. Hatch) An American Policy in Asia, 1955, (with M.F. Millikan) A Proposal: Key to an Effective Foreign Policy, 1957, The United States in the World Arena, 1960, The Stages of Economic Growth, 1960, 2d edit., 1971, 3d edit., 1990, A View from the Seventh Floor, 1964, A Design for Asian Development, 1965, (with William E. Griffith) East-West Relations: Is Detente Possible?, 1969, Politics and the Stages of Growth, 1971, The Diffusion of Power, 1972, How It All Began, 1975, The World Economy: History and Prospect, 1978, Getting From Here to There, 1978, Why the Poor Get Richer and the Rich Slow Down, 1980, Pre-Invasion Bombing Strategy: General Eisenhower's Decision of March 25, 1944, 1981, British Trade Fluctuations, 1868-1896: A Chronicle and a Commentary, 1981, The Division of Europe After World War II: 1946, 1981, Europe After Stalin: Eisenhower's Three Decisions of March 11, 1953, 1982, Open Skies: Eisenhower's Proposal of July 21, 1955, 1982, The Barbaric Counter-Revolution: Cause and Cure, 1983, Eisenhower, Kennedy, and Foreign Aid, 1985, The United States and the Regional Organization of Asia and the Pacific: 1965-1985, 1986, Rich Countries and Poor Countries, 1987, Essays on a Half Century: Ideas, Policies and Action, 1988, History, Policy, and Economic Theory, 1989, Theorists of Economic Growth From David Hume to the Present with a Perspective on the Next Century, 1990; editor: The Economics of Take-Off Into Sustained Growth, 1963. Maj. OSS, AUS, 1942-45. Decorated Legion of Merit, Hon. Order Brit. Empire (mil.); recipient Presdl. Medal of Freedom with distinction; Rhodes scholar Balliol Coll., 1936-38, Outstanding Work in Social Scis. award Assn. Am. Pubs., 1990. Mem. Am. Acad. Arts and Scis., Am. Philos. Soc., Mass. Hist. Soc., Tex. Philos. Soc., Cosmos Club, Elizabethan Club. Clubs: Cosmos (Washington); Elizabethan (New Haven). Home: 1 Wildwind Pt Austin TX 78746-2434

ROSTROPOVICH, MSTISLAV LEOPOLDOVICH, musician; b. Baku, USSR, Mar. 27, 1927; s. Leopold and Sofia (Fedotova) R.; m. Galina Pavlovna Vishnevskaya; children: Olga, Elena. Grad., Moscow Conservatory 1948; numerous hon. doctorate degrees. Faculty mem. Moscow Conservatory, 1953, prof., 1960; head cello and double-bass dept., formerly prof. Leningrad Conservatory; music dir., conductor Nat. Symphony Orch., Washington, 1977-94; hon. prof. Cuban Nat. Conservatory, 1960-78; pres. Evian Internat. Music Festival. Debut as violoncellist, 1935; performer world concert tours, Moscow Philharm. Orch.; recordings include (with various artists) Mstislav Rostropovich Melodiya Recordings, 1949-56, 48-59, The Young Rostropovich: Rare Recordings for the 1950-52 Years. Decorated Hon. Knight of the Brit. Empire, 1987; Commdr. French Legion of Honor, 1987; Officer's Cross of Merit, Fed. Republic Germany, 1987; recipient Stalin prize, 1951, 53, Lenin prize, 1963, Life in Music prize, 1984, Albert Schweitzer Music award, 1985, Grammy awards, 1970, 77, 80, 84, Presdl. Medal Freedom, 1987, Ditson Condr.'s award, Columbia U., 1990, Four Freedoms award Franklin and Eleanor Roosevelt Inst., 1992; named Musician of Yr., Mus. Am., 1987. Mem. Am. Acad. Arts and Scis., Union Soviet Composers, Brit. Royal Acad. Music (hon.), Acad. Arts of French Inst.-Forty Immortals. Office: c/o Columbia Artists Mgmt 165 W 57th St New York NY 10019 also: CAMI 165 W 57th St New York NY 10019

ROSZKOWSKI, STANLEY JULIAN, federal judge; b. Booneville, N.Y., Jan. 27, 1923; s. Joseph and Anna (Christkowski) R.; m. Catherine Mary Claeys, June 19, 1948; children: Mark, Gregory, Dan, John. BS, U. Ill., 1949, JD, 1954. Bar: Ill. 1954. Sales mgr. Warren Petroleum Co., Rockford, Ill., 1954; ptnr. Roszkowski, Paddock, McGreevy & Johnson, Rockford, 1955-77; judge U.S. Dist. Ct. (we. dist.), Rockford, Ill., 1977—; pres. First State Bank, Rockford, 1963-75; chmn. bd. First State Bank, 1977—. Chmn. Fire and Police Commn., Rockford, 1967-74, commr., 1974—; chmn. Paul Simon Com., 1972; active Adlai Stevenson III campaign, 1968-71, Winnebago County Citizens for John F. Kennedy, 1962, Winnebago County Dem. Cen. Com., 1962-64; bd. dirs. Sch. of Hope, 1960—; mem. Ill. Capital Devel. Bd., 1974—. With USAAF, 1943-45. Decorated Air medal with 2 oak leaf clusters.; recipient Pulaski Nat. Heritage award Polish Am. Congress, Chgo., 1982. Mem. ABA, Ill. Bar Assn., Fla. Bar Assn., Winnebago County Bar Assn., Am. Coll. Trial Lawyers, Am. Judicature Soc., Assn. Trial Lawyers Am., Ill. Trial Lawyers Assns., Am. Arbitration Assn. (arbitrator), Fed. Judges Assn. (bd. dirs. 1988—), Forest Hills Country Club (Rockford). Office: US Dist Ct 211 South Court St Rockford IL 61101-1201*

ROSZTOCZY, FERENC ERNO, business executive; b. Szeged, Hungary, Aug. 16, 1932; came to U.S., 1957, naturalized, 1962; s. Ferenc Lipot and Edith Jolan (Kunzl) R.; m. Diane Elder, Dec. 21, 1963; children: Thomas Ferenc, Robert Anthony, Stephanie Elder, Edward Joseph. MS, U. Szeged, 1955; PhD, U. Calif., Berkeley, 1961. Phys. chemist Stanford Research Inst., Menlo Park, Calif., 1961-64; mem. tech. staff Bell Labs., Murray Hill, N.J., 1964-68; mgr. semicondr. materials Bell & Howell, Pasadena, Calif., 1968-69; mgr. semicondr. crystal growth and device engring. Varian Assos., Palo Alto, Calif., 1969-75; dir. Ariz. Machinery Co., Avondale, 1974—, pres., 1975—, chmn. bd., 1976—; pres. Stotz Farms, Inc., 1979—; dir. Ariz. Indsl. Machinery Co., 1975-91; cons. Siltec Corp., Menlo Park, Calif., 1971-72; mem. agribusiness adv. bd. 1st Interstate Bank Ariz., 1995-96. Bd. trustees Agua Fria High Sch., 1981-89, pres. 1986-87. Mem. United Dairymen Ariz. (dir. 1985—). Roman Catholic. Club: Wigwam Country. Contbr. articles to profl. jours. Patentee in field. Home: 1010 E Acacia Cir Litchfield Park AZ 85340-4529 Office: Ariz Machinery Co 11111 W McDowell Rd Avondale AZ 85323

ROTBERG, EUGENE HARVEY, investment banker, lawyer; b. Phila., Jan. 19, 1930; s. Irving Bernard and Blanche Grace (Levick) R.; m. Iris Sybil Comens, Aug. 29, 1954; children—Diana Golda, Pamela Lynn. B.S., Temple U., 1951; LL.B., U. Pa., 1954; PhD (hon.), Salem-Teikyo U., 1992. Chief counsel Office Policy Research Securities and Exchange Commn., Washington, 1963-66; v.p., treas. World Bank, Washington, 1969-87; exec. v.p. Merrill Lynch & Co., N.Y.C., 1987-90. Served with U.S. Army, 1954-55. Decorated King Leopold II medal (Belgium); recipient Disting. Svc. award Securities and Exch. Commn., 1968; named Alumnus of Yr., Temple U., 1969. Home: 7211 Brickyard Rd Potomac MD 20854-4808 Office: Washington Harbour 3050 K St NW Washington DC 20007-5108

ROTBERG, IRIS COMENS, social scientist; b. Phila., Dec. 16, 1932; d. Samuel Nathaniel and Golda (Shuman) Comens; m. Eugene H. Rotberg, Aug. 29, 1954; children: Diana Golda, Pamela Lynn. BA, U. Pa., 1954, MA, 1955; PhD, Johns Hopkins U., Balt., 1958. Research psychologist Pres.'s Commn. on Income Maintenance Programs, Washington, 1968-69, Office Planning, Research and Evaluation, Office Econ. Opportunity, Washington, 1970-73; dep. dir. compensatory edn. study Nat. Inst. Edn., Washington, 1974-77, dir. Office Planning and Program Devel., 1978-82; program dir. NSF, Arlington, Va., 1985-87, 89-91, 1993—; tech. policy fellow Com. on Sci., Space and Tech., U.S. Ho. of Reps., Washington, 1987-89; sr. social scientist RAND, Washington, 1991-93. NSF fellow, 1956-58. Home: 7211 Brickyard Rd Potomac MD 20854-4808

ROTCH, WILLIAM, business administration educator; b. Cambridge, Mass., Nov. 19, 1929; s. Charles Morgan and Helen Aldis (Bradley) R.; m. Jane Coolidge Whitehill, Dec. 20, 1952; children: Jane Revere, William Jr., Sarah Aldis. AB, Harvard U., 1951, MBA, 1956, DBA, 1959. Asst. auditor Ga. R.R. Bank, Augusta, 1953-54; rsch. assoc. Harvard Bus. Sch., Boston, 1956-57; mem. faculty Colgate Darden Grad. Sch. Bus. Adminstrn. U. Va., Charlottesville, 1959—, now Johnson and Higgins prof. bus. adminstrn.; vis. assoc. prof. Amos Tuck Sch., Dartmouth Coll., 1966-67; vis. prof. IMEDE Mgmt. Devel. Inst., Lausanne, Switzerland, 1973-75. Co-author: Executives Guide to Management Accounting and Control, 5th edit., 1993, Cases in Management Accounting and Control Systems, 3d edit., 1995. Vestryman St. Paul's Meml. Ch., Charlottesville, 1962-89; trustee World Learning, Brattleboro, Vt., 1957—, chmn. bd., 1988—. 2d lt. Signal Corps, U.S. Army, 1951-53. Recipient Experiment citation Experiment in International Living, 1986. Mem. Am. Acctg. Assn. (mem. various coms.), Inst. Mgmt. Accts., Somerset Club (Boston), Harvard Club (N.Y.). Avocations: sailing, photography. Home: 808 Fendall Ter Charlottesville VA 22903-1653 Office: U Va Darden Grad Bus Sch 520 Massie Rd Charlottesville VA 22906

ROTE, NELLE FAIRCHILD HEFTY, business consultant; b. Watsontown, Pa., May 23, 1930; d. Edwin Dunkel and Phebe Hill (Fisher) Fairchild; m. John Austin Hefty, Mar. 20, 1948 (div. June 1970); children: Harry E. Hefty, John B. Hefty, Susan E. Hefty DeBartolo; m. Keith Maynard Rote, Dec. 16, 1983 (dec. Aug. 1985). Student, Bucknell U., 1961, Williamsport Sch. of Commerce, 1968-69, Pa. State U., 1971-72, 83, Susquehanna U., 1986. Typesetter, page designer Colonial Printing House, Inc., Lewisburg, Pa., 1970-76; account exec. Sta. WTGC Radio, Lewisburg, 1976-78; co-owner Colonial Printing Co., Lewisburg, 1978-83; temp. HATS-Temps, Lewisburg, 1980-89; artist, editor Create-A-Book, Inc., Milton, Fla., 1980-92; census crew leader, spl. svc. Dept. Commerce, Washington, 1990; cons. Personalized Books, John B. Hefty Pub. Co., Inc., Gulf Breeze, Fla., 1991—; ind. living skills instr. Ctr. Ind. Living, Lewisburg, Pa., 1989-95. Artist: Children's Playmate Mag., 1942, Christmas Wish, Big Parade, 1989-90. Vol. proofreader Lewisburg Bicentennial Commn., 1976; editor-poet Holiday Newspaper Bus. Assn., Lewisburg, 1987; charter mem. Women's Art Mus., Washington; charter sponsor Women in Mil. Svc. Meml., Washington, 1991; chmn. Rooftop Garden Project Evang. Hosp., Pa., 1995—, Nelle Fairchild Rote Book Fund, Union County Libr.; vol. birdwatcher House for Finch Disease Survey program Lab. Ornithology, Cornell U., Ithaca, N.Y. Recipient Humanitarian award Union County Fedn. Women's Clubs, Pa., 1965, Grand Prize in Cooking, Milton Std., 1966, Most Profl. Photo award, Lewisburg Festival of Arts, 1980, Hon. Mention award Women in Arts, Harrisburg, Pa., 1981, Photo Contest award Congressman Allen Ertel, Washington, 1981, Photo awards 2d and 3d place Union County Fair, Laurelton, Pa., 1981, Hon. Mention Photo award Susquehanna Art Soc., Pa., 1981, Silver award for poetry World of Poetry, 1990. Mem. DAR (nat. def. reporter Shikelimo chpt. 1989-95, sec. 1992-95, regent 1995—), Civic Club Lewisburg (v.p. 1994-96), Orgn. United Environment, Nat. Wildlife Fedn. Assn. (cert.), Inst. Lifelong Learning Susquehanna U., Marine Corps League Aux. (life), Union County Hist. Soc. Republican. Avocations: family, reading, nutritional cooking, crossword puzzles. Home: 1015 Saint Paul St Lewisburg PA 17837-1213

ROTELL, THOMAS M., publishing executive. Dir. U of Penn. Press, Phila.; now dir. Texas A & M Press. Office: Texas A&M Press Lindsey Bldg Drawer C College Station TX 77843

ROTEMBERG, JULIO JACOBO, economist, educator, consultant; b. Buenos Aires, Argentina, Sept. 26, 1953; came to U.S., 1972; s. Salomon and Ellen (Wolf) R.; m. Analisa Lattes, Nov. 8, 1982; childrenL Veronica M., Martin S. BA, U. Calif., Berkeley, 1975; PhD, Princeton U., 1981. Researcher Banco Cen. De La Republica Argentina, Buenos Aires, 1976; from asst. prof. to assoc. prof. econs. Sloan Sch. Mgmt. MIT, Cambridge, 1980-89, prof., 1989—; rsch. assoc. Nat. Bureau of Econ. Rsch., Cambridge, 1986—; vis. prof., bus. adminstrn. Harvard Bus. Sch., Boston, 1994-95. Mem. bd. editors Rev. Econ. Studies, 1985-88, Econometrica, 1987—, Quarterly Jour. Econs., 1989—; contbr. articles to profl. jours. Fellow Econometric Soc.; mem. Am. Econ. Assn. Avocations: skiing, bicycling. Office: MIT Sloan Sch Mgmt Cambridge MA 02139

ROTENBERG, MANUEL, physics educator; b. Toronto, Ont., Can., Mar. 12, 1930; came to U.S., 1946; s. Peter and Rose (Plonzker) R.; m. Paula Weissbrod, June 23, 1952; children: Joel, Victor. BS, MIT, 1952, PhD, 1956. Mem. staff Los Alamos (N.Mex.) Nat. Lab., 1955-58; instr. physics Princeton (N.J.) U., 1958-59; asst. prof. U. Chgo., 1959-61; prof. applied physics U. Calif., San Diego, 1961-93, dean grad. studies and research, 1975-84, chmn. dept. elec. engring. and computer engring., 1988-93, rsch. prof., 1993—. Author: The 3-j and 6-j Symbols, 1959; founding editor: Methods of Computational Physics, 1963, Jour. of Computational Physics, 1962; editor: Biomathematics and Cell Kinetics, 1981. Fellow Am. Phys. Soc.; mem. AAAS, Sigma Xi. Office: U Calif San Diego La Jolla CA 92093-0407

ROTENBERG, SHELDON, violinist; b. Attleboro, Mass., Apr. 11, 1917; s. Joseph and Jennie (Almer) R.; m. Hilde Sussmann, Jan. 29, 1950; children: David, Steffi. A.B., Tufts U., 1939, grad. student, 1939-40; violin pupil of, Felix Winternitz, Georges Enesco, Maurice Hewitt. Tchr. violin, 1947—; music adviser, cons. pub. schs., Brookline, Mass.; archivist, cons. Boston Symphony Orch., 1992-93. Concertized extensively with the Boston String Quartet sponsored by Elizabeth Sprague Coolidge, including concerts and rec. at the Libr. of Congress, 1948-52, occupies endowed Kasdon-Paley chair, 1st violin sect., Boston Symphony Orch., 1948-91, solo performances with Boston Pops Orch., 1939-41; Boston Symphony rep. as soloist, tchr., mem. orch. in State Dept. cultural exch. program with Japan Philharm., Tokyo, 1968-69; mem. faculty Boston U. Tanglewood Inst., 1979—. Served to capt. AUS, 1942-46. Mem. Harvard Mus. Assn., Tufts U. Alumni Assn. Home: 60 Browne St Brookline MA 02146-3441 Office: care Boston Symphony Orch Symphony Hall Boston MA 02115

ROTENBERRY, CLINTON GRICE, state representative, real estate broker; b. Mendenhall, Miss., Jan. 12, 1953; s. Clinton Grice and Ethel Jane (Cobb) R.; m. Christy Ann Stephens, Aug. 14, 1976; children: Jennifer Christine, Rebecca Kathleen, Natalie Jane. BA, Belhaven Coll., Jackson, Miss., 1975; postgrad., La. State U., 1976. Sales clk., buyer Stephens of Mendenhall, 1977-79; salesman, realtor Scothye Hooker Real Estate, Jackson, Miss., 1980-88; broker Rotenberry Realty, Mendenhall, 1988—; rep. Miss. Ho. of Reps., Jackson, 1992—; sec. pub. utilities com. Miss. Ho. Reps., Jackson, 1993—, sec. constn. com., 1995—, Banks & Banks. Youth vol. 1st Bapt. Ch., Mendenhall, 1977-80; pres. Mendenhall Jaycees, Mendenhall, 1980; grad. Simpson County Leadership, Mendenhall, 1993, Miss. Econ. Coun. Leadership, Jackson, 1994; mem. nat. policy forum Nat. Rep. Party, 1994—. Mem. Nat. Conf. State Legislators, So. Legis. Conf., Am. Legis. Exch. Coun. (comms. com. 1996—), Miss. Craftsman's Arts Guild (bd. dirs. 1994—). Baptist. Avocation: golf. Home: Rte 5 Box 56 Mendenhall MS 39114 Office: Rotenberry Realty PO Box 818 Mendenhall MS 39114

ROTENSTREICH, JON W., insurance company executive; b. 1943. Ptnr. Salomon Bros., N.Y.C., 1972-82; v.p., treas. Internat. Bus. Machines Corp., 1982-86; pres., chief investment officer, dir. Torchmark Corp., Birmingham, Ala., 1986-91; pres., CEO, dir. United Investors Mgmt. Corp. subs. Torchmark Corp., 1986-91; pres. Jon Rotenstreich Consultants, 1991-93; chmn., CEO TIG Holdings, Inc., N.Y.C., Calif., 1993—. Office: TIG Holdings Inc 65 E 55th New York NY 10022-3613*

ROTERT, DENISE ANNE, occupational therapist, army officer, educator; b. Sioux Falls, S.D., Nov. 18, 1949; d. Leonard Joseph and Irene Winifred (Jennings) R. BS, U. Puget Sound, 1971; MA, U. No. Colo., 1975. Commd. 2d lt. Med. Specialist Corps, U.S. Army, 1970, advanced through grades to lt. col. , 1990; staff occupational therapist Tripler Army Med. Center, Honolulu, 1973-76, officer in charge occupational therapy sect. Ireland Army Hosp., Fort Knox, Ky., 1976-77; clin. supr. occupational therapy sect. Letterman Army Med. Center, Presidio of San Francisco, 1977-79; chief instr. occupational therapy asst. course Acad. Health Scis., Ft. Sam Houston, Tex., 1979-84; chief occupational therapy Tri-Service Alcohol Recovery Dept., Naval Hosp., Bethesda, Md., 1984-89, Womack Army Hosp., Ft. Bragg, N.C., 1989-90, ret., 1990; mem. faculty U. S.D., 1991—. Recipient Myra McDaniel Writer's award, 1989. Mem. Am. Occupational Therapy Assn., World Fedn. Occupational Therapists, S.D. Occupational Therapy Assn. Roman Catholic. Home: 2609 S Prairie Ave Sioux Falls SD 57105-4626 Office: USDSM OT Dept 414 E Clark St Vermillion SD 57069-2307

ROTH, ALAN J., lawyer, congressional aide; b. Bklyn., Feb. 18, 1955; s. Benjamin and Naomi (Wisler) R. BA, Am. U., 1976; JD, N.Y.U., 1979. Bar: Conn. 1979, U.S. Dist. Ct. Conn. 1979, D.C. 1980, U.S. Ct. Appeals (D.C. cir.) 1980, U.S. Ct. Appeals (2d cir.) 1982, U.S. Supreme Ct. 1983. Law clk. to Hon. M. Joseph Blumenfeld U.S. Dist. Ct., Hartford, Conn., 1979-80; assoc. Tyler, Cooper & Alcorn, New Haven, Conn., 1980-84; counsel com. energy and commerce U.S. Ho. of Reps., Washington, 1985-92, chief counsel com. energy and commerce, 1992, staff dir., chief counsel, 1993-95, minority staff dir., chief coun. com. on commerce, 1995—; adj. professorial lectr. sch. pub. affairs Am. U., Washington, 1989-92. Democrat. Jewish. Office: Commerce Com US Ho of Reps Washington DC 20515

ROTH, ALLAN ROBERT, lawyer, educator; b. Newark, June 7, 1931; s. Michael H. and Belle F. (Rosenberg) R.; m. Deborah R. Comerford, Feb. 29, 1976; children: Joseph (dec.), Alexander, Charles (dec.), Sarah. AB, Rutgers U., 1953; LLB, Harvard U., 1956. Bar: D.C. 1956, N.J. 1959, N.Y. 1965. Assoc. Toner, Crowley, Woelper & Vanderbilt, Newark, 1956-61; staff atty. for Gen. Counsel, SEC, Washington, 1962-64; dir. legal and govt. affairs dept. Am. Stock Exch., N.Y.C., 1964-68; prof. grad. sch. mgmt. Rutgers U., Newark, 1969—; dir. Internat. Bus. Inst., 1969-87; coord. Rutgers U. programs in China, 1993—; mem. legal adv. coun. Mid-Atlantic Legal Found., 1978-81; cons. IFC, 1972, Asian Devel. Bank, 1990, 91, 93, AID, 1965, 67, 71, 72, 94, World Bank, 1994; cons. to fgn. govts., 1965—; UN advisor to Pakistan, 1968-69; Fulbright prof. scholar to Thailand, 1988; mem. adv. bd. BNA Direct Investment in N.Am., 1988-95; mem. N.Am. Free Trade and Investment Report, 1995—; mem. book rev. panel Am. Jour. Internat. Law, 1978. Edtl. bd. Jour. Internat. Bus. Studies, 1975-85; contbg. editor: Corp. Law Review, 1977-86; contbr. chpts. to books, articles to profl. jours. With U.S. Army, 1956-58. Mem. ABA (staff dir. study of regulation of fgn. investment in U.S. 1975-79, 87—), Soviet-Am. Securities Law Working Group, Am. Soc. Internat. Law, Am. Law Inst., Phi Beta Kappa. Home: 630 Prospect St Maplewood NJ 07040-2724 Office: Rutgers U Grad Sch Mgmt 180 University Ave Newark NJ 07102-1803

ROTH, ALVIN ELIOT, economics educator; b. N.Y.C., Dec. 18, 1951; s. Ernest and Lillian (Caesar) R.; m. Emilie Matarasso, May 22, 1977; children: Aaron Leon, Benjamin Nathaniel. B.S., Columbia U., 1971; M.S., Stanford U., 1973, Ph.D., 1974. Asst. prof. dept. bus. adminstrn. and dept. econs. U. Ill., Urbana, 1974-77, assoc. prof., 1977-79, prof., 1979-82; A.W. Mellon prof. econs. U. Pitts., 1982—. Author: Axiomatic Models of Bargaining, 1979, Game-Theoretic Models of Bargaining, 1985, Laboratory Experimentation in Economics, 1987, The Shapley Value, 1988; (with M. Sotomayor) Two-Sided Matching: A Study in Game Theoretic Modeling and Analysis, 1990; (with J. Kagel) Handbook of Experimental Economics, 1995. Recipient Founders' prize Tex. Instruments Found., 1980; Guggenheim fellow, 1983; A.P. Sloan research fellow, 1984; 10 Outstanding Young Ams. award, 1984; Lanchester prize Ops. Rsch. Soc. Am., 1991. Fellow Econometric Soc.; mem. AAAS, Am. Econ. Assn., Inst. Mgmt. Scis. Jewish. Home: 2061 Beechwood Blvd Pittsburgh PA 15217-1705 Office: U Pitts Dept Econs Pittsburgh PA 15260

ROTH, ANN, costume designer. Student, Carnegie-Mellon U. costume designer Am. Conservatory Theatre, San Francisco, McCarter Theatre Co., Princeton, Am. Ballet Theatre, Am. Shakespeare Festival, Stratford, Kennedy Ctr. for Performing Arts, Minneapolis Opera, San Francisco Opera, Hartman Theatre Co., Stanford, Long Wharf Theatre, New Haven. Costume designer: (theatre) Maybe Tuesday, 1958, Make a Million, 1958, The Disenchanted, 1958, Edward II, 1958, A Desert Incident, 1959, The Cool World, 1960, Gay Divorcee, 1960, Ernest in Love, 1960, Face of a Hero, 1960, The Pleasure of His Company, 1960-61, A Far Country, 1961, Purlie Victorious, 1961, Look: We've Come Through, 1961, This Side of Paradise, 1962, Isle of Children, 1962, Venus at Large, 1962, A Portrait of the Artist as a Young Man, 1962, The Barroom Monks, 1962, We Comrades Three, 1962, Natural Affection, 1963, Hey You, Light Man!, 1963, Children from Their Games, 1963, A Case of Libel, 1963, The Last Analysis, 1964, Slow Dance on the Killing Ground, 1964, I Had a Ball, 1964, In the Summer House, 1964, The Odd Couple, 1965, 85, Mrs. Dally, 1965, The Impossible Years, 1965, Romeo and Juliet, 1965, The Wayward Stork, 1966, The Star-Spangled Girl, 1966, The Beard, 1967, Something Different, 1967, The Deer Park, 1967, Happiness Is Just a Little Thing Called a Rolls Royce, 1968, Play It Again, Sam, 1969, My Daughter, Your Son, 1969, Tiny Alice, 1969, The Three Sisters, 1969, Gantry, 1970, Purlie, 1970, What the Butler Saw, 1970, The Engagement Baby, 1970, Father's Day, 1971, Prettybelle, 1971, Fun City, 1972, Roseboom, 1972, Twelfth Night, 1972, Children! Children!,

1972, 6 Rms Riv Vu, 1972, Enemies, 1972, The Merchant of Venice, 1973, Seesaw, 1973, The Women, 1973, The Royal Family, 1975, 85 (Tony award nomination best costume design 1985), The Heiress, 1976, The Importance of Being Earnest, 1977, Do You Turn Somersaults?, 1978, The Best Little Whorehouse in Texas, 1978, The Crucifer of Blood, 1978 (Tony award nomination best costume design 1979), First Monday in October, 1978, They're Playing Our Song, 1979, Strangers, 1979, Lunch Hour, 1980, Gardenia, 1982, Kaufman at Large, 1982, Present Laughter, 1982, The Misanthrope, 1983, Yankee Wives, 1983, Open Admissions, 1984, Hurlyburly, 1984, Design for Living, 1984, Biloxi Blues, 1984, 85, Arms and the Man, 1985, Juno's Swans, 1985, Singin' in the Rain, 1985, Social Security, 1986, The House of Blue Leaves, 1986-87 (Tony award nomination best costume design 1987), Light Up the Sky, 1986, Woman in Mind, 1988, O Pioneers!, 1989-90, Elliot Loves, 1990, Square One, 1990, Road to Nirvana, 1991, Any Given Day, 1993, (films) The World of Henry Orient, 1964, A Fine Madness, 1966, Up the Down Staircase, 1967, Pretty Poison, 1968, Sweet November, 1968, Midnight Cowboy, 1969, The Owl and the Pussycat, 1970, Jenny, 1970, The People Next Door, 1970, Klute, 1971, The Pursuit of Happiness, 1971, They Might Be Giants, 1971, The Valachi Papers, 1972, Law and Disorder, 1974, The Day of the Locust, 1975, The Happy Hooker, 1975, Mandingo, 1975, Murder by Death, 1976, Burnt Offerings, 1976, Independence, 1976, The Goodbye Girl, 1977, California Suite, 1978, Coming Home, 1978, Nunzio, 1979, Promises in the Dark, 1979, Hair, 1979, The Island, 1980, Dressed to Kill, 1980, Nine to Five, 1980, Honky Tonk Freeway, 1981, Only When I Laugh, 1981, Rollover, 1981, Blow Out, 1981, The World According to Garp, 1982, The Man Who Loved Women, 1983, Silkwood, 1983, The Survivors, 1983, Places in the Heart, 1984 (Academy Award nomination best costume design 1984), Sweet Dreams, 1985, The Slugger's Wife, 1985, Maxie, 1985, Jagged Edge, 1985, Heartburn, 1986, The Morning After, 1986, Biloxi Blues, 1988, Funny Farm, 1988, The Unbearable Lightness of Being, 1988, Stars and Bars, 1988, Working Girl, 1988, The January Man, 1989, Her Alibi, 1989, Family Business, 1989, Everybody Wins, 1990, Q & A, 1990, Pacific Heights, 1990, Postcards from the Edge, 1990, The Bonfire of the Vanities, 1990, Regarding Henry, 1991, Consenting Adults, 1992, The Mambo Kings, 1992, School Ties, 1992, A Stranger Among Us, 1992, Dennis the Menace, 1993, Dave, 1993, Guarding Tess, 1993, Wolf, 1994, (TV movies) The Silence, 1975, The Rivalry, 1975, Strangers: The Story of a Mother and Daughter, 1979, A Good Sport, 1984, (TV spls.) The House of Blue Leaves, PBS, 1987, O Pioneers!, PBS, 1991; costume design cons.: (TV spl.) Roanoak, 1986 (Emmy award nomination outstanding costume design 1986). Office: care United Scenic Artists 575 Fifth Ave New York NY 10018*

ROTH, BERNARD, mechanical engineering educator, researcher; b. N.Y.C., May 28, 1933; s. Morris Michael and Sara (Goldfarb) R.; m. Ruth Ochs, June 24, 1954; children: Steven Howard, Elliot Marc. BS, CCNY, 1956; MS, Columbia U., 1958, PhD, 1962. Engr. Ford Instrument Co., L.I., N.Y., 1955, Lockheed Aircraft Co., Van Nuys, Calif., 1956, Atlantic Design Co., Newark, 1958; lectr. CCNY, 1956-59; rsch. asst. Columbia U., N.Y.C., 1959-62; prof. Stanford (Calif.) U., 1962—; guest prof. U. Paris, 1988-90; expert, team leader UN Devel. Orgn., Vienna, Austria, 1986-88; mem. tech. adv. bd. Adept Tech., Inc., San Jose, Calif., 1983—; mem. adv. bd. Ctr. for Econ. Conversion, Mountain View, Calif., 1988—; bd. dirs. Peace Rev. Jour., Palo Alto, Calif., 1988-93. Co-author: Theoretical Kinematics, 1979, 2d edit., 1990; contbr. numerous articles on kinematics, robotics and design to profl. jours. Recipient Joseph F. Engelberger award Robotics Industries Assn., 1986. Fellow ASME (Melville medal 1967, Best Papers award mechanism conf. 1978, 80, 82, 92, 94, Mechanisms Coms. award 1982, Machine Design award 1984, chair design engring. divsn. 1981-82), Japanese Soc. for Promotion Sci.; mem. IEEE, Internat. Fedn. for Theory of Machines and Mechanisms (pres. 1980-83, hon. chmn. 7th World Congress 1987). Office: Stanford U Dept Mech Engring Stanford CA 94305

ROTH, CAROLYN LOUISE, art educator; b. Buffalo, June 17, 1944; d. Charles Mack and Elizabeth Mary (Hassel) R.; m. Charles Turner Barber, Aug. 4, 1991. Student, Art Student's League N.Y., 1965, Instituto Allende, San Miguel de Allende, Mex., 1966; BFA, Herron Sch. Art, 1967; MFA, Fla. State U., 1969. Asst. prof. art U. Tenn., Chattanooga, 1969-72; lectr. art So. Ill. U., Carbondale, 1973-75; asst. prof. art U. Evansville, Ind., 1975-80; lectr. art U. So. Ind., Evansville, 1984—; exhbn. coord., gallery dir. Krannert Gallery, U. Evansville, 1977-79; exhbn. coord., conf. advisor Ind. Women in Arts Conf., Ind. Arts Commn., Evansville, 1978. One woman shows include Wabash Valley Coll., Mt. Carmel, Ill., 1994, So. Ind. Ctr. for Arts, Seymour, Ind., 1996; exhibited in group shows Liberty Gallery, Louisville, 1992, Artlink Contemporary Art Gallery, Ft. Wayne, Ind., 1994, S.E. Mo. Coun. on Arts, Cape Girardeau, 1994, Lexington (Ky.) Art League, 1996, Mills Pond Horse Gallery, St. James, N.Y., 1996, SOHO Gallery, Pensacola, Fla., 1996; works appeared in Contemporary Batik and Tie-Dye, 1973, Kalliope: A Journal of Women's Art, vol. XIV, no. 1, 1992, Jour. Am. Vet. Med. Assn., vol. 203, no. 3, 1993. Mem. Nat. Mus. Women in Arts, Met. Mus. Art, J. B. Speed Mus., Evansville Mus. Arts and Sci., New Harmony Gallery of Contemporary Art. Democrat. Mem. Unity Ch. Avocation: travel to study art works in museums and galleries in Europe and Mex. Home: 10801 S Woodside Dr Evansville IN 47712-8422 Office: U So Ind 8600 University Blvd Evansville IN 47712-3534

ROTH, CLIFFORD, insurance company executive. Sr. v.p., regional mgr. The Segal Co. Office: 1 Park Ave Fl 8 New York NY 10016

ROTH, DANIEL BENJAMIN, lawyer, business executive; b. Youngstown, Ohio, Sept. 17, 1929; s. Benjamin F. and Marion (Benjamin) R.; m. Joann M. Roth; children: William M., Jennifer A., Rochelle. BS in Fin., Miami U., Oxford, Ohio, 1951; JD, Case-Western Res. U., 1956. Bar: Ohio 1956, D.C. 1983. Pres. Roth, Stephens, Blair, Roberts & Co., Youngstown, 1969—; co-founder, vice chmn. Nat. Data Processing Corp., Cin., 1961-69, Torent, Inc., Youngstown, 1971—; vice chmn. Morrison Metalweld Process Corp., 1979—, McDonald Steel Corp., 1980—, Torent Oil & Gas Co., 1979—, Vaughn Indsl. Car & Equipment Co., 1988—, DTS Explosive Hardening Co., 1988—; bd. dirs., exec. com. Mahoning Nat. Bank, Gasser Chair Co., Jarret Corp. Profl. singer: appearances including Steve Allen Show, 1952. bd. dirs. Youngstown Symphony, Stambaugh Auditorium; bd. dirs. Youngstown Playhouse, v.p., 1991-93; pres. Rodef Sholom Temple, Youngstown, 1982-84. 1st lt. USAF, 1951-53, lt. col. Res., ret. Recipient Mgr. of Yr. award Mahoning Valley Mgmt. Assn., 1989, Man of Yr. award Youngstown YWCA, 1995. Mem. ABA, D.C. Bar Assn., Ohio Bar Assn., Mahoning County Bar Assn., Lawyer-Pilots Bar Assn., Nat. Assn. Corp. Dirs., Soc. Benchers of Case Western Res. U. Law Sch., Youngstown Club, Squaw Creek Country Club, Pelican Isle Yacht Club (Naples, Fla.), Zeta Beta Tau (nat. v.p. 1964-66), Omicron Delta Kappa, Phi Eta Sigma, Tau Epsilon Rho. Jewish. Home: PO Box 959 Canfield OH 44406-0959 Office: Bank One Bldg Youngstown OH 44503

ROTH, EDWIN MORTON, manufacturing executive; b. Cleve., Oct. 15, 1927; s. Bernath and Lottie (Klafter) R.; m. Sarah Kennedy; children: Lacey Jan Roth, Alden Hope Guren, Corey Bruce, Cullen Andrew. Student, Ohio State U., 1946-47; B.B.A., Case Western Res. U., 1949. With Weather-Proof Co., Cleve., 1949-50; pres. E.M. Roth & Assocs., Cleve., 1950-52; sales mgr. Garland Co., Cleve., 1952-54, PlastiKote, Inc., Cleve., 1954-56; v.p. ITT Consumer Services, Cleve., 1967-75; pres., dir. ITT Service Industries, Cleve., 1970-75, Yellow Cab Co., Kansas City, Mo., 1968-75; v.p., dir. Abbey Casualty Ins. Co., Washington, 1968-75; chmn., chief exec. officer APCOA, Inc., 1975-87; pres. APCOA B.V., Amsterdam, 1979-87; chmn., pres. Momentum, Inc., Cleve., 1982-92; chmn., CEO Splty. Chem. Resources Inc., 1992—; bd. dirs. Working Walls Inc., Ludlow Composites, Inc., Mat-Tech, Inc. Trustee Cleve. Am. Jewish Com., Cleve. Mus. Art, 1994—, Jewish Cmty. Fedn., exec. com.; chmn. bd. dirs. Mt. Sinai Hosp., Cleve., 1979-82; bd. dirs. Menorah Park Home for Aged, No. Ohio coun. Camp Fire Girls, Cleve Ballet, United Way of Cleve., Playhouse Sq. Found., Joint Distbn. Com., Bellefaire Children's Home, pres., 1975-78; bd. overseers Case We. Res. U. With USNR, 1945-46. Mem. Nat. Parking Assn. (pres. 1976-78, chmn. 1978-80), Musical Arts Assn. Cleve., No. Ohio Tennis Assn. Jewish (trustee, v.p. synagogue). Clubs: Union, Oakwood Country (Cleve.), Palm Beach Country. Home: 1 N Breakers Row Palm Beach FL 33480-3252 Office: Splty Chem Resources Inc 9100 Valley View Rd Macedonia OH 44056-2035

ROTH, ERIC, screenwriter. screenplays include: The Nickel Ride, 1975, The Concorde - Airport '79, 1979, Suspect, 1987, Memories of Me, 1988 (with Billy Crystal), Mr. Jones, 1993, Forrest Gump, 1994 (Acad. award Best Adapted Screenplay). Office: care CAA 9830 Wilshire Blvd Beverly Hills CA 90212-1804*

ROTH, EVELYN AUSTIN, elementary school educator; b. Coronado, Calif., May 31, 1942; d. Robert Emmett and Marjorie Eastman (Rice) Austin; m. John King Roth, June 25, 1964; children: Andrew Lee, Sarah Austin. BA, San Diego State U., 1964; MA, U. of LaVerne, Calif., 1984; postgrad., U. Calif., Riverside, 1985. Cert. elem. tchr., Calif. Elem. tchr. Poway (Calif.) Unified Schs., 1964, Wallingford (Conn.) Unified Schs., 1964-66, Ontario (Calif.) Montclair Sch. Dist., 1982-88, Claremont (Calif.) Unified Schs., 1966-67, 83-93, Foothill Country Day Sch., Claremont, 1993—. Pres., bd. trustees Friends of Stone Libr., Claremont, 1993-94. Mem. AAUW, NEA, Calif. Tchrs. Assn., Internat. Reading Assn. (treas. Foothill Reading Coun. 1985-86), Delta Kappa Gamma (v.p. 1991-92). Republican. Presbyterian. Avocations: travel, reading, gardening.

ROTH, GEORGE STANLEY, research biochemist, physiologist; b. Honolulu, Aug. 5, 1946; s. George Frederick and Laura Ann (Zembrzuski) R.; m. Mary Jane Fletcher, Mar. 11, 1972; children: Susan Marie, George William. BS, Villanova U., 1968; PhD, Temple U., 1971. Postdoctoral fellow Fels Rsch. Inst., Phila., 1971-72; staff fellow Gerontology Rsch. Ctr. NIH, Balt., 1972-76, rsch. chemist, 1976—, chief molecular physiology and genetics sect., 1984—; vis. prof. Mehary Med. Coll., Nashville, 1983; Alpha Omega Alpha prof. U. P.R. Med. Sch., San Juan, 1986; chmn. Gordon Rsch. Conf. on Biology of Aging, Oxnard, Calif., 1985; rsch. cons. George Washington U., 1977-82; lectr. Med. Sci. Ctr. Student Sci. Program, 1980, Sandoz lectr. gerontology, Basel, Switzerland, 1984, 86, 94, also various other nat. and internat. meetings and workshops including Gordon confs., NATO workshops, internat. congresses, etc. Contbr. numerous articles and papers to profl. publs.; editor Exptl. Gerontology, Exptl. Aging Rsch., Proc. Soc. Exptl. Biology and Medicine; co-editor Chem. Rubber Co. Press Series in Aging, 1981—; assoc. editor The Ency. of Aging, 1987—. V.p. Community Coalition Harford County, Bel Air, Md., 1988-90, bd. dirs., 1990-92; co-dir. Ea. Harford County Civic Assn., Bel Air, 1981—. Recipient Ann. Rsch. award Am. Aging Assn., 1981, Sandoz prize for gerontol. rsch. Sandoz Ltd., Basel, 1989, Third Age award Internat. Assn. Gerontology, 1989, Spl. award Balt. Longitudinal Study on Aging, 1991; Sigma Chi scholar in residence Miami U., Oxford, Ohio, 1989. Fellow Gerontol. Soc. Am. (chair biol. scis. sect. 1975-76, chair rsch. com. 1978-79, chair fellowship com. 1986-87); mem. Soc. Exptl. Biology and Medicine. Republican. Roman Catholic. Avocations: basketball, fishing, hiking, canoeing. Office: Gerontology Rsch Ctr Molecular Physiology & Gen Hopkins Bayview Campus Baltimore MD 21224

ROTH, HADDEN WING, lawyer; b. Oakland, Calif., Feb. 10, 1930; s. Mark and Jane (Haley) R.; m. Alice Becker, Aug., 1987; 1 child, Elizabeth Wing. AA, Coll. Marin, 1949; BA, U. Calif., Berkeley, 1951; JD, U. Calif., San Francisco, 1957. Bar: Calif. 1958, U.S. Dist. Ct. (no. dist.) Calif. 1958, U.S. Ct. Appeals (9th cir.) 1958, U.S. Supreme Ct. 1966. Pvt. practice San Rafael, 1970—; dep. city atty. City of San Rafael, 1958-60, City of Sausalito and Mill Valley, Calif., 1964-66; dep. dist. atty. County of Marin, 1960-63; judge Marin County Mcpl. Ct., 1966-70; spl. cons. Marin Muni Water Dist., Corte Madera, Calif., County of Marin; atty. Bolinas Pub. Utility Dist., Ross Valley Fire Svc., Ross Valley Paramedics, Town of Ross and San Anselmo, Calif.; hearing officer dist. hosps., 1981—; lectr. law Golden Gate Coll. Law, San Francisco, 1971-73. Chmn. Marin County prison task force, 1973; bd. dirs. Marin Gen. Hosp., 1964-66. Cpl. U.S. Army, 1952-54. Named Outstanding Citizen of Yr., Coll. Marin, 1972. Mem. ABA, Calif. and Marin County Bar Assns., Assn. Bus. Trial Lawyers. Avocations: running, weights, reading. Home: 343 Fairhills Dr San Rafael CA 94901-1110 Office: 1050 Northgate Dr San Rafael CA 94903-2544

ROTH, HAROLD, architect; b. St. Louis, June 30, 1934; s. Samuel and Dorothy (Yawitz) R.; m. Dvora Feigon, Dec. 6, 1959; children: Elizabeth, David. AB, Washington U., 1956; MArch, Yale U., 1957. Designer Warner Burns Toan & Lunde, N.Y.C., 1957; sr. designer Eero Saarinen & Assocs., Roche Dinkeloo & Assocs., Hamden, Conn., 1959-65; ptnr. Harold Roth - Edward Saad, Hamden, Conn., 1965-72; sr. ptnr. Roth & Moore Architects, New Haven, 1973—; critic archtl. design Yale U. Sch. Architecture, New Haven, 1964—; pres., trustee Perspecta, Yale Archtl. Jour. Trustee Long Wharf Theatre, New Haven, 1972—, Conn. Trust for Hist. Preservation, 1983-90; pres. bd. trustees Conn. Architecture Found., 1990-93. Officer U.S. Army, 1957-59, Korea. Recipient Design award Nat. Coun. Religious Arch., 1970, Design award New Haven Preservation Trust, 1978, 88, Tucker award Bldg. Stone Inst., 1983, 88, Honor award Concrete Reinforcing Steel Inst., 1983, Design award Portland Cement Assn., 1984, Design award Archtl. Record, 1970, 80, Design award AIA/ALA, 1983, Faculty Design award Assn. Collegiate Schs. of Arch., 1988, Healthcare Facilities Design award Boston Soc. Archs., 1992; fellow Pierson Coll., Yale U., 1978—. Fellow AIA (chmn. nat. com. on design 1990, bd. dirs. 1992-94, mem. Conn. chpt., bd. dirs. Conn. chpt. 1982-85, Design award Conn. chpt. 1974, 78, 83, 86, 88, 90, 92, 93, Design award New Eng. chpt. 1968, 84, 92)); mem. Elihu Club, Yale Club N.Y. Home: 37 Autumn St New Haven CT 06511-2220 Office: Roth & Moore Architects 108 Audubon St New Haven CT 06510-1206

ROTH, HAROLD PHILMORE, physician; b. Cleve., Aug. 2, 1915; s. Abraham J. and Ida (Harris) R.; m. Kelly Cecile Rabinovitch, Dec. 9, 1952; children: Anita Alix, Edward Harris. B.A., Western Res. U., Cleve., 1936, M.D., 1939; M.S. in Hygiene, Harvard U., 1967. Diplomate Am. Bd. Internal Medicine, Am. Bd. Gastroenterology. Intern Cin. Gen. Hosp., 1939-40; house officer Boston City Hosp., 1940-42; asst. resident in medicine Barnes Hosp., St. Louis, 1942-43; clin. instr. Western Res. U., Cleve., 1949-52; sr. clin. instr. Western Res. U., 1953-55, asst. prof., 1955-63, assoc. prof., 1963—; assoc. prof. dept. community health Case Western Res. U., 1971-74; chief gastroenterology service VA Hosp., Cleve., 1947-74; dir. gastroenterology tng. program Univ. Hosps. and VA Hosp., 1963-74; assoc. physician Univ. Hosps. of Cleve., 1969-74; cons., asst. physician Highland View Hosp.; vis. physician in gastroenterology dept. medicine Cleve. Met. Gen. Hosp.; assoc. dir. for Digestive Diseases and Nutrition Nat. Inst. Arthritis, Diabetes, Digestive and Kidney Disease, NIH, Bethesda, Md., 1974-85, dir. div. Digestive Disease and Nutrition, 1983-85, epidemiology and data systems program dir., div. digestive diseases and nutrition, 1985-91, sr. gastroenterologist emeritus, 1991—; mem. Nat. Commn. on Digestive Diseases, Nat. Digestive Diseases Adv. Bd. Contbr. articles to med. jours. Served with AUS, 1943-46. USPHS spl. fellow, 1966-67; awards from Coalition of Digestive Disease Orgns., 1984, and Am. Gastroent. Assn., 1984. Mem. Am. Gastroenterol. Assn., Am. Assn. Study of Liver Disease, Central Soc. Clin. Rsch., ACP, Soc. Clin. Trials (pres. 1978-80), Phi Beta Kappa. Home: 10319 Gary Rd Potomac MD 20854-4102 Office: NIH 9000 Rockville Pike Rm 9A47 Bethesda MD 20892-0001 *Fifty years ago when I graduated from medical school, the practice of medicine was primarily an art. The physician had a limited number of useful diagnostic tests and procedures and an even more limited number of effective treatments. Since then new diagnostic tests and procedures have been developed that make diagnosis more precise, and new treatments such as the antibiotics still seem miraculous. I was fortunate to have an opportunity to become involved in some of these developments in medicine.*

ROTH, HARVEY PAUL, publisher; b. N.Y.C., Feb. 20, 1933; s. Lewis Theodore and Harriet (Wallow) R.; m. Tanya Cohen; children by previous marriage: Andrea, Matthew Jay; stepchildren: Laura Meryl, Matthew Robert. A.B., Bklyn. Coll., 1954; LL.B., N.Y. U., 1957. Bar: N.Y. bar 1959. Editor West Pub. Co., N.Y.C., 1959-61; pres. BFL Communications, Inc., Plainview, N.Y., 1961-76, Roth Pub., Inc., Great Neck, N.Y., 1976—; chmn. Alcove Press, London, 1970-75, Nash Pub. Corp., Los Angeles, 1971-75. Served with U.S. Army, 1957-58. Office: Roth Pub Inc 185 Great Neck Rd Great Neck NY 11021-3312

ROTH, HERBERT, JR., corporate executive; b. South Bend, Ind., Oct. 7, 1928; s. Gilbert and Vita (Augustienovicz) Shoemaker; m. Dolores Maloney, June 5, 1951; children: Christine, Diane, Carla. B.S., U.S. Mil. Acad., 1951; M.S., Newark Coll. Engring., 1959. Sr. product planner EDP div. RCA, 1956-61; v.p. Nuclear Corp. Am., Phoenix, 1961-62, GCA Corp., Bedford, Mass., 1962-66; pres., chief exec. officer Anelex Corp., Boston, 1966-67; dir., chmn. exec. com. Mohawk Data Scis., Corp., Boston, 1967-68; pres., chief exec. officer, dir. LFE Corp., Clinton, Mass., 1968-85; dir. Boston Edison Co., Landauer Inc., Tech/OpsSevcon Inc., Phoenix Mut. Life Ins. Co., Mark IV Ind. and Phoenix Series Funds. Served with U.S. Army, 1951-55. Mem. Boston C. of C. (pres. 1980-81).

ROTH, JACK JOSEPH, historian, educator; b. Dec. 17, 1920; s. Max and Dinah (Kraus) R.; m. Sheilagh Goldstone. B.A., U. Chgo., 1942, Ph.D., 1955; postgrad., Inst. d'Études Politiques, Paris, 1949-50. Mem. faculty Roosevelt U., 1951-68, prof. history, chmn. dept., 1960-68; prof. history Case Western Res. U., Cleve., 1968—; chmn. dept. Case Western Res. U., 1968-73; vis. asso. prof. history U. Chgo., 1962, professorial lectr. history, 1968; vis. prof. history U. Wis., 1964-65. Project dir.: The Persistence of Surrealism, Nat. Endowment for Humanities, festival, 1979, film, 1982; Translator: (Georges Sorel): Reflections on Violence, 1951, Sorel und die Totalitären Systeme, 1958, Revolution and Morale in Modern French Thought: Sorel and the Sorelians, 1963, The First World War: A Turning Point in Modern History, 1967, The Roots of Italian Fascism, 1967, Georges Sorel: on Lenin and Mussolini, 1977, The Revolution of the Mind: The Politics of Surrealism Reconsidered, 1977, The Cult of Violence: Sorel and the Sorelians, 1980; Contbr. articles to profl. jours., chpts. to books. Served with AUS, 1942-46. Recipient Penrose Fund award Am. Philos. Soc., 1964. Home: 24301 Bryden Rd Beachwood OH 44122-4038 Office: Dept History Case Western Res U Cleveland OH 44106

ROTH, JAMES FRANK, manufacturing company executive, chemist; b. Rahway, N.J., Dec. 7, 1925; s. Louis and Eleanor R.; m. Sharon E. Mattes, June 20, 1969; children by previous marriage: Lawrence, Edward, Sandra. B.A. in Chemistry, U. W.Va., 1947; Ph.D. in Phys. Chemistry, U. Md., 1951. Research chemist Franklin Inst., Phila., 1951-53, mgr. chemistry lab., 1958-60; chief chemist Lehigh Paints & Chems. Co., Allentown, Pa., 1953-55; research chemist GAF Corp., Easton, Pa., 1955-58; with Monsanto Co., St. Louis, 1960-80, dir. catalysis research, 1973-77, dir. process sci. research, 1977-80; corp. chief scientist Air Products and Chems., Inc., Allentown, 1980-91; indsl. cons., 1991—. Contbr. articles to profl. jours.; mem. editl. bd. Jour. Catalysis, 1976-85, Catalysis Revs., 1973-93, Applied Catalysis, 1981-85; editor for Ams., 1985-88, assoc. editor, 1988-95. With USN, 1943-46. Recipient Richard J. Kokes award Johns Hopkins U., 1977, Chem. Pioneer award Am. Inst. Chemists, 1986, Perkin medal Soc. Chem. Industry, 1988. Mem. NAE, Am. Chem. Soc. (St. Louis sect. St. Louis award 1975, E.V. Murphree nat. award 1976, Indsl. Chemistry award 1991), Catalysis Soc. N.Am. (E.J. Houdry award 1991), Catalysis Club of Phila. (award 1981). Inventor process biodegradable detergents, for acetic acid; U.S., fgn. patents in field. Home: 4436 Calle Serena Sarasota FL 34238-5641

ROTH, JANE RICHARDS, federal judge; b. Philadelphia, Pa., June 16, 1935; d. Robert Henry Jr. and Harriett (Kellond) Richards; m. William V. Roth Jr., Oct. 9, 1965; children: William V. III, Katharine K. BA, Smith Coll., 1956; LLB, Harvard U., 1965; LLD (hon.), Widener U., 1986, U. Del., 1994. Bar: Del. 1965, U.S. Dist. Ct. Del. 1966, U.S. Ct. Appeals (3d cir.) 1974. Adminstrv. asst. various fgn. service posts U.S. State Dept., 1956-62; assoc. Richards, Layton & Finger, Wilmington, Del., 1965-73, ptnr., 1973-85; judge U.S. Dist. Ct. Del., Wilmington, 1985-91, U.S. Ct. Appeals (3d cir.), Wilmington, 1991—; adj. faculty Villanova U. Sch. Law. Hon. chmn. Del. chpt. Arthritis Found., Wilmington; bd. overseers Widener U. Sch. Law; bd. consultors Villanova U. Sch. Law; trustee Hist. Soc. Del. Recipient Nat. Vol. Service citiation Athritis Found., 1982. Fellow Am. Bar Found.; mem. ABA, Fed. Judges Assn., Del. State Bar Assn. Republican. Episcopalian. Office: US Ct House J Caleb Boggs Fed Bldg 844 N King St Rm 5100 Wilmington DE 19801-3519

ROTH, JOE, motion picture company executive; b. 1948. Prodn. assistant various commls. and feature films, San Francisco; also lighting dir. Pitchel Players, San Francisco; then producer Pitchel Players, L.A.; co-founder Morgan Creek Prodns., L.A., 1987-89; chmn. 20th Century Fox Film Corp., L.A., 1989-92; founder Caravan Pictures, L.A., 1992-94; chmn. Walt Disney Motion Pictures Group, Burbank, 1994—. Prodr. numerous films including Tunnelvision, Cracking Up, Americathon, Our Winning Season, The Final Terror, The Stone Boy, Where the River Runs Black, Bachelor Party, Off Beat, Streets of Gold (dir. debut), Revenge of the Nerds II (also dir.); exec. prodr. Young Guns, Dead Ringers, Skin Deep, Major League, Renegades, Coupe de Ville (also dir.), Enemies: A Love Story: Caravan Pictures releases include Walt Disney's The Three Musketeers, Angie, Angels in the Outfield, I Love Trouble, A Low Down Dirty Shame, Houseguest, The Jerky Boys, Heavyweights, Tall Tale, While You Were Sleeping. Office: Walt Disney Studio 500 S Buena Vista St Burbank CA 91521-1060

ROTH, JOHN KING, philosopher, educator; b. Grand Haven, Mich., Sept. 3, 1940; s. Josiah V. and Doris Irene (King) R.; m. Evelyn Lillian Austin, June 25, 1964; children: Andrew Lee, Sarah Austin. BA, Pomona Coll., 1962; student, Yale U. Div. Sch., 1962-63; MA, Yale U., 1965, PhD, 1966; LHD, Ind. U., 1990. Asst. prof. philosophy Claremont McKenna Coll., Calif., 1966-71, assoc. prof., 1971-76, Russell K. Pitzer prof. philosophy, 1976—; vis. prof. philosophy Franklin Coll., Lugano, Switzerland, 1973; Fulbright lectr. Am. studies U. Innsbruck, Austria, 1973-74; vis. prof. philosophy Doshisha U., Kyoto, Japan, 1981-82; vis. prof. Holocaust studies U. Haifa, Israel, 1982; Fulbright lectr. in Am. studies Royal Norwegian Ministry of Edn., Oslo, Norway, 1995—. Author: Freedom and the Moral Life, 1969, Problems of the Philosophy of Religion, 1971, American Dreams, 1976, A Consuming Fire, 1979, (with Richard L. Rubenstein) Approaches to Auschwitz, 1987, (with Frederick Sontag) The American Religious Experience, 1972, (with Frederick Sontag) The Questions of Philosophy, 1988, (with Robert H. Fossum) The American Dream, 1981, (with Fossum) American Ground, 1988, (with Rubenstein) The Politics of Latin American Liberation Theology, 1988, (with Michael Berenbaum) Holocaust: Religious and Philosophical Implications, 1989, Ethics, 1991, (with Carol Rittner) Memory Offended, 1991, (with Creighton Peden) Rights, Justice, and Community, 1992, (with Carol Rittner) Different Voices, 1993, American Diversity, American Identity, 1995. Spl. advisor U.S. Holocaust Meml. Coun., Washington, 1980-85, mem., 1995—. Danforth grad. fellow, 1962-66; Graves fellow, 1970-71; NEH fellow, 1976-77; Faculty Pairing grantee Japan-U.S. Friendship Commn., 1981-83; named U.S. Prof. of Yr. Coun. Advancement and Support of Edn. and Carnegie Found. Advancement of Tchg., 1988. Mem Am. Philos. Assn., Am. Acad. Religion, Am. Studies Assn., Calif. Coun. for Humanities, Phi Beta Kappa. Presbyterian. Home: 1648 N Kenyon Pl Claremont CA 91711-2905 Office: Claremont McKenna Coll 850 Columbia Ave Claremont CA 91711-3901

ROTH, J(OHN) REECE, electrical engineer, educator, researcher-inventor; b. Washington, Pa., Sept. 19, 1937; s. John Meyer and Ruth Evangeline (Iams) R.; m. Helen Marie DeCrane, Jan. 14, 1972; children: Nancy Ann, John Alexander. S.B. in Physics, MIT, 1959; Ph.D., Cornell U., 1963. Engring. aide Aerojet-Gen. Corp., Azusa, Calif., 1957, 58; aerospace engr. N.Am. Aviation, Canoga Park, Calif., 1959; prin. investigator NASA Lewis Research Ctr., Cleve., 1963-78; prof. elec. engring. U. Tenn., Knoxville, 1978—; hon. prof. U. Electronic Sci. and Tech. of China, Chengdu, 1992—; prin. investigator Office Naval Rsch., Washington, 1980-89, Air Force Office Sci. Rsch., Washington, 1981-95, Army Rsch. Office, 1988-93, NASA Langley Rsch. Ctr., Hampton, Va., 1995—, March Instruments, Inc., Concord, Calif., 1996—; cons. TVA, Chattanooga, 1982-84, BDM Corp., 1987-88, Tenn. Eastman, 1989-90, March Instruments, 1995—; speaker at profl. meetings; mem. NAS-NRC Com. on Aneutronic Fusion, 1986-87. Author: Industrial Plasma Engineering, Introduction to Fusion Energy; contbr. articles to profl. jours. Sloan scholar, 1955-59; Ford fellow, 1961-62. Fellow IEEE, AIAA (assoc.); mem. Am. Phys. Soc., Am. Nuclear Soc. (exec. com. No. Ohio sect. 1975-78), Nuclear and Plasma Scis. Soc., Am. Soc. Engring. Edn., Knoxville Art Gallery, East Tenn. Soc. of Archaeol. Inst. Am., Sigma Xi (pres. U. Tenn. Knoxville chpt. 1985-86). Club: U. Tenn. Faculty (Knoxville). Home: 12359 N Fox Den Dr Farragut TN 37922 Office: U Tenn Dept Elec Engring Knoxville TN 37996-2100

ROTH, JOHN ROGER, geneticist, biology educator; b. Winona, Minn., Mar. 14, 1939; s. Frederick Daniel and Louise Mae (Wirt) R.; m. Uta Goetz (div.); children: Katherine Louise, Frederick Phillip; m. Sherylynne Harris,

Jan. 4, 1986. BA, Harvard U., 1961; PhD, John Hopkins U., 1965. From asst. prof. molecular biology to prof. molecular biology U. Calif., Berkeley, 1967-76; prof. biology U. Utah, Salt Lake City, 1976—. Recipient Disting. Prof. award, 1990, Rosenblatt award, 1990. Mem. NAS, Am. Soc. for Microbiology, Genetics Soc. Am. Office: U Utah Dept Biology Salt Lake City UT 84112

ROTH, JUDITH SHULMAN, lawyer; b. N.Y.C., Apr. 25, 1952; d. Mark Alan and Margaret Ann (Podell) Shulman; m. William Hartley Roth, May 30, 1976; children: Andrew Henry, Caroline Shulman. AB, Cornell U., 1974; JD, Columbia U., 1977. Bar: N.Y. 1978, U.S. Dist. Ct. (ea. dist.) N.Y. 1978, U.S. Dist. Ct. (so. dist.) N.Y. 1978, U.S. Ct. Appeals (2d cir.) 1993. Assoc. Phillips Nizer Benjamin Krim & Ballon, N.Y.C., 1978-87, ptnr., 1988—; lectr. CLE Fordham Law Sch., N.Y.C., 1990. Mem. Cosmopolitan Club. Jewish. Avocations: reading, tennis, golf, art, gardening. Office: Phillips Nizer Benjamin Krim & Ballon 666 Fifth Avenue New York NY 10103

ROTH, KATHRYN GAIE, government executive; b. Torrejon, Spain, Mar. 19, 1964; came to U.S., 1964; d. Edwin Isaac and Deborah (Weissman) R. BA, Bryn Mawr Coll., 1987; MPA, Princeton U., 1991. Founder, editor-in-chief Jour. for Pub. and Internat. Affairs, Princeton, N.J., 1989-91; asst. sec. to bd., dir. spl. projects Nathan Cummings Found., N.Y.C., 1991-92; assoc. dir. presdl. advance White House, Washington, 1993-95; v.p. Revlon Found. MacAndrews & Forbes Holding, Inc., N.Y.C., 1995-96; exec. dir. U.S. Dept. of Defense Industrial Affairs and Installation, 1996—; polit. cons. Mondale Campaign, Dukakis Campaign, Simon Campaign, Clinton for Pres. Campaign and Transition. Contbg. author: Public Opinion in U.S. Foreign Policy: The Controversy Over Contra Aid, 1994; contbr. articles to profl. publs. Mem. Dem. Bus. Coun. Women's Leadership Forum; bd. dirs. N.Y. Dem. Leadership Coun. Recipient Conf. Paper award Assn. Profl. Schs. of Internat. Affairs, 1991; Woodrow Wilson fellow, 1989-91. Mem. Women in Philanthropy, Coun. Fgn. Rels. (team member), Dem. Bus. Coun. N.Y., Dem. Leadership Coun. Democrat. Jewish. Avocations: travel, art, scuba diving, flying. Home: 525 E 86th St Apt 10B New York NY 10028-7515 Office: McAndrews and Forbes Inc 38 E 63d St New York NY 10021

ROTH, LAURA MAURER, physics educator, researcher; b. Flushing, N.Y., Oct. 11, 1930; d. Keith Langden and Ruth (Oliphint) Maurer; m. Willard Dale Roth, June 6. 1952; children: Andrew Eric, Karen Elsa. AB, Swarthmore Coll., 1952; AM, Radcliffe Coll., 1953, PhD, 1957. Staff physicist Lincoln Lab., MIT, Lexington, Mass., 1956-63; lectr. Harvard U., Cambridge, Mass., summer 1959; assoc. prof., prof. physics Tufts U., Medford, Mass., 1963-67; physicist GE R & D Ctr., Schenectady, N.Y., 1967-72; lectr. Inst. for Theoretical Physics, U. Colo., Boulder, Colo., summer 1969; Abbey Rockefeller Mauze vis. prof. physics MIT, Cambridge, Mass., 1972-73; rsch. prof. SUNY, Albany, 1973-77, prof. physics, 1977-95, prof. emerita, 1995—; cons. Lincoln Lab., MIT, 1963. Co-author: Women in Physics, 1975; co-editor: Fundamental Questions in Quantum Mechanics, 1984; editor: Dharma Paths, 1993; contbr. 80 articles to physics jours., 1956—. Dir. Karma Thegsum Choling Buddhist Ctr., Albany, N.Y., 1979—; program dir. for publs. Karma Kagyu Inst., Woodstock, N.Y., 1988—. Recipient medal Radcliffe Grad. Soc., 1962; grantee Sloan Found., Tufts U., 1963-65, NSF, SUNY, Albany, 1976-81. Democrat. Buddhist. Home: 1270 Ruffner Rd Niskayuna NY 12309-4601 Office: SUNY Albany Dept Physics 1400 Washington Ave Albany NY 12222-0001

ROTH, LAWRENCE MAX, pathologist, educator; b. McAlester, Okla., June 25, 1936; s. Herman Moe and Blanche (Brown) R.; m. Anna Berit Katarina Sundstrom, Apr. 3, 1965; children—Karen Esther, David Josef. B.A., Vanderbilt U., 1957; M.D., Harvard U., 1960. Diplomate Am. Bd. Pathology. Rotating intern U. Ill. Research and Ednl. Hosps., Chgo., 1960-61; resident in anat. pathology Washington U. Sch. Medicine, St. Louis, 1961-64; resident in clin. pathology U. Calif. Med. Ctr., San Francisco, 1967-68; asst. prof. pathology Tulane U. Sch. Medicine, New Orleans, 1968-71; assoc. prof. pathology Ind. U. Sch. Medicine, Indpls., 1971-75, prof., 1975—, dir. div. surg. pathology. Series editor: Contemporary Issues in Surgical Pathology; mem. editl. bd. Am. Jour. Surg. Pathology, Human Pathology, Seminars in Diagnostic Pathology, Internat. Jour. Gynecol. Pathology, Endocrine Pathology; contbr. articles to med. jours. Served to capt. U.S. Army, 1965-67. Mem. Am. Assn. Investigative Pathologists, U.S. and Can. Acad. Pathology, Am. Soc. Clin. Pathologists, Internat. Soc. Gynecol. Pathologists, Arthur Purdy Stout Soc. Surg. Pathologists, Assn. Dirs. Anatomic and Surg. Pathology. Home: 7898 Ridge Rd Indianapolis IN 46240-2538 Office: 550 University Blvd Indianapolis IN 46202-5270

ROTH, LOREN H., psychiatrist; b. May 9, 1939; m. Ellen A. Roth; children: Jonathan, Alexandra, Elizabeth. BA in Philosophy, Cornell U., 1961; MD cum laude, Harvard U., 1966, MPH, 1972; postgrad., Am. U., 1972-73. Diplomate Am. Bd. Psychiatry and Neurology; lic. physician, Conn., Md., Mass., Pa. Med. intern Univ. Hosps., Western Res. U., Cleve., 1966-67; resident psychiatry Yale U., New Haven, 1969-70, Mass. Gen. Hosp., Boston, 1970-72; staff psychiatrist Ctr. for Studies Crime and Delinquency, NIMH, Rockville, Md., 1972-74; co-dir., dir. law and psychiatry program Western Psychiat. Inst. and Clinic/U. Pitts., 1974—, chief adult clin. svcs., 1983-87, 88-89, chief clin. svcs., 1989-95, co-dir., dir. law and psychiatry program, 1974-94; vice-chmn. dept. psychiatry U. Pitts., 1988—, asst. prof., 1974-78, assoc. prof., 1978-82, prof., 1982—; v.p. for Managed Care U. Pitt. Med. Ctr., 1993—; assoc. vice chancellor for edn., health scis. U. Pitts. Sch. Medicine, 1995—; med. staff Presbyn.-Univ. Hosp., Pitts., 1983—; gen. med. officer Fed. Penitentiary, Lewisburg, Pa., 1967-69; William E. Schumacher disting. lectr. Maine Dept. Mental Health and Mental Retardation, Portland, 1982; mem. commn. on mentally disabled ABA, Washington, 1987; cons. law and psychiatry Dept. Welfare, Commonwealth Pa., 1974; cons. reviewer, site visitor crime and delinquency sect. NIMH, 1977; examiner Am. Bd. Psychiatry and Neurology, 1985. Author: (with others) Informed Consent: A Study of Decisionmaking in Psychiatry, 1984; editor: (with others) Psychiatry, Social, Epidemiologic and Legal Psychiatry, Vol. 5, 1986; contbr. articles to profl. jours., chpts. to books; editorial bd. Criminology, 1974-78, Law and Human Behavior, 1980-85, Internat. Jour. Law and Psychiatry, 1980-88, Behavioral Scis. and the Law, 1987-95; assoc. editor Am. Jour. Psychiatry, 1982-90; cons. editor Criminal Justice and Behavior, 1982-85. Lt. comrd. USPHS Res., 1967—. Recipient Steve Allen award United Mental Health, Inc., 1990; grantee NIMH, 1979, 80-81, 89, Founds. Fund for Rsch. in Psychiatry, 1980-82. Fellow Am. Psychiat. Assn. (Isaac Ray award 1988), Am. Coll. Utilization Rev. Physicians, Am. Coll. Psychiatrists; mem. AMA, Am. Acad. Psychiatry and Law (pres. 1983-84), Group for Advancement Psychiatry (com. on psychiatry and law 1979-80, chmn. 1981-84), Am. Soc. Criminology, Am. Soc. Law and Medicine (bd. dirs. 1982-85), Internat. Acad. Law and Mental Health (bd. dirs.), Am. Psychopath. Assn., Phi Beta Kappa, Phi Kappa Phi. Home: 6820 Edgerton Ave Pittsburgh PA 15208-2803 Office: Western Psychiat Inst 3811 Ohara St Pittsburgh PA 15213-2593

ROTH, MICHAEL, lawyer; b. N.Y.C., July 22, 1931; s. Philip Arthur and Mollie (Breitenbach) R.; m. Jeanny Macoir, Nov. 24, 1957; 3 children. B.A., Yale Coll., 1953; J.D., Columbia U., 1956, M. Internat. Affairs, 1964. Bar: N.Y. 1956. Law assoc. Stroock & Stroock & Lavan, N.Y.C., 1956-63; ptnr. Roth, Carlson, Kwit & Spengler, N.Y.C., 1964-74; chmn. N.Y. State Liquor Authority, N.Y.C., 1974-77; ptnr. Shea & Gould, N.Y.C., 1979-89; of counsel Rosenman & Colin, N.Y.C., 1989—. Mem. U.S. del. to UN Population Commn., 1969; Rep.-Conservative candidate for N.Y. State atty. gen., 1978; mem. Pres.' Task Force on Internat. Pvt. Enterprise, 1983-84, Pres.' Commn. on Mgmt. AID Programs, 1991-92. Mem. ABA, N.Y. State Bar Assn., Assn. of Bar of City of N.Y. Republican. Clubs: Yale (N.Y.C.); Sunningdale Country (Scarsdale, N.Y.).

ROTH, MICHAEL I., lawyer, financial executive; b. Bklyn., Nov. 22, 1945; s. Harry A. and Sally (Kutin) R.; m. Carole A. Snofsky, Aug. 10, 1968; children—Barrie, Marc, Andrew. BS, CCNY, 1967; JD, Boston U., 1971; LL.M., NYU, 1973. Bar: N.Y. 1971. CPA: N.Y. 1973, Conn. 1973. With Coopers & Lybrand, N.Y.C., 1969-76; ptnr. Stamford, Conn., 1976-82; exec. v.p. corp. fin., tax and adminstrn. Primerica Corp. (formerly Am. Can Co.), Greenwich, Conn., 1982-87, exec. v.p., 1987, chief fin. officer, 1987-88; exec. v.p., chief fin. officer MONY Fin. Svcs., N.Y.C., 1989-91; pres., COO, MONY-Mut. Ins. Co., N.Y.C., 1991-94, also bd. dirs., chmn. bd. dirs., CEO, 1994—; bd. dirs. Mut. of N.Y. Bd. dirs. Child Guidance Ctr., Stamford, 1984-85; trustee Temple BethEl, Stamford, 1984-85. Mem. Am. Inst. CPA's, Conn. Soc. CPA's, Stamford Tax Assn. (pres. 1981-82). Office: MONY Fin Svcs 1740 Broadway New York NY 10019-4315*

ROTH, OLIVER RALPH, radiologist; b. Cumberland, Md., Nov. 30, 1921; s. DeCoursey Andrew and Mabel (Lathrum) R.; BS, Frostburg (Md.) State Coll., 1942, DSc (hon.), 1980; MD, U. Md., 1950; m. Virginia McBride, June 2, 1943; 1 child, Tiija. Diplomate Am. Bd. Radiology. Resident, Johns Hopkins Hosp., Balt., 1954-57; cancer research fellow Middlesex Hosp., London, 1957-58; founder dept. radiation oncology Presbyn. Hosp., Charlotte, N.C., 1958-62; attending radiologist King's Daus. Hosp., Ashland, Ky., 1962-80; radiologist Our Lady of Bellefonte Hosp., 1981-86; mem. faculty Sch. of Allied Health Shawnee State U., Portsmouth, Ohio, 1986-90; prof. radiology Sch. Medicine Marshall U., Huntington, W.Va., 1990—; mem. adv. com. Ky. Cancer Commn., 1978; bd. dirs. Boyd County chpt. Am. Cancer Soc., 1978. With USN, 1942-45. Commanded to Buckingham Palace, June 17, 1958; recipient Disting. Alumni award Frostburg State U., 1979. Mem. AMA, Am. Coll. Radiology, Radiol. Soc. N.Am., Am. Radium Soc., Royal Faculty Radiology, Brit. Inst. Radiology. Democrat. Lutheran. Club: Shriners (Cumberland, Md.). Book reviewer Radiology, 1954-55. Home: 2912 Cogan St Ashland KY 41102-5230

ROTH, PAMELA JEANNE, marketing professional, web site developer; b. Huntington, N.Y., Sept. 9, 1955; d. Julius Leo and Constance Abby (Gettenberg) R. BA with honors, New Coll. Hofstra U., 1975; MS, Rensselaer Inst. Tech., 1977; JD, New England Sch. Law, 1983; postgrad., Sandler Sales Inst., 1996. Assoc. editor Functional Photography, Hempstead, N.Y., 1976; documentation specialist Allendale Ins., Johnston, R.I., 1977-78; systems analyst Comml. Union Ins., Boston, 1978-79; sr. software writer NEC Info. Systems, Lexington, Mass., 1979-82; pres. TEKDOC Tech. Communications, North Andover, Mass., 1978-86; sr. tech. writer Software Internat., Andover, Mass., 1983; pres., CEO SPIRAL Communications, Inc., SPIRAL Group, SPIRAL Books, Manchester, N.H., 1986—; developer Ofcl. Olympic Torch Relay web site, Nashua, N.H., 1996; presenter in field. Author: The First Book of Adam, 1984, The Second Book of Adam, 1984, Using the PFS Family, 1985; editor: Data Warehousing and Decision Support-The State of the Art, 1995, The Internet and Data Warehousing, 1996; contbr. articles to profl. jours. Gen. mgr. ImprovBoston, 1986. Mem. Women Owners Network. Avocations: sporting clays, travel, bicycling, dog training. Office: SPIRAL Comms Inc Stark Mill Bldg Ste 401 500 Commercial St Manchester NH 03101-1151

ROTH, PAMELA SUSAN, lawyer; b. N.Y.C., Nov. 23, 1961; d. Edward Abraham and Susan Violet (Castro) R. BS in Biology, Adelphi U., 1982, MBA, 1986; JD, Pace U., 1990. Bar: N.Y. 1991, U.S. Dist. Ct. (ea. and so. dists.) N.Y. 1991, U.S. Ct. Appeals (10th cir.) 1993, Colo. 1995, U.S. Dist. Ct. Colo. 1995, U.S. Supreme Ct. 1995. Asst. gen. counsel N.Y.C. Dept. Probation, Bklyn., 1990-91; asst. dist. atty. Kings County Dist. Atty., Bklyn., 1992-93; assoc. Law Firm of Portales & Assocs., Denver, 1993-95; pvt. practice N.Y.C., 1995—; gen. counsel Hispano Crypto-Jewish Rsch. Ctr., Denver, 1994—. Mem. ABA, Am. Soc. Internat. Law, Hispanic Nat. Bar Assn., Bklyn. Bar Assn., Internat. Assn. Jewish Lawyers and Jurists, Kings County Criminal Bar Assn. Avocations: aerobics, skiing, roller blading, gourmet cooking. Office: 26 Court St Ste 2003 Brooklyn NY 11242

ROTH, PAUL NORMAN, lawyer; b. N.Y.C., May 4, 1939; s. Sol and Florence (Glassman) R.; m. Ellen Joan Lipp, May 24, 1964; children: Stefanie H., Jessica A. AB, Harvard U., 1961, LLB, 1964. Bar: N.Y. 1966, U.S. Ct. Appeals (2d cir.) 1966, U.S. Dist. Ct. (so. and ea. dists.) N.Y. 1967, U.S. Supreme Ct. 1975. Assoc. Cleary, Gottlieb, Steen & Hamilton, N.Y.C., 1965-69; ptnr. Schulte Roth & Zabel, N.Y.C., 1969--. Trustee Ctrl. Synagogue, N.Y.C., 1987-95. Fulbright fellow, Netherlands, 1965. Mem. ABA, N.Y. State Bar Assn., Assn. of Bar of City of N.Y. (com. on securities regulation 1982-85, chmn. 1989-92), Harvard Law Sch. Assn. N.Y. (trustee 1987-90, v.p. 1992-93), Century Country Club. Office: Schulte Roth & Zabel 900 3rd Ave New York NY 10022-4728

ROTH, PHILIP, writer; b. Newark, Mar. 19, 1933; s. Herman and Bess (Finkel) R.; m. Margaret Martinson, Feb. 22, 1959 (dec. 1968); m. Claire Bloom, Apr. 29, 1990. Student, Newark Coll. of Rutgers U., 1950-51; AB, Bucknell U., 1954; MA, U. Chgo., 1955. Tchr. English U. Chgo., 1956-58; faculty Iowa Writers Workshop, 1960-62; writer in residence Princeton U., 1962-64; adj. prof. U. Pa., 1967-77; disting. prof. Hunter Coll. CUNY, 1989-92. Short story writer, novelist; works pub. in Harper's, New Yorker, Epoch, Commentary, others; reprints in Best Am. Short Stories of 1956, 59, 60, O'Henry Prize Stories of 1960; author: Goodbye, Columbus, 1959 (Nat. Book award), Letting Go, 1962, When She Was Good, 1967, Portnoy's Complaint, 1969, Our Gang, 1971, The Breast, 1972, The Great American Novel, 1973, My Life as a Man, 1974, Reading Myself and Others, 1975, The Professor of Desire, 1977, The Ghost Writer, 1979, A Philip Roth Reader, 1980, Zuckerman Unbound, 1981, The Anatomy Lesson, 1983, The Prague Orgy, 1985, Zuckerman Bound, 1985, The Counterlife, 1987 (Nat. Book Critics Circle award for fiction, 1988), The Facts, 1988, Deception, 1990, Patrimony, 1991 (Nat. Book Critics Circle award for biography/autobiography 1992), Operation Shylock, 1993 (PEN-Faulkner award for fiction 1993), Sabbath's Theater, 1995 (Nat. Book Fiction award 1995). Recipient prize for fiction Paris Rev., 1958, Nat. Inst. Arts and Letters award, 1960, Daroff award Jewish Book Coun. Am., 1960, Medal of Honor for Lit., Nat. Arts Club, 1991, Karel Capek prize Czech Republic, 1994, Nat. Book award in Fiction, 1995; Guggenheim fellow, 1959-60, Rockefeller fellow, 1966. Office: 250 Melins Rd Cornwall Bridge CT 06754

ROTH, PHILLIP JOSEPH, retired judge; b. Portland, Oreg., Feb. 29, 1920; s. Harry William and Minnie Alice (Segel) R.; m. Ida Lorraine Thomas, Feb. 22, 1957 (div. 1977); children: Phillip Joseph, David William; m. Allison Blake Ramsey, Feb. 14, 1978 (div. 1994). BA cum laude, U. Portland, 1943; JD, Lewis and Clark Coll., 1948. Bar: Oreg. 1948, U.S. Dist. Ct. Oreg. 1949, U.S. Ct. Appeals (9th cir.) 1959, U.S. Supreme Ct. 1962. Dep. atty. City of Portland, 1948-50; dep. dist. atty. Multnomah County, Portland, 1950-52; sole practice Portland, 1952-64; cir. judge Multnomah County State of Oreg., Portland, 1964-94, presiding cir. judge, 1970-71, 76-78; adj. prof. Lewis & Clark U. Law Sch., Portland, 1978-80, mem. standing com., 1972-90; mem. exec. com. Nat. Conf. State Trial Judges, 1980-91. Author: Sentencing: A View From the Bench, 1973; co-author: The Judicial Immunity Doctrine Today: Between the Bench and a Hard Place, 1984, The Brief Jour.; The Dangerous Erosion of Judicial Immunity, 1989. Mem. Oreg. Legislature, 1952-54; Rep. nominee for Congress, 1956; chmn. Oreg. Rep. Ctrl. Com., 1962-64; mem. adv. bd. Portland Salvation Army, 1976—; mem. bd. overseers Lewis and Clark Coll., 1972-90. Named Alumnus of Yr. U. Portland, 1963; named Alumnus of Yr. Lewis & Clark Law Sch., 1973. Fellow Am. Bar Found.; mem. ABA (chmn. jud. immunity com. jud. adminstrn. divsn. 1982-90, mem. commn. on standards jud. adminstrn. divsn. 1973-77, chmn. conf. state trial judges 1990-91, chmn. jud. adminstrn. divsn. 1994-95), Oreg. Bar Assn. (bd. govs. 1961-64), Multnomah County Bar Assn. (pres. 1959), Am. Judicature Soc., Oreg. Cir. Judges Assn. (pres. 1988-89), U. Portland Alumni Assn. (pres. 1967), Lewis and Clark Coll. Alumni Assn. (prs. 1974-76, 80-81), Multnomah Law Libr. Assn. (bd. dirs.), City Club, Univ. Club, Masons, Shriners, Rotary, B'nai B'rith, Delta Theta Phi. Jewish. Home: 2495 SW 73d Ave Portland OR 97225

ROTH, RICHARD J., marketing and advertising consultant; b. N.Y.C., Feb. 11, 1936; s. Aaron and Eleanor (Oppenheim) R.; m. Leslie B. Roth, Sept. 27, 1970; children: Erik, Gregory, Nickolas. BS, Dartmouth Coll., 1958; MBA, Amos Tuck Sch. Bus., 1959. With Burlington Industries, 1959-60, Gen. Foods., 1960-64, Grey Advt., 1964-74; exec. v.p. Scali McCabe Sloves, Inc., N.Y.C., 1974-85; pres. Richard Roth Assocs., Chappaqua, N.Y., 1987—.

ROTH, ROBERT ALLEN, research and development company executive; b. Chgo., Oct. 26, 1947; s. Ralph Robert and Lucile Emily (Hence) R.; m. Betty Rae Wooten, July 23, 1968 (div. June 1975); children: Robert Allen III, Anna Katherine; m. Carolyn McConnell, Aug. 23, 1980. AA, St. Johns River Jr. Coll., Palatka, Fla., 1967; B Gen. Studies, Rollins Coll., 1969; MBA, U. North Fla., 1974. Cert. sys. profl., computing profl. Various positions, 1968-80; systems mgr. Charter Oil Co.-Alaska Oil Co., Jacksonville, Fla., 1980-81; project leader, lead analyst Halliburton Svcs., Duncan, Okla., 1982; mgr. data adminstrn. and software quality assurance Comm. Satellite Corp., Washington, 1982-83; div. mgr. Automated Scis. Group, Inc., Fairfax, Va., 1983-86; div. dir. Inf. Sys. and Networks (ISN) Corp., Sarasota, Fla., 1986-87; pres., owner, operator ROMAC Enterprises, Sarasota, 1987-93; hdqs. div. mgr. COMPEX Corp., Sarasota, 1987, v.p., gen. mgr. S.E. region, 1991-92; pres. Advanced Tech. Group, Sarasota, Fla., 1992—. Mem. Rotary (v.p. Sarasota 1991-92, pres. 1992-93, Paul Harris fellow 1992). Avocations: car rallies, golf, tennis, boating, shooting. Home: 3692 East Wexford Hollow Rd Jacksonville FL 32224-6678 Office: Advanced Tech Group PO Box 17014 Jacksonville FL 32245-7014

ROTH, ROBERT AUGUST, university administrator; b. Cleve., Jan. 26, 1943; s. August Joseph and Carmel Maria (Narducci) R.; children: Rob Eugene, Todd Jason, Tracy Lynn. BA, Hiram Coll., 1964; MEd, Pa. State U., 1967; PhD, Kent State U., 1970; postgrad., Rutgers U., 1972-73. Cert. tchr. Tchr., coach Kirtland (Ohio) Schs., 1965-67, Cuyahoga Heights High Sch., Cleve., 1968-69; mem. edn. faculty, dir. performance project State of N.J. Rutgers U., New Brunswick, N.J., 1971-73; state supr. State of Mich. Dept. Edn. Certification, Lansing, 1974-79, state dir., 1979-83; dir. Ctr. for Rsch. on Teaching and Human Resources Devel. U. So. Fla., Tampa, 1985-86; dir., chmn., edn. tchr. Calif. State U., Long Beach, 1987—. Contbr. over 150 books and articles to profl. jours. recipient Resolution of Tribute Mich. Legislature, 1983, Resolution of Recognition of Leadership Mich. State Bd. Edn., 1982, 84; named Disting. Leader in Tchr. Edn. in U.S., 1990, Univ. Disting. Faculty scholar, Calif. State U. at Long Beach, 1990. Mem. Assn. Tchr. Educators of Mich. (Leadership award 1979, past pres.), Nat. Assn. State Dirs. of Edn. (past nat. pres., Disting. Leadership award 1984), Assn. Tchr. Educators (past nat. pres., Leadership award 1985, Disting. mem. 1988, Disting. Tchr. Educator State of Calif. 1992), Phi Delta Kappa. Avocations: photography, sports. Office: Calif State U Coll Edu 1250 N Bellflower Blvd Long Beach CA 90840-2201

ROTH, ROBERT EARL, environmental educator; b. Wauseon, Ohio, Mar. 30, 1937; s. Earl Jonas and Florence Lena (Mahler) R.; m. Carol Sue Yackee, Aug. 8, 1959; children: Robin Earl, Bruce Robert. BSc, Ohio State U., Columbus, 1959, BSc in Secondary Sci. Edn., 1960, MSc in Conservation Edn., 1960; PhD in Environ. Edn., U. Wis., Madison, 1969. Supr. conservation edn. Ethical Culture Schs., N.Y.C., 1961-63; naturalist, sci. tchr. Lakeside Sch., Spring Valley, N.Y., 1963-65; instr. No. Ill. U.-Oregon, 1965-67; asst. prof. Ohio State U., Columbus, 1969-73, assoc. prof., 1973-78, prof. environ. edn. and sci. edn., 1978—, chmn. div., 1973-84, coord. Office of Internat. Affairs, 1985-89, asst. dir., sch. sec., Sch. Natural Resources Coop. Extension Svc. 1989-93, acting dir. Sch. Natural Resources, 1993-94, assoc. dir., 1994—, state extension specialist Environ. Edn., 1993—; R&D assoc. Moseley & Assocs., Columbus, 1986-89; project cons. NARMA project, U.S. Agy. Internat. Devel., Santo Domingo, Dominican Rep., 1982-87; cons. Richard Trott and Assocs., 1988-90, Kinzelman and Kline, 1990-94, Midwest Consortium Internat. Activity, 1995; workshop leader Carribean Conservation Assn., Bridgetown, Barbados, 1981-83; vis. scholar Indonesian Second U. Devel. project, Jakarta, 1988; vis. scholar Uganda Makerere U., 1989, Pacific Cultural Found., Taipei, Taiwan, 1989; AID lectr., Thesolonika, Greece, 1992. Exec. editor Jour. Environ. Edn., 1974-91, Pub.'s prize 1970; contbr. article to profl. jours. Committeeman Boy Scouts Am., 1983-86; adv. council McKeever Environ. Learning Ctr., Pa., 1977-83. Recipient Pomerene Teaching Enhancement award, Ohio State U., 1986, 95, Environ. Edn. award Ohio Alliance for the Environ., 1992. Mem. N. Am. Assn. Environ. Edn. (life mem., bd. dirs. 1972-82, pres. 1977-78, Walt Jeske award 1988), Nat. Sci. Tchrs. Assn. (life), Sch. Nat., Resource Alumni Assn. (inducted hon. 100), Agrl. Faculty Coun. (elect-pres. 1989, pres. 1990), TBDBITL Alumni Club, Phi Beta Delta, Gamma Sigma Delta (treas. 1987-88, sec. 1988-89, pres.-elect. 1989-90, pres. 1990-91), Sigma Xi. Avocations: swimming, canoeing, camping, fishing, travel. Home: 570 Morning St Columbus OH 43085-3775 Office: Ohio State U Environ Edn Sch Natural Resources Columbus OH 43210

ROTH, SANFORD HAROLD, rheumatologist, health care administrator, educator; b. Akron, Ohio, June 12, 1934; s. Charles and Rose Marie (Zelman) R.; m. Marcia Ann, June 9, 1957; children: Shana Beth, Sari Luanne. B.Sc., Ohio State U., 1955, M.D., 1959. Intern Mt. Carmel, Columbus, Ohio, 1959-60; fellow Mayo Grad. Sch. Medicine, 1962-65; pvt. practice medicine specializing in rheumatology Phoenix, 1965—; med. dir. Arthritis Ctr., Ltd., Phoenix, 1983—; dir. Arthritis Program Healthwest Regional Medical Ctr., Phoenix, 1987-89; med. dir. Arthritis/Orthopedic Ctr. for Excellence Humana Hosp., Phoenix, 1989—; dir. arthritis rehab. program St. Luke's Hosp., Phoenix, 1978-87; med. research dir. Harrington Arthritis Research Ctr., Phoenix, 1984-88; prof., dir. aging and arthritis program Coll. Grad. Program, Ariz. State U., Tempe, 1984—; dir. medicine Ariz. Insts., Phoenix, 1985—; past state chmn. Gov.'s Conf. on Arthritis in Ariz., 1967; cons., rep. arthritis adv. com. FDA, 1982—, chmn. anti-rheumatic new drug guidelines, 1984—; cons. Ciba-Geigy, 1983—, Upjohn, 1985-87, Pennwalt, 1985-88, Arthritis Found. Clinics, 3M-Riker Labs, Inc., 1981-89, VA, 1970-87, FTC, 1980—, Boots Pharm. Co., 1980-87, Greenwich Pharm., 1986-87, Hoffman-LaRoche, 1986—, FDA Office Compliance, 1987—, G.D. Searle, 1987—; prin. investigator Coop. Systematic Studies of Rheumatic Diseases; vis. scholar in rheumatology Beijing Med. Coll., People's Republic China, 1982; proctor, vis. scholar program U.S.-China Edn. Inst., 1982—; med. research dir., exec. bd., trustee Harrington Arthritis Research Ctr., 1983-88; co-chair PANLAR Collaborative Clin. Epidemiol. Group, 1989—; mem. commn. on revision U.S. Pharmacopeial Conv., 1990—; mem. antirheumatic drug task force WHO-Internat. League Against Rheumatism, 1991—. Author: New Directions in Arthritis Therapy, 1980; Handbook of Drug Therapy in Rheumatology, 1985; med. contbg. editor RISS, Hosp. Physician, 1960-68, Current Prescribing, 1976-80; hon. internat. cons. editor Drugs, 1977—; editor in chief Arthron, 1982-85; editor, contbg. author: Rheumatic Therapeutics, 1985; med. cons. editor Update: Rheumatism, 1985, AMA Drug Evaluations, 6th edit., 1986, 7th edit., 1990; mem. editorial bd. VA Practitioner, 1985—, Comprehensive Therapy, 1987; mem. internat. editorial bd. Jour. Drug Devel., 1988—, Practical Gastroenterology, 1989—; contbr. numerous articles to profl. jours., chpts. to books. Fellow Am. Coll. Rheumatology (founding, liaison com. to regional med. program 1974-76, co-dir. med. info. system ARAMIS, computer com., chmn. antiinflammatory drug study club 1974—, com. on clubs and councils 1977-80, western regional co-chmn. 1977—, therapeutic and drug com. 1979—, glossary com. 1981-83, ad hoc com. on future meeting sites 1983); mem. AMA, ACP (regional program com., ann. Philip S. Hench lectureship chmn. 1978-79), Arthritis Found. (dir. central Ariz. chpt. 1982-83, past chmn. med. and sci. com. 1967-72), Lupus Found. Am. (bd. 1981—), Internat. Soc. Rheumatic Therapy (sec.-gen. 1990—, bd. dirs. 1987—, pres. 1992—), Maricopa County Med. Soc. (rehab. com.), Am. Soc. Clin. Rheumatology (past pres. exec. council), Am. Coll. Clin. Pharmacology, Soc. Internal Medicine, Mayo Clinic Alumni Assn., Mayo Clinic Fellows Assn. (sec. 1964-65), Argentine Rheumatology Soc. (hon.), Mayo Clinic Fellows Rheumatology Soc. (pres. 1964-65), Mayo Clinic Film Soc. (bd. dirs. 1964-65), Pan Am. League Against Rheumatism (chmn. clin. trials com. 1987—). Office: Arthritis Ctr Ltd 3330 N 2nd St Ste 601 Phoenix AZ 85012-2371 *To reconcile research of the boundless limits of our restless science with the legacy of our ancient art as to be healer, educator, organizer--all the while blessed by the joys of family love and community service. We create our destiny not alone but with individual dedication.*

ROTH, SANFORD IRWIN, pathologist, educator; b. McAlester, Okla., Oct. 14, 1932; s. Herman Moe and Blanche (Brown) R.; m. Kathryn Ann Corliss, Sept. 3, 1961; children: Jeffrey Franklin, Elisabeth Francyne, Gregory James, Suzannah Joan. Student, Vanderbilt U., 1949-52; MD, Harvard U., 1956. Intern Mass. Gen. Hosp., Boston, 1956-57; resident in pathology Mass. Gen. Hosp., 1957-60, pathologist, 1962-75; pathologist Armed Forces Inst. Pathology, 1960-62; asst. prof. Med. Sch. Harvard U., 1962-69, assoc. prof. Med. Sch., 1969-75; pathologist, prof., chmn. dept. Coll. Medicine U. Ark., Little Rock, 1975-81; prof. Med. Sch. Northwestern U., Chgo., 1981—; chief lab. svc. VA Lakeside Med. Ctr., Chgo., 1981-86; attending pathologist Northwestern U. Hosp., 1981—. With M.C. U.S. Army, 1960-62. Mem. AMA, AAAS, Internat. Acad. Pathologists, Am. Assn. Pathologists, Am. Soc. Cell Biology, Coll. Am. Pathology. Home: 920 Forest Glen Dr W Winnetka IL 60093-1430 Office: 303 E Chicago Ave Chicago IL 60611-3008

ROTH, SOL, rabbi; b. Rzeszow, Poland, Mar. 8, 1927; came to U.S., 1934, naturalized, 1939; s. Joseph and Miriam (Lamm) R.; m. Debra H. Stitskin,

Nov. 26, 1957; children: Steven, Michael, Sharon. B.A., Yeshiva U., 1948, D.D. (hon.), 1977; M.A., Columbia U., 1953, Ph.D., 1966; Rabbi, Yeshiva U. Theol. Sem., 1950. Ordained rabbi Orthodox Jewish Congregations, 1950; pres. Rabbinical Council Am., 1980-82, N.Y. Bd. Rabbis, 1976-79; chmn. Israel Commn. Rabbinical Council Am., 1976-78; dean Chaplaincy Sch., N.Y. Bd. Rabbis, 1976-79; Samson R. Hirsch prof. dept. philosophy Yeshiva U., N.Y.C.; rabbi Jewish Ctr. Atlantic Beach, N.Y., 1956-86; Fifth Ave Synagogue, 1986—; pres. Religious Zionists Am., 1991-94. Author: Science and Religion, 1967, The Jewish Idea of Community, 1977, Halakhah and Politics: The Jewish Idea of a State, 1988 (Samuel Belkin Meml. Lit. award 1989); editor: Morasha. Recipient award Synagogue Adv. Council United Jewish Appeal, 1975. The Rabbi Dr. Sol Roth Chair in Talmud and Contemporary Halakha established at Yeshiva U., 1989. Home: 30 East 62 St New York NY 10021 Office: Yeshiva U Dept Philosophy 500 W 185th St New York NY 10033-3201

ROTH, SUSAN KING, design educator; b. Millville, N.J., Nov. 13, 1945; d. Frank N. and Ruth (Ludlam) King; m. Richard L. Roth, Sept. 17, 1973; 1 child, Justin King Roth. BFA, Cooper Union, 1968; MA, Ohio State U., 1988. With advt. prodn. Mayer/Martin, Inc., N.Y.C., 1968-70; dir. graphics N.Y.C. Parks, Recreation and Cultural Affairs Adminstrn., 1970-73; designer Whole Earth Epilog, Sausalito, Calif., 1974-75; asst. art dir. TV Guide mag., Radnor, Pa., 1975-77; design cons. various orgns., Chgo., 1978-80; instr., tchg. assoc. Ohio State U., Columbus, 1985-88, assoc. prof., 1988—; vis. designer Sch. Art Inst., Chgo., 1980-81, Ohio Wesleyan U., Delaware, 1982-84; co-founder, co-dir. Ctr. for Interdisciplinary Studies, Columbus, 1992—; vis. evaluator Nat. Assn. Schs. Art and Design, Reston, Va., 1994—; mem. faculty adv. com. to chancellor Ohio Bd. Regents, 1994—; cons. Elections Adminstrn., Ohio Sec. of State, Columbus, Franklin County Bd. Elections, Columbus, 1993-96. Consulting editor Jour. Visual Literacy, 1992—; contbr. articles to profl. jours. Battelle grantee Battelle Endowment for Tech. & Human Affairs, 1993-94. Mem. Am. Ctr. Design, Assn. Computing Machinery, Graphic Design Edn. Assn., Internat. Visual Literacy Assn., Indsl. Designers Soc. Am. (mem. edn. bd. 1993-95). Home: 3158 Glenrich Pky Columbus OH 43221-2639 Office: Ohio State U 380 Hopkins Hall Columbus OH 43210

ROTH, SUZANNE ALLEN, financial services agent; b. Santa Monica, Calif., May 31, 1963; d. Raymond A. and Ethel Allen; m. Steve Milstein Roth, Dec. 27, 1992. BA, U. Calif., Santa Cruz, 1986; student, Calif. State U., L.A., 1987-93, Art Ctr. Sch. Design, Pasadena, Calif., 1994—. Cert. tchr., Calif.; lic. real estate agt., Calif. Interviewer L.A. Times Newspaper, 1986-88; educator L.A. Unified Sch. Dist., 1987-90; educator Burbank (Calif.) Unified Sch. Dist., 1990-94, vol., 1994—; ptnr. fin. svcs. Roth & Assocs./N.Y. Life, L.A., 1993—. Mem. NEA, Burbank Tchrs. Union. Avocations: painting, illustrating, writing, weight training, running.

ROTH, THOMAS, marketing executive. Grad., Western Mich. U. With Tarkenton and Co., Atlanta; with Wilson Learning Corp., Eden Prairie, Minn., v.p. product mgmt. in global R & D, 1992-94, v.p. product mgmt. and tng. group, 1994—, v.p. strategic implementation group; founder Nat. Edn. Tng. Group, 1988-92; cons. IBM, AT&T, Ford Motor Co., Gen. Motors, E.I. DuPont, Am. Express, Dow Chem., Hughes Aircraft, Eli Lily, Colgate-Palmolive, Honeywell, others; spkr. in field. Co-author: Creating the High Performance Team, 1987. Office: Wilson Learning Corp 7500 Flying Cloud Dr Eden Prairie MN 55344*

ROTH, TIM, actor; b. London, 1961. With Glasgow Citizen's Theatre, The Oval House, The Royal Ct. Appeared in play Metamorphosis; films include The Hit, 1985, A World Apart, 1988, The Cook, the Thief, His Wife and Her Lover, 1990, Vincent and Theo, 1990, Rosencrantz and Guildenstern Are Dead, 1991, Jumpin' at the Boneyard, 1992, Reservoir Dogs, 1992, Backsliding, 1993, Bodies, Rest and Motion, 1993, Pulp Fiction, 1994, Rob Roy, 1995 (Acad. award nominee for best supporting actor 1996), Little Odessa, 1995, Four Rooms, 1995; TV movies include Meantime, Made in Britain, Metamorphosis, Knuckle, Yellow Backs, King of the Ghetto, The Common Pursuit, Murder in the Heartland, 1993.

ROTH, TOBY, congressman; b. Strasburg, N.D., Oct. 10, 1938; s. Kasper and Julia (Roehrich) R.; m. Barbara Fischer, Nov. 28, 1964; children: Toby Jr., Vicky, Barbie. B.A., Marquette U., 1961. Mem. 96th-104th Congresses from 8th Wis. dist. 96th-103rd Congresses from 8th Wis. dist., Washington, D.C., 1979—; mem. banking, fin., urban affairs com., subcoms. fin. instns. and consumer credit, internat. rels. com., chmn. econ. policy, trade coms., Africa. Served to 1st lt. USAR, 1962-69. Named Wis. Legislator of Yr. Wis. Towns Assn., 1978. Republican. Clubs: VFW (hon.), Optimists (hon.), Kiwanis (hon.). *

ROTH, WILLIAM GEORGE, manufacturing company executive; b. Lamberton, Minn., Oct. 3, 1938; s. Euclair Ford and Kathryn (Kluegel) R.; m. Patricia Elizabeth Gibson, Aug. 27, 1960; children: William, David. B.S.M.E., U. Notre Dame, 1960; MS in Indsl. Adminstrn., Purdue U., 1961. With The Trane Co., LaCrosse, Wis., 1961-85, v.p., gen. mgr., 1973-77, dep. chmn., 1977-78, chmn., chief exec. officer, 1978-85; pres. Am. Standard, Inc., N.Y.C., 1985-87; pres., chief exec. officer Dravo Corp., Pitts., 1987-89, chmn. bd., 1990-93; bd. dirs. Amcast Indsl., Dayton, Cimflex Teknowledge, Pitts. Mem. NAM (bd. dirs. 1978-87). Republican. Roman Catholic. Office: Dravo Corp 1 Oliver Plz Pittsburgh PA 15222-2620

ROTH, WILLIAM STANLEY, hospital foundation executive; b. N.Y.C., Jan. 12, 1929; s. Sam Irving and Louise Caroline (Martin) R.; m. Hazel Adcock, May 6, 1963; children: R. Charles, W. Stanley. AA, Asheville-Biltmore Jr. Coll., 1948; BS, U. N.C., 1950. Dep. regional exec. Nat. council Boy Scouts Am., 1953-65; exec. v.p. Am. Humanics Found., 1965-67; dir. devel. Bethany Med. Ctr., Kansas City, Kans., 1967-74; exec. v.p. Geisinger Med. Ctr. Found., Danville, Pa., 1974-78; found. pres. Baptist Med. Ctrs., Birmingham, Ala., 1978—; sec. Western Med. Systems, Cherokee Cmty. Homes, Cullman Sr. Housing, Dekalb Sr. Housing, Limestone Sr. Housing, Oxford Sr. Housing. Mem.-at-large Nat. council Boy Scouts Am., 1972-86; chmn. NAHD Ednl. Fund, 1980-82; ruling elder John Knox Kirk, Kansas City, Mo., Grove Presbyn. Ch., Danville, Pa. Recipient Silver award United Methodist Ch., 1970, Mid-West Health Congress, 1971; Seymour award for outstanding hosp. devel. officer 1983. Fellow Assn. for Healthcare Philanthropy (life, nat. pres. 1975-76); mem. Nat. Soc. Fund Raising Execs. (pres. Ala. chpt. 1980-82, nat. dir. 1980-84, mem. ethics bd. 1993—, advanced cert. fund raising exec., Outstanding Fund Raising Exec., Ala. chpt. 1983), Mid-Am.Hosp. Devel. Assn. (pres. 1973-74), Mid-West Health Congress (devel. chmn. 1972-74), Am. Soc. for Hosp. Mktg. and Pub. Rels., Ala. Soc. for Sleep Disorders, Ala. Heart Inst., Ala. Assn. Healthcare Philanthropy (pres. 1991-93, chmn. bd. 1993-94), Ala. Planned Giving Coun. (bd. dirs. 1991—, pres. 1994-95), Alpha Phi Omega (nat. pres. 1958-62, dir. 1950—, Nat. Disting. Service award 1962), Delta Upsilon (pres. N.C. Alumni 1963-65). Clubs: Rotary (pres. club 1976-77), Relay House, Summit, Green Valley (bd. govs.), Elks, Order Holy Grail, Order Golden Fleece, Order of The Arrow (Nat. Disting. Service award 1958). Editor Torch and Trefoil, 1960-61. Home: 341 Laredo Dr Birmingham AL 35226-2325 Office: 3500 Blue Lake Dr Ste 101 Birmingham AL 35243-1908

ROTH, WILLIAM V., JR., senator; b. Great Falls, Mont., July 22, 1921; m. Jane K. Richards; children: William V. III, Katharine Kellond. BA, U. Oreg., 1944; MBA, Harvard U., 1947, LLB, 1949. Bar: Del., U.S. Supreme Ct., Calif. Mem. 90th-91st congresses at large from, Del., 1967-71; senator State of Del., 1971—; chmn. senate fin. com., former chmn govt affairs com.; chmn. Del. Rep. State Com., 1961-64; mem. Rep. Nat. Com., 1961-64. Served to capt. AUS, 1943-46. Decorated Bronze Star medal. Mem. ABA, Del. Bar Assn. Episcopalian. Office: US Senate 104 Hart Senate Bldg Washington DC 20510

ROTHBAUM, IRA, retired advertising and marketing executive; b. Phila.; s. Samuel and Charlotte (Gross) R.; m. Eileen Glickfeld, Dec. 26, 1972; children: Stephen Ira, Peggy Ann, John E. A.B. in Journalism, U. N.C., 1947; student, Columbia U., 1944. Copywriter RCA Victor, 1947-49, advt. and sales promotion mgr., 1949-50; divisional sales mgr. RCA Service Co., 1953; instr. Tulane U., 1952; copywriter N.W. Ayer, Phila., 1953-56; account exec., account supr. N.W. Ayer, Detroit, 1956-63; v.p., sr. v.p., mgmt. supr. N.W. Ayer, N.Y.C., 1963-71; sr. v.p., mgmt. supr. SSC & B, 1971-77; asst. to pres. W.B. Doner & Co., Southfield, Mich., 1977-80; pres. Wingfoot Mktg. Co., Boynton Beach, Fla., 1980-83; sr. broker Alan Bush Brokerage Co., Delray Beach, Fla.; v.p. investments Gruntal & Co. Inc., Boca Raton, Fla.; v.p. J.W. Charles Securities, Boca Raton, 1989-94; v.p. investments Stock Depot Inc., Delray Beach, Fla., 1994-96; ret., 1996; adj. prof. Fla. Atlantic U., Boca Raton. Served with USNR, 1943-46, 50-52. Home: 6109 Old Court Rd Boca Raton FL 33433-7844

ROTHBERG, ABRAHAM, author, educator, editor; b. N.Y.C., Jan. 14, 1922; s. Louis and Lottie (Drimmer) R.; m. Esther Conwell, Sept. 30, 1945; 1 son, Lewis Josiah. A.B., Bklyn. Coll., 1942; M.A., U. Iowa, 1947; Ph.D., Columbia U., 1952. Chmn. editorial bd. Stateside (mag.), N.Y.C., 1947-49; instr. English, creative writing Columbia U., N.Y.C., 1948; instr. English, humanities Hofstra Coll., Hempstead, N. Y., 1947-51; prof. English St. John Fisher Coll., 1973-83, chmn. dept. English, 1981-82; disting. writer-in-residence, vis. prof. Wichita State U., 1985; Ford Found. fellow, N.Y.C., 1951-52; editor-in-chief Free Europe Press, N.Y.C., 1952-59; mng. editor George Braziller, Inc., N.Y.C., 1959, New Leader (mag.), N.Y.C., 1960-61; cons. editor New Jewish Ency., 1960-62; writer, editorial cons.; European corr. Nat. Observer, Washington, Manchester (Eng.) Guardian, 1962-63; sr. editor Bantam Books, Inc., N.Y.C., 1966-67; Cons. editor The New Union Prayer Book, N.Y.C., 1975. (Recipient John H. McGinnis Meml. award for short story 1970, John H. McGinnis Meml. award for essay 1973-74, Lit. award Friends of Rochester Library 1980); Author: Abraham, Eyewitness History of World War II, 1962, The Thousand Doors, 1965, The Heirs of Cain, 1966, The Song of David Freed, 1968, The Other Man's Shoes, 1969, The Boy and the Dolphin, 1969, The Sword of the Golem, 1971, Aleksandr Solzhenitsyn: The Major Novels, 1971, The Heirs of Stalin: Dissidence and the Soviet Regime, 1953-1970, 1972, The Stalking Horse, 1972, The Great Waltz, 1978, The Four Corners of the House, 1981; Editor: U.S. Stories, 1949, Flashes in the Night, 1958, Anatomy of a Moral, 1959, A Bar-Mitzvah Companion, 1959, Great Adventure Stories of Jack London, 1967; Contbr. articles, essays, stories, poems to various publs., anthologies, collections. Served with AUS, 1943-45. Home: 340 Pelham Rd Rochester NY 14610-3355

ROTHBERG, GERALD, editor, publisher; b. Bklyn., Oct. 29, 1937; s. Abraham and Pauline Rothberg; m. Glenda Fay Morris, June 18, 1970 (div. 1988); children: Laura, Abigail. B.A., Bklyn. Coll., 1960; postgrad., Dickinson Law Sch., 1962. Spl. projects editor Esquire (mag.), 1963-66; owner, editor, pub., founder Circus (mag.), N.Y.C., 1966—; owner, founder, editor Sci. and Living Tomorrow, 1980—, Who's In, 1981; founder, editor Sports Mirror mag., 1983—, MGF mag., 1985—; Country Mirror mag., 1994—. Author: (novels) Composition 36, 1993, The Six-Hour Song, 1994, Redeeming Esau, 1995. Mem. Periodical and Book Assn. Am. (pres.). Office: Circus Mag 6 W 18th St New York NY 10011-4608

ROTHBERG, JUNE SIMMONDS, retired nursing educator, psychotherapist, psychoanalyst; b. Phila., Sept. 4, 1923; d. David and Rose (Protzel) Simmonds; m. Jacob Rothberg, Sept. 7, 1952; children: Robert, Alan. Diploma in nursing, Lenox Hill Hosp., 1944; BS, N.Y. U., 1950, MA, 1959, PhD (NIH fellow), 1965; Diploma in Psychotherapy and Psychoanalysis, Adelphi U., Inst. for Advanced Psychol. Studies, 1987. USPHS traineeship N.Y. U., 1957-59; sr. public health nurse Bklyn. Vis. Nurse Assn., 1951-53; prin. investigator in nursing, homestead study project Goldwater Hosp. and N.Y. U., 1959-61; instr. N.Y. U., 1964-65, asst. prof., 1965-68, assoc. prof., 1968-69, project dir. grad. program rehab. nursing, 1964-69, prof., 1969-87, prof. emeritus, 1987—; dean Adelphi U., Garden City, N.Y., 1969-85; v.p. acad. adminstrn. Adelphi U., 1985-86; pvt. practice West Hempstead, N.Y., 1993—; pres. David Simmonds Co. Inc., Med. Supply Co., 1982-89; dir., chmn. compensation com. Quality Care, Inc.; cons. to various ednl. and svc. instns.; cons. region 2 Bur. Health Resources Devel., HHS.; speaker on radio and TV; bd. dirs., mem. audit com. Ipco Corp. (formerly Sterling Optical Corp.), 1991. Contbr. articles to profl. jours. Mem. pres's coun. N.Y. U. Sch. Edn., 1973-75; treas. Nurses for Polit. Action, 1971-73; trustee Nurses Coalition for Action in Politics, 1974-76; bd. visitors Duke Med. Ctr., 1970-74; mem. governing bd. Nassau-Suffolk Health Systems Agy., 1976-79; leader People-to-People Internat. med. rehab. del. to People's Republic of China, 1981; mem. com. for the study pain disability and chronic illness behavior Inst. Medicine, 1985-86, com. on ethics in rehab. Hastings Ctr., 1985-87; trustee Paget's Disease Found., 1987-89. Recipient Disting. Alumna award NYU, 1974, recognition award Am. Assn. Colls. Nursing, 1976, Achievers award Ctr. for Bus. and Profl. Women, 1980. Fellow Am. Acad. Nursing (governing coun. 1980-82); mem. Nat. League Nursing (exec. com. coun. of baccalaureate and higher degree programs 1969-73), Am. Nurses Assn. (joint liaison com. 1970-72), Commn. Accreditation of Rehab. Facilities, Am. Congress Rehab. Medicine (pres. 1977-78, chmn. continuing edn. com. 1979-86, 34th Ann. John Stanley Coulter Meml. lectr. 1984, Gold Key award 1984, Edward W. Lowman award 1990), Am. Assn. Colls. Nursing (pres. 1974-76), L.I. Women's Network (pres. 1980-81), Kappa Delta Pi, Sigma Theta Tau, Pi Lambda Theta. June S. Rothberg collection in Nursing Archives, Mugar Meml. Library, Boston U. Home and Office: 305 Elm St West Hempstead NY 11552-3224

ROTHBLATT, DONALD NOAH, urban and regional planner, educator; b. N.Y.C., Apr. 28, 1935; s. Harry and Sophie (Chernofsky) R.; m. Ann S. Vogel, June 16, 1957; children: Joel Michael, Steven Saul. BCE, CUNY, 1957; MS in Urban Planning, Columbia U., 1963; Diploma in Comprehensive Planning, Inst. Social Studies, The Hague, 1964; PhD in City and Regional Planning, Harvard U., 1969. Registered profl. engr. N.Y. Planner N.Y.C. Planning Commn., 1960-62, N.Y. Housing and Redevel. Bd., 1963-66; research fellow Ctr. for Environ. Design Studies, Harvard U., Cambridge, Mass., 1965-71; teaching fellow, instr., then asst. prof. city and regional planning Harvard U., 1967-71; prof. urban and regional planning, chmn. dept. San Jose State U., Calif., 1971—; Lady Davis vis. prof. urban and regional planning Hebrew U., Jerusalem and Tel Aviv U., 1978; vis. scholar Indian Inst. ARchitects, 1979; vis. scholar, rsch. assoc. Inst. Govtl. Studies, U. Calif., Berkeley, 1980—; cons. to pvt. industry and govt. agys. Author: Human Needs and Public Housing, 1964, Thailand's Northeast, 1967, Regional Planning: The Appalachian Experience, 1971, Allocation of Resources for Regional Planning, 1972, The Suburban Environment and Women, 1979, Regional-Local Development Policy Making, 1981, Planning the Metropolis: The Multiple Advocacy Approach, 1982, Comparative Suburban Data, 1983, Suburbia: An International Assessment, 1986, Metropolitan Dispute Resolution in Silicon Valley, 1989, Good Practices for the Congestion Management Program, 1994, Activity-Based Travel Survey and Analysis of Responses to Increased Congestion, 1995, An Experiment in Sub-Regional Planning: California's Congestion Management Policy, 1995, Estimating the Origins and Destinations of Transit Passengers from On/Off Counts, 1995, Changes in Property Values Induced by Light Transit, 1996; editor: National policy for Urban and Regional Development, 1974, Regional Advocacy Planning: Expanding Air Transport Facilities for the San Jose Metropolitan Area, 1975, Metropolitan-wide Advocacy Planning; Dispersion of Low and Moderate Cost Housing in the San Jose Metropolitan Area, 1976, Multiple Advocacy Planning: Public Surface Transportation in the San Jose Metropolitan Area, 1977, A Multiple Advocacy Approach to Regional Planning: Open Space and Recreational Facilities for the San Jose Metropolitan Area, 1979, Regional Transpotation Planning for the San Jose Metropolitan Area, 1981, Planning for Open Space and Recreational Facilities in the San Jose Metropolitan Area, 1982, Regional Economic Development Planning for the San Jose Metropolitan Area, 1984, Planning for Surface Transportation in the San Jose Metropolitan Area, 1986, Expansion of Air Transportation Facilities in the San Jose Metropolitan Area, 1987, Provision of Economic Development in the San Jose Met. Area, 1988, Metropolitan Governance: American/Canadian Intergovernmental Perspectives, 1993; contbr. numerous articles to profl. jours.; dir.: Pub. TV series Sta. KTEH, 1976. Mem. adv. coun. Bay Area Met. Transp. Commn., 1995—. Served to 1st lt. C.E., U.S. Army, 1957-59. Rsch. fellow John F. Kennedy Sch. Govt. Harvard U., 1967-69; William F. Milton rsch. fellow, 1970-71; faculty rsch. grantee, NSF, 1972-82, Calif. State U., 1977-78; grantee Nat. Inst. Dispute Resolution, 1988-88, Can. Studies Enrichment Program, 1989-90, Can. Studies Rsch. Program, 1992-93, Univ. Rsch. and Tng. Program grantee Calif. Dept. Transp., 1993-96; recipient Innovative Teaching award Calif. State U. and Coll., 1975-79; co-recipient Best of West award Western Ednl. Soc. for Telecommunication, 1976; recipient award Internat. Festival of Films on Architecture and Planning, 1983, Meritorious Performance award San Jose State U., 1986, 88, 90. Mem. Assn. Collegiate Schs. of Planning (pres. 1975-76), Am. Inst. Cert. Planners, Am. Planning Assn., Planners for Equal Opportunity, Internat. Fedn. Housing and Planning, AAUP, Calif. Edn. Com. on Architecture and Landscape, Architecture and rban and Regional Planning (chmn. 1973-75). Office: Urban and Regional Planning Dept San Jose State U San Jose CA 95192-0185 *My basic view is that we should try to develop ourselves fully and help others do the same, so that we will be able to live in harmony with, and contribute to, our world community.*

ROTHCHILD, HOWARD LESLIE, advertising executive; b. Burlington, Vt., June 14, 1929; s. Daniel and Florence (Agel) R.; m. Sheila Segelman, June 3, 1973; children—Staci, Erik, Jessica. B.S., U. Vt., 1951; M.Litt., U. Pitts., 1952. Account exec. Lando Advt., Inc., Pitts., 1957-64; v.p. Goldman, Shoop & Rothchild, Inc., Pitts., 1964-67, Marc & Co., Inc., Pitts., 1967-72; chmn. bd. Rafshoon Shivers Tolpin, Inc., Atlanta, 1972-81; exec. v.p. Garber, Goodman & Rothchild Advt., Inc., Miami, Fla., 1981-87; pres. The Rothchild Group, Inc., Miami, 1987-89; chmn., pres., chief exec. officer The Rothchild Cos., Inc., Miami, 1989-93; dir. account devel. Gold Coast Advt. Assoc. Inc., Miami, 1994—; instr. U. Pitts. Grad. Sch. Bus., 1964-71. Bd. dirs. Big Bros. Am., Pitts., 1967-71, Lucky Acorns, Miami, 1991—. Served with AUS, 1952-54. Recipient Top Radio Comml. of Yr. award Nat. Retail Mchts. Assn. Mem. Am. Mktg. Assn., Bus./Profl. Advt. Assn., Advt. Fedn. Miami, Fla. Advt. Golf Assn. (founding dir.). Office: Gold Coast Advt Assoc Inc 4141 NW 2d Ave Miami FL 33137

ROTHENBERG, ADAM LEIGH, lawyer; b. Chgo., Sept. 9, 1963; s. Philip Burton and Roberta Lynn (Keylin) R.; m. Christie Curry, Sept. 23, 1989; children: Alexa Leigh, Zachary Ryan. Student, Tulane U., 1981-83; BABA, U. Wash., 1987; JD, Seton Hall U., 1993. Bar: N.J. 1993, U.S. Dist. Ct. N.J. 1993. Law clk. Blume Vazquez Goldfaden Berkowitz & Donnelly, Newark, 1992-93; assoc. Levinson Axelrod Wheaton & Grayzel, Edison, N.J., 1993—. Mem. Assn. Trial Lawyers Am., N.J. ATLA (bd. govs. 1996), Middlesex County Bar Assn., Middlesex County Trial Lawyers, Essex County Bar Assn. Avocations: tennis, golf, sailing. Office: Levinson Axelrod Wheaton & Grayzel 2 Lincoln Hwy Edison NJ 08818-2905

ROTHENBERG, ALAN I., lawyer, professional sports association executive; b. Detroit, Apr. 10, 1939; m. Georgina Rothenberg; 3 children. B.A., U. Mich., 1960, J.D., 1963. Bar: Calif. 1964. Assoc. O'Melveny & Myers, L.A., 1963-66; ptnr. Manatt Phelps Rothenberg & Phillips, L.A., 1968-90, Latham & Watkins, L.A., 1990—; instr. sports law U. So. Calif., 1969, 76, 84, Whittier Coll. Law, 1980, 84; pres., gen. counsel L.A. Lakers and L.A. Kings, 1967-79, L.A. Clippers Basketball Team, 1982-89; pres. U.S. Soccer Fedn., Chgo., 1990—. Soccer commr. 1984 Olympic Games; chmn., pres., CEO 1994 World Cup Organizing Com., 1990-94; founder, chmn. Major League Soccer, 1994—; bd. dirs., pres. Constl. Rights Found., 1987-90. Mem. aBA, State Bar Calif. (pres. 1989-90), Los Angeles County Bar Assn., L.A. Bar Assn., Nat. Basketball Assn. (bd. govs. 1971-79, 82-89), N.Am. Soccer League (bd. govs. 1977-80, Major League Soccer mgmt. com. 1994—), Order of Coif. Office: Latham & Watkins 633 W 5th St Ste 4000 Los Angeles CA 90071-2005

ROTHENBERG, ALBERT, psychiatrist, educator; b. N.Y.C., June 2, 1930; s. Gabriel and Rose (Goldberg) R.; m. Julia C. Johnson, June 28, 1970; children: Michael, Mora, Rina. A.B., Harvard U., 1952; M.D., Tufts U., 1956. Diplomate: Am. Bd. Psychiatry and Neurology. Intern Pa. Hosp., Phila., 1956-57; resident in psychiatry Yale U., West Haven (Conn.) VA Hosp., 1957-58, Grace-New Haven Hosp., 1958-59; resident in psychiatry Yale Psychiat. Inst., New Haven, 1959-60, chief resident, 1960-61; practice medicine specializing in psychiatry New Haven, 1960-61, 1963-75; chief neuropsychiatry Rodriguez U.S. Army Hosp., San Juan, P.R., 1961-63; practice medicine specializing in psychiatry Farmington, Conn., 1975-79, Stockbridge, Mass., 1979-94, Chatham, N.Y., 1994—, Great Barrington, Mass., 1994—; dir. rsch. Austen Riggs Center, Stockbridge, Mass., 1979-94; asst. dir. Yale Psychiat. Inst., 1963-64, sr. staff mem., 1964-83; mem. staff Yale-New Haven Med. Ctr., West Haven VA Hosp., U. Conn. Health Ctr., Farmington; cons., mem. editorial bd. various jours. in psychiatry and psychology; instr. dept. psychiatry Yale U. Sch. Medicine, 1960-61, 63-64, asst. prof., 1964-68, assoc. prof., 1968-74, clin. prof., 1974-84; prof. psychiatry U. Conn. Sch. Medicine, Farmington, 1975-79, dir. residency tng., 1976-78, dir. clin. svcs., 1975-78; prin. investigator Studies in the Creative Process, 1964—; vis. prof. Pa. State U., 1971, adj. prof., 1971-78; vis. prof. dept. Am. studies Yale U., 1974-76; lectr. dept. psychiatry Harvard U. Med. Sch., 1982-86, clin. prof., 1986—; researcher in psychotherapy. Author: (with B. Greenberg) Index of Scientific Writings on Creativity: Creative Men and Women, 1974, Index of Scientific Writings on Creativity: General 1566-1974, 1976; (with C.R. Hausman) The Creativity Question, 1976; The Emerging Goddess: The Creative Process in Art, Science and Other Fields, 1979; The Creative Process of Psychotherapy, 1988; Adolescence: Psychopathology, Normality, and Creativity, 1990; Creativity and Madness: New Findings and Old Stereotypes, 1990; contbr. numerous articles on the creative process, schizophrenia, anorexia nervosa, and psychotherapy to profl. and popular jours. Researcher on creativity in the arts, sci. and tech. Served with M.C. U.S. Army, 1961-63. Recipient Tufts Med. Alumni award 1956, Rsch. Scientist Career Devel. award NIMH 1964, 69, Golestan Found. award 1991, 92; Guggenheim Meml. fellow 1974-75, Ctr. Adv. Study in Behavioral Studies fellow 1986-87, Netherlands Inst. for Adv. Study in Humanities and Social Scis. fellow, 1992-93. Fellow Am. Psychiat. Assn. (life), Am. Coll. Psychoanalysts; mem. AAAS, Mass. Psychiat. Soc., Am. Soc. Aesthetics, Sigma Xi. Democrat. Home: PO Box 236 52 Pine Ridge Rd Canaan NY 12029

ROTHENBERG, ELLIOT CALVIN, lawyer, writer; b. Mpls., Nov. 12, 1939; s. Sam S. and Claire Sylvia (Feller) R.; m. Sally Smayling; children: Sarah, Rebecca, Sam. BA summa cum laude, U. Minn., 1961; JD, Harvard U. (Fulbright fellow), 1964. Bar: Minn. 1966, U.S. Dist. Ct. Minn. 1966, D.C. 1968, U.S. Supreme Ct. 1972, N.Y. 1974, U.S. Ct. Appeals (2d cir.) 1974, U.S. Ct. Appeals (8th cir.) 1975. Assoc. project dir. Brookings Inst., Washington, 1966-67; fgn. svc. officer, legal advisor U.S. Dept. State, Washington, 1968-73; Am. Embassy, Saigon; U.S. Mission to the UN; nat. law dir. Anti-Defamation League, N.Y.C., 1973-74; legal dir. Minn. Pub. Interest Rsch. Group, Mpls., 1974-77; pvt. practice law, Mpls., 1977—; adj. prof. William Mitchell Coll. Law, St. Paul, 1983—; faculty mem. several nat. communications law and First Amendment seminars. State bd. dirs. YMCA Youth in Govt. Program, 1981-84; v.p. Twin Cities chpt. Am. Jewish Com., 1980-84; mem. Minn. House of Reps., 1978-82, asst. floor leader (whip), 1981-82; pres., dir. North Star Legal Found., 1983—; Legal affairs editor Pub. Rsch. Syndicated, 1986—; briefs and oral arguments published in full Landmark Briefs and Arguments of the Supreme Court of the U.S., Vol. 200, 1992; Mem. citizens adv. com. Voyageurs Nat. Park, 1979-81. Fulbright fellow, 1964-65; recipient Legis. Evaluation Assembly Legis. Excellence award, 1980, Vietnam Civilian Service medal US Dept. State, 1970, North Star award, U. Minn., 1961. Mem. Am. Bar Assn., Harvard Law Sch. Assn., Minn. Bar Assn., Am. Legion, Mensa, Phi Beta Kappa. Jewish. Contbr. articles to profl. and scholarly jours. and books, newspapers, popular magazines; author: (with Zelman Cowen) Sir John Latham and Other Papers, 1965. Avocations: long distance running, classical music, baseball. Home and Office: 3901 W 25th St Saint Louis Park MN 55416-3803

ROTHENBERG, GUNTHER ERICH, history educator; b. Berlin, July 11, 1923; came to U.S., 1949, naturalized, 1952; s. Erich and Lotte Rothenberg; m. Ruth Gillah Smith, June 19, 1969 (dec. 1992); children: Judith, Laura, Georgia; m. Eleanor Iris Margarete Hancock, Apr. 2, 1995. B.A., U. Ill., 1954, Ph.D., 1958; M.A., U. Chgo., 1956. Asst. prof. history So. Ill. U., 1958-63; assoc. prof. U. N.Mex., 1963-69, prof., 1969-73; prof. mil. history Purdue U., 1973—; lectr. U.S. Army Command and Gen. Staff Coll., U.S. Army War Coll., USAF Acad., USAF War Coll., U.S. Mil. Acad., USMC Command and Gen. Staff Coll., disting. chair mil. affairs 1992—. Author: The Military Border in Croatia, 1740-1882, 1960, The Austrian Military Border in Croatia, 1522-1747, 1966, The Army of Francis Joseph, 1976, The Art of Warfare in the Age of Napoleon, 1978, The Anatomy of the Israeli Army, 1979, Napoleon's Great Adversaries, 1981; also others. With Brit. Army, 1941-48. Guggenheim fellow, 1962-63; Fullbright fellow, vis. prof. Royal Mil. Coll., Duntroon, Australia, 1985. Jewish. Home: 210 E Lutz Ave West Lafayette IN 47906-3015 Office: Purdue U Dept History West Lafayette IN 47907

ROTHENBERG, JEROME, author, visual arts and literary educator; b. N.Y.C., Dec. 11, 1931; s. Morris and Estelle (Lichtenstein) R.; m. Diane Brodatz, Dec. 25, 1952; 1 son, Matthew. B.A., CCNY, 1952; M.A., U. Mich., 1953. With Mannes Coll. Music, N.Y.C., 1961-70; Mannes Coll. Music, N.Y.C., 1961-70; vis. prof. U. Calif., San Diego, 1971, 77-84, U. Wis.-Mils., 1974-75, San Diego State U., 1976-77, U. Calif., Riverside, 1980, U. Okla., Norman, 1984; vis. Aerol Arnold prof. English U.So. Calif., 1983; vis. eriter in residence SUNY, Albany, 1986, prof. English SUNY, Binghamton, 1986-88; prof. visual arts and lit. U. Calif., San Diego, 1989—, chmn. visual arts, 1990-93; head, creative writing, 1994-95. Poet, freelance writer, 1956—; author: numerous books of poetry and prose including Between, 1967, Technicians of the Sacred, 1968, Poems for the Game of Silence, 1971, Shaking the Pumpkin, 1972, America a Prophecy, 1973, Revolution of the Word, 1974, Poland/1931, 1974, A Big Jewish Book, 1978, A Seneca Journal, 1978, Vienna Blood, 1980, Pre-Faces, 1981, Symposium of the Whole, 1983, That Dada Strain, 1983, New Selected Poems, 1986, Khurbn, 1989, Exiled in the Word, 1989, The Lorca Variations I-VIII, 1990, Apres le jeu de silence, 1991, The Lorca Variations (complete), 1993, Gematria, 1994, An Oracle for Delfi, 1995, Poems for The Millennium, vol. 1, 1995; editor, pub. Hawk's Well Press., N.Y.C., 1958-65, Some/Thing mag., 1966-69, Alcheringa: Ethnopoetics, 1970-76, New Wilderness Letter, 1976-86. Served with AUS, 1953-55. Recipient award in poetry Longview Found., 1960, Am. Book award, 1982, PEN Ctr. USA West award, 1994, PEN Oakland Josephine Miles award, 1994; Wenner-Gren Found. grantee-in-aide for rsch. in Am. Indian poetry, 1968; Guggenheim fellow in creative writing, 1974; NEA poetry grantee, 1976. Mem. P.E.N. Am. Center, New Wilderness Found. Office: c/o New Directions 80 8th Ave New York NY 10011-5126

ROTHENBERG, JOSEPH HOWARD, federal agency administrator; b. N.Y.C., Dec. 23, 1940; s. Abe Arthur and Nevia Theresa (Vuotto) R.; m. Frances Bernice Albano, Feb. 1, 1964; children: Edward, Joyce, Annette. BS Engring. Sci., SUNY, Farmingdale, 1964; MS Mgmt. Engring., C.W. Post Coll., 1973, MS, 1977. Project engr. Grumman Aerospace, Bethpage, N.Y., 1964-78, mgr. solar Max Mission Ops., 1978-81; mgr. ops. and test projects Computer Tech., Assocs., Englewood, Colo., 1981-83; space telescope ops. mgr. NASA, Goddard Space Flight Ctr., Greenbelt, Md., 1983-87, chief, mission ops. div., 1987-89; dep. dir. mission ops. and data systems directorate, 1989-90, assoc. dir. flight projects Hubble Space Telescope, 1990-94; exec. v.p. space systems divsn. CTA Inc., 1994-95; dir. NASA Goddard Space Flight Ctr., 1995—. With USN, 1957-62. Recipient Laurel award Space/Missiles, Aviation Week & Space Tech., 1993, Collier trophy, 1994, Disting. Svc. medal NASA, 1994, Robert H. Goddard Astronautics award Am. Inst. of Aeronautics and Astronautics, 1994. Mem. AIAA (Robert H. Goddard Astronautics award 1994), Instrument Soc. Am. (pres. L.I. sect. 1968-69). Avocations: sailing, skiing, music. Office: NASA Goddard Space Code # 100 Greenbelt MD 20771

ROTHENBERG, LESLIE STEVEN, lawyer, ethicist; b. Wheeling, W.Va., June 22, 1941; s. Emil and Lucie (Kern) R.; m. Rose-Emily Horkheimer, Dec. 22, 1963; children—Joshua Samuel. B.S., Northwestern U., 1963; M.A., Stanford U., 1964; J.D., UCLA, 1968. Bar: Calif. 1969, U.S. Supreme Ct. 1972. Spl. asst. to pres. U. Calif. and to chancellor UCLA, 1968-69; exec. sec. Los Angeles County Employee Relations Commn., 1969; assoc. firm Kaplan, Livingston, Goodwin, Berkowitz & Selvin, Beverly Hills, Calif., 1969-71; dep. dir. Los Angeles Legal Aid Found., 1971-73; acting prof. law Loyola U., Los Angeles, 1973-77; vis. prof. law U. Calif., Berkeley, 1977-78; pvt. practice, L.A., 1978-84; pres. Leslie Steven Rothenberg A.P.C., Pacific Palisades, Calif., 1984—; adj. asst. prof. medicine UCLA Med. Sch., 1980-87, adj. assoc. prof. medicine, 1987-91, assoc. prof. clin. medicine, 1991—; dir. program in med. ethics UCLA Med. Ctr., 1984—; cons. ethics, 1979—; fellow The Hastings Ctr., Briarcliff Manor, N.Y. Author: The Draft and You, 1968; contbr. articles to profl. jours. Bd. govs. U. Judaism, Los Angeles, 1980-88. Woodrow Wilson fellow, 1963-64. Mem. AAAS, ABA, L.A. County Bar Assn. (trustee 1979-80), Bar Assn. San Francisco, State Bar Calif., Am. Soc. Human Genetics, European Soc. Human Genetics, Assn. Jewish Studies, Soc. Christian Ethics, Soc. Values in Higher Edn., Soc. Health and Human Values, N.Y. Acad. Scis., Can. Bioethics Soc., Soc. Bioethics Consultation, Assn. Practical and Profl. Ethics, Soc. for Bus. Ethics, European Bus. Ethics Network. Jewish. Office: 16751 Edgar St Pacific Palisades CA 90272-3226

ROTHENBERG, PETER JAY, lawyer; b. N.Y.C., Apr. 3, 1941; s. Max and Judith (Berkowitz) R.; m. Laraine H. Silver, Aug. 29, 1970; children: Daniel, Jason. AB, Harvard U., 1961, LLB, 1964. Bar: N.Y. 1965, U.S. Tax Ct. 1969. Dep. counsel judiciary sub. com. on jud. machinery U.S. Senate Com., Washington, 1965-66; assoc. Paul, Weiss, Rifkind, Wharton & Garrison, N.Y.C., 1969-73, ptnr., 1974—. Served to capt. U.S. Army, 1966-69. Mem. N.Y. State Bar Assn. (exec. com. tax sect. 1979-87), Assn. Bar City N.Y. (tax com. 1977-79, com. on taxation of internat. transactions 1990-93), Internat. Fiscal Assn. Democrat. Jewish. Home: 895 Park Ave New York NY 10021-0327 Office: Paul Weiss Rifkind Wharton & Garrison 1285 Avenue Of The Americas New York NY 10019-6028*

ROTHENBERG, ROBERT EDWARD, physician, surgeon, author; b. Bklyn., Sept. 27, 1908; s. Simon and Caroline A. (Baer) R.; m. Lillian Lustig, 1933 (dec. 1977); m. Eileen Fein, 1977 (dec. 1987); children: Robert Philip, Lynn Barbara Rothenberg Kay; m. Florence Richman, 1989. A.B., Cornell U., 1929, M.D., 1932. Diplomate Am. Bd. Surgery. Intern Jewish Hosp., Bklyn., 1932-34; attending surgeon Jewish Hosp., 1955-82; postgrad. study Royal Infirmary, Edinburgh, 1934-35; civilian cons. U.S. Army Hosp., Ft. Jay, N.Y., 1960-66; attending surgeon French Polyclinic Med. Sch. and Health Center, N.Y.C., 1964-76; pres., 1973-76, trustee, 1972-76; attending surgeon Cabrini Health Care Center, 1976-86; cons. surgeon Cabrini Med. Ctr., 1986—, dir. surg. research, 1981—; clin. asst. prof. environ. medicine and community health State U. Coll. Medicine, N.Y.C., 1950-60; clin. prof. surgery N.Y. Med. Coll., 1981-86, prof. emeritus, 1986—; pvt. practice, 1935-86; chmn. Med. Group Coun. Health Ins. Plan of Greater N.Y., 1947-64; cons. Office and Profl. Employees Internat. Union (Local 153) Health Plan, 1960-82, United Automobile Workers (Local 259) Health Plan, 1960-86, Sanitationmen's Security Benefit Fund, 1964-83; dir. Surgery Internat. Ladies Garment Workers Union, 1970-85; med. adv. bd. Hotel Assn. and Hotel Workers Health Plan, 1950-60, Hosp. Workers Health Plan, 1970-76; past bd. dirs. Health Ins. Plan of Greater N.Y. Author and/or editor: Group Medicine and Health Insurance in Action, 1949, Understanding Surgery, 1955, New Illustrated Med. Ency., 4 vols., 1959, New Am. Med. Dictionary and Health Manual, 1962, Reoperative Surgery, 1964, Health in Later Years, 1964, Child Care Ency., 12 vols., 1966, Doctor's Premarital Medical Adviser, 1969, The Fast Diet Book, 1970, The Unabridged Medical Encyclopedia, 20 vols., 1973, Our Family Medical Record Book, 1973, The Complete Surgical Guide, 1973, What Every Patient Wants to Know, 1975, The Complete Book of Breast Care, 1975, Disney's Growing Up Healthy, 4 vols., 1975, First Aid—What to Do in an Emergency, 1976, The Plain Language Law Dictionary, 1980; contbr. articles to med. jours. Served to lt. col. M.C., AUS, 1942- 45. Recipient Cabrini Gold medal, 1986. Fellow ACS; mem. AMA, Bklyn. Surg. Assn., N.Y. County Med. Soc., Alpha Omega Alpha. Home: 35 Sutton Pl New York NY 10022-2464 also: Monterosso, Camaiore Italy *Truly great ideas are had by a large number of people. Success, however, is limited to the very few who have the ability to carry them out.*

ROTHENBERG, ROBERT PHILIP, public relations counselor; b. N.Y.C., June 5, 1936; s. Robert Edward and Lillian Babette (Lustig) R. BA, Cornell U., 1956; MS, Boston U., 1958. With publicity dept. Columbia Pictures Corp., N.Y.C., 1959-60; asst. to pres., pub. rels. dir. Harry N. Abrams Pub. Co., N.Y.C., 1960-62; press sec. to gubernatorial candidate William R. Anderson Tenn., 1962; with Rowland Co., N.Y.C., 1963-70, v.p., 1965-67, sr. v.p., 1967-70; ptnr., exec. v.p. Robert Marston and Assocs., N.Y.C., 1970-88, sr. exec. v.p., 1978-88, also bd. dirs.; ptnr., pres. Marston and Rothenberg Pub. Affairs, Inc., N.Y.C. and Washington, 1977-88; chmn., pres. Rothenberg Pub. Rels. Comms. Counsel, N.Y.C., 1988—; v.p. Medbook Publs., Inc., 1995—. Trustee Mus. of Holography, N.Y.C.; bd. dirs. Found. to Save African Endangered Wildlife; assoc. Nat. Park Found.; counselor Am. Bus. Cancer Rsch. Found., Southport, Conn.; bd. dirs. World Rehab. Fund, N.Y.C.; fellow Met. Mus. of Art, 1990—; pres., chmn., bd. trustees St. Bartholomew's Preservation Found., 1992-95; mem. Blue Hill Troupe, Ltd. With USAFR, 1959-65. Mem. Internat. Soc. Poets, Pride and Alarm Soc. Unitarian. Home and Office: Ste 29B 400 E 54th St Apt 29B New York NY 10022-5169

ROTHENBERGER, DAVID ALBERT, surgeon; b. Sioux Falls, S.D., 1947. MD, Tufts U., 1973. Cert. colon and rectal surgery. Intern St. Paul-Ramsey Med. Ctr., 1973-74, resident gen. surgery, 1974-78; fellow colon rectal surgery U. Minn., Mpls., 1978-79; mem. staff United Hosp., St. Paul; cln. prof. surgery U. Minn., Mpls., chief divsn. colon and rectal surgery. Fellow ACS; mem. Am. Soc. Colon and Rectal Surgeons (exec. coun.), CICD, SSAT, WSA. Office: 299 Fort Rd Med Bldg Minneapolis MN 55102-2409*

ROTHER, JOHN CHARLES, association executive, lawyer; b. Springfield, Mo., Apr. 18, 1947; s. Charles C. and Eleanor J. (Morrison) R. BA with honors, Oberlin Coll., 1969; JD with honors, U. Pa., 1975. Bar: Pa. 1975, D.C. 1977. Appellate litigator NLRB, Washington, 1975-77; counsel Senator Jacob Javits U.S. Senate labor & human resources commn., Washington, 1977-81; staff dir., chief counsel spl. commn. on aging U.S. Senate, Washington, 1981-84; dir. legislation and pub. policy Am. Assn. Retired Persons, Washington, 1984—; co-chmn. Generations United; founder Long-Term Care Campaign; founding mem. Nat. Acad. Social Ins. Bd. dirs. Corp. for Nat. and Cmty. Svc.; mem. nat. com. for quality assurance Nat. Sr. Citizens Law Ctr. Named One of 150 Who Make A Difference, Nat. Jour., Washington, 1986. Mem. D.C. Bar, Gerontol. Soc. Am. Office: Am Assn of Retired Persons 601 E St NW Washington DC 20049-0001

ROTHERHAM, LARRY CHARLES, insurance executive; b. Council Bluffs, Iowa, Oct. 22, 1940; s. Charles Sylvester and Edna Mary (Sylvanus) R.; m. Florene F. Black, May 29, 1965; children: Christopher Charles, Phillip Larry, Kathleen Florene. Student, Creighton U., 1959-61; BSBA, U. Nebr., 1965; postgrad., Am. Coll., Bryn Mawr, Pa., 1985, 87. CPCU, CLU, ARM. Claims rep. and underwriter Safeco Ins. Co., Albuquerque, New Mex., 1965-69; br. mgr. Ohio Casualty Group, Albuquerque, 1969—; assoc. in risk mgmt. Ins. Inst. Am., 1976—. Mem. PTA Collet Park Elem. Sch., Albuquerque, 1963-82, Freedom H.S., Albuquerque, 1982-86; bd. chmn. N.M. Property Ins. Program. Mem. New Mex. Soc. Chartered Property & Casualty Underwriters (charter mem., pres. 1975-77), New Mex. Soc. Chartered Life Underwriters, New Mex. Ins. Assn. Democrat. Roman Catholic. Avocations: race walker, swimming, taxidermist, hiking, camping. Home: 2112 Gretta St NE Albuquerque NM 87112-3238 Office: Ohio Casualty Group 10400 Academy Rd NE Ste 200 Albuquerque NM 87111-1229

ROTHERMEL, DANIEL KROTT, lawyer, holding company executive; b. West Reading, Pa., Mar. 21, 1938; s. Daniel Grim and Ruth Elizabeth (Krott) R.; m. Sarah Finch, July 9, 1960; children: Anne, Daniel F., K. Melissa. BS, Pa. State U., 1960; JD, Am. U., 1966. Bar: D.C. 1967. Acct. Lukens Steel Co., Coatesville, Pa., 1960-61; pvt. practice Reading, Pa., 1966-68; atty. Carpenter Tech. Corp., Reading, 1968-70, resident counsel, 1970-78, asst. sec., 1972-73, sec., 1973-88, v.p., gen. counsel, sec., 1978-88; pres., chief exec. officer Cumru Assocs. Inc., Reading, Pa., 1989—; bd. dirs. Sovereign Bank, Sovereign Bancorp, Inc. Mem. Inst. Cmty. Affairs, Pa. State U., 1974-78; bd. dirs. Berks County chpt. ARC, 1983-86; mem., chmn. adv. bd. Berks campus Pa. State U., 1982—; ch. lay leader. Lt. USNR, 1961-66. Mem. ABA, D.C. Bar Assn., Am. Soc. Corp. Secs., U.S. C. of C., Pa. C. of C., Reading-Berks C. of C., Rotary. Republican. Lutheran. Home: 20 Glenbrook Dr Reading PA 19607-9645 Office: Cumru Assocs Inc PO Box 6573 Reading PA 19610-0573

ROTHERMEL, JOAN MARIE, occupational health nurse; b. Reading, Pa., Mar. 4, 1940; d. Andrew and Marie (Hilbert) Kuzan; m. James Carlton Rothermel, Dec. 15, 1965; 1 child, Wayne Lee. RN, Capitol City Sch. Nursing/, D.C. Gen. Hosp., 1960; BS, St. Joseph Coll., North Windham, Maine, 1983. Cert. occupational health nurse. Nurse Profl. Arts Ctr., Norwalk, Calif., 1962-64; pvt. duty nurse Reading (Pa.) Hosp. Med. Ctr., 1964-67; staff nurse/charge nurse Maple Farm Nursing Home, Akron, Pa., 1969-70; indsl. nurse Hamilton Tech., Lancaster, Pa., 1970-71; indsl. nurse/personnel sec. Rutt Custom Kitchens, Goodville, Pa., 1974-77; dir. nursing Ephrata (Pa.) Nursing Home, 1977-80; occupational health nurse C&D Batteries/Allied Corp., Leola, Pa., 1980-83, R.R. Donnelley & Sons, Lancaster, Pa., 1983-86; coord. occupational health svcs. Lancaster Gen. Hosp., 1986—. Profl. adv. com. March of Dimes, Lancaster, 1984-87; instr. CPR, standard first aid, ARC, Lancaster, 1983—. Mem. Ctrl. Pa. Assn. Occupl. Health Nurses (dir. 1985-88, 1st v.p. 1988-90), Pa. Assn. Occpl. Health Nurses (bd. dirs. 1988-90, chmn. 1991-94). Republican. Avocations: Lionel trains, music, garden, reading, travel. Home: 126 W Metzler Rd PO Box 44 Brownstown PA 17508 Office: Lancaster Gen Hosp Corp Care/Box 10547 1866 Colonial Village Ln Lancaster PA 17605

ROTHFIELD, LAWRENCE I., microbiology educator; b. N.Y.C., Dec. 30, 1927; s. Joseph and Henrietta (Brown) R.; m. Naomi Fox, Sept. 18, 1953; children: Susan Anne, Lawrence, Jane, John. BA, Cornell U., 1947; MD, NYU, 1951. Intern, then resident Bellevue, Presbyn. hosps., N.Y.C., 1951-53, 55-57; successively instr., clin. asst. prof., asst. prof. NYU Sch. Medicine, 1957-64; from asst. prof. to assoc. prof. Albert Einstein Coll. Medicine, N.Y.C., 1964-68; prof. U. Conn. Sch. Medicine, Farmington, 1968—, chmn. dept. microbiology, 1968-80; mem. molecular biology rev. panel NIH, 1970-75, microbiology and immunology adv. com. Pres.'s Biomed. Rsch. Panel, 1975, molecular biology rev. panel NSF, 1979-83; mem. microbial physiology and genetics rev. panel NIH, 1990-94, chairperson, 1991-93. Author: Structure and Function of Biological Membranes, 1972; mem. editorial bd. Jour. Membrane Biology, 1969-83, Jour. Biol. Chemistry, 1974-80. With M.C. U.S. Army, 1953-55. Mem. Am. Soc. Biol. Chemists, Am. Soc. Microbiology (chmn. microbial physiology div. 1975). Home: 540 Deercliff Rd Avon CT 06001-2859 Office: U Conn Health Center Farmington CT 06032

ROTHFUS, JOHN ARDEN, chemist; b. Des Moines, Dec. 25, 1932; s. Truman Clinton and Beatrice (Keeney) R.; m. Paula Kay Harris, Sept. 26, 1959; children: Lee Ellen, David Merrill. B.A., Drake U., 1955; Ph.D., U. Ill., 1960. Asst. biochemistry U. Ill., Urbana, 1955-59; instr. U. Utah Coll. Medicine, Salt Lake City, 1961-63; asst. prof. U. Calif. Med. Sch., Los Angeles, 1963-65; prin. research chemist U.S Dept. Agr., Peoria, Ill., 1965-70, investigations head, 1970-74, research leader, 1974-90, lead scientist, 1990—. Proctor & Gamble Co. fellow, 1957-58; USPHS postdoctoral fellow, 1959-61, archer Daniels Midland award in chem. & nutrition Am. Oil Chemists Soc., 1996. Mem. Am. Chem. Soc., AAAS, N.Y. Acad. Scis., Am. Oil Chemists Soc., Am. Soc. Plant Physiologists, Jojoba Soc., Phi Beta Kappa, Sigma Xi, Phi Lambda Upsilon, Omicron Delta Kappa, Alpha Chi Sigma. Home: 5615 N Sherwood Ave Peoria IL 61614-4148 Office: 1815 N University St Peoria IL 61604-3902 *Science and technology are stewardships passed to each generation. To preserve and nurture the spirit of inquiry and innovation that is their foundation while extending human opportunity and perspective, even incrementally, is to pass these stewardships successfully.*

ROTHHOLZ, PETER LUTZ, public relations executive; b. Berlin, June 23, 1929; came to U.S., 1945, naturalized, 1947; s. Alfred and Bertha (Isner) R.; m. Paula Trachtman, Sept. 16, 1951; 1 dau., Amy Elisabeth (dec.); m. Barbara Peters Margules, July 4, 1971; stepchildren: David, Thomas. B.A., Queens Coll., 1950; postgrad., N.Y. U., 1956-60; certificates, U. London, 1949, McGill U., 1950. With Lissone-Lindeman U.S., Inc., N.Y.C., 1953-56, KLM Royal Dutch Airlines, N.Y.C., 1956-61; exec. v.p. Simmons Tours, Inc., N.Y.C., 1961-62; pres., prin. Peter Rothholz Assocs., Inc., N.Y.C., 1962—; mem. faculty div. bus. mgmt. Sch. Continuing Edn. N.Y. U., 1969-70; mem. faculty Queens Coll., 1992—; former mem. exec. com. pacific Asia Travel Assn., Caribbean Tourism Orgn. Contbr. articles to various publs. Bd. dirs. Queens Coll. Found., 1973-94, Nat. Coun. on Aging. With U.S. Army, 1951-52. Fellow Inst. Certified Travel Agts; mem. Pub. Relations Soc. Am., Soc. Am. Travel Writers, Queens Mus. (pres. 1977-78, chmn. 1978-80), Queens Coll. Alumni Assn. (pres. 1973-75), Phi Alpha Theta. Club: N.Y. Publicity (past v.p., dir.). Home: 55 Squaw Rd East Hampton NY 11937-4510 Office: Peter Rothholz Assocs Inc 360 Lexington Ave New York NY 10017

ROTHING, FRANK JOHN, government official; b. Chgo., July 4, 1924; s. Frank Joseph and Eva A. (Buhl) R.; m. Carita Reiss Corbett, June 16, 1951; children: Frank John, Reginald, Peter, James, Richard, Joseph, Thomas, Carita Ann. B.S., U. Notre Dame, 1948. C.P.A., U. Ill., 1954. Pub. accountant Arthur Young & Co., Chgo., 1948-55; v.p. Midwest Stock Exchange, 1955-60, v.p., treas., 1960-66, sr. v.p., 1966-71; exec. v.p., sec., dir. Ill. Co., 1971-74; v.p. 1st Nat. Bank Chgo., 1974-75; exec. v.p. Front St. Securities, Inc., 1975-78; mem. Chgo. Office SEC, 1978, ret., 1989; chmn. bd. Chgo. Bd. Options Exchange Clearing Corp.; mem. Chgo. Bd. Trade. Adviser Jr. Achievement Chgo.; bd. dirs. St. Elizabeth's Hosp., Chgo.; mem. citizens bd. U. Chgo.; Bd. dirs., mem. exec. bd. North Shore Area Boy Scouts Am.; chmn. bd. trustees St. Mary of Woods Coll., Terre Haute, Ind. Served to 1st lt. USAAF, 1943-45. Decorated D.F.C., Air medal. Mem. Am. Inst. Accountants, Ill. Soc. C.P.A.s, Am. Accounting Assn., Newcomen Soc., Navy League U.S. Clubs: Michigan Shores; Bond of Chicago (dir.), Economic, Chgo. Athletic, Notre Dame (dir.), Attic (Chgo.).

ROTHKOPF, ARTHUR J., college president; b. N.Y.C., May 24, 1935; s. Abraham and Sarah (Mehlman) R.; m. Barbara Sarnoff, Dec. 25, 1958; children: Jennifer, Katherine. AB, Lafayette Coll., 1955; JD, Harvard U., 1958. Bar: N.Y. 1959, D.C. 1967. Atty. U.S. Dept. Treasury, N.Y.C., 1958-60, SEC, Washington, 1960-63; assoc. tax legis. counsel U.S. Dept. Treasury, Washington, 1963-66; ptnr. Hogan & Hartson, Washington, 1967-91; gen. counsel U.S. Dept. Transp., Washington, 1991-92, dep. sec., 1992-93; pres. Lafayette Coll., Easton, Pa., 1993—. Trustee Fed. City Coun., Washington, 1983-91; dep. counsel Rep. Nat. Com., Washington, 1990-92; dir. Lehigh-Northampton (Pa.) Airport Authority; dir. Pa. Commn. on Ind. Colls. and Univs.; dir. Easton (Pa.) Econ. Devel. Corp., 1993—, Lehigh Valley Econ. Devel. Corp., 1995—. Mem. Met. Club of Washington, Chevy Chase Club, 1925 F St. Club, Harvard Club of N.Y.C. Jewish. Home: 515 College Ave Easton PA 18042 Office: Lafayette Coll 316 Markle Hall Easton PA 18042

ROTHKOPF, DAVID JOCHANAN, federal official; b. Urbana, Ill., Dec. 24, 1955; s. Ernst Zacharias and Carol Louise (Zeman) R.; m. Jane Octavia Prelinger, Dec. 14, 1985; children: Joanna Susan, Laura Madeleine. BA, Columbia U., 1977, postgrad., 1977-78. Press sec. Office of Congressman Stephen J. Solarz, Washington, 1979-80; sr. v.p. Tilley, Marlieb & Alan, Inc., N.Y.C., 1980-82; coord. prodr. TV Series-Omni: The New Frontier, N.Y.C., 1980-82; exec. prodr. PBS Series-Flashpoint, Newark, 1984; v.p. Fin. World Mag., N.Y.C., 1984-85; v.p., pub. spl. pubs. Instnl. Investor, Inc., N.Y.C., 1985-87; chmn., CEO Internat. Media Ptnrs., Inc., N.Y.C., 1987-93; dep. under sec. commerce for internat. trade policy devel. U.S. Dept. Commerce, Washington, 1993-95, acting under sec. commerce for internat. trade, 1995-96; mng. dir. Kissinger Assocs., Inc., N.Y.C. and Washington, 1996—; adj. prof. internat. affairs Columbia U. Sch. of Internat. and Pub. Affairs, 1996—; vis. assoc. Carnegie Endowment for Internat. Peace, 1996—; CEO, chmn., The CEO Insts., N.Y.C., 1987-93. Author: The Common Market, 1978; editor Global Money Mgmt. Forum, 1986-87, Global Capital Markets Forum, 1986-87; editor-in-chief CEO/Internat. Strategies Mag., 1989-93, Emerging Markets Newspapers, 1987-93, World Market Outlook, 1991-93, Nat. Conv. News, 1992. Mem. Coun. Fgn. Rels. Democrat. Jewish. Office: 350 Park Ave New York NY 10022 also: 1800 K St Washington DC 20007

ROTHLISBERG, ALLEN PETER, librarian, educator, deacon; b. Jamaica, N.Y., Nov. 15, 1941; s. Allen Greenway and Agnes Clare (Donohoe) R.; m. Linda Lee Lillie, Oct. 17, 1964; children: Bethanie Lynn, Craig Allen. AB, San Diego State U., 1963; MLS, Our Lady of the Lake U., 1970. Cert. tchr., Ariz.; ordained deacon Episcopal Ch., 1989. Libr. dir. Prescott (Ariz.) Pub. Libr., 1963-75; dir. learning resources, head libr. Northland Pioneer Coll., Holbrook, Ariz., 1975-92; libr. dir. Chino Valley (Ariz.) Pub. Libr., 1992—; libr. media instr. Northland Pioneer Coll., Holbrook, Ariz., 1978—. Author: Dance to the Music of Time: Second Movement, 1972; contbr. articles to profl. publs. Recreation dir. Town of Chino Valley, 1993—, pub. access TV dir., 1993—; Episcopal deacon St. George's Ch., Holbrook, 1989-92, St. Luke's, Prescott, 1992—. Recipient Libr. of Yr. Ariz. State Libr. Assn., 1966. Mem. Elks, Masons. Democrat. Episcopalian. Avocations: reading, writing, music, theatre. Office: Chino Valley Pub Libr PO Box 1188 Chino Valley AZ 86323-1188

ROTHMAN, BERNARD, lawyer; b. N.Y.C., Aug. 11, 1932; s. Harry and Rebecca (Fritz) R.; m. Barbara Joan Schaeffer, Aug. 1953; children: Brian, Adam, Helene. BA cum laude, CCNY, 1953; LLB, NYU, 1959. Bar: N.Y. 1959, U.S Dist. Ct. (ea. and so. dists.) N.Y. 1962, U.S. Ct. Apls. (2d cir.) 1965, U.S. Supreme Ct. 1966, U.S. Tax Ct. 1971. Assoc. Held, Telchin & Held, 1961-62; asst. U.S. atty. U.S. Dept. Justice, 1962-66; assoc. Edward Gettinger & Peter Gettinger, 1966-68; ptnr. Schwartz, Rothman & Abrams, P.C., 1968-78; ptnr. Finkelstein, Bruckman, Wohl, Most & Rothman, N.Y.C., 1978—; acting judge Village of Larchmont, 1982-88, dep. Village atty., 1974-81, former arbitrator Civil Ct. N.Y.C., family disputes panel Am. Arbitration Assn., guest lectr. domestic rels. and family law on radio and TV, also numerous legal and mental health orgns. Author: Loving and Leaving-Winning at the Business of Divorce, 1991; co-author: Family Law Sect. Syracuse Law Rev., 1992, Leaving Home Family Law Review, 1987; contbr. articles to profl. jours. Mem. exec. bd., past v.p. Westchester Putnam coun. Boy Scouts Am., 1975—; past mem. nat. coun., 1977-81; mem. N.Y. State PEACE Adv. Commn., 1991—. Recipient Silver Beaver award Boy Scouts Am., Wood Badge award; pres. Congregation B'nai Israel, 1961-63, B'nai Brith, Larchmont chpt., 1981-83. Fellow Am. Acad. Matrimonial Lawyers (bd. govs. N.Y. chpt. 1986-87, 91-93), Interdisciplinary Forum on Mental Health and Family Law (co-chair 1986—); mem. ABA (family law sect.), N.Y. State Bar Assn. (exec. com. family law sect. 1982—, co-chmn. com. on mediation and arbitration 1982-88, 93—, com. on legis. 1978-88, com. on child custody 1985-88, com. alternative dispute resolution, peace adv. com.), Assn. of Bar of City of N.Y., N.Y. State Magistrate Assn., Westchestr Magistrate Assn., N.Y. Road Runners Club, Limousine 6 Track Club. Democrat. Office: Finkelstein Bruckman Wohl Most & Rothman LLP 575 Lexington Ave New York NY 10022-6102

ROTHMAN, DAVID J., history and medical educator; b. N.Y.C., Apr. 30, 1937; s. Murray and Anne (Beier) R.; m. Sheila Miller, June 26, 1960; children: Matthew, Micol. B.A., Columbia U., 1958; M.A., Harvard U., 1959, Ph.D., 1964. Asst. prof. history Columbia U., N.Y.C., 1964-67; assoc. prof. Columbia U., 1967-71, prof., 1971—, Bernard Schoenberg prof. social medicine, dir. Ctr. for Study of Society and Medicine; Fulbright-Hayes prof. Hebrew U., Jerusalem, 1968-69, India, 1982; vis. Pinkerton Prof. Sch. Criminal Justice, State U. N.Y., at Albany, 1973-74; Samuel Paley lectr. Hebrew U., Jerusalem, 1977; Mem. Com. for Study of Incarceration, 1971-74; co-dir. Project on Community Alternatives, 1978-82; chmn. adv. bd. on criminal justice Clark Found., 1978-82; mem. bd. advisors The Project on Death in Am., Open Soc. Inst., 1995—. Author: Politics and Power, 1966, The Discovery of the Asylum, 1971; co-author: Doing Good, 1978, Conscience and Convenience: The Asylum and its Alternatives in Progressive America, 1980, (with Sheila M. Rothman), The Willowbrook Wars, 1984, Strangers at the Bedside, 1991; Editor: The World of the Adams Chronicles, 1976, (with Sheila M. Rothman) On Their Own: The Poor in Modern America, 1972, The Sources of American Social Tradition, 1975, (with Stanton Wheeler) Social History and Social Policy, 1981, (with Norval Morris) The Oxford History of the Prison, 1995, (with Steven Marcus and Stephanie Kiceluk) Medicine and Western Civilization, 1995. Bd. dirs. Mental Health Law Project, 1973-80, 82—. Recipient Albert J. Beveridge prize Am. Hist. Assn., 1971. Mem. Am. Hist. Assn., Orgn. Am. Historians, N.Y. Acad. Medicine, Phi Beta Kappa. Office: Columbia U Coll Physicians and Surgeons Ctr Study Soc and Medicine 630 W 168th St New York NY 10032-3702

ROTHMAN, FRANK, lawyer, motion picture company executive; b. Los Angeles, Dec. 24, 1926; s. Leon and Rose (Gendel) R.; m. Mariana Richardson, Aug. 7, 1985; children: Steven, Robin, Susan. B.A., U. So. Calif., 1949, LL.B., 1951. Bar: Calif. 1952, D.C., U.S. Dist. Ct. (cen. dist.) Calif. 1951. Dep. city atty. City of Los Angeles, 1951-55; mem. law firm Wyman, Bautzer, Rothman, Kuchel & Silbert, Los Angeles, 1956-82; chmn. bd., chief exec. officer MGM-UA Entertainment Co., Culver City, Calif., 1982-86; ptnr. Skadden Arps Slate, L.A., 1986—. Bd. editors U. So. Calif. Law Rev., 1948. Served with USAAF, 1945-46. Fellow Am. Coll. Trial Lawyers; mem. L.A. Bar Assn., Calif. Bar Assn., Univ. Club. Democrat. Home: 10555 Rocca Pl Los Angeles CA 90077-2904 Office: Skadden Arps Slate 300 S Grand Ave Bldg 3400 Los Angeles CA 90071-3144

ROTHMAN, FRANK GEORGE, biology educator, biochemical genetics researcher; b. Budapest, Hungary, Feb. 2, 1930; came to U.S., 1938; s. Stephen and Irene Elizabeth (Manheim) R.; m. Joan Therese Kiernan, Aug.22, 1953; children: Michael, Jean, Stephen, Maria. BA, U. Chgo., 1948, MS, 1951; PhD, Harvard U., 1955. Postdoctoral fellow NSF, U. Wis., MIT, 1956-58, Am. Cancer Soc., MIT, Cambridge, 1958-59; postdoctoral assoc. MIT, Cambridge, 1957-61; asst. prof. Brown U., Providence, 1961-65, assoc. prof., 1965-70, prof., 1970—, dean of biology, 1984-90, provost, 1990-95. Contbr. articles to profl. jours. Served with U.S. Army, 1954-56. Spl. fellow USPHS, U. Sussex, Eng., 1967-68; NSF grantee, 1961-84. Fellow AAAS; mem. Genetics Soc. Am. Office: Brown U Box G-J119 Providence RI 02912

ROTHMAN, HENRY ISAAC, lawyer; b. Rochester, N.Y., Mar. 29, 1943; s. Maurice M. and Golde (Nusbaum) R.; m. Golda R. Shatz, July 3, 1966; children: Alan, Miriam, Cheryl, Suri. BA, Yeshiva U., 1964; JD, Cornell U., 1967. Bar: N.Y. 1967. Trial atty. SEC, N.Y.C., 1967-69; ptnr. Booth, Lipton & Lipton, N.Y.C., 1969-87, Parker, Chapin, Flattau & Klimpl, N.Y.C., 1987—. Bd. dirs. Camp Morasha, Lake Como, Pa., 1982—, vice chmn., 1992—; bd. dirs. Assn. of Jewish Sponsored Camps, Inc., 1986—; bd. dirs. Yeshiva U. High Schs., N.Y.C., 1984—, vice chmn. bd., 1990-91, chmn. bd., 1992-95; v.p. Manhattan Day Sch., N.Y.C., 1985—; assoc. v.p. Orthodox Union, N.Y.C., 1990—. Mem. ABA (com. on fed. regulation of securities), N.Y. State Bar Assn., Assn. of Bar of City of N.Y., Nat. Assn. Hebrew Day Schs., Yeshiva U. Alumni Assn. (pres. 1986-88, hon. pres. 1988-90). Office: Parker Chapin Flattau & Klimpl 1211 Avenue Of The Americas New York NY 10036-8701

ROTHMAN, HOWARD JOEL, lawyer; b. N.Y.C., July 10, 1945; s. Samuel and Avy (Avrutin) R.; m. Joan Andrea Solomon, July 2, 1967; children: Samantha, Rodney. BA, CCNY, 1967; JD, Bklyn. Law Sch., 1971; LLM, NYU, 1972. Bar: N.Y. 1972. From assoc. to ptnr. Marshall, Bratter, Greene, Allison & Tucker, N.Y.C., 1972-82; ptnr. Rosenman & Colin, N.Y.C., 1982—; mem. adv. panel Commr. Fin. of City of N.Y., 1981-83. Author profl. books and articles. Bd. dirs. Alliance Resident Theatres N.Y., 1989-96, Alliance for Young Artists and Writers, 1994—). Mem. ABA (corp. taxation com. 1980—), Internat. Bar Assn., N.Y. State Bar Assn. (corps. com. 1979-87, partnerships com. 1979—, N.Y.C. tax matters com. 1977—, income from real property com. 1987—), Bur. Nat. Affairs (real estate jour. 1984—, tax mgmt. adv. bd. 1979—). Office: Rosenman & Colin 575 Madison Ave New York NY 10022-2511

ROTHMAN, JUDITH ELLEN, associate dean; b. Bklyn., Sept. 12, 1946; d. Benjamin and Shirley (Finkelstein) Siegel; m. Elliott charles Rothman, Jan. 1, 1983; children by previous marriage: Reed Adam Slatas, Kimberly Joy Slatas. BS in Acctg., Fairleigh Dickinson U., 1976, postgrad., 1976-77; postgrad., UCLA, 1986-87. Acct. Interpace Corp., Parsippany, N.J., 1976-77; mgr. fin. planning Blue Cross So. Calif., Woodland Hills, 1977-82; asst. dir. fin. Cedars-Sinai Med. Ctr., L.A., 1982-87; assoc. dean fin. and bus. affairs, Sch. Medicine UCLA, Westwood, 1987-94; sr. assoc. dean fin. and adminstrn. Sch. Medicine UCLA, L.A., 1994—. Mem. Calif. Abortion Rights Action League, Friends of Calif. Spl. Olympics. Mem. NAFE, Assn. Am. Med. Colls. (region sec. 1992, region pres. 1993), Med. Group Mgmt. Assn., UCLA Anderson Mgmt. Alumni Assn. Avocations: hiking, tennis. Office: UCLA Sch Medicine 12-138CHS 10833 Le Conte Ave Los Angeles CA 90024

ROTHMAN, MELVIN L., judge; b. Montreal, Que., Can., Apr. 6, 1930; s. Charles and Nellie (Rosen) R.; m. Joan Elizabeth Presant, Aug. 4, 1954; children: Ann Elizabeth, Claire Presant, Margot Sneyd. B.A., McGill U., 1951, B.C.L., 1954. Bar: Que. 1954. Practice law Montreal, 1954-71; mem. Phillips, Vineberg, Goodman, Phillips & Rothman; judge Superior Ct., Dist. of Montreal, 1971-83, Ct. Appeal of Que., 1983—. Mem. Jr. Bar of Montreal (pres. 1963-64), Bar of Montreal (council 1964-65), Institut Philippe Pinel (sec., dir. 1965-70). Home: 487 Argyle Ave, Westmount, PQ Canada H3Y 3B3 Office: Que Ct of Appeal, Court House, 10 St Antoine St E, Montreal, PQ Canada

ROTHMAN, MICHAEL JUDAH, lawyer; b. Mpls., June 7, 1962; s. Harvey Michael and Elaine Louise (London) R.; m. Shari Latz, Aug. 1, 1993. BA, Carleton Coll., 1984; JD, U. Minn., 1988. Bar: Minn. 1988, U.S. Dist. Ct. Minn. 1988, Calif. 1993, U.S. Dist. Ct. (ctrl. dist.) Calif. 1993, U.S. Ct. Appeals (9th cir.) 1995, U.S. Supreme Ct. 1995. Law clk. to J. Gary Crippen Minn. Ct. of Appeals, St. Paul, 1988-89; adminstrv. asst. Minn. State Senate, St. Paul, 1989-92; assoc. Rubenstein & Perry, L.A., 1993-95, Loeb & Loeb, LLP, L.A., 1995—. Vol. atty. F.A.M.E., Chgo. and Temple Isaiah Legal Project, L.A., 1994-96. Recipient Best Brief award Regional Internat. Moot Ct. Competition, Colo., 1988. Mem. ABA, Calif. Bar Assn., L.A. County Bar Assn. Democrat. Avocations: golf, running, reading. Office: Loeb & Loeb LLP 1000 Wilshire Blvd Ste 1800 Los Angeles CA 90017

ROTHMAN-BERNSTEIN, LISA J., operating room nurse; b. Toledo, Dec. 29, 1949; 1 child, Daniel Karvinen. Diploma, Mercy Hosp. Sch. Nursing, Toledo, 1974; B Individualized Studies magna cum laude, Lourdes Coll., Sylvania, Ohio, 1989; AS in Bus., U. Toledo, 1970; student, U. Florence, Italy, 1972. Buyer Lamson's of Toledo; owner/designer FUNKtional Art, Inc.; owner/baker Tres Bon Cheesecakes, Inc., Margate, Fla.; cruise ship nurse Costa Cruise Line, Miami, Fla.; home health nurse Upjohn, Ft. Lauderdale, Fla.; patient svcs. coord. Fla. Med. Ctr., Lauderdale Lakes, Fla.; vol. nurse in ob-gyn. Yoseftal Hosp., Eilat, Israel; staff nurse in ob-gyn. Mt. Sinai Med. Ctr., Miami Beach, Fla.; staff nurse on eye svc., oper. rm. St. Vincent Med. Ctr., Toledo; nursing and healthcare recruiter, customer svc. advocate emergency dept. Co-chmn. Lourdes Coll. Red Cross Blood Drive, 1988-89; publicity chairperson St. Vincent Med. Ctr. 1993 Nurses' Week. Mem. Assn. Operating Rm. Nurses, Nat. Assn. of Health Care Recruiters, Kappa Gamma Pi.

ROTHMEIER, STEVEN GEORGE, merchant banker, investment manager; b. Mankato, Minn., Oct. 4, 1946; s. Edwin George and Alice Joan (Johnson) R. BBA, U. Notre Dame, 1968; MBA, U. Chgo., 1972. Corp. fin. analyst Northwest Airlines, Inc., St. Paul, 1973, mgr. econ. analysis, 1973-78, dir. econ. planning, 1978, v.p. fin., treas., 1978-82, exec. v.p., treas., dir., 1982-83, exec. v.p. fin. and adminstrn., treas., dir., 1983, pres., chief operating officer, 1984, pres., chief exec. officer, 1985-86, chmn., chief exec. officer, 1986-89, also bd. dirs.; pres. IAI Capital Group, Mpls., 1989-93; chmn., CEO Great No. Capital, St. Paul, 1993—; bd. dirs. Honeywell Inc., Precision Castparts, E.W. Blanch Holdings Inc., Dept. 56 Inc. Chmn. St. Agnes Found., Channel 53 Cath. TV Minn. Decorated Bronze Star. Republican. Roman Catholic. Clubs: Mpls.; Minn. Office: Great Northern Capital 332 Minnesota St Ste W 1295 Saint Paul MN 55101-1305 *Success is not an accident; it is a habit. Success is the result of desire, dedication, sacrifice, mental toughness, hard work—and prayer. And you are not successful until you can share your success with others.*

ROTHSCHILD, ALAN FRIEND, lawyer; b. Columbus, Ga., Aug. 15, 1925; s. Irwin Bernard and Aleen (Samuels) R.; m. Eva Garrett Pound, Sept. 21, 1957; children: Alan Friend, William Garrett, Elizabeth Pound. B.S. in Commerce, U. Va., 1945, LL.B., 1947. Bar: Ga. bar 1948. Partner Rosenstrauch & Rothschild, Columbus, 1948-51; assoc. Hatcher, Stubbs, Land, Hollis & Rothschild (and predecessor), Columbus, 1951-57; ptnr. Hatcher, Stubbs, Land, Hollis & Rothschild (and predecessor), 1957—. Mem. Gov.'s Commn. on Revision Appellate Cts. Ga., 1976-80; mem. Ga. Bd. Bar Examiners, 1980-84, chmn., 1984; mem. bd. commrs. Med. Ctr., 1958-74, chmn., 1973-74; pres. Cmty. Counseling Ctr., 1960-62; local co-chmn. NCCJ, 1958; active Boys Club, Jr. Achievement; trustee Springer Opera House; trustee St. Francis Hosp., chmn., 1979-90; past trustee Three Arts League, Brookstone Sch.; life trustee Columbus Mus.; bd. dirs. Walter Alan Richards Found., Anne Elizabeth Shepherd Home; pres. Columbus Legal Aid Soc., 1971-73. Fellow Am. Coll. Trusts and Estates Counsel, Am. Bar Found., Ga. Bar Found.; mem. ABA, Ga. Bar Assn., Columbus Bar Assn. (pres. 1967), Ga. Hosp. Assn. (trustee). Jewish. Home: 2328 Fairway Ave Columbus GA 31906-1018 Office: 500 Corporate Center Columbus GA 31902

ROTHSCHILD, AMALIE RANDOLPH, filmmaker, producer, director; b. Balt., June 3, 1945; d. Randolph Schamberg and Amalie Getta (Rosenfeld) R. BFA, R.I. Sch. Design, 1967; MFA in Motion Picture Production, NYU, 1969. Spl. effects staff in film and photography Joshua Light Show, Fillmore E. Theatre, NYC, 1969-71; still photographer TWA Airlines Pub. Relations Dept., Village Voice newspaper Rolling Stone magazine, Newsweek magazine, After Dark, N.Y. Daily News, numerous others, 1968-72; co-founder, partner New Day Films, distbn. coop., 1971—; owner, operator Anomaly Films Co., NYC, 1971—; mem., co-founder Assn. of Independent Video and Filmmakers, Inc., NYC, 1974, bd. dirs., 1974-78; instr. in film and TV, N.Y. U. Inst. of Film and TV, 1976-78; cons. in field to various organizations including Youthgrant Program of Nat. Endowment for Humanities, Washington, 1973-76; motion pictures include: Woo Who? May Wilson, 1969; It Happens to Us, 1972; Nana, Mom and Me, 1974; Radioimmunoassay of Renin, Radioimmunoassay of Aldosterone, 1973; Conversations with Willard Van Dyke, 1981; Richard Haas: Work in Progress, 1984; Painting the Town: The Illusionistic Murals of Richard Haas, 1990 (Emily award Am. Film and Video Festival 1990); editor: Doing It Yourself, Handbook on Independent Film Distribution, 1977. Mem. Community Planning Bd. 1, Borough of Manhattan, N.Y.C., 1974-86. Recipient spl. achievement award Mademoiselle mag., 1972; independent filmmaker grant, Am. Film Inst., 1973; film grantee N.Y. State Coun. on the Arts, 1977, 85, 87, Nat. Endowment Arts, 1978, 85, 87, Md. Arts Coun., 1977, Ohio Arts and Humanities Couns., 1985. Mem. Assn. Ind. Video Filmmakers (bd. dirs. 1974-78) Univ. Film and Video Assn., N.Y. Women in Film, Ind. Documentary Assn., Laboratorio Immagine Donna. Democrat. Address: 135 Hudson St New York NY 10013-2102 also: Via delle Mantellate 19, Rome 00165, Italy

ROTHSCHILD, AMALIE ROSENFELD, artist; b. Balt., Jan. 1, 1916; d. Eugene Isaac and Addye (Goldsmith) Rosenfeld; m. Randolph S. Rothschild, Aug. 3, 1936; children: Amalie R., Adrien R. Diploma, Md. Inst. Coll. Art, 1934, BFA (hon.), 1996; student, N.Y. Sch. Fine and Applied Art, 1934. Instr. painting Met. Sch. Art, Balt., 1956-59; lectr. fine arts Goucher Coll., 1960-68. One-woman shows include Balt. Mus. Art, 1971, NAS, Washington, 1975, Kornblatt Gallery, Balt., 1978, 80, travelling retrospective exhbn., 1984, C. Grimaldis Gallery, Balt., 1985, 88, 91, Md. Inst. Coll. Art, 1985, Franz Bader Gallery, Washington, 1989, 91, Artist's Pavillion, Tel Aviv, 1990, Gomez Gallery, Balt., 1993, 95, Art Rsch. and Tech., Lancaster, Pa., 1993; group shows include Jewish Mus., N.Y.C., 1952, Corcoran Gallery Art, Washington, 1958-59, Pub. Art Trust, Washington, 1985, Elements of Style, Md. Inst. Coll. Art, 1986, Internat. Sculpture Ctr. Conf. Exhbn. Sculptors Inc., Phila., 1992, Sculptors Guild N.Y., 1994-95, George Mason U., Fairfax, Va., 1995; represented in permanent collections Corcoran Gallery Art, Phillips Collection, Washington, Peale Mus. Balt., Balt. Mus. Art, Honolulu Acad. Arts, Fed. Res. Bank, Richmond, Va., Md. Sci. Ctr., corp. and univ. collections; commns. include archtl. panels Martin Luther King, Jr. Elem. Sch., Balt., 1969, wall hanging Walters Art Gallery, Balt., 1974, plexiglass window wall, Forest Park H.S., Balt., 1981. Chmn. artists com. Balt. Mus. Art, 1956-58, trustee, 1977-83, mem. accessions com., 1980-83; trustee Md. Inst. Coll. Art., 1991—. Recipient Disting. Alumni award Md. Inst. Coll. Art, 1985. Mem. Artists Equity Assn. (bd. dirs. Md. chpt. 1977-83), Sculptors Inc., Internat. Sculpture Ctr., New York Sculptor's Guild. Democrat. Jewish. Address: 2909 Woodvalley Dr Baltimore MD 21208-1915 *The definition of talent as power of mind and body committed to one for use and improvement describes my purpose in life. Late intellectual motivation followed early practical preparation for commercial art. Continuing self-education through multi-disciplinary reading, directing of energy into daily art-related endeavor, expecting integrity of performance in myself and others—these are my criteria for pursuit of excellence and fulfillment.*

ROTHSCHILD, BERYL ELAINE, mayor; m. Edmund W. Rothschild; children: Margaret, Dan. BS in Journalism, Ohio U., 1951. Councilman City of University Heights, Ohio, 1968-78, mayor, 1979—; sec. Regional Coun. of Govts. Former mem. legis. policy com. Ohio Mcpl. League; past mem. exec. bd. N.E. Ohio Areawide Coord. Agy.; former trustee Citizens League Greater Cleve. and Citizens League Rsch. Inst., YWCA (Metro) Cleve., Meridia Suburban Hosp., 1987-90, chmn., Meridia Health System, 1987-90; bd. dirs. Cuyahoga County Nursing Home; mem. community adv. bd. Coop. Human Tissue Network, Case Western Res. U.; mem. adv. bd. Adult Basic and Literacy Edn.; charter mem., v.p. Ind. Living Experience Achievement Program; mem. adv. com. John Carroll U. Edn. Dept., 1988-90; past mem. com. on svcs. to the disabled Jewish Community Fedn. of Cleve., special needs adv. com. Jewish Community Ctr., advanced program employer adv. coun. Jewish Vocat. Svcs.; active mem. Learning Disabilities Assn. of Greater Cleve., Friends of the Cleveland Heights-Univ. Heights Libr. System, Hadassah, Pioneer Women, Coun. of Jewish Women, Heights Y, Univ. Heights Club 100, Fairmount Temple, Women's Com. of The Cleve. Orchestra, Cleve. Mus. Art. Recipient Career Woman of Achievement award Cleve. YWCA, 1986, Woman of Achievement Recognition award Greater Cleve. chpt. Hadassah, Recognition cert. Cleveland Heights-University Heights Bd. Edn., 1980-81, City of Peace award State of Israel Bonds, 1984, Kenneth R. Oldman Meml. award (with husband) Cleve. Assn. for Children and Adults with Learning Disabilities, 1988; named one of Outstanding Women of Yr. Greater Cleve. State of Israel Bonds, 1988. Mem. Nat. League of Cities and U.S. Conf. of Mayors, Cuyahoga County Mayors and Mgrs. Assn. (exec. bd., waste mgmt. com., legis. com., cable TV com.), Women in Comms., Inc., Alpha Sigma Nu (hon.). Office: City of University Heights 2300 Warrensville Center Rd University Heights OH 44118-3825

ROTHSCHILD, DIANE, advertising agency executive; b. Apr. 11, 1943; d. Morton Royce and Marjorie Jay (Simon) R.; 1 child, Alexandra Rothschild Spencer. B.A., Aldephi U., 1965. Copywriter Doyle Dane Bernbach Advt., Inc., N.Y.C., 1967-73, v.p., 1973-79, sr. v.p., assoc. creative dir., 1979-85, exec. v.p., creative dir., 1985-86; pres. Grace and Rothschild, N.Y.C., 1986—. Recipient maj. advt. awards. Mem. YWCA Acad. Women Achievers. Office: Grace & Rothschild 114 5th Ave New York NY 10011-5604

ROTHSCHILD, DONALD PHILLIP, lawyer, arbitrator; b. Dayton, Ohio, Mar. 31, 1927; s. Leo and Anne (Office) R.; m. Ruth Eckstein, July 7, 1950; children: Nancy Lee, Judy Lynn Hoffman, James Alex. AB, U. Mich., 1950; JD summa cum laude, U. Toledo, 1965; LLM, Harvard U., 1966. Bar: Ohio 1966, D.C. 1970, U.S. Supreme Ct. 1975, R.I. 1989. Teaching fellow Harvard U. Law Sch., Cambridge, Mass., 1965-66; instr. solicitor's office U.S. Dept. Labor, Washington, 1966-67; vis. prof. U. Mich. Law Sch., Ann Arbor, 1976; prof. law George Washington U. Nat. Law Ctr., Washington, 1966-89, emeritus, 1989; prof. law N.Y. Law Sch., 1989—; dir. Consumer Protection Ctr., 1971—; dir. Inst. Law and Aging, Washington, 1973-89, Ctr. for Community Justice, Washington, 1974-88, Nat. Consumers League, Washington, 1981-87; v.p. Regulatory Alternatives Devel. Corp., Washington, 1982—; cons. Washington Met. Council Govt., 1979-82; mayoral appointee Adv. Com. on Consumer Protection, Washington, 1979-80; chmn. bd. dirs. D.C. Citizens Complaint Ctr., Washington, 1980; counsel Tillinghast, Collins & Graham, Providence, 1989-95, chair human resource group. Co-author: Consumer Protection Text and Materials, 1973; Collective Bargaining and Labor Arbitration, 1979; Fundamentals of Administrative Practice and Procedure, 1981. Contbr. numerous articles to profl. publs. Mem. Fed. Trade Commn. Adv. Council, Washington, 1970. Recipient Community Service award Television Acad., Washington, 1981. Mem. Nat. Acad. Arbitrators, Fed. Mediation and Conciliation Service, Am. Arbitration Assn., ABA, D.C. Bar Assn., Phi Kappa Phi. Jewish. Office: Shadow Farm Way Unit 4 Wakefield RI 02879-3631

ROTHSCHILD, JOSEPH, political science educator; b. Fulda, Germany, Apr. 5, 1931; came to U.S., 1940, naturalized, 1945; s. Meinhold and Henriette (Loewenstein) R.; m. Ruth Deborah Nachmansohn, July 19, 1959; children: Nina, Gerson. A.B. summa cum laude, Columbia U., 1951, A.M., 1952; D.Phil. (Euretta J. Kellett fellow), Oxford U., 1955. Instr. dept. polit. sci. Columbia, N.Y.C., 1955-58; asst. prof. Columbia, 1958-62, asso. prof., 1962-68, prof., 1968—, Class of 1919 endowed prof., 1978—, chmn. dept., 1971-75, 81-82, 89-91; Vice chmn., mem. exec. com. Am. Profs. for Peace in Mid. East, 1975-90. Author: The Communist Party of Bulgaria, 1959, Introduction to Contemporary Civilization in the West, 3d edit, 1960, Chapters in Western Civilization, 3d edit, 1962, Communist Eastern Europe, 1964, Pilsudski's Coup d'Etat, 1966, East Central Europe Between the Two World Wars, 1974, Ethnopolitics: A Conceptual Framework, 1981 (transl. into Italian 1984, Japanese 1989), Return to Diversity: A Political History of East Central Europe Since World War II, 1989; contbr. articles to profl. jours. Recipient Mark Van Doren Great Tchr. award Columbia Coll., 1991; Social Sci. Rsch. Coun. fellow, 1963-64, J.S. Guggenheim fellow, 1967-68, Am. Coun. Learned Socs. fellow, 1971-72, Chamberlain sr. fellow, 1974, Ford rsch. fellow, summer 1976, NEH fellow, 1978-79, Lehrman Inst. fellow, 1979-80, Ford Found.-Am. Coun. Learned Socs. rsch. fellow, 1985-87, Woodrow Wilson fellow, 1994. Mem. Polit. Sci. Acad., Am. Assn. for Advancement Slavic Studies, Polish Inst. Arts and Scis. in Am., Phi Beta Kappa. Home: 445 Riverside Dr New York NY 10027-6842

ROTHSCHILD, MICHAEL, economics educator; b. Chgo., Aug. 2, 1942; s. Edwin Alfred and Ann (Meyer) R.; m. Linda Preiss, Sept. 7, 1969 (div. 1991); m. Lynn Kay Greenberg, May 1, 1994; children: David, Daniel. B.A., Reed Coll., 1963; M.A., Yale U., 1965; Ph.D., MIT, 1969. Asst. prof. econs. Harvard U., 1969-73; lectr. Princeton U., 1972-74, assoc. prof., 1974-75, prof., 1975-76; then prof. U. Wis., Madison, 1976-83; prof. U. Calif.-San Diego, 1983-95, divisional dean social scis., 1985-95; dean Woodrow Wilson Sch. Pub./Internat. Affairs, Princeton U., 1995—. Editor: (with Peter Diamond) Uncertainty in Economics, 1978, (with Charles T. Clotfelder) Studies of Supply and Demand in Higher Education, 1993. Guggenheim fellow, 1978-79. Fellow Am. Acad. Arts and Scis., Econometric Soc.; mem. Am. Econ. Assn. Office: Woodrow Wilson Sch Robertson Hall Princeton U Princeton NJ 08544-1013

ROTHSCHILD, STEVEN JAMES, lawyer; b. Worcester, Mass., Mar. 23, 1944; s. Alfred and Ilse (Blumenfeld) R. B.A., U. Vt., 1965; J.D., Georgetown U., 1968. Bar: D.C. 1968, Del. 1969, N.Y. 1992. Ptnr. Skadden Arps Slate Meagher & Flom, Wilmington; mem. Del. Bd. Bar Examiners, 1979-83; chmn. Del. Citizens Conf. on Adminstrn. of Justice, 1982; mem. Del. Bd. on Profl. Responsibility, 1992—, vice chmn., 1993, chmn., 1994—; vice chmn. rules com. Del. Supreme Ct., 1991-94; chmn. Del. Gov.'s Commn. on Major Comml. Litigation Reform, 1993-94. Bd. dirs. United Way Del., 1978-85, 93—, v.p., 1981-84, chmn. 1994-95; bd. dirs. Milton and Hattie Kutz Home, 1972—, pres., 1982-84; bd. dirs. Del. region NCCJ, 1981-92, Hebrew Immigrant Aid Soc., 1986-91, Jewish Fedn. Del., 1988-91; trustee Del. Art Mus., 1986-92, pres., 1990-92. Mem. ABA, Bar Assn. D.C., Assn. of Bar of City of N.Y., Del. Bar Assn. Office: Skadden Arps Slate Meagher & Flom One Rodney Sq PO Box 636 Wilmington DE 19899

ROTHSTEIN, ASER, radiation biology educator; b. Vancouver, B.C., Can., Apr. 29, 1918; emigrated to U.S., 1940, naturalized, 1955; s. Samuel and Etta (Wiseman) R.; m. Evelyn Paperny, Aug. 18, 1940; children: Sharon Leslie, David Michael, Steven Jay. B.A. in Zoology, U.B.C., 1938; student, U. Calif. at Berkeley, 1938-40; Ph.D., U. Rochester, 1943, D.Sc. (hon.), 1983. With atomic energy project U. Rochester, 1948—, co-dir., 1965—; mem. faculty U. Rochester (Med. Sch.), 1946—, prof. radiation biology, 1959—, co-chmn. dept., 1965—; dir. Rsch. Inst. Hosp. for Sick Children, Toronto, Ont., 1971-87, dir. emeritus, 1987—; prof. med. biophysics U. Toronto Med. Sch., 1972-87, prof. emeritus, 1987—, Univ. prof., 1980; vis. prof. Eidgenossische Technische Hochschule, Zurich, 1977; U.S. del. UNESCO Conf., Paris, France, 1957; NSF sr. postdoctoral fellow U. Bern, Switzerland, 1959-60. Recipient Wightman award Gairdner Found., 1986. Fellow AAAS, Royal Soc. Can. Home: 33 Harbour Sq #2018, Toronto, ON Canada M5J 2G2

ROTHSTEIN, BARBARA JACOBS, federal judge; b. Bklyn., Feb. 3, 1939; d. Solomon and Pauline Jacobs; m. Ted L. Rothstein, Dec. 28, 1968; 1 child, Daniel. B.A., Cornell U., 1960; LL.B., Harvard U., 1966. Bar: Mass. 1966, Wash. 1969, U.S. Ct. Appeals (9th cir.) 1977, U.S. Dist. Ct. (we. dist.) Wash. 1971, U.S. Supreme Ct. 1975. Pvt. practice law Boston, 1966-68; asst. atty. gen. State of Wash., 1968-77; judge Superior Ct., Seattle, 1977-80; judge Fed. Dist. Ct. Western Wash., Seattle, 1980—, chief judge, 1987-94; faculty Law Sch. U. Wash., 1975-77, Hastings Inst. Trial Advocacy, 1977, N.W. Inst. Trial Advocacy, 1979—; mem. state-fed. com. U.S. Jud. Conf., chair subcom. on health reform. Recipient Matrix Table Women of Yr. award Women in Communication, Judge of the Yr. award Fed. Bar Assn., 1989; King County Wash. Women Lawyers Vanguard Honor, 1995. Mem. ABA (jud. sect.), Am. Judicature Soc., Nat. Assn. Women Judges, Fellows of the Am. Bar, Wash. State Bar Assn., U.S. Jud. Conf. (state-fed. com., health reform subcom.), Phi Beta Kappa, Phi Kappa Phi. Office: US Dist Ct 705 US Courthouse 1010 5th Ave Seattle WA 98104-1130

ROTHSTEIN, GERALD ALAN, investment company executive; b. Bklyn., Oct. 18, 1941; s. Manuel and Gertrude (Buxbaum) R.; m. Cynthia Bea Pincus, June 11, 1967; children: Michael Neil, Lori Pamela, Meryl Patricia. BBA, City Coll. N.Y., 1962; MBA, U. Pa., 1965. 1st v.p. Shearson Hammill & Co., N.Y.C., 1966-74, Shearson Hayden Stone, N.Y.C., 1974-75; v.p. William D. Witter, Inc., N.Y.C., 1975-76; v.p. Oppenheimer & Co., N.Y.C., 1976-79, sr. v.p., 1979-83, mng. dir., 1983—; dir. internat. rsch., 1991-95, internat. investment banker, 1995—; bd. dirs. Midway Guaranty S.A., (Chile), Pathfinder Investment Co. Ltd. (India). Mem. N.Y. Soc. Security Analysts, Inst. Chartered Fin. Analysts, Coun. of the Americas, Internat. Soc. Fin. Analysts. Office: Oppenheimer & Co Inc Oppenheimer Tower World Fin Ctr New York NY 10281

ROTHSTEIN, MORTON, historian, retired educator; b. Omaha, Jan. 8, 1926; s. Joseph Isadore and Rose (Landman) R.; m. Frances Irene Lustig, Nov. 18, 1950; children: Laurence, Eric, David. Student, Bklyn. Coll., 1952-54; Ph.D., Cornell U., 1960; postgrad., London Sch. Econs., 1956-57. Instr. U. Del., 1958-61; asst. prof. U. Wis.-Madison, 1961-65, assoc. prof., 1965-69, prof. history and agrl. econs., 1969-84, chmn. history dept., 1969-72; prof. history U. Calif., Davis, 1984-94; emeritus prof. U. Calif., Davis, 1994—; vis. prof. London Sch. Econs., 1970-77; mem. acad. adv. bd. Eleutherian Mills-Hagley Found., 1970-74; mem. Wis. Humanities Com., 1978-84, chmn., 1980-82, Calif. Coun. Humanities, 1985-90, chmn. 1988-90. Editor: Explorations in Economic History, 1970-73, Agricultural History, 1984-94; co-editor: Outstanding In His Field: Essays in Honor of Wayne D. Rasmussen, 1993, Quantification in Agrarian History: Essays by American and Soviet Historians, 1994; contbr. articles to profl. jours. Social Sci. Research Council fellow, 1956-57, 67-68; NEH fellow, 1976-77, 83. Mem. Orgn. Am. Historians, Agrl. History Soc. (pres. 1975-76), Bus. History Conf. (pres. 1985-86), Econ. History Assn., Econ. History Soc. (U.K.), So. History Assn., We. History Assn., Calif. Hist. Soc. (trustee 1989-90). Jewish. Home: 3417 Seabright Ave Davis CA 95616-5641 Office: U Calif Dept History Davis CA 95616 *The example of teachers who were thoroughly engaged in research, and generated excitement from it, has informed my own efforts at writing and in the classroom. A professor must have something to profess. Openness and generosity has benefited me, and taught me never to count other people's money, or to fear doing someone a favor.*

ROTHSTEIN, PAUL FREDERICK, lawyer, educator; b. Chgo., June 6, 1938. B.S., Northwestern U., 1958, LL.B., 1961. Bar: Ill. 1962, D.C. 1967, U.S. Supreme Ct. 1975. Instr. U. Mich. Law Sch., 1963; assoc. prof. law U. Tex., 1964-67; mem. Surrey, Karasik, Gould & Greene, Washington, 1967-70; prof. Georgetown U. Law Ctr., Washington, 1970—ABA (chmn. rules of evidence and criminal procedure com., criminal justice sect. 1984—), univs.; spl. counsel U.S. Senate Jud. Com. Subcom. on Criminal Laws and Procedures, 1975-77, U.S. Ho. of Reps. Jud. Com. Subcom. on Criminal Law, 1980; cons. Treasury, 1967-74, HEW, 1970, Commrs. on Uniform State Laws, 1969-75, Nat. Acad. Scis., 1976-77, D.C. Law Revision Commn., 1976-78; speaker, coordinator numerous legal edn. seminars for judges and lawyers, 1970—. Recipient U. Iowa Legal Edn. award 1974, Disting. Pub. Service award Crime Victims Compensation Bd., 1978; other civic and profl. awards; Fulbright scholar, Oxford, Eng., 1962-63. Mem. Fed. Bar Assn. (chmn. fed. rules of evidence com. 1974-77, Disting. Service award 1975 nat. council 1976—, chmn. continuing legal edn. com. 1980), D.C. Bar (continuing legal edn. bd. 1980—), ABA (chmn. rules of evidence and criminal procedure com., criminal justice sect. 1984—), Assn. Am. Law Schs. (sec. evidence sect. 1976, chmn. 1977), Nat. Assn. Criminal Injuries Compensations Bds. (sec. 1977—), Internat. Assn. Criminal Injuries Compensation Bds. Author: Evidence in a Nutshell, 1970, 2d edit., 1981; Understanding the New Federal Rules of Evidence, 1973, 74, 75; Federal Rules of Evidence with Practice Comments and Annotations, 1978, 2d edit., 1981; Cases, Materials and Problems in Evidence, 1986; contbr. articles on evidence and trial to profl. jours.; editor-in-chief Northwestern U. Law Rev., 1960-61.

Office: Georgetown U Law Ctr 600 New Jersey Ave NW Washington DC 20001-2075

ROTHSTEIN, RONALD, professional basketball coach; b. Bronxville, NY, Dec. 27, 1942; m. Olivia Pierorazio; children: David, Dana. Grad., U. R.I., 1964; M degree, CCNY. Asst. coach Upsala Coll., 1974-75; high sch. coach, 1976-79; northeastern regional scout Atlanta Hawks, 1979-82, asst. coach, 1983-86; asst. coach Detroit Pistons, 1986-88, head coach, 1992-93; head coach Miami Heat, 1988-91; scout N.Y. Knicks, 1982-83; asst. coach Cleveland Cavaliers, 1993—. Office: care Cleveland Cavaliers 1 Center Ct Cleveland OH 44115-4001*

ROTHSTEIN, RUTH M., hospital adminstrator. Dir. Cook County Hosp., Chgo.; chief Cook County Bur. of Health Svcs. Mailing: Cook County Hosp 1835 W Harrison St Chicago IL 60612-3701*

ROTHSTEIN, SAMUEL, librarian, educator; b. Moscow, Jan. 12, 1921; arrived in Can., 1922, naturalized, 1929; s. Louis Israel and Rose (Checov) R.; m. Miriam Ruth Teitelbaum, Aug. 26, 1951; children: Linda Rose, Sharon Lee. BA, U. B.C., 1939, MA, 1940; grad. student, U. Calif., Berkeley, 1941-42, U. Calif., Berkeley, 1946-47; BLS, U. Calif., Berkeley, 1947; student, U. Wash., 1942-43; PhD (Carnegie Corp. fellow 1951-54), U. Ill., 1954; DLitt, York U., 1971. Teaching fellow U. Wash., 1942-43; prin. libr. asst. U. Calif., Berkeley, 1947; mem. staff U. B.C. Libr., Vancouver, Can., 1946-51, 54-62; acting univ. libr. U. B.C., Vancouver, Can., 1961-62, prof. libr. sci., 1961-86, prof. emeritus, 1986—, dir. Sch. Librarianship, 1961-70; vis. prof. U. Hawaii, 1969, U. Toronto, 1970, 79, Hebrew U., Jerusalem, 1973; mem. Commn. Nat. Plan Libr. Edn., 1963—; mem. assoc. com. sci. info. Nat. Rsch. Coun. Can., 1962-69; councillor B.C. Med. Libr. Svc., 1971; mem. exec. com. Pacific divsn. Can. Jewish Congress, 1962-69, Internat. House Assn. B.C., 1959-60; mem. Can. Adv. Bd. Sci. and Tech. Info.; mem. cabinet Combined Jewish Appeal of Greater Vancouver, 1992-95; pres. Vancouver Pub. Libr. Trust, 1987-88. Author: The Development of Reference Services, 1955, (with others) Training Professional Librarians for Western Canada, 1957, The University-The Library, 1972, Rothstein on Reference..., 1989; also articles.; co-editor: As We Remember It, 1970. Life mem. bd. dirs. Jewish Cmty. Ctr. of Greater Vancouver, pres., 1972-74; bd. dirs. Jewish Fedn. of Greater Vancouver, 1993—. Recipient Helen Gordon Stewart award, 1970, ALISE award Assn. Library Info. Sci. Edn., 1987, Beta Phi Mu award ALA, 1988. Mem. Can. Libr. Assn. (hon. life), Assn. Am. Libr. Schs. (pres. 1968-69), Can. Assn. Libr. Schs. (hon. life, pres. 1982-84), ALA (coun. 1963-69, Beta Phi Mu award 1988), B.C. Libr. Assn. (hon. life, pres. 1959-60), Pacific N.W. Libr. Assn. (pres. 1963-64, hon. life), Can. Libr. Assn. (hon. life, coun. 1958-60, Outstanding Svc. to Librarianship award 1986), Bibliog. Soc. Can. (coun. 1959-63), Can. Assn. Univ. Tchrs. Home: 1416 W 40th Ave, Vancouver, BC Canada

ROTHWELL, ALBERT FALCON, retired lawyer, retired natural resource company executive; b. N.Y.C., Sept. 2, 1926; s. Albert Cyril and Finita Maria (Falcon) R.; m. Jane Thomas, June 4, 1949 (dec. Dec. 1994); children: Susan, Peter, Anne, James. AB, Princeton U., 1948; LLB, Columbia U., 1951, postgrad., 1956-58. Bar: N.Y. Assoc. Sullivan & Cromwell, N.Y.C., 1951-56; chief exec. officer Nat. Potash Co., N.Y.C., 1972-75; v.p. Freeport Minerals Co., N.Y.C., 1975-81; sr. v.p., treas. Freeport-McMoRan Inc., N.Y.C., 1981-86, ret., 1986. Pres. Quioque Assn., Westhampton Beach, N.Y., 1982-83, Citizens for Good Schs., Glen Ridge, N.J., 1973-74; vice chmn. civic conf. com., Glen Ridge, 1970-71. Served with USN, 1944-46. Mem. Quantuck Yacht Club (commodore 1969-70), Quantuck Beach Club (Westhampton Beach, N.y., pres. 1989-92). Avocations: fishing, photography.

ROTHWELL, ROBERT CLARK, agricultural products executive; b. St. Louis, Dec. 7, 1939; s. Fountain and Frances Marie (Bickell) R.; m. Virginia Warren Hubbard, Apr. 18, 1961; children: Sharon Lee, James Clark, Janice Lynn, David Matthews. BSBA, U. Mo., 1967. CPA, Mo. Staff auditor Arthur Andersen & Co., Kansas City, Mo., 1967-71; internal auditor MFA, Inc., Columbia, Mo., 1971-75, mgr. auditing, 1975-79, contr., 1979-81, v.p. fin., 1981-88, treas., 1987—, sr. v.p. fin., 1988—; treas. Agmo Corp., Columbia, Morris Farms, Inc., Columbia, MFA of Okla., Columbia; mem. investment com. MFA Found., Columbia, MFA Employees Retirement Plan, Columbia; advisor U. Mo. Sch. Accountancy, Columbia, 1987-91. Author various presentations on fin. mgmt. Instr. Mo. Inst. Cooperation, Columbia, 1987-91; bd. dirs. Coop. Buyers Assn., Stuttgart, Ark., Inst. Coop. Fin. Officers, Mo. Coun. on Econ. Edn., Mid-Mo. Alzheimer's Assn., 1995—. Mem. AICPA, Mo. Soc. CPAs, Fin. Execs. Inst., Nat. Assn. Accts. for Coops., Nat. Coun. Farmer Coops. Republican. Office: MFA Inc 615 Locust St Columbia MO 65201-4831

ROTHWELL, TIMOTHY GORDON, pharmaceutical company executive; b. London, Jan. 8, 1951; came to us., 1966; s. Kenneth Gordon Rothwell and Jean Mary (Stedman) Davey; m. Joanne Claire Fleming; children: Tiffany, Heather. BA, Drew U., 1972; JD, Seton Hall U., 1976; LLM, NYU, 1979, MBA, 1983. With Sandoz Pharms., East Hanover, N.J., 1972—, patent atty., 1974-77, patent and trademark counsel, 1980-82, mng. ops. planning and adminstrn., 1982-84, dir. mktg. ops., 1984-85, exec. dir. field ops., 1985-86, v.p. field ops., 1986-87, pres. profl. bus. ops., 1987-88, corp. v.p., chief oper. officer, 1988-89; sr. v.p. sales Squibb Pharm. Group, Princeton, N.J., 1989-95; pres. Rhone, Poulenc, Rorer PharmaceuticalCo., Collegeville, PA, 1995—. Patentee in field. Mem. N.J. State Bar Assn., N.Y. State Bar Assn., Am. Soc. for Pharmacy Law, Nat. Health Care Quality Coun., Am. Found. for Pharm. Exec. (bd. dirs.), N.J. Patent Law Assn. (pres. 1986). Republican. Episcopalian. Avocations: philately, coaching youth soccer, golf, tennis. Office: Rhone, Poulenc, Rorer Pharmaceutical Co. 500 Arcola Rd Collegeville PA 19426*

ROTI, THOMAS DAVID, lawyer, food service executive; b. Evanston, Ill., Jan. 20, 1945; s. Sam N. and Theresa S. (Salerno) R.; m. Donna Sumichrast, July 22, 1972; children: Thomas S., Kyle D., Rebecca D., Gregory J. BS, Loyola U., Chgo., 1967, JD cum laude, 1970. Bar: Ill. 1970, U.S. Dist. Ct. (no. dist.) Ill. 1971, U.S. Ct. Appeals (7th cir.) 1971. Sr. law clk. to presiding justice U.S. Dist. Ct. No. Dist. Ill., 1971-72; assoc. Arnstein, Gluck & Lehr, Chgo., 1972-73, Boodell, Sears et al., Chgo., 1973-75; asst. gen. counsel Dominick's Finer Foods, Inc., Northlake, Ill., 1975-77, v.p., gen. counsel, 1977—; mem. lawyers & econs. com. Food Mktg. Inst., Washington, 1987—, legis. com. Ill. Retail Mchts. Assn., Chgo., 1987—. Trustee Joint Civic Com. Italian Ams., Chgo., 1986—; mem. Chgo. Coun. EDU-CARE Scholarship Program, 1988. Maj. U.S. Army, 1967-83. Recipient Am. Jurisprudence award, 1970; Alumni Assn. award Loyola U., 1970. Mem. ABA, Ill. Bar Assn., Chgo. Bar Assn., Am. Corp. Counsel Assn., Chgo. Zool. Soc., Loyola Alumni Assn., Art Inst. Chgo., Phi Alpha Delta, Alpha Sigma Nu. Roman Catholic. Home: 1141 Hunting Palatine IL 60067 Office: Dominick's Finer Foods Inc 333 Northwest Ave Northlake IL 60164-1604

ROTMAN, MORRIS BERNARD, public relations consultant; b. Chgo., June 6, 1918; s. Louis and Etta (Harris) R.; m. Sylvia Sugar, Mar. 1, 1944; children: Betty Ruth, Jesse, Richard. Student, Wright Jr. Coll., 1936-37, Northwestern U., 1937-39. Editor Times Neighborhood publs., Chgo., 1938-40; asst. editor City News Bur., 1940-42; mng. editor Scott Field Broadcaster, USAAF, 1942-43; publicity dir. Community and War Fund of Met. Chgo., 1943-45; v.p. William R. Harshe Assocs., 1945-49, pres., 1949-66; chmn. bd., chief exec. officer (name changed to Harshe-Rotman & Druck, Inc.), 1966-81; pres. Ruder Finn & Rotman, Inc. (merger of Harshe-Rotman & Druck and Ruder & Finn), 1982, ret.; founder Morris B. Rotman & Assocs., Chgo., 1989—; adj. prof. Coll. of Desert, Palm Desert, Calif. Chmn. solicitations pub. rels. div. Community Fund Chgo., 1948-49, spl. events chmn., 1953; chmn. communications div. Jewish Fedn. Chgo., 1965, Combined Jewish Appeal,1 966; life dir. Rehab. Inst. Chgo.; U.S. dir. The Shakespeare Globe Centre (N.Am.) Inc.; trustee Roosevelt U. (emeritus). Recipient Prime Minister Israel medal, 1969. Mem. Pub. Rels. Soc. Am. (past dir.), Chgo. Presidents' Orgn. (pres. 1970-71), Acad. Motion Picture Arts and Scis. (assoc.), Chief Execs. Orgn., Chgo. Press Vets. Assn., Standard Club, Tamarisk Country Club, Headline Club, Desert Rats (chair), Sigma Delta Chi. Home (winter): 3 Columbia Dr Rancho Mirage CA 92270-3149 Home (summer): 2650 N Lakeview Ave Apt 1701 Chicago IL 60614-1819

ROTT, NICHOLAS, fluid mechanics educator; b. Budapest, Hungary, Oct. 6, 1917; came to U.S. 1951; s. Alexander and Margaret (Pollak) R.; m. Rosanna Saredi, Sept. 30, 1944; children: Paul, Kathy. Diploma in Mechanical engring., Swiss Fed. Inst. Tech., Zurich, 1940; PhD, ETH, Zurich, 1944. Rsch. asst., pvt. dozent Aerodynamics Inst., Zurich, 1944-51; prof. Grad. Sch. Aeronautical Engring. Cornell U., Ithaca, N.Y., 1951-60; prof. UCLA, 1960-67, ETH, Zurich, 1967-83; vis. prof. Stanford (Calif.) U., 1983—. Fellow AIAA, Am. Phys. Soc.; mem. NAE, Acoustical Soc. Am. Home: 1865 Bryant St Palo Alto CA 94301 Office: Stanford U Aero Astro Dept Stanford CA 94305

ROTTER, PAUL TALBOTT, retired insurance executive; b. Parsons, Kans., Feb. 21, 1918; s. J. and LaNora (Talbott) R.; m. Virginia Sutherlin Barksdale, July 17, 1943; children—Carolyn Sutherlin, Diane Talbott. B.S. summa cum laude, Harvard U., 1937. Asst. mathematician Prudential Ins. Co. of Am., Newark, 1938-46; with Mut. Benefit Life Ins. Co., Newark, 1946—; successively asst. mathematician, asso. mathematician, mathematician Mut. Benefit Life Ins. Co., 1946-59, v.p., 1959-69, exec. v.p., 1969-80, ret., 1980. Mem. Madison Bd. Edn., 1958-64, pres., 1959-64; Trustee, mem. budget com. United Campaign of Madison, 1951-55; mem. bd., chmn. advancement com. Robert Treat council Boy Scouts Am., 1959-64. Fellow Soc. Actuaries (bd. govs. 1965-68, gen. chmn. edn. and exam. com. 1963-66, chmn. adv. com. edn. and exam. 1969-72); mem. Brit. Inst. Actuaries (asso.), Am. Acad. Actuaries (v.p. 1968-70, bd. dirs., chmn. edn. and exam. com. 1965-66, chmn. rev. and evaluation com. 1968-74), Asso. Harvard Alumni (regional dir. 1965-69), Actuaries Club N.Y. (pres. 1967-68), Harvard Alumni Assn. (v.p. 1964-66),Am. Lawn Bowls Assn. (pres. SW div.), Phi Beta Kappa Assos., Phi Beta Kappa. Clubs: Harvard N.J. (pres. 1956-57); Harvard (N.Y.C.); Morris County Golf (Convent, N.J.); Joslyn-Lake Hodges Lawn Bowling (pres. 1989-90). Home: 18278 Canfield Pl San Diego CA 92128-1002

ROTTER, STEPHEN A., film editor. Editor: (films) Night Moves, 1975, (with Dede Allen and Jerry Greenberg) The Missouri Breaks, 1976, (with Ronald Roose) The World According to Garp, 1982, (with Glenn Farr, Lisa Fruchtman, Douglas Stewart, and Tom Rolf) The Right Stuff, 1983 (Academy award best film editing 1983), (with Richard P. Cirincone) Target, 1985, Heaven Help Us, 1985, (with Cirincone and William Reynolds) Ishtar, 1987, (with William Scharf) Dirty Rotten Scoundrels, 1988, (with Vivien Hollgrove Gilliam and B.J. Sears) The Unbearable Lightness of Being, 1988, (with Scharf) An Innocent Man, 1989, My Blue Heaven, 1990, (with Robert Reitano) True Colors, 1991, Prelude to a Kiss, 1992, (with Scharf) Rising Sun, 1993, (with Scharf) Cops and Robbersons, 1994. Address: 40 W 86th St Ste 6B New York NY 10024

ROTTMAN, ELLIS, public information officer; b. Balt., Apr. 5, 1930; s. Abraham Isaac and Sadie (Harris) R.; m. Carol Parker Donovan, May 30, 1965; children—Marcus, Lisa, Jason, Adam. B.S., U. Md., 1952. Assoc. editor Army Times Pub. Co., Washington, 1956-59; editor, dir. pub. relations Am. Fedn. Govt. Employees, AFL-CIO, 1959-65; pub. info. officer U.S. Post Office Dept., 1966-69; editor Manpower mag. Dept. Labor, 1969-75; editor, publs. dir. FDA, Rockville, Md., 1975-78; public info. dir. Labor-Mgmt. Services Adminstrn. Dept. Labor, 1978-84; pub. info. officer Office Sec. of Labor, 1984-94. Served with AUS, 1952-54. Recipient Journalism award Internat. Labor Press Assn., AFL-CIO, 1959, 60, 61, 62, 64; award merit Fed. Editors Assn., 1974, 75, 77, 78. Jewish. Home: 901 N Belgrade Rd Silver Spring MD 20902-3247 Office: 2nd St and Constitution Ave NW Washington DC 20210

ROTTMANN, LEON HARRY, psychologist, educator; b. Table Rock, Nebr., Feb. 14, 1927; s. John Henry and Minnie Anna (Huntemann) R.; m. Clara Thoren, 1959 (div. 1967). BS, U. Nebr., 1955, MA, 1957, PhD, 1960. Lic. psychologist, Nebr.; cert. tchr., Nebr., Iowa. Asst. dir. guidance Albuquerque Pub. Schs., 1959-60; asst. prof. U. Minn., Mpls., 1960-67; lectr. U. Nebr., Omaha, 1968-75; ext. specialist in human devel., prof. U. Nebr., Lincoln, 1975-94, prof. emeritus, 1994—; del. Wellness Coun. of Midlands, Omaha, 1980-94. Editor Wellness Perspectives, 1984-89, consulting editor, 1989-92. Mem. APA, Am. Assn. Suicidology (exec. dir. 1982—), Celiac Sprue Assn. U.S.A. (editor Lifeline newsletter 1982—). Republican. Lutheran. Avocations: gardening, dachshunds. Home: 745 N 58th St Omaha NE 68132-2003

ROTUNDA, DONALD THEODORE, public relations consultant; b. Blue Island, Ill., Feb. 14, 1945; s. Nicholas and Frances (Manna) R. B.A., Georgetown U., 1967; M.A., London Sch. Econs., 1968, Ph.D., 1972. Analyst NASA, Washington, 1972; lectr. in econs. U. D.C., 1973; legis. asst. Ho. of Reps., Washington, 1974-76, economist budget com., 1977; mgmt. analyst Office Mgmt. and Budget, Washington, 1977-81; cons., 1981-82; mgr. editorial svcs. United Technologies Corp., Hartford, Conn., 1982-87, Pepsico, Inc., Purchase, N.Y., 1987-89, Union Carbide Corp., Danbury, Conn., 1989-90; dir. editorial svcs. Martin Marietta, Bethesda, Md., 1990-92; cons. pub. rels., 1992—. Contbr. numerous articles to Washington Post, New Republic, Saturday Rev. Roman Catholic. Home: 4431 Klingle St NW Washington DC 20016-3578

ROTUNDA, RONALD DANIEL, law educator, consultant; b. Blue Island, Ill., Feb. 14, 1945; s. Nicholas and Frances (Manna) R.; m. Marcia Ann Mainland, June 21, 1969; children—Nora, Mark. A.B. magna cum laude, Harvard U., 1967, J.D. magna cum laude, 1970. Bar: N.Y. 1971, U.S. Ct. Appeals (2d cir.) 1971, U.S. Ct. Appeals (D.C. cir.) 1971, U.S. Ct. Appeals (7th cir.) 1990, U.S. Supreme Ct. 1974, Ill. 1975. Law clk. U.S. Ct. Appeals (2d cir.), 1970-71; assoc. Wilmer, Cutler & Pickering, Washington, 1971-73; asst. majority counsel Watergate Com., U.S. Senate, Washington, 1973-74; asst. prof. U. Ill. Coll. Law, Champaign, 1974-77, assoc. prof., 1977-80, prof., 1980-93, Albert E. Jenner, Jr. prof. of law, 1993—; vis. prof. law European U. Inst., Florence, Italy, 1981; mem. profl. responsibility exam. com. Nat. Conf. Bar Examiners, 1980-87; constl. advisor Supreme Nat. Coun. Cambodia, 1993; cons. Supreme Ct. Modova, 1996. Author: (with Morgan) Problems and Materials of Professional Responsibility, 1976, 6th edit., 1996; (with Nowak and Young) Constitutional Law, 1978, (with Nowak) 2d edit., 1983, 3d edit., 1986, 4th edit., 1991, 5th edit., 1995, Modern Constitutional Law: Cases and Materials, 1981, 5th edit., 1995. Fulbright research scholar, Italy, 1981, Venezuela, 1986. Fellow Am. Bar Found. (life), Ill. Bar Found. (life); mem. Am. Law Inst. Roman Catholic. Office: U Ill Coll Law Rm 216 504 E Pennsylvania Ave Champaign IL 61820

ROTUNNO, GIUSEPPE, cinematographer; b. Rome, Italy, Mar. 19, 1923. Camera operator: (films) Senso, 1954; cinematographer: (films) Pane amore e..., 1955, Tosca, 1956, The Monte Carlo Story, 1957, Le notti bianche, 1957, Anna of Brooklyn, 1958, La Maja desnuda, 1958, La ragazza del palio, 1959, (with Daniel Fapp) On the Beach, 1959, (with Robert Gerardi) La grande guerra, 1959, The Angel Wore Red, 1960, Five Branded Women, 1960, Rocco e i suoi fratelli, 1960, The Best of Enemies, 1962, Boccaccio '70 ("The Job"), 1962, Cronaca familiare, 1962, Le guepard, 1963, I compagni, 1963, Ieri, oggi e domani, 1963, The Bible...In the Beginning, 1966, Lo straniero, 1967, Le streghe, 1967, Anzio, 1968, (with Aldo Graziata and Robert Krasker) Senso, 1968, Candy, 1968, Fellini Satyricon, 1969, The Secret of Santa Vittoria, 1969, Histoires extraordinaires ("Never Bet the Devil Your Head"), 1968, Sunflower, 1969, Carnal Knowledge, 1971, Man of La Mancha, 1972, Roma, 1972, Film d'amore e d'anarchia, 1973, Amarcord, 1974, Il bestione, 1974, Tutto a posto e niente in ordine, 1974, Il Casanova di Federico Fellini, 1976, Sturmtruppen, 1976, Divina Creatura, 1976, The End of the World in Our Usual Bed in a Night Full of Rain, 1978, Prova d'orchestra, 1978, All That Jazz, 1979 (Academy award nomination best cinematography 1979), La Citta delle donne, 1980, Popeye, 1980, (with William Garroni) Rollover, 1981, Bello mio bellezza mia, 1982, Five Days One Summer, 1982, E la nave va, 1983, American Dreamer, 1984, Non ci resta che piangere, 1984, Desiderio, 1984, The Assisi Underground, 1985, Red Sonja, 1985, Hotel Colonial, 1986, Julia and Julia, 1987, Rent-a-Cop, 1988, Haunted Summer, 1988, The Adventures of Baron Munchausen, 1989, Rebus, 1989, Regarding Henry, 1991, Once Upon a Crime, 1992, Wolf, 1994, (TV movies) The Scarlet and the Black, 1983. Office: The Gersh Agency 232 N Canon Dr Beverly Hills CA 90210-5302

ROTZOLL, KIM BREWER, advertising and communications educator; b. Altoona, Pa., Aug. 21, 1935; s. Fredrick Charles and Anna (Brewer) R.; m. Nancy Benson, Aug. 26, 1961; children: Keith, Kristine, Amanda, Jason. BA in Advt., Pa. State U., 1957, MA in Journalism, 1965, PhD in Sociology, 1971. Account exec. Ketchum, Macleod and Grove, Pitts., 1957-61; instr. advt. Pa. State U., University Park, 1961-71; asst. prof. advt. U. Ill, Urbana, 1971-72, assoc. prof., 1972-78, prof., 1978—, rsch. prof., head advt. dept., 1983-92; dean Coll. Comms., 1992—; lectr. in People's Republic of China, Bahrain. Author, co-author, editor: Is There Any Hope for Advertising, 1986, Advertising in Contemporary Society, 1990, Media Ethics, 1995, The Book of Gossage, 1995, Last Rights: Revisiting Four Theories of the Press, 1995. Named Disting. Advt. Educator of Yr. by Am. Advt. Fedn., 1992. Fellow Am. Acad. Advt. (pres. 1991); mem. Am. Advt. Found., Nat. Advt. Rev. Bd., Alpha Kappa Delta, Phi Kappa Phi. Democrat. Presbyterian. Avocations: reading, films, cycling. Office: U Ill 119 Gregory Hall 810 S Wright St Urbana IL 61801-3611

ROUB, BRYAN R(OGER), financial executive; b. Berea, Ohio, May 1, 1941; s. Bernard Augustus and Pearl Irene (Koeblitz) R.; m. Judith Elaine Penman, June 19, 1965; children: Paul, Bradley, Michael. Student, Ohio Wesleyan U., 1959-62; BS, Ohio State U., 1966; MBA, U. Pa., 1978. Mem. audit staff Ernst & Ernst, Cleve., 1966-70; asst. contr. Midland-Ross, Cleve., 1970-73, contr., 1973-81, v.p., 1977-81, sr. v.p., 1981-82, exec. v.p. fin., 1982-84; sr. v.p. fin. Harris Corp., Melbourne, Fla., 1984-93, sr. v.p., CFO, 1993—; mem. fin. coun. II Machinery and Allied Products Inst., Washington, 1978-84, coun. I, 1984—, vice chmn., 1994—, mem. conf. bd. coun. of CFO's, 1993—. Mem. adv. coun. Coll. Adminstrv. Scis., Ohio State U., 1978-81; mem. citizen's adv. coun. Westlake (Ohio) Schs., 1981-83; trustee Alcoholism Svcs. Cleve., 1982-84; mem. devel. bd. St. John's Hosp., 1983-84; pres. Westridge Homeowners' Assn., 1977; dir., treas. Tortoise Island Homeowners' Assn., 1988-90; bd. dirs. Easter Seal Soc. of Brevard County, 1993—. Mem. AICPA, Ohio Soc. CPAs, Fin. Execs. Inst. (treas. N.E. Ohio chpt. 1976-78, bd. dirs. 1980-81, 83-84, v.p. 1981-82, pres. 1982-83, bd. dirs. Orlando chpt. 1984—, v.p. 1985-86, pres. 1986-87, nat. bd. dirs. 1987-90, area v.p. 1990-91, chmn. budget and fin. com. 1988-89), Fin. Execs. Rsch. Found. (trustee 1994—, chmn. planning com. 1995—), Westwood Country Club, Eau Gallie Yacht Club (bd. govs., treas. 1990-92). Home: 556 Lanternback Island Dr Satellite Beach FL 32937-4712 Office: Harris Corp 1025 W Nasa Blvd Melbourne FL 32919-0001

ROUBOS, GARY LYNN, diversified manufacturing company executive; b. Denver, Nov. 7, 1936; s. Dorr and Lillian Margaret (Coover) R.; m. Terie Joan Anderson, Feb. 20, 1960; children: Lyndel, Leslie. BSChemE with high honors, U. Colo., 1959; MBA with distinction, Harvard U., 1963. With Boise Cascade Corp., 1963-71, Dieterich Standard Corp., Boulder, Colo., 1971-76; exec. v.p., then pres. Dieterich Standard Corp. (co. acquired by Dover Corp. 1975), 1975-76; exec. v.p. Dover Corp., N.Y.C., 1976, pres., 1977-93, chief exec. officer, 1981-94, chmn., 1989—; bd. dirs. Omicron Inc., N.Y.C., Bell & Howell Co., Skokie, Ill., Dovatron Internat. Inc., Boulder, Colo., Kimberly-Clark; trees. Fund, Darien, Conn.; mem. adv. bd. U. Colo. Envring. Devel. Coun. 1990—. 1st lt. C.E., U.S. Army, 1959-61. Mem. North River Yacht Club, Winged Foot Golf Club, Boulder Country Club, Phine Valley Golf Club, Econ. Club N.Y. Office: Dover Corp 280 Park Ave New York NY 10017-1216

ROUDANE, CHARLES, metal and plastics products company executive; b. Los Angeles, July 16, 1927; s. Rudolph and Irene (Warner) R.; BSME, Tulane, 1950; m. Orient Fox, Aug. 20, 1948; children: Mark, Matthew. Gen. mgr. Master div. Koehring Co., Chgo., 1955-67; gen. sales mgr. Wilton Corp., Schiller Park, Ill., 1967-70; dir. mktg. Flexonics div. UOP Inc., Bartlett, Ill., 1970-73, v.p., gen. mgr. div., 1973-83; pres., chief exec. officer Resistoflex Co. div. Crane Co., Marion, N.C., 1983-93; chmn., CEO ASM Corp., Chgo., 1993—; dir. Center Indsl. Mktg. Planning, Inc., PowRhouse Products, Inc. Served with AUS, 1945-46. Elected to Inaugural Hall of Fame, Am. Mgmt. Assn., 1978. Mem. Am. Mgmt. Assn. (former trustee, chmn. mktg. council, mem. internat. coun.), Chgo. Pres. Assn., ASME, Newcomen Soc. Gt. Britain. Republican. Presbyterian.

ROUDYBUSH, FRANKLIN, diplomat, educator; b. Washington, Sept. 17, 1906; s. Rumsey Franklin and Frances (Mahon) R.; student U. Vienna, 1925, Ecole National des Langues Orientales Vivantes, Paris, 1926, U. Paris, 1926-28, U. Madrid, 1928, Academie Julian, Paris, 1967; B.Fgn. Svc., 1930; postgrad. Harvard U., 1931; MA, George Washington U., 1944; PhD, U. Strasbourg (France), 1953; m. Alexandra Brown, May 22, 1941. Dean Roudybush Fgn. Svc. Schs., Washington, L.A., Phila., N.Y.C., 1932—. Prof. internat. econ. rels. Southeastern U., Washington, 1938-42; dir. Pan Am. Inst., Washington, 1934, London Econ. Conf., 1934, Internat. Textile Conf., Washington, 1935; editor Affairs, 1934-45; v.p. France Libre, Washington; censor Diplomatic Pouch World War II; commodity economist, statistician Dept. State, 1945; with Fgn. Svc. Inst., Dept. State, 1945-48, Council of Europe, Strasbourg and the Saar, Germany, 1948-54, Saar, 1949, Am. Embassy, Paris, 1954, Pakistan, 1955, Dublin, 1956; consular Acad. Vienna, 1925; mem. Punjab U., Lahore, Pakistan, 1954; mem., broadster Washington Pub. Affairs Forum, 1935-40. Creator: the cultural pouch for cultural attachees, 1957. Recipient prize Julian painting, Paris. Mem. Am. Soc. Internat. Law, Brit. Inst. Internat. and Comparative Law (London), Delta Phi Epsilon. Clubs: Assns. des Amis du Salon d'Automne (Paris); France Amerique; English Speaking Union (London); Nat. Press (Washington); Harvard (Paris), Royal Aberdeen Golf; Miramar Golf (Oporto, Portugal), Yacht (Angiers, France); Pormarnock Golf (Dublin); Les Societe des Artistes Independants Grand Palais (Paris). Author: The Twentieth Century; The Battle of Cultures; Diplomatic Language; Twentieth Century Diplomacy; The Present State of Western Capitalism, 1959; Diplomacy and Art, French Educational System, 1971; The Techniques of International Negotiation, 1979; The Diplomacy of the Cardinal, Duke de Richilieu, 1980, From Calcutta to Chungking, 1982, The Mysteries of Marsailles, 1983, Tea for Two, 1984, The Fromme Family, 1985, Casino Protocol, 1987, Talleyrand - The Diplomat, 1989, The French Government Political Science School, 1989, History of a Family During the XXth Century, 1990, The Flying Dutchman, 1990, Monsieur Fedeaux, 1990, Death in Darjeeling, 1991, The Alsatians, 1991, The Oriental Express to Constantinople and On To Teheran, 1992, The Elegant Facade of Macaó, 1992, Café Royal, 1993, The Roman Holiday, 1992, The Burlington Sisters, 1993, The Strange Fate of Madame Tarleton, 1980, Rendezvous in Basle, 1989, From Naples to Buenos Aires, 1977, Drawn Blinds, 1972. Home: Villa St Honoré, Moledo do Minho, Minho Portugal also: Sauveterre de Rouerque, 12800 Aveyron France

ROUECHE, JOHN EDWARD, II, education educator, leadership program director; b. Statesville, N.C., Sept. 3, 1938; s. John Edward and Mary (Harris) R.; m. Suanne Davis; 1 stepchild, Robin Sue Maca; children by previous marriage: Michelle Renee, John Edward III. BA, Lenoir Rhyne Coll., Hickory, N.C., 1960; MA, Appalachian Coll., Boone, N.C., 1961; PhD, Fla. State U., 1964. Dean Gaston Coll., Gastonia, N.C., 1964-67; assoc. rsch. educator U. Calif., L.A., 1967-69; dir. jr. coll. div. Nat. Lab. Higher Edn., 1968-71, also assoc. prof. edn. Duke U.; prof. edn., dir. c.c. leadership program U. Tex., Austin, 1971—, Sid W. Richardson regents chair, 1987—; mem. chancellor's coun. U. Tex. System, 1990—, U. Tex. Littlefield Soc., 1992—; lectr. Earl Pullias lectr. U. So. Calif., 1992, Coll. Bd. Disting. Lectr. N.Y.C., 1993, Frances Crain Cook Disting. Lectr. U. Tex., 1994; chmn. nat. ednl. adv. bd. Great Am. Res. Ins. Co., 1991-95; bd. dirs. Acordia Collegiate Benefits, Inc.; co-chair, Nat. Adv. Bd. for C.C.s, Invest Learning Corp., 1993—. C.C. editor Jossey-Bass Pubs., 1971-82; editor Creative Teaching Series, Media Systems Corp., 1980-85; mem. editorial bd. C.C. Times, C.C. Jour., 1990-94, others; author 33 books, including Profiles of Excellence in America's Schools, 1986, Access With Excellence, 1987, Shared Vision, 1989, Teaching As Leading, 1990, Under-representation: A Question of Diversity, 1991, Between a Rock and a Hard Place, 1993, The Company We Keep, 1995, Strangers in Their Own Land: Part Time Faculty, 1995, over 100 articles and monographs. Chmn. nat. community coll. adv. bd. Invest Learning Corp.; pres. Doss Sch. PTA, 1974-75; chmn. bd. N.W. Hills United Meth. Ch., 1973-76. Recipient Disting. Svc. award A.M.E. Ch., 1971, Disting. Rsch. award Nat. Coun. Univs. and Colls., 1990, Disting. Rsch. Publ. award, 1990, Outstanding Alumnus award Appalachian State U., 1979, Disting. Grad. award Fla. State U., 1981, Teaching Excellence award U. Tex., 1982, Outstanding Researcher award, 1985, Excellence award for outstanding learned article U.S. Edn. Press Assn., 1983, Disting. Rsch. award Nat. Assn. Devel. Edn., 1984, 86, Disting. Rsch. Publ. award Nat. Coun.

Student Devel., 1987, Disting. Rsch. award Nat. Coun. Staff, Program, and Orgn. Devel., B. Lamar Johnson Nat. Leadership award, 1988, Disting. Svc. & Leadership award, CCP, INC., 1993—; Disting Faculty award U. Texas, 1994; named lifetime ambassador for N.C., 1978; Kellogg fellow, 1962-64. Mem. Am. Assn. Community and Jr. Colls. (bd. dirs. 1989-94, Nat. Leadership award 1986, 1994, Disting. Rsch. award coun. univs. 1990, dist. rsch. sr. scholar award 1994, 96, nat. student devel. inter-assn. rsch. award 1995-96), Am. Assn. Higher Edn., Coun. Univs. and Colls. (past pres., bd. dirs.), Phi Beta Kappa, Phi Delta Kappa. Home: 6804 Edgefield Dr Austin TX 78731-2906 Office: U Tex Austin Coll Education Ste 348 Austin TX 78712

ROUGEOT, HENRI MAX, medical imaging engineer, physicist; b. Paris, Nov. 22, 1934; arrived in U.S., 1989; s. Henri Felix and Yvette Therese (Ferreira) R.; m. Fanny Astrid Brebion, July 11, 1960; children: Claire, Anne, Pierre, Helene. BSc, Acad. Paris, 1954; degree in math., physics and chemistry, U. Sorbonne, Paris, 1957, M in Physics, 1962; degree in physics of accelerators, Orsay (France) U., 1968. Rsch. engr. Nat. Ctr. Scientific Rsch., Strasbourg, France, 1962-64, Corp. Rsch. Lab., Orsay, 1964-69; project mgr. Thomson-CSF Electron Tube, Grenoble, France, 1969-74; engring. mgr. x-ray II Thomson CSF, Grenoble, 1974-85, tech. dir., 1985-89; program mgr. G.E. Corp. Rsch. & Devel., Schenectady, N.Y., 1989—. Author: Negative Election Affinity, Digital Imaging in Medicine, 1993. With Artillery, 1959-62, Algeria. Recipient grant Nat. Cancer Inst., 1993. Mem. Am. Assn. Physicists in Medicine. Roman Catholic. Achievements include development and promotion of fifth generation high resolution image intensifiers at Thomson-CSF standard in medical industry since 1989; initiation of concept and launching of panel digital radiography image detector at Thomson-CSF and development of a full field digital Mammography system at GE. Home: 2120 Van Antwerp Rd Schenectady NY 12309-1126 Office: Gen Elec River Rd Schenectady NY 12309

ROUGH, HERBERT LOUIS, insurance company executive; b. N.Y.C., Jan. 19, 1935; s. Albert and Jean (Bendeth) R.; m. Fern Sadkin Schultz; children: Lee Michael, Lisa Joi. BS, NYU, 1956. CLU, ChFC. From agt. to dist. mgr. Equitable Life Assurance Soc., N.Y.C., 1961-69; brokerage mgr. Bernard Bergen Cos., Inc., N.Y.C., 1969-73; pres., gen. agt. Rough Agy. Inc., Great Neck, N.Y., 1973—, Comprehensive Planning--Goodman, LLC, Hicksville, N.Y., 1988—, Rough Agy. Inc. of Fla., Ft. Lauderdale, 1991—; pres., mem. field adv. coun. Am. Gen. Life Ins. Co. of N.Y., Syracuse, 1978-83, Madison Life Ins. Co., N.Y.C., 1974-77; guest spkr. in field; instr. continuing edn. Broward c.C., Fla. Treasurer Gray Wig Repertory Theatre, Hofstra U., Uniondale, N.Y., 1981-84; pres. Heart Assn. of Great Neck, 1977. Capt. USAF, 1956-59. Mem. Life Underwriters Assn., Gold Coast Assn. of Health Underwriters (exec. bd. dirs.), Nat. Assn. Ind. Life Brokerage Agys., CLU Assn., Knickerbocker Yacht Club, Kiwanis (pres. Great Neck chpt. 1977—). Democrat. Jewish. Avocations: racquetball, tennis, singing. Office: Comprehensive Planning Group Ltd 99 N Broadway Hicksville NY 11801-2905

ROUGIER-CHAPMAN, ALWYN SPENCER DOUGLAS, furniture manufacturing company executive; b. Ostende, Belgium, Feb. 19, 1939; came to U.S., 1970; s. Douglas Alwyn and Simone (Stiernet) Rougier-C.; m. Christine Hayes, Mar. 14, 1964; children—Andrew Douglas, Duncan Peter. Chartered Acct., City of London Coll., 1963. Chartered acct., Eng. and Wales; C.P.A., Mich. Articled clk. Spain Bros., London, 1958-64; mgr. Deloitte & Co., Brussels, 1964-70; ptnr. Seidman & Seidman, Grand Rapids, Mich., 1970-81; v.p. planning Steelcase Inc., Grand Rapids, Mich., 1981-83, sr. v.p. fin., 1983—; dir. Meijer, Inc. Pres. French Soc., Grand Rapids, Mich., 1974-75; treas., vice chmn. Opera Grand Rapids, 1981-86, pres., 1987-89; treas. Grand Rapids Symphony, 1991—; bd. trustees Blodgett Meml. Hosp., 1989—; bd. dirs. Fin. Execs. Inst., Western Mich., 1988—, pres., 1991-92. Fellow Inst. Chartered Accts. Eng. and Wales; mem. Am. Inst. C.P.A.s (computer exec. com. 1977-81), Mich. Assn. C.P.A.s (auditing standards com. 1973-78). Roman Catholic. Clubs: Cascade Country, Peninsular (Grand Rapids). Avocations: golf; tennis; squash; travel; music (symphony and opera). Home: 2018 San Lu Rae Dr SE Grand Rapids MI 49506-3473 Office: 901 44th St SE Grand Rapids MI 49508-7575*

ROUHANA, WILLIAM JOSEPH, JR., business executive; b. Bklyn., June 23, 1952; s. William Joseph and Anna Freida (Stephan) R.; m. Claudia Caruso, Aug. 27, 1972; children: Timothy, Rosemary. BA, Colby Coll., 1972; JD, Georgetown U., 1976. Bar: N.Y. 1977, U.S. Dist. Ct. (so. and ea. dists.) N.Y. 1977. Founding ptnr. Beinhauer, Rouhana & Pike, N.Y.C., 1977-80; sole practice N.Y.C., 1980-81; ptnr. Rouhana and Trinko, P.C., N.Y.C., 1981-85, Baer, Marks & Upham, N.Y.C., 1985-86; pres. WinStar Corp., N.Y.C., 1984-90; chief exec. officer WinStar Ptnrs., N.Y.C., 1989-90, WinStar Oil Ptnrs., N.Y.C., 1990-91; chmn. Manson Internat., L.A., 1986-87; vice chmn. Mgmt. Co. Entertainment Group, Inc., L.A., 1987-90; bd. dirs., chmn., CEO Win Star Comm., Inc., 1989—; bd. dirs. Lancit Media Prodns., Ltd., 1991-94, TII Industries, Inc., 1992—, Found. Emmes, 1991-92; bd. overseers Colby Coll., 1987-90; bd. dirs., chmn. CEO WinStar Cos., Inc., 1990-94; vice chmn. UN Assn., 1996—, bd. govs., 1992—. Adv. bd. Nassau County Dem. Com., Jericho, N.Y., 1984, Bus. Execs. Nat. Security, 1991—. Grantee NSF, 1968, Thomas J. Watson Found., 1972-73. Mem. UN Assn. (bd. govs. 1992—, vice chmn. 1996—), Phi Beta Kappa. Democrat. Roman Catholic. Office: WinStar Communications Inc 230 Park Ave Fl 31 New York NY 10169-3199

ROUKEMA, MARGARET SCAFATI, congresswoman; b. Newark, N.J., Sept. 19, 1929; d. Claude Thomas and Margaret (D'Alessio) Scafati; m. Richard W. Roukema, Aug. 23, 1951; children—Margaret, Todd (dec.), Gregory. B.A. with honors in History and Polit. Sci, Montclair State Coll., 1951, postgrad. in history and guidance, 1951-53; postgrad. program in city and regional planning, Rutgers U., 1975. Tchr. history, govt., public schs. Livingston and Ridgewood, N.J., 1951-55; mem. 97th-103rd Congresses from 5th N.J. dist., Washington, D.C., 1981—; mem. Banking, Fin. Urban Affairs com., subcom. Housing, Community devel., Internat. devel., Fin., Trade, Monetary Policy, Econ. Growth on; mem. Credit formation, Edn. Labor com., subcom. labor mgmt. rels., elementary, sec., vocat. edn., post-secondary edn. tng.; vice pres. Ridgewood Bd. Edn., 1970-73; bd. dirs., co-founder Ridgewood Sr. Citizens Housing Corp.; chairwoman Fin. Inst. and Consumer Credit Sub. Com. U.S. Congress; sponcer Family Med. Leave U.S. Congress. Trustee Spring House, Paramus, N.J.; trustee Leukemia Soc. No. N.J., Family Counseling Service for Ridgewood and Vicinity; mem. Bergen County (N.J.) Republican Com.; NW Bergen County campaign mgr. for gubernatorial candidate Tom Kean, 1977. Mem. Bus. and Profl. Women's Orgn. Clubs: Coll. of Ridgewood, Ridgewood Rep. Office: US Ho of Reps 2469 Rayburn Bldg Washington DC 20515-0005 *I have served in several roles in my life. Wife, mother, teacher, public servant. All are personally rewarding; each affords the opportunity to help others in need and to enrich the lives of those around you. As a member of Congress, I find the most rewards are in the knowledge that I can truly make a difference and improve the lives of thousands of people. The challenges are frequently insurmountable, but the rewards are incalculable.**

ROULAC, STEPHEN E., real estate consultant; b. San Francisco, Aug. 15, 1945; s. Phil Williams and Elizabeth (Young) R.; children: Arthur, Fiona. BA, Pomona Coll., 1967; MBA with distinction, Harvard Grad. Sch. Bus. Adminstrn., 1970; JD, U. Calif., Berkeley, 1976; PhD, Stanford U., 1978. CPA, Hawaii. Asst. constrn. supt., foreman, adminstr. Roulac Constrn. Co., Pasadena, Calif., 1963-66; rsch. asst. Econs. Rsch. Assocs., L.A., 1966-67; assoc. economist Urbanomics Rsch. Assocs., Claremont, Calif., 1967; acquisition auditor Litton Industries Inc., Chgo., Beverly Hills, 1967-68; tax cons. Lybrand, Ross Bros. and Montgomery, L.A., 1968; cons. to constrn. group and corp. planning dept. Owens-Corning Fiberglas Corp., Toledo, 1969-70; CEO Questor Assocs., San Francisco, 1972-83; chmn. nat. mgmt. adv. svcs. Kenneth Leventhal & Co., 1983-84; pres. Stephen E. Roulac & Co., 1985-86; mng. ptnr. Roulac Group of Deloitte Haskins & Sells (Deloitte & Touche), 1987-91; CEO The Roulac Group, Larkspur, Calif., 1992—; strategic and fin. econ. cons.; expert witness, preparer econ. analyses for legal matters including civil trial of Irvine Co., Jewell et. al. vs. Bank of Am., Tchrs. vs. Olympia & York, Calif. Legis., Calif. Corps. Dept., Midwest Securities Commrs. Assn., Nat. Assn. Securities Dealers, SEC, Dept. of Labor, HUD; advisor to investment arm of Asian country, Calif. Pub. Employees Retirement System, U.S. Dept. Labor, numerous others; adj. prof. Tex. A&M U., 1986, U. Chgo., 1985, UCLA, 1983-84, Stanford Grad. Sch. Bus., 1970-79, Pacific Coast Banking Sch., 1978, Hastings Coll. Law, 1977-78, U. Calif., Berkeley, 1972-77, Calif. State U., 1970-71, Northeastern U., 1969-70; keynote speaker, instr. continuing edn. sessions, program chmn., corps., orgns. Author: Real Estate Syndications Digest: Principles and Applications, 1972, Case Studies in Property Development, 1973, Syndication Landmarks, 1974, Tax Shelter Sale-Leaseback Financing: The Economic Realities, 1976, Modern Real Estate Investment: An Institutional Approach, 1976, (with Sherman Maisel) Real Estate Investment and Finance, 1976 (1976 Bus. Book of Yr. The Libr. Jour.); editor-in-chief, pub. Calif. Bicyclist, 1988—, Tex. Bicyclist, 1989—, Roulac's Strategic Real Estate, 1979-89; columnist Forbes, 1983, 84, 87, 92, 93; mem. editorial adv. bd. Am. Real Estate and Urban Econs. Assn. Jour., 1977-81, Housing Devel. Reporter, 1978-80, Fin. Edn. Jour., 1976-70; contbg. editor Real Estate Law Jour., 1973-78, Real Estate Rev., 1973-75; spl. issue editor Calif. Mgmt. Rev., 1976; editor: Real Estate Syndication Digest, 1971-72, Notable Syndications Sourcebook, 1972, Real Estate Securities and Syndication: A Workbook, 1973, Due Diligence in Real Estate Transactions, 1974, Real Estate Venture Analysis, 1974, Real Estate Securities Regulation Sourcebook, 1975, Questor Real Estate Investment Manager Profiles, 1982, Questor Real Estate Securities Yearbook, 1980-85, Retail Giants and Real Estate, 1986, Roulac's Top Real Estate Brokers, 1984-88; contbr. articles to profl. jours., newspapers; cassettes; frequent appearer on TV shows including MacNeil/Lehrer Newshour, 1986, Cable News Network, 1987, ABC TV, 1987, KCBS Radio, 1986, WABC Radio, Dallas, 1986. Mem. real estate adv. com. to Calif. Commr. Corps., 1973, Calif. Corp. Commr.'s Blue Ribbon Com. on Projections and Track Records, 1973-74; mem. adv. bd. Nat. Bicycle Month, League of Am. Wheelmen, Ctr. for Real Estate Rsch. Kellogg Grad. Sch. Mgmt., Northwestern U. Named Highest Instr. Student Teaching Evaluations, Schs. Bus. Adminstrn., U. Calif., Berkeley, 1975-76; named to Pomona Coll. Athletic Hall of Fame, 1981; W.T. Grant fellow Harvard U., 1969-70,; George F. Baker scholar Harvard Grad. Sch. Bus. Adminstrn., 1970; Stanford U. Grad. Sch. Bus. fellow, 1970-71. Mem. Strategic Mgmt. Soc., Acad. Mgmt., Am. Real Estate and Urban Econs. Assn., Intuition Network, World Future Soc. (exec. com. and adv. bd. World 2000), Am. Econ. Assn., Am. Real Estate Soc. (pr), Noetic Soc., Nat. Bur. Real Estate Rsch. (founder, bd. dirs.), Harvard Club N.Y., L.A. Adventures Club. Avocations: arts, antiquarian books, reading, bicycle racing (U.S. team 1990), outdoor activities. Office: The Roulac Group 900 Larkspur Landing Cir Larkspur CA 94939-1723

ROULEAU, REYNALD, bishop; b. St.-Jean-de-Dieu, Que., Can., Nov. 30, 1935. Ordained priest, 1963, bishop, 1987. Bishop Churchill-Hudson Bay, 1987—. Office: Diocese of Churchill-Baie D'Hudson, C P 10, Churchill, MB Canada R0B 0E0

ROULSTON, THOMAS HENRY, investment adviser; b. N.Y.C., Apr. 6, 1933; s. Henry Davies and Marjorie (Heather) R.; m. Lois Mueller, July 31, 1954; children: Scott Davies, Thomas Henry III, Heather Ettinger. BA, Dartmouth, 1955. Vice pres. Gunn, Carey & Roulston (stockbrokers), Cleve., 1960-63; pres. Roulston & Co., Inc., Cleve., 1963-90, chmn., 1990—; vice chmn. Bank Roulston Ltd., Zurich, Switzerland, 1972-76; pres., chmn. Investment Guidance Fund, 1967-80; chmn., dir. Womens Fed. Savs. Bank, 1983-93; chmn. bd. dirs. MJM Industries, 1994—, Defiance, Inc., 1990—, Continental Pharmacy, 1994, Ramwear, 1994—, Roulston Investment Capital Corp., Roulston Capital Ltd.; chmn. Roulston Investment Trust, Roulston Venture Fund; bd. dirs. City Life Inc.; dir., chmn. bd. RB Mfg. Co., 1995-96. Mem. Ohio Criminal Justice Supervisory Commn., 1970-73; chmn. Adminstrn. of Justice Com., 1968-70; past trustee Soc. for Crippled Children, Hill House, Health Hill Hosp., Cleve. Coun. World Affairs, Choate Rosemary Hall, Lakeview Cemetery Assn.; trustee, mem. exec. com. Univ. Circle, Inc.; trustee, chmn. Bluecoats Inc., State Troopers; vice chmn. Midtown Corridor, 1981-84; past trustee Cleve. State U. Devel. Found. Capt. USAF, 1955-58. Mem. World Bus. Coun., Chief Execs. Orgn., Union Club, Country Club, Pepper Pike Club, Univ. Club (chmn.), Country Club of the Rockies. Home: 2627 Fairmount Blvd Cleveland Heights OH 44106-3601 Office: 4000 Chester Ave Cleveland OH 44103-3612

ROUMAN, JOHN CHRIST, classics educator; b. Tomahawk, Wis., May 1, 1926; s. Christ and Soteria (Dedes) R. BA in Greek, Carleton Coll., 1950; MA in Greek, Columbia U., 1951; student, Rutgers U., 1951-53, U. Kiel, Germany, 1956-57, U. Minn., Mpls., 1959-60; PhD in Classics, U. Wis., 1965. German tchr. Seton Hall Preparatory Sch., South Orange, N.J., 1954-56; ancient history tchr. Malverne (N.Y.) High Sch., 1957-59; tchg. asst. in ancient history U. Wis., Madison, 1960-61, rsch. asst. in ancient history, 1961-65; rsch. asst. in Greek epigraphy Inst. Advanced Study, Princeton, N.J., 1962-63; asst. prof. Classics U. N.H., Durham, 1965-71, assoc. prof., 1971-91, prof., 1991—; examiner N.H. State Bd. Edn. in Latin and Greek, 1979-80; judge Warren H. Held Jr. Exam-Contests in Latin and Mythology, 1988—; cons. Nat. Classical Greek Examination, 1980; presenter, lectr. in field. Active Colovos Rd. Com., 1981-82. With USN, 1944-46. Fulbright scholar U. Kiel, 1956-57; recipient Disting. Tchg. award U. N.H. Alumni Assn., 1985, Pericles award Am. Hellenic Ednl. Progressive Assn. and Daus. of Penelope, 1993. Mem. Am. Classical League (rep. to TCNE at ann. meeting 1978, mem. fin. com. 1981-82, treas. 1982-83), Am. Philol. Assn. (Nat. Excellence in Teaching Classics award, 1991), Archaeol. Inst. Am., Classical Assn. Can., Classical Assn. New Eng. (mem. exec. com. at-large 1981-84, mem. nominating com. 1983-84, 86-87, pres. 1987-88, Barlow-Beach award 1991, mem. ad hoc com. on elections and appointments), Medieval Acad. Am., Modern Greek Studies Assn., Nat. Assn. Advisors for Health Professions, N.H. Classical Assn. (mem. exec. com. 1965—, chair nominating com. 1986—), Strafford County Greco-Roman Found. (pres. 1978—), Vergilian Soc. Am., Phi Kappa Theta (faculty advisor, 1982—, chmn. nat. bd., 1993—). Office: U NH Dept Spanish and Classics 209G Murkland Hall Durham NH 03824-3596

ROUND, ALICE FAYE BRUCE, school psychologist; b. Ironton, Ohio, July 19, 1934; d. Wade Hamilton and Martha Matilda (Toops) Bruce; children: Leonard Bruce, Christopher Frederick. BA, Asbury Coll., 1956; MS in Sch. Psychology, Miami U., Oxford, Ohio, 1975. Cert. tchr., sch. psychologist, supr., Ohio; cert. tchr., Calif. Tchr. Madison County (Ohio) Schs., 1956-58, Columbus (Ohio) Pub. Schs., 1958, San Diego Pub. Schs., 1958-60, Poway (Calif.) Unified Sch. Dist., 1960-64; substitute tchr. Princeton City Schs., Cin., 1969-75; sch. psychologist, intern Greenhills/Forest Park City Schs., Cin., 1975-76; sch. psychologist Fulton County Schs., Wauseon, Ohio, 1976-77, Sandusky (Ohio) pub. and Cath. schs., 1977-96; tchr. art cmty. group and pvt. lessons, Sandusky, 1962, Springdale, Ohio, 1962-69; mem. Youth Svcs. Bd., Sandusky, 1978-88; bd. dirs., cons. Sandusky Sch. Practical Nursing, 1983-91; presenter suicide prevention seminars for mental health orgns.; speaker at ch., civic and youth orgns., local radio and TV programs; cons. on teen pregnancy to various schs., health depts. Mem. Huron (Ohio) Boosters Club, 1978-92, Vols. in Action, Sandusky, 1987—. Mem. NAACP, NEA, Nat. Sch. Psychologist Assn., Ohio Sch. Psychologist Assn., Maumee Valley Sch. Psychologist Assn., Ohio Edn. Assn., Sandusky Edn. Assn., Phi Delta Kappa (historian 1984-88, Most Innovative Preservation of History award 1988). Home: 821 Seneca Ave Huron OH 44839-1842 Office: Sandusky Bd Edn 407 Decatur St Sandusky OH 44870-2442

ROUNDS, DONALD EDWIN, cell biologist; b. Maywood, Ill., Jan. 17, 1926; s. Howard Gilmore and Dorothy May (Stucker) R.; m. Helen Lorraine Cann, Mar. 16, 1951 (dec. 1986); children: Robin Anne, Wendy Jeanne; m. Janice Mary Price, Oct. 17, 1987. BA, Occidental Coll., 1951; PhD, UCLA, 1958. Research asso. med. br. U. Tex., Galveston, 1958-59; dir. dept. cell biology Pasadena Found. for Med. Research, Calif., 1959-65; research coordinator Pasadena Found. for Med. Research, 1965-72, sr. research investigator, dir. carcinogenesis lab., 1972-82; dir. cell biology and laser labs. Huntington Med. Research Insts., 1982-90; chief scientist Advanced Med. Diagnostics Ltd., 1990-94, dir., cons., 1995—; prof. Loma Linda Med. Sch., 1974—; adj. prof. U. So. Calif. Med. Sch. Contbr. numerous articles to profl. jours., also chpts. books.; Reviewing editor: In Vitro, 1970-83. Served with U.S. Army, 1945-47. Mem. AAAS, Am. Soc. Zoologists, Tissue Culture Assn., Am. Soc. Cell Biologists, Am. Film Assn., Am. Inst. Biol. Scis., Sigma Xi. Home: 3111 NW Norwood Pl Corvallis OR 97330-1150

ROUNDS, DONALD MICHAEL, public relations executive; b. Centralia, Ill., May 9, 1941; s. Donald Merritt and Alice Josephine (Soulsby) R.; m. Alma Genevieve Beyer, Dec. 13, 1975. BS in History, Polit. Sci., Colo. State U., 1963. Police reporter, night city editor The Rocky Mountain News, Denver, 1960-70; mgr. Don M. Rounds Co., Denver, 1970-75; sr. editor Western Oil Reporter, Denver, 1975-80; energy writer The Rocky Mountain News, Denver, 1980-87; sr. media rels. advisor Cyprus Minerals Co., Englewood, Colo., 1987-92; media and community rels. mgr., 1992-93; media and community rels. mgr. Cyprus Amax Minerals Co., Englewood, 1994-95, dir. coms., 1995—; adv. bd Colo. State Minerals, Energy, and Geology (appointed by gov.), 1992—. Contbr. articles to mags. and newspapers. Sec. covenant com. Ken Caryl Ranch Master Assn., Littleton, Colo., 1980-84. Recipient MerComm Mercury Gold award, 1995, MerComm Silver award (Denver Post), 1995, 1st pl. spl. news series AP, 1987, 1st pl. news sweepstakes, 1987, Margolin award U. Denver Coll. Bus., 1986, Betty McWhorter Commendation of Honor Desk & Derrick Club of Denver, 1987, Journalism award Rocky Mountain Assn. Geologists, 1985, Citizen Svc. award Denver Police Dept., 1969, Pub. Svc. award Englewood Police Dept., 1967. Mem. Nat. Mining Assn. (pub. rels. com.), Soc. Profl. Journalists, Sigma Delta Chi, Denver Press Club (bd. dirs. 1987). Republican. Methodist. Avocations: scuba diving, skiing, hiking, photography. Home: 8220 S San Juan Range Rd Littleton CO 80127-4011 Office: Cyprus Amax Minerals Co 9100 E Mineral Cir Englewood CO 80112-3401

ROUNICK, JACK A., lawyer, company executive; b. Phila., June 5, 1935; s. Philip and Nettie (Brownstein) R.; BBA, U. Mich., 1956; JD, U. Pa., 1959; m. Noreen A. Garrigan, Sept. 4, 1970; children: Ellen, Eric, Amy, Michelle. Bar: Pa. 1960, U.S. Dist. Ct. (ea. dist.) Pa., 1960. Spl. asst. atty. gen., 1963-71; ptnr. Israelit & Rounick, 1960-67, Moss & Rounick, 1968-69, Moss, Rounick & Hurowitz, Norristown, Pa., 1969-72, Moss & Rounick, Norristown, 1972-73; ptnr. Pechner, Dorfman, Wolffe, Rounick and Cabot, Norristown, 1973-87; pres., CEO Think Big!, Inc., 1992-96; v.p., gen. counsel Martin Lawrence Ltd. Edits., Inc., 1987-93; dir. Martin Lawrence Ltd. Edits., Inc., 1984—, Deb Shops, Inc., 1974—. Fin. chmn. Pa. Young Rep., 1964-66, treas., 1966-68, chmn., 1968-70; supporting assoc. Solomon R. Guggenheim Foun. Recipient Boss of Yr. award Montgomery County Legal Secs. Assn., 1970, Cert. of appreciation Pa. Bar Inst., 1980. Fellow Internat. Acad. Matrimonial Lawyers, Am. Acad. Matrimonial Lawyers (pres. Pa. chpt. 1982-84, gov. 1983-85, v.p. 1985-87); mem. ABA (coun. family law sect. 1982-87), Pa. Bar Assn. (past chmn. family law sect., Spl. Achievement award 1979-80), Montgomery Bar Assn., Am. Friends of the Hebrew U. (v.p. 1990-91, bd. dirs. 1987-93, Nat. Coun. Trustees 1987-93, pres. Phila. chpt. 1988-91). Republican. Jewish. Author: Pennsylvania Matrimonial Practice, 6 vols., 1982; editor Pa. Family Lawyer, 1980-87. Office: 516 Swede St Norristown PA 19401

ROUNTREE, ASA, lawyer; b. Birmingham, Ala., Aug. 9, 1927; s. John Asa and Cherokee Jemison (Van de Graaff) R.; m. Elizabeth Rhodes Blue, Aug. 11, 1951; children—Robert B., John A. A.B., U. Ala., 1949; LL.B., Harvard U., 1954. Bar: Ala. 1954, U.S. Dist. Ct. (no. dist.) Ala. 1954, U.S. Ct. Appeals (5th cir.) 1955, N.Y. 1962, U.S. Dist. Ct. (so. dist.) N.Y. 1963, U.S. Ct. Appeals (2d cir.) 1963, U.S. Supreme Ct. 1972. Assoc. Cabaniss & Johnston, Birmingham, Ala., 1954-60, ptnr., 1960-62; assoc. Debevoise & Plimpton, N.Y.C., 1962-63, ptnr., 1963-91; mem. Maynard, Cooper, & Gale, P.C., Birmingham, 1991—. Bd. dirs. U. Ala. Law Sch. Found. Served with U.S. Army, 1945-46, to lt., 1951-53. Mem. ABA (chmn. litigation sect. 1980-81), Ala. Bar Assn., N.Y. State Bar Assn., Assn. Bar City N.Y., Am. Law Inst., Am. Coll. Trial Lawyers, Am. Bar Found. Episcopalian. Clubs: River (N.Y.C.); Mountain Brook (Birmingham). Office: Maynard Cooper Gale PC 2400 AmSouth/Harbert Plz 1901 6th Ave N Birmingham AL 35203-2618

ROUNTREE, GEORGE DENTON, health services management consultant; b. Houston, Mar. 14, 1937; s. George Washington and Verda Mae (Wagnon) R. B.S., Lamar U., 1960; M.H.A., Washington U., St. Louis, 1963; postgrad. Grad. Sch. Bus. and Public Health, Harvard U., 1976. Vice pres. Methodist Hosp., Houston, 1963-75; pres. Quadrus Internat. Inc. Tex., Houston, 1977—. Adj. asst. prof. Washington U. Med. Sch., St. Louis, 1978-85; adj. prof. U. Istanbul, Turkey; guest lectr. U. Tex. Health Sci. Ct., Houston, 1983. Contbr. articles to profl. jours. Mem. profl. adv. com. Mental Health Assn. Houston and Harris County; adv. and instl. rep. Boy Scouts Am. Served with USNR, 1956-63. Fellow Am. Coll. Hosp. Adminstrs.; mem. Houston C. of C. (chmn. art com. Ronald McDonald House), Am. Assn. Hosp. Planning, Greater Houston Hosp. Council, Nat. Council Internat. Health, Assn. Univ. Programs in Health Adminstrn. Club: Rotary. Home: 1101 Post Oak Blvd Ste 9B Houston TX 77056-3105 Office: Am Hosp Istanbul, Guzelbahce Sokak Nisantasi, 80220 Istanbul Turkey

ROUNTREE, JANET CARYL, astrophysicist; b. Chgo., Aug. 14, 1937; d. Ernest Alonzo and Frances Careta (Vogel) R.; m. J. Harold Lesh, Apr. 19, 1960 (div. 1971); 1 child, Kathryn Frances; m. Morris L. Aizenman, June 24, 1977. A.B., Cornell U., 1958; postgrad., U. Paris, 1958-60; Ph.D., U. Chgo., 1967. Sci. officer Leiden (Netherlands) Obs., 1968-70; astronomer adjoint Meudon (France) Obs., 1970-71; vis. fellow U. Colo., 1971-72; research astronomer, lectr. astronomy U. Denver, 1972-77, dir. obs. ops., 1974-77; rsch. prof. of elec. and computer engring. U. Ariz., 1994—; NASA-NRC sr. resident research asso. Goddard Space Flight Center, 1977-79; phys. scientist Dept. Air Force, 1979-93; cons., sr. scientist Sci. Applications Internat. Corp., 1993—. English lang. editor, translator: Astronomy and Astrophysics: A European Jour, 1969-71; Contbr. numerous articles to profl. publs.; translator books from French, numerous articles from French and German. Fulbright fellow, 1958-60. Mem. Internat. Astron. Union (commn. mem.), Am. Astron. Soc., Royal Astron. Soc., Fulbright Alumni Assn. (dir. 1978-83, nat. capital area, treas. 1991-93), Phi Beta Kappa, Sigma Xi, Phi Kappa Phi. Achievements include visible and ultraviolet classification systems for early-type stars. Office: PO Box 65285 Tucson AZ 85728-5285

ROUNTREE, LINDA SUE, special education educator; b. Marshall, Mo., Oct. 14, 1947; d. Thomas Arnel and Helen Louise (Ray) Meads; m. Thomas Tipton, May 14, 1983; 1 child, Lisa Susanne Meads Adkins. AA, Longview Community Coll., Lee's Summit, Mo., 1987; BS in Edn. cum laude, Cen. Mo. State U., Warrensburg, 1990; student, Mo. Valley Coll., Marshall, Mo., 1966-67. Technician AT&T, Lee's Summit, Mo., 1969-87; tchr. spl. edn. Lee's Summit Sch. Dist., 1990, Midway Sch. Dist., Cleveland, Mo., 1990—; discussion leader Student Teaching conf., Warrensburg, Mo., 1990; guest speaker on the impact of HIV/AIDs on families. Recipient Crystal Apple award for excellence in teaching, 1995. Mem. Coun. Exceptional Children, Learning Disabilities Assn., Kappa Delta Pi, Phi Kappa Phi. Home: 202 18th Ave N Greenwood MO 64034-9673 Office: Midway Sch Dist Cleveland MO 64734

ROUNTREE, NEVA DIXON, public relations executive; b. Jacksonville, Fla., Dec. 13, 1943; d. Jarma E. and Helen (McIlvaine) Dixon; m. Don C. Rountree, Mar. 23, 1941; 1 child, Don C. III. AB in Journalism, U. Ga., 1964, MA, 1979. Press sec. Underwood for U.S. Senate, Atlanta, 1979-80; account exec. Cohn & Wolfe, Atlanta, 1980-81; v.p. Carl Byoir & Assocs., Atlanta, 1981-84; pres. Rountree Group, Inc., Atlanta, 1985—. Co-chmn. Leadership Sandy Springs, Ga., 1985-86, trustee, 1986—; adv. bd. Northside Found., 1994—; comm. com. Atlanta Com. for Olympic Games, 1990-92. Recipient 1 of 3 Best Run Agys. award Atlanta Bus. Chronicle, 1988, 89; named 25 Hot Smaller Pub. Rels. Agys. by Inside Pub. Rels., 1992, named Best Mktg. Driven Pub. Rels. by Atlanta Bus. Chronicle, 1991, 92. Mem. Pub. Rels. Soc. Am. (Counselors Acad., pres. Ga. chpt. 1994—, George Goodwin award 1992), Pub. Rels. Exch. (bd. dirs. 1987—), U. Ga. Journalism Alumni Assn. (v.p., pres. 1986-89). *

ROUPE, JAMES PAUL, accountant; b. Havre de Grace, Md., Apr. 20, 1957; s. Paul Clyde and Shirley Louise (Trivette) R. AA, Harford C.C., Bel Air, Md., 1977; BS, Towson State U., 1979. CPA, Md. Mgmt. asst. Loyola Fed. Savings and Loan, Balt., 1979-81; asst. treas. Legum Chevrolet-Nissan, Balt., 1983-89; contr. Bob Bell Chevrolet/Nissan, Inc., Balt., 1989-92, corp. sec.-treas., 1992—; sr. controller Bob Bell Chevrolet Geo of Bel Air (Md.) Inc., 1991-92, corp. sec.-treas., 1992—; corp. sec.-treas. Bob Bell of Upper Marlboro (Md.), L.C., 1995—. Recipient Bus. Mgmt. Excellence award Nissan Motor Corp., 1990-95. Mem. AICPA, Md. Assn. CPAs, Inst. Mgmt. Accts., Chevrolet Coun. Bus. Acctg. Mgrs., Soc. for Preservation and Encouragement of Barbershop Quartet Singing in Am., Inc. (Dundalk, Md.

chpt., mem. Midnight Run barbershop quartet). Republican. Baptist. Office: Bob Bell Chevrolet Nissan 7900 Eastern Ave Baltimore MD 21224-2125

ROURKE, MICKEY (PHILIP ANDRE ROURKE, JR.), actor; b. Miami, Fla., 1956; m. Debra Feuer (div.); m. Carre Otis. Appearences include (films) including 1941, 1979, Heaven's Gate, 1980, Fade to Black, 1980, Body Heat, 1981, Diner, 1982, Rumblefish, 1983, The Pope of Greenwich Village, 1984, Year of the Dragon, 1985, Eureka, 1985, 9 1/2 Weeks, 1985, Angel Heart, 1987, A Prayer for the Dying, 1987, Barfly, 1987, Homeboy (also screenwriter), 1988, Johnny Handsome, 1989, Wild Orchid, 1990, The Desperate Hours, 1990, Harley Davidson and the Marlboro Man, 1991, White Sands, 1992, (TV movies) Act of Love, 1980, City in Fear, 1980, Rape and Marriage: The Rideout Case, 1980. *

ROUS, STEPHEN NORMAN, urologist, educator; b. N.Y.C., Nov. 1, 1931; s. David H. and Luba (Margulies) R.; m. Margot Woolfolk, Nov. 12, 1966; children: Benjamin, David. A.B., Amherst Coll., 1952; M.D., N.Y. Med. Coll., 1956; M.S., U. Minn., 1963. Diplomate: Am. Bd. Urology. Intern Phila. Gen. Hosp., 1956-57, resident, 1959-60; resident Flower-Fifth Ave. and Met. Hosp., N.Y.C., 1957-59, Mayo Clinic, Rochester, Minn., 1960-63; practice medicine specializing in urology San Francisco, 1963-68; assoc. prof. urology N.Y. Med. Coll., N.Y.C., 1968-72; assoc. dean N.Y. Med. Coll., 1970-72; prof. surgery, chief div. urology Mich. State U., East Lansing, 1972-75; prof., chmn. dept. urology Med. U. S.C., Charleston, 1975-88; urologist-in-chief Med. U. S.C. and County hosps., Charleston, 1975-88; editorial dir. Norton Med. Books div. W.W. Norton and Co., 1988-94, editorial cons., 1994—; clin. prof. surgery Uniformed Svcs. U. of Health Scis., Bethesda, Md., 1992—; adj. prof. urology Med. U. S.C., 1988—, adj. prof. surgery Dartmouth Med. Sch., 1988-91, prof. surgery (urology), 1991—; staff urologist Dartmouth-Hitchcock Med. Ctr., 1991—; cons. urologist Saginaw VA Hosp., 1971-75, Charleston VA Hosp., 1975-88; hon. cons. St. Peter's Hosp., London, 1981-82; sr. vis. fellow Inst. Urology, London, 1981-82; mil. cons. in urology USAF Surgeon Gen., 1982-85; chmn. alumni devel. com. Mayo Clinic, 1979-82; hon. staff The Exeter Hosp., N.H., 1988—; mem. nat. bd. visitors N.Y. Med. Coll., 1988—; chief urology VA Med. Ctr., White River Junction, Vt., 1991—. Author: Understanding Urology, 1973, Urology in Primary Care, 1976, Spanish edit., 1978, Russian edit., 1979, Urology: A Core Textbook, 1985, 2d edit., 1996, The Prostate Book, 1988, latest rev. edit., 1995, (with Judge Hiller B. Zobel) Doctors and the Law: Defendants and Expert Witnesses, 1993; editor Urology Ann., 1987—, Stone Disease: Diagnosis and Management, 1987; mem. editl. bd. Mil. Medicine, 1984-94; contbr. articles to med. jours. Mem. East Lansing (Mich.) Planning Commn., 1974-75; vestryman, jr. warden All Saints Episcopal Ch., East Lansing, 1973-75, lay reader, mem. diocesan com. on continuing edn., 1975-86; vestryman St. Michael's Episc. Ch., 1979-82, Charleston, S.C., chmn. every mem. canvas, 1979-80, chmn. lay readers, 1983-86; mem. fin. com., lay reader Christ Episc. Ch., Exeter, N.J., 1989-91; lector St. Thomas Episc. Ch., Hanover, N.H., 1991—, vestryman, 1992-96, stewardship chmn., 1992-94, jr. warden, 1994-96; mem. selectman's alt. Hampton Falls Planning Bd., 1989-91. Col. USAFR, 1981-85, col. USAR, 1985—. Recipient "A" designator in urology, U.S. Army Surgeon Gen., 1986. Fellow ACS, Am. Acad. Pediatrics; mem. AMA, Soc. Univ. Urologists, Internat. Soc. Urology, Am. Urol. Assn., Nat. Urologic Forum, Soc. Pediatric Urology, Brit. Assn. Urol. Surgeons, German Urol. Assn. (hon.), Mayo Alumni Assn. (v.p. 1979-81, pres. 1983-85), Army and Navy Club (Washington), Lotos Club (N.Y.C.), Sigma Xi, Alpha Omega Alpha (hon.). Republican. Home: 6 Partridge Rd Etna NH 03750-0354 Office: Dartmouth Hitchcock Med Ctr Sect Urology Lebanon NH 03756

ROUSAKIS, JOHN PAUL, former mayor; b. Savannah, Ga., Jan. 14, 1929; s. Paul V. and Antigone (Alexopoulos) R.; m. Elizabeth Lattimore, Oct. 24, 1987; children: Rhonda, Paul, Thea, Tina. B.B.A., U. Ga., 1952. Commr. Chatham County, Ga., 1965-69; vice chmn. Chatham County, 1969-70; mayor of Savannah, 1970-92; ins. broker Savannah, 1956—. Past pres. Nat. League Cities. With AUS, 1953-56. Named Outstanding Young Man of Savannah, Outstanding Young Man of Ga., 1962, Archon Greek Orthodox Ch., 1988, Outstanding City Ofcl., State of Ga.; recipient Tree of Life award Jewish Nat. Fund, 1983, Pres.'s award Nat. League of Cities, 1991. Mem. Ga. Mcpl. Assn. (past pres.), Am. Legion, Ahepa, Masons, (Shriner, Knight Comdr. 32d deg.). Office: 24 E Liberty St Savannah GA 31401

ROUSE, CHRISTOPHER CHAPMAN, III, composer; b. Balt., Feb. 15, 1949; s. Christopher Chapman Jr. and Margery (Harper) R.; m. Ann Jensen, Aug. 28, 1983; children: Jillian, Alexandra, Adrian; 1 stepchild, Angela. MusB, Oberlin Conservatory, 1971; MFA, DMA, Cornell U., 1977. Asst. prof. composition U. Mich., Ann Arbor, 1978-81; asst. prof. composition Eastman Sch. Music, Rochester, N.Y., 1981-85, assoc. prof. composition, 1985-91, prof. composition, 1991—; composer-in-residence Balt. Symphony Orch., 1986-89; writer numerous musical subjects; historian rock music. Composer for numerous renowned soloist and ensembles including Yo-Yo Ma, Charles Castleman, James VanDemark, Jan de Gaetani, Leslie Guinn, Carol Wincenc, Cho-Liang Lin, William Albright, Soc. New Music, Blackearth Percussion Group; commd. composer Atlanta Symphony, Phila. Orch., N.Y. Philharm., L.A. Philharm., Balt. Symphony, Houston Symphony, Detroit Symphony, St. Louis Symphony, Rochester Philharmonic, Cleve. Quartet, Boston Musica Viva, Aspen Music Festival, Chamber Music Soc. Lincoln Ctr., N.Y. Internat. Festival of Arts, Chamber Music Am., New England Conservatory Music, Nonesuch Records; orchestral works programmed by Berlin, Stockholm, N.Y.C., Buffalo, L.A., Rochester Philharmonics, Orchestre Nat. de France, also Philharmonia Chgo., Boston, St. Louis, Detroit, Balt., Nat. Pitts., Houston, Denver, Milw., Cleve., Minn., Phila., Oakland, Cin., Atlanta, Indpls., Memphis, San Francisco, Dallas Symphony Orchs. Recipient awards from Guggenheim Found., League Composers/ISCM, NEA, Rockefeller Found., Am. Music Ctr., Warner Bros. Record Co., BMI and Pitney Bowes, Friedheim 1st prize Kennedy Ctr., 1988, Pulitzer prize for music, 1993, Acad. award Am. Acad. Arts and Letters, 1993. Home: 15 Surrey Hill Ln Pittsford NY 14534 Office: Eastman Sch Music 26 Gibbs St Rochester NY 14604-2505

ROUSE, DORIS JANE, physiologist, research administrator; b. Greensboro, N.C., Oct. 3, 1948; d. Welby Corbett and Nadia Elizabeth (Grainger) R.; m. Blake Shaw Wilson, Jan. 6, 1974; children: Nadia Jacqueline, Blair Elizabeth. B.A. in Chemistry, Duke U., 1970, Ph.D. in Physiology and Pharmacology, 1980. Tchr. sci. Peace Corps, Tugbake, Liberia, 1970-71; research scientist Burroughs Wellcome Co., Research Triangle Park, N.C., 1971-76; sr. physiologist Rsch. Triangle Inst., 1976-83, ctr. dir., 1980—, also dir. NASA tech. application team, 1980—; adminstr. ANSI Tech. Adv. Group for Wheelchairs, N.Y.C., 1982-86; adj. asst. prof. Sch. Medicine U. N.C., 1983—; chair Instl. Rev. Bd., Profl. Devel. Award Com., Rsch. Triangle Inst.; mem. adv. bd. Assistive Tech. Rsch. Ctr., 1994—. Mem. adv. bd. Assn. Retarded Citizens, Arlington (Tex.), 1981-88, Western Gerontology Soc., San Francisco, 1982-85; bd. dirs. Simon Found., Chgo. 1983—; mem. spl. rev. com. small bus. applications; Nat. Forum on Tech. and Aging. Recipient Group Achievement award NASA, 1979. Mem. Rehab. Engring. Soc. N.Am. (chmn. wheelchair com. 1981-86), Am. Soc. on Aging, Rehab. Engring. Soc. N.Am., Tech. Transfer Soc., Assn. Fed. Tech. Transfer Execs., Nat. Space Soc. Club: Triangle Dive. Home: 2410 Wrightwood Ave Durham NC 27705-5802 Office: Research Triangle Inst PO Box 12194 Durham NC 27709-2194

ROUSE, GREGORY STANLEY, international marketing consultant; b. Cin., Sept. 29, 1954; s. Stanley Harry and Virginia (Richardson) R. BA, Ga. State U., 1981; student, U. San Diego, 1972-76. Instl. sales mgr. Audio Brandon, Inc., Atlanta, 1980-84; ops. mgr. Chemray Corp., Inc., Atlanta, 1984-87; pres. The Rouse Co., Inc., Marietta, Ga., 1987—; cons. Travel Industry Assn. of Ga., 1987—. Editor (travel newspaper) Dispatches, 1988—. With USAR, 1987-92. Mem. S.E. Direct Mktg. Assn., Sportslife. Republican. Presbyterian. Avocations: Central American studies, distance running, cinema history, martial arts, computers. Office: The Rouse Co Inc 4880 Lower Roswell Rd Ste 102 Marietta GA 30068-4375

ROUSE, IRVING, anthropologist, emeritus educator; b. Rochester, N.Y., Aug. 29, 1913; s. Benjamin Irving and Louise Gillespie (Bohachek) R.; m. Mary Uta Mikami, June 24, 1939; children: Peter, David. BS, Yale U., 1934, PhD, 1938; D in Philosophy and Letters (hon.), Centro de Estudios Avanzados de Puerto Rico y el Caribe, 1990. Asst. anthropology Yale Peabody Museum, 1934-38, asst. curator, 1938-47, assoc. curator, 1947-54, research assoc., 1954-62, curator, 1977-85, emeritus curator, 1985—; instr. anthropology Yale U., 1939-43, asst. prof., 1943-48; assoc. prof. Yale, 1948-54; prof. Yale U., 1954-69, Charles J. MacCurdy prof. anthropology, 1969-84, prof. emeritus, 1984—. Author monographs on archaeology of Fla., Cuba, Haiti, P.R., Venezuela. Recipient Medalla Commemorativa del Vuelo Panamericano pro Faro de Colon Govt. Cuba, 1945, A. Cressy Morrison prize in natural sci. N.Y. Acad. Sci., 1951, Viking fund medal Wenner-Gren Found., 1960, Wilbur Cross medal Yale U., 1992; Guggenheim fellow, 1963-64. Mem. Am. Anthrop. Assn. (pres. 1967-68), Eastern States Archeol. Fedn. (pres. 1946-50), Assn. Field Archaeology (pres. 1977-78), Soc. Am. Archaeology (editor 1946-50, pres. 1952-53), Nat. Acad. Scis., Am. Acad. Arts and Scis., Internat. Assn. Caribbean Archaeology (hon. mem.), Soc. Antiquaries (London). Office: Yale U Dept Anthropology PO Box 208277 New Haven CT 06520-8277

ROUSE, JEFF, Olympic athlete, swimmer. Olympic swimmer Barcelona, Spain, 1992. Recipient 100m Backstroke Silver medal Olympics, Barcelona, 1992, 4*100 Medley Relay Gold Medal Olympics, Barcelona, 1992. World record holder 100m backstroke long course and short course, 1992. Address: 3831 E Camelback Rd # 106 Phoenix AZ 85018 Address: 4 Britanny Mdws Atherton CA 94027-4101*

ROUSE, JOHN WILSON, JR., research institute administrator; b. Kansas City, Mo., Dec. 7, 1937; s. John Wilson and Gail Agnes (Palmer) R.; m. Susan Jane Davis, May 3, 1981; 1 son, Jeffrey Scott. A.S., Kansas City Jr. Coll., 1957; B.S., Purdue U., 1959; M.S., U. Kans., 1965, Ph.D., 1968. Registered profl. engr., Mo., Tex. Engr. Bendix Corp., Kansas City, Mo., 1959-64; rsch. coord. Ctr. for Rsch., U. Kans., Lawrence, 1964-68; prof. elec. engring., dir. remote sensing ctr. Tex. A&M U., College Station, 1968-78; Logan prof. engr., chmn. elec. engring. U. Mo., Columbia, 1978-81; dean engring. U. Tex., Arlington, 1981-87; pres. So. Rsch. Inst., Birmingham, Ala., 1987—; mgr. microwave program NASA Hdqrs., Washington, 1975-77; bd. dirs. Protective Life Corp., Ala. Power Co.; chmn. bd. So. Rsch. Techs. Inc. Contbr. articles to profl. jours. Recipient Outstanding Tchr. award Tex. A&M U., 1971; Outstanding Prof. award U. Mo., 1980; Engr. of Yr. Tex. Soc. Profl. Engrs., 1983. Mem. IEEE, Nat. Soc. Profl. Engrs., Am. Soc. Engring. Edn., Internat. Bus. Fellows, Internat. Union Radio Sci., Sigma Xi, Eta Kappa Nu., Tau Beta Pi. Home: 2004 Bridgelake Dr Birmingham AL 35244-1421 Office: Southern Research Institute PO Box 55305 2000 9th Ave S Birmingham AL 35205-2708

ROUSE, RICHARD HUNTER, historian, educator; b. Boston, Aug. 14, 1933; s. Hunter and Dorothee (Hüsmert) R.; m. Mary L. Ames, Sept. 7, 1959; children: Thomas, Andrew, Jonathan. B.A., State U. Iowa, 1955; M.A., U. Chgo., 1957; Ph.D., Cornell U., 1963. Mem. faculty UCLA, 1963—, prof. history, 1975—; assoc. dir. Ctr. Medieval and Renaissance Studies, 1966-67, acting dir., 1967-68; dir. Summer Inst. in Paleography, 1978, chair grad. coun., 1989-90; adv. bd. Hill Monastic Microfilm Libr., St. John's U., Collegeville, Minn., Ambrosiana Microfilm Library, Notre Dame (Ind.) U., Corpus of Brit. Medieval Libr. Catalogues, Brit. Acad. Author: Serial Bibliographies for Medieval Studies, 1969, (with M.A. Rouse) Preachers, Florilegia and Sermons: Studies on the Manipulus Florum of Thomas of Ireland, 1979; (with others) Texts and Transmission, 1983; (with C.W. Dutschke) Medieval and Renaissance Manuscripts in the Claremont Libraries, 1986; (with M.A. Rouse) Cartolai, Illuminators and Printers in Fifteenth-Century Italy, 1988; (with L. Bataillon and B. Guyot) La Production du livre universitaire au moyen age, exemplar et pecia, 1988, (with others) Guide to Medieval and Renaissance Manuscripts in the Huntington Library, 1989, (with M. Ferrari) Medieval and Renaissance Manuscripts at the University of California, Los Angeles, 1991, (with M.A. Rouse and R.A.B. Mynors) Registrum de libris doctorum et auctorum veterum, 1991, (with M.A. Rouse) Authentic Witnesses: Approaches to Medieval Texts and Manuscripts, 1991; co-editor: Viator: Medieval and Renaissance Studies, 1970—; mem. editorial bd. Medieval and renaissance manuscripts in Calif. libraries, Medieval Texts, Toronto; Medieval Texts, Binghamton, Library Quar., 1984-88, Speculum, 1981-85, Revue d'histoire des Textes, 1986—, Cambridge Studies in Paleography and Codicology, 1990—, Catalogue of Medieval and Renaissance Manuscripts in the Beinecke Rare Book and Manuscript Library Yale University, 1984—. Am. Coun. Learned Socs. fellow, 1972-73, fellow All Souls Coll., Oxford, 1978-79, Guggenheim fellow, 1975-76, Rosenbach fellow in bibliogrpahy U. Pa., 1976, NEH fellow, 1981-82, 84-85, 94-96, Inst. for Advanced Studies fellow Jerusalem, 1991; J.R. Lyell reader in bibliogrpahy U. Oxford, 1991-92; vis. fellow Pembroke Coll., U. Oxford, 1992. Fellow Royal Hist. Soc., Medieval Acad. Am.; mem. Medieval Assn. Pacific (councillor 1965-68, pres. 1968-70), Medieval Acad. Am. (councillor 1977-80), Comité international de paléographie (treas. 1985-90), Comité international du vocabulaire des institutions et de la communication intellectuelles au moyen age, 1987—, Societa internazionale per lo studio del medioevo latino, 1988—. Home: 11444 Berwick St Los Angeles CA 90049 Office: Univ Calif Dept History Los Angeles CA 90024

ROUSE, ROBERT SUMNER, former college official; b. Northampton, Mass., Sept. 2, 1930; s. Charles Edward and Laura Elisabeth (Rowbotham) R.; m. children: R. Daniel, Roland, James, Katherine; m. Mary Ellen Morgan, Dec. 5, 1992; children: Morgan, Laura; stepchildren: Matthew, James, Joseph. B.S., Yale U., 1951, M.S., 1953, Ph.D. in Chemistry, 1957. Lab. asst., then asst. in instrn. Yale, 1951-56; asst. prof. chemistry Lehigh U., 1956-62; group leader, plastics div. Allied Chems. Corp., 1962-66, tech. supr., 1966-67; prof. chemistry Monmouth U., West Long Branch, N.J., 1967—; chmn. chemistry dept. Monmouth Coll., 1967-73, asso. dean faculty, 1968-73, dean faculty, v.p. acad. affairs, 1973-80, provost and v.p. acad. affairs, 1980-81, chmn. faculty coun., 1990-93; mem. licensure adv. and approval bd. N.J. Dept. Higher Edn., 1973-82, chmn., 1980-81; bd. dirs. Assn. Ind. Colls. and Univs. N.J., 1978-81. Author: (with Robert O. Smith) Energy: Resource, Slave, Pollutant-A Physical Science Text, 1975. Recipient Disting. Tchr. award Monmouth Coll., 1991. Fellow N.Y. Acad. Scis.; mem. Am. Chem. Soc., AAUP, Sigma Xi. Home: 482 Cedar Ave West Long Branch NJ 07764

ROUSE, ROSCOE, JR., librarian, educator; b. Valdosta, Ga., Nov. 26, 1919; s. Roscoe and Minnie Estelle (Corbett) R.; m. Charlie Lou Miller, June 23, 1945; children: Charles Richard, Robin Lou. BA, U. Okla., 1948, MA, 1952; MALS, U. Mich., 1958, PhD, 1962; student (Grolier Soc. scholar), Rutgers U., 1956. Bookkeeper C & S Nat. Bank, Valdosta, Ga., 1937-41; draftsman R.K. Rouse Co. (heating engrs.), Greenville, S.C., 1941-42; student asst. U. Okla. and Rice U., 1947-48; asst. librarian Northeastern State Coll., Tahlequah, Okla., 1948-49; acting librarian, instr. library sci. Northeastern State Coll., 1949-51; circulation librarian Baylor U., 1952-53, acting univ. librarian, 1953-54, univ. librarian, prof., 1954-63, chmn. dept. library sci., 1956-63; dir. libraries State U. N.Y. at Stony Brook, L.I., 1963-67; dean libr. svcs., prof. Okla. State U., Stillwater, 1967-87, univ. libr. historian, 1987-92; chmn. dept. libr. edn. Okla. State U., 1967-74; Vis. prof. U. Okla. Sch. Library Sci., summer 1962, N. Tex. State U., summer 1965; acad. library cons.; mem. AIA-Am. Library Assn. Library Bldg. Awards Jury, 1976; bd. dirs. Fellowship Christian Libr. and Info. Specialists. Author: A History of the Baylor University Library, 1845-1919, 1962; editor: Okla. Librarian, 1951-52; co-author: Organization Charts of Selected Libraries, 1973; A History of the Okla. State U. Library, 1992; contbr. articles, book revs., chpts. to publs. in field. Bd. dirs. Okla. Dept. Librs., 1989-92, chmn., 1990-92. 1st lt. USAAF, 1942-45. Decorated Air medal with 4 oak leaf clusters; recipient citation Okla. State Senate, 1987, Rotary Outstanding Achievement award, 1996; named in 150 Prominent Individuals in Baylor's History. Mem. ALA (life, mem. coun. 1971-72, 76-80, 83-84, 84-88, chmn. libr. orgn. and mgmt. sect. 1973-75, planning and budget assembly 1978-79, coun. com. on coms. 1979-80, bldgs. and equipment sect. exec. bd. 1979-80, chmn. bldgs. for coll. and univ. librs. com. 1983-85, chmn. nominating com. libr. history roundtable 1993-94), Okla. Libr. Assn. (life, pres. 1971-72, ALA coun. rep. 1976-80, 83-84, OLA Disting. Svc. award 1979, Spl. Merit award 1987), S.W. Libr. Assn. (chmn. coll. and univ. div. 1958-60, chmn. scholarship com. 1968-70), Internat. Fedn. Libr. Assns. (standing com. on libr. bldgs. and equipment 1976-88), Assn. Coll. and Rsch. Librs. (chmn. univ. librs. sect. 1969-70, mem. exec. bd. and rep. to ALA Coun., 1971-72), U. Mich. Sch. Libr. Sci. Alumni Soc. (pres. 1979-80, Alumni Recognition award 1988), mem. Alumni Found. Com., 1992—, Payne County Ret. Educators Assn. (v.p., pres. elect 1991-92, pres. 1992-93), Okla. Hist. Soc. (com. on Okla. Higher Edn. mus. 1985—), Beta Phi Mu. Baptist (chmn. bd. deacons 1973). Clubs: Archons of Colophon, Stillwater Rotary (dir. 1978-82, pres. 1980-81). *It is sometimes a hidden influence in our lives which drives us toward a set goal. We ourselves may not recognize the real source of that urge to fulfill a dream. Only after many years was I able to look back and discern the factors in my youth that pushed me toward my goal of attaining a good education. They grew out of the influence that the Great Depression had on my early life. Because of that experience the preparation for a career became my first goal in life, yet the ways and means for achieving it were virtually nonexistent. It was to be, however, and I was fortunate to realize that goal. It causes me to think now that perhaps the degree of determination and endurance one possesses is paced more by adverse condition than by times of comfort and ease.*

ROUSE, ROY DENNIS, retired university dean; b. Andersonville, Ga., Sept. 20, 1920; s. Joseph B. and Janie (Wicker) R.; m. Madge Mathis, Mar. 6, 1946; children—David Benjamin, Sharon. Student, Ga. Southwestern Coll., 1937-39; B.S. in Agr, U. Ga., 1942, M.S., 1947; Ph.D., Purdue U., 1949. Asst. prof. agronomy and soils Auburn (Ala.) U., 1949-50, assoc. prof., 1950-56, prof., 1956-66, assoc. dir., asst. dean Sch. Agr. and Agrl. Expt. Sta., 1966-72, dean, dir., 1972-81, emeritus, 1981—; mem. Com. of Nine, Dept. Agr., 1970-74. Contbr. articles to profl. jours. Pres. Auburn Beautification Coun., 1987-88. Capt. USN, 1942-46, PTO; USNR, 1946-67, ret. Recipient Leadership award Farm-City Com. Ala., 1975, Disting. Svcs. award Catfish Farmers Am., 1976, Disting. Svcs. award Ala. Vocat.-Agrl. Tchrs. Assn., 1976, Man of Yr. in Agr. award Progressive Farmer, 1977, Aeolian award Ga. Southwestern Coll., 1981, Charles W. Summerour award Ala. Soil Fertility Soc., 1987, Conservation medal Nat. Soc. DAR, 1993; named Hon. State Farmer Future Farmers Am., 1976, Man of Yr. Crop Improvement Assn., 1981, Hon. County Agt., 1981; named to Ala. Agrl. Hall of Honor, 1985; R. Dennis Rouse Life Sciences Bldg. named in honor Auburn U., 1993. Fellow Am. Soc. Agronomy, Soil Sci. Soc. Am., Am. Rhododendron Soc. (pres. Chattahoochee chpt. 1993); mem. Am. Assn. Ret. Persons (pres. Lee County chpt. 1989-91), So. Assn. Agrl. Scientists (pres. 1976), Assn. So. Agrl. Expt. Sta. Dirs. (chmn. 1974), Assn. Univs. and Land-Grant Colls (chmn. expt. sta. com. on orgn. and policy 1977), Men's Camellia Club (pres. 1965-66, 82-83), Outing Club, Lions (pres. Auburn 1993-94, Melvin Jones fellow 1994), Sigma Xi, Alpha Zeta, Phi Kappa Phi, Xi Phi Xi. Presbyterian. Home: 827 Salmon St Auburn AL 36830-5930

ROUSE, WILLIAM BRADFORD, systems engineering executive, researcher, educator; b. Fall River, Mass., Jan. 20, 1947; s. Gaylor Louis Rouse and Barbara (Peirce) Rouse Sherman; m. Sandra Howard Kane, Sept. 8, 1968; children: Rebecca Kane, William Howard. B.S.M.E., U. R.I., 1969; S.M., MIT, 1970, Ph.D., 1972. Postdoctoral research assoc. MIT, Cambridge, 1972; asst. prof. Tufts U., Medford, Mass., 1973; prof. U. Ill., Urbana, 1974-81; adj. prof. indsl. and systems engring. Ga. Inst. Tech., Atlanta, 1981—; CEO Enterprise Support Syss., Inc., Norcross, Ga., 1995—. Author/editor 18 books including: Start Where You Are, 1996; also numerous chpts., articles. Recipient O. Hugo Schuck award Am. Automatic Control Council, 1979. Fellow IEEE (Centennial medal 1984), Human Factors Soc.; mem. NAE, Systems, Man and Cybernetics Soc. of IEEE (pres. 1982-83, Norbert Wiener award 1986), Am. Inst. Indsl. Engrs. (sr.), Unitarian-Universalist Assn. Home: 2389 Little Brooke Dr Atlanta GA 30338-3187 Office: Enterprise Support Syss 4898 S Old Peachtree Rd Ste 106 Norcross GA 30071-4707

ROUSH, DOROTHY EVELYN, medical laboratory educator, consultant; b. Flatwoods, Ky., July 16, 1930; d. William Arch and Mary Jane (Frasure) Salyers; m. Gilbert Riley Dush, Aug. 26, 1951 (div. 1972); m. Virgil Bernard Roush, Nov. 18, 1972. Med. tech. degree, Clin. Lab., Mt. Vernon, Ohio, 1953; student, Ohio State U., 1967-72. Registered med. tech. Med. tech. Hosp. & Tb Hosp., Newark, Ohio, 1953-60; office nurse various physicians, Newark and Columbus, Ohio and Seattle, 1960-93; nursing home coord. Med. Lab., Seattle, 1980-89; sr. phlebotomist Roche BioMed. Lab., Burlington, N.C., 1990-95; nurse, phlebotomist ARC Blood Program, Columbus, Ohio, 1961-72; instr. in field; cons. in field. Contbr. articles to profl. jours. Vol. ARC, 1957-72, Boulder (Colo.) County Foster Parents, 1976, Cath. Shared Missions, Seattle, 1987. Recipient Appreciation award Gt. Brit. Red Cross Nursing Svc., 1969, Internat. Cancer Congress, 1982. Mem. Am. Assn. Med. Assts., Am. Med. Techs. (chairperson com., sci. chairperson Ariz. chpt., expert adhoc rev. com. 1994-95, Disting. Achievement award 1991), Wash. State Soc. Am. Tech. (sec., v.p., Tech. of Yr. 1989, 90), Am. Legion Aux. (pres.). Roman Catholic. Avocations: reading, writing poetry, travelling, golfing, tennis. Home and Office: 18002 N Hyacinth Dr Sun City West AZ 85375-5348

ROUSH, EDWARD WESLEY, JR., lawyer; b. Clinton, Ind., Feb. 16, 1957; s. Edward Wesley and Sue Ann (Campbell) R.; m. Cathy Leigh Sarver, Sept. 10, 1983; children: Andrew Wesley, Caroline Elizabeth, Alexa Faith. BA in History, U. Tex., Dallas, 1980; JD, St. Mary's Law Sch., San Antonio, 1983. Bar: Tex., 1983. Pvt. practice Dallas, 1986-88; atty. Lynch Chappell Allday, Austin, Tex., 1983-84; v.p., gen. counsel The Bargo Group, Inc., Laredo, Tex., 1984-86; sr. atty. Malouf, Roush & Dickenson, Dallas, 1988-89; assoc. atty. Milgrim Thomajan & Lee, Dallas, 1989-90; sr. atty. Roush & Assocs., Dallas, 1990-93; chmn., chief exec. officer Continental Investment Corp., Atlanta, 1991, Blue Cactus Post, Dallas, 1994—, Ancarlex Entertainment, Dallas, 1995—; bd. dirs. Data Processing Security, Inc., Ft. Worth. Named one of Outstanding Young Men Am., 1985. Mem. Univ. Club Dallas. Republican. Office: Dallas Comm Complex Bldg 4 6305 N O'Connor Blvd Ste 103 Irving TX 75039

ROUSH, G. JON, consultant. PhD in English, U. Calif., Berkeley, 1965. Pres. The Wilderness Soc., Washington, 1994-96; asst. prof. lit. and humanities Reed Coll.; program officer Carnegie Corp., N.Y.; pres. Canyon Consulting, 1988-94. Contbr. articles to profl. jours., chpts. to books. Past chmn. bd. dirs., exec. v.p. Nature Conservancy; past bd. dirs. Conservation Fund, No. Rockies Action Group, No. Lights Inst., Mont. Land Reliance. Office: 2326 20th St NW Washington DC 20009

ROUSH, WILLIAM R., chemistry educator. BS in Chemistry, UCLA, 1974; PhD in Chemistry, Harvard U., 1977. Disting. prof. chemistry dept. Ind. U., Bloomington. Recipient Arthur C. Cope Scholar award Am. Chem. Soc., 1994, Alan R. Day award Phila. Organic Chemist's Club, 1992. Office: Indiana U Dept Chemistry Bloomington IN 47405-4000

ROUSS, RUTH, lawyer; b. Des Moines, May 21, 1914; d. Simon Jacob and Dora (Goldin) R.; m. Dennis O'Rourke, Jan. 21, 1940; children: Susan Jerene, Kathleen Frances, Brian Jay, Dennis Robert, Ruth Elizabeth, Dolores Ann. B.A., Drake U., 1934, J.D., 1937. Bar: Iowa bar 1937, U.S. Supreme Ct. bar 1945, Colo. bar 1946, D.C. bar 1971. Legal counsel to Jay N. Darling, Des Moines, 1937-38; atty. Office of Solicitor, Dept. Agr., 1938-45, asst. to solicitor, 1940-45; practice law Colorado Springs, Colo., 1946—; mem. firm Williams & Rouss, 1946-50, individual practice law, 1950-69; of counsel firm Sutton, Shull & O'Rourke, Colorado Springs and Washington, 1969-72; mem. firm Rouss & O'Rourke, Colorado Springs and Washington, 1972—; dir., sec.-treas. ManExec., Inc. Mem. cast chorus, Colo. Opera Festival, 1976, 78; mem., Colorado Springs Chorale, 1976—. Bd. dirs. Human Relations Commn. City Colorado Springs, 1968-73, chmn., 1971-72; bd. dirs., sec. Colorado Springs Community Planning and Research Council, 1972-78; bd. dirs. Logos, Inc., Colorado Springs, 1972-78, sec., 1976-77, v.p., 1977-78; bd. dirs. Colorado Springs Opera Festival, Colorado Springs World Affairs Council, Urban League of Pikes Peak Region; mem. com. protection human rights Penrose Hosp., adv. council Am. Lung Assn. of Colo., Pikes Peak region; dir. Joseph Henry Edmondson Found.; adv. bd. Care Castle Divsn. Pikes Peak Seniors,El Paso County, Colo. Mem. El Paso County (Colo.) Bar Assn., Colo. Bar Assn., D.C. Bar Assn., Am. Law Inst. (life), Internat. Fedn. Women Lawyers, Women's Forum Colo., Phi Beta Kappa. Home: 8 Heather Dr Colorado Springs CO 80906-3114 Office: Rouss & O'Rourke Box 572 231 E Vermijo Ave Colorado Springs CO 80901

ROUSSEAU, EUGENE ELLSWORTH, musician, music educator, consultant; b. Blue Island, Ill., Aug. 23, 1932; s. Joseph E. and Laura M. (Schindler) R.; m. Norma J. Rigel, Aug. 15, 1959; children—Lisa-Marie, Joseph. B of Mus Edn., Chgo. Mus. Coll., 1953; MusM, Northwestern U., 1954; student, Paris Conservatory of Music, 1960-61; PhD, U. Iowa, 1962. Instr. Luther Coll., 1956-59; asst. prof. Cen. Mo. State Coll., 1962-64; prof.

music Ind. U., Bloomington, 1964-88, disting. prof. music, 1988—; guest prof. U. Iowa, 1964, Hochschule fur Musik, Veinna, Austria, 1981-82, Ariz. State U., 1984, Prague Conservatory Music, 1985; tchr. U. Wis.-Ext., 1969—; chief adviser for design and mfg. saxophones Yamaha, 1972—, R & D of saxophone mouthpieces; music arranger; svc. on numerous acad. coms.; tchr. 1st course in saxophone Mozarteum in Salzburg, Austria, 1991—; mem. jury Munich Internat. competitions, 1987, 90, pres. of juries, 1991-92; first saxophonist to perform on Prague Spring Festival, 1993; mem. jury Can. Nat. Music competition, 1994. Worldwide concert saxophonist; Carnegie Hall debut, 1965; author: Marcel Mule: His Life and the Saxophone, 1982, Saxophone High Tones, 1978, Method for Saxophone (2 vols.), 1975; performer 1st solo saxophone recitals, several European cities, 1st Am. solo saxophone performance in Japan, 1984; 1st to record concert saxophone on compact disc (Delos); radio broadcasts in Berlin, Bremen, London, Montreal, Ostrava, Paris, Prague, Toronto, Vienna; saxophone recs. for Deutsche Gramophon, Golden Crest, Coronet, Delos, Liscio, ALM and McGill. Instr., asst. band leader 25th Infantry Div. U.S. Army, 1954-56. Grantee Fulbright Found., 1960-61, Rsch. and Exch. Bd., 1985, NEA, 1986; named hon. prof. music Prague Conservatory, 1993—; recipient Edwin Franko Goldman award ABA, 1995. Mem. N.Am. Saxophone Alliance (pres. 1978-80), Comite Internat. de Saxophone (pres. 1982-85), Coll. Music Soc., Clarinet and Saxophone Soc. (U.K.), Music Tchrs. Nat. Assn. (Tchr. of Yr. award for Ind. 1993), Fulbright Assn. (life), World Saxophone Congress (co-founder 1969). Office: Indiana U Sch Music Bloomington IN 47405

ROUSSEAU, GEORGE SEBASTIAN, eighteenth century studies educator, chamber musician; b. N.Y.C., Feb. 23, 1941; s. Hyman Victoire and Esther (Zacuto) R. B.A., Amherst Coll., 1962; diploma, Am. Sch. Classical Studies, Athens, 1963; M.A., Princeton U., 1964, Ph.D., 1966. Instr. English Harvard U., Cambridge, Mass., 1966-68; asst. prof. UCLA, 1968-70, prof. English, 1970-79, prof. 18th Century studies, 1980-94; Regius prof. English U. Aberdeen, Scotland, 1994—; dir. Sir Thomas Reid Inst. Rsch. in Humanities, Scis., Medicine, 1994—; vis. fellow Magdalen Coll., Oxford, 1993-94; Fulbright vis. prof. U. Lausanne, 1994. Author: (with Marjorie Hope Nicolson) This Long Disease, My Life: Alexander Pope and the Sciences, 1968, The Rape of the Lock: Twentieth-Century Interpretations, 1969, The Augustan Milieu: Essays Presented to Louis A. Landa, 1970, (with Neil Rudenstine) English Poetic Satire: Wyatt to Byron, 1972, (with P.G. Boucé) Tobias Smollett: Bicentennial Essays Presented to L.M. Knapp, 1971, Organic Form: The Life of an Idea, 1972, Goldsmith: The Critical Heritage, 1974, (with Roy Porter) The Ferment of Knowledge: Studies in the Historiography of Science, 1980, The Letters and Papers of Sir John Hill, 1982, Tobias Smollett: Essays of Two Decades, 1982, (with Roy Porter) Sexual Underworlds of the Enlightenment, 1987, Exoticism in the Enlightenment, 1989, The Languages of Psyche: Mind and Body in Enlightenment Thought, 1990, Enlightenment Crossings, Perilous Enlightenment, Enlightenment Borders: Pre- and Post-Modern Discourses, 3 vols., 1991 (with others) Hysteria Beyond Freud, 1993; mem. editorial bd. The Eighteenth Century, 1974—, Eighteenth-Century Life, 1980—, Literature and Medicine, 1983—, History of Psychiatry, 1990—; contbr. The Crisis in Modernism: Bergson and the Vitalist Tradition, 1992. Osgood fellow in lit. Princeton U., 1965-66; Am. Council Learned Socs. fellow, 1970; vis. fellow commoner Trinity Coll., Cambridge U., 1982; sr. Fulbright research prof. Sir Thomas Browne Inst., Leiden, Netherlands, 1983; Clark Library prof. U. Calif., 1985-86; sr. research fellow NEH, 1986-87. Mem. Am. Soc. 18th-Century Studies, MLA, History of Sci. Soc., Am. Hist. Assn. (1972), Am. Assn. History of Medicine, Royal Soc. Arts, Royal Soc. Medicine. Home and Office: Taylor Bldg, Univ Aberdeen, Aberdeen AB24 3UB, Scotland

ROUSSEAU, IRENE VICTORIA, artist, sculptor; m. Denis Lawrence Rousseau; children: Douglas, Scott. BA, Hunter Coll., N.Y.C.; MFA, Claremont (Calif.) Grad. Sch., 1969; PhD, N.Y. U., 1977. Tenured prof. William Paterson Coll., Wayne, N.J., 1970-74; invited spkr. Coll. Art Assn./Women Caucus on Art Conf., L.A., 1985, N.J. Ctr. for Visual Arts, Summit, N.J., 1985, Noyes Mus., 1994, Mus. African Art, 1994. Exhbns. include Betty Parsons Gallery, N.Y.C., Claremont Colls., State Mus. Sci. and Industry, L.A., Morris Mus. Arts and Scis., Morristown, N.J., The Bronx Mus. of Art, Galleri Sci. Agnes, Copenhagen/Roskilde, Denmark, Sculptors 5, Madison, N.J., Edmund Sci. Co., Barrington, N.J., AT&T World Hdqrs., Basking Ridge, N.J., N.J. Ctr. for Visual Arts, The Brotherhood Synagogue Holocaust Meml. Gramercy Pk. (mosaic), N.Y.C., 1986, 1st Internat. Art Biennale, Malta, 1995, painted aluminum wall reliefs Capital Sports, Inc., hdqrs. Sports in Action, Stamford, Conn., 1989, mosaic mural Spiriling Light, Overlook Hosp., Summit, N.J., 1993, Nayes Mus., N.J., 1994; represented in permanent collections Brit. Mus., Met. Mus., Guggenheim Mus., Walker Art Ctr., Nat. Mus. Am. Art, Smithsonian Instn.; commn. of mosaic murals concert hall LaRoche, Switzerland, 1995-96. Recipient seven 1st prize awards for creative work in N.J., ER Squibb and Sons Sculpture award, AIA N.J. Presentation Design award, 1995. Mem. AIA (profl. affiliate N.J., N.Y., chmn. architecture dialogue com. Presentation award 1995), Internat. Sculptors Assn., Am. Abstract Artists (exhbn. chmn. 1978-79, pres. 1979-82), Fine Arts Fedn. (bd. dirs.), Coll. Art Assn., Women's Caucus on Art (conf. spkr.), Phi Delta Kappa. Home: 41 Sunset Dr Summit NJ 07901-2322

ROUSSEAU, RONALD WILLIAM, chemical engineering educator, researcher; b. Bogalusa, La., Sept. 28, 1943; s. Ivy John and Dorothy Dean (Talley) R.; m. Tess Marie McKinney, Aug. 5, 1963 (div. June 1978); children: Ronald William Jr., David Patrick, Brett Charles; m. Sandra Barbara Geller, Sept. 2, 1978. BS, La. State U., 1966, MS, 1968, PhD, 1969. Registered profl. engr., N.C. Prof. N.C. State U., Raleigh, 1969-86; prof., dir. Sch. Chem. Engring. Ga. Inst. Tech., Atlanta, 1987—; vis. prof. Princeton U., 1983-84; cons. numerous chem. cos., 1969—. Co-author: Elementary Principles of Chemical Processes, 1978, 2d edit., 1986; editor: Handbook of Separation Process Technology, 1987; contbr. over 120 articles to profl. publs. Mem. AIChE (bd. dirs. 1990-92, Outstanding Chem. Engr. award Ea. N.C. sect. 1986), Am. Chem. Soc., Coun. Chem. Rsch. (bd. govs. 1994-97, 2d vice-chmn. 1995). Democrat. Roman Catholic. Home: 4288 Conway Valley Ct NW Atlanta GA 30327-3602 Office: Sch Chem Engring Ga Inst Tech Atlanta GA 30332

ROUSSEL, LEE DENNISON, economist; b. N.Y.C., May 15, 1944; d. Ethan Allen and Frances Isabel (Ferry) Dennison; m. Andre Homo Roussel, Sept. 6, 1980; children: Cecilia Frances, Stephanie Anne. AB, Wellesley Coll., 1966; MA, Northeastern U., 1973. Mgmt. intern U.S. Dept. HEW, 1966-68; with Planning Office Commonwealth of Mass., 1968-70; exec. dir. Gov.'s Commn. Citizen Participation, Boston, 1973; with Boston Area Office U.S. Dept. HUD, 1970-78; fgn. svc. officer USAID, 1978—; with Housing and Urban Devel. Office USAID, Washington and Tunis, 1978-82; chief Housing and Urban Devel. Office for C.Am. USAID, Honduras, 1982-87; asst. dir. Office Housing and Urban Programs USAID, Washington, 1987-91; country rep. for Czech and Slovak Fed. Rep. USAID, 1991-92, country rep. for Czech Rep., 1993-94; min. counselor, U.S. rep. to Devel. Assistance Com. OECD, Paris, 1994—. Episcopalian. Office: USOECD, 19 rue de Franqueville, 75016 Paris France also: OECD/USAID PSC 116 APO AE 09777-9998

ROUSSELOT, PHILIPPE, cinematographer; b. Meurthe et Moselle, France, 1945. Attended, Vaugirard Film Sch., Paris. Camera asst. (to Nestor Almendros): My Night at Maud's, Claire's Knee, Love in the Afternoon; cinematographer: (films) Absences Repetees, 1972, Il pleut toujours ou c'est mouille, 1974, Pour Clemence, 1977, Pauline et l'Ordinateur, 1977, Paradiso, 1977, Diabolo Menthe, 1977, Adom ou le sang d'abel, 1977, Le Couple Temoin, 1977, Peppermint Soda, 1977, La Drolesse, 1979, Cocktail Molotov, 1980, La Provinciale, 1980, Diva, 1980 (Cesar award Nat. Soc. of Film Critics 1980, Moscow award 1980), The Roads of Exile, 1981, La Gueule du Loup, 1981, Gut de Maupassant, 1982, Nemo, 1983, The Girl from Lorraine, 1983, Thieves After Dark, 1983, The Moon in the Gutter, 1983, Dream One, 1984, Les voleurs de la nuit, 1984, La nuit magique, 1985, The Emerald Forest, 1985, Night Music, 1985, Therese, 1986 (Cesar award Nat. Soc. of Film Critics 1986), (with John Harris) Hope and Glory, 1987 (Academy award nomination best cinematography 1987), Dangerous Liaisons, 1988, The Bear, 1989 (Outstanding Achievement award Am. Soc. of Cinematographers 1990), Too Beautiful for You, 1989, We're No Angels, 1989, Henry and June, 1990 (Academy award nomination best cinematography 1990), The Miracle, 1991, Merci, la vie, 1991, A River Runs Through It, 1992 (Academy award best cinematography 1992), Sommersby, 1993, Flesh and Bone, 1993, Interview with the Vampire, 1994, (TV miniseries) Les Chemins de l'exil, ou les dernieres de Jean Jacques Rousseau, 1978. Office: The Gersh Agency 232 N Canon Dr Beverly Hills CA 90210-5302

ROUSSEY, ROBERT STANLEY, accountant, educator; b. N.Y.C., July 20, 1935; s. George Albert and Estelle (Smegelski) R.; m. Jeanne Archer, May 8, 1965; children: Robert Scott, John Stephen. BS, Fordham U., 1957. CPA, N.Y., Japan. Staff acct. Arthur Andersen & Co., N.Y.C., 1957-63; mgr. Arthur Andersen & Co., N.Y.C. and Tokyo, 1964-69; ptnr. Arthur Andersen & Co., N.Y.C. and Chgo., 1969-92, dir. auditing procedures, 1977-92; prof. acctg. U. So. Calif., L.A., 1992—; adj. prof. auditing Northwestern U. Kellogg Grad. Sch. Mgmt., 1990, 91. Edit. cons. Handbook of Corporate Finance, 1986, Handbook of Financial Markets and Institutions, 1987; mem. edit. bd. Advances in Accounting, 1987—, Jour. Internat. Acctg. Auditing and Taxation, 1991—, Auditing: A Journal of Theory and Practice, 1994—; mem. adv. bd.: Internat. Jour. Auditing; contbr. articles to profl. jours. Treas., bd. dirs. Kenilworth (Ill.) Community House, 1979-81, Troop 13 Boy Scouts Am., Kenilworth, 1978-80, St. Joseph's Ch. Men's Club, Bronxville, N.Y., 1971-73. With U.S. Army, 1958, 61-62. Mem. AICPA (chmn. EDP auditing stds. com. 1978-81, auditing stds. bd. 1986-90, MAS practice stds. and adminstrn. com. 1990-93), Am. Acctg. Assn. (v.p. auditing sect. 1987-90, pubs. com. 1993—), Info. Systems Audit and Control Assn. (stds. bd. 1986—), Ill. State Soc. CPAs, N.Y. State Soc. CPAs, Inst. Internal Auditors (bd. rsch. advisors 1986—), Internat. Fedn. Accts. (internat. auditing practices com. 1990—, chmn. 1995—, EDP audit com. 1980-88), Met. Club (gov. 1977-78), Tokyo-Am. Club (life), Union League Club, Beaver Creek Club, Beta Alpha Psi, Beta Gamma Sigma. Republican. Roman Catholic. Avocations: skiing, sailing, tennis, karate. Office: U So Calif Dept Acctg Los Angeles CA 90089-1421

ROUSUCK, J. WYNN, theater critic; b. Cleve., Mar. 19, 1951; d. Morton I. and Irene Zelda (Winograd) R.; m. James William Cox, Jr., May 8, 1983. BA with honors, Wellesley Coll., 1972; MS, Columbia U., 1974. Assoc. editor, program guide, Sta. WCLV-FM, Cleve., 1972-73; theater and film reviewer Cleve. Press, 1973; gen. assignment arts reporter Balt. Sun, 1974-84, theater critic, 1984—; instr. English Goucher Coll., Towson, Md., 1981; master critic Nat. Critics Inst., Waterford, Conn., 1990—; theater critic Md. Pub. TV., 1986; spkr. in field. Recipient Dog Writers Assn. Am. awards 1977, 79, Md. chpt. 1st Place Arts Reporting award Soc. Profl. Journalists, 1993; NEH journalism fellow U. Mich., 1979-80; Durant scholar Wellesley Coll., 1972. Fellow Nat. Critics Inst.; mem. Balt. Bibliophiles (bd. dirs. 1982-83), Octavo Plus, Walters Art Gallery, Balt. Wellesley Club (pres. 1978-79). Jewish. Avocations: rare books, art, dogs. Office: The Baltimore Sun 501 N Calvert St Baltimore MD 21278

ROUTH, DONALD K(ENT), psychology educator; b. Oklahoma City, Mar. 3, 1937; s. Ross Holland and Fay (Campbell) R.; m. Marion Starbird Wendler, Sept. 10, 1960; children—Rebecca Ann (dec.), Laura Diane. B.A., U. Okla., 1962; Ph.D., U. Pitts., 1967. Diplomate Am. Bd. Profl. Psychology; lic. psychologist, Fla. Asst. prof. psychology and pediatrics U. Iowa, Iowa City, 1967-70; prof. U. Iowa, 1977-85; assoc. prof. psychology Bowling Green State U., Ohio, 1970-71; assoc. prof. U. N.C., Chapel Hill, 1971-77; prof. psychology and pediatrics U. Miami, Coral Gables, Fla., 1985—; Chmn. behavioral medicine study sect. NIH, 1983-85. Editor Jour. Pediatric Psychology, 1976-82, Jour. Clin. Child Psychology, 1987-91, Jour. of Abnormal Child Psychology, 1992—; contbr. numerous articles to profl. jours., books. Pres. Eno River Unitarian Universalist Fellowship, 1976-77. Recipient award for disting. contbn. Soc. Pediatric Psychology, 1981, Presidential award, 1988; Fla. Psychol. Assn. Research Psychologist of Yr. award, 1987. Mem. APA (pres. div. child, youth and family services, 1984, pres. div. on mental retardation 1987), Disting. Profl. Contbns. to Clin. Psychology (sect. on clin. child psychology 1989, div. clin. psychology, 1992, Nicholas Hobbs award, div. child youth and family services, 1996). Democrat. Home: 9394 SW 77th Ave Apt F-7 Miami FL 33156 Office: Dept Psychology Univ Miami PO Box 249229 Miami FL 33124-9229

ROUTIEN, JOHN BRODERICK, mycologist; b. Mt. Vernon, Ind., Jan. 23, 1913; s. William Evert and Frances Lolita (Broderick) R.; m. Helen Harrison Boyd, Mar. 11, 1944 (dec. 1965); m. Constance C. Connolly, Feb. 22, 1967 (dec. 1996). B.A., DePauw U., 1934; M.A., Northwestern U., 1936; Ph.D., Mich. State Coll., 1939. Instr. botany U. Mo., 1939-42; mycologist Pfizer, Inc., N.Y.C., 1946-77; research adviser Pfizer, Inc., 1974-77. Editorial bd.: Applied Microbiology, 1964-71, Antimicrobial Agts. and Chemotherapy, 1974-77. Recipient Comml. Solvents award in antibiotics, 1950. Mem. Mycol. Soc. Am., Bot. Soc. Am., Soc. Am. Bacteriologists, Soc. Indsl. Microbiology. Research on molds producing new antibiotics, strain improvement of cultures, identification of fungi. Home: 318 Grassy Hill Rd Old Lyme CT 06371-3312 Office: Pfizer Inc Groton CT 06340

ROUVELAS, EMANUEL LARRY, lawyer; b. Seattle, Sept. 10, 1944; s. Larry E. and Mary (Derezes) R.; m. Marilyn S. Edmunds, Jan. 23, 1967; children: Eleftherios, Mary. BA, U. Wash., 1965; JD, Harvard U., 1968. Bar: Ill. 1968, D.C. 1973. Assoc. Kirkland & Ellis, Chgo., 1968-69; counsel U.S. Senate Com. on Commerce, Washington, 1969-73; chief counsel U.S. Senate Mcht. Marine and Fgn. Commerce Subcoms., Washington, 1969-73; ptnr. Preston, Gates, Ellis, Rouvelas & Meeds, Washington, 1974—; advisor to two Presdl. transitions and bi-partisan congl.caucus; bd. dirs. OMI Corp. Trustee Am. Coll. of Greece, 1993—. Office: Preston Gates Ellis Et Al 1735 New York Ave NW Washington DC 20006-5209

ROUX, MILDRED ANNA, retired secondary school educator; b. New Castle, Pa., June 1, 1914; d. Louis Henri and Frances Amanda (Gillespie) R. BA, Westminster Coll., 1936, MS in Edn., 1951. Tchr. Farrell (Pa.) Sch. Dist., 1939-55; tchr. Latin, English New Castle (Pa.) Sch. Dist., 1956-76; ret., 1976; chmn. sr. high sch. fgn. lang. dept. New Castle Sch. Dist., 1968-76, faculty sponsor sch. fgn. lang. newspapers, 1960-76, 71-76, Jr. Classical League, 1958-76. Mem. Lawrence County Hist. Soc., Am. Classical League, 1958-76. Mem. AAUW (chmn. publicity, chmn. program com. Lawrence County chpt. 1992-96), Am. Assn. Ret. Persons, Nat. Ret. Tchrs. Assn., Pa. Assn. Sch. Retirees (chmn. cmty. participation com. Lawrence County br. 1976-81), Coll. Club New Castle (chmn. sunshine com. 1989-91, social com. 1991-92), Woman's Club New Castle (chmn. pub. affairs com. 1988-90, internat. affairs com. 1990-92, program com. 1990-92, telephone com. 1992-95). Republican. Roman Catholic. Avocations: church choir, reading, civic interests. Home: 6 E Moody Ave New Castle PA 16101-2356

ROVELSTAD, MATHILDE VERNER, library science educator; b. Kempten, Germany, Aug. 12, 1920; came to U.S., 1951, naturalized, 1953; d. George and Therese (Hohl) Hotter; m. Howard Rovelstad, Nov. 23, 1970. Ph.D., U. Tubingen, 1953; M.S. in L.S, Catholic U. Am., 1960. Cataloger Mt. St. Mary's Coll., Los Angeles, 1953; sch. librarian Yoyogi Elem. Sch., Tokyo, 1954-56; mem. faculty Cath. U. Am., 1960-90, prof. library sci., 1975-90, prof. emeritus, 1990—; vis. prof. U. Montreal, 1969. Author: Bibliotheken in den Vereinigten Staaten, 1974; translator Bibliographia, an Inquiry into its Definition and Designations (R. Blum), 1980, Bibliotheken in den Vereinigten Staaten von Amerika und in Kanada, 1988; contbr. articles to profl. jours. Research grantee German Acad. Exch. Svc., 1969, Herzog August Bibliothek Wolfenbüttel, Germany, 1995. Mem. ALA (internat. relations com. 1977-80), Internat. Fedn. Library Assns. and Instns. (standing adv. com. on library schs. 1975-81), Assn. for Library and Info. Sci. Edn. Home: PO Box 111 Gibson Island MD 21056-0111 Office: Cath U Am Sch Libr & Info Sci Washington DC 20064

ROVER, EDWARD FRANK, lawyer; b. N.Y.C., Oct. 4, 1938; s. Frederick James and Wanda (Charkowski) R.; m. Maureen Wyer, June 15, 1968; children: Elizabeth, Emily, William. AB, Fordham U., 1961; JD, Harvard U., 1964. Bar: N.Y. 1964, U.S. Tax Ct. 1968, U.S. Dist. Ct. (so. dist.) N.Y. 1975, U.S. Supreme Ct. 1994. Assoc. White & Case, N.Y.C., 1964-71, ptnr., 1972—; bd. dirs. Cranshaw Corp., N.Y.C., The Brearley Sch., N.Y.C., Harvard-Mahoney Neuroscience Inst., Boston, Waterford Sch., Sandy, Utah, E.N. Dana Inst., N.Y.C., Norton Simon Art Mus., L.A., Rumsey-Carter Found., Geneva, Charles A. Dana Found. Mem. ABA, N.Y. Bar Assn., N.Y. County Lawyers Assn., Assn. Bar City N.Y., Century Assn., Scarsdale Golf Club, Harvard Club. Avocations: sailing, skiing. Home: 1111 Park Ave New York NY 10128-1234 Office: White & Case 1155 Avenue Of The Americas New York NY 10036-2711

ROVERA, GIOVANNI AURELIO, medical educator, scientist; b. Cocconato, Italy, Sept. 23, 1940; came to U.S., naturalized, 1984.; Student, Liceo Classico Valsalice, Torino, Italy, 1955-58; MD summa cum laude, U. Torino, 1964, postgrad., 1965-68. Diplomate Am. Bd. Anatomic Pathology; lic. physician, Italy, Pa. Postdoctoral fellow Fels Rsch. Inst. Temple U. Sch. of Medicine, Phila., 1968-70, resident in anatomic pathology, 1970-72, chief resident in pathology, 1972; asst. prof. pathology Sch. Medicine Temple U., Phila., 1972-75; assoc. prof. Wistar Inst., Phila., 1975-78, prof., 1979—, assoc. dir., 1988-91, dir., 1991—; Wistar Inst. prof. pathology and lab. medicine Sch. Medicine U. Pa., Phila., 1984—; Wistar Inst. prof. pediatrics U. Pa. Sch. of Medicine, Phila., 1987—; mem. promotion coms. U. Pa. Sch. of Medicine, The Wistar Inst., 1979—; chmn. grad. tng. program The Wistar Inst., 1981-91; mem. sci. adv. com. Leukemia Soc. Am., 1983-88, Am. Cancer Soc., 1986-90; mem. ad hoc sci. adv. com. Nat. Cancer Inst., 1985—. Editor: (with H. Koprowski) Current Opinion in Immunology: Cancer and Immunology, 1990; assoc. editor Proceedings Soc. Exptl. Biol. Medicine, 1975-78, Jour. Cellular Physiology, 1978—, Leukemia, 1988—, Haematologica Pathology, 1990—; mem. editorial adv. bd. Haematologica, 1989—. Fellow EURATOM, 1965-66, Ministero della Publica Istruzione, 1966-67; scholar Leukemia Soc., 1974-79. Achievements include development of techniques of monitoring the extent of residual leukemia in B and T lineage malignancies. Home: 933 Wootton Rd Bryn Mawr PA 19010-2227 Office: The Wistar Inst 3601 Spruce St Philadelphia PA 19104-4205

ROVERE, ROBERT JOHN, secondary school language educator; b. N.Y.C., Jan. 4, 1943; s. Emilio and Clelia (Garlasco) R. BA, Seton Hall U., 1964; MA, NYU, 1968. Cert. nursery, elem., secondary tchr., ednl. adminstr. and supr., N.J. French tchr. St. Mary H.S., Jersey City, 1964-67; French and Italian tchr. North Bergen (N.J.) H.S., 1967-94, chair dept. langs., 1994—; mem. Nat. Honor Soc. selection com. North Bergen H.S., 1988—; mem. staff devel. com., 1990—, fundraiser project graduation com., 1992—. V.p. North Bergen Fedn. Tchrs., 1974-75; draft counselor Peace and Freedom House, Jersey City, 1968-69; rep. to United Farm Workers, AFL-CIO, North Bergen, 1971-72; bioregional connector Creation Spirituality Mag., Oakland, Calif., 1988-90. Mem. NEA, ASCD, Am. Coun. of Tchr. Fgn. Langs., Am. Assn. Tchrs. of French, Am. Assn. Tchrs. Italian, Fgn. Lang. Educators N.J. Democrat. Avocations: creation spirituality, shamanism, birding, cross-country skiing. Office: North Bergen HS 7417 Kennedy Blvd North Bergen NJ 07047-4014

ROVERUD, ELEANOR, pathologist, neuropathologist; b. Spring Grove, Minn., Oct. 24, 1912; d. Henry S. and Sigrid (Bakken) R.; m. Stuart Henry Nam (dec. Nov. 1986); adopted children: Sue, Kay, Becky, Howard, Signe, Sonia, Tom, Ted, Kurt. Diploma, Kahler Sch. Nursing, Rochester, Minn., 1934; BS in Nursing Edn., U. Minn., 1940; MD, Med. Coll. Pa., 1947. Intern Swedish Hosp., Mpls., 1947-48; resident in pathology, resident instr. Sch. of Tropical Medicine U. P.R., San Juan, 1949-52; fellow in Neuropathology Columbia U., Presbyn. Hosp., N.Y.C., 1952-54; neuropathologist Wayne County Gen. Hosp., Eloise, Mich., 1954-59; assoc. prof. Woman's Med. Coll./Med. Coll. Pa., Phila., 1959-61; pathologist Women's Hosp., Phila., 1961-62, St. Anthony Regional Hosp., Carroll, Iowa, 1962-77; cons. in pathology Carroll, Iowa, 1977-87, Spring Grove, 1987—; expert witness forensic cases Carroll County, Iowa, 1962-77. Chmn., v.p., sec. Carroll chpt. ARC, 1968-75. Mem. AMA, Am. Assn. Neuropathologists, Iowa Med. Soc. (life), Carroll County Med. Assn. (sec. 1968-74), Am. Med. Women's Assn., Zumbro Valley Med. Soc., Minn. Med. Assn. Democrat. Lutheran. Office: PO Box 706 Spring Grove MN 55974-0706

ROVETO, CONNIE IDA, financial services executive; b. Montreal, Que., Can.; d. Charles and Angela (Difruscia) R. BA in English Lang. & Lit., U. Toronto, Ont., Can., 1972, BEd, 1973. Cert. officer/dir. Investment Dealers Assn. Can. Mgr. human resources Can. Permanent Trust, Toronto, 1980-81, mgr. orgn. planning, 1981-82, mgr. trust bus. systems, 1982-84, project dir., 1984-85; asst. v.p. Can. Trust, Toronto, 1986; v.p. Cen. Guaranty Trust, Toronto, 1988, Cen. Capital Mgmt. Inc., Toronto, 1986-89; exec. v.p. United Fin. Mgmt. Ltd., Toronto, 1989-93; pres., CEO United Fin. Mgmt. Ltd., 1993-95; also bd. dirs.; COO, sr. v.p. asset mgmt. svcs. Trust Co. of the Bank of Montreal, 1996—; bd. dirs. Ont. Film Devel. Corp. Mem. senate U. St. Michael's Coll., Toronto, 1989—, mem. acad. planning com., 1991—, mem. capital campaign com., 1987—; mem. com. health care planning Archdiocese Toronto, 1986-90; bd. dirs. Queen Elizabeth Hosp. Found. Mem. Can. Club of Toronto (bd. dirs. 1994), Investment Funds Inst. Can. Avocations: films, reading, tennis, fitness.

ROVINE, ARTHUR WILLIAM, lawyer; b. Phila., Apr. 29, 1937; s. George Isaac and Rosanna (Lipsitz) R.; m. Phyllis Ellen Hamburger, Apr. 7, 1963; children: Joshua, Deborah. AB, U. Pa., 1958; LLB, Harvard U., 1961; PhD, Columbia U., 1966. Bar: D.C. 1964, N.Y. 1984. Assoc. Curtis, Mallet-Prevost, Colt & Mosle, N.Y.C., 1964-66; asst. prof. Cornell U., Ithaca, N.Y., 1966-72; editor Digest of U.S. Practice in International Law U.S. Dept. State, Washington, 1972-75, asst. legal adviser, 1975-81; agt. U.S. Govt. to Iran-U.S. Claims Tribunal U.S. Dept. State, The Hague, Netherlands, 1981-83; of counsel Baker & McKenzie, N.Y.C., 1983-85, ptnr., 1985—; adj. prof. law Georgetown U., Washington, 1977-81. Author: The First Fifty Years: The Secretary-General in World Politics, 1920-1970, 1970; editor: Digest of U.S. Practice in International Law, 1973, 74; co-editor: The Case Law of the International Court of Justice, 1968, 1972, 1974, 1976; bd. editors Am. Jour. Internat. Law, 1977-87; also articles on internat. law. Mem. panel on settlement of transnat. bus. disputes, N.Y. panel Ctr. for Pub. Resources; chmn. law subcom. of internat. adv. coun. on profl. edn. Coun. on Internat. Ednl. Exch.; mem. Coun. on Fgn. Rels. Mem. ABA (chmn. internat. law sect. 1985-86, del. to Ho. of Dels. 1988-90), Am. Soc. Internat. Law (cert. of merit 1974, exec. coun. 1975-77), U.S. Coun. for Internat. Bus. (arbitration com.), Am. Arbitration Assn. (panel of arbitrators), Assn. Bar City of N.Y. (coun. on internat. affairs). Home: 150 E 61st St New York NY 10021-8529 Office: Baker & McKenzie 805 3rd Ave New York NY 10022-7513

ROVINSKY, JOSEPH JUDAH, obstetrician, gynecologist; b. Phila., Sept. 4, 1927; s. Israel and Sarah (Blackman) R.; m. Judith S. Levin, June 24, 1964; children: Audrey, John, Jill, Michael, Paul, David. B.A., U. Pa., 1948, M.D., 1952. Diplomate Am. Bd. Ob-Gyn. Intern U. Pa. Hosp., Phila., 1952-53; resident in ob-gyn Mt. Sinai Hosp., N.Y.C., 1953-58; practice medicine specializing in ob-gyn, 1958—; chmn. dept. ob-gyn City Hosp. Center, Elmhurst, N.Y., 1964-74; prof. ob-gyn Mt. Sinai Sch. Medicine, N.Y.C., 1969-74; prof., chmn. dept. ob-gyn Sch. Medicine Health Scis. Center, SUNY, Stony Brook, 1975-79, prof., 1975-89; chmn. dept. ob-gyn L.I. Jewish Med. Center, 1973-92; prof. ob-gyn. Albert Einstein Coll. Medicine, 1989-94; dir. dept. ob/gyn. New Rochelle (N.Y.) Hosp. Med. Ctr., 1992—; mem. obstetric adv. com. N.Y.C. Dept. Health, 1964-92. Author: Medical, Surgical and Gynecological Complications of Pregnancy, 1961, 2d edit., 1965; editor: Davis' Gynecology and Obstetrics, 1968-73. Served to capt., M.C. USAF, 1964-66. Mem. ACS, Am. Coll. Obstetricians and Gynecologists, Am. Soc. Reproductive Medicine, Am. Uro-Gynecologic Soc., N.Y. Acad. Medicine, N.Y. Obstetrical Soc., N.Y. Gynecol. Assn., Med. Soc. State N.Y. Jewish. Office: New Rochell Hosp Med Ctr 16 Guion Pl New Rochelle NY 10801-5503

ROVIRA, LUIS DARIO, state supreme court justice; b. San Juan, P.R., Sept. 8, 1923; s. Peter S. and Mae (Morris) R.; m. Lois Ann Thau, June 25, 1966; children—Douglas, Merilyn. B.A., U. Colo., 1948, LL.B., 1950. Bar: Colo. 1950. Chief justice Colo. Supreme Ct., Denver., 1990-95; ret., 1995; mem. Pres.'s Com. on Mental Retardation, 1970-71; chmn. State Health Facilities Council, 1967-76. Bd. dirs Children's Hosp.; trustee Temple Buell Found., Denver Found. With AUS, 1943-46. Mem. ABA, Colo. Bar Assn., Denver Bar Assn. (pres. 1970-71), Colo. Assn. Retarded Children (pres. 1968-70), Alpha Tau Omega, Phi Alpha Delta. Clubs: Athletic (Denver), Country (Denver). Home: 4810 E 6th Ave Denver CO 80220-5137

ROVISON, JOHN MICHAEL, JR., chemical engineer; b. North Tonawanda, N.Y., June 15, 1959; s. John Michael and Veronica Marie (Donat) R.; m. Beverly Jean Farinet, Sept. 6, 1986 (div. Oct. 1989); m. Janet Marie Konieczny, Apr. 27, 1991; 1 child, Kevin Michael (dec.). BA in Biology, BSChemE, Washington U., 1982; MS in Cancer Biology, Niagara U., 1986.

Physics tchr. North Tonawanda High Sch., 1985; assoc. process engr. Ag Chem. Group FMC Corp., Middleport, N.Y., 1982-83, process engr. Ag Chem. Group, 1983-84, sr. process engr. Ag Chem. Group, 1986-90; sr. process engr. divsn. peroxygen chem. FMC Corp., Buffalo, 1990-91, process group leader divsn. peroxygen chem., 1992-93, prod. area supr. divsn. peroxygen chem., 1993-94, prodn. mgr. PXD, 1994—; mem. new products evaluation bd. Chem. Engring. McGraw Hill, 1983-84; tech. cons. Ag Chem. Group FMC Corp., Middleport, 1985. Mem. Resolve through Sharing Parents Group, Williamsville, N.Y., 1992. Mem. Am. Inst. Chem. Engrs., Am. Chem. Soc. Roman Catholic. Achievements include redesigning Furadan Milling Plant to reduce N@ usage, persulfate caking issues and development of mineral peroxides; design and installation of process ventilation system for phosplant; originated mathematical system to study S1 endonuclease activity on plasmids in alcohol environments using hyperchromic shifts; helped lead effort for plant ISO 9002 certification, implemented first self-directed union workforce in FMC. Home: 1394 Saybrook Ave North Tonawanda NY 14120-2359 Office: FMC Corp Sawyer Ave And River Rd Tonawanda NY 14150

ROVNER, DAVID RICHARD, endocrinology educator; b. Phila., Sept. 20, 1930; s. Arthur and Rae Theresa (Lieb) R.; m. Margaret McCann, Jan. 15, 1987; children: Arthur, Daniel, Gregory, Robert, Paul, Jessica. AB in Chemistry with distinction, Temple U., 1951, MD, 1955. Diplomate Am. Bd. Internal Medicine. Resident, fellow in internal medicine U. Mich., Ann Arbor, 1956-61, from instr. to assoc. prof. endocrinology and metabolism, 1961-71, prof., 1971; prof. medicine, chief endocrinology and metabolism Mich. State U., East Lansing, 1971-96, asst. to dean for tech., 1996—, assoc. chmn. dept. medicine, 1975-77, acting chmn., 1976-77; chmn. dept. medicine Ingham Med. Ctr., Lansing, Mich., 1984-86. Contbr. articles to profl. jours. Pres. PTO, Ann Arbor, 1966-71; pilot Civil Air Patrol, Lansing, 1975-87. Served to capt. USAFR, 1960-70. Fellow ACP (sec., treas., various coms.); mem. Mich. State Med. Soc. (chmn. continuing edn. com.), Am. Diabetes Assn. (pres. Mich. affiliate 1990-92), Am. Heart Assn., Alpha Omega Alpha. Avocations: electronics, computers. Office: Mich State Univ Dept of Medicine East Lansing MI 48824

ROVNER, ILANA KARA DIAMOND, federal judge; b. Aug. 21, 1938; came to U.S., 1939; d. Stanley and Ronny (Medalje) Diamond; m. Richard Nyles Rovner, Mar. 9, 1963; 1 child, Maxwell Rabson. AB, Bryn Mawr Coll., 1960; postgrad., U. London King's Coll., 1961, Georgetown U., 1961-63; JD, Ill. Inst. Tech., 1966; LittD (hon.), Rosary Coll., 1989, Mundelein Coll., 1989; DHL (hon.), Spertus Coll. of Judaica, 1992. Bar: Ill. 1972, U.S. Dist. Ct. (no. dist.) Ill. 1972, U.S. Ct. Appeals (7th cir.) 1977, U.S. Supreme Ct. 1981, Fed. Trial Bar (no. dist.) Ill. 1982. Jud. clk. U.S. Dist. Ct. (no. dist.) Ill., Chgo., 1972-73; asst. U.S. atty. U.S. Atty.'s Office, Chgo., 1973-77; dep. chief of pub. protection, 1975-76, chief pub. protection, 1976-77; dep. gov., legal counsel Gov. James R. Thompson, Chgo., 1977-84; dist. judge U.S. Dist. Ct. (no. dist.) Ill., Chgo., 1984-92; cir. judge U.S. Ct. Appeals (7th cir.), Chgo., 1992—. Trustee Bryn Mawr Coll., Pa., 1983-89; mem. bd. overseers Ill. Inst. Tech./Kent Coll. Law, 1983—; trustee Ill. Inst. Tech., 1989—; mem. adv. coun. Rush Ctr. for Sports Medicine, Chgo., 1991-96; civil justice reform act adv. com. for the 7th cir., Chgo., 1991-95; bd. vis. No. Ill. U. Coll. Law, 1992-94; vis. com. Northwestern U. Sch. Law, 1993—, U. Chgo. Law Sch., 1993-96, 7th cir. race and gender fairness com., 1993—, U.S. Ct. Appeals (7th cir.) fairness com., 1996—, 7th cir. gender study task force, 1995—. Recipient Spl. Commendation award U.S. Dept. Justice, 1975, Spl. Achievement award 1976, Ann. Nat. Law and Social Justice Leadership award League to Improve the Cmty., 1975, Ann. Guardian Police award, 1977, Profl. Achievement award Ill. Inst. Tech., 1986, Louis Dembitz Brandeis medal for Disting. Legal Svc. Brandeis U., 1993, 1st Woman award, Valparaiso U. Sch. Law, 1993, ORT Women's Am. Cmty. Svc. award, 1987-88, svc. award Spertus Coll. of Judaica, 1987, Ann. award Chgo. Found. for Women, 1990; named Today's Chgo. Woman of Yr., 1985, Woman of Achievement Chgo. Women's Club, 1986, more. Mem. ABA, Fed. Bar Assn. (jud. selection com. Chgo. chpt. 1977-80, treas. Chgo. chpt. 1978-79, sec. Chgo. chpt. 1979-80, 2d v.p. Chgo. chpt. 1980-81, 1st v.p. Chgo. chpt. 1981-82, pres. Chgo. chpt. 1982-83, 2d v.p. 7th cir. 1983-84, v.p. 7th cir. 1984-85), Fed. Judges Assn., Nat. Assn. Women Judges, Ill. Bar Assn., Women's Bar Assn. Ill. (ann. award 1989, 1st Myra Bradwell Woman of Achievement award 1994), Chgo. Bar Assn. (commendation def. of prisoners com. 1987), Chgo. Coun. Lawyers, Decalogue Soc. (citation of honor 1991), Kappa Beta Pi, Phi Alpha Delta (hon.). Republican. Jewish. Office: 219 S Dearborn St Ste 2774 Chicago IL 60604-1803

ROW, PETER LYMAN, musician, educator. Student, Rabindra Bharati U., Calcutta; BM, Prayag Sangit Samiti, Allahabad, India, 1968; MM, Prayag Sangit Samiti, 1970, DM, 1973. Rsch. assoc. Harvard U., Cambridge, Mass., 1973-74; mgt. devel. program Inst. for Ednl. Mgmt. Harvard U., 1986; acad. educator, provost New Eng. Conservatory Music; lectr. on Indian music nationwide; cons. on Asian music Smithsonian Instn. Performed as sitarist throughout U.S., India; appeared on TV, radio show numerous times. Mem. Soc. Ethnomusicology (former pres. N.E. chpt.). Office: New Eng Conservatory 290 Huntington Ave Boston MA 02115-5018

ROWAN, CARL THOMAS, columnist; b. Ravenscroft, Tenn., Aug. 11, 1925; s. Thomas David and Johnnie (Bradford) R.; m. Vivien Louise Murphy, Aug. 2, 1950; children: Barbara, Carl Thomas, Geoffrey. Student, Tenn. State U., 1942-43, Washburn U., 1943-44; A.B. in Math, Oberlin Coll., 1947, D.Litt., 1962; M.A. in Journalism, U. Minn., 1948; D.Litt., Simpson Coll., 1957, Hamline U., 1958, Coll. Wooster, 1968, Drexel Inst. Tech., 1969; L.H.D., Washburn U., 1964, Talladega Coll., 1965, St. Olaf Coll., 1966, Knoxville Coll., 1966, R.I. Coll., 1970, U. Maine, 1971, Am. U., 1980; LL.D., Howard U., 1964, Alfred U., 1964, Temple U., 1964, Atlanta U., 1965, Allegheny Coll., 1966, Colby Coll., 1968, Clark U., 1971; D. Pub. Adminstrn., Morgan State Coll., 1964. Copywriter Mpls. Tribune, 1948-50, staff writer, 1950-61; dep. asst. sec. State for pub. affairs Dept. of State, 1961-63; U.S. ambassador to Finland Helsinki, 1963-64; dir. USIA, Washington, 1964-65; syndicated columnist News Am. Syndicate (formerly Field Syndicate); now panelist Inside Washington, Washington, D.C.; now syndicated columnist King Features, N.Y. Author: South of Freedom, 1953 (named to A.L.A. ann. list best books), The Pitiful and the Proud, 1956 (A.L.A. ann. list best books), Go South to Sorrow, 1957, Wait Till Next Year, 1960, Just Between Us Blacks, 1974, Breaking Barriers: A Memoir, 1991, Dream Makers, Dream Breakers: The World of Justice Thurgood Marshall, 1993. Recipient Sidney Hillman award for best newspaper reporting, 1952; selected one of 10 outstanding young mem of Am. U.S. Jr. C. of C., 1954; award for best gen. reporting on segregation cases pending before U.S. Supreme Ct. Sigma Delta Chi, 1954; fgn. corr. medallion for articles on India, 1955; fgn. corr. medallion for articles on S.E. Asia, coverage of Bandung Conf., 1956; Distinguished Achievement award Regents; Distinguished Achievement award U. Minn., 1961; Communications award in Human Relations Anti- Defamation League B'nai B'rith, 1964; Contbns. to Am. Democracy award Roosevelt U., 1964; Nat. Brotherhood award Nat. Conf. Christians and Jews, 1964; Liberty Bell award Howard U., 1965; George Foster Peabody award for TV spl. Race War in Rhodesia, 1978. Address: 3251 Sutton Pl NW # C Washington DC 20016-3507 also: King Features Inc 235 E 45th St New York NY 10017-3305

ROWAN, GERALD BURDETTE, insurance company executive, lawyer; b. Powersville, Mo., Feb. 9, 1916; s. M. C. and Blanch (Spidle) R.; m. Mary Elizabeth Turner, Dec. 24, 1939; children: Sandra Josephine, Roger Turner. A.B., N.W. Mo. State Coll., 1937; LL.B., Mo. U., 1940. Bar: Mo. bar 1940. Practice in Marble Hill, 1940-49, Cape Girardeau, 1949-59, Kansas City, 1959-81, Eagle Rock, Mo., 1981—; mem. firm Frye & Rowan, 1940-42, 46-49, Oliver & Oliver, 1949-59; with legal dept. Kansas City Life Ins. Co., 1959-76, sr. v.p. tech. services, 1976-81, also dir.; pros. atty., Bollinger County, 1946-49; city atty., Cape Girardeau, 1954-59. Pres. Jackson County unit Am. Cancer Soc., 1963-65, 70-73; chmn. Mo. div. Am. Cancer Soc., 1974-76; mem. Mo. Park Bd., 1965-77. Served with F.A. AUS, 1943-45, MTO. Mem. Mo. Bar Assn. (com. chmn.), World Assn. Lawyers, Assn. Life Ins. Counsel, State City Attys. Assn. (past pres.), Mo. Law Sch. Alumni Assn. (past pres.), Order of Coif, Sigma Tau Gamma. Republican. Methodist. Home: PO Box 135 Eagle Rock MO 65641-0135

ROWAN, JOHN ROBERT, medical center director; b. Joliet, Ill., Aug. 19, 1919; s. Hugh Hamilton and Elizabeth Margaret (Maloney) R.; m. Ruth Elaine Boyle, June 17, 1944; 1 child, Robert J. Student, Butler U., 1952-53, Ind. U., 1953-54. Personnel specialist VA Br. Office 7, Chgo., 1946; personnel officer VA Hosp., Ft. Benjamin Harrison, Ind., 1946-51, Indpls., 1951-56; asst. dir. VA Hosp., 1960-67; asst. mgr. VA Hosp., Iron Mountain, Mich., 1956-60; hosp. adminstrn. specialist VA Central Office, Washington, 1967-69; dir. VA Hosp., Manchester, N.H., 1969-71, Buffalo, 1971-72; dir. VA Med. Center, Lexington, Ky., 1972-88, Montgomery, Ala., 1988—, VA Med. Dist. 11, 1975-86. Bd. dirs. Marion County (Ind.) unit Am. Cancer Soc., 1960-67, pres., 1964-66, bd. dirs. Ind. div., 1966-67; bd. dirs. Western N.Y. Regional Med. Program, 1971-72, Eastern Ky. Health Systems Agy., 1976-79, United Way of Bluegrass, 1976-79, 82-85; mem. regional advisory council Ohio Valley Regional Med. Program, 1972-76; mem. State Health Planning Bd., 1982-88; bd. dirs. Hosp. Hospitality House of Lexington, 1981; mem. adv. coun. Cen. Ala. Aging Consortium, 1991; chmn. Montgomery Area Combined Fed. Campaign, 1991. Served in USAAF, 1942-46. Decorated Bronze Star; recipient Meritorious Svc. citations Ind. dept. DAV, 1964, Meritorious Svc. citations Ky. dept. Am. Legion, 1975, Meritorious Svc. citations Ky. dept. VFW, 1976, Meritorious Svc. citations Eastern Ky. U., 1974, Meritorious Svc. citations Ky. dept. DAV 1978, Spl. Recognition award VFW, 1982, cert. of Merit, DAV, 1982; recipient Dedicated Svc. to Vets. award DAV, 1984, Meritorious Svc. to Vets. award, Am. Legion, 1985, Meritorious Svc. award, Chpt. I, Ky. DAV, 1988, VA Performance award, 1990, Joint Fed. Campaign Meritorious Svc. award, 1990, Dedicated Svc. award DAV, 1992, McClusky award Ala. State Nurses Assn., 1993. Fellow Am. Coll. Healthcare Execs.; mem. Am. Hosp. Assn., Ala. Hosp. Assn. (profl. standards and quality assurance com. 1991—), Ctrl. Ala. Hosp. Coun., Ala. Assn. Hosp. Execs., Assn. Mil. Surgeons U.S., Fed. Hosp. Inst. Alumni Assn. Roman Catholic. Home: 2213 Walbash Dr Montgomery AL 36116-2220 Office: Va Med Ctr 215 Perry Hill Rd Montgomery AL 36109-3725

ROWAN, RICHARD LAMAR, business management educator; b. Guntersville, Ala., July 10, 1931; s. Leon Virgle and Mae (Williamson) R.; m. Marilyn Walker, Aug. 3, 1963; children: John Richard, Jennifer Walker. A.B., Birmingham-So. Coll., 1953; postgrad., Auburn U., 1956-57; Ph.D., U. N.C., 1961. Instr. Auburn (Ala.) U., 1956-57, U. N.C., Chapel Hill, 1958-59, 60-61; lectr. U. Pa., Phila., 1961-62, asst. prof., 1962-66, asso. prof. industry, 1966-73, prof. industry, 1973—; dir. indsl. research unit, 1989-91; co-dir. Ctr. for Human Resources, 1991—; visitor to Faculty Econs. and Politics Cambridge (Eng.) U., 1972; pvt. sector advisor U.S. State Dept. Com. on Internat. Investment and Multinational Enterprises, OECD, 1982-89; chmn. Labor Relations Council, 1985—. Author: (with H.R. Northrup) The Negro and Employment Opportunity, 1965, Readings in Labor Economics and Labor Relations, 5th edit., 1984, The Negro in the Steel Industry, 1969, The Negro in the Textile Industry, 1970, (with others) Studies of Negro Employment, 1970, Educating the Employed Disadvantaged for Upgrading, 1972, Collective Bargaining: Survival in the 1970's, 1972, Opening the Skilled Construction Trades to Blacks, 1972, The Impact of Government Manpower Programs, 1975, International Enforcement of Union Standards in Ocean Transport, 1977, The Impact of OSHA, 1978, Multinational Bargaining Attempts: The Record, the Cases, and the Prospects, 1980; (with H.R. Northrup) Employee Relations and Regulations in the 80s, 1982; (with others) Multinational Union Organizations in the Manufacturing Industries, (with D.C. Campbell) The Multinational Enterprises and the OECD Industrial Relations Guidelines, 1984, Trade Union Clout Erodes, But For How Long?, 1985, Employee Relations Trends and Practices in the Textile Industry, 1986; contbr. articles to profl. jours. Mem. personnel com. Del. Valley Settlement Alliance, 1966-68. Served with Transp. Corps U.S. Army, 1953-56. Mem. Indsl. Rels. Rsch. Assn. (sec. Phila. 1964-65), Acad. Internat. Bus., The Penn Club, The Carolina Club. Democrat. Episcopalian. Home: 113 Blackthorn Rd Wallingford PA 19086-6046 Office: U Pa Wharton Sch 3733 Spruce St Philadelphia PA 19104-6358

ROWARK, MAUREEN, fine arts photographer; b. Edinburgh, Midlothian, Scotland, Feb. 28, 1933; came to U.S., 1960, naturalized, 1970; d. Alexander Pennycook and Margaret (Gorman) Prezdpelski; m. Robert Rowark, May 3, 1952 (div. July 1965). 1 child, Mark Steven. Student, Warmington Bus. Coll., Royal Leamington Spa, Eng., 1950-51, Royal Leamington Spa Art Sch.; diploma, Speedwriting Inst., N.Y.C., 1961; AS in Edn., St. Clair County Community Coll., Port Huron, Mich., 1977, AA, 1978. Supr. proof reading Nevin D. Hirst Advt., Ltd., Leeds, Eng., 1952-55; publicity asst. Alvis Aero Engines, Ltd., Coventry, Eng., 1955-57; adminstrv. asst. Port Huron Motor Inn, 1964-66; adminstrv. asst. pub. rels. dept. Geophysics and Computer Svcs., Inc., New Orleans, 1966-68; sales mgr. Holiday Inn, Port Huron, 1968-70; adminstrv. asst. Howard Corp., Port Huron, 1971-73; sales and systems coord. Am. Wood Products, Ann Arbor, Mich., 1973-74; systems coord. Daniels & Zermack Architects, Ann Arbor, 1974; systems coord., cataloger fine arts dept. St. Clair County Community Coll., Port Huron, 1976-79; freelance fine arts photographer Port Huron, 1978—; photographer Patterns mag. front cover, 1978, Erie Sq. Gazette, 1979, Bluewater Area Tourism Bur. brochure, 1989, Port Huron, Can. Legion, Wyo., Ont. Br., 1987, 88—, Grace Episcopal Ch. Mariner's Day, Port Huron, 1987, 92, 93, 94, 95, Homes mag., 1989. One-woman shows at Grace Episcopal Ch., 1995, Port Huron Mus., 1995; exhibited in internat. shows at Ann. Ea. Mich. Internat. Exhbn., 1982, 83, 84 (awards of excellence 1982, 83, Best Photography award 1995), St. Clair County C.C., 1983, 86 (award of excellence), Sarnia (Ont.) Gallery, 1983-92, 94, Bluewater Bridge Exhibit, 1988, Kaskilaaksontie Exhibit, Finland, 1991 (Par Excellence award), others; contbr. short stories to mags. Cons., buyer interior decor Grace Episcopal Ch., 1994; active Port Huron Mus., 1985—. Recipient Hon. Mention award Sarnia Art Gallery, 1981; named Best Photographer, Sarnia Art Gallery, 1988; winner 2d and 3d Pl. awards Times Herald Newspaper, 1988. Mem. St. Clair County C.C. Alumni Assn., Phi Theta Kappa, Lambda Mu. Democrat. Episcopalian. Avocations: costumes and interior design, travel, theater, ballroom dancing, gardening. Home and Office: 2005 Riverside Dr #15 Port Huron MI 48060-2677

ROWDEN, MARCUS AUBREY, lawyer, former government official; b. Detroit, Mar. 13, 1928; s. Louis and Gertrude (Lifsitz) Rosenzweig; m. Justine Leslie Bessman, July 21, 1950; children: Gwen, Stephanie. B.A. in Econs, U. Mich., Ann Arbor, 1950, J.D. with distinction, 1953. Bar: Mich. 1953, D.C. 1978. Trial atty. Dept. Justice, 1953-58; legal advisor U.S. Mission to European Communities, 1959-62; solicitor, assoc. gen. counsel, gen. counsel AEC, 1965-74; commr., chmn. U.S. NRC, Washington, 1975-77; 2tnr. Fried, Frank, Harris, Shriver and Jacobson, Washington, 1977—. Served with AUS, 1946-47. Decorated officer Order Legion of Honor Republic of France; Recipient Disting. Service award AEC, 1972. Mem. Am., Fed., Mich., D.C. bar assns., Internat. Nuclear Law Assn., Order of Coif. Home: 7937 Deepwell Dr Bethesda MD 20817-1927 Office: Fried Frank Harris Shriver and Jacobson 1001 Pennsylvania Ave NW Washington DC 20004-2505

ROWDEN, WILLIAM HENRY, naval officer; b. Woodsville, N.H., May 12, 1930; s. Henry Thomas and Kathleen M. (Gochey) R.; m. Sarah Sumner, Apr. 14, 1956; children: Sarah Jane, Thomas Sumner, John William. B.S., U.S. Naval Acad., 1952, U.S. Naval Postgrad. Sch., 1963. Commd. ensign U.S. Navy, 1952, advanced through grades to vice adm., 1980; comdr. cruiser-destroyer group 3 U.S. Navy, San Diego, 1977-79; staff chief naval ops. U.S. Navy, Washington, 1979-81; comdr. 6th Fleet U.S. Navy, 1981-83, comdr. Mil. Sealift Command, 1983-85; comdr. Naval Sea Systems Command U.S. Navy, Washington, 1985-88, ret., 1988; Disting. fellow Ctr. for Naval Analyses, Alexandria, Va., 1988—. Decorated D.S.M., Legion of Merit, Bronze Star. Mem. Naval Inst. Presbyterian. Avocations: walking, sailing. Home: RR 1 Box 818 Lancaster VA 22503-9739 Office: Ctr for Naval Analyses Alexandria VA 22302

ROWDER, WILLIAM LOUIS, lawyer; b. Chgo., Aug. 21, 1937; s. John Joseph and Theresa Veronica (Major) R.; m. Josephine M. Laurino, Apr. 20, 1940; children: Lauren, Lisa, Jessica, William. BA, DePaul U., 1961, JD, 1965. Bar: Ill. 1965, U.S. Dist. Ct. (no. dist.) Ill. 1967. Atty. Kirkland & Ellis, Chgo., 1965-76; sr. ptnr. estate planning dept. Kirkland & Ellis, 1979-87; mem. Pope, Ballard, Shephard & Fowle, 1976-79; sr. ptnr. estate planning dept. Coffield, Ungaretti, Harris & Slavin, Chgo., 1987-90, of counsel, 1990—; of counsel Coffield, Ungaretti & Harris, Chgo.; dir. Forest Park Nat. Bank; adj. prof. law DePaul U. Contbr. articles to profl. jours. Village trustee Village of River Forest, 1975-76. Fellow Am. Coll. Trust & Estate Counsel; mem. ABA, Ill. Bar Assn., Chgo. Bar Assn., Chgo. Athletic Club, The Law Club. Office: Coffield Ungaretti & Harris 3500 Three 1st National Plz Chicago IL 60602

ROWE, ALLAN DUNCAN, food products executive; b. Corner Brook, Nfld., Can., Feb. 23, 1951. B in Commerce, Dalhousie U., 1974; MBA, U. Western Ont., 1978. V.p. fin. B.F. Goodrich Can. Inc., Kitchener, Ont., 1978-87; chief fin. officer Sobeys Inc., Stellarton, N.S., Can., 1987—. Mem. Fin. Execs. Inst. Office: Sobeys Inc, 115 King St, Stellarton, NS Canada B0K 1S0

ROWE, CHARLES ALFRED, artist, designer, educator; b. Great Falls, Mont., Feb. 7, 1934; s. Alfred Lewis and Alice Lillian (Ledbetter) R.; m. Eugenia Dean, July 5, 1958; children: Allison Rene, Jon Garner, Dorian Leigh. Student, Mont. State U., 1952-53, So. Meth. U., 1956-57, U. Chgo., 1959-60; BFA, Sch. Art Inst., Chgo., 1960; MFA, Tyler Sch. Art, 1968. Prin. Charles Rowe Advt., Chgo., 1957-60; graphic designer Am. Can Co., Bellwood, Ill., 1960-62, Abrams-Bannister Engraving, Inc., Greenville, S.C., 1962-64; prof. art U. Del., Newark, 1964—. One-man shows include Tyler Sch. Art, Phila, 1968, C.M. Russell Mus., Gt. Falls, 1972-73, 81, 92, Mickelson Gallery, Washington, 1970, 74, Pleiades Gallery, N.Y.C., 1977, 81, Vision of La Herradura, Almuñecar, Spain, 1988, USAF exhbn. Soc. Illustrators, N.Y.C., 1989, 91, West Chester (Pa.) U., 1992, Soc. Illustrators, N.Y.C., 1993; exhibited in group shows at C.M. Russell Mus., 1974, 76, 78, 80, 82-83, Am. Painters in Paris, 1976, Monac-Western Art Exhbt. Spokane, Wash., 1977-78, Easton (Md.) Waterfowl Festival, 1981-82, USAF Nat. Collection, 1989, 91; group shows in Artrium Gallery, N.Y.C., 1995, numerous others; represented in permanent collections U. Del., Mont. State Collection, Mont. State U., Del. State Collection, Gt. Falls Pub. Schs., Michael Landon Prodns., Calif., Collection Knissel, Austria, Archives Victoria and Albert Mus., London; artists USAF Nat. Collection, Washington, 1989, 91, NASA Space Mus., 1992, Hauptman and Greenwood Collections, N.Y.C., 1994, Vera Haas, Dallas, Baker, Honolulu; fabric designer Galleon Fabrics, Inc., N.Y.C., Jones of N.Y., Saks Fifth Ave.; designed graphics Mont. State Arts Coun. With inf. U.S. Army, 1954-56. Ctr. for Advanced Study fellow, 1981-82; grantee U. Del., 1964-79, Nat. Endowment for Arts and Humanities, 1972-73, U. Del. Bicentennial, 1976. Mem. AAUP. Home: Chapel Hill 133 Aronimink Dr Newark DE 19711-3802 Office: U Delaware Dept Art Newark DE 19711 *In my paintings and other artforms I strive for perfection, uniqueness, and a special inner beauty, but more than that, I try to create art that has a universal quality. This universality makes an artform communicate beyond a specific locale, continent or a limited time reference. All great works of art have this special element regardless of when they were created.*

ROWE, CHARLES SPURGEON, newspaper publishing and broadcasting executive; b. Fredericksburg, Va., May 28, 1925; s. Josiah Pollard and Genevieve Sinclair (Bailey) R.; divorced; children: Ashley K. Rowe Gould, Charles Spurgeon, Timothy D. AB, Washington and Lee U., 1947, postgrad. Law Sch., 1947-49. Editor, co-pub. Free Lance-Star, Fredericksburg, 1949—, mng. editor, 1949-76; pres. Free Lance-Star Pub. Co. (newspaper and radio stas. WFLS AM-FM, WYSK-FM), Fredericksburg, 1949—; dir. AP, 1976-85, vice chmn., 1983-85, dir. Fredericksburg Savs. & Loan Assn.; trustee Washington and Lee U., 1984-94; former mem. bar news media rels. com. Va. State Bar, 1969-85, co-chmn., 1981-85. Chmn. bd. trustees Cen. Rappahannock Regional Libr., 1969-75; Pulitzer Prize juror, 1982-83, 92-93. Lt. (j.g.) USNR, 1943-46, now capt. Res. ret. Recipient George Mason award, 1974; named Outstanding Young Man of 1958 Fredericksburg Jaycees; named to Va. Communication Hall of Fame, 1989. Mem. A.P. Mng. Editors Assn. (pres. 1969, chmn. regents 1973-75), Am. Soc. Newspaper Editors (dir. 1971-77, 79-84), Newspaper Assn. Am. (dir. 1985-93, chmn. found. 1991-92), So. Newspaper Pubs. Assn. (dir. 1984-87), Va. Press Assn. (dir. 1977-83), World Press Freedom Com. (exec. com.), Soc. Profl. Journalists, Phi Beta Kappa, Omicron Delta Kappa, Phi Delta Phi, Delta Tau Delta. Episcopalian. Clubs: Nat. Press, Fredericksburg Country, Dominion, John's Island. Home: PO Box 754 Fredericksburg VA 22404-0754 Office: The Free Lance-Star 616 Amelia St Fredericksburg VA 22401-3887

ROWE, CLARENCE JOHN, psychiatrist; b. St. Paul, May 24, 1916; s. Clarence John and Sayde E. (Mabin) R.; m. Patricia A. McNulty, Jan. 15, 1945; children: Padraic, Rory, Kelly Michael. B.A., Coll. St. Thomas, 1938; M.B., U. Minn., 1942, M.D., 1943; M.D. fellow in psychiatry, 1946-49. Intern St. Joseph's Hosp., St. Paul, 1942-43; resident VA Hosp., Mpls., U. Minn. Hosps., Mpls., 1946-49; instr., asst. prof. U. Minn., 1949-54; dir. Hamm Meml. Psychiat. Clinic, St. Paul, 1954-57; pvt. practice psychiatry St. Paul, 1957—; from clin. asst. prof. to clin. assoc. prof. U. Minn., 1954-64; cons. 3M Co., 1957-72, Ramsey County Municipal Ct., 1958-80, Constance Bultman Wilson Center, Faribault, Minn., 1973—; clin. prof. psychiatry U. Minn. Med. Sch., 1964—; adj. faculty mem. Antioch Coll., 1974-86; cons. St. Thomas Acad., 1970—; chmn. Minn. Mental Health Planning Council, 1963-69. Author: An Outline of Psychiatry, 10th edit., 1993, The Mentally Ill Employee, 1965; editor: (with A.W. Richard Sipe) Psychiatry, Ministry and Pastoral Counseling, 1984. Mem. Mayor's Com. on Drug Use and Abuse, 1969-71; mem. Gov.'s Council on Employment of Handicapped, 1954-65; mem. adv. bur. hearing and appeals Social Security Adminstrn., 1965—; trustee St. Thomas Acad., 1970-76; bd. dirs. St. Johns U. Inst. Mental Health, Collegeville, Minn., 1954-78. Served with M.C., U.S. Army, 1943-46. Mem. AMA (chmn. mental health in industry com. 1965-71), Group for Advancement Psychiatry (com. on psychiatry in industry), Am. Psychiat. Assn. (com. on occup. psychiatry 1959-65), Minn. Psychiat. Soc. (pres. 1973-75), Minn. Soc. Adolescent Psychiatry (pres. 1978-79), St. Paul Soc. Psychiatry and Neurology (pres. 1978-79), Town and Country Club. Roman Catholic. Home: 1770 Colvin Ave Saint Paul MN 55116-2709

ROWE, DAVID JOHN, physics educator; b. Totnes, Devonshire, Eng., Feb. 4, 1936; came to Can., 1968; s. Herbert Tyack and Marguerite Ella (Whitehead) R.; m. Una Mary Dawson, Oct. 4, 1959; children: Mark Jørgen Dawson, Jacqueline Amanda. BA, Cambridge (Eng.) U., 1959; MA, DPhil, Oxford (Eng.) U., 1959-62. Research assoc. U. Rochester, N.Y., 1966-68; assoc. prof. U. Toronto, Ont., Can., 1968-74, prof., 1974—. Author: Nuclear Collective Motion, 1970; editor: Dynamic Properties of Nuclear States, 1972; mem. editorial bd. (jour.) Phys. Rev., 1983-86, Jour. Phys. G., 1988-92, assoc. editor, 1992; contbr. articles to profl. jours. Dir. Mont Tremblant Internat. Summer Sch., 1971. Served to cpl. RAF, 1954-56. Ford Found. fellow, 1962-63, U.K. Atomic Energy Authority fellow, 1963-66, Sloan Found. fellow, 1972-74, Isaac Walton Killam rsch. fellow, 1990-92. Fellow Royal Soc. Can. (Rutherford Meml. medal and prize 1983); mem. Can. Assn. Physicists (chmn. theoretical physics div. 1970-710. Avocations: piano, woodworking, skiing. Office: U Toronto Physics Dept, Toronto, ON Canada M5S 1A7

ROWE, EDWARD LAWRENCE, JR., graphic designer; b. Bridgeport, Conn., Nov. 5, 1940; s. Edward L. Sr. and Elvera Rowe; m. Elayne Bassler, Oct. 24, 1964; children: Heather, Jonathan David. Assoc., U. Bridgeport, 1960, BS, 1963. Graphic designer Lester Beall, Brookfield, Conn., 1965-69; graphic design cons. Stead Young & Rowe, New Milford, Conn., 1969-87, Rowe & Ballantine, Brookfield, Conn., 1987—; design cons. Atlas Corp., Allied Signal, Borden, Caterpillar Tractor Co., Com. for Econ. Devel., Internat. Paper, Martin Marietta, N.Y. Clearing House, Otis Elevator. Design cons. Literacy Vols. N.Y., N.Y.C., 1990, Harlem R.B.I. (Returning Baseball to Inner Cities), N.Y.C., 1993. With U.S. Army, 1963-65. Recipient award Jour. Am. Inst. Graphic Arts, 1967, 68, Indsl. Design Mag., 1969, Packaging Design Mag., 1969, 74, Fin. World Merit award, 1978, Design Excellence award, 1991, Mohawk Paper Merit award, 1993, cert. spl. merit 53d Ann. Graphic Arts Exhbn., 1995, cert. of merit award Printing Industries Am. Mem. Conn. Art Dirs. Club. Avocatins: scuba diving, photography, architecture, jazz music. Office: Rowe & Ballantine 8 Galloping Hl Brookfield CT 06804-3611

ROWE, EDWARD THOMAS, university administrator, educator; b. Plymouth, Mich., May 14, 1937; s. Milton Sterling and Ruth Elizabeth (Leonard) R.; m. Mary Jane Price, Sept. 15, 1956 (div. Mar. 1985); children: Rebecca, Jennifer. BA, U. Mich., 1959; MA, U. Calif., Berkeley, 1961, PhD, 1966. Instr., asst. prof. U. Conn., Storrs, 1963-90; asst. prof. Va. Poly. Inst.

and State U., Blacksburg, 1970-74; assoc. prof. U. Denver, 1974—, dean Grad. Sch. of Internat. Studies, 1987—; dir. Social Sci. Found., 1987—; vis. prof. U. Tübingen, 1988; mem. nat. policy and planning bd. Pub. Policy and Internat. Affairs Program, Washington, 1994—; exec. bd. dirs. Denver Com. on Fgn. Rel.; project dir. Nat. Resource Ctr. in Internat. Studies, U.S. Dept. Edn., 1991—. Author: Strengthening the United Nations, 1975; co-author: (report) International Disaster Response, 1976; contbr. articles to profl. publs. including Relaciones Internacionales, Internat. Orgn., Jour. Conflic Resolution, Internat. Studies Quar. Grantee U.S. Inst. Peace, Ford Found., Pew Charitable Trusts, Woodrow Wilson Found., U.S. Info. Agy., U.S. Agy. for Internat. Devel., U.S. State Dept., others, 1970—. Mem. Internat. Studies Assn., Am. Polit. Sci. Assn., Colo. Coun. on Internat. Orgns. (exec. bd. dirs. 1994—), Assn. Profl. Schs. in Internat. Affairs (chmn. minority affairs task force 1991—). Home: 2270 Albion St Denver CO 80207 Office: U of Denver Social Sci Found Univ Park Campus Grad Sch of Internat Studies Univ Of Denver CO 80208

ROWE, ELIZABETH WEBB, paralegal administrator; b. Canton, Ohio, Dec. 2, 1957; d. Thomas Dudley Webb and Verity Elizabeth (Voight) O'Brien; m. David Lee Rowe, June 21, 1986; children: Schuyler Jourdan, Thomas Prentiss. AB in History, Mt. Holyoke Coll., 1979. Legal asst. Willkie Farr & Gallagher, N.Y.C., 1979-82; legal asst. supr., 1983-88, adminstrv. asst., 1988-89; outreach dir. St. Bartholomew's Ch., 1989-93, dir. comm., 1991-93; paralegal mgr. Patterson, Belknap, Webb & Tyler LLP, N.Y.C., 1993—; legal asst. Cmty. Law Offices, N.Y.C., 1980-82; clerical asst. 17th Precinct Police Detective, N.Y.C., 1981-82. Chair homeless shelter St. Bartholomew's Ch., N.Y.C., 1984-85; vol. Breakfast Feeding Program, 1983-92, mem. Community Ministry Coun., 1986-88, 93—; mem. N.Y. Jr. League, 1979-94; Pres.'s Coun. Mt. Holyoke Coll., 1988-91; rep. Mt. Holyoke Coll. Alumnae Fund, 1986-89, 94—, class officer, 1989-94; bd. dirs. 509 E 83d St Corp., E 67th St. Owners, Inc. Recipient Mary Lyon award Mt. Holyoke Coll., 1994. Home: 133 E 80th St Apt 2C New York NY 10021-0332 Office: Patterson Belknap Webb & Tyler LLP 1133 Ave of the Americas New York NY 10036

ROWE, ERNEST RAS, education educator, academic administrator; b. Hot Springs, Ark., July 19, 1933; s. Stephen Paul and Emma Leathia (Martin) R.; m. Carla True Dirk, May 27, 1996. BS with distinction, Ariz. State U., 1955, MEd, 1962, EdD, 1965; postgrad., Gonzaga U., 1975, Dublin City U., Ireland, 1989. Tchr. Madison Sch. Dist., Phoenix, 1960-61, Garden Grove (Calif.) Unified Sch. Dist., 1964-66; cons. spl. edn. Ariz. Dept. Pub. Instrn., Phoenix, 1966-67; asst. prof. Idaho State U., Pocatello, 1967-70, assoc. prof., 1970-74, prof. edn., 1974-95, interim chmn. dept. edn., summer 1992; adminstrv. intern Cen. Adminstrn., 1982-83, 94-95; vis. prof. edn. Calif. State U., Long Beach, 1965; adv. mem. Idaho Task Force on Higher Edn., 1982-83; gov. apptd. Idaho commr. to Edn. Commn. of the States, 1979-93, rep. to steering com., 1989-93; elected chmn. Idaho State U. Faculty Senate, 1969, 70, 71-72, 86-87. Contbr. articles to profl. jours. Bd. dirs. Bannock Meml. Hosp., 1975-78; mem. Idaho Bd. Medicine pre-litigation panel for malpractice hearings, 1980-95. 1st lt. U.S. Army, 1955-57. Mem. AAUP, Nat. Soc. Study Edn., Am. Inst. Parliamentarians (univ. parliamentarian, gov. N.W. region 1992-94), Rotary (pres. 1981-82), Mason, Phi Delta Kappa, Phi Kappa Phi (pres. 1972-73, 87-88). Episcopalian. Avocations: music, reading, photography, golf. Home: 678 N Poplar Ct Chandler AZ 85226 *Initiative and responsibility are cornerstones of a meaningful personal and professional life. Sadly they are missing in much of contemporary society. Apathy and self-indulgence appear most prominently at the turn of the century.*

ROWE, GEORGE GILES, cardiologist, educator; b. Vulcan, Alta., Can., May 17, 1921; came to U.S., 1923, naturalized, 1929; s. James Giles and Cora (Blotz) R.; m. Patsy Barnett, Sept. 12, 1947; children—George Lee, James Andrew, Jane Ellen. B.A., U. Wis., Madison, 1943, M.D., 1945. Diplomate: Am. Bd. Internal Medicine. Intern Phila. Gen. Hosp., 1945-46; resident U. Wis., 1950-52; instr. in anatomy Washington U., St. Louis, 1948-50; Am. Heart Assn. rsch. fellow cardiovascular rsch. lab. U. Wis., 1952-54, rsch. assoc. in medicine, 1954-55, asst. prof. medicine, 1957-59, assoc. prof., 1959-64, prof., 1964-89, prof. emeritus, 1989—, lab. dir., 1969-76, Markle scholar in med. sci. dept. medicine, 1955-60; vol. research asso. Hamersmith Hosp., London, 1956-57. Contbr. numerous articles on congenital and acquired heart disease to profl. pubs.; co-editor: Cardiovascular Nursing, 1968-71. Served with M.C. U.S. Army, 1946-48. Mem. Wis. Heart Assn. (pres. 1969-70), Am. Heart Assn., Assn. Univ. Cardiologists (pres. 1974-75), Central Clin. Research Club (pres. 1968-69), Am. Physiol. Soc., Am. soc. Pharmacology, and Exptl. Therapeutics. Home: 5 Walworth Ct Madison WI 53705-4805 Office: 600 Highland Ave Madison WI 53792-0001

ROWE, GILBERT THOMAS, oceanography educator; b. Ames, Iowa, Feb. 7, 1942; s. Charles Gilbert and Catherine (Corkery) R.; m. Judith Lee Ingram, Nov. 27, 1962; 1 child, Atticus Ingram. BS in Zoology, Texas A&M U., 1964, MS in Oceanography, 1966; PhD in Zoology, Duke U., 1968. From asst. to assoc. scientist Woods Hole (Mass.) Oceanographic Inst., 1968-79; oceanographer Brookhaven Nat. Lab., Upton, N.Y., 1979-87; prof., head dept. oceanography Tex. A&M U., College Station, 1987-93. Editor: (books) The Sea, 1983, Deep-Sea Food Chains, 1992; U.S. editor: Jour. Marine Systems. Fellow AAAS. Office: Texas A&M U Dept Oceanography College Station TX 77843

ROWE, HERBERT JOSEPH, retired trade association executive; b. Granite City, Ill., Mar. 25, 1924; s. Herbert Bernard and Maude (Klein) R.; m. Ann Muter, Dec. 2, 1950; children: Douglas H., Stephen F., James D., Edith L. Student, U. Tex., 1942-43, Purdue U., 1943-44; BS in Mgmt.; BS in Mktg., U. Ill., 1948; LittD (hon.), London Inst. for Applied Research, 1975. With Edward Valves, Inc. (subs. Rockwell Mfg. Co.), 1948-50; with Muter Co., Chgo., 1952-71, v.p., 1957-64, pres., 1964-71, treas., 1964-67, chmn. bd., 1965-71, also dir., 1957-71; pres., treas., dir. Wescoil Co., 1964-66, Tri-Axial Corp., 1966-67; v.p., treas. Gen. Magnetic Corp., 1965-67, chmn. bd., 1967-70, dir., 1964-70; chmn. bd., dir; Pemcor, Inc., Westchester, Ill., 1971-75; assoc. adminstr. external affairs NASA, 1975-78; sr. v.p. Electronic Industries Assn., 1978-89; chmn. Famro Corp., 1989-90; pres. Internat. Electronics Fedn., 1989-90; sec.-treas. Englewood Elec. Supply Wis., Inc., 1972-75, Rahr's Inc., 1972-75; pres. Enclave of Naples, Inc., 1992-94, treas., 1994-96; bd. dirs. Aerovox Corp.; pres. Rowe Corp., 1994—; treas. Quality wholesale Foods of S.W. Fla., 1994—. Pres. Pokagon Trails coun. Boy Scouts Am., 1964-66, pres. Calumet coun., 1966-68, region 7 exec. com., 1966-72, vice chmn., 1971-72, bd. dirs. East Ctrl. region, 1972-75, mem. nat. program com., 1970-78, 90-94, nat. Cub Scout com., 1970-80, chmn., 1990-94, S.E. regional exec. com., 1975-78, So. regional exec. bd., 1993—, bd. dirs. Nat. Capital Area coun., 1978-90, adv. bd., 1990-94, mem. exec. bd. S.W. Fla. coun., 1992—, mem. nat. exec. com. and exec. bd., 1990-95, nat. adv. bd., 1995—; membership chmn. Nat. Eagle Scouts Assn., 1976-80; corp. campaign chmn. Chgo. Met. Crusade Mercy, 1964-68; chmn. Bd. Edn. Caucus, Flossmoor, Ill., 1962; mem. bd. Flossmoor United Party, 1963-68; mem. U. Ill. Found., 1967—; mem. adv. com. U. Ill. Coll. Commerce and Bus. Adminstrn., 1968-78; bd. dirs. Electronic Industries Found., 1974-94; mem. adv. bd. Air and Space Mus., Smithsonian Inst., 1975-78; active Moorings Presbyn. Ch., Naples, Fla. With USMCR, 1942-46, 50-52. Recipient Silver Beaver award Boy Scouts Am., 1966, Silver Antelope award, 1969, Silver Buffalo award, 1994; NASA team award Bicentennial Expo on Sci. and Tech., Exceptional Svc. medal, 1978, Baden-Powell fellow World Scout Found., 1992. Mem. AIAA, AAAS, Electronic Industries Assn. (hon., bd. dirs. 1967-69, bd. govs. 1969-75, exec. com. parts divsn. 1966-75, vice chmn. parts divsn. 1970-74, 74-75, bd. dirs. consumer electronics divsn. 1972-75, chmn. world trade com. 1968-78, vice chmn. 1970-73, chmn. membership and scope com. 1972-74, Disting. Svc. award 1989), Am. Loudspeaker Mfrs. Assn. (v.p., dir. 1967-68, pres., bd. dirs. 1968-70), Assn. Electronic Mfrs. (bd. dirs. 1970-73), Nat. Space Club, Nat. Space Inst., Am. Acad. Polit. Social Sci., Am. Soc. Assn. Execs. (vice chmn. internat. sect. 1986-87, chmn. 1987-88), U.S. Naval Inst., Field Mus. Natural History, European Soc. of Assn. Execs., Greater Washington Soc. Assn. Execs., Chgo. Art Inst., Beta Gamma Sigma, Alpha Phi Omega, Sigma Chi (dir. Kappa Kappa corp. 1954-75, sec. 1971-73, pres. 1973-75, Charles J. Kiler award 1975, Grand Consul's citation 1976), Am. Legion, Chaine des Rôtisseurs, Order Mondial, English Speaking Union (pres. 1996—), Naples Conservancy. Home: 4601 Gulf Shore Blvd N Apt 12 Naples FL 33940-2214

ROWE, JACK FIELD, retired electric utility executive; b. Minn., May 10, 1927; s. William F. and Anna (Stenborg) R.; m. Mary E. Moen, Mar. 26, 1955; 1 dau., Lizette Ann. B.E.E., U. Minn., 1950. Registered profl. engr., Minn., Wis. With Minn. Power and Light Co., Duluth, 1950-89; asst. to pres. Minn. Power and Light Co., 1966-67, v.p., 1967-68, exec. v.p., 1969-74, pres., 1974-84, chief exec. officer, 1978-89, chmn., 1969-93, bd. dirs.; chmn. bd., CEO FiberCore, Inc., Minn. Paper, Inc., So. States Utilities, Universal Telephone, Inc., Topeka Group, Inc., NorLight, Inc.; mem. exec. bd. Nat. Electric Reliability Coun., 1970-73; vice chmn. Mid-Continent Area Reliability Coun., 1970-71, chmn., 1972-73; mem. bus. and econs. adv. bd. U. Minn., Duluth, 1980; bd. dirs. Na Tec, Inc., Houston. Past bd. dirs., v.p. Duluth Jr. C. of C.; mem. exec. bd. Lake Superior coun. Boy Scouts Am., 1967-75, chmn. Explorers, 1968-72; comml. chmn. Duluth United Fund, 1960-61; vice chmn. Duluth United Way, 1975, chmn., 1976, U.S. Savs. Bond chmn., St. Lois County, Minn., 1974-77; chmn. St. Louis County Heritage and Arts Ctr., 1979-81; pres. NE Minn. Devel./Assn., 1981-83; mem. Minn. Bus. Partnership, 1979-88; bd. dirs. Minn. Safety Coun., 1979-85, pres., 1983-84, chmn., 1984-85; bd. dirs. Duluth Downtown Devel. Corp., 1979-81, Duluth Growth Co., 1984-85, Greysolon Mall Corp., 1980-86, Duluth Superior Area Cmty. Found., 1984-86, Duluth Clin. Edn. and Rsch. Found., 1985-86, Benedictine Health Sys., 1985-88; mem. adv. bd. exec. program U. Minn., 1979; adv. coun. Inst. Tech., 1979; mem. Minn. High Tech. Coun., 1982-87. With USNR, 1945-46. Recipient Distinguished Service award Duluth Jr. C. of C., 1960, Outstanding Leadership award in energy conversion scis. N.Y.C. sect. ASME, 1980, Outstanding Achievement award U. Minn. Alumni Assn., 1986, Bronze Chief Exec. Officer of Decade award Fin. World Mag., 1989; named Chief Exec. Officer of Yr., Fin. World mag., 1986, 89; Jack F. Rowe Chair of Engring. named in his honor U. Minn., Duluth, 1986. Mem. NAM (dir. 1975-78), IEEE, Electric Info. Coun. (pres. 1978-82), North Cen. Electric Assn., Duluth C. of C. (pres. 1972-73, exec. com., bd. dirs.), Mpls. Club, Engrs. Club (Duluth), Northland Country Club (Duluth), Quail Creek County Club (Naples), Naples Yacht Club, Kitchi Gammi (Duluth) (dir. 1979-87, pres. 1985-87), Rotary Club (Duluth) (pres. 1974-75), Masons, Shriners, Jesters, Kappa Eta Kappa. Lutheran. Home: 4735 Villa Mare Ln Naples FL 33940-3473

ROWE, JAMES W., food chain executive; b. Chattanooga, Dec. 28, 1923; s. John Howard and Anne Lou (Borders) R.; m. Doris Eileen Carlton, Feb. 19, 1946; children: Carlton, Leigh Anne. Student advanced mgmt, Northeastern U., 1976. Vice pres., sec. Colonial Stores, Atlanta, 1970-77, sr. v.p. adminstrn., 1978, pres., 1979-80; sr. v.p., asst. to chief exec. officer Grand Union Co., Elmwood Park, N.J., 1979; exec. v.p., asst. chief exec. officer Gt. Atlantic & Pacific Tea Co., Inc., Montvale, N.J., 1980-82, vice chmn., chief adminstrn. officer, asst. chief exec. officer, 1982-88; vice chmn. bd. and exec. com. Gt. Atlantic and Pacific Tea Co., Inc., Montvale, N.J., 1988—; bd. dirs. Colonial Stores, Grand Union Co., Gt. Atlantic and Pacific Tea Co. Served with AUS, 1942-45. Republican. Home: 4070 Ridgehurst Dr Smyrna GA 30080-3107 Office: Great Atlantic & Pacific Tea Co Box 418 2 Paragon Dr Montvale NJ 07645*

ROWE, JOHN HOWLAND, anthropologist, educator; b. Sorrento, Maine, June 10, 1918; s. Louis Earle and Margaret Talbot (Jackson) R.; m. Barbara Bent Burnett, June 6, 1942; children: Ann Pollard, Lucy Burnett; m. Patricia Jean Lyon, Apr. 24, 1970. A.B., Brown U., 1939, L.H.D. (hon.), 1969; M.A. in Anthropology, Harvard U., 1941, Ph.D. in Latin Am. History and Anthropology, 1947; Litt.D. (hon.), U. Nacional del Cuzco, Peru, 1954; student, U. Paris, France, 1945-46. Field supr. So. Peru, Inst. Andean Research, 1941-42; prof. archaeology dir. Sect. Archaeology U. Nacional del Cuzco, 1942-43; rep. in Colombia, Inst. Social Anthropology, Smithsonian Instn., also tchr. U. del Cauca, Popayán, 1946-48; mem. faculty U. Calif., Berkeley, 1948—, prof. anthropology, 1956-88, prof. emeritus, 1988—, chmn. dept., 1963-67; curator S. Am. archaeology Mus. Anthropology, 1949—; cons. UNESCO, Cuzco, Peru, 1975; sr. fellow Dumbarton Oaks, 1984-90; field rsch. in Maine, 1938, 40, Mass., 1939-41, Fla., 1940, Guambia and Popayan, Colombia, 1946-48, Peru, 1939, 41-43, 46, 54, 58, 59, 61-78, 80-90, 92-95; hon. prof. U. del Cauca, 1947; rsch. prof. Mil. Inst. Basic Rsch. Sci., U. Calif., Berkeley, 1964-65. Author: An Introduction to the Archaeology of Cuzco, 1944, Max Uhle, 1954, Chavin Art, 1962, (with Menzel and Dawson) The Paracas Pottery of Ica, 1964; Editor: (with Patricia Lyon) Nawpa Pacha, 1963—. Served with AUS, 1944-46, ETO. Recipient Diploma de Honor Soc. Cientifica del Cuzco, 1954, Prémio de Honor Concejo Provincial de Ica, Peru, 1958; ofcl. Orden El Sol del Peru, 1968; Diploma de Honor Concejo Provincial del Cuzco, Peru, 1974; Gran Cruz Orden Al Merito por Servicios Distinguidos, Peru, 1981, Medalla de la Ciudad, Municipalidad del Qosqo, Peru, 1993; Guggenheim fellow, 1958. Mem. Archaeol. Inst. Am., Soc. Am. Archaeology, Soc. des Americanistes de Paris, Soc. Antiquaries London, German Archaeol. Inst., Am. Anthropl. Assn., Acad. Nacional de la Historia (Peru), Soc. History Tech., Inst. Andean Studies (pres. 1960—). Home: 1029 Cragmont Ave Berkeley CA 94708-1411

ROWE, JOHN STANLEY, conservationist, past Canadian provincial official; b. Hardisty, Alta., Can., June 11, 1918. BSc in Botany, U. Alta., Edmonton, 1941; MSc, Nebr. U., 1948; PhD in Botany, U. Man., 1956. Forest engr. Can. Dept. Forestry, Winnipeg, 1948-57, 1957-67; tchr. wildland ecology dept. plant ecology U. Sask., 1967; trustee Can. Parks & Wilderness Soc., trustee emeritus; chmn. sci. com. Can. Coun. on Ecol. Areas; chmn. Can. Com. on Ecol. Land Classification, chmn. subcom. on methodology/philosophy; chmn. Sask. Environ. Adv. Coun.; vice-chmn. Can. Environ. Adv. Coun. mem. editl. collective Newest Rev.; book rev. editor Musk-Ox; author: Home Pl.; contbr. articles to profl. jours. Office: 1012 Josephine St, New Denver, BC Canada V0G 1S0*

ROWE, JOHN WALLIS, medical school president, hospital administrator; b. Jersey City, June 20, 1944; s. Albert Wallis and Elizabeth (Lynch) R.; m. Valerie Ann DelTufo, Aug. 10, 1968; children: Meredith, Abigail, Rebecca. BS with honors, Canisius Coll., 1966; MD with distinction, U. Rochester, 1970. Diplomate Am. Bd. Internal Medicine, Am. Bd. Nephrology. Resident in internal medicine Harvard Med. Sch., Beth Israel Hosp., Boston, 1970-72; clin. assoc. Nat. Inst. Child Health and Human Devel., Balt., 1972-74; rsch., clin. fellow Harvard Med. Sch., Mass. Gen. Hosp., Boston, 1974-75; from instr. to prof. Harvard Med. Sch., Boston, 1976-88; pres. Mt. Sinai Sch. Medicine and Mt. Sinai Hosp., N.Y.C., 1988—, prof. geriatrics and medicine, 1988—; trustee N.Y. Acad. Medicine, 1989—, Buck Ctr. for Rsch. in Aging, Marin, Calif., 1989—. Editor: Health and Disease in Old Age, 1982, Geriatric Medicine, 1988, Handbook of the Biology of Aging, 1990, Geriatric Neurology, 1991; contbr. articles to jours. in field. Lt. comdr. USPHS, 1972-74. MacArthur Found. grantee, 1985—. Mem. NAS Inst. Med., Gerontol. Soc. Am. (pres. 1988), Am. Fedn. for Aging Rsch. (pres. 1988), N.Y. Yacht Club, Century Assn. Roman Catholic. Avocation: sailing. Home: 300 Central Park W New York NY 10024-1513 Office: Mt Sinai Med Ctr Fifth Ave & 100th St New York NY 10029

ROWE, JOHN WESTEL, retired organic chemist; b. Forest Hills, N.Y., Sept. 3, 1924; s. John Edward and laura Robinson (Willoughby) R.; m. Mary Dorothy Lowens, June 26, 1949; children: Peter Willoughby, William Westel, Michael Delano. B.S., MIT, 1948; M.S., U. Colo., 1952; Sc.D., Swiss Fedn. Inst. Tech., Zurich, 1956. With Forest Products Lab., Forest Service, USDA, 1957-89; project leader Forest Products Lab., Forest Service, USDA, Madison, Wis., 1966-84; also supervisory research chemist Forest Products Lab., Forest Service, USDA; lectr. U. Wis. Editor: Natural Products of Wood Planets, 1989; contbr. articles on wood and natural products chemistry to profl. jours. Active Boy Scouts Am., 1962-74. Served with USN, 1942-44. Recipient Wood Salutes award Wood & Wood Products, 1975. Fellow Internat. Acad. Wood Sci., AAAS, Am. Inst. Chemists; mem. Soc. Econ. Botany, Phytochem. Assn. N.Am., Am. Chem. Soc. (chmn. Wis. sect. 1968, 69, alt. counselor 1976-78), Am. Soc. Pharmacology, Forest Products Research Soc., Internat. Assn. for Biomass Utilization, TAPPI,. Republican. Unitarian. Home: 1001 Tumalo Trl Madison WI 53711-3024

ROWE, JOHN WILLIAM, utility executive; b. Dodgeville, Wis., May 18, 1945; s. William J. and Lola (Rule) R.; m. Jeanne M.; 1 son, William John. BS, U. Wis., 1967, JD, 1970. Bar: Wis. 1970, Ill. 1970, U.S. Supreme Ct. 1979, Pa. 1982. Assoc. Isham, Lincoln & Beale, Chgo., 1970-77, ptnr., 1978-80; counsel to trustee Chgo. Milw. St. Paul & Pacific R.R., Chgo., 1979-80; v.p. law Consol. Rail Corp., Phila., 1980-82, sr. v.p. law, 1982-84; pres., chief exec. officer Cen. Maine Power Co., Augusta, 1984-89; pres., chief exec. officer New Eng. Elec. System, Westboro, Mass., 1989—, also bd. dirs.; bd. dirs. UNUM Corp., Bank of Boston Corp. Trustee Pa. Ballet, 1982-84, Bryant Coll.; chmn. Ft. Western Endowment Fund, 1987-88; co-chmn. Maine Aspirations Compact, 1988; bd. dirs. USS Constitution Mus., Jobs for Mass., Edison Electric Inst., Worcester C. of C., Dana Farber Cancer Inst.; pres. Worcester Mcpl. Rsch. Bur. Mem. Mass. Bus. Roundtable (chmn.), R.I. Commodores, Order of Coif, Chgo. Club, Worcester Club, Framingham Country Club, Phi Beta Kappa. Home and Office: New England Electric System 25 Research Dr Westborough MA 01582-0001

ROWE, JOSEPH EVERETT, electrical engineering educator, administrator; b. Highland Park, Mich., June 4, 1927; s. Joseph and Lillian May (Osbourne) R.; m. Margaret Anne Prine, Sept. 1, 1950; children: Jonathan Dale, Carol Kay. BSEE, U. Mich., 1951, BS Engring. in Math., 1951, MSEE, 1952, PhD, 1955. Mem. faculty U. Mich., Ann Arbor, 1953-74; prof. elec. engring. U. Mich., 1960-74, dir. electron physics lab., 1958-68, chmn. dept. elec. and computer engring., 1968-74; vice provost, dean engring. Case Western Res. U., Cleve., 1974-76; provost Case Inst. Tech., 1976-78; v.p. tech. Harris Corp., Melbourne, Fla., 1978-81; v.p., gen. mgr. Controls divsn. Harris Corp., 1981-82; exec. v.p. rsch. and def. Gould Inc., 1982, vice chmn., chief tech. officer, 1983-87; sr. v.p., chief technologist Inst. Rsch., Ill. Inst. Tech., Chgo., 1987; v.p. and chief scientist PPG Industries, Inc., Pitts., 1987-92; v.p., dir. Rsch. Inst., U. Dayton, Ohio, 1992—; cons. to industry; mem. adv. group electron devices Dept. Def., 1966-78, 93—; bd. govs. Rsch. inst. of Ill. Inst. Tech.; chmn. Coalition for Advancement of Indsl. Tech., U. Ill.; mem. indsl. adv. bd. U. Ill. at Chgo.; mem. Army Sci. Bd., 1985-91, 93—. Author: Nonlinear Electron-Wave Interaction Phenomena, 1965, also articles. Fellow AAAS, IEEE (chmn. adminstrv. com. group electron devices 1968-69, editor procs. 1971-73, Harrell V. Nobel award 1994); mem. NAE, Am. Phys. Soc., Am. Soc. Engring. Edn. (Curtis McGraw Rsch. award 1964), Am. Mgmt. Assn. (R&D), Sigma Xi, Phi Kappa Phi, Tau Beta Pi, Eta Kappa Nu. Office: U Dayton 300 College Park Ave Dayton OH 45469-0001

ROWE, KEVIN S., banker; b. Seldom come bye, Nfld., Can., Feb. 14, 1938; m. Valma Jean Rowe, Aug. 28, 1958; children: Todd, Michelle, Natalie, Scott. Student, Curtis Acad., St. Johns, Nfld. With The Bank of N.S., various locations, Can., U.S. and abroad, 1955-70; agt. N.Y.C., 1970-73; area mgr. V.I. and P.R., 1973-77; v.p., gen. mgr. Pacific Regional Office Manila, 1977-83; exec. v.p., gen. mgr. internat. Bank of N.S., Toronto, Ont., Can., 1983-86, exec. v.p. Pacific Region, 1987—; bd. dirs. BNS Internat. (Hong Kong) Ltd., The Bank of Nova Scotia Asia Ltd., The Bank of Nova Scotia Berhad, Solidbank Corp., Poonpipat Fin. & Securities Co. Ltd. Office: Bank of NS, United Centre 25th Fl, 95 Queensway, Hong Kong Hong Kong

ROWE, LISA DAWN, computer programmer/analyst, computer consultant; b. Kenton, Ohio, Feb. 2, 1966; d. Daniel Lee and Frances Elaine (Johnson) Edelblute; m. Jeffrey Mark Rowe, Feb. 13, 1982; children: Anthony David, Samantha Paige Elizabeth. Student, Inst. of Lit., 1988-90, Acad. Ct. Reporting, 1988, Marion Tech. Coll., 1991-92; postgrad., Ohio State U., 1993—. Writer, model Newslife, Marion, Ohio, 1982-83; bookkeeper Nat. Ch. Residences, Columbus, Ohio, 1985, Insty-Prints, Columbus, 1985; asst. editor Columbus Entertainment, 1984-85; book reviewer, writer Columbus Dispatch, 1989-91; writer Consumer News, Delaware, Ohio, 1989-90; computer programmer, supr. Dyserv, Inc., Columbus, 1986-92; bookkeeper, acct., office mgr. Marion Music Ctr., Inc., 1990; computer programmer EBCO Mfg., Columbus, 1992-93; sr. programmer/analyst Borden, Inc., Columbus, 1993-94; computer cons. System X, Columbus, 1994-95, LDA Syss., Dublin, Ohio, 1995—; v.p. Jones, Mitchell, Rowe & Assoc., Worthington, Ohio, 1996—. Editor newsletter Assn. System Users, 1989-90; contbr. articles and revs. to profl. jours. Mem. NAFE, MADD, DAV (chaplain 1990). Republican. Mormon. Avocations: horseback riding, swimming, camping, fishing, reading. Home: 1150 Toulon Ave Marion OH 43302 Office: Jones Mitchell Rowe & Assoc 6788 N High St Worthington OH 43085

ROWE, MARY P., academic administrator, management educator; b. Chgo., Feb. 18, 1936; married; children: Katherine, Susannah, Timothy. BA in History, Swarthmore Coll., 1957; PhD in Econs., Columbia U., 1971; LLD (hon.), Regis Coll., 1975. With World Council of Chs./Office of UN High Commr. for Refugees, Salzburg and Vienna, Austria, 1957-58; research asst. Nat. Bur. Econ. Research, N.Y.C., 1961; economist planning bd. Office of Gov., V.I., 1962-63; free-lance cons. Nigeria, 1963-66, Boston, 1967-69; cons., sr. economist with Ctr. for Ednl. Policy Research, Harvard U. Harvard U., Cambridge, Mass., 1970, cons., sr. economist with Abt Assocs., 1970; tech. dir. early edn. project Harvard U., 1971-72, cons. economist with Abt Assocs., 1971; dir. Carnegie Corp. Grant Radcliffe Inst., Cambridge, 1972; spl. asst. to pres., ombudsperson MIT, Cambridge, 1973—, adj. prof. Sloan Sch. Mgmt., 1985—; mem. steering com., program on negotiations Harvard U., 1995—. Mem. editorial bd. Negotiation Jour., 1985—, Alternative Dispute Resolution Report, 1987—; contbr. articles to profl. jours. Trustee Cambridge Friends Sch., 1969-75; mem. bd. advisors Brookline Children's Ctr., 1971-76; mem. Cambridge Friends Meeting and Com. on Clearness, 1971-78, New Eng. Concerns Com., 1973—, Mass. Policy Adv. Com. on Child Abuse/Neglect, 1977-79, Mass. State Youth Council, 1978-83; mem. Mass. State Employment and Tng. Council, 1975-83, chair, 1980-83. mem. nat. adv. Com. Black Women's Ednl. Policy and Research Network Project/Wellesley Coll. Ctr. for Research on Women, 1980-83; bd. dirs. Bay State Skills Commn., 1980-81, Wellesley Women's Research Ctr., 1984-87; sec. bd. dirs. Bay State Skills Corp., 1981-90; mem. panel on employment disputes Ctr. for Pub. Resources, 1986—. Recipient Meritorious Civilian Svc. award Dept. of Navy, 1993. Mem. Am. Econs. Assn., Soc. Profls. in Dispute Resolution (chair com. on ombudspersons 1982—, com. law and pub. policy in employment disputes), Calif. Caucus Coll. and Univ. Ombudsmen, Univ. and Coll. Ombudsman Aassn., Corp. Ombudsman Assn. (pres. 1985-87, program on negotiation steering com. 1995—, Disting. Neutral Ctr. for Pub. Resources 1990—). Office: MIT 10-213 77 Massachusetts Ave Cambridge MA 02139

ROWE, MAX L., lawyer, corporate executive, management consultant, judge; b. Dallas City, Ill., Aug. 14, 1921; s. Samuel Guy and Nellie (Moyes) R.; m. Maxine Marilyn Gladson, May 23, 1944; children: Melody Ann (Mrs. Gunn), Susan Elaine, Joyce Lynn, Andrew Blair. Student, Knox Coll., Galesburg, Ill., 1939-40; A.B., U. Ill., 1943, J.D., 1946; M.B.A., U. Chgo., 1952. Bar: Ill. 1947, Ind. 1954, also U.S. Supreme Ct. 1964. Pvt. practice in Aurora and Urbana, 1947; asst. to sec., asst. treas. Elgin Nat. Watch Co., 1948-50; gen. atty., asst. to pres.-treas. Rival Packing Co., 1950- 51; gen. counsel, asst. sec.-treas. Victor Mfg. & Gasket Co., Chgo., 1951-54; sec. Mead Johnson & Co., Evansville, Ind., 1954-55; assoc. counsel Caterpillar Tractor Co., 1955-62; assoc. gen. counsel, sec., asst. treas. Thomas J. Lipton, Inc. and subs., 1962-68; v.p., treas. Seeburg Corp., Chgo., 1968-69; v.p. fin., law and adminstrn. Nightingale Conant Corp., Chgo., 1970-71; pvt. legal practice, also mgmt. cons., 1968—; v.p. law, sec. Ward Foods, Inc., Wilmette, Ill., 1972-76; mem. firm Kirkland & Ellis, Chgo., 1978-87; atty. Ill. Dept. Profl. Regulation, Chgo. and Springfield, 1987-92; adminstrv. law judge State of Ill., 1993—; dir. Ward-Johnston, Inc., Ward Internat., Inc., Superior Potato Chips, Inc., Quinlan Pretzel Co., Honiron-Philippines, Inc.; instr. extension div. U. Ill., 1960-61, eve. div. Fairleigh Dickinson U., 1966-68; leader Am. Mgmt. Assn., other corp. seminars, 1966-87. actor various TV, radio and print commercials, 1992—. Treas. Peoria County (Ill.) Republican Central Com., 1958-62; Rep. precinct committeeman, Peoria County, 1958-62, Bergen County, N.J., 1966-68, del., Rep. Nat. Conv., 1980; elder Presbyterian Ch., 1975—; mem. nat. adv. council SBA, 1976-78; chmn., mem. adv. bd. Ill. Dept. Personnel, 1979-82; mem. Ill. Compensation Rev. Bd., 1984-87; mem. Pres. Reagan's Nat. Commn. for Employment Policy, 1984-88; mem. U. Ill. Found. and Pres.'s Council, 1979—, bd. visitors Coll. of Law, 1993—; dir., mem. exec. com., chmn. Outreach and Devel., World Heritage Mus., 1992—; mem. bd. dirs. Oak Ridge Cemetary, 1994—. Served to 2d lt. AUS, 1943-45. Named Alumni of Month, U. Ill. Coll. Law, 1982; inductee Sr. Illinoisans Hall of Fame, 1995. Mem. Am. Mgmt. Assn., Conf. Bd., Am., Ill., Chgo. bar assns., Am. Soc. Corp. Secs., Phi Gamma Delta. Republican. Clubs: Union League (Chgo.), Execs. (Chgo.). Office: 49 Inverness Rd Springfield IL 62704-3110

ROWE, PETER A., newspaper columnist; b. Walnut Creek, Calif., Sept. 7, 1955; s. Raymond Alan and Marion (Green) R.; m. Lynn Hanson, Aug. 13, 1977; children: Kyle, Reid, Alec. BA in History, U. Calif., Berkeley, 1977, BA in Journalism, 1977; MSJ, Northwestern U., 1981. Reporter Argus, Fremont, Calif., 1977-80, Va.-Pilot, Norfolk, 1981-84; reporter San Diego Union, 1984-87, asst. features editor, 1987-88, features editor, 1988-92; columnist San Diego Union-Tribune, 1992—. Bd. dirs., mem. adv. bd. St. Didacus Sch., San Diego, 1992-95; coach Mid-City Little League, San Diego, 1993—. Recipient 1st pl. series award Va. Press Assn., 1984, 1st pl. feature story award Copley Newspapers, 1987, 1st place columns award Soc. Profl. Journalists, 1992; Gannett fellow Northwestern U., 1980-81. Roman Catholic. Office: San Diego Union Tribune PO Box 191 San Diego CA 92112-4106

ROWE, PETER GRIMMOND, architecture educator, researcher; b. Wellington, New Zealand, June 28, 1945; came to U.S., 1969; s. Leslie Grimmond and Dorothy Olive (Perkins) R.; m. Lauretta Vinciarelli, Oct. 18, 1993; 1 child, Anthony. BArch, Melbourne (Australia) U., 1969; MArch in Urban Design, Rice U., 1971; AM (hon.), Harvard U., 1986. Asst. prof. architecture Rice U., Houston, 1973-78, assoc. prof., 1978-85, dir. Sch. Architecture, 1981-85; Raymond Garbe prof. architecture and urban design Grad. Sch. Design, Harvard U., Cambridge, Mass., 1985—, chmn. dept. urban planning and design, 1989-92, dean Grad. Sch. Design, 1992—; program dir. S.W. Ctr. Urban Rsch., Houston, 1974-78; rsch. dir. Rice Ctr., Houston, 1978-81, v.p., 1979-81; prin. Environ. Planning and Design, Houston, 1980-86. Author: Principles for Environmental Management, 1978, Design Thinking, 1987, Making a Middle Landscape, 1991, Modernity and Housing, 1993. Mem. Boston Soc. Architects (hon.). Office: Harvard U Grad Sch Design 48 Quincy St Cambridge MA 02138-3000

ROWE, RICHARD HOLMES, lawyer; b. Waltham, Mass., Jan. 2, 1937; s. Robert C. Rowe and Roberta (Holmes) Hayes; m. Sylvia C. Barrow, Aug. 23, 1963; children: Elizabeth C., Dorothy H., Christopher H. AB, Bates Coll., 1957; JD, Harvard U., 1964. Bar: D.C. 1965, N.Y. 1980. Atty., exec. SEC, Washington, 1964-69, 70-79; v.p. Shareholders Mgmt. Co., L.A., 1969-70; ptnr. Proskauer Rose Goetz & Mendelsohn, Washington, 1979—. 1st lt. USMCR, 1957-60. Mem. ABA, FBA, D.C. Bar Assn., Assn. Bar City of N.Y. Democrat. Office: Proskauer Rose Goetz & Mendelsohn 1233 20th St NW Ste 800 Washington DC 20036-2304

ROWE, RICHARD R., on-line information and management services company executive; b. Burlington, Iowa, Apr. 14, 1933; s. Charles Ronald and Elva Margaret (Gilliland) R.; children: Katherine, Susannah, Timothy, Christopher, Jonathan. B.A. in Psychology, UCLA, 1955; S.T.B. in Psychology of Religion, Boston U., 1958; Ph.D. in Psychology, Columbia U., 1963. Cert. and lic. psychologist, Mass. Dir. test devel. and research West African Exams. Council, 1963-67; assoc. dean Grad. Sch. Edn., Harvard U., Cambridge, Mass., 1967-73; dir. program in clin. psychology and pub. practice Harvard U., 1967-73; v.p. Am. Inst. for Research, Cambridge, 1973-79; pres., chief exec. officer The Faxon Co., Westwood, Mass., 1979-93; pres., CEO RoweCom, Inc., 1994—; chmn. Serials Industry Systems Adv. Com.; mem. State Bd. edn., Mass., 1990-95, chmn., Mass. Edn. Reform Implementation Task Force, 1993—. Pres. Statewide Adv. Council to Office for Children, Mass., 1980-87, chmn., 1983-87; mem. K-12 computer literacy com. Mass. High Tech Council, 1983-84; spl. adviser Mass. Legis. Com. on Ednl. Excellence, 1983-84; mem. Mass. Legis. Commn. Early Edn., 1988—. Mem. Am. Psychol. Assn., ALA, Library and Info. Tech. Assn. Club: Harvard (N.Y.C.). Home: 37 Goden St Belmont MA 02178-3002 Office: RoweCom 37 Goden St Ste 100 Belmont MA 02178-3002

ROWE, SANDRA MIMS, newspaper editor; b. Charlotte, N.C., May 26, 1948; d. David Lathan and Shirley (Stovall) Mims; m. Gerard Paul Rowe, June 5, 1971; children—Mims Elizabeth, Sarah Stovall. BA, East Carolina U., Greenville, N.C., 1970; postgrad., Harvard U., 1991. Reporter to asst. mng. editor The Ledger-Star, Norfolk, Va., 1971-80, mng. editor, 1980-82; mng. editor The Virginian-Pilot and The Ledger Star, Norfolk, Va., 1982-84, exec. editor, 1984-86, v.p., exec. editor, 1986-93; editor The Oregonian, Portland, 1993—; mem. Pulitzer Prize Bd., 1994—. Bd. visitors James Madison U., Harrisonburg, VA., 1991-95. Named Woman of Yr. Outstanding Profl. Women of Hampton Rds., 1987. Mem. Am. Soc. Newspaper Editors (bd. dirs. 1992—, v.p. 1996), Va. Press Assn. (bd. dirs. 1985-93). Episcopalian. Office: The Oregonian 1320 SW Broadway Portland OR 97201-3469

ROWE, SHERYL ANN, librarian; b. Stephenville, Tex., Sept. 29, 1946; d. Horace Milton and Letha Faye (Hensley) Hughes; m. Darrell Vanoy Rowe, Nov. 27, 1969; children: Jason Burt, Shelley Jean. BA in English, Tarleton State U., Stephenville, 1967; MS in Libr. Sci., Tex. Women's U., Denton, 1986. Cert. tchr. secondary edn. Tchr. Lake Worth (Tex.) H.S., 1967-69; tchr. Aledo (Tex.) H.S., 1967-73, 78-84, libr., 1984—. Mem. Tex. Libr. Assn., Region XI Librs. Assn. (treas. 1984—). Office: Aledo High School 412 FM1187 S Aledo TX 76008

ROWE, THOMAS DUDLEY, JR., law educator; b. Richmond, Va., Feb. 26, 1942; s. Thomas Dudley and Georgia Rosamond (Stripp) R. BA, Yale U., 1964; MPhil, Oxford U., Eng., 1967; JD, Harvard U., 1970. Bar: D.C. 1971, N.C. 1976. Law clk. to assoc. justice Potter Stewart U.S. Supreme Ct., 1970-71; asst. counsel adminstrv. practice subcom. U.S. Senate, 1971-73; assoc. Miller, Cassidy, Larroca & Lewin, Washington, 1973-75; assoc. prof. Duke U. Sch. Law, Durham, N.C., 1975-79, prof., 1979-96, Elvin R. Latty prof., 1996—, assoc. dean for rsch., 1981-84, sr. assoc. dean acad. affairs, 1995-96; vis. prof. Georgetown U. Law Ctr., Washington, 1979-80, U. Mich. Law Sch., Ann Arbor, fall 1985, U. Va. Law Sch., Charlottesville, fall 1991; atty. Munger, Tolles & Olson, L.A., 1991; mem. adv. com. on rules of civil procedure U.S. Jud. Conf., 1993—; chmn. adv. com. on rules and procedures U.S. Ct. Appeals (4th cir.), 1994—. Author: (with M. Gerhardt) Constitutional Theory: Arguments and Perspectives, 1993; contbr. articles to profl. jours. Fellow U.S. Dept. Justice, Washington, 1980-81; Rhodes scholar, 1964-67; recipient Disting. Teaching award Duke Bar Assn., 1985. Mem. ABA, Am. Law Inst. Democrat. Office: Duke U Sch Law Durham NC 27708-0360

ROWE, VICKIE CALDWELL, reading resource educator; b. Roanoke, Va., Dec. 18, 1951; d. Charles Ray and Della Alice Caldwell; m. Howard William Rowe Jr., June 16, 1974; 1 child, Scott Allen. BS, Longwood Coll., 1974; M of Liberal Studies, Hollins Coll., 1978. Tchr. Roanoke City Schs., 1974—, tchr., team leader, 1982-87, 95—, tchr., relief prin., 1987-89, reading resource tchr., 1989-94. Dir. Vacation Bible Sch., Fairview United Meth. Ch., Roanoke, 1979, 80, 92, asst. dir. Vacation Bible Sch., 1990, 91, 93, chairperson Coun. on Ministries, 1991, 92, chairperson PPR, 1993, 94, 95. Roanoke City Schs. grantee, 1990-91, 91-92, others. Mem. NEA, Va. Edn. Assn., Roanoke Edn. Assn., Roanoke Valley Reading Assn., Internat. Reading Assn. Home: 2412 Olde Salem Dr Salem VA 24153-6667 Office: Grandin Court Elem Sch 2815 Spessard Ave SW Roanoke VA 24015-4215

ROWE, WILLIAM DAVIS, financial services company executive; b. Hibbing, Minn., June 5, 1937; s. Richard Lawrence and Alicia (Davis) R.; m. Bobbie Grace Childress, Apr. 20, 1963; children—Lisa, William. BA in Psychology, U. Minn, 1959, postgrad. in indsl. relations and bus. adminstrn., 1960; grad. exec. devel. program, Northeastern U., 1975; grad. Advanced Mgmt. Program, Harvard U., 1980. Dir. personnel, adminstrn. EDP Control Data Corp., Mpls., 1964-70; with Comml. Credit Co. subs. Control Data Corp, 1971-84, 85—; sr. v.p. consumer group Balt., 1975-81, sr. v.p. consumer realty services, 1981-83, sr. v.p. consumer banking services, 1983-84; v.p. market devel. Computer Service Co., Control Data Corp., Mpls., 1984; sr. v.p., chief adminstrv. officer Comml. Credit Co., Balt., 1985-87, officer, 1985-87; pres. Enterprise Bank Network Bank Svcs. Co., Atlanta, 1988-91; exec. mng. dir., vice chmn. Foster Ptnrs. Inc., Peat Marwick Alliance Co., 1991—; lectr. in field. Mem. Mayor's Vol. Council of Equal Opportunity, Balt.; trustee St. Paul's Sch. for Girls, Brooklandville, Md., 1981—; bd. dirs. Boy Scouts Am. Served to capt. USMC, 1960-63. Mem. Am. Fin. Services Assn. (bd. dirs. and mem. exec. com. 1980-84, consumer banking adv. com. 1983-84), Am. Mgmt. Assn. (pres.'s roundtable 1976). Republican. Avocations: hunting, skiing, cattle ranching.

ROWE, WILLIAM JOHN, newspaper publishing executive; b. Detroit, Jan. 11, 1936; s. Howard Tiedeman and Thelma Irene (Fox) R.; m. Ellen McCabe, Nov. 28, 1959; children: Peter William, Susan Victoria. BA in Journalism and Advt., Mich. State U., 1958. With Chgo. Tribune, 1958-79; pres., gen. mgr. area publs. Suburban Trib., 1977-79; pres., gen. mgr. Merrill Printing Co., Chgo., 1977-79; pres., CEO Peninsula Times Tribune, Palo Alto, Calif., 1979-84; exec. v.p., COO Times Mirror Nat. Mktg., N.Y.C., 1984-85, pres., CEO, 1985-86; pres., pub., CEO Adv. and Greenwich Time, Stamford, Conn., 1986—. Bd. dirs. United Way, Greenwich, Conn., 1986—. 2d lt. inf. USAR, 1950. Mem. Newspaper Assn. Am., New England Newspaper Assn. (bd. dirs.), Indian Harbor Yacht Club (bd. dirs.), Landmark Club (bd. dirs.). Office: Advocate So Conn Newspapers Box 9307 75 Tresser Blvd Stamford CT 06901-3300

ROWELL, CHARLES FREDERICK, chemistry educator; b. Lowville, N.Y., May 29, 1935; s. Erwin Charles and Winifred Jane (Manning) R.; m. JoAnn Cowling, June 19, 1955; children: Mark Edward, Jan Ellen. BS, Syracuse U., 1956; MS, Iowa State U., 1959; PhD, Oreg. State U., 1963. From. asst. to assoc. prof. U.S. Naval Postgrad. Sch., Monterey, Calif., 1962-75; field scientist Office Naval Research, Chgo., 1975-76; prof. U.S. Naval Acad., Annapolis, Md., 1976—, chmn. dept. chemistry, 1984-88; scientist Forensic Techs. Internat., Annapolis, 1980—. Mem. AAAS, Am. Chem. Soc. (counselor 1980—, sect. chair 1982-83, nat. sec. membership affairs com. 1988-90, chmn. admissions com. 1989-91, chmn. constitution and bylaws com. 1994—), Royal Soc. Chemistry, Sigma Xi (sec. chpt. 1972-73, v.p. 1973-74). Presbyterian. Home: 900 Randell Rd Severna Park MD 21146-4726 Office: US Naval Acad Dept Of Chemistry Annapolis MD 21402

ROWELL, EDWARD MORGAN, retired foreign service officer, lecturer; b. Oakland, Calif., Oct. 13, 1931; s. Edward Joseph and Mary Helen (Mohler) R.; m. Lenora Mary Wood, Aug. 23, 1957; children: Edward Oliver, Karen Elizabeth Schuler, Christopher Douglas. B.A. in Internat. Relations, Yale U., 1953; postgrad., Stanford U., 1964-65, Stanford Bus. Sch., 1970-71. Fgn. service insp. U.S. Govt., Washington, 1971-74; dep. dir., econ. officer Office Iberian Affairs, Washington, 1974-75; dep. dir. Office West European Affairs, Washington, 1975-76, dir., 1977-78; minister-counselor U.S. Embassy, Lisbon, Portugal, 1978-83; dep. asst. sec. Bur. Consular Affairs, Washington, 1983-85; U.S. amb. to Bolivia La Paz, 1985-88; U.S. amb. to Portugal Lisbon, 1988-90; U.S. amb. to Luxemburg, 1990-94; assoc. Global Bus. Access, Ltd., 1994—; bd. dirs. F.Y.I. Inc., Dallas. Treas. Cleveland Park Congl. Ch., Washington, 1984-85; bd. dirs. Luso-Am. Devel. Found., 1988-90; mem. adv. bd. Portuguese-Am. Leadership Coun. of U.S. Cpl. U.S. Army, 1953-55. Recipient Bolivian Condor of the Andes, Grand Cross, 1988, Luxembourg Oaken Crown, Grand Cross, 1994, Superior Honor award, 1983,91, Presdl. Honor award, 1988, scholar Yale U., 1994, 50, 51, 52; U. Calif. fellow, 1953; Una Chapman Cox Found. grantee, 1984. Mem. Am. Fgn. Svc. Assn. (v.p. 1995—), Stanford U. Alumni Assn., Yale U. Alumni Assn., Arena Stage Assocs., Smithsonian Assocs., The Phillips Collection, Friends of Kennedy Ctr. Avocations: photography, tennis, music. Home: 5414 Newington Rd Bethesda MD 20816-3316

ROWELL, HARRY BROWN, JR., technology company executive; b. Roberta, Ga., Sept. 21, 1941; s. Harry Brown Sr. and Essie Jewel (Sloan) R.; m. Mary Jeanette Hancock, Sept. 18, 1961; children: Harry Brown III, T. Scott. BBA, U. Ga., 1963, MA, 1964. Dir. cosmic U. Ga., Athens, 1964-69; dir. ops. Carnegie Mellon U., Pitts., 1969-74; v.p., treas. U. Bridgeport, Conn., 1974-79; v.p. corp. planning and devel., group v.p. Hubbell, Inc., Orange, Conn., 1985—; also exec. v.p. Hubbell, Inc., Orange, 1988—; bd. dirs. The Bank Mart, Bridgeport. Bd. dirs. Goodwill Industries, Bridgeport, 1976-87. Mem. Fin. Execs. Inst., Assn. for Corp. Growth. Club: Brokklawn Country (Fairfield, Conn.). Office: Hubbell Inc 584 Derby Milford Rd Orange CT 06477-2204*

ROWELL, JOHN MARTIN, research physicist, science administrator; b. Linslade, Eng., June 27, 1935; married, 1959; 3 children. BS, Oxford (Eng.) U., 1957, MA, PhD in Physics, 1961. Mem. staff Bell Labs., 1961-69, dept. head, 1969-81, dir., 1981-83; asst. v.p. Bellcore, 1983-89; chief tech. officer Conductus Inc., Sunnyvale, Calif., 1989-91, pres., 1991—; vis. prof. Stanford U., 1975. Recipient Fritz London Meml. Low Temperature Physics prize, 1978. Fellow Am. Phys. Soc., Royal Soc. London; mem. NAS. Achievements include research in superconductivity and tunneling; tunneling spectroscopy. Office: Conductus Inc 969 W Maude Ave Sunnyvale CA 94086*

ROWELL, LESTER JOHN, JR., insurance company executive; b. Cleve., Apr. 2, 1932; s. Lester John and Francis Laureen (Corbett) R.; m. Patricia Ann Loesch, Jan. 16, 1953 (div. Sept. 1970); children: Deborah, Cynthia, Gregory, Maureen, Diane; m. Carol Ann Jankowski, Sept. 26, 1970. BS, Pa. State U., 1955; grad. Advanced Mgmt. Program, Harvard U. Bus. Sch., 1971. CLU. Second v.p., field mgmt. Mut. Life Ins. Co. N.Y., N.Y.C., 1969-70, v.p. agys., 1970-72, v.p. sales, 1972-78, sr. v.p., 1978-80; exec. v.p. Provident Mut. Life Ins. Co., Phila., 1980-84, pres., 1984-86, pres., chief oper. officer, 1987, pres., chief exec. officer, 1991-93, chmn., pres., chief exec. officer, 1993—; bd. dirs. Provident Mut. Life Ins. Co., Provident Mut. Life and Annuity Co. Am., Sigma Am. Corp. Chmn. advt. book campaign and bd. dirs. Southeastern Pa. chpt. ARC, 1989; bd. dirs., Paoli Meml. Hosp., Phila. Drama Guild, Internat. Ins. Soc., Inc., Pa. State U. Am. Coun. Life Ins., Ins. Fedn. of Pa., The PMA Group. Cpat. USMC, 1953-62. Recipient Alumni award Pa. State U., 1972, Disting. Alumni award Pa. State U., 1988; Alumni Fellow Pa. State U., 1987. Mem. Life Ins. Mktg. and Rsch. Assn. (dir. 1980-83, mem. strategic mktg. issues com. 1987—), NALU, Agy. Officers Round Table (chmn. 1980-81), Life Underwriters Tng. Coun. (past trustee), Greater Phila. C. of C. (bd. dirs.). Republican. Office: Provident Mut Life Ins Co 1050 Westlakes Dr Berwyn PA 19312*

ROWE-MAAS, BETTY LU, real estate investor; b. San Jose, Calif., Apr. 2, 1925; d. Horace DeWitt and Lucy Belle (Spiker) Rowe; children: Terry Lee, Clifford Lindsay, Craig Harrison, Joan Louise. Real estate investor, Saratoga, Calif., 1968—. Mem. Nat. Trust Hist. Preservation, Smithsonian Instn., Archeol. Inst. Am., Santa Barbara Hist. Soc., Goleta Valley Hist. Soc., Santa Barbara Zool. Gardens, Santa Barbara Mus. Natural History, Santa Barbara Mus. Art, Santa Barbara Symphony League, Santa Barbara City Coll. Theater Group, Loberro Theatre Found., Arlington Theater Restoration Fund; bd. dirs. Valley Inst. Theatre Arts; mem. Route 85 Task Force, 1978—, treas., 1984-89; mem. Saratoga Good Govt., 1970-89; treas. Traffic Relief for Saratoga. Mem. LWV, Commonwealth of Calif. Club (life), Santa Barbara Rep. Club, Toastmasters (past treas. Santa Barbara club #5). Home: 4563 Carriage Hill Dr Santa Barbara CA 93110-2072

ROWEN, DANIEL, architect; b. Washington, Oct. 10, 1953; s. Hobart Quentin and Alice Brooks (Stadler) R.; m. Coco Myers, June 26, 1993; 1 child, Max. BA magna cum laude, Brown U., 1975; MArch, Yale U., 1981. Prin. Daniel Rowen Architects, N.Y.C. Prin. works include Gagosian Gallery, N.Y.C., 1991, 93, Coca-Cola Co. Offices, N.Y.C., 1994, Martha Stewart Living, 1994, 96. Recipient citation N.Y. State Assn. Architects, 1991. Mem. AIA, (citation N.Y.C. chpt. 1990, 91, award 1991), Archtl. League N.Y. Office: 448 W 37th St Apt 12 B New York NY 10018-4027

ROWEN, HAROLD CHARLES, shoe company executive; b. Lincoln, Nebr., Oct. 31, 1931; s. Paul Dale Rowen and Martha Mary (Brocker) Haines; m. Mary Lou Kennison, Nov. 16, 1953; children: Michael, Margaret, Ron, Roger, Joan, Janet. Student, U. Nebr., 1948-50. Salesman Kinney Shoes, Lincoln, Nebr., Topeka, and Des Moines, 1946-54; mgr. Kinney Shoes, L.A., 1955-58; dist. divisional mgr. Kinney Shoes, L.A., Chgo., 1959-70; sales mgr. Kinney Shoe Corp., N.Y.C., 1971-74, gen. mgr., 1975-78, sr. exec. v.p., 1979-88, pres., 1989—. V.p. Two/Ten Nat. Found., 1980-85, pres. 1986-87. Served with U.S. Army, 1951-53, Korea. Republican. Roman Catholic. Lodge: KC. Avocations: running, boating. Office: Kinney Shoe Corp 233 Broadway New York NY 10279-0001 Office: Kinney Service Corporation 3453 Simpson Ferry Rd Camp Hill PA 17011

ROWEN, HENRY STANISLAUS, economics educator; b. Boston, Oct. 11, 1925; s. Henry S. and Margaret Isabelle (Maher) R.; m. Beverly Camille Griffiths, Apr. 18, 1951; children: Hilary, Michael, Christopher, Sheila Jennifer, Diana Louise, Nicholas. BS, MIT, 1949; M in Philosophy, Oxford (Eng.) U., 1955. Economist Rand Corp., Santa Monica, Calif., 1950-61, pres., 1967-72; dep. asst. sec. internat. security affairs Dept. Def., Washington, 1961-64; asst. dir. Bur. Budget, Washington, 1965-66; prof. pub. policy Stanford (Calif.) U., 1972-95, dir. pub. policy program, 1972-75; sr. fellow Hoover Inst., Stanford, Calif., 1983—; Edwin B. Rust prof. pub. policy Stanford (Calif.) U., 1986-95; asst. sec. internat. security affairs Dept. Def., Washington, 1989-91; chmn. nat. intelligence coun. CIA, Washington, 1981-83. Author: (with R. Imai) Nuclear Energy and Nuclear Proliferation, 1980; (with C. Wolf Jr.) The Future of the Soviet Empire, 1987; editor: Options for U.S. Energy Policy, 1977, (with C. Wolf Jr.) The Impoverished Super power, 1990; contbr. numerous articles to profl. jours. Chmn. chief naval ops. exec. panel USN, Washignton, 1972-81, mem., 1983-89, 91-93; mem. def. sci. bd. Dept. Def., Washington, 1983-89, chmn. Def. Policy Bd., 1991-94. With USN, 1943-46, PTO. Mem. Internat. Inst. Strategic Studies. Republican. Roman Catholic. Office: Hoover Inst Hoover Tower Rm 1005 Stanford CA 94305-5015

ROWEN, MARSHALL, radiologist; b. Chgo.; s. Harry and Dorothy (Kasnow) R.; m. Helen Lee Friedman, Apr. 5, 1952; children: Eric, Scott, Mark. AB in Chemistry with highest honors, U. Ill., Urbana, 1951; MD with honors, U. Ill., Chgo., 1954, MS in Internal Medicine, 1954. Diplomate Am. Bd. Radiology. Intern Long Beach (Calif.) VA Hosp., 1955; resident in radiology Los Angeles VA Hosp., 1955-58; practice medicine specializing in radiology Orange, Calif., 1960—; chmn. bd. dirs. Moran, Rowen and Dorsey, Inc., Radiologists, 1969—; asst. radiologist L.A. Children's Hosp., 1958; assoc. radiologist Valley Presbyn. Hosp., Van Nuys, Calif., 1960; dir. dept. radiology St. Joseph Hosp., Orange, 1961—, v.p. staff, 1972; dir. dept. radiology Children's Hosp. Orange County, 1964—, chief staff, 1977-78, v.p., 1978-83, v.p., trustee, 1990-91, 92-95; asst. clin. prof. radiology U. Calif., Irvine, 1967-70, assoc. clin. prof., 1979-72, clin. prof. radiology and pediatrics, 1976-95, pres. clin. faculty assn., 1980-81; trustee Choc. Padrinos; sec. Choco Health Svcs., 1987-89, v.p., 1990-93, trustee, 1995—; trustee Found. Med. Care Orange County, 1972-76, Calif. Commn. Adminstrn. Svcs. Hosp., 1975-79, Profl. Practice Systems, 1990-92, Med. Specialty Mgrs., 1990—, St. Joseph Med. Corp., 1993—; v.p. Found. Med. Care Children's Hosp., 1988-89; v.p., sr. v.p., bd. dirs. St. Joseph Med. Corp. IPA, 1995-96; bd. dirs. Orange Coast Managed Care Svcs., 1995, sr. v.p., 1995-96, Paragon Med. Imaging, 1993—, Calif. Managed Imaging, 1994—, Alliance Premier Hosps., 1995-96; chmn. bd. dirs. Children's Healthcare of Calif., 1995-96; corp. mem. Blue Shield Calif., 1995-96. Mem. editorial bd. Western Jour. Medicine; contbr. articles to med. jours. Founder Orange County Performing Arts Ctr., mem. Laguna Art Mus., Laguna Festival of Arts, Opera Pacific, S. Coast Reportory, Am. Ballet Theater, World Affairs Council. Served to capt. M.C., U.S. Army, 1958-60. Recipient Rea sr. med. prize U. Ill, 1953; William Cook scholar U. Ill., 1951. Fellow Am. Coll. Radiology; mem. AMA, Am. Heart Assn., Soc. Nuclear Medicine (trustee 1961-62), Orange County Radiol. Soc. (pres. 1968-69), Calif. Radiol. Soc. (pres. 1978-79), Radiol. Soc. So. Calif. (pres. 1976), Pacific Coast Pediatric Radiologists Assn. (pres. 1971), Soc. Pediatric Radiology, Calif. Med. Assn. (chmn. sect. on radiology 1978-79), Orange County Med. Assn. (chmn. UCI liaison com. 1976-78), Cardioradiology Soc. So. Calif., Radiol. Soc. N.Am., Am. Roentgen Ray Soc., Am. Coll. Physician Execs., Soc. Chmn. Radiologists Children Hosp., Center Club, Phi Beta Kappa, Phi Eta Sigma, Omega Beta Phi, Alpha Omega Alpha. Office: 1201 W La Veta Ave Orange CA 92668-4213

ROWEN, ROBERT G., savings and loan executive. Pres., CEO Bell Bancorp. Office: Bell Bancorp Inc 79 W Monroe St Chicago IL 60603-4901

ROWEN, RUTH HALLE, musicologist, educator; b. N.Y.C., Apr. 5, 1918; d. Louis and Ethel (Fried) Halle; m. Seymour M. Rowen, Oct. 13, 1940; children: Mary Helen Rowen, Louis Halle Rowen. B.A., Barnard Coll., 1939; M.A., Columbia U., 1941, Ph.D., 1948. Mgmt. ednl. dept. Carl Fischer, Inc., N.Y.C., 1954-63; assoc. prof. musicology CUNY, 1967-72, prof., 1972—, mem. doctoral faculty in musicology, 1967—. Author: Early Chamber Music, 1948, reprinted, 1974; (with Adele T. Katz) Hearing-Gateway to Music, 1959, (with William Simon) Jolly Come Sing and Play, 1956, Music Through Sources and Documents, 1979, (with Mary Rowen) Instant Piano, 1979, 80, 83; contbr. articles to profl. jours. Mem. ASCAP, Am. Musicol. Soc., Music Library Assn., Coll. Music Soc., Nat. Fedn. Music Clubs (nat. musicianship chmn. 1962-74, nat. young artist auditions com. 1964-74, N.Y. state chmn. Young Artist Auditions 1981, dist. coord. 1983, nat. bd. dirs. 1989—, rep. UN 1991—), N.Y. Fedn. Music Clubs (pres.), Phi Beta Kappa. Home: 115 Central Park W New York NY 10023-4153
Opportunity grows with each constructive thought.

ROWLAND, ARTHUR RAY, librarian; b. Hampton, Ga., Jan. 6, 1930; s. Arthur and Jennie (Goodman) R.; m. Jane Thomas, July 1, 1955; children: Dell Ruth, Anna Jane. A.B., Mercer U., Macon, Ga., 1951; M. Librarianship, Emory U., 1952. Circulation asst. Ga. State Coll. Library, 1952, circulation librarian, 1952-53; librarian Armstrong Coll., Savannah, Ga., 1954-56; head circulation dept. Auburn U. Library, 1956-58; librarian, asso. prof. library sci. Jacksonville U., 1958-61; librarian, asso. prof. library sci. Augusta Coll., 1961-76, prof., libr., 1976-91, libr. emeritus, 1991—; lectr. libr. edn. U. Ga., 1962-66; trustee Augusta-Richmond County Pub. Libr., 1980-93, pres. bd. trustees, 1983-85, v.p. bd., 1988-91; trustee Augusta Regional Libr., chmn., 1984-85; trustee East Cen. Ga. Regional Libr., 1987-93, chmn., 1988-91; chmn. Gov.'s Conf. on Ga. Librs. and Info. Svcs., 1977; del. White House Conf. on Librs. and Info. Sci., 1979; cons. on libr. mgmt. to Govt. of Indonesia, 1986. Author: Bibliography of the Writings of Georgia History, 1966, A Guide to the Study of Augusta and Richmond County, Georgia, 1967, (with Helen Callahan) Yesterday's Augusta, 1976, (with James E. Dorsey) A Bibliography of the Writings on Georgia History 1900-1970, rev. edit., 1978, (with Marguerite F. Fogleman) Reese Library Genealogical Resources, 1988, supplement, 1990, Goodman Cousins, 1988, Rowland Cousins, 1990, New Guide to the Study of Augusta, 1990, Index to City Directory of Augusta, Georgia, 1841-1879, 1991, More Goodman Cousins, 1993, My Fair Grandmother, 1994, Distant Cousins, The Huguenots Connecting Rowland, Bulloch, de Bourdeaux, DeVeaux and Roosevelt Families of S.C., N.C. and Ga., 1995, The Bessent Family of Georgia, 1995, Reeves Family of Georgia, 1996, Descendants of Wiley Reeves, 1996; editor: Reference SErvices, 1964, Historical Markers of Richmond County, Georgia, rev. edit., 1971, The Catalog and Cataloging, 1969, The Librarian and Reference Service, 1977, Reminiscences of Augusta Marines, 1985; supervising editor (with Heard Robertson) Jour. Archibald Campbell, 1981; contbr. to profl. jours. V.p. Ga. Libr. Assn. Trustees and Friends, 1989-91. With USN, 1948-49. Recipient Nix-Jones award for disting. service Ga. Library Assn., 1981,,Town and Gown award Augusta Coll. Alumni Assn., 1985. Mem. ALA, Am. Assn. State and Local History, Bibliog. Soc. Am., Southeastern Libr. Assn. (hon. life, exec. bd. 1971-72), Ga. Libr. Assn. (hon. life, 2d v.p. 1965-67, 71-73, 1st v.p., pres.-elect 1973-75, pres. 1975-77, chmn. budget com. 1977-79, adv. to pres. 1979-83, 85-92), Ctrl. Savannah River Area Libr. Assn. (past pres., editor union list of serials 1967), Duval County Libr. Assn. (past v.p.), Nat. Geneal. Soc., Ga. Geneal. Soc., N.C. Geneal. Soc., Va. Geneal. Soc., Augusta Geneal. Soc., Richmond County Hist. Soc. (curator 1964-91, pres. 1967-69, founder, editor Richmond County History), Ga. Hist. Soc. (curator emeritus), Ga. Bapt. Hist. Soc., Nat., Young Men's Libr. Assn. (v.p. 1988-91), Ga. Trusts for Hist. Preservation, Hist. Augusta (trustee emeritus), Soc. Ga. Archivists, Kappa Phi Kappa. Baptist. Address: One Seventh St Ste 603 Augusta GA 30901

ROWLAND, CECILIA STUDLEY, information systems specialist; b. Cin., Dec. 1, 1953; d. George David and Dorothy Mae (Fehder) Studley; m. Earl Lester, Aug. 27, 1984 (div. 1993). AS in Ornamental Horticulture, Cin. Tech. Coll., 1977; BS, U. Toledo, 1986. Acctg. coord. Burke Mktg. Svcs., Inc., Cin., 1978-81, programmer/analyst, 1981-83, personal computer specialist, 1983-84; CATI systems supr. NFO Rsch., Inc., Toledo, Ohio, 1984-88, microcomputer systems specialist, 1988-89, systems/ops. supr., 1989-93; mem. LUG steering com. Digital Equipment Corp., 1989—. Republican. Roman Catholic. Avocation: photography.

ROWLAND, DAVID JACK, academic administrator; b. Columbus, Ohio, June 17, 1921; s. David Henry and Ethel (Ryan) R.; m. Mary Ellen Stinson, Apr. 8, 1944; children: David Allen, Ryan Stinson, Sue Ellen Rowland Summers. BS, Ohio U., 1949; MA, U. Ala., 1951; LittD (hon.), Athens State Coll., 1967; LLD (hon.), Jacksonville State U., 1969. Pres. Walker Coll., Jasper, Ala., 1956-88, chancellor, 1988-95; interim pres. U. Ala./Walker Coll., 1995-96; bd. dirs. First Nat. Bank, Jasper, first Comml. Bancshares, Birmingham, Ala.; chmn. Ala. ACT Bd., Tuscaloosa, 1968—; real estate developer. Chmn. Jasper Indsl. Bd., 1987—; commr. Ala. Mining commn., Jasper, 1976—; mem. Ala. Employer Guard Res. commn., Birmingham, 1988—; trustee Walker Coll.; chmn. adv. bd. Jasper Salvation Army. Col. U.S. Army, 1942-46, ATO. Decorated Legion of Merit; recipient Silver Beaver award Boy Scouts Am., 1972. Mem. Res. Officers Assn. (pres. Jasper chpt.), Summit Club, Met. Dinner Club, Rotary (pres. Jasper 1967-68, Paul Harris fellow), Masons. Avocations: tree farmer, growing Christmas trees, wildfowl carver. Home: 1005 Valley Rd Jasper AL 35501-4964 Office: Walker Coll Office of President UAB/Walker College Jasper AL 35501

ROWLAND, ESTHER E(DELMAN), college dean, retired; b. N.Y.C., Apr. 12, 1926; d. Abraham Simon and Ida Sarah (Shifrin) Edelman; m. Lewis P. Rowland, Aug. 31, 1952; children: Andrew, Steven, Judith. B.A., U. Wis., 1946; M.A., Columbia U., 1948, M.Phil., 1984. Instr. in polit. sci. CCNY, 1947-51, Mt. Holyoke Coll., South Hadley, Mass., 1948-49; dir. health professions adv. bd. U. Pa., Phila., 1971-73; adviser to pre-profl. students Barnard Coll., N.Y.C., 1974-79, dean for pre-profl. students, 1980-93, assoc. dean studies, 1989-95; ret., 1995—. Mem. exec. com. Nat. Emergency Civil Liberties Com., N.Y.C., 1975-90; mem. exec. com. Women's Counseling Project, 1981-86. Mem. N.E. Assn. Health Professions Advisers (exec. com. 1973-74), N.E. Assn. Pre Law Advisors (exec. com. 1981-83, 85-86), Neurol. Inst. Aux. Home: 404 Riverside Dr New York NY 10025-1861

ROWLAND, FRANK SHERWOOD, chemistry educator; b. Delaware, Ohio, June 28, 1927; m. Joan Lundberg, 1952; children: Ingrid Drake, Jeffrey Sherwood. AB, Ohio Wesleyan U., 1948; MS, U. Chgo., 1951, PhD, 1952, DSc (hon.), 1989; DSc (hon.), Duke U., 1989, Whittier Coll., 1989, Princeton U., 1990, Haverford Coll., 1992; LLD (hon.), Ohio Wesleyan U., 1989, Simon Fraser U., 1991. Instr. chemistry Princeton (N.J.) U., 1952-56; asst. prof. chemistry U. Kans., 1956-58, assoc. prof. chemistry, 1958-63, prof. chemistry, 1963-64; prof. chemistry U. Calif., Irvine, 1964—, dept. chmn., 1964-70, Aldrich prof. chemistry, 1985-89, Bren prof. chemistry, 1989-94, Bren rsch. prof., 1994—; Humboldt sr. scientist, Fed. Republic of Germany, 1981; chmn. Dahlem (Fed. Republic of Germany) Conf. on Changing Atmosphere, 1987; vis. scientist Japan Soc. for Promotion Sci., 1980; co-dir. western region Nat. Inst. Global Environ. Changes, 1989-93; del. Internat. Coun. Sci. Unions, 1993—; fgn. sec. NAS, 1994—; lectr., cons. in field. Contbr. numerous articles to profl. jours. Mem. ozone commn. Internat. Assn. Meteorology and Atmospheric Physics, 1980-88, mem. commn. on atmospheric chemistry and global pollution, 1979-91; mem. acid rain peer rev. panel U.S. Office of Sci. and Tech., Exec. Office of White House, 1982-84; mem. vis. com. Max Planck Insts., Heidelberg and Mainz, Fed. Republic Germany, 1982—; ozone trends panel mem. NASA, 1986-88; chmn. Gordon Conf. Environ. Scis.-Air, 1987; mem. Calif. Coun. Sci. Tech., 1989—, Exec. Com. Tyler Prize, 1992—. Recipient numerous awards including John Wiley Jones award Rochester Inst. of Tech., 1975, Disting. Faculty Rsch. award U. Calif., Irvine, 1976, Profl. Achievement award U. Chgo., 1977, Billard award N.Y. Acad. Sci., 1977, Tyler World Prize in Environment Achievement, 1983, Global 500 Roll of Honor for Environ. Achievement UN Environment Program, 1988, Dana award for Pioneering Achievements in Health, 1987, Silver medal Royal Inst. Chemistry, U.K., 1989, Wadsworth award N.Y. State Dept. Health, 1989, medal U. Calif., Irvine, 1989, Japan prize in Environ. Sci., 1989, Dickson prize Carnegie-Mellon U., 1991; Guggenheim fellow, 1962, 74, Albert Einstein prize of World Cultural Coun., 1994, Nobel Prize in Chemistry, 1995, Roger Revelle medal Am. Geophysical Union, 1994. Fellow AAAS (pres. elect 1991, pres. 1992, chmn. bd. dirs. 1993), Am. Phys. Soc. (Leo Szilard award for Physics in Pub. Interest 1979), Am. Geophys. Union (Roger Revelle medal 1994); mem. NAS (bd. environ. studies and toxicology 1986-91, com. on atmospheric chemistry 1987-89, com. atmospheric scis., solar-terrestial com. 1979-83, co-DATA com. 1977-82, sci. com. on problems environment 1986-89, Infinite Voyage film com. 1988-92, Robertson Meml. lectr. 1993, chmn. com. on internat. orgns. and programs 1993—, chmn. office of internat. affairs 1994—), Am. Acad. Arts and Scis., Am. Chem. Soc. (chmn. divsn. nuclear sci. and tech. 1973-74, chmn. divsn. phys. chemistry 1974-75, Tolman medal 1976, Zimmerman award 1980, E.F. Smith lectureship 1980, Environ. Sci. and Tech. award 1983, Esselen award 1987, Peter Debye Phys. Chem. award 1993), Am. Philos. Soc., Inst. Medicine. Home: 4807 Dorchester Rd Corona Del Mar CA 92625-2718 Office: U Calif Irvine Dept of Chemistry 571 PS1 Irvine CA 92717

ROWLAND, HOWARD RAY, mass communications educator; b. Eddy County, N.Mex., Sept. 9, 1929; s. Lewis Marion and Ursula Lorene (Hunt) R.; m. Meredith June Lee, Apr. 19, 1951; children: Runay Ilene Smith, Rhonda Lee Fisher. B in Journalism, U. Mo., 1950; MS in Journalism, So. Ill. U., 1959; PhD, Mich. State U., 1969. Feature writer Springfield (Mo.) Newspapers, Inc., 1954; newspaper editor Monett (Mo.) Times, 1954-55; editorial writer So. Ill. U., Carbondale, 1955-59; pub. rels. dir. St. Cloud (Minn.) State U., 1959-86, asst. dean, 1986-87, 88-90; dir. Ctr. for British Studies, Alnwick, Eng., 1987-88, 90-91; adj. prof. Mass Comms., St. Cloud State U., 1986—; cons. Conf. of Campus Ombudsmen, Berkeley, 1971; recorder Seminar on Fund Raising, Washington, 1985; bibliographer Higher Edn. Bibliography Yearbook, 1987. Author: American Students in Alnwick Castle, 1990, St. Cloud State University--125 Years, 1994; editor: Effective Community Relations, 1980; sect. editor: Handbook of Institutional Advancement, 1986; author book revs. Chair All-Am. City Com., St. Cloud, 1973-74. With U.S. Army, 1951-53. NDEA doctoral fellowship Mich. State U., 1967-69; recipient Appreciation award Mayor of St. Cloud, 1974, Disting Svc. award Coun. for Advancement and Support of Edn., 1985. Mem. Soc. of Profl. Journalists (Minn. chpt. pres. 1963-64, dep. dir. 1965-67), Coun. for Advancement and Support of Edn. (dist. 5 chair 1977-79, Leadership award 1979), Rotary Internat., Phi Delta Kappa (Mich. State U. chpt. pres. 1968-69, St. Cloud State Univ. chpt. pres. 1978-79). Presbyterian. Avocations: writing, fishing, travel, photography, antiques. Home: 29467 Kraemer Lake Rd Saint Joseph MN 56374-9646 *Striving to achieve is more rewarding than striving to succeed. Achievement brings personal satisfaction more fulfilling than recognition and compensation.*

ROWLAND, JAMES RICHARD, electrical engineering educator; b. Muldrow, Okla., Jan. 24, 1940; s. Richard Cleveland and Imogene Beatrice (Angel) R.; m. Jonell Condren, Aug. 24, 1963 (dec. May 1991); children: Jennifer Lynn, Angela Janel; m. Mary Anderson, Jan. 2, 1995. BSEE, Okla. State U., 1962; MSEE, Purdue U., 1964, PhD in Elec. Engring., 1966. Registered profl. engr., Okla. Instr. Purdue U., West Lafayette, Ind., 1964-65; from asst. to assoc. prof. Ga. Inst. Tech., Atlanta, 1966-71; from assoc. to full prof. Okla. State U., Stillwater, 1971-85; prof., chmn. dept. elec. and computer engring. U. Kans., Lawrence, 1985-89, prof., 1985—; cons. Lockheed-Ga. Co., Marietta, 1966-71, U.S. Army Missile Command, Huntsville, Ala., 1969-79, Sandia Nat. Labs., Albuquerque, 1979, Puritan-Bennett, Lenexa, Kans., 1992. Author: Linear Control Systems, 1986; mem. editorial adv. bd. Computer and Elec. Engring., 1971—; co-contbr. 50 articles to profl. jours. Fellow IEEE (edn. soc. pres. 1982-83, Centennial medal 1984, edn. soc. achievement award 1986, edn. conf. award 1988), Am. Soc. Engring. Edn. (dir. grad. div. 1987-89), Eta Kappa Nu (dir. 1989-91). Republican. Methodist. Lodge: Kiwanis. Avocations: golf, gardening. Home: 2424 Free State Ct Lawrence KS 66047-2831 Office: U Kans Dept Elec Engring & Computer Sci 1013 Learned Hall Lawrence KS 66045-2228

ROWLAND, JOHN ARTHUR, lawyer; b. Joliet, Ill., Mar. 6, 1943; s. John Fornof and Grace Ada (Baskerville) R.; m. Lana D. Lee, Sept. 8, 1984; children: Sean B., Keira L. B.A., U. Notre Dame, 1965; J.D., U. San Francisco, 1968. Bar: Calif. 1969, U.S. Dist. Ct. (no. dist.) Calif. 1982. Asst. dist. atty. San Francisco Dist. Atty.'s Office, 1971-81; assoc. Ropers, Majeski, Kohn and Bentley, San Francisco, 1982—, ptnr., 1985—. Pres., South of Market Boys, San Francisco, 1981; bd. dirs. Former San Francisco Asst. Dist. Attys., 1984. Served to capt. U.S. Army, 1969-71, Korea. Recipient Commendation San Francisco Bd. Suprs., 1981, Merit award Mayor of San Francisco, 1982. Roman Catholic. Office: 670 Howard St San Francisco CA 94105-3916

ROWLAND, JOHN G., governor, former congressman; b. Waterbury, Conn., May 24, 1957; s. Sherwood L. and Florence (Jackson) R.; m. Deborah Nabhan; children: Kirsten Elizabeth, Robert John, Julianne Marie. B.S. in Bus. Adminstrn., Villanova U., 1979. Former mem. Conn. Ho. of Reps.; mem. 99th-101st Congress from 5th Conn. dist., 1985-91; governor Conn., 1995—; pres. Rowland Assocs. Ambassador, St. Mary's Hosp., Waterbury; bd. dirs. Am. Cancer Soc., Waterbury. Recipient Disting. Service award VFW, Holy Cross Alumni Assn. Republican. Home: 990 Prospect Ave Hartford CT 06105*

ROWLAND, LANDON HILL, diversified holding company executive; b. Fuquay Springs, N.C., May 20, 1937; s. Walter Elton and Elizabeth Carr (Williams) R.; m. Sarah Fidler, Dec. 29, 1959; children: Sarah Elizabeth, Matthew Hill, Joshua Carr. B.A., Dartmouth Coll., 1959; LL.B., Harvard U., 1962. Bar: Mo. Assoc. Watson, Ess, Marshall & Enggas, Kansas City, Mo., 1962-70; ptnr. Watson, Ess, Marshall & Enggas, 1970-80; v.p. Kansas City So. Industries, Inc., 1980-83, pres., chief oper. officer, 1983-86, pres., chief exec. officer, 1987—, also bd. dirs.; pres., chief exec. officer Kansas City So. Ry. Co., 1990-91, chmn., 1990—; lectr. antitrust law U. Mo. Kansas City; chmn. DST Systems, 1983—. Co-author West's Mo. Practice Series. Trustee Midwest Rsch. Inst., Kansas City, Mo.; chmn. bd. dirs. Swope Ridge Health Care Ctr.; bd. dirs. Lyric Opera of Kansas City, Am. Royal, Jacob L. & Ella C. Loose Found.; chmn. Met. Performing Arts Fund. Mem. ABA, Mo. Bar Assn., Phi Beta Kappa. Clubs: Kansas City Country, Kansas City, River. Home: Ever Glades Farm 12717 NE Mt Olivet Rd Kansas City MO 64166-1236 Office: Kans City So Industries Inc 114 W 11th St Kansas City MO 64105-1804*

ROWLAND, LEWIS PHILLIP, neurologist, medical editor, educator; b. Bklyn., Aug. 3, 1925; s. Henry Alexander and Cecile (Coles) R.; m. Esther Edelman, Aug. 31, 1952; children: Andrew Simon, Steven Samuel, Joy Rosenthal. B.S., Yale U., 1945, M.D., 1948; hon. doctorate, U. Aix-Marseilles, France, 1986, U. Padua, 1996. Diplomate: Am. Bd. Psychiatry and Neurology. Intern New Haven Hosp., 1949-50; asst. resident N.Y. Neurol. Inst., 1950-52, fellow, 1953; clin. assoc. NIH, Bethesda, Md., 1953-54; practice research medicine, specializing in neurology N.Y.C., 1954-67, Phila., 1967-73, N.Y.C., 1973—; asst. neurologist Montefiore Hosp., N.Y.C., 1954-57; vis. fellow Nat. Inst. Med. Research, London, 1956; from asst. prof. to prof. neurology Columbia Coll. Physicians and Surgeons, 1957-67, prof., chmn. dept. neurology, 1973—; prof., chmn. dept. neurology U. Pa., Med. Sch., 1967-73; from asst. neurologist to attending neurologist Presbyn. Hosp., 1957-67; co-dir. Neurol. Clin. Research Center, 1961-67, dir. neurology service, 1973—, pres. med. bd., 1991-94; cons. Harlem Hosp., 1973—; mem. med. adv. bd. Myasthenia Gravis Found., pres., 1971-73; med. adv. bd. Muscular Dystrophy Assocs., Nat. Multiple Sclerosis Soc., Com. to Combat Huntington's Disease; pres. Parkinson's Disease Found., 1979—; mem. tng. grants com. Nat. Inst. Neurol. Diseases and Stroke, NIH, 1971-73, bd. sci. counselors, 1978-83, chmn., 1981-83, nat. adv. council, 1986-90. Editorial bd.: Archives of Neurology, 1968-76, Advances in Neurology, 1969—, Italian Jour. Neurol. Sci., 1979—, Handbook of Clin. Neurology, 1982—, New England Jour. Medicine, 1990—, Medical Letter, 1990—, Jour. Neurol. Sci., 1991—, Jour. Neuromuscular Disorders, 1991—; editor-in-chief: Neurology, 1977-87. Served with USNR, 1942-44; with USPHS, 1953-54. Mem. Am. Neurol. Assn. (pres. 1980, hon. mem. 1989—), Am. Acad. Neurology (pres.-elect 1987-89, pres. 1989-91), Phila. Neurol. Soc. (pres. 1972), Assn. Research Nervous Mental Disease (pres. 1969, trustee 1976—, v.p. 1980, chmn. bd. trustees 1992—), Assn. Univ. Profs. Neurology (sec. 1971-74, pres. 1978), Eastern Pa. Multiple Sclerosis Soc. (chmn. med. adv. bd. 1969-73); hon. mem. Neurol. Socs. France, Poland, Can., Europe, Italy, Gt. Britain, Spain, Japan; mem. N.Y.C. Multiple Sclerosis Soc. (chmn. med. adv. bd. 1977-92). Home: 404 Riverside Dr New York NY 10025-1861 Office: Columbia-Presbyn Med Ctr Neurological Inst 710 W 168th St New York NY 10032-2603

ROWLAND, RALPH THOMAS, architect; b. Elizabeth, N.J., Oct. 10, 1920; s. Thomas Aloysius and Anna Frances (McQuaid) R.; m. Bernice Barbara Cannizzo, Sept. 7, 1946; children: Glenn Thomas, Mark Louis, Roy Joseph, Lisa Rowland Majewski. Student, Manhattan Coll., 1937-38, Columbia U., 1945-49. Archtl. field supr., specifier Voorhees Walker Foley & Smith, N.Y.C., 1945-50; specifier, project mgr. Sargent Webster Crenshaw & Folley, Watertown, N.Y., 1951-53; individual archtl. practice Hamden, Conn., 1958-65; field supr. Fletcher Thompson, Inc., Bridgeport, Conn., 1954-56; project mgr. Fletcher Thompson, Inc., 1957, 65-73, asso., 1969-73, v.p., 1973-81, dir. archtl. research, 1981-85, also dir., 1973-93; cons. Cheshire, Conn., 1981—; chmn. Conn. Bldg. Code Standards Com., 1978-82; vice chmn. Conn. State Codes and Standards Com., 1982-86. Editorial chmn.: Conn. Architect Mag., 1966-74; project mgr. design, St. Vincents Med. Center, Bridgeport. Mem. Cheshire Planning Commn., 1966-72, chmn., 1967-68; pres. Hamden C. of C., 1964, New Eng. Bldg. Code Assn., 1989; mem. Cen. Naugatuck Valley Regional Planning Agy., 1966-74, chmn., 1969; mem. Cheshire Democratic Town Com., 1960-70, treas., 1963-69; mem. Conn. Archtl. Sch. Task Force, 1987-88. With USN, 1942-45. Fellow AIA; mem. AIA Conn. (past pres.), AARP (pres. Cheshire chpt. 1995), Bridgeport Assn. Architects (past sec.), Bldg. Ofcls. and Code Adminstrs. Internat., Conn. Bldg. Ofcls. Assn., Cheshire C. of C. Roman Catholic. Home and Office: 201 N Rolling Acres Rd Cheshire CT 06410-2119

ROWLAND, ROBERT CHARLES, clinical psychotherapist, writer, researcher; b. Columbus, Ohio, Jan. 18, 1946; s. Charles Albert and Lorene Bernadine (Friedlinghaus) R.; m. Saundra Marie Gardner, Dec. 21, 1968 (div. Mar. 1987); children: Carrie Ann, Marcus Jules Harrad, Heather Renée. BS in Physiol. Psychology, Ohio State U., 1971, MSW, 1981. Cert. marital and family therapist; cert. in drug and alcohol treatment; cert. sex therapist; cert. hypnotist. Respiratory therapist Mt. Carmel Med. Ctr., Columbus, Ohio, 1965-68; adj. prof. Columbus Ctr. Sci. and Industry, Columbus, Ohio, 1968-71; researcher in tetrahydrocannabinol/learning experiments Ohio State U. Rsch. Ctr., 1970-71; secondary tchr. Columbus (Ohio) Pub. Schs., 1971-73; case cons. Bur. Disability Determination, Columbus, 1973-80; clin. social worker Clarke County Out-Patient Mental Health Ctr., Springfield, Ohio, 1979-80, Upham Hall, Ohio State U. Hosps., 1980-81; clin. psychotherapist Psychol. Systems, Inc., Columbus, 1981-84; psychotherapist, cons. Columbus, 1974-87, 94—, Delray Beach, Fla., 1987-93; dir. social svc. and cmty. rels. Apple Creek (Ohio) Devel. Ctr., 1981-82; pres., rsch. dir. Neurosocial Scis. Inst., Delray Beach, 1987-93, Columbus, 1994. Author: Brain Wars-The End of the Drug Game, 1991; contbr. articles to profl. jours. Adv. Neighbor to Neighbor, Delray Beach, 1991-93. Recipient scholarship grant, Ohio State U. Coll. of Social Work, 1980-81. Mem. AAAS, NASW (chmn. Ohio Pace chpt., lobbyist 1980-81, Excellence award 1981, mem. Fla. chpt.), Fla. Freelance Writer's Assn., Union of Concerned Scientists, Palm Beach County Scis. Jour. Club, Alpha Delta Mu. Avocations: rockhounding, scuba diving, tennis, music, chess. Home: 6378 Busch Blvd Apt 386 Columbus OH 43229

ROWLAND, ROBERT E., secondary school principal. Prin. Danville (Ky.) High Sch. Recipient Blue Ribbon award U.S. Dept. Edn., 1990-91. Office: Danville High Sch 203 E Lexington Ave Danville KY 40422-1519

ROWLAND, (JAMES) ROY, congressman; b. Wrightsville, GA, Feb. 3, 1926; s. J. Roy and Jerradine R.; m. Luella Price, July 28, 1924; children: Lou Rowland Neal, Jane, Jim. Student, Emory U., 1943, South Ga. Coll., 1946, U. Ga., 1946-48; M.D., Med. Coll. Ga., 1952. Intern Macon Hosp., Ga., 1952-53, resident in family practice, 1953-54; practice medicine specializing in family practice Dublin, Ga., 1954-82; state rep. Ga. Ho. of Reps., Atlanta, 1976-82; mem. 98th-103rd Congresses from 8th Ga. Dist., 1983—; mem. Energy, Commerce com., subcom. Health and Environ., veteran's affairs com., subcom. hosp. and health care, oversight and investigations, house Dem. steering and policy com. Served with U.S. Army, 1944-46, ETO. Decorated Bronze Star. Democrat. Methodist. Office: 1801 Kay St NW Ste 901 L Washington DC 20004*

ROWLAND, THEODORE JUSTIN, physicist, educator; b. Cleve., May 15, 1927; s. Thurston Justin and Lillian (Nesser) R.; m. Janet Claire Millar, June 28, 1952 (div. 1967); children: Theodore Justin, Dawson Ann, Claire Millar; m. Patsy Marie Beard, Aug. 21, 1968. BS, Western Res. U., 1948; MA, Harvard U., 1949, PhD, 1954. Rsch. physicist Union Carbide Metals Co., Niagara Falls, N.Y., 1954-61; prof. phys. metallurgy U. Ill., 1961-92, asst. dean Coll. Engring., acting assoc. dean Grad. Coll., 1990-91, prof. emeritus, 1992—; pres., dir. Materials Cons., Inc.; cons. physicist, 1961—; cons. metallurgist, 1976—. Editor 2 books; author monograph; contbr. articles to profl. jours. Fellow Am. Phys. Soc.; mem. AIME, AAAS, AAUP (pres. U. Ill. chpt.), Phi Beta Kappa, Sigma Xi. Achievements include initial verification of charge density waves in dilute alloys; original contributions to theory and experiment in nuclear magnetic resonance in metals. Home: 805 Park Lane Dr Champaign IL 61820-7613 Office: U Ill Dept Materials Sci and Engring 1304 W Green St Urbana IL 61801-2920

ROWLANDS, BETH ANA, advertising executive; b. Quincy, Ill., Jan. 15, 1957; d. Robert Marlin and Peggy Jean (Murphy) Bohnenlcamp; m. Robert John Rowlands, Dec. 1, 1979 (div. July 1987); 1 child, Blake; m. Michael Joseph Kopp, Oct. 27, 1995; 1 stepchild, Kahli. Student, U. Mo., 1975-76, Columbia Coll., 1977-78. Media analyst SCG Advt., Kansas City, Mo., 1980-83; media buyer/planner Mktg. Resources, Kansas City, 1983-84; sr. media buyer/planner Bernstein-Rein, Kansas City, 1984-85, media supr., 1985-87, assoc. media dir., 1987-94, v.p., assoc. media dir., 1994—; bd. dirs. exec. com. Bernstein Rein Advt., Kansas City, 1994. Bd. mem. Am. Diabetes Assn., Kansas City. Avocations: aerobics, running, skiing, reading, family activities. Office: Bernstein Rein Advt Ste 1500 4600 Madison Ave Kansas City MO 64112

ROWLANDS, DAVID THOMAS, pathology educator; b. Wilkes-Barre, Pa., Mar. 22, 1930; s. David Thomas and Anna Jule (Morgan) R.; m. Gwendolyn Marie York, Mar. 1, 1958; children: Julie Marie, Carolyn Jane. M.D., U. Pa., 1955. Diplomate: Am. Bd. Pathology, Am. Bd. Allergy and Immunology. Intern Pa. Hosp., Phila., 1955-56; resident Cin. Gen. Hosp., 1956-60; asst. prof. U. Colo., 1962-64, Rockefeller U., 1964-66; assoc. prof. Duke U., Durham, N.C., 1966-70; prof. pathology U. Pa., Phila., 1970-82; chmn. dept. pathology U. Pa., 1973-78, prof. medicine, 1979-82; prof., chmn. dept. pathology U. So. Fla., Tampa, 1982-91; assoc. dean U. So. Fla., 1983-84, prof. pediatrics, 1986-91; med. dir. Lifelink Tissue Bank, 1991-93. Mem. editorial bd.: Am. Jour. Pathology, 1971-81, Developmental and Comparative Immunology, 1977-79. Served with USNR, 1960-62. Recipient Lederle Med. Faculty award U. Colo., 1964, Jacob Ehrenzeller award Pa. Hosp., 1976. Mem. Am. Assn. Pathologists, Internat. Acad. Pathology, Am. Soc. Clin. Pathology, Am. Assn. Immunologists, Coll. Am. Pathologist, Arthur Purdy Stout Soc. Presbyterian. Home: 13804 Cypress Village Cir Tampa FL 33624-4406

ROWLANDS, GENA, actress; b. Cambria, Wis., June 19, 1936; d. Edwin Merwin and Mary Allen (Neal) R.; m. John Cassavetes (dec.); children: Nicholas, Alexandra, Zoe. Student, U. Wis., Am. Acad. Dramatic Art, N.Y.C. Theatrical appearance include The Middle of the Night, 1956; films include The High Cost of Loving, 1958, Lonely Are The Brave, 1962, A Child is Waiting, 1962, Spiral Road, 1962, Faces, 1968, At Any Price, 1970, Minnie and Moscowitz, 1971, Woman Under the Influence, 1973, Two Minute Warning, 1976, Opening Night, 1977, The Brinks Job, 1978, One Summer Night, 1979, Gloria, 1980, Tempest, 1982, Love Streams, 1983, Light of Day, 1987, Another Woman, 1988, Once Around, 1990, Ted and Venus, 1991, Night on Earth, 1992; TV movies A Question of Love, 1978, Strangers, 1979, Thurday's Child, 1983, Early Frost, 1986, The Betty Ford Story, 1987, Montana, Face of a Stranger, 1991 (Emmy award, Leading Actress in a Mini-Series or Special, 1992), Parallel Lives, 1994; numerous other TV appearances. Mem. Actors Equity Assn., Screen Actors Guild, AFTRA, Am. Guild Variety Artists. *

ROWLANDS, MARVIN LLOYD, JR., publishing and communications consultant; b. Wellington, Kans., Apr. 30, 1926; s. Marvin Lloyd and Opal Mary (Pilant) R. BS in Journalism, U. Kans., 1950. Wire editor Manhattan (Kans.) Mercury, 1950-51; reporter Leavenworth (Kans.) Times, 1951-56, Topeka (Kans.) Daily Capital, 1956-57, Cin. Times-Star, 1957-58; assoc. editor The Am. Med. News (Chgo., 1958-61, mng. editor, 1961-65, editor, 1965-75; editor-in-chief Modern Healthcare, Chgo., 1975-76; editor Contemporary Surgery and Contemporary Ob/Gyn, N.Y.C., 1976-77; dir. devel. McGraw-Hill Publs. Co., N.Y.C., 1978-84, dir. planning, 1984-85, v.p. planning, 1985-86, v.p. editorial, planning and devel., 1986-88; v.p. editorial McGraw-Hill Fin. Services Co., N.Y.C., 1988-89; sr. v.p. comm. McGraw-Hill Fin. Svcs. Co., N.Y.C., 1989-90; pub., communications cons., N.Y.C., 1990-92, North Chatham, Mass., 1992—. Mem., chmn. bd. dirs. Rush Dance, A Found., Inc., N.Y.C., 1980—. Served with USNR, 1944-46. Mem. Omicron Delta Kappa. Baptist. Home and Office: PO Box 757 52 Spring Hill Rd North Chatham MA 02650

ROWLANDS, ROBERT EDWARD, engineer, educator; b. Trail, B.C., Can., July 7, 1936; s. Edward and Eda May (Randell) R.; m. Mary Roma Ranaghan, Nov. 14, 1959; children: Robert Philip, Edward Hugh. BA. Sc., U. B.C., Vancouver, 1959; MS, U. Ill., 1964, PhD, 1967. Engr. mechanics MacMillan & Bloedel, Powell River, B.C., 1959, Ill. Inst. Tech. Rsch. Inst., Chgo., 1967-74; asst. prof. engring. U. Wis., 1974-76, assoc. prof. engring., 1976-79, prof. engring., 1979—, dir. structural and materials testing lab., 1983-90; vis. scholar People's Republic China, 1985; Clark C. Heritage vis. scientist USDA Forest Products Lab., 1987; vis. scholar Gadjah Mada U., Yogyakarta, Indonesia, 1991; lectr. in field; cons. to rsch. insts., engring. orgns., instrument mfrs., ins. cos., auto, farm-implement, food processing, paper products, foresty, composite, plastics, petroleum and mining industries; expert witness law firms; internat. tech. travel, Scandanavia, Europe, U.K., Japan, Spain, Portugal, Australia, China, and former USSR. Registered profl. engr., Wis. Fellow ASME; mem. Soc. Exptl. Mechanics (mem. papers rev. com. 1967—, mem. editorial com. 1976—, book rev. editor 1976—, chmn. composite com. 1977-79, tech. chmn. 1975, also chmn. various tech. sessions, Hetényi award 1970, 76, fellow 1982, Frocht award 1989), Am. Acad. Mechanics. Author chpt. Handbook of Composite Materials, Handbook of Experimental Mechanics; contbr. over 130 articles to profl. jours. Home: 5401 Russett Rd Madison WI 53711-3564 Office: Dept Mechanical Engring U Wisc 1415 Engineering Dr Madison WI 53706-1691

ROWLENSON, RICHARD CHARLES, lawyer; b. Camden, N.J., Dec. 27, 1949; s. Alton Joseph and Margaret (Mietzelfeld) R.; m. Frances Ambury, July 28, 1979; children: Mary, Anne. BS, Georgetown U., 1971, JD, 1975. Bar: D.C. 1975, U.S. Ct. Appeals (D.C. cir.) 1975, U.S. Supreme Ct. 1979. Atty. Hennessey, Stambler & Siebert, Washington, 1975-87; sr. v.p., gen. counsel Vanguard Cellular Systems Inc., Greensboro, N.C., 1987—. Mem. ABA, Bar Assn. D.C., Greensboro Bar Assn., Fed. Communications Bar Assn., Sherwood Swim and Racquet Club (Greensboro). Office: Vanguard Cellular Systems 2002 Pisgah Church Rd Ste 300 Greensboro NC 27455-3318

ROWLETT, RALPH MORGAN, archaeologist, educator; b. Richmond, Ky., Sept. 11, 1934; s. Robert Kenny and Daisy (Mullikin) R.; m. Elsebet Sander-Jorgensen, Aug. 25, 1963 (div. Jan. 1986); children: Rolf Arvid, Erik Kenneth; m. Elizabeth Helen Dinan, Apr. 21, 1989 (div. Oct. 1995); 1 child, Helen Holly. Student, U. Ky., 1952-53; BA summa cum laude, Marshall U., 1956; postgrad., U. London, 1962-63; PhD, Harvard U., 1968. Instr. anthropology U. Mo., Columbia, 1965-67, asst. prof., 1967-69, assoc. prof., 1969-75, prof., 1975—; postdoctoral fellow Ghent U., 1969. Co-author: Neolithic Levels on the Titelberg, Luxembourg, 1981; anthropology editor Random House Unabridged Dictionary of English, 1980—; editor: Horizons and Styles, 1993, Horizons and Styles in West Eurasiatic Archaeology; developer thermoluminescence dating of flint, 1972; co-developer electron spin resonance dating of flint, 1981. 1st lt. arty., U.S. Army, 1956-58. Decorated officer Legion de Merit (Luxembourg); named Ky. col., 1976; grantee NSF, 1973-75, 76-79, 82-83, Svc. Archeologique de Neuchatel, 1989, British Coun., 1993. Fellow Am. Anthrop. Assn.; mem. AAAS, Archaeol. Inst. Am., Soc. Am. Archaeology, Prehistory Soc., Societe Prehistorique de Luxembourg, Societe Archeologique Champenoise, English Heritage, Palomino Horse Breeders Assn. Democrat. Mem. Christian Ch. (Disciples of Christ). Home: Hollywell Hill 1197 State Rd WW Fulton MO 65251-9805 Office: Univ Mo Dept Anthropology Columbia MO 65211

ROWLEY, BEVERLEY DAVIES, medical sociologist; b. Antioch, Calif., July 28, 1941; d. George M. and Eloise (DeWhitt) Davies; m. Richard B. Rowley, Apr. 1, 1966 (div. 1983). BS, Colo. State U., 1963; MA, U. Nev., 1975; PhD, Union Inst., 1983. Social worker Nev. Dept. Pub. Welfare, Reno, 1963-65, Santa Clara County Dept. Welfare, San Jose, Calif., 1965-66; field dir. Sierra Sage Council Camp Fire Girls, Sparks, Nev., 1966-70; program coord. div. health scis. sch. medicine U. Nev., 1976-78, program coord., health analyst office rural health, 1978-84, acting dir. office rural health, 1982-84; exec. asst. to pres. Med. Coll. of Hampton Rds., Norfolk, Va., 1984-87; rsch. mgr. Office Med. Edn. Info. AMA, Chgo., 1987-88, dir. dept. data systems, 1988-91; dir. med. edn. Maricopa Med. Ctr., Phoenix,

1992—; v.p. Med. Edn. and Rsch. Assocs., Inc., Phoenix, Chgo., 1992—; various positions as adj. prof. and lectr. in health scis. U. Nev. Sch. of Medicine, 1972-75; lectr. Dept. of Family and Community Medicine, U. Nev., 1978-84, asst. dir., evaluator Health Careers for Am. Indians Programs, 1978-84; cons. Nev. Statewide Health Survey, 1979-84; interim dir. Health Max, 1985-86; asst. prof. dept. of family and community medicine Med. Coll. of Hampton Rds., Norfolk, Va., 1985-87; v.p., treas. Systems Devel. Assocs., Reno, 1981-84. Editor of five books; contbr. numerous articles to profl. jours; developer three computer systems including AMA-FREIDA. Mem. Am. Sociol. Assn., Nat. Rural Health Assn. (bd. dirs. 1986-88), Assn. Behavioral Sci. and Med. Edn. (pres. 1986), Assn. Am. Med. Colls. (exec. coun. 1993-95), Coun. Acad. Scis. (adminstrv. bd. 1992—), Delta, Delta, Delta. Avocations: hiking, skiing, gardening, sewing, ceramics. Office: Maricopa Med Ctr Dept Acad Affairs 2601 E Roosevelt St Phoenix AZ 85008-4973

ROWLEY, FRANK SELBY, JR., artist; b. N.Y.C., Aug. 2, 1913; s. Frank Selby and Caroline Estelle (Bremmer) R.; m. Dorothy Folger, June 30, 1942. Student, Art Students League, N.Y.C., 1934, Nassau Inst. of Art, Hempstead, N.Y., 1935-38, U. Richmond, Va., 1952. Designer, illustrator Nina Robinson Studio, Hempstead, 1938-41; designer, muralist, 1946-49; tchr. comml. art John Marshall High Sch., Richmond, 1949-57; lectr. various art orgns. 1957—; judge art exhbns., 1957—. Exhibited in group shows at Portraits Inc., N.Y.C., 1959-87, Gallery Mayo, Richmond, Va., 1975—, Va. Mus. of Fine Arts; represented in permanent collections Va. Mus. of Fine Arts, State of Va., City of Richmond, Richmond Meml. Hosp., Va. Fedn. Womens Clubs and numerous pvt. collections. Founder Richmond Concert Band, 1970; music dir., conductor Richmond Pops Band, 1977—; pres., chmn. bd. Richmond Band Assn., 1977—; vol. art tchr. Va. Home, 1989—. Sgt. U.S. Army, 1941-45. Mem. Lions. Avocations: water color painting, music. Home: 8909 Elm Rd Richmond VA 23235-1427

ROWLEY, GEOFFREY HERBERT, management consultant; b. Harrow, Middlesex, Eng., Nov. 10, 1935; s. Herbert and Muriel Jessie (Nicolls) R.; came to U.S., 1962; BA, Bristol U. (Eng.), 1958; Certificate of Indsl. Adminstrn., Glasgow U., 1962; MBA, Harvard U., 1964. Purchasing officer Pirelli Ltd., London, 1958-61; rsch. assoc. Assn. for Internat. Rsch., Inc., Cambridge, Mass., 1964-68, v.p., dir., 1968—, cons. in expatriate compensation, 1964—; lectr. in field, dir. U. Bristol Found., Inc. Served with Royal Navy, 1953-55. Mem. Am. Compensation Assn., Inst. for Human Resources, Brit. Inst. Mgmt. Club: Harvard. Contbr. articles to profl. jours. Home: 11 Berkeley Pl Cambridge MA 02138-3411 Office: care AirInc 1100 Massachusetts Ave Cambridge MA 02138-5241

ROWLEY, JANET DAVISON, physician; b. N.Y.C., Apr. 5, 1925; d. Hurford Henry and Ethel Mary (Ballantyne) Davison; m. Donald A. Rowley, Dec. 18, 1948; children: Donald, David, Robert, Roger. PhB, U. Chgo., 1944, BS, 1946, MD, 1948; DSc (hon.), U. Ariz., 1989, U. Pa., 1989, Knox Coll., 1991, U. So. Calif., 1992. Cert. Am. Bd. Med. Genetics. Rsch. asst. U. Chgo., 1949-50; intern Marine Hosp., USPHS, Chgo., 1950-51; attending physician Infant Welfare and Prenatal Clinics Dept. Pub. Health, Montgomery County, Md., 1953-54; rsch. fellow Levinson Found., Cook County Hosp., Chgo., 1955-61; clin. instr. neurology U. Ill., Chgo., 1957-61; USPHS spl. trainee Radiobiology Lab. The Churchill Hosp., Oxford, Eng., 1961-62; rsch. assoc. dept. medicine and Argonne Cancer Rsch. Hosp. U. Chgo., 1962-69, assoc. prof. dept. medicine and Argonne Cancer Rsch. Hosp., 1969-77, prof. dept. medicine and Franklin McLean Meml. Rsch. Inst., 1977-84; Blum-Riese Disting. Svc. prof., dept. medicine and dept. molecular genetics and cell biology, 1984—; mem. Nat. Cancer Adv. Bd., 1979-84; bd. sci. counsellors Nat. Ctr. for Human Genome Rsch., NIH, 1994—, chmn., 1994—; Bernard Cohen Meml. lectr. U. Pa., 1993, Katherine D. McCormick Disting. lectr. Stanford U., 1994; Donald D. Van Slyke lectr. Brookhaven Nat. Lab., 1994. Co-founder, co-editor Genes, Chromosomes and Cancer; mem. editl. bds. Oncology Rsch., Cancer Genetics and Cytogenetics, Internat. Jour. Hematology, Genomics, Internat. Jour. Cancer, Leukemia; past mem. editorial bd. Blood, Cancer Rsch., Hematol. Oncology, Leukemia Rsch.; contbr. chpts. to books., articles to profl. jours. Mem. Bd. Sci. Counsellors, Nat. Inst. Dental Rsch., NIH, 1972-76, chmn., 1974-76; mem. Nat. Cancer Adv. Bd. Nat. Cancer Inst., 1979-84; mem. adv. com. Frederick Cancer Rsch. Facility, 1983-85; mem. adv. bd. Leukemia Soc. Am., 1979-84; mem. MIT Corp. vis. com. Dept. Applied Biol. Scis., 1983-86; mem. selection com. scholar award in Biomed. Sci., Lucille P. Markey Charitable Trust, 1984-87; trustee Adler Planetarium, Chgo., 1978—; bd. dirs. am. Bd. Med. Genetics, 1982-83, Am. Bd. Human Genetics, 1985-88; bd. sci. cons. meml. Sloan-Kettering Cancer Ctr., 1988-90; nat. adv. com. McDonnell Found. Program for Molecular Medicine in Cancer Rsch., 1988—; adv. com. Ency. Britannica U. Chgo., 1988—; mem. adv. bd. Howard Hughes Med. Inst., 1989-94; adv. com. for career awards in biomed. scis. Burroughs Wellcome Fund, 1994—. Recipient First Kuwait Cancer prize, 1984, Esther Langer award Ann Langer Cancer Rsch. Found., 1983, A. Cressy Morrison award in natural scis. N.Y. Acad. Scis., 1985, Past State Pres.' award Tex. Fedn. Bus. and Profl. Women's Clubs, 1986, Karnofsky award and lecture Am. Soc. Clin. Oncology, 1987, prix Antoine Lacassagne Lique Nationale Francaise Contre le Cancer, 1987, King Faisal Internat. prize in medicine (co-recipient), 1988, Katherine Berkan Judd award Meml. Sloan-Kettering Cancer Ctr., 1989, (co-recipient) Charles Mott Prize GM Cancer Rsch. Found., 1989, Steven C. Beering award U. Ind. Med. Sch., 1992, Robert de Villiers award Leukemia Soc. Am., 1993, Kaplan Family prize for cancer rsch. excellence Oncology Soc. Dayton, 1995, Cotlove award and lecture Acad. Clin. Lab. Physicians and Scientists, 1995, Nilsson-Ehle lecture Mendelian Soc. and Royal Physiograhic Soc., U. Lund, 1995, The Gardner Found. award, 1996. Mem. NAS (chmn. sect. 41 1995—), Am. Acad. Arts and Scis., Am. Philos. Soc., Am. Soc. Human Genetics (pres.-elect 1992, pres. 1993, Allen award and lectr. 1991), Genetical Soc. (Gt. Britain), Am. Soc. Hematology (Presdl. Symposium 1982, Dameshek prize 1982, Ham-Wasserman award 1995), Am. Assn. Cancer Rsch. (G.H.A. Clowes Meml. award 1989), Inst. Medicine (coun. 1988-90), Sigma Xi (William Proctor prize for sci. achievement 1989), Alpha Omega Alpha Alumnus. Episcopalian. Home: 5310 S University Ave Chicago IL 60615-5106 Office: U Chgo 5841 Maryland Ave MC 2115 Chicago IL 60637

ROWLEY, PETER TEMPLETON, physician, educator; b. Greenville, Pa., Apr. 29, 1929; s. George Hardy and Susan Mossman (Templeton) R.; m. Carol Stone, Mar. 19, 1967; children: Derek Stone, Jason Templeton. AB magna cum laude, Harvard U., 1951; MD, Columbia U., 1955. Diplomate: Am. Bd. Internal Medicine. Intern med. service N.Y. Hosp.-Cornell Med. Center, 1955-56; clin. assoc. Nat. Inst. Neurol. Disease and Blindness, NIH, 1956-58; asst. resident, then resident Harvard Med. Service, Boston City Hosp.; asst. in medicine Harvard U. Med. Sch. and researcher Thorndike Meml. Lab., 1958-60; hon. research asst. dept. eugenics, biometry and genetics Univ. Coll., U. London, 1960-61; postdoctoral fellow dept. microbiology NYU Sch. Medicine, 1961-63; asst. prof. medicine Stanford U., 1963-70; assoc. prof. medicine pediatrics and genetics U. Rochester, 1970-75, prof. medicine, pediatrics, genetics and microbiology, 1975—, prof. oncology, 1991—, chmn. div. genetics, 1990—; physician, pediatrician Strong Meml. Hosp., 1970—; mem. N.Y. State Exec. and Adv. Coms. on Genetic Disease, 1979—; WHO vis. scholar Inst. Biol. Chemistry, U. Ferrara, Italy, 1970. Editor: (with M. Lipkin Jr.) Genetic Responsibility: On Choosing Our Children's Genes, 1974. With USPHS, 1956-58. Recipient Excellence in Teaching award U. Rochester Class of 1976, 1973; NRC fellow, 1960-63; Buswell research fellow, 1970-71, 71-72. Fellow ACP, Am. Coll. Genetics; mem. Am. Fedn. Clin. Rsch., Am. Soc. Hematology, Am. Soc. Human Genetics (social issues com. 1980-89, program com. 1993-96). Office: U Rochester Med Sch Div Genetics PO Box 641 601 Elmwood Ave Rochester NY 14642-0001

ROWLEY, ROBERT DEANE, JR., bishop; b. Cumberland, Md., July 6, 1941; s. Robert Deane Sr. and Alice Marquerite (Wilson) W.; m. Nancy Ann Roland, June 27, 1964; children: Karen Gordon Rowley Butler, Robert Deane III. BA, U. Pitts., 1962, LLB, 1965; LLM, George Washington U., 1970; MDiv, Episcopal Sem. of S.W., 1977, DD (hon.), 1989. Ordained deacon Episcopal Ch., 1977; priest, 1978; bishop, 1989. Bar: Pa. 1965, U.S. Supreme Ct. 1970. Dean of students St. Andrew's Priory Sch., Honolulu, 1977-80; canon St. Andrew's Cathedral, Honolulu, 1979-81; rector St. Timothy's Episcopal Ch., Aiea, Hawaii, 1981-83; canon to bishop Diocese of Bethlehem (Pa.), 1983-89; bishop Diocese of Northwestern Pa., Erie, 1989—; pres. 3rd prov., 1993—. Capt. USN, 1966-92. Mem. Erie County Bar Assn., Erie Club, Lake Shore Country Club. Home: 810 Huntington Dr Erie PA 16505-1087 Office: Diocese of Northwestern Pa 145 W 6th St Erie PA 16501-1001

ROWLEY, WILLIAM ROBERT, surgeon; b. Omaha, June 7, 1943; s. Robert Kuhlmeyer and Dorothy Eleanor (Larson) R.; m. Eileen Ruth Murray, Aug. 11, 1968; children: Bill II, Jeff, Jill. BA in Psychology, U. Minn., 1966, MD, 1970. Diplomate Am. Bd. Surgery. Commd. lt. USN, 1972, advanced through grades to rear admiral, 1994; intern U. Calif., San Diego, 1970-71, gen. surgery resident, 1971-72; gen. surgery resident Naval Regional Med. Ctr., Phila., 1973-76; peripheral vascular surgery fellow Naval Regional Med. Ctr., San Diego, 1977-78; staff surgeon Naval Regional Med. Ctr., Phila., 1977; staff vascular surgeon Naval Regional Med. Ctr., San Diego, 1978-85, chmn. dept. surgery, 1985-88, dir. surg. svcs., 1987-88; asst. chief of staff for plans and ops. Naval Med. Command S.W. Region, San Diego, 1988-89; dep. comdr. Nat. Naval Med. Ctr., Bethesda, Md., 1989-91; comdg. officer Naval Hospital, Camp Pendleton, Calif., 1991-93; dep. asst. chief for health care ops. Navy Bur. of Medicine and Surgery, Washington, 1993-94, asst. chief for plans, analysis and evaluation, 1994-95; commdr. Naval Med. Ctr., Portsmouth, Va., 1995—; program dir. vascular surgery fellowship Naval Hosp., San Diego, 1980-85, gen. surgery residency, 1985-89; assoc. prof. surgery Uniformed Svcs. U. for Health Scis., Bethesda, 1985—. Fellow ACS; mem. AMA, Am. Coll. Physician Execs., Am. Coll. Healthcare Execs. Avocations: backpacking, boating. Home: 580 Williamson Dr Portsmouth VA 23704 Office: Naval Med Ctr 620 John Paul Jones Cir Portsmouth VA 23708-5000

ROWLINGSON, JOHN CLYDE, anesthesiologist, educator, physician; b. Syracuse, N.Y., Aug. 3, 1948; s. John Winthrop and Genevieve Estelle (Mahan) R.; m. Rosemary Colette Laney, Oct. 26, 1974 (div. 1992); children: Kristen, Andrew. BS, Allegheny Coll., 1970; MD, SUNY, Buffalo, 1974. Intern Millard Fillmore Hosp., Buffalo, 1974-75; resident in anesthesiology U. Va., Charlottesville, 1975-77; fellow in anesthesia pain mgmt. U. Va. Med. Ctr., 1977-78; asst. prof. anesthesiology U. Va. Sch. Medicine, Charlottesville, 1978-82, assoc. prof., 1982-86, prof., 1986—, tenured prof., 1995—; assoc. dir. Pain Mgmt. Ctr., U. Va. Health Sci. Ctr., 1978-79, dir., 1980—. Author: Regional Anesthesia, 1984; co-editor: Handbook of Critical Care Pain Management, 1993. Nat. Inst. Handicapped Rsch. fellow, 1983-87, Pain fellow 1977-78. Felllow Am. Coll. Anesthesiology; mem. Am. Soc. Anesthesiologists, Am. Soc. Regional Anesthesia (rsch. grantee 1977, pres. 1996—), Am. Pain Soc., Internat. Assn. Study of Pain, Am. Acad. Pain Medicine (editl. bd. Anesthesia Analog 1996—). Methodist. Avocations: running, tennis, skiing, biking. Home: 1255 Hunters Ridge Ln Earlysville VA 22936-9571 Office: U Va Health Sci Ctr Anesthesiology PO Box 238 Charlottesville VA 22908-0238

ROWND, ROBERT HARVEY, biochemistry and molecular biology, molecular medicine and genetics educator; b. Chgo., July 4, 1937; s. Walter Lemuel and Marie Francis (Joyce) R.; m. Rosalie Anne Lowery, June 13, 1959; children: Jennifer Rose, Robert Harvey, David Matthew. BS in Chemistry, St. Louis U., 1959; MA in Med. Scis, Harvard U., 1961, PhD in Biophysics, 1964. Postdoctoral fellow Med. Rsch. Coun., NIH, Cambridge, Eng., 1963-65; postdoctoral fellow Nat. Acad. Scis.-NRC, Institut Pasteur, Paris, 1965-66; prof., chmn. molecular biology and biochemistry U. Wis., Madison, 1966-81; John G. Searle prof., chmn. molecular biology and biochemistry Med. and Dental Schs., Northwestern U., Chgo., 1981-90; leader cancer molecular biology program Cancer Ctr.Northwestern U., Chgo., 1982-89; prof. biochemistry, dir. Ctr. for Molecular Biology Wayne State U., Detroit, 1990-94, interim chair dept. molecular biology and genetics, 1993-94; dir., prof. Ctr. for Molecular Medicine and Genetics Wayne State U. Sch. Medicine, Detroit, 1994—, prof. internal medicine, 1994—; vice chmn. Gordon Rsch. Conf. Extrachromosomal Elements, 1984, chmn., 1986; hon. rsch. prof. Biotech. Rsch. Ctr., Chinese Acad. Agrl. Scis., Beijing, 1987—. Contbr. numerous articles to sci. jours. and books; mem. editorial bd. Jour. of Bacteriology, 1975-81, editor, 1981-90; assoc. editor Plasmid, 1977-87. Mem. troop com., treas. Four Lakes Coun. Boy Scouts Am., Madison, 1973-77, mem. People to People Program del. of microbiologists to China, 1983; mem. Nat. Acad. Scis./Nat. Rsch. Coun. Com. on Human Health Effects of Subtherapeutic Antibiotic Use in Animal Feeds, 1979-81; sr. tech. adv. recruitment cons. UN Devel. Program in China, 1987. NSF fellow, NIH fellow, 1959-66, rsch. grantee, 1966-92, tng. grantee, 1970-79, 83-91; USPHS Rsch. Career Devel. awardee, 1968-73; recipient Alumni Merit award St. Louis U., 1984. Mem. NIH (microbial genetics study sect. 1978-82, spl. study sect. 1971, 73, 74, 75, 78, 79, 82, chmn. 1983, 84-86, 88, 89, 90, 93-95, dir. med. scientist tng. program 1982-90, adv. panel Nat. Rsch. Coun. 1974-77, chmn. 1976-77, adv. panel for devel. biology NSF, 1968-71, NSF adv. panel NATO postdoctoral fellowships in sci. program 1979), Am. Soc. Microbiology, Assn. Harvard Chemists, Am. Soc. Biol. Chemists, Am. Acad. Microbiology, N.Y. Acad. Scis. Home: 14010 Harbor Place Dr Saint Clair Shores MI 48080-1528

ROWSEY, MICHAEL, printing company executive; b. 1954. BS in Zoology, Marshall U., 1975; grad. Advanced Exec. Program, Kellogg Grad. Sch. Mgmt., 1988. Sales rep. Carnation Co., 1975-79; dealer sales rep. Boise Cascade Office Products, W.Va., 1979-84; sales mgr. Boise Cascade Office Products, Cin., 1984-86, gen. mgr., 1986-87; gen. mgr. Boise Cascade Office Products, Columbus, Ohio, 1987-89, Columbus and Cleve., 1989-90; from north regional mgr. to pres. Associated Stationers, Inc., Itasca, Ill., 1990-95; exec. v.p. United Stationers, Des Plaines, Ill., 1995—. Office: United Stationers 2200 E Golf Rd Des Plaines IL 60016*

ROWSON, RICHARD CAVANAGH, publisher; b. Hollywood, Calif., Apr. 7, 1926; s. Louis Cavanagh and Mable Louise (Montney) R.; m. Elena Louisa Costabile, Nov. 22, 1952; children: Peter Cavanagh, John Cummings. A.B., U. Calif., Berkeley, 1946; certificate, Sorbonne, 1949; M.I.A., Columbia U., 1950. Trainee Fgn. Policy Assn., 1950; dir. World Affairs Council R.I., 1951-52; with Fgn. Policy Assn., 1951-62, dir. finance and devel., 1960-62; with Radio Free Europe, 1962-69, dir. policy and planning, 1964-69; dir. spl. studies Praeger Pubs., Inc., N.Y.C., 1969-77; pres. Praeger Pubs., Inc., 1975-77, Pergamon Press, 1977-80, R.R. Bowker, 1980; info. and pub. cons., 1981; dir. Duke U. Press, 1981-90, sr. cons. editor, 1990-91; dir. Am. U. Press, 1989-91, cons. acquisitions, 1992-94, cons. pub., 1994—, dir.; pub. Woodrow Wilson Ctr. Press, 1992-93; lectr., condr. workshops in field. Contbr. articles to profl. jours. Served to lt. (j.g.) USNR, 1944-47. Mem. Am. Assn. Advancement Slavic Studies, N.Y. Acad. Scis., Soc. for Scholarly Pub., U. Calif. Alumni Assn., Columbia U. Pomona Alumni Assn. Democrat. Clubs: Century Assn., Overseas Press (N.Y.C.). Home: 4701 Connecticut Ave NW Washington DC 20008-5630 also: Am U Press 350 McKinley 4400 Massachusetts Ave NW Washington DC 20016-8001

ROXE, JOSEPH, insurance company executive; b. 1936. Grad., Princeton U., 1958; MBA, Harvard U. With Mobil Oil Corp., N.Y.C., 1965-87; treas. A. Foster Higgins & Co. Inc., N.Y.C., 1988—. Lt. USN, 1958-62. Office: A Foster Higgins & Co Inc 125 Broad St New York NY 10004

ROXIN, EMILIO OSCAR, mathematics educator; b. Buenos Aires, Apr. 6, 1922; came to U.S., 1960; s. Emil Karl and Ullranda Hildegard (Loebel) R.; m. Gudrun D. Kappus, 1962 (div. 1983); children: Ursula R., Walter E. Diploma in engring., U. Buenos Aires, 1947, PhD in Math., 1958. Mem. faculty U. Buenos Aires, 1947-62; researcher Rsch. Inst. Advanced Study, Balt., 1960-64; prof. math. U. R.I., Kingston, 1960-92, prof. emeritus, 1992—; researcher, AEC of Argentina, Buenos Aires, 1956-59. Author: Differential Equations, 1972, Some Applications of Control Theory, 1996; contbr. to sci. publs. Mem. Am. Math. Soc., Math. Assn. Am., Soc. Indsl. and Applied Math., Union Math. Argentina, AAAS. Home: 31 Nichols Rd Kingston RI 02881-1803 Office: U RI Dept Math Kingston RI 02881

ROY, CATHERINE ELIZABETH, physical therapist; b. Tucson, Jan. 16, 1948; d. Francis Albert and Dorothy Orme (Thomas) R.; m. Richard M. Johnson, Aug. 31, 1968 (div. 1978); children: Kimberly Anne, Troy Michael. BA in Social Sci. magna cum laude, San Diego State U., 1980; MS in Phys. Therapy, U. So. Calif., 1984. Staff therapist Sharp Meml. Hosp., San Diego, 1984-89, chairperson patient and family edn. com., 1986-87, chairperson sex edn. and counselling com., 1987-89, chairperson adv. bd. for phys. therapy, asst. for edn. program, 1987-89; mgr. rehab. phys. therapy San Diego Rehab. Inst., Alvarado Hosp., 1989-91; dir. therapeutic svcs. VA Med. Ctr., San Diego, 1991—; lectr. patient edn., family edn., peer edn.; mem. curriculum rev. com. U. So. Calif. Phys. Therapy Dept., 1982; bd. dirs. Ctr. for Edn. in Health; writer, reviewer licensure examination items for phys. therapy Profl. Examination Services.. Tennis coach at clinics Rancho Penasquitos Swim and Tennis Club, San Diego, 1980-81; active Polit. Activities Network, 1985; counselor EEO, 1992-95. Mem. Am. Phys. Therapy Assn. (rsch. presenter nat. conf. 1985, del. nat. conf. 1986-94, rep. state conf. 1987-89, 92-94, Mary McMillan student award 1984, mem. exec. bd. San Diego dist. 1985-88, 92-94), AAUW, NAFE, Am. Congress Rehab. Medicine, Phi Beta Kappa, Phi Kappa Phi, Chi Omega. Avocations: tennis, reading, piano, travel, puzzles. Home: 5067 Park West Ave San Diego CA 92117-1048 Office: San Diego VA Med Ctr Spinal Cord Injury Svc 3350 La Jolla Village Dr San Diego CA 92161-0002

ROY, CHUNILAL, psychiatrist; b. Digboi, India, Jan. 1, 1935; came to Can., 1967, naturalized, 1975; s. Atikay Bandhu and Nirupama (Devi) R.; m. Elizabeth Ainscow, Apr. 15, 1967; children: Nicholas, Phillip, Charles. MB, BS, Calcutta Med. Coll., India, 1959; diploma in psychol. medicine, Kings Coll., Newcastle-upon-Tyne, Eng., 1963. Intern Middlesborough Gen. Hosp., Eng., 1960-61; jr. hosp. officer St. Luke's Hosp., Middlesborough, Eng., 1961-64, sr. registrar, 1964; sr. hosp. med. officer Parkside Hosp., Macclesfield, Eng., 1964-66; sr. registrar Moorehaven Hosp., Ivybridge, Eng., 1966; reader, head dept. psychiatry Maulana Azad Med. Coll., New Delhi, 1966; sr. med. officer Republic of Ireland, County Louth, 1966; sr. psychiatrist Sask. Dept. Psychiat. Services, Can., 1967-68; regional dir. Swift Current, Can., 1968-71; practice medicine specializing in psychiatry Regina, Sask., Can., 1971-72; founding dir., med. dir. Regional Psychiat. Ctr., Abbotsford, B.C., Can., 1972-82; with dept. psychiatry Vancouver Gen. Hosp., 1987—; cons. to prison adminstrs.; hon. lectr. psychology and clin. prof. dept. psychiatry U. B.C.; ex-officio mem. Nat. Adv. Com. on Health Care of Prisoners in Can.; cons. psychiatrist Vancouver Hosp.; advisor Asian chpt. Psychosomatic Medicine, World Congress of Law and Medicine, New Delhi, 1985. Author: (with D.J. West and F.L. Nichols) Understanding Sexual Attacks, 1978; co-author: Oath of Athens, 1979; mem. editorial rev. bd. Evaluation, 1977—; assoc. editor Internat. Jour. Offender Therapy and Comparative Criminology, 1978—; mem. Bd. Internat. Law Medicine, 1979—; field editor Jour. of Medicine and Law; contbr. articles to profl. jours. Recipient merit awards Dept. Health, Republic of Ireland, 1966, Can. Penitentiary Svc., 1974, Correctional Svcs. Can., 1983, citation by pres. U. B.C., 1983; knighted by order of St. John Ecumenical Found., 1993; winner Latten Saugstad Found. prize 1995. Fellow Royal Coll. Psychiatry (Can.), Royal Coll. Psychiatry (Eng.), Pacific Rim Coll. Psychiatrists (founder); mem. World Psychiat. Assn. (sec., vice chmn. forensic psychiatry 1983), World Fedn. Mental Health, Internat. Coun. Prison Med. Svcs. (founding sec.-gen. 1977), Can. Med. Assn., Can. Psychiat. Assn., Amnesty Internat., Internat. Acad. Legal Medicine and Social Medicine, Indian Psychiat. Assn. (life), Can. Assn. Profl. Treatment Offenders (founding dir. 1975), Assn. Physicians and Surgeons Who Work in Can. Prisons (founding pres. 1974), Internat. Found. for Tng. in Penitentiary Medicine and Forensic Psychiatry (founding pres. 1980, vice-chmn., sec.), World Psychiatry Assn., Australian Acad. Forensic Sci. (corr.), Can. Physicians Interested in South Asia (v.p. 1989, pres. 1990), Internat. Coll. Psychosomatic Medicine (adv. Asian chpt.), Internat. Conf. on Health, Culture and Contemporary Soc. (chief advisor Bombay, India 1989, v.p. 1989, pres. 1990), Internat. Coun. Penitentiary Medicine (founding sec., bd. dirs.), World Psychiat. Assn. (vice chmn. forensic psychiat. sect. 1989), Order of St. John (knight 1992), Vancouver MultiCultural Soc. (bd. dirs. 1992-93), B.C. Psychiat. Assn. (pres.-elect 1995). Home: 2439 Trinity St, Vancouver, BC Canada V5K 1C9 Office: 1417-750 W Broadway, Vancouver, BC Canada V5Z 1J4

ROY, CLARENCE LESLIE, landscape architect; b. Ironwood, Mich., Mar. 6, 1927; s. Theodore Gideon and Myrtle May (Mathews) R.; m. Ruth Serou, Nov. 11, 1959. B.S. in Landscape Architecture, U. Mich., 1951. Landscape architect Lambert Assoc. Cos., Dallas, 1951-59; assoc. Eichstedt-Johnson Assoc., Grosse Pointe, Mich., 1960; prin. Johnson Johnson & Roy/inc., Ann Arbor, Mich., 1961-81, Dallas, 1982-92, ret.; dir. The Smith Group, Detroit, 1979-82. Founder Old West Assn., Ann Arbor, 1966, pres., 1968-73; pres. Ann Arbor Tomorrow, 1978-79. Served with USN, 1945-46. Fellow Am. Soc. Landscape Architects; mem. Am. Planners Assn., U. Mich. Alumni Assn. (bd. dirs. 1976-79), Tau Sigma Delta, Alpha Rho Chi. Home: 4039 Travis St Dallas TX 75204

ROY, DAVID TOD, Chinese literature educator; b. Nanking, China, Apr. 5, 1933; s. Andrew Tod and Margaret (Crutchfield) R.; m. Barbara Jean Chew, Feb. 4, 1967. AB, Harvard U., 1958, AM, 1960, PhD, 1965. Asst. prof. Princeton U., 1963-67; assoc. prof. U. Chgo., 1967-73, prof., 1973—, chmn. com. on Far Eastern Studies, 1968-70, chmn. dept. Far Eastern Langs. and Civilizations, 1972-75. Author: Kuo Mo-jo: The Early Years, 1971; contbr.: How to Read the Chinese Novel, 1990; co-editor: Ancient China: Studies in Early Civilization, 1978; translator: The Plum in the Golden Vase or Chin P'ing Mei, 1993. Served with U.S. Army, 1954-56. Ford Found. fellow, 1958-60, Jr. fellow Harvard Soc. Fellows, 1960-63, fellow Fulbright-Hays Commn., 1967, Chgo. Humanities Inst. fellow, 1994-95; grantee Am. Coun. Learned Socs., 1976-77, NEH, 1983-86, 95-96. Mem. Am. Lit. Translators Assn., Am. Oriental Soc., Assn. for Asian Studies, Chinese Lang. Tchrs. Assn. Democrat. Club: Quadrangle (Chgo.). Home: 5443 S Cornell Ave Chicago IL 60615-5603 Office: U Chgo 1050 E 59th St Chicago IL 60637-1512

ROY, ELMON HAROLD, minister; b. Russell Springs, Ky., Dec. 17, 1924; s. Leslie C. and Olza (Gosser) R.; m. Retha Adkins; children: Joel, Michael. BA in Theology, So. Missionary Coll., 1953; MA, Belin U., 1958, Spalding U., 1970; PhD in Theology, Pacific We. U., 1966; postgraduate, Andrews Theol. Seminary, 1959; LLD, Coll. St. Thomas, 1982. Ordained to ministry, 1950. Assoc. pastor Bucyrus, Ohio, 1955-56, Akron, Ohio, 1956-57; pastor East Liverpool, Ohio, 1957-60, Coudersport, Pa., 1960-64, Huntsville, Ala., 1964-65, Louisville, Ky., 1965-71; chaplain Pleasant Grove Hosp., Louisville, Ky., 1965-71; pastor Springfield, Ohio, 1975-85, Wooster, Ohio, 1985-88; chaplain Louisville, Ky., 1989—; cons. religious liberty, 1983-88; chaplain Jefferson County Ct. Author: In Remembrance of Redemption, Courage for Hospital Days, Earth's Coming Events, Israel's Early Leaders, Moments of Meditation, The Word for These Times, Morning is Coming, Something to Live By, Prescription for Personal Peace; contbr. numerous articles to mags. Pres. South Oldham Ch. Coun., 1971-72; mem. Ohio conf. bd. edn., 1985-88. With USN, 1943-46. Recipient Outstanding Cmty. Svc. award Pleasant Grove Hosp., Commrs. Commendation award Wayne County, Ohio Senate Commendation award, Gov.'s Outstanding Kentuckian award; decorated six battle stars, knight Sovereign Order of St. John of Jerusalem, Knights of Malta, Hospitallers, comdr. Star of Peace Fedn. des Combattants En Europe, Tenn. Col., Ky. adm.; named hon. citizen of Tenn., hon. sheriff Clark County, Ohio, hon. Ky. Sec. of State, Ky. amb. Fellow Philos. Soc. Gt. Britain, Huguenot Soc., Royal Soc. Arts; mem. SAR (chaplain Louisville-Thruston chpt. 1974-75), Am. Acad. Religion, Ky. Hist. Soc., Order Founders and Patriots of Am., East Liverpool Ministerial Assn. (sec., treas. 1960), Coudersport Ministerial Assn. (sec., treas. 1963). Address: 2417 West Highway 22 Crestwood KY 40014-9774

ROY, ELSIJANE TRIMBLE, federal judge; b. Lonoke, Ark., Apr. 2, 1916; d. Thomas Clark and Elsie Jane (Walls) Trimble; m. James M. Roy, Nov. 23, 1943; 1 son, James Morrison. JD, U. Ark., Fayetteville, 1939; LLD (hon.), U. Ark., Little Rock, 1978. Bar: Ark. 1939. Atty. Rose, Loughborough, Dobyns & House, Little Rock, 1940-41, Ark. Revenue Dept., Little Rock, 1941-42; mem. firm Reid, Evrard & Roy, Blytheville, Ark., 1945-54, Roy & Roy, Blytheville, 1954-63; law clk. Ark. Supreme Ct., Little Rock, 1963-65; assoc. justice Ark. Supreme Ct., 1975-77; U.S. dist. judge then sr. judge Ea. and We. Dists. Ark., Little Rock, 1977—; judge Pulaski County (Ark.) Cir. Ct., Little Rock, 1966; asst. atty. gen. Ark., Little Rock, 1967; sr. law clk. U.S. Dist. Ct., Little Rock and Ft. Smith, 1967-75; Mem. med. adv. com. U. Ark. Med. Center, 1952-54; Committeewoman Democratic Party 16th Jud. Dist., 1940-42; vice chmn. Ark. Dem. State Com., 1946-48; mem. chmn. com. Ark. Constnl. Commn., 1967-68. Recipient disting. alumnae citation U. Ark., 1978, Gayle Pettus Pontz award, 1986, Brooks Hays Meml. Christian Citizenship award, 1994; named Ark. woman of yr., Bus. and Profl. Women's Club, 1969, 76, outstanding appellate judge, Ark. Trial Lawyers Assn., 1976-77, Delta Theta Phi mem. of yr. 1989; named among top 100 women in Ark. bus., 1995; Paul Harris fellow Rotary Club Little Rock, 1992. Recipient disting. alumnae citation U. Ark.,

1978, Gayle Pettus Pontz award, 1986, Brooks Hays Meml. Christian Citizenship award, 1994; named Ark. Woman of Yr., Bus. and Profl. Women's Club, 1969, 76, Outstanding Appellate Judge, Ark. Trial Lawyers Assn., 1976-77, Mem. of Yr., Delta Theta Phi, 1989; named among top 100 women in Ark. bus., 1995, Ark. Bus. Top 100 Women in Ark., 1995; Paul Harris fellow Rotary Little Rock, 1992. Office: US Dist Ct 600 W Capitol Ave Rm 423 Little Rock AR 72201-3326

ROY, J(AMES) STAPLETON, ambassador; b. Nanking, China, June 16, 1935; s. Andrew Tod and Margaret (Crutchfield) R.; m. Elissandra Nicole Fiore, Jan. 27, 1968; children—Andrew, David, Anthony. B.A. magna cum laude, Princeton U., 1956; postgrad., U. Wash., 1964-65, Nat. War Coll., 1974-75. Dep. dir. Office of Soviet Union Affairs Dept. of State, Washington, 1972-74, dep. dir. Office of Chinese Affairs, 1975-78; minister counselor U.S. Embassy, Beijing, Peoples Republic of China, 1978-81, Bangkok, Thailand, 1981-84; U.S. amb. to Singapore, 1984-86; dep. asst. sec. Bur. East Asian and Pacific Affairs Dept. of State, 1986-89, spl. asst. to sec. and exec. sec., 1989-91; U.S. amb. to People's Republic of China Beijing, 1991-95; U.S. amb. to Indonesia, 1995—. Recipient Presdl. Meritorious Service award Pres. of U.S., 1983, 88, 90, Superior Honor award Dept. State, 1977, 80. Mem. Am. Fgn. Svc. Assn., Phi Beta Kappa. Avocations: swimming; jogging; chess; computers. Office: US Embassy, Jl Medan Merdeka Selatan 5, Jakarta 10110, Indonesia

ROY, KENNETH RUSSELL, educator; b. Hartford, Conn., Mar. 29, 1946; s. Russell George and Irene Mary (Birkowski) R.; BS, Central Conn. State Coll., New Britain, 1968, MS, 1974; 6th yr. degree in profl. edn. U. Conn., 1981, Ph.D., 1985; m. Marisa Anne Russo, Jan. 27, 1968; children: Lisa Marie, Louise Irene. Tchr. sci. Rocky Hill (Conn.) High Sch., 1968-73, N.W. Cath. High Sch., West Hartford, Conn., 1973-74; sci. and math. coord. Bolton (Conn.) High Sch., 1974-78; chmn. scis. Bacon Acad., Colchester, Conn., 1978-81; K-12 dir. sci. Glastonbury (Conn.) Pub. Schs., 1981—; mem. adj. faculty Manchester C.C., 1976-90, Tunxis C.C., 1975-90; instr. U. Conn. Coop. Program, 1974-78; cons./adv. Project Rise, 1978-81; lectr., sci. curriculum cons. various Conn. sch. dists.; nat. dir. Nat. Sci. Suprs. Assn., 1988-91, exec. dir. Leadership Inst. Cen. Conn. State U., New Britain, 1989-91; exec. dir. Nat. Sci. Suprs. Assn., 1992-95; bd. dirs. Lab. Safety Workshop Nat. Ctr., 1995—, Conn. United for Rsch. Excellence, 1995—. Co-editor Conn. Jour. Sci. Edn., 1984-88; editor Sci. Leadership Trend Notes, 1989-91; contbr. articles to profl. jours. Mem. St. Christopher Sch. Bd., 1982-83. Recipient Disting. Educator's and Conn. Educator's awards Milken Family Found., 1989; named Tchr. of Yr., Colchester, 1980; NSF grantee, 1968, staff devel. grantee, 1979, 80, Nat. Sci. Supr. Leadership Conf. grantee, 1980. Mem. ASCD, AAAS, Nat. Sci. Tchrs. Assn., Nat. Sci. Suprs. Assn. (pres.-elect 1986-87, pres. 1987-88), Conn. Sci. Tchrs. Assn., Conn. Sci. Suprs. Assn. (pres. 1985-86), Conn. Assn. Profl. Devel., Conn. Assn. Supervision and Curriculum Devel., Glastonbury Adminstrs. and Suprs. Assn., Nat. Ctr. Improvement Sci. Teaching and Learning (mem. adv. bd. 1988-91), Internat. Council Assns. Sci. Edn. (nat. rep. 1987-88, N.Am. region rep. and exec. com. mem. 1989—), Phi Delta Kappa. Roman Catholic. Office: Glastonbury Pub Schs Glastonbury CT 06033

ROY, MELINDA, dancer; b. Lafayette, La.. Student, Sch. Am. Ballet. Mem. corps de ballet N.Y.C. Ballet, 1978—, soloist, 1984, prin., 1989—. Dancer in ballets including The Nutcracker, Symphony in C (third movement), Symphony in Three Movements, Apollo (polyhymnia), Brahms-Schoenberg Quartet (first movement), Who Cares, the rubies sect. of Jewels, Divertimento no. 15, Serenade, Western Symphony (first movement), Chaconne (first pas de deux), Tschaikovsky suite no. 3 (Scherzo), Stars and Stripes, Tschaikovsky pas de Deux, Walpurgisnacht ballet, Golberg Variations, The Concert, Gershwin Concerto, Fanfare, Interplay, The Four Seasons (spring), The Unanswered Questions, Behind the China Dogs, The Waltz Project, Seven by Five, N.Y.C. Ballet's Balanchine Celebration, 1993; performed in Spain, Italy, Denmark, Eng., France, Germany, China, Japan. Office: NYC Ballet Inc NY State Theater Lincoln Ctr Plz New York NY 10023

ROY, P. NORMAN, manufacturing company executive; b. Fitchburg, Mass., Nov. 25, 1934; s. Joseph and Della (Lavoie) R.; m. Mary Elizabeth Duggan, May 30, 1959; children: Mary Eileen, Ann Elizabeth, Kathleen Theresa, Michele Ann, Ellen Marie, Paul Norman. B.S.B.A. in Acctg. with honors, Boston Coll., 1956; M.B.A., Babson Inst., 1967. C.P.A., Mass. With Gen. Electric Co., Pittsfield, Mass., 1956-62; auditor Arthur Andersen & Co., Boston, 1962-65; ops. analyst Barry Wright Corp., Newton Lower Falls, Mass., 1965-68, mgr. internal audit, 1968-70, asst. to pres., 1970, treas., 1971-73, v.p. fin., treas., 1973-75, v.p. fin. and adminstrn., 1975-76, dir., 1973—, exec. v.p. fin. and adminstrn., 1976-80, exec. v.p., 1980—; bd. dirs., chmn. examining com., mem. exec. com. Baybanks Middlesex, Burlington, Mass., 1982—; dir., mem. exec. com., mem. Loan rev. com. Mass. Bus. Devel. Corp., Boston, 1982—; dir., mem. exec. com., mem. nominating com., mem. budget com., asst. treas. Assoc. Industries of Mass., Boston, 1984—; dir., chmn. audit com. Kronos Inc., Waltham, Mass., 1984—; dir. Mass. Indsl. Devel. and Employment Commn., Boston;. Trustee, bd. govs. Newton Wellesley Hosp., Mass., 1978-83, overseer, 1983-84; trustee Emmanuel Coll., Boston, 1976-78, overseer, 1983—; dir. adv. bd. Nat. Com. on Fraudulent Fin. Reporting, Washington, 1984—; trustee, mem. adminstrn. and Fin. Com., St. Elizabeth's Hosp. of Boston, 1988—. Served to 1st lt. U.S. Army, 1956-58. Recipient Knight award Equestrian Order Holy Sepulchre Jerusalem, 1984. Fellow Am. Inst. C.P.A.s; mem. Fin. Execs. Inst. (chmn. 1984-85, nat. dir. 1980-87), Mass. Soc. C.P.A.s, Machinery and Allied Products Inst. (fin. council), Watertown C. of C. (v.p., dir. 1978-81), Am. Mgmt. Assn., Nat. Assn. Mfrs. (steering com.). Republican. Roman Catholic. Clubs: Brae Burn Country (Newton); Ancient Order Beefeaters (N.Y.C.); Treas., Hundred (Boston). Avocations: sailing, cross country skiing, woodcrafts, bicycling, fishing. Office: Fin Execs Inst PO Box 1938 10 Madison Ave Morristown NJ 07962-1938*

ROY, PATRICK, professional hockey player; b. Quebec City, Que., Can., Oct. 5, 1965. Goaltender Montreal Canadiens, 1984-95, Colo. Avalanche, 1995—; mem. Stanley Cup Championship teams, 1986, 93, 96. Recipient Conn Smythe trophy as playoff MVP, 1986, William M. Jennings trophy 1986-89, 91-92, Trico Goaltender award, 1988-89, 89-90, Georges Vezina trophy, 1988-89, 89-90, 91-92; named to NHL All-Rookie Team, 1985-86, NHL All-Star Second Team, 1987-88, 90-91, NHL All-Star First Team, 1988-89, 89-90, 91-92., Sporting News All-Star Team, 1988-89, 89-90, 91-92. Played in Stanley Cup Championships, 1986, 93. Office: Colo Avalanche 1635 Clay St Denver CO 80204*

ROY, RAYMOND, bishop; b. Man., Can., May 3, 1919; s. Charles-Borromé e and Zephirina (Milette) R. B.A. in Philosophy and Theology, U. Man., 1942; student, Philos. Sem., Montreal, 1942-43, Major Sem., Montreal, 1943-46, Major Sem. St. Boniface, 1946-47. Ordained priest Roman Catholic Ch. 1947. Asst. pastor, then pastor chs. in Man., 1947-50, 53-66; chaplain St. Boniface (Man.) Hosp., 1950-53; superior Minor Sem., St. Boniface, 1966-69; pastor Cathedral Parish, St. Boniface, 1969-72; ordained bishop, 1972; bishop of St. Paul, Alta., Can., 1972—. Club: K.C. Address: 4410 51st Ave Box 339, Saint Paul, AB Canada T0A 3A0

ROY, RAYMOND CLYDE, anesthesiologist; b. 1944. PhD in Chemistry, Duke U., 1971; MD, Tulane U., 1974. Resident Hosp. U. Pa.; prof., chair dept. anesthesia & perioperative medicine Med. U. S.C.; dir. Am. Bd. Anesthesiology. Office: 171 Ashley Ave Chapel Hill SC 29425-2207

ROY, RICHARD E., lawyer; b. Portland, Oreg., July 7, 1939; s. Leighton Eugene and Dorris Mary (Scott) R.; m. Jeanne Beverly Hawley, June 9, 1962; children: Bradley Scott, Jeffrey Alan, Melinda Louise. BS in Engring., Oreg. State U., 1961; MS in Engring., Stanford State U., 1966; JD, Harvard U., 1970. Bar: Oreg. 1970, U.S. Dist. Ct. Oreg. 1970. Assoc. Stoel, Rives, Boley, Fraser & Wyse, Portland, 1970-76; ptnr. Stoel, Rives, Portland, 1976-94; exec. dir. N.W. Earth Inst., 1993—; mem. corp. commrs. task force corp. law, chmn. 1985; mem. model bus. corp. Act Task Force, 1986-88. Editor: Advising Oregon Businesses, 5 vols., 1984-93. Chmn. Oreg. Water Policy Rev. Bd., Salem, 1975-77; mem. Oreg. Bd. of Forestry, Salem, 1987-95; pres., bd. dirs. Oreg. Scholastic Chess Found., Portland, 1983—. Served to lt. USN, 1961-65. Mem. Oreg. State Bar Assn. (chmn. bus. and corp. sect. 1982-83), Profl. Engrs. Soc. of Oreg. Democrat. Club: City (Portland). Avocations: music, backpacking. Home: 2420 SW Boundary St Portland OR 97201-2025 Office: Stoel Rives 900 SW 5th Ave Portland OR 97204-1235

ROY, ROB J., biomedical engineer, anesthesiologist; b. Bklyn., Jan. 2, 1933; m. Carole Ann Roy, Aug. 1, 1959; children: Robert Bruce, David John, Bruce Glenn. BSEE, Cooper Union, N.Y.C., 1954; MSEE, Columbia U., 1956; DEngSc, Rensselaer Poly. Inst., 1962; MD, Albany (N.Y.) Med. Coll., 1976. Profl. engr., N.Y.; diplomate Am. Bd. Anesthesiology. Prof. elec. engrin. dept. Rensselaer Poly. Inst., Troy, N.Y., 1962, prof. elec. engring. dept., 1980—, head biomed. engring. dept., 1985-94; prof. anesthesiology Albany (N.Y.) Med. Ctr., 1979—. Author: State Variables for Engineers, 1965; author 150 papers in field. Sr. mem. IEEE; mem. Am. Soc. Anesthesiologists, Sigma Xi. Home: 565 Highwood Cir Albany NY 12203 Office: Albany Med Ctr Dept Anesthesiology 47 New Scotland Ave Albany NY 12208

ROY, RUSTUM, interdisciplinary materials researcher, educator; b. Ranchi, India, July 3, 1924; came to U.S., 1945, naturalized, 1961; s. Narendra Kumar and Rajkumari (Mukherjee) R.; m. Della M. Martin, June 8, 1948; children: Neill, Ronnen, Jeremy. BS, Patna (India) U., 1942; MS, Patna (India) U., India, 1944; Ph.D., Pa. State U., 1948; DSc (hon.), Tokyo Inst. Tech., 1987, Alfred U, 1993. Research asst. Pa. State U., 1948-49, mem. faculty, 1950—, prof. geochemistry, 1957—, prof. solid state, 1968—, chmn. solid state tech. program, 1960-67, chmn. sci. tech. and soc. program, 1977-84, dir., 1984—, dir. materials research lab., 1962-85, Evan Pugh prof., 1981—; sr. sci. officer Nat. Ceramic Lab., India, 1950; mem. com. mineral sci. tech. Nat. Acad. Scis., 1967-69, com. survey materials sci. tech., 1970-74; exec. com. chem. div. NRC, 1967-70, nat. materials adv. bd., 1970-77, mem. com. radioactive waste mgmt., 1974-80, chmn. panel waste solidification, 1976-80; chmn. com. NRC, USSR and Eastern Europe, 1976-81; mem. com. material sci. and engring. NRC, 1986-89; mem. Pa. Gov.'s Sci. Adv. Com.; chmn. materials adv. panel Gov.'s Sci. Adv. Com., 1965; mem. adv. com. on engring. NSF, 1968-72, adv. com. to ethical and human value implications sci. and tech., 1974-76, adv. com. div. materials rsch., 1974-77; Hibbert lectr. U. London, 1979; bd. dirs. Kirkridge, Inc., Bangor, Pa.; cons. to industry; mem. adv. com. Coll. Engring., Stanford U., 1984-86. Author: Honest Sex, 1968, Crystal Chemistry of Non-metallic Materials, 1974, Experimenting with Truth, 1981, Radioactive Waste Disposal, Vol. 1, the Waste Package, 1983, Lost at the Frontier, 1985; also articles.; editor-in-chief: Materials Research Bull, 1966—, Bull. Sci. Tech. and Soc, 1981—. Chmn. bd. Dag Hammarskjold Coll., 1973-75; chmn. ad hoc com. sci., tech. and ch. Nat. Council Chs., 1966-68. Sci. policy fellow Brookings Instn., 1982-83. Fellow Indian Acad. Scis. (hon.); mem. AAAS (chmn. chemistry sect. 1985), NAE, Nat. Rsch. Coun. (internat. sci. lectr. 1991-92), Royal Swedish Acad. Engring. Scis. (fgn.), Indian Nat. Acad. Sci. (fgn.), Engring. Acad. Japan, Fedn. Materials Socs. (Nat. Materials Advancement award 1991), Ceramic Soc. Japan (Centennial award 1991, hon. mem. 1991), Mineral Soc. Am. (award 1957), Fine Ceramics Assn. Japan (Internat. award), Am. Chem. Soc. (Petroleum Rsch. Fund award 1960, Dupont award for Chem. of Materials 1993), Acad. Natural Scis. (chem. sect., elected fgn. mem. 1995), Am. Ceramic Soc. (Sosman lectr. 1975, Orton lectr. 1984, disting. life mem. 1993, Educator of Yr. 1993), Am. Soc. Engring. Educators (Centennial medal 1993, named to Hall of Fame 1993), Materials Rsch. Soc. (founder, pres. 1976). Home: 528 S Pugh St State College PA 16801-5312 Office: 102 Materials Rsch Lab University Park PA 16802 *My major responsibility to the increasingly unified world culture, as a scientist supported largely by the public, is to integrate into its emerging radically pluralist yet globally unifying Religion, the insights from Science and the impact of Technology on the human condition. As a Christian Radical Pluralist, I am committed to presenting to my fellow humans—expecially all non-scientists, from Presidents and CEOs to the person in the street—an accurate picture of the whole truth aboyt my scientific "advances" and those of others—their limited and ambivalent nature and their relatively minor position in the sum total of human concerns.*

ROY, WILLIAM ROBERT, physician, lawyer, former congressman; b. Bloomington, Ill., Feb. 23, 1926; s. Elmer Javan and Edna Blanche (Foley) R.; m. Jane Twining Osterhoudt, Sept. 1947; children: Robin Jo, Randall Jay, Richelle Jane, William Robert, Renee Jan, Rise Javan. B.S., Ill. Wesleyan U., 1946; M.D., Northwestern U., 1949; J.D. with honors, Washburn U., 1970. Mem. 92d-93d congresses from 2d Dist. Kans.; dir. Sentry Ins.; Democratic candidate for U.S. Senate, 1974, 78. Mem. Inst. Medicine of Nat. Acad. Scis. Democrat. Methodist. Home: 6137 SW 38th Ter Topeka KS 66610-1307

ROYAL, DARRELL K., university official, former football coach; b. Hollis, Okla., July 6, 1924; s. Burley Ray and Katy Elizabeth (Harmon) R.; m. Edith Marie Thomason, July 26, 1944; children: Marian (Mrs. Abraham Kazen III) (dec.), Mack, David (dec.). B.S. in Bus, U. Okla., 1950. Former head football coach, then dir. athletics U. Tex., now asst. to univ. pres. Author: Darrell Royal Talks Football, 1963. Named Coach of Yr., Football Coaches Assn., 1963, 70, Tex. Sports Writers, 1961, 63, 69, 70, Southwesterner of Yr., 1961, 62, 63; named to U. Tex. Longhorn Hall of Fame, 1976, Tex. Sports Hall of Fame, 1976, Jim Thorpe Okla. Hall of Fame, 1977, Nat. Football Hall of Fame, 1983, Coach of Decade for 1960's, ABC; recipient Horatio Alger award, 1996. Mem. Delta Upsilon. Presbyterian. Office: SRH2.101 Univ Tex Austin TX 78712

ROYAL, HENRY DUVAL, nuclear medicine physician; b. Norwich, Conn., May 14, 1948. MD, St. Louis U., 1974. Diplomate Am. Bd. Internal Medicine; Am. Bd. Nuclear Medicine. Intern R.I. Hosp., Providence, 1974, resident internal medicine, 1975-76; resident nuclear medicine Harvard Med. Sch., Boston, 1977-79; assoc. Barnes Hosp., St. Louis, 1987—, Children's Hosp., St. Louis, 1987—, Jewish Hosp., St. Louis, 1993—; prof. Washington U., St. Louis, 1993—; co-team leader health effects sect. Internat. Atome Energy Agy. Internat. Chernobyl Project, 1990; bd. dirs. Am. Bd. Nuclear Medicine; mem. com. on assessment of CDC radiation studies NRC/NAS, 1993—; mem. sci. com. Nat. Coun. on Radiation Protection and Measurements, 1993—; mem. coun. Nat. Coun. on Radiation Protection, 1996—. Contbr. more than 100 articles to profl. jours. Mem. Soc. Nuclear Medicine (chair tech. and outcomes assessment com. 1994—), Alpha Omega Alpha. Office: Acad Faculty Mallinkrodt Inst Radiology 510 S Kingshighway Blvd Saint Louis MO 63110

ROYAL, RICHARD, artist; b. Bremerton, Wash., July 19, 1952. One-man shows include Richard Ian Green Gallery, Seattle, 1985, Foster/White Gallery, Seattle, 1986, 87, 89, 91, 94, The Glass Gallery, Bethesda, Md., 1988, 90, Vespermann Gallery, Atlanta, 1989, 91, 94, Brendan Walter Gallery, L.A., 1989, Holt Gallery, Olympia, Wash., 1990, Grohe Gallery, Boston, 1991, Christy Taylor Gallery, Boca Raton, Fla., 1991, Lyons/Matric Gallery, Austin, Tex., 1992, Maveety Gallery, Gleneden Beach, Oreg., 1992, Lewallen Gallery, Sante Fe, N.Mex., 1993, Friesen Fine Art, Sun Valley, Idaho, 1993, 94, Margo Jacobsen Gallery, Portland, 1993, Elaine Horwich Gallery, Scottsdale, Ariz., 1995, Grand Ctrl. Gallery, Tampa, Fla., 1995; group shows include William Traver Gallery, Washington, 1978-93, G.H. Dalsheimer Gallery, Balt., 1986, Joanne Lyons Gallery, Aspen, Colo., 1987, Am. Embassy, Prague, Czech Rep., 1988, Sun Valley Ctr. for Arts, 1989, Art Work for AIDS, Seattle, 1990, Johnson County C.C., Overland Park, Kans., 1991, Lewallen Gallery, 1992, Whatcom Mus. History and Art, Bellingham, Wash., 1992-95, others; represented in permanent collections at Nicolaysen Art Mus., Casper, Wyo., Bellevue (Wash.) Art Mus., Calif. Coll. Arts and Crafts, Oakland, Albany (Ga.) Mus. Art, others; contbr. articles to profl. jours.

ROYALL, ROBERT VENNING, JR., banker; b. Mt. Pleasant, S.C., Dec. 11, 1934; s. Robert Venning and Eleanor (Williams) R.; m. Edith Gregorie Frampton, July 30, 1955; children: Eleanor, Margaret, Edith. AB, U. S.C., 1956; postgrad., Stonier Grad. Sch. Banking, Rutgers U., 1969; grad. advanced mgmt. program, Harvard U., 1975. Chmn. NBSC Corp. and Nat. Bank S.C., Columbia, 1991—; sec. commerce State of S.C.; bd. dirs. Blue Cross-Blue Shield S.C. Trustee Sch. Bus. U. S.C., U. S.C. Bus. Partnership, S.C. Ednl. Comms. Inc.; mem. bd. visitors Coll. Charleston; chmn. S.C. Coord. Coun. for Econ. Devel. Capt USMCR, 1956-59. Mem. Young Man of Yr. Jr. C. of C., 1961, 65, Outstanding Man of Yr., 1968, 1 of 3 Outstanding Young Men in S.C., 1968, Outstanding Young Banker S.C., 1971, Amb. of Yr. Columbia C. of C., 1986, S.C. Bus. Man of Yr. S.c. State C. of C., 1992. Mem. S.C. Bankers Assn. (state legis. com., pres. 1985-86). Episcopalian (past trustee diocese S.C., vestryman). Home: 4632 Perry Ct Columbia SC 29206-4516 Office: Nat Bank of SC PO Box 1457 Columbia SC 29202-1457

ROYALTY, KENNETH MARVIN, lawyer; b. Cin., Nov. 1, 1940; s. Maurice K. and Frances G. (Budd) R.; div. 1991; children by previous marriages: Ted, Sara. BA, Ohio State U., 1962, JD summa cum laude, 1970. Bar: Ohio 1970. From assoc. to ptnr. Vorys, Sater, Seymour & Pease, Columbus, Ohio, 1970-77, 81—; assoc. regional counsel Prudential Ins. Co. Am., Cin., 1977-81; spl. counsel Ohio Divsn. Securities, Columbus, 1973. Contbr. articles to profl. jours.; presenter in field. Lt. USN, 1962-67, Vietnam. Mem. ABA, Ohio State Bar Assn., Columbus Bar Assn.

ROYBAL-ALLARD, LUCILLE, congresswoman; b. Boyle Heights, Calif., June 12, 1941; d. Edward Roybal; m. Edward T. Allard; 4 children. BA, Calif. State U., L.A. Former mem. Calif. State Assembly; mem. 103rd Congress from 33rd Calif. dist., 1993—; mem. Banking and Fin. Svcs., Budget Com. Office: Ho of Reps 324 Cannon Washington DC 20515*

ROYCE, BARRIE SAUNDERS HART, physicist, educator; b. Eng., Jan. 10, 1933; came to U.S., 1957, naturalized, 1978; s. Vincent Pateman Hart and Kathlene (Saunders) R.; m. Dominique J.M. Vallee, May 7, 1964; children: Vincent Rene Hart, Marc Edward Hart. BSc in Physics, King's Coll., U. London, 1954; PhD, U. London, 1957. Rsch. assoc. Carnegie Inst. Tech., 1957-60; rsch. assoc. Princeton U., 1960-61, mem. faculty, 1961—, prof. applied physics and materials scis., 1978—; master of Dean Mathey Coll. Dean Mathey Coll., 1986-94. Editorial adv. bd.: Jour. Photoacoustics, to 1984, Crystal Lattice Defects. Mem. Princeton Borough Zoning Bd. Adjustment, 1980-93, chair, 1993—. Grantee NSF; Grantee Air Force Office Sci. and Rsch.; Grantee Army Rsch. Office. Mem. Am. Phys. Soc., Sigma Xi. Office: Princeton U D416 Duffield Hall (EQ) Princeton NJ 08544

ROYCE, EDWARD R. (ED ROYCE), congressman; b. Los Angeles, Oct. 12, 1951; m. Marie Porter. BA, Calif. State U., Fullerton. Tax mgr. Southwestern Portland Cement Co.; mem. Calif. Senate, 1983-93, 103rd Congress from 39th dist. Calif., 1993—; vice chmn. Public Employment and Retirement Com.; mem. Bus. and Profs. com., Indsl. Rels. com.; legis. author, campaign co-chmn. Proposition 15 Crime Victims/Speedy Trial Initiative; author nation's 1st felony stalking law, bill creating Foster Family Home Ins. Fund, legis. creating foster parent recruitment and tng. program; mem. Banking and Fin. Svcs. Com., Internat. Rels. Com. Named Legis. of Yr. Orange County Rep. Com., 1986, Child Adv. of Yr. Calif. Assn. Svc. for Children, 1987. Mem. Anaheim C. of C. Republican. Office: US Ho of Reps 1113 Longworth Ho Office Bldg Washington DC 20515-0539*

ROYCE, MARY WELLER SA'ID, artist, poet; b. Tupper Lake, N.Y., July 9, 1933; d. Gerard Charles and Mary Weller (McCarthy) de Grandpré; m. Majed Farhan Sa'id, Nov. 19, 1960 (dec. 1966); children: Mary Weller Richardson, Emily Ann Bacon; m. William Ronald Royce, Sept. 2, 1974. AA with honors, Georgetown Visitation Jr. Coll., 1953; BS cum laude, Georgetown U., 1960; MA in Italian, Middlebury Coll., 1968. Writer, artist, 1954—; translator, adminstrv. asst. U.S. Army, Orleans, France, 1956-58; tchg. asst. dept. Italian Rutgers U., New Brunswick, N.J., 1968-70; translator N.J., Ariz., 1971-84; owner, designer The Stamp Act, Rockville, Md., 1990-93. Groups shows include Rockville (Md.) Arts Pl., 1992—, Rockville Art League, 1993—, Montpelier Cultural Arts Ctr., Laurel, Md., 1994—, Strathmore Hall Arts Ctr., North Bethesda, Md., 1994—; poetry collected in anthologies. Coord. Equal Rights Coalition, Utah, 1975; ACLU rep. So. Ariz. Coalition for ERA, Tucson, 1975-78; mem. steering com. Ariz. ERA, 1976-78; Md. state activist Caths. for a Free Choice, 1991-93; mem. The Alliance of Rockville Citizens, 1995—. Fulbright grantee, 1960. Mem. Acad. Am. Poets (assoc.), Nat. Mus. Women in Arts (charter), Washington Project for Arts, Rockville Art League, Strathmore Hall Arts Ctr., Rockville Arts Pl., Arlington Arts Ctr., Montpelier Cultural Arts Ctr. Avocations: photography, jazz, swimming.

ROYCE, PAUL CHADWICK, medical administrator; b. Mpls., July 2, 1928. BA, U. Minn., 1948, MD, 1952; PhD, Case Western Res. U., 1959. Diplomate Am. Bd. of Internal Medicine. Intern U. Chgo. Clinics, 1952-53; fellow NSF Case Western Res. U., Cleve., 1953-54, 56-58, Upjohn fellow, 1958-59; resident internal medicine Bronx Mcpl. Hosp., N.Y., 1959-61; asst. prof. of medicine Albert Einstein Coll. of Med., N.Y.C., 1961-69; sr. staff endocrinologist Guthrie Clinic, Sayre, Pa., 1970-81; assoc. prof. of medicine Hahnemann Med. Sch., Phila., 1973-81; emeritus prof. medicine Med. Coll. Pa./Hahnemann U., 1996—; dean and prof. clin. sci. and physiology Sch. Medicine U. Minn., Duluth, 1981-87; sr. v.p., clin. dir. Monmouth Med. Ctr., Long Branch, N.J., 1987-94; med. dir. The Segal Co. N.Y., 1995—; prin. Royce Assocs., Atlantic Highlands, N.J., 1995—. Producer, host TV prgram Doctors on Call, 1983-87 (Nat. Friends of Pub. Broadcasting Hill award 1987). Lt. USNR, 1954-56. Mem. Harvey Soc., Am. Physiol. Soc., Fedn. Am. Scientists, Physicians for Social Responsibility, Am. Coll. Physician Execs., Sigma Xi, Alpha Omega Alpha. Avocations: skiing, cycling, canoeing. Office: Royce Associates 9 Prospect Rd Atlantic Highlands NJ 07716-1721

ROYCE, RAYMOND WATSON, lawyer, rancher, citrus grower; b. West Palm Beach, Fla., Mar. 5, 1936; s. Wilbur E. and Veda (Watson) R.; m. Catherine L. Setzer, Apr. 21, 1979; children: Raymond, Steven, Nancy, Kathryn, Ryan. BCE, U. Fla., 1958, JD, 1961. Bar: Fla. 1961, U.S. Dist. Ct. (so. dist.) Fla. 1961, U.S. Ct. Appeals (5th cir.) 1961, U.S. Ct. Appeals (11th cir.) 1981. Assoc. William W. Blakeslee, Palm Beach, Fla., 1961-62; with Scott, Royce, Harris & Bryan P.A., Palm Beach, Fla., 1962-94; pres. Scott, Royce, Harris, Bryan, Barra and Jorgensen, P.A., Palm Beach Gardens, Fla., 1982—. Bd. suprs. No. Palm Beach County Water Control Dist. Mem. Fla. Bar (bd. govs. 1974-78), Fla. Citrus Mut., Fla. Cattleman's Assn., Fla. Blue Key, Phi Delta Phi. Democrat. Presbyterian. Home: 5550 Whirlaway Rd West Palm Beach FL 33418-7735 Office: Scott Royce Harris Bryan Barra and Jorgensen PA 4400 P G A Blvd Ste 800 West Palm Beach FL 33410-6562

ROYCHOUDHURI, CHANDRASEKHAR, physicist; b. Barisal, Bengal, India, Apr. 7, 1942; s. Hiralal and Amiyabala (Sengupta) R.; children: Asim, Onnesha. BS in Physics, Jadavpur U., India, 1963; MS in Physics, Jadavpur U., 1965; PhD in Optics, U. Rochester, 1973. Asst. prof. U. Kalyani, West Bengal, India, 1965-68; sr. scientist Nat. Inst. Astrophysics, Puebla, Mex., 1974-78; sr. staff scientist TRW Inc., Redondo Beach, 1978-86; mgr. laser systems Perkin-Elmer, Danbury, Conn., 1986-89; chief scientist Optics & Applied Tech. Lab. United Technologies Optical Systems, West Palm Beach, Fla., 1990-91; dir. Photonics Rsch. Ctr. U. Conn., Storrs, 1991—. Author: chpt. Optical Shoptesting, 1978; contbr. articles to profl. jours. Fulbright scholar U. Vt., 1968. Fellow Conn. Acad. Sci. and Engring.; mem. IEEE, Optical Soc. Am., Soc. Photo-optical Instrumentation, Am. Phys. Soc. (life). Avocations: hiking, spl. edn. programs for children.

ROYCROFT, EDWARD J., publishing company executive. Sr. v.p. sales Reed Reference Pub., New Providence, N.J. Office: Reed Reference Pub 121 Chanlon Rd New Providence NJ 07974-1541*

ROYCROFT, HOWARD FRANCIS, lawyer; b. Balt., Sept. 9, 1930; s. Howard F. and Bessie (Weaver) R.; B.A., U. Md., 1953; LL.B., Georgetown U., 1958; m. Barbara Lee Seal, Mar. 20, 1954; children: Suzanne Carol Roycroft Soderberg, Nancy Lee Roycroft Branigan. Admitted to D.C. bar, 1958, since practiced in Washington; mem. firm Hogan & Hartson, 1958, ptnr., 1965-87, mem. exec. com., 1970-73, counsel, 1987—; dir. United TV, Inc., 1982—, U TV San Francisco, Inc., 1983; mng. ptnr., dir. WIJY, Inc., Hilton Head, S.C.; lectr. Howard U. Sch. Law, 1973-74; guest lectr. U. Tex., 1980; mem. Met. Washington Bd. Trade. Bd. dirs. YMCA Met. Washington, 1974-76. Served to 1st lt. USMC, 1953-55. Mem. ABA, Va. Bar Assn., Fed. Communications Bar Assn., Bar Assn. D.C., Nat. Broadcasters Club, Barristers, Aircraft Owners and Pilots Assn., Nat. Acad. TV Arts and Scis., Broadcast Pioneers, Kappa Alpha, Beta Kappa, Delta Theta Phi. Republican. Methodist. Clubs: Bryce Mountain Ski and Country (dir., pres. 1974-87, 82-87), Mt. Vernon Country, Old Dominion Boat, Washington Tennis Patrons, Army-Navy, Chaine des Rotisseurs Gastronome, Skull Creek Yacht Club. Office: Hogan & Hartson 555 13th St NW Washington DC 20004-1109 also: WIJY 2 Park Ln Hilton Head Island SC 29928-3420

ROYER, CATHERINE A., pharmacologist educator; b. Sept. 13, 1957. D.E.U.G. in Natural Scis., U. Pierre et Marie Curie, 1978, Lic. in Biochemistry, 1979; PhD in Biochemistry, U. Ill., 1985; postgrad., U. Paris VII, 1986. Rsch. assoc. U. Paris VII, 1985-86; rsch. assoc. Laboratoire d'Enzymologie Centre Nat. pour la Recherche Scientifique, Gif-sur-Yvette, France, 1986-87; user coord. Lab. Fluorescence Dynamics, rsch. physicist U. Ill., Urbana-Champaign, 1987-90, adj. asst. prof. biochemistry, 1988-90; asst. prof. pharmacy, pharmaceutics U. Wis., Madison, 1990-95, assoc. prof., 1995—; spkr. various meetings and confs.; mem. spl. panel for grad. rsch. tng. proposals NSF, 1992, external reviewer panel mem. biophysics program, 1994—; mem. spl. study sect. for instrumentation NIH, 1992, spl. site visit study sect., 1991. Peer reviewer Biochemistry, Jour. Biol. Chemistry, Analytical Biochemistry, Biophys. Jour., Analytical Chemistry, VCH Pubs., Jour. Molecular Biology, PNAS, FASEB Jour., Jour. Phys. Chemistry; asst. editor Archives of Biochemistry and Biophysics. Recipient U.S./France postdoctoral award NSF, 1985-86; grantee NIH, 1988-94, U. Wis. Grad. Sch., 1991-92, 92-93, 93—, Whitaker Found., 1993-96. Mem. AAAS, Biophys. Soc. (co-chair fluorescence subgroup, co-chair com. on profl. opportunities for women), Am. Soc. Biochemistry and Molecular Biology, Protein Soc. Office: U Wis-Madison Sch Pharmacy 425 N Charter Madison WI 53706

ROYER, KATHLEEN ROSE, pilot; b. Pitts., Nov. 4, 1949; d. Victor Cedric and Lisetta Emma (Smith) Salway; m. Michael Lee Royer, June 6, 1971 (div. Aug. 1975). Student, Newbold Coll., 1968-69; BS, Columbia Union Coll., 1971; MEd, Shippensburg U., 1974; student, Lehigh U., 1974-75. Cert. tchr. Pa. Music tchr. Harrisburg (Pa.) Sch. Dist., 1971-77; flight instr. Penn-Air, Inc., Altoona, Pa., 1977; capt., asst. chief pilot Air Atlantic Airlines, Centre Hall, Pa., 1977-80; capt., chief pilot Lycoming Air Svc., Williamsport, Pa., 1980-81; govs. pilot Commonwealth of Pa., Harrisburg, 1981-87; flight engr. Pan-Am, N.Y.C., 1987-91; pilot, 1st officer B737 United Airlines, Chgo., 1992-96; 1st officer B767 United Airlines, N.Y.C., 1996—; first woman pilot/engr. crew mem. on 747, 1989-91, chief pilot, cons. Mem. Internat. Soc. Women Airline Pilots, Flight Engrs. Internat. Assn. (scheduling rep. 1989, scheduling dir. 1990, 1st vice chmn., mem. bd. adjustments 1989, v.p., dir. scheduling 1991), UAL-Airline Pilots Assn. (coord. critical incident stress program 1994—), 99's (local chair Ctrl. Pa. chpt. 1987-92), Whirley-Girls (Washington), Hershey Country Club. Republican. Avocations: skiing, computers, golf. Home: 2047 Raleigh Rd Apt D Hummelstown PA 17036-8709 Office: United Airlines PO Box 66140 O'Hare Internat Airport Chicago IL 60666

ROYER, ROBERT LEWIS, retired utility company executive; b. Louisville, Jan. 2, 1928; s. Carl Brown and Martha Helen (Garrett) R.; m. Carol Jean Pierce, June 24, 1950; children: Jenifer Lea, Todd Pierce, Robert Douglas. BS in Elec. Engring., Rose Hulman Inst. Tech., 1949. Registered profl. engr., Ky. With Louisville Gas and Electric Co., 1949-91, asst. v.p. ops., 1962-63, asst. v.p., asst. gen. supt., 1963-64, v.p., gen. supt., 1964-69, v.p. ops., 1969-78, exec. v.p., 1978, pres., chief exec. officer, 1978-89; chmn., 1989-91; dir. Louisville Gas and Electric Co., 1972-91, chmn. emeritus, 1991—; dir. LG8E Energy Corp., 1990-91; mem. exec. bd. East Cen. Area Reliability Coun., 1978-89; mem. Ky. Energy Resources Commn., 1975-79; mem. energy task force Gov.'s Econ. Devel. Commn., 1976-79; mem. Ky. Energy Rsch. Bd., 1978-88; v.p. Ind.-Ky. Electric Corp., 1979-89; dir. Ohio Valley Transmission Corp., 1978-90, Ohio Valley Electric Corp., 1979-89, Citizens Fidelity Corp. & Citizens Fidelity Bank and Trust Co., 1976-90. Mem. exec. bd. Old Ky. Home Coun. Boy Scouts Am., v.p. dist. ops., 1970-75, 79-80, 1st v.p., 1981-82, pres., 1982-84, commr., 1975-79, rep. to nat. coun., 1975-84, 95—, mem. regional bd., 1985—, S.E. region area pres., 1988-93; bd. dirs. East End Boys Club, 1975-78, Louisville Indsl. Found., 1980-86, Ky. Coun. Sci. and Tech., 1987-92; trustee Spirit of Louisville Found., 1978-90, J. Graham, Brown Found., 1980—; bd. mgrs. Rose Hulman Inst. Tech., 1979—; bd. dirs. Ky. Derby Mus., 1991-93, Leadership Louisville Found., 1985-91, Alliant Health Sys., 1989-94; mem. Louisville Devel. Com., 1979-83. Served with U.S. Army, 1953-55. Recipient Silver Beaver award Boy Scouts Am., 1975, Disting. Eagle award, 1989, Silver Antelope award, 1990. Mem. IEEE, Execs. Club Louisville (dir. 1980-83), Louisville Automobile Club (dir. 1974—, treas. 1977-79, v.p. 1979-81, pres. 1981-83, nat. adv. coun. 1982-86), Louisville Area C. of C. (dir. 1978-80), Hurstbourne Country Club, Pendennis Club, Rotary. Methodist. Home and Office: 4014 Norbourne Blvd Louisville KY 40207-3806

ROYER, THOMAS JERRY, financial planner; b. Coshocton, Ohio, June 17, 1943; s. Walter H. Sr. and Francis (Guerke) R.; m. Felipa T. Pagal, Dec. 24, 1965; children: Matthew Vincent, Brian Eugene, Nicholas Alexander. Student, Xavier U., 1979, Coll. for Fin. Planning, Denver, 1986. Cert. fin. planner. Agt. Met. Life Ins. Co., N.Y.C., 1966-68, mgr., 1968-70; gen. agt. Summit Nat. Life Ins. Co., Akron, Ohio, 1970—, Community Nat., Worthington, Ohio, 1989, Life USA, 1990; prin. Royer & Co., Fairfield, Ohio, 1985-88; founder, pres. Group-10 Fin., Fairfield, 1988—; founder, CEO United Group Mktg., Cin., 1993. Mem. Inst. Cert. Fin. Planners, Nat. Exchange Club. Republican. Roman Catholic. Avocations: golf, swimming, physical fitness. Office: Group-10 Fin 4050 Executive Park Dr Apt 406 Cincinnati OH 45241-2020

ROYHAB, RONALD, journalist, newspaper editor; b. Lorain, Ohio, Oct. 6, 1942; s. Halim Farah and Elizabeth Della (Naiser) R.; m. Roberta Lee Libb, Apr. 20, 1969; children: David Libb, Aaron Nicholas. Student, Lorain County (Ohio) Coll., Kent State U.; postgrad., Am. U., Washington. Reporter Lorain Jour., 1966-69; chief bur. Scripps Howard Ohio Bur., Columbus, 1975-78; reporter spl. assignment Scripps Howard Cin. Post, 1971-72; investigative reporter Scripps Howard Cleve. Press, 1972-75; chief bur. Scripps Howard Ohio Bur., Columbus, 1975-78; asst. mng. editor Scripps Howard News Svc., Washington, 1978-81; mng. editor Scripps Howard El Paso (Tex.) Herald Post, 1981-83; asst. mng. editor Scripps Howard Pitts. Press, 1983-92; assoc. editor Pitts. Post Gazette, 1992-93; mng. editor Toledo Blade, 1993—; bd. dirs. Toledo Blade Co. Bd. dirs. Am. Lebanese Congress. With USAR, 1964-70. Recipient 7 awards for Excellence Cleve. Newspaper Guild, 1972-75; Spl. Sect. awards Pa. Newspaper Pubs. Assn., 1985, 86, 88; fellow Am. Polit. Sci. Assn., 1970-71. Mem. AP Mng. Editors Assn., AP Soc. Ohio. Eastern Orthodox. Home: 27262 Fort Meigs Rd Perrysburg OH 43551-1230 Office: Toledo Blade 541 N Superior St Toledo OH 43660-1000

ROYKO, MIKE, newspaper columnist; b. Chgo., Sept. 19, 1932; s. Michael and Helen (Zak) R.; m. Carol Joyce Duckman, Nov. 7, 1954 (dec. Sept. 1979); children: M. David, Robert F.; m. Judith Arndt, May 21, 1985; children: Samuel, Katherine. Student, Wright Jr. Coll., 1951-52. Reporter Chgo. North Side Newspapers, 1956; reporter, asst. city editor Chgo. City News Bur., 1956-59; reporter, columnist Chgo. Daily News, 1959-78, assoc. editor, 1977-78; reporter, columnist Chgo. Sun-Times, 1978-84; columnist Chgo. Tribune, 1984—. Author: Up Against It, 1967, I May Be Wrong But I Doubt It, 1968, Boss-Richard J. Daley of Chicago, 1971, Slats Grobnik and Some Other Friends, 1973, Sez Who? Sez Me, 1982, Like I Was Sayin', 1984, Dr. Kookie, You're Right!, 1989. Served with USAF, 1952-56. Recipient Heywood Broun award, 1968, Pulitzer prize for commentary, 1972, H.L. Mencken award, 1981, Ernie Pyle award, 1982; medal for svc. to journalism U. Mo. Sch. Journalism, 1979, Lifetime Achievement award Nat. Press Club, 1990; named Best Newspaper Columnist in Am., Washington Journalism Rev., 1985, 87, 88, 90; named to Chgo. Press Club Journalism Hall of Fame, 1980. Club: LaSalle St. Rod and Gun. Office: Chgo Tribune Co 435 N Michigan Ave Chicago IL 60611-4001

ROYSE, MARY KAY, judge; b. Hutchinson, Kans., Oct. 3, 1949; d. J.R. and Patricia Ann (Lambert) R. BS in Edn., Emporia State U., 1970, MA, 1972; JD, Kans. U., 1978. Instr. Miami U., Hamilton, Ohio, 1972-75; assoc. atty. Foulston & Siefkin, Wichita, 1978-82, Law Offices Bryson E. Mills, Wichita, 1982-86; judge Dist. Ct. (18th dist.) Kans., Wichita, 1986-93, Kans. Ct. Appeals, Topeka, 1993—; mem. Kans. Jud. Coun. Com. Pattern Instructions Kans., 1989—. Bd. dirs. Work Option Women, Wichita, 1980, Emporia State U. Alumni Assn., 1982-85, Kans. Dialysis Assn., Wichita, 1986-93. Named Woman Achievement, Women in Communications, Wichita, 1988, Disting. Alumni, Emporia State U., 1990. Mem. ABA, Kans. Bar Assn., Kans. Commn. Bicentenial U.S. Constitution, Kans. Bar Assn. Commn. Status of Women in Profession, Wichita Bar Assn. Avocations: travel, movies, reading.

ROYSTER, VERMONT (CONNECTICUT), journalist; b. Raleigh, N.C., Apr. 30, 1914; s. Wilbur High and Olivette (Broadway) R.; m. Frances Claypoole, June 5, 1937; children: Frances Claypoole, Sara Eleanor. Grad., Webb Sch., Bellbuckle, Tenn., 1931; A.B., U. N.C., 1935, LL.D., 1959; Litt.D., Temple U., 1964, Williams Coll., 1979; L.H.D., Elon Coll., 1968; LL.D., Colby Coll., 1976. Reporter N.Y.C. News Bur., 1936; reporter Wall St. Jour., 1936, Washington corr., 1936-41, 45-46, chief Washington corr., 1946-48, editorial writer and columnist, 1946-48, assoc. editor, 1948-51, sr. assoc. editor, 1951-58, editor, 1958-71, contbg. editor, columnist, 1971—, editor emeritus, 1993—; sr. v.p. Dow Jones & Co., Inc., 1960-71; William Rand Kenan prof. journalism and pub. affairs U. N.C., Chapel Hill, 1971-86; regular commentator pub. affairs CBS Radio and TV, 1972-77; appears on pub. affairs programs on TV and radio.; sr. fellow Inst. Policy Scis., Duke, 1973-85; mem. adv. com. Pulitzer prizes Columbia, 1967-76; mem. Nat. Commn. Hist. Publs., 1974-76. Author: (with others) Main Street and Beyond, 1959, Journey Through the Soviet Union, 1962, A Pride of Prejudices, 1967, (memoirs) My Own, My Country's Time, 1983, The Essential Royster (ed. Edmund Fuller), 1985 contbr. numerous articles on financial and econ. subjects to periodicals. Bd. dirs. Newspaper Fund, Inc.; trustee St. Augustine Coll., Raleigh, N.C. Commd. ensign USNR, 1940; active duty 1941-46, Atlantic, Caribbean, Pacific; exec. officer USS LaPrade comdg. officer USS Jack Miller, USS PC-1262 lt. comdr. Res. Recipient Pulitzer prize for editorial writing, 1953, Pulitzer prize for commentary, 1984; medal for distinguished service in journalism Sigma Delta Chi, 1958; William Allan White award for distinguished service to journalism, 1971; Loeb Meml. award for contbn. to econ. journalism UCLA, 1975; Elijah Lovejoy award Colby Coll., 1976; Fourth Estate award Nat. Press Club, Washington, 1978; Presdl. Medal of Freedom, 1986; named to N.C. Journalism Hall of Fame, 1980. Mem. Am. Soc. Newspaper Editors (pres. 1965-66), Nat. Conf. Editorial Writers (chmn. 1957), Phi Beta Kappa Assos., Phi Beta Kappa. Episcopalian. Clubs: University (N.Y.C.); Nat. Press (Washington). Home: 806 Springmoor Cir # 132P Raleigh NC 27615-5703 *Although mankind forgets old lessons to its pain, just as young people do those of their fathers, it always relearns them. It's comforting to remember that the Dark Ages lasted only 500 years.*

ROZEBOOM, JOHN A., religious organization administrator. Dir. Christian Ref. Home Missions. Office: Christian Ref Ch in N Am 2850 Kalamazoo Ave SE Grand Rapids MI 49508-1433

ROZEL, SAMUEL JOSEPH, lawyer; b. Louisville, Apr. 22, 1935; s. Sam and Anna (Sessmer) R.; m. Jeanne Frances Foulkes, July 3, 1965; children: Brooke Jane, John Samuel. BSL, U. Louisville, 1955, LLB, 1957; grad., Advanced Mgmt. Program, Harvard U., 1979. Bar: Ky. 1958, D.C. 1962, Minn. 1968, Ind. 1970, N.Y. 1983. Atty. FTC, Washington, 1962-67; antitrust counsel Honeywell, Inc., Mpls., 1967-69; atty. Magnavox Corp., Ft. Wayne, Ind., 1969-71, gen. counsel, 1971, v.p., 1972-75, sec., 1973-75; v.p. U.S. Philips Corp., N.Y.C., 1975-77, sr. v.p., 1977—; assoc. gen. counsel Philips Electronics N.Am. Corp., N.Y.C., sec. exec. mgmt. com., 1980—; v.p., sec., gen. counsel, dir. Phillips Electronics N.Am. Corp., N.Y.C., 1987-91, sr. v.p., sec., gen. counsel, mem. exec. com. bd. dirs., 1991—; bd. dirs. Philips Electronics N.Am. Corp., Std. Communications Corp. Served to capt. JAGC, AUS, 1957-62. Mem. ABA, Fed. Bar Assn., Ky. Bar Assn., Ind. Bar Assn., N.Y. Bar Assn., Harvard Club (N.Y.C.), Met. Club (Washington). Home: 215 S Bald Hill Rd New Canaan CT 06840-2908 Office: Philips Electronics N Am 125 Park Ave New York NY 10017-5529

ROZELLE, LEE THEODORE, physical chemist; b. Rhinelander, Wis., Mar. 9, 1933; s. Theodore and Alice (Omholt) R.; m. Barbara J. Ingli, June 21, 1955; children—David, Steven, Carolyn, Ann, Kenneth. B.S., U. Wis., 1955, Ph.D., 1960. Rsch. chemist DuPont Corp., Circleville, Ohio, 1960-63; prin. scientist-tech. coord. Honeywell Corp., Mpls., 1963-67; dir. chemistry div. North Star Rsch. Inst., Mpls., 1967-74; v.p. R&D USCI div. C.R. Bard, Billerica, Mass., 1974-77; dir. engring. tech. div. Mellon Inst., Pitts., 1977-78; dir. rsch. and devel. Permutit Co., Monmouth Junction, N.J., 1978-80; v.p. rsch. and devel. Gelman Scis., Inc., Ann Arbor, Mich., 1980-82; v.p. sci. and tech. Culligan Internat. Co., Northbrook, Ill., 1982-87; assoc. dir. rsch. Olin Chems. Rsch. div. Olin Corp., Cheshire, Conn., 1987-92; cons. in water treatment tech., mktg. and mgmt., 1992—; pres., cons. Water Solutions, Inc., 1995—; v.p., mng. ptnr. Puraq Water Systems, Inc., 1996—; cons. in field; mem. Nat. Drinking Water Adv. Council EPA, 1987-90. Contbr. chpts. to books, numerous articles to profl. jours. Bd. dirs. Unitarian Ch., Andover, Mass., 1974-77. NIH fellow, 1958-60; recipient Spl. Hominum award Nat. Sanitation Found., 1988. Fellow Am. Inst. Chemists; mem. AAAS, Am. Chem. Soc., Am. Soc. Artificial Internal Organs, Health Industry Mfrs. Assn. (chmn. spl. activities com.), Water Pollution Control Fedn., Water Quality Assn. (chmn. sci. adv. com., Award of Merit 1989), Am. Water Works Assn., Assn. Met. Water Agencies, Filtration Soc., Pacific Water Quality Assn. (bd. dirs. 1987-90, Robert Gans award 1988), Am. Soc. Agrl. Engring., Internat. Water Supply Assn., European Membrane Soc., N.Am. Membrane Soc., Asociacion Interamericano De Ingenieria Sanaitaria y Ambiental, Sigma Xi, Eta Phi Alpha, Phi Lambda Upsilon. Home and Office: 626 23rd St N La Crosse WI 54601-3825 *My professional goal has always been to make significant contributions to the well being of our society through science. Goals have been accomplished from contributions to water purification to health care.*

ROZELLE, PETE (ALVIN RAY ROZELLE), former commissioner athletic league; b. South Gate, Calif., Mar. 1, 1926; s. Raymond Foster and Hazel Viola (Healey) R.; 1 dau., Ann Marie. B.A., U. San Francisco, 1950. Athletic news dir. U. San Francisco, 1948-50, asst. athletic dir., 1950-52; pub. relations dir. Los Angeles Rams Football Club, 1952-55; partner Internat. Bus. Relations (pub. relations), San Francisco, 1955-57; gen. mgr. Los Angeles Rams Football Club, 1957-60; commr. NFL, N.Y.C., 1960-89. Served with USNR, 1944-46. Mem. Pro Football Hall of Fame. Office: care Commr's Office NFL 410 Park Ave New York NY 10022-4407*

ROZEN, JEROME GEORGE, JR., research entomologist, museum curator and research administrator; b. Evanston, Ill., Mar. 19, 1928; s. Jerome George and Della (Kretchmar) R.; m. Barbara L. Lindner, Dec. 18, 1948; children—Steven George, Kenneth Charles, James Robert. Student, U. Pa., 1946-48; B.A., U. Kans., 1950; Ph.D., U. Calif.-Berkeley, 1955. Entomologist in taxonomy U.S. Dept. Agr., 1956-58; asst. prof. entomology Ohio State U., 1958-60; assoc. curator hymenoptera, dept. entomology Am. Mus. Natural History, N.Y.C., 1960-65, curator hymenoptera, 1965—, chmn. dept. entomology, 1960-71, dep. dir. research, 1972-86; field expdns. in U.S., Europe, Mex., Trinidad, Argentina, Chile, Brazil, Peru, Venezuela, Morocco, Pakistan, Republic of South Africa, Namibia, Egypt; adj. prof. CUNY, 1968—. Contbr. numerous sci. articles on bees (Apoidea) and beetles (Coleoptera). Fellow AAAS; mem. Am. Inst. Biol. Scis., Entomol. Soc. Am. (editor misc. publs. 1959-60), Soc. Study of Evolution, Soc. Systematic Biology, N.Y. Entomol Soc. (pres. 1964-65), Washington Entomol. Soc., Pacific Coast Entomol. Soc., Kans. Entomol. Soc., Orgn. Biol. Field Stas. (pres. 1990), Internat. Soc. Hymenopterists. Home: 55 Haring St Closter NJ 07624-1709 Office: Am Mus Natural History Central Park West New York NY 10024-5192

ROZENBAUM, NAJMAN, languages educator, counselor; b. Panama, Apr. 29, 1945; s. Hersz Mayer and Ana (Baitel) R.; 1 child, Nataniel. BA, Fla. State U., 1972; MA, U. of the Pacific, 1974, EdS, 1975; DLitt, World U., 1986; PhD, Calif. U. for Advanced Studies, Petaluma, 1987. Cert. tchr., counselor N.C., N.Y., Calif. Prof. English Assn. Panama-N.Am., Panama, 1967-70, Colegio Javier High Sch., Panama, 1970, Inst. Alberto Einstein High Sch., Panama, 1971, 72, Inst. Normal Rubiano, Panama, 1973; teaching asst. Spanish U. of the Pacific, Stockton, fall 1973; teaching asst., prof. techniques of rsch. courses in edn. U. Santa Maria, Panama, 1975-76; prof. English and Spanish YMCA, Balboa, 1975-76; instr. English and Spanish various mil. bases, C.Z., 1976; prof. English and Spanish YMCA/ACJ de Balboa, Panama, 1978-94; prof. English Univ. of the Isthmus, 1995—; instr. English Panama Canal Commn., 1980; pvt. practice counselor. Author: Anxieties in Adolescents, 1981, (monograph) Einstein as a Jew, 1966, ,(short story) The Crime, 1963; newspaper columnist Star and Herald, La Estrella de Panama. Pres. Jewish Nat. Fund, Panama, 1964-67. Mem. Nat. Geographic Soc. Avocations: reading short stories and books social issues; originator/devel. Theory of the Belts or the Bio-Social Theory of Learning, Theory of Number Nine. Home and Office: Apartado 850133, Panama City 5, Panama

ROZMAN, GILBERT FRIEDELL, sociologist, educator; b. Mpls., Feb. 18, 1943; s. David and Celia (Friedell) R.; m. Masha Dwosh, Jan. 25, 1945; children: Thea Dwosh, Noah Dwosh. B.A., Carleton Coll., Northfield, Minn., 1965; Ph.D. (Woodrow Wilson fellow 1965-66), Princeton U., 1971. Mem. faculty Princeton U., 1970—, prof. sociology, 1979—, Musgrave prof. sociology, 1992—, dir. Internat. Studies Program, 1993—; dir. Coun. on Regional Studies, 1993—; mem. com. studies Chinese civilization Am. Council Learned Socs., 1975-80; mem. U.S.-USSR Bi-Nat. Commn. Humanities and Social Scis., 1978-86. Author: Urban Networks in Ch'ing China and Tokugawa Japan, 1973, Urban Networks in Russia, 1750-1800, and Premodern Periodization, 1976, Population and Marketing Settlements in Ch'ing China, 1982, A Mirror for Socialism: Soviet Criticisms of China, 1985, The Chinese Debate About Soviet Socialism 1978-85, 1987, Japan's Response to the Gorbachev Era, 1985-1991: A Rising Superpower Views a Declining One, 1992; co-author: The Modernization of Japan and Russia, 1975; editor: The Modernization of China, 1981, Soviet Studies of Premodern China: Assessments of Recent Scholarship, 1984, Japan in Transition: From Tokugawa to Meiji, 1986, The East Asian Region: Confucian Heritage and Its Modern Adaptation, 1991, Dismantling Communism: Common Causes and Regional Variations, 1992. Guggenheim fellow, 1979-80; grantee NSF, NEH, Social Sci. Rsch. Coun., Nat. Coun. for Soviet and E. European Studies, U.S. Inst. Peace, Woodrow Wilson Internat. Ctr. Mem. Assn. Asian Studies, Am. Sociol. Assn., Am. Assn. Advancement Slavic Studies. Home: 20 Springwood Dr Trenton NJ 08648-1048 Office: Princeton U 2-N-2 Green Hall Princeton NJ 08544

ROZOF, PHYLLIS CLAIRE, lawyer; b. Flint, Mich., Aug. 3, 1948; d. Eugene Robert and Loveta Lucille Greenwood; m. Robert James Rozof, July 17, 1970 (dec. Oct. 1995); children: Nathan, Zachary. AB with high distinction, U. Mich., 1970, JD magna cum laude, 1977. Bar: Mich. 1977, Fla. 1978. Assoc. Honigman Miller Schwartz and Cohn, Detroit, 1977-81, ptnr., 1982—. Mem. Comml. Real Estate Women Detroit (pres. 1992-93). Office: Honigman Miller Schwartz & Cohn 2290 1st National Bldg Detroit MI 48226

ROZZELL, SCOTT ELLIS, lawyer; b. Texarkana, Tex., Apr. 12, 1949; s. George M. and Dora Mae (Boyett) R.; m. Jackie Golden, June 1, 1996; children by previous marriage: Stacey Elizabeth, Kimberly Marie. BA, So. Meth. U., 1971; JD, U. Tex., 1975. Bar: Tex. 1975, U.S. Dist. Ct. (so. dist.) Tex. 1975, U.S. Dist. Ct. (no. dist.) Tex. 1977, U.S. Ct. Appeals (1st, 3d, 9th cirs.) 1977, U.S. Ct. Appeals (5th and D.C. cirs.) 1976. Assoc. Baker & Botts, Houston, 1975-82, ptnr., 1983—. Bd. dirs. Houston Vol. Lawyers, 1984-86, 91-93; vice chair Cancer Counseling Inc., Houston, 1991-92; mem. devel. bd. U. Tex. Houston Health Sci. Ctr., 1994—. Fellow Tex. Bar Found. (life), Houston Bar Found. (life, bd. dirs. 1991-93, chair 1993), Am. Bar Found.; mem. ABA, Houston Bar Assn. (pres. 1996—), Fed. Energy Bar Assn., Houston Young Lawyers Assn. (pres. 1983-84). Republican. Presbyterian. Avocation: flying old airplanes. Home: 5 Long Timbers Ln Houston TX 77024-5445 Office: Baker & Botts 3000 One Shell Plz 910 Louisiana St Houston TX 77002

RUA, MILTON FRANCISCO, retired lawyer; b. San German, P.R., Dec. 8, 1919; s. Urbano F. and Josefa A. (Gonzalez-Ferrer) R.; BA cum laude, U. P.R., 1941, LLB, 1943; m. Barbara Ann Becher (dec. Nov. 1989); children by previous marriage: Milton J., Jaime L. Admitted to P.R. bar, 1943; legal counsel Dept. Finance of P.R., 1943-46; sr. partner Rivera-Zayas, Rivera-Cestero & Rua, San Juan, P.R., 1950-73; founder Milton F. Rua Law Offices, San Juan, P.R., 1973-86; founder, counsellor Banco Mercantil de P.R., Rio Piedras, 1966—, chmn. bd. dirs., 1975—; founder Asso. Ins. Agencies, Inc., San Juan, 1972, Fajardo Fed. Savs. & Loan Assn., 1972—. Mem. bar exam. com. Supreme Ct. P.R., 1955-56; spl. counsel com. natural resources and beautification P.R. Ho. of Reps., 1967-68; mem. citizens com. nuc. plants Environ. Quality Bd. of P.R., 1972; chmn. Electoral Reform Commn., 1973-74; mem. organizing com. First Latin Am. Biennal Graphic Arts, P.R., 1970; bd. dirs. Casa el Libro, chmn., 1960-70; bd. dirs. Inst. of Culture of P.R., 1968-79, Students Art League of San Juan, Mus. P.R., P.R. Found. for Humanities, 1981-84; trustee Advance Ctr. for Studies P.R. and Caribbean, 1986—. Mem. Found. Bar Assn. P.R. (hon. pres. 1976-78), Bar Assn. P.R., Am., Inter-Am. bar assns., Iberoamerican Inst. Aero. Law. Clubs: Bankers, Union League (N.Y.C.), Elks. Address: Calle Candina # 10 Candina 10 San Juan PR 00907-1455

RUAN, JOHN, transportation executive; b. Beacon, Iowa, Feb. 11, 1914; s. John Arthur and Rachel Anthony (Llewellyn) R.; m. Rose Duffy, July 10, 1941 (dec. May 1943); 1 child, John III; m. Elizabeth J. Adams, Sept. 6, 1946; children: Elizabeth Jayne Ruan Fletcher, Thomas Heyliger. Student, Iowa State U., 1931-32. Pres. The Ruan Cos., Des Moines, 1932-86, chmn., 1986—; chmn. Ruan Transp. Corp., Ruan Leasing Co., Ruan Aviation Corp., Ruan Fin. Corp., Ruan Ctr. Corp.; pres. and treas. City Ctr. Corp.; chmn. bd. dirs. and chmn. exec. com. Bankers Trust Co.; bd. dirs. Heritage Communications, Inc., Northwestern States Portland Cement Co. Mem. Des Moines Devel. Corp.; past pres. Greater Des Moines Com., Iowa State Engring. Coll. Adv. Council; fin. chmn., exec. com. Northwestern U. Transp. Ctr.; bd. govs. Iowa State U. Found.; bd. dirs. Des Moines Area Council on Alcoholism, Living History Farms; trustee Hoover Presidential Library Assns., Inc. Named Des Moines Citizen Yr., Des Moines City Council, 1981; elected to Iowa Bus. Hall of Fame, 1982; recipient Disting. Iowa Citizen award Mid-Iowa Council Boy Scouts Am., 1985, Humanitarian award Variety Club of Iowa, 1986, People With Vision award Iowa Soc. Prevent Blindness, 1986. Mem. Am. Trucking Assns., Inc. (treas., exec. com., chmn. fin. com.), Am. Trucking Assns. Found. (trustee), Iowa Assn. Bus. and Industry (bd. dirs.), Des Moines C. of C. (bd. dirs.). Republican. Methodist. Clubs: Wakonda, Des Moines; Lost Tree, Old Port Yacht (North Palm Beach, Fla.); Rancho LaCosta (Carlsbad, Calif.). Avocations: golf, mushroom hunting. Home: 23 34th St Davenport IA 52806 Office: Ruan Fin Corp 666 Grand Ave Des Moines IA 50309-2502 Office: Ruan Cos 3200 Ruan Ctr Des Moines IA 50309-2535*

RUANE, JOSEPH WILLIAM, sociology educator; b. Lansdowne, Pa., Feb. 23, 1933; s. Joseph William and F. Viola (Davis) R.; m. Nancy Di Pasquale, Nov. 25, 1971; 1 child, Krista. Student St. Joseph's U., 1951-53, 68-69, B.A. in Philosophy, St. Charles Sem., 1958; M.A. in Sociology, Temple U., 1971; Ph.D. in Sociology, U. Del., 1978. Ordained priest Roman Catholic Ch., 1962. Asst. pastor, priest Archdiocese, Phila., 1962-68; tchr. social studies Sch. Dist. of Phila., 1968-71; asst. prof. sociology Phila. Coll. Pharmacy and Sci., 1971-77, assoc. prof., 1977—; mem. adj. faculty Gt. Lakes Colls. Assn., Phila., 1983-90; interim chmn. dept. humanities and social scis. Phila. Coll. Pharmacy and Sci., 1984-86, chair dept. social science, 1989-96; dir. West Phila. Mental Health Consortium, 1985-86, Health Svcs. Group, Inc., 1986—, vice chair 1987—; dir. West Phila. C. of C., 1993—, ARC, West Phila., 1990—; dir., exec. com., chmn. urban com. West Phila. Partnership, 1975—. Contbr. articles to profl. jours. Co-editor, prin. author Pub. Edn. Platform of W. Wilson Goode, 1983. Founding dir. West Phila. Community Fed. Credit Union, 1980-88, pres., 1982-88; bd. dirs. University City Clean, Phila., 1981-87, Friends of Clark Park, Phila., 1982-86; dir. Green to Green, 1995—, Spruce Hill Cmty. Assn., 1995. Decorated Legion of Honor Chapel of Four Chaplains, 1967; Lilly fellow, 1980. Mem. Am. Acad. Polit. and Social Scis., Am. Sociol. Assn., Eastern Sociol. Soc., Pa. Sociol. Soc. (chmn. long range planning com. 1982-86, pres. 1989-90, exec. com. 1987—), Global Edn. Assocs., Fedn. Christian Ministries (v.p. Middle Atlantic 1981-84, pres. 1988-92, chmn. bd. dirs. 1992-96), Corps of Res. Priests U.S. (regional coordinator 1984—), AAUP, Sigma Xi. Democrat. Clubs: Vesper (Phila); Westwood (Split Rock, Pa.). Avocations: basketball; attending theatre; travel. Home: 4226 Regent Sq Philadelphia PA 19104-4439 Office: Phila Coll Pharmacy and Sci 43d and Kingsessing Mall Philadelphia PA 19104

RUANE, MAUREEN MURIEL, labor union official; b. Oceanside, N.Y., June 8, 1945; d. Joseph William and Muriel Helen (Bennett) Murphy; m.

Martin Conrad Ruane, July 15, 1967 (div. May 1992). Grad. high sch., Valley Stream, L.I., N.Y. Sec. Local 854 IBT, H&W Benefits Plan, Valley Stream, N.Y., 1971-81; fund mgr. Local 854 Pension Fund Health & Welfare Benefits Plan, Valley Stream, N.Y., 1981-89; bus. agt. Local 854 I.B. of T., Valley Stream, N.Y., 1989, pres., 1990—; dir. Labor Edn. and Community Svc. Agy. Inc., Westbury, N.Y., 1988—; trustee Local 854 Health and Welfare and Pension Fund, Valley Stream, 1990—; del. Eastern Conf. Teamsters, Bethesda, Md., 1990—, Joint Coun. #16, N.Y.C., 1990—, indsl. trade divsn. Internat. Brotherhood of Teamsters, 1992—; area v.p. Internat. Teamsters' Women's Caucus, 1992—; adv. bd. Nat. Conf. Unions and Employees Benefit Funds, 1992—; commr. Teamsters Human Rights Com. and Joint Coun. 16 (rep. women's issues). Mem. Internat. Found. of Employee Benefits Plans, Assn. Benefit Adminstrs., N.Y. Inst. Technol., Indsl. Rels. Rsch. Assn., Ednl. Conf. Health and Welfare and Pension Plans. Lutheran. Avocations: exercise, sewing, decorating & modeling.

RUBARDT, PETER CRAIG, conductor, educator; b. Oakland, Calif., Aug. 7, 1958; s. Kenneth and Betty (Maspero) R.; m. Hedi Salanki; 1 child, Daniel. BA, U. Calif., Berkeley, 1981; M of Music, SUNY, Stony Brook, 1984; student, Hochschule fur Musik, Vienna, 1984-86; D Mus. Arts, Julliard Sch., 1989. Prof., conductor SUNY, Purchase, 1989-90, Rutgers U., New Brunswick, N.J., 1991—; resident conductor N.J. Symphony, Newark, 1990-93; assoc. conductor Syracuse (N.Y.) Symphony, 1993—; guest conductor various orchs. Condr. rec. Bach Concerti, 1988. Fullbright fellow USIA, 1984-86; Bruno Walter scholar, Julliard Sch., 1986-88. Mem. Am. Symphony Orch. League, Condrs. Guild. Democrat. Office: Syracuse Symphony Orch 411 Montgomery St Syracuse NY 13202-2930

RUBAYI, SALAH, surgeon, educator; b. Baghdad, Iraq, Oct. 1, 1942; came to U.S., 1981; s. Abdulla Mossa Rubayi and Fatma (Ibriham) Al-Jarah; m. Cecile-Rose, June 23, 1985. MD, U. Baghdad, Iraq, 1966; LRCP and LRCS, Royal Coll. Surgeons and Physicians, Scotland, 1974. Surgeon burn and reconstructive surgery Birmingham Accident Hosp., Eng., 1978-81; fellow burn unit Los Angeles County/U. So. Calif. Med. Ctr., 1981-82; fellow plastic surgery Rancho Los Amigos Med. Ctr., Downey, Calif., 1982-85, mem. attending staff in plastic and reconstructive surgery, chief pressure ulcer mgmt. service, 1985—; chmn. Laser Safety Com. Rancho Los Amigos Med. Ctr., 1985—; asst. prof. surgery U. So. Calif. Contbr. articles to profl. jours. Fellow ACS, Internat. Coll. Surgeons, Am. Soc. Laser Medicine and Surgery; mem. Internat. Soc. Burn Injury, Am. Burn Assn., Internat. Soc. Paraplegia. Avocations: art, travel, museums, swimming, walking. Office: Rancho Los Amigos Med Ctr HB121 7601 Imperial Hwy # Hb121 Downey CA 90242-3456

RUBBERT, PAUL EDWARD, engineering executive; b. Mpls., Feb. 18, 1937; s. Adolf Christian and Esther Ruth Rubbert; m. Mary Parpart, Oct. 6, 1958 (div. 1985); children: Mark, David, Stephen; m. Rita Monica Saiia, Oct. 7, 1989. BS with high distinction, U. Minn., 1958, MS in Aero. Engring., 1960; PhD in Aerodyn., MIT, 1965. Rsch. engr. The Boeing Co., Seattle, 1960-62, 65-72, unit chief aerodyns rsch., comml. airplane group, 1972—; cons. NASA, 1989—, aeronautics adv. com., aerospace rsch. and tech. sub-coms.; corp. vis. com. MIT, 1990—; served on various coms. Nat. Rsch. Coun. Panel; aerodyns. cons. GM; speaker in field. Contbr. articles to profl. jours. Recipient Arch T. Colwell Merit award Soc. Automotive Engrs., 1968, Wright Brothers Lectureship in Aeronautics Am. Inst. of Aeronautics and Astronautics, 1994. Fellow AIAA (Outstanding Tech. Mgmt. award Pacific Northwest sect., disting. lectr., assoc. editor jour., past mem. fellow selection com., dir., chmn. various workshops and coms.); mem. NAE. Achievements include three patents in field. Office: Boeing Comml Airplane Group MS 67-UC P O Box 3707 Seattle WA 98124-2207 Home: 20131 SE 23rd Pl Issaquah WA 98029

RUBEL, ARTHUR JOSEPH, anthropologist, educator; b. Shanghai, China, Aug. 29, 1924; came to U.S., 1924; s. Arthur John and Marcella (Crohn) R.; m. Phyllis Lavern Howard, Apr. 22, 1954 (dec.); 1 child, Laura; m. Carole H. Browner, Jan. 1, 1986. B.A., Mexico City Coll., 1949; M.A., U. Chgo., 1958; Ph.D., U. N.C., Chapel Hill, 1962. Behavioral scientist behavioral sci. br. USPHS, 1962-63; asst. prof. U. N.C., Greensboro, 1963-64, U. Tex., Austin, 1964-66; asso. prof. U. Notre Dame, Ind., 1966-68; prof. U. Notre Dame, 1968-73; population program adv. Ford Found., Mexico City, Mex., 1969; prof. anthropology Mich. State U., East Lansing, 1973-83; behavioral sci. coordinator Mich. State U. (Coll. Human Medicine), 1975-77; prof. anthropology U. Calif.-Irvine, 1983—, rsch. prof., 1994—; cons. Ford Found.; reviewer social sci. rev. panel NIMH; Disting. vis. prof. Instituto de Investigación Antropológica, Nat. U. Mex., 1980-81; alt. U.S. del. Pan Am. Inst. Geography and History, 1980-83. Author: Across the Tracks: Mexican-Americans in a Texas City, 1966, (with others) Susto, a Folk Illness, 1984; contbr. articles to profl. jours. Served with USNR, 1942-46. NIMH fellow, 1960-63; grantee, 1969-71; NSF grantee, 1994-95. Fellow Am. Anthrop. Assn., Soc. Applied Anthropology, Soc. Med. Anthropology (pres. 1976), Latin Am. Studies Assn. Office: U Calif Dept Family Medicine Irvine CA 92717

RUBELI, PAUL E., gaming company executive; b. 1943; married. BS, U. Notre Dame; MBA, Columbia U., 1967. Assoc. A.T. Kearney Inc., Chgo., 1969-73; v.p., gen. mgr. Bunker-Ramo Corp., 1973-76; group v.p. Baker Industries, Parsippany, N.J., 1976-79; exec. v.p. and pres. Ramada Inns Inc., Phoenix, 1979-89; pres., CEO Aztar Corp., Phoenix, 1989—; chmn. Aztar Corp., 1991—. Served to 1st lt. AUS, 1967-69. Office: Aztar Corp 2390 E Camelback Rd Ste 400 Phoenix AZ 85016-3452*

RUBELLO, DAVID JEROME, artist; b. Detroit, Sept. 3, 1935; s. Ludovico and Girolama (Trupiano) R.; m. Mary Anne Keithan, Oct. 14, 1978. BFA, Am. Acad. Art, Rome, 1961; MFA, U. Mich., 1972; cert., Acad. Fine Art, Copenhagen, 1966. Lect. art U. Mich., Ann Arbor, 1973-74; asst. prof. art Pa. State U., University Park, 1974-80; assoc. prof. art Towson (Md.) State U., 1980-81; assoc. prof. U. Mich., Ann Arbor, 1988-90. One man shows include Cade Gallery, Royal Oak, Mich., 1987; exhibited in group shows at Detroit Inst. Art, 1987, GMB Gallery Internat., Bloomfield Hills, Mich., 1991, Kresge Art Inst., 1989, Kalamazoo Art Inst., 1990, 91, Photo Nat. 2, Ella Sharp Mus., Jackson, Mich., BBAA, Birmingham, Mich., Arts Coun., Traverse City, Mich., 1995-96; exhibited Null Dimension, Fulda, Germany, 1988, Systematica Constructive Art, Madrid, 1989, B4 Pub. Invitational, London, 1990, Archive 90s, Amsterdam and London, Konkrete Miniatures Invitational, Amsterdam, 1991.

RUBEN, ALAN MILES, law educator; b. Phila., May 13, 1931; s. Maurice Robert and Ruth (Blatt) R.; m. Betty Jane Willis, May 23, 1965. A.B., U. Pa., 1953, M.A., 1956, J.D., 1956. Bar: Pa. 1957, Ohio 1972. Law clk. Supreme Ct. Pa., 1956-58; pvt. practice Phila., 1958-65; assoc. counsel Aetna Life & Casualty Co., Hartford, Conn., 1965-69; corp. counsel Lubrizol Corp., Cleve., 1969-70; prof. Cleve.-Marshall Coll. Law, Cleve. State U., 1970—; adv. prof. law Fudan U., Shanghai, People's Republic of China, 1993—; dep. to city solicitor Phila., 1958-61; dep. atty. gen. State of Pa., 1961-65; spl. counsel to U.S. Senate Subcom. on Nat. Stockpile, 1962; commentator Higher Edn. Issues Sta. WCLV-FM, Cleve., 1975-87; mem. nat. panel labor arbitrators Nat. Acad. Arbitrators, Fed. Mediation and Conciliation Svc. and Am. Arbitration Assn., Ohio State Employment Rels. Bd.; lectr. law U. Conn. Law Sch., 1968; vis. prof. law FuDan U., Shanghai, Peoples Republic of China, 1988-89; cons. Shanghai Law Office for Fgn. Economy and Trade, Peoples Republic of China, 1991—. Author: The Constitutionality of Basic Protection for the Automobile Accident Victim, 1968, Unauthorized Insurance: The Regulation of the Unregulated, 1968, Arbitration in Public Employee Labor Disputes: Myth, Shibboleth and Reality, 1971, Illicit Sex of Campus: Federal Remedies for Employment Discrimination, 1971, Model Public Employees Labor Relations Act, 1972, Sentencing the Corporate Criminal, 1972, Modern Corporation Law, supp. edit., 1978, An American Lawyer's Observations on the Inauguration of the Shanghai Stock Exchange, 1989, Ohio Limited Partnership Law, 1992—, Practice Guides, Ohio Limited Liability Company, Law, 1995—; contbr.: With an Eye to Tomorrow: The Future Outlook of the Life Insurance Industry, 1968, The Urban Transportation Crisis: The Philadelphia Plan, 1961, Philadelphia's Union Shop Contract, 1961, The Administrative Agency Law: Reform of Adjudicative Procedure and the Revised Model Act, 1963, The Computer in Court: Computer Simulation and the robinson Patman Act, 1964, State Ltd. Partnership Laws, 1993. Bd. dirs. U.S. Olympic Com., 1968-73; chmn. U.S. Olympic Fencing Sport Com., 1969-73; pres. U.S. Fencing Assn., 1968-73; capt. U.S. Pan-Am. Fencing Team, 1971, U.S. Olympic Fencing Team, 1972; bd. dirs. Legal Aid Soc. Cleve., 1973-77. Winner Internat. Inst. Edn. Internat. Debate Championship, 1953; recipient Harrison Tweed Bowl and Am. Law Inst. prizes Nat. Moot Ct. Competition, 1955; named Guggenheim scholar, 1949-53, Fulbright scholar FuDan U., Shanghai, 1993-94. Mem. ABA, Phila. Bar Assn., Ohio Bar Assn. (corp. law and profl. responsibility com.), Cleve. Bar Assn. (Securities Law Inst.), Assn. Am. Law Schs. (chmn. sect. law and edn. 1976-78), Internat. Indsl. Rels. Rsch. Assn., Internat. Soc. Labor Law, AAUP (pres. Ohio conf. 1974-75), Phi Beta Kappa, Pi Gamma Mu. Home: 9925 Lake Shore Blvd Bratenahl OH 44108-1052 Office: Cleve State U 18th St And Euclid Ave Cleveland OH 44115

RUBEN, ARTHUR DARRELL, financial planner; b. Bklyn., Feb. 23, 1952; s. Irving Rabinowitz and Cecile (Sternberg) Ruben; m. Wendy Mittelman, June 28, 1976 (div. Sept. 1979); m. Barbara Kleine, May 30, 1981; 1 child, Joshua. BS, Am. U., 1974, M Pub. Fin. Mgmt., 1978; MSW, Cath. U. Am., 1976. CFP. Social worker Arlington (Va.) County Govt., 1976-77; program dir. Barrett-Crittenton Residential Treatment Ctr., Washington, 1977-79, clin. dir., 1979-81; ins. agt. Prin. Mut. Life, Rockville, Md., 1981-84; fin. planner Mut. of N.Y./Mid-Hudson Assocs., Kingston, N.Y., 1985—; new agt. cons. Mut. of N.Y., 1994. Contbr. articles to profl. publs. Mem. Life Underwriters PAC, Washington, 1982—. Mem. Inst. CFPs (internat. bd. 1989—), Nat. Assn. Life Underwriters, Million Dollar Round Table (Top of the Table 1989, life and qualifying mem. 1993—). Avocations: weightlifting, swimming, running, piano, guitar. Office: Mid-Hudson Assocs 500 Washington Ave Kingston NY 12401-2947

RUBEN, BRENT DAVID, communication educator; b. Cedar Rapids, Iowa, Oct. 17, 1944; s. Nate and Ruth (Subotnik) R. m. Jann M., Oct. 3, 1967; children, Robbi Lynn, Marc David. BA in Psychology and Advt., U. Iowa, 1966, MA in Mass Communication Rsch., 1968, PhD in Communication, 1970. Instr. to asst. prof. mass communication U. Iowa, 1969-71; asst. to assoc. prof. communication Rutgers U., New Brunswick, N.J., 1971-80, chmn. dept., 1980-84, prof., 1980-87, mem. exec. com. faculty profl. studies, 1981-82, mem. exec. com. PhD program in info. and libr. studies, 1981-83; fellow Rutgers Coll., New Brunswick, N.J., 1982—; dir. PhD program Sch. Communication, Inf. and Libr. Studies Rutgers U., New Brunswick, N.J., 1984-93; exec. dir. univ. program for organizational quality and comm. improvement, 1993—; mem. Inst. for Health, Health Policy and Aging Rsch. Rutgers U., New Brunswick, N.J., 1986—, 1986—, Disting. prof. communication, 1987—; co-project dir. adv. bd. Nat. Survey Pub. Perceptions of Digestive Health and Disease and Louis Harris & Assocs., 1982-84; chmn. steering com. nat. digestive disease edn. program, NIH, 1983-84; sr. cons. grants Fund for Improvement Post-Secondary Edn., 1984-86; mem. nat. digestive diseases adv. bd. HHS, 1982-84; spl. cons. Can. Royal Commn. on Conditions Fgn. Svc., 1980-81; mem. Malcolm Baldrige Nat. Quality Awards Examination Com., 1994—; chmn. conf. bd. Higher Edn. Nat. Quality Coun., 1995-96; invited lectr. Yale U., W.Va. U. Med. Sch., Pitts. U., Duquesne U., Drake U., James Madison U., Columbia-Free State Health System, NIH, others; cons. Johnson & Johnson, Humana Hosp.-Sunrise, N.J. Bell, Bell Can., AT&T, Can. Agy. Internat. Devel., U.S. AID, Merck Sharpe & Dohme, Morristown Meml. Hosp., Cathedral Health Care Systems, York Rehab. Hosp. Chilton Meml. Hosp. Author: (with Richard W.Budd) Human Communication Handbook: Simulations and Games, Vol. 1, 1975, (with John Y. Kim) General Systems and Human Communication Theory, 1975, Human Communication Handbook: Simulations and Games, Vol. 2, 1978, (with Budd) Beyond Media: New Approaches to Mass Communication, 1979, Vol. 2, 2d rev. edit., 1988, Communication and Human Behavior, 1984, 2d rev. edit., 1988, 3rd rev. edit., 1992, Non-Verbal Codes: Appearance, Action, Space and Time, 1985 (Japanese adaptation 1984, 95), The Bottom Line: A Patient Relations Training Program, 1985, 2d rev. edit, 1988, (with Hunt) Mass Communication: Producers and Consumers, 1993, Communicating with Patients, 1992, (with Nurit Guttman) Caregiver-Patient Communication: Readings, 1993; author, editor: (with Budd) Approaches to Human Communication, 1972; (with John Kim) General Systems Theory and Human Communication, 1975; Communication Yearbook 1, 1977 (also founding editor), Communication Yearbook 2, 1978, Interdisciplinary Approaches to Human Communication, 1979, Information and Behavior, Vol. 1, 1985, Vol. 2, 1988, (with Leah Lievrouw) Vol. 3, 1990, Vol. 4 (with Jorge Schement), 1993, Quality in Higher Education, 1995; cons. editor: Hayden Communication and Human Behavior Series, 1978-78; Ablex, Communication: The Human Context Series, 1986—; mem. editl. bd. Internat. and Intercultural Communication Annual, 1980-86, Jour. Communication Therapy, 1982-86, Society, 1983-86, Communication Quar., 1979—; rev. editor Behavioral Sci., 1974-77; cons. editor Internat. Jour. Intercultural Rels., 1983—; reviewer Jour. Am. Soc. Info. Sci.; contbr. numerous articles, book revs., essays, conf. papers to profl. jours., chpts. to books. Mem. Franklin County, (N.J.) Twp. Human Rels. Commn., 1973-75; spl. cons. Ctr. for Disease Control, N.J. Collegiate Consortium for Health in Edn., 1981-82, chair Univ. Community Affairs and Outreach Com., 1992-93, Univ. Sen. Com. Rutgers and the Pub., 1992-93. Recipient Disting. Svc. award Coalition Digestive Disease Orgns., 1984; grantee , project co-dir. Nat. Assn. Broadcasters, 1970, U.S. Office Edn., 1970, Rutgers U., 1973-74, 74-75. Mem. Internat. Communication Assn.ubs. com., conf. site selection com.), Ea. Communication Assn. (pubs. com., adv. bd.), Speech Communication Assn., Am. Soc. Info. Sci., Am. Hosp. Assn., Am. Soc. Patient Representation and Consumer Affairs, Am. Soc. Health Edn. and Tng., Assn. Libr. and Info. Sci Educators (rsch. com. 1988-89), Kappa Tau Alpha, Alpha Kappa Psi. Office: Univ Office of Quality & Comm Improvement 4 Huntington St New Brunswick NJ 08901-1071

RUBEN, GARY A., marketing and communications consultant; b. Cochem, Germany, Jan. 1, 1924; came to U.S., 1939, naturalized, 1943; s. Jules and Erna (Hirsch) R.; m. Irene Jehle, Aug. 12, 1962; 1 child, Monique L. Student, Acad. Comml. Art, Indpls., 1940-41. With advt. dept. Indpls. News, 1940-41; advt. mgr. Greater Indpls. Amusement Corp., 1941-42; pres. Ruben Advt. Agy., Indpls., 1948-68; chmn. bd. Ruben, Montgomery & Assos., 1968-76; pres. Prestige Program Sales Inc., 1973-76, Gary A. Ruben Inc. (advt. and mktg. cons.), Indpls., 1976—; past lectr. advt. Northwood Inst.; past pres. Nat. Fedn. Advt. Agys., 1971; bd. dirs. Connor Prairie Settlement, Noblesville, Ind., Acordia Sr. Benefits Corp. Hon. trustee Indpls. Children's Mus. With Combat Engrs. AUS, 1943-46. Home: 11812 Forest Dr Carmel IN 46033-4345 Office: Ste 206 931 E 86th St Indianapolis IN 46240 *It was years ago, in the late 30's in Vienna, that the cry "Lebensraum" echoed across yet another land. And, a family, judged comfortable by most standards, scattered to the four winds, leaving behind all things material, but salvaging the will to survive and to commence once again in a new land. To a boy in his teens and still dressed in European-style short pants upon arrival in this country, the emotion, the sights, the sounds, and the smells were overwhelming and exciting to say the least. . .so began another chapter in my life. In the ensuing years, I learned the true meaning of individual freedom. And while the echoes of Vienna have become dim, that dim sound will continue to remind me that all worthwhile things in life are earned—not given, and even in adversity, there is opportunity.*

RUBEN, IDA GASS, state senator; b. Washington, Jan. 7, 1929; d. Sol and Sonia E. (Darman) Gass; m. L. Leonard Ruben, Aug. 29, 1948; children: Garry, Michael, Scott, Stephen. Del. Md. Ho. of Dels., Annapolis, 1974-86; mem. Md. Senate, Annapolis, 1986—, majority whip, 1995—; chair Montgomery County House Delegation, 1981-86, Montgomery County Senate Delegation, 1987—; mem. house econ. matters com., 1974-85, house ways and means com., 1985-86, legis. policy com., 1991—, senate budget and taxation com., joint budget and audit com., 1991—, exec. nominations com., 1991—, joint protocol com., 1991—, chair subcom. on pub. safety, transp., econ. devel. and natural resources, 1995—, mem. joint com. on spending affordability, 1995—, mem. capital budget subcom., 1995—; mem. Gov.'s Motor Carrier Task Force, 1989—; conv. chair Nat. Order Women Legislators, 1980. Chair Women Legislators Caucus Md., 1982-84; trustee Adventist Health Care Mid-Atlantic, Takoma Park, Md.; bd. dirs. Ctrs. for Handicapped, Silver Spring, Md.; former internat. v.p. B'nai Brith Women. Recipient Cert. of Appreciation Ctrs. for Handicapped, 1987, Meritorious Svc. award Safety and Survival, 1989, Cover Those Trucks award AAA Potomac, 1989, Leadership Laurel award Safety First Club Md., 1989, Woman of Valor award B'nai B'rith Women, 1991, Pub. Affairs award Planned Parenthood Md., 1992, ESOL support recognition Montgomery County Pub. Schs., 1992, Appreciation award Fraternal Order Police, 1992, John Dewey award Montgomery County Fedn. Tchrs., 1992, Appreciation award ARC of Md., 1992, Safety Leader award Advocates for Hwy. and Auto Safety, 1993, Disting. Svc. award Gov.'s Commn. Employment of People with Disabilities, 1993, award Faculty Guild U. Md. for support of faculty and univ., 1993, Sincere Appreciation award for commitment to Md.'s youth Md. Underage Drinking Prevention Coalition, 1994, Faithful Svc. to citizens of Montgomery County award Montgomery County Assn. of Realtors, 1994; named Most Effective Pub. Ofcl. by residents of Silver Spring, 1990, One of 100 Most Powerful Women in Washington Metro Area by Washingtonian Mag., 1994, Legislator of Yr. award Nat. Commn. Against Drunk Driving, 1995, Legislator of Yr. award Montgomery County Med. Soc., 1995, Carmen S. Turner Achievement in Cmty. Svc. award Montgomery County Dept. Transp., 1995; inducted into Washington, Md., Del., Pa. Svc. Sta. Assn. Hall of Fame, 1994. Mem. Coun. State Govts. (com. on suggested legislation), Hadassah. Democrat. Jewish. Home: 11 Schindler Ct Silver Spring MD 20903-1329 Office: Md State Senate 204 James Senate Off Bldg 110 College Ave Annapolis MD 21401-8012

RUBEN, LEONARD, retired art educator; b. St. Paul, June 3, 1921; s. Theodore and Elizabeth (Hauchman) R.; m. Sue Levey; children: James M., Elizabeth A., Nancy L., Thomas C. Diploma with hon., Pratt Inst., 1948, BFA, 1952; MA, Columbia Tchrs. Coll., 1961; PhD, NYU, 1970. Designer L.W. Frolich, N.Y.C., 1949-52; art dir. Young & Rubicam, N.Y.C., 1952-60; art group head North Advt., N.Y.C., 1960-62; instr. Columbia U. Tchrs. Coll., N.Y.C., 1962-63; assoc. creative dir. Compton Advt., N.Y.C., 1962-64; v.p. assoc. creative dir. J.M. Mathes, N.Y.C., 1964-68; exec. creative dir. Lake Spiro Shurman, Memphis, 1968-69; asst. prof. art Northeast La. U., Monroe, 1969-71; asst. prof. art U. Tex., Austin, 1971-74, assoc. prof., 1974-79, prof. art, 1979-82, F.J. Heyne Centennial Prof. in Communication, 1983-87; design cons. B.B. Martin Pub. Co., Austin, 1978; creative dir. Heart Assn., Austin, 1973. Precinct chmn. Dems., Lake Travis, Tex., 1979; chmn. advt. com. Austin Community Coll., 1980-84. 1st lt. U.S. Army, 1940-46, ETO, PTO. Decorated Bronze Arrowhead, Presdl. Unit emblem; recipient numerous awards including Advt. Appreciation award City of Houston, 1980, Thomas McCartin Tchg. Excellence award, 1983, Founders Day award NYU, 1971; Leo Burnet Creative Excellence Endowment, 1986, Frank Rizzo Meml. Creative grant Tracy-Locke, 1986. Mem. 27th Infantry Div. Assn., 105th (226th) Field Arty Assn., Dallas Soc. Visual Communication. Jewish. Home: 1102A Locust Ave Charlottesville VA 22901-4034

RUBEN, ROBERT JOEL, physician, educator; b. N.Y.C., Aug. 2, 1933; s. Julian Carl and Sadie (Weiss) R.; children—Ann, Emily, Karin, Arthur. A.B., Princeton U., 1955; M.D., Johns Hopkins U., 1959. Intern Johns Hopkins Hosp., Balt., 1959-60; resident Johns Hopkins Hosp., 1960-64, dir. neurophysiology lab., div. otolaryngology, 1958-64; practice specializing in pediatric otorhinolaryngology N.Y.C., 1964—; asst. prof. otorhinolaryngology N.Y. U. Sch. Medicine, 1966-68; mem. staff hosps. Montefiore Med. Ctr., Bronx Med. Hosp. Ctr., N. Cen. Bronx Hosp., Montefiore Med.; prof., chmn. Montefiore Med. Ctr., Bronx Mcpl. Hosp. Ctr., N. Cen. Bronx, Bronx, N.Y., 1979—; prof. pediatrics Albert Einstein Coll. Medicine, Bronx, 1983—; assoc. prof. otorhinolaryngology Albert Einstein Coll. Medicine, N.Y.C., 1968-70, prof., chmn. dept. otolaryngology, 1970—; prof. pediatrics Albert Einstein Coll. Medicine and Montefiore Med. Ctr., 1983—; chmn. Nat. Com. for Rsch. and Neurol. and Communicative Disorders, pres., 1982-84; bd. dirs. Am. Bd. Otolaryngology-Head and Neck Surgery, 1989—; chmn. ENT devices com. FDA, 1993—. Editor-in-chief: Internat. Jour. Pediatric Otorhinolaryngology, 1979—. Bd. dirs. N.Y. League Hard of Hearing, 1969-75, 76-85. Served to surgeon USPHS, 1964-66. Recipient Rsch. award Am. Acad. Ophthalmology and Otolaryngology, 1962, Edmund Prince Fowler award Am. Rhinological-Laryngological-Otological Assn., 1973, Gold medal Best Didactic Film, IX World Congress Otorhinolaryngology, 1977, Pres.'s award Am. Acad. Otolaryngology-Head and Neck Surgery, 1992, Johns Hopkins U. Soc. of Scholars, 1993. Fellow ACS, N.Y. Acad. Medicine; mem. AMA, Am. Assn. Anatomists, Audiology Study Group N.Y. (pres. 1964-66), Acoustical Soc. Am., Am. Acad. Ophthalmology and Otolaryngology, Soc. Univ. Otolaryngologists, Am. Otol. Soc. (sec.-treas. rsch. fund 1979—), Soc. for Ear, Nose and Throat Advances in Children (pres. 1973), Assn. for Rsch. in Otolaryngology (pres. 1985-86), Am. Acad. Pediat. (chmn. otol. bronchoesphology 1983-85), Am. Soc. Pediat. Otolaryngology (historian 1986—), Am. Soc. Pediat. Otolaryngologists (historian 1986-93, pres.-elect 1993-94, pres. 1994-95), Nat. Inst. Deafness and Other Comm. Disorders (adv. coun. 1989-93), Am. Laryngol. Soc. Home: 1025 Fifth Ave Apt 12C S New York NY 10028-0134 Office: Montefiore Med Ctr 111 E 210th St Bronx NY 10467-2401

RUBEN, ROBERT JOSEPH, lawyer; b. N.Y.C., Apr. 9, 1923; s. Ira Herbert and Kathleen Marie (Murphy) R.; m. Audrey H. Zweig, Nov. 20, 1949; children: Pamela Joan, James Bradford. B.S., Columbia U., 1943; M.A., Harvard U., 1948; LL.B., Fordham U., 1953. Bar: N.Y. 1954. Exec. trainee Chase Nat. Bank, N.Y.C., 1948-49; economist, 1949-53; assoc. Milbank, Tweed, Hope & Hadley, N.Y.C., 1953-55; assoc., then ptnr. Shea & Gould, N.Y.C., 1955-90; sec. Gen. Battery Corp., Reading, Pa., 1963-73, Fiat Metal Mfg. Co., Inc., Plainview, N.Y., 1961-64, Filtors, Inc., East Northport, N.Y., 1961-64, Trans-Industries, Inc., 1969—; asst. sec. Elgin Nat. Industries, 1975-88; asst. judge City Ct., Rye, N.Y., 1977-90; arbitrator Nat. Assn. Securities Dealers, 1990—, Pacific Stock Exch., 1992—, Am. Arbitration Assn., 1990—, N.Y. Stock Exch., 1994—. Trustee Rye Hist. Soc.; bd. dirs. Carver Center, Port Chester, N.Y., 1972-90. Served with AUS, 1943-46. Decorated Combat Inf. medal. Mem. ABA, N.Y. State Bar Assn., Assn. Bar of City of N.Y., Am. Arbitration Assn., Harvard Club (N.Y.C.), Harvard-Radcliffe Club So. Calif., Columbia U. Club So. Calif., Beta Gamma Sigma, Zeta Beta Tau. Home: 21285 Amora Mission Viejo CA 92692-4930

RUBEN, WILLIAM SAMUEL, marketing consultant; b. N.Y.C., June 23, 1927; s. Nathaniel Benjamin and Bertha Teresa (Stein) R.; children: Michaele, Marc. B.B.A., Syracuse U., 1950. Exec. trainee, buyer Dey Bros., Syracuse, N.Y., 1950-54; staff asst.-sr. v.p. Allied Stores Corp., N.Y.C., 1954-58; with Jordan Marsch-Fla., Miami, 1958—; gen. mdse. mgr. Jordan Marsch-Fla., 1962-64, mng. dir., 1964-66, pres., 1966-79, chmn. bd., 1979-83; pres. Bonwit Teller, N.Y.C., 1983-89, William Ruben, Inc., N.Y.C., 1989—; bd. dirs. Carnival Cruise Lines Inc. Pres. United Way of Dade County, 1979; mem. stategic planning com. United Way Am.; chmn. Dade County Co-ordinating Council, 1979—; mem. Gov.'s Revitalization Bd., 1980—; bd. dirs. Fla. Philharm., 1980-81; bd. overseers Parsons Sch. of Design, 1986—; chmn. Nat. Found. for Advancement in the Arts, 1983-88; bd. dirs. Theatre for a New Audience, Concordia Chamber Symphony. Served with USMCR, 1945-46. Recipient Silver medallion NCCJ, 1978, Humanitarian award Nat. B'nai B'rith, 1980, Outstanding Citizen award Dade County B'nai B'rith, 1979, Parsons Fashion award, 1983. Mem. Fla. Retail Fedn., Greater Miami C. of C. (v.p. 1979—). Jewish. Clubs: Standard, Sky, Jockey, New World Center. Office: William Ruben Inc 40 E 88th St New York NY 10128-1176

RUBENFELD, STANLEY IRWIN, lawyer; b. N.Y.C., Dec. 7, 1930; s. George and Mildred (Rose) R.; m. Caryl P. Ellner, June 8, 1952; children: Leslie Ann, Lise Susan, Kenneth Michael. B.A., Columbia U., 1952, J.D., 1956. Bar: N.Y. 1956. Practice law N.Y.C., 1956-65, 68—, 1965-68; assoc. Shearman & Sterling, 1956-65; ptnr. Shearman & Sterling, Paris, 1965-68; ptnr. Shearman & Sterling, N.Y.C., 1968-93, of counsel, 1994—crw; mediator U.S. Fed. Ct. Editor-in-chief Columbia Law Rev., 1955-56; contbr. articles to profl. jours. Bd. dirs., past pres. Port Washington (N.Y.) Comty. Chest; former bd. dirs. Residents for a More Beautiful Port Washington. Lt. (j.g.) USNR, 1952-54. Stone scholar, 1951-52, 54-55, 55-56; Rockefeller Found. grantee, 1955. Mem. ABA, N.Y. State Bar Assn. (past chmn. fgn. activities com., reorgn. corp.), Assn. Bar City N.Y. (tax com., past chmn. com. on recruitment lawyers), Nat. Assn. Law Placement (past bd. dirs., exec. com.), Columbia U. Law Sch. Alumni Assn. (bd. visitors, adviser past bd. dirs.), Columbia Coll. Alumni Assn., Tax Club (past chmn.), Phi Delta Phi, Tau Epsilon Phi (past pres.). Home: 41 Longview Rd Port Washington NY 11050-3039 Office: Citicorp Ctr 153 E 53rd St New York NY 10022-4602

RUBENS, SIDNEY MICHEL, physicist, technical advisor; b. Spokane, Wash., Mar. 21, 1910; s. Max Zvoln and Jennie Golda (Rubinovich) R.; m. Julienne Rose Fridner, May 11, 1944; 1 dau., Deborah Janet. BS, U. Wash.,

1934, PhD, 1939. Instr. U. So. Calif., 1939-40; research assoc. UCLA, 1940-41; physicist Naval Ordnance Lab., Washington, 1941-46; physicist Engring. Research Assos., St. Paul, 1946-52; mgr. physics Univac div. Sperry Rand, St. Paul, 1958-61, dir. research, 1961-66, staff scientist, 1969-71, dir. spl. projects, 1971-75; cons., 1975-81; technical advisor Vertimag Systems Corp., 1981—, Advanced Research Corp., 1986—; lectr. U. Pa., 1960-61; mem. adv. subcom. on instrumentation and data processing NASA, 1967-69, panel on computer tech. Nat. Acad. Sci., 1969. Hon. fellow U. Minn., 1977—. Fellow IEEE (magnetic soc. info. storage award 1987); mem. AAAS, N.Y. Acad. Sci., Am. Phys. Soc., Am. Geophys. Union, Acad. Applied Sci., Minn. Acad. Sci., Am. Optical Soc., Phi Beta Kappa, Sigma Xi, Pi Mu Epsilon. Patentee in magnetic material and devices. Author: Amplifier and Memory Devices, 1965. Contbr. articles to profl. jours. Home: 1077 Sibley Hwy Apt 506 Saint Paul MN 55118-3616 Office: Advanced Rsch Corp 815 14th Ave SE Minneapolis MN 55414-1515

RUBENSTEIN, ALBERT HAROLD, industrial engineering and management sciences educator; b. Phila., Nov. 11, 1923; s. Leo and Jean (Kaplan) R.; m. Hildette Grossman, Sept. 11, 1949; children—Michael Stephen, Lisa Joan. B.S. magna cum lauda in Indsl. Engring. (Sr. prize econs.), Lehigh U., 1949; M.S. in Indsl. Engring, Columbia, 1950, Ph.D. in Indsl. Engring. and Mgmt, 1954; DEng (hon.), Lehigh U., 1993. Asst. to pres. Perry Equipment Corp., 1940-43; research assoc. Columbia U., 1950-53; asst. prof. indsl. mgmt. MIT, 1954-59; prof. indsl. engring. and mgmt. scis. Northwestern U., 1959—, Walter P. Murphy prof., 1986—, dir. Ctr. for Info. Tech., 1986—; pres. Internat. Applied Sci. and Tech. Assos., 1977—; vis. prof. U. Calif., Berkeley; pres. Sr. Strategy Group, 1995—; cons. to govt. and industry. Dir. Narragansett Capital Corp. Author books and articles in field. Served with inf. AUS, World War II. Decorated Purple Heart, Combat Inf. badge.; Recipient Lincoln Arc Welding Found. prize paper, 1948, Pioneer in Innovation Mgmt. award Ctr. Innovation Mgmt., 1992; Omicron Delta Kappa annual fellow, 1949-50; Fulbright research fellow, 1955. Fellow IEEE (editor trans. 1959—, Engring. Mgr. of Yr. award 1992), Soc. Applied Anthropology; sr. mem. Inst. Mgmt. Scis. (dir. studies for coll. on research and devel. 1960—, v.p. research and edn. 1966-68). Home: 2348 Ridge Ave Evanston IL 60201-2600

RUBENSTEIN, ARTHUR HAROLD, physician, educator; b. Johannesburg, South Africa, Dec. 28, 1937; came to U.S., 1967; s. Montague and Isabel (Nathanson) R.; m. Denise Hack, Aug. 19, 1962; children: Jeffrey Lawrence, Errol Charles. MB, BChir, U. Witwatersrand, 1960. Diplomate Am. Bd. Internal Medicine. Intern, then resident Johannesburg Gen. Hosp., 1961, 63-65, 66-67; fellow in endocrinology Postgrad. Med. Sch., London, 1965-66; fellow in medicine U. Chgo., 1967-68, asst. prof., 1968-70, assoc. prof., 1970-74, prof., 1974—, Lowell T. Coggeshall prof. med. sci., 1981—, assoc. chmn. dept. medicine, 1975-81, chmn., 1981—, dir. Diabetes Rsch. and Tng. Ctr., 1986-91; attending physician Mitchell Hosp., U. Chgo., 1968—; mem. study sect. NIH, 1973-77, Hadassah Med. Adv. Bd., 1986—, adv. council Nat. Inst. Arthritis, Metabolism and Digestive Diseases, 1978-80; chmn. Nat. Diabetes Adv. Bd., 1982, mem., 1981-83. Mem. editorial bd. Diabetes, 1973-77, Endocrinology, 1973-77, Jour. Clin. Investigation, 1976-81, Am. Jour. Medicine, 1978-81, Diabetologia, 1982-86, Diabetes Medicine, 1987-91, Annals of Internal Medicine, 1991—, Medicine, 1992—; contbr. articles to profl. jours. Mem. Gov.'s Sci. Adv. Coun. State of Ill., 1989-94. Recipient David Rumbough Meml. award Juvenile Diabetes Found., 1978. Master ACP (John Phillips Meml. award 1995); fellow South African Coll. Physicians, Royal Coll. Physicians (London); mem. Am. Soc. for Clin. Investigation, Am. Diabetes Assn. (Eli Lilly award 1973, Banting medal 1983, Solomon Berson Meml. lectr. 1985), Brit. Diabetes Assn. (Banting lectr. 1987), Endocrine Soc., Am. Fedn. Clin. Rsch., Ctrl. Soc. Clin. Rsch. (v.p. 1988, pres. 1989), Assn. Am. Physicians (treas. 1984-89, councillor 1989-94, v.p. 1994-95, pres. 1995-96), Am. Bd. Internal Medicine (bd. govs. 1985-93, exec. com. 1990-93, chmn. 1992-93), Residency Rev. Com., Am. Acad. Arts and Scis., Inst. Medicine (coun. 1991—), Assn. Profs. Medicine (councillor 1991-94, v.p. 1994-95, pres. 1995-96). Home: 5517 S Kimbark Ave Chicago IL 60637-1618 Office: U Chgo Dept of Medicine 5841 S Maryland Ave Chicago IL 60637-1463

RUBENSTEIN, BERNARD, orchestra conductor; b. Springfield, Mo., Oct. 30, 1937; s. Milton and Evelyn Marion (Friedman) R.; m. Ann Warren Little, Aug. 28, 1961; children: Tanya, Stefan Alexei. B.Mus. with distinction, Eastman Sch. Music, U. Rochester, 1958; M.Mus., Yale U., 1961. Assoc. prof. conducting, dir. orch. orgns. Northwestern U., Evanston, Ill., 1968-80. Asst. condr. R.I. Philharm. Orch., 1961-62; condr. music dir. Santa Fe Symphony Orch., 1962-64; condr. Greenwood Chamber Orch., Cummington, Mass., 1968-79; asst. condr. Stuttgart Opera, 1966-68; condr., music dir. Music for Youth, Milw., 1970-80; assoc. condr. Cin. Symphony Orch., 1980-86; music dir. Tulsa Philharm., 1984-96, condr., 1996&; guest condr. numerous orchs. including Milw. Symphony Orch., St. Paul Chamber Orch., Guadalajara Symphony Orch., Berlin Radio Orch., Frankfurt Radio Orch., Grant Park Orch., Chgo., die reihe, Vienna, Austrian Radio Orch., Eastman Philharm., Halle Symphony Orch., E. Ger., Warsaw Philharm., St. Louis Little Symphony, W. German Radio Orch., Palazzo Pitti Orch. Florence, Italy, Frankfurt Opera, Tonkuenstler Orch., Vienna, S.W. German Radio Orch., Baden-Baden, Jerusalem Symphony, Anchorage, Hamilton, Ont., Hartford Conn., L.A. Chamber Orch., Austin (Tex.) Symphony, Am. Composers Orch. N.Y.C. Winner internat. conducting competition Serate Musicale Fiorentine, 1965; Fulbright scholar, 1964-66; recipient Charles Ditson award Yale U., 1961, Martha Baird Rockefeller award, 1966-68. Mem. Am. Symphony Orch. League. Office: 1070 Gov Dempsey Dr Santa Fe NM 87501

RUBENSTEIN, BONNIE SUE, fraternal organization executive; b. Shreveport, La., Feb. 7, 1961; d. David Ochs and Marilyn Sue (Goldstein)R. BBA, Emory U., Atlanta, 1983. Office adminstr. Sanger-Harris, Dallas, 1983-85; asst. buyer Sanger-Harris, 1985-87, Foley's, Houston, 1987-88; exec. dir. Alpha Epsilon Phi Sorority, Columbus, Ohio, 1988—; province dir., pledge programming chmn. Alpha Epsilon Phi Sorority, 1985-87, nat. v.p. collegiate chpts., 1987-88; dir. devel. Alpha Epsilon Phi Found., 1992—; mem. Fraternity Ins. Purchasing Group, 1991—, bd. dirs., 1994—. Contbr. articles to profl. jours. Tchr. religious sch. Temple Israel, Columbus, 1989—, pres. young adults congregation, 1991-93, bd. dirs., 1990-93, bd. dirs. sisterhood, 1991—, also mem. dues revision com. and recruitment com., search com., ritual com. Mem. Assn. Frat. Advisors, Ctrl. Office Execs. Assn. (sec. 1993-94), Frat. Execs. Assn. (bus. mgr. 1993-94), Order of Omega, Women's Am. ORT (activities chmn. 1986-87). Republican. Jewish. Avocations: needlework, reading, cooking, travel. Home: 5616B Hibernia Dr Columbus OH 43232-8502

RUBENSTEIN, EDWARD, physician, educator; b. Cin., Dec. 5, 1924; s. Louis and Nettie R.; m. Nancy Ellen Millman, June 20, 1954; children: John, William, James. MD, U. Cin., 1947. House staff Cin. Gen. Hosp., 1947-50; fellow May Inst., Cin., 1950; sr. asst. resident Ward Med. Service, Barnes Hosp., St. Louis, 1953-54; chief of medicine San Mateo County Hosp., Calif., 1960-70; assoc. dean postgrad. med. edn., prof. medicine Stanford (Calif.) U., 1971—, emeritus, active; mem. faculty Stanford Photon Research Lab.; affiliated faculty mem. Stanford Synchortron Radiation Lab., 1971—; mem. maj. materials facilities com. Nat. Research Council, 1984-85, Nat. Steering Com. 6 GeV Electron Storage Ring., 1986—. Author: (textbook) Intensive Medical Care; editor-in-chief: (textbook) Sci. Am. Medicine, 1978-94; editor: Synchotron Radiation Handbook, 1988, vol. 4, 1991; editor Synchotron Radiation in the Biosciences, Molecular Medicine; mem. editorial adv. bd. Sci. Am., Inc., 1991-94. Served with USAF, 1950-52. Recipient Kaiser award for outstanding and innovative contbns. to med. edn., 1989, Albion Walter Hewlett Award, 1993. Fellow AAAS, Royal Soc. Medicine; mem. APS, ACP (master), Inst. Medicine, Calif. Acad. Medicine, Western Assn. Physicians, Soc. Photo-Optical Engrs., Am. Clin. and Climatol. Assn., Alpha Omega Alpha. Research on synchrotron radiation. Office: Stanford Medical Center Dept of Medicine Stanford CA 94305

RUBENSTEIN, HOWARD JOSEPH, public relations executive; b. N.Y.C., Feb. 3, 1932; s. Samuel and Ada (Sall) R.; m. Amy Forman, Dec. 17, 1959; children: Roni, Richard, Steven. A.B., U. Pa., 1953; student law, Harvard, 1953; LL.B. (Dean's scholar), St. Johns Sch. Law, 1959, LLD (hon.), 1990. Bar: N.Y. State bar 1960. Pres. Rubenstein Assocs., Inc. pub. rels. cons., N.Y.C., 1954—; asst. counsel judiciary com. U.S. Ho. of Reps., 1960; cons. U.S. Fgn. Claims Commn., 1961-62; cons. joint legis. com. child care needs N.Y., 1965-66; adviser SBA,, 1965-66. Mem. Gov.'s Com. on Sale of World Trade Ctr., 1981, Mayor's Com. on Holocaust Commemoration, 1981—, N.Y. State Task Force on Energy Conservation, Dept. Housing, 1981-83, Mayor's Coun. Econ. Bus. Advisors, 1991-93; co-chmn. Holocaust Commn., 1993—; v.p. Jewish Cmty. Rels. Coun., 1988-94, adv. 1995—; past dir. Brownsville Boys Club; bd. dirs. Provide Addict Care Today, Police Athletic League, N.Y. chpt. March of Dimes; mem. U.S. Internat. Coun., 1977-81, Commn. on Status of Women, 1982-89, N.Y.C. Commn. Operation Welcom Home, 1991-92; trustee Ctrl. Park Conservancy; mem. Mayor's Bus. Adv. Coun., 1996—; advisor N.Y. Commn. on Status of Women, 1995—; comm. advisor Gov.'s Com. Jerusalem 3000, 1996—. Mem. Assn. Better N.Y. (mem. exec. com. 1972—), Phi Beta Kappa, Beta Sigma Rho. Jewish (dir. congregation). Home: 993 5th Ave New York NY 10028-0105 Office: Rubenstein Assoc Inc 1345 Avenue Of The Americas New York NY 10105

RUBENSTEIN, JEROME MAX, lawyer; b. St. Louis, Feb. 16, 1927; s. Jacob J. and Anne (Frankel) R.; m. Judith Hope Grand, July 31, 1954; children—Edward J., Emily Rubenstein Muslin, Daniel H. A.B., Harvard U., 1950, LL.B., 1955. Bar: Mo. 1956, U.S. Dist. Ct. (ea. dist.) Mo. 1956, U.S. Ct. Appeals (8th cir.) 1956. Mem. English lit. faculty U. So. Philippines, Cebu, 1950-51; law clk U.S. Dist. Ct., St. Louis, 1955-56; assoc. Lewis, Rice, Tucker, Allen & Chubb, St. Louis, 1956-64; assoc. Grand, Peper & Martin, St. Louis, 1964-65, ptnr., 1965-66; jr. ptnr. Bryan, Cave, McPheeters & McRoberts, St. Louis, 1966-67, sr. ptnr., 1968—; dir. Commerce Bank of St. Louis, N.A. Bd. dirs. Independence Ctr., St. Louis, 1985-88, The Arts and Edn. Coun. Greater St. Louis, 1991—. Served with USN, 1945-46. Bd. dirs. Independence Ctr., St. Louis, 1985. Served with USN, 1945-46. Mem. ABA, Mo. Bar Assn., St. Louis Bar Assn., Mo. Athletic Club, Harvard Club of St. Louis (pres. 1982-83, bd. dirs. 1983-90). Jewish. Avocations: jogging; tennis. Home: 7394 Westmoreland Dr Saint Louis MO 63130-4240 Office: Bryan Cave 1 Metropolitan Sq Saint Louis MO 63102-2750

RUBENSTEIN, JOSHUA SETH, lawyer; b. Bklyn., Aug. 5, 1954; s. Seth and Elaine (Freedman) R.; m. Marta Johnson: children: Mary-Jane, Kenan, Rebecca, Marlena. BA magna cum laude, Columbia U., 1976, JD, 1979. Bar: N.Y. 1980, N.J. 1980, U.S. Dist. Ct. (ea. dist.) N.Y. 1980, U.S. Dist. Ct. (so. dist.) N.Y. 1980, U.S. Dist. Ct. N.J. 1980, U.S. Tax Ct. 1986. Assoc. Fried, Frank, Harris, Shriver & Jacobson, N.Y.C., 1979-82; assoc. Rosenman & Colin, N.Y.C., 1982-88, ptnr., 1988—; mgmt. com. Rosenman & Colin, N.Y.C., 1994—, chmn. trusts & Estates dept., 1995—; adv. bd. TE/DEC Systems, Inc., Jour. N.Y. Taxation; lectr. in field. Contbr. articles to legal publs. Pres. Brasch Farms Civic Assn., Middletown, N.J., 1982-84, 340 E. 74th St. Owners Corp., 1990-91; dir., sec. Irvington Inst. Med. Rsch., 1991, treas., 1991-92, sec., 1992-93, co-pres., 1993-94, pres., 1994—; chmn. estates and trust splty. group, chmn. splty. group; task force, mem. exec. com. lawyers divsn. United Jewish Appeal-Fedn., 1989—; mem. legis. com., devel. com., bd. governance com., Madeleine Borg com., chmn., mem. exec. com., 1994—; trustee Jewish Bd. Family and Children's Svcs., 1991—. Recipient James H. Fogelson award Lawyer's divsn. United Jewish Appeal-Fedn., 1993; named to Best Lawyers in N.Y., N.Y. Mag. Fellow Am. Coll. Trusts and Estate Counsel (state laws com.), N.Y. State Bar Found.; mem. ABA (real property and probate sect.), Practising Law Inst. (estate adv. com., lectr. 1984—, Hadassah estate planning seminar faculty and adv. bd. 1993—), N.Y. State Bar Assn. (trust and estate law sect., lect. 1984—, vice chmn. legis. com. 1988, chmn. 1988-91, co-chmn. ad hoc com. to rev. proposals of EPTL adv. com. of N.Y. State 1991—, mem.-at-large exec. com. 1992-95, liaison to legis. policy com. 1995—, Pres.'s Pro Bono Svc. award 1991, Exec. Com. award, 1992, 95), N.J. Bar Assn. adv. com. rels. with legis. and exec. brs., real property and probate sect.), Assn. of Bar of City of N.Y, Phi Beta Kappa. Democrat. Jewish. Office: Rosenman & Colin 575 Madison Ave New York NY 10022-2511

RUBENSTEIN, LEONARD SAMUEL, communications executive, ceramist, painter, sculptor, photographer; b. Rochester, N.Y., Sept. 22, 1918; s. Jacob S. and Zelda H. (Gordon) R.; widowed May 28, 1983; children—Carolinda, Eric, Harley. B.F.A. cum laude, Alfred U., 1939; student Western Reserve, 1938; postgrad. U. Rochester, 1940-41. Creative dir. Henry Hempstead Advt. Agy., Chgo., 1949-55; v.p., exec. art dir. Clinton E. Frank Advt. Agy., Chgo., 1955-63; v.p., nat. creative dir. Foster & Kleiser div. Metromedia, Inc., Los Angeles, 1967-73, v.p. corp. creative cons., Metromedia, Inc., Los Angeles, 1973-88; guest lectr. U. Chgo.; instr. Columbia Coll., Chgo.; past pres. Art Dirs. Club Chgo. (spl. citation); instr. Fashion Inst., Los Angeles; lectr. in field. Mem. Soc. Typog. Arts (past dir.), Am. Ceramic Soc. (design chpt.), Am. Craft Coun., Inst. Outdoor Advt. (past plans bd.), Los Angeles County Mus. Art, Mus. Contemporary Art of L.A. (charter), Palos Verdes (Calif.) Art Ctr., Phi Epsilon Pi. Lodge: B'nai B'rith. Author: (with Charles Hardison) Outdoor Advertising; contbr. articles in field to profl. publs. One-man show: Calif. Mus. Sci. and Industry, 1970; two-person exhibition of porcelains, Palos Verdes Art Ctr., 1987; numerous juried nat. and regional group shows; creator concept for Smithsonian exhibition Images of China: East and West, 1982; writer-producer (ednl. video) Paul Soldner, Thoughts on Creativity, 1989, (video documentary) High-Tech/Low-Tech: The Science and Art of Ceramics, 1994; porcelains in permanent collections of 3 mus., 1992. Home and Office: 30616 Ganado Dr Palos Verdes Peninsula CA 90275 *Personal philosophy: I have a disdain for the trendy, the superficial and the transient.*

RUBENSTEIN, LOUIS, lawyer; b. Cin., Nov. 19, 1953; s. Eli and Phyllis Rubenstein; m. Christine Rubenstein; children: Michael, Randall, Jeffrey. BA, U. Cin., 1975; JD, U. Dayton, 1978. Bar: Ohio, U.S. Dist. Ct. Ohio, U.S. Ct. Appeals (6th cir.). Law clk. Mcpl. Prosecutors Office, Cin., 1975-78; mediation hearing officer Mcpl. Ct. Dispute Settlement Program, Cin., 1975-78; lectr. in field. Group leader, coach Montgomery-Sycamore Baseball Assn., Cin., 1989—. Mem. Nat. Assn. Criminal Def. Lawyers, Ohio Assn. Criminal Def. Lawyers, Greater Cin. Criminal Def. Lawyers Assn. (pres. 1993-94, chmn. bd. dirs. 1994-95), Ohio State Bar Assn., Cin. Bar Assn. (criminal law com.).

RUBENSTEIN, RICHARD LOWELL, theologian, educator; b. N.Y.C., Jan. 8, 1924; s. Jesse George and Sara (Fine) R.; m. Betty Rogers Alschuler, Aug. 21, 1966; children by previous marriage: Aaron, Nathaniel (dec.), Hannah Rachel, Jeremy. Student, Hebrew Union Coll., Cin., 1942-45; AB, U. Cin., 1946; MHL rabbi, Jewish Theol. Sem., N.Y.C., 1952; DHL (honoris causa), Jewish Theol. Sem., 1987; STM, Harvard U., 1955, PhD, 1960. Rabbi in Brockton, Mass., 1952-54, Natick, Mass., 1954-56; chaplain to Jewish students Harvard U., 1956-68; univ. chaplain to Jewish students U. Pitts. and Carnegie Inst. Tech., 1958-70; adj. prof. humanities U. Pitts., 1969-70; prof. religion Fla. State U., Tallahassee, 1970-77; Disting. prof. religion Fla. State U., 1977-81, Robert O. Lawton Disting. prof. religion, 1981-95; pres. U. Bridgeport, Conn., 1995—; cor. Inst. for Humanities/Fla. State U., 1980-95; pres. Washington Inst. for Values in Pub. Policy, 1982-95; Edgar M. Bronfman vis. prof. U. Va., 1985; adv. bd. Washington Times, 1982-91, chmn. editl. adv. bd., 1991—; exec. adv. bd. The World and I mag., 1986—; exec. com. Internat. Jour. of the Unity of Scis., 1987—; adv. bd. Inst. for Study of Am. Wars, 1989-92; mem. presiding coun. Internat. Religious Fedn. for World Peace, 1991—; chmn. bd. trustees U. Bridgeport, 1994—; bd. dirs. Nostalgia TV Network, 1994. Author: After Auschwitz: Radical Theology and Contemporary Judaism, 1966, The Religious Imagination, 1968 (Portico d'Ottavia lit. prize for Italian transl. 1977), Morality and Eros, 1970, My Brother Paul, 1972, Power Struggle: An Autobiographical Confession, 1974, The Cunning of History, 1975, The Age of Triage, 1983, (with John K. Roth) Approaches to Auschwitz, 1986, After Auschwitz: History, Theology and Contemporary Judaism, Johns Hopkins U. Press, 1992; editor: Modernization: The Humanist Response to Its Promise and Problems, 1982, Spirit Matters: The Worldwide Impact of Religion on Contemporary Politics, 1987, The Dissolving Alliance: The United States and the Future of the NATO Alliance, 1987, In Depth: A Journal of Values in Public Policy, 1991-94; regular columnist Sekai Nippo, Tokyo, 1987-94. Trustee Greater Bridgeport Regional Bus. Coun., 1996—. Recipient Portico d' Ottavia lit. prize Rome, 1977; John Phillips fellow Phillips Exeter Acad., 1970; postdoctoral fellow Soc. Religion in Higher Edn.; Nat. Humanities Inst. fellow Yale U., 1976-77; Rockefeller Found. fellow Aspen Inst. for Humanistic Studies, 1979. Mem. Rabbinical Assembly Am., Am. Acad. Religion, Soc. Sci. Study Religion, Profs. World Peace Acad. (exec. com. 1980—, pres. 1981-82), Internat. House of Japan, Conn. Acad. Arts and Scis., Harvard Club at Nat. Press Club, Cosmos Club, Rotary. Office: Univ Bridgeport Office of Pres Bridgeport CT 06601

RUBENSTEIN, STANLEY ELLIS, public relations consultant; b. Balt., July 25, 1930; s. Albert B. and Lee (Goodman) R.; m. Ruth Anne Zinder, Feb. 8, 1953; children: Deborah C., Steven M., Michael L., Kenneth J., Andrew L. BA, U. Md., 1953. Writer, researcher Bozell & Jacobs, Inc., N.Y.C., 1953-54; reporter Jour. of Commerce, N.Y.C., 1954-56; writer, account exec. Ruder & Finn, Inc., N.Y.C., 1956-60; founder, prin. Rubenstein, Wolfson & Co., Inc., N.Y.C., 1960-91; pub. rels. cons. S. E. Rubenstein, N.Y.C., 1991—. Mem. Bd. Edn. Gt. Neck (N.Y.) Pub. Sch., 1968-74, pres. 3 yrs. Served with USN, 1948-49. Mem. Pub. Relations Soc. Am., N.Y. Fin. Writers Assn. (assoc.). Jewish. Clubs: Nat. Press; World Trade (N.Y.C.). Avocations: photography, travel. Home: 51 Colgate Rd Great Neck NY 11023-1519 Office: 420 Lexington Ave Rm 300 New York NY 10170-0399

RUBENSTEIN, STEVEN PAUL, newspaper columnist; b. L.A., Oct. 31, 1951; s. Victor Gerald and Florence (Fox) R.; m. Caroline Moira Grannan, Jan. 1, 1989; children: William Laurence, Anna Katherine. BA, U. Calif., Berkeley, 1977. Reporter L.A. Herald Examiner, 1974-76; reporter San Francisco Chronicle, 1976-81, columnist, 1981—. Office: San Francisco Chronicle 901 Mission St San Francisco CA 94103-2905

RUBEO, BRUNO, production designer. Art dir.: (films) Spring Fever, 1983; prodn. designer: (films) Platoon, 1986, Salvador, 1986, Walker, 1987, Talk Radio, 1988, Blood Red, 1988, Born on the Fourth of July, 1989, Driving Miss Daisy, 1989 (Academy award nomination best art direction 1989), (with Stuart Wurtzel) Old Gringo, 1989, Kindergarten Cop, 1990, Sommersby, 1992, (with Marek Dobrowolski) Blood In Blood Out, 1993, The Client, 1994, Dolores Claiborne, 1995. Office: Sandra Marsh Mgt 9150 Wilshire Blvd Ste 220 Beverly Hills CA 90212-3429

RUBERG, ROBERT LIONEL, surgery educator; b. Phila., July 22, 1941; s. Norman and Yetta (Wolfman) R.; m. Cynthia Lief, June 26, 1966; children: Frederick, Mark, Joshua. BA, Haverford (Pa.) Coll., 1963; MD, Harvard U., 1967. Diplomate Am. Bd. Surgery, Am. Bd. Plastic Surgery. Instr. surgery U. Pa., Phila., 1972-75; asst. prof. Ohio State U., Columbus, 1975-81, assoc. prof., 1981-88, prof., 1988—; bd. dirs. Am. Bd. Plastic Surgery, 1991—, vice-chair, 1996—; chmn. curriculum com. Coll. Medicine, Ohio State U., 1984—; chief plastic surgery Ohio State U. Hosps., 1985—. Plastic Surgery Ednl. Found. research grantee, 1976, 78. Fellow ACS; mem. Am. Assn. Plastic Surgeons, Assn. Acad. Chairmen of Plastic Surgery (sec.-treas. 1990-93, pres. 1994-85). Avocations: basketball, bicycling. Home: 100 Walnut Woods Ct Gahanna OH 43230-6200 Office: Ohio State U Hosps 410 W 10th Ave # 809 Columbus OH 43210-1240

RUBIN, A. LOUIS, advertising executive; b. Paterson, N.J., Jan. 15, 1954; m. Jeanne Stark, Jan. 21, 1978; 1 child, Matthew. BA, Clark U., 1976; MEd, Harvard U., 1977. Project dir. Benton & Bowles, N.Y.C., 1977-79; account exec. Dancer Fitzgerald Sample, N.Y.C., 1979-81; product mgr. Gen. Foods, White Plains, N.Y., 1981-84; account supr. Scali McCabe Sloves, N.Y.C., 1984-85; v.p., mgmt. dir. FCB/Leberkatz Ptnrs., N.Y.C., 1985-88; sr. v.p., mgmt. dir. Scali McCabe Sloves, N.Y.C., 1988-92; exec. v.p. Y & R Inc., LD & P, N.Y.C., 1992-96; exec. v.p., dir. mktg. planning Doremus, N.Y.C., 1996—. Home: 15 Whig Rd Scarsdale NY 10583-3013

RUBIN, ALAN A., pharmaceutical and biotechnology consultant; b. N.Y.C., July 10, 1926; s. Harry and Gertrude R.; m. Helen M. Feinstein; children: Jeffrey, Ronald, Howard. B.S., NYU, 1950, M.S., 1953, Ph.D., 1959. Pharmacologist Schering Corp., Bloomfield, N.J., 1954-64; dir. pharmacology Endo Labs., Garden City, N.Y., 1964-70, v.p. research, 1970-74; dir. research DuPont Pharms., Wilmington, Del., 1974-82, dir. sci. info. and tech., 1982-87; dir. licensing tech. DuPont Merck Pharms., Wilmington, Del., 1987-91; cons. ARA Assoc., Rockland, Del., 1991—. Editor: Search for New Drugs, 1972, New Drugs: Discovery and Development, 1978; contbr. articles to profl. jours. Served with U.S. Army, 1944-46. Mem. AAAS, Am. Soc. Pharmacology and Exptl. Therapeutics, Soc. Exptl. and Biol. Medicine, Am. Heart Assn. Home: 207 Hitching Post Dr Wilmington DE 19803-1914 Office: ARA Assoc PO Box 244 Rockland DE 19732-0244

RUBIN, ALAN J., environmental engineer, chemist; b. Yonkers, N.Y., Mar. 20, 1934; s. Jerome and Lydia R.; m. Ann Kopyt, June 17, 1962; 1 dau., Sara. B.S. in Civil Engring, U. Miami (Fla.), 1959; M.S. in San. Engring, U. N.C., Chapel Hill, 1962, Ph.D. in Environ. Chemistry, 1966. Civil engr. FAA, Ft. Worth, 1959-60; asst. prof. U. Cin., 1965-68; prof. civil engring. Ohio State U., Columbus, 1968-91, prof. emeritus, 1991—; with U.S. Geol. Survey, Columbus, 1991-93; vis. prof. Technion, Haifa, 1984. Editor 4 books on environ. chemistry; contbr. articles profl. jours. Served with AUS, 1953-55. Mem. Am. Chem. Soc., Am. Water Works Assn., Water Pollution Control Fedn., Internat. Assn. Water Pollution Research. Achievements include research on giardia cysts, metal ion chemistry, flotation techniques, disinfection, flocculation, coagulation, adsorption, and other physical-chemical treatment processes. Home: 1438 Sherbrooke Pl Columbus OH 43209 Office: Ohio State Univ Dept of Civil Engring Columbus OH 43210-1058

RUBIN, ALBERT LOUIS, physician, educator; b. Memphis, May 9, 1927; s. Malcolm M. and Sarah Anne (Bryan) R.; m. Carolyn M. Diehl, Sept. 28, 1953; 1 child, Marc. Student, Williams College, 1944-45, MIT, 1945-56; MD, Cornell U., 1950. Diplomate Am. Bd. Internal Medicine. Intern Bellevue Hosp., N.Y.C., 1950-51, resident internal medicine, 1951-54, fellow nephrology, 1954-55; physician-in-charge Bellevue Hosp., 1953-61; established investigator Am. Heart Assn., N.Y.C., 1958-63; dir. Rogosin Labs., Cornell U. Med. Coll., N.Y.C., 1963—, The Rogosin Kidney Ctr., N.Y.C., 1971—, The Rogosin Inst., N.Y.C., 1983—; prof. biochemistry, surgery, medicine Cornell U. Med. Coll., N.Y.C., 1969—; surgeon The N.Y. Hosp., N.Y.C., 1969—; mem. com. on sci. and tech. aspects of processing materials in space NRC, N.Y.C.; dir. affiliations and patient referrals N.Y. Hosp.-Cornell Med. Ctr., 1977-80; bd. dirs., bd. incorporators neurosci. rsch. program MIT. Author: Physical Diagnosis: A Textbook and Workbook in Methods of Clinical Examination, 1972, Humoral Aspects of Transplantation, 1976, Manual of Clinical Nephrology, 1980; cons. editor Am. Jour. Medicine; med. editl. cons. Time mag., 1983-94. With USN, 1944-45. Recipient Hoeing award Nat. Kidney Found., 1982. Mem. ACP, AAAS, Am. Soc. for Artificial Internal Organs, Transplantation Soc., Sigma XI. Home: 220 Allison Court Englewood NJ 07631 Office: The Rogosin Inst 505 E 70th St HT-230 New York NY 10021

RUBIN, ARNOLD JESSE, aeronautical engineer; b. Bklyn., Sept. 30, 1924; s. Jack and Birdie (Reiss) R.; B. Aero. Engring., N.Y.U., 1949; postgrad. U. Va., 1950, Poly. Inst. Bklyn., 1960-62; m. Gloria Form, June 19, 1949; children—Jacqueline Sue, Mitchell Myles. Aero. research scientist Langley Research Center, NASA, Hampton, Va., 1949-51; with Fairchild Republic Co., Fairchild Industries, Inc., Farmingdale, N.Y., 1951-87, prin. aerodyn. engr., 1979-82, chief aerodyns., T-46A, 1982-87. Served with USAAF, 1943-45. Fellow AIAA (asso.); mem. Soc. Flight Test Engrs., N.Y.U. Alumni Assn. Club: Huron. Home: 106 Sprucewood Dr Levittown NY 11756-3837

RUBIN, BARRY MITCHEL, foreign policy analyst, writer; b. Washington, Jan. 28, 1950; s. David and Helen Victoria (Segal) R.; m. Judith Colp; 1 child, Gavriella. BA, Richmond Coll., 1972; MA, Rutgers U., 1974; PhD, Georgetown U., 1978. Sr. fellow CSIS, Washington, 1978-85, Washington Inst. Near East Policy, Washington, 1988-91; congl. fellow Coun. Fgn. Rels., Washington, 1985-86; fellow Johns Hopkins SAIS, Washington, 1986-93, prof., 1986-93; sr. fellow Hebrew U. Harry S. Truman Inst., 1989—, U. Haifa Jewish-Arab Ctr., 1993—, Bar-Ilan U. BESA Ctr., 1994—; adj. prof. Johns Hopkins SAIS, Washington, 1986-93, dir. SAIS project polit. study terrorism; mem. fgn. policy staff U.S. Senate, 1985-86; prof. Hebrew U., 1994-95. Author: Paved with Good Intentions, 1980, The Arab States and the Palestine Conflict, 1982, Secrets of State, 1985, Modern Dictators, 1987, Istanbul Intrigues, 1989, Islamic Fundamentalists in Egyptian Politics, 1991, Cauldron of Turmoil, 1992, Resolution Until Victory?: The Politics of the PLO, 1994, Assimilation and its Discontents, 1995; editor: (with others) The Human Rights Reader, 1979, The Israel-Arab Reader, 1984, 95, Central

American Crisis Reader, 1987, The Politics of Terrorism, 3 vols., Iraq's Road to War, 1994. Internat. affairs fellow Coun. on Fgn. Rels., 1984-85, Fulbright fellow, 1990-91; grantee U.S. Inst. of Peace, 1989-91, Davis Inst., 1994; Harry Guggenheim fellow, 1990. Mem. Assn. Israel Studies (v.p. 1984-89). Address: Haim ve-Elisha 16, Tel Aviv Israel 64288

RUBIN, BONNIE MILLER, journalist; b. Chgo., Aug. 17, 1951; d. George and Florence Ila (Rubin) Miller; m. David Rubin, June 30, 1974; children: Michael, Alyssa. BA, Drake U., 1973. Sports reporter Quad City Times, Davenport, Iowa, 1973-75; community rels. asst. dir. Metropolitan Med. Ctr., Minn., 1975-77; reporter Minneapolis Star Tribune, 1977-85; features editor Post Tribune, Gary, Ind., 1985-90; home editor Chgo. Tribune, 1990-93, met. reporter, 1993—. Author Time Out, 1987, Great Escapes from Chicago, 1992. Mem. Am. Assn. Sunday and Feature Editors. Office: Chgo Tribune Co 435 N Michigan Ave Chicago IL 60611-4001

RUBIN, BRUCE ALAN, lawyer; b. Pitts., Sept. 12, 1951; s. Stanley and Elaine (Roth) R.; m. Suzanne Kay Boss, Aug. 23, 1975; children: Daniel, Jay. BA, Yale U., 1973; JD, Stanford U., 1976. Bar: Oreg. 1976, U.S. Dist. Ct. Oreg. 1976, U.S. Ct. Appeals (9th cir.) 1976. Atty. Miller, Nash, Wiener, Hager & Carlsen, Portland, 1976—; bd. dirs. Classroom Law Project, Portland, 1990-94. Author: Wrongful Discharge in Oregon, 1988. Mem. Oreg. State Bar (disciplinary coun. 1990—), Jewish Community Ctr. Avocation: competitive long distance running. Office: Miller Nash Wiener Hager & Carlsen 111 SW 5th Ave Portland OR 97204-3604

RUBIN, BRUCE JOEL, screenwriter, director, producer; b. Detroit, Mar. 10, 1943; s. Jim and Sondra R.; m. Blanche Mallins; children: Joshua, Ari. Student, Wayne State U., 1960-62; grad. film sch., NYU, 1965. Former asst. film editor NBC News; mem. film dept. Whitney Mus., assoc. curator. Screenwriter: (with Robert Statzel and Phillip Frank Messina) Brainstorm, 1983, Deadly Friend, 1986, Ghost, 1990 (Academy award best original screenplay 1990), Jacob's Ladder, 1990; writer, dir., prodr. My Life, 1993. Office: care Geoffrey Sanford 1015 Gayley Ave Fl 3 Los Angeles CA 90024-3424

RUBIN, BRUCE STUART, public relations executive; b. Miami, Fla., June 28, 1947; s. Earl Myron and Claire (Malbin) R.; m. Cheryl Joy Cunningham, Aug. 1, 1980. BA in Journalism, U. Miami, 1969. Reporter The Miami News, 1969; v.p. Ronald Levitt Assocs., Inc., Coral Gables, Fla., 1970-75; pres. Bruce Rubin & Assocs., Miami, 1975-94; chmn. bd. Rubin Barney & Birger, Inc., Miami, 1994—; chmn. Counselors Acad., 1987. Recipient Exec. Achievement in Pub. Rels. award O'Dwyer's Directory of Pub. Rels. Execs., 1991, 94. Mem. Pub. Rels. Soc. Am. (accredited, pres. Miami chpt., counselor of pub. rels. 1978). Home: 8065 SW 86 Ter Miami FL 33143 Office: 255 Alhambra Cir Ste 500 Miami FL 33134-7404

RUBIN, CHANDA, professional tennis player; b. Lafayette, La., Feb. 18, 1976; d. Edward and Bernadette Rubin. Grad., Episcopal Sch. Acadiana, 1993. Mem. USTA Jr. Devel. Team, 1989, USTA Nat. Team, 1990; prof. tennis player, 1991—; player 17 tournaments with 28 wins, 17 loses, 1994, named to Olympic Team, Atlanta,1996,. Recipient 3 U.S. Jr. Titles, 12 Singles, 1988, 14 Singles, 1989, 16 Indoor Doublles, 1989; winner U.S. nat. title and Rolex Orange Bowl 12s crown, 1988, 14 Nat., 1989, 16 Indoor Doubles, 1989. Office: USTA 1212 Ave of the Americas New York NY 10036*

RUBIN, CHARLES ELLIOTT, lawyer, sports agent; b. Kansas City, Mo., May 28, 1947; s. Irving C. and Anna Lee (Strauss) R.; m. Linda Jean Nichols, Aug. 6, 1973; children: Aaron Matthew, Joanne Michelle. BSBA, U. Mo., 1969, JD, 1972. Bar: Mo. 1973, U.S. Dist. Ct. (we. dist.) Mo. 1973, U.S. Tax Ct. 1974, U.S. Ct. Appeals (8th cir.) 1974, U.S. Supreme Ct. 1976. Ptnr. Pummil & Rubin, Kansas City, 1973—; chmn. Assured Mgmt. Co., Westwood, Kans., 1990—. Mem. Kansas City Bd. Zoning Adjustment, 1981-84; bd. dirs. New Reform Temple, Kansas City, 1985—, Menorah Med. Ctr., Kansas City, 1987—, Children's Mercy Hosp., Kansas City, 1988—. Mem. ABA, Kansas City Bar Assn., Am. Judicature Assn., Oakwood Country Club (bd. dirs.), Shadow Glen Club. Avocations: outdoor activities, golf, scuba diving. Office: Assured Mgmt Co 1901 W 47th Pl Ste 200 Shawnee Mission KS 66205-1834

RUBIN, DAVID LEE, French literature educator, critic, editor, publisher; b. Indpls., Sept. 30, 1939; s. Ira Bertram and Jeanne Iva (Gamso) R.; m. Carolyn Dettman, June 12, 1965; 1 child, Timothy Craig. BA, U. Tenn., 1962; cert., U. Paris, 1963; MA, U. Ill., 1964, PhD, 1967. Instr. French U. Ill., Urbana, 1966-67; asst. prof. U. Chgo., 1967-69; asst. prof. U. Va., Charlottesville, 1969-74, assoc. prof., 1974-82, prof. French, 1982—; seminar dir. Folger Inst., 1989; founder Rookwood Press, 1992—; cons. Can. Coun., Etudes littéraires françaises, NEH, numerous univ. presses; lectr., spkr. in field. Author: Higher Hidden Order, 1972, The Knot of Artifice, 1981, A Past with Silence, 1991; editor: The Selected Poetry and Prose of John T. Napier, 1972, La poésie française du premier 17e siècle, 1986, Sun King, 1991; co-editor: La Cohérence Intérieure, 1977, Convergences, 1989, The Ladder of High Designs, 1991, The Fulbright Difference, 1993; founding editor Continuum, 1989-93, EMF; Studies in Early Modern France, 1994, EMF Monographs, 1994; mem. editl. bd. Purdue Monographs, 1975—, Oeuvres et Critiques, 1976—, French Rev., 1986-94; Am. corr. Cahiers Maynard, 1973—, Cahiers Tristan L'Hermite, 1989; contbr. articles to profl. jours., chpts. to books. U.S. State Dept. Fulbright fellow, 1962-63, Woodrow Wilson Found. fellow, 1963-64, Guggenheim Found. fellow, 1980-81. Mem. MLA, ACLU, Farmington Club, Boar's Head Club, Phi Beta Kappa. Avocations: reading, travel, fitness. Home: 520 Rookwood Pl Charlottesville VA 22903-4734 Office: U Va French Dept 302 Cabell Hall Charlottesville VA 22903

RUBIN, DONALD BRUCE, statistician, educator, research company executive; b. Washington, Dec. 22, 1943; s. Allan A. and Harriet (Schainis) R.; m. Kathryn M. Kazarow; children: Scott Wilk, Paul Stuart. AB magna cum laude, Princeton U., 1965; MS, Harvard U., 1966, PhD, 1970. Rsch. statistician Ednl. Testing Svc., Princeton, N.J., 1971-75, chmn. stats., 1975-79, sr. statis. advisor, 1979-81; pres. Datametrics Rsch. Inc., Waban, Mass., 1981—; prof. U. Chgo., 1982-84; prof. Harvard U., Cambridge, Mass., 1984—, chmn. stats., 1985-94. Author: Handling Nonresponse in Sample Surveys by Multiple Imputation, 1980, Multiple Imputation for Nonresponse in Surveys, 1987; author: (with others) Incomplete Data in Sample Surveys (Vol. 2): Theory and Bibliography, 1983; co-author: (with R.J.A. Little) Statistical Analysis With Missing Data, 1987, (with A. Gelman, J. Cavlin. H. Steven) Bayesian Data Analysis, 1995; co-editor: (with P.W. Holland) Test Equating, 1982; contbr. over 200 articles to profl. jours. Recipient Parzen prize for statis. innovation, 1996; Woodrow Wilson Grad. fellow, 1965; NSF Grad. fellow, 1965, 68, John Simon Guggenheim fellow, 1977-78. Fellow AAAS (chmn. stats. 1992), Am. Statis. Assn. (editor jour. 1980-82, dir. 1980-82, statistician of yr. Boston chpt. 1995, S.S. Wilkes medal 1995, Parzen prize for statis. innovation), Inst. Math. Stats. (coun. mem. 1990-92); mem. NAS (com. on nat. stats. 1989-92, mem. panel on confidentiality data 1989-92, panel on bilingual edn. 1990-92, working group on statis. analysis of com. on basic rsch. in behavioral and social scis. 1985-86, panel statis. in 21st century 1995, other coms.), N.Y. Acad. Sci., Biometric Soc., Internat. Assn. Survey Statisticians, Internat. Statis. Inst., Psychometric Soc., Royal Statis. Soc. Office: Harvard U Dept Statistics Cambridge MA 02138

RUBIN, ELAINE, service industry executive, marketing professional; b. Manhasset, N.Y., 1963. B in Mktg., Emory U., 1985. Account exec. Basinger & Assocs., Atlanta, 1985-88; account supr., divsn. mgr. Baslinger & Assocs, Atlanta, 1989-92; account exec. MGA Advt., N.Y.C., 1988-89; devel. mgr. 800-Flowers, Westbury, N.Y., 1992-94, gen. mgr. interactive svcs., 1994—. Office: 800-Flowers 1600 Stewart Ave Westbury NY 11590*

RUBIN, EMANUEL, pathologist, educator; b. N.Y.C., Dec. 5, 1928; s. Jacob and Sophie R.; m. Barbara Kurn, Mar. 27, 1955 (div. 1985); children: Raphael, Jonathan, Daniel, Rebecca; m. Linda A. Haegele, Oct. 13, 1985; children: Ariel, Ethan. B.S., Villanova U., 1950; M.D., Harvard U., 1954. Intern Boston City Hosp., 1954-55; resident Children's Hosp. of Phila., 1957-58; research fellow in pathology Mt. Sinai Hosp., N.Y.C., 1958-62, asst. attending pathologist, 1962-64, assoc. attending pathologist, 1964-68; attending pathologist, dir. hosp. pathology services Mt. Sinai Hosp., 1968-72, pathologist-in-chief, 1972-76; dir. labs. Hahnemann Hosp., Phila., 1977-86; physician-in-chief pathology Thomas Jefferson U. Hosp., 1986—; prof. pathology Mt. Sinai Sch. Medicine, CUNY, 1966-72, Irene Heinz and John LaPorte Givien prof. pathology, chmn. dept., 1972-76; prof., chmn. dept. pathology and lab. medicine Hahnemann U. Sch. Medicine, Phila., 1977-86; Gonzalo Aponte prof. pathology, chmn. dept. pathology and cell biology Thomas Jefferson U. Coll. Medicine, Phila., 1986-94, chmn. dept. pathology, anatomy and cell biology, 1994—; adj. prof. biochemistry and biophysics U. Pa. Sch. Medicine, Phila., 1977-88. Author: (with J.L. Farber) Pathology, 1988, 94; (with K.W. Miller and S.H. Roth) Cellular and Molecular Mechanisms of Alcohol and Anesthetics, 1991; editor-in-chief Lab. Investigation, 1982-96; pathology editor: Fedn. Proc., 1982-86, J. Stud Alc, 1982-94. Served with USN, 1955-57. Mem. ACP, Am. Soc. Investigative Pathology, Internat. Acad. Pathology, U.S.-Can. Acad. Pathology, Am. Soc. Biol. Chemists and Molecular Biology, Am. Assn. Study of Liver Diseases, Am. Gastroent. Assn., Internat. Assn. Study of the Liver, Am. Coll. Toxicology. Home: 1505 Monk Rd Gladwyne PA 19035-1316 Office: 1020 Locust St Philadelphia PA 19107-6731

RUBIN, E(RWIN) LEONARD, lawyer; b. Chgo., Jan. 11, 1933; s. Samuel and Frances Birdie (Rabin) R.; m. Stephanie Siegel, Mar. 4, 1961 (div. Dec. 1981); children: Matthew, Suzanne; m. Audrey Gay Holzer, May 8, 1983; children: Margot, Bette. Student, U. Ill., Urbana, 1948-51; AB, U. Miami, 1956, JD, 1959. s. N.Y. 1960, Ill. 1962, U.S. Dist. Ct. (no. dist.) Ill. 1962, U.S. Ct. Appeals (7th cir.) 1990. Assoc. Hays, St. John A&H, N.Y.C., 1960-62, Devoe, Shadur, Mikva & P., Chgo., 1962-65; gen. counsel Playboy Enterprises, Inc., Chgo., 1965-78; ptnr. E. Leonard Rubin Law Offices, Chgo., 1978-81, Epton, Mullin & Druth Ltd., Chgo., 1981-86, Brinks, Hofer, Gilson & Lione, Chgo., 1986—; adj. prof. U. Ill., John Marshall Law Sch. Pres. Lawyers for Creative Arts, Chgo., 1983-85; chmn. bd. dirs. Mus. Holography; bd. dirs. Wisdom Bridge Theatre, Chgo., 1983-85. Cpl. U.S. Army, 1953-5, ETO. Mem. ABA, Ill. Bar Assn., Chgo. Bar Assn. (bd. mgrs. 1983-85, chmn. various coms., dir. Christmas Spirits Satire Show 1965—), Union Internat. Des Avocats (v.p. intellectual property commn.), Copyright Soc. Am. (trustee, pres. midwest chpt.). Jewish. Home: 270 Sunset Dr Northfield IL 60093-1047 Office: Brinks Hofer Gilson & Lione 455 N Cityfront Plaza Dr Chicago IL 60611-5503

RUBIN, GUSTAV, orthopedic surgeon, consultant, researcher; b. N.Y.C., May 19, 1913; s. William and Rose (Strongin) R.; m. Mildred Synthia Holtzer, July 4, 1946 (dec. Dec. 1964); m. Esther Rosenberg Partnow, July 23, 1965; 1 stepchild, Michael Partnow. B.S., NYU, 1934; M.D., SUNY-Downstate Med. Ctr., 1939. Diplomate Am. Bd. Orthopedic Surgery. Intern Maimonides Hosp., Bklyn., 1939-41; resident in orthopedics Hosp. for Joint Diseases, N.Y.C., 1941-42, 1946; practice medicine specializing in orthopedics Bklyn., 1947-56; from orthopedic surgeon to dir. clinic VA Clinic, Bklyn., 1956-70; chief Spl. Prosthetic Clinic VA Prosthetics Ctr., N.Y.C., 1970-85, dir. spl. team for amputations, mobility, prosthetics/orthotics, 1985-87, mem. chief med. dir. adv. group on prosthetics services, rehab. research and devel., 1985-87, orthopedic cons., 1970-87, ret., 1987; pvt. practice N.Y.C., 1987—; med. advisor prosthetic rsch. com. N.Y. State DAV, 1970—; lectr. prosthetics NYU, 1972-89; clin. prof. orthopedics N.Y. Coll. Podiatric Medicine, 1980—; orthopedic cons. Internat. Ctr. for the Disabled, N.Y.C., 1987—. Contbr. book chpts., articles to profl. jours.; contbr. article on amputations Ency. for Disability and Rehab., 1995. Capt. U.S. Army, 1943-46. Recipient Nat. Comdrs. award DAV, 1968, Amvets award for outstanding service, 1969, award for Service to Veterans Allied Veterans Meml. Com., 1970, Eastern Paralyzed Veterans Assn. award, 1977, award for Service to Israeli Wounded Israeli Govt. Dept. Rehab., 1981, Cert. of Merit, Nat. Amputation Found., 1972, Olin E. Teague award VA, 1984, Physician of Yr. award Pres.'s Commn. on Employment of People with Disabilities, 1984. Fellow Am. Acad. Orthopedic Surgeons, ACS, Am. Acad. Neurol. and Orthopedic Surgeons; mem. Alumni Assn. Hosp. Joint Disease, Sigma Xi. Jewish. Avocations: sculpting; oil painting. Home: PO Box 572 15 Circle Dr Moorestown NJ 08057 Office: 304 E 24th St New York NY 10010

RUBIN, HARRIS B., psychology educator; b. Jersey City, May 12, 1932; s. Eli L. and Doris R.; m. Angela Battaglia, June 11, 1960; children: Amy L., Chad A., Thea F., Garth A. B.A. in Psychology, So. Ill. U., 1959; Ph.D., U. Chgo., 1965. Research scientist behavior research lab. Anna State Hosp., Ill., 1965-72; asst. prof. rehab. inst. So. Ill. U., Carbondale, 1966-71, assoc. prof. behavioral sci. Sch. Medicine and Rehab. Inst., 1972-78, prof., 1978-95, interim asst. dean student affairs, 1994-96, prof. emeritus, 19965—; cons. Ill. Dept. Corrections, Ill. Dept. Mental Health. Bd. editors Jour. Applied Behavior Analysis, 1972-75, Jour. Exptl. Analysis of Behavior, 1973-75, The Behavior Analyst, 1986-90; adv. editor various jours.; contbr. articles to profl. jours. Mem. Carbondale Human Relations Com., 1968-73, chmn., 1969-72. Served with U.S. Army, 1952-54. Fellow APA, Am. Psychol. Soc., Am. Assn. Applied and Preventive Psychology; mem. Assn. Behavior Analysis, Midwest Psychol. Assn., Behavior Analysis Soc. Ill. (pres. 1989-90). Office: So Ill U Sch Medicine Carbondale IL 62901

RUBIN, HARRY MEYER, entertainment industry executive; b. N.Y.C., Dec. 21, 1952; s. Martin J. and Helene Rubin; children: Gabriella, James. B.A., Stanford U., 1974; M.B.A., Harvard U., 1976. Investment banker Wertheim & Co., Inc., N.Y.C., 1976-77; fin. mgr. Am. Airlines, Inc., N.Y.C., 1977-79; dir. fin. planning-entertainment, electronics groups RCA Corp., N.Y.C., 1979-81, chief fin. officer RCA Videodiscs, 1981-82, chief fin. officer RCA video and cable ops., 1982-86, group fin. exec. RCA entertainment ops., 1984-86, v.p. strategic planning and video ops., 1983-87; gen. mgr. Home Video Gen. Electric Co., 1986-87; v.p., gen. mgr. home video ops. NBC, Inc., 1988-93; exec. v.p. GT Interactive Software Corp., 1994—; dir., co-head exec. com. RCA/Columbia Pictures Home Video and Internat. Video; dir. Genisco Tech. corp.; founding ptnr. Samuel Adams Beer; dir. Arts & Entertainment Network. Mem. Phi Beta Kappa, 22 Club. Avocations: travel, foreign languages. Home: 784 Park Ave New York NY 10021

RUBIN, HOWARD JEFFREY, lawyer; b. Phila., Apr. 8, 1947; s. Martin C. and Natalie S. (Lerner) R.; m. Nan H. Foster, June 30, 1974; children: Jacob S., Leslie D. BA, Colgate U., 1969; JD, Columbia U., 1972. Bar: N.Y. 1973, U.S. Dist. Ct. (so. and ea. dists) N.Y. 1974, U.S. Ct. Appeals (2d cir.) 1975, U.S. Supreme Ct. 1985. Staff atty. N.Y.C. Dept. Consumer Affairs, 1972-73; co-dir. employment rights project, lectr. in law Sch. of Law Columbia U., N.Y.C., 1974-79; ptnr., chmn. litigation dept., mgmt. com. Davis & Gilbert, N.Y.C., 1979—. Co-author: Fair Employment Litigation, 1975, Fair Employment Litigation Manual, 1977, N.Y. State Department of Human Rights Litigation Manual, 1978. Bd. dirs. U.J.A. Fedn. of N.Y., 1986-92; pres. Town & Village Synagogue, N.Y.C., 1990-92; chmn. Prozdor H.S., N.Y.C., 1994—. Mem. ABA, Assn. of Bar of City of N.Y. Home: 1035 Park Ave New York NY 10028 Office: Davis & Gilbert 1740 Broadway New York NY 10019

RUBIN, IRVING, editor; b. N.Y.C., Apr. 7, 1916; s. Julius and Sadie (Seidman) R.; m. Florence Podolsky, Mar. 12, 1949; children: Joanne, Saul Robert. PhG, Bklyn. Coll. Pharmacy, 1936; BA, Bklyn. Evening Coll., 1948; PharmD (hon.), Mass. Coll. Pharmacy, 1973; DSc (hon.), Union U., 1986; DHL (hon.), L.I. U., 1986; DSc (hon.), St. John's U., 1989. With retail pharmacies N.Y.C., 1933-38; assoc. editor, then mng. editor Pharmacy, Am. Druggist mag.; editorial dir. Blue Price Book, 1938-60; editor, v.p., publ. dir. Pharmacy Times (and predecessors), Port Washington, N.Y., 1960-86; pub. Pharmacy Times (and predecessors), Port Washington, 1984, editor-in-chief, pub., 1987, editor-at-large, 1988-93; pharmacy cons. Resident and Staff Physician mag., 1978—; mem. consumer interest/health edn. panel U.S. Pharmacopeial Conv., Inc., 1991-95; mem. dean's adv. bd. steering com. Coll. Pharmacy and Allied Health Professions, St. John's U. Author: The Pharmacy Graduate's Career Guide, 1970; editor Wellcome Trends in Pharmacy, 1990-93; editor-in-chief emeritus Pharmacy Times, 1994—; chmn. editl. adv. bd. Glaxo Wellcome Trends in Pharmacy, 1996—. Trustee Arnold and Marie Schwartz Coll. Pharmacy, Bklyn.; del. leader People to People Internat., People's Republic China, 1988, USSR, 1990, Great Britain and Ireland, 1992; also addressed about 150 mems. of the Supreme Soviet in the Kremlin about the Chernobyl disaster, 1990. With AUS, 1941-46, ETO. Decorated Bronze Star; recipient Alumni Achievement award Alumni Assn. Bklyn. Coll. Pharmacy, 1963, Editorial Achievement award Alpha Zeta Omega, 1968, Am. Cancer Soc., 1964, Gold medal Nicholas S. Gesoalde Pharm. Econ. Research Found., 1972, J. Leon Lascoff award Am. Coll. Apothecaries, 1977, Presdl. citation ADA, 1982, Disting. Journalism award Pharm. Soc. State N.Y., 1984, Citation Merit, Nat. Assn. Chain Drug Stores, 1986, Spl. Journalism award Nat. Assn. Chain Drug Stores, 1987; named Man of Yr. Pharmacy, B'nai B'rith, 1973, Man of Yr., Empire State Pharm. Soc., 1985; established Irving Rubin scholarship Arnold and Marie Schwartz Coll. of Pharmacy and Health Scis., L.I. U., 1988. Fellow N.Y. Acad. Pharmacy; mem. Am. Coll. Pharmacists (hon. life), Am. Inst. History of Pharmacy (coun. 1982-88), Nat. Assn. Retail Druggists (award 1987), Am. Pharm. Assn. (pres. N.Y. chpt. 1955-56, ho. of dels., Remington Honor medal 1986), NARD Found. (John W. Dargavel Outstanding Svc. medal 1995), Am. Soc. Hosp. Pharmacists, Am. Found. for Pharm. Edn. (exec. com., bd. dirs. 1988—), Okla. Pharm. Assn. (hon.), Alumni Assn. Bklyn. Coll. Pharmacy (prs. 1946-48), Alpha Zeta Omega, Rho Pi Phi, Delta Sigma Theta, Rho Chi, Kappa Psi, Phi Delta Chi (hon.), Phi Lambda Sigma (hon., Nat. Leadership award 1993). Jewish. Home: 39 Ruxton Rd Great Neck NY 11023-1514 Office: Irv Rubin Assocs 39 Ruxton Rd Great Neck NY 11023-1514

RUBIN, JACOB CARL, mechanical research engineer; b. N.Y.C., Nov. 22, 1926; s. Abraham and Bessie (Tockman) R.; m. Nancy Jean Weinstein, Aug. 2, 1952; children: Sara Lee, Jeffrey Daniel. BSME, CUNY, 1945; MMechE, NYU, 1947; MS of Applied Statistics, Rochester (N.Y.) Inst. Tech., 1969, MSEE, 1971, MS in Imaging Sci., 1975. Registered profl. engr., N.Y., D.C. Design group leader MacDonnell Aircraft Corp., St. Louis, 1955-56; mem. research staff U. Mich., Ann Arbor, 1956-57; staff engr. IBM, Vestal, N.Y., 1957-58; engr. advance design GE, Johnson City, N.Y., 1958-60; program engr. GE, Phila., 1960-62; mgr. standards engring. Martin-Marietta Corp., Balt., 1962-63; mgr. product design dept. Am. Car & Foundry Co., Rockville, Md., 1963-64; cons. reliability NASA, Greenbelt, Md., 1964-65; project engr. Eastman Kodak Co., Rochester, 1965-75, sr. rsch. assoc., 1975-90; staff mech. engr. Med. Lab. Automation, Inc., Pleasantville, N.Y., 1990-91; prin. engr. instrument div. Dresser Industries, Stratford, Conn., 1992; sr. mech. engr. Materials Rsch. Corp., Congers, N.Y., 1993; sr. mech. design engr. Electronics Retailing Sys. Inc., Wilton, Conn., 1993-94; mfg. engr. Contact Sys. Inc., Danbury, Conn., 1995; sr. mech. engr. Barnes engring. divsn. EDO Corp., Shelton, Conn., 1995—; course dir. Ctr. Profl. Advancement, East Brunswick, N.J., 1975—; adj. faculty Rochester Inst. Tech., 1965-90; assoc. prof. mech. engring. Bridgeport Engring. Inst., 1991-94; assoc. prof. mech. engring. Fairfield U., 1994—. Patentee artificial kidney, piezo-electric generator. Pres. Grove Place Neighborhood Assn., Rochester, 1984. Mem. NSPE (life), N.Y. State Soc. Profl. Engrs. Republican. Jewish. Avocations: teaching Sunday sch., music appreciation, theater, travel. Home: 161B Heritage Vlg Southbury CT 06488-1433 Office: EDO Corp Barnes Engring Divsn 88 Long Hill Cross Rd Shelton CT 06484-0867

RUBIN, JANE LOCKHART GREGORY, lawyer, foundation executive; b. Richmond, Va., May 27, 1944; d. Phillip Henry and Jane Ball (Lockhart) Gregory; m. Reed Rubin, Jan. 22, 1966; children: Lara Ross, Maia Ayers, Peter Lyon. BA, Vassar Coll., 1965; JD, Columbia U., 1975; LLM in Taxation, NYU, 1984. Bar: N.Y, 1976. Assoc. Coudera & Brothers, N.Y.C., 1977-84; of counsel Lankenau, Kouner & Kurtz, N.Y.C., 1985-95; dir. Interamericas, N.Y.C., 1992—; bd. dirs., treas. Reed Found., N.Y.C., 1985—; mem. adv. bd. Vt. Studio Ctr., 1985—; mem. Mcpl. Archives Reference and Rsch. Adv. Bd., 1991-94; mem. N.Y.C. Commn. for Cultural Affairs, 1992-94; mem. profl. adv. coun. Lincoln Ctr. for the Performing Arts, 1994—; mem. bd. visitors Columbia Law Sch., 1994—. Author: intro. and catalog for exhibit Temple of Justice: The Appellate Divsion Court House; (with others) The Art World and the Law, 1987. Bd. dirs., vice chair Vol. Lawyers for the Arts; mem. profl. advisors coun. Lincoln Ctr. for the Performing Arts, 1994—; bd. govs. The John Carter Brown Libr. Harlan Fiske Stone scholar Columbia U. Sch. Law. Mem. ABA (sect. real property and probate law, sect. internat. law and practice), N.Y. Bar Assn., Union Internationale des Avocats, Assn. Bar City of N.Y. (com. on non-profit orgns. 1984—), Copyright Soc. of U.S.A. Office: Inter Americas 162 East 78 St New York NY 10021 Home: 135 Central Park West New York NY 10023

RUBIN, JEAN ESTELLE, mathematics educator; b. Bklyn., Oct. 29, 1926; d. Leonard Lewis and Phyllis Irma (Mann) Hirsh; m. Herman Rubin, Mar. 23, 1952; children: Arthur Leonard, Leonore Anne Rubin Findsen. B.S., Queens Coll., 1948; M.A., Columbia U., 1949; Ph.D., Stanford U., 1955. Instr. Queens Coll., 1949-51, Stanford U., 1953-55; lectr. U. Oreg., 1955-59; asst. prof. Mich. State U., 1960-67; asso. prof. math. Purdue U., West Lafayette, Ind., 1968-75; prof. Purdue U., 1975—. Author: Set Theory for the Mathematician, 1967, Mathematical Logic: Applications and Theory, 1990; co-author: (with H. Rubin) Equivalents of the Axiom of Choice, 1963, Equivalents of the Axiom of Choice II, 1985. Vol. West Lafayette Libr., 1981—; bd. dirs. Lafayette Symphony Orch., Inc., 1987-93, Friends of West Lafayette Libr., 1993—. Mem. Am. Math. Soc., Assn. Symbolic Logic, Math. Assn. Am. (vis. lectr. 1976-86), Purdue Staff Aero Club Inc. (bd. dirs. 1975-90). Home: 1214 Sunset Ln West Lafayette IN 47906-2429 Office: Purdue U Math Dept Lafayette IN 47907-1395

RUBIN, JOEL EDWARD, consulting company executive; b. Cleve., Sept. 5, 1928; s. Morris and Pearl (Jacobs) R.; m. Lucille Schutmaat, Dec. 18, 1953; children: Brian G., Jennifer L., Rebecca R. BS, Case Inst. of Tech., 1949; MFA, Yale U., 1951; PhD, Stanford U., 1960. Exec. v.p. Kliegl Bros. Lighting, N.Y.C., 1954-85; prin. cons. Joel E. Rubin & Assocs., N.Y.C., 1985—; sr. advisor theater planning, mng. dir. Artec Cons., Inc., N.Y.C., 1993—. Co-author: Theatrical Lighting Practice 1954; author: Technological Development of Stage Lighting 1960. Member Coll. of Fellows of Am. Theatre, John F. Kennedy Ctr. for the Performing Arts, Washington. Recipient Golden Triaga, Prague Quadrennial, 1987, Zlatou medal, 1991, 1st time award Bus. Com. for the Arts, Forbes Mag., 1987, Founders' award U.S. Inst. for Theatre Tech., 1972, 79, U.S. Inst. Tech. Nat. award, 1990, USITT lifetime hon. membership award, 1996, Spl. citation, 1996. Fellow Am. Theatre Assn. (v.p. 1961-63), U.S. Inst. of Theatre Technology (pres. 1963-64); mem. Am. Nat. Theatre Acad. (bd. dirs. 1971-75), Internat. Theatre Inst. of the U.S. (bd. dirs. 1975-79), Nat. Coun. of Arts and Govt. (bd. dirs. 1975-79), Internat. Orgn. Theatre Architects and Scenographers (U.S. chmn., rep. 1968—, pres. 1971-79, Gold medal award 1996), Illuminating Engring. Soc. Avocations: collecting books, stage design, Lincolniana. Home: 24 Edgewood Ave Hastings Hdsn NY 10706-2024 Office: Artec Cons 114 W 26th St New York NY 10001

RUBIN, JUDITH DIANE, medical educator; b. Pitts., 1944. MD, U. Pa., 1969. Diplomate Am. Bd. Pediatrics, Am. Bd. Preventive Medicine. Intern in pediats. Children's Hosp., Phila., 1969-70; resident in pediats. Pahlavi U., Shiraz, Iran, 1970-71; resident in pediats. U. Md. Hosp., Balt., 1975-76, resident preventive medicine, 1973-77; fellow in pub. health Johns Hopkins Sch. Pub. Health, Balt., 1974-75; assoc. prof. U. Md. Sch. Medicine. Contbr. numerous articles to profl. jours. Fellow Am. Acad. Pediatrics, Am. Coll. Preventive Medicine; mem. Am. Bd. Preventive Medicine (trustee). Office: U Md Sch Med Epid & Prev Medicine 132 E Howard Hall 660 W Redwood St Baltimore MD 21201-1596

RUBIN, KENNETH ALLEN, lawyer; b. Rockville Centre, N.Y., Nov. 24, 1947; s. Albert Alton and Marion (Osterweis) R.; m. Susan Kurman, Sept. 14, 1980; children: Jennifer, Kelly. BS, Cornell U., 1969, MS, 1971, JD, 1973. Bar: D.C. 1974, N.Y. 1974, U.S. Ct. Appeals (D.C. crct.) 1974, U.S. Ct. Appeals (5th crct. 1975, U.S. Ct. Appeals (4th, 9th and 10th crct.) 1976, U.S. Ct. Appeals (3d, 8th and 11th crcts.) 1986, U.S. Supreme Ct. 1992. Trial atty. Dept. Justice, Washington, 1973-74; ptnr. Morgan, Lewis & Bockius, Washington, 1974—; adj. prof. USDA Grad. Sch., Washington, 1977-85, U. Ala., Huntsville, 1978-91, Antioch U., Washington, 1978; lectr. Cornell U., Ithaca, N.Y., 1979—. Author: What the Business Executive Needs To Know about U.S. Environmental Laws and Liabilities, 1991. Mem. adv. com. Cornell Ctr. for Environment. Mem. ABA, Am. Water Works Assn., Swiss Club Washington, Cornell Club Washington. Office: Morgan Lewis & Bockius 1800 M St NW Washington DC 20036-5802

RUBIN, LAWRENCE GILBERT, physicist, laboratory manager; b. Bklyn., Sept. 17, 1925; s. Harry E. and Ruth (Feirberg) R.; m. Florence Ruth Kagan, Feb. 11, 1951; children: Michael G., Richard D., Jeffrey N. Student, Cooper Union, N.Y.C., 1943, 46-47; B.S. in Physics, U. Chgo., 1949; M.A.

in Physics, Columbia U., 1950. Staff mem., physicist research div. Raytheon Co., Waltham, Mass., 1950-64; group leader Nat. Magnet Lab., MIT, Cambridge, Mass., 1964-78, divsn. head high magnetic field facility, 1978-93; advisor to high magnetic field facility, 1994-95; vis. scientist MIT, 1996—; mem. NAS adv. panel Nat. Bur. Standards, 1976-82, 85-90; bd. dirs. Lake Shore Cryotronics, Inc., Columbus, Ohio; gen. chmn. 6th Internat. Temperature Symposium, Washington, 1982, 7th Internat. Temperature Symposium, Toronto, Ont., Can., 1992; chmn. adv. com. Physics Today Buyers' Guide; part time staff Am. Physical Soc. Tutorial program. Mem. editorial bd. Rev. Sci. Instruments, 1968-70, 79-81; assoc. editor Ency. Scientific Instrumentation, 1992; contbr. articles to physics jours. With U.S. Army, 1943-46, ETO. Fellow IEEE (life), Am. Phys. Soc. (organizer and 1st chmn. instrument and measurement sci. group 1985); mem. Instrument Soc. Am. (sr.), Am. Vacuum Soc. Jewish. Home: 1504 Centre St Newton MA 02159-2447 Office: MIT Bldg NW14 1209 Bldg NW 14 170 Albany St Cambridge MA 02139-4208

RUBIN, LOUIS DECIMUS, JR., English language and literature educator, writer, publisher; b. Charleston, S.C., Nov. 19, 1923; s. Louis Decimus and Janet (Weinstein) R.; m. Eva M. Redfield, June 2, 1951; children: Robert Alden, William Louis. Student, Coll. of Charleston, 1940-42, LittD (hon.), 1989; AB, U. Richmond, 1946, LittD (hon.), 1972; MA, Johns Hopkins U., 1949, PhD, 1954; LittD (hon.), Clemson U., 1986, U. of the South, 1991; U. N.C. at Asheville, 1993, U. N.C., Chapel Hill, 1995. Instr. Johns Hopkins U.; editor Hopkins Rev., 1950-54; fellow criticism Sewanee Rev., 1953-54; exec. sec. Am. Studies Assn., asst. prof. Am. civilization U. Pa., 1954-56; assoc. editor Richmond (Va.) News Leader, 1956-57; assoc. prof. English Hollins Coll., 1957-60, prof., chmn. dept., 1960-67; prof. English U. N.C., 1967-73, Univ. Disting. prof., 1973-89, prof. emeritus, 1989—; editor Hollins Critic, 1963-68; vis. prof. history La. State U., 1957; Fulbright lectr. U. Aix-Marseille, 1960; lectr. Breadloaf Writer's Conf., 1961; vis. prof. U. N.C., 1965, Harvard U., 1969; lectr. Am. studies seminars Kyoto (Japan) U., 1979; pub., editl. dir. Algonquin Books Chapel Hill, 1982-91. Author: Thomas Wolfe: The Weather of His Youth, 1955, No Place on Earth, 1959, The Golden Weather, 1961, The Faraway Country, 1963, The Teller in the Tale, 1967, The Curious Death of the Novel, 1967, George W. Cable, 1969, The Writer in the South, 1972, William Elliott Shoots A Bear, 1975, Virginia: A History, 1977, The Wary Fugitives, 1978, Surfaces of a Diamond, 1981, A Gallery of Southerners, 1982, The Even-Tempered Angler, 1983, The Edge of the Swamp, 1989, The Algonquin Literary Quiz Book, 1990, The Mockingbird in the Gum Tree, 1991, Small Craft Advisory, 1991, The Heat of the Sun, 1995, Babe Ruth's Ghost, 1996; editor: South Renascence, 1953, The Lasting South, 1957, Teach the Freeman: R.B. Hayes and the Slater Fund for Nego Education, 1959, The Idea of an American Novel, 1961, South: Modern Southern Literature in Its Cultural Setting, 1961, Bibliographical Guide to the Study of Southern Literature, 1969, The Comic Imagination in American Literature, 1973, The Literary South, 1978, The American South, 1980, The History of Southern Literature, 1985, An Apple for My Teacher, 1987, A Writer's Companion, 1995; co-editor: So. Lit. Jour., 1968-69; contbr. articles to periodicals. Served with AUS, 1943-46. Guggenheim fellow, 1958-59, fellow Am. Coun. Learned Socs., 1964. Fellow So. Writers (chancellor 1991-93); mem. Soc. Study So. Lit. (pres. 1975-76), Phi Beta Kappa. Address: 702 Gimghoul Rd Chapel Hill NC 27514-3811

RUBIN, MELVIN LYNNE, ophthalmologist, educator; b. San Francisco, May 10, 1932; s. Morris and May (Gelman) R.; m. Lorna Isen, June 21, 1953; children: Gabrielle, Daniel, Michael. AA, U. Calif., Berkeley, 1951, BS, 1953; MD, U. Calif., San Francisco, 1957; MS, State U. Iowa, 1961. Diplomate Am. Bd. Ophthalmology (bd. dirs. 1977-83, chmn. 1984). Intern U. Calif. Hosp., San Francisco, 1957-58; resident in ophthalmology State U. Iowa, 1958-61; attending surgeon Georgetown U., Washington, 1961-63; asst. prof. surgery U. Fla. Med. Sch., Gainesville, 1963-66; assoc. prof. ophthalmology U. Fla. Med. Sch., 1966-67, prof. ophthalmology, 1967—, chmn. dept. ophthalmology, 1978-95; eminent scholar U. Fla. Med. Sch., Gainesville, 1989—; research cons. Dawson Corp.; ophthalmology cons. VA Hosp., Gainesville. Author: Studies in Physiological Optics, 1965, Fundamentals of Visual Science, 1969, Optics for Clinicians, 1971, 2d edit., 1974, 25th ann. edit., 1995, The Fine Art of Prescribing Glasses, 1978, 2d edit., 1991; editor: Dictionary of Eye Terminology, 1984, 3d edit., 1996, Eye Care Notes, 1989; mem. editorial bd. Survey Ophthalmology; contbr. more than 100 articles to profl. jours. Co-founder Gainesville Assn. Creative Arts, Citizens for Pub. Schs., Inc., ProArteMusica Gainesville, Inc., 1969, pres., 1971-73; mem. Thomas Ctr. Adv. Bd. for the Arts, 1978-84, nat. sci. adv. bd. Helen Keller Eye Rsch. Found., 1989—; bd. dirs. Hippodrome State Theater, 1981-87; bd. trustees U. Fla. Performing ARts Ctr., 1995—, Friends of Photography Ansel Adams Ctr., 1991—. With USPHS, 1961-63. Recipient Best Med. Book for 1978 award Am. Med. Writers Assn., 1979, Shaler Richardson award for svc. to medicine Fla. Soc. Ophthalmology, 1995; M.L. Rubin Ann. Lectureship established in his honor by Fla. State Ophthalmology, 1993. Fellow ACS, Am. Acad. Ophthalmology (sec., dir. 1978-92, pres. 1988, Sr. Honor award 1987. Guest of Honor 1992), Found. Am. Acad. Ophthalmology (bd. trustees, 1988-95, chmn., 1992-94), Joint Commn. on Allied Health Pers. in Ophthalmology (Statesman of Yr. award 1987); mem. Assn. Rsch. in Vision and Ophthalmology (trustee 1973-78, pres. 1979), Retina Soc., Macula Soc., Club Jules Gonin, N.Y. Acad. Sci., Fla. Soc. Ophthalmology, Am. Ophthal. Soc., Pan Am. Soc. Ophthalmology, Ophthalmic Photographers Soc., Alachua County Med. Soc., Fla. Med. Assn., AMA (editorial bd. Archives of Ophthalmology 1975-85), Sigma Xi, Alpha Omega Alpha, Phi Kappa Phi. Office: U Fla Med Ctr PO Box 100284 Gainesville FL 32610-0284

RUBIN, MICHAEL, lawyer; b. Boston, July 19, 1952; m. Andrea L. Peterson, May 29, 1983; children: Peter, Eric, Emily. AB, Brandeis U., 1973; JD, Georgetown U., 1977. Bar: Calif. 1978, U.S. Dist. Ct. (no. dist.) Calif. 1978, U.S. Ct. Appeals (9th cir.) 1978, U.S. Ct. Appeals (5th, 7th, 10th cirs.) 1982, U.S. Supreme Ct. 1984, U.S. Ct. Appeals (D.C. cir.) 1984, U.S. Ct. Appeals (11th cir.) 1987. Teaching fellow Law Sch. Stanford (Calif.) U., 1977-78; law clerk to Hon. Charles B. Renfrew U.S. Dist. Ct. (no. dist.) Calif., San Francisco, 1978-79; law clerk to Hon. James R. Browning U.S. Ct. Appeals (9th cir.), San Francisco, 1979-80; law clerk to Hon. William J. Brennan, Jr. U.S. Supreme Ct., Washington, 1980-81; assoc. Altshuler & Berzon, San Francisco, 1981-85, ptnr., 1985-89; ptnr. Altshuler, Berzon, Nussbaum, Berzon & Rubin, San Francisco, 1989—. Office: Altshuler Berzon Nussbaum Berzon & Rubin 177 Post St Ste 300 San Francisco CA 94108-4700

RUBIN, NORMAN JULIUS, public relations consultant; b. New Haven, May 22, 1923; s. Louis and Ida (Levine) R. BA, Yale U., 1948. City hall-police reporter Meriden (Conn.) Record, 1948-50; assoc. editor Meriden Jour., 1950-53; reporter news bur. Yale U., 1953-55, asst. dir. news bur., 1955-58; dir. pub. rels. New York Tuberculosis Health Assn., N.Y.C., 1958-61; pub. affairs assoc. Western Electric Co., N.Y.C., 1961-64, asst. mgr., pub. affairs, 1964-80; asst. mgr. community rels., 1980-86; asst. sec. Western Electric Fund, N.Y.C., 1974-80; mgr., com. rels. Western Electric Co., N.Y.C., 1980-86; columnist N.Y. Newsday, N.Y.C., 1986-95. With Infantry U.S. Army, 1943-46, ETO. Recipient Media award United Way N.Y.C., 1995; cited for successfully promoting N.Y.C.'s non-profit sector by Non-profit Coord. Com. N.Y., 1992. Mem. Pub. Rels. Soc. Am. (accredited mem.), Yale Club, Grads. Club. Avocations: squash tennis, ballet. Home: 115 E 9th St Apt 14E New York NY 10003-5429

RUBIN, PATRICIA, internist; b. Apr. 27, 1962. MD, Wright State U., 1988. Cert. internal medicine. Resident in internal medicine U. Cin., 1988-91; fellow in cardiology U. Hosp., Cleve., 1991; rsch. fellow in cardiology U. Wash. Sch. Medicine, Seattle, 1993—. Recipient Clinician Scientist award Am. Heart Assn., 1995-96. Mem. ACP, AMA, ACC. Office: U Wash Sch Medicine Box 8086 660 S Euclid Seattle WA 63119*

RUBIN, RICHARD ALLAN, lawyer; b. N.Y.C., June 19, 1942; s. Louis Max and Ruth Ann (Goldman) R.; m. Susan Deborah Levitt, June 18, 1966; children: Karen, Jill. BS, Queens Coll., 1964; JD, Bklyn. Law Sch., 1967; LLM, NYU, 1968. Bar: N.Y. 1967. Assoc. Schwartz and Frank, N.Y.C., 1968-69, Javits and Javits, N.Y.C., 1969-71; ptnr. Wolf Haldenstein Adler Freeman Herz & Frank, N.Y.C., 1972-76, Parker Chapin Flattau & Klimpl, N.Y.C., 1977—; lectr. Am. Mgmt. Assn., N.Y. Bar Assn. Mem. ABA. Office: Parker Chapin Flattau & Klimpl 1211 Avenue Of The Americas New York NY 10036-8701

RUBIN, RICK, record producer; b. Long Beach, N.Y., Mar. 10, 1963; s. Mickey and Linda (Tomberg) R. BFA, NYU, 1985. Owner, founding pres. DEF JAM Recordings, N.Y.C., 1984-88, Am. (formerly DEF Am.) Recordings, L.A., 1988—; producer recordings including: L.L. Cool J. Radio, 1985 (Gold), Beastie Boys License to Kill, 1986 (4x Platinum), Run DMC Raising Hell, 1986 (4x Platinum), The Cult Electric, 1987 (Gold), sound track Less Than Zero, 1988 (Gold), Andrew Dice Clay, 1989 (Gold), Red Hot Chili Peppers Blood Sugar Sex Magic; exec. producer recordings Public Enemy It Take A Nation, 1988 (Platinum); dir., co-producer movie Tougher than Leather, 1987. Named Hot Producer of Yr. Rolling Stone Mag., 1988; recipient Joel Weber award New Music Seminar, 1990.

RUBIN, ROBERT E., federal official; b. N.Y.C., Aug. 29, 1938; s. Alexander and Sylvia (Seiderman) R.; m. Judith Leah Oxenberg, Mar. 27, 1963; children: James Samuel, Philip Matthew. AB summa cum laude, Harvard U., 1960; postgrad., London Sch. Econs., 1960-61; LLB, Yale U., 1964. Bar: N.Y. 1965. Assoc. Cleary, Gottlieb, Steen & Hamilton, N.Y.C., 1964-66; assoc. Goldman Sachs & Co., N.Y.C., 1966-70, ptnr., 1971, mem. mgmt. com., 1980, vice chmn., co-chief oper. officer, 1987-90, co-sr. ptnr., co-chmn., 1990-93; asst. to Pres. Clinton for econ. policy The White House, Washington, 1993-95, lead nat. econ. coun. Exec. Office of Pres., 1993-95; sec. U.S. Dept. of Treasury, Washington, 1995—; ptnr., bd. dirs. N.Y.C. Partnership, Inc., 1991-93; mem. Pres.'s Adv. Com. for Trade Negotiations, Washington, 1980-82, mem. adv. com. on tender offers SEC, Washington, 1983, Gov.'s Commn. on Trade Competitiveness, 1987, regulatory adv. com. N.Y. Stock Exch., 1988-90, adv. com. internat. capital markets Fed. Res. Bank N.Y., 1989-93; mem. Securities and Exch. Commn. Market Oversight and Fin. Svcs. Adv. Com., 1991-93; Gov.'s Adv. Panel on Fin. Svcs., 1988-89; bd. dirs. Ctr. for Nat. Policy, 1982-93, vice chmn., 1984; trustee Sta. WNET-TV, 1985-93; mem., trustee Carnegie Corp. of N.Y., 1990-93; mem. Mayor's Coun. Econ. Advisors, 1990, Gov.'s Coun. on Fiscal and Econ. Priorities, 1990-92. Trustee Am. Ballet Theatre Found., Inc., N.Y.C., 1969-93, Collegiate Sch., 1978-84; mem. bd. overseers' com. to visit econs. dept. Harvard U., 1981-87, com. on univ. resources, 1987-92; mem. fin. com. N.Y. campaign Mondale for Pres., 1983-84; mem. investment adv. coun. N.Y.C. Pension Fund, 1980-89; chmn. Dem. Congl. Dinner, Washington, 1982; Dems. for the 80s, 1985-89, Dems. for the 90s, 1989-90; chmn. N.Y.C. host com. 1992 Dem. Conv., 1989-92; mem. Commn. Nat. Elections. Recipient award Nat. Assn. of Christians and Jews, N.Y.C., 1977. Mem. Phi Beta Kappa, Harvard Club (N.Y.C.), Century Country Club (Purchase, N.Y.). Jewish. Office: Dept of Treasury Office of the Sec 1500 Pennsylvania Ave NW Washington DC 20220

RUBIN, ROBERT J., lawyer; b. Chgo., Apr. 13, 1947. BA, U. Wis., 1969, JD, 1972. Bar: Wis. 1972, Ill. 1974. Ptnr. Altheimer & Gray, Chgo.; instr. law Ind. U., 1972-73. Ford fellow, 1971. Mem. ABA, Ill. State Bar Assn., Chgo. Bar Assn., State Bar Wis. Office: Altheimer & Gray 10 S Wacker Dr Ste 4000 Chicago IL 60606-7407*

RUBIN, ROBERT JOSEPH, physician, health care consultant; b. Bklyn., Feb. 7, 1946; s. B. Norman and Suzanne (Fried) R.; m. Fran Auerbach, June 14, 1970; children: Elyse Beth, David Jon. AB, Williams Coll., 1966; MD, Cornell U., 1970. Diplomate Am. Bd. Internal Medicine. Intern New England Med. Ctr. Hosps., Boston, 1970-71, resident, 1971-72, 74-76; epidemic intelligence officer, respiratory disease and spl. pathogens, divsn. viral diseases Ctr. for Disease Control, 1972-74; asst. dean govt. affairs Tufts U., 1979-84, assoc. prof. medicine, 1981-84; chief renal divsn. Lemuel Shattuck Hosp., Boston, 1979-81; asst. sec. planning and evaluation U.S. HHS, Washington, 1981-84; clin. assoc. prof. Georgetown U., Washington, 1984-95, clin. prof., 1995—; exec. v.p. ICF, Inc., 1984-88; pres. Health and Scis. Internat., 1988-92, Lewin ICF Inc., 1992, Lewin-VHI, Inc., 1992-96, Lewin Group, 1996—. Contbr. articles to profl. jours. With USPHS, 1972-74. Robert Wood Johnson Health Policy fellow, 1977. Mem. ACP, AMA, Am. Soc. Nephrology, Internat. Soc. Nephrology, Am. Fedn. Clin. Rsch., Mass. Med. Soc., Kenwood Club, Potomac Club, Williams Club, Maugus Club, Phi Beta Kappa. Republican. Jewish. Office: 9302 Lee Hwy Ste 500 Fairfax VA 22031-1214

RUBIN, ROBERT SAMUEL, investment banker; b. Boston, Sept. 22, 1931; s. Jesse Abraham and Rose (Solomon) R.; m. Martha Lucy Adams, Dec. 15, 1956; children: Rebecca, David, James, Nathaniel. BA, Yale U., 1953; MBA, Harvard Coll., 1955. With Lehman Bros., 1958-70, ptnr., 1967-70; mng. dir., bd. dirs. Lehman Bros. Kuhn Loeb, Inc., N.Y.C., 1970-84; mng. dir. Smith Barney, Inc., N.Y.C., 1989—. Trustee Bklyn. Hosp.; chmn. Bklyn. Mus.; treas. N.Y. Mcpl. Arts Soc.; bd. dirs. St. Ann's Sch. 2nd lt. AUS, 1955-58. Home: 218 Columbia Hts Brooklyn NY 11201-2105 Office: Smith Barney Inc 390 Greenwich St New York NY 10013

RUBIN, SAMUEL HAROLD, physician, consultant; b. N.Y.C., July 24, 1916; s. Joseph and Esther (Goldfarb) R.; m. Audrey Arndt, Nov. 20, 1943; children: James E., David A. A.B., Brown U., 1938; M.D., St. Louis U., 1943; M.S., U. Chgo., 1957. Diplomate: Am. Bd. Internal Medicine. Intern Jewish Hosp., St. Louis, 1943-44; resident St. Louis U. Group Hosp., 1944-45, St. Mary's Hosp., Kansas City, Mo., 1945-46; practice medicine Asbury Park, N.J., 1948-61; vol. faculty mem. N.Y. Med. Coll., 1948-61, assoc. prof. dept. medicine, 1962-65, prof., 1965—, dir. Inst. Human Values in Med. Ethics, 1984-86; chief med. service N.Y. Med. Coll.-Met. Hosp. Center, 1966-71, assoc. dean, 1971-72, exec. dean, 1972-74, dean, v.p. acad. affairs, 1975, provost, dean, 1977-83, provost, dean emeritus, 1983—, cons., 1983—; cons. medicine Jersey Shore Med. Ctr., 1962—; mem. bd. trustees St. Clares' Hosp., N.Y.C., 1985—, N.Y. Med. Coll., 1988-94. Contbr. articles to med. jours. With M.C. AUS, 1946-48. NIH program dir. grantee, 1966-71. Fellow A.C.P.; mem. N.Y. Acad. Sci. Home: 425E Heritage Hills Dr Somers NY 10589-1912

RUBIN, SANDRA MENDELSOHN, artist; b. Santa Monica, Calif., Nov. 7, 1947; d. Murry and Freda (Atliss) Mendelsohn; m. Stephen Edward Rubin, Aug. 6, 1966. BA, UCLA, 1976, MFA, 1979. Instr. Art Ctr. Coll. Design, Pasadena, Calif., 1980, UCLA, 1981. One-woman exhbns. include L.A. County Mus. Art, 1985, Fischer Fine Arts, London, 1985, Claude Bernard Gallery, N.Y.C., 1987, L.A. Louver Gallery, L.A., 1992; group exhbns. include L.A. County Mus. Artm 1977, 82, 83, L.A. Mcpl. Art Gallery, 1977, 83, 93, L.A. Contemporary Exhbns., 1978, L.A. Inst. Contemporary Arts, 1978, Newport Harbor Art Mus., Newport Beach, Calif., 1981, Odyssia Gallery, N.Y.C., 1981, Nagoya (Japan) City Mus., 1982, Long Beach (Calif.) Mus. Art, 1982, Brooke Alexander Gallery, N.Y.C., 1982, Laguna Beach (Calif.) Mus. Art, 1982, Jan Baum Gallery, L.A., 1984, San Francisco Mus. Art, 1986, Claude Bernard Gallery, 1986, Struve Gallery, Chgo., 1987, Boise (Idaho) Mus., 1988, Judy Youen's Gallery, London, 1988, Tatistscheff Gallery, Inc., Santa Monica, Calif., 1989, Tortue Gallery, Santa Monica, 1990, Contemporary Arts Forum, Santa Barbara, Calif., 1990, San Diego Mus. Art, 1991, Fresno (Calif.) Met. Mus., 1992, Jack Rutberg Fine Arts, L.A., 1993. Recipient Young Talent Purchase award L.A. County Mus. Art, 1980; Artist's Fellowship grant NEA, 1981, 91. Avocations: gardening, exercise, reading, singing.

RUBIN, SEYMOUR JEFFREY, judge, lawyer, educator; b. Chgo., Apr. 6, 1914; s. Sol and Sadie (Bloom) R.; m. Janet Beck, Mar. 26, 1943. BA, U. Mich., 1935; LLB magna cum laude, Harvard U., 1938, LLM, 1939. Bar: Ill. 1939, D.C. 1941. Mem. U.S. Reparations Del., 1945, Inter-Am. Conf. on Problems of War and Peace, 1945; chief U.S. Delegation on Post-War Problems, Portugal, Spain, Sweden, 1946; asst. legal adviser econ. affairs Dept. State, 1946-48; legal adviser U.S. dels. to organizing confs. GATT, 1947-48; practiced law Washington, 1948-61; mem. Spl. Presdl. Mission to Bolivia, 1961; personal rep. Pres. to Bolivia wih rank of spl. ambassador, 1962; gen. counsel ICA and AID, 1961-62; U.S. rep. Devel. Assistance Com., 1962-64; U.S. rep. to spl. com. UN Security Council, 1964-65; counsel Surrey, Karasik & Morse, 1964-75; U.S. rep. UN Commn. on Internat. Trade Law, 1967-69; prof. law sch. Am. U., Washington, 1973-85, prof. emeritus, 1985—; exec. v.p. Am. Soc. Internat. Law, 1975-85; mem. Inter Am. Juridical Commn., 1974-94, chmn., 1988; U.S. rep. UN Commn. on Transnat. Corps., 1975-87; hon. mem. Inter Am. Juridical Commn., 1995—; mem. U.S. del. UNCTAD Tech. Transfer Conf., 1978; mem. panel of conciliators Internat. Centre for Settlement of Investment Disputes, 1981—; prof. emeritus in residence Am. Univ. Law Sch., Washington; judge adminstrv. tribunal Inter-Am. Devel. Bd., 1994—; cons. U.S. Dept. State, Brookings Instn., 1948-49; chief U.S. del. negotiating Marshall Plan Agreements, 1951-52; dep. adminstr. Mut. Def. Assistance Control Act, 1952-53; pub. mem. Commn. on Internat. Rules of Jud. Procedure, 1961-62; adj. prof. Georgetown U. Law Ctr., Washington, 1964-72; lectr. Sloan Sch. Bus. Adminstrn., MIT, Cambridge, 1969; pres. InterAm. Legal Svcs. Assn., 1980-82; sr. cons. Am. Soc. Internat. Law; lectr. in field various univs. worldwide, 1949—; chmn. Bellagio Trade Conf., 1985, Symposium on U.S.-European Cmty. Trade Issues, Boston, 1987; chmn. U.S. Govt. Constitution Com. on Dem. Instns., 1987—; cons. legal issues of trade and investment. Author: Private Foreign Investment, 1956, The Conscience of the Rich Nations - The Common Aid Effort and the Development Assistance Committee, 1966, (with others) The International Corporation, 1970, Global Companies, 1975, Emerging Standards for Internat. Trade and Investment, 1983, Managing Trade Relations in the 1980s, 1984; editor, contbr.: Foreign Development Lending—Legal Aspects, 1971, Environment and Trade, 1981; editor: Avoidance and Settlement of International Trade Disputes, 1986; contbr. (with others) articles in field to profl. jours. Mem. bd. Inst. Internat. Law, Consumers for World Trade. Recipient Sesquicentennial award U. Mich., 1967, Grand Silver medal Austria, 1967, Cert. of Honor from U.S. Dept. State, 1994. Mem. Am. Soc. Internat. Law (sr. advisor), Internat. Law Assn., Washington Inst. Fgn. Affairs, ABA, Coun. Fgn. Affairs, Am. Law Inst., Am. Judicature Soc., InterAm. Bar Assn. (trustee), Soc. Internat. Devel., Washington Fgn. Law Soc. (bd. dirs.). Democrat. Home: 1675 35th St NW Washington DC 20007-2335 Office: American Univ Law School 4801 Massachusetts Ave NW Washington DC 20016

RUBIN, STANLEY CREAMER, producer; b. N.Y.C., Oct. 8, 1917; s. Michael Isaac and Anne (Creamer) R.; m. Elizabeth Margaret von Gerkan (actress Kathleen Hughes), July 25, 1954; children: John, Chris, Angela, Michael. Student, UCLA, 1933-37. Writer Universal Studios, Universal City, Calif., 1940-42, Columbia Pictures, Los Angeles, 1946-47; writer, producer NBC-TV, Burbank, Calif., 1948-49; theatrical film producer various studios, 1949-55, Rastar Prodns., Columbia Pictures, 1988-91; TV producer CBS-TV, Los Angeles, 1956-59, Universal Studios, Universal City, 1960-63, 20th Century-Fox, Los Angeles, 1967-71, MGM Studios, Culver City, Calif., 1972-77; pres. TBA Prodns., Los Angeles, 1978—. Producer theatrical films including The Narrow Margin, 1950, My Pal Gus, 1950, Destination Gobi, 1951, River of No Return, 1952, Promise Her Anything, 1966, The President's Analyst, 1967, Revenge, 1989; co-producer White Hunter, Black Heart, 1990; TV prodns. include G.E. Theatre, 1959-63, Ghost and Mrs. Muir, 1968-69, Bracken's World, 1969-71; writer, producer TV film The Diamond Necklace, 1948 (Emmy award 1949); producer TV films including Babe, 1975 (Hollywood Fgn. Press Golden Globe award, Christopher medal), And Your Name is Jonah, 1978 (Christopher medal 1979), The Story of Satchel Paige, 1980 (Image award 1981); exec. producer TV prodn. Escape from Iran: The Canadian Caper, 1981. Producer spl. programming Dem. Nat. Conv., San Francisco, 1984, Columbia Pictures and Rastar Prodns., 1988-91. 1st lt. USAAF, 1942-46. Mem. Writers Guild Am. (dir. 1941-42), Producers Guild Am. (bd. dirs. 1968-74, pres. 1974-79, v.p. 1987-94, bd. dirs. 1994—), Acad. Motion Picture Arts and Scis., Acad. TV Arts and Scis. (bd. govs. 1971, 73), Phi Beta Kappa. Home and Office: 8818 Rising Glen Pl Los Angeles CA 90069-1222 *I'm still too young to sum up my life, but here's a thought in progress: Stay curious.*

RUBIN, STANLEY GERALD, aerospace engineering educator; b. Bklyn., May 11, 1938; s. Harry Jack and Cele (Sake) R.; m. Carol Ruth Kalvin, Sept. 29, 1963; children—Stephany, Elizabeth, Barbara. B.Ae.E., Poly Inst. Bklyn., 1959; Ph.D., Cornell U., 1963. Asst. prof. to prof. aerospace engring. Poly. Inst. N.Y., Farmingdale, 1964-79, Assoc. dir. aerodynamic labs., 1977-79; prof. aerospace engring. and engring. mechanics U. Cin., 1979—, head dept., 1979-89, dir. NASA Univ. Space Engring. Ctr. on Health Monitoring Space Propulsion Systems, U. Cin., 1988-91; cons. Aerospace Corp., NASA, Allison (GM), others; mem. adv. com. Inst. for Computational Methods in Propulsion, NASA; speaker 9th Internat. Conf. Numerical Methods in Fluid Mechanics, Saclay, France. Chief editor Internat. Jour. Computers and Fluids, 1978—; contbr. articles to profl. jours. and Ann. Rev. Fluid Mechanics, 1992. NSF fellow, 1963-64; grantee Office Naval Research, 1978-88, AFOSR 1968-92, NASA, 1973—, others. Fellow AIAA (assoc.); mem. ASME, Soc. Indsl. and Applied Math., Am. Soc. Engring. Edn., Sigma Xi, Sigma Gamma Tau, Tau Beta Pi. Home: U Cin PO Box 210070 761 Baldwin Hall Cincinnati OH 45221-0070 Office: U Cin ML 070 761 Baldwin Hall Cincinnati OH 45221

RUBIN, STEPHEN CURTIS, gynecologic oncologist, educator; b. Phila., May 24, 1951; s. Alan and Helen (Metz) R.; m. Anne Loughran, May 30, 1985; children: Michael, Elisabeth. BS, Franklin & Marshall U., 1972; MD, U. Pa., 1976. Diplomate Am. Bd. Ob-Gyn., Nat. Bd. Med. Examiners. Intern in ob.-gyn. Hosp. of Univ. of Pa., Phila., 1976-77, residency in ob.-gyn., 1977-80, fellow in gynecologic oncology, 1980-82; asst. prof. of ob-gyn Med. Coll. of Pa., Phila., 1982-85, dir. surg. gynecology, 1982-85, chief gynecol. oncology, 1984-85; asst. mem. gynecol. staff Meml. Sloan-Kettering Hosp., N.Y.C., 1985-90, assoc. mem., 1990-93; asst. prof. ob-gyn Cornell U. Med. Coll., N.Y.C., 1985-90, assoc. prof., 1990-93; prof. ob-gyn., dir. gynecologic oncology U. Pa., Phila., 1993—. Editor: Ovarian Cancer, Cervical Cancer, Chemotherapy of Gynecologic Cancer; contbr. over 150 articles to profl. publs. Recipient Career Devel. award Am. Cancer Soc., 1987, Boyer award Meml. Sloan-Kettering, award Gynecologic Cancer Found., 1996; Nat. Cancer Inst. grantee, 1991, 96. Mem. ACS, Am. Coll. Ob-Gyn., Am. Soc. Clin. Oncology, Soc. Gynecol. Oncologists (Pres.'s award 1993), Soc. Gynecologic Investigation, Soc. Pelvic Surgeons, Gynecol. Cancer Found. (Karin Smith award 1996). Office: U Pa Med Ctr 3400 Spruce St Philadelphia PA 19104

RUBIN, STEPHEN EDWARD, editor, journalist; b. N.Y.C., Nov. 10, 1941; s. Irving and Evelyn (Halprin) R. B.A., NYU, 1965; M.S., Boston U., 1966. Editor UPI, N.Y.C., 1966-69; freelance writer N.Y.C., 1969-82; founder, dir. Writers Bloc, N.Y.C., 1976-82; editor Vanity Fair Mag., N.Y.C., 1982-83; exec. editor Bantam Books, N.Y.C., 1984-85, v.p., editorial dir., 1985-88, sr. v.p., editor-in-chief adult fiction and non-fiction, 1987-88, sr. v.p., pub., editor-in-chief adult fiction and non-fiction, 1988-90; pres., pub. Doubleday divsn. Bantam Doubleday Dell Pub. Group, N.Y.C., 1990-95; chmn., CEO Bantam Doubleday Dell Internat. Divsn., London, 1995—. Author: The New Met in Profile, 1974. Avocations: listening to musical performances, collecting records, tapes and cds, reading, exercising. Office: Bantam Doubleday Dell 1540 Broadway New York NY 10036-4039

RUBIN, STEPHEN WAYNE, lawyer; b. N.Y.C., Mar. 29, 1951; s. Oscar R. and Irene J. (Widelok) R.; m. Eileen Grossman, Sept. 23, 1978; children: Ashley G., Camner G. BS, Cornell U., 1973; JD, Columbia U., 1976. Bar: N.Y. 1977, U.S. Dist. Ct. (so. dist.) N.Y. 1977. Assoc. Gordon, Hurwitz & Butowsky, N.Y.C., 1976-79; assoc. Feit & Ahrens, N.Y.C., 1979-84, ptnr., 1984-88; ptnr. Proskauer Rose Goetz & Mendelsohn, N.Y.C., 1989—; lectr. grad. sch. bus., NYU, 1985-92. Co-contbr. law articles to profl. jours. Nat. pres., sec. Friends of Israel Def. Forces, N.Y.C., 1985—. Mem. ABA, N.Y. State Bar Assn., Assn. of Bar of City of N.Y. Office: Proskauer Rose Goetz Mendelsohn 1585 Broadway New York NY 10036-8200*

RUBIN, THEODORE ISAAC, psychiatrist; b. Bklyn., Apr. 11, 1923; s. Nathan and Esther (Marcus) R.; m. Eleanor Katz, June 16, 1946; children: Jeffrey, Trudy, Eugene. B.A., Bklyn. Coll., 1946; M.D., U. Lausanne, Switzerland, 1951; grad., Am. Inst. Psychoanalysis, 1964. Resident psychiatrist Los Angeles VA Hosp., 1953, Rockland (N.Y.) State Hosp., 1954, Bklyn. State Hosp., 1955, Kings County (N.Y.) Hosp., 1956; chief psychiatrist Women's House of Detention, N.Y.C., 1957; mem. faculty Downstate Med. Sch., N.Y. State U., 1957-59; pvt. practice N.Y.C., 1956—; tng. and supervising psychoanalyst Am. Inst. for Psychoanalysis of Karen Horney Clinic and Ctr.; mem. faculty Am. Inst. Psychoanalytic Psychoanalysis, 1962—; pres. emeritus bd. trustees Am. Inst. Psychoanalysis. Author: Jordi, 1960, Lisa and David, 1961, Sweet Daddy, 1963, In The Life, 1964, Platzo and the Mexican Pony Rider, 1965, The Thin Book by a Formerly Fat Psychiatrist, 1966, The 29th Summer, 1966, Cat, 1966, Coming Out, 1967, The Winner's Note Book, 1967, The Angry Book, 1969, Forever Thin, 1970, Emergency Room Diary, 1972, Doctor Rubin Please Make Me Happy, 1974,

Shrink, 1974, Compassion and Self-Hate, An Alternative to Despair, 1975, Love Me, Love My Fool, 1976, Reflections in a Goldfish Tank, 1977, Alive and Fat and Thinning in America, 1978, Reconciliations, 1980, Through My Own Eyes, 1982, One to One, Understanding Personal Relationships, 1983, Not to Worry, The American Family Book of Mental Health, 1984, Overcoming Indecisiveness, 1985, Lisa and David, The Story Continues, 1986, Miracle at Bellevue, 1986, Real Love, 1990, Child Potential, 1990, Anti-Semitism: A Disease of the Mind, 1990; mem. editorial bd. Am. Jour. Psychoanalysis; also articles, columns. Served as officer USNR, World War II. Recipient Adolf Meyer award Assn. Improvement Mental Health, 1963. Fellow Am. Acad. Psychoanalysis; mem. N.Y. County Med. Soc., Am. Psychiat. Assn., Assn. Advancement Psychoanalysis, Authors Guild. Office: 219 E 62nd St New York NY 10021-7685

RUBIN, VERA COOPER, research astronomer; b. Phila., July 23, 1928; d. Philip and Rose (Applebaum) Cooper; m. Robert J. Rubin, June 25, 1948; children: David M., Judith S. Young, Karl C., Allan M. BA, Vassar Coll., 1948; MA, Cornell U., 1951; PhD, Georgetown U., 1954; DSc (hon.), Creighton U., 1978, Harvard U., 1988, Yale U., 1990, Williams Coll., 1993. Research assoc. to asst. prof. Georgetown U., Washington, 1955-65; physicist U. Calif.-LaJolla, 1963-64; astronomer Carnegie Inst., Washington, 1965—; Chancellor's Disting. prof. U. Calif., Berkeley, 1981; vis. com. Harvard Coll. Obs., Cambridge, Mass., 1976-82, 92—, Space Telescope Sci. Inst., 1990-92; Beatrice Tinsley vis. prof. U. Tex., 1988; Commonwealth lectr. U. Mass., 1991, Yunker lectr. Oreg. State U., 1991, Bernhard vis. fellow Williams Coll., 1993, Oort vis. prof. U. Leiden, The Netherlands, 1995; lectr. in field, U.S., Chile, Russia, Armenia, India, Japan, China, Europe; trustee Associated Univs., Inc., 1993—. Assoc. editor: Astrophys. Jour. Letters, 1977-82; editorial bd.: Sci. Mag., 1979-87; contbr. numerous articles sci. jours.; assoc. editor: Astron. Jour., 1972-77. Pres.'s Disting. Visitor, Vassar Coll., 1987. Recipient Gold medal Royal Astron. Soc. London, 1996, Weizmann Women and Sci. award, 1996; President's disting. visitor Vassar Coll., 1987; mem. President's Commn. To Select U.S. Nat. Medal Sci. Awardees; named Henry Norris Russell lectr. Am. Astron. Soc., 1994. Mem. NAS (space sci. bd. 1974-77, chmn. sect. on astronomy 1992-95), Am. Astron. Soc. (coun. 1977-80, Russell prize lectr. 1994), Internat. Astron. Union (pres. Commn. on Galaxies 1982-85), Assn. Univ. Rsch. in Astronomy (trustee 1973-76, 94—), Am. Philos. Soc., AAAS, Commn. Nat. Med. Sci., Phi Beta Kappa (scholar 1982-83). Democrat. Jewish. *As an observational astronomer, it is my aim to obtain data of highest quality in order to answer questions concerning the universe in which we live. In spite of our enormous ignorance, each day offers exciting opportunities to learn a little more. This is the real joy of doing science.*

RUBIN, WILLIAM, editor; b. N.Y.C., Jan. 10, 1928; s. Herman and Molly (Goodman) R.; m. Claire Levine, Aug. 30, 1953; children: Deborah E., Joan S., Howard I. BA, Bklyn. Coll., 1953. Tech. editor Drug Trade News, N.Y.C., 1952-63; dir. pub. info. Nat. Vitamin Found., N.Y.C., 1958-61; editorial dir. FDC Reports & Drug Rsch. Reports, Washington, 1963-64; proprietor Sci. Reports and Projects, Bethesda, MD., 1964-67; editor Internat. Med. News Group, Rockville, Md., 1967-91; editorial cons., 1992—. Editor Clin. Psychiatry News, Family Practice News, Internal Medicine News, Ob-Gyn. News, Pediatric News, Skin & Allergy News, Internat. Med. News Group. Adminstr. Washington chpt. Am. Suicide Found.; chmn. Md. State Adv. Coun. on Arthritis and Related Diseases; bd. dirs. Reginald Lourie Ctr. for Infants and Young Children Speakers Bur.; mem. Met. Washington chpt. Arthritis Found. With USAAF, 1946-47. Mem. Nat. Assn. Sci. Writers (life), Am. Med. Writers Assn., N.Y. Acad. Scis., Nat. Press Club. Avocations: book accumulating, reading history, woodworking. Office: 6808 Greyswood Rd Bethesda MD 20817-1541

RUBIN, ZICK, psychology educator, lawyer, writer; b. N.Y.C., Apr. 29, 1944; s. Eli and Adena (Lipschitz) R.; m. Carol Moses, June 21, 1969; children—Elihu James, Noam Moses. BA, Yale U., 1965; PhD, U. Mich., 1969; JD, Harvard U., 1988. Bar: Mass., 1988. Asst. to assoc. prof. Harvard U., Cambridge, Mass., 1969-76; Louis and Frances Salvage prof. social psychology Brandeis U., Waltham, Mass., 1976-89, adj. prof. psychology, 1989—; law clk. chief judge U.S. Ct. Appeals (1st cir.), 1988-89; assoc. Palmer & Dodge, Boston, 1990-93, counsel, 1994—; chmn. com. behavioral scis. Yale U. Coun., New Haven, 1981-86; mem. adv. bd. Palmer & Dodge Agy., 1994—. Author: Liking and Loving, 1973, Children's Friendships, 1980; co-author: Psychology, 1993; editor: Doing Unto Others, 1974, Relationships and Development, 1986; contbg. editor: Psychology Today, 1980-85; editorial bd.: Harvard Law Rev., 1986-88. Recipient Socio-Psychol. prize AAAS, 1969, Nat. Media award Am. Psychol. Found., 1980; grantee NSF, NIMH, Ford Found., Social Sci. Research Council, Found. Child Devel. Mem. ABA, Mass. Bar Assn., Boston Bar Assn., Am. Psychology-Law Soc., Authors Guild, Text and Acad. Authors Assn. (mem. coun. 1994-95), Soc. Exptl. Social Psychology, Phi Beta Kappa. Jewish. Club: Elihu (New Haven).

RUBINE, ROBERT SAMUEL, lawyer; b. Rockaway, N.Y., Feb. 28, 1947; s. George and Beatrice (Simon) R.; m. Marilyn Goldberg Rubine, Aug. 15, 1970; children: Seth B., Marisa H. BA, Queens Coll., 1968; JD, Syracuse U., 1971. Bar: N.Y. 1972, Fla. 1975; U.S. Dist. Ct. (ea. and so. dists.) N.Y., 1976; U.S. Supreme Ct. 1976. Trial atty. Legal Aid Soc. Nassau County, Mineola, N.Y., 1971-77; atty. Reifman and Rubine, Jericho, N.Y., 1977-79; ptnr. Stein, Rubine and Stein, Mineola, 1979-94, Rubine and Rubine, Mineola, 1995—; adj. prof. C.W. Post Coll., Greenvale, N.Y., 1979-82. Author: (chpt.) Criminal and Civil Investigation Handbook, 1981. Pres. Legal Aid Soc. Nassau County, 1994—; dir. Legal Aid Soc., Nassau County, 1989—. Avocation: golf. Home: 5 Woodland Rd Oyster Bay NY 11771 Office: Rubine and Rubine Attys at Law PLLC 114 Old Country Rd Mineola NY 11771-3910

RUBINFIEN, LEO H., photographer, filmmaker; b. Chgo., Aug. 16, 1953. Student, Reed Coll.; BFA, Calif. Inst. Arts, 1974; MFA, Yale U., 1976. Instr. in photography Swarthmore Coll., 1977, Sch. Visual Arts, N.Y.C., 1978-87; assoc. prof. art Fordham U., 1981-87; represented by Robert Mann Gallery, N.Y.C.; vis. lectr. Cooper Union, 1982. One man shows include Gastelli Gallery, N.Y., 1981, Fraenkel Gallery, San Francisco, 1982, 86, Robert Mann Gallery, N.Y.C., Met. Mus. Art, N.Y.C., 1992, Seibu Art Forum, Tokyo, 1993, Cleve. Mus. Art, 1994, Seattle Art Mus., 1994, Robert Mann Gallery, N.Y.C.; exhibited in group shows at Internat. Ctr. Photography, N.Y., 1981, Inst. Contemporary Arts, London, 1981, San Francisco Mus. Modern Art, 1981, George Eastman House, Rochester, N.Y., 1981, Corcoran Gallery, Washington, 1981, Mus. Modern Art, N.Y., 1984; dir., co-author (film) The Money Juggler, 1988, My Bed in the Leaves, 1990; author: (books) A Map of the East, 1992, 10 Takeoffs 5 Landings, 1994, (essays) A Love-Hate Relations, Artforum, 1978. Fellow Guggenheim Found., 1982-83, Asian Cult Coun., 1984. Home: 1 Furnace Dock Rd Croton On Hudson NY 10520-1406

RUBINO, VICTOR JOSEPH, law institute executive; b. N.Y.C., Dec. 25, 1940; s. Joseph V. and Olympia (Gayda) R.; 1 child, Victor Gayda. BA in Govt., Cornell U., 1962, LLB, 1965. Bar: N.Y. 1965, U.S. Dist. Ct. (so. dist.) N.Y. 1969. Staff atty. Westchester Legal Svcs., White Plains, N.Y., 1968-71; assoc. Squadron Ellenoff Plesent & Lehrer, N.Y.C., 1971; treas., program officer Council on Legal Edn., N.Y.C., 1971-79; assoc. dir. Practising Law Inst., N.Y.C., 1979-83, exec. dir., 1983—. Democratic candidate for N.Y. State Assembly, 1970, chmn. Rye (N.Y.) Human Rights Commn., 1975-76. Served to capt. U.S. Army, 1966-68. Mem. ABA, Assn. Bar City N.Y. Office: Practising Law Inst 810 7th Ave New York NY 10019

RUBINOFF, IRA, biologist, research administrator, conservationist; b. N.Y.C., Dec. 21, 1938; s. Jacob and Bessie (Rose) R.; m. Roberta Wolff, Mar. 19, 1961; 1 son, Jason; m. Anabella Guardia, Feb. 10, 1978; children: Andres, Ana. B.S., Queens Coll., 1959; A.M., Harvard U., 1960, Ph.D., 1963. Biologist, asst. dir. marine biology Smithsonian Tropical Research Inst., Balboa, Republic of Panama, 1964-70; asst. dir. sci. Smithsonian Tropical Research Inst., 1970-73, dir., 1973—; assoc. in ichthyology Harvard U., 1965—; courtesy prof. Fla. State U., Tallahassee, 1976—; mem. sci. adv. bd. Gorgas Meml. Inst., 1964-88; trustee Rare Animal Relief Effort, 1976-85; bd. dirs. Charles Darwin Found. for Galapagos Islands, 1977—; chmn. bd. fellowships and grants Smithsonian Instn., 1978-79; vis. fellow Wolfson Coll., Oxford (Eng.) U., 1980-81; vis. scientist Mus. Comparative Biology-Harvard U., 1987-88. Author Strategy for Preservation of Moist Tropical Forests; contbr. articles to profl. jours. Vice chmn. bd. dirs. Panama Canal Coll., 1989-93; bd. dirs. Internat. Sch. Panama, 1983-85, 90-93, Fundacion Natura, sec., bd. dirs., 1991—; bd. dirs. Earthwatch, 1995—; hon. dir. Instituto Latino Americano de Estudios Avanzados. Awarded Order of Vasco Nunez de Balboa of Republic of Panama. Fellow Linnean Soc. (London), AAAS, Am. Acad. Arts & Scis.; mem. Am. Soc. Naturalists, Soc. Study of Evolution, N.Y. Acad. Scis., Ancon Panama (bd. dirs.). Club: Cosmos (Washington). Home: Box 2072, Balboa Panama Office: Smithsonian Tropical Rsch Inst Unit 0948 APO AA 34002-0948

RUBINOFF, ROBERTA WOLFF, government administrator; b. N.Y.C., Aug. 26, 1939; d. Leon and Leah (Landauer) W.; m. Ira Rubinoff, 1961 (div. 1975); 1 child, Jason. BS, Queens Coll., 1959; Masters of Environ. Mgmt., Duke U., 1981. Biologist Smithsonian Tropical Rsch. Inst., Balboa, Canal Zone, 1966-75, marine sci. coord., 1975-79; asst. dir. Office Fellowships and Grants Smithsonian Instn., Washington, 1980-84, acting dir. Office Fellowships and Grants, 1984-85, dir. Office Fellowships and Grants, 1985—. Mem. AAAS, Am. Soc. Zoologists, Am. Inst. Biol. Sci. Office: Smithsonian Instn Office Fellowships & Grants 955 Lenfant Plz SW Ste 7000 Washington DC 20024-2119

RUBINOVITZ, SAMUEL, diversified manufacturing company executive; b. Boston, Dec. 26, 1929; s. Benjamin Ephraim and Pauline (Kaufman) R.; m. Phyllis Ann Silverstein; children: David Jay, Robert Neal. BS, MIT, 1951, MS, 1952. Sales engr. Clevite Transistor Products, Waltham, Mass., 1954-63; sales mgr. EG&G Inc., Wellesley, Mass., 1963-72, div. mgr., 1972-79, v.p., 1979-86, sr. v.p., 1986-89, exec. v.p., 1989-94; ret.; bd. dirs. KLA Instruments, Inc., Santa Clara, Calif., Richardson Electronics Ltd., Chgo., Kronos Inc., Waltham, Temptronic Corp., Newton, Mass., EG&G Inc., Wellesley, Mass., LTX Corp., Westwood, Mass. Served to 1st lt. USAF, 1952-54. Democrat. Jewish. Office: EG & G Inc 45 William St Wellesley MA 02181-4004

RUBINOWITZ, LEONARD S., lawyer, educator; b. 1943. BA, U. Wis.-Madison, 1965; LLB, Yale U., 1968. Bar: Conn. 1968. Spl. asst. to adminstr. HUD, Chgo., 1969-72; rsch. assoc. Ctr. for Urban Affairs, Northwestern U., Chgo., 1972-75, assoc. prof. law and urban affairs, 1975-80; prof., 1980—; Field assoc. Brookings Inst., 1975—. Author: Low Income Housing: Suburban Strategies, 1974. Office: Northwestern U Sch Law 375 E Chicago Ave Chicago IL 60611-3008*

RUBINROIT, HOWARD J., lawyer; b. Newark, Apr. 23, 1944. BA, Rutgers U., 1966; LLB, U. Pa., 1969. Bar: N.J. 1969, Calif. 1971. Law clk. to Hon. Nathan Jacobs N.J. Supreme Ct., 1969-70; ptnr. Sidley & Austin, L.A. Office: Sidley & Austin 555 W 5th St Fl 40 Los Angeles CA 90013-1010

RUBINS, ALEX, physical education educator; b. Cleve., Feb. 26, 1926; s. Harry and Nellie (Cutler) R.; m. Betty Buller, May 19, 1946; children: Ira Marc, Jan Merl, Brett Cory. BS in Phys. Edn. and Math., Case Western Res. U., 1949, MA in Ednl. Adminstrn., 1950, PhD in Ednl. Adminstrn., 1971. Tchr. math., athletic dir. Cleve. Pub. Schs., 1950-58, tchr. math. and adult edn., 1966; prof. phys. and health edn. and math. Cuyahoga Community Coll., Cleve., 1966—; pres. Keystone Mortgage Corp. and CCC Ins. Agy. Cleve., 1958-63; broker Realty Mortgage Svc., 1958-63; regional mgr. World Book Ency., 1963-66; football and basketball ofcl., 1946—; adminstr. religious sch. Fairmount Temple, Cleve., 1978—; dir. Red Wing Day Camp, summers 1950--58; visitor, evaluator community colls., Calif., 1978. Author: Programmed Learning Activities for Fencing, 1973. Tchr. religious sch. Park Synagogue, Heights Temple, Community Temple, Cleve., 1946-78; coach Little League Baseball, Cleveland Heights, Ohio, 1962-67; tchr. Cleve. Soc. for Blind, 1971—, County Jail, Cleve., 1981-85; reader Cleve. Soc. for Blind, 1971—; pub. speaker to community orgns., 1967—; lectr. Coun. Gardans Retirement Home, Cleve., 1985—; program dir. Elders Hostel, 1980—; div. head Jewish Welfare Fund, Cleve., 1970—. Master sgt. AUS, 1944-46, CBI. Named Advisor of Yr., Cuyahoga Community Coll., 1971; named to Founders wall as ofcl. Basketball Hall of Fame, 1974. Mem. AAUP, AAHPER and Dance, Midwest Alliance Health, Phys. Edn., Recreation and Dance, Ohio Assn. Health, Phys. Edn., Recreation and Dance (bd. dirs. 1980-85, Mentoring award 1990), Internat. Assn. Approved Basketball Ofcls., Ohio High Sch. Athletic Assn., Ohio Assn. 2-Yr. Colls. (past pres., bd. dirs.), Greater Cleve. Football Ofcls. Assn. (pres., bd. dirs., Outstanding Football Ofcl. award 1985), Jewish War Vets., B'nai B'rith. Avocations: bridge, crossword puzzles, jogging, writing poetry, sketching. Home: 1112 Rutherford Rd Cleveland OH 44112-3654 Office: Cuyahoga Community Coll 2900 Community College Ave Cleveland OH 44115-3123

RUBINSTEIN, AARON, lawyer; b. N.Y.C., Nov. 15, 1950; s. Jacob and Golda Rubinstein; m. Carri Sue Zogan, Mar. 3, 1974; children: David Michael, Jennifer Lauren. BA magna cum laude, Cornell U., 1972; JD, NYU, 1975. Bar: N.Y. 1976, U.S. Dist. Ct. (so. and ea. dists.) 1976, U.S. Supreme Ct. 1986. Assoc. Kaye, Scholer, Fierman, Hays & Handler, N.Y.C., 1975-84, ptnr., 1985—. Mem. ABA, N.Y. State Bar Assn., Ass. of Bar of City of N.Y., Order of Coif. Office: Kaye Scholer Fierman et al 425 Park Ave New York NY 10022-3506 also: KPMG Peat Marwick 365 Park Ave New York NY 10022-6009

RUBINSTEIN, ALVIN ZACHARY, political science educator, author; b. Bklyn., Apr. 23, 1927; s. Max and Sylvia (Stone) R.; m. Frankie Kimmelman, Nov. 12, 1960. BBA, CCNY, 1949; MA, U. Pa., 1950, PhD, 1954. Mem. faculty U. Pa., 1957—, prof. polit. sci., 1966—; vis. lectr. Queen Coll., 1959; vis. prof. U. Calif. at Santa Barbara, summer, 1968, Am. U., Cairo, 1971, Lehigh U., spring, 1973, U. Va., spring 1977, 80; chmn. grad. program internat. relations U. Pa., 1966-70; dir. Anspach Inst. Diplomacy and Fgn. Affairs, 1968-70; cons. Inst. Def. Analysis, 1966-70, Inst. for Fgn. Policy Analysis, 1976-81; vis. assoc. Russian Research Center, Harvard, 1956-57. Author: Communist Political Systems, 1966, (with P. Berton) Soviet Writings on Southeast Asia, 1968, The Soviets in International Organizations, 1964, The Foreign Policy of the Soviet Union, 3rd edit., 1972, Yugoslavia and the Nonaligned World, 1970; editor: Soviet and Chinese Influence in the Third World, 1975, Red Star on the Nile: The Soviet-Egyptian Influence Relationship Since the June War, 1977, The Great Game: Rivalry in the Persian Gulf and South Asia, 1983, The Arab-Israeli Conflict: Perspectives, 2nd edit., 1991, Moscow's Third World Strategy, 1988 (Marshall Shulman prize Am. Assn. Slavic Studies 1989); co-editor: Soviet and American Policies in the United Nations: A Twenty-Five Year Perspective, 1971, Soviet Foreign Policy Toward Western Europe, 1978, Soviet Foreign Policy Since World War II: Imperial and Global, 4th edit., 1992, Soviet Policy Toward Turkey, Iran and Afghanistan, 1982, Anti-Americanism in the Third World, 1985, Perestroika at the Crossroads, 1991, Russia and America: From Rivalry to Reconciliation, 1993, America's National Interest in a Post Cold War World, 1994, Regional Power Rivalries in the New Eurasia, 1995; book rev. editor Current History, 1959-69, mem. bd. editors, 1968—; mem. editl. bd. Studies in Comparative Communism, 1973-89, ORBIS, 1974, Soviet Union, 1974-80. Mem. bd. advisors Naval War Coll., 1983-85. Lt. USNR, 1954-56. Ford Found. fellow, 1956-57; Rockefeller Found. grantee, 1961-62; Guggenheim fellow, 1965-66; grantee Am. Philos. Soc., 1958, 59, 68, 73; NSF travel grant, 1970-71; Barra Found. research grant, 1970-71; resident scholar Bellagio Study and Conf. Center, Rockefeller Found., Italy, 1974; Earhart Found. research grantee, 1974; Joint Com. on Soviet Studies of Am. Council Learned Socs. and Social Sci. Research Council grantee, 1975; vis. fellow Clare Hall, Cambridge (Eng.) U., 1974-75; NATO research fellow, 1977; Earhart Found. research grantee, 1979, 81; sr. fellow Fgn. Policy Research Inst., 1981—; sr. assoc. St. Anthony's Coll., Oxford U., spring 1985. Home: The Mermont Apt 503 Bryn Mawr PA 19010 Office: Univ Pa Dept Polit Sci SH 217 Philadelphia PA 19104-6215

RUBINSTEIN, ARTHUR B., composer. Scores include (films) The Great Bank Hoax, 1978, On the Right Track, 1981, Whose Life Is It Anyway?, 1981, Fake Out, 1982, Deal of the Century, 1983, Blue Thunder, 1983, Wargames, 1983, Lost in America, 1985, Hyper Sapien, 1986, The Best of Times, 1986, Stakeout, 1987, Defense Play, 1988, The Hard Way, 1991, Another Stakeout, 1993, (TV movies) The Prince of Central Park, 1977, Portrait of a Stripper, 1979, Aunt Mary, 1979, The Great American Traffic Jam, 1980, Portrait of a Rebel: Margaret Sanger, 1980, The Phoenix, 1981, Rivkin, Bounty Hunter, 1981, Not Just Another Affair, 1982, Skeezer, 1982, It Came Upon the Midnight Clear, 1984, Sins of the Past, 1984, The Parade, 1984, The Cartier Affair, 1984, Murder in Space, 1985, Doubletake, 1985, Doing Life, 1986, Love Among Thieves, 1987, Roses Are for the Rich, 1987, The Betty Ford Story, 1987, Once Upon a Texas Train, 1988, Inherit the Wind, 1988, Internal Affairs, 1988, Where the Hell's That Gold?!!, 1988, Nightmare at Bitter Creek, 1988, Indiscreet, 1988, Agatha Christie's The Man in the Brown Suit, 1989, Unconquered, 1989, Gideon Oliver: Sleep Well, Professor Oliver, 1989, Baywatch: Panic at Malibu Pier, 1989, Guts and Glory: The Rise and Fall of Oliver North, 1989, Line of Fire: The Morris Dees Story, 1991, Crazy From the Heart, 1991, Fatal Friendship, 1991, Danielle Steel's Secrets, 1992, When No One Would Listen, 1992, Deep Trouble, 1993, Caught in the Act, 1993, Hart to Hart Returns, 1993, Hart to Hart: Crimes of the Hart, 1994. Office: Gorfaine Schwartz Agency 3301 Barham Blvd Ste 201 Los Angeles CA 90068-1477

RUBINSTEIN, EVA (ANNA), photographer; b. Buenos Aires, Argentina, 1933; d. Arthur and Aniela (Mlynarska) R.; m. William Sloane Coffin Jr., 1956 (div. 1968); children: Amy, Alexander (dec.), David. Ballet tng., Paris, N.Y.C., Calif., 1938-53; student, Scripps Coll., 1950-51, UCLA, 1952-53; student in photography, Lisette Model, 1969, Jim Hughes, 1971, Ken Heyman, 1970, Diane Arbus, 1971. lectr. numerous workshops, seminars, confs.; instr. photo seminars Lodz Film Sch., Poland, 1986, 86-87. Dancer, actress: off-Broadway and Broadway, including original prodn. The Diary of Anne Frank, 1955-56; European dance tour, 1955; one-person shows of photographs include Underground Gallery, N.Y.C., 1972, Dayton Art Inst., Ohio, 1973, Arles Festival, France, 1975, Canon Photo Gallery, Amsterdam, 1975, Neikrug Gallery, N.Y.C., 1975, 79, 81, 82, 85, La Photogalerie, Paris, 1975, Friends of Photography, Carmel, Calif., 1975, Galerie 5.6, Ghent, Belgium, 1976, Gallery Trochenpresse, Berlin, 1977, Frumkin Gallery, Chgo., 1977, Galeria Sinisca, Rome, 1979, Hermitage Found. Mus., Norfolk, Va., 1982, Photographers Gallery, London, 1983, Galerie Forum Labo, Arles, France, 1983, Galerie Nicephore, Lyon, France, 1983, Image Gallery, Madrid, 1984, Muzeum Sztuki, Lodz, Poland, 1984, Il Diaframma/Canon Gallery, Milan, 1984, A.R.P.A. Gallery, Bordeaux, 1984, Chateau d'Eau, Toulouse, France, 1985, Galerie Demi-Teinte, Paris, 1985, Associated Artist Photographers galleries in Warsaw, Krakow, Lodz, Katowice and Gdansk, Poland, 1985-86, Foto/Medium/Art Gallery, Wroclaw, Poland, 1986, Visions Gallery, San Francisco, 1986, Canon Galerie, Paris, 1986, Salone Internat. SICOF, Milan, 1987, St. Krzysztof Gallery, Lodz, 1987, L'Image Fixe, Lyon, 1988, Artotheque, Grenoble, 1988, Neikrug Photographica, N.Y.C., 1989, Heuser Art Ctr. Gallery, Bradley U., Peoria, Ill., 1989, 3-os Encontros da Imagem, Braga, Portugal, 1989, Bibliotheque Nat. Galerie Colbert, Paris, 1989, Galerie Picto-Bastille, Paris, 1989-90, Portfolio Gallery, London, 1990, Vaison-La-Romaine, France, 1990, Hist. Mus. of City of Lodz, 1990, Galerie Artem, Quimper, France, 1993, Galerie F.N.A.C. Etoile, Paris, 1994, other F.N.A.C. galleries (France, Belgium, Spain), 1994—, Galerie Augustus, Berlin, 1995, L'Imagerie, Lannion, France, 1995, Zacheta Gallery, Warsaw, 1996; group shows include, Internat. Salon, Krakow, Poland, 1971, Delgado Mus., New Orleans, 1972, Neikrug Gallery, 1972, 73, 75, Salone Internationale, Milan, Italy, 1973, Photo-OVO, Montreal, Que., Can., 1974, Nat. Portrait Gallery, London, 1976, Hera Gallery, R.I., 1977, Musee National d'Art Moderne Georges Pompidou, Paris, 1977, Centre Culturel de l'ouest Aquitain, Bordeaux, France, 1978, Fotografiska Museet, Stockholm, 1978, Nat. Arts Club, N.Y.C., 1979, Chrysler Mus., Norfolk, 1979, Maine Photog. Gallery, 1981, Floating Found. Photography, N.Y.C., 1970, 71, 72, 73, 79, 82, Ffoto Gallery, Cardiff, Wales, 1983, Musée d'Art Moderne de la Ville de Paris, 1987-88, Boca Raton (Fla.) Mus., 1989, Galerie PICTO Bastille, Paris, 1989, Galerie Arena, Arles, 1989-90, Settimana della Fotografia, Palermo, 1990, Festival de l'Image, Le Mans, France, 1993, Quimper (France), 1995, Galerie Camera Obscura, Paris, 1996; represented: in permanent collections Library of Congress, Washington, Met. Mus. Art, N.Y.C., Bibliotheque Nationale, Paris, Musee Reattu, Arles, France, Kalamazoo Inst. Arts, Israel Mus., Jerusalem, Fotografiska Museet, Stockholm, Muzeum Sztuki, Lodz, Poland, Histo Mus. of City of Lodz, others; author 2 monographs, 2 ltd. edit. portfolios with introductions by John Vachon and André Kertész; contbr. photographs in various books, mags., profl. jours. *Making photographs is my way of exploring the questions that keep me alive by ever leading to further questions.*

RUBINSTEIN, FREDERIC ARMAND, lawyer; b. Antwerp, Belgium, Apr. 20, 1931; came to U.S., 1942; s. Samuel N. and Steffa (Warrenreich) R.; m. Susan August, Dec. 24, 1968; 1 child, Nicolas Eric August Rubinstein. BA, Cornell U., 1953, JD, 1955. Bar: N.Y. 1955. Assoc. Law Offices of I. Robert Feinberg, N.Y.C., 1955-60; assoc. Guggenheimer & Untermyer, N.Y.C., 1960-65, ptnr., 1965-85; ptnr. Kelley Drye & Warren, N.Y.C., 1985—. Vice chmn. zoning & planning com. Local Community Bd. # 6, N.Y.C., 1980-86. Mem. ABA (bus. law sect., emerging growth ventures subcom., chmn. 1988—), Cornell Club of N.Y. Office: Kelley Drye & Warren 101 Park Ave New York NY 10178

RUBINSTEIN, JACK HERBERT, health center administrator, pediatrics educator; b. N.Y.C., Aug. 4, 1925; s. Saul David and Anna (Gordon) R.; m. Thelma Regenstreif, Nov. 22, 1952 (dec. June 1988); m. Marlene Florence Tibbs, Sept. 1, 1990. AB, Columbia U., 1947; MD, Harvard U., 1952. Diplomate Am. Bd. Pediatrics. Intern in pediatrics Beth Israel Hosp., Boston, 1952-53; intern in pediatrics Mass. Gen. Hosp., Boston, 1953-54, sr. asst. resident, 1954-55; sr. asst. resident Children's Hosp. Med. Ctr., Cin., 1955-56, asst. med. dir., fellow pediatrics outpatient dept., 1956-57, attending pediatrician, 1957—; instr., asst. prof., assoc. prof. U. Cin., 1956-70, prof., 1970—; dir. Univ. Affiliated Cin. Program for Mentally Retarded, Cin., 1967-74, Univ. Affiliated Cin. Ctr. for Devel. Disorders, Cin., 1974—; dir. Hamilton County Diagnostic Clinic for Mentally Retarded, Cin., 1957-74, Children's Neuromuscular Diagnostic Clinic, Cin., 1962-74. Contbg. author: Medical Aspect of Mental Retardation, 1965, 2d edit., 1978; also articles. Mem. Ohio Devel. Disabilities Planning Coun., Columbus, Ohio Maternal and Child Health Block Grant Cons. Group, Columbus. With USAAF, 1944-46, ETO. Recipient longterm svc. award Children's Hosp. Med. Ctr., 1989, Founder's award Cin. Pediatric Soc., 1989. Fellow Am. Acad. Pediatrics; mem. Am. Pediatric Soc., Cin. Pediatric Soc., Teratology Soc., Am. Assn. on Mental Retardation, Am. Assn. Univ. Affiliated Programs for Persons with Devel. Disabilities (pres. 1978-79), Phi Beta Kappa, Alpha Omega Alpha. Achievements include reporting Rubinstein-Taybi syndrome, 1963. Home: 541 Ludlow Ave Cincinnati OH 45220-1581 Office: Univ Affiliated Cin Ctr for Devel Disorders 3333 Burnet Ave Cincinnati OH 45229-3026

RUBINSTEIN, MOSHE FAJWEL, engineering educator; b. Miechow, Poland, Aug. 13, 1930; came to U.S., 1950, naturalized, 1965; s. Shlomo and Sarah (Rosen) R.; m. Zafrira Gorstein, Feb. 3, 1953; children—Iris, Dorit. B.S., UCLA, 1954, M.S., 1957, Ph.D., 1961. Designer Murray Erick Assos. (engrs. and architects), Los Angeles, 1954-56; structural designer Victor Gruen Assos., Los Angeles, 1956-61; asst. prof. U. Calif. at Los Angeles, 1961-64, assoc. prof. dept. engring., 1964-69, prof., 1969—, chmn. engring. systems dept., 1970-75, program dir. modern engring. for execs. program, 1965-70; cons. Pacific Power & Light Co., Portland, Oreg., Northrop Corp., U.S. Army, NASA Research Center, Langley, Tex. Instruments Co., Hughes Space System Div., U.S. Army Sci. Adv. Com., Kaiser Aluminum and Chem. Corp., IBM Corp., TRW. Author: (with W.C. Hurty) Dynamics of Structures, 1964 (Yugoslavian transl. 1973), Matrix Computer Analysis of Structures, 1966 (Japanese transl. 1974), Structural Systems, Statics Dynamics and Stability, 1970 (Japanese transl. 1979), Patterns of Problem Solving, 1975, (with K. Pfeiffer) Concepts in Problem Solving, 1980, Tools for Thinking and Problem Solving, 1986; IEEE Press Videotapes; Models for People Driven Quality, 1991, Quality through Innovation, 1991, Creativity for Ongoing Total Quality, 1993, Relentless Improvement, 1993, (with I.R. Firstenberg) Patterns of Problem Solving, 2d edit., 1995. Recipient Disting. Tchr. award UCLA Acad. Senate, 1964, Western Electric Fund award Am. Soc. Engring. Edn., 1965, Disting. Tchr. trophy Engring. Student Soc., UCLA, 1966; Sussman prof. for disting. visitor Technion-Israel Inst. Tech., 1967-68; named Outstanding Faculty Mem., UCLA Engring. Alumni award, 1979, Outstanding UCLA Civil Engring. Alumni award, 1990, Outstanding Faculty Mem., State of Calif. Command Coll., 1987, 88, 89, 94, 95; Fulbright-Hays fellow, Yugoslavia and Eng., 1975-76. Mem. ASCE, Am. Soc. Engring. Edn., Seismol. Soc. Am., Sigma Xi, Tau Beta Phi. Research in use of computers in structural systems, analysis and synthesis; problem solving and decision theory. Home: 10488 Charing Cross Rd Los

Angeles CA 90024-2646 Office: UCLA Sch Engring and Applied Sci Los Angeles CA 90024

RUBINSTEIN, ROBERT LAWRENCE, anthropologist, gerontologist; b. Bklyn., Jan. 3, 1951; s. Jack Rubinstein and Enid Farley; m. Susan Hersker, Feb. 13, 1980; children: Lily, Gabriel. BA, Case Western Res. U., 1972; MA, Bryn Mawr Coll., 1974, PhD, 1978. Rsch. anthropologist Polisher Rsch. Inst. of the Phila. Geriatric Ctr., 1981-89, asst. dir. rsch., 1989-91, assoc. dir. rsch., 1991-92, dir. rsch., 1992—. Author: Singular Paths: Old Men Living Alone, 1986, Elders Living Alone, 1992. NIH grantee. Fellow Gerontol. Soc. Am.; mem. Am. Anthrop. Assn. Achievments include research on old age and aging, older men, childless elders, home environments of older people. Office: Polisher Rsch Inst Phila Geriatric Ctr 5301 Old York Rd Philadelphia PA 19141-2912

RUBINSTEIN, SIDNEY JACOB, orthopedic technologist; b. Boston, July 4, 1936; s. Harry and Shirley (Block) R.; m. Sheila Ruby Goldstein, Sept. 1, 1955 (div. 1974); children: Ronda, Barry, Terry, Debra, Neysa; m. Margaret Catherine Burns, Nov. 19, 1976; 1 stepchild, Jerry Hiltonen. Cert., Dimock Ctr., Boston, 1971. Cert. Nat. Bd. of Cert. of Orthopaedic Technologists. Chief orthopaedic technologist Beverly (Mass.) Hosp., 1971-82; orthopaedic technologist Beverly Orthopaedic Assoc., 1982—; owner Orthotics Lab., Danvers, Mass., 1993—. Mem. Nat. Assn. Orthopaedic Technologists (pres. 1992—), Can. Soc. Orthopaedic Technologists, Venezuela Soc. Orthopaedic Technologists, New Eng. Soc. Orthopaedic Technologists (pres. 1988-92). Democrat. Jewish. Avocations: music, traveling, theater, literature. Office: Orthotic Lab 74 Elm St Danvers MA 01923

RUBIO, SUZANNE SARAH, ballet dancer; b. Montreal, Que.. Grad., Nat. Ballet Sch., Toronto, Ont., 1983. Mem. corps de ballet Royal Winnipeg Ballet, Man., 1985-90, soloist, 1990-94, prin. dancer, 1994—; invited guest artist Dance in Canada Gala, Calgary, Alta., 1989. Stage appearances include (musicals) Kismet, 1984, Mame, 1985, (film) The Big Top, Flamenco at 5:15; prin. roles in The Nutcracker, Rodeo, Swan Lake, The Dream, The Sleeping Beauty, Romeo and Juliet, Tarantella, Ballo Della Regina, Allegro Brillante, Piano Variations III, 5 Tangos, Four Last Songs, others. Recipient Can. Coun. Arts grant, 1984, 2nd prize Helsinki Internat. Ballet Competition, 1991. Mem. Can. Actors Equity Assn., Alliance Can. Cinema, TV & Radio Artists. Office: Royal Winnipeg Ballet, 380 Graham Ave, Winnipeg, MB Canada R3C 4K2

RUBIO-LOTVIN, BORIS, obstetrician-gynecologist; b. Toluca, Mexico, Mar. 26, 1927; s. Leon and Elena (Lotvin) R.; m. Paulina Freidberg, June 24, 1951; children: Martha, Luis, Susana. BS, Scientific Literary Inst., 1942; MD, Nat. U. Mexico, 1949. Intern Gen. Hosp., Mexico City, 1947-48; resident Beth Israel Hosp., Boston, 1949-54; chief clin. rsch. Red Cross Hosp., Mexico City, 1961-63, chief dept. gynecology, 1963-68; prof. ob.-gyn. Nat. U. Mexico Sch. Medicine, Mexico City, 1966—, prof. endocrinology of reproduction, 1968—; chief ob.-gyn. Am. British Cowdray Hosp., Mexico City, 1970-71, chief rsch. and teaching, 1971-74. Author: Endocrinology, 1964, Hormones in Gynecology (Spanish), 1996; editor numerous books; contbr. articles to profl. jours. Recipient Gold Medal of Honor Mex. Red Cross, 1967. Mem. Mex. Philatelic Soc. (pres. 1983-84), Mex. Soc. Geography and History, Rotary, Ars Medici (pres. 1962-64). Home: Apt 602, Sierra Vertientes 345, 11000 Mexico City Mexico

RUBLE, RANDALL TUCKER, theologian, educator, academic administrator; b. Greenville, Va., Apr. 15, 1932; s. William Cecil and Carrie Mae (Connor) R.; m. Martha L. Grant, Sept. 6, 1958; children: John, Jeffrey, Ellen. A.B., Erskine Coll., 1958, B.D., 1961; Th.M., Princeton Theol. Sem., 1962; Ph.D., U. Edinburgh, 1964. Prof. Hebrew and Old Testament Erskine Sem., Due West, S.C., 1965—, v.p., dean, 1976—; supply pastor Abbeville (S.C.) Assoc. Ref. Presbyn. Ch., 1967—; chmn. N.Am. and Carribean area World Alliance of Reformed Chs., 1979-80. Author: The Ten Commandents For Our Day, 1971; contbr. articles to jours., mags. Mem. Town Council, Due West, 1972-75; chmn. Christian Prison Ministries, 1987—. Served with USAF, 1951-55. Mem. Soc. Bibl. Lit., Brit. Old Testament Soc., Nat. Assn. Profs. of Hebrew, S.C. Acad. Religion, Atlanta Theol. Assn. (pres. 1990—). Presbyterian. Home and Office: PO Box 172 Due West SC 29639-0172

RUBOTTOM, DONALD JULIAN, management consultant; b. Tulsa, Sept. 29, 1926; s. George William and Nellie Dorcas (Core) R.; m. Wanda Mae Stockton, Apr. 29, 1951; children: Rinda Louise, Joy Lynn, Donald Jay, Jill Anna. BS in Fin., Okla. State U., 1951; postgrad., Tulsa U. Chartered fin. analyst; cert. mgmt. cons. V.p., trust officer 1st Nat. Bank & Trust Co., Tulsa, 1955-56; exec. v.p., trust officer, dir. F&M Bank & Trust Co., Tulsa, 1966-68; pres. Rubottom, Dudash & Assocs., Tulsa, 1968—; tchr. Boston Ave. United Meth. Ch., Tulsa, 1962—. With U.S. Army, 1945-46. Mem. Inst. Mgmt. Cons., Nat. Assn. Bus. Economists, CFA Inst., Okla. Soc. Fin. Analysts, S.W. Regional Assn., Small Bus. Investments Cos. (pres. 1979), Tulsa Knife and Fork Club (pres. 1985-86), Tulsa So. Tennis Club, Rotary (pres. 1988-89, dist. gov. 1993-94). Avocations: tennis, skiing, gardening. Home: 2450 E 47th Pl Tulsa OK 74105-5112 Office: Rubottom Dudash & Assocs Inc 4870 S Lewis Ave Ste 180 Tulsa OK 74105-5172

RUBOTTOM, ROY RICHARD, JR., retired diplomat and educator, consultant; b. Brownwood, Tex., Feb. 13, 1912; s. Roy Richard and Jennie Eleanor (Watkins) R.; m. Billy Ruth Young, Dec. 23, 1938; children: Eleanor Ann Rubottom Odden, Frank, John. BS, So. Meth. U., 1932, MA, 1933; postgrad., U. Tex.; LLD, Southwestern Coll., Winfield, Kans., 1968, Cen. Meth. Coll., Fayette, Mo., 1985. Asst. dean student life U. Tex., 1937-41; apptd. fgn. service officer, 1947; sec. of embassy and consul Bogota, Colombia, 1947-49; officer-in-charge Mex. affairs State Dept., 1950, dep. dir. Middle Am. Affairs, 1951, dir., 1952-53; 1st sec. embassy Madrid, 1953, counselor of embassy, 1954, dir. U.S. Ops. Mission, 1954-56; asst. sec. of state for inter-Am. affairs, 1957-60, U.S. Ambassador to Argentina, 1960-62; advisor Naval War Coll., Newport, R.I., 1962-64; v.p. So. Meth. U., Dallas, 1964-71, prof. polit. sci. emeritus, 1975—; dir. Ctr. of Ibero-Am. Civilization, 1975-77; pres. U. Americas, Puebla, Mex., 1971-73; dir. Office Internat. Affairs, Dallas, 1985-87; sr. fgn. rels. advisor Dean Internat., Dallas, 1996—. Co-author: Spain and the U.S. Since W.W. II, 1984. Active Scouting U.S.A. Served with USNR, 1941-46. Recipient Silver Beaver award Boy Scouts Am., 1975, Inter-Am. award Boy Scouts Am., Silver Buffalo, 1993. Mem. Lambda Chi Alpha, Pi Sigma Alpha. Methodist. Lodge: Rotary. Office: 3429 University Blvd Dallas TX 75205-1833

RUBOW, W. STEVEN, food company executive; b. Chgo., July 15, 1941; s. Walter Franklin and Lorna (Neeley) R.; m. Sharon Jean Matheson, Nov. 22, 1961; children: Steven, Tamara, Brian, Starley, Jennifer, Adam, Neeley, Jonathan, Angela, Mary. BA, Brigham Young U., 1963; MS, Lake Forest Coll., 1973. V.p. merchandising Jewel Food Stores, Chgo., 1972-82; v.p. mktg. Star Market, Boston, 1982-87; v.p. perishables Topco Assocs., Inc., Skokie, Ill., 1987-90, sr. v.p. perishables, 1990, exec. v.p., 1991, pres., CEO, 1992—, also bd. dirs. Bishop L.D.S. Ch., 1984-87, counselor stake presidency, 1988—. Mem. Midwest Frozen Food Assn. (pres. 1972-73). Republican. Avocations: reading, genealogy. Office: Topco Assocs Inc 7711 Gross Point Rd Skokie IL 60077-2615*

RUBRIGHT, JAMES ALFRED, oil and gas company executive; b. Phila., Dec. 17, 1946; s. James Alfred and Helen Lucille (Evans) R.; children: Noah Michael, Benjamin James, Jaime Anne, Nathaniel Drew, James McCurdy; m. Mary Elizabeth Angelich, Dec. 30, 1988. BA, Yale U., 1969; JD, U. Va., 1972. Bar: Ga. 1972. Ptnr. King & Spalding, Atlanta, 1972-94; sr. v.p., gen. counsel Sonat Inc., Birmingham, 1994—. Mem. ABA. Office: Sonat Inc 1900 5th Ave N Birmingham AL 35203-2610 also: Sonat Inc PO Box 2563 Birmingham AL 35202-2563

RUBRIGHT, ROYAL CUSHING, lawyer; b. Denver, Nov. 27, 1909; s. John Compton and Marie (Popovich) R.; m. Dorothy Kelley, Jan. 4, 1985; 1 child, Lynnell. BA, LLB, U. Colo., 1932, LLM, 1933. Bar: Colo. 1933. Pvt. practice law Denver, 1933-40; ptnr. Fairfield & Woods, P.C., Denver, 1940-90; ret., 1990; part-time instr. law U. Denver; spl. lectr. law U. Colo. Recipient William Lee Knous award U. Colo. Law Sch. Mem. ABA, Colo. Bar Assn. (mem. award deserving sect.), Denver Bar Assn. (pres., award of merit), City Club, Rotary, Masons, Pi Kappa Alpha. Home: 7877 E Mississippi Ave Apt 601 Denver CO 80231-2035

RUBY, BURTON BENNETT, men's apparel manufacturer; b. Chgo., Oct. 27, 1919; s. Jacob M. and Fay S. (Silver) R.; m. June Stinnett Zylstra, Sept. 13, 1975; children: Thomas M., Patricia Ruby Sinervo, Roger J., Pamela J. Karger, Kirk D. Zylstra, Julie B. Zylstra, John A. Zylstra. B.S., U. Wis., 1941; LLD (hon.), Purdue U., 1987. With Jaymar-Ruby, Inc., Michigan City, Ind., 1940—; plant supt., then v.p. Jaymar-Ruby, Inc., 1946-54, exec. v.p., 1954-57, pres., chief exec. officer, 1957-81, chmn., 1981—, chief exec. officer, 1981-85; bd. dirs. Hartmarx Inc., Horizon Bankcorp, Ruby Chevrolet Inc., Nixon Newspapers, Inc.; past adv. bd. Fashion Inst. Tech., midwest Liberty Mut.; chancellor's adv. bd. Purdue NC. Chmn. bd. Meml. Hosp. of Michigan City Found., 1962; bd. dirs. Michigan City YMCA, pres., 1952. Served with AUS, 1943-45. Decorated Bronze Star; recipient Brotherhood award NCCJ, 1979, Disting. Service award Michigan City Jaycees, 1949, Sagamor of Wabash, 1985. Mem. Men's Fashion Assn. (adv. bd. dirs.), Am. Apparel Mfrs. Assn. (dir., sec.chmn. 1987), Trouser Inst. Am. (pres. 1954), World Bus. Council (sec., dir.), Chgo. Presidents Orgn., Am. Legion. Clubs: Standard, Chicago Yacht; Pottawattomie Country (Michigan City), Michigan City Yacht (Michigan City); B'nai B'rith (pres. 1949, lodge Humanitarian of Year award 1980). Lodges: Rotary (Paul Harris fellow 1978); Elks. Patentee garment constrn. Office: Jaymar-Ruby Inc 5000 South Ohio St Michigan City IN 46360-7740*

RUBY, CHARLES LEROY, law educator, lawyer, civic leader; b. Carthage, Ind., Dec. 28, 1900; s. Edgar Valentine and Mary Emma (Butler) R.; certificate Ball State U., 1921-22; AB, Cen. Normal Coll., 1924, LLB, 1926, BS, 1931, BPE, 1932; MA, Stanford, 1929; JD, Pacific Coll. of Law, 1931; PhD, Olympic U., 1933; m. Rachael Elizabeth Martindale, Aug. 30, 1925; children: Phyllis Arline (Mrs. Norman Braskat), Charles L., Martin Dale. Prin., Pine Village (Ind.) High Sch., 1923-25; Glenwood (Ind.) Pub. Schs., 1925-26; tchr. El Centro (Calif.) Pub. Sch., 1926-27, Fresno Cen. (Calif.) Union High Sch., 1927-29; prof. law Fullerton Coll., 1929-66; prof. edn. Armstrong Coll., summer 1935, Cen. Normal Coll., summers 1929-33; admitted to Ind. bar, 1926, U.S. Supreme Ct. bar, 1970; pres. Ret. Service Vol. Program, North Orange County, Calif., 1973-76, 83-84; dir. North Orange County Vol. Bur., Fullerton Sr. Citizens Task Force. Life trustee, co-founder Continuing Learning Experiences program Calif. State U., Fullerton, hon. chmn. fund com. Gerontology Bldg; founder, dir. Fullerton Pub. Forum, 1929-39; founder Elks Nat. Found.; co-founder, benefactor Gerontology Ctr. Calif. State U., Fullerton; pres. Fullerton Rotary, 1939-40, hon. mem., 1983—; mem. U.S. Assay Commn., 1968—; mem. Orange County Dem. Cen. Com., 1962-78; bd. dirs. Fullerton Sr. Multi-purpose Ctr., 1981—; bd. dirs. Orange County Sr. Citizens Adv. Council; mem. pres.'s com. Calif. State U., Fullerton. Recipient Medal of Merit, Am. Numis. Assn., 1954, Spl. Commendation Calif. State Assembly, 1966, 88, Calif. State Senate, 1978, 86, Commendation Ind. Sec. of State, 1984, Commendation Bd. Suprs. Orange County, 1985, Commendation Fullerton City Council, 1986, 88, Commendation Orange County Bd. Supervisors, 1986, Commendation Calif. State Senate, 1986, Commendation Exec. Com. Pres. Calif. State U., Fullerton, 1986, Commendation Calif. gov., 1988; Charles L. and Rachael E. Ruby Gerontology Ctr. named in his and late wife's honor, Calif. State U., Fullerton. Fellow Ind. Bar Found.; mem. Pres. Assocs. Calif. State U. Fullerton, Fullerton Coll. Assocs. (named Spl. Retiree of Yr. 1986, Commendation 1986), Calif. (life, pres. So. sect. 1962-63, treas. 1964-65, pres. 1960-61, dir. 1956-65), pres. Fullerton Secondary Tchrs. Assn., Orange County Tchrs. Assn. (pres. 1953-55), Fullerton Coll. (pres. 1958-60) Tchrs. Assn., NEA (life), Ind. Bar Assn., Stanford U. Law Soc., Calif. State Council Edn., Am. Numismatic Assn. (gov. 1951-53, life adv. bd.), Ind. Bar Assn. (hon. life, Golden Career award 1983), Calif. Bus. Educators Assn. (hon. life), Calif. Assn. Univ. Profs., Pacific S.W. Bus. Law Assn. (pres. 1969-70, life), Numismatic Assn. So. Calif. (life, pres. 1961), Calif. Numis. Assn., Indpls. Coin Club (hon. life), Los Angeles Coin Club (hon. life), U.S. Supreme Ct. Hist. Soc., Calif. Town Hall, North Orange County Mus. Assn. (life, benefactor dir.), Stanford U. Alumni Assn. (life), Old Timers Assay Commn. (life), Fullerton Archeology (hon. life, benefactor dir.). Methodist. Clubs: Elks, Fullerton Coll. Vets. (hon. life). Contbr. articles in field to profl. jours. Home: 308 N Marwood Ave Fullerton CA 92632-1139

RUBY, MICHAEL, magazine executive. Editor U.S. News and World Report, Washington. Office: US News & World Report 2400 N St NW Washington DC 20037-1153*

RUBY, RALPH, JR., vocational business educator; b. Newburgh, N.Y., Apr. 11, 1944; m. Dorothy Nelle Privette; children: Laconya Dannet, Ralph III, Vanessa Rae. AAS, Orange County C.C., 1968; BS, U. Tenn., Knoxville, 1969, MS in Bus. Edn., 1972; EdD, U. Mo., Columbia, 1975. Cert. tchr., adminstr., N.Y. Tchr. keyboarding, bus. law Valley Cen. High Sch., Montgomery, N.Y., 1969-76, chair bus. dept., 1974-75; asst. prof. vocat. bus. edn. U. Ark., Fayetteville, 1976-79; from asst. prof. to prof. bus. edn., coord. vocat. bus. edn. Ark. State U., State University, 1979—; mem. ednl. adv. com. 26th Congl. Dist., N.Y.; vis. prof. McGill U., Montreal, Que., Can., 1977; acctg. author Gregg divsn. McGraw-Hill Book Co., 1978—; presenter workshops, tngs. programs. Author: Rough Draft Typing Practice, 1980, Target Type!: Improving Speed and Accuracy, 1987, Word Processing and Editing Techniques, 1988, Real Life Keyboarding Applications: (Word Processor, Data Base, Spreadsheet), 1990, Top Row Target Type, 1991, Starship Speller, 1991, Number Pad Tutor, 1991, Lotus in Your Classroom, 1991, WordPerfect in Your Classroom, 1992, Microsoft Works in Your Classroom, 1993, The Big Board Stock Market (simulation), 1993, PageMaker in Your Classroom, 1993, MS-DOS Made Easy, 993, WordPerfect for Desktop Publications, 1993, Microsoft Windows in Your Classroom, 1994, Mystery at Laser Age Hardware, 1994, The Class Works, 1994, WordPerfect in Your Classroom Using the MacIntosh, 1994, PageMaker in Your Classroom for Windows, 1996, WordPerfect for Desktop Publishing, 1996, Quattao Pao in Your Classroom, 1996, Espionage at International Electronics, 1996; editor Jour. Edn. for Bus, 1980—, also others. Mem. Am. Vocat. Assn. (life), Nat. Bus. Edn. Assn., So. Bus. Edn. Assn., Nat. Assn. Tchr. Edn. for Bus. and Office Edn. (life), Delta Pi Epsilon, Kappa Delta Pi, Phi Delta Kappa (life). Office: Ark State U Coll Bus State University AR 72467

RUBY, RUSSELL (GLENN), lawyer; b. Albany, Mo., Nov. 19, 1911; s. Gordon Romeo and Minnie (Hazelrigg) R.; m. Elizabeth Bradford Popkin, Feb. 11, 1939 (dec. Aug. 1967); children: Michael Gordon, Adrienne Elizabeth, Glenn Russell; m. Dorothea King, 1972 (dec. Dec. 1991). Student, Palmer Coll., 1929-31; B.J., U. Mo., 1933; LL.B., Tulsa U., 1939. Bar: Okla. 1939, U.S. Dist. Ct. (ea. dist.) Okla. 1941, U.S. Supreme Ct. 1957. Pvt. practice, Muskogee, 1939—; spl. agt. FBI, 1942-47; pres. Mandire Corp., 1974—. Mem. Okla. Ho. of Reps., 1955-66; mem. Muskogee City Coun., 1968-72, 76-88, vice mayor, 1968-72, dep. mayor, 1976-83, 84-88, mayor, 1983-84; chmn. Muskogee City-County Port Authority, 1974-76; mem. Muskogee Met. Planning Commn., 1968-72, 76-88, chmn., 1978-79; mem. small cities adv. com. Nat. League Cities, 1980-84; trustee Okla. Mcpl. Pension Fund, 1980-84; bd. dirs. Muskogee Community Concert Assn., Kate Frank Manor, Family Guidance Center; chmn. bd. trustees Muskogee Pub. Libr., 1986-88. Named Outstanding Older Oklahoman Eastern Okla. Devel. Dist., 1984. Mem. ABA, Okla. Bar Assn. (50 Yr. plaque 1989), Muskogee Bar Assn. (past pres., 50 Yr. plaque 1989), Assn. Fed. Attys., Soc. Former Agts. FBI, SAR, Masons, Shriners (potentate 1970), Jesters, Elks. Democrat. Episcopalian. Address: 4500 Girard St Muskogee OK 74401-1543

RUCH, CHARLES P., academic administrator; b. Longbranch, N.J., Mar. 25, 1938; s. Claud C. and Marcella (Pierce) R.; m. Sally Joan Brandenburg, June 18, 1960; children: Cheryl, Charles, Christopher, Cathleen. BA, Coll. of Wooster, 1959; MA, Northwestern U., 1960, PhD, 1966. Counselor, tchr. Evanston (Ill.) Twp. High Sch., 1960-66; asst. prof. U. Pitts., 1966-70, assoc. prof., dept. chmn., 1970-74; assoc. dean sch. edn. Va. Commonwealth U., Richmond, 1974-76, dean sch. edn., 1976-85, interim provost, v.p., 1985-86, provost, v.p., 1986-93; pres. Boise (Idaho) State U., 1993—; cons. various univs., govtl. agys., ednl. founds. Author or co-author over 50 articles, revs., tech. reports. Mem. Am. Psychol. Assn., Am. Ednl. Research Assn., Phi Delta Kappa. Office: Boise State U 1910 University Dr Boise ID 83725-0001

RUCH, RICHARD HURLEY, manufacturing company executive; b. Plymouth, Ind., Apr. 15, 1930; s. Dallas Claude and Mabel (Hurley) R.; m. Patricia Lou Overbeek, June 27, 1931; children: Richard, Michael, Christine, Douglas. BA, Mich. State U., 1952. Stores acctg. supr. Kroger Inc., Grand Rapids, Mich., 1954-55; chief acct. Herman Miller Inc., Zeeland, Mich., 1955-58, controller, 1958-63, dir. mfg., 1963-67, v.p. mfg., 1967-77, v.p. adminstrn., 1978, v.p. corp. resources, 1979-85, chief fin. officer, sr. v.p., 1985-87, chief exec. officer, 1988-92, pres, chief exec. officer, 1990-92, also vice chair bd. dirs., 1992-95; chmn. of bd., 1995—. Active Hope Coll., Twentieth Century Club, Holland, Mich.; formerly active Holland C. of C., Zeeland Planning Com. Mem. Scanlon Plan Assocs. (bd. dirs., past pres.). Avocations: tennis, running. Office: Herman Miller Inc 855 E Main Ave Zeeland MI 49464-1366

RUCH, WILLIAM VAUGHN, writer, educator, consultant; b. Allentown, Pa., Sept. 29, 1937; s. Weston H. and Dorothy D. (Daubert) R. BA, Moravian Coll., 1959; MA in Comm., Syracuse U., 1969; MBA, Fairleigh Dickinson U., 1972; PhD, Rensselaer Poly. Inst., 1980; JD, Western State U. Coll. Law, 1983. Reporter Call-Chronicle Newspapers, Allentown, Pa., 1959-60; tchr. English conversation Jonan Sr. High Sch., Matsuyama, Japan, 1960-62; asst. editor Dixie News, Am. Can Co., Easton, Pa., 1964-65; fin. editor Pa. Power & Light Co., Allentown, 1967-69, advt. asst., 1966-67, sales promotion writer, 1965-66; tech. writer, editor Space Tech. Ctr., GE Co., King of Prussia, Pa., 1969; asst. editor Bell System Tech. Jour., Bell Telephone Labs., Murray Hill, N.J., 1969-71; field rep. N.W. Ayer & Son, Inc., N.Y.C., 1972-73; asst. prof. bus. communication Fairleigh Dickinson U., Madison, N.J., 1974-75, Bloomsburg (Pa.) State Coll., 1975-76; lectr. Sch. Bus. and Pub. Adminstrn., Calif. State U., Sacramento, 1977-79; asst. prof. bus. communication Coll. Bus. Adminstrn., San Diego (Calif.) State U., 1979-84; lectr. European div. U. Md., 1984-85; prof. mgmt. Monmouth Coll., West Long Br., N.J., 1985-88; cons. Corp. Communication, 1988-91; pres., owner WVR Assocs., 1991—; founder, exec. dir. Internat. Inst. of Corp. Communication, 1992—; adj. prof. orgnl. commn., N.Y.U., 1993—. Author: Corporate Communications: A Comparison of Japanese and American Practices, 1984, Business Reports: Written and Oral, 1988, International Handbook of Corporate Communication, 1989, Business Communication, 1990, The Manager's Complete Handbook of Communication, 1992, Business Reporting in the Information Age, 1994, (novel) Infinity/Affinity, 1994, Effective Business Reports, 1995, (novel) It Takes Great Strive, 1996. Named Outstanding Prof. of Yr. San Diego State U., 1983. Mem. Acad. Mgmt., Assn. for Bus. Communication, Internat. Assn. Bus. Communicators, Internat. Platform Assn. Republican. Mem. United Ch. of Christ. Home: PO Box 517 Rockaway NJ 07866-0517

RUCKELSHAUS, WILLIAM DOYLE, waste disposal services company executive; b. Indpls., July 24, 1932; s. John K. and Marion (Doyle) R.; m. Jill Elizabeth Strickland, May 11, 1962; children: Catherine Kiley, Mary Hughes, Jennifer Lea, William Justice, Robin Elizabeth. B.A. cum laude, Princeton U., 1957; LL.B., Harvard U., 1960. Bar: Ind. 1960. Atty. Ruckelshaus, Bobbitt & O'Connor, Indpls., 1960-68; dep. atty.-gen. Ind., 1960-65, chief counsel office atty.-gen. Ind., 1963-65; minority atty. Ind. Senate, 1965-67; mem. Ind. Ho. of Reps., 1967-69, majority leader, 1967-69; asst. atty.-gen. charge civil div. Dept. Justice, 1969-70; adminstr. EPA, Washington, 1970-73; acting dir. FBI, 1973; dep. atty. gen. U.S., 1973; mem. firm Ruckelshaus, Beveridge, Fairbanks & Diamond, Washington, 1974-76; sr. v.p. law and corp. affairs Weyerhaeuser Co., Tacoma, 1975-85; adminstr. EPA, Washington, 1983-85; pres. William D. Ruckelshaus Assocs., 1985-88; mem. firm Perkins Coie, Seattle, 1985-88; chmn. bd., CEO Browning-Ferris Industries, Inc., Houston, 1988—; bd. dirs. Cummins Engine Co., Monsanto Co., Nordstrom, Inc., Tex. Commerce Bancshares, Inc., Weyerhaeuser Co., Inc.; chmn., chief exec. officer Browning-Ferris Industries, Houston. Rep. nominee for U.S. Senate, Ind., 1968. With AUS, 1953-55. Mem. Fed. Bar Assn., Ind. Bar Assn., D.C. Bar Assn., Indpls. Bar Assn. Office: Browning-Ferris Ind Inc 757 N Eldridge Pky Houston TX 77079-4435*

RUCKENSTEIN, ELI, chemical engineering educator; b. Botosani, Romania, Aug. 13, 1925; came to U.S., 1969; m. Velina Rothstein, May 15, 1948; children: Andrei, Lelia. BSChemE, Poly. Inst., Bucharest, Romania, 1949, PhD in Chem. Engring., 1967; doctor honoris causa, Tech. U. Bucharest, 1993. Prof. Poly. Inst., Bucharest, 1949-69; vis. prof. U. London, 1969; NSF sr. scientist Clarkson Coll. Tech., Potsdam, N.Y., 1969-70; prof. U. Del., Newark, 1970-73; prof. SUNY, Buffalo, 1973-81, disting. prof., 1981—; vis. Humbolt prof. Bayreuth U., Fed. Republic Germany, 1986; Gulf vis. prof. Carnegie Mellon U., Pitts., 1988-89; disting. lectr. U. Waterloo, 1985, U. Mo., 1983; Fair Meml. lectr. U. Okla., 1987, Colburn Symposium lectr. U. Del., 1988, Van Winkle lectr. U. Tex., 1989. Contbr. articles, papers to profl. jours. Recipient Nat. award Romanian Dept. Edn., 1958, 64, Teaching award, 1961, George Spacu award Romanian Acad. Sci., 1963, Sr. Humbolt award Alexander von Humbolt Found., 1985, Creativity award NSF, 1985. Mem. NAE, AIChE (Alpha Chi Sigma award 1977, Walker award 1988), Am. Chem. Soc. (Kendall award 1986, Jacob F. Schoellkopf medal 1991, Langmuir Disting. Lectr. award 1994, E.V. Murphree award 1996). Office: SUNY Dept Chem Engring Buffalo NY 14260

RUCKER, CHARLES THOMAS, science facility administrator; b. Augusta, Ga., June 30, 1931; s. Julius Thornton and Ida (Johnson) R.; m. Mary Laura Underwood, June 20, 1959; children: Julie Ann, Patricia Lynn. BEE, Ga. Inst. Tech., 1957. Mem. engring. staff Sperry Rand Corp., Clearwater, Fla., 1957-71, cons. Sperry Microwave Electronics Electron Tube div., Gainesville, Fla., 1971-73; prin. rsch. engr. Ga. Inst. Tech., Atlanta, 1973-88, assoc. dir. Microelectronics Rsch. Ctr., 1988-95; prin. rsch. engr., 1995; cons. USAF, 1987-89; univ. rep. Coun. on Rsch. and Tech., Washington, 1989. Patentee in field. With USN, 1950-54, Korea. Fellow IEEE (Centennial medal 1985); mem. IEEE Microwave Theory and Techniques Soc. (pres. 1983, Disting. Svc. award 1991). Baptist. Avocations: woodworking, mechanical repair, tennis, boating.

RUCKER, KENNETH LAMAR, public administrator, educator; b. Atlanta, July 16, 1961; s. Jack Lamar and Priscilla Anne (Anderson) R.; m. Kerri Lynn Hairston; 1 child, Kenneth Lamar II. BSBA, Brenau U., 1991; MPA in Pub. Mgmt., Ga. State U., 1993; postgrad., U. Ga., 1993—. Cert. peace officer, supr., Ga. Law enforcement officer Met. Atlanta Rapid Transit Authority, 1984-93; sch. resource officer Fulton County Bd. Edn., Atlanta, 1993-95; field facilitator Cmtys. in Schs. of Ga., Inc., Atlanta, 1995—, field facilitator Cross Roads program, 1995—; bd. dirs. Benefactors of Edn., Inc., Atlanta; cons. pub. security Fulton County Bd. Edn., Atlanta, 1993-95. Sunday sch. tchr. Simpson St. Ch. of Christ, Atlanta, 1991—; youth motivator Atlanta Pub. Schs., 1988—; bd. dirs. Benefactors Edn., Inc., 1996—. Commd. officer Supply Corps, USNR, 1995—. Doctoral fellow U. Ga. Mem. Am. Soc. Pub. Adminstrn., Nat. Orgn. Black Law Enforcement Execs., Conf. on Minority Transp. Ofcls., Nat. Forum Black Pub. Adminstrs., Internat. Platform Assn., Benefactors of Edn., Inc. (bd. dirs. 1996—), Brenau U. Alumni Club, Ga. State U. Alumni Club, U.S. Naval Inst., Naval Res. Assn., Res. Officer's Assn., Pi Alpha Alpha, Pi Sigma Alpha, Omicron Delta Kappa (cir. pres. 1992-93). Avocations: computer tech., reading, photography, classical music, fitness. Home: 1823 Tiger Flowers Dr NW Atlanta GA 30314-1833 Office: Cmtys in Schs of Ga Inc c/o Ga Dept Edn 1852 Twin Towers East Atlanta GA 30334

RUCKER, THOMAS DOUGLAS, purchasing executive; b. Ottumwa, Iowa, Aug. 30, 1926; s. Everett Henry and Harriett Mary (Evans) R.; A.B., Loyola U., 1951; postgrad. St. Patrick's Coll., 1950-52; m. Rita Mary Rommelfanger, Apr. 18, 1953; children—David, Theresa, Martin, Paul. Asst. purchasing agt. Radio TV Supply, Los Angeles, 1952-53; buyer Consol. Western Steel div. U.S. Steel, Commerce, Calif., 1953-64, S.W. Welding & Mfg. Co., Alhambra, Calif., 1964-70; dir. purchasing Southwestern Engring., Commerce, Calif., 1970-87, ret. Served with USAAF, 1945-46. Home: 330 W Central Ave Brea CA 92821-3029 Office: Southwestern Engring 5701 S Eastern Ave Ste 300 Los Angeles CA 90040-2934

RUCKERT, EDWARD M., lawyer; b. N.Y.C., Aug. 26, 1950. BA, Georgetown U., 1972; JD, U. Toledo, 1975. Bar: N.Y. 1976, D.C. 1982. Trial atty. Office Gen. Counsel USDA, Washington, 1976-81; ptnr. McDermott, Will & Emery, Washington. Mem. ABA (chmn. agrl. com., mem. adminstrv. law sect. 1983-85), Fed. Bar Assn., D.C. Bar Assn. Office: McDermott Will & Emery 1850 K St NW Washington DC 20006-2213*

RUDAWSKI, JOSEPH GEORGE, educational administrator; b. Nanticoke, Pa., Feb. 22, 1942; s. Nicholas Rudawski and Pauline Zelek; m. Regina Marie Jamiolkowski, Aug. 19, 1967; children: Joseph, Tamra, Valerie, Jeanne. BA, King's Coll., Wilkes-Barre, Pa., 1963; MS in Counseling Psychology, U. Scranton, 1967; postgrad., East Stroudsburg State Coll., summer 1981, Pa. State U., summer 1988. Cert. tchr. math. and English, Pa.; instrnl. II cert. secondary sch. guidance counselor, Pa. Counselor, caseworker Kis-Lyn Indsl. Sch. for Boys, Drums, Pa., 1963-64, adminstrv. caseworker, 1964; math. and psychology instr. MMI Prep. Sch., Freeland, Pa., 1964-67, math. and psychology instr., guidance dir., 1967-71, psychology instr., guidance dir., dean students and faculty, 1971-73, guidance dir., pres., 1973—; guidance counselor Luzerne Intermediate Unit, Kingston, Pa., 1974-84; rep. Bd. of Coll. Bd., 1976—, Bd. Coll. Scholarship Svc., Pa. Assn. Ind. Schs., 1973—; rep. Nat. Assn. Ind. Schs., 1982—, pres., 1986; rep. Mid. States Assn. Colls. and Secondary Schs., 1970—, vice-chmn. evaluating com., 1991. Dir. Freeland YMCA, 1973—, pres. bd. dirs. 1981-83, chmn. budget com., mem. bldg. com., 1984—, svc. award 1983; bd. dirs. United Way, 1975-86; bd. v.p., chmn. coms. Hazleton-St. Joseph Med. Ctr., 1984-92, chmn. nuclear task force com., 1992; comml. div. chmn. United Way Campaign, Hazleton, 1985-86; facilitator edn. program Leadership Hazleton, 1986—; mem. Freeland Indsl. Corp., 1981—; vice-chmn. Sophia G. Coxe Charitable Trust, 1987—; mem. adv. bd. WOLF-TV, 1988—; bd. mem. Luth. Welfare Svc., 1991-93, chmn. resource devel. com., 1992—; bd. dirs. Luth. Welfare Svc. Found., 1993—. Recipient Appreciation award Ea. Pa. chpt. Arthritis Found., 1983, Svc. award YMCA, Freeland, 1983, Cmty. award VFW, Freeland, 1988, Declaration of Achievement Pa. Senate, Harrisburg, 1988; named Citizen of Yr. Freeland Sons of Erin, 1996. Mem. Pers. and Guidance Assn., Pa. Sch. Counselors Assn., Luzerne County Counselors Assn. (pres. 1975-76, Outstanding Svc. award 1976), Freeland Rotary Club Pres. 1976-77, 96—). Office: MMI Prep Sch 154 Centre St Freeland PA 18224-2117

RUDBACH, JON ANTHONY, biotechnical company executive; b. Long Beach, Calif., Sept. 23, 1937; s. John Alexander and Lola (Whitcomb) R.; m. Inge Clye Steincke, July 4, 1959; children: Lucy Trine, Karl Kristian. BA, U. Calif., Berkeley, 1959; MS, U. Mich., 1961, PhD, 1964; MBA, Lake Forest Coll., 1986. Rsch. scientist Rocky Mountain Lab., Hamilton, Mont., 1964-70; prof. microbiology U. Mont., Missoula, 1970-77; mgr. exploratory rsch. Abbott Labs., North Chicago, Ill., 1977-79; dir. Stella Duncan Meml. Rsch. Inst., Missoula, 1979-82; head infectious disease rsch. Abbott Labs., Missoula, 1982-85; v.p. rsch. and devel. Ribi Immunochem Rsch., Inc., Hamilton, 1985-95; pres. TRI, Ltd., Hamilton, 1995—. Contbr. articles to profl. jours.; author 2 books; patentee in field. Mem. Bitterroot Community Bd., Hamilton, 1988—. USPHS grantee, 1970-79, fellow, 1964-66. Mem. Am. Assn. Immunologists, Am. Soc. Microbiology, Soc. for Exptl. Biology and Medicine, Soc. for Biol. Therapy, Lions (local pres. 1993-94, bd. dirs. 1987—). Republican. Congregationalist. Avocations: skiing, fishing, hunting, hiking, band. Home: 243 Hilltop Dr Hamilton MT 59840-9317 Office: TRI Ltd PO Box 527 Hamilton MT 59840

RUDCZYNSKI, ANDREW B., academic administrator, medical researcher; b. Nottingham, England, Sept. 7, 1947; came to U.S., 1951; s. Richard B. and Krystyna Z. (Stachlewska) R.; m. Andrea Skalny, Oct. 16, 1976 (div. Oct. 1990); children: Christina, Thomas. BSc in Biology/Biochemistry, McGill U., 1969; PhD in Immunology, Syracuse U., 1974; MBA in Adminstrn., So. Ill. U., 1984. Prin. investigator scrub typhus project divsn. Rickettsiology U.S. Army Med. Rsch. Infectious Diseases, Ft. Detrick, Md., 1974-76; rsch. assoc. dept. Biology Mich. Cancer Found., Detroit, 1976-77, rsch. scientist dept. Immunology, unit chef immunology unit Breast Cancer Prognostic Study, 1977-80; asst. dir. Office Rsch. and Grants U. Md. Ea. Shore, Princess Anne, 1980-83; extramural assoc. Office Extramural Rsch. and Tng., Office of Dir. NIH, 1981-82; asst. dir. Office Rsch. & Sponsored Programs Rutgers U., Piscataway, N.J., 1983-84, dir., 1984—, asst. v.p. rsch. adminstrn., 1985-93, assoc. v.p. rsch. policy and adminstrn., 1993—; field reader strengthening devel. instns. program U.S. Dept. Edn., 1990; mem. Chancellor's task force instrn. and rsch. infrastructure support N.J. Dept. Higher Edn., 1992. Contbr. articles, abstracts to profl. jours. Capt. U.S. Army Med. Svc. Corps, 1974-76. Recipient traineeship award NSF, 1969-71; predoctoral fellow NIH, 1973-74. Mem. AAAS, Nat. Coun. Univ. Rsch. Adminstrs. (profl. devel. com. 1988-90, region II program com. 1989-90, chmn. region II 1990-92, nat. program com. 1994-95), Coun. Govtl. Rels. (fed. mgmt. devel. com. 1989-90), Soc. Rsch. Adminstrs., Assn. Univ. Tech. Mgrs., Beta Gamma Sigma, Sigma Xi. Roman Catholic. Home: 2 Carina Dr Milltown NJ 08850-1640 Office: Rutgers U Office Rsch/Sponsored Programs Adminstrv Svcs Bldg 123 Annex II PO Box 1179 Piscataway NJ 08855-1179

RUDD, ELDON, retired congressman, political consultant; b. Camp Verde, Ariz.; m. Ann Merritt. B.A., Ariz. State U., 1947; J.D., U. Ariz., 1950. Bar: Ariz. 1949, U.S. Supreme Ct. 1953. Pvt. practice Tucson, 1950; spl. agt.-diplomatic assignment principally Latin Am. FBI, 1950-70; mem. Maricopa County (Ariz.) Bd. Suprs., 1972-76; bd. dirs. Ariz.-Mex. Commn., 1972-92; with U.S.-Mex. Interparliamentary Com., 1976-84; mem. 95th-99th Congresses from 4th Dist. Ariz., 1976-87; of counsel Shimmel, Hill, Bishop & Gruender, P.C., Phoenix, 1987-93; pres. Eldon Rudd Consultancy, Scottsdale, Ariz., 1993—; bd. dirs. Salt River Project; chmn. Phoenix chpt. Soc. Former Spl. Agts. FBI, 1995-96. Author: World Communism-Threat to Freedom, 1987. Mem. numerous pub. svc. orgns., including energy and water, mil. and internat. affairs. Fighter pilot USMCR, 1942-46. Mem. Fed. Bar Assn. (chpt. pres. 1976), Ariz. Bar Assn., Maricopa County Bar Assn., Scottsdale Bar Assn., Paradise Valley Country Club (bd. dirs. 1989-92), Phi Delta Phi, Blue Key. Republican. Roman Catholic. Home: PO Box 873 Scottsdale AZ 85252-0873 Office: 6909 E Main St Scottsdale AZ 85251-4311

RUDD, LYNN EUGENE, JR., industrial hygienist; b. Plainfield, N.J., Nov. 24, 1958; s. Lynn E. and Suzanne (Kish) R. BS in Biology, Albright Coll., Reading, Pa., 1981; MS in Biology, Fairleigh Dickinson U., 1984. Diplomate Am. Bd. Indsl. Hygiene. Occupl. safety and environ. specialist RCA Svc. Co., Ft. Monmouth, N.J., 1984-86; sr. indsl. hygienist U.S. Dept. Def., Ft. Monmouth, 1986-88; regional safety and health rep. NUS Corp. and EPA Region II, Edison, N.J., 1988-89; sr. indsl. hygienist, group head Clayton Environ., Edison, 1989-91; sr. indsl. hygienist Exxon Biomed. Scis. Inc, Houston, 1991—. Mem. Am. Indsl. Hygiene Assn., Am. Soc. Safety Engrs., Am. Acad. Indsl. Hygiene (diplomate), Am. Conf. Govtl. Indsl. Hygienists. Office: Exxon Biomed Scis Inc Lonestar Bldg Ste 220 1501 I-10 East Fwy Baytown TX 77521

RUDD, NICHOLAS, marketing communications company executive; b. N.Y.C., Mar. 18, 1943; s. Emmanuel and Lucie Lia Rudd; children: Alexis Henry, Kenneth Charles. B.A., Columbia U., 1964, M.B.A., 1967. Mem. pub. relations staff Ford Motor Co., N.Y.C., 1964-65; account mgr. Young & Rubicam Inc., N.Y.C., 1968-75, v.p., mgmt. supr., 1975-80, sr. v.p. mgmt. svcs., 1980-90, chief info. officer, 1990-95; chief knowledge officer Wunderman Cato Johnson, N.Y.C., 1996—; cons. Nat. Neurofibromatosis Found., Inc., 1981—; bd. dirs. Vol. Cons. Group, Inc., N.Y.C., 1987. Bd. dirs. Nat. Choral Coun., chmn., 1993-95, Veritas Therapeutic Cmty. Found., Conductor's Circle, Am. Symphony Orch. Mem. Beta Gamma Sigma. Office: Wunderman Cato Johnson 675 Avenue of Americas New York NY 10010

RUDDER, CATHERINE ESTELLE, political science association administrator; b. Atlanta, Dec. 16; d. James M. and Virginia Rudder. BA, Emory U., 1969; MA, Ohio State U., 1972, PhD, 1973. Asst. prof. U. Ga., Athens, 1973-77; chief staff to Rep. W. Fowler, Jr. U.S. House Reps., Washington, 1978-81, assoc. dir., 1983-87; exec. dir. Am. Polit. Sci. Assn., Washington, 1987—. Office: Am Polit Scis Assn 1527 New Hampshire Ave NW Washington DC 20036-1206

RUDDON, RAYMOND WALTER, JR., pharmacology educator; b. Detroit, Dec. 23, 1936; married, 1961; three children. BS, U. Detroit, 1958; PhD in Pharmacology, U. Mich., 1964, MD, 1967. Teaching fellow in chemistry U. Detroit, 1958-59; from instr. to prof. pharmacology U. Mich., Ann Arbor, 1964-76; dir. biol. marker program Nat. Cancer Inst., Frederick, Md., 1976-81; Maurice H. Seevers prof., chmn. dept. pharmacology U. Mich. Med. Sch., Ann Arbor, 1981-90; dir. Eppley Inst. for Rsch. in Cancer and Allied Diseases U. Nebr. Med. Ctr., Omaha, 1990—; Eppley prof. oncology U. Nebr. Med. Ctr. NIH predoctoral fellow, 1959-64; Am. Cancer Soc. scholar, 1964-67. Mem. AAAS, Am. Soc. Pharmacology and Exptl. Therapeutics, Am. Assn. Cancer Rsch., Am. Soc. Biochemistry and Molecular Biology, Endocrine Soc. Research in field of biol. markers of neoplasia; glycoprotein hormones; protein folding. Office: U Nebr Med Ctr Eppley Inst Rsch in Cancer & Allied Dise 600 S 42nd St Omaha NE 68198-6805

RUDDY, FRANK S., lawyer, former ambassador; b. N.Y.C., Sept. 15, 1937; s. Francis Stephen and Teresa (O'Neil) R.; m. Kateri Mary O'Neill, Aug. 29, 1964; children—Neil, David, Stephen. A.B., Holy Cross Coll., 1959; M.A., NYU, 1962, LL.M., 1967; LL.B., Loyola U., New Orleans, 1965; Ph.D., Cambridge U., Eng., 1969. Bar: D.C., N.Y., Tex., U.S. Supreme Ct. Faculty Cambridge U., 1967-69; asst. gen. counsel USIA, Washington, 1969-72, 73-74; sr. atty. Office of Telecommunication Policy, White House, Washington, 1972-73; counsel Exxon Corp., Houston, 1974-81; asst. adminstr. AID (with rank asst. sec. state) Dept. State, Washington, 1981-84; U.S. ambassador to Equatorial Guinea, 1984-88; gen. counsel U.S. Dept. Energy, Washington, 1988-89; v.p. Sierra Blanc Devel. Corp., Washington, 1989-92; prin. Law Offices of Frank Ruddy, Washington, 1992-94; vis. scholar Johns Hopkins Sch. Advanced Internat. Studies, 1990—; dep. chmn. UN Referendum for Western Sahara, 1994, Johnston, Rivlin & Foley, Washington, D.C., 1995—. Author: International Law in the Enlightenment, 1975; editor: American International Law Cases (series), 1972—; editor in chief Internat. Lawyer, 1978-83; contbr. articles to legal jours. Bd. dirs. African Devel. Found., Washington, 1983-84. Served with USMCR, 1956-61. Mem. ABA (chmn. treaty compliance sect. 1991—), Am. Soc. Internat. Law, Internat. Law Assn., Hague Acad. Internat. Law Alumni Assn., Oxford and Cambridge Club (London), Conservative Club, Internat. Club, Dacor House. Republican. Roman Catholic. Home: 5600 Western Ave Chevy Chase MD 20815-3406 Office: Johnston Rivlin & Foley Ste 400 1025 Connecticut Ave Ste200 Washington DC 20036

RUDDY, JAMES W., lawyer; b. 1949. AB, U. Mich., 1971; JD, Wayne State U., 1973. Bar: Wash. 1974, Mich. 1974. Assoc. gen. counsel Safeco Corp., 1984-89, v.p., gen. counsel, 1989—, now sr. v.p. , gen. counsel. Office: Safeco Corp Safeco Plz Seattle WA 98185*

RUDE, BRIAN DAVID, state legislator; b. Viroqua, Wis., Aug. 25, 1955; s. Raymond and Conelee (Johnson) R.; m. Karen Thulin; children: Erik, Nels. BA magna cum laude, Luther Coll., 1977; MA, U. Wis., Madison, 1994. Mem. Wis. Assembly, Madison, 1982-84; mem. Wis. Senate, Madison, 1984—, asst. minority leader, 1989-93; pres. Wis. State Sen., 1993—; with corp. communications The Trane Co., La Crosse, Wis., 1981-85. Bd. advisers Nat. Trust Historic Preservation, 1990—. Mem. Lions, Sons of Norway, Norwegian-Am. Hist. Assn. (trustee). Republican. Lutheran. Avocations: reading, gardening, traveling, fishing. Home: 307 Babcock St PO Box 367 Coon Valley WI 54623-0367 Office: Wis State Senate State Capitol Rm 239-S PO Box 7882 Madison WI 53703

RUDEE, MERVYN LEA, engineering educator, researcher; b. Palo Alto, Calif., Oct. 4, 1935; s. Mervyn C. and Hannah (Mathews) R.; m. Elizabeth Eager, June 20, 1958; children: Elizabeth Diane, David Benjamin. BS, Stanford U., 1958, MS, 1962, PhD, 1965. Asst. prof. materials sci. Rice U., Houston, 1964-68, assoc. prof., 1968-72, prof. materials sci., 1972-74; prof. U. Calif. San Diego, La Jolla, 1974—, founding provost Warren Coll., 1974-82, founding dean Sch. Engring., 1982-93, coord. grad. program on materials sci., 1994—; interim dean engring. U. Calif., Riverside, 1995—; vis. scholar Corpus Christi Coll., Cambridge, Eng., 1971-72; CFO, prin. Univ. Planning Assocs., Inc.; vis. scientist IBM Thomas J. Watson Rsch. Ctr., Yorktown Heights, N.Y., 1987. Pres., bd. trustees Mus. Photographic Art, San Diego, 1995-96. Lt. (j.g.) USN, 1958-61. Guggenheim fellow, 1971-72. Mem. Electron Microscope Soc. Am., Materials Rsch. Soc., Am. Physics Soc., Tex. Soc. Electron Microscopy (hon., pres. 1966), Sigma Xi, Tau Beta Pi. Home: 1745 Kearsarge Rd La Jolla CA 92037-3829 Office: Univ Calif San Diego Dept Elec & Cptr Engring La Jolla CA 92093-0407

RUDEL, JULIUS, conductor; b. Vienna, Austria, Mar. 6, 1921; came to U.S., 1938, naturalized, 1944; s. Jakob and Josephine (Sonnenblum) R.; m. Rita Gillis, June 24, 1942 (dec. May 1984); children: Joan, Madeleine, Anthony Jason. Student, Acad. Music, Vienna; diploma in conducting, Mannes Coll. Music, 1942; diploma hon. doctorates, U. Vt., 1961, U. Mich., 1971; doctorates hon. causa, Pace Coll., Manhattan Coll., 1994, Mannes Coll. Music, 1994, Manhattanville Coll., 1994, Manhattan Sch. Music, 1996. With N.Y. City Opera, 1943-79, debut, 1944, gen. dir., 1957-79, 3rd St. Music Sch. Settlement, 1945-52, mus. dir. Chautauqua Opera Assn., 1958-59, Caramoor Festival, Katonah, N.Y., 1964-76, Cin. May Festival, 1971-72, Kennedy Ctr. Performing Arts, 1971-75; music advisor Wolf Trap Farm Pk., 1971, Phila. Opera, 1978-81; condr. Spoleto (Italy) Festival, 1962-63; music dir. Buffalo Philarm. Orch., 1979-85, debut as condr. Met. Opera, 1978, San Francisco Opera, 1979, Vienna State Opera, 1976, Royal Opera, Covent Garden, 1984, Rome Opera, 1987, Opera de la Bastille, 1992, Teatro Colon, Buenos Aires, 1992, Royal Danish Opera, Copenhagen, 1993, L.A. Opera, 1995; dir. prodn.: Kiss Me Kate, Vienna Volksoper Opera, 1956; guest condr. Chgo. Symphony, Phila. Orch., N.Y. Philharm., Boston Symphony, Detroit Symphony, Israel Philharm., Paris Opera, Munich Opera, Hamburg State Opera, Vienna State Opera, other symphonic, operatic orgns. in U.S. and Europe. Decorated Croix du Chevalier in arts and letters France; recipient gold medal Nat. Arts Club, 1958, citation Nat. Assn. Am. Composers and Conductors, 1958, citation Nat. Fedn. Music Clubs, 1959, Ditson award Columbia, 1959, Page One award in music Newspaper Guild, 1959, hon. insignia for arts and sci. Govt. of Austria, 1961, Handel medal for music City N.Y., 1965, citation Nat. Assn. Negro Musicians, 1965, citation Nat. Opera Assn., 1971, comdr.'s Cross German Order Merit, 1967, hon. lt. Israeli Army, 1969, Julius Rudel award for young condrs., Pan Am./Pan African award for humanism, 1981, Peabody award, 1985. Office: c/o Shuman Assocs 120 W 58th St Apt 8D New York NY 10019

RUDELIUS, WILLIAM, marketing educator; b. Rockford, Ill., Sept. 2, 1931; s. Carl William and Clarissa Euclid (Davis) R.; m. Jacqueline Urch Dunham, July 3, 1954; children: Robert, Jeanne, Katherine, Kristi. B.S. in Mech. Engring., U. Wis., 1953; M.B.A., U. Pa., 1959, Ph.D. in Econs., 1964. Program engr., missile and space vehicle dept. Gen. Electric Co., Phila., 1956-57, 59-61; sr. research economist North Star Research Inst., Mpls., 1964-66; lectr. U. Minn., Mpls., 1961-64; asst. prof. mktg. Coll. Bus. Adminstrn. U. Minn., 1964, assoc. prof., 1966-72, prof., 1972—. Co-author: (with W. Bruce Erickson) An Introduction to Contemporary Business, 1973, rev. 4th edit., 1985, (with Eric N. Berkowitz, Roger A. Kerin and Steven W. Hartley) Marketing, 1986, rev. 4th edit., 1994, (with Krzysztof Przybytowski, Roger A. Kerin and Steven W. Hartley) Marketing na Przykładach, 1994; contbr. articles to profl. jours. Served with USAF, 1954-55. Home: 1425 Alpine Pass Minneapolis MN 55416-3560 Office: Carlson Sch Mgmt U Minn 271 19th Ave S Minneapolis MN 55455-0430

RUDELL, MILTON WESLEY, aerospace engineer; b. Rice Lake, Wis., July 9, 1920; s. George C. and Edna (Bjoraa) R.; m. Doris Lorraine Shella, Nov. 30, 1941; children: Helen, Geoffrey, Lynn, Deborah, Leah, Andrea, Kessea, Eric, Erin. B in Aerospace Engring., U. Minn., 1946. Registered profl. engr. Chief tool engr. Boeing Aircraft Corp., Wichita, Kans. and Seattle, 1941-43, stateside and overseas field engr., 1943-45; chief fueling systems engr. N.W. Airlines, Mpls., 1946-50; pres. Rumoco Co., Frederic, Wis., 1950-68; registrar ECPI-Nat. IBM computer sch., Mpls., 1968-69; pres. Life Engring. Co., Milw. and Frederic, Wis., 1969—. Designer original med. surg. suture tape, 1951; designer 1st match-book cover with strike plate on rear side for safety, 1942; pioneered high-speed underwing fueling systems for comml. aircraft and 1st hydrant ground fueling systems for comml. aircraft; co-author Ops. & Maintenance Manual for B-29 aircraft, 1943. Founder Frederic Found. for Advanced Edn. Recipient WWII Aeronautical Engring. Citation from Pres. Eisenhower, 1944. Mem. Exptl. Aircraft Assn., Wis. Aviation Hall of Fame, Northwestern Wis. Mycol. Soc. (charter). Lutheran. Home and Office: 501 Wisconsin Ave N Frederic WI 54837-0400 *We shall pass through this world but once. Any good therefore that we can do or any kindness that we can show to any human being, let us do it now. Let us not defer nor neglect it, for we shall not pass this way again.*

RUDENSTINE, NEIL LEON, academic administrator, educator; b. Ossining, N.Y., Jan. 21, 1935; s. Harry and Mae (Esperito) R.; m. Angelica Zander, Aug. 27, 1960; children: Antonia Margaret, Nicholas David, Sonya. B.A., Princeton U., 1956; B.A. (Rhodes Scholar), Oxford U., 1959, M.A., 1963; Ph.D., Harvard U., 1964. Instr. dept. English Harvard U., Cambridge, Mass., 1964-66; asst. prof. Harvard U., 1966-68; assoc. prof. English Princeton (N.J.) U., 1968-73, prof. English, 1973-88, dean of students, 1968-72, dean of Coll., 1972-77, provost, 1977-88; exec. v.p. Andrew W. Mellon Found., N.Y.C., 1988-91; pres. Harvard U., Cambridge, Mass., 1991—, prof. English, 1991—. Author: Sidney's Poetic Development, 1967, (with George Rousseau) English Poetic Satire, 1972, (with William Bowen) In Pursuit of the PhD, 1992. Served to 1st lt. arty. AUS, 1959-60. Hon. fellow New Coll., Oxford U. Fellow Am. Acad. Arts and Scis.; mem. Am. Philos. Soc., Coun. on Fgn. Rels., Com. for Econ. Devel. Office: Harvard U Office of Pres Massachusetts Hall Cambridge MA 02138

RUDER, DAVID STURTEVANT, lawyer, educator, government official; b. Wausau, Wis., May 25, 1929; s. George Louis and Josephine (Sturtevant) R.; m. Susan M. Small; children: Victoria Chesley, Julia Larson, David Sturtevant II, John Coulter; m stepchildren: Elizabeth Frankel, Rebecca Wilkinson. BA cum laude, Williams Coll., 1951; JD with honors, U. Wis., 1957. Bar: Wis. 1957, Ill. 1962. Of counsel Schiff Hardin & Waite, Chgo., 1971-76; assoc. Quarles & Brady, Milw., 1957-61; asst. prof. law Northwestern U., Chgo., 1961-63, assoc. prof., 1963-65, prof., 1965—, assoc. dean Law Sch., 1965-66, dean Law Sch., 1977-85; chmn. Securities and Exch. Commn., Washington, 1987-89; ptnr. Baker & McKenzie, Chgo., 1990-94, sr. counsel, 1994—; cons. Am. Law Inst. Fed. Securities Code; planning dir. Corp. Counsel Inst., 1962-66, 76-77, com. mem., 1962-87, 90—; cons. Ray Garrett Jr. Corp. and Securities Law Inst., 1980-87, 90—; vis. lectr. U. de Liege, 1967; vis. prof. law U. Pa., Phila., 1971; faculty Salzburg Seminar, 1976; mem. legal adv. com. bd. dirs. N.Y. Stock Exch., 1978-82; mem. com. profl. responsibility Ill. Supreme Ct., 1978-87; adv. bd. Securities Regulation Inst., 1978—, chmn., 1994—; bd. govs. Nat. Assn. Securities Dealers, 1990-93, chmn. Legal Adv. Bd., 1993-96, Arbitration Policy Task Force, 1994—. Editor-in-chief: Williams Coll. Record, 1950-51, U. Wis. Law Rev, 1957; editor: Proc. Corp. Counsel Inst, 1962-66; contbr. articles to legal periodicals. 1st lt. AUS, 1951-54. Fellow Am. Bar Found.; mem., com. chmn. ABA (coun. sect. corp. banking and bus. law 1970-74), Chgo. Bar Assn., Wis. Bar Assn., Am. Law Inst., Order of Coif, Comml. Club of Chgo., Econ. Club of Chgo., Gargoyle Soc., Phi Beta Kappa, Phi Delta Pi, Zeta Psi. Home: 325 Orchard Ln Highland Park IL 60035-1939 Office: Northwestern U Sch Law 357 E Chicago Ave Chicago IL 60611-3008 also: Baker & McKenzie One Prudential Pla 130 E Randolph St Chicago IL 60601

RUDER, MELVIN HARVEY, retired newspaper editor; b. Manning, N.D., Jan. 19, 1915; s. Moris M. and Rebecca (Friedman) R.; m. Ruth Bergan, Feb. 10, 1950; 1 dau., Patricia E. Morton. B.A., U. N.D., 1937, M.A., 1941; grad. student, Northwestern U., 1940. Asst. prof. journalism U. N.D., 1940; indsl. relations specialist Westinghouse Electric Co., Sharon, Pa., 1940-41; pub. relations with Am. Machine & Foundry Co., N.Y.C., 1946; founder, editor Hungry Horse News, Columbia Falls, Mont., 1946-78; editor emeritus Hungry Horse News, 1978—. Chmn. adv. coun. Flathead Nat. Forest, Dist. 6 Sch. Bd., 1967-70. Served to lt. (s.g.) USNR, 1942-45. Recipient Pulitzer prize for gen. local reporting, 1965. Mem. Mont. Press Assn. (pres. 1957), Flathead Associated C. of C. (pres. 1971), Glacier Natural History Assn. (pres. 1983). Home: Buffalo Hill Terr 40 Claremont Kalispell MT 59901

RUDER, WILLIAM, public relations executive; b. N.Y.C., Oct. 17, 1921; s. Jacob L. and Rose (Rosenberg) R.; m. Betty Ott, May 23, 1980; children—Robin Ann, Abby, Brian, Michal Ellen, Eric. B.S.S., City Coll., N.Y., 1942. With Samuel Goldwyn Prodns., 1946-48; pres. Ruder & Finn, Inc., N.Y.C., 1948-80, William Ruder Inc., 1981—; asst. sec. commerce, 1961-62; Tobe lectr. Harvard Grad. Sch. Bus., 1962; mem. grad. adv. bd. City Coll. N.Y., Baruch Sch. Bus., N.Y.C.; cons. State Dept.; bd. dirs. W.P. Carey & Co., Inc. Author: The Businessman's Guide to Washington. Bd. dirs. Bus. Com. for Arts, Jewish Bd. Guardians, Chamber Music Soc. Lincoln Ctr., Fund for Peace, Project Return Found.; exec. com. United Way Am.; trustee, chmn. Manhattanville Coll., Purchase, N.Y., 1974-75; bd. overseers Wharton Sch. U. Pa.; mem. pres.'s coun. Meml. Sloan-Kettering Cancer Ctr.; chmn. bd. ACCESS. Capt. USAAF, 1941-45. Mem. UN Assn. U.S.A. (nat. policy panel dir.). Home: 430 E 86th St New York NY 10028-6441 Office: Ruder Finn Inc 301 E 57th St New York NY 10022-2900

RUDERMAN, ARMAND PETER, health economics educator, consultant, volunteer; b. N.Y.C., Nov. 19, 1923; s. Louis and Lillian (Prigohzy) R.; m. Alice Helen Holton, June 17, 1948; children: Ann, Mary, William, John. SB, Harvard U., 1943; MA, 1946, PhD, 1947; MBA, U. Chgo., 1944. Instr. econs. various U.S. univs., 1946-50; statistician, economist ILO, Pan.-Am. Health Orgn., WHO, 1950-67; chmn. sci. working group on social and econ. aspects of tropical disease research WHO/TDR, 1979-83; prof. health adminstrn. U. Toronto, Ont., Can., 1967-75; founding dean adminstrv. studies Dalhousie U., N.S., Can., 1975-80, prof. health adminstrn., 1981-89, prof. emeritus, 1989—; vis. prof. Nat. U. Singapore, 1982-83; cons. in field. Contbr. articles to profl. jours. and books. Bd. dirs. Northwood Home Care, 1987-89, Northwestern Gen. Hosp., Toronto, 1991-96; mem. Etobicoke Bd. Health, 1991-95; mem. cmty. adv. com. Toronto Hosp., 1992-95; mem. regional 3 exec. com. Ont. Hosp. Assn., 1994-96. Mem. Can. Pub. Health Assn., Royal Econ. Soc.

RUDGE, NANCY KIM, critical care nurse; b. Woodbury, N.J., June 3, 1958; d. Richard Raymond and Margery Arline (Brush) R. BSN, U. Tenn., 1980. CCRN, BLS. Staff RN Meth. Hosp., Memphis, 1980-84; nurse clinician II Bapt. Meml. Hosp., Memphis, 1984-89, nurse clinician III, 1989-90, nurse clinician IV, 1990-91, unit supr., 1991—; BLS instr. Am. Heart Assn., Memphis, 1991—. Choir officer Bellevue Bapt. Ch., Memphis, 1988—. Named one of top 100 nurses in Shelby and Fayette counties Celebrate Nursing, 1991. Mem. AACN. Baptist. Avocations: singing, gardening, sailing, cooking, playing piano. Office: Bapt Meml Hosp 899 Madison Ave Memphis TN 38103-3405

RUDIN, ANNE NOTO, former mayor, nurse; b. Passaic, N.J., Jan. 27, 1924; m. Edward Rudin, June 6, 1948; 4 children. BS in Edn., Temple U., 1945, RN, 1946; MPA, U. So. Calif., 1983; LLD (hon.), Golden Gate U., 1990. RN, Calif. Mem. faculty Temple U. Sch. Nursing, Phila., 1946-48; mem. nursing faculty Mt. Zion Hosp., San Francisco, 1948-49; mem. Sacramento City Council, 1971-83; mayor City of Sacramento, 1983-92; ind. pub. policy cons. Pres. LWV, Riverside, 1957, Sacramento, 1961, Calif., 1969-71, Calif. Elected Women's Assn., 1973—; bd. trustees Golden Gate U.; adv. bd. U. So. Calif., Army Depot Reuse Commn.; bd. dirs. Sacramento Theatre Co., Sacramento Symphony, Calif. Common Cause, Japan Soc. No. Calif., Sacramento Edn. Found. Recipient Women in Govt. award U.S. Jaycee Women, 1984, Woman of Distinction award Sacramento Area Soroptimist Clubs, 1985, Civic Contbn. award LWV Sacramento, 1989, Woman of Courage award Sacramento History Ctr., 1989, Peacemaker of Yr. award Sacramento Mediation Ctr., 1992, Regional Pride award Sacramento Mag., 1993, Humanitarian award Japanese Am. Citizen's League, 1993, Outstanding Pub. Svc. award Am. Soc. Pub. Adminstrn., 1994; named Girl Scouts Am. Role model, 1989.

RUDIN, SCOTT, film and theatre producer; b. N.Y.C., July 14, 1958. Prodn. asst., asst. to theatre prodrs. Kermit Bloomgarden and Robert Whitehead; casting dir. motion pictures and theatre, prodr. with Edgar Scherick, exec. v.p. prodn. 20th Century Fox, 1984-86, pres. prodn., 1986-87; founder Scott Rudin Prodns., 1990—. Prodr.: (films) He Makes Me Feel Like Dancing, 1982 (Outstanding Children's Program Emmy award 1982, Feature Documentary Acad. award 1982), Mrs. Soffel, 1984, Flatliners, 1990, Pacific Heights, 1990, Regarding Henry, 1991, Little Man Tate, 1991, The Addams Family, 1991, White Sands, 1992, Sister Act, 1992, Jennifer Eight, 1992, Life With Mikey, 1993, The Firm, 1993, Searching for Bobby Fischer, 1993, Sister Act 2, 1993, Addams Family Values, 1993, I.Q., 1994, Nobody's Fool, 1994, Sabrina, 1995, Clueless, 1995, Up Close and Personal, 1996, Ransom, 1996, Marvin's Room, 1996; (theatre) Passion, 1994 (Best Musical Tony award 1994). Office: Paramount Pictures DeMille 200 5555 Melrose Ave Los Angeles CA 90038-3149*

RUDING, HERMAN ONNO, banker, former Dutch government official; b. Aug. 15, 1939; m. Renee V.M. Hekking; 2 children. MA in Econs., Netherlands Sch. Econs. (Erasmus U.), 1964, PhD in Econs. cum laude, 1969. Head div. internat. monetary affairs Treas. Gen. of Ministry of Fin., The Hague, Netherlands. 1965-70; joint gen. mgr. Amsterdam-Rotterdam Bank N.V., Amsterdam, 1971-76; exec. dir. IMF, Washington, 1977-80; bd. mng. dirs. Amsterdam-Rotterdam Bank N.V., 1981-82; minister of fin. Netherlands, The Hague, 1982-89; chmn. Netherlands Christian Fedn. Employers, The Hague, 1990-92; vice chmn., bd. dirs. Citicorp, N.Y.C., 1992—. Contbr. articles to profl. jours. Bd. dirs. Foster Parents Plan Internat., 1981-82, Mt. Sinai Hosp., N.Y.C. Mem. Christian Democratic Alliance, Com. Monetary Union of Europe, Trilateral Commn. Office: Citibank 399 Park Ave New York NY 10022-4614

RUDINS, LEONIDS (LEE RUDINS), retired chemical company executive, financial executive; b. Linava, Latvia, Dec. 15, 1928; came to U.S., 1949; s. Leonids and Aleksandra (Zimins) R.; m. Galina Zakidalski, July 24, 1960; 1 child, Andrew. BS in Commerce, Rider Coll., 1953; MBA, Seton Hall U., 1967, cert. of internat. bus., 1968. Acct. Johnson & Johnson, New Brunswick, N.J., 1957-58; mgr. budget and cost LePage's, Johnson & Johnson, Gloucester, Mass., 1958-60; plant contr. Permacel, Johnson & Johnson, Decatur, Ill., 1960-62; asst. contr. Permacel, Johnson & Johnson, New Brunswick, 1962-63, treas., contr., 1963-70; div. contr. Titanium Pigments, NL Industries, Inc., Sayreville, N.J., 1970-71, group contr., 1971-76; dir. fin. and adminstrn. NL Pigments-U.S., NL Industries, Inc., Sayreville, N.J., 1976-77; dir. fin. and planning NL Pigments-Worldwide, NL Industries, Inc., Sayreville, N.J., 1977-79; v.p. fin., chief fin. officer NL Chemicals, Inc., Hightstown, N.J., 1979-89; pres. Internat. Bus. Mgmt. Assocs., Inc., Princeton, 1990-91; bd. dirs. Robertson-CECO Corp., Boston, Benton-Chemie, Nordenham, Germany, Abbey Chems., Ltd., Livingston, Eng., Enenco, Inc., Memphis, Tenn. Solicitor, budget com. mem., United Fund, New Brunswick, 1962-69; bd. dirs. St. Vladimir Russian Cath. Soc., 1992—. With U.S. Army, 1953-56, Korea. Mem. Nat. Assn. Accts., Fin. Exec. Inst., Forsgate Club, Battleground Club. Republican. Greek/Russian Orthodox. Avocations: golf, stamp collecting, hiking. Home: 28 Tamarack Dr Englishtown NJ 07726-2734

RUDINSKI, MICHAEL J., lawyer; b. Williamsport, Pa., Jan. 29, 1954; s. Edward Paul and Ruth Mary (Nittinger) R.; m. Mary M. Gardner, Jan. 22, 1993; children: Anthony, Jeffrey, Scott. A in Bus., Williamsport (Pa.) Area C.C., 1974; B in Psychology, Lycoming Coll., 1976; JD, Thomas M. Cooley Law Sch., 1982. Assoc. Campana and Campana, Williamsport, 1982-83; ptnr. Campana, Rudinski & Groulx, Williamsport, 1984-94; pvt. practice Williamsport, 1994—; solicitor Borough of DuBoistown, Pa., 1987-94. Bd. dirs. Newberry Little League, Williamsport, 1974-76, Little Mountaineer Little League, South Williamsport, Pa., 1983-90. Mem. Am. Trial Lawyers Assn., Nat. Assn. Criminal Def. Lawyers, Pa. Assn. Criminal Def. Lawyers. Avocations: jet skiing, golf, baseball, weight lifting. Office: 339 1/2 Market St Williamsport PA 17701

RUDISILL, ROBERT MACK, JR., lawyer; b. Charlotte, N.C., Apr. 15, 1945; s. Robert Mack and Lucretia Rose (Hall) R.; m. Frances Barbara McMillan, Aug. 17, 1968 (div. June 1983); children: David Stuart, Michael Joseph; m. Deborah June Olive Baker, Oct. 28, 1989. Cert., U. Geneva, Switzerland, 1965; BA, U. Fla., Gainesville, 1967; cert., Hague Acad., Netherlands, 1969; JD, Duke U., 1970. Bar: Mich. 1970, U.S. Ct. Claims 1971, U.S. Supreme Ct. 1977, Fla. 1978. Assoc. Warner, Norcross & Judd, Grand Rapids, Mich., 1970-75; asst. counsel Mellon Bank, N.A., Pitts., 1975-76; dir. affiliate legal affairs Southeast Banking Corp., Miami, Fla., 1976-81; v.p., gen. counsel Sun Banks, Inc., Orlando, Fla., 1981-86; ptnr. Smith, Mackinnon, Mathews, Harris & Christiansen, Orlando, Fla., 1986-88, Foster & Kelly, Orlando, 1988-90; v.p. regulatory compliance Kirchman Corp., Orlando, 1990—; mem. adv. coun. Banking Law Inst., N.Y., 1984-90; co-founder So. Bank Counsel Group, Miami, 1979; co-founder, dir. Corp. Counsel Assn., Miami, 1978; instr. Am. Bankers Assn. Nat. Comml. Lending Sch., Norman, Okla., 1989-90, Sch. Banking of the South, Baton Rouge, 1984-86, Fla. Sch. Banking, Gainesville, 1980—; moderator Robert Morris Assocs. nat. workshops on comml. loan documentation, Phila., 1978-94; adj. prof. Valencia Community Coll., 1990-92. With USAFR, 1963-69. Mem. ABA, Fla. Bar Assn. (chmn. corp. counsel com. 1980-82, co-chmn. fin. instns. com. 1988-89), Grand Rapids C. of C. (chmn. urban mass transit com.), Mensa. Republican. Episcopalian. Avocations: sailing, underwater photography, playing guitar. Office: Kirchman Corp 711 E Altamonte Dr Altamonte Springs FL 32701-4804

RUDLIN, DAVID ALAN, lawyer; b. Richmond, Va., Nov. 4, 1947; s. Herbert and Dorothy Jean (Durham) R.; m. Judith Bond Faulkner, Oct. 4, 1975; 1 child, Sara Elizabeth. BA with high distinction, U. Va., 1969, JD with honors, 1973. Bar: Va. 1973, U.S. Dist. Ct. (ea. dist.) Va. 1975, U.S. Ct. Appeals (4th cir.) 1975, U.S. Ct. Appeals (10th cir.) 1980, U.S. Ct. Appeals (2d cir.) 1983, U.S. Supreme Ct. 1979. Assoc. gen. counsel U.S. Commn. on Orgn. of Govt. for Conduct of Fgn. Policy, Washington, 1973-75; assoc. Hunton & Williams, Richmond, 1975-82, ptnr., 1982—; adj. faculty William and Mary Coll., Marshall-Wythe Sch. Law, Williamsburg, Va., 1982—, U. Richmond, 1993—; faculty mem. Boulder and S.E. Regional programs Nat. Inst. Trial Advocacy; vis. lectr. U. Va. Sch. Law, Charlottesville, 1980—; mem. dispute resolution svcs. adv. coun. Supreme Ct. Va. Bd. dirs., ex officio mem. Cystic Fibrosis Found., Richmond; alumni Metro Leadership Richmond, 1988-89; mem. bd. editorial advisors The Environmental Counselor, Chesterland, Ohio, 1989—, The Toxics Law Reporter, Washington, 1988—; bd. dirs., apt. special adv., adv. com. Richmond Juvenile and Domestic Rels. Ct., 1990-94. Author: (book chpts.) Toxic Torts: Litigation Of Hazardous Substances Cases, 1983, 2nd edit., 1992, Federal Litigation Guide, 1989, Corporate Counselor's Guide To Environmental Law, 1989, Sanctions: Rule 11 and Other Powers, 1992; contbr. articles to profl. jours. and mags, chpts. to books. Mem. ABA (chmn. litigation sect. environ. litigation com. 1985-88, co-chmn. litigation sect. liaison with jud. com. 1988-91, vice-chmn. toxic and hazardous substances and environ. law com. tort and ins. practice sect., 1988-91, co-liaison to standing com. on environ. law from environ. litigation com. litigation section, 1988-92, dir. divsn. IV litigation sect. 1991-95, litigation sect. co-chair programs subcom. first amendment & media litigation com. 1993—, mem. litigation sect. task force on specialization 1994—, mem. litigation sect. task force on justice sys. 1994—, litigation sect. liaison to ABA jud. adminstrn. divsn. task force on reduction of litigation cost and delay 1995—, chair litigation sect. 1997 ann. meeting Washington 1995—), Va. Bar Assn. (chair joint com. on alternative dispute resolution with Va. State Bar 1991—), Va. Trial Lawyers Assn., Richmond Bar Assn. (chmn. membership com. 1988-91, mem. judiciary com. 1991-94, mem. continuing legal edn. com. 1994—), Va. Assn. Def. Attys., Ctr. Pub. Resources (products liability com. 1988—, judge Ann. Awards in Alternative Dispute Resolution 1990—). Office: Hunton & Williams Riverfront Pla E Tower 951 E Byrd St Richmond VA 23219-4074

RUDMAN, HERBERT CHARLES, education educator; b. N.Y.C., July 29, 1923; s. Abraham and Celia (Factor) R.; m. Florence Bromberg, Dec. 22, 1923; 1 child, Jane Ann (Mrs. Robert Schumacher). B.S., Bradley U., 1947; M.S., U. Ill., 1950, Ed.D., 1954. Tchr., asst. to prin. Peoria (Ill.) Bd. Edn., 1946-51; instr. U. Ill., 1951-53; chmn. dept. elementary edn. U.S.C., 1954-56; prof. adminstrn. and higher edn. Mich. State U., East Lansing, 1956-83, prof. ednl. measurement, evaluation and research design, 1983-93, prof. emeritus, 1993—; admissions testing cons. Nat. U. Sci. and Tech., Pakistan, 1992; chmn. tchr. testing tech. adv. coun. State of Mich., 1989-91. Author: (with Truman Kelly, Richard Madden and Eric Gardner) Stanford Achievement Tests, 1964, (with Richard Featherstone) Urban Schooling, 1968, (with Donald J. Leu) Preparation Programs for School Administrators, 1968, (with Frederick King, Herbert Epperly) Concepts in Social Science, 1970, School and State in the USSR, 1967, (with others) Stanford Achievement Tests, 1973, (with Frederick King) Understanding People, 1977, Understanding Communities, 1977, Understanding Regions, 1978, Understanding Our Country, 1979, Understanding Our World, 1979, tests for At Your Best, 1977, Toward Your Future, 1977, Balance In Your Life, 1977; (with others): Stanford Achievement Tests, 1982; editor: Measurement in Education, 1979-82; guest editor: Bull. Nat. Secondary Sch. Prins., 1986; contbr. articles to profl. jours. Assoc. bd. trustees Bradley U., 1992—. With USAAF, 1942-46. Recipient Outstanding Leadership award Mich. Assn. Elem. Prins., 1972; resolution for contbns. to ednl. measurement Mich. Senate, 1980; named Outstanding Prof. of Yr., Mich. State U. Alumni Assn., 1980; Ford Found. fellow USSR, 1958; head U.S. dep. to USSR for U.S. State Dept., 1963-64. Office: Mich State U Coll Edn 463 Erickson Hall East Lansing MI 48824-1034 *I have, all of my life, valued integrity and truth above all else. Without these two values all relationships—professional and personal—mean little. While I have valued excellence in professional conduct and commitment to professional goals, I have rarely lost perspective concerning my commitment to family and community. While honors, such as this one, are appreciated and valued by me, the greatest honor is that of watching our daughter grow into a fine young woman who, in turn, has developed many of the same values in her professional and personal life, and who now passes them on to her son and daughter.*

RUDMAN, JOAN ELEANOR, artist, educator; b. Owensburg, Ind., Oct. 7, 1927; d. William Hobart and Elizabeth Joaquin (Edington) Combs; m. William Rudman, June 9, 1951; children: Mary Beth, Pamela Ann. BA, Mich. State U., 1949, MA, 1951. tchr. Arlington Jr. and High Sch., Poughkeepsie, N.Y., Rippowam High Sch., Stamford, Conn., North Branch Club, West Dover, Vt., Greenwich (Conn.) Art Soc.; lectr., demonstrator Round Hill Community House, Greenwich; artist-in-residence So. Vt. Art Ctr., Manchester; arts reporter to 42 newspapers, N.Y., N.J. and Conn.; jurist of selection Hudson Valley Art Assn., 1971—; selection and awards jurist 2d Bergen County Mus. Open Mems. Juried Awards-Allied Artist, N.Y.; dir. Watercolor Workshops, Greenwich; liaison to Metro. Mus. Catharine Lorillard Wolfe Art Club; watercolor lectr. and demonstrator tri-state area. One-woman shows include Burning Tree Country Club, Greenwich, Town and Country Club, Hartford, Conn., U. Conn., Stamford, Conn. Valley Art Gallery, New Milford, So. Vt. Art Ctr., Manchester, The Nathaniel Witherall Gallery, Greenwich, Burke Rehab. Ctr., White Plains, N.Y.; exhibited in group shows at Wadsworth Antheneum, 1970, Mus. of Am. Art, New Britain, Conn., So. Vt. Art Ctr., Manchester, 1980-81, Nature Ctr., Westport, Conn., 1979-80, Mus. Fine Arts, Springfield, Mass., 1977, Wadsworth Antheneum, 1970, Mus. Am. Art, New Britain, Conn., Nat. Arts Club Open Show, 1969, 78, 79, 81, 82, Salmagundi Club, N.Y.C., 1978, 79, 80, 82, Am. Watercolor Soc., N.Y.C., 1974, 77, 82, Nat. Acad. Design, 1986, 94; represented in permanent collection Kresge Mus., East Lansing, Mich., numerous others; contbr. chpts. to books. Active North Stamford Congl. Ch. Recipient Nat. Art League awards, 1969, 71, 72, 73, Art Soc. Old Greenwich award, 1989, 94, Windsor Newton award, 1982, YWCA Greenwich Contemporary Women's Art Exhibit award, 1985, Best in Show award Art Soc. Old Greenwich, 1991, 1st Prize Graphics award Art Soc. Old Greenwich, 1994, 2nd Prize award Watercolor. Mem. Am. Watercolor Soc. (bd. dirs., asst. editor newsletter), Acad. Artists, Inc., Hoosier Salon (awards 1975, 76), Am. Artists Profl. League (50th Nat. Exhbn. award 1978), Hudson Valley Art Assn. (bd. dirs., publ. rels. editor, awards 1970, 80-90), Conn. Watercolor Soc. (award 1978), Conn. Artists 33, Whiskey Painters Am. (award 1978), Conn. Women Artists, Catharine Lorillard Wolfe Art Club (awards 1989, 90, chmn. 1989-90, co-chair 1994), Pen and Brush (award 1977-78), Nat. League Am. Pen Women (awards 1967, 69, 76-87), Nat. Press Club, Round Hill Community Guild (art dir.), New Canaan - Am. Assn. Univ. Women, Columbia U. Alumni Club (hon.), Nat. Soc. Daus. Am. Revolution (mem. Stamford chpt., historian), Mich. State Alumni Club, Delta Phi Delta (hon.), Phi Kappa Phi (hon.), Alpha Xi Delta. Republican. Home: 274 Quarry Rd Stamford CT 06903-5004

RUDMAN, MARK, poet, educator; b. N.Y.C., Dec. 11, 1948; s. Charles Kenneth and Marjorie Louise (Levy) R.; m. Madelaine Bates, Dec. 28, 1977; 1 child, Samuel. BA, New Sch. Social Rsch., 1971; MFA, Columbia U., 1974. With Tchrs. and Writers Collaborative, 1971-72, Poetry in the Schs. Program, 1974-80; adj. lectr. Queens Coll., CUNY, Flushing, 1980-81; poet-in-residence, assoc. prof. York Coll., CUNY, Jamaica, 1984-88; adj. prof., asst. dir. grad. creative writing program NYU, 1986—; adj. prof. creative writing sch. gen. studies Columbia U., 1988—, adj. prof. sch. of the arts, 1992; writer-in-residence U. Hawaii, Manoa, 1978, Wabash Coll., 1979, SUNY, Buffalo, 1979; lectr. Parsons Sch. Design, 1983; poet in residence SUNY, Purchase, 1991; lectr. in field. Author: Robert Lowell: An Introduction to Poetry, 1983, The Mystery in the Garden, 1985, The Ruin Revived, 1986, Literature and the Visual Arts, 1990, Diverse Voices: Essays on Poetry, 1993, Rider, 1994 (Cir. award Nat. Book Critics 1995), Realm of Unknowing: Mediatations on Art, Suicide, Uncertainty, and Other Transformations, 1995 (poems) IN the Neighboring Cell, 1982, By Contraries and Other Poems, 1970-84, Selected and New, The Nowhere Steps, 1990, The Millennium Hotel, 1996; translator (with Bohdan Boychuk) Square of Angels: The Selected Poems of Bohdan Antonych, 1977, Orchard Lamps (Ivan Drach), 1978, My Sister--Life (Boris Pasternak), 1983, rev. edit., 1993, The Sublime Malady (Boris Pasternak), 1983; editor and co-translator: Memories of Love: The Selected Poems of Bohdan Boychuk, 1981; editor: Secret Destinations: Writers on Travel, 1986; poetry and criticism editor Pequod, 1975—, editor-in-chief, 1984—; contbr. poems, tranls. of poems and essays to anthologies and profl. jours. Recipient Acad. Am. Poets award, 1971, Hackney award Birmingham Arts Festival, 1972, Max Hayward award Columbia U. Translation Ctr., 1985, Editor's award N.Y. Coun. Arts, 1986; Internat. P.E.N. fellow, 1976-77, Yaddo fellow, 1977, 83, Coordinating Coun. for Literary Mags. fellow, 1981-82, Ingram Merrill fellow, 1983-84, N.Y. Found. Arts fellow, 1988, fellow in poetry NEA, 1994, Guggenheim fellow in poetry, 1996—. Mem. Internat. P.E.N., Poetry Soc. Am. (mem. bd. govs. 1984-88), Nat. Book Critics Circle. Office: 817 W End Ave New York NY 10025-5370 also: New York Univ Dept of English New York NY 10003

RUDMAN, SOLOMON KAL, magazine publisher; b. Phila., Mar. 6, 1930; s. Benjamin and Lena (Holtzman) R.; m. Lucille Steinhauer, June 29, 1958; 1 child, Mitchell. BS in Edn., U. Pa., 1951; MS in Edn., Temple U., 1957. Chmn. dept. spl. edn. Franklin D. Roosevelt Sch., Bristol Twp., Pa., 1960-68; pub. premier record/ radio trade Fri. Morning Quarterback, Cherry Hill, Pa., 1968—; bd. dirs. Variety Club, NARAS; co-host Merv Griffin TV Show, 1981-82; music expert Today Show, 1981-82, Tomorrow Show, 1981-82, Tom Snyder TV Show; creator-sponsor high sch. piano competition, Phila. and suburbs of Pa.; sponsor-host Phial. Franklin Inst. of Sci. and Fels Planetarium mobile sci. programs, top-level entertainment shows to most Phila.-N.J. Sr. Citizens' homes, children's and vets. hosps.; co-host, talent booker Easter Seals Telethon. Bd. dirs. Phila. Broadcast Pioneers. Recipient Lifetime Achievement award in music Phila. Music Conf., Lifetime Music Achievement award Delaware Valley Music Poll. Mem. Phila. Music Alliance (bd. dirs.), Nat. Arthritis Found. (bd. dirs.), Nat. Acad. Arts and Sci. (bd. dirs.), Masons. Office: Friday Morning Quarterback 1930 Marlton Pike E Cherry Hill NJ 08003-2150

RUDMAN, WARREN BRUCE, former senator, lawyer, think tank executive; b. Boston, May 18, 1930; s. Edward G. and Theresa (Levenson) R.; m. Shirley Wahl, July 9, 1952; children: Laura, Alan, Debra. B.S., Syracuse (N.Y.) U., 1952; LL.B., Boston Coll., 1960. Bar: N.H. 1960, D.C. Mem. firm Rudman & Gormley, Nashua, N.H., 1960-69; counsel to Gov. Walter Peterson, Concord, N.H., 1970; atty. gen. State of N.H., Concord, 1970-76; mem. firm. Sheehan Phinney Bass & Green, 1976-80; U.S. Senator from N.H., 1981-92; co-founder Concord Coalition, 1992—; ptnr. Paul, Weiss, Rifkind, Wharton & Garrison, N.Y.C., Washington, 1993—; deputy chmn. Fed. Reserve Bank of Boston. 1993, mem. bd. dirs. Chubb Corp., 1993—, Raytheon Corp., 1993—, Dreyfus Corp., 1993—. Founder, chmn. bd. trustees Daniel Webster Jr. Coll., 1965—, trustees Boston Coll., Aspen Inst., Valley Forge, Mil Acad.; chmn., founder New Eng. Aero. Inst., v. chmn. Pres. Fgn. Intelligence adv. bd.; sr. adv. com. Inst. of Politics John F. Kennedy Sch. Capt. AUS, 1952-54, Korea. Decorated Bronze Star, Combat Inf. Badge. Mem. Am. Legion. Republican. Office: Paul Weiss Rifkind Wharton & Garrison 1615 L St NW Ste 1300 Washington DC 20036-5694*

RUDMANN, SALLY VANDER LINDEN, medical technology educator; b. Rochester, N.Y., Sept. 10, 1942; d. Egbert W. and Mildred M. (Schrader) Vander Linden; m. Ronald J. Rudmann, June 4, 1964 (div.); children: Daniel G., Stephen M.; m. James G. Barlow, Mar. 31, 1980. BA, Russell Sage Coll., 1964; MS, Wright State U., 1980; PhD, Ohio State U., 1986. Lic. med. technologist, Calif.; registered med. technologist; cert. Nat. Agy. Med. Lab. Pers.; CPR instr., ARC. Intern in med. tech. South bay Hosp., Redondo Beach, Calif., 1965-66; med. technologist Green Meml. Hosp., Xenia, Ohio, 1968-72; med. technologist Community Blood Ctr., Dayton, Ohio, 1974-75, intern, 1975-76; tech. supr. Greene Meml. Hosp., Xenia, 1976-78; tech. dir. Brown Labs., Columbus, Ohio, 1979-82; med. technologist Drs. Hosp. North, Columbus, Ohio, 1982-84; instr med. tech. Ohio State U., Columbus, Ohio, 1984-87, from asst. prof. to assoc. prof. med. tech., 1987—, dir. med. tech., 1987—; lect. and cons. in field. Editor: Textbook of Blood Banking and Transfusion Medicine, 1994; cons. MacMillan Pub. Co., 1984; editl. assoc. procs., editl. rev. Modern Blood Banking and Transfusion Practice, 1987, 88; cons. editor Clin. Lab. Sci., 1987—, editor-in-chief, 1988; profl. adv. panel Med. Lab. Observer, 1989-90; contbr. numerous articles to profl. jours. Mem. Am. Assn. Blood Banks (abstract rev. com., inspector inspection and accreditation program, sci. and tech. workshop com.), Am. Soc. Clin. Lab. Sci. (planning com. region IV 1985), Am. Soc. Clin. Pathologists (R&D com., cons., lic. specialist in blood banking), Am. Soc. Allied Health Professions, Ohio Soc. Allied Health Professions, Ohio Soc. Med. Tech., Ohio Assn. BLood Banks (chairperson awards com. 1990-92, mem. award com. 1982—), Dayton Area Blood Bankers (pres. 1976), Phi Kappa Phi. Avocations: hiking, fitness, photography. Office: Ohio State U Med Tech Divsn 1583 Perry St Columbus OH 43210-1234

RUDNER, SARA, dancer, choreographer; b. Bklyn., Feb. 16, 1944; d. Henry Nathaniel and Jeannette (Smolensky) R.; 1 child, Eli Rudner Marschner. A.B. in Russian Studies, Barnard Coll., 1964. Dancer Sansardo Dance Co., N.Y.C., 1964-65, Am. Dance Co. at Lincoln Ctr., N.Y.C., 1965, Shakespeare Festival Touring Children's Show, N.Y.C., 1966; featured dancer Twyla Tharp Dance Found., N.Y.C., 1966-85; artistic dir., dancer 18th St. Dance Found., N.Y.C., 1977—; guest dancer Joffrey Ballet, N.Y.C., 1973, Pilobolus Dance Theatre, N.Y.C., 1975, Lar Lubovitch Dance Co., N.Y.C., 1975-76; guest lectr., choreographer grad. dance dept. UCLA, 1975; tchr. master workshop NYU Theater Program, 1988, 89, 90. Choreographer: Palm Trees and Flamingoes, 1980, Dancing for an Hour or So, 1981, Minute by Minute, 1982, Eight Solos, 1991, Heartbeats, Inside Out, 1993 (with Jennifer Tipton and Dana Reitz) Necessary Weather, 1994. Grantee Creative Artists Pub. Svc. Program, N.Y., 1975-76, N.Y. State Coun. on Arts, 1975-78, Nat. Endowment for Arts, 1979-81, 91-92, 94-97; Guggenheim fellow, 1981-82; recipient N.Y. Dance and Performance award, 1984.

RUDNEY, HARRY, biochemist, educator; b. Toronto, Ont., Can., Apr. 14, 1918; came to U.S., 1948, naturalized, 1956; s. Joshua and Dina (Gorback) R.; m. Bernice Dina Snider, June 25, 1946; children—Joel David, Paul Robert. B.A., U. Toronto, 1947, M.A., 1948; Ph.D., Western Res. U., 1952. Faculty Western Res. U., Cleve., 1952-67; prof. biochemistry Western Res. U., 1965-67; prof., dir. dept. biochemistry and molecular biology U. Cin. Coll. Medicine, 1967-89, Andrew Carnegie Found. prof. biol. chemistry, 1967-89, prof. emeritus, 1989—; vis. prof. Case Inst. Tech., Cleve., 1965-66; mem. rsch. adv. panel N.E. Ohio Heart Assn., 1966-67; mem. panel metabolic biology NSF, 1968-71; rsch. career award com. NIH, 1969-73; mem. biochemistry test com. Nat. Bd. Med. Examiners, 1974-77; co-chair Instnl. Rev. Bd., U. Cinn. Med. Ctr., 1994—, interim chair dept. ph armecology, 1994—. Mem. editorial bd. Archives of Biochemistry and Biophysics, 1965-89, Jour. Biol. Chemistry, 1975-80; contbr. articles profl. jours. Recipient USPHS Research Career award, 1963-67; Am. Cancer Soc. scholar, 1954-56; NSF Sr. Research fellow U. Amsterdam, Netherlands, 1957. Mem. Am. Soc. Biol. Chemists, Am. Chem. Soc., Am. Soc. Microbiology, Biochem. Soc. (Eng.), Sigma Xi. Home: 4040 Winding Way Cincinnati OH 45229-1919

RUDNICK, ELLEN AVA, health care executive; b. New Haven; d. Harold and C. Vivian (Soybel) R.; children from previous marriage: Sarah, Noah; m. Paul W. Earle. BA, Vassar Coll., 1972; MBA, U. Chgo., 1973. Sr. fin. analyst Quaker Oats, Chgo., 1973-75; various positions Baxter Internat., Deerfield, Ill., 1975-80, dir. planning, 1980-83, corp. v.p., 1985-1990; pres. Baxter Mgmt. Svcs., Deerfield, 1983-1990, HCIA, Balt., 1990-92, CEO Advs., Northbrook, Ill., 1992—; prin., chmn. Pacific Biometrics, Irvine, Calif., 1993—; bd. dirs. NCCI. Chief crusader Met. Chgo. United Way, 1982-85; pres. coun. Nat. Coll. Edn., Evanston, Ill., 1983—; cir. of friends Chgo. YMCA, 1985-89; bd. dirs. Highland Park Hosp., 1990—, NCCI. Mem. Chgo. Network, Econs. Club Chgo. (officer, bd. dirs.). Office: CEO Advs 255 Revere Dr Ste 111 Northbrook IL 60062-1595

RUDNICK, IRENE KRUGMAN, lawyer, former state legislator, educator; b. Columbia, S.C., Dec. 27, 1929; d. Jack and Jean (Getter) Krugman; AB cum laude, U. S.C., 1949, JD, 1952; m. Harold Rudnick, Nov. 7, 1954; children: Morris, Helen Gail. Admitted to S.C. bar, 1952; individual practice law, Aiken, S.C., 1952—, now ptnr. Rudnick & Rudnick; instr. bus. law, criminal law U. S.C., Aiken, 1962—; tchr. Warrenville Elem. Sch., 1965-70; supt. edn. Aiken County, 1970-72; mem. S.C. Ho. of Reps., 1972-78, 80-84, 86-94; pres. Adath Yeshurun Synagogue; active Aiken County Dem. Party, S.C. Dem. Party, Network Aiken; hon. mem. Aiken Able-Disabled. Recipient Citizen of Yr. award, 1976-77, Bus. and Profl. Women's Career Woman of Yr., 1978, 94, Aiken County Friend of Edn. award, 1985, 93, Outstanding Legis. award Disabled Vets., 1991, Citizen of the Yr. award Planned Parenthood, 1994, Sertoma Svc. to Mankind award, 1996. Mem. NEA, S.C. Tchrs. Assn., Aiken County Tchrs. Assn., Am. Bar Assn., Aiken County Bar Assn., Nat. Order Women Legislators, AAUW, Network Aiken, Aiken Able-Disabled (hon.), Alpha Delta Kappa. Jewish. Clubs: Order Eastern Star, Hadassah, Am. Legion Aux. Office: PO Box 544 135 Pendleton NW Aiken SC 29802

RUDNICK, PAUL, playwright, screenwriter; b. Piscataway, N.J., 1957. Attended, Yale U. Author: (novels) Social Disease, 1986, I'll Take It, 1989; (plays) Poor Little Lambs, 1982 (Outer Critics Cirle award 1983), Cosmetic Surgery, 1983, I Hate Hamlet, 1991, Jeffrey, 1993 (Obie award for outstanding playwriting 1994, Outer Drama Critics Cirle award 1994, John Gassner Playwriting award 1994), The Naked Truth, 1994; (screenplays) (with others as Joseph Howard) Sister Act, 1992, Addams Family Values, 1993; columnist: (as Libby Gelman-Waxer) "If You Ask Me", Premiere mag., 1989—. Office: CAA 9830 Wilshire Blvd Beverly Hills CA 90212-1804

RUDNICK, PAUL DAVID, lawyer; b. Chgo., May 15, 1940; s. Harry Louis and Cele (Gordon) R.; m. Hope Korshak, June 13, 1963; children: William A., Carolyn. BS, Tulane U., 1962; JD cum laude, Northwestern U., 1965. Bar: Ill. 1965, Colo. 1994, U.S. Dist. Ct. (no. dist.) Ill. Assoc. Schiff, Hardin & Waite, Chgo., 1965-66; ptnr. Rudnick & Wolfe, Chgo., 1966—. Editor Northwestern U. Law Rev., 1964-65; co-editor, author: Illinois Real Estate Forms, 1989. Mem. Am. Coll. Real Estate Lawyers, Internat. Found. Employee Benefits, Tavern Club, Order of Coif. Avocations: skiing, music. Office: Rudnick & Wolfe 203 N La Salle St Ste 1800 Chicago IL 60601-1210

RUDNICK, REBECCA SOPHIE, lawyer, educator; b. Bakersfield, Calif., Nov. 26, 1952; d. Oscar and Sophie Mary (Loven) R.; m. Robert Anthoine, Dec. 2, 1990. BA, Willamette U., Salem, Oreg., 1974; JD, U. Tex., 1978; LLM, NYU, 1984. Bar: Tex. 1978, La. 1979, N.Y. 1980, Calif. 1980. Law clk. to Hon. Charles Schwartz, Jr. U.S. Dist. Ct., New Orleans, 1978-79; assoc. Winthrop, Stimson, Putnam & Roberts, N.Y.C., 1979-85; spl. counsel N.Y. Legis. Tax Study Commn., N.Y.C., 1983-84; asst. prof. law Ind. U., Bloomington, 1985-90; assoc. prof. of law Ind. U. Sch. of Law, Bloomington, 1990-94; assoc. prof. law London Law Consortium, Eng., 1994; vis. assoc. prof. law U. Conn., Hartford, 1984-85; vis. asst. prof. law U. Tex., Austin, 1988; vis. assoc. prof. law U. N.C., Chapel Hill, 1991, Boston U., 1994-95, U. Pa., Phila., 1995-96; prof.-in-residence, IRS, 1991-92; vis. scholar NSW, Australia, 1994, U. Sydney, Australia, 1994; vis. prof. law Seattle U., 1996—. Contbr. articles to various profl. jours. and publs. Dir., gen. counsel Project GreenHope: Svcs. for Women, N.Y.C., 1980-83; advisor, tech. asst. Internat. Monetary Fund, Washington, 1994. Mem. ABA (tax sect. 1982—, sec. tax sect. passthrough entities task force 1986-88, subcom. chairs for incorps. and CLE/important devel. tax sect., 1989—, corp. tax com. 1989—, tax sect. task force on integration 1990—), Am. Assn. Law Schs. (editor tax sect. newsletter 1987—), Assn. Bar of City of N.Y. (admiralty com. 1982-85), Internat. Fiscal Assn., Internat. Bar Assn. Office: Seattle U Sch Law 950 Broadway Plz Tacoma WA 98402

RUDNICKA, ANNA RUTH, physician; b. Cieszyn, Poland, Nov. 9, 1915; d. Jacob and Charlotte (Gutmann) Huppert; m. Ian Levi, Aug., 1939 (dec. Jan. 1942); 1 child, Yoram Levi; m. Eduard Rudnicki, 1977 (dec.). MD, U. Cracow Med. Sch., Poland, 1948. MD, head of ward for pulmonary diseases Hosp. Cieszyn, Poland, 1946-51; chief physician of hosp. Katowice, Poland, 1951-57; family practitioner Kupat-Holim Med. Inst., Jerusalem, Israel, 1977; pvt. practice Jerusalem, Israel, 1977—, nat. ins. inst., 1977—; med. bd. Israel, 1988—. Mem. Internat. Assn. for Med. Law, Internat. Assn. for Vol. Effort, Soroptimist Internat. European Fedn. (pres. Israel union 1982-84).

Avocations: swimming, walking, photography. Home: 26/10 Eshkol Blvd, Jerusalem 97764, Israel Office: Medical Centre, Paran Str, Jerusalem Israel

RUDNICKI, JOHN WALTER, engineering educator; b. Huntington, W.Va., Aug. 12, 1951; s. John Walter Francis and Helen (Nadenichek) R.; m. Joan Weston, June 11, 1977; children: Ellen (dec.), Jean, Stephen, Christopher. BS, Brown U., 1973, MS, 1974, PhD, 1977. Rsch. fellow Seismological Lab. Calif. Inst. Tech., Pasadena, 1977-78; asst. prof. dept. theoretical and applied mechanics U. Ill., Urbana, 1978-81; assoc. prof. dept. civil engring. Northwestern U., Evanston, Ill., 1981-90, prof. dept. civil engring., 1990—, prof. dept. mech. engring. and dept. geol. sci., 1991—; mem. U.S. Nat. Com. on Rock Mechanics, 1996—; adv. bd. Mechanics of Cohesive-Frictional Material and Structures, An Internat. Jour. on Experiments, Modelling and Computations; cons. Sandia Nat. Labs., Albuquerque, 1982-92, SAIC, 1990-91, Amoco, 1995—. Contbr. articles to Jour. Geophys. Rsch., Jour. Applied Mechanics, Pure and Applied Geophysics, Ann. Rev. Earth and Planetary Sci., Jour. Applied Mechanics, 1988-94; assoc editor: Jour. Geophys. Rsch., 1986-88. Recipient Outstanding Rsch. in Rock Mechanics award U.S. Nat. Com. on Rock Mechanics, 1977. Mem. AAAS, ASME, ASEE, Am. Geophys. Union, Seismol. Soc. Am., Sigma Xi. Achievements include discovery of solutions for cracks and dislocations in porous elastic solids and application of same to the study of faults in the Earth's crust. Office: Northwestern U Dept Mechanical Engring 2145 Sheridan Rd Evanston IL 60208-0834

RUDO, MILTON, retired manufacturing company executive, consultant; b. Balt., Jan. 17, 1919; s. Saul E. and Bertha (Berkowitz) R.m. Roslind Mandel, Mar. 27, 1943; children: Stephanie Ellen, Neil Dennis. BA, Johns Hopkins U., 1940; AMP, Harvard U., 1964. With Brunswick Corp., Skokie, Ill., 1940-84, beginning as sales rep., Balt., successively br. mgr., Pitts., billiard mdse. mgr., Chgo., bowling and billiard products mdse. mgr., Chgo., sales v.p. Ea. region, Harrisburg, Pa., div. sales v.p., gen. sales mgr., Chgo., mktg. v.p., Chgo., pres. Bowling div., corp. v.p., Chgo., pres. Bowling div., Chgo., 1940-74, group v.p. recreation bus., 1974-84, ret., 1984, cons. to chief exec. officer, 1984-87; dir., cons. to chief exec., Donlen Leasing Corp, Skokie, Ill., 1986-90. Pres. Nat. Bowling Hall of Fame and Mus., 1979. Capt. AUS, 1942-45, ETO. Recipient ann. award N.Y. Mktg. Club, 1960, Industry Service award, 1973; named to Bowling Hall of Fame, 1984. Mem. Nat. Bowling Council (pres. 1972), Briarwood Country Club, Hamlet Country Club (Delray Beach, Fla.). Office: 1777 Balsam Rd Highland Park IL 60035-4343

RUDOFF, SHELDON, lawyer, former religious organization executive; b. Bklyn., May 29, 1933; s. Raphael and Goldie (Gorelick) R.; m. Hedda Muller, Nov. 22, 1964; children: Shaindy, Sara, Simone. BA cum laude, Yeshiva Coll., 1954; JSD cum laude, NYU, 1958; ordination, RIETS, 1957. Bar: N.Y. 1958, U.S. Dist. Ct. (so. and ea. dists.) N.Y. 1958, U.S. Supreme Ct. 1978. Ptnr. Shatzkin, Cooper & Rudoff, N.Y.C., 1970-84, Goodkind, Labaton, Rudoff & Sucharow, N.Y.C., 1984—; hon. pres. Union Orthodox Jewish Congregation Am., 1990-94. V.p. Yeshiva Coll. Alumni, N.Y.C., 1962-64; pres. Young Israel West Side, N.Y.C., 1969-72; sec. Orthodox Union, 1972-76, v.p., 1976-78, sr. v.p., 1978-84, chmn. bd., 1984-90, pres. 1990—, mem. exec. com. World Zionist Orgn.; bd. dirs. Am. Zionist Movement; trustee United Israel Appeal, Fedn. Jewish Philanthropies, 1980-91, United Jewish Appeal, Ctrl. Claims Conf. Recipient Pres.'s award Orthodox Union, N.Y.C., 1972, Nat. Leadership award Nat. Conf. Synagogue Youth, N.Y.C., 1974, Kesser Shem Tov award Ortohdox Union, 1995. Mem. ABA, N.Y. State Bar Assn., N.Y. City Bar Assn. (transp. com. 1976—). Home: 110 Riverside Dr New York NY 10024-3715 Office: Goodkind Labaton Rudoff & Sucharow 100 Park Ave New York NY 10017-5516

RUDOLPH, ABRAHAM MORRIS, physician, educator; b. Johannesburg, Republic of South Africa, Feb. 3, 1924; s. Chone and Sarah (Feinstein) R.; m. Rhona Sax, Nov. 2, 1949; children: Linda, Colin, Jeffrey. M.B.B.Ch. summa cum laude, U. Witwatersrand, Johannesburg, 1946, M.D., 1951. Instr. Harvard Med. Sch., 1955-57, assoc. pediatrics, 1957-60; assoc. cardiologist in charge cardiopulmonary lab. Children's Hosp., Boston, 1955-60; dir. pediatric cardiology Albert Einstein Coll. Medicine, 1960-66; prof. pediatrics, assoc. prof. physiology Albert Einstein Coll. Medicine, N.Y.C., 1962-66; vis. pediatrician Bronx Mcpl. Hosp. Ctr., N.Y.C., 1960-66; prof. pediatrics U. Calif., San Francisco, 1966—, prof. physiology, 1974-88, Neider prof. pediatric cardiology, prof. ob-gyn and reproductive scis., 1974—, chmn. dept. pediatrics, 1987-91; practice medicine, specializing in pediatric cardiology San Francisco.; mem. cardiovascular study sect. NIH, 1961-65, mem. nat. adv. heart council, 1968-72; established investigator Am. Heart Assn., 1958-62; career scientist Health Research Council, City N.Y., 1962-66; Harvey lectr., Oxford, Eng., 1984; inaugural lectr. 1st Nat. Congress Italian Soc. Perinatal Medicine, 1985. Mem. editorial bd. Pediatrics, 1964-70; assoc. editor Circulation Research, 1965-70; mem. editorial bd. Circulation, 1966-74, 83—; Am. Assoc. editor Pediatric Research, 1970-77; contbr. articles profl. jours. Recipient Merit award Nat. Heart, Lung and Blood Inst., 1986, Arvo Yllpo medal Helsinki U., Finland, 1987, Jonxis medal Children's Hosp. Groningen, 1993. Fellow Royal Coll. Physicians (Edinburgh), Royal Coll. Physicians (London); mem. NAS Inst. Medicine, Am. Acad. Pediatrics (E. Mead Johnson award for research in pediatrics 1964, Borden award 1979, past chmn. sect. on cardiology, Lifetime Med. Edn. award 1992, Joseph St. Geme leadership award Pediatrics 1993), Am. Phys. Soc., Soc. for Clin. Investigation, Soc. for Pediatric Research (coun. 1961-64), Am. Pediatric Soc. (coun. 1985-92, v.p. 1992-93, pres. 1993-94), Am. Heart Assn. (Rsch. Achievement award 1991). Office: U Calif Cardiovascular Rsch Inst Calif Rm 1403 Hse San Francisco CA 94143

RUDOLPH, ALAN, film director; b. Los Angeles, Dec. 18, 1943; s. Oscar Rudolph. asst. dir.: The Long Goodbye, 1973, California Split, 1974, Nashville, 1975; co-writer: Buffalo Bill and the Indians, 1976; dir., screenwriter: Premonition, 1972, Welcome to L.A., 1977, Remember My Name, 1979, Endangered Species, 1982, Choose Me, 1984, The Moderns, 1988, Love at Large, 1990, Equinox, 1993, Mrs. Parker and the Vicious Circle, 1994; dir., story: Roadie, 1980; dir.: Return Engagement, 1983 (film documentary), Songwriter, 1984, Made in Heaven, 1987, Mortal Thoughts, 1991; actor: The Rocket Man, 1954, The Player, 1992. Mem. Dirs. Guild Am. Office: William Morris Agency Inc 151 S El Camino Dr Beverly Hills CA 90212-2704

RUDOLPH, CHARLES HERMAN, retired computer software development executive; b. Balt., Mar. 14, 1953; s. Charles Henry and Margaret Theresa (McCarron) R.; m. Terri Gay; 1 child, Kristin Margaret. B.S. summa cum laude, King's Coll., 1975. Asst. mgr. product mktg. Datapoint Corp., San Antonio, 1977-78, mgr. systems planning, 1978-79, mgr. software devel., 1979-82, dir. software devel., 1982-84; sr. dir. Custom Systems, San Antonio, 1984-85; dir. engring. Digital Communications Assocs., Atlanta, 1985-88; v.p. mktg. Crosstalk Communications, Roswell, Ga., 1988-89, pres., 1989-90; pres. Pacific Data Producers, San Diego, 1990-93; v.p. Peregrine Sys. Inc., San Diego, Calif., 1994—. Republican. Lutheran. Home: 13814 Lake Poway Rd Poway CA 92064-2278 Office: Peregrine Sys Inc 12670 High Bluff Dr San Diego CA 92130

RUDOLPH, FREDERICK, history educator; b. Balt., June 19, 1920; s. Charles Frederick and Jennie Hill (Swope) R.; m. Dorothy Dannenbaum, June 18, 1949; children: Marta R. MacDonald, Lisa R. Cushman. B.A., Williams Coll., 1942, Litt.D., 1985; M.A., Yale U., 1949, Ph.D., 1953; LHD, U. Rochester, 1994. Instr. history Williams Coll., 1946-47; asst. instr. Yale, 1949-50; mem. faculty Williams Coll., 1951—, prof., 1961—, Mark Hopkins prof. history, 1964-82, emeritus, 1982—, chmn. Am. civilization program, 1971-80; Williams Coll. marshal, 1978-87; vis. lectr. history and edn. Harvard U., 1960, 61; vis. prof. Sch. Edn., U. Calif.-Berkeley, 1983; mem. commn. plans and objectives Am. Council Edn., 1963-66; mem. study group on postsecondary edn. Nat. Inst. Edn., 1980-83; mem. com. on baccalaureate degrees Assn. Am. Colls., 1981-85; vis. assoc. Ctr. Studies in Higher Edn., U. Calif.-Berkeley, 1983. Author: Mark Hopkins and the Log, 1956, The American College and University: A History, 1962, rev. edit., 1990, Curriculum: A History of the American Undergraduate Course of Study Since 1636, 1977, rev. edit., 1993; editor: Essays on Education in the Early Republic, 1965, Perspectives: A Williams Anthology, 1983; exec. editor: Change, 1980-84, cons. editor, 1985-92. Founding mem. Berkshire County Hist. Soc., 1962, v.p., 1962-66, pres., 1966-68, bd. dirs., 1974-76; trustee Hancock-Shaker Cmty. Inc., 1974-91, Wyoming Sem., 1976-79, Bennington Mus., 1985-95; bd. dirs. Armand Hammer United World Coll. Am. West, 1993—. Capt. AUS, 1942-46. Guggenheim fellow, 1958-59, 68-69; recipient Frederic W. Ness award Assn. Am. Colls., 1980, Rogerson cup Williams Coll., 1982, Disting. Svc. award Wyo. Seminary, 1986. Mem. Nat. Acad. Edn., Mass. Hist. Soc., Am. Hist. Assn., Am. Studies Assn., Orgn. Am. Historians, AAUP, Phi Beta Kappa. Democrat. Home: 234 Ide Rd Williamstown MA 01267-2800

RUDOLPH, FREDERICK BYRON, biochemistry educator; b. St. Joseph, Mo., Oct. 17, 1944; s. John Max and Maxine Leah (Wood) R.; m. Glenda M. Myers, June 18, 1971; children: Anna Dorine, William K. BS in Chemistry, U. Mo., Rolla, 1966; PhD in Biochemistry, Iowa State U., 1971. Prof. biochemistry Rice U., Houston, 1972—, chair biochemistry and cell biology, 1995—, dir. Lab. for Biochem. and Genetic Engring., 1986—, exec. dir. Inst. Bioscience and Bioengineering, 1993—; chair dept. biochemistry and cell biology, 1995—, chair Dept. Biochemistry Cell Biology, 1995—; cons. World Book, Chgo., 1972—; mem. biochemistry study sect. NIH, Bethesda, Md., 1983-87; bd. dirs. S.W. Assn. Biotech. Cos., Houston, 1990-93. Contbr. over 160 articles to profl. jours. including Jour. Biol. Chemistry, Biochemistry, Transplantation, Exptl. Hematology, Jour. Parenteral and Enteral Nutrition, Jour. Molecular Biology, Applied and Environ. Microbiology, Life Scis., Archives Biochem. Biophysics, Critical Care Medicine, Archives Surgery, Sci.; also chots. to books. Recipient Disting. Alumnus award Iowa State U., 1980. Mem. Am. Chem. Soc., Am. Soc. for Biochemistry and Molecular Biology. Achievements include research on dietary requirements for immune function, new techniques for protein purification, new methods for kinetic analysis of enzymes, structure and function of various enzymes. Office: Rice U Dept Biochemistry PO Box 1892 Houston TX 77251-1892

RUDOLPH, FREDERICK WILLIAM, contractor; b. Wood County, Ohio, July 10, 1929; s. John William and Verna Sophia (Libbe) R.; m. Marilyn Louise Early, Jan. 31, 1954; children—Gail Susan, William David, Frederick John, John Douglas. B.S., Bowling Green State U., 1951. Constrn. supt. V. N. Holderman, Columbus, Ohio, 1951-54, United Constrn., Winona, Minn., 1954-55; pres. Rudolph-Libbe, Inc., Walbridge, Ohio, 1955—; dir. Trustcorp Bank, Ohio; dir. N.W. Ohio Bank, 1978-81. Named Concrete Man of Yr., Concrete Improvement Assn., 1977. Mem. Young Pres.'s Orgn., World Bus. Council, Associated Gen. Contractors (chpt. pres. 1975). Republican. Lutheran. Clubs: Belmont Country, Sigma Alpha Epsilon. Home: 6486 Latcha Rd Walbridge OH 43465-9738 Office: Rudolph/Libbe Inc 6494 Latcha Rd Walbridge OH 43465-9738*

RUDOLPH, GILBERT LAWRENCE, lawyer; b. L.A., Aug. 23, 1946; s. Martin Muttel and Marion (Perlman) R.; Susan Ilene Fellenbaum, Sept. 18, 1983; children: Samara Lisa, Felicia Beth. BA, Ariz. State U., 1967; postgrad., Am. U., Washington, 1967-69; JD, U. Cin., 1973. Bar: D.C. 1973, U.S. Dist. Ct. D.C. 1974, U.S. Ct. Appeals (D.C. cir.) 1974, Ariz. 1975, U.S. Dist. Ct. Ariz. 1975, Calif. 1979. Assoc. Streich, Lang, Weeks & Cardon, P.A., Phoenix, 1975-78; prin. Gilbert L. Rudolph, P.C., Phoenix, 1978-87; sr. mem. O'Connor, Cavanagh, Anderson, Killingsworth & Beshears, P.A., Phoenix, 1987—; lectr. on lending issues. Bd. dirs. Make-A-Wish Found. of Am., 1984-89, Aid to Adoption of Spl. Kids, Ariz., 1995—. Mem. ABA (com. on consumer fin. svcs. bus. law sect. 1981—, com. on comml. fin. svcs. 1989—, mem. com. on uniform comml. code 1992—), Conf. on Consumer Fin. Lqaw (governing com. 1986—), Ariz. Consumer Fin. Assn. (regulatory counsel 1996—). Republican. Jewish. Office: O'Connor Cavanagh Anderson Killingsworth & Beshears PA 1 E Camelback Rd Ste 1100 Phoenix AZ 85012-1656

RUDOLPH, JAMES FRANCIS, financial planner; b. Columbus, Ohio, Aug. 25, 1940; s. Harold Francis and Edna Louise (Johnson) R.; m. Patricia E. Scott, Aug. 31, 1963; children: Joseph, Jason and Jon (twins). BA, Ohio State U., 1967. Coord. product design Gen. Fireproof Ins. Co., Youngstown, Ohio, 1967-71; salesman Mut. N.Y., Columbus, 1971-74, Columbus Life, 1974-78, Guardian Life, Columbus, 1978-82; bus. coord. Northwestern Mut., Columbus, 1982-85; sales mgr. John Hancock Life, Columbus, 1986-87; seminar specialist Ctrl. Life Iowa, Columbus, 1987—; sr. cons. Dome Fin. Svcs., Westerville, Ohio, 1987—. Meem. adv. bd. James Cancer Hosp., Columbus, Am. Life Assn., Columbus; deacon Worthington (Ohio) Presbyn. Ch., 1983-85. Mem. Internat. Assn. Fin. Planners, Columbus Assn. Life Underwriters, Million Dollar Roundtable (life, qualifying, various internal coms. 1976—), Ohio State U. Alumni Assn. Republican. Avocations: golf, reading, outdoor sports. Office: Dome Fin Svcs 68 Westerview Dr Westerville OH 43081-2682

RUDOLPH, JEFFREY N., museum director. Exec. dir. California Museum of Science and Industry, Los Angles, Calif. Office: Calif Mus Sci & Industry 700 State Dr Los Angeles CA 90037-1237

RUDOLPH, LAVERE CHRISTIAN, library director; b. Jasper, Ind., Dec. 24, 1921; s. Joseph Frank and Rose (Stradtner) R. A.B., DePauw U., 1948; B.D., Louisville Presbyn. Sem., 1951; Ph.D., Yale, 1958; student, U. Zurich, Switzerland, 1960; M.L.S., Ind. U., 1968. Ordained to Ministry Presbyn. Ch., 1950; pastor in Ind. and Conn., 1950-54; mem. faculty Louisville Presbyn. Sem., 1954-69, prof. ch. history, 1960-69; lectr. history U. Louisville, 1965-69; rare books bibliographer Van Pelt Library U. Pa.; head tech. services Lilly Library, Ind. U., 1970-78, curator of books, 1978-86, librarian emeritus, 1987—. Author: Hoosier Zion, 1963 (Thomas Kuch award Ind. U. Writers Conf. 1964), Story of the Church, 1966, Francis Asbury, 1966, Indiana Letters, 1979, Religion in Indiana, 1986, Hoosier Faiths, 1995. Served to capt. USAAF, 1940-46. Mem. Am. Soc. Ch. History, ALA, Assn. Coll. and Research Libraries, Presbyn. Hist. Soc., Phi Beta Kappa. Democrat. Home: 1509 E Dunstan Dr Bloomington IN 47401-8607 Office: Ind U Library Bloomington IN 47405

RUDOLPH, MALCOLM ROME, investment banker; b. Balt., Sept. 22, 1924; s. Louis and Sara E. (Rome) R.; m. Zita Herzmark, July 1, 1956 (div. 1979); children: Madelon R. II, Margot R.; m. Barbara J. Girson, 1979. AB, Harvard U., 1947; postgrad., Grenoble U., France, 1948, Hayden Stone Mgmt. Sch., 1965. With div. internat. confs. U.S. Dept. State, Paris, 1949; registered rep. trainee Orvis Bros. & Co., N.Y.C., 1949, rep., asst. mgr., acting mgr., 1950-64; mgr. Hayden Stone Inc., Washington, 1964-68, ptnr., 1968-69; chmn. bd. Donatelli, Rudolph & Schoen Inc., Washington, 1970-74; chmn. bd. Multi-Nat. Fin. Group, Inc., Washington, 1974-79, pres., 1979-86; chmn. Multi-Nat. Precious Metals Corp., 1974-75; chmn. bd. Multi-Nat. Money Mgmt. Co. Inc., 1974-79, pres., 1979—; pres. Rudolph & Schoen Inc., 1975-85; sr. v.p., dir. Laidlaw Adams & Peck Inc., 1975-79; pres. Laidlaw Resources Inc., 1976-95, Sutton Energy, Inc., 1976-90, DeRand Resources Corp., 1979-88; sr. v.p., dir. DeRand Corp. Am., 1979-88; chmn. bd. Arlington Energy Corp., 1980-88; mem. Phila.-Balt.-Washington Stock Exch., 1972-75; pres. Rome Resources Corp., 1982—, Investment Bankers and Cons.; assoc. mem. Pitts., Boston, Montreal stock exchs., 1972-75; allied mem. N.Y. Stock Exch., 1975-79. Mem. Presdl. Inaugural Com., 1960, 64; mem. select com. Palm Beach County Coop Ext. Svc., 1993, U. Fla. Inst. Food and Agrl. Scis. ext. 2000 Select Com.; treas. and dir. Friends of the Mounts Bot. Garden, West Palm Beach, 1994; v.p., dir. Hort. Soc. South Fla., 1994. Mem. Assn. Investment Brokers Met. Washington (v.p. 1965-66, pres. 1967), Bond Club Washington, Ohio Oil and Gas Assn., Ind. Oil and Gas Assn. W.Va., Ind. Petroleum Assn. Am., Southeastern Ohio Oil and Gas Assn., Washington Met. Bd. Trade, Internat. Assn. Fin. Planners, Internat. Club of Washington, Hasty-Pudding Inst. 1770, Harvard Club of Washington (asst. treas. 1957-60, treas. 1960-64, exec. com. 1957-67), Harvard Club Palm Beaches, Nat. Aviation Club, Club Colette (Palm Beach), Palm Beach Yacht Club, Poinsiana Club (Palm Beach). Home: 1333 N Lake Way Palm Beach FL 33480-3109

RUDOLPH, WALLACE MORTON, law educator; b. Chgo., Sept. 11, 1930; s. Norman Charles and Bertha (Margolin) R.; m. Janet L. Gordon, Feb. 14, 1964; children: Alexey, Rebecca, Sarah. B.A., U. Chgo., 1950, J.D., 1953. Bar: Ill. 1953, U.S. Ct. Mil. Appeals 1954, U.S. Supreme Ct. 1954, Nebr. 1962, Wash. 1978, also others. Research assoc. Ford Found., 1953-54, Ford Found. (Project in Law and Behavior Sci.), 1954-55; instr. U. Chgo. Law Sch., 1959; assoc. firm Antonow & Fink, Chgo., 1960-61; asst. prof. law U. Nebr., Lincoln, 1961-63; assoc. prof. U. Nebr., 1963-64, prof., 1965-76; prof. U. Puget Sound Sch. Law, 1976-94, dean, 1976-80; prof. Sch. of Law Seattle U., 1994—; vis. prof. law U. Wis., 1980-81, U. Ill., 1984; chair excellence in law Memphis State U. Law Sch., 1991; mem. Commrs. Uniform State Law, 1973-77; judge Ct. Indsl. Rels., Nebr., 1975-77; mem. Wash. Jud. Coun. and COm. II, 1976-80, Pub. Employment Rels. Commn., Wash., 1977—. Author: Handbook for Correctional Law; contbr. articles to profl. jours.; author: Model Criminal Procedure Code, 1975, Model Sentencing and Corrections Act, 1978, Amicus Curiae Brief, Wash. State Supreme Ct, 1979. Bd. dirs. LIMIT, 1992-94, Nebr. chpt. ACLU, 1965-72; mem. Nebr. Dem. Contact Com., 1973-74, 75-76; chmn. Firt Congl. Dist. Dem. Party, 1975-76; mem. exec. com. Unitarian Ch., Lincoln, 1965-67. Served with JAGC, U.S. Army, 1954-57. Mem. AAUP, Soc. Criminology, ABA Am. Law Inst., Am. Arbitration Assn. Office: Seattle U Sch Law 950 Broadway Tacoma WA 98402-4405

RUDOWSKI, MICHAEL HENRY, secondary school educator; b. Jersey City, Aug. 7, 1950; s. Henry Joseph and Violet (KosoBucki) R.; m. Elena Eloise Testa, Aug. 2, 1980; 1 child, David Michael. BA, Rutgers U., 1972; MA, Jersey City State Coll., 1974. Cert. secondary sch. tchr., N.J. Tchr. comm. arts St. Aloysius H.S., Jersey City, 1975-76; tchr. lang. arts Jersey City Bd. Edn., Jersey City, 1977—. Mem. NEA, Jersey City Edn. Assn. (bd. dirs. 1982—). Democrat. Avocations: raquetball, golf, photography, programming, stamp collecting.

RUDSTEIN, DAVID STEWART, law educator; b. Leeds, Eng., Sept. 27, 1946. B.S., U. Ill., 1968, LL.M., 1975; J.D., Northwestern U., 1971. Bar: Ill. 1971, U.S. Supreme Ct. 1977. Teaching asst. U. Ill. Coll. Law, 1971-72; law clk. to Justice Walter V. Schaefer Supreme Ct. Ill., Chgo., 1972-73; asst. prof. law Ill. Inst. Tech.-Chgo. Kent Coll., 1973-76, assoc. prof., 1976-79, prof., 1979—, assoc. dean, 1983-87. Mem. ABA, Chgo. Council Lawyers, Order of Coif. Office: Ill Inst Tech-Chgo 565 W Adams St Chicago IL 60661-3601

RU DUSKY, BASIL MICHAEL, cardiologist; b. Wilkes-Barre, Pa., July 27, 1933; s. Michael and Anne RuD.; m. Bernadine RuDusky, 1957; children: Daryl, Bryan. B.A., Va. Mil. Inst., 1955; M.D., U. Pitts., 1959. Diplomate Am. Bd. Forensic Medicine. Intern, Martin Army Hosp., Ft. Benning, Ga., 1959-60; resident Youngstown (Ohio) Hosp. Assn., 1962-63, Temple U. Hosp., 1963-66; practice medicine specializing in internal medicine, cardiovascular medicine and forensic medicine, Wilkes-Barre, Pa., 1966—; mem. staff Mercy Hosp., 1966—, chief of medicine, 1966-70, dir. ICU AND CCU, 1966-70, dir. phonocardiography lab., 1966-70; dir. N.E. Cardiovascular Clinic and Research Inst.; mem. staff Wilkes-Barre Gen. Hosp.; cons. cardiology Armed Forces Examining Service; sr. cons. Social Security Adminstrn., HEW; sr. cons. physician Met. Ins. Co. Am., Liberty Mut. Ins. Co., Aetna Ins. Co.; cons. internal medicine and cardiology Retreat State Hosp.; dir. Northeast Cardiovascular Clinic and Research Inst.; clin. instr. medicine Temple U., 1966-70. Served to capt. M.C., U.S. Army, 1959-62. Diplomate Am. Bd. Internal Medicine, Am. Bd. Forensic Medicine, Am. Bd. Forensic Examiners (fellow). Fellow ACP, Am. Coll. Angiology (bd. govs. Eastern Pa.), Am. Coll. Chest Physicians, Am. Coll. Cardiology; mem. Am. Soc. Internal Medicine, AMA, Am. Coll. Occupl. and Environ. Medicine, Nat. Rehab. Assn., N.Y. Acad. Scis., Am. Geriatrics Soc., Assn. Mil. Surgeons U.S., Pan-Am. Med. Assn., Amateur Fencers League Am. Home: 7 Pine Tree Rd Wilkes Barre PA 18707-1707 Office: Bicentennial Bldg 15 Public Sq Wilkes Barre PA 18701-1702

RUDY, DAVID ROBERT, physician, educator; b. Columbus, Ohio, Oct. 19, 1934; s. Robert Sale and Lois May (Arthur) R.; m. Rose Mary Sims; children by previous marriages: Douglas D., Steven W., Katharine L., Hunter A. Elam. BSc, Ohio State U., 1956, MD, 1960, MPH Med. Coll. Wis., 1995. Intern, Northwestern Meml. Hosp., Chgo., 1960-61; resident in internal medicine Ohio State U. Hosp., 1963-64; resident in pediatrics Children's Hosp., Columbus, Ohio, 1964; practice medicine specializing in family practice, Columbus, 1964-75; dir. Family Practice Center and residency program Riverside Meth. Hosp., Columbus, 1975-85; dir. Family Practice Ctr. and residency Monsour Med. Ctr., Jeannette, Pa., 1985-88; dir. Family Practice Ctr. and residency Bon Secours Hosp., Grosse Pointe, Mich., 1988-91; prof., dept. chmn. Finch U. Health Scis., Chgo. Med. Sch., 1991-95; prof., Pomerene chair family medicine Ohio State U., 1995—; former clin. assoc. prof. Ohio State U., Penn. State U., Wayne State U. Dept. Family Medicine. Contbr. articles to profl. jours. Served as capt., flight surgeon, M.C., USAF, 1961-63; lt. col. Ohio Air N.G. Recipient USAF Commendation medal. Diplomate Am. Bd. Family Practice (charter). Fellow Am. Acad. Family Physicians; mem. AMA, Ohio State Med. Assn., Central Ohio Acad. Family Practice (pres. 1979), Pa. Acad. Family Physicians (bd. dirs. 1985-88, treas. 1988), Columbus Maennerchor, Chgo. Coun. on Fgn. Rels. Republican. Office: Ohio State U Dept Family Medicine Thomas E Rardin Family Practice Ctr 2231 N High St Columbus OH 43210

RUDY, JAMES FRANCIS XAVIER, lawyer; b. N.Y.C., Feb. 1, 1954; s. Bertrand Robert and Margaret Eleanor (Campiglia) R.; m. Mary Elizabeth Haas, Aug. 17, 1978; children: Lauren Elizabeth, James F.X. Jr. BA, U. Ariz., 1976; JD, Fordham U., 1979. Bar: N.Y. 1980, N.J. 1981, U.S. Dist. Ct. (so. dist.) N.Y. 1980, U.S. Dist. Ct. N.J. 1981, U.S. Supreme Ct. 1985. Assoc. Briger & Assocs., N.Y.C., 1979-81, Katzenbach, Gildea & Rudner, Trenton, N.J., 1981-84; ptnr. Katzenbach, Gildea & Rudner, Lawrenceville, N.J., 1984-93, Fox, Rothschild, O'Brien & Frankel, Lawrenceville, 1993—; chmn. health law group Fox, Rothschild, O'Brien & Frankel, Lawrenceville, 1994—; twp. atty. Ewing Twp., N.J., 1992-93, atty. Rent Control Bd., 1992-93, atty. Ethical Stds. Bd., 1992-93, atty. Condemnation Bd., 1992-93. Author: University of San Francisco Law Review, 1991. Legal counsel Ewing Rep. Club, 1991-93; mem. Washington Twp. Planning Bd., Robbinsville, N.J., 1993—; wrestling coach Washington Twp. Recreation, Robbinsville, 1993—; dist. committeeperson Ewing Twp. Rep. Com., Ewing, 1990-92. Mem. Nat. Health Lawyers Assn., Assn. of Bar City of N.Y., N.J. State Bar Assn. , Mercer County C. of C. (bus. com. 1993—), Ewing Twp. Kiwanis Club (dir. 1994—), Phi Beta Kappa. Republican. Roman Catholic. Avocations: golf, home improvement, gardening, wrestling, rollerblading. Home: 8 Barto Way Robbinsville NJ 08691 Office: Fox Rothschild OBrien & Frankel 997 Lenox Dr Lawrenceville NJ 08648

RUDY, LESTER HOWARD, psychiatrist; b. Chgo., Mar. 6, 1918; s. Sol and Mildred (Weinzimmer) R.; m. Ruth Jean Schmidt, Nov. 25, 1950; 1 dau., Sharon Ruth. B.S., U. Ill., 1939, M.D., 1941; M.S. in Hosp. Adminstrn, Northwestern U., 1957. Diplomate: Am. Bd. Psychiatry and Neurology (exec. dir. 1972-86). Intern Cedars of Lebanon Hosp., Los Angeles, 1941-42; resident in psychiatry VA Hosp., Downey, Ill., 1946-48; staff psychiatrist VA Hosp., 1948-52, chief service, 1952-54; supt. Galesburg (Ill.) State Research Hosp., 1954-58; practice medicine specializing in psychiatry Chgo.; supt. Ill. State Psychiat. Inst., Chgo., 1958-61; dir. Ill. State Psychiat. Inst., 1961—, Ill. Mental Health Insts., Chgo., 1967-75; prof. psychiatry U. Ill. Coll. Medicine, 1971-88, emeritus, 1988—, head dept. psychiatry, 1975-88, pres. hosp. staff, 1979-80; dir. U. Ill. Hosp., 1981-82; sr. med. dir. Health Care Compare, 1988—; Chmn. research rev. com. mental health services NIMH, 1972-73; AMA commr. Joint Commn. on Accreditation of Hosps., 1967-75; sr. cons. VA; cons. adv. bd. Chgo., Police Dept.; lectr. dept. psychiatry and neurology Loyola U., 1968-75; mem. Ill. Gov.'s Com. Competency to Stand Trial, 1968. Contbr. articles to profl. jours. Served to col. AUS, 1942-46. Decorated Bronze Star with two oak leaf clusters. Fellow Am. Psychiat. Assn. (chmn. ethics com. 1963, Simon Bolivar award 1985), Am. Coll. Psychiatrists (charter, Bowis award 1979); mem. Am. Acad. Psychoanalysis (sci. assoc.), Ill. Psychiat. Soc. (pres. 1962-63), U. Ill. Med. Alumni Assn. (ann. outstanding achievement award 1980). Home: 6343 Collingswood Ct Rockford IL 61103-8961 Office: 912 S Wood St Chicago IL 60612-7325

RUDY, RAYMOND BRUCE, JR., retired food company executive; b. L.A., Apr. 24, 1931; s. Raymond Bruce and Wrena Margaret (Higgins) R.; m. Kathleen Vermeulen; children: Bruce Calvin, Alice M.R. Price, Barbara R. Frith. BS, UCLA, 1953; MBA, Xavier U., Cin., 1960. Brand mgr. Procter & Gamble, Cin., 1956-62; product mgr. Hunt-Wesson Foods, Fullerton, Calif., 1962-63; group v.p. Gen. Foods Corp., White Plains, N.Y., 1963-79; pres. Oroweat Foods Co. subs. Continental Grain Co., N.Y.C., 1979-83; chmn., pres. Arnold Foods Co., Inc., Greenwich, Conn., 1984-86; pres. Affiliates of Best Foods subs. CPC Internat., Englewood Cliffs, N.J., 1987-89; ret., 1989; chmn., CEO, New Hampton, Inc., 1993-94; dep. chmn. Snapple Natural Beverages, Inc., 1992-94; mng. dir. J.W. Childs Assn., 1995—; chmn. Personal Care Group, Inc., 1996—; bd. dirs. Brownstone Studios, Inc., Widmer Brothers Brewing, Inc., Personal Care Group, Inc.; advisor Desai Capital Mgmt., Inc., Kirshenbaum Bond & Ptnrs., Advt. With U.S. Army, 1954-56. Mem. Greenwich Country Club, Dorset Field Club. Congregational.

RUDY, WILLIS, historian; b. N.Y.C., Jan. 25, 1920; s. Philip and Rose (Handman) R; B.S.S., CCNY, 1939; M.A., Columbia U., 1940, Ph.D., 1948; m. Dorothy L. Richardson, Jan. 31, 1948; children: Dee Dee, Willis Philip, Willa. Instr. Coll. City N.Y., 1939-49; instr., lectr. Harvard U., 1949-53, 57-58; prof. Mass. State Coll., Worcester, 1953-63; prof. history Fairleigh Dickinson U., Teaneck, N.J., 1963-82, prof. emeritus, 1982—; mem. editorial bd. Fairleigh Dickinson U. Press, 1966-77. Mem. Orgn. Am. Historians, Phi Beta Kappa. Author: The College of the City of New York, A History, 1847-1947, 1949; 1976; The American Liberal Arts College Curriculum, 1960; Higher Education in Transition, 1958, 68, 76; Schools in an Age of Mass Culture, 1965; The Universities of Europe: a History, 1984; Total War and Twentieth Century Higher Learning, 1991, The Campus and a Nation in Crisis: From the Revolution to Vietnam, 1996. Home: 161 W Clinton Ave Tenafly NJ 07670-1916 Office: Fairleigh Dickinson U Dept Of Hist Teaneck NJ 07666 *As a teacher, my greatest reward has been to see people get involved in the sheer joy of learning new things and seeking answers to the big questions that life proposes. As a writer, my enduring satisfaction has come from the opportunity to explore the seemingly chaotic events on human history in the hope of finding ameaningful and instructive pattern.*

RUEBHAUSEN, OSCAR MELICK, lawyer; b. N.Y.C., Aug. 28, 1912; s. Oscar and Eleonora J. (Melick) R.; m. Zelia Krumbhaar Peet, Oct. 31, 1942. AB summa cum laude, Dartmouth Coll., 1934; LLB cum laude, Yale U., 1937. Bar: N.Y. 1938, U.S. Supreme Ct., 1945. Assoc. Debevoise, Stevenson, Plimpton & Page, N.Y.C., 1937-42, Lend-Lease Adminstrn., Washington, 1942-44; gen. counsel Office Sci. Rsch. and Devel., Washington, 1944-46; ptnr. Debevoise and Plimpton, 1946-84, presiding ptnr., 1972-81, of counsel, 1984-87; counselor to ednl. instn., 1988—. Editor: Pension and Retirement Policies in Colleges and Universities, 1990; contbr. articles to profl. jours. Chmn. Commn. on Coll. Retirement, 1984-93; spl. adviser atomic energy to gov. N.Y. State, 1959; vice chmn. N.Y. State adv. com. on atomic energy, 1959-62; chmn. N.Y. State Gov.'s Task Force on protection from radioactive fallout, 1959; mem. Pres.'s Task Force on Sci. Policy, 1969-70, Pres.'s Sci. Adv. Com. Panel on Chems. and Health, 1970-72, Commn. on Critical Choices for Am., 1973-77, adv. com. Carnegie Commn. on Sci., Tech. and Govt., 1988-93; chmn. UN Day, N.Y. State, 1962, chmn. Spl. N.Y. Com. on Ins. Holding Cos., 1967-68; mem. U.S. govt. panel on Privacy and Behavioral Rsch., 1965-66; mem. presdl. panel Chronic Renal Disease, 1966-67; sec., dir. Fund Peaceful Atomic Devel., Inc., 1954-72; dir. Carrie Chapman Catt Meml. Fund, 1948-58; chmn. bd. Bennington Coll., 1957-61, 62-67; trustee Hudson Inst., Inc., 1961-71; trustee Russell Sage Found., chmn. bd., 1965-80; vice-chmn. N.Y.C. Univ. Constrn. Fund, 1966-69; mem. Coun. on Fgn. Rels., nat. com. on U.S.-China rels., Rockefeller U. Coun.; bd. dirs. Greenwall Found., 1956-95, chmn., 1982-91, chmn. emeritus, 1991—; chmn. Scripps Clinic and Rsch. Found, 1983-89. Recipient U.S. Presdl. Cert. of Merit, 1948. Mem. ABA, N.Y. State Bar Assn., Yale Law Sch. Assn. (exec. com. and pres. 1960-62, chmn. 1962-64), Assn. of Bar of City of N.Y. (pres. 1980-82, pres. and bd. dirs. fund 1980-82), Order of Coif, Phi Beta Kappa, Sigma Phi Epsilon, Sigma Xi (hon.). Clubs: Century (N.Y.C.), River (N.Y.C.); Rancho Santa Fe Assn. (Calif.); Rockefeller Ctr.(N.Y.C.). Home: 450 E 52nd St New York NY 10022-6448

RUECK, JON MICHAEL, manufacturing executive; b. Riley, Kans., Oct. 23, 1940; s. G.M. Karl and Esther Margaret (Jones) R.; m. Connie Lee Dick Rueck, Apr. 14, 1962; children: Michael Jon, Robin Renee. BS in Nuclear Engring., Kans. State U., 1964, MS in Mech. Engring., 1971. Registered profl. engr., KS, Ohio. Radiation safety trainee Argonne Nat. Lab., Lemont, Ill., 1962; tech. sales trainee Owens-Corning Fiberglas Corp., Granville, Ohio, 1964-65; tech. sales Owens-Corning Fiberglas Corp., Mpls., 1965-66; customer svc. engr. Owens-Corning Fiberglas Corp., Granville, Ohio, 1966-67; environ. engr. Owens-Corning Fiberglas Corp., Toledo, 1971-75; dir. plant ops. Leila Y. Post Montgomery Hosp., Battle Creek, Mich., 1975; environ. engr. Thompson Dehydrating Co., Topeka, 1976, Kans. Dept. Health Environ., Topeka, 1976-77; v.p. Hosp. Instrument Svc. Co., Silver Lake, Kans., 1977-80; supr. air pollution source monitoring Kans. Dept. of Health and Environ., 1979-85; chmn. Rueck Assocs., Silver Lake, Kans., 1985—; pres. Computer Et Cetera, Silver Lake, 1995—; cons. to Nat. Coun. Examiners for Engring. and Surveying, 1993—. Co-author: Environmental Engineering Examination Guide & Handbook, 1996. Res. police officer St. Mary's (Kans.) Police Dept., 1981-86; cert. lay speaker Kans. East Conf., United Meth. Ch., 1979—, vol. coord. Topeka dist. disaster response, 1993, coord., 1994—; merit badge counselor Boy Scouts Am., Silver Lake, 1988—; del. candidate for Robertson for Pres., Shawnee County, Kans., 1988; coord. Kans. Interfaith Disaster Recovery, 1993. Mem. Am. Acad. Environ. Engrs. (diplomate, chmn. admissions com. Annapolis, Md. 1986-90, state rep. Kans. 1990—), Midwest Air and Waste Mgmt. Assn. (officer 1987-90), Kaw Valley Bicycle Touring Club (Topeka), Lions. Republican. United Methodist. Avocations: bicycling, vocalist, amateur radio, computers. Home: 617 Walnut St Silver Lake KS 66539-9467 Office: Rueck Assocs 617 Walnut St Silver Lake KS 66539-9467

RUECKERT, ROLAND RUDYARD, virologist, educator; b. Rhinelander, Wis., Nov. 24, 1931; s. George Leonard and Monica Amelia (Seiberlich) R.; m. Ruth Helen Ullrich, Sept. 5, 1959; 1 child, Wanda Lynne. BS in Chemistry, U. Wis., 1953, PhD in Oncology, 1960. Fellow Max Planck Inst. for Biochemistry, Munich, 1960-61, Tübingen, Fed. Republic Germany, 1961-62; asst. rsch. virologist virus lab. U. Calif., Berkeley, 1962-65; asst. prof. biophysics lab. U. Wis., Madison, 1965-69; assoc. prof. biophysics lab. U. Wis., 1969-73; prof. Inst. for Molecular Virology, Madison, 1973-85; dist. rsch. prof. Inst. for Molecular Virology, 1985—. Mem. virology study sect. NIH, Bethesda, Md., 1981-85; pres. Am. Soc. Virology, 1989-90. With U.S. Army, 1953-55. Recipient William D. Stovall award U. Wis., 1953, Marie Christine Kohler award U. Wis., 1959, Rsch. Career Devel. award, 1966, Faculty rsch. award Am. Cancer Soc., 1972; named Hilldale Disting. prof. 1988. Achievements include research in dodecahedral model for picornavirus structure and assembly, molecular biology of picornaviruses (polio 8 common cold), structure 8 biology of small insect viruses, mechanism of neutralization by antibodies and antivirals. Home: 2234 W Lawn Ave Madison WI 53711-1952 Office: U Wis Inst Molecular Biology 1525 Linden Dr Madison WI 53706-1534

RUECKERT, RONALD FRANK, engineering executive; b. Shawano, Wis., Aug. 19, 1947; s. Frank William and Meta Marie (Karstedt) R.; m. Annette Marion Mulay; children: Douglas, Stacy, Nicholas, Amanda. BSEE, Devry Inst. Tech., 1967. Calibration technician Lockheed Missiles & Space Co., Sunnyvale, Calif., 1967-70; sr. test technician Burroughs Bus. Machines, Mission Niejo, Calif., 1970-71; sr. technician Telex Direct Access Divsn., Santa Clara, Calif., 1971-73; staff engr. Storage Tech., Louisville, Colo., 1973-76, Memorex, Santa Clara, 1976-78; program mgr. Priam, Inc., San Jose, Calif., 1978-82, Seagate Tech., Scotts Valley, Calif., 1991-93, Mini Scribe, Longmont, Colo., 1982-91; dir. engring. Maxtor, Longmont, Colo., 1993—. Avocations: skiing, fishing, woodworking, electronics tinkering. Home: 2621 Danbury Dr Longmont CO 80503

RUEGER, LAUREN JOHN, retired physicist, consultant; b. Archbold, Ohio, Dec. 30, 1921; s. Edwin Z. and Hazel Lulu (Fisher) R.; m. Florence Marian Scott, July 30, 1944; children: Carol, Beth, Lauren A., Mary. BS in Engring. Physics, Ohio State U., 1943, MS in Physics, 1947. Advanced tech. planner Johns Hopkins U. Applied Physics Lab., Laurel, Md., 1953-88; project leader Nat. Bur. Standards, Washington, 1948-52; research assoc. Battelle Meml. Inst., Columbus, Ohio, 1946-48; staff MIT Radiation Lab., 1943-45; U.S. del. Internat. Radio Cons. Com., Geneva, 1978, 80, 81, 83, 85, 88; tech. program com. Frequency Control Symposium, Phila., 1976-78, 84-88; com. co-chmn. Internat. Time and Frequency Symposium, Helsinki, Finland, 1978; exec. com. Conf. on Precision Electromagnetic Measurements, Delft, Holland, 1984, Braunschweig, Fed. Republic of Germany, 1980, Tsukuba, Japan, 1988; cons. in precision frequency measurements Rueger Enterprises, Silver Spring, Md., 1989—. Patentee in field. Fellow IEEE; mem. Am. Phys. Soc., Photog. Soc. Am. Avocation: photography. Home: 1415 Glenallan Ave Silver Spring MD 20902-1360

RUEGG, DONALD GEORGE, retired railway company executive; b. LaJunta, Colo., Sept. 11, 1924; s. George Albert and Cecilia Corrine (Decker) R.; m. Ruth Carson, June 27, 1946 (dec. 1963); m. Mary Ann Eichelberger, June 24, 1964. B.A., Dartmouth Coll., 1947; M.B.A., U. Chgo., 1972. Stenographer Atchison, Topeka & Santa Fe Ry. Co., Pueblo, Colo., 1942-51; supr., trainmaster Atchison, Topeka & Santa Fe Ry. Co., various locations, 1951-68; asst. to v.p. info. systems Atchison, Topeka & Santa Fe Ry. Co., Topeka, 1968-69; asst. to v.p. ops. Atchison Topeka & Santa Fe Ry. Co., Chgo., 1969-72; gen. mgr. Atchison Topeka & Santa Fe Ry. Co., Los Angeles, 1972-73; asst. v.p. ops. Atchison, Topeka & Santa Fe Ry. Co., Chgo., 1973-78, v.p. ops., 1978-83, exec. v.p., 1983-86. Served with USN, 1943-46. Republican. Roman Catholic.

RUEGGER, PHILIP T(HEOPHIL), III, lawyer; b. Plainfield, N.J., Oct. 14, 1949; s. Philip T. Jr. and Gloria Marie (McLaughlin) R.; m. Rebecca Lee Huffman, Aug. 3, 1974; children: Sarah, Brittain, Michael. AB, Dartmouth Coll., 1971; JD, U. Va., 1974. Bar: N.Y. 1975. Assoc. Simpson Thacher & Bartlett, N.Y.C., 1974-81, ptnr., 1981—. Chmn. Rye Edn. Fund, Inc.; bd. dirs. Port Chester Carver Ctr. Mem. Assn. of Bar City N.Y., Phi Beta Kappa. Clubs: Manursing Island (Rye, N.Y.), Apawamis (Rye). Avocation: sports. Home: 275 Grace Church St Rye NY 10580-4201 Office: Simpson Thacher & Bartlett 425 Lexington Ave New York NY 10017-3903

RUEHL, MERCEDES, actress; b. Queens, N.Y.. BA in English, Coll. of New Rochelle; studied acting with Uta Hagen, Tad Danielewski. Appearances include (theatre) Vanities, 1977-78, Billy Irish, 1980, Much Ado About Nothing, Misalliance, Androcles and the Lion, Tartuffe, Medea, 1980-82, Three Sisters, 1982-83, The Day They Shot John Lennon, 1982-83, Flirtation, 1983, June Moon, 1983-84, Monday After the Miracle, 1983-84, Coming of Age in Soho, 1985, The Marriage of Bette and Boo, 1985, I'm Not Rappaport, 1985 (Obie Award), American Notes, 1988, Other People's Money, 1989, Lost in Yonkers, 1991 (Tony award, 1991, Drama Desk award, 1991, Outer Critics Circle award 1991), The Shadow Box, 1994 (Tony nominee - Featured Actress in a Play, 1995), The Rose Tattoo, 1995, (film) The Warriors, 1979, Four Friends, 1981, Heartburn, 1986, 84 Charing Cross Road, 1987, Leader of the Band, 1987, The Secret of My Success, 1987, Radio Days, 1987, Big, 1988, Married to the Mob, 1988, Slaves of New York, 1989, Crazy People, 1990, Another You, 1991, The Fisher King, 1991 (Academy award Best Supporting Actress 1991), Lost in Yonkers, 1993, Last Action Hero, 1993, (TV movie) Indictment, 1995. Recipient Nat. Film Critics Circle award, 1988, Clarence Derwent award, 1989.

RUEHLE, DIANNE MARIE, retired elementary education educator; b. Detroit, Aug. 14, 1943; d. Richard Francis and Luella Mary (Kopp) R. BS, Ea. Mich. U., 1966, MA, 1971, adminstrv. cert., 1990, renewed adminstrv. cert., 1995. Cert. tchr., adminstr., Mich. Tchr. Cherry Hill Sch. Dist., Inkster, Mich., 1966-85; tchr. elem. sch. Wayne-Westland (Mich.) Community Schs., 1985-95; dist. com. Pub. Act 25 for State of Mich., Westland, 1990-93, chair bldg., 1991-95. Improvement Instrn. grantee Wayne Westland Found., 1992-94. Mem. ASCD, NEA, Mich. Edn. Assn. Avocations: reading, golf, photography, travel. Home: 26117 La Salle Ct Roseville MI 48066-3285

RUELLAN, ANDREE, artist; b. N.Y.C., Apr. 6, 1905; d. André and Louise (Lambert) R.; m. John W. Taylor, May 28, 1929. Student, Art Students League, 1920-22; art schs., France and Italy. guest instr. Pa. State Coll., summer 1957. One-man shows include Paris, 1925, Weyhe Galleries, N.Y.C., 1928, 31, Maynard Walker Galleries, 1937, 40, Kraushaar Galleries, 1945, 52, 56, 63, 80-81, Phila. Art Alliance, 1955, S.I. Mus., 1958, nat. exhbns., Carnegie Inst., Whitney Mus., Art Inst. Chgo., Corcoran Gallery, Internat. Expn., San Francisco, Artists for Victory Exhbn., N.Y.C., other cities U.S.; retrospective exhbns., Storm King Art Ctr., Mountainville, N.Y., 1966, Lehigh U., 1965, Woodstock Artists Assn., 1977, Ga. Mus. of Art, 1993, Hyde Collection, Glens Falls, N.Y., 1993, Gibbs Mus of Art, Charleston, S.C., 1993, Prints Gallery at Parkbest, Kingston, N.Y., 1995; drawing retrospective Kaushaar Galleries, 1990, 93, Ga. Mus. Art, Athens, 1993, The Hyde Collection, Glen Falls, N.Y., 1993, Gibbs Mus. Art, Charleston, S.C., 1993, Butler Inst., 1996; executed murals in Emporia, Va., Lawrenceville, Ga.; represented in permanent collections at Met. Mus. Art, Whitney Mus. Am. Art, N.Y.C., Fogg Mus., Harvard U., Phila. Mus., Storm King Art Ctr., William Rockhill Nelson Mus., Kansas City, Mo., Duncan Phillips Gallery, Washington, Springfield Mus., Norton Gallery, Art Mus., New Britain, Conn., Libr. of Congress, Ency. Brit., IBM Collections, Art Inst., Zanesville, Ohio, U. Ga., S.I. Mus., Butler Inst., Pa. State U., Lehigh U., Columbia (S.C.) Mus. Art, The Whatcom Mus., Washington, Springville (Utah) Mus. Art, S.C. State Mus., Wichita Art Mus., drawing retrospective Butler Inst. Am. Art, 1996; also numerous pvt. collections. Recipient 3d prize for painting Charleston Worcester Mus. Biennial, Jan. 1938; 1,000 grant in arts Am. Acad. and Inst. Arts and Letters, 1945; Pennell medal Pa. Acad., 1945; medal of Honor and purchase Pepsi-Cola Paintings of Year, 1948; Dawson Meml. medal Pa. Acad., 1950; Purchase award N.Y. State Fair, 1951; Drawing award Ball State Tchrs. Coll.; Guggenheim fellow, 1950-51; recipient Kuniyoshi award, 1994. Mem. Woodstock Artists Assn. (Sally Jacobs award 1981), Art Students League (life), Nat. Mus. Women in Arts. Home: RR 2 Box 154 Shady NY 12409-9510

RUELLO, SAMUEL ANGUS, management consultant; b. Atlantic City, Apr. 26, 1931; s. John and Catherine (Buchanan) R.; B.A., Bklyn. Coll., 1954; M.B.A., Temple U., 1961; m. Brenda Tausend, May 2, 1976; children—Nicole, Jeffrey. Chief indsl. engr. Philco Ford Lansale div. (Pa.), 1959-63; pres. Par Technology and sr. v.p. Booz-Allen & Hamilton, N.Y.C., 1963-73; exec. v.p. Bradford Nat. Corp., N.Y.C., 1973-77; mng. partner Coopers & Lybrand, N.Y.C., 1977—, now CEO Meritus Cons. Svc., N.Y.C.; speaker; sr. v.p., mem. exec. com. N.Y. Bd. Trade, 1979—. Served in U.S. Army, 1954-56; Korea. Registered prof. engr., Calif. Mem. N.Am. Soc. Corp. Planning, Am. Inst. Indsl. Engring. Home: 165 E 66th St New York NY 10021-6132 Office: Meritus Cons Svc 400 Park Ave 22 Fl New York NY 10022*

RUEPPEL, MELVIN LESLIE, environmental research director and educator; b. Rolla, Mo., Sept. 18, 1945; married; three children. BS, U. Mo., 1966; PhD in Chemistry, U. Calif., Berkeley, 1970. NIH fellow biochemistry Cornell U., Ithaca, N.Y., 1970-71; sr. rsch. chemist metab. Monsanto Co., 1971-75, group leader, 1975-77, rsch. mgr. environ. process, 1977-80, rsch. dir. synthesis, 1980-82, rsch. dir. process technology, 1982-85, tech. adv. patent litigation, 1982-86, dir. plant protection, 1985-86, dir. herbicide technology, 1986-89, dir. global product devel., 1989-90, dir. technology Roundup Divsn., 1991-93; dir. Ctr. Environ. Sci. and Technology & Lab. Trace Subs. U. Mo., Rolla, 1993—; prin. Rueppel Consulting, 1993—. Mem. AAAS, Am. Chem. Soc., Am. Mgmt. Assn., Weed Sci. Soc., Internat. Union Pure and Applied Chemicals, Sigma Xi. Office: U of Missouri Rolla 1870 Miner Cir Rolla MO 65409 Office: 1904 Grassy Ridge Rd St Louis MO 63122

RUESCH, JANET CAROL, federal magistrate judge; b. New Brunswick, N.J., May 9, 1943. AB in Polit. Sci., Gettysburg Coll., 1965; JD, Ind. U., 1970. Bar: Tex. 1971, U.S. Dist. Ct. (we. dist.) Tex. 1973, U.S. Ct. Appeals (5th cir.) 1975, U.S. Dist. Ct. (so. dist.) Tex. 1977, U.S. Supreme Ct. 1979. Law clk. Malcolm McGregor and Mark Howell, El Paso, Tex., 1970-71; ptnr. Malcolm McGregor, Inc., El Paso, 1971-78; substitute mcpl. ct. judge City of El Paso, 1977-78; asst. U.S atty. Western Dist. Tex., El Paso, 1978-79; U.S. magistrate judge El Paso divsn. U.S. Dist. Ct. (we. dist.) Tex., 1979—. Bd. dirs. El Paso County Gen. Assistance Agy., 1977-79; past mem. profl. adv. bd. El Paso Mental Health Assn.; v.p. El Paso Women's Pol. Caucus, 1977, program chair, 1976, pub. chair, 1975. Mem. Tex. Bar Assn., El Paso Bar Assn. (pres. 1984), El Paso Women's Bar Assn. (pres. 1975). Office: 206 US Courthouse 511 E San Antonio Ave El Paso TX 79901-2401

RUESCHEMEYER, DIETRICH, sociology educator; b. Berlin, Aug. 28, 1930; came to U.S., 1966; s. Philipp and Eufemia (Ross) R.; m. Marilyn R. Schattner, June 14, 1962; children: Julia Yael, Simone Margalit. Degree, U. Cologne, 1953, PhD in Sociology, 1958; postgrad., Columbia U., U. Chgo., U. Calif. Berkeley, 1960-61. Postdoctoral fellow Rockefeller Found., 1960-61; asst. prof. Dartmouth Coll., Hanover, N.H., 1962-63; from asst. prof. to assoc. prof. U. Toronto, 1963-66; assoc. prof. Brown U., Providence, R.I., 1966-71, prof. sociology, 1971—, Asa Messer Prof., 1995—; vis. assoc. prof. Hebrew U. of Jerusalem, 1969, vis. fellow, 1990; dir. Ctr. Comparative Study of Devel., Brown U., 1989—; mem. selection com. Berlin program for Advanced German and European Studies, 1986-91; mem. rsch. planning com. on states and social structures Social Sci. Rsch. Coun., N.Y., 1983-90, now Working Group on States and Social Structures, Russell Sage Found., 1990—; acad. vis. Nuffield Coll., Oxford, 1979, Wolfson Coll., Oxford, 1982. Author: Lawyers and Their Society, 1973, German edit., 1976, Power and the Division of Labour, 1986, (with others) Capitalist Development and Democracy (Outstanding Book award Am. Sociological Assn. 1991-92); editor, co-editor: Das Interview: Formen, Technik, Auswertung, 2d edit., 1957, Beitrage zur soziologischen Theorie, 1964, Bringing the State Back In, 1985, States Vs. Markets in the World System, 1985, State and Market in Development: Synergy or Rivalry?, 1992; cons. editor Am. Jour. Sociology, 1977-79, Geschichte und Gesellschaft: Zeitschrift fuer historische Sozialwissenschaft, 1975—; assoc. editor Sociological Forum, 1985-92; mem. editorial bd. Am. Bar Found. Rsch. Jour., 1987, now Law and Social Inquiry, 1991-94, Sociological Theory, 1980-83; editor Working Papers on Comparative Development, 1983—; contbr. articles to profl. jours., book chpts.; presenter papers in field; speaker in field. Rsch. fellow Can. Coun., 1966; Faculty fellow Ford Found., 1968-69; Inst. Advanced Study Berlin fellow, 1987-88, Swedish Collegium for Advanced Study in the Social Scis. fellow Uppsala, 1992; recipient Torgny T. Segerstedt Professorship of Swedish Coun. for Studies in Higher Edn., 1992, Fgn. Franqui Chair of Belgium Free U. Brussels, 1987. Mem. Am. Sociol. Assn., Internat. Sociol. Assn., Am. Polit. Sci. Assn. Home: 60 Oriole Ave Providence RI 02906-5528 Office: Brown U Dept Sociology 79 Waterman St Providence RI 02912-9079

RUESINK, ALBERT WILLIAM, biologist, plant sciences educator; b. Adrian, Mich., Apr. 16, 1940; s. Lloyd William and Alberta May (Foltz) R.; m. Kathleen Joy Cramer, June 8, 1963; children: Jennifer Li, Adriana Eleanor. B.A., U. Mich., 1962; M.A., Harvard U., 1965, Ph.D., 1966. Postdoctoral fellow Swiss Fed. Inst. Tech., Zurich, 1966-67; prof. biology Ind. U., Bloomington, 1967—. Recipient Amoco Teaching award Ind. U., 1980. Mem. AAUP (pres. chpt. 1978-79, 90-91), Am. Soc. Plant Physiologists, Bot. Soc. Am. Democrat. Mem. United Ch. of Christ. Home: 2605 E 5th St Bloomington IN 47408-4286 Office: Ind U Dept Biology Bloomington IN 47405

RUF, JOHN FREDERIC, banker; b. Madison, Wis., May 9, 1937. BS, Lawrence U., 1959; JD, U. Wis., 1964. Bar: Wis. 1964. Asst. cashier Continental Ill. Bank, Chgo., 1964-68; v.p. M&I Marshall & Ilsley, Mllw., 1968-81; pres. RBP Chem. Corp., Mllw., 1981-84, First Interstate Bank of Wis., Mllw., 1984-90; chair A.C. Battery, 1990—; mem. legis. coun. Wis. Bankers Assn., Madison, 1974-81, 88-90; bd. dirs., pres. TYME Corp., Milw., 1974-90; dep. sec. State of Wis. Dept. Devel., 1991-93; chmn. Omnion Power Engring. Corp., 1993. Sec.-treas. Inland Lake Yachting Assn., Lake Geneva, Wis.; trustee Lawrence U., Appleton, Wis.; exec. dir. Wis. Housing and Econ. Devel. Authority, 1995—; dir. Great Am. Children's Theater. Mem. Lawrence U. Alumni Assn. (pres.). Clubs: Kettle Moraine Curling (Hartland, Wis.) (pres.); Pewaukee Yacht (Wis.) (commodore). Home: 2772531 NW Rocky Rd Pewaukee WI 53072

RUFA, ROBERT HENRY, writer, editor, photographer, artist; b. Bklyn., Jan. 11, 1943; s. Joseph Simon and Alma (Weinbrecht) R.; m. Barbara LeeJohnson, June 25, 1971 (div. Oct. 1980); 1 child, Eric; m. Donnita Butler Dicus, June 27, 1990 (div. Aug. 1994). Grad. high sch. Tech. editor Tele-Signal Corp., Woodbury, N.Y., 1968; assoc. editor Tobacco Leaf mag., Rockville Centre, N.Y., 1969; mem. staff Travel mag., Floral Park, N.Y., 1969-76; mng. editor Travel mag., 1973-74, editor, 1975-76; artist, writer, photographer, 1976—; mng. editor The Pinehurst Outlook, 1977-78, 88; columnist Moore County Citizen News-Record, 1987-88; columnist The Pilot, 1988—, feature writer, 1990-93; feature writer Stringer News and Observer, Raleigh, 1990-91; dir. publs. Asheville-Buncombe Discovery, Asheville, N.C., 1991-92; arts & features editor Green Line/Mountain Xpress, Asheville, N.C., 1992-95. With USAF, 1961-65. Home: 59 Watauga St Apt 8 Asheville NC 28801-1048

RUFEH, FIROOZ, high technology company executive; b. Isfahan, Iran, Feb. 15, 1937; s. Eberhim and Marian R. Rufeh; m. Heide Marie Haseruck, June 12, 1965; children: Bejan Renard, Jiela Mariam. BS in Chemistry, Cornell U., 1959; MS in Nuclear Engring., U. Calif., Berkeley, 1963. Rsch. scientist Thermo Electron Corp., Waltham, Mass., 1963-67, mgr. rsch. dept., 1967-75, dir. energy conservation and rsch., 1975-79, pres. R & D, new bus. div., 1979-84, group exec., 1984-86, v.p., 1986—; CEO, pres., bd. dirs. Thermotrex Corp., San Diego, 1995—; bd. dirs. Thermo Lase Corp., Thermo Trex Med. Corp., Inc. Office: Thermo Trex Corp 101 1st Ave 9550 Distribution Ave San Diego CA 92121

RUFENACHT, ROGER ALLEN, accounting educator; b. Waldron, Mich., Dec. 17, 1933; s. Alphus Leroy and Frieda (Aschliman) R.; m. Carol Carnahan, June 13, 1965; children: Jeffrey, Jonathan. BS, Mich. State U., 1959, MS, 1965. Cert. tchr., Fla. Tchr. Madison High Sch., Adrian, Mich., 1959-61; bus. edn. instr. Charlotte High Sch., Rochester, N.Y., 1961-62; bus. edn. instr. Edgewater High Sch., Orlando, Fla., 1962-68, chmn. bus. dept., 1965-68; instr. in acctg. Orlando Vo Tech. Ctr. (formerly Orlando Vocat. Sch.), 1968-94, chmn. bus. dept., 1980-85; ret., 1994. Bd. dirs., v.p. Winter Park Jaycees, 1963-68; asst. coach, scorekeeper N.W. Little League; chmn. adv. com. local PTA, 1973-83; pres. Bandboosters 1985-86; cub scout den leader, com. chmn., mem. dist. com., mem. coms. Boy Scouts Am.; adminstrv. bd. local Meth. Ch., 1965—. Recipient Scouters Tng. award, Ten Yr. Vet. award Boy Scouts Am., 1991. Mem. NEA, Am. Vocat. Assn., Fla. Vocat. Assn. (registration com. ann. conf., pres.'s reception planning com.), Orange County Classroom Tchrs. Assn. (bd. dirs., bldg. rep.), Orange County Credit Union (rep.), Orange County Vocat. Assn. (bd. dirs., Pres.'s award 1988-89, Outstanding Vocat. Educator Bus. Edn. award 1988-89), Fla. Bus. Edn. Assn. (chmn., mem. various coms.), Orange County Bus. Edn. Assn. (pres. 1968, 76, chmn., mem. various coms.). Republican. Avocations: reading, gardening, golf. Home: 9510 Bear Lake Rd Apopka FL 32703-1917

RUFF, DAN GEORGE, academic administrator; b. Columbia, S.C., June 16, 1950; s. Dan George and Marguerite (Johnson) R.; m. Shirley Paul, Nov. 20, 1977; children: Jennifer, Jessica. AB in Polit. Sci., Newberry (S.C.) Coll., 1972; MA in Govt., U. S.C., 1975, MPA, 1980, postgrad., 1990—. Planner cmty. devel. divsn. S.C. Gov.'s Office, Columbia, 1975-76, planner employment/tng. divsn., 1976-83; dir. planning and analysis Midlands Tech. Coll., Columbia, 1983-85; trainee, intern and cons. Am. Campaign Acad., Arlington, Va., 1986-87; dir. instnl. planning and rsch. U. S.C.-Salkehatchie, Allendale, 1987—; adj. prof. U. S.C., Allendale and Walterboro, 1987—, Golden Gate U., Shaw AFB Campus, Sumter, S.C., 1985; cons. St. Andrews Middle Sch., Columbia, 1985, S.C. Regional Housing Authority #3, Barnwell, 1994; lectr. in field. Contbr. articles to profl. jours. Bd. dirs. Citizens for the Advancement of Physically Handicapped. Mem. Assn. for Instnl. Rsch., So. Assn. for Instnl. Rsch., Southeastern Assn. for Cmty. Coll. Rsch., Soc. for Coll. and Univ. Planning, Southeastern Employment and Tng. Assn., Am. Soc. for Pub. Adminstrn., Am. Polit. Sci. Assn., So. Polit. Sci. Assn., S.C. Polit. Sci. Assn., Ga. Polit. Sci. Assn., World Future Soc. (S.C. chpt. steering com. on employment and edn.), Cayce-West Columbia Kiwanis (bd. dirs.). Methodist. Home: 3418 Heyward St Columbia SC 29205-2756

RUFF, LORRAINE MARIE, public relations executive; b. Washington, Feb. 13, 1947; d. William Stanley and Jeanne Ann (Murray) Charlton; m. R. Eugene Ruff, July 17, 1968; 1 child, David Michael. BS in Liberal Arts, Oreg. State U., 1976. Reporter The Oregonian, Corvallis, Oreg., 1976-79, Union-Bull., Walla Walla, Wash., 1979-80; dir. pub. rels. Strategic Mktg., Corvallis, 1980-82; gen. mgr. Campaigns Northwest, Corvallis, 1982-84; account supr. Arthur D. Little, Inc., Cambridge, Mass., 1985-87, mgr. corp. ID, 1988-89; dir. biotechnology New Eng. Hill and Knowlton, Waltham, Mass., 1989, v.p., dir. biotechnology, 1990-91, dir. internat. biotechnology practice, 1990-91, sr. v.p., gen. mgr., 1991-93; sr. v.p., mng. dir. divsn. biosci. comm. Stoorza, Ziegaus & Metzger, San Diego, 1993-94, dir.

life scis. practice, 1993-94; owner Charlton Ruff Comm., Puyallup, Wash., 1994—; mem. bd. dirs. Coll. Liberal Arts Devel. Coun., Oreg. State U. Bd. dirs. Wash. State Biotech. & Biomed Assn., Oreg. State U. Coll. Liberal Arts Devel. Coun. Mem. Pub. Rels. Soc. Am., Nat. Investor Rels. Inst., Oreg. Biotech. Assn., Wash. State Biotech. and Biomed. Assn. (bd. dirs.), B.C. Biotech. Alliance, Coll. Club Seattle, Rotary (univ. dist. chpt.). Republican. Avocations: collecting antique ivories, international cuisine, gardening, writing. Office: Charlton Ruff Comm 12124 138th Ave E Puyallup WA 98374-4536

RUFF, ROBERT LOUIS, neurologist, physiology researcher; b. Bklyn., Dec. 16, 1950; s. John Joseph and Rhoda (Alpert) R.; m. Louise Seymour Acheson, Apr. 26, 1980. BS summa cum laude, Cooper Union, 1971; MD summa cum laude, U. Wash., 1976, PhD in Physiology, 1976. Diplomate Am. Bd. Neurology and Psychiatry. Asst. neurologist N.Y. Hosp., Cornell Med. Sch., N.Y.C., 1977-80; asst. prof. physiology and medicine U. Wash., Seattle, 1980-84; assoc. prof. neurology Case Western Res. Med. Sch., Cleve., 1984-92, prof. neurology and neuroscis., 1993—, vice chair neurology dept., 1995—; chief dept. neurology Cleve. VA Med. Ctr., 1984—; adv. Child Devel. and Mental Retardation Ctr., Seattle, 1980-84, Burien Devel. Disability Ctr., Wash., 1982-84; mem. med. adv. bd. Muscular Dystrophy Assn., Seattle, 1984, NE Ohio chpt. Multiple Sclerosis Soc., 1986—; mem. adv. bd. for Neurology Dept. Vets. Affairs, 1989—; chmn. med. adv. bd. N.E. Ohio chpt. Myasthenia Gravis Found., 1987—, bd. trustees, 1993—, nat. med. adv. bd., 1988—, grant and fellowship com., 1990—. Assoc. editor: Neurology, 1994—; ad hoc reviewer various profl. and sci. jours.; contbr. articles to profl. jours. and chpts. to books. Nat. bd. dirs. Myasthenia Gravis Found., 1994—. Recipient Tchr. Investigator award NIH; NSF fellow, 1971; NIH grantee, Muscular Dystrophy Assn. grantee, Dept. Vets. Affair grantee; N.Y. State Regents med. scholar, 1971. Fellow Am. Heart Assn. (stroke coun.), Am. Acad. Neurology (scientific issues com., legis. action com.); mem. AMA, Am. Physics Soc., Neurosci. Soc., Biophys. Soc., Am. Neurol. Assn., N.Y. Acad. Sci., Am. Geriatrics Soc., Sigma Pi Sigma (v.p. 1970-71), Alpha Omega Alpha (v.p. 1975-76). Home: 2572 Stratford Rd Cleveland OH 44118-4063 Office: VA Med Ctr 10701 East Blvd Ste 127W Cleveland OH 44106-1702

RUFFER, DAVID GRAY, museum director, former college president; b. Archbold, Ohio, Aug. 25, 1937; s. Lawrence A. and Florence A. (Newcomer) R.; m. Marilyn Elaine Taylor, Aug. 23, 1958; children: Rochelle Lynne, Robyn Lynne, David Geoffrey. B.S., Defiance Coll., 1959; M.A., Bowling Green State U., 1960; Ph.D., U. Okla., 1964. Spl. instr. U. Okla., 1963-64; asst. prof. biology Defiance Coll., 1964-68, asso. prof., 1968-73, faculty dean, 1969-73; provost Elmira (N.Y.) Coll., 1973-78; pres. Albright Coll., Reading, Pa., 1978-91, U. Tampa, Fla., 1991-94; exec. dir. Dayton (Ohio) Soc. Natural History, 1995—. Author: Exploring and Understanding Mammals, 1971; contbr. articles to profl. jours. NSF grantee, 1965, 67; Ohio Biol. Survey grantee, 1968-69. Fellow AAAS; mem. Am. Assn. Higher Edn., Animal Behavior Soc., Am. Soc. Mammalogists, Sigma Xi. Methodist. Club: Rotary. Home: 3700 Wales Dr Dayton OH 45405 Office: Dayton Mus Natural History 2600 DeWeese Pkwy Dayton OH 45414

RUFFER, MICHAEL R., hotel company executive. Exec. v.p., gen. mgr. Residence Inn, by Marriott Inc., Washington. Office: Residence Inn By Marriott Inc 1 Marriott Dr Washington DC 20058-0001*

RUFFIN, SHIRLEY ANN, federal financial director; b. Tokyo, Japan, Sept. 1, 1955; (parents Am. citizens); d. Alfred Lewis and Linda Eiko (Yokomura) R. BSBA in Acctg., George Mason U., 1977; MBA in Fin., Am. U., 1982. Cert. in Procurement Mgmt. Staff acct., auditor EPA, Def. Contract Audit Agy., Dept. Agriculture, Dept. Navy, Washington, 1973-86; chief accounts payable, travel mgmt. sect. EPA, 1986-87, chief quality assurance staff, 1987-89; assoc. dir. acctg. ops. Comptroller of the Currency, Washington, 1989-91; acting dir. sys. and acctg. standards divsn. IRS, Washington, 1991-93; dir. fin. mgmt. policy Dept. Health and Human Svcs., Washington, 1993—; adj. faculty U.Va., Falls Ch., 1985-87. Sec./v.p. Lyongate Owners Assn., Arlington, Va., 1993—; mem. fin. com. Arlington Village Condo Assn., 1985-86. Mem. Assn. Govt. Accts. (Appreciation award 1988), Annandale Bus. & Profl. Women (corr. sec. 1990-91, Young Careerist award 1990). Avocations: skiing, runnning, cycling.

RUFFING, ANNE ELIZABETH, artist; b. Bklyn.; d. John Paul and Ruth Elizabeth (Price) Frampton; m. George W. Ruffing, Mar. 29, 1967; 1 dau., Elizabeth Anne. B.S., Cornell U., 1964; postgrad., Drexel Inst. Tech., 1966. One-woman exhbns. include, IBM, 1966, Hall of Fame, Goshen, N.Y., 1971, group exhbns. include, Internat. Women's Arts Festival, World Trade Center, N.Y.C., 1975-76, Berkshire Mus., Pittsfield, Mass., 1965, 76, Cooperstown (N.Y.) Mus., 1969; represented in permanent collections, Met. Mus. Art, Bklyn. Mus., Library of Congress, Harvard U., Smithsonian Instn., N.Y. Hist. Soc. Johnston Hist. Mus., Atwater Kent Mus., Albany Inst. History and Art, Whitney Mus. Am. Art, Boston Public Library. Recipient 1st place Eric Sloane award, 1974; Internat. Women's Year award Internat. Women's Art Festival, 1976. Address: PO Box 125 Bloomington NY 12411-0125

RUFFLE, JOHN FREDERICK, banker; b. Toledo, Mar. 28, 1937; s. Matthew Frederick and Hazel Ruth (Johnson) R.; m. Eleanor Grace Loock, Nov. 19, 1960; children: Donald Alan, William Charles, John Garrett. B.A., Johns Hopkins, 1958; M.B.A., Rutgers, 1963. C.P.A., N.J. With Price Waterhouse & Co., N.Y.C., 1958-65; sr. accountant Price Waterhouse & Co., 1962-65; asst. treas. Internat. Paper Co., N.Y.C., 1965-70; comptroller Morgan Guaranty Trust Co. N.Y., N.Y.C., 1970-80; exec. v.p. Morgan Guaranty Trust Co. N.Y., 1980-85, vice chmn. bd., 1985-93, ret., 1993; cons. J.P. Morgan & Co., Inc., N.Y.C., 1993—; bd. dirs. Am. Shared Hosp. Svcs., Inc., Bethlehem Steel Corp., Trident Corp. JPM Advisor Funds. Trustee Johns Hopkins U., Balt., 1990—. With AUS, 1959-60. Mem. AICPA, Fin. Execs. Inst. (chmn. bd. 1983-84), N.J. Soc. CPAs, Fin. Acctg. Found. (trustee 1984-90, pres. 1989-90). Office: 23 Wall St New York NY 10260-1000

RUFFNER, CHARLES LOUIS, lawyer; b. Cin., Nov. 7, 1936; s. Joseph H. and Edith (Solomon) R.; m. Mary Ann Kaufman, Jan. 30, 1966 (div. 1993); children: Robin Sue, David Robert; m. Nanette Diemer, Feb. 26, 1995. BSBA in Acctg., U. Fla., 1958; JD cum laude, U. Miami, 1964. Bar: Fla. 1964, U.S. Dist. Ct. (so. and mid. dists.) Fla. 1964, U.S. Ct. Appeals (5th cir.) 1964, U.S. Ct. Appeals (11th cir.) 1984, U.S. Claims Ct. 1966, U.S. Tax Ct. 1966, U.S. Supreme Ct. 1968. Cert. in taxation. Trial atty. tax div. Dept. Justice, Washington, 1964-67; pres. Forrest, Ruffner, Traum & Hagen, P.A., Miami, Fla., 1967-78; pres. Ruffner, Hagen & Rifkin, P.A., Miami, 1978-81; tax ptnr. Myers, Kenin, Levinson, Ruffner, Frank & Richards, Miami, 1982-84; pres. Charles L. Ruffner, P.A., 1984—; lectr. Fla. Internat. U., Miami. Author: A Practical Approach to Professional Corporations and Associations, 4 edits., 1970, (column) Tax Talk, Miami Law Rev.; editor: Miami Law Rev., 1963-64; contbr. numerous articles on taxation to law jours. Mem. ABA, Fed. Bar Assn., Fla. Bar (exec. council tax sect. 1967-92, 95-96, amicus curiae in test case of validity profl. corps.), Dade County Bar Assn., South Fla. Tax Litigation Assn. (chmn. 1986-96), Phi Alpha Delta, Phi Kappa Phi. Office: Courvoisier Centre II 601 Brickell Key Dr Ste 507 Miami FL 33131-2650

RUFFNER, FREDERICK G., JR., book publisher; b. Akron, Ohio, Aug. 6, 1926; s. Frederick G. and Olive Mae (Taylor) R.; m. Mary Ann Evans, Oct. 8, 1954; children: Frederic G. III, Peter Evans. B.S., Ohio State U., 1950. Advt. mgr. Jim Robbins Co., Royal Oak, Mich., 1950-52; research mgr. Gen. Detroit Corp., 1953-54; pres. Gale Research Co., Detroit, 1954-87, Omnigraphics, Inc., 1987—. Editor: Ency. of Assns, 1956-68, Code Names Dictionary, 1963, Acronyms and Initialisms Dictionary, 1965, Allusions Dictionary, 1985; pub. Gold Coast Mag., 1992—; patentee in field. Bd. dirs. Friends of Detroit Pub. Libr., pres., 1975-76; mem. exec. bd. Detroit coun. Boy Scouts Am., 1974—, v.p., 1976-82; pres. Coun. for Fla. Librs., 1979—; trustee Bon Secours Hosp., Grosse Pointe, Mich., 1980-81; v.p. Etruscan Found., Florence, Italy, 1980—; pres. Mich. Ctr. for the Book, 1990, Literary Landmarks Assn., Gold Coast Jazz Soc., Ft. Lauderdale, 1992—; bd. dirs. Ohio State U. Found., Bonnet House, Ft. Lauderdale, 1992. 1st lt. AUS, 1944-46. Decorated Bronze Star, Combat Inf. award; recipient Centennial award Ohio State U., 1970, Benjamin Creativity award Assn. Am. Pubs., 1985, Career medal Ohioana Libr. Assn., 1988, Lifetime Achievement award Am. Libr. Trustees Assn., 1992; named to Entrepreneurs Hall of Fame, Nova U. Mem. Am. Antiquarian Soc., ALA (hon. life), Am. Mgmt. Assn., Am. Assn. Mus., Detroit Hist. Soc., Am. Hist. Print Collectors Soc., Bibliog. Soc. Am., Sierra Club, Pres. Assn., Audubon Soc., Am. Name Soc., Early Am. Industries Assn., Ephemera Soc., Johnny Appleseed Soc., Navy League, Newcomen Soc., Cen. Bus. Dist. Assn. Detroit (vice-chmn. 1985-87), Jazz Forum (Grosse Pointe Farms, Mich., pres. 1989—), Nat. Trust Hist. Preservation, Fairfield Heritage Soc., Archives Am. Art, Pvt. Librs. Assn., Friend Ft. Lauderdale Pub. Libr. (pres. 1974-78), Phileas Soc. (pres. 1985—), Ohio State U. Club (pres. Detroit club 1958, nat. chmn. Ohio State U. campaighn, 1985-88), Masons, Shriners, Book Club, Detroit Athletic Club, Econ. Club, Prismatic Club (pres. 1990), Fontenada Soc. (pres. 1990-91), Detroit Club, Country Club Detroit, Ocean Reef Club, Grosse Pointe Yacht Club, Coral Ridge Yacht Club, Lauderdale Yacht Club, Princeton Club, Salmagundi Club, Grolier Club, Century Assn., Marco Polo Club, Faculty Club Ohio State U., Old Club, Tau Kappa Epsilon. Republican. Methodist. Home: 221 Lewiston Rd Grosse Pointe Farms MI 48236-3519 also: 1000 Flamingo Isle Dr Fort Lauderdale FL 33301-2670 Office: Omnigraphics Inc 2500 Penobscot Bldg Detroit MI 48226 also: 901 E Las Olas Blvd Fort Lauderdale FL 33301-2320

RUFFNER, JAY STURGIS, lawyer; b. Washington, Pa., June 22, 1941; s. Hugh Lewis And Eleanore (Burchinal) R.; m. Mary Eleanor Glass, Oct. 3, 1966; children: Jay S. Jr., Megan L., Stephanie B. BA, Hobart Coll., 1963; JD, U. Pitts., 1966; LLM, NYU, 1972. Ptnr. Lewis and Roca Law Firm, Phoenix, 1972-93; assoc. Meyer, Hendricks, Victor, Osborn & Maledon, Phoenix, 1993-95; ptnr. Meyer, Hendricks, Victor, Ruffner & Bivens, Phoenix, 1995-96, Fennemore Craig, PC, 1996—. Bd. dirs. The Flinn Found., Phoenix, 1979—, Phoenix Art Mus., 1991—, Blood Sys., Inc., 1995—. Mem. ABA, Am. Soc. Corp. Secs. (former chmn. membership com., corp. practices com., audit com., former bd. dirs., chmn. budget com., edn. com., securities industry com.), Stockholder Rels. Soc. N.Y. (past pres. and dir.), Westchester Clubmen (pres.), Phi Delta Phi, Sigma Pi Phi, Alpha Phi Alpha. Office: Fennemore Craig, PC 2 N Central Ave 22d Fl Phoenix AZ 85004

RUFFOLO, MARILYN CLAIRE, primary education educator; b. Harvey, Ill., Aug. 2, 1952; d. Carmen Anthony and Helen Elaine (Welch) R. AA with high honors, Thornton C.C., 1972; BS in Edn. with high honors, Ill. State U., 1974; MEd, Nat.-Louis U., 1990. Cert. K-9, Ill. Tchr. kindergarten Primary Acad. Ctr., Markham, Ill., 1976-91, tchr. K-3, 1991—. Ill. State scholar, 1969. Mem. Ill. Edn. Assn. (assn. rep. 1976-88), Kappa Delta Pi, Phi Theta Kappa. Republican. Avocations: music, travel. Home: 2522 183rd St Homewood IL 60430-3037 Office: Prairie-Hills Prim Acad Ctr 3055 W 163rd St Markham IL 60426-5626

RUGABER, WALTER FEUCHT, JR., newspaper executive; b. Macon, Ga., Nov. 29, 1938; s. Walter Feucht and Edith Almeda (Maynard) R.; m. Sally Sanford, Oct. 6, 1962; children—Leslie, Christopher, Mark. B.S., Northwestern U., 1960. Corr., editor N.Y. Times, 1965-78; v.p., exec. editor Greensboro Daily News & Record, N.C., 1978-82; pres., pub. The Roanoke Times, Va., 1982—; pres. Landmark Pub. Group; mem. Pulitzer Prize Bd. Bd. dirs. United Way of Roanoke Valley, 1982-88, Roanoke Symphony Soc., 1985—, pres., 1986-88; trustee Hollins Coll. Mem. Am. Newspaper Pubs. Assn., Am. Soc. Newspaper Editors, So. Newspaper Pubs. Assn. Office: Times World Corp PO Box 2491 201-209 W Campbell Ave Roanoke VA 24010

RUGALA, KAREN FRANCIS, television producer, painter; b. Memphis, Apr. 27, 1950; d. Ben Porter and Marguerite K. Higginbotham; children: Sarah Helfinstein, Ben Helfinstein. BA in Communication Arts, Rhodes Coll., 1971; MA, U. Mo., 1973. Cert. tchr., Tenn. Secondary sch. tchr. Memphis City Schs., 1971-72; speech tchr. U. Ga., Athens, 1973-75; dir. computer systems installations Planning Rsch. Corp., McLean, Va., 1976-78; dir. account mgmt. TDX Systems, Cable & Wireless, Vienna, Va., 1978-80; cons. telecommunications MCI, Washington, 1985-87; producer Fairfax Cable Access, Merrifield, Va., 1991—; owner Art Promotions, McLean, 1989—. Exhibited paintings in numerous group and one-woman shows including Clark & Co. Gallery, Washington, 1994, McLean Project for Arts, 1992, Hospice of No. Va. Auction Gala, 1992, Touchstone Gallery Benefit Auction, McLean, 1991, Great Falls Art Ctr., Va., 1990, many others; paintings represented in numerous pvt. collections. Active Family AIDS Housing Found., 1992, Hospice No. Va., 1991, 92, Friends of Vietnam Vets. Meml., 1992; founding bd. mem. Jobs for Homeless People, 1988-90. Avocations: tennis, bridge, skiing. Office: Art Promotions PO Box 3104 Mc Lean VA 22103-3104

RUGE, DANIEL AUGUST, retired neurosurgeon, educator; b. Murdock, Nebr., May 13, 1917; s. August Daniel and Mary Louise R.; m. Greta Piper, June 12, 1942; children: Charlotte, Thomas. B.A., N. Central Coll., Naperville, Ill., 1939, Sc.D., 1971; M.D., Northwestern U., 1945, Ph.D., 1961. Intern Wesley Meml. Hosp., Chgo., 1945-46; resident Wesley Meml. Hosp., 1949-50, Passavant Meml. Hosp., Chgo., 1946-49, VA Hosp., Hines, Ill., 1950-52; practice medicine specializing in neurosurgery Chgo., 1952-76; prof. surgery Northwestern U., Chgo., 1973-76; professorial lectr. George Washington U., Washington, 1976-86, ret., 1986; dep. dir. spinal cord injury service VA Central Office, Washington, 1976-80; dir. VA Central Office, 1980-81, 85-86, ret., 1986; physician to pres. U.S., White House, 1981-85. Author: Spinal Cord Injuries, 1969, Spinal Disorders: Diagnosis and Treatment, 1977; editor: Jour. Am. Paraplegia Soc., 1976-88. Trustee North Cen. Coll., 1960—, chmn. bd., 1974-77. Lt comdr. USN, 1954-56. Recipient Service award Northwestern U., 1966, Merit award Northwestern U., 1983; Outstanding Alumnus award N. Central Coll., 1978, Meritorious Service award VA, 1986. Fellow A.C.S.; mem. AMA, Am. Assn. Neurol. Surgeons, Central Surg. Assn., James IV Assn. Surgeons. Republican. Presbyterian. Home: 240 S High St Denver CO 80209-2628

RUGER, WILLIAM BATTERMAN, firearms manufacturing company executive; b. Bklyn., June 21, 1916; s. Adolph and May R.; m. Mary Thompson, Aug. 26, 1938 (dec.); children: William Batterman, Carolyn Amalie Ruger Vogel, James Thompson (dec.). Student, U. N.C. Firearms design engr. U.S. Armory, Springfield, Mass., 1939-40; machine gun designer Auto Ordnance Corp., Hartford, Conn., World War II; founder, pres. Ruger Corp. (hand tool mfrs.), Southport, Conn., 1946-48; co-founder, 1948; since pres., chmn. bd., treas. Sturm, Ruger & Co., Inc., Southport; v.p. Sporting Arms and Ammunition Inst., 1978—; past bd. dirs. Nat. Shooting Sports Found. Author, editor; patentee in field. Trustee Salisbury (Conn.) Sch., 1970-75, Naval War Coll. Found., Buffalo Bill Hist. Ctr. Recipient Nat. Leadership award Hunting Hall of Fame, 1979; named Handgunner of Year Am. Handgunner Found., 1975. Mem. NRA (past bd. dirs.), Blue Mountain Forest Assn., Vintage Sports Car Club Am., Auburn-Cord-Duesenberg, Rolls Royce Owners Club, Rolls Royce Silver Ghost Assn., Am. Bugatti Club, Bugatti Owners' Club, Vet. Motor Club, Stutz Club, Ferrari Club Am., Campfire Club, Pequot Yacht Club, N.Y. Yacht Club, Boone and Crockett Club, Cat Cay Club, Clambake Club, Delta Kappa Epsilon. Lutheran. Office: Sturm Ruger & Co 1 Lacey Pl Southport CT 06490-1241

RUGGE, HENRY FERDINAND, medical products executive; b. South San Francisco, Oct. 28, 1936; s. Hugo Heinrich and Marie Mathilde (Breiholz) R.; m. Sue Callow, Dec. 29, 1967. BS in Physics, U. Calif., Berkeley, 1958, PhD in Physics, 1963. Sr. physicist Physics Internat. Co., San Leandro, 1963-68; dir. adminstrn. and fin. Arkon Sci. Labs., Berkeley, Calif., 1969-71; v.p. Norse Systems, Inc., Hayward, Calif., 1972-74; v.p. Rasor Assocs., Inc., Sunnyvale, Calif., 1974-81, v.p., gen. mgr., 1983-87, exec. v.p. fin., 1988-89, pres., chief exec. officer, 1990—; chmn. UltraVision, Inc., Calgary, Alta., Can., 1993—, also bd. dirs., 1993—; pres. Berlinscan, Inc., Sunnyvale, 1981-82; cons. The Rugge Group, Berkeley, 1987-90; bd. dirs. Rasor Assocs., Inc., Space Power Inc., Analatom, Inc. Patentee in area med. devices. U. Calif. scholar, 1954-58. Mem. Am. Heart Assn., Berkeley Bicycle (treas. 1983-84), Phi Beta Kappa. Avocations: bicycle racing, wine, food. Home: 46 Hiller Dr Oakland CA 94618 Office: Rasor Assocs Inc 5670 Stewart Ave Fremont CA 94538

RUGGE, HUGO ROBERT, physicist; b. South San Francisco, Calif., Nov. 7, 1935; s. Hugo Heinrich and Marie (Breiholz) R.; m. Coral Loy Irish, Dec. 28, 1969; children—Leslie Anne, Robert David. A.B., U. Calif.-Berkeley, 1957, Ph.D., 1962. Research physicist Lawrence Berkeley Lab., 1961-62; mem. tech. staff Aerospace Corp., Los Angeles, 1962-68, dept. head, 1968-79, prin. dir., 1979-81, lab. dir., 1981-89, v.p. lab. ops., 1989-91, v.p. tech. ops., 1991—. mem. mission systems panel AGARD/NATO. Contbr. numerous articles on space sci. and astrophysics to profl. jours. Fellow Am. Phys. Soc.; mem. Am. Astron. Soc., Am. Geophys. Union, Internat. Astron. Union, Phi Beta Kappa, Sigma Xi.

RUGGERI, RICCARDO, automotive sales executive. Chmn. bd., CEO Ford New Holland (Pa.), Inc.; COO N.H. Geotech N.V., London. Office: New Holland Fiat Spa, Viale Delle Nozioni 55, San Matteo 41100, Italy*

RUGGIERO, LAURENCE JOSEPH, museum director; b. Paterson, N.J., Mar. 25, 1948; s. Salvatore Joseph and Grace Marie (Williams) R.; m. Virginia Frances Fornaci, Mar. 7, 1970; 1 child, John Laurence. BA, U. Pa., 1969, MA, 1979, PhD, 1975; MBA, Boston U., 1978. Asst. prof. history of architecture U. Ill., Chgo., 1973-77; fin. analyst Met. Mus. Art, N.Y.C., 1979-80, asst. to pres., 1980-81; exec. dir. Oakland (Calif.) Mus. Assocs., 1981-85; dir. John and Mable Ringling Mus., Sarasota, Fla., 1985-92; assoc. dir. Charles Hosmer Morse Mus. Am. Art, Winter Park, Fla., 1992—, dir., 1995—; adj. prof. Ringling Sch. Art and Design, Sarasota, 1986-92. Kress Found. fellow, 1971-73. Mem. Fla. Art Mus. Dirs. Assn. (treas. 1987-92), Coll. Art Assn. Am., Am. Assn. Mus., Il Cenacolo (San Francisco). Office: 445 Park Ave N Winter Park FL 32789

RUGGIERO, MATTHEW JOHN, bassoonist; b. Phila., Sept. 18, 1932; s. Pompeo and Theresa (Ciampa) R.; m. Nancy Cirillo, Apr. 2, 1961; children: Eleanor, Claudia, Lisa. Diploma, Curtis Inst. Music, 1957; AA, Harvard U., 1982, BA cum laude, 1984, MA, 1987; PhD, Boston U., 1993. Second bassoonist Nat. Symphony Orch., Washington, 1957-60; asst. prin. bassoonist Boston Symphony Orch., 1961-89; prin. bassoonist Boston Pops Orch., 1974-89; ret., 1989; mem. faculty Boston U., 1963—, New Eng. Conservatory Music, 1963—. Served with U.S. Army, 1954-57. Boston U. Profs. Program scholar and fellow, 1989.

RUGGIERO, THOMAS WILLIAM, lawyer; b. Glen Cove, N.Y., Dec. 2, 1946; s. Philip P. and Virginia M. Ruggiero; m. Patricia Williams, Aug. 7, 1971; 2 children. AB in Hist., St. Michael's Coll., 1968; JD, Boston Coll., 1971. Bar: N.Y. 1972. Ptnr. LeBoeuf, Lamb, Greene and MacRae, N.Y.C., 1983—. Office: LeBoeuf Lamb Greene & MacRae 125 W 55th St New York NY 10019-5369*

RUGGILL, SOLOMON P., psychologist; b. N.Y.C., Sept. 29, 1906; s. Abraham and Sarah (Silverberg) R.; m. Sophie Stock, June 8, 1938; children: Robert Zachary, Peter Alan. BS, CCNY, 1927; MA in Edn., Columbia U., 1930, PhD in Psychology, 1934. Lic. psychologist, N.Y. Tchr. elem. and jr. high sch. Bd. of Edn. of N.Y.C., 1929-59, psychologist, Bur. of Child Guidance, 1959-62; psychologist Baro Civic Ctr. Clinic, Bklyn., 1961-62; assoc. prof. L.I. U., Bklyn., 1962-69, prof., 1969-79, prof. emeritus, 1979—, acting chmn. dept. guidance and counseling, 1972-73; dir. Flatback Progressive Sch., Bklyn., 1943-45, Camp Kinderwelt, Fraternal Order Farband, N.Y.C., 1959-60; lectr. in gerontology to various orgns., Tucson, 1980—, Keeping Mentally Alert classes Sr. Day Ctrs., 1985—. Pres. Chancy Meml. Found., N.Y.C., 1961-63; mem. adv. council Pima Council on Aging, Tucson, 1987—. Mem. N.Y. Acad. Pub. Edn., N.Y. State Guidance Assn., Jewish Tchrs. Assn. (life). Jewish. Home: 425 W Paseo Redondo Apt 7E Tucson AZ 85701-8262

RUGGLES, RUDY LAMONT, JR., investment banker, consultant; b. Evanston, Ill., Nov. 11, 1938; s. Rudy Lamont and Ruth (Cain) R.; m. Cecelia Ann Consorte, July 20, 1974; children—Rudy, Christopher, Daniel, Andrew. B.A., Harvard U., 1960, M.B.A., 1966. Sr. assoc. physicist IBM Labs., Poughkeepsie, N.Y., 1960-64; corp. planning cons. corp. hdqrs. IBM, Armonk, N.Y., 1966-71; sr. mem. profl. staff Hudson Inst., Croton-on-Hudson, N.Y., 1971-75; pres. Hudson Inst., 1975-79, also dir.; prin. Cresap, McCormick & Paget, Inc., 1979-82; ptnr. The Phila. Mgmt. Cons. Group, Inc., 1982—; mng. dir. New China Group, Inc., 1982—. Chmn. residential solicitation United Fund, Pound Ridge, N.Y., 1969; mem. parents com. St. Paul's Sch., Concord, N.H.; dir. Danbury Hosp. and Danbury Hosp. Devel. Fund, Conn., 1978—, also mem. med. affairs com.; chmn. fin. com. Pound Ridge Community Ch., 1969-70; bd. dirs. Harry Frank Guggenheim Found., 1982—; bd. visitors Sch. Langs. and Linguistics Georgetown U.; trustee New Canaan Country Sch. With C.E., U.S. Army, 1962. Fellow Explorers Club; mem. Hudson Inst. (hon.), N. Am. Soc. Corp. Planning (dir. 1966-72), Sci. Rsch. Soc. Am. (hon.), Internat. Inst. Strategic Studies, Ends of the Earth (hon.), U.S.-China Bus. Coun., Harvard Club of N.Y.C., Silver Spring Country Club. Office: Big Shop Ln Ridgefield CT 06877

RUGH, WILLIAM ARTHUR, diplomat; b. N.Y.C., May 10, 1936; s. Roberts and Harriette (Sheldon) R.; m. Andrea Scott Bear, July 12, 1958; children—David William, Douglas Edward, Nicholas Alexander. Student, Hamburg U., Germany, 1958-59; B.A., Oberlin Coll., 1958; M.A., Johns Hopkins U., 1961; Ph.D., Columbia U., 1967. Near East policy dir. USIA, Washington, 1971-72, dep. asst. dir., 1973-76; pub. affairs counsellor U.S. Embassy, Cairo, 1976-81; dep. chief of mission U.S. Embassy, Damascus, Syria, 1981-84; amb. U.S. Embassy, Sanaa, Yemen, 1984-87; diplomat in residence Fletcher Sch. Tufts U., Medford, Mass., 1987-89; dir. Near East, North Africa, South Asia divs. USIA, Washington, 1989-92; U.S. amb. to United Arab Emirates, Abu Dhabi, 1992-95; pres. America-Mideast Edn. and Tng. Svcs., Inc., Washington, 1995—. Author: Riyadh, a History, 1969; The Arab Press, 1979, 87; also contbr. articles and chpts. to books. Coun. on Fgn. Rels. fellow, 1972-73; recipient Presdl. award U.S. Pres., 1983. Mem. Middle East Inst., Middle East Studies Assn. Home: 10113 Montrose Ave Garrett Park MD 20896-0141 Office: Amideast 1730 M St NW Washington DC 20521-6010

RUHLMAN, TERRELL LOUIS, business executive; b. Warren, Pa., Nov. 13, 1926; s. Ross L. and Gertrude R.; m. Phyllis E., Jan. 15, 1951; children: Robyn Ruhlman Dempsey, Randall L., Heather Ruhlman Martin, Mark A. BS, Pa. State U., 1949; JD, George Washington U., 1954; postgrad., Duquesne U. Grad. Bus. Sch., 1966-68. Bar: D.C. bar. Patent counsel Joy Mfg. Co., Pitts., 1954-59; gen. counsel Joy Mfg. Co., 1959-62, asst. to pres., 1962-69; v.p. oilfield ops. Joy Mfg. Co., Houston, 1969-73; gen. mgr. Reed Tool Co., Houston, 1973-74; pres., COO Reed Tool Co., 1974-76, dir., 1975-76; v.p., dir. Baker Internat. Corp., 1975-76, pres. mining group, 1976; pres., CEO, dir. Ansul Co., Marinette, Wis., 1976-80; pres. Wormald Americas, Inc., Scottsdale, Ariz., 1980-88; chmn., CEO Cade Industries, Inc., Scottsdale, 1988—, also bd. dirs.; chmn., bd. dirs. Environ. Engring. Concepts Inc. With USAF. Served with USAF. Home: 9710 E La Posada Cir Scottsdale AZ 85255-3716 Office: # 114 8711 E Pinnacle Peak Rd # 114 Scottsdale AZ 85255-3555

RUHRUP, CLIFTON BROWN, sales executive; b. Jacksonville, Fla., Nov. 9, 1916; s. Ernest Alfred and Elizabeth L. (Garrett) R. Student, U. Okla., 1934-35, Oklahoma City U., 1946-48; cert. sales mgmt., U. Okla., 1962. From intern trainee to asst. sales mgr. Dolese Bros. Co., Oklahoma City, 1950-54, gen. sales mgr. aggregate div., 1955-61, gen. sales mgr. aggregate and prestress div., 1966—, asst. sec., 1971—. Chmn. bd. dirs. Cen. YMCA, Oklahoma City, 1973-78, named Outstanding Vol. of Yr., 1978, fellow mem., 1978—; bd. dirs. Better Bus. Bur., 1992—; mem. assoc. bd. Associated Bd. Contractors Okla. S/Sgt. USAAF, 1943-46, PTO. Mem. Oklahoma City C. of C., Toastmasters (pres. 1968), Rotary (editor newspaper 1972-76, contbg. editor 1988—, Paul Harris fellow), Phi Eta Sigma. Republican. Mem. First Christian Ch. Avocations: photography, fishing, travel, real estate. Office: Dolese Bros Co 20 NW 13th St Oklahoma City OK 73103-4806 *Success in life does not come because you wish for it; success in life comes because you want and work for it.*

RUI, HALLGEIR, cancer researcher; b. Rissa, Norway, Dec. 13, 1961; came to U.S., 1989; s. Tarald Martin and Gerd (Neverlien) R. MD, U. Oslo (Norway), 1987, PhD in Pathology, 1988. Lic. med. doctor, Norway. Clin. resident Notodden (Norway) Hosp., 1987-89; postdoctoral fellow U. South Fla., Tampa, 1989-91; scientist Nat. Cancer Inst., Frederick, Md., 1991-95; asst. prof. USUHS Sch. Medicine, Bethesda, Md., 1995—. Contbr. over 70 articles to profl. jours. Norwegian Sci. Coun. fellow, 1983-87, Fulbright fellow, 1989, Fogarty fellow, 1989-95. Mem. AAAS, N.Y. Acad. Sci., Endocrine Soc., Norwegian Med. Assn. Achievements include cloning of rat Jak2 tyrosine kinase and demonstrating that prolactin activates Jak-Stat and Shc-Ras signaling pathways. Avocations: skiing, running, hiking.

RUIBAL, CHARLES ADRIAN, chemical company executive; b. Habana, Cuba, Mar. 5, 1947; came to U.S., 1961; s. Evelino Arsenio and Maria Gloria (de Puzo) R.; m. Geraldine Catherine McNabb, Aug. 31, 1968; children: Gloria Lynne, Michael Charles. BSChemE, Villanova U., 1968. With Am. Cyanamid Co., 1968-93; process engr. indsl. chems. div. Am. Cyanamid Co., Linden, N.J., 1968-69; tech. sales rep. paper chems. dept. Am. Cyanamid Co., Pittsfield, Mass., 1969-72, Montgomery, Ala., 1972-74; asst. to mktg. mgr. paper chems. dept. Am. Cyanamid Co., Wayne, N.J., 1974-75; dist. sales mgr. paper chems. dept. Am. Cyanamid Co., Ft. Washington, Pa., 1975-77; nat. sales mgr. paper chems. dept. Am. Cyanamid Co., Wayne, N.J., 1977-78, mktg. mgr. paper chems. dept., 1978-80, mktg. mgr. water treating chems. dept., 1980-81, dept. mgr. specialty polymers dept., 1981-83, dept. mgr. crop protection chems. dept., 1983-84, v.p. agrl. div., 1984, pres. indsl. products div., 1984-89, pres. indsl. and performance products div., 1990-92; group v.p. Cytec Industries (bus. unit of Am. Cyanamid Co.), West Paterson, N.J., 1992-93; exec. v.p. Cytec Industries Inc., West Paterson, 1994—; bd. dirs. Am. Indsl. Health Coun., 1987-92, vice chmn. bd. dirs., 1990, chmn., 1991; vice-chmn., bd. dirs. CYRO Industries, 1995. Chmn. bd. dirs. United Way Passaic Valley; bd. dirs. N.C. State U. Pulp and Paper Found. Mem. Soc. Chem. Industry. Republican. Roman Catholic. Office: Cytec Industries Inc 5 Garret Mountain Plz West Paterson NJ 07424-3360

RUINA, JACK PHILIP, electrical engineer, educator; b. Rypin, Poland, Aug. 19, 1923; came to U.S., 1927; naturalized, 1932; s. Michael and Nechuma (Warshaw) R.; m. Edith Elster, Oct. 26, 1947; children: Ellen, Andrew, Rachel. BEE, CCNY, 1944; MEE, Poly. Inst. Bklyn., 1949, DEE, 1951. Rsch. fellow Microwave Rsch. Inst., Poly. Inst. Bklyn., 1948-50; from instr. to assoc. prof. elec. engring. Brown U., 1950-54; rsch. assoc. prof. coordinated sci. lab. U. Ill., 1954-59, rsch. prof., prof. elec. engring., 1959-63; prof. elec. engring. MIT, 1963—, v.p. for spl. labs., 1966-70; U.S. observer Antarctica, 1964; on leave to U.S. Govt., 1959-63, pres. Inst. Def. Analysis, 1964-66; dep. for rsch. to asst. sec. air force, 1959-60; asst. dir. for def. rsch. and engring. Office Sec. Def., 1960-61; dir. Advanced Rsch. Projects Agy., Dept. Def., 1961-63; mem. panel Presdl. Sci. Adv. Commn., 1963-72, sci. adv. bd. USAF, 1964-67, adv. bd. and panels for Dept. Def., HEW, Dept. Transp., ACDA, Office Tech. Assessment, NSF, NSC, 1963—; mem. gen. adv. com. ACDA, 1969-74; sr. cons. Office Sci. and Tech. Policy, The White House, 1977-80; chmn. com. on environ. decision making NAS, 1974-77; bd. dirs. Mitre Corp. Recipient Fleming award, 1962, Disting. Alumnus award Poly. Inst. Bklyn., 1970, One Hundred and Twenty Fifth Anniversary medal CCNY, 1973. Fellow IEEE, AAAS, Am. Acad. Arts and Scis.; mem. Inst. Strategic Studies, Coun. on Fgn. Rels., Internat. Sci. Radio Union, Sigma Xi. Home: 130 Mount Auburn St Apt 409 Cambridge MA 02138-5779 Office: MIT Dept Elec Engring 292 Main St Cambridge MA 02142-1014

RUIZ, PEDRO, psychiatrist; b. Cuba, Dec. 31, 1936. MD, U. Paris VI, 1964. Intern Jackson Meml. Hosp., Miami, Fla., 1965, resident in psychiatry, 1966-68; prof. psychiatry U. Tex./Houston Health Sci. Ctr. Office: U Tex/Houston Health Sci Ct Mental Sci Inst 1300 Moursund Houston TX 77030

RUIZ, RAMON EDUARDO, history educator; b. La Jolla, Calif., Sept. 9, 1921; s. Ramon and Dolores (Urueta) R.; m. Natalia Marrujo, Oct. 14, 1944; children—Olivia, Maura. BA, San Diego State Coll., 1947; MA, Claremont Grad. Sch., 1948; PhD, U. Calif., Berkeley, 1954. Asst. prof. U. Oreg., Eugene, 1955-57, So. Meth. U., Dallas, 1957-58; prof. Smith Coll., Northampton, Mass., 1958-69; prof. Lat. Am. history U. Calif. at San Diego, 1969-91; prof. emeritus, 1991—; chmn. dept. history U. Calif. at San Diego, 1971-76, div. humanities, 1972-74; mem. project grant com. NEH, 1972-73, 75-77, dir. public programs div., 1979-80; vis. prof. Facultad de Economia, Univ. de Nuevo Leon, Mexico, 1965-66, Coll. de Sonora, Mexico, summer 1983, Pomona Coll., 1983-84, Coll. de Michoacan, Mexico, summer 1986, 87, Univ. Nacional Autonoma de Mexico, fall 1992; scholar-in-residence Colegio de la Frontero Norte, Mexico, 1994-96; mem. project grant com. Ford Found. Author: Cuba: The Making of A Revolution, 1968 (One of Best History Books, Book World Washington Post 1968), Mexico: The Challenge of Poverty and Illiteracy, 1963, An American in Maximillians's Mexico, 1865-1866, 1959; (with James D. Atwater) Out From Under; Benito Juarez and Mexico's Struggle for Independence, 1969; (with John Tebbel) South by Southwest: The Mexican-American and His Heritage, 1969, Interpreting Latin American History, 1970, Labor and the Ambivalent Revolutionaries: Mexico, 1911-23, 1975, The Mexican War: Was it Manifest Destiny?, 1963, The Great Rebellion: Mexico, 1905-1924, 1980 (Hubert C. Herring prize), The People of Sonora and Yanqui Capitalists, 1988, Triumphs and Tragedy: A History of the Mexican People, 1992 (named One of Five Best History Books 1991-92, L.A. Times, Gold Medal award Commonwealth Club San Francisco 1993); (with Olivia Teresa Ruiz) Reflexiones Sobre la Identidad de los Pueblos, 1996. Served to lt. USAAF, 1943-46. William Harrison Mills traveling fellow in internat. relations, 1950; John Hay Whitney Found. fellow, 1950; Fulbright fellow Mex., 1965-66; fellow Ctr. for Advanced Study in Behavioral Scis., 1984-85, Ena H. Thompson lectureship, Pomona Coll., 1995;recipient Am. Philos. Soc. grant in aid, 1959. Mem. Am. Hist. Assn., Conf. Latin Am. History, Chicano-Latino Faculty Assn. U. Calif. (pres. 1989-91), Phi Beta Kappa, Sigma Delta Pi. Home: PO Box 1775 Rancho Santa Fe CA 92067-1775 Office: Univ Calif San Diego Dept History La Jolla CA 92093

RUIZ, VANESSA, judge; b. San Jaun, P.R., Mar. 22, 1950; D. Fernando and Irma (Bosch) Ruiz-Suria; m. Eduardo Elejalde, Feb. 11, 1972 (div. Jan. 1982); children: Natalia, Alexia; m. David E. Birenbaum, Oct. 22, 1983; stepchildren: Tracy, Matthew. BA, Wellesley Coll., 1972; JD, Georgetown U., 1975. Bar: D.C. 1972, U.S. Supreme Ct. 1981. Assoc. Fried, Frank, Harris, Shrives & Kampelman, Washington, 1975-83; sr. mgr., counsel Sears World Trade Inc., Washington, 1983-94; assoc. judge D.C. Ct. of Appeals, 1994—; speaker in field. Mem. ABA, Inter-Am. Bar Assn. Office: 500 Indiana Ave NW Washington DC 20001 also: Pepper Hamilton & Scheetz 1300 19th St NW Washington DC 20036-1609*

RUIZ, VICKI LYNN, history educator; b. Atlanta, May 21, 1955; d. Robert Paul and Erminia Pablita (Ruiz) Mercer; m. Jerry Joseph Ruiz, Sept. 1, 1979 (div. Jan. 1990); children: Miguel, Daniel; m. Victor Becerra, Aug. 14, 1992. AS in Social Studies, Gulf Coast Community Coll., 1975; BA in Social Sci., Fla. State, 1977; MA in History, Stanford U., 1978, PhD in History, 1982. Asst. prof. U. Tex., El Paso, 1982-85; asst. prof. U. Calif., Davis, 1985-87, assoc. prof., 1987-92; Andrew W. Mellon prof. Claremont (Calif.) Grad. Sch., 1992-95, chmn. history dept., 1993-95; prof. women's studies and history Ariz. State U., Tempe, 1995—; dir. Inst. of Oral History, U. Tex., El Paso, 1983-85, minority undergrad. rsch. program U. Calif., Davis, 1988-92. Author: Cannery Women, Cannery Lives, 1987; co-editor: Women on U.S.-Mexican Border, 1987, Western Women, 1988, Unequal Sisters, 1990, 2d edit., 1994. Mem. Calif. Coun. for Humanities, 1990-94, vice chmn., 1991-93. Fellow Univ. Calif. Davis Humanities Inst., 1990-91, Am. Coun. of Learned Socs., 1986, Danforth Found., 1977. Mem. Orgn. Am. Historians (chmn. com. on status of minority history 1989-91, nominating com. 1987-88, exec. bd. 1995—), Immigration History Soc. (exec. bd. 1989-91), Am. Studies Assn. (nominating bd. 1992-94), Western History (nominating bd. 1993-95). Democrat. Roman Catholic. Avocations: walking, needlework. Office: Ariz State U Dept Women's Studies Tempe AZ 85287

RUIZ-PETRICH, ELENA, biophysicist; b. Mendoza, Argentina, Nov. 19, 1933; widowed. MD, U. Cuyo, 1959, DSc (hon.), 1976. Sr. instr. physiololy, Faculty Medicine U. Cuyo, 1959-63; gellow Argentina Nat. Coun. Sci. and Technol. Investment, 1960-62; fellow heart electrophysiology U. So. Calif., 1963-65; fellow Can. Heart Found., 1969-70, rsch. scholar, 1971-75; from asst. prof. to assoc. prof. U. Sherbrooke, Chemin Stokes, Que., Can., 1968-77, chmn. dept. biophysics, 1978-84, prof. biophysics, 1977—, chmn. dept. physiol. biophysics, 1987—. Grantee Argentina Nat. Coun. Sci. and Technology, 1966-67, Med. Rsch. Coun. Ottawa, 1967-71, Que Heart Found., 1969-73. Mem. Internat. Soc. Heart Rsch., Can. Physiol. Soc., Am. Physiol. Soc. Office: Electrophysiology Rsch Group, Sherbrooke U / Faculte de med, Sherbrooke, PQ Canada J1H 5N4 Office: Faculty Med, Dept Physiol & Biophys, Univ Sherbrooke, Quebec, Chemin Stokes, Canada*

RUIZ SACRISTÁN, CARLOS, Mexican government official; b. Mexico City, Oct. 27, 1949. BA in Bus. Adminstrn., Anahuac U.; MA in Fin., Northwestern U., Chgo. From chief of currency exch. to mgr. internat. ops. Bank of Mex., 1974-86; dir. Commn. on Exch. Rate Risk Ins., 1986-88; gen. dir. pub. credit Secretarian of Fin. and Pub. Credit, 1988-92, dep. sec. expenditures, 1993; dir. Gen. Mex. Petroleum "Pemex", 1994; sec. comm. and transport Govt. Mex., 1994—. Office: Xola esq Au Universidad, Cuerpu c 1er piso, 03028 Mexico City Mexico

RUKEYSER, LOUIS RICHARD, economic commentator; b. N.Y.C., Jan. 30, 1933; s. Merryle Stanley and Berenice Helene (Simon) R.; m. Alexandra Gill, Mar. 3, 1962; children: Beverley Jane, Susan Athena, Stacy Alexandra. AB, Princeton U., 1954; LittD (hon.), N.H. Coll., 1975; LLD (hon.), Moravian Coll., 1978, Mercy Coll., 1984, Am. U., 1991; DBA (hon.), Southeastern Mass. U., 1979; LHD (hon.), Loyola Coll., 1982, Johns Hopkins U., 1986, Western Md. Coll., 1992. Reporter Balt. Sun newspapers, 1954-65; chief polit. corr. Evening Sun, 1957-59; chief London bur. The Sun, 1959-63, chief Asian corr., 1963-65; sr. corr., commentator ABC News, 1965-73, Paris corr., 1965-66, chief London bur., 1966-68, econ. editor, commentator, 1968-73; host Wall St. Week With Louis Rukeyser PBS-TV, 1970—; nationally syndicated econ. columnist McNaught Syndicate, 1976-86, Tribune Media Services, 1986-93; frequent lectr. Author: How to Make Money in Wall Street, 1974, 2d edit., 1976 (Literary Guild selection 1974, 76), What's Ahead for the Economy: The Challenge and the Chance, 1983, 2d edit., 1985 (Literary Guild selection 1984), Louis Rukeyser's Business Almanac, 1988, 2d edit., 1991; editor-in-chief monthly newsletters, Louis Rukeyser's Wall Street, 1992—, Louis Rukeyser's Mutual Funds, 1994—. With U.S. Army, 1954-56. Recipient Overseas Press Club award, 1963, Overseas Press Club citation, 1964, G.M. Loeb award U. Conn., 1972, Janus award for excellence in fin. news programming, 1975, George Washington Honor medal Freedoms Found., 1972, 78, N.Y. Fin. Writers Assn. award, 1980, Free Enterprise Man of the Yr. award Tex. A&M U. Ctr. for Edn. and Research in Free Enterprise, 1987, Women's Econ. Round Table award, 1990. Office: 586 Round Hill Rd Greenwich CT 06831-2724

RUKEYSER, M. S., JR., television consultant, writer; b. N.Y.C., Apr. 15, 1931; s. Merryle Stanley and Berenice (Simon) R.; m. Phyllis L. Kasha, May 16, 1975; children: Jill Victoria, Patricia Bern. Student, U. Va., 1948-52. Reporter Albany (N.Y.) Times-Union, 1949, Internat. News Service, N.Y.C., 1951; TV publicist Young & Rubicam, Inc., N.Y.C., 1952-57; with NBC, 1958-80, 81-88; dir. news info. NBC, Washington, 1962; v.p. press and publicity NBC, N.Y.C., 1963-72; v.p. corp. info. NBC, 1972-74, v.p. pub. info., 1974-77, exec. v.p. pub. info., 1977-80, 81-84, exec. v.p. corp. communications, 1984-88; v.p. comm. Newsweek Inc., 1980-81; sr. v.p. GTG Entertainment, N.Y.C., 1988-90; pres. Rukeyser Communications, N.Y.C., 1990—; sr. fellow Freedom Forum Media Ctr., 1991-92. Author: (with Grant Tinker) Tinker in Television: From General Sarnoff to General Electric, 1994. Mem. adv. coun. Ctr. for Media in the Pub. Interest. Served with U.S. Army, 1953-54. Home and Office: 2434 NW 59th St Apt 1404 Boca Raton FL 33496-2830 also: RR 1 Box 1036 Waymart PA 18472-9712

RUKEYSER, ROBERT JAMES, manufacturing executive; b. New Rochelle, N.Y., June 26, 1942; s. Merryle Stanley and Berenice Helene (Simon) R.; m. Leah A. Spiro, July 26, 1964; children: David Bern, Peter Lloyd. BA, Cornell U., 1964; MBA with distinction, N.Y.U., 1969. Mcpl. services analyst Dun & Bradstreet, N.Y.C., 1964-65; bond analyst Standard & Poors, N.Y.C., 1965-66; mktg. rep. data processing div. IBM, N.Y.C., 1967-72, regional mktg. staff, 1973-74, mktg. mgr., 1974-76; corp. mgr. internal communications IBM, Armonk, N.Y., 1976-79; mgr. communication ops. IBM, Franklin Lakes, N.J., 1979-81; pub. affairs dir., asst. to chmn. Am. Brands, Inc., N.Y.C., 1981-83, v.p. pub. affairs, asst. to chmn., 1983-85; v.p. office products Am. Brands, Inc., Old Greenwich, Conn., 1986-87, v.p. ops., 1987-89, sr. v.p. corp. affairs, 1990—; bd. dirs. Am. Brands Internat. Co., JBB Worldwide, Inc., Acushnet Co., MasterBrand Industries, Acco World Corp. Mem. communications com. Boy Scouts Am., 1982-86; personal solicitation chair Cornell U., 1985-87; bd. dirs., mem. fin. and devel. com. The Hole in the Wall Gang Camp.; bd. dirs. Stamford Ctr. for Arts. Mem. Bus. Products Industry Assn. Office: Am Brands Inc 1700 E Putnam Ave Old Greenwich CT 06870-1321

RUKEYSER, WILLIAM SIMON, journalist, business executive; b. N.Y.C., June 8, 1939; s. Merryle Stanley and Berenice (Simon) R.; m. Elisabeth Mary Garnett, Nov. 21, 1963; children: Lisa Rukeyser Burn, James William. A.B., Princeton U., 1961; student, Christ's Coll., Cambridge (Eng.) U., 1962-63. Copyreader Wall St. Jour., 1961-62; staff reporter Wall St. Jour., Europe, 1963-67; assoc. editor Fortune mag., 1967-71, mem. bd. editors, 1971-72; mng. editor Money mag., N.Y.C., 1972-80, Fortune mag., 1980-86; dir. internat. bus. devel. Time Inc., 1986-88; editor in chief, exec. v.p. Whittle Communications, Knoxville, Tenn., 1988-91; chmn., chief exec. officer Whittle Books, Knoxville, 1991-94; pres. William Rukeyser, Inc., Knoxville, 1994—; contbg. editor CNNFn, 1995—; commentator Good Morning America, ABC-TV, 1978-85, CBS Radio Stas. News Svc., 1979-86; bd. dirs. Computational Systems, Inc., Tri-Media Comm., Inc. Mem. jud. com. Union County (N.J.) Med. Soc., 1977-80; co-chair capital campaign Nat. Mental Health Assn., 1984-85; dir., mem. exec. com. Knoxville Mus. Art, Knoxville Symphony Orch.; mem. liaison com. U. Tenn. Med. Ctr.; mem. adv. coun. U. Tenn. Coll. Bus. Adminstrn.; dir. Bijou Theatre Ctr., Knoxville. Home: 1509 Rudder Ln Knoxville TN 37919-8437

RULAND, RICHARD EUGENE, English and American literature educator, critic, literary historian; b. Detroit, May 1, 1932; s. Eugene John and Irene (Janette) R.; m. Mary Ann Monaghan; children: Joseph, Michael, Paul, Susan; m. Birgit Noll. BA, Assumption Coll. U. Western Ont., Can., 1953; MA, U. Detroit, 1955; PhD, U. Mich., 1960. Instr., then asst. prof. English and Am. studies Yale U., New Haven, 1960-67, Morse rsch. fellow, 1966-67; prof. English and Am. lit. Washington U., St. Louis, 1967—, chmn. dept. English, 1969-74; chmn. comparative lit. program, 1993-94; vis. Bruern prof. Am. lit. Leeds (Eng.) U., 1964-65; vis. Fulbright prof. U. Groningen, The Netherlands, 1975, Sch. of English and Am. Studies U. East Anglia, Eng., 1978-79; vis. disting. prof. Am. lit. Coll. of William and Mary, 1980-81. Author: The Rediscovery of American Literature: Premises of Critical Taste, 1900-1940, 1967, America in Modern European Literature: From Image to Metaphor, 1976, (with Malcolm Bradbury) From Puritanism to Postmodernism: A History of American Literature, 1991 (paperback 1992), translation into Czech and Hungarian, 1996; editor: Walden: A Collection of Critical Essays, 1967, The Native Muse: Theories of American Literature, Vol. I, 1972, 76, A Storied Land: Theories of American Literature, Vol. II, 1976; contbr. articles to profl. jours. Guggenheim Rsch. fellow, 1982-83. Mem. Assn. Depts. English (pres. 1974). Avocation: jazz musician. Office: Washington U Dept English Saint Louis MO 63130

RULAU, RUSSELL, numismatic consultant; b. Chgo., Sept. 21, 1926; s. Alphonse and Ruth (Thorsen) R.; student U. Wis., 1946-48; m. Hazel Darlene Grizzell, Feb. 1, 1968; children by previous marriage: Lance Eric, Carla Rae, Russell A.W., Marsha June, Scott Quentin, Roberta Ann, Kyle Christopher, Yvonne Marie; 1 step-dau., Sharon Maria Kenowski. With U.S. Army, 1944-1950, master sgt. USAF, 1950-62; resigned active duty, 1962; asst. editor Coin World newspaper, Sidney, Ohio, 1962-74, editor World Coins mag., 1964-74, Numis. Scrapbook mag., 1968-74; editorial coordinator How to Order Fgn. Coins guidebook, 1966-74; editor in chief World Coin News newspaper, 1974-84, Bank Note Reporter, 1983-84; fgn. editor Numis. News newspaper, 1974-77; cons. editor Standard Catalog of World Paper Money, 1975-83; contbg. editor Standard Catalog of World Coins, 1974-81; pres. House of Rulau, 1984—, Alpha Enterprises Inc., 1989—; v.p. Keogh-Rulau Galleries, Dallas, 1984-85, Pobjoy Mint Ltd., Iola, Wis., 1985-96; U.S. agent Christie's Pty. Ltd, 1992-95. Recipient Clemy Literary award 1993, Smedley Lifetime Achievement award, 1994, Numiasmatic Ambassador award, 1995. Mem. U.S. Assay Commn., 1973. Sec., Numismatic Terms Standardization Com., 1966-74; vice-chmn. Waupaca County Republican party, 1977-79, 1988-89, chmn., 1979-82; chmn. county chairmen, 3d vice chmn. Wis. Rep. Party, 1981-83; del. Rep. Nat. Conv., 1980; exec. com. 6th Wis. Dist. Rep. Com., 1984-87 . Fellow Royal Numis. Soc., Am. Numis. Soc. (assoc.); mem. Token and Medal Soc. (editor 1962-63), Am. Numis. Assn. (Merit medal 1995), Canadian, S. African numis. assns., Mont. Hist. Soc., Am. Vecturist Assn., Numis. Lit. Guild (dir. 1974-78, editor 1984-86), VFW (post commdr. 1985-89, 96—), Am. Legion. Lutheran. Author: (with George Fuld) Spiel Marken, 1962-65, American Game Counters, 1972; World Mint Marks, 1966; Modern World Mint Marks, 1970; (with J. U. Rixen and Frovin Sieg) Seddelkatalog Slesvig Plebiscit Zone I og II, 1970; Numismatics of Old Alabama, 1971-73; Hard Times Tokens, 1980; Early American Tokens, 1981; U.S. Merchant Tokens 1845-1860, 1982; U.S. Trade Tokens 1866-1889, 1983, Tokens of the Gay Nineties, 1987, Discovering America: The Coin Collecting Connection, 1989, Latin American Tokens, 1992; (with George Fuld) Medallic Portraits of Washington, 1985, Standard Catalog of U.S. Tokens 1700-1900, 1994; contbr. numis. articles to profl. jours. Home: N7747 County J Iola WI 54945 Office: Pobjoy Mint USA Ltd PO Box 153 Iola WI 54945-0153

RULE, CHARLES FREDERICK (RICK RULE), lawyer; b. Nashville, Apr. 28, 1955; s. Frederick Charles and Mary Elizabeth (Malone) R.; m. Ellen Friedland, May 13, 1976. BA, Vanderbilt U., 1978; JD, U. Chgo., 1981. Bar: U.S. Ct. Appeals. (D.C. cir.) 1983. Law clk. U.S. Ct. Appeals (fed. cir.), Washington, 1981-82; spl. asst. to asst. atty. gen. Antitrust div. Dept. Justice, Washington, 1982-83, dep. asst. atty. gen. policy planning, 1984-85, acting asst. atty. gen., then dep. asst. atty. gen. regulatory affairs, 1985-86, asst. atty. gen., 1986-89; ptnr. Covington & Burling, Washington, 1989—; legal, econ. analyst Lexecon, Inc., Chgo., 1979-80. Mem. Bar of D.C. Ct. Appeals, Phi Beta Kappa, Phi Eta Sigma. Republican. Presbyterian. Office: Covington & Burling PO Box 7566 Rm 915B 1200 Pennsylvania Ave NW Washington DC 20004-2411

RULE, DANIEL RHODES, opera company executive; b. L.A., Aug. 25, 1940; s. Rhodes Elmore and Maud Justice (Edwards) R. BA, Occidental Coll., 1962. Asst. music adminstr. N.Y.C. Opera, 1965-70, assoc. mng. dir., 1970-79, mng. dir., 1980-83; gen. mgr. Central City Opera, Denver, 1984—; cons. Ohio State Arts Coun., Columbus, 1984, 86. Bd. dirs. Colo. Children's Chorale, Denver, Colo. Lawyers for Arts. Ford Found. fellow, N.Y., 1966-68. Mem. Am. Guild Mus. Artists (employer chmn. pension and health fund), Denver Athletic Club. Republican. Mem. Christian Ch. (Disciples of Christ). Avocations: travel, violin. Office: Central City Opera House Assn 621 17th St Ste 1601 Denver CO 80293-1601

RULE, JOHN CORWIN, history educator; b. Evanston, Ill., Mar. 2, 1929; s. Corwin V. and Elaine (Simons) R. A.B., Stanford U., 1951, M.A., 1952; M.A., Harvard U., 1955, Ph.D., 1958. Tutor and fellow Harvard U., Cambridge, Mass., 1956-58; instr. Northeastern U., Boston, 1955-56; from instr. to prof. history Ohio State U., Columbus, 1958—; vis. asst. prof. Western Res. U., Cleve., 1961; vis. prof. Johns Hopkins U., Balt., 1968. Editor and contbg. author: Louis XIV and the Craft of Kingship, 1970; editor: Louis XIV, 1974, Letters from the Hague and Utrecht, 1711-1712, 1979, The Reign of Louis XIV, 1990. Folger Shakespeare Library fellow, 1968,, 1970; Huntington Library fellow, 1978; Am. Council Learned Socs. fellow, 1981. Fellow Royal Hist. Soc. (London); mem. Soc. for French Hist. Studies (sec. 1963-70, assoc. editor jour. 1975-86, co-pres. 1989-91), Signet Soc., Crichton Club. Democrat. Home: 118 E Beck St Columbus OH 43206-1110 Office: Dept History Ohio State U 230 W 17th Ave Columbus OH 43210-1311

RULIS, RAYMOND JOSEPH, manufacturing company executive, consultant; b. New Britain, Conn., June 2, 1924; s. James Alexander and Eva (Ragauskas) R.; m. Thelma Pelchat, June 16, 1949; children: Elaine, Jeffery, Catherine, Elizabeth, Amy, Daniel, Jean. BSME, U. Conn., 1949; postgrad., U. Conn., Ohio State U., Northeastern U., 1949-58; student, Fed. Exec. Inst., Charlottesville, Va., 1976. Devel. engr. Hamilton Standard, U.T.C., Windsorlocks, Conn., 1951-55; mgr. fuel controls Lycoming Textron, Stratford, Conn., 1955-59; mgr. controls and accessories GE, Lynn, Mass., 1959-62; successively program mgr. spacecraft, chief spacecraft engr., chief launch vehicle engr., chief engring design, program mgr. QCSEE program NASA Lewis Rsch. Ctr., Cleve., 1962-81; v.p. rsch. and. devel. Textron Turbocomponents Group, Walled Lake, Mich., 1981-92; cons., 1992—; cons. Joint FAA/NASA Civil Aero Rsch. Document Study, 1972, Cruise Missile PRogram, 1977-78, C-17 Aircraft Source Selection Bd., 1978, Tri-Svcs. Propulsion Group, 1976-78; chmn. Conf. on Short Haul Systems, NASA, 1976; mem. exec. coun. Aerospace Industries Tech. Coun., 1988-89. Contbr. articles to profl. jours.; patentee in field. Chmn. Boy Scouts Am. Fund Drives, Cleve., 1976-78; mem. Coun. on World Affairs, Cleve., 1976-81. Mem. Am. Helicopter Soc. (chmn. tech. session 1970), AIAA (chmn. tech. session 1965), Detroit Engring Soc., KC. Roman Catholic. Avocation: golf. Office: RJR Cons 9 Outpost Ln Hilton Head Island SC 29928

RULON, RICHARD R., lawyer; b. Phila., 1943. BA, Brown U., 1964; JD, U. Pa., 1967. Bar: Pa. 1967. Ptnr. Dechert Price & Rhoads, Phila. Office: Dechert Price & Rhoads 4000 Bell Atlantic Tower 1717 Arch St Philadelphia PA 19103-2713*

RUMBAUGH, CHARLES EARL, lawyer, corporate executive; b. San Bernardino, Calif., Mar. 11, 1943; s. Max Elden and Gertrude Maude (Gulker) R.; m. Christina Carol Pinder, Mar. 2, 1968; children: Eckwood, Cynthia, Aaron, Heather. BS, UCLA, 1966; JD, Calif. Western Sch. Law, 1971; cert. in Advanced Mgmt., U. So. Calif., 1993. Bar: Calif. 1972, U.S. Dist. Ct. (cen. dist.) Calif. 1972, U.S. Ct. Appeals (9th cir.) 1972. Engr. Westinghouse Electric Corp., Balt., 1966-68; legal counsel Calif. Dept. of Corps., L.A., 1971-77; legal counsel Hughes Aircraft Co., L.A., 1977-84, asst. to corp. dir. contracts, 1984-89, asst. to corp. v.p. contracts, 1989-95; corp. dir. contracts/pricing Lear Astronics Corp., 1995—; arbitrator comml., franchise, real estate and constrn. panels Am. Arbitration Assn., L.A., 1989—; mem. arbitration and mediation panels Franchise Arbitration and Mediation, Inc., 1994—, Arbitration and Mediation Internat., 1994—, Ctr. for Conflict Resolution, L.A., 1990—, ADR Group Internat., Los Angeles County Superior Ct., 1993; spkr. to profl. and trade assns.; adj. prof. West Coast U. Contbr. articles to profl. jours. Counselor Boy Scouts Am., L.A., 1976—; mem. City of Palos Verdes Estates (Calif.) Citizen's Planning Com., 1986-90; judge pro tem Los Angeles County Superior Ct., L.A., 1991—. Fellow Nat. Contract Mgmt. Assn. (cert. profl. contracts mgr., nat. bd. advisors, nat. v.p. southwestern region 1993-95, nat. dir. 1992-93, pres. L.A./South Bay chpt. 1991-92, Outstanding Fellows award 1994); mem. ABA (forum on franchising, forum on constrn. industry), Nat. Security Indsl. Assn. (vice chmn. west coast legal subcom. 1994—), Fed. Bar Assn. (pres. Beverly Hills chpt. 1992-93), State Bar Calif. (franchise law com. 1992-95, Wiley W. Manual award 1992), Los Angeles County Bar Assn., South Bay Bar Assn., Soc. Profls. in Dispute Resolution, Aerospace Industries Assn. (chmn. procurement techniques com. 1987-88, 93-94), Christian Legal Soc. Avocations: camping, skiing, jogging, equestrian. Office: PO Box 2636 Rolling Hills Estates CA 90274

RUMBAUGH, MAX ELDEN, JR., professional society administrator; b. Ada, Okla., Dec. 11, 1937; s. Max E. and Gertrude (Gulker) R.; m. Joan E. Brockway; children: Maria Rumbaugh Gross, Max E. III. BS in Engring., U.S. Mil. Acad., 1960; MS in Engring. Scis., Purdue U., 1965, MBA, 1972. Instr. Purdue U., West Lafayette, Ind., 1964-65; corp. officer Midwest Applied Sci. Corp., West Lafayette, 1965-72; chief engr. advanced tech. Schwitzer div. Wallace-Murray Corp., Indpls., 1972-77, dir. research, 1977-81; mgr. engring. activities div. Soc. Automotive Engrs., Warrendale, Pa., 1981-84, v.p., asst. gen. mgr., 1984-86, exec. v.p., 1986—; pres. Performance Rev. Inst., 1991—; pres. Soc. Rsch. Adminstrs. Internat., 1973-74; chmn. Ind. sect. Soc. Automotive Engrs., 1978-79; bd. dirs., exec. com. Am. Nat. Standards Inst., N.Y.C., 1986—; bd. dirs. Intelligent Transp. Soc. of Am., 1992—. Author mag. column Focus, 1986—. Bd. dirs. Jr. Achievement Western Pa., Pitts., 1986-95, YMCA, North Hills, Pitts., 1985-94. 1st lt. U.S. Army, 1960-63,. Mem. ASME, Coun. Engring. and Sci. Soc. Execs. (bd. dirs. 1990—, sec. 1993-94, v.p. 1994-95, pres. 1995—), Rotary (bd. dirs. 1982-84, 93—, v.p. 1994-95, pres. 1995—). Avocations: skiing, photography. Home: 2274 Wood Acre Ct Pittsburgh PA 15237-1524 Office: Soc of Automotive Engrs Inc 400 Commonwealth Dr Warrendale PA 15086-7511

RUMBAUGH, MELVIN DALE, geneticist, agronomist; b. Pella, Iowa, Sept. 13, 1929; s. Herbert Robert and Lena (Schakel) R.; m. Annabelle Eis, July 5, 1953; children: Alan Lee, Rosemary Ann, David James, Steven Thomas. BS, Cen. Coll., Pella, 1951; MS, U. Nebr., 1953, PhD, 1958. Prof.

agronomy Colo. State U., Ft. Collins, 1958; prof. plant sci. S.D. State U., Brookings, 1959-77; rsch. scientist USDA-Agrl. Rsch. Svc., Logan, Utah, 1977-92; pvt. cons. Humboldt, Nebr., 1993—; participant plant germplasm collection Can., China, Bolivia, Peru, Ecuador, USSR, Morocco, Pakistan, Spain, Romania; exch. scientist People's Republic of China, 1987, 90, 91; mem. joint U.S.-Russian expdn. to inventory and collect legumes in Caucasus Mountains Nat. Park, 1995. Contbr. 250 articles to profl. jours., chpts. to books, sci. papers; inventor superior methods to genetically improve rangeland plant species; authority plant growth on saline soils. Cpl. U.S. Army, 1953-55. Fellow Am. Soc. Agronomy, Crop Sci. Soc. Am.; mem. Soc. Range Mgmt. Republican. Avocations: genealogy, history, fishing. Home: RR 3 Box 125 Humboldt NE 68376-9352

RUMBOUGH, STANLEY MADDOX, JR., industrialist; b. N.Y.C., Apr. 25, 1920; s. Stanley Maddox and Elizabeth (Colgate) R.; m. Nedenia Hutton, Mar. 23, 1946 (div. 1966); children: Stanley H., David P. (dec.), Nedenia Colgate; m. Margaretha Wagstrom, Dec. 21, 1967 (div. 1990); m. Janna Herlow, Mar. 8, 1990. A.B., Yale U., 1942; postgrad. in bus. adminstrn., NYU, 1947-51. Vice pres., dir. Willis Air Service, Teterboro, N.J., 1946-47; v.p., dir. White Metal Mfg. Co., Hoboken, N.J., 1945-61; pres. White Metal Mfg. Co., 1960-61; pres., dir. Metal Container Corp., 1950-59, Am. Totalisator, Balt., 1956-58; chmn. bd. Extrusion Devel. Corp., 1959-61; co-founder, chmn. bd. Elec. Engring. Ltd., 1960-69; chmn. bd. Wallace Clark & Co., 1962-69; co-founder, dir. Trinidad Flour Mills, 1961-72, Jamaica Flour Mills, 1963-66; dir. Telemedia Inc., 1980-89; dir. Dart Industries, 1961-80, ABT Family of Funds, 1983-95; bd. dirs. Internat. Flavors and Fragrances, CUC Internat., Inc.; spl. asst. to sec. Dept. Commerce, 1953; spl. asst. White House charge exec. bd. liaison, 1953-55. Chmn. U.S. Com. for UN, 1957-58; co-founder Citizens for Eisenhower, 1951; vice chmn. Citizens for Eisenhower-Nixon Com., 1952; trustee Young Pres. Found., 1957-70, pres., 1962-65; bd. dirs. N.Y. World's Fair Corp., 1961-70, Nat. Conf. on Citizenship, 1973—, Population Resource Ctr., 1978-92, Planned Parenthood of Palm Beach Area, 1979-95, Planned Parenthood Fedn. Am., 1981-84, Kravis Ctr. Performing Arts, Palm Beach Civic Assn.; trustee Libr. for Presdl. Papers, 1966-70, Internat. House, 1959—, Fgn. Policy Assn., 1961-70, Am. Health Found., 1972-76. Capt. USMCR, 1942-46. Decorated Air medal (8), D.F.C. (2). Mem. Chief Execs. Orgn., World Pres.'s Orgn., Def. Orientation Conf. Assn., Racquet and Tennis Club, Internat. Lawn Tennis Club, Maidstone Club, Seminole Club, Bath and Tennis Club, Beach Club, Everglades Club, Nat. Golf Links Am. Club, Zeta Psi. Republican. Home: 655 Island Dr Palm Beach FL 33480-6121 Office: 280 Sunset Ave Palm Beach FL 33480-3815

RUMER, RALPH RAYMOND, JR., civil engineer, educator; b. Ocean City, N.J., June 22, 1931; s. Ralph Raymond and Anna (Hibbard) R.; m. Shirley Louise Haynes, Nov. 30, 1953; children: Sherri, Sue, Sandra, Sarah. BS. in Civil Engring, Duke U., 1953; M.S., Rutgers U., 1959; Sc.D. (ASCE research fellow), M.I.T., 1962. Lic. prof. engr., N.Y. With Lukens Steel Co., Coatesville, Pa., 1953-54; instr. dept. civil engring. Rutgers U., New Brunswick, N.J., 1956-59; civil engr. U.S. Dept. Agr., New Brunswick, summer 1957-59; research asst. Hydrodynamics lab. M.I.T., Boston, 1961-62; asst. prof. dept. civil engring. M.I.T., 1962-63; assoc. prof. dept. civil engring. SUNY, Buffalo, 1963-69; prof. SUNY, 1969-76, 78—, acting head, 1966-67, chmn., 1967-73, 84-87; dir. SUNY (Gt. Lakes Program), 1986-90, acting provost engring. and applied scis., 1974-75; prof., chmn. dept. civil engring. U. Del., Newark, 1976-78; dir. N.Y. Ctr. Hazardous Waste Mgmt., 1987-95; tech. cons. to govt. and industry in hydraulics, water resources and environ. engring.; mem. water resources rsch. com. Nat. Acad. Sci., 1985-86; mem. water mgmt. adv. com. N.Y. State Dept. Environ. Conservation, 1988-93; chmn. sci. adv. com. EPA regions 1 & 2 Hazardous Substance Rsch. Ctr., N.J. Inst. Tech., 1989—; mem. sci. adv. com. Gulf Coast States Hazardous Substance Rsch. Ctr., Lamar U., Tex., 1991—. Contbr. research articles in field to profl. jours. Served with U.S. Army, 1954-56. Recipient Educator of Yr. award Erie-Niagara chpt. N.Y. State Soc. Profl. Engrs., 1989, Excellence award N.Y. State/United Univ. Professions, 1990; Ford fellow, 1962-63; sr. rsch. fellow Calif. Inst. Tech., 1970-71. Fellow ASCE (dir. Buffalo sect., pres. Buffalo sect. 1984-85); mem. Internat. Assn., Hydraulic Rsch., Am. Geophys. Union, Internat. Assn. Gt. Lakes Rsch., Sigma Xi, Tau Beta Pi, Chi Epsilon. Home: 821 Eggert Rd Buffalo NY 14226-4135

RUMFORD, LEWIS, III, real estate company executive; b. Balt., Dec. 21, 1947; m. Frances Rosenfeld. BA, Wesleyan U., 1972; MBA, Harvard U., 1977. Asst. v.p. The Rouse Co., Columbia, Md., 1972-75; ptnr. The JBG Cos., Washington, 1977—. Office: The JBG Cos Ste 500 1250 Connecticut Ave NW Washington DC 20036-2603

RUMLER, DIANA GALE, geriatrics nurse; b. Manchester, Tenn., Feb. 23, 1943; d. Donald Yale and Thelma Irene (Beach) Miller; m. Herschel Hinkle, Aug. 1961 (div. Jan. 1978); children: David, John, Jody Hinkle West; m. Lester Rumler, Jr. (div. June 1984). AA in Nursing, Ind. U.-Purdue U., Indpls., 1974; BS in Pub. Health-Journalism-Psychology, Ball State U., Muncie, 1983. RN; cert. ACLS, BLS. Psychiat. nurse Meth. Hosp., Indpls., 1974-78; women's infant and children's coord. Cmty. & Family Svcs. Inc., Portland, Ind., 1978-81, Ball Meml. Hosp., Muncie, Ind., 1981-84; pub. health nurse Health & Rehab. Svcs., Ft. Lauderdale, Fla., 1984; med.-surg. nurse Holy Cross Hosp., Ft. Lauderdale, 1985; pre-op/post-op nurse VA Med. Ctr., Nashville, 1986-89; nurse vascular, orthopedics, intensive care, telemetry, tchg VA Med. Ctr., Tucson, 1990—; WIC advocate hearings/radio show, Ind., 1978-81; health vol. outreach clinic St. Mary's Hosp., Tucson, 1993-94; vol. Hospice Family Care, Tucson. Contbr. articles to profl. jours. Mem. Nurses of Vet. Affairs, Am. Fedn. Govt. Employees, Ladies' Hermitage Assn. Democrat. Roman Catholic. Avocations: ceramics, crossstitch, health club activities, travel. Home: PO Box 17764 Tucson AZ 85731-7764 Office: VA Med Ctr S 6th Ave Tucson AZ 85723

RUMLER, ROBERT HOKE, agricultural consultant, retired association executive; b. Chambersburg, Pa., Apr. 4, 1915; s. Daniel Webster and Jennie (Sellers) R.; m. Frances Jeannette Montgomery, June 7, 1939 (dec. 1983); children: Craig M., Karen A. Loden; m. Hazel Miller-Karper, Aug. 23, 1986. B.S., Pa. State U., 1936. Asst. county agt. U. Mo., 1936-37; county agrl. agt. Pa. State U., 1937-45; asst. mgr., editor agrl. promotion div. E. I. duPont de Nemours & Co., Inc., Wilmington, Del., 1945-48; asst. exec. sec. Holstein-Friesian Assn. Am., 1948-53, 53-75, exec. sec., chief exec. officer, 1975-81, exec. chmn., 1981-82, chmn. emeritus, 1982—; pres. Holstein-Friesian Svcs., Inc., 1968-81; agribus. cons., 1982—; hon. mem. Holstein-Firesian de Mex. (C.A.); bd. dirs., chmn. Vt. Nat. Bank, Vt. Fin. Svcs., Inc., 1957-88; mem. U.S./USSR Joint Com. Agrl. Cooperation; past chmn. U.S. Agrl. Export Devel. Coun., FAS-USDA; mem. coordinating group Nat. Coop. Dairy Herd Improvement program USDA, 1964-80; mem. agrl. policy adv. com. USTR/USDA Multilateral Trade Negotiations, 1973-87, mem. agrl. tech. adv. com., 1987-95. Contbg. editorial writer Holstein World. Trustee Ea. States Expn., trustee emeritus, 1993—; trustee Assoc. Industries Vt.; past bd. dirs. Internat. Stockmans Ednl. Found.; chmn. adv. bd. Pa. State U., Mont Alto, 1990-94; bd. advisors Pa. State U., Harrisburg. Recipient Disting. award Nat. Dairy Herd Improvement Assn., 1974, Disting. Svc. award Nat. Agrl. Mktg. Orgn., 1977, Disting. Svc. award Holstein Assn., 1985; named Disting. Alumnus Pa. State U., 1978, Dairy Industry Man of Yr., 1979, Headliner-of-Yr. Livestock Publs. Coun., 1995; named to Internat. Livestock Hall of Fame, 1987; Robert H. Rumler scholar. Fellow Agr. Adventures; mem. Purebred Dairy Cattle Assn. (dir., exec. com.), Nat. Soc. Livestock Record Assns. (past pres., dir., Disting. Svcs. award 1981), Am. Dairy Sci. Assn. (Disting. Svc. award 1977), Agri-Bus. Found. (All-Time Gt. award 1981), Nat. Dairy Shrine (Dairy Hall of Fame 1976), N.E. Master Farmers Assn. (hon. master farmer), U.S. Animal Health Assn., Kiwanis, Masons, Elks, Alpha Zeta, Gamma Sigma Delta. Mem. United Ch. of Christ. Home: 937 Wallace Ave Chambersburg PA 17201-3884 Office: PO Box 945 Chambersburg PA 17201-0945

RUMMAN, WADI (SALIBA RUMMAN), civil engineer; b. Beit-Jala, Palestine, Sept. 7, 1926; came to U.S., 1948, naturalized, 1959; s. Saliba Y. and Miladeh (Nasrallah) R.; m. Doris E. Reed, Sept. 6, 1955; children—Mary Elaine, Linda Jean. B.S.E., U. Mich., 1949, M.S.E., 1953, Ph.D., 1959. Field engr. Finkbeiner Pettis and Strout, Toledo, 1949; structural engr. Vogt, Ivers, Seaman and Assos., Cin., 1950-51, Giffels and Vallet, Inc., Detroit, 1951-52; instr. U. Mich., 1952-59, asst. prof. civil engring., 1959-64, assoc. prof., 1964-75, prof., 1975-88, prof. emeritus, 1988—; cons. on design of reinforced concrete chimneys and other tower structures to industry and other agys. Author: Engineering, 1974, 3d edit., 1991. Fellow Am. Concrete Inst.; mem. ASCE (life), Am. Soc. Engring. Edn. (life), Internat. Assn. Bridge and Structural Engring., Sigma Xi, Chi Epsilon, Phi Kappa Phi. Home: 709 Woodhill Dr Saline MI 48176-1708 Office: U Mich Dept Civil Engring Ann Arbor MI 48109

RUMMEL, HAROLD EDWIN, real estate development executive; b. Youngstown, Ohio, Oct. 4, 1940; s. Harold Edward and Florence Louise (Hill) R.; children: Timothy B., Jonathan S., Briana. BS, U. Fla., 1963. Writer, editor various newspapers, Fla., 1958-70; polit. campaign mgr. various state campaigns, Tallahassee, Fla., 1971-79; sr. v.p. Fla. Fed. Sav. Bank, St. Petersburg, 1979-86; pres., chief exec. officer Rummel Cos., St. Petersburg, 1986—. Active in civic and polit. orgns. Democrat. Home: 1682 Oceanview Dr Tierra Verde FL 33715-2500 Office: Rummel Cos 5401 Central Ave Saint Petersburg FL 33710-8049

RUMMEL, ROBERT WILAND, aeronautical engineer, author; b. Dakota, Ill., Aug. 4, 1915; s. William Howard and Dora (Ely) R.; m. Marjorie B. Cox, Sept. 30, 1939; children—Linda Kay, Sharon Lee, Marjorie Susan, Robert Wiland, Diana Beth. Diploma aeronautical engring., Curtiss Wright Tech. Inst. Aeros., 1935. Stress analyst Hughes Aircraft Co., Burbank, Calif., 1935-36, Lockheed Aircraft Corp., Burbank, 1936; draftsman Aero Engring. Corp., Long Beach, Calif., 1936, Nat. Aircraft Co., Alhambra, Calif., 1936-37; chief engr. Rearwin A/C & Engines, Inc., Kansas City, Kans., 1937-42; chief design engr. Commonwealth A/C, Inc., Kansas City, Kans., 1942-43; v.p. engring. Trans World Airlines, Inc., Kansas City, Mo., 1943-59; v.p. planning and research Trans World Airlines, Inc., 1959-69, v.p. tech. devel., 1969-78; pres. Robert W. Rummel Assos., Inc., Mesa, Ariz., 1978-87; aerospace cons., 1987—; commnr. Presdl. Commn. Space Shuttle Challenger Accident, 1986; chmn. nat. rsch. coun. Aero Space Engring. Bd. Fellow Inst. Aero. Scis., Soc. Automotive Engrs.; mem. NAE, Masons (32 deg.), Shriners. Home and Office: PO Box 7330 Mesa AZ 85216-7330

RUMMERFIELD, BENJAMIN FRANKLIN, geophysicist; b. Denver, May 25, 1917; s. Lawrence L. and Helen A. (Roper) R.; Engr. Geology, Colo. Sch. Mines, 1940; grad. Harvard U. Advanced Mgmt. Program, 1947, Aspen Inst. Humanistic Studies, 1958, Indsl. Coll. Armed Forces, 1963; m. Mary Merchant, Feb. 16, 1979; children: Ann S., Michael J., Benjamin F., Mary Susan, Sonya, Karim. Asst. mgr. Seismograph Service Corp., Mexico City, 1947-50, Venezuela and Colombia, 1945-47; exec. v.p. U.S. and Can. ops. Century Geophys. Corp., Tulsa, 1950-60, also dir.; pres. GeoData Corp., Tulsa, 1960—, Gulf Coast GeoData, Houston, 1962—; dir. Permian Exploration, Custom Data Services; cons. Petróleos Mexicanos. Bd. dirs. YMCA, Tulsa, 1955—, pres., 1956-59. Recipient Outstanding Service award YMCA, Tulsa, 1958, 63, Disting. Achievement medal Colo. Sch. Mines, 1978, hon. mention for painting Philbrook Art Mus., 1961. Mem. Tulsa Geol. Soc., Colo. Sch. Mines Alumni Assn. (pres. 1953), Asociación Mexicana de Geólogos Petróleos, Am. Assn. Petroleum Geologists, Soc. Exploration Geophysicists (life, nat. v.p. 1958), Sigma Gamma Epsilon. Clubs: Tulsa, Harvard (Tulsa). Contbr. numerous articles to profl. jours. Home: 6787 Timberlane Rd Tulsa OK 74136-4518 Office: care GeoData Corp 211 S Cheyenne Ave Tulsa OK 74103-3009

RUMPF, JOHN LOUIS, civil engineer, consultant; b. Phila., Feb. 21, 1921; s. Harry L. and Emma S. R.; m. Grace Willis, Apr. 1, 1944 (dec.); children—Jonathan, Christopher; m. Patricia E. Burkitt, June 20, 1970. B.S.C.E., Drexel U., 1943; M.S.C.E., U. Pa., 1954; Ph.D. in Civil Engring. (NSF fellow), Lehigh U., 1960. Structural engr. Belmont Iron Works, Phila., 1946; instr. Drexel U., 1947-50, asst. prof. civil engring., 1950-54, assoc. prof., 1954-56, prof., head dept. civil engring., 1960-69; research instr. Fritz Engring. Lab., Lehigh U., 1956-60; dean Coll. Engring. and Architecture Temple U., Phila., 1969-76; v.p. acad. affairs Temple U., 1976-82, exec. v.p., 1982-84, prof. civil engring., 1984-86; cons. engr. for bldg. and bridge design and investigations, 1947—. Author: Plastic Design of Braced Multistory Steel Frames, 1968; contbg. author Structural Steel Design, 1974. Mem. Lower Moreland Twp. (Pa.) Zoning Bd., 1953-56; mem. Lower Moreland Twp. Sch. Dist. Authority, 1962-70; bd. dirs. Abington Meml. Hosp. (Pa.), 1982-88. Served to capt. C.E. U.S. Army, 1943-46. Decorated Army Commendation medal.; Named Engr. of Yr. Tech. Socs. of Delaware Valley, 1975. Fellow ASCE; mem. Am. Soc. Engring. Edn., Nat. Soc. Profl. Engrs., Research Council for Structural Connections, Am. Concrete Inst., Sigma Xi, Tau Beta Pi, Phi Kappa Phi, Chi Epsilon. Club: Engrs. of Phila. (George Washington medal 1979). Research, publs. on structural connections and members, 1956-69. Home: 1213 Red Rambler Rd Jenkintown PA 19046-2916 Office: Temple U Coll Engring Philadelphia PA 19122

RUMSEY, VICTOR HENRY, electrical engineering educator emeritus; b. Devizes, Eng., Nov. 22, 1919; s. Albert Victor and Susan Mary (Norman) R.; m. Doris Herring, Apr. 2, 1942; children: John David, Peter Alan, Catherine Anne. B.A., Cambridge U., 1941, D.Sc. in Physics, 1972; D.Eng., Tohoku U., Japan, 1962. With U.K. Sci. Civil Service, 1941-48; asst. to asso. prof. Ohio State U., 1948-54; prof. U. Ill., 1954-57, U. Calif., Berkeley, 1957-66; prof. elec. engring. and computer scis. U. Calif., San Diego, 1966-87, prof. emeritus, 1987—; dept. chmn. U. Calif., 1977-81. Author 1 book in field; contbr. articles to profl. jours. Guggenheim fellow.; recipient George Sinclair award Ohio State U., 1982. Fellow IEEE (Morris Liebman prize), Union Radio Scientifique Internationale, Internat. Astron. Union; mem. Nat. Acad. Engring. Patentee in field. Home: PO Box 400 Occidental CA 95465-0400

RUMSFELD, DONALD HENRY, former government official, corporate executive; b. Chgo., July 9, 1932; s. George Donald and Jeannette (Husted) R.; m. Joyce Pierson, Dec. 27, 1954; 3 children. A.B., Princeton U., 1954; hon. degree, De Paul U. Coll. Commerce, Ill. Coll., Lake Forest Coll., Park Coll., Tuskegee Inst., Nat. Coll. Edn., Bryant Coll., Claremont (Calif.) Grad. Sch., Ill. Wesleyan U., Rand Grad. Sch. Adminstrv. asst. U.S. Ho. of Reps., 1958-59; with A.G. Becker & Co., Chgo., 1960-62; mem. 88th-91st Congresses from 13th Ill. dist., Pres. Richard Nixon's Cabinet, 1969-73; dir. OEO, asst. to pres., 1969-70; counsellor to Pres., dir. econ. stabilization program, 1971-72; U.S. ambassador and permanent rep. to NATO, 1973-74; White House chief of staff for Pres. Gerald Ford, 1974-75; sec. Dept. Def., 1975-77; pres., chief exec. officer, then chmn. G.D. Searle & Co., Skokie, Ill., 1977-85; spl. envoy of Pres. Ronald Reagan to Mid. East, 1983-84; sr. advisor William Blair & Co., Chgo., 1985-90; chmn., chief exec. officer General Instrument Corp., Chgo., 1990-93; bd. dirs. Metricom, Kellogg Co., Tribune Co., Gilead Scis., Inc., Amylin Pharms., Inc., Sears, Roebuck & Co.; chmn. bd. trustees RAND Corp. Naval Aviator USN, 1954-57. Recipient Presdl. Medal of Freedom, George Catlett Marshall award, Woodrow Wilson award, Dwight David Eisenhower medal. Office: 400 N Michigan Ave Ste 405 Chicago IL 60611-4102

RUND, DOUGLAS ANDREW, emergency physician; b. Columbus, Ohio, July 20, 1945; s. Carl Andrew and Caroline Amelia (Row) R.; m. Sue E, Padavana, 1980; children: Carie, Emily, Ashley. BA, Yale U., 1967; MD, Stanford U., 1971. Lic. physician, Ohio; Diplomate Nat. Bd. Med. Examiners, Am. Bd. Family Practice, Am. Bd. Emergency Medicine (pres., 1995—). Intern in medicine U. Calif., San Francisco-Moffett Hosp., 1971-72; resident in gen. surgery Stanford U., 1972-74; Robert Wood Johnson Found. clin. scholar in medicine Stanford U., 1974-76; med. dir. Mid-Peninsula Health Svc., Palo Alto, Calif., 1975-76; clin. instr. dept. medicine and preventive medicine Stanford U. Med. Sch., 1975-76; assoc. prof., dir. div. emergency medicine Ohio State Coll. Medicine, 1982-87; dir. emergency medicine residency program, assoc. prof. dept. family medicine, 1976-87, prof., chmn. dept. preventive medicine, 1988-90, prof., chmn. dept. emergency medicine, 1990—, prof., interim chmn. dept. family medicine, 1994-95; attending staff Ohio State U. Hosps., 1976—; med. dir. CSCC, Emergency Med. Svcs. Dept.; pres. Internat. Rsch. Inst. Emergency Medicine; med. dir. Internat. Soc. for Emergency Med. Svcs.; sr. rsch. fellow NATO: Health and Med. Aspects of Disaster Preparedness, 1985-87; bd. dirs. ABEM, 1988—, sr. editor in tng. exam., 1989—; on profl. leave epidemiology and injury control, U. Edinburgh, Scotland, 1987. Fellow Am. Coll. Emergency Physicians (task force on substance abuse and injury control); Mem. Nat. Inst. on Alcohol Abuse and Alcoholism, IAAA, Assn. Acad. Chairs Emergency Medicine (pres. 1992-93), Soc. Acad. Emergency Medicine (chmn. internat. com. 1991—), Columbus Medical Forum (pres. 1993), Alpha Omega Alpha. Author: Triage, 1981; Essentials of Emergency Medicine, 1982, 2nd edit., 1986; Emergency Radiology, 1982; Emergency Psychiatry, 1983; Environmental Emergencies, 1985; editor: Emergency Medicine Ann., 1983, 84; Emergency Medicine Survey, Annals of Emergency Medicine; editor-in-chief Ohio State Series on Emergency Medicine, Emergency Medicine Observer, 1986-87; guest editor Annals of Emergency Medicine Symposium, 1986; mem. editorial bd. Physician, Sports Medicine, Emergency Med. Svcs.; contbr. chpt. to Family Medicine Principles and Practice, 1978, 2d edit., 1983; contbr. articles to profl. jours. Office: Ohio State U Rm 005 Upham Hall 473 W 12th Ave Columbus OH 43210-1228 also: Ohio State U B0902B Univ Hosps Clinic 456 W 10th Ave Columbus OH 43210-1240

RUNDELL, ORVIS HERMAN, JR., psychologist; b. Oklahoma City, June 16, 1940; s. Orvis Herman and Virginia Reid (George) R.; BS, U. Okla., 1962, MS, 1972, PhD, 1976; m. Jane Shannon Brians, June 25, 1966; children: Leslie Jane, Anne Reid. Lab. mgr. Okla. Center Alcohol and Drug-Related Studies, Oklahoma City, 1969-76, staff scientist, 1974—; asst. prof. psychiatry and behavioral scis. U. Okla. Health Sci. Center, 1976—; dir. clin. physiology and sleep disorders ctr. Presbyterian Hosp., Oklahoma City, 1982—; clin. dir. Diagnostic Sleep Ctr. of Dallas, 1989-93; mem. Sleep Medicine Assocs., 1994—; cons. in field; mem. instl. rev. bd. U. Okla. Health Sci. Ctr., 1989—. Bd. dirs. Hist. Preservation, Inc., Oklahoma City, 1978-90. Served with USAR, 1963-69. Grantee Nat. Inst. Drug Abuse, Nat. Inst. Alcohol Abuse and Alcoholism, Kerr Found. Fellow Am. Sleep Disorders Assn.; mem. Am. Psychol. Assn., N.Y. Acad. Scis., Psi Chi, Phi Gamma Delta. Author articles, papers in field, chpts. in books; asst. editor Alcohol Tech. Reports, 1976—; cons. editor Psychophysiology, 1974—. Home: 431 NW 20th St Oklahoma City OK 73103-1918 Office: 700 NE 13th St Oklahoma City OK 73104

RUNDGREN, TODD, musician, record producer; b. Upper Darby, Pa., June 22, 1948; 3 children. Solo artist, 1970—; mem. mus. groups Nazz, 1967-69, Utopia, 1973— ; record producer for numerous mus. groups including Badfinger, Paul Butterfield, Grand Funk, Hall & Oates, New York Dolls, The Band, Patti Smith, The Tubes, The Pursuit of Happiness, XTC; numerous recs. and compositions including Can We Still be Friends, Hello, It's Me, Up Against It, 1989; albums include Another Life, 1975, (with The Nazz) Nazz, 1968, Nazz Nazz, 1969, Nazz III, 1970, (with Utopia) Todd Rundgren's Utopia, 1974, Oops! Wrong Planet, 1987, Adventures in Utopia, 1980, Deface the Music, 1980, Swing to the Right, 1982, Utopia, 1982, Anthology, 1989; solo albums include Runt, 1970, Something/Anything, 1972, Initiation, 1975, Faithful, 1976, Hermit of the Mink Hollow, 1978, Back to the Bars, 1978, Healing, 1981, A Capella, 1985, Nearly Human, 1989, -2nd Wind, 1991, No World Order, 1993, The Best of Todd Rundgren, 1994; composer TV mus. scores Crime Story, Pee-wee's Playhouse, theatre musical score Up Against It, 1990. Office: care Bearsville Warner Bros Record 3300 Warner Blvd Burbank CA 91505-4632

RUNDIO, LOUIS MICHAEL, JR., lawyer; b. Chgo., Sept. 13, 1943; s. Louis Michael Sr. and Germaine Matilda (Pasternack) R.; m. Ann Marie Bartlett, July 10, 1971; children: Matthew, Melissa. BS in Physics, Loyola U., Chgo., 1965, JD, 1972. Bar: Ill. 1972, U.S. Dist. Ct. (no. dist.) Ill. 1972, U.S. Ct. Appeals (7th cir.) 1974, U.S. Dist. Ct. (ea. dist.) Mich. 1983. Assoc. McDermott, Will & Emery, Chgo., 1972-77, ptnr., 1978—. Served to 1st lt. U.S. Army, 1965-68, Vietnam. Mem. ABA, Chgo. Bar Assn. Home: 676 Skye Ln Barrington IL 60010-5506 Office: McDermott Will & Emery 227 W Monroe St Chicago IL 60606-5016

RUNDQUIST, HOWARD IRVING, investment banker; b. Winona, Minn., Mar. 21, 1929; s. Howard Wadsworth and Delilah Jeanette (Erickson) R.; m. Nancy Evelyn Hood, July 30, 1980; children: Sarah Louise, Beth Anne, Peter Hood, Susan Jenniffer, Rebecca Jane. AB, Gustavus Adolphus Coll., 1951; MBA, Harvard U., 1958. Mem. staff MIT Lincoln Lab., Lexington, Mass., 1954-56, 58-60; sr. v.p. Aubrey G. Lanston Co. Inc., N.Y.C., 1960-92; ret., 1992. Investment advisor bd. pensions Evang. Luth. Ch. in Am., 1992—. Lt. USNR, 1951-54. Mem. Webhanet Golf Club, Edgcomb Tennis Club (Kennebunk, Maine). Republican. Lutheran.

RUNFOLA, SHEILA KAY, nurse; b. Canton, Ohio, Feb. 8, 1944; d. Benjamin and M. Suzanne (deBord) Suarez; m. Steven Joseph Runfola, Aug. 17, 1968; children: Michael, Janine, Christine; stepchildren: Stephanie Bufalini, Darlene Teran. BS in Nursing, St. John Coll. Cleve., 1966; teaching credential jr. coll. nursing, UCLA Ext., San Diego, 1973. RN, Calif.; cert. occupational health nurse, cert. pub. health nurse. Staff nurse emergency rm. Leland Meml. Hosp., Riverdale, Md., 1966-67; staff nurse/team leader med./surg. Mercy Hosp., San Diego, 1967-68; staff nurse, charge nurse emergency dept., dept. radiology U. Calif.-San Diego Med.Ctr., 1968-76; staff devel./asst. dir. nurses TLC Nursing Home, El Cajon, Calif., 1978-80; staff nurse/charge nurse emergency dept. Kaiser Permanente Hosp., San Diego, 1980-89; staff nurse emergency dept. Kaiser Permanente Hosp., Sacramento, Calif., 1989-90; house supr. Kaiser Permanente Hosp., Sacramento, 1992-94, case mgr. occupational medicine, 1995—; health svcs. nurse U.S. Automobile Assn., Sacramento, 1990-95. Contbr. articles to profl. jours. Leader Girls Scouts Am., San Diego and Sacramento, 1982-91, treas., local svc. team, 1986-89, 90; parent rep. Elk Grove (Calif.) Sch. Bd. for Elk Grove H.s., 1994, co-chair Sober Grad. Night, 1993-95. Mem. Sacramento Valley Occupational Health Nurses (v.p. 1992-95), Newcomers Club. Democrat. Roman Catholic. Avocations: crafts (crewel), piano, reading, cooking, boating. Office: Kaiser Permanente Dept Occupl Med 6600 Bruceville Rd Sacramento CA 95823

RUNG, RICHARD ALLEN, lawyer, retired air force officer, retired educator; b. Rome, N.Y., Dec. 16, 1929; s. George Stuart and Ruth Marie (Henderberg) R.; m. Yolande Moalli, June 15, 1957; children: Michael, Bruce, Colette. B.A. summa cum laude, St. Michael's Coll., 1957; J.D., Syracuse U., 1960. Bar: N.Y. 1961. Law partner Lawler & Rung, DeWitt, N.Y., 1960-61; law assoc. J. F. Ferlo Law Office, Rome, N.Y., 1961-63; commd. 2d lt. USAF, 1952, advanced through grades to col., 1979; USAF fighter pilot, 1952-55; USAF fighter pilot and flight comdr. La., Spain, Vietnam, N.Y., 1963-74; USAF flight safety evaluator and cons. Norton AFB, Calif., 1974-79; prof. aerospace studies, Air Force ROTC detachment comdr. U. Ill., Champaign-Urbana, 1979-82; commandant AFJROTC Pompano Beach High Sch., (Fla.), 1982-85, Northeast High Sch., (Fla.), 1985-92. Decorated Legion of Merit, DFC, Air medal with 7 oak leaf clusters; recipient award Aerospace Safety Hall Fame, 1979, Disting. Svc. award Am. Vets., 1980, Citation Am. Legion, 1984, Citizenship medal SAR, 1989, Citation Air Force Assn. Fla., 1990. Mem. Delta Epsilon Sigma, Sigma Nu, Phi Delta Phi. Roman Catholic. Home: 2672 Emerald Way N Deerfield Beach FL 33442-8640 *The human being, a magnificent creation, remains obscure if the element of motivation lies dormant. The human will is the key to personal achievement. Discipline is the remedy for what besets many of our American institutions, including our public schools, our criminal justice system, our transportation system, the professions, industry and government. Discipline is simply making good laws and rules and enforcing them. Without discipline, our institutions are fostering dysfunction.*

RUNGE, DE LYLE PAUL, retired library director, consultant; b. Madison, Wis., Feb. 3, 1918; s. Charles Delial and Josephine Ida Clara (Niebuhr) R.; m. Ethelyn Fay Green, Sept. 26, 1943; children: Richard Rene, Willa Dee, Robert Roy. BA in Commerce, U. Wis., 1940, BSLS, 1943. Dir. pub. rels., coord. ref. svcs. Grand Rapids (Mich.) Pub. Libr., 1946-53; libr. dir. St. Petersburg (Fla.) Pub. Libr., 1953-82; cons. on libr. bldgs., 1964—; mem. Fla. State Libr. Adv. Coun., 1973-82. With AUS, 1943-46, ETO, lt. col. USAR. Mem. ALA, Fla. Libr. Assn. (pres. 1968-69, exec. bd. 1969-70), Southeastern Libr. Assn., ASPA, Am. Philatelic Soc., St. Petersburg Stamp Club, Kiwanis, Beta Phi Mu. Home: 4520 Cortez Way S Saint Petersburg FL 33712-4029

RUNGE, DONALD EDWARD, food wholesale company executive; b. Milw., Mar. 20, 1938; s. Adam and Helen Teresa (Voss) R.; divorced; children: Roland, Richard, Lori. Grad., Spencerian Coll., Milw., 1960. Fin. v.p. Milw. Cheese Co., Waukesha, Wis., 1962-69; dir. Farm House Foods Corp., Milw., 1966-89, pres., 1966-89, chief exec. officer, treas., 1984-89, chmn., pres., 1985-89; chmn., chief exec. officer Retailing Corp. Am., Milw.,

1982-89; chief exec. officer, treas. Drug Systems Inc., Milw., 1984-89; chmn. Drug Systems Inc. (now Retailing Corp. of Am.), Milw., 1985-89; pres. TDC, 1987-89; chmn., pres. Runge Industries, Gen. Growth, Inc., 1989—; bd. dirs. Convenient Food Mart, CasaBlanca Industries, Inc., City of Industry, Calif.; sec. The Diana Corp., Milw., 1985-86, treas. 1986—, pres. 1987—; chmn. Economy Dry Goods Co. Inc.; treas. Fairbanks Farms Inc. Adventist. *I believe there is very little in life that cannot be accomplished if a person truly wants to attain the goal.*

RUNGE, KAY KRETSCHMAR, library director; b. Davenport, Iowa, Dec. 9, 1946; d. Alfred Edwin and Ina (Paul) Kretschmar; m. Peter S. Runge Sr., Aug. 17, 1968; children: Peter Jr., Katherine. BS in History Edn., Iowa State U., 1969; MLS, U. Iowa, 1970. Pub. service librarian Anoka County Library, Blaine, Minn., 1971-72; cataloger Augustana Coll., Rock Island, Ill., 1972-74; dir. Scott County Library System, Eldridge, Iowa, 1974-85, Davenport (Iowa) Pub. Libr., 1985—; bd. dirs. Brenton Bank. Bd. dirs. River Ctr. for Performing Arts, Davenport, 1983—, Am. Inst. Commerce, 1989—, Quad-Cities Conv. and Visitors Bur., 1991—, Quad-Cities Grad. Study Ctr., 1992—, Downtown Davenport Devel. Corp., 1992—, Hall of Honor Bd. Davenport Ctrl. H.S., 1992-95, Brenton Bank, 1996—; mem. steering com. Quad-Cities Visions for the Future, 1987-91; bd. govs. Iowa State U. Found., 1991—. Recipient Svc. Key award Iowa State U. Alumni Assn., 1979. Mem. ALA (chmn. library adminstrs. and mgrs. div., fundraising section 1988), Iowa Library Assn. (pres. 1983), Pub. Library Assn. (bd. dirs. 1990-96), Iowa Edn. Media Assn. (Intellectual Freedom award 1984), Alpha Delta Pi (alumni state pres. 1978). Lutheran. Office: Davenport Pub Libr 321 N Main St Davenport IA 52801-1409

RUNGE, PATRICK RICHARD, lawyer; b. Iowa City, Iowa, Oct. 25, 1969; s. Richard Gary and Sally Louise (Cozzolino) R.; m. Kimberly Marie Hansen, Mar. 16, 1996. BSBA in Econs., U. Nebr., Omaha, 1991; JD, Creighton U., 1994. Bar: Nebr. 1994, U.S. Dist. Ct. Nebr. 1994. Prodn. editor U.N.O. Gateway, Omaha, 1990-91; graphic designer Omaha (Nebr.) Pub. Power Dist., 1991—; intern U.S. Dist. Ct., Omaha, 1993; rsch. asst. Creighton U., Omaha, 1993; sr. cert. law student Creighton Legal Clinic, Omaha, 1994; atty. Runge Law Office, Omaha, 1994-95, Runge & Chase, Omaha, 1995—. Disting. scholar Omaha (Nebr.) World-Herald, 1987-91; Merit scholar Creighton Law Sch., Omaha, 1991-94. Democrat. Roman Catholic. Home: 7710 Howard St # 7 Omaha NE 68114 Office: Runge & Chase Ste 218 1941 S 42D St Omaha NE 68105

RUNGE, PAUL EDWARD, baseball umpire, realtor; b. St. Catherine's, Ont., Can., Oct. 20, 1940; came to U.S., 1947; s. Edward Paul and Viola Irene (Meek) R.; m. Anastasia Mouzas, Oct. 17, 1965; children: Brian Edward, Reneé Dyann. Student, San Diego City Coll., 1959-61; BA in Edn. and Bus., Ariz. State U., 1964. Lic. real estate broker. Umpire Nat. League of Profl. Baseball. Mem. Helenic Cultural Soc. Baseball scholar Ariz. State U., 1961; named Umpire of Yr. by Harry Wendelsted Sch. of Umpiring, 1993; inducted Hall of Fame San Diego H.S., 1991. Mem. Major League Umpires Assn. Union (pres., v.p., bd. dirs.), San Diego Bd. Realtors, Ariz. State U. Alumni Assn., Phi Delta Theta. Republican. Mem. New Apostolic Ch. Umpire All-Star games, San Diego, Houston, Pitts., 1978, 86, 94, Championship Series, 1977, 81, 82, 85, 88, 90, World Series, 1979, 84, 89, 93. Home: 649 Calle De La Sierra El Cajon CA 92019-1243 Office: Major League Umpires Assoc 1735 Market St Ste 3420 Philadelphia PA 19103*

RUNKLE, MARTIN DAVEY, library director; b. Cin., Oct. 18, 1937; s. Newton and Ilo (Neal) R.; m. Nancy Force, Aug. 7, 1965; children: Seth, Elizabeth. BA, Muskingum Coll., 1959; MA, U. Pitts., 1964, U. Chgo., 1973. Library systems analyst U. Chgo., 1970-75, head cataloging librarian, 1975-79, asst. dir. tech. services, 1979-80, dir. library, 1980—; sr. lectr. grad. library sch. U. Chgo., 1977-90. Fulbright grantee, 1965. Mem. ALA, Univ. Club Chgo. Office: U Chgo 1100 E 57th St Chicago IL 60637-1502

RUNNALLS, (OLIVER) JOHN (CLYVE), nuclear engineering educator; b. Barrie Island, Ont., Can., June 26, 1924; s. John Lawrence and Ethel May (Arnold) R.; m. Vivian Constance Stowe, Sept. 13, 1947; children: David John, Catherine Ruth. B.A.Sc., U. Toronto, 1948, M.A.Sc., 1949, Ph.D., 1951. Registered profl. engr., Ont. Research and devel. scientist Atomic Energy of Can., Ltd., Chalk River, Ont. and Paris, 1951-71; sr. adviser uranium and nuclear energy Energy, Mines and Resources Can., Ottawa, Ont., 1971-79; prof. energy studies U. Toronto, 1979-89, chmn. Ctr. Nuclear Engring., 1983-89; prof. emeritus nuclear engring. and energy studies, 1989—; chmn. bd. Inst. Hydrogen Systems, 1983-89; pres. O.J.C. Runnalls & Assocs., Ltd.; bd. dirs. Rio Narcea Gold Mines Ltd., Toronto. Contbr. articles to profl. jours.; patentee in field. Decorated Queen's Silver Jubilee medal, 1977; recipient B.T.A. Bell Commemorative medal Can. Mining Jour., 1979, Ian F. McRae award Can. Nuclear Assn., 1980. Fellow Royal Soc. Can., Can. Acad. Engring.; mem. Assn. Profl. Engrs., Can. Nuclear Assn. (bd. dirs., past chmn.), Can. Nuclear Soc. Home and Office: 170 Lytton Blvd, Toronto, ON Canada M4R 1L4

RUNNELLS, DONALD DEMAR, geochemist, consultant; b. Eureka, Utah, Dec. 30, 1936; s. Raymond DeMar and Cleo Cecil (Beckstead) R.; m. Erika Anna Bahe, Sept. 3, 1958; children: Timothy, Suzanne. BS with high honors, U. Utah, 1958; MA, Harvard U., 1960, PhD, 1963. Rsch. geochemist Shell Devel. Co., Houston and Miami, 1963-67; asst. prof. U. Calif.-Santa Barbara, 1967-69; assoc. prof. geochemistry U. Colo., Boulder, 1969-75, prof., 1975-92, chair dept. geol. sci., 1990-92; pres. Shepherd Miller, Inc., Ft. Collins, Colo., 1993—. cons. geochemistry to cos., and govt. agys. Mem. water sci. and tech. bd. NRC/NAS, 1989-92. Contbr. articles to profl. publs. NSF fellow, 1958-62. Fellow Geol. Soc. Am.; mem. Am. Chem. Soc., Assn. Exploration Geologists (pres. 1990-91), Geochemical Soc., Assn. Ground Water Scientists and Engrs. Home: 8032 Allott Ave Fort Collins CO 80525-4269 Office: Shepherd Miller Inc 3801 Automation Way Fort Collins CO 80525-4311

RUNNICLES, DONALD, conductor; b. Edinburgh, Scotland, Nov. 16, 1954. Student, Edinburgh U., Cambridge U., London Opera Ctr. Repetiteur Mannheim, Germany, Nat. theatre, from 1980, Kapellmeister, from 1984; prin. condr. Hanover, from 1987; numerous appearances with Hamburg Staatsoper; former gen. music dir. Stadtische Buhnen, Freiburg/Breisgau; mus. dir. San Francisco Opera, 1992—; appearances with Met. Opera include Lulu, 1988, The Flying Dutchman, 1990, Teh Magic Flute; condr. Vienna Staatsoper, 1990-91; debut at Glyndebourne with Don Giovanni, 1991; condr. London Symphony Orch., Orch. de Paris, Israel Philharm., Rotterdam Philharm., Seattle Symphony, Pitts. Symphony, Chgo. Symphony, 2 complete ring cycles with Wiener Staatsoper; rec. Hansel and Gretel (Humperdinck), Gluck's Orphée with San Francisco Opera Orch., 1995, Tannhäuser-Bayreuth Festspick, 1995; also numerous symphonic engagements; opened Edinburgh Festival, 1994, 96. Office: San Francisco Opera War Meml Opera House San Francisco CA 94102 also: Stadtische Buhnen, Bertoldstr 46, W-7800 Freiburg/Breisgau Germany

RUNNING, NELS, career officer; b. Missoula, Mont.. BS, USAF Acad., 1964; postgrad., George Washington U., 1978-79. Commn. 2d lt. USAF, 1964, advanced through grades to maj. gen., 1992; pilot F4E, left wing position, ops. officer USAF Thunderbirds, 1973-74; comdr. 26th tactical fighter aggressor squadron USAF, Clark AB, The Philippines, 1980-81; dep. comdr. ops., vice comdr. 8th tactical fighter wing USAF, Kunsan AB, Korea, 1981-82; chief ho. liaison officer Office of Sec. USAF, Washington, 1982-84; dir. inspection, hdqs. Pacific Air Forces USAF, Hickam AFB, Hawaii, 1984-85; comdr. 8th tactical fighter wing USAF, Kunsan AB, Korea, 1985-86; dep. dir. internat. programs, hdqs. USAF, Washington, 1986-88, dep. dir. internat. negotiations The Joint Staff, 1988-90; dir. plans, policy, doctrine, simulations and analysis U.S. Spl. Ops. Command, MacDill AFB, Fla., 1990-92; dep. chief of staff UN Command, Seoul, Korea, 1992-95; vice commdr. 12th Air Force and Air Force Component U.S. So. Command, Davis-Monthan AFB, Ariz., 1995—. Mem. Air Force Assn., Air Force Acad. Alumni Assn. (bd. dirs. 1971-75), Korean Am. Friendship Assn. (dir. 1994-95), Order of Daedalians, Red River Valley Fighter Pilots Assn. Avocations: racquetball, skiing, running, hunting, golf. Office: Ste 218 2915 S Twelfth Air Force Dr Davis Monthan AFB AZ 85707

RUNNION, HOWARD J., JR., banker; b. Hot Spring, N.C., May 23, 1930; s. Howard Jackson and Blanche Mae (Elam) R.; m. Betty Ann Bishop, June 30, 1951; children: Debra Joy Sizemore, Jill Marie Faust. BS, U. N.C., 1952. Various postions Wachovia Bank and Trust Co.-Wachovia Corp., Winston-Salem, N.C., 1952—; ret. vice chmn., former dir. Depository Trust Co., N.Y.C., 1985-95; chmn. bd. PSA Treasury Com, 1984-85; ret. exec. v.p. First Wachovia Corp.; bd. dirs. Cardinal Bancshares, Lexington, Ky.; dir. T.R.I.F.I.D. Inc., St. Louis, Security First Network Bank, Pinville, Ky. Chmn. bd. trustees Coll. Found. Raleigh, 1978—. Mem. Res. City Bankers Assn., Pub. Securities Assn. (dir. 1976-79, 84-85). Republican. Presbyterian. Clubs: Forsyth Country, Roaring Gap. Lodge: Elk. Avocation: golf. Home: 3521 York Rd Winston Salem NC 27104-1346 Office: 1st Wachovia Corp PO Box 3099 Winston Salem NC 27102-3099

RUNQUIST, LISA A., lawyer; b. Mpls., Sept. 22, 1952; d. Ralf E. and Violet R. BA, Hamline U., 1973; JD, U. Minn., 1976. Bar: Minn. 1977, Calif. 1978, U.S. Dist. Ct. (ctrl. dist.) Calif. 1985, U.S. Supreme Ct. 1995. Assoc. Caldwell & Toms, L.A., 1978-82; ptnr. Runquist & Flagg, L.A., 1982-85; pvt. practice Runquist & Assocs., L.A., 1985—; mem. adv. bd. Exempt Orgn. Tax Rev., 1990—. Calif. State U. L.A. Continuing Edn. Acctg. and Tax Program, 1995—. Mem. editorial bd. ABA Bus. Law Today, 1995—; contbr. articles to profl. jours. Mem. ABA (bus. law sect. coun. 1995—, com. on nonprofit corps. 1986—, chair 1991-95, subcom. current devels. in nonprofit corp. law 1989—, chair 1989-91, subcom. rels. orgns. 1989—, chair 1987-91, subcom. legal guidebook for dirs. 1986—, subcom. model nonprofit corp. act, partnerships and unincorp. bus. orgns. com. 1987—, state regulation of securities com. 1988—, tax law sect. exempt orgns. com. 1987—, subcom. religious orgns. 1989—, co-chair 1995—), Calif. Bar Assn. (bus. law sect., nonprofit and unincorp. orgns. com. 1985-92, 93—, chair 1989-91), Christian Legal Soc., Ctr. Law and Religious Freedom, Christian Mgmt. Assn. (dir. 1983-89). Office: 10821 Huston St North Hollywood CA 91601-4613

RUNTE, ROSEANN, academic administrator; b. Kingston, N.Y., Jan. 31, 1948; arrived in Can., 1971, naturalized, 1983; d. Robert B. and Anna Loretta (Schorkopf) O'Reilly; m. Hans-Rainer Runte, Aug. 9, 1969. BA summa cum laude, SUNY-New Paltz, 1968; MA, U. Kans., 1969, PhD, 1974, DLitt (hon.), Acadia U., 1989, Meml. U., 1990, U. de Vest Timisoarã, 1996. Lectr. Bethany Coll., W.Va., 1970-71; lectr. adult studies St. Mary's U., Halifax, N.S., Can., 1971-72; from lectr. to assoc. prof. Dalhousie U., Halifax, 1972-83, asst. dean, 1980-82, chmn. dept. French, 1980-83; pres. Universite Sainte-Anne, Pointe-de-l'Eglise, N.S., Can., 1983-88; prin. Glendon Coll., Toronto, 1988-94; pres.,Victoria U., 1994—. Author: Brumes bleues, 1982; Faux-Soleils, 1984, Birmanie Blues, 1993; editor: Studies in 18th Century Culture, vols. VII, VIII, IX, 1977, 78, 79; co-editor: Man and Nature, 1982, Le Développement régional, 1986, 87, From Orality to Literature/de L'Oralite á la littérature, 1991, Lectures canadiennes, 1993, Visions of Beauty, 1994; rev. editor French Rev., 1988-94; editor Lit. Rsch., 1994—; co-translator Local Development, 1987. Bd. dirs. Assn. Med. Svcs., 1989-92; adv. bd. Nat. Libr., 1984-91; v.p. Can. Commn. for UNESCO, 1991-92, pres., 1992-96; vice chair exec. bd. Found. for Internat. Tng., 1994—, 95—, chair exec. bd. Found. for Inst. Tng., 1995—; chair Gottschalk Prize Com., 1994; chairwoman publs. com. Hannah Found, 1989-92; internat. adv. bd. Expo. 2000, 1995—. Decorated Ordre du Mérite; recipient Prix Fr. Coppée French Acad., 1989; regents scholar SUNY-New Paltz, 1965; NDEA Title IV grantee U. Kans., Lawrence, 1968; Acad. Palmes, 1986. Mem. Internat. Soc. 18th Century Studies (assoc. treas. 1983-87), Internat. Assn. of Comparative Lit. (treas. 1985-91, sec. 1991-94), Can. Fedn. Humanities (pres. 1982-84), Atlantic Soc. 18th Century Studies (pres. 1972-76), Canadian Soc. 18th Century Studies (pres. 1975-76), Soc. for Study Higher Edn. (bd. dirs. 1988-90), Found. Internat. Tng. (bd. dirs. 1992), Knights of Malta (grande dame 1991—), Delta Kappa Gamma, Phi Delta Kappa, Club of Rome. Home: 44 Charles St W # 3803, Toronto, ON Canada M4Y 1R8 Office: 73 Queen's Park Crescent, Toronto, ON Canada M5S 1K7

RUNYAN, JOHN WILLIAM, JR., medical educator; b. Memphis, Jan. 23, 1924; s. John William and Lottie (Roberts) R.; m. Barbara Ruth Zerbe, July 16, 1949; children: John William III, Scott Baylor, Keith Roberts. A.B., Washington and Lee U., 1945; M.D., Johns Hopkins, 1947. Diplomate: Am. Bd. Internal Medicine (examiner 1967-72). Intern Johns Hopkins Hosp., 1947-48; asst. to chief resident medicine Albany (N.Y.) Hosp., 1948-50; research fellow Harvard Med. Sch., 1950-53, also Thorndike Meml. Lab., Boston City Hosp.; instr., then asso. prof. medicine Albany Med. Coll., 1953-60; mem. faculty U. Tenn. Med. Sch., 1960—, prof. medicine, 1964—, chief sect. endocrinology, 1963-72, dir. div. health care scis., chmn. dept. community medicine, 1972-87, prof., chmn. preventive medicine, 1987-94, Univ. Disting. prof., 1988—; assoc. med. dir. Family Care Healthplan, 1994—; chief med. svc. John Gaston Hosp., Memphis, 1965-72; cons. endocrinology Memphias VA Hosp., 1962—, USPHS, 1962-70; chmn. Nat. Heart, Blood, Lung Inst. com. on Diabetes and Hypertension, 1985-87; chmn. Generalist and Curriculum Reform Task Force U. of Tenn., 1992-94. Author: Primary Care Guide, 1975, Problem Oriented Primary Care, 1982. Served with AUS, 1951-53. Commonwealth Fund fellow, 1950; recipient John D. Rockefeller III Public Service award in health, 1977; Upjohn award, 1981. Fellow ACP (Rosenthal award 1980, Laureate award Tenn. chpt. 1991, named master 1993); mem. AMA, Am. Fedn. Clin. Rsch., Am. Diabetes Assn. (Outstanding Physician Educator in Diabetes 1981), Tenn. Med. Soc., Memphis Med. Soc., Tenn. Diabetes Soc. (pres. 1968-69). Home: 5496 S Angela Ln Memphis TN 38120-2208

RUNYON, KEITH LESLIE, lawyer, newspaper editor; b. Louisville, Oct. 3, 1950; s. Leslie Thomas and Marjorie Fillmore (Fisher) R.; m. Amelia Payne Sweets, Dec. 29, 1979; children; Amelia Brown Payne, Keith Leslie Jr. Student, U. London, 1971; BA cum laude, U. Louisville, 1972, JD, 1982. Staff writer Courier-Jour., Louisville, 1972-77, staff atty., 1984-86; staff atty., assoc. editor Louisville Times and Courier Jour., 1977-86, forum editor, 1986-90; editorial page editor, 1990-92, editor opinion pages, 1992—. Nat. bd. dirs. English-Speaking Union U.S., N.Y., 1976-79, pres. Ky. br., Louisville, 1986-87, U. Louisville Alumni Assn., 1987-93; mem. exec. com. Louisville com. on fgn. rels., 1985-87, Leadership Louisville, 1990-91; clk. Session Calvin Presbyn. Ch., Louisville, 1986-88. Recipient William E. Leidt award The Episc. Ch. of U.S., 1975, Roy Howard award (shared) Scripps Howard Journalists Nat. for Pub. Svc., 1976; named Alumnus of Yr., U. Louisville, 1991; Ctr. Fgn. Journalists fellow, 1993, Bingham fellow, 1995-96. Mem. ABA, Ky. Bar Assn., Louisville Bar Assn., Nat. Conf. Edit. Writers (editor The masthead, 1994-96), Soc. Profl. Jours. (Outstanding Editl. Writing award, 1983, 84, 85. Home: Nitta Yuma Harrods Creek KY 40027 Office: Courier-Jour and Louisville Times Co 525 W Broadway Louisville KY 40202-2206

RUNYON, MARVIN TRAVIS, postmaster general; b. Ft. Worth, Sept. 16, 1924; s. Marvin T. and Lora Lee (Whittington) R.; children: Marvin, Elizabeth Anne, Paul, James. BS in Mgmt. Engring., Tex. A&M U., 1948. Staff mem. mfg. engring. areas assembly plants Ford Motor Co., 1943-60, asst., plant mgr. various assembly plants, 1960-70; mgr. assembly engring. automotive assembly div. gen. office Ford Motor Co., Dearborn, Mich., 1970-72; gen. mgr. automotive assembly div. Ford Motor Co., 1972-73, v.p. body and assembly ops., 1973-77, v.p. powertrain and chassis ops., 1977-78, v.p. body and assembly ops., 1979-80; pres., chief exec. officer Nissan Motor Mfg. Corp. U.S.A., Smyrna, Tenn., 1980-87; chmn. bd. TVA, Knoxville, Tenn., 1988-92; postmaster gen. U.S. Postal Svc., Washington, 1992—; mem. at large Nuclear Power Oversight Com., 1991-92. Bd. dirs. United Way Knoxville, 1988-92, mem. campaign adv. com. 1990; bd. dirs. Downtown Orgn., Knoxville, 1988-92, Tenn. Tech. Found., 1982, NCCJ, 1985-88, Nashville-Davidson County unit Am. Cancer Soc., 1986-88, United Way Rutherford County, 1986-89, Cumberland Mus., Nashville, 1986; participant Leadership Nashville Assn., 1982—, pres., 1986, Leadership Knoxville, 1989, Leadership Memphis, 1990-91; hon. chmn. Clinic Bowl, Nashville, 1986; mem. devel. adv. bd. Ctr. for Internat. Bus. Studies Tex. A&M U., 1987, mem. coll. bus. adminstrv. devel. coun., 1984-87; mem. outreach com. Knoxville Bicentennial '91 Coord. Coun.; mem. adv. bd. Inroads/Nashville, Inc., 1983—; mem. devel. adv. bd. Nashville State Tech. Inst., 1987; chmn. corp. adv. com. Middle Tenn. Regional Minority Purchasing Coun., 1982-83; mem. gov.'s adv. bd. to S.E./U.S. Japan Assn., 1981; gen. campaign chmn. United Way Nashville and Middle Tenn., 1985-86, trustee, 1984-86; trustee Automotive Hall of Fame, 1985—; chmn. Tenn. Minority Bus. Opportunity Fair, 1987-89, 1992 Trade Fair, Midsouth Minority Purchasing Coun., 1991-92;, Sr. Ptnrs. Bd. for May 1992 World Congress of Indsl. Devel. Rsch. Coun., 1991-92; bd. dir. Memphis in May Internat. Festival Inc., 1991-92, Met. Nashville Pub. Edn. Found., 1991-92; mem. U. Tenn. Devel. Coun., 1990—, Nucleus Fund Com. and Internat. Programs Resource Devel. Com., Tex. A&M U. Named Outstanding Man of Year Soc. Advanced Mgmt., 1968, Pres. slot on 1985 Model Yr. Automotive News All-Star Team, Automotive News; recipient Mgr. of Yr. award Avco Aerostructures chpt. Nat. Mgmt. Assn., 1985, CEO of Yr., Advantage mag., 1985, Disting. Service citation Automotive Hall of Fame, 1986, Salesman of Yr., Nashville chpt. Sales and Mktg. Exec. Club, 1985, award Tenn.-Japan Friends in Commerce, 1989; hon. gen. com. Internat. Fedn. Automotive Engring. Socs. 1988 Congress; recipient Human Rels. award NCCJ Nashville chpt., 1990, Spl. Recognition award Minority Bus. Devel. Agy., 1990, Gold Knight of Mgmt. award Nat. Mgmt. Assn., 1992, Exec. of Yr. award Nat. Mgmt. Assn., 1992, Adv. Mail Mktg. Assns. J. Edward Day award, 1993. Mem. Soc. Automotive Engrs., Engring. Soc. Detroit, Nashville Area C. of C. (bd. govs. 1983-85), Knoxville C. of C. (bd. dirs. 1988-92), Memphis C. of C. (bd. dirs. 1990-92), Tenn. Assn. Bus. (bd. dirs.), Soc. Internat. Bus Fellows, Belle Meade Country Club (Nashville). Episcopalian. Office: US Postal Svc Office of Postmaster Gen 475 Lenfant Plz SW Washington DC 20260-0004

RUOFF, ARTHUR LOUIS, physicist, educator; b. Ft. Wayne, Ind., Sept. 17, 1930; s. Louis A. and Wilma (Rall) R.; m. Enid Frances Seaton, Jan. 24, 1954; children—William Louis, Stephen Arthur, Rodney Scott, Jeffrey Kevin, Kenneth James. B.S., Purdue U., 1952; Ph.D., U. Utah, 1955. Asst. prof. materials sci. and engring. Cornell U., 1955-58, asso. prof., 1958-65, prof., 1965—, Class of 1912 prof. engring., 1978—, chmn. dept. materials sci. and engring., 1978-88, dir. Cornell ceramics program, 1987—. Author: Introduction to Materials Science, 1972, Materials Science, 1973, Introductory Materials Science, 1973, Concepts of Packaged Courses, 1973. Pres. Ithaca (N.Y.) Youth Hockey, 1972-73. Named Engr. of Distinction Engrs. Joint Coun., 1970; recipient Bridgman award Internat. Assn. Advancement of High Pressure Sci. and Tech., 1993. Fellow Am. Phys. Soc., Böehmlische Physicalische Soc.; mem. N.Y. Acad. Scis., Assn. Internat. Pour L'Avancement De La Recherche Et De La Technologie Aux Hautes Pressions (pres. 1995—). Office: Materials Sci and Engring Bard Hall Cornell U Ithaca NY 14853

RUOFF, CYNTHIA OSOWIEC, foreign language educator; b. Chgo., Mar. 1, 1943; d. Stephen R. and Estelle (Wozniak) O.; m. Gary Edward Ruoff, June 5, 1965; children: Gary S., Laura A. AB, Loyola U., 1965; MA, Western Mich. U., 1973; PhD in French Lang. and Lit., Mich. State U., 1992. Tchr. Kalamazoo (Mic.) Pub. Schs., 1965-68; instr. Western Mich. U., Kalamazoo, 1980—; nat. and internat. spkr. in field. Contbr. articles to profl. jours. Mem. MLA, N.Am. Soc. Seventeenth-Century French Lit., Am. Assn. Tchrs. of French, Mich. Fgn. Lang. Assn., Internat. Soc. Phenomenology and Lit., L'Alliance Française, Soc. Interdisciplinary French Seventeenth-Century Studies, Phi Sigma Iota, Pi Delta Phi. Avocations: piano, skiing. Office: Dept Fgn Langs & Lit Western Mich Univ Kalamazoo MI 49008 *Reach beyond intelligence and reason by experiencing the beauty, harmony, grandeur, and mystery of the cosmos..to achieve a higher understanding and truth.*

RUOHO, ARNOLD EINO, biochemical pharmacology educator; b. Thunder Bay, Ont., Can., Nov. 26, 1941; s. Eino Armas and Toini Helen (Kuusisto) R.; m. Marjorie Denise Anderson, Aug. 21, 1965; children—David, Daniel, Jonathon. B.S. in Pharmacy, U. Toronto, Ont., Can., 1964; Ph.D. in Physiol. Chemistry, U. Wis.-Madison, 1970. Helen Hay Whitney postdoctoral fellow U. Calif.-San Diego, 1971-74; asst. prof. pharmacology U Wis.-Madison, 1974-80, assoc. prof., 1980-84, prof., 1984—; cons. NIH, Bethesda, Md., 1984—. Editor: International Encyclopedia of Pharmacology and Experimental Therapeutics, 1984—; contbr. articles to profl. jours., chpts. to books. Den leader local council Boy Scouts Am., Madison, 1975-77, mem. at large, 1979—; hockey coach, 1983—. Grantee March of Dimes, 1975-78, Pharm. Mfrs., 1975-76, NIH, 1975—. Mem. AAAS, N.Y. Acad. Scis. Lutheran.

RUOSLAHTI, ERKKI, medical research administrator; b. Puumala, Finland. B.Medicine, U. Helsinki, Finland, 1961, MD, 1965, Dr.Medicine, 1967; Dr.Medicine (hon.), U. Lund, Sweden, 1991. Rsch./teaching asst. dept. serology and bacteriology U. Helsinki, 1964-66; head blood group dept. State Serum Inst., Helsinki, 1966-68; NIH rsch. fellow Calif. Inst. Tech., 1968-70; asst. prof., acting assoc. prof. dept. serology U. Helsinki, 1970-75; prof. bacteriology and serology U. Turku, Finland, 1975-76; sr. rsch. scientist dept. immunology City of Hope, Duarte, Calif., 1976; dir. immunobiology divsn. immunology City of Hope Nat. Med. Ctr., Duarte, 1978-79; assoc. sci. dir. La Jolla (Calif.) Cancer Rsch. Found., 1979-80, v.p., COO, 1982-89, sci. dir., 1980—, pres., CEO and dir. Cancer Ctr., 1989—; adj. prof. dept. pathology U. Calif., San Diego, 1980—; mem. sci. adv. bd. Helen Keller Eye Rsch. Found., Birmingham, Ala., 1989—; mem. pathobiochemistry study sect. Nat. Cancer Inst., 1981-85; Robert and Estelle Stadtler lectr. U. Tex., Sys. Cancer Ctr., 1984, Burton L. Baker Meml. lectr. U. Mich., Ann Arbor, 1987, Harvey Soc. lectr., 1988, Jeanette Piperno Meml. lectr. Temple U., Phila., 1989, G.H.A. Clowes award and lectr. Am. Assn. Cancer Rsch., 1990, Karl H. Beyer lectr. U. Wis., 1990, Walter Hubert lectr. 33d Ann. Meeting, Brit. Assn. for Cancer Rsch., 1992. Contbr. over 300 articles to profl. jours.; editl. bd. mem. Matrix, 1991—, Internat. Jour. Cancer, 1979—, Ann. Rev. of cell Biology, 1987-90, Jour. Cell Biology, 1987-89, Jour. Biol. Chemistry, 1985-88, Cancer Rsch., 1979-82; reviewing editor Science, 1989—; editor-in-chief Cell Regulation, 1989-91. Recipient Barbara Robert Meml. medal French Soc. of Connective Tissue, 1988, Outstanding Investigator award Nat. Cancer Inst., 1986-93, Robert J. and Claire Pasarow Found. award, 1991, Lella Gruber Cancer Rsch. award Am. Acad. Dermatology, 1993, Abbott award Internat. Soc. for Oncodevelopmental Biology and Medicine, 1995. Fellow Am. Acad. Arts and Scis.; mem. Finnish Acad. Scis. Office: LaJolla Cancer Res Fnd 10901 N Torrey Pines Rd La Jolla CA 92037-1005*

RUOTSALA, JAMES ALFRED, historian, writer; b. Juneau, Alaska, Feb. 17, 1934; s. Bert Alfred and Eva (Karppi) E.; m. Janet Ann Whelan, July 31, 1987; stepchildren: Theresa Cowden, Douglas Whelan, Peggy MacInnis, Michael Whelan, Bruce Whelan. Student, U. Md., 1960-61, Basic Officers Sch., Maxwell AFB, 1964, Air U., Maxwell AFB, 1985; AA, U. Alaska, Kenai, 1990. Asst. div. mgr. Macmillan Pub. Co., 1964-80; mgr. Denny's Restaurants, 1980-82; dir. mktg. and sales Air Alaska, 1982-89; state security supr., lt. Knightwatch Security, Juneau, Alaska, 1990-96; ret., 1996; archival dir. Alaska Aviation Heritage Mus., 1987-90. Author: Lockheed Vegas in Southeast Alaska, 1980, We Stand Ready, 1986, Eielson, Father of Alaskan Aviation, 1986; Alaska's Aviation Heritage Air Alaska newspaper; contbr. articles to profl. jours. Journalist 1st cl. USN, 1951-56; sgt. U.S. Army, 1958-64; 1st sgt. USAR, 1983-94; ret. USAR, 1994; lt. col. ASDF, 1985—. Decorated Korean Svc. medal with 2 combat stars, Korean Presdl. unit citation, UN Svc. medal, Nat. Def. Svc. medal, Vietnam Svc. medal, Meritorious Svc. medal with 2 oak leaf clusters, Army Commendation medal with 4 oak leaf clusters; recipient USAF Brewer Aerospace award, Grover Leoning award, Paul E. Garber award, 1984-85, State of Alaska Gov.'s Cert. Appreciation, 1983, Mayor's Pub. Svc. award, Anchorage, 1985, Commendation from Gov. of Alaska, 1993, 94, 18th Session Alaska Legis. Cert. Recognition, 1993, 94. Mem. VFW (sr. vice comdr. 1995), Res. Officers Assn. (pub. affairs officer 1985—), U.S. Naval Inst., Aviation and Space Writers Assn., Am. Aviation Hist. Soc., Am. Legion (historian), Pioneers of Alaska (sec. 1988, v.p. 1989, pres. 1990, Igloo 33, treas. 1994-95, Igloo 6, Cert. Appreciation 1988), Rotary. Methodist. Home: 2723 John St Juneau AK 99801-2020

RUPAUL (ANDRE CHARLES), model, singer; b. New Orleans. on-air reporter Manhattan Cable, England. Albums include RuPaul is Star Booty, Supermodel of the World; formed groups RuPaul and the U-Hauls, Wee Wee Pole; appearances include (TV) The Am. Music Show, (video) B-52's Love Shack. Office: C/O Tommy Boy Records 902 Broadway Fl 13 New York NY 10010-6002*

RUPERT, DANIEL LEO, elementary education administrator; b. Waynoka, Okla., Nov. 12, 1953; s. Robert Anthony and Georgia Yvonne (Lewis) R.; m. Emily Carol Lummus, June 12, 1977; 1 child, Joshua Daniel. AA, Miss. County C.C., 1979; BA in Social Psychology, Park Coll., 1981; MDiv, New Orleans Bapt. Theol. Sem., 1985; EdS, Miss. State U., Starkville, 1991. Chaplain East Miss. State Hosp., Meridian, 1985-87; dir. of rsch. Am.

Family Assn., Tupelo, Miss., 1988-89; cons. Rupert & Assocs., Tupelo, 1989-93; guidance counselor Okolona (Miss.) Elem. Sch., 1993-94, guidance counselor, asst. prin., chpt. 1 coord., 1994—; computer cons. Lee County Schs., Tupelo, 1990. Author: Selected Poems by Author, 1990; co-author: (state core objectives) Health Education Core Objectives for the State of Mississippi, 1991. Prt-time pastor Koinonia Bapt. Mission, Mooreville, Miss., 1992—; mem. Christian Bus. Men's Com., Tupelo, 1989-94. With USAF, 1976-82; capt. USAFR, 1983-91, ret., 1995. Mem. ASCD, Am. Assn. Christian Counselors, United Am. Karate Assn., Christian Martial Arts Instrs. Assn. (bd. dirs.), Miss. Counseling Assn., Tupelo Martial Arts Acad., Luncheon Civitan Club, Chi Sigma Iota. Republican. Southern Baptist. Avocations: Karate, writing, singing, playing guitar, spending time with family. Home: 1931 E Main St Tupelo MS 38802 Office: Okolona Elem Sch 411 W Main St Okolona MS 38860-1307

RUPERT, DONALD WILLIAM, lawyer; b. Clearfield, Pa., Oct. 15, 1946; s. Donald Lee and Dorothy Mae (Bonsall) R.; m. Patricia A. Rupert, June 21, 1969. BS in Chemistry, Miami U., Ohio, 1968; JD, Washburn U., Topeka, 1976. Bar: Tex. 1976, Ill. 1978, U.S. Ct. Appeals (Fed. cir.) 1978, U.S. Dist. Ct. (so. dist.) Tex. 1977, U.S. Ct. Appeals (7th cir.) 1981, U.S. Dist. Ct. (no. dist.) Ill. 1979, U.S. Supreme Ct., 1992. Assoc. Arnold, White & Durkee, Houston, 1976-78, Kirkland & Ellis, Chgo., 1978-83, ptnr., 1983-86; ptnr. Neuman, Williams, Anderson & Olson, Chgo., 1986-90; founding ptnr. Roper & Quigg, 1990-93; ptnr. Keck, Mahin & Cate, Chgo., 1993-96; ptnr. Mayer, Brown & Platt, Chgo., 1996—; cons. USAF, Dayton, Ohio, 1974-81. Contbr. articles to profl. jours. Served to capt. USAF, 1968-74. Miami U. Undergrad. Rsch. fellow, 1967, Grad. Rsch. fellow, 1968. Mem. ABA, Am. Intellectual Property Law Assn., Tex. Bar Assn., Phi Kappa Phi. Democrat. Presbyterian. Home: 2519 Park Pl Evanston IL 60201-1315 Office: Mayer, Brown & Platt 190 S LaSalle St Chicago IL 60603-3441

RUPERT, ELIZABETH ANASTASIA, retired university dean; b. Emlenton, Pa., July 12, 1918; d. John Hamilton and Eva Blanche (Elliott) R. Diploma, Altoona Sch. Commerce, 1936; BS in Edn., Clarion State Coll., 1959; MSLS, Syracuse U., 1962; PhD, U. Pitts., 1970. Sec. Quaker State Oil Refining Corp., 1939-56; tchr., libr. Oil City Area Schs., 1959-61; libr. Venango campus Clarion (Pa.) U., 1961-62; prof. Coll. Libr. Sci. Clarion (Pa.) U., Clarion, 1962-70; dean Sch. Libr. Sci., Coll. Libr. Sci. Clarion (Pa.) U., 1971-85; prof. emeritus, 1994; interim pres. Clarion U., spring 1977; acct. William Rupert Mortuary, Inc., 1948-88. Author: Pennsylvania Practicum Program for School Librarians: An Appraisal, 1970; mem. ad hoc edit. com. Pa. Media Guidelines, Pa. Dept. Edn., 1976, author (with others) Encylopedia of Library and Information Science, 1984. Bd. dirs. Knox Pub. Libr.; mem. Abscurf Sec. Ch. Orgns.; active Knox Civic Club. Recipient Disting. Faculty award Clarion U. Alumni Assn., 1976, Disting. Alumni award, 1987. Mem. ALA, Zonta Internat. (Women of Achievement award 1987), Beta Phi Mu, Pi Gamma Mu. Republican. Home: PO Box H Knox PA 16232-0608

RUPERT, (LYNN) HOOVER, minister; b. Madison, N.J., Nov. 3, 1917; s. Lynn Hoover and Hazel L. (Linabary) R.; m. Hazel Pearl Senti, June 22, 1941; children—Susan (Mrs. Max Unland), Elizabeth (Mrs. Warren W. Wright). A.B., Baker U., 1938; A.M., Boston U., 1940, M.Div. cum laude, 1941; student (summers), Garrett Bibl. Inst. and Northwestern U., 1942, Union Theol. Sem., 1943; D.D., Adrian Coll., 1952, Baker U., 1966; L.H.D., Milliken U., 1974. Ordained to ministry Methodist Ch., 1940; asst. pastor First Meth. Ch., Baldwin, Kans., 1936-38, St. Mark's Meth. Ch., Brookline, Mass., 1938-41; pastor Thayer-St. Paul, Kans., 1941-43, First Ch., Olathe, Kans., 1943-45; dir. youth dept. Gen. Bd. Edn. Meth. Ch., Nashville, 1945-50; pastor 1st Meth. Ch., Jackson, Mich., 1950-59; pastor 1st United Meth. Ch., Ann Arbor, Mich., 1959-72, Kalamazoo, 1972-83; faculty dept. religion Fla. So. Coll., Lakeland, 1983-89; adj. faculty Wesley Theol. Sem., Washington, 1989-93; dean Mich. Meth. Pastors Sch., 1959-65; mem. Jud. Council United Meth. Ch., 1968-88 , sec., 1976-88, sec. emeritus, 1988. Author: Prayer Poems on the Prayer Perfect, 1943, Christ Above All (editor), 1948, Youth and Evangelism, 1948, Youth and Stewardship, rev. edit., 1960, Your Life Counts (editor), 1950, What Methodists Believe, rev. edit., 1959, John Wesley and People Called Methodists, 1953, I Belong, 1954, And Jesus Said, 1960, Enjoy Your Teen-Ager, 1962, A Sense of What is Vital, 1964, The Church in Renewal, 1965, My People are Your People, 1968, Where is thy Sting?, Christian Perspectives on Death, 1969, What's Good About God?, 1975 God Will See You Through, 1976, An Instrument of Thy Peace, 1982, The High Cost of Being Human, 1986, Why Didn't Noah Swat Both Mosquitoes, 1993, Up to Your Armpits in Alligators, 1996; writer, syndicated weekly mag. column Accent on Living; newspaper feature Talking to Teens; other publs., periodicals, and newspapers. Trustee Bronson Hosp., 1972-88, Adrian Coll., Asbury Meth. Village, 1996—; pres., bd. dirs. Youth for Understanding, 1970-83, Ann Arbor United Fund, YMCA-YWCA. Recipient Distinguished Alumnus award Boston U., 1969; Lucinda Bidwell Beebe fellow Boston U., 1941. Mem. World Meth. Council, Nat. Council Chs., Mark Twain Soc., Nat. Forensic League, Pi Kappa Delta, Alpha Psi Omega. Lodges: Mason, Rotary (Paul Harris fellow 1983). Home: 403 Russell Ave Gaithersburg MD 20877-2811

RUPERT, JOHN EDWARD, retired savings and loan executive, business and civic affairs consultant; b. Cleve., Oct. 19, 1927; s. Edward J. and Emma (Levegood) R.; m. Virginia Carlson, Oct. 27, 1951; children: Kristen, Karen Rupert Keating, David. B.A., Cornell U., 1949, LL.B., 1951; certificate, Grad. Sch. Savs. & Loan, Ind. U., 1958. With Broadview Savs. & Loan Co., Cleve., 1953-86; v.p. Broadview Savs. & Loan Co., 1964-74, mng. officer, 1965-86, pres., chief exec. officer, 1974-86, chmn., 1979-86. Mem. Cleve. Real Estate Bd., 1955-86; mem. Lakewood (Ohio) Bd. Edn., 1971-77, pres., 1975-77; v.p., trustee Lakewood Hosp., 1966-71; trustee exec. com. of Cleve. Zool. Soc., pres., 1987-92, chmn., 1992—; trustee Cleve. Orch., WVIZ Ednl. TV; bd. dirs. West Side YMCA; mem. Greater Cleve. Literacy Coalition, 1991—; mem. Cornell U. Coun., 1971—, pres., 1977; trustee Med. Ctr. Corp., 1987—, chair, 1990—; trustee Internat. Ctr. for Preservation of Wild Animals, 1991—. With USAF, 1951-53. Mem. Cleve. Interfaith Housing Corp. (pres. 1971—), Inst. Fin. Edn. (pres. 1970), Cleve. Real Property Inventory (pres. 1976—), Ohio Motorists Assn., Delta Kappa Epsilon, Phi Delta Phi, Sphinx Head Soc. Clubs: Cleve. Yachting, Cornell (Cleve.) (trustee); Cornell (N.Y.C.). Home and Office: 18129 W Clifton Rd Cleveland OH 44107-1037

RUPKE, BONNIE JO, nurse; b. Hays, Kans., Mar. 19, 1958; d. Lloyd John and Maxiline Deloris (Huser) Kisner; m. Robert James Rupke, Sept. 17, 1977; children: Dustin James, Daisha Marie, Nichole Ann. AAS, Pratt CC, 1990; AAS, ADN, Barton County C.C., 1992; student, Ft. Hays State U. LPN, Kans. Nursing asst. Medicine Lodge (Kans.) Meml. Hosp., 1989-90; RN charge skilled care unit, rehab. unit Hays (Kans.) Med. Ctr., 1990-93; dir. nursing Hays (Kans.) Good Samaritan Hosp., 1993-94; tchr., trainer Medstaff Temp Personal, 1995—; adminstr. blood pressure clinics area health fairs. Office: Hays Good Samaritan Ctr 27th and Canal Hays KS 67601

RUPP, FRANK A., III, association executive; b. Syracuse, N.Y., Sept. 29, 1947; s. Frank A. and Marilyn June (Mammerle) R.; m. Cynthia Marie Montague, Oct. 8, 1993; twins: Peter and Colin; children from previous marriage: Frank A. IV, Jason W. BS, Rutgers U., 1970, postgrad., 1970-72. Environ. engr. City of Raleigh, N.C., 1972-75, State of Ill., Chgo., 1975-85; mng. dir. Chgo. Historic Races, 1985-87; pres. Sportscar Vintage Racing Assn., Charleston, S.C., 1988-89, 91—, Racing Ventures, Charleston, 1989-90. Avocations: vintage car racing, wooden boats, electronics. Office: Sportscar Vintage Racing PO Box 489 N Atlantic Whorf Charleston SC 29402

RUPP, GEORGE ERIK, academic administrator; b. Summit, N.J., Sept. 22, 1942; s. Gustav Wilhelm and Erika (Braunoehler) R.; m. Nancy Katherine Farrar, Aug. 22, 1964; children: Katherine Heather, Stephanie Karin. Student, Ludwig Maximilians U., Munich, Germany, 1962-63; A.B., Princeton U., 1964; B.D., Yale U., 1967; postgrad., U. Sri Lanka, Peradeniya, 1969-70; PhD, Harvard U., 1972. Ordained to ministry Presbyn. Ch. U.S.A., 1971; faculty fellow in religion, vice chancellor Johnston College, U. Redlands, Redlands, Calif., 1971-74; asst. prof. Harvard Divinity School, Harvard U., Cambridge, Mass., 1974-76, assoc. prof., 1976-77, prof., dean, 1979-85; prof., dean acad. affairs U. Wis., Green Bay, 1977-79; prof., pres. Rice U., Houston, Tex., 1985-93, Columbia U., N.Y.C., 1993—; bd. dirs. Com. for Econ. Devel., Freedom Forum Media Studies Ctr., Martel Found., N.Y. Partnership. Author: Christologies and Cultures: Toward a Typology of Religious Worldviews, 1974, Culture Protestantism: German Liberal Theology at the Turn of the Twentieth Century, 1977, Beyond Existentialism and Zen: Religion in a Pluralistic World, 1979, Commitment and Community, 1989; contbr. articles to profl. jours. Bd. dirs. Amigos de las Americas, Am. Assembly, Assn. Am. Univs., Cathedral Ch. St. John Divine, Commn. on Ind. Colls. and Univs., Inst. Internat. Edn, The Presbyn. Hosp., YMCA of Am. Danforth Grad. fellow, 1964-71. Mem. AAAS, Am. Acad. Religion, Soc. for Values in Higher Edn. Office: Columbia Univ 202 Low Libr New York NY 10027

RUPP, JOHN NORRIS, lawyer; b. Seattle, Mar. 18, 1913; s. Otto Burton and Edith Cornelia (Norris) R.; m. Elizabeth Milner McElroy, Aug. 31, 1937; children: Joanne (Mrs. George Crispin), William John, Elizabeth (Mrs. Brian Fulwiler), James McElroy. A.B., U. Wash., 1934, J.D., 1937. Bar: Wash. 1937. Law clk. to chief justice Wash. State Supreme Ct., Olympia, 1937-38; atty. McMicken, Rupp & Schweppe, Seattle, 1939-62; v.p., gen. counsel Pacific N.W. Bell Telephone Co., 1962-75; of counsel Schweppe, Krug & Tausend, Seattle, 1975-90, Preston Gates and Ellis, Seattle, 1990-95. Mem. Wash. State Bd Edn., 1957-67; mem. Seattle Transit Commn., 1957-62, Wash. State Hwy. Commn., 1967-73. Served from ensign to lt. (j.g.) USNR, 1944-46. Decorated Bronze Star. Mem. ABA (ho. dels. 1964-68), Wash. Bar Assn. (hon., pres. 1966-67), Seattle Bar Assn. (pres. 1956-57), Seattle C. of C. (gen. counsel 1960-62), Mcpl. League of Seattle (pres. 1948-50), Seattle Hist. Soc. (pres. 1978-79), Rainier Club, Monday Club, Harbor Club, Seattle Yacht Club, Order of Coif, Phi Gamma Delta, Phi Delta Phi. Clubs: Rainier, Monday, Harbor, Seattle Yacht. Home: 6403 Sand Point Way NE Seattle WA 98115-7915

RUPP, MARK EDMUND, medical educator. BSChemE, U. Tex., 1981; MD, Baylor Coll. Medicine, 1984. Diplomate Am. Bd. Internal Medicine, Am. Bd. Infectious Diseases. Postdoctoral fellow dept. microbiology and immunology Baylor Coll. Medicine, Houston, 1985; intern in internal medicine Med. Coll. Va./Va. Commonwealth U., Richmond, 1985-86, resident in internal medicine, 1986-88, infectious disease fellow, 1988-91, instr. internal medicine, 1991-92; asst. prof. dept. medicine and med. microbiology Sch. Medicine Creighton U., Omaha, 1992—; asst. prof. dept. internal medicine U. Nebr. Med. Ctr., Omaha, 1992—, asst. prof. dept. pathology and microbiology, 1993—; attending physician McGuire Vets Affairs Med. Ctr., Richmond, 1991-92, St. Joseph's Hosp., Omaha, 1992—, Omaha Vets Affairs Med. Ctr.; spkr. in field; instr. physical diagnosis Med. Coll. Va., Va. Commonwealth U., 1991, U. Nebr. Med. Ctr., 1993; guest, invited lectr. univs., confs., med. socs., med. schs. Contbr. book chpts., abstracts, articles to profl. jours.; patentee. Recipient Young Investigators award Nat. Found. Infectious Diseases, 1993, Nat. Rsch. Svc. award NIH, 1991; Am. Heart Assn. grantee, 1993, 95, 96, Rsch. Project grantee, So. Med. Assn., 1991, Collaborative Rsch. grantee NATO, 1993. Fellow ACP; mem. Infectious Diseases Soc. Am., Am. Soc. Microbiology, Soc. Healthcare Epidemiology of Am. Office: U Nebraska Med Ctr Dept Internal Med 600 S 42nd St Omaha NE 68198-5400

RUPP, RALPH RUSSELL, audiologist, educator, author; b. Saginaw, Mich., Apr. 12, 1929; s. Martin Carl and Veronica Marie (Riethmeier) R. B.A., U. Mich., 1951, M.A., 1952; Ph.D., Wayne State U., 1964. Speech and hearing cons. Detroit Pub. Schs., 1955-60; exec. dir. Detroit Hearing and Speech Center, 1960-62; assoc. in audiology Henry Ford Hosp., Detroit, 1962-65; prof. audiology U. Mich., Ann Arbor, 1965-89; coordinator audiology Eastern Mich. U., 1985-93; cons. St. Joseph Mercy Hosp., Ann Arbor, Ann Arbor VA Hosp., Mott Children's Health Ctr., Flint, Mich., Pontiac (Mich.) Gen. Hosp., U. Mich. Health Svcs.; pres. Detroit Hearing Ctr., 1966. Author: (with James Maurer) Hearing and Aging: Tactics for Intervention, 1979, (with Kenneth Stockdell) Speech Protocols in Audiology, 1980; contbr. articles to profl. jours. Served with Med. Service Corps, U.S. Army, 1953-55. Named Disting. Alumnus, Saginaw High Sch., 1981, Outstanding Grad., Wayne State U. Fellow Am. Speech, Lang. and Hearing Assn. (Editor's award); mem. Acad. Rehab. Audiology (past editor Jour.), Mich. Speech and Hearing Assn. (pres. 1954, Disting. Service award, past editor Jour, honor award). Home: 1395 Laurel View Dr Ann Arbor MI 48105-9412

RUPP, SHERON ADELINE, photographer, educator; b. Mansfield, Ohio, Jan. 14, 1943; d. Warren Edmund Rupp and Frances Adeline (Hanson) Christian. BA in Sociology and Psychology, Denison U., 1965; MFA in Photography, U. Mass., 1982. Teaching asst. in photography Hampshire Coll., Amherst, Mass., 1981; instr. photography Northfield (Mass.) Mt. Hermon Sch., 1982-83, U. Mass., Amherst, 1984, Holyoke (Mass.) Community Coll., 1986, 87-88; vis. asst. prof. photography Hampshire Coll., 1985, 87; vis. lectr. photography Amherst (Mass.) Coll., 1994; guest artist, lectr. Boston Mus. Sch., Portland (Maine) Sch. Art, NYU, U. Mass., Deerfield (Mass.) Acad., Hartford Sch. Art/U. Hartford-Conn., Springfield Mus. Fine Arts, Mass., Bard Coll, N.Y., Mass. Coll. Art, Boston, others. Exhibited in one-person shows at Tisch Sch. Arts NYU, 1987, Portland Sch. Art, 1989, Hart Gallery, Northampton, Mass., 1992, O.K. Harris Gallery, N.Y.C., 1992; exhibited in group shows at Zone Art Ctr., N.Y.C., 1987, Mus. Modern Art, N.Y.C., 1991, Springfield Mus. Fine Art, 1993, U. Mass., Amherst, 1993, Dirs. Guild, L.A., 1994, Manchester (N.H.) Inst. Arts and Scis., 1995, Weber State U., Utah, 1995, Grand Ctrl. Terminal, N.Y.C., 1995, Photographic Resource Ctr. 3d Biennial, Boston, 1995; represented in collections at Mus. Modern Art, N.Y.C., Fogg Art Mus. at Harvard U., Mus. Fine Arts, Boston, Rose Art Mus. Brandeis U., Mead Art Mus. Amherst Coll., Smith Coll. Mus. Art, Danforth Mus. Art, Springfield Tech. C.C. Found., Carpenter Ctr. for Visual Arts Harvard U. Bd. dirs., mem. artistic com. Zone Art Ctr., 1987-94. Recipient Mass. Fellowship award in photography Artist Found., 1984, 87; visual arts fellow Nat. Endowment for the Arts, 1986; Guggenheim fellow, 1990, visual artist fellowship Nat. Endowment for Arts, 1994. Avocations: gardening, bicycling, writing. Home and Office: 100 Chestnut St Northampton MA 01060-1407

RUPP, WILLIAM JOHN, architect; b. Phila., Aug. 25, 1927; s. Frank Julius and Sara Viola (Hibbs) R.; m. Gwendolyn O'Rourke, May 10, 1956; children: Susan Hibbs, Molly O'Rourke, Vein Franz. B.Arch., U. Fla., 1953. Draftsman Paul Rudolph, Architect, Sarasota, Fla., 1953-55; pvt. practice architecture Sarasota and Naples, Fla., 1956-67; asso. Morris Ketchum, Jr. & Assos., Architects, N.Y.C., 1968-72; mem. firm Callister, Payne & Bischoff (architects and community planners), Amherst, Mass., 1972-75; pvt. practice architecture and planning, 1975—; vis. lectr. U. Mass., 1976-78, asst. prof., 1978-84, assoc. prof., 1984-91, prof., 1991-95, prof. emeritus, 1995—. Author: (with A.W. Friedmann) Construction Materials for Interior Designers, 1989; contbr. articles to jours. With AUS, 1945-46, 2d lt., 1952. Recipient Archtl. Record award for Housing Design, 1960; Progressive Architecture Design award, 1961. Corp. mem. AIA (N.Y. chpt. 1st award for House Design 1964). Home: 128 Dry Hill Rd Montague MA 01351-9555 Office: U of Mass Fine Arts Center Amherst MA 01003

RUPPE, LORET MILLER, former ambassador; b. Milw., Jan. 3, 1936; d. Frederick C. Miller and Adele (Kanaley) O'Shaughnessy; m. Philip E. Ruppe, Nov. 30, 1957; children: Antoinette B., Adele E., Loret M., Katherine T., Mary Speed. D Pub. Svc. (hon.), No. Mich. U., 1981; LHD (hon.), Marymount Coll., 1981, Luther Coll., 1990; HHD (hon.), Wheeling Coll., 1982, Loyola U., 1987; DCL (hon.), Marquette U., 1983, U. Notre Dame, 1984; hon. degree, Nebr. Wesleyan U., Augustana Coll., Concordia Coll., 1993, St. Bonaventure, 1994, Pace U., Concordia Coll., 1985. Chair Bush Campaign Com., Mich., 1980; co-chair Reagan-Bush Com., Mich., 1980; dir. Peace Corps, Washington, 1981-89; amb. to Norway U.S. Embassy, Oslo, 1989-93. Chair Vice Presdl. Inaugural Reception, 1981; trustee U. Notre Dame, 1988—; bd. dirs. Save the Children, The Hewlett Found., The Shriver Ctr. Decorated Grand Cross Royal Norwegian Order of Merit, Dame of Sovereign Mil. Order Malta. Mem. LWV, Internat. Neighbor's Club IV, Coun. Am. Ambs., The Explorer's Club, Sons of Norway. Roman Catholic. Avocations: reading, tennis. Office: 1 Darby Ct Bethesda MD 20817-2910

RUPPEL, GEORGE ROBERT, accountant; b. N.Y.C., Jan. 6, 1911; s. George W. and Cornelia (Klein) R.; m. Eleanor Holton, Apr. 4, 1941; children—Sandra, Shirley, Lorraine. Grad., St. John's U., 1933. C.P.A., N.Y. State. Chief accountant Am. Agrl. Chem. Co., 1930-36; financial supr. Am. Water Works & Electric Co., 1936-44; v.p., treas., dir. MBS, Inc., 1944-57; v.p., treas. RKO Gen., Inc., 1957-60; treas. Visual Drama, Inc., 1957-60; v.p. finance, dir. Hwy. Trailer Industries, Inc.; v.p., treas. Clinton Engines Corp., 1960-63; pres. Tomahawk Enterprises, Inc., 1963-94, Gehar Co., 1963—; financial cons. Treas. RKO Teleradio Found., 1957-60. Mem. Tax Execs. Inst. (past pres., dir. N.Y. chpt.), Fin. Execs. Inst., N.Y. State Soc. CPAs, Inst. of Mgmt. Accts., Nat. Tax Assn. Address: Pound Ridge Rd Bedford NY 10506

RUPPEL, HOWARD JAMES, JR., sociologist, sexologist, educator; b. Orange, N.J., July 22, 1941; s. Howard J. and Lillian M. (Wordley) R.; m. Barbara Margaret Wiedemann, June 3, 1967. BA, St. Joseph's Coll., Ind., 1963; MA, No. Ill. U., 1968; postgrad. U. Iowa, 1968-76; EdD Inst. for Advanced Study of Human Sexuality, San Francisco, Ca., 1993; PhD 1994. Diplomate Am. Bd. Sexology. Instr. social sci. St. Francis High Sch., Wheaton, Ill., 1963-65, debate coach, 1963-65; instr. sociology St. Dominic Coll., St. Charles, Ill., 1966-67; instr. sociology Cornell Coll., Mt. Vernon, Iowa, 1969-70, asst. prof., 1970-72, lectr., 1972-73; rsch. dir. Social Sci. Rsch. Assos., Cedar Rapids, Iowa, 1973-80; founder, co-dir. Center for Sexual Growth and Devel., Mt. Vernon, 1980—; instr. Sch. Social Work, U. Iowa, 1976-78, adj. asst. prof., 1979-81, adj. assoc. prof., 1981—; exec. dir. Soc. for Sci. Study of Sexuality, 1988—, Found. for the Sci. Study of Sexuality, 1989—; cons. Iowa Dept. Social Svcs., Families Inc., West Branch; bd. dirs. The Human Outreach and Achievement Inst., Boston, 1988-90, Inst. Advanced Study Human Sexuality, 1995—; NSF fellow, 1968. Cert. sexologist Am. Coll. Sexologists. Mem. Am. Sociol. Assn., Nat. Coun. Family Rels., Iowa Coun. Family Rels. (sec. 1983-84, treas. 1985), Changing Family Conf. (bd. dirs. 1983-87), Soc. Sci. Study of Sex Inc. (bd. dirs. 1983-88, pres. Midcontinent Region, 1984-85, treas. 1986-88, chmn. membership com. 1983-85, chmn. exhibits com. 1983-88, ann. meeting chmn. 1986), Am. Assn. Sex Educators, Counselors and Therapists, Soc. Sex Therapy and Rsch. (rsch. mem.), Harry Benjamin Internat. Gender Dysphoria Assn., Coun. Assns. for Sexual Sci., Health and Edn. (del.), Nat. Forensic League, No. Ill. U. Alumni Assn., Alpha Kappa Delta, Alpha Sigma Lambda (hon.). Democrat. Co-editor: Sexuality and the Family Life Span, 1983; assoc. editor: Annual Review of Sex Research, 1992, 93, 94, 95, 96; contbr. articles on complex orgns., marriage and the family, sexual attitudes and behavior, childhood and preadolescent sexuality, methodology and child care theory to profl. publs. Home: 608 5th Ave N Mount Vernon IA 52314-1107 Office: 103 A Avenue S Ste 2-B Mount Vernon IA 52314

RUPPERT, JOHN LAWRENCE, lawyer; b. Chgo., Oct. 7, 1953; s. Merle Arvin and Loretta Marie (Ford) R.; m. Katharine Marie Tarbox, June 5, 1976. BA, Northwestern U., 1975; JD, U. Denver, 1978; LLM in Taxation, NYU, 1979. Bar: Colo. 1978, U.S. Dist. Ct. Colo. 1978, Ill. 1979, U.S. Tax Ct. 1981. Assoc. Kirkland & Ellis, Denver, 1979-84, ptnr., 1984-88; ptnr. Ballard, Spahr, Andrews & Ingersoll, Denver, 1988—; lectr. U. Denver Coll. Law, fall 1984-92; adj. prof. law grad. tax program, 1993-94; sec. Capital Assocs., Inc., 1989-96, acting gen. counsel, 1989-90; sec. and spl. counsel to the bd. dirs. Bros. Gourmet Coffees, Inc., 1995—. Contbr. articles to profl. jours. Mem. ABA, Colo. Bar Assn. (exec. coun. tax sect. 1985-89), Denver Bar Assn., Equipment Leasing Assn. Am. Office: Ballard Spahr Andrews & Ingersoll 1225 17th St Ste 2300 Denver CO 80202-5523

RUPPERT, MARY FRANCES, management consultant, school counselor; b. Flushing, N.Y., May 14; d. Raymond Edward and Mary Josephine (Reilly) R.; m. Donald Francis O'Brien (div.); children: Donald Francis O'Brien III, Kevin Raymond O'Brien; m. Patrick J. Falzone, July 31, 1993. BA in English, Loyola Coll.; MS in Psychology, Counseling, Queens Coll., 1965. Counselor Plainview (N.Y.)-Old Bethpage Schs., 1965—; trainer, cons. stress mgmt., time mgmt., comm., pres. Productivity Programs, Huntington, N.Y., 1975—. Contbr. articles in field; author audiotapes on stress mgmt., 1975—; appearances radio and TV. Mem. ASTD (pres. 1988, chmn. bd. dirs. 1989-95), AAUW, N.Y. State Counselors Assn., Nassau Counselors Assn. Avocations: photography (awards), tennis, golf, reading, wine tasting. Office: 20 Richard Ln Huntington NY 11743-2354

RUPPERT, MICHAEL GEORGE, lawyer; b. Lafayette, Ind., Aug. 15, 1952; s. John Joseph and Jane Ellen (Martin) R.; m. Anita Ruth Wylie, Dec. 31, 1974 (div. Jan. 1984); 1 child, Erin; m. Nancy Louise Cross, Apr. 19, 1986; children: Alexander, Nicholas. BA, Ind. U., 1974; JD, Cleve. State U., 1977; postgrad., Nat. Inst. Trial Advocacy, 1983. Bar: Ind. 1978, U.S. Dist. Ct. (so. dist.) Ind., 1978, U.S. Ct. Appeals (7th cir.) 1978. Editor-in-chief The Gavel (newspaper), 1976-77; legal intern Cleve. Legal Aid Soc., 1977-78; staff atty. children's rights project Legal Svcs. Orgn. Ind., Inc., 1978-81; assoc. Ancel, Miroff & Frank, P.C., 1981-84, Barteau & Deal, 1984-86; ptnr. Ruge & Ruppert, 1986-91; of counsel Miroff, Cross, Ruppert & Klineman, Indpls., 1991—; lectr. in field. Author: Indiana Law Review, Vol. 22, 1989, Vol. 23, 1990; co-author: Indiana Law Review, Vol. 24, 1991, Vol. 25, 1992, Vol. 26, 1993. Mem. ABA (family law sect.), Am. Trial Lawyers Assn., Nat. Orgn. Social Security Claimants Reps., Nat. Assn. Counsel for Children, Ind. Bar Assn. (family law sect.), Ind. Trial Lawyers Assn., Indpls. Bar Assn. (exec. com., family law sect.), Indpls. Athletic Club, Jordan YMCA, Riviera Club. Avocations: handball, racquetball, boating, water skiing. Office: Miroff Cross Ruppert & Klineman 251 E Ohio St Ste 1000 Indianapolis IN 46204-2133

RUPPRECHT, CAROL SCHREIER, comparative literature educator, dream researcher; b. Stafford Springs, Conn., June 30, 1939; d. William Joseph and Caroline Brown (Comstock) Schreier; divorced; children: Jody Francine, Whitney Glenn; m. Richard P. Suttmeier, May 8, 1987. BS, U. Va., 1962; MA, Yale U., 1963, M in Philosophy, 1973, PhD, 1977. Teaching fellow Yale U., 1973; asst. prof. Kirkland Coll., Clinton, N.Y., 1974-78; asst. prof. Hamilton, Coll., Clinton, 1978-81, assoc. dean, 1981-82, assoc. prof. comparative lit., 1982-89; prof., 1989—, chmn. dept., 1984-89; lectr. Switzerland, Israel, The Netherlands, Ireland, People's Republic China, Eng., Japan. Author, editor: The Dream and the Text: Essays on Literature and Language, 1993; co-editor and author: Feminist Archetypal Theory, 1985; sr. editor, cons. editor Dreaming; contbr. articles to profl. jours., chpts. to books. NEH fellow Dartmouth Dante Inst., 1986. Founding mem. Assn. for Study Dreams, 1983, Conn. Assn. Jungian Psychology, 1981. Merrill fellow Bunting Inst., 1970-72. Mem. MLA, Am. Comparative Lit. Assn., Shakespeare Soc., Assn. Study of Dreams (pres., v.p. bd. dirs., mem. editorial bd.), Conn. Assn. for Jungian Psychology (bd. dirs.). Avocations: sports; wilderness activities. Address: 198 College Hill Rd Clinton NY 13323-1218

RUSAW, SALLY ELLEN, librarian; b. Potsdam, N.Y., Apr. 24, 1939; d. Ralph Clinton and Marion Ellen (Jenack) R. BS in Edn., Potsdam Coll., 1964; MLS, SUNY, Albany, 1975. Cert. libr. media specialist, pub. libr., permanent tchr. N-6, N.Y. Tchr. grade 7th-9th Diocese of Ogdensburg, N.Y., 1960-74, cons. office edn., 1975-78; assoc. libr. Mater Dei Coll., Ogdensburg, 1974-89, head libr., 1989—. Vol. Ogdensburg Correctional Facility, 1982, Riverview Correctional Facility, Ogdensburg, 1987—; lector, Eucharistic min. Rite for Christian Initiation of Adults catechist St. Mary's Cathedral; vol. Ogdensburg Cath. Ctrl. Sch., sch. bd., 1995—. Named Vol. of Yr. Ogdensburg Correctional Facility, 1985, Outstanding Vol. Riverview Correctional Facility, 1991; Nat. Def. Edn. Act grantee, 1965. Mem. ALA, N.Y. Libr. Assn., North Country 3Rs Coun., North Country Ref. and Rsch. Resources Coun. (trustee 1994—). Roman Catholic. Avocations: music, reading, berrying, outdoor activities, swimming. Office: Mater Dei Coll Augsbury Meml Libr Ogdensburg NY 13669-9669

RUSCH, HUGH LEONARD, corporate executive; b. Reedsville, Wis., May 5, 1902; s. Albert H. and Ernstena (Seybold) R.; m. Cynthia Katherine VanTuyl, Aug. 30, 1928; children: Willard, Cynthia, Stephen. B.S. in Elec. Engring., U. Wis., 1923. Instr. physics U. Wis., 1921-23, instr. elec. engring., 1923-24; eastern dist. mgr. A.C. Nielsen Co., Chgo., 1924-28; exec. v.p. A.C. Nielsen Co., 1938-46; supr. tech. data Johns-Manville Corp., N.Y.C., 1928-32; v.p., eastern mgr. No. Pump Co., Mpls., 1932-37; v.p. Opinion Research Corp., Princeton, N.J., 1946-66; pres. Hugh Rusch & Assos., Inc., 1967—. Contbr. to: Atlantic Salmon Jour., Readers Digest, Sci. Am., Forbes mag. Co-chmn. N.J. Gov.'s Fluoridation Commn.; Bd. dirs. Insts. of Religion and Health. Recipient Disting. Service award U. Wis., 1959; named Man of Yr., Greater N.Y. Alumni Club U. Wis., 1976. Mem. Pub. Relations Soc. Am., IEEE, Am. Mktg. Assn., Tau Beta Pi, Phi Kappa Phi, Eta Kappa Nu, Alpha

Kappa Lambda. Clubs: University (N.Y.); Nassau, Springdale Golf, Old Guard (Princeton); Union League (Chgo.), Rotary (Princeton). Inventor patented devices as hydraulic transmission, electrohydraulic motor, graphic recorder for measuring radio and TV listening. Home: Pine Run Community Apt Y-12 Doylestown PA 18901

RUSCH, PAMELA JEAN, middle school educator; b. Berwyn, Ill., Mar. 1, 1949; d. James M. and Arlene A. (Meyer) Sanders; m. Steven Paul Rusch, Dec. 23, 1973. BFA, U. Denver, 1971; MA, Lesley Coll., Cambridge, Mass., 1983. Art tchr. Jefferson County Pub. Schs., Lakewood, Colo., 1971—; area coord. Lesley Coll. Outreach Program, Denver, 1981-84; cons. Standard Based Edn., Jefferson County, 1993—. Author curricula. Mem. ASCD, Nat. Mid. Sch. Assn., Colo. Art Edn. Assn. Lutheran. Avocations: flower arranging, skiing, water sports, painting, travel. Home: 7746 Orion St Arvada CO 80007

RUSCH, THOMAS WILLIAM, manufacturing executive; b. Alliance, Nebr., Oct. 3, 1946; s. Oscar William and Gwen Falerne (Middleswart) R.; m. Gloria Ann Sutton, June 20, 1968 (div. Oct. 1979); children: Alicia Catherine, Colin William; m. Lynn Biebighauser, Jan. 17, 1981. BEE, U. of Minn., 1968, MSEE, 1970, PhD, 1973; MS in Mgmt. of Tech., U. Minn., 1993. Sr. physicist cen. rsch. 3M Co., St. Paul, 1973-77, rsch. specialist cen. rsch., 1977-79; project scientist phys. electronics div. Perkin Elmer Corp., Eden Prairie, Minn., 1979-83, sr. project scientist phys. electronics div., 1983-85, lab mgr. phys. electronics div., 1985-87, product mgr. phys. electronics div., 1987-88, sr. product mgr. phys. electronics div., 1988-93; v.p. product devel. Chorus Corp., St. Paul, 1993-94; pres. Creekside Techs. Corp., Plymouth, Minn., 1994—. Editor: X-rays in Materials Analysis, 1986; co-author: Oscillatory Ion Yields, 1977; patentee in field. Recipient IR100 award for transfer vessel Rsch. and Devel. mag., 1981, IR100 award for energy analyser, 1985. Office: 2405 Annapolis Ln Plymouth MN 55441

RUSCH, WILLIAM GRAHAM, religious organization administrator; b. Buffalo, Dec. 23, 1937; s. William Godfrey and Hope (French) R.; m. Thora Joan Ellefsen, Sept. 2, 1967. BA, SUNY, Buffalo, 1959, MA in Classical Langs., 1960; MDiv, Luth. Theol. Sem., Phila., 1963; PhD, Oxford (Eng.) U., 1965; DD (hon.), Yale U., 1995. Ordained to ministry Evang. Luth. Ch., 1966. Assoc. pastor Evang. Luth. Ch. of the Holy Trinity, N.Y.C., 1966-68; asst. prof., chmn. dept. classical langs. Augsburg Coll., Mpls., 1968-71; assoc. exec. dir. div. Theol. Studies Luth. Coun. in the USA, 1971-78; adj. prof. The Gen. Theol. Sem., N.Y.C., 1978-82, 95; exec. dir., asst. to Bishop Evang. Luth. Ch. in Am., Chgo., 1987-96; dir. Commn. on Faith and Order Nat. Coun. of Chs. of Christ USA, N.Y.C., 1996—; vis. lectr. Waterloo Luth. Theol. Sem., 1969; adj. prof. theology Fordham U., N.Y.C., 1984-86; mem. cen. com. World Coun. Chs., 1991—, mem. standing com. faith and order commn., 1991—. Author: The Trinitarian Controversy, Ecumenism: A Movement Toward Church Unity; contbr. articles to profl. jours. Samuel Trexler fellow of N.Y. Synod Luth. Ch. in Am., 1964, 65. Mem. Am. Acad. Religion, Am. Soc. Christian Ethics, Am. Soc. Ch. History, Internat. Assn. Coptic Studies, Gen. Bd. Nat. Coun. Chs. Avocations: book collecting, chess, tennis. Office: Nat Coun of Chs of Christ USA 475 Riverside Dr New York NY 10115-0050

RUSCHA, EDWARD, artist; b. Omaha, Dec. 16, 1937; m. Danna Knego, 1967; children: Edward Joseph. Studied at, Chouinard Art Inst., Los Angeles, 1956-60. Numerous vis. artist positions including UCLA, 1969-70. Author: Twentysix Gasoline Stations, 1962, Various Small Fires, 1964, Some Los Angeles Apartments, 1965, The Sunset Strip, 1966, Thirtyfour Parking Lots, 1967, Royal Road Test, 1967, Business Cards, 1968, Nine Swimming Pools, 1968, Crackers, 1969, Real Estate Opportunities, 1970, Records, 1971, A Few Palm Trees, 1971, Colored People, 1972, Hard Light, 1978; noted for numerous graphite, gunpowder and pastel drawings, over 200 limited-edit. prints; producer, dir.: films Premium, 1970, Miracle, 1974; works include (paintings) Standard Station, Amarillo, Tex., 1963; Annie, 1963, Smash, 1963, Electric, 1964, (mural) Miami-Dade Pub. Library, Fla., 1985; one-man exhbns. include Minn. Inst. Arts, 1972, Nigel Greenwood Ltd., London, 1970, 73, 80, Leo Castelli Gallery, N.Y.C., (10 shows) 1973—, Albright-Knox Art Gallery, Buffalo, 1976, Stedelijk Mus., Amsterdam, 1976, Ft. Worth Art Mus., 1977, San Francisco Mus. Modern Art, 1982, Whitney Mus. Am. Art, 1982, Vancouver Art Gallery, 1982, Contemporary Arts Mus., Houston, 1983, Los Angeles County Mus. Art, 1983, James Corcoran Gallery, Los Angeles, 1985, also others; exhibited in group shows at 64th Whitney Biennial, 1987, Centre Pompidou, Paris, 1989, Mus. Boymans—van Beuningen, Rotterdam, The Netherlands, 1990, Ghislaine Hussenot, Paris, 1990, Fundacio Caixa, Barcelona, Spain, 1990, Serpentine Gallery, London, 1990, Mus. Contemporary Art, L.A., 1990-91, Robert Miller Gallery, N.Y.C., 1992, Thaddaeus Ropac, Salzburg, Austria, 1992; represented in permanent collections including Mus. Modern Art, Los Angeles County Mus. Art, Whitney Mus., Hirshhorn, Washington, Miami-Dade Pub. Libr., Denver Pub. Libr., also others. Guggenheim fellow; Nat. Endowment Arts grantee. Office: care Leo Castelli 420 W Broadway New York NY 10012-3764

RUSE, STEVEN DOUGLAS, lawyer; b. Wichita, Kans., Mar. 8, 1950; B.A., U. Kans., 1972; J.D., Creighton U., 1975. Bar: Mo. 1975, U.S. Dist. Ct. (we. dist.) Mo. 1975, Kans. 1982, U.S. Dist. Ct. Kans. 1982. Law clk. to dist. justice U.S. Dist. Ct. Mo., Kansas City, 1975-77; assoc. Shughart, Thomson & Kilroy, Kansas City, 1977-81, ptnr., 1981—. Mem. ABA, Mo. Bar Assn., Kans. Bar Assn. Office: Shughart Thomson & Kilroy 9225 Indian Creek Pky Overland Park KS 66210-2009

RUSH, ANDREW WILSON, artist; b. Detroit, Sept. 24, 1931; s. Harvey Ditman and Mary Louise (Stalker) R.; m. Jean Cochran, Apr., 1957; children: Benjamin, Samuel, Joseph, Margaret; m. Ann Woodin, Oct., 1978. B.F.A. with honors, U. Ill., 1953; M.F.A., U. Iowa, 1958. Asso. prof. art U. Ariz., 1959-69; co-dir. Rockefeller Found. Indian Arts Project, 1960-64; vis. artist, artist-in-residence Ohio State U., 1970, U. Ark., 1972, Colo. Coll., 1973-74; resident mem. Rancho Linda Vista, Community of the Arts, Oracle, Ariz., 1969—. One-man shows include Carlin Galleries, Ft. Worth, 1973, Graphics Gallery, Tucson, 1972, 75, Tucson Art Inst., 1984; exhibited in group shows at World's Fair, N.Y.C., 1964, USIS exhbns., Europe, Latin Am., 1960-65; represented in permanent collections Libr. of Congress, Uffizi Mus., Dallas Mus., Ft. Worth Mus., Seattle Mus., Free Libr., Phila.; illustrator: Andrew Rush on Oliver Wendell Holmes, 1973, Rule of Two (Ann Woodin), 1984, Voice Crying in the Wilderness (Edward Abbey), 1990, Ask Marilyn, 1992. Served with USMC, 1953-55. Fulbright grantee, 1958-59. Address: Rancho Linda Vista O M Star Rte 2360 Oracle AZ 85623

RUSH, BOBBY L., congressman; b. Ga., Nov. 23, 1946; m. Carolyn Rush; 5 children. BA in Polit. Sci., Roosevelt U., 1974; MA in Polit. Sci., U. Ill., 1992. Fin. planner Sanmar Fin. Planning Corp.; assoc. dean Daniel Hale Williams U.; ins. agent Prudential Ins. Co.; city alderman Chgo., 1984-93; democratic committeeman Chgo. 2nd ward, 1984, 88, Central Ill., 1990; dep. chmn. Ill. Democratic Party, 1990; mem. 103d Congress from 1st Ill. Dist., 1993—; chmn. Environ. Protection, Energy and Pub. Utilities com., Budget and Govt. Operations com., Capitol Devel. com., Hist. Landmark Preservation Com.; mem. Commerce com. Former mem. Student Non-Violent Coordinating com.; founder Ill. Black Panther Party; past coord. Free Breakfast for Children, Free Med. Clinic. With US Army, 1963-68. Recipient Ill. Enterprise Zone award Dept. Commerce and Community, Operation PUSH Outstanding Young Man award, Henry Booth House Outstanding Community Svc. award, Outstanding Bus. and Profl. Achievement award South End Jaycees, Chgo. Black United Communities Disting. Polit. Leadership award. Office: US Ho of Reps 131 Cannon Ho Office Bldg Washington DC 20515-1301*

RUSH, DAVID, medical investigator, epidemiologist; b. N.Y.C., May 3, 1934; s. Samuel Hersh and Fannie (Dubin) R.; m. Catharine Ireland Dawson, June 24, 1957; children: Naomi Rush Olson, Hannah M., Leah D. BA cum laude, Harvard U., 1955, MD, 1959. Diplomate Am. Bd. Pediatrics. Resident in medicine U. Ill. Hosp., Chgo., 1959-61; resident in pediatrics Children's Hosp., Boston, 1963-65; registrar in pediatrics St. Mary's Hosp. Med. Sch., London, 1964-65; rsch. fellow, Harvard U. Med. Sch., Boston, 1965-66; asst. prof. preventive medicine and pediatrics, U. Rochester (N.Y.), 1967-69; asst. prof. pub. health (epidemiology) and pediatrics Columbia U., N.Y.C., also dir. prenatal project, 1969-76, assoc. prof., 1976-82; prof. pediatrics, social medicine and ob-gyn Albert Einstein Coll. Medicine, Bronx, N.Y., 1983-88; dir. epidemiology program USDA, Human Nutrition Research Ctr. on Aging, prof. nutrition, community health, pediatrics Tufts U., Boston, 1988—; mem. human devel. and aging study sect. NIH, USPHS, 1982-86; prin. investigator nat. evaluation of spl. supplemental food program for women, infants and children U.S. Dept. Agr., 1981-86. Author: Diet in Pregnancy, 1980, Dead Reckoning, 1992; assoc. editor Medicine and Global Survival; mem. editorial bd. Am. Jour. Pub. Health; contbr. articles to profl. jours. Trustee, chmn. health services com. Children's Aid Soc., N.Y.C., 1971-86. Served as surgeon USPHS, 1961-63; capt. Res. Recipient career investigator award N.Y.C. Health Research Council, 1977; sr. internat. fellow Fogarty Ctr., NIH, USPHS, U. Bristol, Eng., 1977-78, U. Paris, 1984-85; research grantee Nat. Inst. Child and Human Devel., NIH, 1979-86. Fellow Am. Pub. Health Assn. (governing council 1976-79); mem. Soc. for Epidemiologic Research (pres. 1980-81), Soc. for Pediatric Research, Internat. Epidemiologic. Assn., Am. Epidemiol. Soc., Am. Pediatric Soc., Perinatal Research Soc., Am. Inst. of Nutrition, Am. Soc. Clin. Nutrition, Am. Coll. of Epidemiology. Office: Human Nutrition Rsch Ctr 711 Washington St Boston MA 02111-1524

RUSH, DOMENICA MARIE, health facilities administrator; b. Gallup, N.Mex., Apr. 10, 1937; d. Bernardo G. and Guadalupe (Milan) Iorio; m. W. E. Rush, Jan. 5, 1967. Diploma, Regina Sch. Nursing, Albuquerque, 1958. RN N.Mex.; lic. nursing home adminstr. Charge nurse, house supr. St. Joseph Hosp., Albuquerque, 1958-63; dir. nursing Cibola Hosp., Grants, 1960-64; supr. operating room, dir. med. seminars Carrie Tingley Crippled Children's Hosp., Truth or Consequences, N.Mex., 1964-73; adminstr. Sierra Vista Hosp., Truth or Consequences, 1974-88, pres., 1980-89; clin. nursing mgr. U. N.Mex. Hosp., 1989-90; adminstr. Nor-Lea Hosp., Lovington, N.Mex., 1990-94; with regional ops. divsn. Presbyn. Healthcare Svcs., Albuquerque, 1994—, regional ops., 1994—; adminstr. Sierra Vista Hosp., Truth or Consequences, N.Mex., 1995—; bd. dirs. N.Mex. Blue Cross/Blue Shield, 1977-88, chmn. hosp. relations com., 1983-85, exec. com. 1983—; bd. dirs. Region II Emergency Med. Svcs. Originating bd. SW Mental Health Ctr., Sierra County, N.Mex., 1975; chmn. Sierra County Personnel Bd., 1983—. Named Lea County Outstanding Woman, N.Mex. Commn. on Status of Women; Woman of Yr. for Lea County, N.Mex., 1993. Mem. Am. Coll. Health Care Adminstrs., Sierra County C. of C. (bd. dirs. 1972, 75-76, svc. award 1973, Businesswoman of the Yr. 1973-74), N.Mex. Hosp. Assn. (bd. dirs., sec.-treas., pres.-elect, com. chmn., 1977-88, pres. 1980-81, exec. com., 1980-83, 84-85, recipient meritorius svc. award 1988), N.Mex. So. Hosp. Coun. (sec. 1980-81, pres. 1981-82), Am. Hosp. Assn. (N.Mex. del. 1984-88, regional adv. bd. 1984-88). Republican. Roman Catholic. Avocations: raising thoroughbred horses, cooking. Home: 1100 N Riverside Truth or Consequence NM 87901 Office: 800 E 9th Truth or Consequence NM 87901

RUSH, FLETCHER GREY, JR., lawyer; b. Orlando, Fla., Dec. 28, 1917; s. Fletcher Grey and Elizabeth (Knox) R.; m. Lena Mae Willis, June 6, 1942; children: Patricia Rush White, Richard Fletcher. BSBA, JD with honors, U. Fla., 1942; LLD (hon.), Fla. So. Coll., 1975. Bar: Fla. 1942. Practice in Orlando, 1946—; pres. firm Rush, Marshall, Reber & Jones, P.A., 1957-91, of counsel, 1991—; Trustee Lawyers Title Guaranty Fund, 1953-65, chmn. bd., 1962-63, gen. counsel, 1968-90; v.p., dir., gen. counsel Orlando Fed. Savs. & Loan Assn., 1955-75; dir. Trust Co. Fla., 1974-82; mem. jud. nominating council Supreme Ct. Fla., 1972-73, jud. nominating commn., 1983-87. Contbr. articles to legal jours. Mem. Orlando Municipal Planning Bd., 1961-63; mem. Orlando Loch Haven Park Bd., 1973-81, vice chmn., 1978-81; bd. regents State Fla. Colls. and Univs., 1965; trustee Coll. Orlando, 1960-71, Fla. House, Inc., Washington, 1974-76, Fla. Supreme Ct. Hist. Soc., 1988-91; mem. president's council U. Fla., 1970—; v.p., exec. com. U. Fla. Found., 1973-75, bd. dirs., 1971-75; bd. dirs. Inst. for Study of Trial, Central Fla. U., 1978-80; mem. president's council Nat. Meth. Found., 1977-82. Served as officer F.A. AUS, 1942-46, ETO. Recipient Distinguished Service award Stetson U., 1967; Outstanding Alumnus award John Marshall Bar Assn. U. Fla. Coll. Law, 1971; Distinguished Alumnus award U. Fla., 1976. Fellow Am. Coll. Trust and Estate Counsel, Am. Bar Found., Fla. Bar Found.; mem. ABA (ho. of dels. 1967-85, adv. bd. jour. 1968-71, chmn. standing com. on legislation 1973-75, on lawyers title guaranty funds 1979-83), Orange County (Fla.) Bar Assn. (pres. 1960-61), Fla. Bar (bd. govs. 1959-67, pres. 1966-67), Am. Judicature Soc. (dir. 1968—, exec. com. 1972, treas. 1973-75, v.p. 1975-77, pres. 1977-79), U. Fla. Law Center Assn. (trustee, exec. com., chmn. bd. trustees 1973-75), Blue Key (pres. Fla. 1941), Phi Kappa Phi, Alpha Tau Omega, Phi Delta Phi. Republican. Methodist (chmn. ch. adminstrv. bd. 1961-63, 75-76, trustee 1968-74, 77-80, trustee Fla. Conf., 1973-76). Clubs: Country, Univ. (Orlando) Orange County Old Timers (pres. 1986-87). Lodge: Kiwanis (pres. North Orlando club 1954). Home: 1105 Edgewater Dr Orlando FL 32804-6311 Office: Rush Marshall Reber & Jones Magnolia Pl 5th Fl 109 E Church St Orlando FL 32801

RUSH, HERMAN E., television executive; b. Phila., June 20, 1929; s. Eugene and Bella (Sacks) R.; m. Joan Silberman, Mar. 18, 1951; children: James Harrison, Mandie Susan. BBA, Temple U., 1950. With Ofcl. Films, 1951-57; owner Flamingo Films, 1957-60; with Creative Mgmt. Assos., N.Y.C., 1960-71; pres. TV div. Creative Mgmt. Assos., 1964-71, exec. v.p. parent co., dir., 1964-71; ind. producer, 1971-75; producer Wolper Orgn., 1975-76; pres. Herman Rush Assos., Inc. (Rush-Flaherty Agy. subs.), 1977-78, Marble Arch TV, Los Angeles, 1979-80, Columbia Pictures TV, Burbank, Calif., 1980-87; chmn., chief exec. officer Coca-Cola Telecommunications, 1987-88, Rush Assocs., Inc., Burbank, 1988—, Katz/Rush Entertainment, Beverly Hills, Calif., 1990—; chmn. Entertainment Industries Council. Trustee Sugar Ray Robinson Youth Found., 1967-75; pres. Retarded Infant Services, N.Y.C., 1957-63; bd. dirs. U.S. Marshall's Service Found., Just Say No Found.; conferee White House Conf. for a Drug Free America, 1987, 88. Mem. Acad. TV Arts and Scis., Hollywood Radio and TV Soc., Producers Caucus. Clubs: Friars, Filmex. Office: Katz/Rush Entertainment 345 N Maple Dr Ste 205 Beverly Hills CA 90210-3827

RUSH, NORMAN, author; b. San Francisco, Oct. 24, 1933; s. Roger and Leslie (Chessé) R.; m. Elsa Scheidt, July 10, 1955; children: Jason, Liza. BA, Swarthmore Coll., 1956. Dealer antiquarian books, 1960-78; instr. English, history Rockland C.C., Suffern, N.Y., 1973-78; co-dir. Peace Corps, Botswana, 1978-83; freelance writer, 1983—. Author: Whites, 1986, Mating, 1991 (Nat. Book award for fiction 1991, Internat. Fiction prize Irish Times and Aer Lingus 1992). Mem. lit. com. War Resisters League, N.Y.C., 1985—; bd. dirs. A.J. Muste Inst., N.Y.C., 1988-92; sec. Rockland County, N.Y. chpt. Amnesty Internat., 1990—. Recipient Rosenthal award Nat. Acad. and Inst. Arts and Letters, 1987, Nat. Book award for fiction, 1991, internat. fiction prize Aer Lingus/Irish Times, 1992; fellow Nat. Endowment for Arts, 1986, Guggenheim fellow, 1987, Bellagio residency fellow Rockeller Found., 1990. Mem. PEN Am. Ctr.

RUSH, RICHARD HENRY, financier, writer, lecturer; b. N.Y.C., Mar. 6, 1915; s. Henry Frederick and Bessie (Vreeland) R.; m. Julia Ann Halloran, Aug. 15, 1956; 1 dau., Sallie Haywood. B.A. summa cum laude, Dartmouth Coll., 1937, M.C.S., 1938; M.B.A., Harvard U., 1941, D.C.S. (Littauer fellow), 1942. Dir. aviation U.S. Bur. Fgn. and Domestic Commerce, 1945-46; chief economist, chmn. planning com. All Am. Aviation (U.S. Air), 1943-45; dir. aircraft div. Nat. Security Resources Bd., 1948-51; Washington rep. to J. Paul Getty, 1951-52; partner Rush & Halloran (finance and ins.), 1953-58; pres., chmn. bd. N.Am. Acceptance Corp., Atlanta, also Washington, 1956-59; owner Richard H. Rush Enterprises, Greenwich, Conn., also Washington, 1953-73; prof., chmn. dept. finance and investments Sch. Bus. Adminstrn., Am. U., Washington, 1967-70, 77-79. Author: 12 books, including Art as an Investment, 1961, A Strategy of Investing for Higher Return, 1962, The Techniques of Becoming Wealthy, 1963, Antiques as an Investment, 1968, The Wrecking Operation: Phase One, 1972, Investments You Can Live With and Enjoy, 1976, Techniques of Becoming Wealthy, 1977, Automobiles as an Investment, 1982, Selling Collectibles, 1982, Collecting Classic Cars for Profit and Capital Gain, 1984; contbr. over 700 articles to newspapers, mags. and profl. jours.; editor series of books on starting businesses for U.S. Dept. Commerce; contbg. editor Wall St. Transcript, 1971—, Art/Antiques Investment Report, 1972—. Trustee, mem. exec. com. Finch Coll., 1968-72. Mem. Am. Mktg. Assn. (chmn. nat. com.), Am. Econ. Assn., Am. Statis. Assn., Internat. Platform Assn., AAUP, Harvard Club (N.Y.C.), BocaWest Club (Boca Raton), Royal Palm Yacht Club (Ft. Myers), Phi Beta Kappa, Phi Kappa Phi, Omicron Delta Kappa. Episcopalian. *Strive to your best, get the best education you can and the world will open up to you. Three graduate degrees opened the door to success for me, but to get the top education, all else must be put aside. Also know the reality and strength of good and keep your thought on positive goals.*

RUSH, RICHARD P., chamber of commerce executive; b. Chgo., Apr. 2, 1945; s. Frederick William and Virginia (Predmore) R.; m. Jennifer Amy Mosetick, Dec. 18, 1965; children: Jennette Marie, Dawn Essence, Adam Justin. BS in Communications, So. Ill. U., 1968. Cert. chamber exec. Entertainment editor Life Printing & Pub. Co., Berwyn, Ill., 1970-71; dir. nat. advtg. Fred Harvey, Inc., Brisbane, Calif., 1971-72; assoc. pub. Hudson Home Publs., Los Altos, Calif., 1972-73; asst. mgr. membership San Francisco C. of C., 1973-74; exec. v.p. San Rafael (Calif.) C. of C., 1974-77; dir. small bus. dept. Calif. C. of C., Sacramento, 1977-81; regional mgr. U.S. C. of C., Dallas, 1981-86; pres., chief exec. officer Okla. State C. of C. and Industry, Oklahoma City, 1986—; cons. Zimbabwe Nat. C. of C., Harare, 1985; vice chmn. Coun. State Cs. of C., Washington, 1986—; bd. mem. Am. C. of C. Execs., Alexandria, Va., 1988—, mem. ChamberNet, 1990—; mem. Okla. 2000, Oklahoma City, 1986—; mem. exec. com. Okla. Coun. on Econ. Edn., 1986—; bd. mem. Okla. Good Rds. and Sts. Assn., 1988—; chmn. state C. of C. task force U.S. C. of C., 1988—; mem. Okla. Congl. Econ. Devel. Task Force, 1988—. Contbr. numerous articles to profl. jours. Bd. mem. Okla. Alliance Against Drugs, Oklahoma City, 1989—; charter class mem. Leadership Okla., Oklahoma City, 1987-88; mem. interagy. coun. Okla. Futures, Oklahoma City, 1989; mem. exec. com. S.W. Ctr. for Human Rels. Studies, Norman, Okla., 1988—; mem. adv. bd. Keep Okla. Beautiful, 1988; mem. adv. com. Okla. Ctr. for Advancement of Sci. and Tech., 1989—. With U.S. Army, 1968-70. Decorated Bronze Star; recipient William E. Hammond award Calif. Assn. Chamber Execs., 1975; named resource person White House Conf. on Small Bus., 1980, adv. bd. mem. Ctr. for Internat. Trade Devel., 1988-90, del. head Gov.'s Internat. Team, 1988; Okla. State C. of C. and Industry named 1st accredited State C. of C. in nation while under his leadership by U.S. C. of C., 1990. Baha'i'. Avocations: parenting, pub. speaking, bowling, bridge, photography. Office: Okla State C of C Industry 330 NE 10th St Oklahoma City OK 73104-3220

RUSH, RICHARD R., academic administrator. Pres. Mankato (Minn.) U. Office: Mankato State U South Rd And Ellis Ave Mankato MN 56001

RUSH, WILLIAM JOHN, newspaper executive; b. Alliance, Ohio, Nov. 11, 1936; s. Serle Emmons and Doris Esther (Crider) R.; BA in Journalism, Ohio State U., 1958; m. Ruth Ann Lee, Feb. 29, 1972; children—Kayci, Wendy, Nathan, Jenny, Molly. Mgr., The Madison Press, London, Ohio, 1960-62; adv. mgr. Times Pub. Co., New Milford, Conn., 1962-65; asst. to pub. N.Adams (Mass.) Transcript, 1965-69; asst. to pub. Horvitz Newspapers, 1969-70; gen. mgr. Lake City (Ohio) News-Herald, 1970-72; v.p./gen. mgr. Times Record, Troy, N.Y., 1972-82; assoc. pub., v.p. Times Record and News Jour., Mansfield, Ohio, 1982-86; pub. Warren (Ohio) Tribune-Chronicle, 1986-89, Lorain (Ohio) Morning Jour., 1989-90; pub., chief exec. New Haven (Conn.) Register, 1990—; v.p. Jour. Register Co., 1995—. Bd. dirs. Long Wharf Theater, Conn. Policy and Econ. Coun., Inc., Regional Leadership Coun., United Way; bd. govs. U. New Haven. Mem. Conn. Daily Newspaper Assn. (v.p.), Nat. Co. Mil. Historians, Gateway C. C. Found., Habitat for Humanity, Pine Orchard Yacht and Country Club, Quinnipiac Club, Ohio State U. Alumni Assn., Hon. Order of Ky. Cols., Masons, Shriners, Elks, Theta Chi. Episcopalian. Office: New Haven Register Inc Long Wharf 40 Sargent Dr New Haven CT 06511-5918

RUSHER, WILLIAM ALLEN, writer, commentator; b. Chgo., July 19, 1923; s. Evan Singleton and Verna (Self) R. AB, Princeton, 1943; JD, Harvard U., 1948; DLit (hon.), Nathaniel Hawthorne Coll., 1973. Bar: N.Y. bar 1949. Assoc. Shearman & Sterling & Wright, N.Y.C., 1948-56; spl. counsel fin. com. N.Y. Senate, 1955; assoc. counsel internal security subcom. U.S. Senate, 1956-57; pub., v.p. Nat. Review mag., N.Y.C., 1957-88, also bd. dirs.; Disting. fellow The Claremont Inst, 1989—; mem. Adv. Task Force on Civil Disorders, 1972. Author: Special Counsel, 1968, (with Mark Hatfield and Arlie Schardt) Amnesty?, 1973, The Making of the New Majority Party, 1975, How to Win Arguments, 1981, The Rise of the Right, 1984, The Coming Battle for the Media, 1988; editor: The Ambiguous Legacy of the Enlightenment, 1995; columnist Universal Press Syndicate, 1973-82, Newspaper Enterprise Assn., 1982—; played role of Advocate in TV program The Advocates, 1970-73. Bd. dirs. Media Rsch. Ctr., Washington; chmn. bd. advisors Ashbrook Ctr., Ashland, Ohio; past vice chmn. Am. Conservative Union; past trustee Pacific Legal Found., Sacramento; trustee, treas. Wilbur Found., Santa Barbara. Recipient Disting. Citizen award NYU Sch. Law, 1973. Mem. ABA, U. Club (N.Y.C. and San Francisco), Met. Club (Washington). Anglican. Home and Office: 850 Powell St San Francisco CA 94108-2051

RUSHING, BYRON DOUGLAS, state legislator; b. N.Y.C., July 29, 1942; s. William and Linda (Turpin) R.; (div. 1972); 1 child: Osula Evadne. AA (hon.), Roxbury (Mass.) Community Coll, 1989; DD (hon.), Episcopal Divinity Sch., 1994. Pres. Mus. Afro Am. History, Boston, 1972-85; state rep. Commonwealth of Mass., Boston, 1983—, chair ins., vice chair redistricting, 1993—; former chair Com. on Local Affairs, Com. on Counties, chair pub. svc. com.; mem. Congl. Redistricting com. Active St. John's St. James's Parish, Roxbury, Mass.; past pres. Episc. Urban Caucus, Episc. City Mission; mem. standing com. Diocese of Mass.; lay dep. to gen. conf. Episc. Ch., 1973—; chaplain Ho. of Deps., 1994; former mem. program, budget and fin. com., com. on status of women Epis. Div. Sch., Cambridge, Mass., mem. planning and arrangements com.; lectr. in studies in contemporary soc. Mem. ACLU of Mass. (bd. dirs.), Roxbury Hist. Soc. (pres. 1969—), Roxbury Heritage State Park Adv. Bd. (vice chmn.), Environ. Diversity Forum (bd. dirs.). Episcopalian. Office: Mass House Reps State House Boston MA 02133

RUSHING, JANE GILMORE, writer; b. Pyron, Tex., Nov. 15, 1925; d. Clyde Preston and Mabel Irene (Adams) Gilmore; m. James Arthur Rushing, Nov. 29, 1956; 1 son, James Arthur. BA, Tex. Tech U., 1944, MA, 1945, PhD, 1957. Reporter Abilene (Tex.) Reporter-News, 1946-47; tchr. Tex. high schs., 1947-54; instr. U. Tenn., 1957-59; instr. to asst. prof. Tex. Tech U., intermittently, 1959-68. Author: Walnut Grove, 1964, Against the Moon, 1968, Tamzen, 1972, Mary Dove, 1974, The Raincrow, 1977, Covenant of Grace, 1982, Winds of Blame, 1983, Starting from Pyron, 1992; co-author (with Kline A. Nall) Evolution of a University, Texas Tech's First Fifty Years, 1975. Vassie James Hill fellow of AAUW, 1956-57; recipient Emily Clark Balch prize, 1961; LeBaron R. Barker, Jr., Fiction award, 1975; Tex. Lit. award for fiction, 1984. Mem. Tex. Inst. Letters. Methodist. Home: 3809 39th St Lubbock TX 79413-2521

RUSHMORE, STEPHEN, hotel consulting and appraisal specialist; b. Glen Cove, N.Y., Mar. 18, 1945; s. Leon A. and Caroline (Jackson) R.; m. Judith Ruth Kellner, June 10, 1967; children: Cynthia Ruth, Stephen Jr. BA, Cornell U., 1967; MBA, U. Buffalo, 1971. Lic. real estate broker; cert. gen. appraiser. Active real estate Helmsley-Spear Hospitality Svcs., Inc., N.Y.C., 1971-74, 77-80; appraiser, active hotel operations, mortgage banking James E. Gibbons Assocs., Garden City, N.Y., 1974-77; hotel/motel valuations and investment counselor Hospitality Valuation Svcs. (divsn. Hotel Appraisals, Inc.), Mineola, N.Y., 1980—; appraiser, evaluator hotels and motels throughout U.S. and world; affiliated ownership interest includes Hospitality Valuation Svcs., San Francisco, Miami, Fla., Vancouver, Can., London, Hospitality Equity Investors, Inc., Trumbull Marriott Hotel, Princeton (N.J.) Hotel Assocs., Seaview Golf Resort Assocs., Abescon, N.J., Shelton (Conn.) Hotel Assocs., Danbury (Conn.) Hotel Assocs., Prudential-Hei Joint Venture, Atlanta, Delaware Hotel Assocs., Wilmington, Del., Hospitality Valuation Software, Inc., HVS Eco Svcs., HVS Exec. Search; adj. asst. prof. real estate NYU; hon. faculty Mich. State U.; lectr. in field. Author: (textbooks) The Valuation of Hotels and Motels, 1978, Hotels, Motels and Restaurants: Valuations and Market Studies, 1983, How to Perform an Economic Feasibility Study of a Proposed Hotel/Motel, 1986, Hotel Investments: A Guide for Owners and Lender, 1990, supplement, 1992, 93, The Computerized Income Approach to Hotel Market Studies and Valuations, 1990, Hotels and Motels: A Guide to Market Analysis and Investment Analysis and Valuations, 1992; author manuals and chpts. to books; contbr. articles to profl. jours. Mem. adv. bd. NYU Master's in Hospitality Mgmt. Mem. Am. Soc. Real Estate Investors (bd. govs.), Am. Hotel and Motel

Assn. (mem. industry real estate financing adv. coun., cert. hotel adminstr.), Am. Arbitration Assn. (mem. nat. real estate valuation coun.), Appraisal Inst. (devel., instr. hotel investment and valuation seminar, hotel computer valuation seminar), Internat. Soc. Hospitality Cons., Foodservice Cons. Soc. Internat., Cornell Soc. Hotelmen, Beta Gamma Sigma. Avocations: comml. pilot, instrument, multi-engine; sailing, skiing. Office: Hospitality Valuation Services 372 Willis Ave Mineola NY 11501-1818*

RUSHNELL, SQUIRE DERRICK, television executive; b. Adams Center, N.Y., Oct. 31, 1938; s. Reginald Grant and Erica Mifanwy Redwood Sedgemore (Squire) R.; m. Jinny Schreckinger, Feb. 29, 1980; 1 child, Squire Grant Sedgemore; children by previous marriage: Robin Tracy, Hilary Adair. Ed., Syracuse U., 1956-60. Disc jockey Stas. WOLF, WHEN and WFBL, Syracuse, N.Y., 1958-61, Sta. WTRL, Bradenton, B, 1961-62; exec. prodr. Sta. WBZ AM-TV, Boston, 1962-67; program dir. KYW News-Radio, Phila., 1968; exec. prodr. Kennedy & Co. Sta. WLS-TV, Chgo., 1969-71, program dir., 1971-73; v.p. programs ABC-owned TV stas., N.Y.C., 1973-74; v.p. children's TV ABC Entertainment Network, N.Y.C., 1974-78; v.p. Good Morning Am. and children's programs ABC-TV Network, N.Y.C., 1978-81, v.p. long range planning and children's TV, 1981-87; v.p. late night and children's TV ABC Entertainment, N.Y.C., 1987-89; pres. Rushnell Co., 1990-92, Rushnell Comm. & Pub., Inc., 1993—. Author: The Kingdom Chums Greatest Stories, 1986, Read to Me, Sing to Me Stories, 1993; co-author: Broadcast Programming, 1981, Broadcast/Cable Programming, 1985, rev. edit., 1989, 93. Recipient Emmy awards, 1975-88, TV Critics Circle award, 1976, all for outstanding children's TV programming, Am. Children's TV Festival award, 1985, 87. Mem. NATAS, Nat. Acad. Arts and Scis., Internat. Radio and TV Soc., Action for Children's TV (award for outstanding children's TV programming). Office: Rushnell Comm & Pub Inc 640 Fifth Ave 5th FL New York NY 10019-6102

RUSHTON, BRIAN MANDEL, chemical company executive; b. Sale, Cheshire, Eng., Nov. 16, 1933; came to U.S., 1957; s. Ronald Henry and Edith (Slater) Riley; m. Jean Wrigley, Apr. 1, 1958; children: Jacqueline, Lisa, Amy. A.R.I.C. in Chemistry, U. Salford, Eng., 1957; M.S. in Phys. Organic Chemistry, U. Minn., 1959; Ph.D. in Phys. Organic Chemistry, U. Leicester, Eng., 1963; postgrad. Sr. Exec. program, MIT, 1972. Prodn. mgr. trainee 3M Co. U.K., 1959-60; sr. research chemist Petrolite Corp., 1963-65, group leader, 1965-66; sect. mgr. Ashland Chem. Co., 1966-69; corp. research mgr. Hooker Chem. Corp. subs. Occidental Petroleum, 1969-72, dir. polymer and plastics research and devel., 1972-74, v.p. research and devel. chem. and plastics div., 1974-75; pres. Celanese Research Corp., 1975-80; corp. v.p. tech. Celanese Corp.; also pres. Celanese Research Corp., 1980-81; v.p. research and devel. Air Products & Chem., Inc., Allentown, Pa., 1981-92, sr. v.p. rsch. and devel., 1992-94; pres., mem. exec. com., bd. dirs. Indsl. Rsch. Inst., 1990-94, chmn. plans and policies com., 1988-90; bd. dirs. Mallinckrodt, Inc., Petrolite Corp., Inc.; mem. chem. vis. com. Lehigh U., 1992—; mem. exec. master sci.-in-engring. adv. coun. U. Pa., 1992-94. Contbr. articles to profl. jours.; patentee in field. Mem. life scis., vis. com. Lehigh U., chmn. surface sci. vis. com., 1983-86; bd. dirs. WLVT Channel 39, Bethlehem, Pa., 1992-95; trustee Summit YMCA, N.J., 1976-79; mem. nat. materials bd. NRC, 1980-84. Mem. Coun. Chem. Rsch. (dir., treas.), Am. Chem. Soc. (pres.-elect 1994, pres. 1995), Soc. Chem. Industry, Am. Mgmt. Assn., Saucon Valley Country Club. Episcopalian. Home: 3366 Bingen Rd Bethlehem PA 18015-5715

RUSHTON, WILLIAM JAMES, III, insurance company executive; b. Birmingham, Ala., Apr. 23, 1929; s. William James and Elizabeth (Perry) R.; m. LaVona Price, Aug. 19, 1955; children: William James IV, Deakins Ford, Tunstall Perry. B.A. magna cum laude, Princeton U., 1951; LL.D. (hon.), Birmingham So. Coll., 1981. Asso. actuary Protective Life Ins. Co., Birmingham, Ala., 1954-59; dir. Protective Life Ins. Co., 1956—, agt., 1959-62, v.p., 1962-63, agy. v.p., 1963-67, pres., from 1967, pres., chief exec. officer, 1969-82, chmn., 1982—; pres. Protective Life Corp., Birmingham, 1981-82, CEO, chmn., 1982-92, chmn., 1992—; dir. Ala. Power Co., The Southern Co., Amsouth Bank N.A., Amsouth Bancorp. Trustee So. Rsch. Inst., Children's Hosp., Birmingham So. Coll., Highland Day Sch.; mem., deacon 1 st Presbyn. Ch., Birmingham, chmn. bd. deacons, 1960—; chmn. United Way campaign, 1977, pres., 1986, life mem., 1993; chmn. Leadership Birmingham, United Appeal, Indsl. Health Coun.; mem. adv. com. Meyer Found., Greater Birmingham Found. Capt. arty., U.S. Army, Korea. Decorated Bronze Star; named to Ala. Acad. of Honors, 1979; recipient Disting. Eagle Scout award Boy Scouts Am., 1980, Brotherhood award NCCJ, 1990. Fellow Soc. Actuaries; mem. Am. Council Life Ins. (dir.), Am. Life Conv. (state v.p. 1975), Am. Life Ins. Assn. (Ala. v.p. 1975), Health Ins. Assn. Am. (dir. from 1982), Million Dollar Round Table, Birmingham C. of C. (dir.). Clubs: Rotary (bd. dirs. 1973-74, treas. 1978-79, pres. 1988-89), Mountain Brook Country, Summit, Birmingham Country, The Club, Redstone. Office: Protective Life Corp 2801 Highway 280 S Birmingham AL 35223-2407*

RUSIN, EDWARD A., banker; b. Fenton, Mich., June 10, 1922; s. Andrew Stephen and Anna Maria (Kostka) R.; m. Virginia Ruth Ware, May 14, 1953; children: Gregory, Stephen, Valerie, Lisa, Tracey. Student, Ohio Wesleyan U. and Carroll Coll., 1942; BA, Mich. State U., 1948, MA, 1955. With Citizens Comml. Bank and Trust, Flint, Mich., 1953-55; examiner Fed. Res. Bank of Chgo., 1955-60; rev. examiner Fed. Res. Bd. Govs., Washington, 1961-62; pres., chmn. Mich. Nat. Bank-North Metro, Troy, 1962-87; chmn. Mich. Nat. Bank-Sterling, Sterling Heights, Mich., 1980-87, Mich. Nat. Bank-Macomb, Warren, Mich., 1985-87; sr. v.p. Mich. Nat. Corp., Farmington Hills, 1987-88. Mem. Troy Master Plan Commn., 1963; pres., founder Troy C. of C., 1964-65; chmn. Troy Comml./Indsl. Devel. Commn., 1963-65; bd. dirs. Oakland County Traffic Safety Com., Pontiac, Mich., 1975-86, P.I.M.E. Missionaries, Detroit, 1968-95. Served with U.S. Naval Air Corps, 1942-45, PTO. Recipient Toppers award Detroit area Boy Scouts Am., 1964, Troy Sesquicentennial Commn. award, 1971, Outstanding Svc. award Troy C. of C., 1984; named Outstanding Citizen of Troy, 1993. Mem. Red Run Golf club (Royal Oak, Mich.), Stoneybrook Golf and Country Club (Sarasota, Fla.). Republican. Roman Catholic. Avocations: golf, collecting classic golf clubs, fishing, swimming. Home (summer): 912 Robinhood Rd Bloomfield Hills MI 48304-3760 also (winter): Villas of Deer Creek 4420 Deer Trail Blvd Sarasota FL 34238

RUSINKO, FRANK, JR., fuels and materials scientist; b. Nanticoke, Pa., Oct. 12, 1930; s. Frank Sr. and Eva (Ruduski) R.; m. Lucy Geryak, June 1, 1957; children: Nancy, Lawrence. BS, Pa. State U., 1952, MS, 1954, PhD, 1958. Vice-pres., tech. dir. Airco Carbon, St. Mary's, Pa., 1959-76; pres. Electrotools Inc., Broadview, Ill., 1976-89, Intech EDM Electrotools, Broadview, Ill., 1989-91; sr. scientist, dir. Carbon Rsch. Ctr. Pa. State U., University Park, 1991—; dir. Anthracite Inst., dir. coop. program in coal rsch. Carbon Rsch. Ctr., Pa. State U., University Park, 1991—; bd. dirs., bd. chmn. transor Filter USA, Elk Grove Village, Ill., C-Cor Electronics State Coll., Pa.; cons. in field, 1996—. Contbr. articles to profl. jours. Mem. Hinsdale (Ill.) Plan Commn., 1986; mem. Region Campaign Pa. State U., 1989; pres. Sch. Bd. Edn., St. Marys, Pa., 1965-76. Fellow Pa. State Alumni Assn. (indsl. cons.); mem. Am. Chem. Soc., Am. Carbon Soc., N.Y. Acad. Sci., Sigma Xi. Orthodox. Home: 2392 Pine Hurst Dr State College PA 16803-3385 Office: Pa State U Carbon Rsch Ctr C204 Coal Utilization Lab University Park PA 16802

RUSKIN, JOSEPH RICHARD, actor, director; b. Haverhill, Mass., Apr. 14, 1924; s. Ely and Betty Edith (Chaimson) Schlafman; m. Barbara Greene; 1 child, Alicia. Grad., Carnegie Inst. Tech., 1949. Founder Rochester (N.Y.) Arena Theatre, 1949-52. Actor N.Y. stage plays, 1952-58, Theatre Group, UCLA, Mark Taper Forum, 1959—, (films) Fall of Legs Diamond, 1959, Magnificient Seven, 1960, Escape from Zahrein, 1963, Robin and the Seven Hoods, 1965, Prizzi's Honor, 1985, Longshot, 1987, regular appearances various TV programs, 1952—; dir. Houston Alley, 1965-69; freelance dir., 1969—. Served with USNR, 1943-46. Mem. AFTRA, SAG (nat. bd. dirs.), Actors Equity Assn. (nat. coun.). Home: 1326 Devon Ave Los Angeles CA 90024-5346

RUSMISEL, STEPHEN R., lawyer; b. N.Y.C., Jan. 27, 1946; s. R. Raymond and Esther Florence (Kutz) R.; m. Beirne Donaldson, Sept. 6, 1980 (div. Jan. 1984); 1 child, Margo Alexander; m. Melissa J. MacLeod, Aug. 24, 1985; children: Benjamin William, Eric Scot Kunze, Erin Lea Kunze. AB, Yale U., 1968; JD, U. Va., 1971. Bar: N.Y. 1972, U.S. Ct. Appeals (2d cir.) 1974, U.S. Dist. Ct. (so. dist.) N.Y. 1975. Assoc. Winthrop, Stimson, Putnam & Roberts, N.Y.C., 1971-80, ptnr., 1980—. Aux. officer Bedminster Twp. (N.J.) Police, 1976—. Mem. Practicing Law Inst., Am. Arbitration Assn. (arbitrator 1976—), Far Hills Polo Club (Annandale, N.J.), Ausable Club (St. Huberts, N.Y.), Phi Delta Phi. Republican. Avocations: polo, flying, carpentry, gardening, poetry. Home: Shadowline Farm Bedminster NJ 07921 Office: Winthrop Stimson Putnam & Roberts One Battery Park Plz New York NY 10004-1490

RUSNAK, MICHAEL, bishop; b. Beaverdale, Pa., Aug. 21, 1921; arrived in Can., 1951; s. Andrew and Maria (Sotak) R. Student, Slovak U. Bratislava, Oberište. Ordained priest Slovak Cath. Byzantine Rite Ch., 1949, joined Redemptorist Fathers, 1949. Founder Maria publ., 1953; dean Slovak parishes Byzantine Rite, Ukrainian Eparchy Toronto, Can., 1957; apptd. titular bishop Diocese of Cernik, 1964; apptd. apostolic visitator for Slovak Caths. of Byzantine Rite in Can., 1964, consecrated bishop, 1965; named eparch Diocese of Sts. Cyril and Methodius, Slovak Byzantine Cath. Eparchy in N.Am., Can., 1980. Address: Slovak Cath Ch in Can, 223 Carlton Rd, Unionville, ON Canada L3R 2L8

RUSS, CHARLES PAUL, III, lawyer, corporate executive; b. N.Y.C., Aug. 24, 1944; s. Charles Paul Jr. and Dorothea (von Frieling) R.; m. Dianne P. McLaughlin, June 24, 1969; children: Alexander Peter, Andrew William. B.A., Amherst Coll., 1966; J.D., Columbia U., 1969. Bar: N.Y. 1970, Ga. 1973. Assoc. Sullivan & Cromwell, N.Y.C., 1969-72; assoc. Gambrell & Mobley, Atlanta, 1972-74, ptnr., 1974; sr. atty. Stauffer Chem. Co., Westport, Conn., 1975-78; asst. gen. counsel Geo Internat. Corp., Stamford, Conn., 1978-80, v.p., gen. counsel, 1980-84; v.p., sec., gen. counsel NCR Corp., Dayton, Ohio, 1984-92; exec. v.p., sec., gen. counsel U.S. West, Inc., Englewood, CO, 1992—. Harlan Fiske Stone scholar Columbia U., 1969. Mem. ABA, Am. Corp. Counsel Assn., Ohio State Bar Assn., Assn. Gen. Counsel. Clubs: Dayton Country, Miami Valley Hunt and Polo, NCR Country, Seabrook Island Ocean. Home: 88 Glenmoor Pl Englewood CO 80110-7122 Office: US West Inc 7800 E Orchard Rd Ste 200 Englewood CO 80111-2533*

RUSS, JOANNA, writer, English language educator; b. N.Y.C., Feb. 22, 1937; d. Everett and Bertha (Zinner) R. B.A. in English with high honors, Cornell, U., 1957; M.F.A. in Playwriting and Dramatic Lit, Yale U., 1960. Lectr. in English Cornell U., 1967-70, asst. prof., 1970-72; asst. prof. English, Harpur Coll., State U. N.Y. at Binghamton, 1972-75, U. Colo., 1975-77; asso. prof. English, U. Wash., 1977-90, prof., 1984-90. Author: Picnic on Paradise, 1968, And Chaos Died, 1970, The Female Man, 1975, We Who Are About To, 1977, Kittatinny: A Tale of Magic, 1978, The Two of Them, 1978, On Strike Against God, 1980, The Adventures of Alyx, 1983, The Zanzibar Cat, 1983, How To Suppress Women's Writing, 1983, Extra (Ordinary) People, 1984, Magic Mommas, Trembling Sisters, Puritans and Perverts: Feminist Essays, 1985, The Hidden Side of the Moon, 1987; also numerous short stories. Mem. Sci. Fiction Writers Am. (Nebula award for best short story 1972, Hugo award for best novella 1983). Address: 8961 E Lester St Tucson AZ 85715-5568

RUSSEL, RICHARD ALLEN, telecommunications consultant, aerospace engineer, nuclear engineer, electrical engineer, retired naval officer; b. Shreveport, La., Jan. 24, 1958; s. Robert Lee and Gloria Jeanette (Gile) R.; m. Kathryn Joy Koehler, Dec. 30, 1983; children: Richard Allen Russel Jr., Kammie Joyce Jeanette, Jonathan Mark, Katie Jacqueline Keala, Stephen Sungmin. BSEE, U. N.Mex., 1980; MS Astronautics, Aero./Astro. Engring., Naval Postgrad. Sch., Monterey, Calif., 1994, postgrad., 1994. Commd. ensign, nuclear submarine officer USN, 1980, advanced through grades to lt. comdr., 1990; main propulsion analyst USS Puffer, Pearl Harbor, Hawaii, 1981-85; antisubmarine analyst, nuclear engr., comdr. 3d fleet USN, Pearl Harbor, 1985-87; combat systems officer USS TAUTUG, Pearl Harbor, 1987-89; navigator, ops. officer USS Indpls., Pearl Harbor, 1989-92; UHF/EHF satellite navy rep. PEO-SCS USN, El Segundo, Calif., 1994-96; project mgr. for spacecraft comms. Boaz-Allen and Hamilton, Inc., San Diego, 1996—. Contbr. articles to profl. jours. Sch. bd. mem. Our Savior Luth. Sch., Aiea, Hawaii, 1986; den leader webelos Boy Scouts Am., 1995—. Fellow Inst. for the Advancement of Engring.; assoc. fellow AIAA (vice-chair edn. L.A. sect. 1991—, dep. dir. edn. region VI 1994—); mem. Space Nuclear Thermal Propulsion, Eta Kappa Nu. Republican. Lutheran. Achievements include design of predictive control system for thermoacoustic refrigerator, 3D laser range and orientation measuring system, navy satellite/computer secure communications systems. Home: 7405 Andasol St San Diego CA 92126

RUSSELL, ALLAN DAVID, lawyer; b. Cleve., May 6, 1924; s. Allan MacGillivray and Marvel (Codling) R.; m. Lois Anne Robinson, June 12, 1947; children: Lisa Anne, Robinson David, Martha Leslie. B.A., Yale U., 1945, LL.B., 1951. Bar: N.Y. 1952, Conn. 1956, Mass. 1969, U.S. Supreme Ct. 1977. Atty. Sylvania Electric Products, Inc., N.Y.C., 1951-56; div. counsel Sylvania Electric Products, Inc., Batavia, N.Y., 1956-65; sr. counsel Sylvania Electric Products, Inc., 1965-71; sec., sr. counsel GTE Sylvania Inc., Stamford, Conn., 1971-76; asst. gen. counsel GTE Service Corp., 1976-80, v.p., assoc. gen. counsel staff, 1980-83; sole practice law Redding, Conn., 1983—; sec., dir. mktg. subs. Sylvania Entertainment Products Corp., 1961-67; sec. Wilbur B. Driver Co. Dist. leader Rep. Party, New Canaan, Conn., 1955-56; sec. bd. dirs. Youth Found., Inc., 19812-83, bd. dirs., 1985—; mem. planning commn., Redding, Conn., 1987-89; mem. Redding Bd. Ethics, 1990—, chmn., 1992—; warden Christ Ch. Parish, Redding, 1987-89; bd. dirs. Mark Twain Libr., 1988-94, v.p., 1988-89, pres., 1990-92. With USAAF, 1943-46. Mem. SAR, Assn. of Bar of City of N.Y., Conn. Bar Assn. (exec. com. corp. counsel sect. 1986-90), Am. Soc. Corp. Secs., St. Nicholas Soc., Collie Club Am. Found., Inc. (v.p., dir. 1986-89, pres. 1989-90), Soc. Colonial Wars, Yale Alumni Assn. (sec. local chpt. 1953-56), Yale Club of Danbury (pres. 1990—), Phi Delta Phi. Home: 9 Little River Ln Redding CT 06896-2018

RUSSELL, ALLEN STEVENSON, retired aluminum company executive; b. Bedford, Pa., May 27, 1915; s. Arthur Stainton and Ruth (Stevenson) R.; m. Judith Pauline Sexauer, Apr. 5, 1941. B.S., Pa. State U., 1936, M.S., 1937, Ph.D., 1941. With Aluminum Co. Am., 1940-82, assoc. dir. research, 1973-74; v.p. Alcoa, Pa., 1974-78; v.p. sci. and tech. Pitts., 1978-81, v.p., chief scientist, 1981-82; adj. prof. U. Pitts., 1981-86. Contbr. articles to profl. jours. Named IR-100 Scientist of Yr., 1979; Pa. State U. alumni fellow, 1980; K.J. Bayer medalist, 1981; recipient chem. Pioneer award Am. Inst. Chemists, 1983. Fellow Am. Soc. Metals (Gold medal 1982), AIME (James Douglas gold medal 1987), Am. Inst. Chemists; mem. NAE (coun. 1978-84), Am. Chem. Soc., Sigma Xi. Republican. Presbyterian. Patentee in field. Home: 9 N Calibogue Cay Rd Sea Pines Plantation Hilton Head Island SC 29928

RUSSELL, ANDREW GEORGE ALEXANDER, author, naturalist; b. Lethbridge, Alta., Can., Dec. 8, 1915; s. Harold George and Lorenda Scarlett (McTavish) R.; m. Anna Kathleen Riggall, Nov. 1, 1936; children: Richard, Charles, John, Gordon, Anne. Grad. high sch., Lethbridge; LLD (hon.), U. Lethbridge, 1978, U. Calgary, Alta., 1978. Rocky Mountain guide, author, photographer, cinematographer, Alta., 1936—, rancher, lectr., 1936—. Author: Grizzy Country, 1964, Trails of a Wilderness Wanderer, 1971, Horns in the High Country, 1973, The High West, 1974, The Rockies, 1975, Wild Animals, 1977, Men of the Saddle, 1978, Alpine Canada, 1979, Memoirs of a Mountain Man, 1984, Life of a River, 1987, The Canadian Cowboy, 1993; contbr. articles to mags.; columnist; prodr. 3 feature films; writer radio scripts. Liberal candidate for Parliament, 1972. Decorated Order of Can.; recipient commemorative medal Confedn. of Can., 1992. Mem. Explorers Club. Avocations: fly fishing, target shooting, corresponding. Office: Box 68, Waterton Lakes Park, AB Canada T0K 2M0

RUSSELL, ANDREW MILO, music educator; b. Fredericksburg, Tex., July 16, 1948; s. Daniel Louden and Evelyn Sarah (Allen) R.; m. Sharon Anne Shelburne, June 2, 1968 (div. June 1994); children: Emily Christine, Andrea Layne, Dana Leslie. MusB, U. Houston, 1974; performance cert., Ind. U., 1974; MusM, Ind. U., Bloomington, 1975. Asst. prof. Baylor U., Waco, Tex., 1975-79; assoc. prof. U. Tex., Arlington, 1979—; cons. Tex. Commn. on Arts, Austin, 1985—. Performer numerous concerts, recitals nationwide, 1968--. E-5 with U.S. Army, 1971-74. Mem. Internat. Trombone Assn. (Emory B. Remington award), Am. Fedn. Musicians, Tex. Music Educators Assn., Chgo. Chamber Brass. Democrat. Baptist. Home: 1213 Scott Dr Hurst TX 76053-4223 Office: U Tex PO Box 19105 Arlington TX 76019

RUSSELL, ATTIE YVONNE, academic administrator, dean, pediatrics educator; b. Washington, Aug. 10, 1923; d. George and Kathleen L. (Milliner) Werner; m. Rex Hillier, Apr. 19, 1954 (dec.); m. Henry J. Russell, 1960 (div. 1971); children: Richard Russell, Margaret Jane Russell-Harde; m. Harry F. Camper, Sept. 2, 1984. BS, Am. U., 1944; PhD, State U. Iowa, 1952; MD, U. Chgo., 1958. Intern Phila. Gen. Hosp., 1958-59; resident in pediatrics Bronx (N.Y.) Mcpl. Hosp., 1960-61, Del. Hosp., Wilmington, 1962-63; dir. maternal and child health, crippled children's svcs. Del. State Bd. Health, Dover, 1963-68; asst. dean community health affairs, assoc. prof. pediatrics U. Cin. Coll. Medicine, 1968-71; clin. assoc. prof. pediatrics Med. Coll. Pa., Phila., 1966-68, 71-74; dep. dir. div. pub. health State of Del., Dover, 1971-74; dir. Santa Clara Valley Med. Ctr., San Jose, Calif., 1974-79; assoc. dean, clin. prof. pediatrics, family medicine Stanford (Calif.) U. Sch. Medicine, 1974-79; dir. USPHS Hosp., Boston, 1979-81, Balt. City Hosps., 1981-82; asst. v.p. community affairs, prof. pediatrics U. Tex. Med. Br., Galveston, 1982-87, asst. v.p. student affairs, dean students, prof. pediatrics, 1987-92, clin. prof. pediatrics, 1992—; reviewer Coun. for Internat. Exchange of Scholars, Washington, 1987-94; dir. III Symposium on Health and Human Svcs. in the U.S.-Mex., Brownsville, 1988; mem. sci. coun. Am. Fedn. for Aging Rsch., Inc., 1983-86. Contbr. articles and abstracts to profl. jours. Mem. budget com. United Way, Galveston, 1982-84; mem. Mayor's Adv. Com. for Sr. Citizens and Handicapped Persons for the City of Galveston, 1983-85; bd. dirs. Galveston County Coordinated Community Clinics, 1983-87; bd. advisors Galveston Hist. Found., 1983-88; mem. Com. for Coop. Action Planning, 1983-88, Houston-Galveston Health Promotion Consortium, 1983-88, Injury Control Prevention (Houston), 1984-89, aging programs adv. com. Houston-Galveston Area Coun., 1985-92. Recipient Disting. Alumni award Am. U., 1984. Fellow Am. Acad. Pediatrics, Am. Pub. Health Assn.; mem. AMA, Am. Coll. Preventive Medicine, Soc. for Adolescent Medicine, Am. Physiol. Soc., Am. Fedn. for Aging Rsch., Am. Geriatrics Soc., Mass. State Med. Soc., Galveston Med. Soc., Tex. Med. Assn., Tex. Pediatric Soc., Galveston C. of C. (legis. com. 1983-88), Order of Eastern Star, Sigma Xi, Alpha Omega Alpha.

RUSSELL, BILL, former professional basketball team executive, former professional basketball player; b. Monroe, La., Feb. 12, 1934. Grad., San Francisco State Coll., 1956. Player, NBA Boston Celtics Profl. Basketball Club, 1956-69, coach, 1966-69; sportscaster ABC-TV, 1969-80, CBS-TV, 1980-83; coach NBA Seattle Supersonics, 1973-77; coach NBA Sacramento Kings, 1987-88, v.p. basketball ops., then exec. v.p., 1988-89; mem. U.S. Olympic Basketball Team (Gold medal), 1956. Appeared in: TV series Cowboy in Africa; also commls.; co-host: The Superstars, ABC-TV, 1978-79; Author: Second Wind: Memoirs of an Opinionated Man, 1979. Inducted into Basketball Hall of Fame, 1974; mem. 11 NBA championship teams.

RUSSELL, CAROL ANN, personnel service company executive; b. Detroit, Dec. 14, 1943; d. Billy and Iris Koud; m. Victor Rojas (div.). BA in English, CUNY-Hunter Coll., 1993. Registered employment cons. Various positions in temp. help cos. N.Y.C., 1964-74; v.p. Wollborg-Michelson, San Francisco, 1974-82; co-owner, pres. Russell Staffing Resources, Inc., San Francisco and Sonoma, 1983—; media guest, spkr., workshop and seminar leader in field; host/cmty. prodr. Job Net program for Viacom Cable T.V.; pres. bd. Russell Ctr. for Career Skills. Pub. Checkpoint Newsletter; contbr. articles to profl. publs. Named to the Inc. 500, 1989, 90. Mem. Am. Women in Radio & TV, Soc. to Preserve and Encourage Radio Drama Variety and Comedy, No. Calif. Human Resources Coun., Soc. Human Resource Mgmt., Calif. Assn. Pers. Cons. (pres. Golden State chpt. 1984-85), Calif. Assn. Temp. Svcs., Bay Area Pers. Assn. (pres. 1983-84), Pers. Assn. Sonoma County. Office: Russell Pers Svcs Inc 120 Montgomery St San Francisco CA 94104-4303

RUSSELL, CHARLES, film director, producer. films include: (dir.): Nightmare on Elm Street III, 1987 (also co-writer), The Blob, 1988 (also co-writer), The Mask, 1994 (also exec. prodr.); (prodr.): Cheerleaders' Wild Weekend, 1979, Hell Night, 1981, The Seduction, 1982, Body Rock, 1984, Dreamscape, 1984 (also co-writer), Girls Just Want to Have Fun, 1985, Back To School, 1986. Address: Bldg 81 4000 Warner Blvd Room 205 Burbank CA 91522

RUSSELL, CHARLES F., newspaper publishing executive. V.p. technology The Wall Street Journal, N.Y.C. Office: Wall Street Journal 200 Liberty St New York NY 10281-1003

RUSSELL, CHARLES ROBERTS, chemical engineer; b. Spokane, Wash., July 13, 1914; s. Marvin Alvin and Dessie Corselia (Price) R.; m. Dolores Kopriva, May 17, 1943; children—Ann E., John C., David F., Thomas R. B.S. in Chem. Engring, Wash. State U., 1936; Ph.D. in Chem. Engring. (Procter and Gamble Co. fellow 1940-41), U. Wis., 1941. Egr. div. reactor devel. AEC, Washington, 1950-56; engr. Gen. Motors Tech. Center, Warren, Mich. and Santa Barbara, Calif., 1956-68; assoc. dean engring. Calif. Poly. State U., San Luis Obispo, 1968-73; prof. mech. engring. Calif. Poly. State U., 1973-80; mem. nuclear standards bd. Am. Nat. Standards Inst., 1956-78; cons., 1980—; sec. adv. com. reactor safeguards AEC, 1950-55. Author: Reactor Safeguards, 1962, Elements of Energy Conversion, 1967, Energy Sources, Ency. Britannica. Served with USNR, 1944-46. Mem. Am. Chem. Soc. Republican. Roman Catholic. Club: Channel City (Santa Barbara). Home and Office: 3071 Marilyn Way Santa Barbara CA 93105-2040

RUSSELL, CHARLOTTE SANANES, biochemistry educator, researcher; b. N.Y.C., Jan. 4, 1927; d. Joseph and Marguerite (Saltiel) Sananes; m. Joseph Brooke Russell, Dec. 20, 1947; children: James Robert, Joshua Sananes. BA, Bklyn. Coll., 1946; MA, Columbia U., 1947, PhD, 1951. Asst. prof. biochemistry CCNY, N.Y.C., 1958-68, assoc. prof., 1968-72, prof., 1972—; peer reviewer NSF, NIH; ad hoc reviewer sci. jours. including Jour. Bacteriology, Biochemistry. Contbr. articles to profl. jours. Mem. AAAS, AAUP, AAUW (internat. fellowship panel 1986-89), Am. Soc. Biochemistry and Molecular Biology, Am. Chem. Soc., Amnesty Internat., Urgent Action Network, Sigma Xi. Office: CCNY Dept Chemistry 138th St & Convent Ave New York NY 10031

RUSSELL, CLIFFORD SPRINGER, economics and public policy educator; b. Holyoke, Mass., Feb. 11, 1938; s. Kenneth Clifford and Helen Alwilda (Springer) R.; m. Louise Pancoast Bennett, Feb. 3, 1965 (div. June 1985); m. Susan Vanston Reid, Sept. 7, 1985; stepchildren: Timothy Taylor Greene, Elizabeth Claussen Greene. BA, Dartmouth Coll., 1960; PhD, Harvard U., 1968. Sr. rsch. assoc. Resources for the Future, Washington, 1968-70, fellow, 1970-73, sr. fellow, 1973-85, div. dir., 1981-85; prof. econs. and pub. policy Vanderbilt U., Nashville, 1986—, dir. Vanderbilt Inst. for Pub. Policy Studies, 1986—. Author: Drought and Water Supply: Implications of the Massachusetts Experience for Municipal Planning, 1970, Residuals Management in Industry: A Case Study of Petroleum Refining, 1973, Steel Production: Processes, Products and Residuals, 1976, Environment Quality Management: An Application to the Lower Delaware Valley, 1976, Freshwater Recreational Fishing: The National Benefits of Water Pollution Control, 1982, Enforcing Pollution Control Laws, 1986; contbr. articles to profl. jours. Trustee, treas. Environ. Def. Fund, N.Y.C., and Washington, 1973-85; mem. Tenn. Gov.'s Energy Adv. Bd., Nashville, 1989-94; trustee Tenn. Environ. Coun., Nashville, 1989-96; pres. 1992-95. Lt. USN, 1960-63. Mem. Assn. Environ. and Resource Econs. (bd. dirs. 1983-85, chmn. workshop com., pres. 1993-94). Avocations: tennis, fly fishing, sailing, boat building. Home: 122 Clifftee Dr Brentwood TN 37027-4105 Office: Vanderbilt Inst Pub Policy Studies 1207 18th Ave S Nashville TN 37212-2807

RUSSELL, DAN M., JR., federal judge; b. Magee, Miss., Mar. 15, 1913; s. Dan M. and Beulah (Watkins) R.; m. Dorothy Tudury, Dec. 27, 1942; children—Ronald Truett, Dorothy Dale, Richard Brian. B.A., U. Miss., 1935, LL.B., 1937. Bar: Miss. bar 1937. Practice in Gulfport and Bay St. Louis, Miss.; U.S. judge So. Dist. Miss., 1965—; now sr. judge; Dir. So. Savs. & Loan Assn., Gulfport, Miss. Chmn. Hancock (Miss.) Civic Action

Assn., 1964—; Democratic presdl. elector, 1964; chmn. Hancock County Election Commn., 1959-64. Served to lt. comdr. USNR, 1941-45. Mem. Miss. Bar Assn., Hancock County Bar Assn. (v.p. 1964-65), Hancock County C. of C. (pres. 1946), Tau Kappa Alpha, Scribblers. Club: Rotarian (pres. Bay St. Louis, Miss. 1946). Office: US Dist Ct PO Box 1930 Gulfport MS 39502-1930*

RUSSELL, DANIEL FRANCIS, hospital administrator; b. Tiskilwa, Ill., Oct. 8, 1940; married. BA, U. Miami, 1963; MA, Washington U., 1966. Adminstrv. intern James M. Jackson Meml. Hosp., Miami, Fla., 1963-64; adminstrv. resident Rush Presbyn. St. Luke's Med. Ctr., Chgo., 1965-66, adminstrv. asst., 1966-68; asst. adminstr. St. Joseph's Hosp. & Med. Ctr., Phoenix, 1968-70, assoc. adminstr., 1970-74; pres. St. Joseph Hosp. & Med. Ctr., Tacoma, 1974-86, Ea. Mercy Health System, Radnor, Pa., 1986—. Mem. Am. Hosp. Assn., Washington Hosp. Assn. (bd. dirs.). Office: Ea Mercy Health System 100 Matsonford Rd Wayne PA 19080-0001*

RUSSELL, DAVID EMERSON, consulting mechanical engineer; b. Jacksonville, Fla., Dec. 20, 1922; s. David Herbert and Wilhelmina (Ash) R.; B.Mech. Engring., U. Fla., 1948; postgrad. Oxford (Eng.) U. Mech. engr. United Fruit Co., N.Y.C., 1948-50, U.S. Army C.E., Jacksonville, 1950-54, Aramco, Saudi Arabia, 1954-55; v.p. Beiswenger Hoch and Assocs., Inc., Jacksonville, 1955-57; owner, operator David E. Russell and Assos., cons. engrs., Jacksonville, 1957—. Chmn. Jacksonville Water Quality Control Bd., 1969-73; bd. dirs. Jacksonville Hist. Soc., 1981-82; mem. Jacksonville Bicentennial Commn., 1973-79. Served to 2d lt. AUS, 1943-46. Recipient Outstanding Service award City of Jacksonville, 1974. Registered profl. engr., Fla., Ga. Mem. ASME (chmn. N.E. Fla. 1967-68), Nat. Soc. Profl. Engrs., ASHRAE, Fla. Engring. Soc. Episcopalian. Club: University (Jacksonville). Contbr. articles to profl. jours.; holder of 5 U.S. patents. Avocations: world travel, boating, classical music. Home: 4720 Timuquana Rd Jacksonville FL 32210-8231 Office: 110 Riverside Ave Jacksonville FL 32202-4906

RUSSELL, DAVID L., federal judge; b. Sapulpa, Okla., July 7, 1942; s. Lynn and Florence E. (Brown) R.; m. Dana J. Wilson, Apr. 16, 1971; 1 child, Sarah Elizabeth. BS, Okla. Bapt. U., 1963; J.D., Okla. U., 1965. Bar: Okla. 1965. Asst. atty. gen. State of Okla., Oklahoma City, 1968-69, legal adviser to gov., 1969-70; legal adviser Senator Dewey Bartlett, Washington, 1973-75; U.S. atty. for Western dist. Okla. Dept. Justice, 1975-77, 81-82; ptnr. Benefield & Russell, Oklahoma City, 1977-81; chief judge U.S. Dist. Ct. (we. dist.) Okla., Oklahoma City, 1982—. Lt. comdr. JAGC, USN, 1965-68. Selected Outstanding Fed. Ct. Trial judge Okla. Trial Lawyers Assn., 1988. Mem. Okla. Bar Assn., Fed. Bar Assn. (pres. Oklahoma City chpt. 1981). Republican. Methodist. Office: US Dist Ct 3321 US Courthouse 200 NW 4th St Oklahoma City OK 73102-3003

RUSSELL, DAVID L(AWSON), psychology educator; b. Apr. 1, 1921; m. Jean Williams; children: David W., Nancy K. B.A. in Psychology with honors, Wesleyan U., 1942; postgrad., Columbia U., summers 1942, 46; Ph.D. in Psychology, U. Minn., 1953. Lic. psychologist, Ohio. Adminstrv. fellow Office Dean of Students, U. Minn., Mpls., 1947; teaching asst. dept. psychology U. Minn., 1947-48; clin. fellow Student Counseling Bur., 1948-50; dir. student counseling Bowdoin Coll., Brunswick, Maine, 1950-59; instr. Bowdoin Coll., 1950-54, asst. prof. psychology, 1954-59; assoc. prof. Ohio U., 1959-67, prof., 1967-91, asst. chmn. dept. psychology, 1968, chmn., 1969-72, prof. emeritus, 1991—; vis. prof. U. N.H., summer 1958; mem. faculty NDEA Counseling and Guidance Inst. at Ohio U., 1961, 63, 65, 1966-67; pres. Maine Psychol. Assn., 1956-57; chmn. Maine Bd. Examiners Psychologists, 1959; cons. Div. Undergrad. Edn. in Sci., NSF, 1965, 70, 71; sec. Nat. Coun. Chmns. Grad. Depts. Psychology, 1971-72. Author: (with others) Applied Psychology, 1966; contbr. articles to profl. publs. Mem. Superintending Sch. Com., Topsham, Maine, 1953-59, chmn., 1953-54, 56-57, mem. sch. bldg. com., 1953-55, com. chmn., 1953-55; sec. Joint-Com. Maine Sch. Union 46, 1953-59; mem. Topsham Zoning Com., 1956-57; bd. dirs. United Srs. of Athens County, 1987-91; mem. adv. bd. Athens County Dept. Human Services, 1987-94, pres. 1993-94; mem. Buckeye Hills—Hocking Valley Regional Devel. Dist. area agy. on aging, adv. coun. on aging, 1988-94; mem. Athens County Coun. on Aging, 1988-94, pres., 1990-93. Lt. USCGR, 1943-52. Mem. AAUP, VFW, Am. Psychol. Assn., Midwestern Psychol. Assn., Am. Ednl. Rsch. Assn., Mass. Audubon Soc., Hocking Valley Audubon Soc., Buckeye Trail Assn., Vergilian Soc., Athens League of Women Voters, Athens County Humane Soc., Columbus Urban League, Orleans Hist. Soc., Ohio U. Soc. Alumni Friends of Coll. Arts and Scis. (exec. sec. 1985-90), Athens County Hist. Soc., Sierra Club, Appalachian Mountain Club, Sigma Xi (pres. Ohio U. chpt. 1972-73), Psi Chi, Sigma Phi Omega. Home: 41 Elmwood Pl Athens OH 45701-1905 Home (summer): PO Box 727 112 Main St Orleans MA 02653

RUSSELL, DAVID WILLIAMS, lawyer; b. Lockport, N.Y., Apr. 5, 1945; s. David Lawson and Jean Graves (Williams) R.; AB, Dartmouth Coll., 1967, MBA, 1969; JD cum laude, Northwestern U., 1976; m. Frances Yung Chung Chen, May 23, 1970; children: Bayard Chen, Ming Rennick. Bar: Ill. 1976, Ind. 1983. English tchr. Talledega (Ala.) Coll., summer 1967; math. tchr. Lyndon Inst., Lyndonville, Vt., 1967-68; instr. econs. Royalton Coll., South Royalton, Vt., part-time 1968-69; asst. to pres. for planning Tougaloo (Miss.) Coll., 1969-71, bus. mgr., 1971-73; mgr. will and trust rev. project Continental Ill. Nat. Bank & Trust Co. Chgo., summer 1974; law clk. Montgomery, McCracken, Walker & Rhoads, Phila., summer 1975; with Winston & Strawn, Chgo., 1976-83; ptnr. Klineman, Rose, Wolf & Wallack, Indpls., 1983-87, Johnson, Smith, Pence, Densborn, Wright & Heath, 1987—; cons. Alfred P. Sloan Found., 1972-73; dir. Forum for Internat. Profl. Svcs., 1985—, sec., 1985-88, pres. 1988-89; U.S. Dept. Justice del. to U.S. China Joint Session on Trade, Investment & Econ. Law, Beijing, 1987; lectr. internat. Law, Gov's Ind. Trade Mission to Japan, 1986, bus. law Ind. Continuing Legal Edn. Forum, 1986-94, chmn., 1987, 89, 91; adj. prof. internat. bus. law Ind. U., 1993—; bd. dirs. Ind. ASEAN Coun., Inc., 1988—; nat. selection com. Woodrow Wilson Found. Adminstrv. Fellowship Program, 1973-76; vol. Lawyers for Creative Arts, Chgo., 1977-83; dir. World Trade Club of Ind., 1987-93, v.p., 1987-91, pres., 1991-92; dir. Ind. Swiss Found., 1991—; dir. Ind. Soviet Trade Consortium, 1991—, sec., 1991-92; v.p., bd. dirs. Ind. Sister Cities, 1988—; dir. Internat. Ctr. Indpls., 1988-92, v.p. 1988-89; Ind. dist. enrollment dir. Dartmouth Coll., 1990—; bd. dirs. Indpls. Sister Cities, 1992—, Carmel Sister Cities, 1993—, v.p. 1995—; v.p. gen. coun. Lawrence Durrell Soc., 1993—; mem. bd. advisors Ctr. for Internat. Bus. Edn. and Rsch. Krannert Grad. Sch. Mgmt. Purdue U., 1995—. Woodrow Wilson Found. Adminstrv. fellow, 1969-72. Mem. ABA, ACLU, Ill. Bar Assn., Ind. Bar Assn. (vice chmn. internat. law section, 1988-90, chmn. 1990-92), Indpls. Bar Assn., Dartmouth Lawyers Assn., Indpls. Assn. Chinese Ams., Chinese Music Soc., Dartmouth Club of Ind. (sec. 1986-87, pres. 1987-88), Zeta Psi. Presbyterian. Home: 10926 Lakeview Dr Carmel IN 46033-3937 Office: Johnson Smith Pence Densborn Wright & Heath 1800 NBD Tower One Indiana Sq Indianapolis IN 46204

RUSSELL, DONALD STUART, federal judge; b. Lafayette Springs, Miss., Feb. 22, 1906; s. Jesse and Lula (Russell) R.; m. Virginia Utsey, June 15, 1929; children: Donald, Mildred, Scott, John. AB, U. S.C., 1925, LLB, 1928; postgrad., U. Mich., 1929; LLD (hon.), Wofford Coll., Lander Coll., The Citadel, U.S.C., Emory U., Clemson U., C.W. Post Coll. Bar: S.C. 1928. Pvt. practice law Spartanburg, 1930-42, 1938-42, 47-51, 57-63; with Nicholls, Wyche & Byrnes, Nicholls, Wyche & Russell, and Nicholls & Russell, 1930-42; mem. Price Adjustment Bd., War Dept., Washington, 1942; asst. to dir. econ. stabilization, 1942, asst. to dir. war mobilization, 1943; dep. dir. Office War Mobilization Reconversion, 1945; asst. sec. state, 1945-47; pres. U. S.C., 1951-57; gov. S.C., 1963-65, mem. U.S. Senate from S.C., 1965-66, U.S. Dist. Ct. judge, 1967-71; judge U.S. Ct. Appeals, Spartanburg, S.C., 1971—. Mem. Wriston Com. on Reorgn. Fgn. Service, 1954; trustee emeritus Emory U., Atlanta, Converse Coll., Spartanburg, S.C., Benedict Coll., Columbia, S.C. Served as maj. AUS, 1944, SHAEF, France. Mem. ABA, Am. Law Inst., S.C. Bar Assn., Spartanburg County Bar Assn., Phi Beta Kappa. Methodist. Office: US Ct Appeals 4th Ct PO Box 1985 Spartanburg SC 29304-1985

RUSSELL, ELBERT WINSLOW, neuropsychologist; b. Las Vegas, N.Mex., June 4, 1929; s. Josiah Cox and Ruth Annice (Winslow) R.; children from previous marriage: Gwendolyn Marie Harvey, Franklin Winslow, Kirsten Nash, Jonathan Nash; m. Sally Lynn Kolitz, Apr. 2, 1989. BA, Earlham Coll., Richmond, Ind., 1951; MA, U. Ill., 1953; MS, Pa. State U., 1958; PhD, U. Kans., 1968. Clin. psychologist Warnersville (Pa.) State Hosp., 1959-61; clin. neuropsychologist VA Med. Ctr., Cin., 1968-71; dir. neuropsychology lab. VA Med. Ctr., Miami, Fla., 1971-89, rsch. psychologist, 1989—; adj. prof. Nova U., Ft. Lauderdale, 1980-87, U. Miami Med. Sch., 1980-94, U. Miami, 1979—. Author: (with C. Neuringer and G. Goldstein) Assessment of Brain Damage, 1970; (with R.I. Starkey) Halstead Russell Neuropsychology Evaluation System (manual and computer program), 1993; contbr. articles to profl. jours. Fellow APA, Am. Psychol. Soc., Nat. Acad. Neuropsychology; mem. Sigma Xi. Democrat. Soc. of Friends. Home: 6091 SW 79th St Miami FL 33143-5030 Office: 6262 Sunset Dr Ste PH 228 Miami FL 33143

RUSSELL, FRANCIA, ballet director, educator; b. Los Angeles, Jan. 10, 1938; d. W. Frank and Marion (Whitney) R.; m. Kent Stowell, Nov. 19, 1965; children: Christopher, Darren, Ethan. Studies with, George Balanchine, Vera Volkova, Felia Doubrouska, Antonina Tumkovsky, Benjamin Harkarvy; student, NYU, Columbia U. Dancer, soloist N.Y.C. Ballet, 1956-62, ballet mistress, 1965-70; dancer Ballets USA/Jerome Robbins, N.Y.C., 1962; tchr. ballet Sch. Am. Ballet, N.Y.C., 1963-64; co-dir. Frankfurt (Fed. Republic Germany) Opera Ballet, 1976-77; dir., co-artistic dir. Pacific N.W. Ballet, Seattle, 1977—; dir. Pacific N.W. Ballet Sch., Seattle; affiliate prof. of dance U. Wash. Dir. staging over 100 George Balanchine ballet prodns. throughout world, including the Soviet Union and People's Republic of China, 1964—. Named Woman of Achievement, Matrix Table, Women in Comm., Seattle, 1987, Gov.'s Arts award, 1989, Dance Mag. award, 1996. Mem. Internat. Women's Forum. Home: 2833 Broadway E Seattle WA 98102-3935 Office: Pacific NW Ballet 301 Mercer St Seattle WA 98109-4600

RUSSELL, FRANK ELI, newspaper publishing executive; b. Kokomo, Ind., Dec. 6, 1920; s. Frank E. and Maude (Wiggins) R.; children: Linda Carole Russell Atkins, Richard Lee, Frank E. III, Rita Jane Russell Eagle, Julie Beth Russell Smith; m. Nancy M. Shover, Oct. 5, 1991. AB, Evansville Coll., 1942; JD, Ind. U., 1951; LLD (hon.), U. Evansville, 1985; HHD (hon.), Franklin Coll., 1989. Bar: Ind. 1951; CPA, Ind. Ptnr. George S. Olive & Co., Indpls., 1947-53; exec. v.p. Spickelmier Industries, Inc., Indpls., 1953-59; bus. mgr. Indpls. Star & News, 1959-77; v.p., gen. mgr. New Ctrl. Newspapers, Inc., Indpls., 1977-79, pres., 1979-95, chmn., bd. dirs., 1996—; pres. Ctrl. Newsprint, also bd. dirs.; pres. Bradley Paper Co., also bd. dirs.; sec.-treas., bd. dirs. Phoenix Newspapers Inc., Indpls., Newspapers, Inc., Muncie Newspapers, Inc., Ctrl. Newspapers Found., Indpls.; past chmn. adv. bd. Met. Indpls. TV Assn., Inc.; trustee retirement trust Ctrl. Newspapers, Inc.; bd. dirs. Newspaper Advt. Bur.; chmn. retirement com. Hoosier State Press. Bd. dirs. Ariz. Cmty. Found., 1992—, Eiteljorg Mus., 1994—. Recipient Life Salvation award Salvation Army, 1989, Disting. Alumni award Ind. U. Sch. Law, 1989, Life Trustee award U. Evansville, 1991. Mem. ABA, AICPA, Ind. Bar. Assn., Indpls. Bar Assn. (past bd. dirs., past treas.), Ind. Assn. CPAs (past dir.), Tax Execs. Inst. (past pres.), Ind. Assn. Credit Mgmt. (dir., v.p.), Inst. Newspaper Controllers and Fin. Officers (dir., past pres.), Ind. Acad. Ind. Assn. Colls., Midwest Pension Conf. (Ind. chpt.), Newspaper Advt. Bur. (bd. dirs.), Salvation Army (life mem. award), Order of Coif, Phi Delta Phi, Sigma Alpha Epsilon. Methodist. Clubs: Indpls. Athletic, Columbia, Meridian Hills Country, Skyline. Lodges: Masons, Shriners. Office: Indianapolis Star-News 307 N Pennsylvania St Indianapolis IN 46204-2400

RUSSELL, FRED MCFERRIN, journalist, author, lawyer; b. Nashville, Aug. 27, 1906; s. John E. and Mabel Lee (McFerrin) R.; m. Katherine Wyche Early, Nov. 2, 1933; children: Katherine (Mrs. Earl Beasley), Ellen (Mrs. Robert Sadler), Lee (Mrs. John Brown, Carolyn Russell. Student, Vanderbilt U., 1923-27. Bar: Tenn. 1928. Atty. Real Estate Title Co., 1928; reporter Nashville Banner, 1929, sports editor, 1930-69, sports dir., 1969-87, v.p., 1955—; chmn. honors ct. Nat. Football Found. and Hall of Fame, 1967-92; So. chmn. Heisman Trophy Com., 1946-92. Author: 50 Years of Vanderbilt Football, 1938, I'll Go Quietly, 1944, I'll Try Anything Twice, 1945, Funny Thing About Sport, 1948, Bury Me in an Old Press Box, 1957, Big Bowl Football, 1963; contbr. to mags. including Saturday Evening Post, 1939-63. A founder Harpeth Hall Sch., 1951, trustee, 1951-55; nat. pres. Vanderbilt Alumni Assn., 1960-61; dir. Children's Regional Med. Center, 1970-72. Recipient Nat. Headliners award, 1936; Grantland Rice award for sports writing, 1955; Jake Wade award, 1966; Coll. Football Centennial award, 1969; writing award Golf Writers Assn. Am., 1972; award for disting. journalism U.S. Olympic Com., 1976; Disting. Am. award Nat. Football Found. and Hall of Fame, 1980; Amos Alonzo Stagg award Am. Football Coaches Assn., 1981; award Nat. Turf Writers Assn., 1983; Red Smith award AP Sports Editors, 1984; named to Tenn. Sports Hall of Fame, 1974, Nat. Sportscasters and Sportswriters Hall of Fame, 1988. Mem. Football Writers Assn. Am. (pres. 1960-61), Sigma Delta Chi, Kappa Sigma (nat. man of yr. 1983), Omicron Delta Kappa. Methodist. Clubs: Belle Meade Country, Univ. Lodges: Masons (33 degree), Shriners. Office: Nashville Banner 1100 Broad St Nashville TN 37203 *There is a close affinity between sport and humor, and a sportswriter can provide a good measure of entertainment just by putting into print some of the humor he sees and hears along the way.*

RUSSELL, FREDERICK WILLIAM, Canadian provincial official; b. St. John's, Nfld., Can., Sept. 10, 1923; s. Herbert J. and Jean (Campbell) R.; m. Margaret M. Cross, June 15, 1946; children: Douglas, Janice, James, Peter. Student, Prince of Wales Coll., St. John's, Dalhousie U., Halifax, N.S., Can.; LLD (hon.), Meml. U. Nfld., St. John's, 1976. Pres. Blue Peter Steamships, St. John's, 1949-72, Terra Nova Motors Ltd., St. John's, 1962-79, Gen. Industries, St. John's, 1980-88, Delta Holdings Ltd., St. John's, 1980-88, Fremar Investments Ltd., St. John's, 1980-91; lt. gov. Province of Nfld., St. John's, 1991—; mem. Royal Trust Adv. Bd., St. John's, 1980-91. Mem. Nfld. Labour Rels. Bd., St. John's 1953-89; chmn. United Ch. Sch. Bd., St. John's, 1958-67; chmn. bd. regents Meml. U. Nfld., 1974-82; bd. dirs. Atlantic Can. Opportunities Agy., Moncton, N.B., Can., 1986-91. Decorated Order of Can.; knight of justice Order of St. John; recipient Can. Forces Decoration, 1995; apptd. HCol of 5 Wing Goose Bay, Nfdl., 9 Wing Gander, Nfdl., 1995. Mem. Rotary (bd. dirs. St. John's). Mem. United Ch. of Canada. Avocations: skiing, boating, salmon fishing. Home and Office: Govt House, Military Rd PO Box 5517, Saint John's, NF Canada A1C 5W4

RUSSELL, GEORGE ALBERT, university president; b. Bertrand, Mo., July 12, 1921; s. George Albert and Martha (Cramer) R.; m. Ruth Ann Ashby, Nov. 11, 1944; children: George Albert, Frank Ashby, Ruth Ann, Cramer Anderson. B.S. in Elec. Engring, Mass. Inst. Tech., 1947; M.S., U. Ill., 1952, Ph.D. in Physics, 1955. Assoc. prof. So. Ill. U., 1960-62; faculty U. Ill., Urbana, 1962-72, prof. physics, 1963-72, assoc. dir. Materials Research Lab., 1963-68, assoc. head physics dept., 1968-70, assoc. dean Grad. Coll., 1970-72, vice chancellor research, dean Grad. Coll., 1972-77; chancellor U. Mo.-Kansas City, 1977-91; pres. U Mo. system admin., Columbia, Mo., 1991—; cons. Office Naval Research, 1961-76; dir. Microthermal Applications Inc.; dir. Kansas City Power and Light Co.; mem. adv. bd. dirs. Boatman's First Nat. Bank Kansas City; mem. acad. adv. panel Com. on Exchanges. Vice chmn. Illini Union Bd., 1970; pres. Levis Faculty Center, 1972; chmn. bd. trustees AUA, 1977; mem. Mo. Sci. and Tech. Corp.; trustee Midwest Research Inst.; bd. dirs. Edgar Snow Meml. Fund, Inc. Served with USN, World War II. Mem. Am. Assn. Physics Tchrs., Am. Phys. Soc. Clubs: Champaign Country (pres. 1972), Mission Hills Country, Rockhill Tennis. Home: 1900 S Providence Rd Columbia MO 65203-3544 Office: U of Mo 321 University Hall Columbia MO 65211

RUSSELL, GEORGE ALLEN, composer, musicologist; b. Cin., June 23, 1923; s. Joseph and Bessie (Sledge) R.; 1 son, Jock Millgardh; m. Alice Norbury, Aug. 4, 1981. Student, Wilberforce U. High Sch., 1940-43; pupil composition, Stephan Volpe, 1949. Pvt. tchr. concept N.Y.C., 1953-68, also confs. and festivals; apptd. mem. faculty New Eng. Conservatory Music, 1969; also tchr. in Sweden, Norway and Finland; Mem. panel Nat. Endowment of Arts, 1975-76. Published concept, 1953, composer (with Dizzy Gillespie); 1st composition featuring jazz and Latin influences Cubana-Be, Cubana Bop; presented Carnegie Hall, 1947; performed John F. Kennedy's People to People Music Festival, Washington, 1962, Philharmonic Hall, Lincoln Center, 1963, tours of Europe with Newport Jazz Festival, 1964, jazz orchestras 1970—; performed original compostions with large and small European ensembles for radio, TV and new music socs., in Scandinavia, Italy, Sweden, W.Ger., also other parts Europe, 1964-70; condr. seminars on Lydian Chromatic concept, N.Y.C., 1975, Carnegie Hall performance, 1975; participant 1st White House Jazz Festival, 1978; recs. for RCA Records, Decca, Prestige, Capitol, Atlantic, Columbia, Contemporary, Blue Note, Soul Note, numerous others.; commd. composer maj. jazz work, Brandeis U., 1957, Norwegian TV; other commns. include original music for ballet Othello, 1967, Norwegian Cultural Fund, 1st choral work Listen to the Silence, 1971, Columbia Recs., Living Time for big band featuring Bill Evans, 1975, Swedish Radio for orch., 1977, 81, 83, Mass. Council on the Arts, 1983, Boston Musica Viva, 1987, work for orch. New Eng. Presentors, 1988, work for Relache New Music Ensemble, 1989; Composer jazz and electronic music.; author George Russell's Lydian Chromatic Concept of Tonal Orgn.; sponsor Am. Music Week, 1985, 86; artist-in-residence Glasgow Internat. Festival, 1990, Ezz-thetics with Don Ellis, Dave Baker, et al, N.Y. Big Band, New York, N.Y., Electronic Sonata for Souls Loved By Nature, The Essence of George Russell, Listen to the Silence with Bjornar Andresen et al, 1994; tours of U.K., Europe with George Russell Living Time Orch., 1986-95; co-commn. Swedish Concert Inst. and Brit. Coun., 1995; recordings Label Bleu, 1989, 96; seminars: Paris Conservatoire Nat. Superier, Royal Coll. Music, Stockholm, Huddersfield Contemporary Music Festival, Guildhall, others, 1986-96. Recipient Outstanding Composer award Metronome mag., 1958, New Star Composer award Downbeat mag., 1961, Nat. Endowment of the Arts award, 1969, 76, 80, 81, Jazz Masters fellow, 1989; recipient Nat. Music award Am. Music Conf., 1976, numerous awards for recs.; Guggenheim fellow, 1969, 72; Nat. Endowment for Arts grantee, 1979; MacArthur Found. fellow, 1989. Mem. Internat. Soc. Contemporary Music, Norwegian Soc. New Music, Am. Fedn. Musicians. Formed principles of Lydian Chromatic concept of tonal orgn., 1945-46. Address: care Concept 1770 Massachusetts Ave Ste 182 Cambridge MA 02140-2808

RUSSELL, GLEN ALLAN, chemist, educator; b. Johnsonville, N.Y., Aug. 23, 1925; s. John Allen and Marion (Cottrell) R.; m. Martha Ellen Havill, June 6, 1953; children: Susan Ann, June Ellen. B.S., Rensselaer Poly Inst., 1947, M.S., 1948; Ph.D., Purdue U., 1951. Research assoc. Gen. Electric Research Lab., Schenectady, 1951-58; assoc. prof. Iowa State U., Ames, 1958-61, prof., 1961—, disting. prof. scis. and humanities, 1972—; vis. prof. Chemistry Rsch. Promotion Ctr., Taiwan, 1994, Korean Soc. Advanced Sci., 1993, U. Grenoble, France, 1985; mem. adv. panel Petroleum Research Fund, 1964-67; vis. prof. U. Würzburg, Fed. Republic Germany, 1966; Reilly lectr. U. Notre Dame, 1966. Edit. adv. bd. Jour. Organic Chem., 1985-89. Recipient Iowa Gov.'s medal for sci. achievement, 1988; Guggenheim fellow Centre d'Etude Nucleaires de Grenoble, France, 1972; Alfred P. Sloan Found. fellow, 1959-63; Fulbright-Hayes lectr., 1966. Fellow AAAS, Japan Soc. for Promotion of Sci.; mem. Am. Chem. Soc. (award in petroleum chemistry 1965, Iowa medal 1971, Midwest award 1974, James Flack Norris award 1983, mem. editorial adv. bd. Jour. Am. Chem. Soc. 1966-76), AAUP, Chem. Soc. (London). Research, numerous publs. on directive effects in aliphatic substitutions occurring via free radicals, photochlorination, oxidation, bromination, solvent effects, application of E.S.R. spectroscopy to problems of structure and conformation, mechanism of autoxidation of organic substances in basic solution. Home: 1014 Murray Dr Ames IA 50010-5151 Office: Iowa State U Dept Chemistry Ames IA 50011

RUSSELL, H. DIANE, museum curator, educator; b. Kansas City, Mo., Apr. 8, 1936; d. Harry Fay Russell and Georgia Mae (Canfield) Haeberle. AB, Vassar Coll., 1958; PhD, Johns Hopkins U., 1970; postgrad., Inst. for Advanced Study, Princeton, N.J., 1980-81. Mus. curator Nat. Gallery Art, Washington, 1964-90, curator of Old Master Prints, 1990—; professorial lectr. The Am. U., Washington, 1966-82, adj. prof. Art History, 1982—. Author: Rare Etchings of G.B. and G.D. Tiepolo, 1972, Jacques Callot, 1975, Claude Lorrain, 1982 (Barr award 1984), EVA/AVE: Woman in Renaissance and Baroque Prints, 1990. Woodrow Wilson Foun. fellow, 1958-59; Univ. fellow, Johns Hopkins U., 1961-63; Kress Found. fellow, 1973; Nat. Endowment for Arts fellow, 1980-81. Mem. Coll. Art Assn., Renaissance Soc. Am., Print Coun. Am., Vassar Club. Avocations: gardening, walking, poodles. Office: Nat Gallery Art 4th & Constitution Ave NW Washington DC 20565-0001

RUSSELL, HAROLD LOUIS, lawyer; b. Abingdon, Va., July 1, 1916; s. Harold L. and Bess N. (Kinzel) R.; m. Katherine C. (Thompson) May 19, 1939; 1 child, Katherine T. Russell Prophet; m. Mildred Baggett Roach, Sept. 5, 1970. AB, Hendrix Coll., 1937; JD, Columbia U., 1940. Bar: N.Y. 1941, Ga. 1942, U.S. Ct. Appeals (1st, 2d, 3d, 5th, 11th and D.C. cirs.), U.S. Supreme Ct. 1950, D.C. 1972. Assoc. Gambrell & Russell and predecessors, Atlanta and N.Y.C., 1941-47, ptnr., 1947-84; ptnr. Smith, Gambrell & Russell, 1984—. Bd. dirs. Atlanta Fed. Defender Program, 1973-80, pres. 1978-79; bd. visitors, Columbia Law Sch., 1959—; mem. council Adminstrv. Conf. of U.S., 1968-76; bd. legal advisers Southeastern Legal Found., 1976—. Recipient Alumni Fedn. medal Columbia U., 1965; Disting. Alumnus award, Hendrix Coll., 1969. Fellow Am. Coll. Trial Lawyers, Am. Bar Found.; mem. ABA (past chmn. pub. utilities law sect., past chmn. spl. com. on legal service procedure, past chmn. adminstrv. law sect., ho. of dels. 1983-96), D.C. Bar Assn., Fed. Bar Assn., Atlanta Bar Assn., Atlanta Lawyers Club, Assn. Bar City of N.Y., Columbia Law Sch. Assn. (nat. pres. 1973-75), Atlanta C. of C., Phi Delta Phi. Democrat. Clubs: Capital City, Piedmont Driving. Home: 3999 Parian Ridge Rd NW Atlanta GA 30327-3029 Office: Smith Gambrell & Russell 3100 Promenade II 1230 Peachtree St NE Atlanta GA 30309-3592

RUSSELL, HARRIET SHAW, social worker; b. Detroit, Apr. 12, 1952; d. Louis Thomas and Lureleen (Hughes) Shaw; m. Donald Edward Russell, June 25, 1980; children: Lachante Tyree, Krystal Lanae. BS, Mich. State U., 1974; AB, Detroit Bus. Inst., 1976; BA in Pub. Adminstrn., Mercy Coll. Detroit, 1988; MSW, Wayne State U., 1992. Factory employee Gen. Motors Corp., Lansing, Mich., 1973; student supr. tour guides State of Mich., Lansing, 1974; mgr. Ky. Fried Chicken, Detroit, 1974-75; unemployment claims examiner State of Mich. Dept. Labor, Detroit, 1975-77, asst. payment worker, 1977-84, social svcs. specialist, 1984-90; ind. contractor Detroit Compact pres. Victory Enterprises, 1991; sch. social worker Detroit Bd. of Edn., 1992—; moderator Michigan Opportunity Skills and Tng. Program, 1985-86. Vol. Mich. Cancer Soc., East Lansing, 1970-72, Big Sisters/Big Bros., Lansing, 1972-73; elected rep. Mich. Coun. Social Svcs. Workers; speaker Triumphant Bapt. Ch., Detroit, 1976-80; chief union steward Mich. Employees Assn., Lincoln Park, 1982-83; leader Girl Scouts U.S.A.; area capt. Life Worker Project Program. Recipient Outstanding Work Performance Merit award Mich. Dept. Social Services, 1979; grad. profl. scholar, 1990-91, Dean's scholar, 1991-92; elected to Wayne State Sch. Social Work Bd., 1992—. Mem. NAFE, Am. Soc. Profl. and Exec. Women, Assn. Internat. Platform Speakers, Mich. Coun. Social Svcs. Workers, Nat. Fedn. Bus. and Profl. Women's Clubs, Inc. U.S.A. (elected del. to China), Nat. Assn. Black Social Workers, Wayne State U. Social Work Alumni Assn. (bd. dirs. 1992—), Delta Sigma Theta. Democrat. Baptist. Office: PO Box 361 Lincoln Park MI 48146-0361

RUSSELL, HENRY GEORGE, structural engineer; b. Tewkesbury, Eng., June 12, 1941; came to U.S., 1968. BE, Sheffield U., Eng., 1962, PhD, 1965. Registered structural engr., Ill.; registered profl. engr., Wash., Minn. Rsch. fellow Bldg. Rsch., Eng., 1965-68; structural engr. Constrn. Tech. Labs., Inc. (formerly Portland Cement Assn.), Skokie, Ill., 1968-74, mgr., 1974-79, dir., 1979-88, pres., 1989-91, v.p. 1991-94; v.p. Henry G. Russell, Inc., Glenview, Ill., 1994-95. Contbr. articles to profl. jours. Named one Those Who Made Marks in 1992, Engring. News Record. Fellow Am. Concrete Inst. (Delmar L. Bloem award 1986, Wason medal 1992, Anderson award 1994); mem. Prestressed Concrete Inst. (Martin P. Korn award 1980). Office: 720 Coronet Rd Glenview IL 60025-4457

RUSSELL, HERMAN JEROME, business executive; b. Atlanta, Dec. 23, 1930; s. Rogers and Maggie (Goodson) R.; m. Otelia Hackney, Aug. 18, 1956; children: Donata C., Jerome, Michael. Student, Tuskegee Inst., 1949-53. Chmn. bd., chief exec. officer H.J. Russell & Co., Atlanta, 1952—, Concessions Internat. Inc., Los Angeles, 1959—; bd. dirs. Citizens Trust Co. Bank, Atlanta (chmn.), Ga. Power Co., Wachovia Corp. Bd. dirs. Butler St. YMCA, Tuskegee U.; trustee Morris Brown Coll., Atlanta; nat. adv. bd. Ga. Inst. Tech., Ga. State U. Coll. Bus. Adminstrn. Recipient Meritorious

Alumni award Tuskegee Inst. Alumni Assn., 1967, Black Enterprise mag. ann. achievement award, 1978, Top Hat award New Pittsburg Courier, 1980, award for outstanding achievement in breaking new ground on road to democracy in housing Nat. Assn. Real Estate Brokers, 1980, Disting. Humanitarian award Nat. Jewish Ctr. for Immunology and Respiratory Medicine, 1986, Chief Exec. Officer of Yr. award Atlanta Bus. League, 1986, Tree of Life award Jewish Nat. Fund, 1985, Bus. and Youth award Jr. Achievement, 1979, Nat. Alumni award Tuskegee U., 1968, Equal Opportunity Day award Atlanta Urban League, 1972; Drum Major for Justice award in Bus. Ga. State U. Coll. Bus. Adminstrn., 1982; named to Pres.'s Club, Morehouse Sch. Medicine, 1986, Nat. Black Coll. Alumni Hall of Fame, 1986, Bus. Hall of Fame, Ga. State U. Coll. of Bus. Aminstrn., 1985, Entrepreneurs Hall of Fame, Atlanta U. Sch. Bus., 1982, Dow Jones Entrepreneurial Excellence award Dow Jones & Co. Inc. and Wall Street Journal, 1992, Atlanta Bus. Hall of Fame award Junior Achievement, 1992, Horatio Alger award, Horatio Alger Assn. Am., Entrepreneur of Yr. award Nat. Black and Ga. MBA assn., 1991. Mem. Atlanta C. of C. (bd. dirs., past pres. 1981), U.S. C. of C., NAACP (life), Cen. Atlanta Progress, Atlanta Commerce Club, Atlanta Action Forum, Phi Beta Sigma. Mem. African Meth. Episcopal Ch. Office: H J Russell & Co Inc 504 Fair St SW Atlanta GA 30313

RUSSELL, JAMES ALVIN, JR., college administrator; b. Lawrenceville, Va., Dec. 25, 1917; s. Dr. James Alvin and Nellie M. (Pratt) R.; m. Lottye J. Washington, Dec. 25, 1943; children: Charlotte Justyne, James Alvin III. BA, Oberlin Coll., 1940; BS, Bradley U., 1941, MS, 1950, spl. insts.; EdD, U. Md., 1967; spl. insts., Wayne U., U. Mich., U. Ill., NSF. Prof., dir. div. engring., also prof. edn. div. grad. studies Hampton Inst., 1950-71; pres. St. Paul's Coll., Lawrenceville, 1971-81; dir. instructional programs and student services Va. C.C. System, 1981-82; chmn. div. profl. studies W.Va. State Coll., 1982-86, acting pres., 1986-87, exec. asst. to pres., 1987-88; pres. So. W.Va. C.C., 1988-89, ret., 1989. Pres. Peninsula Council Human Relations, 1961-65. United Negro Coll. Fund fellow, 1966-67. Mem. IEEE, Am. Soc. Engring. Edn., Am. Assn. Univ. Adminstrs., Am. Vocat. Assn., Am. Tech. Edn. Assn., Nat. Assn. Indsl. Tech., Am. Assn. for Higher Edn., Nat. Assn. for Equal Opportunity in Edn., Brunswick C. of C., Sigma Pi Phi, Alpha Kappa Mu, Iota Lambda Sigma, Omega Psi Phi. Home: 811 Grandview Dr Dunbar WV 25064-1175

RUSSELL, JAMES BRIAN, broadcast executive; b. Hartford, Conn., Jan. 30, 1946; s. Seymour and Marian (Kamins) R.; m. Kathleen Anne Schardt, Dec. 28, 1968; children: Theodore, Jennifer, Kimberly. BA in Journalism, Am. U., 1968; postgrad., U. Pa., Stanford U. News dir. Sta. WPIK-AM, Arlington, Va., 1965-66; editor, anchorman Sta. WAVA-AM/FM, Washington, 1966-68; editor, corr. UPI, Washington, Cambodia and, Vietnam, 1968-71; from reporter to exec. prodr. All Things Considered Nat. Pub. Radio, Washington, 1971-78; sta. dir., sr. v.p. programming Stas. KTCA/KTCA-TV, Mpls./St. Paul, 1978-88; v.p. nat. prodns., exec. prodr. Marketplace USC Radio, U. So. Calif., L.A., 1988—; mem. media leader's forum La. State U.; cons. Corp. Pub. Broadcasting, Nat. Endowment Arts, Sta. WNET-TV, N.Y.C., Sta. WGBH-TV, Boston, Nat. Pub. Radio, Am. Pub. Radio, Pub. Radio Internat., Am. Documentary Consortium, The Learning Channel, The Pacific Rim Consortium, Internat. Pub. TV Conf., Audible Words Corp. Columnist pub. broadcasting's Current newspaper. Mem. prison visitor program AMICUS, St. Paul, 1984-85. Postgrad. fellow U. Mich.; recipient Nat. Headliner award 1972, 74, Ohio State award, 1973, 75, duPont Columbia awards Columbia U., 1979, 81, Peabody award, Nat. TV Emmy award Acad. TV Arts and Scis., 1989. Home: 3820 Gundry Ave Long Beach CA 90807 Office: Marketplace U So Calif Radio 3716 S Hope St Los Angeles CA 90007-4344

RUSSELL, JAMES DONALD MURRAY, hospital administrator; b. Madison, Wis., Feb. 6, 1934; s. Roger Bridgford and Margaret (Murray) R.; m. Charlotte Russell. BS, U. Wis., 1956; MA, State U. Iowa, 1961. Asst. adminstr. Luther Hosp., Eau Claire, Wis., 1960-70, adminstr., 1970-77; adminstr. St. Mary's Hosp., Pierre, S.D., 1978—; chief exec. officer St. Mary's Hosp., Maryhouse Nursing Home and Parkwood Apts., Pierre, 1990—. Bd. dirs. S.D. Delta Dental Plan, 1990—, Pierre Econ. Devel. Corp., S.D. and Western Iowa Blue Cross, 1980-87; sec. bd. dirs. Capital U. Ctr., Pierre. Fellow Am. Coll. Healthcare Execs.; mem. Am. Hosp. Assn., S.D. Hosp. Assn. (chmn. 1985-86, bd. dirs. 1981-87, 90-92). Office: St Marys Healthcare Ctr 800 E Dakota Ave Pierre SD 57501-3313

RUSSELL, JAMES FRANKLIN, lawyer; b. Memphis, Mar. 21, 1945; s. Frank Hall and Helen (Brunson) R.; m. Marilyn Land, June 1, 1968 (div. May 1976); children: Mary Helen, Myles Edward; m. Linda Hatcher, July 9, 1977; 1 child, Maggie Abele. BA, Rhodes Coll., 1967; JD, Memphis State U., 1970. Bar: Tenn. 1971, U.S. Dist. Ct. (we. dist.) Tenn. 1971, U.S. Ct. Appeals (6th cir.) 1971, U.S. Dist. Ct. (no. dist.) Miss. 1976, U.S. Ct. Appeals (5th cir.) 1977, U.S. Ct. Appeals (8th cir.) 1987. Assoc. Nelson, Norvell, Wilson, McRae, Ivy & Sevier, Memphis, 1971-75; ptnr. Stanton, Russell & Challen, Memphis, 1975-78, Russell, Price, Weatherford & Warlick, Memphis, 1978-82, Price, Vance & Criss, Memphis, 1982-85, Apperson, Crump, Duzane & Maxwell, Memphis, 1985—. V.p. mid-south chpt. Am. Red Cross, Memphis, 1992-94; treas. Epilepsy Found. West Tenn., Memphis, 1992-94. Mem. ABA, Nat. Assn. R.R. Trial Counsel, Internat. Assn. Def. Counsel, Tenn. Bar Assn., Tenn. Def. Lawyers Assn., Memphis Bar Assn. (pres. 1992). Episcopalian. Avocations: golf, snow skiing. Home: 1792 Autumn Ave Memphis TN 38112-5310 Office: Apperson Crump Duzane and Maxwell 2110 One Commerce Sq Memphis TN 38103

RUSSELL, JAMES H., lawyer; b. Oak Park, Ill., Aug. 22, 1943. BA, Ohio Wesleyan U., 1965; JD, Ohio State U., 1969. Bar: Ill. 1970, Fla. 1982, Ohio 1985. Ptnr. Winston & Strawn, Chgo. Contbr. articles to profl. jours. Mem. ABA, Ohio State Bar Assn., The Fla. Bar, Chgo. Bar Assn. Office: Winston & Strawn 35 W Wacker Dr Chicago IL 60601-1614*

RUSSELL, JAMES WEBSTER, JR., newspaper editor, columnist; b. Shreveport, La., Nov. 30, 1921; s. James Webster and Aline (Faulk) R.; m. Jean Buck, June 29, 1949; children: Nancy Russell Dearr, Eileen Russell Goure. B.A., La. State U., 1942. Fla. mgr. Internat. News Service, 1946-51; bur. chief UPI, Tallahassee, 1951-52; regional editor U.P.I., Atlanta, 1953-57; asst. city editor Miami (Fla.) Herald, 1957-58, bus.-fin. editor, 1958-74, fin.-econ. columnist, 1974—; guest lectr. U. Miami, Fla. Internat. U., Miami-Dade Community Coll., La. State U. Contbr. articles to: Fla. Trend, Times of London, N.Y. Times, Gentlemen's Quar. Trustee Fla. So. Coll. Served with USAAF, 1942-45. Recipient Eagle award Invest-in-Am. Nat. Council, 1976; Decorated Air medal with eleven oak leaf clusters. Mem. Soc. Am. Bus. Writers, Lambda Chi Alpha, Sigma Delta Chi. Republican. Methodist (chmn. ch. council on ministries 1971-72). Home: 4800 SW 64th Ct Miami FL 33155-6133 Office: 1 Herald Plz Miami FL 33132-1609

RUSSELL, JEFFREY BURTON, historian, educator; b. Fresno, Calif., Aug. 1, 1934; s. Lewis Henry and Ieda Velma (Ogborn) R.; m. Diana Emily Mansfield, June 30, 1956; children: Jennifer, Mark, William, Penelope. A.B., U. Calif., Berkeley, 1955, A.M., 1957; Ph.D., Emory U., 1960. Asst. prof. U. N.Mex., Albuquerque, 1960-61; jr. fellow Soc. of Fellows, Harvard U., Cambridge, Mass., 1961-62; mem. faculty U. Calif., Riverside, 1962-75; prof. dept. history U. Calif., 1969-75, assoc. dean grad. div., 1967-72; dir. Medieval Inst.; Michael P. Grace prof. medieval studies U. Notre Dame, South Bend, Ind., 1975-77; dean grad. studies Calif. State U., Sacramento, 1977-79; prof. history U. Calif., Santa Barbara, 1979—, prof. religious studies, 1994—. Author: Dissent and Reform in the Early Middle Ages, 1965, Medieval Civilization, 1968, A History of Medieval Christianity: Prophecy and Order, 1968, Religious Dissent in the Middle Ages, 1971, Witchcraft in the Middle Ages, 1972, The Devil: Perceptions of Evil from Antiquity to Primitive Christianity, 1977, A History of Witchcraft: Sorcerers, Heretics, and Pagans, 1980, Medieval Heresies: a Bibliography, 1981, Satan: The Early Christian Tradition, 1981, Lucifer: The Devil in the Middle Ages, 1984, Mephistopheles: The Devil in the Modern World, 1986, The Prince of Darkness, 1988, Ruga in Aevis, 1990, Inventing the Flat Earth: Columbus and the Historians, 1991, Dissent and Order in the Middle Ages, 1992; contbr. articles in field to profl. jours. Fulbright fellow, 1959-60; Am. Council Learned Socs. grantee, 1965, 70; Social Sci. Research Council grantee, 1968; Guggenheim fellow, 1968-69; Nat. Endowment for Humanities sr. fellow, 1972-73. Fellow Medieval Acad. Am.; mem. Medieval Assn. of Pacific, Am. Soc. Ch. History, Am. Acad. Religion, Sierra Club. Home: 4796 Calle Camarada Santa Barbara CA 93110-2053 Office: U Calif Dept History Santa Barbara CA 93106

RUSSELL, JERRY LEWIS, public relations counselor, political consultant; b. Little Rock, July 21, 1933; s. Jerry Lewis and Frances (Lieb) R.; m. Alice Anne Cason, Feb. 14, 1969; children—Leigh Anne, Andrew J. III, Christopher R.; children by previous marriage—Jerry Lewis III, Susan Frances. B.A. in Journalism, U. Ark., 1958; postgrad. in history U. Central Ark., 1978-82. Pub. relations dir. Little Rock C. of C., 1958; editor, pub. The Visitor, Little Rock, 1959-60; sec.-mgr. Ark. Press Assn., Little Rock, 1960-61; account exec. Brandon Agy., Little Rock, 1961-65; founder, pres. Guide Advt. (now part of River City Enterprises, Inc.), also River City Pubs., Little Rock 1965-70, 72—; pres. River City Enterprises, Inc., 1974—; dir. pub. relations services S.M. Brooks Agy., Little Rock, 1970-72; founder, pres. Campaign Cons., 1974—; pub., editor Grass Roots Campaigning newsletter, 1979—. With AUS, 1953-56. Mem. Ark. Advt. Fedn. (pres. 1967-68), Pub. Relations Soc. Am. (pres. Ark. chpt. 1974), Am. Assn. Polit. Cons., Orgn. Am. Historians, Co. Mil. Historians, Western Hist. Assn., Custer Battlefield Hist. and Mus. Assn. (bd. dirs. 1988-90), Custer Battlefield Preservation Com. (bd. dirs. 1989—), Ft. Laramie Hist. Assn., Council on Am.'s Mil. Past (state dir. 1979—), So. Hist. Soc., Little Big Horn Assos., Ark. Hist. Soc., Pulaski County Hist. Soc., Civil War Round Table Ark. (charter pres. 1964-65), Civil War Round Table Assos. (founder 1968, nat. chmn.), Order Indian Wars (founder 1979, nat. chmn.), Circus Fans Assn. Am. (pres. Little Rock chpt. 1981-83), Westerners Internat. (charter pres. Little Rock Corral 1974—), Confederate Hist. Inst. (founder 1979, nat. chmn.), Soc. Civil War Historians (founder 1984, exec. dir.), Ft. Phil Kearny Bozeman Trail Assn. (bd. dirs. 1985-95), Friends of Ft. Davis. Home: 9 Lefever Ln Little Rock AR 72227-3303

RUSSELL, JOHN CLARENCE, investment management professional; b. Marlow, Okla., Dec. 22, 1917; s. John Clarence Russell and Effie Lee Howard; m. Betty Lou Rice, Nov. 28, 1943; children: Susan Russell Vivoli, John Robert. BA, U. Tex., 1938; postgrad., U. Okla., 1938-39, Ohio State U., 1968-69. Regional mgr. Am. Optical Co., L.A., Atlanta, 1946-70; broker Sweney Cartwright, Columbus, Ohio, 1970-78; CFO, pres. Tex. Constrn. Assocs., Brownsville, San Antonio, 1978-81; investment counselor E.F. Hutton, Harlingen, Tex., 1981-85, Merrill Lynch, Brownsville, 1985-88; CEO, pres. John C. Russell Investment Mgmt. Inc., Brownsville, 1988—; CEO, pres. Water Purifiers, Inc., Brownsville, 1992—, Russell-Morgan Co., 1994—. Author monthly personal investment letter, 1972-78. Served in U.S. Army Air Corps, 1942-45. Mem. Super Srs. of Brownsville, Nat. Assn. Securities Dealers (bd. arbitrators 1995—). Avocations: tennis, bridge, history. Address: 7 Mcfadden Hut Dr Brownsville TX 78520-8905

RUSSELL, JOHN DAVID, English literature educator; b. Chgo., Dec. 12, 1928; s. John David and Charlotte Rita (Graf) R.; m. Mary Elizabeth Need, Aug. 20, 1954; 1 child, Ryan. AB, Colgate U., 1951; MA, U. Wash., Seattle, 1956; PhD, Rutgers U., 1959. Prof. English U. S.C., 1958-69, U. Md., College Park, 1969—. Author: Henry Green, 1960, Anthony Powell, 1970, Style in Modern British Fiction, 1978, Honey Russell: Between Games, Between Halves, 1986. Served to lt. USNR, 1952-55. Recipient award for criticism, Explicator Mag., 1961, Russell Research award, U.S.C., 1962; Fulbright grantee Brazil, 1966, Portugal, 1984. Home: 3112 Landfall Ln Annapolis MD 21403-4312 Office: Dept English Univ of Maryland College Park MD 20742

RUSSELL, JOHN ST. CLAIR, JR., lawyer; b. Albany, N.Y., Mar. 21, 1917; s. John St. Clair and Hazel (Barbiers) R.; m. Betty Kixmiller, Sept. 12, 1941; children: Patricia Russell, John St. Clair III (dec.), David K. AB cum laude, Dartmouth Coll., 1938; LLB, Yale U., 1941. Bar: N.Y. 1942, D.C. 1965. Mem. Hale Russell & Gray (and predecessors), N.Y.C., 1948-85; mem. Winthrop, Stimson, Putnam & Roberts, N.Y.C., 1985-90, sr. counsel, ret. ptnr., 1991—. Mem. Irvington (N.Y.) Zoning Bd. Appeals, 1955-89; chmn. Raoul Wallenberg Com. of U.S., 1985-90; exec. trustee Am.-Scandinavian Found.; mem. alumni coun. Dartmouth Coll., 1994—. Maj. USMCR, OSS, 1942-46. Decorated Order of Vasa Sweden; recipient medal of merit Swedish Red Cross. Mem. ABA, Assn. of Bar of City of N.Y., Dartmouth Club, Downtown Assn. (N.Y.C.), Phi Beta Kappa, Phi Sigma Kappa. Office: Winthrop Stimson Putnam and Roberts One Battery Park Pla New York NY 10004-1490

RUSSELL, JOSIAH COX, historian, educator; b. Richmond, Ind., Sept. 3, 1900; s. Elbert and Lieuetta (Cox) R.; m. Ruth Winslow, Sept. 15, 1924 (dec. Apr. 1966); children: Elbert Winslow, Walter Howard, Joan (dec.). A.B., Earlham Coll., 1922; M.A., Harvard U., 1923, Ph.D., 1926. Asst. in history Radcliffe Coll., 1923-24, Harvard U., 1924-26; asst. prof. Colo. Coll., 1927-29; prof. history and head social sci. dept. N.Mex. Highlands U., 1929-31; instr. to assoc. prof. U. N.C., 1931-46; chmn. history dept. U. N.Mex., 1946-53, prof., 1946-65; prof. emeritus U. N. Mex., 1965—; prof. Tex. A & I U., 1965-71, Piper prof. (hon.), 1971. Author: Dictionary of Writers of Thirteenth Century England, 1936, British Medieval Population, 1948, Late Ancient and Medieval Population, 1958, Medieval Regions and Their Cities, 1972, Twelfth Century Studies, 1978, Control of Late Ancient and Medieval Population, 1985, Medieval Demography, 1987; contbr. chpt. to Fontana Economic History of Europe, Historia Universal, Salvat, vol. IV; author: (with others) Ever Since Eve: Archaeology, 1994; contbr. numerous articles to profl. jours. Chmn. Orange Dist. com. Boy Scouts Am., 1945-46. Fulbright lectr. Univ. Coll., Wales, 1952-53; research grantee Guggenheim Found., 1930-31, Am. Council Learned Socs., summers 1933, 34, Social Sci. Research Council, summers 1938, 49, 51, Am. Philos. Soc., 1938-39, 61; fellow Islamic Seminar Princeton, summer 1935; cons. Fulbright Brit. Empire Prof. Selection, 1955. Fellow Mediaeval Acad. Am.; mem. Am. Hist. Assn. (mem. Pacific Coast council 1964-65), Soc. of Friends, AAUP (state chmn. 1951-52, nat. council 1953-56), Phi Alpha Theta. Address: 116 Southwind Cir Saint Augustine FL 32084-5352 *My darling wife, our 72 years of life together have been the happiest part of our life. Guggenheim, Fulbright, Piper (Texas) - bright spots. TB, down's syndrome, alzheimers - low spots, awful periods. We had our chance - and we played it.*

RUSSELL, JOYCE ANNE ROGERS, librarian; b. Chgo., Nov. 6, 1920; d. Truman Allen and Mary Louise (Hoelzle) Rogers; m. John VanCleve Russell, Dec. 24, 1942; children: Malcolm David, John VanCleve. Student, Adelphi Coll., 1937; B.S. in Chemistry, U. Ky., 1942; M.L.S., Rosary Coll., 1967; postgrad., Rutgers U., 1970-71. Research chemist Sherwin Williams Paint Co., Chgo., 1942-45; reference librarian Chicago Heights (Ill.) Pub. Library, 1959-61; librarian Victor Chem. Works, Chicago Heights, 1961-62; lit. chemist Velsicol Chem. Corp., Chgo., 1964-67; chemistry librarian U. Fla., Gainesville, 1967-69; interim assoc. prof. U. Fla., 1967-69; librarian Thiokol Chem. Corp., Trenton, N.J., 1969-73; supr. library operations E.R. Squibb Co., Princeton, N.J., 1973-80, sr. research info scientist, 1980-91; mem. library adv. commn. Mercer Community Coll., 1979—; adv. asso. Rutgers U. Grad. Sch. Library and Info. Scis., 1978—. Editor: Bibliofile, 1967-69; contbr. articles to profl. jours. Mem. PTA, 1950-66; den mother Cub Scouts, 1952-59. Mem. Spl. Libraries Assn. (sec., dir., v.p., pres. Princeton-Trenton 1971, 75-80), Am. Chem. Soc. (bus. mgr., sec., dir. Trenton sect. 1969-78), AAUW, Mortar Board, Beta Phi Mu, Sigma Pi Sigma, Chi Delta Phi, Pi Sigma Alpha. Home: 1189 Parkside Ave Trenton NJ 08618-2625

RUSSELL, JOYCE WEBER, principal; b. Detroit, Feb. 21, 1948; d. Ronald Robert and Eleanor Treva (Burns) Weber; m. James Edward Russell, Mar. 25, 1970; 1 child, Jennifer Eileen. AA, Palm Beach C.C., Lake Worth, Fla., 1968; BA, Fla. Atlantic U., 1970, MA, 1975. Cert. tchr., prin. Tchr. Palm Beach County Sch. Bd., West Palm Beach, Fla., 1970-79, staff devel. specialist, 1979-84; asst. prin. Allamanda Elem., 1984-88; prin. Addison Mizner Elem., Boca Raton, Fla., 1988-90, South Olive Elem., West Palm Beach, 1990-95; adminstr. Safe Schs. AFTER Sch. Programs, Sch. Police, 1995—. Chairperson Vision 2000 Good Shepherd Meth. Ch., West Palm Beach, 1990-95; mem. Leadership Palm Beach County, 1990-96. Mem. NAESP, ASCD, Fla. Assn. Sch. Administrs., Palm Beach County Adminstr. Assn., Phi Delta Kappa. Avocations: singing in chancel choir, water sports, geneology, creating curriculum, writing poetry, computers. Office: Sch Bd Palm County Dept Sch Police # 121B 3330 Forest Hill Blvd West Palm Beach FL 33405-4769

RUSSELL, KEN (HENRY KENNETH ALFRED RUSSELL), film and theatre director; b. Southampton, Eng., July 3, 1927; s. Henry and Ethel (Smith) R.; m. Shirley Kingdon, Feb. 3, 1957 (div.); 5 children; m. Vivian Jolly, June 10, 1984; children: Molly, Rupert. Student, Walthamstow Art Sch., Internat. Ballet Sch. Formerly dancer, actor, still photographer, BBC documentary film maker; feature film dir.; feature films include French Dressing, 1964, Billion Dollar Brain, 1967,Women in Love, 1970, The Music Lovers, 1970, The Boy Friend, 1971, The Devils, 1971, Savage Messiah, 1972, Mahler, 1975, Tommy, 1975, Lizstomania, 1975, Altered States, 1980, Crimes of Passion, 1984, Gothic, 1986, Salome's Last Dance, 1986, Aria, 1987, The Lair of the White Worm, 1988, The Rainbow, 1989, Whore, 1991, Lady Chatterly, 1993; dir., writer: film Valentino, 1977; actor, The Russia House, 1990; dir.: operas Rakes Progres, 1982, Die Soldaten, 1983, Madame Butterfly, Spoleto and Melbourne; La Boheme, Macenata; Faust, Vienna; Mephisto, Rhodes and Genoa. Served with Mcht. Navy, 1945; Served with also RAF. Recipient Screen writers Guild award for TV films Elgar, Debussy, Isadora, Dante's Inferno; Delius award (Merit Scroll); award Guild TV Producers and Dirs., 1966; Desmond Davis award, 1968. Office: care Peter Rawley Internat Creative Mgmt 8942 Wilshire Blvd Beverly Hills CA 90211 Office: 16 Salisbury Pl, London W1H 1FH, England

RUSSELL, KENNETH CALVIN, metallurgical engineer, educator; b. Greeley, Colo., Feb. 4, 1936; s. Doyle James and Jennie Frances (Smith) R.; m. Charlotte Louise Wolf, Apr. 13, 1963 (div. 1978); children: David Allan, Doyle John. Met.E., Colo. Sch. Mines, 1959; Ph.D., Carnegie Inst. Tec., 1963. Engr. Westinghouse Research and Devel. Center, 1959-61; NSF postdoctoral fellow Physics Inst., U. Oslo, 1963-64; asst. prof. metallurgy M.I.T., Cambridge, 1964-69; assoc. prof. M.I.T., 1969-78, prof. metallurgy, 1978—, prof. nuclear engring., 1979—. Contbr. articles to profl. publs. Served as 2d lt. U.S. Army, 1959-60. DuPont fellow, 1961-62; NSF grad. fellow, 1962-63. Mem. AIME, Am. Phys. Soc., Am. Soc. for Metals. Office: MIT Rm 8-411 Cambridge MA 02139

RUSSELL, KENT, hospital administrator. With Arthur Andersen Accounting Firm, L.A., 1968-1972, AMI, Beverly Hills, Calif., 1972-1976, St. Joseph Hospital, Tacoma, Wa., 1976-1986; exec. v.p., cfo Eastern Mercy Health System, Wayne, Pa., 1986—. Office: Eastern Mercy Health System 100 Matsonford Rd 3 Radnor Corp Ctr Ste 220 Radnor PA 19087-4592*

RUSSELL, KURT VON VOGEL, actor; b. Springfield, Mass., Mar. 17, 1951; s. Bing Oliver and Louise Julia (Crone) R.; m. Season Hubley, Mar. 17, 1979 (div.), 1 son, Boston; 1 son (with Goldie Hawn), Wyatt Russell. Student, pub. schs. Profl. baseball player, 1971-73. Actor in numerous films including The Absent Minded Professor, 1961, It Happened at the World's Fair, 1963, Follow Me Boys, 1966, The One and Only Genuine Original Family Band, 1968, The Horse in the Grey Flannel Suit, 1968, The Computer Wore Tennis Shoes, 1970, The Barefoot Executive, 1971, Fools' Parade, 1971, Now You See Him Now You Don't, 1972, Charley and the Angel, 1972, Superdad, 1974, The Strongest Man in the World, 1975, Used Cars, 1980, Escape from New York, 1981, The Thing, 1982, Silkwood, 1983, Swing Shift, 1984, The Mean Season, 1985, The Best of Times, 1986, Big Trouble in Little China, 1986, Overboard, 1987, The Winter People, 1988, Tequila Sunrise, 1988, Winter People, 1989, Tango and Cash, 1989, Backdraft, 1991, Unlawful Entry, 1992, Captain Ron, 1992, Tombstone, 1993, Stargate, 1994; TV series include Travels with Jamie McPheeters, 1963-64, The New Land, 1974, The Quest, 1976; TV movies include Search for the Gods, 1975, The Deadly Tower, The Quest (pilot), 1975, Christmas Miracle in Caulfield USA, 1977, Elvis, 1979, Amber Waves, 1988; TV guest appearences include The Fugitive, Daniel Boone, Gilligan's Island, Lost in Space, The FBI, Love American Style, Gunsmoke, Hawaii Five-O. Served with Calif. Air N.G. Recipient numerous auto racing trophies, 10 baseball awards, 5 acting awards, 1 golf championship. Mem. Profl. Baseball Players Assn., Stuntman's Assn. World championship Class Modified Stock, 1959 Race of Champions, Las Vegas. Office: Creative Artists Agy 9830 Wilshire Blvd Beverly Hills CA 90212-1804*

RUSSELL, LEONARD ALONZO, dentist; b. Paris, Ky., Dec. 27, 1949; s. Joseph Bailey and Celia Russell. BS in Indsl. Edn., Eastern Ky. U., 1971; BS in Biology, Cen. State U., Wilberforce, Ohio, 1978; DDS, Case Western Res. U., 1982. Indsl. arts tchr. Dayton (Ohio) Bd. Edn., 1972-76; assoc. Hawes Realty, Dayton, 1974-83; resident in dentistry Med. Coll. of Ohio, Toledo, 1982-83; gen. practice dentistry Shaker Heights, Ohio, 1983-84, Cleveland Heights, Ohio, 1984—. Recipient Kenneth W. Clement award Cleve. City COuncil, 1981; named one of Outstanding Young Men of Am., U.S. Jaycees, 1984. Office: 2204 S Taylor Rd Cleveland Heights OH 44118

RUSSELL, LIANE BRAUCH, geneticist; b. Vienna, Austria, Aug. 27, 1923; came to U.S., 1941; d. Arthur and Clara (Starer) B.; m. William Lawson Russell, Sept. 23, 1947; children: David Lawson, Evelyn Ruth. AB, Hunter Coll., 1945; PhD, U. Chgo., 1949. Fellow U. Chgo., 1945-46, teaching asst., 1946-47; research asst. Jackson Lab., Bar Harbor, Maine, 1945, 46; research staff mem. Oak Ridge (Tenn.) Nat. Lab., 1947-75, sect. head., 1975-95, disting. research staff mem., 1983—; sci. advisor U.S. Del. at 1st Atoms for Peace Conf., Geneva, Switzerland, 1955; mem. numerous sci. bds. including Nat. Research Council com. on energy and environment, 1975-77, com. on biol. effects of ionizing radiation, 1977-80, bd. on environ. studies and toxicology, 1981-90, Nat. Council on Radiation Protection and Measurement Task Group, Washington, 1975-77, Genetox Program EPA, Washington, 1979—, Internat. Com. for Protection Against Environ. Mutagens and Carcinogens, Lausanne, Switzerland, 1977-83, Internat. com. on standardized genetic nomenclature for mice, 1977-91, office of tech. assessment, scientific adv. panel, 1985-86; mem. task group Internat. Agy. for Research on Cancer, Hanover, Fed. Republic of Germany, 1979, EPA review panel on mutagenicity guidelines, 1985-86. Assoc. editor: Mutation Research, 1976—, Environ. Mutagenesis, 1980-83; editor: TCWP Newsletter, 1966—; editor: (book) Genetic Mosaics and Chimeras, 1979; contbr. over 135 articles in field to profl. jours. Founder Tenn. Citizens for Wilderness Planning, Oak Ridge, 1966, pres. 1967-70, 86-87; active numerous environ. groups. Corp. fellow Union Carbide, 1983; corp. fellow Martin Marietta, 1985, sr. corp. fellow, 1988; recipient Merit award Mademoiselle, 1955, Roentgen medal City of Remscheid-Lennep, 1973, Disting. Assoc. award U.S. Dept. Energy, 1987; named to Hall of Fame Hunter Coll., 1979, Sol Feinstone Environ. Achievement award, N.Y., 1987, Tenn. Environ. Coun. Lifetime Achievement award, 1990, Oak Ridge Rotary Club Vocational Svc. award, 1992, Marjorie Stoneman Douglas award Nat. Parks & Conservation Assn., 1993, Enrico Fermi award U.S. Dept. Energy, 1994. Fellow AAAS, Environ. Health Inst.; mem. Nat. Acad. Scis. (elected 1986), Environ. Mutagen Soc. (EMs award 1993, pres. 1984-85), Genetics Soc. Am. (presdl. nominee 1979). Avocation: environ. acitivism. Office: Oak Ridge Nat Lab Biol Divsn PO Box 2009 Oak Ridge TN 37831-8077

RUSSELL, LILLIAN, medical, surgical nurse; b. N.Y.C., Feb. 21, 1942; d. Joserelle Russell; 1 child, Evan Gregory. AAS, N.Y.C. Community Coll., 1973; BS, St. Xavier Coll., Chgo., 1986; MS, Spertus Coll. of Judaica, Chgo., 1989. Staff/charge nurse Beth Israel Med. Ctr., N.Y.C., 1973-76; charge nurse Roosevelt Hosp., N.Y.C., 1977-78; staff/charge nurse U. Ill. Hosp., Chgo., 1979—; asst. adminstrv. coord. Bethany Hosp., Chgo., 1990-91; adminstv. nurse I Mile Square Health Ctr. & U. Ill. Hosp., Chgo., 1991-95; asst. dir. nursing Mile Square Health Ctr., Chgo., 1995—; mem. instnl. rev. com. Bethany Hosp., 1987—; adj. asst. prof. Trinity Christian Coll., Palos Heights, Ill., 1996—. Mem. Great Cities Com., Chgo., 1994—. Mem. ANA, NAFE, AAUW, Ill. Nurses Assn., Res. Officers Assn. Home: 1342 N Oakley Blvd Chicago IL 60622-3048 *Everyone is born a genius. Some are recognized and nurtured to greatness; some are ignored and the genius withers and fades. The rest of us are fortunate to have a teacher or mentor who finds our special genius and makes it shine so everyone we encounter sees it too.*

RUSSELL, LOUISE, educator, folklorist; b. Stratford, Okla., Aug. 9, 1931; d. Virgel Wylie and Louise J. (Hayden) R. BA magna cum laude, Oklahoma City U., 1953; MA, Northwestern U., 1955; PhD, Ind. U., 1977; postgrad. Ea. N.Mex. U., Ruidoso, 1992-93. Sterling, Colo., 1958-59, Washington-Lee High Sch., Arlington, Va., 1959-62, John Handley High Sch., Winchester, Va., 1962-63, Weld Sch. Dist. No. 6, Greeley, Colo., 1963-68, 72-87, Colegio Internacional, Valencia, Venezuela, 1968-69, Holmdel Schs., N.J., 1971-72; chmn. staff devel. team, English and basic skills, subject specialist Northland

Pioneer Coll., Holbrook, Ariz., 1987-91; instr. English humanities Ea. N.Mex. U., 1992-93; with Dulce (Ind. Sch. Dist., 1994—. Author: Understanding Folklore, 1975, Understanding Folk Music, 1977; also articles. Named Tchr. of Yr. Masons; Grant dir. Title V Indian Edn., 1994—. Mem. MLA, Am. Anthrop. Assn., Am. Folklore Soc., Nat. Coun. Tchrs. English, Apache County Hist. Soc. (mus. bd.), Kiwanis, Phi Delta Kappa. Office: Dulce Ind Sch Dist PO Box 547 Dulce NM 87528-0547

RUSSELL, LOUISE BENNETT, economist, educator; b. Exeter, N.H., May 12, 1942; d. Frederick Dewey and Esther (Smith) B.; m. Robert Hardy Cosgriff, May 3, 1987; 1 child, Benjamin Smith. BA, U. Mich., 1964; PhD, Harvard U., 1971. Economist Social Security Adminstrn., Washington, 1968-71, Nat. Commn. on State Workmen's Compensation Laws, Washington, 1971-72, Dept. Labor, Washington, 1972-73; sr. economist Nat. Planning Assn., Washington, 1973-75; sr. fellow Brookings Instn., Washington, 1975-87; rsch. prof. Inst. for Health, Health Care Policy and Aging Rsch. Rutgers U., New Brunswick, N.J., 1987—, prof. econs., 1987—; chmn. health care policy divsn. Rutgers U., 1988—; mem. tech. bd. Milbank Fund, 1993-95. Author: Technology in Hospitals, 1979, The Baby Boom Generation and the Economy, 1982, Is Prevention Better Than Cure, 1986, Evaluating Preventive Care: Report on a Workshop, 1987, Medicare's New Hospital Payment System: Is It Working, 1989, Educated Guesses: Making Policy About Medical Screening Tests, 1994; also numerous articles. Mem. U.S. Preventive Svcs. Task Force, 1984-88; co-chair Panel on Cost Effectiveness in Health and Medicine DHHS, ODPHP, 1993—. Mem. Inst. Medicine of NAS (com. to study future pub. health 1986-87, bd. on health scis. policy 1989-91, com. on clin. practice guidelines 1990-91, com. on setting priorities for practice guidelines 1994). Office: Rutgers U Inst for Health Care Policy 30 College Ave New Brunswick NJ 08903

RUSSELL, LYNN DARNELL, mechanical engineer, educator; b. Pontotoc, Miss., Nov. 1, 1937; s. Clyde Austin and Clytee Lora (Faulkner) R.; m. Elaine Lowery, June 16, 1963; children—Kathy, Brent, Mark, Jeffrey. B.S., Miss. State U., 1960, M.S., 1961; Ph.D., Rice U., 1966. Profl. engr. Ala., Miss., Tenn. Engr. NASA Marshall Space Flight Ctr., Johnson Spacecraft Ctr., 1961-64; research scientist Lockheed, Huntsville, Ala., 1966-67; mem. tech. staff TRW, Huntsville, 1967-69; dean engring. U. Tenn.-Chattanooga, 1969-79; prof. mech. engring. Miss. State U., 1979-87, dean Coll. Engring., U. Ala., Huntsville, 1987—; energy cons. Recipient numerous fellowships and grants. Mem. Chattanooga Engrs. Club (pres. 1975); pres. Tenn. Soc. Profl. Engrs., 1978-79. Mem. ASME, Nat. Soc. Profl. Engrs., Ala. Soc. Profl. Engrs., Am. Soc. Engring. Edn., Internat. Solar Energy Soc., Sigma Xi, Pi Tau Sigma (past pres. Miss. chpt.). Contbr. articles to profl. jours. Office: U Ala 300 Sparkman Dr NW Huntsville AL 35899

RUSSELL, MARGARET JONES (PEG RUSSELL), secondary school educator; b. Durham, N.C., Apr. 25, 1938; d. Roderic O. and Margaret (Moore) Jones; m. Michael Morgan Russell; children: Lauren Skinner, Carol Martin, Seth Russell, Jay Russell. BA, Muskingum Coll., 1961. Ordained deacon Presbyn. Ch., 1970. Tchr. Sarasota (Fla.) County Sch. Bd., 1962—, Sarasota H.S., 1982—; sponsor literary mag. Quest, 1988—. Editor newsletter The Mainsail, 1989-95; contbr. poems to Fla. English Jour., Light Years Anthology; contbr. articles to newsletters and newspapers. ARC vol. Sarasota Meml. Hosp., 1966-83, aux. vol., 1994—; reader Fla. Studio Theatre, Sarasota, 1980—. Sarasota Herald Tribune scholar, 1993; Fla. Writing Project fellow, 1990. Mem. Nat. Coun. Tchrs. English, Fla. Coun. Tchrs. English (presenter), Fla. Freelance Writers, Light Verse Workshop, Sarasota Fiction Writers, Meadows Country Club, Alpha Gamma Delta. Republican. Presbyterian. Home: 1150 Willis Ave Sarasota FL 34232-2148 Office: Sarasota HS 1000 S School Ave Sarasota FL 34237-8016

RUSSELL, MARIANNE, human resources manager; b. Kansas City, Mo., Oct. 9, 1963; d. William Howard and Linda Lee (Chinn) Chenault; m. Michael Robert Ludy, Nov. 30, 1985 (div. Feb. 1991); 1 child, Elliott Tyler Ludy; m. Gary William Russell, Sept. 5, 1992; 1 child, Shannon Kathleen. BA, Park Coll., 1991; postgrad., Ottawa U., 1993—. Cert. profl. human resources mgr. Benefits adminstr. Borden, Inc., Liberty, Mo., 1983-84; mktg. svcs. adminstr. Western Water Mgmt., North Kansas City, Mo., 1984-87, mktg. svcs. mgr., 1988—; human resources mgr. Western Water Mgmt., North Kansas City, 1992—. Mem. siltation control com. Weatherby Lake (Mo.) Improvement Co., 1993; vol. Platte County (Mo.) 4-H, 1992—; recreation chmn. Renner Elem. PTA, Kansas City, Mo., 1993—. Mem. Am. mgmt. Assn., Soc. Human Resource Mgmt., Human Resource Mgmt. Assn. of Kansas City, Job Svc. Employer's Com. (hospitality com. 1992—), NAFE. Republican. Roman Catholic. Home: 8111 NW Miami St Weatherby Lake MO 64152 Office: Western Water Mgmt 1345 Taney St Kansas City MO 64116

RUSSELL, MARJORIE ROSE, manufacturing company executive; b. Welcome, Minn., Sept. 3, 1925; d. Emil Frederick and Ella Magdalene (Sothman) Wohlenhaus; m. Kenneth Kollmann Russell, Sept. 15, 1947 (div. May 1973); children: Jennie Rose, Richard Lowell, Laura Eloise, James Wesley. Student, Northwestern Sch., Mpls., 1944-45, St. Paul Bible Inst., 1946-47. Cook U. Minn., Mpls., 1943-45; maintenance person U. Farm Campus/N.W. Schs., St. Paul, 1945-46; clk. Kresge Corp., Mpls., 1945; cook, waitress, mgr. Union City Mission Bible Camp, Mpls., 1944-47; caterer for v.p. Gt. No. R.R., St. Paul, 1947; custodian Old Soldiers Home, St. Paul, 1946; nurse Sister Elizabeth Kenney Polio Hosp., St. Paul, 1946; seamstress Hirsch, Weis, White Stag, Pendleton, Mayfair, Portland, Oreg., 1960-72; owner, operator, contract mgr., creative designer The Brass Needle, Portland, 1972—; contractor Forrester's Sanderson Safety, Scotsco, Nero & Assocs., Gara Gear, Portland, 1972—, Columbia Sportswear; tchr. Indo Chinese Cultural Ctr., Portland, 1982; mfr. of protective chaps and vests for the Pacific Northwest hogging industry. Designer, producer Kisn Bridal Fair, 1969; composer: He Liveth in Me, 1968; prodr. Safety Chaps for Loggers. Sec. Model Cities Com., Portland, 1969; com. mem. Neighborhood Black Christmas Parade, Portland, 1970; custume designer Local Miss Jr. Black Beauty Contest, Portland, 1973; nominating com. Nat. Contract Mgmt. Assn., Portland, 1978; mem. nominating com. Multi-Cultural Sr. Adv. Com., 1988-91. Mem. NAFE, Urban League, Urban League Guild (historian 1991-92), Am. Assn. Ret. Persons, Nat. Contract Mgmt. Assn. Democrat. Mem. United Ch. of Christ. Avocations: music, swimming, painting, gardening, arts. Home and Office: The Brass Needle 2809 NE 12th Ave Portland OR 97212-3219

RUSSELL, MARK, comedian; b. Buffalo, Aug. 23, 1932; s. Marcus Joseph and Marie Elizabeth (Perry) Ruslander; m. Alison Kaplan, Dec. 17, 1978; children: Monica, John, Matthew. Student, George Washington U., 1952; LittD, Union Coll., 1987; LHD, Canisius Coll., 1988; LHD (hon.), Goucher Coll., 1990. lectr., public speaker. Polit. comedian, featured performer Shoreham Hotel, Washington, 1961-81; prin. Mark Russell Comedy Spls., Pub. Broadcasting Svc., 1975—; host Mark Russell's England, PBS-TV, 1988, Mark Russell's Irish Fling, 1993, Mark Russell's Great Ala. Trek, 1994, Mark Russell's Tour de France, 1995, Mark Russell's Viva Italia, 1996; co-host NBC's Real People, 1979-84; regular contbr. Good Morning Am., ABC-TV, Inside Politics Weekend, CNN; author: Presenting Mark Russell, 1980; syndicated columnist via L.A. Times Syndicate, 1975. Served with USMC, 1953-56. Recipient Mark Twain award Internat. Platform Assn., 1980, 86, 4th Ann. Lucy award Shea's Buffalo, 1992, Nat. Humor Treasure award Nat. Humor Conf., 1995, SOAR St. Elizabeth Ann Seton award Washington, 1995, Washingtonian of the Yr. Washington Mag., 1996. Mem. AFTRA, Am. Fedn. Musicians. Office: 2800 Wisconsin Ave NW Washington DC 20007-4703

RUSSELL, MARY WENDELL VANDER POEL, non-profit organization executive, interior; b. N.Y.C., Feb. 6, 1919; d. William Halsted and Blanche Pauline (Billings) Vander Poel; m. George Montagu Miller, Apr. 5, 1940 (div. 1974); children: Wendell Miller Steavenson, Gretchen Miller Elkus; m. Sinclair Hatch, May 14, 1977 (dec. July 1989); m. William F. Russell, June 24, 1995 (dec. Apr. 1996). Pres. Miller Richard, Inc., Interior Decorators, Glen Head, N.Y., 1972—; bd. dirs. Eye Bank Sight Restoration, N.Y.C., 1975—, pres., 1980-88, hon. chair, 1988—; bd. dirs. Manhattan Eye Ear and Throat Hosp., N.Y.C., 1966-92, v.p., 1978-90; sec. Cold Spring Harbor Lab., N.Y., 1985-89, 92—, bd. dirs., 1985-90; chair DNA Learning Ctr., 1991—; bd. dirs. Cold Spring Harbor Lab, 1991—, sec., 1992—. V.p. North Country Garden Club, Nassau County, N.Y., 1979-81, 1983-85; dir. Planned Parenthood Nassau County, Mineola, N.Y., 1982-84, Hutton House C.W.Post Coll.,Greenvale, N.Y., 1982—; chair Hutton House, 1992-94. Recipient Disting. Trustee award United Hosp. Fund, 1992. Mem. Colony Club (N.Y.C.), Church Club (N.Y.C.), Piping Rock Club (Long Island), Order St. John Jerusalem (N.Y.C.). Republican. Episcopalian. Home: Mill River Rd # 330 Oyster Bay NY 11771-2733

RUSSELL, MICHAEL JAMES, lawyer; b. Northampton, Mass., May 19, 1958; s. John Michael and Celia (Jaskolka) R. Cert. in German, U. Vienna, 1979; BA summa cum laude, Gettysburg Coll., 1980; MA, JD, Vanderbilt U., 1984. Bar: Pa. 1984, D.C. 1985. Rsch. asst. Vanderbilt U., Nashville, 1982-84; legal intern U.S. State Dept., Washington, 1982; law clk. Stewart, Estes & Donnell, Nashville, 1983; atty. U.S. Dept. Agr., Washington, 1984-85; majority counsel subcom. on juvenile justice senate judiciary com. U.S. Senate, Washington, 1985-86, minority gen. counsel subcom. on constn., 1987, legis. dir. to Senator Arlen Specter, 1987-90; senate staff mem. Congrl. Crime Caucus, 1987-90; dep. dir. Nat. Inst. Justice U.S. Dept. Justice, Washington, 1990-93, acting dir., 1993-94; pres. Russell & Assocs., Washington, 1994-96; sr. pub. safety advisor Corp. Nat. Svc., Washington, 1994-96; dep. chief of staff to Senator Ben Nighthorse Campbell, 1996—. Editorial staff Vanderbilt Jour. Transnat. Law, Nashville, 1982-83, contbr., 1983, rsch. editor, 1983-84 (editor award 1984). Mem. senate staff club, 1985-90, Bush/Quayle Campaign's Crime Adv. Com., 1988, Friends of the Nat. Parks at Gettysburg, Pa., 1989—; bd. fellows Gettysburg Coll., 1990—; vol. Nat. Constrn. Ctr., Phila., 1990; mem. Bush/Quayle Adminstrn. S.E.S. Assn., 1990-92; Eisenhower Leadership Prize Dinner Com., Eisenhower World Affairs Inst., 1992, 93, mem. com. to celebrate bicentennial of constn., Northampton, Mass., 1987; mem. Bush/Quayle Alumni Assn., 1993—. Recipient Voluntary Svc. award VA, Northampton, 1978, Trustees award Forbes Libr., Northampton, 1989, cert. of appreciation Correctional Edn. Assn., 1991, Phi Alpha Delta, 1989, Fed. Bur. Alcohol, Tobacco and Firearms, 1989, Gettysburg Coll. Career Svcs. Office, 1992, Young Alumni Achievement award Gettysburg Coll., 1992, Wasserstein Fellowship Harvard Law Sch. Office of Pub. Interest Adv., 1995-96. Mem. ABA, Am. Soc. Internat. Law, Pa. Soc. of Washington, Phi Beta Kappa, Psi Chi (jr. award 1979). Avocations: racquetball, politics, community svc. Office: Office Senator Ben Nighthorse Campbell 380 Russell Senate Office Bldg Washington DC 20510

RUSSELL, NEWTON REQUA, state senator; b. L.A., June 25, 1927; s. John Henry and Amy (Requa) R.; m. Diane Henderson, Feb. 12, 1953; children: Stephen, Sharon, Julia. BS, U. So. Calif., 1951; postgrad. UCLA, Georgetown U. Spl. agt. Northwestern Mut. Life Ins. Co., Calif., 1954-64; mem. Calif. State Assembly, 1964-74, Calif. Senate, 1974—; vice-chmn. com. on energy, utilities and comm., mem. com. on local govt., mem. com. on fin. and investment, internat. trade, mem. com. on transp., com. ins., joint com. on rules, select com. on Calif.'s wine industry, mem. Com. on Legis. Ethics, Joint Oversight Com. on Lowering the Cost of Electric Svcs, chmn. senate select com. mediation. Mem. Rep. State Central Com. Served with USN, 1945-46. Recipient Outstanding Legislator award Calif. Rep. Assembly, 1968, 76, 81, Mayor's commendation City of Burbank, 1978, Disting. Service award County Suprs. Assn. Calif., 1980, Nat. Rep. Legislator of Yr., 1981, Legislator of Yr. award Los Angeles County Fedn. Rep. Women, 1982, Legislator of Yr. award Calif. Credit Union League, 1983, Paul Harris Fellow award Rotary Found. Rotary Internat., numerous honors from cmty. orgns. and instns. Mem. Rotary Internat., Am. Legion, Delta Tau Delta, Alpha Kappa Phi. Mem. Church on the Way. Office: Office of State Senate 401 N Brand Blvd Ste 424 Glendale CA 91203-2307

RUSSELL, PAUL EDGAR, electrical engineering educator; b. Roswell, N.Mex., Oct. 10, 1924; s. Rueben Matthias and Mary (Parsons) R.; m. Lorna Margaret Clayshulte, Aug. 29, 1943; children: Carol Potter, Janice Russell Cook, Gregory. BSEE, N.Mex. State U., 1946, BSME, 1947; MSEE, U. Wis., 1950, PhDEE, 1951. Registered elec. engr., Ariz., Minn., S.C. From instr. to asst. prof. elec. engring. U. Wis., Madison, 1947-52; sr. engr., design specialist Gen. Dynamics Corp., San Diego, 1952-54; from prof. to chmn. elec. engring. dept. U. Ariz., Tucson, 1954-63; dean engring. Kans. State U., Manhattan, 1963-67; prof. Ariz. State U., Tempe, 1967-90; dir. engring. Ariz. State U. West, Phoenix, 1985-88; dir. Sch. Constrn. and Tech. Ariz. State U., Tempe, 1988-90; cons. in field, 1954—; programs evaluator, mem. engring. commn. Accreditation Bd. for Engring. and Tech., N.Y.C., 1968-81. Contbr. articles to jours. and chpts. to books. Served as sgt. U.S. Army, 1944-46. Recipient Disting. Service award N.Mex. State U., 1965. Fellow IEEE (life, chmn. Ariz. sect. 1960), Accreditation Bd. Engring. and Tech.; mem. Am. Soc. Engring. Educators. Home: 5902 E Caballo Ln Paradise Valley AZ 85253

RUSSELL, PAUL FREDERICK, lawyer; b. Kansas City, Mo., Feb. 3, 1948; s. Walter Edward and Dorothy Marie (Sickels) R.; m. Kerry Diann Anderson, June 2, 1973; children: Philip, Erin, Shannon, Kelsey, Scott. BA, Northwestern, 1970; JD, U. Mich., 1973. Bar: Ill. 1973, U.S. Dist. Ct. (no. dist.) Ill. 1973. Assoc. Vedder, Price, Kaufman & Kammholz, Chgo., 1973-79, ptnr., 1980—. Mem. ABA, Chgo. Bar Assn., Ill. State Bar Assn., Midwest Benefits Coun., University Club (Chgo.), Mich. Shores Club. Office: Vedder Price Kaufman & Kammholz 222 N La Salle St Chicago IL 60601-1003

RUSSELL, PAUL SNOWDEN, surgeon, educator; b. Chgo., Jan. 22, 1925; s. Paul Snowden and Carroll (Mason) R.; m. Allene Lummis, Sept. 24, 1952; children—Katherine Swift, Paul Snowden, Allene, Laura Rice. Student, Groton (Mass.) Sch., 1939-41; Ph.B., U. Chgo., 1944, B.S., 1945, M.D., 1947; M.A. (hon.), Harvard U., 1962. Diplomate: Am. Bd. Surgery, Am. Bd. Thoracic Surgery. From surg. intern, to resident Mass. Gen. Hosp., 1948-56, asst. surgery, 1957-60, chief gen. surg. services, 1962-69, vis. surgeon, 1969—, chief transplantation unit, 1969-90, chmn. com. on research, 1973-76; postdoctoral fellow USPHS, 1954-55; successively teaching fellow, instr., clin. asso. surgery Harvard Med. Sch., 1956-60, John Homans prof. surgery, 1962—; asso. prof. surgery Columbia Coll. Phys. and Surg., 1960-62; asso. attending surgeon Presbyn. Hosp., N.Y.C., 1960-62; assoc. vis. surgeon Francis Delafield Hosp., N.Y.C., 1960-62, 74-94; bd. dirs. Warner Lambert Co.; mem. com. tissue transplantation NRC-Nat. Acad. Scis., 1963-71, com. trauma, 1963-68; ad hoc com. to study clin. investigation and edn. in USN, 1971-73; allergy and immunology study sect. USPHS, 1963-65, chmn. allergy and immunology study sect. B, 1965-67; mem. transplantation and immunology com. Nat. Inst. Allergy and Infectious Diseases, 1967-69, chmn., 1970; mem. com. on cancer immunotherapy Nat. Cancer Inst., 1974-79. Contbr. papers in field.; Editorial bd.: Archives Surgery, 1963-72, Surgery, 1963-71, Transplantation, 1965-79, Annals of Surgery, 1966—, Transplantation Procs, 1966—, Jour. Immunology, 1977-80. Trustee Pine Manor Coll., Chestnut Hill, Mass., 1963-76, Groton Sch., 1964-79; bd. dirs. Boston Fulbright Com., 1968, pres., 1980; bd. governing trustees Jackson Lab.; bd. trustees Worcester Found. for Biomed. Rsch. With USAF, 1951-53. Fellow ACS, Royal Soc. Medicine; mem. AAAS, Am. Acad. Arts and Scis., Assn. Immunologists, N.Y. Acad. Scis., Mass. Med. Soc., New Eng. Surg. Soc., Boston Surg. Soc. (pres. 1994), Soc. Univ. Surgeons, Soc. Exptl. Biology and Medicine, Halsted Soc., Whipple Soc., Internat. Soc. Surgery, Am. Surg. Assn., Transplantation Soc. (pres. 1970), Polish Acad. Sci. (fgn.), Sigma Xi. Home: 32 Lawrence Rd Chestnut Hill MA 02167-1230 Office: Dept Surgery Mass Gen Hosp Boston MA 02114

RUSSELL, PEGGY TAYLOR, soprano, educator; b. Newton, N.C., Apr. 5, 1927; d. William G. and Sue B. (Cordell) Taylor; Mus.B. in Voice, Salem Coll., 1948; Mus.M., Columbia U., 1950; postgrad. U. N.C., Greensboro, 1977; student Am. Inst. Mus. Studies, Austria, 1972, 78; student of Clifford Bair, Nell Starr, Salem Coll., Winston-Salem, N.C., Edgar Schofield, Chloe Owen, N.Y.C.; student opera-dramatics Boris Goldovsky, Southwestern Opera Inst., Ande Andersen, Max Lehner, Graz, Austria; m. John B. Russell, Feb. 23, 1952; children: John Spotswood, Susan Bryce. Mem. faculty dept. voice Guilford Coll., Greensboro, 1952-53, Greensboro Coll., 1971-72; pvt. tchr. voice, Greensboro, 1963—; co-founder, v.p. sales, mktg. Russell Textiles, Inc., 1988; vis. instr. in voice U. N.C., Chapel Hill, 1973-77; founding artistic dir., gen. mgr. Young Artists Opera Theatre, Greensboro, 1983; staged and produced 18 operatic prodns., 1983-91; guest lectr. opera workshop U. N.C., Greensboro, 1990-91; lectr. opera Friends of Weymouth, So. Pines, N.C., 1994; lectr. on music history and opera, High Point, N.C., Center for Creative Leadership, Greensboro, 1979-80, First Presbyn. Ch., 1982; debut in light opera as Gretchen in The Red Mill, Winston-Salem Opera Assn., 1947; debuts include: Rosalinda in Die Fledermaus, Piedmont Festival Opera Assn., 1949, Lola in Cavalleria Rusticana, Greensboro Opera Assn., 1951, Violetta in La Traviata, Greensboro Opera Assn., 1953, Fiordiligi in Cosi fan tutte, Piedmont Opera Co., 1956; appeared as Marguerite in Faust, Brevard Music Center Resident Opera Co., 1967, First Lady in The Magic Flute, Am. Inst. Mus. Studies, Graz, Austria, 1972; mem. Greensboro Oratorio Soc., 1955-59, soprano soloist in The Messiah, 1952, 58, The Creation, 1955, Solomon, 1958; soprano soloist Presbyterian Ch. of the Covenant, Greensboro, 1958-71; guest appearances Sta. WFMY-TV, Greensboro, 1958-62; soprano soloist with Greensboro Symphony Orch., 1964, 80, Eastern Music Festival Orch. 1965, Greensboro Civic Orch., 1980; soloist in numerous recitals including: Wesleyan Coll., 1964, Roanoke Symphony Guild, 1967, Am. Inst. Mus. Studies, Austria, 1972, 78, U. N.C., Chapel Hill, 1974, 75, 76, 77, N.C. Mus. of Art, 1978; recital, masterclass Mars Hill Coll., 1981. Bd. dirs. Music Theater Assocs., Greensboro Friends of Music, N.C. Lyric Opera; judge Charlotte Opera Guild Auditions, 1994. Mem. Friendship Force of Guilford County, Holland, 1985, No. Germany, 1987. scholarship grantee N.C. Arts Council and Nat. Endowment for the Arts, 1991. Mem. Nat. Opera Assn. (chmn. regional opera cos. com. 1985-91, judge vocal competition auditions 1991, 92, 94, chmn. trustees Cofield Endowment 1991), Central Opera Service, Nat. Assn. Tchrs. of Singing (state gov. 1976-82, coordinator Regional Artist Contest 1982-84), N.C. Fedn. Music Clubs (dir. 1956-58), Music Educators Nat. Conf., Greensboro Music Tchrs. Assn. (pres. 1966-67), Symphony Guild (dir. 1977-78), Broadway Theater League (chmn. 1961-63), Atlanta Opera Guild, Civic Music Assn. (chmn. 1963-64), English Speaking Union (bd. dirs. Greensboro chpt., chmn. Shakespeare competition 1995), N.C. Symphony Soc., Piedmont Triad Coun. Internat. Vis. (Appreciation award Nat. Coun. Internat. Visitors 1994), Greensboro Preservation Soc., Guilford County Planning/Devel. Office (Forecast 2015 Com.). Presbyterian. Clubs: Sherwood Swim and Racquet, The Greensboro City. Home: 3012 W Cornwallis Dr Greensboro NC 27408-6730

RUSSELL, RALPH ERNEST, librarian, educator; b. Bradenton, Fla., Jan. 25, 1938; s. Wilbur Lee and Beatrice (Parrish) R.; m. Linda Dee Sherman, June 16, 1962; 1 child, Lauren Susan Russell Fallon. BA in English, Fla. State U., 1960, MLS, 1961, PhD in Libr. Sci., 1973; MA in English, NYU, 1962. Br. reference libr. Queens Borough Pub. Libr., N.Y.C., 1961-62; asst. circulation libr., asst. acquisitions libr. U. So. Calif., L.A., 1964-66; head libr. Fla. Jr. Coll., Jacksonville, 1966-68; sci. libr. U. Ga., Athens, 1968-71; dir. libr. svcs. East Carolina U., Greenville, N.C., 1973-75; libr. Ga. State U., Atlanta, 1975—; cons. Xavier U., 1990, U. Wis.-Oshkosh, 1991, S.C. Commn. Higher Edn., 1992; bd. dirs. Southeastern Libr. Network, chmn. bd. dirs., nominating com., 1977, chair, 1982; bd. trustees OCLC, 1988-94, audit com. 1989, personnel and compensation com. 1990; chair Regents' Acad. Com., 1988-89; adv. coun. State of Ga. Libr. Svcs. and Constrn. Act., 1981-83; mem. exec. bd. dirs. Friends of the Atlanta-Fulton Pub. Libr., 1981-85, chair exec. bd. dirs., 1985-87; mem. libr. coun. U. Ctr. in Ga., Inc. Contbr. articles to profl. jours. Mem. presdl. inaugural commn. Ga. State U., 1993, chair com. on inaugural pub. events and ceremonies; program chair Ga. Gov.'s Conf. on Librs. and Info. Svcs., 1990; elected Ga. del. to 1991 White House Conf. on Librs. and Info. Svcs. With USN, 1962-64. Coun. on Libr. Resources grantee, 1977-78, NEH grantee, 1990-94; named Acad./Rsch. Libr. of Yr. ACRL, 1996. Mem. ALA (coun.), Southeastern Libr. Assn. (chair coll. and u. sect. 1978-80, hdqrs. com. 1983-85, chair program com. 1986), Ga. Libr. Assn. (2nd v.p. 1986-87), Met. Atlanta Libr. Assn. (v.p. 1976-77, pres. 1977-78), Omicron Delta Kappa, Beta Phi Mu, Phi Kappa Phi. Republican. Presbyterian. Avocations: running, swimming, piano, trashy ficion. Home: 96 Spring Lake Pl NW Atlanta GA 30318-1646 Office: Ga State U U Libr 100 Decatur St SE Atlanta GA 30303-3202

RUSSELL, RICHARD, religious organization adminstrator. Moderator North Am. Baptist Conf., Villa Park, Il. Office: North American Baptist Conf 1 S 210 Summit Ave Villa Park IL 60181

RUSSELL, RICHARD DONCASTER, geophysicist, educator, geoscientist; b. Toronto, Ont., Can., Feb. 27, 1929; s. Richard Douglas and Ada Gwennola (Doncaster) R.; m. Virginia Ann Reid Clippingdale, Aug. 11, 1951; children: Linda Jean, Morna Ann, Mary Joyce. BA, U. Toronto, 1951, MA, 1952, PhD, 1954. Asst. prof. physics U. Toronto, 1956-58, prof., 1962-63; asso. prof. physics U. B.C., Vancouver, 1958-62; prof. geophysics U. B.C., 1963-91, prof. emeritus, 1991—, head dept. geophysics, 1968-72, head dept. geophysics and astronomy, 1972-79, bd. govs., 1978-81, assoc. dean sci., 1980-83, assoc. v.p. acad., 1983-86; sec.-gen. Inter-Union Commn. on Geodynamics, 1976-80; profl. geoscientist. Author textbooks.; Contbr. articles to profl. jours. Fellow Royal Soc. Can.; mem. Am. Geophys. Union, Can. Geophys. Union (J. Tuzo Wilson medal 1992). Home: 226-4955 River Rd, Delta, BC Canada V4K 4V9 Office: Dept Earth and Ocean Scis U BC, Vancouver, BC Canada V6T 1Z4

RUSSELL, RICHARD OLNEY, JR., cardiologist, educator; b. Birmingham, Ala., July 9, 1932; s. Richard Olney and Louise (Taylor) R.; m. Phyllis Hutchinson, June 15, 1963; children: Scott Richard, Katherine Hutchinson, Meredith Cooper, Stephen Wilbon. A.B., Vanderbilt U., 1953, M.D., 1956. Diplomate Am. Bd. Internal Medicine, Am. Bd. Cardiovascular Disease. Intern Peter Bent Brigham Hosp., Boston, 1956-57; resident Peter Bent Brigham Hosp., 1959-60, 63-64; fellow in cardiology Med. Coll. Ala., Birmingham, 1960-62; instr. Med. Coll. Ala., 1962-63; instr. medicine U. Ala., Birmingham, 1964-65; asst. prof. U. Ala., 1965-70, assoc. prof., 1970-73, prof., 1973-81, clin. prof., 1981—; practice medicine specializing in cardiology Birmingham, 1981—; Mem. Jefferson County Bd. Health, 1977-81, chmn., 1979. Author: (with Charles Edward Rackley) Hemodynamic Monitoring in a Coronary Intensive Care Unit, 1974, 2d rev. and enlarged edit., 1981, Coronary Artery Disease: Recognition and Management, 1979, (with others) Radiographic Anatomy of the Coronary Arteries: An Atlas, 1976, Acute Ischemic Syndromes in American College of Cardiology Self Assessment Program, 1993; mem. editorial bd. Circulation, 1976-80, Am. Jour. Cardiology, 1977-82, Heart and Lung, 1978-83, Chest, 1978-83, Ala. Jour. Med. Scis, 1977-80, Jour. Am. Coll. Cardiology, 1987-90; contbr. articles to profl. jours. Distbn. com. Greater Birmingham Found., 1984-90; exec. bd. Birmingham area coun. Boy Scouts Am., 1987—, v.p., 1990-96, coun. commr., 1996—, vice chmn. Vulcan dist., 1988-89, chmn., 1989-91, bd. dirs. S.E. region, 1990-92, bd. dirs. southern region, 1992—; bd. dirs. Ctrl. Ala. United Way, 1988-92; mem. Newcomen Soc., 1988—; chmn. exec. com. Birmingham Bapt. Med. Ctr., Montclair, 1995. Decorated Commendation medal; recipient Dist. Award of Merit, Boy Scouts Am., 1991, Silver Beaver award, 1990; NIH rsch. fellow, 1966-67. Fellow ACP, Am. Coll. Cardiology (bd. govs. 1979-81, trustee 1984-85, 89-94, ann. sci. session program chmn. 1994); mem. Am. Heart Assn. (pres. Ala. affiliate 1975-76, v.p. so. region 1986-87), Am. Coll. Chest Physicians (bd. regents 1985-91), Am. Fedn. Clin. Rsch., Am. Bd. Cardiovascular Disease, So. Soc. Clin. Investigation, Jefferson County Med. Soc. (v.p. 1982, pres. 1984), Birmingham Cardiovascular Soc. (pres. 1981), Med. Assn. State Ala. (speaker house counselors dels. 1989-94), Leadership Birmingham, Kiwanis (Birmingham sec. 1984-85, pres. 1994-95), Phi Beta Kappa, Alpha Omega Alpha, Omicron Delta Kappa. Home: 4408 Kennesaw Dr Birmingham AL 35213-1826 Office: Ala Heart Inst 880 Montclair Rd 1st Fl Birmingham AL 35213

RUSSELL, RICHARD R., chemicals executive. CEO Gen. Chem. Group, Hampton, N.H. Office: General Chemical Group Liberty Ln Hampton NH 03842*

RUSSELL, ROBERT C., plastic surgeon; b. Mansfield, Ohio, July 13, 1945. MD, Ind. U., 1972. Diplomate Am. Bd. Plastic Surgery. Intern Wishard Meml. Hosp., Indpls., 1972; resident gen. surgery Ind. U. Sch. Medicine, Indpls., 1973-75, resident plastic surgery, 1975-76; fellow plastic surgery St. Vincent's Hosp., Indpls., 1974, 76-77; resident Southern Ill. U. Sch. Medicine, Springfield, Ill., 1977-79; plastic surgeon St. John's Hosp., Springfield, Ill.; prof surg. divsn. plastic surgery Southern Ill. U., Springfield. Mem. AMA, Am. Assn. Hand Surgeons, Am. Soc. Plastic and Reconstructive Surgery, Am. Soc. Surgery for the Hand. Office: So Ill Sch Medicine PO Box 19230 747 N Rutledge St 3d Fl Springfield IL 62781

RUSSELL, ROBERT GILMORE, lawyer; b. Detroit, May 22, 1928; s. William Gilmore and Esther Marion (Redmond) R.; m. Martha Jones, July

9, 1955; children: Robin Russell Millstein, Julie Russell Smith. AB, U. Mich., 1951, JD, 1953. Bar: Mich. 1954. Atty. Kerr, Russell & Weber (and predecessors), Detroit, 1953—; ptnr. Kerr, Russell & Weber (and predecessors), 1959-93, of counsel, 1994—; instr. Wayne State U. Law Sch., 1954-60. Assoc. editor Mich. Law Rev., 1952-53. Fellow Am. Coll. Trial Lawyers, Am. Bar Found. (sustaining life), Mich. Bar Found. (charter); mem. ABA, ABOTA (advocate, charter mem. Mich. chpt.), Mich. Bar assn. (chair negligence coun. 1988-89), Detroit Bar Assn. (dir. 1977—, pres. 1981-82), Am. Judicature Soc., Am. Arbitration Assn., Internat. Assn. Def. Counsel, Assn. Def. Trial Counsel Detroit (pres. 1973-74), U.S. Supreme Ct. Hist. Soc., Mich. Supreme Ct. Hist. Soc., Nat. Conf. State Trial Cts. (mem. lawyers com.), Def. Rsch. Inst. Barristers, Order of Coif, Mimes, Theta Xi, Phi Delta Phi, Phi Eta Sigma, Thomas Colley Club. Home: 879 Sunningdale Dr Grosse Pointe MI 48236-1629 Office: Kerr Russell & Weber 500 Woodward Ave Detroit MI 48226-3423

RUSSELL, ROBERT HILTON, Romance languages and literature educator; b. Oak Park, Ill., Dec. 26, 1927; s. Melvin Alvord and Gladys (Hilton) R.; m. June Adele Thayer, Oct. 27, 1956. A.B., Knox Coll., 1949; A.M., Harvard U., 1950, Ph.D., 1963; A.M., Dartmouth Coll., 1968. Instr. Romance langs. and lits. Dartmouth Coll., 1957-61, asst. prof., 1961-63, assoc. prof., 1963-67, prof., 1967-91, prof. emeritus, 1991—; vis. prof. Spanish, U. San Diego, 1989, 90, 91, Knox Coll., 1993; guest lectr. Trinity Coll., Dublin, 1967, U. Salamanca, 1977, U. Leeds, 1978, Oxford U., 1978, U. P.R., 1987. Author: The Christ Figure in Misericordia, 1968; translator: Our Friend Manso, 1987. Corporate mem. United Ch. Bd. Homeland Ministries, 1963-69; N.H. del. Gen. Synod, United Ch. Christ, 1973, 75; corporator Internat. Inst. in Spain. Mem. MLA, Asociación Internacional de Hispanistas, Asociación Internacional de Galdosistas, Phi Beta Kappa. Democrat. Home: 14 Allen St Hanover NH 03755-2005 Office: 6072 Dartmouth Hall Hanover NH 03755-3511

RUSSELL, SALLY LYNN KOLITZ, clinical and neuropsychologist; b. Jersey City, Mar. 31, 1943; d. Norman and Sylvia (Goldstein) Ostrow; m. Elbert W. Russell, Apr. 2, 1989; 1 child, Brent Kolitz. BA, Vanderbilt U., 1965; MEd, U. Fla., 1967; PhD in Clin. Psychology, U. Miami (Fla.), 1986. Lic. psychologist, Fla.; diplomate Am. Bd. Profl. Disability Cons. Tchr. Bronson (Fla.) High Sch., 1965-66; dir. counseling Chamberlayne Jr. Coll., Boston, 1967-68; indsl. psychologist Gillette Co., Boston, 1968-69; dir. family life edn. Family Svc., Miami, 1971-75; researcher, grantee Am. Heart Assn., Miami, 1978-80; pvt. practice psychology Miami, 1986—. Author: Psychology of the Cardiac Patient, 1980, 88. Mem. APA, Nat. Acad. Neuropsychologists, Internat. Neuropsychology Soc., Sigma Xi. Office: 6262 Sunset Dr Ph 228 Miami FL 33143-4843

RUSSELL, STANLEY G., JR., accountant. Formerly dep. mng. ptnr. Deloitte and Touche, Wilton, Conn.; mng. ptnr. Deloitte and Touche, Pitts., 1992—. Office: Deloitte and Touche 2500 One PPG Pl Pittsburgh PA 15222*

RUSSELL, THEODORE EMERY, diplomat; b. Madras, India, Nov. 21, 1936; s. Paul Farr and Phyllis Hope (Additon) R.; m. Sara Mather (Stedman) Russell, Sept. 3, 1960; children: Douglas Richmond Russell, Richard Mather Russell. BA, Yale U., 1958; MA, Fletcher Sch. Law & Diplomacy, 1960, MALD, 1961; sr. tng., Nat. War Coll., 1980-81. Fgn. svc. officer Dept. State, Italy, Czechoslovakia, Washington, 1963-80; dep. office dir. (EUR/RPE) Dept. State, Washington, 1981-83; dep. chief mission Dept. State, Copenhagen, 1983-87, Prague, Czechoslovakia, 1988-91; dep. asst. adminstr. for internat. activities EPA, Washington, 1992-93; ambassador to Slovak Republic Bratislava, Slovakia, 1993-96; dep. comdt. internat. affairs Army War Coll., Carlisle, Pa., 1996—. Sch. bd. chmn.Internat. Sch. of Prague, Czechoslovakia, 1988-91; pres. Dept Chief of Mission Club, Prague, Czechoslovakia. 1990-91. Councillor Atlantic Coun.; mem. Army-Navy Club, Fgn. Svc. Assn., Nat. War Coll. Alumni Assn. Avocations: hiking, fishing, history, numismatics, philately. Home and Office: 3 Garrison Ln Carlisle PA 17013

RUSSELL, THERESA LYNN, actress; b. San Diego, Mar. 20, 1957; d. Jerry Russell Paup and Carole (Mall) Platt; m. Nicholas Jack Roeg, Feb. 12, 1986; children: Statten Jack, Maximilian Nicolas Sextus. Appeared in films including The Last Tycoon, 1976, Straight Time, 1977, Blind Ambition, 1978, Bad Timing, 1980, Eureka, 1981, Razor's Edge, 1983, Insignificance, 1985, Aria, 1984, Black Widow, 1985 (Nat. Assn. Theater Owners award 1985), Track 29, 1986 (Newcomer of Yr. award), Physical Evidence, 1987, Impulse, 1988, Cold Heaven, 1989 (Best Actress award Viareggio Film Festival 1991), Whore, 1990, Kafka, 1990, Thicker Than Water, 1992, Flight of the Dove, 1994, The Trade Off, 1994, (narrator) Being Human, 1994, Grotesque, 1995; TV movies Blind Ambition, 1979, Women's Guide to Adultery, 1993; BBC radio play Double Indemnity, 1993. *

RUSSELL, THOMAS, British government official; b. Melrose, Scotland, May 27, 1920; s. Thomas and Margaret Thomson (Wilkie) R.; m. Andrée Irma Désfossés, Jan. 2, 1951 (dec. May 1989). MA, St. Andrews U., Scotland, 1941; diploma in anthropology, Cambridge (Eng.) U., 1947. Dist. commr. Colonial Adminstrv. Svc., Solomon Islands, 1948-51, 54-56; asst. sec. Western Pacific high commn. Colonial Adminstrv. Svc., 1951-54; adminstrv. officer on secondment to col. Office, London, 1956-57; dep. fin. sec. Western Pacific high commn. Colonial Adminstrv. Svc., Solomon Islands, 1956-65, fin. sec., 1965-70, chief sec., 1970-74; gov. Cayman Islands, 1974-81; Cayman Islands govt. rep. U.K., 1982—. Capt. Brit. armed forces, 1940-46, North Africa and Italy, prisoner of war, Germany. Named Comdr. of Order of Brit. Empire, The Queen of England, 1970, Companion of the Order of St. Michael and St. George, The Queen of England, 1980. Fellow Royal Anthropol. Inst. (hon.); mem. Commonwealth Parliamentary Assn. (pres. Cayman Islands br. 1974-81, hon. mem.), Brit. Commonwealth Ex-Svcs. League (mem. coun. 1982—, chmn. welfare com. 1993—), Pacific Islands Soc. (mem. coun. 1989—, past chmn.), Caledonian Club, Commonwealth Trust. Mem. Ch. of Scotland. Avocations: archaeology, anthropology. Home: 6 Eldon Dr Frensham Rd, Farnham GU10 3JE, England Office: Cayman Islands Govt Office, 6 Arlington St, London SW1A 1RE, England

RUSSELL, THOMAS J., critical care supervisor; b. Meriden, Conn., July 30, 1954; s. Joseph George and Anna M. (Rusczek) R. BS in Immunology, Kans. State U., 1977; BS in Microbiology, U. New Haven, 1981; MS, Yale U., 1984; cert. EMT-P, Norwalk Community Coll. Instr. in biology U. New Haven, West Haven, Conn., So. Conn. State U., New Haven; PALS instr, ACLS instr., PHTLS instr. Yale U.; ops. supr. New Eng. Ambulance, Shelton, Conn., New Haven Ambulance; instr. EMS, Conn.; EMS coord. Bradley Meml. Hosp., Southington, Conn.; mem. pre-hosp. pediatric task force State of Conn. Mem. Nat. Assn. EMT's, Nat. Paramedic Assn., N.Y. Acad. Scis., Nat. Acad. Scis., Am. Soc. Microbiology, Am. Soc. Immunology, Conn. Soc. Paramedics, Conn. CISD Team, Conn. EMS-C Com., Conn. Spl. Olympics World Games Med. Team Leader, Phi Beta Kappa, Tau Kappa Epsilon (Teke of Yr.), Beta Beta Beta. Home: 129 Tuttle Rd Durham CT 06422-2208

RUSSELL, THOMAS WILLIAM FRASER, chemical engineering educator; b. Moose Jaw, Saskatchewan, Can., Aug. 5, 1934; s. Thomas D. and Evelyn May (Fraser) R.; m. Shirley A. Aldrich, Aug. 1956; children: Bruce, Brian, Carey. BS, U. Alberta, Edmonton, Can., 1956, MS, 1958; PhD, U. Del., 1964. Registered profl. engr., Del. Asst. prof. U. Del., 1964-67, assoc. prof., 1967-70, prof., 1970-81, assoc. dean, 1974-77, acting dean, 1978-79, dir. Inst. of Energy Conversion, 1979-95, Allan P. Colburn prof., 1981—, chmn. chem. engring. dept., 1986-91; cons. E.I. duPont de Nemours & Co., Inc., Wilmington, Del., 1968—. Author 2 books; contbr. articles to profl. jours., patentee in field. Mem. NAE, Am. Inst. Chem. Engring. (Thomas H. Chilton award 1988, Chem. Engring. Practice award 1987), Am. Chem. Soc., Am. Soc. Engring. Edn. (3M Lecture award chem. engring. divsn. 1984). Avocations: wind surfing, hiking, skiing. Home: 46 Darien Rd Newark DE 19711-2024 Office: U Del Inst Energy Conversion Wyoming Rd Newark DE 19716-3820

RUSSELL, THOMAS WRIGHT, JR., retired manufacturing executive; b. Hartford, Conn., July 19, 1916; s. Thomas Wright and Dorothy (Mason) R.; m. Mary Ferguson, Feb. 16, 1946; children: Thomas Wright 3d, Jennifer, Sarah. B.A., Yale U., 1939; student, Advanced Mgmt. Program, Harvard U., 1955. With Am. Brake Shoe Co. (now Abex Corp.), 1945-70, dir., 1966-70, pres., 1968-70, chmn., chief exec. officer, 1970, cons., dir., 1971-90. Bd. dirs. Met. Opera Assn. Served from pvt. to capt. AUS, 1941-45, PTO. Mem. Yale Assn. Class Officers (pres. 1955-57), Council Fgn. Relations, Delta Kappa Epsilon. Republican. Presbyterian (elder, trustee). Clubs: Yale, Century Assn.; Hay Harbor (Fishers Island). Home: J-4 Heritage Cove 85 River Rd Essex CT 06426-1334

RUSSELL, WILLIAM FLETCHER, III, opera company director; b. Denver, Aug. 31, 1950; S. William Fletcher Jr. and Ruth Talcott (Kenyon) R. MusB, U. Colo., 1973; MBA, UCLA, 1981. Singer various opera cos. including N.Y. Met. Opera, 1956-78; asst. bus. mgr. San Francisco Opera Co., 1980-84; mng. dir. The Washington Opera, 1984-87, L.A. Music Ctr. Opera, 1987-88; gen. dir. Anchorage Opera Co., 1988-92, Opera/Columbus, Ohio, 1991—; cons. NEA, Washington, 1984—; dramatic coach Anchorage Opera Co., 1988-92. Actor: (TV film) Disappearance of Aimee, 1976, (film) Duchess and Dirtwater Fox, 1977; assoc. prodr.: (TV operas) La Gioconda, 1979, Samson et Dalila, 1982, Pavarotti in Concert, 1983 (Emmy award 1983), Aida, 1984; prodr.: (TV opera) Goya, 1986 (Emmy award 1987). Mem. Anchorage East Rotary. Avocation: ski jouring. Home: 1779 N Galena Rd Sunbury OH 43074-9588 Office: Opera/Columbus 177 E Naghten St Columbus OH 43215-2613

RUSSELL, WILLIAM JOSEPH, educational association administrator; b. Boston, Sept. 23, 1941; s. Stanley Whiteside and Helen Rita R.; m. Frances Marie Chapdelaine, June 25, 1967; 1 son, Scott David. B.S., Boston Coll., 1963; M.Ed., Northeastern U., 1966; Ph.D., U. Calif., Berkeley, 1971. Head math. dept. Oceana, Pacifica, Calif., 1966-71; asst. for fed. and profl. affairs Am. Ednl. Research Assn., Washington, 1971-73; dep. exec. officer Am. Ednl. Research Assn., 1973-74, exec. officer, 1974—; adv. bd. Edn. Resource Info. Center Ednl. Testing Center, Princeton, N.J., 1975-87; exec. officer Nat. Council on Measurement in Edn., Internat. Assn. Computing in Edn., 1987-89. Editor: Ednl. Researcher, 1979-90. Mem. Am. Ednl. Research Assn., Phi Delta Kappa. Roman Catholic. Home: 1443 Creekside Ct Vienna VA 22182-1701 Office: AERA 1230 17th St NW Washington DC 20036-3003

RUSSELL, WILLIAM STEVEN, finance executive; b. Evanston, Ill., Aug. 5, 1948; s. John W. and Lillian H. Russell; m. Susan M. Hanson, Aug. 20, 1972. BS, So. Ill. U., 1970. CPA, Ill. Sr. staff auditor Arthur Andersen & Co., Chgo., 1972-76; acctg. mgr., controller, asst. sec. and treas. Lawter Internat., Inc., Northbrook, Ill., 1976-86, treas., sec., 1986-87, v.p. fin., treas. and sec., 1987—. Served with U.S. Army, 1970-72. Mem. Am. Inst. CPA's, Beta Alpha Psi, Beta Gamma Sigma. Roman Catholic. Home: 2690 Edgewood Ct Deerfield IL 60015-1906 Office: Lawter Internat Inc 990 Skokie Blvd Northbrook IL 60062-4005

RUSSELL-HUNTER, GUS W(ILLIAM) D(EVIGNE), zoology educator, research biologist, writer; b. Rutherglen, Scotland, May 3, 1926; came to U.S., 1963, naturalized, 1968; s. Robert R. and Gwladys (Dew) R-H.; m. Myra Porter Chapman, Mar. 22, 1951 (dec. 1989); 1 child, Peregrine D. BSc with honors, U. Glasgow, 1946, PhD, 1953, DSc, 1961. Sci. officer Bisra, Brit. Admiralty, Millport, Scotland, 1946-48; asst. lectr U. Glasgow, Scotland, 1948-51, univ. lectr. in zoology, 1951-63; examiner in biology Pharm. Soc. Gt. Britain, Edinburgh, 1957-63; chmn. dept. invertebrate zoology Marine Biol. Lab., Woods Hole, Mass., 1964-68, trustee, 1967-75, 77-87, trustee emeritus, 1989—; prof. zoology Syracuse (N.Y.) U., 1963-90, emeritus prof., 1990—, continuing rsch. fellow in biology, 1990—; cons. editor McGraw-Hill Encys., 1977—; bd. dirs. Upstate Freshwater Inst., Syracuse, 1981—. Author: Biology of Lower Invertebrates, 1967, Biology of Higher Invertebrates, 1968, Aquatic Productivity, 1970, A Life of Invertebrates, 1979, The Mollusca: Ecology, 1983; mng. editor: Biol. Bull. Woods Hole, Mass., 1968-80; contbr. over 120 articles to sci. jours. William Wasserstrom award Syracuse U., 1988; Carnegie and Browne fellow, 1954; rsch. grantee NIH, 1964-70, NSF, 1971-81, U.S. Army C.E., 1985-87; confirmed Scottish armiger, 1967. Fellow AAAS, Linnean Soc. London, Royal Soc. Edinburgh, Inst. Biology U.K.; mem. AAUP, Ecol. Soc. Am., Soc. Internat. Limnology, Am. Malacological Union, Malacological Soc. London, Soc. Sys. Biol. Avocations: book collecting, small boat sailing, model railroading, painting (oils and acrylics). Home: 711 Howard St Easton MD 21601-3934 Office: Syracuse U 026C Lyman Hall Syracuse NY 13244 *Having a sufficiency of books around one results in more than mere contentment. Many of us who come from a more literate pre-electronic civilization cannot imagine - if we exclude only the counterchanging transports of sex - any bliss superior to that of living surrounded by books.*

RUSSELL-WOOD, ANTHONY JOHN R., history educator; b. Corbridge-on-Tyne, Northumberland, Eng., Oct. 11, 1939; came to U.S., 1971; s. James and Ethel Kate (Roberts) R.-W.; m. Hannelore Elisabeth Schmidt, May 19, 1972; children: Christopher James Owen, Karsten Anthony Alexander. Diploma in Portuguese studies, Lisbon U., Portugal, 1960; BA with honors, Oxford (Eng.) U., 1963, MA, DPhil., 1967. Lectr. Portuguese lang. and lit. Oxford U., 1963-64; rsch. fellow St. Antony's Coll., Oxford, 1967-70; vis. assoc. prof. Johns Hopkins U., Balt., 1971-72, assoc. prof., 1972-76, prof., 1976—, chmn. dept. history, 1984-90, 96—; chmn. Albert Beveridge award and the Dunning prize coms., 1986-87; mem. U.S. Commn. Maritime History, 1977—. Author: Manuel Francisco Lisboa: A Craftsman of the Golden Age of Brazil, 1968, Fidalgos and Philanthropists: The Santa Casa da Misericordia of Bahia, 1550-1755, 1968, The Black Man in Slavery and Freedom in Colonial Brazil, 1982; Society and Government in Colonial Brazil, 1500-1822, 1992; A World on the Move: The Portuguese in Africa, Asia and America 1415-1808, 1992; co-author: From Colony to Nation: Essays on the Independence of Brazil, 1975; general editor: An Expanding World: The European Impact on World History, 1450-1800, 1995—; mem. editorial com. L.Am. Studies, Tsukuba, Japan, 1989—. Chmn. CLAH Columbus Quincentennial Com., 1987-90, Md. State Humanities Coun., 1980-82; mem. Md. Heritage Com., 1982-85, Balt. County Commn. Arts and Scis., 1982-84. Recipient Bolton Meml. prize Conf. Latin Am. Hist., 1969, Whitaker prize Middle-Atlantic Coun. Latin Am. Studies, 1983, Dom João de Castro prize Portuguese Nat. Commn. for Commemoration of Discoveries, 1993. Fellow Royal Geog. Soc. (life), Instituto Historico e Geografica da Bahia (corr.); mem. Brazilian Studies Assn., Forum on European Expansion and Global Interaction, Latin Am. Studies Assn., Conf. on Latin Am. History, European Acad. Scis. and Arts (Vienna, elected mem.). Avocations: squash, hiking, cycling. Home: 113 Belmore Rd Lutherville Timonium MD 21093-6111 Office: Johns Hopkins Univ Dept Of History Baltimore MD 21218

RUSSERT, TIMOTHY JOHN, broadcast journalist, executive; b. Buffalo, N.Y., May 7, 1950; m. Maureen Orth; 1 child, Luke. BA, John Carroll U., 1972; JD, Cleve. State U., 1976; LHD (hon.), Canisius Coll., Marist Coll., D'Youville Coll.; LLD (hon.), Albany Law Sch. Bar: N.Y., D.C. Spl. counsel, then chief of staff U.S. Senator Daniel Patrick Moynihan, 1977-82; counselor N.Y. Gov. Mario M. Cuomo, 1983-84; with NBC News, 1984—; moderator Meet the Press, 1991—; anchor The Tim Russert Show CNBC, 1994—; sr. v.p., Washington bureau chief NBC News; nat. polit. analyst Today program and NBC Nightly News with Tom Brokaw; supr. NBC News Today program live broadcasts from Rome, 1985; overseer prodn. prime time spl. A Day in the Life of President Bush, 1990, A Day in the Life of President Clinton, 1993; has covered 8 U.S./Russian Summits, Geneva, Malta, Washington, Moscow, Vancouver; lectr. at more than 30 univs. Recipient Alumni Spl. Achievement award Cleve.-Marshall Coll. Law, Pres.'s medal Trocaire Coll., Dean's award Cleve.-Marshall Coll. Law, John Peter Zenger award N.Y. State Bar Assn., 1992, Disting. Grad. award Nat. Cath. Educator's Assn., 1995, Spl. Achievement Alumni medal John Carroll U. Fellow Comm. European Communities. Office: NBC News Meet the Press 4001 Nebraska Ave NW Washington DC 20016-2733

RUSSETT, BRUCE MARTIN, political science educator; b. North Adams, Mass., Jan. 26, 1935; s. Raymond Edgar and Ruth Marian (Martin) R.; m. Cynthia Margaret Eagle, June 18, 1960; children: Margaret Ellen, Mark David, Lucia Elizabeth, Daniel Alden. BA magna cum laude, Williams Coll., 1956; diploma in econs., Cambridge (Eng.) U., 1957; MA, Yale U., 1958, PhD, 1961. Instr. MIT, Cambridge, 1961-62; asst. prof., then assoc. prof. Yale U., New Haven, 1961-68, prof., 1968—, Dean Acheson prof. internat. rels. and polit. sci., 1985—, chair dept. polit. sci., 1990-96, dir. UN studies, 1993—; vis. prof. Columbia U., 1965, U. Mich., 1965-66, U. Libre Brussels, 1969-70, U. N.C., 1979-80, Richardson Inst., London, 1973-74, Netherlands Inst. Advanced Study, 1984, Tel Aviv U., 1989; prin. cons. pastoral letter on peace Nat. Conf. Cath. Bishops, Washington, 1981-83; co-dir., secretariat ind. working group Future of the UN, 1993—. Author: World Handbook of Political and Social Indicators, 1964, What Price Vigilance?, 1970 (Kammerer award Am. Polit. Sci. Assn. 1971), Interest and Ideology (with E. Hanson), 1975, Controlling the Sword, 1990, Grasping the Democratic Peace, 1993, others; editor: Jour. Conflict Resolution, 1972—; contbr. articles to profl. jours. Grantee NSF, 1964, 65, 69, 77, 79, 85, 88, 89, 90, 95, Ford Found., 1993, 94, John and Catherine MacArthur Found., 1988; Fulbright-Hayes fellow, Belgium and Israel, 1969, 89; John Simon Guggenheim Found. fellow, 1969, 77; German Marshall Fund fellow, 1977. Fellow Am. Acad. Arts and Scis.; mem. AAUP, Am. Polit. Sci. Assn. (coun. 1984-86), Internat. Studies Assn. (pres. 1983-84), Peace Sci. Soc. Internat. (pres. 1977-79), Internat. Polit. Sci. Assn. (chair N.Am. adv. coun. 1977-80), Fedn. Am. Scientists. Avocations: tennis, classical music, hiking. Home: 70 Martin Ter Hamden CT 06517-2333 Office: Yale U Dept Polit Sci PO Box 208301 New Haven CT 06520-8301

RUSSIANO, JOHN See MILES, JACK

RUSSIN, JONATHAN, lawyer, consultant; b. Wilkes-Barre, Pa., Oct. 30, 1937; s. Jacob S. and Anne (Wartella) R.; m. Antoinette Stackpole, Oct. 6, 1962; children: Alexander, Andrew, Benjamin, Jacob. BA, Yale U., 1959, LLB., 1963. Bar: D.C. 1963. Guide interpreter Am. Nat. Exhibit, Moscow, 1959; rsch. asst. Law Faculty, U. East Africa, Dar es Salaam, Tanganyika, 1961-62; regional legal adviser for Caribbean, AID, 1967-69; ptnr. Kirkwood, Kaplan, Russin & Vecchi, Santo Domingo, Dominican Republic, 1969-74, Washington, 1974-78; ptnr. Kaplan Russin & Vecchi, Madrid, 1978-81, Washington, 1981-92; ptnr. Russin & Vecchi, 1992—; cons. on financing worker's housing in less developed countries of Latin Am., 1991; Washington rep. for Moscow Patriarchate of Russian Orthodox Ch.; convener adv. coun. Inst. for European, Russian and Eurasian Studies, George Washington U.; mem. adv. bd. Caribbean Am. Directory; trustee St. Nicholas Cathedral, Washington, St. Vladimir's Orthodox Theol. Sem., Crestwood, N.Y., 1985-93; legal adviser Orthodox Ch. in Am.; bd. dirs. Delphi Rsch. Assocs., Washington; Dominican Am. Cultural Inst., Santo Domingo, Dominican Republic, 1988-92, Nat. Coun. Internat. Visitors, Washington, 1987-93, Fund for Democracy and Devel., Washington, 1993—. Recipient Order of St. Vladimir, Moscow Patriarchate, Russian Orthodox Ch., 1991. Mem. Latin Am. Studies Assn., Caribbean Studies Assn., ABA, Inter-Am. Bar Assn. Republican. Clubs: Yale of N.Y., Yale of Washington. Contbr. articles to profl. jours. Office: 815 Connecticut Ave NW Ste 650 Washington DC 20006

RUSSIN, ROBERT ISAIAH, sculptor, educator; b. N.Y.C., Aug. 26, 1914; s. Uriel and Olga (Winnett) R.; m. Adele Mutchnick, May 21, 1937; children: Joseph Mark, Lincoln David, Uriel Robin. BA, CCNY, 1933, MS, 1935; postgrad. (Inst. fellow), Beaux Arts Inst. Design, 1935-36. Tchr. sculpture Copper Union Art Inst., N.Y.C., 1944-47; prof. art U. Wyo., Laramie, 1947-86; prof., artist-in-residence U. Wyo., 1976-85, Disting. prof. emeritus, 1985—. One-man shows Tucson Fine Arts Ctr., 1966, Colorado Springs (Colo.) Fine Arts Ctr., 1967, Palm Springs (Calif.) Desert Mus., Chas. G. Bowers Meml. Mus., Judah L. Magnes Meml. Mus., Berkeley, Calif.; retrospective one-man exhbn. Nat. Gallery Modern Art, Santo Domingo, Dominican Republic, 1976, Tubac Ctr. of the Arts, Ariz., 1987, Old Town Gallery-Park City, Ut., Riggins Gallery, Scottsdale, Ariz., 1989, Fine Arts Mus., U. Wyo., 1991; sculpture commns. include 2 8-foot metal figures, Evanston (Ill.) Post Office, 1939, three life-size carved figures, Conshohocken (Pa.) Post Office, 1940, Benjamin Franklin Monument, U. Wyo., 1957, Bust of Lincoln, Lincoln Mus., Washington, (now in Gettysburg Mus.), 1959, Lincoln Monument atop summit Lincoln Hwy., (now U.S. Interstate 80), Wyo, 1959, monumental bas-relief bronze Cheyenne (Wyo.) Fed. Bldg, 1966, two carved wood walls, Denver Fed. Bldg., 1966, monumental fountain, City of Hope Med. Ctr., Los Angeles, 1966-67, statue, Brookhaven (N.Y.) Nat. Lab., 1968, life-size bronze sculpture fountain, Pomona Coll., 1969, monumental bronze sculpture Prometheus Natrona County (Wyo.) Pub. Library, 1974, Man and Energy, Casper (Wyo.) C. of C., 1974, 12-foot marble carving Menorah Med. Ctr., Kansas City, Mo., 1975, Einstein and Gershwin medals Magnes Meml. Mus, Berkeley, Nat. Mus. Art, Santo Domingo, Dominican Republic, 1975, monumental fountain, Galleria d'Arte Moderna, Santo Domingo, 1977, Duarte Monument, Santo Domingo, 1977, 30 foot steel and water fountain monument City Hall, Casper, 1980, marble and bronze monument, Lincoln Centre, Dallas, 1982, acrylic steel and bronze monument, Herschler State Office Bldg., Cheyenne, 1984, marble monument, U. Wyo., Laramie, 1985, portrait head Charles Bluhdorn, chmn. Gulf & Western, 1975, portrait bust Pres. J. Balaguer of Dominican Republic, 1975, portrait head G. Wilson Knight, Shakespearean actor and scholar, 1975, 2 12-foot bronze figures The Greeting and the Gift for Bicentennial Commn., Cheyenne, 1976, monumental marble head of Juan Pablo Duarte liberator Dominican Republic, Santo Domingo, 1976, marble sculpture Trio, U. Wyo., 1985, Isaac B. Singer medal for Magnes Mus., 1983, monumental Holocaust Figure Tucson Jewish Community Ctr., 1989, granite monument Chthonodynamis, Dept. Energy Bldg., Washington, 1992, bust Hon. Milward Simpson, 1993, bust James Forest U. Wyo., 1993, bronze statue Univ. Med. Ctr., Tuscon, Head, Gov. Stanley Hathway, Cheyenne, Wy. 1995; contbr. articles to profl. jours.Head, Pres. Franklin D. Roosevelt, Rotunda (pres.hosp. Bethsda, Md.). Recipient awards sec. fine arts U.S. Treasury, 1939, 40, Lincoln medal U.S. Congress, 1959, Alfred G.B. Steel award Pa. Acad. Fine Arts, 1961, medal of Order of Duarte Sanchez y Mella, Dominican Republic, 1977; Ford Found. fellow, 1953. Mem. Nat. Sculpture Conf. (exec. bd.), Sculptors Guild, Nat. Sculpture Soc., AIA, AAUP, Coll. Art Internat. Inst. Arts and Letters, Phi Beta Kappa (hon.). Home: 61 N Fork Rd Centennial WY 82055 also: 1160 Placita Salubre Green Valley AZ 85614

RUSSMAN, THOMAS ANTHONY, philosophy educator; b. Pitts., June 20, 1944; s. Joseph Anthony and Mary Virginia (LaGuardia) R. BA, St. Fidelis Coll., 1967; MA in Philosophy, Cath. U. of Am., 1971; M of Theology, Capuchin Coll., 1971; PhD, Princeton U., 1976. Asst. prof. Cath. U. Am., Washington, 1976-83; assoc. prof. U. St. Thomas, Houston, 1983-90, dept. chmn., dir. PhD and MA programs, 1987—, dir. Ctr. for Thomistic Studies, 1987—, prof., 1990—; fin. cons., portfolio mgr. St. Augustine Province of Capuchin Order, Pitts., 1986—; bd. dirs. San Antonio Law Ctr., 1995—. Author: Prospectus for Triumph of Realism, 1987; editor: Thomistic Papers V, 1990, Thomistic Papers VI, 1994, Studies in Thomistic Theology, 1996; contbr. articles to profl. jours. Mem. Am. Philos. Assn., Am. Cath. Philos. Assn. (treas. 1977-83), Metaphys. Soc. Avocations: performing arts, hiking, canoeing, Bridge, trail riding. Office: U St Thomas 3800 Montrose Blvd Houston TX 77006-4626

RUSSO, ALEXANDER PETER, artist, educator; b. Atlantic City, June 11, 1922; s. Peter Joseph and Lillian Mary (Soma) R.; 1 child, Eugenie. Student, Pratt Inst., 1940-42, Swarthmore Coll., 1946-47; S.S., Bard Coll., 1947; B.F.A. (Breevort-Eickenmeyer fellow), Columbia U., 1952; postgrad., Acad. Fine Arts, Rome, 1952-54, Inst. Advanced Fine Arts, 1977-79. Instr. New Orleans Acad. Art, 1948-49; asst. prof. art U. Buffalo, 1955-58; instr. in graphic design Parsons Sch. Design, 1958-60; chmn. dept. drawing and painting Corcoran Sch. Art, 1961-70, chmn. faculty, acting dean, 1967-70; lectr., thesis adv. George Washington U., 1961-70; prof. Hood Coll., Frederick, Md., 1970-90, prof. emeritus, 1990—, chmn. dept. art, 1970-87; vis. guest prof. art Instituto Allende, San Miguel de Allende, Mexico, 1993-94; panelist Md. State Coun. Arts, Balt., 1981-82; reviewer art programs Md. State Bd. Edn., 1981—; guest art critic Southampton Press, N.Y., 1989, 91; cons. in field. One-man shows include Corcoran Gallery Art, Washington, 1946, 64, Chiurazzi Gallery, Rome, 1953, Cavallino Gallery, Venice, Italy, 1954, U. So. Ill., 1955, Frank Rehn Gallery, N.Y.C., periodic exhbns., 1954-74, Phoenix II Gallery, Washington, 1983, Ingber Gallery, N.Y.C., 1983, Washington Gallery Art, 1963, Franz Bader Gallery, Washington, 1967, Internat. Monetary Fund, Washington, 1968, 79, Agra Gallery, Washington, 1971, Benson Gallery, Bridgehampton, L.I., 1976, Phoenix Fine Arts, Frederick, 1981, Benton Gallery, Southampton, N.Y., 1985, 86, 88, 90, 91, Arlene Bujese Gallery, East Hampton, N.Y., 1994, 95, Hood Coll., Frederick, Md., 1991, Western Md. Coll., Westminster, 1991, Bell Gallery, Seattle, 1991, 92, Gettysburg (Pa.) Coll., 1989; group exhbns. include Salon de la Marne, Paris, 1945, Met. Mus. Art, N.Y.C., 1948, Bordighera Internat., Italy, 1953-54 (hon. mention), Mus. Modern Art, Madrid, 1953, Sala di Esposizione delle Biblioteca Americano, Rome, 1953,

Whitney Mus. Am. Art, N.Y.C., 1960, Mus. Modern Art, N.Y.C., 1969, Guild Hall, East Hampton, N.Y., 1976, East Hampton Avant-Garde, A Salute to the Signa Gallery, 1990, NAS, Washington, 1984, Bell Gallery, Seattle, 1990, Illustrator's Club, N.Y.C., 1991, Armory Exhbn., N.Y.C., 1991, Instituto Alleude, San Niguel de Allende, Mex., 1994, Josh Kligerman Gallery, San Miguel de Allende, Mex., 1994; represented in permanent collections Albright-Know Gallery, Buffalo, Columbia U., N.Y.C., Delgado Mus. Art, New Orleans, Corcoran Gallery Art, Fiat Automobile Co., Rome, Nat. Collection Smithsonian Inst., Washington, Fed. Ins. Deposit Corp., Washington, Gettysburg Coll. of Pa.; author: Profiles on Women Artists, 1985, The Challenge of Drawing, 1986. Served with USNR, 1942-46. Fellow Guggenheim Found., 1947-48, 49-50,Edward McDowell Found., 1956, Hood Coll. Hodson teaching fellow, 1983; Fulbright grantee for painting and research, Rome, 1952-54, U.S.-Indo Subcommn. on Edn. and Culture grantee, India, 1984. Office: PO Box 1377 Wainscott NY 11975-1377 also: Arlene Bujese Gallery 66 Newtown Ln East Hampton NY 11937 *Success is an equivocal matter. "Outward success", no doubt, is meaningful and necessary to most people in terms of fulfilling goals or for some similar reason. "Interior success" is more difficult to achieve, for it means the labor of a developing soul, and, more often than not, the relinquishing of what most would consider to be "material success." Whatever I have achieved in the way of outward or material success, therefore, is but a minute reflection of that which I would wish to achieve on the spiritual level. There is a long way to go.*

RUSSO, ANGELA BROWN, assistant principal; b. Balt., Apr. 21, 1948; d. Johnny Jeff and Lavonia Vernette (Davis) Royster; m. James Elton Brown, Oct. 5, 1975 (div. Aug. 1993); 1 child, Tiffany Lavonne; m. John Russo, Nov. 26, 1993. BS in Health Edn., Morgan State U., Balt., 1971; MS in Adult Edn., Kans. State U., 1977; postgrad., Charles County C.C., LaPlata, Md., 1983. Tchr. Harlem Park Jr. H.S., Balt., 1972-73, St. Maur's Internat. Sch., Yokohama, Japan, 1973-74, Herring Run Jr. H.S., Balt., 1974-75; Homebound tchr. Geary County Unified Schs., Junction City, Kans., 1975-77; counselor/head counseling dept. Dededo (Guam) Jr. H.S., 1977-79; tchr. Walker Mill Jr. H.S., Capitol Heights, Md., 1979-82; asst. dir./instr. pre-employment tng. program Charles County C.C., LaPlata, 1982-84; ednl. dir., counselor Odyssey Alternative Sch. Utah State Employment, Salt Lake City/Clearfield, 1984-85; tchr. North Davis Jr. H.S., Ogden, Utah, 1985-87; prin. Island Paradise Sch., Honolulu, 1989-90; asst. prin. C.W. Woodbury Mid. Sch., Las Vegas, 1994—; tchr. Mahlon Brown Jr. H.S., Las Vegas, Nev., 1990-91; adminstrv. dean Green Valley H.S., Las Vegas, 1992-93, asst. prin., 1994—; asst. prin. Becker Mid. Sch., Las Vegas, 1993-94; part-time coord./counselor Sinajaha (Guam) Adult Basic Edn. Program, 1978. Foster parent; vol. Juvenile Ct. Recipient Pub. Svc. Commendation, U.S. Dept. Commerce. Mem. AAUW, ASCD, Phi Delta Gamma, Alpha Kappa Alpha, Phi Delta Kappa. Avocations: travel, community choir. Home: 128 Shadow Ln Las Vegas NV 89106-4304 Office: Las Vegas High Sch 6500 E Sahara Ave Las Vegas NV 89122-2800

RUSSO, ANTHONY JOSEPH, public relations professional; b. N.Y.C., Oct. 23, 1953; s. Lucio and Tina (Iarossi) R. BA cum laude, Alfred U., 1974; MA, Columbia U., 1975; PhD, Claremont Grad. Sch., 1982. Asst. to chmn. Mocatta Metals, N.Y.C., 1982-83; account exec. Gavin Anderson and Co., N.Y.C., 1983-85; sr. account exec. Adams and Reinhart, N.Y.C., 1985; dir. corp. rels. Geto and DeMilly, N.Y.C., 1985-86; v.p. Cameron Assocs., N.Y.C., 1986-88; CEO Noonan/Russo Communications, N.Y.C., 1988—; chmn. Noonan/Russo Ltd., London, 1995—. Mem. Am. Psychol. Assn., Pub. Rels. Soc. Am., Psi Chi. Democrat. Home: 10 W 15th St Apt 1914 New York NY 10011-6829 Office: Noonan/Russo Comm 220 5th Ave New York NY 10001-7708 Also: Noonan/Russo Ltd, 3 Olaf St, London W11 4BE, England

RUSSO, BARBARA LEWIS, financial planner, asset manager; b. Richmond, Va., Mar. 4, 1933; d. Parker Burdette Lewis and Evelyn Chadwick Lewis Edmonds; m. Sabatino A. Russo, Jr., Sept. 5, 1953 (dec. Jan. 1984); children: Burdette, Sab, Chris, Nick, John; m. Frederic E. Fischer, Apr. 21, 1990. BFA, Stephens Coll., Columbia, Mo., 1953. Cert. fin. planner. Profl. photographer Turner-Russo Photography, Hopewell, N.J., 1967-84; in ins. N.Y. Life Ins. Co., Lawrenceville, N.J., 1985-93; in securities N.Y. Life and Annuity Corp., Lawrenceville, 1985-93; fin. planner, asset mgr. Capital Planning Adv. Group, Princeton, N.J., 1993—; talk show host On Your Own, Princeton, 1994—. Bd. dirs. Homeowners Assn., Princeton, 1993—. Mem. Inst. Cert. Fin. Planners, Princeton C. of C., The Exch. Club Greater Princeton (bd. dirs. 1989—). Office: Capital Planning Adv Group 711 Executive Dr Princeton NJ 08540-1529

RUSSO, D. CHRISTINE FIORELLA, elementary education educator, English educator; b. N.Y.C., July 24, 1931; d. Anthony Joseph and Assunta Mary (Moroni) Fiorella; m. Victor Donald Russo, Jr., Apr. 30, 1960. BA, Marymount Manhattan Coll.; MS, Fordham U., 1959; diploma in reading, Hofstra U., 1978, PhD, 1987, postgrad., 1987—; cert. in litigation, Adelphi U. and Nat. Ctr. for Paralegal Tng., 1980. Cert. elem. and secondary English tchr., N.Y., reading specialist, N.Y. Tchr. St. Margaret's Sch., Bronx, N.Y., 1955-56, Sacred Heart, Manhattan, N.Y., 1956-57, Bd. Edn., N.Y.C., 1957-60, Harborfields Dist. 6, L.I., 1960—; 1st v.p. Marymount Manhattan Coll.; English instr. Marymount Manhattan Coll., N.Y., 1st v.p. Bd. dirs. Marymount Alumnae Adv. Coun., N.Y., 1985—, Fordham U. Pres.'s Coun., Bronx, 1985-87, Fordham U. Recruitment Program, Bronx, 1983-87; mem. adv. bd. Fordham U.; campaign worker Dem. Party, N.Y.C., 1990, 92, 94, 96; Marymount rep. N.Y. State Bundy/Affairs Fund, 1982-83; L.I. rep. Marymount Recruitment Program, 1992; chmn. Ft. Salonga Assn., L.I., 1979-83; vol. St. John's Hosp., L.I.; co-dir. Just Say No Thomas J. Lahey Sch.; active Suffolk Reading Coun., 1991-96. Recipient Tchr.-Student Participation award Suffolk Reading Coun., 1991-96, Tchr.-Student Participation award 3d, 4th and 5th ann. N.Y. Senate Earth Day Competition, 1994, 95, 96. Mem. APA, Guilford Internat. Soc. Intelligence Edn. (v.p. 1991—, bd. dirs. 1990—), N.Y. Acad. Scis., N.Y. Orton Dyslexia Soc., Nat. Dyslexia Rsch. Found., Coun. for Exceptional Children, World Coun. for Gifted and Talented Children, Am. Assn. Higher Edn., Marymount Manhattan Coll. Alumnae Assn. (1st v.p. 1995—), Fordham U. Alumni Assn. (bd. dirs. adv. coun. Sch. Edn. 1995), Children and Adults with Attention Deficit Disorders. Roman Catholic. Home: 7 Bonnie Dr Northport NY 11768-1448

RUSSO, GREGORY THOMAS, lawyer; b. Bellerose, N.Y., Dec. 19, 1949; s. Albert Thomas and Geraldine Ann (Norton) R.; m. Helen Mary Shannon, Dec. 29, 1973; children: Deirdre Leslie, Nicholas Shannon, Barbara Celeste. AB, Georgetown U., 1971; JD, Cath. U. Am., 1974. Bar: N.Y. 1975, D.C. 1977, U.S. Supreme Ct. 1979. Sr. counsel, v.p. corp. staff, corp. sec. Merrill Lynch & Co., Inc., N.Y.C., 1974—. Capt. USAR, 1975. Mem. ABA. Republican. Roman Catholic. Avocation: golf. Office: Merrill Lynch & Co Inc 100 Church St New York NY 10007-2601

RUSSO, IRMA HAYDEE ALVAREZ DE, pathologist; b. San Rafael, Mendoza, Argentina, Feb. 28, 1942; came to U. S., 1972; d. Jose Maria and Maria Carmen (Martinez) de Alvarez; m. Jose Russo, Feb. 8, 1969; 1 child, Patricia Alexandra. BA, Escuela Normal MTSM de Balcarce, 1959; MD, U. Nat. of Cuyo, Mendoza, 1970. Diplomate Am. Bd. Pathology. Intern Sch. of Medicine Hosps., Argentina, 1969-70; resident in pathology Wayne State U. Sch. Medicine, Detroit, 1976-80; rsch. asst. and instr. Inst. of Histology and Embryology Sch. Medicine U. Nat. of Cuyo, 1963-71, assoc. prof. histology Faculty of Phys., Chem. and Math. Scis., 1970-72; rsch. assoc. Inst. for Molecular and Cellular Evolution, U. Miami, Fla., 1972-73; rsch. assoc. exptl. pathology lab. div. biol. scis., Mich. Cancer Found., Detroit, 1973-75, rsch. scientist, 1975-76, vis. rsch. scientist, 1976-82, asst. mem., pathologist, 1982-89, assoc. rsch. mem., 1989-91, co-dir. pathology reference lab., 1982-86, chief exptl. pathology lab., 1989-91; co-dir. Mich. Cancer Found. Lab. Svcs., 1986-91; mem. Dept. Pathology Fox Chase Cancer Ctr., 1991—, dir. anatomic pathology, 1991-92; dir. Lab. Svcs., 1992-94; chief molecular endocrinology sect. Breast Cancer Rsch. Lab. Fox Chase Cancer Ctr., 1994—; mem. dept. pathology Fox Chase Cancer Ctr., Phila., 1992—; chief resident physician dept. pathology Wayne State U. Sch. Medicine, 1978-80, asst. prof., 1980-82; mem. staff Harper-Grace Hosps., Detroit, 1980-82; adj. prof. Pathology and Cell Biology Jefferson Sch. of Medicine/Thomas Jefferson Univ., 1992—; mem. endocrinology peer rev. com. breast cancer rsch. program U.S. Army R&D Command, 1994, 95; ad-hoc mem. biochem. endocrinology study sect. NIH, DHHS, 1994; mem. bd. scientific counselor, sec. of health & human svcs. Nat. Toxicology Program Bd., 1994—; mem. Internat. Life Scis. Inst.-Risk Sc. Inst. Mammary Working Group, 1992—; pres., founder League of Women Against Cancer, Rydal, Pa., 1994—. Rockefeller grantee, 1972-73; Nat. Cancer Inst. grantee, 1978-81, 84-87, 1994—; Am. Cancer Soc. grantee 1988-89, 91-94, U.S. Army Med. R&D Command grant, 1994—; Recipient Shannon award Nat. Cancer Inst./NHHSS, 1992-94. guest lectr. dept. obstetrics Sch. Medicine U. Nat. of Cuyo, 1965-71. Mem. AAAS, Nat. Cancer Inst. (breast cancer working group, breast cancer program 1984-88), Nat. Alliance Breast Cancer Orgns. (med. adv. bd. N.Y.C. chpt. 1986—), Eastern Coop. Oncology Group, 1992—, Coll. Am. Pathologists, Am. Soc. Clin. Pathologists, Am. Assn. for Cancer Research, Mich. Soc. Pathologists, Am. Assn. Clin. Chemistry, Electron Microscopy Soc. Am., The Endocrine Soc, Internat. Assn. Against Cancer, Mich. Electron Microscopy Forum, Sigma Xi. Roman Catholic. Contbr. numerous articles on pathology to profl. jours. Office: Fox Chase Cancer Ctr 7701 Burholme Ave Philadelphia PA 19111-2412

RUSSO, JOSE, pathologist; b. Mendoza, Argentina, Mar. 24, 1942; came to U.S., 1971; s. Felipe and Teresa (Pagano) R.; m. Irma Haydee, Feb. 8, 1969; 1 child, Patricia Alexandra. BS, Agustin Alvarez Nat. Coll., 1959; MD, U. Nat. Cuyo, 1967. Instr. Inst. Gen. and Exptl. Pathology Med. Sch., Mendoza, 1961-66; asst. prof. Inst. Histology and Embryology, 1967-71; Rockefeller Found. postdoctoral fellow Inst. Molecular and Cellular Evolution U. Miami, 1971-73; chief exptl. pathology lab. Mich. Cancer Found., Detroit, 1973-81; assoc. clin. prof. pathology Wayne State U., Detroit, 1979-91, chmn. dept. pathology, 1981-91; chmn. dept. pathology, sr. mem. Fox Chase Cancer Ctr., Phila., 1991-94, sr. mem., dir. Breast Cancer Rsch. Lab., 1994—; mem. Mich. Cancer Found., 1982-91; adj. prof. pathology Jefferson Sch. Medicine, Univ. Penn. Sch. Medicine, Phila. Author: Tumor Diagnosis by Electron Microscopy, vol. 1, 1986, vol. 2, 1988, vol. 3, 1990, Immunocytochemistry in Tumor Diagnosis, 1985; contbr. over 200 articles to profl. jours. USPHS grantee, 1978, 80, 84, 88, 90, 93, 94, 95, grantee Am. Cancer Soc., 1982; NRC Argentina fellow, 1967-71. Mem. Am. Assn. Cancer Rsch., Am. Soc. Cell Biology, Soc. Exptl. Biology and Medicine, Tissue Culture Assn., Am. Soc. Clin. Pathology, Internat. Acad. Pathology, Am. Coll. Pathology, Sigma Xi. Roman Catholic.

RUSSO, JOSEPH FRANK, former college president; b. Pitts., Jan. 11, 1924; s. Joseph and E. Carmella (Sanseverino) R.; m. Jean Montierth, Mar. 26, 1947; children: Joseph Gary, Nancy Louise Russo Cook. BA, U. Ariz., 1953; MA, Ariz. State U., 1961, EdD, 1969. Tchr.-coach to prin. Prescott (Ariz.) High Sch., 1953-68; asst. supt. schs. Prescott, 1968; dean student personnel services, then dean instrn. Yavapai Coll., Prescott, 1968-74; pres. Yavapai Coll., 1974-84, pres. emeritus, 1984—; faculty assoc. Ariz. State U., 1960-63, No. Ariz. U., 1972, 73, 78; mem. Ariz. Commn. Post-Secondary Edn., 1976-83; interim pres. Burlington County Coll., Pemberton, N.J., 1986; adj. prof. history Embry-Riddle Aero. U., Prescott, Ariz., acting chancellor acads., 1985-86. Contbr. articles to profl. jours. Mem. Prescott Charter Rev. Com., 1975; bd. dirs. Prescott Salvation Army, 1970-73. With U.S. Army, 1944-46. Far Eastern Studies scholar Harvard U., 1955; recipient Builder Greater Ariz. award Ariz. Savs. and Loan Assn.-Sta. KTAR, Phoenix, 1967. Mem. Phi Delta Kappa. Republican. Roman Catholic. Home: 628 Cypress Dr Prescott AZ 86303-4905 Office: 1100 E Sheldon St Prescott AZ 86301-3220

RUSSO, KATHLEEN MARIE, art educator; b. Worcester, Mass., Jan. 14, 1947; d. Cornelius Joseph and Miriam Nancy (Bradford) Lucey; m. Don Albert Russo, Apr. 12, 1969 (div. Apr. 1988). BA, U. Miami, Coral Gables, Fla., 1968, MA, 1971; PhD, Fla. State U., 1976. Prof. art history Fla. Atlantic U., Boca Raton, 1976—, chair art dept., 1988—. Co-author: International Dictionary of Art and Artists, 1990, Eros in the Minds Eye, 1985, Encyclopedia of Architects, 1982, The Symbolism of Vanitas in the Arts, Literature and Music, 1992. Summer fellow Nat. Endowment for the Humanities, 1979, 83. Mem. Am. Soc. Archtl. Historians, S.E. Soc. Archtl. Historians (Fla. rep. 1985-92), Coll. Art Assn., Am. Soc. 18th Century Studies, Am. Assn. Italian Studies, Phi Kappa Phi. Home: 925 Iris Dr Delray Beach FL 33483-4810 Office: Fla Atlantic U Art Dept Boca Raton FL 33431

RUSSO, LAURA, gallery director; b. Waterbury, Conn., Mar. 7, 1943; d. Lawrence and Lillian A. (Russo) Kaplan; m. John I. Lawrence, May 6, 1962 (div. 1974); children: Maia Giosi, Dylan Russo. Cert., Pacific N.W. Coll. Art, 1975. Art instr. Tucker Maxon Oral Sch., Portland, Oreg., 1970-74, Pacific N.W. Coll. of Art, Portland, 1977-78; assoc. dir. Fountain Fine Arts, Seattle, 1981-82; asst. dir. The Fountain Gallery of Art, Portland, 1975-86; owner, dir. The Laura Russo Gallery, Portland, 1986—; lectr. Seattle Art Mus., 1987, Portland State Coll., 1992; juror Oreg. Sch. Design, Portland, 1988, Western Oreg. State Coll. 1992, Beaverton Arts Commn., 1992; com. mem. Oreg. Com. for Nat. Mus. Women in Arts, 1988; lectr. Oregon Hist. Soc., 1990. Mem. com. awards and grants Met. Arts Commn., Portland, 1988, 89; mem. P.N.C.A.; juror Art in Pub. Schs. Program, 1990; juror ArtQuake, Portland, 1994; juror Carvallis (Oreg.) Art Ctr., 1995. Mem. Alumni Friends, Contemporary Arts Coun. (program chmn., v.p. 1989-91), Portland Art Mus. (search com. 1993-94), Oreg. Art Inst., Friends Print Soc., Oreg. Art Inst., L.A. Mus. Contemporary Art, Seattle Art Mus. Democrat. Office: Laura Russo Gallery 805 NW 21st Ave Portland OR 97209-1408

RUSSO, PIERANTONIO, pediatric cardiac surgeon; b. Bergamo, Italy, Apr. 5, 1954; came to U.S., 1988; s. Vincenzo and Bianca (Raneri) R. Classic Liceum, Collegio San Luigi, Bologna, Italy, 1972; MD cum laude, Bologna U., 1978. Lic. physician, Italy, Pa., Eng. Intern in gen. surgery Castel-San Pietro Hosp., Bologna, 1979-80; intern in emergency medicine Univ. Hosp., Bologna, 1980-81; asst. dept. surgery Bologna Med. Sch., 1981-82; surg. fellow Cardiothoracic Inst., U. London, 1982-84; rsch. fellow dept. pediatrics Cardiothoracic Inst., Brompton Hosp., London, 1982-84; fellow cardiothoracic and cardiovascular surgery Mayo Clinic and Mayo Found., Rochester, Minn., 1984-86; surg. sr. registrar Cardiothoracic Unit Hosp. for Sick Children, London, 1986-87; dir. CICU and dir. heart transplant program St. Christopher's Hosp. for Children, Phila., 1988—; dir. surg. divsn. Pediatric Heart Inst. Temple U., Phila., 1988—, chief pediatric cardiothoracic surgery and assoc. prof., 1988—; surgical dir.heart ctr. for children St. Christopher Hosp. for Children; dir. fetal rsch. lab. Temple U., 1989—; attending surgeon cardiothoracic surgery Temple U. Hosp.; hon. mem. acad. staff dept. physiology U. Reading, U.K., 1987-88; hon. fellow pediatric cardiology Inst. of Child Health, U. London, 1987-88; vis. prof. cardiothoracic surgery U. Ark., Little Rock, 1992, Bologna Med. Sch., 1992; vis. prof. Baltic Soc. of Cardiac Surgery, Riga, Latvia, 1993; vis. surgeon cardiothoracic surgery, Riga, 1993; lectr. in field; assoc. prof. Cardiothoracic Surgery Med. Coll. Hahnemann U., 1995. Contbr. numerous articles, abstracts to profl. jours., chpts. to books. Recipient Princeps Studiorium aaward in Classic Studies, Bologna, Italy, 1972, Award Gran Croce Al Merito della Sanita, Acad. Internat. Sci. Econ. Sociali, and others, 1986; grantee Brit. Heart Found., 1987, Temple U., 1982. Fellow Internat. Coll. Surgeons, Soc. Acad. Surgeons, Am. Coll. Angiology; mem. AAAS, AMA, Internat. Soc. Heart and Lung Transplantation, Greater Delaware Valley Soc. Transplant Surgeons, N.Y. Acad. Sci., STS, Mayo Alumni Assn., Italian Med. Soc. Roman Catholic. Avocations: music, reading, tennis. Office: St Christophers Hosp Front St/Eric Ave Philadelphia PA 19134-1095

RUSSO, ROY LAWRENCE, electronic design automation engineer, retired; b. Kelayres, Pa., Nov. 6, 1935; s. Peter John and Mary (Fudge) R.; m. Elizabeth Jean Tautkus, Dec. 26, 1959; children: Mark, Keith, Aileen, Linda. B.S.E.E., Pa. State U., 1957, M.S.E.E., 1959, Ph.D.E.E., 1964. Asst. prof. elec. engring. Pa. State U., University Park, 1964-65; mgr., staff mem. IBM Research, Yorktown Heights, N.Y., 1965-77, mem. research staff, 1983-85; mgr. design automation lab. IBM Research, 1985-94; sr. engr. Gen. Tech. div. IBM, Hopewell Junction, 1977-81; mgr. strategy Gen. Tech. div. IBM, 1981-82; cons. prof. elec. engring Stanford U., 1982-83; retired, 1994. Editor-in-chief IEEE Computer Soc., 1983-85; co-inventor ink jet printer correction system. Treas. St. Patrick's Ch., Yorktown Heights, 1975-77. Recipient Invention Achievement award IBM, 1978, Outstanding Contbn. award IBM, 1968, 89, Outstanding Writing award Pa. State U., 1967. Fellow IEEE (dir. computer disvn. 1989); mem. IEEE Computer Soc. (pres. 1986-87, Svc. award, Centennial medal 1984, Richard E. Merwin award 1992), Eta Kappa Nu.

RUSSO, ROY R., lawyer; b. Utica, N.Y., July 26, 1936; s. Chester F. and Helen L. (Gacek) R.; m. Ann M. Obernesser, Sept. 19, 1959; children: Andrew F., Susan Elizabeth. BA, Columbia U., 1956; LLB cum laude, Syracuse U., 1959. Bar: N.Y. 1959, D.C. 1967, U.S. Supreme Ct. 1969. Pvt. practice law, Washington, 1959—; atty. FCC, Washington, 1959-66; ptnr. Cohn and Marks, Washington, 1966—; spl. counsel Nat. Cath. Conf. for Interracial Justice, Washington, 1984—. Mem. editl. adv. com. The Communications Act: A Legislative History of the Major Amendments 1934-96; mem. adv. bd. Pike and Fischer Comms. Regulation. Founding chmn. Commn. on Social Ministry, Richmond (Va.) Diocese, 1970-74; v.p., bd. dirs. St. Mary's Housing Corp., Annandale and Manassas, Va., 1971—; pres., bd. dirs. Caths. for Housing, Inc., 1979-84, Cath. Charities, Arlington (Va.) Diocese, 1980-84. With USAF, 1960-61. Recipient Alumni medal Alumni Fedn. Columbia U., 1994. Mem. ABA, Fed. Communications Bar Assn. (co-chair mass media practice com. 1988-91, nominations com. 1991-92), Computer Law Assn., Internat. Inst. Communications, John Jay Assocs., Soc. Columbia Grads., Columbia U. Club of Washington (sr. v.p. 1989-91, pres. 1991-95), Order of Coif, Phi Alpha Delta. Democrat. Club: Columbia Coll. (Washington) (mem. steering com. 1985—, chmn. Deans' Day program 1988—). Home: 6528 Bowie Dr Springfield VA 22150-1309 Office: Cohn & Marks 1333 New Hampshire Ave NW Washington DC 20036-1511

RUSSO, THOMAS ANTHONY, lawyer; b. N.Y.C., Nov. 6, 1943; s. Lucio F. and Tina (Iarossi) R.: m. Nancy Felipe, June 18, 1966 (div. 1974); m. Janice Davis, June 10, 1977 (div. 1979); m. Marcy C. Applebaum, June 16, 1985; children: Morgan Danielle and Alexa Anne (twins), Tyler James. BA, Fordham U., 1965; MBA, Cornell U., 1969, JD, 1969. Bar: N.Y., 1970, U.S. Ct. Appeals (2d cir.) 1971, U.S. Dist. Ct. (so. and ea. dists.) N.Y. 1971, U.S. Ct. Appeals (7th cir.) 1982. Staff atty. SEC, Washington, 1969-71; assoc. Cadwalader, Wickersham & Taft, N.Y.C., 1971-75; dir. div. trading and markets Commodity Futures Trading Commn., Washington, 1975-77; ptnr. Cadwalader, Wickersham & Taft, N.Y.C., 1977-92; mgmt. com., 1984-92; mng. dir., mem. op. com. Lehman Bros., N.Y.C., 1993—; bd. dirs. Futures Industry Inst., Rev. Securities and Commodities Regulation, N.Y.C., Futures Internat. Law Letter, N.Y.C. Author: Regulation of the Commodities Futures and Options Markets; co-author: Regulation of Brokers, Dealers and Securities Markets, Supplement Markets; editorial bd. mem. Jour. Fin. Regulation and Compliance; practitioner bd. advisors Stanford Jour. of Law. Mem. ABA (mem. futures regulations, exec. coun., adv. com. on fed. regulation of securities, past co-chmn. derivative instruments subcom. of com. on fed. regulation), Assn. of Bar of City of N.Y. (chmn. internat. law sub com. of the com. on commodities regulation 1984-85, chmn. com. commodities regulations 1981-82), D.C. Bar Assn. Office: Lehman Bros Inc 10th Fl 200 Vesey St New York NY 10285-1000

RUSSO, THOMAS JOSEPH, hospitality and consumer durables industry executive; b. Stamford, Conn., Sept. 15, 1941; s. Thomas and Ann (Petrozzi) R.; m. Wendy Fenwick, May 2, 1964; children: Michelle, Matthew. BS, Fordham U., 1963; postgrad., Chewton Pl., Bristol, Eng., 1980; D of Bus. Adminstrn. in Hospitality Mgmt. honoris causa, Johnson and Wales U., 1990. Div. gen. mgr. Howard Johnson Co., Wilmington, Del., 1974-76; v.p. Howard Johnson Co., Braintree, Mass., 1976-78, group v.p., 1978-80, sr. v.p., 1980-82, exec. v.p., 1982-83, pres., 1983-85; pres., chief exec. officer Ponderosa Steakhouse div., 1984-87; group chmn., CEO Hanson Industries Housewares Group, Framingham, Mass., 1987-94; chmn., CEO, pres. Miami Subs Corp., Ft. Lauderdale, Fla., 1994—; bd. dirs. Summit Family Restaunts, Inc., The Ground Round Inc., Legal Sea Foods, Inc. Trustee Framingham Union Hosp., 1981—. Mem. Nat. Restaurant Assn. (bd. dirs. 1982-83), Mass. Restaurant Assn., Del. Restaurant Assn. (bd. dirs. 1974-76), Rotary. Roman Catholic. Home: 2650 Edgewater Dr Fort Lauderdale FL 33332 Office: Miami Subs Corp 6300 NW 31st Ave Fort Lauderdale FL 33309-1633

RUST, EDWARD BARRY, JR., insurance company executive, lawyer; b. Chgo., Aug. 3, 1950; s. Edward Barry Sr. and Harriett B. (Fuller) R.; m. Sally Buckler, Feb. 28, 1976; 1 child, Edward Barry III. Student, Lawrence U., 1968-69; BS, Ill. Wesleyan U., 1972; JD, MBA, So. Meth. U., 1975. Bar: Tex. 1975, Ill. 1976. Mgmt. trainee State Farm Ins. Cos., Dallas, 1975-76; atty. State Farm Ins. Cos., Bloomington, 1976, sr. atty., 1976-78, asst. v.p., 1978-81, v.p., 1981-83, exec. v.p., 1983-85, chmn., 1987—; pres., CEO State Farm Life Ins. Cos., Bloomington, 1985—; now also pres., CEO, chmn. State Farm Mutual Auto Ins. Co.; pres. and bd. dirs. State Farm Investment Mgmt. Corp., State Farm Internat. Services, Inc., State Farm Cos. Found.; chmn. State Farm Mut. Automobile Ins. Co., 1987; bd. dirs. exec. and investment coms. State Farm Annuity and Life Ins. Co., State Farm Mut. Automobile Ins. Co., State Farm Life Ins. Co., State Farm Fire and Casualty, State Farm Gen. Trustee Ill. Wesleyan U., 1985—; mem. adv. coun. Grad. Sch. Bus. Stanford U.; mem. bus. adv. coun. Coll. Commerce and Bus. Adminstrn. U. Ill. Mem. ABA, Am. Enterprise Inst., Bus. Roundtable, Tex. State Bar Assn., Ill. Bar Assn., Am. Inst. Property and Liability Underwriters (trustee 1986—), Ins. Inst. Am. (trustee 1986—). Office: State Farm Ins Cos 1 State Farm Plz Bloomington IL 61701-4300*

RUST, JOHN LAURENCE, manufacturing company executive; b. Normal, Ill., June 23, 1925; married. Student, Ill. Wesleyan U., 1943; BA, U.S. Mil. Acad., West Point, N.Y., 1949. Enlisted U.S. Army, 1943, advanced through grades to capt., 1954; resigned from active duty Ill. Army N.G., 1954; owner, mgr. Chevrolet dealership, Bloomington, Ill., 1954-60; pres. Rust Tractor Co., Albuquerque, 1960—; bd. dirs. Sunwest Bank Albuquerque, Mountain States Mut. Casualty Co., Fed. Home Loan Bank Dallas. Campaign chmn. United Cmty. Fund, Albuquerque, 1965, pres., 1967-68; bd. regents N.Mex. Mil. Inst., Roswell, 1962-74; vice chmn. Presbyn. Healthcare Svcs., Albuquerque, 1968-82, chmn., 1982-95; pres. U. N.Mex. Found., Inc., 1980—. Col. USAR, ret. Home: 3550 Tucson Ct NW Albuquerque NM 87120-1124 Office: Rust Tractor Co 4000 Osuna Rd NE Albuquerque NM 87109-4423

RUST, ROBERT WARREN, lawyer; b. Jamaica, N.Y., Aug. 16, 1928; s. Adolf Harry and Helen Margaret (Dauth) R.; m. Mary Ruth Duncan, Jan. 28, 1953 (dec. Aug. 1981); children: Benjamin, Lani, Debra, Bonnie, Randall, Wendy; m. Theresa Maria Nagymihaly, Dec. 18, 1982; 1 stepchild, Brandon. Student, St. Lawrence U., 1946-48; JD, U. Miami, Coral Gables, Fla., 1954; postgrad., Naval War Coll., 1975. Bar: Fla. 1954, U.S. Supreme Ct. 1960. Police officer City of Miami (Fla.) Police Dept., 1953-54; asst. auditor First Nat. Bank, Miami, 1954-56; assoc. Smathers, Thompson & Dyer, Miami, 1956-57; asst. U.S. atty. Dept. of Justice, Miami, 1957-61; assoc. Shutts & Bowen, Miami, 1961-63; asst. county solicitor Palm Beach County, West Palm Beach, Fla., 1963-66; state rep. Fla. Legislature, Palm Beach, Fla., Martin County, Fla., 1966-68; chief counsel House Crime Com., Tallahassee, Fla., 1968-69; U.S. atty. So. Dist. Fla., Miami, 1969-77; ptnr. Rust & Rust, Miami, 1977—, ret. Col. USMCR, 1947-80, Ret. Recipient award of merit for assisting in preventing assassination Pres. of U.S., Sec. of Treasury and Chief U.S. Secret Svc., 1964, Outstanding Legislator award St. Petersburg Times, 1967, Fla. lodge Fraternal Order Police, 1967. Mem. NRA, Fla. Bar, Navy League, Marine Corps Res. Officers Assn. (pres. West Palm Beach chpt. 1964-65), Am. Legion, Mil. Order World Wars, Res. Officers Assn., Key Biscayne Yacht Club, Capitol Hill Club, Coconut Grove Sailing Club, Rotary. Republican. Presbyterian. Avocations: sailing, shooting, skiing, dog sledding. Office: 1700 S Bayshore Ln Apt 2A Miami FL 33133-4041 Home: PO Box 7339 0251 Gold Nugget Dr Breckenridge CO 80424

RUST, WILLIAM JAMES, retired steel company executive; b. Newark, Mar. 21, 1929; s. William G. and Anna (Glavin) R.; m. Adele M. Laubner, July 29, 1950; 1 dau., Rita Marie. B.S. in Math. magna cum laude, Boston Coll., 1953; M.B.A. with high distinction, Harvard, 1955. With Nat. Cash Register Co., 1955-68, dir. distbn. and material, 1964-68; v.p., treas. Indian Head, Inc., 1968-72, v.p. planning and fin., 1972-77; v.p. fin. Nat. Steel Co., Pitts., 1977-84, ret., 1984. Pres. Social Health Agy., Dayton, Ohio, 1966-68; chmn. United Fund campaigns, Dayton, 1962-68; Bd. dirs. Good Samaritan Hosp., 1965-68. Served with USAAF, 1946-49. Mem. Nat. Assn. Accountants (bd. dirs. Dayton 1960-63), Fin. Execs. Inst. Clubs: Duquesne, Fox Chapel Golf. Home: 117 Haverford Rd Pittsburgh PA 15238-1639

RUSTEN, JON E., financial planner; b. Bagley, Minn., Feb. 14, 1943; s. Elmer R. and Doris Olga (Hudspeth) R.; m. Kay Diane Dale, Dec. 27, 1968; children: Chad, Kyle, Shanna. BS in Bus., Moorhead State U., 1966; MS in Bus., Bemidji State U., 1985; postgrad., Drake U., 1969-70. CFP. Bus. instr. Gen. Learning Corp., Clinton, Iowa, 1968-69, Des Moines Pub. Schs., 1969-71, N.W. Tech. Coll., Minn., 1971-72; owner, mgr. Ben Franklin Store, Park Rapids, Minn., 1972-81; dist. rep. Luth. Brotherhood, Bemidji, Minn., 1981-88; advanced mktg. specialist Luth. Brotherhood, Grand Forks, N.D., 1988—; mem. planning coun. Red River Valley Estate Planning Coun., Fargo, N.D., 1989-96; bd. dirs. North Valley Underwriters, Grand Forks, 1989-91; pres. Northwest Minn. Life Underwriters, Bemidji, 1985-86; pub. rels. dir. N.D. Life Underwriters, Bismark, 1992-96. Regional dir. Girl Scouts U.S., Grand Forks, 1993-96; mem. sml. bus. advisory, Grand Forks C. of C., 1990-93; bd. dirs. Sharon Luth., Grand Forks, 1992-96; mem. govtl. affairs coun. Grand Forks Chamber, 1991-93; bd. dirs. Willow Bible Camp, 1990-96. Named to White House Sml. Bus. Conf., U.S. Govt., Washington, 1980. Mem. Jaycees (named one of 10 Outstanding Minnesotians 1978), Rotary 9bd. dirs. 1971-92, Outstanding Project award 1979), Million Dollar Round Table. Republican. Avocations: winter skiing, tennis, sailing, golf, restore automobiles. Office: Rusten Fin Group 416 Demers Ave Grand Forks ND 58201-4508

RUSTHOVEN, PETER JAMES, lawyer; b. Indpls., Aug. 12, 1951; s. Richard and Henrietta (Iwema) R.; children from previous marriage: Julia Faith, David James; m. Linda C. Bennett, Dec. 28, 1987; children: Mark Bennett, Matthew Boyd. A.B. magna cum laude, Harvard U., 1973, J.D. magna cum laude, 1976. Bar: Ind., 1976. Assoc. Barnes, Hickam, Pantzer & Boyd, Indpls., 1976-81; assoc. counsel to Pres. of U.S. White House, Washington, 1981-85; of counsel Barnes & Thornburg, Indpls., 1985-86, ptnr., 1987—; counsel Presdl. Commn. on Space Shuttle Challenger cident, 1986; spl. cons. U.S. Atty. Gen.'s Adv. Bd. on Missing Children, 1988; adj. fellow Hudson Inst., 1989-91, adj. sr. fellow, 1991—; sr. fellow Ind. Policy Rev. Found., 1991—; bd. advisors Indpls. Lawyers Chpt. Federalist Soc., 1993—, mem. nat. practitioners coun., 1995—. Contbr. monthly column The Am. Spectator mag., 1973-79; mem. bd. editors Harvard Law Rev., 1974-76, case editor, 1975-76; contbr. articles to nat. mags. Bd. dirs. Ednl. Choice Charitable Trust, 1994—, Legal Svcs. Orgn. Indpls., 1977-79; precinct committeeman Marion County Rep. Ctrl. Com., Indpls., 1978-81; state media dir. Ind. Reagan for Pres. Com., 1979-80, Ind. Reagan-Bush Com., 1980; speechwriter nat. Reagan for Pres. Campaign, 1980; mem. legal policy adv. bd. Washington Legal Found., 1989—. Grantee Inst. Politics, Harvard U., 1972. Mem. ABA, Ind. Bar Assn., Indpls. Bar Assn., Phi Beta Kappa. Roman Catholic. Avocations: golf; contract bridge; baseball memorabilia. Office: Barnes & Thornburg 1313 Merchants Bank Bldg 11 S Meridian St Indianapolis IN 46204-3506

RUSTIN, DOWSE BRADWELL, III, credit union executive; b. Charleston, S.C., Sept. 14, 1950; s. Dowse Bradwell, Jr. and Mary Bill (Griffin) R.; m. Ruth Ann Johnson, June 26,1976; children: Dowse Bradwell IV, Sarah Caroline. BS, Coll. of Charleston, 1975; postgrad., U. N.C., 1982. Internal auditor Wachovia Bank & Trust Co. N.A., Winston-Salem, N.C., 1975; retail loan officer, banking officer Wachovia Bank & Trust Co. N.A., Eden, N.C., 1978-81; city office mgr., asst. v.p. Wachovia Bank & Trust Co. N.A., Graham, N.C., 1981-85; pres. Charleston Area Fed. Credit Union, S.C., 1985—; bd. dirs. S.C. Credit Union League, Columbia, 1992-94, treas. bd. dirs., 1994; mem. supervisory com. Carolina Corp. Credit Union, Columbia, 1991-92; treas. Charleston Area Chpt. Credit Unions, 1990-93, pres., 1994; faculty mem. S.C. Credit Union Lending Sch., Columbia, 1989—; regional spkr. on banking, econs. and disaster recovery planning. Mem. exec. bd. Coll. of Charleston Alumni Assn., 1992; mem. allocations bd. Trident United Way, Charleston, 1991-92. Served with USNR, 1968-74. Mem. S.C. Credit Union Mgmt. Assn., Charleston Trident C. of C. (speakers bur. 1987—), Masons (master mason), Charleston Rod and Reel Club (pres. 1991-92). Republican. Methodist. Avocations: golf, gardening, boating. Office: Charleston Area Fed Credit Union 1845 Sam Rittenberg Blvd Charleston SC 29407-4870

RUTENBERG-ROSENBERG, SHARON LESLIE, journalist; b. Chgo., May 23, 1951; d. Arthur and Bernice (Berman) Rutenberg; m. Michael J. Rosenberg, Feb. 3, 1980; children: David Kaifel and Jonathan Reuben (twins), Emily Mara. Student, Harvard U., 1972; B.A., Northwestern U., 1973, M.S.J., 1975; cert. student pilot. Reporter-photographer Lerner Home Newspapers, Chgo., 1973-74; corr. Medill News Service, Washington, 1975; reporter-newsperson, sci. writer UPI, Chgo., 1975-84. Interviewer: exclusives White House chief of staff, nation's only mother and son on death row; others. Vol. Chgo.-Read Mental Health Ctr. Recipient Peter Lisagor award for exemplary journalism in features category, 1980, 81; Golden Key Nat. Adv. Bd. of Children's Oncology Service Inc., 1981; Media awards for wire service feature stories, 1983, 84, wire service news stories, 1983, 84, all from Chgo. Hosp. Pub. Relations Soc. Mem. Profl. Assn. Diving Instrs., Nat. Assn. Underwater Instrs., Hon. Order Ky. Cols., Hadassah, Sigma Delta Chi, Sigma Delta Tau. Home: 745 Marion Ave Highland Park IL 60035-5123

RUTES, WALTER ALAN, architect; b. N.Y.C., Sept. 21, 1928; s. Jack and Sarah (Ogur) R.; m. Helene Darville, Apr. 2, 1952; children: Daniel J., Linda Lee. B.Arch. (Sands Meml. medal 1950), Cornell U., 1950; fellow city planning, MIT, 1951; postgrad., Harvard U. Grad. Sch. Design, 1978. Cert. Nat. Council Archtl. Registration Bds. Assoc. ptnr. Skidmore, Owings & Merrill, N.Y.C., 1951-72; v.p. John Carl Warnecke & Assocs., N.Y.C., 1972-74; staff v.p. Intercontinental Hotels Corp., N.Y.C., 1974-80; dir. architecture Holiday Inns, Inc., Memphis, 1980-83; dir. design The Sheraton Corp., Boston, 1983-85; chmn 9 Tek Ltd. Hotel Cons., 1985—; chmn. adv. bd. Hult Fellowships for Constrn. Industry, 1968-75, Architects and Engrs. Com. New Bldg. Code, 1968; mem. zoning adv. com. N.Y.C. Planning Commn., 1970; lectr. in field, 1968—; mem. steering com. UNESCO Council Tall Bldgs. and Urban Habitat, 1980—; vis. prof. Cornell-Essec Grad. Program; vis. prof. Nova U. Author: Hotel Planning and Design, New Trends in Resort Design and Development; (software system) SHAPE, Megatrends and Marketecture; contbr. articles to profl. jours.; prin. works include Lincoln Center Library for Performing Arts, N.Y.C., 1967, Am. Republic Ins. Co. Nat. Hdqrs., Des Moines, 1967, HUD Apts., Jersey City, 1972, Merrill Lynch Bldg., N.Y.C., 1973, Tour Fiat, Paris, 1974, Aid Assn. for Luths. Nat. Hdqrs., Appleton, Wis., 1976, Semiramis Intercontinental Hotel, Cairo, 1985, Intercontinental, Jeddah, 1983, Embassy Suites Internat., 1985, Universal City Hotel Complex, L.A., 1986, TechWorld Conv. Hotel, Washington, 1986, Sheraton Fairplex Conv. Ctr., L.A., 1992, Orlando Conv. Ctr. Hotel, 1993, Winter Olympiad Media Complex, Norway, 1993, Ephesus Resort Complex, Turkey, 1986, Royal Christiania Hotel, Oslo, Norway, 1991, EuroFrance Leisure Park Complex, Cannes, 1993, Kuna Hills Multi Resort, Guam, 1994. Recipient Platinum Circle award Hotel Design Industry, 1988. Fellow AIA; mem. Ethical Culture Soc. Office: 8501 N 84th Pl Scottsdale AZ 85258-2419 also: 25 Richbell Rd White Plains NY 10605-4110

RUTFORD, ROBERT HOXIE, geoscience educator; b. Duluth, Minn., Jan. 26, 1933; s. Skuli and Ruth (Hoxie) R.; m. Marjorie Ann, June 19, 1954; children: Gregory, Kristian, Barbara. B.A., U. Minn., 1954, M.A., 1963, Ph.D., 1969; DSc (hon.), St Petersburg State Tech U., Russia, 1994. Football and track coach Hamline U., 1958-62; research fellow U. Minn., 1963-66; asst. prof. geology U. S.D., 1967-70, asso. prof., 1970-72, chmn. dept. geology, 1968-72, chmn. dept. physics, 1971-72; dir. Ross Ice Shelf Project U. Nebr., Lincoln, 1972-75; dir. divsn. Polar Programs NSF, Washington, 1975-77; vice chancellor for research and grad. studies, prof. geology U. Nebr., 1977-82, interim chancellor, 1980-81; pres. U. Tex., Dallas, 1982-94, Excellence in Edn. Found. prof. of geoscis., 1994—; U.S. del. to Scientific Com. on Antarctic Rsch., 1986—; chmn. NRC Polar Rsch. Bd., 1991-95. Mem. editl. bd. Issues in Sci. and Tech., 1991-94. Trustee Baylor Coll. Dentistry, 1989—. 1st lt. U.S. Army, 1954-56. Recipient Antarctic Svc. medal, 1964, Disting. Svc. award NSF, 1977, Ernie Gunderson award for svc. to amateur athletics S.D. AAU, 1972, Outstanding Achievement award U. Minn., 1993, Lifetime Achievement award, 1995. Fellow Geol. Soc. Am.; mem. Antarctican Soc. (pres. 1988-90), Arctic Inst. N.Am., Explorers Club, Am. Polar Soc., Philos. Soc. Tex., St. Petersburg Acad. Engring. (Russia), Cosmos Club, Sigma Xi. Lutheran. Home: 1882 Quail Ln Richardson TX 75080-3456 Office: Univ Tex Dallas Geosciences Program Richardson TX 75083-0688

RUTGERS, KATHARINE PHILLIPS (MRS. FREDERIK LODEWIJK RUTGERS), dancer; b. Butler, Pa., Sept. 2, 1910; d. Thomas Wharton and Alma (Sherman) Phillips; m. Frederik Lodewijk Rutgers, Feb. 2, 1942; children: Alma, Corinne Tolles. Diploma Briarcliff Coll., 1928; student L'Hermiage, Versailles, France, 1929-30; pupil ballet Vera Trefilova, Paris, Carl Raimund, Vienna, Varga Troyanoff, Budapest; pupil modern dance with Iris Barbura, Bucharest Ballet, Vincenzo Celli, N.Y.C., Igor Schwezoff, N.Y.C., Jean Yazvinsky, N.Y.C. Performed dance concerts Bucharest, 1937-40, U.S., 1941—; repertoire includes patriotic, dramatic, poetical dances, religious interpretations; dance therapist St. Barnabas Hosp., N.Y.C., 1965-70; author numerous pamphlets on dance, verses for choreographies. Chmn. ethnol. dance dept. Bruce Mus. Assocs., Greenwich, Conn., 1970—. Bd. dirs. Bruce Mus. Recipient citation for promoting culture with dance programs Nat. Fedn. Music Clubs, 1973. Mem. DAR, Conn. Fedn. Music Clubs (chmn. dance dept. 1965-66), Nat. League Am. Pen Women (local pres. 1973-78), Alliance Francaise, Mayflower Soc., Colonial Dames Am., Federated Music Club N.Y.C. (dir., dance chmn.), Met. Farm and Garden Club (dir.), Indian Harbor Club. Home: 9 Riversville Rd Greenwich CT 06831-3666

RUTH, ALPHEUS LANDIS, dairy farmer; b. Souderton, Pa., Sept. 6, 1915; s. Henry M. and Mary (Landis) R.; m. Miriam D. Rittenhouse, Sept. 26, 1936; children: Esther R., Mary Ellen, Samuel, Joseph, Phoebe. Student, pub. schs. Sunday sch. supt. Oley Mennonite Sunday Sch., Fleetwood, Pa., 1954-64; dir. Lehigh Valley Coop., Allentown, Pa., 1969—; lay minister Oley Mennonite Ch., 1977—; dir. Berks Lehigh Fed. Land Bank Bd., 1960—; diary farmer; treas. Hope Christian Ctr., South Bronx, N.Y., 1975—; pres. Lehigh Valley Farmers, Lansdale, Pa., 1978—; chmn. bd. Atlantic Processing, Inc., Allentown, Pa., 1978—; sales exec. Prudential Rittenhouse Realty Group, Harleysville, Pa.; mem. North Penn. Bd. of Realtors, 1992—. Active N.E. Dairy Coord. Com., 1985—, Berks County Farm Land Preservation Task Force, 1986-92; pres. Dock Woods Residence Coun. Named to Pa. Holstein Hall of Fame, 1989. Mem. Nat. Holsten Club, Pa. Holstein Club, Nat. Holstein Assn., Berks County Soil Conservation, Pa. Farmer Assn. Republican. Office: Prudential Rittenhouse 418 Main St Harleysville PA 19438-2350

RUTH, BETTY MUSE, school system administrator; b. Florence, Ala., Oct. 24, 1943; d. Paul and Mary Lucille (Gresham) Muse; m. Thomas Gary Ruth, Dec. 17, 1965 (div. Sept. 1979); 1 child, Thomas Paul; m. Charles Larry Oliver, Jr., Mar. 10, 1990. BSBA, Athens State Coll., 1982; MBA, U. N.Ala., 1986. Sec., bookkeeper Anderson News Co., Florence, 1963-65; acct. receivable bookkeeper McConnell AFB, Wichita, Kans., 1967-68; legal sec. Reynolds Law Firm, Selmer, Tenn., 1973-74; subs. tchr. Athens (Ala.) City Schs., 1974-78, dir. RSVP, 1978—; del. White House Conf. on Aging, 1995; mem. Nat. Coun. on Aging, 1985—. Active United Way, Athens, 1990-94; sec. Gov.'s Commn. Nat. and Comty. Svc., Ala, 1994; vice chair Tenn. Valley Exhibit Commn., Ala., 1984—; past pres. Athens-Limestone County Beautification Bd., 1991-94; People-to-People internat. del. to People's Republic of China, 1994. Named outstanding project dir. Action, Atlanta, 1985, outstanding woman of Ala., 1989. Mem. NEA, Ala. Edn. Assn., Nat. Assn. RSVP Dirs. (v.p., treas., del. 1985—, svc. award 1993), Region IV Assn. RSVP Dirs. (pres., v.p., treas. 1979—, svc. award 1989), Ala. Assn. RSVP Dirs. (v.p., sec., treas. 1978—, Citizens award 1991), Athens State Coll. Alumni Assn. (bd. dirs. 1993—). Mem. Ch. of Christ. Avocations: reading, traveling, volunteerism. Home: 15705 Kings Dr Athens AL 35611 Office: Athens State Coll PO Box 852 Athens AL 35612-0852

RUTH, BRYCE CLINTON, JR., lawyer; b. Greenwood, Miss., Dec. 19, 1948; s. Bryce Clinton and Kathryn (Arant) R.; m. Martha M. Ruth; children: Lauren Elizabeth, Bryce Clinton III. BS, Delta State U., 1970; JD, Memphis State U., 1979. Bar: Tenn., 1979, U.S. Dist. Ct. (mid. dist.) Tenn. 1979, U.S. Ct. Mil. Appeals 1991, U.S. Ct. Appeals (6th cir.), 1994. Criminal investigation spl. agt. IRS, Memphis and Nashville, 1971-82; asst. dist. atty. Dist. Atty. Office, Gallatin, Tenn., 1982-89; asst. pub. defender Pub. Defender's Office, Gallatin, 1989-90; pvt. practice White House, Tenn., 1989—; judge City of Cross Plains, Tenn., 1992—; juvenile ct. referee judge Robertson County, Tenn., 1995—; mem. dist. investigating com. dist. VI Tenn. Bd. Law Examiners, 1989—; mem. child enforcement steering com. Asst. Dist. Atty. Office, 1983-84, chmn. legis. subcom., 1985; lectr. in field. Chmn. fin. com. White House First United Meth. Ch., 1983-88, trustee, 1988-90, chmn., 1990; trustee Vol. State Coll. Found., 1993—; bd. dirs. Crime Stoppers of Sumner County, 1989-94; bd. dirs. White House Youth Soccer, 1992-93, coach, 1987-91; bd. dirs. Sumner County CASA, 1992-93; coach Jr. Pro Football, 1980-85; video cameraman for football team White House H.S., 1991—; mem. Leadership Sumner, 1989; bd. dirs. White House Men's Club, 1981-83, 85-88, v.p., 1984, 88, pres., 1985. Maj. USAR, JAGC, 1983—. Recipient Disting. Expert award for pistol marksmanship U.S. Treasury, Disting. Svc. award City of White House. Mem. NRA, Tenn. Bar Assn. (del. 1993—), Sumner County Bar Assn. (chmn. domestic rels. com. 1984-85), White House Area C. of C. (bd. dirs. 1990—, pres. 1993-94). Avocations: scuba diving, skeet, golf, hunting, pistol shooting. Office: 3210 Hwy 31W PO Box 68 White House TN 37188

RUTH, CAROL A., public relations executive; b. N.Y.C., June 19, 1942; d. Edward McDonald and Dorothea (Beauman) Smith. BBA, CUNY, 1979. Sr. v.p. Hill and Knowlton, Inc., N.Y.C., 1968-86; pres., chief exec. officer Dewe Rogerson, Inc., N.Y.C., 1986—, also bd. dirs.; Dewe Rogerson Group, London; exec. dir. Dewe Rogerson Asia. Recipient Woman Achievers award YWCA of N.Y. 1985, bd. dirs. 1991—. Mem. Nat. Investors Rels. Inst. (bd. dirs. 1981-85, chmn. bd. 1984-85). Office: Dewe Rogerson Inc 850 3rd Ave New York NY 10022-6222

RUTH, DANIEL JOHN, journalist; b. Akron, Ohio, Sept. 16, 1949; s. John Edgar and Ruth (Motz) R.; m. Barbara Verde, July 10, 1980 (div. June 1988); m. Angela Pecoulas, July 31, 1992. BA in Polit. Sci., Gannon U., 1972. Reporter, critic Tampa (Fla.) Tribune, 1973-81; v.p., pub. Group W Satellite Com., Stamford, Conn., 1981-84; reporter, critic, columnist Chgo. Sun-Times, 1984-91; editor The Big Guava Mag., Tampa, Fla., 1991-92; columnist Tampa (Fla.) Tribune, 1992—; critic Sta. WMAQ, Chgo., 1988-91; tchr. Columbia Coll., Chgo., 1988-90. Pres. Hillsborough County (Fla.) Suicide and Crisis Ctr., Tampa, 1979-80. Recipient 1st place in commentary Fla. chpt. Sigma Delta Chi, 1980, Peter Lisagor award Chgo. chpt., 1985. Roman Catholic. Home: 10706 N Rome Ave Tampa FL 33612-6577

RUTH, EDWARD B., principal; b. Lancaster, Pa., Aug. 23, 1943; s. Edward B. and Jeanne L. (Schaeffer) R.; m. Betsy A. Lorenz, Aug. 28, 1965; 1 child, Heather L. BS in Biology, Lebanon Valley Coll., Annville, Pa., 1965; MEd, Millersville (Pa.) U., 1970; cert. secondary prin., Temple U., 1990. Cert. secondary prin., secondary tchr. gen. sci., biology. Sci. tchr. Milton Hershey (Pa.) Sch., 1965-87, mid. sch. asst. prin., 1987-92, mid. sch. prin., 1992—, asst. athletic dir., 1983-87; recreation supr., Milton Hershey Sch.; mgr. Palmyra Swimming Pool, summers; mem. evaluation team Pa. Assn. Pvt. Acad. Schs., 1991; mem. planning com. Pa. Commonwealth Partnership, F&M Coll., Lancaster, Pa., 1987; mem. biol. safety and recombinant DNA com. Hershey Med. Ctr., 1987—; mem. union negotiations team Milton Hershey Sch., 1994—; judge regional and state meetings Pa. Jr. Acad. Sci., Capital Area Sci. and Engring. Fairs, Pa. Coll. Energy Debates. Author, editor: Energy Teaching Units Energy Concepts, 1982; tech. writer Harrisburg Energy Edn. Adv. Coun.; author: (flow chart) Summary: Modern Interpretation of the Central Dogma (Watson & Crick's DNA Model), 1983; reviewer pre-publ. articles, books, audio-visual materials Am. Biology Tchr. Mem. camping program com. Keystone Area Boy Scouts, Harrisburg, Pa., 1994; chmn. Derry Twp. Environ. Adv. Coun., Hershey, Pa., 1993-94; deacon, choir mem. Presbyn. Ch. Mem. Nat. Assn. Biology Tchrs. (Outstanding Pa. Biology Tchr. 1984), Nat. Assn. Secondary Sch. Prins., Pa. Assn. Secondary Sch. Prins., Nat. Eagle Scout Assn., Lancaster County Conservancy. Avocation: distance running. Home: 356 William Dr Hershey PA 17033-1859 Office: Milton Hershey Sch PO Box 830 Hershey PA 17033-0830

RUTH, JAMES PERRY, financial planning executive; b. Washington, Feb. 27, 1946; s. Robert Walker and Virginia Null Ruth; m. Kathleen McHugh, Aug. 10, 1968; children: Heather Lynn, Michael James. BS in Bus. and Public Adminstrn., U. Md., 1970; postgrad. Am. Coll., Bryn Mawr, Pa., 1971-83; CLU, CFP, chartered fin. cons. agt., Northwestern Mutual Life Ins. Co., Washington, 1967-74; gen. agt. Indpls. Life, Rockville, Md., 1974-82; partner Fox, Ruth & Middledorf, Rockville, 1975-82; mgr. Mfrs. Fin. Svcs., Rosslyn, Va., 1982-84; pres. Potomac Fin. Group, 1984—. Past pres. Jelleff Boys' Club; past pres. Montgomery County Police Boys' and Girls' Club; bd. dirs. Boys' Clubs Greater Washington. Named Outstanding Young Man Am., U.S. Jaycees, 1979. Mem. Nat. Assn. Life Underwriters, Nat. Assn. Securities Dealers, Suburban Md. Life Underwriters Assn. (past pres.; H.L. Meyer Meml. award 1980), Internat. Assn. Fin. Planning, Suburban Md. Estate Planning Coun. (past pres.), Million Dollar Round Table, Md. State Life Underwriters Assn. (pres. 1995-96). Lutheran. Contbr. articles to profl. publs; quoted in N.Y. Times, U.S. News and World Report, USA Today, others. Home: 7920 Warfield Rd Gaithersburg MD 20882-4409 Office: Ste 420 18310 Montgomery Village Ave Gaithersburg MD 20879-3551

RUTH, THOMAS GRISWOLD, history educator; b. Benton Harbor, Mich., Nov. 7, 1940; s. John Griswold and Ruth Margery (Hopkins) R. BA, U. Mich., 1963; MA, U. Tex., 1968. Instr. Am.-Nicaraguan Sch., Managua, 1965-67; instr. history (Ind. Found. Teaching Endowment) The Hill Sch., Pottstown, Pa., 1968—. Mem. Assn. Am. Historians, Sloan Club (London). Avocations: travel, coin collecting, ancient map collecting. Home and Office: The Hill Sch Pottstown PA 19464

RUTHCHILD, GERALDINE QUIETLAKE, training and development consultant, writer, poet; d. Nathan and Ruth (Feldman) Stein; m. Neil Wolinsky, Dec. 31, 1993. BA summa cum laude, Queens Coll., 1977; MA in Am. Lit., Johns Hopkins U., 1980, PhD in Am. Lit., 1983. Asst. prof. Albion (Mich.) Coll., 1982-84; assoc. Investor Access Corp., N.Y.C., 1984-85; program dir. Exec. Enterprises, Inc., N.Y.C., 1985-86; pres. Ruthchild Assocs., N.Y.C., 1987-90, Exemplar, N.Y.C., 1991-95, Examplar, Ltd., N.Y.C., 1995—; cons. J.P. Morgan & Co., Inc., Bankers Trust Co., Chase Manhattan Bank N.A., Merill Lynch, NatWest Bank, U.S.A., Citibank N.A., Robert Morris Assocs., Goldman, Sachs & Co., Dean Witter Reynolds, Inc., also others, 1987—. Contbr. articles, poems to profl. and lit. jours. Vol. handicapped children N.Y. Foundling Hosp., N.Y.C., 1988-90, Fgn. Visitors Desk, Met. Mus. Art, N.Y.C., 1989—. Hopkins fellow Johns Hopkins U., 1979-80, Andrew Mellon Found. fellow, 1980-81, 81-82. Mem. ASTD, Assn. Bank Trainers and Cons., Internat. Soc. Philos. Enquiry, Phi Beta Kappa. Avocations: foreign languages, needlework, house plants. Office: Exemplar 501 E 87th St Fl 12 New York NY 10128-7665

RUTHERFOORD, REBECCA HUDSON, computer science educator; b. Elkhart, Ind., Feb. 24, 1948; d. Charles Melvin Hudson and Eunice Klaire (Lund) Edmonds; m. James Kincanon Rutherford, Aug. 31, 1968; children: James Kincanon Jr., Charles Penn. BS, Ind. State U., Terre Haute, Ind., 1971, MS, 1972, EdD, 1975; MS in Computer Sci., So. Coll. Tech., Marietta, Ga., 1995. Cert. data processor. Staff asst. Ind. State U., Terre Haute, 1969-71; vocal music tchr. S.W. Parke Schs., Rockville, Ind., 1971-73; fellowship asst. Ind. State U., Terre Haute, 1974-75; vocal music tchr. Slidell (La.) High Sch., 1977-78; programmer, analyst La. State U., Baton Rouge, 1978-79, dir. computer rehab. program, 1979-80; programmer, analyst Hanes Corp., Atlanta, 1980-81; asst. prof. Devry Inst., Atlanta, 1981-83; acting dept. chair So. Coll. Tech., Marietta, Ga., 1989-92; prof. computer sci. So. Coll. Tech., Marietta, 1983—; cons. The Assocs. Group, Inc., Roswell, Ga., 1986-88, Crawford Communications, Atlanta, 1987; adj. prof. Cobb County Bd. Edn., Marietta, Ga., 1985-87, Joseph T. Walker Sch., Marietta, 1985-86; vis. prof. Leicester (U.K.) Polytechnic, 1990. Choir dir. St. Peter and Paul Episcopal Ch., Marietta, 1981-85, choir mem., 1992—; Christian edn. dir. St. Francis Episcopal Ch., Denham Springs, La., 1978-80; choir mem. St. David's Episcopal Ch., Roswell, 1985-92; bd. dirs., mem. Cherokee Comty. Habitat for Humanity, 1994—. Mem. Data Processing Mgmt. Assn., Assn. Computing Machinery, Sigma Alpha Iota. Republican. Avocations: boating, reading. Office: So Coll Tech 1100 S Marietta Pky Marietta GA 30060-2855

RUTHERFORD, JIM, professional sports team executive; b. 1948; m. Heidi Rutherford; 1 child, Andrea. Goal tender Detroit Red Wings, Pitts., Toronto, L.A. profl. hockey teams, 1969-82; dir. hockey ops Compuware Sports Corp., 1982-94; gen. mgr. Windsor (Ont.) Spitfires, 1984-88, head coach, 1986-87; dir. hockey ops. Detroit Ambassadors, 1989-91, coach, dir. hockey ops., 1991-92; coach, dir. hockey ops. Detroit Jr. Red Wings (formerly Ambassadors), 1992-94; COO KTR Hockey Ltd. Partnership, Hartford, Conn., 1984—; pres., gen. mgr. Hartford Whalers, 1994—; mem. Team Can. hockey world championships Vienna, 1977, Moscow, 1979; Red Wings' player rep. 5 seasons. Recipient Exec. of Yr. award Ont. Hockey League, Can. Hockey League, 1993, Ont. Hockey League, 1994. Achievements include directing Windsor Spitfires to 1988 Meml. Cup finals, leading Detroit Ambassadors to first-ever playoff in 1992, winning Emms Divsn. championship with Jr. Red Wings in 1994, bringing 1st Am.-based Ont. Hockey League franchise to Detroit, 1989, securing Nat. Hockey League approval of KTR purchase of Hartford Whalers from Conn. Devel. Authority, 1994. Office: Hartford Whalers 242 Trumbull St Hartford CT 06103*

RUTHERFORD, JOHN SHERMAN, III (JOHNNY RUTHERFORD), professional race car driver; b. Coffeyville, Kans., Mar. 12, 1938; s. John Sherman and Mary Henrietta (Brooks) R.; m. Betty Rose Hoyer, July 7, 1963; children: John Sherman, Angela Ann. Student, Tex. Christian U., 1956. Profl. race car driver, 1959-94, ret., 1994, driver super-modified race cars, sprint cars, stock cars, midgets, sports cars, Indy cars, Trans-Am cars and formula 5000; mem. Indy Car Racing Inc.; appointed spl. events coord. Indy Racing League, 1995—; pace car driver for CART, 1992-95; lectr. in field. Host: TV show The Racers; race commentator TV show, NBC, ESPN, CBS, ABC; appeared in numerous TV commercials; art work included in traveling exhbn. Art and Athletes; TV and radio pub. services messages for Nat. Safety Council, Calif. Hwy. Patrol, U.S. Marines, Muscular Dystrophy Assn., Cystic Fibrosis Assn., Boy Scouts, Camp Fire, Shriner's Hosp., Tex. Soc. to Prevent Blindness, Air N.G. Hon. state chmn. Am. Cancer Soc., Tex., Tarrant County Soc. to Prevent Blindness, Emergency Medicine Found., Ft. Worth Kidney Assn., Ft. Worth Burn Ctr.; Ind. chmn. Am. Heart Assn. Named Ft. Worth Newsmaker of Yr., 1974, Driver of Yr. Sport Mag., 1976, Driver of Yr. Auto Race Writers and Broadcasters Am., 1974, 80, Olsonite Driver of Yr., 1980, Corvette Challenge's Sportsman of Yr., 1988, Motorsports amb., 1993; recipient Jim Clark award, 1969, Extra Mile award, 1973, Mim Malloy award, 1974, Eddie Sachs award, 1975, Louie Meyer award, 1992; chosen for Internat. Race of Champions, 1974, 76, 77, 78, 79, 84, chosen Fast Masters, 1993; elected to Tex. Sports Hall of Fame, 1981, Indy 500 Hall of Fame, 1987, Boys Clubs Am.'s Celebrity Hall of Fame, 1987, Tex. Auto Racing Hall of Fame, 1988, Nat. Sprint Car Hall of Fame, 1995, Internat. Motorsports Hall of Fame, 1996, Motorsports Hall of Fame, 1996. Mem. Fedn. Internat. Automobile, Internat. Motors Sports Assn., Exptl. Aircraft Assn., Warbirds of Am., Confederate Air Force, Internat. Aerobatic Club, League Auto Racing (sec., bd. dirs.), Championship Drivers Assn. (bd. dirs.), Nat. Rifle Assn., Air Force Assn., Air Power Coun., Blue Angels Assn., Ft. Worth Boat Club, Shady Oaks Country Club, Lions. Winner 27 championship car races; winner Indianapolis 500, 1974, 76, 80, second place, 1975; set new world's record for stock cars, Daytona Beach, Fla., 1963; set record at Indpls. 500, 1973; at Mich. Internat. Raceway, 1984; U.S. Auto Club Nat. Sprint Car champion, 1965; Nat. Driving champion USAC and CART, 1980; oldest driver (48) to win a 500 mile Indy Car Race, 1986. *I am a firm believer in the fact that a person can do anything in this world he or she wants to as long as you have desire. People have to set goals, things to achieve. No one ever remembers who finished second. Luck is where preparation meets opportunity.*

RUTHERFORD, MARY JEAN, laboratory administrator, science educator; b. Webb City, Mo., Apr. 23, 1935; d. John Edward and Martha Rose (Hare) R. AA, Joplin Jr. Coll., 1955; BS, Northwestern U., 1957; MEd, Drury Coll. Cert. med. technologist, specialist in chemistry. Med. technologist Northwestern U., Chgo., 1957-60; lab. supr., instr. St. Louis U. Hosp.-Med. Tech., 1961-67; supr. in chemistry, instr. U. Ill. R & E Hosp., Chgo., 1967-68; teaching supr. in chemistry L.E. Cox Med. Ctr. Sch. of Med. Tech., Springfield, Mo., 1968-86; asst. prof., mem. faculty Ark. State U., Jonesboro, 1986-90, program dir. clin. lab. scis., asst. prof., 1990—; mem. adv. bd. Springhouse (Pa.) Pub., 1992—; mem. rev. com. Nat. Accrediting Agy. for Clin. Lab. Scis., Chgo., 1993-94. Author: Inorganic Chemistry-Applied Science Review, 1992. Pres. LWV, Jonesboro, 1991-92. Mem. Am.

Soc. Clin. Lab. Scis., Ark. Soc. Med. Technologists, Ark. Clin. Lab. Educator's Forum (chair 1993-94), Ark. Coalition of Lab. Profls. (treas. 1992—). Avocations: travel, photography, needlecrafts. Office: Ark State U PO Box 69 State University AR 72467-0069

RUTHERFORD, PAUL HARDING, physicist; b. Shipley, Yorkshire, Eng., Jan. 22, 1938; came to U.S., 1965, naturalized, 1976; s. Joseph William and Annie (Harding) R.; m. Audrey Jones Irvine, Oct. 31, 1959; children—Andrea Christine, Julia Irvine. B.A., Cambridge (Eng.) U., 1959, M.A., 1963, Ph.D., 1963. Research asso. Princeton (N.J.) U. Plasma Physics Lab., 1962-63, mem. research staff, 1965-68, research physicist, 1968-71, sr. research physicist, 1971—, head theoretical div., 1972-80, dep. asso. dir. for research, 1978-80, asso. dir. research, 1980—; chair tech. adv. com. Internat. Thermonuclear Exptl. Reactor, 1992—; research asso. U.K. Atomic Energy Authority Culham (Berkshire, Eng.) Lab., 1963-65; lectr. astrophys. scis. Princeton U. Co-author: (with R.J. Goldston) Introduction to Plasma Physics, 1995; mem. bd. assoc. editors Physics of Fluids, 1973-75; mem. editl. bd. Nuclear Fusion, 1980—. Recipient E.O. Lawrence award U.S. Dept. Energy, 1983. Fellow Am. Phys. Soc. Home: 192 Bertrand Dr Princeton NJ 08540-2904 Office: Plasma Physics Lab PO Box 451 Princeton NJ 08544-0999

RUTHERFORD, ROBERT BARRY, surgeon; b. Edmonton, Alta., Can., July 29, 1931; s. Robert Lyon and Kathleen Emily (Gunn) R.; m. Beulah Kay Folk, Aug. 20, 1955; children: Robert Scott, Lori Jayne, Holly Anne, Trudy Kaye, Jay Wilson. BA in Biology, Johns Hopkins U., 1952, MD, 1956. Surgeon U. Colo. Health Sci. Ctr., Denver; cons. EndoVascular Techs., Menlo Park, Calif., 1989; mem. adv. bd. Med. Edn. Collaborative, Lakewood, Colo., 1989; bd. dirs. Am. Bd. Surgery. Editor: (texts) Management of Trauma, 1968, 4 edits., Vascular Surgery, 1978, 4 edits, An Atlas of Vascular Surgery, 1993; editor quar. rev. Seminars in Vascular Surgery. Mem. Internat. Soc. for Cardiovascular Surgery, Phi Beta Kappa, Alpha Omega Alpha. Republican. Unitarian. Avocations: skiing, biking, wind surfing, sailing. Office: U Colo Dept Vascular Surgery 4200 E 9th Ave # C-312 Denver CO 80220-3706

RUTHERFORD, THOMAS TRUXTUN, II, state senator, lawyer; b. Columbus, Ohio, Mar. 3, 1947; s. James William and Elizabeth Whiting (Colby) R.; m. Linda Sue Rogers, Aug. 28, 1965 (div.); 1 child, Jeremy Todd. BBA, U. N.Mex., 1970, JD, 1982. Page, reading clk. N.Mex. State Legislature, 1960-65; mem. N.Mex. Atty. Gen. Environ. Adv. Commn., 1972; radio broadcaster Sta. KOB Radio and TV, 1963-72; mem. N.Mex. Senate, Albuquerque, 1972-96, majority whip, 1978-88, chmn. rules com., 1988—, chmn. econ. devel. and new tech. interim com., mem. sci. and new tech. oversight com., majority fl. leader; pres. Rutherford & Assocs., Albuquerque, 1978-83; pvt. practice, Albuquerque, 1983—; commr.-elect Bernalillo County Commn., 1996; former bd. dirs. Union Savs. Bank, Albuquerque; past chmn. Albuquerque Cable TV adv. bd.; mem. Southwest Regional Energy Council, N.Mex. Gov.'s Commn. on Public Broadcasting; bd. dirs., v.p. Rocky Mountain Corp. for Pub. Broadcasting; mem. Am. Coun. Young Polit. Leaders, del. mission to Hungary, Austria, Greece, 1983; mem. Fgn. Trade Adv. Com. Bd. Econ. Devel. and Tourism; trade del. to People's Republic of China, 1985. N.Mex. Broadcasting Assn. scholar, 1970. Home: 4719 Marquette Ave NE Albuquerque NM 87108-1267 also: PO Box 1610 Albuquerque NM 87103-1610

RUTHERFORD, VICKY LYNN, special education educator; b. Florence, S.C., Sept. 12, 1947. BS, Hampton U., 1969, MA, 1971; PhD, Mich. State U., 1991. Cert. tchr. French, spl. edn., reading specialist, Va., tchr. spl. edn., S.C. Social worker day care Hampton (Va.) Dept. Social Svc., 1970-72; reading therapist, asst. dir., dir. Bayberry Reading Clinic, Hampton, 1973-77; tchr. reading, English, counselor York County Schs., Yorktown, Va., 1977-85; staff advisor, asst. to course coord. Mich. State U., East Lansing, 1985-90; tchr. autistic Florence (S.C.) Dist. 1 Sch. Sys., 1992—. Instrnl. designer: Addiction Severity Index #1, 1987, #2, 1988, Managing a Diverse Workforce, 1990; designer, trainer: Project Teach, 1991; designer, developer: (video) Camp Takona Summer Experience, 1992. Bass guitarist, Sun. sch. sec., youth worker, Sun. sch. supt. Progressive Ch. of Jesus, Florence, 1992—. Fellow Mich. Dept. Edn., 1987-89. Mem. Internat. Reading Assn. Office: Theodore Lester Elem Sch 3501 E Palmetto St Florence SC 29506-4015

RUTHERFORD, WILLIAM DRAKE, investment executive, lawyer; b. Marshalltown, Iowa, Jan. 14, 1939; s. William Donald and Lois Esther (Drake) R.; m. Janice W. Rutherford, Feb. 4, 1965 (div. Mar. 1982); children: Wayne Donald, Melissa Drake; m. Karen Anderegg, Jan. 2, 1994. BS, U. Oreg., 1961; LLB, Harvard U., 1964. Bar: Oreg. 1964, U.S. Dist. Ct. Oreg. 1966. Assoc. Maguire, Kester & Cosgrave, Portland, Oreg., 1966-69; house counsel May & Co., Portland, 1969-70, pvt. practice, 1970-71; pvt. practice McMinnville, Oreg., 1971-84; mem. Oreg. Ho. of Reps., Salem, 1977-84; state treas. State of Oreg., Salem, 1984-87; chmn. Oreg. Investment Coun., Salem, 1986-87; exec. v.p., dir. U.S. and Australia ops. ABD Internat. Mgmt. Corp., N.Y.C., 1987-88, pres., chief exec. officer, bd. dirs., 1988-89; pres., bd. dirs. Societé Gen. Touche Remnant, 1990-93; dir. spl. projects Metallgesellschaft Corp., N.Y.C., 1994-95; mng. dir. Macadam Capital Ptnrs., Portland, 1995—; bd. dirs. Metro One Telecomms. Bd. dirs. Portland Opera Assn. 1st lt. U.S. Army, 1964-66. Recipient Contbn. to Individual Freedom award ACLU, 1981. Mem. Internat. Bar Assn., Nat. Assn. State Treas. (exec. v.p. 1985, 86, pres. western region 1985, 86), Nat. Assn. State Auditors, Comptr. and Treas. (exec. com. 1987). Republican. Home and Office: 6978 SW Foxfield Ct Portland OR 97225-6054

RUTHERGLEN, GEORGE A., law educator; b. Portland, Oreg., Sept. 12, 1949; s. John Alfred and Helen Kathleen (Bero) R.; m. Jessica Rosalind Feldman, Apr. 25, 1975; children: Susannah Kathleen, Michael Francis. AB, U. Calif., 1971, JD, 1974. Bar: Va. 1979, U.S. Dist. Ct. (we. dist.) Va. 1980, U.S. Ct. Appeals (4th cir.) 1980, U.S. Supreme Ct. 1988. Law clk. to judge J. Clifford San Diego, 1974-75; law clk. to justices William O. Douglas, John Paul Stevens Washington, 1975-76; prof. law U. Va., Charlottesville, 1976—; supervising atty. Post-Conviction Assistance Project, 1980—; cons. standing com. on fed. jud. improvements ABA, Chgo., 1988-89. Author: Major Issues in the 1983 Federal Law of Employment Discrimination, 1988. Mem., chair adv. com. 4th Cir. Rules, Richmond, Va., 1988—. Mem. Order of Coif, Phi Beta Kappa. Democrat. Home: 1698 Rugby Ave Charlottesville VA 22903-5141 Office: U Va Sch Law 580 Massie Rd Charlottesville VA 22903-1738

RUTHVEN, DOUGLAS MORRIS, chemical engineering educator; b. Ernakulum, India, Oct. 9, 1938; arrived in Can., 1966; s. Joseph Morris and Beryl (Mackay) R.; m. Patricia Evelyn Goodwin, July 20, 1968; 1 child, Fiona Beryl. BA, U. Cambridge, Eng., 1960, MA, 1963, PhD, 1966, ScD, 1988. Design engr. Davy Power Gas Corp., Stockton-on-Tees, Eng., 1961-63; asst. prof. dept. chem. engring. U. N.B., Fredericton, Can., 1966-72, assoc. prof., 1973-74, prof., 1975-95; prof., chair chem. engring. U. Maine, Orono, 1995—. Author: Principles of Adsorption and Adsorption Processes, 1984; co-author: Diffusion in Zeolites, 1992, Pressures Swing Adsorption, 1994; contbr. numerous articles to profl. jours. Recipient Max Planck rsch. prize, 1993. Fellow Royal Soc. Can.; mem. Am. Inst. Chem. Engrs. Avocation: Scottish country dancing. Home: 2650 Bennoch Rd Old Town ME 04468 Office: Univ Maine Dept Chem Engring Orono ME 04469

RUTISHAUSER, URS STEPHEN, cell biologist; b. Pasadena, Feb. 27, 1946; s. Hans and Elsa (Riese) R.; m. Stephanie Waddey, June 23, 1990; children: Justin, Emily, Stephen. ScB, Brown U., 1967; PhD, Rockefeller U., 1973. Asst. to assoc. prof. cell biology Rockefeller U., N.Y.C., 1973-83; prof. cell biology Case Western Res. U., Cleve., 1983—. Assoc. editor Jour. Neurosci., 1990—, European Jour. of Cell Biology, 1991—; contbr. over 100 articles to profl. jours. NIH grantee, 1975—; McKnight scholar, 1979-82; Jane Coffin Childs fellow, 1973-74. Mem. AAAS, Am. Soc. Cell Biology, Soc. for Neurosci., Soc. for Developmental Biology. Achievements include co-discovery of first cell adhesion molecule (CAM). Office: Case Western Res Univ Sch Medicine 2109 Adelbert Rd Cleveland OH 44106-2624

RUTKIN, SEYMOUR, architect; b. Weehawken, N.J., Oct. 22, 1927; s. Herman Irving and Dora (Oltarsh) R. B.S. in Architecture, Ill. Inst. Tech., 1949; certificate arts and architecture, Cooper Union. Apprentice with R.M. Schindler (architect), L.A. One-man show projected designs, Peter Cooper Gallery, N.Y.C., 1957; presented new shell designs and theories, World Conf., San Francisco, 1962, Internat. Congress IASS, Mexico City, 1967, Internat. Colloquim, Madrid, 1969; group juried art show, East Islip (N.Y.) Arts Coun., 1984, exhibited, 1985-90 (honorable mention water colors); two-person architecture show of new designs Storefront for Art and Architecture Gallery, N.Y.C., 1985; new prototype design concrete shell, residence under construction, 1995-96; prin. works include schs., hotels, 42 story office bldg., hosp., shell bldg. design, dormitories, residential, and interiors; patentee in field; contbr. articles to profl. jours. Schweinburg scholar Cooper Union; recipient Art in Am.-New Talent USA award, 1959. Address: 445 E 65th St New York NY 10021-6912

RUTKOFF, ALAN STUART, lawyer; b. Chgo., May 31, 1952; s. Roy and Harriet (Ruskin) R.; m. Mally Zoberman, Dec. 22, 1974; children: Aaron Samuel, Jordana Michal, Robert Nathaniel. BA with high distinction, U. Mich., 1973; JD magna cum laude, Northwestern U., 1976. Bar: Ill. 1976, U.S. Dist. Ct. (no. dist.) Ill. 1976, U.S. Ct. Appeals (7th cir.) 1977, U.S. Ct. Appeals (3d cir.) 1978, U.S. Supreme Ct. 1981, U.S. Ct. Appeals (5th cir.) 1983, U.S. Ct. Appeals (8th cir.) 1990. Assoc. Altheimer & Gray, Chgo., 1976-80; ptnr. Kastel & Rutkoff, Chgo., 1980-83, Holleb & Coff Ltd., Chgo., 1983-84, McDermott, Will & Emery, Chgo., 1984—. Mem. ABA, Chgo. Bar Assn., Order of Coif. Home: 801 Timberhill Rd Highland Park IL 60035-5148 Office: McDermott Will & Emery 227 W Monroe St Chicago IL 60606-5096

RUTKOWSKI, JAMES ANTHONY, state legislator; b. Milw., Apr. 6, 1942. BS in Bus., Marquette U., 1964, JD, 1966. Former instr. Marquette U., Milw.; asst. instr. U. Wis., Milw.; state legis. State of Wis., Madison, 1970. With USAR, 1966-72. Recipient Clean 16 award, 1982, 88, 90, 94, Wis. Man of Achievement award, 1976. Mem. KC, Greendale Jaycee Roosters. Home: 4550 S 117th St Greenfield WI 53228-2451 Office: State Capitol 216 North PO Box 8953 Madison WI 53708

RUTLAND, JOHN DUDLEY, lawyer; b. Austin, Tex., Jan. 4, 1931; s. Jesse Blake and Myrtle Estelle (Miller) R.; m. Eva Lou Smith, Jan. 1, 1953 (div.); 1 child, Joseph Blake; m. Beryl Ann Beebe, Apr. 25, 1985. B Bus., U. Tex., 1956; JD, U. Houston, 1961. Bar: Tex. 1961, U.S. Supreme Ct. 1971. With Gibraltar Savs. Assn., Houston, 1956-64, Southwestern Life Ins. Co., Dallas, 1964-67; sole practice, Beaumont, Tex., 1967—; cons. oil mktg. Mem. ABA, Fed. Bar, Tex. Bar Assn., Jefferson County Bar Assn., Port Arthur Bar Assn., Photog. Soc. Am. Episcopalian. Club: Beaumont Camera Club. Lodge: Rotary (past pres. West End, Beaumont).

RUTLAND-AMAGLIANI, CAROL ELAINE, music director, educator; b. Memphis, Aug. 11, 1952; d. Charles Wesson and Evelyn (Matthew) Rutland; m. Malcolm Brown Futhey (div. Mar. 1986); children: Malcolm Brown III, Meredith Elaine; m. Michael Lewis Amagliani, July 1993; 1 child, Christopher Ian Amagliani. Cert. in theory teaching/piano pedagogy, St. Louis Inst. Music, 1970, 71; BS in Edn., Memphis State U., 1989. Cert. in theory and piano, Tenn. Pvt. tchr. piano, voice and keyboard Memphis, 1970—; lower sch. music coord. Evangelical Christian Sch., Memphis, 1983—; judge piano competitions, drama tchr. and choreographer; fgn. study culture and music and missions trip, Papua, New Guinea, 1990. Keyboard accompanist, voice tchr. various chs., Memphis; mem. King's Daughter Women's Fellowship. Mem. Tenn. Counseling Assn., Women's Fellowship, Kings Daus., Pi Mu Beta. Avocations: gardening, music groups.

RUTLEDGE, CHARLES OZWIN, pharmacology educator; b. Topeka, Oct. 1, 1937; s. Charles Ozwin and Alta (Seaman) R.; m. Jane Ellen Crow, Aug. 13, 1961; children: David Ozwin, Susan Harriett, Elizabeth Jane, Karen Ann. BS in Pharmacy, U. Kans., 1959, MS in Pharmacology, 1961; PhD in Pharmacology, Harvard U., 1966. NATO postdoctoral fellow Gothenburg U., Sweden, 1966-67; asst. prof. U. Colo. Med. Ctr., Denver, 1967-74, assoc. prof., 1974-75; prof., chmn. dept. pharmacology U. Kans., Lawrence, 1975-87; dean, prof. pharmacology Purdue U., West Lafayette, Ind., 1987—. Contbr. articles on neuropharmacology to profl. jours. Grantee: NIH, 1970, Kans. Heart Assn., 1978. Mem. Am. Soc. Pharmacology and Exptl. Therapeutics (councillor 1982-84, sec.-treas. 1990-93, pres. 1996—), Am. Assn. Coll. Pharmacy (chmn. biol. scis. sect. 1983-84, chmn. council of faculties 1986-87, chmn. coun. deans, 1993-94, commn. implement change pharm. edn. 1989-92, pres. 1996—), Soc. for Neurosci., Am. Pharm. Assn. AAAS. Avocations: gardening; skiing. Home: 40 Brynteg E West Lafayette IN 47906-5643 Office: Purdue U Office of Dean Sch Pharmacy 1330 R Heine Pharm Bldg West Lafayette IN 47907-1330

RUTLEDGE, GLORIA JUDITH, property manager; b. Jackson, Tenn., Nov. 22, 1961; d. Rustico Dizon and Kathryn Lillian (Crump) Garcia; m. Corey Neal Rutledge, Oct. 28, 1983. Student, Okla. A&M Coll., 1979-80; AAS, San Jacinto Coll., 1986; AA, Austin C.C., 1991; postgrad., St. Edwards U., 1994—. Asst. mgr. Southland Corp., Norman, Okla., 1980-81; hydrologic rsch. asst. U.S. Geol. Survey, Oklahoma City, 1982-83; service adminstr. Berkey Mktg. Co., N.Y.C., 1983; exec. adminstr. First Computer Corp., Houston, 1984; mktg. support asst. IBM/NYNEX, Houston, 1984-86; exec. adminstr. Coulson and Assocs. Engrs., Houston, 1987-89; pres. Quality, Time & Money, Austin, 1988—. Author: (short story) Inverted Origins, 1980. Asst., Rep. Campaign, Houston, 1984; vol. Hospice Austin, Muscular Dystrophy Assn., Am. Cancer Soc., United Jewish Appeal, 1979—; pres. Camp Fire, 1976-80, Horizon Rep., 1977, congress rep. 1979-80. Named Mgr. of Yr., Austin Apt. Assn., 1994. Mem. B'nai Brith, Alpha Sigma Epsilon (named Outstanding Pledge 1982). Avocations: flying, real estate investing, antique collecting, cycling. Home and Office: 121 Woodward St Apt 114 Austin TX 78704-7274 Office: Quality Time & Money PO Box 218586 Houston TX 77218-8586

RUTLEDGE, IVAN CATE, retired legal educator, arbitrator; b. White Pine, Tenn., Dec. 24, 1915; s. Wiley Blount and Tamsey (Cate) R.; children: Ann, Thomas Carroll. BA, Carson-Newman Coll., 1934; MA, Duke U., 1940, LLB, 1946; LLM, Columbia U., 1952. Bar: Ga. 1946, Wash. 1951, Ohio 1966. Asst. prof. law Mercer U., Macon, Ga., 1946-47; from asst. prof. to prof. law U. Wash., Seattle, 1947-54; prof. law Ind. U., Bloomington, 1954-63; prof. law Ohio State U., Columbus, 1963-79, dean, 1965-70; Walter F. George prof. law Mercer U., Macon, 1979—, prof. emeritus, 1986—. Home: 3188 Vista Cir Macon GA 31204-1960

RUTLEDGE, JOHN WILLIAM, former watch company executive; b. Eureka, Calif., Mar. 12, 1923; s. William Eugene and Ellen Agnes (Jordan) R.; m. Mary Jo McKinley, Nov. 23, 1951; children: Ellen, John William, Amy. B.S., Northwestern U., 1943; M.B.A., Harvard U., 1947; MA. in Archaeology, Yale U., 1985. Tchr. Charlestown State Penitentiary, Boston, 1946-47; salesman Lahey Fargo & Co., 1947-48; asst. controller Lehigh Coal & Navigation Co., 1948-54; sr. v.p., dir. Xerox Corp., Stamford, Conn., 1954-71; sr. v.p. home furnishings group, dir. Magnavox Co., N.Y.C., 1971-73; pres., dir. Bulova Watch Co., N.Y.C., 1973-79; dir. Nat. Telecommunications and Tech., Network Controls, Nat. Aviation & Tech. Corp., Orion Capital Corp. Served to lt. USNR. Mem. Sigma Alpha Epsilon. Clubs: Harvard (N.Y.C.), N.Y. Athletic (N.Y.C.). Home: 127 Dunning Rd New Canaan CT 06840-4011 also: 893 S County Rd Palm Beach FL 33480-4908

RUTLEDGE, PAUL E., III, insurance company executive; b. 1953. Grad., Duke U. With Torch Cos., Birmingham, Ala., 1975-91, pres., COO, 1991—; pres. Life Ins. Co. of Va., Richmond. Office: Life Ins Co of Va 6610 W Broad St Richmond VA 23230-1702*

RUTLEDGE, WILLIAM P., manufacturing company executive; b. 1942. BS, Lafayette Coll., 1963; MS, George Washington U., 1967. With Bethlehem Steel Corp., 1963-68, foreman; with Stamco Sales Co., 1968-71, sales engr.; successively bus. planner, works mgr., dir. planning, div. mgr. FMC Corp., 1971-86; with Teledyne Inc., 1986—, group exec., v.p., 1987-88, sr. v.p., 1988-90, pres., 1990-91, pres., CEO, 1991—, now also chmn., bd. dirs. Office: Teledyne Inc 2049 Century Park E Los Angeles CA 90067-6001*

RUTMAN, MARK CHARLES, public relations executive; b. N.Y.C., Sept. 3, 1930; s. Nathan and Sarah Barbara (Korman) R.; m. Geraldine N. Leitner, Jan. 31, 1954; children: Lee, Lisa, Neil. B.A., NYU, 1952; M.S. in Journalism, Columbia U., 1953. Account exec., then v.p., gen. mgr. Affiliated Public Relations Agy., N.Y.C., 1956-60; pres., owner Nat. Public Relations Counsel, N.Y.C., 1960-78; exec. v.p. Grey & Davis Inc., N.Y.C., 1978; pres. Grey & Davis Inc., 1979-84; chmn. Grey Com Inc., 1984-85; sr. assoc. Fred Rosen Assocs., Inc., 1985-90; mng. dir. LH&H Pub. Rels., N.Y.C., 1990—. Served with Ordnance Corps AUS, 1953-55. Recipient Freedoms Found. medal, 1955. Jewish. Club: Overseas Press (N.Y.C.). Home: 9 Crossway Scarsdale NY 10583-7136 Office: 866 3rd Ave New York NY 10022-6221

RUTMAN, ROBERT JESSE, biochemist, educator; b. Kingston, N.Y., June 23, 1919; s. Leon and Anne (Porringer) R.; B.S., Pa. State U., 1940; postgrad. U. Idaho, 1942, U. Calif., Berkeley, Ph.D., 1950; M.S., U. Pa., 1975; m. Geraldine Burwell, Jan. 1971; children—Rose, Randy, Steven, Brian, David, Ellen. Mem. teaching rsch. staffs Jefferson U., Phila., 1950-53; rsch. assoc. chemistry dept. U. Pa., 1954-60, assoc. prof., 1961-68, prof. biochemistry and molecular biology Sch. Vet. Medicine, 1968-87, prof. emeritus, 1987—, chmn. dept. biochemistry, 1976-80; vis. prof. U. Ibadan (Nigeria); coord. U. Pa.-U. Ibadan Exch. Agreement; expert witness on carcinogenesis; cons. on environ. contamination. Mem. nat. steering com. Am. Found. Negro Affairs, also co-chmn. sci. and tech. div.; pres. C.W. Henry Home and Sch. Assn., 1960; pres. Phila. Citizens Com. on Pub. Edn., 1963; campaign fin. mgr. Mayoralty Campaign, Phila., 1978; bd. dirs. S.E. Pa. region Leukemia Soc., Southeastern Pa. Anti-Drug Symposium; chmn. bd. Ile-Ife Ctr. for Humanities, Parkside Human Svcs., Inc., corp. sec.; v.p. Phila. region Martin Luther King Jr. Ctr., Pa. State Commn. Martin Luther King Celebration; bd. dirs. Earth Regeneration Soc., adv. bd. dirs., Univ. Conversion Project; chmn. bd. dir. WACI-TV Channel 62, Atlantic City, N.J., chair Del. Valley Rain Forest Action Group, 1995—; chair conf. com. Nat. Black Leadership Initiative on Cancer; bd. dirs. Nat. Conf. Christians/Jews. Served to capt. C.E., AUS, 1944-48, PTO. USPHS grantee, 1960-82. Mem. AAAS, AAUP, Am. Soc. Biol. Chemistry, Am. Chem. Soc., Am. Assn. Cancer Rsch., Phila. Cancer Club, Vet. Oncology Soc., Am. Assn. Vet. Educators, Phila. Biochemists Club (pres.), U.S. Fedn. Sci. Scholars (exec. bd.), World Fedn. Sci. Workers (exec. com.). Office: 3900 Ford Rd Apt PH-P Philadelphia PA 19131

RUTSALA, VERN A., poet, English language educator, writer; b. Feb. 5, 1934; s. Ray Edwin and Virginia Mae (Brady) R.; m. Joan Merle Colby, Apr. 6, 1957; children: Matthew, David, Kirsten. BA, Reed Coll., 1956; MFA, U. Iowa, 1960. Instr. Lewis and Clark Coll., Portland, 1961-64, asst. prof., 1964-69, assoc. prof., 1969-76, prof., 1976—; vis. prof. U. Minn., Mpls., 1968-69, Bowling Green (Ohio) State U., 1970; writer-in-residence U. Idaho, Moscow, 1988, Redlands (Calif.) U., 1979; chair English dept. Lewis and Clark, Portland, 1986-89. Author: The Window, 1964, Laments, 1975, The Journey Begins, 1976, Paragraphs, 1978, Walking Home from the Icehouse, 1981, Backtracking, 1985, Ruined Cities, 1987, Selected Poems, 1991, Little-Known Sports, 1994. With U.S. Army, 1956-58. GUggenheim Found. fellow, 1982-83, NEA fellow, 1975, 79, Masters fellow Oreg. Arts Commn., 1990; recipient Carolyn Kizer prize Western Oreg. State Coll., 1988, N.W. Poets prize N.W. Rev., 1975, Hazel Hall award Oreg. Inst. Lit. Arts, 1992, Juniper prize U. Mass. Press, 1993, Duncan Lawrie prize Arvon Found., 1994. Mem. AAUP, AWP, PEN, Poetry Soc. Am. Avocations: drawing, painting, watching the ocean, sports. Office: Lewis and Clark Coll Dept English Portland OR 97212

RUTSTEIN, STANLEY HAROLD, apparel retailing company executive; b. Wilkes-Barre, Pa., July 1, 1941; s. Sydney D. and Bessie H. (Cohen) R.; m. Jo Ella Rutstein; children—Wendy Sue, Michael Scott, Lynne Elizabeth. Student, Wilkes Coll., 1959-61; grad., Advanced Mgmt. Program, Harvard U., 1975. Buyer Barbara Lynn Stores, Inc., N.Y.C., 1961-63; buyer, then mdsg. mgr. Casual Corner div. U.S. Shoe Corp., Enfield, Conn., 1963-71; pres. Casual Corner div. U.S. Shoe Corp., 1971-76; pres., cons., dir. U.S. Shoe Corp., Cin., 1976-79; pres. Commonwealth Trading, Inc., Stoughton, Mass., 1979-85, Chadwick's of Boston Ltd., 1983-85; cons. Commonwealth Trading, Inc., 1985—; pres. Trim Trends, Inc., Boston, 1986-87, chmn., 1987-91; chmn., chief exec. officer, pres. Narragansett Clothing Co., Tiverton, R.I., 1987-90, also bd. dirs.; bd. dirs. Reynolds Bros. Inc., 1989-95; pres., chief exec. officer S/J Designs Inc., 1989—; pres., chief exec. officer DBA, Northeast Knitters; bd. dirs. The Icing, Inc., Sycamore Shops, Inc. Bd. dirs. Ptnrs. for Disabled Youth, 1992. Mem. Young Pres. Orgn. Home: 18 Charles River Sq Boston MA 02114-3266 Office: 560 Harrison Ave Boston MA 02118-2436

RUTTAN, VERNON WESLEY, agricultural economist; b. Alden, Mich., Aug. 16, 1924; s. Ward W. and Marjorie Ann (Chaney) R.; m. Marilyn M. Barone, July 30, 1945; children: Lia Marie, Christopher, Alison Elaine, Lore Megan. BA, Yale U., 1948; MA, U. Chgo., 1950, PhD, 1952; LLD (hon.), Rutgers U., 1978; D Agrl. Sci. ((hon.), U. Kiel, Germany, 1986, Purdue U., 1991. Economist TVA, 1951-54; prof. agrl. econs. Purdue U., 1954-63; staff economist President's Council Econ. Advisers, 1961-63; economist Rockefeller Found., 1963-65; head dept. agrl. econs. U. Minn., St. Paul, 1965-70, Regent's prof., 1986—; pres. Agrl. Devel. Council, N.Y.C., 1973-77. Author: (with Y. Hayami) Agricultural Development: An International Perspective, 1971, 85, Agricultural Research Policy, 1982, Aid and Development, 1989, Agriculture, Environment and Health, 1994, U.S. Development Assistance Policy, 1996. Recipient Alexander von Humboldt award, 1985. Fellow AAAS, Am. Acad. Arts and Scis., Am. Agrl. Econs. Assn. (pres. 1971-72, Publ. award 1956, 57, 62, 66, 67, 71, 79, 85); mem. NAS. Home: 2381 Commonwealth Ave Saint Paul MN 55108-1605 Office: Dept Agrl Econs U Minn Saint Paul MN 55108

RUTTENBERG, CHARLES BYRON, lawyer; b. Reading, Pa., Nov. 16, 1922; s. Abraham David and Mollie Belle (Rabinowitz) R.; m. Arden Honore Suk, July 29, 1955; children—Victoria Arden, Valerie Honore, Alexandra Anne. B.A., U. Va., 1946; LL.B., U. Pa., 1949. Bar: D.C. With Covington & Burling, Washington; gen. counsel NSF, Washington, Nat. Found. Arts and Humanities, Washington, 1949-69; ptnr. Arent, Fox, Kintner, Plotkin & Kahn, Washington, 1969—; chmn. Legis. Bur., mem. exec. com., bd. dirs., gen. counsel Greater Washington Bd. of Trade, 1983-92. Co-chmn. U. Pa. Law Sch. Alumni Fund, Washington, 1983-91, chmn. lawyers com. D.C. Commn. on Arts, 1972-75; gen. counsel People to People Music Program, Washington, 1970-91; trustee, gen. counsel Wolf Trap Found. Performing Arts, Vienna, Va., 1981-91, Nat. Inst. Music Theatre, Washington, 1969-90; bd. dirs. Washington Area Lawyers for Arts, 1984-95, Greater Washington Rsch. Ctr., Washington, 1980-95. With USAAF, 1942-46, capt. USAFR, 1946-55. Recipient Outstanding Service awards U.S. Govt., 1967, 68. Mem. ABA, U. Pa. Law Alumni Assn. (pres. 1967-71, bd. dirs. 1967-78), Arts Internat. (gen. counsel), Phi Beta Kappa. Clubs: Cosmos, St. Alban's, Mitchell Law, Washington Athletic (bd. govs. 1969-74). Home: 4735 Butterworth Pl NW Washington DC 20016-4459 Office: Arent Fox Kintner Plotkin & Kahn 1050 Connecticut Ave NW Washington DC 20036-5303

RUTTENBERG, HAROLD JOSEPH, manufacturing executive; b. St. Paul, May 22, 1914; s. Charles H. and Fannie R. (Weinstein) R.; m. Katherine Monori, Sept. 23, 1936; children: Charles L. (dec.), James E., Edward F., Ellen Ruttenberg Rabin. B.A., U. Pitts., 1935. Research dir. United Steelworkers Am., 1936-46; asst. dir. steel div. WPB, 1942-44; exec. v.p. Portsmouth Steel Co., Ohio, 1946-49; pres. Harkit Corp., Pitts., 1949-51; pres., chmn. bd. Stardrill-Keystone Co., Beaver Falls, Pa., 1951-59; mng. dir. Humanation Assos., Pitts., 1959-64; chmn. bd., pres. United Steel & Wire Co., Battle Creek, Mich., 1964-68; chmn. Rehovoth Instruments Co., Israel, 1968-78; chmn. bd., pres. AVM Corp. (name changed to Am. Locker Group Inc. 1985), Pitts., from 1973, now chmn. bd., chief exec. officer, treas.; chmn., treas. Rollform of Jamestown (N.Y.), Inc. Author: (with C.S. Golden) Dynamics of Industrial Democracy, 1942, Self-Developing America, 1960. Democrat. Jewish. Home: 307 S Dithridge St Apt 814 Pittsburgh PA 15213-3519 Office: 300 S Craig St Pittsburgh PA 15213-3707

RUTTENBERG, STANLEY HARVEY, economist; b. St. Paul, Mar. 19, 1917; s. Charles and Fannie (Weinstein) R.; m. Gertrude Bernstein, Nov. 28, 1940; children: Joel, Ruth, Charles. Student, Massanutten Mil. Acad., Woodstock, Va., 1929-33; B.S., U. Pitts., 1937. Asst. to dir. Hull House, Chgo., 1938-39; with CIO, 1937-55; organizer and field rep. in Ohio Valley

CIO, Cin., 1937-38; assoc. dir. research CIO, Washington, 1939-48; dir. dept. edn. and research CIO, 1948-55; dir. dept. research AFL-CIO, 1955-62; spl. asst. to sec. of labor, 1963-65, manpower adminstr., 1965-69, asst. sec. labor, manpower adminstr., 1966-69; pres. Stanley H. Ruttenberg Assos. Inc., 1969-82; chmn. bd. RFK & A, Inc., 1982—; bd. dirs. Nat. Planning Assn.; dir. Nat. Bur. Econ. Res., 1940-41, 48-62; exec. com. U.S. nat. commn. UNESCO, 1948-53, vice chmn., 1952; spl. adviser to (Am. del. 4th and 5th Internat. Confs.), 1949, 50; del. to Internat. Labor Orgn. Conf., Geneva, 1952; dir. Resources for the Future, Inc., 1952-79; pub. mem. Fgn. Service Selection Bd., 1950; mem. Presdl. Price Adv. Com., 1979-80. Author: (with Jocelyn Gutchess) Manpower Challenge of the 1970s: Institutions and Social Change, 1970, The Federal-State Employment Service: A Critique, 1970. Served as 1st lt. AUS, 1943-46, PTO. Mem. Am. Econ. Assn., Am. Statis. Assn., Indsl. Relations Research Assn. (exec. bd. 1953). Home: 6310 Maiden Ln Bethesda MD 20817-5610 Office: 1211 Connecticut Ave NW Washington DC 20036-2701

RUTTER, FRANCES TOMPSON, publisher; b. Arlington, Mass., Apr. 12, 1920; d. Harold F. and Mildred F. (Wheeler) Tompson; m. John H. Ottemiller, Mar. 24, 1943; children: Joan Tompson, John Tompson; m. William D. Rutter, Oct. 26, 1970. AB magna cum laude, Pembroke Coll., Brown U., 1941; postgrad., Mt. Holyoke Coll., 1942-43. Res. book librarian Brown U., 1941-42; annotator ship's papers John Carter Brown Library, Providence, 1943-44; librarian Sci. Service, Washington, 1944-45; ptnr. Shoe String Press, Hamden, Conn., 1952-58; sec., treas. Shoe String Press, Inc., 1958-68, pres., treas., 1968-80, also bd. dirs.; sec.-treas., dir. Tompson-Malone, Inc., book mfrs., 1967-80; pres., treas., dir. Tompson & Rutter, Inc., 1980-89. V.p. class 1941 Pembroke Coll., 1967-73, 76—, pres., 1973-76, head class agt., 1979-85, bequests and trust chmn., 1979-90, 40th reunion gift com., 1980, co-chair 50th reunion gift com., 1990-91, 55th reunion gift com., 1995-96; spl. projects adv. panel N.H. Commn. on Arts, 1980-84; mem. natural resources com. Grantham, 1980; mem. Grantham Planning Bd., 1981-87, sec., 1981-83, chmn., 1985-87; chmn. Grantham Recycling Com., 1988-89, Grantham Hist. Soc., 1992-96, Habitat for Humanity-Kearsarge/Sunapee chpt., 1989-94; mem. Diocesan Altar Guild Bd., 1990-93, sec., 1991-92; vol. Mary Hitchcock Meml. Hosp. Aux., 1991—. Mem. Friends of Fernald Libr. of Colby-Sawyer Coll., ACLU (life), LWV (editor newsletter 1987-89), Assoc. Alumni Brown U. (bd. dirs. 1981-83), Nicholas Brown Soc., Pembroke Ctr. Assocs. (coun. 1984-86), Soc. for Preservation N.H. Forests, Episcopal Peace Fellowship, River City Arts Club, Assocs. of Holy Cross, Phi Beta Kappa. Episcopalian. Home: 19 The Gardens White River Junction VT 05001-3344

RUTTER, JEREMY BENTHAM, archaeologist, educator; b. Boston, Mass., June 23, 1946; s. Peter and Nancy Kendall (Comstock) R.; m. Sarah Robbins Herndon, Jan. 31, 1970; children: Benjamin Ryerson, Nicholas Kendall. BA Classics with honors, Haverford Coll., 1967; PhD Classical Archaeology, U. Pa., 1974; MA, Dartmouth Coll., 1993. Vis. asst. prof. dept. classics U. Calif., L.A., 1975-76, from asst. prof. to prof. dept. classics, 1976—; participant excavations West Germny, 1966, Italy, 1968-69, Greece, 1972, 73-74, 75, 77, 78, 80-81, 84-86, 88-89, 91—. Author: Lerna III: The Pottery of Lerna IV, 1995; publ. com. Am. Sch. Classical Studies at Athens; contbr. numerous articles, reviews to profl. jours. With U.S. Army, 1969-71, Vietnam. Woodrow Wilson fellow, 1967-68; NDEA fellow U. Pa., 1968-69, 71-73; Olivia James Traveling fellow Archeol. Inst. Am., 1974-75; NEH rsch. grantee, 1979-81; travel grantee Am. Coun. Learned Socs., 1982; sr. faculty grantee, 1985-86, 91-92. Mem. Archaeol. Inst. Am. (numerous coms.), Classical Assn. New England, Phi Beta Kappa. Home: 47 Eagle Ridge Dr Lebanon NH 03766-1900 Office: Dept Classics Dartmouth College Hanover NH 03755

RUTTER, MARSHALL ANTHONY, lawyer; b. Pottstown, Pa., Oct. 18, 1931; s. Carroll Lennox and Dorothy (Tagert) R.; m. Winifred Hitz, June 6, 1953 (div. 1970); m. Virginia Ann Hardy, Jan. 30, 1971 (div. 1992); children: Deborah Frances, Gregory Russell, Theodore Thomas; m. Terry Susan Knowles, Dec. 19, 1992. BA, Amherst (Mass.) Coll., 1954; JD, U. Pa., 1959. Bar: Calif 1960. Assoc. O'Melveny & Myers, Los Angeles, 1959-65; assoc. Flint & MacKay, Los Angeles, 1965-67, ptnr., 1967-72; ptnr. Rutter, Greene & Hobbs, Los Angeles, 1973—. Gov. The Music Ctr. of L.A. County, 1978-86, 89-92; dir. Music Ctr. Operating Co., 1992—; bd. dirs. Chorus Am., Phila., 1987—, pres., 1993-95; bd. dirs., pres. L.A. Master Chorale Assn., 1963-92, chmn., 1992—; vestryman All Saints Ch., Beverly Hills, Calif., 1983-86, 88-90. Mem. ABA, Assn. Bus. Trial Lawyers (bd. dirs. 1980-82), L.A. County Bar Assn., Beverly Hills Bar Assn., Century City Bar Assn., Pasadena Bar Assn., English-Speaking Union (various offices L.A. chpt. 1963-91), L.A. Jr. C. of C. (bd. dirs. 1964-67). Democrat. Episcopalian. Avocations: classical music, tennis, golf. Home: 460 S Oakland Ave Apt 112 Pasadena CA 91101-4003 Office: Rutter Greene & Hobbs Ste 2700 1900 Avenue Of The Stars Los Angeles CA 90067-4508

RUTTER, MICHAEL LLEWELLYN, child psychiatry educator; b. Brummanna, Lebanon, Aug. 15, 1933; s. Llewellyn Charles and Winifred Olive (Barber) R.; m. Marjorie Heys, Dec. 27, 1958; children: Sheila Carol, Stephen Michael, Christine Ann. MBChB, U. Birmingham, 1955; DPM, U. London, 1961; MD with honors, U. Birmingham, 1963; degree (hon.) U. Leiden, 1985, Catholic U., 1990, U. Birmingham, 1990, U. Edinburgh, 1990, U. Chgo., 1993, U. Minn., 1993, U. Ghent, 1994, U. Jyvaskyla, 1996. Various tng. positions in pediatrics, neurology and internal medicine, 1955-58; registrar then sr. registrar Maudsley Hosp., London, 1958-62; mem. sci. staff MRC Social Psychiatry Research Unit, London, 1962-65; sr. lectr., then reader U. London Inst. Psychiatry, 1966-73, prof. child psychiatry, 1973—, hon. dir. MRC Child Psychiatry unit, 1984—, Social Genetic and Devel. Psychiatry Rsch. Ctr., 1994; Nuffield med. travelling fellow, Albert Einstein Coll. Medicine, N.Y.C., 1961-62; fellow Ctr. for Advanced Study in Behavioral Scis., Stanford, Calif., 1979-80. Author: Helping Troubled Children, 1975; Maternal Deprivation Reassessed, 2nd edit. 1981; (with Henri Giller) Juvenile Delinquency: Trends & Perspectives, 1983, (with Marjorie Rutter) Developing Minds: Challenge and Continuity Accross the Lifespan, 1993; co-editor: Child and Adolescent Psychiatry: Modern Approaches, 3d edit., 1994, Stress, Risk and Resilience In Children and Adolescents: Processes, Mechanisms and Interventions, 1994, Psychosocial Disorders in Young People: Time Trends & Their Causes, 1995; Autism: A Reappraisal of Concepts and Treatment, 1978, Development Through Life: A Handbook For Clinicians, 1994; editor: Scientific Foundations of Developmental Psychiatry, 1980, Developmental Neuropsychiatry, 1983. Belding travelling scholar, 1963; Goulstonian lectr., Royal Coll. Physicians, 1973; Am. Assn. Mental Deficiency rsch. award, 1975; Rock Carling fellow, 1979; Salmon lectr. N.Y. Acad. Medicine, 1979; C. Anderson Aldrich award Am. Acad. Pediatrics, 1981; Adolf Meyer ward lectr. APA, 1985, Disting. Sci. Contbn. award APA, 1995, Castilla del Pino prize for achievement in psychiatry, Spain, 1995; Royal Soc. fellow, 1987. Fellow Royal Soc. Medicine (London, hon.); mem. AAAS (fgn. hon.), U.S. Nat. Acad. Edn. (fgn. assoc.), Brit. Paediatric Assn. (hon.), Assn. Child Psychology and Psychiatry (chmn. 1973-74), Brit. Psychol. Soc. (hon. fellow), Am. Acad. Child Psychiatry (hon. membership), NAS (fgn. assoc. Inst. Medicine), Soc. Research in Adolescence (John P. Hill award for excellence in theory devel. and rsch. 1992, hon. fellow 1996), Internat. Acad. Rsch. in Learning Disabilities, Academia Europaea (founding mem.). Home: 190 Court Ln, London SE21 7ED, England Office: Inst Psychiatry, DeCrespigny Park, London SE5 8AF, England

RUTTER, NATHANIEL WESTLUND, geologist, educator; b. Omaha, Nov. 22, 1932; s. John Elliot and Karleen (Ludden) R.; m. Mary Marie Munson, Sept. 11, 1961; children: Todd, Christopher. B.S., Tufts U., 1955; M.S., U. Alaska, 1962; Ph.D., U. Alta., 1965. Geologist Venezuelan Atlantic Refining Co., 1955-58; research scientist Geol. Survey Can., Calgary, Alta., 1965-74; head urban projects sect Geol. Survey Can., Ottawa, Ont., 1974; environ. advisor Nat. Energy Bd., Ottawa, 1974-75; assoc. prof. dept. geology U. Alta., Edmonton, 1975-77, 77-80, prof., chmn. dept., 1980-89, 77—; mem. Can. nat. com. Internat. Geol. Correlation Program, UNESCO, 1986—; pres. Internat. Union Quaternary Rsch. Congress, 1982-87; mem. Internat. Geosphere-Biosphere Program: A Study of Global Change; mem. rsch. com. Can. Global Change Program, 1992-94; chmn. global change com. INUQA, 1991—; hon. prof. Chinese Acad. Sci., Beijing, 1994—; nat. lectr. Sigma Xi, 1995—. Contbr. numerous articles to profl. jours.; assoc. editor Arctic, Geosci. Can. Quaternary Rsch.; mem. editorial bd. Quaternary Sci. Revs.; editor in chief Quaternary Internat. Grantee Natural Scis. and Engring. Research Council of Can.; grantee Energy, Mines and Resources. Fellow Royal Soc. Can.; mem. Assn. Profl. Engrs., Geologists and Geophysicists of Alta., Internat. Union Quaternary Research (v.p. 1982-87, pres. 1987-91), Can. Quaternary Assn. (v.p. 1981-82), Geol. Soc. Am. (mgmt. bd. dirs. quaternary geol. and geomorphology div. 1982-84). Clubs: Explorer's, Cosmos. Home: Rural Route 3, Stony Plain, AB Canada T7Z 1X3 Office: Dept Earth and Atmospheric, Scis, U Alta, Edmonton, AB Canada T6G 2E3

RUTTINGER, GEORGE DAVID, lawyer; b. Detroit, Jan. 17, 1948; s. George Jacob and Margaret Mary (Smith) R.; m. Camille Ann Larson, Oct. 4, 1975; children: Jacob Charles, David Hayes, Philip George. AB with high distinction and honors, U. Mich., 1970, JD magna cum laude, 1973. Bar: Calif. 1975, D.C. 1975, U.S. Dist. Ct. D.C. 1975, U.S. Dist. Ct. Md. 1987, U.S. Ct. Appeals (D.C. and 4th cirs.) 1984, U.S. Ct. Appeals (1st cir.) 1988, U.S. Supreme Ct. 1984. Law clk. to Hon. Malcolm R. Wilkey U.S. Ct. Appeals, Washington, 1973-74; assoc. Latham & Watkins, L.A., 1974; assoc. Crowell & Moring (formerly Jones, Day, Reavis & Pogue), Washington, 1975-79, ptnr., 1980—. Author: (with others) Containing Legal Costs: ADR Strategies for Corporations, Law Firms and Government, 1988; contbr. articles to profl. jours. Office: Crowell & Moring 1001 Pennsylvania Ave NW Washington DC 20004-2505

RUTZ, RICHARD FREDERICK, physicist, researcher; b. Alton, Ill., Feb. 9, 1919; s. Erwin William and Esther Norma (Brooks) R.; m. Mary Lamsom Lambert, June 10, 1945; children—Frederick R., Carl R., William L. BA, Shurtleff Coll., Alton, Ill., 1941; MS, State U. Iowa, 1947. Staff mem. Sandia Corp., Albuquerque, 1948-51; mem. staff, mgr. IBM T.J. Watson Sr. Rsch. Ctr., Yorktown Heights, N.Y., 1951-87. Contbr. articles to profl. jours.; patentee numerous semicond. devices. With U.S. Maritime Svc., 1941-42, USAAF, 1942-46. Fellow IEEE; mem. Am. Phys. Soc. Home: 9 Burgundy Ct Grand Junction CO 81503

RUTZEN, ARTHUR COOPER, JR., investment company executive; b. Chgo., Nov. 18, 1947; s. Arthur Cooper and Helen Doyle Rutzen; children: Sandy, Arthur C., Judy. BS in Bus. and Econs., Lehigh U., 1970, MBA, 1972; postgrad. in advanced mgmt. Stanford U., 1982. Account exec. Merrill Lynch Pierce Fenner & Smith, N.Y.C., 1971-75; mgr. bus. analysis and mktg. positions Union Carbide Corp., N.Y.C., 1975-77, San Francisco and Los Angeles, 1977-83; dir. nat. accounts Liquid Air Corp., San Francisco, 1979-83; v.p., dir. investment mktg. Security Pacific Nat. Bank, Pacific Century Advisors, San Francisco, 1983-85, sr. v.p., 1985-86, exec. v.p., Calif. Group head, 1986-88; mng. dir., sr. v.p. Asset Mgmt. div. Wells Fargo Bank, 1988—; participant nat. accounts mgmt. study Mktg. Sci. Inst., Harvard U. Sch. Bus., 1980—. Trustee Am. Conservatory Theater, 1991—. Mem. Nat. Accounts Mktg. Assn. (former dir., v.p.), Merrill Lynch Exec. Club, Bay Area Sales and Mktg. Execs. Assn. (div. 1981—, v.p. 1982—), Golden Gateway Tennis Club, Villa Taverna Club, Lehigh U. Alumni Club, The Family Club. Home: 2275 Broadway St San Francisco CA 94115-1284

RUTZICK, MARK CHARLES, lawyer; b. St. Paul, Sept. 6, 1948; s. Max Arthur and Bertha (Ward) R.; children from a previous marriage: Elizabeth Leslie, Karen Deborah; m. Cynthia Lombardi Jan. 16, 1994. B.A., U. Mich., 1970; J.D., Harvard U., 1973. Bar: N.Y. 1974, U.S. Supreme Ct. 1977, U.S. Ct. Appeals (9th cir.) 1982, Oreg. 1984, Wash. 1987. Spl. asst. corp. counsel N.Y.C. Housing Adminstrn., 1973-75; assoc. Alexander Hammond P.C., N.Y.C., 1975-76; asst. atty. gen. N.Y. State Atty. Gen., N.Y.C., 1976-78; atty. Dept. Justice, Washington, 1978-82, spl. litigation counsel, 1982-83, atty.-in-charge field office, Portland, Oreg., 1983-86; counsel Preston, Thorgrimson, Shidler, Gates & Ellis, Portland, 1986-87, ptnr. 1988-94; shareholder Mark C. Rutzick Law Firm, P.C., 1994—. Mem. ABA, Oreg. State Bar Assn., Wash. State Bar Assn. Home: 3450 SW Downs View Ter Portland OR 97221-3173 Office: 500 Pioneer Tower 888 SW 5th Ave Portland OR 97204-2012

RUUD, CLAYTON OLAF, engineering educator; b. Glassgow, Mont., July 31, 1934; s. Asle and Myrtle (Bleken) R.; children: Kelley Astrid, Kirsten Anne; m. Paula Kay Mannino, Feb. 24, 1990. BS in Metallurgy, Wash. State U., 1957; MS in Matl. Sci., San Jose State U., 1967; PhD in Materials Sci., U. Denver, 1970. Registered profl. engr., Calif., Colo. Asst. remelt metallurgist Kaiser Aluminum & Chem. Corp., Trentwood, Wash., 1957-58; devel. engr. Boeing Airplane Co., Seattle, 1958-60; mfg. rsch. engr. Lockheed Missiles & Space Corp., Sunnyvale, Calif., 1960-63; rsch. engr. FMC Corp., San Jose, 1963-67; sr. rsch. scientist U. Denver, 1967-79; prof. indsl. engring. Pa. State U., University Park, 1979—; cons. in field; bd. dirs. Denver X-Ray Inst. Inc., Altoona, Pa. Editor series of books: Advances in X-Ray Analysis, Vol. 12-22, 1970-80, Nondestructive Character of Materials, Vol. 1-6, 1983—; editor X-Ray Spectometry, 1975-87; editl. com. Nondestructive Testing and Evaluation, 1991—. Mem., chmn. Nat. Acad. Sci. Safe Drinking Water Com., Washington, 1976-78. Recipient IR 100 award, 1983, Gov.'s New Product Award, Pa. Soc. Profl. Engrs., 1988. Mem. ASM Internat. (chmn. Resid. Stress Conf. 1989-91), Internat. Ctr. for Diffraction Data, Soc. Mfg. Engrs., Metall. Soc. of AIME. Achievements include patent on Method for Determining Internal Stresses in Polycrystalline Solids; patent on Stress-Unstressed Standard for X-Ray Stress Analysis; invention of a Fiber Optic Based Position Sensitive Scintillation X-Ray Detector; invention of an instrument for simultaneous stress and phase composition measurement; development of an X-ray diffraction instrument for manufacturing process quality control. Office: Pa State U 207 Hammond Bldg University Park PA 16802

RUUD, MILLARD HARRINGTON, former legal association administrator, retired educator; b. Ostrander, Minn., Jan. 7, 1917; s. Mentor L. and Helma M. (Olson) R.; m. Barbara W. Dailey, Aug. 28, 1943; children: Stephen D., Christopher O., Michael L. B.S. in Law, U. Minn., 1942, LL.B., 1947; LL.D., Georgetown U., 1980, U. Pacific, 1981, New Eng. Sch. Law, 1981, Southwestern U., 1983, Widener U., 1987, John Marshall Law Sch., 1987. Bar: Minn. 1947, Tex. 1956. Asst. prof. law U. Kans., Lawrence, 1947-48; assoc. prof. U. Tex., Austin, 1948-52, prof., 1952-78, 80-83, prof. emeritus, 1983—; asst. exec. dir. Tex. Legis. Council, 1950-52; exec. dir. Assn. Am. Law Schs., Washington, 1973-80, 83-87; mem. Tex. Commn. Uniform State Laws, 1967—; cons. legal edn. Am. Bar Assn., 1968-73; chmn. Law Sch. Admission Council, 1966-69, Council on Legal Edn. Opportunity, 1968. Bd. visitors U. Miami, 1980-94, McGeorge Sch. Law, U. of Pacific, 1985-92, U. Minn., 1994—. Recipient Disting. Grad. award U. Minn., 1980. Mem. ABA (Robert J. Kutak award for disting. svc. to legal edn. and profession 1988), Tex. Bar Assn., Am. Law Inst., Order of Coif (nat. sec.-treas. 1981-83). Club: Cosmos. Home: 3416 Foothill Ter Austin TX 78731-5836 Office: U Tex Sch Law 727 E 26th St Austin TX 78705-3224

RUVANE, JOHN AUSTIN, pharmaceutical industry consultant; b. Jersey City, N.J., Nov. 27, 1935; s. Joseph Jerome and Anne Agnes (Sullivan) R.; m. Anne Patricia Beebe, Apr. 13, 1957; children: Anne Julie, Kathleen Kearney Vrabel, Molly Vaughn Kamensky, Alice Regan, John Austin, Susan Sullivan D'Avanzo. A.B. in Econs., Princeton U, 1957; postgrad., NYU, 1958-60. Salesman Ayerst Co., N.Y.C., 1960-65; asst. to v.p. McCann-Erickson Co., N.Y.C., 1965-70; pres., chief exec. officer J.R. Druid-Ruvane-Leverte, N.Y.C., 1970-83; chmn., bd. dirs. Bozell & Jacobs Co., N.Y.C., 1983-85; pres. JARCOM Inc., N.Y.C., 1985—; bd. dirs. Pharm. Advt. Coun., N.Y.C., 1974-86, pres., 1983; mem. adv. coun. Health Care Expo, N.Y.C., 1984-88. Contbr. articles to profl. jours., newsletter. mem. fin. coun. St. Rose of Lima Parish Coun., Short Hills, N.J., 1974-76; chmn., interviewer Princeton Schs. & Scholarship Commn., Short Hills; jazz pianist, choral singer Univ. Glee Club N.Y.C.; pres., bd. dirs. Buck Hill Lot and Cottage Assn., Buck Hills Falls, Pa., 1988-94. Recipient numerous advt. awards. Mem. Pharm. Advt. Council (pres. 1983), Med. Advt. Agy. Assn. Republican. Roman Catholic. Clubs: Princeton (N.Y.C.); Canoe Brook Country (committeeman 1980-87, Summit, N.J.), Buck Hill Golf Club. Avocations: music; golf. Home: PO Box 275 64 Hemlock Ln Buck Hill Falls PA 18323 Office: Jarcom Inc 304 Park Ave S New York NY 10010-5302*

RUWART, DAVID PETER, lawyer; b. Balt.; s. William M. and Inez W. (Wilder) R.; m. Susan J. Collins, Oct. 15, 1960; children: Carole, Sharon, Peter, Denise. B.A., Xavier U., Cin., 1954; J.D., U. Detroit, 1956; LL.M. in Taxation, NYU, 1957. Bar: Mich. 1956, U.S. Dist. Ct. (ea. dist.) Mich. 1957. Sole practice, Detroit, 1957-81; prin. in charge bus. law sect. Plunkett & Cooney P.C. and predecessor firms, Detroit, 1982—; mem. faculty U. Detroit Law Sch., 1969-74, Wayne State U., 1966-69, U. Mich., 1964-66. Mem. ABA, Mich. State Bar Assn., Detroit Bar Assn., Fed. Bar Assn., Am. Judicature Soc., Assn. For Corp. Growth (bd. dirs. 1986—, Detroit chpt. pres. 1990-92, intergrowth chmn. 1995), Internat. Assn. Fin. Planners (bd. dirs. 1982-86), Am. Law Firm Assn. (chmn. 1987-89). Roman Catholic. Home: 43 Deming Ln Grosse Pointe MI 48236-3742 Office: Plunkett & Cooney 243 W Congress St Detroit MI 48226

RUWE, ROBERT P., federal judge; b. 1941. Grad., Xavier U., 1963; JD, No. Ky. U., 1970. Chief counsel IRS Dept. Treasury, 1970-87; judge U.S. Tax Ct., Washington, 1987—. Office: US Tax Ct 400 2nd St NW Washington DC 20217-0001*

RUXIN, PAUL THEODORE, lawyer; b. Cleve., Apr. 14, 1943; s. Charles and Olyn Judith (Koller) R.; m. Joanne Camy, May 25, 1965; children: Marc J., Sarah. BA, Amherst Coll., 1965; LLB, U. Va., 1968. Bar: Ill. 1968, Ohio 1977, U.S. Dist. Ct. (no. dist.) Ill. 1968, U.S. Ct. Appeals D.C. 1972. Assoc. Isham, Lincoln & Beale, Chgo., 1968-73, ptnr., 1974-77; ptnr., chmn. energy utilities sect. Jones, Day, Reavis & Pogue, Cleve., 1977—. Mem. Hudson Archtl. and Hist. Bd. Rev., 1981-91; exec. bd. Greater Cleve. Boy Scouts Am., 1978-90; bd. dirs. ARC Cleveland Chpt., 1991—. Mem. ABA, Ohio State Bar Assn. (pub. utilities sect.), Bar Assn. Greater Cleve., Fed. Energy Bar Assn. (com. chmn. 1981), Western Res. Hist. Soc. (collections com. Cleve. chpt.), Club at Soc. Ctr., Rowfant Club. Home: 40 Wellgate Dr Hudson OH 44236-3143 Office: Jones Day Reavis & Pogue 901 Lakeside Ave E Cleveland OH 44114-1116

RUYTER, NANCY LEE CHALFA, dance educator; b. Phila., May 23, 1933; d. Andrew Benedict Chalfa and Lois Elizabeth (Strode) McClary; m. Ralph Markson (div.); m. Hans C. Ruyter, Dec. 7, 1968. BA in History, U. Calif., Riverside, 1964; PhD in History, Claremont Grad. Sch., 1970. Tchr. theater dept. Pomona Coll., 1965-72; instr. dance program U. Calif., Riverside, 1972-76, acting chair dance program, 1974-75; instr. dance dept. UCLA, 1976; instr. phys. edn. dept. Orange Coast Coll., 1976-77; asst. prof. dept. phys. edn. and dance Tufts U., 1977-78; asst. prof. phys. edn. dept. Calif. State U., Northridge, 1978-82; asst. prof., then assoc. prof. dance dept. U. Calif., Irvine, 1982—, assoc. dean Sch. Fine Arts, 1984-88, 95-96, chair dept. dance, 1989-91; presenter in field. Appeared with Jasna Planina Folk Ensemble, 1972-77, 78-79, Di Falco and Co., 1955-57; choreographer, dir. numerous coll. dance prodns.; contbr. articles, revs. to profl. publs.; author: Reformers and Visionaries: The Americanization of the Art of Dance, 1979. Mem. Am. Soc. Theatre Rsch., Bulgarian Studies Assn., Congress on Rsch. in Dance (bd. dirs. 1977-80, pres. 1981-85), Folk Dance Fedn., Internat. Fedn. Theatre Rsch., Soc. Dance Rsch., Soc. Ethnomusicology, Soc. Dance History Scholars (steering com. 1980-81), Spanish Dance Soc., Theatre Libr. Assn. Office: U Calif-Irvine Dept Dance Irvine CA 92717

RYABOV, ALEXANDER A., health services professional, consultant; b. Russia, Feb. 25, 1941; came to U.S., 1972; s. Alexander S. and Daria A. (Molankin) R. Diploma, U. Tashkent Law Sch., 1971; student, Columbia U., 1977-80. Mine engr. Abashevskaya 3-4 Coal Mine, Siberia, USSR, 1960-62; legal counsel Tashkent (USSR) State Constrn. Co., 1970-72; translator N.Y.C., 1972-77; technician Meml. Sloan-Kettering Cancer Ctr., N.Y.C., 1977-78; pres. Arithmoi Cons. Internat., N.Y.C., 1981—; dir. Internat. Inst. of Geneonomics and Pub. Philosophy, N.Y.C., 1987—. With Russian Mil., 1962-65. Russian Orthodox. Office: Arithmoi Consultants Internat PO Box 1882 Cathedral Station New York NY 10025-1882

RYALL, A(LBERT) LLOYD, horticulturist, refrigeration engineer; b. Phoenix, June 25, 1904; s. Lloyd Oliver and Kate Florence (Southam) R.; m. Mary Elizabeth Newton, Dec. 26, 1928; children: Patricia June, Philip Lloyd, Pamela Kate, Peter Newton. BS, N.D. Agrl. Coll., 1926; MS, Oreg. Agrl. Coll., 1928. Jr. pomologist USDA, Yakima, Wash., 1928-41; assoc. horticulturist USDA, Harlingen, Tex., 1942-49; horticulturist USDA, Fresno, Calif., 1949-57; sr. horticulturist USDA, Beltsville, Md., 1957-62; prin. horticulturist, br. chief USDA, Washington, 1962-69; asst. prof. N.Mex. State U., Las Cruces, 1971-75; hort. cons. various produce and transp. cos., 1970-82. Author: (with others) Handling, Transportation and Storage, Vol. 1, Vegetables and Melons, 1981, Handling, Transporatation and Storage, Vol. 2, Fruits and Tree Nuts, 1983; contbr. over 90 articles to profl. jours. Fellow AAAS, Am. Soc. Hort. Sci. (chmn. Pacific chpt. 1956); mem. ASHRAE, Am. Inst. Biol. Sci., Alpha Zeta, Phi Kappa Phi, Lambda Kappa Delta. Achievements include development of advanced applications in precooling, special storage requirements, packaging and transportation services for fresh fruits and vegetables. Home: 6101 Camelot Dr Harlingen TX 78550

RYALL, JO-ELLYN M., psychiatrist; b. Newark, May 25, 1949; d. Joseph P. and Tekla (Paraszczuk) R.; BA in Chemistry with gen. honors, Douglass Coll., Rutgers U., 1971; MD, Washington U., St. Louis, 1975. Diplomate Am. Bd. Psychiatry and Neurology. Resident in psychiatry Washington U., 1975-78, psychiatrist Student Health, 1980-84, clin. instr. psychiatry, 1978-83, clin. asst. prof. psychiatry, 1983—; inpatient supr. Malcolm Bliss Mental Health Ctr., St. Louis, 1978-80, psychiatrist outpatient clinic, 1980-82; pvt. practice medicine specializing in psychiatry, St. Louis, 1980—. Bd. dirs. Women's Self Help Ctr., St. Louis, 1980-83. Fellow APA, Soc. (pres. Ea. Mo. Dist. Br. 1983-85, sect. coun. AMA 1986—, dep. rep. to assembly 1994—); mem. AMA (alt. del. Mo. 1988-90, 93-94, del. 1995—), Am. Med. Women's Assn. (pres. St. Louis Dist. br. 1981-82, 92, regional gov. VIII 1986-89, spkr. house of dels., 1993—), St. Louis Met. Med. Soc. (del. to state conv. 1981-86, 93—, councilor 1985-87, v.p. 1989), Mo. State Med. Assn. (vice speaker ho. of dels. 1986-89, speaker 1989-92), Manic Depressive Assn. St. Louis (chmn. bd. dirs. 1985-89), Washington U. Faculty Club. Office: 9216 Clayton Rd Saint Louis MO 63124-1560

RYALS, CLYDE DE LOACHE, humanities educator; b. Atlanta, Dec. 19, 1928; s. Chester A. and Ruth C. (de Loache) R.; m. Hildegard Thun Scheffey Ellerkmann, Sept. 4, 1971. A.B., Emory U., 1947, M.A., 1949; Ph.D., U. Pa., 1957. Instr. U. Md., 1956-57; instr. U. Pa., Phila., 1957-60; asst. prof. U. Pa., 1960-64, assoc. prof., 1964-69, prof. English, 1969-73, grad. chmn. dept. English, 1969-72; prof. English Duke U., Durham, N.C., 1973—, chmn. dept., 1979-82; exec. dir. Carlyle Letters Project, 1980—; mem. Christian Gauss Award Com., 1989-91. Author: Theme and Symbol in Tennyson's Poetry to 1850, 1964, From the Great Deep, 1967, Browning's Later Poetry, 1871-1889, 1975, Becoming Browning: The Poems and Plays of Robert Browning, 1833-46, 1983, A World of Possibilities: Romantic Irony in Victorian Literature, 1990, The Life of Robert Browning: A Critical Biography, 1993, paperback edit. 1996; editor: Tennyson's Poems, Chiefly Lyrical, 1966, Mrs. Humphry Ward's Robert Elsmere, 1967, Nineteenth-Century Literary Perspectives, 1974, The Collected Letters of Thomas and Jane Welsh Carlyle, 1980—; mem. editl. bd.: Victorian Poetry, 1964—, South Atlantic Quar., 1975-87, Nineteenth Century Lit., 1986—, Studies in Browning and His Circle, 1987—, Jour. Narrative Lit., 1986-90, South Atlantic Rev., 1988-90, The Carlyle Ann., 1989-93, Carlyle Studies Ann. 1993—, Victorian Literature and Culture, 1991—; contbr. articles to profl. jours. Guggenheim fellow, 1972-73; fellow Beinecke Libr., Yale U., 1994; recipient Pa. Tchg. award 1964. Mem. MLA, Am. Soc. for Aesthetics, Century Assn. N.Y., Chi Phi. Democrat. Episcopalian. Home: 1620 University Dr Durham NC 27707-1629

RYAN, ALLAN ANDREW, JR., lawyer, author, lecturer; b. Cambridge, Mass., July 3, 1945; s. Allan Andrew and Anne (Conway) R.; m. Nancy Foote, June 30, 1978; children: Elisabeth, Andrew. AB, Dartmouth Coll., 1966; JD magna cum laude, U. Minn., 1970. Bar: D.C. 1972, Mass. 1985. Law clk. to assoc. justice Byron R. White U.S. Supreme Ct., 1970-71; assoc. Williams, Connolly & Califano, Washington, 1974-77; asst. to Solicitor Gen. U.S., Washington, 1977-80; dir. office of spl. investigations, Dept. Justice, Washington, 1980-83, spl. asst. to atty. gen., 1983; pvt. practice law, 1983-85; with office of gen. counsel, Harvard U., 1985—; presenting counsel Internat. Commn. Inquiry on Kurt Waldheim, London, 1988; adj. prof. Law Sch., Boston Coll., 1989—. Author: Quiet Neighbors: Prosecuting Nazi War Criminals in America, 1984. pres., editor-in-chief: Minn. Law Rev., 1969-70. Mem. adv. bd. holocaust and human rights rsch. project Boston Coll. Law Sch., 1984—; bd. dirs. Facing History and Ourselves Nat. Found., 1985-92; mem. exec. com. New Eng. region Anti-Defamation League, 1990—. Capt. USMC, 1971-74. Recipient Internat. Human Rights award B'nai B'rith,

1986. Mem. ABA, Boston Bar Assn. Office: Harvard U Office Gen Counsel 1350 Massachusetts Ave Ste 980 Cambridge MA 02138-3846

RYAN, ARTHUR FREDERICK, insurance company executive; b. Bklyn., Sept. 14, 1942; s. Arthur Vincent and Gertrude (Wingert) R.; m. Patricia Elizabeth Kelly; children: Arthur, Kelly Ann, Kevin, Kathleen. BA in Math., Providence Coll., 1963. Area mgr. Data Corp., Washington, 1965-72; project mgr. Chase Manhattan Corp. and Bank, N.Y.C., 1972-73, 2d v.p., 1973-74, v.p., 1974-75, from 1978, former ops. exec., from 1978, former exec. v.p., from 1982, former vice-chmn., then pres., chief operating officer, 1990-94; chmn., CEO Prudential Ins. Co. Am., Newark, N.J., 1994—; mem. policy and planning com.; bd. dirs., chmn. audit com. Depository Trust Co.; past mem. exec. com., Cedel (European Depository); past chmn. steering com., program mgr. CHIPS Same Day Settlement, N.Y. Clearing House. Past bd. dirs. Urban Acad. N.Y.C. Lt. U.S. Army, 1963-65. Mem. Am. Bankers Assn. (vice chmn. ops. and automation div. and govt. rels. coun., past chmn. internat. ops. com.). Home: 144 The Helm East Islip NY 11730-2918 Office: Prudential Ins Co Am 213 Washington St Newark NJ 07102-2917*

RYAN, BARBARA ANN, church official; b. East Saint Louis, Mo., Nov. 1, 1951; d. Paul Charles and Blanche Vernie (Hamblin) Becker; divorced; children: Nicole, McKenzie C. AS in Bus. Adminstrn., Belleville Jr. Coll., 1989; postgrad., Webster U. Officer, congl. sec. Luth. Ch.-Mo. Synod, 1992, 93, lay del. SID conv., 1994, dir. human resources. Mem. Concordia Mut. Life Assn. (bd. dirs., vice chair 1991—). Office: Luth Ch-Mo Synod 1333 S Kirkwood Rd Saint Louis MO 63122-7226

RYAN, BARBARA DIANE, management information systems director; b. Phila., Nov. 3, 1950; d. Joseph Wayne and Elsie Elaine (Schafer) Hart; m. Dennis M. Ryan, Mar. 20, 1976; 1 child, Christine Susan. BA in Math., Eastern Coll., St. Davids, Pa., 1972. Computer programmer H. F. Michel, King of Prussia, Pa., 1972-73, L. P. Muller, King of Prussia, 1973-77, Hajoca Corp., Ardmore, Pa., 1977-78; MIS dir. Hajoca Corp., Ardmore, 1978—; pvt. practice installing, setting up and tng. for home personal computers, 1991—. Vol. chmn. publicity com. Trinity Luth. Ch., 1985-87, supt. Sunday sch., 1986-88, vol. Sunday sch. tchr., 1988-91, chmn. staff support Cong. Coun. 1988-91, v.p. Congl. Coun., 1991-92, sec. Congl. Coun., 1992-94, chmn. Evangelism, 1992-94, mem. 1995-96, co-chmn. fall holiday bazaar, 1994, fin. rec. sec., 1995—; mem. Haverford Band & Orch. Parents, 1994—, treas., 1994—. Mem. Llanerch Civic Assn., Ea. Coll. Alumni Assn. Republican. Avocations: cooking, gardening, traveling, walking on the beach. Office: Hajoca Corp 127 Coulter Ave Ardmore PA 19003-2410

RYAN, BONNIE MAE, business office technology educator; b. Wooster, Ohio, May 26, 1953; d. Clarence Roger and Dorothy Mae Reynolds; m. Richard Dean Ryan, May 4, 1974; children: Sean Patrick Ryan, Heather Marie Ryan. AS, Sauk Valley C.C., Dixon, Ill., 1979; BA, Western Ill. U., 1980; MS in Bus. Edn., So. Ill. U., 1982. Sec. to dir. of admissions Sauk Valley C.C., 1973-74, sec. to dean of students, 1974-76, ednl. specialist, 1976-84; office tech. instr. Highland C.C., Freeport, Ill., 1984—; adv. bd. Stephenson Area Career Ctr., Freeport, 1984-86. Religion tchr. St. Patrick's Cath. Ch., Dixon, 1986; v.p. Al Morrison Baseball Ladies Aux., Dixon, 1986. Mem. ASCD, AFT, Nat. Bus. Edn. Assn., Ill. Bus. Edn. Assn., Ill. Vocat. Assn., No. Ill. Bus. Edn. Assn. (pres. 1991-92, v.p. 1990-91, sec. 1988-90), Profl. Secs. Internat., Delta Pi Epsilon (2d v.p. 1994-95). Roman Catholic. Avocations: reading, swimming, refinishing furniture. Home: 711 E Chamberlin St Dixon IL 61021-2225 Office: Highland C C 2998 W Pearl City Rd Freeport IL 61032-9338

RYAN, BUDDY (JAMES RYAN), professional football coach; b. Frederick, Okla., Feb. 17, 1931; m. Doris Ward (div. 1966); children: Jim, Rex, Rob; m. Joanie Clark. Ed., Okla. State U. Football coach, athletic dir. Gainesville, H.S., Gainesville, Okla., 1959-60; defensive coordinator U. Buffalo, 1961-65, Vanderbilt U., Nashville, 1965-66, U. of Pacific, Stockton, Calif., 1966-67; mem. defensive staff N.Y. Jets, 1968-75; defensive line coach Minn. Vikings, 1976-77; defensive coordinator Chgo. Bears, 1978-86; head coach Phila. Eagles, 1986-91; defensive coordinator Houston Oilers, 1993-94; head coach, gen. manager Arizona Cardinals, 1994—; horse breeder Lawrenceburg, Ky., 1977—. Master Sergeant, US Army, Korean War. former Baptist, now Roman Catholic. Coached in Super Bowls III (1969) and XX (1986). Office: Arizona Cardinals PO Box 888 Phoenix AZ 85001-0888

RYAN, CARL RAY, electrical engineer; b. Gateway, Ark., Mar. 3, 1938; s. Clarence and Stella (Schnitzer) R.; m. Arline Walker; children: Carline, Julie. BSEE, U. Ark., 1962; MSEE, Iowa State U., 1963; PhD in Elec. Engring., U. Mo.-Rolla, 1969, profl. degree Elec. Engring., 1994. Instr. U. Mo.-Rolla, 1968-69; sr. engr. Govt. Electronics Group, Motorola Inc., Scottsdale, Ariz., 1969-72, mem. tech. staff, 1972-76, sr. mem. tech. staff, chief engr., 1979-89, v.p. tech. staff, 1989-90, dir. communication systems tech., 1990—; prof. Mich. Tech. U., 1976-79; adj. prof. Ariz. State U., Tempe, 1980-89; panel mem. Internat. Solid States Circuits Conf., Phila., 1977; session chmn. Future Space Communications Tech. Workshop, Pasadena, Calif., 1980; external advisor Mich. Technol. U. Contbr. articles to profl. jours.; patentee in field. Assoc. Motorola Sci. Adv. Bd. Served with USAF, 1956-60. Fellow IEEE (communications tech., solid state circuits, accreditation com., Dan Nobel fellow, chmn. Phoenix chpt. 1981-82, program chmn. 1989, gen. chmn. Phoenix Conf. on computers and communication 1988).

RYAN, CHARLES EDWARD, public relations executive, advertising executive; b. Cumberland, Md., Feb. 28, 1940; s. William Donaldson and Mabel Thestle (Miner) R.; children: Elizabeth Shandon, Margaret Amy. AA, Potomac State Coll., Keyser, 1960; BS in Journalism, W.Va. U., Morgantown, 1962. Announcer, disc jockey Sta. WKYR Radio, Keyser, 1957-60; announcer, newsman Sta. WCLG Radio, Morgantown, 1960; news dir., newsman Sta. WAJR Radio, Morgantown, 1960-62; reporter Sta. WSAZ-TV, Charleston, W.Va., 1962-65, 66-67; news editor Sta. WSAZ-TV, Charleston, 1968-69; state broadcast editor AP, Charleston, 1965-66; news reporter Sta. KTVI-TV, St. Louis, 1967-68; news dir. Sta. WCHS-TV, Charleston, 1969-74; pres. Charles Ryan Assocs., Inc., Charleston, 1974—; prin. Ryan-McGinn pub. rels. firm, Arlington, Va., Ryan-McGinn-Samples rsch. firm, Charleston and Arlington; lectr. in field. Bd. dirs. YMCA, Charleston, 1983-86, Charleston Symphony, 1983-86, State Spl. Olympics, Parkersburg, W.Va., 1984-86, Faculty Merit Found., Charleston, 1985—, W.Va. State Coll. Found., 1991—. Recipient Alumni Achievement award Potomac State Coll., 1985, Profl. Achievement award Perley Isaac Reed Sch. Journalism Alumni Assn., 1989. Mem. Nat. Pub. Rels. Soc. Am. (accredited, bd. dirs. 1986—), W.Va. State Pub. Rels. Soc. Am. (honoree 1983), Nat. Counselors Acad., W.Va. C. of C. (bd. dirs. 1985—), Advt. Club, Edgewood Country Club (bd. dirs. 1993), Rotary (bd. dirs. 1987—). Democrat. Methodist. Avocations: squash, tennis, golf, running. Office: Charles Ryan Assocs Inc 1012 Kanawha Blvd E Charleston WV 25301-2809*

RYAN, CHARLOTTE MURIEL, oncology nurse; b. Beedeville, Ark., Sept. 2, 1939; d. Eugene Sanford and Edith Elizabeth (Goforth) Breckenridge; children: Russell Kent, Cary Randall, Molly Renee. BSN cum laude, Calif. State U., Fresno, 1991, MSN, 1996. OCN cert. nurse. Psychiat. technician Porterville (Calif.) State Hosp., 1959-67; tchr. developmentally disabled Ariz. Tng. Ctr., Coolidge, 1967-71; Montessori tchr. Tucson, 1972-77; tchr. developmentally disabled Heartland Opportunity Ctr., Madera, Calif., 1977-79; med. office mgr. office of orthopedic surgeon, Madera, 1979-83, office mgr., x-ray technician, 1983-87; staff nurse in oncology St. Agnes Med. Ctr., Fresno, 1991—; instr. nursing dept. Calif. State U., Fresno, 1992, 93, 95. Treas. Hospice of Madera County, 1990-92, bd. dirs., 1992; peer counselor Calif. State U., Fresno, 1989-91; pres. bd. dirs. Easter Seals Soc., Madera, 1981. Mem. Oncology Nursing Soc., Nightingale Soc., Golden Key, Sigma Theta Tau (chair pub. com., editor MUNEWS newsletter 1994-95). Republican. Avocations: reading, improving quality of life for cancer patients. Home: 4544 N Barton Fresno CA 93726 Office: St Agnes Med Ctr 1303 E Herndon Ave Fresno CA 93720-3309

RYAN, CHRISTOPHER RICHARD, construction company executive; b. Ft. Dix, N.J., Jan. 18, 1948; s. Albert John and Pamela Joan (Hudson) R.; m. Mary Lasky, Sept. 8, 1979; children: Patrick Hudson, Peter Dacey, Katelyn Christine. BS Civil Engring., MIT, 1969, MS Civil Engring., 1972. Registered profl. engr., Pa. Project mgr. Engineered Construction Internat., Pitts., 1972-79; pres. Geo-Con, Monroeville, Pa., 1979—; spkr. in field. Contbr. articles to profl. jours. Bd. dirs. Three Rivers Rowing Assn., Pitts., 1989-93. Named Entrepreneur of Yr. Arthur Anderson, Western Pa., 1988. Mem. Am. Soc. Civil Engrs., Am. Inst. Entrepreneurs, Young Pres. Orgn., Moles, Longue Vue Country Club. Republican. Presbyterian. Avocations: rowing, skiing, golf. Office: Geo-Con Inc 4075 Monroeville Blvd Monroeville PA 15146-2529

RYAN, CLARENCE AUGUSTINE, JR., biochemistry educator; b. Butte, Mont., Sept. 29, 1931; s. Clarence A. Sr. and Agnes L. (Duckham) R.; m. Patricia Louise Meunier, Feb. 8, 1936; children: Jamie Arlette, Steven Michael (dec.), Janice Marie, Joseph Patrick (dec.). BA in Chemistry, Carroll Coll., 1953; MS in Chemistry, Mont. State U., 1956, PhD in Chemistry, 1959. Postdoctoral fellow in biochemistry Oreg. State U., Corvallis, 1959-61, U.S. Western Regional Lab., Albany, Calif., 1961-63; chemist U.S. Western Regional Lab., Berkeley, Calif., 1963-64; asst. prof. biochemistry Wash. State U., Pullman, 1964-68, assoc. prof., 1968-72, prof., 1972—, Charlotte Y. Martin disting. prof., 1991—, chmn. dept. agrl. chemistry, 1977-80, fellow Inst. Biol. Chemistry, 1980—; faculty athletics rep. to PAC-10 & NCAA Wash. State U., 1991-94; vis. scientist dept. biochemistry U. Wash., 1981, Harvard U. Med. Sch., 1982; cons. Kemin Industries, Des Moines, 1981—, Plant Genetics, Davis, Calif., 1987-89; research adv. bd. Frito-Lay, Inc., Dallas, 1982, Plant Genetic Engring. Lab., N.M. State U., Las Cruces, 1986-89; mem. NRC rev. bd. Plant Gene Exptl. Ctr., Albany, Calif., 1990-93; mgr. biol. stress program USDA Competitve Grants Program, Washington, 1983-84; former mem. adv. panels for H. McKnight Found., Internat. Potato Ctr., Lima, Peru, Internat. Ctr. Genetic Engring. and Biotech., New Delhi, Internat. Ctr. Tropical Agr., Cali, Columbia, Internat. Tropical Agr., Ibandan, Africa; mem. grant rev. panels NSF, USDA, DOE, NIH; co-organizer Internat. Telecommunications Symposium on Plant Biotech. Mem. edit. bd. several biochem. and plant physiology jours.; contbr. articles to profl. publs., chpts. to books; co-editor 2 books. Grantee USDA, NSF, NIH, Rockefeller Found., McKnight Found.; recipient Merck award for grad. rsch. Mont. State U., 1959, career devel. awards NIH, 1964-74, Alumni Achievement award Carroll Coll., 1986, Pres.'s Faculty Excellence award in rsch. Wash. State U., 1986; named to Carroll Coll. Alumni Hall of Fame, 1981, Carroll Coll. Basketball Hall of Fame, 1982. Mem. AAAS, Nat. Acad. Scis. (elected 1986), Am. Chem. Soc. (Kenneth A. Spencer award 1992), Am. Soc. Plant Physiologists (Steven Hales Prize 1992), Am. Soc. Exptl.Biology, Biochem. Soc., Internat. Soc. Chem. Ecology, Internat. Soc. Plant Molecular Biology (bd. dirs.), Phytochem. Soc. N.Am., Nat. U. Continuing Assn. (Creative Programming award 1991), Phi Kappa Phi (Recognition award 1976, selected 1 of 100 centennial disting. alumni Mont. State U. 1993). Democrat. Avocations: fishing, basketball, golf. Office: Wash State Univ Inst Biol Chemistry Pullman WA 99164

RYAN, CORNELIUS O'BRIEN, lawyer; b. Abilene, Tex., Oct. 15, 1917; s. William Cornelius and Joanna Genevieve (Morris) R.; m. Mary Anne Kelley, Mar. 24, 1942; children: Elisabeth Ryan Goldstein, Robert C., Carl E., William E., Joseph W., Mary Louise Ryan Ray. BA, Rice U., 1937; LLB, So. Meth. U., 1940. Bar: Tex. 1940. Mem. firm Kelley & Ryan, Houston, 1951—; v.p., gen. counsel Tex. United Corp., 1982-88. Bd. dirs. Am. Irish Found., 1977-90, hon. life trustee, 1990—. Lt. USNR, 1942-46. Decorated knight grand cross Order Holy Sepulchre Knight of Malta. Mem. Am., Houston bar assns., Tex. State Bar, Am. Judicature Soc., Phi Beta Kappa, Phi Delta Theta, Phi Alpha Delta. Republican. Roman Catholic. Clubs: Houston (Houston), Serra (Houston). Home: 3107 Newcastle Dr Houston TX 77027-5507 Office: Kelley & Ryan 5847 San Felipe St Ste 4295 Houston TX 77057-3011

RYAN, DANIEL LEO, bishop; b. Mankato, Minn., Sept. 28, 1930; s. Leonard Bennett and Irene Ruth (Larson) R. BA, Ill. Benedictine Coll., 1952; JCL, Pontificia Università Lateranense, Rome, 1960. Ordained priest Roman Cath. Ch., 1956, consecrated bishop, 1981. Parish priest Roman Cath. Diocese, Joliet, Ill, 1956-82, chancellor, 1965-78, vicar gen., 1977-79, aux. bishop, 1981-84; bishop Roman Cath. Diocese, Springfield, Ill., 1984—. Office: Diocese of Springfield PO Box 3187 1615 W Washington Springfield IL 62708-3187

RYAN, DANIEL NOLAN, financial corporation executive; b. N.Y.C., Sept. 28, 1930; s. Thomas Francis and Helen Grace (Nolan) R.; m. Hope Lang, Dec. 21, 1973; children: Christine, Pamela, Anne Marie. BS, Fordham U., 1960. With Citicorp, N.Y.C., 1944-55, Credit Am. Corp., N.Y.C., 1955-58, James Talcott, Inc., N.Y.C., 1958-63, Comml. Alliance Corp. (name changed to ORIX Comml. Alliance Corp. subs. ORIX Corp., 1989), N.Y.C., 1963—, pres., 1987—; pres., chmn. ORIX Credit Alliance, Inc., 1989—; bd. dirs. ORIX Comml. Alliance Corp.; mem. N.Am. adv. bd. OIRX, 1990—. Signal Corps U.S. Army, 1951-54. Mem. Ea. Assn. Equipment Lessors (bd. dirs. 1982-86, treas. 1984-86), Am. Assn. Equipment Lessors, Western Assn. Equipment Lessors, Beta Alpha Psi. Avocations: owner race horses, gourmet cooking. Home: 800 Palisade Ave Fort Lee NJ 07024-4111 Office: Orix Credit Alliance Inc 300 Lighting Way Secaucus NJ 07094-3622

RYAN, DAVID ALAN, computer specialist; b. Cin., Nov. 13, 1961; s. James Patrick and Virginia Ann (Stewart) R. BS, Wright State U., 1983; MS, Tex. A&M U., 1988. Statistician U.S. Bur. of Census, Washington, 1988-92, computer specialist, 1992—. Vol. math. modeling Soil Conservation Svc., Washington, 1991—; date modeling vol. Washington Opera, 1992—; data entry/programming vol. Opera Am., Washington, 1990-91; hist. rschr. Gasby's Tavern Mus., Alexandria, Va., 1991—; mem. Bravo! for the Washington Opera, 1991-95. Recipient Vol. Svc. award Soil Conservation Svc., 1992, 93. Mem. Am. Statis. Assn., Capitol PC Users Group, Ballston-Va. Square Civic Assn. (exec. com. 1995—). Avocations: classical music, ethnomusicology, history, geography, travel. Office: US Bur of Census Econ Planning Coord Divsn Ctr for Econ Studies Washington DC 20233-6101

RYAN, DAVID THOMAS, lawyer; b. Torrington, Conn., Apr. 18, 1939; s. Edward John and Margaret (Murphy) R.; m. Dale Anderson, Aug. 21, 1965; children: Rachael Anderson, Conor Anne. BS, U. Md., 1961; LLB, Georgetown U., 1965. Bar: Conn. 1966, U.S. Dist. Ct. Conn. 1967, U.S. Ct. Appeals (2d cir.) 1969, U.S. Ct. Appeals (fed. cir.) 1982, U.S. Claims Ct. 1983, U.S. Supreme Ct. 1992. Ptnr. Cooney, Scully & Dowling, Hartford, Conn., 1966-77, Robinson & Cole, Hartford, 1977—. Fellow Am. Coll. Trial Lawyers; mem. Am. Bd. Trial Advs. Home: 126 Westerly Ter Hartford CT 06105-1117 Office: Robinson & Cole 1 Commercial Plz Hartford CT 06103-3512

RYAN, DEBBIE, university athletic coach. B.Phys. Edn., Ursinus Coll., 1975; M.Phys. Edn., U. Va., 1977. Asst. basketball and field hockey coach U. Va., Charlottesville, 1975-77, head women's basketball coach, 1977—; lectr. in field; adv. coach Nike; head coach U.S. Jr. Nat. Team, 1988, Jr. World Championship Team, 1989; mem. U.S.A. Basketball Women's Games Com. for 189-92 quadrennium; dir. West team U.S. Olympic festival, Chapel Hill, N.C., 1987 (gold medal). Author: Virginia Defense, Virginia Summer Development Program, Women's Basketball Drills-Conditioning. Recipient ACC Coach of the Yr. award, 19884, 86, 87, 91, 93, 95; named Outstanding Woman of the Yr. Va. Women's Forum, 1991, Converse Dist. III Coach of the Yr., 1985-86, Nat. Coach of the Yr., Shreveport Jour., 1986, Natsmith Coach of the Yr., Atlanta Tipoff club, 1991. Avocations: fishing, golf. Office: University of Virginia University Hall PO Box 3785 Charlottesville VA 22903

RYAN, DESMOND, film critic; b. London, May 30, 1943; came to U.S., 1967; s. Christopher and Evelyn (Daley) R.; m. Patricia Mazer, Jan. 27, 1967; 1 child, Christopher. B.A. with honors, New Coll., Oxford U., Eng., 1965, M.A., 1968. Reporter Phila. Inquirer, 1969-74, film critic, 1974—, columnist mag., 1975-82. Author: (novels) Helix, 1979, Deadlines, 1984 (Athanaeum award 1984); (video capsule revs.) Guide to 3000 Movies, 1985. Office: Phila Inquirer 400 N Broad St Philadelphia PA 19130-4015

RYAN, EARL M., public affairs analyst; b. Detroit, Oct. 23, 1942; s. Thomas M. and Margaret L. (Halsey) R.; m. Jo Ellen Junod, July 3, 1965; children: Andrew M., Jeffrey A. BA in Polit. Sci., U. Mich., 1964; MA in Polit. Sci., Wayne State U., 1968. Dir. rsch. Detroit Urban League, 1965-67; resch. assoc. Citizens Rsch. Coun. Mich., Lansing, 1967-70; budget analyst Dept. Social Svcs., Lansing, 1970-71; dir. rsch. Health Impact Project, Lansing, 1971, Office of Program Effectiveness Rev., Lansing, 1971-74, Legis. Program Effectiveness Rev., Lansing, 1974-77, Citizens Rch. Coun. Mich., Detroit, 1977-84; pres. Pub. Affairs Rsch. Coun. La., Baton Rouge, 1984-87, Ind. Fiscal Policy Inst., Indpls., 1987-94; exec. dir. Citizens Rsch. Coun. of Mich., 1994—; polit. analyst Sta. WWL-TV, New Orleans, 1986; mem. blue ribbon panel Indpls. Bus. Jour., 1992-94. Recipient disting. achievement award grad. program pub. adminstrn. Wayne State U., Detroit, 1991. Mem. Govtl. Rsch. Assn. (pres. 1985-86, Disting. rsch. award 1977), Govtl. Fin. Officers Assn. Avocations: photography, Anthony Trollope novels. Home: 40292 Woodside Dr N Northville MI 48167-3431 Office: Citizens Rsch Coun Mich 625 Shelby St Ste 1B Detroit MI 48226-3206

RYAN, EDWARD W., economics educator; b. Plainfield, N.J., Aug. 23, 1932; s. Edward A. and Helen R. (Shannon) R.; m. Georgian Hurley, Dec. 17, 1966; children: Sarah, Jennifer. BS, U. Pa., 1955; MA, Duke U., 1957. Lectr. Fordham U., N.Y.C., 1956-57; instr. Iona Coll., New Rochelle, N.Y., 1958-60; prof. econs. Manhattanville Coll., Purchase, N.Y., 1958—; dir. Econ. Freedom Inst. Author: In the Words of Adam Smith: The First Consumer Advocate, 1990. Mem. Am. Econ. Assn., Indsl. Rels. Rsch. Assn., Pub. Choice Assn., Econ. History Assn. Roman Catholic. Home: 25 Jefferson Rd Scarsdale NY 10583-6411 Office: Manhattanville College 2900 Purchase St Purchase NY 10577-2628

RYAN, ELLEN BOUCHARD, psychology educator, gerontologist; b. Holyoke, Mass., Jan. 11, 1947; emigrated to Can., 1982; d. Raoul Rosario and Etiennette Marie (Morin) Bouchard; m. Patrick J. Ryan, July 12, 1969; children: Lorraine Yvette, Dennis Patrick, Kevin Myles. BA, MA, Brown U., 1968; PhD, U. Mich., 1970. Asst. prof. psychology U. Notre Dame, 1970-76, assoc. prof., 1976-81, prof., 1981-82, chmn. dept., 1978-82; prof. psychiatry McMaster U., Hamilton, Ont., Can., 1982—, dir. Office Gerontol. Studies, 1985-95. Editor: Attitudes Toward Language Variation, 1982, Language Communication and The Elderly, 1986, Intergenerational Communication, 1994, Language Attitudes, 1994, Communication, Aging and Health, 1996. Grantee NICHD, 1972-75, NSF, 1976-79, Nat. Inst. Edn., 1979-82, Natural Scis. and Engring. Rsch., 1983-89, Gerontol. Rsch. Coun. of Ont., 1983-85, Ont. Ministry Health, 1986-89, Soc. Sci. and Humanities Rsch. Coun., 1986—. Fellow APA, Gerontol. Soc. Am., Can. Psychol. Assn.; mem. Internat. Comm. Assn., Can. Assn. Gerontology. Roman Catholic. Home: 346 Brookview Ct, Ancaster, ON Canada L9G 4C2 Office: McMaster U Dept Psychiatry, 1200 Main St W, Hamilton, ON Canada L8N 3Z5

RYAN, ELLEN MARIE, elementary education and gifted education educator; b. Flushing, N.Y.; d. Francis and June Marie Ryan. BA in Elem. Edn., Queens Coll., 1971; MA in Edn., Adelphi U., 1974; MEd in Adminstrn., Stetson U., 1982; postgrad., Fla. Tech., 1988—. Cert. tchr. N.Y.C.; profl. cert. N.Y., Pa., Fla.; cert. tchr., elem. edn. adminstr., early childhood, gifted tchr.; cert. sch. site trainer in tech. Miami Mus. Sci. Tchr. grade 3 Park View Elem Kings Park (N.Y.) Sch. Dist., 1971-75; tchr. grade 6 So. Lehigh Sch. Dist., Center Valley, Pa., 1975-77; resource tchr. grades K-6 North Penn Sch. Dist., Lansdale, Pa., 1977-79; tchr. grade 1 Holland Elem., Brevard County Schs., Satellite Beach, Fla., 1979-81; tchr. gifted student program Surfside Elem., Satellite Beach; tchr. grades K-6 Brevard County Schs., 1981—; grant writer, reviewer Grantsmanship Cadre, Brevard Schs., Fla., 1992—; cons. multimedia presentation NSF, State Systemic Initiative, Surfside Elem., Fla. Tech., Melbourne, 1994; cons., trainer, spkr. Surfside Elem., Satellite Beach, 1994, 95; presenter in field. Dir., prodr., photographer various prodns., 1992. Treas. Melbourne (Fla.) Panhellenic, 1987, yearbook chairperson, 1988, installation banquet chair, 1989; publicity chair Holy Name of Jesus Fall Festival, Indialantic, Fla., 1991. Fla. Instrnl. Tech. grantee Fla. Tech., 1991-93, Creative Tchg. grantee Brevard Schs. Found., Fla. Found., Melbourne, 1993, Tchrs. and Tech. Measuring Math Meaningfully Project-NSF grantee, 1993-95, Multimedia Life Sci. mini grantee Fla. Assn. for Gifted, Fla., 1994, Tech. Apprentice Program grantee Bell South Found., 1994—. Mem. Fla. Assn. Computer Educators (integrating tech. into the curriculum 1994—), Fla. Edn. Tech. Conf. (workshop presenter 1994), Delta Kappa Gamma (Beta Sigma chpt. yearbook chairperson, membership chair 1994—), Phi Delta Kappa (Creative Tchg. grants Cape Kennedy chpt. 1993). Office: Brevard County Schs Surfside Elem 475 Cassia Blvd Melbourne FL 32937

RYAN, FREDERICK JOSEPH, JR., lawyer, public official; b. Tampa, Fla., Apr. 12, 1955; s. Frederick Joseph and Cordelia Beth (Hartman) R.; m. Genevieve Ann McSweeney, Dec. 28, 1985; children: Genevieve Madeline, Madeline Elizabeth. BA, U. So. Calif., 1977, JD, 1980. Bar: Calif. 1980, D.C. 1986. Assoc. Hill, Farrer and Burrill, Los Angeles, 1980-82; dep. dir. then dir. presdl. appointments and scheduling The White House, Washington, 1982-87, dir. pvt. sector initiatives, 1985-87, asst. to the Pres., 1987-89; chief of staff Office of Ronald Reagan, L.A., 1989-95; vice chmn. Allbritton Comm. Co., Washington, 1995—; bd. cons. Riggs Bank Washington, 1995—; mem. staff Reagan-Bush Campaign, Los Angeles, 1980; dir. Internat. Conf. on Pvt. Sector Initiatives, Paris, 1986, Italian-Am. Conf. on Pvt. Sector Initiatives, 1987, Brit.-Am. Conf. on Pvt. Sector Initiatives, 1988. Author (column) Legal Briefs, 1980-82; editor: Ronald Reagan: The Wisdom and Humor of the Great Communicator, 1995. Chmn. Monterey Park (Calif.) Cmty. Rels. Commn., 1977-78; bd. dirs. Ford's Theater, Washington, Town Hall of Calif., L.A., Nancy Reagan Found.; trustee Ronald Reagan Presdl. Found.; mem. bd. advisors Ronald Reagan Inst. for Emergency Medicine, George Washington U. Med. Ctr. Recipient Presdl. Commendation for pvt. sector initiatives Pres. Ronald Reagan, 1986, Medal of Arts and Letters, Govt. of France, 1986, Golden Ambrosiana medal of Milan, Italy, 1987, The Lion of Venice medal, Italy, 1987, comdr. Order of Merit of Republic of Italy, 1992, comdr. Ouissam Alaouite of Morocco, 1995. Mem. ABA, Jonathan Club (L.A.), Metro. Club (Washington). Presbyterian. Avocations: Karate, tennis, skiing. Office: Allbritton Comm Co 800 17th St NW Washington DC 20006-3903

RYAN, GEORGE H., state government official, pharmacist; b. Maquoketa, Iowa, Feb. 24, 1934; s. Thomas J. and Jeanette (Bowman) R.; m. Lura Lynn Lowe, June 10, 1956; children: Nancy, Lynda, Julie, Joanne, Jeanette, George. BS in Pharmacy, Ferris State Coll., Big Rapids, Mich. Mem. Ill. Ho. of Reps., 1973-82, minority leader, 1977-80, speaker, 1981-82; lt. gov. State of Ill., 1983-91, sec. of state, 1991—. Mem. Kankakee County Bd., 1966-72, chmn., 1971-72; chmn. Ill. Literacy Coun., 1991—. With U.S. Army, Korea. Recipient Humphrey award Am. Pharm. Assn., 1980, Top award Ill. chpt. DARE, 1989, Govt. Leadership award Nat. Commn. Against Drunk Driving and MADD Govt. Leader Against Drunk Driving award, 1994-95, City Club of Chgo. Man of Yr. award, 1995. Mem. Am. Pharm. Assn., Ill. Pharm. Assn., One Hundred Club, Masons (33d degree). Republican. Methodist. Lodges: Elks, Moose, Shriners.

RYAN, GERALD ANTHONY, financial adviser, venture capitalist; b. Milw., Oct. 24, 1935; s. Gerald Edward and Frances (Dierksmeier) R.; m. Carole Lesley Schuster, May 19, 1956; children: Karen P., Kevin M., Kimberly F., Kendra A., Keith A. B.S.M.E., MIT, 1957. Engr., Johnson Controls, Buffalo, 1958-61; mgr. Johnson Controls, Erie, Pa., 1961-73; pres. TEI Corp., Erie, 1973-75; chmn., CEO Erie Bus. Mgmt. Corp., 1975—; chmn., CEO Skinner Engine Co., 1986—; pres. Ryco Holding Ltd., 1986—; chmn. bd. Automated Indsl. Sys., Fairview, Pa., 1981—, Spectrum Control, Inc., Erie, Personal Svc. Corp., 1974-82, Rent-Way, Inc., 1981—. Mem. Kahkwa Club. Republican. Roman Catholic. Home: 10 Peninsula Dr Erie PA 16505 Office: EBMC PO Box 6242 Erie PA 16512-6242

RYAN, GERARD SPENCER, inn executive; b. N.Y.C., June 10, 1926; s. Gerard Aloysius and Helen (Kirwan) R.; m. Barbara Battle, May 3, 1952; children—Jerry, Catherine, Janet, Mary Ellen, Barbara, Elizabeth, David, Peter. B.A., Georgetown U., 1950. Dir. fund raising Georgetown U., 1950-51; sales rep. McGraw Hill Pub. Co., Chgo., 1951-53; mgr. Pitts. Chem. Engring. Dist., 1953-68; sales mgr. Power Mag., N.Y.C., 1968-73; SLS mgr. Elec. Constrn. and Maintenance and Elec. Wholesaling mags., N.Y.C., 1973-74; pub. Elec. Constrn. and Maintenance and Elec. Wholesaling mags., 1974-85; propr. Arrowhead Inn, Durham, N.C., 1985—. Pres. South Hills Assn. Racial Equality, Pitts., 1966-68, Debra, Montclair, N.J., 1981-83. Served with USN, 1944-46. Mem. N.C. Bed and Breakfast Assn. (past pres.).

Democrat. Roman Catholic. Home and Office: Arrowhead Inn 106 Mason Rd Durham NC 27712-9201

RYAN, HALFORD ROSS, speech educator; b. Anderson, Ind., Dec. 29, 1943. AB, Wabash Coll., 1966; MA, U. Ill., 1968, PhD, 1972. Prof. Washington and Lee U., Lexington, Va., 1970—. Author: FDR's Rhetorical Presidency, 1988, Harry Emerson Fosdick, 1989, Henry Ward Beecher, 1990, Classical Communication for the Contemporary Communicator, 1992, Harry S. Truman, 1993; editor: Oratorial Encounters, 1988, Inaugural Addresses of Twentieth-Century American Presidents, 1993, U.S. Presidents as Orators, 1995; also articles. Recipient awards Eleanor Roosevelt Inst., 1979, Herbert Hoover Inst., 1986, Maurice Mednick Found., 1991; Rockefeller Theol. fellow, 1967. Mem. Speech Communication Assn. Office: Washington and Lee U Robinson Hall Lexington VA 24450

RYAN, HOWARD CHRIS, retired state supreme court justice; b. Tonica, Ill., June 17, 1916; s. John F. and Sarah (Egger) R.; m. Helen Cizek, Oct. 16, 1943; children: John F., Elizabeth Ellen, Howard Chris. B.A., U. Ill., 1940, LL.B., J.D., 1942; LL.D. (hon.), John Marshall Law Sch., 1978. Bar: Ill. 1942. Practice in Decatur, 1946-47, Peru, 1947-57; asst. state's atty. LaSalle County, 1952-54, county judge, 1954-57, circuit judge, 1957-68; chief judge, 1964-68; judge appellate ct. 3d Jud. Dist. Ill., 1968-70; justice Ill. Supreme Ct., 1970-90, chief justice, 1981-84; of counsel Peterson & Ross, Chgo., 1990-93. Served with USAAF, 1942-45. Mem. ABA, Ill. Bar Assn., LaSalle County Bar Assn., Am. Legion, Masons, Elks, Odd Fellows, Phi Alpha Delta. Republican. Methodist. Home: PO Box 397 Tonica IL 61370-0397

RYAN, J. BRUCE, health care management consulting executive; b. Southbridge, Mass., Mar. 28, 1944; s. Charles J. and Doris (Olney) R.; m. Sarah E. Pattison, Aug. 16, 1993. BSBA in Fin., U. Mass., 1972, MSBA, 1974; MA in Econs., U. Wash., 1976. Regional v.p. Amherst Assocs. Inc., Atlanta, 1976-85; exec. v.p. Jennings Ryan & Kolb, Inc., Atlanta, 1985—; mem. managed care adv. bd. St. Anthony Pub. Mem. editl. rev. bd. Healthcare Fin. Mgmt.; contbr. articles to profl. jours. With U.S. Army, 1968-70. Mem. Healthcare Fin. Mgmt. Assn. (Helen M. Yerger/L. Van Seawell best article award 1990), Soc. for Healthcare Planning & Mktg., Fin. Mgmt. Assn., Am. Assn. Physician-Hosp. Orgns. Avocation: sailing. Home: 1060 Kentucky Ave NE Atlanta GA 30306-3534 Office: Jennings Ryan & Kolb Inc # 500 17 Executive Park Dr NE Atlanta GA 30329-2222

RYAN, J. PATRICK, fund raising consulting company executive; b. Sandusky, Ohio, Nov. 2, 1940; s. James E. and Dorothy G. (McNeil) R.; m. Mary Anne Moore, Dec. 27, 1968 (div. 1986); children: J. Michael, McNeil T., Mark M., J. Matthew. BA in Philosophy, U. Ky., 1963; postgrad. in bus., U. So. Calif., 1966. Asst. dean U. So. Calif., L.A., 1966-68; alumni dir. Lambda Chi Alpha Frat., Indpls., 1969-70; cons., ptnr. Marts & Lundy, Inc., N.Y.C., 1971-75; devel. dir. Archdiocese of Cin., 1976-77; sr. ptnr. Staley-Robeson-Ryan-St. Lawrence, Inc., Cin., 1978-85, pres., 1985—; joint mng. dir. Downes/Ryan Internat., Washington, 1988—. Chmn. Mt. Lookout Civic Assn., Cin., 1982. Mem. Nat. Soc. Fund Raising Execs. (chmn. Found. 1987-89, bd. dirs., Fund Raising Exec. of Yr. award Cin. 1985), Questover Hounds Hunt Club, Bankers Club Cin. (life), World Fundraising Coun. (chair 1995—), Am. Assn. Fund-Raising Coun. (chair 1993-95). Republican. Roman Catholic. Home: 2943 Mt Pisgah Rd New Richmond OH 45157-9731 Office: Staley Robeson Ryan & St Lawrence Inc 635 W 7th St Cincinnati OH 45203-1513

RYAN, J. RICHARD, lawyer; b. N.Y.C., Oct. 23, 1929; s. Peter Leon and Mary Martha (Franklin) R.; m. Diana Louise Gambarelli, Nov. 6, 1954 (dec. Feb. 1988); children: Christopher, Claudia; m. Joan Frances Revelle, Jan. 21, 1995. BA, Georgetown U., 1951, JD, Fordham U., 1954. Bar: N.Y. 1956, U.S. Dist. Ct. (so. dist.) N.Y., 1957, U.S. Supreme Ct., 1987. Assoc. Engel, Judge, Miller, Sterling & Reddy, N.Y.C., 1956-63, ptnr., 1963-66; ptnr. Kantor, Shaw & Ryan, N.Y.C., 1966-71; ptnr. Ryan & Silberberg, N.Y.C., 1971-84, Ryan & Fogerty, 1984-88, Ryan, Botway, Reddy and Mesrop, 1988-90; sole practice, 1990—. Bd. dirs. Guiding Eyes for the Blind, Inc., pres., 1973-77, Am. Health Capital Ins. Co.; trustee Cooper Inst. for Advanced Studies in Medicine and Humanities. Mem. Bar Assn. City N.Y. (Young Lawyers Com. 1957-60), N.Y. State Bar Assn., ABA, The Soc. of the Friendly Sons of St. Patrick, Copyright Soc. Candidate for mayor, Pelham, N.Y., 1963. Served with AUS, 1954-56. Clubs: Pelham Country (past pres.), Union League, Winged Foot Golf Club. Office: 516 5th Ave New York NY 10036-7501

RYAN, JACK, physician, hospital corporation executive; b. Benton Harbor, Mich., Aug. 26, 1925; s. Leonard Joseph and Beulah (Southworth) R.; m. Lois Patricia Patterson; children: Michele, Kevin, Timothy, Sarah, Daniel. AB, Western Mich. U., 1948; postgrad., U. Mich. Law Sch., 1949-50, Emory U., 1950-51; MD, Wayne State U., 1955. Intern St. Luke's Hosp., Saginaw, Mich., 1955-56; pres. Meml. Med. Ctr., Warren, Mich., 1956-77; v.p. med. affairs Detroit-Macomb Hosps. Corp., 1976-77, pres. and chief exec. officer, 1977—; assoc. prof. medicine Wayne State U., Detroit, 1974—. Recipient Disting. Alumnus award Wayne State U. Med. Sch., 1974, Wayne State U., 1979, Western Mich. U., 1989, Disting. Key award Mich. Hosp. Assn., 1986. Fellow Am. Coll. Family Physicians, Am. Coll. Physician Execs., Detroit Acad. Medicine; mem. Internat. Health Econs. and Mgmt. Inst. (charter), Econ. Club Detroit, Detroit Athletic Club, Renaissance Club, Red Run Club. Avocations: Civil War, history, golf, tennis. Home: 175 Hendrie Blvd Royal Oak MI 48067-2412 Office: Detroit-Macomb Hosp Corp 12000 E 12 Mile Rd Warren MI 48093-3570

RYAN, JAMES, insurance company executive; b. Pittsburgh, Pa., Jan. 21, 1937; s. Martin Charles and Lucy Elizabeth (Misklow) r.; m. Marlene Sullivan Ryan, Jan. 27, 1973. BA, U. Pitts., U. Louisville. Cert. ins. wholesaler. Chmn. Market Finders Ins. Corp., Louisville, 1972—; com. chmn. Am. Assn. Mng. Gen. Agts., 1988-89; pres. Ky. Lloyd's Agts. Assn., 1985—; bd. dirs. Nat. Assn. Profl. Surplus Lines Office, Inc., 1983-86; pres. Ky. Surplus Lines Assn., Louisville, 1988-89; mem. adv. coun. Essex Ins. Co., 1991-93. Pub. in Best Rev., 1995. Mem. Ky. Thoroughbred Owners & Breeders, Inc., Hon. Order of Blue Goose Internat., Kosair Shrine Temple, Hon. Order of Ky. Col. Named Adv. Coun. Colony Ins. Co., Glen Allen, Va., 1991-93, Hamilton Ins. Co., 1993, Cardinal Ins. Co., 1991-93. Mem. Profl. Ins. Agts., Ind. Ins. Agts. Assn., Am. Assn. Mng. Gen. Agts. (cert., chmn. adv. com. 1991-92, bd. dirs. 1994-96, v.p. zone 3 1995-96), Nat. Assn. Profl. Surplus Lines Offices (chmn. legis. com. 1988-89, Published Best Rev. 1995). Republican. Roman Catholic. Avocations: breeding and racing Thoroughbred horses, golf.

RYAN, JAMES E., attorney general; married; 6 children. BA in Polit. Sci., Ill. Benedictine Coll., 1968; JD, Ill. Inst. Tech., 1971. Bar: Ill. 1971. Asst. state's atty. criminal divsn. DuPage County State's Atty.'s Office, 1971-74, 1st. asst. state's atty., 1974-76; founder Ryan & Darrah; state's atty. DuPage County State's Atty.'s Office, 1984-94; atty. gen. State of Ill., 1994—. Recipient numerous awards from various orgns. including Nat. Assn. Counties, Alliance Against Intoxicated Motorists. Republican. Office: Office of Atty General 500 S Second St Springfield IL 62706*

RYAN, JAMES EDWIN, industrial arts educator; b. Pittsburg, Kans., Oct. 21, 1919; s. James Joseph and Eva May (Bates) R.; m. Carol Floella Nowell, June 15, 1941; 1 child, Carol Jean. B.S., Kans. State Coll., 1940; M.A., Calif. State Coll., Long Beach, 1954; Ed.D., UCLA, 1964. High sch. tchr. Mo. and Kans., 1940-43; journeyman printer Long Beach (Calif.) Ind. Press-Telegram, 1947-54; mem. faculty Calif. State U., Long Beach, 1954-83; prof. indsl. arts Calif. State U., 1964-83, prof. emeritus, 1983—, chmn. acad. senate, 1976-78; mem. acad. senate Calif. State Univs. and Colls., 1979-83; mem. graphic arts adv. com. Downey (Calif.) City Schs., 1966-83, Golden West Coll., 1970-83; mem. visitation team accreditation council Calif. Assn. Schs. Cosmetology, 1965-83; judge tech. exhibits Gt. Western Exposition, Los Angeles, 1962-83; cons. in field. Contbr. articles to profl. jours. Served with AUS, 1943-46. Mem. Soc. History Tech., Am. Indsl. Arts Assn., Assn. Calif. State Univ. Profs. (past officer), Am. Coun. Indsl. Arts Tchr. Educators, Calif. Indsl. Edn. Assn. (life), Congress Faculty Assn. (v.p. 1976-79, treas. 1979-81), Calif. Colls. Univ. Faculty Assn. (chpt. pres. 1977-79), Calif. State U. Long Beach Emeritus and Ret. Faculty Assn. (pres. 1988-89, 92-93), Calif. State U. Emeritus and Ret. Faculty Assn. (v.p. 1992—), Epsilon Pi Tau (Laureate citation 1960), Phi Kappa Phi, Phi Delta Kappa. Home: 13952 Falmouth Walk Westminster CA 92683-3432

RYAN, JAMES FRANKLIN, retail executive; b. London, Ont., Can., July 21, 1948; s. Patrick and Helen Anne (Wenechuk) R.; m. Dora Lee Ballan, Mar. 17, 1979 ; children: Christine, Carol. BS, U. Western Ont., London, 1970; MBA, York U., Toronto, Ont., 1972. Various mgmt. positions Shell Can. Ltd., Toronto, 1972-84; mgr. retail Shell Can. Ltd., Calgary, 1984-85; dir. mktg. svcs. Petro-Can., Inc., Toronto, 1985-86; pres. Pyne Mgmt., Inc., Toronto, 1986-88, Can. Tire Petroleum, Toronto, 1988-92; sr. v.p. dealer rels. Can. Tire Corp., Toronto, 1992—. Avocation: tennis. Home: 9 Ferndell Circle, Unionville, ON Canada L3R 3Y7 also: 28 Weatherstone Ct, Niagara-on-the-Lake, ON Canada L0S 1J0 Office: Can Tire Corp, 2180 Yonge St, Toronto, ON Canada M4S 2B9

RYAN, JAMES JOSEPH, lawyer; b. Cin., June 17, 1929; s. Robert J. and Marian (Hoffman) R.; m. Mary A. Noonan, Nov. 25, 1954; children: Kevin, Timothy, Nora, Daniel. AB, Xavier U., 1951, JD, U. Cin., 1954. Bar: Ohio 1954. Teaching assoc. Northwestern U., Chgo., 1954-55; ptnr. Dolle, O'Donnell & Cash, Cin., 1958-71, Taft, Stettinius & Hollister, Cin., 1971—; lectr. U. Cin. Coll. Law, 1960-65. Chmn. Health Planning Assn. Ohio River Valley, Cin., 1978-85; bd. dirs. Hamilton County Bd. of Mentally Retarded, 1968-80; trustee Resident Home for Mentally Retarded, 1980—, St. Francis-St. George Hosp. Devel. Coun., 1989—. Mem. ABA, Ohio Bar Assn., Cin. Bar Assn. Republican. Roman Catholic. Clubs: Queen City, Western Hill. Avocations: reading, sports. Home: 5316 Cleves Warsaw Pike Cincinnati OH 45238-3602 Office: 1800 Star Bank Ctr 425 Walnut St Cincinnati OH 45202-3904

RYAN, JAMES LEO, federal judge; b. Detroit, Mich., Nov. 19, 1932; s. Leo Francis and Irene Agnes R.; m. Mary Elizabeth Rogers, Oct. 12, 1957; children: Daniel P., James R., Colleen M. Hansen, Kathleen A. LL.B., U. Detroit, 1956, BA, 1992; LL.D. (hon.), Madonna Coll., 1976, Detroit Coll. Law, 1978, Thomas M. Cooley Law Sch., Lansing, Mich., 1986, U. Detroit Sch. Law, 1986. Justice of peace Redford Twp., Mich., 1963-66; cir. judge 3d Jud. Circuit Mich., 1966-75; justice Mich. Supreme Ct., 1975-86; judge U.S. Ct. Appeals (6th cir.), 1986—; faculty U. Detroit Sch. Law, Nat. Jud. Coll., Reno, Am. Acad. Jud. Edn., Washington, Thos M.Cooley Law Sch. Contbr. article to legal jour. Served with JAGC, USNR, 1957-60; to capt. JAGC, mil. judge Res., 1960-92, ret., 1992. Mem. Naval Res. Lawyers Assn., Nat. Conf. Appellate Ct. Judges, Fed. Judges Assn., State Bar Mich., Fed. Bar Assn., KC. Office: US Ct Appeals 611 US Courthouse Detroit MI 48226

RYAN, JAMES WALTER, physician, medical researcher; b. Amarillo, Tex., June 8, 1935; s. Lee W. and Emma E. (Haddox) R.; children: James P.A., Alexandra L.E., Amy J.S. A.B. in Polit. Sci., Dartmouth Coll., 1957; M.D., Cornell U., 1961; D.Phil., Oxford U. (Eng.), 1967. Diplomate: Nat. Bd. Med. Examiners. Intern, Montreal (Que.) Gen. Hosp., McGill U., Can., 1961-62; asst. resident in medicine Montreal (Que.) Gen. Hosp., McGill U., 1962-63; USPHS research asso. NIMH, NIH, 1963-65; guest investigator Rockefeller U., N.Y.C., 1967-68; asst. prof. biochemistry Rockefeller U., 1968; asso. prof. medicine U. Miami (Fla.) Sch. Medicine, 1968-79, prof. medicine, 1979-95; prof. anesthesiology, pharmacology and toxicology Med. Coll. Ga., Augusta, 1995—; sr. scientist Papanicolaou Cancer Rsch. Inst., Miami, 1972-77; hon. med. officer to Regius prof. medicine Oxford U., 1965-67; vis. prof. Clin. Rsch. Inst. Montreal, 1974; mem. vis. faculty thoracic disease divsn., dept. internal medicine Mayo Clinic, 1974; cons. Hycor, Inc., Chugai Pharm. Co., Ltd., Tokyo, Apotex, Inc., Toronto. Contbr. numerous articles on biochem. research and pathology to sci. jours.; patentee in field. Rockefeller Found. travel awardee, 1962; William Waldorf Astor travelling fellow, 1966; USPHS spl. fellow, 1967-68; Pfizer travelling fellow, 1972; recipient Louis and Artur Luciano award for research of circulatory diseases McGill U., 1984-85. Fellow Am. Inst. Chemists; mem. Am. Chem. Soc., Biochem. Soc., Am. Soc. Biol. Chemists, Am. Heart Assn. (mem. council cardiopulmonary diseases 1972—, Council for High Blood Pressure Research 1976—), Microcirculatory Soc., So. Soc. Clin. Investigation, AAAS, N.Y. Acad. Scis., Sigma Xi. Baptist. Club: United Oxford and Cambridge U. (London). Home: 3047 Lake Forest Dr Augusta GA 30909-3027 Office: Med Coll Ga Vascular Biology Ctr Augusta GA 30912

RYAN, JERRY WILLIAM, lawyer; b. Highland Park, Mich., Mar. 18, 1928; s. Jeremiah Ryan and Irene (Evans) R. BA, U. Mich., 1949, JD, 1952; postgrad., Inst. Universitaire des Hautes Etudes Internat., Geneva, Switzerland, 1954, 55. Bar: Mich. 1952, N.Y. 1958, D.C. 1966. Field atty. VA, Detroit, 1953-54; atty. Pan Am. World Airways Inc., N.Y.C., 1956-66; ptnr. Pogue & Neal, Washington, 1966-67, Jones, Day, Reavis & Pogue and predecessor firm Reavis, Pogue, Neal & Rose, Washington, 1967-79, Crowell & Moring, Washington, 1979—; arbitrator U.S. and internat. arbitrations; speaker Inst. Continuing Edn., U. Mich., 1989-90. Capt. USAF, 1952-53. Mem. ABA (speaker 1985), Assn. of Bar of City of N.Y., Sky Club (N.Y.C.), Metropolitan Club (washington). Office: Crowell & Moring 1001 Pennsylvania Ave NW Washington DC 20004-2505

RYAN, JOAN, sportswriter; b. Sept. 20, 1959; m. Barry Tompkins; 1 child. BS in Journalism with honors, U. Fla., 1981. Copy editor Orlando (Fla.) Sentinel, 1981-82, copy editor sports, 1982-83, sports writer, 1983-85; sports columnist San Francisco Examiner, 1985—. Recipient Fla. Sports Columnist of Yr. award, 1984, numerous AP Sports Editors awards, AP 1st place enterprise reporting award, 1993, Nat. Headliner award sports writing, 1990, Women's Sports Found. Journalism award, 1992. Office: San Francisco Examiner PO Box 7260 110 5th Ave San Francisco CA 94120

RYAN, JOHN DUNCAN, lawyer; b. Portland, Oreg., Dec. 20, 1920; s. Thomas Gough and Virgian Abigail (Hadley) R.; m. Florence A. Ryan, Jan. 30, 1970 (dec. 1987). BS, Fordham U., 1943; JD, Lewis & Clark Coll., Portland, 1950. Bar: Oreg. 1950. Private practice Portland, 1950—; adj. instr. Northwestern Sch. Law Lewis & Clark Coll., 1953-70. Author: (poems) Expressions, 1993. Sgt. Air Corps, U.S. Army, 1942-46, ETO. Recipient St. Thomas More award Catholic Lawyers for Social Justice, 1993. Mem. ABA (Oreg. delegate 1985-93, chmn. spl. com. on law & literacy 1991-93), Am. Coll. Trial Lawyers, Am. Trial Lawyers Assn., Oreg. State Bar (bd. govs. 1963-67), Oreg. Trial Lawyers Assn. (Trial Lawyer of Yr. 1993), Multnomah Bar Assn., Washington County Bar Assn. Home and Office: 1760 SW 90th Ave Portland OR 97225-6509

RYAN, JOHN EDWARD, federal judge; b. Boston, Jan. 22, 1941; s. Howard Frederick and Mary (Burke) R.; m. Terri Reynolds; children: Valerie, Jennifer, Keely. BSEE, U.S. Naval Acad., 1963; LLB, Georgetown U., 1972; MS, Pacific Christian U., 1979. Assoc. Hale and Dorr, Boston, 1972-76, C.F. Braun, Alhambra, Calif., 1976-77; gen. counsel Altec Corp., Anaheim, Calif., 1977-79; v.p., sr. atty. Oak Industries, San Diego, 1979-82; sr. v.p. Oak Media, San Diego, 1982-84; ptnr. Dale and Lloyd, La Jolla, Calif., 1984-85, Jennings, Engstrand and Henrikson, San Diego, 1985-86; bankruptcy judge U.S. Bankruptcy Ct., Santa Ana, Calif., 1986—; ex officio dir. Orange County Bankruptcy Forum; exec. com. 9th Cir. conf. With USN, 1963-69. Fellow Am. Coll. Bankruptcy; mem. Mass. Bar Assn., Calif. Bar Assn., Orange County Bar Assn., Bankruptcy Judges Assn. Republican. Roman Catholic. Avocations: tennis, camping, basketball. Home: 3155 Summit Dr Escondido CA 92025-7529 Office: US Bankruptcy Ct PO Box 12600 Santa Ana CA 92712-2600

RYAN, JOHN FRANKLIN, multinational company executive; b. Huntington, W.Va., Apr. 10, 1925; s. Oscar F. and Mamie J. (Tyler) R.; m. Renee B. Bourn, June 17, 1948; children—Carolyn, Linda, Elizabeth. Student, Emory and Henry Coll., 1943-44; B.S., Marshall U., 1948. Data processing sales mgr. IBM, Phila., 1958-60; dir. worldwide integrated data systems ITT, Washington, 1960-62, dept. dir., 1962-72, dir. corp. relations, 1972-87, v.p., 1981-87; cons., 1987—. Mem. Bus.-Govt. Relations Council, pres. 1978; bd. dirs. Pub. Affairs Council. Served with USNR, 1943-45. Clubs: Carlton (pres. 1982), Burning Tree. Home: 8447 Portland Pl Mc Lean VA 22102-1707

RYAN, JOHN MICHAEL, landscape architect; b. Chgo., Sept. 27, 1946; s. Terrance Joseph and Norma (Morris) R.; m. Victoria Jean Wheetley, June 26, 1986; children: Micheline Giannasi-Mennecke, Tony Giannasi, Nick Giannasi, Andrew Morris Jennings, Melissa Contance Victoria, Cameron Michael Montgomery. B in Landscape Architecture, U. Ill., 1969. Registered landscape architect, Ill., Mich., Ariz.; cert. CLARB. Assoc. landscape architect Carl Garnder & Assocs., Inc., Chgo., 1969-71; sr. landscape architect Collaborative Rsch. & Planning, Chgo., 1971-73; v.p. Michael L. Ives & Assocs., Inc., Downers Grove, Ill., 1973-84; pres. Ives/Ryan Group, Inc., Naperville, 1984—. Prin. works include renovation of Old Orchard Shopping Ctr., Skokie, Ill., Lake Katherine Nature Preserve, Palos Heights, Ill., Crystal Tree Residential Golf Course Cmty., Orland Park, Ill., Corporetum Office Campus, Lisle, Ill. Crew chief search and rescue USCG Aux., 1980—. Recipient Nat. Landscape award Am. Assn. Nurserymen, 1988, 92, Key award in landscape arch. Home Bldrs. Assn. Greater Chgo., 1981, 84, 90. Mem. Am. Assn. Landscape Archs. (Merit award 1991, 94, 96), Ill. Landscape Contractors Assn. (Gold award 1991, 96, Silver award 1986, 90, 93, Merit award 1988, 91), Chgo. Hort. Soc., Perennial Plant Assn. (Nat. Honor award 1993), Morton Arboretum. Avocations: competitive volleyball, golf, gardening, travel. Office: Ives/Ryan Group Inc 1801 A North Mill St Naperville IL 60563 *My life is committed to raising my dear children as best I can, which I believeto be my true purpose for being here. As a professional landscape architect, if I can enhance or imporve the environment for my children and their children, I have made a worthwhile professional contribution to my perceived purpose in life.*

RYAN, JOHN WILLIAM, retired university president; b. Chgo., Aug. 12, 1929; s. Leonard John and Maxine (Mitchell) R.; m. D. Patricia Goodday, Mar. 20, 1949; children: Kathleen Elynne Ryan Acker, Kevin Dennis Mitchell, Kerrick Charles Casey. BA, U. Utah, 1951; MA, Ind. U., 1958, PhD, 1959, LLD (hon.), 1988; LLD (hon.), U. Notre Dame, 1978, Oakland City Coll., 1981, St. Joseph Coll., 1981, Hanover Coll., 1982, DePauw U., 1983, U. Ma., 1983, Manchester Coll., 1983, U. Evansville, 1985, Wabash Coll., 1986, Ind. U., 1988; DLitt (hon.), U. St. Thomas, 1977; D Pub. Adminstrn., Nat. Inst. Devel. Adminstrn., Thailand, 1991; LLD (hon.), U. Md., 1994. Rsch. analyst Ky. Dept. Revenue, Frankfort, 1954-55; vis. rsch. prof. U. Thammasat, Bangkok, Thailand, 1955-57; asst. dir. Inst. Tng. for Pub. Svc. Ind. U., 1957-58; successively asst. prof., assoc. prof. polit. sci., assoc. dir., Bur. Govt. U. Wis., 1958-62; exec. asst. to pres., sec. of univ. U. Mass., Amherst, 1962-63; chancellor U. Mass., Boston, 1965-68; v.p. acad. affairs Ariz. State U., 1963-65; v.p., chancellor regional campuses Ind. U., Bloomington, 1968-71, pres., 1971-87, prof. polit. sci., 1968-95, prof. pub. and environ. affairs, 1981-95, prof. emeritus, 1995—; cons. AID, 1991-92; cons. AID, 1991-92; interim pres. Fla. Atlantic U., 1989, U. Md., Balt., 1994; bd. dirs. Ind. U. Found., chmn. 1972-87; chmn. Nat. Adv. Bd. on Internat. Edn. Programs, 1985-89. Contbr. articles to profl. jours. Bd. govs. Pub. Broadcasting Svc., 1973-82; bd. visitors Air U., 1974-81; chmn. Air Force Inst. Tech Subcom., 1976-81; mem. univ. adv. com. Am. Coun. Life Ins.; bd. dirs. Corp. Community Coun., 1976; mem. nat. adv. coun. Pan Am. Games, 1985; mem. adv. bd. Assocs. for Religious and Intellectual Life, 1984—; active United Way Ind. Centennial Commn. Mem. Am. Soc. Pub. Adminstrn. (pres. Ind. chpt. 1969-70, nat. chpt. 1972-73, nat. coun. from 1970, Ind. Soc. Chgo. (non-resident v.p. from 1976, Am. Polit. Sci. Assn., Assn. Asian Studies, Am. Coun. Edn., Am. Judicature Soc., Assn. Am. Univs. (exec. com. from 1978, chmn. com. on coms. 1984, health edn. com. from 1978, chmn. 1981-82), Ind. Soc. N.Y.C., Ind. Soc. Washington, Nat. Acad. Public Adminstrn., Ind. Acad., Explorers Club, Adelphia (hon.), Circumnavigators Club (N.Y.C.), Columbia Club (Indpls.), Skyline Club, Cosmos Club (Washington), St. Botolph (Boston), K.C, Elks, Phi Kappa Phi, Phi Alpha Theta, Pi Sigma Alpha, Beta Gamma Sigma, Kappa Sigma (worthy grand master 1985-87). Office: Ind U Spea # 316 Bloomington IN 47405

RYAN, JOHN WILLIAM, educational association administrator; b. Manchester, N.H., Sept. 16, 1937; s. William Charles and Mary Ann (Marcoux) R.; m. Carol Jean Battaglia, Sept. 17, 1960; children: James, Kathleen, John, Michael. A.B., St. Anselm Coll., 1959; M.A., Niagara U., 1960; Ph.D., St. John's U., 1965. Asst. prof. history Gannon U., Erie, Pa., 1965-66; edn. specialist, div. grad. programs U.S. Office Edn., Washington, 1966-68; regional coordinator, grad. acad. programs U.S. Office Edn., 1968-70; dir. univ. programs Univ. Assos., Inc., Washington, 1970-72; asst. to pres., sec. Council of Grad. Schs. in U.S., Washington, 1972-80; exec. v.p. Renewables Research Inst., Annandale, Va., 1980-81; exec. dir. Worcester (Mass.) Consortium Higher Edn., 1981-89, N.H. Coll. and Univ. Coun., Manchester, 1989-93; cons.; exec. dir. Mass. Vet. Med. Assn., Marlborough, Mass., 1995—. Contbr. articles to profl. jours. Mem. Am. Soc. Assn. Execs. Office: 169 Lakeside Ave Marlborough MA 01752

RYAN, JOSEPH, lawyer; b. Seattle, Feb. 11, 1942; s. John Joseph and Jane (Wing) R.; m. Mary Katherine Gavin, Aug. 10, 1963; children: Michael Gavin, Kathleen Ann, Jennifer Jo. BA, U. Washington, 1964; JD, Columbia U., 1967. Bar: Calif. 1968, N.Y. 1983, D.C. 1983. Ptnr. O'Melveny & Myers, Los Angeles, 1976-94; exec. v.p., gen. counsel Marriott Internat., Inc., Washington, 1994—; teacher, lecturer N.Y. Law Jour. Author: Stating Your Case--How To Interview for a Job as a Lawyer, 1982, Take or Pay Contracts: Alive and Well in California, vol. 192, 1987, Current Investment Banking Activities in the United States, vol. 2, #15 M&A Report, 1988; co-author (with Lorin Fife) The Urban Lawyer, 1987; contbr. articles to law publs. Bd. dirs. Pasadena Playhouse, L.A., 1981-92, Planetary Soc., Pasadena, 1981, Westridge Sch., L.A., 1982-91, Natural History Mus. Los Angeles County, 1988-93. Capt. U.S. Army, 1968-70. Mem. ABA, N.Y. Bar Assn., D.C. Bar Assn., Calif. Bar Assn., Nat. Assn. Bond Lawyers (legis. com.). Republican. Roman Catholic. Avocations: running, biking, camping, hunting and fishing, boating. Home: 10836 Alloway Dr Potomac MD 20854-1503 Office: Marriott Internat Inc Dept 52/923 Marriott Dr Washington DC 20058

RYAN, JUDITH LYNDAL, German language and literature educator; b. Sydney, Australia, Apr. 6, 1943; came to U.S., 1967; d. William Matthew and Kathleen (Ferris) O'Neil; m. Lawrence Ryan, Feb. 24, 1964 (div. 1985); children: Antony Lawrence, Vanessa Lyndal; m. Lawrence A. Joseph, Sept. 26, 1986. B.A. with honors, U. Sydney, 1964; Dr. Phil., U. Munster, Westfalia, W. Ger., 1970. Research student U. Sydney, 1965; instr., asst. prof. then assoc. prof. German Smith Coll., Northampton, Mass., 1967-79; prof. German German Smith Coll., 1979—, Doris Silbert prof. humanities, 1982-85; prof. German and comparative lit. Harvard U., Cambridge, 1985-90, Robert K. & Dale J. Weary prof. German and comparative lit., 1990—, chmn. dept. comparative lit., 1988-93, chair dept. Germanic langs. and lits., 1993-96; vis. assoc. prof. Brown U., Providence, 1978-79. Author: Umschlag und Verwandlung, 1972, The Uncompleted Past, 1983 (Basilius award 1983), The Vanishing Subject, 1991; mem. editorial bd. German Quar., 1983-90; mem. adv. bd. German Studies Rev., 1983-87, PMLA, 1984-87. NEH fellow, 1978; Humboldt-Stiftung grantee, 1970-71. Mem. MLA (del. 1973-75, 77-79, programs com. 1980-83, exec. coun. 1987-90, nominating com. 1994-95, editorial bd. Texts and Translations Series, 1991-94), AAUP (pres. Smith Coll. chpt. 1982-83). Office: Harvard U Dept German Cambridge MA 02138

RYAN, JUDITH W., geriatrics nurse, adult nurse practitioner, educator, researcher; b. Waterbury, Conn., Dec. 8, 1943; d. James Patrick Ryan and Edna (Swanson) Billings. BS, U. Conn., 1965; MS, Boston U., 1967; PhD, U. Md., 1984. RN, Md., Conn.; cert. adult nurse practitioner ANA. Instr. U. Conn., Storrs, 1967-69; asst. prof. Ind. U., Purdue U., Indpls., 1969-73; asst. prof. U. Md., Balt., 1973-82, dir. nursing and health care dept. family medicine, supportive care project, 1985-87, asst. prof. sch. nursing, 1987-95; asst. prof. Coll. Notre Dame, Balt., 1982-83; clin. dir. EverCare, Linthicum, Md., 1995—; dir. primary care adult nurse practitioner cert. program U. Md., 1976-82; arbitrator Health Claims Arbitration Program, Md., 1976—; pres. Md. Bd. Nursing, Balt., 1993—; bd. trustees Md. Nurses Assn. Polit. Action Com., Balt., treas., 1989-91. Contbr. articles to profl. jours. Named Distinguished Practitioner Nursing, Nat. Acad. Practice, 1984—. Mem. Md. Nurses Assn. (2d v.p. 1986-88), Md. Gerontol. Assn., Nat. Conf. Gerontol. Nurse Practitioner, Nurse Practitioner Assn. Md., Sigma Theta Tau, Phi Kappa Phi. Home: 622 Lucia Ave Baltimore MD 21229-4516 Office: 849 International Dr # 125 Linthicum Heights MD 21090

RYAN, KENNETH JOHN, physician, educator; b. N.Y.C., Aug. 26, 1926; s. Joseph M. R.; m. Marion Elizabeth Kinney, June 8, 1948; children: Alison

Leigh, Kenneth John, Christopher Elliot. Student, Northwestern U., 1946-48; MD, Harvard U., 1952. Diplomate Am. Bd. Ob-Gyn. Intern, then resident internal medicine Mass. Gen. Hosp., Boston, also Columbia-Presbyn. Med. Center, N.Y.C., 1952-54, 56-57; resident in ob-gyn. Boston Lying-in Hosp., also Free Hosp. for Women, Brookline, Mass., 1957-60; prof. ob-gyn., dir. dept. Med. Sch. Western Res. U., 1961-70; prof. reproductive biology, dept. ob-gyn. U. Calif. San Diego, La Jolla, 1970-73; chief of staff Boston Hosp. for Women, 1973-80; chmn. dept. ob-gyn. Brigham Women's Hosp., Boston, 1980-93; instr. ob-gyn. Harvard U., also dir. Fearing Rsch. Lab., 1960-61, Kate Macy Ladd prof., chmn. dept. ob-gyn. Med. Sch., 1973-93, dir. Lab. Human Reprodn. and Reproductive Biology, 1974-93, Disting. prof., 1993-96, prof. emeritus, 1996—; chief staff Boston Hosp. for Women, 1973-80; chmn. dept. ob-gyn. Brigham Women's Hosp., Boston, 1980-93. Chmn. Nat. Commn. for Protection of Human Subjects Biomed. and Behavioral Rsch., 1974-78. Recipient Schering award Harvard Med. Sch., 1951, Soma Weis award, 1952, Bordon award, 1952; Ernst Oppenheimer award, 1964; Max Weinstein award, 1970; fellow Mass. Gen. Hosp., 1954-56. Fellow Am. Cancer Soc.; mem. ACOG, Am. Soc. Biol. Chemists, Endocrine Soc., Soc. Gynecol. Investigation, Am. Gynecol. Soc., Am. Soc. Clin. Investigation, Mass. Med. Soc., Alpha Omega Alpha. Office: Brigham & Women's Hosp 75 Francis St Boston MA 02115-6110

RYAN, KEVIN WILLIAM, research virologist, educator; b. Fort Dodge, Iowa, Dec. 8, 1952; s. Joseph Michael Ryan and Etoile Evelyn Werth; m. Mary Ellen Lyman, June 1, 1974; children: Matthew Lyman, Mark Joseph. BS, U. Iowa, 1978; PhD, U. Mich., 1984. Staff fellow Nat. Inst. of Allergy and Infectious Diseases/NIH, Bethesda, Md., 1984-86; rsch. asst. dept. virology and molecular biology St. Jude Children's Rsch. Hosp., Memphis, 1986-89, asst. mem., 1989—; asst. prof. pathology U. Tenn. Coll. Medicine, Memphis, 1994—. Contbr. articles to profl. jours., chpts. to tech. manuals. Predoctoral fellow Mich. Cancer Rsch. Inst., U. Mich., Ann Arbor, 1982; prin. investigator grantee Nat. Inst. Allergy and Infectious Diseases, 1992—. Mem. AAAS, Am. Soc. for Virology (co-chair pub. affiars com. 1995-96), Am. Soc. Microbiology, Soc. Gen. Microbiology, Radiol. Soc. N.Am., Sigma Xi. Roman Catholic. Avocations: golf, chess. Office: St Jude Children Rsch Hosp Children Rsch Hosp 332 N Lauderdale Memphis TN 38101

RYAN, LEHAN JEROME, lawyer; b. Des Moines, July 30, 1935; s. Lehan T. and Hannah (Cody) R.; m. Carol F. Crawford, Feb. 22, 1958; children: Dennis M., David L. BS, U. Iowa, 1957, JD, 1964. Bar: Minn. 1964, U.S. Dist. Ct. Minn. 1964, U.S. Ct. Appeals (8th cir.) 1964. Assoc. Oppenheimer, Wolff & Donnelly, St. Paul, 1964-68, ptnr., 1969—. Pres. St. Paul Jaycees, 1970; v.p. St. Paul Winter Carnival, 1974; bd. trustees U. Iowa Law Sch. Found., 1990—, U. Minn. Med. Found., 1991— . 1st lt. USAF, 1958-61. Recipient Ted Christian award St. Paul Jaycees, 1982. Fellow Am. Coll. Trust and Estate Counsel (Minn. state chmn. 1986-91); mem. Minn. Bar Assn. (chmn. legal edn. com. 1980, chmn. probate and trust law com. 1982-83, bd. govs. 1988-90), Ramsey County Bar Assn. (pres. 1987-88), St. Paul Area C. of C. (bd. dirs. 1987-91, sec. 1989), Gyro Club (bd. dirs., treas. 1985-88), St. Paul Alea YMCA (bd. dirs. 1993—, chair fin. com., treas., 1995—), St. Paul Rotary (v.p. 1996-97). Democrat. Office: Oppenheimer Wolff & Donnelly 1700 1st Bank Bldg Saint Paul MN 55101

RYAN, LEO VINCENT, business educator; b. Waukon, Iowa, Apr. 6, 1927; s. John Joseph and Mary Irene (O'Brien) R. BS, Marquette U., 1949; MBA, DePaul U., 1954; PhD, St. Louis U., 1958; postgrad., Catholic U. Am., 1951-52, Bradley U., 1952-54, Northwestern U., 1950; LLD, Seton Hall U., 1988. Joined Order Clerics of St. Viator, Roman Cath. Ch., 1950. Mem. faculty Marquette U., Milw., 1957-65; dir. continuing edn. summer sessions, coord. evening divs. Marquette U., 1959-65, prof. indsl. mgmt., 1964; prof. and chmn. dept. mgmt. Loyola U., Chgo., 1965-66; adj. prof. mgmt. Loyola U., 1967-69; dep. dir. Peace Corps, Lagos, Nigeria, 1966-67; dir. Western Nigeria Peace Corps, Ibadan, 1967-68; asst. superior gen. and treas. gen. Clerics of St. Viator, Rome, 1968-69; dir. edn. Am. province Clerics of St. Viator, Arlington Heights, Ill., 1969-74; pres. St. Viator High Sch., 1972-74; dean, prof. mgmt. Coll. Bus. Adminstrn. U. Notre Dame, Ind., 1975-80; dean Coll. Commerce DePaul U., 1980-88, prof. mgmt. Coll. Commerce, 1980—, Wicklander prof. profl. ethics, 1993—; dir. Peace Corps tng. programs Marquette U., 1962-65; adj. prof. human devel. St. Mary's Coll., Winona, Minn., 1972-74; mem. sch. bd. Archdiocese Chgo., 1972-75, vice chmn., 1973-75, mem. nat. edn. com. U.S. Cath. Conf., 1971-75, mem. exec. com., 1973-75; mem. nat. adv. bd. Benedictine Sisters of Nauvoo, 1973-83; mem. nat. adv. coun. SBA, 1982-85, vice chmn. minority bus., 1982-85, exec. com. Chgo. chpt., 1982-84; vis. prof. U. Ife, Ibadan, 1967-68; mem. adv. bd. 1st Bank-Milw., 1991-93, chmn. trust audit com., 1980-85, chmn. audit and examination com., 1985-90, mem. bus. adv. coun., 1991-93; bd. dirs. Vilter Mfg. Co., external dir. Vilter ESOP, Filbert Corp., Vilter Internat. (now Vilter Export Corp.), Henricksen & Co., Inc.; mem. fin. commn. Clerics of St. Viator, 1978—, mem. provincial chpt., 1985—; cons. Pontifical Commn. on Justice and Peace, 1968-70; vis. prof. Helsinki Sch. Econs., Mikkeli, Finland, 1990, 91, 94, 96, Poznan (Poland) Sch. Mgmt., 1991, 92, 93; coord. Polish Am. summer program in econs. Acad. Econs., Poznan, 1991; Fulbright prof. Adam Mickiewicz U., Poland, 1993, 94, 95; co-chair bus. and profl. com. Archdiocese of Chgo. Sesquetennial Com. Out Reach Divsn. Ctrl. Planning Group, 1993-94. Mem. editl. bd. Internat. Jour. Value Based Mgmt., European Bus. Jour., Bus. Ethics Quar. Mem. Pres.'s Com. on Employment Handicapped, 1959-65, Wis. Gov.'s Com. on Employment Handicapped, 1959-65, Wis. Gov.'s Com. on UN, 1961-64, Burnham Park Planning Commn., 1982-88; bd. dirs. Ctr. Pastoral Liturgy U. Notre Dame, 1976-79, Lake Forest Grad. Sch. Mgmt., 1989-91; trustee St. Mary of Woods Coll., 1978-81; regent Seton Hall U., 1981-87, mem. acad. affairs com., 1981-87, chmn., 1983-87; trustee Cath. Theol. Union, U. Chgo., 1992-95; dir. Ctr. for Enterprise Devel., 1992-95; fellow St. Edmonds Coll. Cambridge U., 1992; mem. Cath. Commn. Intellectual and Cultural Affairs, 1992—, Cath. Campaign for Am., 1994—; bd. dirs. Internat. Bus. Ethics Inst., Am. Grad. Sch. Internat. Mgmt., 1995—, Assn. Profl. Ethics, 1995—; mem. adv. coun. Mgmt. Edn. in Poland, U. Md., College Park, 1995—. Recipient Freedom award Berlin Commn., 1961, chieftancy title Asoju Atoaja of Oshogbo Oba Adenle I, Yorubaland, Nigeria, 1967, B'nai B'rith Interfaith award, Milw., 1963, Disting. Alumnus award Marquette U., 1974, DePaul U., 1976, Tchr. of Yr. award Beta Alpha Psi, 1980, Centennial Alumni Achievement award Marquette U., 1981, Boland Meml. Disting. Alumni award, St. Louis, 1989, Disting. Alumni and Bicentennial awards Jesuit Bus. Schs., 1989, Pres.' award St. Viator H.S., 1992, Medal of Merit Adam Mickiewicz U., 1995, Excellence in Teaching award DePaul U., 1995; Brother Leo V. Ryan award created in his honor Cath. Bus. Edn. Assn., 1962; Ryan Scholars in Mgmt. established in his honor DePaul U., 1989, Outstanding Svc. award, 1991-93; named Man of Yr. Jr. C. of C., Milw., 1959, Marquette U. Bus. Adminstrn. Alumni Man1974, Tchr. of Yr. U. Notre Dame, 1980; Milw. Bd. Realtors traveling fellow, 1964, Nat. Assn. Purchasing Agts. faculty fellow, 1958, German Am. Acad. Exch. Coun. fellow, summer 1983, Presdl. fellow Am. Grad. Sch. Internat. Mgmt., 1989, vis. scholar, 1995, Malone fellow in Islamic studies, 1990, fellow Kosciuszko Found. Adam Mickiewicz U., 1990; scholar-in-residence Mgmt. Sch. Imperial Coll. Sci. and Tech. U. London, 1988; vis. scholar U. Calif., Berkeley, spring 1989; USIA Acad. Specialists grantee (3), Poland, 1991, 92, 93; fellow St. Edmund's Coll. Cambridge U., 1992; named vis. rsch. fellow Von Hugel Inst., 1992-93; scholar-in-residence Am. Grad. Sch. Internat. Mgmt., 1995; guest scholar Kellogg Inst. Internat. Studies U. Notre Dame, 1997. Mem. Cath. Bus. Edn. Assn. (nat. pres. 1960-62, nat. exec. bd. 1960-64), Assn. Sch. Bus. Ofcls. (nat. com. chmn. 1965-67), Am. Assembly Collegiate Schs. Bus. (com. internat. affairs 1977-84, chmn. 1981-84, bd. dirs. 1981-87, program chmn. 1979-80, exec. com., chmn. projects/svc. mgmt. com. 1984-86), Am. Fgn. Svc. Assn., Am. Assn. Profl. Ethics (bd. dirs. 1996—), Allamakee County Hist. Soc. (charter life), Acad. Internat. Bus., Acad. Mgmt. (social issues div., chmn. membership com. 1990-91), Nat. Returned Peace Corps Assn., Atomic Vets. Assn., August Derleth Soc., Chgo. Area Return Peace Corps Vols., Econ. Club Chgo., Chgo. Coun. Fgn. Rels., Coun. Fgn. Rels. (Chgo. com.), European Found. Mgmt. Edn., European Bus. Ethics Network, Soc. Bus. Ethics (mem. exec. com. 1991—, pres. 1993-94, adv. bd. 1995—), Assn. Social Econs. (life), Assn. Christian Economists, Inst. Global Ethics, Inst. Internat. Ethics (adv. bd.), Dubuque County Hist. Soc., Iowa Hist. Soc., Fulbright Assn. (life), Internat. Assn. for Bus. and Soc. (founder), Internat. Soc. for Bus., Econs. and Ethics (charter), Internat. Trade and Fin. Assn. (founder, bd. dirs. 1989-92, 96—, v.p. membership 1991-92), Internat. Assn. Environ. Ethics, Internat. Learned Soc. Praxiology, Milw. Press Club (hon.), USS Mt. McKinley Reunion Assn. (hon. chaplain AGC-7 1989-96, Disting. Svc. award 1991), Alpha Sigma Nu, Alpha Kappa Psi (bd. dirs. found. 1985-91, vice chmn. 1987-91, chmn. scholarship com. 1987-91, chmn. devel. com. 1987, mem. exec. com. 1990-91, Bronze Disting. Svc. award 1949, Silver Disting. Svc. award 1958), Beta Alpha Psi, Beta Gamma Sigma (co-chair 75th Anniversary com. Ill., faculty advisor DePaul chpt. 1986-92), Delta Mu Delta, Pi Gamma Mu, Tau Kappa Epsilon.

RYAN, LEONARD EAMES, judge; b. Albion, N.Y., July 8, 1930; s. Bernard and Harriet Earle (Fitts) R.; m. Ann Allen, June 18, 1973; 1 child, Thomas Eames Allen-Ryan. Grad., Kent Sch., 1948; AB, U. Pa., 1954; JD, NYU, 1962. Bar: D.C. 1963, N.Y. 1963, U.S. Ct. Appeals (D.C. cir.) 1963, U.S. Dist. Ct. (so. and ea. dists.) N.Y. 1965, U.S. Ct. Appeals (2nd cir.) 1966, U.S. Supreme Ct. 1967. Reporter Upper Darby (Pa.) News, 1954; newsman AP, Pitts., Phila., Harrisburg, N.Y.C., 1955-62; reporter, spl. writer on law N.Y. Times, 1962-63; info. adviser corp. hdqrs. IBM, N.Y.C., 1963; trial atty. firm Perrell, Nielsen & Stephens, N.Y.C., 1964-66; trial atty. civil rights div. Dept. Justice, Washington, 1966-68; asst. to dir. bus. affairs CBS News, N.Y.C., 1968; program officer Office Govt. and Law, Ford Found., N.Y.C., 1968-74; pvt. practice law, cons. pub. affairs N.Y.C., 1974-91; v.p., sec. W. P. Carey & Co., Inc., Investment Bankers, N.Y.C., 1976-81; hearing examiner Family Ct. of State of N.Y., 1981-82; adminstrv. law judge N.Y. State Div. Human Rights, 1976-91, N.Y. State Dept. Health, 1982-91; adminstrv. law judge Office of Hearings and Appeals, San Rafael, Calif., 1991-93, Phila., 1993-94, N.Y.C., 1994—; impartial hearing officer Edn. for All Handicapped Children Act of 1975, 1976-91; hearing officer N.Y. State Dept. Agr. and Markets, 1987-91, N.Y. State Office Mental Retardation and Devel. Disabilities, 1989-91; arbitrator Small Claims Ct., N.Y.C., 1974-84; bd. dirs. Community Action for Legal Svcs. Inc., N.Y.C., 1971-77, vice-chmn., 1975-77; co-chmn. Citizens Com. to Save Legal Svcs., N.Y.C., 1975-76; bd. dirs. Lower East Side Svc. Ctr., N.Y.C., 1977-89. Author: (with Bernard Ryan Jr.) So You Want to Go Into Journalism, 1963; contbr. articles to profl. jours. Served with USAR, 1950-57. Mem. Am. Judicature Soc., Assn. of Bar of City of N.Y., N.Y. State Bar Assn., St. Elmo Club (Phila.), Heights Casino (Bklyn.). Home: 32 Orange St Brooklyn NY 11201-1634

RYAN, MARK ANTHONY, architect; b. Council Bluffs, Iowa, Sept. 6, 1964; s. Paul Elmer and Darreline Kay (Wyland) R.; m. Shelli Ann Hagerbaumer, Sept. 26, 1992. BA in Architecture with distinction, Iowa State U., 1987. Registered profl. architect, Wis. Project architect U.S. Army Corps. of Engrs., Omaha, 1987-90, architect, security engr., 1990-91, environ. project mgr., 1991—; owner Ryan Designs, Omaha, 1987—, The Ryan Co., Omaha, 1994—; bd. advisors Fitness Plus, Council Bluffs, Iowa, 1990-92; expert witness for pvt. attys., Iowa and Nebr., 1991—. Chmn. City Devel. Commn., Council Bluffs, 1992; bd. trustees San. and Improvement Dist. No. 142, Douglas County, Nebr., 1995-96. State of Iowa scholar, 1982. Mem. AIA (sec. S.W. Iowa sect. 1991, treas. 1992, v.p. 1993, pres. 1994-96), Soc. Am. Mil. Engrs., Nat. Trust for Hist. Preservation, Golden Key, Phi Kappa Phi, Tau Sigma Delta. Avocations: archl. restoration, biking, freshwater aquatics. Home: 9030 Raven Oaks Dr Omaha NE 68152-1759 Office: US Army Corps of Engrs 215 N 17th St Omaha NE 68102-4910

RYAN, MARLEIGH GRAYER, Japanese language educator; b. N.Y.C., May 1, 1930; d. Harry and Betty (Hurwick) Grayer; m. Edward Ryan, June 4, 1950; 1 child, David Patrick. B.A., NYU, 1951; M.A., Columbia U., 1956, Ph.D., 1965; Cert., East Asian Inst., 1956; postgrad., Kyoto U., 1958-59. Research assoc. Columbia U., N.Y.C., 1960-61, lectr. Japanese, 1961-65, asst. prof., 1965-70, assoc. prof., 1970-72; vis. asst. prof. Yale U ., New Haven, 1966-67; assoc. prof. U. Iowa, Iowa City, 1972-75, prof., 1975-81, chmn. dept., 1972-81; prof. Japanese SUNY, New Paltz, 1981—, dean liberal arts and scis., 1981-90; vice chmn. seminar on modern Japan, Columbia U., 1984-85, chmn., 1985-86; co-chmn. N.Y. State Conf. on Asian Studies, 1986, editor, 1993—, mem. exec. com., 1993-96, sec., 1993—. Co-author: (with Herschel Webb) Research in Japanese Sources, 1965; author: Japan's First Modern Novel, 1967, The Development of Realism in the Fiction of Tsubouchi Shoyo, 1975; assoc. editor: Jour. Assn. Tchrs. Japanese, 1962-71, editor, 1971-75. East Asian Inst. fellow Columbia U., 1955; Ford Found. fellow, 1958-60; Japan Found. fellow, 1973, Woodrow Wilson Ctr. Internat. Scholars fellow, 1988-89; recipient Van. Am. Disting. Book award Columbia, 1968. Mem. MLA (sec. com. on teaching Japanese Lang. 1962-68, mem. del. assembly 1979-87, mem. exec. com. div. Asian lit. 1981-86), Assn. Tchrs. Japanese (exec. com. 1969-72, 74-77), Assn. Asian Studies (bd. dirs. 1975-78, coun. of confs., 1993—), Midwest Conf. Asian Studies (pres. 1980-81). Office: SUNY Ft # 414 New Paltz NY 12561 *Studying the most difficult language in the world has taught me patience and tact. One learns what it is to sit completely still at the Japanese No theatre and absorb wondrous sights and sounds in an atmosphere of absolute peace. Discovering the stillness in movement is perhaps the most important lesson we in the West can derive from our Asian experience.*

RYAN, MARY A., diplomat; b. New York, N.Y., Oct. 1, 1940. B.A., St. John's Univ., 1963, M.A., 1965. With Foreign Service, Dept. of State, 1966—; consular and adminstrv. officer Naples, Italy, 1966-69; personnel officer Am. Embassy, Tegucigalpa, Honduras, 1970-71; consular officer Am. Consulate Gen., Monterrey, Mexico, 1971-73; adminstrv. officer Bur. of African Affairs, Dept. of State, Washington, 1973-75, post mgmt. officer, 1975-77; career devel. officer Bur. of Personnel, Dept. of State, 1977-80; adminstrv. counselor Abidjan, Ivory Coast, 1980-81, Khartoum, Sudan, 1981-82; inspector, Office of Insp. Gen. Dept. of State, Washington, 1982-83, exec. dir. Bur. of European and Can. Affairs, 1983-85, exec. asst. to Under Sec. of State for Mgmt., 1985-88; ambassador to Swaziland, 1988-90; dep. asst. sec. Bur. of Consular Affairs, Washington, 1990; dir. Kuwait task force, 1990-91, ops. dir. UN spl. commn. on elimination of Iraqi weapons, 1991; dep. asst. sec. Bur. European & Can. Affairs, Washington, 1991-93; asst. sec. Bur. of Consular Affairs, Washington, 1993—. Office: Dept State Bureau of Consular Affairs 2201 C St NW Washington DC 20520-0001*

RYAN, MARY CATHERINE, pediatrician; b. N.Y.C., Mar. 22, 1938; d. Thomas Michael and Catherine (Scullin) McLaughlin; m. Enda Kieran Ryan, Feb. 8, 1969; children: Denise Marie, Kathleen May. BS in Chemistry, St. John's U., Bklyn., 1959; MD, NYU, 1963. Diplomate Am. Bd. Pediatrics. Cons. Hampton health dept. Va. State Dept. Health, 1969-71; med. coord. N.Y.C. Bur. Handicapped, 1971-72; asst. prof. pediatrics L.I. Coll. Hosp., Bklyn., 1972-73; pub. health clinician Fairfax County Health Dept., Fairfax, Va., 1973—; pvt. contractor pediatrics PHP Health-care Corp., Fairfax, 1987-93. Tchr. religious edn. St. Thomas à Becket Ch., Reston, Va., 1978-81. Maj. M.C., U.S. Army, 1969. Fellow Am. Acad. Pediatrics; mem. AMA, Med. Soc. Va., No. Va. Pediatric Soc., Fairfax County Med. Soc., Soc. Devel. Pediatrics. Avocation: gardening. Home: 1423 Aldenham Ln Reston VA 22090-3903 Office: Fairfax County Health Dept 1850 Cameron Glen Dr Ste 100 Reston VA 22090-3310

RYAN, MARY NELL H., training consultant; b. Milw., Oct. 17, 1956; d. Robert Healey and Elizabeth Anne (Schulte) R.; 1 child, Katharine Scarlett. BA, Marquette U., 1979; MS, U. Wis., Milw., 1991. Tchr. St. Francis Borgia Sch., Cedarburg, Wis., 1979-81; dir. pub. rels. Aerobics West Club, N.Y.C., 1981; unit head, team leader Northwestern Mut. Life Ins. Co., Milw., 1982-84, asst. supr., 1984-86, tng. coord., 1986-87, mgr. tng., 1987-92; tng. cons. for ins. industry Workplace Learning, Inc., Milw., 1992—; cons. Aetna Life and Casualty Co., Hartford, Conn., 1988, Robertson-Ryan & Co., Milw., 1989, Blue Cross/Blue Shield United of Wis., Northwestern Mut. Life Ins. Co., CMI Group, Inc., Homes for Ind. Living, Inc., Aurora Health Care, Literacy Svcs. Wis., Executrain, Inc., Milw. First in Quality, Wis. Quality Network, United Wis. Svcs., Inc., Ameritech, Milw. Art Mus., Blood Ctr. Southeastern Wis., Meretz, Inc., Radiology Assocs. Wis., Deluxe Data, Inc., Portable Solution, Inc., Hewlett-Packard Users Group of Wis., Miller Brewing Co.; guest lectr. U. Wis., Milw., 1989, Milw. Area Tech. Coll., 1990, Marquette U., 1990; speaker confs., developer/trainer workshops. Mem. exec. com. Lakefront Festival Arts, Milw., 1985—, vol. com. chair, silent auction chair; exec. fundraiser United Performing Arts Fund, Milw., 1986; com. chmn. Jr. League Milw., 1983-87; fundraiser YMCA Ptnr. Youth, Milw. 1987-88; tutorHead Start Read with Me program, 1993—. Recipient gold medal Life Communicators Assn., 1987. Mem. ASTD (bd. dirs. Wis. chpt., membership com. 1989-90, chmn. Train Am.'s Workforce and comty. svcs. 1992-94), Milw. Mgmt. Support Orgn. (bd. dirs. 1988), Wis. Ins. Club (spkr.), InRoads (bd. dirs. Wis. chpt.), Phi Kappa Phi. Avocations: reading, tennis, swimming, theatre, travel. Office: Workplace Learning Inc 1426 W Westport Cir Mequon WI 53092-5753

RYAN, MEG, actress; b. Fairfield, Conn., Nov. 19, 1961; m. Dennis Quaid, 1991; 1 child, Jack Henry. Student, NYU. Appearences include (TV) One of the Boys, 1982, As The World Turns, 1982-84, Wild Side, 1985, (films) Rich and Famous, 1981, Amityville 3-D, 1983, Top Gun, 1986, Armed and Dangerous, 1986, Innerspace, 1987, Promised Land, 1987, D.O.A., 1988, The Presidio, 1988, When Harry Met Sally, 1989, Joe Versus the Volcano, 1990, The Doors, 1991, Prelude to a Kiss, 1992, Sleepless in Seattle, 1993, Flesh and Bone, 1993, When a Man Loves a Woman, 1994, Restoration, 1994, I.Q., 1994, French Kiss, 1995, Two for the Road, 1996, Courage Under Fire, 1996; owner Prufrock Pictures movie prodn. co. Recipient Golden Apple award Hollywood Women's Press Club, 1989. Office: care ICM 8942 Wilshire Blvd Beverly Hills CA 90211*

RYAN, MICHAEL BEECHER, lawyer, former government official; b. Chgo., Aug. 20, 1936; s. Walter Joseph and Mary Agnes (Beecher) R.; m. Maria Chantal Wiesman, June 1, 1963; children—Mary, Catherine, Matthew. B.S. in Labor Relations, Manhattan Coll., 1957; J.D., U. Notre Dame, 1964. Bar: N.Y. 1964, Ill. 1991. With NLRB, 1964-91; sr. trial atty. NLRB, Peoria, Ill. region, 1968-74, dep. officer in charge, 1974-78, regional atty., 1978-91; exec. v.p. NLRB Union, 1968-69, pres., 1969-71; mem. Peoria Planning Commn., 1977-89, chmn., 1979-89; sole practice Peoria; adj. prof. labor relations Bradley U., 1972-74. Mem. Tri-County Land Use Adv. Com., 1978-82; Pres. Catholic Interracial Council Peoria, 1971-72, North Sterling Homeowners Assn., 1973-77. Served with AUS, 1958-61, Korea. Mem. Regional Attys. Guild (chmn. 1982-88), Wedgewood Country Club. Roman Catholic. Home: 3438 W Villa Rdg Apt A Peoria IL 61604-1739 also: E-9 Plantation Hale Kapaa Kauai HI 96746

RYAN, MICHAEL LEE, lawyer; b. N.Y.C., Feb. 23, 1951; s. William Francis and Helen (Lee) R.; m. Julia A. Smith, Dec. 1, 1979; children: Matthew, Rachel. BA, Harvard U., 1973; JD, NYU, 1978. Bar: N.Y. 1979, Mass. 1980. Sr. editor E.P Dutton, N.Y.C., 1974-77; assoc. Cleary, Gottlieb, Steen & Hamilton, N.Y.C., 1978-80, 83-86, ptnr., 1986—; assoc. Ropes & Gray, Boston, 1980-82. Articles editor NYU Law Rev., 1977-78. Dir. Pub. Interest Law Found. NYU. Named Urban Fellow Office of Mayor, N.Y.C. 1973. Mem. Order of Coif.

RYAN, MILES FRANCIS, III, lawyer; b. Washington, July 31, 1963; s. Miles Francis Jr. and Vernance Dolores (Beste) R. AB cum laude, Harvard U., 1986; JD, Columbia U., 1990. Bar: Pa. 1991, U.S. Ct. Fed. Claims 1995, U.S. Tax Ct. 1995, U.S. Ct. Appeals for Armed Forces 1995, U.S. Ct. Vets. Appeals 1995, U.S. Supreme Ct. 1995. Staff mem. U.S. Senator William Proxmire, Washington, 1980, 82, 83; intern U.S. Senator Tom Harkin, Washington, 1989; law clerk U.S. Dept. Commerce Office of Gen. Counsel's Honors Program, Washington, 1990-91, atty.-advisor, 1991-92; atty.-advisor U.S. Dept. Commerce Office Gen. Counsel's Office of Chief Counsel for Econ. Affairs, Washington, 1992—; mem. U.S. Dept. Commerce Office of Gen. Counsel's Law Libr. Com., Washington, 1992, 93; key worker U.S. Dept. Commerce's Combined Fed. Campaign, Washington, 1992, 93. Mem. Harvard-Radcliffe Dem. Club, Cambridge, Mass., 1983-86; vol. Joe Kennedy for Congress Campaign, Cambridge, 1986; at-large mem., treas. Columbia U. Law Sch. Student Senate, N.Y.C., 1987-90, 89-90. Jaffin Pub. Interest and Student Funded Fellowship grantee Columbia U. Sch. Law, 1989, John Harvard scholar Harvard U., 1983-86. Mem. ABA, FBA (D.C. chpt., bd. dirs., alt. nat. del., elected sec.), Columbia U. Law Sch. Alumni Assn., Columbia U. Club, Harvard U. Club Washington, KC (local coun. co-comty. activities dir. 1982). Democrat. Roman Catholic. Avocations: reading historical, political and current affairs books and articles, attending public policy and historical lectures, visiting museums, attending the theater and concerts, travel. Home: 12502 Two Farm Dr Silver Spring MD 20904-2931 Office: US Dept Commerce Office Gen Counsel Rm 3077 Fed Bldg 3 Suitland & Silver Hill Rds Suitland MD 20233

RYAN, NOEL, librarian, consultant; b. St. John, N.B., Canada, May 27, 1925; s. Fergus James and Evelyn Grace (Hayes) R.; m. Doreen Lillian Allison, Dec. 19, 1950; children: Colin Allison, Karen Jennifer. B.A., Sir George Williams U., Montreal, 1964; M.L.S., McGill U., 1967; M.B.A., Northland U., Toronto, 1983. Vice-pres. Temco Electric Mfg. Co., Montreal, 1949-57; owner, operator photo finishing co. Local Photo, Montreal, 1957-67; chief librarian Dorval (Que.) Pub. Library, 1967-69, Brampton (Ont.) Pub. Library, 1969-71; chief librarian Mississauga (Ont.) Library System, 1971-87, bldg. projects mgr., 1987-89. Joint author: Juxtaposited, 1974. Served with Can. Army, 1944-46, ETO. Mem. Toronto Black Watch Assn. Avocations: painting, making pots, writing poetry. Home and Office: 55 Falconer Dr Apt 35, Mississauga, ON Canada L5N 1B3

RYAN, NOLAN, former professional baseball player; b. Refugio, Tex., Jan. 31, 1947; s. Lynn Nolan and Martha (Hancock) R.; m. Ruth Elsie Holdruff, June 26, 1967. Student, Alvin (Tex.) Jr. Coll., 1966-69. Pitcher N.Y. Mets, N.Y.C., 1966-71, Calif. Angels, 1972-79, Houston Astros, 1980-88, Texas Rangers, 1989-93; mem. Am. League All-Star Team, 1972, 73, 75, 79, Nat. League All-Star Team, 1981, 85. Author: (with Steve Jacobson) Nolan Ryan: Strike-Out King, 1975, (with Bill Libby) Nolan Ryan: The Other Game, 1977, (with Joe Torre) Pitching and Hitting, 1977, (with Harvey Frommer) Throwing Heat: The Autobiography of Nolan Ryan, 1988, (with Tom House) Nolan Ryan's Pitcher's Bible, 1991, (with Jerry Jenkins) Miracle Man: Nolan Ryan, The Autobiography, 1992, (with others) Kings of Hill, 1992. Served with AUS, 1967. Named Sporting News AL pitcher of yr., 1977. Holds over 50 Major League records including most seasons pitched (27), most strikeouts (5,714) and most no-hit games (7). Address: care Texas Rangers Arlington Stadium PO Box 1111 Arlington TX 76004

RYAN, PATRICK G., insurance company executive; b. Milw., May 15, 1937; m. Shirley Welsh, Apr. 16, 1966; children: Patrick Jr., Robert J., Corbett M. BS, Northwestern U., 1959. Sales agt. Penn Mut., 1959-64; Pat Ryan & Assocs. Penn Mut., Chgo., 1964-71; chmn., pres. Ryan Ins. Group Inc., Chgo., 1971-82; pres., chief exec. officer Combined Internat. Corp. (now Aon Corp.), Northbrook, Ill., 1982—, bd. dirs., 1982—; chmn., pres., chief exec. officer Aon Corp., Chgo., 1990—; bd. dirs. First Chgo., NBD Corp., Chgo. Trustee Rush-Presbyterian-St. Luke's Med. Ctr., Chgo., chmn. bd. trustees; trustee Northwestern U., Field Mus. Natural History, Chgo. Office: Aon Corp 123 N Wacker Dr 30th Flr Chicago IL 60606-1700

RYAN, PATRICK J., electric utility company executive; b. Chgo., July 31, 1938; s. Phillip W. and Estelle F. Ryan; m. Grace M. Marko, Sept. 5, 1959; children: Rachel, Nicole. BS in Elect. Engring., U. Okla. 1961; hon. degree in mgmt. Edison Electric Inst., 1976. Registered profl. engr., Okla Western div. service mgr. Okla. Gas and Electric, Oklahoma City, 1971-73, chief environ. affairs, 1973-76, asst. treas., 1976-78, treas., 1978-80, v.p. and treas., 1980-81, sr. v.p. and treas., 1981-84, exec. v.p. fin. and adminstrn., 1984-86, exec. v.p. and chief oper. officer, 1986-94, vice chmn. 1994—; bd. dirs. St. Anthony Hosp. Found., Inc., ARC, Oklahoma City, 1981-91, Last Frontier coun. Boy Scouts Am., 1985-91, United Way Cen. Okla., Blue Cross and Blue Shield Okla.; bd. visitors Coll. Engring. U. Okla.; bd. dirs. Funds IV, Witicha, Kans. Served with U.S. Army, 1962. Mem. U. Okla. Assocs., Okla. Soc. Profl. Engrs., NSPE, Okla. City C. of C. (bd. dirs.). Republican. Episcopalian. Clubs: Oklahoma City Golf and Country, Petroleum. Office: Okla Gas & Electric Co 101 N Robinson Ave Oklahoma City OK 73102-5504

RYAN, PATRICK MICHAEL, lawyer; b. Chgo., May 26, 1944; s. Edward Michael and Kathleen Teresa (Crimmins) R.; m. Holly Ann Daleske, Aug. 31, 1968; children: Rebecca Eileen, Brendan Patrick, Abigail Christine, Lucas Christopher. BA, St. Mary's Coll., Winona, Minn., 1966; JD, Marquette U., 1969. Bar: Wis. 1969. Law clk. Wis. Supreme Ct., Madison, 1969-70; ptnr. Quarles & Brady, Milw., 1970—; dir. and officer several pvt. bus. corps. Mem. ABA, Wis. Bar Assn., Milw. Bar Assn., University Club. Avocations: reading, sports. Home: 363 Huntington Dr Cedarburg WI 53012-9507 Office: Quarles & Brady 411 E Wisconsin Ave Milwaukee WI 53202-4409

RYAN, RANDEL EDWARD, JR., airline pilot; b. N.Y.C., Jan. 11, 1940; s. Randel Edward and Ann Augusta (Horwath) R.; m. Pamela Michael Wiley, May 12, 1962; children: Katherine, Gregory. BS in Sci., Trinity Coll., 1961. Quality control supr. Ideal Toy Corp., Jamaica, N.Y., 1961-62; airline pilot United Airlines, San Francisco, 1967—. Editor: The Lowdown, 1980-83. Pres., Highlands Community Assn., San Mateo, Calif., 1975; chmn. Com. to Re-elect County Supr., San Mateo, 1976; mediator San Mateo County, 1986-95; arbitrator Better Bus. Bureau, 1988-95; rep. Highlands Community Assn., San Mateo, 1970-86; coach Little League and Babe Ruth Baseball, San Mateo, 1979-83. Served to capt. USAF, 1962-68. Recipient Vandor award San Mateo PTA, 1976, awards of merit United Airlines, San Francisco, 1975, 79. Mem. Air Line Pilots Assn. (chmn. speakers panel 1983-86, community rels com. 1983-86, bd. dirs. 1986-89, 91-93, chmn. coun. 34 1991-93, vice-chmn. 1986-89, editor newspaper The Bayliner 1984-86, mem. contract study com. 1984-86, vice-chmn. MEC grievance com. 1989-91, chmn. MEC grievance rev. 1993—, mem. nat. hearing bd. 1994—).Democrat. Club: Midtown Tennis (Chgo.). Home: 175 N Harbor Dr # 5402 Chicago IL 60601 Office: United Airlines O Hare Internat Airport Chicago IL 60601

RYAN, RAY DARL, JR., academic administrator; b. Joliet, Ill., Dec. 2, 1945; s. Ray D. and Oral Ada (Smiley) R.; m. Marianne Ryan, Aug. 28, 1965; children: Kimberley, Kristin, Matthew. BS, U. Wis., Menomonie, 1970; MEd, U. Mo., 1973, EdD, 1975. Cert. vocat./tech. tchr., adminstr., chief sch. officer. Dep. supt. pub. instrn. Nev. Dept. Edn., Carson City; dep. supt. spl. programs Ariz. Dept. Edn., Phoenix, state dir., vocat. educator; exec. dir. Ctr. Edn. and Tng. for Employment Ohio State U., Columbus, assoc. dean rsch., internat. affairs; vice-chair Coun. Ednl. Devel. and Rsch., bd. dirs.; bd. advisors Marquis Who's Who, New Providence, N.J., rep. at large. Mem. OTT, Am. Vocat. Assn., ASTD, Omicron Tau Theta. Home: 1080 Kirk Ave Columbus OH 43085-2925 Office: Ohio State U Ctr Edn and Tng Employment 1900 Kenny Rd Columbus OH 43210-1016

RYAN, RAYMOND D., retired steel company executive, insurance and marketing firm executive; b. Big Timber, Mont., Feb. 7, 1922; s. Robert Allen and Elsie (Beery) R.; m. Eunice Dale Burnett, Jan. 17, 1943; children: Raymond Brant, Brenda Ruth, Ronald Dale. BA, U. Mont., 1948, JD (hon.), 1970; LLM, NYU, 1949. Bar: Mont. 1948. Tax acct. Geneva Steel, Provo, Utah, 1949-50; tax supr., asst. compt. Orinoco Mining Co., Puerto Ordaz, Venezuela, 1950-58; compt. Oliver Iron Mining Co. div. U.S. Steel, Duluth, Minn., 1958-61; v.p. U.S. Steel, Pitts., 1968-74; v.p. U.S. Steel, Caracas, 1974-75, v.p., treas., 1975-83; pres. The Evergreen Group Inc., Stamford, Conn., 1984-94, chmn., 1995-96. With mil. police AUS, 1943-45, ETO. Mem. ABA, Duquesne Club (Pitts.), Allegheny County Club (Sewickley), Metropolitan Club, Phi Sigma Kappa, Phi Delta Phi. Office: 300 Atlantic St Ste 301 Stamford CT 06901-3522 *Although luck and ambition are the basis of many apparently successful careers, true success comes from hard work, ethical relationships, dedication, and a willingness to accept responsibility.*

RYAN, REGINA CLAIRE (MRS. PAUL DEUTSCHMAN), editor, book packager, literary agent; b. N.Y.C., June 19, 1938; d. Edward F.X. and Kathryn Regina (Gallagher) R.; m. Paul Deutschman, Apr. 11, 1970. B.A., Trinity Coll., 1960; postgrad., New Sch. for Social Research, 1960-61, N.Y. U. Film Sch., 1961, N.Y. U. Grad. Sch. English, 1962-63. Copywriter trainee, sec. J. Walter Thompson Co., N.Y.C., 1960-64; asst. to mng. editor Alfred A. Knopf, Inc., N.Y.C., 1964-67; editor Alfred A. Knopf, Inc., 1967-75; editor-in-chief, v.p. Gen. Books div. Macmillan Pub. Co., N.Y.C., 1975-76; pres. Regina Ryan Pub. Enterprises, Inc., N.Y.C., 1976—. Co-author: Janice LaRouche's Strategies for Women at Work, 1984, 1987. Active Larchmont-Mamaroneck Young Reps., 1960-64; campaign worker, speech writer mayoralty campaign, Larchmont, 1962, 64; mem. Manhattan Women's Polit. Caucus, 1972-74; mem. com. Jimmy Carter Presdl. Campaign; mem., chmn. Sherman Dem. Town Com., 1985-86; Justice of the Peace, Sherman Ct., 1986—; mem. Jewish Cmty. Ctr. for Sherman. Mem. PEN Am. Ctr., Women's Forum (bd. dirs. 1976-77, co-chair issues com. 1990-92), Am. Book Prodrs.' Assn. (pres. 1985-86, dir. 1985-88, 93-96), Women's Media Group, Nat. Women's Health Network, Nat. Abortion Rights Action League, Internat. Women's Com. on Human Rights, Planned Parenthood of Conn., The Mad Gardeners. Democrat. Office: 251 Central Park W New York NY 10024-4134 also: 3 Coburn Rd W Sherman CT 06784-2218

RYAN, RICHARD E., painter; b. London, Feb. 14, 1950; s. Richard E. and Arlene Ryan. BA with distinction, Stanford U., 1972; MFA, Yale U., 1979. Vis. asst. prof. Sch. Art Ind. U., Bloomington, 1979-82; asst. prof. art dept. Vassar Coll., Poughkeepsie, N.Y., 1982-86; artist in residence Queens Coll., U. Melbourne, Australia, 1991-92; assoc. prof. painting and printmaking Yale U. Sch. Art, New Haven, 1986-93, sr. critic painting and printmaking, 1993; adj. faculty Hartford (Conn.) Art Sch., 1994—; instr. Yale U. Summer Sch. Music and Art, Norfolk, Conn., 1985-86, 88, 89, co-dir., 1991-94; vis. artist Amherst Coll, U. Houston, San Francisco Art Inst., U. Pa., Williams Coll., Boston U., Brandeis U., R.I. Sch. Art. Artist, pub.: XXII, 1992; one-man shows include Robert Schoelkopf Gallery, N.Y.C., 1984, 89, Ghirgis and Klymn Gallery, Melbourne, 1992, The Contemporary Realist Gallery, San Francisco, 1994; exhibited in group shows at Aldrich Mus., Ridgefield, Conn., 1977, Alpha Gallery, Boston, 1981, 88, Indpls. Art League, 1981, Depauw U. Art Gallery, Greencastle, Ind., 1982, Vassar Coll. Art Gallery, Poughkeepsie, 1983, Robert Schoelkopf Gallery, N.Y.C., 1984, Aldrich Mus., Ridgefield, 1985, 87, Am. Acad. Arts and Letters, N.Y.C., 1986, Calif. Palace of the Legion of Honor, San Francisco, 1989, Maxwell Davidson Gallery, N.Y.C., 1990, First St. Gallery, N.Y.C., 1991, Sacramento (Calif.) State U., 1991, Wiegand Gallery, 1990, Yale Art Gallery, New Haven, 1993, Littlejohn Steinaur Gallery, N.Y.C., 1994, Eli Marsh Gallery, Amherst (Mass.) Coll., 1994, Fogg Mus. Art, Cambridge, Mass., 1994. Recipient Eli Harwood Schless award for excellence in painting Yale U. Sch. Art, New Haven, 1979, Richard and Hinda Rossenthal Found. award Am. Acad. and Inst. Arts and Letters, N.Y.C., 1986; Ford Found. grantee, 1980, Ingram Merrill Found. grantee in aid, 1985, Louis Comfort Tiffany Found. grantee in aid, 1986, NEA fellowship grantee, 1993. Home: 106 Exchange St New Haven CT 06513

RYAN, ROBERT, consulting company executive; b. Columbus, Ohio, July 25, 1922; s. Howard L. and Jannie Gertrude (McComis) R.; m. Esther Lee Moore, Mar. 15, 1947; children: Phillip Craig, Lynda Joyce, Lois Jean. BS in Indsl. Engring, Ohio State U., 1947. Registered profl. engr., Ohio, Ind. Maintenance foreman Internat. Harvester Co., Richmond, Ind., 1947-52; prin. welding engr. Battelle Meml. Inst., Columbus, 1952-55; dir. engring. Columbia Gas System, Columbus, 1955-67; sr. v.p. Columbia Gas System, Pitts., 1967-73; sr. v.p., dir. Columbia Gas Cos. in, Pa., W.Va., Md., N.Y., 1973-75; dir. Columbia Gas Distbn. Cos., N.Y., Md., Ky., Ohio, W.Va., Va., Ohio Energy and Resource Devel. Agy., 1975-76, Ohio Dept. Energy, 1977-80; mem. Gov.'s Cabinet; pres. Robert S. Ryan & Assocs., 1981—; chmn. bd. dirs. Resource Gen. Corp., Columbus, 1995—. Contbr. articles profl. jours. Served to capt. U.S. Army, 1943-46, Japan. Recipient Disting. Alumnus award Ohio State U. Coll. Engring., 1970. Mem. NSPE, Am. Gas Assn., Pa. Gas Assn. (pres. 1974), Capital Club (Columbus). Republican. Methodist. Avocation: golf. Home: 6566 Plesenton Dr S Columbus OH 43085-2931 Office: Robert S Ryan & Assocs 6566 Plesenton Dr S Columbus OH 43085-2931

RYAN, ROBERT COLLINS, lawyer; b. Evanston, Ill., Sept. 15, 1953; s. Donald Thomas and Patricia J. (Collins) R.; m. Joanne Kay Holata, Nov. 5, 1983. BA in Econs., BSIE with high honors, U. Ill., 1976; JD, Northwestern U., 1979. Bar: Ill. 1979, U.S. Dist. Ct. (no. dist.) Ill. 1980, U.S. Ct. Appeals (Fed. cir.) 1982, U.S. Supreme Ct. 1984. Assoc., Allegretti, Newitt, Witcoff & McAndrews, Ltd., Chgo., 1979-83, ptnr. 1983-88; founding ptnr. McAndrews, Held & Malloy, Ltd., Chgo., 1988—; lectr. engring. law Northwestern U. Tech. Inst., Evanston, Ill., 1981-85, adj. prof. engring. law, 1985-90; lectr. patent law & appellate practice John Marshall Law Sch., 1991-93, adj. prof. patent law & appellate advocacy, 1993—. Exec. editor Northwestern Jour. Internat. Law & Bus., 1978-79. Contbr. articles to profl. jours. James scholar U. Ill., 1976. Mem. ABA, Fed. Cir. Bar Assn., Intellectual Property Law Assn. Chgo., Licensing Execs. Soc., Tau Beta Pi, Phi Eta Sigma, Alpha Pi Mu, Phi Kappa Phi. Home: 61 Hawkins Cir Wheaton IL 60187-8464 Office: McAndrews Held & Malloy Ltd Citicorp Ctr 34th Fl 500 W Madison St Chicago IL 60661-2511

RYAN, ROBERT JOHN, JR., agricultural cooperative executive; b. Boston, July 31, 1944; s. Robert John and Marjorie MacFarland (Collins) R.; m. Linda Marie Villa, Dec. 28, 1968; children—Robert, Melissa. B.S. in Mech. Engring., U. Vt., 1966; M.B.A., Cornell U., 1971. Asst. treas. Agway, Inc., Syracuse, N.Y., 1971-79, treas., 1979-82, v.p., treas., 1982—; dir. Curtice Burns, Inc., Rochester, N.Y., Blue Cross, Syracuse; adv. bd. Marine Midland Bank, Syracuse, 1980—. Pres. Syracuse Boys Club, 1983—. Served to lt. USN, 1967-70, Vietnam. Mem. Fin. Mgmt. Assn. Democrat. Roman Catholic. Avocations: skiing; golf.

RYAN, STEPHEN COLLISTER, funeral director; b. Salina, Kans., Jan. 10, 1942; s. Kenneth Richard and Janys (Collister) R.; m. Lynne Katheryn Slease, June 18, 1966; children: Scott Richard, Carrie Anne. BS in Bus. Adminstrn., U. Kans., 1964; Cert. in Mortuary Sci., Kans. U. Med. Ctr., 1965. Cert. funeral svc. practitioner; lic. funeral dir. and embalmer. Sec.-treas. Ryan Mortuary, Inc., Salina, 1969-80, pres., COO, 1980—. Contbr. articles to profl. jours. Mem., chmn. City Planning Commn., Salina, 1981-85; mem. Salina City Commn., 1985-93, mayor, 1987-88, 91-92; chmn. Govt. Bldg. Authority, Salina, 1990-91, 92-93. Capt. USAF, 1965-69. Mem. Nat. Selected Morticians (bd. dirs. 1993—, pres. 1995—), Nat. Funeral Dirs. Assn. (Spl. Recognition award 1991), Kans. Funeral Dirs. Assn. (bd. dirs. 1984-92, pres. 1990-91), Morticians of the S.W. (Kans. Funeral Dir. of Yr. 1991), Salina Area C. of C. (bd. dirs. 1982-85, 94—, vice chair 1984-85, sec. treas. 1994-95, chmn. 1996—) Lions, Masons (Knight Cmmdrs. Ct. of Honor, 32 KCCH), Shriners, Phi Gamma Delta. Republican. Lutheran. Avocations: golf, nautilus exercise. Home: 2313 Melrose Ln Salina KS 67401-3546 Office: Ryan Mortuary Inc 137 N 8th St Salina KS 67401-2686

RYAN, STEPHEN J., academic dean. Dean U. So. Calif. Sch. Medicine, L.A. Office: U So Calif Sch Medicine 1450 San Pablo St Los Angeles CA 90033

RYAN, STEPHEN JOSEPH, JR., ophthalmology educator, university dean; b. Honolulu, Mar. 20, 1940; s. S.J. and Mildred Elizabeth (Farrer) F.; m. Anne Christine Mullady, Sept. 25, 1965; 1 dau., Patricia Anne. A.B., Providence Coll., 1961; M.D., Johns Hopkins U., 1965. Intern Bellevue Hosp., N.Y.C., 1965-66; resident Wilmer Inst. Ophthalmology, Johns Hopkins Hosp., Balt., 1966-69, chief resident, 1969-70; fellow Armed Force Inst. Pathology, Washington, 1970-71; instr. ophthalmology Johns Hopkins U., Balt., 1970-71, asst. prof., 1971-72, assoc. prof., 1972-74; prof., chmn. dept. ophthalmology Los Angeles County-U. So. Calif. Med. Ctr., L.A., 1974-95, prof. dept. ophthalmology, 1974—; acting head ophthalmology div., dept. surgery Children's Hosp., L.A., 1975-77; med. dir. Doheny Eye Inst. (formerly Estelle Doheny Eye Found.), L.A., 1977-86; chief of staff Doheny Eye Hosp., L.A., 1985-88; dean U. So. Calif. Sch. Medicine, L.A., 1991—; mem. advisory panel Calif. Med. Assn., 1975—. Editor: (with M.D. Andrews) A Survey of Ophthalmology--Manual for Medical Students, 1970, (with R.E. Smith) Selected Topics on the Eye in Systemic Disease, 1974, (with Dawson and Little) Retinal Diseases, 1985, (with others) Retina, 1989; assoc. editor: Ophthalmol. Surgery, 1974-85; mem. editorial bd. Am. Jour. Ophthalmology, 1981—, Internat. Ophthalmology, 1982—, Retina, 1983—, Graefes Archives, 1984—; contbr. articles to med. jours. Recipient cert. of merit AMA, 1971; Louis B. Mayer Scholar award Research to Prevent Blindness, 1973; Rear Adm. William Campbell Chambliss USN award, 1982. Mem. Wilmer Ophthal. Inst. Residents Assn., Am. Acad. Ophthalmology and Otolaryngology (award of Merit 1975), Am. Ophthal. Soc., Pan-Am. Assn. Ophthalmology, Assn. Univ. Profs. of Ophthalmology, L.A. Soc. Ophthalmology, AMA, Calif. Med. Assn., Los Angeles County Med. Assn., Pacific Coast Oto-Ophthal. Soc., L.A. Acad. Medicine, Pan Am. Assn. Microsurgery, Macula Soc, Retina Soc., Nat. Eye Care Project, Rsch. Study Club, Jules Gonin Club, Soc. Scholars of Johns Hopkins U. (life). Office: U So Calif Sch of Medicine 1450 San Pablo St Los Angeles CA 90033

RYAN, STEPHEN MICHAEL, JR., professional hockey team executive; m. Marie Ryan; 1 child. BS, Fordham U., 1964. Br. mgr., sales mgr. Maxwell House divsn. Gen Foods Corp., 1965-72; sr. mgr. Marriott Corp., 1972-75, Am. Brands Corp., 1975-77; v.p., chief mktg. officer Paddington Corp., 1978-81; v.p. mktg. and pub. rels. NHL Enterprises, 1981-86, pres. CEO, 1986-95; pres., COO Pitts. Sports Assocs. Holding Co., 1995—; dir. Hockey Hall of Fame Entertainment Complex, 1990. Creator The NHL TV Awards: A Celebration of Excellence; establisher NHL All-Star Weekend, 1990. Mem. USO World Bd., Washington; nat. bd. dirs. Boys Home, St. Louis; mem. Bus. Coun. for UN and Cardinals's Com. of Laity; past trustee Dominican Coll., Blauvelt, N.Y., chmn. devel. and pub. rels. com. Office: Pitts Penguins Civic Arena Gate No 9 Pittsburgh PA 15219

RYAN, SYLVESTER D., bishop; b. Catalina Island, Calif., Sept. 3, 1930. Grad., St. John's Sem., Camarillo, Calif. Ordained priest Roman Cath. Ch., 1957, titular bishop of Remesiana. Aux. bishop L.A., 1990-92; bishop Monterey, Calif., 1992—. Office: Chancery Office PO Box 2048 580 Fremont St Monterey CA 93940-3216*

RYAN, TERESA WEAVER, obstetrical nurse; b. Dallas, July 18, 1956; d. J.E. and Mary (Davis) Weaver; m. Patrick Hallaron Ryan, Apr. 7, 1991. BS, Troy State U., 1983; BSN, Tex. Christian U., 1987; MSN, U. South Ala., 1994; postgrad., La. State U. RN, Fla.; cert. maternal-newborn nurse ANCC. Intelligence analyst USN, Dallas, 1983-87; enlisted USAF, 1987, advanced through grades to capt. (obstetrical nurse), 1987—; childbirth educator USAF, 1988—. Mem. NOW, Assn. Women's Health, Obstetrical and Neonatal Nurses, Nat. Humane Soc. Educators, People for the Ethical Treatment of Animals, Sigma Theta Tau (sec. 1987—, rsch. grant 1987), Phi Kappa Phi. Roman Catholic. Avocations: aerobics, nursing history, gourmet cooking, animal welfare. Home: 35 Imperial Woods Dr Harahan LA 70123

RYAN, THOMAS F., lawyer; b. Detroit, Nov. 4, 1943. BS, Ferris State U., 1965; JD magna cum laude, Wayne State U., 1971. Bar: Ill. 1972, U.S. Supreme Ct. 1978. Ptnr. Sidley & Austin, Chgo.; mem. adv. com. cir. rules 7th Fed Ct. Appeals. 1st lt. U.S. Army, 1966-68. Mem. Chgo. Bar Assn. (mem. jud. evaluation com.), 7th Cir. Bar Assn. (bd. govs. 1986-89, 2nd v.p. 1990-91, pres. 1991-92). Office: Sidley & Austin 1 First Nat Plz Chicago IL 60603*

RYAN, THOMAS J., lawyer; b. Waltham, Mass., Sept. 10, 1945; s. Joseph H. and Mary (Murphy) R.; m. Margaret Atkins, June 21, 1969. BA, St. Lawrence U., 1968; JD with honors, Suffolk U., 1974; LLM in Trade Regulation, NYU, 1977; PMD, Harvard U. , 1982. Bar: Mass. 1974, N.Y 1975, Wis. 1984. Sales rep. Gen. Foods Corp., New Haven, 1969-71, atty., White Plains, N.Y., 1974-76, sr. atty., 1976-77, counsel, 1977-80, sr. counsel, 1980-83; dir. legal svcs. Oscar Mayer Foods Corp., Madison, Wis., 1983-84, v.p., gen. counsel, sec., 1984-94; v.p., gen. counsel Pillsbury Brands, Mpls., 1994—; bd. dirs. Oscar Mayer Found., Madison, 1984-86; mem. allocations com. Dane County United Way, 1984-88, co-chair, 1987-88, bd. dirs. 1991-94; chmn. legal com. Pet Food Inst., 1978-80; chmn. legal com. Am. Meat Inst., 1987-90. Trustee law alumni Suffolk U., 1982-85; alumni rep., admissions office St. Lawrence U., Canton, N.Y., 1983—; v.p. exec. com., bd. dirs. Madison Repertory Theatre, 1989-94, pres., 1993-94; bd. dirs. Red Cross Dane County, 1991-94, Ronald McDonald House, 1992-94, Children's Theatre Co. of Mpls., 1994—, Greater Mpls. Red Cross, 1995—. Mem. ABA (anti-trust and corp. sects., corp. counseling com., Robinson-Patman com.), Am. Corp. Counsel Assn., Wis. State Bar, Sigma Chi (chpt. trustee 1970-83), Harvard Club of N.Y.C., Madison Club, Mpls. Athletic Club, Wayzata Country Club. Office: The Pillsbury Co 200 S 6th St Minneapolis MN 55402

RYAN, TIMOTHY CHRISTOPHER, anchor, reporter; b. Albany, N.Y., Mar. 7, 1955; s. Donald H. and Maureen (Fitzsimmons) R.; m. Beth Hunt, Oct. 7, 1984; children: Meghan, Patrick. BS in Mass Comm. with honors, Ariz. State U., 1976. Anchor, reporter Sta. KPNX-TV, Phoenix, 1977-81; reporter Sta. KTRK-TV, Houston, 1981-83, Sta. WLS-TV, Chgo., 1983-89; reporter Sta. KDFW-TV, Dallas, 1989-94, anchor, reporter, 1995—; news dir. Sta. KSTU-TV, Salt Lake City, 1994-95. Recipient Chgo. Emmy award, 1988. Mem. Radio-TV News Dir. Assn. (Edward R. Murrow award 1995). Office: Sta KDFW-TV 400 N Griffin Dallas TX 75202

RYAN, TODD MICHAEL, corporate finance consultant; b. Milw., Oct. 8, 1947; s. William George and Virginia Mary (Jurcek) R.; m. Margaret Ellen Schantz, Oct. 7, 1967; 1 child: Jennifer Ann. BA, U. Wis., Milw., 1970, BS, 1971, MSc, 1974. Fin. analyst The Falk Corp., Milw., 1969-74; mgr. sales, services and devel. Miller Brewing Co. div. Philip Morris, Milw., 1974-79; dir. planning Seven-Up div. Philip Morris, St. Louis, 1979-85; ptnr. Arthur Andersen, Chgo., 1985—. Mem. Assn. Corp. Growth, Coun. on Fgn. Rels., Chgo. United, Ducks Unltd., Inc., Halter Wildlife Club, Ruffed Grouse Soc., Mich. Shores Club, Fedn. Fly Fishermen, Univ. Club of Chgo., Angler's Club of Chgo., Pere Marquette Rod and Gun Club. Avocations: fishing, tennis, skiing, hunting, golf. Office: care Arthur Andersen & Co 33 W Monroe St Chicago IL 60603-5302

RYAN, TOM KREUSCH, cartoonist; b. Anderson, Ind., June 6, 1926; s. Francis Gavin and Mary Katherine (Kreusch) Ryan Smith; m. Joanne Faulkner, Dec. 19, 1947; children—Linda, Tim, Dan, Diane. Student, U. Notre Dame, 1945, U. Cin., 1946-47. Artist Del. Engraving Co., Muncie, Ind., 1950-54, Robinson Agy., Muncie, 1954-60; free-lance artist, 1960-65. Author: Best of Tumbleweeds, 1993; syndicated cartoonist Tumbleweeds, Lew Little Syndicate, 1965—; pub. 20 paperback book compilations of strips, 1970-87; created Tumbleweeds Gulch, a sect. MGM Grand Theme Park, Las Vegas. Named Hon. Old Master Purdue U., 1978. Mem. Nat. Cartoonists Soc. (Outstanding Cartoonist cert. 1970, 80), Graphic Artists Guild. Roman Catholic.

RYAN, WILLIAM FRANCIS, priest; b. Renfrew, Ont., Can., Apr. 4, 1925; s. William Patrick Ryan and Helen Mary Doneg. BA, Montreal U., 1951; MA in Labor Rels., St. Louis U., 1953; postgrad., Heythrop Coll., Oxon, Eng.; STL, St. Albert Coll., Louvain, 1958; PhD in Econs., Harvard U., 1964. Ordained priest Roman Catholic Ch., 1957. Asst. prof. econs. Loyola Coll., Montreal, Que., Can., 1963-65; nat. dir. Social Justice Office Can. Conf. Cath. Bishops, Ottawa, Ont., 1964-70, gen. sec., 1984-90; founding dir. Ctr. of Concern, Washington, 1970-78; nat. supr. Jesuit Order, Toronto, Ont., Can., 1978-84; chancellor Sch. Theology Regis Coll., Toronto, 1978-84; vis. sr. rsch. fellow Can. Inst. for Internat. Peace and Security, Ottawa, 1990-91; chair on Cath. social thought St. Paul U., Ottawa, 1991-92; dir. Jesuit Project on Ethics in Politics, Ottawa, 1992—; exec. sec. Inter-religious Peace Colloquium, Washington, 1975-78; bd. dirs. Roncalli Internat. Found., Montreal, 1979-83, North/South Inst., Ottawa, 1979-91; spl. advisor to Internat. Devel. Rsch. Ctr., Ottawa, 1993—; lectr. in field. Author: The Clergy and Economic Growth in Quebec, 1966, Culture, Spirituality and Economic Development—Opening a Dialogue, 1995; co-author: Religious as Contemplatives in the 80's, 1984; translator: The Primacy of Charity in Moral Theology, 1961; contbr. articles to profl. jours. Mem. Am. Econs. Assn. Avocations: hiking; skiing. Office: 169 Sunnyside Ave, Ottawa, ON Canada K1S 0R2

RYAN, WILLIAM J., bank executive; b. 1943. With All Allstate, White Plains, N.Y., 1964-72, Essex Bank, Peabody, Mass., 1973-82, Bank New Eng. Corp., 1982-89; with People's Heritage Bank, Portland, Maine, 1989-90, pres., CEO, 1990—. Office: Peoples Heritage Fin Group 1 Portland Sq Portland ME 04101-4057*

RYAN, WILLIAM JOSEPH, communications company executive; b. Nyack, N.Y., Apr. 14, 1932; s. William Joseph and Elizabeth (Langley) R.; m. Jane Householder, June 27, 1970; children: Ashley Allison, William Joseph, III. BA, U. Notre Dame, 1954. TV producer Jules Power Prodn., Chgo., 1954-56; pres., gen. mgr. Radio Naples, Naples, Fla., 1956-70; gen. mgr. Radio Naples (Fla.) div. Palmer Broadcasting, 1970-73; v.p., cable-radio Palmer Broadcasting, Fla. and Calif., 1973-80; v.p. cable Palmer Communications, Naples, 1980-82; pres. Palmer Communications, Inc., Des Moines, 1982-84, pres., chief exec. officer, 1984-95; pres. CEO Palmer Wireless Inc., 1995—; bd. dirs. Norwest Bank, Des Moines, C&S Bank, Ft. Myers, Fla., Naples Cmty. Hosp. State committeeman Rep. Com., Collier County, Fla., 1970-72; pres. Navy League, Naples, local chpt. Am. Cancer Soc.; chmn. Collier County Econ. Devel. Coun.; bd. dirs. Philharm. Ctr. Arts, Naples Philharm., N. Collier Hosp. Recipient Walter Kaitz award Nat. Cable TV Assn. Mem. Cable Advt. Bur. (founding chmn., bd. dirs.), Econ. Develop. Coun. (chmn.), So. Cable Assn. (pres.), Fla. Cable Assn. (pres.), Fla. Assn. Broadcasters (pres.), Cable TV Pioneers, Broadcast Pioneers, Cable TV Adminstrn. and Mktg. Soc. (Grand Tammy award 1981), Cellular Telephone Industry Assn. (bd. dirs.), Naples C. of C. (pres.), Royal Poinciana Club, Rotary, KC (grand knight). Office: Palmer Comm Inc 12800 University Dr Ste 500 Fort Myers FL 33907-5337

RYAN, WILLIAM MATTHEW, state legislator, safety educator; b. Great Falls, Mont., June 28, 1955; s. William Duncan and Jeanette Rosette (Merrill) R.; m. Elaine Louise Brastrup, Jan. 19, 1974; children: Jennifer, Kelli, Katie. Grad., Great Falls. Cert. journeyman, lineman. Meter reader Mont. Power Co., Great Falls, 1973, head meter reader, 1974, dispatcher, 1975, groundman, 1976-79, apprentice, 1979-82, lineman, 1982—; mem. Ho. of Reps. Mont. State Legislature, Helena, 1993—; instr. Mont. Power Apprentice Program, 1982—. Recipient Medal of Valor State of Mont., 1995. Mem. NAACP, Internat. Brotherhood Elec. Workers (local 44, unit v.p. 1984—, officer exam bd. 1988—, sec. Joint Apprenticeship Tng. Com. 1988—), Rocky Mountain Coord. Assn., Russell Country Sportsman, Walleyes Unlimited. Democrat. Roman Catholic. Avocations: rose gardening, fishing, hunting, youth coach. Home: 8 18th Ave S Great Falls MT 59405-4113 Office: Montana Electric Coop Assoc 501 Bay Dr Po Box 59403 Great Falls MT 59404-2880

RYAN-JOHNSON, DEBORAH, principal. Prin. West Ridge Elem. Sch., Greece, N.Y. Office: West Ridge Elem Sch 200 Alcott Rd Greece NY 14626-2424

RYANS, YVONNE, principal. Prin. Richland High Sch., Wash., 1994—. Office: Richland High Sch 930 Long Ave Richland WA 99352-3311

RYBAK, JAMES PATRICK, engineering educator; b. Cleve., Mar. 16, 1941; s. John Anthony and Irene Marcella (Kovar) R.; m. Linda Louise Watkins, Oct. 12, 1968. BSEE, Case Western Res. U., 1963; MS, U. N.Mex., 1965; PhD, Colo. State U., 1970. Registered profl. engr., Colo. Mem. tech. staff Sandia Nat. Labs., Albuquerque, 1963-66; rsch. asst., NDEA fellow Colo. State U., Ft. Collins, 1966-70, postdoctoral fellow, 1970-72; prof. engring. and math. Mesa State Coll., Grand Junction, Colo., 1972—, asst. v.p. acad. affairs, 1986-88, v.p. acad. affairs, 1988—. Contbr. articles to profl. publs. including IEEE Transactions, Engring. Edn., Popular Electronics. Mem. adv. bd. Grand Mesa Youth Svcs., Grand Junction, 1986-88; bd. dirs. Hilltop Rehab. Hosp., Grand Junction, 1989-93, Salvation Army, Grand Junction, 1993—. NEDA fellow, 1968-70, THEMIS fellow, 1970-72. Mem. IEEE, Am. Soc. Engring. Edn. (vice chmn. Rocky Mountain sect. 1974-75, chmn. 1975-76). Avocation: amateur radio. Home: 314 Quail Dr Grand Junction CO 81503 Office: Mesa State Coll 1175 Texas Ave Grand Junction CO 81501

RYBCZYNSKI, WITOLD MARIAN, architect, educator, writer; b. Edinburgh, Scotland, Mar. 1, 1943; emigrated to Can., 1953; s. Witold Kasimir and Anna Jadwiga (Hofman) R.; m. Shirley Hallam, Nov. 15, 1974. Diploma, Loyola Coll., Montreal, 1960; B.Arch., McGill U., 1966, M.Arch., 1972. Pvt. practice architecture Montreal, 1970-82; research assoc. McGill U., Montreal, 1972-75, asst. prof. architecture, 1975-80, assoc. prof., 1980-86, prof., 1986-93; Meyerson prof. of Urbanism U. Pa., 1994—; cons. UN, Manila, 1976, Internat. Devel. Research Ctr., Ottawa, 1977, Banco de Mex., 1979-80. Author: Paper Heroes: A Review of Appropriate Technology, 1980, Taming the Tiger: The Struggle to Control Technology, 1983, Home: A Short History of an Idea, 1986, The Most Beautiful House in the World, 1989, Waiting for the Weekend, 1991, Looking Around: A Journey Through Architecture, 1992, A Place for Art, 1993, City Life, 1995; contbg. editor: Saturday Night, 1990—; adv. bd. Encyclopedia Americana. Recipient QSPELL lit. prize for nonfiction, 1988, 89, Prix Paul-Henri Lapointe, 1988, Progressive Architecture Design award, 1991, Alfred Jurzykowski Found. award, 1993; Ballard Real Estate scholar, 1994-95.

Fellow AIA (hon.); mem. Authors Guild. Home: 230 Rex Ave Philadelphia PA 19118-3719 Office: Grad Sch Fine Arts U Pa 215 Meyerson Hall Philadelphia PA 19104

RYBURN, SAMUEL MCCHESNEY, marketing executive; b. Morristown, Tenn., Oct. 25, 1914; s. Samuel McChesney and Mary Belle (Whittaker) R.; m. Margaret Beverly Huse, June 5, 1943; children: John Huse, Marie DuPlessis. B.S., U. Ala., 1936; postgrad., U. Vienna, Austria, 1937-38; M.B.A., Boston Coll., 1962. Vice pres. Boston Capital Corp., 1960-72; v.p. Urban Nat. Corp., Boston, 1972-73, Am. Research and Devel. Co., Boston, 1973-77; pres. Textron Adv. Group Inc., Providence, 1977-80; advisor Egypt-Sudan Integration Fund, Cairo, 1985; advisor FocoInsa S.A., Guadalajara, Mexico, 1982, Consomado S.A. Panama, 1984, Mohammad Ali Habib Group, Karachi, Pakistan, 1986, Capital Markets Authority Govt. of Egypt, 1987, agy. for investment and free zones Govt. of Egypt, 1988, Phatra Thanakit Co. Ltd., Bangkok, 1988-89, Kenya Capital Corp., 1989, Adv. Jamaica Capital Corp., 1992. Pres. bd. trustees Charles River Sch., Dover, Mass., 1961-64; trustee Hale Reservation, Boston, 1963-69; v.p. Dover Found., 1965-67, Nat. Inst. Campus Ministries, Boston, 1980-81. Lt. comdr. USN, 1941-45, PTO. Recipient Gamma Sigma Epsilon award, Internat. Scholarship award. Mem. Am. Chem. Soc., Nat. Venture Capital Assn., Am. Rock Garden Soc. (chmn. New Eng. chpt.), Phi Gamma Delta. Roman Catholic. Clubs: Dedham Country and Polo, Marshall St. Hist. Home: 33 Wilsondale St Dover MA 02030-2260

RYCE, DONALD THEODORE, lawyer; b. New Orleans, Dec. 15, 1943; s. Donald Theodore and Martha (Herndon) R.; m. Claudine Dianne Walker, July 8, 1984; children: Ted, Martha, Jimmy. BA, U. Fla., 1966, JD, 1968. Bar: Fla. 1968, U.S. Dist. Ct. (so. dist.) Fla. 1972, U.S. Ct. Appeals (5th and 11th cirs.) 1973; approved arbitrator Broward County Sheriff's Office. Jud. law clk. Fla. Dist. Ct. Appeals (4th cir.), West Palm Beach, 1968-70; ptnr. Hogg, Allen, Ryce, Norton & Blue, Miami, Fla., 1970-89; pvt. practice Miami, 1989—; co-chmn. liaison com. labor and employment sect. NLRB, Fla., 1990—, mem. publs. com., 1990—, exec. coun. labor and employment sect. Mem. Fla. Police Chiefs Edn. Rsch. Found. (Leadership award 1993). Mem. ABA, Miami Rotary Club, Microcomputer Edn. for Employment of the Disabled (bus. adv. coun.), Winter Haven C. of C. (Cmty. Leadership award 1994). Episcopalian. Avocations: tennis, gourmet cooking. Home: 23700 SW 162nd Ave Homestead FL 33031-1310 Office: Seacoast Towers Ste 1036 5151 Collins Ave Miami FL 33140

RYCHETSKY, STEVE, civil and environmental engineer, consultant; b. Phoenix, Oct. 9, 1951; s. Edward and Maria (Zabroni) R.; m. Dawna Marie Strunk, June 10, 1972 (div. Oct. 1985); children: Brian, Melissa; m. Michaele Ann Turner, Dec. 28, 1986; children: Mike, Kristi, Jaye, Karly. AA in Engring., Oreg. Inst. Tech., 1972, BTech, 1976. Registered profl. civil engr., Oreg., Calif. Mgr. sales engring. Varcopruden, Turlock, Calif., 1976-79, AMCA Internat., Winston-Salem, N.C., 1979-82; civil engr. USDA Natural Resources Conservation Svc., Klamath Falls, Oreg., 1983-85; tech. advisor USDA Soil Conservation Service, Klamath Falls, Oreg., 1983-88; civil engr., tech. advisor USDA Natural Resources Conservation Svc., Tillamook, Oreg., 1985—; private cons. engr. Tillamook, Oreg., 1985—. Active vol. cons. svcs. for environ. handicapped and children projects. Democrat. Roman Catholic. Avocation: outdoor activities. Home: PO Box 1457 Redmond OR 97756 Office: USDA Nat Resources Cons Svc Ste A-3 20350 Empire Ave Bend OR 97701

RYCHLAK, JOSEPH FRANK, psychology educator, theoretician; b. Cudahy, Wis., Dec. 17, 1928; s. Joseph Walter and Helen Mary (Bieniek) R.; m. Lenora Pearl Smith, June 16, 1956; children: Ronald, Stephanie. B.S., U. Wis., 1953; M.A., Ohio State U., 1954, Ph.D., 1957. Diplomate Am. Bd. Examiners in Profl. Psychology. Asst. prof. psychology Fla. State U., Tallahassee, 1957-58, Washington State U., Pullman, 1958-61; assoc. prof., then prof. psychology St. Louis U., 1961-69; prof. psychology Purdue U., West Lafayette, Ind., 1969-83, interim dept. head, 1979-80; prof. Loyola U. Chgo., 1983—, Maude C. Clarke prof. humanistic psychology, 1983—; dir. Human Relations Ctr., Pullman, Wash., 1958-61; research cons. AT&T, 1957-82. Author: The Psychology of Rigorous Humanism, 1977, 2d edit., 1988, Discovering Free Will and Personal Responsibility, 1979, A Philosophy of Science for Personality Theory, 2d edit., 1981, Personality and Life Style of Young Male Managers, 1982, (with N. Cameron) Personality Development and Psychopathology, 2d edit., 1985, Artificial Intelligence and Human Reason: A Teleological Critique, 1991; assoc. editor Psychotherapy: Theory, Research and Practice, 1965-76, Jour. Mind and Behavior, 1985-94, Logical Learning Theory: A Human Teleology and Its Empirical Support, 1994. With USAF, 1946-49. Named Outstanding Contbr. to Human Understanding, Internat. Assn. Social Psychiatry, 1971. Fellow Am. Psychol. Assn. (div. 24 pres. 1977-78, 86-87), Am. Psychol. Soc.; mem. Soc. Personality Assessment, Phi Beta Kappa. Roman Catholic. Home: 916 Michigan Ave Apt 2 Evanston IL 60202-1463 Office: Loyola U Chgo Dept Psychology 6525 N Sheridan Rd Chicago IL 60626-5311 *From my father I learned to have a sense of purpose, work hard, and assume responsibility. From my mother I learned not to take myself too seriously, and to realize that my achievements are never entirely up to me.*

RYCKMAN, DEVERE WELLINGTON, consulting environmental engineer; b. South Boardman, Mich., May 27, 1924; s. Seymour Willard and LaVerne Eliza (Jenkins) R.; m. Betty Jane Rendall, May 28, 1949; children—Mark, Jill, Stewart. Student, U. Maine at Orono, 1941-43; B.S. in Civil Engring, Rensselaer Poly. Inst., 1944; M.S. in Civil Engring, Mich. State U., 1949; Sc.D., Mass. Inst. Tech., 1956. Diplomate: Am. Acad. Environ. Engrs. Cons. san. engr. Frank R. Theroux & Assos., East Lansing, Mich., 1946-53; environ. engr., research asst. Mass. Inst. Tech., 1953-56; A.P. Greensfelder prof. environ. engring. Washington U., St. Louis, 1956-69; founder, pres. Ryckman/Edgerley/Tomlinson & Assocs., St. Louis, 1956-75; pres., dir. Reta/Nolte & Assocs., San Francisco, 1974-76; founder, mem. bd. dirs. D.W. Ryckman & Assocs., St. Louis, 1975—; also Ryckman's Emergency Action and Cons. Team (REACT); asst. prof. Mich. State U., 1946-53; vis. prof. U. Hawaii, Honolulu, 1962-63; pres., dir. Environ. Triple S Co., St. Louis, 1969-75. Contbr. articles to profl. jours. Mem., dir. Mo. Gov.'s Sci. Adv. Bd., 1959-66; mem. Washington Arch. and Engrs. Pub. Affairs Conf., 1969-75; founder grad. program environ. engring. Washington U.; mem. adv. bd. Salvation Army, 1987—; bd. dirs. Ctr. for Biology, Washington U., 1964-70, Arts and Edn. Fund, St. Louis, 1970-75; chmn. Salvation Army Bequest & Endowment Fund, 1991—; mem. U.S. EPA Rsch. Rev. Bd. With USNR, 1944-46, capt. USPHS Res., 1946—. Mem. ASCE (Profl. Recognition award 1991), MIT Alumni (dir. leadership fund 1970-74), Am. Water Works Assn. (Man of Yr. 1965), Engrs. Club St. Louis (award of merit 1970, Hon. Mem. award 1993), Cons. Engring. Coun. U.S. (Grand Conceptor award for excellence in design 1969), Cons. Engrs. Coun. Mo. (dir. 1971-75, pres. 1973-75), Nat. Soc. Profl. Engrs., Air Pollution Control Assn., Water Environment Fedn., Assn. Environ. Engring. Profls., Sigma Xi, Tau Beta Pi, Chi Epsilon, Lambda Chi Alpha. Republican. Congregationalist (chmn. exec. com., bd. deacons, bd. Christian edn. 1960-72, chmn. stewardship campaign 1992-93). Clubs: Washington U. Century, Masons, Shriners, Rotary (mem. program and membership coms.). Patentee in field. Address: 1733 S Vandeventer Saint Louis MO 63110

RYCROFT, DONALD CAHILL, insurance executive; b. Chgo., Jan. 3, 1938; s. Ernest C. and Helen C. (Cahill) R.; m. Sabina Bielawski; children—Deborah, Laura, Taylor, Elliot. B.S., Northwestern U., 1960. Chartered financial analyst. Sales rep. Penn Mut. Life Ins. Co., Chgo., 1960-62; investment analyst Continental Assurance Co., Chgo., 1962-67; asst. treas. Continental Assurance Co., 1967-70, treas., 1970-75, v.p., dir. investments, 1973—; also chmn. com. for separate account B; asst. treas. Continental Casualty Co., 1967—; v.p., dir. in investments, 1973—; treas. Valley Forge Life Ins. Co., 1970-75; pres., dir. CNA Income Shares Inc.; sr. v.p., treas. Continental Assurance and Continental Casualty Co., Chgo., 1993—. Alumni adviser Phi Delta Theta, Northwestern U., 1965-70. Served with U.S. Army, 1961. Mem. Transp. Securities Club of Chgo. (past pres.), Investment Analysts Soc. Chgo., Sunset Ridge Country Club (Winnetka, Ill.). Home: 1133 Taylorsport Ln Winnetka IL 60093-1543 Office: Continental Assurance Co CNA Plz Chicago IL 60685

RYCUS, MITCHELL JULIAN, urban planning educator, urban security and energy planning consultant; b. Detroit, June 20, 1932; s. Samuel Israel and Esther (Mitnick) R.; m. Carole Ann Lepofsky, Aug. 31, 1958; children: Lisa Karen Rycus Mikalonis, Peter Todd. BS in Math., U. Mich., 1958, MS in Math., 1961, MS in Physics, 1965, PhD in Urban and Regional Planning, 1976. Asst. rsch. scientist radiation lab. U. Mich., Ann Arbor, 1958-61, pvt. cons. extension gaming svc., 1972-77, rsch. assoc. Mental Health Rsch. Inst., 1977-80; asst. prof. Coll. Architecture and Urban Planning, Ann Arbor, 1980-83; assoc. prof. U. Mich., Ann Arbor, 1983-86; chmn. Coll. Architecture and Urban Planning, Ann Arbor, 1986-92; prof. Coll. Architecture and Urban Planning, 1989—; co-dir. Studies in Urban Security Group U. Mich., Ann Arbor, 1985—; mathematician Bendix Corp. & Rocketdyne, Ann Arbor, 1961-62; group scientist Conductron Corp., Ann Arbor, 1962-70; project assoc. Mich. State C. of C., Lansing, 1970-72; cons. Community Systems Found., Ann Arbor, 1985—. Contbr. rsch. reports, articles. Advisor assessment com. United Way of Washtenaw County, Ann Arbor, 1988-89. With USN, 1950-54. Recipient Faculty Recognition award U. Mich., 1982-83. Mem. AAAS, Am. Planning Assn. Democrat. Jewish. Avocation: computer applications to planning. Office: U Mich Coll Architecture & Urban Planning Ann Arbor MI 48109-2069

RYDELL, AMNELL ROY, artist, landscape architect; b. Mpls., Sept. 17, 1915; s. John S. and Josephine Henrietta (King) R.; m. Frances Cooksey, Jan. 24, 1942. BFA, U. So. Calif., 1937; postgrad., Atelier 17, Paris, 1938, U. Calif., Berkeley, 1939-40, U. Calif., Santa Cruz, 1988. Instr. engring. Douglas Aircraft, El Segundo, Calif., 1940-46; ind. artist, designer San Francisco, 1946-48; ind. artist, designer Santa Cruz, 1948—, ind. landscape architect, 1958-91. Author, cons.: Low Maintenance Gardening, 1974; restoration design Sesnon House Garden Cabrillo Coll., 1995. Pres. Santa Cruz Hist. Soc., 1978-79, Rural Bonny Doon Assn., 1955-56, Santa Cruz Orgn. for Progress and Euthenics, 1977-78; mem. vision bd. City of Santa Cruz, 1991-92; mem. task force Ctr. for Art and History, 1986-94; bd. dirs. Santa Cruz Hist. Trust, 1978-94, Art Mus. Santa Cruz County, 1982-94; donor advisor Roy and Frances Rydell Visual Arts Fund, Greater Santa Cruz County Cmty. Found.; archivist pers. hist. archives, spl. collections Libr. U. Calif., Santa Cruz. Mem. Am. Soc. Landscape Architects (emeritus), William James Assn. (vice chair bd. 1979-95, chair 1995-96), Art Forum (chair 1983-90), Art League (Disting. Artist 1996), Friends of Sesnon Gallery U. Calif., Santa Cruz. Avocation: gardening. Home: 201 Pine Flat Rd Santa Cruz CA 95060-9708

RYDELL, MARK, film director, producer, actor; b. N.Y.C., Mar. 23; s. Sidney and Evelyn R.; children: Christopher, Amy. Student, NYU, The Julliard Sch. Bd. dirs. Actors Studio. Actor TV series As the World Turns, play Seagulls Over Sorrento, films Crime in the Streets, The Long Goodbye; dir. motion pictures The Fox, 1968, The Reivers, 1970; producer, dir.: motion pictures The Cowboys, 1972, Cinderella Liberty, 1974; dir. motion pictures Harry and Walter Go to N.Y., 1976, The Rose, 1979, On Golden Pond, 1980 (nominated for Acad. award for best dir.), The River, 1984, For the Boys, 1991, Intersection, 1993; producer: The Man in the Moon, 1991. Mem. Dirs. Guild Am. Office: Concourse Prodns Formosa Bldg 3110 Main St Ste 220 Santa Monica CA 90405-5353 also: ICM 8942 Wilshire Blvd Beverly Hills CA 90211

RYDEN, JOHN GRAHAM, publishing executive; b. N.Y.C., Dec. 19, 1939; s. Albert Graham and Margaret Keating (Bastable) R.; m. Barbara Dee Kelly, June 19, 1962; children: Linda, Patricia. A.B., Harvard U., 1961. Sales rep. McGraw-Hill Book Co., 1965-68; editor coll. dept. Harper & Row, 1968-71, editor in chief coll. dept., 1971-74; editor in chief, asst. dir. U. Chgo. Press, 1974-78, assoc. dir., 1978-79; dir. Yale U. Press, New Haven, 1979—; chmn. bd. trustees Yale Univ. Press, London, 1981—; mem. adminstr. bd. The Papers of Benjamin Franklin, 1979—; chmn. adv. bd. Beacon Press, 1983—. Mem. editl. bd. Public Historian, 1980-86, Scholarly Publishing, 1992-95, The Yale Editions of the Private Papers of James Boswell, 1993—; adv. bd. The Yale Review, 1992—. Trustee Orch. New Eng., 1980—, pres., 1983-86, chmn., 1995—; bd. dirs. Fund for Free Expression, 1990—; mem. Helsinki Watch Com., 1992—. With USNR, 1962-65. Berkeley Coll. fellow Yale U. Mem. Assn. Am. Publs. (bd. dirs. 1990-94), Assn. Am. U. Presses (bd. dirs. 1980-83, 87-90, pres. 1988-89), Conn. Acad. Arts and Scis., Internat. Assn. Scholarly Pubs., Grads. Club, New Haven Lawn Club, Hasty Pudding Club (Cambridge, Mass.), Yale Club (N.Y.C.), Century Assn. (N.Y.C.). Office: Yale Univ Press PO Box 209040 New Haven CT 06520-9040 also: Yale U Press 302 Temple St New Haven CT 06511-6601

RYDER, DAVID R., lawyer; b. Hinsdale, Ill., Oct. 8, 1946. BA, DePauw U., 1968; JD, U. Mich., 1971. Bar: Ill. 1971, Fla. 1977. Ptnr. McDermott, Will & Emery, Chgo. Mem. Ill. State Bar Assn., Fla. Bar. Office: McDermott Will & Emery 227 W Monroe St Fl 57 Chicago IL 60606-5016*

RYDER, GENE ED, retired United States Air Force training administrator; b. Canyon, Tex., Sept. 19, 1932; s. Johnny Allen and Rilda (New) R.; m. Mary Louise Wilson, Feb. 16, 1958; children: Carlyn, Katherine, Anita, Valerie. BA in Govt. cum laude, St. Mary's U., 1965; MEd, Our Lady of the Lake U., 1968; PhD in Adminstrn., The Union Inst., 1979. Instr. USAF, Scott, Keesler & Lackland AFB, 1958-65; tng. specialist USAF, Lackland AFB, Tex., 1965-69, tng. evaluator, 1969-72, curriculum coord., 1972-75, supr. curriculum devel., 1975-78, supr. tng. evaluation, 1978-83, tng. advisor, 1983-92; chief tng. policy USAF, Randolph AFB, Tex., 1992-95; ret., 1995; chmn. affiliated schs. adv. panel C.C. of Air Force, Maxwell AFB, Ala., 1984-88; co-chmn. USAF Tng. and Instrnl. Sys. Career Program, Randolph AFB, 1992-95; apptd. to Tex. State Bd. Profl. Counselors, 1995—. Author: Basics of Sunday School Leadership: A Guide for Lay Leaders, 1982. Dir. edn. Calvary Hills Bapt. Ch., San Antonio, 1981-94; coord. state scripture Gideons Internat., Nashville, 1991-94; elected mem. Tex. State Rep. Exec. Com., 1994—. With USAF, 1953-56. Mem. Phi Delta Kappa. Home: 1502 Copperfield Rd San Antonio TX 78251-3324

RYDER, GEORGIA ATKINS, university dean, educator; b. Newport News, Va., Jan. 30, 1924; d. Benjamin Franklin and Mary Lou (Carter) Atkins; m. Noah Francis Ryder, Sept. 16, 1947; children: Olive Diana, Malcolm Eliot, Aleta Renee. B.S., Hampton (Va.) Inst., 1944; Mus.M., U. Mich., 1946; Ph.D., NYU, 1970. Resource music tchr., Alexandria, Va., 1945-48; faculty music dept. Norfolk State U., 1948—, prof., 1970—, head dept., 1969-79, dean Sch. Arts and Letters, 1979-86. Contbr. articles to profl. jours, contbr. chpts. to books. Trustee Va. Symphony, Va. Wesleyan Coll.; bd. dirs. Black Music Rsch. Ctr., Columbia Coll., Chgo., Nat. Assn. Negro Musicians, Southeastern Va. Arts Assn.; mem. advisory com. Norfolk chpt. Young Audiences, Va. Coalition for Mus. Edn., Gordon Inst. Music Learning, Temple U. Grantee So. Fellowship Fund, 1967-69, Consortium Rsch. Tng., 1973; recipient Norfolk Com. Improvement Edn. award, 1974, People's Acad. of Arts award, 1985, City of Norfolk award, 1989, Nat. Assn. Negro Musicians award, 1989, Nat. Conf. Christians and Jews award, 1990, Va. Laureate in Music award, 1992, Cultural Alliance award Greater Hampton Roads, 1992, Disting Alumni award Hampton U., 1993, Norfolk State U. Alumni. award, 1994, MECA Found. award, 1995. Mem. Music Educators Nat. Conf., Coll. Music Soc., Intercoll. Music Assn., Va. Music Educators Assn., Delta Sigma Theta.

RYDER, HARL EDGAR, economist, educator; b. Mt. Vernon, Ill., July 11, 1938; s. Harl Edgar and Pearl (Kirkpatrick) R.; m. Mary Irene Kingsolver, June 30, 1970; children—Jonathan Harl, David Eugene, Benjamin James. A.A., Mt. Vernon Community Coll., 1958; B.A., U. Ill., 1960, M.S., 1961; Ph.D., Stanford U., 1967. Asst. prof. econs. Brown U., Providence, 1965-69; assoc. prof. Brown U., 1969-73, prof., 1973—, chmn. dept. econs., 1974-81. Mem. Am. Econ. Assn., Econometric Soc. Office: Brown Univ Dept Econs 79 Waterman St Providence RI 02912-9079

RYDER, HENRY C(LAY), lawyer; b. Lafayette, Ind., Feb. 18, 1928; s. Raymond Robert and Mina Elizabeth (Arnold) R.; m. Ann Sater Clay, Nov. 29, 1952 (dec.); children: David C., Sarah Paige Hugon, Anne M.; m. Velma Iris Dean, Aug. 27, 1976. BS, Purdue U., 1948; LLB, U. Mich., 1951. Bar: Mich. 1951, Ind. 1952, U.S. Dist. Ct. (so. dist.) Ind. 1953, U.S. Ct. Appeals (7th cir.) 1957, U.S. Supreme Ct. 1981. Assoc. Buschmann, Krieg, DeVault & Alexander, Indpls., 1953-57, ptnr., 1957-60; ptnr. Roberts & Ryder and successor firms, Indpls., 1960-86, of counsel, 1996—; ptnr. Barnes & Thornburg (merger), Indpls., 1987-95, of counsel, 1996—; bd. dirs. Peoples Bank and Trust Co., Idpls., 1985—. Pres. Ind. State Symphony Soc. Inc., 1979-82, bd. dirs., 1972-91, trustee, 1991—; chmn. United Way of Greater Indpls., 1984; vice chmn. Greater Indpls. Progress Com., 1979-86, chmn., 1987-89, mem. exec. com., 1979—; trustee Purdue U., 1983-89, Hanover Coll., 1979, chmn., 1988—; bd. dirs. Hist. Landmark Found. of Ind., 1985-96, chmn., 1992-95; bd. dirs. Purdue Rsch. Found., 1992—; hon. v.p. Ind. Soc. Chgo. Lt. U.S. Army, 1951-53. 'ecipient Jefferson award Indpls. Star, 1983, Whistler award Greater Indpls. Progress Com., 1989; named Man of Yr., B'nai B'rith Soc., 1984. Fellow Am. Bar Found., Ind. Bar Found.; mem. ABA, Ind. Bar Assn., Indpls. Bar Assn., Purdue U. Alumni Assn. (pres. 1975-77, Alumni Svc. award 1982, Citizenship award 1989), Ind. C. of C. (bd. dirs. 1991-94), Lawyers Club (pres. Indpls. 1966), U.s. Automobile Club (sec., bd. dirs., Pres.'s award 1989), USAC Properties (sec., bd. dirs.), Columbia Club (bd. dirs. 1987-90, sec. 1988, pres. Found. 1990-95, Benjamin Harrison award 1983), Kiwanis (pres. Indpls. 1983, Civic award 1981). Republican. Presbyterian. Office: Barnes & Thornburg 1313 Merchants Bank Bldg 11 S Meridian St Indianapolis IN 46204-3506

RYDER, JACK MCBRIDE, educational consultant; b. Newport, Ky., Dec. 2, 1928; s. Amon McBride Ryder and Esther Mabel (Harris) Ryder Rachford; m. Roberta Joyce Hayward, Mar. 17, 1951 (div. 1964); children: Joyce Ann (dec.), Constance Lynn, Judith Louise, John McBride; m. Lila Joan Baker, Oct. 2, 1964; 1 child, Suzanne Carol. BS in Biology, Mich State U., East Lansing, 1952; MA in Sch. Adminstrn., Mich State U., 1955, PhD in Ednl. Adminstrn., 1962; LLD (hon.), Saginaw Valley State U., 1992. Tchr. Anglo-Am. Schs., Athens, Greece, 1952-54; supt. of schs. Brady Community Schs., Oakley, Mich., 1955-57, Cassopolis (Mich.) Pub. Schs., 1957-61; assoc. instr. Coll. Edn. Mich. State U., East Lansing, 1961-62; asst. to dean univ. extension adminstrn. Purdue U., W. Lafayette, Ind., 1962-63; interim dir. (on loan) Ind. Vocat. Tech. Coll., Indpls., 1964-65; dir., dean and dir. Purdue U., Indpls., 1963-69; vice chancellor, dean for adminstrv. affairs Indiana U. and Purdue U., Indpls., 1969-74; prof. edn., pres. Saginaw Valley State U., University Center, Mich., 1974-89, prof. edn., 1989-92; pres. J&L Assoc. Internat. Ednl. Cons., 1992—; bd. dirs. Saginaw, Second Nat. Bank, Saginaw; chmn. Valley Libr. Consortium, Saginaw, 1981-89, Saginaw Valley R&D Corp., Univ. Ctr., 1982-89; vis. prof., cons. Fedn. Universitaire ET PolyTechnique, De Lille, France, 1989. Mem. Saginaw Area Growth Alliance, 1989; bd. dirs. Saginaw Future, 1989, St. Luke's Healthcare Assn., Saginaw, 1981-89; mem. Leadership Bay County, Bay City, Mich., 1988; bd. dirs., 1st vice chmn. Saginaw Valley State U. Found., 1974-89; pres. emeritus Saginaw Valley State U. Bd. Control, 1992. Recipient Albert Community Svc. award Saginaw Area C. of C., 1989, Disting. Contbr. of Svc. award Delta Coll., Bay City, 1989, Leadership and Svc. award Saginaw Valley State U., 1989, Saginaw Valley State U. Found., 1989; Ryder Ctr. for Health and Phys. Edn. named in honor of him and his wife Saginaw Valley State U.; Paul Harris fellow Rotary Internat., 1988. Mem. Am. Assn. State Colls. and Univs. (Disting. Leadership award 1988), President's Coun. State Univs. (chmn. 1984-86, Leadership and Svc. award 1989), Internat. Torch Club (bd. dirs. Chgo. 1988-89), Phi Delta Kappa. Avocations: fishing, spectator sports, gardening, walking, tennis.

RYDER, THOMAS MICHAEL, newspaper editor; b. East Chicago, Ind., May 17, 1934; s. Thomas Henry and Margaret (Lauber) R.; m. George-Anne Richmond, Sept. 22, 1962. B.S. in Journalism, Marquette U., 1956. Reporter Daily Dispatch, Moline, Ill., 1956-60; reporter The Press, Evansville, Ind., 1960-62, Tri-state editor, 1962-64, city editor, 1969-83; editor The Sunday Courier & Press, Evansville, 1983-86; asst. mng. editor Evansville Courier, 1986—; adj. prof. Ind. State U., Evansville, 1984. Contbr. articles to mags. Served with U.S. Army, 1967-69. Mem. Soc. Profl. Journalists, Stamp Club (pres. 1966). Roman Catholic. Club: Meml. Patrons (pres. 1983). Office: The Courier 300 E Walnut St Evansville IN 47708-1239

RYDER, WINONA (WINONA LAURA HOROWITZ), actress; b. Winona, Minn., Oct. 29, 1971; d. Michael and Cynthia (Istas) Horowitz. Films include: Lucas, 1986, Square Dance, 1987, 1969, 1988, Beetlejuice, 1988, Great Balls of Fire, 1989, Heathers, 1989, Edward Scissorhands, 1990, Mermaids, 1990, Welcome Home, Roxy Carmichael, 1990, Night On Earth, 1992, Bram Stoker's Dracula, 1992, Age of Innocence, 1993 (Golden Globe for Best Supporting Actress, 1994, Academy award nominee, Best Supporting Actress, 1993), The House of the Spirits, 1994, Reality Bites, 1994, Little Women, 1994 (Acad. Awd. nom., Best Actress), Boys, 1995, How to Make An American Quilt, 1995, Looking for Richard, 1995, The Crucible, 1996, Boys, 1996. Office: c/o Carole Obie Arts Entertainment 9460 Wilshire Blvd 7th Fl Beverly Hills CA 90210*

RYDHOLM, RALPH WILLIAMS, advertising agency executive; b. Chgo., June 1, 1937; s. Thor Gabriel and Vivian Constance (Williams) R.; m. Jo Anne Beechler, Oct. 5, 1963; children: Kristin, Erik, Julia. B.A., Northwestern U., 1958, postgrad. in bus. adminstrn, 1958-59; postgrad. Advanced Mgmt. Program, Harvard U., 1982. Acct. trainee, copywriter Young & Rubicam Advt., Chgo., 1960-63; copywriter Post-Keyes-Gardner Advt., Chgo., 1963, E. H. Weiss Advt., Chgo., 1963-65; copy group head BBDO Advt., Chgo., 1965-66; with J. Walter Thompson Advt., Chgo., 1966-86; creative dir., v.p. J. Walter Thompson Advt., 1969-76, exec. creative dir., 1976-86, sr. v.p., 1972-80, exec. v.p., dir., 1980-86; exec. v.p., chief creative officer, dir. Ted Bates Worldwide, N.Y.C., 1986-87; mng. ptnr., chmn. mgmt. com., chief creative officer, chmn., CEO Tatham EURO RSCG Advt., Chgo., 1987—; bd. dirs., ops. com., chmn. creative com., vice chmn., 1996, 4A's, guest spkr. Ad Age Workshop, 1969, 77, 86, Adweek Seminar, 1993; keynote spkr. Stephen B. Kelly Awards, 1993. Mem. assoc. bd. Newberry Libr. Assn. With USAFR, 1959-65. Recipient Clio awards, Internat. Broadcast award, Lion awards, Cannes Film Festival, Addy awards; named one of Top 100 Creative Ad People Ad Daily, 1972, Advt. Exec. of Yr. Adweek, 1991, Best Man in Advt. McCalls and Adweek, 1992, Creative Leader Wall St. Jour., 1994. Mem. ASCAP, Chgo. Advt. Fedn., Saddle and Cycle Club, Econ. Club Chgo. (bd. dirs.), Northwestern Club Chgo., Harvard Club Chgo., Exec.'s Club Chgo., Tavern Club, Carlton Club, Chikaming Country Club (Mich.), Dunes Club (Mich.), Phi Delta Theta. Office: Tatham EURO RSCG 980 N Michigan Ave Chicago IL 60611-4501

RYDSTROM, CARLTON LIONEL, chemist, paint and coating consultant; b. Indpls., Dec. 4, 1928; s. Carlton Lionel and Sara Ann (McNeese) R.; m. Kathleen O'Leary, Oct. 21, 1954 (dec.); children: Carlton L. III, Michael, Mary (dec.), Leslie, Patricia, Timothy, Molly; m. Mary L. Murphy, June 13, 1992. BS in Polymer Chemistry, N.D. State U., 1951; MS in Phys. Chemistry, U. Puerto Rico, Rio, Piedras, 1953. Chemist Am. Marietta Co., Kankakee, Ill., 1951-52; chemist, plant mgr. Chinamel Paints, Hato Rey, Puerto Rico, 1952-53; tech. mgr. Midwest Synthetics (Valspar), Rockford, Ill., 1953-55; mng. ptnr. Norcote Co., St. Petersburg, Fla., 1955-71; pres. C.M. Industries, Inc., St. Petersburg, 1971-74, Tuf-top/Norcote Coatings, Inc., St. Petersburg, 1974-80; owner Rydstrom Lab., Inc., St. Petersburg, 1980—; bd. dirs. Stacote Finishes, Ltd., W.I.; cons. Sch. Bds. State of Fla., 1981—, paint and adhesive industries. Pres. parish coun. St. Jude Cath. Cathedral Parish, 1977-78, 78-79, St. Vincent de Paul Pinellas Dist., St. Petersburg, 1988-91; nat. secretariat Cursillo Movement, Roman Cath. Ch., Dallas, 1985-88; dir. Cursillo Movement, Diocese of St. Petersburg, 1995—; dir. St. Vincent de Paul Food Ctr., St. Petersburg, 1988—; chmn. Waterfront Planning Com., St. Petersburg, 1959; mem. bd. dirs. St. Petersburg Cath. H.S., 1977-80. Fellow N.Y. Acad. Sci.; mem. Nat. Assn. Corrosion Engrs., Soc. Coatings Tech. (chmn./pres. 1958-59, Disting. Svc. award 1975), Fla. Paint and Coating Assn. (treas., dir. 1959-75), St. Vincent dePaul Soc. (Top Hat award 1991), Jr. C. of C. (DSA 1960). Republican. Roman Catholic. Avocations: golf, gardening, travel, public speaking, working with needy. Home and Office: 6300 25th Ave N Saint Petersburg FL 33710-4128

RYDZ, JOHN S., manufacturing executive; b. Milw., May 7, 1925; s. John M. and Victoria A. (Kosse) R.; m. Clare L. Steinke, May 18, 1946; children: John A., Karen E. BS in Physics, MIT, 1952; MS in Physics, U. Pa., 1956; postgrad., Case Western Res. U., 1965-70. Mem. staff of sr. exec. v.p. RCA, N.Y.C., 1952-61; exec. v.p. Nuclear Corp. Am. (NUCOR), Phoenix, 1961-63; dir. research Adressograph/Multigraph, Cleve., 1963-65; v.p. Diebold Inc., Canton, Ohio, 1965-70; v.p., chief tech. officer The Singer Co., N.Y.C., 1970-80; corp. v.p. Emhart Corp., Farmington, Conn., 1980-89; pres. Music Memories Inc., Avon, Conn., 1989—; vis. prof. U. Conn., 1988—; mem. engring. adv. com. NSF, Washington, 1986—. Author: Managing Innovation and Common Sense Manufacturing Management, 1986; contbr. articles to profl. jours.; patentee in field. Mem. MIT Lab. for Mfg. and Productivity,

Cambridge, Mass., 1975—, U. Hartford Engring. Exec. Council, West Hartford, Conn., 1982—, Worcester (Mass.) Poly. Inst. Mech. Engring. Adv. Com., 1980—; chmn. engring adv. com. U. Conn., Storrs, 1986—. Served with USN, 1943-46, WWII. Mem. Soc. Mfg. Engrs., IEEE, Indsl. Research Inst. Avocations: astronomy, swimming.

RYDZEL, JAMES A., lawyer; b. Worcester, Mass., Nov. 13, 1946; s. Joseph S. and Shirley F. Rydzel; m. Mary C. Chandler; 1 child, Molly. BA, St. Louis U., 1968; JD, Duke U., 1971. Bar: Ohio, 1972, Fla. 1975, U.S. Dist. Ct. (no. dist.) Ohio, U.S. Dist. Ct. (ea. dist.) Mich., U.S. Ct. Appeals (2d, 3d, 4th and 6th cirs.). Ptnr. Jones, Day, Reavis & Pogue, Cleve., 1972—; adj. prof. law Case Western Res. U. Bd. dirs. New Orgn. Visual Arts, 1990, Greater Cleve. Growth Assn., Citizens League. Mem. ABA (litigation labor and employment law com.), Ohio State Bar Assn., Fla. Bar Assn., Def. Rsch. Inst. Office: Jones Day Reavis & Pogue 901 Lakeside Ave E Cleveland OH 44114-1116

RYERSON, PAUL SOMMER, lawyer; b. Newark, Oct. 2, 1946; s. Robert Paul and Audrey Mae (Sommer) R.; m. Susan Jean Duckrow, Aug. 7, 1971 (div. Apr. 1995); children: James Sommer, Jill Carin. BA, Wesleyan U., 1968; JD, Columbia U., 1971. Bar: N.Y. 1972, D.C. 1972, U.S. Ct. Appeals (D.C. cir.) 1973, U.S. Dist. Ct. D.C. 1973, U.S. Supreme Ct. 1976, U.S. Ct. Appeals (5th cir.) 1979, U.S. Ct. Appeals (4th cir.) 1980. Law clk. to judge Jack B. Weinstein U.S. Dist. Ct. ea. dist. N.Y., 1971-72; assoc. Arnold & Porter, Washington, 1972-79, ptnr., 1980-89; ptnr. Jones, Day, Reavis & Pogue, Washington, 1989—. Contbr. articles to profl. publs. Mem. ABA, D.C. Bar Assn. Home: 4903 Edgemoor Ln Bethesda MD 20814 Office: Jones Day Reavis & Pogue 1450 G St NW Washington DC 20005-2001

RYGIEWICZ, PAUL THADDEUS, plant ecologist; b. Chgo., Feb. 19, 1952; s. Sigismund Thaddeus and Regina (Korpalski) R. BS in Forestry, U. Ill., 1974; MS in Wood Sci., U. Calif., Berkeley, 1976; PhD in Forest Resources, U. Wash., 1983. Research wood technologist ITT Rayonier, Inc., Shelton, Wash., 1977; research assoc. Centre National de Recherches Forestières, Nancy, France, 1983-84; research soil microbiologist U. Calif., Berkeley, 1984-85; rsch. ecologist, global climate change project leader EPA, Corvallis, Oreg., 1985—; asst. prof. dept. forest sci. Oreg. State U., 1987—. Contbr. articles to profl. jours.; rsch. on reforestation of tropical forests in Brazil, global climate changes on forests. Vol. Big Bros. of Am., Urbana, Ill., 1972-74. Fellow Regents U. Calif., Berkeley, 1973-74, Weyerhaeuser U. Calif., Berkeley, 1978-79, Inst. Nat. de la Recherche Agronomique, France, 1983-84, French Ministry of Fgn. Affairs, 1983-84. Mem. Ecol. Soc. Am., Soil Ecology Soc., Forestry Club, Sigma Xi, Gamma Sigma Delta, Xi Sigma Pi (officer 1973-74). Avocations: bicycling, skiing, mountain climbing, camping, hiking. Office: EPA 200 SW 35th St Corvallis OR 97333-4902

RYGOR, STANLEY, advertising executive; b. N.Y.C., Apr. 9, 1926; s. Harry and Marie (Maugeri) R.; children: Robert, Brenda, Daniel, Kathleen, Valerie. Student, Hunter Coll., 1947-50. Advt. account exec. Doremus Advt. Agy., N.Y.C., 1947—. Home: 32-37 34th St Long Island City NY 11106-1801 Office: Doremus & Co 200 Varick St New York NY 10014-4810

RYKER, CHARLES EDWIN, former aerospace company executive; b. Baxter Springs, Kans., Mar. 17, 1920; s. Herbert Earl and Nellie (Sims) R.; m. Evelyn Maude Fairchild, July 28, 1943; children: Patricia Evelyn, Charles Franklyn. Student, San Diego State Coll., 1937-38; B.S. cum laude, U. So. Calif., 1947. C.P.A., Calif. Sr. accountant Arthur Andersen & Co., Los Angeles, 1947-49; auditor Airquipment Co., Burbank, Calif., 1949-50; accounting mgr. Hughes Aircraft Co., Culver City, Calif., 1950-52; with N.Am. Aviation, Inc., Los Angeles, 1952-67; v.p., controller Los Angeles airplane div. N.Am. Aviation, Inc., 1959-62, asst. corp. controller, asst. corp. treas., 1962-67; controller Rockwell Internat. Corp. (merger N.Am. Aviation, Inc. and Rockwell-Standard Corp.), 1967-73, staff v.p. controller's office Western region, 1973-75, v.p., controller, 1975-81, v.p. corp. fin.-major programs, 1981-84; fin. cons., 1984-86. Served to lt. USNR, 1941-45, PTO. Mem. Fin. Execs. Inst., Am. Inst. C.P.A.'s, Calif. Soc. C.P.A.'s, Nat. Assn. Accountants, Beta Gamma Sigma, Beta Alpha Psi, Phi Kappa Phi, Chi Phi. Home: 248 Rocky Point Rd Palos Verdes Peninsula CA 90274-2622

RYKER, NORMAN J., JR., retired manufacturing company executive; b. Tacoma, Dec. 25, 1926; s. Norman Jenkins and Adelia Gustine (Macomber) R.; m. Kathleen Marie Crawford, June 20, 1947 (div. 1983); children: Jeanne Ryker Flores, Christina, Vickie Ryker Risley, Norman Jenkins, Kathy; m. Judith Kay Schneider, Dec. 18, 1983. B.S., U. Calif.-Berkeley, 1949, M.S., 1951; postgrad. Advanced Mgmt. Program, Harvard U., 1973. Asst. chief engr. space divsn. Rockwell Internat., Downey, Calif., 1962-68, v.p. rsch. engring. and testing, 1968-70, v.p. rsch. and engring. graphic systems group, 1970-74, v.p., gen. mgr. Webb divsn., 1974, v.p., gen mgr. transp. and equipment divsn., 1974-76; pres. Rocketdyne divsn. Rockwell Internat., Canoga Park, Calif., 1976-83; sr. v.p. aerospace and indsl. group Pneumo Corp., Boston, 1983-84, exec. v.p., COO, 1984-85; pres., CEO Pneumo Corp. subs. IC Industries, 1985-86, Pneumo Abex Corp., 1986-88; vice chmn., CEO Cross & Trecker Corp., 1989-91; lectr. in field. Contbr. articles to profl. jours. Served with U.S. Army, 1944-46. Recipient cert. of appreciation NASA, 1969, merit award, 1979, Disting. Pub. Svc. medal, 1981, Silver Knight award Nat. Mgmt. Assn., 1979, Tech. Mgmt. award Calif. Soc. Profl. Engrs., 1979. Fellow Inst. Advancement Engring., AIAA; mem. ASCE, Am. Astronautical Soc., Nat. Mgmt. Assn., Instn. Prodn. Engrs. (elected companion). Republican. Address: 15233 Jarrettsville Pike Monkton MD 21111-2402

RYKWERT, JOSEPH, architecture and art history educator; b. Warsaw, Poland, Apr. 5, 1926; arrived in Eng., 1939; s. Szymon Mieczyslaw and Elizabeth (Melup) R.; m. Anne-Marie Sandersley, Feb. 14, 1972; 1 child from previous marriage, Simon Sebastian; 1 stepchild, Marina Joanna Engel. Student, Archtl. Assn., London, 1944-47; MA, U. Cambridge, London; PhD, Royal Coll. Art, London, 1970; MA (hon.), U. Pa., 1988; DSc (hon.), U. Edinburgh, Scotland, 1995. Libr., tutor Royal Coll. Art, 1960-67; prof. art, chmn. dept. U. Essex, Colchester, Eng., 1967-81; Slade prof. fine arts U. Cambridge, 1980, reader in architecture, 1981-87; Paul Philippe Cret prof. architecture, prof. art history U. Pa., Phila., 1988—, also chmn. PhD program in architecture; Andrew Mellon prof. Cooper Union, N.Y.C., 1977; George Lurcy prof. Columbia U., N.Y.C., 1986; commr. Venice (Italy) Biennale, 1974-77; mem. jury Parc de la Villette Competition, Paris, 1982, Wolf Found. Prize, Jerusalem, 1983; trustee Cubitt Trust, London, 1986—; sr. scholar Getty Ctr. for History Art and Humanities, 1992, 93; co-editor catalogue, curator Alberti Exhbn., Mantua, Italy, 1994. Author: The Golden House, 1947, The Idea of a Town, 1963, 76, 88, Church Building, 1966, On Adam's House in Paradise, 1972, 82, The First Moderns, 1980, 84, The Necessity of Artifice, 1982, (with Anne-Marie Rykwert) The Brothers Adam, 1985; editl. transl.: One the Art of Building (L.B. Alberti), 1989, 91, The Dancing Column, 1996; editor Res. jour., Peabody Mus., Cambridge, Mass., 1979—. Mem. steering com. UNESCO Conf. on Urbanism, 1989—. Decorated Chevalier des Arts et des Lettres, Govt. of France, 1985; recipient Alfred Jurzykowski Found. award, 1990, Accademia di San Luca, 1993. Mem. Coll. Art Assn., Comite Internat. des Critiques d'Arch. (pres.), Savile Club (London). Office: U Pa Dept Architecture 210 S 34th St 102 Meyerson Hall Philadelphia PA 19104-6311

RYLAND, DAVID RONALD, lawyer; b. Ashland, Ohio, Mar. 22, 1945; s. Willis A. and Lois Eleanor (Landis) R.; m. Rita Ann Cooney, Jan. 20, 1973. BA, Coll. of Wooster, 1967; JD, Columbia U., 1970. Bar: Calif. 1970. Assoc. U. of Calif., Berkeley, 1970-71; from assoc. to ptnr. Severson, Werson, Berke & Melchior, San Francisco, 1971-82; ptnr. Sheppard, Mullin, Richter & Hampton, San Francisco, 1982—. Home: 3 Edgewater Rd Belvedere CA 94920-2315 Office: Sheppard Mullin Richter & Hampton 4 Embarcadero Ctr Ste 1700 San Francisco CA 94111-4158

RYLAND, G(REANER) NEAL, financial executive; b. Richmond, Va., June 26, 1941; s. William Bradford and Elizabeth (Neal) R.; m. Marjorie Kane Gerry II, Aug. 18, 1978; children: Averell, Elizabeth Bradford, Alexandra, Nelson. BA, Harvard U., 1963; MBA, NYU, 1967. With Bank of N.Y., N.Y.C., 1964-67; treas. Ea. Gas & Fuel Assn., Boston, 1967-78; sr. v.p., chief fin. officer Courier Corp., Lowell, Mass., 1979-85, Kenner Parker Toys Inc., Beverly, Mass., 1985-88; exec. v.p., CFO The Boston Co., Boston, 1988-93, New Eng. Investment Cos., L.P., Boston, 1993—. Editor: The American Business Corporation, 1972. Pres. bd. trustees Shore Country Day Sch., Beverly, 1987; trustee Trustees of Reservation; chmn. fin. com., trustee Mass. Gen. Hosp.

RYLANDER, HENRY GRADY, JR., mechanical engineering educator; b. Pearsall, Tex., Aug. 23, 1921; married; 4 children. B.S., U. Tex., 1943, M.S., 1952; Ph.D. in Mech. Engring., Ga. Inst. Tech., 1965. Design engr. Steam Div., Aviation Gas Turbine Div., Westinghouse Elec. Corp., 1943-47; from asst. to assoc. prof. mech. engring. U. Tex., Austin, 1947-68, research scientist, 1950, prof. mech. engring., 1968—, Joe J. King prof. engring., 1980—; cons. engr. TRACOR, Inc., 1964-69; founding dir. Ctr. for Electromechanics, U. Tex., 1977-85, chmn., mech. engring. dept., 1976-86. Named Disting. Grad. Coll. Engring., U. Tex., Austin, 1989. Fellow ASME (Leonardo da Vinci award 1985); mem. ASME. Office: U Tex Coll Engring Austin TX 78712

RYLANT, CYNTHIA, author; b. Hopewell, Va., June 6, 1954; d. John Tune and Leatrel (Rylant) Smith; 1 child, Nathaniel. BA, Morris Harvey Coll., 1975; MA, Marshall U., 1976; MLS, Kent State U., 1982. English instr. Marshall U., Huntington, W.Va., 1979-80, U. Akron, Ohio, 1983-84; children's libr. Akron (Ohio) Pub. Libr., 1983; part-time lectr. Northeast Ohio Univs. Coll. Medicine, Rootstown, Ohio, 1991—. Author: (picture books) When I Was Young in the Mountains, 1982 (Caldecott Honor book 1983, English Speaking Union Book-Across-the-Sea Amb. of Honor award 1984, Am. Book award nomination 1983), Miss Maggie, 1983, This Year's Garden, 1984, The Relatives Came, 1985 (Horn Book Honor book 1985, Children's Book of Yr. Child Study Assn. Am. 1985, Caldecott Honor Book 1986), Night in the Country, 1986, Birthday Presents, 1987, All I See, 1988, Mr. Grigg's Work, 1989, An Angel for Solomon Singer, 1992, The Everyday Town, 1993, The Everyday School, 1993, The Everyday House, 1993, The Everyday Garden, 1993, The Everyday Children, 1993, The Everyday Pets, 1993, Mr. Putter and Tabby Pour the Tea, 1994, Mr. Putter and Tabby Walk the Dog, 1994, The Old Woman Who Named Things, 1994, The Blue Hill Meadows and the Much Loved Dog, 1994, Gooseberry Park, 1995; (Henry and Mudge series) Henry and Mudge: The First Book of Their Adventures, 1987, Henry and Mudge in Puddle Trouble, 1987, Henry and Mudge in the Green Time, 1987, Henry and Mudge Under the Yellow Moon, 1987, Henry and Mudge in the Sparkle Days, 1988, Henry and Mudge and the Forever Sea, 1989, Henry and Mudge Get the Cold Shivers, 1989, Henry and Mudge and the Happy Cat, 1990, Henry and Mudge and the Bedtime Thumps, 1991, Henry and Mudge Take the Big Test, 1991, Henry and Mudge and the Long Weekend, 1992, Henry and Mudge and the Wild Wind, 1993, Henry and Mudge and the Careful Cousin, 1994, Henry and Mudge and the Best Day Ever, 1995; (poetry) Waiting to Waltz ... a Childhood, 1984 (Nat. Coun. for Social Studies Best Book 1984), Soda Jerk, 1990, Something Permanent, 1994; (novels) A Blue-Eyed Daisy, 1985 (Children's Book of Yr. Child Study Assn. Am. 1985), A Fine White Dust, 1986 (Newbery Honor Book 1987), A Kindness, 1988; (stories) Every Living Thing, 1985, Children of Christmas: Stories for the Season, 1987, A Couple of Kooks: And Other Stories About Love, 1990; (autobiography) But I'll Be Back Again: An Album, 1989, Best Wishes, 1992; (other) Appalachia: The Voices of Sleeping Birds, 1991 (Boston Globe/Horn Book Honor book for nonfiction 1991), Missing May, 1992 (John Newbery medal 1992), I Have Seen Castles, 1993, The Dreamer, 1993. Office: PO Box 368 Kent OH 44240-0007

RYLE, JOSEPH DONALD, public relations executive; b. Stamford, Conn., Aug. 19, 1910; s. Joseph P. and Vivian (Sander) R. B.S., NYU, 1933. With pub. relations dept. Joseph D. Ryle, N.Y.C., 1933-41; dir. pub. relations Am. Overseas Airlines, London, 1946-50, Am. Airlines, N.Y.C., 1950-52; exec. v.p. Fedn. Ry. Progress, Washington, 1953-55, vice chmn., 1955—; pres. Nat. Transit Ads., 1955-57; exec. v.p. pub. relations Thomas J. Deegan Jr., Inc., now dir.; pub. relations cons., N.Y.C.; promotion cons. Met. Mus. Art. Exec. dir. Gov.'s Com. for the Centennial of Thoroughbred Racing at Saratoga; v.p., bd. dirs. East Side Settlement House; adv. com. Am. Folk Art Mus.; chmn. emeritus Winter Antiques Show; trustee Hancock (Mass.) Shaker Village; bd. dirs. Isabel O'Neil Sch., N.Y.C. Served with USAAF, 1942-45; dep. to Gen. H. H. Arnold, pub. relations. Decorated Legion of Merit. Mem. Air Transport Assn. (past chmn. pub. relations com.), Newcomen Soc., Irish Georgian Soc. (bd. dirs.). Clubs: Nat. Press (Washington), Army Navy (Washington); Overseas Press (N.Y.C.), Wings (N.Y.C.); Squadron A; Reading Room (Saratoga, N.Y.). Home: 455 E 51st St New York NY 10022-6474 also: The Academy Remsenburg NY 11960

RYLES, GERALD FAY, private investor, business executive; b. Walla Walla, Wash., Apr. 3, 1936; s. L. F. and Janie Geraldine (Bassett) R.; m. Ann Jane Birkenmeyer, June 12, 1959; children—Grant, Mark, Kelly. B.A., U. Wash., 1958; M.B.A., Harvard U., 1962. With Gen. Foods Corp., White Plains, N.Y., 1962-65, Purex Corp., Ltd., Lakewood, Calif., 1966-68; cons. McKinsey & Co., Inc., Los Angeles, 1968-71; with Fibreboard Corp., San Francisco, 1971-79, v.p., 1973-75, group v.p., 1975-79; with Consol. Fibres, Inc., San Francisco, 1979-88, exec. v.p., 1979-81, pres., dir., 1981-86, chief exec. officer, 1986-88; cons. Orinda, Calif., 1988-90; with Interchecks Inc., 1990-92, pres., CEO, 1990-92; bus. exec., pvt. investor, 1992-94; chmn. bd., CEO Microserv, Inc., Kirkland, Wash., 1994—; bd. dirs. Morning Sun, Inc., Tacoma, Wash. Mem. adv. com. entrepreneur and innovation program U. Wash. Bus. Sch. Served to capt. U.S. Army, 1958-66. Mem. Harvard Bus. Sch. Assn., Univ. Wash. Alumni Assn., World Trade Club (San Francisco), Wash. Athletic Club. Republican. Episcopalian. Home: 2625 90th Ave NE Bellevue WA 98004-1601

RYLL, FRANK MAYNARD, JR., professional society administrator; b. St. Petersburg, Fla., Jan. 22, 1942; s. Frank Maynard and Laura Marjorie (Howarth) R.; m. Patti Sue Craig, Mar. 2, 1984; children: Christopher E. Gibson, Rebekah H. Gibson. BA, Fla. State U., 1964. Office mgr. So. Bell Telephone, Miami Beach, Fla., 1966-67; account exec. Francis I. DuPont & Co., St. Petersburg, 1967-68, Merril Lynch, St. Petersburg, 1969-74; mgr. news and info., exec. dir. Sarasota (Fla.) County C. of C., 1974-76; dir. fin. Greater Greenville (S.C.) C. of C., 1976-77, mgt. govt. affairs, 1977-78, gen. mgr., 1978-80; staff v.p. govt. affairs Fla. C. of C., Tallahassee, 1980-83; pres. Fla. C. of C., 1983—, treas., 1994—. Exec. com. Greenville chpt. ARC, 1979; active Tallavana Community Ch. Served with U.S. Army, 1965-69, Vietnam. Mem. Am. C. of C. Execs. (bd. dirs.), U.S. C. of C. (bd. dirs.), Coun. State Chambers (chmn.), Fla. State U. Alumni Assn. (v.p. 1982-85), Pi Kappa Phi. Republican. Avocation: tennis. Home: 3916 Leane Dr Tallahassee FL 32308-2211 Office: Fla C of C 136 S Bronough St Tallahassee FL 32301-7706

RYMAN, ROBERT TRACY, artist; b. Nashville, May 30, 1930; s. William Tracy and Nora (Boston) R.; m. Lucy Lippard, 1961 (div. 1966); children: Ethan, Ryman; m. Merrill Wagner, Jan. 31, 1969; children: William Tracy, George Corydon. Exhibited one man shows: Paul Bianchini Gallery, 1967, Solomon R. Guggenheim Mus., N.Y.C., 1972, Kunsthalle, Basel, Switzerland, 1975, Palais des Beaux-Arts, Brussels, 1974, Stedelijk Mus., Amsterdam, Netherlands, 1974, Whitechapel Gallery, London, 1977, Centre Pompidou, Paris, 1981, Sidney Janis Gallery, N.Y.C., 1981, Kunsthalle, Dusseldorf, Germay, 1982, Bonnier Gallery, N.Y.C., 1983, Daniel Weinberg Gallery, L.A., 1983, Galerie Maeght LeLong, Paris, 1984, Rhona Hoffman Gallery, Chgo., 1985, Leo Castelli Gallery, N.Y.C., 1986, Galerie Maeght LeLong, N.Y.C., 1986, Pace Gallery, N.Y.C., 1990, DIA Art Found., N.Y.C., 1988-89, Konrad Fischer Gallery, Dusseldorf, Fed. Republic Germany, 1987, Pace Gallery, N.Y., Tate Gallery, London, MMA, N.Y., San Francisco Mus. Modern Art, Walker Arts Ctr., Mpls.; group shows: Biennal Whitney Mus. Am. Art, N.Y.C., 1977, Stedelijk Mus., Amsterdam, 1978, Art of the 70's, Venice Bernnale, Italy, 1980, Haus der Kunst, Munich, 1981, Stedelijk Mus., Amsterdam, 1983, Whitney Mus. Am. Art, 1983, Skowhegan Sch. of Painting and Sculpture Medal, 1987, Whitney Biennal Exhbn, 1987; Mus. Modern Art, N.Y.C., 1985, Carnegie International, 1985; represented permanent collections: Mus. Modern Art, N.Y.C., Milw. Art Center, Stedelijk Mus., Amsterdam, Whitney Mus. Am. Art, pvt. collections; apptd. commr. City of N.Y. Art Comm. Mem. AAAL, Mcpl. Art Soc. N.Y. (bd. dirs. 1991—). Home: 17 W 16th St New York NY 10011-6301 Studio: 637 Greenwich St New York NY 10014-3306 *There is never a question of what to paint, but only how to paint. The "how" of painting is the image, the end product.*

RYMAN, RUTH (STACIE) MARIE, primary education educator; b. Moline, Ill., July 22, 1952; d. Henry Joseph and Gladys Julia (Campbell) DeKeyzer; m. Phillip DeForrest Ryman, Aug. 14, 1976; children: Michelle, Daniel, Jennifer. BA, Augustana Coll., 1974; MA, U. Denver, 1988. Cert. tchr. Resource tchr. Notre Dame Sch., Denver, 1986-91, 2nd grade tchr., 1991—; cons. Notre Dame Sch., Denver, 1991—. mem. Nat. Cath. Edn. Assn., Nat. Coun. Tchrs. Math. Office: Notre Dame Sch 2165 S Zenobia St Denver CO 80219-5058

RYMAR, JULIAN W., manufacturing company executive; b. Grand Rapids, Mich., June 29, 1919; student Grand Rapids Jr. Coll., 1937-39, U. Mich., 1939-41, Am. Sch. Dramatic Arts, 1946-47, Wayne U., 1948-52, Rockhurst Coll., 1952-53; Naval War Coll., 1954-58; m. Margaret Macon Van Brunt, Dec. 11, 1954; children: Margaret Gibson, Gracen Macon, Ann Mackall. Entered USN as aviation cadet, 1942, advanced through grades to capt., 1964; chmn. bd., chief exec. officer, dir. Grace Co., Belton, Mo., 1955—; chmn. bd. dirs. Shock & Vibration Research, Inc., 1956-66; chmn. bd., CEO Bedtime Story Fashions; bd. dirs. Am. Bank & Trust; comdg. officer Naval Air Res. Squadron, 1957-60, staff air bn. comdr., 1960-64. Mem. Kansas City Hist. Soc.; bd. dirs. Bros. of Mercy, St. Lukes Hosp.; adv. bd. dirs. St. Joseph Hosp.; trustee Missouri Valley Coll., 1969-74; pres. Rymar Found. Active Sch. Am. Rsch., Inst. Am. Arts, Mus. N.Mex. Found., Spanish Colonial Art Soc. Mem. Mil. Order World Wars, Navy League U.S. (pres. 1959-60, dir. 1960-70), Rockhill Homes Assn. (v.p.) Friends of Art (pres., chmn. bd. govs. 1969-70, exec. bd. 1971-74), Soc. of Fellows of Nelson Gallery Found. (exec. bd. 1972-77), Soc. Profl. Journalists, Press Club, Univ. of Mich. Club, Arts Club of Washington, Sch. of Am. Rsch., Santa Fe Symphony, Inst. Am. Indian Art, Mus. NMex. Found., Mus. Indian Arts & Culture, Mus. Internat. Folk Art, Mus. Fine Arts, Spanish Colonial Arts Soc., Quiet Birdman Club, Sigma Delta Chi. Episcopalian (dir., lay reader, lay chalice, vestryman, jr. warden, sr. warden, diocesan fin. bd., parish investment bd.).

RYMER, PAMELA ANN, federal judge; b. Knoxville, Tenn., Jan. 6, 1941. AB, Vassar Coll., 1961; LLB, Stanford U., 1964; LLD (hon.), Pepperdine U., 1988. Bar: Calif. 1966, U.S. Ct. Appeals (9th cir.) 1966, U.S. Ct. Appeals (10th cir.), U.S. Supreme Ct. V.p. Rus Walton & Assoc., Los Altos, Calif., 1965-66; Assoc. Lillick McHose & Charles, L.A., 1966-72, ptnr., 1973-75; ptnr. Toy and Rymer, L.A., 1975-83; judge U.S. Dist. Ct. (cen. dist.) Calif., L.A., 1983-89, U.S. Ct. Appeals (9th cir.), L.A., 1989—; faculty The Nat. Jud. Coll., 1986-88; mem. com. summer ednl. programs Fed. Jud. Ctr., 1987-88; chair exec. com. 9th Cir. Jud. Conf., 1990; mem. com. criminal law Jud. Conf. U.S., 1988-93, Ad Hoc com. gender-based violence, 1991-94, fed.-state jurisdiction com., 1993—. Mem. editorial bd. The Judges' jour., 1989-91; contbr. articles to profl. jours. and newsletters. Mem. Calif. Postsecondary Edn. Commn., 1974-84, chmn., 1980-84; mem. L.A. Olympic Citizens Adv. Commn.; bd. visitors Stanford U. Law Sch., 1986—, chair, 1993-96, exec. com.; bd. visitors Pepperdine U. Law Sch., 1987—; mem. Edn. Commn. of States Task Force on State Policy and Ind. Higher Edn., 1987-89; bd. dirs. Constnl. Rights Found., 1985; Jud. Conf. U.S. Com. Fed.-State Jurisdiction, 1993, Com. Criminal Law, 1988-93, ad hoc com. gender based violence, 1991-94; chair exec. com. 9th cir. jud. conf., 1990-94. Recipient Outstanding Trial Jurist award L.A. County Bar Assn., 1988. Mem. ABA (task force on civil justice reform 1991—), State Bar Calif. (antitrust and trade regulation sect., exec. com. 1990-92), L.A. County Bar Assn. (chmn. antitrust sect. 1981-82), Assn. of Bus. Trial Lawyers (bd. govs. 1990-92), Stanford Alumni Assn., Stanford Law Soc. Soc. Calif., Vassar Club So. Calif. (past pres.). Office: US Ct Appeals 9th Cir 304 US Court of Appeals Bldg 125 S Grand Ave Pasadena CA 91105-1652*

RYMER, RANDAL EUGENE, chemical engineer; b. Youngstown, Ohio, Jan. 19, 1964; s. Rodney Eugene Rymer and Carol Jean (Sandusky-Rymer) Stahl; m. Amy Sue Williams, Sept. 13, 1986; children: Ashley Mae, Rachel Irene. B of Engring., Youngstown State U., 1986. Chem. loss prevention cons. IRI, Cleve., 1986-90; supr. dist. loss prevention IRI, Chgo., 1990-92, account cons., 1992-94; engr. Starr Tech. Risks Agy., Chgo., 1994—. Mem. PTA, Aurora, Ill., 1993—; instr., coach Young Am. Bowling Alliance, Youngstown and Naperville, Ill., 1985-86, 94—. Recipient Dow Rsch. award Dow Chem. Co., 1986. Mem. AIChE, Soc. of Fire Protection Engrs., Nat. Fire Protection Assn., Am. Bowling Congress (league pres., treas. 1981—). Republican. Presbyterian. Achievements include rsch. in adsorptive seperation of carbon monoxide/nitrogen for groundwork in alterative fuel development with carbon monoxide and hydrogen or replacing oxygen with compressed air. Home: 3150 Compton Rd Aurora IL 60504-4205 Office: Starr Risks Agy Inc Ste 1000 500 W Madison Chicago IL 60661-2511

RYMER, S. BRADFORD, JR., retired appliance manufacturing company executive; b. Cleveland, Tenn., May 30, 1915; s. S. Bradford and Clara Ladosky (Gee) R.; m. Anne Roddye Caudle, Nov. 7, 1942; children: Anita Elise, S. Bradford III. Grad., Fishburne Mil. Sch., 1933; BS in Indsl. Mgmt, Ga. Inst. Tech., 1937; D of Bus. Adminstration (hon.), Tenn. Wesleyan Coll. Indsl. engr. Dixie Foundry Co., Inc., Cleveland, Tenn., 1937-40, sec.-treas., dir. prodn., 1940-50; pres. Dixie Foundry Co., Inc. (name changed to Magic Chef Inc. 1961), Cleveland, Tenn., 1950-61; pres., chmn. Magic Chef Inc., Cleveland, 1961-87; chmn. Magic Chef Inc. div. Maytag Corp., Cleveland, 1986-87, ret., 1987; past chmn. Dixie-Narco, Inc., Ranson, W. Va.; forum dir. Munford Co.; former dir. Provident Life and Accident Ins. Co., Citizens & So. Nat. Bank, Atlanta. Past pres. Cleveland Asso. Industries; past trustee Tenn. Wesleyan Coll., Ga. Tech. Found.; past bd. dirs. Bradley County Meml. Hosp., Allied Arts of Chattanooga; past nat. dir. Jr. Achievement; trustee Fishburne Mil. Sch.; trustee Hiwassee Coll., John Templeton Found., 1993—. War Tng. Svc. flight instr. World War II. Recipient Palm Beach Atlantic Colleges Am. Free Enterprise medal. Mem. Am. Gas Assn. (past exec. com., dir.), NAM (past dir.), Chief Execs. Orgn. (pres. 1971, dir.), Gas Appliance Mfrs. Assn. (pres. 1965), Young Pres. Orgn. (past dir., area v.p., chmn. Rebel chpt.), Ga. Tech. Nat. Alumni Assn. (past trustee), Toastmasters (bd. dirs. 1992—), Phi Gamma Delta. Methodist (past chmn. bd. trustees). Home: 28 Stonedge 100 Scenic Hwy Lookout Mountain TN 37350-1267 also: 1326 Lake Worth Ln Lost Tree Village North Palm Beach FL 33408 *No man is a success unto himself; for his success has been wrought with the help and talents of many associates.*

RYMER, WILLIAM ZEV, research scientist, administrator; b. Melbourne, Victoria, Australia, June 3, 1939; came to U.S., 1971; s. Jacob and Luba Rymer; m. Helena Bardas, Apr. 10, 1961 (div. 1975); children: Michael Morris, Melissa Anne; m. Linda Marie Faller, Sept. 5, 1977; 1 child, Daniel Jacob. MBBS, Melbourne U., 1962; PhD, Monash U., Victoria, 1971. Resident med. officer dept. medicine Monash U., Victoria, 1964-66; Fogarty internat. fellow NIH, Bethesda, Md., 1971-74; rsch. assoc. Johns Hopkins U. Med. Sch., Balt., 1975-76; asst. prof. SUNY, Syracuse, 1976-78; asst. prof. Northwestern U., Chgo., 1978-81, assoc. prof., 1981-87, prof., 1987—; rsch. dir. Rehab. Inst. Chgo., 1989—. Contbr. articles to profl. jours. Grantee NIH, VA, Dept. of Def., Nat. Inst. Disability Rehab. Rsch., pvt. founds. Fellow Royal Australian Coll. Physicians; mem. Soc. Neurosci., Am. Soc. Biomechanics. Democrat. Avocations: tennis, racquetball. Office: Rehab Inst Chgo 345 E Superior St Chicago IL 60611-3015

RYN, CLAES GÖSTA, political science educator, author, research institute administrator; b. Norrköping, Sweden, June 12, 1943; permanent resident of U.S., 1979; s. Gösta Karl and Cecilia Edit (Blom) R.; m. Marianne Carin Tedhagen, Aug. 30, 1969; children: Charlotte, Viveka, Elisabet. Fil.kand. (MA), Uppsala (Sweden) U., 1967, postgrad., 1969-71; postgrad., Syracuse U., 1968-69; PhD, La. State U., 1974. Asst. prof. politics Cath. U. Am., Washington, 1974-78, assoc. prof. politics, 1978-82, prof. politics, 1982—; asst. dean Sch. Arts and Scis., Catholic U. Am., Washington, 1977-79; chmn. dept. politics Catholic U. Am., Washington, 1979-85; vis. assoc. prof. U. Va., Charlottesville, 1981; co-founder, chmn. Nat. Humanities Inst., Washington, 1984—; referee, evaluator NEH, Dept. Edn., USIA, others; dir. several scholarly confs. and lecture series; mem. Richard M. Weaver fellowship selection com., 1980—; faculty sponsor Earhart Found., 1989—; mem. awards com. Ingersoll Prizes, 1990; mem. Salvatori doctoral fellowship selection com. Intercollegiate Studies Inst., 1990—. Author: (with Bertil Häggman) Nykonservatismen i USA, 1971, Democracy and the Ethical Life, 1978, 2nd expanded edit., 1990, Will, Imagination and Reason, 1986, Individualism och Gemenskap, 1986, The New Jacobinism, 1991; editor: Humanitas, 1992—; co-editor (with George Panichas), author (with others):

Irving Babbitt in Our Time, 1986; editor, author introduction for other volumes; contbr. numerous articles to profl. jours. and collective vols.; mem. editorial adv. bd. Modern Age, 1981—; editorial advisor Marknadsekonomisk Tidskrift, Sweden, 1986-92; mem. editorial bd. This World, 1992—. Mem. vestry St. Francis Episcopal Ch., Potomac, Md., 1986-88. Served with Swedish Army, Royal Life Company, 1963, Signal Corps, 1967-68. Rsch. fellow various orgns., including Earhart Found., 1980-81, 87-88, Wilbur Found., 1980-81, 90, 93-94; recipient award King of Sweden, 1983; named Outstanding Grad. Prof., Cath. U. Am., 1992. Episcopalian. Home: 10008 Crestleigh Ln Potomac MD 20854-1820 Office: Cath Univ Am Dept Politics Washington DC 20064

RYNEAR, NINA COX, retired registered nurse, author, artist; b. Cochranville, Pa., July 11, 1916; d. Fredrick Allen and Nina Natalie (Drane) Cox; m. Charles Spencer Rynear, Aug. 22, 1934 (dec. May 1941); children: Charles Joseph, Stanley Spencer. RN, Coatesville Hosp. Sch. Nursing, 1945; BS in Nursing Edn., U. Pa., 1954. Interviewer Nat. Opinion Rsch. Ctr., U. Denver, Colo., 1942-47; sch. nurse West Goshen Elem. Sch., West Chester, Pa., 1946-47; pub. health nurse Pa. Dept. Health Bur. Pub. Health Nursing, Harrisburg, 1947-51; staff nurse V.A. Hosp., Coatesville, Pa., 1951-54; staff nurse, asst. head nurse V.A. Hosp., Menlo Park, Calif., 1954-56; asst. chief nursing svc. Palo Alto and Menlo Park VA Hosps., Palo Alto, Menlo Park, Calif., 1956-76; self employed Reno, Nev., 1976—. Author: (poems, musical compositions) Old Glory and the U.S.A., 1989, Mister Snowman, 1988, Dawn Shadow of Lenape, 1988; (poem and song compilation) This Side of Forever, 1990; (musical compositions) Blessed Are Those Who Listen, What Can I Leave, The Hobo's Promise; (childrens' stories) Wilyum of Orange 1st, Lady Harley and Pepper, 1995; contbr. sonnets to Newsletter of N.Am. Acad. Esoteric Studies; monthly contbr.; paintings represented in numerous pvt. collections. Pres. Chester County Pub. Health Nurses Assn., 1950. Staff nurse Cadet Corps, 1944-45. Mem. VFW Aux. (patriotic instr. 1989-90, chmn. safety div. Silver State #3396 chpt. 1990-91), New Century Rebekah Lodge #244. Methodist. Home and Office: 3476 Harbor Beach Dr Lake Wales FL 33853-8082

RYNEARSON, W. JOHN, foundation administrator; b. Grosse Point, Mich., Oct. 10, 1948; s. William J. and Anna Lee (Hutto) R.; m. Justine M. Pointer, Aug. 28, 1971; children: Jill, Amy, Julie. Cert. in French, Sorbonne U., Paris, 1967; BA in Mktg., Jacksonville U., 1970, MA in Teaching, 1973. Instr. Duval County Schs., Jacksonville, Fla., 1970-73, Fla. Jr. Coll., Jacksonville, 1973-74; territory mgr. Burroughs Corp., Jacksonville, 1974-76; Mideast, Far East sales administr. Coleman Co., Wichita, Kans., 1976-77; Asia sales mgr. Coleman Co., Wichita, 1977-79, Asia, Europe mktg. mgr., 1979-82; v.p. mktg. O'Brien Co. div. Coleman Co., Seattle, 1982-84; pres., gen. mgr. Knight Internat., Seattle, 1984-85; exec. v.p., found. sec., bd. dirs. Civitan Internat., Birmingham, 1985—; com. chmn. Shoreline Community Coll. Internat. Studies, Seattle, 1984-85. Author: Yankee Traveler, 1986. Sunday sch. tchr., dir. youth program Emmanual Bapt. Ch., Jacksonville, 1975-76; bd. dirs., missions bd. Faith Chapel, Wichita, 1976-82, bd. mgr., 1976-82, Redmond (Redmond) Assembly of God, 1982-85. Mem. Am. Soc. Assn. Execs. (cert. assn. exec. 1991), Am. Mktg. Assn. Republican. Pentacostal. Lodges: Civitan. Avocations: sailing, snow skiing. Home: 3404 Field Stone Ln Birmingham AL 35242-3936 Office: Civitan Internat 1 Civitan Pl Birmingham AL 35213-1983

RYNKIEWICZ, STEPHEN MICHAEL, journalist; b. Sheboygan, Wis., Oct. 20, 1955; s. Walter Paul and Ruth Catherine (Van Hercke) R.; m. Brenda Gail Russell, Sept. 27, 1986. BA, U. Wis., 1976. Various staff assignments Chgo. Sun-Times, 1979—, real estate editor, 1990—; pres. Ill. Freedom of Info. Coun., 1991-93, Chgo. Headline Club, 1991-92; sec.-treas. Soc. Profl. Journalists, 1995—, exec. com., 1995—, regional dir., 1992-95. Office: Chicago Sun-Times 401 N Wabash Ave Chicago IL 60611-3532

RYNN, NATHAN, physics educator, consultant; b. N.Y.C., Dec. 2, 1923; s. Meyer and Rose (Wolkerwiczer) Rynkowsky; m. Glenda Brown, June 24, 1989; children by previous marriage: Jonathan, Margaret, David. BSEE, CCNY, 1944; MS, U. Ill., 1947; PhD, Stanford U., 1956. Rsch. engr., RCA Labs., Princeton, 1947-52; rsch. asst. Stanford U., 1952-56, rsch. assoc., 1958; mem. tech. staff Ramo-Woolridge, L.A., 1956-57; supr. Huggins Labs., Menlo Park, Calif., 1957-58; rsch. staff physicist Princeton U., 1958-65; prof. physics U. Calif.-Irvine, 1965-94, prof. physics emeritus, rsch. prof. physics, 1994—; vis. prof. Ecole Polytechnique Fed. of Lausanne, Switzerland, 1984-90, Ecole Polytechnique, Paris, and other European univs. and labs., 1973-80; indsl. sci. advisor/cons., 1964—; com. mem. Plasma Sci. Com. Nat. Rsch. Coun. Contbr. articles and revs. to profl. jours. Founder and leader plasma physics research facility. With USN, 1944-46. Grantee NSF, U.S. Dept. Energy, Air Force Geophys. Lab.; Fulbright sr. fellow, 1978. Fellow Am. Phys. Soc., IEEE, AAAS. Office: U Calif Dept Physics and Astronomy Irvine CA 92717-4575

RYPIEN, MARK ROBERT, professional football player; b. Calgary, Alta., Can., Oct. 2, 1962. Student, Wash. State U. With Washington Redskins, 1987-94, Cleve. Browns, 1994—. Named to Pro Bowl team, 1989, 91; recipient Most Valuable Player award Superbowl, 1992. Office: Cleve Browns 80 1st Ave Berea OH 44017-1238

RYSANEK, LEONIE, soprano; b. Vienna, Austria, Nov. 14, 1926; d. Peter and Josefine (Hoeberth) R.; m. Ernst-Ludwig Gausmann, Dec. 23, 1968. Student, Vienna Conservatory, 1947-49. First singing engagements include Bayreuth, (Sieglinde-Die Walkure), 1951, San Francisco Opera, (Senta-Der Fliegende Hollaender), 1956, Met. Opera, (Lady Macbeth), 1959; now appears in world's foremost opera houses, N.Y.C., Vienna, Milan, San Francisco, London, Paris, (Chrysothemis-Elektra 1973), Berlin, (Gioconda 1974), Munich, Hamburg, Budapest, Moscow, (Parsifal 1975), and festivals of Salzburg, (Kaiserin-Die Frau Ohne Schatten 1974), Bayreuth, Orange, (Salome 1974), Sieglinde-Die Walkuere, 1975, Aix en Provende, Athens, (Medea 1973), Edinburgh recordings for RCA Victor, Deutsche Grammophon, London Records, EMI and Phillips, Kundry, Parsifal (Stuttgart 1978), Kammersangerin of Austria and Bavaria, Kostelnicka, Jenufa, Australian Opera, 1985, Vienna, 1986, San Francisco, 1986, N.Y. Carnegie Hall, 1988; only artist to sing three major roles in opera Elektra on videocassette; debut Spain, Sieglinde in Die Walküre, Kostelnicka in Janufa, Carnegie Hall, 1988, Liceo, Barcelona, Spain, 1989, Kabanicha in Katya Kabanova, Paris and L.A., 1988, Klytaemnesha in Elektra, Marseille, France, 1989, Orange, 1991, Met. Opera, N.Y.C., 1992, 95-96, Old Countess, Queen of Spades, Barcelona, 1992, San Francisco, 1994, S.Am. Teatro Color, Buenos Aires, 1995, Rio de Janeiro, 1996, Operate Farewell Salzburg Festival, Elektra, 1996; Met. Farewell, 1996. Recipient Chappel Gold medal of singing London; Silver Rose Vienna Philharmonic; Austrian Gold Cross 1st class for arts and scis.; San Francisco medal. Hon. mem. Vienna Staatsoper. Office: Merle Hubbard Mgmt 133 W 71st St Ste 8A New York NY 10023

RYSCAVAGE, RICHARD JOSEPH, Jesuit priest, social services administrator; b. Pa., Mar. 25, 1945; s. Edward Thomas and Kathleen (Loftus) R. AB, Assumption Coll., 1967; MA, Boston Coll., 1972; M in Intercultural Adminstrn., Sch. Internat. Tng., Brattleboro, Vt., 1973; MDiv, Weston Sch. Theology, Cambridge, Mass., 1977; M of Law & Diplomacy, Tufts U., 1977. Ordained Jesuit priest, 1977, Md. Pres. Cath. Legal Immigration Network, Inc., Washington; exec. dir. migration and refugee svcs. U.S. Cath. Conf., Washington, 1990-94; Arrupe tutor, Oxford rsch. assoc. Refugee Studies Program Oxford U., Eng., 1995—; v.p. Internat. Cath. Migration Commn., Geneva, 1993—; chmn. com. on migration and refugee affairs, Interaction, Washington, 1993—; bd. dirs. Ctr. for Migration Studies, N.Y.C., Nat. Forum, Washington, Nat. Coalition for Haitian Refugees, N.Y.C.; mem. adv. bd. Refugee Policy Group, Washington, 1991—. Home: Oxford U, Campion Hall, Oxford OX1 1QS, England Office: Refugee Studies Program, Queen Elizabeth Ho 21 St Giles, Oxford OX1 3LA, England

RYSER, PAMELA HORTON, small business owner; b. Grove Hill, Ala., June 13, 1952; d. Glover Wade and Gwendolyn (Finch) Horton; m. William Edward Ryser; children: William Joseph, Edward Wade. AA, Ala. So. Coll.; student, U. S. Ala. Cert. accomplishment H&R Block. Head teller Merchants Bank, Jackson, Ala., 1972-79; sec., bookkeeper McLain Constrn. Co., Jackson, 1978-80, Melton DuBose, P.A., Jackson, 1982-84; pres., owner McLain Hardware, Inc., Jackson, 1984—. Den leader Cub Scouts Am., Jackson, 1988-89; Sunday Sch. tchr. Goodsprings Bapt. Ch. Mem. NAFE, Jackson C. of C. (vice chair Christmas Parade 1993, chair 1994), Downtown Merchants Assn., Phi Theta Kappa. Avocations: horseback riding, cross stitch, tennis, swimming, four-wheeler riding. Home: RR 1 Box 52-f Jackson AL 36545-9801 Office: McLain Hardware Inc 108 Carroll St Jackson AL 36545-2710

RYSKAMP, BRUCE E., publishing executive; b. Grand Rapids, Mich., 1941. AB, Calvin Coll., 1962; MBA, Mich. State U., 1964. With R. H. Donnelly Corp., 1964-82; with Zondervan Pub. House Zondervan Corp., Grand Rapids, 1983—, v.p. book and bible pub. Zondervan Pub. House, 1986—. Office: Zondervan Pub House 5300 Patterson Ave SE Grand Rapids MI 49512-9659

RYSKAMP, CHARLES ANDREW, museum executive, educator; b. East Grand Rapids, Mich., Oct. 21, 1928; s. Henry Jacob and Flora (DeGraaf) R. A.B., Calvin Coll., 1950; M.A., Yale U., 1951, Ph.D., 1956; postgrad., Pembroke Coll., Cambridge U., 1953-54; Litt.D., Trinity Coll., Hartford, 1975; L.H.D., Union Coll., 1977. Nathan Hale fellow Yale U., 1954-55; instr. English Princeton U., 1955-59, asst. prof., 1959-63, assoc. prof., 1963-69; curator English and Am. lit. Univ. Library, 1967-69, prof., 1969—; Procter & Gamble faculty fellow, 1958-59; jr. fellow Council of Humanities, 1960-61, John E. Annan preceptor, 1961-64; dir. Pierpont Morgan Library, N.Y.C., 1969-87, Frick Collection, N.Y.C., 1987—; mem. adv. bd. Skowhegan Sch. Painting and Sculpture, Private Papers of James Boswell, Yale U. Author: William Cowper of the Inner Temple, Esq, 1959, William Blake, Engraver, 1969; editor: (with F.A. Pottle) Boswell: The Ominous Years, 1963, The Cast-Away, 1963, Wilde and the Nineties, 1966, William Blake: The Pickering Manuscript, 1972, (with J. King) The Letters and Prose Writings of William Cowper, vol. I, 1979, vol. II, 1981, vol. III, 1982, Vol. IV, 1984, Vol. V, 1986, (with R. Wendorf) The Works of William Collins, 1979, (with J. Baird) The Poetical Works of William Cowper, vol. I, 1980, vols. II-III, 1995, (with J. King) William Cowper: Selected Letters, 1989, Report to the Fellows of the Pierpont Morgan Library, vols. 16-21, 1969-89. Trustee, mem. exec. com. Mus. Broadcasting, 1977-87; trustee Andrew W. Mellon Found., John Simon Guggenheim Meml. Found., Corning Mus. Glass, Amon Carter Mus.; mem. adv. coun. art mus. Princeton U.; mem. vis. com. dept. paintings conservation Met. Mus. Art; patron William Blake Trust; mem. bd. mgrs. Lewis Walpole Libr., Yale U.; bd. dirs., v.p. Gerard B. Lambert Found.; v.p. Frederick R. Koch Found.; v.p. Giannalisa Feltrinelli Found. Decorated Order St. John of Jerusalem, comdr. Order Orange Nassau, The Netherlands, officer Order Leopold II, Belgium, comdr. Order of Falcon, Iceland; recipient Peter Stuyvesant award Dutch Am. West-India Co., 1987, Gold medal Holland Soc., 1991. Mem. Am. Acad. Arts and Scis., Am. Philosphical Soc., Museums Coun. N.Y.C. (past v.p.), Royal Soc. Arts London, Keats-Shelley Assn. Am. (past v.p.), Master Drawings Assn. (pres.), Met. Opera Assn. (bd. advisors), Drawing Soc. (nat. com.), Bibliog. Soc. Am., Acad. Am. Poets, Am. Antiquarian Soc., Assn. Art Mus. Dirs. (past pres.), N.Y. Geneal. and Biog. Soc. (spl. corr.), Cowper Soc., Assn. Internationale de Bibliophilie (com. of Honor), Found. French Mus. (adv. bd.), Royal Soc. Arts (London), Wordsworth Rydel Mount Trust, Pilgrims, Grolier Club, Century Assn., Lotos Club (N.Y.C.), Elizabethan Club (New Haven), Roxburghe Club (London). Office: The Frick Collection 1 E 70th St New York NY 10021-4907

RYSKAMP, KENNETH LEE, federal judge; b. 1932; m. Karyl Sonja Ryskamp; 1 child, Cara Leigh. AB, Calvin Coll., 1955; JD, U. Miami, 1956. Bar: Fla. 1956, Mich. 1957, U.S. Supreme Ct. 1970. Law clk. to presiding judge Fla. Ct. Appeals 3d Dist., 1957-59; pvt. practice law Miami, Fla., 1959-61; ptnr. Goodwin, Ryskamp, Welcher & Carrier, Miami, 1961-84; mng. ptnr. Squire, Sanders & Dempsey, Miami, 1984-86; judge U.S. Dist. Ct. (so. dist.) Fla., Miami, 1986—. Office: US Dist Ct 701 Clematis St Fl 4 West Palm Beach FL 33401-5101

RYU, DEWEY DOO YOUNG, biochemical engineering educator; b. Seoul, Korea, Oct. 27, 1936; came to U.S., 1955; s. Hansang and Sonam (Kim) R.; children: Mina L., Regina P. BSChemE, MIT, 1961, PhD in Biochemical Engring., 1967. Sr. rsch. engr. Sqibb Inst. for Med. Rsch., New Brunswick, N.J., 1967-72; adj. prof. Rutgers U., New Brunswick, 1968-72; prof., chmn. Korea Advanced Inst. Sci., Seoul, 1973-81; prof., dir. biochemical engring. program U. Calif., Davis, 1982—, SUNY, Buffalo, 1991-92; vis. prof. MIT, Cambridge, 1972-73; com. mem. UN Indsl. Devel. Orgn. & Food and Agr. Orgn./UN, N.Y.C., 1981-86, NAS-NRC/Bioprocess Engring., Washington, 1991-92. Contbr. over 170 sci. articles to profl. jours. Recipient Nat. Order Civil Merit/Presdl. Medal Hon., Pres. of Korea, Korea, 1981. Fellow Am. Inst. Med. and Biological Engring. Socs.; mem. AAAS, AICE, Am. Chem. Soc., Am. Soc. for Microbiology. Achievements include 18 patents in the areas of bioprocess engineering and biotechnology. Home: 658 Portsmouth Ave Davis CA 95616-2738 Office: U Calif Dept Chem Engring Davis CA 95616

RYU, EDWIN KYU SUNG, investment advisor and financial planner; b. Monterey, Calif., Nov. 24, 1951; s. Henry H. and Helen K. (Lee) R.; m. Julie Satake; children: Nicole, Danielle. BA in Econs., Stanford U., 1976. CPA. Supr., mgr. Touche Ross & Co. (noe Deloitte & Touche), San Francisco, 1979-84; v.p. fin. Van Kasper & Co., San Francisco, 1984-86; pres., prin. Ryu & Co. (now Kendrick, Stimpfig & Ryu, Ltd.), San Francisco, 1985—; also chmn. bd. Ryu & Co. (now Kendrick, Stimpfig & Ryu, Ltd.); instr. Golden Gate U., San Francisco, 1986-89; spl. advisor Pacific West Partnership, Inc., L.A., 1987—; bd. dirs. Willow Tree Invest, Inc., 1991—. Co-author (Grad. Sch. Course) Internat. Investment & Taxation, 1986-89; founder, editor-in-chief (newsletter) Medwatch, 1995—. Bd. dirs. Stonestown YMCA, San Francisco, 1989-92, Midpeninsula YMCA, Mountain View, 1995—. Mem. Stanford Alumni Assn. Avocations: basketball, travel. Office: Kendrick Stimpfig & Ryu Ltd 2001 Gateway Pl Ste 340 E San Jose CA 95110

RZECINSKI, DOREEN ANN, preschool educator; b. Morristown, N.J., Jan. 16, 1971; d. George John and Eileen Dorothy (Sexton) R. AA in Liberal Arts, County Coll. of Morris, Randolph, N.J., 1992, group tchr. cert., 1992. Pre-sch. tchr. Teddy and Me Day Care, Morristown, N.J., 1988—. Mem. Nat. Child Care Assn. (cert.). Roman Catholic.

SA, JULIE, mayor, restaurant chain owner; b. Korea, Dec. 15, 1950; came to US, 1970:; married;. Degree in Polit. Sci., Dong-A U., Korea. Owner restaurant chain; councilwoman City of Fullerton, Calif., 1992-94, mayor, 1994—; rep. bd. Orange County Sanitation Dists. Mem. Fullerton C. of C., Orange County Korean C. of C., Orange County Chinese C. of C. Office: Office of the Mayor 303 W Commonwealth Ave Fullerton CA 92632*

SAAD, THEODORE SHAFICK, retired microwave company executive; b. Boston, Sept. 13, 1920; s. Wadie Assad and Mary (Shalhoub) S.; m. Afeefi Abdelnour, May 5, 1943; children: Karen Jeanne, Janet Elaine. BSEE, MIT, 1941. Engr. Sylvania Electric Products, Danvers, Mass., 1941-42; rsch. assoc. radiation lab. Radiation Lab. MIT, Cambridge, 1942-45; sr. engr. Submarine Signal Co., Boston, 1945-49; v.p., chief engr. Microwave Devel. Labs., Waltham, Mass., 1949-53; engring. specialist Sylvania Electric Products, Woburn, Mass., 1953-55; pres., chmn. Sage Labs. Inc., Natick, Mass., 1955-93; ret., 1993; cons. Horizon House Microwave, Norwood, Mass., 1958—. Editor: Microwave Engineers Handbook, 1971, Historical Perspectives of Microwave Technology, 1984; patentee in microwavetech. and passive components fields. Fellow IEEE (life; Richard M. Emberson award 1996), AAAS; mem. Microwave Soc. of IEEE (hon. life; nat. lectr. 1972, Disting. Svc. award 1983, Centennial medal 1984, Career award 1992). Avocations: photography, reading, travel, music. Home: 52 Doublet Hill Rd Weston MA 02193-2331

SAADA, ADEL SELIM, civil engineer, educator; b. Heliopolis, Egypt, Oct. 24, 1934; came to U.S., 1959, naturalized, 1965; s. Selim N. and Marie (Chahyne) S.; m. Nancy Helen Hernan, June 5, 1960; children: Christiane Mona, Richard Adel. Ingénieur des Arts et Manufactures, École Centrale, Paris, 1958; M.S., U. Grenoble, France, 1959; Ph.D. in Civil Engring, Princeton U., 1961. Registered profl. engr., Ohio. Engr. Société Dumez, Paris, 1959; research assoc. dept. civil engring. Princeton (N.J.) U., 1961-62; asst. prof. civil engring. Case Western Reserve U., Cleve., 1962-67; asso. prof. Case Western Reserve U., 1967-72, prof., 1973—, chmn. dept. civil engring., 1978—, Frank H. Neff prof. civil engring., chmn. dept., 1987; R.J. Carroll Meml. lectr. Johns Hopkins U., 1990; cons., lectr. soil testing and properties Waterways Expt. Sta. (C.E.), Vicksburg, Miss., 1974-79; cons. to various firms, 1962—. Author: Elasticity Theory and Applications, 1974, 2d edit., 1993; contbr. numerous articles on soil mechanics and foundation engring. to profl. jours. Recipient Telford Prize Instn. of Civil Engrs., U.K., 1995. Fellow ASCE (Civil Engr. of Yr. Cleve. sect. 1992); mem. Internat. Soc. Soil Mechanics, ASTM, One Two One Athletic Club. Inventor pneumatic analog computer and loading frame. Home: 3342 Braemar Rd Cleveland OH 44120-3332 Office: Case Western Res U Dept Civil Engring Case Sch Engring Cleveland OH 44106

SAALFELD, FRED ERICH, naval researcher; b. Joplin, Mo., Apr. 9, 1935; s. Eric Arthur and Milla (Kessler) S.; m. Elizabeth Renner, Nov. 22, 1958; 1 child, Fred E. Jr. (dec.). BS cum laude, So. East Mo. State U., 1957; MS in Chemistry, Iowa State U., 1959, PhD in Physical Chem., 1961. Instructor Iowa State U., Ames, 1961-62; chemist Naval Rsch. Lab, Washington, 1962-63, head mass spectrometry sect., 1963-74, head physical chm. br., 1974-76, supt. chem. divsn., 1976-82; chief scientist Office Naval Rsch., London, 1979-80; dir. rsch. Office Naval Rsch., Arlington, Va., 1982-87, dir., 1987-93, dep. chief naval rsch., tech. dir., 1993—. Author more than 500 publications, reports, presentations on applications of mass spectrometry to fields of combustion, laser, environ. analysis. Recipient Disting. Rank award Pres., Washington, 1989, Meritorious Rank award Pres., Washington, 1986, Robert Conrad award Sec. U.S. Navy, Washington, 1988; named Fed. Exec. of Yr. Fed. Exec. Inst., Washington, 1991. Fellow AAAS; mem. Am. Chem. Soc. (councilor 1973-89), Am. Soc. Mass Spectrometry (sec. 1970-74), Combustion Inst., Chem. Soc. Washington (pres. 1972). Achievements include provision for science base for life support systems used in all U.S. submarines; development of educational programs used by USN for scientist training. Avocations: history, woodworking, sports. Office: Office of Naval Rsch 800 N Quincy St Arlington VA 22217-5660

SAAR, ALISON, sculptor; b. L.A., Feb. 5, 1956. BA, Scripps Coll., 1978; MFA, Otis Art Inst., 1981. One-woman shows include Bellevue (Wash.) Art Mus., 1992, Neuberger Mus., Purchase, N.Y., 1992, Cleve. Ctr. Contemporary Art, 1992, High Mus., Atlanta, 1993, Hirshhorn Mus., Washington, 1993, Freedman Gallery, Allbright Coll. Ctr. Arts, Reading, Pa., 1993, Va. Mus. Fine Arts, 1994, Otis Art Inst. Jan Baum Gallery, L.A., 1993, Laguna Gloria Art Mus., Austin, 1993, Whitney Mus. Am. Art, 1993, Clar Humanities Mus., Scipps Coll., Pomona, Calif., 1994, Denver Art Mus., 1994, Columbus Mus. Art, 1994, Jan Baum Gallery, L.A., 1994, San Francisco Cmty. Arts, Hines Internat. Ltd., L.A., 1994; commd. bronze gates Metro Transit Authority, N.Y., 1990-91; exhibited works at Met. Mus. Art, N.Y., 1987, Whitney Mus. Am. Art, N.Y., 1988, Met. Mus. Art, N.Y., 1988, Aldrich Mus., 1991. Recipient awards Nat. Endowment Arts, 1985, 88, John Solomon Guggenheim award, 1989. Office: c/o Jan Baum Gallery 170 S La Brea Ave Los Angeles CA 90036

SAAR, BETYE (IRENE SAAR), artist; b. L.A., July 30, 1926; d. Jefferson Maze and Beatrice Lillian (Parson) Brown; m. Richard W. Saar, Sept. 16, 1952 (div. 1968); children: Lesley Irene, Alison Marie, Tracye Ann. BA, UCLA, 1949. Instr. art Calif. State U., Hayward, 1971, Northridge, 1973-74; instr. art Otis Art Inst., L.A., 1976-83; lectr., free-lance designer for films, 1970-75—; costume designer Inner City Cultural Ctr., Napa Valley Theatre Co., 1968-73. One-woman exhbns. include Monique Knowlton, N.Y.C., 1976, 81, Calif. State U. Gallery, L.A., 1972, Whitney Mus. Art, N.Y.C., 1975, Jan Baum, L.A., 1977, 79, 81, Maneville Art Gallery, U. Calif., San Diego, 1979, Quay Gallery, San Francisco, 1982, Mus. Contemporary Art, L.A., 1984, Pa. Acad. Art, Phila., 1987, MIT, Cambridge, Mass., 1987, Calif. State U., Fullerton, 1988, also galleries in Manila, Kuala Lumpur, Malaysia, Taichung, Taiwan, 1988, Aukland and Wellington, New Zealand, 1988, 89, Montgomery Art Gallery Pomona Coll., 1991, U. Hartford (Conn.) Art Gallery, 1992, Fresno (Calif.) Art Mus., 1993, U. Ctrl. Fla. Art Gallery, Orlando, 1994, Santa Monica (Calif.) Mus. Art, 1994; two-woman exhbns. San Francisco Mus. Modern Art, 1977, Wight Gallery, UCLA, 1990; group exhbns. include Small Environments, Univ. Galleries, So. Ill. U., 1972, 20th Century Black Am. Art, San Jose (Calif.) Mus., 1976, San Francisco Mus. Modern Art, 1977, Smithsonian Instn.; touring exhbn. with daughter Alison Saar, 1990—, Netherlands Textile Mus., Tilburg, 1993, Mus. Applied Arts, Helsinki, Finland, 1993, Ctr. for Arts at Yerba Buena Gardens, San Francisco, 1993, Mus. Modern Art, Sao Paulo, 1994, Wilfredo Law Ctr., Havana, Cuba, 1994. NEA grantee, 1974, 84, James Van Der Zee grantee, 1992; J. Paul Getty fellow, 1990, Guggenheim Found. fellow, 1991. Mem. L.A. Inst. Contemporary Art. Democrat.

SAARI, DONALD GENE, mathematician; b. Ironwood, Mich., Mar. 9, 1940; s. Gene August and Martha Mary (Jackson) S.; m. Lillian Joy Kalinen, June 11, 1966; children: Katri, Anneli. BS, Mich. Tech. U., 1962; PhD, Purdue U., 1967, DSc (hon.), 1989. Research astronomer Yale U., New Haven, 1967-68; prof. dept. math. Northwestern U., Evanston, Ill., 1968—, prof. econs., 1988—, Pancoe prof. math., 1995—, chmn. dept., 1981-84; prof. U. Nanjing (China), 1995; cons. Nat. Bur. Standards, Gaithersburg, Md., 1979-86, Commn. 9, Internat. Astron. Union, 1985-91. Assoc. editor Jour. Econ. Behavior and Orgn., 1988-94, Celestial Mechanics and Dynamical Astronomy. 1989-95, Econ. Theory, 1990—. Recipient Duncan Black award, Pub. Choice Soc., 1991, Chauvenet prize Mathematical Assn. of Am., 1995; Guggenheim fellow, 1988-89. Mem. Am. Math. Soc., Math. Assn. Am. (Chauvenet prize 1995), Am. Astron. Soc., Soc. Indsl. and Applied Math. (editor jour. 1981-88), Econometric Soc. Office: Dept Math Northwestern U Evanston IL 60208-2730

SAARI, JOHN WILLIAM, JR., lawyer; b. Jersey City, Oct. 12, 1937; s. John William Sr. and Ina Marie (Bain) S.; m. Susan Jo Olson, Aug. 27, 1967 (div. June 1971); m. Marjorie Ann Palm, Nov. 16, 1973. Student, Duke U., 1955-58, U. N.C., 1962-63; JD with honors, Ill. Inst. Tech., Chgo., 1972. Bar: Ill. 1972, U.S. Dist. Ct. (no. dist.) Ill. 1972, Wis. 1980, U.S. Dist. Ct. (ea. and we. dists.) Wis. 1980, U.S. Ct. Appeals (7th cir.) 1972. Assoc. Yates, Goff, Gustafson & Been, Chgo., 1972-76, Hubbard, Hubbard, O'Brien & Hall, Chgo., 1976-78; atty. Ill. Bell Telephone Co., Chgo., 1978-79; assoc. Cirilli Law Office, Rhinelander, Wis., 1979-83; pvt. practice Rhinelander, 1983-90; ptnr. Rodd, Mouw, Saari & Krueger, Rhinelander, 1990—. Bd. dirs. Northwoods United Way, 1980-88, pres., 1983-84. With U.S. Army, 1958-61, ETO. Mem. ABA, Ill. Bar Assn., Wis. Bar Assn., Oneida-Vilas-Forest Bar Assn. (pres. 1996—), Lions (pres. Sugarcamp 1983-84). Avocations: hunting, fishing, baseball, reading, golf. Home: 7279 Arbutus Dr Eagle River WI 54521-9249 Office: Rodd Mouw Saari & Krueger 8A W Davenport St Rhinelander WI 54501-0757

SAARI, JOY ANN, family nurse practitioner, geriatrics and medical/surgical nurse; b. Chippewa Falls, Wis., July 14, 1953; d. Harry R. and Hilda R. (Christianson) Harwood; m. Allan A. Saari, Dec. 31, 1973 (dec.); children: Christopher, Erik. BSN summa cum laude, U. Wis., Eau Claire, 1978; postgrad., Blue Ridge Community Coll., Verona, Va., 1987; MSN, FNP, George Mason U., 1995; MSN. RN, Mich., Wis., Va.; FNP, Va.; cert. BLS instr., ACLS. Staff nurse Portage View Hosp., Hancock, Mich., 1979-80; evening supr., asst. dir. nursing Chippewa Manor, Chippewa Falls, 1980-86; staff nurse Bridgewater (Va.) Home, Inc., 1986-90; p.m. charge nurse Medicalodge Leavenworth, Kans., 1990-91; outdoor edn. nurse Montgomery County (Md.) Schs., 1991-93; FNP Leesburg/Sterling Family Practice, 1995—. Capt. USAR Nurse Corps. Mem. Am. Acad. Nurse Practitioners, Nat. League of Nursing, No. Va. Nurse Practitioner Assn., Res. Officer Assn., Am. Legion Aux., Phi Kappa Phi.

SAAVEDRA, CHARLES JAMES, banker; b. Denver, Nov. 2, 1941; s. Charles James and Evangeline Cecilia (Aragon) S.; m. Ann Helen Taylor, 1967; children: Michael, Kevin, Sarah. BSBA, Regis U., Denver, 1963; postgrad. U. Calif., San Francisco, 1964-66. Vice-pres., Western States Bankcard Assn., San Francisco, 1969-77; dir. info. systems World Airways, Inc., Oakland, Calif., 1977-79; v.p. computer services First Nationwide Bank, San Francisco, 1979-83; sr. v.p. Wells Fargo Bank, San Francisco, 1983-92; sr. v.p. Union Bank of Calif., San Francisco, 1992—; instr. Programming & Systems Inst., San Francisco, 1968-69; lectr. Am. Mgmt. Assn., 1984—; pres. Right Direction Project of Contra Costa County; bd. dirs. No. Calif. Family Ctr. With USNR, 1963-64. Mem. Data Processing Mgrs. Assn. (bd. dirs., chmn. program com. 1981), Am. Nat. Standards Inst., Am. Bankers Assn., San Francisco Jaycees, Alpha Delta Gamma. Clubs: Commonwealth of

Calif., Lake Lakewood Assn. Home: 210 Lakewood Rd Walnut Creek CA 94598-4826 Office: Union Bank 350 California St San Francisco CA 94104-1402

SABANAS-WELLS, ALVINA OLGA, orthopedic surgeon; b. Riga, Latvia, Lithuania, July 30, 1914; d. Adomas and Olga (Dagilyte) Pipyne; m. Juozas Sabanas, Aug. 20, 1939 (dec. Mar. 1968); 1 child, Algis (dec.); m. Alfonse F. Wells, Dec. 31, 1977 (dec. 1990). MD, U. Vytautas The Great, Kaunas, Lithuania, 1939; MS in Orthopaedic Surgery, U. Minn., 1955. Diplomate Am. Bd. Orthopaedic Surgery. Intern Univ. Clinics, Kaunas, 1939-40; resident orthopaedic surgery and trauma Red Cross Trauma Hosp., Kaunas, 1940-44; orthopaedic and trauma fellow Unfall Krankenhous, Vienna, Austria, 1943-44; intern Jackson Park Hosp., Chgo., 1947-48; fellow in orthopaedic surgery Mayo Clinic, Rochester, Minn., 1952-55; assoc. orthopaedic surgery Northwestern U., 1956-72; asst. prof. orthopaedic surgery Rush Med. Sch., 1973-76; pvt. practice orthopaedic surgery Sun City, Ariz., 1976-89; pres. cattle ranch corp. Contbr. articles to profl. jours. Fellow ACS; mem. Am. Acad. Orthopaedic Surgery, Physicians Club Sun City, Mayo Alumni Assn. Mem. U. Minn. Alumni Assn., Ruth Jackson Orthopedic Soc. Republican. Mem. Evang. Reformed Ch. Avocations: art, antiques, environment. Home: 3101 Skipworth Dr Las Vegas NV 89107-3241

SABAROFF, ROSE EPSTEIN, retired education educator; b. Cleve., Sept. 4, 1918; d. Hyman Israel and Bertha (Glaser) Epstein; m. Bernard Joseph Sabaroff, Dec. 28, 1940; children: Ronald Asher, Katya Nina. B.A., U. Ariz., 1941; M.A., San Francisco State U., 1954; Ed.D., Stanford U., 1957. Tchr. Presidio Hill Elem. Sch., San Francisco, 1951-55; asst. prof. edn. Oreg. State U., Corvallis, 1958-61; asst. dir., then dir. elem. edn. Harvard Grad. Sch. Edn., Cambridge, Mass., 1961-66; prof. edn., head elem. edn., head reading program Va. Poly. Inst. and State U., Blacksburg, 1967-82; dir. Grad. Edn. Ctr. Calif. Luth. Coll., North Hollywood, 1982-84; reading specialist How to Learn, Inc., West Los Angeles, Calif., 1983-88. Author: (with Hanna, Davies, Farrar) Geography in the Teaching of Social Studies, 1966, (with Mary Ann Hanna) The Open Classroom, 1974, Teaching Reading with a Linguistic Approach, 1980, Developing Linguistic Awareness, 1981; contbr. articles to profl. jours. Recipient Disting. Research award Va. Edn. Research Assn., 1977; Phi Delta Kappa grantee, 1980. Mem. AAUP, Internat. Reading Assn., NEA, Va. Edn. Assn., Va. Coll. Reading Educators (pres. 1976-77), Va. Reading Assn., Phi Delta Kappa, Pi Lambda Theta, Gamma Theta Upsilon. Democrat. Jewish. Conducted 15 month study abroad comparing ednl. systems in 4 European countries with differing social-econ. systems. Home: 23826 Villena Mission Viejo CA 92692-1818

SABAT, RICHARD J., lawyer; b. Nov. 24, 1947. BA, SUNY Binghamton, 1970; JD, Syracuse U., 1973. Bar: Pa. 1973. Ptnr. Morgan, Lewis & Bockius, Phila. Office: Morgan Lewis & Bockius 2000 One Logan Sq Philadelphia PA 19103*

SABAT, ROBERT HARTMAN, magazine editor; b. Newark, Aug. 28, 1957; s. Charles and Marilyn Ruth (Hartman) S.; m. Jessica Schilling Fine, Oct. 15, 1989; 1 child, Nathaniel. BA, Brandeis U., 1980. Mng. editor Penthouse mag., N.Y.C., 1986-91, Lear's mag., N.Y.C., 1992-94, Interview, N.Y.C., 1994-95, Smart Money mag., N.Y.C., 1995—, Connoisseur mag., N.Y.C., 1991-92. Mem. Am. Soc. Mag. Editors. Office: Smart Money 1790 Broadway New York NY 10019

SABATH, LEON DAVID, internist, educator; b. Savannah, Ga., July 24, 1930; s. Sholom and Sarah (Cherkas) S.; children—Natasha, Joanna, Rachel. A.B. magna cum laude, Harvard U., 1952, M.D., 1956. Diplomat Am. Bd. Internal Medicine, Am. Bd. Infectious Disease. Intern Peter Bent Brigham Hosp., Boston, 1956-57; sr. resident in medicine Peter Bent Brigham Hosp., 1962-63; jr. resident in medicine Bellevue Hosp., N.Y.C., 1959-60; fellow in infectious disease Harvard U. and Thorndike Meml. Lab., Boston City Hosp., 1960-62; fellow in antibiotic resistance Sir William Dunn Sch. Pathology, Oxford U., Eng., 1963-65; mem. faculty dept. medicine Harvard U., also; staff physician Boston City Hosp., 1965-74; asst. Harvard Med. Sch., 1965-67, asst. prof., 1967-70, asso. prof., 1970-74; head sect. infectious diseases U. Minn., Mpls., 1974-83; prof. medicine U. Minn., 1974—; chmn. coms. U. Minn. Hosps.; adj. faculty Rockefeller U., 1990-91. Editor: Pseudomonas aeruginosa, 1980, Antibiotic Action in Patients, 1982; editl. bd. Clin. Pharmacology and Therapeutics, 1978-80; contbr. articles on antibiotics and their use, bacterial resistance to antibiotics chlamydia and death associated wiht exercise to profl. jours. Trustee E.P.A. Cephalosporin Fund, Oxford U., 1970—. Capt. M.C. AUS, 1957-59. NIH spl. fellow, 1963-65; recipient Career Devel. award NIH, 1968-72. Fellow ACP, Infectious Disease Soc. Am.; mem. Am. Soc. Clin. Investigation, Am. Soc. Microbiology (vice chmn. div. antimicrobial chemotherapy 1976-77, chmn. 1977-78), Am. Soc. Clin. Pharmacology and Theapeutics, Central Soc. Clin. Research, Am. Fedn. Clin. Research, Soc. Gen. Microbiology, Mass. Med. Soc., Soc. Exptl. Biology and Medicine, Brit. Soc. Antimicrobial Chemotherapy, Sigma Xi. Home: 2504 Washburn Ave S Minneapolis MN 55416-4351 Office: Phillip Wangenstean Bldg 14-168A University of Minn Hospitals Minneapolis MN 55455

SABATINI, DAVID DOMINGO, cell biologist, biochemist; b. Bolivar, Argentina, May 10, 1931; m. Zulema Lena Sabatina, 1960; children: Bernardo L., David M. MD, Nat. U. Litoral, 1954; PhD in Biochemistry, Rockefeller U., 1966. Instr., lectr., assoc. prof. histiology Inst. Gen. Anatomy and Embryology, U. Buenos Aires, 1957-60; dir. admissions Med. Sch. U. Buenos Aires, 1957-60; Rockefeller Found. fellow Med. Sch. Yale U., 1961, Rockefeller Inst., 1961-62; rsch. assoc. cell biol. lab Rockefeller U., N.Y.C., 1961-63, from asst. prof. to assoc. prof. cell biology, 1960-72; prof. cell biology and biochemistry NYU, 1972-74, Frederick L. Ehrman prof., chmn. dept. cell biol. Sch. Med., 1975—, dir. MD-PhD program, 1987—; Wendell Griffith Meml. lectr. St. Louis U., 1977; Mary Peterman Meml. lectr. Meml.-Sloan Kettering Inst., N.Y., 1977; 25th Robert J. Terry lectr. Wash. U., 1978; 7th Ann. Kenneth F. Naidorff Meml. lectr. Columbia U., 1989; fellow Nat. Acad. Medicine, Argentina, 1956; UNESCO fellow Biophysics Inst., Rio de Janeiro, 1957; Pfizer traveling fellow, 1972; mem. molecular biology study sect. NIH, 1973-77, chmn., 1976-77; mem. bd. basic biology Nat. Rsch. Coun., 1986—. Editor Jour. Cellular Biochemistry, 1980-84, Molecular & Cellular Biology, 1980-82, Biol. Cell, 1986—, Current Opinions Cell Biology, 1990—. Recipient Samuel Roberts Noble Rsch. Recognition award, 1980. Fellow AAAS, N.Y. Acad. Sci.; mem. NAS, Am. Soc. Cell Biology (pres. 1978-79, coun. mem. 1974-77, E. B. Wilson award 1986), Harvey Soc. (v.p. 1985-86, pres. 1986-87). *

SABATINI, GABRIELA, tennis player; b. Buenos Aires, May 16, 1970; d. Osvaldo and Beatriz S. Winner French Jr. Open, 1984, Italian Jr. Open, 1984, Japan Open, 1985, Tokyo Open, 1987, Brighton Open, 1987, Italian Open, 1988, 1989, 1991, 1992, Virginia Slims Championship, 1988, 94, U.S. Open, 1990; Silver medalist in Tennis, 1988 Summer Olympics.

SABATINI, LAWRENCE, bishop; b. Chgo., May 15, 1930; s. Dominic and Ada (Piloi) S. Ph.L., Gregorian U., Rome, 1953, S.T.L., 1957, J.C.D., 1960; M.S. in Edn., Iona Coll., 1968. Ordained priest, Roman Catholic Ch., 1957, bishop, 1978. Prof. canon law St. Charles Sem., S.I., N.Y., 1960-71; pastor St. Stephen's Parish, North Vancouver, B.C., Canada, 1970-78; provincial superior Missionaries of St. Charles, Oak Park, Ill., 1978; aux. bishop Archdiocese Vancouver, B.C., Can., 1978-82; bishop Diocese Kamloops, B.C., Can., 1982—; procurator, adviser Matrimonial Tribunal, N.Y.C., 1964-71; founder, dir. RAP Youth Counseling Service, S.I., N.Y., 1969-71; vice ofcl. Regional Matrimonial tribunal of Diocese Kamloops, 1978-82; chmn. Kamloops Cath. Pub. Schs., 1982—. Named Man of Yr. Confratellanza Italo-Canadese, 1979. Mem. Can. Canon Law Soc., Canon Law Soc. Am., Can. Conf. Cath. Bishops. Office: Diocese of Kamloops, 635A Tranquille Rd, Kamloops, BC Canada V2B 3H5*

SABATINI, NELSON JOHN, government official; b. Rochester, N.Y., Jan. 20, 1940; s. John R. and Ida M. (Ceconi) S.; m. Marilyn Jean Gromala, Jan. 19, 1963; children—John Nelson, Michael Christopher. Student, Lewis Coll., Lockport, Ill., 1958-62; B.A. in Psychology, George Washington U., 1971, postgrad. Claims rep. Social Security Adminstrn., Chgo., 1962-65; various positions Social Security Adminstrn., Balt., 1965-79, dep. dir. disability programs, 1979-81, exec. asst. to commr., 1981-82, assoc. commr., 1982—, dep. commr., 1983-88; dep. sec. health and mental hygiene State of Md., 1988, sec. health and mental hygiene, 1991—; v.p. U. Md. Med. System, 1995—. Named Disting. Marylander of Yr. 1993; recipient Sec.'s cert. HHS, 1975; Commr.'s citation Social Security Adminstrn., 1977, 81; Presdl. Merit Rank award Pres. of U.S., 1984. Roman Catholic. Avocations: sailing; tennis.

SABATINI, SANDRA, physician; b. N.Y.C., Dec. 1, 1940. BS in Chemistry, Millsaps Coll., 1962; MS in Pharmacology, Marquette U., 1966; PhD in Pharmacology, U. Miss., 1968; MD in Internal Medicine, Tex. Med. Sch., 1974. Lic. physician, Ill., Tex. Intern in medicine U. Ill. Hosp., Chgo., 1974-75; asst. prof. U. Tex. Med. Sch., San Antonio, 1968-70; assoc. dir. U. Ill. Hosp., Chgo., 1977-78; asst. prof. U. Ill. Coll. of Medicine, Chgo., 1977-83, assoc. prof. medicine and physiology, 1983-84; attending physician in nephrology VA, Chgo., 1977-84; med. dir. Dialysis Unit U. Ill., Chgo., 1978-84; prof. internal medicine and physiology Tex. Tech. U. Health Sci. Ctr., Lubbock, 1985—, chmn. dept. physiology, 1993—; attending physician in nephrology U. Med. Ctr., Lubbock, 1985—; lab. instr. Millsaps Coll., Jackson, Miss., 1961-62; instr. in pharmacology, Bapt. Hosp. Sch. Nursing, Jackson, 1966-68; merit rev. mem. NSF, 1987, 91, 92; rev. mem. several orgns. including Chgo. Heart Assn., 1984, NIH, 1982, 86, 89-93, Nat. Kidney Found., 1987, 89—, Am. Heart Assn., 1981-84, others. Editorial referee Am. Jour. Kidney Disease, Am. Jour. Physiology, Am. Jour. Nephrology, Annals of Internal Medicine, others; editorial bd. Am. Jour. Nephrology, 1989-93, Seminars in Nephrology, 1984—; ; author numerous publs. and abstracts in field; contbr. articles to profl. jours. Recipient predoctoral fellowship tng. grant, Marquette U., 1963-66, pub. health predoctoral fellow U. Miss. Med. Sch., 1967-69, gen. medicine sci. rsch. grant U. Tex. Med. Sch., 1968-70, post-grad. fellowship award Karolinska Inst., Swedish Med. Coun., 1971, 73, NIH grants, 1979-82, 1984—, Chgo. Heart Assn. grant-in-aid, 1979-85, Nat. Eye Inst. grant, 1979-80, Banes Charitable Trust award U. Ill.,1984-85, U.S. Olympic Com. Rsch. Found. Clin. Study, 1986-87, numerous others awards in field. Fellow Am. Coll. Physicians; mem. AAAS, AAUP, Am. Fedn. Clin. Rsch., Am. Heart Assn., Am. Physiol. Soc., Am. Soc. Nephrology, Am. Soc. Pharmacology and Exptl. Therapeutics, Am. Soc. Renal Biochemistry and Metabolism (pres. elect 1994), Cen. Soc. Clin. Rsch., Ill. Kidney Found., Internat. Soc. Nephrology, Italian-Am. Nephrologists, Inc., Nat. Kidney Found. (numerous offices including chmn. several coms.), Nat. Kidney Found. of West Tex. (bd. dirs. 1993—), Alpha Omega Alpha, numerous others. Office: Tex Tech U Health Sci Ctr 3601 4th St Lubbock TX 79430-0001

SABATO, LARRY JOSEPH, political science educator; b. Norfolk, Va., Aug. 7, 1952; s. N.J. and Margaret F. (Simmons) S. BA, U. Va., 1974; postgrad. Princeton U., 1974-75; DPhil, Oxford U., 1977. Lectr. politics New Coll., Oxford U., 1977-78; Robert Kent Gooch prof. Govt. and Foreign Affairs, U. Va., Charlottesville, 1978—; guest scholar Brookings Instn., 1980; Thomas Jefferson vis. prof. Downing Coll., Cambridge U., 1982; Danforth fellow, 1975; Kellogg fellow, 1983; Rhodes scholar. Mem. Am. Polit. Sci. Assn., Phi Beta Kappa. Author: The Rise of Political Consultants: New Ways of Winning Elections, 1981, Goodbye to Goodtime Charlie: The American Governorship Transformed, 1983, PAC Power: Inside the World of Political Action Committees, 1984, The Party's Just Begun: Shaping Political Parties for America's Future, 1988, Feeding Frenzy: How Attack Journalism Has Transformed American Politics, 1991, American Government: Roots and Reform, 1992, Dirty Little Secrets: The Persistence of Corruption in American Politics, 1996. Office: U Va Dept Govt 232 Cabell Charlottesville VA 22901

SABAT-RIVERS, GEORGINA, Latin American literature educator; b. Santiago, Oriente, Cuba; came to U.S., 1962; d. José and Balbina (Mercadé) Sabat; m. Armando A. Guernica (div.); children: Armando A., Antonio J., Rodolfo M., Georgina M.; m. Elias L. Rivers, Sept. 19, 1969. MA in Romance Langs., Johns Hopkins U., 1967, PhD in Romance Langs., 1969. Instr. U. Oriente, Santiago de Cuba, 1956-61; asst. prof. Georgetown Visitation Coll., Washington, 1962-63; asst. prof. Western Md. Coll., Westminster, 1963-69, assoc. prof., 1969-73, prof., 1973-78, chair dept., 1974-78; assoc. prof. SUNY, Stony Brook, 1978-86, prof., 1986—, chair dept., 1981-84; vis. prof. U. Calif., Irvine, 1989, U. Iowa, Iowa City, 1994, UNAM, Mexico City. Author: El Sueño de Sor Juana Inés de la Cruz tradiciones literarias y originalidad, 1976, Sor Juana Inés de la Cruz Inundación castálida, 1982, Literatura Femenina conventual: Sor Marcela de San Félix Hija de Lope, 1992, others; mem. editl. bd. Colonial L.Am. Rev., 1990—, Calíope; contbr. articles to profl. jours. Fellow NEH, 1984-85, Fulbright, 1987; Soviet Union Internat. Rsch. and Exch. Bd. grantee, 1986, Summer seminar grantee NEH, 1995. Fellow Am. Philos. Soc.; mem. MLA (del. 1988-93), AAUW, Assn. Internat. Hispanistas, Assn. Internat. Siglo de Oro, Assn. Internat. Cervantes, Inst. Internat. Revista Iberoamericana Lit. (editl. bd. 1987-90).

SABBAGHA, RUDY E., obstetrician, gynecologist, educator; b. Tel Aviv, Oct. 29, 1931; s. Elias C. and Sonia B. S.; m. Asma E. Sahyouny, Oct. 5, 1957; children: Elias, Randa. BA, MD, Am. U., Beirut. Sr. physician Tapline, Saudi Arabia, 1958-64, ob-gyn specialist, 1969-70; teaching fellow U. Pitts., 1965-68; asst. prof. ob-gyn, 1970-75; prof. Northwestern U., Chgo., 1975—; obstetrician, gynecologist Prentice Women's Hosp., Chgo. Author: Ultrasound-High Risk Obstetrics, 1979; editor: Ultrasound Applied to Obstetrics and Gynecology, 1980, 2d edit., 1987; contbr. articles to profl. jours. Fellow Am. Coll. Obstetricians and Gynecologists; mem. Soc. Gynecol. Investigation, Am. Gynecol. and Obstet. Soc., Central Assn. Obstetricians and Gynecologists, Assn. Profs. Ob-Gyn, Am. Inst. Ultrasound in Medicine. Research on diagnostic ultrasound, obstetrics and gynecology.

SABEL, BRADLEY KENT, lawyer; b. Charleston, Ill., Oct. 6, 1948; s. Walter Bernard and Charlotte (Ahlstrom) S.; m. Nancy Jean Parker, Apr. 4, 1984. B.A., Vanderbilt U., 1970; J.D., Cornell U., 1975; M.S. in Bus. Policy, Columbia U., 1983. Bar: N.Y. 1976. Atty. Fed. Reserve Bank of N.Y., 1975-80; asst. counsel Fed. Reserve Bank of N.Y., 1980, sec., asst. counsel, 1981-85, assoc. counsel, 1985-87, counsel, 1988-93, counsel, v.p., 1993-94; counsel Shearman & Sterling, N.Y.C., 1994—. Contbr. numerous articles to profl. jours. Bd. dirs., treas. N.Y. Chamber Orch., N.Y.C., 1985-87; Served with U.S. Army, 1970-72. Home: 2 Midland Gdns Apt 4E Bronxville NY 10708-4727 Office: Shearman & Sterling 599 Lexington Ave New York NY 10022-6030

SABERHAGEN, BRET WILLIAM, professional baseball player; b. Chicago Heights, Ill., Apr. 13, 1964; s. Bob Saberhagen; m. Janeane Saberhagen; children—Drew, William. Pitcher Kansas City Royals, 1982-91, N.Y. Mets, 1991—, Colorado Rockies, Denver, 1995—. Recipient Cy Young award Baseball Writers' Assn. Am., 1985, 89, Gold Glove award, 1989; named Am. League Pitcher of the Year Sporting News, 1985, 89; pitched no-hit game, 1991; mem. All-Star team, 1987, 90, named AL Comeback Player of the Year, 1987; named to The Sporting News Am. League All-Star Team, 1985, 89. Office: Colorado Rockies 2001 Blake St Denver CO 80205*

SABERS, RICHARD WAYNE, state supreme court justice; b. Salem, S.D., Feb. 12, 1938; s. Emil William and Elrena Veronica (Godfrey) S.; m. Colleen D. Kelley, Aug. 28, 1965; children: Steven Richard, Susan Michelle, Michael Kelley. BA in English, St. John's U., Collegeville, Minn., 1960; JD, U. S.D., 1966. Bar: S.D. 1966, U.S. Dist. Ct. S.D. 1966, U.S. Ct. Appeals (8th cir.) 1983. From assoc. to ptnr. Moore, Rasmussen, Sabers & Kading, Sioux Falls, S.D., 1966-86; justice Supreme Ct. S.D., Pierre and Sioux Falls, 1986—. Mem. editorial bd. U. S.D. Law Rev., 1965-66. State rep. March of Dimes, Bismarck, N.D., 1963; bd. dirs. St. Joseph Cathedral, Sioux Falls, 1971-86; trustee, bd. dirs. O'Gorman Found., Sioux Falls, 1978-86; active sch. bd. O'Gorman High Sch., Sioux Falls, 1985-86. Lt. U.S. Army, 1960-63. Named Outstanding Young Religious Leader, Jaycees, Sioux Falls, 1971. Mem. ABA, S.D. Bar Assn., Inst. Jud. Adminstrn., St. John's Alumni Assn. (pres. Sioux Falls chpt. 1975-91). Republican. Roman Catholic. Avocations: tennis, skiing, sailing, sports. Home: 1409 E Cedar Ln Sioux Falls SD 57103-4514 Office: SD Supreme Ct 500 E Capitol Ave Pierre SD 57501-5070

SABERSKY, ROLF HEINRICH, mechanical engineer; b. Berlin, Germany, Oct. 20, 1920; came to U.S., 1938, naturalized, 1944; s. Fritz and Berta (Eisner) S.; m. Bettina Sofie Schuster, June 16, 1946; children—Carol, Sandra. B.S., Calif. Inst. Tech., 1942, M.S., 1943, Ph.D., 1949. Devel. engr. Aerojet Gen. Co., 1943-46, regular cons., 1949-70; asst. prof. Calif. Inst. Tech., Pasadena, 1949-55, asso. prof., 1955-61, prof. mech. engring., 1961-88, prof. emeritus, 1988—; cons. various indsl. orgns. Author: Engineering Thermodynamics, 1957, Fluid Flow, 3d edit., 1989; contbr. articles to profl. jours. Fellow ASME (Heat Transfer Meml. award 1977, 50th anniversary award Heat Transfer Div 1988); mem. Sigma Xi, Tau Beta Pi. Home: 1060 Fallen Leaf Rd Arcadia CA 91006-1903 Office: Div Engring and Applied Sci Calif Inst Tech Pasadena CA 91125

SABHARWAL, RANJIT SINGH, mathematician; b. Dhudial, India, Dec. 11, 1925; came to U.S., 1958, naturalized, 1981; s. Krishan Ch and Devti (An) S.; m. Pritam Kaur Chadha, Mar. 5, 1948; children—Rajinderpal, Amarjit, Jasbir. B.A. with honors, Punjab U., 1944, M.A., 1948; M.A. U. Calif, Berkeley, 1962; Ph.D., Wash. State U., 1966. Lectr. math. Khalsa Coll., Bombay, India, 1951-58; teaching asst. U. Calif., Berkeley, 1958-62; instr. math. Portland (Oreg.) State U., 1962-62, Wash. State U., 1963-66; asst. prof. Kans. State U., 1966-68; mem. faculty Calif. State Hayward, 1968—, prof. math., 1974—. Author papers on non-Desarguesian planes. Mem. Am. Math. Soc., Math. Assn. Am., Sigma Xi. Address: 27892 Adobe Ct Hayward CA 94542-2102

SABIN, JAMES THOMAS, publisher; b. Toledo, June 23, 1943; s. Siegfried S. and Pauline R. (Lewis) S.; m. Anna Helen Greenhut, Oct. 1, 1971; children: David Michael, Karla Karen. BS, Georgetown U., 1965; MA (cert. in African studies), Columbia U., 1967, PhD, 1974. Writer, cons. Funk & Wagnalls Inc., N.Y.C., 1967-83; asst. editor Macmillan Inc., N.Y.C., 1969-70; social sci. editor Am. Book co., N.Y.C., 1971-73; sr. editor Greenwood Press Inc., Westport, Conn., 1973-74, exec. editor, 1974-75, v.p., editorial, 1975-84, exec. v.p., 1984—; cons. NAS; cons./referee NEH; cons./del. People to People Book Publ. Del. to Peoples Republic of China, 1987. Contbr. more than 200 articles to books and encys. Alumni admissions interviewer Georgetown U., Washington, 1988—; mem. nat. adv. bd. Ctr. for Black Music Rsch., Columbia Coll., Chgo., 1988—. African Inst. fellow Columbia U., 1965-67, Nat. Def. Fgn. Lang. fellow (Hausa) Columbia U., 1965-69. Democrat. Avocations: travel, music. Home: 459 Barrack Hill Rd Ridgefield CT 06877-2301 Office: Greenwood Publ Group Inc 88 Post Rd W Westport CT 06880-4208

SABIN, WILLIAM ALBERT, editor; b. Paterson, N.J., May 29, 1931; s. David and Esther (Goodman) S.; m. Marie Frances Noonan, May 31, 1958; children—Margaret, John, Katherine, Christopher, James. B.A. in English, Yale Coll., 1952; M.A. in English, Yale U., 1956. Pub. bus. and office edn. McGraw Hill Book Co., N.Y.C., 1973-78, editor in chief bus. books, 1979-86, pub. bus. books, 1987-90. Author: The Gregg Reference Manual, 8th edit., 1996; co-author: College English: Grammar and Style, 1967. Served as cpl. U.S. Army, 1952-54, ETO. Home: 38 Afterglow Way Montclair NJ 07042-1712

SABINE, GORDON ARTHUR, educator, writer; b. Brockton, Mass., Feb. 10, 1917; s. Charles Arthur and Esther (Carey) S.; m. Lois Eleanor Freiburg, June 26, 1941 (div. 1973); children: Ellen Jean, Gordon Arthur, Robert Allan, Roger Malcolm; m. Patricia Lundblade Williams, May 15, 1980; children: Patricia Glyn Williams Rhodes, John Paul, Nina Lynn Williams Keenan, Janet Anne Williams Maxim. A.B., U. Wis., 1939, M.A., 1941; Ph.D., U. Minn., 1949. Reporter, Lynchburg (Va.) News, 1931-35; reporter, copy editor Wis. State Jour., 1939-42; corr. UP, 1946-47; grad. asst. journalism U. Wis., 1939-41; instr., later asst. prof. journalism U. Kans., 1945-47; lectr. journalism U. Minn., 1947-48; asst. prof. U. Oreg., 1948-50, asso. prof., 1950-52, prof. journalism, 1952-55, dean Sch. Journalism, 1950-55; prof. communication arts, dean Coll. Communication Arts, Mich. State U., East Lansing, 1955-60; prof. Coll. Communication Arts, Mich. State U., 1955-72, v.p. spl. projects, 1960-71; v.p. asst. to pres. Ill. State U., 1971-72; dir. Sch. Journalism, U. Iowa, 1972-75; prof. journalism Va. Poly. Inst. and State U., 1975-84; prof. journalism Ariz. State U., 1985, spl. asst. to univ. libr. dean, 1986-93; dir. Nat. Project in Agrl. Communication, 1960-62, GI Project MEMO, 1969-70; prof.-in-residence Time, Inc., 1951; Bd. dirs. Oregon Newspaper Pubs. Assn., 1950-55. Contbr. articles to nat. mags. and newspapers, 1938—; writer syndicated newspaper column Youthpoll America, 1976-77, Books That Made the Difference project Ctr. for the Book, Libr. of Congress, 1980-81; author: When You Listen, This Is What You Can Hear, 1971, How Students Rate Their Schools and Teachers, 1971, Teachers Tell It like It Is, Like It Should Be, 1972, The Folks in the Newsroom, 1977, Broadcasting in Virginia: Benchmark '79, 1980; (with Patricia L. Sabine) Books That Made the Difference: What People Told Us, 1983, Monsignor Donohoe, 1988; (with Donald Riggs) Libraries in the '90s: What the Leaders Expect, 1988, Tom Chauncey, A Memoir, 1989, Rabbi Plotkin, A Memoir, 1992, G. Homer, A Biography of Arizona State University President G. Homer Durham, 1992, Culver Bill Nelson, 1992, Phyllis B. Steckler and the Oryx Press, 1993, "... a damn beautiful butterfly": The Memoir of the Rev. William Lee Burkhardt, 1993, Nan Pyle: Payson's Unhappy Millionaire, 1993, Father Jack: Physician to the Soul, 1993, The Memoir of a Book: The Norton Reader of Expository Prose, 1993; prodr. The Evolution of a Dream, 1996. Mem. Gov.'s Commn. on Employment of Handicapped, 1958-59; mem. rsch. com. Am. Coun. Edn. for Journalism, 1951-53; founder (with Patricia L. Sabine) FRIENDS of the AZ Talking Book Libr., 1995. 1st lt. AUS, 1942-45, Iceland. Carnegie Corp. fellow, 1953; FAE-NAEB scholar TV, 1954; sr. postdoctoral research fellow Am. Coll. Testing Program, 1970-71. Mem. Assn. Edn. in Journalism, Assn. Accredited Schs. and Depts. Journalism (pres. 1954-55), Am. Polit. Sci. Assn., Sigma Delta Chi (nat. research com. 1949-51), Omicron Delta Kappa. Home: 2625 E Southern Ave C-102 Tempe AZ 85282

SABINSON, HARVEY BARNETT, cultural organiztion administrator; b. N.Y.C., Oct. 24, 1924; s. Samuel and Sarah Sabinson; m. Sarah S. Sabinson, Aug. 15, 1944; children: Eric, Allen. BS, Queens Coll., 1947. Freelance publicist N.Y., 1946-73; dir. spl. projects League Am. Theatres & Producers, N.Y.C., 1976-82, exec. dir., 1982-95; vis. prof. theatre adminstrn. Yale U. Sch. of Drama, New Haven, 1966-70. Author: Darling, You Were Wonderful, 1977. Recipient Lifetime Achievement award United Jewish Appeal Fedn., 1990, Lifetime Achievement Tony award, 1995, Theatre Hall of Fame Founder's award, 1996. Mem. Actor's Fund of Am. (trustee 1990—), Broadway Assn. (bd. dirs. 1977—), Theater Devel. Fund (bd. dirs. 1992-96), Mayor's Midtown Citizens Com. Avocation: theatre.

SABINSON, MARA BETH, theatre educator, director, actress; b. N.Y.C., Mar. 1, 1946; d. Lee S. and Belle M. (Lindenauer) S.; m. John David Bergman, Sept. 6, 1987. BA, U. Calif., Berkeley, 1968; postgrad., Dartmouth Coll.; acting studies with Joseph Chaikin, Herbert Berghoff, Carl Weber, directing studies with Aaron Frankel, Jan Kott, Augusto Boal, voice and singing studies with Kristin Linklater and Mark Zeller. Mem. faculty Dell'Arte Sch. of Mime and Comedy, Blue Lake, Calif., 1978-81; acting coach N.Y.C., 1982-84; assoc. prof. drama/film studies, dir. theatre, dept. chair Dartmouth Coll., Hanover, N.H., 1984—; tchr. numerous workshops and programs including Mark Taper Forum, L.A., Sanford U., U. Calif. Berekely, Santa Cruz and Irvine, San Jose State U., Calif. State U. at Hayward, San Francisco State U., Laney Coll., U. San Francisco, Studiejamfrandet, Stockholm, Humboldt State U., Geese Theatre Co., Berkshire Theatre Festival; vis. faculty Calif. State Coll. of the Redwoods, 1980, Dell'Arte Sch. Phys. Theatre, 1990; extensive adminstrn. and prodn. experience. Co-author: (plays) Profiles in Porridge, 1972, Clowns, 1973, Ever Since Felix Moved to New Zealand, 1974, Phenoxy Follies, 1979, Intrigue at Ah-Pah, 1979, Whiteman Meets Bigfoot, 1980, The Gump Show, 1985, The Fall and Rise of Roger Gump, 1987; dir. plays including Orestes, 1967, Clowns, 1974, Jim Doodle Dandy, 1976, Space Bondage, 1979, Italian Detectives, 1981, We Are Not From Here, 1982, Judy's Floating Head, 1984-85, Female Transport, 1987, Cruel and Unusual Couples, 1988, Finale, 1988, Lone Star, 1989, The Taming of the Shrew, 1989, Cloud 9, 1990, numerous others; stage appearances include The Fool of the World, 1972, Human Rites, 1975, And Still I Rise, 1976, Music for Homemades, 1983, Canaries and Sitting Ducks, 1984, Heartbreak House, 1985, A Streetcar Named Desire, 1989, In the Jungle of Cities, 1991, God, 1991, numerous others; TV appearances on Sid Caesar's Show of Shows, 1956, The Immigrants, 1979, September Song: An American Autumn, 1987; film appearances include The Projectionist, 1975, History Book: Part I, 1975, Family Plot, 1976, The Killer Elite, 1976, The Reunion, 1976, Shaping Things, 1977, The Great Weirton Steel, 1984; also radio appearances, commls., theatrical adaptations, interviews, play readings; editorial contbr. various publs.; contbr. photographs and articles to numerous jours. and publs. Grantee Nat. Endowment for the Arts, Calif. State Arts Coun., Berkeley City Arts Coun., Roseberg Found.; recipient Bay Area Critics' Circle award, Critic's Choice/Best Bets citations, Lila Wallace/Reader's Digest Found. Arts Ptnrs. award, 1990, Marion and Jasper Whiting Found. fellowship, 1993. Home: RR 2 Box 312 Cornish NH 03745-9720 Office: Dartmouth Coll Dept Drama Hanover NH 03755

SABIO, JOHN MANUEL, satellite communications engineering executive; b. Bklyn., Dec. 1, 1955; s. David and Lily May (Cantero) S. BSC, Fla. Internat. U., 1978; MBA, Barry U., 1980. Chief engr. Sheraton Hotels Corp., Miami, Fla., 1973-83; pres., chmn. SAT/Com., Inc. (Satellite Communications Internat. Corp.), Miami, 1983—; CEO, chmn. Digital Satellites Comm. Co., Orlando, Fla., 1993—; pres. SAT/Com. SA, Spain, 1985—, v.p. SAT/Com. Venezuela, 1986—; pres. SAT/Com. Enterprises, Inc., Miami, 1986—; bd. dirs. SAT/Com. Ltd., Israel, 1985—. Mem. Satellite Comm. Assn. Am. (charter), Greater Miami C. of C., Hialeah Dade C. of C., Spain-U.S. C. of C., Orlando C. of C., Caribbean C. of C., Coral Ridge Yacht Club (Ft. Lauderdale), Citrus Club. Roman Catholic. Clubs: Miami Shores (Fla.) Country; Turnberry Yacht and Beach; Regines Worldwide. Home: Bay Hill Country Club PO Box 618640 Orlando FL 32861-8640 Office: Digital Satellite Comm 7448 Republic Dr Orlando FL 32819

SABISTON, DAVID COSTON, JR., surgeon, educator; b. Onslow County, N.C., Oct. 4, 1924; s. David Coston and Marie (Jackson) S.; m. Agnes Foy Barden, Sept. 24, 1955; children: Anne Sabiston Leggett, Agnes Sabiston Butler, Sarah Coston. BS, U. N.C., 1944; MD, Johns Hopkins U., 1947; DSc (hon.), U. Madrid. Diplomate: Am. Bd. Surgery (chmn. 1971-72). Successively intern, asst. resident, chief resident surgery Johns Hopkins Hosp., 1947-53; successively asst. prof., assoc. prof., prof. surgery Johns Hopkins Med. Sch., 1955-64, Howard Hughes investigator, 1955-61; Fulbright research scholar U. Oxford, Eng., 1960; research assoc. Hosp. Sick Children, U. London, Eng., 1961; James B. Duke prof. surgery, chmn. dept. Duke Med. Sch., 1964-94; chief of staff Duke U. Med. Ctr., Durham, N.C., 1994-96, dir. internat. programs, 1996—; chmn. Accreditation Council for Grad. Med. Edn., 1985-86. Editor: Textbook of Surgery, Essentials of Surgery, Atlas of General Surgery, Atlas of Cardiothoracic Surgery, A Review of Surgery; co-editor: Gibbon's Surgery of the Chest, Companion Handbook to Textbook of Surgery; chmn. editl. bd. Annals of Surgery; mem. editl. bd. Annals Clin. Rsch., ISI Atlas of Sci.: The Classics of Surgery Libr., Surgery, Gynecology and Obsetrics, Jour. Applied Cardiology, Jour. Cardiac Surgery, World Jour. Surgery, Jour. Served to capt., M.C. AUS, 1953-55. Recipient Career Rsch. award NIH, 1962-64, N.C. award in Sci., 1978, Disting. Achievement award Am. Heart Assn. Sci. Coun., 1983 Michael E. DeBakey award for Outstanding Achievement, 1984, Significant Sigma Chi award, 1987, Coll. medalist Am. Coll. Chest Physicians, 1987, Disting. Tchr. award Alpha Omega Alpha, 1992; named Disting. Physician, U.S. VA, 1995. Mem. ACS (chmn. bd. govs. 1974-75, regent 1975-82, chmn. bd. regents 1982-84, pres. 1985-86), NAS Inst. Medicine, Am. Surg. Assn. (pres. 1977-78), So. Surg. Assn. (sec. 1969-73, pres. 1973-74), Am. Assn. Thoracic Surgery (pres. 1984-85), Soc. Clin. Surgery, Internat. Soc. Cardiovascular Surgery, Soc. Vascular Surgery (v.p. 1967-68), Soc. Univ. Surgeons (pres. 1968-69), Halsted Soc., Surg. Biology Club II, Soc. Thoracic Surgery, Soc. Surgery Alimentary Tract, Johns Hopkins U. Soc. Scholars, Soc. Surg. Chairmen (pres. 1974-76), Soc. Thoracic Surgeons Great Britain and Ireland, Soc. Internat. De Chirurgie, James IV Assn. Surgeons (bd. dirs. U.S. chpt.), Ill. Surg. Soc. (hon.), Phila. Acad. Surgery (hon.), Royal Coll. Surgeons Edinburgh (hon., editl. bd. jour.), Royal Coll. Surgeons Eng. (hon.), Asociación de Cirugía del Litoral (Argentina) (hon.), Royal Coll. Physicians and Surgeons Can. (hon.), Royal Coll. Surgeons Ireland (hon.), Royal Australasian Coll. Surgeons (hon.), German Surgical Soc. (hon.), Colombian Surg. Soc. (hon.), Brazilian Coll. Surgeons (hon.), Japanese Coll. Surgeons (hon.), French Surg. Assn. (hon.), Surg. Congress Assn. Espanola de Cirujanos (hon.), Philippine Coll. Surgeons (hon.), Phi Beta Kappa, Alpha Omega Alpha. Clubs: Cosmos (Washington), Hope Valley Country Club (Durham), Treyburn City Club (Durham). Home: 1528 Pinecrest Rd Durham NC 27705-5817 Office: Duke U Med Ctr PO Box 2600 MSRB Durham NC 27710

SABL, JOHN J., lawyer; b. L.A., June 16, 1951. AB with distinction, Stanford U., 1973, JD, 1976. Bar: Calif. 1976, Ill. 1977. Ptnr. Sidley & Austin, Chgo. editorial bd. Stanford U. Law Review, 1974-75, assoc. mng. editor, 1975-76. Mem. Chgo. Bar Assn. (chmn. securities law com. 1985-86), Legal Club Chgo. Office: Sidley & Austin 1 First National Plz Chicago IL 60603-0001

SABLE, BARBARA KINSEY, former music educator; b. Astoria, L.I., N.Y., Oct. 6, 1927; d. Albert and Verna Rowe Kinsey; B.A., Coll. Wooster, 1949; M.A., Tchrs. Coll. Columbia U., N.Y.C., 1950; D.Mus., U. Ind., 1966; m. Arthur J. Sable, Nov. 3, 1973. Office mgr., music dir. sta. WCAX, Burlington, Vt., 1954; instr. Cottey Coll., 1959-60; asst. prof. N.E. Mo. State U., Kirksville, 1962-64; asst. prof. U. Calif., Santa Barbara, 1964-69; prof. music U. Colo., Boulder, 1969—, prof. emeritus, 1992—. Author: The Vocal Sound, 1982; contbr. poetry to literary jours. Mem. Nat. Assn. Tchrs. Singing (past state gov., asso. editor bull.), AAUP, Colo. State Music Tchrs. Assn. Democrat. Avocation: poetry. Home: 3430 Ash Ave Boulder CO 80303-3432 Office: U Colo Coll Music Campus Box 301 Boulder CO 80309

SABLIK, MARTIN JOHN, research physicist; b. Bklyn., Oct. 21, 1939; s. Martin C. and Elsie M. (Fuzia) S.; m. Beverly Ann Shively, Nov. 26, 1965; children: Jeanne, Karen, Marjorie, Larry. BA in Physics, Cornell U., 1960; MS in Physics, U. Ky., 1965; PhD, Fordham U., 1972. Jr. engr. The Martin Co., Orlando, Fla., 1962-63; half-time instr. U. Ky., Lexington, 1963-65; rsch. assoc. Fairleigh Dickinson U., Teaneck, N.J., 1965-67, instr. physics, 1967-1972, asst. prof., 1972-76, assoc. prof., 1976-80; sr. rsch. scientist Southwest Rsch. Inst., San Antonio, 1980-87, staff scientist, 1987—; local chmn. Intermag. Conf., San Antonio, 1995. Mem. editorial bd. Nondestructive Testing and Evaluation, 1989—; mem. adv. bd. Conf. on Properties and Applications of Magnetic Materials, 1990—, Workshop on Advances in Measurement Techniques and Instrumentation for Magnetic Properties Determination, 1993—; contbr. articles to profl. jours.; referee, patentee in field. Recipient Imagineer award Mind Sci. Found., 1989. Mem. Am. Phys. Soc., Am. Geophys. Union, Am. Soc. Nondestructive Testing (chmn. So. Tex. sect. 1983-84), IEEE, Am. Assn. Physics Tchrs. Roman Catholic. Office: SW Rsch Inst PO Box 28510 San Antonio TX 78228-0510

SABLOFF, JEREMY ARAC, archaeologist; b. N.Y.C., Apr. 16, 1944; s. Louis and Helen (Arac) S.; m. Paula Lynne Weinberg, May 26, 1968; children: Joshua, Saralinda. A.B., U. Pa., 1964; M.A., Ph.D., Harvard U., 1969. Asst. prof., asso. prof. Harvard U., Cambridge, Mass., 1969-76; asso. prof. anthropology U. Utah, Salt Lake City, 1976-77; curator anthropology Utah Mus. Natural History, Salt Lake City, 1976-77; prof. anthropology U. N.Mex., Albuquerque, 1978-86; chmn. dept. U. N.Mex., 1980-83; Univ. prof. anthropology and the history and philosphy of sci. U. Pitts., 1986-94, chmn. dept. anthropology, 1990-92; Charles K. Williams II dir. U. Mus., U. Mus. Term prof. anthropology, curator Mesoamerican archaeology U. Pa., Phila., 1994—; sr. fellow for Pre-Columbian Studies, Dumbarton Oaks, 1986-92, chmn. 1989-92. Author: (with G.R. Willey) A History of American Archaeology, 1974, 2d edit., 1980, 3d edit., 1993, Excavations at Seibal: Ceramics, 1975, (with C.C. Lamberg-Karlovsky) Ancient Civilizations: The Near East and Mesoamerica, 1979, 2nd edit., 1995, (with D. A. Freidel) Cozumel: Late Maya Settlement Patterns, 1984, The Cities of Ancient Mexico, 1989, The New Archaeology and the Ancient Maya, 1990, (with G. Tourtellot) The Ancient Maya City of Sayil: The Mapping of a Puuc Region Center, 1991; editor(with C.C. Lamberg-Karlovsky) The Rise and Fall of Civilizations, 1974, Ancient Civilization and Trade, 1975, (with W.L. Rathje) A Study of Changing Pre-Columbian Commercial Systems, 1975, American Antiquity, 1977-81, (with G.R. Willey) Scientific American Readings in Pre-Columbian Archaeology, 1980, Simulations in Archaeology, 1981, Supplement to the Handbook of Middle American Indians: Archaeology, 1981, Archaeology: Myth and Reality: A Scientific American Reader, 1982, Analyses of Fine Paste Ceramics, 1982, (with D. Meltzer and D. Fowler) American Archaeology: Past and Future, 1986, (with E.W. Andrews V) Late Lowland Maya Civilization: Classic to Postclassic, 1986, (with J.S. Henderson) Lowland Maya Civilization in the Eighth Century A.D., 1993. Nat. Geog. Soc. grantee, 1972-74; NSF grantee, 1983-88; NEH grantee, 1990-91. Fellow Am. Anthrop. Assn., AAAS (sec. H. chair 1994-95), Royal Anthrop. Inst., Soc. Antiquaries London; mem. Nat. Acad. Sci., Am. Phil. Soc., Soc. Am. Archaeology (pres. 1989-91), Prehist. Soc., Internat. Soc., Comparative Study of Civilizations, Sigma Xi. Office: U Pa Mus Archaeology and Anthropology 33d and Spruce Sts Philadelphia PA 19104-6324

SABO, MARTIN OLAV, congressman; b. Crosby, N.D., Feb. 28, 1938; s. Bjorn O. and Klara (Haga) S.; m. Sylvia Ann Lee, June 30, 1963; children: Karin, Julie. BA cum laude, Augsburg Coll., Mpls., 1959; postgrad., U. Minn., 1961-62. Mem. Minn. Ho. of Reps. from 57B Dist., 1960-78, minority leader Dem.-Farmer-Labor party, 1969-72, speaker, 1973-78; mem. 96th to 104th U.S. Congresses from 5th Minn. Dist., 1979—; chmn. Dem. Study Group 96th to 101st Congresses; dep. majority whip 96th to 103rd Congresses, mem. appropriations com.; mem. permanent select com. on intelligence 102d Congress; chmn. Ho. Budget Com. 103d Congress; former mem. Nat. Adv. Commn. on Intergovtl. Rels.; past pres. Nat. Legis. Conf.; bd. regents Augsburg Coll. Mgr., player Dem. Congl. Baseball Team, 1987—. Recipient Disting. Alumni citation Augsburg Coll., Arms Control Leadership award Employees Union, Local 113, SEIU, AFL-CIO; named One of 200 Rising Young Leaders in Am. Time mag., 1974; Man of Yr. Mpls. Jr. C. of C., 1973-74, One of Ten Outstanding Young Men of Yr. Minn. Jr. C. of C., 1974; inducted Scandinavian Am. Hall of Fame, 1994. Mem. Nat. Conf. State Legis. Leaders (past pres.). Office: 2336 Rayburn Bldg Office B Washington DC 20515-0005

SABO, RICHARD STEVEN, electrical company executive; b. Walkertown, Pa., Jan. 1, 1934; s. Alex S. and Elizabeth (Haluska) S.; m. Gail P. Digon, Feb. 15, 1954; children: Gailyn J., Richard A., Kerry S., Dale A. BS in Edn., California (Pa.) U., 1955; MS in Edn., Edinboro (Pa.) U., 1965. Tchr. Northwestern Sch. Dist., Albion, Pa., 1955-65; prodn. technician The Lincoln Electric Co., Cleve., 1965-66, staff asst. mktg., 1966-70, mgr. pub. rels., 1971-86, asst. to chmn., 1986—, dir. cop. comms. and investor rels.; also exec. dir. James F. Lincoln Arc Welding Found. Editor: The Procedure Handbook of Arc Welding, 1994, 10 other books on arc welding; contbr. numerous articles to profl. jours. Chmn. Area Recreation Bd., Chesterland, Ohio, 1970, West Geauga Boosters, Chesterland, 1973-77; mem., bd. dirs. Profit Sharing Coun. Am., 1991—. Recipient Svc. award Future Farmers Am., 1970—, Svc. award U.S. Skill Olympics, 1980, Lakeland Community Coll. award, 1990, Ohio State U. Hon. Welding Engring. Alumni award, 1990, Calif. U. (Pa.) medallion of Distinction, 1990. Mem. Am. Welding Soc. (vice chmn. edn. and fin. com., mem. fin. com. 1988—, speaker, various awards, Plummer lectr. 1992), Am. Soc. for Engring. Edn., Am. Inst. Steel Cons. (mem. edn. com. 1986—), Steel Plate Fabricators Assn. (past chmn. promotions com., mem. bd. dirs.s profit sharing coun. 1991—), California U. Alumni Assn. (trustee 1983—). Republican. Presbyterian. Lodge: Masons. Avocations: golf, hunting, fishing, classical music. Office: The Lincoln Electric Co 22801 Saint Clair Ave Cleveland OH 44117-2524

SABOSIK, PATRICIA ELIZABETH, publisher, editor; b. Newark, Aug. 25, 1949; d. George Aloysius and Elizabeth Ann (Simko) S.; m. Kenneth Donald Gursky, Apr. 21, 1972 (div. 1980). BA in English, Kean Coll. N.J., 1976; MBA in Mktg., Seton Hall U., 1984; cert. advanced study in fin., Fairfield U., 1989. Proofreader Baker & Taylor, Somerville, N.J., 1969-71, database coordinator, 1971-74, prodn. editor, 1974-77, publs. mgr., editor, 1977-82; dir. mktg. services H.W. Wilson Pub. Co., Bronx, N.Y., 1982-84; editor, pub. Choice mag. Am. Library Assn., Middletown, Conn., 1984-94; project dir. Books for Coll. Librs. Am. Library Assn., Middletown, 1985-88, project dir. Guide to Ref. Books, 1988-94; v.p. electronic text Booklink Technologies, Wilmington, Mass., 1994; v.p. Linked Media, Navi Soft Divsn. Am. Online, Inc., Needham, Mass., 1994-96; editor in chief Whole Internet Catalog, GNN an Am. Online, Inc. Co., 1996—; membership chmn. Serials Industry Systems Adv. Com., 1983-89, vice chmn., 1985-86, newsletter editor, 1986-87. Editor-in-chief Whole Internet Catalog, 1995—; contbr. articles to profl. jours. Party rep. Twp. Com. Cranford, N.J., 1977-79; hon. bd. advisors U. Conn. Women's Ctr., 1989-91; mem. Conn. Women's Edn. and Legal Fund; nat. bd. dirs. Literacy Vols. of Am., 1992-94, also chair pub. and mktg. com. Mem. ALA (coms., editorial bd. Choice), AAUW, Assn. Coll. and Rsch. Librs. (publs. com.), Soc. for Scholarly Pub. (membership com., editor newsletter 1988-91, budget and fin. com. 1990-92, sec.-treas. 1994—, bd. dirs. 1994—), Appalachian Mountain Club, Women's Outdoors Club (newsletter editor 1984-86, regional rep. 1986-87). Republican. Roman Catholic. Office: Am Online Inc 75 2d Ave Ste 710 Needham MA 02194

SABOT, RICHARD HENRY, economics educator, researcher, consultant; b. N.Y.C., Feb. 16, 1944; s. Arnold G. and Victoria (Gomberg) S.; m. Judith A. Plunkett, Sept. 9, 1969; children: Diana, Christopher, Oliver, Julia. BA, U. Pa., 1966, Oxford U., 1968; MA, Oxford U., 1970, DPhil, 1973. Rsch. officer Inst. Econs. and Stats. Oxford (Eng.) U., 1972-74; rsch. economist World Bank, Washington, 1974-84; John J. Gibson prof. econs. Williams Coll., Williamstown, Mass., 1984—; econ. advisor Office of the Exec. Vice Pres., Interam. Devel. Bank, Washington, 1994—; sr. rsch. fellow Internat. Food Policy Rsch. Inst., Washington, 1987-92; sr. rsch. fellow policy rsch. dept. World Bank, 1992—; cons. OECD Devel. Ctr., Paris, 1971-74, Internat. Inst. Applied Sys. Analysis, Vienna, Austria, 1982-83, Harvard Inst. Internat. Devel., Cambridge, Mass., 1985-88, World Bank, 1985—. Author: Economic Development and Urban Migration, 1979, Education Productivity and Inequality, 1990, The East Asian Miracle, 1993; editor: Migration and the Labor Market in Developing Countries, 1982, Unfair Advantage, 1991; contbr. numerous articles to scholarly jours. Mem. Nat. Panel on the Econ. of Ednl. Reform, Pew Found., 1991-95; trustee Nat. Child Rsch. Ctr., Washington, 1978-81; mem. nat. bd. Fund for Improvement Post-Secondary Edn., Washington, 1987-91. Rsch. grantee Ford Found., Mellon Found., Rockefeller Found., World Bank; Fulbright fellow, Thouron fellow, Danforth fellow. Mem. Am. Econ. Assn., Royal Econ.l Soc., United Oxford and Cambridge U. Club (London), Williams Club (N.Y.C.), Mt. Greylook Ski Club (bd. dirs. 1984-85). Avocations: hiking, yoga, cross country skiing, chess. Home: Birch Hollow Oblong Rd Williamstown MA 01267 Office: Williams Coll Fernald House Williamstown MA 01267

SABSAY, DAVID, library consultant; b. Waltham, Mass., Sept. 12, 1931; s. Wiegard Isaac and Ruth (Weinstein) S.; m. Helen Glenna Tolliver, Sept. 24,1 966. AB, Harvard U., 1953; BLS, U. Calif., Berkeley, 1955. Circulation dept. supr. Richmond (Calif.) Pub. Library, 1955-56; city libr. Santa Rosa (Calif.) Pub. Library, 1956-65; dir. Sonoma County Library, Santa Rosa, 1965-92; libr. cons., 1992—; coordinator North Bay Coop. Library System, Santa Rosa, 1960-64; cons. in field, Sebastopol, Calif., 1968—. Contbr. articles to profl. jours. Commendation, Calif. Assn. Library Trustees and Commrs., 1984. Mem. Calif. Library Assn. (pres. 1971, cert. appreciation 1971, 80), ALA. Club: Harvard (San Francisco). Home and Office: 667 Montgomery Rd Sebastopol CA 95472-3020

SABSHIN, MELVIN, psychiatrist, educator, medical association administrator; b. N.Y.C., Oct. 28, 1925; s. Zalman and Sonia (Barnhard) S.; m. Edith Goldfarb, June 12, 1955; 1 child, James K. BS, U. Fla., Gainesville, 1944; MD, Tulane U., New Orleans, 1948. Diplomate Am. Bd. Psychiatry and Neurology. Assoc. dir. Michael Reese Hosp. Psychosomatic and Psychiat. Inst., Chgo., 1953-61; prof., head dept. psychiatry U. Ill. Coll. Medicine, Chgo., 1961-74; med. dir. Am. Psychiat. Assn., Washington, 1974—. Author Depression, 1960, Psychiatric Ideology, 1961; Normality, 1978; Normality and Life Cycle, 1984. Served with U.S. Army, 1944. Recipient Bowen award Am. Coll. Psychiatrists, 1978, Disting. Psychiatrist award, 1985. Mem. Am. Coll. Psychiatrists (pres. 1974-75). Home: 2801 New Mexico Ave NW Washington DC 20007-3921 Office: Am Psychiat Assn 1400 K St NW Washington DC 20005-2403

SABY, JOHN SANFORD, physicist; b. Ithaca, N.Y., Mar. 21, 1921; s. Rasmus S. and Maude Emily (Sanford) S.; m. Mary Elizabeth Long, June 9, 1945; children: Arthur D., Thomas S., Joseph A., Jean E. B.A., Gettysburg (Pa.) Coll., 1942, Sc.D. (hon.), 1969; M.S., Pa. State U., 1944, Ph.D., 1947. Lab. instr. Gettysburg Coll., 1940-42; instr. Cornell U., 1947-50; with Gen. Electric Co., 1951-82; mgr. semicondr./solid state Gen. Electric Co., Syracuse, N.Y., 1954-56; mgr. lamp phenomena research Gen. Electric Co., Cleve., 1956-82; cons., 1982—; mem. vis. com. biol. and phys. scis. Case Western Res. U., chmn., 1969. Co-author: Principles of Transistor Circuits, 1953. Fellow IEEE (past com. officer); mem. Am. Phys. Soc., Cleve. Assn. Research Dirs. (pres. 1963-64), Am. Watchmakers Inst., Nat. Assn. Watch and Clock Collectors, Phi Beta Kappa, Sigma Xi, Phi Kappa Phi, Phi Sigma Kappa. Patentee in field. Home: 8 Tamarac Ter Hendersonville NC 28701-9770

SACCA, HARRIET WANDS, music educator; b. Pittsfield, Mass; d. Harry J. and Anna F. (Mara) Wands; BS, Coll. St. Rose, 1939, MA, 1962; student SUNY, Albany, Oneonta. Tchr. pub. schs., Albany, N.Y., 1942-66; instr. Coll. St. Rose, 1962-63; dir. music edn. Albany (N.Y.) Bd. Edn., 1966—; bur. assoc. examiner personnel N.Y. State Dept. Edn. Past pres. Soroptimist Internat., 1969-70, City Club Albany, Inc., 1974-75; active Albany County Dem. Com., 1962—; jud. del. 3d Jud. Dist. N.Y. State, 1975-96; mem. Albany Local Devel. Corp.; bd. dirs. St. Joseph's Housing Corp., Albany Tulip Festival; mem. adv. bd. capital Region Ctr. Arts in Edn., 1983—, Albany County Alteratives to Incarceration, 1983-96, chair sub com., 1985—; bd. dirs. Coop. Extension Community Resources Devel., 7 County Youth Symphony Orch., 1970-84; project dir. N.Y. Council on Arts; chair festival N.Y. Sch. Music, 1988; mem. com. of 5 appointed select name for 16, 000 seat Civic Arena; trustee assoc. Coll. of St. Rose, 1996—; mem. exec. bd. N.Y.S. Coun. Music Adminstrs., 1996—; area 3 rep. N.Y. State Coun. Music Adminstrs., 1995—. Recipient Citizen of Yr. award Ford Motor Co., 1971; Women Helping Women award Soroptimist, 1975; Disting. Service award N.Y. State PTA, 1985. Fellow Harry Truman Library; mem. Nat. Coun. Music Adminstrs., Music Educators Nat. Conf., N.Y. State Sch. Music Assn., Capitol Hill Choral Soc. (dir.), N.Y. St. Council Arts Award Childrens Opera (dir. project), Albany Adminstrs. Assn., Albany Civic Auditorium (dir.), Delta Kappa Gamma, Delta Epsilon. Democrat. Roman Catholic. Clubs: Bus. and Profl. Women's, Soroptimist, Club of Albany, Cath. Women's Service League, Coll. St. Rose Alumni, Pres.'s Soc. Home: 226 Morris St Albany NY 12208-3525 Office: Albany Bd Edn Acad Park Albany NY 12207

SACCHET, EDWARD M., foreign service officer; b. Bklyn., Sept. 28, 1936; m. Elizabeth Priore. BA in Internat. Affairs, George Washington U., 1958; postgrad., Sch. Advanced Internat. Studies, Johns Hopkins U., Bologna, Italy, 1958-59; MA in Internat. Affairs, Sch. Advanced Internat. Studies, Johns Hopkins U., 1960; postgrad., U. Oslo, Norway, 1959. Labor economist U.S. Dept. of Labor, Washington, 1961-63; mem. U.S. Fgn. Service-Dept. of State, Washington, 1963—; internat. economist White House Office of Spl. Trade Rep., Washington and Geneva, 1964-67; sec., econ. comml. officer Am. Embassy, Tananarive, Madagascar, 1967-69; consul, econ. comml. officer Am. Consulate Gen., Naples, Italy, 1969-72; 1st sec., fin. economist Am. Embassy, Rome, Italy, 1972-75; congl. fellow U.S. State Dept.-U.S. Congress, 1975-76; econ. officer Bur. Econ. and Bus. Affairs-U.S. Dept. State, 1976-78; career devel. and assignments officer Bur. of Personnel-U.S. Dept. State, 1978-80; consul gen. Am. Consulate Gen., Marseille, France, 1980-84; Pearson fellow, spl. advisor to Gov. of Fla. for Internat. Issues Tallahassee, 1984-85; fgn. svc. inspector Office Inspector Gen. Fgn. Svc.-U.S. Dept. State, Washington, 1985-87; U.S. consul gen. Am. Consulate Gen., Martinique, French W. Indies, 1987-88; spl. asst. Office Exec. Dir., Bur. Econ. and Bus. Affairs-Dept. State, 1987; acting ambassador U.S. Embassy, Antigua, W.I., 1988; cons. Bur. Adminstrn., info. mgmt. system and diplomatic security U.S. Dept. State, 1989—; lectr. in field. George Washington U. scholar, 1954-58, Johns Hopkins Sch. Internat. Studies scholar, Washington and Bologna, Italy, 1958-60; State Dept. fellow, 1980, Pearson fellow Office of Gov. Fla., 1984, Congl. fellow Am. Polit. Sci. Assn., 1980. Mem. Am. Fgn. Svc. Assn., Johns Hopkins U. Alumni Assn., Army-Navy Club of Washington. Home: 118 Monroe St Apt 907 Rockville MD 20850-2513 also: 13167 La Lique Ct Palm Bch Gdns FL 33410-1417

SACCO, FRANK VINCENT, hospital administrator; b. Akron, Ohio, June 28, 1947; married. BA, U. Miami, 1970; MA, Fla. Internat. U., 1978. Various positions Meml. Hosp., Hollywood, Fla., 1973-78, adminstrv. asst., 1978-79, asst. adminstr., 1979-84, sr. assoc. adminstr., 1984-85, sr. assoc. adminstr., COO, 1985-87, adminstr., CEO, 1987—; adj. educator in field. Home: 3120 Peachtree Cir Fort Lauderdale FL 33328-6705 Office: Meml Hosp 3501 Johnson St Hollywood FL 33021-5421*

SACCO, ROBERT ANTHONY, financial executive; b. N.Y.C., Oct. 24, 1944; s. Amerigo and Margaret (McCarthy) S.; children—Stephanie, Robert. Student U. Miami, 1962-64; B.S., Monmouth Coll., 1966; M.B.A., NYU, 1968. C.P.A., N.Y. Staff acct. J.H. Cohn & Co., Newark, 1969; supr. Rudolf, Cinamon & Calafato, Ocean, N.J., 1969-78; mgr. M. Sternlieb & Co., Hackensack, N.J., 1978-79; chief fin. officer Conf. Environs. Corp., N.Y.C., 1979—; dir., officer Cox Hotel Corp., Long Branch, N.J., Twin Gardens Condo Assn., Long Branch; mng. dir. East Beach Ocean Front, N.Y., 1983—; prof. acctg. Monmouth Coll., 1974-79; treas. dir. Horizon Hotels, Ltd., N.Y.C. Mem. N.J. Soc. C.P.A.s, Am. Inst. C.P.A.s, NYU Alumni Assn. Roman Catholic. Address: Horizon Hotels Ltd 442 State Highway 35 South Eatontown NJ 07724*

SACCOMAN, STEFANIE ANN, secondary school educator; b. San Francisco, Dec. 13, 1953; d. Frank and Jacqueline (Collier) S. BS in Biology, Calif. Poly. U., 1976, MA in Edn., 1980; postgrad., Calif. State U., L.A., Calif. Coast U. Environ. scientist Engring.-Sci. Inc., Arcadia, Calif., 1978-83; sci. tchr. Pasadena (Calif.) H.S., 1983-90; sci. and math curriculum specialist Pomona (Calif.) Unified Sch. Dist., 1990—; instr. sci. edn. for secondary tchrs. La. State U., Baton Rouge, summer 1990, 91. Contbr. (lab. manual) Cal Poly University Institute for Cellular and Molecular Biology Experiments for Science Teachers, 1985. Spkr. on math curriculum Rotary Club, Pomona, 1993; spkr. on sci. instrn. and student self esteem Human Rights Conf., Pomona, 1994. Recipient Calif. Congress of Parents, Tchrs., Students Svc. award PTA, Pasadena, 1987, Disting. Tchr. award Verdugo Hills Hosp., Glendale, 1988; named Outstanding Young Woman of Am., 1981. Mem. ASCD, Nat. Coun. Tchrs. Math., N.Y. Acad. Sci. Avocations: traveling, gardening, nature study. Office: Pomona Unified Sch Dist 800 S Garey Ave Pomona CA 91766-3325

SACERDOTE, MANUEL RICARDO, banker; b. Buenos Aires, Feb. 20, 1943; s. Ricardo Edmundo and Ana Maria (Devoto) S.; m. Nora Alejandrina Mascarenhas, Aug. 24, 1966; children: Juan Martin, Diego Raul, Andrea Maria, Matías. E.E., U. Buenos Aires, 1966; M.B.A., Harvard U., 1968. Treas., Chrysler Argentina, Buneos Aires, 1969-71; gen. mgr. Sasin S.A., Buenos Aires, 1971-74; pres. Banco de Boston, Buenos Aires, 1974—; pres. Bank of Boston Found., Buenos Aires; dir. La Continental Ins. Co., Buenos Aires, Pfizer S.A., Buenos Aires, Swift Armour S.A., Buenos Aires. Mem. Argentine Bankers Assn. (bd. dirs. 1976—, vice chmn. 1989—, chmn. 1987-89), Argentine Bus. Coun., Latin Am. Found. Econ. Research (bd. dirs. 1983—). Clubs: Martindale, Belgrano Athletic, Harvard of Argentina (pres. 1979-80). Avocations: tennis, swimming, reading. Office: First Nat Bank of Boston, Florida 99, Buenos Aires 1005, Argentina

SACERDOTE, PETER M., investment banker; b. Turin, Italy, Oct. 15, 1937; came to U.S., 1940; s. Giorgio S. and Luciana (Levi) S.; m. Bonnie Lee Johnson, June 18, 1967; children: Alisa, Alexander, Laurence. B.E.E., Cornell U., 1960; M.B.A., Harvard U., 1964. Assoc. investment banking div. Goldman, Sachs & Co., N.Y.C., 1964-69, v.p. investment banking div., 1969-73, gen. ptnr., 1973-90, ltd. ptnr., 1990—; bd. dirs. Weis Markets, Inc., Sunbury, Pa., Qualcomm, Inc., San Diego, Franklin Resource, San Mateo, Calif.; in charge Pvt. Fin. Dept., 1974-80, The Corp. Fin. Dept., 1980-87, Merch Bank, 1987-90; chmn. Committments, Credit and Investment Cons., 1987-90, GS Capital Partnership; adj. prof. Columbia Grad. Sch. Bus., 1984-86; nat. chmn. HBSFD, Milton (Mass.) Acad. Trustee Day Sch., N.Y.C., 1980—; chmn. Alumni Bd. Harvard Bus. Sch., 1990; bd. visitors Fuqua Sch. Duke U., 1990; bd. overseers Cornell Med. Coll. Served to lt. (j.g.) USNR, 1960-62. Mem. Harvard Club N.Y.C., River Club N.Y.C., Downtown Assn., Nantucket Yacht Club, Stanwich Golf Club, Country Club of the Rockies, Sankaty Head Golf Club (Siasconset, Mass.). Office: Goldman Sachs & Co 85 Broad St New York NY 10004-2434

SACHA, ROBERT FRANK, osteopathic physician, allergist; b. East Chicago, Ind., Nov. 29, 1946; b. S. Frank John and Ann Theresa Sacha; m. Linda T. Le Page, 1988; children: Joshua Jude, Josiah Gerard, Anastasia Levon, Jonah Bradley. BS, Purdue U., 1969; DO, Chgo. Coll. Osteo. Medicine, 1975. Diplomate Am. Bd. Pediatrics, Am. Bd. Allergy and Immunology. Pharmacist, asst. mgr. Walgreens Drug Store East Chicago, Ind., 1969-75; intern David Grant Med. Ctr., San Francisco, 1975-76, resident in pediatrics, 1976-78; fellow in allergy and immunology Wilford Hall Med. Ctr., 1978-80; staff pediatrician, allergist Scott AFB (Ill.), 1980-83; practice medicine specializing in allergy and immunology Cape Girardeau, Mo., 1983—; assoc. clin. instr. St. Louis U., 1980—; clin. instr. Purdue U., 1971-72, Pepperdine U., 1975-76, U. Tex.-San Antonio, 1978-80, assoc. clin. instr. So. Ill. U. Pres., Parent Tchrs. League. Maj. M.C., USAF, 1975-83, comdr., USNR. Fellow Am. Coll. Allergy, Am. Coll. Chest Physicians, Am. Acad. Pediatrics, Am. Acad. Allergy-Immunology, Am. Assn. Cert. Allergists; mem. AMA, Am. Acad. Allergy, Assn. Mil. Allergists, ACP, Am. Coll. Emergency Physicians, Mil. Surgeons and Physicians. Republican. Lutheran.

SACHAR, DAVID BERNARD, gastroenterologist, medical educator; b. Urbana, Ill., Mar. 2, 1940; s. Abram Leon and Thelma (Horwitz) S.; m. Joanna Maud Belford Silver, Aug. 29, 1961; children: Mark Benson, Kenneth Hulbert Belford (dec.). AB magna cum laude, Harvard U., 1959, MD cum laude, 1963. Diplomate Bd. Gastroenterology Am. Bd. Internal Medicine. Intern medicine Beth Israel Hosp., Boston, 1963-65, resident, 1967-68; asst. chief clin. rsch. Pakistan-SEATO Cholera Rsch. Lab., Dhaka, Bangladesh, 1965-67; resident in gastroenterology Mt. Sinai Hosp., N.Y.C., 1968-70; from instr. to prof. medicine Mt. Sinai Sch. Medicine, CUNY, N.Y.C., 1970-92, 1st Burrill B. Crohn prof. medicine, 1992—; dir. div. gastroenterology Mt. Sinai Hosp., N.Y.C., 1983—, vice chmn. dept. medicine, 1992—; co-chmn. work group on inflammatory bowel disease NIH, 1973-75; expert adv. panel on gastroenterology and nutrition U.S. Pharmacopeial Conv., 1980-85; chmn. rsch. devel. com. Nat. Found. for Ileitis and Colitis, 1984-89; co-founder, sec.-treas. Burrill B. Crohn Rsch. Foun., N.Y.C., 1984—; K.H. Koster Meml. lectr. Danish Soc. of Gastroenterology, 1992; Internat. State of the Art lectr. Brit. Soc. Gastroenterology, 1995, Falk Symposium, Germany, 1996; mem. Gastroenterology Leadership Coun. Task Force on Fellowship Curriculum, 1994. Author over 130 articles and chpts. on natural history and treatment of inflammatory bowel disease; editor 7 books and monographs on gastroenterology. Trustee Bangladesh Coun. of the Asia Soc., N.Y.C., 1972-75, Bd. Edn., Englewood Cliffs, N.J., 1973-75. Sr. surgeon, comdr. USPHS,1965-67. Recipient Jacobi medallion for Disting. Achievement Mt. Sinai Alumni Assn., 1994, Alexander A. Richman Commemorative award for Humanism in Medicine, 1996. Fellow ACP, Am. Coll. Gastroenterology (program dirs. com. 1991—, Henry Baker Presdl. lectr. 1989); mem. Am. Gastroent. Assn. (chmn. subcom. on cert. 1987, 1st chmn. clin. tchg. project 1984-90, nominating com., chmn. Immunology-Microbiology-Inflammatory Disorders sect. 1995, Disting. Educator award 1996), Crohn's and Colitis Found. Am. (grants rev. com. and coun. 1990-94, Disting. Svc. award 1991, N.Y. Govs.' medal 1992, chmn. clin. rsch. subcom. Disease Classification and Measurement 1994), Internat. Orgn. for Study of Inflammatory Bowel Disease (1st Am. elected chmn. 1989-92), Phi Beta Kappa, Alpha Omega Alpha. Achievements include co-development of oral rehydration therapy for diarrhea; development of resources and standards for clinical teaching in gastroenterology. Office: Mt Sinai Med Ctr One Gustave L Levy Pl New York NY 10029

SACHDEV, MOHINDAR SINGH, engineering educator; b. Amritsar, Punjab, India, Apr. 1, 1928; naturalized Can. citizen; s. Khushal Singh and Kishen Kour (Chawla) S.; m. Joginder Kour, Feb. 4, 1951; children—Narinder P., Mandhir, Sukhbir, Sukhvinder. B.Sc., Benares Hindu U., Varanasi, India, 1950; M.Sc., Panjab U., Chandigarh, India, 1965, U. Sask., 1967; Ph.D., U. Sask., 1969; DSc, U. Sask, 1994. Registered profl. engr., Sask.; chartered engr. U.K. Asst. engr. Pub. Works Dept., Amritsar, India, 1950-59; exec. engr. Pub. Works Dept., Nangal, India, 1960-61; assoc. prof. Punjab Engring. Coll., Chandigarh, India, 1961-65; supt. engr. State Electricity Bd., Patiala, India, 1968-69; asst. to assoc. prof. U. Sask., Saskatoon, 1969-76; prof. U. Sask., 1976-95, prof. emeritus, 1995—, head elec. engring. dept., 1988-93; cons., lectr. in field; chmn. Can. subcom. Internat. Electrotech. Commn., 1975-85, mem. 1985-90; mem. grant selection com. Nat. Sci. and Rsch. Coun. Can., 1991-94, chmn., 1993-94. Coordinator/author: (IEEE Course text) Computer Relaying, 1979, Microprocessor Relays and Protection Systems, 1988. Instr. def. driving courses Can. Safety Council, Ottawa, Ont., 1973-84; bd. dirs. Sask. Safety Council, 1976-81, chmn. traffic div., 1979-80. Recipient Cert. of Appreciation, Punjab State Electricity Bd., India, 1962; Sci. Research Council sr. vis. fellow, U.K., 1980. Fellow IEEE (chmn. western Can. coun. 1984-86, awards com. 1989-91, Outstanding Engring. Educator award IEEE Can. 1994), Instn. Engrs. India, Instn. Elec. Engrs. (U.K.), Engring. Inst. Can.; mem. Can. Elec. Assn. (vice chmn. power sys. planning and operation sect. 1989-92, chmn. 1993-96). Sikh. Office: Dept Elec Engring, 57 Campus Dr, Saskatoon, SK Canada S7N 5A9

SACHEDINA, ABDULAZIZ, religious studies educator; b. Lindi, Tanzania, May 12, 1942; came to U.S., 1976; s. Abdulhussein and Hamida (Shariff) S.; m. Fatima Akbar Takim, Aug. 14, 1967; children: Alireza, Muhammadreza. BA, Aligarh (India) Muslim U., 1966; BA in Persian Lang. and Literature, U. Mashad, Iran, 1971; MA in Islamic Studies, U. Toronto, Can., 1972, PhD, 1976. Instr. English Jorjani Nursing Sch., Mashhad, Iran, 1968-71; rsch. asst. dept. Mid. East and Islamic studies U. Toronto, 1971-72; asst. prof. dept. history, asst. prof. dept. French and gen. linguistics U. Va., 1977-78, asst. prof. dept. religious studies, oriental langs., 1978-82, assoc. prof., 1982-88, prof., 1988—; vis. lectr. dept. religious studies U. Waterloo, Ont., Can., 1975, dept. religion and culture Wilfrid Laurier U., Waterloo, 1975-76; vis. asst. prof. dept. religious studies U. Va., 1976-77; vis. prof. Faculty Shari'a U. Jordan, Amman, 1986; Margaret Gest vis. prof. religion Haverford (Pa.) Coll., 1987-88; adj. prof. dept. religion Temple U., Phila., 1987-88; vis. scholar U. Jordan, Amman, 1990-91; mem. editl. bd. Ency. Modern World Islam Oxford U. Press Project, Al-Mizan Translation Project Alawi Found. N.Y.; mem. adv. bd. law and religion Emory U., Atlanta; coord. Islamic Med. Ethics Network Internat. Assn. Bioethics; lectr. in field. Author: Islamic Messianism: The Idea of the Mahdi in Twelver Shi'ism, 1980, The Just Ruler in Twelver Shi'ism: The Comprehensive Authority of the Jurist in Imamite Jurisprudence, 1988; author: (with others) Human Rights and the Conflict of Cultures: Western and Islamic Perspectives on Religious Religion Liberty, 1988; contbr. articles to profl. jours., chpts. to books; contbr. articles to reference books. Religious scholar East African Fedn. of Shia Ithnashery Jamaats, 1963-66, Cultural scholar Govt. Iran, 1967-71; Grad. fellow Province of Ont., 1972-73, Open fellow U. Toronto, 1973-75, Rsch. fellow Ferdowsi U., 1973-74, Rsch. fellow Muhammedi Trust, 1978-79, Rsch. fellow Sesquicentennial, 1983; Summer Rsch. grantee U. Va., 1978, 80, 81, 83, Rsch. in Iran grantee, 1982-83. Mem. Am. Acad. Religion (editl. bd. jour.), Am. Oriental Soc., Mid. East Studies Assn., Iranian Studies Assn. Home: 698 Highland Ave Charlottesville VA 22903-4033 Office: U Va Dept Religious Studies Charlottesville VA 22903

SACHER, BARTON STUART, lawyer; b. Birmingham, Ala., Apr. 9, 1948; s. Martin R. and Inez (Zuckerman) S.; 1 child, Joseph Alan; m. Susan Angela Anton, Sept. 30, 1976. BBA, U. Ala., 1970, JD, 1973. Law clk. to judge J. Pointer U.S. Dist. Ct., Birmingham, 1973-74; assoc. Berkkowitz, Lefkowitz & Patrick, Birmingham, 1974-77; atty. investigations, trial counsel SEC, Washington, 1977-79; chief of investigations and enforcement SEC, Atlanta Region, 1979-85; ptnr. Tew, Jorden, Schulte & Beasley, Miami, 1986-90; pres., dir., ptnr. Hornsby, Sacher, Zelman, Stanton, Paul & Beiley, P.A., Miami, 1990—. Vice chmn. bd. dirs. Atlanta Fantasy Fair Inc., 1982—; v.p., trustee Temple Israel of Greater Miami, Inc.; v.p., dir. Alex Muss H.S., Israel; regional dir. ADL, Nat. Fin. Com., Dem. Party, Dem. Leadership Coun. Mem. ABA, Fed. Bar Assn., Fla. Bar Assn., D.C. Bar Assn., Ala. State Bar Assn., Greater Miami C. of C. (trustee), Grove Isle Club, Brickell Club. Jewish. Office: Hornsby Sacher Zelman Stanton Paul & Beiley PA 1401 Brickell Ave 7th Fl Miami FL 33131

SACHER, STEVEN JAY, lawyer; b. Cleve., Jan. 28, 1942; s. Albert N. and Cecil P. (Chessin) S.; m. Colleen Marie Gibbons, Nov. 28, 1970; children—Alexander Jerome, Barry Elizabeth, William Paul. B.S., U. Wis., 1964; J.D., U. Chgo., 1967. Bar: D.C. 1968. Assoc. solicitor Employee Retirement Income Security Act U.S. Dept. Labor, Washington, 1974-77; spl. counsel com. on labor and human resources U.S. Senate, Washington, 1977-79, gen. counsel, 1980-81; ptnr. Pepper, Hamilton & Scheetz, Washington, 1982-88; shareholder Johnson & Wortley, Washington, 1988-94; ptnr. Kilpatrick & Cody, Washington, 1994—; adj. prof. law Georgetown U. Law Ctr., 1977; co-chair sr. editors Employee Benefits Law and Annual Supplements, Bur. Nat. Affairs, Washington, 1991—. Mem. adv. bd. BNA Pension and Benefits Reporter; mem. editorial bd. Benefits Law Jour., Jour. Pension Planning and Compliance, Jour. Taxation of Employee Benefits. Founding mem. ERISA Roundtable, Washington. Mem. ABA (mgmt. co-chmn. com. on employee benefits, sect. on labor and employment law 1988-91, chmn. prohibited trans. subcom., com. on employee benefits, sect. on taxation 1986-91), Fed. Bar Assn., D.C. Bar Assn. Office: Kilpatrick & Cody 700 13th St NW Ste 800 Washington DC 20005-3960

SACHS, ALAN ARTHUR, lawyer, corporate executive; b. Bklyn., Feb. 7, 1947; s. Herman and Clara Ethel (Treinkman) S.; m. Marilyn Neda Mushlin, May 19, 1974; children: David Henry, Stephen Edward. B.A., Columbia U., 1967; J.D., Harvard U., 1970. Bar: N.Y. 1971, U.S. Dist. Ct. (ea. and so. dists.) N.Y. 1972, U.S. Ct. Appeals (2d cir.) 1973, U.S. Dist. Ct. (no. dist.) N.Y. 1977, Wis. 1983, Mo. 1989. Law clk. to judge U.S. Dist. Ct. (ea. dist.) N.Y., 1970-71; assoc. Cleary, Gottlieb, Steen & Hamilton, N.Y.C., 1971-79, Paskus, Gordon & Hyman, N.Y.C., 1979-81; sec., gen. counsel The Trane Co., LaCrosse, Wis., 1981-85; exec. v.p., gen. counsel, sec. Edison Bros. Stores Inc., St. Louis, 1985—, also bd. dirs. Mem. ABA, Am. Soc. Corp. Secs. Office: Edison Bros Stores Inc 501 N Broadway Saint Louis MO 63102-2102

SACHS, DAVID, lawyer; b. N.Y.C., Aug. 4, 1933; s. Morris and Fannie R. (Kaplan) S.; m. Frumet P. Lome, July 7, 1957; children: Diane R., Daniel L., Francine E. BS, U. Pa., 1954; JD, Harvard U., 1957. Bar: N.Y. 1958, U.S. Tax Ct. 1959, U.S. Ct. Fed. Claims 1960, U.S. Ct. Appeals (2d cir.) 1960, U.S. Supreme Ct. 1967. Assoc. White & Case, N.Y.C., 1957-68, ptnr., 1968-88, ret. ptnr., 1988—. Fellow Am Coll. Tax Counsel, N.Y. Bar Found.; mem. ABA, N.Y. Bar Assn. (chmn. tax sect. 1980), N.Y.C. Bar Assn. (chmn. com. on taxation 1986-89, mem. coun. on taxation 1990-96). Office: White & Case 1155 Avenue Of The Americas New York NY 10036-2787

SACHS, HOWARD F(REDERIC), federal judge; b. Kansas City, Mo., Sept. 13, 1925; s. Alex F. and Rose (Lyon) S.; m. Susanne Wilson, 1960; children: Alex Wilson, Adam Phinney. B.A. summa cum laude, Williams Coll., 1947; J.D., Harvard U., 1950. Bar: Mo. 1950. Law clk. U.S. Dist. Ct., Kansas City, Mo., 1950-51; pvt. practice law Phineas Rosenberg, Kansas City, 1951-56; with Spencer, Fane, Britt & Browne, 1956-79; U.S. dist. judge Western Dist. Mo., Kansas City, 1979—, chief dist. judge, 1990-92, now sr. judge. Contbr. articles to various publs.; contbr. chpt. to Mid-America's Promise, 1982. Mem. Kansas City Commn. Human Rels., 1967-73; chmn. Jewish Community Rels. Bur., 1968-71, Kansas City chpt. Am. Jewish Com., 1963-65; mem. exec. com. Nat. Jewish Community Rels. Adv. Coun., 1968-71; pres. Urban League Kansas City, 1957-58, Kansas City chpt. Am. Jewish Congress, 1974-77; co-chmn. Kansas City chpt. NCCJ, 1958-60; mem. Kansas City Sch. Dist. Desegregation Task Force, 1976-77; pres. Jackson County Young Democrats, 1959-60; treas. Kennedy-Johnson Club, Jackson County, 1960. Served with USNR, 1944-46. Mem. ABA, Mo. Bar, Kansas City Bar Assn., Am. Judicature Soc., Lawyers Assn. Kansas City, Dist. Judges Assn. (8th cir., pres. 1992-94), Phi Beta Kappa. Office: US Dist Ct US Courthouse 811 Grand Ave Rm 716 Kansas City MO 64106-1909

SACHS, JERRY, professional basketball team executive; b. Balt.; m. Joyce; children: Gene, Barbara. Pub. rels. asst. Balt Orioles, 1959-62, pub. rels. dir., 1962-65; dir. advt. mktg. and pub. rels. Atlanta Braves, 1965-70; gen. mgr. Balt. Bullets, 1970-73; former exec. v.p., now vice chmn. Washington Bullets NBA; pres. Capital Centre, 1974—. Office: Washington Bullets USAir Arena Landover MD 20785*

SACHS, JOHN PETER, carbon company executive; b. Duesseldorf, Germany, 1926; married. BAChemE, Ill. Inst. Tech., 1948, MAChemE, 1950, PhDChemE, 1952. Various mgmt. positions in research and devel., engring. and ops. Union Carbide Corp., 1951-66; v.p. ops. then group v.p. Great Lakes Carbon Corp., N.Y.C., 1966-78; pres., chief exec. officer Gt. Lakes Carbon Corp., N.Y.C., 1978-86, now bd. dirs.; chmn. bd., dir. Gen. Refractories Co., 1978-85; ptnr. J.P. Sachs Assocs., Mgmt. Cons., New Canaan, Conn., 1987—. Trustee Fairfield U., 1978-92; bd. dirs. Kneissl-Dachstein 1992—, Peridot, 1989—. Mem. Am. Inst. Chem. Engrs. (pres. 1985). Home and Office: JP Sachs Assocs 67 Dunning Rd New Canaan CT 06840-4009

SACHS, LLOYD ROBERT, entertainment critic, writer; b. Flushing, N.Y., Dec. 3, 1950; s. Sidney Howard Sachs and Eleanor Sachs Brown. BA in English, Marietta Coll., 1972; MSJ, Northwestern U., 1974. Reporter, critic Variety, Chgo., 1975-76; pop culture columnist The Reader, Chgo., 1976-80; pop music reviewer USA Today, Washington, 1983-84; entertainment critic Chgo. Sun-Times, 1984—; vis. lectr. in journalism U. Ill., Chgo., 1983. Trustee The Ragdale Found., Lake Forest, Ill., 1985—; vol. The Peace Mus., Chgo., 1984—. Grantee Ill. Arts Coun., Chgo., 1985. Democrat. Jewish. Office: Chgo Sun-Times Inc 401 N Wabash Ave Chicago IL 60611-3532

SACHS, MARILYN STICKLE, author, lecturer, editor; b. N.Y.C., Dec. 18, 1927; d. Samuel and Anna (Smith) Stickle; m. Morris Sachs, Jan. 26, 1947; children: Anne, Paul. BA, Hunter Coll., 1949; MSLS, Columbia U., 1953. Children's libr. Bklyn. Pub. Libr., 1949-60, San Francisco Pub. Libr., 1961-67. Author: Amy Moves In, 1964, Laura's Luck, 1965, Amy and Laura, 1966, Veronica Ganz, 1968, Peter and Veronica, 1969, Marv, 1970, The Bears' House, 1971 (Austrian Children's Book prize 1977, Recognition of Merit award George C. Stone Ctr. for Children's Books 1989), The Truth About Mary Rose, 1973 (Silver Slate Pencil award 1974), A Pocket Full of Seeds, 1973 (Jane Addams Children's Book Honor award 1974), Matt's Mitt, 1975, Dorrie's Book, 1975 (Silver State Pencil award 1977, Garden State Children's Book award 1978), A December Tale, 1976, A Secret Friends, 1978, A Summer's Lease, 1979, Bus Ride, 1980, Class Pictures, 1980, Fleet Footed Florence, 1981, Hello...Wrong Number, 1981, Call Me Ruth, 1982 (Assn. Jewish Librs. award 1983), Beach Towels, 1982, Fourteen, 1983, The Fat Girl, 1984, Thunderbird, 1985, Underdog, 1985 (Christopher 1986), Baby Sister 1986, Almost Fifteen, 1987, Fran Ellen's House, 1987 (award Bay Area Book Reviewers Assn. 1988, Recognition of Merit award George C. Stone Ctr. for Children's Books 1989), Just Like A Friend, 1989, At the Sound of the Beep, 1990, Circles, 1991, What My Sister Remembered, 1992, Thirteen, 1993, Ghosts in the Family, 1995; co-editor: (with Ann Durell) Big Book for Peace, 1990 (Calif. Children's Book award 1991, Jane Addams Children's Book prize 1991); reviewer books N.Y. Times, San Francisco Chronicle, 1970—. Mem. PEN, ACLU, SANE-Freeze, Sierra Club, Authors' Guild, Soc. Children's Bookwriters. Democrat. Jewish. Avocations: reading, hiking, baseball. Home: 733 31st Ave San Francisco CA 94121

SACHS, MURRAY B., audiologist, educator. BS, MIT, 1962, MS, 1964, PhD in Elec. Engring., 1966. From asst. prof. to assoc. prof. biomed. engring. Johns Hopkins U., Balt., 1970-80, dir. Ctr. Hearing Sci., 1986-91, Massey prof., dir. dept. biomed. engring., 1991—; mem. com. communication and control Internat. Union Pure and Applied Biophysics, 1975-80; mem. communication disease panel and basic sci. task force Nat. Inst. Neurol. and Communicative Disorders and Stroke NIH, 1977-78, chmn. communicative disease rev. com., 1977-79, ad hoc adv. com., 1979-86, sci. program adv. com., 1984-86; prof. biomed. engring. Johns Hopkins U., 1980—, prof. neurosci., 1981—, prof. otolaryngology-head and neck surgery, 1982-85. Mem. Inst. Medicine-Nat. Acad. Sci., Sigma Xi. Office: Johns Hopkins U Sch Medicine Ctr for Hearing Scis 720 Rutland Ave Baltimore MD 21205-2109*

SACHS, ROBERT GREEN, physicist, educator, laboratory administrator; b. Hagerstown, Md., May 4, 1916; s. Harry Maurice and Anna (Green) S.; m. Selma Solomon, Aug. 28, 1941; m. Jean K. Woolf, Dec. 17, 1950; children: Rebecca, Jennifer, Jeffrey, Judith, Joel; m. Carolyn L. Wolf, Aug. 21, 1968; stepchildren: Thomas Wolf, Jacqueline Wolf, Katherine Wolf. Ph.D., Johns Hopkins U., 1939; D.Sc. (hon.), Purdue U., 1967, U. Ill., 1977, Elmhurst Coll., 1987. Research fellow George Washington U., 1939-41; instr. physics Purdue U., 1941-43; on leave as lectr., research fellow U. Calif. at Berkeley, 1941; sect. chief Ballistic Rsch. Lab., Aberdeen Proving Ground, Md., 1943-46; dir. theoretical physics divsn. Argonne (Ill.) Nat. Lab., Ill., 1946-47; asso. prof. physics U. Wis., 1947-48, prof., 1948-64; assoc. dir. Argonne Nat. Lab., 1964-68, dir., 1973-79; prof. physics U. Chgo., 1964-86, prof. emeritus, 1986—; dir. Enrico Fermi Inst., 1968-73, 83-86; Higgins vis. prof. Princeton U., 1955-56; vis. prof. U. Paris, 1959-60, Tohoku U., Japan, 1974; cons. Ballistic Research Labs., 1945-59, Argonne Nat. Lab., 1947-50, 60-64; cons. radiation lab. U. Calif. at Berkeley, 1955-59; adv. panel physics NSF, 1958-61; mem. physics survey com., chmn. elem. particle physics panel Nat. Acad. Scis., 1969-72; high energy physics adv. panel div. research AEC, 1966-69; mem. steering com. (Sci. and Tech., A Five Year Outlook), 1979; mem. DOE task force on energy rsch. priorities, 1991-93. Author: Nuclear Theory, 1953, The Physics of Time Reversal, 1987; chief editor: High Energy Nuclear Physics, 1957; editor: National Energy Issues: How Do We Decide, 1980, The Nuclear Chain Reaction--Forty Years Later, 1984. Recipient Disting. Svc. to Engring. citation U. Wis., 1977; Guggenheim fellow, 1959-60. Fellow Am. Phys. Soc. (coun. 1968-71, regional sec. Cen. States 1964-69), Am. Acad. Arts and Scis. (v.p. Midwest Ctr. 1980-83); mem. NAS (chmn. physics sect. 1977-80, chmn. Class I Math. and Phys. Scis. 1980-83), AAAS (v.p., chmn. physics sect. 1970-71), Am. Inst. Physics (mem. gov. bd. 1969-71), Phi Beta Kappa, Sigma Xi. Achievements include research in theoretical particle, nuclear and solid state physics, terminal ballistics, nuclear power reactors. Office: U Chicago Enrico Fermi Inst Enrico Fermi Inst 5640 Ellis Ave Chicago IL 60637

SACHS, SAMUEL, II, museum director; b. N.Y.C., Nov. 30, 1935; s. James Henry and Margery (Fay) S.; m. Susan McAllen (div.); children: Katherine, Eleanor; m. Jerre S. Hollander (div.); 1 child, Alexander; m. Elizabeth M. Gordon; 1 child, Hadley Elizabeth. BA cum laude, Harvard U., 1957; MA, NYU Inst. Fine Arts, 1962. Asst. in charge prints and drawings Mpls. Inst. Arts, 1958-60; asst. dir. U. Mich. Mus. of Art, Ann Arbor, 1963-64; chief curator Mpls. Inst. Arts, 1964-73, dir., 1973-85; dir. Detroit Inst. Arts, 1985—. Bd. dirs. Ctr. for Creative Studies, Detroit, Univ. Liggett Sch., Grosse Pointe. Decorated knight 1st class Order North Star (Sweden); Order of Dannebrog (Denmark). Mem. Am. Assn. Museums, Coll. Art Assn., Assn. Art Mus. Dirs. Clubs: Detroit, Century Assn, Harvard, Grosse Pointe. Home: 19344 Cumberland Way Detroit MI 48203-1456 Office: Detroit Inst Arts 5200 Woodward Ave Detroit MI 48202-4008

SACHS, STEPHEN HOWARD, lawyer; b. Balt., Jan. 31, 1934; s. Leon and Shirley (Blum) S.; m. Sheila Kleinman, Sept. 4, 1960; children: Elisabeth Leon. BA, Haverford Coll., 1954; postgrad., New Coll., Oxford, Eng., 1954-55; LLB, Yale U., 1960. Bar: Md. 1960, D.C. 1988, U.S. Supreme Ct. 1965. Law clk. U.S. Ct. Appeals, Washington, 1960-61; asst. U.S. atty. Dist. of Md., 1961-64, U.S. atty., 1967-70; pvt. practice law Balt., 1970-78; atty. gen. State of Md., Balt., 1979-87; with firm Wilmer, Cutler & Pickering, Washington, 1987—. Served with U.S. Army, 1955-57. Fulbright scholar, 1954-55. Fellow Am. Coll. Trial Lawyers; mem. ABA, Md. Bar Assn., Balt. Bar Assn., Fed. Bar Assn., Nat. Urban Coalition and Lawyers Com. for Civil Rights Under the Law. Democrat. Jewish. Home: 5 Roland Mews Baltimore MD 21210-1560 Office: Wilmer Cutler & Pickering 2445 M St NW Washington DC 20037-1435

SACK, BURTON MARSHALL, restaurant company executive; b. Melrose, Mass., Dec. 13, 1937; s. Samuel and Bertha (Gersin) S.; m. Susan Lightbown, June 9, 1963 (dec.); children: Brian, David, Scott; m. Gail Summerfield, June 17, 1990. B.S., Cornell U., 1961; P.M.D., Harvard Bus. Sch., 1967. With Howard Johnson's, 1951-83, successively dishwasher, counter-man, cook, and asst. mgr., to 1955, advt. asst., 1961, asst. dir. mktg., 1961-62, dir. public relations, 1962-67, gen. mgr. fast food service div., 1967-70; gen. mgr. Ground Round Restaurant div., 1970-73, v.p. splty. restaurants, 1973-76, group v.p. corp. devel., 1976-81, sr. v.p. corp. devel., 1981-83; pres. Exeter Hospitality Group, Boston, 1983-87, Pub Ventures of New Eng., Braintree, Mass., 1984-94; exec. v.p. Applebees Internat., Inc., 1994—; lectr. Cornell U., Wharton Sch. Bus. U. Pa., Cape Cod C.C., Babson Coll.; bd. dirs. Bay St. Restaurants; mem. bd. advisors Restaurant Assocs. Chmn. fund raising Greater Boston Assn. Retarded Citizens. With USMC, 1955-58. Mem. Nat. Restaurant Assn. (past chpt. pres., dir., bd. dirs.), Nat. Assn. Corp. Real Estate Execs., Broadcasting Execs. of New Eng. (past dir.), Mass. Restaurant Assn. (1st v.p., mem. bd. dirs.), Cornell Soc. Hotelmen (past pres. New Eng. chpt., past nat. pres.). Home: 415 L'Ambiance Dr PH-D Longboat Key FL 34228 Office: Applebee's Internat Inc 4551 W 107th St Overland Park KS 66207

SACK, EDGAR ALBERT, electronics company executive; b. Pitts., Jan. 31, 1930; s. Edgar Albert and Margaret Valentine (Engelmohr) S.; m. Eugenia Ferris, June 7, 1952; children: Elaine Kimberley, Richard Warren. B.S., Carnegie-Mellon U., 1951, M.S., 1952, Ph.D., 1954. Dept. mgr. Westinghouse Research Lab., Pitts., 1960-63; engring. mgr. Westinghouse Microelectronics, Balt., 1963-65; operations mgr. Westinghouse Microelectronics, 1965-67, div. mgr., 1967-69; div. v.p. Gen. Instrument Corp., Hicksville, N.Y., 1969-73; group v.p. Gen. Instrument Corp., 1973-77, sr. v.p., 1977-84; pres., chief exec. officer Zilog Inc., Campbell, Calif., 1984—, also chmn. bd. dirs.; vis. com. elec. engring. dept. Carnegie-Mellon U., 1969-74; bd. dirs. Catalyst Semiconductor, Inc.; mem. indsl. adv. council SUNY, Stony Brook, 1979-83; mem. Adv. Com. on Solid State Electronics for Poly. Inst. Tech., 1981-83. Author: Forward Controllership Business Management System, 1989, 2nd edit., 1993. Mem. Action Com. Long Island, 1982-84. Recipient 2nd Ann. Hammerschlag Disting. Lectr. award Carnegie Mellon U., 1995. Fellow IEEE, Poly. Inst. Tech.; mem. Semicondr. Industry Assn. (dir. 1982-85); mem. Carnegie Mellon Alumni Assn. (Merit award 1981), Eta Kappa Nu (Outstanding Young Elec. Engr. 1959), Huntington Yacht Club (vice comdr. 1977), Tau Beta Pi (finalist San Francisco Entrepreneur of Yr. award 1991), Phi Kappa Phi. Patentee in field. Home: 21412 Sarahills Ct Saratoga CA 95070-4814 Office: Zilog Inc 210 E Hacienda Ave Campbell CA 95008-6617

SACK, JAMES MCDONALD, JR., radio and television producer, marketing executive; b. London, Ky., Oct. 11, 1948; s. James McDonald and Ruth Elmore (Bryant) S.; m. Cheryl S. Gremaux, July 13, 1969 (div. June 1974); 1 child, Graehm McDonald. BA in History, Ind. U., 1975, MS in Telecommunications, 1976. Coordinator Latin Am. Ednl. Ctr., Ft. Wayne, Ind., 1979-81, Mayor's Office, Ft. Wayne, 1981-83; producer WMEE-WQHK Radio, Ft. Wayne, 1983-85; owner, operator Festival Mgmt. and Devel., Ft. Wayne, 1984—; ptnr. Lily Co., Fort Wayne, 1991—; v.p. communications, mktg. United Way of Allen County, Ft. Wayne, Ind., 1989—; owner The Sack Co., 1992; owner The Lily Co.; pub. affairs prodr. WBYR, Ft. Wayne; dir. Cable Access, Inc. Producer radio documentary, 1985 (First Place award Ind. Broadcasters Assn., 1985), producer WFWA-PBS Eye on the Arts, 1987-89. Founder, pres. Germanfest of Ft. Wayne, 1981-92; pres. cable TV program adv. coun. City of Ft. Wayne, mktg. dir., 1996; founder Ft. Wayne-Gera (Germany) Sister City Affilation; commr. Ind. Hoosier Celebration, 1988; dir. Ind. Highland Games, 1992, cons., 1993—. Named Ky. Col., 1991. Mem. German Heritage Soc. (founder, bd. dirs. 1986—), Ind. German Heritage Soc. (founder, bd. dirs. 1986-92, Gov.'s Commendation award 1983), N.Am. Sängerbund (sec. 1985-86), Männerchor Club (Ft. Wayne), Ft. Wayne Sport Club (sec. 1985-86, trustee 1987-89). Lutheran. Avocations: fencing, canoeing, flying, politics, linguistics. Home and Office: 2502 S Harrison St Fort Wayne IN 46807-1318

SACK, ROBERT DAVID, lawyer; b. Phila., Oct. 4, 1939; s. Eugene J. and Sylvia I. (Rivlin) S.; div.; children: Deborah Gail, Suzanne Michelle, David Rivlin; m. Anne K. Hilker, 1989. B.A., U. Rochester, 1960; LL.B., Columbia U., 1963. Bar: N.Y. 1963. Law clk. to judge Fed. Dist. Ct., Dist. of N.J., 1963-64; assoc. Patterson, Belknap & Webb, N.Y.C., 1964-70; ptnr. Patterson, Belknap, Webb & Tyler, N.Y.C., 1970-74, 74-86, Gibson, Dunn & Crutcher, N.Y.C., 1986—; sr. assoc. spl. counsel U.S. Ho. of Reps. Impeachment Inquiry, 1974; lectr. Practising Law Inst., 1973—; mem. adv. bd. Media Law Reporter. Author: Libel, Slander and Related Problems, 1980, 2nd edit., 1994, CD-Rom edit., 1995, N.Y.C. Commission on Public Information and Communication, 1995; mem. adv. bd. Media Law Reporter BNA; contbr. articles to legal jours. Chmn. bd. dirs. Nat. Council on Crime and Delinquency, 1982-83; trustee Columbia seminars on media and society Columbia U. Sch. Journalism, 1985-92; v.p., dir. William F. Kerby and Robert S. Potter Fund. Mem. ABA (bd. govs. forum com. on communications law 1980-88), N.Y. State Bar Assn., Assn. Bar City N.Y. (chmn. communications law com. 1986-89). Office: Gibson Dunn & Crutcher 200 Park Ave 47th Fl New York NY 10166-0193

SACK, SYLVAN HANAN, lawyer; b. Phila., Dec. 26, 1932; s. Isidore F. and Mollye (Bellmore) S.; m. Ellen L. Foreman, Aug. 13, 1972; children:

Reuben H., Sara I. M.S. in Bus. Adminstrn, Pa. State U., 1956; J.D., U. Balt., 1964. Bar: Md. 1964, U.S. Tax Ct. 1967, U.S. Supreme Ct. 1970; C.P.A., Md. Pvt. practice Balt., 1967—; assoc. counsel Safety First Club of Md., 1975-78, spl. counsel, 1979—; gov. Md. chpt. Retinitis Pigmentosa Found., 1974-75. Contbr. articles to profl. jours. Chmn. Indsl. Toxicology NIOSH Function, 1977, Occupational Disease Forum, 1979, OSHA and Diseases in Workplace Seminar, 1981. Mem. Fed. Bar Assn. (gov. chpt. 1968—, chmn. bd. govs. 1969-70, chmn. environ. law program 1984), ABA (chmn. subcom. sect. taxation 1972-75), Md. Bar Assn., Assn. Trial Lawyers Am.; mem. Md. Trial Lawyers Assn. (lectr. toxic torts 1983 conv.). Home: 27 Brightside Ave Baltimore MD 21208-4802 Office: 2404 Saint Paul St Baltimore MD 21218-5118

SACKEIM, HAROLD, psychologist; b. Hackensack, N.J., July 13, 1951; s. Alexander and Ruth (Frymer) S.; m. Donna Zucchi, Oct. 9, 1977. BA, Columbia U., 1972; BA, MA, Oxford (Eng.) U., 1974; PhD, U. Pa., 1977. Asst. prof. psychology Columbia U., N.Y.C., 1977-79, lectr. psychiatry Coll. Physicians and Surgeons, 1980-87; asst. prof. psychology N.Y.U., N.Y.C., 1979-81, assoc. prof., 1981-87; assoc. prof. dept. psychiatry Columbia U., N.Y.C., 1987-90, prof. dept. psychiatry, 1990—, chief dept. biol. psychiatry, 1991—; assoc. attending psychologist N.Y. State Psychiat. Inst., N.Y.C., 1980—, rsch. sci. and dep. chief dept. biol. psychiatry, 1980-91, chief dept. biol. psychiatry, 1991—; cons. WNET, 1978, 85; pvt. practice psychology, N.Y.C., 1977—. NIMH grantee, 1981—, NYU Rsch. Challenge Fund grantee, 1981-82, McGraw-Hill grantee, 1979-80, NIA grantee, 1985—; recipient Rsch. Excellence award N.Y. Office Mental Health, 1995. Fellow Am. Psychiat. Assn. (hon.); mem. AAAS, APA, Am. Coll. Neuropsychopharmacology (Joel Elkes Internat. award 1994), Am. Psychopathol. Assn., Internat. Neuropsychol. Soc., Soc. Biol. Psychiatry. Assoc. editor Jour. Social and Clin. Psychology, 1982-87; cons. editor jour. Imagination, Cognition and Personality, 1981—, Convulsive Therapy, 1985—, Neuropsychiatry, Neuropsychol. and Behavior Neurology, 1987—; contbr. numerous articles to profl. jours. Office: Columbia U Dept Psychiatry 722 W 168th St # 72 New York NY 10032-2603

SACKETT, DIANNE MARIE, city treasurer, accountant; b. Oil City, Pa., Dec. 29, 1956; d. Clarence Benjamin and Donna Jean (Grosteffon) Knight; m. Mark Douglas Sackett, May 26, 1984; children: Jason Michael, Cory James. BBA, Ea. Mich. U., 1979, MBA, 1986. Accounts payable supr. Sarns, Inc., Ann Arbor, Mich., 1979-81; cost acct. Simplex Products Divsn., Adrian, Mich., 1981-83, gen. acctg. supr., 1983-88; city treas. City of Tecumseh, Mich., 1991—. Mem. Mich. Mcpl. Treas.' Assn., Mich. Mcpl. Fin. Officers Assn., Mcpl. Treas.' Assn. of the U.S. and Can. Pentecostal. Office: 309 E Chicago Blvd Tecumseh MI 49286-1550

SACKETT, JOSEPH FREDERIC, radiologist, educator, administrator; b. Cleve., Jan. 16, 1940; s. George Leslie and Cora Lenore (Hurst) S.; children: Joseph Frederic, Samson Occom, Penelope Cora. B.A., Dartmouth Coll., 1962; M.D., Tulane U., 1966. Diplomate Am. Bd. Radiology. Intern Mary Hitchcock Meml. Hosp., Hanover, N.H., 1966-67; resident Dartmouth Coll.-Hitchcock Hosp., Hanover, 1969-72; fellow in neuroradiology Ulleval Hosp., Oslo, 1972-73, N.Y. Hosp.-Cornell U., N.Y.C., 1973-74; asst. prof. radiology U. Wis.-Madison, 1974-78, assoc. prof., 1978-81, chmn. dept., prof., 1981—; vis. prof. U. Nebr.-Omaha, 1977, Dartmouth Med. Sch., 1977, 82, U. Calif.-San Francisco, 1977, Med. Coll. Wis., Milw., 1977, Cleve. Clinic, 1978, Case Western Res. Sch. Medicine, 1978, UCLA, 1978, U. Kans., 1979, U. Cin., 1979, Rutgers Med. Sch., New Brunswick, N.J., 1979, Cornell U. Med. Ctr., 1980, U. Louisville, 1981, others; lectr. in field. Author: New Techniques in Myelography, 1979; editor: Digital Subtraction Angiography, 1981; contbr. numerous articles to profl. jours. Served to capt. M.C., U.S. Army, 1967-69, Vietnam. Fellow Am. Coll. Radiology; mem. Assn. Univ. Radiologists (fin. chmn. 1984—), Radiol. Soc. N.Am., Am. Soc. Neuroradiology, Rotary Internat. Republican. Avocations: sailing; yacht racing. Home: 3100 Lake Mendota Dr Madison WI 53705-1481 Office: Clin Sci Ctr 600 Highland Ave Madison WI 53792-0001

SACKETT, ROSS DEFOREST, publisher; b. Chgo., Mar. 26, 1930; s. DeForest and Margaret (Ross) S.; m. Marvyda Wild, Sept. 1, 1951; children: David, Scott, Cynthia, Amy, Stuart. BA, Lawrence Coll., 1951. Editor in chief Charles Merrill Books, Inc., Columbus, Ohio, 1959-61; gen. mgr., v.p., exec. v.p., dir. Holt, Rinehart & Winston, N.Y.C., 1961-67, pres., dir., 1967-70, chmn. bd., 1970-72; pres. CBS Edn. Pub. Group, 1970-72, Ency. Brit. Ednl. Corp., 1972-76; chmn. Crescent Park Press, Angeles Toy Corp., Childs/Play, Inc.; chmn. bd. Big Toys Inc.; pres., chmn. bd. Kompan Holdings; dir. Ency. Brit. Corp., Kompan, Inc.; former dir. CBS. Trustee Highscope Ednl. Rsch. Found. Mem. Assn. Am. Pubs. (chmn.), Civil War Round Table, Delta Tau Delta, Eta Sigma Phi. Episcopalian. Office: PO Box 448 Eureka Springs AR 72632-0448

SACKETT, SUSAN DEANNA, film and television production associate, writer; b. N.Y.C., Dec. 18, 1943; adopted d. Maxwell and Gertrude Selma (Kugel) S. B.A. in Edn., U. Fla., 1964, M.Ed., 1965. Tchr. Dade County Schs., Miami, Fla., 1966-68, L.A. City Schs., 1968-69; asst. publicist, comml. coordinator NBC-TV, Burbank, Calif., 1970-73; asst. to creator of Star Trek Gene Roddenberry, 1974-91; prodn. assoc. Star Trek: The Next Generation TV Series, 1987-91; writer Star Trek: The Next Generation, 1990-92; lectr. and guest speaker STAR TREK convs. in U.S., Eng., Australia, 1974-93. Author and editor: Letters to Star Trek, 1977; co-author: Star Trek Speaks, 1979; The Making of Star Trek-The Motion Picture, 1979; You Can Be a Game Show Contestant and Win, 1982, Say Goodnight Gracie, 1986; author: The Hollywood Reporter Book of Box Office Hits, 1990, 2nd edit., 96, Prime Time Hits, 1993, Hollywood Sings, 1995. Mem. ACLU, Writers Guild Am., Am. Humanist Assn., Mensa, Sierra Club. Democrat. Address: PO Box 3372 Carefree AZ 85377

SACKHEIM, ROBERT LEWIS, aerospace engineer, educator; b. N.Y.C., N.Y., May 16, 1937; s. A. Frederick and Lillian L. (Emmer) S.; m. Babette Freund, Jan. 12, 1964; children: Karen Holly, Andrew Frederick. BSChemE, U. Va., 1959; MSChemE, Columbia U., 1961; postgrad., UCLA, 1966-72. Project engr. Comsat Corp., El Segundo, Calif., 1969-72; project mgr. TRW, Redondo Beach, Calif., 1964-69, sect. head, 1972-76, dept. mgr., 1976-81, mgr. new bus., 1981-86, lab. mgr., 1986-90, dep. ctr. dir., 1990-93, ctr. dir., 1993—; instr. UCLA engring. ext., 1986; mem. adv. bds. NASA, Washington, 1989—; mem. peer rev. bd. various univs. and govtl. agys., 1990—; mem. Nat. Rsch. Coun./Aeronautics and Space Engring. Bd., 1994—; guest lectr. various univs. and AIAA short courses. Author: Space Mission Analysis and Design, 1991, Space Propulsion Analysis and Design, 1995; contbr. over 70 papers to profl. jours., confs. Mem. adv. bd. L.A. Bd. Edn., 1990-92; fund raiser March of Dimes, L.A., 1970-90, YMCA, San Pedro, Calif., 1974-86. Capt. USAF, 1960-63. Recipient Group Achievement award NASA, 1970, 78, 86. Fellow AIAA (chmn. com. 1980-83, J.H. Wyld Propulsion award 1992, Shuttle Flag award 1984). Achievements include 4 patents for spacecraft propulsion systems, devices and components. Office: TRW Space & Elects Group Bldg 01/RM 2010 1 Space Park Blvd Rm 2010 Redondo Beach CA 90278-1001

SACKLER, ARTHUR BRIAN, lawyer; b. Utica, N.Y., June 9, 1950; s. Joseph Leon and Leonore (Guttman) S.; m. Linda J. Cimarusti, May 27, 1979; children: Joshua Michael, Jenna Rachel. B.A., Syracuse U., 1970, J.D., 1973; LL.M., Georgetown U., 1979. Bar: N.Y. 1974, D.C. 1975, U.S. Dist. Ct. D.C. 1979, U.S. Supreme Ct. 1979, U.S. Ct. Appeals (D.C. cir.) 1981. Appeals examiner U.S. Civil Service Commn., Washington, 1973-75, atty. advisor, 1975-76, trial atty., 1976-79; gen. counsel Nat. Newspaper Assn., Washington, 1979-82; dir. pub. policy devel. Time Warner, Washington, 1982-92, v.p. law and pub. policy, 1992—; mng. dir. Mailers Coun., 1990—; mem. Joint Washington Media Com., 1979—, Am. Copyright Council, Washington, 1984-86; faculty communications law Practicing Law Inst., 1980, forum com. on communications law seminar, 1980; instr. Am. Press Inst., 1980-82. Editor and contbr.: Federal Laws Affecting Newspapers, 1981; founder, editor newsletter News Media Update, 1979-82; contbr. articles to profl. jours., newspapers. Pres. Birnam Wood Community Assn., Potomac, Md., 1983-84; sec., treas. Potomac Springs Community Assn., Potomac, Md., 1986-87. Mem. ABA (chmn. postal matters com., adminstrv. law sect.), D.C. Bar Assn., Fed. Communications Bar Assn., Fed. Bar Assn., Mag. Pubs. Am. (govt. rels. coun. N.Y.C. 1982-85, 92—), Am. Advt. Fedn. (govt. relations com. Washington 1984—), Direct Mktg. Assn. (govt. relations com. 1986—), Am. Tort Reform Assn. (bd. dirs. 1987-88, corp. steering com. 1986-88), Assn. Am. Pubs. (postal com. N.Y.C. 1983—). Jewish. Clubs: Nat. Press, Bethesda Country. Office: Time Warner Inc 800 Connecticut Ave NW Ste 800 Washington DC 20006-2718

SACKLOW, STEWART IRWIN, advertising executive; b. Albany, N.Y., July 29, 1942; s. Jacob David and Freda Ruth (Pearlman) S.; A.A.S., N.Y.C. C.C., 1962; BS, Western Mich. U., 1965; m. Harriette Lynn Cooperman, July 2, 1967; 1 son, Ian Marc. Asst. dist. office Humble Oil & Refining Co., Inc., Albany, 1963-65; dir. advt. and sales promotion Albany Pub. Markets div. Weiss Foods, 1965-68; Golub Corp., v.p. and dir. advt. Price Chopper Discount Foods, Schenectady, 1968-78; pres., creative dir. Wolkcas Advt., Inc., 1978-93, pres., CEO, 1993-95; pres. Wolkens Comms. Group, 1995—; exec. dir. Ski the Catskills, 1982-84; pres. Broadcast Creations, 1985—; pres. Testimonials, Inc., 1991-93. Mem. Dist. Atty.'s readiness team; active Albany County Cerebral Palsy Telethons, 1966-68; mem. fund drive com. Sta. WMHT-TV ednl. TV, 1967-74; bd. dirs. N.E. Cystic Fibrosis Found., Video Spirit; bd. dirs., mem. exec. com. Upstate Leukemia Assn.; mem. bd. Gov. Clinton council Boy Scouts Am., leader, Voorheesville, N.Y.; chmn. N.Y. State Arbor Day Com., 1990-96; pres. Takundewide Home Owners Assn., 1991-92; key market coord. Partnership Drug Free Am.; coord. Drug Free N.Y. State. Recipient certificate merit Nat. Research Bur., 1966, Freedoms Found., 1966, Amsterdam Recorder, 1968, Retail Advt. Conf., 1969, 70, Woman's Day Mag., 1971, 72, 73, 74, 75, 76; Grand Nat. award Am. Dairy Assn., 1969, Hunt Wesson Foods, 1970; recipient 4 1st place awards Am. Advt. Fedn., 1972, Crystal Prism award, 1973; Effie award Am. Mgmt. Assn., 1972; Silver medal award Am. Advt. Fed., 1973, Addy award, 1973, 74, 75; award excellence Retail Advt. Conf., 1971; Best 15 Internat. Ads award Internat. Newspaper Advt. Execs., 1972, Gold Leaf award Interant. Arborist Soc., 1993. Mem. N.Y. Art Dirs. Club, Ad Club N.Y. (bd. dirs. 1974-79, 93-94, pres. 1976-77), Am. Advt. Fedn. (bd. govs. 1975), Profl. Pub. Rels. Coun. Albany Execs. Assn. Mem. B'nai B'rith (bd. dir. housing 1992-93), N.Y. Art Dirs. Club, Capital Dist. Creative Club, Mohawk Antique Auto Club, Albany Yacht Club, Schenectady Racquet Club, KP. Home: 716 St Marks Ln Niskayuna NY 12309-4843

SACKNER, MARVIN ARTHUR, physician; b. Phila., Feb. 16, 1932; s. Albert B. and Goldie Mildred (Haber) S.; m. Ruth Karsch, June 24, 1956; children: Sara, Deborah, Jonathan. BS, Temple U., 1953; MD, Jefferson Med. Coll., 1957. Diplomate Am. Bd. Internal Medicine. Intern Phila. Gen. Hosp., 1957-58, med. resident, 1958-61; ACP rsch. fellow U. Pa., Phila., 1961-64; chief pulmonary disease Mt. Sinai Hosp., Miami Beach, Fla., 1964-74, dir. med. svcs., 1974-91; dir. med. svcs. emeritus Mt. Sinai Hosp., Fla., 1992—; prof. medicine U. Miami, Fla., 1973—; gov., chmn. pulmonary disease exam. bd. Am. Bd. Internal Medicine, 1977-80; chief exec. officer Non-Invasive Monitoring Systems, Inc., Miami Beach, Fla., 1986—. Author: Scleroderma, 1966; editor: Diagnostic Techniques in Pulmonary Disease, Parts I and II, 1980; mem. editorial bd. Fla. Med. Assn., 1974, Am. Rev. Respiratory Physiology, 1976-80, Jour. Applied Physiology, 1976-80, Annals Internal Medicine, 1979; patentee in field; contbr. articles to profl. jours. Pres. Art in Pub. Places, Inc., 1975-78; co-dir. Ruth and Marvin Sackner Archive of Concrete and Visual Poetry, 1979—; bd. dirs. Ctr. for Book Art, N.Y.C., 1987-93; mem. libr. com. Mus. Modern Art, N.Y.C., 1990-94. NEA grantee, 1977-78, Nat. Heart, Lung and Blood Inst. grantee, 1966—, others. Fellow ACP, Am. Coll. Chest Physicians; mem. Am. Thoracic Soc. (pres.1980), Am. Physiol. Soc., Grolier Club N.Y.C. Jewish. Office: 1840 West Ave Miami FL 33139-1432

SACKS, ARTHUR BRUCE, environmental and liberal arts educator; b. N.Y.C., Apr. 21, 1946; s. Fred and Lillian Pearl (Levy) S.; m. Normandy Roden, May 17, 1987; children: Rachel, Erica. BA, Bklyn. Coll., 1967; MA, U. Wis., 1968, PhD, 1975. Teaching asst. dept. English, U. Wis., Madison, 1968-72, asst. to assoc. dean for student acad. affairs, 1972-76, lectr. dept. English, 1975, sr. lectr. Inst. for Environ. Studies, 1976-90, coord. acad. programs, 1976-78, asst. to dir., asst. dir., then assoc. dir., 1983-85, acting dir., then dir., 1985-90, assoc. mem. dept. urban and regional planning, 1985-93, adminstr. acad. programs, 1978-85; sr. spl. asst. to dean grad. sch. U. Wis., 1990-93; assoc. mem. Russian and East European studies U. Wis., Madison, 1992-93, acting dir. internat. faculty and staff svcs., 1993; dir., prof. internat. studies Colo. Sch. Mines, Golden, 1993—; mem. adj. faculty Ohio State U., Columbus, 1992-94; prof. environ. sci. Internat. U., Moscow, 1992—. Bd. dirs. Friends of Waisman Ctr. on Mental Retardation and Human Devel., 1991-93; mem. Emergency Med. Svcs. Commn., 1992-93. Recipient blue ribbon for poetry Am. Assn. Interpretive Naturalists, 1983. Mem. AAAS, Am. Assn. Higher Edn., N.Am. Assn. Environ. Edn. (adv. group internat. rels. com. 1991-94, rep. to jour. 1988—, nominating com. 1989-90, pres. 1984-85, pres.-elect 1983-84, sec. 1982-83, exec. com. 1982-86, chmn. devel. com. 1986-94, liaison to Friends of the UN Environ. Programme, chmn. participation World Decade of the Environ., 1982-92, bd. dirs., 1980-84, chmn. environ. studies sect. 1980-82, program com. confs., publs. com. 1978-83, chmn. 1981-83, polit. strategies com. 1982-83, sec.-treas. environ. studies sect. 1978-80, chmn. com. on establishing jour. environ. studies 1978, mem. spl. task force on mission, membership and orgnl. structure 1977-78, mem. planning group nat. com. environ. edn. rsch. 1979-80), Internat. Soc. Environ. Edn., World Conservation Union, Russian Acad. Edn. (fgn.). Office: Colo Sch Mines 301 Stratton Hall Golden CO 80401

SACKS, DAVID ARNOLD, lawyer; b. Balt., Feb. 14, 1940; s. Jerome and Jennie (Lieben) S.; m. Lois Resnick, June 29, 1963; children: Darrin, Jill. JD, Georgetown U., 1967. Bar: Md. 1967, D.C. 1968. Ptnr. Foley & Lardner, Washington. Office: Foley & Lardner 3000 K St NW Washington DC 20007-5109*

SACKS, DAVID G., retired distilling company executive, lawyer; b. N.Y.C., Jan. 6, 1924; s. Irving and Jeannette (Greenhoot) S.; m. Naomi Gostin, Oct. 12, 1947; children: Jonathan E., Deborah A., Judith A., Joshua M. A.B., Columbia U., 1944, LL.B., 1948. Ptnr. Simpson Thacher & Bartlett, N.Y.C., 1961-67, sr. ptnr., 1967-76, counsel, 1981-83; chief adminstrv. officer Lehman Bros., Inc., N.Y.C., 1976-81; exec. v.p. fin. adminstrn. The Seagram Co. Ltd., Montreal, Que., Can., 1983-86, pres., chief operating officer, 1986-89, also bd. dirs.; exec. v.p. fin. adminstrn. Joseph E. Seagram & Sons, N.Y.C., 1983-86, pres., chief operating officer, 1986-89; vice chmn. The Seagram Co. Ltd. and Joseph E. Seagram & Sons, Inc., Montreal and N.Y.C., 1989-91. Pres. United Jewish Appeal, Fedn. Jewish Philanthropies, N.Y.C., 1989-92. Cpl. USAAF, 1943-46. Club: Beach Point (Mamaroneck, N.Y.). Office: 375 Park Ave 4th Fl New York NY 10152

SACKS, HERBERT SIMEON, psychiatrist, educator, consultant; b. N.Y.C., Nov. 29, 1926; s. Maxwell Lawrence and Anne (Edelstein) S.; m. Helen Margery Levin, Dec. 26, 1948; children—Eric Livingston, Katharine Bird, Douglas Lowell, Russell Avery. A.B. magna cum laude, Dickinson Coll., 1948; M.D., Cornell U., 1952. Diplomate Am. Bd. Psychiatry and Neurology and subspecialty Child and Adolescent Psychiatry. Clin. assoc. Western New Eng. Psychoanalytic Inst., New Haven, 1955-63; intern in pediatrics Yale-New Haven Med. Ctr., 1952-53; jr. asst. resident in psychiatry Yale Psychiat. Inst., 1953-54; sr. asst. resident in psychiatry, USPHS fellow Yale-New Haven Med. Ctr., psychiat. out patient dept., 1954-55; USPHS fellow in child psychiatry Yale U. Child Study Ctr., 1955-57; clin. dir. Mid-Fairfield Child Guidance Ctr., Norwalk, Conn., 1957-59; cons. Expt. in Internat. Living, Putney, Vt., 1962-69; sr. cons. U.S. Peace Corps, Washington, 1962-69; cons. AID, U.S. Dept. State, Office of Sahel, West Africa, 1974-84, Neurosci. Consultation Group, Grosse Point Farms, Mich., 1984-94; clin. prof. child and adolescent psychiatry Child Study Ctr., Yale U. Sch. Medicine, New Haven; co-investigator, co-dir. Senegal River pilot health research program, New Haven and West Africa, 1976-78, co-investigator, co-dir. health sector, design team Senegal River integrated devel. project, 1981-83; vis. lectr. Yale Coll., 1969-71; mem. com. reviewers Dept. Commerce Nat. Bur. Standards, Inst. for Computer Scis. and Tech., Washington, 1975-77; mem. exec. com. Nat. Commn. on Confidentiality of Health Records, 1975-80. Author: Hurdles: The Admissions Dilemma in American Higher Education, 1978; contbg. author chpts. in books, articles on confidentiality, juvenile justice, higher edn., issues of youth in transition, other topics; author monographs. Mem. Conn. Juvenile Justice Commn., Hartford, 1975-80; bd. advisors Dickinson Coll., Carlisle, Pa., 1980-85. Served to lt. (j.g.) U.S. Navy, 1944-46; PTO. Fellow AMA, ACPO, Am. Psychiat. Assn. (trustee 1988-94, v.p. 1994-96, pres.-elect 1996—), Am. Acad. Child and Adolescent Psychiatry, Am. Orthopsychiat. Assn., Am. Coll. Psychiatrists; mem. Conn. Psychiat. Soc. (pres. 1976-77), Conn. Coun. Child and Adolescent Psychiatrists (pres. 1972-73), World Fedn. for Mental Health, Phi Beta Kappa. Avocations: farming, photography, fishing, lawn bowling. Home: 110 Laurel Rd New Haven CT 06515-2426 Office: 260 Riverside Ave Westport CT 06880-4804 also: Yale U Child Study Ctr PO Box 207900 New Haven CT 06520

SACKS, IRA STEPHEN, lawyer; b. N.Y.C., Dec. 6, 1948; s. Marvin Leonard and Mildred (Finkelstein) S.; children: Jennifer, Allison, Gillian. BS, MIT, 1970; JD, Georgetown U., 1974. Bar: N.Y. 1975, U.S. Dist. Ct. (so. and ea. dists.) N.Y. 1975, U.S. Ct. Appeals (2d cir.) 1975, U.S. Ct. Appeals (3d cir.) 1984, U.S. Supreme Ct. 1985, U.S. Ct. Appeals (9th cir.) 1986, U.S. Ct. Appeals (11th cir.) 1987, U.S. Ct. Appeals (D.C. and fed. cirs.) 1993. Assoc. Kaye, Scholer, Fierman, Hays & Handler, N.Y.C., 1974-82, ptnr., 1983-87; ptnr. Fried, Frank, Harris, Shriver & Jacobson, N.Y.C., 1988—. Contbr. articles to profl. jours. NSF fellow, 1970. Mem. ABA, Supreme Ct. Hist. Soc., N.Y. State Bar Assn., Assn. of Bar of City of N.Y. Democrat. Jewish. Avocations: tennis, skiing, softball. Home: 105 Old Colony Rd Hartsdale NY 10530-9999 Office: Fried Frank Harris Shriver & Jacobson 1 New York Plz 24 Flr New York NY 10004

SACKS, OLIVER WOLF, neurologist, writer; b. London, July 9, 1933; Came to U.S., 1960; s. Samuel and Muriel Elsie (Landau) S. BA, U. Oxford, 1954; MA, BM, BCh, Middlesex Hosp., London, 1958; DHL (hon.), Georgetown U., 1990, Coll. Staten Island, CUNY, 1991; DS (hon.), Tufts U., 1991, N.Y. Med. Coll., 1991. Intern in medicine, surgery and neurology Middlesex Hosp., 1958-60; rotating intern Mt. Zion Hosp., San Francisco, 1961-62; resident in neurology UCLA, 1962-65; I.D. fellow in neuropathology and neurochemistry Albert Einstein Coll. Medicine, N.Y.C., 1965-66, instr. neurology, 1966-75, asst. prof., 1975-78, assoc. prof., 1978-85, clin. prof. neurology, 1985—; cons., speaker, lectr. in field; hon. lectureships in field. Author: Migraine, 1970, Awakenings, 1973, rev. paperback edit., 1990 (Hawthornden prize 1975), A Leg To Stand On, 1984, The Man Who Mistook His Wife for a Hat, 1985, Seeing Voices: A Journey into the World of the Deaf, 1989, An Anthropologist on Mars, 1995. Recipient Felix Mart-Ibanez book award MD mag., 1987, Oskar Pfister award APA, 1988, Harold D. Vursell Meml. award Am. Acad. and Inst. Arts and Letters, 1989, Odd Fellows book award, 1990, Scriptor award U. So. Calif., 1991, profl. support award Nat. Headache Found., 1991; open scholar in biology Queen's Coll., Oxford U., 1950, Theodoe Williams scholar in anatomy, 1953, med. rsch. scholar, 1954; Guggenheim fellow, 1989. Mem. Am. Acad. Neurology (presdl. citation 1991), N.Y. State Med. Soc., N.Y. Inst for the Humanities, Alpha Omega Alpha. Office: 299 W 12th St Apt 14C New York NY 10014-1823

SACKS, PATRICIA ANN, librarian, consultant; b. Allentown, Pa., Nov. 6, 1939; d. Lloyd Alva and Dorothy Estelle (Stoneback) Stahl; m. Kenneth LeRoy Sacks, June 27, 1959. A.B., Cedar Crest Coll., 1959; M.S. in L.S., Drexel U., 1965. News reporter Call-Chronicle, Allentown, 1956-59, 1961-63; reference librarian Cedar Crest Coll., Allentown, 1964-66, head librarian, 1966-73; dir. libraries Muhlenberg and Cedar Crest Colls., Allentown, 1973-94; dir. libr. svcs. Cedar Crest Coll., 1994; sr. fellow Lehigh Valley Assn. Ind. Colls., 1994—. del. On Line Computer Library Ctr. Users Council, Columbus, Ohio, 1977-84; cons. colls./health care orgns., libr. orgns. 1981—. Author: (with Whildin Sara Lou) Preparing for Accreditation: A Handbook for Academic Librarians, 1993; mem. editorial bd. Jour. Acad. Librarianship, 1982-84. Trustee Cedar Crest Coll., 1985-89. Mem. United Way Lehigh Valley Coms., 1993—; bd. dirs. John and Dorothy Morgan Cancer Ctr., 1994—. Named Outstanding Acad. Woman, Lehigh Valley Assn. for Acad. Women, 1984, Muhlenberg Coll. Outstanding Adminstr., 1987, Alumni Tricorn award Muhlenberg Coll., 1989, Alumnae Achievement award Cedar Crest Coll., 1994. Mem. ALA (chmn. copyright com. 1985-87), Assn. Coll. and Research Libraries (chmn. standards and accreditation com. 1976-78, 81-84), Lehigh Valley Assn. Ind. Colls. (chmn. librarians sect. 1967-81, 88-92), AAUW, LWV Lehigh Valley Conservancy, Appalachian Mountain Club, Phi Alpha Theta, Phi Kappa Phi, Beta Phi Mu. Democrat. Home: 2997 Fairfield Dr Allentown PA 18103-5413 Office: Lehigh Valley Assn Ind Colls 119 W Greenwich St Bethlehem PA 18018

SACKS, TEMI J., public relations executive; b. Phila.; d. Jule and Adeline (Levin) S. BA, Temple U. Pubs. editor Del. Valley Regional Planning Commn., Phila.; communications assoc. Fedn. Jewish Agys., Phila.; pres. T. J. Sacks Pub. Relations, Phila.; exec. v.p., mng. dir. healthcare div. Lobsenz-Stevens Inc., N.Y.C.; guest lectr. Temple U. Sch. Communications. Mem. Healthcare Businesswomen's Assn., Pharm. Advt. Coun., Women Execs. in Pub. Rels. Avocations: skiing, Americana antiques, jewelry design. Home: 142 W End Ave New York NY 10023-6103 Office: 460 Park Ave S New York NY 10016-7301

SACKSTEDER, FREDERICK HENRY, former foreign service officer; b. N.Y.C., July 12, 1924; s. Frederick H. and Denise (Dorin) S.; m. Evelyn M. Blickensderfer, Oct. 14, 1977; children by previous marriage: Frederick Henry, III, Timothy W. B.A., Amherst Coll., 1947; postgrad., Sch. Advanced Internat. Studies, Washington, 1947. Asst. to exec. v.p. Internat. Standard Electric Corp., N.Y.C., 1948-49; joined U.S. Fgn. Service, 1950; Kreis resident officer U.S. High Commn. for Germany, 1950-52; vice consul, consul, sec. Am. embassy, Lyon, France, 1952-55, Madrid, 1959-61, Barcelona, Spain, 1962-65, Tunis, Tunisia, 1967-69; internat. relations officer Dept. State, 1955-59; 65-67; mem. U.S. Mission to UN, 1969-72, Internat. Boundary and Water Com., El Paso, Tex., 1972-75; consul gen. Hermosillo, Sonora, Mexico, 1975-79; bd. examiners Fgn. Service, Dept. State, 1979-81, expert cons. Bur. Personnel, 1981-86; mem. U.S. del. to UN Gen. Assembly, N.Y.C., 1969-71. Mem. UN Trusteeship Coun., 1970-71, U.S. rep., 1971; pres. El Paso chpt. UN Assn., 1973-75. Lt. (j.g.) USNR, 1943-46. Mem. Fgn. Service Assn., Diplomatic and Consular Officers Ret., Council Fgn. Relations (chmn. Charlottesville com.). Lodge: Rotary (local club pres. 1988-89). Home: The Westchester 4000 Cathedral Ave NW # 344-b Washington DC 20016-5249

SACKTON, FRANK JOSEPH, public affairs educator; b. Chgo., Aug. 11, 1912; m. June Dorothy Raymond, Sept. 21, 1940. Student, Northwestern U., 1936, Yale, 1946, U. Md., 1951-52; B.S., U. Md., 1970; grad., Army Inf. Sch., 1941, Command and Gen. Staff Coll., 1942, Armed Forces Staff Coll., 1949, Nat. War Coll., 1954; M.Pub. Adminstrn., Ariz. State U., 1976. Mem. 131st Inf. Regt., Ill. N.G., 1929-40; commd. 2d lt. U.S. Army, 1934, advanced through grades to lt. gen., 1967; brigade plans and ops. officer (33d Inf. Div.), 1941, PTO, 1943-45; div. signal officer, 1942-43, div. intelligence officer, 1944, div. plans and ops. officer, 1945; sec. to gen. staff for Gen. MacArthur Tokyo, 1947-48; bn. comdr. 30th Inf. Regt., 1949-50; mem. spl. staff Dept. Army, 1951; plans and ops. officer Joint Task Force 132, PTO, 1952; comdr. Joint Task Force 7, Marshall Islands, 1953; mem. gen. staff Dept. Army, 1954-55; with Office Sec. Def., 1956; comdr. 18th Inf. Regt., 1957-58; chief staff 1st Inf. Div., 1959; chief army Mil. Mission to Turkey, 1960-62; comdr. XIV Army Corps, 1963; dep. dir. plans Joint Chiefs Staff, 1964-66; army general staff mil. ops., 1966-67, comptroller of the army, 1967-70, ret., 1970; spl. asst. for fed./state relations Gov. Ariz., 1971-75; chmn. Ariz. Programming and Coordinating Com. for Fed. Programs, 1971-75; lectr. Am. Grad. Sch. Internat. Mgmt., 1973-77; vis. asst. prof., lectr. public affairs Ariz. State U., Tempe, 1976-78; founding dean Ariz. State U. Coll. Public Programs, 1979-80; prof. public affairs Ariz. State U., 1980—, finance educator, v.p. bus. affairs, 1981-83, dep. dir. intercollegiate athletics, 1984-85, dir. strategic planning, 1987-88. Contbr. articles to public affairs and mil. jours. Mem. Ariz. Steering Com. for Restoration of the State Capitol, 1974-75, Ariz. State Personnel Bd., 1978-83, Ariz. Regulatory Coun., 1981-93. Decorated D.S.M., Silver Star, also Legion of Merit with 4 oak leaf clusters, Bronze Star with 2 oak leaf clusters, Air medal, Army Commendation medal with 1 oak leaf cluster, Combat Inf. badge. Mem. Ariz. Acad. Public Adminstrn., Pi Alpha Alpha (pres. chpt. 1976-82). Clubs: Army-Navy (Washington); Arizona (Phoenix). Home: 1200 N 90th St Apt 3072 Scottsdale AZ 85260-8600 Office: Ariz State U Sch Pub Affairs Tempe AZ 85287

SADAO, SHOJI, architect; b. Los Angeles, Jan. 2, 1927; s. Riichi and Otatsu (Kodama) S.; m. Tsuneko Sawada, Apr. 8, 1972. B.Arch., Cornell U., 1954; Fulbright scholar, Waseda U., Tokyo, 1956-57. Designer Geodesics, Inc., Raleigh, N.C., 1954-56; job capt. Edison Price, Inc., N.Y.C., 1959-64; v.p. Fuller & Sadao (P.C.), Long Island City, N.Y., 1965—; assoc. prof. archtl. design Sch. Architecture and Environ. Design, SUNY, Buffalo, 1976-77. Works include Dymaxion World Map, 1954; co-designer works include, U.S. Pavilion at Montreal Expo 67. Trustee and exec. dir. Isamu Noguchi Found., Long Island City, N.Y., 1989—. With AUS, 1945-49. Mem. Japan Soc., Yamashita Sekkei Archs. and Engrs. (U.S. rep. 1989—), The Century Assn. Address: Fuller & Sadao 32-37 Vernon Blvd Long Island City NY 11106-4926

SADDLEMYER, ANN (ELEANOR SADDLEMYER), educator, critic, theater historian; b. Prince Albert, Sask., Can., Nov. 28, 1932; d. Orrin Angus and Elsie Sarah (Ellis) S. BA, U. Sask., 1953, DLitt, 1991; MA, Queen's U., 1956, LLD (hon.), 1977; PhD, U. London, 1961; DLitt (hon.), U. Victoria, 1989, McGill U., 1989, Windsor U., 1990. Lectr. Victoria (B.C.) Coll., 1956-57, instr., 1960-62, asst. prof., 1962-65; assoc. prof. U. Victoria, 1965-68, prof. English, 1968-71; prof. English Victoria Coll. U. Toronto, 1971-95; prof., dir. grad. ctr. for study of drama Grad. Ctr. Study of Drama, U. Toronto, 1972-77, 85-86; sr. fellow Massey Coll., 1975-88, master, 1988-95, master emeritus, prof. emeritus, 1995—; Berg prof. NYU, 1975. Dir. Theatre Puls, 1972-84; dirl. Colin Smythe Pubs.; author: The World of W.B. Yeats, 1965, In Defence of Lady Gregory, Playwright, 1966, Synge and Modern Comedy, 1968, J.M. Synge Plays Books One and Two, 1968, Lady Gregory Plays, 4 vols., 1970, Letters to Molly: Synge to Maire O'Neill, 1971, Letters from Synge to W.B. Yeats and Lady Gregory, 1971, Collected Letters of John Millington Synge, Vol. 1, 1983, vol. II, 1984, Theatre Business, The Correspondence of the First Abbey Theatre Directors, 1982, (with Colin Smythe) Lady Gregory Fifty Years After, 1987, Early Stages: Theatre in Ontario, 1980-1914, 1990; (with Richard Plant) Later Stages: Theatre in Ontario, 1914-1970s, 1996; co-editor Theatre History in Canada, 1980-86; editorial bds. Modern Drama, 1972-82, English Studies in Can., 1973-83, Themes in Drama, 1974—, Shaw Rev., 1977—, Research in the Humanities, 1976-90; Irish Univ. Rev., 1970—, Yeats Ann., 1982-86; Studies in Contemporary Irish Lit., 1986—; contbr. articles to profl. jours. Recipient Brit. Acad. Rose Mary Crawshay award, 1986, Disting. Svc. award Province of Ont., 1985, U. Toronto Alumni award of excellence, 1991; named Disting. Dau. of Pa., 1992, Women of Distinction in Letters, Toronto, YWCA, 1994; Officer of Order of Can., 1995; Can. Coun. scholar, 1958-59, fellow, 1968, Guggenheim fellow, 1968, 77, sr. rsch. fellow Connaught, 1985. Fellow Royal Soc. Can., Royal Soc. Arts; mem. Internat. Assn. Study Anglo-Irish Lit. (chmn. 1973-76), Assn. Can. Theatre History (pres. 1976-77), Can. Assn. Irish Studies, Assn. Can. Univ. Tchrs. English, Can. Assn. Univ. Tchrs., Assn. Can. and Que. Lit. Home: 100 Lakeshore Rd E Apt 803, Oakville, ON Canada L6J 6M9

SADDLER, DONALD EDWARD, choreographer, dancer; b. Van Nuys, Calif., Jan. 24, 1920; s. Elmer Edward and Mary Elizabeth (Roberts) S. Student, Los Angeles City Coll., 1939; dance pupil of, Carmalita Maracci, Anton Dolin, Anthony Tudor, Madame Anderson Ivantzova. Mem. Ballet Theatre, N.Y.C., 1940-43, 46-47; asst. dir., then artistic dir. Harkness Ballet, N.Y.C., 1964-70; exec. v.p. Rebekah Harkness Found., 1967-69; mem. exec. bd. Internat. Ballet Corp., 1979; prodr. N.Y. Dance Festival, Delacorte Theatre; guest artist Valerie Bettis Co. Stage appearances include Grand Canyon Suite, 1937, High Button Shoes, 1947, Dance Me A Song, 1950, Bless You All, 1950, The Song of Norway, 1951, Winesburg, Ohio, 1958, The Golden Round, 1960, The Castle Period, 1961, Happy Birthday, Mr. Abbot!, 1987, (with the Ballet Theatre, N.Y.C.) Bluebeard, Billy the Kid, Swan Lake, Aurora's Wedding, Les patineurs, Lilac Garden, Gala Performance, Romeo and Juliet, Peter and the Wolf, (television) Holiday Hotel, 1950; choreographer: (theatre) Blue Mountain Ballads, 1948, Wish Your Were Here, 1952, Wonderful Town, 1952 (Tony award for choreography 1953), 55, John Murray Anderson's Almanac, 1953, Tobia la Candida Spia, 1954 (Maschera d'Argento 1954), La patrona di raddio di luna, 1955, Shangri-La, 1956, Buona notte Bettina, 1956, L'adorabile Giulio, 1957, Winesburg, Ohio, 1958, This Property is Condemned, 1958, Un trapezio per Lisistrata, 1958, When in Rome, 1959, Un manderino per Teo, 1959, Dreams of Glory, 1961, Milk and Honey, 1961, Sophie, 1963, Morning Sun, 1963, To Broadway, With Love, 1964, No, No, Nanette, 1971 (Tony award for choreography 1971, Drama Desk award for choreography 1971), 73, Much Ado About Nothing, 1972 (Tony award nomination for choreography 1973), Fanfare Gala, 1973, Good News, 1973, Tricks, 1973, The Merry Wives of Windsor, 1974, Miss Moffat, 1974, A Midsummer Night's Dream, 1975, A Doll's House, 1975, A Gala Tribute to Joshua Logan, 1975, Rodgers and Hart, 1975, The Robber Bridegroom, 1975, 1976, Koshare, 1976, Vaudeville, 1976, Dear Friends and Gentle Hearts, 1976, Icedancing, 1978, The Grand Tour, 1979, A Long Way to Boston, 1979, Happy New Year, 1980, Hey Look Me Over!, 1981, Pardon, Monsieur Moliere, 1982, On Your Toes, 1983 (Tony award nomination for choreography 1983), The Loves of Anatol, 1985, The Golden Land, 1985, Broadway, 1987, The Student Prince, 1987, Teddy and Alice, 1987, My Fair Lady, 1993, The Boys from Syracuse, Aida, La Perichole, The Merry Widow, Tropicana, (tours) We Take This Town, 1962, Knickerbocker Holiday, 1971, No, No, Nanette, 1971-73, Good News, 1973-74, Hellzapoppin', 1976-77, On Your Toes, 1984, (films) April in Paris, 1952, By the Light of the Silvery Moon, 1953, Young at Heart, 1954, The Main Attraction, 1963, The Happy Hooker, 1975, Radio Days, 1987, (television) Holiday Hotel, 1950, The Perry Como Show, 1950, Canozionissima, 1959-60, Bell Telephone Hour, 1961-64, Much Ado About Nothing, 1973, Tony award broadcasts, 1973, 75-78, 83, Verna: U.S.O. Girl, 1978; dir., choreographer: (theatre) Wonderful Town, 1955, (tour) Oh, Kay!, 1978, A Celebration for Sir Anton Dolin, 1984, 100 Years of Performing Arts at the Metropolitan, 1984, Kiss Me Kate, 1989, American Ballet Theatre's Fortieth Anniversary, Tribute to Lucille Lortel, Tribute to Richard Rodgers, Merman-Martin Gala, Tribute to Cy Coleman, An Evening with Kurt Weill, Jo Sullivan in Concert, Tribute to George Abbott, Tribute to Lerner and Loewe, Stratford Shakespeare Festival Gala, American Guild of Musical Artists 100th Anniversary Gala, (operas) Bitter Sweet, Weiner Blut, Abduction fron the Seraglio, Washington Opera Follies; dir.: (theatre) Berlin to Broadway with Kurt Weill, 1972, George Abbott...A Celebration, 1976, Life with Father, 1982, I Hear Music...of Frank Loesser and Friends, 1984, State Fair Music Hall, Dallas, 1957, 59, Carousel Theatre, Framingham, Mass., 1958, Stratford Shakespeare Festival, 1979; prodr.: (theatre) The Sol Hurok Birthday Gala, 1973, The 30th Anniversary of City Center Theatre, 1975, (with Martin Feinstein) The Pre-Inaugural Ballet-Opera Gala, 1981, The Dance Collection Gala, 1972, The 35th Anniversary of the American Ballet Theatre, 1975, The Cynthia Gregory Gala. Recipient Dance Mag. award, 1984. Address: Coleman-Rosenberg 155 E 55th St Apt 5D New York NY 10022-4039*

SADE (HELEN FOLASADE ADU), singer, songwriter; b. Ibadan, Nigeria, 1959; d. Adebisi Adu and Anne. BA, St. Martin's Coll. of Art, London, 1979. Mem. band Sade; recording artist Epic, A Division of Sony Music, N.Y.C. Albums include Diamond Life, 1984, Promise, 1985, Stronger Than Pride, 1988, Love Deluxe, 1992; singles include Smooth Operator, 1984. Recipient Grammy award Best New Artist, 1986, Best R&B duo or group performance for "No Ordinary Love", 1994.

SADE, DONALD STONE, anthropology educator; b. Charleston, W.Va., July 17, 1937; s. Samuel and Charlotte Tracy (Stone) S.; m. Bonita Diane Chepko, Dec. 24, 1971 (div. Feb. 1994); children: Irony Cuervo del Norte, Omen Ondatra; m. Kerry L. Knox, Nov. 24, 1994. Grad., N.Y. State Ranger Sch., 1957; student, Hamilton Coll., 1957-60; A.B., U. Calif., Berkeley, 1963, Ph.D., 1966. Instr. anthropology Northwestern U., Evanston, Ill., 1965-66; asst. prof. Northwestern U., 1966-70, asso. prof., 1970-75, prof., 1975-95; scientist-in-charge Cayo Santiago, U. P.R., 1970-77; founder, pres. North Country Inst. for Natural Philosophy, Inc., Mexico, N.Y., 1980—. Sr. author: Basic Demographic Observations on Free-Ranging Rhesus Monkeys, 3 vols., 1985; editor: The North Country Naturalist, Vol. 1, 1987. NSF grantee, 1967—. Mem. AAAS, Am. Assn. Phys. Anthropologists, Am. Soc. Mammalogists, Animal Behavior Soc. Office: North Country Inst for Natural Philosophy Inc 18 Emery Rd Mexico NY 13114 *I have never given undue heed to the opinions of others regarding my work or character.*

SADEGH, ALI M., mechanical engineering educator, researcher, consultant; b. Tehran, Iran, Sept. 1, 1950; came to U.S., 1974; s. Saleh S. Mir-Mohamad-Sadegh and Asam Lotfi; m. Guita Miremadi, July 10, 1980; children: Mietra, Cameron, Mona, Jasmin, David. Postdoctoral tng., U. Mich., 1979; BS in Mech. Engring., Arya-Mehr U. Tech., Tehran, 1972; MS in Mech. Engring., Mich. State U., 1975, PhD in Mechanics, 1978; postdoctoral, U. Mich., 1979. Registered profl. engr., Mich.; cert. mfg. engr. Design engr. Nat. Radio engring. sect., Tehran, 1972-74; rsch. and teaching asst. Mich. State U., East Lansing, 1975-78; postdoctoral scholar U. Mich., Ann Arbor, 1978-79; asst. prof. Arya-Mehr U. Tech., 1979-81; vis. asst. prof. Mich. State U., 1981-82; asst. prof. CUNY, N.Y.C., 1982-87, assoc. prof., 1987-91, prof., 1991—, chmn. dept. mech. engring., 1992—, tchr. courses in solid mechanics, design and CAD/CAM; cons. Devel. Iranian Heavy Industries, Tehran, 1979-81; tech. cons. AC Rochester Gen. Motors Co., 1986-92; cons. to numerous industries, 1988—; expert witness, 1990—. Contbr. some 80 articles to profl. and sci. jours., 43 tech. reports, also presentations to nat. and internat. confs.; holder 3 U.S. patents. Recipient 27 rsch. awards NSF, AT&T Found., PSC-CUNY, others. Mem. ASME (Best Paper award 1992, Melville medal 1993), Am. Acad. Mechanics, Biomed. Engrs. Soc., Soc. Mfg. Engrs. (chmn. chpt. 320), Sigma Xi. Avocations: tennis, swimming, soccer. Home: 33 Greenway Ct Closter NJ 07624-2201 Office: CUNY 140th St and Convent Ave New York NY 10031

SADEGHI-NEJAD, ABDOLLAH, pediatrician, educator; b. Meshed, Iran, Apr. 29, 1938; s. Abdolhossein and Azizeh (Jabbari) S.-N.; m. Marion M. Marguardt, Jan. 26, 1974; children; Nathan R., Adrienne R. BA, Beloit Coll., 1960; MS in Pathology, U. Chgo., 1964, MD, 1964. Diplomate Am. Bd. Pediatrics. Intern then resident U. Chgo., 1964-67; fellow pediatric endocrinology New Eng. Med. Ctr., Boston, 1967-69, U. Calif., San Francisco, 1969-70; from asst. prof. to prof. pediatrics Tufts U., Boston, 1970—; chief pediatric endocrinology and metabolism divsn. New Eng. Med. Ctr., Boston, 1989—. Author and co-author books and articles. Mem. town meeting Town of Brookline, Mass., 1987—, mem. adv. com., 1993—; founder, mem. Friends of Lost Pond. Fellow Am. Acad. Pediatrics; mem. Am. Pediatric Soc., Am. Diabetes Assn., Endocrine Soc., European Soc. Pediatric Rsch., Lawson Wilkins Pediat. Endocrine Soc., Soc. Pediat. Rsch. Office: New Eng Med Ctr 750 Washington St Boston MA 02111-1533

SADER, CAROL HOPE, former state legislator; b. Bklyn., July 19, 1935; d. Nathan and Mollie (Farkas) Shimkin; m. Harold M. Sader, June 9, 1957; children: Neil, Randi Sader Friedlander, Elisa. BA, Barnard Coll., Columbia U., 1957. Sch. tchr. Bd. Edn., Morris, Conn., 1957-58; legal editor W. H. Anderson Co., Cin., 1974-78; freelance legal editor Shawnee Mission, Kans., 1978-87; mem. Kans. Ho. of Reps., 1987-94; chair Ho. Pub. Health and Welfare Com., 1991-92; chair Joint Ho. and Senate Com. on Health Care Decisions for the 90's, 1992; vice chair Ho. Econ. Devel. Com., 1991-92; policy chair Ho. Dem. Caucus, 1993-94. Dem. candidate for Kans. Lt. Gov., 1994; chmn. bd. trustees Johns County C.C., Overland Park, Kans., 1984-86, trustee Johnson County Cmty. Coll., 1981-86; pres. League of Women Voters, Johnson County, 1983-85; State of Kans. League of Women Voters Bd, 1986-87; bd. dirs. United Cmty. Svcs. of Johnson County Shawnee Mission, 1984-92, Jewish Vocat. Svc. Bd., 1983-92; chmn. Kans. State Holocaust Commn., 1991-94; pres. Mainstream Coalition of Johnson County, 1995-96. Recipient Trustee award Assn. of Women in Jr. and C.C., 1985, awards Kans. Pub. Transit Assn., 1990, AARP, 1992, Assn. Kans. Theater, 1992, Nat. Coun. Jewish Women, 1992, Kans. Assn. Osteo. Medicine, 1992, Kans. Chiropractic Assn., 1992, United Com. Svcs. Johnson County, 1992, Disting. Pub. Svcs. award Johnson County, 1993, Hallpac Kans. Pub. Svc. award Hallmark Cards, Inc., 1993. Mem. Coun. Women Legislators, Phi Delta Kappa. Democrat. Avocations: lakehouse, theatre, travel. Home: 8612 Linden Dr Shawnee Mission KS 66207-1807

SADIK, MARVIN SHERWOOD, art consultant, former museum director; b. Springfield, Mass., June 27, 1932; s. Harry Benjamin and Florence (Askinas) S. A.B. magna cum laude, Harvard U., 1954, A.M., 1960; D.F.A. (hon.), Bowdoin Coll., Brunswick, Maine, 1978. Curatorial asst. Worcester (Mass.) Art Mus., 1955-57; curator Mus. Art Bowdoin Coll., 1961-64, dir., 1964-67; dir. Mus. Art U. Conn. at Storrs, 1967-69, Nat. Portrait Gallery, Washington, 1969-81; cons. Am. and European art, 1981—; mem. Pres.'s com. on Arts and the Humanities, 1990—; bd. visitors Edmund S. Muskie Inst. of Pub. Affairs, U. So. Maine, bd. dirs. The Osher Map Libr. U. So. Maine. Author: Colonial and Federal Portraits at Bowdoin College, 1966, The Drawings of Hyman Bloom, 1968, The Paintings of Charles Hawthorne, 1968, Christian Gullager: Portrait Painter to Federal America, 1976; co-author: American Portrait Drawings, 1980. Decorated knight Order Dannebrog Denmark; recipient Maine State Art award, 1975, gold medal for exceptional svc. Smithsonian Instn., 1981; Harris fellow, 1957-61; Barr fellow, 1957-61. Fellow Pierpont Morgan Library; mem. Am. Antiquarian Soc., Colonial Soc. Mass. (corr.). Clubs: Century Assn, Grolier. Home: PO Box 6360 Scarborough ME 04070-6360

SADLER, DAVID GARY, business executive; b. Iowa City, Mar. 14, 1939; s. Edward Anthony and Elsie June (Sherman) S.; m. Karen Sadler. Student, St. Ambrose Coll., 1957-59; BS in Indsl. Adminstrn. and Prodn., Kent State U., 1961. Various mgmt. positions Ford Motor Co., Lorain, Ohio, 1962-67, Sperry-New Holland, Lebanon, Ohio, 1967-71; mgr. mfg. Allis Chalmer, Springfield, Ill., 1971-72; dir. mfg. Purolator, Inc., Fayetteville, N.C., 1972-73; v.p. mfg. farm equipment and ops. truck div. White Motor Co., Eastlake, Ohio and Chgo., 1973-78; corp. v.p. mfg. Massey Ferguson Ltd., Toronto, Ont., Can., 1978-80; corp. v.p. mfg. Internat. Harvester, Chgo., 1980-81, sr. v.p. ops. staff, 1981-82, v.p. bus. devel., 1982, pres. diversified group, 1982-83, pres. internat. group, 1983-85; pres. AMI, Inc., Chgo., 1985-86; vice chmn., chief exec. officer Savin Corp., Stamford, Conn., 1986, chmn., chief exec. officer, 1986-89, also bd. dirs.; pres. Asset Mgmt. Internat., Westport, Conn., 1989-95; chmn., CEO, Rowe Internat., Grand Rapids, Mich., 1995—, also bd. dirs. Bd. dirs. greater Chgo. Safety Coun., 1981-84; mem. adb. bd. Hellmond Assocs. Opportunity Fund II. Roman Catholic. Home: 751 Bradford Farms Ln NE Grand Rapids MI 49546 Office: Rowe International 1500 Union Ave SE Grand Rapids MI 49507

SADLER, ERIC, recording industry executive; b. Hempstead, N.Y., Sept. 18, 1960; s. Donald Joseph and Lygia Ann (Wilson) S.; m. Karen Ann Francis Douglas, Nov. 10, 1990; 1 child, Karis Leigh. Student, Hempstead (N.Y.) High, 1978. Composer, assoc. Cassad Studios, Hempstead, 1981-87; producer, assoc. Greene St. Recording Inc., N.Y.C., 1987-89; pres. Street Element Inc., N.Y.C., 1989—. Grantee NEA, 1990; recipient 3 platinum, 5 gold albums CBS Records, 1988-90, 1 platinum, 1 gold album, MCA, Virgin & Priority Records, 1990; grammy nominee Nat. Acad Recording Arts and Scis., 1990.

SADLER, GRAHAM HYDRICK, library administrator; b. Sikeston, Mo., Aug. 17, 1931; s. Philip Landis and Montie Pearl (Hydrick) S.; m. Betty A. Grugett, Nov. 22, 1950; children—Graham Hydrick, Lee, Susan, Harrison. B.S., S.E. Mo. State Coll., 1952; M.L.S., Emory U., 1957. Asst. libr. S.E. Mo. State Coll., Cape Girardeau, 1954-61; adminstrv. libr. Kinderhook Regional Libr., Lebanon, Mo., 1961-66; dir. Fort Lewis Coll. Libr., Durango, Colo., 1966-67; assoc. prof. librarianship Kans. State Tchrs. Coll., Emporia, 1967-69; asst. libr., dir. community svc. Denver Pub. Libr., 1970-77; dir. County of Henrico Pub. Libr., Richmond, Va., 1978-94, ret., 1994; mem. adv. com. Office of Library Service to Disadvantaged, 1978-91. Mem. ALA (membership com. 1989-92).

SADLER, LUTHER FULLER, JR., lawyer; b. Jacksonville, Fla., Apr. 10, 1942; s. Luther Fuller and Jane Grey (Lloyd) S.; children: Catherine Winchester, Anna Stephenson Lloyd. BA, Yale U., 1964, LLB, 1967. Bar: Fla. 1967. Ptnr. Mahoney, Hadlow, Chambers & Adams, Jacksonville, 1967-81, Commander, Legler, Werber, Dawes, Sadler & Howell, Jacksonville, 1982-91, Foley & Lardner, Jacksonville, 1991—; gen. counsel Jacksonville C. of C., 1987. Trustee Jacksonville Art Mus., 1984-94, Episcopal Child Care and Devel. Ctrs., Inc., 1990-94. Lt. USNR, 1967-73. Mem. ABA, Fla. Bar Assn. (chmn. corp. banking and bus. law sect. 1979-80), Timuquana Country Club. Episcopalian. Office: Foley & Lardner PO Box 240 200 N Laura St Jacksonville FL 32202-3528

SADLER, M. WHITSON, petroleum company executive. Pres., chief exec. officer Soltex Polymer Corp., Houston. Office: Soltex Polymer Corp 3333 Richmond Ave Houston TX 77098-3007*

SADLER, ROBERT LIVINGSTON, banker; b. Beloit, Kans., Dec. 19, 1935; s. D.M. and Retha (Livingston) S.; m. E. Elllen Lewis, July 14, 1957; children: Diane, Julia. AB, Baker U., 1958; MBA, Ind. U., 1959; student, Stonier Grad. Sch. Banking, Rutgers U., 1970. Dir. alumni relations Baker U., Baldwin, Kans., 1957-58; indsl. engr. Colgate-Palmolive Co., N.Y.C., 1958-60, pers. mgr., 1961-64, product mgr., 1964-65; v.p. pers. and adminstrv. svcs. Old Kent Bank & Trust Co., Grand Rapids, Mich., 1965-72, exec. v.p., 1972-86; exec. v.p. Old Kent Fin. Corp., Grand Rapids, 1972-89, vice chmn., 1989—; pres. Old Kent Bank, Grand Rapids, 1995—. Pres. Grand Rapids Jr. Achievement, 1976; pres. United Way Kent County, 1982; chmn. Grand Rapids Found., 1987; Davenport Coll. Bus., Grand Rapids. Mem. Am. Bankers Assn. (chmn. communications council 1980—, dir. 1982-83), Sigma Iota Epsilon, Delta Mu Delta. Republican. Methodist. Clubs: Cascade Country (dir. 1978-80); University (Grand Rapids). Office: Old Kent Fin Corp 1 Vandenburg Ctr NW Grand Rapids MI 49503-2402*

SADLER, THEODORE R., JR., thoracic and cardiovascular surgeon; b. St. Louis, Mar. 26, 1930; s. Theodore R. and Nellie R. (Guffey) S.; m. Roberta Cary Moody, Nov. 26, 1953; children: Michael, Patrick, Susan, Daniel, Shelley. AB, U. Mo., 1951, BS in Medicine, 1954; MD, Washington U., 1956. Diplomate Am. Bd. Thoracic and Cardiovascular Surgery. Commd. U.S. Army, 1956, advanced through grades to brig. gen., 1990; chief of surgery Noble Army Hosp., Ft. McClellans, Ala., 1964-66; comdr. 3d Surgery Hosp., Vietnam, 1966-67; chief thoracic surgery Fitzsimmons Army Hosp., Denver, 1968-71; resigned U.S. Army, 1971, with Res., 1971-82; comdr. 181st Thoracic Detachment, 1971-73, 5502d U.S. Army Hosp. Augmentation Fitzsimmons Army Hosp., Denver, 1974-77; brig. gen. 2d Hosp. Ctr., Hamilton AFB, Calif., 1977-81; ret. Res. U.S. Army, 1990; rotating intern Walter Reed Hosp., Washington, 1956-57; resident in gen. surgery Brooke Gen. Hosp., San Antonio, 1958-61, resident thoracic and cardiovascular surgery, 1964-66; practice medicine specializing in thoracic and cardiovascular surgery St. Joseph's Hosp. and Presbyn. Hosp., Denver, 1971-88; comdr. 147th U.S. Army Hosp. Colo. N.G., 1987-90; mem. staff St. Mary' Hosp., Grand Junction, 1988—, Community Hosp., Hilltop Rehab. Hosp., 1989—; ret.; cons. to surgeon gen. Fitzsimmons Army Hosp., 1983—, VA Hosp., Grand Junction, 1989—; past pres. bd. dirs. St. Joseph's Hosp. Contbr. articles to profl. jours. Vice chmn. Bd. of Health and Hosps., 1982-88; mem. Commn. Mental Health, Denver, 1985-88. Fellow ACS, Am. Coll. Chest Physicians; mem. Soc. Thoracic Surgeons, Western Thoracic Assn., AMA, Colo. Med. Soc. (pres.-elect 1986, bd. dirs., house speaker, pres. 1987-88), Denver Med. Soc. (bd. dirs., past pres.), Mesa County Med. Soc. (bd. dirs. 1989—), Rocky Mounty Individual Physicians Assn. (bd. dirs. 1990—). Republican. Presbyterian. Clubs: Denver Athletic, Bookcliff Country, Metropolitan. Avocations: golf, sports, stamp collecting. Home: 2680 Kimberly Dr Grand Junction CO 81506-1850 Office: 425 Patterson # 506 Grand Junction CO 81506-1935

SADOCK, BENJAMIN JAMES, psychiatrist, educator; b. N.Y.C., Dec. 22, 1933; s. Samuel William and Gertrude S.; m. Virginia Alcott, Oct. 20, 1963; children: James William, Victoria Anne. A.B., Union Coll., 1955; M.D., N.Y. Med. Coll., 1959. Rotating intern Albany (N.Y.) Hosp., 1959-60; resident Bellevue Psychiat. Hosp., N.Y.C., 1960-63; instr. psychiatry Southwestern Med. Sch., Dallas, 1964-65, N.Y. Med. Coll., N.Y.C., 1965-67; asst. prof. N.Y. Med. Coll., 1967-71, assoc. prof., 1972-74, prof., 1975-80, dir. student health psychiatry, 1980—; prof. psychiatry NYU Sch Medicine, 1981—, vice chmn. dept. psychiatry, 1984—; attending psychiatrist Tisch Univ. Hosp. of NYU Med. Ctr., Bellevue Hosp.; cons. psychiatrist Franklin Delano Roosevelt VA Hosp., 1970-78, U.S. Dept. State, 1980-81, P.R. Inst. Psychiatry, 1976-80; examiner Am. Bd. Psychiatry and Neurology, 1970—; mem. conf. on recert. Am. Bd. Med. Spltys.-Am. Psychiat. Assn., 1974; mem. Commn. on Continuing Edn. in Psychiatry, NIMH-Am. Psychiat. Assn., 1974-75. Co-author: Comprehensive Group Psychotherapy, 1971, 3d edit., 1993, Synopsis of Psychiatry, 1972, 4th edit., 1985, 5th edit., 1989, 6th edit., 1991, 7th edit., 1994, The Sexual Experience, 1976, Study Guide Modern Synopsis of Psychiatry, 1983, 2d edit., 1985, 3d edit., 1989, 4th edit., 1991, 5th edit., 1994, Comprehensive Textbook of Psychiatry, 5th edit., 1988, 6th edit., 1995, Pocket Handbook of Clinical Psychiatry, 1991, 2d edit., 1995, Comprehensive Glossary of Psychiatry and Psychology, 1991, Pocket Handbook of Drug Treatment in Psychiatry, 1992, 2d edit., 1995, Pocket Handbook of Psychiatric Emergency Medicine, 1993; contbr. articles on psychiat. edn., individual and group psychotherapy, diagnosis and treatment psychiat. and sexual disorders to med. jours.; contbr. to Ency. Americana. Fellow Am. Psychiat. Assn. (treas. N.Y. County dist. br. 1973-76, mem. conf. on psychiatry and med. edn. 1967), N.Y. Acad. Medicine, A.C.P.; mem. AMA, Med. Soc. County and State N.Y., N.Y. Acad. Scis., AAAS, Am. Group Psychotherapy Assn., World Psychiat. Assn., Am. Public Health Assn., Royal Soc. Medicine (London), Psychiat. Soc. N.Y. Med. Coll. (founder, pres. 1975-79), N.Y. Med. Coll. Alumni Assn. (gov. 1965-90), NYU-Bellevue Psychiat. Soc. (pres. 1981—), Alpha Omega Alpha. Office: 4 E 89th St New York NY 10128-0636 also: NYU Med Ctr 550 1st Ave New York NY 10016-6481

SADOFF, ROBERT LESLIE, psychiatrist; b. Mpls., Feb. 8, 1936; s. Max and Rose C. (Karroll) S.; m. Joan A. Handleman, June 21, 1959; children—Debra, David, Julie, Sherry. B.A., U. Minn., 1956, B.S., 1957, M.D., 1959; M.S., UCLA, 1963. Intern Los Angeles VA Hosp., 1959-60; resident UCLA, 1960-63; asst. prof. psychiatry Temple U., Phila., 1966-72; clin. prof. psychiatry U. Pa., Phila., 1972—; lectr. in law Villanova U., 1972-85. Author: (with Marvin Lewis) Psychic Injuries, 1975; Forensic Psychiatry, 1975, 2d edit., 1988; Legal Issues in the Care of Psychiatric Patients, 1982, Violence and Responsibility, 1988; (with Robert I. Simon) Psychiatric Malpractice, 1992; editor: Psychiatric Clinics of North America, 1984. Bd. dirs. Joseph T. Peters Inst., Phila., 1980—. Served to capt. U.S. Army, 1963-65. Recipient Earl Bond award U. Pa., 1979, VIIth Annual Nathaniel Winkelman award Phila. Psychiat. Ctr., 1988, Manfred Guttmacher award Am. Psychiat. Assn., 1992. Fellow Am. Psychiat. Assn., Am. Coll. Psychiatrists, Am. Coll. Legal Medicine; mem. AMA, Am. Acad. Psychiatry and Law (pres. 1971-73), Internat. Soc. for Philos. Enquiry (mentor 1987—), Am. Red Magen David for Israel (nat. pres. 1987—), Internat. Acad. Law and Mental Health (bd. dirs. 1989—, Philippe Pinel award 1995) . Avocation: collecting antique books in law and medicine. Office: Benjamin Fox Pavilion Ste 326 Jenkintown PA 19046

SADOSKI, MARK CHRISTIAN, education educator; b. Bristol, Conn., June 2, 1945; s. Waldmyr John Sadoski and Ruth Elaine (Gustafson) Kantorski; m. Carol Ann Bove, June 28, 1969; 1 child, Thomas Christian. BS, So. Conn. State U., 1968, MS, 1973; PhD, U. Conn., 1981. Cert. reading, English, social studies tchr. Tchr., reading cons. Milford (Conn.) Pub. Schs., 1968-81; assoc. faculty So. Conn. State U., New Haven, 1978-81; prof. edn. Tex. A&M Univ., College Station, 1981—. Mem. editl. bd. Reading Reasearch Quarterly, 1989—, Jour. Reading Behavior, 1990-95, Reading Psychology, 1990—, Jour. Literacy Rsch., 1995—; contbr. over 50 articles to profl. jours. Accident prevention counselor S.W. region FAA, 1989-91. Recipient Disting. Alumnus award So. Conn. State U., 1994. Mem. Internat. Reading Assn. (outstanding dissertation award com. 1983-85, finalist Outstanding Dissertation award 1982), Nat. Reading Conf., Am. Ednl. Rsch. Assn. (outstanding book award com. 1994—), Soc. for Sci. Study of Reading (chair pubs. com. 1996—). Avocations: reading, cinema. Office: Tex A&M Univ Dept EDCI College Station TX 77843

SADOULET, BERNARD, astrophysicist, educator; b. Nice, France, Apr. 23, 1944; s. Maurice and Genevieve (Berard) S.; m. Elisabeth M.L. Chaine, Apr. 27, 1967; children: Loic, Helene, Samuel. Lic. in Physics., U. Paris, 1965; diploma, Ecole Polytechnique, Paris, 1965; Diploma in Theoretical Physics, U. Orsay, France, 1966, PhD in Phys. Scis., 1971. Fellow CERN, Berkeley, Calif., 1966-73; physicist, then sr. physicist CERN, France, 1976-84; postdoctoral fellow Lawrence Berkeley (Calif.) Nat. Lab., 1973-76; mem. faculty U. Calif., Berkeley, 1984—, prof. physics, 1985—, dir. Ctr. Particle Astrophysics, 1988—; mem. commn. astrophysics Internat. Union Pure and Applied Physics, 1991—; vis. com. Max Planck Inst., Heidelberg, Germany, 1991—, Fermilab, 1992—, Lawrence Livermore Nat. Lab., 1992—; mem. program initiation com. NAS, 1992; internat. adv. com. various profl. confs. Contbr. to Sky and Telescope, The Early Universe Observable from Diffuse Backgrounds, other profl. publs. Fellow Am. Phys. Soc., U.S. Nat. Res. Coun. (com. on astronomy & astrophysics 1992). Achievements include work on the problem of the dark matter which constitutes more than 90% of the mass of the universe; devel. of a high-pressure gas scintillation drift chamber; search for WIMPs using cryogenic detectors of phonons and ionization. Office: Univ Calif Berkeley Ctr Particle Astrophysics 301 Le Conte Hall Berkeley CA 94720

SADOVE, STEPHEN IRVING, consumer products company executive; b. Washington, July 25, 1951; s. A. Robert and Harriet (Tenenbaum) S.; m. Sandra Rozenberg, Feb. 24, 1982; children: Stacy, David, Laurie. BA, Hamilton Coll., 1973; MBA, Harvard U., 1975. Asst. product mgr. Gen. Foods Corp.-Desserts Div., White Plains, N.Y., 1975-76; assoc. product mgr. Gen. Foods Corp.-Desserts Div., White Plains, 1976-77, product mgr., 1977-80, group product mgr., 1980-82, category mgr., 1982-84; mktg. mgr. Gen. Foods Corp.-Meals Div., White Plains, 1984-86, bus. unit mgr., 1986-88, v.p., gen. mgr., 1988-89; exec. v.p., gen. mgr. Gen. Foods Corp.-Desserts Div., White Plains, 1989-91; pres. Clairol, Inc., 1991—; alumni coun. Hamilton Coll., Clinton, N.Y. Bd. trustees, exec. com. Coun. for Arts in Westchester, White Plains, 1990—; bd. trustees Caramoor, Hazeldon. Avocations: tennis, golf, reading, arts. Home: 6 Crest Ct Armonk NY 10504-2901 Office: Clairol Inc 345 Park Ave New York NY 10154-0004*

SADOW, HARVEY S., health care company executive; b. N.Y.C., Oct. 6, 1922; s. Nat. and Frances Donna (Saveth) S.; m. Sylvia June Riber, Dec. 22, 1944 (div. 1966); children: Harvey Jr., Suzanne Gail, Todd Forrest, Gay Summer; m. Jacqueline Lucille Clavel, Jan. 24, 1969 (div. 1993); 1 adopted child, Daniel Jean marie; m. Mary Morrissey McSwiggan, July 13, 1995. BS, Va. Mil. Inst., Lexington, 1947; MS, U. Kans., 1949; PhD, U. Conn., 1953. Intelligence officer CIA, Washington, 1951-53; assoc. dir. rsch. Lakeside Labs., Inc., Milw., 1953-56; med. rsch. cons. Milw., 1956; dir. clin. rsch. U.S. Vitamin & Pharm. Corp., N.Y.C., 1957-64, v.p. rsch. and devel., 1964-68; sr. v.p. scientific affairs USV Pharm./Revlon Corp., N.Y.C., 1969-71; pres., CEO Boehringer Ingelheim, Ltd. (named changed to Boehringer Ingelheim Pharms., Inc. 1984), Ridgefield, Conn., 1971-88; pres., CEO Boehringer Ingelheim Corp., Ridgefield, 1984-88, chmn. bd., 1988-90; chmn. bd. Roxane Labs., Inc., Columbus, Ohio, 1981-88, Boehringer Ingelheim Animal Health, Inc., St. Joseph, Mo., 1981-88, Henley Co., N.Y.C., 1986-88, U. Conn. Rsch. and Devel. Corp., Storrs, 1984-87; bd. dirs. Cortex Pharms., Inc., Irvine, Calif., 1989—, chmn. bd., 1991—; bd. dirs. Cholestech Corp., Hayward, Calif., chmn. bd. 1992—; bd. dirs. Cytel Corp., San Diego, Anika Rsch. Corp.; mem. adv. bd. Salk Inst. Biotechnology-Indsl. Assocs., Inc., La Jolla, 1988-90. Co-author: Oral Treatment of Diabetes, 1967; author, co-author 23 papers on intermediary metabolism, diabetes, obesity and cardiovascular disease., 1963-72. Bd. dirs. Pharm. Mfrs. Assn., 1983-90; chmn. Pharm. Mfrs. Assn. Found., 1988-90; bd. dirs. Conn. Bd. Higher Edn., Hartford, 1977-83, Govs. Tech. Adv. Bd., Hartford, 1984-87; mem. Conn. Commn. on Bus. Opportunity, Def. Diversification and Indsl. Policy, 1991-93; mem. bd. visitors Va. Mil. Inst., Lexington, 1987—, pres. bd., 1991-95; chmn. bd. Comm. Law Enforcement Found., Hartford, 1981-86, 92—, U. Conn. Found., Storrs, 1984-87; chmn., pres.' coun. Am. Lung Assn., N.Y.C., 1986-87, York Sch., Monterey, Calif., 1988-89; trustee Conn. Coll., Groton, 1991-96, ALdrich Mus. Contemporary Art, Ridgefield, Conn., 1991—. Decorated Disting. Svc. Cross, Fed. Republic of Germany, 1987; recipient Univ. medal U. Conn., 1987, Recognition award Nat. Hypertension Assn., 1990, Humanitarian award Am. Lung Assn. Conn., 1993, Disting. Svc. award, 1996. Mem. Am. Soc. for Clin. Pharmacology and Therapeutics, Am. Fedn. for Clin. Rsch., Am. Diabetes Assn., Danbury C. of C. (Abraham Ribicoff Community Svc. award City of Danbury 1987, bd. dirs. 1978-81), Union League (N.Y.C.), Landmark Club (Stamford, Conn.), Masons, Sigma Xi, Sigma Pi Sigma, Phi Lambda Upsilon. Avocations: art collecting, photography, music, writing, golfing. Home and Office: 120-36 Prospect St Ridgefield CT 06877-4648

SADOWAY, DONALD ROBERT, materials science educator; b. Toronto, Mar. 7, 1950; s. Donald Anthony and Irene Mary (Romanko) S.; m. Sandra Lynn Mary Babij, Sept. 8, 1973; children: Steven, Laryssa, Andrew. BASc, U. Toronto, 1972, MASc, 1973, PhD, 1977. Cert. in chem. metallurgy. Asst. prof. materials engring. MIT, Cambridge, 1978-82, assoc. prof., 1982-92, prof. materials chemistry, 1992—; MacVicar faculty fellow MIT, 1995—. Contbr. over 75 articles on electro and phys. chemistry to profl. jours.; patentee in field, U.S., Can., and Europe. Recipient Grad. Student Coun. Teaching award MIT, 1982, 84, 87, 88, 93, Prof. T.B. King Meml. award dept. materials sci. and engring. undergrad. students MIT, 1986; NATO postdoctoral fellow Nat. Rsch. Coun. Can., 1977; AT&T Faculty Fellow in Indsl. Ecology, 1993-95, MacVicar Faculty fellow, 1995—. Mem. AAAS, Minerals, Metals and Materials Soc., Electrochem. Soc., Internat. Soc. Electrochemistry. Home: 100 Memorial Dr Apt 5-23B Cambridge MA 02142-1329 Office: MIT # 8-109 77 Massachusetts Ave Cambridge MA 02139-4307

SADOWSKI, CAROL JOHNSON, artist; b. Chgo., Mar. 20, 1929; d. Carl Valdamar Johnson and Elizabeth Hilma (Booth) Johnson-Chellberg; m. Edmund Sadowski, July 9, 1949; children: Lynn Carol Mahoney, Christie Sadowski Cortez. AAS, Wright-Ill. Coll., 1949. Tchr. art Malverne (N.Y.) High Sch., 1968-69; artist Valley Stream, N.Y., 1968-76, Hollywood, Fla., 1976—; guest speaker Mus. Art Ft. Lauderdale, Fla., 1991, others; TV appearances on WCGB, Gainesville, WSVN, Miami, Storer and Hollywood Cable, others. One-person shows include Mus. Fla. History, 1984, 85, 87, Hist. Mus. South Fla., Miami, 1986, Thomas Ctr. Arts, Gainesville, Gla., 1985, 87, Hist. Mus. South Fla., Miami, 1986, Thomas Ctr. Arts, Gainesville, Gla., 1985, 87, Elliott Mus., Stuart, Fla., 1987, Hemingway Mus. & Home, Key West, Fla., 1986, Mus. Fla. History, Tallahassee, 1985, 87, Alliance Francaise de Miami, 1995; commd. painting St. Agustin Antigua Found., St. Augustine, Fla., 1985, Atlantic Bank, Ft. Lauderdale, Fla., Bonnet House Fla. Trust, Ft. Lauderdale, Tropical Art Gallery, Naples, Fla., 1981, 82, 83, Tequesta (Fla.) Art Gallery, 1985, 86, 87, 88, 89, Gingerbread Square Gallery, Key West, 1990-96, Patricia Cloutien Gallery, Tequesta, 1993-96. Recipient Hemingway medal Ernest Hemingway Mus., Cuba, 1990, appreciation award City of Hollywood. Mem. Broward Art Guild, Fla. Hist. Assn., Ernest Hemingway Soc., Chopin Found., Am. Inst. for Polish Culture, Alliance Francaise de Miami, Internat. Platform Assn. Avocations: travel, hiking, biking, swimming, reading. Home and Studio: 1480 Sheridan St Apt B-17 Hollywood FL 33020-2295 *I try to do my best at what I love to do, not for money or fame, but for self satisfaction.*

SADRUDDIN, MOE, oil company executive, consultant; b. Hyderabad, India, Mar. 3, 1943; came to U.S., 1964; m. Azmath Oureshi, 1964; 3 children. BSME, Osmania U., Hyderabad, 1964; MS in Indsl. Engring., NYU, 1966; MBA, Columbia U., 1970. Cons. project engr. Ford, Bacon & Davis, N.Y.C., 1966; staff indsl. engr. J.C. Penney, N.Y.C., 1966-68; sr. cons. Drake, Sheahan, Stewart & Dougall, N.Y.C., 1968-70, Beech-Nut Inc. subs. Squibb Corp., N.Y.C., 1970-72; founder, pres. Azmath Constrn. Co., Englewood, N.J., 1972-77; crude oil cons., fgn. govt. rep., 1977—; pres. A-One Petroleum Co., Fullerton, Calif., 1985—; govt. advisor Puerto Rico, 1980-82, Dominica, 1983-84, St. Vincent, 1981-82, Kenya, 1983-84, Belize 1984-85, Costa Rica 1983-86, Paraguay 1984-87. Chmn. Azhar Found., 1989—; bldg. 6 charitable hosps. in India; mem. L.A. World Affairs Coun. Mem. Internat. Platform Assn. Address: A-One Petroleum Co 2656 N Camino Del Sol Fullerton CA 92633-4806 *Personal philosophy: I learned from a young age that acquisition of knowledge, developing honesty and integrity and service to humanity in the form of charity, love and struggle to help the poor and needy, are the main foundation stones of a successful life. I believe that acquisition of wealth is only a means to an end and not an end in itself. With accumulation of wealth, one has to care for the underprivileged and try to improve their lot.*

SADUN, ALBERTO CARLO, astrophysicist, physics educator; b. Atlanta, Apr. 28, 1955; s. Elvio Herbert and Lina (Ottolenghi) S.; m. Erica Liebman. BS in Physics, Mass. Inst. Tech., 1977; PhD in Physics, MIT, 1984. Asst. prof. Agnes Scott Coll., Decatur, Ga., 1984-90, assoc. prof., 1990—, dir. Bradley Obs., 1984—; adj. prof. Ga. State U., Atlanta, 1986—; rsch. affiliate NASA/Caltech Jet Propulsion Lab., Pasadena, Calif., 1988-90, summer faculty fellow, 1987, 88. Contbr. articles to Nature, Astrophys. Jour., Astron. Jour., Publ. Aston. Soc. of the Pacific, Astrophys. Letters and Communications. Mem. Am. Jewish Com., Atlanta, 1984—. Fellow Royal Astron. Soc.; mem. Internat. Astron. Union, Am. Astron. Soc., N.Y. Acad. Scis. Achievements include relocation of Agnes Scott College's telescope to Hard Labor Creek Observatory. Home: 4739 Springfield Dr Dunwoody GA 30338 Office: Agnes Scott Coll 141 E College Ave Decatur GA 30030-3770

SADUN, ALFREDO ARRIGO, neuro-ophthalmologist, scientist, educator; b. New Orleans, Oct. 23, 1950; s. Elvio H. and Lina (Ottoleghi) S.; m. Debra Leigh Rice, Mar. 18, 1978; children: Rebecca Eli, Elvio Aaron, Benjamin Maxwell. BS, MIT, 1972; PhD, Albert Einstein Med. Sch., Bronx, N.Y., 1976, MD, 1978. Intern Huntington Meml. Hosp. U. So. Calif., Pasadena, 1978-79; resident Harvard U. Med. Sch., Boston, 1979-82, HEED Found. fellow in neuro-ophthalmology Mass. Eye and Ear Inst., 1982-83, instr. ophthalmology, 1983, asst. prof. ophthalmology, 1984; dir. residential tng. U. So. Calif. Dept. Ophthalmology, L.A., 1984-85, 90—; asst. prof. ophthalmology and neurosurgery U. So. Calif., L.A., 1984-87, assoc. prof., 1987-90; full prof. U. So. Calif., 1990—, mem. internal review bd.; prin. investigator Howe Lab. Harvard U., Boston, 1981-84, E. Doheny Eye Inst., L.A., 1984—; examiner Am. Bd. Ophthalmology; mem. internal rev. bd. U. So. Calif. Author: Optics for Opthalmologists, 1988, New Methods of Sensory Visual Testing, 1989; contbr. articles to profl. jours. and chpts. to books. James Adams scholar, 1990-91; recipient Pecan D. award, 1988-92. Fellow Am. Acad. Ophthalmology Neuro-Ophthalmologists; mem. NIH (Med. Scientists Tng. award 1972-78), Am. Assn. Anatomists, Assn. Univ. Prof. Ophthalmology (assoc.), Am. Bd. Ophthalmology (rep. to residency rev. com. 1994—), Soc. to Prevent Blindness, Nat. Eye Inst. (New Investigator Rsch. award 1983-86, rsch. grants 1988-91, 93—), Soc. Neuroscis., Assn. Rsch. in Vision and Ophthalmology, N.Am. Neuro-Ophthal. Soc. (chmn. membership com. 1990—, v.p. 1994—). Avocation: writing. Home: 2478 Adair St San Marino CA 91108-2610 Office: U So Calif E Doheny Eye Inst 1450 San Pablo St Los Angeles CA 90033-4615

SADUN, LORENZO ADLAI, mathematician; b. Silver Spring, Md., Nov. 3, 1960; s. Elvio Herbert and Lina Amelia (Ottolenghi) S.; m. Anita Elizabeth Glazer, Sept. 4, 1988; children: Rina Ellen, Allan Elvio. BS, MIT, 1981; MA, U. Calif., 1982, PhD, 1987. Rsch. instr. Calif. Tech. Math. Dept., Pasadena, 1987-89; Courant instr. Courant Inst. Math. Scis., N.Y.C., 1989-91; asst. prof. U. Tex., Austin, 1991—. Contbr. articles to profl. publs. Home: 1706 W 30th St Austin TX 78703-1824 Office: U Tex Math Dept Austin TX 78712

SAEED, MOHAMMED, Islamic historian, eqyptologist, educator; b. El Paso, Tex., Aug. 15, 1948; s. Willard Wood and Grace Margaret (Weddle) W.; m. Jeanne Burger, Apr. 2, 1970 (div. 1979); children: Grace Ann, Annabelle Jane; m. Katleen M. D'Annette, Dec. 12, 1992. Student, Fullerton Coll., 1973-76; AA, Wichita State U., 1983, BS, 1983; MA, Emporia State U., 1989; student, Am. U., Cairo, Egypt. Rschr. Lawrence (Kans.) Islamic Student Assn., 1989-92, Islamic Studies Student Assn., Lawrence, 1992—. Author: The Jayhawk Nazi, 1983, Perceptions: Vietnam Veterans, 1989, Allah, The Glorious Quran and the Muslim Family, 1995; contbr. articles to profl. jours. Mem. DAV, World Wildlife Fund, Nat. Parks and Conservation Assn., Blinded Veterans Assn., Nat. Wildlife Fedn., Nat. Audubon Soc., Hist. Preservation Soc., Emporia State Alumni Assn., Greenpeace, Amnesty Internat., Disabled Am. Blind Vets., Archeol. Inst. Am., Egypt Exploration Soc. Moslem. Avocations: travel, Middle Eastern cooking, model trains, reading, classical music. Home: 1611 W 8th Tr # 2 Lawrence KS 66044-2450

SAEKS, ALLEN IRVING, lawyer; b. Bemidji, Minn., July 14, 1932; m. Linda J. Levin; 1 child, Adam Charles. BS in Law, U. Minn., 1954, JD, 1956. Bar: Minn. 1956, U.S. Dist. Ct. Minn. 1956, U.S. Ct. Appeals (8th cir.) 1957, U.S. Ct. Appeals (fed. cir.) 1959, U.S. Supreme Ct. 1959; cert. civil trial specialist. Asst. U.S. atty. Dept. Justice, St. Paul, 1956-57; assoc. Leonard Street & Deinard, Mpls., 1960-63, ptnr., 1964—; adj. prof. law U. Minn. Law Sch., 1960-65; chmn. Lawyer Trust Account Bd., Interest on Lawyers Trust Accounts., 1984-87. Chmn. Property Tax Com., 1986-87; bd. dirs. Citizens League, Mpls., 1984-87; pres. Jewish Cmty. Rels. Coun. of Minn. and the Dakotas, 1994—. Served to 1st lt. JAGC, U.S. Army, 1957-60. Fellow Am. Bar Found.; mem. Hennepin County Bar Assn. (pres. 1983-84), ABA (commn. on interest on lawyers trust accts. 1990-93), Minn. State Bar Assn. (cert. trial specialist 1988), Order of Coif, Phi Delta Phi. Office: Leonard Street and Deinard 150 S 5th St Ste 2300 Minneapolis MN 55402-4223

SAEKS, RICHARD EPHRAIM, electrical engineer; b. Chgo., Nov. 30, 1941; s. Morris G. and Elsie E. S. B.S., Northwestern U., 1964; M.S., Colo. State U., 1965; Ph.D., Cornell U., 1967. Elec. engr. Warwick Mfg. Co., Niles, Ill., 1961-63; asst. prof. dept. elec. engring. U. Notre Dame, 1967-71, asso. prof., 1971-73; asso. prof. depts. elec. engring., math. Tex. Tech U., Lubbock, 1973-77; prof. Tex. Tech U., 1977-79, Paul Whitfield Horn prof. elec. engring., math., computer sci., 1979-82; prof., chmn. elec. engring. Ariz. State U., 1983-88; dean Armour Coll. Engring. Ill. Inst. Tech., 1988-91, Motorola prof., 1991-92; v.p. engring. Accurate Automation Corp., 1992—; cons. Research Triangle Inst., 1978-80, Marcel Dekker Inc., 1978-80. Author: Generalized Networks, 1972, Resolution Space Operators and Systems, 1973, Interconnected Dynamical Systems, 1981, System Theory: A Hilbert Space Approach, 1982; contbr. articles to profl. jours.; Editor: Large-Scale Dynamical Systems, 1976, Rational Fault Analysis, 1977, The World of Large Scale Systems, 1982. Recipient Disting. Faculty Research award Tex. Tech U., 1978. Fellow IEEE.

SAENGER, EUGENE LANGE, radiology educator, laboratory director; b. Cin., Mar. 5, 1917; s. Eugene and Therese (Lange) S.; m. Sue Reis, June 18, 1941 (dec.); children: Katherine Saenger Soodek (dec.), Eugene Lange. A.B., Harvard U., 1938; M.D., U. Cin., 1942. Diplomate: Am. Bd. Radiology, Am. Bd. Nuclear Medicine. Intern Cin. Gen. Hosp., 1942-43, resident in radiology, 1943-46; asst. prof., then assoc. prof. radiology U. Cin. Med. Ctr., 1949-62, prof., vice chmn. dept., 1962-87, prof. radiology emeritus, 1987—; radiation therapist Children's Hosp., Cin., 1947-87; dir. E.L. Saenger Radioisotope Lab., U. Cin., 1950-87; cons. AEC and NRC, 1962-88, to med. liaison EPA, 1968—; dir. Nat. Coun. Radiation Protection, 1967—; mem. Internat. Com. on Radiation Protection, 1977-84. Author: Medical Aspects of Radiation Accidents: A Handbook for Physicians, Health Physicists and Industrial Hygienists, 1963. Trustee Cin. Community Chest and Council, 1964-70. Served to maj. M.C. U.S. Army, 1953-55. Mem. Soc. Med. Decision Making (pres., co-founder 1979-80), Nat. Coun. Radiation Protection (hon. mem.), Queen City Club, Literary Club (Cin.), Cosmos Club (Washington), Optimists Club. Jewish. Home: 9160 Given Rd Cincinnati OH 45243-1148 Office: Eugene L Saenger Radioisotope Lab U Cin Hosp ML 569 Cincinnati OH 45267-0569

SAENZ, MICHAEL, college president; b. Laredo, Tex., Oct. 25, 1925; s. C. A. and Pola R. Saenz; B.S. with honors in Accounting, Tex. Christian U., 1949, M.Ed., 1952; Ph.D. in Econs., U. Pa., 1961; m. Nancy Elizabeth King; children—Michael King, Cynthia Elizabeth. Dep. collector IRS, Ft. Worth, Dallas, 1949-52; adminstr. United Christian Missionary Soc., Bayamon, P.R., 1954-57, 59-65, exec. sec., Indpls., 1965-71; acad. dean Laredo Jr. Coll., 1971-74; pres. N.W. campus Tarrant County Jr. Coll., 1975—; founder Nat. Comm. Coll. Hispanic coun., 1985, bd. dirs. 1985— (pres. 1989-91); founder, co-dir. Nat. Hispanic Leadership Inst., 1989—; trustee Tex. Christian U., Brite Div. Sch., 1973—. Bd. dirs. Civic Ballet of Laredo (Tex.), Ft. Worth chpt. NCCJ, Juliette Fowler Homes, Dallas; chmn. Aztec Dist., dir. Gulf Coast council Boy Scouts Am., 1971-75; gov. Career Devel. Center, Arlington, Tex.; chmn. Laredo's Bicentennial Com., 1973-76; trustee, bd. dirs. United Way Ft. Worth, 1979—; mem., vice moderator gen. bd. Christian Ch. (Disciples of Christ), 1991-93. Mem. Am. Assn. Cmty. Colls.(bd. dirs., 1991-94), Commn. Internat. Edn. Am. Coun. Edn, Tex. Jr. Coll. Tchrs. Assn., Tex. Assn. Jr. Coll. Instructional Adminstrs., Am. Acad. Polit. and Social Scis., Urban Ministries in Higher Edn, Civic Music Assn. Laredo, N. Ft. Worth C. of C. (dir. 1978—). Lodge: Rotary (North Ft. Worth). Home: 4427 Tamworth Rd Fort Worth TX 76116-8127 Office: Tarrant County Jr Coll 1500 Houston St Fort Worth TX 76102-6524

SAETA, PHILIP MAX, judge; b. L.A., Feb. 21, 1931; s. Maurice and Elizabeth (Jacobs) S.; m. Joanne Edith Hixson, Aug. 28, 1954; children: David, Peter, Sandra. AB, Stanford U., 1953, LLB, 1957. Bar: Calif. 1958, U.S. Dist. Ct. (cen. dist.) Calif. Assoc., ptnr. Beardsley, Hufstedler & Kemble, L.A., 1964-75; judge Mcpl. Ct., L.A., 1964-75; judge L.A. County Superior Ct., L.A., 1975-91, ret., 1991; pvt. judge, 1991—. With U.S. Army, 1953-55. Mem. ABA, Calif. Judges Assn. (Jefferson award 1987), L.A. County Bar Assn. Democrat. Jewish. Avocation: music. Home and Office: 2036 Oak St South Pasadena CA 91030-4954

SAFA, BAHRAM, civil engineer; b. Abadan, Iran, May 15, 1941; came to U.S., 1970; s. Ghassem Safa and Sekineh Bigom Khaki; m. Nahid Araji, Apr. 1, 1966; children: Shahrzad, Sarah, Susan, Cyrus. BSC, Abadan Inst. Tech., 1965; MBA, SUNY, Albany, 1976; grad. cert., UCLA, 1983; post-grad., U. Calif. San Diego, 1994-95. Profl. engr., Calif., Nev. Project engr. Myrick and Chevalier, Albany, 1971-75; project mgr. Internat. Housing Ltd., Westport, Conn., 1975-77, asst. v.p., 1977-79; constrn. coord. Security Pacific Bank, L.A., 1979-80; design engr. VTN Engrs., L.A., 1980-84, project mgr., 1984-85; sr. civil engr. City of Simi Valley, Calif., 1985-88, prin. engr., 1988-92; sr. civil engr. San Diego County Water Authority, 1992-96; pres. Water Svcs. Internat., 1996—; mng. dir. Internat. Housing Iran, Tehran, 1978-79. Sustaining mem. Ronald Reagan Presdl. Found., L.A., 1989-92. Mem. NSPE, ASCE, Am. Water Works Assn., Internat. Water Supply Assn. Republican. Avocations: reading, research, cultural activities. Office: Water Svcs Internat PO Box 26897 San Diego CA 92196-6897

SAFAN, CRAIG ALAN, film composer; b. L.A., Dec. 17, 1948; s. Eugene Leroy and Betty Lou (Torchin) S.; m. Linda Sue McClelland, Aug. 27, 1978; children: Alec, Kira. BA, Brandeis U., 1970. Film composer, 1973—. Composer film scores The Great Texas Dynamite Chase, 1976, The Bad News Bears in Breaking Training, 1977, Corvette Summer, 1978, Good Guys Wear Black, 1978, The Great Smokey Roadblock, 1978, Roller Boogie, 1979, Fade to Black, 1980, Die Laughing, 1980, T.A.G.: The Assassination Game, 1982, Nightmares, 1983, Angel, 1984, The Last Starfighter, 1984, The Legend of Billie Jean, 1985, Remo Williams: The Adventure Begins, 1985, Warning Sign, 1985, Lady Beware, 1987, The Stranger, 1987, Stand and Deliver, 1988, A Nightmare on Elm Street IV: The Dream Master, 1988, Money for Nothing, 1993, Major Payne, 1995, Mr. Wrong, 1995, TV scores Cheers, 1983-94, Life Goes On, 1990-94, Hope and Gloria, 1995. Fellow Watson Found., 1970-71. Mem. NARAS, ASCAP (award for Cheers 1987-93), Acad. Motion Picture Arts and Scis. (exec. music com. 1987-95). Avocation: collecting American sheet music. Office: MSK Agy 4146 Lankershim Blvd Ste 401 North Hollywood CA 91602-2832

SAFARS, BERTA See FISZER-SZAFARZ, BERTA

SAFDIE, MOSHE S., architect; b. Haifa, Israel, July 14, 1938; s. Leon S.; m. Nina Nusynowicz, Sept. 6, 1959 (div. 1981); children: Taal, Oren; m. Michal Ronnen, June 7, 1981; children: Carmelle, Yasmin. BArch, McGill U., 1961; LLD (hon.), 1982; DSc (hon.), Laval U., 1988; DFA (hon.), U. Victoria, 1989. With H.P.D. Van Ginkel (architect), Montreal, Que., Can., 1961-62, then Louis I. Kahn, Phila., 1962-63; assoc. David, Barrott and Boulva, Montreal, 1964; pvt. practice Boston, 1964—; with brs. in Toronto, Ont., Jerusalem, Toronto, Can., Jerusalem; prof. architecture and urban design, dir. urban design program Harvard U. Grad. Sch. Design, 1978-84, Ian Woodner Studio prof. architecture and urban design, 1984-89. Prin. works include Skirball Cultural Ctr., L.A., Vancouver (B.C., Can.) Libr. Sq., Ford Ctr. for Performing Arts, Vancouver, Mamilla Jaffa Gate Parking and Transp. Terminal, Jerusalem, Mamilla David's Village, phases I, II and III, Jerusalem, Rosovsky Hall, Harvard-Radcliffe Hillel, Harvard U., Manchat, Israel, Yeshiva Aish Hatorah, Jerusalem, Ottawa (Ont.) City Hall, Morgan Hall and Class of 1959 Chapel, Bus. Sch. Harvard U., Mus. des Beaux-Arts Montreal, Nat. Gallery Can., Ottawa, Mus. de la Civilisation, Quebec City, Que., Cambridge (Mass.) Ctr. Master Plan and Office/Hotel Complex, Columbus Ctr., N.Y.C., Esplanade, Cambridge, Hewbre Union Coll., Jerusalem, Yad Vashem Children's Holocaust Meml., Jerusalem, Porat Yosef Rabbinical Coll., Jerusalem, Mammila Ctr., Jerusalem, Mamilla Hilton, Jerusalem, Modi'in, Israel, Elwyn Inst., Jerusalem. Recipient Massey medal in architecture, Lt. Gov. Can. gold medal, urban design concept award HUD, 1980, internat. design award in urban design Am. Soc. Interior Designers, 1980, Prix d'Excellence in architecture Que. Order Architects, 1988, Gov. Gen.'s medal for architecture, 1992, Richard J. Neutra award, 1993, RAIC Gold medal Royal Architectural Inst. of Canada, 1995. Fellow Royal Inst. Architects Can. (Gold Medal 1995), Order of Can.; mem. AIA, Order Architects Province Que., Ont. Assn. Architects. Office: 100 Properzi Way Somerville MA 02143-3740 also: 165 Avenue Rd Ste 501, Toronto, ON Canada M5R 2H7 also: 4 Ha'emek St, Jerusalem Israel 94106

SAFER, JAY GERALD, lawyer; b. Jacksonville, Fla., Oct. 11, 1946; s. Moe B. and Rubye (Lipsitz) S.; m. Annette Fashing, Nov. 26, 1970; children: Michelle Laurie, Ellie Renee. BA, Vanderbilt U., 1968; JD, Columbia U., 1971. Bar: N.Y. 1972, U.S. Dist. Ct. (so. and ea. dists.) N.Y. 1973, U.S. Dist. Ct. Conn. 1984, U.S. Ct. Appeals (2d cir.) 1974, U.S. Supreme Ct. 1992. Assoc. Paul, Weiss, Rifkind, Wharton & Garrison, N.Y.C., 1971-75, Hardee, Barovick, Konecky & Braun, N.Y.C., 1975, LeBoeuf, Lamb, Leiby & MacRae, N.Y.C., 1975-80; ptnr. LeBoeuf, Lamb, Greene & MacRae, L.L.P., N.Y.C., 1980—. Contbr. articles to profl. jours. Served to capt. U.S. Army, 1972. Harlan Fiske Stone scholar, Columbia U., 1971. Mem. ABA, N.Y. State Bar Assn., Assn. Bar City N.Y. Office: LeBoeuf Lamb Greene and MacRae LLP 125 W 55th St New York NY 10019-5369

SAFER, JOHN, artist, lecturer; b. Washington, Sept. 6, 1922; s. John M. and Rebecca (Herzmark) S.; m. Joy Scott; children: Janine Whitney, Thomas. AB, George Washington U., 1947; LLB, Harvard, 1949. chmn. NationsBank/D.C., 1980-92; chmn. exec. com. Fin. Gen. Bankshares, 1977-80. Represented in permanent collections at Balt. Mus. Art, Corocoran Gallery Art, Nat. Air and Space Mus., Washington Tennis Ctr., Washington High Mus. Art, Atlanta, Milw. Mus. Art, Harvard Law Sch., Harvard Bus. Sch., Phila. Mus. Art, San Francisco Mus. Art, Georgetown U., George Washington U., Williams Coll., Mus. Fine Arts, Caracas, Venezuela, Duke Med. Ctr., Royal Collection, Madrid, Am. Hosp., Paris, Embassy of U.S., London, Beijing Royal Collection, Amman; pub. sculpture includes World Series of Golf Trophy, Timepiece (World's Largest Clock - Guiness Book of Records), Christa McAuliffe Meml., Bowie, Md. Served as 1st lt. USAAF, 1942-46. Clubs: Cosmos, Burning Tree, Harvard, Woodmont (Washington); Harvard (N.Y.); Lyford Cay (Nassau); Mid-Ocean (Bermuda); Linville Ridge (N.C.). Office: PO Box 30163 Bethesda MD 20824-0163

SAFER, MORLEY, journalist; b. Toronto, Ont., Can., Nov. 8, 1931; came to U.S., 1964; s. Max and Anna (Cohn) S. Student, U. Western Ont., 1952. With Reuters, London, Eng., 1955; corr., producer Canadian Broadcasting Corp., 1955-60, writer, London corr., 1961-64; corr., producer BBC, 1961; Vietnam corr. CBS, 1964-71; co-host 60 Minutes news program CBS-TV, 1971—; writer-corr. news documentary The Second Battle of Britain, 1976. Author: Flashbacks: On Returning to Vietnam, 1990. Recipient Polk award L.I.U., 1965, Overseas Press Club award, 1965, 66, Sigma Delta Chi award, 1965, Peabody award, 1965, Paul White award Radio and TV, News Dirs. Assn., 1966, 4 Emmy awards, 1981, 82, 3 Emmy awards, 1985, George Foster Peabody award, 1983, 3 prestigious awards, George Foster Peabody, Alfred I. duPont-Columbia U., Emmy for "Lenell Geter's in Jail", 60 Min. broadcast, 1984. Fellow Royal Coll. Bloviation (Edinburgh). Office: care CBS News 60 Minutes 555 W 57th St New York NY 10019-2925

SAFERITE, LINDA LEE, library director; b. Santa Barbara, Calif., Mar. 25, 1947; d. Elwyn C. and Polly (Frazer) S.; m. Andre Doyon, July 16, 1985. BA, Calif. State U., Chico, 1969; MS in Library Sci., U. So. Calif., 1970; cert. in Indsl. Relations, UCLA, 1976; MBA, Pepperdine U., 1979. Librarian-in-charge, reference librarian Los Angeles County Pub. Libr. System, 1970-73, regional reference librarian, 1973-75, sr. librarian-in-charge, 1975-78, regional adminstr., 1978-80; libr. dir. Scottsdale (Ariz.) Pub. Libr. System, 1980-93, Fort Collins (Colo.) Pub. Libr., 1993—; task force del. White House Conf. on Libr. and Info. Svcs., 1992—, rep. Region V, 1982-94. Bd. dirs. Scottsdale-Paradise Valley YMCA, 1981-86, Ariz. Libr. Friends, 1990-92; bd. dirs. AMIGOS, 1990, chmn., 1992-93; mem. Class 5, Scottsdale Leavership, 1991. Recipient Cert. Recognition for efforts in civil rights Ariz. Atty. Gen.'s Office, 1985, Libr. award Ariz. Libr. Friends, 1988, Women of Distinction award for Edn., 1989, State Project of Yr. award, 1995, Ariz. Disting. Svc. award, 1993; named State Libr. of Yr., 1990. Mem. ALA, Ariz. State Libr. Assn. (pres. 1987-88), Ariz. Women's Town Hall Alumni-Assn., Met. Bus. and Profl. Women (Scottsdale, pres. 1986-87), Soroptimist (pres. 1981-83). Republican. Avocations: mountain jaunts, reading, ballroom dancing, photography. Office: Fort Collins Pub Libr 201 Peterson St Fort Collins CO 80524-2919

SAFF, EDWARD BARRY, mathematics educator; b. N.Y.C., Jan. 2, 1944; s. Irving H. and Rose (Koslow) S.; m. Loretta Singer, July 3, 1966; children:

Lisa Jill, Tracy Karen, Alison Michelle. BS with highest honors, Ga. Inst. Tech., 1964; PhD, U. Md., 1968. Asst. prof. U. Md., 1968; post-doctoral researcher Imperial Coll., London, 1968-69; asst. prof. math. U. South Fla., 1969-71, assoc. prof., 1971-76, prof., 1976-86, disting. rsch. prof., 1986—, dir. Ctr. for Math. Svcs., 1978-83, dir. Inst. for Constructive Math., 1985—; sr. vis. fellow Oxford U., 1978. Author: (with A.D. Snider) Fundamentals of Complex Analysis, 1976, (with A.W. Goodman) Calculus, Concepts and Calculations, 1981, (with A. Edrei and R.S. Varga) Zeros of Sections of Power Series; editor (with R.S. Varga) Pade and Rational Approximation: Theory and Applications, 1977, (with R.K. Nagle) Fundamentals of Differential Equations, (with R.K. Nagle) Fundamentals of Differential Equations and Boundary Value Problems, 1993, (with D.S. Lubinsky) Strong Asymptotics for Extremal Polynomials Associated with Weights on R., 1988; editor-in-chief Constructive Approximation Jour., 1983—; editor Jour. Approximation Theory, 1990—, Cambridge Univ. Press, 1995—. Fulbright fellow, 1968-69, Guggenheim fellow, 1978; NSF grantee, 1970-72, 80—; Hon. prof. Zhejiang Normal U. Mem. Am. Math. Soc., Math. Assn. Am., Sigma Xi. Home: 11738 Lipsey Rd Tampa FL 33618-3620 Office: U South Fla Dept Math Tampa FL 33620

SAFFELS, DALE EMERSON, federal judge; b. Moline, Kans., Aug. 13, 1921; s. Edwin Clayton and Lillian May (Cook) S.; m. Margaret Elaine Nieman, Apr. 2, 1976; children by previous marriage: Suzanne Saffels Gravitt, Deborah Saffels Godowns, James B.; stepchildren: Lynda Cowger Harris, Christopher Cowger. AB, Emporia State U., 1947; JD cum laude, LLB cum laude, Washburn U., 1949. Bar: Kans. 1949. Pvt. practice law Garden City, Kans., 1949-71, Topeka, 1971-75, Wichita, Kans., 1975-79; U.S. dist. judge Dist. of Kans., Topeka, 1979—; county atty. Finney County, Kans., 1951-55; chmn. bd. Fed. Home Loan Bank Topeka, 1978-79; mem. Jud. Conf. Com. on Fin. Disclosure, 1993—. Mem. bd. govs. Sch. Law Washburn U., 1973-85; pres. Kans. Dem. Club, 1957; Dem. nominee Gov. of Kans., 1962; mem. Kans. Ho. of Reps., 1955-63, minority leader, 1961-63; mem. Kans. Corp. Commn., 1967-75, chmn., 1968-75; mem. Kans. Legis. Coun., 1957-63; Kans. rep. Interstate Oil Compact Commn., 1967-75, 1st vice chmn., 1971-72; pres. Midwest Assn. Regulatory Commn., 1972-73, Midwest Assn. R.R. and Utilities Commrs., 1972-73; trustee Emporia State U. Endowment Assn.; bd. dirs. Nat. Assn. Regulatory Utility Commrs., 1972-75. Maj. Signal Corps U.S. Army, 1942-46. Fellow Am. Bar Found., Kans. Bar Found.; mem. ABA, Kans. Bar Assn., Wichita Bar assn., Am. Judicture Soc., Delta Theta Phi. Lutheran. Home: 2832 SW Plass Ave Topeka KS 66611-1630 Office: US Dist Ct 420 Federal Bldg 444 SE Quincy St Topeka KS 66683

SAFFER, ALFRED, retired chemical company executive; b. N.Y.C., Dec. 3, 1918; s. Louis and Ruth (Mirkis) S.; m. Ruth Lillian Rudow, Jan. 31, 1942 (dec. Dec. 1983); children: Anita Carolyn Horowitz, Martin Kenneth; m. Doris Barbara Graubard, June 18, 1985. AB in Chemistry, NYU, 1939, MS in Chemistry, 1941, PhD, 1943. Research chemist Princeton (N.J.) U., 1943-46; sr. research assoc. Firestone Tire and Rubber Co., Akron, Ohio, 1946-48; dir. research Sci. Design Co., Inc., N.Y.C., 1948-57, v.p. mfg.; pres. Catalyst Devel. Corp., Little Ferry, N.J., 1957-69; exec. v.p. Halcon Internat., Inc., N.Y.C., 1963-69; vice chmn. ret. Halcon SD Group, Inc., N.Y.C., 1978-81; exec. v.p. Oxirane Corp, Princeton, 1969-76; pres. Oxirane Internat., Princeton, 1976-78; bd. dirs. Norwood Venture Co., N.Y.C. Contbr. articles to profl. jours.; patentee in field. Trustee Internat. Ctr. for Disabled, N.Y.C., 1978—; assoc. trustee North Shore U. Hosp., Manhasset, N.Y., 1981—; active instl. rev. bd. Boca Raton (Fla.) Community Hosp., 1992—. Fellow Am. Inst. Chemists (Chem. Pioneer award, 1982); mem. Nat. Acad. Engring., Am. Chem. Soc., Soc. Chem. Industry. Clubs: Glen Oaks (Old Westbury, N.Y.); Delaire Country (Delray Beach, Fla.). Avocation: golf. Home: 16629 Ironwood Dr Delray Beach FL 33445-7050

SAFFER, AMY BETH, foreign language educator; b. N.Y.C., Apr. 19, 1950; d. William and Evelyn (Yankowitz) S. BA, Fairleigh Dickinson U., 1972, MA, 1983; postgrad., Jersey City State Coll., 1983-84. Cert. tchr. Spanish K-12, N.J. Tchr. Madison (N.J.) High Sch., 1973, Livingston (N.J.) High Sch., 1973—; mem. faculty and dist. coms. Livingston Sch. Dist., 1975—; advisor to class of 1977, Livingston High Sch., 1975-77, chair mid. states subcom., 1990. Inducted Livington H.S. Alumni Hall of Fame, 1993. Mem. NEA, Am. Assn. Tchrs. of Spanish and Portuguese, N.J. Edn. Assn., Fgn. Lang. Educators of N.J., Livingston Edn. Assn. (negotiations rep. 1980—), Essex County Edn. Assn. Office: Livingston High Sch Livingston NJ 07039

SAFFERMAN, ROBERT SAMUEL, microbiologist; b. Bronx, N.Y., Dec. 19, 1932; s. Irving and Rose (Schuler) S.; m. Jewel S. Reisman, June 7, 1958; children—Karen M., Sharon L., Steven I. B.S., Bklyn. Coll., 1955; Ph.D., Rutgers U., 1960. With USPHS, Cin., 1959-64; with Dept. Interior, Cin., 1964-70, U.S. EPA, Cin., 1970—; chief virology sect. Environ. Monitoring and Support Lab. EPA, Cin., 1974-88, chief virology br. Environ. Monitoring Systems Lab., 1988-94; chief virology and parasitology br. Environ. Monitoring Sys. Lab., Cin., 1994-95; chief biohazard assessment rsch. br. Nat. Exposure Rsch. Lab., 1995—; mem. Internat. Com. on Taxonomy of Viruses. Recipient Spl. Service award San. Engring. Ctr., USPHS, 1963; Gans medal Soc. Water Treatment and Examination, Eng., 1970; named Fed. Employee of Yr., Cin., 1974. Fellow Am. Acad. Microbiology; mem. ASTM, Am. Soc. Microbiology, Phycological Soc. Am., Sigma Xi. Home: 1669 Locksley Dr Cincinnati OH 45230-2220 Office: 26 Martin Luther King Dr W Cincinnati OH 45268

SAFFIOTTI, UMBERTO, pathologist; b. Milan, Jan. 22, 1928; came to U.S., 1960, naturalized, 1966; s. Francesco Umberto and Maddalena (Valenzano) S.; m. Paola Amman, June 21, 1958; children: Luisa M., Maria Francesca. MD cum laude, U. Milan, 1951, splty. diploma occupational medicine cum laude, 1957. Intern Inst. Pathol. Anatomy U. Milan, 1951-52, asst. to chmn. occupational medicine, chief lab. pathology, Inst. Occupational Medicine, 1956-60, fellow Inst. Gen. Pathology, 1957-60; rsch. asst. oncology, rsch. assoc. Chgo. Med. Sch., 1952-55, from asst. prof. to prof. oncology, 1960-68; mem. staff Nat. Cancer Inst., NIH, Bethesda, Md., 1968—, assoc. dir. carcinogenesis, 1968-76, chief lab. exptl. pathology, 1974—, acting head Registry of Exptl. Cancers, 1988—; mem. pathology B study sect., NIH, 1964-68; mem. various adv. coms. govt. agys.; mem. cancer prevention com. Internat. Union Against Cancer, 1959-66, panel on carcinogenicity, 1963-66; chmn. ad hoc com. evaluation low levels environ. carcinogens HEW, 1969-70. Co-editor books; contbr. articles to profl. jours. Bd. dirs. Rachel Carson Trust, 1976-79. Recipient Career Devel. award NIH, 1965-68, Superior Svc. Honor award HEW, 1971, Pub. Interest Sci. award Environ. Def. Fund, 1977, Spl. Recognition award USPHS, 1980. Fellow NYAS; mem. AAAS, Am. Assn. Cancer Rsch. (pres. Chgo. chpt. 1966-67), Am. Soc. Investigative Pathology, Internat. Commn. Occupational Health, Soc. Occupational and Environ. Health (councillor 1972-76, v.p. 1976-78, pres. 1978-82), Soc. Toxicology, Sigma Xi. Democrat. Home: 5114 Wissioming Rd Bethesda MD 20816-2259 Office: NIH Nat Cancer Inst Lab Exptl Pathology Bldg 41 Bethesda MD 20892-0041

SAFFIR, HERBERT SEYMOUR, structural engineer, consultant; b. N.Y.C., Mar. 29, 1917; s. A.L. and Gertrude (Samuels) S.; m. Sarah Young, May 9, 1941; children: Richard Young, Barbara Joan. BS in Civil Engring. cum laude, Ga. Inst. Tech., 1940. Registered profl. engr., Fla., N.Y., Tex., P.R., Miss. Civil engr. TVA, Chattanooga, 1940, NACA, Langley Field, Va., 1940-41; structural engr. Ebasco Services, N.Y.C., 1941-43, York & Sawyer & Fred Severud, N.Y.C., 1945; engr. Waddell & Hardesty, Cons. Engrs., N.Y.C., 1945-47; asst. county engr. Dade County, Miami, Fla., 1947-59; cons. engr. Herbert S. Saffir, Coral Gables, Fla., 1959—; adj. prof. civil engring. Coll. Engring., U. Miami, 1964—; adviser civil engring. Fla. Internat. U., 1975-80; cons. on bldg. codes Govt. Bahamas; cons. on engring. in housing to UN; mem., chmn. Met. Dade County Unsafe Structures Bd., 1977-92; mem. Bldg. Code Evaluation Task Force after Hurricane Andrew; mem. Am. Nat. Stds. Inst. Commn. Bldg. Design Loads, Nat. Adv. Group on Glass Design, Dade County Bldg. Code Com. 1993—; mem. U. Miami/Coral Gables Community Rels. Com., 1993—; cons. to govt. and industry, condr. seminars, Australia; reviewer for NSF; mem. bd. adjustment Coral Gables, 1994—. Author: Housing Construction in Hurricane Prone Areas, 1971, Nature and Extent of Damage by Hurricane Camille, 1972, Evaluation of Structural Damage Caused by Hurricanes, 1993; contbg. author: Wind Effects on Structures, 1976; editor: Wind Engr., 1986-92; contbr. articles to profl. jours.; designer Saffir/Simpson hurricane scale. With N.Y. Guard, 1942-43, AUS, 1943-44. Recipient Outstanding Service award Fla. Profl. Engrs., 1954, Pub. Service award Nat. Weather Service, 1975, Disting. Service award Nat. Hurricane Conf., 1987; named Miami Engr. of Year, 1978, 94, Gov.'s Design award, 1986, Gov. Gilchrist award for Profl. Excellence, 1988, Albert H. Friedman Community Svc. award, 1992; named to Ga. Tech. Engring. Hall of Fame, 1995. Fellow ASCE (past pres., sec., aerodynamics com. 1983—, mem. mitigation of wind damage com. 1985—, chmn. com. on damage investigation 1989—, mem. com. A7 on design loads for bldgs. 1972—), Fla. Engring. Soc. (award for outstanding tech. achievement 1973, Cmty. Svc. award 1980); mem. Soc. Am. Mil. Engrs., Am. Concrete Inst., ASTM (mem. com. performance bldg. constrn.), Prestressed Concrete Inst., Internat. Assn. for Bridge and Structural Engring., Colegio de Ingenieros P.R., Am. Meterol. Soc., Am. Arbitration Assn., Wind Engring. Rsch. Coun. (past bd. dirs., Svc. award 1990), Coral Gables C. of C. (bd. dirs., past pres., past chmn.), Tau Beta Pi, Chi Epsilon (hon.). Club: Country of Coral Gables. Home: 4818 Alhambra Cir Coral Gables FL 33146-1615 Office: 350 Sevilla Ave Ste 210 Coral Gables FL 33134-6617

SAFFIR, LEONARD, public relations executive; b. N.Y.C., Apr. 19, 1930; s. Abraham and Gertrude (Samuels) S.; m. Patricia Roemer (div. 1980); children: Andrew, Michelle; m. Wendy McConaughy (div. 1992); 1 child, Samantha. Student, Syracuse U., 1948-51. Editor, bur. chief Internat. News Service, Dallas, Tokyo, 1953-58; producer Eng., Australia, Asia, 1958-60; ptnr. Haft, Saffir, Siegel Polit. Pub. Relations & Advt., N.Y.C., 1960-64; cons. Ferdinand Marcos, 1964; pub. Latin Am. Times, N.Y.C., 1965; exec. v.p. Franchises Internat., N.Y.C., 1965-69; chief of staff to Senator James Buckley U.S. Senate, Washington, 1970-76; pub., editor The Trib, N.Y.C., 1977-78, The Sun, Bridgehampton, N.Y., 1978-84; exec. v.p. Porter/Novelli, N.Y.C., 1984-90; pres. Jay DeBow & Ptnrs., 1990—, PR/E, 1990—, Sports Experience Internat., 1995—. Chmn. Marchi for Mayor, N.Y.C., 1973, Buckley for Senator, N.Y., 1976. Served as sgt. USMC, 1951-53. Recipient Silver Anvil and Big Apple awards Pub. Rels. Soc. Am., Mayor's award City of N.Y., others. Mem. Overseas Press Club (pres. 1988-89). Home: 11181 Boca Woods Ln Boca Raton FL 33428-1840

SAFFMAN, PHILIP G., mathematician; b. Leeds, Eng., Mar. 19, 1931; s. Sam Ralph and Sarah (Rebecca) S.; m. Ruth Arion, Sept. 2, 1954; children—Louise J., Mark E., Emma E. B.A., Trinity Coll., Cambridge U., 1953; M.A., Cambridge U., 1956, Ph.D., 1956. Asst. lectr. applied math. Cambridge U., 1958-60; reader in applied math. Kings Coll., London U., 1960-64; prof. fluid mechanics Calif. Inst. Tech., Pasadena, 1964-69; prof. applied math. Calif. Inst. Tech., 1969-95, Theodore von Kármán prof. applied math. and aeros., 1995—. Contbr. articles to profl. jours. Trinity Coll. fellow, 1955-59; recipient Otto Laporte award, Am. Physical Soc., 1994, Fluid Dynamics Award, Am. Inst. Aeronautics and Astronautics, 1995. Fellow Am. Acad. Arts and Scis., Royal Soc. London. Office: 217-50 Firestone Calif Inst Tech Pasadena CA 91125

SAFFORD, FLORENCE VIRAY SUNGA, travel agent and consultant; b. Masantol, Pampanga, Luzon, Philippines, Mar. 19, 1932; came to U.S., 1953; d. Filomeno Garcia and Dominga (Viray) Sunga; m. Francis Ingersoll Safford, Aug. 4, 1979; children: H. Robert, Erlinda Ann, Ruben Michael. BS in Edn., Adamson U., Manila, 1952; student Hotel Mgnt., Political Sci., Kapiolani C.C., Honolulu, 1975; student, Am. Travel Sch., Honolulu, 1977. Tchr. Cecilio Apostolic Elem. Sch., Manila, 1949-51, St. Michael Acad., Masantol, 1951-52; social worker Cath. Social Svc., Honolulu, 1970-77; cons. Travel Cons. of the Pacific, Honolulu, 1977—. Exec. bd. dirs. Oahu Cmty. Coun., 1994—; elected to Neighborhood Bd., 1982-84, 93-95; apptd. by mayor of Honolulu to Ethics Commn., 1986-95. Named Most Outstanding Leader of the Community, Filipino Jaycees of Honolulu, 1976. Mem. Women's Cmty. Action League of Hawaii (pres. 1972-96, Outstanding Pres. 1992), Filipino C. of C. of Hawaii (treas., bd. dirs. 1994, Outstanding award 1991-92), Aloha Bus. and Profl. Women's Club (treas., Outstanding award 1981-89). Republican. Roman Catholic. Avocations: counseling, dancing. Office: Travel Cons of Pacific PO Box 1238 Honolulu HI 96807

SAFFRAN, BERNARD, economist, educator; b. Bklyn., May 13, 1936; s. Isidore and Goldie (Bleeker) S.; m. Eleanor Meyerowitz, Aug. 23, 1959; children: Jenny, Linnea (dec.). BA, CCNY, 1956; PhD, U. Minn., 1963. Asst. prof. econs. U. Calif., Berkeley, 1961-67; assoc. prof. Swarthmore Coll., Pa., 1967-73, prof., 1973—, Franklin and Betty Barr prof. econs., 1989, chmn. dept. econs., 1976-83; sr. staff economist Coun. Econ. Advisors, Washington, 1971-72; vis. lectr. London Sch. Econse., 1979-80, CED Rsch. Adv. bd., 1992-96. Assoc. editor Jour. Econ. Perspectives, 1987—. Home: 201 Garrett Ave Swarthmore PA 19081-1433 Office: Swarthmore Coll Dept Econs Swarthmore PA 19081

SAFFRAN, KALMAN, engineering consulting company executive, entrepreneur; b. Boston, Dec. 28, 1947; s. Max and Marion (Patick) S. B.A., Northeastern U., 1971; postgrad. MIT, 1971-72. Lic. real estate broker, Mass. Mgr. systems MIT, 1972-76; corp. cons. United Brands Co., Boston, 1977-78; chief exec. officer Monitrex Corp., Boston, 1977-82; pres. Kalman Saffran Assocs., Inc., Newton, Mass., 1978—; bd. advisors Blackstone Bank and Trust Col, Boston; mem. network implementation panel U.S. Energy Research and Devel. Adminstrn., Washington, 1975-76; mem. computer com. MIT Lab. for Nuclear Sci., 1975-76. Mem. Data Processing Mgmt. Assn., Assn. Computing Machinery, Soc. for Info. Mgmt., IEEE, Mensa. Republican. Jewish. Home: 1564 Commonwealth Ave Newton MA 02165-2806 Office: Kalman Saffran Assocs Inc 1841 Commonwealth Ave Newton MA 02166-2725

SAFFRAN, MURRAY, biochemist; b. Montreal, Oct. 30, 1924; s. Isidore Irving and Rebecca Reva (Elimelech) S.; m. Judith Cohen, June 8, 1947; children—Michael David, Wilma Anne, Arthur Martin, Richard Eli. B.Sc., McGill U., 1945, M.Sc., 1946, Ph.D., 1949. Mem. faculty depts. psychiatry and biochemistry McGill U., Montreal, 1948-69; prof. McGill U., 1966-69; prof. biochemistry Med. Coll. Ohio, Toledo, 1969—, chmn. dept., 1969-80, asst. dean Med. Edn., 1992—; Dozor vis. prof. biochemistry Ben Gurion U., Israel, 1981; vis. prof. Inst. Biochemistry, Armenian Acad. Scis., Yerevan, 1988, U. Autonom, Guadalajara, 1991-94. Mem. editl. bd. Biochem. Edn., Med. Biochemistry Question Bank, Drug Delivery; contbr. articles to profl. jours. Recipient Ayerst-Squibb award Endocrine Soc., 1968. Fellow AAAS, Ohio Acad. Sci.; mem. Am. Soc. Biochemistry and Molecular Biology, Endocrine Soc., Internat. Brain Rsch. Orgn., Alpha Omega Alpha. Home: 2331 Hempstead Rd Toledo OH 43606-2447 Office: Med Coll Ohio PO Box 10008 Toledo OH 43699

SAFIAN, GAIL ROBYN, public relations executive; b. Bklyn., Dec. 12, 1947; d. Jack I. and Harriet S.; m. Jay Mark Eisenberg, Jan. 6, 1979; children: Julia, Eric. BA, SUNY, Albany, 1968; MBA, NYU, 1982. Reporter Albany (N.Y.)-Knickerbocker News/Times-Union, 1969, Athens (Ohio) Messenger, 1969-71; pub. relations asst. Mountainside Hosp., Montclair, N.J., 1971-74; dir. pub. relations Riverside Hosp., Boonton, N.J., 1974-78; consumer affairs coordinator Johnson & Johnson Personal Products Div., Milltown, N.J., 1978-79; v.p., group mgr. Harshe Rotman & Druck, N.Y.C., 1979-82; exec. v.p., dir. Health Care Div. Ruder Finn & Rotman, N.Y.C., 1982-84; v.p., mgr. client services Burson-Marsteller, N.Y.C., 1984-86; v.p., group mgr. health care Cohn & Wolfe, N.Y.C., 1986-90; exec. v.p., gen. mgr. MCS, Summit, N.J., 1990-94; pres. Safian Comm. Inc., Maplewood, N.J., 1994—. Mem. devel. com. Cancer Care, N.Y.C., 1985—. Recipient MacEachern award Am. Hosp. Assn., 1974, Communications Award Internat. Assn. Bus. Communicators, 1976, Creativity in Pub. Rels. award Inside PR, 1992, 93. Mem. N.Y. Acad. Scis., Drug Info. Assn., Women in Communications (Clarion award 1974), Healthcare Businesswomen's Assn. (mem. bd. dirs.). Jewish. Home: 31 Hickory Dr Maplewood NJ 07040-2107 Office: Safian Comm Inc 31 Hickory Dr Maplewood NJ 07040-2107

SAFIAN, KEITH FRANKLIN, hospital administrator; b. Bklyn., June 22, 1950; s. Jack I. and Harriet S. (Cohen) S.; m. Ellen Rita Babat, May 18, 1974; children: Elizabeth Anne, Alexander William. BS in EE and Indsl. Engring., SUNY, Buffalo, 1972; MBA, U. Pa., 1974. Asst. dir. Kings County Hosp. Ctr., Bklyn., 1974-76; asst. adminstr. NYU Med. Ctr., N.Y.C., 1977-80, assoc. adminstr., 1981-84, sr. assoc. adminstr., 1984-85; adminstr. St. John's Episcopal Hosp., Far Rockaway, N.Y., 1985-89; pres., CEO Phelps Meml. Hosp. Ctr., North Tarrytown, N.Y., 1989—. Bd. dirs. Addabbo Family Health Ctr., Arverne, N.Y., 1987-89, Rockaway Devel. and Revitalization Corp., Far Rockaway, 1988-89, chmn., 1995—; bd. dirs. The ExcelCare Sys., Bronxville, N.Y., 1993—, chmn. 1995—; chmn. No. Met. Hosp. Assn., Newburgh, N.Y., 1996. Fellow Am. Coll. Healthcare Execs.; mem. Hosp. Adminstrs. Club of N.Y. Home: 16 Brokaw Ln Great Neck NY 11023 Office: Phelps Memorial Hosp 701 N Broadway Tarrytown NY 10591

SAFIOL, GEORGE E., electronics company executive; b. Bklyn., Apr. 23, 1932; s. Charles and Effie (Patika) S.; m. Demetra Karambelas, July 12, 1958; children: Olympia Safiol Twomey, Peter, Christina. BS in Engring., NYU, 1954; postgrad. Sch. Engring., Columbia U., 1954-55. V.p., gen. mgr. No. Am. Telecom, ITT, Memphis, 1957-69; exec. v.p., chief operating officer Sycor, Inc., Ann Arbor, Mich., 1969-70; v.p. investments Heizer Co., Chgo., 1970-71; sr. v.p. Gen. Instrument Corp., Chicopee, Mass., 1971-77; pres., chief exec. officer Am. Biltrite, Framingham, Mass., 1977-83; various sr. exec. positions Gen. Instrument Corp., N.Y.C., 1984-87, chief operating offficer, pres., 1987—, also dir.; pvt. practice mgmt. cons., 1983-84. Served to 1st lt. U.S. Army, 1955-57. Mem. Alpha Omega. Republican. Greek Orthodox. Club: Metropolitan (N.Y.C.). Avocations: racquetball, golf, reading. Home: 64 Juniper Rd Weston MA 02193-1358

SAFIR, HOWARD, fire commissioner; b. N.Y.C., Feb. 24, 1942; s. George and Rose (Weiner) S.; m. Carol Ferrara, Nov. 21, 1965; children: Jennifer, Adam. BA in History and Polit. Sci., Hofstra U., 1963; postgrad., Bklyn. Law Sch., 1963-65; cert., Harvard U., 1988, 89. Spl. agent Fed. Bur. Narcotics; dep. chief spl. projects Bur. Narcotics and Dangerous Drugs, 1970-72; asst. regional dir. Drug Enforcement Administrn., 1972-74, spl. asst. for organized crime, 1974-75, chief spl. enforcement programs, 1975-76, dep. regional dir., 1976-77, asst. dir., 1977-79; chief witness security divsn. U.S. Marshals Svc., 1979-81, asst. dir. ops., 1979-84, assoc. dir. ops., 1984-90; pres. Safir Assocs. Ltd., 1990—; fire commr. N.Y.C. Fire Dept., 1994—; del. Interpol Gen. Assembly, 1981-88, Nat. Drug Policy Bd., 1986-88, Nat. Office Drug Policy; directed Warrant Apprehension Narcotic Team Program, 1989; dir. security Pres. Task Force on Victims of Crime, 1982; operational dir. security force fgn. delegations UN Gen. Assembly, 1979-89; nat. coord. Spl. Op. Mex. Nat. Heroin Interdiction Program, 1975, Spl. Op. SE Asia Interdiction Program, 1971; rep. Pres. Law Enforcement Com. Domestic Coun. Drug Abuse Task Force, 1975; mem. steering com. Nat. Conf. Organized Crime, 1975; dir. spl. investigations. Served USMCR, 1960-66. Mem. Internat. Assn. Chiefs of Police (chmn. N.Am. subcom., chmn. internat. adv. com. 1988-90 , Internat. Assn. Intelligence Analysts, Am. Soc. Indsl. Security, Pi Delta Epsilon. Office: Fire Dept 250 Livingston St Brooklyn NY 11201-5881

SAFIRE, WILLIAM, journalist, author; b. N.Y.C., Dec. 17, 1929; s. Oliver C. and Ida (Panish) S.; m. Helene Belmar Julius, Dec. 16, 1962; children: Mark Lindsey, Annabel Victoria. Student, Syracuse U., 1947-49. Reporter N.Y. Herald Tribune Syndicate, 1949-51; corr. WNBC-WNBT, Europe and Middle East, 1951; radio-TV producer WNBC, N.Y.C., 1954-55; v.p. Tex McCrary, Inc., 1955-60; pres. Safire Pub. Relations, Inc., 1960-68; spl. asst. to Pres. Nixon, Washington, 1969-73; columnist N.Y. Times, Washington, 1973—. Author: The Relations Explosion, 1963, Plunging into Politics, 1964, Safire's Political Dictionary, 1968, rev. edit., 1972-78, Before the Fall, 1975, Full Disclosure, 1977, Safire's Washington, 1980, On Language, 1980, What's the Good Word?, 1982, (with Leonard Safir) Good Advice on Writing, 1982, I Stand Corrected, 1984, Take My Word for It, 1986, Freedom, 1987, You Could Look It Up, 1988, Words of Wisdom, 1989, (with Leonard Safir) Leadership, 1990, Language Maven Strikes Again, 1990, Fumblerules, 1990, Coming to Terms, 1991, The First Dissident, 1992, Lend Me Your Ears, 1992, Good Advice on Writing, 1992, Quoth the Maven, 1993, Safire's New Political Dictionary, 1993, In Love with Norma Loquendi, 1994, Sleeper Spy, 1995. Served with AUS, 1952-54. Recipient Pulitzer prize for Disting. Commentary, 1978. Mem. Pulitzer Bd. Republican. Office: NY Times 1627 I St NW Washington DC 20006-4085

SAFLEY, JAMES ROBERT, lawyer; b. Cedar Rapids, Iowa, Sept. 19, 1943; s. Robert Starr and Jean (Engelman) S.; m. Dianne Lee McInnis; children: Anne Michele, Jamie Leigh. BA, U. Iowa, 1965; JD, Duke U., 1968. Bar: Minn. 1968, U.S. Ct. Appeals (4th, 6th, 8th and 9th cirs.), U.S. Supreme Ct. Law clk. U.S. Dist. Ct. Minn., Mpls., 1968-69; assoc. Robins, Kaplan, Miller & Ciresi, Mpls., 1969-74, ptnr., 1974—. Mem. adv. coun. Women's Intercollegiate Athletics, U. Minn., 1988-94; mem. Minn. Fed. Bar Assn. Commn. on ADR, 1995—. Mem. ABA, Minn. State Bar Assn. (antitrust sect. chmn. 1985-87), Hennepin County Bar Assn., Phi Beta Kappa. Office: Robins Kaplan Miller & Ciresi 2800 LaSalle Pla 800 Lasalle Ave Minneapolis MN 55402-2006

SAFONOV, MICHAEL GEORGE, electrical engineering educator, consultant; b. Pasadena, Calif., Nov. 1, 1948; s. George Michael and Ruth Garnet (Ware) S.; m. Nancy Kelshaw Schorn, Aug. 31, 1968 (div. Oct. 1983); 1 child, Alexander; m. Janet Sunderland, Feb. 25, 1985; 1 child, Peter. BSEE, MSEE, MIT, 1971, EE, 1976, PhDEE, 1977. Electronic engr. Air Force Cambridge Rsch. Lab., Hanscom AFB, Mass., 1968-71; rsch. asst. MIT, Cambridge, 1975-77; prof. elec. engring. U. So. Calif., L.A., 1977—, assoc. chmn. dept., 1989-93; vis. scholar Cambridge (Eng.) U., 1983-84, Imperial Coll., London, 1987, Calif. Inst. Tech., Pasadena, 1990-91; cons. Honeywell Systems and Rsch. Ctr., Mpls., 1978-83, Space Systems div. TRW, Redondo Beach, Calif., 1984, Northrop Aircraft, Hawthorne, Calif., 1985-91, also numerous others. Author: Stability and Robustness of Multivariable Feedback Systems (hon. mention Phi Beta Kappa 1981); co-author: (book and software) Robust-Control Toolbox, 1988; assoc. editor IEEE Trans. on Automatic Control, 1985-87, Internat. Jour. Robust and Nonlinear Control, 1989-93, Sys. and Control Letters, 1995—. Awards com. chair Am. Automatic Control Coun., 1993-95. Lt. (j.g.) USNR, 1972-75. Rsch. grantee Air Force Office Sci. Rsch., 1978—, NSF, 1982-84. Fellow IEEE; mem. AIAA (sr.), Common Cause. Democrat. Office: U So Calif Dept EE-Systems MC-2563 3740 Mcclintock Ave # 310 Los Angeles CA 90007-4012 *Consider first only the very simplest problem--but strive for a representation of the simplest problem that generalizes easily.*

SAFRAN, CLAIRE, writer, editor; b. N.Y.C.; d. Simon and Flora (R) S.; m. John Milton Williams, June 8, 1958; 1 son, Scott Edward. B.A. in English cum laude, Bklyn. Coll., 1951. News editor Photo Dealer mag., 1951-53; assoc. editor TV Radio Mirror, 1954-58; mng. editor Photoplay mag., 1958-61; editor TV Radio Mirror, 1961-65, IN mag., 1965-67; assoc. editor Family Weekly mag., 1967-68; editor Coronet mag., 1968-71; contbg. editor Redbook, 1974-77; exec. editor, 1977-78, contbg. editor, 1979-81; roving editor Reader's Digest, 1983-88; contbg. editor Woman's Day, 1988-91. Author: New Ways to Lower Your Blood Pressure, 1984, Secret Exodus, 1987; contbr. to maj. nat. mags., 1972—. Recipient Media award Am. Psychol. Found., 1977; finalist Penney-Missouri Mag. Awards, 1977, Merit award in journalism Religious Pub. Rels. Coun., 1978, hon. mention journalism awards Am. Acad. Pediatrics, 1979, 1st pl. nat. editorials Odyssey Inst. Media Awards, 1979, 80, 86, Matrix award Women in Comm., 1982, 83, 84, William Harvey award, 1984, 91, Journalism award Am. Acad. Family Physicians, 1984, Investigative Journalism citation Deadline Club, 1993, Cert. of Merit Cmty. Action Network, 1995. Mem. Am. Soc. Journalists and Authors (Outstanding Mag. Article award 1984, pres. 1996-97). Home: 53 Evergreen Ave Westport CT 06880-2563

SAFRAN, EDWARD MYRON, financial service company executive; b. Boston, Oct. 9, 1937; s. Morris and Sophie (Radin) S.; m. Harriet Reva Podolsky, Jan. 15, 1966; children: Steven, Rebecca. BS in Metall., MIT, 1959; MBA, Harvard U., 1961. Pres. Suncrest Corp., Worcester, Mass., 1962-65; exec. asst. Am. Metal Climax, N.Y.C., 1966; sr. auditor Gen. Electric Co., Lynn, Mass., 1966-68; fin. analyst Polaroid Corp., Cambridge, Mass., 1968-70, mgr. banking and investments, 1970-84, asst. treas., 1984-87; pres. Merganser Capital Mgmt. Corp., Cambridge, 1984—; chmn. Direct Fed. Credit Union, Needham, Mass., 1986—. Gleason Works fellow Harvard U., 1959-60. Mem. Fin. Execs. Inst., Bond Analysts Soc. of Boston. Home: 37 Barney Hill Rd Wayland MA 01778-3601 Office: Merganser Capital Mgmt Corp One Cambridge Ctr Cambridge MA 02142

SAFT, STUART MARK, lawyer; b. N.Y.C., Feb. 17, 1947; s. Stanley and Dorothy (Ligerman) S.; m. Stephanie C. Optekman, June 6, 1970; children:

Bradley S., Gordon D. BA, Hofstra U., 1968; JD, Columbia U., 1971. Bar: N.Y. 1972, Fla. 1975, U.S. Dist. Ct. (so. dist.) N.Y. 1975, U.S. Supreme Ct. 1990. Asst. gen. counsel Joseph Bancroft & Son Co., N.Y.C., 1972-74; ptnr. Brauner, Baron, Rosenzwerz, Kligler & Sparber, N.Y.C., 1974-81, Powsner, Saft & Powsner, N.Y.C., 1981-84, Goldschmidt & Saft, N.Y.C., 1984-88; Wolf Haldenstern Adler Freeman & Herz, N.Y.C., 1988—; chmn., bd. dirs. Coun. of N.Y. Coops., N.Y.C., 1981—; bd. dirs. Pvt. Industry Coun. of N.Y.C., Am. Women's Econ. Devel. Corp.; adj. asst. prof. NYU, Real Estate Inst. Author: Commercial Real Estate Forms, 3 vols., 1987, Commercial Real Estate Transactions, 1989, Commercial Real Estate Workouts, 1991, Real Estate Development: Strategies for a Changing Market, 1990, Commercial Real Estate Leasing, 1992, Real Estate Investor's Survival Guide, 1992, Commercial Real Estate Financing, 1993, Commercial Real Estate Forms, 2d edit., 5 vols., 1994, Commercial Real Estate Transactions, 2d edit., 1995, Commercial Real Estate Workouts, 2d edit., 1996; contbg. editor: The Real Estate Finance Jour., 1989—; contbr. articles to profl. jours. Served to capt. USAR, 1968-76. Mem. ABA, N.Y. Bar Assn., Fla. Bar Assn. Office: Wolf Haldenstein Adler Freeman & Herz 270 Madison Ave New York NY 10016-0601

SAGALKIN, SANFORD, lawyer; b. N.Y.C., June 24, 1942; s. Nathan and Blanche (Hoffner) S.; m. Monda E. Fifield, Aug. 25, 1969; children: Nicholas, Amy. BA, Queens Coll., 1964; LLB, Columbia U., 1967. Bar: N.Y. 1967, Alaska 1969, D.C. 1980, Md., 1986. Staff atty. N.Y. Mental Health Info. Service, N.Y.C., 1967-69; mem. firm Faulkner, Banfield, Doogan, Gross and Holmes, Juneau, Alaska, 1969-74; firm Ely, Guess & Rudd, Juneau, 1974-75; asst. atty. gen. Atty. Gen.'s Office, State of Alaska, 1975-77; dep. asst. atty. gen. Dept. Justice, Washington, 1977-80; mem. firm Ely, Guess & Rudd, Washington, 1980-82; pvt. practice Sharpsburg, Md., 1982-86; assoc. gen. counsel CIA, Washington, 1986—. Mem. Juneau Parks and Recreation Com., 1972-74; bd. dirs. Defenders of Wildlife, 1986-90. Mem. Alaska Bar Assn., D.C. Bar Assn., Md. Bar Assn. Democrat. Jewish. Office: CIA Washington DC 20505

SAGAMI, KIM, dancer; b. Inglewood, Calif.. Scholarship student, The Joffrey Ballet Sch. Dancer Am. Ballet Theatre II, N.Y.C., 1981-82, Garden State Ballet, 1982, The Joffrey Ballet, N.Y.C., 1983—. Office: The Joffrey Ballet 130 W 56th St New York NY 10019-3818

SAGAN, CARL EDWARD, astronomer, educator, author; b. N.Y.C., Nov. 9, 1934; s. Samuel and Rachel (Gruber) S.; m. Ann Druyan; children: Alexandra, Samuel; children by previous marriages: Dorion, Jeremy, Nicholas. AB with gen. and spl. honors, U. Chgo., 1954, BS, 1955, MS, 1956, PhD, 1960; ScD (hon.), Rensselaer Poly. Inst., 1975, Denison U., 1976, Clarkson Coll. Tech., 1977, Whittier Coll., 1978, Clark U., 1978, U. S.C., 1984, Hofstra U., 1985, L.I. U., 1987, Tuskegee U., 1988, Lehigh U., 1990, Wheaton Coll., 1993, SUNY, Albany, 1994; DHL (hon.), Skidmore Coll., 1976, Lewis and Clark Coll., 1980, Bklyn. Coll., CUNY, 1982; LLD (hon.), U. Wyo., 1978, Drexel U., 1986, Queens U., 1993; DScL (hon.), U. Ill., 1990; LHD (hon.), U. Hartford, 1991. Miller research fellow U. Calif.-Berkeley, 1960-62; vis. asst. prof. genetics Stanford Med. Sch., 1962-63; astrophysicist Smithsonian Astrophys. Obs., Cambridge, Mass., 1962-68; asst. prof. Harvard U., 1962-67; mem. faculty Cornell U., 1968—, prof. astronomy and space scis., 1970—, David Duncan prof., 1976—, dir. Lab. Planetary Studies, 1968—, assoc. dir. Center for Radiophysics and Space Research, 1972-81, Johnson Disting. lectr. Johnson Grad. Sch. Mgmt., 1985; pres. Carl Sagan Prodns. (Cosmos TV series), 1977—; nonresident fellow Robotics Inst., Carnegie-Mellon U., 1982—; NSF-Am. Astron. Soc. vis. prof. various colls., 1963-67, Condon lectr., Oreg., 1967-68; Holiday lectr. AAAS, 1970; Vanuxem lectr. Princeton U., 1973; Smith lectr. Dartmouth Coll., 1974, 77; Wagner lectr. U. Pa., 1975; Bronowski lectr. U. Toronto, 1975; Philips lectr. Haverford Coll., 1975; Disting. scholar Am. U., 1976; Danz lectr. U. Wash., 1976; Clark Meml. lectr. U. Tex., 1976; Stahl lectr. Bowdoin Coll., 1977; Christmas lectr. Royal Instn., London, 1977; Menninger Meml. lectr. Am. Psychiat. Assn., 1978, Adolf Meyer lectr., 1984; Carver Meml. lectr. Tuskegee Inst., 1981; Feinstone lectr. U.S. Mil. Acad., 1981; Pal lectr. Motion Picture Acad. Arts and Scis., 1982; Dodge lectr. U. Ariz., 1982; Disting. lectr. USAF Acad., 1983; Lowell lectr. Harvard U., 1984; Poynter fellow, Schultz lectr. Yale U., 1984; Disting. lectr. Fla. State U., 1984; Jack Disting. Am. lectr., Ind. U., Pa., 1984; Keystone lectr. Nat. War Coll., Nat. Def. U., Washington, 1984-86; Marshall lectr. Nat. Resources Def. Coun., Washington, 1985; Gifford lectr. in natural theology U. Glasgow, 1985; Lilenthal lectr. Calif. Acad. Sci., 1986; Dolan lectr. Am. Pub. Health Assn., 1986; von Braun lectr. U. Ala., Huntsville, 1987; Gilbert Grosvenor Centennial lectr. Nat. Geog. Soc., Washington, 1988; Murata lectr., Kyoto, Japan, 1989; Bart Bok Centennial lectr. Astron. Soc. of the Pacific, 1989, James R. Thompson Leadership lectr. Ill. Math. and Sci. Acad., 1991, Nehru Meml. lectr. New Delhi, 1991, Boyer lectr. Stanford U., 1993, Robert Resnick lectr. in physics Rensselaer Poly. Inst., 1993; other lectureships; mem. various adv. groups NASA and Nat. Acad. Scis., 1959—; mem. council Smithsonian Instn., 1975-80; vice chmn. working group moon and planets, space orgn. Internat. Council Sci. Unions, 1968-74; lectr. Apollo flight crews NASA, 1969-72; chmn. U.S. del. joint conf. U.S. Nat. and Soviet Acads. Sci. on Communication with Extraterrestrial Intelligence, 1971; responsible for Pioneer 10 and 11 and Voyager 1 and 2 interstellar messages; judge Nat. Book Awards, 1975; mem. fellowship panel Guggenheim Found., 1976—; disting. vis. scientist Jet Propulsion Lab., Calif. Inst. Tech., 1986—; researcher physics and chemistry of planetary atmospheres and surfaces, origin of life, exobiology, Mariner, Viking, Voyager amd Galileo spacecraft observations of planets, long-term consequences nuclear war. Author: Atmospheres of Mars and Venus, 1961, Planets, 1966, Intelligent Life in the Universe, 1966, Planetary Exploration, 1970, Mars and the Mind of Man, 1973, The Cosmic Connection, 1973, Other Worlds, 1975, The Dragons of Eden, 1977, Murmurs of Earth: The Voyager Interstellar Record, 1978, Broca's Brain, 1979, Cosmos, 1980, (novel) Contact, 1985, (with Ann Druyan) Comet, 1985, (with Richard Turco) Path Where No Man Thought: Nuclear Winter and the End of the Arms Race, (with Ann Druyan) Shadows of Forgotten Ancestors: A Search for Who We Are, 1993, Pale Blue Dot, 1994; also numerous articles; editor: Icarus: Internat. Jour. Solar System Studies, 1968-79, Planetary Atmospheres, 1971, Space Research, 1971, UFOs: A Scientific Debate, 1972, Communication with Extraterrestrial Intelligence, 1973; editorial bd.: Origins of Life, 1974-84, Icarus, 1962—, Climatic Change, 1976-90, Science 80, 1979-82. Mem. bd. advisors Children's Health Fund, N.Y.C., 1988—. Recipient Smith prize Harvard U., 1964, NASA medal for exceptional sci. achievement, 1972, Prix Galabert, 1973, John W. Campbell Meml. award, 1974, Klumpke-Roberts prize, 1974, Priestley award, 1975, NASA medal for disting. pub. service, 1977, 81, Pulitzer prize for lit., 1978, Washburn medal, 1978, Rittenhouse medal, 1980, Peabody award, 1981, Hugo award, 1981, Seaborg prize, 1981, Roe medal, 1981, Environment Programme medal UN, 1984, SANE Nat. Peace award, 1984, Regents medal Bd. Regents Univ. of State N.Y., 1984, Ann. award Physicians for Social Responsibility, 1985, Disting. Svc. award World Peace Film Festival, 1985, Honda prize Honda Found., 1985, Nahum Goldmann medal World Jewish Congress, 1986, Ann. award of merit Am. Cons. Engrs. Coun., 1986, Maurice Eisendrath award Cen. Conf. Am. Rabbis and Union Am. Hebrew Congregations, 1987, In Praise of Reason award Com. for Sci. Investigation of Claims of the Paranormal, 1987, Konstantin Tsiolkovsky medal Soviet Cosmonautics Fedn., 1987, George F. Kennan Peace award SANE/Freeze, 1988, Roger Baldwin award Mass. Civil Liberties Union, 1989, Oersted medal Am. Assn. Physics Tchrs., 1990, Ann. award for Outstanding TV Script Writers Guild Am., 1991, UCLA medal UCLA, 1991, Disting. Leadership award Nuclear Age Peace Found., 1993, 1st Carl Sagan Pub. Understanding of Sci. award Coun. Sci. Soc. Pres., 1993, 1st Isaac Asimov award Com. Sci. Investigation of Claims of Paranormal, 1994, Public Welfare medal NAS, 1994, award for Pub. Understanding of Sci. and Tech. AAAS 1995; named Humanist of Yr. by Am. Humanist Assn., 1981; NSF fellow, 1955-60, Sloan research fellow, 1963-67. Fellow AAAS (chmn. astronomy sect. 1975, John Wesley Powell Meml. lectr. Tucson, 1992, Award for Public Understanding of Science and Technology, 1995), AIAA, Am. Geophys. Union (pres. planetology sect. 1980-82), Am. Astronautical Soc. (council 1976-81, Kennedy award 1983), Brit. Interplanetary Soc., Explorers Club (75th Anniversary award 1980); hon. mem. NAS, mem. Am. Phys. Soc. (Leo Szilard award 1985), Am. Astron. Soc. (councillor, chmn. div. for planetary scis. 1975-76, Masursky award 1991, Annenberg Found. prize 1993), Fedn. Am. Scientists (council 1977-81, bd. sponsors 1988—, Ann. award 1985), Soc. Study of Evolution, Genetics Soc. Am., Internat. Astron. Union, Internat. Acad. Astronautics, Internat. Soc. Study Origin of Life (council 1980—), Planetary Soc. (pres. 1979—), Authors Guild, Astron. Soc. of the Pacific, Coun. Fgn. Rels., Coun. Econ. Priorities, Phi Beta Kappa, Sigma Xi. Office: Cornell U Space Sci Bldg 302 CRSR Ithaca NY 14853*

SAGAN, HANS, mathematician, educator, author; b. Vienna, Austria, Feb. 15, 1928; came to U.S., 1954, naturalized, 1960; s. Hans and Josefa (Seif) S.; m. Ingeborg Ulbrich, Mar. 20, 1954; 1 child, Ingrid. Ph.D. in Math., U. Vienna, 1950. Asst. prof. U. Tech., Vienna, 1950-54; asst. prof. Mont. State U., Bozeman, 1954-57; assoc. prof. U. Idaho, Moscow, 1957-61, prof., head dept., 1961-63; prof. N.C. State U., Raleigh, 1963-94, prof. emeritus, 1994—; vis. prof. U. Tech., Munich, 1964, U. Vienna, 1972, 95; vis. lectr. Math. Assn. Am., 1963-73, 77—; assoc. editor Math. Mag., 1963-73; mem. sci. adv. bd. Monatshefte für Mathematik, 1994—. Co-author: Die Laplace Transformation and Ihre Anwendung, 1953; author: Boundary and Eigenvalue Problems in Mathematical Physics, 1961, Integral and Differential Calculus-an Intuitive Approach, 1962, Introduction to the Calculus of Variations, 1969, Advanced Calculus, 1974, Beat the Odds, 1980, Calculus-Accompanied on the Apple, 1984, Space-Filling Curves, 1994; co-author: Ten Easy Pieces, 1980; also articles in field. Recipient Outstanding Faculty award U. Idaho, 1959-60; Poteat award N.C. Acad. Sci., 1966. Mem. Math. Assn. Am., AAUP, Oesterreichische Mathematische Gesellschaft, Sigma Xi. Avocations: swimming; sailing; horseback riding; fishing.

SAGAN, JOHN, former automobile company executive; b. Youngstown, Ohio, Mar. 9, 1921; s. John and Mary (Jubinsky) S.; m. Margaret Pickett, July 24, 1948; children: John, Linda, Scott. B.A. in Econs, Ohio Wesleyan U., 1948; M.A., U. Ill., 1949, Ph.D., 1951; Fellow, Ohio Wesleyan U., 1946-48; scholar, fellow research, U. Ill., 1948-51. Various positions Ford Motor Co., Dearborn, Mich., 1951-66; v.p., treas. Ford Motor Co., 1966-86; pres. John Sagan Assocs., Dearborn, 1986—; bd. dirs. Telident Corp., Chartwell Corp., SBCM Derivatives Products, Ltd. Trustee Ohio Wesleyan U., 1964—, Com. Econ. Devel. U.S.A., Oakwood Hosp., Dearborn, Mich., YMCA Found., Detroit Fund for Henry Ford Hosp. Served with USNR, 1943-46. Mem. Am. Econ. Assn., Phi Beta Kappa, Phi Kappa Phi, Delta Sigma Rho. Home and Office: 22149 Long Blvd Dearborn MI 48124-1104

SAGANSKY, JEFF, broadcast executive. BA, Harvard U., MBA. Fin. analyst CBS-TV, 1976-77; mgr. film programs NBC-TV, 1977, dir. dramatic devel. entertainment div., 1978, sr. v.p. series programming, 1982-85; v.p. devel. David Gerber Co., 1979-82; pres. prodn., then pres. Tri-Star Pictures Inc., 1985-90; pres. CBS Entertainment Divsn., 1990-94; exec. v.p. Sony U.S., 1994—. Office: Sony Corp Am 550 Madison Ave New York NY 10022

SAGAWA, SHIRLEY SACHI, lawyer; b. Rochester, N.Y., Aug. 25, 1961; d. Hidetaka H. and Patricia (Ford) S.; m. Gregory A. Baer; children: Jackson Ford Baer, Matthew Sagawa Baer. AB, Smith Coll., 1983; MSc, London Sch. Econs., 1984; JD, Harvard U., 1987. Bar: Md. 1988. Chief counsel youth policy, labor and human resources com. U.S. Senate, Washington, 1987-91; sr. counsel and dir. family and youth policy Nat. Women's Law Ctr., Washington, 1991-93; spl. asst. to Pres. Clinton for domestic policy, 1993; exec. dir., mng. dir., exec. v.p. Corp. for Nat. and Comty. Svc., Washington, 1993—. Mem. exec. bd. Orgn. for Pan-Asian Am. Women, Washington, 1987-89; mem. Women of Color Leadership Coun., 1991-92; vice chair, bd. dirs. Nat. Community Svc. Commn., 1991-93. Recipient Philip V. McGance award Coun. for Advancement of Citizenship, 1991, cert. of recognition Nat. Coun. Jewish Women, 1989, Alexandrine medal Coll. St. Catherine, St. Paul, 1995; Harry S. Truman scholar, 1981; Smith Coll. Alumnae Assn. fellow, 1983, AAUW fellow, 1986. Mem. Md. Bar Assn. Democrat. Episcopalian. Office: Corp for Nat and Community Svc 1201 New York Ave NW Washington DC 20005-3917

SAGAWA, YONEO, horticulturist, educator; b. Olaa, Hawaii, Oct. 11, 1926; s. Chikatada and Mume (Kuno) S.; m. Masayo Yamamoto, May 24, 1962 (dec. Apr. 1988); children: Penelope Toshiko, Irene Teruko. AB, Washington U., St. Louis, 1950, MS, 1952; PhD, U. Conn., 1956. Postdoctoral research assoc. biology Brookhaven Nat. Lab., Upton, N.Y., 1955-57; guest in biology Brookhaven Nat. Lab., 1958; asst. prof., then assoc. prof. U. Fla., 1957-64; dir. undergrad. sci. ednl. research participation program NSF, 1964; cons. biosatellite project NASA, 1966-67; prof. horticulture U. Hawaii, 1964—; dir. Lyon Arboretum, 1967-91; assoc. dir. Hawaiian Sci. Fair, 1966-67, dir., 1967-68; research assoc. in biology U. Calif., Berkeley, 1970-71; rsch. assoc. Bishop Mus., Honolulu, 1992—, Botanical Rsch. Inst. of Tex., 1993—; external assessor U. Pertanian, Malaysia, 1994—; mem. Internat. Orchid Commn. on Classification, Nomenclature and Registration; fellow Inst. voor Toepassing van Atoomengerie in de Landbouw, U. Agr., Wageningen, The Netherlands, 1979-80; mem. sci. adv. bd. Nat. Tropical Bot. Garden, Kawai, Hawaii; councilor Las Cruces Bot. Garden, Costa Rica; cons. FAO, Singapore, 1971, USAID-Agribusiness Assistance Program, Vols. in Overseas Cooperative Assistance, UN Devel. Program-UN Internat. Short Term Advisory Resources; dir. Hawaii Tropical Bot. Garden. Editor: Hawaii Orchid Jour., 1972—, Pacific Orchid Soc. Bull., 1966-71; mem. editl. bd.: Allertonia, 1976; contbr. numerous articles to profl. jours. Trustee Friends of Honolulu Bot. Gardens, 1973—. Recipient Disting. Svc. award South Fla. Orchid Soc., 1968, Cert. of Achievement Garden Club Am., 1995; grantee Am. Orchid Soc., AEC, NIH, HEW, IMS, Stanley Smith Hort. Trust, Honolulu Orchid Soc. Fellow Am. Orchid Soc. (hon. life); mem. AAAS, Internat. Assn. Hort. Sci., Am. Assn. Hort. Sci., Am. Inst. for Biol. Scis., Bot. Sco. Am., Hawn Bot. Soc. (past v.p.), Internat. Assn. Plant Tissue Culture, Internat. Palm Soc., Am. Anthurium Soc. (hon. life), Pacific Orchid Soc. (trustee 1994), Kaimuki Orchid Soc. (hon. life), Honolulu Orchid Soc. (hon., life), Lyon Arboretum Assn. (trustee 1974-91), Garden Club Honolulu (hon., life), Aloha Bonsai Club, Atomic Energy Commn., Inst. Mus. Svcs., Sigma Xi, Gamma Sigma Delta, Phi Kappa Phi (past pres., v.p., councillor Va. chpt.). Democrat. Office: U Hawaii Horticulture Rm 102 3190 Maile Way Honolulu HI 96822-2232

SAGE, ANDREW GREGG CURTIN, II, corporate investor, manager; b. Bryn Mawr, Pa., Mar. 11, 1926; s. Henry W. and Eleanor (Purviance) S.; m. Sara Wakefield, Sept. 29, 1956; children: Andrew Gregg Curtin III, Sally. Mem. staff DeCoppet & Doremus (odd lot stock house), N.Y.C., 1946-47, Sage & Co., N.Y. Stock Exchange Specialists, N.Y.C., 1947-48; assoc. Lehman Bros., N.Y.C., 1948-60; gen. partner Lehman Bros., 1960-68, pres., 1970-73, vice chmn., 1973-77, mng. dir., 1977-82; mng. dir. Lehman Bros Kuhn Loeb, Inc., 1977-82; mng. dir. Shearson Lehman Bros., Inc., 1982-87, sr. cons., 1987-90; pres., CEO, dir. Robertson CECO Corp., Boston, 1992-93, chmn. bd. dirs., 1994—; bd. dirs. Fluid Conditioning Products, Lititz, Pa., Tom's Foods, Computervision Corp.; pres., treas. Sage Land Devel. Co.; pres., dir. Sage Capital Corp. Served with USAAF, 1944-46. Home: PO Box 937 Wilson WY 83014-0937

SAGE, ANDREW PATRICK, JR., systems information and software engineering educator; b. Charleston, S.C., Aug. 27, 1933; s. Andrew Patrick and Pearl Louise (Britt) S.; m. LaVerne Galhouse, Mar. 3, 1962; children: Theresa Annette, Karen Margaret, Philip Andrew. BS in Elec. Engring, The Citadel, 1955; SM, MIT, 1956; PhD, Purdue U., 1960; DEng (hon.), U. Waterloo, Can., 1987. Registered profl. engr., Tex. Instr. elec. engring. Purdue U., 1956-60; assoc. prof. U. Ariz., 1960-63; mem. tech. staff Aerospace Corp., Los Angeles, 1963-64; prof. elec. engring. and nuclear engring. scis. U. Fla., 1964-67; prof., dir. Info. and Control Scis. Center, So. Methodist U., Dallas, 1967-74; head elec. engring. dept. So. Meth. U., 1973-74; Quarles prof. engring. sci. and systems U. Va., Charlottesville, 1974-84; chmn. dept. chem. engring. U. Va., 1974-75, chmn. dept. engring. sci. and systems, 1977-84, assoc. dean, 1974-80; First Am. Bank prof. info. tech. George Mason U., Fairfax, Va., 1984—, assoc. v.p. for acad. affairs, 1984-85; dean Sch. Info. Tech. and Engring. George Mason U., 1985—; cons. Martin Marietta, Collins Radio, Atlantic Richfield, Tex. Instruments, LTV Aerospace, Battelle Meml. Inst., TRW Sys., NSF, Inst. Def. Analyses, Planning Rsch. Corp., MITRE, Engring. Rsch. Assocs., Software Productivity Consortium; gen. chmn. Internat. Conf. on Sys., Man and Cybernetics, 1974, 87; mem. spl. program panel on sys. sci. NATO, 1981-82; trustee, cons. Ctr. Naval Analysis, 1990-94. Author: Optimum Systems Control, 1968, 2d edit., 1977, Estimation Theory with Applications to Communications and Control, 1971, System Identification, 1971, An Introduction to Probability and Stochastic Processes, 1973, Methodology for Large Scale Systems, 1977, Systems Engineering: Methodology and Applications, 1977, Linear Systems Control, 1978, Economic Systems Analysis, 1983, System Design for Human Interaction, 1987, Information Processing in Systems and Organizations, 1990, Introduction to Computer Systems Analysis, Design, and Applications, 1989, Software Systems Engineering, 1990, Decision Support Systems Engineering, 1991, Systems Engineering, 1992, Systems Management for Information Technology and Software Engineering, 1995; assoc. editor IEEE Transactions on Systems Sci. and Cybernetics, 1968-72; editor: IEEE Transactions on Systems, Man and Cybernetics, 1972—; assoc. editor: Automatica, 1968-81; editor, 1981—; mem. editl. bd. Systems Engring, 1968-72, IEEE Spectrum, 1972-73, Computers and Elec. Engring., 1972-94, Jour. Interdisciplinary Modeling and Simulation, 1976-80, Internat. Jour. Intelligent Sys., 1986—, Orgn. Sci.-94, 1990; editor Elsevier North Holland textbook series in sys. sci. and engring., 1970-88, John Wiley textbook series on sys. engring., 1989—; co-editor-in-chief Jour. Large Scale Sys.: Theory and Applications, 1978-88, Info. and Decision Technologies, 1988-94, Info. and Sys. Engring., 1995—; contbr. articles on computer sci. and sys. engring. to profl. jours. Recipient Norbert Wiener award, 1980, Joseph G. Wohl career award, 1991, Superior Pub. Svc. award Sec. of the Navy, 1994; Case Centennial scholar, 1980, Award Washington Soc. of Engrs., 1996. Fellow IEEE (M. Barry Carlton award 1970, Centennial medal 1984, Outstanding Contbn. award 1986, Donald G. Fink prize 1994), AAAS (chmn. sect. M 1990), IEEE Sys. Soc.; mem. Man and Cybernetics Soc. (pres. 1984-85, Inst. Mgmt. Scis., Internat. Fedn. Automatic Control (Outstanding Svc. award), Am. Soc. Engring. Edn. (Frederick Emmonds Terman award 1970, Centennial cert. for exceptional contbn. 1993), Washington Soc. Engrs. (award 1996), Inst. for Mgmt. Sci. and Ops. Rsch., Sigma Xi, Eta Kappa Nu, Tau Beta Pi. Home: 8011 Woodland Hills Ln Fairfax VA 22039-2433 Office: George Mason U Sch Info Tech Fairfax VA 22030-4444

SAGER, CAROLE BAYER, lyricist, singer; b. N.Y.C., Mar. 8, 1947; d. Elias and Anita (Nathan) Bayer; m. Burt Bacharach, 1982 (div.); 1 son, Cristopher Elton. B.S. in Speech and Dramatic Art, N.Y. U., 1967. Lyricist numerous songs including Midnight Blue, A Groovy Kind of Love, Don't Cry Out Loud, You're Moving Out Today, Nobody Does It Better, When I Need You, Come In From the Rain, I'm Coming Home Again, I'd Rather Leave While I'm In Love, Heartbreaker, You're the Only One, If You Remember Me, 1979, It's My Turn, 1981, Arthur's Theme (Best that You Can Do) (Academy award 1982) That's What Friends Are For, 1986 (Grammy award 1987; recorded by Dionne Warwick, Elton John, Stevie Wonder, Gladys Knight), On My Own (Patti La Belle and Michael Mac Donald), Love Power, (Dionne Warwick and Jeffrey Osborne), Heartlight (Neil Diamond); Love is My Decision (Chris De Burgh), The Day I Fall in Love (from Beethoven's 2nd, 1993, Academy award nominee, Best Original Song, 1993); lyricist in collaboration with Marvin Hamlisch (Broadway play) They're Playing Our Song, 1979, Dancin', 1978; also movies The Spy Who Loved Me, 1977, Ice Castles, 1979, Arthur, 1981, Continental Divide, 1981, The Devil and Max Devlin, 1981, I Ought to Be in Pictures, 1982, Night Shift, 1982, Making Love, 1983, Tough Guys, 1986, Baby Boom, 1987, Three Men and A Baby, 1987, Arthur 2: On the Rocks, 1988; rec. artist, 1977—; albums include: Carole Bayer Sager, 1977, Carole Bayer Sager, Too, 1979, Carole Bayer Sager/Sometimes Late at Night, 1981 (Voted Best New Artist in France and Germany, German Record Acad. 1977); collaborated with numerous composers including Peter Allen, Marvin Hamlisch, Alice Cooper, Mike MacDonald, Melissa Manchester, Bette Midler, Bruce Roberts, Neil Sedaka, Burt Bacharach; author: (novel) Extravagant Gestures, 1986. Recipient Academy award for best song (Arthur's Theme), 1982; Acad. award nom. Best Original Song ("Look What Love Has Done" from Junior, 1994); Grammy award for song of the yr., (That's What Friends Are For), 1986. Office: care Guttman & Pam 118 S Beverly Dr Ste 201 Beverly Hills CA 90212-3016

SAGER, CLIFFORD J(ULIUS), psychiatrist, educator; b. N.Y.C.; s. Max and Lena (Lipman) S.; m. Anne Scheinman; children by previous marriage: Barbara L., Philip T., Rebecca J., Anthony F. BS, Pa. State U., 1937; MD, NYU, 1941; cert. in psychoanalysis, N.Y. Med. Coll., 1949. Diplomate: Am. Bd. Psychiatry and Neurology. Rotating intern Montefiore Hosp., N.Y.C., 1941-42; resident in psychiatry Bellevue Hosp., N.Y.C., 1942, 46-48; practice medicine specializing in psychiatry N.Y.C., 1946—; dir. therapeutic services, asso. dean Postgrad. Ctr. Mental Health, 1948-60; vis. psychiatrist, med. bd. Flower and Fifth Ave Hosp., 1960-71, Met. Hosp., 1960-71; dir. psychiat. tng. and edn. N.Y. Med. Coll., 1960-71; attending psychiatrist Bird S. Coler Hosp., 1960-71; clin. dir. N.Y. Med. Coll., 1960-63, assoc. prof. psychiatry, 1960-65, prof., 1966-71, dir. partial hosp. programs and family treatment and study unit, 1964-71; clin. prof. psychiatry Mt. Sinai Sch. Medicine, 1971-80; assoc. dir. psychiatry Beth Israel Hosp. for Family and Mental Therapy; chief of psychiatry Gov.'s Hosp., 1970-74; dir. family therapy Mt. Sinai Sch. Medicine, 1974-80; clin. prof. psychiatry N.Y. Hosp.-Cornell Univ. Med. Ctr., 1980—; attending psychiatrist N.Y. Hosp.-Payne Whitney Clinic, 1980—; dir. marital and family clinic N.Y. Hosp., 1991—; attending psychiatrist Mt. Sinai Hosp., 1971-80; chief behavioral scis. Gouverneur Hosp.; chief family treatment unit Beth Israel Med. Ctr., 1970-74, assoc. dir. psychiatry family and group therapy, 1971-74; psychiat. dir. Jewish Family Svc., 1974-77; dir. family psychiatry Jewish Bd. Family and Childrens Svcs., 1978-90; dir. Remarried Consultation Svc., 1976-90; dir. Tng. and Sex Therapy Clinic, 1974-90; founder The Relationship Inst., N.Y.C., 1990—; psychiat. dir. Employee Consultation and Corp. Health Programs, JBFCS, 1980—; faculty , supr. Contemporary Ctr. Advanced Psychoanalytic Studies; chief neuropsychiatry 42d and 312th Gen. Hosp. Author: Marriage Contracts and Couple Therapy, 1976, Intimate Partners, 1979, Treating the Remarried Family, 1983; 4 other books; mem. editorial bd. Am. Jour. Orthopsychiatry, 1960-69, Internat. Jour. Group Psychotherapy, 1968—, Family Process, 1969-92, Divorce and Remarriage, 1977—, Comprehensive Rev. Jour. Family and Marriage, 1978—; cons. Sexual Medicine, 1974-82; co-editor, founder Jour. Sex and Marital Therapy, 1974—; mem. editorial bd.: Jour. Marriage and Family Counseling, 1977—, Internat. Jour. Family Counseling, 1977—; author or contbr. over 88 sci. articles to jours. Capt. M.C. AUS, 1942-46, chief neuropsychiatry 42d and 312th Gen. Hosp. Recipient Am. Family Therapy Assn. award for Outstanding Contribution to Family Therapy 1983, Assn. Marriage and Family Therapists award for Outstanding Contributions to the field of Marital and Family Therapy, 1984. Fellow Am. Psychiat. Assn. (life), Am. Orthopsychiat. Assn. (life), Acad. Psychoanalysis (charter), Am. Group Psychotherapy Assn. (pres. 1968-70, dir. 1962-74), Soc. Med. Psychoanalysts (pres. 1960-61, dir. 1958-62), Am. Assn. Marital and Famiy Therapists; mem. AMA, Am. Soc. Advancement Psychotherapy (dir. 1954-67), N.Y. Soc. Clin. Psychiatry, Soc. for Sex Therapy and Rsch. (pres. 1976-77, bd. dirs. 1953-58) PAIRS Found. (bd. dirs. 1985—). Office: 65 E 76th St New York NY 10021-1844 also: 33 Breeze Hill Rd East Hampton NY 11937-4505

SAGER, DONALD JACK, publisher, former librarian; b. Milw., Mar. 3, 1938; s. Alfred Herman and Sophia (Sagan) S.; m. Sarah Ann Long, May 23, 1987; children: Geoffrey, Andrew. BS, U. Wis., Milw., 1963; MSLS, U. Wis., 1964. Sr. documentalist AC Electronics divsn. GM, Milw., 1958-63; teaching asst. U. Wis., Madison, 1963-64; dir. Kingston (N.Y.) Pub. Libr., 1964-66, Elyria (Ohio) Pub. Libr., 1966-71, Mobile Pub. Libr., 1971-75, Pub. Libr. Columbus and Franklin County, Ohio, 1975-78; commr. Chgo. Pub. Libr., 1978-81; dir. Elmhurst Pub. Libr., Ill., 1982-83, Milw. Pub. Libr., 1983-91; pub. Highsmith Press, Ft. Atkinson, Wis., 1991—; sec. Online Computer Libr. Ctr., 1977-78, disting. vis. scholar, 1982; chmn. mus. com. PLA Pub. Libr., 1989-91, history com., 1993-95, chmn. investment com., 1985-89, chmn. PLA nat. conf. com., 1986-88; bd. dirs. Coun. Wis. Librs., 1982-91, Urban Librs. Coun., 1985-93, sec., 1991-93; adj. faculty U. Wis., Milw., 1984-91; cons. in field. Author: Reference: A Programmed Instruction, 1970, Binders, Books and Budgets, 1971, Participatory Management, 1981, The American Public Library, 1982, Public Library Administrators Planning Guide to Automation, 1983, Managing the Public Library, 1984, 2d rev. edit., 1989, Small Libraries, 1992, 2d rev. edit., 1996; co-editor: Urban Library Management Trends, 1989; contbg. editor: Public Libraries, 1990—; contbr. articles to profs. publs. Bd. dirs. Goethe House, 1985-91; pres. Milw. Civic Alliance, 1990-91; chmn. Milw. United Way Campaign, 1984; pres. Milw. Westown Assn., 1987-90. With inf. AUS, 1956-58. Mem. ALA (coun. mem. 1995—), Pub. Libr. Assn. (bd. dirs., v.p., pres.-elect, pres. 1982-83), Ill. Libr. Assn., Chgo. Book Clinic, Wis. Libr. Assn., Wis. Libr. Assn. Found. (chmn. 1986-88), Libr. Adminstrn. Assn. Wis. (chmn. 1987-88), Exch. Club Milw. (pres. 1988-89). Home: 590 Wilmot Rd Deerfield IL 60015-4206 Office: Highsmith Press 5527W Highway 106 Fort Atkinson WI 53538

SAGER, PHILIP TRAVIS, academic physician, cardiac electrophysiologist; b. N.Y.C., Jan. 23, 1956; s. Clifford Julius and Ruth (Levy) S.; m. Jodi Lauren Halpern, Nov. 29, 1986. BS in Chemistry and Biology, MIT, Cambridge, Mass., 1977; MD, Yale U., New Haven, Conn., 1982, resident, cardiology fellow, 1982-88. Diplomate Am. Bd. Internal Medicine Sch. Cardiology, AM. Bd. Cardiac Electrophysiology. Asst. prof. medicine Sch. Medicine, U. So. Calif., L.A., 1988-90, asst. dir. electrophysiology, 1988-90, dir. Pacemaker Ctr., 1988-90; asst. prof. medicine Sch. Medicine, UCLA, 1990-96; dir. cardiac electrophysiology West L.A. VA Med. Ctr., 1990-96; assoc. prof. medicine Sch. Medicine, UCLA, 1996—; assoc. prof. of medicine UCLA Sch. Medicine, 1996—; mem. cardiology adv. com. VA Adminstrn., Washington, 1990-94; cons. electrophysiology ACGME, Chgo., 1995—; vis. prof. Kern Med. Ctr., Bakersfield, Calif., 1991, 94, U. Iowa Sch. Medicine, 1994, Northwestern U. Sch. Medicine, 1994, Yale U. Sch. Medicine, 1995; invited lectr. Contbr. chpts. to books, numerous articles to profl. jours. grantee AHA, 1996. Fellow Am. Coll. Cardiology, Am. Coll. Physicians; mem. Am. Fedn. Clin. Rsch., Nat. Assn. Pacing and Electrophysiology (program dirs. com. 1992—, govt. com. 1994—), Phi Beta Kappa, Alpha Omega Alpha. Avocations: bicycling, scuba diving, reading history, movies. Office: W LA VAMC/UCLA Dept 111E 11301 Wilshire Blvd Los Angeles CA 90073

SAGER, RODERICK COOPER, retired life insurance company executive; b. Washington, May 25, 1923; s. Theron Parker and Rebecca (Ward) S.; m. Ruth Regina Ross, Sept. 2, 1947; children: Lawrence Cooper, Jonathan Ward, Timothy Charles. A.B., Syracuse U., 1948, J.D., 1950. Bar: N.Y. 1951, U.S. Supreme Ct. 1958; C.L.U., 1969; chartered fin. cons. Assoc. Mackenzie, Smith, Lewis, Michell and Hughes, Syracuse, 1950-62; gen. counsel Farmers and Traders Life Ins. Co., Syracuse, 1962-66, v.p., gen. counsel, 1966-69, sr. v.p., gen. counsel, 1969-74, exec. v.p., gen. counsel, 1974-79, pres., chief exec. officer, 1979-89, also bd. dirs., ret., 1989; chmn. Life Ins. Council, N.Y., 1984. Trustee Jamesville-DeWitt Cen. Sch. Dist., 1956-69, Onondaga Community Coll., 1971-75; bd. dirs. N.Y. State Tchrs. Retirement System, 1977-92, Onondaga Indsl. Devel. Corp., 1984-89, Lit. Vols. of Greater Syracuse, Inc., 1990-91; trustee Rescue Mission Alliance, Syracuse, 1980—, pres., 1985-86. 1st lt. U.S. Army, 1943-46, 51-52. Mem. Onondaga County Bar Assn., Assn. Life Ins. Counsel. Clubs: Century (Syracuse); Onondaga Golf and Country (Fayetteville, N.Y.). Lodge: Rotary. Home: 3 Wynnridge Rd Fayetteville NY 13066-2532

SAGER, THOMAS WILLIAM, statistics research administrator. BA, U. Iowa, 1968, MS, 1971, PhD in Stats., 1973. Asst. prof. stats. Stanford U., 1973-78; vis. asst. prof. math. and bus. U. Tex., Austin, 1978-79, asst. prof., 1979-82, assoc. prof. stats., 1982-93, prof. stats., 1993—. Mem. Inst. Math. Stats., Am. Statis. Assn., Sigma Xi. Office: U Tex Ctr Statis Sci Ctr Statis Scis GSB5.176 & CBA 5.202 Austin TX 78712

SAGER, WILLIAM F., retired chemistry educator; b. Glencoe, Ill., Jan. 22, 1918; s. Fred Anson and Alta (Stansbury) S.; m. Marilyn Olga Williams, Dec. 26, 1941; children: Karen Louise Sager Dickinson, Judith Lynn SagerPeyton), Kathryn Gwen Sager Potts. B.S. in Chemistry, George Washington U., 1939, M.A. in Organic Chemistry, 1941; Ph.D. in Organic Chemistry, Harvard U., 1948. Research chemist The Texas Co., 1941-45; prof. chemistry George Washington U., 1948-65; prof. chemistry U. Ill.-Chgo., 1965-86, prof. emeritus, 1986—, chmn., 1965-80; cons. to govt. and industry, 1952—. Recipient Disting. Service award U. Ill. Alumni Assn.; Guggenheim fellow, 1954-55. Mem. Am. Chem. Soc., Sigma Xi, Alpha Chi Sigma. Home: 1552 John Anderson Dr Ormond Beach FL 32176-3567 Office: Dept Chemistry U Ill-Chicago Chicago IL 60680

SAGERHOLM, JAMES ALVIN, retired naval officer; b. Uniontown, Pa., Dec. 23, 1927; s. Frithiof Norris and Margaret Blocher S.; m. Margaret Ann Herrlich, June 7, 1952; children—Lisa Marie, Ann Denise, Jeannine Louise, Mark Christian. B.S., U.S. Naval Acad., 1952. Commd. ensign U.S. Navy, 1952, advanced through grades to vice admiral, navigator USS Seadragon, 1965, exec. officer blue crew USS Mariano G. Vallejo, 1966-67, commanding officer gold crew USS Kamehameha, 1968-71, head gen. purpose warfare forces group Office of Chief Naval Ops., 1971, dep. exec. dir. Chief Naval Ops. Exec. Panel, 1972, exec. sec. Chief Naval Ops. Exec. Bd., 1973; comdr. Naval Intelligence Support Ctr. U.S. Navy, Washington, 1974-75; dep. dir. naval intelligence Chief Naval Ops. U.S. Navy, 1975-76, comdr. South Atlantic Force, U.S. Atlantic Fleet, 1976-78, dir. Office of Program Appraisal, Office of Sec. Navy, 1978-81; chief naval edn. and tng. U.S. Navy, Pensacola, Fla., 1983-85; exec. dir. Pres. Fgn. Intelligence Adv. Bd. White House, Washington, 1981-82; ret., 1985; chmn. bd. dirs. Piedmont Environ. Coun., 1987-89; v.p. for nat. affairs Gen. George C. Marshall Home Found., 1990-91. Decorated D.S.M., Legion of Merit, Meritorious Service medal. Mem. Naval Submarine League, U.S. Naval Inst., Civil War Soc., K.C. Roman Catholic. Avocations: golf; tennis; Civil War enthusiast. Home: 414 Rockfleet Rd Unit 102 Lutherville MD 21093

SAGET, BOB, actor, comedian. Grad. film studies, Temple U., 1978. Stand-up comedian clubs around country; has performed at Carnegie Hall, also Las Vegas, Lake Tahoe, Atlantic City; did stand-up at The Comedy Store, The Improv, Calif.; actor (film) Critical Condition, 1986, (series) Full House, ABC-TV, 1986-94; co-host The Morning Program, CBS-TV, 1986; host, writer: America's Funniest HomeVideos, ABC-TV, 1989—; dir., writer: HBO Comedy Hour: In The Dream State. Address: care Vin Di Bona Prodns 4151 Prospect Ave Los Angeles CA 90027-4524

SAGETT, JAN JEFFREY, lawyer, former government official; b. Chgo., Dec. 12, 1943; s. Leonard Henry and Carolyn (Zilberman) S.; BS with honors, U. Ill.-Urbana, 1965; JD, U. Chgo., 1968. Bar: Ill. 1969, D.C. 1969, U.S. Supreme Ct. 1972; CPA, Ill. Assoc., McDermott, Will, and Emery, Chgo., 1968-69; spl. asst. to dir. Office of Minority Bus. Enterprise, Washington, 1969; spl. counsel, asst. gen. counsel Office Econ. Opportunity, Washington, 1969-73; legis. counsel Small Bus. Adminstrn., Washington, 1973-74; dep. assoc. commr., legal counsel Social Security Adminstrn., Washington, 1974-81; asst. gen. counsel, asst. treas. Edison Electric Inst., Washington, 1981-94; v.p., mem. trust mgmt. com. First Nat. Bank Md., Balt., 1995—; treas., mem. exec. com., bd. dirs., chmn. audit com. U.S. Energy Assn., 1991-93; mem. bd. dirs Dreyfus Edison Electric Index Fund, 1992-94, mem. industry adv. bd., 1991-94. Contbg. author: Federal Regulatory Process: Agency Practices and Procedures, 1981-84. Ill. State scholar, 1961-65; selected for Sr. Mgrs. in Govt. program Harvard U., 1978. Mem. ABA (taxation sect., employee benefits com.), Washington Met. Area Corp. Counsel Assn., Am. Corp. Counsel Assn., Beta Gamma Sigma, Phi Eta Sigma, Pi Lambda Phi (exec. council 1963-64), Phi Kappa Phi, Beta Alpha Psi. Jewish. Office: First Nat Bank Md 25 S Charles St Baltimore MD 21201

SAGHIR, ADEL JAMIL, artist, painter, sculptor; b. Beirut, Lebanon, May 27, 1930; came to U.S., 1973; s. Jamil Khalil and Aisha Rachid (Mirii) S.; m. Jindriska Antonin Moucka, Aug. 24, 1968; children: Jamil, Ryan. BA, Am. U., Beirut, 1968, diploma in tchg., 1973; MFA, Pratt Inst., 1975; postgrad., NYU, 1976-79. Asst. prof. Fine Arts Inst., Lebanese U., Beirut, 1963-73; lectr. Am. Beirut U. Coll., 1972-73; adj. prof. Western Conn. State U., Danbury, 1988—; instr., sculpture Silvermine Sch. Art, New Canaan, Conn., 1989—. Artist various murals and tapestries. Recipient 4th prize Alexandria Biennale, Egyptian Govt., 1963, 1st prize silk tapestries Nat. Contest Lebanon, 1965, 1st prize major sculpture monuments, 1966, 1st prize City Ctr. Sculpture Contest, 1969; Fine Arts scholar, Germany, Munic Acad., 1958-60; Fulbright-Hayes fellow NYU, N.Y.C., 1973-79. Mem. Internat. Soc. Advancement of Living Traditions in Art, Washington Pl. Artists Assn. (pres. 1977-80), Lebanese Artists Assn. (v.p. 1964-73). Avocations: gardening, fishing, upland hunting. Home: 20 Newfane Rd New Fairfield CT 06812-4721 Office: Western Conn State U 181 White St Danbury CT 06810-6845

SAGMEISTER, EDWARD FRANK, business owner, hospitality industry executive, civic official, retired consultant, fund raiser, career officer; b. N.Y.C., Dec. 10, 1939; s. Frank and Anna (Unger) S.; m. Anne Marie Ducker, Aug. 18, 1962; children: Cynthia Anne, Laura Marie, Cheryl Suzanne, Eric Edward. BS, U. San Francisco, 1962; MBA, Syracuse U., 1968; postgrad., Air Command and Staff Coll., 1977, Air War Coll., 1981. Commd. 2d lt. USAF, 1963, advanced through grades to lt. col., pers. officer, 1963, aide-de-camp, 1965; dir. pers. sys. Alaskan Air Command, 1968; sys. design program analysis officer HQ USAF, The Pentagon, 1971; spl. asst. sec. Air Force Pers. Coun., USAF, 1975; dir. pers. programs and assignments HQUSAF Europe, 1979; Air Force dep. asst. inspector gen., 1982; ret. USAF, 1984; dir. devel. Am. Cancer Soc., Riverside, Calif., 1984-87; cons. Redlands, Calif., 1987-92; chmn. of bd., pres., CEO Hospitality Pub and Grub, Inc., San Bernardino, Calif., 1992—; instr. Am. Internat. U., L.A., 1987; program dir. Am. Radio Network, L.A., 1987; ptnr., owner Midway Med. Ctr., San Bernardino, 1990-91. Foreman pro-tem San Bernardino County Grand Jury, 1990-91; mem. Redlands 2000 Com., 1988; campaign cabinet mem. Arrowhead United Way, San Bernardino, 1986-87, loaned exec., 1985; exec. dir. Crafton hills Coll. Found., Yucaipa, Calif., 1988; vol. San Bernardino County Dept. Probation, 1985-88; mem. Redlands Cmty., Chorus, 1988-90; vice-chmn., charter mem. Redlands Human Rels. Commn., 1994—, chmn., 1996; mem. Redlands Youth Accountability Bd., San Bernardino County, 1994—, treas. 1996; mem. supt.'s human rels. adv. com., Redlands Unified Sch. Dist., 1996—. Mem. San Bernardino C. of C., Redlands C. of C., Ret. Officers Assn., Nat. Soc. Fundraising Execs., (dir., charter mem. Inland Empire chpt. 1987-88), Empire Singers (v.p. 1987). Republican. Roman Catholic. Avocations: travel, music, singing, tennis, reading. Home: 503 Sunnyside Ave Redlands CA 92373-5629 Office: Hospitality Pub and Grub Inc 1987 Diners Ct San Bernardino CA 92408-3330

SAGNESS, RICHARD LEE, education educator, former academic dean; b. Rock Rapids, Iowa, Jan. 9, 1937; s. David Harold and Joyce Morrow (Carlson) S.; m. Donna Jayne Lanxon, Feb. 18, 1956; children: Debbi Van Vooren, Becky Hardy, Beth Sagness Higbee. BA, U. No. Iowa, 1961; MS, Emporia State U., 1965; PhD, Ohio State U., 1970; grad. Inst. for Higher Edn. Mgmt., Harvard Coll., 1977. Tchr. biology Cen. High Sch., Sioux City, Iowa, 1961-66; lectr. biology Emporia (Kans.) State U., 1966-67; info. analyst Ohio State U., 1967-70; asst. prof. sci. edn. U. S.D., Vermillion, 1970-72, assoc. prof., 1972-75, coord. sci. edn., 1970-75; prof. sci. edn., assoc. dean Sch. Edn. U. S.D., Vermillion, 1975-79; prof. edn. Coll. Edn. Idaho State U., Pocatello, 1979—, dean Coll. Edn., 1979-89, dir. clin. experiences and student svcs., 1993—; mem. Idaho Profl. Stds. Commn.; faculty rep. to bd. dirs. Idaho State U. Found., 1992—; mem. Idaho Sch.-to-Work Collaborative Team, 1994—. Contbr. articles to profl. jours. Bd. dirs. Vermillion Devel. Corp., 1974-78, pres., 1976-77; bd. dirs. Pocatello United Fund, 1976-79, 82-83, v.p., 1982-83, pres., 1985-86. With U.S. Army, 1955-57. Mem. Idaho Assn. Colls. Tchr. Edn. (pres. 1984-88), Am. Assn. Colls. of Tchr. Edn. (rep., chairperson govtl. rels. com. 1988-89, bd. dirs. 1988-92), Pocatello C. of C. (bd. dirs. 1983-89, pres. 1987-88), Tchr. Edn. Coun. State Colls. and Univs. (exec. coun. 1988-90), N.W. Assn. Schs. and Colls. (commn. on schs. 1995—), Rotary (bd. dirs. local club 1988-89, team leader study exch. team to Sweden 1991), Masons, Order Eastern Star, Phi Delta Kappa. Office: Idaho State Univ PO Box 8059 Pocatello ID 83209-8059

SAGO, PAUL EDWARD, retired college administrator; b. Mo., July 5, 1931; s. John and Mabel S.; m. Donna; children: Bruce, Brad, Lori. Student, Mineral Area Coll., 1949-51; BS, Findlay Coll., 1953; postgrad., Winebrenner Theol. Sem., 1953-55; MS, St. Francis Coll., 1964; PhD, Walden U., 1976. Dir. devel. Findlay (Ohio) Coll., 1964-67, Hiram (Ohio) Coll., 1967-68; v.p. fin. affairs, treas. Anderson (Ind.) Coll., 1968-76; pres. Azusa Pacific U., Azusa, Calif., 1976-90, Woodbury U., Burbank, Calif., 1990-96; participant seminars and insts. Trustee Findlay Coll., 1958-64; mem. Ind. adv. council SBA, 1972-76. Mem. Assn. Governing Bds., Internat. Platform Assn., Coun. for Advancement and Support Edn., Nat. Assn. Ind. Colls. and Univs., Assn. Ind. Calif. Colls. and Univs., Rotary. Home: 713 E Amberst Dr Burbank CA 91504 Office: Woodbury U 7500 N Glenoaks Blvd Burbank CA 91504-1052

SAGOFF, MARK, philosopher, educator, academic administrator; b. Boston, Nov. 29, 1941; s. Maurice and Hazel Sagoff; m. Kendra Heymann, Oct. 14, 1984; children: Jared, Amelia. AB, Harvard U., 1963; PhD, U. Rochester, 1968. Lectr. dept. philosophy Princeton (N.J.) U., 1968-69; asst. prof. dept. philosophy U. Pa., Phila., 1969-75; vis. asst. prof. dept. philosophy U. Wis., Madison, 1975-76; asst. prof. sci., tech. and soc. program Cornell U., Ithaca, N.Y., 1976-79; rsch. scholar Inst. for Philosophy and Pub. Policy U. Md., College Park, 1979-86; with Inst. for Philosophy and Pub. Policy, College Park, 1986—; dir. Inst. for Philosophy and Pub. Policy, 1988-95; mem. pub. advisor panel Chem. Mfrs. Assn., Washington, 1989-91; mem. adv. panel NSF, Washington, 1991-94; mem. sci. adv. bd. biotech. U.S. EPA, Washington, 1992-95; speaker in field. Author: The Economy of the Earth, 1988; contbr. articles to profl. jours. Pew scholar, 1991-94; NSF grantee, 1981—. Mem. Internat. Soc. Environ. Ethics (pres. 1994—). Democrat. Jewish. Avocations: his children. Home: 6801 Carlynn Ct Bethesda MD 20817-4302 Office: University of Maryland Inst For Philosophy Pu College Park MD 20742

SAHAI, HARDEO, medical statistics educator; b. Bahraich, India, Jan. 10, 1942; m. Lillian Sahai, Dec. 28, 1973; 3 children. BS in Math., Stats. and Physics, Lucknow U., India, 1962; MS in Math., Banaras U., Varanasi, India, 1964; MS in Math. Stats., U. Chgo., 1968; PhD in Stats., U. Ky., 1971. Lectr. in math. and stats. Banaras U., Varanasi, India, 1964-65; asst. stats. officer Durgapur Steel Plant, Durgapur West Bengal, India, 1965; statistician Rsch. and Planning div. Blue Cross Assn., Chgo., 1966; statis. programmer Cleft Palate Ctr., U. Ill., 1967, Chgo. Health Rsch. Found., 1968; mgmt. scientist Mgmt. Systems Devel. Dept. Burroughs Corp., Detroit, 1971-72; from asst. prof. to prof. dept. math. U. P.R., Mayaguez, 1972-82; vis. research prof. Dept. Stats. and Applied Math. Fed. U. of Ceara, Brazil, 1978-79; sr. research statistician Travenol Labs., Inc., Round Lake, Ill., 1982-83; chief statistician U.S. Army Hqrs., Ft. Sheridan, Ill., 1983-84; sr. math. statistician U.S. Bur. of Census Dept. of Commerce, Washington, 1984-85; sr. ops. rsch. analyst Def. Logistics Agy. Dept. Def., Chgo., 1985-86; prof. Dept. Biostats. and Epidemiology U. P.R. Med. Scis., San Juan, 1986—; cons. P.R. Univ Cons., P.R. Driving Safety Evaluation Project, Water Resources Rsch. Inst., Travenol Labs., Campo Rico, P.R., U.S. Bur. Census, Washington, Lawrence Livermore Nat. Lab., Calif., others; vis. prof. U. Granada, Spain, U. Veracruzana, Mex., U. Nacional de Colombia; vis. prof. U. Nacional de Trujillo, Peru, 1993-94, hon. prof. dept. stats., 1994—; adj. prof. dept. math. U. P.R. Natural Scis. Faculty, 1995—. Author: Statistics and Probability: Learning Module, 1984; author: (with Jose Berrios) A Dictionary of Statistical Scientific and Technical Terms: English-Spanish and Spanish-English, 1981, (with Wilfredo Martinez) Statistical Tables and Formulas for the Biological Social and Physical Sciences, 1995, (with Anwer Khurshid) Statistics in Epidemiology: Methods, Techniques and Applications, 1996, (with Satish C. Misra and Michael Graham) Quotations on Probability and Statistics with Illustrations, 1996; mem. editl. bd. Sociedad Colombiana de Matematicas, P.R. Health Scis. Jour.; contbr. editor Current Index to Stats.; reviewer Collegiate Microcomputer, Comm. in Statistics, Indian Jour. Stats., Jour. Royal Statis. Soc. (series D, The Statistician), New Zealand Statistician, Biometrics, Can. Jour. Stats., Technometrics, Problems, Resources and Issues in Math. Undergrad. Studies; contbr. more than 100 articles and papers to profl. and sci. jours., numerous articles to tech. mags. Active Dept. Consumer Affairs Svcs. Commonwealth of P.R., San Juan, Dept. Anti-Addiction Svcs., Commonwealth of P.R., San Juan., Inst. of AIDS, Municipality of San Juan, VA Med. Ctr. of San Juan, Caribbean Primate Rsch. Ctr., Ctr. Addiction Studies Caribbean Ctrl. U. Recipient Dept. Army Cert. Achievement award, 1984, U. Ky. Outstanding Alumnus award, 1993, medal of honor U. Granada, 1994, plaque of honor U. Nacional de Trujillo, 1994; fellow Coun. Sci. and Indsl. Rsch., 1964-65, U. Chgo., 1965-68, Harvard U., 1979, Fulbright Found., 1982; U.P. Bd. Merit scholar, 1957-59, Govt. India Merit scholar, 1959-64; grantee NSF, 1974-77, NIMH, 1987-90, 91—, NIDA, 1991—. Fellow AAAS, Inst. Statisticians (charter statistician), Inst. Math. and Its Applications (charter mathematician), N.Y. Acad. Scis., Royal Statis. Soc.; mem. Internat. Statis. Inst., Internat. Assn. Teaching Stats., Soc. Epidemiol. Rsch., Inst. Math. Stats., Bernouilli Soc. for Math. Stats. and Probability, Internat. Biometric Soc., Am. Soc. for Quality Control, Am. Stats. Assn., Japan Statis. Soc., Can. Statis. Soc., Inter-Am. Statis. Inst., Internat. Assn. Statis. Computing, Sch. Sci. and Math. Assn., Sigma Xi. Avocations: religious studies, philosophy, reading, gardening. Home: Street Dr Gaudier Texidor K-5-B Terrace Mayaguez PR 00680-9998 Office: U PR Grad Sch Pub Health Med Scis Campus Dept Biostats & Epidemiology x 365067 San Juan PR 00936-5067

SAHANEK, TATANA, librarian, editor; b. Prague, Czechoslovakia, Nov. 2, 1922; d. Emanuel and Frances (Blovsky) S.; naturalized, 1969; JUDr., Masaryk U., Brno, Czechoslovakia, 1947; BLS, U. Toronto, Ont., Can., 1953; PhD (Higher Edn. Act fellow), U. Tex., Austin, 1973. Cataloger, Toronto Pub. Libr., 1953-55; law libr., gen. reference libr. Ont. Legis. Libr., Toronto, 1956-61; head catalog and classification divsn. Harvard Law Sch. Libr., Cambridge, Mass., 1962-65; head catalog dept. Law Libr., U. Mich., Ann Arbor, 1965-66; translator, interpreter Dow Chem. Internat., Midland, Mich., 1967-68; libr.-translator Dow Chem. Co., Tex. div., Freeport, 1968-70; asst. libr. Antioch Sch. Law, Washington, 1972-74; editor Index to Legal Priodicals, H.W. Wilson Co., Bronx, N.Y., 1974-78; coordinator Saginaw (Mich.) Med. Ctr., 1978-79; acquisitions libr. Exec. Office of Pres. Info. Ctr., Washington, 1980—. Recipient award U. Tex. Grad. Sch. Subvention Fund, 1972. Mem. ALA, Assn. Am. Law Librs., Spl. Librs. Assn., Can. Libr. Assn., Ont. Libr. Assn., Czechoslovak Soc. Arts and Scis. Club: Worldwide Sportmen's. Author: Entries for Provincial Publications, Province of Ontario, 1867-1960, 1960; editor Index to Legal Periodicals, 1973-79. Home: 205 S Yoakum Pky Apt 1602 Alexandria VA 22304-3840 Office: New Exec Office Bldg Washington DC 20503

SAHATJIAN, MANIK, nurse, psychologist; b. Tabris, Iran, July 24, 1921; came to U.S., 1951; d. Dicran and Shushanig (Der-Galustian) Mnatzaganian; m. George Sahatjian, Jan. 21, 1954; children: Robert, Edwin. Nursing Cert., Am. Mission Hosps.-Boston U., 1954; BA in Psychology, San Jose State U., 1974, MA in Psychology, 1979. RN, Calif., Mass. Head nurse Am. Mission Hosp., Tabris, 1945-46; charge nurse Banke-Melli Hosp., Tehran, 1946-51; vis. nurse Vis. Nurse Assn., Oakland, Calif., 1956-57; research asst. Stanford U., 1979-81, Palo Alto (Calif.) Med. Research Found., 1981-84; documentation supr. Bethesda Convalescent Ctr., Los Gatos, Calif., 1985-86; sr. outreach worker City of Fremont (Calif.) Human Svcs., 1987-90, case mgr., 1990—; guest rsch. asst. NASA Ames Lab., Mountain View, Calif., summers 1978, 79. Author (with others) psychol. research reports. Fulbright scholar, 1951; Iran Found. scholar, 1953. Mem. AAUW, Western Psychol. Assn. Democrat. Mem. St. Andrew Armenian Church. Avocations: oil painting, classic dance. Home: 339 Starlite Way Fremont CA 94539-7642

SAHGAL, RANJIT, financial executive; b. Allahabad, India, Nov. 22, 1951; came to U.S., 1974; s. Gautam and Nayantara (Pandit) S.; m. Franca Dal Bianco, June 10, 1975; children: Gautam Giorgio, Giorgio Gautam. BA with honors in Econs., U. Bombay (India), 1974. With Ciba-Geigy Corp., 1974—; cost adminstr. controller's dept. Ciba-Geigy Corp., Ardsley, N.Y., 1980-81, mgr. fin. controls treas. dept., 1981-84, mgr. treasury planning and analysis, 1984-85, mgr. fin. acctg. and control support, 1985-87, dir. mgmt. acctg. systems and devel., controller's dept., 1987-90; dir. spl. situation analysis Ciba-Geigy Corp., Saronno, Italy, 1990-91; project mgr. Ciba-Geigy Corp., Basle, Switzerland, 1991-92, head fin. and control, Europe, 1992—; head of fin. Ciba-Geigy Corp., Novartis, Italy, 1996—. Mem. Inst. Mgmt. Acctg.

SAHID, JOSEPH ROBERT, lawyer; b. Paterson, N.J., Feb. 14, 1944; s. Joseph James and Helen (Vitale) S.; m. Annunziata Carol Aiello, May 16, 1981 (div.); children: Annuziata, Joe. BS, Rutgers U., 1965; LLB, U. Va., 1968. Bar: N.Y. 1973, U.S. Dist. Ct. (so. dist.) N.Y., U.S. Ct. Appeals (2d and 3d cirs.), U.S. Supreme Ct. Staff mem. Nat. Commn. on Causes and Prevention of Violence, Washington, 1968-69; cons. Pres.'s Commn. on Campus Unrest, Washington, 1970; assoc. Cravath, Swaine & Moore, N.Y.C., 1972-77, ptnr., 1977-93, cons., 1994—; ptnr. Barrack, Rodos & Bacine, N.Y.C., 1994—. Author: Rights in Concord, 1969; co-author: Law and Order Reconsidered, 1969; contbr. articles to profl. jours. Lt. USCG, 1968-72. Office: Barrack Rodos & Bacine 575 Madison Ave Fl 6 New York NY 10022-2511

SAHLI, NANCY ANN, government agency administrator; b. Beaver Falls, Pa., Jan. 4, 1946; d. John Rankin and Betty Melville (McClane) S. AB, Vassar Coll., 1967; MA, U. Pa., 1971, PhD, 1974. Research asst. Drexel U., Phila., 1969-74; archivist Nat. Hist. Publs. and Records Commn., Washington, 1975-81, 83-84, archives cons., 1981-84, archives specialist, 1984-87, dir. records program, 1987-95, program dir., 1991—, acting exec. dir., 1994-95; cons. Princeton Theol. Sem., N.J., 1981-82, Vassar Coll., Poughkeepsie, N.Y., 1981-82, Smithsonian Instn., Washington, 1983. Author: Elizabeth Blackwell, 1982, Women and Sexuality, 1984, MARC for Archives and Manuscripts, 1985 (Coker prize 1986); editor Directory of Archives and Mss. Repos., 1978. NEH grantee, 1981-83; AAUW fellow, 1973-74; recipient Dommendable Svc. award GSA, 1978, GSA citation, 1979, 81, Archivist's Achievement award, 1994, 95. Fellow Soc. Am. ARchivists (cons. 1983-84); mem. Assn. Documentary Editing, Nat. Assn. Govt. Archives and Records Adminstrs., Orgn. Am. Historians (life), Sierra Club (life), Appalachian Trail Conf. Democrat. Buddhist. Avocations: gardening, hiking, traveling. Home: 9 Indian Spring Dr Silver Spring MD 20901-3016 Office: Nat Hist Publs & Records Commn Nat Archives Washington DC 20408

SAHLSTROM, E(LMER) B(ERNARD), lawyer; b. Seattle, Feb. 25, 1918; s. August Waldimer and Alma Carolyn (Ostrom) S.; m. Phyllis May Horstman, June 18, 1946; children: Gary Bernard, Cheryl Linn Sahlstrom Monohan, Gregory Lane. B.S., U. Oreg., 1945, J.D., 1947. Bar: Oreg. 1947, U.S. Dist. Ct. Oreg. 1948, U.S. Dist. Ct. Hawaii, 1961, U.S. Ct. Appeals (9th cir.), 1950, U.S. Supreme Ct. 1977; CPA, Oreg. Acct. Haskins & Sells, N.Y.C., 1941-44; mem. Thompson & Sahlstrom, Eugene, Oreg., 1947-57, Sahlstrom, Lombard, Starr & Vinson, and predecessor, Eugene, 1957-76, Sahlstrom & Lombard, Eugene, 1976-78; sole practice Eugene, 1978-80; ptnr. Sahlstrom & Dugdale, Eugene, 1980—. Bd. visitors U. Oreg. Law Sch., 1977-79, 92—. Mem. ATLA (1st v.p. western regional conf. 1954, 4th v.p. conf. 1956, dir. 1955-56, v.p. Oreg. chpt. 1970-71, pres. So. Oreg. chpt. 1972-74), ABA, Oreg. State Bar (com. taxations, unauthorized practice of law, procedure and practice, CLE, coun. on ct. procedures), Am. Judicature Soc., Assn. Attys. and CPA's, U. Oreg. Sch. Law Alumni Assn. (bd. dirs., pres.), C. of C., Country Club, Town Club (dir. 1970-71, pres. 1978) (Eugene), Multnomah Club (Portland), Elks, Sister Theodore Marie Soc., Order of the Antelope, Order of the Buggy Ride, Phi Alpha Delta, Beta Alpha Psi. Home: 715 Fairoaks Dr Eugene OR 97401-2392 Office: Sahlstrom & Dugdale 915 Oak St Eugene OR 97401-3142

SAHR, MORRIS GALLUP, financial planner; b. Schenectady, Nov. 28, 1928; s. Nathan and Esther (Gallup) S.; m. Sarah Diane Eisenberg, Dec. 23, 1956; children: Evelyn, David, Janet. AB, U. Oreg., 1951, MA, 1953; PhD, Calif. Open U., Oakland, 1978. CFP. Pres. Deposit Mgmt. Svc., Inc., Palmyra, Va., 1978—. Co-author: Your Book of Financial Planning, 1983, Encyclopedia of Financial Planning, 1984, The Financial Planner, 1986, Financial Planning Can Make You Rich, 1987. Chmn. Fairfax County Planning Commn., 1964-68; del. White House Conf. on Aging, 1980, U.S. Congl. Adv. Bd., 1984-87; bd. dirs. Fairfax Indsl. Devel. Authority, 1985-95; dir. Nat. Ctr. Fin. Edn.; adj. instr. Am. Arbitraion Assn. Recipient award Danforth Found.; named 1 of Top 200 Planners in U.S., Money Mag.; hon. fellow Kennedy Libr., 1985; Paul Harris fellow, 1989. Mem. Internat. Assn. Fin. Planning (founder, 1st pres. Metro Washington chpt.), Inst. Cert. Fin. Planners (nat. govt. affairs com.), Am. Assn. Practicing Fin. Planners (past pres.), Rotary (pres. Fairfax 1984-85), Sr. Leadership Coun. Home and Office: DMS Inc 61 Wildwood Dr Palmyra VA 22963

SAHS, MAJORIE JANE, art educator; b. Altadena, Calif., Aug. 27, 1926; d. Grayson Michael and Janie Belle (Aaron) McCarty; m. Eugene Otto Sahs, July 21, 1949; children: Victoria, Stephen, Jeffry. Student, Art Ctr. of L.A., 1943-45, Emerson Coll., Boston, 1945; BA, Sacramento State U., 1970; MA in Art Edn., Calif. State U., Sacramento, 1972, postgrad., 1973-79. Cert. secondary tchr., Calif. Tchr. art Sacramento County Schs., 1971-80; cons. Whole Brain Learning Modes, Sacramento, 1980-84; tng. specialist Art Media, Sacramento, Calif., 1983—; instr. Found. for Continuing Med. Edn., Calif., 1985; presenter Nat. Art Edn. Conf., Chgo., 1992, 93, Asian Pacific Conf. on Arts Edn., Franklin, Australia, Internat. Conf., Montreal, Can., 1993; cons., lectr. in field; judge U.S. Treas., 1994, 95, 96, Dept. of Calif. Student Art. Prodr., writer guide and video Gesture Painting Through T'ai Chi, 1992; editor, pub. Calif.'s state newspaper for art edn., 1987-90; editor: Crocker Mus. Docent Guide, 1990; mem. editl. bd. Jour. for Nat. Art Edn. Assn., 1990—; editor: (newsletter) U.S. Soc. for Edn. Through Art, 1994-96; designer of ltd. edits. scarves and cards for Nat. Breast Cancer Rsch. Fund, Exploration Inspiration '95. Del. Calif. Arts Leadership Symposium for Arts Edn., 1979, Legis. Coalition Through The Arts, Calif., 1989, 95; judge Calif. State Fair Art Show, 1989, 95, Fed. Treasury Poster Contest, 1994, 95, 96;

organizer and host art show and fundraiser for women candidates, 1992. Recipient Patriotic Svc. award Fed. Treasury Dept., 1996, State award of Merit. Mem. Internat. Assn. Edn. through Art, U.S. Soc. Edn. through Art (editor newsletter 1994-96), Nat. Art Edn. Assn. (mem. editl. bd. jour. 1990—, Nat. Outstanding Newspaper Editor award 1988, 89), Calif. Art Edn. Assn. (mem. state coun., mem. area coun., editor state paper, State Award of Merit), Calif. Children's Homes Soc. (pres. Camellia chpt. 1990-91), Asian Pacific Arts Educators Assn., Art Ctr. L.A. Alumni. Avocations: creating art pieces, textile clothing design, writing, designing jewelry, designing greeting cards. Home and Office: 1836 Walnut Ave Carmichael CA 95608-5417

SAIBLE, STEPHANIE, magazine editor; b. Mobile, Ala., Sept. 11, 1954; d. Lewis J. Slaff and Phoebe-Jane (Berse) Deats; m. Mark Saible, May 31, 1981 (div. 1983). Student, Va. Commonwealth U., 1972-75. Editorial asst. Woman's World Magazine, Englewood, N.J., 1980-81, service copywriter, 1981-83, assoc. articles editor, 1983-84, articles editor, 1984-85, sr. editor features dept., 1985-86, sr. editor services dept., 1986, now editor-in-chief. Contbr. articles to Woman's World, Modern Bride, New Body, Celebrity Beauty, Trim & Fit. Named Wonder Woman of the Yr., Bus. Jour. N.J., 1986. Mem. Women in Communications. Office: Woman's World Mag 270 Sylvan Ave Englewood Cliffs NJ 07632

SAID, EDWARD W., English language and literature educator; b. Jerusalem, Palestine, Nov. 1, 1935; s. Wadie A. and Hilda (Musa) S.; m. Mariam Cortas, Dec. 15, 1970; children: Wadie, Najla. A.B., Princeton U., 1957; A.M., Harvard U., 1960, Ph.D., 1964. Tutor history and lit. Harvard U., 1961-63; instr. Columbia U., 1963-65, asst. prof. English, 1965-67, assoc. prof., 1968-70, prof., 1970-77, Parr prof. English and comparative lit., 1977-89, Old Dominion Found. prof. humanities, 1989—; univ. prof., 1992—; vis. prof. Harvard U., 1974, Johns Hopkins, spring 1979, Yale U., fall 1985; fellow Ctr. for Advanced Study in Behavioral Scis., Palo Alto, Calif., 1975-76; Christian Gauss lectr. in criticism Princeton U., spring 1977, T.S. Eliot lectr. U. Kent, Canterbury, U.K., 1985, Messenger lectr. Cornell U., 1986, Little lectr. Princeton U., 1988, Raymond Williams Meml. lectr., London, 1989, Wilson lectr. Wellesley Coll., 1991, Amnesty lectr. Oxford U., 1992, Lord Northcliffe lectr., U. Coll., London, 1993, Reith lectr. BBC, London, 1993, others; Carpenter prof. U. Chgo., 1983; Northrop Frye chair U. Toronto, fall 1986. Author: Joseph Conrad and the Fiction of autobiography, 1966, Beginnings: Intention and Method, 1975, Orientalism, 1978, The Question of Palestine, 1979; editor: Literature and Society, 1979, Covering Islam, 1981, The World, the Text, and the Critic, 1983, After the Last Sky, 1986, Blaming the Victims, 1988, Musical Elaborations, 1991, Culture and Imperialism, 1993, Representations of the Intellecual, 1994, Politics of Dispossession, 1994, Ghazzah-Arihah: Salam Amriki, 1994. Social Sci. Research fellow, 1975; Guggenheim fellow, 1972-73; Recipient Lionel Trilling award Columbia U., 1976, 94. Mem. AAAS, MLA, Assn. Arab Am. U. Grads. (past v.p.), N.Y. Coun. Fgn. Rels., Am. Comparative Lit. Assn. (René Wellek award 1985), PEN (exec. bd. 1989—), Am. Acad. Arts and Scis. Office: Columbia U Dept English 602 Philosophy Hall New York NY 10027

SAID, KAMAL E., accounting educator; b. Cairo, Egypt, May 26, 1937; came to U.S., 1965; s. Mohamed A. and Ehsan (Yasin) S.; m. Sally Sneed, Dec. 22, 1967 (div. 1979); children: Jamal E., Karim E.; m. Maria A. Gruner, Aug. 11, 1984; 1 child, Noelle Rianne. B in Comm., Ain-Shams U., Cairo, 1957; MBA, U. Tex., 1967, PhD, 1971. CPA, Tex., La. Asst. prof. U. Houston, 1971-75, assoc. prof., 1975-76, assoc. prof. acctg., 1978-83; Fulbright prof. U. Khartoum, Sudan, 1976-78; chmn. acctg. dept. King Saud U., Saudi Arabia, 1984-88; prof. acctg. U. Southwestern La., Lafayette, 1988-92; prof. Coll. of Indsl. Mgmt., U. Petroleum & Minerals, Dhahran, Saudi Arabia, 1992—; cons. Nat. Coun. Higher Edn., Khartoum, 1976-78, European Econ. Community, Khartoum, 1977; external examiner U. Calcutta, India, 1978-79. Author: Auditing: Theory and Practice, 1989, Modern Advanced Accounting, 1989, Accounting Information Systems, 1988, Intermediate Accounting, I and II, 1987, The Voice of Music, Inc. Practice Set, 1986, Naggie and Sons, Inc. Practice Set, 1986, Gasseem Sporting Goods, Inc. Practice Set, 1986, Cost Accounting I and II, 1985, Managerial Accounting, 1984, Implementation of Long-Range Plans Through Current Operating Budgets, 1978, A Budgeting Model for Institutions of Higher Education, 1974, others. U. Houston grantee, 1974, 75, 78. Mem. Am. Acctg. Assn. (rschr. 1973-75), Inst. Internal Auditors, Phi Beta Delta, Delta Sigma Pi, Beta Gamma Sigma, Beta Alpha Psi. Avocations: Arabian horse shows, horse-back riding, swimming, racquetball.

SAID, PHYLLIS DIANNE, elementary school educator; b. Muncie, Ind., Aug. 21, 1942; d. Russel Philip and Edna Ann (Kiracofe) Donhauser; m. William Lee Said, Aug. 24, 1963; children: Denise Janine, Douglas James. BS, Ball State U., Muncie, Ind., 1970, MA in Edn., 1976. Kindergarten tchr. Delaware Cmty. Schs., Eaton, Ind., 1970-76, tchr. 1st grade, 1976—. Author/prodr.: (video prodn.) Prime Time - Indiana Dept. of Edn., 1986, 87, 89. Vol. Minnetrista Cultural Ctr., Muncie, Delaware County Coalition for Literacy, Muncie. Lilly Endowment Tchr. Creativity fellow, Indpls., 1992; Ind. Dept. Edn. Tchr. Tech. grantee, 1988, 90, Energy Edn. grantee, 1990, Bell grantee, 1995, Ctrl. Bur. Eng. Enhancement grant, 1996; recipient Fulbright Tchr. Exch. award, Eng., 1995—, Eisenhower Sci. and Math. award, 1995, Ind. Wildlife Fedn. Conservation Educator of Yr., 1995, Nila Purvis Animal Helper of Yr., 1994. Mem. Internat. Reading Assn., Ind. Wildlife Assn., Audubon Soc., Muncie Area Reading Coun., Hoosier Mgrs. (pres. 1993-94), Alpha Delta Kappa (treas. 1992-94). Republican. Methodist. Avocations: reading, herb gardening, quilting, travel.

SAIDMAN, GARY K., lawyer; b. Washington, July 29, 1952; s. Harry and Rose K. (Kruger) S.; m. Suzan R. Kinbar, Mar. 25, 1984; children: Benjamin A., David M. BS, SUNY, Stony Brook, 1974; JD, Emory U., 1978. Bar: Ga. 1978, D.C. 1983, U.S. Dist. Ct. (no. dist.) Ga. 1978, U.S. Ct. Appeals (5th cir.) 1978, U.S. Ct. Appeals (11th cir.) 1981. Assoc. Seward & Kissel, Atlanta, 1978-80; assoc. Kilpatrick & Cody, Atlanta, 1980-86, ptnr., 1986—. Mem. Lawyers Club Atlanta, Ga. State Bar Assn. (chmn. Computer Law Section 1987-88). Office: Kilpatrick & Cody 1100 Peachtree St NE Ste 2800 Atlanta GA 30309-4528

SAIDMAN, LAWRENCE JAY, anesthesiologist; b. Detroit, 1936. MD, U. Mich., 1961. Diplomate Am. Bd. Anesthesiology (v.p. 1992-93, pres. 1993-94). Intern Sinai Hosp., Detroit, 1961-62; resident in anesthesiology U. Calif., San Francisco, 1962-65; fellow Cardiovascular Rsch. Inst., San Francisco, 1963-64; anesthesiologist U. Calif. Med. Ctr., San Diego; prof. U. Calif., San Diego. Editor-in-chief Anesthesiology, 1985—. Mem. Am. Bd. Anesthesiology (bd. dirs.). Office: U Calif at San Diego Sch Medicine T-015 San Diego CA 92110

SAIFER, MARK GARY PIERCE, pharmaceutical executive; b. Phila., Sept. 16, 1938; s. Albert and Sylvia (Jolles) S.; m. Phyllis Lynne Trommer, Jan. 28, 1961 (dec.); children: Scott David, Alandria Gail; m. Merry R. Sherman, June 26, 1994. AB, U. Pa., 1960; PhD, U. Calif., Berkeley, 1966. Acting asst. prof. zoology U. Calif., Berkeley, 1966, postdoctoral fellow, 1967-68; sr. cancer research scientist Roswell Park Meml. Inst., Buffalo, 1968-70; lab. dir. Diagnostic Data Inc., Palo Alto, Calif., 1970-78; v.p. DDI Pharms., Inc., Mountain View, Calif., 1978-94, Oxis Internat., Inc., 1994-95; sci. dir. Mountain View Pharms., Inc., San Carlos, Calif., 1996—. Patentee in field. Mem. AAAS (life), Am. Assn. Pharm. Scientists, Parenteral Drug Assn. Home: 1114 Royal Ln San Carlos CA 94070 Office: Mountain View Pharms Inc 871-L Industrial Rd San Carlos CA 94070

SAIGO, ROY HIROFUMI, academic administrator; b. Aug. 6, 1940. BA, U. Calif., Davis, 1962; PhD, Oreg. State U., 1969. Mem. faculty U. Wis., Eau Claire, 1967-84; intern acad. affairs U. Wis. Sys., Madison, 1976-77, dir. rsch. projects, summer 1976; asst. to dean Coll. Arts and Scis. U. Wis., Eau Claire, 1976-80; asst. dean, 1981-84; dean Coll. Natural Scis. U. No. Iowa, Cedar Falls, 1984-90; provost, v.p. acad. and student affairs Southeastern La. U., Hammond, 1990-94; chancellor Auburn U., Montgomery, Ala., 1994—; mem. bd. Colonial Bank. Recipient Charles E. Bessey award Bot. Soc. Am., Svc. and Contbn. award Am. Inst. Biol. Scis., Disting. Alumni award U. Calif., Davis, 1994. Fellow AAAS; mem. Am. Assn. Higher Edn., Phi Delta Kappa. Office: Auburn U 7300 University Dr Montgomery AL 36117-3531

SAIKI, PATRICIA (MRS. STANLEY MITSUO SAIKI), former federal agency administrator, former congresswoman; b. Hilo, Hawaii, May 28, 1930; d. Kazuo and Shizue (Inoue) Fukuda; m. Stanley Mitsuo Saiki, June 19, 1954; children: Stanley Mitsuo, Sandra Saiki Williams, Margaret C., Stuart K., Laura H. BA, U. Hawaii, 1952. Tchr. U.S. history Punahou Sch., Kaimuki Intermediate Sch., Kalani High Sch., Honolulu, 1952-64; sec. Rep. Party Hawaii, Honolulu, 1964-66, vice chmn., 1966-68, 82-83, chmn., 1983-85; rsch. asst. Hawaii State Senate, 1966-68; mem. Hawaii Ho. of Reps., 1968-74, Hawaii State Senate, 1974-82, 100th-101st Congresses from 1st Hawaii dist., Washington, 1987-91; adminstr. SBA, Washington, 1991-93; mem. Pres.'s Adv. Coun. on Status of Women, 1969-76; mem. Nat. Commn. Internat. Women's Yr., 1969-70; commr. We. Interstate Commn. on Higher Edn.; fellow Eagleton Inst., Rutgers U., 1970; fellow Inst. of Politics, Kennedy Sch. Govt., Harvard U., 1993; bd. dirs. Bank of Am.-Hawaii, Landmark Systems Corp., Internat. Asset Recovery Corp. Mem. Kapiolano Hosp. Aux.; sec. Hawaii Rep. Com., 1964-66, vice chmn., 1966-68, chmn., 1983-85; del. Hawaii Constl. Conv., 1968; alt. del. Rep. Nat. Conv., 1968, del., 1984, Rep. nominee for lt. gov. Hawaii, 1982, for U.S. Senate, 1990, for. gov. Hawaii, 1990; mem. Fedn. Rep. Women; trustee Hawaii Pacific Coll.; st bd. govs. Boys and Girls Clubs Hawaii; mem. adv. coun. ARC; bd. dirs. Nat. Fund for Improvement of Post-Secondary Edn., 1982-85; past bd. dirs. Straub Med. Rsch. Found., Honolulu, Hawaii's Visitors Bur., Honolulu, Edn. Commn. of States, Honolulu, Hawaii Visitors Bur., 1983-85; trustee U. Hawaii Found., 1984-86, Hawaii Pacific Coll., Honolulu. Episcopalian. Avocation: golf. Home: 784 Elepaio St Honolulu HI 96816-4710

SAIMAN, MARTIN S., lawyer; b. N.Y.C., Jan. 27, 1932; s. Adolph and Mary (Kaplan) S.; m. Rita C. Chernick, Apr. 10, 1955; children: Lisa, Richard, Gwen. A.B., Columbia Coll., 1953; LL.B., Columbia U., 1955. Bar: N.Y. 1956. Ptnr. Kaye, Scholer, Fierman, Hays & Handler, N.Y.C., 1971-94, spl. counsel firm, 1995. Bd. dirs. Smalley Found., 1966—. Office: Kaye Scholer Fierman Hays & Handler 425 Park Ave New York NY 10022-3506

SAIN, MICHAEL KENT, electrical engineering educator; b. St. Louis, Mar. 22, 1937; s. Charles George and Marie Estelle (Ritch) S.; m. Frances Elizabeth Bettin, Aug. 24, 1963; children: Patrick, Mary, John, Barbara, Elizabeth. BSEE, St. Louis U., 1959, MSEE, 1962; PhD, U. Ill., 1965. Engr. Sandia Corp., Albuquerque, 1958-61, Vickers Electric Corp., St. Louis, 1962; instr. U. Ill., Urbana, 1962-63; asst. prof. U. Notre Dame (Ind.), 1965-68, assoc. prof., 1968-72, prof., 1972-82, Frank M. Freimann prof. elec. engring., 1982—; vis. scientist U. Toronto, Ont., Can., 1972-73; disting. vis. prof. Ohio State U., Columbus, 1987; cons. Allied-Bendix Aerospace, South Bend, Ind., 1976—, Deere & Co., Moline, Ill., 1981, 82, Garrett Corp., Phoenix, 1984, GM, Warren, Mich., 1984-94; plenary spkr. IEEE Conf. on Decision and Control, 1990. Author: Introduction to Algebraic System Theory, 1981; editor: Alternatives for Linear Multivariable Control, 1978; hon. editor: Ency. of Systems and Control, 1987; editor jour. IEEE Trans. on Automatic Control, 1979-83; contbr. 275 articles to profl. jours., books and refereed proc. Grantee Army Rsch. Office, NSF, Ames Rsch. Ctr., Lewis Rsch. Ctr. NASA, Office Naval Rsch., Air Force Office Sci. Rsch., Law Enforcement Assistance Adminstrn., Clark-Hurth Components. Fellow IEEE (prize papers com. 1992-96, chair 1994-96, awards bd. 1994-96); mem. Control Sys. Soc. IEEE (bd. govs. 1978-84, Disting. Mem. award 1983, Centennial medal 1984, Axelby prize chair 1991-96, awards com. chair 1993-96), Circuits and Sys. Soc. IEEE (co-chair internat. symposium on circuits and sys. 1990, newsletter editor 1990-96, v.p. adminstrn. 1992-93, v.p. tech. activities 1994-95), Soc. Indsl. and Applied Math. Republican. Roman Catholic. Avocations: photography, swimming, jogging. Office: U Notre Dame Dept Elec Engring 275 Fitzpatrick Heights Notre Dame IN 46556-5637

SAINE, BETTY BOSTON, elementary school educator; b. Newton, N.C., Dec. 1, 1932; d. Glenn and Carrie Queen Boston; m. Thomas Paul Saine, Aug. 3, 1968; 1 child, Carrie Ann. BA, Lenoir Rhyne Coll., 1956. Tchr. grade 4 High Point (N.C.) City Schs., 1956-59, Charlotte City Schs./Charlotte-Mecklenburg Schs., 1959-66; art tchr. grades 1-8 Newton-Conover City Schs., 1966-67; tchr. grade 4 Charlotte-Mecklenburg Schs., 1967-68; tchr. grade 6 Lincolnton (N.C.) City Schs., 1968-70; tchr. grades 5 and 6 Lincolnton City Schs./Lincoln County Schs., 1972-90; ret. Historian, publicity chair beautification com. Sunflower Garden Club, Lincolnton, 1976-87. Mem. Alpha Delta Kappa (various offices and coms.). Methodist. Avocations: painting, creative embroidery, horticulture, calligraphy, children's books. Home: 2492 Pickwick Pl Lincolnton NC 28092-7748

SAINER, ARTHUR, writer, theater educator; b. N.Y.C., Sept. 12, 1924; s. Louis and Sadie (Roth) S.; m. Maryjane Treloar, Apr. 18, 1981; children: Douglas M., Stephanie M., Jane M., Ross M. B.A., Washington Sq. Coll., N.Y.C., 1946; M.A., Columbia U., 1948. Tchr. Bennington Coll., Vt., 1967-69, Adelphi U., Garden City, N.Y., 1974-75, S.I. Community Coll., 1974-75; faculty Wesleyan U., Middletown, Conn., 1977-80, Hunter Coll., N.Y.C., 1980-81; assoc. prof. theatre Middlebury Coll., Vt., 1981-83; theater faculty New Sch. for Social Rsch., N.Y.C., 1985—, Sarah Lawrence Coll., Bronxville, N.Y., 1990—; play dir. Boat Sun Cavern Middlebury Coll., Vt., 1983; drama critic Village Voice, N.Y.C., 1961—; play dir. Lord Tom Goldsmith at Theatre for New City, N.Y.C., 1979, Witnesses at Open Space, N.Y.C., 1977, Poor Man Rich Man, Theatre for the New City, 1992. Editor: Village Voice, 1962; author: (plays) The Celebration Reclaimed, 1993-95, Images of the Coming Dead, 1980, After the Baal-Shem Tov, 1979, Carol in Winter Sunlight, 1977, The Children's Army Is Late, 1974, The Burning Out of '82, 1983, Cruising Angel, 1984, Sunday Childhood Journeys to Nobody at Home (Berman award), 1984, Jews and Christians in the End Zone, 1987, (criticisms), The New Radical Theatre Notebook, 1975, 96, The Sleepwalker and the Assassin, 1964; reporter: Nat. Endowment for Arts, Washington, 1979-82. Panelist Vt. Council on the Arts, Montpelier, 1982, 83; panelist N.Y. State Council on the Arts, 1976-78. Ford Found. grantee, 1979, 80; recipient grant Office for Advanced Drama Research, U. Minn., 1967, award for Grab Your Hat John Golden Found., 1946. Address: 565 W End Ave New York NY 10024-2705 *From a work of mine in progress: Francis: But finally, who is going to do my work? No one is going to do it. Lev: Each will do his work. But in the end only God's work amounts to anything. Francis: And does that make you happy? Lev: It makes me useful.*

SAINSBURY OF PRESTON CANDOVER, LORD (JOHN DAVAN SAINSBURY), entrepreneur; b. Nov. 2, 1927; m. Anya Linden, 1963. Student, Oxford U., fellow (hon.), 1982; DSC in Econs. (hon.), Worcester Coll., Oxford, 1985. Vice chmn. J. Sainsbury PLC, 1967-69, chmn., 1969-92; pres. J. Sainsbury plc, 1992—; also bd. dirs. J. Sainsbury PLC. Bd. dirs. Royal Opera House, Covent Garden, Eng., 1969-85, chmn., 1987—; bd. dirs. Royal Opera House Trust, 1974-84, The Economist, 1972-80, chmn. Coun. Friends of Covent Garden, 1969-81, Benesh Inst. Choreology, 1986-87; gov. Royal Ballet Sch., 1965-76; joint hon. treas. European Movement, 1972-75, pres., 1975-89; trustee Nat. Gallery, 1976-83, Westminster Abbey Trust, 1977-83, Tate Gallery, 1982-83, Rhodes Trust, 1984—; active Nat. Com. for Electoral Reform, 1976-85. Named Hon. Bencher Inner Temple, 1985. Fellow Inst. Grocery Distbrs.; mem. Coun. Retail Consortium, Garrick Club, Contemporary Arts Soc. (v.p. 1984—). Office: J Sainsbury PLC, care Stamford House Stamford St, SE1 9LL London England Office: J Sainsbury U S A Inc 140 Laurel St East Bridgewater MA 02333-1764

SAINT, CROSBIE EDGERTON, retired army officer; b. West Point, N.Y., Sept. 29, 1936; s. Frederick Gilman and Jean (Crosbie) Saint Malevich; m. Virginia Fisher Carnahan, Aug. 3, 1961; children: Frederick Gilman II, Mary Elizabeth. B.S., U.S. Mil. Acad., 1958; M.A., Am. U., 1973. Commd. 2d lt. U.S. Army, 1958, advanced through grades to gen.; comdr. 1st Squadron, 1st Cav., Vietnam, 1970; exec. to chief of staff U.S. Army, Washington; comdr. 11th Armored Cav. Regt., Fulda, Germany, 1976-78, 7th Army Tng. Command, Grafenwohr, Germany, 1979-81; dept. comdt. Command and Gen. Staff Coll., Ft. Leavenworth, Kans., 1981-83; comdr. 1st Armored Div., Ansbach, Germany, 1983-85; comdt. 3d Corps and Ft. Hood Tex., 1985-88; comdr. in chief U.S. Army Europe, Heidelberg, Germany, 1988-92; ret. U.S. Army, 1992; v.p. Europe Mil. Profl. Resources, Inc.; cons. Decorated DSM with two oak leaf clusters, DFC, Air medal with V device, Legion of Honor (France), German Armed Forces Gt. Cross of Merit with star, Vietnamese Cross of Gallantry. Mem. Assn. U.S. Army, Armor Assn. Address: 1116 N Pitt St Alexandria VA 22314-1455

SAINT, EVA MARIE, actress; b. Newark, July 4, 1924; d. John Merle and Eva Marie (Rice) S.; m. Jeffrey Hayden, Oct. 28, 1951; children: Darrell, Laurette. BA, DFA, Bowling Green State U., 1946; student, Actors Studio, after 1950. Appeared in various radio and TV dramatic shows, N.Y.C., 1947—; theater roles include The Trip to Bountiful, 1953 (Outer Circle Critics award, N.Y. Drama Critics award, 1953), The Rainmaker, 1953, Winesburg, Ohio, 1970, The Lincoln Mask, 1972, Summer and Smoke, 1973, Desire Under the Elms, 1974, The Fatal Weakness, 1976, Candida, 1977, Mr. Roberts, First Monday in October, 1979, Duet for One, 1982-83, The Country Girl, 1986 (L.A. Dramalogue award 1986), Death of a Salesman, 1994, Love Letters, 1994; appeared in films On the Waterfront, 1954 (Acad. Award for best supporting actress, 1955), Raintree County, 1957, That Certain Feeling, 1956, A Hatful of Rain, 1957, North by Northwest, 1959, Exodus, 1961, All Fall Down, 1962, 36 Hours, 1963, The Sandpiper, 1964, The Russians Are Coming, The Russians Are Coming!, 1965, Grand Prix, 1966, The Stalking Moon, 1969, Loving, 1970, Cancel My Reservation, 1972, Nothing in Common, 1986; TV dramas The Macahans , 1976 (Emmy nom.), The Fatal Weakness, 1976, Taxi!!, 1978 (Emmy nom.), A Christmas to Remember, 1978, When Hell Was in Session, 1980, The Curse of King Tut's Tomb, The Best Little Girl in the World, 1981, Splendor in the Grass, 1981, Love Leads the Way, 1983, Jane Doe, 1983, Fatal Vision, 1984, The Last Days of Patton, 1986, A Year in the Life, 1986, Breaking Home Ties, 1987, I'll Be Home for Christmas, 1988, Voyage of Terror: The Achille Lauro Affair, 1990, People Like Us, 1990 (Emmy award, 1990), Palomino, 1991, Kiss of the Killer, ABC, 1992, documentary Primary Colors: The Story of Corita, 1991, My Antonia, 1994; also appeared in TV series Moonlighting, 1986-89.

ST. AMAND, PIERRE, geophysicist; b. Tacoma, Wash., Feb. 4, 1920; s. Cyrias Z. and Mable (Berg) St. A.; m. Marie Pöss, Dec. 5, 1945; children: Gene, Barbara, Denali, David. BS in Physics, U. Alaska, 1948; MS in Geophysics, Calif. Inst. Tech., 1951, PhD in Geophysics and Geology, 1953; Dr. honoris causa, U. De Los Altos, Tepatitlan, Mex., 1992. Asst. dir. Geophys. Lab., U. Alaska, also head ionospheric and seismologic investigations, 1946-49; physicist U.S. Naval Ordnance Test Sta., China Lake, Calif., 1950-54; head optics br. U.S. Naval Ordnance Test Sta., 1955-58; head earth and planetary sci. div. U.S. Ordnance Test Sta., 1961-78, now cons. to tech. dir., head spl. projects office, 1978-88; fgn. service with ICA as prof. geol. and geophys. Sch. Earth Scis., U. Chile, 1958-60; originator theory rotational displacement Pacific Ocean Basin; pres. Saint-Amand Sci. Services; adj. prof. McKay Sch. Mines, U. Nev., U. N.D.; v.p., dir. Covillea Corp.; v.p., dir. tech. Muetal Corp.; cons. World Bank, Calif. Div. Water Resources, Am. Potash & Chem. Co., OAS; mem. U.S. Army airways communications system, Alaska and Can., 1942-46; cons. Mexican, Chilean, Argentine, Philipines, Can. govts.; mem. Calif. Gov.'s Com. Geol. Hazards; mem. com. magnetic instruments Internat. Union Geodesy and Geophys., 1954-59, Disaster Preparation Commn. for Los Angeles; charter mem. Sr. Exec. Service. Adv. bd. GeoScience News; contbr. 100 articles to scientific jours. Chmn. bd. dirs. Ridgecrest Community Hosp.; chmn. bd. dirs. Indian Wells Valley Airport Dist.; v.p. bd. dirs. Kern County Acad. Decathlon. Decorated knight Mark Twain, Mark Twain Jour.; recipient cert. of merit OSRD, 1945, cert. of merit USAAF, 1946, letter of commendation USAAF, 1948, Spl. award Philippine Air Force, 1969, Diploma de Honor Sociedad Geologica de Chile, Disting. Civilian Svc. medal USN, 1968, L.T.E. Thompson medal, 1973, Thunderbird award Weather Modification Assn., 1974, Disting. Pub. Svc. award Fed. Exec. Inst., 1976, Meritorious Svc. medal USN, 1988, Disting. Alumnus award U. Alaska, 1990; Fulbright rsch. fellow France, 1954-55. Fellow AAAS, Geol. Soc. Am., Earthquake Engr. Rsch. Inst.; mem. Am. Geophys. Union, Weather Modification Assn., Am. Seismol. Soc., Sister Cities (Ridgecrest-Tepatitlan) Assn. (pres.), Rotary (past pres., Paul Harris fellow), Footprinters Internat. (mem. grand bd., pres.), Sigma Xi. Achievements include patents in photometric instrument, weather and ordnance devices, pvt. pilot multi-engine-instruments. Home: 1748 W Las Flores Ave Ridgecrest CA 93555-8635

SAINT-AMAND, PIERRE NEMOURS, humanities educator; b. Port-Au-Prince, Haiti, Feb. 22, 1957; came to U.S., 1978; s. Nemours and Carmen (Clerveaux) Saint-A. BA, U. Montreal, 1978; MA, Johns Hopkins U., 1980, PhD, 1981. Asst. prof. Yale U., New Haven, 1981-82, Stanford (Calif.) U., 1982-86; assoc. prof. Brown U., Providence, 1986-90, prof., 1990—; Francis Wayland prof. Brown U., Providence, R.I., 1996—; vis. prof. Harvard U., Cambridge, Mass., 1992. Author: Diderot, Le Labyrinthe de La Relation, 1984, Seduire Ou La Passion des Lumieres, 1986, Les Lois de L'Hostilite, 1992, The Libertine's Progress, 1994; editor: Diderot, 1984, Le Roman an Dix-huitième siecle, 1987, Autonomy in the Age of the Enlightenment, 1993. Fellow Stanford Humanities Ctr., 1985-86, John Simon Guggenheim Meml. Found., 1989. Office: Brown U Box 1961 French Dept Providence RI 02912

ST. ANTOINE, THEODORE JOSEPH, law educator; b. St. Albans, Vt., May 29, 1929; s. Arthur Joseph and Mary Beatrice (Callery) S.; m. Elizabeth Lloyd Frier, Jan. 2, 1960; children: Arthur, Claire, Paul, Sara. AB, Fordham Coll., 1951; JD U. Mich., 1954; postgrad. (Fulbright grantee), U. London (Eng.), 1957-58. Bar: Mich. 1954, Ohio 1954, D.C. 1959. Assoc., Squire, Sanders & Dempsey, Cleve., 1954; assoc., ptnr. Woll, Mayer & St. Antoine, Washington, D.C., 1958-65; assoc. prof. law U. Mich. Law Sch., Ann Arbor, 1965-69, prof. 1969—; Degan prof. 1981—; dean, 1971-78; pres. Nat. Resource Ctr. for Consumers of Legal Svcs., 1974-78; mem. Pub. Rev. Bd., UAW, 1973—; chmn. UAW-GM Legal Svcs. Plan, 1983-95; Mich. Gov.'s spl. counselor on workers' compensation, 1983-85; reporter Uniform Law Commrs., 1987-92; life mem. Clare Hall, Cambridge (Eng.) U. 1st lt. JAGC, U.S. Army, 1955-57. Mem. ABA (past sec. labor law sect., coun. 1984-92), Am. Bar Found., State Bar Mich. (past chmn. labor rels. law sect.), Nat. Acad. Arbitrators (bd. govs. 1985-88, v.p. 1994—), Internat. Soc. Labor Law and Social Security (U.S. br. exec. bd. 1983—, vice chmn. 1989-95), Indsl. Rels. Rsch. Assn., Order of Coif (life). Democrat. Roman Catholic. Author (with R. Smith, L. Merrifield and C. Craver) Labor Relations Law: Cases and Materials, 4th edit., 1968, 9th edit., 1994; contbr. numerous articles to various profl. jours. Home: 1421 Roxbury Rd Ann Arbor MI 48104-4047 Office: U Mich Law Sch 625 S State St Ann Arbor MI 48109-1215

ST. ARNOLD, DALE S., hospital administrator. Attended, Mich. Tech. U., 1974; BS in Bus. Adminstrn., Pa. State U., 1976; MHA, Washington U., 1986, MBA, 1986. Staff acct. Francis L. Killer & Co., Pub. Accts., Rapid City, S.D., 1976-77; staff acct. Andrew Skeeter, Inc. CPA, Tulsa, 1977, comptroller, adminstrv. mgr., 1978, fin. svcs. mgr., 1979; owner, gen. mgr. Fin. and Acctg. Svcs. of Tulsa, 1980-84; adminstrv. fellow Holy Cross Health System, South Bend, Ind., 1986-87; v.p. ops. St. Benedict's Hosp., Ogden, Utah, 1987-89, pres., chief oper. officer, 1989-91; exec. v.p. Mt. Carmel Health, Columbus, Ohio, 1991; chief oper. officer Mt. Carmel East Hosp., Columbus, 1991; interim pres., chief exec. officer Mt. Carmel Health, 1991-92, pres., chief exec. officer, 1992—; bd. dirs. St. Benedict's Hosp., mem. all bd. coms.; gen. ptnr. mgmt. responsibility Medico Home Health, Ltd., 1987-90. Home: 953 Avir Ct Gahanna OH 43230-3833 Office: Mt Carmel Health 793 W State St Columbus OH 43222-1551*

ST. AUBIN, J. ARTHUR, Canadian federal agency executive; b. Paris, July 2, 1930; m. Doreen Spence Flett, Mar. 10, 1956; children: Robert, Marc, Catherine, Richard. BA, U. Montreal, 1951. Exec. dir. tng. programs Govt. of Can., Ottawa, Ont., 1980-88; asst. commr. corp. mgmt. Correctional Svc. Can., Ottawa, Ont., 1988-90; CEO, pres. Can. Ctr. Occupational Health and Safety, Hamilton, Ont., 1990—. Maj. Gen. Can. Army, 1950-80, Viet Nam, Middle East, Europe. Recipient Centennial medal, Jubilee medal Can. Armed Forces, Order Military Merit. Avocation, fitness tng. Office: Can Ctr for Occupational H & S, 250 Main St East, Hamilton, ON Canada L8N 1H6

ST. CLAIR, CARL, conductor, music director. Music dir. Pacific Symphony Orch., Santa Ana, Calif., 1990—. Office: Pacific Symphony Orch 1231 E Dyer Rd Santa Ana CA 92705-5606

ST. CLAIR, DONALD DAVID, lawyer; b. Hammond, Ind., Dec. 30, 1932; s. Victor Peter and Wanda (Rubinska) Small; m. Sergine Anne Oliver, June

6, 1970 (dec. June 1974); m. Beverly Joyce Tipton, Dec. 28, 1987. BS, Ind. U., 1955, MS, 1963, EdD, 1967; JD, U. Toledo, 1992. Bar: Ohio 1992, U.S. Dist. Ct. (no. dist.) Ohio 1993, U.S. Supreme Ct., 1996. Assoc. prof. Coll. Edn. Western Ky. U., Bowling Green, 1967-68; assoc. prof. U. Toledo, 1968-77, prof., 1977-92; atty., ptnr. Garand, Bollinger, & St. Clair, Oregon, Ohio, 1992—; bd. dirs. Toledo Mental Health Ctr., 1977-79; mem. Ohio Coun. Mental Health Ctrs., Columbus, 1978-79; dir. honors programs U. Toledo. Author: (poetry) Daymarks and Beacons, 1983; contbr. numerous articles to profl. jours. Organizer Students Toledo Organized for Peace, 1970-71; mem. Lucas County Dem. Party, 1990—. With U.S. Army, 1955-57. Mem. ABA, AAU (nat. bd. dirs. 1973-74), Ohio Bar Assn., Toledo Bar Assn., Ohio Acad. Trial Lawyers, Toledo Power Squadron (commdg. officer 1981), Bay View Yacht Club, Masons (32 degree), Shriners, Ancient Order Friars, Phi Alpha Delta Law Soc. Home: 3353 Christie Blvd Toledo OH 43606-2862 Office: Garand Bollinger & St Clair Charlesgate Commons Forum 860 Ansonia Ste 113 Oregon OH 43616

ST. CLAIR, HAL KAY, electrical engineer; b. Los Angeles, Oct. 11, 1925; s. Millard T. and Ruth (McGrew) St. C.; m. Jane Creely, June 24, 1949; children: Gregory, Russell, Elizabeth. Student, U. So. Calif., 1943-44; BS, U. Calif.-Berkeley, 1946, MS, 1948. Research engr. Marchant Calculators, Emeryville, Calif., 1948-52; project engr. RCA, Camden, N.J., 1953-54; program mgr. IBM, San Jose, Calif., 1954-69; tech. staff IBM, Boca Raton, Fla., 1969-72, mgr. input/output devel., 1972-75, mgr. gen. lab. devel., 1975-81, mgr. small comml. systems engring., 1981-83; ergonomics adviser div. hdqrs. staff IBM, White Plains, N.Y., 1983-85, devel. edn. mgr., 1986-88, ret., 1988; instr. U. Calif. Extension Div., 1951-52; tech. adv. U.S. Nat. Com. Internat. Electrotechnical Commn., 1967-69. Mem. Republican Central Com. of Calif., 1962-66. Served to lt. (j.g.) USNR, 1943-46. Mem. IEEE, SAR, Mensa, Phi Beta Kappa, Sigma Xi, Tau Beta Pi, Eta Kappa Nu. Home: 17137 Bernardo Oaks Dr San Diego CA 92128-2104

ST. CLAIR, JAMES DRAPER, lawyer; b. Akron, Ohio, Apr. 14, 1920; s. Clinton Draper and Margaret Joanna (Glenn) St. C.; m. Asenath Nestle, Nov. 25, 1944; children: Margaret Nestle, David Scott, Thomas Bruce. Student, Augustana Coll., 1938-39; AB, U. Ill., 1941; LLB, Harvard U., 1947; LLD, Gettysburg Coll., 1975, New Eng. Sch. Law, 1975, Emerson Coll., 1993. Bar: Mass. Assoc. Hale & Dorr, Boston, 1947-52; jr. ptnr. Hale & Dorr, 1952-56, sr. ptnr., 1956-95; spl. counsel to Pres. Richard Nixon, 1974; lectr. Harvard Law Sch.; asst. counsel to Army, Army-McCarthy Hearings, 1954; co-mng. trustee Amelia Peabody Found., 1985—. Author: (with others) Assignments in Trial Practice, 1960. Mem. Town Meeting, Wellesley, Mass., 1963-73; gen. counsel United Fund, 1966; mem. Town of Wellesley Adv. Com., 1966-69; mem. steering com. Lawyers Com. for Civil Rights Under Law, 1968-73; mem. adv. com. Mass. Jud. Conf. Com. on Criminal Rules Project, 1972-73; Trustee, bd. dirs. Walker Home for Children, 1951-73, 75—; pres. Horizons for Youth, 1981-94, chmn. bd., 1994—; bd. dirs. The Met in Boston, The Boston Opera Assn.; mem. New Eng. Bapt. Health Care Corp., 1991—; chair mgmt. rev. com. Boston Police Dept., 1991-92; mem. Corporation Mass. Gen. Hosp., 1992—. Served to lt. USNR, 1942-45. Mem. ABA (council of litigation sect. 1974—), Boston Bar Assn. (council), Am. Law Inst., Am. Coll. Trial Lawyers, Practising Law Inst. (nat. adv. council 1967-73), New Eng. Law Inst. (adv. council 1970-71), Order of Coif. Republican. Conglist. Clubs: Brae Burn Country, Eastward Ho Country. Office: Hale & Dorr 60 State St Boston MA 02109-1803*

ST. CLAIR, JAMES WILLIAM, lawyer; b. Charleston, W.Va., Apr. 1, 1935; s. James William and Daisy Catherine (Litz) St. C.; m. Doria Diana Arrington, Aug. 10, 1956; children: Patricia A. St. Clair Deford, Laura J. St. Clair Johnson, J. William, Samual A. AB in History, U. Va., 1957, LLB, 1960. Bar: Va. 1960, W.Va. 1960, U.S. Dist. Ct. (no. and so. dists.) W.Va. 1960, U.S. Ct. Appeals 1965, U.S. Supreme Ct. 1970. Ptnr. Marshall Harghbarer & St. Clair, Huntington, W.Va., 1960-70, Marshall & St. Clair, Huntington, 1970-80, Marshall, St. Clair & Levine, Huntington, 1980-89, St. Clair & Levine, Huntington, 1989—; bd. dirs. 1st Huntington Nat. Bank; dir., officer Huntington Realty Corp., Gen. Allied Oil and Gas Corp., Frankfurt, Germany, Town and Country Shopping Ctr., Inc., Huntington. Pres., bd. mem. Cabell Wayne Hist. Soc., Huntington, 1970—, Greater Huntington Pk. Bd., 1973—. 1st lt. U.S. Army, 1957-62. Mem. ABA (law practice mgmt. sect., bd. mem. 1985-91, specialist to Ukraine, Kazakhstan & Kyrgyzstan). Democrat. Presbyn. Avocations: lawn and gardening. Home: 1805 Mccoy Rd Huntington WV 25701-4823 Office: St Clair & Levine 717 6th Ave Huntington WV 25701-2105

ST. CLAIR, JANE ELIZABETH, management executive; b. Concord, Mass., Aug. 15, 1944; d. James F. and Mary E. (Clyne) Connell. BA, Salem State Coll., 1969; MPH, Columbia U., N.Y.C., 1990. Field rep., safety program Am. Red Cross of Greater N.Y., 1971-72; program dir. Bronx Community Coll., N.Y., 1973-75; dir. edn. Council N.Y.C., Inc., 1975-77, asst. exec. dir., 1978; exec. dir. Regional Emergency Med. Services, N.Y., 1979-91; dir. Peace Corps, Kenya, 1991-94, Gulfcoast South Area Health Edn. Ctr., Sarasota, Fla., 1995—; adjunt asst. prof., Hunter Coll. N.Y., 1973-91. Contbr. articles to profl. jours. Mem. Emergency Cardic Care Com. N.Y., Heart Assn., Am. Soc. Safety Engrs., Profl. Edn. Com., Am. Red Cross, First Aid Com. Address: 1749 S Highland Ave Apt 12A Clearwater FL 34616-1869

ST. CLAIR, JESSE WALTON, JR., retired savings and loan executive; b. Phila., Jan. 15, 1930; s. Jesse Walton and Susan Elizabeth (Leath) St. C.; m. Elizabeth Anne Bartlett, Oct. 6, 1951; children: Jesse Walton III, Susan Elizabeth, Bruce Bartlett, Anne Leath. BA, Coll. of William and Mary, 1951; MBA, U. Pa., 1958; postgrad., Harvard U., 1968. Trainee Fed. Res. Bank, Phila., 1955-57; with Girard Trust Bank, Phila., 1957-78; asst. treas. Girard Trust Bank, 1960-64, asst. v.p., 1964-67, v.p., 1967-70, sr. v.p., 1970-75, exec. v.p., 1976-78; pres., chief exec. officer First Nat. Bank of Allentown (Pa.), 1978-82; chmn., chief exec. officer Wilmington Savs. Fund Soc., 1982-90, ret., 1990. Trustee emeritus endowment fund Coll. William and Mary; dir. Del. Mut. Ins. Co.; mem. exec. bd., v.p. fin. Delmarva coun. Boy Scouts Am.; trustee Wesley Coll.; bd. dirs. Ingleside Homes Inc. With USN, 1951-55. Mem. Wilmington Country Club, Theta Delta Chi. Republican. Methodist. Home: 4011 Springfield Ln Greenville Wilmington DE 19807

ST. CLAIR, MICHAEL, art dealer; b. Bradford, Pa., May 28, 1912. Student, Kans. City Art Inst., Colo. Springs Fine Arts Ctr. Instr. Okla. Art Ctr. Sch., Oklahoma City; dir. Babcock Galleries, N.Y.C., 1959—. Named Vanderslice scholar Kansas City Art Inst. Mem. Art Dealers Assn. Am. (founding mem. 1962), Architecture & Am. Art Drawing Soc. Office: Babcock Galleries 724 5th Ave New York NY 10019-4106

ST. CLAIR, ROBERT NEAL, English language and linguistics educator; b. Honolulu, Apr. 24, 1934; divorced; 1 child, Tiffany Neal. BA, U. Hawaii, 1964; MA, U. Wash., 1966, U. Calif., La Jolla, 1970; PhD, U. Kans., 1973. Asst. prof. Calif. State U., L.A., 1966-67; asst. prof. English and linguistics U. Louisville, 1974-75, assoc. prof., 1975-76, prof., 1978—, disting. prof. rsch., 1995—; chmn. Forum for Interdisciplinary Rsch., Cancun, Mex., 1976, Curacao, Antilles, 1978; disting. vis. prof. N.Mex. State U., Las Cruces, 1978, Internat. Christian U., Tokyo, 1979, Josai Internat. U., Chiba, Japan, 1996. Author: Language and Social Psychology, 1976, Social Metaphors, 1990, Languages of the World, 1990, numerous others; editor Lektos, 1974-78; contbr. over 400 articles and revs. to profl. jours. Sgt. U.S. Army, 1957-60. Grantee Philips Found., 1974, NEH, 1975-77, U.S. Office Edn., 1977-79. Mem. MLA, Nat. Coun. Tchrs. English, Coll. Composition Comm. Conf. Office: 9431 Westport Rd Ste 343 Louisville KY 40241-2219

ST. CLAIR, THOMAS MCBRYAR, mining and manufacturing company executive; b. Wilkinsburg, Pa., Sept. 26, 1935; s. Fred C. and Dorothy (Renner) St. C.; m. Sarah K. Stewart, Aug. 1, 1959; children—Janet, Susan, Carol. AB, Allegheny Coll., 1957; MS, MIT, 1958; grad. advanced mgmt. program, Harvard U. With Koppers Co., Inc., Pitts., 1958-88, asst. to gen. mgr. engring. and constrn. div., 1966-69, comptroller, asst. treas., 1969-78, pres. Engineered Metal Products Group, 1978-83, v.p., asst. to chmn., 1983-84, v.p., treas., chief fin. officer, 1984-88; sr. v.p., chief fin. officer Phelps Dodge Corp., Phoenix, 1989—; bd. dirs. Nortrust of Ariz. Bd. dirs., treas. Herberger Theater Ctr., Phoenix; trustee Allegheny Coll. Mem. Fin. Execs. Inst., Duquesne Club (Pitts.), Univ. Club (Pitts. and Phoenix). Presbyterian. Office: Phelps Dodge Corp 2600 N Central Ave Phoenix AZ 85004-3050

ST. CLAIRE, FRANK ARTHUR, lawyer; b. Charlotte, N.C., June 16, 1949. BS, MIT, 1972; JD, NYU, 1975. Bar: Tex. 1975, U.S. Dist. Ct. (no. dist.) Tex. 1985. Assoc. James H. Wallenstein, Dallas, 1975-78; v.p. Wallenstein & St. Claire, Dallas, 1978-81; pres. Frank A. St. Claire, P.C., Dallas, 1981-84; ptnr. St. Claire & Case, P.C., Dallas, 1984-88, pres., 1988—; chmn. bd. Sunbelt Empire Title Co., Dallas, 1983-88; pres. St. Claire & Assocs., Dallas, 1993—; chmn. real estate section Godwin & Carlton, P.C., Dallas, 1994-96; ptnr. bus. and fin. divsn. Strasburger & Price, L.L.P., Dallas, 1996—. Author: Texas Condominium Law, 1986; contbr. articles to profl. jours. Ofcl. del. Dallas to Baltic Legal Conf., Riga, Latvia, 1990. Mem. ABA, Tex. Bar Assn. (study of uniform condominium act com., legis. liaison com. 1981-85, vice chmn. 1981-82, chmn. 1982-85, chmn. condominium and coop. housing com. 1985-89, title ins. com., mem. coun. real estate, probate and trust coun. 1991-95, treas. 1996—), Dallas Bar Assn., Cmty. Assn. Inst. (bd. dirs. Dallas-Ft. Worth chpt. 1984-85, 87-89, pres.-elect 1989-90), Real Estate Fin. Exec. Assn. (asst. sec. 1996—), Real Estate Coun., Am. Coll. Real Estate Lawyers (planning com. 1990—, chmn. practice tech. com. 1993—, mem. common interest ownership com. 1986—, alternative dispute resolution com. 1993-95), Tex. Coll. Real Estate Attys. (chmn. projects com. 1991-92, bd. dirs. 1994—). Episcopalian. Office: NationsBank Plz Ste 4300 901 Main St Dallas TX 75202

ST. CYR, ROGER JOSEPH, banker; b. Burlington, Vt., July 13, 1946; s. Alfred Joseph and Ursula (Paquin) St. Cyr.; m. Sandra Rose Flanagan, June 14, 1975; children: Molly, Maureen, Emelie. ABS, Champlain Coll., Burlington, Vt., 1966; student, U. Md., Heidelburg, Germany, 1966-68; BS Double Major, U. Dayton, Ohio, 1972; MBA, Capital U., Columbus, Ohio, 1980; grad. (with honors), U. Del., 1991. Data processing mgr. Third Nat. Bank, Dayton, Ohio, 1971-74, Bank One, Columbus, Ohio, 1974-75, Blue Shield, Columbus, 1975-76; data processing mgr. BancOhio Nat. Bank, Columbus, 1976-80, sales mgr., cash mgmt., 1980-84; v.p. nat. accounts BancOhio Nat. Bank, 1984-87; v.p. & mgr. nat. accts. Nat. City Trust, Columbus, 1987-91, v.p., sales mgr. institutional trust, 1991—. Author: Thesis-Cash Management, 1985, Thesis-Psychological Study on How Acquisition Targets React to and Adapt to Culture Change, 1991. Chair Sta. WOSU (PBS) Fundraiser - Auction Columbus; sec. Friends of Sta. WOSU (PBS) Columbus. With U.S. Army 1966-69, Fed. Rep. Germany. Mem. Athletic Club of Columbus, Muirfield Country Club. Office: Nat City Trust 155 E Broad St Columbus OH 43251-0050

ST. FLORIAN, FRIEDRICH GARTLER, architect, educator, university dean; b. Graz, Austria, Dec. 21, 1932; came to U.S., 1967, naturalized, 1973; s. Friedrich and Anna Maria (Prassl) G.; m. Livia Campanella, Jan. 12, 1967; children: Alisia, Ilaria. Diploma in architecture, U. Graz, 1958; M.S. in Architecture, Columbia U., 1962. Instr. architecture Columbia U., N.Y.C., 1962-63; asst. prof. R.I. Sch. Design, Providence, 1963-70; assoc. prof. R.I. Sch. Design, 1974-77, prof. architecture, 1980—, chmn. div. archtl. studies, 1977-78, dean of architecture, 1978-88; chief critic European Honors Program R.I. Sch. Design, Rome, 1991-93; vis. asso. prof. MIT, Cambridge, 1970-71, 74-75; prin. St. Florian Assos., architects, Providence, 1978—. Works exhibited Nat. Inst. Architects, Rome, 1967, 14th Triennale, Milan, 1968, Moderna Museet, Stockholm, 1969, Hayden Galelry, MIT, 1973, Mus. Modern Art, N.Y.C., 1975, Drawing Ctr., N.Y.C., 1979, Walker Art Ctr., Mpls., 1980, Georges Pompidou Ctr., Paris, 1994, Centre de Cultura Contemporania, Barcelona, 1994. Recipient Nat. Endowment for Arts award, 1972-73, 76-77, 79, 26th ann. Progressive Architecture Mag. award, 1979; Ctr. for Advanced Visual Studies fellow MIT, 1970-77, Rome Prize fellow, fellow Am. Acad. in Rome, 1985. Mem. AIA. Address: RI Sch Design Arch Dept Providence RI 02903

ST. GEORGE, JUDITH ALEXANDER, author; b. Westfield, N.J., Feb. 26, 1931; d. John Heald and Edna (Perkins) Alexander; m. David St. George, June 5, 1954; children: Peter, James, Philip, Sarah Anne. BA, Smith Coll., 1952. Author: Turncoat Winter, Rebel Spring, 1970, The Girl with Spunk, 1975, By George, Bloomers!, 1976, The Chinese Puzzle of Shag Island, 1976, The Shad Are Running, 1977, The Shadow of the Shaman, 1977, The Halo Wind, 1978, The Halloween Pumpkin Smasher, 1978, Mystery at St. Martin's, 1979, The Amazing Voyage of the New Orleans, 1980, Haunted, 1980, Call Me Margo, 1981, The Mysterious Girl in the Garden, 1981, The Brooklyn Bridge: They Said It Couldn't Be Built, 1982 (Am. Book award), Do You See What I See?, 1982, In The Shadow of the Bear, 1983, What's Happening to My Junior Year?, 1983, Who's Scared? Not Me!, 1984, The Mount Rushmore, 1985 (Christopher award), Panama Canal: Gateway to the World, 1989 (Golden Kite award), The White House, 1990, Mason and Dixon's Line of Fire, 1991, Dear Dr. Bell...Your Friend Helen Keller, 1992, Crazy Horse, 1994; (from filmscript) A View to a Kill, 1985; (from screenscript) Tales of the Gold Monkey, 1983. Mem. adv. coun. on children's lit. Rutgers U., 1977—; chmn. ednl. com. Bklyn. Bridge Centennial Commn., 1981-83. Mem. Soc. Children's Book Writers, Author's Guild. Episcopalian. Avocations: tennis, hiking, travel. Home: 8 Binney Rd Old Lyme CT 06371-1445

ST. GEORGE, NICHOLAS JAMES, lawyer, manufactured housing company executive; b. Waltham, Mass., Feb. 11, 1939; s. Louis and Rose (Argonti) St. G.; B.A. in Econs., Coll. William and Mary, 1960, J.D., 1965; children: Blane Stephen, Nicholas John; m. Eugenia Metzger, July 25, 1987. Trainee, Gen. Electric Co., Schenectady, 1960; admitted to Va. bar, 1965; trust rep. Va. Nat. Bank, Norfolk, 1965-66; group v.p.-in-charge investment banking dept. Ferguson Enterprises, Newport News, Va., 1977-78; pres., chief exec. officer Oakwood Homes Corp., Greensboro, N.C., 1979—, also dir.; dir. Am. Bankers Ins. Group, First Union Nat. Bank Greensboro, Legg Mason, Inc.; dir. Manufactured Housing Inst.; trustee Marshall-Wythe Sch. Law Coll. William and Mary. 1st lt. U.S. Army, 1960-62. Mem. ABA, Va. Bar Assn., Am. Mgmt. Assn. Republican. Roman Catholic. Office: Oakwood Homes Corp 2225 S Holden Rd Greensboro NC 27407-4605

ST. GEORGE, WILLIAM ROSS, lawyer, retired naval officer, consultant; b. Southport, N.C., Nov. 19, 1924; s. William B. and Ila (Ross) St. G.; m. Emma Louise Bridger, June 10, 1950; children—Victoria Butler, William Ross, Susan Bridger. B.S., U.S. Naval Acad., 1946; J.D., George Washington U., 1953. Bar: D.C. 1953, U.S. Supreme Ct. 1964, Calif. 1980. Commd. ensign U.S. Navy, 1946, advanced through grades to vice adm., 1973; comdg. officer U.S.S. Josephus Daniels, 1969-70; comdr. Cruiser-Destroyer Flotilla 11, also comdr. Cruiser-Destroyer Flotilla 3, 1973; dep. and chief staff to comdr.-in-chief U.S. Pacific Fleet, 1973-76; comdr. Naval Surface Force, U.S. Pacific Fleet, 1976-79, ret., 1979; sole practice San Diego, 1980—. Decorated D.S.M. with oak leaf cluster, Legion of Merit, Bronze Star. Presbyterian. Home: 862 San Antonio Pl San Diego CA 92106-3057 Office: 1110 Rosecrans St Fl 2D San Diego CA 92106-2630

ST. GERMAIN, FERNAND JOSEPH, congressman; b. Blackstone, Mass.; s. Andrew Joseph and Pearl (Talaby) St Germain; m. Rachel O'Neill, Aug. 20, 1953; children: Laurene, Lisette. Ph.B. in Social Sci, Providence Coll., 1948, LL.D., 1965; LL.B., Boston U., 1955; J.S.D. (hon.), Suffolk U., 1976; D.C.L. (hon.), Our Lady of Providence Sem., 1968; D.B.A. (hon.), Bryant Coll., 1981; D.Public Service (hon.), Roger Williams Coll., 1981; LL.B., Brown U., 1985. Bar: R.I. 1956, Fed. 1957, U.S. Supreme Ct. 1983. Mem. R.I. Ho. of Reps., 1952-60; mem. 87th to 100th Congresses from 1st R.I. Dist., 1961-1989, chmn. house com. on banking fin. and urban affairs, 1980-88. Served with AUS, 1949-52. Recipient Silver Shingle award for disting. public service Boston U. Sch. Law Alumni Assn., 1981, Alumni award disting. pub. service Boston U. Sch. Law, 1982. Mem. ABA, R.I., Bar Assn. Fed. Bar Assn., alumni assns. Our Lady of Providence Sem., Providence Coll., Boston U. Law Sch., Am. Legion. Office: 7601 Lewinsville Rd Ste 205 Mc Lean VA 22102

ST. GERMAIN, GEORGE, retail executive. With Applebaums Food Markets Inc., Saint Paul, Minn., 1958-78; with Jerry's Enterprises Inc, Mpls., 1978—, now v.p. grocery ops. Office: Jerry's Enterprises Inc 5101 Vernon Ave S Minneapolis MN 55436*

ST. GERMAIN, GERRY, entrepreneur, Canadian senator; b. St. Boniface, Canada, Nov. 6, 1937; s. Michel and Mary Kathleen (James) St. G.; m. Margaret Schilke, Nov. 25, 1961; children: Michele, Suzanne, Jay. Entrepreneur, 1965—; chmn., dir. Brit. Columbia Poultry Industry; mem. parliament House Commons, 1983-88; with Minstry of State (Transport), 1988, Ministry of State (Forestry) Fed. Govt., 1988; apptd. mem. Senate of Can., 1993—; chmn. St. Thomas More Coll. Bd. Pursuit of Excellence. With City of St. Boniface Police Force, 1960. Mem. Can. Broiler Coun. (rep.), Vancouver Golf Club. Avocation: golf. Office: Progressive Conservative Party, 275 Slater St Ste 600, Ottawa, ON Canada K1P 5H9 Office: Senate of Canada, 205 Victoria Bldg Wellington St, Ottawa, ON Canada

ST. GOAR, HERBERT, food corporation executive; b. Hamburg, Germany, Apr. 7, 1916; came to U.S., 1938, naturalized, 1943; s. Otto and Thekla St.G.; m. Maria Karsch, Sept. 3, 1954; children: Edward, Elisabeth. Student schs., Hamburg, Germany; LL.B., Chattanooga Coll. Law, 1943. With Internat. Harvester Co., Hamburg, Germany, 1936-38; with Dixie Saving Stores, Inc., Chattanooga, 1938—; pres. Dixie Saving Stores, Inc., 1969—, chief exec. officer, 1969—. Bd. dirs. Chattanooga Opera Assn., Jr. C. of C., 1945-54; mem. Hamilton County Juvenile Ct. Commn. Served with Intelligence Sect., U.S. Army, World War II. Decorated Bronze Star, Legion of Merit.; Named Disting. Citizen Chattanooga, 1979. Mem. Southeastern Food Coop. Assn. (past pres.), Tenn. Wholesale Grocers Assn. (bd. dirs. 1988-91), Retailer-Owned Food Distrbrs. Assn. (bd. dirs. 1988—), NGA Retailer-Owned Exec. Coun., Asparagus Club. Home: 1502 Hixson Pike Chattanooga TN 37405-2431 Office: PO Box 1637 Chattanooga TN 37401-1637

SAINT-JACQUES, BERNARD, linguistics educator; b. Montreal, Que., Can., Apr. 26, 1928; s. Albert and Germaine (Lefebvre) Saint-J.; m. Marguerite Fauquenoy. M.A., Sophia U., Tokyo, 1962; M.S., Georgetown U., 1964; Doctorat es Lettres and Scis. Humaines, Paris U., 1975. Asst. prof. linguistics U. B.C., Vancouver, 1967-69; assoc. prof. U. B.C., 1969-78, prof., 1978-90, prof. emeritus, 1991—; prof. Aichi U., Japan, 1990—; mem. U.S. Citizen Amb. Program. Author: Structural Analysis of Modern Japanese, 1971, Aspects sociolinguistiques du bilinguisme canadien, 1976, Language and Ethnic Relations, 1979, Japanese Studies in Canada, 1985, Studies in Language and Culture, 1995. Leave fellow Can. Council, 1974; profl. fellow Japan Found., 1981; research fellow French Govt., 1982, Ohira Programme, Japan, 1983. Fellow Royal Soc. Can. Acad.; mem. Sociolinguistic Assn. (co-editor), Linguistic Soc. Am., Can. Soc. Asian Studies, Can. Linguistics Assn. Office: U BC, Dept Linguistics, Vancouver, BC Canada V6T 1Z1 also: Aichi ShuKutoKu U, Katahira NagaKute, NagaKute-cho Aichi-gun Aichi 480-11, Japan

SAINT-JACQUES, MADELEINE, advertising agency executive; b. Montreal, Can., June 27, 1935; d. Henri and Marie-Jeanne (Ostiguy) S.J. BA, U. Montreal, 1972. Writer, producer Young & Rubicam, Montreal, 1955-70, creative dir., 1970-77, exec. v.p., mng. dir., 1977-90, pres., 1990-94, chmn. bd. dirs., 1995; bd. dirs. Télé Métropole Inc., Ultramar Corp., Premier Choix: TVEC Inc.; bd. govs. Inno-Centre Québec; v.p. Soc. d'édition de la revue Forces, La Corp. des Célébrations du 350e anniversaire de Montréal, 1989-93; adv. bd. Guarant Trust, 1979-84. Bd. dirs. Internat. Mag. Mgmt., 1980-92. 1st v.p. Children's Broadcast Inst., 1972-77; grievance com. L'Union des Artistes, 1976-78; gen. v.p. comm. divsn. Centraide campaign, 1980, v.p. bd. dirs. 1983-87; v.p. Coun. Arts Montreal Urban Community, 1979-89; co-pres. Com. Econ. Promotion Montreal, 1981-82; bd. govs. McGill U. 1986-90; bd. dirs. Terry Fox Humanitarian Award Program, St. Mary's Hosp. Found., Can. Mental Health Assn., 1975-79, Soc. Devel. Industries and Culture of Comm. (SDICC), 1979-82, Via Rail Can. Inc., 1977-82, Soc. Devel. Montreal, 1982-88, Found. Films of World Festival, Montreal, 1990-92. Recipient advt. award Assn. Can. Advertisers, 1975, 76, Gold award, 1977, award distinction Faculty commerce and adminstrn. Concordia U., 1992, mgmt. achievement award Mgmt. Undergrad. Soc. McGill U., 1993. Mem. Can. Club Montréal (bd. dirs., pres. 1993—, pres. centennial yr. 1987), Club St.-Denis, Forest and Stream, Publicité Club Montreal (pres. 1972-73). Roman Catholic. Avocations: skiing, tennis, golf. Office: Young & Rubicam 12th Fl, 1600 René Lévesque Blvd W, Montreal, PQ Canada H3H 1P9

ST. JAMES, LYN, business owner, professional race car driver; b. Willoughby, Ohio, Mar. 13, 1947; d. Alfred W. and Maxine W. (Rawson) Cornwall; m. John Raymond Carusso, Dec. 7, 1970 (div. 1979); m. Roger Lessman, Feb. 27, 1993; 1 stepchild, Lindsay. Cert. in piano, St. Louis Inst. Music, 1967. Sec. Cleve. dist. sales office U.S. Steel Corp., 1967-69, Mike Roth Sales Corp., Euclid, Ohio, 1969-70; co-owner, v.p. Dynasales Fla., Hollywood, 1970-79; owner, pres. Autodyne, Ft. Lauderdale, Fla., 1974-91, Creative Images, Inc., 1979—; professional race car driver, 1979—; ranked 11th Indpls. 500, 1992; race car driver Ford Motor Co., Dearborn, Mich., 1981—, spokesperson, cons., 1981—; media spokesperson JC Penney, 1992—. Author: Lyn St. James Car Owner's Manual, 1989; contbg. editor automotive articles Seventeen mag., 1987—, Cosmopolitan mag., 1989-90. Bd. trustees Women's Sports Found., N.Y.C., 1988—. Recipient Rookie of the Year, AutoWeek Magazine, 1984, Woman of Yr. award McCalls mag., 1986, Leadership award Girl Scouts U.S., 1988, Rookie of Yr. at the Indy 500, 1992, Touchstone award Girls Inc. Indpls., 1995; first woman since Janet Guthrie to qualify for the Indpls. 500. Mem. Internat. Motorsports Assn., Sports Car Club of Am. Republican. Avocation: tennis.Only woman winner in the Internat. Motor Sports Assn.'s Camel GTO series; holder of 31 auto racing speed records; first woman to win a professional road race driving solo; first woman to drive over 200 mph on an oval track. Office: Creative Images Ste F 2570 International Speedway Blvd Daytona Beach FL 32114

ST. JEAN, GARRY, professional basketball coach; m. Mary Jane St. Jean; children: Emily, Gregory. B in Phys. Edn., Springfield (Mass.) Coll., 1973, M in Phys. Edn., postgrad. cert. Head coach Chicopee (Mass.) High Sch., 1973-80; coll. scout, asst. bench coach, asst. dir. player pers. Milw. Bucks, 1980-86; asst. coach, asst. player pers. dir. N.J. Nets, 1986-88; asst. coach Golden State Warriors, 1988-92; head coach Sacramento Kings, 1992—. Office: Sacramento Kings One Sports Pkwy Sacramento CA 95834*

ST. JEAN, JOSEPH, JR., micropaleontologist, educator; b. Tacoma, July 24, 1923; s. Joseph Leger and Ruby Pearl (Burg) St. J.; m. Elena Mikhailovna Melnikova, Sept. 22, 1971. B.S., Coll. Puget Sound, 1949; M.A., Ind. U., 1953, Ph.D., 1956. Field asst., party chief Ind. Geol. Survey, summers 1950-53; instr. Kans. State U., Manhattan, 1951-52; instr., asst. prof. Trinity Coll., Hartford, Conn., 1955-57; faculty U. N.C., Chapel Hill, 1957-90; prof. geology U. N.C., 1966-90, gen. coll. advisor, 1979-90, ret., 1990; peer reviewer NSF, 1966—, profl. jours., 1960—. 2d violinist, Durham (N.C.) Symphony Orch., 1977-84; Contbr. sects. to McGraw-Hill Ency. Sci. and Tech; papers to paleontol., biol. jours. Served as Q.M. USNR, 1942-45. Grantee Geol. Soc. Am., 1956-58; Grantee AEC, 1958-60; Grantee NSF, 1960-62; Grantee U. N.C. Faculty Research Council, 1960-62; Grantee Soc. Sigma Xi, 1954-56. Mem. Paleontol. Soc., Soc. Econ. Paleontologists and Mineralogists, Carolina Geol. Soc., Paleontol. Rsch. Instn., N.C. Acad. Scis., Paleontol. Assn. London, Sigma Xi. Home: 1212 Hillsborough Rd Chapel Hill NC 27516-8712 Office: U NC Dept Geology CB #3315 Mitchell Hall Chapel Hill NC 27599-3315

ST. JOHN, ADRIAN, II, retired army officer; b. Ft. Leavenworth, Kans., Nov. 16, 1921; s. Adrian and Marie (McMahon) St John; m. Petronella Elizabeth Durham, Jan. 19, 1943; children: Adrian III, Brian. BS, U.S. Mil. Acad., 1943; M.A., U. Va., 1951; MPA, Am. U., 1981; postgrad., Army War Coll., 1960, U. Hawaii, 1963, Am. U., 1977-82. Commd. 2d lt. U.S. Army, 1943, advanced through grades to maj. gen., 1969, co. comdg. officer 15th Cav., 1943-45; intelligence staff officer U.S. Army, Berlin, 1945-47; China desk officer gen. staff U.S. Army, Washington, 1951-53; bn. comdg. officer 3d Bn., 31st Inf. Regt. U.S. Army, Korea, 1954, comdr. 73d Tank Bn., 1955; mem. faculty Command and Gen. Staff Coll., Ft. Leavenworth, 1956-59; faculty adviser Iranian Def. Coll., 1959; S.E. Asia plans officer G3, U.S. Army-Pacific, 1960-64; long range plans br. Strategic Div., Orgn. Joint Chiefs of Staff, Washington, 1964-66; chief Surface P & O Div. J3, US-MACV, Vietnam, 1966-67; comdg. officer 14th Armored Cav. Regt., Europe, 1967-69; asst. div. comdr. 4th Armored Div., Europe, 1969-70; chief Strategic Plans and Policy Div. J5, Orgn. Joint Chiefs of Staff, Washington, 1970-71; dir. plans gen. staff U.S. Army, Washington, 1971-72; comdg. gen. 1st Armored Div., Europe, 1972-74; vice dir. joint staff Joint Chiefs of Staff, 1974-76; ret., 1976; mem. adv. council on internat. security affairs Republican Nat. Com., 1977-80; del. Va. State Rep. Conv., 1980, 81; sr. mil. adv. U.S. Negotiating Del. Mut. Balanced Force Reductions, Vienna, 1982-88; Joint Chiefs of Staff rep. U.S. Del. Conventional Stability Talks, Vienna,

1987-88, negotiations on Conventional Armed Forces, Europe, 1989-92; del., presenter Congress Arms Control Mid. East, Delphi, Greece, 1994; U.S. del. World Helicopter Championships, Moscow, 1994; chmn. operational working group internat. conf. on arms control in Mid. East, Jordan, 1994; presenter plaques signed by Sec. of Def. to Australian authorities in 6 cities during ceremonies commemorating VJ Day, 1995. Co-chmn. orchestral benefit ball Austrian Embassy, 1993, 94; mem. pres. club Heritage Found. Decorated D.S.M. with oak leaf cluster, Silver Star, Legion of Merit with 3 oak leaf clusters, Bronze Star with V device, Joint Svc. Commendation medal, Army Commendation medal with oak leaf cluster, Joint Meritorious Unit award, French Croix de Guerre with silver star, Vietnamese Gallantry Cross with palm; recipient European Comdr. in Chief's Individual Project partnership award, 1968, Presdl. award Disting. Citizen, 1993, Dept. State Superior honor award, 1989, 91, Dept. of Def. medal for disting. pub. svc., 1992. Mem. Am. Security Coun., Am. Fgn. Affairs Coun., Pres. Club Heritage Found., World Affairs Coun., Pacific-Sierra Rsch. Corp. (cons.). Roman Catholic. Home: # 118 9110 Belvoir Woods Pkwy Fort Belvoir VA 22060-2716 Office: Pentagon Bldg Washington DC 20301 *There are no limits to the heights man can reach so long as he cares not who gets the credit.*

ST. JOHN, BILL DEAN, diversified equipment and services company executive; b. Wewoka, Okla., 1931. BBA, So. Meth. U., 1952. Asst. treas. Seaboard Oil Co., 1954-58; auditor Alford Merony & Co., 1958-60; v.p. fin. Can. Refractories Ltd., 1968; with Dresser Industries Inc., Dallas, 1960—; treas. Ideco div. Dresser Industries, Dallas, 1961-63; fin. contr. Dresser Industries Inc., Dallas, 1970-73, staff v.p. fin. svcs., 1975-76, v.p. acctg., 1976-80; exec. v.p. adminstrn. Dresser Industries, Inc., Dallas, 1980-92, vice chmn., 1992—, CFO, 1993—; Allendale Ins. So. adv. bd., 1995—. With U.S. Army, 1952-54. Mem. AICPA, Mfrs.' Alliance for Productivity and Innovation (fin. coun.), The Conf. Bd. (chief adminstrv. officers coun.), Allendale Ins. So. Adv. Bd. Office: Dresser Industries Inc PO Box 718 2001 Ross Ave Dallas TX 75221-0718

ST. JOHN, BOB, journalist, columnist, author; b. Canton, Okla., Jan. 10, 1937. Sportswriter, sports columnist, until 1978; gen. columnist Dallas Morning News, 1978—. Author: On Down the Road, 1977, Landry: The Man Inside, 1978, Tex, 1988, The Landry Legend, 1990, Sketches, 1981, While The Music Lasts, 1989, South Padre: The Island and Its People, Heart of a Lion, 1991, others; co-author: Straubach: First and Lifetime With Sam Blair, 1974; over 150 radio, TV internviews. Recipient Disting. Alumni award U. North Tes., 1986, two 1st place awards Pro Football Writers Assn. Am., over 40 awards for newspaper writing; named to North Tex. State U. Journalism Hall of Honor, 1986. Office: The Dallas Morning News Communications Ctr PO Box 655237 Dallas TX 75265-5237

ST. JOHN, HENRY SEWELL, JR., utility company executive; b. Birmingham, Ala., Aug. 18, 1938; s. H. Sewell and Carrie M. (Bond) St. J.; student David Lipscomb Coll., 1956-58, U. Tenn., 1958-59, U. Ala., 1962-64; m. J. Ann Morris, Mar. 7, 1959; children: Sherri Ann, Brian Lee, Teresa Lynn, Cynthia Faye. Engring. aide Ala. Power Co., Enterprise, 1960-62, Birmingham, 1962-66; asst. chief engr. Riviera Utilities, Foley, 1966-71, sec.-treas., gen. mgr., 1971—. Deacon, Foley Ch. of Christ, 1975-82, elder, 1983—; active Am. Cancer Soc., chmn. bd. Baldwin County unit, 1977; bd. dirs. AGAPE of Mobile, 1977-80; treas. Christian Care Ctr., Inc., 1981—; bd. dirs. South Baldwin Civic Chorus, pres., 1979-82 . Mem. IEEE., South Ala. Power Distbrs. Assn. (chmn. 1973-74), Ala. Consumer-Owned Power Distbrs. Assn. (chmn. 1974-75, 82-83, vice-chmn. 1981, sec.-treas. 1980), S.E. Electric Reliability Coun. (assoc.), Mcpl. Electric Utility Assn. Ala. (exec. com., dir. 1971—), Ala. Mcpl. Electric Authority (bd. dir. 1981—, vice chmn. 1981-82, chmn. 1983—), Electric Cities Ala. (bd. dirs., exec. com. 1989—), United Mcpl. Distbrs. Group (bd. dirs. 1972—), Am. Pub. Power Assn. (cable communications com.), Pub. Gas. Assn. Ala. (bd. dirs. 1987-88), South Baldwin C. of C. (pres. 1974, dir. 1972-75, 81-90, 92-95). Clubs: Foley Quarterback (sec.-treas. 1984-85); Gulf Shores Golf (dir. 1974-75), Classic Chevy, Internat. (life mem.), Azalea City Classic Chevy (bd. dirs., exec. com. 1989—, v.p. 1991-92, 95—), Chevrolet Nomad Assn. (bd. dirs. 1992—, v.p. 1993—). Rotarian. Home: PO Box 1817 Foley AL 36536-1817 Office: PO Box 550 Foley AL 36536

ST. JOHN, JOHN, food company executive; b. Battle Creek, Mich., Aug. 8, 1921; s. Raymond Martin and Hazel (Eastman) St. J.; m. Lorraine Margaret McCarthy, Feb. 27, 1943; 1 dau., Shannon Elaine. B.A., Mich. State U., 1943. With Minute Maid Co. (and predecessors), 1949—, fin. v.p., 1963-65, pres., 1965-69; v.p. finance and ops. Citrus Central, Inc., Orlando, Fla., 1969-71; exec. v.p. Citrus Central, Inc., 1971-87, mgmt. cons., 1987—; dir., chmn. Farm Credit Capital Corp., Kansas City, Mo., 1985-87; bd. dirs., chmn. Fed. Farm Credit Banks Funding Corp., N.Y., 1983-88; asset mgr. Treasure Coast Citrus, Inc., Ft. Pierce, Fla., 1989—. Past pres., bd. dirs. Central Fla. unit Am. Cancer Soc. Served with USAAF, 1943-46. Mem. Country Club of Orlando, Racquet Club (Winter Park, Fla.), Univ. Club (Lansing, Mich.). Episcopalian. Home: 910 Pace Ave Maitland FL 32751-5768 Office: 2251 Lucien Way Ste 220 Maitland FL 32751-7022

ST. JOHN, RICHARD See HARRIS, RICHARD

ST. LAURENT, DAVID FRANCIS, insurance company executive. With Electric Mut. Liability Ins. Co., Beverly, Mass., 1989—, pres. Office: Electric Ins Co 152 Conant St Beverly MA 01915*

SAINT LAURENT, YVES (HENRI DONAT MATHIEU), couturier; b. Oran, Algeria, Aug. 1, 1936; s. Charles Mathieu and Lucinne-Andree (Wilbaux) Saint L. Student, Lycée d'Oran. Worked with Christian Dior, 1954-57, successor, 1957-60; adminstr. Société Yves Saint Laurent, 1962—. Costume designer (ballets) Cyrano de Bergerac, 1959, Adage et Variations, Notre-Dame de Paris, 1965, Delicate Balance, 1967, Sheherezade, 1973, (films) The Pink Panther, 1962, Belle de Jour, 1967, La Chamade, 1968, La Sirène du Mississippi, 1969, L'Affaire Stavisky, 1974; stage sets and costumes Spectacle Zizi Jeanmaire, 1961, 63, 68, Les Chants de Maldoror, 1962; costume designer for Mariage de Figaro, 1964; illus. La Vilaine Lulu, 1967; exhbns. include Met. Mus. Art, N.Y., 1983, Beijing Mus. Fine Arts, 1985, Musée des Arts de la Mode, Paris, 1986, Ho. Painters USSR, 1986, Hermitage Mus., St. Petersburg, 1987, Art Gallery NSW, Sydney, 1987, Sezon Mus., Tokyo, 1990. Recipient Neiman-Marcus award for fashions, 1958, Oscar from Harper's Bazaar, 1966, Internat. award Coun. Fashion Designers Am., 1982, Best Fashion Designer Oscar, 1985; named Chevalier de la Légion d'Honneur, 1995, promoted de la Légion d'Honneur. Office: 5 ave Marceau, 75116 Paris France

ST. LOUIS, PAUL MICHAEL, foreign language educator; b. Vernon, Conn., Aug. 30, 1946; s. Wilfred Henry and Alice Agnes (Brennan) St. L. Spl. cert. Jr. Yr. Abroad program, U. Louvain, Belgium, 1967; BA, Boston Coll., 1968; MA, Trinity Coll., 1975. Cert. tchr. secondary French, Conn. Tchr. French East Hartford (Conn.) H.S., 1968—, head dept. fgn. lang., 1984-85; advisor to French club East Hartford H.S., 1969-85, jr. class advisor, 1985, 87, 89-90, 92, sr. class advisor, 1986, 88, 90-92, bus. mgr. grades 9-12, 1993—. Vis. com. New England Assn. Schs. and Colls., Milford, Conn., 1980, steering com. for sch. evaluation, 1978, 88. Mem. NEA, Am. Coun. Tchg. of Fgn. Lang., Conn. Edn. Assn., Conn. Coun. Lang. Tchrs. (treas. bd. dirs. 1992—, chairperson registration fall conf. 1989—, co-chairperson fall conf. 1991, cons. poetry recitation contest 1992—), Am. Assn. Tchrs. of French (cons. regional conf. 1990), Mass. Fgn. Lang. Assn., East Hartford Edn. Assn. Avocation: computer technology. Home: 275 Cedar Swamp Rd Monson MA 01057-9303 Office: East Hartford HS 869 Forbes St East Hartford CT 06118-1921

ST.MARIE, SATENIG, writer; b. Brockton, Mass., June 2, 1927; d. Harry and Mary K. Sahjian; m. Gerald L. St. Marie, Dec. 26, 1959. B.S., Simmons Coll., Boston, 1949; M.A., Columbia U., 1959; LL.D. (hon.), N.D. State U., 1976. Extension home economist U. Mass. Extension Service, 1949-52, U. Conn. Extension Service, 1953-56; with J.C. Penney Co., Inc., 1959-87, mgr. endl. and consumer relations, 1967-73, dir. consumer affairs, 1973-87, div. v.p., 1974-87; dir. Nat. Reins. Co.; mem. U.S. Metric Bd. Author: Homes Are For People, 1973, Romantic Victorian Weddings: Then and Now, 1992; pub. J.C. Penney Consumer Edn. Services, 1981-87; lifestyles editor: Victorian Homes Mag., 1987—. Mem. Am. Home Econs. Assn. (past pres.), Antiques Dealers Assn. Am. (exec. dir. 1987—). Office: PO Box 335 Greens Farms CT 06436-0335

ST. MARY, EDWARD SYLVESTER, direct mail marketing company executive; b. Campbellsport, Wis., May 31, 1941; s. Raymond O. and Freida (Beisbier) St. Mary; m. Patricia Dyer, Aug. 5, 1961; children—Todd M., Brian D. B.S. in Bus. Adminstrn, Drake U., Des Moines, 1963. CPA, Wis., Minn. With Gen. Electric Co., 1963-72, mgr. sales analysis and planning, 1972; asst. contr., then contr. and treas. Fingerhut Corp., Minnetonka, Minn., 1972-75; v.p. fin. Fingerhut Corp., Minnetonka, Minn., 1975-80, sr. v.p. adminstrn., CFO, 1981-87; CFO, Hanover (Pa.) House, 1988-90; prin. SEC Cons. Group, Maple Grove, Minn., 1991—; bd. dirs. HomServ Co. Mem. AICPA, Nat. Acctg. Assn., Minn. Soc. CPA's. Roman Catholic. Home and Office: 13831 Tonbridge Ct Bonita Springs FL 33923-2463

ST-ONGE, DENIS ALDERIC, geologist, research scientist; b. Ste-Agathe, Man., Can., May 11, 1929; s. Adolphe and Jeanne M. (Ritchot) St-O.; m. Jeanne Marie Behaegel, Jan. 7, 1955; children—Marc R., Nicole J.M. B.A., Coll. St-Boniface, 1951; Lic. Sci., U. Louvain, Belgium, 1957, D.Sc., 1962; D.Sc. honoris causa, U. Man., 1990. Research scientist Geol. Survey, Ottawa, Ont., Can., 1958-68, sect. head, 1982-85; chief sub. div. Quaternary Geology, 1985-87, dir. terrain scis. div., 1987-91, sci. advisor Polar Continental Shelf Project, 1991—; prof. geography U. Ottawa, 1968-82, chmn. geography, 1974-77, vice dean grad. studies, 1977-80. Author: Geomorphologie Ellef-Ringnes Island, 1965, Quaternary Geology, Inman River Region, N.W.T. Canada, 1995; contbr. articles to profl. jours. Pres. Ont. Francophone PTA, 1967-69. Recipient Medal Queen Elizabeth II, 1989, medal of Honor U. Liege, Belgium, 1980, medal A. Cailleux, 1991, medal Can. 125, 1992, medal Royal Scottish Geog. Soc., 1994; officer Order of Can., 1996. Fellow Geol. Assn. Can. (pres. 1984-85), Royal Can. Geog. Soc. (bd. dirs. 1980-92, pres. 1992—), Arctic Inst. N.Am.; mem. Can. Assn. Geographers (pres. 1979-80), Can. Quaternary Assn., Assn. Quebecoise pour l'etude du Quaternaire (hon.), Internat. Union Quaternay Rsch. (hon. life). Avocations: swimming; skiing; photography. Home: 1115 Sherman Dr, Ottawa, ON Canada K2C 2M3 Office: Polar Continental Shelf Project, 615 Booth St, Ottawa, ON Canada K1A 0E9

ST. PIERRE, CHERYL ANN, mentor and art educator; b. Buffalo, Apr. 26, 1945; d. Guy Thomas and Madeline (Duncan) St. P. BS in Art Edn., SUNY, Buffalo, 1967, MS in Art Edn., 1970; MA in Italian, Middlebury Coll., 1976; PhD in Humanities, NYU, 1992. K-12 art tchr. Kenmore-Town of Tonawanda (N.Y.) Union Free Sch. Dist., 1967—; cooperating tchr. for art student tchrs. SUNY, Buffalo, 1972—; advisor on original multi-media prodn. N.Y. State Coun. for Arts, Tonawanda, 1990—; coord., tchr. Parents As Reading Ptnrs. Artwork, Tonawanda, 1990—; grad. asst. NYU, N.Y.C., 1987-88. Illustrator jour. Italian Americana, 1971-81; designer greeting cards for State of N.Y. and Maine, Am. Lung Assn., 1978-79. Earthwatch vol. Identity through Native Costume, Macedonia, 1995. Mem. N.Y. State United Tchrs., Nat. Art Edn. Assn., N.Y. State Tchrs. Assn., Am. Fedn. Tchrs., Kenmore Tchrs.' Assn. Avocations: travel, photography, film studies, animal rights, reading. Home: 3881 Bailey Ave Buffalo NY 14226-3202

ST. PIERRE, GEORGE ROLAND, JR., materials science and engineering administrator, educator; b. Cambridge, Mass., June 2, 1930; s. George Rol and Rose Ann (Levesque) St. P.; m. Roberta Ann Hansen, July 20, 1956; children: Anne Renee, Jeanne Louise, John David, Thomas George; m. Mary Elizabeth Adams, Dec. 11, 1976. BS, MIT, 1951, ScD, 1954. Rsch. metallurgist Inland Steel Co., 1954-56; mem. faculty Ohio State U., 1956—, prof. metall. engring., 1957-88, assoc. dean Grad. Sch., 1964-66, chmn. Metall. Engring., 1983-88, chmn. mining engring., 1985-92; dir. Ohio Mineral Rsch. Inst., 1984-92, prof., chmn. material sci. and engring., 1988-92, Presdl. prof., 1988-92, chmn., presdl. prof. emeritus, 1992—; chief scientist Materials Directorate, Wright-Patterson AFB, 1995-96; cons. in field, 1957—; vis. prof. U. Newcastle, NSW, Australia, 1975; mem. adv. com. materials sci. MIT, 1990-97; mem. adv. bd. Argonne Nat. Lab., 1994—. Editor: Physical Chemistry of Process Metallurgy, Vols. 7 and 8, 1961, Advances in Transport Processes in Metallurgical Systems, 1992, Transactions Iron and Steel Soc., 1994—; contbr. articles to profl. jours. Bd. dirs. Edward Orton Jr. Ceramic Found., 1989-92. With USAF, 1956-57. Recipient Milton (Mass.) Sci. prize, 1947; MacQuigg award, 1971; Alumni Disting. Tchr. award, 1978; named Disting. scholar Ohio State U., 1988, Presdl. prof. Ohio State U., 1988. Fellow Minerals, Metals & Materials Soc., AIME (bd. dirs. 1988-91, 93-96, Educator award 1996), Am. Soc. Materials Internat. (Bradley Stoughton Outstanding Tchr. award 1961, Gold medal 1987); mem. Am. Inst. Mining Metall. and Petroleum Engrs. (Mineral Industry Edn. award 1987), Iron and Steel Soc. (Elliott lectr. 1994), Am. Contract Bridge League (silver life master), Faculty Club (pres. 1990-92), Sigma Xi. Home: 4495 Carriage Hill Lane Columbus OH 43220-3801 Office: Ohio State U Dept Materials Sci/Engring 2041 N College Rd Columbus OH 43210-1124

SAINT-PIERRE, GUY, engineering executive; b. Windsor Mills, Que., Can., Aug. 3, 1934; s. Arm and Alice (Perra) Saint-P.; m. Francine Garneau, May 4, 1957; children—Marc, Guylaine, Nathalie. B in Applied Sci. in Civil Engring, Laval U., 1957; diploma, Imperial Coll., London, 1958; MSc, U. London, 1959; LLD (hon.), Concordia U., 1992; hon. degree, le Coll. militaire Royal de Saint-Jean, 1993; DSc (hon.), Laval U., 1992; hon. degree Applied Sci., Sherbrooke, 1994; DSe (hon.), Montreal U. Registrar, Corp. Engrs. Que., 1964-66. Dir. Irnes Inc., 1966-67; v.p. Acres Que., 1967-70; minister of edn. Govt. Que., 1970-72, of industry and commerce, 1972-76; asst. to pres. John Labatt Ltd., Montreal, 1977-80; sr. v.p. John Labatt Ltd.; pres., chief operating officer Ogilvie Mills Ltd., Montreal, 1977-80; pres., chief exec. officer, bd. dirs. The SNC-Lavalin Group Inc., 1989-96; chmn. bd. The SNC-Lavalin Group, Inc., 1996—; dir. GM of Can., Royal Bank, BCE Inc., Purolator Can., Alcan Aluminum; chmn. Bus. Coun. Nat. Issues, 1995—. Gov. Conseil de Patronat de Que.; mem. British-N.Am. Com. Served as officer C.E. Can. Army, 1959-64. Decorated officer Order of Can.; named Canada's CEO of Yr., 1994, Canada's Internat. Exec. of Yr., 1996; recipient Sir John Medal, 1993; Engring. Inst. of Can. Mem. Engring. Inst. Can., Can. Mfrs. Assn. (chmn. bd., pres. 1987), Order Engrs. Que., Coun. Can. Unity (v.p.), Mil. and Hospitalier Order St. Lazarus Jerusalem, Met. Montreal C. of C., Can. Club Montreal (adv. com.), Mt. Royal Club, St. Denis Club, Mt. Bruno Club, Forest and Streams Club, Hermitage Club. Liberal. Roman Catholic. Office: SNC-Lavalin Group Inc, 455 Boul René-Lèvesque O, Montreal, PQ Canada H2Z 1Z3

SAINT-PIERRE, JACQUES, statistics educator, consultant; b. Trois Rivières, Que., Can., Aug. 30, 1920; s. Oscar and Lucie (Landreville) St. P.; m. Marguerite Lachaine, July 15, 1947; children: Marc, Guy, Andre, Louis, Francois, Mireille. B.S., U. Montreal, 1948, M.S., 1951; Ph.D., U. N.C., 1954. Mem. faculty U. Montreal, 1947—, prof. stats., 1960-83, prof. emeritus, 1983—, dir. computing center, 1964-71, v.p. planning, 1971-82; cons. statistician, 1954—. Contbr. articles to profl. jours. Mem. Canadian Assn. Univ. Tchrs. (pres. 1965-66). Home: 4949 Earnscliffe, Montreal, PQ Canada H3X 2P4 Office: U Montreal, Box 6128, Montreal, PQ Canada H3C 3J7

ST. PIERRE, RONALD LESLIE, anatomy educator, university administrator; b. Dayton, Ohio, Feb. 2, 1938; s. Leslie Frank and Ruth Eleanor (Rhoten) St.P.; m. Joyce A. Guilford, Apr. 1, 1961; children: Michele Christine, David Bryan. B.S., Ohio U., 1961; M.Sc., Ohio State U., 1962, Ph.D., 1965. Instr. anatomy Ohio State U., Columbus, 1965-67; asst. prof. Ohio State U., 1967-69, assoc. prof., 1969-72, prof., 1972—, chmn. dept. anatomy, 1972-81, assoc. v.p. health scis., 1981-83, assoc. v.p. health scis. and acad. affairs, 1983, assoc. dean coll. medicine, 1987-96; vice dean coll. of medicine, 1996—; dir. Cancer Research Center, 1974-78; vis. research assoc. Duke U., 1966-67; cons. Battelle Meml. Inst., Columbus. Contbr. articles to profl. jours. Chmn. Ohio Gov.'s Com. on Employment of Handicapped, 1970-78; mem. state exec. com. Presdl. Commn. Employment of Handicapped, 1970-78, chmn., 1971-72; mem. planning and adv. council White House Conf. on Handicapped Individuals, 1975-78; mem. Columbus Mayor's Com. on Internat. Yr. of Disabled. Recipient Lederle Med. Faculty award, 1968-71; prize for basic research South Atlantic Assn. Obstetricians and Gynecologists, 1968; Outstanding Individual award Ohio Rehab. Assn., 1969; Gov.'s award for community service, 1973. Mem. Am. Assn. Anatomists, Am. Assn. Immunologists, Soc. Exptl. Biology and Medicine, Sigma Xi (pres. Ohio State chpt. 1979-80). Republican. Presbyterian. Home: 8586 Button Bush Ln Westerville IL 43082 Office: Ohio State U 218 Meiling Hall 370 W 9th Ave Columbus OH 43210-1238

SAISSELIN, REMY GILBERT, fine arts educator; b. Moutier, Bern, Switzerland, Aug. 17, 1925; came to U.S., 1938, naturalized, 1944; s. Paul A. and Jeanne (Nydegger) S.; m. Nicole M. Fischer, May 31, 1955; children: Anne, Juliet, Peter. B.A., Queens Coll., 1951; M.A., U. Wis-Madison, 1952; M.A. in French, U. Wis.-Madison, 1953, Ph.D, 1957. Asst. prof. French Western Res. U., Cleve., 1956-59; asst. curator publs. Cleve. Mus. Art, 1959-65; prof. French lit. U. Rochester (N.Y.), 1965-70, prof. fine arts, 1970-87; prof. humanities Hobart & William Smith Coll., 1987-90. Asst. editor: Jour. Aesthetics and Art Criticism, 1959-62; author: Taste in Eighteenth Centruy France, 1965, Rule of Reason and Ruses of the Heart, 1970, Literary Enterprise in XVIII Century France, 1979, The Bourgeois and the Bibelot, 1984, The Enlightenment Against the Baroque, 1992. Served with U.S. Army, 1944-46. Guggenheim fellow, 1972-73. Mem. Phi Beta Kappa. Home: 117 Westland Ave Rochester NY 14618-1044

SAITO, KIYOMI, investment banking executive; b. Tokyo, Japan, Dec. 1, 1950; d. Genichiro and Kimiko Saito; m. Tsuguo Tadakawa, Aug. 20, 1974 (div. Aug. 1975); m. Kenji Takei, Dec. 3, 1994. BA, Keio U., Tokyo, 1973; MBA, Harvard Bus. Sch., 1981. Staff Nihon Econ. Jour., Tokyo, 1973-74; asst. Sony Corp., Tokyo, 1975-79; account officer, product specialist Bank of Am., Tokyo, 1981-82; mktg. mgr. Elizabeth Arden, Tokyo, 1982-84; v.p. Morgan Stanley Internat., Tokyo, 1984-88, N.Y.C., 1988-89, Morgan Stanley Realty, 1989-91; prin. Rep. Office Morgan Stanley Realty Inc., Tokyo, 1991-92; pres. Pont du Gard Co. Ltd., 1992—. Author: A Woman's New Start, 1984, Women's Era, 1986, Kiyomi's Challenge, 1994.

SAITO, SHUZO, electrical engineering educator; b. Nagoya, Aichi, Japan, Jan. 12, 1924; s. Sukesaburo and Masa Saito; m. Yoko Nakane, Mar. 26, 1953; children: Jun'ichiro, Ken'jiro. BSEE, Nagoya U., 1948, MSEE, 1953, PhD, 1962. Mem. tech. staff Elec. Com. Lab. NT&T, Tokyo, 1953-64, chief rsch. sect., 1964-75, dir. rsch. dept., 1975-79; prof. speech sci. U. Tokyo, 1979-84; prof. elec. engring. Kogakuin U., 1984-92; prof. info. sci. Hokkaido Info. U., 1992—; mem. tech. staff Japanese Patent Agy., Tokyo, 1963; tech. specialist Japanese Ministry Transp., Tokyo, 1982. Author: Fundamental Speech Signal Processing, 1979; contbr. articles to profl. publs.; inventor PARCOR speech synthesis. Recipient Meritorious award Min. Sci. & Tech., Japan, 1977, promotion award Asahi Newspaper Co., 1981. Fellow IEEE (chmn. acoustics, speech and signal processing Tokyo chpt. 1986-88, chmn. tech. program com. internat. conf. on acoustics, speech and signal processing 1986), Acoustical Soc. Am.; mem. Audio and Visual Rsch. Group (hon., pres. 1985-88), Inst. Elec. and Comm. Engrs. Japan (adviser speech rsch. com. and pattern recognition com. 1983, paper award 1970, 71, 79, achievement award 1973), Acoustical Soc. Japan (exec. coun. 1969-83, Sato paper award 1972, meritorious award 1994). Avocations: golf, photography. Home: 1-1-3-38-704 Atsubetsu Chuo, Atsubetsu-ku, Sapporo 004, Japan Office: Hokkaido Info U, Nishinopporo 59-2, Ebetsu Hokkaido 069, Japan

SAITO-FURUKAWA, JANET CHIYO, practitioner facilitator; b. L.A., June 29, 1951; d. Shin and Nobuko Ann (Seki) Saito; m. Neil Yasuhiko Furukawa, June 30, 1990. BS, U. So. Calif., 1973; MA, Mt. St. Mary's Coll., L.A., 1990. Cert. elem. tchr. K-8, adminstrn. 1st tier, lang. devel. specialist, Calif. Tchr. grades four through six Rosemont Elem. Sch., L.A., 1973-80, psychomotor specialist, 1979-80; tchr. mid. sch. lang. arts Virgil, Parkman Mid. Schs., L.A./Woodland Hills, Calif., 1980-87, 87-90, dept. chairperson, 1974-77, 80-84, 1989-90; drama tchr. Virgil Mid. Sch., L.A., 1980-81, dance tchr., 1984-87; mid. sch. advisor L.A. Unified Sch. Dist., Encino, Calif., 1990-91; practitioner facilitator L.A. Unified Sch. Dist., Encino, 1991—; young authors chairperson Parkman Mid. Sch., Woodland Hills, 1988-90; multicultural performance educator, Great Leap, L.A., 1988-93; mentor tchr. L.A. Unified Sch. dist., 1980-90; presenter/cons. in field. Tchr./leader Psychomotor Grant, 1979; writer Level II Teamin' and Theme-in, 1994. Recipient Nancy McHugh English award English Coun. L.A., Woodland Hills, 1987, 88, 91, Outstanding Reading and Lang. Tchr. award L.A. Reading Assn., Woodland Hills, 1991, Apple award L.A. Mayor's Office, 1990, Tchr. of the Month award Phi Delta Kappa, San Fernando, Calif., 1989. Mem. ASCD, Nat. Mid. Schs. Assn. (presenter), Nat. Coun. Tchrs. Math., Calif. Sci. Tchrs. Assn., Nat. Coun. Tchrs. English, The Learning Collaborative. Lutheran. Avocations: volleyball, fishing, reading, skiing. Office: Practitioner Ctr LA Unified Sch Dist 3010 Estara Ave Los Angeles CA 90065-2205

SAITOH, TAMOTSU, pharmacology educator; b. Tokyo, May 29, 1938; s. Jiro and Tayo Saitoh; m. Masako Hayashida, June 4, 1967. PhD, U. Tokyo, 1969. Postdoctoral fellow chemistry dept. UCLA, 1969-71; instr. U. Tokyo, 1968-76; asst. prof. Showa U., Tokyo, 1976-78; prof. Teikyo U., Tokyo, 1978—. Author: Natural Products Chemistry, Vol. 2, 1975, Pharmacognosy, 1983. Avocations: travel, photography, computer programming, painting. Home: 7-13-19 Tsukimino, Yamato 242, Japan Office: Teikyo U, Sagamiko-machi, Tsukui Kanagawa 199-01, Japan

SAIZAN, PAULA THERESA, oil company executive; b. New Orleans, Sept. 12, 1947; d. Paul Morine and Hattie Mae (Hayes) Saizan; m. George H. Smith, May 26, 1973 (div. July 1976). BS in Acctg. summa cum laude, Xavier U., 1969. CPA, Tex.; notary pub. Systems engr. IBM, New Orleans, 1969-71; acct., then sr. acct. Shell Oil Co., Houston, Tex., 1971-76, sr. fin. analyst, 1976-77, fin. rep., 1977-79, corp. auditor, 1979-81, treasury rep., 1981-82, sr. treasury rep., 1982-86; asst. treas. Shell Credit Inc., Shell Leasing Co., Shell Fin. Co. 1986-88, sr. pub. affairs rep., 1988-89, sr. staff pub. affairs rep., 1990-91, program mgr., 1991-96, sr. program mgr., 1996—. Bd. dirs. Houston Downtown Mgmt. Corp., Greater Houston Conv. and Visitors Bur. (exec. com.), St. Joseph Hosp. Found., United Negro Coll. Fund, Children at Risk, Cath. Charities; mem. adv. coun. U.S. SBA region VI, Houston; acctg. dept. adv. bd. Tex. So. U. Mem. AICPA, NAACP, Tex. Soc. CPAs, Leadership Houston, Greater Inwood Partnership, LWV of Houston, Xavier U. Alumni Assn., Nat. Assn. Black Accts., Nat. Coun. Negro Women, Inc., Nat. Political Congress Black Women, Alpha Kappa Alpha, Phi Gamma Nu, Kappa Gamma Pi. Roman Catholic. Home: 5426 Long Creek Ln Houston TX 77088-4407 Office: Shell Oil Co PO Box 2463 Houston TX 77252-2463

SAJAK, PAT, television game show host; b. Chgo., Oct. 26, 1947; m. Lesly Brown, Dec. 31, 1990. Newscaster WEDC-Radio, Chicago, IL; disk jockey WNBS-Radio, Murray, KY; staff announcer, public affairs program host, weatherman WSM-TV, Nashville, TN; weatherman, host The Sunday Show, 1977-81; host Wheel of Fortune, 1981—, The Pat Sajak Show, 1989-90. film appearances include: Airplane II: The Sequel, 1982, Jack Paar is Alive and Well, 1987; NBC television specials, host, The Thanksgiving Day Parade, The Rose Parade. Served with U.S. Army, Vietnam.

SAKAI, AKIYOSHI, urban redevelopment consultant; b. Oguchi, Aichi, Japan, Jan. 1, 1930; s. Hisayoshi and Asako S.; m. Toshiko A. Sakai, Dec. 8, 1956; children: Seiji, Tatsuto. BS, Gitu Agrl. Coll., 1951. Microbiologist Fujisawa Pharm. Co., Ltd., Nagoya, Japan, 1951-59; pres. Takaha Archtl. Engring. Co., Ltd., Nagoya, 1960-73; chmn. Urban Dynamics Inst. Takaha Co. Ltd., Tokyo, 1974—, Toshikagaku Engring. Co., Ltd., Tokyo, 1986—. Author: Shigaichi Saikaihatsu, 1974. Trustee Regional Bus. Devel. Inst., 1994—. Mem. City Planning Assn. Japan, Urban Renewal Coord. Assn. Japan (trustee 1996—). Avocations: new thinking for intelligent creative process by subdivision and digitization. Office: Urban Dynamics Inst Takaha, 1-3-2 Nishiazabu Minato, Tokyo 106, Japan

SAKAI, HIROKO, trading company executive; b. Nishiharu, Aichi-ken, Japan, Jan. 9, 1939; came to U.S., 1956; d. Kichiya and Saki (Shiraishi) S. BA, Wellesley Coll., 1963; MA, Columbia U., 1967, PhD, 1972. Journalist Asahi Evening News, Tokyo, 1963-65; escort interpreter Dept. State, Washington, 1967-68; econ. analyst Port Authority N.Y. and N.J., N.Y.C., 1968-69; sr. cons. Harbridge House, Inc., Boston, 1970-84, Quantum Sci. Corp., White Plains, N.Y., 1984-87; corp. planner ITOCHU Internat. Inc., N.Y.C., N.Y., 1988-92; dir. bus. devel. ITOCHU Internat. Inc., N.Y.C., 1993-94, dir. venture and investment, 1995—. Interpreter Govt. Mass., Boston, 1974. Wellesley Coll. fellow, 1960-63, Columbia U. fellow, 1965-68; Columbia U. grantee, 1969. Mem. Regional Sci. Assn., Assn. Am. Geographers. Buddhist. Avocations: piano, oil painting, tennis. Home: 235 E

51st St Apt 5C New York NY 10022-6523 Office: ITOCHU Internat Inc 335 Madison Ave New York NY 10017-4605

SAKAI, SHINJI, finance company executive. With Toyota Motor Corp., Japan, 1985-1992; pres. and dir. Toyota Motor Sales, USA, Inc., Torrance, Calif., 1992—; pres. Toyota Motor Credit Corp., Torrance, Calif., 1992—. Office: Toyota Motor Credit Corp 19001 South Western Ave Torrance CA 90509*

SAKAI, YOSHIRO, chemistry educator; b. Nagasaki, Japan, Dec. 28, 1935; s. Tsuyoshi and Rei (Ikeno) S.; m. Mutsuko Abe, Oct. 18, 1964; children: Hideaki, Masako. BS, Kyushu U., Fukuoka, Japan, 1958, ScD, 1970. Research fellow Govt. Indsl. Research Inst., Nagoya, Japan, 1958-68; assoc. prof. Ehime U., Matsuyama, Japan, 1968-74, prof. chemistry, 1974—. Mem. Chem. Soc. Japan, Soc. Polymer Sci., Electrochem. Soc. Japan, Japan Assn. Chem. Sensors (pres. 1995—). Avocations: traveling, reading. Home: 225-4 Shin-ishite, Matsuyama 790, Ehime Japan Office: Ehime Univ, Bunkyo-cho Matsuyama, Ehime Japan

SAKAMOTO, RYUICHI, composer. Score include (films) Merry Christmas, Mr. Lawrence, 1983, (with David Byrne and Cong Su) The Last Emperor, 1987 (Academy award best original score 1987), The Handmaid's Tale, 1990, The Sheltering Sky, 1990, Tacones Lejanos, 1991, Emily Bronte's Wuthering Heights, 1992, Little Buddha, 1993, (TV miniseries) Wild Palms, 1993. Office: Creative Artists Agency 9830 Wilshire Blvd Beverly Hills CA 90212-1804

SAKELLARIOS, GERTRUDE EDITH, retired office nurse; b. Lowell, Mass., Mar. 14, 1929; d. William V. and Eileen E. (Hale) Yoachimciuk; m. Angelos D. Sakellarios, Dec. 30, 1966. Diploma, Lowell Gen. Hosp., 1949; student, Boston U., 1949-53, Boston Coll./St. Josephs Hosp., Lowell, 1951. Gen. duty med.-surg. nurse Lowell Gen. Hosp., 1949-50, operating room nurse, 1950-52; office nurse gen. practitioner's office, Lowell, 1952-83. Home: 124 Cashin St Lowell MA 01851-2004

SAKITA, BUNJI, physicist, educator; b. Inami, Toyama-ken, Japan, June 6, 1930; came to U.S., 1956; s. Eiichi and Fumi (Morimatsu) S.; children—Mariko, Taro. B.S., Kanazawa U., 1953; M.S., Nagoya U., 1956; Ph.D., U. Rochester, 1959. Research asso. U. Wis., Madison, 1959-62; asst. prof. U. Wis., 1963-64, prof., 1966-70; assoc. physicist Argonne (Ill.) Nat. Lab., 1964-66; distinguished prof. City Coll. CUNY, N.Y.C., 1970—; vis. prof. IHES, Bures-sur-Yvette, France, 1970-71, Ecole Normale Superieur, Paris, 1979-80, 88, U. Tokyo, 1987. Recipient Nishina prize, 1974; Guggenheim fellow, 1970-71, Japan Soc. Promotion Sci. fellow, 1975, 80, 87, 95. Fellow Am. Phys. Soc. Home: 5 Horizon Rd Apt 2406 Fort Lee NJ 07024-6646 Office: City College CUNY Convent Ave at 138th St New York NY 10031

SAKOWITZ, ROBERT TOBIAS, investor; b. Houston, Oct. 13, 1938; s. Bernard and Ann (Baum) S.; m. Laura Howell, 1984; children: Robert Tobias Jr., Alexandra Noelle, Brittany Ann, Laura Alexis. BA in History and Econs. cum laude, Harvard U., 1960. Exec. trainee Bloomingdales, N.Y.C., 1959-62, Macy's, N.Y.C., 1961-62, Galleries Lafayette, Paris, 1960; buyer Sakowitz, Inc., Houston, 1962-65, exec. v.p., gen. mdse. mgr., 1965-71, pres., 1971-74; pres. Sakowitz, Inc., Ariz., 1974-75; pres. corp., CEO Sakowitz, Inc., 1975-90, chmn., 1981-87; chmn., CEO Sakowitz Ventures, 1990—; chmn. Clean fuels Inc., 1991—; chmn., CEO Hazak Corp., 1986—, Robosak Corp., 1983—; co-mgr. Thunderbird Ranch, 1993—; Bd. dirs. Continental Air Lines, Inc.; dir. Morse Shoe, 1974-87, Tex. Am. Bank-Galleria, 1972-83, Fed. Reserve Bank, Houston br., 1983-85, chmn., 1985—, Societe Viticole, S.A. (Lux.), 1983-87. Mem. exec. com., nat. bd. dirs. Am. Council for Arts, N.Y.C., 1970-83; bd. dirs. Found. for Joffrey Ballet, Houston Internat. Festival, Houston Symphony Soc., NCCJ, Greater Houston Conv. and Visitors Bur., chmn. 1990-92; Houston Econ. Devel. Council, Houston Indsl. Devel. Corp.; co-chmn. Tex. Conf. on Small Bus., 1981; chmn. S.E. del. White House Conf. on Small Bus., 1980; mem. Houston Mcpl. Art Commn., 1965-83, vice chmn., 1972-73, chmn., 1974-75; chmn. Sesquicentennial Commn. State of Tex., Houston and Harris County, 1984-86, Greater Houston Ptnrship.; mem. bd. selectors Am. Inst. for Public Service, Washington; mem. pres. coun. and pub. policy coun. U. Houston; bd. dirs. host com. Rep. Nat. Conv., 1991-92; bd. advisors Edna Gladney Home. Served with USAF, 1961-66. Decorated knight Nat. Order of Merit (France, 1976) (Italy, 1983); recipient Epingle d'Or, French Fashion Fedn., 1972; Am. Acad. Achievement award, 1973; Gt. Texan award Nat. Ileitis and Colitis Found., 1975; Display award Nat. Assn. Display Industries, 1976; Ten Outstanding Nat. Bus. Leaders award Northwood Inst., 1981; named to Internat. Best Dressed List, 1970, 71, 72, 73, 74, 75; named to Hall of Fame, 1975. Mem. Nat. Retail Mchts. Assn. (dir., mem. exec. com., internat. com.), Houston C. of C. (dir., mem. downtown com. 1980-81, chmn. small bus. task force 1978-79, chmn. cultural affairs com. 1971-73), German Am. C. of C. (dir.), German Wine Soc. (chmn. S.W. chpt.), Confrerie des Chevaliers du Tastevin, Brotherhood of Knights of Vine, Confrerie de la Chaine des Rotisseurs, Commanderie de Bordeaux du Texas. Clubs: Houston, Houstonian; Fly (Cambridge, Mass.); Knickerbocker (N.Y.C.). Avocations: skiing, tennis, art, oenology. Office: 3050 Post Oak Blvd Ste 640 Houston TX 77056-6525*

SAKS, ARNOLD, graphic designer; b. N.Y.C., Dec. 21, 1931; s. Alfred and Esther (Barnett) S.; m. Joanna Ernst, Sept. 23, 1959. B.F.A., Syracuse U., 1953; postgrad., Yale U., 1953-54. Exhbn. designer Mus. Natural History, N.Y.C., 1956-57; art dir. Interiors Mag., N.Y.C., 1957-58; ptnr. Ward & Saks, N.Y.C., 1958-68; prin. Arnold Saks, Assocs., N.Y.C., 1968—. Served with U.S. Army, 1954-56. Mem. Alliance Graphique Internationale, Am. Inst. Graphic Arts, Century Assn. Office: Arnold Saks Assocs 350 E 81st St New York NY 10028-3931

SAKS, GENE, theater and film director, actor; b. N.Y.C.. Began career as an actor off-Broadway at Provincetown Playhouse and the Cherry Lane Theatre; played in: Auden's Dog Beneath the Skin, E.E. Cummings' Him, Molière's The Bourgeois Gentilhomme; appeared on Broadway in Mr. Roberts, South Pacific, Middle of the Night, The Tenth Man, A Shot in the Dark, Love and Libel, A Thousand Clowns; debut as dir. on Broadway Enter Laughing, 1963; dir. stage plays Nobody Loves an Albatross, 1964, Half a Sixpense, 1964, Generation, 1965, Mame, 1960, Same Time, Next Year, 1975, California Suite, 1972, I Love My Wife (best dir. of Musical award Drama Desk, Tony), 1967, Brighton Beach Memoirs (best dir. award, Tony), 1983, Biloxi Blues (best dir. of play award, Tony), 1985, The Odd Couple (female version), 1985, Broadway Bound, 1986, A Month of Sundays, 1987, Rumors, 1988, Lost in Yonkers, 1991, Jake's Women, 1992; dir. films Barefoot in the Park, The Odd Couple, Cactus Flower, Last of the Red Hot Lovers, Mame, Brighton Beach Memoirs, A Fine Romance; dir. TV movie Bye, Bye Birdie, 1995; appeared in films including a Thousand Clowns, Prisoner of Second Aveneue, Lovesick, The One and Only, The Goodbye People, 1986, Nobody's Fool, 1994, TQ, 1994. Recipient George Abbott award for lifetime achievement in the theatre, 1990; elected to Theatre Hall of Fame, 1991.

SAKS, MICHAEL JAY, law educator; b. Phila., Mar. 8, 1947; s. Harold and Bella (Pall) S.; m. Roselle Wissler, May 18, 1986. BS in Psychology, BA in English, Pa. State U., 1969; MA in Social Psychology, Ohio State U., 1972, PhD in Social Psychology, 1975; MSL in Law, Yale U., 1983. Prof. psychology Boston Coll., Chestnut Hill, Mass., 1973-88; sr. staff assoc. Nat. Ctr. for State Cts., Williamsburg, Va., 1978-80; vis. prof. law Georgetown U. Law Ctr., Washington, 1985-86; prof. law U. Iowa, Iowa City, 1986—; disting. vis. prof. law grad. program for judges U. Va., Charlottesville, 1981, 83, 85, 87, 89; cons. Office of Tech. Assessment, U.S. Congress, Washington, numerous law firms; chair law sch. admissions coun. grants com. Editor-in-chief Law & Human Behavior, 1985-87; mem. editorial bd. Jour. Personality and Social Psychology, Law & Society Rev., Law & Human Behavior, Law & Policy, Applied Social Psychology Annual, Social Behaviour: An Internat. Jour. Applied Social Psychology, Ethics and Behavior; contbr. articles to profl. jours. Chair bd. Cen. Ohio chpt. Ohio Civil Liberties Union, Columbus, 1972-73; bd. dirs. Civil Liberties Union Mass., Boston, 1984-86, Iowa City Area Sci. Ctr.; mem. subcom. on organ and tissue transplants Mass. Legis., Boston, 1975. U. Iowa Faculty scholar, 1990-93. Fellow Am. Psychol. Assn. (Disting. Contbn. award 1987), Am. Psychology Law Soc. (pres. 1988-89), Soc. for the Psychol. Study of Social Issues (bd. dirs.); mem. Law & Soc. Assn. Office: U Iowa Coll Law Iowa City IA 52242

SAKS, STEPHEN HOWARD, accountant; b. Phila., May 16, 1941; s. Samuel and Edythe (Edelman) S.; m. Ruth Workman, Dec. 22, 1963; children: Amy Meryl, Brian Eric, Joshua Marc. BS in Econs., U. Pa., 1962. CPA, Pa. Staff acct. to ptnr. Peat, Marwick, Mitchell & Co., Phila., 1962-78; ptnr. Laventhol & Horwath, Phila., 1978-91; chief fin. officer Northeastern Health Sys., Phila., 1991—. Bd. dirs. Jewish Family and Children's Agy, Phila,. 1979-88; treas. Jewish Employment and Vocat. Svc., Phila., 1984-88; chmn. bd. overseers Gratz Coll., Melrose Pk., Pa., 1987-90; pres. Beth Sholom Men's Club, Elkins Pk., Pa., 1987-90. Mem. AICPA, Pa. Inst. CPAs, Healthcare Fin. Mgmt. Assn. (advanced). Democrat. Avocations: community activities, travel. Home: 1110 Gypsy Ln Oreland PA 19075-2508 Office: Northeastern Health System 2346 E Allegheny Ave Philadelphia PA 19134-4434

SAKURAI, KIYOSHI, economics educator; b. Tokyo, Aug. 1, 1934; m. Noriko Ogawa, Oct. 22, 1966; children: Misako, Minako. D of Commerce, Meiji U., Tokyo, 1971. Prof. econs. Wako U., Tokyo, 1974—, chmn. dept. econs., 1980-82, dean dept. econs., 1990-93; lectr. Ministry of Fin., Tokyo, 1982-86; dir. Ednl. Institution Wako Gakuen, Tokyo, 1990-93; pres. Japanese Calligraphy Soc., Tokyo, 1970—; curator of the Library of Wako U., Tokyo, 1993—. Author: Historical Studies of the Staple System of England, 1974, Friction Between Japan and the U.S. in the Automobile Industry (Prewar Period), 1987; co-author: Adam Smith and His Age, 1977, Malthus, Ricardo and Their Age, 1981, Mill, Marx and Their Age, 1986, A. Marshall and His Age, 1991. Mem. Soc. Socio-Econ. History, Soc. Finance Theory, Econ. History Assn. Home: 3177-9 Honmachida, Machida-shi, Tokyo 194, Japan Office: 2160 Kanai, Machida-shi, Tokyo 195, Japan

SAKUTA, MANABU, neurologist, educator; b. Ichikawa, Japan, Oct. 31, 1947; s. Jun and Shizuko (Tsuji) S.; m. Yuko Fukushi, June 17, 1973; children: Akiko, Junko, Ken-Ichi. MD, U. Tokyo, 1973, PhD, 1978; MS in Neurology, U. Minn., 1981. Med. diplomate. Diplomat Japanese Bd. Neurology, Japanese Bd. Internal Medicine. Asst. Dept. Neurology U. Tokyo, Japan, 1980; rsch. fellow Dept. Neurology U. Minn., Mpls., 1980-81, asst. prof., 1981-82; head Dept. Neurology Japanese Red Cross Med. Ctr., Tokyo, 1982—; prof. Japanese Red Cross Women's Coll. Sch. Nursing, Tokyo, 1983-85, instr. 1986-88; lectr. dept. neurology, U. Tokyo, 1984—, dept. medicine U. Kobe, 1990—; cons. Nakayama Hosp., Ichikawa, Japan, 1980—. Contbr. articles to profl. jours. Fellow Royal Soc. Medicine (London); mem. AAAS, N.Y. Acad. Sci., Japanese Soc. Internal Medicine (pres. Kanto br. 1992), Japanese Soc. Neurology (mem. coun., 1985—, mem. coun. Kanto Br., 1984—, pres. Kanto Br. 1984, mem. editorial bd. 1988—), Japanese Soc. Diabetology, Japanese Soc. Electroencephalography and Electromyography, Japanese Soc. Autonomic Nervous System (mem. coun.), Clinical Neurology Club, Chevalier Club (pres. internat. com. 1995—), U. Minn. Alumni Club, Tetsumon Club. Democrat. Buddhist. Office: Japanese Red Cross Med Ctr, 4-1-22 Hiroo Shibuya-ku, Tokyo 150, Japan

SAKUTA, MASAAKI, engineering educator, consultant; b. Kagoshima, Japan, Feb. 16, 1929; s. Masanori and Haruko (Oozato) S.; m. Akiko Shimomura, Nov. 4, 1956; children: Shigeru, Mitsuru. B of Engring., Tokyo Inst. Tech., 1952; postgrad, MIT, 1959-60; DEng, Tokyo Inst. Tech., 1966. Cert. oceanic architect, architect-engr., Japan. Rschr. Taisei Constrn. Co. Ltd., Tokyo, 1956-58, chief rschr., 1960-69; mng. dir. Fuyo Ocean Devel. and Engring. Co. Ltd., Tokyo, 1969-77; advisor Taisei Corp. Co. Ltd., Tokyo, 1978-79; prof. Nihon U., Tokyo, 1977—; councilor Archtl. Inst. Japan, Tokyo, 1975-76, dir., 1989-91; vice dean Coll. Sci. and Tech., Nihon U., 1978-94; vice chmn., life mem. Pacific Congress on Marine Sci. and Tech., Japan, 1990—. Author: Transportation in Ocean Space, 1975, Construction Method of Marine Structures, 1976, Introduction of Ocean Development, 1977; patentee in field of Marine structure system with soft-touched basement. Mem. Visualization Soc. Japan, Inc. (pres. 1991-92, Merit award 1992), Rotary (sr., charter). Mem. Liberal Dem. Party. Buddhist. Avocations: hiking, tennis, table tennis, painting, reading. Home: 39-723 2-2 chome Jingumae, Shibuya-ku Tokyo 150, Japan Office: Coll Sci & Tech Narashino Campus, 7-24 Narashinodai, Funabashi, Chiba 274, Japan

SALA, LUIS FRANCISCO, surgeon, educator; b. N.Y.C., Dec. 13, 1919; s. Luis and Josefina (Goenaga) S.; m. Judith Colon, June 5, 1943; children: Luis E., Francisco A., Jorge P., Jose M. B.S. cum laude, Georgetown U., 1939, M.D., 1943; M.Sc. in Surgery, U. Pa., 1951. Diplomate: Am. Bd. Surgery. Intern, resident Presbyn. Hosp., San Juan, P.R., 1943-45; resident Presbyn. Hosp., 1944-45; chief resident Grad. Hosp. U. Pa., 1947-51, instr. surgery, 1950-51; clin. asst. surgery Med. Coll. Pa.; practice medicine, specializing in surgery Ponce, P.R., 1951-91; chmn. dept. surgery Damas Hosp., Ponce, 1955-88; prof. surgery U. P.R. Sch. Medicine, 1968-88; pres., dean, prof. surgery Ponce Sch. of Medicine, 1988-94; del. P.R. Med. Assn., 1960-93, pres., 1965-66; apptd. mem. Med. Examining Bd. by Gov. of P.R., 1995. Author: Consideraciones Basicas para la Acreditacion de Hospitales, 1978; contbr. chpts. to books, articles to profl. jours. Active Boy Scouts Am., 1955-74; pres. adv. com. to pres. Cath. U. P.R., 1963-72; bd. dirs. Boys Home of Ponce, 1966-76; bd. regents Amigos Museo de Arte de Ponce, 1968-73, Cath. U., 1972-93; pres. bd. regents Ponce Med. Sch. Found., 1980-92. Served with M.C. U.S. Army, 1945-47. Recipient Silver Beaver award, 1965, Acad. Médica, Dto. Sur, 1st. Dr. Luis F. Sasa medal, 1995; named lt. P.R. Equestrian Order of Holy Sepulchre of Jerusalem, 1982—. Fellow ACS (gov. for P.R. 1965-74, Disting. Svc. award 1989), Internat. Soc. Surgery, P.R. Med. Assn. (so. dist., Dr. Pila medal for disting. svc. 1991), Indsl. Med. Coun. of SIF (apptd. pres. by Gov. of P.R. 1993-95), P.R. Mfrs. Assn. (Profl. of Yr. in area of svcs. 1994), C. of C. (Profl. of Yr. 1990), State Med. Examining Bd. (appt. by Gov. of P.R. 1995—). Republican. Roman Catholic. Home: 6 Almena Alhambra Ponce PR 00731 Office: 43 Calle Concordia Ponce PR 00731-4984

SALA, MARTIN ANDREW, biophysicist, inventor; b. Buffalo, N.Y., Sept. 6, 1957; s. Paul and Adrienne (Williams) Zahm; m. Erie Anne Wagner-Sala, Nov. 23, 1986; 1 child, Rebeckah. BA in Biophysics, SUNY, Buffalo, 1981. Dir. clin. engring. Buffalo Columbus Hosp., 1982-85; lab. inst. designer Roswell Park Cancer Inst., Buffalo, 1985-89; v.p. for R&D MBS Foundry, Brook's Grove, N.Y., 1989-96; pressetter applications engr. Nationwide Precision Prods., Henrietta, N.Y., 1996—; cons. Lotus Link Found., Buffalo, 1990—, West N.Y. Clin. Engring. Assn., Buffalo, 1989—. Author: Theory & Design of Core Memory, 1979; editor various periodicals, 1970—; inventor, developer Retrospex Sys. for large vehicles. With USN, 1976-81. Grantee NIH, 1990. Mem. Am. Inst. Physics, Instrument Soc. Am., AAAS, Soc. for Advancement Med. Instrument Design. Mem. Anglican Ch. Achievements include patents pending for new surgical measuring tool, facsimile design, canine surgical tool; invention of various novel scientific instruments, Retrospex Rear Vision System, vehicular safety devices. Office: Nationwide Precision Prods 200 Tech Park Dr Henrietta NY 14623

SALAAM, RASHAAN, professional football player; b. San Diego, Oct. 24, 1974; s. Teddy Washington and Dolores Shelly Salaam. Attended, U. Colo., 1992-94. With Chgo. Bears, 1995—; mem. Aloha Bowl, 1992. Recipient Heisman trophy, 1994, Doak Walker award, 1994, Walter Camp Player of Yr. trophy, 1994; named to AP All-Am. Team, 1994. Avocations: rap music, sega. Office: Chgo Bears Halas Hall 250 N Washington Rd Lake Forest IL 60045

SALACUSE, JESWALD WILLIAM, lawyer, educator; b. Niagara Falls, N.Y., Jan. 28, 1938; s. William L. and Bessie B. (Buzzelli) S.; m. Donna Booth, Oct. 1, 1966; children: William, Maria. Diploma U. Paris, 1959; AB, Hamilton Coll., 1960; JD, Harvard U., 1963. Bar: N.Y. 1965, Tex. 1980. Lectr. in law Ahmadu Bello U., Nigeria, 1963-65; assoc. Conboy, Hewitt, O'Brien & Boardman, N.Y.C., 1965-67; assoc. dir. African Law Ctr., Columbia U., 1967-68; prof., dir. Research Ctr., Nat. Sch. Adminstrn., Zaire, 1968-71; Middle East regional advisor on law and devel. Ford Found., Beirut, 1971-74, rep. in Sudan, 1974-77; vis. prof. U. Khartoum (Sudan), 1974-77; vis. scholar Harvard Law Sch., 1977-78; prof. law So. Meth U., Dallas, 1978-80, dean, prof. law, 1980-86; dean, prof. internat. law The Fletcher Sch. Law and Diplomacy Tufts U., Medford, Mass., 1986-94; Henry J. Braker prof. comml. law Fletcher Sch. Law and Diplomacy Tufts U., 1994—; fellow Inst. Advanced Legal Studies, U. London, 1995; vis. prof. Ecole Nat. des Ponts et Chaussées, Paris, 1990—, Instituto de Empressa, U. Bristol, Madrid, 1995—, Sch. Oriental and African Studies U. London, 1995; cons. Ford Found., 1978-82, 93, U.S. Dept. State, 1978-80, U.N. Ctr. on Transnat. Corps., 1988—, Harvard Inst. Internat. Devel., 1990—, Asia Found., 1992, Harvard Law Sch./World Bank Laos Project, 1991-93; with Sri Lanka fin. sector project ISTI/USAID, 1993-94; lectr. Georgetown U. Internat. Law Inst., 1978-94, Universidad Panamericana, Mexico City, 1981; chmn. com. on Middle Eastern law Social Sci. Research Council, 1978-84; chmn. Coun. Internat. Exchange of Scholars, 1987-91; bd. dirs. Boston World Affairs Coun., 1988-95, Emerging Markets Income Funds. I & II, Inc., Global Ptnrs. Income Fund, Inc., Salomon Brothers Worldwide Income Fund, Inc., The Asia Tigers Fund, Inc., The India Fund. Inc., Emerging Markets Floating Rate Fund, Inc., Mcpl. Advantage Fund, Inc., Salomon Bros. High Income Fund; trustee Southwestern Legal Found., 1992—, Am. U. of Paris, 1993; pres. Internat. Third World Legal Studies Assn., 1987-91; chmn. Inst. Transnat. Arbitration, 1991-93; pres. Assn. Profl. Schs. Internat. Affairs, 1988-89. Author: (with Kasunmu) Nigerian Family Law, 1966, An Introduction to Law in French-Speaking Africa, vol. I, 1969, vol. II, 1976, (with Steng) International Business Planning, 1982; Making Global Deals-Negotiating in the International Marketplace, 1991, The Art of Advice, 1994; contbr. articles to profl. jours. Mem. ABA, Dallas Bar Found. (trustee 1983-86), Coun. on Fgn. Rels., Am. Law Inst., Am. Soc. Internat. Law, Cosmos Club (Washington). Home: 220 Stone Root Ln Concord MA 01742-4755 Office: Tufts U Fletcher Sch Law & Diplomacy Medford MA 02155

SALADINO, JOHN F., architect, interior decorator, furniture designer; b. Kansas City, Mo., 1939. BFA, U. Notre Dame, 1960; MFA, Yale U., 1963; pvt. studies with, Piero Sartago, Rome, 1968-69. Prin., architect, decorator, furniture designer John F. Saladino Inc., N.Y.C., 1972—; bd. dirs. Formica Corp. Bd. dirs. Parsons Sch. Design. Recipient 2 Awards of Excellence, Illuminating Engring. Soc., 1976, 2 Best Show awards Daphne, 1981, Design Excellence award Daphne, 1981, 1st Ann. award Chgo. Design Sources Com., 1982, Euster Mdse. Mart award, 1982, Award for Excellence, Chgo. Design Fest, 1983; named Designer of Yr., Interiors Mag., 1980. Mem. Am. Soc. Interior Designers (Designer Disting. 1982). Office: 305 E 63rd St New York NY 10021-7772*

SALAH, JOSEPH ELIAS, research scientist, educator; b. Jerusalem, Feb. 27, 1944; came to U.S., 1961; s. Elias and Souraya (Nesnas) S.; m. Marie Shintani, Jan. 30, 1965; 1 child, Anthony. BSEE, U. Ill., 1965, MSEE, 1966; PhD, MIT, 1972. Staff mem. Lincoln Lab., MIT, Lexington, 1966-76, group leader, 1977-83; sr. lectr. dept. earth, atmospheric and planetary scis. MIT, Cambridge, 1983—, prin. rsch. scientist, 1983—; dir. Haystack Obs. MIT, Westford, 1983—; mem. adv. com. for astron. scis. NSF, Washington, 1985-88, mem. steering com. Coupling, Energetics and Dynamics of Atmospheric Regions, 1987-90; mem. com. on solar terrestrial rsch. NRC-NAS, Washington, 1986-89. Contbr. articles on physics of earth's upper atmosphere and ionosphere to sci. jours. Mem. Am. Geophys. Union, Am. Astron. Soc., Am. Meteorol. Soc., Internat. Union Radio and Sci., Internat. Assn. for Geomagnetism and Aeronomy. Office: MIT Haystack Obs RR 40 Westford MA 01886

SALAH, SAGID, retired nuclear engineer; b. Seoul, Sept. 2, 1932; came to U.S., 1954; s. Galim and Faiza (Sultan) Salahutdin; m. Ravile Almakay, Apr. 2, 1966; children: Shamil, Kamil, Safiye. BChemE, U. Fla., 1958, MS in Nuclear Engring., 1960, PhD in Nuclear Engring., 1964. Nuclear engr. AEC, Bethesda, Md., 1964-66; sr. design engr. Westinghouse Astronuclear Lab., Large, Pa., 1966-70; sr. sys. engr. Westinghouse Nuclear Energy Sys., Pitts., 1970-73; mem. sys. safety engring. staff U.S. Nuclear Regulatory Commn., Bethesda, 1973-93; ret., 1993; nuclear engring. cons. Oak Ridge (Tenn.) Inst. Nuclear Studies, 1963, 64; instr. U. Md., College Park, 1973-76. Contbr. articles to Nuclear Sci. and Engring. Youth coach Nat. Capital Soccer League, Vienna, Va., 1975-85. Mem. Am. Nuclear Soc. (emeritus, reviewer trans. papers 1972), Sigma Tau. Moslem. Achievements include measurements of neutron energy spectra in heterogeneous media using differential and integral methods, neutron energy spectra measurements and analysis in intermediate spectra reactors, three-dimensional transient analysis of boron dilution in PWR reactors. Avocations: astronomy, neurology, financial analysis, tennis, swimming. Home: 9302 Kilport Ct Vienna VA 22182

SALAMA, C. ANDRE TEWFIK, electrical engineering educator; b. Heliopolis, Egypt, Sept. 27, 1938; arrived in Can., 1957; s. Tewfik and Sarine (Bigio) S.; m. Rhoda R. Kurtz, Dec. 19, 1974. BASc with honours, U. B.C., Vancouver, Can., 1961, MASc, 1963, PhD, 1966. Registered profl. engr., Ont. Mem. sci. staff Bell No. Rsch., Ottawa, Ont., Can., 1966-67; asst. prof. elec. engring. U. Toronto, Ont., 1967-70, assoc. prof., 1970-77, prof., 1977-92, univ. prof., 1992—; chmn., bd. dirs. Can. Microelectronics Corp., Kingston, Ont., 1984—; program leader, bd. dirs. Micronet, Toronto, 1990—. Mem. editorial bd. Solid State Electronics, 1982—; contbr. over 200 articles to sci. jours. Recipient Izaak Walton Killam Meml. prize, 1994; Info. Tech. Assn. Can. and Natural Scis. and Engring. Rsch. Coun. fellow U. Toronto, 1989-90. Fellow IEEE (assoc. editor Trans. on Cirs. and Systems 1987-89); mem. Electrochem. Soc., Assn. Profl. Engrs. Ont. Avocations: swimming, sailing, scuba diving, horseback riding, reading. Office: U Toronto, Dept Elec Engring, Toronto, ON Canada M5S 1A4

SALAMAN, MAUREEN KENNEDY, nutritionist; b. Glendale, Calif., Apr. 4, 1936; d. Ted and Elena (Peters) Kennedy; 1 child, Sean. West Coast Report, Sta. WMCA-AM, N.Y.C., 1980—; hostess Maximize Your Life with Maureen Kennedy Salaman, KFCB, Concord, Calif.; pres. Nat. Health Fedn., Monrovia, Calif., 1982—; cons., lectr., rschr. on cancer rsch. and metabolic medicine, nutrition; freedom of choice lobbyist. Author: Foods That Heal, Nutrition: The Cancer Answer, 1983, The Diet Bible, The Light at the End of the Refrigerator, Health Freedom News, 1982-85, Nutrition: The Cancer Answer II, 1995. Contbr. articles to profl. jours.; hostess TV show Maureen Salaman's Maximize Your Life. Developer nutrition programs for radio and TV. Office: Nat Health Fedn PO Box 688 Monrovia CA 91017-0688 also: Maureen Kennedy Salaman Inc 1259 El Camino Real Ste 1500 Menlo Park CA 94025-4227

SALAMATI, FARSHID, environmental engineer, environmental company executive; b. Tehran, Iran, May 30, 1949; came to U.S., 1980; s. Plato and Kharman (Yezeshni) S.; m. Fariba Azari, June 19, 1978; 1 child, Behan. BSEE, U. Tehran, 1974; MS in Eviron. and Energy Mgmt., U. Calif., Berkeley, 1984. Cert. environ. mgr., designer; cert. asbestos cons.; lic. gen., elec. and asbestos contr. Field engr. Shahin Factory, Tehran, 1968-72; supr. Irom Engring., Tehran, 1972-75; proj. mgr., pres. Techno Bond, Tehran, 1975-80; field engr. EAL Corp., Richmond, Calif., 1980-85; CFO, v.p. INOV Corp., Oakland, Calif., 1985-87; CFO, pres. Environ. Innovations Corp., Oakland, 1987—. Mem. Bldg. Owners and Mgrs. Assn., Am. Indsl. Hygiene Assn., Environ. Safety Coun. Am., Fedn. Zoroastrian Assn. N.Am., Nat. Assn. Environ. Profls., Nat. Assn. Gen. Contrs., Nat. Asbestos Coun. (qualified field instr., founding co-chmn. tech./analytical adv. com. Calif. chpt.), Calif. Energy Commn., No. Calif. Electronic Systems Contrs. Assn., Assn. Profl. Energy Mgrs., Asbestos Abatement Coun., Assoc. Bldrs. and Contrs. Inc. (Golden Gate chpt.), Environ. Assessment Assn. Avocations: swimming, tennis, surfing, snorkeling. Office: Environ Innovations Corp 7901 Oakport St # 3100 Oakland CA 94621

SALAMON, LESTER MILTON, political science educator; b. Pitts., Jan. 11, 1943; s. Victor William Salamon and Helen (Sanders) Weiss; m. Lynda Anne Brown, June 27, 1965; children: Noah, Matthew. BA in Econs. and Pub. Policy, Princeton U., 1964; PhD in Govt., Harvard U., 1971. Instr. dept. polit. sci. Tougaloo (Miss.) Coll., 1966-67; asst. prof. Vanderbilt U., Nashville, 1970-73; assoc. prof. policy scis. and polit. sci. Duke U., Durham, N.C., 1973-80, dir. Ctr. for Urban and Regional Devel., 1977-80; dep. assoc. dir. U.S. Office Mgmt. and Budget, Washington, 1977-79; dir. Ctr. for Governance and Mgmt. Rsch., Urban Inst., Washington, 1980-86; prof., dir. Inst. for Policy Studies, Johns Hopkins U., Balt., 1987—. Author: America's Nonprofit Sector: A Primer, 1992, The Emerging Sector: Nonprofit Organizations in Comparative Perspective, 1994, Partners in Public Service: Government Nonprofit Relations in the Modern Welfare State, 1995; editor: The Tools of Government Action, 1989, Human Capital and America's Future, 1991; mem. editl. bd. Adminstrn. and Soc., 1985—, Voluntas, 1988—, Nonprofit and Voluntary Sector Quar., 1990—. Mem. Balt. City

Planning Commn., 1987-95. Recipient Laverne Burchfield award Am. Soc. Pub. Adminstrn., 1977. Mem. Internat. Soc. Third Sector Rsch. (vice chmn. 1991—), Nat. Acad. Pub. Adminstrn. Avocations: tennis, swimming, carpentry. Home: 903 Lynch Dr Arnold MD 21012 Office: Johns Hopkins U Inst Policy Studies 3400 N Charles St Baltimore MD 21218-2608

SALAMON, LINDA BRADLEY, university administrator, English literature educator; b. Elmira, N.Y., Nov. 20, 1941; d. Grant Ellsworth and Evelyn E. (Ward) Bradley; divorced; children: Michael Lawrence, Timothy Martin. B.A., Radcliffe Coll., 1963; M.A., Bryn Mawr Coll., 1964, Ph.D., 1971; Advanced Mgmt. Cert., Harvard U. Bus. Sch., 1978; D.H.L., St. Louis Coll. Pharmacy, 1993. Lectr., adj. asst. prof. Eng. Dartmouth Coll., Hanover, N.H., 1967-72; mem. faculty lit. Bennington Coll., Vt., 1974-75; dean students Wells Coll., Aurora, N.Y., 1975-77; exec. asst. to pres. U. Pa., Phila., 1977-79; assoc. prof. English Washington U., St. Louis, 1979-88, prof., 1988-92, dean Coll. Arts and Scis., 1979-92; prof. English, dean Columbia Sch. Arts and Scis. George Washington U., Washington, 1992-95, interim v.p. for acad. affairs, 1995—; mem. faculty Bryn Mawr Summer Inst. for Women, 1979—. Author, co-editor: Nicholas Hilliard's Art of Limning, 1983; co-author: Integrity in the College Curriculum, 1985; contbr. numerous articles to literary and ednl. jours. Bd. dirs. Assn. Am. Colls., vice chmn., 1985, chmn., 1986; bd. dirs. Greater St. Louis council Girl Scouts U.S.A.; trustee Coll. Bd., St. Louis Coll. Pharmacy. Fellow Radcliffe Coll. Bunting Inst., 1973-74; Am. Philos. Soc. Penrose grantee, 1974; fellow Folger Shakespeare Library, 1986, NEH Montaigne Inst., 1988. Mem. MLA, Cosmos Club, Phi Beta Kappa. Office: George Washington U Off VP Acad Affairs Washington DC 20052

SALAMON, MIKLOS DEZSO GYORGY, mining engineer, educator; b. Balkany, Hungary, May 20, 1933; came to U.S., 1986; s. Miklos and Sarolta (Obetko) S.; m. Agota Maria Meszaros, July 11, 1953; children: Miklos, Gabor. Diploma in Engring., Polytech U., Sopron, Hungary, 1956; PhD, U. Durham, Newcastle, England, 1962; doctorem honoris causa, U. Miskolc, Hungary, 1990. Research asst. dept. mining engring. U. Durham, 1959-63; dir. research Coal Mining Research Controlling Council, Johannesburg, South Africa, 1963-66; dir. collieries research lab Chamber of Mines of South Africa, Johannesburg, 1966-74, dir. gen. research org., 1974-86; dir. Ctr. for Advanced Mining Sys., Golden, 1986—; dir. Ctr. for Advanced Mining Sys. Colo. Sch. Mines, Golden, 1986-94, disting. prof., 1986—, dir. Colo. Mining and Mineral Resources Rsch. Inst., 1990-94; 22d Sir Julius Wernher Meml. lectr., 1988; hon. prof. U. Witwatersrand, Johannesburg, 1979-86; vis. prof. U. Minn., Mpls., 1981, U. Tex., Austin, 1982, U. NSW, Sydney, Australia, 1990, 91—; mem. Presdl. Commn. of Inquiry into Safety and Health in South African Mining Industry, 1994-95. Co-author: Rock Mechanics Applied to the Study of Rockbursts, 1966, Rock Mechanics in Coal Mining, 1976; contbr. articles to profl. jours. Mem. Pres.'s Sci. Adv. Council, Cape Town, South Africa, 1984-86, Nat. Sci. Priorities Com., Pretoria, South Africa, 1984-86. Recipient Nat. award Assn. Scis. and Tech. Socs., South Africa, 1971. Fellow South African Inst. Mining and Metallurgy (hon. life, v.p. 1974-76, pres. 1976-77, gold medal 1964, 85, Stokes award 1986, silver medal 1991), Inst. Mining and Metallurgy (London); mem. AIME, Internat. Soc. Rock Mechanics. Roman Catholic. Office: Colo Sch of Mines Dept Of Mining Engring Golden CO 80401

SALAMON, MYRON BEN, physicist, educator; b. Pitts., June 4, 1939; s. Victor William and Helen (Sanders) S.; m. Sonya Maxine Blank, June 12, 1960; children—David, Aaron. B.S., Carnegie-Mellon U., 1961; Ph.D., U. Calif., Berkeley, 1966. Asst. prof. physics U. Ill., Urbana, 1966-72, assoc. prof., 1972-74, prof., 1974—, program dir. materials research lab., 1984-91; vis. scientist U. Tokyo, 1966, 71, Tech. U. Munich, Fed. Republic Germany, 1974-75; cons. NSF; Disting. Vis. Prof. Tsukuba (Japan) U., 1995-96. Editor: Physics of Superionic Conductors, 1979; co-editor: Modulated Structures, 1979; divisional assoc. editor: Phys. Rev. Letters, 1992-96; contbr. sci. papers to profl. jours. Recipient Alexander von Humboldt Sr. U.S. Scientist award, 1974-75; NSF coop. fellow, 1964-66; postdoctoral fellow, 1966; A.P. Sloan fellow, 1972-73; Berndt Matthias scholar Los Alamos Nat. Lab., 1995—; visiting scientist CNRS and Inst. Laue-Langevin Grenoble, France, 1981-82. Fellow Am. Phys. Soc. Office: U Ill Dept Physics 1110 W Green St Urbana IL 61801-3003

SALAMON, RENAY, real estate broker; b. N.Y.C., May 13, 1948; d. Solomon and Mollie (Friedman) Langman; m. Maier Salamon, Aug. 10, 1968; children: Mollie, Jean, Leah, Sharon, Eugene. BA, Hunter Coll., 1969. Licensed real estate borker, N.J. Mgr. office Customode Designs Inc., N.Y.C., 1966-68; co-owner Salamon Dairy Farms, Three Bridges, N.J., 1968-86; assoc. realtor Max. D. Shuman Realty Inc., Flemington, N.J., 1983-85; pres., chief exec. officer Liberty Hill Realty Inc., Flemington, N.J., 1985—; cons. Illva Saronna Inc. (Illva Group), Edison, N.J. 1985—; real estate devel. joint venture with M.R.F.S. Realty Inc. (Illva Group), 1986—. Mem. Readington twp. Environ. Commn., Whitehouse Sta., N.J., 1978-87, N.J. Assn. Environ. Commrs., Trenton, 1978—; fundraiser Rutgers Prep. Sch., Somerset, N.J., 1984—; bd. dirs. Hunterdon County YMCA, 1987-95. Named N.J. Broker Record, Forbes Inc., N.Y.C. 1987. Mem. Nat. Assn. Realtors, N.J. Assn. Realtors, Hunterdon County Bd. Realtors (mem. chair 1986), Realtor's Land Inst. Republican. Jewish. Office: Liberty Hill Realty Inc 415 US Highway 202 Flemington NJ 08822-6021

SALAMONE, GARY P. (PIKE SALAMONE), newspaper editor-in-chief, cartoonist; b. Rochester, N.Y., Aug. 26, 1950. BA, St. John Fisher Coll., 1972; MA, San Diego State U., 1979. Editor, pub. Inkslinger's Review, San Diego, 1981—; founder, news dir. Continental News Svc., San Diego, 1985—; pub., columnist Continental Newstime, San Diego, 1987—; founder, editor-in-chief Continental Features/Continental News Svc., San Diego and Washington, 1988—; pub., cartoonist Kids' Newstime, San Diego, 1992—. Author: An Examination of Alexander Hamilton's Views on Civil Liberty, 1979. Vol. radio announcer, reader Nat. Pub. Radio Affiliate Sta. KPBS, San Diego, 1976-81; founder Fisher Recycling, Rochester, N.Y., 1971; pres. Young People's Conservation Com., Webster-Penfield, N.Y., 1971; high sch. coord. Ecology Centre, San Diego, 1976; vol. pub. info. asst. Cleve. Nat. Forest, San Diego. Mem. Phi Alpha Theta, Pi Sigma Alpha. Democrat. Office: Continental Features Continental News Svc 341 W Broadway Ste 265 San Diego CA 92101-3802

SALAMONE, JOHN DOMINIC, neuroscientist, educator; b. Bay Shore, N.Y., Oct. 21, 1956; s. Joseph Anthony and Margaret (Silvis) S.; m. Donna Nicholson, Dec. 21, 1983 (div. Apr. 1988); m. Alexandria Roe; 1 child, Isabella Marie. BA, Rockhurst Coll., 1978; MA, Emory U., 1978, PhD, 1982. Rsch. fellow U. Cambridge, Eng., 1982-83; rsch. pharmacolgist Merck, Sharp & Dohme, Harlow, Eng., 1983-86; rsch. fellow U. Pitts., 1986-88; asst. prof., assoc. prof. U. Conn., Storrs, 1988—. Editl. bd. mem. Behavioral Brain Rsch., 1995; contbr. articles to profl. jours. NATO fellow NSF, 1982. Mem. Soc. Neurosci., N.Y. Acad. Scis. Democrat. Roman Catholic. Avocations: astronomy, poetry, cooking. Home: 31 Laurel St Manchester CT 06040 Office: U Conn Dept Psychology 406 Babbidge Rd Storrs CT 06269-1020

SALAMONE, JOSEPH CHARLES, polymer chemistry educator; b. Bklyn., Dec. 27, 1939; s. Joseph John and Angela (Barbagallo) S.; children: Robert, Alicia, Christopher. BS in Chemistry, Hofstra U., 1961; PhD in Chemistry, Poly. Inst. N.Y., 1967. NIH postdoctoral fellow U. Liverpool, Eng., 1966-67; rsch. assoc., Horace H. Rackham postdoctoral fellow U. Mich., Ann Arbor, 1967-70, adminstrv. sec., 1968-70; asst. prof., then assoc. prof. chemistry U. Mass., Lowell, 1970-76, prof., 1976-90, prof. emeritus, 1990—, dean Coll Sci., 1978-84, Disting. Rsch. fellow, 1984-90, chmn. dept. chemistry, 1975-78; pres. Optimers Inc., Lowell, 1985—; bd. dirs. Rochal Industries, Inc., Boca Raton, Fla.; cons. editor CRC Press, Inc., Boca Raton, 1992—. Mem. editl. bd. Polymer, 1976-94, Jour. Macromolecular Sci.-Chemistry, 1985—, Progress of Polymer Sci., 1987—, ChemTech, 1995—; adv. bd. Jour. Polymer Sci., 1974—; editor-in-chief Polymeric Materials Ency., 1993—; contbr. more than 155 articles to profl. jours. Recipient Disting Alumnus award, Poly. Inst. N.Y., 1984. Mem. Am. Chem. Soc. (chmn. div. polymer chemistry 1982), Soc. Plastics Engrs., Polymer Sci., Am. Acad. Ophthalmology (assoc.), Pacific Polymer Fedn. (sec., treas. 1988-90, dep. v.p. 1991-92, v.p., 1993, pres. 1994-95). Office: U Mass Dept Chemistry 1 University Ave Lowell MA 01854-2881

SALANS, CARL FREDRIC, lawyer; b. Chicago Heights, Ill., Mar. 13, 1933; s. Leon and Jean (Rudnick) S.; m. Edith Motel, Sept. 26, 1956; children: Eric Lee, Marc Robert, Christopher John. A.B., Harvard, 1954; B.A., Trinity Coll., Cambridge (Eng.) U., 1956, LL.B., 1958, M.A., 1962; J.D., U. Chgo., 1957. Bar: Ill. 1958, D.C. 1973, U.S. Supreme Ct. 1972, admitted in France as avocat, 1972. With State Dept., 1959-72, dep. legal adviser, 1966-72; practice law Paris, 1972—; legal adviser U.S. del. Vietnam Peace Talks, Paris, 1968-71; assoc. prof. law George Washington U., 1965-66; lectr. on internat. comml. arbitration Inst. Internat. Bus. Law and Practice, Internat. C. of C., Paris, France; arbitrator internat. cases; arbitrator U.S.-Iran Claims Tribunal, The Hague. Mem. ABA (chmn. com. East-West trade and investment 1975-82), Am. Soc. Internat. Law, Am. Arbitration Assn. (panel arbitrators), Am. C. of C. in France (bd. dirs. 1977-87, chmn. laws and pub. affairs com. 1980-85). Home: 18 Ave Raphael, 75016 Paris France Office: Salans Hertzfeld & Heilbronn, 9 Rue Boissy d'Anglas, 75008 Paris France

SALANS, LESTER BARRY, physician, scientist, educator; b. Chicago Heights, Ill., Jan. 25, 1936; s. Leon K. and Jean (Rudnick) S.; m. Lois Audrey Kapp, Dec. 21, 1958; children: Laurence Eliot, Andrea Eileen. B.A., U. Mich., 1957; M.D. with honors, U. Ill., 1961. Internal medicine intern Stanford U. Med. Ctr., 1961, resident, 1962-64; USPHS postdoctoral and spl. fellow Rockefeller U., 1964-67, asst. prof., 1967-68, adj. prof., 1984—; asst. prof. medicine Dartmouth Coll., 1968-70, assoc. prof., 1970-77, adj. prof., 1978-79; assoc. dir. diabetes, endocrinology, metabolism, also chief lab. cellular metabolism and obesity Nat. Inst. Arthritis, Metabolism and Digestive Diseases, NIH, Bethesda, 1976-81; dir. Nat. Inst. Arthritis, Diabetes, Digestive and Kidney Diseases, NIH, 1981-84; v.p., head preclin. rsch. Sandoz Rsch. Inst., 1985-92, v.p. scientific and acad. affairs, 1993—; dean Mt. Sinai Sch. Medicine, 1984, prof. internal medicine, 1984-85, clin. prof. medicine, 1987—; adj. prof. Rockefeller U., 1985—; vis. prof. U. Geneva, Switzerland, 1974-75. Contbr. articles on insulin, diabetes mellitus, obesity to profl. jours., textbooks. Recipient NIH Research Career Devel. award, 1972-76, NIH Dirs. award, 1980, Juvenile Diabetes Fedn Pub. Service award, 1979. Fellow ACP; mem. AAAS, Am. Soc. Clin. Investigation, Am. Fed. Clin. Rsch., Am. Diabetes Soc., Am. Diabetes Assn. (Charles H. Best award 1985), Endocrine Soc., Assn. Am. Physicians, Am. Soc. Clin. Nutrition. Office: Sandoz Rsch Inst 59 Route 10 East Hanover NJ 07936

SALANT, NATHAN NATHANIEL, athletic conference executive; b. Bronx, N.Y., June 25, 1955; s. Benjamin B. and Marilyn (Balterman) S. BA cum laude, SUNY, Albany, 1976; JD, Boston U., 1979. Bar: N.J. 1981. Asst. athletic dir. SUNY, Albany, 1979-80, St. Francis Coll., Bklyn., 1981-85; spl. asst. athletic dir. Adelphi U., Garden City, N.Y., 1985-88; commr. Mid. Atlantic States Collegiate Athletic Conf., Chester, Pa., 1988-92; adj. prof. English Widener U., Chester, 1988-92; commr. Gulf South Conf., Birmingham, Ala., 1992—; mem. men's com. on coms. NCAA, 1993—, mem. D-II men's basketball south ctrl. regional adv. com., 1995—. Author: This Date in New York Yankees History, 1979, 81, 83, Superstars, Stars and Just Plain Heroes, 1982. Head coach Rockland (N.Y.) OTB Pirates Am. Legion Baseball Team, 1974-76, 77—. Named Coach of Yr., Rockland County Big League, 1979-81, 83, 85-86, 87, 89, N.Y. State Am. Legion, 1987, 89-94. Mem. ABA. Avocations: writing, collecting sports memorabilia, stamps and coins. Home: 174 Woodmere Creek Ln Birmingham AL 35226-3561 Office: Gulf South Conf 4 Office Park Cir Ste 218 Birmingham AL 35223-2538

SALANT, WALTER S., economist; b. N.Y.C., Oct. 24, 1911; s. Aaron Bennett and Josephine Adele (Scheider) S.; m. Edna Goldstein, Jan. 25, 1939; children—Michael Alan, Stephen Walter. B.S., Harvard, 1933; A.M., Grad. Sch. Pub. Adminstrn., 1937-38, Ph.D., 1962; postgrad., Cambridge U., Eng., 1933-34. Research, statistics Treasury Dept., 1934-36; research Wall St. firm, 1936; asst. econs. Harvard, 1938; research SEC, 1938-39; mem. sr. staff indsl. econ. div. Office of Sec. Dept. Commerce, 1939-40; head economist research div. OPA (and predecessor agencies), 1940-45; econ. adviser to Econ. Stblzn. Dir., 1945-46, Price Decontrol Bd., 1946; economist Council Econ. Advisers, Exec. Office Pres., 1946-52; cons. econ. and finance div. NATO, 1952-53; vis. prof. Stanford, 1954, 69; sr. fellow Brookings Instn., 1954-76, emeritus, 1977—; cons. to sec. of treasury, 1961—, mem. U.S. econ. survey team to, Indonesia, 1961; cons. AID, 1963-66. Author: (with B.N. Vaccara) Import Liberalization and Employment, 1961, (with others) Indonesia: Perspectives and Proposals for U.S. Economic Aid, 1963, The U.S. Balance of Payments in 1968, 1963, International Monetary Arrangements: The Problem of Choice, 1967, Maintaining and Restoring Balance in International Payments, 1966, International Mobility and Movement of Capital, 1972, European Monetary Unification and Its Meaning for the United States, 1973, Worldwide Inflation: Theory and Recent Experience, 1977, also The Effects of Increases in Imports on Domestic Employment: A Clarification of Concepts, 1978; bd. editors: (with others) Am. Econ. Rev, 1956-58; contbr. (with others) articles to econs. jours. Mem. Univ.-Nat. Bur. Com. Econ. Research, 1956—, mem. exec. com., 1962-74, vice chmn., 1967-74. Mem. Am. Econ. Assn., Royal Econ. Soc., Phi Beta Kappa. Clubs: Cosmos (Washington), Harvard (Washington). Home: 2101 Connecticut Ave NW Washington DC 20008-1728

SALANTRO, MARIA VOGEL, retired art educator; b. N.Y.C., Jan. 25, 1918; d. Salvatore and Marie (Mondello) S.; children: Michele Jolly, Linda Vogel Kelley. Student, Art Students League, N.Y.C., Salmagundi Club, N.Y.C. Art tchr. Mission Hills Mus. Am. Folk Art, N.Y.C., 1979-85, Forest Hills (N.Y.) Sr. Ctr., 1984-87; tchr. art Mission Hills; artist Miniature Art Soc. Fla., 1987-93, O.T.O.W. Art Guild, Clearwater, Fla., 1991-93. Recipient many awards for paintings. Mem. Nat. Mus. Women in Arts. Democrat. Roman Catholic. Home: 1439 Mission Dr W Clearwater FL 34619-2744

SALATHE, JOHN, JR., manufacturing company executive; b. Montreal, Que., Can., Sept. 25, 1928; s. John and Ida (Schenk) S.; m. Harriet Edith Styles; children: Linda Paul, Craig. BSME, San Jose State U., 1950. Gen. mgr. Indsl. Steel Tank & Body Co., Berkeley, Calif., 1958-62; project mgr. Pacific Foundry div. PACCAR Inc., Renton, Wash., 1962-66, prodn. mgr., 1966-70, asst. gen. mgr., 1970-71, gen. mgr., 1971-79; asst. v.p. PACCAR Inc., Bellevue, Wash., 1979-81, v.p., 1981-90; ret., 1991. Bd. dirs. Jr. Achievement, Seattle, 1979-85; mem. adv. bd. Seattle Pacific U., 1985—. Sloan fellow Stanford U., 1970. Mem. Soc. Mfg. Engrs. (sr.), Am. Soc. Quality Control (sr.). Avocations: gardening, boating, reading.

SALATICH, JOHN SMYTH, cardiologist; b. New Orleans, Nov. 28, 1926; s. Peter B. and Gladys (Malter) S.; BS cum laude, Loyola U., New Orleans, 1946; MD, La. State U., 1950; m. Patricia L. Mattison, Sept. 26, 1959; children: John Smyth, Elizabeth, Allison, Stephanie. Intern Charity Hosp., New Orleans, 1950-51, resident, 1951-54; practice medicine, specializing in cardiology and internal medicine, New Orleans, 1954-92, Gen. Internal Med. Clinic Tulane Med. Sch., 1992—; dir. EKG dept. Southeastern La. Hosp., Mandeville, La.; prof. clin. medicine La. State U., 1994; mem. staff Touro Infirmary, St. Charles Gen. Hosp.; chmn. dept. medicine Hotel Dieu, 1974-86 pres., New Orleans Emergency Room Corp., Physician Supplemental Services; adv. bd. Bank La., 1960-89; mem. Pres.'s Coun. Loyola U., 1990-92. Bd. dirs. La. Regional Med. Program, 1972. Served to capt. M.C., AUS, 1954-56; Korea. Decorated Medallion of Greek Army. Diplomate Am. Bd. Internal Medicine. Fellow Am. Coll. Chest Physicians, ACP; mem. Am. Heart Assn., La. Heart Assn., New Orleans Acad. Internal Medicine, La. Soc. Internal Medicine, AMA, La. Med. Soc., Orleans Parish Med. Soc., Theta Beta, Alpha Sigma Nu, Delta Epsilon Sigma. Club: New Orleans Country. Contbr. articles to profl. and bus. jours. Home: 433 Country Club Dr New Orleans LA 70124-1038 Office: Nola 70112 144 Elk Pl Ste 1100 New Orleans LA 70112-2636

SALATKA, CHARLES ALEXANDER, archbishop; b. Grand Rapids, Mich., Feb. 26, 1918; s. Charles and Mary (Balun) S. Student, St. Joseph's Sem., Grand Rapids, 1932-38; M.A., Cath. U. Am., 1941; J.C.L., Inst. Civil and Canon Law, Rome, 1948. Instr. St. Joseph's Sem., Grand Rapids, Mich., 1945; ordained priest Roman Catholic Ch., 1945; assigned chancery office Diocese of Grand Rapids, 1948-54, vice chancellor, 1954-61; aux. bishop, 1961, vicar gen., 1961, consecrated bishop, 1962; pastor St. James Parish, Grand Rapids, 1962-68; titular bishop of Cariana and aux. bishop of Grand Rapids, 1962-68; bishop of Marquette, 1968-77; archbishop of Okla. City, 1977-92; ret., 1992. Mem. Canon Law Soc. Am. *

SALAVERRIA, HELENA CLARA, educator; b. San Francisco, May 19, 1923; d. Blas Saturnino and Eugenia Irene (Loyarte) S. AB, U. Calif., Berkeley, 1945, secondary teaching cert., 1946; MA, Stanford U., 1962. High sch. tchr., 1946-57; asst. prof. Luther Coll., Decorah, Iowa, 1959-60; prof. Spanish, Bakersfield (Calif.) Coll., 1961-84, chmn. dept., 1973-80. Vol., Hearst Castle; mem. srs. adv. group edn. Cuesta Coll. Community Svcs. Mem. AAUW (edn. com.), NEA, Calif. Fgn. Lang. Tchrs. Assn. (dir. 1976-77), Kern County Fgn. Lang. Tchrs. Assn. (pres. 1975-77), Union Concerned Scientists, Natural Resources Def. Coun., Calif. Tchrs. Assn. (chpt. sec. 1951-52), Yolo County Coun. Retarded, Soc. Basque Studies in Am., RSVP, Amnesty Internat., Common Cause, Sierra Club, Prytanean Alumnae, U. Women of Cambria, U. Calif. Alumni Assn., Stanford U. Alumni Assn. Democrat. Presbyterian. Address: PO Box 63 Cambria CA 93428-0063

SALAZAR, ALBERTO, Olympic professional runner; b. Havana, Cuba, Aug. 7, 1958; s. Jose and Marta Galbis (Rigal) S.; m. Molly Morton, Dec. 21, 1981; 1 son, Antonio Roberto. B.A., U. Oreg., 1981. Mem. U.S. Olympic Team, 1980, 1984; cons. Nike Co., 1981—. Record holder N.Y. Marathon, Oct. 25, 1980, winner, 1980-82; winner Boston Marathon, 1982. Mem. Assn. Bd. Racing Athletes. Office: Internat Mgmt Group 1 Erieview Plz Ste 1300 Cleveland OH 44114-1715*

SALAZAR, RAMIRO S., library administrator; b. Del Rio, Tex., Mar. 3, 1954; s. Jesus and Juanita (Suarez) S.; m. Cynthia Castillo, Dec. 19, 1976 (div. 1990); children: Ramiro Orlando, Selinda Yvette. BA, Tex. A&I U., 1978; MLS, Tex. Woman's U., 1979. Asst. libr. dir. Val Verde County Libr., Del Rio, Tex., 1975-76; libr. Robert J. Kleberg Libr., Kingsville, Tex., 1977-78; libr. dir. Eagle Pass Pub. Libr. (Tex.), 1980-84; dir. Main Libr. San Antonio Pub. Lib., 1984-90; dir. librs. El Paso Pub. Libr., 1991-93, Dallas Pub. Libr., 1993—; chmn. Tex. State Libr. Planning Task Force, 1991-92; active Tex. Women's U. Sch. Libr. and Info. Studies Adv. Bd., 1993—, Alliance for Higher Edn. Libr. Dirs. Coun., 1993—; bd. advs. U. N. Tex. Sch. Lib. and Info. Scis., 1993, Booker T. Washington H.S. of Performing and Visual Arts, 1995-96. Chair customer svc. steering com. City of Dallas, 1993—; chair coupon book/ resident privilege card task force City of Dallas, 1995-96; active home instruction program for presch. children Nat. Coun. Jewish Women, 1996—. Recipient H.W. Wilson Staff Devel. award jury, 1995-96. Mem. ALA, Libr. Adminstrn. and Mgmt. Assn. (bldg. and equipment sect., arch. for pub. lib. com. 1993-95, cultural diversity com. 1995—, pres.'s programs com. 1996—), Tex. Mcpl. Libr. Dirs. Assn., Pub. Libr. Adminstrs. North Tex., Reforma (exec. bd. dirs. 1993—), Tex. Lib. Assn. (chmn. pubs. com. 1992-93, legis. com. 1993-95, ad hoc com. value of public libs. 1995—, awards com. 1995—, Tall Tex. Leadership Devel. Inst. mentor, 1996), Jaycees. Democrat. Roman Catholic. Home: PO Box 15031 Dallas TX 75201-0031 Office: Dallas Pub Libr 1515 Young St Dallas TX 75201-5499

SALAZAR-CARRILLO, JORGE, economics educator; b. Havana, Cuba, Jan. 17, 1938; came to U.S., 1960; s. Jose Salazar and Ana Maria Carrillo; m. Maria Eugenia Winthrop, Aug. 30, 1959; children: Jorge, Manning, Mario, Maria Eugenia. BBA, U. Miami, 1958; MA in Econs., U. Calif., Berkeley, 1964, cert. in econ. planning, 1964, PhD in Econs., 1967. Sr. fellow, non-resident staff mem. Brookings Instn., Washington, 1965—; dir., mission chief UN, Rio de Janeiro, Brazil, 1974-80; prof. econs. Fla. Internat. U., Miami, 1980—, chmn. dept. econs., 1980-89; dir. Ctr. Econ. Rsch. & Edn.; mem. coun. econ. advisors State of Fla.; advisor U.S. Info. Agy., advisor, contbg. editor Library of Congress, Washington, 1972—; chmn. program com. Hispanic Profs. of Econs. and Bus.; cons. econs. Agy. for Internat. Devel., Washington, 1979—; council mem. Internat. Assn. Housing, Vienna, 1981—; exec. bd. Cuban Am. Nat. Council, Miami, 1982—; bd. dirs., pres. Fla. chpt. Insts. of Econ. and Social Rsch. of Caribbean Basin, Dominican Republic and Costa Rica, 1983—, U.S.-Chile Council, Miami, 1984—, Fla.-Brazil Inst. Co-author: Trade, Debt and Growth in Latin America, 1984; Prices for Estimation in Cuba, 1985; The Foreign Debt and Latin America, 1983; External Debt and Strategy of Development in Latin America, 1985; The Brazilian Economy in the Eighties, 1987, Foreign Investment, Debt and Growth in Latin America, 1988; World Comparisons of Incomes, Prices, and Product, 1988, Comparisons of Prices and Real Products in Latin America, 1990, The Latin American Debt, 1992; author: Wage Structure in Latin America, 1982, Oil and Development of Venezuela During the Twentieth Century, 1994. Fellow Brit. Council, London, 1960, Georgetown U., Washington, 1961-62, OAS, Washington, 1962-64, Brookings Instn., Washington, 1964-65. Mem. Am. Econ. Assn., Internat. Assn. Research in Income and Wealth, Econometric Soc. Latin Am., N.Am. Econs. and Fin. Assn., Nat. Assn. Cuban Am. Educators (treas. exec. com.), Internat. Assn. Energy Economists (pres. Fla. chpt.), Nat. Assn. Forensic Economists, Assn. for Study Cuban Economy (exec. com., dir. Cuban banking study group), Latin Am. Studies Assn., Knights of Malta. Roman Catholic. Home: 1105 Almeria Coral Gables FL 33134 Office: Fla Internat U Tamiami Campus DM 347 Miami FL 33199

SALBAING, PIERRE ALCEE, retired chemical company executive; b. Lectoure, France, May 8, 1914; emigrated to Can., 1946, naturalized, 1968; s. Jean and Sylvia (LaForgue) S.; m. Genevieve Nehlil, July 18, 1942; children: Michel, Christian, Francois, Patrick. B.A., Caen (France) U., 1931; Engring. Degree, Ecole Polytechnique, Paris, 1937; Naval Architecture Degree, Ecole Genie Maritime, Paris, 1939. With N.Am. dept. Air Liquide, Montreal, Que., Can., 1946-91, asst. gen. mgr., 1957-58, gen. mgr., 1958-60; exec. v.p. Canadian Liquid Air Ltd., Montreal, 1960-62, pres., 1962-82, chmn. bd., 1982-91; vice chmn. bd. Liquid Air Corp N.Am., San Francisco, 1984-91. Served to lt. comdr. French Navy, 1939-46. Decorated Legion of Honour., Nat. Order of Merit. Clubs: Mt. Royal, Montreal Amateur Athletic Assn.

SALCH, STEVEN CHARLES, lawyer; b. Palm Beach, Fla., Oct. 25, 1943; s. Charles Henry and Helen Louise (Alverson) S.; m. Mary Ann Prim, Oct. 7, 1967; children—Susan Elizabeth, Stuart Trenton. B.B.A., So. Meth. U., 1965, J.D., 1968. Bar: Tex. 1968, U.S. Tax Ct. 1969, U.S. Dist. Ct. (so. dist.) Tex. 1969, U.S. Dist. Ct. (ea. dist.) Tex. 1972, U.S. Ct. Appeals (5th cir.) 1969, U.S. Ct. Appeals (fed. cir.) 1982, U.S. Ct. Fed. Claims, 1982. Assoc. Fulbright & Jaworski, Houston, 1968-71, participating assoc., 1971-75, ptnr., 1975—. Co-author: Tax Practice Before the IRS, 1994; contbr. articles to legal jours. Pres. Tealwood Owners Assn., 1982-83, Meml. High Sch. PTA, 1985-86; mem. Tex. PTA (Hon. Life Member award 1986). Mem. ABA (coun. dir. 1985-88, vice chair tax sect. 1988-91, chair elect 1995-96, chair 1996—), State Bar Tex., Houston Bar Assn., Am. Law Inst., Nat. Tax Assn., Am. Coll. Tax Counsel, Internat. Fiscal Assn., Harris County Heritage Soc., Galveston Hist. Found., Smithsonian Assocs., Colonial Williamsburg Found., Am. Bar Found., Southwestern Legal Found., Houston Bar Found., Order of Coif, Beta Alpha Psi, Phi Eta Sigma, Phi Delta Phi. Presbyterian. Clubs: Houston, Cotillion, Lakeside Country, Houston Center, Governor's, Galveston Country, Yacht, Pelican of Galveston, Galveston Artillery. Home: 342 Tamerlaine Dr Houston TX 77024-6147 Office: Fulbright & Jaworski 51st Fl 1301 Mckinney St Fl 51 Houston TX 77010 *Set goals for yourself. Unless you know where you are and where you want to be in life, you will not be able to map a plan to accomplish your goals.*

SALCUDEAN, MARTHA EVA, mechanical engineer, educator; b. Cluj, Romania, Feb. 26, 1934; emigrated to Can., 1976, naturalized, 1979; d. Edmund and Sarolta (Hirsch) Abel. B.Eng., U. Cluj, 1956; postgrad., 1962; PhD, U. Brasov (Romania), 1969; PhD (hon.), U. Ottawa, 1993 ; m. George Salcudean, May 28, 1955; 1 child, Septimiu E. (Tim). Mech. engr. Armatura, Cluj, 1956-63; sr. rsch. officer Nat. Rsch. Inst. Metallurgy, Bucharest, 1963-75; part-time lectr. Inst. Poly., Bucharest, 1967-75; sessional lectr. U. Ottawa (Ont., Can.), 1976-77, asst. prof., 1977-79, assoc. prof., 1979-81, prof., 1981-85; prof., head mech. engring. U. B.C., 1985—, assoc. v.p. rsch., 1993—, acting v.p. rsch. pro-tem, 1995; mem. grant selection com. for mech. engring. Natural Scis. and Engring. Rsch. Coun. Can.; mem. Nat. Adv. Panel to Min. Sci. and Tech. on advanced indsl. materials, Can., 1990; mem. governing coun. Nat. Rsch. Coun.; mem. defense science adv. bd. Dept. Nat. Defense. Recipient Gold medal B.C. Sci. Coun., Killam Rsch. prize U. B.C. Rsch. Coun. Can. grantee, 1978—, Commemorative Medal 125th anniversary Can. Confederation, 1993, Julian C. Smith medal Engring. Inst. Can.,

1994-95. Fellow CSME, Can. Acad. Engring., Royal Soc. Can.; mem. ASME, Assn. Profl. Engrs. Ont. Contbr. numerous articles to profl. jours. Home: 1938 Western Pkwy, Vancouver, BC Canada V6T 1W5

SALE, GEORGE EDGAR, physician; b. Missoula, Mont., Apr. 18, 1941; s. George Goble and Ruth Edna (Polleys) S.; m. Joan M. Sutliff, 1989; children: George Gregory Colby, Teo Marie Jonsson. AB, Harvard U., 1963; MD, Stanford U., 1968. Intern U. Oreg., Portland, 1968-69; sr. asst. surgeon USPHS, Albuquerque, 1969-71; resident in pathology U. Wash., Seattle, 1971-75, instr. pathology, 1975-78, asst. prof., 1978-81, assoc. prof., 1981-88, prof., 1988—; asst. mem. faculty, dept. oncology Hutchinson Cancer Ctr., Seattle, 1975-88, assoc. mem., 1988-91, mem., 1991—. Author, editor: Pathology of Bone Marrow Transplantation, 1984, Pathology of Transplantation, 1990. Mem. AAAS, Internat. Acad. Pathology, Coll. Am. Pathologists, Am. Assn. Investigative Pathologists, Physicians for Social Responsibility. Home: 12146 Sunrise Dr NE Bainbridge Island WA 98110-4304 Office: Fred Hutchinson Cancer Rsh Ctr 1124 Columbia Seattle WA 98104

SALE, (JOHN) KIRKPATRICK, writer; b. Ithaca, N.Y., June 27, 1937; s. William M. Jr. and Helen (Stearns) S.; m. Faith Apfelbaum Sale, June 21, 1962; children: Rebekah Zoe, Kalista Jennings. BA, Cornell U., 1958. Editor The New Leader, N.Y.C., 1959-61; corr. Chgo. Tribune, San Francisco Chronicle, 1961-62; lectr. U. Ghana, Accra, 1963-65; editor N.Y. Times mag., N.Y.C., 1965-68, The Nation, N.Y.C., 1981-82; ind. scholar and writer, 1968—; bd. dirs. PEN Am. Ctr. N.Y.C., The Learning Alliance, N.Y.C. Author: The Land and People of Ghana, 1963, SDS: The Rise of the Students for a Democratic Society..., 1973, Power Shift: The Rise of the Southern Rim and Its Challenge to the Eastern Establishment, 1975, Human Scale, 1980, Dwellers in the Land: The Bioregional Vision, 1985, The Conquest of Paradise: Christopher Columbus and the Columbian Legacy, 1990, The Green Revolution: The American Environmental Movement, 1962-92, 1993, Rebels Against the Future: The Luddites and Their War on the Industrial Recolution: Lessons for the Computer Age, 1995; contbg. editor The Nation; contbr. articles to profl. jours. Bd. dirs. EF Schumacher Soc., Great Barrington, Mass., 1981—; co-dir. Hudson Bioregional Coun., N.Y.C., 1985—. Home: 113 W 11th St New York NY 10011-8325 Office: Joy Harris Agy 156 5th Ave New York NY 10010-7002

SALE, LLEWELLYN, III, lawyer; b. St. Louis, May 19, 1942; s. Llewellyn Jr. and Kathleen (Rice) S.; m. Cynthia Jean Bricker, Aug. 17, 1968 (div. Apr. 1995); children: Allyson J., Erin E. AB cum laude, Yale U., 1964; LLB cum laude, Harvard U., 1967. Bar: Mo. 1967, U.S. Dist. Ct. (ea. dist.) Mo. 1967, U.S. Tax Ct. 1982, U.S. Ct. Claims 1985. From assoc. to ptnr. to mng. ptnr. Husch & Eppenberger, St. Louis, 1967-88; ptnr. Bryan Cave, St. Louis, 1988—. Bd. dirs. Washington U. Child Guidance Clinic, St. Louis, 1978-80, Mental Health Assn. St. Louis, 1988-89. Mem. ABA, Bar Assn. Met. St. Louis (chmn. law econs. subcom. 1982), Media Club, Noonday Club. Avocations: spectator sports, jogging. Office: Bryan Cave 211 N Broadway Ste 3600 Saint Louis MO 63102-2733

SALE, TOM S., III, economist, educator; b. Haynesville, La., July 27, 1942; s. Thomas and Mary Belle (Fagg) S.; divorced; children: Jennifer Elizabeth, Sarah Elaine. BA, Tulane U., 1964; MA, Duke U., 1965; PhD, La. State U., 1972. Mem. faculty La. Tech. U., Ruston, 1965—, prof. econs., 1975—, head dept. econs. and fin., 1974-86, 90-95, dir. grad. studies Coll. Adminstrn and Bus., 1988-89. Chartered fin. analyst. Mem. Am. Econs. Assn., So. Econs. Assns., Southwestern Fin. Assn. (pres. 1985-86), Am. Fin. Assn., Inst. Chartered Fin. Analysts (exam. com. 1983-92, curriculum com. 1993—), SW Fedn. Adminstrv. Disciplines (v.p. 1988-89, pres. 1989-90), Dallas Assn. Fin. Analysts, Omicron Delta Kappa, Omicron Delta Epsilon. Episcopalian. Contbr. articles to profl. jours. Home: PO Box 1365 Ruston LA 71273-1365 Office: La Tech U Ruston LA 71272

SALE, WILLIAM MERRITT, classicist, comparatist, educator; b. New Haven, Nov. 27, 1929; s. William Merritt and Helen (Stearns) S.; m. Marilyn Mills, June 13, 1953 (div. Oct. 1967); children: Elizabeth, David; m. Anne Perkins, May 18, 1991. B.A., Cornell U., 1951, M.A., 1954, Ph.D., 1958. Engr. U.S. Metals Co., Carteret, N.J., 1951-52; instr. in classics Yale U., New Haven, 1957-58; asst. prof., assoc. prof. Washington U., St. Louis, 1958-75, chmn. classics dept., 1961-69, prof. classics and comparative lit., 1975—, chmn. comparative lit. dept., 1981-90. Author: Sophocles' Electra: Commentary with Introduction and Translation, 1970, Existentialism and Euripides, 1977, Homer and the Roland, 1993, The Government of Troy, 1995. Recipient Founder's Day award for Excellence in Teaching Washington U., 1978. Mem. Am. Philol. Assn., London Inst. for Classical Studies. Home: 2342 Albion Pl Saint Louis MO 63104-2524 Office: Washington U Dept Comparative Lit Saint Louis MO 63130

SALEH, BAHAA E. A., electrical engineering educator; b. Cairo, Sept. 30, 1944; came to U.S., 1977.; BS, Cairo U., 1966; PhD, Johns Hopkins U., 1971. Lectr. Johns Hopkins U., Balt., 1969-71; asst. prof. U. Santa Catarina, Brazil, 1971-74; rsch. assoc. Max Planck Inst., Göttingen, Fed. Republic Germany, 1974-76; asst. prof. elec. engring. U. Wis., Madison, 1977-79, assoc. prof., 1979-81, prof., 1981-94, chmn. dept. elec. and computer engring., 1990-94; prof., chmn. dept. elec. computer and systems engring Boston Univ., Boston, 1994—. Author: Photoelectron Statistics, 1978, Fundamentals of Photonics, 1991; also over 150 articles on optics and image processing. Romnes faculty fellow U. Wis., 1981, Guggenheim fellow, 1984. Fellow IEEE, Optical Soc. Am.; Jour Optical Soc. of Am. A., editor-in-chief; mem. Phi Beta Kappa, Sigma Xi. Office: 44 Cummington St Boston MA 02215-2407

SALEM, GEORGE RICHARD, lawyer; b. Jacksonville, Fla., Dec. 24, 1953; s. Kamel Abraham and Margaret Virginia (Bateh) S.; m. Rhonda M. Ziadeh, June 28, 1980; children: James George, Jihan Camille, Laila Suad. BA, Emory U., 1975, JD, 1977; LLM, Georgetown U., 1984. Bar: Ga. 1978, Fla. 1979, D.C. 1981. Ptnr. Thompson, Mann & Hutson, Washington, 1977-85; dep. solicitor U.S. Dept. Labor, Washington, 1985-86, solicitor of labor, 1986-89; ptnr. Akin, Gump. Strauss, Hauer & Feld, Washington, 1990—; bd. dirs. Overseas Pvt. Investment Corp. Contbr. articles to profl. jours. Nat. exec. dir. ethnic voters div. Reagan Bus '84; bd. dirs. United Palestinian Appeal, Inc., 1981-85, 86—, Arab Am. Inst., Jan.-Mar., 1985, Dec. 1986—; chmn. Arab Am. Leadership Coun., 1990—; mem. Am. Arab Anti-Discrimination Com., Interagy. Coordinating Coun.; chmn. Arab-Ams. for Bush-Quayle '88, '92. Recipient Ellis Island Medal of Honor, 1992. Mem. ABA (labor and employment law sect.), Ga. Bar Assn. (labor rels. div.), fla. Bar Assn. (labor rels. div.), D.C. Bar Assn. (labor rels. div.), Nat. Assn. Arab Ams. (bd. dirs. 1987, pres. 1992—), Am. Ramallah Club (pres. D.C. chpt. 1984, Wash. rep. 1982-84), Am. Ramallah Fedn. (chmn. human rights com., Washington rep. 1982-84), Arab Am. Rep. Fedn. (chmn. 1985), Assn. Am. Arab Univ. Grads., Century Club Nat. Rep. Heritage Groups Coun., Delta Theta Phi, Omicron Delta Kappa. Mem. Eastern Orthodox Christian Ch. Office: Akin Gump Hauer & Feld 1333 New Hampshire Ave NW #210 Washington DC 20036-1564

SALEMBIER, VALERIE BIRNBAUM, publishing executive; b. Teaneck, N.J., July 2, 1945; d. Jack and Sara (Gordon) Birnbaum; m. David J. Salembier, June 23, 1968 (div. 1980); m. Paul J. Block, Dec. 9, 1990. B.A., Coll. of New Rochelle, 1973. Merchandising mgr. Life Internat., Time, Inc., N.Y.C., 1964-69; merchandising copywriter Newsweek, Inc., N.Y.C., 1970; promotion prodn. mgr. Newsweek, Inc., 1971, adv. sales rep., 1972-76; advt. dir. Ms. Mag., N.Y.C., 1976-79, assoc. pub., 1979-81; pub. Inside Sports Mag., N.Y.C., 1982; v.p., pub. 13-30 Corp., N.Y.C., 1983; sr. v.p. advt. USA Today, 1983-88; pub. TV Guide, Radnor, PA, 1988-89; pres. N.Y. Post, N.Y.C., 1989-90; pub. Family Circle Mag., N.Y.C., 1991-93; v.p. advt. The N.Y. Times, 1993-94; pres. Quest Mag., 1995-96; v.p. mag. devel. Meigher Comms., 1995-96; pub. Esquire Mag., 1996—; lectr. in field. Trustee Coll. New Rochelle; trustee, exec. com. N.Y.C. Police Found.; mem. exec. com. Women of Distinction, United Jewish Appeal; pres., bd. dirs. Nat. Alliance Breast Cancer Orgns., BOX (Beneficial Orgn. to Aid Ex-Fighters). Mem. C200, Women in Comm., Womens Forum, Nat. Coun. Jewish Women (bd. dirs.). Home: 1075 Park Ave New York NY 10128-1003

SALENTINE, THOMAS JAMES, pharmaceutical company executive; b. Milw., Aug. 8, 1939; s. James Edward and Loretta Marie (Burg) S.; m. Susan Anne Sisk, Apr. 16, 1966; children: Anne Elizabeth, Thomas James Jr. BS in Acctg., Marquette U., Milw., 1961. CPA, Ind., Wis. Sr. audit mgr. Price Waterhouse, Milw., 1961-74; dir. corp. acctg. Ward Foods Inc., Wilmette, Ill., 1974-78; corp. contr. Johnson Controls Inc., Milw., 1984-85; v.p., contr. Stokely Van Camp Inc., Indpls., 1978-87; exec. v.p., chief fin. officer Bindley Western Industries Inc., Indpls., 1987—, also bd. dirs. Chmn. com. United Way, Indpls., 1989-90. Lt. USN, 1962-65. Mem. AICPA, Fin. Execs. Inst. Republican. Roman Catholic. Home: 13540 Brentwood Ln Carmel IN 46033-9488 Office: Bindley Western Industries Ste 300 10333 N Meridian St Indianapolis IN 46290

SALERNO, THOMAS JAMES, lawyer; b. Jersey City, Aug. 30, 1957; s. Thomas E. and Imelda (Gyurik) S.; m. Tricia Joan Neary, Feb. 14, 1982; children: Alissa Lee, Lauren Mae, Thomas James Jr., Laina Hope. BA summa cum laude, Rutgers U., 1979; JD cum laude, U. Notre Dame, 1982. Bar: Ariz. 1982, U.S. Dist. Ct. Ariz. 1982, U.S. Ct. Appeals (9th cir.) 1982. Ptnr. Streich Lang, Phoenix, Ariz., 1982-94, Meyer, Hendricks, Victor, Osborn & Maledon, Phoenix, 1994-95, Squire, Sanders & Dempsey, Phoenix, 1995—; lectr. Profl. Edn. Sys., Inc., Eau Claire, Wis., 1984—, Robert Morris Assn., Phoenix, 1984—, Comml. Law League of Am., 1986—, Am. Law Inst.-ABA, 1990—, Nat. Conf. Bankruptcy Judges, 1991—, Continuing Legal Edn. Satellite Network, 1991; adj. prof. London Inst. Internat. Bus. and Comml. Law, Inns of Ct. Sch. Law, Gray's Inn, London, 1994—; adj. prof. Salzburg (Austria) U., 1995. Co-author: Bankruptcy Litigation and Practice: A Practitioner's Guide, 1988, 2d edit., 1995, Arizona's New Exemption Statute, 1983, Bankruptcy Law and Procedure: A Fundamental Guide for Law Office Professionals, 1989, Troubled Construction Loans: Law and Practice, 1990, In and Outs of Foreclosure, 1989, Advanced Chapter 11 Banktuptcy Practice, 1990, 2d edit., 1996, Norton Bankruptcy Law and Practice, 1993, Chapter 11 Theory and Practice: A Guide to Reorganizations, 1994. Mem. Vol. Legal Svcs. Program. Mem. ABA (bankruptcy com., lectr. 1990—, mem. working group prepackaged plans bus. bankruptcy com. 1991), ATLA, Am. Bankruptcy Bd. of Certification (bd. dirs. 1994—), Ariz. State Bar Assn. (chmn. bankruptcy sect. 1988-90, co-chmn. bankruptcy sect. of continuing legal edn. com. 1988-89, mem. bankruptcy adv. commn. 1992-96), Am. Bankruptcy Inst. (editor jour. 1991—, bd. dirs. 1993—, mem. bd. cert. 1993—), Comml. Law League, Phi Beta Kappa, Pi Sigma Alpha. Avocations: tennis, golf, travel. Home: 9638 N 33rd St Phoenix AZ 85028-4919 Office: Squire Sanders & Dempsey 40 North Central Ave Ste 2700 Phoenix AZ 85004

SALERNO-SONNENBERG, NADJA, violinist; b. Rome, Jan. 10, 1961; came to U.S., 1969; d. Josephine Salerno-Sonnenberg. Grad., Curtis Inst. Music, 1975, Juilliard Sch., 1982. Profl. debut with Phila. Orch., 1971; appearances include Am. Symphony Orch., Balt., Chgo., Cin., Detroit, Houston, Indpls., Milw., Montreal, N.J., Pitts. symphonys, Cleve., L.A. Chamber, Phila., Minn. orchs., New Orleans, N.Y., L.A. philharms.; guest appreareance include Mostly Mozart Festival, Ravinia, Blossom, Meadow Brook, Gt. Woods, Caramoor, Aspen, Hollywood Bowl; internat. appearances include Vienna, Munich, Stuttgart, Frankfurt, Geneva, Rotterdam, Lisbon, Tokyo; featured on 60 Minutes, CBS, CBS Sunday Morning, NBC Nat. News, PBS Live from Lindoln Ctr., Charlies Rose Show; numerous appearances on The Tonight Show with Johnny Carson; rec. artist Angel, 1987, Nonesuch, 1996. Recipient 1st prize Naumburg Violin Competition, N.Y.C., 1981; Avery Fisher Career grantee, N.Y.C., 1983. Mem. AFTRA, Screen Actors Guild. Office: care M L Falcone Pub Rels 155 W 68th St New York NY 10023-5808

SALES, A. R., financial executive; b. Holguin, Oriente, Cuba, Sept. 20, 1948; came to U.S., 1961; s. Angel Alberto and Adeina Rosa (Paneque) S.; m. Barbara Cornell Felix, Aug. 26, 1972; children: Ashley Lynden, Alison Lane. BS, Ind. U., 1972, MBA, 1977. Mgmt. trainee Lincoln Nat. Bank, Ft. Wayne, Ind., 1972-73; asst. v.p. Am. Fletcher Nat. Bank, Indpls., 1973-77; treasury mgr. The Upjohn Co., Kalamazoo, 1977-82, v.p., treas., 1985-90; asst. treas. Midland-Ross Corp., Cleve., 1982-85; treas. Arvin Industries, Inc., Columbus, Ind., 1990—. Bd. dirs. C. Brown Speech and Hearing Ctr., Kalamazoo, 1987-90, treas., 1989; bd. dirs. Columbus Pro Musica Orch., Columbus Regional Hosp. Found., Bartholomew Co. United Way; adv. bd. Ind. U.-Purdue U., Columbus. Mem. Fin. Execs. Inst., Nat. Assn. Corp. Treas., Beta Gamma Sigma. United Methodist. Avocations: tennis, golf, art. Office: Arvin Industries PO Box 3000 Columbus IN 47202-3000

SALES, EUGENIO DE ARAUJO CARDINAL, archbishop; b. Acari, Brazil, Nov. 8, 1920; d. Celso Dantas and Josefa de A. Sales; student Seminary Fortaleza City. Ordained priest Roman Cath. Ch., 1943, consecrated bishop, 1954, elevated to cardinal, 1969; Sede Plena apostolic adminstr., Natal, 1962, Salvador, 1964; archbishop, Salvador, 1968-71, Rio de Janeiro, 1971—. Mem. Congregations, for Divine Cult, clergy, Evangelization, Oriental Chs., Couns. for Social Communication. Editor: The Pastors Voice. Address: Gloria 446, 20241-150 Rio de Janeiro Brazil

SALES, JAMES BOHUS, lawyer; b. Weimar, Tex., Aug. 24, 1934; s. Henry B. and Agnes Mary (Pesek) S.; m. Beuna M. Vornsand, June 3, 1956; children: Mark Keith, Debra Lynn, Travis James. BS, U. Tex., 1956, LLB with honors, 1960. Bar: Tex. 1960. Practiced in Houston, 1960—; sr. ptnr. firm, head litigation dept., mem. exec. com. Fulbright & Jaworski, 1960—; advocate Am. Bd. Trial Advocates; pres. State Bar of Tex., 1988-89. Author: Products Liability in Texas, 1985; co-author: Texas Torts and Remedies, 5 vols., 1986; assoc. editor Tex. Law Rev., 1960; contbr. articles to profl. jours. Trustee South Tex. Coll. Law, 1982-88, 90—, A.A. White Dispute Resolution Ctr., 1991-94; bd. dirs. Tex. Resource Ctr., 1990-95, Tex. Bar Hist. Found., 1990-96. 1st lt. USMCR, 1956-58. Fellow Internat. Acad. Trial Lawyers, Am. Coll. Trial Lawyers (state chmn. 1993-960), Am. Bar Found. (sustaining life, state chmn. 1993—), Tex. Bar Found. (trustee 1991-95, vice-chmn. 1992-93, chmn. 1993-94, chair adv. bd. for planned giving 1994-97, sustaining life mem.), Houston Bar Found. (sustaining life, chmn. bd. 1982-83); mem. ABA (ho. of dels. 1984—, mem. Commn. on IOLTA 1995—), Internat. Assn. Def. Counsel, Nat. Conf. Bar Pres. (coun. 1989-92), So. Conf. Bar Pres., Def. Rsch. Inst., Tex. Law Review (bd. dirs. 1996—), So. Tex. Coll. Trial Advocacy (dir. 1983-87), Fed. Bar Assn., State Bar Tex. (pres. 1988-89, bd. dirs. 1983-87, chmn. bd. 1985-86), Tex. Assn. Def. Counsel (v.p. 1977-79, 83-84), Houston Bar Assn. (pres. 1980-81), Gulf Coast Legal Found. (bd. dirs. 1982-85), Bar Assn. 5th Fed. Cir., The Forum, Westlake Club (bd. govs. 1980-85), Inns of Ct. (bd. dirs. 1981-84), Ramada-Tejas. Roman Catholic. Home: 10803 Oak Creek St Houston TX 77024-3016 Office: Fulbright & Jaworski 1301 Mckinney St Houston TX 77010

SALES, JAMES WILLIAM, chemical engineer; b. Mobile, Ala., May 1, 1958; s. John Wesley and Willean (Bondurant) S.; m. Cynthia Lynn Griffis, Feb. 23, 1980; children: James William Jr., Christopher Brandon, Kimberly Nicole, Rebecca Lynn. AS, Patrick Henry Jr. Coll., 1977; BSChemE, U. Ala., 1979. Registered profl. engr., Tenn. Design engr. Eastman Chem. Co., Kingsport, Tenn., 1979-85; project engr. Ectona polyethylene terethalate project Eastman Chem. Co., London, 1985-88; engring. mgr. filtrate purge project Eastman Chem. Co., Columbia, S.C., 1989-90; engring. mgr. Ectona polyethylene terethalate project Eastman Chem. Co., London, 1990-93; engring. mgr. Mex. polyethylene terethalate project Eastman Chem. Co., Mexico City, 1993-94; bus. devel. mgr. fine chems. bus. orgn. Eastman Chem. Co., Kingsport, 1994—. Chmn. deacons First Bapt. Ch., Kingsport, 1995—, Sunday sch. dir., 1994-95; pres. Tellico Hills Home Owners Assn., Kingsport, 1988-89. Mem. AIChE, Kiwanis (sec. 1981-86), Phi Kappa Sigma (treas. 1978-79), Tau Beta Pi, Alpha Chi Omega. Avocations: golf, tennis. Office: Eastman Chem Co Eastman Fine Chems 1999 E Stone Dr Kingsport TN 37662

SALES, ROBERT JULIAN, newspaper editor; b. N.Y.C., Jan. 1, 1936; m. Naomi Simon, Oct. 11, 1958; children: Jonathan, Marian. B.A., L.I. U., 1957. Reporter Newsday, Garden City, N.Y., 1960-63; N.Y. Herald Tribune, N.Y.C., 1963-66, Boston Globe, 1966-78; editor Boston Phoenix, 1978-79; mng. editor Boston Herald Am., 1979-81; exec. editor Boston Herald, 1981-83, Toledo Blade, Ohio, 1983; mét. editor N.Y. Newsday, N.Y.C., 1984-86; sports editor Boston Herald, 1986—. Urban Journalism fellow Northwestern U., Evanston, Ill., 1973. Club: Univ. Club. (Boston). Office: Boston Herald One Herald Sq Boston MA 02106

SALESSES, JOHN JOSEPH, university administrator; b. Providence, Feb. 13, 1933; s. William Edward and Alice Marie (McConnell) S.; m. Dolores Ann Serbst, Nov. 27, 1954; children: John J., Robert G., Gregory M., Beth Ann. AB, Providence Coll., 1954; MA, U. R.I., 1960, PhD, 1979. Instr. Coll. Steubenville, Ohio, 1960-62; asst. prof. English R.I. Coll., Providence, 1962-79, assoc. prof. English, 1979—, chmn. dept. English, 1976-79, asst. v.p., dean, 1979-90, v.p., 1990—; adj. faculty U.S. Naval War Coll., Newport, R.I., 1963-73; mem. Dept. Def. Res. Forces Policy Bd., Washington, 1985-88. Mem. R.I. Postsecondary Commn. Maj. gen. USMCR, 1954-88. Decorated Disting. Svc. medal; recipient Disting. Svc. award R.I. Coll., 1985; fellow U. R.I., 1958-60. Mem. N.E. MLA, Soc. for Eighteenth Century Studies, Res. Officers Assn., Marine Corps Res. Officers Assn., Renaissance Soc. Am., Barrington Yacht Club (R.I.), Newport Arty. Co. (master gunner) Waneumetonomy Golf Club (R.I.). Roman Catholic. Avocations: running, golf, sailing. Home: 89 Peleg Rd Portsmouth RI 02871-3831 Office: RI Coll 600 Mt Pleasant Ave Providence RI 02908-1924

SALEWSKI, RUBY MARIE GRAF, nursing educator; b. Vernon, Tex., Feb. 22, 1932; d. Albert Carl and Olga Emma (Mertink) Graf; children: Stephen, Elizabeth, Matthew, Rebecca, Deborah. Diploma in nursing, Meth. Hosp. Sch. Nursing, Dallas, 1952; BSN, U. Tex., Galveston, 1956; postgrad., U. Tex., Austin, 1979-82, 87, St. Louis U., 1960-61; MEd in Nursing, U. Minn., 1967, postgrad., 1982. Lic. nurse, Minn., Tex. Mem. nursing faculty U. Tex., Galveston, 1956-59, Luth. Hosp., St. Louis, 1959-60, Anoka-Ramsey Community Coll., Coon Rapids, Minn., 1968-69; faculty prenursing advisor U. Minn., Mpls., 1970, 72, 73-74; mem. nursing faculty Austin (Minn.) C.C., 1975-76; mem. faculty Rochester (Minn) C.C., 1976-90, coord. continuing edn. in nursing, 1981-82; asst. prof. Tex. Tech U. Health Scis. Ctr. Sch. Nursing, Lubbock, 1991—; staff nurse St. John's Hosp., Springfield, Ill.; staff and charge nurse Dist. 1 Hosp., Faribault, Minn., U. Tex. Med. Br. Hosps., Galveston, Meth. Hosp., Dallas, Meml. Hosp., Springfield, Seton Hosp., Austin Tx., St. Mary's Hosp., Rochester. Bd. dirs., coord. Family Edn. Ctr., 1985;; vol. Contact Ministries, 1984-89; mem. organized caring and sharing ministry Good Shepherd Luth. Ch., 1990; parish nurse Hope Luth. Ch., Lubbock, 1991-92. Mem. ANA, LWV (bd. dirs. local chpt. 1985-88), NEA, Mich. Edn. Assn., Minn. Nurses Assn. (govtl. affairs com. 1987-89, chmn. dist. 13 1988), Nat. League for Nursing, Minn. League for Nursing (v.p. 1985-87, founding com. mem. educators coun.), Adlerian Soc., Sigma Theta Tau. Home: 1601 McRae Apt H-6 El Paso TX 79925

SALGADO, LISSETTE, dancer; b. Hialeah, Fla.. Dancer Miami (Fla.) Dance Theater Co., 1980-86, Joffrey II Dancers, N.Y.C., 1986-88, The Joffrey Ballet, N.Y.C., 1988—. Office: The Joffrey Ballet 130 W 56th St New York NY 10019-3818

SALHANI, CLAUDE, photojournalist; b. Cairo, Mar. 25, 1952; s. I. and Edith (Rogalska) S.; m. Cynthia Nuckolls, Dec. 1985; children: Justin Olivier, Isabelle Faustine. Certificate of Edn., U. London, 1969. Freelance war and roving corr. Sygma, 1970-81; dep. news pictures editor for Europe, Africa and Mid. East, Reuters, 1984-91; pres., gen. mgr. U.S. operation Sipa Press, N.Y.C., 1991-92; chief Mid. East photog. corr. UPI, Beirut, 1981-84; chief photographer for Europe, UPI, Brussels, 1983-84; mng. editor UPI NewsPictures, UPI, Washington, 1992—; asst. prof. photojournalism Beirut U. Coll., 1982-83; mem. adv. coun. Am. News Svc. Author: Lebanon, Days of Tragedy, 2 vols., Bravado & Trepidation, A Journalist's Guide to the Middle East-Black September to Desert Storm; photographs on covers Time, Newsweek, also others. Recipient Pulitzer prize nomination for picture of crying U.S. Marine after Beirut barracks bombing. Office: UPI World Hdqs 1400 I St NW Washington DC 20005

SALHANY, LUCILLE S., broadcast executive. Formerly with Paramount Pictures; pres. Paramount Domestic Television, from 1985; chmn. Twentieth Television, a unit of Fox Inc., 1991-92, Fox Broadcasting Co., Beverly Hills, Calif., 1993-94; pres. United ParamountNetwork, 1994—.

SALIBA, JACOB, manufacturing executive; b. East Broughton, Que., Can., June 10, 1913; s. Said and Nazira (David) S.; m. Adla Mudarri, May 31, 1942; children: John, Thomas, Barbara. BS, Boston U., 1941. Sr. supervising engr. Thompson and Lichtner Co., Boston, 1944-49; pres. Kingston Dress Co., Boston, 1949-51, Indsl. & Mgmt. Assocs., Inc., Boston, 1951-54, Maine Dress Co., Cornish, 1948-61; exec. v.p., mem. exec. com. Cortland Corp., Inc. (formerly Brockway Motor Co., Inc.), N.Y.C., 1954-59; exec. v.p. Sawyer-Tower, Inc., Boston, 1955-56, pres., 1956-59; v.p. Farrington Mfg. Co.; exec. v.p. Farrington Packaging Corp., 1959-61, Farrington Instruments Corp.; pres. N.E. Industries, Inc., from 1961, also bd. dirs.; pres. Fanny Farmer Candy Shops, Inc., 1963-66, W.F. Schrafft & Sons Corp., 1967-68; pres. frozen foods div. W.R. Grace & Co., 1966-68; pres. Katy Industries, Inc., Elgin, Ill., 1969-88, chmn., CEO, 1988-94; bd. dirs. Schon & Cie, Emerging Germany Fund, NYSE, Syratech Corp., NYSE, Katy Industries, NYSE; spl. cons. Air Materiel Commmand, USAF, Dayton, Ohio, 1942-43; cons. to chief air staff USAF, 1952-54; co-chmn. Air Force Spare Study Group, 1953. Mem. corp. Mass. Gen. Hosp., Mus. Sci. Mem. Union League Club, Bridgton Club, Highlands Country Club, Palm Beach Yacht Club. Methodist. Office: Katy Industries Inc 6300 S Syracuse Way Denver CO 80111-6723

SALIBA, PHILIP E., archbishop; b. Abou-Mizan, Lebanon, 1931; came to U.S., 1956, naturalized, 1961; s. Elias Abdallah and Salema (Saliba) S. B.A., Wayne State U., 1959; M.Div., D.D., St. Vladimir's Sem., N.Y., 1964; DHL, Wayne State U., 1986. Became sub-deacon Antiochian Orthodox Christian Ch. N.Am., 1945-49, ordained deacon, 1949-59, priest, 1959-66, consecrated archbishop, 1966, now primate; chmn. Standing Conf. Am.-Middle Eastern Christian and Moslem Leaders; chmn. Orthodox Christian Edn. Commn.; vice chmn. Standing Conf. Canonical Orthodox Bishops in Ams. Vice-chmn. St. Vladimir's Orthodox Theol. Sem. Address: 358 Mountain Rd Englewood NJ 07631-3727

SALIGMAN, HARVEY, consumer products and services company executive; b. Phila., July 18, 1938; s. Martin and Lillian (Zitin) S.; m. Linda Powell, Nov. 25, 1979; children: Martin, Lilli Ann, Todd Michael, Adam Andrew, Brian Matthew. BS, Phila. Coll. Textiles and Sci., 1960. With Queen Casuals, Inc., Phila., 1960-88; v.p. Queen Casuals, Inc., 1966-68, pres., chief exec. officer, 1968-81, chmn., 1981-88; pres., chief operating officer Interco Inc., St. Louis, 1981-83, chief exec. officer, 1983-85; chief exec. officer Interco Inc., 1985-89, chmn., 1989-90; bd. dirs. Merc. Bank, Union Electric. Trustee Jewish Hosp., St. Louis, Washington U., St. Louis. Mem. St. Louis Club, Masons. Office: 10 S Brentwood Bvld Ste 408 Saint Louis MO 63105-1694

SALINAS, CARLOS FRANCISCO, dentist educator; b. Iquique, Chile, Apr. 9, 1941; came to U.S., 1972; s. Carlos F. and Victoria (Cerda) S.; m. Maria Asunción Córdova, 1963; children: Carlos Miguel, Claudio Andres, Maria Asunción. BS, U. Chile, Santiago, 1958; DDS, U. Chile, 1963; DMD, Med. U. S.C., 1985. Cert. Fla., 1982, Tenn., 1982, S.C., 1985. Dentist Nat. Health Svc., Viña del Mar, Chile, 1963-65; pvt. practice Viña del Mar, 1963-72; fellow in medicine/genetics Johns Hopkins U., Balt., 1972-74; faculty mem. Med. Univ. S.C., Charleston, 1974-88, assoc. prof., 1988-94, prof., 1994—, dir. divsn. craniofacial genetics, 1981—; dir. craniofacial anomalies and cleft lip palate ctr. Med. U. S.C., Charleston, 1995—; faculty mem. U. Chile, Valparaiso, 1965-74; dentist Dental Ctrl. Clinic for Chilean Navy, Valparaiso, 1964-66; vis. scientist U. Montreal, 1974; internat. cons. Inter-american Coll. Physicians and Surgeons, Ptnrs. of Ams., WHO/Pan Am. Health Orgn. Editor: Genetica Craniofacial, 1979, Craniofacial Anomalies: New Perspectives, 1982, (with R.J. Jorgenson) Dentistry in the Interdisciplinary Treatment of Genetic Diseases, 1980, (with K.S. Brown) Craniofacial Mesenchyme In Morphogensis and Malformations, 1984, (with J.M. Opitz) Recent Advances in Ectodermal Dysplasias, 1988; contbr. articles to profl. jours. Bd. dirs. Ptnrs. Am. (award 1992), East Cooper Cmty. Outreach, S.C. World Trade Ctr., Charleston; chmn. bd. S.C. Hispanic Coalition, 1994—; founder Circulo Hispanoamericano de Charleston, pres. 1978-96; hon. consul of Chile, 1978—. Fogarty Internat. Rsch. fellow; grantee NIH, 1972-74, HEW, 1979-80, 80-81, 81-82, 82-83, 83-84, Dept. Health and Human Svcs., 1983-84, 84-85, March of Dimes Birth Defects Found., 1984-85, S.C. State Health and Human Svcs. Fin. Commn., 1989—. Mem. AAAS, Soc. Craniofacial Genetics (pres. 1985, 92, chmn. membership com.

1993-94), Iberoam. Soc. Human Genetics of N.Am. (v.p. 1992-94, pres. 1994—), Am. Assn. Dental Schs., Am. Soc. Human Genetics, Am. Cleft Palate and Craniofacial Anomalies Assn., Internat. Assn. for Dental Rsch., Am. Assn. for Dental Rsch., Interam. Coll. Physicians and Surgeons (bd. dirs. chpt. faculty and rschrs. 1994—), Incontinentia Pigmenti Found. (sci. adv. coun. 1995—), Med. Assn. P.R. (hon.), Peruvian Soc. Human Genetics (hon.), Med. Soc. Western Dist. P.R. (hon.). Home: 948 Equestrian Dr Mount Pleasant SC 29464-3608 Office: Med Univ SC 171 Ashley Ave Charleston SC 29425-2601

SALINE, LINDON EDGAR, industrial company executive; b. Mpls., Mar. 16, 1924; s. Emil and Anna (Hinz) S.; m. Jane Sprenger, Oct. 14, 1950; children: Sandra, Susan, Jeffrey, Bradley. B.E.E., Marquette U., 1945; M.S. in Elec. Engring., U. Wis., 1948, Ph.D. in Elec. Engring., 1950, Sc.D. hon., 1973. Registered profl. engr., Ariz., Fla., Md., N.Y. With Cutler-Hammer, Milw., 1946-47; with Gen. Electric Co., Fairfield, Conn., 1948-84, tech. and mgmt. positions in power systems, computers, aerospace and def., human resources and health care mgmt.; bd. dirs. St. Francis Med. Ctr., Franciscan Health System, LaCrosse Found., Chileda Habilitation Inst.; adv. com. on sci. edn. NSF; lectr. in field. Contbr. tech. papers and articles to profl. jours. Leader nat. minority engring. effort, chmn. State of Conn. Task Force on Mgmt. Human Resources, 1977-78; exec. dir. Bus. Roundtable on Health Initiatives, 1982-84. Served with USN, 1942-46. Recipient Disting. Service Citation U. Wis., 1973; named Disting. Engring. Alumnus Marquette U., 1981. Fellow IEEE, Am. Soc. Engring. Edn.; mem. AAAS, ASME, Sigma Xi, Tau Beta Pi, Eta Kappa Nu, Pi Mu Epsilon. Republican. Presbyterian. Club: La Crosse Country. Lodge: Rotary. Home: 1874 Mulder Ct Dresbach MN 55947-3013 *Balancing the spiritual, intellectual, and physical aspects of my life has given me the energy, freedom and desire to pursue a wide variety of interests. I am most grateful that somehow, somewhere I "learned how to learn", which gives me the confidence to enjoy and cope with a rapidly changing society.*

SALINGER, JEROME DAVID, author; b. N.Y.C., Jan. 1, 1919; s. Sol and Miriam (Jillich) S.; m. Claire Douglas, 1953 (div. 1967); children: Margaret Ann, Matthew. Student, Valley Forge Mil. Acad., Columbia U. Author: Catcher in the Rye, 1951, Nine Stories, 1953, Franny and Zooey, 1961, Raise High the Roof Beam, Carpenters; and Seymour: An Introduction, 1963; contbr. stories to New Yorker mag. Sgt. AUS, 1942-46. Address: care Harold Ober Assocs 425 Madison Ave New York NY 10017-1110*

SALINGER, PIERRE EMIL GEORGE, journalist; b. San Francisco, June 14, 1925; s. Herbert and Jehanne (Bietry) S.; m. Renee Laboure, Jan. 1, 1947; children: Marc (dec.), Suzanne (dec.), Stephen; m. Nancy Brook Joy, June 28, 1957; m. Nicole Helene Gillmann, June 18, 1965 (div. June 1988); 1 son, Gregory; m. Nicole Beauvillain de Menthon, June 17, 1989. BS, U. San Francisco, 1947. Reporter, night city editor San Francisco Chronicle, 1946-55; guest lectr. journalism Mills Coll., 1950-55; West Coast editor, contbg. editor Collier's mag., 1955-56; investigator select com. to investigate improper activities in labor or mgmt. field U.S. Senate, 1957-59; press sec. U.S. Senator Kennedy, 1959-60, Pres. Kennedy, 1961-63, Pres. Johnson, 1963-64; U.S. Senator from Calif., 1964; v.p. Nat. Gen. Corp., 1965; v.p. internat. affairs Continental Airlines, Inc. and Continental Air Services, Inc. (subsidiary), 1965-68; pres. Gramco Devel. Corp., 1968—; dep. chmn. Gramco (U.K.) Ltd., 1970-71; sr. v.p. AMROP Inc., 1969; L'Express, Paris, 1973-78; contbg. corr. ABC for Europe, 1977—, Paris bur. chief, 1979-87, sr. editor, 1988-90; sr. editor ABC News, 1988-93; vice chmn. Burson Marsteller, Washington, 1993—. Author: With Kennedy, 1966, On Instructions of My Government; editor A Tribute to John F. Kennedy, 1964, A Tribute to Robert F. Kennedy, 1968, Je Suis un Americain, 1975, La France et le Nouveau Monde, 1976, America Held Hostage-The Secret Negotiations, 1981, The Dossier, 1984, Mortal Games, 1988, Secret Dossier--The Hidden Agenda Behind the Gulf Crisis, 1991, PS-A Memoir, 1995. Press officer Calif. Stevenson for Pres. Campaign, 1952, Richard Graves for Gov. Calif. Campaign, 1954; trustee Robert F. Kennedy Meml. Found.; chmn. bd. trustees Am. U. in Paris, 1978-88, hon. chmn., 1988—. With USNR, World War II. Decorated officer Legion of Honor (France); recipient Ellis Island Medal of Honor, 1992. Mem. Nat. Press Club. Office: Burson Marsteller 1801 K St NW Washington DC 20006

SALISBURY, EUGENE W., lawyer, justice; b. Blasdell, N.Y., Mar. 20, 1933; s. W. Dean and Mary I. (Burns) S.; m. Joanne M. Salisbury, July 14, 1950; children: Mark, Ellen, Susan, David, Scott. BA in History and Govt. cum laude, U. Buffalo, 1959, JD cum laude, 1968. Bar: N.Y. 1960, D.C. 1973, U.S. Dist. Ct. (we. and no. dists.) 1961, U.S. Ct. Appeals (2d cir.) 1970, U.S. Ct. Appeals (D.C. cir.) 1973, U.S. Supreme Ct. 1973. Ptnr. Lipsitz, Green, Fahringer, Roll, Salisbury and Cambria, Buffalo, 1960—; justice Village of Blasdell, 1961—; lectr. N.Y. Office Ct. Adminstrn., N.Y.C., 1961—; mem. N.Y. State Commn. on Jud. Conduct, 1989—. Author: Manual for N.Y. Courts, 1973, Forms for N.Y. Courts, 1977. Capt. U.S. Army, 1948-54, Korea. Decorated Bronze Star, Purple Heart. Mem. ABA (del. spl. ct. sect. 1988—), D.C. Bar Assn., Erie County Bar Assn., N.Y. State Bar Assn., World Judges Assn., N.Y. State Magistrates Assn. (pres. 1973, Man of Yr. 1974), N.Y. State Jud. Conf., Upstate N.Y. Labor Adv. Council, 1995—. Office: Lipsitz Green Fahringer Roll Salisbury and Cambria 42 Delaware Ave Ste 300 Buffalo NY 14202-3901

SALISBURY, FRANK BOYER, plant physiologist, educator; b. Provo, Utah, Aug. 3, 1926; s. Frank M. and Catherine (Boyer) S.; m. Lois Marilyn Olson, Sept. 1, 1949; children: Frank Clark, Steven Scott, Michael James, Cynthia Kay, Phillip Boyer (dec.), Rebecca Lynn, Blake Charles; m. Mary Thorpe Robinson, June 28, 1991. BS, U. Utah, 1951, MA, 1952; PhD, Calif. Inst. Tech., 1955. Asst. prof. botany Pomona Coll., Claremont, Calif., 1954-55; faculty Colo. State U., Ft. Collins, 1955-66; prof. plant physiology Colo. State U., 1961-66; plant physiologist Expt. Sta., 1961-66; prof. plant physiology Utah State U., Logan, 1966—, disting. prof. Agr., 1987—, head dept. plant sci., 1966-70; tech. rep. plant physiology AEC, Germantown, Md., 1973-74; vis. prof. U. Innsbruck, Austria; Lady Davis fellow Hebrew U. Jerusalem, 1983; mem. aerospace medicine adv. com. NASA, 1988-93, life scis. adv. com., 1986-88, chmn. NASA Controlled Ecol. Life Support System Discipline Working Group, 1989—. Author: The Flowering Process, 1963, Truth by Reason and by Revelation, 1965, The Biology of Flowering, 1971, The Utah UFO Display, 1974, The Creation, 1976; co-author: (with R.V. Parke) Vascular Plants, Form and Function, 2d edit., 1970, (with C. Ross) Plant Physiology, 1969, 4th edit., 1992; (with W. Jensen) Botany: An Ecological Approach, 1972, Botany, 2d edit., 1984, (with others) Biology, 1977; editor Jour. Plant Physiology, Ams. and the Pacific Rim, 1989—; editor, contbr.: Units, Symbols, and Terminology for Plant Physiology, 1996. Trustee Colo. State U. Rsch. Found., 1959-62; leader People to People bot. del. to Republic South Africa, 1984, Peoples Republic China, 1988, Soviet Union, 1990. NSF sr. postdoctoral fellow Germany and Austria, 1962-63. Fellow AAAS; mem. Am. Soc. for Gravitational and Space Biology (Founders award 1994), Am. Soc. Plant Physiologists (editorial bd. 1967-92), Utah Acad. Sci., Arts and Letters, Am. Inst. Biol. Scis. (governing bd. 1976-79), Bot. Soc. Am. (Merit award), Sigma Xi, Phi Kappa Phi. Mem. LDS Ch. Home: 2020 N 1250 E North Logan UT 84341-2077 Office: Utah State U Dept Plants Soils and Biometeorology Logan UT 84322-4820 *This is an extremely exciting time to live! Science has provided marvelous insight into the cosmos, the earth, and the nature of life. The fact that mankind exists and can contemplate it all cries out that it has purpose and direction. My life is full to overflowing because God's revelation of Himself adds the final capstone to this beautiful structure.*

SALISBURY, FRANKLIN CARY, foundation executive, lawyer; b. Cleve., Sept. 29, 1910. B.A., Yale U., 1932; J.D., Case Western Res. U., 1937; LL.D. (hon.), U. Wales, 1985. Bar: Ohio 1937, D.C. 1947. Adminstrv. asst. to commr. FCC, 1939-40; chief legal div. ammunition br. Office Chief Ordnance, U.S. Army, 1941-45; chief clearance div. WPB, Army Service Forces, 1945; dir. legal div. Office Fgn. Liquidation Commn., Rio de Janeiro, Brazil, 1945-46; asst. solicitor Indian legal activities Dept. Interior, 1956-61; gen. counsel Ams. United for Separation Ch. and State, 1963-72; pres., chief exec. officer Nat. Found. Cancer Research, Bethesda, Md., 1973—; hon. pres., hon. dir. Assn. for Internat. Cancer Research, St. Andrews, Scotland, 1973-95; chmn. Krebsforschung Internat., Dusseldorf, Federal Republic Germany; trustee, counsel Latin Am. Inst., 1943-75; sec., dir. Atlantic Research Corp., 1949-64, Dryomatic Corp., 1950-59; chmn. bd., sec., dir. Orbit Industries, Inc., 1960-68; co-founder, dir. Internat. Sch. Law (now George Mason Law Sch.), 1975-77. Named Pro Universitate Med. U. Debrecen, 1982; recipient Quantum Biology award Internat. Soc. Quantum Biology, 1983, Medal of Merit U. Turin, Italy, 1984; decorated Order of Leopold II (Belgium). Mem. Fed. Bar Assn.; associated fgn. mem. Institut de Biologie Physico-Chimique (Fondation Edmond de Rothschild). Office: NFCR 7315 Wisconsin Ave Rm 500W Bethesda MD 20814

SALISBURY, JUDITH MURIEL, marketing consultant; b. Plainfield, N.J., Aug. 5, 1940; d. James Donald and Gladys Maybelle (Scull) S.; m. Leonard Gordon Hartsoe, July 9, 1966 (div. 1982); 1 child, Allison Lynn Hartsoe. BA in English, Vassar Coll., 1962; MA, Ind. U. Pa., 1972. Cert. paralegal; lic. real estate broker, Pa.; cert. secondary sch. tchr., N.J., Pa. Tchr. Greater Johnstown (Pa.) Pub. Schs., 1967-68, Altoona (Pa.) Area Pub. Schs., 1968-71; instr. Pa. State U., Altoona, 1970-72, C.C. Allegheny County, Pitts., 1973-84; realtor Greater Pitts. Bd. Realtors, 1973-91; instr. La Roche Coll., Pitts., 1974-75; cons. Salisbury Mktg. Assocs., Evans City, Pa., 1991—; mktg. mgr. TRI-V, Inc., 1994—; staff writer Butler (Pa.) Eagle, 1993-94; sales rep. Future Electronics Corp., Westborough, Mass., 1984-87. Vol. Peace Corps, Sierra Leone, West Africa, 1962-64, Butler County Literacy, 1991-94, Neighborhood Legal Svc., Butler, 1993, Butler County Hospice, 1990-94; telephone bank coord. Campaign for State Rep., Butler County, 1992; active pub. rels. LWV, Butler County, 1990-91, AAUW, Pa., 1990-91. Recipient Andron Epiphanon award Greater Pitts. Bd. Realtors, 1975-77, Pa. Gov.'s award Pennserve, 1991; named Top 25 Realtors North Suburban Multi-List, 1974. Mem. Internat. Toastmasters (v.p. pub. rels. 1993-94), West. Pa. Press Club, Returned Peace Corps Vols. Episcopalian. Avocations: genealogy research, history, needlework, poetry. Office: 121 Needle Point Rd Evans City PA 16033-7625

SALISBURY, MARGARET MARY, educator; b. LaGrange, Tex., Oct. 23, 1932; d. Charles Frederick and Hedwig Mary (Fajkus) Meyer; m. Harrison Bryan Salisbury, Jan. 8, 1955; children: Elaine, Kathleen, David, Stephen, Mark, Margaret II. BA, Our Lady of the Lake, San Antonio, 1954; MA, U. Tex., San Antonio, 1975. Lic. elem., secondary edn., English and sch. adminstrn. High sch. tchr. St. Joseph's Sch. for Girls, El Paso, Tex., 1954-55; tchr. 1st grade St. Patricks Cathedral Sch., El Paso, 1955; tchr. 2d grade S.W. Ind. Sch. Dist., San Antonio, 1971-74, tchr. 6th grade, 1974-75, supr. testing, reading, 1975-81, 82-86, jr. high sch. prin., 1981-82, dir. alternative sch., 1986-87, tchr. 3d grade, 1987-96; pres. Cooperating Tchr./Student Tchr. U. at Tex., San Antonio, 1986-87. Mem. AAUW (chairperson pub. policy com. 1995—), Internat. Reading Assn., Tex. State Reading Assn., Alamo Reading Coun., Reading Improvement, Pres. Club. Republican. Roman Catholic. Avocations: gardening, reading, travel, photography. Home: 126 Meadow Trail Dr San Antonio TX 78227-1639 Office: Big Country Elem 11914 Dragon Ln San Antonio TX 78252-2612

SALISBURY, NANCY, convent director. Head Convent of Sacred Heart, N.Y.C. Office: Convent of the Sacred Heart 1 E 93rd St New York NY 10128-0613

SALISBURY, ROBERT HOLT, political science educator; b. Elmhurst, Ill., Apr. 29, 1930; s. Robert Holt and Beulah (Hammer) S.; m. Rose Marie Cipriani, June 19, 1953; children: Susan Marie, Robert Holt, Matthew Gary. A.B., Washington and Lee U., 1951; M.A., U. Ill., 1952, Ph.D., 1955. Mem. faculty Washington U., St. Louis, 1955—; prof. Washington U., 1965—, chmn. dept. polit. sci., 1966-73, 86-92, dir. Center for Study Pub. Affairs, 1974-77, Sidney W. Souers prof. govt., 1982—; vis. prof. State U. N.Y. at Buffalo, 1965, So. Ill. U., Edwardsville, 1975; affiliated scholar Am. Bar Found., 1981—; cons. U.S. Conf. Mayors, 1965, Hartford (Conn.) C. of C., 1964, NSF, 1973. Author: Interest Groups Politics in America, 1970, Governing America, 1973, Citizen Participation in the Public Schools, 1980, Interests and Institutions, 1992, The Hollow Core, 1993; contbr. articles to profl. jours. Mem. St. Louis County Charter Commn., 1967, Gov.'s Commn. on Local Govt., 1968-69. Guggenheim fellow, 1990; Rockefeller Ctr. scholar, 1990. Mem. Mo. Polit. Sci. Assn. (pres. 1964-65), Am. Polit. Sci. Assn. (exec. council 1969-71, v.p. 1980-81), Midwest Polit. Sci. Assn. (pres. 1977-78), Pi Sigma Alpha. Democrat. Methodist. Home: 337 Westgate Ave Saint Louis MO 63130-4710 Office: Washington U Dept Polit Sci Saint Louis MO 63130

SALIT, GARY, lawyer. Sr. v.p., gen. counsel, sec. Bell Howell Co., Skokie, Ill. Office: Bell & Howell Company 5215 Old Orchard Rd Skokie IL 60077-1076*

SALITERMAN, RICHARD ARLEN, lawyer, educator; b. Mpls., Aug. 3, 1946; s. Leonard Slitz and Dorothy (Sloan) S.; m. Laura Shrager, June 15, 1975; 1 child, Robert Warren. BA summa cum laude, U. Minn., 1968; JD, Columbia U., 1971; LLM, NYU, 1974. Bar: Minn. 1972, D.C. 1974. Mem. legal staff U.S. Senate Subcom. on Antitrust and Monopoly, 1971-72; acting dir., dep. dir. Compliance and Enforcement div. Fed. Energy Office, N.Y.C., 1974; mil. atty. Presdl. Clemency Bd., White House, Washington, 1975; sr. ptnr. Saliterman & Siefferman, Mpls., 1975—; adj. prof. law Hamline U., 1976-81. Chmn. Hennepin County Bar Jour., 1985-87; trustee, sec. Hopkins Edn. Found. Author: Advising Minnesota Business Corporations, 4 vols., 1995. Bd. dirs. Mpls. Urban League, 1987-94; pres. Am. Jewish Com., Mpls. St. Paul chpt., 1988-90; v.p., trustee W. Harry Davis Found, 1989—; treas., bd. dirs. Pavek Mus. Broadcasting, 1992—. With USN, 1972-75. Mem. ABA, Minn. State Bar Assn., Hennepin County Bar Assn. (governing council 1987-89), Oakridge Country Club (Hopkins, Minn.), Mpls. Club, Wayzata Yacht Club.

SALJINSKA-MARKOVIC, OLIVERA T., oncology researcher; b. Skopje, Macedonia, Oct. 27, 1938; d. Trajko and Radmila Saljinska; m. Nenad Markovic, July 9, 1961; children: Svetomir, Mila. MD, Med. Faculty, Skopje, 1962; PhD, Med. Faculty, Belgrade, 1977; Specialist Med. Biochemistry, U. Kiril and Metodij, Skopje, 1969. Asst. prof. Med. Faculty, Skopje, 1964-79, assoc. prof., 1979-84; dir. clin. lab. U. Children's Hosp., Skopje, 1974-84; sr. rsch. assoc. Pa. State U., State College, 1984-85; sr. fellow U. Pa., Phila., 1985-88; prof. U. Belgrade, 1988-93; adj. prof. Med. Coll. of Pa., 1993-95; vis. scientist MIAMDH, NIH, Bethesda, 1976-77; vis. scientist ATCC, Rockville, Md., 1995-96; dir. BioSciCon, Md., 1996—; primarius Univ. Children's Hosp., Skopje, 1983-86; head lab. for rsch. and devel., Clin. Ctr., Belgrade, 1990-93; mem. exam. com., State of Macedonia, 1980-90. Author: Quantitative Cytoch of Enzymes, 1986; contbr. articles to profl. jours., publs. Postdoctoral intern rsch. fellowship Fogarty Internat. Ctr., NIH, Bethesda, 1971-73; recipient several rsch. grants NIH, Pharm. Co., 1984-95. Mem. Histochem. Soc., Am. Assn. Clin. Chem., N.Y. Acad. Scis., Am. Assn. Cell Biology. Achievements include inosinic acid dehydrogenase assay patent; patent pending tissue injury protective agt.; new concept for the reversal of multidrug resistance of cancer cells to antineoplast; novel methods for cancer diagnosis and treatment. Home: Apt 602 259 Congressional Ln Rockville MD 20852 Office: BioSciCon Inc Rockville MD 20852

SALKIN, PATRICIA E., law educator; b. Suffern, N.Y., Aug. 18, 1964; d. Stuart David and Sheila Diane (Gustin) S.; m. Howard F. Gross, Aug. 17, 1986. BA, SUNY, Albany, 1985; JD, Albany Law Sch., 1988. Bar: N.J. 1988, N.Y. 1989. Asst. counsel N.Y. State Office of Rural Affairs, Albany, 1988-90; asst. dir. Govt. Law Ctr., Albany, 1990-91, acting dir., 1992, dir., 1992—; mem. adj. faculty Renssalaer Poly. Inst., Troy, N.Y., 1990-93, Albany Law Sch., 1992—, SUNY, Albany, 1993—. Editor: Everything You Wanted to Know About Zoning, 2d edit. 1993; contbr. articles to profl. jours, chpts. to books. Active Albany Civic Forum, 1992—, comty. devel. coun. Ctr. for Econ. Growth, 1992-95; bd. dirs. Albany-Tula Alliance, 1992-94, Homeless and Travelers Aid Soc. of Capital Dist., 1992—, N.Y. Planning Fedn., 1995—. Recipient Pres.'s award for Outstanding Alumni Svc., SUNY, Albany, 1990, Tribute to Women award YMCA, Albany, 1994. Mem. ABA (co-chair state adminstrv. law com. 1993—, chair govt. ops. com. 1992—, editor state and local news, state and local govt. law sect.), Am. Planning Assn. (reporter Land Use Law & Zoning Digest 1992—), N.Y. State Bar Assn. (mem. exec. com. mcpl. law sect. 1993—), Capital Dist. Women's Bar Assn., SUNY Albany Alumni Assn. (bd. dirs., v.p. 1994). Office: Albany Law Sch Govt Law Ctr 80 New Scotland Ave Albany NY 12208-3434

SALKIND, ALVIN J., electrochemical engineer, educator; b. N.Y.C., June 12, 1927; s. Samuel M. and Florence (Zins) S.; m. Marion Ruth Koenig, Nov. 7, 1965; children: Susanne, James. B.Ch.E., Poly. Inst. N.Y., 1949, M.Ch.E., 1952, D.Ch.E., 1958; postgrad. and mgmt. courses, Pa. State U., 1965, Harvard U., 1976. Registered profl. engr., N.Y., N.J. Chem. engr. U.S. Electric Mfg. Co., N.Y.C., 1952-54; sr. scientist Sonotone Corp., Elmsford, N.Y., 1954-56; research assoc. Poly. Inst. N.Y., 1956-58, adj. prof. chem. engring., 1960-70; with ESB-Ray OVAC Co., Yardley, Pa., 1958-79; dir. tech. ESB-Ray OVAC Co., 1971-72, v.p. tech., 1972-79; pres. ESB Tech. Co., 1978-79; prof., chief bioengring. div., dept. surgery UMDNJ-Robert Wood Johnson Med. Sch., Piscataway, N.J., 1970—, vis. prof. chem. engring., 1979-85; prof. biomed. engring. and chem. and biochem. engring Rutgers U., Piscataway, 1985—, dir. Bur. Engring. Rsch., assoc. dean Coll. Engring., 1989—; vis. prof. and exec. officer Case Ctr. for Electrochem. Sci., 1981-82; bd. dirs., cons. various cos., rsch. instns. and govt. orgns. Author: (with S.U. Falk) Alkaline Storage Batteries, 1969, (with Herbert T. Silverman and Irving F. Miller) Electrochemical Bioscience and Bioengineering, 1973; editor: (with E. Yeager) Techniques of Electrochemistry, 1971, vol. 2, 1973, vol. 3, 1978, History of Battery Technology, 1987, (with F. McLarnon and V. Bogatzky) Rechargeable Zinc Electrodes, 1996; contbr. articles to profl. jours. Served with USNR, 1945-46. Recipient Alumnus citation Poly. Inst. N.Y., 1975, award Internat. Tech. Exch. Soc., 1992; Case Centennial scholar Case-Western Res. U., 1980. Fellow Acad. Medicine of N.J., Am. Coll. Cardiology, AAAS; mem. Electrochem. Soc. (past chmn. new tech. com., past chmn. battery div.), Assn. Advancement Med. Instrumentation, Indsl. Research Inst. (emeritus 1979), Internat. Soc. Electrochemistry, N.Y. Acad. Scis., Sigma Xi, Phi Lambda Upsilon. Home: 51 Adams Dr Princeton NJ 08540-5401 Office: Rutgers U Bur Engring Rsch Busch Campus PO Box 909 Piscataway NJ 08855

SALKIND, MICHAEL JAY, technology administrator; b. N.Y.C, Oct. 1, 1938; s. Milton and Esther (Jaffe) S.; m. Miriam E. Schwartz, Aug. 16, 1959 (div. 1979); children: Michael Jay, Elizabeth Jane, Jonathan Hillson, Joshua Isaac; m. Carol T. Gill, Dec. 23, 1990. B in Metall. Engring., Rensselaer Polytech. Inst., 1959, PhD, 1962. Chief advanced metallurgy United Techs. Rsch. Labs., East Hartford, 1964-68; chief structures and materials Sikorsky Aircraft div. United Techs. Corp., 1968-75; dir. product devel. Avco Systems div., 1975-76; mgr. structures NASA, 1976-80; dir. aerospace scis. Air Force Office of Sci. Rsch., 1980-89; pres. Ohio Aerospace Inst., 1990—; adj. faculty metallurgy Trinity Coll., Hartford; adj. faculty aerospace U. Md., 1982-85; adj. faculty materials Johns Hopkins U., 1985-89. Cons. editor Internat. Jour. Fibre Sci. and Tech.; editor Applications Composite Materials, 1973; contbr. to profl. jours. and textbooks. Evaluator Accreditation Bd. Engring. and Tech., 1989—; mem. Daniel Guggenheim Medal Bd. Awards, 1984-90; mem. Spirit of St. Louis Medal Bd., 1984-89. Capt. AUS, 1962-64. Fellow AAAS, AIAA (assoc.); mem. ASME (Disting. lectr. 1989-93), ASTM (chmn. com. D-30 on high modulous fibers and their composites 1968-74), Am. Helicopter Soc., Am. Inst. Mining Metall. and Petroleum Engrs., ASM Internat., Brit. Inst. Metals, Rsch. Soc. Am., Plansee Soc., Cosmos Club, Union Club, Leadership Cleve., Sigma Xi, Alpha Sigma Mu. Office: Ohio Aerospace Inst 22800 Cedar Point Rd Cleveland OH 44142-1012

SALLAH, MAJEED (JIM SALLAH), real estate developer; b. Boston, Aug. 5, 1920; s. Herbert K. and Rose (Karem) S. Student, Gloucester (Mass.) pub. schs.; m. Aline C. Powers, Apr. 10, 1970; children: Christopher M., Melissa Rose. Pres., dir. Glo-Bit Fish Co., Gloucester, 1947-48, Live-Pak of Ohio, Inc., 1947-51, Cape Ann Glass Co., Inc., Gloucester, 1950-72, Cape Ann Realty Corp., Gloucester, 1961—, Marias Restaurant, Gloucester, 1960—; pres., treas., dir. Gloucester Hot-Top Constrn. Co., Gloucester, 1967-75; pres., bd. dirs. SGF Corp., Gloucester, 1983-85, SALFAD, Inc. Rossford, Ohio; pres., treas. Points East, Inc.; trustee Christopher Investment Trust; bd. dirs. Lutsal, Inc.; bd. dirs., ptnr. Barsal, Inc., Toledo, Ohio, Hamsal, Inc., Toledo. Pres. Lebanese-Am. Bus. Men's Club; treas. Lebanese-Maronite Soc. With U.S. Army, 1942-45. Decorated Bronze Star. Mem. Gloucester Assocs., Cape Ann Investment Corp., Am. Legion, Amvets, Gloucester Fraternity Assn., Order Ky. Cols. (hon.), Lions, Elks, Moose. Roman Catholic. Home and Office: PO Box 78 Gloucester MA 01931-0078

SALLAN, STEPHEN E., pediatrician; b. Detroit. MD, Wayne State U., 1967. Cert. pediat. Intern Boston Foundling Hosp., 1967-68; resident in pediatrics Children's Hosp., Phila., 1968-69, Hosp. Sick Children, London, 1969-70; fellow in pediatric oncology Children's Hosp. Med. Ctr./Harvard U., Boston, 1973-75; mem. med. staff Dana Farber Cancer Inst., Boston, chief physician, 1995—; prof. pediatrics Harvard Med. Sch., Boston. Mem. AMA, AACR, ASCO, ASH, SPR. Office: Dana Farber Cancer Inst 44 Binney St Boston MA 02115*

SALLER, RICHARD PAUL, classics educator; b. Ft. Bragg, N.C., Oct. 18, 1952; s. George E. and Arthea E. (North) S.; m. Carol Joann Fisher, Jan. 12, 1974; children: John E., Benjamin T. BA in Greek and History, U. Ill., 1974; PHD in Classics, U. Cambridge, Eng., 1978. Asst. prof. Swarthmore (Pa.) Coll., 1979-84; assoc. prof. U. Chgo., 1984-89, prof., 1990—; dean of social scis., 1994—. Author: Personal Patronage, 1982, Patriarchy, Property and Death in the Roman Family, 1994; co-editor: Economy and Society in Ancient Greece, 1981; co-author: Roman Empire, 1987; editor Classical Philology, 1991-93. Rsch. fellow Jesus Coll., U. Cambridge, 1978-79; Ctr. for Adv. Study fellow, Stanford U., 1986-87; Trinity Coll., U. Cambridge fellow commoner, 1991. Mem. Am. Philol. Assn., Am. Hist. Assn. Office: U Chgo Dept History 1126 E 59th St Chicago IL 60637-1580

SALLEY, JOHN JONES, university administrator, oral pathologist; b. Richmond, Va., Oct. 29, 1926; s. Thomas Raysor and Kathryn (Josey) S.; m. Jean Gordon Cunningham, Dec. 21, 1950; children: Katharine Gordon, John Jones, Martha Cunningham. DDS, Med. Coll. Va., 1951; PhD, U. Rochester, 1954; DSc, Boston U., 1975. Research fellow U. Rochester, 1951-54; from instr. to prof., chmn. dept. oral pathology Med. Coll. Va., 1954-63, prof. emeritus, 1991—; prof. pathology, dean Sch. Dentistry U. Md., 1963-74, dean emeritus Sch. Dentistry, 1977—, ret., 1991; v.p. research and grad. affairs Va. Commonwealth U., Richmond, 1974-85; acting pres. Va. Ctr. for Innovative Tech., 1985, v.p., 1985-87; cons. div. research grants NIH, 1962-66; cons. U.S. Naval Dental Sch., Bethesda, Md., 1966-75; spl. cons. Nat. Inst. Dental Research, NIH, 1957-64; cons. USPHS Hosp., Balt., 1963-74, U.S. Naval Hosp., Portsmouth, Va., VA Hosp., Balt., 1964-74; dental health div. USPHS; mem. Md. Adv. Council Comprehensive Health Planning, 1968-74, Nat. Health Council, 1970-71; pres. Am. Assn. Dental Schs., 1971-72, Conf. So. Grad. Schs., 1983-84; sr. program cons. Robert Wood Johnson Found., 1978-84; mem. career devel. rev. com. VA, 1974-78; mem. com. health care resources in VA, NRC, 1974-77; cons. WHO, 1969-75; mem. Va. Gov.'s Task Force Sci. and Tech., 1982-83, sci. advisor to Gov. of Va., 1984-86; mem. research com. Va. State Council Higher Edn., 1974-84; chmn. task force Council Grad. Schs. in U.S., 1979-82. Contbr. articles in field; editorial rev. bd.: Jour. Dental Edn, 1974-78. Bd. dirs. Md. divsn. Am. Cancer Soc., 1963-70, Am. Fund Dental Health, Nat. Found. Dentistry for the Handicapped, 1986, pres., 1992-94; mem. adv. bd. Va. Inst. for Devel. Disabilities, 1987-91; bd. trustees Middlesex County Pub. Libr., 1994—, pres., 1995—. With USAAF, 1944-46. Recipient Outstanding Civilian Service medal Dept. Army, 1961, Disting. Citizenship award State Md., 1974. Fellow AAAS, Am. Coll. Dentists; mem. ADA, Nat. Conf. Univ. Research Adminstrs., Am. Acad. Oral Pathology, Internat. Assn. Dental Research (Novice award 1953), Internat. Med. Informatics Assn. (chmn. working group 1989-92), Sigma Xi, Sigma Zeta, Omicron Kappa Upsilon. Episcopalian (vestryman). Home and Office: PO Box 838 Urbanna VA 23175-0838

SALLUS, MARC LEONARD, lawyer; b. Washington, Sept. 14, 1954; s. Gerald M. and Bette R. (Rosenthal) S. BA, Claremont Men's Coll., 1976; JD, U. Calif., Hastings, 1979. Bar: Calif. 1979, U.S. Dist. Ct. (no., cen., so. and ea. dists.) Calif. 1980, U.S. Ct. Appeals (9th cir.) 1980. Assoc. Long & Levit, Los Angeles, 1979-80, Overton, Lyman & Prince, Los Angeles, 1980-87, Brobeck, Phleger & Harrison, Los Angeles, 1987-88, Weinstock, Marion, Reisman, Shore & Neumann, L.A., 1989—. Chmn. adv. bd. Nat. Resource Ctr. for Child Advocacy and Protection, Washington, 1985-86, 88-89; bd. dirs. Pub. Counsel. Mem. ABA (chmn. com. for child advocacy and protection young lawyers sect. 1985-86, 88-89, vice chmn. com. awards of achievement 1987-88, parliamentarian of the assembly 1987-91, ho. dels.

1990-91), Los Angeles County Bar Assn. (bd. trustees 1986-88, exec. com. 1986-88, asst. v.p. 1986-88, litigation sect. exec. com. 1987-89, co-chmn. minority employment com. 1986-87, chmn. ABA rels. com. 1990-92, 93—), Los Angeles County Barristers (pres. 1987-88, pres.-elect 1986-87, v.p. 1985-86, exec. com., 1984-88, chmn. child abuse com. 1983-85), Thurston Soc., Calif. CEB (probate and estate planning adv. com. 1985—), Order of the Coif. Democrat. Jewish.

SALMAN, ROBERT RONALD, lawyer; b. N.Y., Dec. 26, 1939; s. Samuel L. and Lillian Gertrude (Sincoff) S.; m. Reva Carol Rappaport, June 16, 1963; children: Elyse D. Spiewak, Suzanne A. BA magna cum laude, Columbia Coll., 1961, LLB cum laude, 1964. Bar: N.Y. 1965, U.S. Supreme Ct. 1974, U.S. Ct. Appeals (2nd cir.) 1967, U.S. Ct. Appeals (3rd cir.) 1993, U.S. Ct. Appeals (11th cir.) 1985, U.S. Ct. Appeals (9th cir.) 1979, U.S. Dist. Ct. so. dist., ea. dist.) N.Y. 1969. Assoc. Proskauer, Rose, Goetz & Mendelsohn, N.Y.C., 1964-67; asst. corp. counsel Law Dept. N.Y., N.Y.C., 1967-69; assoc. Phillips, Nizer, N.Y.C., 1969-73; ptnr. Phillips, Nizer, Benjamin, Krim & Ballon, N.Y.C., 1973-87, Reavis & McGrath, N.Y.C., 1987-88, Carter, Ledyard & Milburn, N.Y.C., 1988-94, Phillips & Salman, N.Y.C., 1994—; adj. prof. Seton Hall Law Sch., Newark, N.J., 1995—. Contbr. articles to profl. jours. Pres., founder The Assn. for A Better N.J. Inc., 1991—; pres. Marlboro Jewish Ctr., 1982-84. Recipient NEGEV Builder award Israel Bonds, 1980, Award of Honor UJA Fedn., 1981. Mem. N.Y. State Bar Assn., ABA. Avocations: charitable and communal work, baseball, reading, writing. Office: Phillips & Salman 111 Broadway New York NY 10006

SALMANS, CHARLES GARDINER, banker; b. Washington, Apr. 23, 1945; s. Marion K. and Agnes A. (Gardiner) S.; m. Robin Elizabeth Wakeman, June 8, 1986; children: Jonathan, Peter, Charles II. BS, Northwestern U., 1967; MBA in Fin., Columbia U., 1970. Account supr. Burson-Marsteller, N.Y.C., 1970-74; v.p. Bankers Trust Co., N.Y.C., 1974-84; sr. v.p., divsn. head Chem. Bank, N.Y.C., 1984-96; global bank mng. dir. Chase Manhattan Bank (merger with Chem. Bank 1996), N.Y.C., 1996—; mem. editl. adv. bd. Grad. Sch. of Bus., Columbia U., N.Y.C., 1984—; chmn. bus. adv. com. Guggenheim Mus., N.Y.C., 1994—. Home: 6 Red Rose Cir Darien CT 06820-4928 Office: Chase Manhattan Bank 270 Park Ave New York NY 10017-2014

SALMELA, DAVID DANIEL, architect; b. Wadena, Minn., Mar. 28, 1945; s. Laurie Fredrich and Lempi Christin (Matti) S.; m. Gladys Elaine Hanka, June 23, 1967; children: Cory, Chad, Tia, Kai, Brit. Grad. high sch., Sebeka, Minn. Registered profl. architect, Minn. Draftsman McKenzie Hague & Gilles, Mpls., 1965-66, A.G. McKee, Hibbing, Minn., 1966, ABI Contracting, Virginia, Minn., 1966-69, Archtl. Resources, Hibbing, 1969-70; designer, arch. Damberg Scott Peck & Booker, Virginia, 1970-89; arch. Mulfinger Susanka, Duluth, Minn., 1989-90; prin. Salmela Fospick Ltd., Duluth, 1990-94, Salmela, Arch., Duluth, 1994—. Recipient Minn. Masonry Inst. award, 1987, citation Am. Wood Coun., 1994. Mem. AIA (Honor award Minn. br. 1985, 87, 90, 92, 93, 94, 95, Honor award Western Rek Cedar Coun./AIA 1994). Office: Architect 852 Grandview Ave Duluth MN 55812

SALMOIRAGHI, GIAN CARLO, physiologist, educator; b. Gorla Minore, Italy, Sept. 19, 1924; came to U.S., 1952, naturalized, 1958; s. Giuseppe Carlo and Dina (Rinetti) S.; m. Eva Tchoukourlieva, Dec. 5, 1970; 1 child, George Charles. MD, U. Rome, 1948; PhD, McGill U., 1959; DSc (hon.), Hahnemann U., 1995. Sr. med. officer Internat. Refugee Orgn., Naples, Italy, 1949-52; research fellow Cleve. Clinic Found., 1952-55; lectr. dept. physiology McGill U., Montreal, Que., Can., 1956-58; from neurophysiologist to dir., div. spl. mental health research NIMH, Washington, 1959-73; assoc. commr. research N.Y. State Dept. Mental Hygiene, Albany, 1973-77; assoc. dir. for research Nat. Inst. Alcohol Abuse, HHS, Bethesda, Md., 1977-84; prof. neurology and physiology Hahnemann U., Phila., 1984-85, vice provost for research affairs, 1984-85, chmn. dept. physiology, asst. v.p sci. affairs, 1986-94; clin. prof. psychiatry George Washington U., 1966-73. Contbr. articles to profl. jours. Recipient Superior Service award HEW, 1970. Fellow Am. Coll. Neuropsychopharmacology; mem. AAAS, Am. Physiol. Soc., Am. Soc. Pharmacology and Exptl. Therapeutics, Internat. Brain Research Orgn., Internat. Soc. Psychoneuroendocrinology, Am. Psychiat. Assn., Soc. Neurosci., Royal Soc. Medicine, Soc. Biol. Psychiat., Assn. Research Neurol. and Mental Disease, Research Soc. Alcoholism, Assn. Chmn. Dept. Physiology, Sci. Research Soc., Sigma Xi. Club: Cosmos (Washington). Home: 8216 Hamilton Spring Ct Bethesda MD 20817-2714

SALMON, EDWARD LLOYD, JR., bishop; b. Jan. 30, 1934; s. Edward Lloyd Sr. and Helen Bernice (Burley) S.; m. Louise Hack, 1972; children: Catherine, Edward III. BA, U. of the South, 1956; BD, Va. Theol. Seminary, 1960. Ordained to deaconate Episc. Ch., 1960, to priesthood, 1961. Vicar St. Andrew's Ch., Rogers, Ark.; rector St. Andrew's Ch., Rogers, 1963-68; vicar St. James Ch., Eureka Springs, Ark., St. Thomas Ch., Springdale, Grace Ch., Siloam Springs; assoc. St. Paul's Ch., Fayetteville, 1968, rector, 1968-78; rector Ch. St. Michael and St. George, St. Louis, 1978-90; elected bishop Diocese S.C., 1990—; chmn. bd. dirs. Speak, Inc., The Anglican Digest; trustee Univ. of South, Nashotah House Seminary, Voorhees Coll., Denmark, S.C.;pres. Kanuga Confs., Inc.; chmn. Anglican Inst. Office: PO Box 20127 Charleston SC 29413-0127

SALMON, JOHN HEARSEY MCMILLAN, historian, educator; b. Thames, New Zealand, Dec. 2, 1925; came to U.S., 1969; s. John Hearsey and Elizabeth (McMillan) S. M.A., U. New Zealand, 1951; M.Litt., Cambridge (Eng.) U., 1957; Litt.D., Victoria U., 1970. Prof. history U. New S. Wales, Sydney, Australia, 1960-65; prof. history, dean humanities U. Waikato, New Zealand, 1965-69; Marjorie Walter Goodhart prof. history Bryn Mawr Coll., 1969-91, prof. emeritus, 1991—. Author: The French Religious Wars in English Political Thought, 1959, A History of Goldmining in New Zealand, 1963, Cardinal de Retz, 1969, Society in Crisis - France in The 16th Century, 1975, Renaissance and Revolt: Essays in the Intellectual and Social History of Early Modern France, 1987; editor: The French Wars of Religion, 1967; co-editor: Francogallia by François Hotman, 1972; contbr. to hist. jours. Fellow Royal Hist. Soc. Home: 1853 County Line Rd Villanova PA 19085-1729 Office: Bryn Mawr Coll Bryn Mawr PA 19010

SALMON, JOSEPH THADDEUS, lawyer; b. Auburn, Ala., Nov. 13, 1927; s. William Davis and Helen (Bowman) S.; m. Mabel Marie Groves, July 7, 1951; children: Joseph Thaddeus Jr., Bruce Groves. B.S., Auburn U., 1949; J.D., U. Ala., 1951. Bar: Ala. 1951. Practice in Montgomery, 1953-93; sec., gen. counsel Alfa Mut. Ins. Co., Alfa Mut. Fire Ins. Co., Alfa Mut. Gen. Ins. Co., Alfa Corp., Alfa Ins. Corp., Alfa Gen. Ins. Corp., Alfa Life Ins. Co.; ret., 1993. Served with USNR, 1946-47; to 1st lt. USAF, 1951-53. Mem. Internat. Assn. Def. Counsel, Ala. Def. Lawyers Assn., Phi Alpha Delta, Kappa Sigma. Episcopalian. Home: 2731 Lansdowne Dr Montgomery AL 36111-1741

SALMON, KATHLEEN A., insurance company executive; b. 1945. With Commonwealth of Penn., Harrisburg, 1967-79, Penn. Blue Shield, Camp Hill, Penn., 1979-83; sr. v.p.-adminstrn. Capital Blue Cross, Harrisburg, Penn., 1983—. Office: Capital Blue Cross 2500 Elmerton Ave Harrisburg PA 17110-9763*

SALMON, MATT, congressman; b. Salt Lake City, Jan. 21, 1958; s. Robert James and Gloria (Aagard) S.; m. Nancy Huish, June, 1979; children: Lara, Jacob, Katie, Matthew. BA in English Lit., Ariz. State U., 1981; MA in Pub. Adminstrn., Brigham Young U., 1986. Mgr. pub. affairs U.S. West, Phoenix, 1988—; mem. Ariz. Senate, Mesa, 1990-94, 104th Congress, Washington, 1995—; congressman, Ariz. U.S. House of Reps., Washington, D.C., 1995—. Bd. dirs. Mesa United Way, 1990—, Ariz. Sci. Mus., 1992—. Recipient Outstanding Svc. award Ariz. Citizens with Disabilities, 1991, Excellence in Govt. award Tempe Ctr. for Handicapped, 1992; named Outstanding Young Phoenician, Phelps Dodge/Phoenix Jaycees, 1990, Outstanding Legislator, Mesa United Way, 1991. Republican. Mormon. Avocations: tennis, racquetball, cycling. Office: 104th Congress Cannon 115 House Office Bldg Washington DC 20515

SALMON, MERLYN LEIGH, laboratory executive; b. Macksville, Kans., June 24, 1924; s. Kenneth Elbert and Inez Melba (Prose) S.; student U. Kans., 1943-44; BS, U. Denver, 1951, MS, 1952; m. Flora Charlotte Sievers, Mar. 20, 1948; children: Charla Lee, Merlyn Leigh. Rsch. engr. Denver Rsch. Inst., U. Denver, 1951-56; owner-operator Fluo-X-Spec Lab., Denver, 1956-92; ret. 1992; cons. in field. With AUS, 1943-45, 45-47. Mem. Am. Chem. Soc., Soc. for Applied Spectroscopy (Outstanding Svc. award 1970), Am. Soc. Metals, Sigma Xi, Tau Beta Pi, Phi Lambda Upsilon. Omicron Delta Kappa. Democrat. Contbr. articles to profl. jours. Address: 718 Sherman St Denver CO 80203

SALMON, RAPHAEL JACK, urban studies and public policy educator; b. Jerusalem, Jan. 29, 1931; came to U.S., 1949; s. Israel and Malka (deToledo) S.; divorced; children: Ron, Daniel, Tamar. BSc, Utah State Coll., 1953; MSPH, U. N.C., 1955; PhD in Health Edn., U. Md., 1970. prof. of Health Adminstrn. Ben-Gurion U., Ber-Sheba, Israel, 1972—. Civil engr. Metro. Engrng. Co., Salt Lake City, 1952-54; pub. health engr., economist Dept. Agrl., Israel, 1954-56, U.S. Dept. Health Edn. Welfare, Washington, 1958-60; exec. dir. Seaboard Z.Y. Commn., Washington, 1959-62; head dept. rsch., health and cmty. devel. No. Mich. U., Marquette, 1962-64; sr. rsch. analyst, economist Rsch. Triangle Inst., Durham, N.C., 1964-66; sr. economist, engr. Battelle Meml. Inst., Columbus, Ohio, 1966-68; dir. health and rehab. svcs., policy analysis and planning Health Edn. and Welfare, Washington, 1968-72; prof. urban studies and pub. policy Rutgers State U. of N.J., Moorestown, 1970—. Contbr. over 80 articles to profl. jours. Fellow APHA (life), AAAS (life); mem. NEA, AAUP, IEEE (sr. mem.), Ops. Rsch. Soc. Am. (sr. mem.), Internat. Health Econ. and Mgmt. Inst., N.Y. Acad. Scis., Am. Econ. Assn., Am. Chem. Soc., Am. Water Works Assn., Nat. Cmty. Devel. Assn., Adult Edn. Assn. Office: Rutgers State U Moorestown NJ 08057

SALMON, SYDNEY ELIAS, medical educator, director; b. S.I., N.Y., May 8, 1936; m. Joan; children: Howard, Julia, Laura, Stewart, Russell. BA cum laude, U. Ariz., 1958; MD, Washington U., St. Louis, 1962. Intern, then resident in medicine Strong Meml. Hosp., Rochester, N.Y., 1962-64; rsch. fellow in immunology dept. pediats. Harvard U. Med. Sch., Boston, 1965-66; rsch. fellow dept. medicine Medicine and Cancer Rsch. Inst. U. Calif., San Francisco, 1966-68, asst. prof. medicine dept. medicine, 1968-72; assoc. prof. medicine U. Ariz., Tucson, 1972-74, head sect. hematology and oncology, 1972-81, prof. medicine, 1974-89, founding dir. Ariz. Cancer Ctr., 1976—, regents prof. medicine, 1989—; NIH spl. fellow Cancer Rsch. Inst., U. Calif., San Francisco, 1966-68, rsch. assoc., 1968-72; mem. nat. cancer adv. bd. Nat. Cancer Inst., 1990—; founding sci. Selectide Corp., 1990; mem. sci. adv. bds. Amplimed Corp., SUGEN Corp.; bd. dirs. Synergen Devel. Corp., Repligen Devel. Corp. Editor: Cloning of Human Tumor Cells, Human Tumor Cloning, Adjuvant Therapies of Cancer, 1982, Clinics of Haematology, 1982; mem. adv. bd. Cancer Treatment Reports, 1979-82; mem. editl. bd. Stell Cells, Jour. Clin. Oncology; patentee in field; contbr. articles to profl. jours. Surgeon USPHS, 1964-66. Recipient Lectureship award Gold Headed Cane Soc., 1979, Alumni Achievement award U. Ariz., 1986. Mem. AAAS, Am. Soc. Hematology, Am. Soc. Clin. Investigation, Am. Soc. Clin. Oncology (pres. 1984-85), Am. Cancer Soc. (bd. dirs. Ariz. divsn.), Leukemia Soc. Am., Am. Assn. Cancer Rsch., Assn. Am. Cancer Insts. (pres. 1988-89). Office: U Ariz Cancer Ctr 1515 N Campbell Ave Tucson AZ 85724-0001

SALMON, TIMOTHY JAMES, professional baseball player; b. Long Beach, Calif., Aug. 24, 1968. Outfielder Calif. Angels, Anaheim, 1992—. Named Minor League Player of Yr. The Sporting News, 1992, Am. League Rookie of Yr., 1993, Pacific Coast League MVP, 1992, Am. League Rookie of Yr. Baseball Writer's Assn. of Am., 1993. Office: Calif Angels 2000 Gene Autry Way Anaheim CA 92806*

SALMON, VINCENT, acoustical consultant; b. Kingston, Jamaica, Jan. 21, 1912; came to U.S., 1914; s. Albert James and Ethlin (Baruch) S.; m. Madeline L. Giuffra, June 11, 1937 (dec. 1977); children—Margaret Elizabeth, Jean Louise. B.A., Temple U., 1934, M.A., 1936; Ph.D., MIT, 1938. Registered profl. engr., Calif. Physicist research and devel. Jensen Mfg. Co., Chgo., 1939-49; mgr. sonics sect. Stanford Research Inst., Menlo Park, Calif., 1949-65; staff scientist SRI Internat., Menlo Park, Calif., 1965-94; acoustical cons., Chgo., 1946-49, Menlo Park, 1949-71, 76—; dir. Acoustical Svcs., v.p., sec. Indsl. Helath, Inc., 1971-76; cons. prof. dept. aeronautics and astronautics Stanford U., Calif., 1977-95. Contbr. articles to profl. jours.; inventor new family of horns, 1942, 46. Pres. Palo Alto Sr. Housing Project, Calif., 1966; v.p. Stebbins Found. for Community Facilities, San Francisco, 1966; pres. Planned Parenthood Assn. of Santa Clara County, 1967, Sr. Coordinating Council of Palo Alto, 1971. Recipient Disting. Alumnus award Temple U., Phila., 1964. Fellow Acoustical Soc. Am. (pres. 1970-71, Biennial award 1946, Silver Medal in engrng. acoustics 84), Audio Engring. Soc. (life charter, western v.p. 1958-59); mem. Chgo. Audio and Acoustical Group (founder, pres. 1948), Inst. Noise Control Engrng. (pres. 1974-75), Nat. Council of Acoustical Cons. (pres. 1969-71). Democrat. Unitarian. Club: Stanford Faculty. Avocations: chamber music; photography; automobile technology. Home: 765 Hobart St Menlo Park CA 94025-5705

SALMON, WILLIAM COOPER, mechanical engineer, engineering academy executive; b. N.Y.C., Sept. 3, 1935; s. Chenery and Mary (Cooper) S.; m. Josephine Stone, Sept. 16, 1967; children—William Cooper, Mary Bradford, Pauline Alexandra. S.B. in Mech. Engring., MIT, 1957, S.M. in Mech. Engring., 1958, Mech. Engr., 1959, S.M. in Mgmt. Sci., 1969. Registered profl. engr., Mass. Research and teaching asst. MIT, Cambridge, 1957-59; sr. engr. Microtech, Cambridge, 1959-60; 1st lt. U.S. Army Ord. C., Aberdeen, Md., 1960; asst. sci. advisor U.S. Dept. State, Washington, 1961-74, sr. advisor for sci. and tech., 1978-86; counselor for sci. and tech. Am. embassy, Paris, 1974-78; exec. officer Nat. Acad. Engring., Washington, 1986—. Recipient Superior Honor award Dept. State, 1984, Meritorious Svc. award Pres. U.S., 1984, Kenneth A. Roe award, 1966; Sloan fellow MIT. Mem. ASME, Nat. Soc. Prof. Engrs., Am. Soc. Engring. Edn., Cosmos Club, Masons. Episcopalian. Office: Nat Acad Engring 2101 Constitution Ave NW Washington DC 20418-0007

SALMONSON, MARTY LEE, stockbroker, consulting engineer; b. Wellsville, N.Y., Sept. 23, 1946; s. John William and Alice May (Olson) S.; Gail White, Sept. 17, 1971; children: René, Marci. AS in Engring. Sci., SUNY, Alfred, 1970; postgrad., SUNY, Buffalo, 1971; BS in Sci. and Bus. Mgmt., Empire State Coll., 1979. Engr. Dresser-Rand, Olean, N.Y., 1974-90, Petro-Marine, Gretna, La., 1990-91; stockbroker Franklin Lord, Scottsdale, Ariz., 1992, Charles Schwab, Phoenix, Ariz., 1993—; cons. engr., Phoenix, 1994—. With U.S. Army, 1967-69, Vietnam. Mem. NSPE, ASME, VFW, Moose. Episcopalian. Achievements include development of state of the art programs for centrifugal compressors. Home: 20620 N 18th Ave Phoenix AZ 85027

SALO, HARRY A., health care executive; b. Rahway, N.J., Jan. 27, 1944; s. E. Arthur and Nina (Hill) S.; m. Karen Waugh, Sept. 7, 1964 (div. 1972); 1 child, Jannine; m. Carol Ann Vath, Mar. 17, 1973; children: Jessica, Adam. BA, Cornell U., 1967; MA, Barry U., 1974; postgrad., Columbia U., 1974, NYU, 1974-75. Tchr. Miami (Fla.) Country Day Sch., 1967-69, Fairfield (Conn.) Country Day Sch., 1968-74; MA Barry U., 1969; dir. admissions Fairfield (Conn.) Country Day Sch., 1972-74; adminstr. Med. Pers. Pool, Cin., 1975-77; v.p. Salo Inc., Cin., 1977-79; v.p., founder T.S.O. Mgmt. Corp., Media, Pa., 1979-84, pres., 1984-90, chmn., 1990—; chmn. bd. dirs. Ind. Franchise Assn., San Francisco; mem. Owners Adv. Coun., Ft. Lauderdale, Fla., 1981-82, chmn., 1993—. Bd. dirs. Women Against Rape, Delaware County, Pa., 1985-88; mem. leadership group, exec. dir.'s adv. coun. Amnesty Internat., N.Y.C., 1989—; fundraiser Berkshire Sch., Sheffield, Mass., 1990; vol. Oxfam Am., N.Y.C., 1991—. Recipient L.E. Dettman Founders award Pers. Pool Am., 1981, Raymond Herrighes Mgmt. award, 1986. Office: TSO Mgmt Corp 113 N Olive St Media PA 19063-2809

SALOMAN, MARK ANDREW, lawyer; b. North Brunswick, N.J., Sept. 12, 1967; s. Josef Goldner and Susan (Lind) S.; m. Laurie Jill Greenwald, Mar. 14, 1993. BA in Am. Studies summa cum laude, Brandeis U., 1989; JD, U. Pa., 1992. Bar: N.J. 1992, U.S. Dist. Ct. N.J. 1992, N.Y. 1993, Pa. 1994, U.S. Ct. Appeals (3d cir.) 1995. Jud. law clk. Superior Ct. N.J., New Brunswick, 1992-93; assoc. Gebhardt & Kiefer, Clinton, N.J., 1993-96, Norris, McLaughlin & Marcus, Somerville, N.J., 1996—. Mem. Hunterdon County Bar Assn. Republican. Jewish. Avocations: alpine skiing, cross training. Home: 178 Locust Ln Basking Ridge NJ 07920 Office: Norris McLaughlin & Marcus PO Box 1018 721 Rte 202-206 Somerville NJ 08876-1018

SALOMON, DARRELL JOSEPH, lawyer; b. San Francisco, Feb. 16, 1939; s. Joseph and Rosalie Rita (Pool) S.; m. Christine Mariscal, Apr. 25, 1992; 1 child, Camilla Lind. Student Georgetown U., 1957-59; BS, U. San Francisco, 1964, JD, 1966. Bar: Calif. 1970, U.S. Dist. Ct. (ctrl. and no. dists.) Calif. 1970, U.S. Supreme Ct. 1971. Assoc., Offices of Joseph L. Alioto, San Francisco, 1970, 73., 1972; dep. city atty. City of San Francisco, 1972; assoc. Salomon & Costello, 1981; ptnr. Hill, Farrer & Burrill, L.A., 1984-87, Arter & Hadden, L.A., 1987-94; assoc. Keck, Mahin & Cate, San Francisco, 1994-96; chmn. Commerce Law Group A Profl. Assn., 1996—; lectr. law Santa Clara U. Mem. Human Rights Commn. City and County of San Francisco, 1975, mem., past pres. Civil Svc. Commn., San Francisco, 1976-84; trustee San Francisco War Meml. and Performing Arts Ctr., 1984-88; bd. dirs. L.A. Symphony Master Chorale, 1985-87, Marin Symphony Assn., 1995—. D'alton-Power scholar Georgetown U., 1957; recipient Disting. Svc. citation United Negro Coll. Fund, 1975. Mem. ABA, Calif. Trial Lawyers Assn. (bd. govs. 1977), Soc. Calif. Pioneers, L.A. Bar Assn., Chit Chat Club, San Francisco Lawyers Club. Office: Commerce Law Group 744 Montgomery St 4th Fl San Francisco CA 94111-2104

SALOMON, FRANK LOEWEN, anthropology educator; b. N.Y.C., Apr. 13, 1946; s. George and Mathilde (Loewen) S.; children: Malka, Abraham. BA, Columbia U., 1968; MA, Cornell U., 1974, PhD, 1978. Vis. asst. prof. U. Ill., Urbana, 1978-82; asst. prof. U. Wis., Madison, 1982-84, assoc. prof., 1984-91, prof. anthropology, 1991—. Author: Native Lords of Quito, 1986, Spanish version, 1981, The Huarochiri Manuscript, 1991; mem. edit. bd. Ethnohistory, 1992-94; contbg. editor Handbook of Latin American Studies, 1980-88. Fellow Am. Anthrop. Assn., Soc. for Ethnohistory. Jewish. Avocation: poetry. Office: Univ Wisconsin Dept Anthro 5240 Social Scis Madison WI 53706

SALOMON, JANET LYNN NOWICKI See LYNN, JANET

SALOMON, MIKAEL, cinematographer, director; b. Copenhagen, Denmark, Feb. 24, 1945. Cinematographer, Zelly and Me, 1988, Torch Song Trilogy, 1988, The Abyss, 1989 (Oscar nomination), Always, 1989, Stealing Heaven, 1989, Arachnophobia, 1990, Backdraft, 1991, Far and Away, 1992; TV, The Man Who Broke 1,000 Chaines, 1987 (ACE award); dir.: (films) A Far Off Place, 1993, (television) Space Rangers, 1993.. Office: Am Soc Cinematographers N Orange Dr Hollywood CA 90028 also: care Spyros Skouras Sanford Skouras Gross & Assocs 1015 Gayley Ave Fl 3 Los Angeles CA 90024-3424

SALOMON, ROGER BLAINE, English language educator; b. Providence, Feb. 26, 1928; s. Henry and Lucia Angell (Capewell) S.; m. Elizabeth Helen Lowenstein, June 14, 1950; children—Pamela, Wendy. B.A., Harvard, 1950; M.A., U. Calif. at Berkeley, 1951, Ph.D., 1957. Instr. Mills Coll., Oakland, Calif., 1955-57; instr., then asst. prof. Yale U., New Haven, 1957-66; mem. faculty Case Western Res. U., Cleve., 1966—, prof. English, 1969—, Oviatt prof. English, 1990, chmn. dept., 1974-80, now part-time prof. English, 1994—; Mem. adv. screening com. Am. lit. Sr. Fulbright-Hayes Program, 1973-76, chmn., 1975; mem. grants-in-aid selection com. Am. Council Learned Socs., 1976-78. Author: Twain and the Image of History, 1961, Desperate Storytelling: Post-Romantic Elaborations of the Mock-Heroic Mode, 1987. Served to 1st lt. USAF, 1952-53. Morse fellow, 1960-61; Guggenheim fellow, 1972-73. Mem. AAUP, MLA. Home: 2830 Coventry Rd Cleveland OH 44120-2231 Office: Case Western Reserve U Dept English Cleveland OH 44106

SALONEN, HEIKKI OLAVI, retired corporate executive; b. Joroinen, Finland, May 12, 1933; s. Viljo Ilmari and Vieno (Valimaa) S.; m. Kirsti-Liisa Koskinen, June 20, 1958; children: Marju, Jyri. BS in Econs., Helsinki (Finland) U., 1958, MS in Econs., 1962. Pres. Finnish Export Inst., Helsinki, 1962-67; exec. v.p. Saastamoinen-Yhtyma oy Teollisuus, Kuopio, Finland, 1968, pres., 1969-72; pres., chief exec. officer Amer Group, Ltd., Helsinki, 1972-86, chmn., chief exec. officer, 1986-91; chmn. bd. Am. Cultural Found., 1978-85, Wilson Sporting Goods Co., USA, Amer Holding Co., USA, numerous others; mem. supervisory bd. Pohjola Group, 1983—, MTV Oy, 1975—, Kansallis-Osake-Pankki, 1986—; mem. adv. bd. Med. Rsch. Found., 1978—; alt. mem. adv. bd. Finnish Export Inst., 1976—; bd. dirs. Found. for Econ. Edn., Mgmt. Study Group. Mem. adv. bd. Helsinki Sch. Econs. and Bus. Adminstrn., 1979—, Scout Found., 1980—, Mannerheim League for Child Welfare, 1979—, Voluntary Def. Promotion, 1979—; vice chmn. bd. Helsinki Rsch. Inst. for Bus. Econs., 1976-78, chmn. bd., 1978-85, bd. dirs., 1985—; bd. trustees World Wildlife Fund of Finland, 1980—; v.p. delegation Valamo Found., 1988—; bd. dirs. Finnish Employers Gen. Group, 1982—, Confederation of Finnish Industries, 1984—; mem. del. Europe Inst., 1988—. Mem. Confederation Finnish Industries (vice mem. bd. 1984—), Employer's Assn. Food Industries (bd. dirs. 1985—), Finnish Heart Assn. (bd. dirs. 1983—). Lutheran. Avocations: literature, fishing. Office: Amer Group Ltd, Makelankatu 91, 00610 Helsinki Finland

SALONER, GARTH, management educator; b. Johannesburg, South Africa, Jan. 18, 1955; came to U.S., 1978; s. Max and Rachel (Aronowitz) S.; m. Marlene Shoolman, Dec. 26, 1978; children: Amber, Romy, Kim. BCom, U. Witwatersrand, S. Africa, 1976; MBA, U. Witwatersrand, 1977; MS in Statistics, Stanford U., 1981, MA in Econs., PhD, 1982. Asst. lectr. U. Witwatersrand, 1977-78; asst. prof. econs. MIT, Cambridge, 1982-86, assoc. prof. econs. and mgmt., 1986-89, prof., 1990; vis. assoc. prof. bus. adminstrn. Harvard Bus. Sch., Boston, 1989-90; vis. asst. prof. Stanford (Calif.) U., 1986-87, prof. strategic mgmt. and econs. Grad. Sch. Bus., 1990—, Robert A Magowan prof., 1993—, dir. rsch. and curriculum devel., 1993—; assoc. dean for acad. affairs, 1994—; rsch. assoc. Nat. Bur. Econ. Rsch., 1991—; bd. dirs. Quick Response Svcs. Inc., 1993—. Assoc. editor Rand Jour. Econs., 1986-88, co-editor, 1988-95; assoc. editor Internat. Jour. Indsl. Orgn., 1988-95, Econs. of Innovation and New Tech., 1988-95, Strategic Mgmt. Jour., 1991-94; contbr. articles to profl. jours. Nat. fellow, Hoover Inst., 1986-87, Sloan fellow, 1987-89; grantee, NSF, 1982, 85, 88. Mem. Am. Econ. Assn., Acad. Mgmt. Jewish. Avocations: bicycling, photography. Home: 4151 Amaranta Ave Palo Alto CA 94306-3903 Office: GSB Stanford U Stanford CA 94305

SALONGA, LEA, actress, singer; b. Manila, Feb. 22, 1971; d. Feliciano Genuino and Maria Ligaya (Imutan) S. Attended, Ateneo De Manila U., 1988-89. Actress, singer The King and I, Manila, 1978, Annie, Manila, 1980, The Rose Tattoo, Manila, 1980, The Bad Seed, Manila, 1981, The Goodbye Girl, Manila, 1982, Paper Moon, Manila, 1983, The Fantasticks, Manila, 1988, Miss Saigon, London, 1989-90 (Outstanding Performance by Actress in Musical Olivier award 1990), Broadway, 1991-92 (Best Actress in Musical Tony award 1991, Best Actress in Musical Drama Desk award 1991, Best Actress in Musical Outer Critics Circle award 1991, Outstanding Debut Theatre World award 1991), Les Miserables, Broadway, 1993, My Fair Lady, Manila, 1994, Into the Woods, Singapore, 1994, also The Sound of Music, Manila, Fiddler on the Roof, Manila, Cat on a Hot Tin Roof; Philippine films include Bakit Labis Kitang Mahal?, Dear Diary, Pik Pak Boom, Captain Barbell, Ninja Kids, Like Father, Like Son, Tropang Bulilit; Philippine TV: (host) Kulit Bulilit, Love Lea, Naku, Ha!, Sunday Special, Iba Ito!, That's Entertainment!, This is It!, (co-host) Patok Na Patok!; opening act for Stevie Wonder, Menudo; concerts: The Filipinos of Miss Saigon, A Miss Called Lea, Lea Salonga in Concert, L.A., San Francisco; recs. include Small Voice, 1981 (gold record), Lea, Happy Children's Club, Christmas Album, We are the World, (debut album) Lea Salonga, 1993, Miss Saigon original London cast rec. (gold record), The King and I, Aladdin, 1992 (singing voice Princess Jasmine, motion picture soundtrack), The Little Tramp; TV films include: Redwood Curtain, 1995. Recipient AWIT award outstanding svc. Philippings Recording Industry, 1993, ASEAN Industry award performing arts, 1992, Ten Outstanding Young Men award outstanding debut, 1991, AWIT award outstanding performer, 1990, Presdl. Award of Merit Pres. Aquino, 1990, Laurence Olivier award best actress musical, 1990, Cecil award best recording by a child, 1984, Tining award one of 10 outstanding singers, 1983, 94, 92, ALIW award best child performer, 1980, 81, 82; named Outstanding Manilan by Govt. City of Manila, 1990. Mem. AFTRA, Actor's Equity Assn. Roman Catholic. Avocations: music, reading, collecting raised-trunk elephants, collecting swatches, working on computers. Office: c/o Jeff Hunter 1325 Ave of the Americas New York NY 10019

SALONY, JOHN, III, banker; b. N.Y.C., July 12, 1947; s. John and Anne (Sokol) S.; m. Betty Charlene McDonald, Aug. 17, 1973; children: John IV, Jason R. BA, Jersey State Coll., 1971; cert. in Adminstrn., U. Md., 1993. Budget analyst Maher Terminals, N.Y.C., 1969-71; sales officer Provident Bank, Jersey City, N.J., 1971-73, Md. nat. Bank, Balt., 1973-77; v.p. Fidelity Fed. Savs., Balt., 1977-78; prin. Bus. Consulting Group, Eldersburg, Md., 1978-83; sr. v.p. Ops., Sales, Adminstrn. Reisterstown (Md.) Fed. Bank, 1983—; pres. Time Fin. Svcs., Inc., Reistertown, 1983—; pres. Reisterstown/Ownings Mills, 1989-90;advisor U.S. Small Bus. Adminstrn., Balt., 1977—. active pub. speaker, contbr. articles to profl. jours. Chmn. bd. Carroll C.C., Westminster, Md., 1982-88; mem. jud. nominating commn. State Md., Annapolis, 1988—; treas. Cystic Fibrosis Fedn., Md., 1977; pres. Houses, Inc., Md., 1994; baseball commr. Reisterstown Recreation, 1991; co-founder Champion Nat. Handicapped Baseball League; founding pres. Carroll C.C. Found., 1994-96; founder Small Bus. Found. USA, 1995, Appalachian Found. USA, 1995. Company comdr. Md. SG, 1988-93. Recipient Balt. is Best award, 1979; Senate citation Md. Senate, 1990; Assembly citation Md. House, 1990; Gov.'s citationMd., 1990. Mem. KC. Democrat. Roman Catholic. Avocations: Bonsai, fly fishing, sailing, book collecting.

SALOOM, JOSEPH A., III, diplomat; b. Urbana, Ill., Apr. 8, 1948; s. Joseph A. and Barbara (Bombard) S.; m. Anne Elizabeth Mayer, Jan. 22, 1972; children: Elizabeth, Shahin, Ilyas. BA in Econs., Georgetown U., 1970; MS, MIT, 1973. Joined Fgn. Svc.; comml. officer U.S. Consulate Gen., Dusseldorf, Germany, 1974-76; econ. officer Am. Embassy, Rabat, Morocco, 1976-78; fin. economist Am. Embassy, Jidda, Saudi Arabia, 1978-80; econ. counselor Am. Embassy, Kinshasa, Zaire, 1983-87; dep. chief mission Am. Embassy, Niamey, Niger, 1987-90; U.S. amb. to Guinea Am. Embassy, Conakry, Guinea, 1993—; transp. economist Dept. State, Washington, 1980-83, dir. office monetary affairs, 1990-91, dep. asst. sec., 1991-93. Office: Am Embassy, BP 603, Conakry Guinea

SALOOM, KALISTE JOSEPH, JR., lawyer, retired judge; b. Lafayette, La., May 15, 1918; s. Kaliste and Asma Ann (Boustany) S.; m. Yvonne Adelle Nassar, Oct. 19, 1958; children: Kaliste III, Douglas James, Leanne Isabelle, Gregory John. BA with high distinction, U. Southwestern La., 1939; JD, Tulane U., 1942. Bar: La. 1942. Atty. City of Lafayette (La.), 1948-52; judge City and Juvenile Ct., Lafayette, 1952-93, ret., 1993; judge pro tempore La. Ct. Appeal 3d Cir., 1992; of counsel Saloom & Saloom, Lafayette, La., 1993—; tech. adviser Jud. Adminstrn. of Traffic Cts.; mem. jud. coun. La. Supreme Ct., 1960-64; bd. dirs. Nat. Ctr. for State Cts., Williamsburg, Va., 1978-84, adv. coun., 1984—, mem. assocs. com., 1986— (Disting. Svc. award Trial Judge on State Level 1988); mem. Nat. Hwy. Traffic Safety Adminstrn. Adv. Com., U.S. Dept. Transp., 1977-80, Nat. Com. on Uniform Traffic Laws, 1986; expert panel Drunk Driving Protection Act U.S. Congress, 1989-91. With U.S. Army, 1942-45. mem. editorial bd. Tulane Law Rev., 1941; contbr. articles to profl. jours. Recipient Civic Cup, City of Lafayette, 1965, Pub. Svc. award U.S. Dept. Transp., 1980, Disting. Jurist award Miss. State U. Pre-Law Soc., 1987, Disting. Svc. award Nat. Ctr. for State Cts., 1988, Disting. La. Jurist award La. State Bar Found., 1992. Mem. ABA (Benjamin Flaschner award 1981, vice chair JAD com. on traffic ct. program 1989-95), Am. Judges Assn. (William H. Burnett award 1982), Nat. Coun. Juvenile Ct. Judges, La. City Judges Assn. (past pres.), La. Juvenile Ct. Judges Assn. (past pres.), Am. Judicature Soc. (panel drafting La. children's code 1989-91), Order of Coif, Equestrian Order of Holy Sepulchre (knight), Oakbourne Country Club, KC. Democrat. Roman Catholic. Home: 502 Marguerite Blvd Lafayette LA 70503-3138 Office: 211 W Main St Lafayette LA 70501-6843

SALOP, STEVEN CHARLES, economics educator; b. Reading, Pa., Dec. 23, 1946; s. Saul Harold and Byrd (Kalish) S.; m. Judith Rebecca Gelman, Mar. 14, 1982; children: Aviva, Ezra, Joshua. BA summa cum laude, U. Pa., 1968; M Phil, Yale U., 1971, PhD, 1972. Economist Fed. Res. Bd., Washington, 1972-77, CAB, Washington, 1977-78; economist FTC, Washington, 1978-79, asst. dir., 1979-80, assoc. dir., 1980-81; prof. econs. and law Georgetown U. Law Ctr., Washington, 1981—; spl. cons., bd. dirs. Charles River Assocs., Boston, 1987—. Editor: Strategic Competition, 1982. Bd. dirs. Lowell Sch., 1989-95. Mem. Am. Econ. Assn., Phi Beta Kappa. Jewish. Office: Georgetown U Law Ctr 600 New Jersey Ave NW Washington DC 20002

SALPETER, ALAN N., lawyer; b. Phila., Oct. 7, 1947. BA with honors, Am. U., 1969; JD, Villanova U., 1972. Bar: Ill. 1972. Ptnr. Mayer, Brown & Platt, Chgo.; lectr. and author in field. Mng. editor Law Rev., Villanova U. Mem. ABA, Chgo. Bar Assn., Chgo. Coun. Lawyers. Office: Mayer Brown & Platt 190 S La Salle St Chicago IL 60603-3410

SALPETER, EDWIN ERNEST, physical sciences educator; b. Vienna, Austria, Dec. 3, 1924; came to U.S., 1949, naturalized, 1953; s. Jakob L. and Frieder (Horn) S.; m. Miriam Mark, June 11, 1950; children—Judy Gail, Shelley Ruth. M.S., Sydney U., 1946; Ph.D., Birmingham (Eng.) U., 1948; DSc, U. Chgo., 1969, Case-Western Reserve U., 1970, U. Sydney, 1994. Research fellow Birmingham U., 1948-49; faculty Cornell U., Ithaca, N.Y., 1949—; now J.G. White prof. phys. scis. Cornell U.; mem. U.S. Nat. Sci. Bd., 1979-85. Author: Quantum Mechanics, 1957, 77; mem. editorial bd. Astrophys. Jour., 1966-69; assoc. editor Rev. Modern Physics, 1971—; contbr. articles to profl. jours. Mem. AURA bd., 1970-72. Recipient Gold medal Royal Astron. Soc., 1973, J.R. Oppenheimer Meml. prize U. Miami, 1974, C. Bruce medal Astron. Soc. Pacific, 1987, A. Devaucouleurs medal, 1992. Mem. NAS, Am. Astron. Soc. (v.p. 1971-73), Am. Philos. Soc., Am. Acad. Arts and Scis., The Royal Soc. (fgn.), Australian Acad. Sci., Deutsche Akademie Leopoldina. Home: 116 Westbourne Ln Ithaca NY 14850-2414 Office: Cornell U Newman Lab Ithaca NY 14853

SALSBERG, ARTHUR PHILIP, publishing company executive; b. Bklyn., Aug. 28, 1929; s. Solomon William and Rae (Miller) S.; m. Rhoda Gelb, Sept. 11, 1960; children: Charles Martin, Solomon William. BBA, CCNY, 1951. Mng. editor Ojibway Press, N.Y.C., 1957-64; advt. and promotion mgr. RCA Corp., Harrison, N.J., 1965-67; editor N.Am. Pub. Co., Phila., 1967-70; v.p., gen. mgr. Lawyers World, Inc., Phila., 1970-72; editorial dir. Ziff-Davis Pub. Co., N.Y.C., 1973-83; editor, assoc. pub. CQ Communications, Inc., Hicksville, N.Y., 1984—; mag. and newspaper pub. cons.; electronics instr.; local campaign publicist, speech writer for town mayor, town coun., libr. bd., sch. bd. Author: Complete Book of Video Games, 1977, Collier's Ency. Yearbook, 1977, 78, 79, 80, 81, 82, First Book of Modern Electronics Fun Projects, 1986, Second Book of Modern Electronics Fun Projects, 1986; editor: Audio Mag, 1967-70, Lawyers World, 1970-72, Popular Electronics, 1973-83, Comm. Handbook, 1973-83, Stereo Directory, 1973-83, Tape Recorder Directory, 1973-83, Citizens Band Handbook, 1976-83, Invitation to Electronics, 1972-83, Modern Electronics, 1984-91, Computer Craft, 1992-93, MicroComputer Jour., 1994-96; assoc. pub.: Amateur Radio Equipment Buyers Guide, 1988, 89, 90, 91, 92, Amateur Radio Antenna Buyers Guide, 1989, 90, 91-92. Publicity chmn. Nassau coun. Boy Scouts Am., 1975; mem. adv. com. Bramson OR Tech. Inst., 1975. With AUS, 1951-53, Korea. Recipient Indsl. Mktg. Mag. award, 1959. Home: 7844A Lexington Club Blvd Delray Beach FL 33446-3401

SALSBURY, STEPHEN MATTHEW, historian, educator; b. Oakland, Calif., Oct. 12, 1931; s. Ralph Thomas and Roma Enola (Connor) S. AB, Occidental Coll., 1953; AM, Harvard U., 1957, PhD, 1961; PhD (hon.), St. Petersburg State U., 1995. Research assoc. Harvard Sch. Bus. Adminstrn., 1961-62; asst. prof. history U. Del., Newark, 1963-68; assoc. prof. U. Del., 1968-70, prof., 1970-77, chmn. history dept., 1974-77; prof. econ. history U. Sydney, Australia, 1977—; also head dept., dean Faculty Econs. U. Sydney, 1980-88, prof., dean Faculty Econs., 1989-90—; vis. asst. prof. Johns Hopkins, 1967-68; vis. scholar La Trobe U., Melbourne, Australia, 1974; Hunter Baillie fellow St. Andrew's Coll., Sydney; vis. prof. history U. Calif., Berkeley, 1987-88; hon. curator Harvard U. Libr., 1989—. Author: The State, The Investor and the Railroad, 1967, (with Alfred D. Chandler, Jr.) Pierre S. duPont and the Making of the Modern Corporation, 1971, Essays on the History of the American West, 1975, No Way to Run a Railroad: The Untold Story of the Penn Central Crisis, 1982, (with Kay Sweeney) The Bull, The Bear and the Kangaroo: The History of the Sydney Stock Exchange, 1988, (with Kay Sweeney) Sydney Stockbrokers: Biographies of the Members of the Sydney Stock Exchange 1871-1987, 1992; assoc. editor: American National Biography, 1992—. Mem. adv. bd. Eleutherian-Mills-Hagley Found., 1975-78, Bus. History Rev., 1981-85. Served with USAF, 1955-57, 62-63. Mem. Am. Hist. Assn., Econ. History Assn. (chmn. com. research 1976-77), Econ. History Assn. Australia and N.Z., Orgn. Am. Historians, Agrl. History Soc., Hist. Soc. Del., AAUP, Assn. Evolutionary Econs., Phi Beta Kappa, Alpha Tau Omega. Congregationalist. Club: Am. Nat. (Sydney), Rotary (Sydney), Union Club (Sydney). Home: 28 Wahroonga Ave, Wahroonga NSW, Australia Office: U Sydney, Dean Faculty Econs, Sydney NSW 2006, Australia

SALTARELLI, EUGENE A., retired engineering and construction company executive, consultant; b. Buffalo, Feb. 22, 1923; s. Joseph A. and Mary (Cataldo) S.; m. Jean Marie Cray, Nov. 25, 1950; children—Margaret, Joseph, Thomas, Paul, Mary, John. B.Mech. Engring., U. Detroit, 1949; M.S. in Mech. Engring., Northwestern U., 1951. Registered profl. engr. Calif., Md., Mich., N.Y., Pa. Tex., Ariz., Ga. Design engr. Bell Aircraft Corp., Buffalo, 1950-56; sr. mgr. Bettis Atomic Power Lab., Pitts., 1956-67; group v.p. NUS Corp., Gaithersburg, Md., 1967-80; sr. v.p., chief engr. power Brown & Root, U.S.A., Inc., Houston, 1980-88; now pvt. cons.; expert witness in power plant engring. and constrn. litigation. Contbr. articles to profl. jours.; patentee in field. Served to 1st lt. USAAF, 1942-46. Mem. ASME (George Westinghouse Gold medal 1985), Atomic Indsl. Forum, Am. Nuclear Soc. (exec. com. power divsn. 1975). Roman Catholic. Club: Montgomery Country Club, Laytonsville, Md. Avocations: woodworking; piano and organ; golf.

SALTEN, DAVID GEORGE, county agency administrator, academic administrator; b. N.Y.C., Aug. 23, 1913; s. Max Elias and Gertrude (Brauer) S.; m. Frances Claire Brown (div. 1983); children: Phoebe, Cynthia, Melissa; m. Adrienne O'Brien, 1989. ScB, Washington Sq. Coll., N.Y.C., 1933; AM, Columbia U., 1939; PhD, NYU, 1944; LLD (hon.), Lynn U., 1976; L.H.D., Nova U., Ft. Lauderdale, Fla., 1983; Sc.D. (hon.), N.Y. Inst. Tech., 1984. Registered psychologist, N.Y. Chemist Almay Cosmetics, 1934-35, City of New York, 1938-40; tchr., chmn. dept., high sch. prin. N.Y.C. Bd. Edn., 1940-50; assoc. prof. Hunter Coll. Grad. Program, 1947-63; supt. of schs. City of Long Beach, N.Y., 1950-62, City of New Rochelle, N.Y., 1962-65; exec. v.p. Fedn. of Jewish Philanthropies, N.Y.C., 1965-69; exec. v.p., provost N.Y. Inst. Tech., Old Westbury, 1969-90; chmn. Nassau County Indsl. Devel. Agy., Mineola, N.Y., 1985—; exec. dir. Nassau County Tax Relief Commn., 1990-93; mem. White House Conf. on Edn., 1955, White House Conf. on Youth, 1960; U.S. resource person on edn. World Mental Health Congress, Paris, 1961; mem. Bd. Edn., Hawthorne, Cedar Knolls, N.Y., 1963-65; mem. adv. council Columbia U. Sch. of Social Work, 1967-69; chmn. adv. council NYU Sch. Edn., 1963-65; chmn. adv. council to Select Com. on Higher Edn. N.Y. Legislature, 1971-73. Author: Mathematics: A Basic Course, 1957. Editor instructional software. Contbr. articles on edn. and ednl. adminstrn. to profl. publs. Vice chmn. N.Y. State Mental Health Council, Albany, 1965-72; pres. N.Y. State Citizens Council, 1957, Nat. Council on Aging, Washington, 1975-77; chmn. Nassau County Local Devel. Agy., 1982—, Nassau County Local Devel. Corp., N.Y., 1982—, pres., 1992—; chmn. Nassau County Cultural Devel. Bd., 1980—; bd. dirs. NAACP Legal Def. Fund, 1964-74; chmn. bd. trustees The Hewlett Sch., 1991—. Recipient citation U.S. Navy, 1947, Mental Health Assn., Nassau County, N.Y., 1955, Long Beach Edn. Assn., N.Y., 1962, Council of City of New Rochelle, N.Y., 1965, Council of Town of Islip, N.Y., 1982. Fellow AAAS, Am. Orthopsychiat. Assn.; mem. Princeton Club (N.Y.C.), Capitol Hill Club (Washington). Avocations: opera, ballet, international travel, photography. Office: Nassau County Indsl Devel Agy 400 County Seat Dr Mineola NY 11501-4825

SALTER, EDWIN CARROLL, physician; b. Oklahoma City, Jan. 19, 1927; s. Leslie Ernest and Maud (Carroll) S.; m. Ellen Gertrude Malone, June 30, 1962; children—Mary Susanna, David Patrick. B.A., DePauw U., 1947; M.D., Northwestern U., 1951. Intern Cook County Hosp., Chgo., 1951-53; resident in pediatrics Children's Meml. Hosp., Chgo., 1956-58, Cook County Hosp., Chgo., 1956-58; practice medicine specializing in pediatrics Lake Forest, Ill., 1958—; attending physician Lake Forest Hosp., 1958—, pres. med. staff, 1981-82; attending physician Children's Meml. Hosp., Chgo.; clin. faculty mem. dept. pediatrics Northwestern U. Med. Sch. Served to capt. M.C., U.S. Army, 1954-56. Mem. AMA, Ill. State Med. Soc., Lake County Med. Soc. (pres. 1984), Phi Beta Kappa. Republican. Methodist. Home: 19 N Maywood Rd Lake Forest IL 60045-3233 Office: 900 N Westmoreland Rd Ste 110 Lake Forest IL 60045-1688

SALTER, KEVIN THORNTON, lawyer; b. N.Y.C., Oct. 21, 1947; s. Hershel Fletcher and Elizabeth (Thornton) S.; m. Eleanor Raftery, Aug. 28, 1982. BA, Iona Coll., 1973; JD, St. John's U., 1977. Bar: N.Y. 1978, U.S. Dist. Ct. (so. and ea. dists.) N.Y., 1978. Atty. Nat. Coun. on Compensation Ins., N.Y.C., 1978-80; coun. James G. Barron, N.Y.C., 1980-81; assoc. St. Regis Paper Co./ Champion Internat., N.Y.C. and Stamford, Conn., 1981-88; sr. ptnr. Kroll & Tract, N.Y.C., 1988-94; ptnr. Peterson & Ross, N.Y.C., 1994—; bd. dirs. Alliance Assurance Co. Am. Inc., N.Y.C., Sea Ins. Co. Am. Inc., N.Y.C., Sun Ins. Office Am. Inc., N.Y.C., London Assurance Co. Am. Inc., N.Y.C., Marine Indemnity Ins. Co. Am., Merc. and Gen. Reins Co. Am., Morristown, N.J., Fortress Ins. Co. Am., N.Y.C. With U.S. Army, 1967-69. Mem. ABA, N.Y. State Bar Assn., Brit. Ins. Law Assn. Office: Peterson & Ross 805 3rd Ave Fl 6 New York NY 10022-7513

SALTER, LANORA JEANETTE, corporate financial officer; b. Omaha, Nebr., June 7, 1964; d. Phillip Ray Sr. and Charlene (Sanford) H.; m. Howard Douglas Salter, March 26, 1964; children: Ryan Douglas, Erin Jeanette, Evan Tainter. AS, Chattohoochee Valley C.C., 1988; diploma, Am. Inst. Banking, 1988, Spring Hill Coll., 1995. Office mgr. Zales, Mobile, Ala., 1983-85; customer svc. rep. Columbus (Ga.) Bank & Trust, 1985-88; adminstrv. asst. First Atlanta Bank, Augusta, Ga., 1988-90; customer svc. specialist Am. South Bank, Mobile, 1990-92; v.p. finance adminstrn. Performance Rehab. Assocs., Inc., Fairhope, Ala., 1992—; treas. bd. dirs. AIB, 1989-90. tutor Am. Literacy Coun., 1994. Republican. Episcopalian. Avocations: biking, sailing. Office: Performance Rehab Assoc Inc 8075 Spring Run Rd Fairhope AL 36532-3821

SALTER, LESTER HERBERT, lawyer; b. Waterbury, Conn., Apr. 26, 1918; s. Nathan M. and Eva G. (Levy) S.; m. Nina P. Scheftel, Sept. 15, 1951; 1 child, Ellen Lee. B.S. in Econs, U. Pa., 1940, LL.B., 1948. Bar: R.I. bar 1948. Trial atty. Office of Chief Counsel, IRS, Newark and Boston, 1949-53; individual practice law Providence, 1953-57; partner firm Salter & McGowan, Providence, 1957-70, Salter, McGowan, Arcaro & Swartz, 1970-74; pres. firm Salter, McGowan, Swartz & Holden, Inc., Providence, 1974-95; pres. Salter, McGowan & Swartz, Inc., Providence, 1995—; lectr. Northeastern U., 1955-56; chmn. U. R.I. Fed. Tax Inst., 1972-77; chmn. disciplinary bd. Supreme Ct., R.I., 1975-81; mem. R.I. Adv. Commn. Jud. Appts., 1978-82, ethics adv. panel Supreme Ct., R.I., 1987-92. Assoc. editor: R.I. Bar Jour, 1961-68. Served with F.A. AUS, 1941-46. Decorated Bronze Star. Fellow Am. Bar Found.; mem. ABA (ho. of dels. 1987), R.I. Bar Assn. (pres. 1986-87), New Eng. Bar Assn. (v.p. 1995—), Am. Judicature Soc., Am. Law Inst. Home: 75 Blackstone Blvd Providence RI 02906-5413 Office: 321 S Main St Providence RI 02903-7108

SALTER, MARY JO, poet; b. Grand Rapids, Aug. 15, 1954; d. Albert Gregory and Lormina (Paradise) S.; m. Brad Leithauser, 1980; children: Emily Salter, Hilary Garner. BA cum laude, Harvard U., 1976; MA, Cambridge U., 1978. Instr. Harvard U., 1978-79; instr. English conversation Japan, 1980-83; lectr. English Mount Holyoke Coll., S. Hadley, 1984—, apptd. Emily Dickinson lectr. in humanities, 1995—; staff editor Atlantic Monthly, 1978-80; poet-in-residence Robert Frost Place, 1981; poetry editor The New Republic, 1992-95. Author: Henry Purcell in Japan, 1985, Unfinished Painting, 1989 (Lamont prize in poetry 1988), The Moon Comes Home, 1989, Sunday Skaters: Poems, 1994 (Nat. Book Critics Circle award nomination 1994); contbr. to periodicals including New Yorker, New Republic, Kenyon Rev. Recipient Discovery prize Nation, 1983; Nat. Endowment for Arts fellow, 1983-84, Guggenheim fellow, 1993. Mem. Internat. P.E.N. Office: care Alfred A Knopf Inc 201 E 50 St New York NY 10022

SALTER, ROBERT MUNDHENK, JR., physicist, consultant; b. Morgantown, W. Va., Apr. 24, 1920; s. Robert Mundhenk and Sara Opal (Godfrey) S.; m. Darlene Jeanette Oliva, Jan. 21, 1977; children by previous marriage: Robert Mundhenk III, Wendy Lou Salter Reynolds, Gary Coddington. BME, Ohio State U., 1941; MA, UCLA, 1957, PhD, 1965. Research engr. Gen. Motors Research Labs., Detroit, 1941-42; research engr. Aerophysics Lab. N.Am. Aviation, Los Angeles, 1946-48; project dir. USAF satellite devel. Rand Corp., Santa Monica, Calif., 1948-54, phys. scientist, 1965-82; project dir. USAF WS-117L satellite devel. Lockheed Aircraft, Palo Alto, Calif., 1954-59; founder, pres. Quantatron, Inc., Pioneer Laser Co., Santa Monica, 1960-62; sci. cons. to various industries, 1962—; chief exec. officer Xerad, Inc., Santa Monica, 1973—. Patentee in field. Founding dir. U.S. chpt. Elsa Wild Animal Appeal, 1968. Lt. USN, 1942-46. Recipient Space Pioneer medal Dept. Def., 1985. Mem. Sigma Xi, Sigma Pi Sigma, Tau Beta Pi. Republican. Presbyterian. Club: Riviera Country. Achievements include design and constrn. of Giga-bit optical CD/rom; and an invention of variable-geometry, moving spike supersonic aircraft diffuser. Home and Office: 12432 Trout Ln Machipongo VA 23405 *My professional goal has been to apply and focus knowledge of new and emerging technologies in the development of large and complex systems to benefit both U.S. defense and the public sector. Examples are the early Air Force Discoverer/Corona and Midas "Spy" satellite programs forerunners to NASA and Planatran, a future ultra high speed subway system magnetically levitated and propelled in evacuated tubeways.*

SALTER, SALLY, reporter. Comml. real estate reporter The Atlanta Jour. Constn., Atlanta. Office: Atlanta Journal & Constitution 72 Marietta St NW Atlanta GA 30303-2804

SALTMAN, STUART IVAN, lawyer; b. Holyoke, Mass., Mar. 16, 1940; s. Abraham and Sidel Esther (Schultz) S.; m. Sandra Lee, Sept. 19, 1964; children: Jason, Michael, Laura. BS in Polit. Sci., U. Mass., 1961; JD, Case Western Res. U., 1964. Bar: Mass. 1965, Ohio 1965, Pa. 1975. Assoc. gen. counsel Internat. Chem. Workers, Akron, Ohio, 1965; assoc. Metzenbaum, Gaines, Krupansky, Finley & Stern, Cleve., 1965-67; staff U.S. Dept. Labor, Cleve., 1967-69; staff NLRB, Cleve., 1969-70; regional atty. EEOC, Cleve., Phila. and Washington, 1970-75; chief labor counsel Westinghouse Electric Corp., Pitts., 1975-88, chmn. labor law sect. Grigsby, Gaca & Davies, Pitts., 1988-90; asst. gen. counsel Asea Brown Boveri Power T & D Inc., Windsor, Conn., 1990—. Recipient Excellence Hon. award in labor law Case Western Res. U. 1965. Mem. ABA, Allegheny County Bar Assn. (chmn. 1986-88). Club: Masons (Holyoke). Home: 23 Ivy Ln Windsor CT 06095 Office: 2000 Day Hill Rd Windsor CT 06095

SALTOUN, ANDRE MEIR, lawyer; b. Baghdad, Iraq, Jan. 21, 1929; came to U.S., 1947; s. Meir and Synthia (Noury) S.; m. Beverly Melnik, 1947 (div. 1959); children: Myra, Cynthia, Julie; m. Francine Klein, Aug. 17, 1960; children: Diane, Josiane, Carol. BA, U. N.C., 1950; JD, U. Wis., 1960. Bar: Ill. 1960, Wis., U.S. Dist. Ct. (no. dist.) Ill. 1960, Calif. 1978, U.S. Ct. Claims 1978, U.S. Tax Ct. 1978, U.S. Ct. Appeals (6th, 7th and 10th cirs.) 1978, U.S. Supreme Ct. 1978. Ptnr. Baker & McKenzie, Chgo. and Palo Alto, 1964—. Contbr. articles to profl. jours. Mem. ABA, Ill. Bar Assn., Calif. Bar Assn., Wis. Bar Assn., Chgo. Bar Assn., Chgo. Assn. Commerce and Industry (exec. com. of bd. dirs.), Plaza Club. Office: Baker & McKenzie PO Box 60309 660 Hanson Way Palo Alto CA 94304*

SALTZ, HOWARD JOEL, newspaper editor; b. Bronx, N.Y., Apr. 11, 1960; s. Fred Raymond and Sheila Lois (Goldberg) S. BA in Liberal Arts, SUNY, Stony Brook, 1983. Reporter Greenwich Time So. Conn. Newspapers, divsn. Times Mirror, 1983-85; with Garden State Newspapers, divsn. MediaNews Group, 1985—; with N.J. Advance, Garden State Newspapers div. MediaNews Group, Dover, 1985-87, editor, 1987-88; editor Hamilton (Ohio) Jour.-News Garden State Newspapers div. MediaNews Group, 1988-89, editor Fremont (Calif.) Argus, 1989-91, editor Johnstown (Pa.) Tribune-Democrat, 1991—; mem. adv. com. dept. journalism Ohlone Coll., Fremont, Calif., 1990-91. Bd. dirs. YMCA of Fremont-Newark, Calif., 1990-91, Johnstown Area Heritage Assn., 1991-93. Mem. Greater Johnstown C. of C. (bd. dirs. 1991—), Soc. Profl. Journalists (bd. dirs. Northern Calif. chpt. 1990-91). Avocations: skiing, travel. Home: 43 Venango St Johnstown PA 15905-2249 Office: The Tribune Democrat 425 Locust St Johnstown PA 15907

SALTZ, RALPH, corporate lawyer; b. May 31, 1948; s. Peter and Eve (Bass) S.; m. Linda Bergman, Mar. 15, 1970; children: Erica, Alan. BA, Queens Coll., 1969; JD, St. John's U., 1972. Bar: N.Y. 1973, N.J. 1975. Atty. The Port Authority of N.Y. and N.J., N.Y.C., 1972-76, The Great Atlantic and Pacific Tea Co., Montvale, N.J., 1976-77; asst. real estate counsel Supermarkets Gen. Corp., Woodbridge, N.J., 1977-82, Toys 'R' Us, Inc., Rochelle Park, N.J., 1982-84; v.p., house counsel, sec. Jamesway Corp., Secaucus, N.J., 1984-94; v.p., gen. counsel Rickel Home Ctrs., Inc., South Plainfield, N.J., 1994—. Mem. ABA. Democrat. Office: Rickel Home Ctrs Inc 200 Helen St South Plainfield NJ 07080-3817

SALTZBURG, STEPHEN ALLAN, law educator, consultant; b. Phila., Sept. 10, 1945; s. Jack Leonard and Mildrid (Osgood) Adelman; m. Susan Lee Saltzburg; children: Mark Winston, Lisa Marie, Diane Elizabeth, David Lee Musseh1. AB, Dickinson Coll., 1967; JD, U. Pa., 1970. Bar: Calif. 1971, D.C. 1972, Va. 1976. Law clk. U.S. Dist. Ct. (no. dist.) Calif., San Francisco, 1970-71, U.S. Supreme Ct., 1971-72; asst. prof. law sch. U. Va., Charlottesville, 1972-74, assoc. prof., 1974-77, prof., 1977-87, Class of 1962 chairholder, 1987-90; Howrey prof. trial advocacy, litigation and profl. responsibility George Washington U. Nat. Law Ctr., Washington, 1990—; reporter Alaska Rules of Evidence, 1976-77, Alaska Civil Jury Instrns., 1979-81, Adv. Com. on Rules of Criminal Procedure, 1984-89, Va. Rules on Evidence, 1984-85, Civil Justice Act Adv. Group, U.S. Dist. Ct. D.C., 1992-93, chmn., 1994—; dep. asst. atty. gen. criminal divsn. U.S. Dept. Justice, 1988-89; mem. adv. com. on Fed. Rules of Criminal Procedure, 1989-95, on Fed. Rules of Evidence, 1992-95; mediator dispute resolution program U.S. Ct. Appeals, 1993—. Author: American Criminal Procedure, 5th edit., 1996, Criminal Law: Cases and Materials, 1994, Federal Rules of Evidence Manual, 6th edit., 1994, A Modern Approach to Evidence, 2d edit., 1982, Federal Criminal Jury Instructions, 2d edit., 1991, Evidence in America, 1987, Military Rules of Evidence Manual, 3d edit., 1991, Basic Criminal Procedure, 1994, Military Evidentiary Foundations, 1994. Mem. ABA (chmn. com. on trial advocacy criminal justice sect. 1992—), Am. Law Inst. Office: George Washington U Nat Law Ctr 720 20th St NW Washington DC 20006-4306

SALTZER, JEROME HOWARD, computer science educator; b. Nampa, Idaho, Oct. 9, 1939; s. Joseph and Helene (Scheuermann) S.; m. Marlys Anne Hughes, June 16, 1961; children—Rebecca, Sarah, Mark. B.S., MIT, 1961, M.S., 1963, Sc.D., 1966. Faculty dept. elec. engring. and computer sci. MIT, Cambridge, Mass., 1966—, now prof. emeritus and sr. lectr.; tech. dir. Project Athena, Cambridge, Mass., 1984-88; cons. Chem. Abstracts Svc., 1968-88, IBM Corp., 1970-84. Mem. Mayor's Cable Adv. Bd., Newton, Mass., 1984—. Fellow AAAS, IEEE; mem. NRC (computer sci. and telecom. bd. 1991-93), Assn. for Computing Machinery (mem. com. on computers and pub. policy 1984—), Eta Kappa Nu, Tau Beta Pi. Home: 54 Gammons Rd Newton MA 02168-1216 Office: MIT Lab Computer Sci 545 Technology Sq Cambridge MA 02139-3539

SALTZMAN, BARRY, meteorologist, educator; b. N.Y.C., Feb. 26, 1931; s. Benjamin and Bertha (Burmil) S.; m. Sheila Eisenberg, June 10, 1962; children—Matthew David, Jennifer Ann. B.S., CCNY, 1952; S.M., Mass. Inst. Tech., 1954, Ph.D., 1957; M.A. (hon.), Yale, 1968. Research staff meteorologist MIT, 1957-61; sr. research scientist Travelers Research Center, Inc., Hartford, Conn., 1961-66, research fellow, 1966-68; prof. geophysics Yale U., 1968—, chmn. dept. geology and geophysics, 1988-91. Editor: Selected Papers on the Theory of Thermal Convection, 1962, Advances in Geophysics, 1977—; asso. editor Jour. Geophys. Research, 1971-74; mem. editorial bd. Climate Dynamics, 1986—, ATMOSFERA, 1987—; co-editor Milankovitch and Climate, 1984; contbr. articles to profl. publs. Fellow AAAS, Am. Meteorol. Soc.; mem. Conn. Acad. Sci. and Engring., Am. Geophys. Union, Acad. Scis. Lisbon (hon. fgn.), European Geophys. Soc., Phi Beta Kappa, Sigma Xi. Home: 9 Forest Glen Dr Woodbridge CT

06525-1420 Office: Yale U Dept Geology and Geophysics PO Box 208109 New Haven CT 06520-8109

SALTZMAN, BENJAMIN NATHAN, retired state health administrator, physician; b. Ansonia, Conn., Apr. 24, 1914; s. Joseph N. and Frances (Levine) S.; m. Ruth Elizabeth Bohan, Dec. 19, 1941 (dec. May 1994); children: Sue Ann, John Joseph, Mark Stephen. B.A., U. Oreg., 1935, M.A., 1936, M.D., 1940; D.Sc., U. Ark., 1989. Diplomate Am. Bd. Family Practice. Intern, then resident Gorgas Hosp., Ancon, Panama, 1940-42; gen. practice medicine Saltzman Clinic, Mountain Home, Ark., Panama Canal Zone, 1946-74; prof. family and community medicine U. Ark. for Med. Scis., Little Rock, 1974-81; prof. emeritus U. Ark. for Med. Scis., 1981—; dir. Ark. Dept. Health, Little Rock, 1981-87; med. dir. Pulaski County unit Ark Dept. Health, Little Rock, 1987-91. Mem. editorial bd. Jour. Ark. Med. Soc., 1989—; contbr. articles to profl. publs. Alderman Mountain Home City Coun., 1947-55; pres. Ark. Brotherhood NCCJ, 1986-88; sr. bd. pres. Florence Crittendon Home Svcs., Ark., 1986-89; v.p. Ark. 4H Found., 1988-89, pres., 1989—. Capt. AUS, 1942-46, lt. col. USAFR, ret. 1973. Recipient Ark. Man of Yr. award Ark. Democrat, 1975, Will Ross award Am. Lung Assn., 1979; Tom T. Ross award Ark. Pub. Health Assn., 1975, Outstanding Achievement award 1975; Ark. Human Rels. award NCCJ, Ark., 1980, Disting. Leadership award Am. Rural Health Assn., 1985; named Arkansan of Yr., Ark. Gerontol. Soc., 1987. Fellow Am. Acad. Family Physicians (chmn. rural health and mental health com. 1956-71), Am. Coll. Preventive Medicine, AMA (chmn. council on rural health 1966-69, 50 yr. club); mem. Ark. Acad. Family Physicians (life mem., pres. 1955-56), Ark. Med. Soc. (life, pres. 1974-75, 50 yr. club), Gerontologic Soc. (life, Arkansan of the Yr. 1987), Mountain Home C. of C. (pres. 1955-68), Am. Lung Assn. (Ark. rep. to bd. 1964-75, pres. bd. Ark. div. 1957-63, hon. life mem. 1991), Am. Cancer Soc. (pres. bd. Ark. div. 1983, hon. life mem. 1991), Sigma Xi. Lodges: Rotary Internat. (bd. dirs. 1961-63, trustee Rotary Internat. Found. 1965-67, bd. dirs. internat. chpt., Rotary Found Citation for Meritorious Svc. 1982-83, Disting. Svc. award 1988-89), Masons (33 degree), Elks (state pres. 1956-59). Avocation: lapidary work. Home: PO Box 823 Mountain Home AR 72653-0823

SALTZMAN, CHARLES MCKINLEY, educational consultant; b. N.Y.C., Apr. 6, 1937; s. Charles Eskridge Saltzman and Gertrude (Lamont) Saltzman Rockwood; m. Cornelia Metz Biddle, Sept. 3, 1965; children: Cornelia Biddle Saltzman Tierney, Charles Eskridge. AB, Harvard Coll., 1959, MA in Teaching, 1962. Cert. prin. and supr., La. Tchr., coach, dorm head St. Albans Sch., Washington, 1962-66, 67-73; tchr., coach Athenian Sch., Danville, Calif., 1966-67; headmaster Hannah More Acad., Reisterstown, Md., 1973-74, Metairie (La.) Park Country Day Sch., 1974-81, Madeira Sch., McLean, Va., 1981-88; cons. Ind. Ednl. Svcs., Princeton, N.J., 1988-95; adj. instr. Gettysburg (Pa.) Coll., 1988—; dir. Upper Adams Sch. Dist., Biglerville, Pa., 1991-95. Capt. U.S. Army, 1959-61. Mem. Country Day Sch. Headmasters Assn. Episcopalian. Avocations: farming, gardening, tennis. Home and Office: 622 Chestnut Hill Rd Aspers PA 17304-9746

SALTZMAN, ELLEN S., lawyer; b. Bklyn., Apr. 6, 1946; d. Joseph and Hilda (Lazar) Estrin; m. Stuart Saltzman, June 25, 1966; children: Todd, Michael. BA in Sociology, L.I. U., 1967; JD, CUNY, 1993. Bar: Pa. 1993, N.J. 1994. Fin. cons. Cigna Fin. Svcs., Syosset, N.Y., 1983-84; pension cons. Pension Svcs. Corp., Port Washington, N.Y., 1984-86, Consulting Actuaries Internat., Inc., N.Y.C., 1986-89; mktg. mgr. New Eng. Life Ins. Co., N.Y.C., 1986-89; atty. Vaccaro & Prisco, Hauppauge, N.Y., 1993-95. Mem. task force Women on the Job, Port Washington, N.Y., 1989—, bd. dirs., 1994—; bd. dirs., chair pub. affairs com. L.I. region March of Dimes, 1994—; mem. N.Y. State legis. com. March of Dimes. Recipient Women of Distinction award March of Dimes, 1994, Spl. Congl. cert., 1994, Nassau County Exec. citation, 1994, Suffolk County Exec. citation, 1994; named to Town of North Hempstead's Women's Roll of Honor, 1995. Mem. ABA, Pa. Bar Assn., Nat. Women's Polit. Caucus, L.I. Ctr. for Bus. and Profl. Women (pres. 1992-94). Home: 28 Driftwood Dr Port Washington NY 11050-1717

SALTZMAN, GLENN ALAN, behavioral sciences educator; b. Findlay, Ohio, Sept. 10, 1935; s. Andrew Frank and Lois Elizabeth (Stahl) S.; m. Ruth Elinor Weaver, June 9, 1957; children—Jeff Alan, Jay Aaron, Jill Lynn. B.S., Ohio State U., 1957, M.A., 1962, Ph.D., 1966. Tchr., counselor Lakota Pub. Schs., Fremont, Ohio, 1960-62; asst. state supr. guidance Ohio Dept. Edn., Columbus, 1962-66; prof., chmn. counseling Kent (Ohio) State U., 1966-76; prof. behavioral scis. Northeastern Ohio Univs. Coll. Medicine, Rootstown, 1976—, chmn. behavioral scis., 1976-83, dir. div. basic med-scis., 1982-95. Author: Career Education (6 vols.), 1978, Midshipman Counseling, 1978, Is Anybody Listening?, 1987; contbr. articles to profl. jours. Lay leader Kent United Meth. Ch., 1974-78; bd. dirs. Am. Cancer Soc., 1974-78; v.p. Am. Heart Assn., 1981-82, pres., 1982-84. With USN, 1957-60, USNR, 1960-85, capt. USNR ret. Recipient Provost's award Northeastern Ohio U. Coll. Medicine, 1988, Olson-Blair award for adminstrv. excellence NEDUCOM, 1995; Paul Harris fellow, 1981. Mem. APA, Assn. Behavioral Scis. in Med. Edn., Am. Pers. and Guidance Assn., Am. Sch. Counselors Assn., Assn. Counselor Edn. and Supervision, Ohio Pers. and Guidance Assn., Ohio Sch. Counselors Assn., Ohio Assn. Counselr Edn. and Supervision, Rotary (pres. 1980-81, pres. Kent Rotary Found. 1985-91, A.Z. Baker Leadership award dist. 663 1981). Office: Northeastern Ohio Univs Coll Medicine PO Box 95 Rootstown OH 44272-0095

SALTZMAN, IRENE CAMERON, perfume manufacturing executive, art gallery owner; b. Cocoa, Fla., Mar. 23, 1927; d. Argyle Bruce and Marie T. (Neel) Cameron; m. Herman Saltzman, Mar. 23, 1946 (dec. May 1986); children: Martin Howard (dec.), Arlene Norma Hanly. Owner Irene Perfume and Cosmetics Lab., Jacksonville, Fla., 1972—, Irene Gallery of Art, Jacksonville, 1973—. Mem. Cummer Gallery of Art, Jacksonville, 1972—, Jacksonville Gallery of Art, 1972—; mem. Jacksonville and Beaches Conv. and Vis. Bur. Mem. Aircraft Owners and Pilots Assn., USAF Assn., Jacksonville C. of C. (mem. downtown coun.), U.S. C. of C., Ret. Judge Advocates Assn. of USAF (hon.), First Coast Women in Internat. Trade, Cosmetic, Toiletry and Fragrance Assn., Jacksonville Navy Flying Club, Ponte Vedra Club. Democrat. Episcopalian. Avocations: aviation, painting, traveling, swimming, golf. Home: 2701 Ocean Dr S Jacksonville FL 32250-5946

SALTZMAN, JOSEPH, journalist, producer, educator; b. L.A., Oct. 28, 1939; s. Morris and Ruth (Weiss) S.; m. Barbara Dale Epstein, July 1, 1962; children: Michael Stephen Ulysses, David Charles Laertes. BA, U. So. Calif., 1961; MS, Columbia U., 1962. Freelance writer, reporter, producer, 1960—; reporter Valley Times Today, Los Angeles, CA, 1962-64; editor Pacific Palisades Palisadian Post, 1964; sr. writer-producer CBS-KNXT TV, Los Angeles, 1964-74; freelance broadcast cons. Los Angeles, 1974—; sr. producer investigative unit Entertainment Tonight, 1983; supervising producer Feeling Fine Prodns., Los Angeles, 1984-92; prof. journalism U. So. Calif., Los Angeles, 1974—. Documentaries include Black on Black, 1968, The Unhappy Hunting Ground, 1971, The Junior High School, 1971, The Very Personal Death of Elizabeth Schell-Holt-Hartford, 1972, Rape, 1972, Why Me?, 1974; spl. producer: Entertainment Tonight, 1983; supervising producer med. films, video, audio, 1984-93; assoc. mass media editor, columnist USA Today, 1983—; syndicated columnist: King Features Syndicate, 1983-92; contbg. editor Emmy Mag., 1986—, Roberts Reviewing Service, 1964—; others. Recipient AP certificates of excellence and merit, 1968, 72, 73, 74, 75, Edward R. Murrow awards for distinguished achievements in broadcast journalism, 1969, 72, Alfred I. duPont-Columbia U. award in broadcast journalism, 1973-74, Silver Gavel award Am. Bar Assn., 1973, Ohio State award Am. Exhbn. Ednl. Radio-Television Programs and Inst. for Edn. by Radio-Television Telecommunications Center, 1974, Broadcast Media awards San Francisco State U., 1974, 75; Media award for excellence in communications Am. Cancer Soc., 1976; awards for teaching excellence U. So. Calif., 1977, 88, 90; Disting. Alumni award U. So. Calif., 1992; Seymour Berkson fellow, 1961; Robert E. Sherwood fellow, 1962; alt. Pulitzer traveling fellow, 1962-63. Mem. Radio-Television News Assn. (Golden Mike awards 1969, 71, 73, 75), Nat. Acad. Television Arts and Scis. (regional Emmy awards 1965, 68, 74, 75), Writers Guild Am., Greater Los Angeles Press Club (awards 1968, 74, 75), Columbia U., U. So. Calif. alumni assns., Skull and Dagger, Blue Key, Phi Beta Kappa, Sigma Delta Chi, Pi Sigma Alpha, Alpha Epsilon Rho. Home: 2116 Via Estudillo Palos Verdes Peninsula CA 90274-1931 Office: U So Calif Sch Journalism Univ Park Los Angeles CA 90007

SALTZMAN, PHILIP, television writer, producer; b. Sonora, Mexico, Sept. 19, 1928; came to U.S., 1929, naturalized, 1948; s. Louis and Vanya (Liberman) S.; m. Caroline Veiller, Jan. 24, 1960; children: Jennifer, Daniel, Anthony. B.A., UCLA, 1951, M.A., 1953. Free lance writer, 1958-68; pres. Woodruff Prodns., Inc. Writer: TV shows Alcoa Goodyear Theater, 1959, Richard Diamond, 1959, Rifleman, 1961, Perry Mason, 1964, Dr. Kildare, 1964, Fugitive, 1964, Twelve O'Clock High, 1966; producer, writer: TV shows Felony Squad, 1966-69, F.B.I, 1969-73, Barnaby Jones, 1973-77; producer, writer, creator Intertect, 1973; producer: TV movie The FBI vs. Alvin Karpis, 1974, Attack on Terror: The FBI vs. the KKK in Mississippi, 1975, Brinks: The Great Robbery, 1976; co-writer: feature film The Swiss Conspiracy, 1975; creator-writer-producer TV movie Crossfire, 1975; exec. producer: TV shows Barnaby Jones, 1978-80, Escapade, 1978, Colorado C-I, 1978, A Man Called Sloane, 1979, The Aliens Are Coming, 1979, Freebie and the Bean, 1980; producer: TV shows Bare Essence, 1982; supervising producer-writer Partners in Crime, 1984; producer-writer Crazy Like a Fox, 1985; producer, co-writer TV movie That Secret Sunday, 1986; exec. supervising producer The New Perry Mason movies, 1987-88; exec. supervising producer, writer Jake and The Fatman, 1987-88; supervising producer Columbo, 1989-90; creator-writer The Caller, 1991. Mem. dean's coun. Coll. Letters and Sci., UCLA, Friends of English, UCLA. Mem. Writers Guild Am., West, Caucus for Writers, Producers, Dirs., Acad. TV Arts and Scis., PEN Ctr. USA West.

SALTZMAN, ROBERT PAUL, insurance company executive; b. Chgo., Oct. 25, 1942; s. Al and Viola (Grossman) S.; m. Diane Maureen Schulman, Apr. 10, 1964; children: Amy, Adam, Suzanne. BA in Math., Northwestern U., 1964. Mgr. Continental Casualty Co., Chgo., 1964-69; sr. v.p. Colonial Penn Group, Phila., 1969-83; pres., CEO Sun Life Ins. of Am. and Anchor Nat. Life Ins. Co., 1985-93; exec. v.p. mktg. Kaufman & Broad (now Broad, Inc.), L.A., 1987-93; pres., CEO Jackson Nat. Life Ins. Co., Lansing, Mich., 1994—. Office: Jackson Nat Life Ins Co 5901 Executive Dr Lansing MI 48911-5333

SALTZMAN, WILLIAM, painter, sculptor, designer; b. Mpls., July 9, 1916. B.S., U. Minn. Asst. dir. U. Minn. Art Gallery, 1946-48; resident artist, also dir. Rochester (Minn.) Art Ctr., 1948-64; vis. prof. art U. Nebr., Lincoln, 1964; vis. prof. art Macalester Coll., St. Paul, 1967-68, assoc. prof. art, 1969-74, prof. art, 1974-83, emeritus, 1983—. One-man shows include St. Olaf Coll., Minn., Rochester Art Ctr., 1948-58, Ctrl. Luth. Ch., Mpls., 1983, Philbrook Art Ctr., Tulsa, Macalester Coll., 1982, Douglas-Baker Gallery, Mpls., 1995, Dorothy Berge Gallery, Stillwater, Minn., 1995, also others; group exhbns. include Calif. Palace Legion of Honor, 1945, St. Paul Art Gallery, 1946, 54, 57, Chgo. Art Inst., 1947, Carnegie Inst., 1952, numerous others; spl. invitational showing nat. conf. Stained Glass Assn. Am., 1980, Artbanque Gallery, Mpls., 1989, S.K. Gallery, Mpls., 1990; major watercolor show Premier Gallery, Mpls., 1991-92, Am. Contemporary Artist Premier Gallery, Mpls., 1992; major works include mural Mayo Clinic Bldg., Rochester, Minn., 1953, stained glass Midwest Fed. Bldg., 1968, glass mobile 1st Bank, Crystal, Minn., 1986, copper relief Nationality Cultural Ctr., Internat. Inst., St. Paul, mixed relief sculpture Bryan Mem. Hosp., Lincoln, Nebr., low relief sculpture Temple of Agron, 1995, numerous other sculptures and stained glass in various corps., chs., pvt. residence, 1994; designer sets and costumes Minn. Opera prodn. The Abduction from the Seraglio (Mozart), 1979. Recipient awards from Mpls. Inst. Art, 1936, Minn. State Fair, 1937, 40, Walker Art Ctr. 1949, 51, Guild for Religious Architecture, 1973, AIA, 1973; honor award for stained glass Interfaith Forum on Religion, Art, and Architecture, 1981, 92; Ford Found. grantee. Mem. Nat. Soc. Mural Painters. Home and Studio: 5916 Walnut Dr Edina MN 55436-1750

SALUJA, SUNDAR S., engineering educator, researcher, consultant; b. Wasu, Punjab, India, June 23, 1927; came to U.S., 1981; s. Wadaya Mal and Gur Devi (Bagga) S.; m. Kamla S. Grover Saluja, Oct. 12, 1953; children: Bhupinder, Urvashi, Dipender. AISM, Indian Sch. of Mines, Dhanbad, India, 1950; postgrad. diploma, U. Sheffield, United Kingdom, 1955; MS, U. Ill., 1961; PhD, U. Wis., 1963. Cert. mine surveyor and mine mgr., India. Mine engr., surveyor Mining Industry, 1950-53, mine mgr., 1953-57; prof. of coal mining Banaras Hindu U., Varanasi, India, 1957-66, head dept of mining engring., 1966-71, prin. coll. mining & met., 1966-68, dean faculty of engring. & tech., 1968-71, dir. inst. tech., 1971-81; prof. mining engring. U. N.D., Grand Forks, 1982—. Co-author: Handbook on Mechanical Properties of Rocks, vol. 1, 1974, translated in Japanese, 1989. Mem. state adv. com. U.S. Commn. on Civil Rights, 1993-95; founder, pres. Gt. Plains Forum, Grand Forks, N.D., 1985—, ROUSE Found. For Reclamation of Our Spiritual Environ.; advisor N.D. State Pub. Svc. Commn., 1983-84. Grad. fellowship, Colombo Plan, 1954-55, fellowship in Engring., Nuffield Found., 1959, Commonwealth U. Tchrs. Exch., Australia, 1960, TCM fellowship, U.S Ag. for Int. Devel., 1961; recipient Dr. R.P. Meml. Gold medal Inst. of Engrs., Calcutta, India, 1978. Mem. AAUP, Mining, Geol. & Met. Inst. of India (coun. mem. 1966-69), Am. Soc. Engring. Edn., Am. Soc. Mining Met. & Exploration, Indian Sci. Congress Assn. (pres. engring. 1979-80). Achievements include pioneer rsch. on roof bolting (1954-66), blasting mechanics (1961-71), mining of thick coal seams (1964-71), airlift pumping (1976-78), Nat. Reconstruction Corps. (1972), architect of engr. clinic c prototype dev. centres (1963-78), Indian Energy Policy (1979-81), World Energy Policy (1982—), leadership role in saving the $ 3.8 billion coal gasification plant in N.D. (1984-86), rsch. in environ. of human mind to improve the quality of life and its impact on soc. (1992—). Avocations: photography, travelling and study of different cultures. Office: U ND Geology/Geological Engr Dept Box 8358 University Station Grand Forks ND 58202

SALVADORI, MARIO, mathematical physicist, structural engineer; b. Rome, Italy, Mar. 19, 1907; came to U.S., 1939; s. Riccardo and Ermelinda (Alatri) S.; m. Giuseppina Tagliacozzo, July 30, 1935 (div. June 1975); 1 child, Vieri R.; m. Carol B. Salvadori, Apr. 5, 1975. DCE, U. Rome, 1930, D of Math. Physics, 1933; DSc, Columbia U., 1977; D of Fine Letters, New Sch. for Social Rsch., 1990; LHD, Lehman Coll., 1994. Prof. U. Rome (Italy) Sch. Engring., 1932-38, Columbia U., N.Y.C., 1940-90; chmn. Weidlinger Assocs., N.Y.C., 1957-90, hon. chmn, 1991—; founder, chmn. Salvadori Ednl. Ctr. on Built Environment, 1975-91, hon. chmn., 1993—. Author of 22 books; contbr. articles to profl. jours. Recipient more than 20 awards from univs., engring. and archtl. socs. and ednl. assns., 1970-95. Fellow ASME, Am. Concrete Inst.; mem. ASCE (hon.), AIA (hon.). Democrat. Achievements include research in applied mathematics and engineering structures; 27 new routes and 3 virgin peaks climbed in the Eastern Alps. Home: 2 Beekman Pl New York NY 10022-8058 Office: Weidlinger Assocs 333 Seventh Ave New York NY 10001

SALVANESCHI, LUIGI, real estate and development executive, business educator; b. Casale, Italy, 1929; arrived in U.S., 1959; s. Ernesto and Carolina (Bassignana) S.; m. Lenore M. Rickels, Aug. 20, 1958; 1 child, Margherita Lina. Classical Maturity, Valsalice, Torino, Italy, 1950; PhD, Vatican U., Rome, 1958; cert. in real estate, UCLA, 1965. Restaurant mgr. McDonalds Co., Chgo., 1959-61; restaurant mgr. and supr. McDonalds Co., Los Angeles, 1961-63, real estate mgr., 1964-68; v.p. real estate McDonalds Co., Oakbrook, Ill., 1969-83; sr. v.p. real estate and constrn. Kentucky Fried Chicken, Louisville, 1983-88; pres., COO, dir. Blockbuster Entertainment, Ft. Lauderdale, Fla., 1988-91; dir. First American Railways Inc., 1995-96; disting. adj. prof. Barry Univ., 1991—; adj. prof. Sch. Bus. U. Louisville, 1987. Served as 2d lt. in Italian Infantry, 1945-46. Recipient Outstanding Italo-Am. award Italian Am. Fedn., 1991; named Colonel of the Commonwealth of Ky., 1984. Mem. Nat. Assn. Real Estate Execs. (co-founder, bd. dirs.). Roman Catholic. Avocations: reading classics in Latin and Greek, mountain hiking. Office: Barry Univ Sch of Bus 11300 NE 2nd Ave Miami FL 33161-6628

SALVENDY, GAVRIEL, industrial engineer; b. Budapest, Hungary, Sept. 30, 1938; came to U.S., 1968; s. Paul and Katarina (Brown) S.; m. Catherine Vivien Dees, Apr. 1, 1966; children: Laura Dorit, Kevin David. MSc in Engring. Prodn, U. Birmingham, Eng., 1966, PhD, 1968; Doctorate (hon.), Academia Sinica, 1995; Chinese Acad. Scis. Asst. prof. indsl. engring. SUNY, Buffalo, 1968-71; mem. faculty Purdue U., 1971—, prof. indsl. engring., chmn. human factors program, 1977, Fulbright distinguished prof., 1979-80, 81-82, NEC prof. indsl. engring., 1984—; chmn. Internat. Commn. on Human Aspects in Computing, Switzerland, 1986-91. Co-author: Prediction and Development of Industrial Work Performance, 1973, Human Aspects of Computer Aided Design, 1987; sr. editor: Machine-Pacing and Occupational Stress, 1981, Social, Ergonomic and Stress Aspects of Work with Computers, 1987, Designing and Using Human-Computer Interfaces and Knowledge Based Systems, 1989; editor: Handbook of Industrial Engineering, 1982, 2d edit., 1992, Human Computer Interaction, 1984, Handbook of Human Factors, 1987, Cognitive Engineering in the Design of Human Computer Interaction and Expert Systems, 1987; founding editor: Internat. Jour. on Human-Computer Interaction, Internat. Jour. Human Factors in Mfg., Internat. Jour. of Cognitive Ergonomics; co-editor: Work with Computers: Organizational Management, Stress and Health Aspects, 1989, Human Computer Interaction: Software and Hardware Interfaces, 1993, Human-Computer Interaction: Applications and Case Studies, 1993, Design of Work and Development of Personnel in Advanced Manufacturing, 1994, Organization and Management of Advanced Manufacturing, 1994; contbr. articles to profl. jours., chpts. to books. Pres. Lafayette Jewish Sunday Sch., 1980-81. Recipient Mikhail Vasilievich Lomonosov medal USSR Acad. Sci., 1991. Fellow APA, Inst. Indsl. Engrs. (sr., Phil Carroll award 1973), Human Factors Soc. (past officer), Ergonomics Soc. (hon., life mem.); mem. NAE. Office: Purdue U Sch Indsl Engring West Lafayette IN 47907

SALVESON, MELVIN ERWIN, business executive, educator; b. Brea, Calif., Jan. 16, 1919; s. John T. and Elizabeth (Green) S.; m. Joan Y. Stipek, Aug. 22, 1944; children: Eric C., Kent Erwin. B.S., U. Calif. at Berkeley, 1941; M.S., Mass. Inst. Tech., 1947; Ph.D., U. Chgo., 1952. Cons. McKinsey & Co., N.Y.C., 1948-49; asst. prof., dir. mgmt. sci. research U. Calif. at Los Angeles, 1949-54; mgr. advanced data systems, cons. strategic planning Gen. Electric Co., Louisville and N.Y.C., 1954-57; pres. Mgmt. Scis. Corp., Los Angeles, 1957-67; group v.p. Control Data/CEIR, Inc., 1967-68; pres. Electronic Currency Corp., 1968—; chmn. OneCard Internat., Inc., 1983-92, Univ. Trans. System Inc., 1992—; founder and pres. Southern Calif. Econ. Alliance, 1992-96, also bd. dirs.; founding chair Am. Soc. for Edn. and Econ. Devel., 1996—; also bd dirs.; exec. dir. Am. Found. for Edn. and Econ. Devel.; bd. dirs. Diversified Earth Scis., Inc., Eco Rx Inc., Excel Enterprise Inc., Veritas et Justus Inc., Algeran, Inc., Electronic Currency Corp.; founder Master Card System, Los Angeles, 1966; chmn. Corporate Strategies Internat.; prof. bus. Pepperdine U. 1972-85; adj. prof. U. So. Calif.; adviser data processing City of Los Angeles, 1962-64; futures forecasting IBM, 1957-61; adviser strategic systems planning USAF, 1961-67; info. systems Calif. Dept. Human Resources, 1972-73, City Los Angeles Automated Urban Data Base, 1962-67; tech. transfer NASA, 1965-70, others; mem. bd. trustees, Long Beach City Coll. Contbr. articles to profl. jours. Served to lt. comdr. USNR, 1941-46. Named to Long Beach City Coll. Hall of Fame; recipient Dist. Alumnus 1992 award Calif. Coll. System, 1992. Fellow AAAS; mem. Inst. Mgmt. Sci. (founder, past pres.). Republican. Club: Founders (Los Angeles Philharmonic Orch.), Calif. Yacht. Home: 130 Marguerita Ave Apt 8 Santa Monica CA 90402-1652

SALYER, STEPHEN LEE, broadcast executive; b. Lexington, Ky., July 20, 1950; s. Ralph Conley Salyer and Margaret (Greenlee) Miles; m. Martha Ingels Ruddy, Apr. 21, 1985; children: Samuel Wilmot, Duncan Davis, Clara Josephine. BA, Davidson Coll., 1972; MPA, Harvard U., 1975. Pres. Citizens' Com. on Population and the Am. Future, Washington, 1972-73; cons. to John D. Rockefeller 3d Rockefeller Family Assocs., N.Y.C., 1973-75; assoc. pub. issues program Population Coun., N.Y.C., 1977-79; asst. to the pres. Ednl. Broadcasting Corp., Sta. WNET TV, N.Y.C., 1975-76, v.p. corp. affairs, 1979-80, v.p. program devel. and mktg., 1981-82, sr. v.p. edn. divsn., 1982-86, sr. v.p. mktg. and comm., 1986-88; pres., CEO Pub. Radio Internat., Mpls., 1988—, also bd. dirs.; bd. dirs. Minn. Meeting; mem. nat. adv. com. Save the Children, 1991—, Nat. Peace Found., 1991—. Co-author: (with James J. Bausch) Toward Safe, Convenient and Effective Contraceptives, 1978. Fellow Japan Soc. U.S.-Japan Leadership, 1996; mem. Nat. Commn. on Population Growth and the Am. Future, Washington, 1970-72. Mem. Harvard Club (N.Y.C.), Mpls. Club. Avocations: tennis, reading. Home: 1801 Irving Ave S Minneapolis MN 55403-2822 Office: Pub Radio Internat 100 N 6th St Ste 900 A Minneapolis MN 55403-1516

SALZBERG, BRIAN MATTHEW, neuroscience and physiology educator; b. N.Y.C., Sept. 4, 1942; s. Saul and Betty Bernice (Jacobs) S. BS, Yale U., 1963; AM, Harvard U., 1965, PhD, 1971. Woodrow Wilson fellow in physics Harvard U., Cambridge, Mass., 1963-64, rsch. asst. in high energy physics, 1964-71; rsch. assoc. physiology Yale Med. Sch., New Haven, 1971-75; asst. prof. physiology U. Pa. Sch. Dental Medicine, Phila., 1975-80; assoc. prof. physiology U. Pa., Phila., 1980-82; prof. physiology U. Pa. Sch. Medicine, Phila., 1982-92, prof. neurosci. and physiology, 1992—; Arthur Rosenblueth vis. prof. CINVESTAV, Mexico City, 1987. Contbr. over 100 sci. articles on neurophysiology and biophysics to profl. jours. Trustee Marine Biol. Lab., Woods Hole, Mass., 1980-84, 87-95. Guest fellow Royal Soc., Cambridge U., 1991, fellow Japan Soc. for Promotion of Sci., Tokyo, 1989, STEPS fellow Marine Biol. Lab., 1977, 78; recipient Marine Biol. Lab. award, 1981. Fellow Am. Phys. Soc., AAAS; mem. Biophys. Soc. (exec. bd. 1987-90), Soc. Gen. Physiology (coun. 1986-88), Phi Beta Kappa, Sigma Xi. Achievements include co-discovery of voltage-sensitive merocyanine, styryl, oxonol and cyanine dyes; application of optical methods to cell physiology and neuroscience. Avocation: marathon runner. Home: 4632 Spruce St Philadelphia PA 19139-4540 Office: U Pa Physiology Dept 234 Stemmler Hall Philadelphia PA 19104-6074

SALZBERG, EMMETT RUSSELL, new product developer; b. N.Y.C., Aug. 15, 1924; s. Herman and Freda (Russell) S.; m. Ilene Roslyn Greenhut, Oct. 29, 1960; children: Shelby Russell, Laurie Russell. Grad., Bronx High Sch. of Sci., 1941; student, Columbia U., CCNY. Pres. Dixey Tapes Corp., Stratford, Conn., 1969-85; sr. product mgr. Tuck Tape, New Rochelle, N.Y., 1986-88; pres. Dixey Tapes Corp., Stratford, 1993—; cons. Tape div. Shuford Mills, Hickory, N.C., 1990-92. Patentee telephone answering equipment. Mem. Trumbull Yr.-Round. Edn. Feasibility Study Com. Served with U.S. Army, 1943-45, PTO. Mem. Mensa (pres. So. Conn. chpt.), Inventors Assn. Conn. (co-founder, past mem. exec. bd.). Democrat. Jewish. Avocations: target shooting, photography. Home: 37 Partridge Ln Trumbull CT 06611-4919 Office: Dixey Tapes Corp 959 Main St Stratford CT 06497-7400

SALZER, JOHN MICHAEL, technical and management consultant; b. Vienna, Austria, Sept. 12, 1917; came to U.S., 1940; s. Siegfried and Rose (Deutsch) S.; m. Eva R. Arvay, Mar. 26, 1944; children: Arleen, Ronald, Myra, Gary. BSEE, Case Inst. Tech., 1947, MSEE, 1948; ScDEE, MIT, 1951. Instr. in mechanics and electronics Case Inst. Tech., Cleve., 1947-48; rsch. assoc. Electronic Computer Lab., MIT, Cambridge, Mass., 1948-51; mem. tech. staff Hughes Aircraft Co., El Segundo, Calif., group mgr., 1951-54; asst. dir rsch. lab. Maganvox Co., L.A., 1954-59, dir. systems, 1959; dir. Intellectronics Labs. TRW Inc., 1959-62, spl. asst. to exec. v.p. corp. planning, 1962-63; v.p. tech. and planning Librascope div. Singer Co. Inc., 1963-69; pres. Salzer Tech. Enterprises Inc., tech. and mgmt. cons., Santa Monica, Calif., 1968—. Author: Evolutionary Design of Complex Systems, 1961, Sampled-Data Theory, 1961. Fellow IEEE, Inst. Advancement Engring; mem. Internat. Soc. Hybrid Microelectronics, Semicondr. Equipment and Materials Inst., Sigma Xi, Tau Beta Pi, Eta Kappa Nu. Office: Salzer Tech Enterprises Inc 909 Berkeley St Santa Monica CA 90403-2307

SALZINGER, MARK ALAN, editor, violinist; b. Cleve., Nov. 20, 1965; s. Carl Benjamin and Margriet Regina Salzinger. BA in Econs. with honors, U. Chgo., 1988; MBA, Cornell U., 1992. Economist U.S. Dept. of Labor, Washington, 1988-89; rschr./writer KCI Comm., Alexandria, Va., 1989-90; investment assoc. J & W Seligman, N.Y.C., 1992-94; sr. analyst Citicorp, N.Y.C., 1994-95; mng. editor Fin. Svcs. Assocs., Alexandria, 1995-96, exec. editor, 1996—; violinist Arlington (Va.) Symphony, 1988-90, 95-96, Fairfax (Va.) Symphony, 1988-90. Intern Voinovich for Senate, Cleve., 1987. Republican. Avocations: violin playing, fantasy football, baseball and basketball, exercise. Home: 820 Bashford Ln Alexandria VA 22314 Office: Financial Services Assocs 1101 King St #400 Alexandria VA 22314

SALZMAN, ARTHUR GEORGE, architect; b. Chgo., June 20, 1929; s. Russell Harvey Salzman and Mildred Olive (Olsen) Erickson; m. Joan Marie Larson, Aug. 16, 1952; children: Lisa Jo Salzman Braucher, David Ralph. BS in Archtl. Engring., U. Ill., 1952; MArch, Ill. Inst. Tech., 1960. Registered architect, Ill., Mich., NCARB. Architect Skidmore, Owings & Merrill, Chgo., 1960, Mies van der Rohe, Arch., Chgo., 1960-69; assoc. The Office of Mies Van Der Rohe, Chgo., 1969-81; v.p. FCL Assocs., Chgo., 1981-86; ex. v.p. Lohan Assocs., Chgo., 1986-91; pvt. practice architecture Evanston, Ill., 1992—; mem. Building Code Restructuring Com., City of Chgo., 1994—. Mem. Chgo. Com. on High Rise Bldgs.; bd. dirs. Savoy Aires, Evanston, 1985-88, 90-93, pres. 1992-93; v.p. Chgo. area Unitarian-Universalist Coun., Chgo., 1974-76. Cpl. U.S. Army, 1952-54. Mem. AIA (bd. dirs. Chgo. chpt. 1992—, sec. 1994—), Constrn. Specifications Inst., Bldg. Ofcls. and Code Adminstrs. Internat. (profl.), Coun. on Tall Bldgs. and Urban Habitat, Wind Engring. Rsch. Coun., Precast-Prestressed Concrete Inst., Cliff Dwellers Club. Avocations: community theater, choral singing, sailing. Home: 1018 Greenwood St Evanston IL 60201-4212 Office: 1569 Sherman Ave Ste 200 Evanston IL 60201-4486

SALZMAN, DAVID ELLIOT, entertainment industry executive; b. Bklyn., Dec. 1, 1943; s. Benjamin and Rose Harriet (Touby) S.; m. Sonia Camelia Gonsalves, Oct. 19, 1968; children: Daniel Mark, Andrea Jessica, Adam Gabriel. B.A., Bklyn. Coll., 1965; M.A., Wayne State U., 1967. Dir. TV ops. Wayne State U., 1966-67; producer Lou Gordon Program, 1967-70; program mgr. Sta. WKBD-TV, Detroit, 1970-71; program mgr. Sta. KDKA-TV, Pitts., 1971-72, gen. mgr., 1973-75; program mgr. Sta. KYW-TV, Phila., 1972-73; chmn. bd. Group W Prodns., N.Y.C and Los Angeles, 1975—; founder, pres. United Software Assocs., 1980-81; creator News Info. Weekly Service, 1981; exec. v.p. Telepictures Corp., 1980-84, vice chmn., 1984; pres. Lorimar Telepictures Corp. (merger Telepictures and Lorimar, Inc.), 1985-90, Lorimar TV, 1986-90; creator Newscope: Nat. TV News Cooperative, 1983; pres., CEO David Salzman Entertainment, Burbank, Calif., 1990-93; co-CEO Quincy Jones-David Salzman Entertainment (QDE), 1993—; exec. prodr. Jenny Jones Show, 1991—; exec. prodr. Mad-TV, In the House, 68th Ann. Acad. awards; co-owner QD7 Interactive, 1994; bd. dirs. Premiere Radio, 1994, 7th Level; guest lectr. at schs.; bd. govs. Films of Coll. and Univ. Students. Contbr. articles to Variety and numerous communications trade publs. Bd. dirs. Pitts. Civic Light Opera, Am. Blood Bank, Pitts., Hebrew Inst., Jewish Community Ctr., Harrison, N.Y., Temple Etz Chaim, USC Sch. Cinema-TV, Emory U. Ctr. for Leadership, Emory Bus. Sch., Bklyn. Coll. Found. Recipient award Detroit chpt. Am. Women in Radio and TV, 1969, award Golden Quill, 1971, award Golden Gavel, 1971, local Emmy award, 1972, award AP, 1974, Gold medal Broadcast Promotion Assn., 1983, Lifetime Achievement award Bklyn. Coll., 1990, Disting. Alumnus award, Golden Plate award Am. Acad. Achievement, 1995; BPME Gold medal San Francisco Film Festival, 1984, N.Y., 1985, Chgo., 1986, Tree of Life award Jewish Nat. Fund, 1988. Mem. Acad. TV Arts and Scis., Nat. Assn. TV Program Execs., Radio-TV News Dirs. Assn., Am. Mgmt. Assn., Am. Film Inst., Brooklyn Coll. Found. Office: QDE Entertainment 3800 Barham Blvd Ste 503 Los Angeles CA 90068 *"Courage is the first of human qualities because it is the quality which guarantees all the others."*

SALZMAN, ERIC, artistic director; b. N.Y.C., Sept. 8, 1933; s. Samuel and Frances (Klenett) S.; m. Lorna Jackson, Dec. 24, 1956; Eva, Stephanie. BA in Music with honors, Columbia U., 1954; MFA, Princeton U., 1956. Music critic N.Y. Times, N.Y.C., 1958-62; dir. music Sta. WBAI-FM, N.Y.C., 1962-63, 68-72; music critic N.Y. Herald Tribune, N.Y.C., 1963-67; asst. prof. Queens Coll. CUNY, Queens, 1966-68; artistic dir. Quog Music Theater, N.Y.C., 1970-80; co-founder, artistic dir. Am. Music Theater Festival, Phila., 1981-93; founder, co-artistic dir. MusicTheater/N.Y., 1994—; mem. guest faculty NYU, Yale U., Banff Ctr. for Arts, Can., Conservatoire Nationale, Lyon, France; organizer ann. conf. Small Scale Opera and Music Theatre, Brussels, 1992, Antwerp, Belgium, 1983, Colmar, 1994. Principal works include: (compositions) String Quartet, 1955, Inventions, 1957, In Praise on the Owl and the Cuckoo, 1963, Foxes and Hedgehogs, 1964, Queens College, 1966, Larynx Music, 1966, Helix, 1971, Fantasy on Lazarus, 1974, Accord, 1975, Variations on Sacred Harp Tunes, 1982, (radio opera) Voices, 1971, (mime-dance prodn.) The Peloponnesian War, 1967, (multimedia participatory work) Feedback 1968, The Nude Paper Sermon, 1969, (multimedia environ. work) Can Man Survive?, 1968, (media poem) Ecolog, 1982, (musical theater prodn.) Saying Something, 1972, Biograffiti, 1972, Lazarus, 1973, (with Michael Stahl) The Conjuror, 1974, Stauf, 1976, Noah, 1978, The Passion of Simple Simon, 1979, Boxes, 1982 (Seagram Prodn. award), (opera buffa) Civilization and its Discontents, 1980 (Prix Italia award Assn European Broadcasters), (with Ned Jackson) Big Jim and the Small-time Investors, 1996, (with Valeria Vasilevski) The Last Words of Dutch Schultz, 1996, (with Michel Rostain) Prières, 1997; (media and live performance piece) Toward a New American Opera, 1985, (adaptations) Strike Up the Band, 1984, Love Life, 1990, The Silent Twins, 1992; prodr., dir. The Unknown Kurt Weill, Silverlake, Civilization and its Discontents, The Tango Project (Record of Yr. award Stereo Rev.), Two to Tango, The Palm Court, The Waltz Project, Moore's Irish Melodies, A Portrait Album, Notebooks of Anna Magdalena Bach, An Old-Fashioned Christmas, Revelation in the Courthouse Park, Casino Paradise; recs. include Civilization and its Discontents, Wiretap, The Nude Paper Sermon, Noah, Accord; author: 20th Century Music: An Introduction, 3d edit., 1989; editor Musical Quar., 1984-91; contbg. editor, critic Stereo Rev., N.Y.C., 1970—; contbr. N.Y. Times, New York Herald-Tribune, N.Y. Mag., others. Fulbright scholar St. Cecilia Acad., 1956-58, Darmstadt Ferienkurse, 1957; recipient Armstrong, Prix Italia radio awards. Mem. Linnaean Soc. (mem. coun.), South Fork Nat. History Soc. (mem. coun.). Avocations: natural history, ornithology. Home: 29 Middagh St Brooklyn NY 11201-1339

SALZMAN, MARILYN B. WOLFSON, service company executive; b. Chgo., Dec. 25, 1943; d. Joseph and Sera (Krol) Wolfson; 1 son, Lawrence Todd. Student, U. Ill., Barat Coll., Lake Forest, Ill., U. Calif., Irvine. Adminstrv. project asst. Sci. Research Assocs., Chgo., 1964-70; reporter Suburban Trib of Chgo. Tribune, 1979-80; pres. MWS Assocs., Los Angeles and Fullerton, Calif., 1980—; exec. adminstrv. dir. Crystal Tips of No. Ill., Inc., 1980-83; dir. adminstrn. Ice Dispensers, Inc., 1981-83, Sani-Serv of Ill., Inc., 1981-83; adminstrv. and organizational cons. 1140 Corp., 1980-83; adminstrv. dir. Iceman's Ico Co., Inc., 1980-83; founder, moderator DWC Workshops, 1984; dir. data processing Florence Crittenton Svs., Orange County, 1984-86, dir. MIS, 1986-88, dir. support svcs., 1988-92, bd. dirs. devel. & ways and means com., 1991—, fin. com., found. com., bd. devel. com., ann. meeting com., 1995—, dir. adminstrn. & contract compliance, 1992-94, dir. devel. & cmty. svcs., 1994—; pres. MWS Prodns., L.A. and Fullerton, Calif., 1990—; exec. producer (TV series) The State of the Child, 1990-91; panelist computers in residential treatment Child Welfare League Am. Biennial Conf. Workshop, 1986; presenter outcomes and svc. evaluation North Am. Out-of-Home Care Conf., 1991, families & children in residential treatment Calif. State U. Child Devel. Conf., Fullerton, 1994, advancing your message Child Welfare League of Am. Nat. Conf., 1995; comm. & Pub. Rels. for Profl., Child Welfare League Am. Nat. Conf., 1996. Active Friends of Fullerton Library, Boy Scouts Am.; panelist Child Welfare League Am., Bienniel Conf. Workshop; chmn. govtl., pub. affairs coms. Orange County Assn. of Children's Svcs.; mem. steering com. Orange County UN Assn. Yr. of Family, 1993-95; mem. com. Internat. Yr. of the Family Exhibit & Celebration, Bowers Mus., 1994; mem. planning com. Orange County Summit for Children, 1994—; mem. exec. com. Anne Frank Orange County Organizing Com., 1994—; mem. adv. com. Child Devel. & Family Life Dept., Fullerton Coll., 1994; mem. bd. mgrs. N. Orange County Family YMCA, 1995—, chmn. child care adv. com., 1995—, mem. sr. care adv. com., exec. dir. selection com., 1996; facilitator Orange County Together, 1994—. Mem. Calif. Assn. Svcs. for Children (rsch. and evaluation com. 1993—), Soroptimist Internat. of Fullerton (TAP chmn. 1995—, v.p. 1996), Mgmt. Forum, Fullerton C. of C. (indsl. com. 1994—, local govt. com. 1995—). Contbr. articles to newspapers and indsl. jours.

SALZMAN, RICHARD WILLIAM, artists' representative; b. Los Angeles, Nov. 22, 1958; s. Paul and Anne (Meyersburg) S.; student public schs., Los Angeles. Stockboy, Marathon Clothing, Los Angeles, 1976-77, salesman, 1977, sales and mgmt. trainee, 1977-78, br. mgr., San Francisco, 1978-80, San Diego, 1980-82; artist rep., 1982—; owner Salzman Internat., San Francisco; dir. Therapy Springs Presents. Tchr. freelance bus. practices San Diego City Coll. Contbr. illustrations Communication Arts mag., 1992, Graphic Arts of the World. Recipient 2 Gold medals N.Y. Soc. Illustrators. Mem. Union of Concerned Scientists, Green Peace, Environ. Def. Fund, Coalition for Non-Nuclear World, Communicating Arts Group San Diego (2 Gold awards 1989), Internat. Assn. Bus. Communicators, Soc. Photographers and Artists Reps., Am. Inst. Graphic Arts (founder, v.p. San Diego chpt., mem. nat. task force), Graphic Artist Guild, Western Art Dirs. Club, San Francisco Creative Alliance. Democrat. Home: 716 Sanchez St San Francisco CA 94114-2929 Office: Salzman Internat 716 Sanchez St San Francisco CA 94114

SALZMAN, ROBERT JAY, accountant; b. Bklyn., Dec. 7, 1941; s. Irving and Sydelle (Feingold) S.; m. Constance A. Freeman, Sept. 16, 1990. BA, Allegheny Coll., Meadville, Pa., 1962; MBA, U. Pa., 1965; JD, N.Y. Law Sch., 1972. Bar: N.Y. 1973; CPA, N.Y. Acct. N.Y.C., 1965—; pvt. practice Robert J. Salzman, CPA, P.C., N.Y.C., 1970—. Home: 10 East End Ave New York NY 10021 also: 82 Sycamore Dr East Hampton NY 11937-1482 also: 2801 NE 183rd St North Miami Beach FL 33160 Office: 845 Third Ave New York NY 10022

SALZSTEIN, RICHARD ALAN, biomedical engineer, researcher; b. Elkins Park, Pa., Sept. 16, 1959; s. Eli and Lorraine (Reese) S.; m. Sharon Lazar; children: Hillary, Lauren. BS in Engring., U. Pa., 1981, MS in Engring., 1982, PhD in Bioengring., 1985. Rsch. fellow U. Pa., Phila., 1981-85; rsch. scientist Hercules, Inc., Wilmington, Del., 1986—. Mem. Soc. for Biomaterials, Orthopaedic Rsch. Soc., Tau Beta Pi. Recipient Kappa Delta award Bioelectrical Repair & Growth Soc., 1985; NSF fellow, 1981-85. Avocations: racquetball, skiing. Office: Hercules Inc Rsch Ctr 500 Hercules Rd Wilmington DE 19808-1599

SAM, DAVID, federal judge; b. Hobart, Ind., Aug. 12, 1933; s. Andrew and Flora (Toma) S.; m. Betty Jean Brennan, Feb. 1, 1957; children: Betty Jean, David Dwight, Daniel Scott, Tamara Lynn, Pamela Rae, Daryl Paul, Angie, Sheyla. BS, Brigham Young U., 1957; JD, Utah U., 1960. Bar: Utah 1960, U.S. Dist. Ct. Utah 1966. Sole practice and ptnr. Duchesne, Utah, 1963-76; dist. judge State of Utah, 1976-85; judge U.S. Dist. Ct. Utah, Salt Lake City, 1985—; atty. City of Duchesne, 1963-72; Duchesne County atty., 1966-72; commr. Duchesne, 1972-74; mem. adv. com. Codes of Conduct of Jud. Conf. U.S., 1987-91, Jud. Coun. of 10th Cir., 1991-93; mem. U.S. Del. to Romania, Aug. 1991. Chmn. Jud. Nomination Com. for Cir. Ct. Judge, Provo, Utah, 1983; bd. dirs. Water Resources, Salt Lake City, 1973-76. Served to capt. JAGC, USAF, 1961-63. Mem. Utah State Bar Assn., Am. Judicature Soc., Supreme Ct. Hist. Soc., Am. Inns of Ct. VII (counselor 1986-89), A. Sherman Christensen Am. Inn of Ct. I (counselor 1989—), Utah Jud. Conf. (chmn. 1982), Utah Dist. Judges Assn. (pres. 1982-83). Mem. LDS Ch. Avocations: beekeeping, reading, sports, cooking chinese food. Office: US Dist Ct 148 US Courthouse 350 S Main St Salt Lake City UT 84101-2106

SAM, DAVID FIIFI, political economist, educator; b. Winneba, Ghana, Sept. 9, 1957; came to U.S., 1975; s. Alfred Sam and Christiana Impraim; m. Juliana Sam, Jan. 3, 1987; children: Michelle Ann Tabirwaa, David Charles Impraim. BA, Ill. State U., 1981; MBA, Northwestern U., 1987; M.A.L.D., Tufts U., 1984, PhD, 1990. Tchg. asst. in polit. sci. Tufts U., Medford, Mass., 1982-84, adminstr. Fletcher Sch., 1983-84; fin. asst. Arthur Andersen & Co., Chgo., 1984-86; assoc. dir. City Colls. of Chgo., 1986-88; asst. prof., coord. Coll. of DuPage, Glen Elyn, Ill., 1988-90; dean natural and social scis. Mott C.C., Flint, Mich., 1990-92, acting exec. v.p., 1992-93; v.p., prof. Harrisburg (Pa.) Area C.C., 1993—; cons. internat. bus. and edn., 1989—. Co-editor: International Business: Designing Effective Programs for Community Colleges, 1988. Bd. dirs. Flint Internat. Inst., 1992-93, Am. Coun. Internat./Intercultural Edn., 1994—, Ill. Consortium for Internat. Studies and Programs, 1987-90. Recipient Martin Luther King Svc. award Ill. State U., 1981. Avocations: reading, travel, sports. Home: 4551 Sequoia Dr # C-275 Harrisburg PA 17109-5137 Office: Harrisburg Area CC One HACC Dr Harrisburg PA 17110

SAM, JOSEPH, retired university dean; b. Gary, Ind., Aug. 15, 1923; s. Andrew and Flora (Toma) S.; m. Frances Adickes, Sept. 11, 1945; children—Sherrie, Joseph A., Suzanne F. Student, Drake U., 1942-43; B.S., U. S.C., 1948; Ph.D., Kans. U., 1951. Sr. research chemist McNeil Labs., Phila., 1951-54; research group leader Bristol Labs., Syracuse, N.Y., 1955-57; sr. scientist E.I. duPont de Nemours & Co., Inc., 1957-59; faculty U. Miss., 1959-86, prof. pharm. chemistry, 1961-68, chmn. dept., 1963-68, dir. univ. research, 1968-81, asso. vice chancellor research, 1981-86; dean U. Miss. (Grad. Sch.), 1968-86; Fulbright lectr. Cairo U., 1965-66. Mem. Am. Pharm. Assn. (found. research achievement award in pharm. and medicinal chemistry 1968), Sigma Xi, Rho Chi, Phi Lambda Upsilon, Phi Kappa Phi. Home: PO Box 351 University MS 38677-0351

SAMAD, NIDAL ABDUL, research scientist; b. Mazraa, Beirut, Lebanon, June 9, 1961; came to U.S., 1985; s. Nadim N. and Dalal N. Samad; m. Soha A., Sept. 9, 1988. BS in Chemistry, Lebanese U., Beirut, 1984; BSChemE with honors, Fla. Inst. Tech., 1987, MSChemE, 1989, MS in Environ. Sci., 1994. Plant operator Cocoa, Fla., 1989-90; grad. rsch. asst. Fla. Inst. Tech., Melbourne, Fla., 1990-92, rsch. cons., 1991-92, rsch. scientist, 1991-93; rsch. scientist Mainstream Engring., Rockledge, Fla., 1993—; rsch. scientist, cons. Fla. Inst. Tech., Melbourne, 1991-93; rsch. scientist Mainstream Engring. Corp., Rockledge, 1993—. Mem. edn. com. UN, Brevard chpt., 1994. Recipient Rsch. assistantship Fla. Inst. Tech., 1997-89, teaching assistantship, 1991. Mem. AIChE, Sigma Xi (assoc.). Achievements include four patents pending, two in the area of water and waste water treatment and two in the area of air conditioning. Home: Apt 108 1470 Malibu Circle NE Palm Bay FL 32905

SAMALIN, EDWIN, lawyer, educator; b. N.Y.C., Sept. 19, 1935; s. Harry Louis and Sydell (Fisher) S.; children: David Seth, Andrew Evan, Jonathan Daniel. B.S., U. R.I., 1957; J.D., N.Y. Law Sch., 1962. Bar: N.Y. 1963, U.S. Supreme Ct. 1976. Tax atty. Electric Bond & Share Co., N.Y.C., 1963; ptnr. Samalin & Sklaver, Yorktown Heights, N.Y., 1969-78; pvt. practice law, Yorktown Heights, 1963-69, 78-84; mng. ptnr. Yorktown Office Park Assocs., Yorktown Heights, 1971—; pres. Samalin & Bock, P.C., Yorktown Heights, 1984—; adj. faculty Mercy Coll., Dobbs Ferry, N.Y., 1974-92; commodity cons. Murlas Commodities, Yorktown Heights, 1982-85; ptnr. Patterson (N.Y.) Realty Assn., 1983—; pres. Sammark Realty Corp., Westchester, N.Y., 1984—, Old Smoke House Realty Corp., 1987—, Atty.'s Asset Mgmt. Corp., Registered Investment Advisors, 1992—; Dem. candidate for County Legislature, 1973. Capt. U.S. Army, 1957-59. Mem. N.Y. State Bar Assn., Westchester County Bar Assn. (dir., former chair atty. client dispute com.), Yorktown Bar Assn. (pres. 1982, Man of Yr. 1983), Am. Arbitration Assn. (arbitrator 1974—), Phi Delta Phi. Home: 951A Heritage Hills Dr Somers NY 10589-1913 Office: Samalin & Bock PC 2000 Maple Hill St Yorktown Heights NY 10598-4122

SAMANIEGO, PAMELA SUSAN, organization administrator; b. San Mateo, Calif., Nov. 29, 1952; d. Armando C. and Harriott Susan (Croot) S. Student, UCLA, 1972, Los Angeles Valley Coll., 1970-72. Asst. new accts. supr. Beverly Hills Fed. Savings, 1970-72; asst. controller Bio-Science Enterprises, Van Nuys, Calif., 1972-74; adminstr. asst. Avery/Tirce Prodns., Hollywood, Calif., 1974-78; sr. estimator N. Lee Lacy and Assocs., Hollywood, 1978-81; head of prodn. Film Consortium, Hollywood, 1981-82; exec. producer EUE/Screen Gems Ltd., Burbank, Calif., 1982-88; advt. agency dir. Barrett & Assocs., Las Vegas, Nev., 1988-90; exec. producer Laguna/Take One, Las Vegas, 1990-93; dir. Sta. KXLY-4 ABC, Spokane, Wash., 1993-94; dir. advt. and mktg. Appaloosa Horse Club, Moscow, Idaho, 1994—. Author: Millimeter & Backstage, 1982-88. Emergency room vol. San Mateo (Calif.) County Hosp., 1968-70; Sunday sch. tchr. Hillsdale Meth. Ch., San Mateo, 1968-70; vol. worker Hillsdale Meth. Ch. Outreach, San Francisco, 1967-70. Recipient CLIO award CLIO Awards, Inc., 1985, ADDY award Las Vegas Advt. Fedn., 1988. Mem. Dirs. Guild Am. (2nd asst. dir. 1987-88), Assn. Ind. Comml. Producers, Am. Horse Show Assn., Internat. Arabian Horse Assn., AHASFV (sec. 1978-79), AHASC (sec. 1978-88). Democrat. Methodist. Avocations: breed and show Arabian horses. Home: 323 E First St Moscow ID 83843 Office: Appaloosa Horse Club 5070 Hwy 8 W Moscow ID 83843

SAMANIEGO BREACH, NORMA, Mexican government official; b. Mexico City, Feb. 24, 1944; married; 1 child. BA in Econ., Autonomous U., Mexico City, 1966; MA in Economic Planning, Inst. Social Studies, The Hague, The Netherlands, 1970. Planning analyst Secretariat of the Presidency Govt. of Mex., 1967-69, dep. dir. rsch. on revenue distbn. and salary Secretariat of, 1974-75, dep. dir. econ. rsch. Nat. Commn. on Minimum Wages, 1975-76, sr. analyst planning Secretariat of Edn., 1977-78; advisor for svcs. Mex. Inst. Social Security, 1978-82, tech. dir. Nat. Commn. on Minimum Wages, 1982-88, pres. Nat. Commn. on Minimum Wages, 1988-90, undersec. "B" Secretariat of Labor and Social Assistance, 1991-94, comptroller gen., 1995—. Author several works on labor market in Mex. Mem. Instl. Revolutionary Party. Office: Embassy of Mexico 1911 Pennsylvania Ave NW Washington DC 20006*

SAMANOWITZ, RONALD ARTHUR, lawyer; b. N.Y.C., June 1, 1944; s. Sam and Thelma (Levin) S.; m. Ann Frieda Weisman, Dec. 18, 1971; 1 child, Samuel. BBA, CUNY, 1965; JD, Bklyn. Law Sch., 1967. Bar: N.Y. 1968, U.S. Dist. Ct. (ea. and so. dists.) N.Y. 1974, U.S. Supreme Ct. 1991. Ptnr. Krakower, Samanowitz & Goldman, N.Y.C., 1968-86, Resnicoff, Samanowitz, Endzweig & Brawer, Great Neck, N.Y., 1986-90, Samanowitz & Endzweig, Great Neck, N.Y., 1990—. Pres. Greater Fresh Meadows Civic Assn., Flushing, N.Y., 1984-85, award for Civic Svc. 1985, Flower Hill Civic Assn., 1992. Mem. N.Y. State Trial Lawyers Assn. (gov. L.I. divsn.), Brandeis Lawyers Assn. (sec. 1985—), Queens Bar Assn. (family law com.), Nassau Bar Assn. (plaintiff roundtable 1988—), Great Neck Lawyers Assn. (past pres., chmn. bd.). Avocation: marathon running. Office: Samanowitz & Endzweig 98 Cuttermill Rd Great Neck NY 11021-3006

SAMARTINI, JAMES ROGERS, retired appliance company executive; b. Cleve., Apr. 13, 1935; s. Leonard Henry and Grace Rogers (Tully) S.; m. Irene Ann Kurnava, Sept. 16, 1961 (dec. June 1994); children: David L., James F., Patrick R. AB, Dartmouth Coll., 1957; MBA, Harvard U., 1961. Fin. supr. Ford Motor Co., Dearborn, Mich., 1966-72; v.p. fin. and adminstrn. Thonet Industries Inc., York, Pa., 1972-74; asst. controller Mead Corp., Dayton, 1974-78, assoc. treas., 1974-78, 1978-79, v.p. fin. resources, 1982-86, v.p., chief fin. officer, 1986-91; exec. v.p., chief adminstrv. officer Whirlpool Corp., Benton Harbor, Mich., 1986-95; ret., 1995; bd. dirs. Peoples State Bank, St. Joseph, Mich. Chmn. bd. trustees Whirlpool Found., 1993-95; trustee Dayton Opera Assn., 1977-86, pres., 1985-86; mem. adv. bd. Salvation Army; bd. dirs. Epilepsy Assn. Western Ohio, 1986, S.W. Mich. Symphony Orch., 1991-93. Mem. Fin. Execs. Inst. (dir. 1983-86). Home: 173 Crossridge Dr Kettering OH 45429

SAMBURG, A. GENE, security company executive; b. Indpls., Apr. 25, 1941; s. A. George and Hermine (Wittgenstein) S.; m. Lorrie Silverman, June 26, 1966; children: Kimberly Jill, Thomas Blair. BEE, Cornell U., 1964; OPM, Harvard U., 1985. Engr. Westinghouse Corp., 1964-72; founder, pres. and CEO Kastle Systems, Inc., 1972—; adv. on bus. programs Cornell U.; spl. lectr. for numerous profl. and ednl. courses in field. Patentee in field. Mem. IEEE, ASME, CPP, Am. Soc. Indsl. Security, Woodmont Country Club, City Club (Washington), Tower Club (McLean, Va.). Home: 1206 Stable Gate Ct Mc Lean VA 22102 Office: Kastle Systems Inc 1501 Wilson Blvd Arlington VA 22209

SAMEK, MICHAEL JOHANN, corporation executive; b. Vienna, Austria, Feb. 26, 1920; came to U.S., 1939; s. Berthold and Leontine (Bruell) S.; m. Edith Raymond, Apr. 1948 (div. 1961); m. Stacy Graham, Dec. 20, 1964 (div. 1974). B.S., Vienna, 1938; postgrad., Columbia U., 1949-51. Pres. Computech Inc., N.Y.C., 1956-60; v.p. Data Systems ITT, Paramus, N.J., 1961-64; mgr. dir. internat. Auerbach Corp., Europe and U.S., 1964-69; v.p. Celanese Corp., N.Y.C., 1969-83; pres. Primary Care Software Inc., Riverhead, N.Y., 1987—; chmn. Am. Mgmt. Assn. Info. Systems and Tech. Council, 1960-83; chmn. adv. com. on data processing City of N.Y., 1963—. Served to lt. col. USAF, 1941-45, ETO. Mem. AAAS, AIAA, Assn. Computing Machinery, N.Y. Acad. Scis.

SAMENT, SIDNEY, neurologist; b. Zagaré, Lithuania, Apr. 25, 1928; came to the U.S., 1964; s. Bernard and Mina Sament; children: Hilary, David, Brian. MB, BCh, Witwatersrand U., 1952. Intern Baragwanath Hosp., Johannesburg, 1953-55, resident, 1955-60; postgrad. tng. various hosps., Great Britain, 1960-64; resident in neurology Jersey City Med. Ctr., 1964-65, New Eng. Med. Ctr., Boston, 1965-67; EEG fellow, asst. in enurology Mass. Gen. Hosp., Boston, 1967-69; in charge EEG Lab. VA Hosp., Boston, 1969-70; asst. prof. neurology Hahnemann Hosp., Phila., 1970-73; pvt. practice Easton, Pa., 1973-88, Visalia, Calif., 1988—. Mem. Calif. Med. Soc. Office: 204 N Floral St Visalia CA 93291-4957

SAMEROFF, ARNOLD JOSHUA, developmental psychologist, educator, research scientist; b. N.Y.C., Apr. 20, 1937; s. Stanley and Zeena (Shapiro) S.; m. Susan C. McDonough, Jan. 2, 1982; children: Shira, Rebecca, Crista, Andrew. BS, U. Mich., 1961; PhD, Yale U., 1965; MA (hon.), Brown U., 1987. Asst. prof. psychology, pediatrics and psychiatry U. Rochester, 1967-70, assoc. prof., 1970-73, prof., 1973-78, dir. developmental psychology tng. program, 1975-78; prof. psychology U. Ill., Chgo., 1978-86, assoc. dir. Inst. for Study Developmental Disabilities, 1978-86; assoc. dir., dir. rsch. Ill. Inst. for Developmental Disabilities, Ill. Dept. Mental Health and Developmental Disabilities, 1978-86; prof. psychiatry and human behavior Brown U., Providence, 1986-92; dir. Developmental Psychopathology Rsch. Ctr., Bradley Hosp., East Providence, 1986-92; prof. psychology, rsch. scientist Ctr. for Human Growth and Devel., U. Mich., Ann Arbor, 1992—; vis. prof. psychology Birkbeck Coll., U. London, 1974-75; vis. scientist Ctr. for Interdisciplinary Rsch., U. Bielefeld, Fed. Republic Germany, 1977-78; W.T. Grant Found. lectr. Soc. for Behavioral Pediatrics, 1984; dir. Summer Inst. on Human Devel. and Psychopathology, Ctr. for Advanced Study in Behavioral Scis., Stanford, Calif., 1989; mem. small grants adv. com. NIH, 1977-81, behavioral scis. assessment panel, 1987-88; mem. organizational planning com. Internat. Conf. for Infant Studies, 1980-84. Editor: (with R.N. Emde) Relationship Disturbances in Early Childhood: A Developmental Approach, 1989, (with F. Kessel and M. Bornstein) Contemporary Constructions of the Child: Essays in Honor of William Kessen, 1991, (with M. Haith) The Five to Seven Year Shift, 1996; also monographs; mem. editl. bds. Devel. and Psychopathology, 1988-94, Jour. Devel. and Behavioral Pediatrics, 1989-93, Jour. Family Psychology, 1990-91, others. Mem. social and behavioral scis. rsch. adv. com. March of Dimes Birth Defects Found., 1977-94, rsch. adv. com. Little City Found., 1986-88; bd. dirs. Nat. Ctr. for Clin. Infant Programs, 1986—; mem. program on successful adolescent devel. among youth in high-risk settings John D. and Catherine T. MacArthur Found., 1986-95, network on early childhood transitions, 1989-92. GE fellow Yale U., 1961; NIMH predoctoral rsch. fellow Yale U., 1962, NIMH postdoctoral rsch. fellow, 1965-67, Ctr. for Advanced Study in Behavioral Scis. fellow Stanford U., 1984-85. Fellow AAAS, Am. Acad. Mental Retardation, Am. Psychol. Soc., Devel. Psychology and Mental Retardation divsn. Am. Psychol. Assn. (mem. program com. devel. psychology divsn. 1978-90, chair 1979, mem. coun. 1980-83, mem.-at-large exec. com. 1985-88, pres. devel. psychology divsn. 1995-96, NIMH Rsch. Scientist award 1994—); mem. AAUP, Soc. for Rsch. in Child Devel. (com. on summer insts. and study groups 1985-88), World Assn. Infant Mental Health, Internat. Soc. for Infant Studies, Soc. for Rsch. on Adolescence.

SAMERS, BERNARD NORMAN, fund raising organization executive; b. N.Y.C., Jan. 25, 1934; s. Abraham and Edith (Slomack) S.; m. Edith Maralyn Rosenblum, Sept. 7, 1958; children: Audrey Meryl, Michael Eric, William David. BS, Queens Coll., 1956; BSIE, Columbia U., 1956; MBA, Harvard U., 1958; Profl. Indsl. Engr., Columbia U., 1968. Registered profl. engr., Calif; Cer: CFRE. Cons. S.B. Littauer & Assocs., N.Y.C., 1956; asst. dir. spl. studies Hudson Pulp & Paper Corp., N.Y.C., 1957; sr. mgmt. scientist Dunlap & Assocs., Inc., Darien, Conn., 1958-66; v.p. Cooper & Co., Mgmt. Cons., Stamford, Conn., 1966-82; v.p. adminstrn. and regional ops. Am. Technion Soc., N.Y.C., 1982-86; exec. v.p. Am. Com. for the Weizmann Inst. of Sci., N.Y.C., 1986—; adj. asst. prof. mgmt. engring. U. Bridgeport, 1972-88; lectr. MBA program U. Conn., 1980-82. Pres. Jewish Edn. in media, N.Y.C., 1978—, United Jewish Fedn. of Stamford, 1978-79; dir. Coun. of Jewish Fedn., 1979-80; committeeman Dem. City Com., Stamford, 1980-82. Mem. Nat. Assn. Fund Raising Execs., Assn. Jewish Community Orgn. Pers., Ops. Rsch. Soc. of Am. Democrat. jewish. Avocation: abstract painting. Home: 180 Big Oak Rd Stamford CT 06903-4608 Office: Am Com Weizmann Inst Sci 51 Madison Ave New York NY 10010-1603

SAMET, ANDREW, government official; b. Boston, June 29, 1957; s. Theodore S. and Elaine S. (Sloane) S.; m. Kennari S. Sargent, May 10, 1986; children: Daniel Jeremy, Hanna Gabrielle. BA, Carleton Univ., 1978; MA, Carleton U., Ottawa, Ont., Can., 1981; JD, Georgetown U., 1983. Bar: D.C. Assoc. Chapman, Duff and Paul, Washington, 1983-85, Mudge Rose Guthrie Alexander & Ferdon, Washington, 1985-87; legis. counsel. Senator Daniel P. Moynihan, Washington, 1987-89, legis. dir., 1989-93; assoc. dep. under sec. for internat. affairs Dept. Labor, Washington, 1993—. Editor: Human Rights Law and Reagan Adminstration, 1984, The U.S.-Israel Free Trade Area Agreement, 1989; contbr. articles to profl. jours. Democrat. Jewish. Office: Dept of Labor Internat Labor Affairs 200 Constitution Ave NW Washington DC 20210-0001

SAMET, DEAN HENRY, safety engineer; b. Elgin, Ill., Mar. 22, 1947; s. Henry Ralph and Ardella Mary (Schiebel) S.; m. Karen Rae Meyer, Feb. 11, 1979; children: Chris, Lisa, Sean. AAS, Elgin C.C., 1972; BS in Engring. Tech., So. Ill. U., 1974. Cert. engring. technologist Nat. Inst. Cert. in Engring. Tech.; cert. healthcare safety profl. Internat. Healthcare Safety Profl. Cert. Bd.; assoc. safety profl. Bd. Cert. Safety Profls. Project engr. McBro Planning & Devel. Co., Grand Island, Nebr., 1974-78; field constrn. engr. Arabian Am. Oil Co., Dhahran, Saudi Arabia, 1978-79; project engr. McCarthy Co., Jeddah, Saudi Arabia, 1979-81; sr. project engr. Univ. Mech., Riyadh, Saudi Arabia, 1981-82; staff engr. Joint Commn., Chgo., 1983-85; chief mech. cons. engr. Architects Collaborative, Baghdad, Iraq, 1985; codes and stds. engr. King Faisal Specialist Hosp., Riyadh, 1985-89; assoc. dir. Joint Commn., Oakbrook Terrace, Ill., 1989—; mem. architecture for health com. AIA, Washington, 1983-85. Co-author: Plant, Technology and Safety Management Handbook, 1985, The 1996 KIPS Survey Guide, 1996. Staff sgt. USAF, 1966-69. Mem. Am. Soc. Hosp. Engring., Nat. Fire Protection Assn., Tenn. Squires Assn. Avocation: playing guitar. Office: Joint Commn 1 Renaissance Blvd Oakbrook Terrace IL 60181-4294

SAMET, JACK I., lawyer; b. N.Y.C., Aug. 6, 1940; s. William and Tillie (Katz) S.; m. Helen Ray, Feb. 12, 1967; 1 son, Peter Lawrence. BA, Columbia U., 1961; JD, Harvard U., 1964. Bar: N.Y. 1964, Calif. 1973. Assoc. Whitman & Ransom, N.Y.C., 1966-69, Hall, Casey, Dickler & Howley, N.Y.C., 1969-73; ptnr. Ball, Hunt, Hart, Brown & Baerwitz, L.A., 1973-81, Buchalter, Nemer, Fields & Younger, L.A., 1981-94, Baker & Hostetler, L.A., 1994—; arbitrator Nat. Assn. Securities Dealers, L.A., 1976—; speaker, panelist Calif. Continuing Edn. of Bar, 1988. Mem. ABA, Sports Club/L.A. Avocations: exercise, reading. Home: 2741 Aqua Verde Cir Los Angeles CA 90077-1502 Office: Baker & Hostetler 600 Wilshire Blvd 12th Fl Los Angeles CA 90017

SAMET, KENNETH ALAN, hospital administrator; b. Bklyn., Mar. 17, 1958; married. BA, Old Dominion U., 1990; MA, U. Mich., 1982. Adminstrv. intern Mt. Vernon Hosp., Fairfax, Va., 1981; adminstrv. resident Washington Hosp. Ctr., 1982-83, pres., 1991—; asst. to pres. Washington Health Care Corp., 1983-85, dir. system devel., 1985-86; v.p. system devel. Medlantic Health Care Group, Washington, 1986-88, exec. v.p. systems, bus. devel., 1988-91; pres. Medlantic Enterprises, Washington, 1988-91. Mem. D.C. Hosp. Assn., Md. Hosp. Assn., Va. Hosp. Assn. (bd. dirs.). Home: 9041 Holly Leaf Ln Bethesda MD 20817-2657 Office: Washington Hosp Ctr 110 Irving St NW Washington DC 20010-2931*

SAMFORD, THOMAS DRAKE, III, lawyer; b. Opelika, Ala., Mar. 4, 1934; s. Thomas Drake and Aileen (Maxwell) S., Jr.; m. Jacqueline Screws, June 7, 1955; children: Thomas Drake IV, Jacquelyn, Robert Maxwell, Richard Drake. A.B. magna cum laude, Princeton U., 1955; J.D., U. Ala., 1961. Bar: Ala. 1961. Owner firm Samford & Samford, 1961-88; judge Mcpl. Ct., Opelika, 1961-88; mem. Ala. Permanent Jud. Commn., 1979-83; gen. counsel Auburn U., 1965-95, gen. counsel emeritus, 1995—; lectr. Ala. Law Inst., 1969, Am. Judicature Soc., 1969—. Editor-in-chief: Ala. Law Rev, 1960-61. Dir., bd. trustees Opelika Comty. Chest, 1965-68, pres., 1966-67; bd. dirs. U. Ala. Law Sch. Found., Jr. Achievement Chattahoochee-Lee; elder Presbyn. ch., 1974-94, Meth. ch., 1994—. Recipient John G. Buchanan prize politics, 1955; Farrah, Order Jurisprudence U. Ala., 1956; named one of four Outstanding Young Men in Ala. Jr. C. of C., 1967. Mem. Opelika C. of C. (dir. 1967, pres. 1968), ABA, Lee County Bar Assn. (pres. 1965), Ala. State Bar, U. Ala. Nat. Alumni Assn. (pres. 1966-67), Phi Beta Kappa, Alpha Tau Omega, Phi Delta Phi, Omicron Delta Kappa. Lodge: Kiwanis (bd. dirs. 1966-67, pres. 1969-70). Home: 805 Ridgewood Ct Opelika AL 36801-3525 Office: Auburn Univ Off Gen Counsel 101 Samford Ave Auburn AL 36830-7415

SAMFORD, YETTA GLENN, JR., lawyer; b. Opelika, Ala., June 8, 1923; s. Yetta Glenn and Mary Elizabeth (Denson) S.; m. Mary Austill, Sept. 6, 1949; children: Mary Austill Lott, Katherine Park Alford, Yetta Glenn III (dec.). BS, Ala. Poly. Inst., 1947; LLB, U. Ala., 1949, LLD (hon.), 1995. Bar: Ala. 1949, U.S. Dist. Ct. (mid. dist.) Ala. 1950, U.S. Ct. Appeals (5th cir.) 1961, U.S. Ct. Appeals (11th cir.) 1981. Since practiced in Opelika; ptnr. Samford, Denson, Horsley, Pettey & Martin (and predecessors), 1949—; mem. Ala. Senate from Lee and Russell counties, 1958-62; bd. dirs. Torchmark Corp., Farmers Nat. Bank Opelika; mem. State of Ala. Bd. of Corrections, 1969-75; mem. adv. bd. State Docks, 1987—. Trustee U. Mobile, 1963-92, life trustee, 1992—, trustee U. Ala., 1972-93, trustee emeritus, 1993—. Mem. Ala. Law Inst. Council (exec. com., v.p.), Ala. Acad. of Honor, Phi Delta Phi, Omicron Delta Kappa, Alpha Tau Omega. Republican. Baptist. Lodge: Masons. Home: 615 Terracewood Dr Opelika AL 36801-3850 Office: Samford Denson Horsley Pettey & Martin PO Box 2345 Opelika AL 36803-2345

SAMII, ABDOL HOSSEIN, physician, educator; b. Rasht, Iran, June 20, 1930; came to U.S., 1947; s. Mehdi Ebtehaj and Zahra (Mojdehi-Akbar) S.; m. Shahla Khosrowshahi; children: Ali, Golnaz. Student, Stanford U., 1947-49; BA, UCLA, 1950, MA, 1952; MD, Cornell U., 1956. Intern N.Y. Hosp., N.Y.C., 1956, asst. in medicine, 1956-58; asst. in physiology Cornell U. Med. Sch., N.Y.C., 1958-59; resident and sr. resident N.Y. Hosp., Peter Bent Brigham Hosp. and Mass. Gen. Hosp., Boston, 1959-61; adj. prof. medicine Cornell U. Med. Sch., 1973-79, prof. clin. medicine, 1979—; rsch. fellow Harvard U., Boston, 1959-60; prof. medicine Nat. Univ. Iran, Tehran, 1963-68; med. dir. Pars Hosp., Tehran, 1968-73; dir. div. medicine N.Y. Hosp.-Cornell Med. Coll., White Plains, 1979—; chancellor Reza Shah Kabir Grad. Univ., Tehran, 1973-78; cons. med. rsch. WHO, Geneva, 1973-79; v.p. Imperial Acad. Sci., Tehran, 1974-78. Gen. editor: International Textbook of Medicine, 1981; author, editor: Medical Clinics of North America, 1983, Textbook of Diagnostic Medicine, 1987. Dep. minister, Ministry of Health, Tehran, 1963-65; minister, Ministry Sci. and Higher Edn., Tehran, 1973-75. Fellow Rockefeller Found., Helen Hay Whitney Found. Fellow Royal Soc. of Medicine; mem. N.Y. Acad. Medicine, Harvey Soc., Internat. Soc. Nephrology, Am. Fed. Clin. Rsch. Avocations: music, antiques. Office: NY Hosp CMC WD 21 Bloomingdale Rd White Plains NY 10605-1504 also: 14 E 63d St New York City NY 10021

SAMINSKY, ROBERT L., lawyer; b. N.Y.C., Nov. 4, 1947; s. Hyman L. and Beatrice (Shatzkin) S.; m. Nancy Ann Epstein, Jan. 23, 1971; 1 son, Heath. BBA, Hofstra U., 1969; MS, CUNY, 1971; JD, St. John's U., Jamaica, N.Y., 1975. Bar: N.Y. 1976. Trial atty. criminal div. N.Y.C. Legal Aid Soc., 1976-77; assoc. Fischer Bros., N.Y.C., 1977-78; ptnr. Brecher, Fishman, Feit, Heller, Rubin, & Tannenbaum, P.C., Hauppauge, 1978—; guest lectr. Suffolk County Acad. of Law, 1989; lectr. N.Y. State Chiropractic Soc., 1992—. Mem. med. authorizations com. N.Y. Worker's Compensation Bd., 1989—. Editor John's Law Sch. Labor Law Jour., 1974. Assoc. Urban Tchr. Corps, N.Y.C., 1970. Mem. Suffolk County Bar Assn., N.Y. State Workers Compensation Bar Assn., N.Y. County Bar Assn., N.Y. State Bar Assn., N.Y. State Trial Lawyers Assn. (community lecturer program 1989—) Labor Law Soc. (v.p. St. Johns Law Sch. chpt. 1974), Lions, Phi Delta Phi. Home: 24 Eva Ln Plainview NY 11803-3015 Office: Brecher Fishman Feit Heller Rubin & Tannenbaum 235 Brooksite Dr Hauppauge NY 11788

SAMIOS, NICHOLAS PETER, physicist; b. N.Y.C., Mar. 15, 1932; s. Peter and Niki (Vatick) S.; m. Mary Linakis, Jan. 12, 1958; children: Peter, Gregory, Alexandra. AB, Columbia U., 1953, PhD, 1957. Instr. physics Columbia U., N.Y.C., 1956-59; asst. physicist Brookhaven Nat. Lab., Upton, N.Y., 1959-62, assoc. physicist, 1962-64, physicist, 1964-68, sr. physicist, 1968—, group leader, 1965-75, chmn. dept. physics, 1975-81, dep. dir. for high energy and nuclear physics, 1981, dir., 1982—; adj. prof. Stevens Inst. Tech., 1969-75, Columbia U., 1970—. Contbr. articles in field to profl. jours. Bd. dirs. Stony Brook Found., 1989, L.I. Assn., 1990, Adelphi U., 1989. Recipient E.O. Lawrence Meml. award, 1980, award in physics and math. scis. N.Y. Acad. Scis., 1980; named AUI Disting. Scientist, 1992, W.K.H. Panofsky prize, 1993. Fellow Am. Phys. Soc. (chmn. divsn. of particles and fields 1975-76, chmn. PEP exptl. program com. 1976-78); mem. Internat. Ctr. Future Acceleration, Akademia Athenon (corr.). Achievements include being an expert in field of high energy particle and nuclear physics. Office: Brookhaven Nat Lab Office of Dir Upton NY 11973

SAMMAN, GEORGE, obstetrician, gynecologist; b. Syria, Dec. 12, 1946; came to U.S., 1971; naturalized, 1981; s. Nicolaki and Antoinette (Charaoui) S.; M.D., Damascus U., 1971; m. Husn Massouh, July 4, 1971; children—Fadi, Luna Miriam. Intern, Washington Hosp. Center, 1971-72, resident in ob-gyn., 1972-75, mem. hosp. staff, 1975—, vice chmn. dept. gynecology, 1980, teaching faculty, 1985-88; practice medicine specializing in ob-gyn, Washington, 1975—, Fairfax, Va., 1980—; mem. staff Providence Hosp., 1975—, Columbia Hosp. for Women. Recipient Best Teaching award Washington Hosp. Ctr., 1985, 88. Diplomate Am. Bd. Ob-Gyn. Fellow Am. Coll. Obstetricians and Gynecologists, Am. Fertility Assn.; mem. Med. Soc. D.C. (maternal health com. 1978-80). Melkite Catholic. Home: 10400 Bit & Spur Ln Potomac MD 20854 Office: 2021 K St NWNW Washington DC 20006-2104

SAMMARCO, PAUL WILLIAM, ecologist; b. Hackensack, N.J., Oct. 18, 1948; s. Giacomo and Esther (Galanti) S.; m. Jean Sogioka, May 29, 1971; children: Mimi Cecile, Dustin Paul, Jack Isao. BA, Syracuse U., 1970, postgrad., 1970-71; cert. Marine Biology Lab., Woods Hole, Mass., 1971, Fairleigh Dickinson U. W.I. Lab., U.S. V.I., 1972; PhD, SUNY-Stony Brook, 1977. Teaching asst. Syracuse (N.Y.) U., 1970-71, Discovery Bay Marine Lab., SUNY-Stony Brook Overseas Acad. Program, Jamaica, 1974, SUNY-Stony Brook, 1971-77; asst. prof. Clarkson U., Potsdam, N.Y., 1977-79; vis. asst. prof. tropical ecology, in St. Croix, V.I., SUNY-Potsdam, 1979; sr. rsch. scientist Australian Inst. Marine Sci., Townsville, Queensland, 1979-89, coord. Shelf Seas Rsch. Program 1985-86; dir. environ. rsch. of Resource Assessment Commn. Prime Minister's commn. on natural resources, Canberra, Australia, 1989-91; exec. dir. La. Univs. Marine Consortium, Chauvin, 1991-95, prof., 1995—; dir. inter-univ. seminar program Assn. Colls. St. Lawrence Valley, Potsdam, 1977-79; adj. prof. La. State U., U. So. La., U. New Orleans, Nicholls State U. Composer ballads, sacred music; former mem. Australian Chamber Choir, Wesley Choir, Canberra; editor (with M.L. Heron) The Bio-Physics of Marine Larval Dispersal, 1994; contbr. numerous articles to profl. jours.; editorial advisor Marine Ecology Progress Series, 1985-93; co-editor Proceedings Inaugural Great Barrier Conf., 1983, Proceedings 6th Internat. Coral Reef Symposium, 1988, Proceedings 8th Internat. Coral Reef Symposium. Recipient Internat. Sci. Exch. award, 1988-89. Mem. chancel choir First United Meth. Ch., Houma, La. Mem. Australian Marine Scis. Assn. (keynote speaker 1981, counselor 1984-89, chmn., organizer nat. conf. 1987, chmn. Australia Acad. Sci. Boden Conf. 1990), Internat. Soc. Reef Studies, Australian Coral Reef Soc., Australasian Performing Rights Assn., Sigma Xi. Democrat. Methodist. Home: 205 Midland Dr Houma LA 70360-6231 Office: La Univs Marine Consortium 8124 Hwy 56 Chauvin LA 70344-2110

SAMMOND, JOHN STOWELL, lawyer; b. Milw., Dec. 27, 1928; s. C. Frederic and Marie (Freitag) S.; m. Cynthia Miller, Feb. 13, 1951 (dec. Dec. 1992); m. Diana Denholm, July 1995; children: Frederic, Christopher, Nicholas, Timothy. BA, Yale U., 1950; SJD, Harvard U., 1955. Bar: Wis. 1955, Fla. 1969, D.C. 1972, Fla. Supreme Ct. as Cir. Ct. mediator, 1990. Assoc. predecessor firm to Quarles & Brady, Milw., 1955-60; ptnr. Quarles & Brady (and predecessor firms), Milw., 1961—, Quarles & Brady, West Palm Beach, Fla., 1969—; bd. dirs. Medalist Industries Inc., Milw., Associated Commerce Bank, Milw., Tropical Plant Rentals Inc., Riverwoods, Ill., Kelley Co. Inc., Milw., others. Bd. dirs., officer Univ. Sch., Milw., Lakeside Children's Ctr., Milw., Palm Beach Habilitation Ctr., Lake Worth, Fla.; sr. warden Christ Episcopal Ch., Whitefish Bay, Wis. Maj. USMCR, 1948-63. Mem. ABA, Wis. Bar Assn., Milw. Bar Assn., Fla. Bar Assn., Palm Beach County Bar Assn., D.C. Bar Assn., Bath and Tennis Club (Palm Beach), Everglades Club (Palm Beach), Milw. Country Club, Milw. Club, Governor's Club (Palm Beach). Republican. Office: Quarles & Brady PO Box 3188 West Palm Beach FL 33402-3188 also: Quarles & Brady 411 E Wisconsin Ave Milwaukee WI 53202-4409

SAMMONS, ELAINE D., corporate executive. Chmn. Sammons Enterprises, Inc., Dallas. Office: Sammons Enterprises Inc 300 Crescent Ave Ste 700 Dallas TX 75201*

SAMMONS, JEFFREY LEONARD, foreign language educator; b. Cleve., Nov. 9, 1936; s. Harold Leonard and Therese (Herrmann) S.; m. Kathryn Josephine Stella, July 1958 (div. 1962); children: Rebecca Kathryn; m. Christa Ann Smith, Oct. 20, 1967; children: Charles Leonard, Harold Hawthorne, Benjamin Gardner. BA, Yale U., 1958, PhD, 1962. Instr., asst. prof. Brown U., Providence, 1961-64; asst. prof. German, Yale U., 1964-67, assoc. prof., 1967-69, prof., 1969—, Leavenworth prof. German, 1979—; mem. editl. bd. Arbitrium, Munich, 1980-87, Mich. Germanic Studies, 1985—. Author: Heinrich Heine: The Elusive Poet, 1969; Six Essays on the Young German Novel, 1972; Literary Sociology and Practical Criticism, 1977; Heinrich Heine: A Modern Biography, 1979, Wilhelm Raabe: The Fiction of the Alternative Community, 1987, The Shifting Fortunes of Wilhelm Raabe, 1992. Guggenheim fellow, 1972-73; Am. Council Learned Socs. fellow, 1977-78, travel grantee, 1983; Duke August Library, Wolfenbuttel Ger. adoptive stipend, 1983. Mem. MLA, Am. Assn. Tchrs. German, Lessing Soc., Goethe Soc. N.Am., Conn. Acad. Arts and Scis., Heinrich-Heine Gesellschaft. Home: 211 Highland St New Haven CT 06511 Office: Yale U Dept German PO Box 208210 New Haven CT 06520-8210

SAMO, AMANDO, bishop; b. Moch Island, Federated States of Micronesia, Aug. 16, 1948; s. Benito and Esiper Samo. BA in Psychology, Chaminade U., 1973; diploma in religious edn., EAPI, Manila, Philippines, 1982. Ordained priest Roman Cath. Ch. Parish priest Cath. Ch., Truk, Federated States of Micronesia, 1977-87; bishop Diocese of the Carolines and Marshalls, Truk, 1987—; founder, bd. dirs. Marriage Encounter-Carolines-Marshalls, Truk, 1982-88; dir. ch. leadership tng. programs, Truk, 1986—; mem. Bishop's Conf. Oceania, 1988, pontificial commn. Cor Unum, Rome, 1995. Chmn. Bishop's commn. justice and devel., 1995. Home: PO Box 250, Chuuk Federated States Micronesia Office: Diocese Caroline Is, PO Box 202, Chuuk Federated States Micronesia

SAMOJLIK, EUGENIUSZ, administrator, medical educator; b. Kuchmy-Bialystok, Poland, Aug. 20, 1933; s. Michael and Anastazia S.; m. Anna Morozewicz, Apr. 10, 1965; children: Dorothy, Michael. BS in Biomedicine, U. Warsaw, 1958, PhD in Reproductive Endocrinology, 1964. Rsch. asst. Maternity Inst. Dept. Pharmacology, Warsaw, 1958-62, sr. asst., 1962-66; asst. prof., chief reproductive pharmacology & toxicology Inst. Pharmacy Dept. Pharmacology, Warsaw, 1966-70; assoc. prof., chief hormone rsch. lab. Med. Acad. Dept. Clin. Endocrinology, Warsaw, 1970-73; staff researcher II Syntex, Inc. Rsch. Divsn., Palo Alto, Calif., 1974-75; asst. prof. physiology, dir. radioimmunoassay lab. Milton S. Hershey (Pa.) Med. Ctr., Divsn. Endocrinology, 1975-80; staff endocrinologist VA Med. Ctr. Dept. Medicine, Sect. Endocrinology, East Orange, N.J., 1980-82; dir. endocrine lab. Newark Beth Israel Med. Ctr., Dept. Medicine, 1982-92; assoc. prof. medicine U. Medicine & Dentistry-N.J. Med. Sch., Newark, 1982—; chief endocrine lab. dept. Labs. NBIMC, 1994-96; vis. researcher UCLA Sch. Medicine, Torrance, Calif., 1973; vis. scientist Nat. Inst. Child Health Human Devel., Reproductive Br., Bethesda, Md., 1973-74; lectr. in field. Mem. internat. adv. bd. Jour. Assisted Reproductive Tech. and Andrology, mem. editorial bd., 1996; contbr. articles to profl. jours. Grantee WHO, 1973-74, Ciba-Geigy, 1982-83, Nat. Cancer Inst., 1983-86, 85-88; tng. program fellow Worcester Found. Experimental Biology, Shrewsbury, Mass., 1967-69. Mem. Am. Soc. Andrology, Am. Assn. Clin. Chemistry, Nat. Acad. Clin. Biochemistry, Acad. Medicine N.J., Endocrine Soc. Home: 73 Sykes Ave Livingston NJ 07039-1318 Office: Newark Beth Israel Med Ctr Endocrine Lab Newark NJ 07112

SAMOLE, MYRON MICHAEL, lawyer, management consultant; b. Chgo., Nov. 29, 1943; s. Harry Lionel and Bess Miriam (Siegel) S.; m. Sandra Rita Port, Feb. 2, 1967; children—Stacey Ann, Karen Lynn, Rena Mara, David Aaron. Student U. Ill., 1962-65; J.D., DePaul U., 1967; postgrad. John Marshall Lawyers Inst., 1967-69. Bar: Ill. 1967, U.S. Dist. Ct. (no. dist.) Ill. 1968, U.S. Dist. Ct. (so. dist.) Fla. 1989, U.S. Ct. Appeals (7th cir.) 1968, Fla. 1981. Pvt. practice, Chgo., 1967-79, Miami, Fla., 1981—; chmn. bd. Fidelity Electronics and subs., Miami, 1969-83; pres. Fidelity Hearing Instruments, Miami, 1984-86, Samole Enterprises, Inc., Miami, 1986—, Fla. Citrus Tower, Inc., Clermont, 1986—; bd. dirs. Enterprise Bank Fla., Miami, 1985-89, The Sports Collection, Inc., Miami, 1987-94; Bd. dirs. South Dade Greater Miami Jewish Fedn., Young Israel of Kendall, Anshe Emes Congregation. Jewish Vocat. Service scholar U. Ill., Champaign, 1962-65. Mem. ABA, Chgo. Bar Assn., Ill. State Bar Assn., Fla. Bar Assn., Kendall Bar Assn., Dade County Bar Assn., Ill. Trial Lawyers Assn., Miami C. of C., Phi Alpha Delta. Democrat. Lodges: Masons, Shriners. Office: 9700 S Dixie Hwy Ste 1030 Miami FL 33156-2865

SAMOUR, CARLOS MIGUEL, chemist. BA in Chemistry, Am. U. Beirut, 1942, MA, 1944; MS in Organic Chemistry, MIT, 1947; PhD, Boston U., 1950. Postdoctoral rsch. fellow Boston U., 1950-52; rsch. chemist The Kendall Co., 1952-57, dir. Theodore Clark Lab., 1957-73, dir. Lexington Rsch. Lab., 1973-81; pres. Samour Assocs., 1981-84; chmn., scientific dir. MacroChem Corp., Lexington, Mass., 1982—; section chmn. Internat. Union Pure and Applied Chemistry, U. Mass., Amherst, 1982; session chmn. Biomaterials, Sardinia, Italy, 1988, internat. conf. MIT, 1982, tech. advisor; pres., chmn. Augusta Epilepsy Rsch. Found., Washington, 1989—; advisor univs. and med. ctrs. Contbr. numerous articles to profl. jours. Mem. Am. Chem. Soc. (cert. merit 1981, adminstr. Kendall award 1964-83), Am. Assn. Pharm. Scis., Controlled Release Soc. Achievements include over 50 U.S. patents and over 200 foreign patents; research in the fields of polymer chemistry, bio-materials, pharmaceuticals, dental materials and transdermal drug delivery systems. Office: Macrochem Corp 110 Hartwell Ave Lexington MA 02173-3134

SAMPAS, DOROTHY M., government official; b. Washington, Aug. 24, 1933; d. Lawrence and Anna Cornelia (Henkel) Myers; m. James George Sampas, Dec. 8, 1962; children: George, Lawrence James. AB, U. Mich., 1955; postgrad., U. Paris, 1955-56; PhD, Georgetown U., 1970; cert., Nat. War Coll., Washington, 1987, Naval Post Grad. Sch., 1993. With Bur. Pub. Affairs Dept. State, Washington, 1958-60, analyst Bur. of Adminstrn., 1973-75, div. chief, dep. chief Office of Position and Pay Mgmt., 1979-83, div. chief Office of Mgmt., 1983-84, dir. Office of Mgmt., 1984-86; vice consul Am. Consulate Gen., Hamburg, Fed. Republic Germany, 1960-62; cons. Trans Century Corp., Washington, 1972; gen. svcs. officer Am. Embassy, Brussels, 1975-79; embassy minister-counselor Am. Embassy, Beijing, 1987-90; minister-counselor U.S. Mission to UN, N.Y.C., 1991-94; Am. ambassador to Islamic Republic of Mauritania, 1994—. Presbyterian. Home: 4715 Trent Ct Chevy Chase MD 20815-5516 Office: Am Embassy Nouakchott Dept State Washington DC 20521-2430 also: Am Embassy, Boite Postale 222, Nouakchott Mauritania

SAMPER, JOSEPH PHILLIP, retired photographic products company executive; b. Salt Lake City, Aug. 13, 1934; s. Juan M. and Harriet (Howell) S.; married; children: Joaquin P., Christopher F. With Eastman Kodak Co., Rochester, N.Y., 1961—; asst. to gen. mgr. mktg. div. Eastman Kodak Co. (U.S. and Can. photog. div.), 1976-77; asst. v.p., asst. gen. mgr. mktg. div. Eastman Kodak Co. (U.S. and Can. photographic div.), 1977-79; v.p., gen. mgr. mktg. div. Eastman Kodak Co., 1979—, exec. v.p., gen. mgr. photographic div., 1983-86, vice chmn., exec. officer, 1986-90; chief exec. officer, pres. Kinder-Care Learning Ctrs., Inc., 1990—; pres. Sun Microsystems Computer Co., 1994-95; chmn., CEO Cray Rsch., Inc., Eagan, Minn., 1995—; bd. dirs. Armstrong World Industries, Inc., Lancaster, Pa., Interpub. Group, N.Y.C., Lifetouch, Inc., Mpls., Sylvan LEarning Systems, Inc., Columbia, Md. Mem. adv. bd. U. Calif. Bus. Sch. With USNR, 1952-56. Recipient Alfred Knight award Am. Grad. Sch. Internat. Mgmt., 1961, Barton Kyle Young award, 1961; Sloan fellow, MIT, 1972-73. Roman Catholic.

SAMPLE, ALTHEA MERRITT, secondary education educator, conductor; b. Miami, Fla., Apr. 6, 1937; d. Otis and Alma (Carter) S. BS in Music Edn., Fla. A&M, 1960; Master in Music Edn., U. Miami, 1971. Tchr. elem. music edn. Dade County, Miami, Fla., 1960-65, dir. jr. h.s. orch., 1965-84, dir. orch. sr. h.s., 1984—; dir. orch. Miami Northwestern Performing Arts Ctr., 1984—; clin. tchr. internship program U. Miami, 1988-90; clinician Broward County Orch. Evaluation, 1986, 87; participant workshops in field, 1965—. Coord. North Area Festival, 1988; conducted Supt.'s Honors Orch., 1988, 92, South Area Festival Orch., 1989, tribute Dr. George Bornoff Concert, 1994, Gov. Fla. Inaugural Concert, 1991; performed Nat. Educator Reception, 1993; sponsor Miami Herald Silver Knight Award winners, 1988, 90, 92. Recipient Black Music Achievement award, 1992, Outstanding Educator award U.S. Rep. Dante Fussell, 1992, Area III Tchr. of Yr., Dade County, 1992. Mem. United Tchrs. Dade, Fla. Orch. Assn., Fla. Music Educators, Dade Music Educators, Nat. Alliance Educators, Eta Phi Beta. Democrat. Episcopalian. Avocations: reading, playing flute, violin, organ, tennis. Home: 15720 E Bunche Park Dr Opa Locka FL 33054-2020

SAMPLE, BETTE JEANE, elementary educator; b. Long Beach, Calif., Oct. 20, 1943; d. Dennis Lynn and Norma Dorothy (Ladner) Hart; m. Ronald Charles Sample, Oct. 7, 1967; children: Jennifer Lynne Sample Amend, Leah Anne. BS, Augustana Coll., Sioux Falls, S.D., 1966; MA in Edn., U. Wyo., 1994. Tchr. Whittier Elem. Sch., Colorado Springs, Colo., 1966-67, North Park Elem. Sch., Columbia Heights, Minn., 1967-68; tchr. Gertrude Burns Elem. Sch., Newcastle, Wyo., 1976-88, 2d grade tchr., 1989-90, 1st grade tchr., 1990-96; instr. Ea. Wyo. Coll., Torrington, 1987-96; tchr. English Newcastle Mid. Sch., 1988-89. Grantee Ency. Brittanica, 1991. Mem. NEA, Wyo. Edn. Assn. (Tchr. of Yr. 1991), Newcastle Edn. Assn. Democrat. Lutheran. Home: PO Box 537 Newcastle WY 82701-0537 Office: Gertrude Burns Elem Sch 116 Casper Ave Newcastle WY 82701-2705

SAMPLE, FREDERICK PALMER, former college president; b. Columbia, Pa., May 22, 1930; s. William Walter and Erna Rebecca (Roye) S.; m. Mary Jane Drager, Aug. 19, 1951; children: Jeffrey Lynn, Roger Lee. AB, Lebanon Valley Coll., 1952; MEd, Western Md. Coll., 1956; DEd, Pa. State U., 1968; D in Pedagogy, Albright Coll., 1968. Tchr. Annville (Pa.) High Sch., 1952-53; tchr. Red Lion Area (Pa.) High Sch., 1953-57, prin., 1957-59, supervising prin., 1959-64; supt. Manheim Twp. Sch. Dist., Neffsville, Pa., 1964-68; pres. Lebanon Valley Coll., Annville, Pa., 1968-83; supt. Bellefonte (Pa.) Area Sch. Dist., 1987-92; ednl. cons.; adminstr. Bucknell U., 1985-87. Mem. Phi Delta Kappa. Republican. Home: PO Box 92 Eagles Mere PA 17731-0092 *Despite failures, difficulties, and disappointments I have tried to find the honorable, responsible, productive, true, and humane solutions to problems and make decisions for progress.*

SAMPLE, JOSEPH SCANLON, foundation executive; b. Chgo., Mar. 15, 1923; s. John Glen and Helen (Scanlon) S.; m. Patricia M. Law, Dec. 22, 1942 (div.); children: Michael Scanlon, David Forrest, Patrick Glen; m. Miriam Tyler Willing, Nov. 19, 1965. B.A., Yale U., 1947. Trainee, media analyst, media dir. Dancer-Fitzgerald-Sample, Inc., advt. agy., Chgo., 1947-50; v.p., media dir. Dancer-Fitzgerald-Sample, Inc., advt. agy., 1952-53; pres. Mont. Television Network KTVQ, Billings, KXLF-AM-TV, Butte, Mont., KRTV, Great Falls, Mont., KPAX-TV, Missoula, Mont., 1955-84. Pres. Greater Mont. Found., 1986—; chmn. Wheeler Ctr. Mont State U., 1988—. Served with AUS, 1943-46. With U.S. Army, 1950-52. Mem. Rotary, Yellowstone Country Club, Port Royal Club, Hole in The Wall Golf Club, Hilands Golf Club, Naples Yacht Club. Home: 606 Highland Park Dr Billings MT 59102-1909 Office: 14 N 24th St Billings MT 59101-2422

SAMPLE, NATHANIEL WELSHIRE, architect; b. Phila., Apr. 3, 1918; s. Nathaniel Welshire Jr. and Evelyn Aldrich (Hope) S.; m. Virginia Bogert, May 19, 1945; children: Peter, Gregory, Deborah, Phoebe, Joan. BA, Dartmouth Coll., 1940; BArch, Ill. Inst. Tech., 1946. Registered architect, Wis. Archtl. designer Shaw Naess & Murphey, Chgo., 1946-47; designer Weiler, Strang & Assocs., Madison, Wis., 1947-51; project mgr. Weiler, Strang & Assocs., Madison, 1951-58, ptnr., 1958-62; ptnr. Sample & Mullins, Madison, 1962-67, Sample & Potter, Inc., Madison, 1967-84; v.p. Design for

Tomorrow, Madison, 1956; pres. Dane County U.N. Assn., Madison, 1965-67; archtl. cons. Mass., N.Y., Ill., 1987—. Prin. works include Sch. Design, a Columbus elem. sch., 1953 (honor award), residence of Shorewood Hills, Wis., 1955 (honor award), Chilren's Treatment Ctr., Madison, 1959, Chgo. Pub. Libr. (1st pl. award nat. competition 1970), design for restoration of 120 Yr. old mansion in Madison for Wis. hdqrs. of Urban League (Preservation award Dane County), 1991. Mem. Dane County Regional Plan Commn., 1981-86, Urban Design Commn., Madison, 1990—; bd. dirs. Madison Downtown Sr. Ctr., 1988—. Lt. (j.g.) USNR, 1942-46, PTO. Fellow AIA; mem. Wis. Soc. Architects (chmn. jury housing for homeless competition 1990, Golden award 1992). Democrat. Mem. Soc. of Friends. Avocations: sports, grandchildren, citizenship. Address: 1105 Rutledge St Madison WI 53703-3825

SAMPLE, STEVEN BROWNING, university executive; b. St. Louis, Nov. 29, 1940; s. Howard and Dorothy (Cunningham) S.; m. Kathryn Brunkow, Jan. 28, 1961; children: Michelle Sample Smith, Melissa Ann. BS, U. Ill., 1962, MS, 1963; DHULL (hon.), Canisius Coll., 1989; PhD, U. Ill., 1965; LLD (hon.), U. Sheffield, Eng., 1991; EdD (hon.), Purdue U., 1994; DHL (hon.), Hebrew Union Coll., 1994; DL (hon.), U. Nebr., 1995. Sr. scientist Melpar Inc., Falls Church, Va., 1965-66; assoc. prof. elec. engring. Purdue U., Lafayette, Ind., 1966-73; dep. dir. Ill. Bd. Higher Edn., Springfield, 1971-74; exec. v.p. acad. affairs, dean Grad. Coll., prof. elec. eng. U. Nebr., Lincoln, 1974-82; prof. elec. and computer engring. SUNY, Buffalo, 1982-91, pres., 1982-91; pres. U. So. Calif., L.A., 1991—, prof. elec. engring., 1991—; bd. dirs. Ind., First Interstate Bancorp, L.A., Presley Cos., Newport Beach, Calif., Western Atlas Inc., Beverly Hills, Calif.; vice chmn., bd. dirs. Western N.Y. Tech. Devel. Ctr., Buffalo, 1982-91; chmn. bd. dirs. Calspan-UB Rsch. Ctr., Inc., Buffalo, 1983-91; mem. Calif. Coun. Sci. and Tech., Irvine, Calif.; cons. in field. Contbr. articles to profl. jours.; patentee in field. Timpanist St. Louis Philharm. Orch., 1955-58; chmn. Western N.Y. Regional Econ. Devel. Coun., 1984-91; trustee U. at Buffalo Found., 1982-91, Studio Arena Theatre, Buffalo, 1983-91, Western N.Y. Pub. Broadcasting Assn., 1985-91; bd. dirs. Buffalo Philharm. Orch., 1982-91, Regenstrief Med. Found., Indpls., 1982—, Rsch. Found. SUNY, 1987-91; chmn. Gov.'s Conf. on Sci. and Engring. Edn., Rsch. and Devel., 1989-91; chair Calif. Bus.-Higher Edn. Forum; bd. dirs. L.A. chpt. World Affairs Coun., Hughes Galaxy Inst. Edn., L.A., 1991-94, Rebuild L.A. Com., L.A., Annenberg Metro Project, Coalition of 100 Club of L.A.; trustee L.A. Ednl. Alliance for Restructuring Now. Recipient Disting. Alumnus award Dept. Elec. Engring. U. Ill., 1980, citation award Buffalo Coun. on World Affairs, 1986, Engr. of Yr. award N.Y. State Soc. Profl. Engrs., 1985, Alumni Honor award Coll. Engring., U. Ill., 1985, Outstanding Elec. Engr. award Purdue U., 1993, Humanitarian award Nat. Conf. Christians and Jews, L.A., 1994, Hollzer Meml. award Jewish Fedn. Coun. Greater L.A., 1994; Sloan Found. fellow, 1962-63, NSF grad. fellow, 1963-65, Am. Coun. Edn. fellow Purdue U., 1970-71, NSF. Mem. AAU (chmn. com. on postdoctoral edn. 1994—), IEEE (Outstanding Paper award 1976), Nat. Assn. State Univs. and Land-Grant Colls. (ednl. telecommunications com., 1982-83, chmn. coun. of pres. 1985-86, edn. and tech. com. 1986-87, exec. com. 1987-89), Coun. on Fgn. Rels., Sigma Xi. Episcopalian. Home: 1550 Oak Grove Ave San Marino CA 91108-1108 Office: U So Calif Office of the Pres University Park ADM 110 Los Angeles CA 90089-0012

SAMPLES, RONALD EUGENE, coal company executive; b. Boonville, Ind., Apr. 23, 1926; s. Harold Forest and Hazel Pearl (Grandstaff) S.; student U. Notre Dame, 1944-46; B.S.E.M., N. Mex. Sch. Mines, 1949; m. Virginia Agnes Derr, Feb. 13, 1950; children—Ronald Eugene, II, Rebecca Lee, Thomas Harold, Susan Ann. With Peabody Coal Co., St. Louis, 1949-66, regional chief engr., 1960-66; with Consol. Coal Co., Pitts., 1966-73, 75—, v.p. engring./exploration, 1973, pres., chief operating officer, 1975-77, chmn., chief exec. officer, 1977—; pres. coal and minerals ops. Conoco Inc., 1980—; sr. v.p ops. Amax Coal Co., Indpls., 1973-75, exec. v.p. engring. ops., exploration, purchasing, 1975. Bd. dirs. United Way, Pitts., 1977—, Regional Indsl. Devel. Corp. Southwestern Pa., 1978-79, Allegheny Trails council Boy Scouts Am., 1978-79; mem. sponsoring com. Penn's S.W. Assn., 1978-79; mem. citizen's sponsoring com. Allegheny Conf. on Community Devel., 1978-79; chmn. sect. coal industry, corp. campaign Boys Clubs Am., 1978-80. Served with USN, 1944-46. Registered profl. engr., Ind., Pa., Ky., Mont., N.Mex., Utah; registered profl. land surveyor, Ind., Ky. Recipient Erskine Ramsay Gold medal SMME, 1994. Mem. Pa. Soc. Profl. Engrs., AIME, Nat. Coal Assn. (chmn. bd.). Democrat. Clubs: King Coal, St. Clair Country, Duquesne, Renaissance, Rolling Rock, Laurel Valley Golf, Elks. Office: Arch Mineral Corp 1 Cityplace Dr Ste 3 Saint Louis MO 63141-7065*

SAMPRAS, PETE, tennis player; b. Washington, Aug. 12, 1971; s. Sam and Georgia Sampras. mem. U.S. Davis Cup team., named to Olympic Team Atlanta, 1996. chairman ATP Tour Charities program, 1992. Winner tournaments including Phila., 1990, Manchester, 1990, U.S. Open, 1990, 1993, Grand Slam Cup, 1990, L.A., 1991, Indpls., 1991, Lyon, 1991, IBM/ATP Tour World Championship-Frankfurt, 1991, 94, U.S. Pro Indoor, 1992, Lipton Internat., 1993, Wimbledon, 1993, 94, 95, Australian Open, 1994, Italian Open, 1994; ranked # 1 during 1993, 94 season, finalist Australian Open, 1995. 1st male to win the U.S Open, Wimbledon, and the Australian Open in succession, mem. U.S. Davis Cup Team, 1991, became only the fourth player to finish as No. 1three (or more) consecutive years, 1st player to surpass $5 million in a season,all-time leader in career earnings, named ATP Tour Player of the Year, 1993-94, Jim Thorpe Tennis Player, 1993. *

SAMPSON, DAPHNE RAE, library director; b. Milw., Aug. 11, 1943; d. Gerald Joseph and Helene Virginia Babbitt; m. Charles Sargent Sampson, Oct. 23, 1971. BA, U. Wis., 1965, MLS, 1966. Reference libr. Def. Intelligence Agy., Washington, 1966-68; sr. reference libr. U.S. Dept. of State, Washington, 1968-78, Exec. Office of the Pres., Washington, 1978-80; chief readers' svcs. Fed. Trade Commn., Washington, 1980-81; chief readers' svcs. U.S. Dept. of Justice, Washington, 1981-84, asst. dir. libr. staff, 1984-86, dep. dir. libr. staff, 1986, acting dir. libr. staff, 1986-87, dir. libr. staff, 1987—, sr. exec. svc., 1995—. Active Berkshire Civic Assn., Alexandria, Va., 1976—. Mem. Am. Assn. Law Librs., Law Librs. Soc. of Washington, Fed. Libr. and Info. Ctr. Com. (bd. mem. 1992). Home: 5838 Wyomissing Ct Alexandria VA 22303-1634 Office: US Dept of Justice Libr Rm 5317 10th & Pennsylvania Ave NW Washington DC 20530

SAMPSON, EARLDINE ROBISON, education educator; b. Russell, Iowa, June 18, 1923; d. Lawrence Earl and Mildred Mona (Judy) Robison; m. Wesley Claude Sampson, Nov. 25, 1953; children: Ann Elizabeth, Lisa Ellen. Diploma, Iowa State Tchrs. Coll., 1943, BA, 1950; MS in Edn., Drake U., 1954; postgrad., No. Ill. U., Iowa State U., 1965-66, 74. Cert. tchr., guidance counselor, Iowa. Tchr. elem. sch. various pub. sch. sys., 1943-48; cons. speech and hearing Iowa Dept. Pub. Instrn., Des Moines, 1950-52; speech therapist Des Moines Pub. Schs., 1952-54, 55; lectr. spl. edn. No. Ill. U., DeKalb, 1964-65; tchr. of homebound Cedar Falls (Iowa) Pub. Schs., 1967-68; asst. prof. edn. U. No. Iowa, Cedar Falls, 1968; asst. prof., counselor Wartburg Coll., Waverly, Iowa, 1968-70; instr. elem. edn., then head of advising elem. edn. Iowa State U., Ames, 1972-82; field supr. elem. edn. U. Toledo, 1988, 89; ind. cons. Sylvania, Ohio, 1989—; cons. Des Moines Speech and Hearing Ctr., 1958-59, bd. dirs., 1962, 63; cons. Sartori Hosp., Cedar Falls, 1967-69; bd. dirs. Story County Mental Health Ctr., Ames, 1972-74. NDEA fellow, 1965. Mem. AAUW, Univ. Women's Club, Zeta Phi Eta. Methodist. Avocations: public speaking on preservation of prose and poetry, reading, music, photography. Home: 4047 Newcastle Dr Sylvania OH 43560-3450 *My creed is based on the words of Edwin Markham: "There is a destiny that makes us brothers; none goes his way alone. All that we send into the lives of others comes back into our own. Just reward came from a former student who stated "I have never known you to compromise your principles".*

SAMPSON, EDWARD COOLIDGE, humanities educator; b. Ithaca, N.Y., Dec. 20, 1920; s. Martin W. and Julia (Pattison) S.; m. Frances P. Hanford, Oct. 26, 1946 (div. 1968); children: Susan S. Wilt, Edward H.; m. Cynthia R. Clark, 1968. BA, Cornell U., 1942, PhD, 1957; MA, Columbia U., 1949. Instr. Hofstra Coll., Hempstead, N.Y., 1946-49; teaching fellow Cornell U., Ithaca, 1949-52; with faculty Clarkson Coll. Tech., Potsdam, N.Y., 1952-69, assoc. prof. humanities, 1957-61, prof., 1961-69; prof. SUNY, Oneonta, 1969-82, ret., 1982. Author: E.B. White, 1974, Afterword, The House of the Seven Gables, 1961. Capt. USAAF, 1942-46. Decorated Bronze Star medal; Fulbright prof. U. Panjab, 1959-60. Fellow Am. Coun. Learned Studies; mem. MLA. Home: 89 Hemlock Dr Killingworth CT 06419-2225

SAMPSON, FRANKLIN DELANO, minister; b. Houston, Jan. 31, 1947; s. Harry Burney and Annie Belle (Lenzia) S.; m. Fannie Marie Iles, Mar. 12, 1972; children: De Anza Michelle, Franklin Delano, Jr., Frederick Dwayne. BA, U. Houston, 1970; D of Ministries (hon.), Mt. Hope Bible Coll., 1978. Ordained to ministry Nat. Bapt. Conv., 1969. Pastor Friendship Missionary Bapt. Ch., Houston, 1972—; moderator Unity Missionary Bapt. Gen. Assn., Houston, 1985—; chmn. Minister's Conf. of Missionary Bapt. Gen. Conv., Dallas, 1987—, Commn. on Orthodoxy of Nat. Bapt. Conv. of Am., Inc., Shreveport, La., 1987—; chief exec. officer Visions of Faith Ministries, Inc., Houston, 1985—. Mem. Bapt. Mins. Assn. of Houston and Vicinity (v.p. 1990—), Unity Missionary Bapt. Gen. Assn. (Houston, moderator 1985-93), Masons. Democrat. Home: 12947 Wincrest Ct Cypress TX 77429-2001 Office: Friendship Missionary Bapt Ch 4812 Bennington St Houston TX 77016-7003

SAMPSON, JOHN DAVID, lawyer; b. Lackawanna, N.Y., Feb. 20, 1955; s. Hugh Albert Sampson and May (Davidson) Sampson Henderson; m. Carol Jasen, July 29, 1978; children: Rachel Henderson, Matthew David. BA, Canisius Coll., Buffalo, 1977; JD, Union U., Albany, N.Y., 1982. Bar: N.Y. 1983, U.S. Dist. Ct. (we. dist.) N.Y. 1983. Assoc. Damon & Morey, Buffalo, 1982-87, Lippes Silverstein Mathias & Wexler, Buffalo, 1987-88; ptnr. Walsh & Sampson, P.C., Buffalo, 1988-93, Jasen, Jasen & Sampson P.C., Buffalo, 1993—. Dir. Edu Kids Early Childhood Ctrs., Inc., Orchard Park, N.Y., 1994—. Mem. ATLA, N.Y. State Bar Assn., Erie County Bar Assn., NFL Players Assn., Rotary of East Aurora (dir. 1993-96, pres. 1995-96). Wesleyan Methodist. Avocations: golf, cycling, skiing. Home: 44 Elmwood Ave East Aurora NY 14052-2610 Office: Jasen Jasen & Sampson PC # 620 3556 Lakeshore Rd Buffalo NY 14219

SAMPSON, JOHN EUGENE, food company executive; b. Lincoln, Nebr., Feb. 25, 1941; s. Delbert John and Mary Etta (Dodrill) S.; m. Mary Margaret Treanor, Aug. 14, 1965; children—J. Mark, Sharon. A.B. with distinction, Nebr. Wesleyan U., 1963; M.B.A., Ind. U., 1964. Mgmt. asst., exec. trainee Office Sec. Def., Washington, 1963-64; mem. staff Com. Econ. Devel., Washington, 1964-69; coordinator environ. planning Gen. Mills Inc., Mpls., 1969-72, mgr. devel. planning, 1972-74; dir. corp. planning Central Soya Co. Inc., Ft. Wayne, Ind., 1974-76, v.p. corp. planning, 1976-80, v.p. corp. planning and devel., 1980-82, v.p. corp. devel., corp. sec., 1982-84; v.p. corp. planning and devel. Internat. Multifoods, Inc., 1984—; pres. Sampson Assocs., Inc., 1994—. Mem. bd. govs. Nebr. Wesleyan U., 1974-80; chmn. bd. trustees St. Joseph United Meth. Ch., Ft. Wayne, 1984; bd. dirs., treas. North Ind. United Meth. Found., 1981-84; lay mem. North Ind. Ann. Conf. United Meth. Ch., 1980-84; bd. dirs. Anthony Wayne coun. Boy Scouts Am., 1984; lay mem. Minn. Ann. Conf. United Meth. Church, 1985-91; chmn. conf. bd. devel. Minn. United Meth. Conf., 1986-91; chmn. bd. trustees Hennepin Ave. United Meth. Ch., Mpls., 1990-92, chair adminstrv. coun., 1993-95, lay leader, 1995—. Mem. Ind. U. Sch. Bus. Alumni Assn. (pres. 1984-85), Interlachen Country Club. Home: 6612 Gleason Ter Minneapolis MN 55439-1131 Office: Internat Multifoods Inc Multifoods Tower Box 2942 33 S 6th St Minneapolis MN 55402-3601

SAMPSON, ROBERT NEIL, natural resources consultant; b. Spokane, Wash., Nov. 29, 1938; s. Robert Jay and Juanita Cleone (Hickman) S.; m. Jeanne Louise Stokes, June 7, 1960; children—Robert W., Eric S., Christopher B., Heidi L. B.S. in Agr, U. Idaho, 1960; M.Public Adminstrn., Harvard U., 1974. Soil conservationist Soil Conservation Service, Burley, Idaho, 1960-61; work unit conservationist Soil Conservation Service, Orofino, Idaho, 1962-65; agronomist Soil Conservation Service, Idaho Falls, Idaho, 1967-68; info. specialist Soil Conservation Service, Boise, 1968-70, area conservationist, 1970-72; land use specialist Soil Conservation Service, Washington, 1974-77; dir. environ. services div. Soil Conservation Service, 1977; land use program mgr. Idaho Planning and Community Affairs Agy., Boise, 1972-73; exec. v.p. Nat. Assn. Conservation Dists., Washington, 1978-84, Am. Forestry Assn., Washington, 1984-95; sr. fellow Am. Forests, Washington, 1995—; pres. The Sampson Group, Inc., 1996—; instr. soils and land use Boise State U., 1972; dir. Am. Land Forum, Washington, 1978-88. Author: Farmland or Wasteland: A Time To Choose, 1981, For Love of the Land, 1985; contbr. articles to profl. and popular publs. Pres. Orofino Golf Assn., 1966, Clearwater County Search and Rescue Unit, 1966-67; chmn. Nat. Commn. on Wildfire Disasters, 1992-94. Recipient President's citation Soil Conservation Soc. Am., 1978; named Boise Fed. Civil Servant of Year Boise Fed. Bus. Assn., 1972. Fellow Soil and Water Conservation Soc. (Hugh Hammond Bennett award 1992); mem. Soc. Am. Foresters, Am. Soc. Assn. Execs. Presbyterian.

SAMPSON, RONALD A., advertising executive; b. Charlottesville, Va., Nov. 13, 1933; s. Percy Thomas Sampson and Lucile (Mills) Martin; m. Norvelle Ann Johnson, Aug. 8, 1959; children: David Alan, Cheryl Ann. BS in Commerce, DePaul U., 1956. Advt. sales rep. Ebony Mag., Chgo., 1959-63; merchandising rep. Foote, Cone & Belding Advt., Chgo., 1963-66; account mgr. Tatham, Laird & Kudner Advt., Chgo., 1966-78; account mgr., exec. v.p. Burrell, Advt., Chgo., 1978-81; advt. agy. account mgr., sr. v.p. Darcy McManus Masius, Chgo., 1981-88, Burrell Comm. Group, Chgo., 1990—; bd. mem. Chgo. Advt. Fedn., 1995—. Bd. mem. Cmty. Renewal Soc., Chgo., 1969-74; deacon Chgo. United, 1992-94. With U.S. Army, 1956-58. Home: 6175 S Oglesby Ave Chicago IL 60602 Office: Burrell Comm Group 20 N Michigan Ave Chicago IL 60602

SAMPSON, RONALD GARY, lawyer; b. Haverhill, Mass., Apr. 8, 1942; s. Courtney Howard and Irene Velma (Sweetser) S. AB, Yale U., 1963; MA, Cambridge U., Eng., 1967; JD, Harvard U., 1968. Bar: Mass. 1969. Asst. prof., asst. dean sch. law U. Conn., 1968-69; assoc. Goodwin, Procter and Hoar, Boston, 1969-75; gen. counsel The Boston Co., 1975-93. Trustee Longy Sch. Music, Cambridge, Mass., 1973—, pres., 1986-91; trustee Kneisel Hall Chamber Music Sch., 1994—; dir. Early Music Am., 1992—. Mem. Harvard Music Assn. (bd. dirs. 1982-94, pres. 1991-94), St. Botolph Club (treas. and gov. 1994—), Longwood Cricket Club, Badminton and Tennis Club.

SAMPSON, SAMUEL FRANKLIN, sociology educator; b. Malden, Mass., Sept. 22, 1934; s. Samuel Daniel and Margaret Louise (Grimes) S.; m. Patricia Katherine Driscoll, Apr. 8, 1972. B.A., U. Okla., 1960, M.A., 1961; Ph.D., Cornell U., 1968. Asst. prof. dept. sociology SUNY, Binghamton, 1965-66; research assoc. dept. sociology Cornell U., Ithaca, N.Y., 1966-67; lectr., chmn. bd. tutors and advs. Harvard U., Cambridge, Mass., 1967-72; assoc. prof. dept. urban studies and planning MIT, Cambridge, 1971-72; prof. sociology U. Vt., Burlington, 1972—, chmn. dept. sociology, 1972-76, 90-96; research and policy cons. Public & Community Agys. and Orgns., 1969—. Gen. editor: Bobbs-Merrill Studies in Sociology, 1970-77; contbr. articles to profl. jours. Served with USAF, 1954-58. Mem. AAUP, AAAS, Internat. Sociol. Assn., Am. Sociol. Assn., Am. Acad. Arts and Scis., Ea. Sociol. Soc., Soc. Study Social Problems, New Eng. Sociol. Assn., Soc. Sci. Study Religion, Internat. Soc. Sociology of Knowledge. Home: 215 S Cove Rd Burlington VT 05401-5445 Office: Univ Vt Dept Sociology 31 S Prospect St Burlington VT 05405-1704

SAMPSON, STEVE, professional soccer coach; b. Salt Lake City, Jan. 19, 1957. Graduate, San Jose State U.; MEd, Stanford U. Soccer coach Foothill Cmty. Coll., Los Altos Hills, Calif.; asst. soccer coach U. Calif., L.A., 1982-85; soccer coach Santa Clara (Calif.) U., 1985-90; asst. coach U.S. Nat. Soccer Team, Chgo., 1993-1995, head coach, 1995—; mem. organizing com. World Cup USA 1990-95, co-chmn. U.S. Soccer Coaching com. 1990-91, v.p. competition mgmt. 1994. Named Nat. Coach of the Yr., 1989; earned All-America honors, Foothill Cmty. Coll., 1976. Office: US Soccer 1801-11 S Prairie Ave Chicago IL 60616*

SAMPSON, WILLIAM ROTH, lawyer; b. Teaneck, N.J., Dec. 11, 1946; s. James and Amelia (Roth) S.; 1 child, Lara; m. Drucilla Jean Mort, Apr. 23, 1988. BA with honors in History, U. Kans., 1968, JD, 1971. Bar: Kans. 1971, U.S. Dist. Ct. Kans. 1971, U.S. Ct. Appeals (10th cir.) 1982, U.S. Ct. Claims 1985, U.S. Ct. Appeals (8th cir.) 1992. Assoc. Turner & Balloun, Gt. Bend, Kans., 1971; ptnr. Foulston & Siefkin, Wichita, Kans., 1975-86; shareholder Shook, Hardy & Bacon, Overland Park, Kans., 1987—; presenter legal edn. seminars and confs.; adj. prof. advanced litig. U. Kans., 1994; mem. faculty trial tactics inst. Emory U. Sch. Law, 1994, 95, 96; lectr. area law schs. Mem. Kans. Law Rev., 1969-71, editor, 1970-71; contbr. articles to legal jours. Chmn. stewardship com. Univ. Friends Ch., Wichita, 1984-86; bd. dirs. Friends U. Retirement Corp., Wichita, 1985-87; chmn. capital fund drives Trinity Luth. Ch., Lawrence, Kans., 1990-93, mem. ch. coun., 1990-92; bd. dirs. The Lied Ctr. of Kans., Lawrence. Lt. USNR, 1971-75. Fellow Kans. Bar Assn. (chmn. Kans. coll. advocacy 1986, long-range planning, CLE com. 1987-88); mem. ABA, Douglas County Bar Assn., Johnson County Bar Assn. (bench-bar com. 1989-96, Boss of Yr. award 1990), Wichita Bar Assn. (bd. dirs. 1985-86), Am. Bd. Trial Advs. (pres. Kans. chpt. 1990-91, nat. bd. mem. 1990-91), Internat. Assn. Def. Coun. (faculty mem. trial acad. 1994), Def. Rsch. Inst. (Kans. chmn. 1990-96, Exceptional Performance Citation 1990, Outstanding State Rep. 1991, 92, 94), Kans. Assn. Def. Counsel (pres. 1989-90, legis. coun. 1991, 93, William H. Kahrs Disting. Achievement award 1994), Kans. U. Law Soc. (bd. govs. 1993—), Am. Inn Ct. (Judge Hugh Means chpt., Master of Bench), Alvamar Country Club, Order of Coif, Delta Sigma Rho, Phi Alpha Theta, Omicron Delta Kappa. Republican. Lutheran. Avocations: jogging, golf, snow skiing, travel, reading. Office: Shook Hardy & Bacon 9401 Indian Creek Pky Overland Park KS 66210-2005

SAMPUGNARO, TRUDY M., principal. Prin. St. Andrew Apostle Sch., Silver Spring, Md. Recipient DOE Elem. Sch. Recognition award, 1989-90. Office: St Andrew Apostle Sch 11602 Kemp Mill Rd Silver Spring MD 20902-1718

SAMRA, HISHAM, pharmaceutical executive. With Ares Serono, Inc., 1988-92; pres. Serono Labs. Inc., Norwell, Mass., 1992—. Office: Serono Labs Inc 100 Longwater Cir Norwell MA 02061-1616*

SAMS, CHARLES E., accounting firm executive. Grad., U. N.C., 1970. Exec. ptnr. Dixon, Odom & Co., LLP, High Point, N.C., 1970—. Office: Dixon Odom & Co PO Box 2646 1208 Eastchester Dr High Point NC 27261

SAMS, JAMES FARID, real estate development company executive; b. Bay City, Mich., Apr. 21, 1932; s. James and Adele (Abuismail) S.; m. Betty Suham Hamady, Aug. 17, 1957; children: James Karl, Alicia Diane, Victoria Saab. BA, Northwestern U., 1954; JD, U. Mich., 1957; LLM, Harvard U., 1959. Com. counsel ABA spl. com. World Peace/Law, Washington, 1960-63; ptnr. Reeves, Harrison, Sams & Revercomb, Washington, 1964-69, Brown & Sams, Washington, 1969-71, Kirkwood, Kaplan, Russin, Veechi & Sams, Beirut, 1971-74; owner, prin. Am. Devel. Services Corp., Washington, 1978—; former chmn. bd. DASI, Inc., Washington, 1974-90; dir. Bristol Compressors, Inc., 1983-86, Nat. Bank Wash., 1986-91; rep. U.S. State Dept. Ams. Abroad, Washington, 1965; del. UN Com. on Internat. Trade Law, N.Y.C., 1970. Contbr. articles to profl. jours. Co-founder, dir. Am. Near East Refugee Aid, Washington, 1968-92; mem. adv. bd. Ctr. for Study of Global South, Am. U., Washington, 1983—; mem. visitors com. U. Mich. Law Sch.; mem. exec. com. Am. Task Force for Lebanon, Washington. Served to lt. U.S. Army, 1957-58. Mem. ABA, Bar Assn. of Washington, Am. Soc. Internat. Law, Nat. Assn. Arab Ams. (pres. 1981, chmn. 1983). Avocations: skiing, sports. Home: 8907 Fernwood Rd Bethesda MD 20817-3015 Office: Am Devel Svcs Corp 5454 Wisconsin Ave Ste 1260 Bethesda MD 20815-6901

SAMS, JOHN ROLAND, retired mission executive, missionary; b. Whatcheer, Iowa, Nov. 1, 1922; s. Bert Willian and and Vesta Leora (Wilkins) S.; m. Frances Elizabeth McCluney, July 3, 1924; children: Phyllis Jean, Georgia Ann, Bert Franklin. BS, Iowa State U., 1949; MA, Drake U., 1952; student, Hartford Sem., 1952-54; MA, Chapman Coll., 1972; HHD (hon.), Philippine Christian U., Manila. Tchr. Paullina (Iowa) Pub. Schs., 1949-51; missionary Christian Ch. (Disciples of Christ), Thailand, 1954-67, Philippines, 1968-71; v.p. Am. Leprosy Missions, N.Y.C., 1972-76; exec. v.p. Am. Leprosy Missions, Bloomfield, N.J., 1976-84; pres. Am. Leprosy Missions, Elmwood Park, N.J., 1984-89. Served with USAAF, 1942-46. Mem. United Ch. of Christ. Avocations: travel, reading.

SAMS, JUDITH ANN, counselor, mental health nurse; b. Akron, Ohio, May 18, 1943; d. Clifford and Virginia (Slider) Starcher; m. Robert E. Sams, Dec. 15, 1963; children: Robert Steven, Patricia Ann, Erik Jason. RN, St. Joseph's Nursing Sch., Parkersburg, W.Va., 1963; BSN cum laude, Ohio U., 1980, MEd, 1991. Cert. counselor. Staff nurse W.Va. U. Med. Ctr. Cancer Rsch., Morgantown, 1963-65; sch. nurse Ea. Sch. Dist., Meigs County, Ohio, 1976-78; psychiat. nurse Worthington Ctr. Inc., Parkersburg, 1990-93, dir. adult mental health, 1993—. Pres. Acad. Parkersburg Med. Aux., 1976. Mem. Ohio Counselors Assn., Chi Sigma Iota. Democrat. Methodist. Avocations: skiing, reading, sewing. Address: 1110 Ann St Parkersburg WV 26101 Office: Worthington Ctr Inc 3199 Core Rd Parkersburg WV 26104-1557

SAMSEL, MAEBELL SCROGGINS (MIDGE SAMSEL), paralegal; b. Yazoo City, Miss., Aug. 15, 1940; d. Robert and Lela Estelle (Hammons) Scroggins; m. John Sanders Swain, Dec. 30, 1960 (div. Oct. 1968); 1 child, Stacy Melissa Swain Ramsey; m. Howard Swinehart Samsel, Oct. 8, 1981. BA, Miss. Coll., 1963. Sec. Standard Life Ins. Co., Jackson, Miss., 1963-64; legal sec. Gray & Montague Law Firm, Hattiesburg, Miss., 1964-65; personnel sec. Adj. Gen.'s Office, State of Miss., Jackson, 1965-70; paralegal State of Miss., Atty. Gen.'s Office, Jackson, 1970-79, 84-86; sales agt. Prudential Ins. Co. Am., Jackson, 1979-84. Chmn. acquisitions Miss. Mus. Art, Jackson, 1983, acquisitions vol., 1982, 89, chmn. Vols. at the Palette Restaurant, 1990-95, music chair Miss. Mus. Art Palette Restaurant, 1996, pres. aux., 1991-92, trustee, 1991-92; mem. Jackson Symphony League, 1988—, Miss. Opera Guild, Jackson, 1991—; bd. dirs. Friends of the Ballet, Internat. Ballet Competition. Named Vol. of the Week, Miss. Mus. Art Palette Restaurant, 1989, Vol. of Yr., Miss. Mus. of Art, 1991-92. Mem. AAUW, Jackson Assn. Legal Secs. (pres. 1975-76, 77-78, del. to nat. convs. 1975-77, Outstanding Legal Sec. of Yr. 1975-76), Miss. Assn. Legal Secs., Nat. Assn. Legal Secs. (chmn. nat. spring bd. mtg. 1980), Miss. Coll. Alumni Assn., Petroleum Aux. (v.p. 1986-87, pres. 1988-89, treas. 1989-90, pres. 1994-96), Revelers Dance Club, Serendipity Bridge Club (treas. 1989-93, v.p. 1991-92, pres. 1992-93), Met. Supper Club. Republican. Baptist. Avocations: fishing, piano, travel. Home: 1206 Bay Vis Brandon MS 39042-8650

SAMSON, ALLEN LAWRENCE, bank executive; b. Milw., Nov. 16, 1939; s. Harry E. and Rose (Landau) S.; m. Vicki Faye Boxer, July 3, 1977; children: Daniel, Rachel; children from previous marriage: Nancy, David. BS, U. Wis., 1962, LLB, 1965. Bar: Wis. 1965. Asst. dist. atty. Milw. County Dist. Attys. Office, 1965-67, dep. dist. atty., 1968-70; assoc. Samson & Nash, Milw., 1967-68; ptnr. Samson, Friebert, Sutton and Finerty, Milw., 1970-73; v.p., sec. Am. Med. Svcs., Inc., Milw., 1973-83, exec. v.p., chief exec. officer, 1983-86, chmn., chief exec. officer, 1986-90; cons. nursing homes Samson Med. Mgmt. Co., Milw., 1990-93; pres. Liberty Bank, Milw., 1993—; pub. mem. nursing home study Wis. Legis. Bur., 1988-89; mem. bd. visitors U. Wis. Law Sch., 1992—; mem. health policy adv. coun. Med. Coll. Wis., 1992—. Trustee Milw. Ballet, 1982-89, Milw. Art Mus., 1985-95, pres. bd. trustees, 1992-95; bd. dirs. Milw. Symphony Orch., 1995—, War Meml. Corp., 1993-95, Jewish Fedn., 1985—, Milw. Jewish Home, 1992—, Jewish Cmty. Ctr., 1985-96; gen. chmn. Wis. Israel Bond Campaign, 1993, chmn., 1996—. Recipient Kaplan prize for econ. devel. Govt. of Israel, 1986. Avocations: tennis, skiing, golf. Office: Liberty Bank 815 N Water St Milwaukee WI 53202-3526 : Liberty Bank 815 N Water St Milwaukee WI 53202-3526

SAMSON, ALVIN, former distributing company executive, consultant; b. N.Y.C., May 2, 1917; s. Morris and Jennie (Buitekant) S.; m. Ann Carol Furmansky, Aug. 15, 1942; children: Leslie Joan, Marla Adriane. Br. mgr. U.S. Hardware and Paper Co., 1947-51; mdse. mgr. U.S. Servateria, 1951-57; dir. purchasing U.S. Consumer Products, Los Angeles, 1959-64; v.p. ops. U.S. Consumer Products, 1964-66, pres., 1966-72; pres. U.S. Consumer Products, San Diego, Bakersfield, Las Vegas, Phoenix, 1966-72, Zelman Co., Los Angeles, San Francisco and Las Vegas, 1968-72, Triple A Corp., Los Angeles, 1966-72, U.S. Consumer Products-West Mdse., Los Angeles, 1972-74; v.p. APL Corp., N.Y.C., 1967-74; pres. USCP-WESCO, 1974-85; cons. A. Samson Cons., Beverly Hills, 1985-92; retired, 1992. Active USCG

Aux., 1981—, divsn. capt., 1992—. With USAAF, 1942-45. Named Man of Year Housewares Club So. Calif., 1965. Mem. Housewares Club So. Calif. (pres. 1957, bd. govs. 1955-56), Nat. Assn. Service Merchandisers (dir. 1982-85).

SAMSON, CHARLES HAROLD, JR. (CAR SAMSON), retired engineering educator, consultant; b. Portsmouth, Ohio, July 12, 1924; s. Charles Harold and Gertrude (Morris) S.; m. Ruth Aileen Baumbach, Sept. 12, 1947; children: Peggy Aileen, Charles Harold III. B.S., U. Notre Dame, 1947, M.S., 1948; Ph.D., U. Mo., 1953. Registered profl. engr., Tex., Ind. Asst. field rep. Loebl, Schlossman and Bennett (architects and engrs.), Chgo., 1948-49; structures engr. Convair Aircraft, Fort Worth, 1951-52; sr. structures engr. Convair Aircraft, 1952-53, project aerodynamics engr., 1956-58, project structures engr., 1958-60; asst. prof. civil engring. U. Notre Dame, 1953-56; office engr. Wilbur H. Gartner & Assocs., South Bend, Ind., 1954; grad. lectr. civil engring. So. Meth. U., Dallas, 1952-53, 56-60; prof. structural engring. and mechanics, depts. aerospace and civil engring. Tex. A&M U., College Station, 1960-64, prof. civil engring., 1964-94; prof. emeritus Tex. A&M, College Station, 1994—; head dept. Tex. A&M U., College Station, 1964-79, assoc. head dept., 1989-92, construction area engring. leader, dir. ctr. construction edn., 1992-93; rsch. engr. Tex. Transp. Inst., Tex. A&M U., 1960-62, head structural research dept., 1962-65, acting pres., 1980-81, v.p. planning, 1981-82; pres. S.W. Athletic Conf., 1979-81; v.p. Nat. Collegiate Athletic Assn., 1981-83, mem. council, 1983-85; cons. systems engring. and quality mgmt. Contbr. articles to profl. jours. Served to ensign USNR, 1943-46. Fellow ASCE (life), Nat. Inst. Engring. Mgmt. and Systems (pres. 1989-90); mem. Am. Soc. Engring. Mgmt., Am. Soc. Engring. Edn., Nat. Soc. Profl. Engrs. (past v.p., chmn. profl. engrs. in edn., pres. 1987-88), Tex. Soc. Profl. Engrs. (past nat. dir., pres. 1973-74), Nat. Assn. Parliamentarians, Internat. Soc. Systems Sci., Order of the Engr. (chmn., bd. govs. 1989-91), Am. Soc. Quality Control, Nat. Coun. on Systems Engring., Nat. Inst. Engring. Ethics, Sigma Xi, Sigma Gamma Tau, Tau Beta Pi, Phi Kappa Phi, Chi Epsilon. Home: 810 Dogwood Ln Bryan TX 77802-1144

SAMSON, FREDERICK EUGENE, JR., neuroscientist, educator; b. Medford, Mass., Aug. 16, 1918; s. Frederick Eugene and Annie Bell (Pratt) S.; m. Camila Albert; children Cecile Samson Folkerts, Julie Samson Thompson, Renée. DO, Mass. Coll. Osteopathy, 1940; PhD, U. Chgo., 1952. Asst. prof. U. Kans., Lawrence, 1952-57, prof. physiology, 1962-73, chmn., prof. dept. physiology and cell biology, 1968-73; prof. physiology U. Kans. Med. Ctr., Kansas City, 1973-89, prof. emeritus, 1989—; dir. Ralph L. Smith Rsch. Ctr. U. Kans., Kansas City, 1973-89; staff scientist neuroscis. rsch. program MIT, Cambridge, Mass., 1968-82, cons., 1982-91; vis. prof. neurobiology U. Catolica de Chile, Santiago, 1972; prof. Inst. de Investigaciones Citologicas, Valenica, Spain, 1981-89; hon. lectr. Mid-Am. State Univs. Assn., 1987. Editor: (with George Adelman) The Neurosciences: Paths of Discovery, II, 1992, (with Merrill Tarr) Oxygen Free Radicals in Tissue Damage, 1993; contbr. articles to profl. publs. Scientist, U.S.A., Spain Friendship Treaty, Madrid and Valencia, 1981. Staff sgt. U.S. Army, 1941-45, PTO. Recipient Rsch. Recognition award U. Kans. Med. Ctr., Kansas City, 1984; Van Liere fellow U. Chgo., 1948; Rawson fellow U. Chgo., 1949-51; USPHS fellow MIT, 1965. Fellow AAAS; mem. Am. Soc. Neurochemistry (chmn. program com. 1980), Am. Soc. Cell Biology (local host com. 1984), Am. Physiol. Soc. (emeritus 1990), Soc. Neurosci. (program com. 1972-73), The Oxygen Soc., N.Y. Acad. Sci., U. Chgo. Kansas City Club (chmn. alumni fund bd. 1975-82, pres. 1979-81), Sigma Xi (regional lectr. 1974-75, pres. Kansas City chpt. 1977-78, pres. neurosci. chpt. 1978). Avocation: hand balancing. Home: 171 Lakeshore Dr S Lake Quivira KS 66106-9516 Office: U Kans Med Ctr Ralph L Smith Rsch Ctr Bldg 37 Kansas City KS 66160

SAMSON, GORDON EDGAR, educator, consultant; b. Waterville, Que., Can., Oct. 25, 1923; came to U.S., 1952; s. Edgar John Knox and Ethel May (Holyon) S. BSc, Bishop's U., 1942, MEd, 1948; PhD, U. Chgo., 1955. Cert. tchr. h.s., 1943. Tchr., prin. various sch. sys. Que., 1943-52; rsch. asst. U. Chgo., 1952-54; exec. asst. Ednl. Policies Commn., NEA, Washington, 1954-57; chmn. dept. edn. Fenn Coll., Cleve., 1957-65; assoc. prof. Cleve. State U., 1965-85, acting dean, 1965-67; vis. scholar Brock U., St. Catharines, Ont., summer 1986, 87, external examiner, 1988. Contbr. articles to profl. jours. Mem. NEA (life), Am. Ednl. Rsch. Assn., Nat. Soc. for Study of Edn., Phi Delta Kappa. Avocations: genealogy, reading. Home: 2636 Haddam Rd Cleveland OH 44120-1532

SAMSON, LINDA FORREST, nursing educator and administrator; b. Miami, Dec. 7, 1949; d. Alvin S. and Grace (Kanner) Forrest; m. Mark I. Samson, Jan. 29, 1972; children: Amy, Josh. BSN, Emory U., 1972, MN, 1973; PhD, U. Pa., 1989. RN, Fla., Ga., N.J., Pa. Nursing instr. Ga. State U., Atlanta, 1974-78; neonatal intensive care nurse Northside Hosp., Atlanta, 1976-78; perinatal clin. specialist Our Lady of Lourdes Med. Ctr., Camden, N.J., 1978-82, per diem staff nurse, ICU nursery, labor and delivery, 1982-88; asst. prof., nursing Kennesaw Coll., Marietta, Ga., 1988-89; asst. prof. Clayton State Coll., Morrow, Ga., 1989-92, head baccalaureate nursing dept., 1991-94, acting dean Sch. Health Scis., 1992-94; dean Sch. Health Scis., 1994—; adj. faculty Gloucester County Coll., 1981-83; adj. clin. preceptor U. Pa. Sch. Nursing, 1981-83, lectr. in perinatal nursing, 1983-88; nursing dir. So. N.J. Perinatal Coop., 1982-84; researcher and lectr. in field. Mem. editorial rev. bds.; contbr. chpts. to textbooks, articles to profl. jours. Bd. dirs., chmn. profl. adv. com. South Jersey chpt. March of Dimes, 1980-85. Named Nurse of Yr. N.J. State Nurses Assn., 1985; recipient Network Edn. grant N.J. State Dept. Health, 1982-84, numerous grants for rsch., 1983-89, Outstanding Svc. award March of Dimes, 1983, Disting. Leadership award March of Dimes, 1984. Mem. ANA (cert. advanced nursing adminstrn., RNC high risk perinatal nursing), AACN (program com. 1987-88, rsch. com. 1988-89, project devel. task force 1989, strategic planning com. 1989, bd. dirs. 1987-90, bd. dirs. certification corp. 1987-90, chair neonatal and pediatric appeal panels 1992), Am. Orgn. Nurse Execs. (planning com. 1994-95), Nat. Assn. Neonatal Nurses (pub. policy and legis. com. 1994-96), Assn. Women's Health, Obstetrics and Neonatal Nurses, Nat. Perinatal Assn. (program planning com. 1983-85, resolutions com. 1984-88, stds. devel. com. spl. interest group task force 1985-88, bd. dirs. 1985-89, chmn. resolutions com. 1988, fin. com. 1989, pub. health policy com.), Ga. Nurses Assn., Ga. Perinatal Assn. N.J. (pres. 1982-86), Sigma Theta Tau. Home: 2915 Four Oaks Dr Atlanta GA 30360-1744 Office: Clayton State Coll Sch Health Scis PO Box 285 Morrow GA 30260-0285

SAMSON, PERRY J., environmental scientist, educator; b. Binghamton, N.Y., May 18, 1950; s. Perry C. and Ann I. Samson; children: Karis, Carla. BS, SUNY, Albany, 1972, MS, 1974; PhD, U. Wis., 1979. Rsch. sci. N.Y. State Dept. Environ. Conservation, Albany, 1973-79; asst. prof. U. Mich., Ann Arbor, 1979-85, assoc. prof., 1985-89, prof., 1989—, Arthur Thurnal prof., 1995—; vis. scientist Nat. Ctr. Atmospheric Rsch., Boulder, Colo., 1985-86, Univ. Corp. Atmospheric Rsch., Boulder, 1994—. Author chpts. to books; contbr. articles to profl. jours. Mem. Am. Geophys. Union, Air and Waste Mgmt. Assn. (mem. TT-3 meteorol com., mem. TE-5 visibility com.). Office: U Mich 1539 Space Rsch Bldg Ann Arbor MI 48109-2143

SAMSON, PETER, lawyer; b. Princeton, N.J., Oct. 26, 1951; s. Hugh and Edith (Willett) S.; m. Lynne W. Coughlin, July 3, 1993; children: David, Brian, Catherine, Molly. BA, U. Pa., 1973; JD, New Eng. Sch. Law, 1976. Bar: Pa. 1976, U.S. Dist. Ct. Pa. 1980, U.S. Ct. Appeals (3d cir.) 1981, U.S. Supreme Ct. 1983. Staff atty. Defender Assn. of Phila., 1976-80; assoc. White & Williams, Phila., 1980-86, ptnr., 1986—; lectr. Temple U. Sch. Law. Mem. Phila. Bar Assn., Pa. Def. Inst., Assn. of Def. Counsel. Democrat. Avocations: skiing, sailing, wind surfing. Home: 215 Lenoir Ave Wayne PA 19087-3908 Office: White & Williams 1800 One Liberty Pl Philadelphia PA 19103-7395

SAMSON, RICHARD MAX, investments and real estate executive; b. Milw., June 13, 1946; s. Harry E. and Rose (Landau) S.; m. Nancy K. Pinter; children: Gina Shoshana, Alayna Tamar; (stepson) Christopher P. BA, U. Wis., 1968. Dir., owner The Puppet Co., Jerusalem, 1972-73; pres. Century Hall, Inc., Milw., 1974-75; dir. purchasing Am. Med. Svcs., Inc., Milw., 1973-74, v.p., 1974-82, exec. v.p., 1982-86, pres., 1986-90; pres. Samson Investments, Milw., 1990—; bd. dirs. Liberty Bank, Milw.; sec. Super Sitters, Mequon, Wis., 1987—. Pres. bd. Theatre X, Milw., 1982, Holton Youth Ctr., Milw., 1994, Children's Outing Assn., 1996; v.p. bd. ArtReach, Milw., 1987; bd. dirs. Pnai Or Religious Fellowship, 1988-93, Milw. Jewish Coun., 1992-94; mem. funding bd. Wis. Cmty. Fund, 1989-93. Recipient Humanitarian Peace award Ecumenical Refugee Coun., 1989. Mem. Ams. for Peace Now (bd. dirs. 1990—). Avocations: chess, comic collecting, puppetry. Office: Samson Investments 100A Pleasant Milwaukee WI 53212

SAMSOT, ROBERT LOUIS, newspaper editor, consultant; b. New Orleans, July 20, 1943; s. Robert Desposito and Mary Helen (Dohan) S.; m. A. Michael Newton, June 9, 1965; children: Kathleen Anderson Samsot English, Robert Dohan. BA in Journalism, U. N.C., Chapel Hill, 1965; cert. in Bus. Adminstrn., Rockhurst Coll., 1982. Reporter Rocky Mountain News, Denver, 1965-67, The Comml. Appeal, Memphis, 1967-72; reporter, editor Newsday, L.I., N.Y., 1972-80; Gannett profl.-in-residence reporter U. Kans., Lawrence, 1980-81; met. editor The Kansas City (Mo.) Times, 1981-84; city editor The Plain Dealer, Cleve., 1984-87; lifestyle editor, dep. editor N.J., dep. editor nat. The Phila. Inquirer, 1987—; cons. W.K. Kellogg Nat. Fellowship, Battle Creek, Mich., 1984-93; freelance writer, 1965—. Youth soccer coach Northport, N.Y., 1976-80, dir., 1979-80, Shaker Heights, Ohio, 1984-87, Swarthmore (Pa.) Recreation Assn., 1987-88; coach Johnson County (Kans.) Soccer League, 1983-84; bd. dirs. Suffolk County Heart Assn., L.I., 1974-75. Mem. Nat. Assn. Hispanic Journalists. Democrat. Roman Catholic. Avocations: travel, fishing, outdoor sports. Home: 610 Strath Haven Ave Swarthmore PA 19081-2307 Office: The Phila Inquirer 400 N Broad St Philadelphia PA 19130-4015

SAMTER, MAX, physician, educator; b. Berlin, Germany, Mar. 3, 1908; came to U.S., 1937; s. Paul and Claire (Rawicz) S.; m. Virginia Svarz Ackerman, Oct. 17, 1947; 1 dau., Virginia Claire. Student, U. Freiburg, Germany, 1926, U. Innsbruck, Austria, 1928; M.D., U. Berlin, 1933. Diplomate: Am. Bd. Internal Medicine (past chmn. bd. allergy), Am. Bd. Allergy and Immunology. Intern, Medizinische Universitätsklinik der Charité, Berlin, 1931-32, resident internal medicine, 1932-33; practice medicine Berlin-Karow, Germany, 1933-37; resident internal medicine & hematology Johns Hopkins Hosp., 1937-39; resident anatomy U. Pa. Sch. Medicine, 1939-43; research asso. dept. biochemistry U. Ill., Chgo., 1946-47, from instr. to full prof. dept. medicine, 1948-69, prof. medicine Coll. Medicine (formerly Abraham Lincoln Sch. Medicine), 1969—, assoc. dean for clin. affairs, 1974-75; vis. scholar, immunology Weizmann Inst. of Sci.; chief staff U. Ill. Hosp., 1974-75; dir. inst. allergy & clin. immunology Grant Hosp., Chgo., 1975-83, sr. cons., 1983-93; rsch. sci. otolaryngology, head & neck surg. U. Ill. Coll. Med., Chgo., 1994—; prof. dept. otolaryngology U. Ill. Hosp., 1994-96; clin. prof. otorhinolaryngology Loyola U. Med. Ctr., Chgo., 1996—; cons. in allergy U.S. VA, 1962—. Editor: American Lectures in Allergy, 1950, (with Oren C. Durham) Regional Allergy, 1954, (with Harry L. Alexander) Immunological Diseases, 1965, 71, 78, 88, Excerpts from Classics in Allergy, 1969, rev. edit. (with Sheldon G. Cohen), 1992; (with Charles W. Parker) Hypersensitivity to Drugs, 1972; also articles in field. Served to capt. M.C. AUS, 1943-46, ETO. Recipient Disting. Faculty award U. Ill. Coll. Med. 1987. Fellow ACP; mem. AMA, Am. Acad. Allergy (past pres.), Internat. Assn. Allergology and Clin. Immunology (past pres., Disting. Svc. award 1991), German Soc. Allergology and Clin. Immunology (hon.), Phila. Coll. Physicians (hon.), Interasma (hon.), Sigma Xi, Alpha Omega Alpha. Home: 645 Sheridan Rd Evanston IL 60202-2533

SAMUEL, ELIZABETH, nurse educator, administrator; b. Gardner, Mass., Feb. 13, 1941. Student, Johnson County Vocat. Nursing, Cleburne, Tex., 1971; BSN, U. Tex., Austin, 1986. Cert. emergency med. technician, BLS, ACLS. Staff nurse Stephenville (Tex.) Gen. Hosp., 1983, Lea Regional Hosp., Hobbs, N.Mex., 1983; staff nurse med.-surg. unit South Austin Community Hosp., Austin, Tex., 1983-86; staff nurse on neuro-respiratory unit Meth. Med. Ctr., Dallas, 1986-87; staff nurse post cardiac unit Mary Washington Hosp., Fredericksburg, Va., 1987-89; staff nurse and night shift supr. Summers County Hosp., Hinton, W.Va., 1990-94; edn. coord., ICU nurse mgr. Summers County ARH, 1994—. Bd. dirs. Tri-County Med. Corp. Suicide Prevention Hotline; bd. dirs., sec. Universal Gospel of Jesus Christ Ministries. Founder fellow the sons ministries Mem. Phi Theta Kappa.

SAMUEL, GERHARD, orchestra conductor, composer; b. Bonn, Germany, Apr. 20, 1924; came to U.S., 1939, naturalized, 1943; s. Arthur and Hilde (Behr) S. Student violin with Samuel Belov, chamber music with Jacques Gordon (scholarship); B.Mus. cum laude, Eastman Sch. Music, 1945; choral conducting with Hermann Genhart, conducting with Paul White and Howard Hanson, 1945; student of Serge Koussevitsky, Tanglewood, Mass., 1945-47; student, also Boris Goldowsky; student of Paul Hindemith (scholarship), Yale U., Mus.M. (Haupt prize), 1947; Ph.D. (hon.), Calif. Coll. Arts and Crafts. Fulbright grantee for study in Europe, 1949; exec. com. San Francisco Composers Forum, 1959-62; mem. composers workshop San Francisco Conservatory Music, 1960; prof. music Calif. Inst. Arts, to 1976; condr. Contemporary Ensemble Concert Series, U. Cin. Coll.-Conservatory of Music, 1976—; lectr. in field; guest condr. Oakland (Calif.) Ballet Co. Condr.: Ballet Ballads, Music Box Theatre, Broadway, 1947-48; rsch. in France and Italy; condr. concerts Am. contemporary music, Paris, 1948-49, Accademia Chigiana (1st prize), Siena, Italy, 1949; assoc. condr. Mpls. Symphony Orch., 1949-59; condr., Ballets Concertants, Mpls., 1950-59, Collegium Musicum, Mpls., 1952-59, Mpls. Civic Opera Co., 1954-59; mus. dir. Grand Marais (Minn.) Music Festival, 1957-59, Minn. Centennial Music Festival, 1958, Oakland (Calif.) Symphony Orch., 1959-71; mus. dir., condr. San Francisco Ballet, 1961-70; founder, condr., Cabrillo Music Festival, 1962-68, West Coast New Music Ensemble, 1968-70, condr., mus. dir. Oakland Chamber Orch., 1963-69; assoc. condr. Los Angeles Philharmonic, 1970-74; mus. dir., condr., Ojai (Calif.) Festival, 1970-71, Pacific N.W. Ballet Co., 1982-83; artistic dir., L.A. Philharmonic Docents; guest condr. Am. Symphony, Lincoln Center, N.Y.C., 1964, Denver Symphony, 1965, San Francisco Spring Opera, 1965, 66, Am. Symphony Orch., 1965, Winnipeg (Can.) Symphony, 1967, Rochester Philharmonic Orch., 1973, Ives-Schoenberg Festival, Washington, 1974, Fresno Philharmonic, San Francisco Symphony, Vancouver Opera Orch., ann. European, Far Eastern and S.Am. concert tours.; condr. Grand Teton Music Festival, 1992; also concerts on TV, with Opera Co. of Phila., youth orchs.; composer numerous works including Twelve on Death and No, In Memoriam D.Q., What of My Music, Into Flight From ..., Looking at Orpheus Looking, On A Dream, Requiem for Survivors, Fortieth Day, Beyond McBean, Au Revoir to Lady R., The Relativity of Icarus, Three Hymns to Apollo, Dirge for John Cage, Left Over Mirrors, Music for Four; commd. major orchs., prominent artists; condr. German premiere Hans Rott's Symphony in E with Sudwestfunk Orch., 1993; dir. orch. activities Coll. Conservatory of Music, Cin., from 1976; music dir., condr. Cin. Chamber Orch., 1983-91, Cin. Philharm. Orch., 1976—; invited participant Lincoln Ctr.'s Mozart Bicentennial Celebration, premiere of Outcries and Consolations, L.A., 1990; conducts and recs. (world premieres) Charles Ives (Larry Austin) Universe Symphony, Schubert's opera Der Graf von Gleichen, 1993—; recs. for CRI, Everest, Laurel, Orion, Hyperion, Desto, Delos, Centaur, ACOMA and Vienna Modern Masters labels. Mem. adv. panel State Dept. Cultural Exchange; mem. music council Young Musicians Found. Recipient Nat. Endowment for Arts Composition award, 1974-75, Composer's Showcase N.Y. award, 1976, 77, 78, Post-Corbett award, 1987, Meet the Composer award, 1990, George Rieveschl prize U. Cin., 1992, Alice M. Ditson award Columbia U., 1994; Rockefeller Found. grantee. Mem. ASCAP (ann. award 1970—), Cin. Composers Guild, Nat. Assn. Composers. Achievements include CD recordings of String Quartets, "Transformations" and Nocturne on and "Impossible Dream", 1996—; concert tour of China, American Music Beijing and Shenyang.Orchestra concerto "In Siardi Words", "The Butterfly", and "Two Moods". Home: 412 Liberty Hill #2-C Cincinnati OH 45210-1498 Office: Coll Conservatory Music Cincnati OH 45221-0003

SAMUEL, HOWARD DAVID, union official; b. N.Y.C., Nov. 16, 1924; s. Ralph E. and Florence (Weingarten) S.; m. Ruth H. Zamkin, Apr. 15, 1948; children: Robert H., Donald F., William H. BA, Dartmouth Coll., 1948. Various positions Amalgamated Clothing and Textile Workers (formerly Amalgamated Clothing Workers Am.), N.Y.C., 1949-60; asst. pres. Amalgamated Clothing and Textile Workers (formerly Amalgamated Clothing Workers Am.), 1960-64, v.p., 1966-77; dep. under sec. Bur. Internat. Labor Affairs Dept. Labor, Washington, 1977-79; pres. indsl. union dept. AFL-CIO, Washington, 1979-92; v.p. New Sch. for Social Rsch., N.Y.C., 1964-65, Econ. Strategy Inst., 1992—; vice chmn. N.Y. Urban Coalition, 1968-74; mem. governing bd. Common Cause, 1971-77; sec. Nat. Com. Full Employment, 1975-77, sec.-treas., 1977-89; mem. Pres.'s Commn. on Indsl. Competitiveness, 1983-85; sr. fellow Coun. on Competitiveness, 1993—, sr. chmn., 1986-92; mem. U.S. Dept. Labor Task Force on Econ. Adjustment, and Worker Dislocation, 1985-87; mem. vis. com. advanced tech. Nat. Inst. Stds. and Tech., 1995—; mem. adv. com. Export-Import Bank. Author: (with Stephen K. Bailey) Congress at Work, 1952; Government in America, 1957; Editor: Toward a Better America, 1968. Mem. Nat. Manpower Adv. Com., 1969-74; mem. Commn. Population Growth and the Am. Future, 1970-72; mem. Def. Mfg. Bd., 1988-89, Def. Sci. Bd., 1989-92; chmn. White Plains Dem. Com., 1960-64; vice-chmn. Westchester County com., 1957-70, alt. del. nat. conv., 1964; mem. Nat. Dem. Charter Revision Com., 1972-73; exec. dir. Nat. Labor Com. McGovern-Shriver, 1972; del. Dem. Conv. on Party Orgn. and Policy, Kansas City, 1974, Nat. Dem. Conv., 1976; trustee Carnegie Corp., 1971-77, Joint Coun. Econ. Edn., 1971-77; bd. dirs. ACLU, 1966-68; trustee Brookings Instn.; overseer RAND Inst. for Civil Justice, 1987-93. With AUS, 1943-46. Mem. Coun. on Fgn. Rels., Phi Beta Kappa. Office: Coun on Competitiveness 900 17th St NW Washington DC 20006-2501

SAMUEL, RALPH DAVID, lawyer; b. Augusta, Ga., May 8, 1945; s. Ralph and Louise Elizabeth (Wurreschke) S.; m. Lynn Christel Malmgren, June 12, 1971; children: Lynn Britt, Ralph Erik. AB, Dartmouth Coll., 1967; JD, Dickinson Sch. of Law, 1972. Bar: Pa. 1972, U.S. Dist. Ct. (ea. dist.) Pa. 1972, U.S. Ct. Appeals (3d cir.) 1973, U.S. Supreme Ct. 1976. Law clk. to hon. judge John P. Fullam U.S. Dist. Ct. (ea. dist.) Pa., Phila., 1972-74; assoc. MacCoy, Evans & Lewis., Phila., 1974-76; ptnr. Samuel and Ballard, P.C., Phila., 1976—; established Samuel Poetry Fellow Dartmouth Coll., Hanover, N.H., 1994. Contbr. articles to profl. jours. Trustee The George Sch., Newtown, Pa., 1983-90; chmn. bd. dirs. Stapeley in Germantown, 1985-90; chmn. budget com. Phila. Yearly Meeting of Friends, 1991-93; bd. dirs., mem. fin. com. Phila. Ranger Corps., 1992-94; pres. Cedar Park Neighbors, Phila., 1975-78, West Mt. Airy Neighbors, Phila., 1981-82. Mem. Pa. Soc., Athenaeum of Phila., Germantown Cricket Club. Mem. Soc. of Friends. Avocations: music, writing, squash, tennis. Office: Samuel and Ballard PC 225 S 15th St Fl 1700 Philadelphia PA 19102-3917

SAMUEL, ROBERT THOMPSON, optometrist; b. Kansas City, Mo., June 27, 1944; s. Manlius Thompson and Helen Evelyn (Syverson) S. B.A., William Jewel Coll., 1966; postgrad. U. Mo.-Kansas City, 1967, M.S. U. Mo., 1968; D. Optometry, U. Tenn.-Memphis, 1971. Cert. optometrist, Mo. Buyer Recco, Inc., Kansas City, Mo., 1963-67; histology lab. instr. William Jewell Coll., Liberty, Mo., 1965-66; pvt. practice optometry Gladstone, Mo., 1972—; panel Dr. Ford Motor Co., Claycomo, Mo., 1985—, Union Pacific R.R., Kansas City, 1985—, TWA Airlines, 1990, Union Carbide, 1990. Publicity coord. Rep. Party, Kansas City, Mo., 1975-76; chmn. Save Your Vision Week, Kansas City, 1977; mem. Theatre League of Kansas City, 1976—, Kansas City Mus., 1986—, Friends of Art, 1985, Friends of Mo. Town 1855, 1980—. Recipient Outstanding Young Men of Am. award Jaycees, 1978, Good Citizens award DAR, 1962. Mem. Am. Optometric Assn., Mo. Optometric Assn., Optometric Soc. Greater Kansas City, Heart of Am. Contact Lens Congress, Am. Acad. Sports Vision, Vol. Optometric Svcs. for Humanity, Smithsonian Assocs, Kappa Alpha Order (treas. 1966). Republican. Lutheran. Lodge: Lions (exec. bd. dirs. Lions Eye Clinic 1974-84, bd. dirs. Lions Eye Clinic 1982—, Outstanding Svc. award 1973, 74, editor Lions Optometric Ctr. Quar., 1974-84). Avocations: photography, music, piano, swimming, travel. Home: 6325 N Monroe Ave Kansas City MO 64119-1923 Office: 2700 NE Kendallwood Pky Ste 109 Kansas City MO 64119-2071

SAMUELI, HENRY, electrical engineering educator; b. Buffalo, Sept. 20, 1954; s. Aron and Sala (Traubman) S.; m. Susan Faye Eisenberg, Aug. 22, 1982; children: Leslie Pamela, Jillian Meryl, Erin Sydney. BS, UCLA, 1975, MS, 1976, PhD, 1980. Staff engr. TRW Inc., Redondo Beach, Calif., 1980-83, section mgr., 1983-85; asst. prof. UCLA, 1985-90, assoc. prof., 1990-94, prof., 1994—; cons. TRW, Inc., Redondo Beach, 1985-89; chief scientist PairGain Techs., Inc., Tustin, Calif., 1989-94; v.p. R & D Broadcom Corp., Irvine, Calif., 1991—. Mem. IEEE, Sigma Xi, Tau Beta Pi. Republican. Jewish. Avocations: skiing, basketball. Office: UCLA Elec Engring Dept 56-125B Engring IV Los Angeles CA 90024

SAMUELS, ABRAM, stage equipment manufacturing company executive; b. Allentown, Pa., Sept. 15, 1920; s. Irving and Ann (Friedman) S.; m. Harriet Ann Goodman, Sept. 1, 1945; children: Margaret A. Samuels Berger, Katherine E., Sally R. Samuels Slifkin, John A., Dorothy M. Samuels Lampl, Caroline J. Samuels Bagli. B.S., Lehigh U., 1942; auditor philosophy, Princeton U., 1962-65. Pres. Automatic Devices Co., Allentown, 1946-75, chmn. exec. com., 1987-92; chmn. bd. Automatic Devices Co., 1975-87, 93—; chmn. bd. Mchts. Bank, 1981-85, chmn. exec. com., 1985-91; past guest lectr. Cedar Crest Coll., 1969-71, 84, Muhlenberg Coll., 1977-82, 92. Author: Where the Colleges Rank, 1973. Pres. Samuels Family Found., 1959—; past pres. Pa. Soc. for Crippled Children and Adults, 1957-58; past pres., hon. bd. dirs. Lehigh County Crippled Children's Soc., 1949-51; past pres. Lehigh County Humane Soc., 1960-64, Cedar Crest Coll. Assocs., 1968-70; bd. dirs. Allentown Hosp., 1977-88, chmn. bd., 1987; vice chmn. Allentown Hosp.-Lehigh Valley Hosp. Ctr., 1988; pres. Lehigh County Hist. Soc., 1976-78; past bd. dirs. Nat. Soc. for Crippled Children and Adults, Pa. Mental Health Assn., Merchants Bank, 1965-91, Lehigh County Indsl. Devel. Corp., Pa. Stage Co., 1983-84, Health East, Inc., 1985-91, Nightingale Awards of Pa., 1989-91; trustee St. Augustine's Coll., 1970-77, 92-95, Allentown YWCA, 1977-83, Cedar Crest Coll., 1996—; bd. dirs. Fund to Benefit Children and Youth of Lehigh Valley Inc., 1992—. With AUS, 1942-46. Recipient Benjamin Rush award Lehigh County Med. Soc., 1954, Allentown Human Relations award, 1979; named Outstanding Young Man of Year Jr. C. of C., 1954. Mem. ASCAP, Hon. First Defenders, C. of C. (past v.p. 1960), Pa. German Soc., Am. Soc. Psychical Rsch. (trustee 1985-91, treas. 1990), Princeton Club (N.Y.C.), Rotary (pres. Allentown club 1955-56, dist. gov. 1964-65). Republican. Office: 2121 S 12th St Allentown PA 18103-4751

SAMUELS, CYNTHIA KALISH, communications executive; b. Pitts., May 21, 1946; d. Emerson and Jeanne (Kalish) S.; m. Richard Norman Atkins, Sept. 12, 1971; children: Joshua Whitney Samuels Atkins, Daniel Jonathan Samuels Atkins. BA, Smith Coll., 1968. Press aide McCarthy for Pres. Campaign, Washington, 1968; assoc. producer Newsroom program Sta. KQED, San Francisco, 1972-73; with CBS News, 1973-80, researcher, Washington, 1969-71, documentary researcher, N.Y.C., 1973-74, asst. fgn. editor, 1974-76, asst. N.Y. bur. chief, 1976-80; writer, field producer Today program NBC News, N.Y.C., 1980-84, polit. producer Today program, 1984-89; planning producer, 1988-89; sr. producer Main Street program NBC News, N.Y.C., 1987; founding exec. producer Channel One Program, 1989-92; exec. v.p. Whittle Communications, N.Y.C., 1989-94; now interactive TV and multi-media cons., 1994—. Author: It's A Free Country!: A Young Person's Guide to Politics and Elections, 1988; contbr. book revs. to N.Y. Times Book Rev., Washington Post Book World. Recipient Emmy award No. Calif. Acad. TV Arts and Scis., 1974, Columbia DuPont citation, 1975, Media Access award Calif. Office of Handicapped, 1991, Silver award Nat. Mental Health Assn., 2 Bronze awards Nat. Assn. Edn. in Film and TV, 1993.

SAMUELS, JOHN STOCKWELL, III, financier, mining company executive; b. Galveston, Tex., Sept. 15, 1933; s. John Stockwell and Helen Yvonne (Poole) S.; children: Evelyn Kathleen, John Stockwell, Ainlay Leontine, Peter Ashton Hayes. AB, Tex. A&M U., 1954, SM, 1954; JD, Harvard U., 1960. Bar: N.Y. 1961. Assoc. Chadbourne, Parke, Whiteside & Wolff, N.Y.C., 1960-73; pres. Internat. Carbon & Minerals, N.Y.C., 1973-78, Carbomin Group, Inc., N.Y.C., 1978—; chmn. bd. United Energy Ltd., Manama, Bahrain, 1987—. Bd. dirs. City Center Music and Drama, Inc., N.Y.C.; chmn. bd. dirs. N.Y.C. Ballet, N.Y.C. Opera, 1976-81, Lincoln Ctr. Theatre, N.Y.C., 1979-81, Lincoln Ctr., N.Y.C. With U.S. Army, 1954-57. Mem. Inst. Petroleum, Century Assn., Southampton Bathing Corp. Democrat. Episcopalian.

SAMUELS, LESLIE B., federal agency administrator, lawyer; b. St. Louis, Nov. 10, 1942; s. Joseph E. and Dorothy J. (Bernstein) S.; m. Judith B.

Thorn, June 19, 1966 (div. Aug. 1976); children: Colin T., Polly B.; m. Augusta H. Gross, Nov. 8, 1980. BS in Econs., U. Pa., 1963; LLB magna cum laude, Harvard U., 1966; postgrad., London Sch. Econs., 1966-67. Bar: N.Y., U.S. Dist. Ct. (so. dist.) N.Y., U.S. Tax Ct.; CPA. Tax analyst Gulf Oil Co., London, 1967-68; assoc. Cleary, Gottlieb, Steen & Hamilton, N.Y.C., 1968-75, ptnr., 1975-93; asst. sec. for tax policy U.S. Dept. Treasury, Washington, 1993—. Editor Law Rev.; contbr. articles to profl. jours. Dir. Lower Manhattan Cultural Coun., N.Y.C., 1981-93; active Carter-Mondale Transition Planning Group, Washington, 1976-77. Fulbright fellow London Sch. Econs., 1966-67. Mem. N.Y. State Bar Assn., Assn. of Bar of City of N.Y., Harvard Club (N.Y.C.). Democrat. Office: US Dept Treasury Office Tax Policy 1500 Penn Ave NW Washington DC 20220-0002*

SAMUELS, RICHARD JOEL, political science educator; b. N.Y.C., Nov. 2, 1951; s. Sidney and Rita (Cohen) S.; m. Debra G., June 11, 1972; children: Bradley M., Alexander J. AB, Colgate U., 1973; MA, Tufts U., 1974; PhD, MIT, 1980. Asst. prof. MIT, Cambridge, Mass., 1980-83, assoc. prof., 1983-87, prof., 1987—, head dept. polit. sci., 1992—; mem. Coun. Fgn. Rels., N.Y.C., 1985—, vice chmn. com. on Japan, 1988—; founding dir. MIT Japan Program, 1981—. Author: Politics of Regional Policy in Japan, 1983, Business of Japanese State, 1987 (Ohira prize 1988), Rich Nation, Strong Army, 1994 (Hall prize 1996); editor: Political Generations and Political Developments, 1977, Political Culture of Foreign Area Studies, 1993. Mem. Am. Polit. Sci. Assn., Assn. Asian Studies. Office: MIT Dept Polit Sci E53-473 Cambridge MA 02142

SAMUELS, SHELDON WILFRED, lecturer, educator, writer; b. St. Johnsville, N.Y., Dec. 7, 1929; s. Max and Ethel (Feynman) S.; m. Morjean Rogoff, July 6, 1952; children: Charles A., Susan L. AB, U. Chgo., 1951, postgrad., 1951-56; postgrad., State U. N.Y., 1964-66, USPHS Tng. Program, 1960-66. Mem. adminstrv. staff U. Chgo., 1952-60; dir. pub. info. Air Pollution Control Bd., N.Y. State Health Dept., 1960-66; pub. health advisor USPHS, Washington, 1967-69; chief field service br. Air Programs Office EPA, Washington, 1970-71; dir. health, safety and environment Indsl. Union Dept. AFL-CIO, Washington, 1971-94; adj. prof. State U. N.Y., 1964-66, U. Cin., 1971-73, Mt. Sinai Sch. Medicine, 1973—, Johns Hopkins U., Balt., 1994—; mem. coun. grad. med. edn. HHS, 1987-88; cons. Carpenter's Safety and Health Fund, 1994—; mem. com. on genetic screening policy Congl. Office of Tech. Assessment, 1988-91; mem. hazardous materials com. Sierra Club, 1985—; exec. v.p. Ramazzin Inst., 1992-94, v.p. policy studies, 1995—. Contbg. editor Am. Jour. Indsl. Medicine; contbr. articles, studies on environ. health, philosophy and pub. policy to lay and profl. jours. Past mem. tech. adv. bd. Dept. Commerce, com. on standards ILO; past mem. nat. cancer adv. bd., chmn. subcom. environ. carcinogenesis, mem. com. on risk assessment, mem. com. on cancer control Nat. Cancer Inst.; past mem. task force on research priorities Nat. Inst. Environ. Health Scis.; past mem. com. on regulating chems., com. on food policy and com. on saccharine Nat. Acad. Scis.; founding officer Workers Inst. for Safety and Health, Occupational Health Legal Rights Found.; exec.v.p. Workplace Health Fund, 1983—; exec. dir. Albert Schweitzer Edn. Found., 1959-60; bd. visitors Chesapeake Biol. Lab., U. Md., 1985-89, Ctr. Environ. Policy, U. Md., 1989-92; mem. Vol. Speakers Program Dept. State and Dept. Labor. Recipient ann. Dubos award René Dubos Ctr., 1989, William Steiger award Am. Conf. Govtl. Indsl. Hygienists, 1987. Fellow N.Y. Acad. Scis., Collegium Ramazzini; mem. Am. Coll. Toxicology (past councilor), Environ. and Occupational Health Sci. Inst. (adv. bd.), Soc. for Philosophy and Pub. Affairs. Home: PO Box 50 Solomons MD 20688-0050 Office: Ramazzini Inst PO Box 1570 Solomons MD 20688-1570

SAMUELS, WILLIAM MASON, physiology association executive; b. Dover, Ohio, Jan. 17, 1929; s. William Mason and Anne Frieda (Fankhauser) S.; m. Joanne Gorenflo, Oct. 2, 1971; children: Robert Lee, Ann Frances. A.B., U. Ky., 1951; postgrad., Georgetown U., 1952. Mng. editor for Ind., Courier-Jour. & Times, Louisville, 1955-65; dir. office of v.p. U. Ky. Med. Center, Lexington, 1965-70; exec. dir. Am. Soc. Allied Health Professions, Washington, 1970-78, Am. Assn. Blood Banks, Washington, 1978-80, Nat. Soc. Med. Research Washington, 1980-84, Am. Physiol. Soc., Bethesda, Md., 1984-92; retired, 1992—. Contbr. articles to profl. jours. Mem. secretariat Nat. Commn. Health Certifying Agys.; v.p. Coalition Health Funding; cons. to fed. agys.; vol. Habitat for Humanity, Boca Raton. With USAF, 1951-53, USAFR, 1954-76, lt. col. ret. Named Ky. Man of Yr. Sigma Phi Epsilon, 1968. Mem. Am. Soc. Assn. Execs., Am. Optometric Assn. (mem. coun. on edn., coun. on optometric clin. care), Health Staff Soc., Washington Soc. Assn. Execs., Pinehurst (N.C.) Country Club, Lions. Presbyterian. Home: 3190 Leewood Ter # L-101 Boca Raton FL 33431-6548 Home (summer): 11700 Happy Choice Ln North Potomac MD 20878-2453

SAMUELSEN, ROY, bass-baritone; b. Moss, Norway, June 12, 1933; came to U.S., 1950, naturalized, 1954; s. Ragnar Andreas and Margaret Olivia (Evensen) S.; m. Mary Lou Thorne, May 25, 1955; children—Eric Roy, Robert Ragnar, Rolf Harold. B.S. in Music Edn, Brigham Young U., 1961; Mus.M. in Performance, Ind. U., 1963; diploma, Acad. of West, Santa Barbara, Calif., 1960; student voice, Joseph Heuler, Lotte Lehmann, Victor Fuchs, Frank St. Leger, Paul Matthen Charles Kullman. Sheet metal worker Utah, 1951-61. Performed with, Norwegian Opera Co., guest soloist, Norwegian Singing Soc. Am. convs., also with, Am. orchs., prof. music, Ind. U. Opera Theatre, Bloomington, 1963—, rec. artist., (regional winner Met. Opera Auditions, 1960, San Francisco Opera Auditions 1961). Served with Mil. Police U.S. Army, 1953-55. Recipient Lotte Lehmann award Acad. of West, 1960. Mem. AAUP, Nat. Assn. Tchrs. of Singing, Am. Guild Mus. Artists. Democrat. Mormon. Home: 3615 S Oakridge Dr Bloomington IN 47401-8931 Office: Ind U Bloomington IN 47401 *My success in life is a direct reflection upon the standards set by my parents during my early life and by trying to live according to the teachings of my adopted church. These influences, along with my wife's total devotion, have encouraged me and continue to encourage me in my private and professional life.*

SAMUELSON, BILLIE MARGARET, artist; b. Long Beach, Calif., Apr. 11, 1927; d. William Christian and Gladys Margaret (Caffrey) Newendorp; m. Fritz Eric Samuelson, Aug. 12, 1950 (div. 1985); children: Craig Eric, Clark Alan, Dana Scott. Student, Long Beach City Coll., 1945-46. Pvt. art tchr. Wycokoff/Allendale, N.J., 1985—; workshop instr. Jane Law Studio, Long Beach Island, N.J., 1990—. Exhibited in solo show at Ridgewood (N.J.) Art Inst., 1985, West Wing Gallery, 1991; group shows include Craig Gallery, Ridgewood, 1979, Charisma Gallery, Englewood, N.J., 1981-83, Custom Gallery, Waldwick, N.J., 1985, Wyckoff (N.J.) Gallery, 1987-90, West Wing Gallery, Ringwood State Park, N.J., 1991, Union Camp Corp., 1992. Recipient 1st in State N.J. Womens Clubs, 1978-80, Watercolor award N.J. Painters and Sculptors, 1981. Mem. DAR, Community Arts Assn. (pres. 1978-79), Am. Artists Profl. League (bd. dirs. 1985-87, watercolor prize 1992), Ringwood Manor Arts Assn. (sr. profl.), Catherine Lorillard Wolfe Art Club (cash award 1993), Salute to Women in the Arts, Art Ctr. Watercolor Affiliates, Nat. Mus. of Women in the Arts. Avocations: bridge, travel, museums, theatre, reading. Home: 1-3 Chestnut Pl Waldwick NJ 07463-1125

SAMUELSON, DERRICK WILLIAM, lawyer; b. Mpls., July 24, 1929; s. Oscar W. and Ruth (Hill) S.; m. Diana L. Webster, Aug. 10, 1957; children: David W., Deirdre W. B.S., U.S. Mil. Acad., 1951; LL.B., Harvard U., 1957. Bar: N.Y. 1958. Assoc. firm Lowenstein, Pitcher, Hotchkiss, Amann & Parr, N.Y.C., 1957-60; staff atty. internat. div. Warner-Lambert Pharm. Co., Morris Plains, N.J., 1960-63; counsel internat. div. Olin Mathieson Chem. Corp., N.Y.C., 1964-65; v.p., gen. counsel ITT World Communications Inc., N.Y.C., 1965-70, ITT Asia Pacific, Inc., N.Y.C., 1970-81; sr. counsel ITT Corp., N.Y.C., 1981-87, asst. gen. counsel, asst. sec., 1987-92; of counsel Mulvaney, Kahan & Barry, San Diego, 1993—; mem. panel of arbitrators Asia Pacific Ctr. Pres. Am-Indonesian C. of C., 1976-79, Smoke Rise Club, 1976-77, 88-89; chmn. Am. ASEAN Trade Coun., Inc., 1978-92. With U.S. Army, 1951-54. Mem. ABA, Am. Arbitration Assn. (panel of neutrals 1995—). Home: 2940 Via Asoleado Alpine CA 91901-3182

SAMUELSON, KENNETH LEE, lawyer; b. Natrona Heights, Pa., Aug. 22, 1946; s. Sam and Frances Bernice (Robbins) S.; m. Marlene Ina Rabinowitz, Jan. 1, 1980; children: Heather, Cheryl. BA magna cum laude, U. Pitts., 1968; JD, U. Mich., 1971. Bar: Md. 1972, D.C. 1980, U.S. Dist. Ct. (trial bar) Md. 1984. Assoc. Weinberg & Green, Balt., 1971-73, Dickerson, Nice, Sokol & Horn, Balt., 1973; asst. atty. gen. State of Md., 1973-77; pvt. practice Balt., 1978; ptnr. Linowes and Blocher, Silver Spring (Md.), Washington, 1979-93, Semmes, Bowen & Semmes, Washington and Balt., 1993-95; Wilkes, Artis, Hedrick & Lane, Chartered, Washington and Md., 1995—. Author in field. Bd. dirs. D.C. Assn. for Retarded Citizens, Inc., 1986—. Mem. ABA (chmn. transfer of interest com. sect. real property, probate and trust law 1993—, moderator programs comml. leases 1987, 88, 89, 90, 91, 92, 94), Am. Coll. Real Estate Lawyers, D.C. Bar (comml.) real estate com., chmn. legal opinions project and speaker programs on real estate 1987, 89, 90), Md. State Bar Assn. (real property, planning and zoning sect., chmn. environ. subcom. legal opinions project 1987-89, litigation sect. 1982-84, chmn. comml. trans. com.), Md. Inst. Continuing Profl. Edn. Lawyers (speaker on article 9 of Uniform Comml. Code, opinion letters, environ. considerations in real estate transactions, easements, enforcement of liens easements, and leasing to profls. 1981, 83, 88, 89, 91, 94), Am. Arbitration Assn. (arbitrator and mediator), Washington D.C. Assn of Realtors, Inc. (moderator of a program on commercial leasing in 1992, program on letters of intent 1996), Apt. and Office Bldg. Assn. Met. Washington (moderator of programs and speaker 1989, 92), East Coast Builders Conf. (moderator program on Asian financing 1990), Internat. Coun. Shopping Ctrs. (organized, co-faculty program "univ." 1988, NAFTA 1992, condemnations 1994), Montgomery County Bar Assn. (jud. selections com. 1988-90), Phi Beta Kappa, Lambda Alpha. Office: Wilkes Artis Hedrick & Lane Ste 1100 1666 K St NW Washington DC 20006

SAMUELSON, MARVIN LEE, veterinarian; b. Oketo, Kans., July 25, 1931; s. Eben R. and Mabel M. (Brown) S.; m. Rubye Rittgers, Aug. 26, 1995; children by previous marriage: Valorie, Vonna, Melanie, John, Jennifer. BS, Kans. State U., 1956, DVM, 1956. Staff veterinarian Carthage (Mo.) Vet. Svcs., 1956, San Pedro (Calif.) Animal Hosp., 1958-61; ptnr., mgr. Clarmar Animal Hosp., Torrance, Calif., 1961-63; owner, dir. South Shore Pet Clinic, San Pedro, Calif., 1963-73; assoc. prof. Coll. Vet. Medicine Kans. State U., Manhattan, 1973-87; dir. Vet. Tchg. Hosp. Tex. A&M U., College Station, 1987-91, asst. to dean pub. programs Coll. Vet. Medicine, 1991-92; dir. Animal Dermatology and Allergy Assocs., Topeka, 1992—. Contbr. book chpts. to vet. textbooks, articles to profl. jours. Mem. Jaycees, San Pedro, 1958-61; pres. Lions Club, 1963-64; v.p. San Pedro C. of C., 1972; precinct committeeman Wildcat Twp., Manhattan, 1985-87. 1st lt. U.S. Army, 1956-58. Recipient Bustad award for Companion Animal Vet. of Yr., 1996. Mem. AVMA (mem. edn. com. vet. fgn. grads. 1994—), Am. Acad. Vet. Dermatology (sec.-treas. 1986-91), Acad. Vet. Allergy (bd. dirs. 1983-91), Am. Assn. Vet. Clinicians (pres. 1990-91), Tex. Vet. Med. Assn., Kans. Vet. Med. Assn. (Kans. Vet. of Yr. 1992), Kans. Bd. Vet. Examiners (pres.), Calif. Vet. Med. Assn., So. Calif. Vet. Med. Assn. (pres. 1972), Soc. for Internat. Vet. Symposium (pres.-elect 1991), Alpha Zeta. Republican. Methodist. Avocation: farming. Office: Animal Dermat Allrgy Assocs 11520 SW 57th Topeka KS 66610

SAMUELSON, PAUL ANTHONY, economics educator; b. Gary, Ind., May 15, 1915; s. Frank and Ella (Lipton) S.; m. Marion E. Crawford, July 2, 1938 (dec.); children: Jane Kendall, Margaret Wray, William Frank, Robert James, John Crawford, Paul Reid.; m. Risha Eckaus, 1981; stepdaughter, Susan Miller. BA, U. Chgo., 1935; MA, Harvard U., 1936, PhD (David A. Wells prize 1941), 1941; LLD (hon.), U. Chgo., Oberlin Coll., 1961, Boston Coll., 1964, Ind. U., 1966, U. Mich., 1967, Claremont Grad. Sch., 1967, Seton Hall U., 1971, U. N.H., 1971, Keio U., 1971, Widener Coll., 1982, Cath. U. at Riva Aguero U., Lima, Peru, 1980, Harvard, 1972, Gustavus Adolphus Coll., 1974, U. So. Calif., 1975, U. Pa., 1976, U. Rochester, 1976, Emmanuel Coll., 1977, Stonehill Coll., 1978, Indiana U. of Pa., 1993; DLitt (hon.), Ripon Coll., 1962, No. Mich. U., 1973, Valparaiso U., 1987, Columbia U, 1988; LHD (hon.), Williams Coll., 1971; DSc (hon.), U. Mass., 1972, U. R.I., 1972, Tufts U., 1988, East Anglia U., Norwich, Eng., 1966; D (hon.), U. Catholique de Louvain, Belgium, 1976, City U., London, 1980, New U. Lisbon, 1985, Univ. Nat. de Educacion a Distancia, Madrid, 1989, Univ. Politecnica de Valencia, Spain, 1991. Prof. econs. MIT, 1940-65, inst. prof., 1966, prof. emeritus, 1986; mem. staff Radiation Lab., 1944-45; prof. internat. econ. relations Fletcher Sch. Law and Diplomacy, 1945; cons. Nat. Resources Planning Bd., 1941-43, WPB, 1945, U.S. Treasury, 1945-52, 61-74, Bur. Budget, 1952, RAND Corp., 1948-75, Fed. Res. Bd., 1965—; council Econ. Advisers, 1960-68; econ. adviser to Pres. Kennedy; sr. adviser Brookings Panel on Econ. Activity; mem. spl. commn. on social scis. NSF, 1967-68; cons. Congl. Budget Office, Federal Reserve Bd., 1965—; Gordon Y Billard Fellow MIT, Boston, 1986—; vis. prof of polit. econ. Ctr. Japan-U.S. Bus. and Econ. Studies, NYU, 1987—; Stamp Meml. lectr., London, 1961, Wicksell lectr., Stockholm, 1962, Franklin lectr., Detroit, 1962; Carnegie Found. reflective year, 1965-66; John von Neumann lectr. U. Wis., 1971; Gerhard Colm Meml. lectr. New Sch. for Social Research, N.Y.C., 1971; Sulzbacher Meml. lectr. Columbia Law Sch., N.Y.C., 1974; J. Willard Gibbs lectr. Am. Math. Soc., San Francisco, 1974; John Diebold lectr. Harvard, 1976; Alice E. Blurneuf lectr. Boston Coll., 1981, Horowitz lectr. Jerusalem and Tel Aviv, 1984, Marschak Meml. lectr. UCLA, 1984, Tennenbaum lectr. Ga. Inst. Tech., 1985, Julis Steinberg Meml. lectr. Wharton Sch., 1986, Godkin lectr. Harvard, 1986, Woodward lectr. U. British Columbia, 1987; lectr. Harvard 350 Symposium, Harvard U., 1986, Olin lectr. U. Va., 1989, Commemorative lectr. Stonehill Coll., 1990, Lionel Robbins Meml. lectr. Claremont Coll., 1991; mem. nat. advisory com. Inst. for Rsch. on Poverty. Author: Foundations of Economic Analysis, 1947, enlarged edit., 1983, Economics, 1948-95, Readings in Economics, 1955-73, (with R. Dorfman and R.M. Solow) Linear Programming and Economic Analysis, 1958, Collected Scientific Papers, 5 vols., 1966, 72, 78, 86; co-author numerous other books; contbr. numerous articles to profl. jours.; columnist Newsweek, 1966-81; assoc. editor Jour. Pub. Econs., Jour. Internat. Econs., Jour. Fin. Econs., Jour. Nonlinear Analysis; adv. bd. Challenge Mag.; editl. bd. Procs. Nat. Acad. Scis. Chmn. Pres.'s Task Force Maintaining Am. Prosperity, 1964; mem. Nat. Task Force on Econ. Edn., 1960-61; econ. adviser to Pres. John F. Kennedy, 1959-63; mem. adv. bd. Nat. Commn. Money and Credit, 1958-60. Hon. fellow London Sch. Econs. and Polit. Sci. Guggenheim fellow, 1948-49; Ford Found. Research fellow, 1958-59; recipient David A. Wells prize Harvard U., 1941, John Bates Clark medal Am. Econ. Assn., 1947, Alfred Nobel Meml. prize, 1970, medal of Honor U. Evansville, Ill., 1970, Albert Einstein Commemorative award, 1971, Alumni medal U. Chgo., 1983, Britannica award, 1989, Gold Scanno prize, Naples, Italy, 1990; Paul A. Samuelson Professorship established in his name, MIT, 1991. Fellow Brit. Acad. (corr. Am. Philos. Soc., Econometric Soc. (v.p. 1950, pres. 1951), Am. Econ. Assn. (hon.; pres. 1961); mem. AAAS, Com. Econ. Devel. (commn. on nat. goals, research adv. bd. 1959-60), Internat. Econ. Assn. (pres. 1966-68, hon. pres.), Nat. Acad. Scis., Leibniz-Akademie der Wissenschaften und der Literatur (corr. mem. 1987—) Nat. Assn. of Investment Clubs (Disting. Svc. award in Investment Edn. 1974), Club of Econ. and Mgmt. (medal, hon. Valencia, Spain 1990), Phi Beta Kappa, Omicron Delta Epsilon (trustee). Home: 94 Somerset St Belmont MA 02178-2010 Office: MIT Dept Econs E52 # 383C Cambridge MA 02139

SAMUELSON, RITA MICHELLE, speech language pathologist; b. Chgo., July 15, 1954; d. Mike Dabetic and Rita Lorraine (Stasny) Dabertin; m. K. Alan Samuelson, May 7, 1977; children: Amber Michelle, April Claire. BS, Ind. U., 1976, MA in Teaching, 1977. Speech lang. therapist East Maine Dist. 63, Des Plaines, Ill., 1977-80, Cmty. Cons. Dist. 59, Elk Grove, Ill., 1980-83, Fenton High Sch. Dist. 100, Bensenville, Ill., 1988-93, Addison (Ill.) Dist. 4, 1993-94, Elgin (Ill.) Dist. U-46, 1994—. Author: Sound Strategist, 1989, The Birthday Party Adventure, 1991, The Lizard Princess Adventure, 1991; contbr. chpt.: Yuletide Reverie, 1993. Mem. Am. Speech Lang. Hearing Assn., DuPage County Speech Hearing Lang. Assn. (v.p. bd. dirs. 1995—), Ill. Speech Lang. Hearing Assn., Villagers Club Bloomingdale, Writer's Workshop of Bloomingdale. Roman Catholic. Avocations: singing in church choir, lectr. in children and humor, doll collecting, antiquing. Home: 156 Longridge Dr Bloomingdale IL 60108-1416 Office: Oakhill Elementary Sch 502 S. Oltendorf Rd Streamwood IL 60107

SAMUELSON, ROBERT JACOB, journalist; b. N.Y.C., Dec. 23, 1945; s. Abraham and Joan (Kahn) S.; m. Judith Herr, July 10, 1983; children: Ruth, Michael, John. AB in Govt., Harvard U., 1967. Reporter Washington Post, 1969-73; free-lance writer Washington, 1973-76; reporter; columnist National Jour. mag., Washington, 1976-84; columnist Newsweek, Washington, 1984—; columnist Washington Post, 1977—. Author: The Good Life and Its Discontents: The American Dream in the Age of Entitlement 1945-1995, 1996.

SAN AGUSTIN, JOE TAITANO, Guam senator, financial institution executive, management researcher; b. Agana, Guam, Oct. 15, 1930; s. Candido S. and Maria P. (Taitano) San A.; m. Carmen Santos Shimizu, June 18, 1955; children: Mary, Ann, Joe, John. BA, George Washington U., 1954, MA, 1965. Chief budget and mgmt. Office of Govt. Guam, Agana, 1966-68; dir. dept. adminstrn. Govt. Guam, Agana, 1968-74; senator Guam Legislature, Agana, 1976—, minority leader 16th Guam Legislature, 1981-82, vice-speaker 17th and 18th Guam Legislature, 1983-86, chmn. com. on ways and means 17th and 18th Guam Legislatures, 1983-86, chmn. com. on health, edn. and welfare 19th Guam Legislature, 1987, chmn. com. on edn., 1991, econ. com.; speaker 20th, 21st, 22nd Guam Legislature, 1989-95, chmn. econ. com. Guam Legis., 1975—. bd. dirs. Bank of Guam, Agana. Democrat. Roman Catholic. Office: 155 Hessler Pl Agana GU 96910-5004

SAN ANTONIO MENDOZA, OSCAR ANIBAL, state legislator; b. Isabela, P.R., Jan. 17, 1945; s. Giordano A. and Maria Teresa (Mendoza) San A.; m. Ana I. Rivero, Jan. 21, 1966; children: Oscar A., Silvia M., Ana Maria. BS, U. Catolica P.R., Ponce, 1966. Med. rep. Merck, Sharp & Dohme, Carolina, 1967-70, Schering Plough P.R. Inc., Carolina, 1970-84; mem. Ho. of Reps., San Juan, 1985—. Treas. Partido Popular Democratico, Isabela, 1982-84, campaign dir. mgr., 1986-94. Mem. Lions, Phi Sigma Alpha. Roman Catholic. Avocations: reading, diving, swimming. Home: Ave Estacion # 61 Isabela PR 00662-2808 Office: Camara de Reps Capitolio San Juan PR 00662

SANBORN, ANNA LUCILLE, pension and insurance consultant; b. Bklyn., Mar. 29, 1924; d. Peter Francis and Matilda M. (Stumpp) Galligen; B.A., Bklyn. Coll., 1945; 1 son, Dean Sanborn. Head dept. benefit and estate planning Union Central Life Ins. Co., N.Y.C., 1949-51; adminstr. employee benefits Seaboard Oil Co., N.Y.C., 1952-56; with Frank J. Walters Assocs., Inc., N.Y.C., 1957—, pres., 1970—. Bd. dirs. Archdiocesan Service Corp. Mem. Am. Acad. Actuaries, Republican. Roman Catholic. Home: 58-11 Seabury St Elmhurst NY 11373-4825 Office: Frank J Walters Assocs 58-13 Seabury St Flushing NY 11373-4825

SANBORN, DAVID, alto saxophonist; b. St. Louis, MO, 1945. Student, Northwestern Univ., Univ. of Iowa. Ind. jazz saxophonist, 1975—. Rec. artist: (with James Taylor) How Sweet It Is, (with David Bowie) Young Americans, (with Gil Evans) Priestess, (with Bob James) Double Vision, (solo albums) Taking Off, 1975, Sanborn, 1976, Promise Me the Moon, 1977, Heart to Heart, 1978, Hideaway, 1980, Voyeur, 1981, Grammy awd., 1981), As We Speak, 1982, Backstreet, 1983, Straight to the Heart, 1984, Close Up, 1988 (Grammy awd., 1989), Upfront, 1992, Hearsay, 1994, Pearls, 1995; music for film: Lethal Weapon 2, 1989; host and co-producer of "The Jazz Show," NBC-Radio; TV appearances: host of Night Music, 1988-89, regular guest on Late Night with David Letterman, 1982-94.

SANBORN, GEORGE FREEMAN, JR., genealogist; b. Laconia, N.H., Jan. 18, 1944; s. George Freeman and Charlotte (Dearborn) S.; m. Melinde Laura Lutz, Mar. 30, 1984; children: Ruth Alice, Lowell Freeman. AB, Boston U., 1967; AM, U. Ill., 1968; MEd, U. N.H., 1981. French tchr. Souris (P.E.I., Can.) Regional H.S., 1968-69; French and occupational studies tchr. Massey-Vanier H.S., Cowansville, Que., Can., 1969-70; French and English tchr. Kings Coll. Sch., Windsor, N.S., Can., 1970-71; translator, revisor Province of N.B., Fredericton, 1971-73; sr. govt. revisor Province of Ont., Toronto, 1973-75; French and Spanish tchr. Tilton (N.H.) Sch., 1978-80; living unit coord. Laconia (N.H.) State Sch., 1982-83; ref. libr. New Eng. Hist. Geneal. Soc., Boston, 1983-85, acquisitions libr. and tech. svcs. dir., 1985—. Editor The N.H. Geneal. Record, 1990-93; compiler Vital Records of Hampton, N.H., 1992; contbr. articles to profl. jours. Fellow Am. Soc. Genealogists; mem. Soc. of the Cin. in the State of N.H., Soc. of Mayflower Descendants in the State of N.H., New Eng. Hist. Geneal. Soc., P.E.I. Geneal. Soc., N.H. Soc. Genealogists (pres. 1988-95), Geneal. Soc. Vt. (chair publs. com. 1992—). Democrat. Presbyterian. Avocations: gardening, bantam raising, Scottish Gaelic language, P.E.I. history, antique glass and china. Home: 24 Thornton St Derry NH 03038-1628 Office: New Eng Hist Geneal Soc Libr 99-101 Newbury St Boston MA 02116

SANBRAILO, JOHN A., mission director; b. San Francisco, July 26, 1943; s. John and Ann (Schonfeld) S.; m. Cecilia Del Pozo, Jan. 12, 1974. B in Econs., U. Calif., Berkeley, 1965; M in Econs., San Francisco State U., 1969; MPA, Harvard U., 1976. Vol. U.S. Peace Corps., Sucre State, Venezuela, 1965-68; credit union and coop. extension agt. U.S. Peace Corps., Washington; internat. devel. intern US AID, Washington, 1969-70; chief project devel. Nicaragua, project devel. officer Ecuador US AID, 1970-75; dir. policy planning and budgeting, chief fin. officer Latin Am. and Caribbean Bur. US AID, Washington, 1976-79; dir. US AID Mission, Quito, Ecuador, 1979-82, 93-96, Lima, Peru, 1983-86, Tequcigalpa, Honduras, 1987-91, San Salvador, El Salvador, 1991-93; career minister US Sr. Fgn. Svc. Decorated Honduran Cong., 1991, Govt. Peru, 1984, 96, Govt. Ecuador, 1982, 96. Office: USAID Quito Ecuador Unit 5330 APO AA 34039

SANCAR, AZIZ, research biochemist. MD, Istanbul Med. Sch., 1969; PhD in Molecular Biology, U. Tex., Dallas, 1977. Assoc. prof. biochemistry U. N.C., Chapel Hill, 1982—. Office: University of N Carolina School of Medicine Dept of Biochem & Biophysics Chapel Hill NC 27599*

SANCETTA, CONSTANCE ANTONINA, oceanographer; b. Richmond, Va., Apr. 17, 1949; d. Anthony Louis and Joyce Louise (Kellogg) S. BA, Brown U., 1971, MSc, 1973; PhD, Oreg. State U., 1976. Rsch. assoc. Stanford (Calif.) U., 1977-78; assoc. rsch. scientist Columbia U., N.Y.C., 1979-84, rsch. scientist, 1985-87, sr. rsch. scientist, 1988-94; assoc. program mgr. divsn. ocean sci. NSF, Washington, 1992—; mem. adv. com. divsn. ocean sci. NSF, 1981-86, 89-92. Editl. bd. Marine Micropaleontology, Oceanography, 1983—; contbr. articles to profl. jours. Fellow AAAS, Geol. Soc. Am.; mem. Am. Quaternary Soc. (councilor 1988-90), Am. Geophys. Union (sec. ocean sci. sect. 1988-90), Oceanography Soc. (councilor 1989-93), Paleontol. Rsch. Instn. (trustee 1991-92). Home: 1637 Irvin St Vienna VA 22182-2119 Office: NSF Assoc Prog Mgr Divsn Ocean Sci 4201 Wilson Blvd Rm 725 Arlington VA 22230

SANCHEZ, DAVID ALAN, mathematics educator; b. San Francisco, Jan. 13, 1933; m. Joan Patricia Thomas, Dec. 28, 1957; children: Bruce, Christina. BS, U. N.Mex., 1955; MS, U. Mich., 1960, PhD, 1964. Instr. U. Chgo., 1963-65; from asst. to assoc. to full prof. UCLA, 1966-77, assoc. dean grad. sch., 1972-73; prof. U. N.Mex., Albuquerque, 1977-86, chmn. dept. math., 1983-86; v.p., provost Lehigh U., Bethlehem, 1986-90; asst. dir. math. and phys. scis. NSF, Washington, 1990-92; dep. assoc. dir. rsch. and edn. Los Alamos (N.Mex.) Nat. Lab., 1992-93; vice chancellor acad. affairs Tex. A&M Sys., College Station, 1993-95; prof. math. Tex. A&M U., College Station, 1996—. Author books; contbr. articles to profl. jours. Served as 1st lt. USMC, 1956-59. Mem. Am. Math. Soc., Math. Assn. Am. Avocations: fishing, bridge. Office: Tex A & M U Dept Math College Station TX 77843-3368

SANCHEZ, GILBERT, retired academic administrator, microbiologist, researcher; b. Belen, N.Mex., May 7, 1938; s. Macedonio C. and Josephine H. Sanchez; m. Lorena T. Tabet, Aug. 26, 1961; children—Elizabeth, Phillip, Katherine. B.S. in Biology, N.Mex. State U., 1961; Ph.D. in Microbiology, U. Kans., 1967. Research asst. U. Kans., Lawrence, 1963-67; research assoc., postdoctoral fellow Rice U., Houston, 1967-68; prof. N.Mex. Inst. Tech., Socorro, 1968-79; dean grad. studies Eastern N.Mex. U., Portales, 1979-83; v.p. acad. affairs U. So. Colo., Pueblo, 1983-85; pres. N.Mex. Highlands U., Las Vegas, 1985-95; cons. NIH, NSF, Solvex Corp., Albuquerque, 1979-83; bd. dirs. Fed. Res. Bank, Denver. Contbr. numerous articles to profl. jours. Patentee in field. Pres. Socorro Sch. Bd., 1974-79, Presbyn. Hosp. Bd., Socorro, 1977-79. Research grantee Dept. Army, 1976-79, N.Mex. Dept. Energy, 1979-83, NSF, 1979. Mem. Am. Soc. Microbiology, Am. Soc. Indsl. Microbiology, AAAS, Am. Assn. Univs. and Colls. (bd. dirs. 1988-90), Hispanic Assn. Univs. and Colls. (pres. 1986-89). Roman Catholic. Lodge: Rotary. Avocations: auto mechanics; welding; woodworking; golf.

SANCHEZ, LEONEDES MONARRIZE WORTHINGTON (DUKE DE LEONEDES), fashion designer; b. Flagstaff, Ariz., Mar. 15, 1951; s. Rafael Leonedes and Margaret (Monarrize) S. BS, No. Ariz. U., 1974; studied, Fashion Inst. Tech., N.Y.C., 1974-75; AA, Fashion Inst. D&M, L.A., 1975; lic., La Ecole de la Chambre Syndical de la Couture Parisian, Paris, 1976-78. Lic. in designing. Contract designer/asst. to head designer House of Bonnet, Paris, 1976—; dress designer-in-residence Flagstaff, 1978—; mem. faculty No. Ariz. U., Flagstaff, 1978-80; designer Ambiance, Inc., L.A., 1985—; designer Interiors by Leonedes subs. Studio of Leonedes Couturier, Ariz., 1977, Calif., 1978, London, Paris, 1978, Rome, 1987, Milan, Spain, 1989; designer Liturgical Vesture subs. Studio of Leonedes Couturier; CEO Leonedes Internat.; owner, COO, designer Leonedes Internat., Ltd., London, Milan, Paris, Spain, Ambian Ariz, Calif., Appolonian Costuming, Ariz., London, Milan, Paris, El Castillo de Leonedes, Sevilla, Spain, Villa Apollonian de Leonedes, Mykonos, Greece; cns. House of Bonnet, Paris, 1976—, Bob Mackie, Studio City, Calif., 1974-75. Bd. dirs. Roman Cath. Social Svcs., 1985-86, Northland Crisis Nursery, 1985—; bd. dirs., chmn. Pine Country Transit, 1986-88; pres. Chicanos for Edn.; active master's swim program ARC, Ariz., 1979—; eucharistic min., mem. art and environ. com., designer liturgical vesture St. Pius X Cath. Ch.; vol. art tchr., instr. St. Mary's Regional Sch., Flagstaff, 1987-90, vol. art dir.; mem. Flagstaff Parks and Recreation Commn., 1994-96, citizens' adv. com. master plan, 1994-96; mem. cmty. bd. adv. com. Flagstaff Unified Sch. Dist., 1995; active Duke de Leonedes Found., The Netherlands, 1994—. Decorated Duke de Leonedes (Spain), 1994; recipient Camellian Design award 1988, Atlanta. Mem. AAU (life, chairperson swiimming Ariz. 1995, vice chairperson physique, mem. citizen adv. bd. parks and recreation), Am. Film Inst., Am. Assn. Hist. Preservation, Costume Soc., Am. Nat. Physique Com., Internat. Consortium Fashion Designers, Nat. Cath. Ednl. Assn., La Legion de Honour de la Mode Parisienne, Social Register Assn., Phi Alpha Theta (historian 1972-73, pres. 1973-74), Pi Kappa Delta (pres. 1972-73, historian 1973-74). Republican. Avocations: body building, swimming. Address: El Castillo de Leonedes, Seville Spain Also: Villia de Apollonian de Leonedes, Mykonos Greece

SANCHEZ, MARY ANNE, secondary school educator; b. Galesburg, Ill., Aug. 4, 1939; d. Stephen Mingare and M. Margaret Kennedy; m. J. Manuel Sanchez, Dec. 26, 1980. BS in Edn., Western Ill. U., 1961; MA, Ill. State U., 1970. Tchr. Montgomery County Bd. Edn., Chevy Chase, Md., Hillsborough County Bd. Edn., Tampa, Fla.; tchr. Stanford, Ill., Titusville, Fla. Mem. Nat. Coun. for Social Studies, Fla. Coun. for Social Studies, Adult Edn. Assn. Home: 2715 W Ivy St Tampa FL 33607-1922

SANCHEZ, RAFAEL CAMILO, physician; b. Tampa, Fla., July 18, 1919; s. Francisco and Catalina (Mateo) S.; children: Stephen Francis, John Thomas, David Lear. B.S., Loyola U., New Orleans, 1940; M.D., La. State U., 1950. Diplomate: Am. Bd. Family Practice (bd. dirs. 1976-79, assoc. exec. dir. 1979-84). Intern U.S. Marine Hosp., New Orleans, 1950-51; gen. practice medicine New Orleans, 1951-72; med. educator, dir. continuing med. edn. La. State U., 1963-77, prof. family medicine, 1979-84; prof. family medicine East Carolina U. Sch. Medicine, Greenville, 1984-90, prof. emeritus, 1990—; dir. family practice residency program Charity Hosp. of Bogalusa, La., 1977-79; dir. Continuing Med. Edn.; med. dir. Nat. Med. Info. Network. Served with AUS, 1940-46. Recipient Recognition award Soc. of Tchrs. of Medicine, 1987, Willard M. Duff award Accreditation Coun. for Continuing Med. Edn. Fellow AMA, Am. Acad. Family Physicians (Thomas W. Johnson award 1978, Presdl. award 1983, Pres.'s award 1989); mem. Network for Continuing Med. Edn. (med. dir.), Nat. Med. Info. Network of the World Med. Comms. Orgns. (med. dir.), Alpha Omega Alpha. Democrat. Roman Catholic. Office: PO Box 20035 Greenville NC 27858-0035

SANCHEZ, ROBERT FORTUNE, archbishop; b. Socorro, N.Mex., Mar. 20, 1934; s. Julius C. and Priscilla (Fortune) S. Student, Immaculate Heart Sem., Santa Fe, 1954, N.Am. Coll., Gregorian U., Rome, 1960. Ordained priest Roman Cath. Ch., 1959; prof. St. Piux X High Sch., Albuquerque, 1960-68; dir. extension lay vols. Archdiocese Santa Fe, 1965-68, chmn. priest personnel bd., 1968-72, vicar gen., 1974, archbishop, 1974-93; rep. instl. ministry pastoral care N.Mex. Council Chs., 1968; pres. Archdiocesan Priests Senate, 1973-74; rep. region X Nat. Fedn. Priests Councils, 1972-73; bd. dirs. Mexican Am. Cultural Center; mem. regional com. Nat. Conf. Cath. Bishops, N.Am. Coll., Rome; pres. N.Mex. Conf. Chs.; gen. sec. U.S. Cath. Conf./Nat. Conf. Cath. Bishops, 1991. Mem. U.S. Cath. Conf. (chmn. ad hoc com. Spanish speaking). Office: Archdiocese Santa Fe The Cath Ctr 4000 Saint Josephs Pl NW Albuquerque NM 87120-1714*

SANCHEZ, ROBERT FRANCIS, journalist; b. Bradenton, Fla., Jan. 1, 1938; s. Robert and Frances Alice (Thompson) S. B.S. in English Edn., Fla. State U., 1959, M.S., 1962, postgrad., 1971-74. Mem. faculty Fla. State U., Tallahassee, 1962-67; mem. faculty Fla. A&M U., Tallahassee, 1968-71; writer, editor Tallahassee Democrat, 1965-74; editorial writer Miami Herald, 1974—. Co-recipient Pulitzer Prize, 1983. Mem. Phi Delta Kappa, Sigma Delta Chi. Republican. Methodist. Home: 7000 Miller Rd Miami FL 33155-5615 Office: Miami Herald 1 Herald Plz Miami FL 33132-1609

SANCHEZ, VICTORIA WAGNER, science educator; b. Milw., Apr. 11, 1934; d. Arthur William and Lorraine Marguerite (Kocovsky) Wagner; m. Rozier Edmond Sanchez, June 23, 1956; children: Mary Elizabeth, Carol Anne, Robert Edmond, Catherine Marie, Linda Therese. BS cum laude, Mt. Mary Coll., 1955; MS, Marquette U., 1957; postgrad., U. N.Mex., 1979-86, U. Del., 1990. Cert. secondary tchr., N.Mex. Chemist Nat. Bur. Standards, Washington, 1958-60; tchr., chmn. sci. dept. Albuquerque Pub. Schs., 1979-94; chmn. pub. info. area conv. Nat. Sci. Tchrs. Assn., 1984, mem. sci. rev. com. Albuquerque Pub. Schs., 1985-86, 92-93, dedication of N.W. Regional Sci. Fair, 1994, Gov.'s Summit on Edn., 1991, 92, Gov.'s Steering Com. Systemic Change in Math. and Sci. Edn. Bd. dirs. Encino House, Albuquerque, 1976-92, treas., 1977-79; leader Albuquerque troop Girl Scouts U.S., 1966-77. Named Outstanding Sci. Tchr., NW Regional Sci. Fair, Albuquerque, 1983, 88, 90; recipient St. George's award N.Mex. Cath. Scouting Com., 1978, Focus on Excellence award ASCD, Albuquerque, 1985, 89, Presdl. awards for excellence in sci. and math., 1989. Mem. AAUW (officer Albuquerque br. 1976-77, N.Mex. divsn. 1977-78), NSTA, N.Mex. Sci. Tchrs. Assn. (treas. 1988-90), Albuquerque Sci. Tchrs. Assn. (treas. 1984-85, v.p., pres.-elect 1986-87, pres. 1987-88, Svc. to Sci. award 1994), N.Mex. Acad. Sci., Am. Coun. on Edn. (math. and sci. edn. nat. com. 1990-92), DuPont Honors Workshop for Tchrs., Albuquerque Rose Soc. (sec. 1962-63). Democrat. Roman Catholic. Avocations: reading, fishing, hiking, needlecraft, camping. Home: 7612 Palo Duro Ave NE Albuquerque NM 87110-2315

SANCHEZ-LLACA, JUAN, hotel executive; b. Oviedo, Spain, Jan. 29, 1960; s. Luis Sanchez and Marina Llaca. Grad. law degree, U. Pontificia de Comillas-ICADE, Madrid, 1983, BA, 1984; M in Tax Law, Centro de Estudios Tributarios y Economicos, Madrid, 1987; Grad. Bus. Sch., Stanford U., Palo Alto, Ca. Cons. Deloitte Haskins & Sells, Madrid, 1984-85, tax sr., 1985-87; internat. tax specialist Deloitte & Touche, L.A., 1988-89; asst. COO Cannon Group/Pathe Metro Goldwyn Mayer Communications, L.A., 1989-90; pres. Imperial Hotel Corp., L.A., 1990-92, Interfly, L.A., 1990-92, Vagabond Inns, Inc., El Segundo, Ca., 1994—. Office: Arquitecto Reguera, 9-7F Oviedo Spain

SAND, LEONARD B., federal judge; b. N.Y.C., May 24, 1928. B.S., NYU, 1947; LL.B., Harvard, 1951. Bar: N.Y. 1953, U.S. Supreme Ct. 1956, D.C. 1969. Clk. to dist. ct. judge N.Y., 1952-53; asst. U.S. atty. So. Dist. N.Y., 1953-54; asst. to U.S. Solictor Gen., 1956-59; mem. firm Robinson, Silverman, Pearce, Aronsohn Sand and Berman, N.Y.C., 1960-78; judge U.S. Dist. Ct. So. Dist. N.Y., 1978—; adj. prof. law NYU. Note editor: Harvard Law Rev, 1950-51. Del. N.Y. State Constl. Conv., 1967; v.p., treas. Legal Aid Soc. Fellow Am. Coll. Trial Lawyers; mem. ABA, Assn. Bar City N.Y. (v.p.), N.Y. State Bar Assn., Fed. Bar Coun. Office: US Dist Ct US Courthouse 500 Pearl St New York NY 10007-1316*

SAND, THOMAS CHARLES, lawyer; b. Portland, Oreg., June 4, 1952; s. Harold Eugene and Marian Anette (Thomas) S.; m. Rhonda Diane Laycoe, June 15, 1974; children: Kendall, Taylor, Justin. Student, Centro des Artes y Lenguas, Cuernavaca, Mex., 1972; BA in English, U. Oreg., 1974; JD, Lewis and Clark Coll., 1977. Bar: Oreg. 1977, U.S. Dist. Ct. Oreg. 1977, U.S. Ct. Appeals (9th cir.) 1984. Assoc. Miller, Nash, Wiener, Hager & Carlsen, Portland, 1977-84, ptnr., 1984—; mem. Oreg. State Bar Com. on Professionalism, 1989, chmn., 1990; dir. young lawyers divsn. Multnomah County Bar Assn., 1980; spl. asst. atty. gen. Wasco County 1983 Gen. Election; speaker in field. Contbr. articles to legal jours. and procs. Mem. U.S. Dist. Ct. of Oreg. Hist. Soc., 1990—; bd. dirs. Portland Area coun. Camp Fire, Inc., 1978-90,pres., 1984-86; bd. dirs. Oreg. Indoor Invitational Track Meet, Inc., 1982-84. Recipient Boss of the Yr. award Portland Legal Secs. Assn., 1989. Mem. ABA (securities litigation com., subcom. on broker-dealer litigation), Oreg. Bar Assn., Multnomah Bar Assn. (bd. dirs. task force on structure and orgn. 1989, chmn. com. on professionalism 1988, nominating com. 1986, participating atty. in N.E. legal clin. Vol Lawyers project, award of merit for svc. to profession 1988), Securities Industry Assn. (compliance and legal divsn.), Northwestern Sch. of Law, Lewis and Clark Coll. Alumni Assn. (bd. dirs. 1992), Valley Comm. Presbyterian Ch., Multnomah Athletic Club, Univ. Club, Portland Golf Club. Avocations: golf, guitar, camping, river rafting, children's sports. Office: Miller Nash Wiener Hager & Carlsen 111 SW 5th Ave Ste 3500 Portland OR 97204-3638

SANDAGE, ALLAN REX, astronomer; b. Iowa City, June 18, 1926; s. Charles Harold and Dorothy (Briggs) S.; m. Mary Lois Connelley, June 8, 1959; children: David Allan, John Howard. AB, U. Ill., 1948, DSc (hon.), 1967; PhD, Calif. Inst. Tech., 1953; DSc (hon.), Yale U., 1966, U. Chgo., 1967, Miami U., Oxford, Ohio, 1974, Graceland Coll., Iowa, 1985; LLD (hon.), U. So. Calif., 1971; D Honoris Causa, U. Chile, 1992. Astronomer Mt. Wilson Obs., Palomar Obs., Carnegie Instn., Washington, 1952—; Peyton postdoctoral fellow Princeton U., 1952; asst. astronomer Hale Obs., Pasadena, Calif., 1952-56; astronomer Obs. Carnegie Instn., Pasadena, Calif., 1956—; sr. rsch. astronomer Space Telescope Sci. Inst. NASA, Balt., 1986—; Homewood Prof. of Physics Johns Hopkins U., Balt., 1987-89; vis. lectr. Harvard U., 1957; mem. astron. expdn. to South Africa, 1958; cons. NSF, 1961-64; Sigma Xi nat. lectr., 1966; vis. prof. Mt. Stromlo Obs., Australian Nat. U., 1968-69; vis. rsch. astronomer U. Basel, 1985-92, vis. prof., 1994; vis. rsch. astronomer U. Calif., San Diego, 1985-86; vis. astronomer U. Hawaii, 1986; Lindsey lectr. NASA Goddard Space Flight Ctr., 1989; Jansky lectr. Nat. Radio Astron. Obs., 1991; Grubb-Parsons lectr. U. Durham, Eng., 1992. Assoc. editor Ann. Rev. Astronomy and Astrophysics, 1990—. With USNR, 1944-45. Recipient Pope Pius XI gold medal Pontifical Acad. Sci., 1966, Rittenhouse medal, 1968, Presdl. Nat. Medal of Sci., 1971, Adon medal Obs. Nice, 1988, Crafoord prize Swedish Royal Acad. Scis., 1991, Tomalla Gravity prize Swiss Phys. Soc., 1993; Fulbright-Hays scholar, 1972. Mem. Lincei Nat. Acad. (Rome), Am. Astron. Soc. (Helen Warner prize 1960, Russell prize 1973), Royal Astron. Soc. (Eddington medal 1963, Gold medal 1967), Astron. Soc. Pacific (Gold medal 1975), Royal Astron. Soc. Can., Franklin Inst. (Elliott Cresson medal 1973), Am. Philos. Soc., Phi Beta Kappa, Sigma Xi. Home: 8319 Josard Rd San Gabriel CA 91775-1003 Office: 813 Santa Barbara St Pasadena CA 91101-1232

SANDAHL, BONNIE BEARDSLEY, pediatric nurse practitioner, clinical nurse specialist, nurse manager; b. Washington, Jan. 17, 1939; d. Erwin Leonard and Carol Myrtle (Collis) B.; m. Glen Emil Sandahl, Aug 17, 1963; children: Cara Lynne, Cory Glen. BSN, U. Wash., 1962, MN, 1974, cert. pediatric nurse practitioner, 1972. Dir. Wash. State Joint Practice Commn., Seattle, 1974-76; instr. pediatric nurse practitioner program U. Wash., Seattle, 1976, course coordinator quality assurance, 1977-78; pediatic nurse practitioner/health coordinator Snohomish County Head Start, Everett, Wash., 1975-77; clin. nurse educator (specialist), nurse manager Harborview Med. Ctr., Seattle, 1978—, dir. child abuse prevention project, 1986—; speaker legis. focus on children, 1987; clin. assoc. Dept. of Pediatrics, U. Wash. Sch. medicine, 1987—, clin. faculty Sch. Nursing. Mem. Task Force on Pharmacotherapeutic Courses, Wash. State Bd. Nursing, 1985-86; Puget Sound Health Systems Agy., 1975-88, pres., 1980-82; mem. child devel. project adv. bd. Mukilteo Sch. Dist., 1984-85; mem. parenting adv. com. Edmonds Sch. Dist., 1985—; chmn. hospice-home health task force Snohomish County Hospice Program, Everett, 1984-85, bd. dirs. hospice, 1985-87, adv. com. 1986-88; mem. Wash. State Health Coordinating Council, 1977-82, chmn. nursing home bed projection methodology task force, 1986-87; mem., interim chair Nat. Council Health Planning and Devel., HHS, 1980-87; mem. adv. com. on uncompensated care Wash. State Legislature, 1983-84; mem. Joint Select Com., Tech. Adv. Com. on Managed Health Care Systems, 1984-85. Pres., Alderwood Manor Community Council, 1983-85; treas. Wash. St. Women's Polit. Caucus, 1983-84; mem. com. to examine changes in Wash. State Criminal Sex Law, 1987; appointee county needs assessment com. Snohomish County Govt. United Way, 1989; chair human svcs. adv. coun. Snohomish County Human Svcs. Dept., chair adv. com., 1992-96. Recipient Golden Acorn award Seattle-King County PTA, 1973, Katherine Rickey Vol. Participation award, 1987. Mem. Am. Nurses Assn. (chmn. pediatric nurse practitioner subcom. Com. Examiners Maternal-Child Nursing Practice, 1986-92, chair Com. Examiners Maternal-Child Nursing Practice 1988-90). Wash. State Nurses Assn. (hon. leadership award 1981, chair healthcare reform task force 1992—), King County Nurses Assn. (Nurse of Yr. 1985, 1st v.p. 1992—, pres. 1996—), Wash. State Soc. Pediatrics, Sigma Theta Tau. Democrat. Methodist. Home: 1814 201st Pl SW Lynnwood WA 98036-7060 Office: Harborview Med Ctr 325 9th Ave # Za-53 Seattle WA 98104-2420

SANDALOW, TERRANCE, law educator; b. Chgo., Sept. 8, 1934; s. Nathan and Evelyn (Hoffing) S.; m. Ina Davis, Sept. 4, 1955; children: David Blake, Marc Alan, Judith Ann. AB, U. Chgo., 1954, JD, 1957. Bar: Ill. 1958, Mich. 1978. Law clk. to judge Sterry R. Waterman U.S. Ct. Appeals (2d cir.), 1957-58; law clk. to justice Potter Stewart U.S. Supreme Ct., Washington, 1958-59; assoc. Ross, McGowan & O'Keefe, Chgo., 1959-61; assoc. prof. law U. Minn., Mpls., 1961-64, prof., 1964-66; prof. law U. Mich., Ann Arbor, 1966—, dean Law Sch., 1978-87, Edson R. Sunderland prof. law, 1987—. Author: (with F.I. Michelman) Government in Urban Areas, 1970, (with E. Stein) Courts and Free Markets, 1982; contbr. to legal jours., periodicals. Mem. Mpls. Commn. Human Relations, 1965-66. Fellow Ctr. Advanced Study in Behavioral Scis., 1972-73; recipient U. Chgo. Alumni Profl. Achievement award. Fellow Am. Acad. Arts Scis.; mem. Order of Coif, Phi Beta Kappa (hon.). Office: U Mich Law Sch 409 Hutchins Hall Ann Arbor MI 48109-1215

SANDBANK, HENRY, photographer, film director; b. Burg, Germany, Mar. 20, 1932; came to U.S., 1939, naturalized, 1950; s. Sylvan and Bella (Spatz) S.; m. Judith Lebow, July 4, 1952; children: Kenneth, Laura, Lisa, David. Ed. pub. schs. Partner Beach & Sandbank, Syracuse, N.Y., 1960-63; sr. ptnr. Sandbank & Ptnrs., N.Y.C., 1963-88; pres., film dir. Sandbank Films Co., Inc., N.Y.C., 1972—; dir. Vantage Films, 1979—; sr. ptnr. Sandbank Kamen & Ptnrs., 1992-94; lectr. Syracuse U., 1972, Mus. Modern Art, 1994, for Eastman Kodak, Tokyo, 1994; cons. Fashion Inst. Tech., 1974-80. Recipient Gold Medal awards Art Dirs. and Copywriters Show, Gold medal Film Festival of the Americas, several Clio and Andy awards, Cannes Festival award, Gold medal for film documentary Houston Internat. Film Festival 1980). Served to sgt. AUS, 1952-54, Korea. Mem. Am. Soc. Mag. Photographers (chmn. exec. com. 1978-79, Outstanding Achievement award 1981), Soc. Photographers in Communications (trustee 1974-81, 2d v.p. 1975-76, 1st v.p. 1977, chmn. exec. com. 1979). Home: 24 Nutmeg Dr Greenwich CT 06831-3211 Office: 140 Old Saw Mill River Rd Hawthorne NY 10532-1515

SANDBERG, IRWIN WALTER, electrical and computer engineering educator; b. N.Y.C., Jan. 23, 1934; s. Ben and Estelle (Hornick) S.; m. Barbara A. Zimmerman, June 15, 1958; 1 dau. Heidi L. Student, CCNY, 1951-53; B.E.E., Poly. Inst. Bklyn., 1955, M.E.E., 1956, D.E.E., 1958. Tech. aid Bell Telephone Labs., Inc., Murray Hill, N.J., summer 1954, mem. tech. staff, 1958-67, head systems theory research dept., 1967-72, mem. math. and statis. research ctr., 1972-86; prof. elec. and computer engring. U. Tex., Austin, 1986—; now holder Cockrell Family Regents Chair in Engring. U. Tex.; engr. Wheeler Labs., Great Neck, N.Y., summer 1955; vis. prof. U. Calif.-Berkeley, 1965; U.S. del. Union Radio Scientifique Internationale, Munich, Germany, 1966; U.S. nat. inst. rep. Advanced Study Inst. on Network and Signal Theory, NATO, Bournemouth, Eng., 1972; lectr. study inst. NATO (Knokke), Belgium, 1966, Copenhagen, 1970; disting. invited spkr. Asilomar Conf., 1973-74; main lectr. European Conf. on Circuit Theory and Design, The Hague, 1981; advisor Inst. Electronics, Info. and Comm. Engrs., Tokyo; advisor Am. Men and Women of Sci., 1993. Patentee (in field). Recipient Best Paper award Asilomar Conf., 1970, Achievement award IEEE Circuits and Systems Soc., 1986, Classic Paper citation ISI press, 1984, Outstanding Alumnus award Poly. U., 1993. Fellow IEEE (adminstrv. com. group circuit theory 1969-70, vice chmn. group circuit theory 1971-72, Centennial medal), AAAS; mem. NAE, Soc. for Indsl. and Applied Math., Eta Kappa Nu, Sigma Xi, Tau Beta Pi. Home: 8505 Hickory Creek Dr Austin TX 78735-1527 Office: Univ Tex Dept Elec Comp Engr Austin TX 78712

SANDBERG, ROBERT ALEXIS, former research organization administrator; b. Spokane, Sept. 20, 1914; s. Robert A. and Faye P. (Davis) S.; m. Ruth Margaret Cheatham, Apr. 1, 1934 (dec. July 1985); children—Robert, Howard, William, Douglas; m. Evelyn M. Lake, May 16, 1987. A.B., Wash. State U., 1936, A.M., 1937; postgrad., Northwestern U., 1937-38, U. Ill., 1939-41. Instr. speech U. Ill., 1939-42; exec. asst. to pres. Wash. State U., 1945-52; v.p. pub. affairs and advt. Kaiser Aluminum and Chem. Corp., Oakland, Calif., 1965-72; sr. v.p. Kaiser Industries, Inc., Oakland, 1972-74; sr. adv. Electric Power Research Inst., Palo Alto, Calif., 1974-80; ret., 1980; cons. in comm. and pub. rels., 1980—. Author: Everyday Business Speech, 1942, Handbook of Public Speaking, 1940, Effective Speaking in Business, 1960. Dir. fund raising Eastern area A.R.C., 1941-45; Trustee Inst. Ednl. Devel.; bd. dirs. Advt. Council. Mem. Pub. Rels. Soc. Am. (accredited, accreditation bd. 1968—), Newcomen Soc., Sigma Delta Chi. Home: 735 Arroyo Ct Lafayette CA 94549-5311

SANDBURG, HELGA, author; b. Maywood, Ill., Nov. 24, 1918; d. Carl and Lilian (Steichen) S.; m. George Crile, Jr., Nov. 9, 1963; children by previous marriage: John Carl Steichen, Paula Steichen Polega. Student, Mich. State Coll., 1939-40, U. Chgo., 1940. Dairy goat breeder, also personal sec. to father, 1944-51; sec. manuscripts div., also for keeper of collections Library of Congress, 1952-56; adminstrv. asst. for papers of Woodrow Wilson, 1958-59; writer, lectr., 1957—. Author: (novels) The Wheel of Earth, 1958, Measure My Love, 1959, The Owl's Roost, 1962, The Wizard's Child, 1967; (non-fiction) Sweet Music, A Book of Family Reminiscence and Song, 1963; (with George Crile, Jr.) Above and Below, 1969; (poetry) The Unicorns, 1965; To A New Husband, 1970, The Age of the Flower, 1994; (young adult novels) Blueberry, 1963; Gingerbread, 1964; (juveniles) Joel and the Wild Goose, 1963; Bo and the Old Donkey, 1965, Anna and the Baby Buzzard, 1970; Children and Lovers: 15 Stories by Helga Sandburg, 1976; (biography) A Great and Glorious Romance: The Story of Carl Sandburg and Lilian Steichen, 1978; "...Where Love Begins", 1989; (with Diane Leslie) Joel and The Wild Goose, Contempory Musical Fantasy, 1991, also numerous short stories; rep. in collections.; contbr.short stories, poems, articles to popular mags. including Seventeen. Recipient Va. Quar. Rev. prize for best short story, 1959, Borestone Mountain poetry award, 1962, Poetry award Chgo. Tribune, 1970; 2d prize 7th Ann. Kans. Poetry Contest, Florence Roberts Head Ohioana Book award, 1990; grantee Finnish Am. Soc. and Svenska Inst., 1961. Mem. Authors Guild, Poetry Soc., Am. Milk Goat Record Assn., Am.-Scandinavian Found., Nat. Nubian Club, Coun. Save the Dunes, Am. Luxembourg Soc., Acad. Am. Poets. Address: 2060 Kent Rd Cleveland OH 44106-3339

SANDDAL, NELS DODGE, foundation executive, consultant; b. Salt Lake City, Feb. 17, 1949; s. James Wesley and Charlotte Jean (Ewer) S.; m. Brenda Kay Lille Griffin, Sept. 27, 1970 (div. June 1990); m. Theresa Louise Knipe, Oct. 12, 1992; 1 child, Jami. BA in English, Carroll Coll., 1966-70; MS in Psychology, Mont. State U., 1996. In-svc. trainer Boulder (Mont.) River Sch. and Hosp., 1974-75; group home mgr. REACH, Inc., Bozeman, Mont., 1975-76; community home trainer Devel. Disabilities Tng. Inst., Helena, Mont., 1976-77; tng. coord. emergency med. svcs. bureau State Dept. Health and Environ. Scis., Helena, 1977-82; cons., lead staff Nat. Coun. State Emergency Med. Svcs. Tng. Coords., Inc., Lexington, Ky., 1981-86; account exec., lead staff Nat. Assn. Emergency Med. Techs., Clinton, Miss., 1986-87; pres., CEO Assn. Mgmt. and Cons., Inc., Boulder, 1983-89; writer, prodr., dir. North Country Media Group, Great Falls, Mont., 1990-91; chief conf. planner S.O.S. Conf. Planning Consortium, Great Falls, 1991-92; exec. dir. Critical Illness & Trauma Found., Big Timber, Mont., 1986-91; season course leader Nat. Outdoor Leadership Sch., Lander, Wyo., 1966-74; mem. exec. com. Nat. Coun. State EMS Tng. Coords., 1977-82, chmn., Lexington, Ky., 1979-81; mem. adv. com. pediatric emergency med. svcs. tng. project Children's Hosp. Nat. Med. Ctr., Washington, 1985-88, pediatrics emergency instr., 1986-90; mem. grant peer rev. com. divsn. injury epidemiology Ctrs. for Disease Control, Atlanta, 1986-87; cons. Emergency Med. Svcs. Bureau, Helena, 1977, Devel. Disabilities Tng. Inst., Helena, 1977-78; mem. injury prevention profls. New Eng. Network to Prevent Childhood Injuries, Newton, Mass., 1988—; mem. core faculty devel. trauma sys. tng. program U.S. Dept. Transp., Washington, 1989, tech. assistance team mem. EMS, 1991-93; EMS instr. and program coord. Great Falls Vocat. Tng. Ctr., 1991-93; rsch. asst. inst. for cmty. studies U. Mo., Kansas City, 1983—; pres. exec. com. Intermountain Regional EMS Children Coord. Coun., Salt Lake City, 1994—. Editor and tech. cons.: Workbook for Prehospital Care and Crisis Interventions, 4th edit., 1992, 5th edit., 1993, Instructor Resource Manual for Prehospital Care and Crisis Intervention, 4th edit., 1992, Workbook for First Responder, 1990; contbg. editor Jour. of Prehospital Care, 1984-85, The EMT Jour., 1980-81; editl. cons. Am. Acad. Orthopaedic Surgeons, 1980-81; contbr. numerous articles to profl. jours.; video prodr. and presenter in field. Mem. Park County DUI Task Force, Livingston, 1993—; inaugural coord. Mont. Safe Kids Coalition, Big Timber, 1988-90; adv. com. Nat. Significance Project for Respite Care, 1977-78; mem. basic life support com. of Mont., Mont. Heart Assn., 1977-82. Recipient Golden award for humanity ARC, 1976, 500 Hour award, 1976, Outstanding Svc. award Nat. Coun. State EMS Tng. Coords., 1979, Leadership award, 1981, Charter Membership award, 1984, J.D. Farrington award for excellence Nat. Assn. Emergency Med. Technicians, 1981, Jeffrey S. Harris award, 1985, Outstanding Svc. award Am. Heart Assn., 1982, Appreciation cert. for paramedic emergency care U.S. Dept. Transp., 1984. Mem. Nat. Registry EMTs, Mont. Bd. Med. Examiners. Democrat. Avocations: mountaineering, hiking, sailing, golf, skiing. Home: 317 N 2nd St Livingston MT 59047-1901 Office: Critical Illness Trauma Found 300 N Willson Ave Ste 3002 Bozeman MT 59715

SANDE, THEODORE ANTON, architect, educator, foundation executive; b. New London, Conn., Nov. 21, 1933; s. Lars Anton and Viola (Edgcomb) S.; m. Solveig Inga-Maj Imselius, Aug. 6, 1960; children: Susanne Ingrid, Lars Michael. BSc in Architecture, R.I. Sch. Design, 1956; MArch, Yale U., 1961; PhD, U. Pa., 1972; grad. Cultural Instns. Mgmt. Program, Mus. Collaborative, 1983; postgrad., Attingham (Eng.) Summer Sch., 1980. Vis. prof. history of architecture Rensselaer Poly. Inst., fall 1973-74, U. Pa., 1976-77; adj. prof. Am. studies and history Case-Western Res. U., 1981—; vis. lectr. in historic preservation Cleve. State U., summer 1994; lectr. art Williams Coll., 1972-75; attended teleconfs. non-profit orgn. mgmt. Drucker Found., 1992. Designer, Arkitekt, Hakon Ahlberg, SAR, Arkitekt, Stockholm, 1960, designer, Washburn, Luther & Rowley, Architects, Attleboro, Mass., 1961-62, Barker & Turoff, Architects, Providence, 1962-63, jr. partner, Turoff Assocs., Architects, 1964-67, partner, Turoff & Sande, Architects, Providence, 1968-70, prin., Ted Sande, Architect, Cranston, R.I., 1970, Cleve., 1993—; author: Industrial Archaeology: A New Look at the American Heritage, 2d edit, 1978; contbg. author: Guidebook to Philadelphia Architecture, 1974; editor: New England Textile Mill Survey, 1971; co-editor: Historic Preservation of Engineering Works, 1981; contbr. articles to profl. jours.; two-man show drawings, Providence Art Club, 1970. Dir. profl. svcs. office hist. properties Nat. Trust Hist. Preservation, Washington, 1975-77, dir. planning and devel., 1977-78, acting v.p. office hist. properties, 1978-79, v.p., 1979-80; mem. Old Georgetown Bd. Nat. Commn. Fine Arts, 1979-81; exec. dir. Western Res. Hist. Soc., Cleve., 1981-93, exec. dir. emeritus, 1993—; cons. architecture Mus. and Hist. Soc. Mgmt., Historic Preservation and Archtl. Hist., 1993—; co-chmn. Conf. Indsl. Archeology, Smithsonian Instn., 1971; active Shaker Heights Landmark Commn., 1982-84, Cleve. Landmarks Commn., 1985—, Leadership Cleve. Class 86/87, Ohio Gov.'s Commn. on the Bicentennials the NW Ordinance and U.S. Const., 1986-89, Cleve. Bicentennial Commn., 1992-94; trustee Univ. Circl Inc., 1981-93, Cemetery Found., 1985—, Nat. Rock and Roll Mus. and Hall Fame, mem. exec. blgd. com., 1993-95, instnl. rep. Cleve. Arts Consortium, 1987-93; pres. Cleve. Restoration Soc., 1994—. Mem. AIA (architect mem., com. hist. resources 1972-74), SAR, Soc. Indsl. Archeology (co-founder, 1st pres. 1971-72, dir. 1973-76, project supr. handbook, gen. chmn. 15th ann. conf.), Soc. Archtl. Historians (preservation com. 1972-74), Internat. Com. for Conservation of Indsl. Heritage (chmn. bd. dirs. 1978-81), Ohio Mus.

Assn. (trustee 1982-87), Am. Assn. Mus., Rowfant Club (coun. fellows), Philos. Club Cleve. (past pres.). Episcopalian. Home: 13415 Shaker Blvd Cleveland OH 44120-1548

SANDEEN, RODERICK COX, newspaper editor; b. Mpls., Apr. 27, 1943; s. Clair William and Mary Ethel (Cox) S.; B.S. in Journalism, U. Colo., 1969; m. Patricia Anne McDermott, June 10, 1972; children—Peter, Mark. Reporter, The New Haven Post-Register, 1969-70; reporter Post-Register, Idaho Falls, Idaho, 1972-73; reporter, editor Idaho Statesman, Boise, 1973-78, mng. editor, 1978—. Office: The Freedom Forum 1101 Wilson Blvd Arlington VA 22209-2248

SANDEFUR, THOMAS EDWIN, JR., tobacco company executive; b. Cochran, Ga., Dec. 4, 1939; s. Thomas Edwin and Elsie (Camp) S.; m. Annette Crawford Meginniss, May 8, 1965. B.S. in Bus. Acctg., Ga. So. U., 1963. Sales and mktg. positions R.J. Reynolds Tobacco Co., Winston-Salem, N.C., 1964-76, sr. v.p. advt. and brand mgmt., 1976-79; sr. v.p. R.J. Reynolds Internat., Winston-Salem, N.C., 1979-81; exec. v.p. Europe, Geneva, 1981-82; sr. v.p. internat. mktg. Brown & Williamson Tobacco Corp., Louisville, 1982-84, exec. v.p., 1984-85, pres., COO, 1985-93, chmn., CEO, 1993—; bd. dirs. Bank Louisville. Bd. dirs. Wesleyan Coll., L.A. Bantle Inst., Greater Louisville Fund for Arts, Cathedral Heritage Found., Boy Scout coun. Louisville; bd. overseers U. Louisville; bd. adv. coun. Ga. So. Coll., Nat. Assn. Mfrs. Mem. Am. Wholesale Marketers Assn.

SANDELL, RICHARD ARNOLD, international trade executive, economist; b. Buenos Aires, Argentina, Oct. 22, 1937; s. Kurd Wolfcang and Isolde Mary (Josevich) S.; m. Phyllis H. Levinson, July 6, 1968; children: Laurie Alyssa, Karyn Joy, Sylvie Jennine. BA in Social Sci., U. Buenos Aires, 1957, JD, 1959; MS in Econs., U. San Marcos, 1960; LLM in Internat. Law, NYU, 1962; Ph.D., Columbia U., 1972, M.B.A., 1977. Dir. bus. planning Guerrero Merc. Internat. Ltd., Buenos Aires, 1954-62; gen. mgr. Acquatronic Universal, Inc., 1965-68; corp. v.p. indsl. econs. Mgmt. Analyst Group, Ins., Van Nuys, Calif., 1968-70; pres., CEO A.I.M. Internat. Corp., Alameda, Calif., 1970-76; pres., CEO, dir. Aurag Internat. Corp. and Aura Tech. Corp., Scarsdale, N.Y., 1979—; bd. dirs. FerroCement Internat. Ltd. of Panama, Consorcio Pesquero Marmesa of Guayaquil, Ecuador, INTEX S.A., Buenos Aires, Export Marketeers Ltd., Auckland, N.Z., Aledo Transnat. Trading Corp., Panama, Geneva, Oakland, Calif., dir. Nexus Corp., Santa Rosa, Calif., Guanabara Mining Co., Rio De Janeiro, Brazil, Primax Electronics Ltd., Aimore Internat. Corp., Stockton, Calif., Premisa, S.A., Venezuela; former cons. U.S. Dept. State, govts. Ecuador, Nicaragua, Guyana, Zaire, Fiji, El Salvador, N.Z., Ghana, currently cons. to Taiwan, Chile, Venezuela, Brazil, 1972—; cons. Nat. Security Coun. during Desert Shield and Desert Storm Campaign, 1990-91; cons. on privatization Govt. Argentina; adj. prof. bus. adminstrn. Elbert Covell Coll. and Coll. Pacific at U. Pacific, 1972-77; adj. prof. internat. bus., mgmt. U. Am. States, Miami, Fla., 1977-79, prof. internat. trade and tech., chair bus. enterprise , 1987—; adj. prof. internat. bus., mgmt. U. Francisco Marroquin, Guatemala City, 1977-79; dir. Grad. Inst. Free Enterprise Studies, prof. internat. bus., govt. Mercy Coll. and L.I.U., Dobbs Ferry, N.Y., 1980-83; prof. internat. fin. and bus., chair bus. enterprise Ramapo Coll. of N.J., Mahwah, 1983-87. Author: The Politics of Marketing in Latin America, 1970, Private Investment in the Andean Block - A Study in Conflicts, 1970, Santa Cruz - Crossroads of Heaven and Hell, 1971, U.S.-Latin America - a Time for Reciprocity, 1972, Use of Consultants - How Valuable an Investment, 1972, The Role of U.S. Multinational Corporation, 1972, Summary of Controls on the International Movement of Capital, 1973, The Effects of Rising Energy Costs on LDC Development, 1974, Trade in the Andean Common Market, 1975, U.S. Private Investment - Its Future Role in Interamerican Development, 1976, Tourism in Latin America - Cornerstone of Development, 1976, Administration of Human Resources - Its Effectiveness in the Modern Organization, 1977, A System Called Capitalism, 1977, Marketing Plague - The Regulators, 1978; Prescription for Survival - Can Free Enterprise Make It?, 1979, The Intellectual Defense of Free Enterprise, 1980, Freedom at Bay - Government Controls in the Economy, 1982, American Values: the Economy, the Polity, the Society, 1986, The Debt Bomb: In the Shadow of Depression, 1987, Finance and Stress: The Market Crash of '87, 1988, Investment in Eastern Europe: Good Politics, Bad Finance! 1989, Socialism: The Accomplishment of a Nightmare, 1990, The House That Lenin Built: The Crash of the USSR, 1991, Special Interests: The Politics of Privilege, 1991, North American Free Trade Area: Road to Prosperity, 1992, The Watermelon Syndrome: Green Outside, Red Inside!, 1992, Highway to World Freedom: The Information Superhighway, 1993, To Clinton's Hammer...Does Gore Add the Sickle?, 1994, Marabunta's Passage: The Legacy of Socialism, 1995; editor Internat. Econ. Journal, Univ. Am. States. Advisor Explorer post Alameda coun. Boy Scouts Am., 1969-71, post com. chmn., 1971-75; bd. dirs. San Francisco-Bay area coun. Girls Scouts U.S.A., 1975-80, v.p., 1978-80; trustee Amigos de las Americas, Houston, 1975-80, U. Am. States, Santiago, 1976-80, Am. Rsch. Inst. for Social Environments, Alameda, 1975-82, Princeton Fund, 1976-82, Found. for F Ent., 1983-87, Aura Tech. Found., 1987—, Electro-Bio-Scis., 1987-89, Am.-Pacific Found., 1989—; mem. Am. Rsch. Inst. for Soc. and Economy, Washington, 1990—, The Maldon Inst. Found., Washington, 1991-95. With U.S. Army, 1962-65. Decorated Bronze Star; decorated Purple Heart; recipient medal Sagitario Found., 1962, Silver Condor award U. Andina, 1969, Kenneth Chilton Meml. award, 1972. Life fellow AAAS; mem. N.Y. Acad. Scis., Am. Numis. Assn., Inst. Mgmt. Cons. (dir., v.p. Latin Am. 1975-80), Am. Econs. Assn., Internat. Inst. Economists, Interam. Soc. Polit. Economists (trustee 1971-81, v.p. 1988-90, pres. 1991-96), Inst. Mgmt. Sci., Internat. Execs. Assn., Fgn. Policy Assn., 2d Amendment Found., Am. Security Coun., Am. Soc. Internat. Execs., N.Am. Corp. Planning Assn., Soc. Internat. Trade Planning (dir. 1989—), Am. Sociol. Assn., Am. Psychol. Assn., Nat. Rifle Assn., Am. Radio Relay League (dir. 1990—), Soc. for Internat. Tech. Assessment, Mensa, many others. Clubs: Commonwealth (San Francisco, chmn. sect. Latin Am. 1969-75); Oakland World Trade. Lodge: Rotary. Office: 441 Central Ave 441 Central Ave PO Box 1367 Scarsdale NY 10583-9367 *Struggling for the preservation of individual freedom is the most noble cause to which I can address my life's endeavor.*

SANDELL, WILLIAM, production designer. Art dir.: (films) Fast Charlie...the Moonbeam Rider, 1979; prodn. designer: (films) The Pack, 1977, The Clones, 1977, Piranha, 1978, The Promise, 1979, Serial, 1980, Blood Beach, 1981, (with Joe Aubel) Dead and Buried, 1981, Airplane II: The Sequel, 1982, Young Lust, 1982, The Wild Life, 1984, St. Elmo's Fire, 1985, Robocop, 1987, Big Business, 1988, Total Recall, 1990, Nothing But Trouble, 1991, Newsies, 1992, Hocus Pocus, 1993, The Flintstones, 1994. Office: care Art Directors Guild 11365 Ventura Blvd Ste 315 Studio City CA 91604-3148

SANDENAW, THOMAS ARTHUR, JR., lawyer; b. Harlowton, Mont., Mar. 17, 1936; s. Thomas A. Sr. S.; m. Colleen A. Andrews, June 3, 1956 (div. May 1981); children: Cheryl Lea, Kevin K., Dana Scott; m. Deborah Rose Hammel, Sept. 26, 1981. BS, Mont. State U., 1958; JD, U. N.Mex., 1967. Bar: N.Mex. 1967, U.S. Dist. Ct. N.Mex. 1968, U.S. Ct. Appeals (10th cir.) 1968. Atty. Wilkinson, Durrett & Conway, Alamogordo, N.Mex., 1968-69, Spence & Sandenaw, Alamogordo, N.Mex., 1969-71, Shipley, Durrett, Conway & Sandenaw, Alamogordo, N.Mex., 1971-77; judge 12th jud. dist. Lincoln and Otero Counties, Alamogordo, N.Mex., 1978-79; atty. Overstreet & Sandenaw, Alamogordo, N.Mex., 1979-82; ptnr. Weinbrenner, Richards, Paulowsky, Sandenaw & Ramirez, Las Cruces, N.Mex., 1982-92; pvt. practice Las Cruces, N.Mex., 1992—. Dir. St. Lukes Health Care, Las Cruces, 1992, Mesilla Valley Hospice, Las Cruces, 1992—. Mem. ABA (law practice mgmt. tort and ins. practice litigation), Am. Bd. Trial Advocates, Am. Bd. Profl. Liability Attys. (diplomat 1993—), Nat. Bd. Trial Advocacy (cert. civil trial practice 1989), State Bar N.Mex. (chmn. pub. rels. com. 1967-68), N.Mex. Def. Lawyers Assn. (sec. 1984-85, v.p., 1985-86, pres. 1987-88, bd. dirs. 1983—, chmn. Amicus Curie com. 1991—), N.Mex. Sr. Lawyers Div., N.Mex. Bench and Bar Com., Dona Ana County Bar Assn., Assn. Def. Trial Attorneys, Rotary (past pres. Rio Grande chpt.; barrister Am. Inn of Courts. Republican. Lutheran. Avocations: skiing, sailing, woodworking. Office: 2951 A Roadrunner Parkway Las Cruces NM 88011

SANDER, DONALD HENRY, soil scientist, researcher; b. Creston, Nebr., Apr. 21, 1933; s. Paul L. and Mable O. (Wendt) S.; m. Harriet Ora Palmateer, Dec. 27, 1953; children: Ben, Joan. BS, U. Nebr., 1954, MS in Agronomy, 1958, PhD in Agronomy, 1967. Soil scientist, researcher USDA Forest Svc., Lincoln, Nebr., 1958-64; asst. prof. agronomy, soil fertility specialist Kans. State U., Manhattan, 1964-67; prof. agronomy U. Nebr., Lincoln, 1967—. Contbr. over 40 articles to jours. including Soil Sci. Soc. Am. Jour. 1st lt. U.S. Army, 1954-56, Korea. Recipient USDA Superior Svc. award, 1987, Soil Sci. Applied Rsch. award, 1989, Great Plains Leadership award, Denver, 1990,. Fellow Am. Soc. Agronomy (Agronomic Achievement award 1985), Soil Sci. Soc. Am.; mem. Gama Sigma Delta, Sigma Xi. Republican. Presbyterian. Avocation: woodworking. Home: 6548 Darlington Ct Lincoln NE 68510-2362 Office: Univ Nebr Dept Agronomy Lincoln NE 68583

SANDER, FRANK ERNEST ARNOLD, law educator; b. Stuttgart, Germany, July 22, 1927; came to U.S., 1940, naturalized, 1946; s. Rudolf and Alice (Epstein) S.; m. Emily Bishop Jones, Apr. 26, 1958; children: Alison Bishop, Thomas Harvey, Ernest Ridgway Sander. A.B. in Math. magna cum laude, Harvard U., 1949, LL.B. magna cum laude, 1952. Bar: Mass. 1952, U.S. Supreme Ct 1952. Law clk. to Chief Judge Magruder U.S. Ct. Appeals, 1952-53; law clk. to Justice Frankfurter, U.S. Supreme Ct., 1953-54; atty. tax div. Dept. Justice, 1954-56; with firm Hill & Barlow, Boston, 1956-59; mem. faculty Harvard Law Sch., 1959—, prof. law, 1962—, Bussey prof., 1981—, assoc. dean, 1987—; spl. fields fed. taxation, family law, welfare law, dispute resolution; chmn. Council on Role of Cts.; mem. panels Am. Arbitration Assn., Fed. Mediation and Conciliation Service; chmn. Council on Legal Edn. Opportunity, 1968-70; cons. Dept. Treasury, 1968; treas. Harvard Law Rev., 1951-52. Author: (with Westfall and McIntyre) Readings in Federal Taxation, 2d edit., 1983, (with Foote and Levy) Cases and Materials on Family Law, 3d edit., 1985, (with Gutman) Tax Aspects of Divorce and Separation, 4th edit., 1985, (with Goldberg and Rogers) Dispute Resolution, 2d edit., 1992. Mem. tax mission Internat. Program Taxation to Republic of Colombia, 1959; mem. com. on civil and polit. rights President's Commn. on Status of Women, 1962-63; trustee Buckingham Browne and Nichols Sch., 1969-75; chmn. Mass. Welfare Adv. Bd., 1975-79. With AUS, 1945-46. Recipient Whitney North Seymour medal Am. Arbitration Assn., 1988, spl. award for disting. svc. to dispute resolution Ctr. for Pub. Resources, 1990. Mem. ABA (chmn. standing com. dispute resolution 1986-89, vice chair Mass. Supreme Jud. Ct. standing com. dispute resolution 1994—, Kutak medal 1993), Boston Bar Assn., Phi Beta Kappa. Home: 74 Buckingham St Cambridge MA 02138-2229 Office: Harvard U Sch of Law Cambridge MA 02138

SANDER, RAYMOND JOHN, government executive; b. N.Y.C., July 4, 1944; s. Raymond John and Rose Marie (Nigrelli) S.; m. Sheryl Swed; children: Raymond Paul, Christy. BS, Fordham Coll., 1965; MA, U. Md., 1971. With CIA, Washington, 1966-73; asst. dir. mgmt. program, budget staff Dept. Justice, Washington, 1973-77; dir. office mgmt. planning Dept. Transp., Washington, 1977-81; exec. dir. Urban Mass Transit Adminstrn., Washington, 1981-88; dir. trade and comml. programs Am. Inst. in Taiwan, Arlington, Va., 1988—. Office: Am Inst in Taiwan 1700 N Moore St Arlington VA 22209-1903

SANDERCOX, ROBERT ALLEN, college official, clergyman; b. Akron, Ohio, May 20, 1932; s. Monroe J. and Elverda (Arnold) S.; m. Nancy Lee Wertz, Sept. 13, 1958; children—Alison Grace, Megan Louise, Robert Philip. B.A., Bethany Coll., W. Va., 1954; M.Div., Yale U., 1957; postgrad., U. Buffalo, W.Va. U.; LittD, Bethany Coll., 1989. Ordained to ministry Christian Ch. (Disciples of Christ). Asst. minister Park Ave Christian Ch., N.Y.C., 1954-57; asst. provost Bethany Coll., 1957-60, v.p., dean students, 1960-75, v.p., dir. devel., 1975-79, interim pres., 1979-80, v.p., provost for coll. advancement, 1980-89, sr. v.p., 1989-95, cons. to the pres., 1995—. Trustee Christian Ch. Disciples of Christ in W.Va., Parkersburg, 1984-88; chmn. Brooke County Landmarks Commn., 1988—, Brooke County Mus. Bd., 1995. Recipient Alumni Disting. Service award Bethany Coll., 1982. Mem. Coun. for Advancement and Support Edn., Duquesne Club (Pitts.), Order of Symposiarch, Rotary, Kiwanis (pres. 1967), Alpha Sigma Phi (nat. treas. 1982-84, v.p. 1984-86, grad. sr. pres. 1986-88, bd. dirs., trustee Ednl. Found. 1982—, chmn. Ednl. Found. 1994—, Delta Beta Xi svc. award 1960). Democrat. Home: Highland Hearth Bethany WV 26032 Office: Bethany Coll. Milsop Ctr Bethany WV 26032

SANDERS, AARON PERRY, radiation biophysics educator; b. Phoenix, Jan. 12, 1924; s. DeWitt and Ruth (Perry) S.; m. Betty Mae Gelein, Aug. 11, 1944 (div.); children: Merle Sanders Ireland, Julie Sanders Jacome, James DeWitt; m. Georgia Anne Bullock, Nov. 26, 1972; 1 dau., Kai Marie. B.S., U. Tex., El Paso, 1950; M.S. (AEC fellow), U. Rochester, 1952; Ph.D., U. N.C., 1964. Diplomate: Am. Bd. Health Physics. Baggage clk., ticket agt. Greyhound Bus Lines, Phoenix, 1942; dispatcher, ticket agt. Greyhound Bus Lines, El Paso, Tex., 1946-50; asso. health physicist Brookhaven Nat. Lab., Upton, N.Y., 1951-53; instr. physics, radiol. safety officer N.C. State Coll., 1953; instr. radiology Duke Med. Center, Durham, N.C., 1953-56; dir. radioisotope lab. Duke Med. Center, 1953-65; asso. in radiology Duke Med. Ctr., 1956-57, asst. prof., 1957-64, assoc. prof., 1964-65, assoc. prof., dir. div. radiobiology, 1965-70, prof., dir. div. radiobiology, 1970-83, prof. emeritus, 1983—; chmn. Biomed. Physics Dept. King Faisal Specialist Hosp., Riyadh, Saudi Arabia, 1984-86; Fulbright sr. lectr. radiol. physics, Argentina, 1958-59; cons. N.C. Bd. Health, 1961-76; mem. N.C. Radiation Protection Commn., 1976-83, chmn., 1978-79. Contbr. articles to profl. jours. Served with USNR, 1942-45. Mem. AAAS, Am. Assn. Physicists in Medicine, AAUP, Soc. Exptl. Biology and Medicine, Health Physics Soc., Soc. Nuclear Medicine, Biophys. Soc., Radiation Research Soc., Undersea Med Soc., Sigma Xi, Sigma Pi Sigma. *Each individual has an obligation to himself and society to pursue an education to his maximum capability. This capability should then be used in his career in an effort to contribute to society as much, or more, than he receives. In work and personal relations you must never deny a man the dignity of his work by ridicule or denigration, and you must never use people.*

SANDERS, ADRIAN LIONEL, educational consultant; b. Paragould, Ark., Aug. 3, 1938; s. Herbert Charles and Florence Theresa (Becherer) S.; m. Molly Jean Zecher, Dec. 20, 1961. AA, Bakersfield Coll., 1959; BA, San Francisco State U., 1961; MA, San Jose State U., 1967. 7th grade tchr. Sharp Park Sch., Pacifica, Calif., 1961-62; 5th grade tchr. Mowry Sch., Fremont, Calif., 1962-64; sci. tchr. Blacow Sch., Fremont, Calif., 1964-76; 5th grade tchr. Warm Springs Sch., Fremont, 1977-87, 5th grade gifted and talented edn. tchr., 1987-94; edn. cons., 1994—. Mem. San Jose Hist. Mus. Assn., 1980—, Nat. Geog. Soc., Washington, 1976—, Alzheimer's Family Relief Program, Rockville, Md., 1986; vol. 7 km. Race for Alzheimer's Disease Willow Glen Founders Day, San Jose, 1988-92. Named Outstanding Young Educator, Jr. C. of C., Fremont, Calif., 1965. Mem. Smithsonian Assocs., U.S. Golf Assn. Avocations: photography, travelling, visiting presidents' birthplaces, collecting license plates, collecting matchbooks worldwide. Home and Office: 15791 Rica Vista Way San Jose CA 95127-2735

SANDERS, ALEXANDER MULLINGS, JR., judge; b. Columbia, S.C., Sept. 29, 1938; s. Alexander Mullings Sr. and Henrietta Courtrier (Thomas) S.; m. Zoe Caroline Dutrow; 1 child, Zoe Caroline. BS, U. S.C., 1960, LLB, 1962; LLM, U. Va., 1990. Bar: S.C. 1962, U.S. Dist. Ct. S.C. 1962, U.S. Supreme Ct. 1975, U.S. Ct. Appeals (4th cir.) 1976. Sr. ptnr. Sanders & Quackenbush, Columbia, 1974-83; of counsel Adams & Quackerbush, Columbia, 1983; chief judge S.C. Ct. Appeals, Columbia, 1983-92; pres. Coll. Charleston, S.C., 1992—; adj. faculty U. S.C., Columbia, 1965-92, Harvard U. Law Sch., Cambridge, Mass., 1983-96. Mem. S.C. Ho. Reps., Columbia, 1966-74, S.C. Senate, Columbia, 1976-83. Served with USAR, 1956. Mem. ABA, S.C. Bar Assn. Office: Coll of Charleston Off of Pres Charleston SC 29424

SANDERS, BARRY, football player; b. Wichita, July 16, 1968; s. William and Shirley Sanders. Student, Okla. State U., 1986-89. With Detroit Lions, 1989—. Recipient Heisman Trophy award, 1988; named Sporting News Coll. Football Player of Yr., 1988, NFL Rookie of Yr., 1990; named to Sporting News Coll. All-Am. team, 1987, 88, All-Pro team, 1989-91, 93, Pro Bowl, 1989-95. Led NFL in rushing, 1990, 94. Office: Detroit Lions 1200 Featherstone Rd Pontiac MI 48342-1938*

SANDERS, BERNARD (BERNIE SANDERS), congressman; b. Bklyn., Sept. 8, 1941; s. Eli and Dorothy (Glassberg) S.; m. Jane O'Meara, 1988; children: Levi, Heather, Carina, David. B.A., U. Chgo., 1964. Freelance writer, carpenter, youth counselor, 1964-76; with Govt. Vt., 1965-66; dir. Am. People's Hist. Soc., Burlington, Vt., 1976-81; mayor of Burlington, 1981-89; mem. U.S. House of Reps. from Vt., 102nd-104th Congresses from Vt., 1991—. Chairperson, Vt. Liberty Union Party, 1975-76, candidate for gov., 1972, 76, 86, U.S. Senate, 1971, 74; mem. Com. on Banking and Fin. Svcs., Com. on Govt. Reform and Oversight. Mem. Vt. League Cities and Towns. Jewish. Author filmstrips and articles on social, hist. and polit. subjects. Office: US Ho of Reps 213 Cannon Washington DC 20515-4501

SANDERS, BRICE SIDNEY, bishop; b. Nashville, Oct. 15, 1930; s. Walter Richard and Agnes Mortimer (Jones) S.; m. Nancy Elizabeth Robinson, Aug. 22, 1953; children—Richard Evan, Robert Wesley, Lynne Elizabeth. B.A., Vanderbilt U., 1952; M.S.T., Episcopal Div. Sch., Cambridge, Mass., 1955; D.D. (hon.), Va. Theol. Sem., 1980, U. South, Sewanee, Tenn., 1984. Ordained to ministry. Rector St. James Ch., Union City, Tenn., 1955-58, Good Shepherd Ch., Knoxville, 1958-61, Eastern Shore Chapel, Virginia Beach, Va., 1961-70; assoc. dean Va. Theol. Sem., Alexandria, 1970-75; dean St. Andrews Cathedral, Jackson, Miss., 1975-79; bishop Diocese of East Carolina, Kingston, N.C., 1979—. Home: 2112 Sparre Dr Kinston NC 28501-1926 Office: Diocese of E Carolina PO Box 1336 Kinston NC 28503-1336

SANDERS, CHARLES ADDISON, physician; b. Dallas, Feb. 10, 1932; s. Harold Barefoot and May Elizabeth (Forrester) S.; m. Elizabeth Ann Chipman, Mar. 6, 1956; children: Elizabeth, Charles Addison, Carlyn, Christopher. MD, U. Tex., 1955. Intern, asst. resident Boston City Hosp., 1955-57, chief resident, 1957-58; clin. and rsch. fellow in medicine Mass. Gen. Hosp., Boston, 1958-60; chief cardiac catheterization lab. Mass. Gen. Hosp., 1962-72, gen. dir., 1972-81, physician, 1973-81, program dir. myocardial infarction rsch. unit, 1967-72; exec. v.p. E.R. Squibb and Sons, 1981-84; exec. v.p. Squibb Corp., 1984-88, vice chmn., 1988-89; chief exec. officer Glaxo Inc., Research Triangle Park, N.C., 1989-94, chmn., 1992-95; assoc. prof. medicine Harvard U. Med. Sch., 1969-80, prof., 1980-83; candidate U.S. Senate, 1996; bd. dirs. Mt. Sinai Med. Ctr., N.Y.C.; chmn. Commonwealth Fund N.Y.C.; mem. Inst. Medicine. Mem. editorial bd. New Eng. Jour. Medicine, 1969-72. Chmn. Project Hope. Capt. USAF, 1960-62. Mem. ACP, Am. Heart Assn., Mass. Med. Soc. Office: Sanders for Senate 100 Europa Dr Ste 170 Chapel Hill NC 27514

SANDERS, CHARLES FRANKLIN, corporate executive; b. Louisville, Dec. 22, 1931; s. Charles Franklin and Maragret Rhea (Timmons) S.; m. Marie Audrey Galuppo, Dec. 29, 1956; children: Karen Lynn, Craig Joseph, Keith Franklin. B.Chem. Engring., U. Louisville, 1954, M.Chem. Engring., 1958; Ph.D., U. So. Calif., 1970. Research engr. Exxon Research and Engring. Co., Linden, N.J., 1955-62; asst. prof. engring. Calif. State U., Northridge, 1962-68, assoc. prof., 1968-71, prof., 1971-82, chmn. dept., 1969-72, dean Sch. Engring. and Computer Sci., 1972-81; pres., chief exec. officer, dir. Rusco Industries, Los Angeles, 1981-82; exec. v.p. Energy Systems Assocs., Tustin, Calif, 1982-89; exec. v.p. Energeo, San Francisco, 1989-95, also bd. dirs.; v.p. tech. Smith-Bellingham Capital, San Francisco, 1989-91; bd. dirs. Advanced Combustion Tech., Kailua-Kona, Hawaii. Bd. dirs. San Fernando Valley Child Guidance Clinic, 1979-81. Served to 1st lt. U.S. Army, 1956-57. NSF fellow, 1965-67. Mem. AIChE, NSPE, Calif. Soc. Profl. Engrs., Am. Soc. for Engring. Edn. Republican.

SANDERS, DAVID G., federal agency administrator. Student, Cambridge U., 1979; BA in Econs. and Philosophy, Coll. William and Mary, 1981; student, Willamette U., Cambridge Acad. Transport, 1992, 94. Sr. fgn. policy cons. Internat. Freedom Found., Washington; dir. rsch., prin. adv. U.S. Rep. Parris; v.p. devel. Nat. Found. Econ. Rsch.; staff dir. subcom. internat. econ. policy and trade U.S. Ho. of Reps. Com. on Fgn. Affairs, Washington; chief of staff Saint Lawrence Seaway Devel. Corp., Washington, 1992, acting adminstr., 1995—; chmn. joint tolls adv. bd. Saint Lawrence Seaway Devel. Corp., 1993. Bd. govs. McLean Cmty. Ctr., Va. Office: Dept Transp Saint Lawrence Seaway Corp 400 7th St SW Washington DC 20590

SANDERS, DAVID P., lawyer; b. Chgo., Sept. 24, 1949. BA with distinction, U. Wis., 1971; JD, Georgetown U., 1974. Bar: Ill. 1974, U.S. Ct. Appeals (7th and 4th cirs.) 1974, U.S. Dist. Ct. (no. dist. trial bar) Ill. 1974. Ptnr. Jenner & Block, Chgo.; adj. prof. trial advocacy Northwestern U., Chgo., 1981-91. Editor Am. Criminal Law Rev., 1974. Mem. ABA, Chgo. Coun. Lawyers (chmn. fed. jud. evaluation com. 1989—, mem. def. counsel sect. libel def. resource ctr.). Office: Jenner & Block One IBM Plz Chicago IL 60611

SANDERS, DEION LUWYNN, baseball and football player; b. Ft. Myers, Fla., Aug. 9, 1967. Student, Fla. State U. Baseball player N.Y. Yankees, 1988-90, Atlanta Braves, 1991-94, Cin. Reds, 1994; football player Atlanta Falcons, 1989-94, San Francisco 49ers, 1994, Dallas Cowboys, 1995—. Named to Sporting News Coll. All-Am. football team, 1986-88, Sporting News NFL All-Pro Football Team, 1991, 92, 94, Pro Bowl team, 1991-94; recipient Jim Thorpe award, 1988. NFL kickoff return leader, 1992, Nat. League Triples Leader, 1992; mem. Championship team Super Bowl XXIX, 1994, Super Bowl XXX, 1995. Address: San Francisco Giants Candlestick Park San Francisco CA 94124*

SANDERS, FRANKLIN D., insurance company executive; b. Newton, Mass., Apr. 24, 1935; s. Franklin and Ethel Shriner (Dulaney) S.; m. Jane Gray Collier, June 18, 1960; children—Cynthia, Franklin D., Nancy, Carolyn. A.B., Amherst Coll., 1957; M.B.A., Harvard U., 1959. With 1st Boston Corp., N.Y.C., 1960-86, mng. dir., 1976-86; pres. Aegis Ins. Services Inc., Jersey City, 1986—; treas., bd. dirs. Assoc. Electric & Gas Ins. Services, Ltd., Hamilton, Bermuda. Chmn. Republican Exec. Com., Bernardsville, N.J., 1965-72, Bernardsville Zoning Bd. of Adjustment, 1966—. Episcopalian. Clubs: Down Town, Harvard (N.Y.C.); Somerset Hills Country (Bernardsville), Mid-Ocean (Bermuda). Avocations: sailing, skiing, golf. Home: RR 2 34 Post Kunhardt Rd Bernardsville NJ 07924-1522 Office: Aegis Ins Svcs Inc Harborside Fin Ctr 10 Exchange Pl Jersey City NJ 07302

SANDERS, FRED JOSEPH, aerospace company executive; b. Tulsa, June 18, 1928; s. Charles Frederick and Mary Ethel (White) S.; m. Marceline Frances Shaw, May 19, 1951; 1 son, Fred William. A.A., Spartan Coll., 1947; M.S.M.E., St. Louis U., 1961. Design engr. McDonnell Aircraft Co., St. Louis, 1947-66; program mgr. Skylab Program, McDonnell Douglas, Huntington Beach, Calif., 1967-74; dir. product devel. McDonnell Douglas, Huntington Beach, 1975-76, v.p., 1977-84; v.p., gen. mgr. McDonnell Douglas Astronautics Co., St. Louis, 1985-88, ret., 1988. Served as cpl. U.S. Army, 1954-56. Recipient Public Service award NASA, 1974. Assoc. fellow AIAA. Roman Catholic. Home: 4 Broadview Farm Rd Saint Louis MO 63141-8501

SANDERS, FREDERICK, meteorologist; b. Detroit, May 17, 1923; s. Frederick William and Dorothy Gail (Martin) S.; m. Nancy Seabury Brown, Nov. 30, 1946; children: Christopher Martin, John Arnold, Frederick Duncan. B.A., Amherst Coll., 1944; Sc.D., M.I.T., 1954. Forecaster U.S. Weather Bur., N.Y.C., 1947-49; teaching asst. MIT, 1949-51, instr. meteorology, 1951-56, asst. prof., 1956-59, asso. prof., 1959-69, prof., 1969-84, prof. emeritus, 1984—; cons. in field. Author: (with H.C. Willett) Descriptive Meteorology, 1955, (with D.M. Houghton) Weather at Sea, 1988; editor Monthly Weather Rev., 1986—; contbr. numerous articles to profl. jours. Served with USAAF, 1942-46. Recipient award for applied research Nat. Weather Assn., 1978; NSF grantee, 1958—; NOAA grantee, 1956-78; Office Naval Research grantee, 1979-92; USAF grantee, 1954-78. Fellow AAAS, Am. Meteorol. Soc.; mem. Royal Meteorol. Soc. (fgn.). Club: Eastern Yacht (Marblehead, Mass.). Home and Office: 9 Flint St Marblehead MA 01945-3716

SANDERS, FREDRIC M., lawyer; b. N.Y.C., Jan. 10, 1941; s. Louis and Ruth (Appel) Samanowitz; m. Susan Sanders, June 11, 1961; children: Lauren, Lawrence. BA, Queens Coll., 1961; JD, Harvard U., 1964. Bar: N.Y. Assoc. Rubin Baum & Levin, N.Y.C., 1964-67, Hess Segall, N.Y.C., 1967-74; ptnr. Hess Segall Guterman Pelz et al (merged with Loeb and Loeb,

1986), N.Y.C., 1974-86, Loeb and Loeb, N.Y.C., 1986—. Mem. ABA, N.Y. State Bar Assn., Assn. of Bar of City of N.Y. Office: Loeb and Loeb 345 Park Ave New York NY 10154-0004

SANDERS, GERALD HOLLIE, communications educator; b. Mt. Vernon, Tex., Dec. 10, 1924; s. Elmer Hugh and Velma Mae (Hollowell) S.; m. Mary Dean Crew, July 18, 1947; children: Michael Dwaine, Rose Ann, Susan Kathleen, Randall Wayne. BA, Southeastern Okla. U., 1947; MA, Tex. Tech U., 1969; PhD, U. Minn., 1974. Program dir. Sta. WEWO, Laurenburg, N.C., 1947-49; sports dir. Sta. KFYO, Lubbock, Tex., 1949-50; gen. mgr. Sta. KLVT, Levelland, Tex., 1950-51, 53-54; sports dir. Sta. KCUL, Ft. Worth, 1954-55; asst. mgr. Sta. KDAV, Lubbock, 1955-57; mgr. Sta. KCBD, Lubbock, 1957-58; owner Sta. KSEL, Lubbock, 1958-67, Sta. KBUY, Amarillo, Tex., Sta. KERB, Kermit, Tex., Sta. KBEK, Elk City, Okla., Sta. KZZN, Littlefield, Tex.; lectr. communications The Coll. of Wooster, Ohio, 1967-68, asst. prof., 1968-75, assoc. prof., 1975-81, chmn. dept. communication, 1974-81; chmn. dept. communication Miami U., Oxford, Ohio, 1981-92, prof. emeritus comm., 1992—; disting. lectr. Jinan U., Zhong Shan U., Fudan U., Nanjing U., Beijing U., China, 1989; cons. in field, Oxford, 1982—; polit. and trial cons., 1996—. Author: Introduction to Comtemporary Academic Debate, 1983; also articles. Active Political Campaigns. Served to col. USMC, 1943-46, PTO, 1951-53, Korea. Recipient Disting. Svc. award Delta Sigma Rho-Tau Kappa Alpha, 1991, Am. Forensic Assn., 1991. Mem. Am. Forensic Assn. (pres. 1978-82), Speech Communication Assn., Speech Communication Assn. of Ohio (pres. 1976-77), Disting. Svc. award 1978), Am. Inst. Parliamentarians, Soc. Trial Cons. Presbyterian. Avocations: sports, political campaigns. Home: 200 Country Club Dr Oxford OH 45056-9002 Office: Advocacy Unltd PO Box 457 Oxford OH 45056

SANDERS, GILBERT OTIS, psychologist, addictions treatment therapist, consultant, educator, motivational speaker; b. Oklahoma City, Aug. 7, 1945; s. Richard Allen and Evelyn Wilmoth (Barker) S.; m. Lidia Julia Grados-Ventura; 1 child, Lisa Dawn Sanders-Coker. AS, Murray State Coll, 1965; BA, Okla. State U., 1967, U. State of N.Y.; MS, Troy State U., 1970; EdD, U. Tulsa, 1974; postdoctoral studies St. Louis U., Am. Tech. U.; grad. U.S. Army Command and Gen. Staff Coll., Ft. Leavenworth, Kas., 1979. Diplomate Am. Bd. Med. Pschotherapist, Am. Bd. Forensic Examiners, Am. Forensic Counselors Assn. Dir. edn. Am. Humane Edn. Soc., Boston, 1975; chmn. dept. computer sci., dir. Individual Learning and Counseling Ctr., asst. prof. pschology and law enforcement Calumet Coll., Whiting, Ind., 1975-78; rsch. psychologist U.S. Army Rsch. Inst., Ft. Hood, Tex., 1978-79; pvt. practice counseling, Killen, Tex., 1978-79; psychologist U.S. Army Tng. and Doctrine Command Sys. Analysis Activity, White Sands Missile Range, N.Mex., 1979-80; project dir. psychologist Applied Sci. Assocs., Ft. Sill, Okla., 1980-81; pvt. practice counseling, Lake St. Louis, 1981-83; assoc. prof. Pittsburg State U., Kans., 1983-85; pres. Applied Behavioral Rsch. Assocs. (formerly Southwestern Behavioral Rsch.), Oklahoma City, 1985-94; pvt. practice counseling Christian Family Counseling Ctr., Lawton, Okla., 1986-87; psychologist, systems analyst U.S Army Field Artillery Sch.-Directorate of Combat Devels., Ft. Sill, Okla., 1987; psychologist U.S. Army Operational Test and Evaluation Agy., Washington, 1988-89; psychologist, drug abuse program dir. Fed. Bur. of Prisons-Fed. Correctional Inst. El Reno, Okla., 1989-91; psychologist, clin. dir. drug abuse program U.S. Penitentiary, Leavenworth, Kans., 1991-94; pvt. practice psychologist MacArthur Med. and Psychotherapy, Inc. and Acad. Christian Counseling Okla., Oklahoma City, 1992—; adj. prof. bus. and psychology Columbia Coll.-Buder Campus, St. Louis, 1982-84; adj. prof. U.S. Army Command Staff and Gen. Coll., 1983-89, Columbia Pacific U., 1984—, Greenwich U., 1990—, U. Alaska S.E., 1995—. Editor: Evaluation for a Manual Backup System for TACFIRE (ARI), 1978, Training/Humane Factors Implications--Copperhead Operational Test II Livefire Phase, 1979, TRADOC Training Effectiveness Analysis Handbook, 1980, Cost and Training Effectiveness Analysis/TEA 8-80/ Patroit Air Defense Missile System, 1980, Cost and Training Analysis/Infantry Fighting Vehicle (Bradley), 1980, Human Factors Implications for the Howitzer Improvement Program, 1989, The Drug Education Handbook, 1995, Therapist Handbook for Drug Treatment, 1996; author research reports. Recipient Kavanough Found. Community Builder award, 1967; named Hon. Col. Okla. Gov. Staff, 1972, Hon. Amb., 1974. Fellow Am. Assn. Psychologists Treating Addictions; mem. APA, ACA, Am. Assn. Marriage and Family Therapists, Am. Mental Health Counselors Assn., Res. Officers Assn., Commd. Officers Assn., U.S. Pub. Health Svc., Pi Kappa Phi, Alpha Phi Omega. Home: 5404 NW 65th St Oklahoma City OK 73132-7747 Office: Mac Arthur Med Inst 7317 N Mac Arthur Blvd Oklahoma City OK 73132

SANDERS, HAROLD BAREFOOT, JR., federal judge; b. Dallas, Tex., Feb. 5, 1925; s. Harold Barefoot and May Elizabeth (Forrester) S.; m. Jan Scurlock, June 6, 1952; children—Janet Lea, Martha Kay, Mary Frances, Harold Barefoot III. BA, U. Tex., 1949, LLB, 1950. Bar: Tex. bar 1950. U.S. atty. No. Dist. Tex., 1961-65; asst. dep. atty. gen. U.S., 1965-66; asst. atty. gen., 1966-67; legis. counsel to President U.S., 1967-69; partner firm Clark, West, Keller, Sanders & Butler, Dallas, 1969-79; U.S. dist. judge for No. Dist. Tex., Dallas, 1979—, chief judge, 1989-95. Mem. Tex. Ho. of Reps., 1952-58; Dem. nominee U.S. Senate, 1972. Lt. (j.g.) USNR, World War II. Mem. ABA (chmn. nat. conf. fed. trial judges 1988-89), Fed. Bar Assn. (Disting. Svc. award Dallas 1964), Dallas Bar Assn., State Bar Tex. (jud. conf. U.S. 1989-92, jud. panel on multidistrict litigation 1992—), Blue Key, Phi Delta Phi, Phi Delta Theta. Methodist. Office: US Courthouse 1100 Commerce St Fl 15 Dallas TX 75242-1027

SANDERS, HOWARD, investment company executive; b. Phila., June 30, 1941; s. Louis and Freda (Liss) S.; m. Dale Rosenberg, Dec. 15, 1963; children: Lee Michael, Kimberly Joy. BS in Acctg., Temple U., 1962; M in Acctg., Ohio State U., 1963. CPA. Acct., Price, Waterhouse & Co., Phila., 1962-65; asst. prof. acctg. Temple U., 1965-72; v.p. Revere Fund, Inc., Phila., 1966-76; pres. Revere Mgmt. Co., Inc., Phila., 1966-72; chmn. bd. Ladies Center of Nebr., Inc., 1976—, Volk Footwear and Findings Co., 1977-78, Mister Plywood Enterprises, Inc., 1970-82; pres. Sanders Fin. Mgmt., Inc., Fort Lauderdale, 1972—; chmn. bd. Am. Carpet Backing Distbg. Inc., 1978-80, Polis-Sanders Real Estate Corp., 1981—; exec. chmn. Humedco Corp., 1995—. Contbg. author: How to Start a Mutual Fund, 1970. Mem. adv. bd. Phila. Assn. for Retarded Children, 1970-72; chmn. bd. Women's Med. Center of Providence, Inc., 1977—, Women's Med. Center of North Jersey, Inc., 1977-82, Women's Med. Center of Atlanta, Inc., 1977—, Cherry Hill Women's Center, Inc., 1978—, Metairie Women's Center of New Orleans, Inc., 1980-84, Hartford Gynecol. Center, 1980—. Kaiser Aluminum and Chem. Co. fellow, 1962-63. Mem. Am. Inst. C.P.A.s, Pa. Inst. C.P.A.s (award for paper 1961), Phila. Jaycees (dir. 1966), Nat. Assn. Accts., B'rith Shalom Assn., Beta Gamma Sigma, Beta Alpha Psi, Tau Epsilon Phi. Home and Office: 410 Sea Turtle Ter Fort Lauderdale FL 33324-2814 *My life has been guided by careful attention to words which are rapidly disappearing from the "Dictionary of American Life". I have concentrated on integrity, prudence, brevity, clarity, ego control and true friendship. In all dealings I insist upon mutual benefit, taking great effort to assure that the opposite party receives a slightly larger gain. My goal is total value received for all. I attempt to mix my love for life and humor in all my relationships.*

SANDERS, IRWIN TAYLOR, sociology educator; b. Millersburg, Ky., Jan. 17, 1909; s. Robert Stuart and Lucy (Taylor) S.; m. Margaret Rydberg, June 23, 1934; children: Gerda S. (Groff), Robert Stuart. Student, Tenn. Mil. Inst., 1920-25; A.B., Washington and Lee U., 1929; student, Theol. Sem., Princeton, 1932-33; Ph.D., Cornell U., 1938; D.Pedagogy (hon.), R.I. Coll., 1981; Litt.D. (hon.), Washington and Lee U., 1981. Instr. American Coll., Sofia, Bulgaria, 1929-32; dean American Coll., 1934-37; asst. prof. sociology Ala. Coll., 1938-40; successively asst. prof., asso. prof., prof., head dept. sociology, distinguished univ. prof. U. Ky., 1940-56; lectr. sociology Harvard Sch. Pub. Health, 1958-62; chmn. dept. sociology and anthropology Boston U., 1960-63, 69-72, prof. sociology, 1972-77, Univ. lectr., 1973-74, also co-dir. community sociology tng. program; research dir. Assos. Internat. Research, Inc., Cambridge, Mass., 1956-60; asso. dir. Internat. Tng. and Research Program, Ford Found., 1962-66; v.p. Edn. and World Affairs, 1967-69; social science analyst Bur. Agrl. Econ., U.S. Dept. Agr., summer 1943; sr. social scientist Bur. Agrl. Econ., U.S. Dept. Agr. (Office Fgn. Agrl. Relations), 1943; social sci. Bur. Agrl. Econ., U.S. Dept. Agr. (Extension Service), summer 1944; agrl. attaché Am. Embassy, Belgrade, Yugoslavia, 1945-46; research assoc. Harvard, 1952-53; cons. rural welfare division FAO. Author: Balkan Village, 1949, The Community, 1958, 3d rev. edit., 1975, Rainbow in the Rock, People of Rural Greece, 1962, Rural Society, 1977; co-author: Alabama Rural Communities, 1940, Sociological Foundations of Education, 1942, Kentucky: Designs for Her Future, 1944, Farmers of the World, 1945, Making Good Communities Better, 1950, Bridges to Understanding: International Programs at U.S. Colleges and Universities, 1970; Editor: Societies Around the World, 1953, Collectivization of Agriculture in Eastern Europe, 1958, The Professional School and World Affairs, 1968; series editor: Social Movements: Past and Present, 1980-95. Bd. dirs. Am. Farm Sch., Thessaloniki, Greece, Sofia Am. Schs., Inc., Assn. for Study Southeastern Europe, Bucharest, Rumania. Decorated Royal Order of Phoenix Greece). Mem. Am. Sociol. Soc. (disting. cmty. sect. award 1983), Eastern Sociol. Soc., So. Siol. Soc. (pres. 1955-56), Rural Sociol. Soc. (pres. 1956-57, Disting. Rural Sociologist 1993), New Eng. Sociological Assn. (Apple award 1993), Am. Assn. Advancement Slavic Studies, Bulgarian-Am. Studies Assn. (hon. pres.), Modern Greek Studies Assn. (council), Am. Assn. for S.E. European Studies (pres. 1980), Société European de Culture (Venice), Rumanian Studies Soc. (council), Bulgarian Acad. Scis. (fgn. mem.), Am. Assn. for Promotion Bulgarian Culture (hon. pres.), Cornell Club (N.Y.), Univ. Club (Boston), Phi Beta Kappa, Omicron Delta Kappa, Kappa Phi Kappa, Delta Sigma Rho, Delta Upsilon. Democrat. Presbyterian. Home: 400 School St Wellesley MA 02181-4715 Office: 96 Cummington St Boston MA 02215-2407

SANDERS, JACK FORD, physician; b. St. Louis, Mich., July 16, 1918; s. Ford and Viva (Marvin) S.; m. Gretchen A. Jellema, Feb. 2, 1945; children: Karen Jean, Vicki Leigh, Mary Beth, Donald Curtis, Wendy Lynn. B.S. summa cum laude, Alma Coll., Mich., 1939; M.D., U. Mich., 1945; LL.D., Northwood U. Diplomate Am. Bd. Internal Medicine; cert. flight instr. aircraft and instruments, airplane single and multi-engine land and sea; flight safety counselor FAA; CAP check pilot; sr. aviation med. examiner. Intern Henry Ford Hosp., 1945-46, resident in internal medicine, 1947-50; practice medicine specializing in internal medicine Alma, Mich.; sr. attending physician internal medicine Butterworth Hosp., Blodgett Hosp., Grand Rapids, Mich.; cons. St. Mary's Hosp., Grand Rapids, Ferguson-Droste-Ferguson Hosp.; med. dir. Mich. Masonic Hosp., Alma, 1960-77; med. dir. rehab. div., chmn. dept. medicine, chief staff Gratiot Community Hosp.; chmn. dept. medicine Tri-County Hosp., Edmore, Mich.; clin. assoc. prof medicine Coll. Human Medicine, Mich. State U.; mem. Com. on Aging, Gov's Adv. Coun. on Heart Disease, Cancer and Stroke; del White Ho. Conf. on Aging; bd. dirs. Mich. Masonic Home and Hosp.; chmn. bd. Cen. Mich. Wendy's, Inc.; sec., treas. Gratiot Aviation, Inc. Contbr. articles to profl. jours. Chmn. bd. govs. Mich.; bd. dirs. Northwood U., Gratiot Cmty. Airport Bd. Instr. ACTS, U.S. Air Corps and lt. (j.g.) M.C., USNR, WWII. Fellow ACP, Am. Geriatrics Soc.; mem. AMA, Mich. State Med. Soc., Gratiot Med. Soc., Kent Med. Soc., Gratiot-Isabella-Clare County Med. Soc. (pres. 1965), Am. Diabetes Assn., Am. Heart Assn., Am. Multiple Sclerosis Soc., Mich. Crippled Children and Adults Soc., East Ctrl. Mich. Health Svc. Assn., Mason (33d degree), Rotary, Phi Sigma Pi (hon.). Home: 250 Purdy Dr Alma MI 48801-2174 Office: Mich Masonic Hosp Alma MI 48801-2174

SANDERS, JACK THOMAS, religious studies educator; b. Grand Prairie, Tex., Feb. 28, 1935; s. Eula Thomas and Mildred Madge (Parish) S.; m. Patricia Chism, Aug. 9, 1959 (dec. Oct. 1973); 1 son, Collin Thomas; m. Susan Elizabeth Plass, Mar. 3, 1979. B.A., Tex. Wesleyan Coll., 1956; M.Div., Emory U., 1960; Ph.D., Claremont Grad. Sch., 1963; postgrad., Eberhard-Karls U., Tuebingen, Germany, 1963-64. Asst. prof. Emory U., Atlanta, 1964-67, Garrett Theol Sem., Evanston, Ill., 1967-68, McCormick Theol. Sem., Chgo., 1968-69; assoc. prof. U. Oreg., Eugene, 1969-75, prof., 1975—, head dept. religious studies, 1973-80, 85-90. Author: The New Testament Christological Hymns, 1971, Ethics in the New Testament, 1975, 2d edit., 1986, Ben Sira and Demotic Wisdom, 1983, The Jews in Luke-Acts, 1987, Schismatics, Sectarians, Dissidents, Deviants: The First One Hundred Years of Jewish-Christian Relations, 1993; editor: Gospel Origins and Christian Beginnings, 1990, Gnosticism and the Early Christian World, 1990; mem. edit. bd. Jour. Bibl. Lit., 1977-83. Mem. policy bd. Dept. Higher Edn. Nat. Council Chs., N.Y.C., 1971-73. NDEA grad. study fellow, 1960-63; Fulbright Commn. fellow, 1963-64; Am. Council Learned Socs. travel grantee, 1981; NEH fellow, 1983-84. Mem. AAUP (chpt. pres. 1981-82), Studiorum Novi Testamenti Soc., World Union Jewish Studies, Assn. for Jewish Studies, Soc. Bibl. Lit. (regional sec. 1969-76, sabbatical rsch. award 1976-77), Archeol. Inst. Am. (chpt. pres. 1988-89), Soc. for Sci. Study of Religion, Assn. for Sociology Religion. Democrat. Home: 2555 Birch Ln Eugene OR 97403-2191 Office: U Oregon Dept Religious Studies Eugene OR 97403

SANDERS, JACQUELYN SEEVAK, psychologist, educator; b. Boston, Apr. 26, 1931; d. Edward Ezral and Dora (Zoken) Seevak; 1 son, Seth. BA, Radcliffe Coll., 1952; MA, U. Chgo., 1964; PhD, UCLA, 1972. Counselor, asst. prin. Orthogenic Sch., Chgo., 1952-65; research assoc. UCLA, 1965-68; cons. Osawatomie State Hosp. (Kans.), 1965-68; asst. prof. Ctr. for Early Edn., L.A., 1969-72; assoc. dir. Sonia Shankman Orthogenic Sch., U. Chgo., 1972-73, dir., 1973-93, dir. emeritus, 1993—; curriculum cons. day care ctrs. L.A. Dept. Social Welfare, 1970-72; instr. Calif. State Coll., L.A., 1972; lectr. dept. edn. U. Chgo., 1972-80, sr. lectr., 1980-93, clin. assoc. prof. dept. psychiatry, 1990-93, emeritus, 1993—; instr. edn. program Inst. Psychoanalysis, Chgo., 1979-82; reading cons. Foreman High Sch., Chgo. Author: Greenhouse for the Mind, 1989; editor: (with Barry L. Childress) Psychoanalytic Approaches to the Very Troubled Child: Therapeutic Practice Innovations in Residential & Educational Settings, 1989, Severly Disturbed Children and the Parental Alliance, 1992, (with Jerome M. Goldsmith) Milieu Therapy: Significant Issues and Innovative Applications, 1993; contbr. articles to profl. jours. Mem. vis. com. univ. sch. rels. U. Chgo. UCLA Univ. fellow, 1966-68; Radcliffe Coll. Scholar, 1948-52; recipient Alumna award Girls' Latin Sch., Boston. Mem. Assn. Children's Residential Ctrs. (past pres.). Clubs: Quadrangle, Radcliffe of Chgo. (sec/treas. 1986-87, pres. 1987-89); Harvard of Chgo. (bd. dirs. 1986—). Home: 5842 S Stony Island Ave Apt 2G Chicago IL 60637-2023

SANDERS, JAMES ALVIN, minister, biblical studies educator; b. Memphis, Nov. 28, 1927; s. Robert E. and Sue (Black) S.; m. Dora Cargille, June 30, 1951; 1 son, Robin David. BA magna cum laude, Vanderbilt U., 1948, BD with honors, 1951; student, U. Paris, 1950-51; PhD, Hebrew Union Coll., 1955; DLitt, Acadia U., 1973; STD, U. Glasgow, 1975; DHL, Coe Coll., 1988, Hebrew Union Coll., 1988. Ordained teacher Presbyn. Ch., 1955; instr. French Vanderbilt U., 1948-49; faculty Colgate Rochester Div. Sch., 1954-65, assoc. prof., 1957-60, Joseph B. Hoyt prof. O.T. interpretation, 1960-65; prof. O.T. Union Theol. Sem., N.Y.C., 1965-70, Auburn prof. Bibl. studies, 1970-77; adj. prof. Columbia, N.Y.C., 1966-77; prof. Bibl. studies Sch. Theology and Grad. Sch., Claremont, Calif., 1977—; ann. prof. Jerusalem Sch. of Am. Schs. Oreintal Rsch., 1961-62; fellow Ecumenical Isnt., Jerusalem, 1972-73, 85; Ayer lectr., 1971, 79, Shaffer lectr., 1972, Fondren lectr., 1975, Currie lectr., 1976, McFadin lectr., 1979, Colwell lectr., 1979; guest lectr. U. Fribourg, Switzerland, 1981, 90, Hebrew Union Coll., 1982, 88, Oral Roberts U., 1982, Tulsa U., 1982, Ind. U., 1982, Coe Coll., 1983, Garrett Sem., 1984, Pepperdine U., 1985, Western Sem., 1985, Bethany Sem., 1986; lectr. Union Sem. Sesquicentennial, 1987, U. Wis., 1987, U. Chgo., 1987; Gray lectr. Duke U., 1988; guest lectr. Notre Dame U., Georgetown U., Tex. Christian U., 1989, Alexander Robertson lectr. U. Glasgow, 1990-91, Gustavson lectr. United Theol. sem., 1991; assoc. program lectr. Smithsonian, 1990, Am. Bible Soc. Sesquicentennial, 1991, U. N.Mex., 1992, 94, Am. Interfaith Inst., 1992, Georgetown U., 1992; Lily Rosmen lectr. Skirball Mus., 1992; vis. prof. U. N.Mex., 1992, Southwestern U., 1992, Calif. Luth. U., 1992, 94, Willamette U., 19923, Peter Craigie lectr. U. Calgary, 1993, U. So. Ariz., 1993; Samuel Iwry lectr. John Hopkins U., 1993; lectr. San Diego State U., 1994, Creighton U., 1995, The Mercantile Libr., N.Y.C., 1995, U. Heidelberg, Germany, 1995, U. Mich., 1995; mem. internt. O.T. text critical com. United Bible Socs., 1969—; exec. officer Ancient Bibl. Manuscript Ctr. for Preservation and Rsch., 1977-80, pres., 1980—. Author: Suffering as Devine Discipline in the Old Testament and Post-Biblical Judaism, 1955, The Old Testament in the Cross, 1961, The Psalms Scroll of Qumran Cave 11, 1965, The Dead Sea Psalms Scroll, 1967, Near Eastern Archaeology in the Twentieth Century, 1970, Torah and Canon, 1972, 74, Identité de la Bible, 1975, God Has a Story Too, 1979, Canon and Community, 1984, From Sacred Story to Sacred Text, 1987, Luke and Scripture, 1993; editor: Paul and the Scriptrues of Israel, 1993; contbr. over 250 articles to profl. jours.; mem. editorial bd. Jour. Bibl. Lit., 1970-76, Jour. for Study Judaism, Bibl. Theology Bull., Interpretation, 1973-78, New Rev. Standard Version Bible Com. Trustee Am. Schs. Oriental Research. Fulbright grantee, 1950-51, Lilly Endowment grantee, 1981, NEH grantee, 1980, 91-92; Lefkowitz and Rabinowitz interfaith fellow, 1951-53, Rockefeller fellow, 1953-54, 85, Guggenheim fellow, 1961-62, 72-73, Human Scis. Rsch. fellow, 1989. Mem. Soc. Bibl. Lit. and Exegesis (pres. 1977-78), Phi Beta Kappa, Phi Sigma Iota, Theta Chi Beta. Home: PO Box 593 Claremont CA 91711-0593 Office: Ancient Bible Manuscript Ctr PO Box 670 Claremont CA 91711-0670

SANDERS, JAMES GRADY, biogeochemist; b. Norfolk, Va., June 10, 1951; s. Allen Buford and Maple Seretha (Myers) S.; m. Carmen Lee Nance, Aug. 19, 1972. BS in Zoology, Duke U., 1973; MS in Marine Scis., U. N.C., 1975, PhD in Marine Scis., 1978. Postdoctoral investigator Woods Hole (Mass.) Oceanographic Instn., 1978-80; vis. scientist Chesapeake Biol. Lab. U. Md., Solomons, 1980-81; asst. curator Benedict (Md.) Estuarine Rsch. Lab. Acad. Natural Scis., 1981-85, assoc. curator Benedict (Md.) Estuarine Rsch. Lab., 1985-89, curator Benedict (Md.) Estuarine Rsch. Lab., 1989—, dir. Benedict (Md.) Estuarine Rsch. Lab., 1983—; cons. EPA Sweden, Stockholm, 1985-90; mem. Md. Sea Grant Adv. Com., College Park, 1983-90, Environ. Commn., Calvert City, Md., 1981-88; mem. environ. biology panel Office R & D EPA, Washington, 1986-95; regional rep. Coastal Resources Adv. Commn., Md., 1983-86. Contbr. over 60 articles to sci. jours. Grantee NOAA, 1981—, EPA, 1983—. Mem. AAAS, Am. Soc. Limnology and Oceanography, Soc. for Environ. Toxicology and Chemistry, Estuarine Rsch. Fedn. (treas. 1993—). Achievements include first identification of relationships between algal growth and chemical transformations of arsenic in aquatic systems. Office: Acad Natural Scis Benedict Estuarine Rsch Ctr 10545 Mackall Rd Saint Leonard MD 20685

SANDERS, JAMES JOSEPH, architect; b. Clearwater, Kans., 1936. BS in Architecture, U. Wash., 1963; MS in Architecture, Columbia U., 1964. Registered arch., Wash., Mont., N.Y.; cert. Nat. Coun. Archtl. Registration Bd. Designer, project arch. Naramore Bain Brady and Johanson, Seattle, 1965-68; asst. prof., lectr. dept. architecture U. Wash., Seattle, 1968-76; prin. James J. Sanders Arch. and Urban Designer, Seattle, 1968-76; project dir., designer TRA Architecture Engrng. Planning Interiors Ltd., Seattle, 1977—; prin. TRA Architecture Engrng. Planning Interiors Ltd., 1991—. Prin. works include Farm Products Rsch. Lab., Wash. State U., Bellevue (Wash.) C.C., Pike Street Hill Climb, Seattle, UNICO, Seattle, Doha (Qatar) Internat. Airport, McCarran Internat. Airport, Las Vegas, Dulles Internat. Airport additions, Washington, Wash. State Conv. and Trade Ctr., Seattle, Providence Conv. Ctr. Planning, New Denver Internat. Airport Concourses, Wash. State Patrol Hdqs. Bldg., Riddel, Williaams, Bullit & Walkinshaw Law Offices, Ruby Spring Lodge, also others. Chmn. Pike Pl. Market Hist. Commn., 1981; past bd. dirs. Allied Arts of Seattle; active Leschi Improvement Coun., Seattle, Madrona Cmty. Coun., Seattle; profl. soccer referee WSSA, 1974-85. Grad. scholar Columbia U. Fellow AIA (past chmn. Honor awrds com., pre. Seattle chpt. 1993-94, recipient Student Gold medal, Scholar for Design, Home awards); mem. Seattle Architecture Found. (bd. dirs.). Office: TRA Seattle 215 Columbia St Seattle WA 98104-1551

SANDERS, JAY WILLIAM, audiology educator; b. Balt., July 26, 1924; s. Jay Will and Mary Magdalene (Fisher) S.; m. Mary Elizabeth St. John, Aug. 27, 1950; children—Mary Jean, John Jay, Elizabeth Ann. A.A., Louisburg Coll., 1948; B.A., U. N.C., 1950; M.A., Columbia U., 1951; Ph.D., U. Mo., 1957; postgrad. (spl. fellow), Northwestern U., 1962-64. Instr. speech U. Mo., Columbia, 1952-57; from asst. prof. to assoc. prof. Trenton (N.J.) State Coll., 1957-62; asst. prof. audiology Vanderbilt U. Sch. Medicine, Nashville, 1964-65, assoc. prof., 1965-71, prof., 1971-87, prof. emeritus, 1987—; chmn. Tenn. State Bd. Examiners for Speech Pathology and Audiology, 1973-79. Contbr. chpts. to textbooks, articles to profl. jours. Served with U.S. Navy, 1942-45. Recipient various awards; Nat. Inst. Neurol. Diseases and Blindness spl. fellow, 1962-64. Fellow Am. Speech and Hearing Assn.; mem. Am. Acad. Audiology, Tenn. Speech-Lang.-Hearing Assn., Phi Beta Kappa. Home: 5518 Vanderbilt Rd Old Hickory TN 37138-1133 Office: Wilkerson Hearing & Speech Ctr 1114 19th Ave S Nashville TN 37212-2110

SANDERS, JIMMY DEVON, university educator; b. Montgomery, Ala., Nov. 6, 1945; s. Harold Wright Sanders and Elsie M. (Huett) Harris; m. Linda Ruth Sweatt, Mar. 25, 1966; children: Richard Devon, Robert Pearson. B Gen. Studies, U. Nebr., Omaha, 1968; MPA, U. Okla., 1973, U. So. Calif., 1988; D Pub. Adminstrn., U. So. Calif., 1989. Commd. officer USAF, 1964, advanced through grades to lt. col., 1985, various health svc. adminstrv. positions, 1964-83; dir. base med. svcs. USAF, San Vito dei Normanni, Italy, 1980-83; sr. health policy analyst Dept. Def., Washington, 1983-88; ret., 1988; assoc. prof. mgmt. and healthcare mgmt. Marymount U., Arlington, Va., 1988-91; dir. Atlantic region Troy State U., Norfolk, Va., 1991-94; dir. Fla. region Troy State U., Ft. Walton Beach, 1995—; health care cons. various hosps. and cities, 1987—, Ret. Officers Assn., Arlington, 1988-90. Fellow Am. Coll. Health Care Execs.; mem. Assn. Mgmt. (dir. orgnl. studies, editor Procs. 1994). Republican. Lutheran. Avocations: walking, reading, golf. Home: Rt 1 Box 342E Montgomery AL 36105 Office: Troy State U PO Box 2829 Fort Walton Beach FL 32549

SANDERS, JOHN LASSITER, retired academic administrator; b. Four Oaks, N.C., June 30, 1927; s. David Hardy and Louie Jane (Lassiter) S.; m. Ann Beal, Aug. 14, 1954; children—Tracy Elizabeth Sanders Justus, Jane Nesbit, William Hardy. A.B., U. N.C., 1950, J.D., 1954. Bar: N.C. 1955. Law clk. to judge U.S. Ct. Appeals, 1954-55; pvt. practice Raleigh, N.C., 1955-56; mem. faculty Inst. Govt., U. N.C., Chapel Hill, 1956-94, dir., 1962-73, 79-92, v.p. planning at univ., 1973-78. Served with USNR, 1945-46. Mem. N.C. Bar Assn. Democrat. Baptist. Home: 1107 Sourwood Dr Chapel Hill NC 27514-4914 Office: U NC Inst Govt Cb 3330 Knapp Bldg Chapel Hill NC 27514

SANDERS, JOSEPH STANLEY, lawyer; b. L.A., Aug. 9, 1942; s. Hays and Eva (Cook) S.; m. Melba Binion, Mar. 17, 1984; children: Alexandria, Chelsea; children by previous marriage: Edward Moore, Justin Hays. BA, Whittier Coll., 1963; BA, MA (Rhodes scholar), Magdalen Coll., Oxford U., 1965; LLB, Yale U., 1968. Bar: Calif. 1969. Dir. summer projects Westminster Neighborhood Assn., Los Angeles, 1966-67; dir. pro tem, instr. polit. sci. Yale U. Transitional Year, 1967-68; staff atty. Western Center on Law and Poverty, Los Angeles, 1968-69; exec. dir. Lawyers Com. for Civil Rights Under Law, Los Angeles, 1969-70; assoc. law firm Wyman, Bautzer, Finell, Rothman & Kuchel, Beverly Hills, Calif., 1969-71; partner Rosenfeld, Lederer, Jacobs & Sanders, Beverly Hills, 1971-72, Sanders & Tisdale, Los Angeles, 1972-78, Sanders & Dickerson, Los Angeles, 1978-92; assoc. Barnes, McGhee & Pryce, L.A., 1992—. Co-founder Watts Summer Festival, 1966; co-chmn. Whittier Coll. Alumni Fund, 1970-71, trustee 1973-90, 93—; mem. Yale Law Alumni Com. on Curriculum Reform, 1970; coord. Calif. Conf. Black Attys., 1969; chmn. membership drive Dist. 8 Boy Scouts Am., L.A., 1971; mem. Coun. on Fgn. Rels., 1994—, L.A. World Affairs Coun., 1970-74, Com. on Fgn. Affairs, 1971-75, L.A. Meml. Coliseum Commn.; bd. dirs. West L.A. United Way, 1970, Black Arts Coun., Econ. Resources Corp., L.A. Beautiful, L.A. Coun. for Internat. Visitors, Cape of Good Hope Found., Overland Park, Kans., Westminster Neighborhood Assn.; trustee Mus. Contemporary Art, NCAA Found., 1991—, bd. dirs.; pres. L.A. Recreation and Parks Commn.; chmn. United Way Task Force on Youth Unemployment, L.A.; mem. adv. bd. Pub. Radio Sta. KCRW, 1991—; dir. met. transp. authority L.A. County, 1993-95. Recipient Ten Outstanding Young Men of Am. award, 1971. Mem. Langston Bar Assn., Los Angeles County Bar Assn. Club: Mason. Home: 2015 Wellington Rd Los Angeles CA 90016-1824 Office: Barnes McGhee & Pryce 333 S Grand Ave Ste 2000 Los Angeles CA 90071

SANDERS, KEITH PAGE, journalism educator; b. Ashland, Ohio, Sept. 25, 1938; s. Merwin Morse and Phyllis Pearl (Snyder) S.; m. Jane Carmel Adams, June 11, 1966; children: Paige Ann, Kevin Scott. BS in Journalism, Bowling Green State U., 1960; MS in Journalism, Ohio U., 1964; PhD in Mass. Comm., U. Iowa, 1967. Sports editor Ashland (Ohio) Times Gazette, 1960-61, Dover (Ohio) Daily Reporter, 1961-62; instr. journalism Bowling Green (Ohio) State U., 1963-64, U. Iowa, Iowa City, 1965-67; prof. journalism U. Mo., Columbia, 1967—, assoc. dean grad. studies Sch. Journalism, 1986-87, 90-91; exec. dir. Kappa Tau Alpha, Columbia, 1991—; cons. in field. Contbr. articles to profl. jours. including Journalism Quar.,

Mass Media Rev., Jour. Broadcasting, Electronic Jour. of Comm.; assoc. editor Mass Comm. Rev., 1981-92, editl. bd., 1972—; editl. bd. Journalism Monographs, 1973-80. Named O.O. McIntyre Disting. Prof., U. Mo., 1993; recipient Award for Outstanding Achievement U. Mo. Alumni Assn., 1986. Mem. Internat. Soc. for Sci. Study of Subjectivity (treas. 1990-95), Assn. for Edn. in Journalism/Mass. Comm. (Trayes Prof. of the Yr. 1987), Soc. of Profl. Journalists, Kappa Tau Alpha, Omicron Delta Kappa. Avocations: bowling, golf, fishing. Home: 6551 N Creasy Springs Rd Columbia MO 65202-8093 Office: Univ of Missouri Sch Journalism Columbia MO 65211

SANDERS, KEITH R., university chancellor; b. Benton, Ill., July 31, 1939; m. Carol Dial, 1961; 1 child, Mark Andrew. BS, So. Ill. U., 1961, MS, 1962; PhD in Communication, U. Pitts., 1968. Asst. prof. speech George Washington U., Washington, 1962-66; instr. So. Ill. U., Carbondale, 1967-68, asst. prof., 1969-72, assoc. prof., 1972-77, prof. speech communications, 1977-89, officer govtl. rels. So. Ill. U. System, 1980-83, prof., dean Coll. Communication and Fine Arts, 1983-89; chancellor U. Wis., Stevens Point, 1989—. Author: (with Lynda Kaid and Robert Hirsch) Political Campaign Communication, 1974; co-editor, contbr.: (with Dan Nimmo) The Handbook of Political Communication, 1981; (with Dan Nimmo and Lynda Kaid) Political Communication Yearbook, 1985; (with Dan Nimmo and Lynda Kaid) New Perspectives on Political Advertising, 1986, (with Lynda Kaid and Jacques Gestle) Mediated Politics in Two Cultures, 1991; founder, editor Polit. Communication Rev., 1974-90; cons. editor Human Communication Rsch., 1976-79, Cen. States Speech Jour., 1979-80; contbg. editor: Communication Yearbook III and IV, 1978-80. Pres. Ill. Arts Alliance, Ill. Arts Alliance Found., 1987-88. Am. Coun. on Edn. fellow, 1980-81; honored by Ill. Gen. Assembly, 1983. Mem. So. Ill. U. Alumni Assn. (pres. 1977-78). Home: 2351 Rainbow Dr Plover WI 54467-2464 Office: U Wis Stevens Point WI 54481-3897

SANDERS, LAWRENCE, author; b. Bklyn., 1920. BA, Wabash Coll., 1940. Staff mem. Macy's Dept. Store, N.Y.C., 1940-43; novelist, 1969—. Author: The Anderson Tapes, 1970 (Edgar award best 1st mystery novel Mystery Writers Am. 1970), The Pleasures of Helen, 1971, Love Songs, 1972, The First Deadly Sin, 1973, The Tomorrow File, 1975, The Tangent Objective, 1976, The Marlow Chronicles, 1977, The Second Deadly Sin, 1977, The Tangent Factor, 1978, The Sixth Commandment, 1978, The Tenth Commandment, 1980, The Third Deadly Sin, 1981, The Case of Lucy Bending, 1982, The Seduction of Peter S., 1983, The Passion of Molly T., 1984, The Fourth Deadly Sin, 1985, The Loves of Harry Dancer, 1986, The Eighth Commandment, 1986, Tales of the Wolf, 1986, The Dream Lover, 1987, Caper, 1987, The Timothy Files, 1987, Timothy's Game, 1988, Capital Crimes, 1989, Stolen Blessings, 1989, Sullivan's Sting, 1990, The Seventh Commandment, 1992, McNally's Luck, 1992, McNally's Secret, 1992, McNally's Risk, 1993, Private Pleasures, 1993, The Great Coaster Ride, 1993, McNally's Caper, 1994, McNally's Trail, 1995; (as Mark Upton) Dark Summer, 1979. Served as sgt. USMC, 1943-46. Office: care Putnam Publishing Group 200 Madison Ave New York NY 10016-3903

SANDERS, LEWIS A., investment research and management executive. Former pres., chief oper. officer Sanford C. Bernstein & Co., Inc., N.Y.C., chmn., CEO, 1993—. Office: Sanford C Bernstein & Co Inc 767 5th Ave Fl 22 New York NY 10153-2299*

SANDERS, MARLENE, anchor; b. Cleve., Jan. 10, 1931; d. Mac and Evelyn (Menitoff) Sanders; m. Jerome Toobin, May 27, 1958 (dec. Jan. 1984); children: Jeff, Mark. Student, Ohio State U., 1948-49. Writer, prodr. Sta. WNEW-TV, N.Y.C., 1955-60, P.M. program Westinghouse Broadcasting Co., N.Y.C., 1961-62; asst. dir. news and public affairs Sta. WNEW, N.Y.C., 1962-64; anchor, news program ABC News, N.Y.C., 1964-68, corr., 1968-72, documentary prodr., writer, anchor, 1972-76, v.p., dir. TV documentaries, 1976-78; corr. CBS News, N.Y.C., 1978-87; host Currents Sta. WNET-TV, N.Y.C., 1987-88; host Met. Week in Review, 1988-90; host Thirteen Live Sta. WNET-TV, 1990-91; prof. dept. journalism NYU, 1991-93; adj. prof. journalism, adminstr. Columbia U. Grad. Sch. Journalism, N.Y.C., 1994-95; tv anchor Prime Life Network, N.Y., 1996—. Co-author: Waiting for Prime Time: The Women of Television News, 1988. Recipient award N.Y. State Broadcasters Assn., 1976, award Nat. Press Club, 1976, Emmy awards, 1980, 81, others. Mem. Am. Women in Radio and TV (Woman of Yr. award 1975, Silver Satellite award 1977), Women in Comm. (past pres.), Soc. Profl. Journalists.

SANDERS, PAUL HAMPTON, lawyer, retired educator, arbitrator/mediator; b. Sherman, Tex., Feb. 26, 1909; s. Jewell Richard and Louisa Jane (Gaskill) S.; m. Pauline Cameron, Feb. 23, 1935. A.B., Austin Coll., 1931, LL.D., 1960; J.D., Duke U., 1934. Bar: Tex. 1934, Ga. 1944, N.C. 1946, Tenn. 1951. Practiced with Leo Brewer, San Antonio, 1934; asst. to dir. of nat. bar program Am. Bar Assn., Chgo., 1934-36; asst. prof. law Duke U., 1936-40, assoc. prof. law, 1940-45, prof. law, from 1946; practiced with firm of Wilson and Sanders, Atlanta, 1946-47; vis. prof. law Sch. Jurisprudence, U. Calif. at Berkeley, 1947-48; prof. law Vanderbilt U., 1948-74, prof. emeritus, 1974—, past lectr. Sch. Medicine, adj. prof. mgmt. Grad. Sch. Mgmt.; regional atty. U.S. Dept. of Labor, 1951-53; prin. mediation officer Nat. War Labor Bd., Washington, 1942; regional atty., hdqrs. Nat. War Labor Bd., Atlanta, 1942-44, regional vice chmn., 1944; regional atty. Nat. Wage Stblzn. Bd., Atlanta, 1946; past lectr. Nashville Sch. Social Work; cons. Fed. Civil Rights Commn., 1958-61; dir. Race Relations Law Reporter, 1955-59; apptd. mem. bd. inquiry, labor disputes in atomic energy installations, Oak Ridge, also Ky.; pub. mem., chmn. Industry Com. on Minimum Wages, Puerto Rico, 1950, 56-58, 60-61, 63, 67, 69, 71, 73, 75, 77; apptd. mem. various Presdl. emergency boards to consider labor disputes. Assoc. editor: Law and Contemporary Problems, 1937-46; editor symposia on Unauthorized Practice of Law, The Wage and Hour Law, Governmental Tort Liability, Alcoholic Beverage Control, Combating the Loan Shark, Labor in Wartime and Labor Dispute Settlement, all in Duke Univ., 1938-46; contbr. articles to profl. jours. Indsl. relations specialist, 12th Naval Dist. 1944-46, San Francisco; lt. USNR, 1945-53. Mem. ABA (council mem., sec. labor relations sect. 1949-52), Am. Law Inst. (life), Nat. Acad. Arbitrators (past mem., past bd. govs., regional chmn. Southeastern states 1968-74), Am. Arbitration Assn. (labor panel), Nat. Conf. Jud. Councils, Soc. Profls. in Dispute Resolution, Scholarship Soc. S., Order of Coif, Pi Gamma Mu, Phi Delta Phi. Democrat. Baptist (vice chmn. Christian Life Commn., So. Bapt. Conv. 1953-59). Club: University (Nashville). Home: 115 Woodmont Blvd Apt 320 Nashville TN 37205-2200 *My primary interests as a law teacher and arbitrator have centered in systematic study of the processes of dispute settlement and conflict resolution, particularly in the labor relations field. This reflects a conviction that building "community" is the essence of civilization and that there needs to be individual and group commitment to understanding and utilizing the arts of peaceful accomodation. Social conflict is as inevitable as change. All too frequently, however, we show that we have not learned to distinguish, and maintain the proper balance, between the productive and counterproductive aspects of such conflict.*

SANDERS, PHAROAH, saxophonist, composer; b. Little Rock, Oct. 13, 1940. Student, Oakland Jr. Coll., Calif. Saxophonist N.Y.C., 1962-66, John Coltrane, 1966-67, Alice Coltrane, 1967-69; leader own group, 1969—. Albums include Jewels of Thought, Journey to the One, Karma, Live, Pharoah, Rejoice, Tauhid, Thembi, Love Will Find a Way, Heart Is a Melody, 1984, Shukuru, Impluse, 1987, Oh Lord, Let Me Do No Wrong, 1989, Moon Child, 1990, Welcome to Love: Pharaoh Sanders Plays Beautiful Ballads, 1991, Shukuru, 1992, A Prayer Before Dawn, 1993; composer: songs, including Prince of Peace, The Creator Has a Master Plan; guest artist Sonny Sharaock's Ask the Ages, 1991. Office: care Ted Kurland Assocs 173 Brighton Ave Allston MA 02134-2003

SANDERS, REGINALD LAVERNE (REGGIE SANDERS), professional baseball player; b. Florence, S.C., Dec. 1, 1967. Student, Spartanburg Meth. Coll., S.C. Outfield Cin. Reds, 1991—. Named Midwest League Most Valuable Player, 1990; selected to N.L All-Star Team, 1995. Office: Cin Reds 100 Riverfront Stadium Cincinnati OH 45202*

SANDERS, RICHARD HENRY, lawyer; b. Chgo., Apr. 10, 1944; s. Walter J. and Marian (Snyder) Sikorski; m. Sharon A. Marciniak, July 8, 1967 (div. Oct. 1979); 1 child, Douglas Bennett. BS, Loyola U., Chgo., 1967; JD, Northwestern U., 1969. Bar: Ill. 1969, Ind. 1990, D.C. 1990, U.S. Dist. Ct. (no. dist.) Ill. 1970, U.S. Dist. Ct. (no. and so. dists.) Ind. 1990, U.S. Ct. Appeals (7th cir.) 1990, U.S. Supreme Ct. 1990. Assoc. Vedder, Price, Kaufman & Kammholz, Chgo., 1969-76, ptnr., 1976—, mem. exec. com., 1991-93; gen. counsel Ancilla Sys. Inc., Chgo., 1985-95; adj. prof. Sch. of Law Northwestern U., 1994—. Mem. adv. coun. campaign com. Greater Chgo. divsn. March of Dimes, 1993—. Mem. ABA, Ill. Bar Assn. (chmn. health sect. 1989-90), Chgo. Bar Assn., Ind. Bar Assn., D.C. Bar Assn., Am. Acad. Hosp. Attys., Cath. Health Attys., Ill. Assn. Hosp. Attys., Chgo. Commons Assn. (adv. bd. dirs., sec. 1989-91), Northwestern U. Sch. Law Alumni Assn. (bd. dirs. 1985-90), Univ. Club, Evanston Golf Club (Skokie). Avocations: skiing, diving, photography, golf. Office: Vedder Price Kaufman & Kammholz 222 N La Salle St Chicago IL 60601-1003

SANDERS, RICHARD KINARD, actor; b. Harrisburg, Pa., Aug. 23, 1940; s. Henry Irvine and Thelma S. BFA, Carnegie Inst. Tech., 1962; postgrad. (Fulbright scholar), London Acad. Music and Dramatic Art, 1962-63. pres. Blood Star, Inc. Mem. various acting cos., Front St., Memphis, Champlain Shakespeare Festival, Vt., Center Stage, Balt., N.Y. Shakespeare Festival, N.Y.C., Chelsea Theater Center, N.Y.C., Mark Taper Forum, Los Angeles, Arena Stage, Washington; appeared on: (Broadway) Raisin; (TV series) Les Nessman on WKRP in Cincinnati and The New WKRP in Cincinnati, Paul Sycamore in You Can't Take It With You, Mr. Beanley in Spenser; writer of many episodes of WKRP and other situation comedies; writer NBC movie Max and Sam; numerous TV and film appearances. Vol. Peace Corps, Northeastern Brazil, 1966-69. Recipient Buckeye Newshawk award, 1974-79, Silver Sow award, 1979. Mem. Writers Guild Am., Screen Actors Guild, AFTRA, Actors Equity Assn. Office: care Blood Star Inc 10866 Wilshire Blvd Ste 1100 Los Angeles CA 90024-4335

SANDERS, RICHARD LOUIS, executive editor; b. Rockville Centre, N.Y., July 14, 1949; s. Louis Chadrone and Grace Marie (Clarke) S.; m. Laurie Anne Miroff, July 24, 1970. BFA in Film, NYU, 1976. Sr. editor Us mag., N.Y.C., 1978-83, exec. editor, 1983-85; sr. editor People mag., N.Y.C., 1985-91; gen. editor Entertainment Weekly, N.Y.C., 1991-92, assistant mng. editor, 1993-95, exec. editor, 1995—. Office: Entertainment Weekly 1675 Broadway New York NY 10019-5820

SANDERS, RICKY WAYNE, professional football player; b. New Orleans, La., Aug. 30, 1966. Student, Southwest Texas State U. With Houston Gamblers, USFL, 1984-86, N.J. Generals, USFL, 1986, Washington Redskins, 1986-94, Atlanta Falcons, 1994—. Played in Super Bowl XXII (1987) and XXVI (1991). Office: Atlanta Falcons 2745 Burnette Rd Suwanee GA 30174-2127

SANDERS, ROBERT MARTIN, commodity trader; b. Amsterdam, The Netherlands, Feb. 8, 1928; came to U.S., 1941, naturalized, 1949; s. Hugo Benjamin and Jean (van der Linden) S.; m. Ingrid Vera Borchardt, Apr. 12, 1959 (dec. Jan. 1993); children: Mark Robert, Steven George. BA, Queens Coll., 1948; MS, Columbia U., 1950; postgrad., New Sch. Social Research, 1953-61. Research asst. The Netherlands Govt., 1948-50; with fgn. acctg. dept. Colgate-Palmolive-Peet, 1950; with A.C. Israel Commodity Co., Inc., N.Y.C., 1952-71, asst. mgr. rubber dept., 1963-67, mgr. rubber dept., 1967-71, asst. v.p., 1967-70, v.p., 1970-71; v.p. ACLI Internat., Inc., 1971-81; pres. A.C. Israel Rubber Co. div., 1971-76, ACLI Rubber Co., 1976-81; v.p. ACLI Commodity Services, Inc., 1975-81; dir. ACLI (Malaysia), Kuala Lumpur, 1975-81; pres. Clinton Internat., Inc., 1982—; mem. N.Y. Cocoa Exchange, 1975-78; U.S. rep. Internat. Natural Rubber Orgn., 1982—. Bd. dirs. Family Resources, 1983—. With AUS, 1950-52. Mem. Internat. Rubber Assn. (pro-tem. com. 1970-71, mgmt. com. 1971-81, dep. chmn. 1974-77), Am.-Indonesian C. of C. (bd. dirs. 1974-80, v.p. 1979-80), Am. Importers Assn. (bd. dirs. 1975-77), Rubber Trade Assn. N.Y. Inc. (bd. dirs. 1970-74, 76-79, 81, v.p. 1971-72, 73-74, pres. 1972, 78-79). Home: 310 Clinton Ave Dobbs Ferry NY 10522-3023 Office: Clinton Internat Inc PO Box 278 Dobbs Ferry NY 10522-0278

SANDERS, ROGER COBBAN, radiologist; b. London, June 17, 1936; s. Douglas William and Angela (Cobban) S.; children—Nicolette, Nigel; m. Barri Standish, May 26, 1991. M.A., Oxford U., 1960; B.M., B.CH., F.R.C.R., 1971. Diplomate: Am. Bd. Radiology. Intern United Oxford (Eng.) Hosp., 1964-65, sr. house officer neurology dept., 1965-66, resident in radiology, 1967-70; mem. faculty Johns Hopkins Hosp., Balt., 1971-89; assoc. prof. radiology Johns Hopkins Hosp., 1975-86, prof. radiology, 1986-89; med. dir. Ultrasound Inst. Balt., 1989—; clin. prof. radiology, ob/gyn. U. Md., 1990—. Author: (with A.E. James) Principles and Practice of Ultrasonography in Obstetrics and Gynecology, 3d edit., 1984, Clinical Sonography, A Practical Guide, 1984, 2d edit., 1992, Atlas of Ultrasonic Normal Variants, 1992; editor: Ultrasound Quarterly. Fellow Royal Coll. Radiologists, Am. Coll. Radiologists (sec. 1984-86), Am. Inst. Ultrasound in Medicine; mem. Soc. Radiologists in Ultrasound (pres. 1976), Brit. Ultrasound Soc., Radiol. Soc. N.Am., Am. Coll. Radiology. Mem. Soc. Friends. Home: 34 E Montgomery St Baltimore MD 21230-3847 Office: Ultrasound Inst Balt # 252 10751 Falls Rd Lutherville MD 21093

SANDERS, RUTH ANN NOMATHEMBA SIDZUMO, social services administrator; b. Johannesburg, South Africa, Feb. 2, 1941; came to U.S., 1969; d. Robert Bantubonke and Miriam Nozipho (Mkhosana) Sidzumo; m. Ferrell Lee Sanders, Sept. 3, 1970 (div. 1978); children: Muzill Lumkile, Valrie Nozipho Vuyo. BA in Social Work, San Francisco State U., 1970; MA in Guidance and Counseling, Wayne State U., 1976, EdS in Adminstrn. and Supervision, 1981, PhD, 1989. Social case worker Quaker Svc. Fund, Johannesburg, 1967; social worker London Borough of Hounslow, 1968-69, San Francisco Housing Authority, 1970; study skills counselor Wayne State U., Detroit, 1973-74; asst. dir. Todd-Phillips Children's Home, Detroit, 1975-84; program dir. Barat Human Svcs., Detroit, 1984-87; project dir. Transformations in Employment, Detroit, 1987-88; contractual family worker Family and Neighborhood Svcs., Detroit, 1988; program dir. Boysville of Mich., Detroit, 1989—; family reunication specialist private consultation lectr. Eastern Mich. U., Ypsilanti, 1989-91; instr. African history Roeper City and County Sch., Birmingham, Mich., 1994—; assoc. prof. sch. social work U. Transkei, South Africa, 1995. Bd. dirs. E.W. Daniel Episcopal Credit Union, Detroit, 1988; fellow mem. Episcopalian Coun. of Women, Detroit, 1980. Recipient Families 1st Program award Mich. Dept. Social Svc. Family Preservation, 1994, Program Mgr. of Yr. award, 1994, various fed. and county grants. Mem. Internat. Assn. Black Social Workers, Nat. Assn. Black Social Workers, Mich. Fedn. Pvt. Agys., Wayne State Alumni Assn., Mich. Assn. Sch. Adminstrs., Child Care Coordinating Coun., NAACP. Home: 800 W Boston Blvd Detroit MI 48202-1408 Office: Boysville of Mich 19403 W Chicago St Detroit MI 48228-1741

SANDERS, SHARON RAYE (SHARRI SANDERS), telecommunications executive, educator; b. Dayton, Ohio, Aug. 25, 1942; d. Robert J. Rapa and Mildred B. Wallace; m. Robert Meredith Sanders, Dec. 28, 1961; children: Robert E., Kenneth B. (dec.). Tchr. cert., U. Tex., 1989, 90. Various positions Rockwell Internat, Bastian-Blessing, others, Mich. and Ill., 1960-79; adminstrv. asst. Tex. Tech. Sch. Medicine, Lubbock, 1980, Thermex Energy Corp., Dallas, 1980-81; exec. asst. Bonser-Philhower Sales, Richardson, Tex., 1982; owner, operator SRS Bus. Svc. Secretarial/Printing, Kaufman, Tex., 1982-89; tchr. Kaufman High Sch., 1989-92; prin. ptnr. MetCom of East Tex., Chandler, Tex., 1993—. Author: What's Cooking?, 1988; contbr. poetry to anthologies; contbg. writer Kaufman Herald, 1988-89, The Secretary mag., 1991. Pres. PTA, Allegan, Mich., 1973, sec., 1974; sec. ladies aux. Forest Grove Property Owners Assn., 1993-94; bd. dirs. Forest Grove Property Owners Assn., 1994—. Recipient Engraved Appreciation award Student Body/Graphic Arts, Kaufman H.S., 1992, 20th Century award for Achievement in Edn., 1994. Mem. NAFE, Nat. League Am. Pen Women (2d place writing contest award 1988), Tex. Printing Instrs. Assn. (sec. 1992), Kaufman C. of C. (bd. dirs. 1983-86), Chandler Lioness Club (co-first v.p., 1995—). Avocations: oil painting, writing, quilting. Office: MetCom of East Tex PO Box 1590 Chandler TX 75758-1590

SANDERS, STEVE, singer; b. Richland, Ga., Sept. 17; s. Herbert and Lorraine Sanders; m. Janet Sanders (div.); 4 children. Mem. Oak Ridge Boys, 1987—, rhythm guitar, now singer. Albums include Heartbeat, 1987, Monongahela, 1988, Unstoppable, 1991, The Long Haul, 1992, Back to Back, 1994; songs written include Live in Love, 1982; appeared in Broadway prodn. The Yearling; appeared in film Hurry Sundown, 1967; TV appearances include Gunsmoke, Noon Wine. Avocations: scuba diving, fishing. Office: The Oak Ridge Boys 329 Rockland Rd Hendersonville TN 37075-3423

SANDERS, STEVEN GILL, telecommunications executive; b. Chgo., Aug. 23, 1936; s. Raymond E. and Mildred (Gostow) S.; m. Gretchen Griffith, Jan. 15, 1959 (div. 1985); children: Steven Gill, Meghan Griffith; m. Nancy Lee Wolf, Sept. 23, 1989. BS, MIT, 1958; postgrad., Rutgers U., 1960-61; PhD, U. S.C., 1965. Instr. mechanics U. S.C., Columbia, 1964-65; asst. prof. So. Ill. U., Edwardsville, 1965-67, assoc. prof., 1969-75, prof. physics, 1975-79, chmn. physics faculty, 1967-71; resident rsch. assoc. Agronne (Ill.) Nat. Lab., 1971-72; pres., gen. mgr. No. Ark. Tel. Co., Flippin, 1977—, Nova Systems, Flippin, 1981-92. Contbr. articles on physics to sci. publs. Fellow NSF, 1971. Mem. AAAS, IEEE (sr.), Am. Phys. Soc., U.S. Tel. Assn. (new svcs. and tech. issues subcom. 1991-92, Supercom program com. 1993-94), Ark. Tel. Assn. (pres. 1992, bd. dirs. 1985—), Western Rural Tel. Assn. (bd. dirs. 1993—, chmn. Western Alliance Universal svc. com. 1994—), Ark. C. of C. (bd. dirs. 1989-94), Sigma Xi. Home: 220 N Cardinal Dr Mountain Home AR 72653-3754 Office: No Ark Tel Co 301 E Main St Flippin AR 72634

SANDERS, SUMMER, Olympic athlete; b. 1972; d. Bob and Barbara S. Gold medalist, 200m Butterfly Barcelona Olympic Games, 1992, Silver medalist, 200m Individual Medley, 1992, Bronze medalist, 400m Individual Medley, 1992. Address: US Olympic Com 1750 E Boulder St Colorado Springs CO 80909-5724*

SANDERS, THURMAN, retired transportation executive; b. Savannah, Ga., Mar. 31, 1937; s. Thurman and Esther (Gibbs) S.; m. Frediebelle Quattlebaum, Nov. 11, 1972 (dec. May 1982); m. Germain Joseph Sanders, Mar. 31, 1986; children: Thurman, Lynda, Mark, Steven, Deborah, Shawn, David. AS, C.C. of Phila., 1984; BS, Temple U., 1987. Registered profl. engr., Pa., Ohio, Ga. Signal repairman Phila. Transp. Co., 1960-74; signal foreman South Ea. Pa. Transp. Authority, Phila., 1974-78, elec. engr. II, 1978-81, signal specialist, 1981-84, project engr., 1984-87, project mgr., 1987-90, program mgr., 1990-93; cons. TXS, Phila., 1993-95. With USN, 1956-60. Avocation: reading. Home: 2007 Pine Cone Dr SW Atlanta GA 30331-2437

SANDERS, TRISHA LYNN, middle school educator; b. Chowchilla, Calif., June 7, 1965; d. Kenneth L. and Karen L. (Lobo) S.; 1 child, Craig. BA in Social Sci., Calif. State U., Stanislaus, 1987; MA in Edn1. Adminstrn., Chapman U., 1992, MA in Curriculum and Instrn., 1992. Cert. tchr., Calif. 6th grade tchr. lang. arts and math. Merced (Calif.) City Sch. Dist., 1988-91, 6th grade tchr. sci. and math., 1991-94, 8th grade sci. tchr., 1994-95; 7th grade tchr. Cruickshank Mid. Sch., Merced, Calif., 1995—; mentor tchr. Merced City Schs., 1993-95, sci. cadre, 1992-95; mem. steering com. Merced High Sch., 1992-95. Mem. ASCD, CUE, Phi Delta Kappa.

SANDERS, WALLACE WOLFRED, JR., civil engineer; b. Louisville, June 24, 1933; s. Wallace Wolfred and Mary Jane (Brownfield) S.; m. Julia B. Howard, June 9, 1956; children—Linda, David. B.C.E., U. Louisville, 1955; M.S., U. Ill., Urbana, 1957, Ph.D., 1960; M.Engring., U. Louisville, 1973. Research asst., then research assoc. U. Ill., 1955-60, asst. prof., 1960-64; mem. faculty Iowa State U., Ames, 1964—; prof. civil engring. Iowa State U., 1970—, assoc. dir. engring. research, 1980-91, assoc. dean research, 1988-91, interim asst. vice provost for research and advanced studies, 1991-92; cons. to govt. and industry. Contbr. numerous papers to profl. jours. Bd. dirs. Northcrest Retirement Cmty., Ames, 1976-82, 92—, pres., 1987-91, 96—. Mem. ASCE (R.C. Reese research prize 1978), Am. Welding Soc. (Adams Meml. membership award 1971), Am. Ry. Engring. Assn., Am. Soc. Engring. Edn. Baptist. Home: 1809 Maxwell Ave Ames IA 50010-5539 Office: Iowa State U 374 Town Engring Bldg Ames IA 50011

SANDERS, WALTER JEREMIAH, III, electronics company executive; b. Chgo., Sept. 12, 1936. BEE, U. Ill., 1958. Design engr. Douglas Aircraft Co., Santa Monica, Calif., 1958-59; applications engr. Motorola, Inc., Phoenix, 1959-60; sales engr. Motorola, Inc., 1960-61; with Fairchild Camera & Instrument Co., 1961-69; dir. mktg. Fairchild Camera & Instrument Co., Mountain View, Calif., 1961-68, group dir. mktg. worldwide, 1968-69; pres. Advanced Micro Devices Inc., Sunnyvale, Calif., until 1987, chmn. bd., chief exec. officer, 1969—; dir. Donaldson, Lufkin & Jenrette. Mem. Semicondr. Industry Assn. (co-founder, dir.), Santa Clara County Mfg. Group (co-founder, dir.). Office: Advanced Micro Devices Inc PO Box 3453 One AMD Pl Sunnyvale CA 94086-3453*

SANDERS, WAYNE R., manufacturing executive; b. Chgo., July 6, 1947; s. Ralph G. and Bernice F. (Swanson) S.; m. Kathleen E. Lessard, Aug. 22, 1970; children: Tracy, Amy, Megan. BCE, Ill. Inst. Tech., 1969; MBA, Marquette U., 1972. Fin. analyst Ford Motor Co., Dearborn, Mich., 1972-75; sr. fin. analyst Kimberly-Clark Corp., Neenah, Wis., 1975, dir. bus. planning internat., 1976-80, dir. bus. planning U.S. consumer bus., 1980-81; v.p. strategic planning Kimberly-Clark of Can., Toronto, Ont., 1981-82, pres., 1982-85; sr. v.p. Kimberly-Clark Corp., Dallas, 1986; pres. infant care sector Kimberly-Clark Corp., Neenah, Wis., from 1987; former pres. personal care div. Kimberly-Clark Corp., pres., chief oper. officer world consumer, nonwovens and svc. and indsl. ops., 1990—; pres., CEO Kimberly-Clark Corp., Dallas, 1990-91, chmn., CEO, 1992—, chmn. bd., CEO, 1992—. Elected mem. Neenah Sch. Bd., 1980-81; nat. trustee Boys and Girls Clubs Am., 1994; trustee Marquette U., Milw. Roman Catholic. *

SANDERS, WILLIAM EUGENE, marketing executive; b. Asheboro, N.C., Nov. 16, 1933; s. Arthur Ira and Picola (Loftin) S.; m. Velna Elizabeth Sumner, June 8, 1957; children: William Eugene Jr., George Herbert Sumner. AB in Polit. Sci., U. N.C., 1956, postgrad. in Law, 1956-57. Marketing rep. Encyclopaedia Britannica, Greensboro, N.C., 1957-60, Am. Pubs., Chgo., 1960-66; pres. S&W Distbrs., Inc., Greensboro, 1966—. Little league coach Civitans, Greensboro, 1967-68. With U.S. Army Res., 1957-63. Named Hon. Amb. Dept. of Labor, Ky., 1976, Ky. Col., 1976, Hon. Mem. La. Lt. Gov. Staff, 1984; recipient Cert. Appreciation Jefferson Davis Parish Libr., Jennings, La., 1986. Mem. State Libr. Assns. Va., W.Va., La., Gen. Alumni Assn. (co-chairman Greensboro chpt. 1979-80), Chi Phi. Democrat. Presbyterian. Avocations: billiards, golf, fishing. Office: S&W Distbrs Inc 1600H E Wendover Ave Greensboro NC 27405-6837 *As a youth, someone told me that it cost not one pennymore to be nice in your dealing with otherr individuals. I have followed this advice.*

SANDERS, W(ILLIAM) EUGENE, JR., physician, educator; b. Frederick, Md., June 25, 1934; s. W(illiam) Eugene and E. Gertrude (Wilburn) S.; m. Christine Culp, Feb. 22, 1974. A.B., Cornell U., 1956, M.D., 1960. Diplomate: Am. Bd. Internal Medicine. Intern Johns Hopkins Hosp., Balt., 1960-61; resident Johns Hopkins Hosp., 1961-62; instr. medicine Emory U. Sch. Medicine, Atlanta, 1962-64; chief med. resident, instr. U. Fla. Coll. Medicine, Gainesville, 1964-65; asst. prof. medicine and microbiology U. Fla. Coll. Medicine, 1965-69, asso. prof., 1969-72; prof., chmn. dept. med. microbiology, prof. medicine Creighton U. Sch. Medicine, Omaha, 1972—; cons.-in-research Fla. Dept. Health and Rehab. Services, 1966—. Editor: Am. Jour. Epidemiology, 1974—; contbr. sci. articles to profl. jours. Served as med. officer USPHS, 1962-64. Recipient NIH Research Career Devel. award, 1968-72; John and Mary R. Markle scholar in acad. medicine, 1968-73. Mem. Am. Soc. for Microbiology, Infectious Diseases Soc. Am., Soc. for Epidemiol. Research, Am. Lung Assn., Thoracic Soc., N.Y. Acad. Scis., Phi Beta Kappa, Sigma Xi, Phi Kappa Phi. Achievements include patent on enocin antibiotic and RBE limonene and perrilyl alcohol. Home: T-1004 Woodcliff RR 2 Fremont NE 68025-9619 Office: Creighton U Sch Medicine Dept Med Microbio Omaha NE 68178 *Each day provides more challenges and more opportunities than the preceding. No individual can possibly cope with each of these in any given day. Success depends upon establishing priorities and maintaining them. Fight only those battles and pursue with fervor only those opportunities that improve both one's self and one's fellow man.*

SANDERS, WILLIAM EVAN, bishop; b. Natchez, Miss., Dec. 25, 1919; s. Walter Richard and Agnes Mortimer (Jones) S.; B.A., Vanderbilt U., 1942; B.D., U. of South, 1945, D.D., 1959; S.T.M., Union Theol. Sem., 1946; m.

Kathryn Cowan Schaffer, June 25, 1951; 4 children. Curate St. Paul's Episcopal Ch., Chattanooga, 1945-46; asst. St. Mary's Cathedral, Memphis, 1946-48, dean, 1948-62; bishop coadjutor Tenn., Knoxville, after 1962, now bishop Eastern Tenn., 1985—

SANDERS, WILLIAM GEORGE, public relations executive; b. Sacramento, Jan. 11, 1932; s. Samuel S. and Alice M. (Trow) S.; m. Teresa Helsel, Oct. 20, 1979. Student, Contra Costa Jr. Coll., 1950-51; B.A. in Journalism, U. Oreg., 1957; postgrad. cinema dept., U. So. Calif., 1962. Reporter Roseburg (Oreg.) News-Rev., 1957; group advt. mgr. Montgomery Ward & Co., Oakland, Calif., 1957-61; advt. public relations dir. Jacuzzi Research, Inc., Berkeley, Calif., 1964-65; asst. v.p. corp. communications Airborne Freight Corp., San Mateo, Calif., 1966-67; sr. editor Motor Trend Mag., Hollywood, Calif., 1967-71; exec. v.p., assoc. pub. Four Wheeler Mag., Canoga Park, Calif., 1971-87; pres. William Sanders & Assocs., Sepulveda, Calif., 1987—; sr. editor Off Road Mag., 1988—. Editor: automotive sect. World Year Book, 1970, 71. Served with Signal Corps U.S. Army, 1952-54, Korea. Decorated U.S. Korean Svc. medal W/1 Bronze Svc. star, U.N. Svc. medal, Nat. Def. Svc. medal, Singman Rhee citation Korea. Mem. Calif. Assn. Four Wheel Dr. Clubs, Specialty Equipment Mfrs. Assn., Am. Automotive Writers and Broadcasters Assn., Chi Psi. Winner Baja 1000 Off Rd. Race for prodn. 4 wheel dr. class, 1973, 4th Pl. Baja 1000, 1979.

SANDERS, WILLIAM JOHN, research scientist; b. Detroit, July 10, 1940; s. John William and Charlotte Barbara (Linsday) Steele; m. Gary Roberts, Sept. 12, 1961; children: Scott David, Susan Deborah. BS, U. Mich., 1962; MSEE, U. Calif., Berkeley, 1964. Sr. rsch. scientist Stanford (Calif.) U., 1967—; pres. Sanders Data Systems, 1991—; pres. Computers in Cardiology, 1990-93, bd. dirs., 1978—. Inventor cardiac probe; contbr. articles to profl. jours. Mem. IEEE Computer Soc., Assn. Computing Machinery. Avocations: bicycling, wind surfing. Home: 3980 Bibbits Dr Palo Alto CA 94303-4531 Office: Stanford U Med Ctr Cardiovasc Medicine Stanford CA 94305

SANDERS CHILDEARS, LINDA, banker; b. Council Bluffs, Iowa, Jan. 25, 1950; d. Nolan Glen and Mary Lucile (Dunken) Jackson. Grad., U. Wis., Am. Inst. Banking; student, U. Colo., U. Denver. Various positions First Nat. Bank Bear Valley (name changed to United Bank Bea, Colo., 1969-79; v.p. adminstrn. First Nat. Bancorp., 1979-83; pres., CEO, Equitable Bank of Littleton, 1983—; founder The Fin. Consortium; pres., CEO, Young Ams. Bank, Denver, 1987—, also vice-chmn. bd. dirs.; chmn. bd., pres. Young Ams. Edn. Found. Contbr. articles to Time and Newsweek. Bd. dirs. Cherry Creek Art Festival, Denver, 1989—; chmn.-elect Grad. Sch. Banking, Colo. Student Loan Program, Denver; chmn. Nat. Assembly; past dir. Jr. Achievement, Panorama Products and Svcs., Mile High United Way; mem. adv. bd. Campfire Coun. Colo., nat. past pres. Named hon. life mem. Nat. CampFire, past chmn., numerous other awards Camp Fire Inc. Mem. Am. Bankers Assn. (past chmn. Edn. Found., edn. coun.), Found. Tchg. Econs. (trustee), Colo. Bankers Assn. Republican. Office: Young Ams Bank 311 Steele St Denver CO 80206-4414

SANDERSON, CATHY ANN, histotechnician, researcher; b. Key West, Fla., Apr. 12, 1954; d. Robert Gary and Cheri Dae (Colin) S.; 1 child, Nichole Renee. Grad. h.s., Phoenix, Ariz., 1972. Histology trainee St. Luke's Medical Ctr., Phoenix, 1972-73, histotechnician, 1973-83; histotechnician/rsch. Harrington Arthritis Rsch. Ctr., Phoenix, 1983-87, Emory U., Atlanta, 1987-88, VA Medical Ctr, Salt Lake City, 1988—; founder, chair hard tissue com. Nat. Soc. Histotech., Bowie, Md., 1989—, editor, 1992—, vet. indsl. rsch. com., 1989—, health and safety com., 1988—, mem. ednl. com., 1989-91; owner Wasatch Histological Cons., 1988—. Mem. editl. bd. Jour. Histotechnology, 1993—; contbr. articles to numerous profl. jours. Organizer Neighborhood Watch, West Valley City, Utah, 1993—. Named Histotechnologist of Yr., Nat. Soc. Histotechnology, 1992; recipient Hacker Instruments; Membership Incentive award, 1991-92, Superior Performance award, 1989-92, 95-96, William J. Hacker award, 1988, Rsch. Technician of Yr. award, 1989. Mem. European Soc. Histotechnology, Nat. Wildlife Fedn., Ga. Soc. Histotechnology, Utah Soc. Histotechnology, Am. Assn. Lab Animal Sci. (bd. dirs. 1989-91), The Cousteau Soc., Inc., Nat. Soc. Histotechnology, Am. Soc. Clinical Pathologists. Achievements include development of Sandersons Rapid Bone Stain and staining protocol for mineralized bone which differentiates mineralized bone from soft tissue and non-mineralized bone. Office: VA Medical Ctr 500 Foothill Blvd 151F Salt Lake City UT 84148

SANDERSON, DAVID R., physician; b. South Bend, Ind., Dec. 26, 1933; s. Robert Burns and Alpha (Rodenberger) S.; divorced, 1978; children: David, Kathryn, Robert, Lisa; m. Evelyn Louise Klunder, Sept. 20, 1980. BA, Northwestern U., 1955, MD, 1958. Cons. in medicine Mayo Clinic, Rochester, Minn., 1965-87, chmn. dept. Thoracic Disease, 1977-87; cons. in medicine Mayo Clinic Scottsdale, Ariz., 1987—, chmn. dept. internal medicine, 1988-96, vice chmn. bd. govs., 1987-94; assoc. dir. Mayo Lung Project, Nat. Cancer Inst., Rochester. Contbr. articles to profl. jours. Recipient Noble award, Mayo Found., Rochester, "Significant Sig" award, Sigma Chi Fraternity, Ill., 1989, Chevalier Jackson award, Am. Bronchoesophagologic Assn., Fla., 1990. Fellow ACP, Am. Coll. Chest Physicians (gov. for Minn. 1981-87); mem. Am. Bronchoesophagologic Assn., World Assn. for Bronchology, Internat. Bronchoesophagologic Assn., Internat. Assn. Study of Lung Cancer, AMA. Presbyterian. Home: 10676 E Bella Vista Dr Scottsdale AZ 85258-6086 Office: Mayo Clinic Scottsdale 13400 E Shea Blvd Scottsdale AZ 85259-5404

SANDERSON, DENNIS CARL, theater director, educator; b. Akron, Ohio, Jan. 20, 1935; s. Carl A. Sanderson and Gladys M. (Minter) Sanderson Buchmiller; m. Carol Ann Heitzman, May 13, 1961; children: Dennis Douglas, Diana Dawn. MA, Kent State U., 1963; PhD, Mich. State U., 1973. Dir. theatre Newberry (S.C.) Coll., 1963-73, Francis Marion U., Florence, S.C., 1973—; chmn. div. humanities Newberry Coll., 1971-73; chair, prof. dept. fine arts Francis Marion U., 1985—, C.B. and Marlene Askins prof. art; chmn. Art's Alive Spring Arts Festival, Florence, 1985-95; cons. in field. Dir. plays including Grease, 1981, Children of a Lesser God, 1983, Hedda Gabler, 1984, The Comedy of Errros, 1985, The Rimers of Eldritch, 1986, Royal Gambit, 1988, South Pacific, 1988, Out Town, 1989, Working, 1990; scenic designer plays Bell, Book, & Candle, 1985, The Foreigner, 1987. Pres. Dem. Com. Precinct 14, Florence, 1980-90. Luth. Ch. Am. fellow, 1966; faculty grantee Newberry Coll., 1970. Mem. Nat. Assn. Schs. of Theatre, Southeastern Theatre Assn., Am. Theatre in Higher Edn., S.C. Theatre Assn. (bd. dirs. 1988), Rotary (bd. dirs. 1987-90), Lions Internat., Sierra Club, Alpha Psi Omega, Phi Delta Theta (treas. 1960-61). Democrat. Lutheran. Avocations: coaching basketball and baseball, wood carving, research. Office: Francis Marion U PO Box 100547 Florence SC 29501-0547

SANDERSON, DOUGLAS JAY, lawyer; b. Boston, Apr. 21, 1953; s. Warren and Edith S. Sanderson; m. Audrey S. Goldstein, June 6, 1982; children: Scott M.G., Phoebe H.G. BA, Trinity Coll., Hartford, Conn., 1974; JD, George Washington U., 1977. Bar: Va. 1977, D.C. 1978, U.S. Dist. Ct. (ea. dist.) Va. 1978, U.S. Ct. Appeals (4th cir.) 1978. Assoc. Bettius, Rosenberger & Carter, P.C., Fairfax, Va., 1977-82; ptnr. Bettius & Sanderson, P.C. and predecessor firms, Fairfax, 1982-86; prin. Miles & Stockbridge P.C., Fairfax, 1986-95; br. head Miles & Stockbridge, Fairfax, 1989-91; co-owner McCandlish & Lillard, P.C., Fairfax, 1995—; trustee Cambridge Ctr. Behavioral Studies, Cambridge, 1981-90. Editor: Consumer Protection Reporting Svc., 1976-77. Bd. dirs. Legal Svcs. No. Va., Inc., 1991—, pres., 1993-95. Mem. ABA, Va. Bar Assn., Fairfax Bar Assn., Ctrl. Fairfax C. of C. (bd. dirs. 1988-93). Avocations: sports, reading. Office: McCandlish & Lillard 11350 Random Hills Ste 500 Fairfax VA 22030

SANDERSON, EDWARD FRENCH, state official; b. Evanston, Ill., June 25, 1947; s. Edward Gatewood and Barbara (French) S.; m. Carol Clo; children: David, Sarah, Katherine. BA, Wesleyan U., 1969; MA, Brown U., 1974. Exec. dir. Providence Hist. Dist. Commn., 1975-80; dep. dir. R.I. Hist. Preservation Commn., Providence, 1980-84, exec. dir., 1984—; sec. Nat. Conf. of State, Washington, 1989-91, dir., 1985-91; bd. dirs. R.I. Hist. Soc., Providence, 1987-93; commr. Blackstone Valley Nat. Heritage Corridor, Washington, 1988—. Author: Providence, R.I., 1986 (Downing Prize 1987). Office: RI Hist Preservation Commn Old State House 150 Benefit St Providence RI 02903-1209*

SANDERSON, ERIC GEORGE (SANDY SANDERSON), broadcast executive; b. Toronto, Ont., Can., Oct. 10, 1948; s. George Douglas and Miriam W. (House) S.; m. Anne Chard, May 23, 1970; children: Timothy, Katherine. Student, U. Toronto, 1965-66, U. Western Ont., 1967-68. Morning announcer, program dir. Radio Sta. CKAR, Huntsville, Ont., 1970-73; prodn. dir. Radio Sta. CJBK, London, Ont., 1973; creative dir. Radio Sta. CKGM, Montreal, Que., Can., 1974-77; asst. program dir. Radio Sta. WABC, N.Y.C., 1977-80; program dir. Radio Sta. WLS, Chgo., 1980-81; dir. programming ABC Radio Network, N.Y.C., 1982; program dir. Sta. CFTR-AM, Toronto, 1983-85, v.p. programming, 1986, sr. v.p., gen. mgr., 1988-90; sr. v.p. programming Rogers Broadcasting Ltd., Toronto, 1987-88, exec. v.p., gen. mgr. stas. CFTR-AM and CHFI-FM, 1990—. Bd. dirs. Found. to Assist Can. Talent on Record, Queen Elizabeth Hosp. Found.; bd. dirs. radio exec. com. Bur. Broadcast Measurement. Mem. Mayfair Lakeshore Tennis Club, Toronto Athletic Club, Greystone Golf and Country Club. Avocations: squash, golf, tennis. Office: Rogers Broadcasting Ltd, 36 Victoria St, Toronto, ON Canada M5C 1H3

SANDERSON, FRED HUGO, economist; b. Germany, Apr. 15, 1914; came to U.S., 1937, naturalized, 1944; s. Siegfried and Maria (Schulze) S.; m. Elisabeth Doepfer, Jan. 3, 1938. Lic.Sc.Econ., U. Geneva, Switzerland, 1935; A.M., Harvard U., 1942, Ph.D., 1943. Research asst. Dept. Agr., 1938-42; research asso. com. on research in social scis. Harvard U., 1938-43, teaching fellow, 1942-43; economist OSS, 1943-45; chief Central European econ. sect. div. research for Western Europe Dept. of State, 1946-48, chief Western European econ. br., 1948-52, chief regional econ. staff, 1952-55, asst. chief div., 1955-57, chief div. of research Western Europe, 1957-58; alt. U.S. rep. European Payments Union, 1958-59; dir. finance div. U.S. Mission to OEEC, Paris, 1959-62; chief foodstuffs div. Dept. State, 1963-67; dir. Office Food Policy and Programs, 1967-69, adviser internat. finance, 1970; detailed to Pres.'s Commn. on Internat. Trade and Investment Policy, 1970-71; mem. planning and coordination staff State Dept., 1971-73; fgn. service officer, 1955-73; sr. fellow Brookings Instn., Washington, 1974-83, Resources for Future, Washington, 1983-92, Nat. Ctr. for Food and Agrl. Policy, Washington, 1992—; on leave under Rockefeller Pub. Svc. award to study econ. effects of European coal and steel cmty., 1956-57; cons. to econ. adviser OMGUS, Berlin, 1948; detailed to Pres.'s Materials Policy Commn., 1951; professorial lectr. Sch. Advanced Internat. Studies Johns Hopkins U., 1973-94. Author: Methods of Crop Forecasting, 1954 (David A. Wells prize), Japan's Food Prospects and Policies, 1978, (with S. Roy) Food Trends and Prospects in India, 1979; contbg. author: Resources for Freedom, Vol. III, 1952, The Struggle for Democracy in Germany (G. Almond, editor), 1949, Strains in International Finance and Trade, 1974, The Great Food Fumble, 1975, U.S. Farm Policy in Perspective, 1983, World Food Prospects to the Year 2000, 1984, Agriculture and International Trade, 1988, The GATT Agreement on Agriculture, 1994, Agriculture and Multilateralism, 1994; co-author/editor: Agricultural Protectionism in the Industrialized World, 1990. Mem. Am. Econ. Assn., Am. Agrl. Econ. Assn. Home: 5017 Westport Rd Chevy Chase MD 20815-3714 Office: Nat Ctr for Food and Agrl Policy Washington DC 20036

SANDERSON, GARY WARNER, food company executive; b. Thermal, Calif., Dec. 17, 1934; s. Syl Z. and Inez (Goodpasture) S.; m. Irene Elizabeth Blocker, Aug. 15, 1953; children: Phillip Paul, Jennifer Ellen Sanderson Bakshi, Peter George, Andrew Forest. BS with honors, U. Calif. at Davis, 1956; PhD, U. Nottingham, 1962. Biochemist, head biochemistry div. Tea Rsch. Inst. of Ceylon, Talawakelle, Sri Lanka, 1963-66; from group leader of tea rsch. sect. to dir. beverage product R&D sect. Thomas J. Lipton, Inc., Englewood Cliffs, N.J., 1966-77; from v.p. rsch. to v.p. techs. Universal Foods Corp., Milw., 1978—; adj. prof. chemistry U. New Rochelle, N.Y., 1985; mem. biology adv. bd. Marquette U., 1987—; bd. adv. Food Rsch. Inst. U. Wisc. Madison, 1990—. Contbr. articles to profl. jours.; patentee in tea processing. Councilman City of Englewood, N.J., 1976-78; pres. City Coun., Englewood, 1977. Woodrow Wilson fellow U. Calif.-Davis, 1957-58; recipient Fulbright scholarship, 1960-62. Mem. Am. Chem. Soc. (chmn. N.Y. sect. 1976-77, treas. midwest regional meeting 1986, 92), Inst. Food Technologists (chmn. biotech. div. 1986-87), Biochem. Soc. (London), Wis. Biotech. Assn. (bd. dirs. 1993—), Wis. Assn. Rsch. Mgmt. (pres. 1992-94, Friends U. Nottingham in Am. (pres. 1994—), Cream City Cycle Club (ride leader 1988—, v.p. 1993—). Democrat. Unitarian. Avocations: bicycling, hiking, camping. Office: Universal Foods Corp 433 E Michigan St Milwaukee WI 53202-5104

SANDERSON, JAMES RICHARD, naval officer, planning and investment company consultant; b. Selma, Calif., Dec. 27, 1925; s. Charles Maxwell and Edith (Wente) S.; m. Betty Lee Bradley, Sept. 19, 1947. Student, U. Calif.-Berkeley, 1943-44, U. Wash., 1944, U. Willamette, 1944-45; grad., USNR Midshipman Sch. at Columbia U., 1945, Nat. War Coll., 1966; student, Gen. Line Sch., Monterey, Calif., 1953, Sr. Officers Ship Material Mgmt. Course, Idaho Falls, Idaho, 1979; B.A. in Internat. Affairs, George Washington U., 1968. Served as enlisted man U.S. Naval Res., 1943-45; commd. ensign USN, 1946, advanced through grades to vice adm., 1980; gunnery officer U.S.S. Mansfield, 1946-47, U.S.S. Bausell, 1947-48; flight trainee Naval Air Sta., Pensacola, Fla., 1949, Corpus Christi, Tex., 1950; served in Attack Squadron 195, Alameda, Calif., 1950-52; flight instr. Naval Air Sta., Pensacola, 1953-55; served in Attack Squadron 16, 1955-57; air ops. officer on staff Comdr. Carrier Div. Four, U.S.S. Forrestal, 1957-60; ops. officer Attack Squadron 43, Naval Air Sta., Oceana, Va., 1960-62; comdg. officer Attack Squadron 76, 1962-63; comdr. Attack Carrier Air Wing Three in U.S.S. Saratoga, 1963-65; spl. support plans officer, Pacific Area Strategic Plans and Policy Div., Office of Chief of Naval Ops., Washington, 1966-67; exec. asst. and sr. aide to dep. chief. naval ops., 1967-69; comdg. officer U.S.S. Ranier, 1969-70; dep. chief of staff for ops. and plans U.S. Sixth Fleet, 1970-71; comdg. officer U.S.S. Saratoga, 1971-73; dep. comdr. Naval Striking and Support Forces, So. Europe, Naples, Italy, 1973-76; vice dir. ops. Joint Chiefs of Staff, Washington, 1976-77; asst. dep. chief naval ops. for plans, policy and ops., 1977-79; comdr. Task Force Sixty, U.S. 6th Fleet, 1979-80, Carrier Group Two, 1979-80, Battle Force Sixth Fleet, 1979-80, Carrier Striking Force So. Region, 1979-80; dep. and chief staff, comdr. in chief Atlantic/U.S. Atlantic Fleet, Norfolk, Va., 1980-83; ret., 1983; exec. cons. Exec. Planning & Investment Co., Inc.,, Virginia Beach, Va., 1983-85; sr. v.p. for corp. ops. Computer Dynamics, Inc., 1984-86; asst. to pres. Eastern Computers, Inc., 1986—; cons., prin. Exec. Planning and Investment Co., Inc., 1986-94; sr. fellow joint and combined warfare course Armed Forces Staff Coll., 1994—. Decorated D.S.M., Legion of Merit with 3 gold stars, D.F.C., Meritorious Service medal, Air medal with 4 gold stars, Navy Commendation medal with combat distinguishing device. Mem. U. Calif. Alumni Assn., George Washington U. Alumni Assn., Nat. War Coll. Alumni Assn., Naval Acad. Athletic Assn., Assn. Naval Aviation, Tailhook Assn., Smithsonian Assn., Nat. Eagle Scout Assn. (regent, Disting. Eagle Scout award 1994), Nat. Skeet Shooting Assn., Eye Found., Nat. Assn. Investment Clubs, Nat. Wildlife Assn., Army Navy Country Club (Arlington, Va.), Masons (33d degree), Masons, Shriners, KT, Sojourners, Order of Eastern Star. Club: Army Navy Country (Arlington, Va.). Lodges: Masons (33 degree), Shriners, Knight Templer, Sojourners. Office: Eastern Computers Inc 596 Lynnhaven Pky Virginia Beach VA 23452-7303

SANDERSON, JEROME ALAN, survey statistician, accountant; b. Nashville, Nov. 18, 1945; s. Bernard and Anna Sanderson; m. Rhona J. Flehinger, Oct. 5, 1990. BSBA, U. Tenn., 1968; MS in Tech. of Mgmt., Am. U., 1974. CPA, Md. Survey statistician Bur. of Census, Washington, 1968-80, U.S. Dept. Energy-Energy Info. Adminstrn., Washington, 1980—; chief minerals & metals sect. Bur. of Census Fgn. Trade Divsn., Washington, 1977-80. Mem. Hexagon, Inc., Washington, 1984—, Camelot Community Neighborhood Watch, Annandale, Va., 1993—. Mem. D.C. Inst. CPAs, Md. Assn. CPAs, Alpha Epsilon Pi. Avocations: amateur radio, philately. Home: 3806 King Arthur Rd Annandale VA 22003-1323 Office: US Dept Energy 950 L'Enfant Plz SW Washington DC 20024

SANDESON, WILLIAM SEYMOUR, cartoonist; b. Mound City, Ill., Dec. 16, 1913; s. William Stephen and Jessie Mae (Mertz) S.; m. Ione Wear, June 4, 1938 (dec. 1975); 1 son, William Scott; m. Ruth Cress, Dec. 31, 1978. Student, Chgo. Acad. Fine Arts, 1931-32. Free-lance cartoonist for nat. mags., 1932-37; editorial cartoonist New Orleans Item-Tribune, 1937-41; cartoonist, picture editor and art dir. St. Louis Star-Times, 1941-51; editorial cartoonist Ft. Wayne (Ind.) News-Sentinel, 1951-82; ret., 1982. Drew daily cartoon feature for, Star-Times, Sketching Up With the News. Recipient Honor medal Freedoms Found., 1952, 53, 56, George Washington Honor medal, 1954, 55, 57, 58, 59, 60, Disting. Service award, 1961-72, cartoon award, 1982;, Ind. Sch. Bell award, 1967, Disting. Service awards, 1971-76, prin. cartoon award, 1977, cartoon award, 1978; co-recipient Pulitzer prize for gen. local reporting, 1982. Mem. Nat. Cartoonist Soc., Assn. Am. Editorial Cartoonists. Congregationalist. Club: Fort Wayne Press (pres. 1965). Home: 119 W Sherwood Ter Fort Wayne IN 46807-2846 Office: Fort Wayne News Sentinel Fort Wayne IN 46802 *Until I'm listed in WHO WAS WHO, I intend to dip my brush in a mixture of self-improvement, stubbornness, and sincere thoughtfulness of my fellow American.*

SANDITEN, EDGAR RICHARD, investment company executive; b. Okmulgee, Okla., Feb. 1, 1920; s. Herman and Anna (Sanditen) S.; m. Isabel Raffkind, Jan. 26, 1945; children: Linda Caryl, Judith Marie, Ellen Jane, Michael Jay. Student, Western Mil. Acad., 1934-37; B.S. in Bus., Okla. U., 1941. With Otasco, Inc., Tulsa, 1941-87, pres., 1974-77, chmn., chief exec. officer, 1977-83, chmn. employees retirement trust, 1983-87; prin., chmn. Sanditen Investments, Ltd., Tulsa, 1987—; bd. dirs. Bank of Okla. Trust Co.; fin. advisor Bank of Okla., 1978-84. Chmn. United Jewish Appeal, Tulsa, 1959; mem. bd. dirs. Jewish Fedn., Tulsa, 1960-62 (Honor award 1960), YMCA, 1966-95, Am. Cancer Soc., 1978-80, Tulsa Met. Ministry, 1977-78, Simon Estes Ednl. Found., 1982—, March of Dimes, 1983—; mem. adv. com. Jr. League, 1977—, Girl Scouts U.S.A., 1987—; chmn. Tulsa Charity Horse Show, 1969-71, 80-84; bd. dirs. Tulsa Opera, 1979—, v.p., 1989 (Champion Fundraiser, 1989-96), Tulsa Ballet Theatre (Dimedici award 1989), Tulsa Econ. Devel. Commn., 1970-84; bd. dirs. Temple Israel Found., 1968-70, chmn., 1979-80; mem. B'nai Emunah Synagogue; pres. Temple Israel, 1968-70; trustee Children's Med. Ctr., 1983—; bd. dirs. St. John Med. Ctr., 1973-82, chmn., 1979-81; bd. dirs. St. John Found., 1983-89, chmn., 1983-85; bd. dirs. Tulsa Jewish Retirement and Health Care Ctr., 1986—, Tulsa Ctr. for Homeless, 1991—, fenster Mus., 1986—, NCCJ, 1983—, pres., 1985-87; mem. adv. bd. dirs. U. Okla. Coll. Bus. Adminstrn., 1986-91; hon. chmn. Ronald McDonald House, 1991. Served with USAAF, 1943-46. Recipient Nat. Humanitarian award Nat. Jewish Hosp., 1987, Brotherhood award NCCJ, 1991, Alfred Aaronson Cmty. Rels. award, 1993; named Boss of Yr., Am. Bus. Women's Assn., 1976; named to Okla. Hall of Fame, 1996. Mem. Tulsa Jr. C. of C. (honor award 1943), Okla. C. of C. (bd. dirs. 1978-87), Tulsa C. of C. (bd. dirs. 1977-83, v.p. 1978-79), Quarter Century Club Automotive Industry, So. Hills Country Club (bd. dirs. 1990-96, fin. chmn., exec. com., v.p. 1992, pres. 1995), Summit Club (bd. dirs. 1971-77). Office: Sanditen Investments Ltd 3314 E 51st St Ste 207K Tulsa OK 74135-3527

SAND LEE, INGER, artist; b. Sauda, Norway, Apr. 8, 1938; came to U.S., 1960; d. Inge Sigvald and Johanne Elise (Hamre) Sand; m. Charles Allen Lee, Aug. 28, 1981. Cert. in decorative art, N.Y. Sch. Interior Design, 1968; BFA, Marymount Manhattan Coll./N.Y. Sch. Interior Design, 1980; cert. completion, Art Students League, 1993; postgrad., Nat. Acad. Design, 1993-94. One-woman shows include Art 54, N.Y.C., 1988, Pyramid Gallery, N.Y.C., 1990, Exhbn. Space, N.Y.C., 1991, Denise Bibro Fine Art, N.Y.C., 1993, 95; selected exhbns. include Lincoln Ctr., N.Y.C., 1988, Avery Fisher Hall, N.Y.C., 1988, Mus. Atheism and Realism, Lviv, USSR, 1990, Lever House, N.Y.C., 1991, Nat. Acad. Mus., N.Y.C., 1994; group exhbns. include Pyramid Gallery, N.Y.C., 1989, 90, 91, Ariel Gallery, N.Y.C., 1991, Broome Street Gallery, N.Y.C., 1992, 93, Ward-Nasse Gallery, N.Y.C., 1992, Hudson Guild Art Gallery, N.Y.C., 1992, Denise Bibro Fine Art, N.Y.C., 1992, 94, 95, Frank Bustamante Gallery, N.Y.C., 1993, Southern Alleghenies Mus. Art, Loretto, Pa., 1994, Edward William Gallery, 1996, Knoxville (Tenn.) Opera Guild, 1996, Fairleigh Dickinson U., 1996; represented in numerous permanent pvt. and pub. collections. Recipient Alumni award N.Y. Sch. Interior Design, 1979; merit scholar Art Student's League, 1991. Mem. Archtl. League N.Y.

SANDLER, ABRAHAM, minister. Missionary Jewish Ministry Dist. of Christian and Missionary Alliance. Office: Jewish Ministry Dist 9820 Woodfern Rd Philadelphia PA 19115-2921

SANDLER, BERNICE RESNICK, women's rights specialist; b. N.Y.C., Mar. 3, 1928; d. Abraham Hyman and Ivy (Ernst) Resnick; children: Deborah Jo, Emily Maud. BA cum laude, Bklyn. Coll., 1948; MA, CCNY, 1950; EdD, U. Md., 1969; LLD (hon.), Bloomfield Coll., 1973, Hood Coll., 1974, R.I. Coll., 1980, Colby-Sawyer Coll., 1984; LHD (hon.), Grand Valley State Coll., 1974; Dr. Pub. Service (hon.), North Adams State Coll., 1985; LLD (hon.), Goucher Coll., 1991; LHD (hon.), Plymouth State Coll., 1992, Wittenberg U., 1993. Research asst., nursery sch. tchr., employment counselor, adult edn. instr., sec.; psychologist HEW, 1970; tchr. psychology Mt. Vernon Coll., 1970; head Action Com. for Fed. Contract Compliance, Women's Equity Action League, 1970-71; edn. specialist U.S. Ho. Reps., Washington, 1970; dep. dir. Womens Action program, HEW, Washington, 1971; dir. project on status and edn. of women Assn. Am. Colls., Washington, 1971-91; sr. assoc. Ctr. for Women Policy Studies, 1991-94; sr. scholar in residence Nat. Assn. Women in Edn., Washington, 1994—; cons., 1991—; expert witness, 1990—; writer, 1971—; vis. lectr. U. Md., 1968-69; adv. bd. Women's Equity Action League Ednl. and Legal Def. Fund, 1980—, trustee, 1974-80, Women's Equity Action League, 1971-78; adv. com. Math./Sci. Network, 1979, Wider Opportunities for Women, 1978-85, Women's Legal Def. Fund, 1978-84; adv. bd. N.J. project Inst. for Rsch. on Women Rutgers U., New Brunswick, 1987—, Nat. Coun. for Alternative Work Patterns Inc., 1978-85, Women's Hdqs. State Nat. Bank for Women's Appointments, 1977-78, and others. Mem. adv. bd. Jour. Reprints Documents Affecting Women, 1976-78, Women's Rights Law Reporter, 1970-80; editor: (newsletters) On Campus With Women, 1971-91, About Women on Campus, 1991—; contbr. articles to profl. jours. Mem. bd. overseers Wellesley Coll. Ctr. for Rsch. on Women, 1975-87; bd. dirs. Ctr. for Women's Policy Studies, 1972-75; mem. exec. com. Inst. for Ednl. Leadership, 1982-87, mem. program adv. com., 1987—, chair bd. dirs., 1981, chair adv. com., 1975-81; mem. affirmative action com., task force on family, nat. affairs commn. Am. Jewish Com., 1978, bd. dirs D.C. chpt.; tech. adv. com. Nat. Jewish Family Ctr., 1980-89; adv. coun. Ednl. Devel. Ctr., 1980-85; adv. bd. Urban Inst., 1981-85, Women Employed Inst., 1981-84, Ex-New Yorkers for N.Y., 1978-79; mem. adv. com. Arthur and Elizabeth Schlesinger Libr. History of Women in Am., 1981-85; nat. adv. com. Shelter Rsch. Inst., Calif., 1980-82; chair adv. panel project on self-evaluation Am. Insts. for Rsch., 1980-82; bd. dirs. Equality Ctr., 1983, Evaluation and Tng. Inst., Calif., 1980, Inst. for Studies in Equality, 1975-77. Recipient Athena award Intercollegiate Assn. Women Students, 1974, Elizabeth Boyer award Women's Equity Action League, 1976, Rockefeller Pub. Svc. award Princeton U., 1976, Women Educators award for activism, 1987, Anna Roe award Harvard U., 1988, Readers Choice honors Washington Woman Mag., 1987, Woman of Distinction award Nat. Assn. Women in Edn., 1991, Georgina Smith award AAUP, 1992, Woman of Achievement Turner Broadcasting System, 1994; named one of 100 Most Powerful Women Washingtonian Mag., 1982, one of the nation's 100 Most Important Women, Ladies Home Jour., 1988. Mem. Assn. for Women in Sci. Found. (bd. dirs. 1977—), Am. Soc. Profl. and Exec. Women (adv. bd. 1980). Avocations: birding, music, swimming, hiking. Office: Nat Assn Women in Edn 1350 Connecticut Ave NW Ste 850 Washington DC 20036-1701

SANDLER, GERALD HOWARD, computer science educator, company executive; b. N.Y.C., Sept. 17, 1934; s. Irving and Sally S.; m. Ann Sandler; children: Eric, Steven. BS, CUNY, 1956, MS, 1957. Past pres. Grumman Data Systems & Svcs., Bethpage, N.Y.; pres. GHS Enterprises; prof. computer sci. Poly. U., Bklyn. Author: System Engineering, 1963. Home: 46 Bonnie Dr Westbury NY 11590-2804

SANDLER, HERBERT M., savings and loan association executive; b. N.Y.C., Nov. 16, 1931; s. William B. and Hilda (Schattan) S.; m. Marion Osher, Mar. 26, 1961. BSS, CCNY, 1951; JD, Columbia U., 1954. Bar: N.Y. 1956. Asst. counsel Waterfront Commn. N.Y. Harbor, 1956-59; partner firm Sandler & Sandler, N.Y.C., 1960-62; pres., dir., mem. exec. com. Golden West Savs. & Loan Assn. and Golden West Fin. Corp., Oakland, Calif., 1963-75; chmn. bd., co-chief exec. officer, dir., mem. exec. com. World Savs. & Loan Assn. and Golden West Fin. Corp., Oakland, 1975—; charter mem. Thrift Instns. Adv. Coun., to Fed. Res. Bd., 1980-81; former chmn. Legis. and Regulation Com. Calif. Savs. and Loan League; former mem. bd. dirs. Fed. Home Loan Bank, San Francisco. Pres., trustee Calif. Neighborhood Services Found.; chmn. Urban Housing Inst.; mem. policy adv. bd. Ctr. for Real Estate and Urban Econs. U. Calif., Berkeley. With U.S. Army, 1954-56. Office: Golden W Fin Corp 1901 Harrison St Oakland CA 94612-3574

SANDLER, IRVING HARRY, art critic, art historian; b. N.Y.C., July 22, 1925; s. Harry and Anna (Robin) S.; m. Lucy Freeman, Sept. 4, 1958; 1 child, Catherine Harriet. BA, Temple U., 1948; MA, U. Pa., 1950; PhD, NYU, 1976. Instr. in art history NYU, 1960-71; prof. art history SUNY, Purchase, 1971—; art critic N.Y. Post, N.Y.C., 1960-65. Author: The Triumph of American Painting: A History of Abstract Expressionism, 1970, The New York School: Painters and Sculptors of the Fifties, 1978, Alex Katz, 1979, Al Held, 1984, American Art of the 1960s, 1988; editor (with Amy Newman) Defining Modern Art: Selected Writings of Alfred H. Barr Jr., 1986. John Simon Guggenheim fellow, 1965; Nat. Endowment for Arts fellow, 1977. Mem. Coll. Art Assn., Internat. Assn. Art Critics. Home: 100 Bleecker St New York NY 10012-2202 Office: SUNY at Purchase Dept Visual Arts 735 Anderson Hill Rd Purchase NY 10577

SANDLER, JENNY, dancer; b. N.Y.C.. Scholarship student, The Joffrey Ballet Sch. Dancer Joffrey II Dancers, N.Y.C., 1988-90, The Joffrey Ballet, N.Y.C., 1990—. Featured in mag. Mirabella, Aug., 1994. Office: 25 E 9th St #7A New York NY 10003

SANDLER, LUCY FREEMAN, art history educator; b. N.Y.C., June 7, 1930; d. Otto and Frances (Glass) Freeman; m. Irving Sandler, Sept. 4, 1958; 1 child, Catherine Harriet. B.A., Queens Coll., 1951; M.A., Columbia U., 1957; Ph.D., NYU, 1964. Asst. prof. NYU, 1964-70, assoc. prof., 1970-75, prof. fine arts, 1975-86, Helen Gould Sheppard prof. art history, 1986—, chmn. dept., 1975-89; editorial cons. Viator, UCLA, 1983—. Author: The Peterborough Psalter in Brussels, 1974, The Psalter of Robert De Lisle in the British Library, 1983, Gothic Manuscripts 1285-1385, 1986, 'Omne Bonum': A Fourteenth-Century Encyclopedia of Universal Knowledge, 1996; editor: Essays in Memory of Karl Lehmann, 1964, Art the Ape of Nature: Studies in Honor of H.W. Janson, 1981, Monograph Series, 1970-75, 86-89, Gesta, 1991-94; asst. editor Art Bull., 1964-67, mem. editl. bd., 1994; mem. editl. bd. Jour. Jewish Art, 1978, Speculum, 1994. Trustee Godwin-Ternbach Mus., Queens Coll., 1982-94. NEH fellow, 1967-68, 77; fellow Pierpont Morgan Library; Guggenheim fellow, 1988-89. Fellow Soc. Antiquaries (London); mem. AAUP, Coll. Art Assn. (pres. 1981-84), Medieval Acad. Am., Internat. Ctr. Medieval Art (adv. bd., bd. dirs. 1976-80, 84-87, 89-92, 95—). Home: 100 Bleecker St Apt 30A New York NY 10012-2207 Office: NYU Dept Fine Arts New York NY 10003

SANDLER, MARION OSHER, savings and loan association executive; b. Biddeford, Maine, Oct. 17, 1930; d. Samuel and Leah (Lowe) Osher; m. Herbert M. Sandler, Mar. 26, 1961. BA, Wellesley Coll., 1952; postgrad., Harvard U.-Radcliffe Coll., 1953; MBA, NYU, 1958; LLD (hon.), Golden Gate U., 1987. Asst. buyer Bloomingdale's (dept. store), N.Y.C., 1953-55; security analyst Dominick & Dominick, N.Y.C., 1955-61; sr. fin. analyst Oppenheimer & Co., N.Y.C., 1961-63; sr. v.p., dir. Golden West Fin. Corp. and World Savs. & Loan Assn., Oakland, Calif., 1963-75, vice chmn. bd. dirs., CEO, mem. exec. com., dir., 1975-80, pres., co- chief exec. officer, dir., mem. exec. com., 1980-93, chmn. bd. dirs., CEO, mem. exec. com., 1993—; pres., chmn. bd. dirs., CEO Atlas Assets, Inc., Oakland, 1987—, Atlas Advisers, Inc., Oakland, 1987—, Atlas Securities, Inc., Oakland, 1987—; mem. adv. com. Fed. Nat. Mortgage Assn., 1983-84. Mem. Pres.'s Mgmt. Improvement Coun., 1980, Thrift Insts. Adv. Coun. to Fed. Res. Bd., 1989-91, v.p., 1990, pres., 1991; mem. policy adv. bd. Ctr. for Real Estate and Urban Econs. U. Calif., Berkeley, 1981—, mem. exec. com. policy adv. bd., 1985—; mem. ad hoc com. to rev. Schs. Bus. Adminstrn. U. Calif., 1984-85; vice chmn. industry adv. com. Fed. Savs. and Loan Ins. Corp., 1987-88, Ins. Corp., 1987-88; bd. overseers NYU Schs. Bus., 1987-89; mem. Glass Ceiling Commn., 1992-93. Mem. Phi Beta Kappa, Beta Gamma Sigma. Office: Golden W Fin Corp 1901 Harrison St Oakland CA 94612-3574

SANDLER, PAUL MARK, lawyer; b. Balt., June 7, 1945; s. Edward Barry and Dorothy (Livingston) S.; m. Margaret Batten, Dec. 29, 1974; children: Douglas, David. BA, Hobart Coll., Geneva, N.Y., 1967; JD, Georgetown U., Washington, 1971. Bar: Md. 1972, D.C. 1972, U.S. Dist. Ct. Md. 1972, U.S. Ct. Appeals (4th cir.) 1972. Assoc. Ulman & Cohan, Balt., 1972-77; ptnr. Freishtat & Schwartz, Balt., 1977, Freishtat & Sandler, Balt., 1978—; adj. prof. appellate practice U. Balt., 1974-84; lectr. in field; mem. Speedy Trial Planning Grp., U.S. Dist. Ct. of Md., mem. adv. com. on admission of attys. to fed. practice. Author: Pattern Examinations of Witnesses for the Maryland Lawyer, 1987, 3d edit., 1996, Pleading Causes of Action in Maryland, 1991, Pleading Causes of Action in Maryland Supplements, 1994, Appellate Practice for the Maryland Lawyer: State and Federal, 1994; editor: The Maryland Appellate Practice Handbook, 1978; mem. bd. editors Trial Diplomacy Jour., 1983-84. Bd. dirs. Easter Seal Soc. of Md., St. Joseph Hosp. Found., 1989—, chmn. fund raising campaign, 1990-93; chmn. V.I.P. Panel, Nat. Easter Seal Telethon, 1988—; bd. trustees Balt. County Community Colls., 1977-80; mem. Balt. County Bd. Social Svcs., 1981-83. With USAFR, 1968-72. Mem. ABA (co-chmn. sect. litigation legis. com. 1989—, other coms. in past), Md. Bar Assn. (founder and 1st chmn. litigation sect. 1980-81, mem. litigation sect. coun. 1981—), J. Dudley Digges Inn of Ct. (master of bench). Avocations: reading, writing, horseback riding, fishing, hiking. Office: Freishtat & Sandler Ste 1500 201 E Baltimore St Baltimore MD 21202-1505

SANDLER, RICHARD JAY, lawyer; b. N.Y.C., Aug. 26, 1947; s. Albert and Ruth (Marcus) S.; m. Ronda Muir, Feb. 27, 1982; children: Elizabeth Muir, Russell Muir. BA summa cum laude, Princeton U., 1969; JD, Harvard U., 1972. Assoc. Davis, Polk & Wardwell, N.Y.C., 1972-79, ptnr., 1979—; ptnr. Davis, Polk & Wardwell, Paris, 1982-85. Mem. ABA. Avocations: collecting art, skiing, tennis, reading, antiques. Office: Davis Polk & Wardwell 450 Lexington Ave New York NY 10017-3911*

SANDLER, ROBERT MICHAEL, insurance company executive, actuary; b. N.Y.C., Apr. 20, 1942; s. Albert and Ruth (Marcus) S.; m. Annette L. Marchese, Aug. 18, 1963; children—David, Glenn. B.A. in Math., Hofstra U., 1963. Various actuarial positions Met. Life, N.Y.C., 1963-68; various actuarial positions Am. Internat., N.Y.C., 1968-80; v.p., casualty actuary American Internat. Group, Inc., N.Y.C., 1980-84, sr. v.p., sr. actuary, sr. claims officer, 1984-95, exec. v.p., 1995—, dir. various subs. Mem. Casualty Acturial Soc. (assoc.), Am. Acad. Actuaries, Internat. Actuarial Assn., Am. Internat. Underwriters (chmn. 1994—). Republican. Home: 3 Crestwood Dr Bridgewater NJ 08807-2209 Office: Am Internat Group 70 Pine St New York NY 10270-0002

SANDLER, ROSS, law educator; b. Milw., Jan. 31, 1939; s. Theodore T. and Laurette (Simons) S.; m. Alice R. Mintzer, Sept. 15, 1968; children: Josephine, Jenny, Dorothy. AB, Dartmouth Coll., 1961; LLB, NYU, 1965. Bar: N.Y. 1965, Fla. 1965. Assoc. atty. Cahill Gordon Reindel & Ohl, N.Y.C., 1965-68; asst. U.S. atty. So. Dist. N.Y., 1968-72; assoc. atty. Trubin Sillcocks Edelman & Knapp, N.Y.C., 1972-75; sr. staff atty. Natural Resources Def. Coun., N.Y.C., 1975-81, 83-86; spl. advisor to mayor City of N.Y., 1981-82; exec. dir. Hudson River Found., N.Y.C., 1983-86; commr. N.Y.C. Dept. Transp., 1986-90; ptnr. Jones Day Reavis & Pogue, N.Y.C., 1991-93; law prof. N.Y. Law Sch., 1993—, dir. Ctr. for N.Y.C. law, 1993—; mem. N.Y.C. Procurement Policy Bd., 1994—; vis. lectr. Yale Law Sch., New Haven, 1977; adj. prof. law NYU Law Sch., 1976—; chair, mem. N.Y.C. Taxi and Limousine Commn., 1980-90. Co-author: A New Direction in Transit, 1978; columnist Environ. Mag., 1976-80; editor: (jour.) City Law; contbr. book chpt., op-ed columns, articles to profl. jours.; lectr. environ. law, spkr. confs. Trustee Woods Hole (Mass.) Rsch. Ctr., 1983—; mem. exec. com. Hudson River Found., 1986—. Recipient Pub. Interest award NYU Law Alumni, 1987, Louis J. Lefkowitz award Fordham Law Sch. Urban Law Jour., 1989. Mem. City Club of N.Y. (chair 1992-93, trustee). Office: NY Law Sch 57 Worth St New York NY 10013-2926

SANDLER, STANLEY IRVING, chemical engineering educator; b. N.Y.C., June 10, 1940; s. Murray C. and Celia M. (Kamenetsky) S.; m. Judith Katherine Ungar, June 17, 1962; children: Catherine Julietta, Joel Abraham, Michael Howard. BChemE, CCNY, 1962; PhD, U. Minn., 1966. NSF postdoctoral fellow Inst. Molecular Physics, U. Md., College Park, 1966-67; successively asst. prof., assoc. prof., prof. dept. chem. engring. U. Del., Newark, 1967-82, H.B. du Pont prof., 1982—, chmn. dept., 1982-86, dir. Ctr. for Molecular and Engring. Thermodynamics, 1992—, interim dean Coll. of Engring., 1992; vis. prof. Imperial Coll., London, 1973-74, U. Nat. del Sur, Bahia Blanca, Argentina, 1985, Tech. U., Berlin, 1981, 88-89, U. Queensland, Brisbane, Australia, 1989, 96, U. Calif., Berkeley, 1995; cons. maj. oil and chem. cos. Author: Chemical and Engineering Thermodynamics, 1977, 2d rev. edit., 1989; editor: Fluid Properties and Phase Equilibria, 1977, Chemical Engineering Education in a Changing Environment, 1989, Kinetic and Thermodynamic Lumping of Multicomponent Mixtures, 1991, Models for Thermodynamic and Phase Equilibria Calculations, 1993; mem. adv. bd. Jour. Chem. Engring. Data, Chem. Engring. Edn., Indsl. Engring. Chem. Rsch., Indian Chem. Engr., Engring. Sci. and Tech. (Malaysia); also numerous articles. Mem. adv. bd. chem. engring. La. State U., Carnegie-Mellon U. Recipient U.S. sr. Scientist award Alexander von Humboldt Found., 1988, Francis Alison award U. Del., 1993, Ashton Cary award Ga. Tech. U., 1994, Phillips Lecture award Okla. State U., 1993. Mem. AIChE (jour. adv. bd., Profl. Progress award 1984), NAE, Am. Chem. Soc. (award Del. sect. 1989), Am. Soc. Engring. Edn. (lectr. chem. engring. div. 1988), Cosmos Club (Washington). Jewish. Avocations: jogging, philately. Home: 202 Sypherd Dr Newark DE 19711-3627 Office: U Del Dept Chem Engring Newark DE 19716

SANDLER, THOMAS R., accountant; b. Mt. Kisco, N.Y., Dec. 16, 1946; s. Louis and Susan (Rosen) S.; m. Alison G. Corneau, Aug. 26, 1972; children—Justin C., Shawn A. B.S. summa cum laude, Ithaca Coll., 1968; M.S., SUNY-Binghamton, 1972. C.P.A., N.Y., Colo. 1982. Asst. acct. KPMG Peat Marwick, White Plains, N.Y., 1972; mgr. KPMG Peat Marwick, Phoenix, 1975; sr. mgr. KPMG Peat Marwick, N.Y.C., 1978; ptnr. KPMG Peat Marwick, Denver, 1981-92; ptnr. in-charge corp. recovery svcs. KPMG Peat Marwick, N.Y.C., 1993-94; mng. ptnr. BDO Seidman, Denver, 1994-95; CFO, treas., sec. Samsonite Corp., Denver, 1995—. Contbr. articles to profl. jours. Past trustee, past pres. Colo. Children's Chorale; treas., past pres., gov., mem. exec. com., committeeman Colo. Golf Assn.; committeeman U.S. Golf Assn. bd. dirs. Pacific Coast GOlf Assn. Served with USMC, 1968-70. Mem. Colo. Soc. C.P.A.s (chmn. real estate and govt. acctg. com.), Am. Inst. C.P.A.s. Clubs: Columbine Country (Littleton, Colo.); Whippoorwill Country (Armonk N.Y.); Bear Creek Golf. Home: 4 Spyglass Dr Littleton CO 80123-6656 Office: Samsonite Corp South Tower 11200 E 45th Ave Denver CO 80239

SANDLOW, LESLIE JORDAN, physician, educator; b. Chgo., Jan. 7, 1934; s. Harry H. and Rose (Ehrlich) S.; m. Joanne J. Fleischer, June 16, 1957; children; Jay, Bruce, Lisa. BS, U. Ill., 1956; MD, Chgo. Med. Sch., 1960. Intern Michael Reese Hosp. and Med. Ctr., Chgo., 1961, med. resident, rsch. fellow gastrointestinal rsch., 1961-64, physician-in-charge clin. gastroenterology lab., 1963-74, asst. attending physician, 1964-67, assoc. attending physician, 1967-72, vice chmn. divsn. gastroenterology, dir. ambulatory medicine, 1968, dir. ambulatory care, 1969-76, attending physician, 1972—, assoc. med. dir., 1972-73; clin. asst. Chgo. Med. Sch., 1963-68, clin. instr., 1966; asst. prof. dept. medicine Pritzker Sch. Medicine, U. Chgo., 1973-76, assoc. prof., 1976-85, prof., 1985-90; prof. clin. medicine and med. edn. U. Ill. Coll. Medicine, Chgo., 1990-91, prof. medicine and med. edn., 1992—, sr. assoc. dean for grad. and continuing med. edn., 1993—, head dept. med. edn., 1993—, sr. assoc. dean for med. edn., 1994—; dep. v.p. profl. affairs Michael Reese Hosp. and Med. Ctr., 1973-78, dir. Office Ednl. Affairs, 1976-81, assoc. v.p. acad. affairs, 1978-82, dir. quality assurance program, 1981-91, v.p. planning, 1982-83, v.p. profl. affairs and planning, 1983-88, dir. divsn. internal medicine, 1986-93, v.p. profl. and acad. affairs, 1988-91, med. dirs. acad. and med. affairs, 1992-94; med. dir. Michael Reese Health Plan, Inc., 1972-74, interim exec. dir., 1976-77; cons. gastroenterologist Ill. Ctrl. Hosp., 1978-80; vis. prof. Pontifica U. Catolica Rio Grande do Sul, Brazil, 1978, U. Fed. Espirito Santo, Brazil, 1978, Nordic Fedn. for Med. Understanding, Akureyri, Iceland, 1978, Seoul Nat. U. Sch. Medicine, 1981, Coll. Physicians and Surgsons, Kharachi, Pakistan, 1994, U. Tex., Ft. Worth, 1977, U. Ariz., Tucson, 1977, Loyola U. Med. Sch., Maywood, Ill., 1979; cons. in field; coord. Health Scis. Librs. in Ill.; mem. Midwest Med. Libr. Network; mem. subcom. on delivery of ambulatory med. care Inst. Medicine Chgo.; mem. cmty. resources task force Interinstnl. Cardiovascular Ctr.; chmn. steering group Ill. Regional Med. Program; past co-chmn. curriculum com. U. Chgo. Reviewer Rsch. in Med. Edn./Assn. Am. Med. Colls., 1985—, Acad. Medicine/Assn. Am. Med. Colls., 1989; contbr. numerous articles to profl. publs. Mem. Skokie (Ill.) Bd. Health, 1973-85, chmn., 1976-85; bd. dirs. Group Health Assn. Am., 1976-78, Portes Ctr., 1980—; bd. dirs. Good Health Program Skokie Valley Hosp., 1978-80; bd. dirs., exec. com. Rsch. and Edn. Found. of Michael Reese Hosp. Med. Staff, 1992—. Recipient numerous grants, including NIH, 1988, Michael Reese Hosp. Found., 1994-95, Chgo. Cmty. Trust, 1994-95. Fellow Am. Coll. Gastroenterology; mem. N.Y. Acad. Scis., Inst. Medicine, Assn. Am. Med. Colls., Am. Coll. Physician Execs. (co-chair resource mgmt. com. of quality assurance forum), Soc. Dirs. Med. Coll. Continuing Med. Edn., Soc. Dir. Rsch. in Med. Edn. Home: 2314 Lincoln Park West Chicago IL 60614 Office: U Ill Coll Medicine Med Edn M/C 784 1819 W Polk St Chicago IL 60612

SANDMAN, DAN D., lawyer. BA, Ohio State U., 1970, JD, 1973. Bar: Ohio 1973, Pa. 1995. Gen. counsel, sec. Marathon Oil Co., 1986-92, USX Corp., Pitts., 1992—. Office: USX Corp 600 Grant St Rm 6118 Pittsburgh PA 15219-4776*

SANDMAN, PETER M., risk communication consultant; b. N.Y.C., Apr. 18, 1945; s. Howard Edwin and Gertrude Leah (Orgel) S.; m. Susan Marie Goertzel, June 18, 1967 (div. 1975); m. Jody Sue Lanard, June 10, 1990; children: Alison, Jennifer; 1 stepchild, James Sachs. BA in Psychology, Princeton U., 1967; MA in Comm., Stanford U., 1968, PhD, 1971. Reporter Toronto (Ont.) Star, Can., 1966; stringer Time, 1966-67; instr. comm. Stanford (Calif.) U., 1968-70; instr. journalism Calif. State Coll., Hayward, 1970; sr. editor The Magazine, 1970; asst. prof. Ohio State U., Columbus, 1971-72; asst. prof. natural resources, journalism U. Mich., Ann Arbor, 1972-75, assoc. prof. natural resources, 1975-77; assoc. prof. comm., coord. Cook Coll. comm. program Rutgers U., New Brunswick, N.J., 1977-83, prof. journalism, 1983-94, prof. dept. human ecology, 1992-94; adj. prof., 1994—; adj. prof. TV, radio Ithaca (N.Y.) Coll., 1976, grad. program in pub. health Rutgers U., 1986—, dept. environ. and cmty. medicine Robert Wood Johnson Med. Sch., Rutgers U., 1987—; adv. com. environ./occupl. health info. program 1984-89; founder, dir. environ. comm. rsch. program N.J. Agrl. Exptl. Sta., Rutgers U., 1986-92; vis. scholar urban and environ. policy Tufts U., Medford, Mass., 1990-91; rsch. prof. George Perkins Marsh Inst., Clark U.; comm. coun. Environ. Def. Fund, 1985—; bd. advisors grad. program in tech. and sci. comm. Drexel U., Phila., 1988—; cons. on comm. ACP, 1976-79, The Cousteau Soc., 1977-79, Pres. Com. on the Accident at Three Mile Island; specialist in comm. coop. ext. svc. U.S. Dept. Agr., 1977-86; cons. risk commn. office policy analysis EPA, 1986-88; exec. com. Sci. Writing Educators Group, 1978-81; cons. ARCO Chem., Boise Cascade, Chevron, Ciba-Geigy, Consumers Power, Dow, Du Pont, Johnson and Johnson, Johnson Wax, Procter and Gamble, Union Carbide, others. Cons. editor Random House, 1982-89, McGraw-Hill, 1989-94, Holt, Rinehart and Winston, 1978-81; contbg. editor Apt. Life, 1971-75; freelance writer, 1966—; editl. bd. Pub. Rels. Rsch. Ann., 1981-91, Jour. Pub. Rels. Rsch., 1991-94; editl. adv. bd. Environ. and Behavior, 1976-86; contbr. articles to profl. jours. Bd. dirs. N.J. Environ. Lobby, 1984-90, Nuclear Dialogue Project, 1985-90, pres. 1986-90; pub. info. com. N.J. chpt., Am. Cancer Soc., 1981-86, vice-chmn., 1983-86; comm. coord. N.J. Campaign for a Nuclear Weapons Freeze, 1982-85; socioeconomic subcom., com. on biotechnology agr. divsn. Nat. Assn. State Univs. and Land Grant Colls., 1988-90; bd. advisors Environ. Scientists for Global Survival, 1988-91; sci. review panel, radium/radon adv. bd. N.J. Dept. Environ. Protection, 1987-88; com. to survey the health effects mustard gas and lewisite Inst. Medicine, NAS, 1992. Mem. AAUP, ACLU (bd. dirs. N.J. chpt. 1984-87), Assn. for Edn. in Journalism and Mass Comm., Environ. Def. Fund, Investigative Reporters and Editors, Nat. Assn. Profl. Environ. Communicators, Sci. Writing Educators Group, Soc. for Risk Analysis, Soc. Environ. Journalists, Soc. Profl. Journalists, Sigma Delta Chi. Home: 54 Gray Cliff Rd Newton Center MA 02159-2017

SANDMEYER, ROBERT LEE, university dean, economist; b. Evansville, Ind., June 12, 1929; s. Orville G. Sandmeyer and Elizabeth Chandler; m. Loretta Mae Jacobs, Aug. 5, 1950; children: Karen, Bridgit, Barbara, Robert C. B.A., Ft. Hays State U., 1956; M.S., Okla. State U., 1958, Ph.D., 1962. Instr. Ft. Hays (Kans.) State U., 1957-58; instr. Iowa State U., 1958-59; asst. prof. econs. Ariz. State U., 1961-62; asst. prof. Okla. State U., 1962-65, assoc. prof., 1965-70, prof., dean Coll. Bus. Adminstrn., 1977-94, dean emeritus Coll. Bus. Adminstrn., 1994—; econ. adv. Ariz. Gov.'s Tax Study Com., 1961-62; adv. Okla. Gov.'s Com. on Mental Health, 1963; bd. dirs. Reading & Bates Corp.; adviser to faculty of econs. and adminstrv. scis. United Arab Emirates U., 1994-95. Contbr. articles to profl. publs. With USN, 1947-51. Mem. So. Econ. Assn., Phi Kappa Phi, Beta Gamma Sigma. Democrat. Roman Catholic. Office: Oklahoma State U 470 Student Union Stillwater OK 74078-7064

SANDOR, GEORGE NASON, mechanical engineer, educator; b. Budapest, Hungary, Feb. 24, 1912; came to U.S., 1938, naturalized, 1949; s. Alexander S. and Maria (Adler) S.; m. Magda Breiner, Dec. 5, 1964; stepchildren: Stephen Gergely, Judith Patricia Gergely (Mrs. J. Peter Vernon). Diploma in Mech. Engring, Poly. U. Budapest, 1934; D. Eng. Sci., Columbia U., 1959; D (hon.), Budapest Technol. U., 1986. Registered profl. engr., Fla., N.J., N.Y., N.C., cert. of qualification Nat. Council Engring. Examiners. Asst. to chief engr. Hungarian Rubber Co., Budapest, 1935-36; mfg. dept. head Hungarian Rubber Co., 1936-38; design engr. Babcock Printing Press Corp., New London, Conn., 1939-44; v.p., chief engr. H.W. Faeber Corp., N.Y.C., 1944-46; chief engr. Time Inc. Graphic Arts Research Labs., Springdale, Conn., 1946-61, Huck Co., Inc., N.Y.C., 1961; assoc. prof. mech. engring. Yale, 1961-66; prof. mech. engring. Rennselaer Poly. Inst., Troy, N.Y., 1966-67; Alcoa Found. prof. mech. design, chmn. machines and structures div. Rennselaer Poly. Inst., 1967-75; rsch. prof. mech. engring. U. Fla., Gainesville, 1976-89, rsch. prof. emeritus, 1989—; dir. mech. engring. design and rotordynamics labs. U. Fla., 1979-87; instr. engring. U. Conn. Extension, New London and Norwich, 1940-44; lectr. mech. engring. Columbia U., N.Y.C., 1961-62; dir. Huck Design Corp., Huck Co., Inc., Montvale, N.J., 1964-70; cons. engr., printing equipment and automatic machinery, mech. engring. design, 1961—; cons. NSF Departmental and Instl. Devel. Program, 1970-72; cons. nat. materials adv. bd. Nat. Acad. Scis., 1974; cons. Xerox Corp., Burroughs Corp., Govt. Products div. Pratt & Whitney Aircraft Co., Time Inc., also others, 1961-92; prin. investigator, co-investigator NSF, U.S. Army Research Office and NASA sponsored research at Yale U.; dir. and co-dir. NSF, U.S. Army Research Office and NASA sponsored research at Rensselaer Poly. Inst. and; U. Fla. at Gainesville; chief U.S.A. del. to Internat. Fedn. for Theory Machines and Mechanisms, 1969-75; cons. for materials conservation through design Office Tech. Assessment, Congress U.S., 1977. Author: (with others) Mechanical Design and Systems Handbook, 1964, 2d edit., 1985, Linkage Design Handbook, 1977, Mechanism Design-Analysis and Synthesis, vol. 1, 1984, 2d edit., 1991, Advanced Mechanism Design, Analysis and Synthesis, vol. 2, 1984; mem. editorial bd. Jour. Mechanism, 1966-72, Machine and Mechanism Theory, 1972—, Robotica, 1982—; contbr. articles to profl. jours. Recipient Outstanding Achievement awrd Northctrl. sect. Fla. Engring. Soc., 1983; Fla. Blue Key Leadership award for disting. faculty mem. U. Fla., 1985; elected hon. mem. Internat. Fedn. for Theory Machines and Mechanisms, 1987, Hungarian Acad. Scis., Budapest, 1993. Fellow ASME (life, Machine Design award 1975, mechanisms com. award 1980, hon. mem. 1991); mem. NSPE, Am. Soc. Engring. Edn. (Ralph Coats Roe award 1985), N.Y. Acad. Scis., Am. Acad. Mechanics, Hungarian Acad. Scis. (hon. mem. 1993), Flying Engrs. Internat., Sigma Xi, Tau Beta Pi, Pi Tau Sigma. Achievements include patent for rotary-linear actuator for robotic manipulators, and 5 others. Home: 136 Broadview Acres Highlands NC 28741-9454 *Find out what is expected of you and try to fulfill those expectations to the best of your ability.*

SANDOR, GYORGY, pianist; b. Budapest, Hungary; came to U.S., 1938, naturalized, 1943; s. Ignac and Zsenka (Czipszer) S.; 1 child, Michael. Student, Liszt Ferenc Conservatory, Budapest, 1927-33; studied piano with, Bela Bartok; composition with, Zoltan Kodaly. Mem. piano faculty Julliard Sch., 1982—. Made concert debut, Budapest, 1931; toured, Europe, 1931-38, Am. debut Carnegie Hall, N.Y.C., 1939, touring throughout U.S., Mexico, Can., W.I., North Africa, C.Am., S.Am., Europe, Australia, Far East; rec. with N.Y. Philharm. and Phila. orchs., also solo rec. (Grand Prix du Disque for rec. entire piano repertory of Bela Bartok's works 1964); rec. entire solo piano repertory of Prokofiev, 1967, Kodály, 1973; author: On Piano Playing, 1981; world premiers include Bartok's 3d Piano Concerto, Ormandy and Phila. Orch., 1946, Dance Suite, Carnegie Hall, 1945, Concerto for Orch., piano version by Bartok, 1990, Sony Classical, Vox Candide Turnabout, Columbia Records, Trio, Phillips Records; compact discs include entire solo piano repertory by Bartok and Prokofieff.

SANDOR, RICHARD LAURENCE, financial company executive; b. N.Y.C., Sept. 7, 1941; s. Randolph Henry and Luba (Mirner) S.; m. Ellen Ruth Simon, June 27, 1963; children: Julie, Penya. B.A., CCNY, 1962; Ph.D., U. Minn., 1967. Asst. prof. applied econs. U. Calif, Berkeley, 1966-72; v.p., chief economist Chgo. Bd. Trade, 1972-75; v.p. ContiCommodity Services, Chgo., 1975-82; dir. ContiFin div. ContiCommodity Services, Chgo., 1975-82; sr. v.p. instl. fin. futures Drexel Burnham Lambert, Inc., Chgo., 1982-90; pres., CEO Indosuez Internat. Capital Markets, Chgo., 1990-93; chmn. Indosuez Carr Futures, 1990-91; chmn., CEO Ctr. Fin. Products Ltd., N.Y.C., 1993—; mem. Chgo. Bd. Trade, 1975—, bd. dirs., 1980-82, 90—; exec. mng. dir. Kidder, Peabody Inc., N.Y.C., 1991-93; pres., CEO Centre Fin. Products Ltd., 1993— ; mem. Index and Option Market, 1983—, bd. dirs. Chgo. Mercantile Exchange, 1984-85; vis. scholar Northwestern U., 1972-74; Martin C. Remer vis. Disting. prof. fin. Grad. Sch. Mgmt., 1974-75; cons. agribus. orgns., securities firms, banks, fgn. exchanges, govts., 1969—; mem. faculty NYU, 1964; mem. faculty U. Minn., 1863-67; mem. faculty Stanford U., 1969; disting. adj. prof. Grad. Sch. Bus. Columbia U., 1993; expert advisor UNCTAD; dir. First Fed. Savs. & Loan Assn. of Chgo.; guest lectr. various univs. Contbr. articles to profl. journs., chpts. of books and handbooks. Vice chmn. bd. govs. Sch. of Art Inst. of Chgo.; bd. dirs. Lincoln Park Zool. Soc., 1985—. Summer faculty fellow U. Calif.; NSF grantee. Mem. Am. Econ. Assn., Econometric Soc., Am. Fin. Assn., Am. Agrl. Econs. Assn. Club: Union League of Chgo. Home: 1301 N Astor St Chicago IL 60610-2186 Office: One Chase Manhattan Plz 42nd fl New York NY 10005

SANDOR, THOMAS, biochemist; b. Budapest, Hungary, Nov. 3, 1924; emigrated to Can., 1950; s. Miksa and Iren (Forstner) S.; m. Vera Varkonyi, July 5, 1949; 1 dau., Catherine-Susanne. Dipl. Chem., U. Budapest, 1948; Ph.D., U. Toronto, 1960. Attaché de recherche Inst. A. Fournier, Paris, 1949-50; rsch. fellow Hosp. for Sick Children, U. Toronto, Ont., 1951-56; rsch. biochemist Hotel Dieu Hosp., Montreal, Que., Can., 1956-59; sr. rsch. assoc., endocrinology lab. Hosp. Notre Dame, Montreal, 1959-93; rsch. asst. prof. medicine U. Montreal, 1961-67, rsch. assoc. prof., 1967-70, rsch. prof., 1970-92; hon. prof. McGill U., Montreal, 1969-92; career investigator Med. Research Council of Can., 1962-91; rsch. prof. emeritus Louis C. Simard Rsch. Ctr., Hosp. Notre Dame, U. Montreal, 1993—; vis. prof. zoology U. Sheffield, Eng., 1970-71, 79-80; vis. prof. biochemistry U. Buenos Aires, 1974; lectr. numerous univs., symposia, Can., U.S., U.K., France, Italy, Ger., Spain, India, Hong Kong. Corr. editor: Jour. Steroid Biochemistry, 1970-79; Mem. editorial bd.: Gen. and Comparative Endocrinology, 1974-81; Contbr. chpts. on steroid biochemistry to books, articles to profl. jours. Gouverneur à vie Hôpital Notre-Dame, Montreal. Recipient Nuffield Found. Travelling Fellowship, 1964; recipient Schering Travelling Fellowship, 1966, Science Research Council (U.K.) sr. vis. research fellowship, 1970-71, 79-80. Fellow Royal Soc. Can.; mem. can. Biochem. Soc., Endocrine Soc. (emeritus mem., Travelling Fellowship 1968), Biochem. Soc. (Gt. Britain), Soc. for Endocrinology (Gt. Britain), Am. Soc. Zoologists (emeritus mem.), European Soc. Comparative Endocrinologists (founder mem.), AAAS, Order Chemists of Que., Canadians for Health Rsch. (bd. dirs. 1976-79, 82-86). Home: 5194 W Broadway, Montreal, PQ Canada H4V 2A2 Office: Hôpital Notre Dame, CP 1560 Succ C, Montreal, PQ Canada H2L 4K8

SANDORFY, CAMILLE, chemistry educator; b. Budapest, Hungary, Dec. 9, 1920; emigrated to Can., 1951, naturalized, 1957; s. Kamill and Paula (Fenyes) S.; m. Rolande Cayla, Aug. 24, 1971. B.Sc., U. Szeged, Hungary, 1943, Ph.D., 1946; D.Sc., Sorbonne, U. Paris, 1949; PhD (hon.), U. Moncton, N.B., Can., 1986, U. Szeged, Hungary, 1988. Attache de recherches Centre National de la Recherche Scientifique, Paris, France, 1947-51; postdoctoral fellow Nat. Research Council of Can., 1951-53; asst. prof. chemistry U. Montreal, Que., Can., 1954-56; assoc. prof. U. Montreal, 1956-

59, prof., 1959—; vis. prof. U. Paris, 1968, 74, univs. in Naples, Italy, 1969, Rio de Janeiro, Brazil, 1970, 82, Lille, France, 1987. Author: Les Spectres Electroniques en Chimie Theorique, 1959, Electronic Spectra and Quantum Chemistry, 1964; (with R. Daudel) Semi-empirical Wave-Mechanical Calculations on Polyatomic Molecules, 1971. Recipient Prix Marie-Victorin Que., 1982, medal Chem. Inst. Can., 1983, Sci. prize of Que., 1964, Herzberg medal, 1980, Killam meml. scholar, 1978, Compagnon de Lavoisier (Que.), 1992, Heyrovsky gold medal Czech Acad. Sci., 1993; decorated Officer of Order of Can., 1995, Chevalier, Ordre du Quebec, 1995. Fellow Royal Soc. Can., Internat. Acad. Quantum Molecular Sci., Hungarian Acad. Sci. Rsch. over 250 publs. in chemistry. Address: 5050 Roslyn, Montreal, PQ Canada H3W 2L2

SANDOVAL, ARTURO, jazz musician; b. Havana, Cuba, Nov. 6, 1949; came to U.S., 1990; s. Arturo and Cira (Arocha) S.; m. Carmen Marianela, Oct. 17, 1975; 1 child, Arturo Jr. Prof. Fla. Internat. U.; lectr. in field; featured artist Dizzy Gillespie UN Orch., Live at Royal Festival Hall album (Grammy 1991). Performed with Cuban Orch. Modern Music; guest artist BBC Symphony, London, Leningrad Symphony; founding mem. Irakere mus. group; albums include Flight to Freedom, I Remember, Clifford (2 Grammy nominations), Dream Come True, Danzon (Dance On), Tumbaito. Recipient Grammy award for Irakere, 1980, also 4 Grammy nominees; named Cuba's Best Instrumentalist, 1982, 83, 84, Golden Feather Artist of Yr., L.A. Times, 1991. Roman Catholic. Home: 101 S Royal Poinciana Blvd Miami FL 33166-6134

SANDOVAL, ARTURO ALONZO, art educator, artist; b. Espanola/Cordova, N.Mex., Feb. 1, 1942; s. Lorenzo Sandoval and Cecilia Eulalia (Archuleta) Harrison; (div. Sept. 1982); 1 child, Avalon Valentine Galaglorial. Student, U. Portland, 1959; BA, Calif. State Coll., L.A., 1964, MA, 1969; MFA, Cranbrook Acad. Art, Bloomfield Hills, Mich., 1971. Designer, illustrator Western Lighting Corp., L.A., 1964-66; advt. designer, adult edn. instr. spl. svcs. USN, Yokosuka, Japan, 1966; interior designasst. Walter B. Broderick & Assocs., La Mesa, Calif., 1967; asst. prof. art dept. U. Ky., Lexington, 1974-76, assoc. prof., 1976-86, full prof., 1986—, dir. art dept. Barnhart Gallery, 1976—, curator, 1979—; teaching asst. Calif. State Coll., L.A., 1969, Cranbrook Acad. Art, Bloomfield Hills, 1970; fiber art demonstrator Mus. Art, Grand Rapids, Mich., 1970; batik and tie-dye demonstrator Gwynn's Fabric Shop, Birmingham, Mich., 1970; instr. Calif. State Coll., L.A., 1970, So. Ill. U., Carbondale, 1971, Edwardsville, 1971, 72; presenter various lectures and workshops throughout the U.S., 1973—; juror Mo.Women Festival Arts, St. Louis, So. Ill. U., East St. Louis, 1974, Paramount Arts Assn., Ashland, Ky., 1975, Ind. Weavers Guild, Indpls., 1979, Fed. Corrections Inst., Lexington, 1979, Hawaii Craftsman Hui and Art Dept. U. Hawaii, Manoa, Honolulu, 1982, art dept. Va. Intermont Coll., Bristol, 1982, Arrowmont Sch. Arts and Crafts, Gatlinburg, Tenn., 1984, Ctr. Contemporary Art, U. Ky., Lexington, 1984, Guild Greater Cin.,Carnegie Art Ctr., Covington, Ky., 1989, S.C. Arts Commn., Charleston, 1990, Adams Art Gallery, Dunkirk, N.Y., 1994; visual arts cons. Ky. Arts Commn., Frankfort, 1977; curator Visual Arts Ctr. Alaska, Anchorage, 1982, Ky. Art and Crafts Found., Inc., Louisville, 1985; mem. artist adv. panel Ky. Art and Crafts Found., Louisville, 1986, 87, 92, 93, 94; visual arts cons. Arts Midwest, 1987; artistic advisor Ky. Guild Mktg. Bd., Lexington, 1988, 91, 92, 93; bd. mem. Ky. Guild Mktg. Bd., 1992; vis. artist/critic Allen R. Hite Inst., U. Louisville, 1992; vis. artist Coll. Human Environ. Scis., U. Ky., Lexington, 1993; vis. artist/ lectr. fiber dept. Cranbrook Acad. Art, Bloomfield Hills, Mich., 1994. Exhibited in group shows at Yeiser Art Ctr., Paducah/Paramount Arts Ctr., Ashland/S.E. Cmty. Coll., Cumberland, 1994, Textile Arts Centre, Chgo., 1994, Winnipeg (Man., Can.) Art Gallery, 1994, Riffe Gallery, Ohio Arts Coun., Columbus, 1994, Royal Hiberian Acad., Gallagher Gallery, Dublin, Ireland, Cooper Gallery, Barnsley, South Yorks, Gt. Britain, Shipley Art Gallery,Gateshead, Gt. Britain, 1994, Grand Rapids (Mich.) Art Mus., 1994, Whatcom Mus. History and Art, Bellingham, Wash., The Rockwell Mus., Corning, N.Y., Mus. Art, Washington State U., Pullman,The Hyde Collection, Glen Falls, N.Y., 1994, U. Art Galleries, U. S.D., Vermillion, 1994, Barnhart Gallery, U. Ky., Lexington, 1994, Sawtooth Ctr. Visual Art, 1994, Santa Fe Gallery, Santa Fe Cmty. Coll., Gainesville, Fla., 1994, Liberty Gallery, Louisville, 1994, Asahi Shimbun Gallery, Tokyo, Takashimaya Gallery, Osaka, 1994, Minn. Mus. Art, Landmark Ctr., St. Paul, 1994, S.C. State Mus., Columbia, 1994, Galbreath Gallery, Lexington, 1994, others; represented in permanent collections at Wabash Coll., Crawfordsville, Ind., Greenville County Mus. Art, Greenville, S.C., Mus. Modern Art, N.Y.C., St. Mary's Coll., Notre Dame, Ind., Coll. St. Rose, Albany, N.Y., Bowling Green (Ohio) StateU., U. Notre Dame, Transylvania U., Lexington, U. Ky. Mus. Art, Lexington, Mid-Am. Rare Coin Auction Galleris, Lexington, Henry Luce Found., N.Y.C., Lexington Ctrl. Libr., others. Recipient Alexandra Korsakoff Galston Meml. prize St. Louis Artist's Guild, 1971, Mus. Merit award Mus. Arts and Scis., Evansville, 1972, Creative Rsch. Grant So. Ill. U.-Edwardsville Rsch. Found., 1972, Craftsman fellowship Nat. Endowment for Arts, Washington, 1973, Friend of Mus. award Mus. Arts and Scis., Evansville, 1973, Clay Eugene Jordan ann. beq prize for crafts St. Louis Artist's Guild, 1973, Teaching Improvement grant U. Ky. Rsch. Found., 1974, Travel grant U. Ky. Rsch. Found., 1977, Judges Choice award Berea (Ky.) Coll., 1978, Handweaver's Guild Am. award, 1978, Fiber award LeMoyne Art Found., Tallahassee, 1981, Elise Strout Merit award Mus. Arts and Scis., Evansville, 1981, Handweavers Guild Am. award, 1983, Martha Ryan Merit award Mus. Arts and Scis., Evansville, 1984, Best of Show award Gayle Willson Galleries, Southampton, 1984, Juror's merit award Brenau Coll., Gainesville, Ga., 1985, Installation Grant Ind. Arts Commn., Ft. Wayne, 1985, All Smith fellowship Ky. Arts Coun., Frankfort, 1987, Merit award Renwick Gallery, Tuscaloosa, Ala., 1988, Merit award Mus. Arts and Scis., Evansville, 1989, Design Grant, Arts and Cultural Coun. for O.A. Singletary Ctr. for Arts, Lexington, 1990, Visual Arts fellowship Nat. Endowment for Arts, Washington, 1992, Hon. award Ky. Crafts Mktg. Bd., Frankfort, 1994. Mem. Lexington Fiber Guild Inc., Louisville Visual Arts Assn., Ky. Art and Craft Found., Inc., Ky. Guild Artists and Craftsmen, Am. Craft Coun. Home: PO Box 237 Lexington KY 40584 Office: U Ky Dept Art 207 Fine Arts Bldg Lexington KY 40506

SANDOVAL, MONA LISA, daycare provider, educator; b. Wilmington, Calif., Aug. 2, 1965; d. Alfred Rudy and Lita Candelaria (Machado) S. AA, Trinidad State Jr. Coll., 1992, 1993. Tchr. asst. Trinidad (Colo.) State Jr. Coll., 1992-93; infant/toddler tchr. Alta Vista Preschool, Trinidad, 1993; preschool tchr. Headstart, Trinidad, 1994—; mem. Child Daycare Task Force, Trinidad, 1992-93; participant Workshop in Early Child Devel., Trinidad, 1993. Editor: (newspaper) Trojan Tribune, 1993, cartoonist, 1992-93. Rep. State Supervisory Adv., Denver, 1993, State Bd. for C.C.s, Denver, 1992-93. Recipient scholarship in edn., Delta Kappa Gamma, 1991, sign lang. tng., Amy Martin, Trinidad State, 1994. Mem. ASCD, Colo. Assn. for Edn. Young Children. Democrat. Roman Catholic. Avocations: sign language, spl. edn., children's book writer. Office: Headstart 415 S Indiana Ave Trinidad CO 81082-3126

SANDOVAL IÑIGUEZ, JUAN CARDINAL, archbishop; b. Yahualica, Mar. 28, 1933. Archbishop of Guadalajara Mexico; created and proclaimed cardinal, 1994. Office: Arzobispado Guadalajara, Arzobispado Liceo 17 Apdo 1-331, 44100 Guadalajara Jal, Mexico

SANDOZ, WILLIAM CHARLES, lawyer; b. Opelousas, La., Aug. 23, 1928; s. Lawrence Broussard and Cecelia (Boagni) S.; m. Jane Simmons, Apr. 29, 1950; children: Yvonne Marie, William Simmons, Charles Jeffrey. Student, La. State U., 1945-47, U. Southwestern La., 1945-47; JD, La. State U., 1950. Bar: La. 1950, U.S. Dist. Ct. (we. dist.) 1950, U.S. Dist. Ct. (ea. dist.) La. 1972, U.S. Dist. ct. (mid. dist.) La. 1972, U.S. Ct. Appeals (5th cir.) 1963. Pvt. practice Opelousas, 1950-54, 83-87; ptnr. Sandoz & Sandoz, Opelousas, 1954-60, Sandoz, Sandoz & Schiff, Opelousas, 1960-83, Law Offices William C. Sandoz and W. Simmons Sandoz, Opelousas, 1983—; also Alexandria, Baton Rouge, Houma, Lafayette, Lake Charles, Monroe, New Orleans, and Shreveport; bd. dirs. Church Point (La.) Bank & Trust Co.; lectr. profl. assns. Mem. La. Law Rev., 1948. Named to Hall of Fame, La. State U. Law Sch., 1987. Mem. ABA, La. Bar Assn., St. Landry Parish Bar Assn., Assn. Trial Lawyers Am., La. Trial Lawyers Assn., Nat. Assn. Bankruptcy Trustees, Am. Bankruptcy Inst., Comml. Law League Am., KC (rec. sec. Opelousas 1950-52) Elks, Order of Colf, Delta Kappa Epsilon, Phi Delta Phi. Republican. Roman Catholic. Office: Sandoz & Sandoz 435 S Union St Opelousas LA 70570-6119

SANDQUIST, ELROY CHARLES, JR., lawyer; b. Chgo., Dec. 18, 1922; s. Elroy Carl and Lillian (Peterson) S.; m. Sally Patricia Dunham, Mar. 15, 1945; children: Deirdre, Elroy Charles III, Peter, Ellen. BS, U.S. Naval Acad., 1943; JD, Northwestern U., 1950. Bar: Ill. 1950. Assoc. Peterson, Ross, Schloerb & Seidel, Chgo., 1950-57, ptnr., 1960—; asst. state's atty. County of Cook, Ill., 1957-60; mem. Ho. of Reps. State of Ill., Springfield, 1977-83; legis. coord. County of Cook, 1983-91. Pres. Child Svc., Park Ridge, Ill., 1985-88. Lt. USN, 1943-46. Mem. City Club Chgo. (pres. 1966-68). Republican. Methodist. Home: 353 W Belden Ave Chicago IL 60614-3817 Office: Peterson Ross Schloerb 200 E Randolph Dr # 7300 Chicago IL 60601-6401

SANDQUIST, GARY MARLIN, engineering educator, researcher, consultant, author; b. Salt Lake City, Apr. 19, 1936; s. Donald August Sandquist and Lillian (Evaline) Dunn; m. Kristine Powell, Jan. 17, 1992; children from previous marriage: Titia, Julia, Taunia, Cynthia, Carl; stepchildren: David, Michael, Scott, Diane, Jeff. BSME, U. Utah, 1960, PhD in Mech. Engring., 1964, MBA, 1995; MS in Engring. Sci., U. Calif., Berkeley, 1961; postdoctoral fellow MIT, 1969-70. Registered profl. engr., Utah, N.Y., Minn., Calif.; cert. health physicist, cert. quality auditor. Staff mem. Los Alamos (N.Mex.) Sci. Lab., 1966; rsch. prof. surgery Med. Sch., U. Utah, Salt Lake City, 1974—, prof., dir. nuc. engring., mech. engring. dept., 1975—, acting chmn. dept., 1984-85; expert in nuclear sci. Internat. Atomic Energy Agy., UN, 1980—; chief sci. Rogers and Assocs. Engring. Corp., Salt Lake City, 1980—; vis. sci. MIT, Cambridge, Mass., 1960-70; advisor rocket design Hercules, Inc., Bachus, Utah, 1962; sr. nuc. engr. Idaho Nat. Engring. Lab., Idaho Falls, Idaho, 1963-65; cons. various cos.; cons. nuclear sci. State of Utah, 1982—. Author: Geothermal Energy, 1973; Introduction to System Science, 1985. Comdr. USNR, 1954-56, Korea. Recipient Glen Murphy award in nuclear engring. Am. Soc. Engring. Edn., 1984. Fellow ASME, Am. Nuclear Soc.; mem. Am. Soc. Quality Control (sr.), Am. Health Physics Soc., Alpha Nu Sigma of Am. Nuclear Soc., Sigma Xi, Tau Beta Pi, Pi Tau Sigma. Republican. Mormon. Home: 2564 Neffs Cir Salt Lake City UT 84109-4055 Office: U Utah 1206 Merrill Engring Bldg Salt Lake City UT 84112

SANDRICH, JAY H., television director; b. L.A., Feb. 24, 1932; s. Mark R. and Freda (Wirtschafter) S.; m. Nina Kramer, Feb. 11, 1952 (div.); children: Eric, Tony, Wendy; m. Linda Green Silverstein, Oct. 4, 1984. BA, UCLA, 1953. Producer (TV show) Get Smart, 1965; dir. (TV shows) He and She, 1967, Mary Tyler Moore Show, 1970-88, Soap, 1977-79, Cosby Show, 1984-92; dir. (films) Seems Like Old Times, 1980, For Richer, For Poorer (HBO), 1992, Neil Simon's London Suite, 1996. Served to 1st lt. Signal Corps U.S. Army, 1952-55. Mem. Dirs. Guild Am. (award 1975, 85, 86), TV Acad. Arts and Scis. (Emmy award 1971, 73, 85, 86).

SANDRIDGE, WILLIAM PENDLETON, JR., lawyer; b. Winston-Salem, N.C., Jan. 27, 1934; s. William Pendleton and Kathryn (Mosby) S.; m. Jane Carolyn Yeager, Dec. 10, 1966; children: Jane, William. AB, U. N.C., 1956; LLB, U. Va., 1961. Bar: N.C. 1961. Ptnr. Womble Carlyle Sandridge & Rice, Winston-Salem, 1962—. Chmn., bd. dirs. Horizons Residential Care Ctr., 1980, Food Bank N.W. N.C., Inc., 1988-89, Data Max Corp., 1996. Mem. ABA. Office: Womble Carlyle Sandridge & Rice PO Box 84 1600 One Triad Pk Winston Salem NC 27102

SANDROK, RICHARD WILLIAM, lawyer; b. Evergreen Park, Ill., July 8, 1943; s. Edward George and Gertrude Jeanette (Van Stright) S.; m. Rebecca Fitzz, June 9, 1973; children: Richard William Jr., Alexander Edward, Philip Robert, Erika Joy. BA, Wheaton (Ill.) Coll., 1965; JD, U. Ill., 1968. Bar: Ill. 1968, U.S. Dist. Ct. (no. dist.) Ill. 1971. Assoc. Hinshaw Culbertson Moelmann Hoban & Fuller, Chgo. and Wheaton, 1971-75; ptnr. Hinshaw Culbertson Moelmann Hoban & Fuller, Wheaton, 1976-89, Lisle, Ill., 1989—. Reviewer: Legal Checklists. Capt. U.S. Army, 1969-71. Mem. ABA, Ill. Bar Assn., Chgo. Bar Assn., Am. Arbitration Assn. (arbitrator), DuPage County Bar Assn. (chmn. med./legal com. 1978-79), Assn. Def. Trial Attys., Def. Rsch. Inst. Home: 818 Revere Rd Glen Ellyn IL 60137-5537 Office: Hinshaw & Culbertson 4343 Commerce Ct Ste 415 Lisle IL 60532-3617

SANDS, AMY CATHERINE, nursing administrator, educator; b. Rochester, Minn., Mar. 16, 1968; d. Byron James and Lorraine Ann (Volmer) Reha; m. Todd Michael Sands, June 22, 1991; children: Jessica, Emily. BA in Nursing, Luther Coll., 1990. RN, Minn. Pediatric nurse, RN United Med. Ctr., Moline, Ill., 1990-92; pediatric home care RN Kimberly Quality Care, Moline, 1990-92; asst. DON Samaritan Bethany Home Health Svcs., Rochester, 1992—; program coord. 25 Hour Home Health Aide Tng. Program, 1995—; home health aide instr. Riverland Tech. Coll., Rochester, 1992—, alt. adv. bd., 1993—, cert. nursing asst., home health aide state examiner, 1994—; asst. dir. tng., program coord., cons. Samaritan Bethany Home Health Svcs., 1994—; program coord. home health aide-nurse asst. tng. program Minn. Home Care Agy. Program, 1994—; instr., coord. care giver classes to Rochester Cmty. Fellowship vol. Zumbro Luth. Ch., Rochester, 1993—. Recipient Small Bus. award Rochester C. of C., 1994. Mem. Minn. Home Care Assn. Avocations: crafts, hiking, traveling, movies. Home: 1401 48th St NW Rochester MN 55901-0490

SANDS, DONALD EDGAR, chemistry educator; b. Leominster, Mass., Feb. 25, 1929; s. George and Emily (Parker) S.; m. Elizabeth Stoll, July 28, 1956; children: Carolyn Looff, Stephen Robert. BS in Chemistry, Worcester Poly. Inst., 1951; PhD in Phys. Chemistry, Cornell U., 1955. Sr. chemist Lawrence Livermore (Calif.) Lab., 1956-62; asst. prof. chemistry U. Ky., Lexington, 1962-65, assoc. prof., 1965-68, prof., 1968—, dir. gen. chemistry, 1974-75, assoc. dean arts and scis., 1975-81, acting dean, 1978, 80-81, assoc. v.p., 1981-82, assoc. vice chancellor, 1982-84, vice chancellor acad. affairs, 1984-89; sect. head sci. and engring. edn. dept. NSF, 1989-91; mem. staff dept. chemistry U. Ky., Lexington, 1991—, chmn. dept. chem., 1993—. Author: Introduction to Crystallography, 1969, Vectors and Tensors in Crystallography, 1982. Mem. Am. Chem. Soc. (chmn. Lexington 1972), Am. Crystallographic Assn., AAAS, N.Y. Acad. Scis., Sigma Xi (chmn. Lexington 1975), Omicron Delta Kappa. Democrat. Avocations: reading, hiking, music, art. Home: 335 Cassidy Ave Lexington KY 40502-2559 Office: U Ky Dept Chemistry Lexington KY 40506

SANDS, EDITH SYLVIA ABELOFF (MRS. ABRAHAM M. SANDS), finance educator, author; b. Bklyn.; d. Louis and Jennie (Goldstein) Abeloff; m. Abraham M. Sands, June 5, 1932; children: Stephanie Lou Sands Fersko, John Eliot. B.A., Adelphi Coll., 1932; M.B.A., Baruch Sch. Bus. Adminstrn., CCNY, 1956; Ph.D., NYU, 1961; cert. fin. planner, Adelphi U., 1985. Asst. prof. L.I. U., Bklyn., 1961-65, assoc. prof., 1965-69, prof., 1969-81, prof. fin. emeritus, 1981—, chmn. dept. finance, 1962-72; prof. fin., cons. Touro Coll., N.Y.C., 1981—, chmn. dept. fin.; participant in person-to-person citizen ambassador program, China, 1987. Author: How to Select Executive Personnel, 1963; contbr. articles to profl. jours.; editor jour. industry studies for investment decisions. Corr. sec. Welfare Council Bklyn. Cancer Com., 1956-58; mem. council Friends of Adelphi Coll. Library, 1955-60; pres. Foster Care Aux., 1959-61; bd. dirs. Nat. Council Jewish Women, 1935-38; mem. community com. Bklyn. Mus., 1950-52; mem. women's aux. Prospect Heights Hosp., 1954-56, Bklyn. Eye and Ear Hosp., 1950-53; mem. asso. bd. Jewish Child Care Assn., 1959-61; chmn. bd. dirs. Friends Bklyn. Center Libraries, L.I. U. Recipient Alumni Achievement award Baruch Alumni Assn., CCNY, 1969; L.I. U. Alumni Assn. award of appreciation, 1978. Mem. AAUW, AAUP, Nat. Assn. Pers. Fin. Advs., Am. Econ. Assn., Met. Econ. Assn., Fedn. Woman Shareholders (exec. com.), Econ. History Assn., Am. Fin. Assn., Acad. Mgmt., Assn. Investment Mgmt. and Rsch., Soc. Advancement Mgmt., Am. Mgmt. Assn., N.Y. Soc. Security Analysts (Vol. of Yr. award 1990-91), Am. Statis. Assn., Fin. Mgmt. Assn., met. Econs. Assn., Inst. Cert. Fin. Planners, Internat. Assn. for fin. Planning (registered/lic. fin. planner, registered investment adviser), Acad. Fin. Svcs., City Coll. Alumni Assn., NYU Grad. Sch. Bus. Adminstrn. Alumni Assn. (dir. 1968-85, treas. 1975-77), Adelphi Coll. Alumnae Assn. (chpt. pres. 1957-59), Nat. N.Y. assns. bus. economists, Prospect Park Alliance, Park-slope Civic Coun., Money Marketeers NYU (dir. 1973-75), Women's City Club, City Coll. Club, The Exec. Forum of NYU (v.p. 1973-75), Money Marketeers, Exec. Forum, NYU Club, Princeton in N.Y. (guest mem.), Beta Gamma Sigma Alumni N.Y. (pres. 1967-70), Beta Gamma Sigma (nat. exec. com. 1972-76), Phi Sigma Sigma (chpt. archon 1931-32). Home: 874 Carroll St Brooklyn NY 11215-1702

SANDS, I. JAY, corporate executive, business, marketing and real estate consultant, lecturer, realtor, analyst; b. N.Y.C.. B.A., NYU; J.D., Columbia U. Bar: N.Y., U.S. Supreme Ct. Mng. partner Korvette Bldg. Assocs., N.Y.C.; mng. dir., founder, chmn. bd. dirs., sec. First Republic Corp. Am.; chief exec. officer, sec. First Republic Corp., N.Y.; gen. partner Velvex Mid-City Parking Center, N.Y.C., Manhattan Parking Assocs.; dir., chmn. First Republic Underwriters, Inc.; pres., dir. Waltham Mgmt. Inc., Mass.; partner Cypress Parking Assocs., Cypress Plaza Shopping, Pompano Beach, Fla.; partner Sheraton Hotel Randolph House Co., Syracuse, N.Y.; partner Beau Rivage Hotel Co., Bal Harbour, Fla., Gulf Assocs., Fla., Sahara Motel Assocs., Miami Beach, Fla.; chmn. Waltham (Mass.) Engring. & Research Co.; gen. partner Allstate Ins. Bldg. Co., N.Y.C., Fairfax Bldg. Assocs., Kansas City, Mo., Engring. Bldg. Assocs., Chgo., Manhattan Parking Co., Williamsbridge Assocs., N.Y.C., First Republic Funding Life Ins. Agy., N.Y.C.; gen. partner Chateau Motel Atlantic Co., Miami Beach; gen. partner Syracuse-Randolph House Hotel, N.Y.C., Marchwood Realty Co., Phila., Video Film Center Assocs., N.Y.C., Hempstead Real Estate Enterprises, N.Y.C., Imperial Sq. Assocs., N.Y.C., DeMille Theatre Co., N.Y.C., Ohio Indsl. Assocs., Cleve., Pelham Park Assocs., Phila., Peoria (Ill.) Parking Assocs.; chmn., dir. Triple P Parking Corp., Peoria, Ill., Square Mgmt. Corp., N.Y.C., Park Circle Apts., Inc., N.Y.C., Holme Circle Apts., Inc., Phila.; pres., dir., sec. F.S. Mgmt. Corp., N.Y.C.; founder, chmn. exec. com., sec., dir. Imperial Sq. Mgmt. Corp., Hempstead, N.Y.; chmn. bd., chmn. exec. com., sec., dir. Nat. Med. Industries, Inc., Health Insts. Leasing Corp., Am. Med. Computer Corp.; pres. Med. Contract Supply Corp., City Capital Corp., N.J., Claredon Co., N.Y.C.; vis. lectr., instr. entrepreneurship, real estate, comml. mktg. NYU, New Sch. for Social Research, U. Fla.; gen. agt. Northeastern Life Ins. Co., Patriot Life Ins. Co., Citizens Life Ins. Co.; expert witness in corp. and securities litigations. Past trustee Baldwin Sch., N.Y.C.; hon. trustee Pres. Harry S. Truman Libr. Served with AUS. Harlan Fiske Stone fellow Columbia U., 1975; named Man of Yr., Real Estate Weekly. Mem. Nat. Real Estate Club, N.Y. Real Estate Bd., Columbia U. Law Sch. Alumni Assn. (class chmn. 1978). Clubs: Shriners, Masons (32 deg.).

SANDS, MARVIN, wine company executive; b. Cleve., Jan. 28, 1924; s. Mack E. and Sally (Kipnis) S.; m. Marilyn Alpert, May 30, 1947; children: Laurie, Richard, Robert. BSBA, U. N.C., 1946. Chmn., dir. Canandaigua Wine Co., Inc., N.Y., 1945—; pres., dir. Tenner Bros., Inc., Patrick N.C., 1965—, Roberts Trading Corp., Canandaigua, 1959—; v.p., dir. Bisceglia Bros. Wine Co., Madera, Calif., 1975—. Pres. F.F. Thompson Health System, Inc., 1990—; past pres., dir. F.F. Thompson Hosp., Canandaigua, 1970—, Finger Lakes Area Hosp. Corp., Geneva, N.Y., 1980—; trustee YMCA, Canandaigua. Served with USN, 1943-46. Mem. Nat. Wine Assn. (treas., dir.), N.Y. State Finger Lakes Wine Growers Assn. (past pres., bd. dirs. 1979—), Assn. Am. Vintners (bd. dirs.). Office: Canandaigua Wine Co Inc 116 Buffalo St Canandaigua NY 14424-1012

SANDS, MATTHEW LINZEE, physicist, educator; b. Oxford, Mass., Oct. 20, 1919; m. Freya Kidner, 1978; children: Michael, Richard, Michelle. B.A., Clark U., 1940; M.A., Rice Inst., 1941; Ph.D., MIT, 1948. Physicist U.S. Naval Ordnance Lab., 1941-43, Los Alamos Sci. Lab., 1943-46; research asso., then asst. prof. physics Mass. Inst. Tech., 1946-50; sr. research fellow, asso. prof., prof. physics Calif. Inst. Tech., 1950-63; prof., dep. dir. Linear Accelerator Center, Stanford, 1963-69; prof. physics U. Calif.-Santa Cruz, 1969-85, prof. emeritus, 1985—, fellow Kresge Coll.; vice chancellor for sci., 1969-72; pres. Sands-Kidner Assocs., Inc., 1986-90; vis. prof. U. Paris-Sud, spring 1976; mem. Commn. Coll. Physics, 1960-66, chmn., 1964-66; cons. Office Sci. and Tech., ACDA, Inst. Def. Analyses, 1962-67; mem. Pugwash Conf. Sci. and World Affairs, 1960-63; cons. on accelerator physics, 1975-93. Author: (with W.C. Elmore) Electronics-Experimental Techniques, 1948, (with R.P. Feynman and R.B. Leighton) The Feynman Lectures on Physics, 3 vols, 1965, (with others) Physical Science Today, 1973; also articles.; Mem. editorial bd.: Il Nuovo Cimento, 1972-85. Fulbright scholar Italy, 1952-53. Fellow Am. Phys. Soc.; mem. Am. Assn. Physics Tchrs. (Disting. Service award 1972), Fedn. Am. Scientists, AAAS. Spl. research electronic instrumentation for nuclear physics, cosmic rays, accelerators, high-energy physics, sci. edn., sci. and public affairs, electron storage rings. Office: 160 Michael Ln Santa Cruz CA 95060-1704

SANDS, MIRIAM LINDA, special education educator; b. Claxton, Ga., June 12, 1954; d. Luther and Juanita (Clark) Morris; m. Carson Sands Jr., Mar. 27, 1971; children: Sallie, Charles, Sarah. BS in Edn. magna cum laude, Ga. So. U., 1994. Cert. tchr., Ga. Tchr. Meth. Ch., Claxton, 1978-83, Presch. Intervention Program, Collins, Ga., 1989-94; spl. edn. tchr. Claxton Elem. Sch., 1994—. Fellow Coun. for Exceptional Children, Ga. Assn. Educators, Phi Kappa Phi. Republican. Baptist. Avocation: writing short stories. Home: PO Box 26 Daisy GA 30423-0026

SANDS, RICHARD E., food products executive; b. Canandaigua, N.Y., Mar. 3, 1951; s. Marvin Sands and Marilyn Alpert; m. Sharon Gillick, Apr. 1991. BA in Psychology, U. Vt.; postgrad., U. Calif.; M, PhD, U. N.C. Teaching rsch. asst. psychology dept. U. N.C., Chapel Hill, 1974-79; exec. trainee Canandaigua Wine Co. Inc., 1979-82, exec. v.p., 1982-86, pres., chief oper. officer, 1986—; now CEO Canadaigua Wine Co. Inc., 1993—. Office: Canandaigua Wine Co Inc 116 Buffalo St Canandaigua NY 14424-1012*

SANDS, ROBERTA ALYSE, real estate investor; b. N.Y.C., Oct. 7, 1937; d. Harry and Irene (Mytelka) S. BEd, U. Miami, 1960; postgrad., U. Oslo, 1960. Cert. secondary educator biology, Mass. Phys. edn. instr. Key Biscayne and Ludlam Elem. Sch., Miami, 1961-63; sci. tchr. Plantation (Fla.) Mid. Sch., 1969-71, Rickards Middle Sch., Ft. Lauderdale, Fla., 1972-76; founder U. Miami Diabetes Rsch. Inst., 1989. Author: Biology on the Secondary Level, 1970. Vol. Douglas Garden Retirement Home, Miami, 1988-92, Mus. of Art, Ft. Lauderdale, 1988-92, Imperial Point Hosp., Ft. Lauderdale, 1981-83. Mem. AAUW (rec. sec. 1988-92, cultural chair 1993-94, legis. chair Ft. Lauderdale br. 1994-95, women's issue chair Ft. Lauderdale br. 1995, Recognition of Significant Svc. award 1983). Avocations: oil painting, golf, embroidery, travel. Home: 4250 Galt Ocean Dr Fort Lauderdale FL 33308-6138

SANDS, SHARON LOUISE, graphic design executive, art publisher, artist; b. Jacksonville, Fla., July 4, 1944; d. Clifford Harding Sands and Ruby May (Ray) MacDonald; m. Jonathan Michael Langford, Feb. 14, 1988. BFA, Cen. Washington U., 1968; postgrad, UCLA, 1968. Art dir. East West Network, Inc., L.A., 1973-78, Daisy Pub., L.A., 1978; prodn. dir. L.A. mag., 1979-80; owner, creative dir. Carmel Graphic Design, Carmel Valley, Calif., 1981-85; creative dir., v.p. The Video Sch. House, Monterey, Calif., 1985-88; graphic designer ConAgra, ConAgra, Nebr., 1988; owner, creative dir. Esprit de Fleurs, Ltd., Carmel, Calif., 1988—; lectr. Pub. Expo, L.A., 1979, panelist Women in Mgmt., L.A., 1979; redesign of local newspaper, Carmel, Calif., 1982. Contbr. articles to profl. mags. Designer corp. ID for Carmel Valley C. of C., 1981, 90, redesign local newspaper, Carmel, Calif., 1982. Recipient 7 design awards Soc. Pub. Designers, 1977, 78, Maggie award, L.A., 1977, 5 design awards The Ad Club of Monterey Peninsula, 1983, 85, 87, Design awards Print Mag. N.Y., 1986, Desi awards, N.Y., 1986, 88. Mem. NAFE, Soc. for Prevention of Cruelty to Animals, Greenpeace. Democrat. Avocations: publishing art, oil painting, cactus growing, interior decorating. Home and Office: 15489 Via La Gitana Carmel Valley CA 93924-9669

SANDS, WILLIE LOUIS, federal judge; b. 1949. BA, Mercer U., 1971, JD, 1974. Chief legal asst. to dist. atty. Macon Jud. Cir., 1974, asst. dist. atty., 1975-78; asst. U.S. atty. U.S. Dist. Ct. (mid. dist.) Ga., 1978-87; with Mathis, Sands, Jordan & Adams, Macon, 1987-91; judge superior ct. Macon Jud. Cir., 1991-93; dist. judge U.S. Dist. Ct. (mid. dist.) Ga., Albany, 1994—; ptnr. Investors Ltd., 1984-91; mem. task force substance abuse Ga. Supreme Ct., 1991—, mem. com. gender equality, 1993—; bd. dirs. Bank Corp. Ga./1st South Bank, N.A. Organist/min. music, officer Steward Chapel AME Ch., 1976—; active Cmty. Found. Ga., Inc.; mem. 30th anniversary planning com. Mercer U., mem. bd. visitors Walter F. George sch. law, 1994—; v.p. Ga. Commn. Family Violence, 1992—; bd. dirs. Macon Symphony, 1992—. 2d lt. Signal Corps, U.S. Army, 1971, res. Acad. scholar Mercer U.; grad. Leadership Macon, 1985, Leadership Ga., 1986.

Mem. ABA, Am. Judicature Soc., State Bar Ga. (mem. bench and bar com. 1991—), Macon Bar Assn. (pres. 1991-92), Coun. Superior Ct. Judges (mem. bench and bar com. 1991—), Walter F. George Sch. Law Alumni Assn. (bd. dirs.), Scabbard and Blade Mil. Honor Soc., Alpha Phi Alpha, Sigma Pi Phi, Homosophian Club. Office: 11th Circuit Court PO Box 1705 Albany GA 31702-1705

SANDSON, JOHN I., physician, educator, retired university dean; b. Jeannette, Pa., Sept. 20, 1927; s. Abraham and Dora (Whitman) S.; m. Hannah E. Ney, June 17, 1957; children: Jennifer, Thomas. BS, St. Vincent Coll., Latrobe, Pa., 1949; MD, Washington U., St. Louis, 1953. Diplomate Am. Bd. Internal Medicine. Resident in internal medicine Columbia-Presbyn. Med. Ctr., N.Y.C., 1953-56; chief resident Bronx (N.Y.) Mcpl. Hosp. Ctr., 1956-57; from instr. to prof. medicine Albert Einstein Coll. Medicine, Bronx, 1957-74, from asst. to assoc. dean, 1969-74; med. dir. Hosp. Albert Einstein Coll. Medicine, Bronx, 1969-74; prof. medicine Boston U., 1974—, dean Sch. Medicine, 1974-88, dean emeritus, 1988—; mem. Mass. Health Coordinating Com., Boston, 1984-87. Mem. pub. com. New Eng. Jour. Medicine, 1977-89, advisor, 1990—. Trustee Univ. Hosp., Boston, 1974-88, Louis E. Wolfson Found., Boston, 1984—, Whitaker Health Sci. Fund, Cambridge, Mass., 1977-91; pres. Mass. chpt. Arthritis Found., 1990-91, chmn., 1991-93. Served with U.S. Army, 1946-47. Recipient Doris Carr award Health Planning Council, 1981, Maimonides award Anti-Defamation League, 1986, Mayor's award for Disting. Svc. to Boston City Hosp., 1991. Fellow Am. Rheumatism Assn. (founding); mem. AMA, AAAS (study group project on liberal edn. in sci. 1987-90), Am. Soc. for Clin. Investigation, Assn. Am. Physicians, Mass. Med. Soc., Mass. Soc. Med. Rsch. (pres. Waltham 1987-91, chmn.-elect 1991, chmn. 1993—), Alzheimer's Disease and Related Diseases Assn. (bd. dirs. 1989-91), Alpha Omega Alpha, Saint Botolph Club (Boston). Avocation: gardening. Office: Boston U Sch of Medicine Office of the Dean Emeritus 80 E Concord St Boston MA 02118-2307

SANDSTEAD, HAROLD HILTON, medical educator; b. Omaha, May 25, 1932; s. Harold Russel and Lula Florence (Hilton) S.; m. Kathryn Gordon Brownlee, June 6, 1959 (dec. May 13, 1989); m. Victoria Regan Liddle, Feb. 14, 1990 (div. Oct. 1993); children: Eleanor McDonald, James Brownlee, William Harold. BA, Ohio Wesleyan U., 1954; MD, Vanderbilt U., 1958. Diplomate Am. Bd. Internal Medicine, Am. Bd. Nutrition. Intern, asst. resident in internal medicine Barnes Hosp. Washington U., St. Louis, 1958-60; asst. resident in pathology Vanderbilt Hosp., Nashville, 1960-61; asst. surgeon USPHS U.S. NAMRU 3, Cairo, Egypt, 1961-63; asst. resident in internal medicine Thayer VA Hosp. Vanderbilt, Nashville, 1963-64; chief resident in internal medicine Vanderbilt Hosp., Nashville, 1964-65; instr. internal medicine, asst. prof. biochemistry Med. Sch. Vanderbilt U., Nashville, 1965-70, asst. prof. internal medicine, assoc. prof. nutrition, 1970-71; dir. USDA-ARS Human Nutrition Rsch. Ctr., Grand Forks, N.D., 1971-84; adj. prof. biochemistry and internal medicine Sch. Medicine U. N.D., Grand Forks, 1971-84; dir. USDA-ARS Human Nutrition Rsch. Ctr. on Aging, Boston, 1984-85; prof. nutrition Tufts U., Medford, Mass., 1984-85; prof. preventive medicine and community health U. Tex. Med. Br., Galveston, 1985—; chmn. preventive medicine and community health Med. Br. U. Tex., Galveston, 1985-90, prof. internal medicine, human biol. chemistry & genetics, 1986—; cons. NAS, NRC, NIH, WHO, USDA; Joseph Goldberger vis. prof. AMA, 1976, Ellen Swallow Richards Meml. lectr., 1984; W.O. Atwater lectr. USDA, 1984; Sam E. and Mary F. Roberts lectr., 1985, Raymond Ewell Meml. lectr., 1985; Welcome prof. in basic sci. Fedn. Am. Socs. Exptl. Biology, 1988. Contbr. articles to profl. jours. Recipient Future Leader award Nutrition Found., 1968-70, Hull Gold medal AMA, 1970. Fellow ACP; mem. Am. Inst. Nutrition (Mead Johson award 1972), Cen. Soc. Clin. Rsch., Am. Soc. Clin. Nutrition (various office including pres.), So. Soc. Clin. Investigation, Alpha Omega Alpha. Avocations: gardening, fishing, reading. Office: U Tex Med Br Ewing Bldg K09 Galveston TX 77555-1109

SANDSTROM, DALE VERNON, state supreme court judge; b. Grand Forks, N.D., Mar. 9, 1950; s. Ellis Vernon and Hilde Geneva (Williams) S.; m. Gail Hagerty, Mar. 27, 1993; children: Carrie, Anne; 1 stepchild, Jack. BA, N.D. State U., 1972; JD, U. N.D., 1975. Bar: N.D. 1975, U.S. Dist. Ct. N.D. 1975, U.S. Ct. Appeals (8th cir.) 1976. Asst. atty. gen., chief consumer fraud and antitrust div. State of N.D., Bismarck, 1975-81, securities commr., 1981-83, pub. svc. commr., 1983-92, pres. commn., 1987-91, justice Supreme Ct., 1992—; chair N.D. Commn. on Cameras in the Courtroom, 1993—, Joint Procedure Com., 1996—; mem. exec. com. N.D. Jud. Conf., 1995—; mem. Gov.'s Com. on Security and Privacy, Bismarck, 1975-76, Gov.'s Com. on Refugees, Bismarck, 1976; chmn. Gov's Com. on Comml. Air Transp., Bismark, 1983-84. Mem. platform com. N.D. Reps., 1972, 76, exec. com., 1972-73, 85-88, dist. chmn., 1981-82; former chmn. bd. deacons Luth. Ch.; mem. ch. coun., chair legal and constl. rev. com. Evang. Luth Ch. Am., 1993—. Mem. ABA, N.D. Bar Assn., Big Muddy Bar Assn., Nat. Assn. Regulatory Utility Commrs. (electricity com.), N.A. Assn. Securities Adminstrs., Order of De Molay (grand master 1994-95, mem. Internat. Supreme coun., Legion of Honor award), Nat. Eagle Scouts Assn., Shriners, Elks, Eagles, Masons (chmn. grand youth com. 1979-87, Youth Leadership award 1986). Office: State ND Supreme Court Bismarck ND 58505

SANDSTROM, DEBORAH SNAPP, sales executive; b. Bethesda, Md., June 24, 1946; d. Roy Baker and Dorothy (Loftis) Snapp; m. Roy Sandstrom, Oct. 1, 1983. BA, Wake Forest U., 1968; MA, Tulane U., 1970. Educator Old Lyme (Conn.) Pub. Schs., 1974-80; fed. account mgr. NBI, Arlington, Va., 1981-88; nat. account mgr. Apple Computer, Reston, Va., 1988—. Mem. Columbia Country Club (Washington), Mortar Board. Presbyterian. Avocations: flying, skiing, sailing, traveling. Home: 9724 Brimfield Ct Potomac MD 20854-4338 Office: Apple Computer 1892 Preston White Dr Reston VA 22091-4325

SANDSTROM, SVEN, federal agency administrator. BA, U. Stockholm; MBA, Stockholm Sch. Econs.; DSc in Civil Engring., Royal Inst. Tech., Stockholm. Cons. Sweden, 1966-68; rsch. asoc. MIT and Harvard Bus. Sch., 1969-72; with World Bank, Washington, 1972—, dir. South African dept., 1987-90, dir. office of pres., 1990-91, mng. dir., also chair policy rev. com., 1991—. Office: IBRD World Bank 1818 H St NW Washington DC 20433*

SANDWEISS, MARTHA A., museum director, author, American studies educator; b. St. Louis, Mar. 29, 1954; d. Jerome Wesley and Marilyn Joy (Glik) S. BA magna cum laude, Radcliffe Coll., 1975; MA in History, Yale U., 1977, MPhil in History, 1981, PhD, 1985. Smithsonian-Nat. Endowment Humanities fellow, Nat. Portrait Gallery, Washington, 1975-76; curator photographs Amon Carter Mus., Ft. Worth, 1979-86, adj. curator photographs, 1987-89; dir. Mead Art Mus. Amherst Coll., 1989—, adj. assoc. prof. of fine arts and Am. studies, 1989-94, assoc. prof. Am. studies, 1994—. Author: Carlotta Corpron: Designer with Light, 1980, Masterworks of American Photography, 1982, Laura Gilpin: An Enduring Grace, 1986, (catalogue) Pictures from an Expedition: Early Views of the American West, 1979; co-author: Eyewitness to War: Prints and Daguerreotypes of th Mexican War, 1989; editor: Historic Texas: A Photographic Portrait, 1986, Contemporary Texas: A Photographic Portrait, 1986, Denizens of the Desert, 1988, Photography in Nineteenth Century America, 1991; co-editor: Oxford History of the American West, 1994. Fellow Ctr. for Am. Art and Material Culture, Yale U., 1977-79, NEH, 1988, Am. Coun. Learned Socs., 1996—. Office: Amherst Coll Mead Art Mus Amherst MA 01002

SANDY, ROBERT EDWARD, JR., lawyer; b. Libertyville, Ill., Feb. 16, 1943; s. Robert Edward and Elizabeth Ann (Carroll) S.; m. Joan Mary Phillips, Apr. 19, 1969; children: Mary Rosanne Phillips-Sandy, John Robert Phillips-Sandy. AB, Harvard U., 1965; JD, U. Chgo., 1968. Bar: Mass. 1969, Maine 1972, U.S. Dist. Ct. Mass. 1970, U.S. Dist. Ct. Maine 1972, U.S. Ct. Appeals (1st cir.) 1994, U.S. Supreme Ct. 1980. Atty. Boston Redevel. Authority, 1969-72; ptnr. Sandy and Sandy, Waterville, Maine, 1972-83, Sherman and Sandy, Waterville, 1983-87; sr. ptnr. Sherman, Sandy and Lee, Waterville, 1987—. Mem. Waterville Bar Assn., Maine Bar Assn., Maine Trial Lawyers Assn., ABA. Avocations: boating, skiing, community theater. Home: Greenwood Park Waterville ME 04901 Office: Sherman Sandy and Lee 74 Silver St Waterville ME 04901

SANDY, STEPHEN, writer, educator; b. Mpls., Aug. 2, 1934; s. Alan Francis and Evelyn Brown (Martin) S.; AB, Yale U., 1955; AM, Harvard U., 1958, PhD, 1963; m. Virginia Scoville, 1969; children: Nathaniel Merrill, Clare Scoville. Instr., Harvard U., 1963-67; vis. prof. U. Toyko, 1967-68; asst. prof. Brown U., Providence, 1968-69; mem. faculty Bennington (Vt.) Coll., 1969—; McGee prof. of writing Davidson (N.C.) Coll., 1994; lectr. U. R.I., 1969; prof. Harvard U. Summer Sch., 1986, 87, 88; poetry workshop dir. Chautauqua Instn., 1975, 77, Johnson (Vt.) State Coll., 1976, 77, Bennington Coll., summers 1978-80, 1989, Bennington Writing Seminars Program, 1994—, Wesleyan Writers Conf., 1981; councillor for English, Harvard Grad. Soc. Coun., 1969-74. With U.S. Army, 1955-57. Dexter fellow, 1961; Yaddo fellow, 1963-68, 76, 93; Huber Found. grantee, 1973; Vt. Coun. Arts grantee, 1974; recipient Fulbright postdoctoral award, 1967-68; invited poetry fellow Breadloaf Writers Conf., 1968; nominee for Pulitzer prize, 1971. Fellow Ingram Merrill Found., 1985, MacDowell Colony fellow, 1986, 93, Blue Mt. Ctr. fellow, 1985, 88, creative writing fellow Nat. Endowment for the Arts, 1988, Vt. Coun. on Arts fellow, 1988—; mem. Signet Soc., Elizabethan Club. Author: Stresses in the Peaceable Kingdom, 1967, Roofs, 1971, End of the Picaro, 1977, The Hawthorne Effect, 1980, The Raveling of the Novel: Studies in Romantic Fiction from Walpole to Scott, 1980, Riding to Greylock, 1983, To a Mantis, 1987, Man in the Open Air, 1988, The Epoch, 1990, Thanksgiving Over the Water, 1992; translator Seneca's Hercules Oetaeus, 1994. Home: W St Box 524 North Bennington VT 05257 Office: Bennington Coll Bennington VT 05201

SANDY, WILLIAM HASKELL, training and communications systems executive; b. N.Y.C., Apr. 28, 1929; s. Fred and Rose S.; AB, U. Md., 1950, JD, 1953; postgrad. Advanced Mgmt. Program, Harvard Bus. Sch., 1970-71; m. Marjorie Mazor, June 15, 1952; children: Alan, Lewis, Barbara. Admitted to Md. bar, 1953; planner-writer, account exec., account supr. Jam Handy Orgn., Detroit, 1953-64, v.p., 1964-69, sr. v.p., 1969-71; pres. Sandy Corp., Troy, Mich., 1971-88; chmn., 1988—. Author: Forging the Productivity Partnership, 1990. Bd. govs. Northwood Inst., 1976-80; bd. dirs. Cranbrook Sci. Inst., Met. Ctr. High Tech., 1993; pres. Graphic Arts Coun., 1992-93; trustee Detroit Inst. Arts, 1992-93; v.p. nat. exec. coun. Harvard Bus. Sch., 1985-89; mem. Bloomfield Hills Zoning Bd., Walsh Coll. President's Adv. Coun.; city commr. City of Bloomfield Hills, Troy Downtown Devel. Authority. Mem. Am. Mktg. Assn. (pres. Detroit chpt. 1975), Am. Soc. Tng. and Devel., Southeastern Mich. Better Bus. Bur. (bd. dirs.), Adcraft Club, Nat. Assn. Ednl. Broadcasters. Clubs: Harvard Bus. Sch. (pres. Detroit club 1983-85), The Hundred. Home: 596 Rudgate Rd Bloomfield Hills MI 48304-3355 Office: Sandy Corp 1500 W Big Beaver Rd Troy MI 48084-3526

SANETO, RUSSELL PATRICK, pediatrician, neurobiologist; b. Burbank, Calif., Oct. 10, 1950; s. Arthur and Mitzi (Seddon) S.; m. Kathleen D. Saneto. BS with honors, San Diego State U., 1972, MS, 1975; PhD, U. Tex. Med. Br., 1981; DO U. Osteo. Medicine and Surgery, 1994. Teaching asst. San Diego State U. 1969-75; substitute tchr. Salt Lake City Sch. Dist., 1975; teaching and rsch. asst. U. Tex. Med. Br., 1976-77, NIH predoctoral fellow, 1977-81, postdoctoral fellow, 1981; Jeanne B. Kempner postdoctoral fellow UCLA, 1981-82, NIH postdoctoral fellow, 1982-87; asst. prof. Oreg. Regional Primate Rsch. Ctr. div. Neurosci., Beaverton, 1987-89; asst. prof. dept. cell biology and anatomy Oreg. Health Scis. U., Portland, 1988-90, U. Osteo. Medicine & Surgery, 1991-94, Cleve. Clinic, 1994—; lectr. rsch. methods Grad. Sch., 1982; vis. scholar in ethics So. Baptist Theol. Sem., Louisville, 1981. Contbr. articles to profl. jours. Recipient Merit award Nat. March of Dimes, 1978; named one of Outstanding Young Men in Am., 1979, 81, one of Men of Significance, 1985. Mem. AAAS, Am. Acad. Pediats., Bread for World, Save the Whales, Sierra Club, Am. Soc. Human Genetics, Winter Confs. Brain Rsch., Neuroscis. Study Program, N.Y. Acad. Scis., Am. Soc. Neurochem., Soc. Neurosci., Am. Soc. Neurochemistry, Soc. Neurosci., World Runners Club, Sigma Sigma Phi. Democrat. Mem. Evangelical Free Ch.

SANETTI, STEPHEN LOUIS, lawyer; b. Flushing, N.Y., June 25, 1949; s. Alfred Julius Sanetti and Yolanda Marie (DiGioia) Boyes; m. Carole Leighton Koller, Sept. 21, 1974; children: Christopher Edward, Dana Harrison. B.A. in History with honors, Va. Mil. Inst., 1971; J.D., Washington and Lee U., 1974. Bar: Conn. 1975, U.S. Ct. Mil. Appeals 1975, U.S. Dist. Ct. Conn. 1978, U.S. Ct. Appeals (2d cir.) 1979, U.S. Supreme Ct. 1980. Litigation atty. Marsh, Day & Calhoun, Bridgeport, Conn., 1978-80; gen. counsel Sturm, Ruger & Co., Southport, Conn., 1980—; v.p. Sturm, Ruger & Co., 1993—; dir. Product Liability Adv. Coun. Tech. advisor Assn. Firearm and Toolmark Examiners; chmn. legis. & legal affairs com. Sporting Arms & Ammunition Mfrs. Inst. Served to capt., chief criminal law 1st Cavalry Div. Staff Judge Advocate, U.S. Army, 1975-78. Mem. Am. Acad Forensic Sci., Def. Rsch. Inst., Phi Delta Phi. Republican. Roman Catholic. Office: Sturm Ruger & Co Inc 1 Lacey Pl Southport CT 06490-1241

SANFELICI, ARTHUR H(UGO), editor, writer; b. Haledon, N.J., May 23, 1934; s. Hugo and Anna (Schilder) S.; m. Betty Louise Van Riper, Aug. 10, 1957; children: Brian Arthur, Amy Elizabeth, Gary Hugh, Bruce Richard. Attended, Lehigh U., 1952-55. Assoc. editor Flying Mag., N.Y.C., 1961-64; mng. editor Am. Aviation Mag., Washington, 1964-68; dist. sales mgr. Gates Learjet Co., N.Y.C., 1969-71; exec. editor Airport World Mag., Westport, Conn., 1971-74; spl. project editor Aircraft Owners & Pilots Assn., Washington, 1974-75, mng. editor Pilot mag., 1975-79, editor AOPA Newsletter, AOPAirport Report, Gen. Aviation Nat. Report, 1979-88; pub. cons., 1989-90; sr. editor Flight Safety Found., Washington, 1989-92; editor S-Cubed divsn. Maxwell Labs., Alexandria, Va., 1992-95; comms. dir. Helicopter Assn. Internat., Alexandria, 1996—. Editor, compiler: Yesterday's Wings; Editor Aviation History Mag., Leesburg, Va., 1990—. Served with USAF, 1955-60. Mem. Nat. Aeronautic Assn., Washington Ind. Writers, Aero Club of Washington, Soc. Aerospace Comms. Home: 5 Oak Shade Rd Sterling VA 20164-1163

SANFELIPPO, PETER MICHAEL, cardiac, thoracic and vascular surgeon; b. Milw., Nov. 1, 1938; s. Michael L. and Genevieve M. (Gagliano) S.; m. Cecelia Monica Reuss, May 25, 1968. MD, Marquette U., Milw., 1965; MS in Surgery, U. Minn., 1976. Diplomate Am. Bd. Surgery, Am. Bd. Thoracic Surgery, Am. Bd. Gen. Vascular Surgery. Intern Sacred Heart Hosp., Spokane, Wash., 1965-66; gen. surgery fellow Mayo Grad. Sch. Medicine, Rochester, Minn., 1966, 69-73; residency in thoracic surgery USAF Med. Ctr., Lackland AFB, Tex., 1973-75; thoracic surgeon USAF Med. Corps, various locations, 1966-78; pvt. practice cardiac, thoracic and vascular surgery Ohio Heart & Thoracic Surgery Ctr., Columbus, 1978-91; prof. cardiothoacic and vascular surgery U. Tex. Health Ctr., Tyler, Tex., 1991—. Contbr. articles to profl. jours. Lt. col. USAF, 1966-78. Decorated Air Force Commendation medal. Fellow ACS, Am. Coll. Cardiology, Am. Coll. Angiology, Am. Coll. Chest Physicians; mem. AMA. Avocations: scouting, camping, photography, gardening.

SANFILIPPO, ALFRED PAUL, pathologist, educator; b. Racine, Wis., Aug. 30, 1949; s. Paul Joseph and Therese (Rhode) S.; m. Janet Lee Thompson, 1973; children: Lisa, Joseph. Student, Max Planck Inst. Exptl. Med., Gottingen, Germany, 1966-68, U. Pa., 1969-70; BA and MS in Physics, U. Pa., 1970; postgrad., Duke U., 1972-75, PhD in Immunology, 1975, MD, 1976. Diplomate Am. Bd. Pathology; lic. physician N.C., Md. Postdoctoral rschr. divsn. tumor virology dept. surgery, 1976-79; intern in anatomic pathology Duke U. Hosp., 1976-77, resident in anatomic and clin. pathology, 1977-79; asst. prof. pathology and exptl. surgery, lectr. immunology Duke U., Durham, 1979-84, from assoc. prof. to prof. pathology, 1984-93, from assoc. prof. to prof. exptl. surgery, 1985-93, prof. immunology, 1990-93; attending pathologist Duke U. and Durham VA Hosps., 1979-93; staff mem. Duke Surg. Pvt. Diagnostic Clinic, 1979-93; dir. Transplantation Lab. Durham VA Hosp., 1979-93; dir. immunopathology Duke U. Med. Ctr., 1982-93, exec. com. dept. pathology, 1989-91; pathologist-in-chief Johns Hopkins Hosp., Balt., 1993—; Baxley prof., dir. dept. pathology Johns Hopkins U., Balt., 1993—; adj. prof. pathology and immunology Duke U., 1993—, clin. rsch. unit sci. adv. com., 1988-91, at-large rep. basic sci. faculty steering com., 1989-91, dir. interdisciplinary program in transplantation, 1991-93; mem. Duke Comprehensive Cancer Ctr., 1979-93; chmn. comprehensive transplant ctr. planning com. Johns Hopkins Med. Instns., 1993—, mem. physician coun. for Atlantic Alliance, 1994—; med. bd. Johns Hopkins Hosp., 1993—, strategic planning work group, 1993—, quality assessment and improvement coun., 1994—, re-engring. steering com., 1994—; Osler prof., dir. medicine search com. Johns Hopkins U. Sch. Medicine, 1994—, DeVelbiss fund com., 1994—, Clayton fund com., 1993—, Shelley vis. prof. com., 1993—, faculty compensation com., 1993—, bd. dirs. clin. practice assn., 1993—; mem. orgn. student reps. Assn. Am. Med. Colls., 1973-75; sec. Carolina Organ Procurement Agy., 1987-89, exec. com., 1987-93, v.p., 1989-91, pres., 1991-93; com. med. student affairs N.C. Med. Soc., 1972-76, del. Durham County, 1974; cons. Battelle Human Affairs Rsch. Ctrs., Seattle, 1985-93, NSF of Switzerland, 1992-93, also numerous U.S. govt. adv. coms.; speaker and presenter in field. Guest editor: Human Immunology, Vol. 14, 1987; mem. editl. bd. Transplantation, 1985—, Pathobiology, 1989—, Transplantation Now (Japan) 1989—, Pathology, Rsch. and Practice, 1990—, Human Immunology, 1992—, Lab. Investigation, 1993—, Xeno, 1994—; reviewer Am. Jour. Kidney Diseases, Am. Jour. Ophthalmology, Am. Jour. Pathology, Hepatology, Jour. of AMA, Jour. Am. Soc. Nephrology, Jour. Clin. Investigation, Jour. Leukocyte Biology, Kidney Internat., others; contbr. numerous articles to profl. jours. Recipient Kermit G. Osserman award Myasthenia Gravis Found., 1976, Wiley D. Forbus award N.C. Soc. Pathologists, 1979, Reach for Sight Physician Investigator award, 1990; NIH predoctoral fellow Duke U., 1970-76, fellow in exptl. pathology Duke U., 1978-79; numerous rsch. grants. Fellow Coll. Am. Pathologists, Am. Soc. Clin. Pathologists (coun. on edn. and rsch. 1994—); mem. AMA (Physician Recognition award 1979-84), Am. Assn. Immunologists, Am. Soc. Investigative Pathology, U.S.-Can. Acad. Pathology, Southeastern Organ Procurement Found. (sci. projects and publs. com. 1980—, organ preservation com. 1981-83, exec. com. 1992—, sec. 1992-93, treas. 1993-94, v.p. 1994-95, bd. dirs. med. svcs. 1992—, pres. med. svcs. 1994-95), Transplantation Soc., Am. Soc. Histocompatibility and Immunogenetics (chmn. clin. affairs com. 1987-90, chmn. cornea transplant standards subcom. 1985-86), Assn. for Rsch. in Vision and Ophthalmology, Am. Soc. Transplant Physicians (pres.-elect 1984-85, pres. 1985-86, chmn. sci. studies com. 1991-92), Am. Soc. Nephrology, N.C. Kidney Coun. (rep. histocompatibility 1981-92), Md. Soc. Pathologists, Assn. Pathom. grad. med. edn. 1994—), Alpha Omega Alpha. Office: Johns Hopkins Med Insts Dept Pathology 415 600 N Wolfe St Baltimore MD 21287

SANFILIPPO, JOSEPH SALVATORE, physician, reproductive endocrinologist, educator; b. Bklyn., Feb. 28, 1948; s. Joseph Philip and Elena Teresa (Canepa) S.; m. Patricia M. Cantwell, June 21, 1974; children: Angela, Andrea, Luke. BS, St. John's U., N.Y.C., 1969; MD, Chgo. Med. Sch., 1973. Diplomate Am. Bd. Ob-Gyn., spl. qualification in reproductive endocrinology. Intern Milwaukee County Gen. Hosp.; resident in ob-gyn. SUNY Upstate Med. Ctr., Syracuse; instr. dept. ob-gyn. U. Louisville Sch. Medicine, 1977-79, asst. prof., 1979-83, assoc. prof., 1983-89, prof., 1989—, dir. div. reproductive endocrinology, 1993—; pres. med. staff Alliant Health System/Norton Hosp. and Alliant Med. Pavilion, Louisville, 1994—; dir. gynecology Kosair-Children's Hosp., Louisville, 1979—. Editor: Pediatric and Adolescent Obstetrics and Gynecology, 1985, Operative Gynecologic Endoscopy, 1988, Pediatric and Adolescent Gynecology, 1994; editor-in-chief Adolescent and Pediatric Gynecology, 1989—. Mem. parish coun. Holy Trinity Roman Cath. Ch., Louisville, 1988-92; mem. prin.'s adv. coun. Sacred Heart Acad., Louisville, 1993-94. Named Disting. Alumnus, Chgo. Med. Sch., 1990. Fellow Am. Fertility Soc. (dir. postgrad. program), N.Am. Soc. for Pediatric Adolescent Gynecology (founding mem.); mem. Am. Coll. Ob-Gyn. (tech. bull. com.), Alpha Omega Alpha. Avocations: jogging, boating, fishing, ham radio. Home: 5505 Apache Rd Louisville KY 40207-1613 Office: U Louisville Sch Medicine Dept Ob-Gyn ACB Bldg 550 S Jackson St Louisville KY 40202-1622

SANFORD, BRUCE WILLIAM, lawyer; b. Massena, N.Y., Aug. 5, 1945; s. Doris (Suhrland) Sanford; m. Marilou Green, May 17, 1980; children: Ashley Anne, Barrett William. BA, Hamilton Coll., 1967; JD, NYU, 1970. Bar: N.Y. 1970, Ohio 1971, D.C. 1981, Md. 1985. Staff reporter Wall St. Jour., 1966-67; assoc. Baker and Hostetler, Washington, 1971-79, ptnr., 1979—. Author: Sanford's Synopsis Law of Libel and Privacy, rev. edit., 1991, Libel and Privacy, 2nd edit., 1991. Trustee Nat. Symphony Orch. Assn.; bd. dirs. Thomas Jefferson 1st Amendment Ctr., U. Va., Charlottesville. Mem. ABA (governing bd., forum com. on communication law, chmn. defamation torts com. 1985-86). Office: Baker & Hostetler 1050 Connecticut Ave NW Washington DC 20036-5303

SANFORD, CHARLES STEADMAN, JR., banker; b. Savannah, Ga., Oct. 8, 1936; s. Charles Steadman and Ann (Lawrence) S.; m. Mary McRitchie, June 19, 1959; children: Ann Whitney, Charles Steadman III. BA, U. Ga., 1958; MBA, U. Pa., 1960. V.p. nat. div., relationship mgr. Bankers Trust Co., N.Y.C., 1961-68, 1st v.p., asst. to head resources mgmt., 1969-71, sr. v.p., 1973, head resources mgmt., from 1972, exec. v.p., 1974, pres., 1983-86, dep. chmn., from 1986, chmn., chief exec. officer, 1987-96; ret., 1996; mem. mgmt. com. Bankers Trust Co., N.Y.C., 1979-96; ret., 1996; chmn. N.Y. Clearing House Com., 1987-88; bd. dirs. J.C. Penney Co., Mobil Corp. Mem. Bus. Roundtable; bd. overseers Wharton Sch., U. Pa. With arty. U.S. Army, 1958-59. Mem. Coun. Fgn. Rels. Office: Bankers Trust NY Corp 130 Liberty St New York NY 10006-1105

SANFORD, DAVID BOYER, writer, editor; b. Denver, Mar. 4, 1943; s. Filmore Bowyer and Alice Irene (Peterson) S. B.A. with honors, U. Denver, 1964; M.S. in Journalism with honors, Columbia U., 1965. With New Republic mag., Washington, 1965-76; mng. editor New Republic mag., 1970-76, Politics Today (formerly Skeptic), Santa Barbara, Calif., 1976-78; contbg. editor Politics Today (formerly Skeptic), 1978-79; editorial writer Los Angeles Herald Examiner, 1978-79; mng. editor Harper's mag., N.Y.C., 1979-80; editor Wall St. Jour. mag., 1980-81; sr. spl. writer Wall Street Jour., 1981—; syndicated columnist, 1970-71; commentator Can. Broadcasting Corp., 1967-76; judge Heywood Broun award Newspaper Guild, 1971; mem. print screening com. Champion-Tuck awards, 1985, 86, Judge Wuxtry award, 1990. Author: Who Put the Con in Consumer?, 1972, Me and Ralph, 1976; editor, co-author: Hot War on the Consumer, 1970. Centennial scholar, 1960-64; N.Y. Newspaper Guild fellow, 1964-65; recipient Sackett Law prize Columbia, 1965, Eckenberg prize, 1965; Gold award N.Y. Art Dirs. Club, 1977; Wuxtry award for disting. achievement in headline writing, Internat. Soc. for Gen. Semantics, 1989. Mem. Phi Beta Kappa, Omicron Delta Kappa. Democrat. Home: 118 Prospect Park W Brooklyn NY 11215-4270

SANFORD, DAVID HAWLEY, philosophy educator; b. Detroit, Dec. 13, 1937; s. Hawley Seager and Alice Katherine (Brown) S.; m. Anne Irene Zeleney, July 10, 1965; children: Daria Margaret, Katherine Eugenia. Student, Oberlin Coll., 1955-57; B.A., Wayne State U., 1960; Ph.D., Cornell U., 1966. Instr., asst. prof. philosophy Dartmouth Coll., Hanover, N.H., 1963-70; assoc. prof. Duke U., Durham, N.C., 1970-78; prof. Duke U., 1978—, chmn. dept., 1986-89; vis. faculty U. Oreg., U. Mich., Dalhousie U. Author: If P, then Q: Conditionals and the Foundations of Reasoning, 1989, paperback edit., 1992; contbr. articles to profl. jours. Samuel S. Fells fellow, 1962-63, NEH fellow, 1974-75, 82-83, 89-90, Nat. Humanities Ctr. fellow, 1989-90. Mem. Am. Philos. Assn. (exec. com. Eastern div. 1979-81), N.C. Philos. Soc. (pres. 1983-85), Soc. for Philosophy and Psychology, Phi Beta Kappa. Home: 2227 Cranford Rd Durham NC 27706-2507 Office: Duke Univ Dept Philosophy Durham NC 27708

SANFORD, FREDERIC GOODMAN, career officer; b. Williamsport, Pa.; m. Mary Jane Sharpless. BA, Haverford Coll., 1962; MD, U. Pa., 1966. Diplomate Am. Bd. Radiology. Commd. ensign USN, 1962, advanced through grades to rear adm., 1991; intern Robert Packer Hosp., Guthrie Clinic, Sayre, Pa., 1966-67; bn. surgeon 11th Engrs. Bn. 3d Marine Div., Republic of Vietnam, 1967-68; gen. med. officer San Francisco Bay Naval Dispensary, Hunter's Point, 1968-69; resident in radiology Naval Hosp., Bethesda, Md., 1969-72; head radiation therapy div. Naval Hosp., Portsmouth, Va., 1972-73; fellow in radiation therapy Med. Coll. Va., Richmond, 1973-74; head radiation therapy div., program dir. therapeutic radiology tng. program, chmn. radiology dept., dir. ancillary svcs., exec. officer Naval Hosp., San Diego, until 1986; comdg. officer Naval Hosp., Newport, R.I., 1986-88; mem. staff Surgeon Gen.'s Office, Washington, 1988-89, med. insp. gen., 1991-92; comdg. officer Naval Hosp., Long Beach, Calif., 1989-91; med. officer USMC, 1992-93; comdr. Naval Med. Ctr., Oakland, Calif., 1993-94; asst. chief operational medicine and fleet support Bur. Medicine and Surgery, Washington, 1994—. Decorated Legion of Merit, Meritorious Svc. medal, Vietnamese Cross Gallantry, Combat Action ribbon, other awards.

Fellow Am. Coll. Radiology; mem. AMA, Radiol. Soc. N.Am., Am. Radium Soc. Office: Bureau of Medicine & Surgery Navy Dept Washington DC 20372

SANFORD, JAMES KENNETH, public relations executive; b. Clyde, N.C., Jan. 23, 1932; s. James Edward S. and Bernice (Crawford) Peebles; m. Alice Pearl Reavis, Sept. 22, 1957; children: Timothy, Scott, Jeannette. AA, Mars Hill (N.C.) Coll., 1952; AB, U. N.C., 1954, MA, 1958. Pub. rels. officer Asheville (N.C.) United Appeal, 1954; reporter, copy editor Winston-Salem (N.C.) Jour., 1957-59, asst. state editor, 1959-61, news editor, 1961-63, editorial writer, 1963-64; dir. pub. info. and publs. U. N.C., Charlotte, 1964-94; pub. rels. cons. Charlotte, N.C., 1994—; cons. Commn. on Future of Mars Hill Coll., 1990-91, City of Charlotte, 1991. Author: Charlotte and UNC Charlotte: Growing Up Together, 1996; co-author: Fifty Favored Years, 1972; contbr. numerous articles to mag. and newspapers. Active attractions com. Charlotte Conv. and Visitors Bur., 1994—, Internat. House Bd., 1995, adv. com. Sta. WTVI Pub. TV, Charlotte, 1986-94; chmn. bd. deacons local ch., 1994-95. With U.S. Army, 1954-56. Elected to N.C. Pub. Rels. Hall of Fame, 1995. Fellow Pub. Rels. Soc. Am. (chmn. S.E. dist. 1991); mem. Coll. News Assn. Carolinas (Lewis Gaston award 1982), Charlotte Pub. Rels. Soc. (pres. 1974, Infinity award 1986), Coun. for Advancement and Support Edn. (asst. dist. chmn. 1975-76), Phi Kappa Phi. Baptist. Avocations: writing, hiking, photography. Home and Office: 1216 Braeburn Rd Charlotte NC 28211-4769

SANFORD, JAY PHILIP, internist, educator; b. Madison, Wis., May 27, 1928; s. Joseph Arthur and Arlyn (Carlson) S.; m. Lorraine Burklund, Apr. 7, 1950; children—Jeb, Nancy, Sarah, Philip, Catherine. M.D., U. Mich., 1952; D of Mil. Medicine (hon.), Uniformed Svcs. U. Health Sci., 1991. Intern Peter Bent Brigham Hosp., Boston, 1952-53; research fellow Harvard Med. Sch., Boston, 1953-54; resident Duke U. Hosp., Durham, N.C., 1956-57; practice medicine specializing in internal medicine Dallas, 1957-75; mem. faculty U. Tex. Southwestern Med. Sch. at Dallas, 1957-75; prof. internal medicine, 1965-75; dean F. Edward Hebert Sch. Medicine, Uniformed Services U. Health Scis., Bethesda, Md., 1975-90; pres. Uniformed Services U. Health Scis., 1981-90, dean emeritus, 1990—; clin. prof. internal medicine U. Tex. Southwestern Med. Sch., 1992—; chief microbiology lab. Parkland Meml. Hosp., Dallas, 1957-75, pres. med. staff, 1968-69, mem. attending staff; mem. adv. coun. Dallas Health and Sci. Mus., 1968-75; chmn. Am. Bd. Internal Medicine, 1978-79, Gov.'s Commn. Phys. Fitness, 1971-75; bd. regents Nat. Libr. Medicine, 1984-90; mem. Accreditation Coun. on Grad. Med. Edn., 1987-92, chmn. transitional year residency rev. com., 1989-92, chmn., 1990-91; mem. bd. on army sci. and tech. NRC, 1995—; cons. Dallas VA Ctr. Contbr. articles to profl. jours. With M.C., U.S. Army, 1954-56; col. Res., 1983—. Decorated Medal of Honor du Service de Sante des Armees, France, 1991; recipient cert. of award Div. Health Moblzn. USPHS, 1963, 64, Prizer award for CD, 1965, Presdl. citation for Health Moblzn. Planning, 1970, Disting. Pub. Svc. medal Dept. Def., 1982, 91. Fellow Am. Acad. Microbiology, ACP (master); mem. Inst. Medicine of NAS, Assn. Am. Physicians, Nat. Inst. Allergy and Infectious Diseases (chmn. tng. grant com. 1971, adv. coun. 1979-90), Am. Fedn. Clin. Research (pres. 1968-69), Am. Soc. Microbiology, Central Soc. Clin. Rsch., Soc. Exptl. Biology and Medicine, Am. Soc. Clin. Investigation, Soc. Med. Consultants to Armed Forces (pres. 1976-77, John R. Seal award 1988, 91), Am. Thoracic Soc., Infectious Disease Soc. Am. (pres. 1978-79, Bristol award 1981, E.H. Kass lectr. 1994), Sigma Xi, Alpha Omega Alpha, Phi Kappa Phi. Home: 4509 Edmondson Ave Dallas TX 75205-2605 Office: 5910 N Central Expy Ste 1955 Dallas TX 75206-5151

SANFORD, KATHERINE KOONTZ, cancer researcher; b. Chgo., July 19, 1915; d. William James and Alta Rachel (Koontz) S.; m. Charles Fleming Richards Mifflin, Dec. 11, 1971. BA, Wellesley Coll., 1937; MA, Brown U., 1939, PhD, 1942; DSc (hon.), Med. Coll. Pa., 1974, Cath. U. Am., 1988. Teaching asst. Brown U., Providence, 1937-39, rsch. asst., 1939-41; instr. biology Western coll., Oxford, Ohio, 1941-42, Allegheny Coll., Meadville, Pa., 1942-43; asst. dir. Johns Hopkins Nursing Sch., Balt., 1943-47; rsch. biologist Nat. Cancer Inst. NIH, Bethesda, Md., 1947-74; head cell physiology and oncogenesis sect. Lab. Biochemistry, Bethesda, 1974-77; chief in vitro carcinogenesis sect. Nat. Cancer Inst. NIH, Bethesda, 1979—. Contbr. 150 articles to profl. jours. Ross Harrison fellow, 1954. Mem. Phi Beta Kappa, Sigma Xi. Home: 101 Stuart Dr Dover DE 19901-5817 Office: Nat Cancer Inst In Vitro Carcinogenesis Bethesda MD 20892

SANFORD, LEROY LEONARD, rancher; b. Sanford Ranch, Wyo., June 24, 1934; s. Claude Leonard and Herminnie May (Brockmeyer) S.; m. Barbara Jo Shackleford, June 15, 1965 (dec. Oct. 1965); stepchildren: Christina Pedley, Marlena McCollum, Diana Sumners; 1 foster child, Catherine Frost. Cert. satellite geodesy, Johns Hopkins U., 1971; cert. astron. geodesy, U.S. Geol. Survey-Branch R & D, 1971. Cert. Geodesic Surveyor. Rancher Sanford Ranch, Douglas, Wyo., 1952-57; topographer, photogrametrist U.S. Geol. Survey-Topog. Divsn.-Hdqs., Denver, 1957-81; rancher Sanford Ranch, Douglas, 1981—; speaker various schs. and community orgns. Congl. Svc. medal U.S. Congress, 1972. Mem. NRA (endowment), Am. Solar Energy Soc., Antarctican Soc., Wyo. Farm Bur. Republican. Avocation: photography. Home: 400 Windy Ridge Rd Douglas WY 82633-0145 *Early on I ran across this saying; author unknown to me, "Why is there never enough time to do it right, but always enough time to do it over?" I feel that anyone's time spent "doing it over" is wasted unless it is to do something better in light of new knowledge. Anything I build now will last longer than me and I want it to survive until the next technological leap forward.*

SANFORD, MARSHALL (MARK SANFORD), congressman; b. Ft. Lauderdale, Fla., May 28, 1960; m. Jenny Sullivan; 3 children. BA, Furman U., 1983; MBA, U. Va., 1988. With Goldman Sachs, 1988, CRC Realty, 1988-89; prin. Southeastern Ptnrs., 1989—, Norton & Sanford, 1993—; mem. 104th Congress from 1st Dist. S.C., 1995—. Republican. Office: US Ho of Reps Washington DC 20515

SANFORD, RICHARD D., computer company executive; b. 1944. With Arthur Andersen Co., N.Y.C., 1968-77; exec. v.p. Commodore Internat. Ltd., 1977-81; chmn., CEO, former pres. Intelligent Electronics Inc., Exton, Pa., 1982—. With USMC, 1964-68. Office: Intelligent Electronics Inc 411 Eagleview Blvd Exton PA 19341-1117*

SANFORD, SARAH J., healthcare executive; b. Seattle, July 20, 1949; d. Jerome G. and Mary L. (Laughlin) S. BS in Nursing, U. Wash., 1972, MA in Nursing, 1977. Cert. in advanced nursing adminstrn. Critical care staff nurse Valley Gen. Hosp., Renton, Wash., 1972-75, Evergreen Gen. Hosp., Kirkland, Wash., 1975-76; instr. nursing Seattle Pacific U., 1977-79; with Overlake Hosp. Med. Ctr., Bellevue, Wash., 1979-88, critical care coord., 1979-80, dir. acute care nursing, 1980-82, assoc. adminstr., 1982-83, sr. v.p. patient care, 1983-88; exec. dir. AACN, Aliso Viejo, Calif., 1988-90, CEO, 1990—; bd. dirs. Partnership for Organ Donation, Boston, Am. Soc. of Assn. Execs. Found., Washington. Co-editor: Standards for Nursing Care of the Critically Ill, 1989; contbr. articles to books and jours. Fellow Am. Acad. Nursing; mem. AACN (pres. 1984-85, bd. dirs. 1981-83), ANA, Soc. for Critical Care Medicine, Am. Orgn. Nurse Execs., Sigma Theta Tau. Office: AACN 101 Columbia Aliso Viejo CA 92656-1491

SANFORD, TERRY, lawyer, educator, former United States Senator, former governor, former university president; b. Laurinburg, N.C., Aug. 20, 1917; s. Cecil and Elizabeth (Martin) S.; m. Margaret Rose Knight, July 4, 1942; children: Elizabeth Knight, Terry. AB, U. N.C., 1939, JD, 1946; 30 hon. degrees from colls. and univs. Bar: N.C. 1946, D.C. 1979. Asst. dir. Inst. Govt., U. N.C., 1940-41, 46-48; spl. agt. FBI, 1941-42; pvt. practice Fayetteville, 1948-60; ptnr. Sanford, Adams, McCullough & Beard, Raleigh, N.C. and Washington, 1965-86; gov. State of N.C., 1961-65; pres. Duke U., Durham, N.C., 1969-85, prof. pub. policy, 1992—; mem. U.S. Senate 99th-102d Congresses from N.C., Washington, 1986-93; ptnr. The Sanford Law Firm, PLLC, Raleigh, 1993—; prof. of practice, public policy Duke U., 1992—; pub. gov. Am. Stock Exchange, 1977-83; dir. Study of Am. States, Duke U., 1965-68; mem. Carnegie Commn. Ednl. TV, 1964-67; pres. Urban Am., Inc., 1968-69; chmn. ITT Internat. Fellowship Com., 1974-86, Am. Coun. Young Polit. Leaders, 1976-86; pres. U.S. Del. Inter-Parliamentary Union, 1988-90. Author: But What About the People?, 1966, Storm Over the States, 1967, A Danger of Democracy, 1981. Sec.-treas. N. C. Port Authority, 1950-53; mem. N.C. Senate, 1953-54; pres. N.C. Young Dem. Clubs, 1949-50; del. Nat. Dem. Conv., 1956, 60, 64, 68, 72, 84, 88, 92; chmn. Nat. Dem. Charter Commn., 1972-74; mem. governing bd. Nat. Com. for Citizens in Edn., Am. Art Alliance; trustee Am. Council Learned Socs., 1970-73, Nat. Humanities Center, 1978-86, Meth. Coll., 1958-94, Howard U., 1968-86; chmn. N.C. Mus. Art, 1993—; bd. dirs. Children's TV Workshop, 1967-71, Council on Founds., 1971-76, N.C. Outward Bound, 1981-88; chmn. bd. trustees U. N.C., 1961-65; chmn. So. Regional Edn. Bd., 1961-63, Sta. ACSN (The Learning Channel), 1980-86, Assn. Am. Univs., 1980-81, Nat. Civic League, 1985-86. Served to 1st lt. AUS, 1942-46. Mem. ABA, Am. Acad. Polit. and Social Sci., Coun. Fgn. Rels., Am. Judicature Soc., Nat. Acad. Pub. Adminstrn., AAAS, Phi Beta Kappa. Methodist. Office: Sanford Law Firm 234 Fayetteville St Raleigh NC 27601-1867

SANFORD, WILBUR LEE, elementary education educator; b. Lexington, Ky., Aug. 2, 1935; s. Lloyd Daniel and Catherine (Kirtley) S.; m. Dorothy Moore; children: James, Venessa. BA, Ky. State Coll., 1958; MA in Adminstrn., Xavier U., 1969, cert. elem. counselor, 1973. Cert. elem. counselor, Ohio; cert. elem. tchr. and prin., Ohio. Elem. tchr. North Coll. Hill (Ohio) Sch., 1960-65, Cin. Pub. Schs., 1965-73, St. Joseph Elem. Sch., Cin., 1993—; adminstrv. intern Cin. Pub. Schs., 1983-85, asst. prin., 1975-80, elem. prin., 1980-92; cons. PTA, Cin., 1989-92, GED program, Cin., 1990-91; prin./instrnl. leader Windsor Sch. Meritorious Achievement, Cin., 1985-86; dir. After Sch. Evening Tutorial, Cin., 1988-92. Leader 4-H Club, Cin., 1991-92, Boy Scouts Am., Cin., 1985-89; mem. Walnut Hills Victory Community Coun., Cin., 1985-89, Avondale Community Coun., Cin., 1990-92; mem. Sinai Temple. Recipient Notable Recognition award Youth Crime Intervention, Cin., 1991, Community Svc. award So. Bapt. Ch., Cin., 1991, Outstanding Svc. award Cincinnatians Active to Support Edn., 1989. Mem. Ohio Assn. Elem. Sch. Adminstrs. (Exemplary Svc. award 1987), Cin. Assn. Adminstrs. and Suprs., Cin. Assn. Elem. Prins. Democrat. Methodist. Avocations: music, reading, dancing, gardening, traveling. Home: 6748 Stoll Ln Cincinnati OH 45236-4039 Office: St Joseph Elem Sch 745 Ezzard Charles Dr Cincinnati OH 45203-1410

SANGER, ALEXANDER CAMPBELL, family planning executive; b. N.Y.C., Nov. 25, 1947; s. Grant and Marjery Edwina (Campbell) S.; m. Lisa-Margaret Stevenson, Oct. 31, 1970, (div. July, 1978); m. Jeannette Kittredge Watson, Dec. 21, 1978; children: Ralph, Andrew, Matthew. AB, Princeton U., 1969; MBA, JD, Columbia U., 1974; LLM, NYU, 1985. Bar: N.Y. 1974, Fla. Ptnr., assoc. White and Case, N.Y.C., 1974-88; CEO Sanger Plastics, Union, N.J., 1988-90, Old Line Plastics, Forest Hill, Md., 1990; pres., CEO Planned Parenthood of N.Y.C., 1991—. bd. dirs. Planned Parenthood of N.Y.C., 1984-90, Pierpont Morgan Libr., 1988-90; active alumni coun. Princeton (N.J.) U., 1984-89. Sgt. Air N.G., 1969-70. Mem. Unitarian Ch. Office: Planned Parenthood NYC 26 Bleecker St New York NY 10012-2413

SANGER, GAIL, lawyer; b. N.Y.C., Feb. 4, 1945; d. Maury Daniel and Ethel (Seley) S.; m. Albert M. Fenster, June 16, 1985; children: Robert Jonathan Fenster, Amanda Ruth Fenster. BA cum laude, Bryn Mawr Coll., 1965; LLB cum laude, U. Pa., 1968. Bar: N.Y. 1968. Assoc. Hughes Hubbard & Reed, N.Y.C., 1968-72; assoc. Proskauer Rose Goetz & Mendelsohn, N.Y.C., 1972-76, ptnr., 1976—. Editor: University of Pennsylvania Law Review, 1966-68; contbr. articles to profl. jours. Bd. overseers U. Pa. Law Sch., 1988-91. Mem. ABA, Assn. Bar City N.Y., N.Y. County Lawyers Assn. (chair corp. law com. 1990-93), Order of Coif. Avocation: dressage riding. Office: Proskauer Rose Goetz & Mendelsohn 1585 Broadway New York NY 10036-8200*

SANGER, STEPHEN W., consumer products company executive; b. 1945. With General Mills, Inc., Mpls., 1974—; v.p., gen. mgr. Northstar Divsn. General Mills, Inc., 1983, v.p., gen. mgr. new bus. devel., 1986, pres. Yoplait USA, 1986, pres. Big G Divsn., 1988, sr. v.p., 1989, vice chmn. bd., 1992—, pres., 1993—; bd. dirs. Donaldson Co., Inc., Mpls. Treas. Guthrie Theatre Found., Mpls. Office: Gen Mills Inc One General Mills Blvd Minneapolis MN 55426-1347*

SANGERMAN, HARRY M., lawyer; b. Chgo., Ill., Jan. 13, 1941. BS, U. Ill., 1962; JD, Northwestern U., 1965. Bar: Ill. 1965. Ptnr. McDermott, Will & Emery, Chgo. Mem. ABA, Chgo. Bar Assn. Office: McDermott Will & Emery 227 W Monroe St Chicago IL 60606-5016*

SANGIULIANO, BARBARA ANN, telecommunications industry executive; b. Bronx, N.Y., Dec. 28, 1959; d. Patrick John and Mildred (Soell) Gallo; m. John Warren Sangiuliano, Aug. 28, 1982. BA, Muhlenberg Coll., 1982; MST, Seton Hall U., 1989. CPA, N.J.; CMA. Sr. tax mgr. KPMG Peat Marwick, Short Hills, N.J., 1988-92; sr. tax analyst Allied Signal, Morristown, N.J., 1992-93; tax mgr. AT&T, Morristown, 1993-96, Lucent Techs., Morristown, 1996—. Mem. N.J. Soc. CPAs (dir. Union County chpt.), AICPA, Inst. Mgmt. Accts., Mensa, Omicron Delta Epsilon, Phi Sigma Iota. Republican. Roman Catholic. Avocations: reading, bicycling. Home: 340 William St Scotch Plains NJ 07076-1430 Office: Lucent Techs Inc 412 Mount Kemble Ave Morristown NJ 07962

SANGMEISTER, GEORGE EDWARD, congressman, lawyer; b. Joliet, Ill., Feb. 16, 1931; s. George Conrad and Rose Engaborg (Johnson) S.; m. Doris Marie Hinspeter, Dec. 1, 1951; children: George Kurt, Kimberley Ann. BA, Elmhurst Coll., 1957; LLB, John Marshall Law Sch., 1960, JD, 1970. Bar: Ill. 1960. Ptnr. McKeown, Fitzgerald, Zollner, Buck, Sangmeister & Hutchison, 1969-89; justice of peace, 1961-63; states atty. Will County, 1964-68; mem. Ill. Ho. of Reps., 1972-76, Ill. Senate, 1977-87, 101st-103rd Congresses from 4th (now 11th) Dist. Ill., 1989-95; ret., 1995. Chmn. Frankfort Twp. unit Am. Cancer Soc., Will County Emergency Housing Devel. Corp.; past trustee Will County Family Svc. Agy.; past bd. dirs. Joliet Jr. Coll. Found., Joliet Will County Ctr. for Econ. Devel., Silver Cross Found., Silver Cross Hosp. With inf. AUS, 1951-53. Mem. ABA, Ill. Bar Assn., Assn. Trial Lawyers Am., Am. Legion, Frankfort (past pres.), Mokena C. of C., Old Timers Baseball Assn., Lions. Home: 20735 Wolf Rd Mokena IL 60448-8927

SANGREE, WALTER HINCHMAN, social anthropologist, educator; b. N.Y.C., June 15, 1926; s. Carl Micheal and Constance (LaBoiteaux) S.; m. Mary Lucinda Shaw, June 14, 1952 (div. Jan. 1986); children: Margaretta Elizabeth, Mary Cora; m. Ilse Michaelis, Dec. 31, 1988. A.B., Haverford Coll., 1950; M.A., Wesleyan U., 1952; Ph.D., U. Chgo., 1959. Asst. prof. anthropology U. Rochester, N.Y., 1957-64; assoc. prof. U. Rochester, 1964-73, prof., 1973-95, prof. emeritus, 1995—, chmn. dept. anthropology, 1974-77, acting chmn. dept., 1990; vis. scholar dept. anthropology Harvard U., 1979-80; vis. scholar Ctr. for Population Studies, Harvard U., 1986-87. Author: Age, Prayer & Politics in Tiriki, Kenya, 1966; contbr. articles to profl. jours. Co-clk. Rochester Friends Meeting, 1977-79. Fulbright scholar U.K. and Kenya, 1954-56; NSF research fellow Nigeria, 1963-65. Mem. AAAS, Am. Anthrop. Assn., Internat. African Inst., Royal Anthropol. Soc. Gt. Britain and Ireland, Sigma Xi. Democrat. Mem. Soc. of Friends. Home: PO Box 1290 65 Meadow View Dr Nantucket MA 02554 Office: U Rochester Dept Anthropology Rochester NY 14627

SANI, ROBERT LEROY, chemical engineering educator; b. Antioch, Calif., Apr. 20, 1935; m. Martha Jo Marr, May 28, 1966; children: Cynthia Kay, Elizabeth Ann, Jeffrey Paul. B.S., U. Calif.-Berkeley, 1958, M.S., 1960; Ph.D., U. Minn., 1963. Postdoctoral researcher dept. math Rensselaer Poly. Inst., Troy, N.Y., 1963-64; asst. prof. U. Ill., Urbana, 1964-70, assoc. prof., 1970-76; prof. chem. engring. U. Colo., Boulder, 1976—; co-dir. Ctr. for Low-g Fluid Mechanics and Transport Phenomena, U. Colo., Boulder, 1986-89, dir., 1989—; assoc. prof. French Ministry Edn., 1982, 84, 86, 92, 94, 95; cons. Lawrence Livermore Nat. Lab., Calif., 1974—. Contbr numerous chpts. to profl. publs.; mem. editorial bd. Internat. Jour. Numerical Methods in Fluids, 1981—, Revue Européenne des Éléments Finis, 1990—,. Guggenheim fellow, 1970. Mem. AICE, Soc. for Applied and Indsl. Math., World User Assn. in Applied Computational Fluid Dynamics (bd. dirs.). Democrat. Office: U Colo Dept Chem Engring Campus Box 424 Boulder CO 80309

SANKOVITZ, JAMES LEO, development director, lobbyist; b. St. Paul, July 3, 1934; s. John L. and Mabel A. (Hanrahan) S.; m. Margaret E. Mathews, Aug. 3, 1957; children: Richard, Therese, Patrick, Margaret, Katherine. BS in Journalism, Marquette U., 1956; MA in Speech, U. Denver, 1963. Dir. pub. rels. Coll. of St. Mary of the Wasatch, Salt Lake City, 1956-57; dir. pub. info. Colo. Sch. of Mines, Golden, 1957-63; assoc. dir. devel. Marquette U., Milw., 1963-66, dir. alumni fund, 1966-67, dir. alumni rels., 1967-69, asst. v.p. univ. rels., 1969-70, v.p. univ. rels., 1970-78, v.p. govtl. rels., 1978-86, v.p. govtl. and community affairs, 1986—. Contbr. articles to profl. jours. Founding dir. Univ. Nat. Bank, Milw., 1971-74; bd. dirs. St. Coletta Sch., Jefferson, Wis., 1970-76, 86-93, chair, 1974-76. Mem. Nat. Assn. for Ind. Colls. and Univs. (bd. dirs. Washington 1986-90), Disting. Svc. award 1986), Assn. Jesuit Colls. and Univs. (fed. affairs cons. Washington 1974-90), Assn. Cath. Colls. and Univs. (fed. affairs cons. Washington 1974-85, Blue Key, Alpha Sigma Nu. Roman Catholic. Avocations: woodworking, reading. Home: 4057 N Prospect Ave Milwaukee WI 53211-2121 Office: Marquette U 1324 W Wisconsin Ave Milwaukee WI 53233-2241

SANKS, CHARLES RANDOLPH, JR., clergyman, psychotherapist; b. Yonkers, N.Y., Feb. 14, 1928; s. Charles Randolph and Myrtle Elizabeth (Bunn) S.; m. Jacquelyn Gibson, Nov. 11, 1949; children: Charlene Cynthia Saunders, Valeri Ann. BA cum laude, Stetson U., 1956; BDiv, Southeastern Sem., 1960; ThM, Union Sem., 1961; postgrad., U. Salamanca, Spain, 1975; DMinistry, Wesley Theol. Sem., 1977. Ordained to ministry Baptist Ch., 1957. Minister Judson Meml. Bapt. Ch., Fayetteville, N.C., 1957-60; interim minister First Bapt. Ch. of South Miami, Fla., 1961-62, Sunset Heights Bapt. Ch., Hialeah, Fla., 1962; sr. minister Starling Ave. Bapt. Ch., Martinsville, Va., 1963-69; assoc. pastor 1st Bapt. Ch., Washington, 1969-82, minister to Pres. U.S., 1976-80; developer ministry to community foster-care patients, 1975; dir. Pastoral Counseling Ctr. Greater Marlboro, Md., 1982-87; sr. counselor Washington Pastoral Counseling Svc., 1982-95; dir. clin. mgmt. Washington Pastoral Counseling Svc., 1988-91; ptnr. Pastoral Psychotherapy Assocs., Washington, 1984-91; fellow Am. Assn. Pastoral Counselors, 1984—; trainer Journeyman Program, Fgn. Mission Bd., So. Bapt. Convention, 1968; mem. exec. com. D.C. Bapt. Conv., 1971-77; leader, speaker in liturgics and worship N.C. Bapt. Conv. Conf., 1972, 75; cons. Pastoral Psychotherapy Assocs., Washington, 1981-84; lectr. on worship and liturgics So. Bapt. Theol. Sem., Louisville, 1978; lectr. Stetson U., Deland, Fla., 1978, So. Ecumenical Conf., Atlanta, 1978. Bd. dirs. Uplift House, Washington, 1970-73, Day Care Ctr., Martinsville, Va., 1963-69, Big Brother Orgn. and Sheltered Workshop, Martinsville, Va., 1963-69. Served to cpl. USMC, 1946-49. Fellow Interpreters' House, Lake Junaluska, N.C., 1968-79; guest Oxford U., Eng., 1981. Mem. Am. Digestive Disease Soc. (bd. dirs. 1979-87). Democrat. Baptist. Avocations; travel; horseback riding; music; art. Home: 3087 Oak Chase Dr Roswell GA 30075-5457

SANKS, ROBERT LELAND, environmental engineer, emeritus educator; b. Pomona, Calif., Feb. 19, 1916; s. John B. and Nellie G. (Church) S.; m. Mary Louise Clement, May 16, 1946 (dec. Oct. 1994); children: Margaret Nadine, John Clement. Registered profl. engr., Mont. Draftsman City of La Habra Calif., 1940; asst. engr. Alex Morrison cons. engr., Fullerton, Calif., 1941; jr. engr. U.S. Army Engrs., Los Angeles, 1941-42; asst. research engr. dept. civil engring. U. Calif.-Berkeley, 1942-45; structural engr. The Austin Co., Oakland, Calif., 1945-46; instr. dept. civil engring. U. Utah, Salt Lake city, 1946-49; asst. prof. U. Utah, Salt Lake City, 1949-55, assoc. prof., 1955-58; structural engr. The Lang Co., Salt Lake City, 1950; instrument man Patti McDonald Co., Anchorage, 1951; checker Western Steel Co., Salt Lake City, 1952; structural engr. Moran, Proctor, Meuser and Rutledge, N.Y.C., 1953, F.C. Torkelson Co., Salt Lake City, 1955; soils engr. R.L. Sloane & Assocs., Salt Lake City, 1956; prof., chmn. dept. civil engring. Gonzaga U., Spokane, Wash., 1958-61; prof. dept. civil engring.-engring. mechanics Mont. State U., Bozeman, 1966-82, prof. emeritus, 1982—; vis. prof. U. Tex.-Austin, 1974-75; part-time sr. engr. Christian, Spring, Sielbach & Assoc., Billings, Mont., 1974-82; cons. engr., 1945—; lectr. at pumping sta. design workshops, 1988—; assoc. specialist San. Engring. Research Lab., 1963-65, research engr., 1966. Author: Statically Indeterminate Structural Analysis, 1961; co-author: (with Takashi Assano) Land Treatment and Disposal of Municipal and Industrial Wastewaters, 1976, Water Treatment Plant Design for the Practicing Engineer, 1978; editor-in-chief: Pumping Station Design, 1989 (award Excellence profl. & scholarly pub. div. Assn. Am. Pubs. 1989); contbr. articles on civil engring. to profl. publs. Named to Wall of Fame, Fullerton High Sch., 1987; NSF fellow, 1961-63. Fellow ASCE (chmn. local qualifications com. intermountain sect. 1950-56, pres. intermountain sect. 1957-58); mem. Am. Water Works Assn. (life, pres. Mont. sect. 1981-82, George Warren Fuller award), Mont. Water Environ. Fedn., Assn. Environ. Engring. Profs., Rotary, Sigma Xi, Chi Epsilon. Home: 411 W Dickerson St Bozeman MT 59715-4538 Office: Mont State U Dept Civil Engring Bozeman MT 59717 *True happiness is achieved by dedicating a large share of one's time and effort to promoting the welfare of others. For me, that consists of masterminding the book "Pumping Station Design" for the good of engineers with royalties to the university.*

SANLI, NEVIN, financial executive; b. Izmir, Turkey, Aug. 9, 1962; came to U.S., 1982; s. Nadir and Sunay (Gurtin) S. JD, Lycee Francais de Brussels, Belgium, 1982; BA in Econs., U. Calif., Irvine, 1986, Econs. Degree (hon.), 1986. Accredited sr. appraiser. Investment analyst Unireal Investments, Irvine, 1986-89; analyst Micronomics, Inc., L.A., 1989-90; sr. analyst Desmond, Marcello & Amster, 1990-92; prin., co-founder, pres. Sanli, Pastore & Hill, Inc., L.A., 1992—; bd. dirs. Sanli, Pastore & Hill, U. Calif. Irvine, Step-Up on 2nd, Santa Monica, Calif.; dir. Polit. Action Com. of the Calif. Redevel. Assn. Editor: (newsletter) Valorem Principia, 1992—. Bd. dirs. CRA/PAC, Sacramento, 1994—; mem. Internat. Right-of-Way Assn., L.A., 1993—, San Diego, Calif., 1993—. Mem. Am. Soc. Appraisers. Avocations: Polo, speaking four langs., golf, internat. travel. Office: Sanli Pastore & Hill 3679 Motor Ave Ste 201 Los Angeles CA 90034-5701

SAN MARTIN, ROBERT L., federal official. MME, PhDME, U. Fla. Prof. mech. engring. N.Mex. State U.; past dir. N.Mex. Solar Energy Inst., N.Mex. Energy Inst.; dep. asst. sec. renewable energy, solar energy, field ops. Office Conservation and Renewable Energy, Washington, 1978-89; dep. asst. sec. utility techs. Office Energy Efficiency and Renewable Energy (formerly Office Conservation and Renewable Energy), Washington, 1990-95; acting asst. sec. Office Energy Efficiency and Renewable Energy, 1993-95; chief scientist Office Energy Efficiency and Renewable Energy, Washington, 1995—; past chariperson Renewable Energy Working Party Internat. Energy Agy. Mem. ASME (former chair solar divsn.), Am. Solar Energy Soc. (past bd. dirs.). Office: US Dept Energy Efficiency & Renewable Energy 1000 Independence Ave SW Washington DC 20585-0001

SAN MIGUEL, MANUEL, painter, historian, composer, poet; b. Guayama, P.R., Sept. 29, 1930; s. Manuel and Luisa (Griffo) San M.; m. Sandra Bonilla, July 12, 1969; children: Manuel, Ana. Educated, U. P.R., 1947-51, U. Pa., 1966-68, Arts Students League, N.Y.C., 1968-69. Historian, San Juan Nat. Historic Site, Nat. Park Svc., 1953-63; exec. sec. Acad. Arts and Scis., San Juan, 1963-64; founder of mus. and study collection El Morro Castle San Juan Nat. Hist. Site (U.S. Recipient Commendable Svc. award, 1964, citation for commendable svc. in field of hist. rsch. and interpretation, 1964); painter, writer, musician, 1964—; cons. in field. Exhibited in U. P.R., 1958, 62, Ateneo de P.R., 1962, Pan-Am. Union, Washington, 1963, Bienal Mexico, 1972, Bienal Rio de Janeiro, 1976, Orange County Schs. Mus. Art, Orlando, Fla., 1992, Mus. Modern Art, Paris, 1994, and numerous other nat. and internat. exhbns.; contbr. monographs on historical work in San Juan Nat. Historic Site to U.S. Nat. Archives, Washington; contbr. poetry to anthologies including Anthology of Latin American Poets, vol. III, 1987; rec. artist popular music of P.R. Capt. U.S. Army, 1951-53, Korea. Decorated Bronze Star with valor clasp and oakleaf cluster, Purple Heart, Combat Infantryman Badge, others; recipient citation Nat. Park Svc., 1964, Lifetime Achievement award in cultural arts Govt. of Puerto Rico and Spanish Heritage Found., 1996; named One of Ten Outstanding Hispanic Men, Orlando, Fla., 1991. Mem. VFW (life), Disables Am. Vets. (life), Am. Legion, Acad. Arts and Scis., Ateneo de P.R. (bd. govs. 1959-60), Am. Biog. Inst. (bd. advisors, life mem. bd. govs.), Am. Philatelic Soc. (postal commemorative soc.), Inst. Puerto Rican Culture (cons.), Puerto Rican Philatelic Assn., Internat. Platform Assn., Lions (Lion of Yr. 1962-63). Achievements include documentary research in the restoration of Castillo San Marcos, St. Augustine, Fla., Castillo San Felipe de Barajas, Colombia, South Am. Home: 1214 Howell Creek Dr Winter Springs FL 32708-4516

SAN MIGUEL, SANDRA BONILLA, social worker; b. Santurce, P.R., May 23, 1944; d. Isidoro and Flora (Carrero) Bonilla; m. Manuel San Miguel, July 12, 1969. BA, St. Joseph's Coll., 1966; MS in Social Work, Columbia U., 1970. Case worker Dept. Labor, Migration Div., N.Y.C., 1966-68; clin. social worker N.Y.C. Housing Authority, N.Y.C., 1968-69, Children's Aid Soc., N.Y.C., 1969-71; sr. social worker Traveler's Aid Soc., San Juan, P.R., 1971-74; coord., supr. Dept. Addiction Control Svcs., San Juan, P.R., 1974-77; substance abuse div. dir. Seminole County Mental Health Ctr., Altamonte Springs, Fla., 1978-81; cons. pvt. practice Hispanic Cons. Svcs., Winter Springs, Fla., 1982—; adj. prof. Seminole Community Coll., Lake Mary, Fla., 1986-90; sch. social worker I Seminole County Pub. Schs., Sanford, Fla., 1986-91, lead sch. social worker, 1991—; mem. pres.'s minority adv. coun. U. Ctrl. Fla., 1982—, vice-chair, 1982-86, chair, 1986-90; mem. bd. regents EEO adv. com. State Univ. System Fla., 1985-89; bd. dirs. Seminole Cmty. Mental Health Ctr., 1986-94, 95—, v.p. 1988-90, pres., 1990-91; mem. Fla. Consortium on Tchr. Edn. for Am. Minorities, 1990—; mem. local com. Hispanic Info. and Telecomms. Network, 1990-93, mem. Seminole County (Fla.) Juv. Justice Coun., 1993—; mem. Devereux Found.'s Ctrl. Fla. adv. bd., 1993—; mem. statewide student svcs. adv. com. Dept. Edn., Fla., 1993—; mem. South Seminole Hosp.'s Women's adv. com., 1994—; women's adv. bd. South Seminole Hosp., Fla., 1994—. Mem. NASW, Fla. Assn. Sch. Social Workers (co-founder minority caucus 1988, columnist quar. newsletter Minority Corner 1988-92, bd. dirs. 1989—, sec. 1990-92, v.p. 1992-93, pres. 1993-94), Collegiate Social Workers P.R., Columbia U. Alumni Assn., St. Joseph's Coll. Alumni Assn., Sch. Social Work Assn. of Am., Fla. Assn. of Student Svcs. Adminstrs. Home: 1214 Howell Creek Dr Winter Springs FL 32708-4516 Office: Seminole County Pub Schs 1401 S Magnolia Ave Sanford FL 32771-3400

SANNEH, LAMIN, religion educator; married; 2 children. MA in Arabic and Islamic Studies, U. Birmingham, Eng., 1968; postgrad., Near East Sch. Theology, Beirut, 1968-69; PhD in African Islamic History, U. London, 1974. Resident tutor Ctr. for Study of Islam and Christianity, Ibadan, Nigeria, 1969-71; vis. scholar U. Sierra Leone, Freetown, 1974-75; lectr. U. Ghana, Legon, 1975-78, U. Aberdeen, Scotland, 1978-81; asst. prof., then assoc. prof. history of religion Harvard U., Cambridge, Mass., 1981-89; prof., chmn. Coun. on African Studies Yale U., New Haven, 1989—; cons. World Coun. Chs., 1974-79, The Africans TV series, PBS, 1986, Program on Christian-Muslim Rels. in Africa, 1988—, Prof. Lamin Sanneh Found., Banjul, The Gambia; instr. San Francisco Theol. Sem., San Anselmo, Calif., 1987, Iliff Sch. Theology, Denver, 1988, Disting. Staley Christian lectr. Mennonite Brethern Bible Coll., Winnipeg, Can., 1988; lectr. Princeton (N.J.) Theol. Sem., 1988; guest lectr. Haverford (Pa.) Coll., 1988; Mars lectr. Northwestern U., 1988, Spriggs lectr. Protestant Episcopal Theol. Sem., Alexandria, Va., 1990; Cullum lectr. Augusta Coll., U. Ga., 1990; life fellow Clare Hall, Cambridge (Eng.) U., 1995; participant various acad. confs. Author: West African Christianity: The Religious Impact, 1983, Translating the Message: The Missionary Impact on Culture, 1989, The Jakhanke Muslim Clerics: A Religious and Historical Study of Islam in Senegambia (c. 1250-1905), 1990, Encountering the West: Christianity and the Global Cultural Process, 1993, The Crown and the Turban, 1996; also articles; co-editor Jour. Religion in Africa, 1979-84; mem. adv. bd. Studies in Interreligious Dialogue; editor-at-large The Christian Century; contbg. editor Internat. Bull. Missionary Rsch. Decorated comdr. de l'Ordre Nat. du Lion (Senegal); recipient award Theol. Edn. Fund, 1971-74, award U. London, 1972, Carnegie Truste of Univs. of Scotland, 1980. Mem. Internat. Acad. Union (consultative mem. Africa com.), Ecumenical Assn. African Theologians (exec. com.), Royal African Soc. Home: 47 Morris St Hamden CT 06517-3426 Office: Yale U Div Sch 409 Prospect St New Haven CT 06511-2167

SANNER, KENNETH LEROY, quality systems analyst; b. Smithton, Pa., Apr. 26, 1952; s. Kenneth James and Esther (Lebe) S.; m. Dianna Lee Lynn, Nov. 24, 1971. A of Engring. Tech., Grantham Coll., 1988. NDT tech. Bucyrus Engring., Glassport, Pa., 1971-73, metallurgy lab. tech., 1973-75, metallurgy lab. supr., 1975-81; supr. NDT Latrobe (Pa.) Steel Co., 1981-83, NDT specialist, 1983-86, supr. NDT, 1986-87, supr. NDT, Lims, 1987-90, inspection systems analyst, 1990-96; mgr. Quality Systems, 1996—. Mem. Am. Soc. Nondestructive Testing, Am. Soc. Quality Control, Am. Soc. Testing & Materials, NRA, Masons. Avocations: aviation, ham radio, computers, hunting, shooting. Home: Rd 3 Box 195A Belle Vernon PA 15012 Office: Latrobe Steel Co PO Box 31 Latrobe PA 15650

SANNER, ROYCE NORMAN, lawyer; b. Lancaster, Minn., Mar. 9, 1931; s. Oscar N. and Clara (Hermanson) S.; m. Janice L. Sterne, Dec. 27, 1972; children—Michelle Joy, Craig Allen. BS, Moorhead State U., 1953; LLB cum laude, U. Minn., 1961. Bar: Minn. 1961, U.S. Dist. Ct. Minn. 1961, U.S. Supreme Ct. 1981. Tchr. English Karlstad (Minn.) High Sch., 1955-57; counsel IDS Life Ins. Co., Mpls., 1961-68; v.p., gen. counsel IDS Life Ins. Co., 1969-72, exec. v.p., gen. counsel, 1972-77; dir. corp. devel. Investors Diversified Svcs., Inc., Mpls., 1968-69; v.p., gen. counsel Investors Diversified Svcs., Inc., 1975-78; v.p. Investors Diversified Svcs., Inc. (Benefit Plans Svc. Group), 1978-80, v.p., gen. counsel, 1980-82; v.p. law Northwestern Nat. Life Ins. Co., Mpls., 1982-83, sr. v.p., gen. counsel, sec., 1983—; sr. v.p., gen. counsel, sec. ReliaStar Fin. Corp. (formerly known as NWNL Cos., Inc.), Mpls., 1988-96; with Maslon, Edelman, Borman & Brand, Mpls., 1996—; bd. dirs. Riverside Med. Ctr., Friendship Ventures, Inc.; chmn. bd. dirs. Fairview Hosp. and Healthcare Svcs. Served with U.S. Army, 1953-55. Mem. ABA, Am. Soc. Corps. Secs., Minn. Bar Assn., Hennepin County Bar Assn., Fed. Bar Assn., Assn. of Life Ins. Counsel, Minn. Corp. Counsel Assn., Mpls. Club, Rotary. Home: 4811 Westminster Rd Minnetonka MN 55345-3723 Office: Maslon Edelman Borman & Brand 3300 Norwest Ctr 90 S 7th St Minneapolis MN 55402-4140

SAN NICOLAS, HENRY DELEON GUERRERO, territory senator; b. Rota, No. Mariana Islands, Dec. 9, 1955; s. Jose Mendiola and Vicenta (Deleon Guerrero) San N.; m. Estella Lizama cruz, Feb. 12, 1977; children: Hilbert Henry, Sharon Esther, Eric Henry, Jamaima Esther, Jonathan Henry. Student, No. Marianas Coll., Saipan, U. Guam Ext., Saipan, Internat. Bus. Coll., Agana, Guam, 1974. Tchr. Tinian (No. Mariana Islands) Elem. and Jr. H.S., 1975-80; govt. acct., certifying officer Dept. Fin., Tinian, 1980-83, resident dir. fin., 1983-84; spl. asst. to mayor Office of Mayor, City of Tinian, 1983, 88-90; econ. specialist Commonwealth Devel. Authority, Saipan, 1984-87; mem. No. Marianas Commonwealth Senate, Saipan, 1990—, v.p., 1990-92, 94—; asst. instr. Internat. Bus. Coll., 1975; gen. mgr., fin. cons. Day's Splty. Svcs., Tinian, 1979-86; assoc. instr. San Jose State U., Saipan, 1982. Chmn. Tinian Legis. Del., 1994-96. Recipient certs. of acctg. and bus. math. Internat. Bus. Coll., 1975; cert. for human rels. No. Marianas Govt., 1980, advanced supervisory and mgmt. award, 1981. Mem. Calif. Astrology Assn. Home: San Jose Vlg Tinian MP 96952 Office: 9th No Marianas Commonwealth Legis Capitol Hill PO Box 129 Saipan MP 96950-0129

SANNUTI, PEDDAPULLAIAH, electrical engineering educator; b. Rajupalem, Andhra-Pradesh, India, Apr. 2, 1941; came to U.S., 1965; m. 1965; children: Aruna, Arun. PhD, U. Ill., Urbana, 1968. Asst. prof. dept. elec. and computer engring. Rutgers U., Piscataway, N.J., 1968-71, assoc. prof., 1971-76, prof., 1976—. Fellow IEEE. Office: Rutgers Univ Dept Elec & Computer Engring Piscataway NJ 08855-0909

SANNWALD, WILLIAM WALTER, librarian; b. Chgo., Sept. 12, 1940; s. William Frederick and Irene Virginia (Stanish) S.; children: Sara Ann, William Howard. B.A., Beloit Coll., 1963; M.A.L.S., Rosary Coll., River Forest, Ill., 1966; M.B.A., Loyola U., Chgo., 1974. Mktg. mgr. Xerox Univ. Microfilms, 1972-75; assoc. dir. Detroit Public Library, 1975-77; dir. Ventura (Calif.) County Library, 1977-79; city libr. San Diego Public Libr., 1979—; vis. instr. mktg. San Diego State U. Author: Checklist of Library Building Considerations, 2d edit., 1992; chairperson editorial adv. bd. Pub. Librs. Pres. Met. Libraries Sect., 1989. Recipient Outstanding Prof. award and Outstanding Mktg. Prof. award, 1985; Award of Merit AIA San Diego chpt., 1988, Irving Gill award for Architecture and Mgmt., 1995. Mem. ALA, Calif. Library Authority for Systems and Services (pres. congress of mems. 1980), Calif. Library Assn., Libr. Admintrn. and Mgmt. Assn. (pres. 1995—). Roman Catholic. Home: 3538 Paseo Salomoner La Mesa CA 91941 Office: San Diego Pub Libr 820 E St San Diego CA 92101-6416

SANO, EMILY J., museum director; b. Santa Ana, Calif., Feb. 17, 1942; d. Masao and Lois Kikue (Inokuchi) S. BA, Ind. U., 1967; MA, Columbia U., 1970, MPhil, 1976, PhD, 1983. Lectr. Oriental Art Vassar Coll., Poughkeepsie, N.Y., 1974-79; curator Asian Art, asst. dir. programs Kimbell Art Mus., Ft. Worth, 1979-89; dep. dir. collections and exhbns. Dallas Mus. Art, 1989-92; dep. dir., chief curator Asian Art Mus., San Francisco, 1993-95, dir., 1995—. Author: Great Age of Japanese Buddhist Sculpture, 1982; editor: The Blood of Kings, 1986, Weavers, Merchants and Kings, 1984, Painters of the Great Ming, 1993. Bd. dirs. Coll. Art Assn., N.Y.C., 1990-94. Woodrow Wilson Fellow, 1966-67; grantee Carnegie, 1963-64, Fulbright-Hays, 1977-78. Office: Asian Art Mus Golden Gate Park San Francisco CA 94118

SANO, ROY I., bishop. Ordained to ministry United Meth. Ch., later consecrated bishop; appointed Bishop Rocky Mountain Conf., United Meth. Ch., Denver. Office: PO Box 6006 Pasadena CA 91102-6006*

SANSBURY, BLAKE EDWARD, product development engineer; b. Louisville, Jan. 6, 1957; s. Edward R. and Marilyn M. (Blake) S.; m. Amy S. Zeldin, June 12, 1994. BS in mech. engring., U. Louisville, 1982. Cert. mfg. tech., 1985. Intern mfg. engring. TubeTurns, Inc., Louisville, 1980-82; tooling engr. Square D Co., Oxford, Ohio, 1982-85; engring. mgr. Dayton-Walther Corp., Dayton, Ohio, 1985-87; process engr. U.S. Precision Lens, Inc., Cin., 1987-89, product devel. engr., 1989—. Author: (manual) Curve-Master, 1989, (handbook) O-Ring Coupler Guidelines for Design, 1992. Asst. scoutmaster Boys Scouts Am., eagle scout, 1974. Mem. Nat. Mgmt. Assn. (outstanding new mem. award 1984), Machining Tech. Assn., Soc. Plastics Engrs., Soc. Mfg. Engrs., Sigma Phi Epsilon (pres. 1981-82). Achievements include U.S. patent for focus adjustment assembly for projection TV. Home: 901 Old Orchard Rd Cincinnati OH 45230 Office: US Precision Lens Inc 3997 McMann Rd Cincinnati OH 45245

SANSEVERINO, RAYMOND ANTHONY, lawyer; b. Bklyn., Feb. 16, 1947; s. Raphael and Alice Ann (Camerano) S.; m. Karen Marie Mooney, Aug. 24, 1968 (dec. 1980); children: Deirdre Ann, Stacy Lee; m. Victoria Vent, June 6, 1982 (div. 1995). AB in English Lit., Franklin & Marshall Coll., 1968; JD cum laude, Fordham U., 1972. Bar: N.Y. 1973, U.S. Dist. Ct. (so. dist. and ea. dist.) N.Y. 1973, U.S. Ct. Appeals (2d cir.) 1974, U.S. Supreme Ct. 1986. Assoc. Rogers & Wells, N.Y.C., 1972-75, Corbin & Gordon, N.Y.C., 1975-77; ptnr. Corbin Silverman & Sanseverino, N.Y.C., 1978—, mng. ptnr., 1985—. Contbr. articles to profl. jours.; articles editor Fordham Law Rev., 1971-72. Recipient West Pub. Co. prize, 1972. Mem. ABA, Assn. Bar City of N.Y., N.Y. State Bar Assn., Twin Oaks Swim and Tennis Club (bd. dirs. 1981—, pres. 1993—). Republican. Roman Catholic. Office: Corbin Silverman & Sanseverino 805 3rd Ave New York NY 10022-7513

SANSOM, ANDREW, federal agency administrator; b. Hawthorne, Nev., Oct. 10, 1945; s. Ernest Samuel and Imo Leone (Heacock) S.; m. Nona Wood, Dec. 30, 1966; children: Andrew Wood, April Claire. BS cum laude, Tex. Tech. U., 1968. Environ. coord. White House Conf. Youth, Washington; spl. asst. Office Sec. Interior, Washington; dir. conservation edn. Fed. Agy. Adminstrn., Washington, 1974-76; dep. dir. Energy Inst. U. Houston, 1976-80; v.p. devel. Old River Co.; exec. dir. Tex. Nature Conservancy; coord. land acquisition and mgmt. Tex. Parks and Wildlife, Austin, exec. dir., 1991—. Author: Texas Lost, 1995; contbr. articles to Tex. Monthly mag., The Tex. Observer, Houston City Mag., Politics Today, Tex. Hwys., Tex. Parks and Wildlife. Commr. Brazoria County Parks Bd.; founder Cradle Tex. Conservancy; trustee Tex. Hist. Found., Bat Conservation Internat.; del. Rep. Nat. Conv., 1980; chmn. State Senate campaign Buster Brown; county chmn. George Bush campaign; co-chmn. Gov. Clements Brazoria county campaign; appt. Gov.'s Task Force on Flooding and Flood Control, 1981. Recipient Conservationist of Yr. Sportsmans Clubs Tex., Conservation award Chevron, 1990, Cornelius Amory Pugsley medal Nat. Parks Found., 1993. Chuck Yaeger award Nat. Fish and Wildlife Found., 1995. Office: Tex Parks & Wildlife Dept 4200 Smith School Rd Austin TX 78744-3218

SANSONE, PAUL J., automotive executive; b. 1955. CEO Sansone Auto Network, Avenel, N.J., 1980—. Home: 100 Route 1 Avenel NJ 07001

SANSONE, TORRY MARK, association executive; b. Chgo., Oct. 12, 1940; s. Vincent Anthony and Dorothy Ann (Scolaro) S. BA, St. Mary's Sem., Perryville, Md., 1963; postgrad., De Andreis Inst. Theology, Lemont, Ill., 1964-67; STL, Lateran U., Rome, 1968. Dean of men St. John's Sem., Camarillo, Calif., 1968-71; exec. dir. Am. Student Dental Assn., Chgo., 1972-80, Emergency Nurses Assn., Chgo., 1981-89, Soc. Nuclear Medicine, Reston, Va., 1989—. Mem. Am. Soc. Assn. Execs. Office: Soc Nuclear Medicine 1850 Samuel Morse Dr Reston VA 22090-5316

SANSTEAD, WAYNE GODFREY, state superintendent, former lieutenant governor; b. Hot Springs, Ark., Apr. 16, 1935; s. Godfrey A. and Clara (Buen) S.; m. Mary Jane Bober, June 16, 1957; children: Timothy, Jonathan. B.A. in Speech and Polit. Sci, St. Olaf Coll., 1957; M.A. in Pub. Address, Northwestern U., 1966; Ed.D., U. N.D., 1974. Tchr. Luverne, Minn., 1959-60; dir. forensics Minot (N.D.) High Sch., 1960-71, tchr. social sci., 1960-78; mem. N.D. Ho. of Reps., 1965-70, 83-85, N.D. Senate, 1971-73; lt. gov. N.D. Bismarck, 1973-81; supt. pub. instrn. N.D., Bismarck, 1985—. Served with AUS, 1957-59. Recipient Disting. Alumnus award St. Olaf Coll., 1991; named Outstanding Freshman Senator A.P., 1971, Outstanding Young Educator, N.D. Jr. C. of C., 1967, Outstanding Young Man, Minot Jr. C. of C., 1964; Coe Family Found. scholar, 1963, Eagleton scholar Rutgers U., 1969. Mem. N.D. Edn. Assn., NEA (legis. com. 1969—), Central States Speech Assn., Am. Forensic Assn., Jr. C. of C., Sons of Norway. Democrat. Lutheran (chmn. Western N.D. research and social action com. 1962-68). Clubs: Elk, Toastmaster. Home: 1120 Columbia Dr Bismarck ND 58504-6514 Office: Dept Pub Instrn 600 E Boulevard Ave Bismarck ND 58505-0660*

SANSWEET, STEPHEN JAY, journalist, author; b. Phila., June 14, 1945; s. Jack Morris and Fannie (Axelrod) S. BS, Temple U., 1966. Reporter Phila. Inquirer, 1966-69; reporter Wall Street Jour., Phila., 1969-71, Montreal, Que, Can., 1971-73; reporter Wall Street Jour., L.A., 1973-84, dep. bur. chief, 1984-87, bur. chief, 1987—; lectr. bus. journalism U. So. Calif., L.A., 1984-87. Author: The Punishment Cure, 1976, Science Fiction Toys and Models, 1981, Star Wars: From Concept to Screen to Collectible, 1992, Tomart's Guide to Worldwide Star Wars Collectibles, 1994; consulting editor: Star Wars Galaxy, 1993, 2d series, 1994, 3d series, 1995. Recipient award for best fire story Phila. Fire Dept., 1968, Pub. Svc.-Team Mem. award Sigma Delta Chi, 1977; finalist Loeb award, 1990. Mem. Soc. Profl. Journalists. Avocation: collecting toys and movie memorabilia. Office: Wall Street Jour 6500 Wilshire Blvd Ste 1500 Los Angeles CA 90048-4935 also: The Wall Street Journal 200 Liberty St New York NY 10281-1003

SANT, JOHN TALBOT, lawyer; b. Ann Arbor, Mich., Oct. 7, 1932; s. John Francis and Josephine (Williams) S.; m. Almira Steedman Baldwin, Jan. 31, 1959; children: John Talbot Jr., Richard Baldwin, Frank Williams. AB, Princeton U., 1954; LLB, Harvard U., 1957. Bar: Mo. 1957. Assoc. Thompson, Mitchell, Douglas & Neill, St. Louis, 1958-60; atty. McDonnell Aircraft Co., St. Louis, 1960-61, asst. sec., 1961-62, sec., 1962-67; sec. McDonnell Douglas Corp., St. Louis, 1967-76, asst. gen. counsel, 1969-74, corp. v.p. legal, 1974-75, corp. v.p., gen. counsel, 1975-88, bd. dirs. 1978-82, sr. v.p., gen. counsel, 1988-91; ptnr. Bryan Cave, 1991—. Vestry of St. Michael and St. George, St. Louis, 1979-82, 87-90, 93-95; bd. dirs. Grace Hill Neighborhood Svcs. Inc., St. Louis, 1987-93; pres. Grace Hill Settlement House, 1996—; mem. transition task force Supt. Elect of St. Louis Pub. Schs., 1996. Mem. ABA (pub. contracts sec., coun. 1987-91), Am. Law Inst., Mo. Bar. Assn., St. Louis Bar Assn. Home: 9 Ridgewood St Saint Louis MO 63124-1849 Office: Bryan Cave 1 Metropolitan Sq Saint Louis MO 63102-2750

SANTA, DONALD F., JR., federal agency administrator; m. Karen Santa; 1 child, Madelyn. AB, Duke U., 1980; JD, Columbia U., 1983. Assoc. atty. Andrews & Kurth, Washington, 1983-85, Van Nes, Feldman, Sutcliffe & Curtis, P.C., Washington, 1985-89; counsel U.S. Senate com. on Energy and Natural Resources; mem. Fed. Energy Regulatory Commn., 1993—. Co-author: (with Patricia J. Beneke) Federal Natural Gas Policy and the Energy Policy Act of 1992, 1993, (with Clifford S. Sikora) Open Access and Transition Costs: Will the Electric Industry Track the Natural Gas Industry Restructuring?, 1994; contbr. articles to law jours. Mem. Nat. Assn. Regulatory Utilities Commrs. (com. on gas). Office: Fed Energy Regulatory Commn 825 N Capitol St NE Washington DC 20426

SANTACANA, GUIDO E., physiology educator; b. Placetas, Las Villa, Cuba, Dec. 25, 1952; came to U.S., 1964; s. Guido and Concepcion (Sanchez) S.; m. Maria E. Laffitte, May 27, 1978; 1 child, Guido E. BS, Coll. Agrl. and Mech. Arts, Mayaguez, P.R., 1975; PhD, Med. Sci. Campus, San Juan, P.R., 1982. Instr. dept. nat. sci. Sacred Heart U., Santurce, P.R., 1976-84, asst. prof. dept. natural sci., 1982-84; instr. dept. physiology S.J.B. Sch. Med., Hato Rey, P.R., 1981-83; asst. prof. dept. physiology Universidad Central del Caribe Sch. Medicine, Bayamon, P.R., P.R., 1984-86; prof., chmn. dept. physiology Universidad Central del Caribe Sch. Medicine, Bayamon, P.R., 1986-95, dir. grad. program, 1994-95; chmn. dept. physiology Ponce Sch. Medicine, 1995—. Contbr. articles to sci. jours. Recipient Sci. award Bausch & Lomb, San Juan, P.R., 1971, Rsch. Ctr. for Minority Instns. rsch. grant NIH, Bayamon, P.R., 1986—, Minority Access to Rsch. Careers Program faculty fellowship NIH, San Juan, 1979-82. Mem. AAVSO Assn. (Boston), Am. Physiol. Soc. (Porter physiology devel. grants com.), Am. Assn. Chmn. Depts. Physiology, Soc. Exptl. Biology and Medicine, Alpha Omega Alpha. Roman Catholic. Avocations: amateur radio, astronomy. Office: Ponce Sch Medicine Dept Physiology PO Box 7004 Ponce PR

SANTA-COLOMA, BERNARDO, secondary school educator, counselor; b. N.Y.C., May 31, 1934; s. Bernardo Santa-Coloma Sr. and Belma Remotti; m. Sofia A. Santa-Coloma, Dec. 22, 1981; children: Ananda, Anita. BA in Humanistic Psychology, U. Calif., Santa Cruz, 1973; MA in Integral Counseling Psychology, Calif. Inst. Integral Studies, San Francisco, 1976; MEd in Secondary Edn., U. Nev., Las Vegas, 1979; 3 level cert., Feuerstein's Instrumental, Enrichment Program; postgrad., U. Sarasota. Cert. secondary edn. tchr. ESl, history, English, Tex.; cert. guidance counselor Tex. Edn. Assn., lic. marriage and family therapist, Tex.; nat. cert. counselor. Mem. tchr. corps., vol. VISTA, Las Vegas, Nev., 1976-79; family counselor, English tutor Diocese of Matamoros and Valle Hermoso Tamps, Mexico, Cath. Family Svcs. and Vol. Ednl. and Social Svcs., Amarillo, Tex., 1980-82; grad. asst. Pan Am. U., Brownsville, Tex.; at-risk program, low-level reading instr. Brownsville Ind. Sch. Dist., 1984-94; basic skills instr. James Pace High Sch., Brownsville; counselor and psychotherapist Family Effectiveness and Devel. Program, Kids in Crisis Teenage Crisis Hotline, La Casa Esperanza Home for Boys; basic adult reading instr. Southmost Coll., ESL Alternative Ctr.; tchr., pvt. practice counselor, Brownsville Ind. Sch. Dist. Alternative Ctr. Contbr. articles to profl. jours. in U.S. and Mex. including Integracion Integral, Journey in Matamoros. Vol. VISTA, 1976-79, VISTA Tchr. Corps, Las Vegas, Peace Corps, Thailand, 1979, Vol. Edn./Soc. Svc., Tex., Mex., 1980-82. With USN, 1952-56, medic neuropsychiatric wards San Diego and Guam. Recipient scholarship U. Calif.-Santa Cruz, 1971-73, U. Nev. tchr. corps, 1977-79; named grad. asst. Calif. Inst. Integral Studies, 1974-76. Home: PO Box 3941 Brownsville TX 78523-3941 also: Country Club 2009 Madero Dr Brownsville TX 78521-1734 *Waking up is really the seed of perfection, of personal and transpersonal realization - involution precedes evolution! To be is to do and to do IS. In the final analysis, final judgement, what shall we - yes, you and I contribute to our fellowman, to posterity? - we often die before giving birth to ourselves - truly to be reborn is not easy; we create, instead, an intense paradox.*

SANTA MARIA, PHILIP JOSEPH, III, lawyer; b. Ft. Lauderdale, Fla., Oct. 10, 1945; s. Philip Joseph Jr. and Margaret Elizabeth (Hillard) S.; m. Gail Suzanne Claussen, Aug. 23, 1969; children: Todd, Carly. AB, Gettysburg (Pa.) Coll., 1967; JD, Am. U., 1970. Bar: Md. 1970, U.S. Ct. Mil. Appeals 1971, U.S. Supreme Ct. 1975, D.C. 1976, Calif. 1976, U.S. Dist. Ct. Md. 1977, U.S. Ct. Appeals (4th cir.) 1977. Assoc. Simpson & Simpson, Rockville, Md., 1974-75; sole practice Gaithersburg, Md., 1975-79; ptnr. Haight, Rosfeld, Noble & Santa Maria, Gaithersburg, 1980-81, Santa Maria & Weiss, Chartered, Gaithersburg, 1981—. Mem. editorial bd. Am. U. Law Rev., 1969; author pamphlet What To Do. Mem. Standby Selective Service Local Bd. 69, Montgomery County, Md., 1981-83, Standby Selective Service Bd. of Appeals, Md., 1983-92, Met. Wash. YMCA Trustee's Coun., 1990-93. Served to capt. USAF, 1970-74. Named one of Outstanding Young Men in Am., 1971. Mem. ABA, Calif. Bar Assn., D.C. Bar Assn., Montgomery County Bar Assn., Md. Trial Lawyers Assn. Clubs: Montgomery Soccer, Inc. (league commr. 1985); Gaithersburg Tennis Assn. (pres. 1976); Snowbird Youth Ski (Md.) (pres. 1975-76). Home: 10319 Royal Woods Ct Gaithersburg MD 20879-1027 Office: Santa Maria & Weiss Chartered 18522 Office Park Dr Gaithersburg MD 20879-2500

SANTANA, CARLOS, guitarist; b. Autlan de Navarro, Mexico, July 20, 1947. prin. Guts and Grace Records, 1993. Played guitar in Tijuana nightclubs; recorded with Mike Bloomfield and Al Kooper's Super Session; founder, guitarist: rock band Santana, 1966—; appeared at Woodstock Festival, 1969; rec. artist, Columbia Records, 1969—; albums include: Santana, 1968, Abraxas, 1970, Santana III, 1972, Caravanserai, 1972, Welcome, 1973, Greatest Hits, 1974, Barboletta, 1974, Lotus, 1975, Amigos, 1976, Festival, 1977, Moonflower, 1977, Inner Secrets, 1979, Marathon, 1979, Swing of Delight, 1980, Zebop, 1981, Shango, 1982, Havana Moon, 1983, Beyond Appearances, 1985, Freedom, 1987, Viva Santana!, 1988, Doin' It, 1990, Spirits Dancing In the Flesh, 1990, Milagro, 1992, Brothers, 1994, Sacred Fire: Live in South America, 1995; solo albums include Devadip Carlos-Oneness: Silver Dreams, Golden Reality, 1979, Blues for Salvador, 1987; world-wide concert tours with Santana Band; performed and recorded with Buddy Miles, Herbie Hancock, McCoy Tyner, John McLaughlin, Jose Feliciano, Wayne Shorter and Alice Coltrane, Aretha Franklin, Olatunji . Recipient Gold Medal award, 1977, Grammy award, 1989. Office: Santana Mgmt PO Box 881630 San Francisco CA 94188-1630 *Keep an open heart, focus on the positive, be true to your innermost feelings, but most of all make time to visit the Lord within.*

SANTANA, ROBERT RAFAEL, lawyer; b. Bklyn., Apr. 22, 1961; s. Carlos Roberto and Hilda Eva (Cabrera) S.; 1 child, Robert Jr. BBA, Fordham U., 1985; JD, NYU, 1990. Bar: N.Y. 1992, U.S. Dist. Ct. (ea. dist.) 1992, U.S. Dist. Ct. (so. dist.) 1993. Police officer N.Y.C. Police Dept., 1981-93, sgt., 1993—; assoc. Morales & Silva, P.C., N.Y.C., 1992-94, ptnr., 1995-96; ptnr. Morales & Assocs., 1996—. Mem. ABA, N.Y. State Bar Assn., N.Y. County Lawyers Assn., Puerto Rican Bar Assn., Hispanic Nat. Bar Assn. Democrat. Roman Catholic. Avocations: basketball, football, baseball, travel, reading. Office: Morales & Assocs 11 Park Pl Ste 909 New York NY 10007

SANTANGELI, FRANK, financial services company executive; b. Liverpool, Eng., June 20, 1934; s. Louie and Ellen S.; m. Anne Gauge, Dec. 21, 1957; children: Susan, David, Peter. Grad., Sch. Slavonic Studies, Cambridge (Eng.) U., 1954. C.L.U., Can., U.S. Asst. gen. mgr. for Can. Occidental Life Ins. Co. Calif., 1958-69; with Sun Life Assurance Co. Can., Toronto, 1970—, mgmt. services officer, then corp. sec., 1977-79, v.p. mktg., 1979-84; pres., chief exec. officer Finsco Svcs. Ltd., Toronto, 1988—; chmn. Investment Funds Inst. Can.; pres., bd. dirs. Jarilowsky Finsco. Mem. York Downs Golf and Country Club (Toronto), Nat. Club. Home: 80 Front St E # 511, Toronto, ON Canada Office: Finsco Svcs Ltd, 110 Yonge St Ste 500, Toronto, ON Canada M5C 1T4

SANTANGELO, MARIO VINCENT, dental association executive, educator; b. Youngstown, Ohio, Oct. 5, 1931; s. Anthony and Maria (Zarlenga) S.; student U. Pitts., 1949-51; D.D.S., Loyola U. (Chgo.), 1955, M.S., 1960. Instr. Loyola U., Chgo., 1957-60, asst. prof., 1960-66, chmn. dpt. radiology, 1962-70, dir. dental aux. utilization program, 1963-70, assoc. prof., 1966-70, chmn. dept. oral diagnosis, 1967-70, asst. dean, 1969-70; practice dentistry, Chgo., 1960-70; cons. Cert. Bd. Am. Dental Assts. Assn., 1967-76, VA Research Hosp., 1969-75, Chgo. Civil Service Commn., 1967-75; counselor Chgo. Dental Assts. Assn., 1966-69; mem. dental student tng. adv. com. Div.

Dental Health USPHS, Dept. Health, Edn. and Welfare, 1969-71; cons. dental edn. rev. com. NIH, 1971-72; cons. USPHS, HEW, Region IV, Atlanta, 1973-76, Region V, Chgo., 1973-77; mem. Commn. on Dental Edn. and Practice, Fedn. Dentaire Internationale, 1984-92. Bd. visitors Sch. Dental Medicine, Washington U., St. Louis, 1974-76. Served to capt. USAF, 1955-57. Recipient Dr. Harry Strusser Meml. award NYU Coll. Dentistry, 1985. Fellow Am. Coll. Dentists; mem. AMA (mem. edn. work Group 1982-86), Assembly Specialized Accrediting Bodies (council on postsecondary accreditation 1981-92, award of Merit 1992), Am. Assn. Dental Schs., Odontographic Soc. Chgo., Am. (asst. sec. council dental edn. 1971-81, acting sec. 1981-82, sec. 1982-90, dir., 1990-92, asst. sec. commn. on dental accreditation 1975-81, acting sec. 1981-82, sec. 1982-90, dir., 1990-92, acting sec. commn. on continuing dental edn. 1981-82, sec. 1982-85), Ill., Chgo. dental assns., Am. Acad. Oral Pathology, Am. Acad. Dental Radiology, Canadian Dental Assn. (commission on dental accreditation award of merit 1992), Am. Acad. Oral Medicine, Am. Assn. Dental Examiners (hon. 1993), Omicron Kappa Upsilon (pres. 1967-68), Blue Key, Xi Psi Phi. Contbr. articles to profl. jours. Home: 1440 N Lake Shore Dr Chicago IL 60610

SANTANIELLO, ANGELO GARY, retired state supreme court justice; b. New London, Conn., May 28, 1924; s. Samuel C. and Katie Santaniello; m. Catherine A. Driscoll, June 1948 (dec.); children—Samuel Gary, Lisa Mary; m. Catherine M. Cooper, Sept. 27, 1968; 1 child, Maria Roberta. B.A., Coll. Holy Cross, 1945; JD, Georgetown U., 1950. Bar: Conn. 1950, U.S. Dist. Ct. Conn. Sole practice, New London, 1950-53; sr. ptnr. Santaniello & Satti, 1953-61, Santaniello Satti Wilensky & Schwartz, 1962-65; judge Conn. Cir. Ct., 1966-71, Conn. Ct. Common Pleas, 1971-73; judge Conn. Superior Ct., 1973-85, adminstrv. judge, 1978-85, chief adminstrv. judge, civil divsn., 1979-85; assoc. justice Conn. Supreme Ct., Hartford, 1985-87, sr. assoc. justice, 1987-95; asst. prosecuting atty. New London Police Ct., 1951-55. Trustee, New London Pub. Library, Mitchell Coll., Lawrence and Meml. Hosp.; bd. dirs. Holy Cross Alumni, Am. Cancer Soc., New London Fed. Savs. and Loan; chmn. New London Republican Party, 1956-65; nat. committeeman Conn. State Young Reps., 1959-61; legal counsel Conn. State Senate Rep. Minority, 1961-65; campaign mgr. to gubernatorial candidate, 1962; mem. athletic council Holy Cross Coll., 1971-77, chmn., 1972-73; bd. of trustees Mitchell Coll., 1976-89, chmn., 1988-91. Served to lt. (j.g.) USNR, 1942-46. Recipient Columbus award Italian-Am. Civic Assn., 1964; In Hoc Signo award Holy Cross Coll., 1976; 1st Humanitarian award Eastern Conn. chpt. March of Dimes, 1983. Mem. New London Bar Assn., Conn. Bar Assn., Am. Justinian Soc., Holy Cross Alumni Assn. (pres. 1981-82). Roman Catholic. Home: 25 Shirley Ln New London CT 06320-2929 Office: 70 Huntington St New London CT 06320-6113 also: 70 Huntington St New London CT 06320-6113

SANTE, WILLIAM ARTHUR, II, aerospace and manufacturing company executive; b. N.Y.C., July 16, 1943; s. William Arthur and Grace Elizabeth (Burnat) S.; m. Kathleen Margaret Rourke, July 2, 1966; children: Jennifer, William, Timothy. BS, U. Detroit, 1965; MBA, U. Pitts., 1981. CPA, Mich. Mgr. Deloitte & Touche, Detroit, 1965-78; gen. auditor Rockwell Internat., Pitts., 1978—. Mem. Am. Inst. CPA's, Mich. Assn. CPA's, Inst. Internal Auditors. Republican. Roman Catholic. Clubs: Shannopin (Pitts.), Rivers (Pitts.). Office: Rockwell Internat Corp 625 Liberty Ave Pittsburgh PA 15222-3110

SANTEN, ANN HORTENSTINE, broadcasting executive; b. New Orleans, May 23, 1938; d. Jacob L. and Martha Taylor (Grace) Hortenstine; m. Harry H. Santen, Oct. 4, 1958; children: Edward, Sally, Matthew. Student Smith Coll., 1956-58; BFA, U. Cin., 1979. Assoc. producer Sta.-WGUC, Cin., 1974-77, chief music producer, 1977-79, music dir., 1977-89, internat. coordinator, 1981-89, exec. dir., gen. mgr., 1989—; cons. Radio Nederland, The Netherlands, 1978-94, Deutsche Welle, Fed. Republic Germany, 1980-95; v.p., dir. Am. Music. Ctr.; producer radio series Festival! (Oebie award 1982). Adviser Cin. Composers Guild League, 1979-94; head media panel Ohio Arts Coun., Columbus, 1987-88; trustee Cin. Opera, 1980-84; panelist Ohio Arts Coun., 1985-88; mem. radio projects adv. panel NEA, 1987, 88, 93. Named Producer of Yr., Ohio Ednl. Broadcasters, 1983; recipient Deems Taylor Broadcast award ASCAP, 1989. Mem. Am. Assn. Advancement Edn., Coll. Conservatory Music Alumni Assn. (trustee 1981-85), Taft Mus. (bd. overseers 1991—). Avocations: skiing, climbing. Office: Sta WGUC-FM 1223 Central Pky Cincinnati OH 45214-2812

SANTER, RICHARD ARTHUR, geography educator; b. Detroit, Sept. 26, 1937; s. Arthur James and Hazel Luella (Houghten) S.; m. Ruth Margaret Boyce, Aug. 29, 1959; children: Carolyn M., Catherine R. BS, Ea. Mich. U., 1959, MS, 1965; PhD, Mich. State U., 1970. Cert. secondary tchr., Mich. Tchr. geography Wyandotte (Mich.) Pub. Schs., 1963-66; prof. geography Ferris State U., Big Rapids, Mich., 1969—; cons. Graphic Learning Corp., Tallahassee, 1983, Humanities Coun. West Cen. Mich., Big Rapids, 1987—; coord. govs. conf. Upper Great Lakes Commn., Bid Rapids, 1980. Author: Michigan: Heart of Great Lakes, 1977, Geography of Michigan and the Great Lakes Basin, 1993, (atlas) Green Township Atlas, 1974; contbg. author: Michigan Visions of Our Past, 1989; co-editor, team leader: The Autobiography of Woodbridge N. Ferris, 1995. Mem., mapper Green Twp. Plan Commn., Paris, Mi., 1973-74; co-chmn. Mecosta County Bicentennial Commn., Big Rapids, 1974-75; mem. Mecosta County Zoning Commn., Big Rapids, 1978-81; bd. dirs., elder United Ch., Big Rapids, 1970-81; mem. Mich. conf. United Ch. of Christ, Commn. of Ch. and Pastoral Ministries, 1988-91; chmn. 1993 commn. Ferris State U., 1990-93; mem. bd. of trust Hist. Soc. Mich., 1993—. 1st Lt. U.S. Army, 1959-62. Recipient Recognition award Population Action Coun., 1983, Certs. of Appreciation, Mich. Sesquicentennial Commn., 1987, The Population Inst., 1987, Nat. Geography Bee, 1989-95. Mem. Assn. Am. Geographers, Nat. Coun. for Geog. Edn. (Mich. coord. 1970-74), Mich. Acad. Sci., Arts and Letters (sect. chmn. 1974-75, 94-95, instn. rep. 1988-89), Phi Delta Kappa (chmn. 1990-91). Presbyterian. Avocation: outdoor nature recreation. Office: Ferris State Univ Dept Social Scis Geography 901 S State St Big Rapids MI 49307-2251

SANTIAGO, BENITO RIVERA, professional baseball player; b. Ponce, P.R., Mar. 9, 1965; m. Bianca Santiago; 1 child, Benny Beth. Baseball player San Diego Padres, 1982-92, Florida Marlins, 1992-94, Cininnati Reds, 1995—. Named Nat. League Rookie of Yr. Baseball Writers' Assn. Am., 1987, Sporting News All-Star Team, 1987, 89, 91, 92; recipient Gold Glove award, 1988-90, Silver Slugger award, 1987-88, 90-91; holder maj. league rookie record for most consecutive games batted safely. Office: Cincinnati Reds 100 Riverfront Stadium Cincinnati OH 45202*

SANTIAGO, CARLOS, minister. Supt. Ea. Spanish Ministry Dist. of the Christian and Missionary Alliance. Office: Ste 3000 6220 S Orange Blossom Trl Orlando FL 32809-4630

SANTIAGO, JUAN JOSE, secondary school president; b. San Juan, P.R., July 8, 1931; s. Juan Jose and Mercedes (Asenjo) S. BA and BS, Colegio de Belen, Habana, Cuba, 1957; licensee in philosophy, Cath. U., Quito, Ecuador, 1958; licensee in theology, Woodstock Coll., 1965; D in Missiology, Gregorian U., Rome, 1988. Prof. Interdiocesan Seminary, Aibonito, P.R., 1958-59, Colegio San Ignacio, Rio Piedras, P.R., 1959-61; spiritual dir. Interdiocesan Seminary, Aibonito, 1966-67, Major Seminary, Ponce, P.R., 1967-68; vocation dir. Soc. of Jesus, San Juan, 1969-74; pres. Colegio San Ignacio, Rio Piedras, 1972-78, 88—, prof., 1983-84, prin., 1984-88; Pres. adv. bd. P.R. Symphony Orch., 1986-92. Author: Frutos de Soledad, 1978, Y el rio sigue fluyendo, 1989; contbr. articles to profl. jours. Mem. Am. Soc. for Psychical Rsch., Soc. for Psychical Rsch. (assoc.), Acad. Cath. Hispanic Theologians of the U.S., Cath. Theol. Soc. Am., Internat. Yoga Tchrs. Assn. (Australia). Roman Catholic. Avocations: reading, music, photography, writing. Home and Office: Urb Santa Maria 1940 Sauco St San Juan PR 00927-6718

SANTIAGO, JULIO VICTOR, medical educator, researcher, administrator; b. San German, Puerto Rico, Jan. 13, 1942. BS, Manhattan Coll., 1963; MD, U. Puerto Rico, 1967. Diplomate Am. Bd. of Internal Medicine, 1975. Fellow in metabolism and endocrinology Washington U., St. Louis, 1972-74; chief resident Barnes Hosp., St. Louis, 1974-75; dir. divsn. of endocrinology and metabolism Dept. of Pediatrics, 1984—; program dir., Diabetes Rsch. and Tng. Ctr. Wash. U. Sch. Medicine, 1987—, prof. of medicine, pediatrics, 1983—. Assoc. editor Diabetes, 1977-79, 91-95, editor, 1995—. Mem. Am. Soc. for Clin. Investigation, Soc. for Pedatric Rsch., Am. Diabetes Assn. Home: 4 Forest Parkway Dr Ballwin MO 63021-5553 Office: Washington U Sch Medicine St Louis Hosp 1 Childrens Place Saint Louis MO 63110

SANTIAGO-HUDSON, RUBEN, actor. Appeared in Broadway play Jelly's Last Jam; appeared in off-Broadway plays including East Texas Hot Links, Measure for Measure, Ceremonies in Dark Old Men; appeared in plays including Seven Guitars (Tony award winner 1996); appeared in films including Blown Away, Solomon and Sheba; appeared on TV shows including NYPD Blue, NY Undercover, Law & Order, The Cosby Mysteries, Another World, The Return of the Hunter, Dear John. Office: Hardin & Curtis 850 7th Ave Ste 405 New York NY 10019*

SANTILLAN, ANTONIO, financial company executive; b. Buenos Aires, May 8, 1936; naturalized, 1966; s. Guillermo Spika and Raphaella C. (Abaladejo) S.; children: Andrea, Miguel, Marcos. Grad., Morgan Park Mil. Acad., Chgo., 1954; BS in Psychology, Coll. of William and Mary, 1958. Cert. real estate broker. Asst. in charge of prodn. Wilding Studios, Chgo., 1964; pres. Adams Fin. Services, Los Angeles, 1965—. Writer, producer, dir. (motion pictures) The Glass Cage, co-writer Dirty Mary/Crazy Harry, Viva Knievel; contbg. writer Once Upon a Time in America; TV panelist Window on Wall Street; contbr. articles to profl. fin. and real estate jours. Served with USNR, 1959. Recipient Am. Rep. award San Francisco Film Festival, Cork Ireland Film Fest, 1961. Mem. Writer's Guild Am., L.A. Bd. Realtors, Beverly Hills Bd. Realtors (income/investment divsn. steering com.), Westside Realty Bd. (bd. dirs.), L.A. Ventures Assn. (bd. dirs.), Jonathan Club (L.A.), Rotary, Roundtable, Toastmasters Internat. Avocations: golf, tennis, skiing. Office: Adams Fin Svcs Inc 425 N Alfred St West Hollywood CA 90048-2504

SANTINI, JOHN AMEDEO, educational consultant; b. Detroit, Nov. 4, 1926; s. Amedeo Enrico and Ida Mercurio (LaFata) S.; m. Mary Beverly Bergman, Aug. 11, 1956 (div. 1982); m. Deborah Sewell Stogner, Apr. 28, 1996; children: Maria Bettina, Lucia Bianca, John Amedeo. B.A., U. Chgo., 1948; J.D., Wayne State U., 1953; M.A., U. Mich., 1960; Ed.D., Harvard, 1965. Bar: Mich. 1954. Prodn. engr. Fisher body div. Gen. Motors Corp., 1949-51; pvt. practice Detroit, 1954-56; tchr. elem. and middle grades St. Clair Shores and Grosse Pointe, Mich., 1956-60; elem. sch. prin. Chagrin Falls, Ohio, 1960-62; dir. curriculum study Brockton, Mass., 1963-64; supt. schs. Farmington, Conn., 1964-66, New Haven, 1966-69; prof. edn., chmn. dept. edn. Conn. Coll., New London, 1969-85, edn. cons., 1985—; lectr. edn. Western Res. U., 1962; vis. prof. edn. adminstrn. U. Bridgeport, 1971, U. Conn., 1974; cons. edn., Sarasota (Fla.) County, 1963—, Walpole, Mass., 1964, West Hartford, Conn., 1973. Mem. Old Lyme Park and Recreation Commn.; bd. mgrs. Old Lyme-P.G. Noyes Library, 1980—; mem. arbitration panel Conn. Dept. Edn., basic skills adv. com., 1980—, tchr. prep. program rev. com., 1979—. Served with USAAF, World War II. Mem. ABA (adv. commn. on youth edn. for citizenship), Mich. Bar Assn., Am. Fedn. Musicians, Am., Conn., New Eng. assns. sch. supts., Nat., Conn., Mich. edn. assns., Nat. Orgn. Legal Problems of Edn., AAUP, Conn. Assn. Colls. and Univs. for Tchr. Edn. (pres. 1973-74), Conn. Profs. Ednl. Adminstrn. (pres. 1973-74), Phi Kappa Phi, Phi Delta Kappa. Presbyn. (deacon). Home: 110 Tremain St N Mount Dora FL 32757-5678

SANTLOFER, JONATHAN, artist, educator; b. N.Y.C., Apr. 26, 1946; s. Louis and Edith (Brill) S.; m. Joy Katzman; 1 child, Doria. BFA, Boston U., 1967; MFA, Pratt Inst., 1969. Head art dept. Tower Hill Sch., Wilmington, Del., 1969-73; instr. studio and art history Jersey City (N.J.) State Coll., 1974-80; instr. drawing and painting Columbia U., N.Y., 1988-90; resident painter, instr. Vt. Studio Ctr., 1991; instr. drawing and painting Lacoste Sch. of Arts, 1992; mem. humanities faculty art history New Sch. for Social Rsch., 1976—; resident artist Am. Acad. in Rome, Italy, 1989-90; Yaddo residency Yaddo Colony, Saratoga Springs, N.Y., 1995. One-man shows include Inst. Contemporary Art, Tokyo, 1978, 85, Franklin & Marshall Coll., Pa., 1981, Betsy Rosenfield Gallery, Chgo., 1982, Pam Adler Gallery, N.Y.C., 1982, 83, 85, Lawrence Oliver Gallery, Phila., 1983, Graham Modern, N.Y.C., 1986, 88, 90, Klein Gallery, Chgo., 1986, 89, The Heckscher Mus., Huntington, N.Y., 1987, Nina Freudenheim Gallery, Buffalo, N.Y., 1987, Ruth Bachofner, L.A., 1991, Galleriea Peccolo, Italy, 1992, James Graham and Sons, N.Y.C., 1994; exhibited in group shows at Graham Modern, N.Y.C., 1988-89, 90-91, 92, Galleria Peccolo, Italy, 1988-89, Andre Zarre, N.Y.C., 1988-89, The Jewish Mus., N.Y.C., 1988-89, Gallery Urban, N.Y.C., 1988-89, PPOW, N.Y.C., 1988-89, Richard Green Gallery, L.A., 1988-89, Barbara Toll Fine Arts, N.Y.C., 1988-89, 92, Nina Freudenheim, Buffalo, 1990-91, Lennon/Weinberg Gallery, N.Y.C., 1993, Santa Monica Mus., 1994, The Drawing Ctr., N.Y.C., 1994, Adam Baumgold Fine Arts, N.Y.C., 1994, others; represented in permanent collections Art Inst. Chgo., Ill., AT&T, Am. Can Co., Amoco Products Co., Boston (Mass.) U. Mus. and Gallery Collection, Buscaglia-Castellani Mus./Gallery, Niagara Falls, N.Y., Chase Manhattan Bank, NA, Chem. Bank, Continental Group, Cooke & Bieler, Pa., Grand Rapids (Mich.) Mus. Art, Grahan Gund, Mass., Indpls. (Ind.) Mus. Art, Inst. Contemporary Art, Japan, others; contbr. articles to profl. jours. Painting grantee Nat. Endowment for the Arts, 1981, 89. Office: c/o James Graham & Sons 1014 Madison Ave New York NY 10021

SANTMAN, LEON DUANE, lawyer, former federal government executive; b. Phila., July 29, 1930; s. Elmer William and Anna Mary (Moffitt) S.; m. Juliet Gloria Peacock, June 16, 1952; 1 dau., Lorri Leigh Santman Myers. BS, U. S., COAST Guard Acad., 1952; LLB, U. Houston, 1953; LLM, George Washington U., 1968. Bar: Tex. 1963, Md. 1974. Commd. ensign U.S. Coast Guard, 1952, advanced through grades to comdr., 1967, ret., 1972; assoc. gen. counsel Cost of Living Council, Washington, 1972-74; asst. gen. counsel U.S. Dept. Transp., Washington, 1974-77, dir. Materials Transp. Bur., 1977-85; dir. ship ops. Maritime Adminstrn., 1985-88. Episcopalian.

SANTNER, THOMAS, statistics educator, consultant, researcher; b. St. Louis, Aug. 29, 1947; s. Joseph Frank and Margaret Ann (Dolak) S.; m. Gail DeFord, Aug. 29, 1970; children—Emily, Matthew, Abigail, Dominick. BS, U. Dayton, 1969; MS, Purdue U., 1971, PhD, 1973. Asst. prof. Cornell U., Ithaca, N.Y., 1973-80, assoc. prof., 1980-86, prof., 1986-89, dir. stats. ctr., 1982-86; prof. Ohio State U., 1990—, chair dept. statistics, 1992—; cons. Hosp. for Spl. Surgery, N.Y.C., 1983—. Co-author: The Statistical Analysis of Discrete Data, 1989, Design and Analysus if /experiments for Statistical SElection, Screening, and Multiple Comparisons, 1995; co-editor: Design of Experiments: Ranking and Selection, 1984. Contbr. articles to prof. jours. NSF fellow; recipient numerous grants. Mem. Inst. Math. Stats., Biometric Soc., Am. Statis. Assn. Home: 1042 Putney Dr Columbus OH 43085-2903 Office: Ohio State U Dept Stats Columbus OH 43210

SANTOMERO, ANTHONY M., business educator; b. N.Y.C., Sept. 29, 1946; s. Camillo and Jean (Oddo) S.; m. Marlena Belviso, Aug. 21, 1971; children: Jill Renee, Marc Anthony. AB, Fordham U., 1968; PhD, Brown U., 1971; EDhe (hon.), Stockholm Sch. Econs., 1992. Successively asst. prof., assoc. prof., prof. fin. Wharton Sch., U. Pa., Phila., 1972-84, R.K. Mellon prof. fin., 1984—, vice dean, dir. grad. div., 1984-87, dep. dean, 1990-94; dir. Wharton Fin. Instns. Ctr., 1995—; asst. prof. econs. Baruch Coll., CUNY, 1971-72; vis. prof. European Inst. Advanced Studies in Mgmt., Brussels, 1977-78, Stockholm Sch. Econs., 1989-90, Gothenberg U., 1989-90, U. Rome, 1994, vis. prof. fin., Tor Vergata, 1994; formerly vis. prof. Ecole Superieure des Sciences Economiques and Commerciales, France, 1977-78; bd. dirs. The Zweig Fund, The Zweig Total Return Fund, Temp. Investment Fund Inc., PNC Fubd; bd. trustees Trust Fed. Securities, 1991—, Mcpl. Fund for Temp. Investment, 1991—, Portfolios for Diversified Investment, 1991—; rsch. assoc. NYU Ctr. for Japan-U.S. Bus. and Econ. Studies, 1989—. Author: Current Views on Bank Capital, 1983; assoc. editor Jour. Fin., Jour. Banking and Fin., 1978—, Jour. Money, Credit and Banking, 1980—, Jour. Eocns. and Bus., 1979—, Jour. Econs. and Bus., 1979—, Jour. Bank Rsch., Jour. Fin. Rsch., Jour. Fin. Svc. Rsch., 1992—; contbr. numerous articles to profl. jours. Mem. European Fin. Assn. (exec. com. 1984-87), Am. Fin. Assn., Am. Econs. Assn. Roman Catholic. Home: 310 Keithwood Rd Wynnewood PA 19096-1224 Office: U Pa Wharton Sch Philadelphia PA 19104

SANTONI, RONALD ERNEST, philosophy educator; b. Arvida, Que., Can., Dec. 19, 1931; s. Fred Albert and Phyllis (Tremaine) S.; m. Marguerite Ada Kiene, June 25, 1955; children: Christina, Marcia, Andrea, Juanita, Jonathan, Sondra. BA, Bishop's U., Lennoxville, Que., 1952; MA, Brown U., 1954; PhD, Boston U., 1961; postgrad., U. Paris-Sorbonne, 1956-57. Asst. prof. philosophy U. Pacific, Stockton, Calif., 1958-61; postdoctoral fellow Yale U., New Haven, 1961-62; asst. prof. philosophy Wabash Coll., Crawfordsville, Ind., 1962-64; mem. faculty Denison U., Granville, Ohio, 1964—; prof. philosophy Denison U., 1968—, chmn. dept., 1971-73, 82-84, 92—, Maria Teresa Barney chair in philosophy, 1978—; Peace lectr. Bethel Coll., 1985; vis. scholar Cambridge U., Eng., 1986, 90, 94, also vis. lectr. in philosophy, 1990; vis. fellow Clare Hall, Cambridge U., 1986, 90; vis. fellow in philosophy Yale U., 1975, 81, 93; keynote speaker 2d Internat. Conf. on Nuclear Free Zones, Cordoba, Spain, 1985; speaker World Cong. Philosophy, Montreal, Can., 1982, Brighton, U.K., 1988, Internat. Studies Assn., London, 1989, speaker and U.S.A. co-chair Internat. Conf. Internat. Philosophers for Prevention of Nuclear Omnicide, Moscow, 1990; speaker World Congress Universalism, Warsaw, Poland, 1993; del. and raporteur UN meeting of Peace Messenger Orgns., Dagomys, Sochi, USSR, 1991; invited plenary speaker 2d Internat. Cong. Violence and Co-existence, Montreal, Can., 1992; invited participant Colloquium on Technological Risks to Environment, Montreal, Can., 1993; participant, spkr. numerous profl. confs. Contbg. author: Current Philosophical Issues, 1966, Towards an Understanding and Prevention of Genocide, 1984, Nuclear War: Philosophical Perspectives, 1985, Encyclopedic Critical Bibliography of Genocide, 1988, Just War, Nonviolence and Nuclear Deterrence: Philosophers on War and Peace, 1992, The Institution of War, 1991; author: Bad Faith, Good Faith and Authenticity in Sartre's Early Philosophy, 1995; editor, contbr. Religious Language and the Problem of Religious Knowledge, 1968; co-editor Social and Political Philosophy, 1963; contbg. editor Internet on the Holocaust and Genocide; contbr. over 120 articles and revs. to profl. jours., also to The Progressive, The Human Quest, Churchman; bd. editors Jour. Peace and Justice Studies. V.p. NAACP, Licking County, 1967; active ACLU; organizer Crawfordsville Human Rels. Coun., 1962-64; mem. nat. exec. com. Episcopal Peace Fellowship, 1968-78; mem. internat. coun. Internat. Inst. on the Holocaust and Genocide, 1985—; mem. nat. coun. Fellowship of Reconciliation, 1988-89; trustee Margaret Hall Sch., Versailles, Ky., 1972-74; nat. bd. dirs. Promoting Enduring Peace, 1982—. Canadian Govt. Overseas fellow Royal Soc. Can., 1956-57; Church Soc. for Coll. Work faculty fellow, 1961-62; Soc. for Religion postdoctoral fellow, 1972—; Yale rsch. fellow, 1975; Yale postdoctoral rsch. fellow, 1961-62; guest fellow Berkeley Coll., Yale U., 1975, 81, 93-94, elected assoc. fellow, 1994—; vis. fellow in philosophy Yale U., 1981, 93-94; Robert C. Good faculty fellow Denison U., 1985-86, Robert C. Good Faculty Rsch. fellow, 1993-94; elected life mem. Clare Hall, Cambridge (Eng.) U., 1986; recipient Mellon award for disting. faculty Denison U., 1972, Crossed Keys Faculty of Yr. award Denison U., 1986-87. Mem. Am. Philos. Assn., Ch. Soc. for Coll. Work, Soc. for Phenomenology and Existential Philosophy, Internat. Philosophers for Prevention of Nuclear Omnicide (v.p. 1983-85, v.p. cen. div. 1990-91, internat. pres. 1991-96), Sartre Soc. of N.Am. (exec. com. 1994—), Sartre Circle, Gandhi-King Soc., War Resisters League, Union of Bi-Nat. Profls. Against Omnicide (v.p. 1978—), Concerned Philosophers for Peace (coord., pres. 1996-97). Episcopalian. Home: 500 Burg St Granville OH 43023 *Gratitude for what one has been given, commitment to personal growth and integrity, some gracious gall, listening to the world's humiliated, and a recognition that any genuine success is a gift of grace, never fully merited.*

SANTORE, CARRIE-BETH, computer management professional; b. Torrington, Conn., July 28, 1953; d. Michael and Dolores Leonard S. BA History and Am. Studies cum laude, Conn. Coll., 1975; MA History, U. Conn., 1977; MBA Mktg., Va. Polytechnic Inst., 1988. Analyst CIA, Washington, 1980-90; prin. tng. specialist Quality Sys., Inc., Fairfax, Va., 1990-93, dep. dir. ops. programs, 1993-95; mgr. Proposal Ctr. Quality Systems, Inc., Fairfax, Va., 1995-96; tech. publs. mgr. Sci. & Tech. Analysis Corp., Fairfax, Va., 1996—; Lotus cert. cons., 1994. Bd. dirs., sec. Seminary Walk Condo Assn., Alexandria, Va., 1987-88, editor newsletter, 1986-87; vol. Alexandria Waterfront ARC, 1989-90; mem. com. to devel. internat. studies program Conn. Coll., New London, 1988-89. Mem. SALT, Balt. Washington Info. Systems, AAUW, Women's Nat. Book Assn., Assn. Proposal Mgmt. Profls., Phi Alpha Theta. Avocations: golf, hiking, reading, baseball, travel. Office: Sci & Tech Analysis Corp Ste 300 11250 Waples Mill Rd Fairfax VA 22030

SANTORO, ANTHONY RICHARD, academic administrator; b. Feb. 2, 1939; m. Carol Lynne; 1 child, Melissa. AB, Coll. of the Holy Cross, 1960; MA, U. Calif., 1962; PhD, Rutgers U., 1978. Instr. history Monmouth Coll., West Long Branch, N.J., 1963-67; v.p. for adminstrn., chair depts history and philosophy, registrar Briarcliff Coll., Briarcliff Manor, N.Y., 1967-77; v.p. Devel. and Coll. Rels. Ladycliff Coll., Highland Falls, N.Y., 1977-88; pres. St. Joseph's Coll., Standish, Maine, 1979-87; pres. Christopher Newport U., Newport News, Va., 1987-96, pres. emeritus, disting. prof. history, 1996—. Author: Theophanes Chronograhia: A Chronicle of 8th Century Byzantium, 1982; co-author: An Eyewitness to History: The Short History of Nikephoros the Patriarch of Constantinople, 1991. Office: Christopher Newport U Smith Hall 164 Newport News VA 23606-2998

SANTORUM, RICK, senator; b. Winchester, Va., May 10, 1958; s. Aldo and Catherine (Dughi) S.; m. Karen Garver, June 2, 1990; children: Elizabeth Anne, Richard John, Daniel James. BA with honors, Pa. State U., State College, 1980; MBA, U. Pitts., 1981; JD, Dickinson Sch. Law, 1986. Bar: Pa. 1986. Adminstrv. asst. State Sen. Doyle Corman, Harrisburg, Pa., 1981-86; exec. dir. local govt. com. Pa. State Senate, Harrisburg, 1981-84, exec. dir. transp. com., 1984-86; assoc. atty. Kirkpatrick and Lockhart, Pitts., 1986-90; mem. 102nd-103rd Congresses from 18th Pa. dist., Washington, D.C., 1991-95; U.S. Senator from Pa., 1995—; mem. Agr. Com., Armed Svcs. Com., Rules and Adminstrn. Com., Spl. Com. on Aging. Bd. dirs. Mt. Lebanon Extended Day Program, 1987-91; mem. Child Advocacy Project, 1987-91. Mem. Allegheny County Bar Assn., Tyrolean Soc. Western Pa., Italian Sons and Daus. Assn., Rotary. Republican. Roman Catholic. Avocations: golf, cross country skiing, racquet sports. Home: 127 Seminole Dr Pittsburgh PA 15228-1528 Office: US Senate 120 Russell Senate Office Bldg Washington DC 20510-3803*

SANTOS, ADELE NAUDE, architect, educator; b. Cape Town, South Africa, Oct. 14, 1938; came to U.S., 1973; d. David Francois Hugo and Aletta Adèle Naudé. Student, U. Cape Town, South Africa, 1956-58; Diploma, Archtl. Assn., 1961; MArch in Urban Design, Harvard U., 1963; M in City Planning, U. Pa., 1968, MArch, 1968. Pvt. practice architecture with Antonio de Souza Santos, 1966-73; ptnr. Interstudio, Houston, 1973-79; assoc. prof. architecture Rice U., Houston, 1973-78, prof., 1979; prof. architecture and urban design, dept. architecture U. Pa., Phila., 1981-90; founding dean Sch. Architecture U. Calif., San Diego, 1990-94; pvt. practice architecture and urban design Adele Naude Santos, Architect, Phila., 1979-90, Adele Naude Santos and Assocs., San Diego and Phila., 1991—; prof. architecture Coll. Environ. Design U. Calif., Berkeley, 1994—; founding dean Sch. of Architecture, U. Calif., San Diego, 1990—. Project dir., co-filmmaker for 5 part series, 1979-80. Wheelwright Travelling fellow, Harvard U., 1968; NEA grantee, 1976, Tex. Com. for Humanities grantee, 1979; recipient (with Hugo Naudé) Bronze medal for House Naudé Capt. Inst. South African Architects, 1967, award for public TV program So. Ednl. Communications Assn., 1980, 3d place award Inner city Infill Competition, 1986; winner Internat. Design Competition, Hawaii Loa Coll., hon. mention Cin. Hillside Housing Competition and City Visions, Phila., 1986; winner competition for Franklin/La Brea Affordable Housing Project Mus. Comtemporary Art and Community Redevel. Agy. City L.A., 1988, Pa. Soc. Architects design award for Franklin/La Brea Multi-Family Housing, 1988; winning entry collaborative competition for amphitheater, restaurant and natural history mus., Arts Pk., La., 1989; winner competition for 24-unit residential devel., City of Camden, N.J., 1989, for New Civic Ctr., City of Perris, Calif., 1991. Office: 2527 South St Philadelphia PA 19146-1037 also: 629 J St Ste 102 San Diego CA 92101

SANTOS, GEORGE WESLEY, physician, educator; b. Oak Park, Ill., Feb. 3, 1928; s. George and Emma (Gast) S.; m. Joanne Agnes Corrigan, June 7, 1952; children: Susan Elizabeth, George Wesley II, Kelly Anne, Amy Coburn. SB, MIT, 1951, MS in Phys. Biology, 1951; MD, Johns Hopkins U., 1955; Doctoris Medicinae Gradum Honoris Cause, U. Munich, Fed. Republic Germany, 1989. Intern Johns Hopkins Hosp., Balt., 1955-56, asst. resident, 1958-60; scholar Leukemia Soc., N.Y.C., 1961-66; mem. faculty

Johns Hopkins Sch. Medicine, Balt., 1962—, assoc. prof. medicine, 1968-73, prof. oncology and medicine, 1973-94; prof. emeritus, 1994—; asst. physician in chief Balt. City Hosp., 1963-77; mem. Cancer Clin. Investigative Rev. Com., 1969-73; mem. extramural sci. adv. bd. Meml. Sloan-Kettering Cancer Ctr., 1977-79; mem. Immunology-Epidemiology Spl. Virus Cancer Program, 1969-73; chmn. bone marrow transplant registry ACS, 1969-73; mem. Internat. Com. Organ Transplant Registry ACS, 1969-73; mem. cell biology-immunology-genetics rsch. evaluation com. VA, 1969-71. Assoc. editor Cancer Rsch., 1978-81; mem. bd. editorial advisors Jour. Immunopharmacology, 1978—; mem. editorial bd. Blood, 1983—. With USNR, 1956-58. Recipient Disting. Achievement in Cancer Rsch. award Bristol Meyers, 1988. Mem. Am. Soc. Hematology, Transplantation Soc. (counselor 1971-73), Am. Assn. Immunologists, Leukemia Soc. Am. (bd. dirs. 1973—), Internat. Soc. Exptl. Hematology (councillor 1973, pres. 1981), Am. Assn. Cancer Rsch., Am. Soc. Clin. Investigation, Nat. Multiple Sclerosis Soc. (chmn. adv. com. on drug devel. 1981-82, mem. adv. com. on drug devel. 1981—). Home: 3078 Mariners Point Hilton Head Island SC 29926-1213

SANTOS, HERBERT JOSEPH, JR., lawyer; b. Reno, Feb. 17, 1963; s. Herbert Joseph Sr. and Jeanette Dorothy Santos; m. Kimberly Ellen Saylors, Mar. 8, 1986; children: Herbert Joseph III, Jarred Adam, Hannah McKenzie. BA in Sociology, U. Nev., Las Vegas, 1985; JD, U. of the Pacific, 1991. Bar: Nev. 1991, Calif. 1992, U.S. Dist. Ct. Nev. 1992. Head social worker Cmty. Welfare, Inc., Reno, 1986-87; inspector Nev. Athletic Commn., Reno, 1986-87; sr. legal rsch. asst. County Sacramento, Calif., 1987-91; assoc. Law Offices of Terry A. Friedman, Ltd., Reno, 1991—. Author (instrn. manual) ORR, County of Sacramento Bankruptcy Forms and Procedures Manual with Practice Pointers, 1990. Mem. Cmty. Coalition, Reno, 1986-87; mentor U. Nev., Reno, 1993—. Recipient Am. Jurisprudence award, 1991. Mem. ATLA, Nev. Trial Lawyers Assn., State Bar Nev. (exec. coun. mem. young lawyers sect. 1993—, pres. young lawyers sect. 1996-97), Washoe County Bar Assn., Am. Inns of Ct. (Hon. Bruce Thompson chpt. 1995—). Republican. Roman Catholic. Avocations: family, boxing, basketball. Office: Law Offices of Terry A Friedman 527 S Arlington Ave Reno NV 89509

SANTOS, LEONARD ERNEST, lawyer; b. Caracas, Venezuela, Aug. 5, 1946; s. Paul Joseph and Frieda (Epstein) S.; m. Jeannie Bernadette Niedermeyer, Oct. 28, 1978; children: Jonathan, Matthew, Andrew. BA cum laude, Tufts U., 1967; JD, NYU, 1971. Bar: Ariz. 1972, D.C. 1972, U.S. Dist. Ct. D.C. 1972, U.S. Ct. Appeals (9th and 5th cirs.) 1972, U.S. Supreme Ct. 1972. Law clk. to cir. judge U.S. Ct. Appeals (9th cir.), San Francisco, 1971-72; assoc. Hogan & Hartson, Washington, 1972-76; sr. atty. internat. affairs U.S. Dept. Treasury, Washington, 1976-83; internat. trade counsel U.S. Senate Fin. Com., Washington, 1983-87; ptnr. Verner, Liipfert, Bernhard, McPherson & Hand, Washington, 1987-89, Perkins Coie, Washington, 1989—. Note and comment editor NYU Law Jour., 1970; contbr. legal publs. Exec. dir. Dole for Pres. campaign, Washington, 1988, 96. Mem. NAFTA (mem. 19 dispute settlement panels). Republican. Roman Catholic. Avocations: architecture, economics. Office: Perkins Coie 607 14th St NW Washington DC 20005-2007

SANTOS, LISA WELLS, critical care nurse; b. Richardson, Tex., Oct. 25, 1963; d. Malcolm R.N. and Maitland Anne (MacIntyre) Wells; m. Ignacio Santos, Jr., Dec. 17, 1988. Cert. med. asst., x-ray-lab. technician, Tex. Coll. Osteopathy, 1983; ASN, El Centro Coll., 1988; postgrad., U. North Tex.; BS in Bus. Mgmt., Le Tourneau U., 1993; postgrad., U. Phoenix, 1995—. RN, Tex.; cert. in CPR; cert. case mgr., cert. profl. in health care quality; advanced competency certification in continuity of care; assoc. cert. mgr. Med. technologist Family Med. Ctr., Dallas, 1984-85, Beltline Med. Clinic, Dallas, 1985-86; nurse, lab. technician Primacare, Dallas, Plano, Richardson, Tex., 1986-88; charge nurse telemetry unit NME Hosp.-RHD Meml. Hosp., Denton, Tex., 1988-89; nurse ICU Denton (Tex.) Regional Med. Ctr.; nurse Angel Touch, Dallas, 1989; nurse cons. Travelers Ins., Richardson, Tex., 1990-91; med. rev. specialist Nat. Group Life, Las Colinas, Tex., 1991-94; mgr. coordinated care Nat. Group Life, 1994-95; pres. San Cal Health Care Options, Lewisville, Tex., 1994-95; clin. dir. PRN Associated Care, Dallas, 1995—. Contbr. articles to profl. jour. Mem. AACN, NAFE, Nat. Assn. Health Care Quality, Nat. Assn. Quality Assurance Profls., Assn. Nurses in AIDS Care, Case Mgmt. Soc. Am., Am. Assn. Law Ethics and Medicine, Am. Assn. Continuity of Care, Alpha Epsilon Delta, Alpha Beta Kappa, Gamma Beta Phi.

SANTOS, ROBERT DAVID, health and fitness educator, consultant; b. Chalan, Pago, Guam, Jan. 1, 1952; s. Joaquin L. G. and Carmen I. (Pinaula) S.; m. Elaine Marie Pudwill, Sept. 1, 1975; children: Zane, Deylene, Makao, Shane. AAS in Gen. Studies, Pierce County C.C., Wash., 1973; EdB in Physical Edn., Ctrl. Wash. U., 1975; MPE, U. Oreg., 1979; PhD in Higher Edn. Administrn. and Adult Edn., U. North Tex., 1990; ABD in Adminstrn. in Kinesiology, Tex. Woman's U. Cert. tchr. Physical edn. tchr. George Washington H.S., Guam, 1975-76, John F. Kennedy H.S., Guam, 1978-80; math, physical edn., health tchr. Battle Mt. H.S., Battle Mt., Nev., 1981-82; math. tchr. E.C. Best Jr. H.S., Fallon, Nev., 1982-83; rsch. cons. Sitterly Mgmt. and Cons. Firm, Ft. Worth, Tex., 1986-87; health tchr. S. Sanchez H.S., Guam, 1989-91; dir., mem. gov.'s cabinet Guam Health Planning and Devel. Agy., 1991-93; lectr. divsn. health, physical edn. and athletics Western Oreg. State Coll., Monmouth, 1993—; instr. dept. physical edn. and health Linn-Benton C.C., Albany, Oreg., 1994—; pvt. personal fitness instr., 1992-95; dir. fundraiser Sports Medicine Design by Guam--A Wholistic Approach, 1992; dir. 1st Ann. Gov.'s Health Task Forces' Forum, 1992; rsch. dir. Gov.'s 21st Century Health Work Force Survey, 1991-93; wellness cons. Clark Hatch Health and Fitness Ctr., 1992-93; fitness cons. Gold's Gym, 1992-93; coaches' lectr., cons. athletic injuries Oreg. H.S., 1977-79; student teaching asst. supr. U. Nev.-Reno, 1981; wellness instr. U. North Tex., 1986-90, adj. prof. kinesiol. studies, 1986-90;. Co-author: (with John Eddy) Circle of Excellence: Basketball, 1986; contbr. articles to profl. jours. Clinic dir. Albany Boys and Girls Club, 1993; mem. fellowship com. WHO; hon. amb.-at-large Gov. Joe Ada, Guam, 1991. Recipient Coat of Arms, Mayor of Rutherford, Eng., 1991. Mem. AAHPERD, Internat. Coun. for Health, Phys. Edn., Recreation, Sport and Dance (dir. philosophy edn. and sport commn.), Am. Assn. for Wellness Edn., Counseling & Rsch., Oreg. Athletic Trainer's Soc., Nat. Athletic Trainers Assn. (cert.). Roman Catholic.

SANTSCHI, PETER HANS, marine sciences educator; b. Bern, Switzerland, Jan. 3, 1943; came to U.S., 1976; s. Hans and Gertrud (Joss) S.; m. Chana Hoida, Mar. 28, 1972; children: Rama Aviva, Ariel Tal. BS, Gymnasium, Bern, 1963; MS, U. Bern, 1971, PhD summa cum laude, 1975; Privatdozent, Swiss Fed. Inst. Tech., Zurich, Switzerland, 1984. Lectr. chemistry Humboltianum Gymnasium, Bern, 1968-70; teaching rsch. asst. U. Bern, 1970-75; rsch. scientist Lamont-Doherty Geol. Obs., Columbia U., Palisades, N.Y., 1976-77; rsch. assoc. Lamont-Doherty Geol. Obs. Columbia U., Palisades, N.Y., 1977-81; sr. rsch. scientist Lamont-Doherty Geol. Obs., Columbia U., Palisades, N.Y., 1981-82, Swiss Inst. Pollution Control, Zurich-Duebendorf, Switzerland, 1982-88; prof. oceanography Tex. A&M U., College Station, 1988—; prof. marine scis. Tex. A&M U., Galveston, Tex., 1988—; sect. head chem. oceanography dept. oceanography Tex. A&M U., College Station, 1990—; head isotope geochemistry and radiology sect. Swiss Inst. Water Resources and Water Pollution Control, Zurich, 1983-88; mem. rev. panel on chem. oceanography NSF, 1990-91. Contbr. articles to profl. jours. Cpl. Swiss Army, 1964-65. Mem. AAAS, Am. Chem. Soc., Am. Geophys. Union, Oceanography Soc., Am. Soc. Limnology and Oceanography. Avocation: swimming. Office: Tex A&M U Oceanography Dept Galveston TX 77553-1675

SANTULLI, THOMAS VINCENT, surgeon; b. N.Y.C., Mar. 16, 1915; s. Frank and Amalia (Avagliano) S.; m. Dorothy Muriel Beverly, Apr. 10, 1941 (dec.); children: Thomas Vincent Jr., Robert B.; m. Patricia Rita, May 28, 1982. B.S., Columbia, 1935; M.D., Georgetown U., 1939. Intern N.Y. Polyclinic Hosp., 1939-41, resident, 1941-44; prof. surgery Columbia U., N.Y.C., 1967-81, prof. emeritus, 1981—; chief pediatric surg. service emeritus Babies Hosp., Columbia-Presbyn. Med. Center, N.Y.C., 1955-81; attending surgeon emeritus Presybn. Hosp., Columbia-Presbyn. Med. Center. Mem. Am. Surg. Assn., Am. Pediatric Surg. Assn. (pres. 1980-81), A.C.S., British Assn. Pediatric Surgeons, N.Y. Pediatric Surg. Soc. (pres. 1967-69). Office: Babies Hosp Babies Hosp 3959 Broadway New York NY 10032-3784

SANWICK, JAMES ARTHUR, mining executive; b. Balt., Feb. 15, 1951; s. Alfred George and Catherine Anne (von Sas) S.; m. Brenda Julia Tietz, Sept. 20, 1980; children: Luke Graham, Sierra Catherine. AS, Catonsville (Md.) Community Coll., 1975; BS, U. No. Colo., 1976; M in Pub. Administn., U. Alaska S.E., 1985. Recreation therapist Md. Sch. for the Blind, Balt., 1974; dir. camp New Horizon United Cerebral Palsy Md., Balt., 1975; sub-dist. mgr. Nat. Park Svc., various, 1976-82; freelance mgmt. cons. Juneau, Alaska, 1982-84; regional mgr. div. labor standards Alaska Dept. Labor, Juneau, 1983-88; adj. faculty sch. bus. and pub. administrn. U. Alaska S.E., Juneau, 1985-93; mgr. Alaska Productivity Improvement Ctr., Juneau, 1989-93; mgr. human resources and pub. affairs Greens Creek Mining Co., Juneau, 1989-93; mgr. human resources, securities and pub. affairs Rawhide Mining Co., Fallon, Nev., 1993—; owner Sierra Bldg. Alternatives, 1995—; bd. dirs. Gov.'s Com. on Employment Disabled Persons, Alaska Acad. Decathalon Inc.; chmn. Job Svc. Employer Com., Alaska, 1989-93; bd. advisors Inst. Mine Tng. U. Alaska S.E., 1989-93. Co-author: (info. phamphlet) Blue Water Paddling in Alaska, 1980; editor: (film) Green's Creek Project, 1990; photographic editor: Inside Passage Mag., 1982, 83; photographer: (book) Death Valley, 1977. Patrolman Nat. Ski Patrol System, Juneau, 1978-83; instr., trainer ARC, Alaska, Utah, Ariz., 1979-82; v.p. bd. dirs. Alaska Acad. Decathlon. Sgt. USMC, 1970-73. Recipient Nat. New Svc. award United Cerebral Palsey, 1975; named Candidate of Yr. Nat. Ski Patrol System, 1979. Mem. Nev. Mining Assn. (human resources com. 1993—), Soc. Human Resources Mgmt., Juneau Ski Club. Avocations: skiing, hiking, scuba diving, guitar, tennis. Office: Rawhide Mining Co PO Box 2070 Fallon NV 89407-2070

SANYOUR, MICHAEL LOUIS, JR., financial services company executive; b. Richmond, Va., Aug. 24, 1930; s. Michael Louis, Sr. and Betty (Toobert) S.; m. Therese Marie McCarthy, June 1, 1951; children: Jeffrey, Mark, Jennifer, Florence, Norman, Ned. A.A., Union Coll., 1952; S.B., Rutgers U., 1954, postgrad., 1978-82; M.B.A., Harvard U., 1956; postgrad., Am. Coll., 1987-92. CLU, ChFC. Vice pres. Harbridge House, Inc., Boston, 1956-63; also dir; corp. v.p. mktg. Volkswagen of Am., Inc., Englewood Cliffs, N.J., 1963-70; pres., chief exec. officer Subaru of Am., Pennsauken, N.J., 1970-75, also dir.; exec. v.p., dir. Sci. Mgmt. Corp., 1975-82; pres., chief exec. officer Wofac Co., Bridgewater, N.J., 1975-82; pres., chief exec. officer, dir. Metrologic Instruments Inc., Bellmawr, N.J., 1982-85; pres., chief operating officer, dir. Avant-Garde Computing, Inc., Mt. Laurel, N.J., 1985-86; principal, dir. CMS Cos., Phila., 1986—; bd. dirs. CSS Industries Inc., Gordon Wahls Co. Contbr. to: Chief Executive's Handbook, 1975, Am. Mgmt. Assn.'s Publs., 1990. Trustee, pres. West Jersey Chamber Music Soc., 1987-88; councilman Moorestown, N.J., 1988—; bd. dirs. Union League of Phila., Meml. Health Alliance, ARC of Burlington County, 1989-94, Coriell Inst. for Med. Rsch., World Affairs Coun. Phila., 1992—; bd. dirs. Phila. Pres.'s Orgn., vice chmn., 1992-93, chmn., 1993-94; class sec. HBS Class of '56, 1986—. With USNG, 1948-56. Recipient Alumni award Rutgers U., 1954, awards Am. Cancer Soc., 1978, 79. Mem. World Pres.'s Orgn., Legatus, Am. Mensa Ltd., Automotive Orgn. Team, World Affairs Coun. Phila., South Jersey C. of C. (v.p., dir.), Beta Gamma Sigma, Delta Sigma Pi. Clubs: Harvard (N.Y.C.); Union League (Phila.), Harvard Bus. Sch. (Phila.) (pres. 1980-81, chmn. 1983-84, dir. 1984—); Moorestown Rotary (pres.1987-88, dir.). Home: 201 E Maple Ave Moorestown NJ 08057-2011 Office: 1926 Arch St Philadelphia PA 19103-1444

SANZO, ANTHONY MICHAEL, health care executive; b. Bayonne, N.J., June 13, 1954; married. BA, Allegheny Coll., 1976; MA, Duke U., 1978. Dir. ambulatory care svcs. Meml. Hosp. Burlington County, Mt. Holly, N.J., 1979; adminstrv. resident Presbyn. U. Hosp., Pitts., 1978-79, asst. dir., 1980-82, v.p., 1982-84, sr. v.p., COO, 1985-86; sr. v.p., COO Allegheny Gen. Hosp., Pitts., 1986-87, pres., CEO, 1988—; adj. educator in field. Contbr. articles to profl. jours. Home: Blackburn Rd Sewickley PA 15143-8386 Office: Allegheny Gen Hosp 320 E North Ave Pittsburgh PA 15212-4772*

SANZONE, DONNA S., editor-in-chief; b. Bklyn., Apr. 4, 1949; d. Joseph J. Seitz and Faye (Brooks) Rossman; m. Charles F. Sanzone, Jan. 2, 1972; children: Danielle, Gregory. BA magna cum laude, Boston U., 1970; MA, Northeastern U., 1979. Grad. placement specialist Inst. Internat. Edn., N.Y.C., 1970-72; adminstr. AFS Internat. Scholarships, Brussels, 1972-74; editor Internat. Ency. Higher Edn., Boston, 1974-76; editor G.K. Hall & Co., Pubs., Boston, 1977-81, exec. editor, 1981-91, editor-in-chief, 1991—. Contbg. author: Access to Power, 1981. Mem. ALA, Assn. Am. Pubs., Assn. Coll. and Rsch. Librs., Libr. and Info. Tech. Assn. Office: G K Hall & Co 18 Pine St Weston MA 02193-1116

SAPER, CLIFFORD BAIRD, neurobiology and neurology educator; b. Chgo., Feb. 20, 1952; s. Julian and Susan Menkin S.; m. Barbara Susan Farby, Aug. 26, 1973; children: Rebecca Michelle, Leah Danielle, Sean Zachary. BS, U. Ill., 1972, MS, 1972; MD, Washington U., 1977, PhD, 1977. Diplomate Am. Bd. Psychiatry and Neurology. Intern Jewish Hosp., St. Louis, 1977-78; resident New York Hosp., N.Y.C., 1978-81; asst. prof. Washington U., St. Louis, 1981-84, assoc. prof., 1984-85; assoc. prof. U. Chgo., 1985-88, prof., 1988-92, chmn. com. on neurobiology, 1987-92; James Jackson Putnam prof. neurology and neurosci. Harvard Med. Sch., 1992—; chmn. dept. neurology Beth Israel Hosp., Boston, 1992—. Editor-in-chief Jour. of Comparative Neurology, 1994—; contbr. articles to profl. jours. Mem. Am. Neurol. Assn., Am. Acad. Neurology, Am. Physiol. Soc., Soc. for Neurosci. Office: 330 Brookline Ave Boston MA 02215-5400

SAPERS, CARL MARTIN, lawyer; b. Boston, July 16, 1932; s. Abraham E. and Anne (Herwitz) S.; m. Judith H. Thompson, Nov. 29, 1959; children: Jonathan Simonds, Rachel Elizabeth, Benjamin Lovell. AB, Harvard U., 1953, JD, 1958. Bar: Mass. 1958. Assoc. Hill, Barlow, Goodale & Adams, Boston, 1958-65; ptnr. Hill & Barlow, Boston, 1965—; counsel Mass. Crime Commn.; spl. asst. atty. gen. criminal divsn. Commonwealth of Mass., 1963-65; adj. prof. Harvard Grad. Sch. Design, 1983—; spl. cons. Mass. Ethics Commn., 1978-79; mem. Mass. Bd. Registration in Medicine, 1995—. Moderator Town of Brookline, 1982-91; trustee Nat. Bldg. Mus., 1990—; bd. dirs. Boston Archtl. Ctr., 1993—. With U.S. Army, 1953-55. Mem. AIA (hon., Allied Professions medal 1975), Boston Bar Assn. (coun. 1970-73, 91-94), Am. Arbitration Assn. (bd. dirs. 1987—, Whitney North Seymour medal 1991), Am. Coll. Constrn. Lawyers (bd. govs. 1989—, pres. 1993), Handel & Haydn Soc. (bd. govs. 1988—). Home: 26 Chesham Rd Brookline MA 02146-5811 Office: Hill & Barlow One International Pl Boston MA 02110

SAPERSTEIN, DAVID ALLAN, novelist, screenwriter, film director; b. N.Y.C.; s. Louis and Celia S.; m. Ellen Mae Bernard; children: Ivan, Ilena. Student, CCNY Film Inst., CCNY. With CBS-TV Ed Murrow Show-Person To Person; writer, prodr., dir. Skyline Films, Inc., 1963-83; asst. prof. film NYU Grad. Sch., Tisch Sch. Arts, 1992-93; instr. screenwriting Manhattan Marymount Coll., 1996. Lyricist 70 pub. songs; theatrical prodns. include musicals Blue Planet Blue, Clowns; author: Cocoon, 1985 (Best seller), Fatal Reunion, 1987, Metamorphosis, 1988, Red Devil, 1989, Funerama, 1994; movies include Cocoon (Best Original Story for Screen 1985, 2 Acad. awards); writer, dir. My Sister's Keeper, Personal Choice (Beyond the Stars), Hearts & Diamonds; writer Torch, Sara Deri, Queen of America, Italian Ices, Joshua's Golden Band, Roamers, Vets, Do Not Disturb, Snatched, Jack in the Box, School House, Point of Honor, Roberto!, The John Gill Story: In Defense of Ivan the Terrible, Joshua's Golden Band, Fighting Back, Babs' Labs; writer, dir. music videos Dr. Bill, Teenage Mutant Ninja Turtles, Fallow Angel, Wowii; segment prodr. for Northstar Ent./PBS Poppies; dir. over 300 TV commls.; writer, dir. over 200 documentaries, corp. and indsl. films, videos including Dance of the Athletes (Emmy nomination), Explorers in Aqua-Space, Rodeo: A Matter of Style. Recipient Cine Golden Eagle award, N.Y. Film Festival award, San Francisco Film Festival award, Venice Film Festival award, Melbourne Film Festival award, N.Y. Art Dirs. award, Chgo. Film Festival award. Mem. Writer Guild of Am., Dir. Guild of Am. Office: Ebbets Field Prodns Ltd Wykagyl Station PO Box 42 New Rochelle NY 10804-0042

SAPERSTEIN, GUY T., lawyer; b. June 20, 1943. AB, U. Calif., Berkeley, 1966, JD, 1969. Bar: Colo. 1969, Calif. 1970, U.S. Dist. Ct. Colo., U.S. Dist. Ct. (no., ea. and ctrl. dists.) Calif., U.S. Ct. Appeals (9th and 10th cirs.), U.S. Supreme Ct. Ptnr. Saperstein, Mayeda & Goldstein, Oakland, Calif. Contbr. articles to profl. jours. Reginald Heber Smith fellow, 1969-71. Mem. ABA (labor and employment law sect.), State Bar Calif., Calif. Trial Lawyers Assn. Office: Saperstein Mayeda & Goldstein 1300 Clay St Fl 11 Oakland CA 94612-1425*

SAPERSTEIN, LEE WALDO, mining engineering educator; b. N.Y.C., July 14, 1943; s. Charles Levy and Freda Phyllis (Dornbush) S.; m. Priscilla Frances Hickson, Sept. 16, 1967; children: Adam Geoffrey, Clare Freda. BS in Mining Engring., Mont. Sch. Mines, 1964; PhD in Engring. Sci., Oxford U., 1967. Registered profl. engr., Ky., Mo., Pa. Laborer, miner, engr. The Anaconda Co., Butte, Mont., and N.Y.C., 1963-64; asst. prof. mining engring. Pa. State U., University Park, 1967-71; assoc. prof. Pa. State U., 1971-78, prof., 1978-87, sect. chmn., 1974-87; prof., chmn. dept. mine engring. U. Ky., Lexington, 1987-93; dean, prof. mining engring. Sch. Mines and Metallurgy U. Mo., Rolla, 1993—; chmn. engring. accreditation commn., 1989-90, bd. dirs. Accreditation Bd. for Engring. and Tech., 1992—, sec. of bd., 1995-96, ABET fellow. Contbr. articles to refereed jours. Rhodes scholar Oxford U., 1967. Mem. NSPE, ASEE, AIME, Soc. Mining Engrs. (disting. mem. AIME-Soc. Mining Engrs.), Am. Assn. Rhodes Scholars. Home: 801 Laurel Dr Rolla MO 65401-3841 Office: U Mo 305 V H Mc Nutt Hall Rolla MO 65409-0810

SAPERSTEIN, MARC ELI, religious history educator, rabbi; b. N.Y.C., Sept. 5, 1944; s. Harold Irving and Marcia Belle (Rosenblum) S.; m. Roberta Shapiro, June 17, 1970; children: Sara Michal, Adina Ruth. AB, Harvard U., 1966, PhD, 1977; student, Pembroke Coll., U. Cambridge, Eng., 1966-67; MA, Hebrew U., Jerusalem, 1971, Hebrew Union Coll., N.Y.C., 1972. Ordained rabbi, 1972. Lectr. in Hebrew lit. Harvard U., Cambridge, Mass., 1977-79; lectr. in Jewish studies Harvard U. Divinity Sch., 1979-81, asst. prof. Jewish studies, 1981-83, assoc. prof., 1983-86; Gloria M. Goldstein prof. Jewish history and thought Washington U., St. Louis, 1986—, chmn. program Jewish and Near Eastern Studies, 1989—; rabbi Temple Beth David, Canton, Mass., 1973-86; mem. exec. bd. Cen. Conf. Am. Rabbis, 1985-87. Author: Decoding the Rabbis, 1980, Jewish Preaching, 1200-1800, 1989, Moments of Crisis in Jewish-Christian Relations, 1989, also articles; editor: Essential Papers on Messianic Movements and Personalities in Jewish History, 1992. Fellow Charles and Julia Henry Fund, 1966-67, Am. Coun. Learned Socs., 1983-84, Inst. Advanced Studies Hebrew U., Jerusalem, 1989, Am. Acad. for Jewish Rsch., 1994—; Danforth Found. Kent fellow, 1973-77. Mem. Assn. Jewish Studies (bd. dirs. 1983—), Phi Beta Kappa. Home: 7445 Oxford Dr Saint Louis MO 63105-2915 Office: Washington U Dept History Saint Louis MO 63130

SAPERSTON, HOWARD TRUMAN, SR., lawyer; b. Buffalo, Oct. 30, 1899; s. Willard W. and Julia (Wilson) S.; m. Nan Basch, Oct. 5, 1937; children: Howard Truman, Willard B. Student, Cornell U., 1917; LLB, Syracuse U., 1921, LLD (hon.), 1969. Bar: N.Y. 1922. Since practiced in Buffalo; mem. Saperston and Day, P.C. Assoc. editor: Cornell U. Daily Sun, 1918. Mem. Nat. coun., mem. exec. com. Buffalo coun. Boy Scouts Am.; pres., gov. United Jewish Fedn., 1948-51; pres. Community Vol. Svc. Bur., 1946-47; bd. dirs. United Fund, 1950-68, 1973-74, trustee, 1950—; bd. dirs. Buffalo chpt. ARC, 1948—; gen. chmn. Community Chest-ARC campaign United Fund, 1955; v.p. Federated Health Fund Buffalo, 1948-49; mem. adv. bd. Cerebral Palsy Assn. Western N.Y., 1953-68; bd. dirs. Buffalo Tennis Found., 1970-72; mem. exec. bd., co-chmn. Buffalo chpt. NCCJ, 1962-65; v.p. Coun. Jewish Fedns. and Welfare Funds for N.Y., Ont., 1935-50; bd. dirs. Jr. Achievement of Niagara Frontier, 1960—, Arthritis Found., 1978-88; pres. United Jewish Fedn., 1952-55, Community Chest, 1956-57; trustee Union of Am. Hebrew Congregations, 1956; pres. Temple Beth Zion, 1953-55; hon. chmn. Temple Beth Zion Endowment Fund; nat. coun. Joint Def. Appeal, Am. Jewish Joint Distbn. Com.; del. bd. Community Welfare Coun.; dir. Western N.Y. Traffic Coun.; N.Y. State assoc. chmn. U.S. Olympic Com., 1976; regent Canisius Coll., 1955-70, trustee, 1970-77; mem. coun. U. Buffalo, 1957-63; chmn. bd. dirs. Chmns. Club of Erie County Rep. Party, 1965-72, pres., 1978-80; bd. visitors Syracuse U. Coll. Law, 1960— mem. deans adv. com. U. Buffalo Coll. Law, 1955-65; bd. dirs. Bradley Sch. Music, 1960-85; trustee Buffalo Gen. Hosp., pres., 1969-72; trustee, mem. adv. com. Children's Hosp., 1962-69; mem. governing com. Buffalo Found., 1960-77, chmn., 1972-75; chmn. United Negro Coll. Fund, 1951-52, gen. chmn., 1953; bd. dirs. Greater Buffalo Devel. Found., 1960-68, Buffalo Urban League, 1942-65, Meals on Wheels, 1981-87; mem. devel. bd. U. Buffalo, 1957-62; mem. Pres.' Assocs. State U. N.Y. at Buffalo; dir. Jewish Ctr. Buffalo, 1940-43; mem. adv. bd. Camp Lakeland, 1950-75; chmn. Erie County Republican Fin. Com., 1954-73, 78-79. Officer U.S. Army, World War I, Officers Tng. Camp. Named one of 6 outstanding citizens Buffalo Eve. News, 1955; recipient Brotherhood award NCCJ, 1956, President's medal Canisius Coll., 1963, Silver Beaver award Boy Scouts Am., 1964, Nat. award NCCJ, 1966, Disting. Citizen's award Canisius Coll., 1968, Chancellor's award SUNY-Buffalo, 1982, Outstanding Citizen's award Syracuse U. Club of Buffalo, 1982, Outstanding Citizen Am. Jewish Comm. 1987, Lawyer of Yr. award Erie County Bar Assn., 1986, Citizen of Yr. award Am. Jewish Com., 1987, Lifetime Svc. award Jr. Achievement of Western N.Y., 1989, Bronze Leadership award, 1989. Mem. Am., N.Y., Erie County bar assns., Lawyers Club Buffalo, Greater Buffalo Advt. Club (sec.-treas. 1934), 100 Club of Buffalo, Am. Legion, C. of C., Am. Arbitration Assn. (dir. 1960-70), Buffalo Hist. Soc., Buffalo Pub. Libr. (life), Buffalo Fine Arts Acad. (life), Buffalo Soc. Natural Scis., Grovesnor Soc., The Soc. of the Buffalo (Ann. award 1989), Cornell Spike Shoe Soc., Zeta Beta Tau. Jewish (temple pres., trustee). Clubs: Mason (Shriner); Wilmont Country (pres. 1936-38, 43), Buffalo, Westwood Country (pres. 1948), Cornell, Syracuse, Automobile, 100, Marshall, Mid-Day, Capitol Hill, Saturn. Home: 226 Depew Ave Buffalo NY 14214-1622 Office: 1100 MIT Ctr 3 Fountain Plz Buffalo NY 14203-1486

SAPICO, FRANCISCO LEJANO, internist, educator; b. Manila, July 18, 1940; came to U.S., 1967; s. Urbano Loyola and Asuncion Limon (Lejano) S.; m. Margaret Mary Armstrong, Nov. 7, 1969; children: Erica Anne, Derek Armstrong. AA, U. Philippines, 1960, MD, 1965. Diplomate Am. Bd. Internal Medicine, Am. Bd. Infectious Diseases. Rotating intern, resident in internal medicine Philippine Gen. Hosp.-U. Philippines, Manila, 1964-67; resident in internal medicine SUNY Upstate Med. Ctr., Syracuse, 1967-69; fellow in infectious diseases UCLA Ctr. for Health Scis., 1969-71; fellow in infectious diseases Wadsworth VA Hosp., L.A., 1971-72, staff physician dept. medicine, 1972-77; physician specialist dept. medicine Rancho Los Amigos Med. Ctr., Downey, Calif., 1977—, chief infectious diseases, 1995—; adj. asst. prof. medicine UCLA Sch. Medicine, 1972-77; asst. prof. medicine U. So. Calif. Sch. Medicine, L.A., 1977-82, assoc. prof., 1982-90, prof., 1990—. Contbr. articles to med. jours., chpts. to books. Judge Fullerton (Calif.) Youth Sci. Fair, 1982-86, Orange County Sci. and Engring. Fair, Fullerton, 1984; coach, asst. coach Fullerton Rangers Youth Soccer Club, 1982-89. Fellow ACP, Infectious Diseases Soc. Am.; mem. Am. Soc. Microbiology, Am. Fedn. Clin. Rsch., Am. Soc. Tropical Medicine and Hygiene, Infections Disease Assn. Calif. Republican. Avocations: soccer, tennis, camping, fishing, photography. Office: Rancho Los Amigos Med Ctr 7601 Imperial Hwy Downey CA 90242-3456

SAPIENZA, CHARLES PAT, JR., lawyer; b. New Castle, Pa., July 12, 1963; s. Charles Pat Sr. and Joyce Elaine (Pacelli) S.; m. Maria Ann Viggiano, June 22, 1985; children: Charles Pat III, Alaina Marie, Rachel Lynn. BA, Westminster Coll., 1985; JD, U. Akron, 1989. Bar: Pa. 1989, U.S. Dist. Ct. (we. dist.) Pa. 1989. Law clerk Lawrence County Ct. Common Pleas, New Castle, 1986; law clerk Luxenberg, Garbett & Kelly, Ellwood City, Pa., 1986-89, assoc. atty., 1989-94; ptnr. Luxenberg, Garbett, Kelly & Sapienza, New Castle, 1994—; solicitor New Castle Airpirt Auth., 1991—, New Castle Red Hurricane Club, 1991—. Mem. ABA, Am. Trial Lawyers Assn., Pa. Bar assn., Pa. Trial Lawyers Assn., Lawrence County Bar Assn. Democrat. Roman Catholic. Avocations: golf, skiing, hunting. Home: 924 Warren Ave New Castle PA 16101-4455 Office: Luxenberg Garbett Kelly & Sapienza PC 101 S Mercer St New Castle PA 16101-3849

SAPIENZA, JOHN THOMAS, lawyer; b. South Orange, N.J., Feb. 26, 1913; s. James C. and Rosalie (Giaimo) S.; m. Virginia H. Gignoux, Feb. 12, 1972; children by previous marriage: John Thomas, James K. A.B. summa cum laude, Harvard U., 1934, LL.B. magna cum laude, 1937. Bar: N.Y. 1938, D.C. 1943. Law clk. Judge A.N. Hand, N.Y.C., 1937-38, Justice Stanley Reed, Washington, 1938-39; assoc. firm Wright, Gordon, Zachry & Parlin, N.Y.C., 1939-41; assoc. firm Covington & Burling, Washington, 1941-48, ptnr., 1949-87, ret. ptnr., 1987—; dir. Hiram Walker-Gooderham &

Worts Ltd., 1971-86, Hiram Walker & Sons, Inc., 1971-86, Hiram Walker Resources Ltd., 1981-86, Wyman Gordon Co., 1973-83; dir. Am. Security Bank, N.A., 1975-83, dir. emeritus, 1983-88. Pres.: Harvard Law Rev, 1936-37. Trustee George Washington U., 1978-88, hon. trustee, 1988—. Served to lt. comdr. USNR, 1943-46. Mem. Am., D.C., Fed. bar assns., Am. Law Inst., Confrerie des Chevaliers du Tastevin, Phi Beta Kappa. Clubs: Burning Tree (Washington), Metropolitan (Washington) ; Farmington Country (Charlottesville, Va.). Home: 635 Worthington Dr Apt 300 Charlottesville VA 22903-4660 Office: Covington & Burling PO Box 7566 1201 Pennsylvania Ave NW Washington DC 20004-2401

SAPINSKY, JOSEPH CHARLES, magazine executive, photographer; b. N.Y.C., Dec. 13, 1923; s. Simon Moses and Janet (Charles) S.; m. Jane Tomney, Oct. 21, 1970; children—Michael Joseph, Jane Anne, Laura Alexandra. Certificate illustration, Pratt Inst., 1943; certificate advt. design, 1947; postgrad., Colgate U., 1943, Cornell U., N.C. U. Art dir. Today's Living, N.Y. Herald Tribune, N.Y.C., 1960-63; art dir. N.Y. Mag., N.Y.C., 1963-65; asso. art dir., dir. photography Sat. Evening Post, N.Y.C., 1965-67; dir. publs. I.O.S., Geneva, 1967-69; art dir. This Week, N.Y.C., 1969, Jock N.Y. mag., N.Y.C., 1970; dir. publs. I.I.G., London, 1970; art dir. Woman's Day mag., N.Y.C., 1971-83; exec. art dir. Woman's Day Spls., N.Y.C., 1983-92; comml. photographer, 1992—; cons. art dir. Infinity mag., N.Y.C., 1971-73; instr. dept. photography Sch. Visual Arts, N.Y.C., New Sch., N.Y.C. Served with USNR, 1943-46; capt. Res. ret. Recipient numerous art dir. awards. Mem. Am. Soc. Mag. Photographers, Soc. Illustrators, Am. Soc. Mag. Editors, Am. Inst. Graphic Arts, Soc. Publ. Designers, Res. Officers Assn. Home: 76 Bank St New York NY 10014-2124

SAPINSLEY, LILA MANFIELD, state official; b. Chgo., Sept. 9, 1922; d. Jacob and Doris (Silverman) Manfield; BA, Wellesley Coll., 1944; D. Pub. Service, U. R.I., 1971; D. Pedagogy, R.I. Coll., 1973, LHD, Brown U., 1993; m. John M. Sapinsley, Dec. 23, 1942; children—Jill Sapinsley Mooney, Carol Sapinsley Rubenstein, Joan Sapinsley Lewis, Patricia Sapinsley Levy. Mem. R.I. Senate, 1972-84, minority leader, 1974-84; dir. R.I. Dept. Community Affairs, 1985; bd. dirs. Lifespan Corp.; chmn. R.I. Housing and Mortgage Fin. Corp., 1985-87; Commr. R.I. Pub. Utilities Commn., 1987-93. Mem. R.I. Gov.'s Commn. on Women; commr. Edn. Commn. of States; pres. bd. trustees Butler Hosp., 1978-84; trustee R.I. State Colls., 1965-70, chmn., 1967-70; trustee U. R.I., R.I. Coll. Found.; bd. dirs. Hamilton House, Trinity Repertory Co., Lincoln Sch., Wellesley Center for Research on Women, 1980, Providence Pub. Libr. Recipient Alumnae Achievement award Wellesley Coll., 1974; Outstanding Legislator of Yr. award Republican Nat. Legislators Assn., 1984. Republican. Jewish. Home: 25 Cooke St Providence RI 02906-2022

SAPOFF, MEYER, electronics component manufacturer; b. N.Y.C., June 2, 1927; s. Benjamin and Mary (Charney) S. Student, Mohawk Coll., 1946-48, Poly. Inst. Bklyn., 1948-50, 52-53; BS in Elec. Engring. magna cum laude, Poly. Inst. Bklyn., 1950, postgrad., 1952-53; postgrad., MIT, 1951, U. Pa., 1951-52; MS in Elec. Engring., Drexel Inst. Tech., 1952. Rsch. engr. Franklin Inst. Labs., Phila., 1950-52; rsch. fellow sr. grade Poly. Inst. Bklyn., 1952-53; dir. rsch. Victory Engring. Corp., Springfield, N.J., 1953-57; dir. engring. Victory Engring. Corp., Springfield, 1957-63, v.p., 1963-69; cons., sr. staff scientist Keystone Carbon Co., St. Mary's, Pa., 1969-70; pres. Thermometrics, Inc., Edison, N.J., 1970-86, chmn. bd. dirs., 1986-93, sr. staff cons., 1993-96; pres. MS Cons., Princeton, 1993—; cons. in field; program com., chmn. E20.08 Med. Thermometry subcom., chmn. session on thermistors 6th Symposium on Temperature, Measurement and Control in Sci. and Industry. Contbr. articles to profl. jours.; patentee in field. Active Citizens League West Orange, 1962-75, West Orange PTA, 1960-76. With USN, 1945-46. Recipient Indsl. Rsch. IR-100 award, 1974; State of NYU scholar, 1948-50; Poly. Inst. Bklyn. fellow, 1953. Mem. IEEE, ASTM, AAAS, Poly. Inst. Bklyn. Alumni Assn., Am. Ceramic Soc., Internat. Orgn. for Legal Metrology, Am. nat. Standards Inst., Am. Vacuum Soc., Tau Beta Pi, Eta Kappa Nu. Home: 1137 Stuart Rd Princeton NJ 08540-1216 Office: 301 N Harrison St Ste 69 Princeton NJ 08540-3512

SAPOLSKY, HARVEY MORTON, political scientist, educator; b. Haverhill, Mass., Feb. 21, 1939; s. Abraham and Anne Betty (Selig) S.; m. Karen P. Stenbo, Aug. 27, 1966. BA, Boston U., 1961; MPA, Harvard U., 1963, PhD, 1967. Mem. faculty MIT, 1966—, prof. polit. sci., 1977—, dir. comm. forum, 1987-95, dir. def. and arms control program, 1989—; dep. dir. Univ. Health Policy Consortium, 1978-83, assoc. chmn. faculty, 1981-83; vis. prof. U. Mich., 1971-72; cons. Artificial Heart Assessment Panel Nat. Heart and Lung Inst., Washington, 1972-73; mem. Ethics and Health Policy Panel Hastings (N.Y.) Ctr., 1979-80; mem. com. on Fed. Rsch. on Effect of Ionizing Radiation NRC, Washington, 1980-81; mem. com. on Risk Perception and Comm. NRC, 1987-88; mem. Sec. of Energy's Task Force on Alternative Futures for Dept. of Energy Labs., 1994-95. Author: The Polaris System Development, 1972, (with D. Altman and Richard Greene) Health Planning and Regulation, 1981, (with A. Drake, S. Finkelstein) The American Blood Supply, 1982, Science and the Navy, 1990; editor: Consuming Fears: The Politics of Product Risks, 1986; co-editor: Federal Health Programs, 1981, (with S. Altman), 1981, (with R. Crane, W.R. Newman and E. Noam) The Telecommunications Revolution, 1992; also articles. Mem. AAAS (sec. sect. social and econ. scis. 1968-73), Am. Polit. Sci. Assn., Nat. Acad. Social Ins., Coun. on Fgn. Rels. Home: 37 Edgemoor Rd Belmont MA 02178-3916 Office: MIT Def Arms Control Studies Pro E38-600 Cambridge MA 02139

SAPOLU, MANASE JESSE, professional football player; b. Laie, Western Samoa, Mar. 10, 1961. Student, U. Hawaii. Guard San Francisco 49ers, 1983—. Selected to Pro Bowl, 1993, 94; mem. San Francisco 49ers Super Bowl Champions XXIII, 1988, XXIV, 1989, XXIX, 1994. Office: San Francisco 49ers 4949 Centennial Blvd Santa Clara CA 95054-1229*

SAPORTA, JACK, psychologist, educator; b. N.Y.C., Oct. 21, 1927; s. David and Victoria (Fils) S.; m. Judith Hammond, May 28, 1967 (div. 1979); children: David, Victoria. AB cum laude, Adelphi U., 1951; PhD, U. Chgo., 1962. Diplomate Am. Bd. Profl. Psychology; lic. clin. psychologist. Pvt. practice, 1962—; supt. Tinley Park (Ill.) Mental Health Ctr., 1975-78; chief manpower tng. and devel. Ill. Dept. Mental Health, Chgo., 1978-82; dean, prof. Forest Inst. Profl. Psychology, Des Plaines, Ill., 1982-85; coord. studies Fielding Inst., Santa Barbara, Calif., 1984—; prof. Ill. Sch. Profl. Psychology, Chgo., 1985—; mem. adj. faculty psychology Lake Forest Grad. Sch. Mgmt., 1987—; mem. Ill. State Clin. Psychology Lic. and Disciplinary Com., Springfield, 1984-93; prof. staff Forest Hosp., Des Plaines, 1977-96; mem. staff Luth. Gen. Hosp., Park Ridge, Ill., 1986—. Served with U.S. Army, 1946-47, Germany. Named Educator of Yr., Forest Inst., 1982, Outstanding Faculty Mem. Lake Forest Grad. Sch. Mgmt. Fellow Acad. Clin. Psychology, NTL-Inst. (faculty); mem. APA (accreditation site vis. team), Ill. Psychol. Assn., Chgo. Psychol. Assn. Avocations: tennis, computers, do-it-yourself home projects. Home: 3201 California Ave Rolling Meadows IL 60008-2226

SAPP, A. EUGENE, JR., electronics executive; b. Winston-Salem, N.C., 1933; married. BEE, Ga. Inst. Tech., 1959. With Tex. Instruments Inc., 1959-62, SCI Systems Inc., Hunstville, Ala., 1962—; v.p. SCI Systems Inc., 1973-80, exec. v.p., 1980—, now pres., chief oper. officer. Office: SCI Systems Inc PO Box 1000 Huntsville AL 35807-4001*

SAPP, DONALD GENE, minister; b. Phoenix, Feb. 27, 1927; s. Guerry Byron and Lydia Elmeda (Snyder) S.; m. Anna Maydean Nevitt, July 10, 1952 (dec.); m. Joann Herrin Mountz, May 1, 1976; children: Gregory, Paula, Jeffrey, Mark, Melody, Cristine. AB in Edn., Ariz. State U., 1949; MDiv, Boston U., 1952, STM, 1960; D Ministry, Calif. Grad. Sch. Theology, 1975. Ordained to ministry Meth. Ch., 1950. Dir. youth activities Hyde Park (Mass.) Meth. Ch., 1950-52; minister 1st Meth. Ch., Peabody, Mass., 1952-54, Balboa Island (Calif.) Community Meth. Ch., 1954-57, Ch. of the Foothills Meth., Duarte, Calif., 1957-63; sr. minister Aldersgate United Meth. Ch., Tustin, Calif., 1963-70, Paradise Valley (Ariz.) United Meth. Ch., 1970-83; dist. supt. Cen. West Dist. of Desert S.W. Conf. United Meth. Ctr., Phoenix, 1983-89. Editor Wide Horizons, 1983-89; contbr. articles to profl. jours. Chaplain City of Hope Med. Ctr., Duarte, 1957-63; trustee Plaza Community Ctr., L.A., 1967-70; corp. mem. Sch. Theology at Claremont, Calif., 1972-80; pres. Met. Phoenix Commn., 1983-85; del. Western Jurisdictional Conf. United Meth. Ch., 1984, 88; bd. dirs. Coun. Chs., L.A., 1963-67, Orange County (Calif.) Human Rels. Coun., 1967-70, Interfaith Counseling Svc. Found., 1982-89, Wesley Community Ctr., Phoenix, 1983-89; mem. gen. conf. United Meth. Ch., 1988. With USN, 1945-46. Mem. Ariz. Ecumenical Coun., Bishops and Exec. Roundtable, Rotary (pres.), Kappa Delta Pi, Tau Kappa Epsilon. Democrat. Avocation: overseas travel. Home: 5225 E Road Runner Rd Paradise Valley AZ 85253

SAPP, JOHN RAYMOND, lawyer; b. Lawrence, Kans., June 18, 1944; s. Raymond Olen and Amy (Kerr) S.; m. Linda Lee Tebbe, July 3, 1965; children: Jeffrey, Jennifer, John. BA, U. Kans., 1966; JD, Duke U., 1969. Bar: Wis. 1969, U.S. Dist. Ct. (ea. dist.) Wis. 1969, U.S. Ct. Appeals (7th cir.) 1974, U.S. Ct. Appeals (4th cir.) 1984, U.S. Supreme Ct. 1974. Assoc. Michael, Best & Friedrich, Milw., 1969-76, ptnr., 1976-90, mng. ptnr., 1990—; dir. Roadrunner Freight Systems, Milw., 1992—, Aarrow Elec. Signs, Inc., Shawno, Wis., 1990. Bd. dirs. Milw. Symphony, 1981—, mem. exec. com., 1993—; bd. dirs. Boy Scouts Am., Milw., 1986—, pres. 1990; mem. Milw. Arts Bd., 1990, Greater Milw. Com.; assoc. bd. dirs. Zool. Soc., 1992—. Avocations: golf, curling, print collecting. Office: Michael Best & Friedrich 100 E Wisconsin Ave Ste 3300 Milwaukee WI 53202-4107

SAPP, MARY ELLEN, state official, educator; b. Bethesda, Md., Aug. 6, 1945; d. Richard Friend and Anne Carr (Garges) S. BA in Math., Incarnate Word Coll., 1968; MS in Health Care Adminstrn., Trinity U., 1972; M in Theol. Studies, Oblate Sch. Theology, San Antonio, 1984. Tchr. Archdiocese of San Antonio, 1965-71; adminstrv. resident Spohn Hosp., Corpus Christi, 1971, Morningside Manor, San Antonio, 1972; exec. dir. St. Benedict Health Care Ctr., San Antonio, 1972-85, Benedictine Health Resource Ctr., Austin/San Antonio, 1985-89, Tex. Dept. Aging, Austin, 1992—; town meeting specialist Alamo Area Coun. of Govts., San Antonio, 1990-91; pres. Tex. Conf. Cath. Health Facilities, Austin, 1980-81; cmty. advisor San Antonio Light Newspaper, 1989-91; mem. adj. faculty Inst. on Aging Incarnate Word Coll., San Antonio, 1991-93; active Tex. Indigent Health Care Task Force, Austin, 1983-84. Recipient Headliners award for pub. endeavors Women in Comm., 1990; named Regional Citizen, Alamo Area Coun. Govts., 1987. Avocations: music, art, poetry, hiking. Office: Tex Dept Aging 1949 IH 35 South Austin TX 78711

SAPP, NEIL CARLETON, pilot; b. Miami, Fla., Nov. 22, 1939; s. Alfred Eli and Vera May (Crowson) S.; m. Peggy Joe Brotherton, June 10, 1962; children: Erin Lynn, Kerrie Ellen. BS, U.S. Naval Acad., 1962; postgrad., U. Miami, Coral Gables, Fla. Commd. ensign U.S. Navy, 1962, advanced through grades to lt.; fighter pilot U.S. Navy, Virginia Beach, Va., 1962-67; resigned U.S. Navy, 1967; capt. Nat. Airlines, Miami, Fla., 1967-80, Pan Am. World Airways, Inc., Miami, 1980-91, Delta Air Lines, Inc., N.Y.C., 1991—; mng. ptnr. Sapp & Slaton Fin. Concepts Group, Coral Gables, Fla., 1981-85; chmn., chief exec. officer, pres. U.S. Indsl. Dynamics Corp., Miami, 1988—; pres., COO Iowa Acquisition Group, Inc., 1990-91; v.p. mktg. and corp. devel. The Systema Group, Inc., Miami, 1993-95; pres. Air Transport Equity Corp., 1996—; past chmn. internat. ops., vice chmn. master exec. coun. Nat. Airlines Pilots Assn., Miami; past chmn. spl. corp. ops. profl. standards, flight standard and tng. Pan Am. N.Y.; bd. dirs. World Export/Import Marts, Ltd., Waterloo, Iowa, 1989-95; bd. advisors The Cesne Inst., Waterloo, 1988—; trustee Pan Am Pilots Retirement Found., Inc., 1996—. Officer affiliate admissions com. U.S. Naval Acad., 1967-95; bd. dirs. St. Thomas Sch., Miami, 1976-77; co-pres. Coral Gables Sr. H.S. PTA, 1983-84; vol. Informed Families of Dade County, Miami, 1984—; vestry St. Thomas Ch., Miami, 1976-79. Mem. Internat. Platform Assn., Delta Airline Pilots Assn. (chmn. profl. stds., flight stds. and tng. 1991-93), Assn. Naval Aviation, Tailhook Assn., U.S. Naval Acad. Alumni Assn., Am. Legion, Naval Inst., Navy League of the U.S., Camarilla Club, Beach Colony Club, Miami Club, Army-Navy Club Washington, Riviera Country Club. Episcopalian. Avocations: reading, tennis, golf, economics, computers. Home: 7201 SW 47th Ct Miami FL 33143-6109

SAPP, WALTER WILLIAM, lawyer, energy company executive; b. Linton, Ind., Apr. 21, 1930; s. Walter J. and Nona (Stalcup) S.; m. Eva Kaschner, July 10, 1957 (dec.); children: Karen Elisabeth, Christoph Walter. AB magna cum laude, Harvard, 1951; JD summa cum laude, Ind. U., 1957. Bar: Ind. 1957, N.Y. 1959, Colo. 1966, U.S. Supreme Ct. 1972, Tex. 1977. Pvt. practice N.Y.C., 1957-60, 63-66; practice in Paris, France, 1960-63, Colorado Springs, 1966-76; assoc. atty. Cahill, Gordon, Reindel & Ohl, Paris, 1960-63, N.Y.C., 1957-60, 63-65; partner Cahill, Gordon, Reindel & Ohl, 1966; gen. counsel Colo. Interstate Corp., 1966-76, v.p., 1968-76, sec., 1971-76, sr. v.p., dir., exec. com., 1973-75, exec. v.p., 1975-76; v.p. Coastal States Gas Corp., 1973-76; sr. v.p., gen. counsel Tenneco, Inc., Houston, 1976-92, sec., 1984-86; pvt. practice Houston, 1992—; Editor-in-chief Ind. U. Law Jour., 1956-57. Trustee Houston Ballet, 1982-85, Awty Internat. Sch., 1989—, vice-chmn., 1994—; bd. dirs. Harris County Met. Transit Authority, 1982-84, Houston Internat. Protocol Alliance, 1992-94, Houston Symphony, 1989—, v.p., 1991-94; adv. bd. Inst. for Internat. Edn. S.W. region, 1987—, chmn., 1992-94, Internat. and Comparative Law Ctr. Southwestern Legal Found., 1976-92. Lt. USNR, 1951-54. Mem. ABA, N.Y. State Bar Assn., Tex. Bar Assn., Assn. Bar City of N.Y., Houston Bar Assn., Order of the Coif, French-Am. C. of C. (bd. dirs. 1987-92), Alliance Francaise Houston (bd. dirs. 1989—, v.p. 1991-94). Mem. United Ch. of Christ. Office: 1 West Loop S Ste 100 Houston TX 77027-9009

SAPPENFIELD, CHARLES MADISON, architect, educator; b. Columbia, S.C., Mar. 17, 1930; s. Charles Madison and Elizabeth Olive (Moss) S.; m. Mary Frances McGowan Dec. 14, 1963 (div. June 1990); children—Charles Ross, Sarah Kathleen. B.Arch., N.C. State U., 1956; Cert., Denmark's Royal Acad., Copenhagen, 1961. Registered architect, Ind., Tenn., N.C. Asst. prof. N.C. State U., Raleigh, 1956-57, asst. prof., 1961-63; head archtl. firm C.M. Sappenfield, Asheville, N.C. and Muncie, Ind., 1961—; assoc. prof. Clemson U., S.C., 1963-65; prof. architecture Ball State U., Muncie, Ind., 1965-94, prof. emeritus, 1994—, dean, 1965-81, dean emeritus, 1994—, dir. Design Indiana, 1983-88; awards juror Interfaith Forum on Religious Art and Architecture, 1981, Am. Cons. Engrs. Council, 1982; mem. accreditation teams Nat. Archtl. Accrediting Bd., 1967-82. Archtl. works include: Dormitories, U. N.C., Gumpert residence, Dave residence. Pres. Asheville Art Mus., N.C., 1964-65; chmn. Ind. Commn. on Aging, Indpls., 1983-85; pres. Alpha Day Care Ctr. for Elderly, Muncie, 1985; mem. State Planning Adv. Commn., Indpls., 1974-82. Served with U.S. Army. Recipient Gold medal for service Ball State U., 1983; named Sagamore of the Wabash, Gov. of Ind., 1982. Fellow AIA (dir. nat. bd. dirs. 1989-92); mem. Ind. Soc. Architects (pres. 1976), Ind. Archtl. Found. (chmn. 1975), Am. Soc. Landscape Architects (awards juror 1983), Danish Fedn. Architects (hon., Aeresmedallion 1987), Fulbright Alumni Assn., Alpha Rho Chi. Republican. Episcopalian. Lodges: Rotary, Civitan. Avocations: bicycling, racquetball, photography. Home and Office: 2900 W Torquay Rd Muncie IN 47304-3229

SAPSOWITZ, SIDNEY H., entertainment and media company executive; b. N.Y.C., June 29, 1936; s. Max and Annette (Rothstein) Sapsowitz; m. Phyllis Skopp, Nov. 27, 1957; children: Donna Dawn Chazen, Gloria Lynn Aaron, Marsha Helene Gleit. BBA summa cum laude, Paterson (N.J.) State Coll., 1980. Various fin. and oper. systems positions Metro Goldwyn Mayer, Inc., N.Y.C., 1957-68; exec. v.p., dir. Penta Computer Assoc. Inc., N.Y.C., 1968-70, Cons. Actuaries Inc., Clifton, N.J., 1970-73; exec. v.p., CFO Am. Film. Theatre, N.Y.C., 1973-76, Cinema Shares Internat Dristb. Corp., N.Y.C., 1976-79; sr. cons. Solomon, Finger & Newman, N.Y.C., 1979-80; exec. v.p., chief fin. officer Metro Goldwyn Mayer, Inc., L.A., 1980-85; various positions leading to exec. v.p. fin. and adminstrn., CFO MGM/UA Entertainment Co., Culver City, Calif., 1985-86; also bd. dirs. MGM/UA Entertainment Co., L.A.; fin. v.p.; chief bus. and ops. officer, Office of Pres., dir. United Artists Corp., Beverly Hills, Calif., 1986-87; chmn. bd., CEO MGA/UA Telecommunications Corp., Beverly Hills, 1986-89; sr. exec. v.p., dir., mem. exec. com. MGA/UA Communications Co., 1986-89; chmn., CEO Sid Sapsowitz & Assocs., Inc., 1989—. Pres., Wayne Conservative Congregation, N.J., 1970-77. Mem. Am. Mgmt. Assn., Am. Film Inst., Acad. Motion Picture Arts and Scis., Fin. Exec. Inst., TV Acad. Arts and Scis., KP (chancellor comdr.).

SAPUTRA, DANIEL, agricultural engineering educator; b. Padangsidempuan, Indonesia, Aug. 9, 1958; s. Adam and Hanna Saputra; m. Liniyanti D. Oswari, Sept. 19, 1984; children: Danny Matthew, Joshua Michael, Irene Ruth. Sarjana, Bogor (Indonesia) Agrl. U., 1982; MS in Agrl. Engring., U. Ky., 1988, PhD, 1992. Site mgr. P.T. Layaniraya, Tarakan, Indonesia, 1982-83; supervision head P.T. Trans Intra Asia, West Aceh, Indonesia, 1983-84; lectr. Coll. Agr. U. Sriwijaya, Palembang, Indonesia, 1985—, head food process engring., 1993—. Contbr. articles to profl. jours.; patentee in field. Mem. Am. Soc. Agrl. Engrs., Indonesian Soc. Agrl. Engrs. Seventh Day Adventist. Office: Indralaya Campus, U Sriwijaya Coll Agr, Palembang 30662, Indonesia

SARACENI, ROCCO, financial planner, educator; b. Orsogna, Chieti, Italy, Apr. 14, 1942; came to U.S., 1956; *; s. Giovanni and Concetta (D'Alleva) S.; m. Rosemarie Abate, June 4, 1966; children: Annmarie, Stephanie. AS, Nassau C.C., Garden City, N.Y., 1984; MBA, Adelphi U., 1986, Adelphi U., 1987. CFP. Real estate mgr., N.Y.C. and Nassau, N.Y., 1974—; acct. and fin. planner D'Angelo & Saraceni, N.Y.C., 1987-88; fin. planner Saracens Cons. Svcs., Inc., Lynbrook, N.Y., 1988—; adj. prof. fin. Hofstra U., Adelphi U., SUNY, N.Y.C., Nassau, 1989—. Mem. Inst. CFP's, Alumni Assn. Nassau C.C. (pres. 1993—), KC, Delta Mu Delta. Republican. Roman Catholic. Home and Office: 7 Huntington Ave Lynbrook NY 11563-3753

SARACHIK, MYRIAM PAULA, physics educator; b. Antwerp, Belgium, Aug. 8, 1933; came to U.S., 1947; d. Solomon and Sarah (Segal) Morgenstein; m. Philip E. Sarachik, Sept. 6, 1954; 1 child, Karen Beth. AB, Barnard Coll., 1954; MS, Columbia U., 1957, PhD, 1960. Rsch. assoc. IBM Watson Labs., Columbia U., N.Y.C., 1960-61; mem. tech. staff Bell Telephone Labs., Murray Hill, N.J., 1962-64; asst. prof. physics CCNY, 1964-67, assoc. prof., 1967-70, prof., 1971—, Disting. prof., 1995—; advisor NSF, NRC. Contbr. over 75 articles to profl. jours. Recipient N.Y.C. Mayor's award for excellence in sci. and tech., 1995. Fellow Am. Phys. Soc. (various offices and coms.), N.Y. Acad. Scis.; mem. NAS. Office: CCNY Physics Dept Convent Ave and 138 St New York NY 10031

SARANDON, SUSAN ABIGAIL, actress; b. N.Y.C., Oct. 4, 1946; d. Phillip Leslie and Lenora Marie (Criscione) Tomalin; m. Chris Sarandon, Sept. 16, 1967 (div. 1979); children: Eva Maria Livia Amurri, Jack Henry Robbins, Miles Guthrie Robbins. B.A. in Drama and English, Cath. U. Am., 1968. Actress: (plays) include An Evening with Richard Nixon, 1972, A Coupla White Chicks Sittin' Around Talkin', 1980-81, A Stroll in the Air, Albert's Bridge, Private Ear, Public Eye, Extremities, 1982, (films) Joe, 1970, Lady Liberty, 1972, The Rocky Horror Picture Show, 1975, Lovin' Molly, 1974, The Front Page, 1974, The Great Waldo Pepper, 1975, Dragon Fly, 1976, Crash, 1976, The Other Side of Midnight, 1977, The Last of the Cowboys, 1978, Checkered Flag or Crash, 1978, Pretty Baby, 1978, King of the Gypsies, 1978, Something Short of Paradise, 1979, Loving Couples, 1980, Atlantic City, 1980 (Prix Genie Best Fgn. Actress award 1981, Acad. award nominee 1981), Tempest, 1982 (Best Actress award Venice Film Festival 1982), The Hunger, 1983, Buddy System, 1984, Compromising Positions, 1985, The Witches of Eastwick, 1987, Bull Durham, 1988, Sweet Hearts Dance, 1988, A Dry White Season, 1989, The January Man, 1989, White Palace, 1990, Thelma and Louise, 1991 (Acad. award nominee for best actress 1992, Golden Globe award nominee 1992), The Player, 1992, Light Sleeper, 1992, Bob Roberts, 1992, Lorenzo's Oil, 1992 (Acad. award nominee 1993), The Client, 1994 (Acad. award nominee for best actress), Little Women, 1994, Safe Passage, 1994, Dead Man Walking, 1995 (Golden Globe award nominee for best actress 1996, Acad. award for best actress 1996); TV appearances The Haunting of Rosalind, 1973, F. Scott Fitzgerald and The Last of the Belles, 1974, Who Am I This Time, 1982, A.D., 1985. Mussolini: The Deline and Fall of Il Duce, 1985, (TV series) A World Apart, 1970-71, Search for Tomorrow, 1972-73. Mem. AFTRA, Screen Actors Guild, Actors Equity, Acad. Motion Picture Arts and Scis., NOW, MADRE, Amnesty Internat., ACLU. Office: Internat Creative Mgmt Martha Luttrell 8942 Wilshire Blvd Beverly Hills CA 90211

SARASON, IRWIN G., psychology educator; b. Newark, Sept. 15, 1929; s. Max and Anna Sarason; m. Barbara June Ryrholm, Sept. 19, 1953; children: Suzanne, Jane, Donald. BA, Rutgers U., Newark, 1951; MS, U. Iowa, 1953; PhD, Ind. U., 1955. Lic. psychologist, Wash. Intern clin. psychology VA Hosp., West Haven, Conn., 1955-56; asst. prof. psychology U. Wash., Seattle, 1956-59, assoc. prof., 1959-65, prof., 1965—. Co-author: Abnormal Psychology, 1972, 8th edit., 1996; editor: Jour. Personality and Social Psychology, 1985-91; author over 250 articles. The Netherlands Inst. for Advanced Study fellow, Wassenaar, 1975, 85. Fellow APA, Japan Soc. for Promotion of Sci., AAAS, Western Psychol. Assn. (pres. 1978-79), Wash. State Psychol. Assn. (pres. 1965). Avocations: travel, music, reading. Home: 13516 42nd Ave NE Seattle WA 98125-3826 Office: U Wash Dept Psychology Seattle WA 98195

SARASTE, JUKKA-PEKKA, conductor; b. Heinola, Finland, 1956. With Finnish Radio Symphony Orch., 1978—, prin. condr., 1987—; prin. condr. Scottish Chamber Orch., 1987-91; music dir. The Toronto Symphony Orch., 1994—. Guest condr. Helsinki Philharm., Beijing Cen. Opera Orch., Symphonic Orch. Chengdu, Rotterdam Philharm. Orch., Chamber Orch. Europe, Bavarian Radio Symphony Orch., Junge Deutsche Philharm., Detroit Orch., Minn. Orch., Vienna Symphony Orch., Rome's Santa Cecilia Orch., others; co-founder Avanti Chamber orch.; condr. more than 39 recs. with Finnish Radio Symphony Orch. and Scottish Chamber Orch. Recipient First prize Scandinavian Conducting Competition, 1981, hon. doctorate fine arts, York U., Toronto, 1995. Office: Radio Symphony Orch, Yleisradio Ja 14, SF-00240 Helsinki 24, Finland also: Toronto Symphony Orch, 212 King St W Ste 550, Toronto, ON Canada M5H 1K5

SARAVANJA-FABRIS, NEDA, mechanical engineering educator; b. Sarajevo, Yugoslavia, Aug. 2, 1942; came to U.S., 1970; d. Zarko and Olga Maria (Majstorovic) Saravanja; m. Gracio Fabris, Nov. 4, 1967; children: Drazen Fabris, Nicole. Diploma in mech. engring., U. Sarajevo, 1965; MSME, Ill. Inst. Tech., 1972, PhD in Mech. Engring., 1976. Lectr. in mech. engring. U. Sarajevo, 1965-70; teaching asst. Ill. Inst. Tech., Chgo., 1970-76; lectr. U. Ill., Chgo., 1974-75; mem. tech. staff Bell Telephone Lab., Naperville, Ill., 1976-79; prof. mech. engring. Calif. State U., L.A., 1979—, chair mech. engring. dept., 1989-92; assoc. researcher Lab. for Machine Tools, Aachen, Fed. Republic Germany, 1966-67; cons. Northrop Corp., L.A., 1984; COO FAS Engring. Inc., Burbank, Calif., 1993—. Contbr. articles to profl. publs. Grantee NSF, 1986, Brown & Sharpe Co., 1989; German Acad. Exch. fellow DAAD, 1966-67, Amelia Earhart fellow Zonta Internat., 1973-74, 75-76; recipient Engring. Merit award San Fernando Valley Engring. Coun., 1990, Disting. Chair award sch. of engring. and tech. Calif. State U., L.A., 1993. Mem. AAUW, Soc. for Engring. Edn., Soc. Women Engrs. (sr.), Soc. Mfg. Engrs. (sr., chpt. v.p. 1984-88). Home: 2039 Dublin Dr Glendale CA 91206-1006 Office: Calif State U 5151 State University Dr Los Angeles CA 90032

SARAZEN, RICHARD ALLEN, media company executive; b. Bklyn., June 27, 1933; s. Nicholas and Anna M. (Isacco) S.; children: Richard, Theresa, Mary, Barbara, David, Russell, Christina, Andrea. B.B.A., Hofstra U., 1955. CPA, N.Y., Pa., Calif. Acct. Arthur Young & Co., N.Y.C., 1955-58; ptnr. Alexander Grant & Co., N.Y.C., 1958-67; v.p. fin. Seeburg Corp., Chgo., 1967-69; mng. ptnr. Alexander Grant & Co., Pitts., Los Angeles, 1969-74; exec. v.p. News Am. Pub., Inc., N.Y.C., 1974-80; chmn. bd. XCor Internat., Inc., N.Y.C., 1980-82; sr. exec. v.p., bd. dir. The News Corp. Ltd., Sydney, Australia, 1982—. Bd. dirs. N.Y.C. Center Found. Mem. AICPA, N.Y. State Soc. CPAs. Republican. Roman Catholic. Club: Chgo. Athletic. Home: 165 Galway Rd Windham NY 12496 Office: News Am Pub Inc 1211 Avenue Of The Americas New York NY 10036-8701

SARAZIN, CRAIG LEIGH, astronomer, educator; b. Milw., Aug. 11, 1950; s. Valley V. and Martha V. (Gustafson) S.; m. Jane Curry, June 12, 1971; children: Stephen N., Andrew T. BS in Physics, Calif. Inst. Tech., 1972; MA in Physics, Princeton U., 1973, PhD in Physics, 1975. Millikan fellow Calif. Inst. Tech., Pasadena, 1975; mem. Inst. Advanced Study, Princeton, N.J., 1975-77; asst. prof. U. Va., Charlottesville, 1977-79, assoc. prof. dept. astronomy, 1979-86, prof., 1986-96, W.H. Vanderbilt prof. astronomy, 1996—, chmn. dept., 1992-95; vis. asst. prof. U. Calif., Berkeley, 1979; vis. scientist Nat. Radio Astronomy Obs., Charlottesville, 1977-82; vis. prof. physics Inst. Advanced Study, 1981-82, Joint Inst. Lab. Astrophysics vis. fellow U. Colo., Boulder, 1985-86; mem. com. on Space Astronomy Astrophysics, Washington, 1984-86, mem. x-ray astronomy working group, 1989-94; mem. Advanced X-ray Astronomy Facility users com., 1993—, Advanced Satellite for Cosmology and Astrophysics users com., 1995—. Author: X-ray Emission from Clusters of Galaxies; contbr. numerous articles to profl. jours. NSF grantee, 1981-86, NASA grantee, 1979-82, 86—; recipient Haren Fischer Physics prize Calif. Inst. Tech., 1971. Mem. Am. Astron. Soc., Internat. Astron. Union. Home: 2574 Kimbrough Cir Charlottesville VA 22901-9516 Office: Leander J McCormick Obs Dept of Astronomy U of Va PO Box 3818 Charlottesville VA 22903-0818

SARBANES, PAUL SPYROS, senator; b. Salisbury, Md., Feb. 3, 1933; s. Spyros P. and Matina (Tsigounis) S.; m. Christine Dunbar, June 11, 1960; children—John Peter, Michael Anthony, Janet Matina. A.B., Princeton, 1954; B.A. (Rhodes scholar), Oxford (Eng.) U., 1957; LL.B., Harvard, 1960. Bar: Md. bar 1960. Law clk. to judge Morris Soper U.S. Ct. Appeals (4th cir.), 1960-61; asso. Piper & Marbury, Balt., 1961-62; adminstrv. asst. Walter W. Heller; chmn. Council Econ. Advisers, 1962-63; exec. dir. Charter Revision Commn., Balt., 1963-64; asso. Venable, Baetjer & Howard, Balt., 1965-70; mem. Md. Ho. of Dels., 1967-71, 92d Congress from 4th Dist. Md., 93d-94th congresses from 3d Dist. Md.; U.S. senator from Md., 1977—. Democrat. Greek Orthodox. Office: US Senate 309 Hart Senate Bldg Washington DC 20510 also: Tower I Ste 100 100 S Charles St Baltimore MD 21201-2725*

SARBIN, HERSHEL BENJAMIN, management consultant, business publisher, lawyer; b. Massillon, Ohio, Dec. 30, 1924; s. Joseph I. and Sarah Charlotte (Reich) S.; m. Susan Challman, July 24, 1973; children by previous marriage: Penelope Sarbin Burke, Richard, Barbara; 1 stepdau., Caroline Cooley. A.B., Western Res. U., 1946; J.D., Harvard U., 1950. Bar: Ill. 1950, N.Y. 1953. Assoc. firm Lewis and MacDonald, N.Y.C., 1953-58; with Ziff-Davis Pub. Co., 1950-81; pub. Popular Photography mag., 1965-66, sr. v.p. co., 1967-74; assoc. pub. Travel Weekly, 1967-68, pub., 1969-74, pres., pub. dir., chief exec. officer photog. div., 1968-69, pres. Pub. Transp. and Travel div., 1970-74; pres. Ziff-Davis Pub. Co., 1974-78; exec. v.p. Ziff Corp., 1978-81, also dir.; chmn., pres. Hershel Sarbin Assocs., Inc., 1981—; vis. assoc. prof. Fla. Internat. U., 1980; mem. exec. com., nat. photography coordinator Pres.'s Council Youth Opportunity, 1968; fed. commr. Nat. Commn. on New Technol. Uses of Copyrighted Works, 1975-78; mem. policy rev. bd. Public Agenda Found.; pres., CEO Cowles Bus. Media, Inc., 1991-95; Sr. Advisor Cowles Media, 1995. Author: (with George Chernoff) Photography and the Law, 1958, rev. edit., 1977. Mem. exec. com. Westchester County (N.Y.) Sch. Bd., 1964-66; mem. ethical practices com. N.Y. Sch. Bd. Assn., 1965-68; pres. Hastings-on-Hudson Bd. Edn., 1966-67. Served with AUS, 1946-47. Mem. Phi Beta Kappa. Clubs: Harvard, Sky (N.Y.C.); Bedford Golf and Tennis (N.Y.). Home: 756 Guard Hill Rd Bedford NY 10506-1042 Office: 6 Riverbend Ctr 911 Hope St Stamford CT 06907-2318

ŠARČEVIĆ, PETAR A., ambassador, educator, lawyer; b. Subotica, Vojvodina, Yugoslavia, Apr. 26, 1941; s. Andrija G. and Marija (Szekely) Š.; m. Susan J. Gooding, Sept. 5, 1970. LLB, Zagreb (Croatia) U., 1965; postgrad. diploma, Europa Inst. U. Amsterdam, 1968; LLD, Johannes Gutenberg U., Mainz, Germany, 1973. Atty. Subotica, Yugoslavia, 1970-77; prof. law Rijeka (Croatia) U. Sch. Law, 1977—, dean, 1986-88; sci. collaborator Swiss Inst. Comparative Law, Lausanne, 1983-86; rector, pres. U. Rijeka, 1989-91; amb. to U.S. Govt. of Republic of Croatia, Washington, 1992—; vis. prof. U. Graz, Austria, 1986, Cath. U. Leuven, Belgium, 1988, U. Fla. Coll. Law, Gainesville, 1988, 90; disting. vis. prof. Case Western Res. Sch. Law, Cleve., 1992; dir. studies Internat. Assn. Legal Sci., Paris, 1990-94; v.p. Internat. Soc. Family Law, London, 1992-94; arbitrator in internat. legal matters. Editor: International Sale of Goods, 1986, International Commercial Arbitration, 1989, International Contracts and Conflicts of Law, 1990, Legal Issues in International Trade, 1990, International Contracts and Payments, 1991, Privatization in Central and Eastern Europe, 1992. Mem. Am. Soc. Internat. Law, Am. Law Inst., Swiss Arbitration Assn., Inst. Internat. Bus. Law and Practice (corr.), Internat. Law Assn. Roman Catholic. Avocations: tennis, skiing, swimming, philately. Home: Ivana Milcetića 12, 51000 Rijeka Croatia Office: Embassy Republic of Croatia 2343 Massachusetts Ave NW Washington DC 20008-2803

SARCHET, BERNARD REGINALD, retired chemical engineering educator; b. Byesville, Ohio, June 13, 1917; s. Elmer C. and Nellie Myrtle (Huff) S.; m. Lena Virginia Fisher, Dec. 13, 1941; children: Renee Erickson, Dawne, Melanie Koewing. BS in Chem. Engring., Ohio State U., 1939; MS in Chem. Engring., U. Del., 1941. From engr. to dir. comml. devel. Koppers Co., Inc., Pitts., 1941-67; prof. and founding chmn. dept. engring. mgmt. U. Mo., Rolla, 1967-88; mgmt. cons. Sarchet Assocs., Rolla, 1975—. Coauthor: Supervisory Management (Essentials), 2nd edit. 1976, Management for Engineers, 1981; contbr. articles to profl. jours. Mem. Planning Commn. Beaver, Pa., 1955-58; dir. Billy Graham Film Crusades, Rolla, 1969-75; area dir. Here's Life America, Rolla, 1977. Recipient Profl. Achievement award U. Del., 1952, Freedom Found. awards, 1974-75, Fellow Mem. awd., Am. Soc. for Engineering Educ., 1992. Fellow Am. Soc. Engring. Mgmt. (founding pres., bd. dirs. 1979—), Am. Soc. Engring. Edn. (chmn. 1976). Achievements include patent on composition for producing detergent polyglycol condensation products; led in developing engineering management for engineers. Home: PO Box 68 Rolla MO 65402-0068

SARD, GEORGE, public relations company executive; b. N.Y.C., May 13, 1953. BA, Clark Univ., 1975. Pub. rels. writer Clark Univ., 1975-78; dir. pub. rels. East N.Y. Svgs. Bank, 1978-80; acct. exec. Adams & Rinehart, Inc. (now Ogilvy Adams & Rinehart), 1980-82, v.p., 1982-86; pres., chief operating officer Adams & Rinehart, Inc. (now Ogilvy Adams & Rinehart), N.Y.C., from 1986; now chmn./N.Y. Ogilvy Adams & Rinehart, N.Y.C.; chmn., CEO Sard Verbinnen & Co., N.Y.C., 1992—. Office: Sard Verbinnen & Co 630 3rd Ave New York NY 10017-6705*

SARDELLA, EDWARD JOSEPH, television news anchor; b. Buffalo, June 2, 1940; s. Joseph Edward and Josephine Jenny (D'Amico) S.; m. Sandra K. Lorenzen, Jan. 17, 1975. BA in Speech Arts, Occidental Coll., L.A., 1962. Radio disc jockey, newsman KWIN/KTIL/KERG, Ashland/Tillamook/Eugene, Oreg., 1966-69; reporter KVAL-TV, Eugene, 1969-70; reporter/anchor KOIN-TV, Portland, Oreg., 1970-72, KMGH-TV, Denver, 1972-74; news anchor/sr. editor KUSA-TV, Denver, 1974—; adj. instr. journalism U. Colo., Boulder, 1984-92. Author: Write Like You Talk, 1984; co-author: The Producing Strategy, 1995. Olympic torchbearer, 1996. Capt. USMC, 1962-66. Recipient Emmy award Nat. Assn. TV Arts and Scis., 1992, 93, 94. Office: KUSA-TV 500 Speer Blvd Denver CO 80206

SARDESON, LYNDA SCHULTZ, nursing, diabetes educator; b. LaPorte, Ind., Nov. 5, 1946; d. Wilbur W. and Helen (Winkfein) Schultz; children: Brian Michael, Eric Matthew. BS, Purdue U., Westville, Ind., 1976. Cert. diabetes educator. Emergency room nurse LaPorte Hosp., inpatient ctr. rep., sr. clin. instr. diabetes edn. program coord.; parish nurse Bethany Luth. Ch., LaPorte. Active N.Am. Cultural Exch. League; pres. People to People Internat., Vietnam Women's Meml.; mem. bd. elders, chmn. svc. divsn. Bethany Luth. Ch. With AUS, 1967-70. Mem. ANA, ADA, Am. Assn. Diabetes Educators, No. Ind. Assn. Diabetes Educators (sec., bd. dirs.), Am. Legion.

SARFATY, SUZANNE, internist and educator; b. Irvington, N.Y., Apr. 11, 1962; d. Sam and Pat (Petrovich) S. BS, Boston U., 1984, MD, 1988, MPH, 1994. Diplomate Am. Bd. Internal Medicine. Intern and resident Boston City Hosp., 1988-91; attending/clin. instr. Boston U., 1991-93, asst. prof. medicine and pub. health, 1995—, asst. dean of student affairs, 1995—. Mem. prof. com. Am. Cancer Soc., Boston, 1991—; mentor Boston Ptnrs. for Edn., 1991—. Recipient Cmty. Svc. award CIBA Geigy, 1986; Dana Farber cancer prevention fellow, 1993-94. Fellow ACP. Avocations: cooking, travel, reading, Spanish language. Home: 11 Verndale St Brookline MA 02146-2423

SARFATY, WAYNE ALLEN, insurance agent, financial planner; b. Rochester, N.Y., Apr. 18, 1951; s. Benjamin and Grace (Rowan) S.; m. Karen Nugent, July 12, 1957, Apr. 18, 1951; children; Melissa A., Gabrielle M. Student, Parsons Coll., 1971-74. Cert. ins. agt. Sales rep. Met. Life, Rochester, N.Y., 1979-81; register rep. Prudential Fin. Svcs., Rochester, 1981-92; owner, broker Wayne A. Sarfaty & Assocs., Rochester, 1992—. Dir. tng. films. Mem. Eagle Club. Recipient Nat. Quality award Nat. Assn. Life Underwriters, 1982-90; named to Million Dollar Round Table, NALU, 1987. Avocations: camping, auto racing, darts. Home: PO Box 182 Cohocton NY 14826-0182

SARFO, KWASI, history and political science educator; b. Acherensua, Ghana, June 2, 1955; arrived in U.S., 1980; m. Monica Sarfo; children: Ama, Akua, Abena. BA with honors, U. Ghana, Accra, 1979; MPA, SUNY, Albany, 1981, PhD, 1985. Lectr. SUNY, Albany, 1985-92; asst. prof. history and political sci. York Coll. of Pa., 1992—; field faculty adv. Vt. grad. program Norwich U., Montpelier, 1986; adj. lectr. Coll. Saint Rose, Albany, 1988-89, Russell Sage Coll., Troy, N.Y., 1988-90; cons., external examiner degrees and exams program Regents Coll., Albany, 1988, 91. Author: Life in the Third World, 1988, Issues in Modern African Politics, 1991, Politics and Government in the 3rd World, 1992, History of Africa, 1993, 95; author 3 other books; contbr. articles to profl. jours. Rsch. and publ. grantee York Coll. Pa., 1993, 95. Mem. Internat. Studies Assn., Am. Polit. Sci. Assn., Am. Soc. Pub. Adminstrn., African Studies Assn., Acad. Polit. Sci. Home: 41 Fox Run Dr York PA 17403 Office: York Coll Pa History Dept Country Club Rd York PA 17405-7199

SARGEANT, ERNEST JAMES, lawyer; b. Spokane, Wash., Sept. 26, 1918; s. Ernest Edward and Louise (McWhinnie) S.; m. Helene Sophie Kazanjian, Jan. 29, 1944. B.A. cum laude, Harvard U., 1940, LL.B. magna cum laude, 1947. Bar: Mass. 1947. Assoc. Ropes & Gray, Boston, 1947, 52-56, ptnr., 1956-90, of counsel, 1991—; lectr. law Harvard U. Law Sch., Cambridge, Mass., 1961-62, 65-92; adj. prof. Boston Coll. Law Sch., 1990—. Grad. treas. Harvard Law Rev., Cambridge, 1971—. Capt. U.S. Army, 1942-46, 51-52. Mem. Am. Law Inst. (council), ABA, Boston Bar Assn. Clubs: Union (Boston); Country (Brookline, Mass.). Home: 24 Highgate Wellesley Hills MA 02181-1420 Office: Ropes & Gray 1 International Pl Boston MA 02110-2600

SARGENT, CHARLES LEE, recreation vehicle and pollution control systems manufacturing company executive; b. Flint, Mich., Mar. 22, 1937; s. Frank T. and Evelyn M. (Martinson) S.; m. Nancy Cook, June 9, 1962; children: Wendy L., Joy A., Candace L. B ME, GM Inst., 1960; MBA, Harvard U., 1962. Reliability engr. AC Spark Plug div. GM, Flint, 1962-63; with Thetford Corp., Ann Arbor, Mich., 1962-95, pres., chmn. bd. dirs., 1974-95; pres., chmn. bd. dirs. Thermassan Corp., 1969-72; chmn. GMI Engring. and Mgmt. Inst., Flint, Fla., 1995—; bd. dirs. First of Am. Bank-Mich., 1995—; trustee Lincoln Cons. Schs., 1973-77; GMI Engring. and Mgmt. Inst., Flint, 1989, chmn. 1995—. Patentee in field. Elder Presbyn. Ch. Recipient Entrepreneurial Achievement award GMI, 1989; named Entrepreneur of the Yr., Harvard Bus. Sch. Club of Detroit, 1981. mem. Barton Hills Country Club (bd. dirs. 1985-87, pres. 1987), Harvard Bus. Sch. Club of Detroit (bd. dirs. 1983-93). Avocations: traveling, golf. Home: 3774 Cracker Way Bonita Springs FL 33923

SARGENT, DAVID JASPER, university official; b. Manchester, N.H., Aug. 5, 1931; s. Merton Jasper and Marguerite (Riley) S.; student U. N.H., 1949-51; J.D. magna cum laude, Suffolk U., Boston, 1954, LL.D. (hon.), 1978; m. Shirley Woodbury Swift, Dec. 21, 1951. Bar: N.H., 1954, Mass., 1954; U.S. Supreme Ct. 1978. Assoc. Kowal and Sargent, Boston, 1954-57; mem. faculty Suffolk U. Law Sch., Boston, 1957-73, prof. law, 1961-73, dean, 1973-89, pres., 1989—; chmn. Chief Justice's Commn. Future of the Cts., 1989; cons. Am. Trial Lawyers Assn., 1957-81; mem. Mass. Jud. Selection Com., 1974-77, Nat. Bd. Trial Advocacy, 1978—. Trustee, Anatolia Coll., Thessaloniki, Greece. Recipient Nat. Service award Am. Trial Lawyers Assn., 1968; Outstanding Alumnus award Suffolk U. Law Sch., 1978; hon. mem. Minn. Bar. Mem. ABA, Am. Law Inst., Mass. Bar Assn. (chmn. com. trial practice 1974-77, chmn. subcom. ct. unification 1976), N.H. Bar Assn. Episcopalian. Club: Masons. Contbr. articles to legal publs. Home: 83 Church St Winchester MA 01890-2545 Office: Suffolk U President's Office 25th Fl 1 Beacon St Boston MA 02108-2770

SARGENT, DIANA RHEA, corporate executive; b. Cheyenne, Wyo., Feb. 20, 1939; d. Clarence and Edith (de Castro) Hayes; grad. high sch.; m. Charles Sargent, Apr. 17, 1975 (div. 1991); children: Rene A. Coburn, Rochelle A. Rollins, Clayton R. Weldy, Christopher J. IBM proof operator Bank Am., Stockton, Calif., 1956-58, gen. ledger bookkeeper, Modesto, Calif., 1963-66; office mgr., head bookkeeper Cen. Drug Store, Modesto, 1966-76; pres. Sargent & Coburn, Inc., Modesto, 1976—, sec.-treas., v.p. Mem. Stanislaus Women's Ctr., NOW, San Francisco Mus. Soc., Modesto Women's Network, Stanislaus County Commn. for Women, Yerba Buena Art Ctr. Office: 1101 Standiford Ave Ste D-2 Modesto CA 95350

SARGENT, JAMES O'CONNOR, freelance writer; b. N.Y.C., June 15, 1918; s. Joseph Hughes and Maryann Josephine (O'Connor) S.; m. Mildred Elizabeth Clark, apr. 19, 1949. Student, British Intelligence Sch., Calcutta, India, summer 1944, Fordham U., 1949-51. Ghostwriter, freelance writer, 1949—; founder Washington Writers Group, Washington, 1960—. Ghostwriter: History of the Helicopter, 1952; author: (novellas) You Don't Bury on Christmas, 1960, Interregnum in a Commune, 1968, The Button Man, 1969, Moon in Pisces, 1970, Death in Saigon, 1971, Last Minuet in Washington, 1973, MWA Anthology Killers of the Dream, 1974; (screenplay) Queen Victoria and Lady Flora, 1993; (play) Loss of Innocence, 1994; pub. over 1500 works. Liaison with Peiping Aviators Assn., 1995-96. Maj. USAF, 1942-47. Decorated Bronze Star, Chinese medal of freedom. Mem. 14th USAF Assn., 528th Fighter Squadron Assn. (officer). Avocations: walking 5 miles per day, genealogy, World War I & II history, friendships. Home: 1019 Stillbrook Rd Pensacola FL 32514-1629

SARGENT, JOSEPH DENNY, insurance executive; b. West Hartford, Conn., Sept. 11, 1929; s. Thomas Denny and Elizabeth (Owen) S.; m. Mary A. Tennant, June 25, 1955; children: Robert Tennant, Thomas Denny II, Mary Diane, Suzanne Davis. Grad., St. Paul's Sch., Concord, N.H., 1948; BA, Yale U., 1952. With Conning & Co., Inc., Hartford, Conn., ptnr., 1957—; mng. ptnr. Conning & Co., Inc., 1986-92; chmn., chief exec. officer Conning & Co., 1986-91, chmn., 1992; chmn. Conning Internat., London, 1986-92; vice chmn. Conning & Co., 1993-95, also bd. dirs., 1993-95; bd. dirs. Beekley Corp., Bristol, Conn., Tenwick Reins., Stamford, Conn., Exec. Risk Ins. Co., Simsbury, Conn., MMI co., Chgo., Blanch, Mpls., Mut. Risk, Bermuda, Policy Mgmt. Sys., Columbia, S.C.; chmn. Conn. Surety Corp., Hartford, Bradley, Foster & Sargent, Hartford, Beazley Furlonge Holdings, Ltd., London; trustee McLean Fund; chmn., treas. SKI Ltd. Past trustee Wadsworth Athenaeum; past trustee Children's Svcs. of Conn.; trustee Hartford Hosp. Mem. Yale Club (Hartford), Hartford Club, Hartford Golf Club. Home: 25 Colony Rd West Hartford CT 06117-2215 Office: City Place II 185 Asylum St Hartford CT 06103-3402

SARGENT, JOSEPH DUDLEY, insurance executive; b. Phila., Apr. 16, 1937; s. Gerald Thomas and Nora (Oliver) S.; m. Sheila Reidy, Apr. 27, 1963; children: Moira, Colleen, Joseph, Sean, Liam, Bridget. AB, Fairfield U., 1959. CLU. Agy. sec. The Guardian Life Ins. Co. Am., N.Y.C., 1959-70, v.p., 1970-79, sr. v.p. health ins., 1980-83, sr. v.p. life ins., 1984-88, exec. v.p., 1989-92, pres., 1993—, pres., CEO, 1996, also bd. dirs.; pres.-guardian Ins. and Annuity Co., 1993. Bd. dirs. Life Ins. Mktg. and Rsch. Inst., Life Office Mgmt. Assn., United Way of N.Y.C. With U.S. Army, 1960-64. Mem. Nat. Assn. Life Underwriters. Republican. Roman Catholic. Avocations: boating, fishing. Home: 231 Balmforth St Bridgeport CT 06605-3508 Office: Guardian Life Ins Co of Am 201 Park Ave S New York NY 10003-1605

SARGENT, LIZ ELAINE (ELIZABETH SARGENT), safety consulting executive; b. Meadville, Pa., Apr. 17, 1942; d. Melvin Ellsworth and Roberta Jean (Beach) Taylor; m. Lawrence Sargent, Sept. 6, 1969; 1 child, Kathy-Dawn. Student, Allegheny Coll., 1964; AA cum laude, Cuyahoga C.C., Cleve., 1987, Assoc. in Transp. cum laude, 1989, BA, Ithaca Coll., 1993. Car distbr. Norfolk and Western R.R., Cleve., 1963-69; account mgr. Ill. Cen. R.R., Cleve., 1970-73; traffic coord. Carlon Pipe, Mantua, Ohio, 1973-75; chief dispatcher X.L. Trucking, Coshocton, Ohio, 1975-77; corp. log auditor Anchor Motor Freight, Beachwood, Ohio, 1977-78; cons. Saf-T, Parma, Ohio, 1978-84; v.p. safety Saf-T, Shaker Heights, Ohio, 1987-91; dir. safety Sherwin Williams, Cleve., 1984-87; pres. Safety Advisors for Transp., Inc., Beachwood, Ohio, 1991—; founder Love Keepers, 1996; speaker Coshocton (Ohio) Traffic Club, 1984, Am. Indsl. Hygiene, Cleve., 1985; founder Love Keepers, 1996. Author: Hall Chemical-Safety Procedures, 1983-84, Progressive Insurance, 1987, RL Lipton Co. manual, 1995; contbr. articles to profl. jours. Chairperson intergenerational com. Ch. in Aurora, Ohio, 1984-86, Valley View Village Ch. libr. chairperson, mem. choir; bd. dirs. Shaker Heights Teen Recreational Com., 1984-87. Delta Nu Alpha scholar, 1977. Mem. Ohio Trucking Assn. (nat. safety coun.), Cleve. Bd. Realtors, Motor Fleet Safety Suprs. (nat. com.), Fleet Maintenance Coun., Phi Theta Kappa. Republican. Avocations: interior design, painting, writing poetry and short stories, dried floral arrangements, hiking. Office: Saf-T 14716 Rockside Rd Maple Heights OH 44137-4016

SARGENT, NOEL BOYD, electrical engineer; b. Cleve., Dec. 5, 1943; s. William Boyd and Jennie Parkin (Wheeler) S.; m. Joan Marie Hodan, Aug. 21, 1965; children: Andrew, Jeffrey. BS in Engring., Cleve. State U., 1970. Broadcast engr. Stas. WVIZ-TV, WERE am-fm, WKSU, Cleve., 1960-65; electronics technician NASA-Lewis Rsch. Ctr., Cleve., 1965-70, engr. aeroacoustics, 1970-76, rsch. engr., 1976-83, sr. engr. launch vehicles, 1983-87, tech. asst., 1988—. Mem. IEEE, Soc. Automotive Engrs. (vice chmn. Com. AE-4, 1992—, sec. Com. AE-4R, 1988-92). Avocations: soccer, amateur radio. Office: NASA-Lewis Rsch Ctr 21000 Brookpark Rd Cleveland OH 44135-3127

SARGENT, PAMELA, writer; b. Ithaca, N.Y., Mar. 20, 1948. BA, SUNY, Binghamton, N.Y., 1968, MA, 1970. Mng. editor, Binghamton, N.Y., 1970-73, asst. editor, 1973-75; Am. editor Bull. Sci. Fiction Writers Am., Johnson City, N.Y., 1983-91. Author: Cloned Lives, 1976, Starshadows, 1977, The Sudden Star, 1979, Watchstar, 1980, The Golden Space, 1982, The Alien Upstairs, 1983, Earthseed, 1983, Eye of the Comet, 1984, Homesmind, 1984, Venus of Dreams, 1986, The Shore of Women, 1986, The Best of Pamela Sargent, 1987, Alien Child, 1988, Venus of Shadows, 1988, Ruler of the Sky, 1993 (Nebula best novelette award 1992, Locus best novelette award 1993), Electric Sci. Fiction award 1993); edit: (anthology) Women of Wonder, 1975, Bio-Futures, 1976, More Women of Wonder, 1976, The New Women of Wonder, 1978, (with Ian Watson) Afterlives, 1986, Women of Wonder, The Classic Years, 1996, Women of Wonder, The Contemporary Years, 1995, Nebula Awards 29, 1995, Nebula Awards 30, 1996. Office: care Richard Curtis Assocs Inc 171 E 74th St New York NY 10021-3221

SARGENT, ROBERT GEORGE, engineering educator; b. Port Huron, Mich., June 14, 1937; s. George O. and Marie L. (Roome) S.; m. Dorothy Baum, 1970; 1 dau., Tiffany. BSE, U. Mich., 1959, MS, 1963, PhD, 1966. Elec. engr. Hughes Aircraft Co., Culver City, Calif., 1959-61; faculty mem. Syracuse U., 1966—, asst. prof., 1966-70, assoc. prof., 1970-81, prof. indsl. engring. and ops. research, 1982—, chmn. dept., 1982-85, prof. elec. and computer engring., 1994—; vis. faculty Cornell U., 1981-82, Ctr. Econ. Rsch. Tilburg U., 1996; bd. dirs. Winter Simulation Conf., 1974-84, chmn. bd., 1979-81, gen. chmn., 1977; chmn. TIMS Coll. on Simulation and Gaming, 1978-80. Dept. editor: Communications of Assn. Computing Machinery, 1980-85; editorial adv. bd. ACM Transactions on Modeling and Simulations, 1989—; contbr. articles to profl. jours. Recipient Service award Winter Simulation Conf., 1984. Mem. Assn. Computing Machinery (nat. lectr. 1985-89, Svc. award 1985), Ops. Rsch. Soc. Am., Inst. Mgmt. Scis. (Disting. Svc. award for Simulation 1985), Inst. Indsl. Engrs. (Svc. award 1985), Soc. Computer Simulation (bd. dirs. 1984-87), Computer Soc. of IEEE (mem. exec. com. simulation 1985—). Office: Syracuse U Dept Indsl Engring and Ops Rsch 439 Link Hall Syracuse NY 13244

SARGENT, THOMAS ANDREW, political science educator, university program director; b. Indpls., Apr. 24, 1933; s. Thomas Edward and Inez (Secrest) S.; m. Cecily Constance Fox-Williams, 1965 (dec.); children: Sarah Beatrice, Andrew Fox; m. 2d Frances Petty, 1987. BA, DePauw U., Greencastle, Ind., 1955; MA, Fletcher Sch. Law and Diplomacy, Tufts U., 1959, MA in Law and Diplomacy, 1968, PhD, 1969. With First Nat. City Bank, N.Y.C., 1959-64, asst. accountant, 1963-64; asst. sec. Irving Trust Co., N.Y.C., 1964-66; mem. faculty Ball State U., Muncie, Ind., 1969-89, dir. London Ctr., 1973-74, chmn. polit. sci. dept., 1977-80, prof. polit. sci., 1979-89, prof. emeritus, 1989—, acting asst. to dean Coll. Scis. and Humanities, 1981-82, assoc. dean Coll. Scis. and Humanities, 1982-85, dir. spl. programs Minnetrista Ctr., 1985-87; dir. E.B. Ball Ctr., Muncie, 1987-89, dir. emeritus, 1989—. Contbg. editor: Ripon Forum, 1973-78. Bd. dirs., exec. v.p. Ea. Ind. Cmty. TV, Muncie, 1974-76, pres., 1976-77; mem. nat. bd. govs. Ripon Soc., Washington, 1976-84; mem. Indpls. Com. Fgn. Rels., 1977—; bd. dirs. Hist. Muncie, Inc., 1979-85, pres., 1980; bd. dirs. Muncie Civic Theatre Assn., 1978-81, 90—, 1st v.p., 1992—; exec. dir. Ind. Consortium for Internat. Programs, 1982-88; mem. Ind. Real Estate Commn., 1983-91; trustee DePauw U., 1983—; bd. dirs. Muncie Symphony Orch., 1985-95, pres., 1991-93; mem. bd. govs. Minnetrista Cultural Ctr., Muncie, 1989-94, chmn., 1992-94; bd. dirs. Arts Ind., Inc., 1992—, Muncie Children's Mus., 1994—, v.p., 1996—. 1st lt. USAF, 1955-58. Named Sagamore of Wabash, 1988. Mem. Am. Polit. Sci. Assn., Am. Acad. Polit. Sci., Delaware County Hist. Alliance (bd. dirs. 1980-86, 87-95, pres., 1987-91), Soc. Profl. Journalists, Delaware Country Club, Muncie Club, Columbia Club (Indpls.), Maxinkuckee Yacht Club (Culver, Ind.), Rotary, Phi Delta Theta. Republican. Methodist. Address: 2207 W Wiltshire Rd Muncie IN 47304-3350

SARGENT, WALLACE LESLIE WILLIAM, astronomer, educator; b. Elsham, Eng., Feb. 15, 1935; s. Leslie William and Eleanor (Dennis) S.; m. Anneila Isabel Cassells, Aug. 5, 1964; children: Lindsay Eleanor, Alison Clare. B.Sc., Manchester U., 1956, M.Sc., 1957, Ph.D., 1959. Research fellow Calif. Inst. Tech., 1959-62; sr. research fellow Royal Greenwich Obs., 1962-64; asst. prof. physics U. Calif., San Diego, 1964-66; mem. faculty dept. astronomy Calif. Inst. Tech., Pasadena, 1966—; prof. Calif. Inst. Tech., 1971-81, Ira S. Bowen prof. astronomy, 1981—; Miller Prof. U. Calif., Berkeley, 1993; Thomas Gold lectr. Cornell U., Ithaca, N.Y., 1994-95; Sackler lectr. Harvard U., Cambridge, Mass., 1995, U. Calif., Berkeley, 1996. Contbr. articles to profl. jours. Alfred P. Sloan fellow, 1968-70. Fellow Am. Acad. Arts and Scis., Royal Soc. (London); mem Am. Astron. Soc. (Helen B. Warner prize 1969, Dannie Heineman prize 1991), Royal Astron. Soc. (George Darwin lectr. 1987), Astron. Soc. Pacific (Bruce Gold medal 1994), Internat. Astron. Union. Club: Athenaeum (Pasadena). Home: 400 S Berkeley Ave Pasadena CA 91107-5062 Office: Calif Inst Tech Astronomy Dept 105-24 Pasadena CA 91125

SARIDIS, GEORGE NICHOLAS, electrical, computers and system engineering educator, robotics and automation researcher; b. Athens, Greece, Nov. 17, 1931; came to U.S., 1961, naturalized, 1971; s. Nicholas and Anna (Tsofa) S.; m. Panayota Dimarogona, Apr. 10, 1985. Diploma in Mech. and Elec. Engring., Nat. Tech. U., Athens, 1955; MS in Elec. Engring., Purdue U., 1962, PhD, 1965. Instr. Nat. Tech. U., 1955-63, Purdue U., West Lafayette, Ind., 1963-65, asst. prof., 1965-70, assoc. prof., 1970-75, prof., 1975-81; prof. elec., computer and system engring. Rensselaer Poly. Inst., Troy, N.Y., 1981—, dir. Robotics and Automation Lab., 1982—; dir. NASA Ctr. for Intelligent Robotic Systems for Space Exploration, 1988-92; engring. program dir. NSF, Washington, 1973; hon. prof. Huazhong U., Wuhan, China. Author: Self-Organizing Control of Stochastic Systems, 1977, Stochastic Processes Estimation and Control, 1995; co-author: Intelligent Robotic Systems: Theory and Applications, 1992; also numerous articles, reports. Co-author: Intelligent Robotic Sys.; co-editor, contbg. author: Fuzzy Automata, 1977; editor, contbg. author: Advances in Automation and Robotics, Vol. 1, 1985, Vol. 2, 1990. Fellow IEEE (founding pres. robotics and automation council 1981-84, Centennial medal 1984, Disting. Mem. award 1989); mem. ASME, Soc. Mfg. Engrs./Robotics Internat.-Machine Vision Assn. (sr.), Am. Soc. Engring. Edn., N.Y. Acad. Scis. Home: 38 Loudonwood E Loudonville NY 12211-1465 Office: Rensselaer Poly Inst Dept Electrical Computer & Sys Engring Sch of Engring Troy NY 12180-3590

SARIS, PATTI B., federal judge; b. 1951. BA magna cum laude, Radcliffe Coll., 1973; JD cum laude, Harvard U., 1976. Law clerk to Hon. Robert Braucher Mass. Supreme Judicial Ct., 1976-77; atty. Foley Hoag & Eliot, Boston, 1977-79; staff counsel U.S. Senate Judiciary Com., 1979-81; atty. Berman Dittmar & Engel, Boston, 1981-82; chief civil divsn. U.S. Atty.'s Office, 1984-86; U.S. magistrate judge U.S. Dist. Ct. Mass., 1986-89; assoc. justice Mass. Superior Ct., 1989-94; dist. judge U.S. Dist. Ct. Mass., 1994—;

mem. com. on civil rules Supreme Judicial Ct. Comments editor civil rights Civil Liberties Law Rev. Bd. trustees Beth Israel Hosp.; active Wexner Heritage Found. Nat. Merit scholar, 1969; recipient award Mothers of Murdered Children, 1993. Mem. Nat. Assn. Women Judges, Am. Jewish Com., Women's Bar Assn. (bd. dirs. 1982-86), Mass. Bar Assn., Mass. Assn. Women Judges, Boston Bar Assn., Boston Inns Ct., Phi Beta Kappa. Office: John W McCormack Courthouse 90 Devonshire St Rm 707 Boston MA 02109-4501

SARJEANT, WALTER JAMES, electrical and computer engineering educator; b. Strathroy, Can., Apr. 7, 1944; s. Walter Burns and Margaret (Laurie) S.; m. Ann Richards, June 30, 1972; children: Eric, Cheryl. BSc in Math, Physics, U. Western Ont., Can., 1966, MSc in Physics, 1967, PhD in Physics, 1971. Asst. dir. R&D Gen-Tec Inc., Quebec City, Que., Can., 1971-73; program mgr. Lumonics Rsch. Ltd., Ottawa, Ont., Can., 1973-75; staff scientist Nat. Rsch. Coun., Ottawa, Ont., Can., 1975-78; project leader Los Alamos (N.Mex.) Nat. Lab., 1978-81; James Clerk Maxwell prof. elec. and computer engring. SUNY, Buffalo, 1981—; dir. High Power Electronics Inst. Author: High Power Electronics, 1989. Fellow IEEE; mem. Electromagnetics Acad., Electrostatics Soc., N.Y. Acad. Scis., Rotary, Eta Kappa Nu. Office: SUNY Elec Engring Dept PO Box 601900 312 Bonner Hall Buffalo NY 14260

SARKIS, J. ZIAD, management consultant; b. Beirut, Lebanon, July 8, 1968; arrived in France, 1975; s. Nicolas Ata and Claude (Moussalli) S. BAS in Anthropology, Econs. and Math. with distinction and honors, Stanford U., 1990, MS in Engring. and Mgmt., 1990. Cons. McKinsey & Co., San Francisco, 1990, N.Y.C., 1991-92, Paris, 1992; prin. fin. svcs. practice AT Kearney & Co., N.Y.C., 1992-94; co-founder, ptnr. Mitchell Madison Group, N.Y.C., 1994—. Gen. sec. Phoenixia-X, Paris, 1993—. Greek Catholic. Office: Mitchell Madison Group 520 Madison Ave New York NY 10022-4213

SARKISIAN, CHERILYN See CHER

SARLE, CHARLES RICHARD, health facility executive; b. Saratoga Springs, N.Y., Sept. 21, 1944; s. John Robert and Marjorie Elizabeth (Swick) S.; m. Marion D. Wallace, June 21, 1968; children: Richard Charles, Robert Edmond. BBA cum laude, Northea. U., 1968; MBA, Babson Coll., 1973. CPA, Mass., Vt.; cert. mental health adminstr. Assn. Mental Health Adminstrs. Staff acct. Price Waterhouse & Co., Boston, 1968-70, George Kanavich, CPA, Wellesley, Mass., 1970-72; controller Human Resource Inst., Boston, 1972-73, adminstr., 1973-77; controller Brattleboro (Vt.) Retreat, 1977-78, dir. adminstrn., 1978-85, v.p., 1985-88, chief exec. officer, 1988—; bd. dirs., treas. Prouty Child Devel. Ctr., Brattleboro, 1983—; speaker in field. Mem. commn. Vt. Health Bldg. Fin. Agy., 1978-90; trustee Austine Sch. for Deaf and Hard of Hearing, 1990—, pres., 1994—; trustee Winston Prouty Ctr. for Child Devel., 1982—, treas., 1983-90, sec., 1991—. Recipient recognition award Brattleboro C. of C., 1985. Fellow AICPA, Mass. Soc. CPAs, Am. Coll. Healthcare Execs. (regent Va. br. 1991-95); mem. Am. Hosp. Assn. (del.-at-large 1988-92, del.-at-large to regional policy bd.), Nat. Assn. Pvt. Psychiat. Hosps. (bd. dirs. polit. action com. 1983-93), Nat. Psychiat. Alliance (trustee 1989-96, pres. 1994-96), Vt. Soc. CPAs (Comty. Svc. award 1984), Hosp. Fin. Mgmt. Assn. (mem. hosp. cost com. 1985—), Rescue, Inc. (trustee 1982-83), New Eng. Healthcare Assembly (trustee 1995—). Republican. Avocations: skiing, fishing, tennis, photography. Home: PO Box 104 Brattleboro VT 05302-0104 Office: Brattleboro Retreat 75 Linden St Brattleboro VT 05301-4807

SARN, JAMES, physician, health association administrator; b. Orange, N.J., July 17, 1941; s. Chester Walter and Grace Marie (Lang) S.; m. Leslie Barton Warren, June 28, 1971; children: Fiona Rachel, Audrey Pearmain, Nicola Warren, Philip Hamilton. BS, U.S. Military Acad., 1963; MPH, U. N.C., 1972; MD, Duke U., 1973. Diplomate Bd. Med. Examiners. Dir. health, nutrition, population USAID, Managua, Nicaragua, 1974-78; dir. disease control Ariz. Dept. Health Svcs., Phoenix, 1978-80, health dir., 1980-83; agency dir. health and population U.S. Agency Internat. Devel., Washington, 1983-85; dir. health, nutrition, population U.S. Agency Internat. Devel., Khartoum, Sudan, 1985-87; dir. health and nutrition U.S. Agency Internat. Devel., Cairo, Egypt, 1987-91; dep. asst. sec. internat. and refugee health Dept. Health and Human Svcs., Washington, 1991-93; dir. health, nutrition and population Save The Children, Westport, Conn., 1993—. Contbr. articles to profl. jours. U.S. delegate Internat. Conf. Nutrition, Rome, Italy, 1992, Pan Am. Health Orgn. Governing Coun., Washington, 1991-93, World Health Assembly, Geneva, 1991-93; mem. bd. Nat. Coun. Internat. Health, Washington, 1984, 85, 91-93. Capt. U.S. Army 1963-68, Vietnam. Recipient Bronze Star U.S. Army, 1965, 68, Medal Honor 1st Class Govt. Vietnam ,1968, Peacemaker medal Govt. Brazil, 1965, Surgeon General's Exemplary Svc. award Pub. Health Svc. Dept. Health and Human Svcs., 1993. Mem. AMA, APHA, Am. Coll. Preventative Medicine, Am. Soc. Tropical Medicine, Nat. Coun. Internat. Health (bd. dirs. 1991—). Home: 426 Judd Rd Easton CT 06612 Office: Save the Children 54 Wilton Rd Westport CT 06880-3108

SARNA, NAHUM MATTATHIAS, biblical studies educator; b. London, Eng., Mar. 27, 1923; came to U.S., 1951, naturalized, 1959; s. Jacob and Milly (Horonzick) S.; m. Helen Horowitz, Mar. 23, 1947; children: David E. Y., Jonathan D. BA, U. London, 1944, MA, 1946; minister's diploma, Jews Coll., London, 1947; PhD, Dropsie Coll., Phila., 1955; D Hebrew Letters (hon.), Gratz Coll., Phila., 1984; LHD (hon.), Hebrew Union Coll.-Jewish Inst. Religion, 1987; D Hebrew Lit., Hebrew Coll., Boston, 1991. Asst. lectr. Hebrew, Univ. Coll., London, 1946-49; lectr. Gratz Coll., Phila., 1951-57; librarian Jewish Theol. Sem.; also asst. prof. Bible Tchrs. Inst., 1957-63, assoc. prof. of Bible, 1963-65; asso. prof. Bibl. studies Brandeis U., Waltham, Mass., 1965-67; Dora Golding prof. Bibl. studies Brandeis U., 1967-85, prof. emeritus, 1985—, chmn. dept. Near Eastern and Judaic studies, 1969-75, chmn. humanities council, 1980-81; vis. prof. Bible, Dropsie Coll., 1967-68; vis. prof. religion Columbia U., 1964-65, 92, Yale U., 1992-94; vis. disting. prof. Fla. Atlantic U., 1995—. Author: Understanding Genesis, 1966, Exploring Exodus, 1986, Commentary to Genesis, 1989, Commentary to Exodus, 1991, Songs of the Heart: An Introduction to the Book of Psalms, 1993; co-author: A New Translation of the Book of Psalms, 1973, The Book of Job, A New Translation with Introductions, 1980; editor, translator: Jewish Publ. Soc. Bible, 1966-85; editorial bd. Jour. Bibl. Lit, 1973-75, Soc. Bibl. Lit. Monograph Series, 1975—; deptl. editor Ency. Judaica; gen. editor Jewish Publ. Soc. Bible Commentary series, 1974—; editor Proceedings of the American Academy for Jewish Research; mem. editorial adv. bd. Biblical Archaeology Rev., Moment Mag.; contbr. to Ency. Judaica, 1972, Ency. Brit., 1974, Ency. Religion, 1986, Anchor Bible Dictionary, 1992, Oxford Companion to the Bible, 1993; also articles to scholarly jours. Assoc. trustee Am. Sch. Oriental Rsch.; trustee, mem. exec. com. Boston Hebrew Coll.; mem. acad. adv. coun. Nat. Found. Jewish Culture; trustee Annenberg Rsch. Inst., 1990-95. Recipient Jewish Book Ann. award, 1967, Jewish Cultural Achievement award in Bibl. scholarship, 1994; Am. Coun. Learned Socs. fellow, 1971-72, Moses A. Dropsie fellow U. Pa., 1993, Inst. Advanced Studies fellow Hebrew U., 1982-83. Fellow Royal Asiatic Soc., Am. Acad. Jewish Research; mem. Soc. Bibl. Lit. and Exegesis, Am. Oriental Soc., Israel Exploration Soc., Archons of Colophon, Palestine Exploration Soc. Bibl. Colloquium, Assn. for Jewish Studies (hon. sec.-treas. 1972-79, pres. 1983-85). Home: 7886 Chula Vista Crescent Boca Raton FL 33433-4101

SARNAT, BERNARD GEORGE, plastic surgeon, educator, researcher; b. Chgo., Sept. 1, 1912; s. Isadore M. and Fanny (Sidran) S.; m. Rhoda Elaine Gerard, Dec. 25, 1941; children: Gerard, Joan. SB, U. Chgo., 1933, MD, 1937; MS, DDS, U. Ill., 1940. Diplomate Am. Bd. Plastic Surgery. Intern Los Angeles County Gen. Hosp., 1936-37; resident oral and plastic surgery Cook County Hosp., Chgo., 1940-41; asst. to Dr. Marshall Davison (gen. surgery), Chgo., 1942-43, Drs. Vilray P. Blair and Louis T. Byars (plastic and reconstructive surgery), St. Louis, 1943-46; practice medicine specializing in plastic surgery Chgo., 1946-56, Beverly Hills, Calif., 1956-91; asst. histology U. Ill. Coll. Dentistry, 1937-40, prof., head dept. oral and maxillofacial surgery, 1946-56; asst. dept. surgery Washington U. Sch. Medicine, St. Louis, 1944-46; prof., dir. dept. oral and plastic surgery St. Louis U. Coll. Dentistry, 1945-46; clin. asst. prof. surgery (plastic surgery) U. Ill. Coll. Medicine, 1949-56; adj. prof. oral biology Sch Dentistry UCLA, 1969—, mem. Dental Rsch. Inst., 1974-95, adj. prof. plastic surgery Sch. Medicine, 1974—; attending staff Cedars-Sinai Med. Ctr., L.A., 1956-91, emeritus, 1991—, mem. staff, sr. rsch. scientist, chief plastic surgery, 1961-81; cons. in gen., plastic and maxillofacial surgery VA Regional Office, Chgo., until 1956; lectr. in field. Sr. author: (with Dr. Isaac Schour) Oral and Facial Cancer, 2d edit., 1957, (with Dr. Daniel Laskin) Surgery of the Temporomandibular Joint, 1964; editor: (with Daniel Laskin) The Temporomandibular Joint A Biological Basis for Clinical Practice, 4th edit., 1991, (with Andrew D. Dixon) Factors and Mechanisms Affecting Growth of Bone, 1982, Normal and Abnormal Bone Growth: Basic and Clinical Research, 1985, Fundamentals of Bone Growth: Methodology and Applications, 1991; contbr. chpts. to textbooks, articles to surg. and sci. jours., other pubs. Co-winner Joseph A. Capps prize for med. rsch., 1940, Frederick B. Noyes prize, 1940; recipient Kerbs award for rsch. plastic and reconstructive surgery, 1950, 1st prize, sr. award Found. Am. Soc. Plastic and Reconstructive surgeons, 1957, Beverly Hills Acad. of Medicine award, 1959, Nat. Achievement award medicine Phi Epsilon Pi, 1964, 1st prize Am. Rhinologic Soc., 1980, medal Hebrew U., Jerusalem, 1985, medal Tel Aviv U., 1985, Disting. Svc. Alumni award U. Chgo. Pritzker Sch. Medicine, 1987, hon. award Am. Soc. Maxillofiacial Surgeons, 1990, Dallas B. Phemister Profl. Achievement award Dept. Surgery U. Chgo., 1993, Disting. Alumnus award U. Ill. Coll. Dentistry, 1994, Craniofacial Biology Rsch. award Internat. Assn. for Dental Rsch., 1995, Disting. Scientist award. Fellow ACS, AAAS, Am. Assn. Plastic Surgeons (hon.); mem. Calif. Med. Soc., L.A. Med. Soc., Am. Soc. Plastic and Reconstructive Surgeons, Plastic Surgery Rsch. Coun. (founding mem. 1955, chmn. 1957), Calif. Soc. Plastic Surgeons, Beverly Hills Acad. Medicine (pres. 1962-63), Internat. Assn. Craniofacial Biology, Am. Assn. Phys. Anthropologists, Internat. Assn. Study Dento-Facial Abnormalities (hon.), Sigma Xi, Omicron Kappa Upsilon, Zeta Beta Tau, Phi Delta Epsilon, Alpha Omega (Internat. Achievement medal 1988). Home: 1875 Kelton Ave Apt 301 Los Angeles CA 90025-4576

SARNELLE, JOSEPH R., electronic publishing specialist, magazine and newspaper editor; b. Bklyn., Aug. 24, 1951; s. Alphonse Louis and Julie Lena (Mingarelli) S.; m. Ruth Patricia Cullen, Aug. 5, 1982; children: Cullen Joseph, D'Arcy Emilie. BA, Cornell U., 1973; postgrad., Sch. Visual Arts, N.Y.C., 1976-77, The New Sch., N.Y.C., 1979-80. Graphic artist Lewahl KC Graphics, N.Y.C., 1974-76; editor United Bus. Publs., N.Y.C., 1976-79; mng. editor Lebhar-Friedman Inc., N.Y.C., 1979-88; assoc. mng. editor HomeOwner Mag., N.Y.C., 1988-90; sr. composition specialist Info. Builders Inc., N.Y.C., 1990—; cons. video Markham-Novelle Pub. Rels., N.Y.C., 1988-89; cons. Best info. Family Media, N.Y.C., 1990-91. Author, dir. (videos) J. Roland Pepe's Guide to New York City, 1980, Underground Roundup, 1981. Recipient McMullen scholar, Cornell U., Regents scholar, State of N.Y., 1969; Best Headline of Year award Lebhar-Friedman Inc., 1982. Office: Info Builders Inc 1250 Broadway New York NY 10001-3701

SARNET, JONATHAN MICHAEL, epidemiologist, educator; b. Va., Mar. 26, 1948. AB in Chemistry and Physics, Harvard Coll., 1966; MD, U. Rochester, 1970; MS in Epidemiology, Harvard Sch. Pub Health, 1977. Diplomate Am. Bd. of Internal Medicine, Nat. Bd. Med. Examiners. Intern in medicine U. Ky. Med. Ctr., Lexington, 1970-71; asst. resident in medicine U. N.Mex. Affiliated Hosps., Albuquerque, 1973-74, sr. resident, 1974-75; rsch. fellow in clin. epidemiology Channing lab. Harvard Med. Sch., Boston, 1975-78, rsch. assoc. in medicine, 1978-83; epidemiologist Cancer Rsch. and Treatment Ctr. U. N.Mex., Albuquerque, 1980—, asst. prof. medicine, 1978-82, assoc. prof. medicine, 1982-88, assoc. prof. family, cmty., and emergency medicine, 1985-88, prof. family, cmty., and emergency medicine, 1986-94, prof. medicine, 1988-94, clin. prof. medicine, 1994—; prof., chmn. dept. epidemiology The Johns Hopkins U., Balt., 1994—, co-dir. risk scis. and pub. policy inst., 1995—; chief pulmonary divsn. U. N.Mex. Hosp., Albuquerque, 1985-94, chief pulmonary and critical care divsn. dept. medicine, 1986-94; mem. indoor air quality and total human exposure com., sci. adv. bd. U.S. EPA, 1987—; chmn. biol. effects of ionizing radiation VI com. Nat. Rsch. Coun., 1994—. Editor pro tem Am. Jour. of Epidemiology, 1991-92, editor, 1992—; assoc. editor Tobacco Control: An Internat. Jour., 1991—; editor Epidemiologic Revs., 1994—. With U.S. Army, 1971-73. Recipient Clinton P. Anderson award Am. Lung Assn. N.Mex., 1988. Fellow AAAS, Am. Coll. Epidemiology; mem. Soc. for Epidemiologic Rsch. (pres.-elect 1988-89, pres. 1989-90, exec. com. 1988-91), Am. Thoracic Soc. (long range planning com. environ. and occupational health assembly 1992—, program com. behavioral scis. sect. 1994-95), N.Mex. Thoracic Soc. (sec.-treas. 1982-83, v.p. 1983-84, pres. 1984-85), Internat. Epidemiol. Assn., Internat. Soc. of Indoor Air Quality and Climate, Md. Thoracic Soc., Alpha Omega Alpha, Delta Omega Alpha. Office: Dept Epidemiology The Johns Hoopkins U 615 N Wolfe St Ste 6030 Baltimore MD 21205-3286

SARNO, MARIA ERLINDA, lawyer, scientist; b. Manila, Philippines, July 26, 1944. BS in Chemistry magna cum laude, U. Santo Tomas, Philippines, 1967; MS in Chemistry summa cum laude, Calif. State U., Long Beach, 1975; JD cum laude, Western State U., 1993. Bar: Calif. 1994, U.S. Patent Office, 1993. Instr. U. Santo Tomas, Philippines, 1967-68; sr. chemist, analytical rsch. and quality assurance Rachelle Labs., Long Beach, Calif., 1969-74; teaching/rsch. asst. Calif. State U., Long beach, 1971-73; mgr. in charge of radioisotope section Curtis Nuclear Lab., L.A., 1974; assoc. chemist, asst. to dir. quality control Nichols Inst., San Pedro, Calif., 1974-75; mgr. rsch. and devel. Baxter Healthcare, Hyland, Calif., 1975-91; legal coord. sci. affairs Immunotherapy div. Baxter Biotech, Irvine, Calif., 1991-93, mgr. regulatory affairs, 1994-95; pvt. law practice, 1994—. Editorial bd: (tech. editor) Western State U. Law Review; Contbr. articles to profl. jours.; patentee in field. Mem. ABA, Orange County Bar Assn., Los Angeles County Bar Assn., Am. Chem. Soc., Am. Intellectual Property Law Assn., Phi Kappa Phi, Phi Delta Gamma. Home: 12541 Kenobi Ct Cerritos CA 90703-7756

SARNO, PATRICIA ANN, biology educator; b. Ashland, Pa.; d. John Thomas and Anna (Harvest) S. BS, Pa. State U., 1966, MEd, 1971; postgrad. Bucknell U., 1967, Bloomsburg U., 1970. Programmer planetarium, tchr. sci. Pottsville (Pa.) High Sch., 1967; tchr. biology Schuylkill Haven (Pa.) Area High Sch., 1967-91, sci. chmn., coord. dist., 1973-91; lead tchr. sci. Pa. Acad. Suprs. and Curriculum Devel. Dist. Pa. Sch., 1991—; cons. Contbr. to profl. jours. Pa. Edn. Dept., career program Pottsville Hosp. Dow Chem. Co. grantee, 1971. Mem. AAAS, AAUW, NEA, Pa. Edn. Assn. (exec. bd.), Nat. Assn. Biology Tchrs., Nat. Tchrs. Assn., Pa. Assn. Supervision and Curriculum Devel., N.Y. Acad. Scis., Pa. Tchrs. Assn., Am. Inst. Biol. Scis., Pa. Acad. Scis., Pa. State U. Alumni Assn., Schuylkill Haven Edn. Assn., Phi Sigma, Delta Kappa Gamma. Discoverer spider species Atypus snetzingeri, 1973. Home: 49 S Balliet St Frackville PA 17931-1703 Office: Schuylkill Haven HS Schuylkill Haven PA 17972

SARNOFF, ALBERT, communications executive; b. N.Y.C., July 19, 1925; s. Morris and Clara (Oppenheimer) S.; m. Nancy Hanak, July 25, 1968; children: Gary, Ken, Doug. B.A., Yale U., 1947. Buyer R.H. Macy & Co., N.Y.C., 1950-52; v.p. Pease & Elliman, N.Y.C., 1952-58; pres. Club Razor Blade Mfg. Co., N.J., 1958-62; sr. v.p., treas. Warner Communications Inc., N.Y.C., 1962-90; sr. cons. Time Warner Inc., 1990—. Mem. Metropolis Country Club, City Athletic Club, El Cabellero. Office: Warner Comm Inc 75 Rockefeller Plz New York NY 10019-6908

SARNOFF, LILI-CHARLOTTE DREYFUS (LOLO SARNOFF), artist, business executive; b. Frankfurt, Germany (Swiss citizen), Jan. 9, 1916; came to U.S., 1940, naturalized, 1943; d. Willy and Martha (Koch von Hirsch) Dreyfus; m. Stanley Jay Saronff, Sept. 11, 1948; children: Daniela Martha Bargezi, Robert L. Grad. Reimann Art Sch. (Germany), 1936, U. Berlin, 1936-38; student U. Florence (Italy), 1948-54. Rsch. asst. Harvard Sch. Pub. Health, 1955-69; rsch. assoc. cardiac physiology Nat. Heart Inst., Bethesda, Md., 1954-59; pres. Rodana Rsch. Corp., Bethesda, 1959; v.p. Catrix Corp., Bethesda, 1958-61; inventor FloLite light sculptures under name Lolo Sarnoff, 1968; one-woman shows include Agra Gallery, Washington, 1969, Corning Glass Ctr. Mus., Corning, N.Y., 1970, Gallery Two, Woodstock, Vt., 1970, Gallery Marc, Washington, 1971, 72, Franz Bader Gallery, Washington, 1976, Gallery K, Washington, 1978, 81, Alwin Gallery, London, 1981, Galerie von Bartha, Basel, Switzerland, 1982, Gallery K, Washington, 1982, 83, 84, 85, 87, 88, 89, 90, 91, La Galerie L'Hotel de Ville, Geneva, Switzerland, 1982, Pfalzgalerie, Kaiserlautern, Fed. Republic of Germany, 1985, Gallery K, Washington, 1987-91, Galerie Les Hirondelles, Geneva, 1988, Rockville (Md.) Civic Ctr., 1988, Washington Square Sculpture Group, 1989, Internat. Sculpture Congress, Washington, 1990; represented in collections: Fed. Nat. Mortgage Assn., Washington, Brookings Inst., Washington, Corning Glass Ctr. Mus., Nat. Air and Space Museum, Washington, Kennedy Ctr., Washington, Nat. Acad. Sci., Chase Manhattan Bank, N.Y.C., Israel Mus., Jerusalem, Nat. Mus. Women in the Arts, Washington, others. Past trustee Nat. Ballet, Mt. Vernon Coll.; founder, pres. Arts for the Aging, Inc., Bethesda, Md., 1988—; active Washington Opera Soc., Washington Ballet Soc.; bd. overseers Corcoran Gallery Art, 1991, Retrospective Show, Gallery K, Washington, 1995. Recipient Gold medal Accademia Italia delle Arti e del Lavoro, 1980, Golda Meir award, 1995. Mem. City Tavern Club (Washington), Cosmos Club. Democrat. Co-inventor electrophrenic respirator; inventor flowmeter. Home: 7507 Hampden Ln Bethesda MD 20814-1331

SARNOFF, MARC DAVID, lawyer; b. Bklyn., Dec. 28, 1959; s. Joel Sarnoff and Alaine (Katz) Stagnitta. BA, U. Tampa, 1981; JD, Loyola U., New Orleans, 1984. Bar: La. 1985, Fla. 1986, U.S. Dist. Ct. (so. dist.) Fla. 1986, D.C. 1987. Assoc. Herman, Herman, Katz & Coller, New Orleans, 1984-85; asst. prosecutor Orleans Parish Dist. Atty. Office, New Orleans, 1985-86; assoc. Christenberry & D'Antoni, New Orleans, 1986-87, Law Offices of Howard D. Dillman, Miami, Fla., 1987-91; ptnr. Goldman, Moore and Sarnoff, Miami, 1991-92, Sarnoff & Bayer, Miami, 1992—. Capt. U. Tampa Swimming Team, 1978. Mem. Million Dollar Advs. Forum, Phi Delta Theta (v.p. 1980, 81). Home: 3197 Virginia St Miami FL 33133 Office: Sarnoff & Bayer 3197 Virginia St Miami FL 33133

SARNOFF, THOMAS WARREN, television executive; b. N.Y.C., Feb. 23, 1927; s. David and Lizette (Hermant) S.; m. Janyce Lundon, May 21, 1955; children: Daniel, Timothy, Cynthia. Grad., Phillips Acad., 1939-43; student, Princeton, 1943-45; B.S. in Elec. Engring., Stanford U., 1948, postgrad. Sch. Bus. Adminstrn., 1948-49; D.H.L., Columbia Coll. Engaged in prodn. and sales with ABC, Inc., 1949-51; prodn. Metro-Goldwyn-Mayer, 1951-52; with NBC, 1952-77; v.p. prodn. and bus. affairs NBC (Pacific div.), 1956-60, v.p. adminstrn. West Coast, 1960-62, v.p. charge West Coast, 1962-65, staff exec. v.p. West Coast, 1965-77; pres. NBC Entertainment Corp., 1972-77, Sarnoff Internat. Enterprises, 1977-81, Sarnoff Entertainment Corp., 1981—; exec. v.p. Venturetainment Corp., 1981-87, pres., 1987—. Exec. producer Bonanza: The Next Generation, 1987, Bonanza: The Return, 1993, Back to Bonanza Retrospective, 1993, Bonanza: Under Attack, 1995. Mem. Calif. Commn. for Reform Intermediate and Secondary Edn. Pres., Research Found., St. Joseph Hosp., Burbank, 1965-73, Permanant Charities Com. of Entertainment Industries, 1971-72; nat. trustee Nat. Conf. Christians and Jews. Served with Signal Corps AUS, World War II. Mem. Acad. TV Arts and Scis. (chmn. bd. trustees 1972-74, chmn. past pres.'s coun. 1989-92), Acad. TV Arts and Scis. Found. (pres. 1990—), The Caucus for Prodrs., Writers and Dirs. Office: 2451 Century Hl Los Angeles CA 90067-3510

SAROKIN, H. LEE, federal judge; b. Perth Amboy, N.J., Nov. 25, 1928; s. Samuel O. and Reebe (Weinblatt) S.; m. Marjorie Lang, Apr. 23, 1971; children: James Todd, Jeffrey Scott, Abby Jane. A.B., Dartmouth Coll., 1950; J.D., Harvard U., 1953. Bar: N.J. 1954. Assoc. Lasser, Lasser, Sarokin & Hochman, Newark, 1955-58; partner Lasser, Lasser, Sarokin & Hochman, 1958-79; asst. county counsel Union County, N.J., 1959-65; U.S. dist. judge Dist. of N.J., Newark, 1979-94; judge U.S. Ct. Appeals (3d cir.), Newark, 1994—. Fellow Am. Bar Assn.; mem. Am. Law Inst.; Mem. N.J. Bar Assn., Essex County Bar Assn., Fed. Bar Assn. Office: US Dist Ct PO & Courthouse PO Box 419 Newark NJ 07101-0419*

SARPY, LEON, lawyer; b. New Orleans, Nov. 25, 1907; s. Henry Leon and Anita Louise (Staigg) S.; m. Courtney Dickinson, July 7, 1938 (dec. Mar. 1945); children: Courtney Anne, H. Leon; m. Eleanor Legier, July 17, 1948; 1 son, John Robert. A.B., Loyola U., New Orleans, 1928, LL.B., 1931, LL.D. (hon.), 1961; LL.M., Georgetown U., 1932. Bar: La. 1931. Practice law New Orleans, 1932; mem. firm Chaffe, McCall, Phillips, Toler & Sarpy, 1948—; lectr. Loyola U. Law Sch., 1934-87, prof., 1992—, Sarpy Endowed prof., 1992—; dist. rent atty. OPA, 1942-43; reporter La. Criminal Code, 1942, La. Code Civil Procedure, 1960. Contbr. to legal jours. Chmn. CSC New Orleans, 1952-63; chmn. civic luncheon for Pres. deGaulle of France, 1960; pres. Asso. Catholic Charities New Orleans, 1953-54; mem. Audubon Park Commn., 1963-70; bd. pres. New Orleans United Fund, 1959-60; bd. dirs. Greater New Orleans Homestead Assn., 1940-87; chmn. adv. bd. Convent Good Shepherd, 1957-58; trustee St. Mary's Dominican Coll., 1963-67; chmn. Community Chest of New Orleans, 1970-73; adv. bd. Loyola U., 1964-72, Tulane Admiralty Inst., 1966-87. Mem. La. N.G., 1925-28; Mem. USCG Temp. Res., 1944-45. Decorated Legion of Honor France; named Outstanding Alumnus, Jesuit High Sch., New Orleans, 1964; recipient Brotherhood award NCCJ, 1964, Gold medal St. Mary's Dominican Coll., 1970, Pres.' medal Loyola U., 1989, Alexis deTocqueville award United Way, 1989; named Rex of New Orleans Mardi Gras, 1972; cert. appreciation Outstanding Community Svc. ARC, 1992. Mem. ABA (ho. dels. 1965-70), La. Bar Assn. (pres. 1964-65), New Orleans Bar Assn. (pres. 1950-51), Am. Law Inst., La. Law Inst. (v.p. 1961-68, pres. 1968-73, chmn. 1980-86), Inst. Jud. Adminstrn. (N.Y.), S.W. Legal Found. (chmn. rsch. fellows 1970-72), Order of Coif, Blue Key, Delta Theta Phi, La. Club, Boston Club (New Orleans), Round Table Club (pres. 1964-66), Serra Club (pres. 1960-61), Order of St. Lazarus. Clubs: Boston (New Orleans), Round Table (New Orleans) (pres. 1964-66), Serra (New Orleans) (pres. 1960-61); Order of St. Lazarus. Home: 455 Walnut St New Orleans LA 70118-4933 Office: 2300 Energy Centre 1100 Poydras St New Orleans LA 70163-1100

SARRIS, ANDREW GEORGE, film critic; b. Bklyn., Oct. 31, 1928; s. George Andrew and Themis (Katavolos) S.; m. Molly Clark Haskell, May 31, 1969. A.B., Columbia, 1951. Film critic Village Voice, N.Y.C., 1960-89, N.Y. Observer, 1989—; editor-in-chief Cahiers du Cinema in English; instr. Sch. Visual Arts, 1965-67; asst. prof. N.Y. U., 1967-69; assoc. prof. films Columbia Sch. Arts, N.Y.C., 1969-81, prof., 1981—. Author: The Films of Josef Von Sternberg, 1966, Interviews with Film Directors, 1967, The Film, 1968 The American Cinema, 1968, Confessions of a Cultist, 1970, The Primal Screen, 1973, The John Ford Movie Mystery, 1976, Politics and Cinema, 1978. Served with Signal Corps AUS, 1952-54. Guggenheim fellow, 1969. Mem. Am. Film Inst. (dir.), Soc. Cinema Studies, Nat. Soc. Film Critics, N.Y. Film Critics. *I keep on working toward that last deadline.*

SARRY, CHRISTINE, ballerina; b. Long Beach, Calif., May 25, 1946; d. John and Beatrice (Thomas) S.; m. Jim Varriale, Sept. 12, 1984; 1 child, Maximilian Sarry Varriale. With Joffrey Ballet, 1963-64; With Am. Ballet Theatre, 1964-68, prin. dancer, 1971-74; leading dancer Am. Ballet Co., 1969-71; ballerina Eliot Feld Ballet, 1974-81; mem. faculty New Ballet Sch., also freelance guest tchr. Performed ballets for Agnes DeMille, Antony Tudor, Jerome Robbins, Eliot Feld; appeared at White House, 1963, 67; U.S. Dept. State tours include, Russia, 1963, 66, S.Am., 1964, 76, various tours of N.Am., Orient, Europe, various appearances U.S. nat. TV; partnered by Mikhail Baryshnikov.

SARSFIELD, LUKE ALOYSIUS, school system administrator; b. Luzerne, Pa., July 29, 1925; s. Luke Aloysius and Margaret Ann (Conahan) S.; m. Nancy Ann Chiavacci, Aug. 19, 1961; 1 child, Luke Aloysius III. BA, King's Coll., Wilkes-Barre, Pa., 1952; MA, Montclair (N.J) State Coll., 1962; PhD, NYU, 1973. Diplomate Ednl. Adminstrn. Tchr. Ogdensburg (N.J) Pub. Schs., 1953-55, Luzerne Pub. Schs., 1955-60; tchr. Rutherford (N.J.) Pub. Schs., 1960-70, adminstrv. asst. to supt., 1970-72, supt. schs., 1972—. Trustee Rutherford Pub. Libr., 1972—, v.p.; trustee Williams Inst. Inc., Rutherford, 1986—, treas.; trustee Bergen County Tenn Arts, 1989—; pres. Jack Frost Jr. Racing Found., White Haven, Pa., 1987-93, South Bergen Jointure Com. With USN, 1943-46. Mem. Am. Assn. Sch. Adminstrs., N.J. Assn. Sch. Adminstrs., Bergen County Supts. Assn. (past pres.), Bergen County Assn. Sch. Adminstrs., Bergen County Audio-Visual Com., King's Coll. Alumni Assn. (past pres.), Rotary (past pres.), Phi Delta Kappa. Roman Catholic. Office: Rutherford Pub Schs 176 Park Ave Rutherford NJ 07070-2310

SARSON, EVELYN PATRICIA See KAYE, EVELYN PATRICIA

SARSON, JOHN CHRISTOPHER, television producer, director, writer; b. London, Jan. 19, 1935; s. Arnold Wilfred and Annie Elizabeth (Wright) S.; m. Evelyn Patricia Kaye, Mar. 25, 1963; children: Katrina May, David Arnold. BA with honors, Trinity Coll., Cambridge, Eng., 1960, MA, 1963.

Dir. Granada TV, Manchester, Eng., 1960-63; producer, dir. Sta. WGBH-TV, Boston, 1963-73; pres. Blue Penguin, Inc., Boulder, Colo., 1974—; v.p. TV programming Sta. WYNC-TV, N.Y.C., 1989-90; dir. Pub. Broadcasting Assocs., Newton, Mass.; cons. to numerous pub. TV stations. Creator, producer MAsterpiece Theatre, PBS, 1970-73, Zoom, PBS, 1971-73; producer Live From the Met, PBS, 1977-79, Kid's Writes, Nickelodeon, 1982-83, American Treasure, a Smithsonian Journey, 1986, Spotlight Colorado, 1991, PArenting Works, 1993, Club 303, 1994. Served with Royal Navy, 1956-57. Recipient Emmy award, 1973, 74, Peabody award Ohio State U., 1978, Internat. Emmy award, 1983, Nat. Acad. TV Arts and Scis. Gov.'s award, 1991. Mem. Dirs. Guild Am., Nat. acad. TV Arts and Scis. (gov. Heartland chpt.). Avocations: music; cooking; gardening; travel. Home and Office: 3031 5th St Boulder CO 80304-2501

SARTAIN, JAMES EDWARD, lawyer; b. Ft. Worth, Feb. 9, 1941; s. James F. and May Belle (Boaz) S.; m. Barbara Hardy, Aug. 17, 1962; 1 child, Bethany Sartain Hughes. BA, Tex. A&M U., 1963; LLB, Baylor U., 1966. Bar: Tex. 1966, U.S. Ct. Mil. Appeals, 1971, U.S. Dist. Ct. (no. dist.) Tex. 1974. Staff atty. Dept. Justice, Washington, 1970-72; staff atty. to U.S. Sen. William L. Scott Fairfax, Va., 1972; pvt. practice Ft. Worth, 1973—; sec. Penrose Lumber Co., Abilene, Tex., 1987—, Esprit Comm. Corp., Austin, Tex.; bd. dirs. Emerald Restoration, Inc., Abilene, Tex.; sec. Esprit Comm. Corp., Austin, Tex. Bd. dirs. Ft. Worth Boys Club, 1980-89, Oakwood Cemetery, Ft. Worth, 1979-84. Capt. arty. U.S. Army, Vietnam. Mem. ABA, Abilene Bar Assn., Baylor Law Alumni Assn., Ft. Worth-Tarrant County Bar Assn., Coll. State Bar Tex., Masons, Petroleum Club, Phi Delta Phi. Republican. Presbyterian. Office: 3880 Hulen St Ste 620 Fort Worth TX 76107-7280

SARTOR, AMELIA ADELAIDE, nursing educator, consultant; b. Charlotte, N.C., Feb. 25, 1921; d. William Charles and Rosa (Williams) Brown; m. John Author Sartor, 1975. Diploma, Good Samaritan Hosp.; BSN, St. Augustine's Coll., 1951; MA, NYU, 1954. RN, N.C.; cert. tchr., N.Y. Staff nurse St. Philip Hosp., Richmond, Va., 1950-51; staff nurse, team leader, clin. instr. N.Y. Hosp., 1954-62; staff nurse, head nurse Mt. Sinai Hosp., N.Y.C., 1962-70; instr., nursing supr. Comty. Hosp., Wilmington, N.C., 1970-83, New Rochelle (N.Y.) Hosp., 1983-87; instr., supr. Meals on Wheels Agy., N.Y.C., 1987-89; prof., asst. to dean Meharry Med. Coll., Nashville, 1989-91; prof. pediats. A&T U., Greensboro, N.C., 1991-92; cons. Bd. of Edn., N.Y.C., 1992—. Co-author: Pediatrics, 1954; pub. bibliography for nursing schs. in U.S., 1962. Mem., active voter registration Bd. Social and Christian Concern-Abyssinian Bapt. Ch., N.Y.C., 1972—; mem. Bd. of Christian and Social Concern. Recipient award for loyal svc. musicdept. woman's chorus, 1985, award for 40 yrs. of svc. in first aid and other svcs., 1994. Mem. ANA (life), N.Y. State Nurses Assn., St. Augustine's Alumni Club, Alpha Kappa Alpha (mem.-at-large). Republican. Avocations: traveling, reading, singing, movies, plays. Home: 65 W 96th St New York NY 10025-6532

SARTOR, ANTHONY JOSEPH, environmental engineer; b. Englewood, N.J., Mar. 28, 1943; s. John and Catherine (Dottino) S. Sr.; m. Maria C. Crisonio, Dec. 26, 1964; children: Lisanne, Colette (twins), John. BS in Engring., Manhattan Coll., 1964; MS in Engring., Mich. U., 1965, PhD, 1968. Devel. engr. Celanese Co., 1968-70; sr. water quality engr. Con Edison, N.Y.C., 1970-72; mgr. environ. affairs N.Y. Power Pool, 1972-74; pres. Sartor Assocs., Warren, N.J., 1974-77; exec. v.p., treas., sec. Paulus, Sokolowski, Sartor, Inc., Warren, 1977—; commr. N.J. Sports and Exposition Authority, 1992. Trustee Richard J. Hughes Found., Inc.; mem. Environ. Commn., Fanwood, N.J.; mem. gov.'s transition team N.J. Dept. Environ. Protection. Recipient Disting. Service award Fanwood-Scotch Plains Jaycees. Mem. Am. Chem. Soc., Am. Inst. Chem. Engrs., Na.t Soc. Environ. Engrs., Jaycees (past bd. dirs., pres.), UNICO (Environ. Sci. award), Italian-Am. Club, Sigma Xi, Phi Lambda Upsilon. Club: Italian-Am. (Fairview, N.J.). Home: 19 Kevin Rd Scotch Plains NJ 07076-2211 Office: PO Box 4039 67A Mountain Boulevard Ext Warren NJ 07059-5626

SARTOR, DANIEL RYAN, JR., lawyer; b. Vicksburg, Miss., June 2, 1932; s. Daniel Ryan and Lucy Leigh (Hubbs) S.; m. Olive Guthrie Moss, Oct. 12, 1957; children—Clara M., Daniel Ryan, Walter M. B.A., Tulane U., 1952, LL.B., 1955. Bar: La. 1955. Instr. Tulane U., New Orleans, 1955-56, asst. prof., 1956-57; ptnr. Snellings, Breard, Sartor, Inabnett & Trascher, Monroe, La., 1957—. Contbr. articles to profl. jours. Fellow Am. Coll. Trust and Estate Counsel, Am. Bar Found., La. Bar Found.; mem. La. State Law Inst. (mem. council 1969—, sec. civil law sect. 1969—), La. State Bar Assn. (chmn. sect. on trust estate, probate and immovable property 1973-74, bd. govs. 1974-75). Democrat. Methodist. Clubs: Lotus (Monroe), Tower. Home: 2405 Pargoud Blvd Monroe LA 71201-2326 Office: Snellings Breard Sartor 1503 N 19th St Monroe LA 71201-4941

SARTORE, JOEL, photojournalist; b. Ponca City, Okla., June 16, 1962; s. John Edward and Sharon Lee (Meese) S.; m. Kathleen Louise Vestecka, June 21, 1985; 1 child, Cole Woodrow. B in Journalism, U. Nebr., 1985. Photo intern The Witchita Eagle, 1984, staff photographer, 1985-88, asst. dir. photography, 1989, dir. photography, 1990; freelance photographer Nat. Geographic, Washington, 1991, contract photographer, 1992—. Recipient Award of Excellence Pictures of the Yr. Competition U. Mo., 1992. Mem. Nat. Press Photographer's Assn. (dir. region 7 1990). Methodist. Avocations: fishing, antique restoration. Office: Nat Geog Soc Photo Dept 1145 17th St NW Washington DC 20036-4701

SARTORE, JOHN THORNTON, lawyer; b. N.Y.C., Nov. 5, 1946; s. Frank Jean and Mary Olive (Wacaser) S.; m. Sally Ann Coppersmith, Feb. 28, 1973; children: Michael, David, Delmy, Jenny. BA, Yale U., 1968; JD, Columbia U., 1971. Bar: Vt. 1972, U.S. Dist. Ct. Vt. 1972, U.S. Ct. Appeals (2d cir.) 1978, N.Y. 1989, U.S. Dist. Ct. (no. dist.) N.Y. 1992. Assoc. Paul, Frank & Collins, Inc., Burlington, Vt., 1971-74, mem., 1974—, pres., CEO, 1994—. Mem. ABA, Am. Coll. Trial Lawyers, Am. Bd. Trial Advocates, Vt. Bar Assn., N.Y. State Bar Assn., Chittenden County Bar Assn., New Eng. Legal Found. (dir.). Office: Paul Frank & Collins Inc One Church St Burlington VT 05402-1307

SARTORELLI, ALAN CLAYTON, pharmacology educator; b. Chelsea, Mass., Dec. 18, 1931; m. Alice C. Anderson, July 7, 1969. B.S., New Eng. Coll. Pharmacy Northeastern U., 1953; M.S., Middlebury (Vt.) Coll., 1955; Ph.D., U. Wis., 1958; M.A. (hon.), Yale U., 1967. Rsch. chemist Samuel Roberts Noble Found., Ardmore, Okla., 1958-60; sr. rsch. chemist Samuel Roberts Noble Found., 1960-61; mem. faculty dept. pharmacology Yale Sch. Medicine, New Haven, Conn., 1961—, prof., 1967—, head devel. therapeutics program Comprehensive Cancer Center, 1974-90, chmn. dept. pharmacology, 1977-84, dep. dir. Comprehensive Cancer Ctr., 1982-84, dir. Comprehensive Cancer Ctr., 1984-93, Alfred Gilman prof. pharmacology, 1987—, prof. epidemiology, 1991—; Charles B. Smith vis. rsch. prof. Meml. Sloan-Kettering Ctr., 1979; William N. Creasy vis. prof. clin. pharmacology Wayne State U., 1983; Mayo Found. vis. prof. oncology Mayo Clinic, 1983; Walter Hubert lectr. Brit. Assn. Cancer Rsch., 1985; Pfizer lectr. in clin. pharmacology U. Conn. Health Ctr., 1985; William N. Creasy vis. prof. clin. pharmacology Bowman Gray Sch. Medicine, 1987; Wellcome vis. prof. basic sci. U. Pitts. Sch. Medicine, 1990; mem. sci. adv. bd. ImmunoGen, Inc., 1981—, U. Ind. Cancer Ctr., 1992, Cancer Inst. N.J., 1993—, Cell Pathways, Inc., 1993—; chmn. cancer sci. adv. bd. ViraChem., Inc., 1986-93, The Liposome Co., 1986—, Vion Pharms., 1993—, bd. dirs.; chmn. vis. sci. adv. com. Columbia U. Comprehensive Cancer Ctr., 1986—; chmn. pres.'s cancer adv. bd. Fox Chase Cancer Ctr., 1992—; mem. cancer clin. investigation rev. com. Nat. Cancer Inst., 1968-72, mem. cons. to dir. divsn. cancer treatment, 1975-77, bd. sci. counselors, divsn. cancer treatment, 1978-81, chmn. com. to establish nat. coop. drug discovery groups, 1982-83, chmn. special review com. Outstanding Investigator grant applications, 1992, chmn. ad hoc contracts tech. rev. group, 1993; mem. instl. rsch. grants com. Am. Cancer Soc., 1971-76, coun. analysis and projection, 1978-79; cons. in biochemistry U. Tex. M.D. Anderson Hosp. and Tumor Clinic, Houston, 1970-76; cons. Sandoz Forschungs-Institut, Vienna, Austria, 1977-80; mem. exptl. therapeutics study sect. NIH, 1973-77, working cadre nat. large bowel cancer project, 1973-76; mem. adv. com. Cancer Rsch. Ctr., Washington U. Sch. Medicine, 1971-75, SLSB Partners, L.P., 1992—; mem. sci. adv. com. U. Iowa Cancer Ctr., 1979-83; mem. external adv. com. Wis. Clin. Cancer Ctr., 1978-79, Duke Comprehensive Cancer Ctr., 1983-94; mem. external adv. bd. U. Ariz. Cancer Ctr., 1982-92, U. So. Calif. Cancer Ctr., 1983-93, Clin. Cancer Rsch. Ctr., Brown U., 1980-86; mem. nat. program com. 13th Internat. Cancer Congress, 1979-81; cons. Bristol-Myers Co., 1982-93, mem. selection com. prize in cancer rsch., 1977-85, chmn., 1979-81, chmn. selection com. award for disting. achievement in cancer rsch., 1989-92; bd. advisors Drug and Vaccine Devel. Corp. (Ctr. for Pub. Resources), 1980-81, Specialized Cancer Ctr., Mt. Sinai Med. Ctr., 1981-90, Grace Cancer Drug Ctr., Roswell Park Meml. Inst., 1986-89; mem. med. and sci. adv. com. grants rev. subcom. Leukemia Soc. Am., 1984-88; bd. dirs. Metastasis Rsch. Soc., 1984-90; mem. program planning com. Mary Lasker-Am. Cancer Soc. Conf., 1986; mem. external sci. rev. com. Massey Cancer Ctr., 1989-94; bd. visitors Moffit Cancer Ctr. U.S. Fla., 1989-94; mem. ad hoc cons. group for cancer ctrs. program Nat. Cancer Adv. Bd., 1989-92; dep. dir. Cancer Prevention Rsch. Unit for Conn., 1989-93, acting dir., 1991-93; mem. nat. bd. Cosmetic Toiletry and Fragnance Assn.'s Look Good...Feel Better Program, 1989-91; mem. organizing com. Conf. on Bioreductive Drug Activation, 1993-94; chmn. bd. special cons. Inst. for Cancer Therapeutics, 1993—. Regional editor Am. Continent Biochem. Pharmacology, 1968—, exec. editor, 1993—; editor-in-chief Cancer Comm., 1969-91, Oncology Rsch., 1993—; editor Handbuch der experimentellen Pharmakologie vols. on antineoplastic and immunosuppressditor series on cancer chemotherapy Am. Chem. Soc. Symposium, 1976; exec. editor Pharmacology and Therapeutics, 1975—; mem. editl. bd. Internat. Ency. Pharmacology and Therapeutics, 1972—, Seminars in Oncology, 1973-83, Chemico-Biol. Interactions, 1975-78, Jour. Meldicinal Chemistry, 1977-82, Cancer Drug Delivery, 1982-85, Jour. Enzyme Inhibition, 1984—, Anti-Cancer Drug Design, 1984—, Jour. Liposome Rsch., 1986-92, In Vivo, 1990—, Cancer Biotherapy, 1992, Cancer Rsch., Therapy, and Control, 1993—, Oncology Reports, 1995—, Molecular and Cellular Differentiation, 1995—; mem. adv. bd. Advances in Chemistry Series, ACS Symposium Series, 1977-80; mem. editl. adv. bd. Cancer Rsch., 1970-71, assoc. editor, 1971-78; assoc. editor Current Awareness in Biol. Scis., Current Advances in Pharmacology and Toxicology, 1983—, Cancer Cells, 1989-91, Jour. Exptl. Therapeutics and Oncology, 1995—; mem. exec. adv. bd. Ency. of Human Biology, 1987-90, Dictionary of Sci. and Tech., 1989-91; editl. cons. Biol. Abstracts, 1984—; contbr. articles to profl. jours. Bd. dirs. Shubert Performing Arts Ctr., 1992—, Shubert Opera Bd., 1991—, chmn., 1993—. Recipient Outstanding Alumni award Northeastern U., 1987, Mike Hogg award M.D. Anderson Cancer Ctr., U. Tex., 1989, Alumni Achievement award Middlebury Coll., 1990. Fellow AAAS, N.Y. Acad. Scis.; mem. Am. Assn. Cancer Rsch. (dir. 1975-78, 84-87, chmn. publs. com. 1981-88, v.p. 1985-86, fin. com. 1985-88, exec. com. 1985-89, chmn. exec. com. 1987, pres. 1986-87, chmn. awards com. 1987, chmn. nominating com. 1993-95, mem. devel. com. 1995—), Am. Chem. Soc., Am. Soc. Microbiology, Am. Soc. Biochemistry and Molecular Biology, Am. Soc. Cell Biology, Am. Soc. Pharmacology and Exptl. Therapeutics (award in exptl. therapeutics 1986, award com. 1988, chmn. 1992), Assn. Am. Cancer Insts. (v.p. 1986, bd. dirs. 1986-89, liaison rep. to Nat. Cancer Inst. 1986, pres. 1987-88, chmn. bd. dirs. 1989), Inst. of Medicine of NAS (com. on govt. industry collaboration in biomed. rsch. and edn. 1989, mem. Forum on Drug Devel. and Regulation 1989—), Conn. Acad. Sci. and Engring., Coun. Biology Editors. Home: 4 Perkins Rd Woodbridge CT 06525-1616 Office: Yale U Dept Pharmacology 333 Cedar St New Haven CT 06510-3206

SARTORI, GIOVANNI, political scientist; b. Florence, Italy, May 13, 1924; s. Dante and Emilia (Quentin) S.; 1 child, Ilaria. PhD, U. Florence, 1956; Doctor honoris causa, U. Genoa, 1992; Georgetown U., 1994. Assoc. prof. U. Florence, 1956-62, prof., 1962-76, dean faculty of polit. scis., 1968-71; prof. polit. sci. Stanford U., 1976-79; Albert Schweitzer prof. in the humanities Columbia U., N.Y.C., 1979—; fellow Ctr. Advanced Study Behavioral Scis., 1971-72; sr. fellow Hoover Instn., 1976-79. Author: Democratic Theory, 1962, Parties and Party Systems: A Framework for Analysis, 1976, La Politica, 1979, The Theory of Democracy Revisited, 1987, Elementi di Teoria Politica, 1990, Seconda Repubblica?, 1992, Democrazia, 1993, Comparative Constitutional Engineering, 1994. Guggenheim fellow, 1979, Russell Sage Found. fellow, 1988-89. Mem. Am. Acad. Arts and Scis, Academia dei Lincei. Home: 25 Central Park W Apt 270 New York NY 10023-7253 Office: Sch Internat Affairs 420 W 118th St Rm 1234 New York NY 10027-7213

SARTORIUS, PETER S., lawyer; b. Jan. 15, 1947. BA, Williams Coll., 1968; JD, U. Va., 1974. Bar: Pa. 1975. Law clk to Hon. Leonard P. Moore U.S. Ct. Appeals (2nd cir.), 1974-75; ptnr. Morgan, Lewis & Bockius, LLP, Phila. Office: Morgan Lewis & Bockius LLP 2000 One Logan Sq Philadelphia PA 19103

SARUBBI, JUDITH ALICE CLEARWATER, guidance counselor; b. Englewood, N.J., Oct. 5, 1956; d. Jasper and Mary (Fadden) Clearwater; m. Edward J. Sarubbi, July 7, 1979; children: Brian, Alyssa, Christopher. BA, William Paterson Coll., 1978; MA, Kean Coll. N.J., 1983. Cert. tchr., spl. edn. tchr., reading specialist, guidance and counseling, N.J. Tchr. Bergen County Bd. Spl. Svcs., Paramus, N.J., 1978-82; asst. dir. Day Camp Oratam, Harriman State Park, N.Y., 1980-82; co-dir. Skyland Learning and Guidance Assocs., Ringwood, N.J., 1985--89; guidance counselor Wharton (N.J.) Borough Pub. Schs., 1992—; cons. Embossography, Paramus, 1979-81. Steering com. Alliance of Wanaque (N.J.) and Ringwood for Edn. and Substance Abuse Prevention, 1989-92. Mem. ASCD, ACA, Pi Lambda Theta. Roman Catholic. Avocations: reading, collecting farm antiques, skiing, crafts, computers. Office: Alfred C MacKinnon Mid Sch 137 E Central Ave Wharton NJ 07885-2431

SARVER, EUGENE, finance educator; b. N.Y.C., July 15, 1943; s. Edmund and Stella (Bodek) S.; m. Vivian J. Ortega, Jan. 1, 1992. BA, Haverford Coll., 1965; MA, Johns Hopkins U., 1967; postgrad., U. N.C., 1967-69; ArtsD, Idaho State U., 1973. Lectr. in polit. sci. U. N.C., Greensboro, 1969-76; chief economist, corp. fin. advisor Credit Lyonnais-U.S. Group (#2 French Bank), N.Y.C., 1974-79; v.p., mgmt. cons. Chemical Bank, N.Y.C., 1979-84; dir. banking programs N.Y. Inst. Fin., N.Y.C., 1984-85; asst. chmn., assoc. prof. fin. Lubin Grad. Sch. Bus., Pace U., N.Y.C., 1985—; vis. prof. Internat. Fin. and Banking U. Malta, 1993; guest lectr. Ind. U. Sch. Bus.; cons. INFORMASI Indonesian Bus. Data Ctr., Jakarta, Malaysian Indsl. Devel. Authority (MIDA), MTB Banking Corp., Republic Nat. Bank of N.Y., Swiss Banking Corp., Bank of Valletta Malta, Chemical, Chase, Citibank, Nomura Securities Internat., Global Mgmt. Inc. (U.S., Russia), Global Interface Group, World Trade Inst. of the Port Authority of N.Y. and N.J.; cross-cultural cons. Moran, Stahl and Boyer Internat. (subs. Prudential Ins. Co.). Author: The Eurocurrency Market Handbook, 1988, 2d edit., 1990; contbr. articles to World Trade Mag. ("Currency Events"), The Malta Bus. Weekly, Third World ann. edit., Bank of Valletta Rev., Currency Forecasters Digest, Jour. of Commerce, The World and I, Money and Investments, Jour. Fin. Planning Treasury Mgr.; TV commentator on Financial Fitness. Active Ptnrs. for Internat. Edn. and Training (providing fin. tng. for U.S. State Dept. AID-selected fgn. nationals); pres. Haverford (Pa.) Young Democrats, 1964-65; candidate City Coun., Greensboro, 1971; elected bd. dirs. Am. Heritage (Mutual) Fund and Am. Heritage Growth Fund; elected gov. The Money Marketeers, 1990-93. Mem. AAUP (pres. Pace chpt. 1990-93), N.Y. Assn. Bus. Economists (chmn. conf. com. 1989), Money Marketeers, Met. Econs. Assn., Assn. Downtown Economists, Am. Arbitration Assn. (panel of comml. arbitrators 1980—), Am. Fin. Assn., Fin. Mgmt. Assn., Mensa, Theodore Roosevelt Assn., Brandford Country Club. Democrat. Avocations: travel, skiing, furniture design. Home: 241 W 97th St Apt 8M New York NY 10025-6209 Office: Pace U Lubin Grad Sch Bus 1 Pace Plz New York NY 10038-1502

SARWER-FONER, GERALD JACOB, physician, educator; b. Volkovsk, Grodno, Poland, Dec. 6, 1924; arrived in Can., 1932, naturalized, 1935; s. Michael and Ronia (Caplan) Sarwer-F.; m. Ethel Sheinfeld, May 28, 1950; children: Michael, Gladys, Janice, Henry, Brian. B.A., Loyola Coll. U., Montreal, 1945, M.D. magna cum laude, 1951; D.Psychiatry, McGill U., 1955. Diplomate: Am. Bd. Psychiatry and Neurology. Intern. Univ. Hosps. U. Montreal Sch. Medicine, 1950-51; resident Butler Hosp., Providence, 1951-52, Hosps. Western Res. U., Cleve., 1952-53, Queen Mary Vets. Hosp., Montreal, 1953-55; lectr. psychiatry U. Montreal, 1953-55; lectr., assoc. prof. McGill U., 1955-70; prof. psychiatry U. Ottawa, Ont., 1971—, prof., chmn. psychiatry, 1974-86; dir. dept. psychiatry Ottawa Gen. Hosp., 1971-87; dir. Lafayette Clinic, Detroit, 1989-92; prof. psychiatry Wayne State U., Detroit, 1989—; cons. in psychiatry Ottawa Gen. Hosp., Royal Ottawa Hosp., Nat. Def. Med. Ctr., Children's Hosp. of Eastern Ont., Ottawa, Windsor (Ont.) Western Hosp. Ctr., Ottawa Sch. Bd.; Z. Lebensohn lectr. Silbey Meml. Hosp. Cosmos Club, Washington,. 1991. Editor: Dynamics of Psychiatric Drug Therapy, 1960, Research Conference on the Depressive Group of Illnesses, 1966, Psychiatric Crossroads-the Seventies, Research Aspects, 1972; editor in chief Psychiat. Jour. U. Ottawa, 1976-90, emeritus editor in chief, 1990—; mem. editorial bds. of numerous internat. and nat. profl. jours.; editor numerous audio-video tapes; contbr. numerous articles to profl. jours. Bd. govs. Queen Elizabeth Hosp., Montreal, 1966-71; life gov. Queen Elizabeth Hosp. Found.; cons. Protestant Sch. Bd., Westmount, Que., 1966-71; advisor Com. on Health, City of Westmount, 1969-71. Served to lt. col. Royal Can. A Med. Corps, 1949-62. Recipient Sigmund Freud award Am. assn. Psychoanalytic Physicians, 1982, William V. Silverberg Meml. award Am. Acad. Psychoanalysis, 1990, Poca award Assn. Psychiat. Out Patient Ctrs. Am., 1990; Simon Bolivar lectr. Am. Psychiat. Assn., New Orleans, 1981; Can. Decoration Knight of Malta. Fellow AAAS, Royal Coll. Physicians and Surgeons (Can., mem. spl. psychiat. com. 1958-64, exec. sec. test psychiat. com. 1987-89), Royal Coll. Psychiatry (Found. fellow), Am. Coll. Neuropsychopharmacology (charter, life), Can. Coll. Neuropsychopharmacology (life, hon. found.), Internat. Coll. Psychosomatic Medicine (sec.-gen. 1979-83), Am. Psychiat. Assn. (life), Am. Orthopsychiat. Assn. (life), Am. Coll. Psychiatrists (bd. regents 1978-80, emeritus fellow), Am. Psychopathol. Assn., Am. Coll. Psychoanalysts (pres. elect 1983, pres. 1984-85, Henry Laughlin award 1986), Am. Coll. Mental Health Adminstrn. (life), Benjamin Rush Soc. (founding mem., councillor), World Psychiat. Assn. (chair Sci. program VI World Congress 1974, v.p. sect. on edn. 1989—, mem. internat. adv. com. 9th World Congress Rio de Janeiro 1993, mem. nominating com.), Collegium Internat. Neuropsychopharmacology; mem. Am. Acad. Psychiatry and the Law (sr., pres. 1977, Silver Apple award), Soc. Bio.. Psychiatry (sr. mem., H. Azina Meml. lectr. 1963, pres. 1983-84), Can. Psychoanalytic Soc. (pres. 1977-81), Can. Assn. Profs. of Psychiatry (pres. 1976-77, 82-86), Am. Assn. for Social Psychiatry (v.p. 1987-89, pres. elect 1990, pres. 1992-94), Mich. Psychoanalytic Soc., Cosmos Club, Royal Can. Mil. Inst. Club. Home and Office: 3220 Bloomfield Shore Dr West Bloomfield MI 48323-3300

SASAHARA, ARTHUR ASAO, cardiologist, educator, researcher; b. Del Rey, Calif., May 11, 1927; s. Harold Hango and Blanche (Takayama) S.; m. Alice Ann Guenther, Apr. 2, 1955; children: Ann Mariko, Claire Michiko, Ellen Reiko, Karen Hideko, Mark Tadao. AB, Oberlin Coll., 1951; MD, Case Western Res. U., 1955; AM (hon.), Harvard U., 1974. Diplomate Am. Bd. Internal Medicine. Intern Boston City Hosp., 1955-56; jr. asst. med. resident Mass. Gen. Hosp., Boston, 1956-57; fellow in cardiology West Roxbury VA Med. Ctr., Mass., 1957-58, Children's Hosp. Med. Ctr., Boston, 1958-59; sr. resident in medicine Yale-New Haven Med. Ctr., 1959-60; asst. chief med. svc., dir. cardiopulmonary lab., dep. chmn. rsch. and edn. com. VA Hosp. West Roxbury, 1960-70, chief cardiopulmonary sect., 1971-74, assoc. chief staff for rsch. and edn., 1970-76, chief med. svc., 1974-82; chief med. svc. West Roxbury-Brockton VA Hosp., 1982-87; prof. medicine Harvard Med. Sch., Boston, 1974-93; prof. emeritus Harvard Med. Sch., 1993—; cons. cardiovascular-pulmonary diseases Boston, 1965-87; cons. pediatric cardiology Children's Hosp. Med. Ctr., Boston, 1976-86; physician Brigham and Women's Hosp., Boston, 1979-82, sr. physician, 1982—; dir. Thrombolytics Rsch. Pharm. Products Divsn. Abbott Labs., Abbott Park, Ill., 1987-95, sr. med. dir., 1995—. Author-editor: Pulmonary Embolic Disease, 1965, Pulmonary Emboli, 1975; contbr. articles to profl. jours.; designer constant infusion med. pump, Harvard Apparatus Co., 1973; editorial bd. Jour. Nuclear Medicine, 1981-83, Am. Jour. Medicine, 1971-72, Circulation, 1973-78, VASA, 1978-85, Jour. Cardiovascular Medicine, 1980-86, Primary Cardiology, 1986-89. With U.S. Army, 1945-47. NIH grantee, 1963-82; VA grantee, 1961-87. Fellow ACP, Am. Coll. Chest Physicians, Am. coll. Cardiology; mem. AAAS, Am. Fedn. Clin. Rsch., Internat. Soc. Thrombosis and Thrombolysis, Alpha Omega Alpha. Democrat. Episcopalian. Home: 1094 Linda Ln Glencoe IL 60022-1147 Office: Abbott Labs R&D D48N AP9 Abbott Park IL 60064

SASAKI, CLARENCE TAKASHI, surgeon, medical educator; b. Honolulu, Jan. 24, 1941; s. Tsutomu and Carla Harumi (Mirikitani) S.; m. Carolyn Elizabeth Lindahl, June 26, 1967; children: Peter Gordon, John Eric. B.A., Pomona Coll., 1962; M.D., Yale U., 1966. Diplomate: Am. Bd. Otolaryngology. Intern San Francisco Hosp., U. Calif., 1966-67; resident in surgery Dartmouth Med. Sch., 1967-68; resident in otolaryngology Yale U. Med. Sch. Hosps., New Haven, 1970-73, faculty mem., 1973—, assoc. prof., 1977-82, prof. surgery, 1982—, chief sect. otolaryngology, 1981—; Charles Ohse prof. surgery Yale U. Med. Sch. Hosps., 1988—. Author: Surgery of the Skull Base, Head and Neck Surgery, Vol. 1 Atlas Otolaryngology, Vocal Fold Physiology, Laryngeal Function in Phonation and Respiration, Neurological Diseases of the Larynx; mem. editorial bd. profl. jours. Served to maj. M.C. U.S. Army, 1968-70. Recipient award Fowler Triological Soc., 1979. Mem. Am. Acad. Otolaryngology (1st prize clin. rsch.), Am. Soc. Head and Neck Surgery (coun.), Assn. Rsch. Otolaryngology, Am. Laryngol. Rhinol. and Otol. Soc. (coun., sec. ea. sect. 1990), New Eng. Otolaryngology Soc. (pres. 1987, coun.), Assn. Acad. Depts. Otolaryngology (coun.), Am. Laryngol. Assn., Pan Pacific Surg. Assn., Soc. for Neurosci., Soc. Neurovascular Surgery, Soc. for Head and Neck Surgeons, Am. Neurotolog. Soc., Pan Am. Assn. Oto-rhino-laryngology and Bronchoesophagology, Conn. Med. Soc., N.Y. Acad. Scis., Soc. Univ. Otolaryngologists, Collegium ORLAS, Cartesian Soc., Am. Bronchoesophagological Assn., N.Am. Skull Base Soc., Laryngeal. Cancer Assn. (Padua), Am. Otol. Soc., Dysphagia Rsch. Soc. (treas., pres.), Lawn Club, Mory's Club, Yale Club, Phi Beta Kappa, Sigma Xi. Office: Yale U Med Sch Dept Surgery PO Box 208041 333 Cedar St New Haven CT 06520-8041

SASAKI, TATSUO, musician; b. Okayama, Japan, Mar. 30, 1944; s. Koichi and Fumiko Sasaki; m. Shigeko Hayashi, Apr. 9, 1972; children: Jun Daniel, Maki Elisabeth. BA in Music, Tokyo U. of Arts, 1965; postgrad., Juilliard Sch. Music, 1965-67. Percussionist Am. Symphony, N.Y.C., 1966-67; solo timpanist Am. Wind Symphony, Pitts., 1966-67; asst. timpanist Israel Philharm. Orch., Tel Aviv, 1967-69; percussionist Japan Philharm. Orch., Tokyo, 1969-72; prin. timpanist Orch. Sinfonica Brazileiro, Rio de Janeiro, 1972-73, San Diego Symphony and San Diego Opera, 1973—; xylophone recitalist in U.S., Europe, Japan; spl. mem. Japan Xylophone Assn., Tokyo, 1971—; dir. Pacific Xylo-Marimba Trio, San Diego, 1974-76; dir., xylophone soloist Internat. Chamber Concert, Dusseldorf, Fed. Republic Germany, 1975—; dir. Sasaki/Rhein Brass Quintet, Dusseldorf, 1988—. Performer (album) Xylophone Artistry, 1983, (compact disk) Xylophone Artistry, Musical Heritage Soc., 1994. Fulbright scholar U.S. govt., 1965-67. Avocations: golfing, skiing, shogi (japanese chess). Home: 5842 Henley Dr San Diego CA 92120-4521 Office: San Diego Symphony 1245 7th Ave San Diego CA 92101-4302

SASENICK, JOSEPH ANTHONY, health care company executive; b. Chgo., May 18, 1940; s. Anthony E. and Caroline E. (Smicklas) S.; m. Barbara Ellen Barr, Aug. 18, 1962; children: Richard Allen, Susan Marie, Michael Joseph. BA, DePaul U., 1962; MA, U. Okla., 1966. With Miles Labs., Inc., Elkhart, Ind., 1963-70; product mgr. Alka-Seltzer, 1966-68, dir. mktg. grocery products div., 1968-70; with Gillette Corp., Boston, 1970-79; dir. new products/new ventures, personal care div. Gillette Corp., 1977; v.p. diversified cos. and pres. Jafra Cosmetics Worldwide, 1977-79; mktg. dir. Braun AG, Kronberg, W. Ger., 1970-73; chmn. mng. dir. Braun U.K. Ltd., 1973-77; with Abbott Labs., North Chicago, 1979-84; corp. v.p., pres. consumer products div. Abbott Labs., 1979-84; pres., chief exec. officer Moxie Industries, 1984-87, Personal Monitoring Technologies, Rochester, N.Y., 1987; pres. Bioline Labs., Ft. Lauderdale, Fla., 1988; mng. dir., ptnr. Vista Resource Group, Newport Beach, Calif., 1988-90; pres., CEO, Alcide Corp., Redmond, Wash., 1991-92, CEO, 1992—. Mem. Knollwood Club, El Niguel Club, Landmark Club, Wash. Athletic Club. Home: 1301 Spring St Seattle WA 98104-1354 Office: Alcide Corp 8561 154th Ave NE Redmond WA 98052-3557

SASLOW, GEORGE, psychiatrist, educator; b. N.Y.C., Dec. 5, 1906; s. Abram and Becky (Zinkoff) S.; m. Julia Amy Ipcar, July 28, 1928; children: Michael G., Rondi, Steven, Marguerite. ScB magna cum laude, Washington Sq. Coll. NYU, 1926; postgrad., U. Rochester, 1926-28; PhD in Physiology, NYU, 1931; MD cum laude, Harvard U., 1940. Instr., asst. prof. biology N.Y. U., 1928-37; vis. research asso. physiology Cornell Med. Coll., 1935-36, U. Rochester Sch. Medicine, 1936-37; research asso. physiology Harvard Sch. Pub. Health, 1937-40; neurology-neurosurgery intern Boston City

Hosp., 1940-41; resident Worcester State Hosp., 1941-42; chief resident psychiatry Mass. Gen. Hosp., Boston, 1942-43; staff Mass. Gen. Hosp., 1955-57; instr., successively asst., asso. prof., prof. pychiatry Washington U. Sch. Medicine, 1943-55; staff Barnes Hosp., St. Louis, 1943-55; practice of psychiatry, 1943—; clin. prof. psychiatry Harvard, 1955-57; prof. psychiatry U. Oreg. Med. Sch., Portland, 1957-74; head dept. U. Oreg. Med. Sch., 1957-73, prof. emeritus, 1979—; chief mental health and behavioral sci. edn., chief psychiatry service VA Hosp., Sepulveda, Calif., 1974-79; prof. psychiatry in residence UCLA, 1974-79; mem. Psychiat. Security Rev. Bd., 1983—. Nat. Tng. Labs. fellow. Fellow Am. Psychiat. Assn. (life; mem. task force on nomenclature and stats.), Am. Coll. Psychiatrists (charter); mem. AMA, Assn. for Advancment of Behavioral Therapy, Delta Soc. (bd. dirs. 1986-89). Home: 02403 SW Greenwood Rd Portland OR 97219-8394

SASMOR, JAMES CECIL, publisher representative, educator; b. N.Y.C., July 29, 1920; s. Louis and Cecilia (Mockler) S.; 1 child from previous marriage: Elizabeth Lynn; m. Jeannette L. Fuchs, May 30, 1965. BS, Columbia U., 1942; MBA, Calif. Western U., 1977, PhD, 1979. Cert. Am. Bd. Med. Psychotherapists, sex educator Am. Assn. Sex Educators, Counselors and Therapists, Healthcare Risk Mgr. Am. Inst. Med. Law, diplomate Am. Bd. Sexology. Advt. sales exec. 1946-59; registered rep. Nat. Assn. Security Dealers, 1956-57; founder, owner J.C. Sasmor Assocs. Publishers' Reps., N.Y.C., 1959-89; co-founder, pres., dir. adminstrn. Continuing Edn. Cons., Inc., 1976—; pub. cons., 1959—; clin assoc., U. So. Fla. Coll. of Medicine, 1987-89; adj. faculty Coll. Nursing, 1980-89, dir. Ednl. Counseling Comprehensive Breast Cancer Ctr., U. So. Fla. Med. Ctr., 1984-89, client librn. mental health inst., 1979-89. Team tchr. childbirth edn. Am. Soc. Childbirth Educators; bd. dirs. Tampa chpt. ARC; pres. Am. Cancer Soc. Sedona, Ariz. Unit, 1995—, co-chmn. adult edn. com.; bd. dirs. Ariz. State Divsn., mem. pub. edn. com.; county nursing ednl. cons. ARC, chmn. instrnl. com. on nursing and health, 1979-85. With USN, 1942-58, PTO; lt. USNR ret. Recipient cert. appreciation ARC, 1979, Dept. Health and Rehab. Svcs. award for Fla. Mental Health Inst. Svc., 1980, Cert. of Appreciation Am. Fgn. Svc. Assn., 1988. Internat. Coun. of Sex Edn. and Parenthood Am. U. fellow, 1981—. Mem. NAACOG (bd. dirs. Tampa chpt.), Nat. Assn. Pubs. Reps. (pres. 1965-66), Am. Soc. Psychoprophylaxis in Obstetrics (dir. 1970-71), Am. Soc. Childbirth Educators (co-founder, dir. 1972—), Internat. Coun. Women's Health Issues (chmn. resources com.), Health Edn. Media Assn., Nursing Educators Assn. Tampa, Lions (bd. dirs. Found. Ariz., pres. Sedona club). Author: Economics of Structured Continuing Education in Selected Professional Journals'; contbr. chpts. to Childbirth Education: A Nursing Perspective; contbr. articles to profl. jours. Home: 235 Arrowhead Dr Sedona AZ 86351-8900 Office: PO Box 2282 Sedona AZ 86339-2282

SASMOR, JEANNETTE LOUISE, educational consulting company executive; b. N.Y.C., May 17, 1943; d. Sol and Willmyra J. (Reilly) Fuchs; m. James C. Sasmor, May 30, 1965. BS, Columbia U., 1966, MEd, 1968, EdD, 1974; adult primary care nurse practitioner, U. Md., Balt., 1982; MBA, U. South Fla., 1990. Cert. adult primary care nurse practitioner; cert. women's health nurse practitioner; cert. risk mgr. Coord. ANA Div. Maternal Child Health, N.Y.C., 1972-73; maternal child health cons. test constrn. div. Nat. League for Nursing, N.Y.C., 1973; prof., dir. continuing nursing edn. U. South Fla., Tampa, 1973-89; v.p. and dir. edn. Continuing Edn. Cons. Inc., Tampa, Fla., 1976-89, Sedona, Ariz., 1989—; coord. maternal child health and 2d yr. nursing curriculum Yavapai Coll., Prescott, Ariz., 1994—; dir. internat. study tours USSR, 1986, New Zealand/Australia, 1990, Scandinavia, 1992, China, 1996; mem. scope practice com. Ariz. Bd. Nursing, 1994—. Author: What Every Husband Should Know About Having a Baby, 1972, Father's Labor Coaching Log and Review Book, 1972, 82, Childbirth Education: A Nursing Perspective, 1979. Del. White House Conf. on Children and Youth, 1970, White House Conf. on Families, 1980; bd. dirs. Ariz. divsn. Am. Cancer Soc., 1992—, sec., 1995-96. Am. Acad. Nursing fellow, 1977, Robert Wood Johnson Nurse faculty fellow in primary care, 1981-82; recipient NEAA Nursing Practice award Tchrs.'s Coll. Columbia U., 1992, Vol. of Yr. award Sedona-Oak Creek unit Am. Cancer. Soc., 1992. Mem. Am. Soc. Childbirth Educators (pres. 1972-78), Fla. Nurses Assn. (pres. dist. 4 1976-77), Ariz. Nurses Assn. (continuing edn. review com. 1990—), Ariz. Bd. Nursing (scope of practice com. 1994—), Lions (treas. Sedona-Oak Creek Canyon Club 1990—, Melvin Jones fellow 1996), One Good Turn Inc. (pres. 1992-95), Phi Theta Kappa (founding pres. Lambda Nu chpt. 1962, faculty advisor Beta Gamma Pi chpt. 1996—), Pi Lambda Theta, Sigma Theta Tau (chpt. treas. 1992-96, newsletter editor 1991-94, Outstanding Cmty. Leader award Lambda Omicron chpt. 1994), Kappa Delta Pi. Avocations: traveling, writing. Office: Yavapai Coll 1100 E Sheldon St Prescott AZ 86301-3220

SASS, ARTHUR HAROLD, educational executive; b. N.Y.C., Nov. 22, 1928; s. Maxwell Sigmund and Alice May (McGillick) S.; m. Eleanore G. Schmidt, Dec. 31, 1949; children: Nancy, Arlene, Susan, Eric. BS, Oswego (N.Y.) State Coll., 1949; EdM, Rutgers U., 1959, postgrad., 1960-68. Cert. chief sch. adminstr. Tchr. Millsboro (Del.) Pub. Sch. System, 1949-51, Eatontown (N.J.) Pub. Sch. System, 1955-66; coord. coop. indsl. edn. Monmouth Regional High Sch., Tinton Falls, N.J., 1966-68; prin. Mt. Holly (N.J.) Pub. Sch. System, 1968-71; supt. schs. Lumberton Twp. (N.J.) Pub. Sch. System, 1971-72, Lacey Twp. (N.J.) Pub. Sch. System, 1972-74; analyst mil. pers. Naval Sea Systems Command, Washington, 1975-79; head employee devel. Naval Rsch. Lab., Washington, 1979-83, 85-90; acad. dir. Naval Res. Engring. Duty Officer Sch., Leesburg, Va., 1983-85; pres. DEVPRO, Inc., Warrenton, Va., 1985—; prin. founder Dept. Def. Sci. and Engring. Apprentice Program; established nation's first fed. svc. high sch. coop. indsl. edn. program, 1967. Author: Guide to the Naval Ammunition Depot, 1967; editor: (brochure) Commodore John Barry-Father of the U.S. Navy, 1976. Chmn. Shade Tree Commn., Little Silver, N.J., 1968-75, Rapidan/Rappahannock (Va.) Cmty. Mental Health Ctrs., 1980-81; deacon Warrenton Ch. of Christ, 1985—, elder, 1995; mem. Va. Gov.'s Adv. Bd. for Emergency Med. Svcs., 1994—. With USN, 1952-55; capt. USNR, 1983-88. Recipient Tng. Officers' Conf. Disting. Svc. award, 1988, Outstanding Contbn. to Engring. Edn. and Rsch award George Washington U., 1991. Mem. Am. Soc. Tng. and Devel., Res. Officers Assn. (v.p. Va. chpt. 1982-83), Naval Res. Assn. (Plimsoll Mark award 1975), Am. Soc. Naval Engrs., Navy League, Wash. Acad. Scis., Tng. Dirs. Forum. Republican. Avocation: outdoor activities. Home and Office: 5268 Ambler Rd Warrenton VA 22186-9201

SASS, DONALD JAY, anesthesiologist; b. Balt., July 12, 1934; s. Albert Roy and Ruth Ellen (Smith) S.; m. Elizabeth Anne Bridges, Aug. 15, 1959 (div. Aug. 4, 1976); children: David J., Christin L. Sass Cross, Elizabeth A.; m. Eleanor Elsie Perry, Oct. 6, 1978. BS, Johns Hopkins U., 1955, MS, 1957; MD, Stanford U. Sch. Medicine, 1964. Diplomate Am. Bd. Anesthesiologists, Nat. Bd. Med. Examiners. Fellow in physiology Mayo Grad. Sch. Medicine, Rochester, Minn., 1968-72; head biophysics dept. Naval Med. Rsch. Inst., Bethesda, Md., 1972-76; resident in anesthesia U.S. Naval Hosp., Bethesda, 1976-78; fellow in cardiac anesthesia Mass. Gen. Hosp., Boston, 1978-79; asst. chief anesthesia U.S. Naval Hosp., 1979-81, chief anesthesia, 1981-84; chief anesthesia Kaiser Permanente Hosp., Oakland, Calif., 1984-94; staff anesthesiologist, sr. physician Kaiser Permanente Hosp., 1994—; assoc. prof. Uniformed Svcs. Health Scis., Bethesda, 1979-84. Capt. U.S. Navy, 1964-84. Mem. Am. Soc. Anesthesiologists, Calif. Soc. Anesthesiologists, Calif. Med. Assn. Republican. Avocations: collecting antique Jaguars and MGs. Home: 6353 Ascot Dr Oakland CA 94611 Office: Kaiser Permanente Hosp 280 W MacArthur Blvd Oakland CA 94611

SASS, RONALD LEWIS, biology and chemistry educator; b. Davenport, Iowa, May 26, 1932; s. Erwin Leese and Flora Alice (Puck) S.; m. Joyce R. Moorhead, 1951 (div. 1968); children: Dennise, Andria; m. Margaret Lee Macy, Apr. 4, 1969; children: Hartley, Dennis. BA, Augustana Coll., Rock Island, Ill., 1954; PhD, U. So. Calif., L.A., 1957. Chemist U.S. Army, Rock Island (Ill.) Arsenal, 1951-54; asst. prof. Rice U., Houston, 1958-62, assoc. prof., 1962-66, prof., 1966—, chmn. biology, 1981-87; co-dir. Rice Ctr. for Edn., Houston, 1988—; chair Rice Earth Sys. Inst., Houston, 1990—, Ecology and Evolutionary Biology, 1995—; cons. EPA, Washington, 1990—, Coll. Bd., N.Y.C., 1988—. Contbr. articles on chemistry, biology and biochemistry to profl. jours. NSF predoctoral fellow U. So. Calif., 1954-57, fellow AEC, 1957-58, Guggenheim fellow, 1965, sr. rsch. fellow NRC, 1988. Mem. Internat. Geospher-Biosphere Program (com. chair 1990—). Avocations: tennis, fishing. Home: 2406 Wordsworth St Houston TX 77030-1834 Office: Rice U Ecology & Evolutionary Biology Houston TX 77251

SASSAMAN, ANNE PHILLIPS, science administrator; b. La Grange, Ga., Jan. 7, 1944; d. Joe and Bessie (Lewis) Phillips; m. John Robert Ball, Aug. 13, 1966 (div.); children: Kristen Anne, John Robert; m. Jan Frederick Sassaman, Oct. 1, 1983. BS with honors, Auburn U., 1965; PhD, Duke U., 1970. Rsch. assoc. depts. surgery, medicine, biochemistry Duke U., Durham, N.C., 1970-74; rsch. chemist FDA, Bethesda, Md., 1974-76; scientist-adminstr. Nat. Heart, Lung & Blood Inst., Bethesda, 1976-79, chief blood diseases br., 1979-86; dir. div. extramural rsch. and tng. Nat. Inst. Environ. Health Scis., NIH, Research Triangle Park, N.C., 1986—. Contbr. rsch. articles on biochemistry of thrombosis and thrombolysis to sci. jours. Mem. exec. com. coun. on thrombosis Am. Heart Assn., Dallas, 1979-86; mem. exec. bd. Am. Field Svc., Chapel Hill, N.C., 1989-92; vol. Am. Heart Assn., March of Dimes. Mem. AAAS, Am. Soc. Hematology, Internat. Soc. Thrombosis and Haemostatis, N.C. Soc. Toxicology, Assn. for Women in Sci., Sigma Xi. Democrat. Methodist. Home: 534 Caswell Rd Chapel Hill NC 27514-2704 Office: Nat Inst Environ Health Scis PO Box 12233 Durham NC 27709-2233

SASSAMAN, PAULA, reading specialist; b. Harrisburg, Pa., Nov. 2, 1943; d. Charles and R. Pauline Huggins; m. James H. Sassaman, Apr. 8, 1967; children: Craig, David, Joseph. BS in Elem. Edn., Millersville (Pa.) U., 1966; MEd, Shippensburg (Pa.) U., 1969. Cert. elem. tchr., reading specalist and supr., reading recovery tchr., Pa. Elem. tchr. Susquenita Sch. Dist., Duncannon, Pa., 1966-69, reading specialist, 1969-71; reading specialist West Perry Sch. Dist., Elliottsburg, Pa., 1987—, reading recovery tchr., 1993—; presenter in field. Sunday sch. thcr., historian Otterbein United Meth. Ch., Duncannon; booster Susquenita H.S. Band, Duncannon, 1988; mem. cmty. liaison adv. com. to Susquenita Sch. Bd.; vol. Alliance for Acid Rain Monitoring, 1986—. Recipient lead tchr. award South Ctrl. Pa. Lead Tchr. Ctr., 1992. Mem. ASCD, NEA, Pa. Edn. Assn., West Perry Edn. Assn., Internat. Reading Assn., Audubon Soc., Perry Historians. Avocations: genealogy, gardening, nature appreciation, reading. Office: Blain Elem Sch Box 38 Main St Blain PA 17006

SASSEEN, ROBERT FRANCIS, university president; b. Bklyn., June 6, 1932; s. Robert B. and Teresa M. (Regan) S.; divorced; children: Robert V., Christopher J., Patricia M., Timothy P., Katherine A. BA in Polit. Sci, U. Notre Dame, Ill., 1957; MA, U. Chgo., 1959, PhD, 1961. Instr. polit. sci. Marquette U., Milw., 1960-62; asst. prof. honors div. U. Santa Clara, Calif., 1962-65; from lectr. to prof. polit. sci. San Jose (Calif.) State U., 1965-72, chmn. dept., 1971-72, assoc. acad. v.p., dean faculty, 1972-81; pres. U. Dallas, 1981—. Author articles in field. With AUS, 1951-54. Mem. Legatus Club. Roman Catholic. Office: U Dallas Office of Pres 1845 E Northgate Dr Irving TX 75062-4736

SASSER, JAMES RALPH (JIM SASSER), ambassador, former senator; b. Memphis, TN, Sept. 30, 1936; s. Joseph Ralph and Mary Nell (Gray) S.; m. Mary Gorman, Aug. 18, 1962; children: Gray, Elizabeth. Student, U. Tenn., 1954-55; BA, Vanderbilt U., 1958, LLB, 1961. Bar: Tenn. 1961. Ptnr. Goodpasture, Carpenter, Woods & Sasser, Nashville, 1961-76; chmn. Tenn. Dem. Party, 1973-76; mem. U.S. Senate from Tenn., 1977-1994; U.S. Ambassador to China U.S. State Dept., Beijing, China, 1996—. Chmn. Tenn. State Dem. Exec. Com., 1973-76; so. vice chmn. Assn. Dem. State Chmn., 1975-76. Served with USMCR, 1958-65. Mem. ABA, NCCJ (dir. Nashville chpt.), UN Assn., Nashville Com. Fgn. Relations, Am. Judicature Soc. *

SASSER, WILLIAM JACK, government official; b. Arcadia, Okla., Aug. 12, 1934; children: Sam, Steve, Susan, Sandra. BS in Sociology and Psychology, Okla. Bapt. U., 1956; postgrad., S.W. Bapt. Sem., 1957-60, George Washington U., 1966. Lic. comml. pilot with instrument rating. Air traffic control specialist S.W. region FAA Air Route Traffic Control Ctr., Ft. Worth, 1963-65, pers. officer, 1970-71; tech. intern FAA, Washington, 1965-66; employee devel. officer S.W. region FAA, Houston and Ft. Worth, 1966-70; chief tng. br. pers. div. Gt. Lakes region FAA, Des Plaines, Ill., 1971-73; with exec. devel. program Gt. Lakes and ctrl. regions FAA, Des Plaines, Kansas City, Mo., 1973-75; asst. chief airports div. ctrl. region FAA, Kansas City, 1975-76, mgr., 1977-87; mgr. airports div. S.W. region FAA, Ft. Worth, 1987-89, dep. regional adminstr. S.W. region, 1989-95; ret. S.W. region, 1995; pvt. cons. Decatur, 1995—. Home: RR 1 Box 314 Decatur TX 76234-9740

SASSO, CASSANDRA GAY, lawyer; b. Washington, Feb. 5, 1946; d. Phillip Francis and Lois Aileen (Ayers) S.; m. David John Stephenson, Jr., Feb. 12, 1982; 1 child, Gabriel David. BS magna cum laude, U. Nebr., 1967; MA, U. Calif., Santa Barbara, 1970; JD, Northwestern U., 1974. Bar: Ill., 1974, Colo., 1976. Law clk. Schiff Hardin & Waite, Chgo., 1973; assoc. Sidley & Austin, Chgo., 1974-75; instr. antitrust and securities U. Denver Law Sch., 1978-79, 1985-87; instr. trial practice U. Colo. Law Sch., Boulder, 1983-86; instr. Nat. Inst. Trial Advocacy, 1985—; ptnr., trial lawyer Sherman & Howard, Denver, 1976-91; ptnr. Kutak Rock, Denver, 1991-96; ptnr. Baker & Hostetler, Denver, 1996—. Bd. dirs. Colo. Jud. Inst., 1982-88, v.p. 1984; bd. dirs. Colo. Lawyers Com., Denver, 1980-82, Legal Aid Soc. of Met. Denver, 1981-83; mem. Denver Com. Fgn. Rels., 1981—; chmn. bd. dirs. Colo. ACLU, Denver, 1982-83; mem. steering com. Colo. Lawyers for Nuclear Arms Edn., Denver, 1982-83. Mem. Colo. Womens Bar Assn., Colo. Bar Assn. (bd. govs. 1980-83, ethics com. 1986-95), ABA (securities litigation com. 1988—), Chgo. Council Lawyers (sec. 1974-75), Denver Bar Assn. (bd. trustees 1978-81), Colo. Trial Lawyers Assn. (bd. dirs. 1984-85), Alpha Omicron Pi, Mortar Bd. Democrat. Presbyterian. Home: 108 S Dexter Denver CO 80222 Office: Baker & Hostetler 303 E 17th Ave Ste 1100 Denver CO 80203

SASSO, SANDY, rabbi; b. Phila., Jan. 29, 1947; d. Israel and Freda (Plotrick) Eisenberg; m. Dennis Sasso, June 25, 1970; children: David Aryeh, Debora Shoshana. BA magna cum laude, Temple U., 1969, MA in Religion, 1972. Ordained rabbi, 1974. Rsch. assoc. Jewish Reconstructionist Found., N.Y.C., 1974-76; rabbi Congregation Beth-El Zedeck, Indpls., 1977—; lectr. Jewish Welfare Bd. Lecture Bur., 1972-77. Bd. dirs. Julian Mission, 1978-79; mem. adm. coun. Women's Health Resource Ctr., 1983—. Recipient Woman of Yr. award Brith Sholom Women, 1975. Mem. Reconstructionist Rabbinical Assn. (pres. Wyncote, Pa. chpt.), Nat. Coun. Jewish Women (edn. and pub. affairs coms.), N.Y. Bd. Rabbis, Coalition for Alternatives in Jewish Edn., NCCJ (exec. bd. 1978-79). Office: Reconstructionist Rabbinical Church Rd Greenwood Ave Wyncote PA 19095

SATA, LINDBERGH SABURO, psychiatrist, physician, educator; b. Portland, Oreg., Jan. 6, 1928; s. Charles Kazuo and Ito (Kojima) S.; m. Yuriko Kodama, Aug. 19, 1956; children: Roberta, Camille, Holly, John. BS, U. Utah, 1951, MD, 1958, MS, 1964. Intern U. Utah Coll. Medicine, Salt Lake Gen. Hosp., 1958-59, resident in psychiatry, 1959-62, chief resident in psychiatry, 1961-62; adminstrv. chief resident neurology U. Utah Coll. Medicine, VA Hosp., Salt Lake City, 1960-61; fellow Inst. for Mental Retardation, Letchworth Village, Thiells, N.Y., 1962; intern Behavioral Sci. Intern Program Nat. Tng. Labs., Bethel, Maine, 1966; instr. U. Utah, 1962-64; asst. prof. The Psychiat. Inst. U. Md., Balt., 1964-67, assoc. prof., 1967-68; assoc. prof. U. Wash., Seattle, 1968-77, asst. dean, 1969-70, prof., 1975-78; prof., chmn. St. Louis U. Sch. Medicine, 1978-94, prof. emeritus, chmn. emeritus, 1994—. Fellow Am. Coll. Psychiatrists, Am. Psychiat. Assn., Pacific Rim Coll. Psychiatrists (founding); mem. Am. Assn. for Social Psychiatry. Office: 1606 Riverview Dr NE Auburn WA 98002-3054

SATCHER, DAVID, public health service officer, federal official; b. Anniston, Ala., Mar. 2, 1941; s. Wilmer and Anna S; m. Nola; children: Gretchen, David, Daraka, Daryl. BS, Morehouse Coll., 1963; MD, PhD, Case Western Reserve Univ., 1970. Pres. Meharry Med. Coll., Nashville; now dir. Centers for Disease Control and Prevention, Atlanta, 1993—. Office: Ctr Disease Control & Prevention 1600 Clifton Rd NE Bdlg 16 Atlanta GA 30333*

SATCHLER, GEORGE RAYMOND, physicist; b. London, June 14, 1926; came to U.S., 1959; s. George Cecil and Georgina Lillie (Strange) S.; m. Margaret Patricia Gibson, Mar. 27, 1948; children: Patricia Ann, Jacqueline Helen. BA, Oxford U., 1951, MA, 1951, D Phil., 1955, DSc, 1989. Research fellow Clarendon Lab., Oxford U., 1954-59, 71; research assoc. physics dept. U. Mich., 1956-57; physicist Oak Ridge Nat. Lab., 1959—, assoc. dir. physics div., 1967-74, theoretical physics dir., 1974-76, distinguished research staff mem., 1976—. Author: (with D.M. Brink) Angular Momentum, 1962, Introduction to Nuclear Reactions, 1980, Direct Nuclear Reactions, 1983; contbr. research articles to profl. jours. Served with RAF, 1944-48. Corp. rsch. fellow, 1976—. Fellow Am. Phys. Soc. (mem. exec. com. nuclear physics div. 1974-75, T.W. Bonner prize 1977). Home: 973 W Outer Dr Oak Ridge TN 37830-8608

SATER, WILLIAM FREDERICK, history educator, writer; b. N.Y.C., Nov. 17, 1937; 1 child, Rachel Mayen. AB in History, Stanford U., 1959; MA, UCLA, 1964, PhD, 1968. Prof. history Calif. State U., Long Beach, 1967—; cons. Rand Corp., Calif., 1977-90, Mellon Fellowship Found., 1982-88, NEH, 1983, ABC Cilo, 1985—, Libr. Congress, 1988—; book rev. editor The New World, 1984-90; guest lectr. Peace Corps, L.A., 1967, U. Chile, Santiago, 1968, UCLA, 1972, U. Concepcion, Chile, 1975, Cath. U., Santiago, 1980, U. Calgary, 1983, 87, 96, Western Can. Mil. Soc., 1983, 96; papers presented at Am. Hist. Assn., 1972, 76, Pacific Coast Conf. L.Am. History, 1972, Nat. Assn. Pvt. Schs., 1983, Conf. on Independence of Mex., U. Calif., Irvine, 1987, Can. Hist. Assn., 1990, 94, Rocky Mountain Conf. L.Am. History, Soc. for Mil. History, Ont., 1993. Editor, assoc. editor, book rev. editor The History Tchr., 1972-85; mng. editor TVI Report, 1984—; author: The Revolutionary Left and Terrorist Violence in Chile, 1986, Puerto Rican Terrorists: A Possible Threat to U.S. Energy Installations?, 1981, The Heroic Image in Chile, 1973, The History Teacher, 1981, The Research Guide to Andean History, 1981, The Southern Cone Nations, 1984, Chile and the War of the Pacific, 1986, Chile and the United States, 1990, A General History of Chile, 1996; contbr. articles to profl. jours. 1st lt. U.S. Army, 1959-60. Fellow U. Calif.-U. Chile, 1965-66, Orgn. Am. States, 1974-75; recipient Barros Arana Internat. Contest on Chilean History, Chilean Hist. Assn., 1984. Mem. Chilean Acad. History (corr.), Pacific Coast of L.Am. Studies (bd. govs., Hubert Herring award), Conf. on L.Am. History (chmn. com. teaching and teaching materials, chmn. andean studies com., acting chmn. Rio de la Plata com.), Am. Hist. Assn. Office: Calif State U Dept History Long Beach CA 90840

SATHE, SHARAD SOMNATH, chemical company executive; b. Bombay, Oct. 10, 1940; came to U.S., 1967; s. Somnath Waman and Kamala S. (Bhave) S. m. Usha Moreshwar Tamhankar, Feb. 6, 1966; children: Vandana, Swapna. BS, U. Bombay, 1960; B in Pharmacy, Banaras Hindu U., 1963; PhD, Ind. U., 1971. Rsch. asst. CIBA Rsch. Ctr., Bombay, 1964-67; postdoctoral fellow Rsch. Triangle Inst., Raleigh, N.C., 1971-73; rsch. chemist Mallinckrodt, Inc., St. Louis, 197-379, tech. supr., 1979-81, group leader, 1981-87, mgr. R & D, 1989-94; assoc. dir. rsch., 1995—. Patentee in field; contbr. articles to profl. jours. Pres. India Student Assn., Bloomington, Ind., 1969-70; mem. bd. of trustees India Assn. of St. Louis, 1980-85; pres. Sangeetha, St. Louis, 1986-87. Fellow Am. Inst. Chemistry, N.Y. Acad. Scis.; mem. Am. Chem. Soc. Avocations: music, tennis, reading. Office: Mallinckrodt Inc 2nd & Mallinckrodt St Saint Louis MO 63147

SATHER, EVERETT NORMAN, accountant; b. Story City, Iowa, July 20, 1935; s. George John and Laura Josephine (Bakka) S.; m. Patricia Ann Johnson, Apr. 24, 1955; children: Kimberly L., Kristine J., Kendall D. Student, Am. Inst. Bus., Des Moines, 1953-55. CPA, Iowa, Nebr., Ill. Office mgr. Story Polk Farm Svc., Nevada, Iowa, 1955-57; office mgr., bookeeper Capital City Electric Co., Des Moines, 1958-59; staff acct. Willard C. Randol, CPA, Des Moines, 1959-60, Ryun, Givens and Co., Des Moines, 1960-63; acct. Everett N. Sather, CPA, Des Moines, 1963-66; acct., ptnr. Denman and Co., Des Moines, 1966—; pres., chmn. Ankeny (Iowa) Nat. Bank, 1972-82; pres. Triple K Ltd., Ankeny, 1983—, Boone (Iowa) Speedways, Inc., 1976—. Active Polk County Bd. Rev., Des Moines, 1970—; chmn. bd. Greater Des Moines Aviation Expo, 1989-95; treas. Des Moines Grand Prix, 1988-94; bd. dirs. Care Initiatives, 1995—. Mem. AICPA, Ill. Soc. CPAs, Iowa Soc. CPAs, Rotary (bd. dirs. 1990-93, pres. 1994-95), Zagszig Shrine, Scottish Rite, MAsons. Lutheran. Avocation: sports. Office: Denman and Co 1601 22nd St Ste 400 West Des Moines IA 50266-1408

SATHER, GLEN CAMERON, professional hockey team executive, coach; b. High River, Alta., Canada, Sept. 2, 1943. Former professional hockey player; pres., gen. mgr. Edmonton Oilers, Nat. Hockey League, Alta., Can., coach, 1977-89, now alt. gov.; coach winning team in Stanley Cup competition, 1987. Recipient Jack Adams Award for NHL Coach of the Yr., 1986. Office: care Edmonton Oilers, Edmonton Coliseum, Edmonton, AB Canada T5B 4M9*

SATHRE, LEROY, mathematics educator, consultant; b. Cleve., June 4, 1936; s. Louis and Hazel Irene (Pletcher) S.; m. B. Ann Sathre, May 30, 1968 (div. May 1983); m. Winona Sechrist, Aug. 30, 1984. BA, DePauw U., 1958; MS, U. Fla., 1960; postgrad., U. Calif., Santa Barbara, 1963-65. Reliability engr. N.Am. Aviation, Downey, Calif., 1960-62; statistician Gen. Electric Co., Daytona Beach, Fla., 1965-67; instr. St. Johns River Jr. Coll., Palatka, Fla., 1968-70; prof. Valencia C.C., Orlando, Fla., 1970-94, dept. chmn., 1994—; pres. faculty senate Valencia City Coll., 1974-75; sec., treas. United Community Coll. Faculty of Fla., Tallahassee, 1976-80; textbook reviewer various pubs. Mem. Math. Assn. Am., Fla. Math. Assn. of Two Yr. Colls., Am. Math. Assn. Two Yr. Colls. Democrat. Methodist. Office: Valencia Community Coll 701 N Econlockhatchee Trl Orlando FL 32825-6404

SATHYAMOORTHY, MUTHUKRISHNAN, engineering researcher, educator; b. Sathanur, Tamil Nadu, India, Feb. 21, 1946; s. Kuppusamy and Visalakshi Muthukrishnan; m. Chitra Subbiah, May 26, 1971; children: Mohanakrishnan, Kumaran. B in Civil Engring., U. Madras, India, 1967; M in Engring. Mechanics, Indian Inst. of Tech., Madras, India, 1969, PhD in Aero. Engring., 1973. Lectr. Indian Inst. of Tech., Madras, India, 1969-74; rsch. fellow U. Birmingham, Eng., 1974-76; asst. prof. Clarkson U., Potsdam, N.Y., 1979-82, assoc. prof., 1982-92, assoc. prof., exec. officer, 1992-94, prof., exec. officer, 1994—; vis. rsch. faculty U. Calgary, Can., 1977-79. Contbn. author: Handbook of Civil Engineering Practice, 1988; editor: Material Nonlinearity in Vibrations, 1985. Recipient Appreciation cert. U.S. Army, 1990, Outstanding Advisor award Clarkson U., 1993. Fellow ASME (mem. nat. student sect. com. 1992-94, mem. gen. awards com. 1994—, Nat. Faculty Advisor award 1993); AIAA (assoc.), Aero. Soc. India. Avocations: overseas travel, camping, photography, fishing. Home: 177 Regan Rd Potsdam NY 13676 Office: Clarkson U Dept Mech & Aeronautical Engr Mech Engring Dept Potsdam NY 13699-5725

SATIN, JOSEPH, language professional, university administrator; b. Phila., Dec. 16, 1920; s. Reuben Philip and Harriet (Price) S.; m. Selma Rosen (dec. 1978); children: Mark, Diane; m. Barbara Jeanne Dodson (dec. 1987); m. Terrye Sagan, 1992. BA, Temple U., 1946; AM, Columbia U., 1948, PhD, 1952. Instr. integrated studies W.Va. U., Morgantown, 1952-54; prof. English and Comparative Lit. Moorhead (Minn.) State U., 1954-63; chmn. dept. English and Journalism Midwestern U., Wichita Falls, Tex., 1963-73; dean Sch. Arts and Humanities Calif. State U., Fresno, 1973-89; mgr. concert series Moorhead State U., 1956-61; mem. nat. bd. cons. NEH, Washington, 1979—; dir. London semester Calif. State U., Fresno, 1982-92, dir. Frank Lloyd Wright Auditorium project. Author: Ideas in Context, 1958, The 1950's: America's "Placid" Decade, 1960, Reading Non-Fiction Prose, 1964, Reading Prose Fiction, 1964, Reading Drama, 1964, Reading Poetry, 1964, Shakespeare and His Sources, 1966, Reading Literature, 1968, The Humanities Handbook (2 Vols.), 1969; editor: Frank Lloyd Wright-Letters to Apprentices, 1982, Letters to Architects, 1984, Letters to Clients, 1986, Treasures of Taliesin, 1985, The Guggenheim Correspondence, 1986, Frank Lloyd Wright: His Living Voice, 1987, Frank Lloyd Wright, The Crowning Decade, 1989; translator: Federico Fellini, Comments on Film, 1987; contbr. to Ency. Internat. Edn., 1978; dir. Univ. Press, Calif. State U., 1982-92. Served with U.S. Army, 1943-46, ETO. Jewish. Avocations: creative writing, music, parcheesi. Home: 65 Maywood Dr San Francisco CA 94127-2007

SATINE, BARRY ROY, lawyer; b. N.Y.C., July 25, 1951; s. Norman S. and Fay (Mekles) S.; m. Janice Bea Halfond, Aug. 4, 1974; children: David,

Leah. B.A., CCNY, 1972; J.D., George Washington U., 1975. Bar: N.Y. 1976, D.C. 1977, U.S. Dist. Ct. (so. dist.) N.Y. 1978, U.S. Supreme Ct. 1979, U.S. Dist. Ct. (ea. dist.) N.Y. 1982, U.S. Ct. Appeals (2d cir.) 1989. Trial atty. U.S. Civil Service Commn., Washington, 1975-78; atty. AT&T, N.Y.C., 1978-81, N.Y. Tel. Co., N.Y.C., 1981-82; mem. assoc. Surrey & Morse, N.Y.C., 1982-84, ptnr., 1985; ptnr. Jones, Day, Reavis & Pogue, 1986—. Mem. ABA (litigation sect., internat. litigation com.), Assn. of Bar of City of N.Y. (litigation com.). Office: Jones Day Reavis & Pogue 599 Lexington Ave New York NY 10022-6030

SATINOVER, JEFFREY B., psychiatrist, health science facility administrator, lecturer, author; b. Chgo., Sept. 4, 1947; s. Joseph and Sena (Rotman) S.; m. Julie Rachel Leff, June 10, 1982; Sarah Katherine, Anne-Rebecca, Jenny Leigh. BS, MIT, 1971; EdM, Harvard U., 1973; MD, U. Tex., 1982; Diplomate, C.G Jung Institute, Zurich, Switzerland, 1976. Diplomate Am. Bd. Psychiatry and Neurology, added qualifications in geriatric psychiatry. Fellow dept. psychiatry and child psychiatry Yale U., New Haven, 1982-86; founder, exec. dir. Sterling Inst., Stamford, Conn., 1985-92; med. dir. Temenos Inst., Westport, Conn., 1984—; pvt. practice, Westport, 1992—; mem. pastoral care ministries, pres., bd. dirs. C.G. Jung Found. N.Y., 1988-92; bd. dirs., mem. catchment area coun. S.W. Regional Mental Health Bd., 1988-92; William James lectr. psychology and religion Harvard U., 1975; mem. Lower Fairfield County Regional Action Coun. Against Substance Abuse, 1990-92. Author: Homosexuality and the Politics of Truth, 1994, The Empty Self: Gnostic Foundations of Modern Identity, 1994, Feathers of the Skylark, 1995; contbg. author: Jungian Psychotherapy, 1984, Science and the Fragile Self, 1990, Jungian Analysis, 1992; contbr. articles to profl. and pub. policy jours. Founder, mem. exec. bd. com. Save Our Schs., 1994—; bd. dirs. Towrd Tradition; trustee, pres. Family Inst. Conn., 1994-96; active nat. physician's resource coun. Focus on Family; bd. dirs. Klingberg Family Ctrs., 1994-96. Capt. USAR N.G., 1989-94; maj. USAR, 1995—. Recipient Seymour Lustman Rsch. award Yale U., 1983, 85. Mem. AMA, Am. Psychiat. Assn. (Burroughs-Wellcome fellow 1983-85), Am. Psychosomatic Soc., Am. Acad. Psychomatics, Internat. Assn. Analytical Psychology (diplomate), Aspetuck Valley Country Club, Alpha Omega Alpha. Republican. Jewish. Avocations: tennis, harpsichord, jazz keyboard. Home: 38 Steep Hill Rd Weston CT 06883-1822 Office: 29 E Main St Westport CT 06880-3749

SATINSKAS, HENRY ANTHONY, airline services company executive; b. Kaunas, Lithuania, Dec. 22, 1936; came to U.S., 1949; s. Henry Francis and Donna (Olechnavicius) S.; m. Lucia Aldona Sestakauskas, Dec. 7, 1963; children: Henry Arnold, Paul Steven (dec.), Laura Monica. Student, Drexel U., 1957-60; BS in Bus. Adminstrn., Temple U., 1963. Mgmt. trainee Pub. Service Coordinated Transp., Maplewood, N.J., 1964; asst. garage supr. Jersey City, 1965-66; charter service mgr. Suburban Transit Corp., New Brunswick, N.J., 1966-68; gen. mgr. Ave B and E Byway Transit Co., N.Y.C., 1968-71, St. John's (Newfoundland, Can.) Transp. Commn., 1971-73; asst. dir. transp. planning Montgomery County Govt., Rockville, Md., 1973-76; gen. mgr. Airway Limousine Service subs. Hudson Gen. Corp., Balt., 1976-78; dir. transp. services Airway Services subs. Hudson Gen. Corp., Jamaica, N.Y., 1978-81; v.p. Hudson Gen. Corp., Great Neck, N.Y., 1981—. Mem. adv. coun. on edn. Province of Newfoundland and Labrador, St. John's, 1972; bd. dirs. Greater Jamaica Devel. Corp., 1987-90. Republican. Roman Catholic. Avocations: reading, gardening, travel, biking. Home: 35 Woodvale Dr Syosset NY 11791-1213 Office: Hudson Gen Corp 111 Great Neck Rd Great Neck NY 11021-5402

SATINSKY, BARNETT, lawyer; b. Phila., June 17, 1947; s. Alex and Florence (Talsky) S.; m. Fredda Andrea Wagner, June 17, 1973; children: Meagen, Sara Beth, Jonathan. AB, Brown U., 1969; JD, Villanova U., 1972. Bar: Pa. 1972, U.S. Dist. Ct. (ea. dist) Pa. 1975, U.S. Dist. Ct. (mid. dist.) Pa. 1975, U.S. Ct. Appeals (3d cir.) 1981. Law clk. Phila. Ct. Common Pleas, 1972-73; dep. atty. gen. Pa. Dept. Justice, Harrisburg, 1973-75; 1st asst. counsel Pa. Pub. Utility Commn., Harrisburg, 1975-77, chief counsel, 1977; assoc. Fox, Rothschild, O'Brien & Frankel, Phila., 1978-81, ptnr., 1981—. Children Svcs. Rev. com., United Way Southeast Pa., 1984-86; bd. dirs. ACLU, Harrisburg, 1973-74, Voyage House, Inc., 1994—. Mem. ABA (pub. utility, labor and employment law sects., employee benefits com. 1984—), Pa. Bar Assn. (labor rels., pub. utility law sects. 1980—, pub. utility law com., governing coun. 1991-93), Phila. Bar Assn. (labor law pub. utility law coms. 1980—, chmn. pub. utility law com. 1988-91), Nat. Assn. Coll. and Univ. Attys., Nat. Assn. Regulatory Commrs. (staff subcom. law 1977), Soc. for Human Resource Mgmt., Tau Epsilon Law Soc. Democrat. Jewish. Office: Fox Rothschild O'Brien & Frankel 2000 Market St Philadelphia PA 19103-3291

SATO, EUNICE NODA, former mayor, consultant; b. Livingston, Calif., June 8, 1921; d. Bunsaku and Sawa (Maeda) Noda; m. Thomas Takashi Sato, Dec. 9, 1950; children—Charlotte Patricia, Daniel Ryuichi and Douglas Ryuji (twins). AA, Modesto Jr. Coll., 1941; BA, U. No. Colo., 1944; MA, Columbia U., 1948. Public sch. tchr. Mastodon Twp. Schs., Alpha, Mich., 1944-47; ednl. missionary Reformed Ch. Am., Yokohama, Japan, 1948-51; coun. mem. City of Long Beach, Calif., 1975-86; mayor, 1980-82; sec. corp. bd. Los Angeles County Health Systems Agy., 1978-79. Monthly contbr. articles to 2 neighborhood papers, 1975-86. Bd. dirs. Long Beach chpt. ARC, 1975—, mem. exec. com., 1978-91, 93—, past pres. and v.p., mem. Calif. state svc. coun., 1995—; bd. dirs. Goodwill Industries, 1978-82 ; trustee St. Mary's Bauer Med. Ctr., 1977—; pres. Industry Edn. Coun., Long Beach, 1984-86, mem. exec. bd., 1984—; bd. dirs. Industry Edn. Coun. of Calif., treas. So. Calif. Consortium of I.E.C., 1986-87, pres., 1988-89; mem. State Adv. Group on Juvenile Justice and Delinquency Prevention, 1983-91, Calif. Coun. Criminal Justice, 1983-95, legis. com. Girl Scout coun. Calif., 1986-92, chair, 1991-92; bd. dirs. Long Beach council Girl Scouts U.S., 1986-92, Region III United Way, 1974-88; mem. Asian Pacific adv. com. Calif. Dept. Rehab., 1985-87, recreation commn. City of Long Beach, 1985-86, pub. safety policy com. League Calif. Cities, 1981-86, community econ. and housing devel. com. So. Calif. Assn. Govts., 1976-86, Calif. Task Force to Promote Self-Esteem and Personal and Social Responsibility, 1987-90; Long Beach chpt. pres. NCCJ, 1987-88; pres. Internat. Community Coun., 1986-87, Japanese Am. Reps., 1987, 88; presdl. appointee Nat. Adv. Coun. Ednl. Rsch. and Improvement, 1991-94; pres. Aux. to Sch. Theology, Claremont, 1990-91, exec. bd. 1989-91; chair selection com. Leadership Long Beach, 1990-91, sec. exec. bd., 1991-92; chair adv. bd. AIESEC, 1990-92, Long Beach Area Rep. Party, 1990-92; mem. cen. com., L.A.; sec.-gen. coun. on fin. and administrn. United Meth. Ch., 1992—; appointed by Gov. to commn. on teacher credentialing State Calif., 1994; chair adminstrv. bd. Leisure World Cmty. Ch., 1996; rep. to South Coast Ecumenical Coun., 1993—. Recipient Outstanding Svc. award Long Beach Coord. Coun., 1969, Mother of Yr. award Silverado United Meth. Ch., 1973, Hon. Svc. award Calif. PTA, 1963, Continuing Svc. award, 1974, hon. life membership award Nat. PTA, 1974, Outstanding Laywoman of Yr. award Long Beach Area Coun. Chs., 1976, Woman of Yr. award State Women's Coun.-C. of C., 1979, Long Beach Iternat. Bus. and Profl. Women's Club, Nat. Merit award DAR, 1982, Citizen of Yr. award Los Altos YMCA, 1982, Calif. Cmty. Pool for Handicapped, 1982, Outstanding Citizen award Torch Club of Long Beach, 1983, W. Odie Wright award Industry Edn. Coun., 1990, Humanitarian award NCCJ, 1992, Vol. of Yr. award ARC, 1st Life Membership award Long Beach chpt. UN Assn. Mem. Alpha Iota (hon.). Republican. Methodist. Home: Bixby Village 551-101 Pittsfield Ct Long Beach CA 90803

SATO, GLENN KENJI, lawyer; b. Honolulu, Jan. 6, 1952; s. Nihei and Katherine (Miwa) S.; m. Donna Mae Shiroma, Apr. 4, 1980 (dec. Aug. 1985); m. Nan Sun Oh, Mar. 27, 1987; children: Gavan, Allison, Garrett. BBA, U. Hawaii, 1975; JD, U. Calif., San Francisco, 1977. Bar: Hawaii 1978, U.S. Dist. Ct. Hawaii, 1978, U.S. Ct. Claims 1990. Assoc. Fujiyama, Duffy & Fujiyama, Honolulu, 1978-80, 83-87, ptnr., 1987-95; stockholder Law Offices of Glenn K. Sato, Honolulu, 1980-82; pres. ISL Svcs., Inc., Honolulu, 1983; ptnr. Sato & Thomas, Honolulu, 1995—; vice chmn. Pattern Jury Instrn. Com., State of Hawaii, Honolulu, 1993. Treas. Polit. Action Com., Honolulu, 1993. Mem. Beta Gamma Sigma. Avocations: golf, hunting, target shooting, surfing. Office: Sato & Thomas Ste 770 1001 Bishop St Honolulu HI 96813-3429

SATO, HIROSHI, materials science educator; b. Matsuzaka, Mie, Japan, Aug. 31, 1918; came to U.S., 1954; s. Masayoshi and Fusae (Ohhara) S.; m. Kyoko Amemiya, Jan. 10, 1947; children: Norie M., Nobuyuki Albert, Erika Michiko. BS, Hokkaido Imperial U., Sapparo, Japan, 1938, MS, 1941; DSc, Tokyo U., 1951. Rsch. assoc. faculty sci. Hokkaido Imperial U., Sapparo, 1941-42, asst. prof. Inst. Low Temperature Sci., 1942-43; rsch. physicist Inst. Phys. and Chem. Rsch., Tokyo, 1943-45; prof. Tohoku Imperial U., Sendai, Japan, 1945-57; rsch. physicist Westinghouse Rsch. Labs., Pitts., 1954-56; prin. scientist Sci. Lab., Ford Motor Co., Dearborn, Mich., 1956-74; prof. materials engring. Purdue U., West Lafayette, Ind., 1974—, Ross Disting. prof. engring., 1984-89; Ross Disting. prof. engring. emeritus Purdue U., West Lafayette, 1989—; affiliate prof. dept. materials sci. U. Washington, Seattle, 1986-89; collaborator Los Alamos (N.Mex.) Nat. Lab., 1989—; vis. prof. U. Grenoble, France, 1967, Tokyo Inst. Tech., 1979, Tech. U. Hannover, Fed. Republic Germany, 1980-81; cons. Oak Ridge (Tenn.) Nat. Lab., 1978, 80. Contbr. over 260 articles to profl. jours., chpts. to books. Recipient U.S. Sr. Scientist award Alexander von Humboldt Found., 1980; fellow John Simon Guggenheim Meml. Found., 1966, Japan Soc. for Promotion Sci., 1979. Fellow Am. Phys. Soc.; mem. Japan Phys. Soc., Am. Ceramic Soc., Metall. Soc.-AIME, Japan Inst. Metals (hon. 1985—, Prize of Merit 1951). Office: Purdue U Sch. Materials Engring 1289 MSEE Bldg West Lafayette IN 47907-1289

SATO, KATSUO, real estate company executive; b. Tokyo, Nov. 29, 1927; s. Katsuji and Toyo (Koide) S.; m. Kimiko Moriyasu, Nov. 9, 1960; children: Takako, Yasuhiro, Genta. BSc, Tokyo Inst. Tech., 1950, postgrad., 1950-52. Mem. transsitor bus. devel. study engring. sect. Hokushin Electric Co., Tokyo, 1952-57; mem. transistor bus. devel. study engring. sect. Nippon Electric Co., Tokyo, 1957-64; supr. engring. sect. semicondr. devel. dept. NEC Corp., Tokyo, 1964-65, sect. mgr. design engring. sect. semicondr. div., 1965-71, dept. mgr. computer-aided design dept. integrated crct. div., 1971-76; lab. mgr. Very Large Scale Integrated Circuit Rsch. Lab. NEC-Toshiba Info. Sys. Inc., Tokyo, 1976-80; dir. NEC IC Microcomputer Sys. Inc., Tokyo, 1980-89, advisor, 1989-92; ret., 1992; chmn. Fujimi Kosan Inc. Ltd., Tokyo, 1992—. Numerous patents for semicondr. device inventions in Japan, U.S., Eng., France, and Germany. Recipient 7 awards for patents, including Dir. Gen. award Govt. Patent Office, 1968, Spl. Invention award Japan Invention Assn., 1968, Invention award, 1969, 82. Mem. IEEE (assoc.), Phys. Soc. Japan, N.Y. Acad. Sci. Avocations: foreign travel, gardening, tennis, skiing. Home and Office: 3-6-21 902 Ohsaki, Shinagawa-ku, Tokyo 141, Japan

SATO, RICHARD MICHIO, consulting engineering company executive; b. Paia, Maui, Hawaii, Dec. 30, 1934; s. Shinichi and Namie (Hanazawa) S.; m. Althea Reiko Ouye; children: Janice Muraoka, Kelvin. BSCE, U. Hawaii, 1956. Registered civil/structural engr., Calif., Hawaii, Guam. Civil and structural engr. Dalton Dalton Assocs., L.A., 1960-62; structural engr. William M. Taggart, SE, L.A., 1962-67; project coord. Office of Univ. Planning U. Hawaii, Honolulu, 1967-69; project engr. T.Y. Lin Hawaii, Honolulu, 1969; pres. Sato & Assocs., Inc. (formerly Richard M. Sato & Assoc. & Sato & Kuniyoshi, Inc.), Honolulu, 1969—. 1st lt. U.S. Army, 1957-59. Mem. Am. Concrete Inst., Prestressed Concrete Inst., Structural Engrs. Assn. Hawaii (pres. 1976), Consulting Engrs. Coun. Hawaii, Hui Kokua Kinipopo (pres. 1993—), U. Hawaii Pres.'s Club, U. Hawaii Alumni Assn., Chi Epsilon. Avocations: golf, sports fan. Office: Sato & Assocs Inc 2046 S King St Honolulu HI 96826

SATO, TADASHI, artist; b. Maui, Hawaii, Feb. 6, 1923. Student, Honolulu Sch. Art, Bklyn. Mus. Art Sch., New Sch. Soc. Rsch. Exhbns. include Guggenheim Mus., N.Y.C., 1954, Honolulu Acad. Arts, 1957, Pacific Heritage Exhibit, L.A., 1963, McRoberts and Tunnard Ltd., London, 1964, White House Festival Arts, Washington, 1965, Berlin Art Festival, 1967, Japanese C. of C., Honolulu, 1993-94, Maui Cmty. and Cultural Assn., 1994; represented in permanent collections Albright-Knox Art Gallery, Buffalo, Guggenheim Mus., Whitney Mus. Am. Art, N.Y.C., Honolulu Acad. Arts, U. Art Gallery, Tucson, (mosaic) Hawaii State Capitol Bldg., State Libr. Aina Haina, Oahu, State Hosp., Kea-lakekua, Hawaii, Wailuku War Meml. Gymnasium, Maui, Krannert Art Mus., Ill., U. Nebr.; executed murals Halekulani Hotel, Honolulu, (mosaic) West Maui Recreation Ctr., (oil) Bay Club, Kapalua, Maui; retrospective Hui No Eau, Makawao, Maui, 1992. Office: PO Box 476 Lahaina HI 96767-0476

SATOLA, JAMES WILLIAM, lawyer; b. Cleve., Aug. 26, 1961; s. William John and Catherine Ann (Recek) S. BS in Zoology, Ohio State U., 1984; JD, Case Western Reserve U., 1989. Bar: Ohio 1989, U.S. Dist. Ct. (no. dist.) Ohio 1990, D.C. 1991, U.S. Ct. Appeals (6th cir.) 1992, U.S. Supreme Ct. 1993. Med. rsch. asst. I U. Hosps. of Cleve., 1985-86; law clk to judge John M. Manos U.S. Dist. Ct. (no. dist.) Ohio, Cleve., 1989-91; assoc. Squire, Sanders & Dempsey, Cleve., 1991—. Articles editor Case Western Reserve Law Rev., Cleve., 1988-89. Mem. Inn of Ct. (assoc.). Republican. Avocations: art, music, golf, landscaping. Home: 2608 Dysart Rd University Heights OH 44118 Office: Squire Sanders & Dempsey 4900 Soc Ctr 127 Public Sq Cleveland OH 44114-1216

SATORIUS, JOHN ARTHUR, lawyer; b. Berwyn, Ill., Aug. 20, 1946; s. Woodrow Wilson and Frances Jane (Embshoff) S.; m. Linda Kay Grove, Dec. 26, 1968; children: Katherine, Joseph. BA summa cum laude, U. Va., 1968; MA, Harvard U., 1972, JD cum laude, 1975, PhD, 1977. Bar: Minn. 1975. Assoc. Fredrikson & Byron PA, Mpls., 1975-81, ptnr., 1981—, also bd. dirs., mem. exec. com.; bd. dirs. Bellcomb Techs., Mpls. Editor Contract Law in Minnesota, 1993. Bd. dirs. Childrens Theater Co., Mpls. With U.S. Army, 1968-70, Vietnam. Named Vol. of Yr. Met. Econ. Devel., 1986. Avocations: wilderness canoe activities, traveling, reading. Office: Fredrikson & Byron PA 1100 International Ctr 900 2nd Ave S Minneapolis MN 55402-3314

SATO-VIACRUCIS, KIYO, inventor, nurse, entrepreneur, consultant; b. Sacramento, May 8, 1923; d. John Shinji and Mary Tomomi (Watanabe) Sato; m. Gene Viacrucis, Aug. 9, 1958 (div. May 1976); adopted children: Cia, Jon, Paul, Tanya. BS, Hillsdale Coll., 1944; MSN, Western Res. U., 1948. Cert. health and devel. specialist, Calif., pub. health nurse, Calif., audiologist. Nursery sch. attendant Poston (Ariz.) II Concentration Camp, 1942; staff nurse U. Hosps., Cleve., 1948; pub. health nurse Sacramento County Health Dept., 1948-50, 52-53; sch. nurse U. Oslo, 1953, Sacramento County Schs., 1954-58; presch. nurse Sacramento City Unified Sch. Dist., 1973-85; pvt. practice cons. Blackbird Vision Screening System, Sacramento, 1985—; cons., speaker Blackbird Vision Screening System, 1973—; cons. state task force Vision Screening Guidelines, 1981. Inventor Blackbird presch. vision screening method; cons. vision screening; contbr. articles to profl. jours. Served to capt. USAF, 1951-52. Recipient Excellence in Nursing award RN Mag. Found., 1983. Mem. Nat. Sch. Nurses Assn., Calif. Sch. Nurses Orgn., Japanese Am. Citizens League (pres. 1950), Am. Assn. Ret. Persons, VFW (pub. rels. com., post surgeon 1985—, cmty. activities 1986—). Democrat. Avocations: writing, pottery, hula dancing, Tai Chi, grandchildren. Home: 9436 Americana Way Sacramento CA 95826-4621 Office: Blackbird Vision Screening PO Box 277424 Sacramento CA 95827-7424

SATOVSKY, ABRAHAM, lawyer; b. Detroit, Oct. 15, 1907; s. Samuel and Stella (Benenson) S.; m. Toby Nayer, Sept. 4, 1938 (dec.); children: Sheldon Baer, James Bennett. B.A., U. Mich., 1928, J.D., 1930. Bar: Mich. 1930, U.S. Supreme Ct. 1930. Assoc. William Henry Gallagher, Detroit, 1930-65; Bldg. chmn. lawyers com. United Found. and Torch Dr. Co-chmn. profl. divsn. Allied Jewish Campaign; adv. coun. United Synagogue Am.; del. Jewish Cmty. Coun. Detroit; v.p. Mosies Chetim Orgn. Detroit; bd. dirs. Detroit Svc. Group, past chmn. fgn. mission; active fund raiser Greater Miami United Jewish Appeal; mem. fund dr. com. U. Mich. Law Sch.; trustee Clover Hill Park Cemetery, 1978-81, trustee emeritus, 1982—; bd. dirs. Congregation Sharrey Zedek, Southfield, Mich., past pres., 1959-62. Recipient Sem. award Jewish Theol. Sem. Am., 1952; citation of merit Jewish Welfare Fedn., Detroit; Jerusalem award State of Israel Bond Orgn.; numerous other awards. Mem. ABA, Mich. Bar Assn., Detroit Bar Assn., Oakland County Bar, Nat. Fedn. Jewish Men's Clubs (founder, past pres., hon. life pres., Gt. Lakes regional award 1977, Ma'Asim Tovim (Good Deeds) award 1989), Am. Arbitration Assn., Jewish Hist. Soc. Mich. (mem. adv. bd.), Am. Jewish Hist. Soc., Am. Judicature Soc., Men's Club Congregation Shaarey Zodek (past pres., hon. life pres.), Standard Club, B'nai B'rith (past pres. Detroit), Hadassah (life), Phi Beta Delta (merged with Pi Lambda Phi). Home: 28455 Northwestern Hwy Southfield MI 48034-1823 also: 20379 W Country Club Dr Aventura FL 33180-1629 Office: 28455 Northwestern Hwy Southfield MI 48034-1823 *With a desire and willingness to improve my profession, my religious beliefs, and help the community, I have devoted a good portion of my time and efforts for those purposes. I, too, have been enriched by the association, have hopefully directed and encouraged others, and hope to continue to do so.*

SATRE, PHILIP GLEN, casino entertainment executive, lawyer; b. Palo Alto, Calif., Apr. 30, 1949; s. Selmer Kenneth and Georgia June (Sterling) S.; m. Jennifer Patricia Arnold, June 30, 1973; children: Malena Anne, Allison Neal, Jessica Lilly, Peter Sterling. BA, Stanford U., 1971; JD, U. Calif.-Davis, 1975; postgrad sr. exec. program MIT, 1982. Bar: Nev. 1975, Calif. 1976. Assoc. Vargas & Bartlett, Reno, 1975-79; v.p., gen. counsel, sec. Harrah's, Reno, 1980-83, sr. v.p., 1983-84, pres. Harrah's East, Atlantic City, 1984; pres., CEO Harrah's Hotels and Casinos, Reno, 1984-91; dir, sr. v.p. Gaming Group The Promus Cos., Inc., Memphis, 1988-91, pres., COO, 1991-94, pres., CEO, 1994-95; pres, CEO Harrahs Entertainment, Inc., 1995—; dir., treas. Nat. Judicial Coll., Reno. Mem. ABA, Nev. Bar Assn., Calif. Bar Assn., Order of Coif, Phi Kappa Phi, Stanford Alumni Assn. (pres. Reno chpt. 1976-77), Young Pres. Orgn.

SATRUM, JERRY R., chemicals company executive; b. 1933. BS, Oreg. State U., 1967. With Ga.-Pacific Corp., Atlanta, 1968-84; v.p., treas. fin. and adminstr. Ga. Gulf Corp., 1984-89, pres., COO, 1989—, now CEO, 1992—, also bd. dirs. Office: Georgia Gulf Corp 400 Perimeter Ctr Ter NE Ste 3595 Atlanta GA 30346-1227*

SATTER, LARRY DEAN, biochemist, scientific research administrator; b. Madelia, Minn., July 30, 1937; m. 1966; 1 child. BS, S.D. State U., 1960; MS, U. Wis., 1962, PhD in Biochemistry and Dairy Sci., 1964. Asst. prof. to assoc. prof. dairy sci. U. Wis., Madison, 1964-73, prof., 1973-81; mem. staff U.S. Dairy Forage Rsch. Ctr., U. Wis., USDA, Madison, 1981-87, dir., 1987—. Recipient Am. Feed Mfrs. award, 1977. Mem. Am. Dairy Sci. Assn., Am. Soc. Animal Sci., Am. Inst. Nutrition, Brit. Nutrition Soc. Office: U Wis USDA Dairy Forage Rsch Ctr 1925 Linden Dr W Madison WI 53706-1108*

SATTERFIELD, CHARLES NELSON, chemical engineer, educator; b. Dexter, Mo., Sept. 5, 1921; s. Charles David and Hermine (Weber) S.; m. Anne Pettingell, July 6, 1946; children—Mark Edward, Joye. B.S. cum laude, Harvard U., 1942; M.S., MIT, 1943, Sc.D., 1946. Registered profl. engr., Mass. Asst. prof. chem. engring. Mass. Inst. Tech., Cambridge, 1946-53; asso. prof. Mass. Inst. Tech., 1953-59, prof., 1959—; Lectr. indsl. chemistry Harvard, 1948-57; cons.on rocket propellants Dept. Def., 1952-60; mem. com. chem. kinetics NRC, 1960-66; chmn. ad hoc panel on abatement nitrogen oxide emissions from stationary sources Nat. Acad. Engring., 1970-72; indsl. cons. to major cos. in petroleum and chem. industries. Co-author: Thermodynamic Charts for Combustion Processes, 1949, Hydrogen Peroxide, 1955 (translated into Russian 1957), Role of Diffusion in Catalysis, 1963; author: Mass Transfer in Heterogeneous Catalysis, 1970 (translated into Russian 1976), Heterogeneous Catalysis in Practice, 1980 (translated into Russian 1984), repub. as Heterogeneous Catalysis in Industrial Practice, 1991, also more than 140 tech. papers; mem. editl. adv. bd. Indsl. and Engring. Chemistry, 1966-68, Advances in Chemistry Series, 1971-73, 82-86, Energy and Fuels, 1990—, Applied Catalysis, 1995—. Fellow Am. Acad. Arts and Scis.; mem. Am. Chem. Soc., Am. Inst. Chem. Engrs. (Wilhelm award 1980), Sigma Xi, Tau Beta Pi. Patentee in field. Home: 38 Tabor Hill Rd Lincoln MA 01773-2906 Office: Dept Chem Engring Mass Inst Tech Cambridge MA 02139

SATTERTHWAITE, CAMERON B., physics educator; b. Salem, Ohio, July 26, 1920; s. William David and Mabel (Cameron) S.; m. Helen Elizabeth Foster, Dec. 23, 1950 (div. July 31, 1979); children: Mark Cameron, Tod Foster, Tracy Lynn, Keith Alan, Craig Evan (dec.). B.A., Coll. Wooster, 1942; postgrad., Ohio State U., 1942-44; Ph.D., U. Pitts., 1951. Chemist Manhattan dist. project Monsanto Chem. Co., Dayton, Ohio, 1944-47; research chemist DuPont, Wilmington, Del., 1950-53; researcher, adv. physicist Westinghouse, Pitts., 1953-61; asso. prof. physics U. Ill., Urbana, 1961-63; prof. U. Ill., 1963-79, prof. emeritus, 1979—; prof. physics Va. Commonwealth U., Richmond, 1979-85; prof. emeritus Va. Commonwealth U., 1985—, chmn. dept. physics, 1979-82; program dir. NSF, 1975-76; field sec. Friends Com. on Nat. Legis., 1988-90. Contbr. articles to profl. jours. Sch. dir., Monroeville, Pa., 1959-61; trustee, mem. fin. com. Southeastern Univs. Research Assn., 1980-85; Democratic nominee for U.S. Congress, 1966; del. to Dem. Nat. Conv., 1968, 72. Fellow Am. Phys. Soc.; mem. Fedn. Am. Scientists (chmn. 1968). Patentee in field. Home: Unit # 1 803 S Coler Ave Urbana IL 61801-4009

SATTERTHWAITE, HELEN FOSTER, retired state legislator; b. Blawnox, Pa., July 8, 1928; d. Samuel J. and Lillian (Schreiber) Foster; B.S. in Chemistry, Duquesne U., 1949; m. Cameron B. Satterthwaite, Dec. 23, 1950 (div. July 1979); children: Mark Cameron, Tod Foster, Tracy Lynn, Keith Alan, Craig Evan (dec.). Biol. technician U.S. Dept. Agr., 1967-68; research asst. Iowa State U. Coll. Agr., 1971; lab. technician U. Ill. Coll. Agr., 1968-70; rsch. chemist E.I. duPont de Nemours & Co., Wilmington, Del., 1951-53; rsch. asst. Gulf R & D, Harmarville, Pa., 1950; natural sci. lab. technician U. Ill. Coll. Vet. Medicine, 1971-74; rep. Gen. Assembly Ill., 1974-92, majority leader, 1991-92, sch. fin. task force, 1990-92, ret., 1993; chairperson House com. on higher edn., 1983-91, vice-chairperson elem. and secondary edn., 1983-91; mem. Commn. on Mental Health and Devel. Disabilities, 1975-85, mem. exec. com., 1977-85, vice chairperson, 1979-85; mem. Commn. to Visit and Examine State Instns., 1977-85, Ill. Coun. Mental Health, 1992-95, task force on global climate change, 1991—, League Women Voters, treas. 1995—, Bus. & Profl. Women's Club, treas. 1993-94, sec. 1994-95. Bd. dirs. East Central Ill. Health Systems Agy., 1977-79, Champaign County Mental Health Ctr. 1993—, Girls Inc. 1992—, Champaign County (Ill.) United Way, 1970-74, mem. budget com., 1973-74, mem. joint rev. com. on funding Champaign County Mental Health Programs, 1973; co-chairperson Task Force on Mental Retardation for Champaign County Mental Health Bd., 1973; mem. Ill. Developmental Disability Advocacy Authority, 1977-85, vice chmn., 1979-80; chairperson Ill. House Democratic Study Group, 1979-81; mem. Edn. Commn. of the States, 1985-92; mem. Nat. Conf. State Legis. Commn. on Labor and Edn., 1985-92. Recipient Freshman Legislator of Yr. award Ill. Edn. Assn., 1975; commendation Ill. State's Attys. Assn., 1975; Best Legislator award Ind. Votors Ill., 1976, 78, 80, 82, 84, 86, 88, 90; cert. honor Assn. Students Govts., 1977; Disting. Service cert. Am. Vets. World War II, Korea and Viet Nam, 1977; Environ. Legis. of Yr. award Ill. Environ. Council, 1977, 79, 81, 83; Meritorious Svc. award Champaign County Council on Alcoholism, 1978, Ill. Community Coll. Trustees Assn., 1986; Perfect Voting Record award Ill. Credit Union League, 1979, Ill. Wildlife Fedn., 1979; cert. spl. recognition Ill. Women's Polit. Caucus, 1979, 80, Public Service award Izaak Walton League, 1980, Friend of Edn. award Ill. State Bd. Edn., 1985, Cert. of Appreciation Champaign County Urban League, 1987, Resolution of Honor Ill. Libr. Assn., 1987, 100 percent award Ill. State Coun. Sr. Citizens Orgns., 1989, Dare to be Great award Ill. Women Adminstrs., 1989; named Person of Yr., Champaign County Mental Health Assn., 1981, Pub. Citizen of Yr., Illini Dist. and Ill. chpt. Nat. Assn. Social Workers, 1981, Legislator of Yr., Ill. Assn. Sch. Social Workers, 1989. Mem. Ill. Conf. Women Legislators (coconvenor 1981-83), Nat. Order Women Legislators (dir. Region IV 1982, treas. 1983-84), Delta Kappa Gamma. Quaker.

SATTERWHITE, WILLIAM T., lawyer, energy company executive; b. Baytown, Tex., 1933. Grad., Baylor U., 1956, LLB, 1958. Now sr. v.p., gen. counsel, chief legal officer ENSERCH Corp., Dallas, 1995—. Office: Enserch Corp 301 S Harwood Dallas TX 75201*

SATTLER, ROLF, plant morphologist, educator; b. Göppingen, Germany, Mar. 8, 1936; arrived in Can., 1962; s. Otto and Emma (Mayer) S.; m. Liv Hamann, May 1, 1963 (div. 1985). PhD, U. Munich, 1961; DS, Colombo U. Asst. prof. McGill U., Montreal, Que., Can., 1964-69, assoc. prof., 1969-77, prof., 1977—. Author: Organogenesis of Flowers, 1973 (Lawson medal 1974), Biophilosophy, 1986; editor: Theoretical Plant Morphology, 1978,

Axioms and Principles of Plant Construction, 1981; contbr. articles to profl. jours. NATO fellow, 1962-64. Fellow Royal Soc. Can., Linnean Soc. London; mem. Can. Bot. Assn., Bot. Soc. Am., Can. Soc. for Theoretical Biology, Internat. Soc. for History, Philosophy and Social Studies of Biology, Sci. and Med. Network, Internat. Assn. for New Sci., Ctr. for Process Studies, Sigma Xi. Office: McGill U, 1205 Dr Penfield Ave, Montreal, PQ Canada H3A 1B1

SATUR, NANCY MARLENE, dermatologist; b. Philipsburg, Pa., Apr. 12, 1953; d. Nicholas and Mary (Kutzer) S.; m. John David Lortscher, Oct. 20, 1979; children: David Nicholas, Glenn William, Stephen John. BS magna cum laude, Pa. State U., 1974; MD, Thomas Jefferson U., 1976. Diplomate Am. Bd. Dermatology. Intern Allentown (Pa.) Gen. Hosp., 1976-77; resident in pathology U. Ill. Hosp., Chgo., 1978-79; resident in dermatology Case Western Res. U. Hosp., Cleve., 1979-82; dermatologist Encinitas, Calif., 1985—; sr. instr. dermatology Case Western Res. U. Hosp., 1982-83, sr. clin. instr. dermatology, 1983-84. Fellow Am. Acad. Dermatology; mem. Am. Soc. Dermatologic Surgery, Am. Soc. Laser Medicine and Surgery, N.Am. Soc. Phlebology, San Diego Dermatologic Soc., Pacific Dermatologic Assn. Office: Ste C308 477 N El Camino Real #C308 Encinitas CA 92024-1331

SATURNELLI, ANNETTE MIELE, school system administrator; b. Newburgh, N.Y., Dec. 1, 1937; d. William Vito and Anna (Marso) M.; m. Carlo F. Saturnelli, Oct. 15, 1960; children: Anne, Karen, Carla. BA, Vassar Coll., 1959; MS, SUNY, New Platz, 1978; EdD, NYU, N.Y.C., 1993. Rsch. chemist Lederle Labs/Am. Cyanamid, Pearl River, N.Y., 1959-64; sci. coord. Marlboro (N.Y.) Cen. Sch. Dist., 1974-84; state sci. supr. N.Y. State Dept. Edn., Albany, 1984-86; dir. sci. edn. Newburgh (N.Y.) City Sch. Dist., 1986—; project dir., proposal reviewer NSF, Washington, 1984—; state coord. N.Y. State Sci. Olympiad, 1985-86; mem. Gov. Cuomo's Task Force on Improving Sci. Edn., Albany, N.Y., 1989—; mem. adv. bd. N.Y. State Systemic Initiative, 1993—, N.Y. State Tech. Edn. Network, 1993—. Author: Focus on Physical Science, 1981, 87; editor: Transforming Testing in New York State--A Collection of Past, Present and Future Assessment Practices, 1994. Recipient Presdl. award Excellence in Sci. Tchg., Washington, 1983; NSF 3-yr. summer sci. camp grantee, 1995, 96, 97, N.Y. State Edn. Dept. Workforce Preparation grantee, 1993-94, N.Y. State Edn. Dept. Sch.-to-Work grantee, 1995-96. Mem. ASCD, Nat. Sci. Tchrs. Assn. (exemplary sci. tchrs. award 1982), N.Y. State Sci. Suprs. (bd. dirs., pres. 1991), Sci. Tchrs. Assn. N.Y. State (outstanding sci. tchrs. award 1983, fellows award 1990, pres. 1993), Phi Delta Kappa. Home: 3 Taft Pl Cornwall On Hudson NY 12520-1713 Office: Newburgh Free Acad 201 Fullerton Ave Newburgh NY 12550-3718

SATYAPRIYA, COMBATORE KESHAVAMURTHY, geotechnical engineering executive; b. Bangalore, Mysore, India, Jan. 27, 1949; came to U.S., 1972; s. C.V. and C.V. (Vedamma) Keshavamurthy; m. Indira Muthanna, Nov. 1, 1976; children: Ajay S., Anand A., Divya S. BCE, Bangalore U., 1969, MCE, 1971; MS, Worcester (Mass.) Poly. Inst., 1972. Registered profl. engr., Ohio, Md., Va., W.Va., Washington, Pa., Ind., Ky., Fla. Staff engr. Mason & Ray Inc., Columbus, Ohio, 1976-77; sr. geotech. engr. Resource Internat. Inc., Columbus, 1977-78; staff engr. CTL Engring. Inc., Columbus, 1978-79, dept. head geotech. engring., 1979-80, v.p., 1981-83, exec. v.p., 1983-86; mgr. ops. Washington Testing, Inc., Fairfax, Va., 1981-82; pres. CTL Engring. Inc., Columbus, 1986—; mem. control group Placement & Improvement, Columbus, 1982—. Contbr. articles to profl. jours. Fellow ASCE (pres. Ctrl. Ohio chpt. 1978-79, tech. com. on placement and improvement of soils 1982—); Mem. ASTM (coms. E-06, D-18, D-20), Indian Geotech. Soc., Rotary, Chi Epsilon. Home: 8015 Flint Rd Columbus OH 43235-6406 Office: CTL Engring Inc 2860 Fisher Rd Columbus OH 43204-3538

SATZ, LOUIS K., publishing executive; b. Chgo., Apr. 28, 1927; s. Harry Addison and Faye (Pollen) S.; m. Adele Wallenstein, Mar. 2, 1976 (dec.); children: Jay, Jonathan. B.S. in Mktg, U. Ill., 1949. Circulation dir. Pubs. Devel. Corp., Chgo., 1953, Guns mag., Jr. Arts and Activities, 1961; wholesaler sales mgr., then v.p., dir. sales Bantam Books, Inc., N.Y.C., 1962-80; sr. v.p., dir. diversified markets Bantam Books, Inc., 1980-84; pub. Passport Books, Lincolnwood, Ill., 1985-88; pres. Louis K. Satz Assocs., Pub. Cons., N.Y.C., 1988-91; ptnr. Scott/Satz Group, Pub. Cons., Walnut Creek, Calif., 1991—; guest lectr. Sarah Lawrence Coll. Pub. Sch., Pace U.; faculty Hofstra U., Denver Pub. Inst.; bd. dirs. N.Y. is Book Country, Brandeis U. Pub. Scholarship Fund, Oscar Dystel Fellowship NYU. Served with AUS, World War II, ETO. Decorated Army Commendation medal. Mem. Am. Assn. Pubs. (chmn. small books mktg. div. 1975). Office: Scott/Satz Group 539 Monarch Ridge Dr Walnut Creek CA 94596-2955

SATZ, MICHAEL ELLIS, insurance executive; b. N.Y.C., Oct. 30, 1948; s. Louis and Rose (Schiff) S.; m. Marietta Maldonado Staples, Mar. 3, 1978; children: William Harrington, Marisa Blanca. BA, Cornell U., 1970; JD, Harvard U., 1974. Bar: N.Y. Assoc. Willkie Farr and Gallagher, N.Y.C., 1974-82; gen. counsel Ambac Indemnity Corp., N.Y.C., 1982-85, chief operating officer, 1985-87; chmn., chief exec. officer Capital Re Corp., N.Y.C., 1987—; founder Assn. Fin. Guaranty Insurors, N.Y.C., 1986; lectr. pub. adminstrn. NYU; panelist Bond Atty.'s Workshop, Chgo., 1979-83, 85-87. Contbr. articles to profl. jours. Bd. advisors Outward Bound U.S.A. Mem. ABA, N.Y. State Bar Assn., Assn. of Bar of City of N.Y., Cornell Club, Harvard Club. Avocations: travel, riding, scuba diving. Office: Capital Re Corp 787 7th Ave New York NY 10019-6018*

SAUCIER, GENE DUANE, state legislator, import/export company executive; b. Dallas, Sept. 25, 1931; s. Albert L. and Myrtle Irene (West) S.; m. Marilyn Emmy Cox, Dec. 27, 1952 (div. Sept. 1980); children: Alan, Steve, Renee; m. Giulia Riga LaCagnina, Nov. 28, 1981. BS in Agronomy Soils, Miss. State U., 1953; MS in Counseling, U. So. Miss., 1970, EdD in Adult Edn., 1978. Builder, developer Saucier Co., Hattiesburg, Miss., 1957-70; dir. admissions U. So. Miss., Hattiesburg, 1970-74, dean spl. acad. svcs., 1974-84, asst. v.p. bus. and fin., 1984-93; rep. Miss. Ho. of Reps., Jackson, 1993—; importer tractors from China. Scoutmaster Boy Scouts Am., 1960-70, chmn. camping and activities Pine Burr Area, 1970. 1st lt. USAF, 1953-56. Named Forrest County Tree Farmer of Yr., 1996. Mem. Res. Officers Assn., Am. Assn. Collegiate Registrars and Admissions Officers (mem. adv. bd. 1985-86), So. Assn. Collegiate Registrars and Admissions Officers (bd. dirs. 1981, local arrangements chmn. 1981, v.p. admissions and fin. aid 1982-83, pres. 1985-86), Miss. Assn. Collegiate Registrars and Admissions Officdrs, Miss. Forestry Assn. (exec. bd. dirs. 1992-94, bd. dirs. 1992-94), Miss. Nature Conservancy, Forrest/Lamar Forestry Assn. (pres. 1989-92), Sigma Chi, ODK, Phi Delta Kappa, Omicron Delta Kappa. Office: 41 Saucier Rd Hattiesburg MS 39402-9138

SAUER, ANNE KATHERINE, glass blower, artist, educator; b. Madison, Wis., Sept. 2, 1958; d. Collin Harold and Margaret (Isabell (Roberts) S. BS, U. Wis., 1982; MFA, Mass. Coll. Art, Boston, 1987. Owner, mgr. Brick House Glass, Madison, 1989; lectr., demonstrator Madison Art Ctr., 1992, Madison East H.S., 1992, Univ. League, 1993. Exhibited in group shows Valperine Gallery, Madison, 1992, City-County Arts, Madison, 1993, Newell Gallery, Waunakee, Wis., 1993, 94, Blue Bird Gallery, Prairie du Sac, Wis., 1994; work represented in various mags. Avocations: playing polo, sail boarding, swimming, running. Home: 3860 N River Hills Dr Tucson AZ 85720 Office: Brick House Glass 6777 E River Rd Tucson AZ 85715-2045

SAUER, CONRAD FREDERICK, IV, food products executive; b. Richmond, Va., May 28, 1949; s. Conrad F. III and Barbara (Boyd) S.; m. Patricia Totty, Nov. 3, 1973; children: Ashley, Jennifer. BA, Hampden-Sydney Coll., 1972. Mgmt. trainee C.F. Sauer Co., Richmond, 1972-80, asst. v.p., officer, 1980-85, officer, dir., v.p., 1985—. Avocations: hunting, fishing, biking, swimming. Office: CF Sauer Co 2000 W Broad St Richmond VA 23220-2006*

SAUER, DAVID ANDREW, writer, computer consultant; b. Urbana, Ill., Feb. 25, 1948; s. Elmer Louis and Frances (Hill) S. BA, Northwestern U., 1970; MS, Simmons Coll., 1975. Reference libr. Boston U., 1976-78, bibliographer, 1978-84, sci. bibliographer, 1984-88, head Stone Sci. Libr., 1988-94; v.p. info. svcs. CyberHelp, Inc., 1995—. Co-author: Internet for Windows, 1994, WinComm Pro: The Visual Learning Guide, 1995, ProComm Plus V2 for Windows: The Visual Learning Guide, 1995, Access for Windows 95: The Visual Learning Guide, 1995, Cruising America Online 2.5, 1995, Internet for Windows: The America Online 2.5 Edition, 1995, Internet for Windows: The Microsoft Network Edition, 1995, Cruising the Microsoft Network, 1996, Cruising CompuServe, 1996;. Mem. S.W. Corridor Project, Boston, 1977-87, Forest Hills Neighborhood Improvement Assn., Boston, 1977-90, Forest Hills/Woodbourne Neighborhood Group, 1991-94. Mem. ALA, Spl. Librs. Assn., Assn. Coll. and Rsch. Librs., Geoscience Info. Soc., San Diego Computer Soc., Highland Casitas Homeowners Assn. (treas. 1995—). Democrat. Home and Office: 1034 La Tierra Dr San Marcos CA 92069-4617

SAUER, ELISSA SWISHER, nursing educator; b. Williamsport, Pa., Jan. 9, 1935; d. Oliver S. and Emily Louisa (Gehron) Swisher; m. Raymond James Sauer, Nov. 27, 1964. Diploma, Reading Hosp. Sch. Nursing, 1957; BS, Albright Coll., Reading, 1958; MS in Nursing, U. Pa., Phila., 1964. Nurse Community Health and Civic Assn., Ardmore, Pa., 1966-67; pub. health coord. Albert Einstein Med. Ctr., 1967-68; pvt. duty nurse, 1968-73; clin. faculty Schuylkill County AVTS, 1973-74; prof. nursing Reading (Pa.) Area Comunity Coll., 1975-80; oncology nurse adminstr.-educator Comprehensive Community Cancer Ctr., Allentown, Pa., 1981-85; exec. dir. Holy Family Home Health Care, Orwigsburg, Pa., 1985-89; dir. nursing program, chair health svcs. div. Reading Area Community Coll., 1989—. Author: Instructor's Manual and Procedure Manual to accompany Fundamentals of Nursing: Human Health and Function, 2d edit., 1996. Mem. Pa. Nurses Assn. (Dist. 2 dir. 1994—, Adminstr. award 1992), Pa. League for Nursing, Sigma Theta Tau. Home: 475 Marshall Dr Orwigsburg PA 17961-1617 Office: Reading Area C C PO Box 1706 10 S 2d St Reading PA 19603-1706

SAUER, GEORGIA BOORAS, newspaper writer; b. Kalamata, Greece, May 9, 1946; came to U.S., 1946; d. Peter P. and Angela (Dimopoulos) Booras; m. Mark Sauer, Jan. 4, 1969; children: Peter, Alexander. BS, U. Ill., 1968. Obituary and feature writer Champaign (Ill.)-Urbana Courier, 1966-68; reporter Times-Democrat, Davenport, Iowa, 1968; reporter, travel writer, copy editor Chgo. Tribune, 1969-70, fashion and feature writer, asst. Lifestyle editor, 1971-75; reporter Home Furnishings Daily, Fairchild Publs., N.Y.C., 1970-71; fashion reporter, Sunday women's editor N.Y. Daily News, N.Y.C., 1975-76; fashion editor St. Louis mag., 1981-86; became feature writer St. Louis Post-Dispatch, 1986-91; fashion editor Pitts. Post Gazette, 1993—. Pres. bd. dirs. Ladue Chapel Nursery Sch.; bd. dirs. Martha's Shelter, St. Louis, 1985-91, DG Found. for Visually Impaired Children, St. Louis, 1985-91, St. Louis Pub. Libr., 1987-91, Payback, St. Louis, 1987-91; mem. Jr. League St. Louis and Pitts.; bd. dirs. Three Rivers South, Pitts., Ozanam Cultural Ctr., mem. bd. parents coun. Shadyside acad., mem. devel. com. Greek Orthodox. Office: Pittsburgh Post-Gazette 34 Blvd Of The Allies Pittsburgh PA 15222-1204

SAUER, GORDON CHENOWETH, physician, educator; b. Rutland, Ill., Aug. 14, 1921; s. Fred William and Gweneth (Chenoweth) S.; m. Mary Louise Steinhilber, Dec. 28, 1944; children: Elisabeth Ruth, Gordon Chenoweth, Margaret Louise, Amy Kieffer.; m. Marion Green, Oct. 23, 1982. Student, Northwestern U., 1939-42; B.S., U. Ill., 1943, M.D., 1945. Diplomate: Am. Bd. Dermatology and Syphilology. Intern Cook County Hosp., Chgo., 1945-46; resident dermatology and syphilology N.Y. U.-Bellevue Med. Center, 1948-51; dermatologist Thompson-Brumm-Knepper Clinic, St. Joseph, Mo., 1951-54; pvt. practice Kansas City, Mo., 1954—; mem. staff St. Luke's, Research, Kansas City Gen. hosps.; asso. instr. U. Kans., 1951-56, vice chmn. sect. dermatology, 1956-58, asso. clin. prof., 1960-64, clin. prof., 1964-93; clin. prof. emeritus, 1993—; head sect. dermatology U. Kans., 1958-70; clin. asso., acting head dermatology sect. U. Mo., 1955-59, cons. dermatology, 1959-67, clin. prof., 1967—; cons. Munson Army Hosp., Ft. Leavenworth, Kans., 1959-68; Mem. dermatology panel, drug efficacy panel Nat. Acad. Sci.-FDA, 1967-69. Author: Manual of Skin Diseases, 1959, 7th edit., 1995, Teen Skin, 1965, John Gould Bird Print Reproductions, 1977, John Gould's Prospectuses and Lists of Subscribers to His Work on Natural History: With an 1866 Facsimile, 1980, John Gould The Bird Man, 1982; editor Kansas City Med. Bull., 1967-69; contbr. articles to profl. jours. Bd. dirs. Kansas City Area coun. Camp Fire Girls Am., 1956-59, Kansas City Lyric Theatre, 1969-74, Kansas City Chamber Choir, 1969-74, Chouteau Soc., 1985—, U. Mo.-Kansas City Friends of Libr., 1988-92; bd. dirs. Mo. br. The Nature Conservancy, 1984-91. Sr. asst. surgeon USPHS, 1946-48. Named Dermatology Found. Practitioner of Yr., 1992. Fellow Am. Acad. Dermatology and Syphilology (dir. 1975-79, v.p. 1980); mem. Mo., Jackson County med. socs., Mo. Dermatol. Soc. (pres. 1974-75), Dermatology Found. (trustee 1978-83), Am. Ornithol. Union, Wilson Ornithol. Soc., Royal Australasian Ornithologists Union, Soc. Bibliography Natural History, Am. Dermatol. Assn., Alpha Delta Phi, Nu Sigma Nu. Presbyterian. Office: 6400 Prospect Ave Kansas City MO 64132-1181

SAUER, HARRY JOHN, JR., mechanical engineering educator, university administrator; b. St. Joseph, Mo., Jan. 27, 1935; s. Harry John and Marie Margaret (Witt) S.; m. Patricia Ann Zbierski, June 9, 1956; children: Harry John, Elizabeth Ann, Carl Andrew, Robert Mark, Katherine Anne, Deborah Elaine, Victoria Lynn, Valerie Joan, Joseph Gerard. B.S., U. Mo.-Rolla, 1956, M.S., 1958; Ph.D., Kans. State U., 1963. Instr. mech. engring. Kans. State U., Manhattan, 1960-62; sr. engr., cons. Midwest Rsch. Inst., Kansas City, Mo., 1963-70; mem. faculty dept. mech. and aerospace engring. U. Mo., Rolla, 1957—, prof., 1966—, assoc. chmn., 1980-84, dean grad. study, 1984-92; cons. in field; mem. Gov.'s Commn. on Energy Conservation, 1977; mem. Mo. Solar Energy Resource Panel, 1979-83. Co-author: Environmental Control Principles, 1975, 4th edit., 1985, Thermodynamics, 1981, Heat Pump Systems, 1983, Engineering Thermodynamics, 1985, Principles of Heating, Ventilating and Air Conditioning, 1991, 2d edit., 1994; contbr. articles to profl. jours. Pres. St. Patrick's Sch. Bd., 1970-72, St. Patrick's Parish Council, 1975-76. Recipient Ralph R. Teetor award Soc. Automotive Engrs., 1968; Hermann F. Spoehrer Meml. award St. Louis chpt. ASHRAE, 1979; also disting. service award, 1981, E. K. Campbell award of merit, 1983. Mem. ASME, ASHRAE, NSPE, Soc. Automotive Engrs., Am. Soc. Engring. Edn., Mo. Soc. Profl. Engrs., Mo. Acad. Sci., Sigma Xi. Roman Catholic. Home: 10355 College Hills Dr Rolla MO 65401-7726 Office: Dept of Mech Engring U Mo Rolla MO 65401

SAUER, KENNETH H., bishop. Bishop Luth. Ch. Am., Columbus, Ohio.

SAUER, NORMAN GARDINER, judge, attorney; b. Independence, Iowa, Aug. 28, 1921; s. Olvin Charles and Dorothy (Geiser) S.; m. Irene Manuth, Sept. 14, 1947; children: Georg, James, Vicki, Douglas. BS, U.S. Mil. Acad., 1945; JD, Gonzaga U., Spokane, Wash., 1975. Atty. pvt. practice, Republic, Wash., 1976-77; prosecuting atty. Ferry County, Republic, Wash., 1977-82; atty. pvt. practice, Republic, Wash., 1983-88; dist. court judge Ferry County, Republic, Wash., 1989-94; pvt. practice as atty. Republic, Wash., 1995—; judge pro tem Ferry County Dist. Ct., Republic, Wash., 1982-88; superior ct. commr. Ferry County Superior Ct., Republic, Wash., 1989-94; mcpl. ct. judge City of Republic, Wash., 1989-92. Chmn. Rep. Ctl. Com., Ferry County, Wash., 1976. Lt. col. USAF, 1964-70. Home: 87 Klondike Rd Republic WA 99166-9701 Office: PO Box 526 Republic WA 99166-0526

SAUER, RICHARD JOHN, developer fundraiser; b. Walker, Minn., Nov. 15, 1939; s. Herman and Katherine Elizabeth (Rieder) S.; m. Elizabeth Louise Hornstein, Aug. 18, 1962; children: Michele, Alison, Maria, Peter. BS in Biology, St. John's U., Collegeville, Minn., 1962; MS in Zoology, U. Mich., Ann Arbor, 1964; PhD in Entomology, N.D. State U., 1967. Asst. prof. biology St. Cloud (Minn.) State U., 1967-68; asst. prof., then assoc. prof. entomology Mich. State U., East Lansing, 1968-76, acting assoc. dir. Mich. Agrl. Expt. Sta., 1975-76; prin. entomologist Coop. State Rsch. Svc., USDA, Washington, 1974-75; prof., head dept. entomology Kans. State U., Manhattan, 1976-80; dir. Agrl. Expt. Sta. U. Minn., St. Paul, 1980-89, v.p. agriculture, forestry and home econs., 1983-89; interim pres. U. Minn., Mpls., 1988-89; pres., CEO Nat. 4-H Coun., Chevy Chase, Md., 1989—. Mem. Entomol. Soc. Am. (pres. N.Cen. br. 1989-90), Am. Soc. Assn. Execs. Roman Catholic. Home: 1523 Ivystone Ct Silver Spring MD 20904-5476 Office: Nat 4-H Coun 7100 Connecticut Ave Chevy Chase MD 20815-4934

SAUER, ROBERT C., religious organization administrator. 3d v.p. Luth. Ch.-Mo. Synod, St. Louis. Office: 1333 S Kirkwood Rd Saint Louis MO 63122-7226

SAUERACKER, EDWARD, academic administrator; b. Bethpage, N.Y., Apr. 20, 1956; s. William Francis and Carol Veronica (Schuyler) S. BS magna cum laude, Hofstra U., 1978; MPh in Econs., CUNY, 1982, PhD in Econs., 1984. Rsch. asst. CUNY Grad. Ctr., 1978-82; asst. prof. econs. and fin. Baruch Coll., CUNY, 1984-86, asst. dir. Ctr. for Study of Bus. and Govt., 1982-86; asst. dean for assessment SUNY Empire State Coll., Old Westbury, N.Y., 1986—, asst. prof. econs., 1990—; asst. dean for assessment Harry Van Arsdale Jr. Sch. Labor Studies SUNY-ESC, N.Y.C., 1994—; adj. instr. dept. econs. and geography Hofstra U., 1979-84, adj. asst. prof., 1987—; editor Baruch Prospectus, Baruch Coll., CUNY, 1984; cons. in field. Author articles and column. N.Y. state rep. Coun. for Adult and Exptl. Learning, 1993-95; founder, mem. steering com. The Learning Collaborative, 1992—; bd. dirs. Help-Aid-Direction, Inc., 1991; sec. Met. Econ. Assn., 1988-91; trustee Hicksville Pub. Libr., 1994—. Unied Hosp. Fund grantee, 1985-86; CUNY fellow, Hofstra scholar, Danforth nominee; named to Outstanding Young Men of Am.; recipient Excellence in Profl. Svc. award SUNY Emprie State Coll. Mem. Kiwanis (pres. 1994—, divsn. circle-K chair 1994—), Phi Beta Kappa, Omicron Kappa Epsilon. Home: 43 Jay St Hicksville NY 11801-5855 Office: SUNY Empire State Coll Long Island Ctr PO Box 130 Old Westbury NY 11568-0130

SAUERBREY, ELLEN ELAINE RICHMOND, radio talk show host; b. Balt., Sept. 9, 1937; d. Edgar Arthur and Ethel Frederika (Landgraf) Richmond; m. Wilmer John Emil Sauerbrey, June 27, 1959. AB summa cum laude in Biology and English, Western Md. Coll., 1959. Biology instr., chmn. sci. dept. Baltimore County Sch. System, 1959-64; dist. mgr. Baltimore County U.S. Census, 1970; Md. Ho. of Dels., Annapolis, 1978-95, minority leader, 1986-95; radio talk show host Sta. WBAL; Rep. candidate for Gov., 1994. Rep. Nat. Committee Woman, Md., 1996—; del. Rep. Nat. Convs., 1968, 76, 84, 88, 92, 96, mem. credentials com., 1984, platform com., chmn. subcom. on economy, 1977; vice chmn. Rep. State Ctrl. Com. of Balt. County, 1966-71; trustee Md. Coun. Econ. Edn., Franklin Sq. Hosp.; founder United Citizens for Md.'s Future; mem. govt. activities com. United Cerebral Palsey Ctrl. Md.; nat. chmn. Am. Legis. exec. Coun., 1990-91. Recipient Pvt. Property award Greater Balt. Bd. Realtors, 1984; named Legislator of Yr., Md. Assn. Builders and Contractors, 1982, Am. Legis. Exec. Coun., 1986, Western Md. Coll. Alum of Yr., 1988, Outstanding Legis. Leader, Am. Legis. Exec. Coun., 1992, Rep. Woman of Yr., Md. Rep. Party, 1995. Mem. DAR, Nat. Fedn. rep. Women (Margaret Chase Smith award 1995), Md. Fedn. Rep. Women, Am. Legis. exch. Coun. (chmn. emeritus), Md. Farm Bur., Md. Conservative Union, Beta Beta, Beta, Phi Beta Kappa. Presbyterian. Avocations: gardening, travel.

SAUERHAFT, STAN, public relations executive, consultant; b. N.Y.C., Nov. 25, 1926; s. Al and Rae S.; m. Rosalie Cynthia Tolkin, Oct. 28, 1951; children: Richard Craig, Douglas Clark, Robert James. BA, U. Mich., 1948, MA, 1949. Editor, scriptwriter Paramount News, 1950-51; scriptwriter Hearst Metrotone News, N.Y.C., 1951-52; editor Food Bus. Mag., N.Y.C., 1952-53; acct. supr. Selvage, Lee & Chase, N.Y.C., 1953-55; v.p., mem. creative plans bd. Communications Counselors, Inc. McCann-Erickson, N.Y.C., 1955-59; pres. Chase and Sauerhaft Assocs., N.Y.C., 1959-65; exec. v.p., dir., mem. mgmt. com. Hill & Knowlton, Inc., N.Y.C., 1965-86; vice chmn. bd. , dir. Burson-Marsteller, U.S., 1987-88; vice chmn., dir. Burson-Marsteller Internat., 1988—; instr., lectr. Columbia U. Grad. Sch., 1962-65, NYU Grad. Bus. Sch., 1984-87. Author: The Merger Game, 1971; co-author: Image Wars, 1989; contbr. bus. articles and chpts. to anthologies. Chmn. West Point Civilian Adv. Com., N.Y., 1980—; mem. exec. com. of bd. Inst. for Pub. Rels. Rsch. and Edn., 1984—, LS&A Coll. of U. Mich., 1990—; mem. adv. bd. U. Mich. Staff sgt. AUS, 1945-46. Coll. of Fellows Pub. Rels. Soc. Am. (nat. accreditation bd. 1981-83), Pub. Rels. Soc. N.Y. (pres. 1983-85); mem. Soc. Profl. Journalists, Authors Guild, Pub. Affairs Coun., Am. Platform Tennis Assn. (v.p.), U. Mich. Alumni Club, Union League Club N.Y. (chmn. pub. affairs com. 1980-84), Burning Tree Country Club (Greenwich, Conn.), Wiindmill Club, Seabrook Island Club (S.C.). Republican. Avocations: golf, platform tennis, bridge. Home: 21 Windmill Pl Armonk NY 10504-2830 Office: Burson-Marsteller 230 Park Ave S New York NY 10003-1513 *A father's advice to his sons: If you can't outthink them, outwork them. But better yet, try to do both. Also, the best luck seems to befall the hardest workers.*

SAUFER, ISAAC AARON, lawyer; b. Bronx, N.Y., June 16, 1953; s. Solomon and Beatrice (Kanofsky) S.; m. Debra Edith Goldberg, June 26, 1977; children: Suzanne, Nancy, Scott, Daniel, Jonathan. BA, Yeshiva U., N.Y.C., 1975; JD, Bklyn. Law Sch., 1978; LLM in Taxation, NYU, 1982. Bar: N.Y. 1979, N.J. 1986, Fla. 1986, Conn. 1987. Summer intern N.Y. County Dist. Attys. Office, N.Y.C., 1976; legal editor Prentice-Hall, Inc., Englewood Cliffs, N.Y., 1979-80; assoc. Kurzman Karelsen & Frank, N.Y.C., 1980-85, ptnr., 1986—; adj. asst. prof. NYU Sch. Continuing Edn., N.Y.C., 1988—; lectr. seminars, 1991, 93, 95. Co-author: (N.Y. real property forms) Bergerman & Roth, 1986-87. Office: Kurzman Karelsen & Frank Ste 2300 230 Park Ave New York NY 10169-0005

SAUFLEY, WILLIAM EDWARD, banker, lawyer; b. Washington, Mar. 7, 1956; s. Franklin Dewit and Ruth Constance (Wright) S.; m. Leigh Ingalls, Jan. 3, 1981. BA, Dartmouth Coll., 1977; JD, U. Maine, 1980. Bar: Maine 1980, U.S. Dist. Ct. Maine 1980. Of counsel Maine Legislature, Augusta, 1981-84; v.p. counsel Maine Savs. Bank, Portland, 1984-88, gen. counsel, sec., 1988-91; corp. sec. The One Bancorp, Portland, 1984-91, gen. counsel, 1989-91; sr. v.p., gen. counsel Fleet Bank of Maine, Portland, 1992-94; of counsel Monaghan, Leahy, Hochadel & Libby, Portland, 1995-96; sr. v.p. Atlantic Bank N.A., Portland, 1996—. Trustee 75 State St Home for Elderly, Portland, 1986-92. Mem. ABA, Maine Bar Assn. (chmn. consumer and fin. instns. law sect.). Democrat. Roman Catholic. Avocations: photography, computers. Home: 51 Bramblewood Dr Portland ME 04103-3796 Office: Atlantic Banak NA 100 Foden Rd South Portland ME 04106

SAUL, B. FRANCIS, II, bank executive; b. Washington, Apr. 15, 1932; s. Andrew Maguire and Ruth Clark (Sheehan) S.; m. Elizabeth Patricia English, Apr. 30, 1960; children: Sharon Elizabeth, B. Francis III, Elizabeth Willoughby, Andrew Maguire II, Patricia English. Grad. Georgetown Prep. Sch., 1950; BS, Villanova U., 1954, DCS (hon.), 1989; LLB, U. Va., 1957. Bar: D.C. 1959. Chmn., pres. B.F. Saul Co., Chevy Chase, Md., 1957—; chmn., trustee B.F. Saul Real Estate Investment Trust Co., Chevy Chase, 1964—; With Chevy Chase Bank, F.S.B., 1969—, chmn., CEO, founder; chmn. Fin. Gen. Bankshares, Inc., 1978-82; chmn., CEO, trustee Saul Ctrs., Inc., 1993—; chmn. bd. dirs. 1st Am. Bankshares, Inc., Washington, 1978-85; dir. Colonial Williamsburg Hotel Properties, Inc., 1983—; fin. cons. Archdiocese of Washington, 1990—; mem. honors com. John F. Kennedy Ctr. Performing Arts, 1995—; dir. bd. vis. and govs. Washington Coll., 1995—; mem. bd. advisors CLW Life and Annuity Acquisition Corp., 1994—. Trustee Fed. City Coun., Nat. Geographic Soc., 1985—, Suburban Hosp., 1972-76; dirs. Wadsworth Preservation Trust, 1983—; trustee Brookings Inst., 1987-93, hon. trustee, 1993—; trustee Corcoran Gallery Art, Washington, 1972-90; mem. vis. com. Sch. Architecture U. Va., 1985—; bd. dirs. Garfinckel, Brooks Bros., Miller & Rhoads, 1970-81, Madeira Sch., Greenway, Va., 1978-88, Portsmouth Abbey Sch., R.I., 1979-84, United World Coll. of Am. West, Montezuma, N.Mex., 1982-85, D.C. Fund for Creative Space, 1980-82, D.C. chpt. ARC, 1964-86; mem. Folger Shakespeare Libr. Com., 1985—; pres. D.C. Soc. for Crippled Children, 1973-75. Mem. Mortgage Bankers Assn. Met. Washington (pres. 1968), Nat. Assn. Real Estate Investment Trusts (pres. 1973-74), Alfalfa Club, Alibi Club, Met. Club, Knights of Malta, Chevy Chase Club, Burning Tree Club, Friendly Sons of St. Patrick (pres. 1992), Wianno Club, The Brook Club, Roman Catholic. Home: 1 Quincy St Chevy Chase MD 20815-4226 Office: BF Saul Co 8401 Connecticut Ave Chevy Chase MD 20815-5803

SAUL, GEORGE BRANDON, II, biology educator; b. Hartford, Conn., Aug. 8, 1928; s. George Brandon and Dorothy (Ayers) S.; m. Sue Grau Williams, Mar. 28, 1953. A.B., U. Pa., 1949, A.M., 1950, Ph.D., 1954. From instr. to assoc. prof. Dartmouth, 1954-67; prof. biology Middlebury (Vt.) Coll., 1967—, chmn. dept., 1968-76, 91-93, v.p. acad. affairs, 1976-79; Research asso. Calif. Inst. Tech., 1964-65; NSF postdoctoral fellow U. Zurich, Switzerland, 1959-60; vis. scientist Boyce Thompson Inst. for Plant Research, Yonkers, N.Y., 1972-73. Author papers in field. Fellow AAAS; mem. Pa. Acad. Sci., Genetics Soc. Am., Am. Genetics Assn., Radiation Research Soc., N.Y. Acad. Scis., Sigma Xi. Club: Lion. Home: Munger St

RR 3 Box 2575 Middlebury VT 05753 Office: Middlebury Coll Dept Biology Middlebury VT 05753

SAUL, JOHN WOODRUFF, III, writer; b. Pasadena, Calif., Feb. 25, 1942; s. John Woodruff and Adeline Elizabeth (Lee) S. Student, Antioch Coll., 1959-60, Cerritos Coll., 1960-61, Mont. State U., Missoula, 1961-62, San Francisco State Coll., 1963-65. In various positions primarily in L.A. and San Francisco, 1965-76. Author: Suffer The Children, 1977, Punish the Sinners, 1978, Cry for the Strangers, 1979, Comes the Blind Fury, 1980, When the Wind Blows, 1981, The God Project, 1982, Nathaniel, 1984, Brainchild, 1985, Hellfire, 1986, The Unwanted, 1987, The Unloved, 1988, Creature, 1989, Second Child, 1990, Sleep Walk, 1990, Darkness, 1991, Shadows, 1992, Guardian, 1993, The Homing, 1994, Black Lightning, 1995; also other novels under pseudonyms. Bd. dirs. Seattle Theatre Arts, 1978-80; bd. govs. Tellurian Communities, Inc., Madison, Wis.; v.p. Chester Woodruff Found., N.Y.C. Mem. Authors Guild. Democrat. Swedenborgian. Office: care Jane Rotrosen 318 E 51st St New York NY 10022-7803 *For a writer, the education of experience is without doubt the best education.*

SAUL, JULIAN, retail executive; b. 1940. CEO Queen Carpet, Dalton, Ga., 1962—. Office: PO Box 1527 Dalton GA 30722

SAUL, KENNETH LOUIS, retired utility company executive; b. Columbus, Ohio, Aug. 29, 1923; s. Aloysius Louis and Ruth Geneva (Duke) S.; m. Shirley Ann Todd, Feb. 14, 1953; children: Carl, Deborah, Kenneth, Mark, Lori, Richard. BBA, Ohio State U., 1949. Various mgmt. positions Columbus & So. Ohio Elec. Co., 1955-70, asst. controller, 1970-74; v.p., controller Tucson Elec. Power, 1974-84, sr. v.p., chief fin. officer, 1984-88, also bd. dirs.; bd. dirs. Ohio Steel Products, Columbus, Engring. Rsch. Assocs., Tucson. Chmn. bd. Bishop Hartley High Sch., Columbus, 1967-73; treas., bd. dirs. United Way, Tucson, 1975-81, Carondelet Health Care, Tucson, 1982-85, St. Joseph's Hosp., Tucson, 1976-82. Staff sgt. USAAF, 1943-45, PTO. Mem. Nat. Assn. Accts., Skyline Country Club (pres. 1979-80), SMOO Investment Club (pres. 1970-73). Republican. Roman Catholic. Avocations: golf, swimming, baseball, football. Home: 6260 E Placita El Vuelo Tucson AZ 85715-1284

SAUL, NORMAN EUGENE, history educator; b. LaFontaine, Ind., Nov. 26, 1932; s. Ralph Odis and Jessie (Neff) S.; m. Mary Ann Culwell, June 27, 1959; children: Alyssa, Kevin, Julia. B.A., Ind. U.- Bloomington, 1954; M.A., Columbia U., 1959, Ph.D., 1965; postgrad., Leningrad State U. (USSR), 1960-61. Instr. history Purdue U., 1962-65; asst. prof. Brown U., 1965-68; vis. assoc. prof. Northwestern U., 1969-70; assoc. prof. U. Kans., Lawrence, 1970-75, prof. history, 1975—, chmn. dept. history, 1981-89. Author: Russia and the Mediterranean 1797-1807, 1970, Sailors in Revolt, 1978, Distant Friends: The United States and Russia, 1763-1867, 1991, Concord and Conflict: The United States and Russia, 1867-1914, 1996. Fulbright scholar, London, 1954-55, Helsinki, 1968-69; Soviet Am. exch. scholar Internat. Rsch. and Exch. Bd., Moscow, 1973-74, 91-92; fellow Ford Found., 1957-59, Kennan Inst., 1976, 84, 91, 95, Hall Ctr. for Humanities, 1989, 95; recipient Byron Caldwell Smith Book award for Distant Friends Hall Ctr. for Humanities, 1993. Mem. Am. Hist. Assn., Am. Assn. Advancement of Slavic Studies, Kans. State Hist. Soc. Home: 1002 Crestline Dr Lawrence KS 66049-2607 Office: Dept of History U of Kans Lawrence KS 66045

SAUL, PETER A., artist, educator; b. San Francisco, Aug. 16, 1934; s. Arthur Charles and Mabel Clare (Kelso) S.; m. Vicki Goorman, Jan. 1960 (div. Aug. 1975); children: Rufin, Leif; m. Sarah Patricia Lutz; 1 child, Gwendolyn. BFA, Washington U., St. Louis, 1956; student, Stanford U., Calif. Sch. Fine Arts. Prof. art U. Tex., Austin. Solo exhbns. include Allan Frumkin Gallery, N.Y.C. and Chgo., Galerie Breteau, Paris, La Tartaruga Gallery, Rome, Reed Coll., Portland, Oreg., Youngstown (Ohio) State U., Frumkin Struve Gallery, Chgo., Tex. Gallery, Houston, Frumkin/Adams Gallery, N.Y.C., Galerie Bonnier, Geneva, Galerie du Centre, Paris, Herbert Palmer Gallery, L.A., Ynglingagatan I, Stockholm; exhibited in group shows at Art Inst. Chgo., U. Mich., Ann Arbor, San Francisco Mus. Modern Art, Rose Art Mus./Brandeis U., Mcpl. Mus., The Hague, Mus. Modern Art, N.Y.C., Mus. Modern Art, Paris, Whitney Mus. Am. Art, Taft Mus., Cin., Chrysler Mus., Norfolk, Va., Mus. Art, Ft. Lauderdale, Fla., Inst. Contemporary Arts, London, R.I. Sch. Design, Providence, U. N.C. at Greensboro, Phyllis Kind Gallery, N.Y.C. and Chgo., Mus. Contemporary Art, L.A., Frumkin/Adams Gallery, Nolan/Eckman, N.Y.C., numerous others; represented in collections at Art Inst. Chgo., Carnegie Inst., Pitts., Centre Pompidou, Paris, Kansas City Art Inst., Met. Mus. Art, N.Y.C., Mus. of Art, Honolulu, Mus. Modern Art, N.Y.C., San Franciso Mus. Modern Art, Stedelijk Mus., Ostende, Belgium, Whitney Mus. Am. Art, others. Office: care Frumkin/Adams Gallery 50 W 57th St New York NY 10019-3914

SAUL, RALPH SOUTHEY, financial service executive; b. Bklyn., May 21, 1922; s. Walter Emerson and Helen Douglas (Coutts) S.; m. Bette Jane Bertschinger, June 16, 1956; children: Robert Southey, Jane Adams. B.A., U. Chgo., 1947; LL.B., Yale U., 1951. Bar: D.C. 1951, N.Y. 1952. With Am. Embassy, Prague, Czechoslovakia, 1947-48; assoc. firm Lyeth & Voorhees, N.Y.C., 1951-52; asst. counsel to Gov. N.Y. State, 1952-54; staff atty. RCA, 1954-58; with SEC, 1958-65, dir. div. trading and markets, 1963-65; v.p. corporate devel. Investors Diversified Services, Inc., Mpls., 1965-66; pres. Am. Stock Exchange, N.Y.C., 1966-71; co-CE, chmn. mgmt. com. First Boston Corp., 1971-74; chmn., chief exec. officer INA Corp., Phila., 1975-82, CIGNA Corp., Phila., 1982-84; bd. dirs. PH-II, Inc., Commonwealth Ventures, Phila. Ventures Liberty Fund, Am. Bldgs. Co., Horace Mann Educators Corp. Trustee Com. for Econ. Devel., Brookings Inst.; chmn. Ednl. Quality Work Force Adv. Bd. With USNR, 1943-46, PTO. Mem. ABA, N.Y. Stock Exch. (regulatory adv. com.), Union League , Merion Golf Club, Links Club. Home: 549 Avonwood Rd Haverford PA 19041-1602 Office: Cigna Corp One Logan Square PO Box 7716 18th and Cherry Sts Philadelphia PA 19192

SAUL, STEPHANIE, journalist; b. St. Louis, Jan. 28, 1954; d. Elmer William and Nancy (Cromer) S.; m. Walt Bogdanich, Jan. 2, 1982; children: Nicholas Walter, Peter Eric. BA, U. Miss., 1975. Reporter New Albany (Miss.) Gazette, 1974, Clarion-Ledger, Jackson, Miss., 1975-80, The Plain Dealer, Cleve., 1980-84; nat. corr. Newsday, Melville, N.Y., 1984—. Recipient Silver Gavel award ABA, 1980, George Polk award for regional reporting, 1981, Nat. Press Club award, 1990, IRE award Investigative Reporters and Editors, 1995, Headliner award Atlantic City Press Club, 1995, Roy Howard award Scripps Howard Found., 1995, Pulitzer prize for investigative reporting, 1995. Office: Newsday 235 Pinelawn Rd Melville NY 11747-4250

SAUL, WILLIAM EDWARD, academic administrator, civil engineering educator; b. N.Y.C., May 15, 1934; s. George James and Fanny Ruth (Murokh) S.; m. J. Muriel Held Eagleburger, May 11, 1976. BSCE, Mich. Tech. U., 1955, MSCE, 1961; PhD in Civil Engring., Northwestern U., 1964. Registerd profl. engr., Wis., Idaho, Mich., profl. structural engr., Idaho. Mech. engr. Shell Oil Co., New Orleans, 1955-59; instr. engring. mechanics Mich. Tech. U., Houghton, 1960-62; asst. prof. civil engring. U. Wis., Madison, 1964-67, assoc. prof., 1967-72, prof., 1972-84; dean Coll. Engring., prof. civil engring. U. Idaho, Moscow, 1984-90; prof. civil engring. Mich. State U., East Lansing, 1990—, chair dept. civil and environ. engring., 1990-95; cons. engr., 1961—; bd. dirs. Idaho Rsch. Found., 1984-90; vis. prof. U. Stuttgart, Fed. Republic Germany, 1970-71. Co-editor Conf. of Methods of Structural Analysis, 1976. Fulbright fellow 1970-71; von Humboldt scholar, 1970-71. Fellow ASCE (pres. Wis. sect. 1983-84); mem. NSPE, Mich. Soc. Profl. Engrs., Internat. Assn. Bridge and Structural Engrs., Am. Concrete Inst., Am. Soc. Engring. Edn., Sigma Xi, Phi Kappa Phi, Tau Beta Pi, Chi Epsilon. Avocations: hiking, reading, travel, gadgets. Home: 1971 Cimarron St Okemos MI 48864-3905 Office: Mich State U A349 Engring Bldg East Lansing MI 48824

SAULMON, SHARON ANN, librarian; b. Blackwell, Okla., June 13, 1947; d. Ellis Gordon and Willa Mae Overman; 1 child, John Henry. AA, No. Okla. Coll., 1967; BA, Ctrl. State U., 1969, MBA, 1987; MLS, U. Okla., 1974; postgrad., Okla. State U., 1982. Children's libr. Met. Libr. Sys., Oklahoma City, 1969-74, coord. pub. svcs., 1974-77, asst. chief ext. svcs., 1977-80; reference/special projects libr. Rose State Coll., Midwest City, Okla., 1980-91, head libr., 1991—; adj. faculty Rose State Coll., 1983—; program chair Global Okla. Multi-Cultural Festival, 1993; mem. nat. adv. panel for assessment of sch. and pupb. librs. in support of nat. edn. goals, 1995—; spkr. various civic and profl. orgns. Contbr. articles to profl. jours. Bd. dirs. Areawide Aging Agy., 1974-77; chair Met. Libr. Commn., 1990—, disbursing agt., chair fin. com., 1986-88, long-range planning com., 1985-87; chair bd. dirs. Met. Librs. Network Ctrl. Okla., 1989-90, chair alternative funding com., 1990—, newsletter editor, 1987-89, chair electronic media com., 1987-89. Recipient Outstanding Contbn. award Met. Libr. Sys., Friends of the Libr., 1990, Disting. Svc. award Okla. Libr. Assn., 1995. Mem. AAUW, Am. Libr. Trustee Assn. (pres. 1994-95, 1st v.p., pres. elect 1993-94, newsletter editor 1989-93, chair publs. com. 1987-92, regional v.p. 1985-88, chair speakers bur. com. 1991-92), Assn. Coll. and Rsch. Librs. (Cmty. and Jr. Coll. sect.), Pub. Libr. Assn., Am. Mktg. Assn., Okla. Libr. Assn. (conf. preview editor 1990-91, chair trustees divsn. 1989-90, mem. coms., disting. svc. award 1995). Democrat. Methodist. Avocations: organist, tennis. Office: Rose State Coll Libr 6420 SE 15th St Midwest City OK 73110-2704

SAULS, DON, religious organization administrator, clergyman; b. Eureka, N.C.; m. Marie Brown; children: Donna, Dale. B in Sacred Lit., Holmes Sch. of the Bible, Greenville, S.C., 1967; MA in Adult Edn., N.C. State U., 1984; postgrad., N.C. Wesleyan Coll. Ordained to ministry Pentecostal Free Will Bapt. Ch., 1966. Pastor Pentecostal Free Will Bapt. Ch., Benson, N.C., 1967-74, gen. dir. Christian Edn. dept., 1971-84, gen. supt., 1984—; tchr. Heritage Bible Coll., Dunn, N.C., 1971—, also trustee; chmn. bd. dirs., sec., mem. bd. adminstrn. Pentecostal Fellowship N.Am., 1988-91, Pentecostal and Charismatic Chs. of N.Am.; lectr. U.S. and abroad. Columnist Messenger, 1984—, now editor-in-chief; contbr. articles to jours. in field. Chmn. bd. dirs. Cape Fear Christian Acad.; pres. Harnett County Helpnet. Mem. Kiwanis (former pres. Dunn club, bd. dirs., dir. children's programs dist. 11). Office: Pentecostal Free Will Bapt Ch PO Box 1568 Dunn NC 28335-1568

SAUMIER, ANDRE, finance executive; b. Montreal, Que., Can., Aug. 26, 1933; s. Robert and Georgette (Sansoucy) S.; children—Sonia, Genevieve, Verushka. BA, U. Montreal, 1950; LTh, Angelicum U., Rome, 1955; MA, U. Chgo., 1958; MBA, Harvard U., 1962. Research assoc. Battelle Inst., Columbus, Ohio, 1962-63; dir. research Urban Affairs Council, Ottawa, Ont., Can., 1963-67; asst. dep. minister rural devel., regional devel., urban affairs Can. Govt., Ottawa, Ont., Can., 1967-75; dep. sec. gen. to cabinet, dep. minister of mines, water & energy Que. Govt., Quebec City, 1975-79; sr. v.p. Richardson Greenshields Co., Montreal, 1979-85; pres., chief exec. officer Montreal Stock Exchange, 1985-87; chmn. Saumier Morrisson & Davidson Inc., Investment Bankers, Montreal, 1987-89, Saumier Freres Conseil, Fin. Advisors, Montreal, 1989—; bd. dirs., chmn. Societe Nat. de L'Amiante, Montreal; chmn. Sebentar Holdings Inc., Unilever Can., Inc., Toronto, Alyvanor Inc., Montreal, Virage Prodns., Inc., Vista Info. Tech. Inc., Minorca Inc., Montreal, Can. ASEAN Ctr., Singapore; advisor World Resources Inst., Washington, Ministry of Fin. of Indonesia, Jakarta, Ministry of Fin. of Gabon, Libreville, Ministry of Fin. of Kazakjstan, Almaty, Office of Prime Min., Govt. of Vietnam, Hanoi; bur. de consultation de Montreal, City of Montreal, Que. Contbg. author books on environment. Bd. govs. Nouveau-Monde Theater, Montreal, 1983—, Quebec Press Coun. Found. Decorated officer Nat. Order of Niger, 1972, Order of St.-Lazarus of Jerusalem, 1987; recipient Merit award Montreal C. of C., 1985, 88. Home: 65 St Paul W Apt 403, Montreal, PQ Canada H2Y 3S5 Office: Saumier Freres Conseil, 5 Place Ville-Marie Ste 1234, Montreal, PQ Canada H3B 2G2

SAUNBY, JOHN BRIAN, petrochemical company executive; b. Hull, Eng., Mar. 7, 1933; came to U.S., 1959; s. Clive Henry and Frances Evelyn (Smith) S.; m. Eileen Mary Hillman, Sept. 1, 1956; children: Carole, Linda. B.S. in Chem. Engring., Birmingham U., Eng., 1954, Ph.D., 1957. Postdoctoral fellow NRC, Ottawa, Can., 1957-59; chem. engr. Union Carbide Corp., South Charleston, W.Va., 1959-65, group leader, 1965-73, assoc. dir., 1973-80, dir. licensing, 1978-80, dir. rsch. and devl., 1980-92; cons. R&D NSF EPSCOR program, 1992—; chmn. NSF Exptl. Program for Stimulation of Competitive Rsch., W.Va., 1980-85, 89-92; W.Va. rep. So. Tech. Coun., 1989-92. Patentee in field. Bd. dirs. Kanawha Valley Youth Orch., Charleston, 1972-78, pres., 1972-78; bd. dirs. W.Va. Opera Theater, Charleston, 1978-79; mem. arts and scis. adv. bd. W.Va. U., 1985-92. Fellow Trinidad Leaseholds Ltd., 1954-56; fellow Shell Petroleum Co., 1956-57. Mem. Am. Inst. Chem. Engrs. Club: Les Amis du Vin (Charleston).

SAUNDERS, ADAH WILSON, physical education educator; b. Balt.; d. William Llewellyn and Irene Bertha (Dorkins) Wilson; 1 child, Leigh Robert. BS, Hampton U., 1967; MS, Columbia U. Teacher's Coll., 1971. Instr. phys. edn. Hunter Coll CUNY, N.Y.C., 1967-68, Bronx C.C., N.Y.C., 1968-69; phys. edn. tchr. N.Y.C. Bd. Edn., 1971—, dean students, 1993—; coach N.Y. Jr. Tennis League. Inventor: (bd. game) The Presidency; patentee: Rollice Shoe, 1991. Grantee N.Y.C. Bd. Edn., The Early Morning Health Club, 1985. Mem. United Fedn. Tchrs., Am. Fedn. Tchrs., Queens C. of C. Home: 41-10 Bowne St Apt 7V Flushing NY 11355-5612 Office: Leonardo Da Vinci Sch 98-50 50th Ave Corona NY 11368-2757

SAUNDERS, ARLENE, opera singer; b. Cleve., Oct. 5, 1935. MusB, Baldwin-Wallace Coll., 1957. Tchr. voice Rutgers U., New Brunswick, N.J., 1987-88; tchr. classical vocal repertoire Abraham Goodman Sch., N.Y.C., 1987-88; advisor, tchr. vocal dept. NYU, 1990—, tchr. master classes, head opera dept., 1990-96; tchr. master classes Baldwin Wallace Coll., Santa Fe Opera Co., etc.; founder, dir. Opera Mobilé, Inc., N.Y.C., 1991—; adjudicator Met. Opera Regional Auditions, Liederkranz Voice Auditions, etc. Debut Milan Opera, 1961; Met. Opera debut in Die Meistersinger, 1976; specializes in Strauss and Wagner; performer with Phila. Opera, Lyric Opera, Houston Opera, Covent Garden, London, Teatro Colon, Buenos Aires, San Francisco Opera, Vienna Staatsoper, Paris Opera, Australian Opera, Sydney, Berlin Deutsche Opera, Munich Staatsoper, Hamburg State Opera, 1963-86, Rome Opera, Brussels Opera, Maggio Musicale, Florence, Italy, Geneva (Switzerland) Opera, Berlin Festival, Lisbon Opera, Glyndebourne Festival Opera, Eng., English Opera North, Boston Opera, N.Y.C. Opera; performed world premieres of Beatrix Cenci, 1971, Jakobowsky und der Oberst, 1965, Help, Help, The Globolinks, 1968, Ein Stern Geht Auf Aus Jaakob, 1970 (Gold medal Vercelli (Italy) voice competition); appeared in opera films including Arabella (title role), Meistersaenger (Eva), Marriage of Figaro (Countess), Help, Help the Globolinks (Mme. Euterpova), Der Freischuetz (Agathe), Gasparone (Carlotta); recs. for Philips and Victor. N.Y.C. Mayor's award, 1962; Kammersängerin Hamburg, 1967. Mem. Pi Kappa Lambda (Epsilon Phi chpt.). Address: 535 E 86th St New York NY 10028-7533

SAUNDERS, BRYAN LESLIE, lawyer; b. Newport News, Va., Apr. 18, 1945; s. Raymond Hayes and Lois Mae (Pair) S.; divorced; children: Kelly Brooke, Justin Lee; m. Anne Mason Dunbar, July 15, 1995. BS, East Tenn. State U., 1967; JD, U. Tenn., 1973. Bar: Va. 1973, U.S. Dist. Ct. (ea. dist.) Va. 1973, U.S. Ct. Appeals (4th cir.) 1991. Lawyer Cogdill & Assocs., Newport News, Va., 1973-76; pvt. practice Newport News, 1976—; commr. in chancery Cir. Ct. of Newport News, 1990—. Sgt. U.S. Army, 1968-71. Decorated Bronze star, 1971; recipient Outstanding Svc. to Law Enforcement Newport News and Police Dept., 1986. Mem. Va. Bar Assn., Nat. Assn. Criminal Def. Lawyers, Va. Coll. Criminal Def. Attys., Pi Kappa Phi, Pi Gamma Mu. Avocations: chess, bridge, bowling. Office: 728 Thimble Shoals Blvd Ste C Newport News VA 23606

SAUNDERS, CHARLES ALBERT, lawyer; b. Boulder, Colo., Jan. 18, 1922; s. Charles and Anna (Crouse) S.; m. Betti Friedel, Oct. 18, 1946; children—Melanie, Stephen, Cynthia, Shelley. BA, U. Houston, 1942; LLB, U. Tex., 1945. Bar: Tex. bar 1945. Since practiced in Houston; partner firm Fulbright & Jaworski, L.L.P., 1959—; dir. Brookside Corp. Editor: How To Live-and Die-With Texas Probate, 8 vols., 1968, Texas Estate Administration, 1975. Bd. dirs. Houston Symphony Soc., 1964—; bd. dirs. Am. Lung Assn., San Jacinto, 1965—, pres., 1972-73. Mem. ABA, State Bar Assn., Houston Bar Assn., Am. Coll. Trust and Estate Coun. (regent 1972-80, pres. 1978-79), Internat. Acad. of Estate and Trust Law, Assn. Cmty. TV (bd. dris. 1970—). Republican. Presbyterian. Home: 19 Willowron Dr Houston TX 77024-7618 Office: Fulbright & Jaworski 1301 Mckinney St Ste 5100 Houston TX 77010-3095

SAUNDERS, CHARLES BASKERVILLE, JR., retired association executive; b. Boston, Dec. 26, 1928; s. Charles Baskerville and Lucy (Carmichael) S.; m. Margaret MacIntire Shafer, Sept. 9, 1950; children—Charles Baskerville III, George Carlton, Margaret Keyser, Lucy C., John R. Grad., St. Mark's Sch., 1946; A.B., Princeton, 1950. News reporter, polit. columnist Ogdensburg (N.Y.) Jour., 1950-51; edn. reporter Hartford (Conn.) Times, 1951-53; asst. dir. pub. relations Trinity Coll., Hartford, 1953-55; asst. dir. pub. info. Princeton, 1955-57; legis. asst. Sen. H. Alexander Smith, 85th Congress, 1957-58; asst. to asst. sec. for legislation HEW, 1958-59; asst. to sec. Arthur S. Flemming, 1959-61, dep. asst. sec. for legislation, 1969-71; asst. to pres. Brookings Instn., 1961-69; dep. commr. of edn. for external affairs U.S. Office Edn., 1971-72; dep. asst. sec. for edn. HEW, 1973-74; dir. govt. relations Am. Council on Edn., 1975-78, v.p. for govt. relations, 1978-87, sr. v.p., 1987-92. Author: Brookings Institution: A Fifty-Year History, 1966, Upgrading the American Police, 1970. Mem. Montgomery County Bd. Edn., 1966-70, Md. Higher Edn. Commn., 1989— (chmn. 1994-95, vice chmn. 1995—); chmn. bd. dirs. Md. Higher Edn. Loan Corp., 1994-95. Republican. Presbyterian. Home: 7622 Winterberry Pl Bethesda MD 20817-4848

SAUNDERS, DAVID ALAN, lawyer; b. Chgo., June 3, 1939; s. Elmer M. and Eleanor (Lindauer) S.; m. Judith Obalil, June 15, 1963; children: Lynn Ellen, Laura Beth. BA, Oberlin Coll., 1961; JD, U. Chgo., 1964. Bar: Ill. 1964, U.S. Dist. Ct. (no. dist.) Ill. 1964, U.S. Ct. Appeals (7th cir.) 1965. Assoc. Hoffman & Davis, Chgo., 1964-69, ptnr., 1969-86; ptnr. Seyfarth, Shaw, Fairweather & Geraldson, Chgo., 1986-; lectr. on pub. fin. for various bar and govt. fin. assns. Active Bd. Ethics, Evanston, Ill., 1986--. Mem. ABA, Chgo. Bar Assn., Nat. Assn. Bond Lawyers, Chgo. Council Lawyers. Home: 1133 Forest Ave Evanston IL 60202-1407 Office: Seyfarth Shaw Fairweather 55 E Monroe St Ste 4200 Chicago IL 60603-5803

SAUNDERS, DEBRA J., columnist; b. Newton, Mass., Dec. 8, 1954. BA in Latin and Greek, U. Mass., Boston, 1980. Asst. dir. Arnold Zenher Assocs., 1982-83; writer/rschr., account exec. Todd Domke Assocs., Sacramento, 1983-84, Russo Watts & Rollins, Sacramento, 1985-86; asst. to Rep. Leader Calif. Legislature, Sacramento, 1987-88; columnist, editl. writer L.A. Daily News, 1988-92; columnist San Francisco Chronicle, 1992—; leader study group on polit. speechmaking Harvard U., Cambridge, Mass., 1984; tchr. editl. and column writing UCLA Ext., 1992. Office: San Francisco Chronicle 901 Mission St San Francisco CA 94103-2905

SAUNDERS, DERO AMES, writer, editor; b. Starkville, Miss., Sept. 27, 1913; s. Madison and Erin (Hearon) S.; m. Beatrice Nair, May 23, 1936; children: David, Richard. A.B., Dartmouth Coll., 1935; A.M., Columbia U., 1938. Lectr., lecture mgr., contbr. to various mgs., 1936-42; with Fgn. Econ. Adminstrn., Washington and Cairo, Egypt, 1943-45; chief Fgn. Econ. Adminstrn. (Middle East div.), 1945; asso. editor Fortune mag., 1945-57; v.p. Med. and Pharm. Info. Bur., 1957-59; lectr. Hunter Coll., 1960-61, 67—; assoc. editor Forbes mag., 1960-62, sr. editor, 1962-66, exec. editor, 1966-81, contbg. editor, 1982—. Contbg. author: Why Do People Buy?, 1953, The Changing American Market, 1954; Editor: The Portable Gibbon, 1952, The Autobiography of Edward Gibbon, 1961; co-editor: The History of Rome, 1958; chmn. editorial bd.: Dartmouth Alumni mag., 1983-85. Pres. Dartmouth Alumni Council, 1970-71; Prin. U.S. civilian rep. Middle East Supply Center, 1945. Clubs: Players (N.Y.C.); Heights Casino (Bklyn.). Home: 446 W 22nd St New York NY 10011-2502 Office: 60 5th Ave New York NY 10011-8802

SAUNDERS, DONALD HERBERT, utility company executive; b. Gallipolis, Ohio, Dec. 1, 1935; s. Clyde Edwin and Daisy Mae (Betz) S.; m. Dolores Marie Martin, Jan. 4, 1958; children: Scott, Glenn, Laura, Ellen. BBA, U. Toledo, 1957, MBA, 1964. Budget and statis. analyst Toledo Edison Co., 1957-60, supr. customer records and acctg., 1960-63, supr. property acctg., 1963-66, mgr. gen. acctg., 1966-68, asst. contr., dir. acctg. records, 1968-71, contr., dir. acctg., 1971-79, treas., 1979-86, v.p. fin. and adminstrn., 1986-90, v.p. adminstrn. and govtl. affairs, 1990, pres., 1990—. Treas. City of Oregon, Ohio, 1972—; mem. adv. bd. St. Charles Hosp., Oregon, 1981—; trustee Metro Toledo YMCA, 1980—, St. Charles and Mercy Hosp., 1989—, United Way, Toledo, 1991, chmn. 1993; bd. dirs. Corp. for Effective Govt., 1987—, Pub. Broadcasting Found. N.W. Ohio, 1991—, Toledo coun. Boy Scouts Am., 1991—, Toledo chpt. ARC, 1991—; mem. Ohio Electric Utility Inst. Bd., 1991—. Named Outstanding Citizen of Oregon, Oregon C. of C., 1983. Mem. Fin. Execs. Inst. (sec. Toledo chpt. 1986-87, treas. 1987-88, 2nd v.p. 1988-89, 1st v.p. 1989-90, pres. 1990-91), Toledo C. of C. (named one of Outstanding Young Men of Toledo 1970), Air Force Assn., N.G. Assn., N.G. Assn. U.S., The Oregonian Club (past. pres.), U. Toledo Alumni Assn., Toledo Automobile (mem. corp. bd. 1984—), Masons, Blue Key. Republican. Avocations: golf, hunting, fishing. Home: 239 Ponderosa Dr Oregon OH 43616-2229 Office: Toledo Edison Co 300 Madison Ave Toledo OH 43652-1000

SAUNDERS, DONALD LESLIE, hotel owner, real estate investor; b. Brookline, Mass., Jan. 28, 1935; s. Irving M. Saunders and Shirley Brown; children: Lisa M., Pamela R. AB in Econs., Brown U., 1957; grad., Inst. Real Estate Mgmt., 1963; LLB (hon.), Pine Manor Coll., 1989. Real estate broker, R.I., Mass. Chmn., CEO Saunders Real Estate Corp., Boston, 1957—; CEO, gen. mgr. Saunders Real Estate, Hotels L.C., Boston; co-owner Boston Pk. Plz. Hotel & Towers, 1976—; gen. ptnr. SaunStar Land Co., LLC; bd. dirs. Hotel Lenox of Boston Inc. Bd. dirs. Park Sch. Corp., Brookline, Mass., Jerusalem Found., Inc., U.S.A.; pres. Farview Inc.; vice chmn. facilities and design com. Brown U., trustee emeritus, 1972—; mem. nat. adv. com. U.s. Com. for UNICEF; trustee Boston Ballet Co.; bd. dirs. Jerusalem Inst. Mgmt. Inc. at Harvard Bus. Sch.; bd. dirs. John Carter Libr. of Americana at Brown U. Recipient Nat. Jewish Hosp. and Research Ctr. Nat. Asthma Ctr. Humanitarian award, 1979, Back Bay Fedn. Community Devel. Ann. award, 1981, Historic Neighborhoods Found. award, 1986. Mem. Internat. Hotel Assn., Inst. Real Estate Mgmt. (key 2299), Nat. Assn. Realtors, Great Boston Real Estate Bd., Ocean Reef Club (Racquet Club), Brown U. Club, Lotos Club, The Players, Union League Club, Hope Club, Boston Tennis and Racquet Club, Ea. Point Yacht Club, Belmont Country Club, Bay Club, Downtown Club, Union Club Boston, Charles River Yacht Club. Office: Saunders Real Estate Corp Statler Bldg 700 20 Park Plz Boston MA 02116-4399

SAUNDERS, DOROTHY ANN, insurance company executive, sales management; b. Roxbury, N.C., Nov. 29, 1932; d. James William and Anna Bell (Wesley) Rice; m. Bernard L. Lewis, June 10, 1950 (dec. Jan. 1957); m. J.R. Saunders, Nov. 26, 1976 (dec. May 1981). Student, Md. U., 1950-53. Bookeeper, office mgr. TTN Cosmetics, Bethesda, Md., 1958; owner, mgr. Donnel's Hall of Gifts, Washington, 1959-63, Gifts, Inc., Washington, 1959-63; with U.S. Govt. Health, Edn., Welfare, Bethesda, 1965-73; owner, mgmt. in sales Dorothy Saunders Ins. Agy., Forest, Va., 1973—; vis. spkr. Bus. & Profl. Woman's Assn., Brookneal, Va., 1986-87; mem. bd. rsch. advisor ABI. Mem. Nat. Trust for Historic Preservation. Fellow Am. Biog. Inst.; mem. Internat. Platform Assn., Am. Lyceum Assn. Democrat. Baptist. Avocation: music. Home and Office: RR 1 Box 166D Huddleston VA 24104-9765

SAUNDERS, GEORGE LAWTON, JR., lawyer; b. Mulga, Ala., Nov. 8, 1931; s. George Lawton and Ethel Estell (York) S.; children: Kenneth, Ralph, Victoria; m. Terry M. Rose. B.A., U. Ala., 1956; J.D., U. Chgo., 1959. Bar: Ill. 1960. Law clk. to chief judge U.S. Ct. Appeals (5th cir.), Montgomery, Ala., 1959-60; law clk to Justice Hugo L. Black U.S. Supreme Ct., Washington, 1960-62; assoc. Sidley & Austin, Chgo., 1962-67, ptnr., 1967-90; founding ptnr. Saunders & Monroe, Chgo., 1990—. With USAF, 1951-54. Fellow Am. Coll. Trial Lawyers; mem. ABA, Ill. State Bar Assn., Chgo. Bar Assn., Order of Coif, Chgo. Club, Tavern Club, Point-O'Woods Club, Quadrangle Club, Law Club, Legal Club, Phi Beta Kappa. Democrat. Baptist. Home: 179 E Lake Shore Dr Chicago IL 60611-1351 Office: Saunders & Monroe 205 N Michigan Ave Chicago IL 60601-5925

SAUNDERS, IRIS ELAINE, social work administrator; b. N.Y.C.; d. Sidney Denison and Viola (Francis) Simon. BA, CUNY, 1946, MSW with honors, 1993. Cert. social worker, N.Y. Case mgr. Dept. Social Svcs., N.Y.C., 1949-51, supr., 1952-60; case supr. Div. Employment and Rehab., N.Y.C., 1960-70; dir. programs Human Resources Adminstrn., N.Y.C., 1970-92; ret., 1993; notary public N.Y. Bd. dirs. Tioga Carver Found.,

N.Y.C., 1989—, mem. dem. club; active M.L. Wilson Boys and Girls Club, N.Y.C., 1986—, The Schomburg Ctr. for Rsch. in Black Culture, 1993—. Recipient cert. of achievement Am. Soc. Profl. and Exec. Women, 1987, Vol. Leadership award united negro Coll. Fund, 1987, Vol. Recognition cert., 1988, 89, 90, Outstanding Fund Raising award M.L. Wilson Boys and Girls Club Harlem, 1991, Recognition for Cmty. Svc., N.Y. Newsday, 1992, cert. of merit Tioga Carver Cmty. Found., 1993, citation in Hunter Coll. Alumni Assn. Pub., 1994, 95. Mem. NASW, NAACP, AAUW, Assn. Black Social Workers, Hunter Coll. Alumni Assn., Nat. Caucus and Ctr. on Black Aged, Coalition 100 Black Women, Smithsonian Instn., Studio Mus. in Harlem. Democrat. Baptist. Avocations: crossword puzzles, music, poetry, creative writing, public spkg.

SAUNDERS, JAMES C., neuroscientist, educator; b. Elizabeth, N.J., May 8, 1941; s. Charles Oliver and Elizabeth Veronica (Drake) S.; m. Elaine Priscilla Edwards, Oct. 14, 1967; children: Breton Morris, Drew Charles. BA, Ohio Wesleyan U., 1963; MA, Conn. Coll., 1965, U. Pa., 1979; PhD, Princeton U., 1968. Lectr. dept. psychology Monash U., Victoria, Australia, 1969-72; rsch. assoc. Cen. Inst. for Deaf, St. Louis, 1972-73; asst. prof., then prof. dept. otorhinolaryngology U. Pa., Phila., 1973-92, acting dir. Inst. Neurol. Scis., 1980-83, prof., 1984—; guest scientist Karolinska Inst., Stockholm, 1984-85; exec. com. CHABA, Nat. Rsch. Coun., Washington, 1986-89; chmn. disorders rev. com. NIDCD, Bethesda, Md., 1987-89; mem. exec. coun. Assn. Rsch. Otolaryngology, Chgo., 1988-91; mem. com. on hearing and bioacoustics Nat. Inst. on Deafness and Other Communications Disorders. Contbr. chpts., rev. papers to books on biology of hearing; contbr. articles on auditory neurobiology to profl. jours; author abstracts of meeting presentations on hearing. Recipient Basic Sci. Rsch. award Am. Acad. Otolaryngology, 1978, 87, Pa. Acad. Otolaryngology, 1982, Basic Sci. Excellence award (Claude Pepper award) NIDCD, 1988, Lindback award for disting. teaching U. Pa., 1992. Mem. AAAS, Acoustical Soc. Am., Soc. Neurosci., N.Y. Acad. Sci., Sigma Xi (legal cons. effects of noise on hearing). Democrat. Office: U Pa 5 Ravdin ORL 3400 Spruce St Philadelphia PA 19104 Home: 417 Bryn Mawr Ave Bala Cynwyd PA 19004-2619

SAUNDERS, KENNETH D., insurance company executive, consultant, arbitrator; b. Chgo., Jan. 4, 1927; s. Maurice and Mildred (Cochrane) S.; m. Jean S. Davies, Dec. 17, 1949; children: Karen Saunders Waugh, William Thomas. A.B., Dartmouth Coll., 1949. With Continental Casualty Co., Chgo., 1949-59; asst. v.p. Continental Casualty Co., 1957-59; exec. asst. Standard Accident Ins. Co., Detroit, 1959-62; with Combined Ins. Co. Am., Chgo., 1962-86; v.p. Combined Ins. Co. Am., 1969-74, sr. v.p., 1974-86; with Rollins, Burdick, Hunter, 1986-87. With USMC, 1945-46. Mem. Health Ins. Assn. Am. (com. leader), Chgo. Group Ins. Assn. (past treas., dir.), Internat. Ins. Soc. (charter mem.), Am. Arbitration Assn. (panel). Clubs: Economic (Chgo.), Tavern (Chgo.), Exmoor Country (Ill.), John's Island (Fla.). Office: 1418 Woodhill Dr Northbrook IL 60062-4661

SAUNDERS, LONNA JEANNE, lawyer, newscaster, talk show host; b. Cleve.; d. Jack Glenn and Lillian Frances (Newman) Slaby. Student, Dartmouth Coll.; AB in Polit. Sci. with hons., Vassar Coll.; JD, Northwestern U., 1981; cert. advanced study in Mass Media, Stanford U., 1992. Bar: Ill. 1981. News dir., morning news anchor Sta. WKBK-AM, Keene, N.H., 1974-75; reporter Sta. KDKA-AM, Pitts., 1975; pub. affairs dir., news anchor Sta. WJW-AM, Cleve., 1975-77; morning news anchor Sta. WBBG-AM, Cleve., 1978; talk host, news anchor Sta. WIND-AM, Chgo., 1978-82; atty. Arvey, Hodes, Costello & Burman, Chgo., 1981-82; host, news anchor WCIU-TV, Chgo., 1982-85; staff atty. Better Govt. Assn., Chgo., 1983-84; news anchor, reporter Sta. WBMX-FM, Chgo., 1984-86; pvt. practice, Chgo., 1985—; news anchor Sta. WKQX-FM, Chgo., 1987; instr. Columbia Coll., Chgo., 1987-90; guest talk host Sta. WMCA, N.Y.C., 1983, Sta. WMAQ, Chgo., 1988, Sta. WLS, Chgo., 1989, Sta. WWWE, Cleve., 1989, Sta. KVI, Seattle, 1994; host, prodr. The Lively Arts, Cablevision Chgo., 1986; talk show host The Lonna Saunders Show, Sta. KIRO, Seattle, 1995—; atty. Lawyers for Creative Arts, Chgo., 1985-91. Columnist Chgo. Life mag., 1986—; editl. bd. Jour. Criminal Law and Criminology, 1979-81; contbr. articles to profl. jours.; creator pub. affairs program WBBM-AM, Chgo., 1985; guest talk host WMAQ-Am, Chgo., 1988, WLS-AM, Chgo., 1989, WWWE-AM, Cleve., 1989, Sta. KVI, Seattle, 1994; talk host The Lonna Saunders Show, KIRO-AM, Seattle, 1995—. Recipient Akron Press Club award for best pub. affairs presentation, 1978; grantee Scripps Howard Found., 1978-81; AFTRA George Heller Meml. scholar, 1980-81. Fellow Am. Bar Found.; mem. ABA (mem. exec. coms. Lawyers and the Arts, Law and Media 1986-92, chmn. exec. com. Law and Media 1990-91, 91-92, Young Lawyers divsn. liaison to Forum Com. on Communications Law 1991-93, Commn. for Partnership Programs 1993-94, regional divsn. chair Forum on Communications Law 1995-96), NATAS, Women's Bar Assn. Ill., Dartmouth Lawyers Assn., Investigative Reporters and Editors, Sigma Delta Chi. Roman Catholic. Avocations: theater, piano. Office: 39 S La Salle St Ste 825 Chicago IL 60603-1603

SAUNDERS, NORMAN THOMAS, military officer; b. Amityville, N.Y., Oct. 19, 1942; s. Norman George and Marjory (Scott) S.; m. Christine Patricia Miller, Feb. 24, 1968; children: Thomas, Carré. BS, USCG Acad., 1964; MS, Naval Postgrad. Sch., Monterey, Calif., 1972; grad., Nat. War Coll., 1985. Commd. officer USCG, 1964, advanced through grades to Radm., 1991; br. chief edn. and tng. div. USCG, Washington, 1972-76; exec. officer USCGC COURAGEOUS, Port Canaveral, Fla., 1976-78; spl. projects officer personnel div. USCG, Washington, 1978-79, br. chief personnel div., 1979-82; comdg. officer USCGC DEPENDABLE, Panama City, Fla., 1982-84; spl. projects officer research and devel. USCG, Key West, Fla., 1985-86; comdr. USCG Group, Key West, 1986-88; chief intelligence and law enforcement br. 7th CG Dist., Miami, Fla., 1988-90; chief, ops. div. 7th USCG Dist., Miami, 1990-91; comdr. 2nd USCG Dist., St. Louis, 1991-93, mil. personnel command, Washington, 1993-94; chief Office of Law Enforcement and Def. Ops., 1994—. Mem. Mil. Order World Wars, Naval Order U.S., Coast Guard Combat VA, Ret. Officers Assn., Sigma Xi. Republican. Methodist. Avocations: running, tennis, fishing, reading. Home: 13479 Point Pleasant Dr Chantilly VA 22021-2446

SAUNDERS, PAUL CHRISTOPHER, lawyer; b. N.Y.C., May 21, 1941; s. John Richard and Agnes Grace (Kelly) S.; m. Patricia Newman, Sept. 14, 1968; children—Paul Christopher, Michael Eagan. A.B., Fordham Coll., 1963; J.D., Georgetown U., 1966; Certificat d'Études Politiques, Institut d'Études Politiques, Paris, 1962. Bar: N.Y. 1966, D.C. 1967, U.S. Supreme Ct. 1969. Assoc. Cravath, Swaine & Moore, N.Y.C., 1971-77, ptnr., 1977—. Mem. bd. editors Georgetown Law Jour., 1965-66; editor-in-chief The Advocate, 1969-70. Trustee Fordham U.; mem. bd. regents Georgetown U., chair bd. visitors Law Ctr.; trustee, vice chmn. Fordham Prep. Sch., 1986-94; v.p., bd. dirs. Legal Aid Soc., 1983-88; co-chair, bd. dirs., trustee Lawyers Com. for Civil Rights Under Law; mem. Cardinal's Com. of Laity, 1982-90. Capt. JAGC, U.S. Army, 1967-71. Decorated Knight of Malta, 1982, Meritorious Svc. medal. Fellow Am. Bar Found.; mem. ABA, N.Y. State Bar Assn., Assn. of Bar of City of N.Y., Phi Beta Kappa, Pi Sigma Alpha. Democrat. Roman Catholic. Clubs: Apawamis, Westchester Country (Rye, N.Y.). Home: 1220 Park Ave New York NY 10128-1733 also: 455 Polly Pk Rd Rye NY 10580-1949 Office: Cravath Swaine & Moore Worldwide Plz 825 8th Ave New York NY 10019-7416

SAUNDERS, PETER PAUL, investor; b. Budapest, Hungary, July 21, 1928; emigrated to Can., 1941, naturalized, 1946; s. Peter Paul and Elizabeth (Halom) Szende; m. Nancy Louise McDonald, Feb. 11, 1956; children: Christine Elizabeth McBride, Paula Marie. Student, Vancouver Coll., 1941-44; B.Com., U. B.C., 1948. Acct. Canadian Pacific Rly. Co., 1948-50; founder, pres. Laurentide Fin. Corp., Ltd., 1950-66, vice chmn., 1966-67; chmn., pres. Coronation Credit Corp. Ltd., Vancouver, B.C., Can., 1968-78, Versatile Corp. (formerly Coronation Credit Corp. and Cornat Industries Ltd.), Vancouver, B.C., Can., 1978-87; prin., pres. Saunders Investment Ltd., Vancouver, 1987—; bd. dirs. Computrol Security Sys. Ltd., Wajax Ltd., Greene Valley Concessions, AXA Pacific Ins. Co., Molnar Capital Corp.; mem. Vancouver adv. bd. Nat. Trust Co. Ltd.; pres., dir. Harlan Fairbanks Co. Ltd. Past pres. Vancouver Symphony Soc., 1968-70, Can. Cancer Soc., B.C. and Yukon Rdgion, 1975-77, Vancouver Art Gallery Assn., 1981-83; chmn. Vancouver Opera Round Table, 1984-92; bd. dirs. B.C. and Yukon Div. Arthritis Soc. Mem. Vancouver Club, Vancouver Lawn Tennis and Badminton Club, Shaughnessy Golf and Country Club, Royal Vancouver Yacht Club, Thunderbird Country Club (Rancho Mirage, Calif.). Avocations: golf, skiing, hunting, boating. Home: 3620 Alexandra St, Vancouver, BC Canada V6J 4B9 Office: Saunders Investment Ltd, PO Box 49352 Bentall Ctr, Vancouver, BC Canada V7X 1L4

SAUNDERS, PHILIP D., professional basketball team executive; b. Cleve., Feb. 23, 1955; m. Debbie Saunders; children: Ryan, Mindy, Rachel and Kimberly (twins). Student, U. Minn. Asst. coach U. Minn Golden Golphers, 1982-86, U. Tulsa, 1986-88; head coach Continental Basketball Assn. Rapid City (S.D.) Thrillers, 1988-89; head coach Continental Basketball Assn. La Crosse (Wis.) Catbirds, 1989-94, gen. mgr., 1991-93, team pres., 1991-94; head coach Continental Basketball Assn. Sioux Falls (S.D.) Skyforce; gen. mgr. Minn. Timberwolves, 1995—. Named CBA Coach of the Yr., 1989, 92. Office: Minn Timberwolves 600 First Ave North Minneapolis MN 55403*

SAUNDERS, RON, lawyer, former state legislator; b. Key West, Fla., Oct. 30, 1954; s. Jack and Edith (Hill) S. BS with high honors, U. Fla., 1976, JD, 1979. Bar: Fla. 1979. Pvt. practice Key West, 1979-94, Tallahassee, 1995—; mem. Fla. Ho. of Reps., 1986-94, chmn. appropriations com., 1990-92, chmn. cmty. affairs com., 1992-94; mem. Fla. Tax and Budget Reform Commn., 1993-94. Pres. Key West Jaycees, 1981-82; chmn. bd. trustees Fla. Keys C.C., 1983-86; pres. Fla. Keys Land and Sea Trust, 1990-91. Named Outstanding Chpt. Pres., Fla. Jaycees, 1982, Outstanding Young Floridian, 1993, Most Effective Mem., Fla. Ho. of Reps., 1991, 92. Mem. Fla. Bar Assn. (bd. govs. young lawyers sect. 1982-86). Democrat. Episcopalian. Address: PO Box 10923 Tallahassee FL 32302-3923

SAUNDERS, RUBIE AGNES, former magazine editor, author; b. N.Y.C., Jan. 31, 1929; d. Walter St. Clair and Rubie Gwendolyn (Ford) S. B.A., Hunter Coll. CUNY, 1950. Editorial sec. Parents Mag. Enterprises, Inc., N.Y.C., 1950-51; editorial asst. Parents Mag. Enterprises, Inc., 1951-53, asst. editor, 1953-54, mng. editor, 1955-60; editor Young Miss mag., 1960-80, editorial dir., 1967-80; instr. Inst. Children's Lit., 1980—. Author: Calling All Girls Party Book, 1966, Marilyn Morgan, R.N., 1969, Marilyn Morgan's Triumph, 1970, Concise Guide to Baby Sitting, 1972, Concise Guide to Smart Shopping and Consumerism, 1973, Quick and Easy Housekeeping, 1977, The Beauty Book, 1983, Good Grooming for Boys, 1989, Good Grooming for Girls, 1989. Bd. dirs. Feminist Press, New Rochelle Coun. on Arts.; mem., pres. New Rochelle Bd. Edn., 1991—. Named Outstanding Grad., 1960, elected to Hunter Coll. Hall of Fame, 1972; recipient 25 Yr. service award Cub Scout Pack 371, Bklyn., 1985. Mem. Westchester-Putnam Sch. Bds. Assn. (exec. com.). Home: 26 Glenwood Ave New Rochelle NY 10801-3602

SAUNDERS, RUSSELL JOSEPH, utility company executive; b. San Mateo, Calif., Oct. 4, 1937; s. Russell Lyall and Beatrice Virginia (Clyne) S.; m. Joan Virginia Donahue, Jan. 6, 1989; children from previous marriage: Shelli Marie, Laura Lee. Student, Stanford, 1955-56, San Mateo Coll., 1956-57, San Jose State Coll., 1957-61; BS in Acctg. and Fin., Grad. Sch. Bus. Adminstrn., Harvard U., 1970. Acct. Consol. Freighways, Inc., Menlo Park, Calif., 1958-66, dir. budgets, 1966; dir. finance Freightliner Corp., Portland, Oreg., 1966-67, v.p., finance, treas., 1967—, sr. v.p., 1973, also bd. dirs.; v.p. fin. Diamond Reo Trucks, Inc., Lansing, Mich., 1974-75; sr. v.p., controller Envirotech Corp., Menlo Park, 1975-82; v.p. fin. Baker Hughes Process Techs., Houston, 1982-91; v.p. fin., CFO, corp. sec. S.W. Water Co., West Covina, Calif., 1992-94, Phase Metrics, Inc., 1994—; dir. Freightliner Can., Ltd., Calif. Domestic Water Co. Mem. Multnomah County Tax Supervising and Conservation Commn., 1973-74; trustee Oreg. Mus. Sci. and Industry, Portland, 1970—, pres., 1973-74; dir. Found. Oreg. Research and Edn., 1973—. Mem. Planning Execs. Inst. (pres. 1965-66), Stanford Alumni Assn., Harvard Bus. Sch. Alumni Assn., Alpha Eta Sigma. Home: 6431 Lago Grande Dr Bonsall CA 92003 Office: 10260 Sorrento Valley Rd San Diego CA 92121

SAUNDERS, SALLY LOVE, poet, educator; b. Bryn Mawr, Pa., Jan. 15, 1940; d. Lawrence and Dorothy (Love) S. Student, Sophia U., Tokyo, Japan, 1963, U. Pa., Columbia; B.S., George Williams Coll., 1965. Tchr. Shipley Sch., Bryn Mawr, 1962-65, Agnes Irwin Sch., Wynnewood, Pa., 1964-65, Montgomery County Day Sch., Wynnewood, 1962, Miquon (Pa.) Sch., Waldron Acad., Merion, Pa., 1965-66, Phelps Sch., Malvern, Pa., 1965-70, Frankford Friends Sch. Phila., 1965-66, Haverford (Pa.) Sch., 1965-66, Friends Sem. Sch., N.Y.C., 1966-68, Ballard Sch., N.Y.C., 1966-67, Lower Merion Sch., Ardmore, Pa., nights 1967-71, Univ. Settlement House, Phila., 1961-63, Navajo Indian Reservation, Fort Defiance, Ariz., 1963, Young Men's Jewish Youth Center, Chgo., 1964-65, Margaret Fuller Settlement House, Cambridge, Mass., 1958-61; poetry therapist Pa. Hosp. Inst., 1969-74; also drug rehab. house Pa. Hosp. Inst., Phila.; poet in residence Tyrone Guthrie Ctr., Newbliss, Ireland, Aug. 1988; poetry workshop leader Pendle Hill Quaker Ctr., Wallingford, Pa., Apr. 1988; poetry week leader Ferry Beach, Saco, Maine, summer 1988; pioneer in poetry therapy. Poet, 1946—; poems pub. in periodicals including others; author: Past the Near Meadows, 1961, Pauses, 1978, Fresh Bread, 1982, Random Thoughts, 1992, Patchwork Quilt, 1993; contbr. poems to newspapers. Mem. Acad. Am. Poets, Nat. Fedn. State Poetry Socs., Am. Poetry League, Nat. League Am. Pen Women, Poetry Therapy Assn. (v.p.), Avalon Orgn., Authors Guild, Nat. Writers Club, Pen and Brush Club, N.H., Pa. poetry socs., Cath. Poetry Soc. (asso.), Fla. State Poetry Soc. (asso.). Episcopalian. Home: 2030 Vallejo St Apt 501 San Francisco CA 94123-4854 Office: 609 Rose Hill Rd Broomall PA 19008-2254 *So often during my life I have found great comfort and strength in writing and reading poetry. With my poetry I want to help others to get in touch with their own powers. Poetry, to me, is a rare and beautiful freedom and this is what I want to share with others.*

SAUNDERS, TERRY ROSE, lawyer; b. Phila., July 13, 1942; d. Morton M. and Esther (Hauptman) Rose; m. George Lawton Saunders Jr., Sept. 21, 1975. BA, Barnard Coll., 1964; JD, NYU, 1973. Bar: D.C. 1973, Ill. 1976, U.S. Dist. Ct. (no. dist.) Ill. 1976, U.S. Ct. Appeals (7th cir.) 1976, U.S. Supreme Ct. 1983. Assoc. Williams & Connolly, Washington, 1973-75; assoc. Jenner & Block, Chgo., 1975-80, ptnr., 1981-86; ptnr. Susman, Saunders & Buehler, Chgo., 1987-94; pvt. practice Law Offices of Terry Rose Saunders, Chgo., 1995—. Author: (with others) Securities Fraud: Litigating Under Rule 10b-5, 1989. Recipient Robert B. McKay award NYU Sch. Law. Mem. ABA (co-chair class actions and derivative suits com. sect. litigation 1992-95, task force on merit selection of judges), Ill. State Bar Assn., Chgo. Bar Assn., NYU Alumni Assn. (bd. dirs. 1985—), Order of Coif, Union League Club. Office: 30 N La Salle St Chicago IL 60602-2508

SAUNDERS, WARD BISHOP, JR., retired aluminum company executive; b. Gilroy, Calif., Nov. 26, 1919; s. Ward Bishop and Lamira (Doan) S.; m. Elaine McDermott, Oct. 11, 1942; children: Douglas L., Myra K., Leslie J. B.S., U. Calif.-Berkeley, 1942; J.D., Stanford U., 1948. Bar: Calif. 1948, U.S. Dist. Ct. (no. dist.) Calif. 1948, U.S. Supreme Ct. 1956. Atty. Kaiser Aluminum & Chem. Corp., Oakland, Calif., 1951-65, div. v.p., 1965-71; v.p. Kaiser Aluminum & Chem. Corp., Oakland, 1971-84; dir. Volta River Authority, Accra, Ghana, Aluminium Bahrain, Manama, Bahrain, Hindustan Aluminium Co., Bombay, India; mng. dir. Volta Aluminium Co. Ltd., Tema, Ghana, 1971-84; pres. Kaiser Aluminum Salaried Retirees Assn., 1991-93. Served to lt. USNR, 1942-46. Mem. State Bar Calif., Alameda County Bar Assn., Kaiser Aluminum Salaried Retirees Assn. (bd. dirs. 1988-94, v.p. 1995—), Commonwealth Club of Calif. Republican. Unitarian. Home: 6123 Estates Dr Oakland CA 94611-3117

SAUNDERS, W(ARREN) PHILLIP, JR., economics educator, consultant, author; b. Morgantown, W.Va., Sept. 3, 1934; s. Warren Phillip and Thelma Marie (Dotson) S.; m. Nancy Lee Trainor, June 16, 1956; children: Kathleen M., Kevin W., Keith A., Kent T., Kristine A. BA, Pa. State U., 1956; MA, U. Ill., 1957; PhD, MIT, 1964. Instr. econs. Bowdoin Coll., Brunswick, Maine, 1961-62; rsch. assoc., from asst. to assoc. prof. econs. Carnegie-Mellon U., Pitts., 1962-70; prof. econs. Ind. U., Bloomington, 1970—; assoc. dean Coll. of Arts and Scis. Ind. U., Bloomington, 1974-78, chmn. dept. econs., 1988-92; cons. Agy. for Instructional Tech., Bloomington, 1976-78, 81-84, 92-93. Author: (books) Political Dimension of Labor-Management Relations, 1986; author, editor: Framework for Teaching Basic Economic Concepts, 1995; (Workbooks) Introduction to Macroeconomics (16th edit.), 1996, Introduction to Microeconomics (16th edit.), 1996; contbr. articles to Am. Econ. Rev., 1964—. Chmn. staff-parish rels. com. First United Meth. Ch., Bloomington, 1982-94. Recipient Vilard award for disting. rsch., Nat. Assn. Econ. Educators, N.Y.C., 1986, Leavey award for edn. Freedoms Found., Valley Forge, Pa., 1986, Disting. Svc. award. Nat. Coun. Econ. Edn., 1995. Mem. Am. Econ. Assn., Midwest Econ. Assn. (1st v.p. 1988-89), Soc. Econs. Educators (pres. 1992-93). Home: 3725 Brownridge Rd Bloomington IN 47401-4209 Office: Ind Univ Dept Econs Bloomington IN 47405

SAUNDERS, WILLIAM HUNDLEY, JR., retired chemist, educator; b. Pulaski, Va., Jan. 12, 1926; s. William Hundley and Vivian (Watts) S.; m. Nina Velta Plesums, June 25, 1960 (dec. June 1982); children: Anne Michele, Claude William. BS in Chemistry, Coll. William and Mary, 1948; PhD in Organic Chemistry, Northwestern U., 1952. Rsch. assoc. MIT, 1951-53; instr. U. Rochester, 1953-56, from. asst. prof. to assoc. prof., 1956-64, prof. chemistry, 1964-91, faculty sr. assoc., 1991-95, chmn. dept., 1991-95, prof. emeritus, 1996—. Author: Ionic Aliphatic Reactions, 1965; (with A.F. Cockerill) Mechanisms of Elimination Reactions, 1973; (with L. Melander) Reaction Rates of Isotopic Molecules, 1980; contbr. numerous articles to profl. jours. With U.S. Army, 1944-45, ETO. Guggenheim fellow, 1960-61; Sloan Found. fellow, 1961-64; NSF sr. postdoctoral fellow, 1970-71. Mem. Am. Chem. Soc., Royal Soc. Chemistry, Phi Beta Kappa, Sigma Xi, Phi Lambda Upsilon. Democrat. Unitarian. Avocations: bicycling, cross country skiing, travel. Home: 15 Parkwood Ave Rochester NY 14620-3401 Office: U Rochester Dept Chemistry River Sta Rochester NY 14627

SAUNDERS, WILLIAM LOCKWOOD, financial consultant; b. Seattle, Dec. 13, 1911; s. William Guy and Elizabeth (Ruggles) S.; m. Marjorie Allen, Nov. 30, 1945 (dec.); 1 dau., Mary Lee; m. Margaret Cella, Feb. 13, 1959. B.A., U. Wash., 1948; M.B.A., Northwestern U., 1950. Resident mgr. Drumheller Ehrlichman & White, Aberdeen, Wash., 1933-36; with W.L. Saunders (investments), 1936-42; sales mgr. H. Irving Lee & Co., San Jose, Calif., 1946; fin. cons., 1946-48; with A.G. Becker & Co., Inc., Chgo., 1949—; v.p. A.G. Becker & Co., Inc., 1951—, dir., 1960—; chmn. Oceanatic Steamship Co., 1958-61; pres. Gisholt Machine Co., Madison, Wis., 1963-66; also dir.; chmn. Long Island Tankers, 1958-60; dir. Oregon Am. Lumber Co., 1951-53, Pacific Far East Line, 1957-61, Gilman Engring. & Mfg., 1963, Enterprises Internat., Inc., 1973—, The George E. Taylor Fgn. Affairs INst., 1986—. Bd. dirs. John A. Johnson Found. Served to lt. comdr. USNR, 1943-46. Mem. Bohemian Club (San Francisco), Lighthouse Point Yacht and Racquet Club (Fla.), Beta Gamma Sigma, Alpha Sigma Phi. Congregationalist. Home: The Highlands Seattle WA 98177 also: # 16 1212 Hwy A-1A Hillsboro Bch FL 33062 Office: PO Box 33250 Seattle WA 98133-0250

SAUNDERSON, WILLIAM, Canadian provincial official; m. Meredith Saunderson; children: Janet, Brian, Pamela. BA in History, U. Toronto; Hon.Doctorate, U. Ottawa, 1994. Chartered acct. With firm Clarkson & Gordon (now Ernst & Young), to 1971; co-founder, v.p. Sceptre Investment Counsel Ltd., from 1971; mem. for Eglinton Can. Parliament; min. econ. devel., trade and tourism Province of Ont., 1995—; fin. comptroller Progressive Conservative Nat. Election Campaigns, 1984 88. Active in fundraising for U. Ottawa, Queen Elizabeth Hosp., Toronto, Scouts Can., Rowing Can. Office: Hearst Block, 900 Bay St, Toronto, ON Canada M7A 2E1*

SAUNDERS-SMITH, GAIL ANN, educational administrator, consultant; b. Pitts., Nov. 23, 1952; d. John E. and Ruth L. Saunders; m. Charles D. Smith, June 21, 1975. BS in Early Childhood Edn., Kent State U., 1974, MA in Early Childhood Edn., 1977; MS in Adminstrn. and Supervision, Youngstown State U., 1981; PhD in Elem. Edn., U. Akron, 1994. Classroom tchr. Youngstown Diocese, Warren, Ohio, 1974-76; cooperating tchr. Kent (Ohio) State U. Lab. Sch., 1976-77; classroom tchr. Maplewood Bd. Edn., Cortland, Ohio, 1977-85; reading/lang. arts supr. Summit County Bd. Edn., Akron, Ohio, 1985-90; reading recovery tchr. leader Summit County Bd. Edn., Akron, 1986-89, coord. state and fed. programs, 1990-94; mgr. cons. svcs. Rigby, Chgo., 1994—; part-time faculty Kent (Ohio) State U., 1986-89; bd. mem. Stark, Summit, U. of Akron (Ohio) Tchrs. Applying Whole Lang. Group, 1987—, Ohio Coun. Tchrs. English Lang. Arts, Columbus, Ohio, 1989-92; bd. mem. edn. com. Akron Symphony Orch., 1993-94. Author: (children's books) Giant's Breakfast, 1993, Half for You, Half for Me, 1993, Worms, 1993, How Dogs and Man Became Friends, 1993, Laughing Giraffes, 1991. Mem. Internat. Reading Assn., AAUW, Nat. Staff Devel. Coun., Phi Delta Kappa, Kappa Delta Pi, Pi Lambda Theta.

SAUNTRY, SUSAN SCHAEFER, lawyer; b. Bangor, Maine, May 7, 1943; d. William Joseph and Emily Joan (Guenter) Schaefer; m. John Philip Sauntry, Jr., Aug. 18, 1968; 1 child, Mary Katherine. BS in Foreign Service, Georgetown U., 1965, JD, 1975. Bar: D.C. 1975, U.S. Dist. Ct. D.C. 1975, U.S. Ct. Appeals (D.C. cir.) 1975, (4th cir.) 1977, (6th cir.) 1978, (10th cir.) 1983, U.S. Supreme Ct. 1983. Congl. relations asst. OEO, Washington, 1966-68; program analyst EEO Com., Washington, 1968-70, U.S. Dept. Army, Okinawa, 1970-72; assoc. Morgan, Lewis & Bockius, Washington, 1975-83, ptnr., 1983-94; of counsel Howe, Anderson & Steyer, PC, Washington, 1994—. Co-author: Employee Dismissal Law: Forms and Procedures, 1986; contbr. articles to profl. jours. Mem. ABA, D.C. Bar Assn., D.C. Women's Bar Assn., Am. Assn. Univ. Women, USA, Phi Beta Kappa, Pi Sigma Alpha. Democrat. Office: Ste 1050 1747 Pennsylvania Ave NW Washington DC 20006-4604

SAUR, KLAUS G., publisher; b. Pullach, Germany, July 27, 1941; s. Karl-Otto and Veronika (Bossmann) S.; m. Lilo Stangel, Oct. 5, 1940; children: Klaus Peter, Annette. Grad. Comml. Coll. Munich; PhD honorus causa Philipps U., Marburg, Simmons Univ. Coll., Boston. Pub. mgr. Vulkan-Verlag, Essen, 1962-63; pub. K.G. Saur Verlag, Munich, 1963-66, pub., pres., 1966—; hon. prof. U. Glasgow; chmn. export com. German Book Trade, Frankfurt, 1979—, dep. chmn. Deutsche Bibliothek German Nat. Libr., Bowker Co., N.Y., bd. dirs. F.A. brockhaus/Bibliographisches Inst. A.G./Mannheim, Reed Reference Pub. Editor, founder World Guide to Libraries. Hon. fellow U. Graz, Austria; hon. senator Ludwig-Maximilian U., Munich. Recipient Munich Honor medal, 1994, Fed. Cross of merit, Hon. medal Fed. Republic of Germany. Mem. German Pubs. Assn. (pres.), Deutsche Bibliothek Frankfurt-Leipzig-Berlin (bd. dirs. 1978, chmn. bd.), Frankfurt Book Fair (chmn. bd.), German Museum Munich (bd. dirs. 1976), Rotary. Office: K G Saur Verlag KG, Ortlerstr 8, D-81373 Munich Germany also: K G Saur 121 Chanlon Rd New Providence NJ 07974-1541

SAURBIER, SCOTT ALAN, lawyer; b. Evergreen Park, Ill., Apr. 14, 1947; s. Richard George and Lois M. (Swisher) S.; m. Catherine Francis Wrobel, June 26, 1981. BS, Cen. Mich. U., 1969; JD, Wayne State U., 1972. Bar: Mich. 1972, U.S. Dist. Ct. (ea. and we. dists.) Mich. 1972. Prin. Scott A. Saubier & Assocs., Detroit; lectr., speaker various hosps., orgns., ins. cos. Author: Keys to 1994 Medicial Malpractice Tort Reform. Mem. ABA, Mich. Bar Assn., Detroit Bar Assn., Am. Soc. of Law and Medicine, Assn. Mich. Hosp. Assn., Mich. Soc. Hosp. Risk Lawmakers, Def. Trial Counsel, Mich. Def. Trial Counsel, Am. Soc. Hosp. Attys. Office: Saurbier Paradiso Davis PLC Ste 402 400 Maple Park Blvd Saint Clair Shores MI 48081

SAUSMAN, KAREN, zoological park administrator; b. Chgo., Nov. 26, 1945; d. William and Annabell (Lofaso) S. BS, Loyola U., 1966; student, Redlands U., 1968. Keeper Lincoln Park Zoo, Chgo., 1964-66; tchr. Palm Springs (Calif.) Unified Sch., 1968-70; ranger Nat. Park Svc., Joshua Tree, Calif., 1968-70; zoo dir. The Living Desert, Palm Desert, Calif., 1970—; natural history study tour leader internat., 1974—; part-time instr. Coll. Desert Natural History Calif. Desert, 1975-78; field reviewer conservation grants Inst. Mus. Svcs., 1987—, MAP cons., 1987—, panelist, 1992—; internat. studbook keeper for Sand Cats, 1988—, for Cuvier's Gazelle, Mhorr Gazelle, 1990—; co-chair Arabian Oryx species survival plan propogation group, 1986—; spkr. in field. Author Survival Captive Bighorn Sheep, 1982, Small Facilities- Opportunities and Obligations, 1983; wildlife illustrator books, mags, 1970—; editor Fox Paws newsletter Living Desert, 1970—, ann. reports, 1976—; natural sci. editor Desert Mag., 1979-82; compiler Conservation and Management Plan for Antelope, 1992; contbr. articles to profl. jours. Past bd. dirs., sec. Desert Protective Coun.; adv. coun. Desert Bighorn Rsch. Inst., 1981-85; bd. dirs. Palm Springs Desert Resorts Convention and Visitors Bur., 1988-94; bd. dirs., treas. Coachella Valley

Mountain Trust, 1989-92. Named Woman Making a Difference Soroptomist Internat., 1989, 93. Fellow Am. Assn. Zool. Parks and Aquariums (bd. dirs., accredation field reviewer, desert antelope taxon adv. group, caprid taxon adv. group, felid taxon adv. group, small population mgmt. adv. group, wildlife conservation and mgmt. com., chmn. ethics com. 1987, mem. com., internat. rels. com., ethics task force, pres'. award 1972-77, outstanding svc. award 1983, 88, editor newsletter, Zool. Parks and Aquarium Fundamentals 1982); mem. Internat. Species Inventory System (mgmt. com., policy adv. group 1980-88), Calif. Assn. Mus., Calif. Assn. Zoos and Aquariums, Internat. Union Dirs. Zool. Gardens, Western Interpretive Assn. (so. Calif. chpt.), Am. Assn. Mus., Arboreta and Botanical Gardens So. Calif. (coun. dirs.), Soc. Conservation Biology, Nat. Audubon. Soc., Jersey Wildlife Preservation Trust Internat., Nature Conservancy, East African Wildlife Soc., African Wildlife Found., Kennel Club Palm Springs (past bd. dirs., treas. 1978-80), Scottish Deerhound Club Am. (editor SCottish Deerhounds in N.A., 1983, life mem. U.K. chpt.). Avocations: pure bred dogs, dressage, painting, photography. Office: The Living Desert 47 900 Portola Ave Palm Desert CA 92260

SAUSVILLE, EDWARD ANTHONY, medical oncologist; b. Albany, N.Y., Apr. 3, 1952; s. Edward Adolphus and Pauline (Zamenick) S.; m. Carol Ann Cassidy, Feb. 1, 1975; children: Justin, Brendan, Elizabeth, Rebecca, Paul. BS, Manhattan Coll., 1973; MD, PhD, Albert Einstein Coll. Medicine, 1979. Med. house staff Brigham & Women's Hosp., Boston, 1979-82; med. staff fellow Nat. Cancer Inst., Bethesda, Md., 1982-85; sr. investigator Nat. Cancer Inst., Bethesda, 1985-88, 90—, assoc. dir. Devel. Therapeutics Program, 1994—; assoc. prof. medicine Georgetown U. Sch. Medicine, Washington, 1988-90. Author: (book chpt.) "Lung Cancer" in Kelley Textbook Internal Medicine, 1989; contbr. articles to New Eng. Jour. Medicine, Jour. Biol. Chemistry, Cancer Rsch. Mem. Am. Assn. Cancer Rsch., Am. Soc. Clin. Oncology, Am. Soc. Biochem. Molecular Biology, Phi Beta Kappa, Alpha Omega Alpha. Achievements include research on mechanisms of bleomycin action; bombesin-related peptide gene expression and response in lung cancer; optimal treatment and staging of cutaneous T-cell lymphoma; preclinical, Phase I and Phase II trials of novel antineoplastic agents. Home: 709 Bonifant Rd Silver Spring MD 20905 Office: Nat Cancer Inst Devel Ther Program EPN 843 Bethesda MD 20892

SAUTER, CATHERINE, computer programmer; b. Balt., Oct. 16, 1969; d. Donald and Anna (Pillar) S. BA in Physics, U. Md., Balt., 1991. Rsch. analyst Areté Assocs., Sherman Oaks, Calif., 1991-93; test engr. Centronic, Inc., Newbury Park, Calif., 1993-94; computer scientist Trandes Corp., San Diego, 1995—. Mem. Am. Phys. Soc., Sigma Pi Sigma, Pi Mu Epsilon. Democrat. Roman Catholic. Avocations: reading, cycling, needlework. Home: 9505 Genesee Ave #519 San Diego CA 92121

SAUTER, MARSHA JEANNE, elementary school educator; b. Ft. Wayne, Ind., Apr. 13, 1951; d. Donald Paul and Juanita Mae (Foltz) Harsch; m. Michael Charles Sauter, Dec. 11, 1971; 1 child, Paul Michael. Student, Ball State U., 1969-71; BS in Edn. summa cum laude, U. Cin., 1974. Cert. tchr., Ohio, Okla. 6th grade tchr. Norwood (Ohio) Schs., 1974-75, 1st grade tchr., 1975-77; kindergarten tchr. Mason (Ohio) Schs., 1979-81; 1st grade tchr. Oak Park Elem. Sch. Bartlesville (Okla.) Schs., 1988—, primary curriculum coord., 1992—, mem. edn. com., 1991—, mem. English/math. textbook selection com., 1992, 93. Jr. H.S. youth advisor Good Shepherd Presbyn. Ch. Bartlesville, 1982-85, Sr. H.S. youth advisor, 1991-92, elder on session, 1985-88, 96—; mem. sunshine squad-crisis line Women Children in Crisis, Bartlesville, 1993—; sec. Bartlesville Cmty. Singers. Grantee Bartlesville Sch. Found., 1992, 94, 95. Mem. NEA, Nat. Coun. Tchrs. Math., Tchrs. Assn. of Whole Lang., Nat. Reading Assn., Okla. Reading Assn., Soc. for Prevention of Cruelty to Animals, Okla. Edn. Assn., Toastmasters (Competent Toastmaster award 1993, sec.-treas. 1994-95, v.p. membership 1995—), Elks. Avocations: singing, church, traveling. Home: 365 Turkey Creek Rd Bartlesville OK 74006-8116 Office: Bartlesville Pub Schs Oak Park Elem 200 Forest Park Rd Bartlesville OK 74003-1503

SAUTER, VAN GORDON, communications executive; b. Middletown, Ohio, Sept. 14, 1935; s. Freeman and Cornelia (Banker) S.; children: Mark Allen, Jeremy Banker. B.A., Ohio U., 1957; M.A., U. Mo., 1959. Reporter, New Bedford (Mass.) Standard-Times, 1959-63; staff writer Detroit Free Press, 1963-67, Chgo. Daily News, 1967-68; news and program dir. WBBM-CBS Radio, Chgo., 1968-71; exec. producer CBS News (radio), 1971; dir. news WBBM-TV, CBS, Chgo., 1972-74; Paris bur. chief CBS News, 1974-76; v.p. program practices CBS TV Network, N.Y.C., 1976-77, 86; v.p., gen. mgr. Sta. KNXT-TV, CBS, Los Angeles, 1977-80; pres. CBS Sports, N.Y.C., 1980-82; pres. CBS News, 1982-83, exec. v.p., 1983-86; exec. v.p. CBS, Inc., 1986; contbr. articles Los Angeles Times, ind. TV project cons., 1986—; pres. Fox News div. Fox Inc., L.A., 1992—. Co-author: Nightmare in Detroit, 1968, Fabled Land, Timeless River, Life Along the Mississippi, 1970. Mem. Radio TV News Dirs. Assn., Sigma Delta Chi.

SAUTNER, BARRY ROBERT, artist; b. Phila., Jan. 20, 1952; s. Alfred Carl and Elva Mae (Ehly) S.; children: Heather Lynn, Jason Barry. First to use sandblasting to create cameo glass, 1979; devel. 3 dimensional undercut cameo glass, 1982, insculpture-diatreta paperweight, 1984; incorporated posts into diatreta design, 1985; creator double diatreta vase, 1987, postless double diatreta vase, 1988; carved vase on entire outside and inside, 1992; exhibited glass carvings in several shows including Bergstrom-Mahler Mus., Neenah, Wis., 1994, Am. Mus. Glass, Millville, N.J., 1993, Mus. Fine Arts, Houston, 1991, Corning (N.Y.) Mus. Glass, 1982, William Traver Gallery, Seattle, 1995, Habatat Gallery, Boca Raton, Fla., 1993, Judy Youens Gallery, Houston, 1993, Georgeo's Collection, Beverly Hills, Calif., 1993, Habatat Gallery, Aspen, Colo., 1993, Sandra Ainsley Gallery, Toronto, 1993, Habatat Gallery, Pontiac, Mich., 1993, Grohe Glass Gallery, Boston, 1993, Leo Kaplan Gallery, N.Y.C., 1995, others. Home: 123 Richardson Rd Lansdale PA 19446-1443

SAUTTER, RICHARD DANIEL, physician, administrator; b. Ord, Nebr., Dec. 30, 1926; s. Daniel August and Theresa May (Ries) S.; m. Rosemary Elizabeth Graham, Aug. 4, 1952; children—Ann Elizabeth, Daniel Richard, Michael Graham, Mark Allen. B.S., U. Nebr., Lincoln, 1948; M.D., U. Nebr., Omaha, 1953. Diplomate Am. Bd. Surgery, Am. Bd. Thoracic Surgery. Intern Highland Alameda County, Oakland, Calif., 1953-54; resident, instr. in gen. surgery State Univ. of Iowa, Iowa City, 1954-61; thoracic and cardiovascular surgeon Marshfield Clinic, Wis., 1961-93, dir. med. edn., 1975-92; exec. dir. Marshfield Med. Research Found., Wis., 1977-93; asst. dean for clin. affairs U. Wis., Madison, 1984-92; resident St. Joseph's Hosp., Marshfield, Wis., 1961-93; mem. alcohol and other drug abuse rsch. adv. com. Dept. Health and Social Svcs., State of Wis., 1985-93. Contbr. numerous articles to profl. jours., chpts. to books; patentee in field; mem. editl. bd. Wis. Med. Jour., 1977-95, assoc. editor, 1986-87, med. editor, 1987-95. Bd. dirs. State Med. Jour. Advt. Bur. Served with U.S. Army, 1944-45; PTO. Grantee NIH, 1968-70, 70-71, Nat. Heart-Lung Inst., 1971, 71-72, 73-83, 74-77, others. Fellow ACS (nat. and Wis. chpt.); mem. Am. Assn. Thoracic Surgery, Soc. Thoracic Surgeons, Central Surg. Assn., Wis. Surg. Soc., Wis. Heart Club, Wood County Med. Soc., Am. Heart Assn. (council on thrombosis), Wis. State Med. Soc., Western Surg. Assn., Soc. for Clin. Trials Inc. Lodge: Elks. Avocations: fishing; gardening. Home: 212 S Schmidt Ave Marshfield WI 54449-5703

SAUVAGE, LESTER ROSAIRE, health facility administrator, cardiovascular surgeon; b. Wapato, Wash., Nov. 15, 1926; s. Lester Richard Sauvage and Laura Marie Brouillard; m. Mary Ann Marti, June 9, 1956; children: Lester Jr., John, Paul, Helen, Joe, Laura, William, Mary Ann. Student, Gonzaga U., 1942-43, DSc (hon.), 1982; MD, St. Louis U., 1948; Honoris Causa (hon.), Seattle U., 1976. Diplomate Nat. Bd. Med. Examiners, Am. Bd. Surgery, Am. Bd. Thoracic Surgery. Intern King County Hosp., Seattle, 1948-49, surg. resident, 1949-50, sr. resident, 1955-56; sr. resident Children's Med. Ctr., Boston, 1956-58; rsch. assoc. dept. surgery U. Wash., Seattle, 1950-52; sr. resident in thoracic surgery Boston City Hosp., 1958; pvt. practice Pediatric and Cardiovascular Surgeons, Inc., Seattle, 1959-91; founder, med. dir. Hope Heart Inst. (formerly Reconstructive Cardiovascular Rsch. Ctr.), Seattle, 1959—; clin. prof. surgery sch. medicine U. Wash.; chmn. dept. surgery, dir. surg. edn. Providence Med. Ctr., Seattle; dir. cardiac surgery Children's Orthopedic Hosp. and Med. Ctr.; presenter in field, 1974—. Author: Prosthetic Replacement of the Aortic Valve, 1972; mem. editorial bd. Annals Vascular Surgery; contbr. over 200 rsch. papers to profl. jours. Capt. M.C., U.S. Army, 1952-54. Recipient Vocat. Svc. award Seattle Rotary Club, 1977, Humanitarian award Human Life Found., 1977, Brotherhood award Nat. Conf. Christians and Jews, 1979, Clemson award Soc. Biomaterials, 1982, Jefferson award Am. Inst. Pub. Svc., Seattle Post-Intelligencer, 1983, Gov.'s Disting. Vol. award, 1983, Spotlight award Am. Soc. Women Accts., 1985, Wash. State Medal of Merit, 1987, Seattle 1st Citizen award, 1992. Mem. AMA, Am. Acad. Pediatrics (surg. sect.), Am. Assn. Thoracic Surgery, Am. Coll. Cardiology, Am. Coll. Chest Physicians, Am. Coll. Surgeons, Am. Heart Assn., Am. Pediatric Surg. Assn., Neurovascular Soc. N.Am. (founding mem.), Wash. State Heart Assn., Wash. State Med. Assn., North Pacific Pediatric Soc., North Pacific Surg. Soc., N.W. Soc. Clin. Rsch., Pacific Assn. Pediatric Surgeons, Pacific Coast Surg. Assn., New Eng. Soc. Vascular Surgery (hon.), Seattle Surg. Soc., King County Med. Soc., Internat. Cardiovascular Soc., Soc. Artificial Internal Organs, Soc. Clin. Vascular Surgery (hon.), Soc. Vascular Surgery, Acad. Surg. Rsch., Alpha Omega Alpha, Alpha Sigma Nu. Roman Catholic. Achievements include research in synthetic blood vessel grafts, vascular surgical techniques, prediction and prevention of thrombotic complications of atherosclerosis, endothelial cell function and vascular autografts.

SAUVAGEAU, PHILIPPE, library director; b. Trois-Rivières, Que., Can., June 11, 1940; s. Lorenzo and Laurette (Forest) S. BA, Seminaire St.-Joseph, Trois-Rivieres, 1961; B of Libr. Scis., U. Montréal, 1962. Assoc. libr. Svc. des Bibliothèque de la Mauricie, Trois-Rivières, 1962-64; adminstr. Bibliothèque Régionale du Nord de l'Outaouais, 1964-70, Bibliothèque Centrale de prêt de l'Outaouais et du Saguenay-Lac, St. Jean, 1971-75; dir. Bibliothèque Que., Can., 1975-80; gen. dir. Institut Canadien de Que., 1980-89; pres. gen. dir. Bibliothèque Nationale du Que., 1989—; cons. various orgns. including Agence de Coopèration Culturelle et Technique, Paris, Benin, Senegal, 1986-87, Bibliothèque de L'Assemblee Nationale, Que., 1983. Author: Comment Diffuser La Culture, 1969; contbr. articles to jours. Pres. Secrétariat Permanent des Peuples Francophones, Que., 1979-89; adminstr. Fest. du Film Que., 1986-87; mem. Conf. Canadienne des Arts, 1970—. Decorated Chevalier de l'Ordre des Arts et des Lettres Min. Culture and Communication of the French Govt., 1988; recipient Prix de Développement Culturel "La Laurentienne", Couns. Culture Que., 1986; named adminstr. of cultural devel. Conseil de la Culture de la Region de Que., 1985. Mem. Le Trident (dir. 1976), Com. Internat. des Bibliothèque Publiques, Assn. L'Avancement Scis. et Tech. de la Docum., Can. Libr. Assn., L'Institut Quebecois de Recherche sur la Culture (adminstr. 1991-93). Club: Garnison. Office: Bibliothèque Nat de Quebec, 125 rue Sherbrooke W, Montreal, PQ Canada H2X 1X4

SAUVÉ, GEORGES, surgeon; b. Paris, Sept. 10, 1925; s. Louis de Gonzague andMarie (Bourdon) S.; m. Monique Lemaigre, June 11, 1955; children: Frédérique, Jacques-Phillipe, Diane, Claire, Marie-Amelie, Bérengère. MD, U. Paris, 1956. Intern Hosp. de Paris, 1952-57, chief of surgery, 1975-62; practice surgery, Laval, France, 1962—. Author: Les fils de Saint Come, 1987, De Louis XV à Poincar"248, 1989, Le Collège Stanislas, 1994. Mem. Internat. Coll. Surgeons, Lauréat Acad. Médecine, Acad. Maine, Acad. Généalogie. Roman Catholic. Avocations: music, art, literature. Home: 22 Place Du Gast, 53000 Laval France Office: Polyclinique du Maine, Ave Francais, Laval France

SAUVEY, DONALD (ROBERT), retired musical instrument company executive; b. Green Bay, Wis., Mar. 15, 1924; s. Irving and Alice (LaBelle) S.; m. Shirley Ann Capelle, Nov. 24, 1949. Student, Am. TV Lab., 1942-43; cert. electronic tech., Milw. Sch. Engring., 1947. Sales mgr. Conn Organ Co., Elkhart, Ind., 1960-65; dir. mktg. Electro Music, Pasadena, Calif., 1965-70; v.p., gen. mgr. Electro Music, 1970-73, Gulbransen Organ Co. subs. CBS, Chgo., 1973-75; pres., chief exec. officer Hammond Organ Chgo., 1975-85; pres., dir. Hammond Internat. Can., Ltd., Agincourt, Ont.; v.p. Organos Hammond de Mex. S.A. de C.V., Mexico City; dir. Hammond Organ U.K. Ltd., Milton Keynes, Eng., Nihon Hammond, Osaka, Japan, Marmon Co. Mem. businessmen's adv. council Forty-Plus of Chgo., Inc., 1977—. Served with USAAF, 1943-46. Mem. Am. Music Conf. (dir.), Nat. Assn. Music Mchts. Republican. Roman Catholic. Patentee in field.

SAVAGE, ARTHUR L., professional hockey team executive; b. Amarillo, Tex., July 3, 1951; s. Kyle and Rhoda Lou (McClendon) S.; m. Susan Elizabeth Black, May 26, 1970; children: Jeffrey Alan, Brent Thomas. BA, Tex. Tech U., 1973. CPA, Calif. Acct. Deloitte Haskins & Sells, L.A. and San Francisco, 1973-79; ptnr. Bunje Dowse & Co., 1979-86; pres. Savage & Assocs., 1986—; pres. Cleve. Cavaliers, 1988-89, also bd. dirs.; pres., chief exec. officer San Jose (Calif.) Sharks, NHL, 1990—; bd. dirs. Nationwide Advt., 1983—. Office: 525 W Santa Clara St San Jose CA 95113-1520*

SAVAGE, BLAIR DEWILLIS, astronomer, educator; b. Mt. Vernon, N.Y., June 7, 1941; s. Rufus Llewellyn and Christine (Burney) S.; m. Linda Jean Wilber, June 25, 1966; children: Reid Hamilton, Keith Wesley. B.Engring. Physics, Cornell U., 1964; M.S., Princeton U., 1966, Ph.D., 1967. Research assoc. Princeton U., 1967-68; asst. prof. U. Wis., Madison, 1968-73, assoc. prof., 1973-78, prof. astronomy, 1978—, chmn. dept., 1982-85; vis. fellow Joint Inst. Lab. Astrophysics, Boulder, Colo., 1974-75; investigator space astronomy projects NASA, 1968—; bd. pres. Wis., Ind., Yale Nat. Optical Astronomy Obs. Telescope Consortium, 1990—. Contbr. articles to profl. jours. Peyton fellow Princeton U., 1964-66; NASA fellow Princeton U., 1966-67; research grantee NASA, NSF, 1968—. Mem. Am. Astron. Soc. (councilor 1994-97), Internat. Astron. Union, Nat. Rsch. Coun. (space sci. bd. mem. 1985-88, chmn. com. for space astronomy and astrophysics 1985-88, astronomy and astrophysics survey com. 1989-90), Assn. for Univ. Rsch. in Astronomy (bd. dirs. 1989-92), Tau Beta Pi. Home: 4015 Hiawatha Dr Madison WI 53711-3037 Office: Dept Astronomy U Wis 475 N Charter St Madison WI 53706-1507

SAVAGE, CHARLES FRANCIS, lawyer; b. Bklyn., Oct. 2, 1942; s. Charles Lincoln and Frances Regis (Moran) S.; m. Maria Ania Bojcun, July 1, 1967; children: Charles F.I., Michael R. BA, Columbia U., 1963, JD, 1966. Bar: N.Y., 1966, Fla. 1977, Colo. 1981. Assoc. Cadwalader, Wickersham & Taft, N.Y.C., 1966-70; sec., gen. counsel Belco Petroleum Corp., N.Y.C., 1970-75, v.p. planning and devel., 1975-77; also bd. dirs. Belco Petroleum Corp.; v.p., gen. counsel Fla. Gas Co., Winter Park, 1977-78; asst. gen. counsel conservation and solar applications U.S. Dept. of Energy, Washington, 1978-79, dep. gen. counsel legal svcs., 1979-81; v.p.-legal, sec. Ensource, Inc., Denver, 1981-86; ptnr. Holland & Hart, Denver, 1986-93, Heppenstall, Savage, Hilyard & Muller, L.L.C., 1993—. Mem. ABA, N.Y. Bar Assn., Fla. Bar Assn., Colo. Bar Assn., Assn. Bar City N.Y., Denver Bar Assn., N.Y. County Lawyers Assn., Fed. Energy Bar.

SAVAGE, EDWARD TURNEY, lawyer; b. Boston, Feb. 14, 1946; s. Arthur Turney and Katrine (Tuttle) S. B.A., Amherst Coll., 1968; M.B.A., Harvard U., 1974, J.D., 1974. Bar: Calif. 1975, N.Y. 1975, U.S. Dist. Ct. (no. dist.) Calif. 1975, U.S. Dist. Ct. (so. dist.) N.Y. 1975, U.S. Ct. Appeals (2nd cir.) N.Y. 1975. Law clk. to presiding judge U.S. Dist. Ct. (no. dist.) Calif., San Francisco, 1974-75; assoc. Cadwalader, Wickersham & Taft, N.Y.C., 1975-77; ptnr. Rosenman & Colin, N.Y.C., 1977-87, Ashinoff, Ross & Korff, N.Y.C., 1988-90, Andrews & Kurth, L.L.P., N.Y.C., 1990—; gen. counsel, v.p. The Marcade Group, Inc., N.Y.C., 1987-88. Pres. Friends of Amherst Athletics, 1979-82. Served to lt. (j.g.) USN, 1968-70; lt. comdr. Res. Recipient Disting. Service award Harvard Bus. Sch., 1974; Amherst Meml. scholar, 1970; Woodroff Simpson fellow, 1971. Mem. Westfield Jaycees. Republican. Presbyterian. Home: 401 E 88th St Apt 16A New York NY 10128-6634 Office: Andrew & Kurth 425 Lexington Ave # 10 New York NY 10017-3903

SAVAGE, EDWARD WARREN, JR., physician; b. Macon, Ga., July 7, 1933; s. Edward Warren and Mildred Eleanor (Goodwin) S.; m. Carole Porter, June 6, 1959; children: Cheryl, Racheal, Edward Warren. A.B., Talladega Coll., 1955; postgrad., St. Louis U., 1955; M.D., Meharry Med. Coll., 1960. Diplomate: Am. Bd. Obstetrics and Gynecology. Intern St. Joseph's Hosp., Syracuse, N.Y., 1960-61; resident Kings County Hosp.-State U. N.Y., Bklyn., 1963-67; USPHS fellow in gynecol. cancer State U. N.Y. Downstate Med. Center, Bklyn., 1967-69; asst. instr. State U. N.Y. Downstate Med. Center, 1964-66, instr., 1966-69; dir. gynecologic oncology U. Ill., Chgo., 1970-73; asst. prof. U. Ill., 1969-73, asso. prof., 1973; med. dir. King/Drew Med. Ctr., L.A., 1993—; assoc. prof. Sch. Medicine Charles R. Drew Med. Sch., L.A., 1973-80, prof., 1980—, dean clin. affairs, 1993—; mem. staff St. Francis Hosp. of Lynwood, Centinela Hosp. Med. Ctr., UCLA Hosps. and Clinics; adj. assoc. prof. UCLA Sch. Medicine, 1977, prof., 1986—. Contbr. numerous articles to profl. publs. Exec. bd. Los Angeles Community Cancer Control., 1977. Served as capt. M.C. USAF, 1961-63. Fellow ACS, Am. Coll. Obstetricians and Gynecologists; mem. Soc. Gynecologic Oncologists, Am., Western Assn. Gynec. Oncologists (pres. 1980-81), Nat., Golden State med. assns., AAUP, Am. Soc. Colposcopy and Cervical Pathology (dir. 1973-80), Chgo. Gynecol. Soc., Am. Cancer Soc., Ill., Los Angeles Obstet. and Gynecol. Socs. (pres. 1989-90), Charles R. Drew Med. Soc. Office: 12021 Wilmington Ave Los Angeles CA 90059-3019 *I am the product of two wonderful parents whose support and ideals, inclusive of a strong work ethic, allowed me to be prepared for the several fortuitous opportunities that presented themselves. My hope is that somehow my life will be a positive statement to those who know me.*

SAVAGE, JAMES CATHEY, III, lawyer; b. Nashville, June 26, 1947; s. James C. Jr. and Mary (Estes) S.; m. Annette Egan, Aug. 5, 1975 (div.); children: Sean Patrick, Catriona Sarah; m. Clara Parra, Nov. 25, 1986; children: James C. IV, Anthony Joseph. BS, Austin Peay St. U., 1968; JD, Memphis State U., 1973; MS in Criminal Justice, Troy State U., 1977; LLM, John Marshall Law Sch., 1978, Georgetown U., 1981; LLD (hon.), North Tenn. Bible Inst., 1981. Bar: Tenn. 1973, U.S. Supreme Ct. 1977, D.C. 1981, Md. 1982; cert. tchr. Commd. 1st lt. U.S. Army, 1973, advanced through grades to lt. col, 1988; enlisted ranger and edn. dir. U.S. Army, Vietnam, 1969-70; ins. adjuster Tenn. Co., Molloy & Leary, Bituminious Casualty, 1971-73; judge adv. U.S. Army, Ga., Germany, 1973-77; vets. and contracts atty. V.A. Gen. Counsel, Washington, 1978-82; fgn. mil. sales atty. USAF Electronic Systems Ctr., Hanscom AFB, Mass., 1983-86; chief counsel U.S. Army Materials Tech. Lab, Watertown, Mass., 1986-92, U.S. Army Rsch. Lab, Watertown, Mass., 1992-95; sr. atty. Soldier Sys. Command, Natick, Mass., 1995—; civilian mem. Army Acquisition Corps, 1995—; army reserve asst. counsel Defense Contract Mgmt., Boston, 1992-96; adj. prof. City Colls. Chgo., Troy State U., Phillips Coll., John Marshall Law Sch., Middlesex, C.C., U. of Andes, 1974-92. Weekly show host Assembly (BCAT-TV), Burlington, Mass., 1989-93; contbr. articles to profl. jours. Dep. dir. Internat. Rescue Com./Army Res. Project Resettlement for Refugees, Washington, 1980-82; canvasser Am. Heart Assn., Burlington, 1989-92; lay min. Christian Chs., 1974—; chmn. bd. deacons, mem. pastor/parish, pers., parish counsel and nomination coms. Burlington Congl. Ch., 1986-95, 1st Congl. Ch., Natick, 1995—; mem. Christian Legal Soc., 1980—, Inst. Religion and Democracy, 1980—, United Ch. Bd. World Ministries, 1993, corp. mem.; active Christian Mil. Fellowship, 1984—; comdr., exec. officer New Eng. Selective Svc. Sys., 1986-92; officer Christian Fellowship, 1988—; mem. Cultural Coun. and Cable TV Adv. Bd., Town of Burlington; mem. Cable TV Adv. Bd., Town of Natick; lt. col. civil air patrol CAP Group I Mass., 1988-93. Decorated Bronze Star and 25 other mil. medals; named Mass. Citizen of Yr. Am. Legion, 1985; recipient Exceptional Profl. award, 1985, Excellence in Govt. and Outstanding Community Svc. awards, Boston, 1987, 92, Fed. Exec. Bd., mil., edn. and community svc. recognition resolution Mass. Ho. of Reps., 1992. Mem. Fed. Bar Assn. (nat. chmn. internat. procurement com. 1985-88, vice-chmn. 1979-90, past pres. Mass. chpt. 1985-86, nat. del., Disting. Svc. award), Assn. U.S. Army, New Eng. Chpt. Judge Advocates Assn. (pres./v.p. 1983-86), Res. Officers Assn. (nat. judge adv. 1993-94, state pres. 1993-94, pres.-elect 1992-93, state v.p. for Army 1990-92, state judge adv. 1985-86, pres. William Tudor and N.E. Civil Affairs chpts. 1984-89, Nat. Disting. Svc. awards), Nat. Civil Affairs Assn. (Nat. Disting. Svc. award), DAV (life, Honor Guard Burlington chpt. 113 1985-93), Natick VFW (life, state judge adv. and sr. vice comdr.-All Am. Post 1982-83), Natick AMVETS (life, post comdr.and state judge adv. 1982-83), Natick Am. Legion, 75th Ranger Regiment Assn. (nat. dir. 1987-90), Vietnam Vets. Am. (life, sec. D.C. chpt. 1980), Phi Delta Kappa (treas. Harvard U. chpt. 1990-92), Phi Alpha Delta. Avocations: computers, and guitar and trumpet playing. Home: 15 Lake Shore Rd Natick MA 01760-2007 Office: US Army Soldier Sys Command Kansas St Legal Office Natick MA 01760-5035

SAVAGE, JAMES FRANCIS, editor; b. Boston, July 23, 1939; s. James and Hanora (Enright) S.; m. Sharon Kaye Base, May 29, 1965; 1 son, Sean. A.A., Boston U., 1959, B.S., 1961. Reporter Quincy (Mass.) Patriot Ledger, 1961-63; reporter Miami (Fla.) Herald, 1963-67, investigative reporter, 1967-78, investigations editor, 1978-84, assoc. editor investigations, 1984—; investigative reporter Boston Herald Traveler, 1967. Served with AUS, 1962. Recipient Nat. Headliners award, 1969, Fla. Press Assn. award, 1972, George Polk Meml. award for investigative reporting, 1973, 80, Pub. Service award Nat. A.P. Mng. Editors, 1974, 80, award Fla. Soc. Newspaper Editors, 1974, 75, Nat. Disting. Service award Sigma Delta Chi, 1979, 87, Pulitzer Prize Staff award for Nat. Reporting, 1987, Outstanding Investigative Reporting award Investigative Reporters and Editors, 1988, Disting. Alumni award Boston U. Coll. Communications, 1990, Pulitzer Prize Staff Pub. Svc. award, 1993; Profl. Journalism fellow Stanford, 1974-75. Home: 1004 Orange Is Fort Lauderdale FL 33315-1651 Office: 1 Herald Plz Miami FL 33132-1609

SAVAGE, JOHN EDMUND, computer science educator, researcher; b. Lynn, Mass., Sept. 19, 1939; s. Edmund J. and Eldora A. (Guay) S.; m. Patricia Joan Landers, Jan. 29, 1966; children: Elizabeth, Kevin, Christopher, Timothy. ScB, MIT, 1962, ScM, 1962, PhD, 1965. Mem. tech. staff Bell Telephone Labs., Holmdel, N.J., 1965-67; prof. computer sci. Brown U., Providence, 1967—, chmn. dept. computer sci., 1985-91; vis. prof. U. Paris, 1980-81, Warwick U., Eng., 1991-92; mem. dept. vis. com. elec. engring. and computer sci. MIT, 1991—; cons. in field. Author: The Complexity of Computing, 1976; (with others) The Mystical Machine, 1986; editor: (with Thomas Knight) Advanced Research in VLSI and Parallel Systems, 1992; chair editl. bd. Computing Rsch. News, 1990—; editl. bd. Jour. Computer and Sys. Scis., 1993—; patentee data scrambler, 1970, means and methods for generating permutation of a square, 1976. Mem. MIT Corp. visiting com. dept. elec. engring. and computer sci. Fulbright-Hays grantee, 1973; NSF fellow, 1961, Guggenheim fellow, 1973. Fellow IEEE, Assn. Computing Machinery; mem. Computing Rsch. Assn. (bd. dirs. 1990—), Sigma Xi, Tau Beta Pi. Avocations: reading, skiing, bicycling. Office: Brown U Dept Computer Sci 115 Waterman St Providence RI 02912-9016

SAVAGE, JOHN PATRICK, provincial official; b. Newport, South Wales, N.S., Can., May 28, 1982; married; 7 children. Grad., Queen's Coll. Med. Sch., Belfast, No. Ireland, 1956. Mayor City of Dartmouth, Can., 1985-92; premier, min. intergovtl. affairs, min. aboriginal affairs, pres. exec. coun. Govt. of Nova Scotia, Halifax, 1993—; co-chair Nova Scotia Round Table on Environment and Economy. Active Dartmouth Sch. Bd., 1978, chair bd. dirs., 1984, 85. Office: Office of the Premier, 1700 Granville St 7th Fl PO Box 726, Halifax, NS Canada B3J 2T3

SAVAGE, M. SUSAN, mayor. Student, U. Aix-Marseilles, Aix-en-Provence, France, 1969, City of London Poly., Eng., 1972; BA in Sociology with honors, Beaver Coll., 1974. Pre-trial rep. Phila. Ct. Common Pleas, 1974-75; criminal justice planner Montgomery County Criminal Justice Unit, 1975-77; exec. dir. Met. Tulsa Citizens Crime Com., 1977-87; vol. coord. Vote Yes For Tulsa, 1987; chief of staff to mayor City of Tulsa, 1988-92, mayor, 1992—. Active Lee Elementary Sch. PTA; bd. dirs., treas. Okla. Crime Prevention Assn.; bd. dirs. Youth Svcs. of Tulsa County, 1984-88, pres., 1986-87; co-chair Safe Streets/Enhanced 911 Steering Com., 1987; mem. C. of C. Task Force/Community Edn. Network, 1983. Office: Office of Mayor City Hall Rm 1115 200 Civic Ctr Tulsa OK 74103-3827*

SAVAGE, MICHAEL PAUL, medicine educator, interventional cardiologist; b. Wilkes-Barre, Pa., Jan. 25, 1955; s. Peter J. and Olga J. (Sekerchek) S.; m. Kathleen A. Gallagher, June 1989; children: Katherine, Andrew. BA, Wesleyan U., Middletown, Conn., 1976; MD, Jefferson Med. Coll., 1980. Diplomate Am. Bd. Internal Medicine, Am. Bd. Cardiovascular Disease, Nat. Bd. Med. Examiners. Intern, then resident New Eng. Deaconess Hosp.-Harvard U. Med. Sch., Boston, 1980-83; fellow Jefferson Med. Coll., Phila., 1983-86, asst. prof. medicine, 1986-91, assoc. prof., 1991—, dir. cardiac catheterization, 1990—; cons. Johnson & Johnson Interventional Sys. Co., Warren, N.J., 1994—; lectr. coronary angioplasty and cardiac catheterization. Contbr. numerous articles to New Eng. Jour. Medicine, Circulation, Am. Jour. Cardiology, Jour. Am. Coll. Cardiology, chpts. to books. Fellow

Am. Coll. Cardiology, Soc. Cardiac Angiography and Interventions, Pa. Med. Soc., Am. Heart Assn., Am. Fedn. for Clin. Rsch. Roman Catholic. Achievements include research in interventional cardiology concerning new techniques in treatment of coronary artery disease, culminating in international, prospective trials demonstrating superiority of implantable coronary stents over conventional balloon angioplasty. Office: Jefferson Med Coll 1025 Walnut St Ste 410 Philadelphia PA 19107

SAVAGE, MICHAEL THOMAS, government office executive; b. Oroville, Calif., Oct. 22, 1934; s. Guy Thomas Savage and Sarah Mery (Bennett) Barber; m. Robin Kendall Ward, Apr. 4, 1966; children: Mark McNeer, Kelly Robin. BA in Polit. Sci., U. Calif., Berkeley, 1956, MA in Polit. Sci., 1959; postgrad., Woodrow Wilson Sch., 1969-70. Field renewal rep. Community Devel. Programs, San Francisco, 1959-64, acting chief, chief of ops. br., 1964-66, dir. field svcs. divsn., 1966-68, deouty regional dir. renewal assistance, 1968-70; various positions Office of Orgn. and Mgmt., Washington, 1970-74, dir. office of mgmt. systems, acting dir., 1974-76, deputy dir. office mgmt., 1976-79; dir. office housint ops. and field monitoring Office of Community Planning and Devel., Washington, 1979-82, program advisor to asst. sec., enterprise zone coord., 1982-86, deputy dir. office block grant assistance and zone coord., 1986—; urban policy advisor Chmn. Ho. Govt. Ops. Com., Washington, 1990-93. Editorial bd.: Econ. Devel. Quar.; contbr. articles to profl. jours. Officer, supporter Great Falls (Va.) Players, 1983-94; co-chair No. Va. alumni recruiting com. Pa. State U., No. Va., 1992-94. 2d lt. U.S. Infantry, 1959. Recipient Mid Career fellowship Nat. Inst. Pub. Affairs, Washington, 1969; named LEGIS fellow Office Pers. Mgmt., Washington, 1990. Avocations: little theater, softball. Home: 436 River Bend Rd Great Falls VA 22066-4017

SAVAGE, NEVE RICHARD, marketing executive; b. Harrow, Eng., Nov. 18, 1944; came to U.S., 1970, naturalized, 1983; s. Richard Marshall and Joan Muriel (Eperon) S.; m. Ann Elizabeth Freeman, Apr. 29, 1972; children: Sarah-Jane, Megan, Truan. B.A., U. Oxford (Eng.), 1966, M.A., 1968. Account supr. Garland-Compton Advt., London, 1966-70; sr. v.p. Compton Advt., N.Y.C., 1970-77; dir. Compton Advt., 1980-83; exec. v.p. Cadwell Davis Savage Advt., N.Y.C., 1977-82; exec. v.p. internat. Wells, Rich, Greene, Inc., N.Y.C., 1983-86; vice chmn. Kornhauser & Calene Inc., 1986-88; exec. group dir. Ogilvy & Mather, 1988-94; v.p. mktg. McCaw Cellular Comm. (name changed to AT&T Wireless Svcs.), Kirkland, Wash., 1994—.

SAVAGE, PHILLIP HEZEKIAH, federal agency administrator; b. Balt., Aug. 13, 1932; s. Abraham and Ivory F. (Robinson) Shpritz; m. Phyllis Millard; children: Kim Yvette, Jan Miriam, Kirk Phillip; m. Diane Bradford Geers, June 24, 1972; children: Rebekah Ann, Elisabeth Bradford. BA, Morgan State U., 1970; MA, Antioch Sch. Law, 1984. Dir. NAACP, N.Y.C. and Phila., 1960-72, ARA Svcs. Inc., 1972-74; mgr. equal employment opportunity tng. project Gen. Acctg. Office, Washington, 1975-76; dir. equal employment opportunity office SEC, Washington, 1976-84; dir. pub. employment divsn. HUD, Washington, 1984-89, exec. asst. to asst. sec., 1989-92, dep. asst. sec. ops. and mgmt., 1992-94; sr. advisor to supt. D.C. Pub. Schs., 1994-95; sr. advisor, asst. sec. HUD, 1995—. Arbitrator Better Bus. Bur., Office Common Ownership Communities and Office Consumer Affairs, Montgomery County, Md.; past chair Partnership Fund for Compensation of Victims of Hate, Violence, Montgomery County; pres. Interracial Family Circle, v.p. Kenwood Park Citizens Assn.; mem. River Rd. Unitarian Ch. With USAF, 1950-53. Recipient Giraffe award, 1988. Avocations: reading, walking, travelling. Home: 7223 Marbury Ct Bethesda MD 20817-6129 Office: HUD Fair Housing and Equal Opportunity 451 7th St SW Washington DC 20410-0001

SAVAGE, RANDALL ERNEST, journalist; b. Commerce, Ga., Mar. 3, 1939; s. Ernest Kyle and Sara Beatrice (Collins) S.; m. Joyce Carol Martin, Nov. 26, 1964 (div. May 1984); children: Kimberly Dawn, Bradley Kyle; m. Mary Elizabeth Hallmark, Aug. 4, 1984; children: Brock Morgan, Laura Marie, Shaw Hamilton. Student, U. Md.-European Div., RAF Bentwaters, Eng., 1967-69; B.A. in Journalism, U. Ga., 1972. Service sta. worker Collins Service Sta., Commerce, Ga., 1958; billing clk. Benton Rapid Express, Atlanta, 1958-61; truck driver So. Oil Co., High Point, NC, 1964-65; reporter Commerce News, Ga., 1972; sr. spl. projects reporter Macon Telegraph and News, Ga., 1972—. Served with U.S. Army, 1961-64; with USAF, 1966-69. Recipient 3rd place in news AP, Atlanta, 1976, 2nd place in news AP, Atlanta, 1976, 1st place in sports AP, Atlanta, 1984; 2d place in news Green Eyeshades award, 1976; Pulitzer prize, 1985, Outstanding Alumnus award Henry W. Grady Coll. of Journalism and Mass Communication, U. Ga., 1989. Baptist. Avocations: jogging; softball; fishing; freelance writing. Home: 3269 Lennox Dr Macon GA 31204-1054 Office: Macon Telegraph & News Po Box 4167 120 Broadway Macon GA 31201-3444

SAVAGE, RICHARD T., manufacturing company executive; b. 1939. BS, Ohio State U., 1961. With Gen. Motors, 1961-70; v.p. mfg. Blackstone Corp., Jamestown, N.Y., 1979-81; with Modine Mfg. Co., 1970-79, v.p., 1981-83, group v.p. original equipment, 1983-89, pres., COO, 1989—, CEO, 1990—. With USAFR, 1956-62. Office: Modine Mfg Co 1500 De Koven Ave Racine WI 53403-2540*

SAVAGE, ROBERT HEATH, advertising executive; b. Chillicothe, Ohio, Nov. 24, 1929; s. Russell Heath and Frances (Hunt) S.; m. Lorna Dale, May 2, 1970. B.A., Principia Coll., 1951; M.B.A., Harvard U., 1956. Brand mgr. Procter & Gamble, Cin., 1956-60; sr. v.p., mgmt. supr., dir. Ogilvy & Mather, Inc., N.Y.C., 1960-71; mktg. mgr. personal products div. Lever Bros., N.Y.C., 1971; exec. v.p. Botsford Ketchum, Inc., San Francisco, 1972, pres., 1972-78, chmn., 1978-81; pres. KM&G Internat., Inc., 1978-81, Saatchi and Saatchi Compton, Inc., N.Y.C., 1981-83; mng. dir. Henson Assocs., N.Y.C., 1983-86; ptnr. CMA Assocs., Fairfield, Conn., 1987—; mngt. cons., sports and video mktg. cons., 1987—. With USMCR, 1951-54. Mem. Am. Assn. Advt. Agys., Gipsy Trail Club, Naples Bath and Tennis Club, Fairfield County Hunt Club, Brooklawn Country Club. Home and Office: 5 Crooked Mile Rd Westport CT 06880-1124

SAVAGE, SCOTT DAVID, broadcast executive; b. Newark, Nov. 10, 1954; s. Philip and Charlotte Jean (Figman) S.; m. Anne Marthine Aldrich, Aug. 24, 1975 (div. Mar. 1992); children: Daniel, Ellen; m. Marilyn Massucci, May 4, 1993. BA, Pa. State U., 1975. Account exec., sales mgr. Stas. WMAJ and WXLR, State College, Pa., 1974-77, Westinghouse Broadcasting Co., Pitts., N.Y.C., Ft. Wayne, Ind., 1977-80; dir. sports mktg. Sta. WTOP, Washington, 1981-84; gen. sales mgr. Sta. WCBM, Balt., 1984-85; sta. mgr., gen. sales mgr. Sta. WNEW, N.Y.C., 1985-88; v.p., gen. mgr. Tex. State Network, Dallas, 1988-90; exec. v.p., chief oper. officer Pinnacle Broadcasting Co., Dallas, 1990-91; Stas. KYNG-FM and KEWS-FM Stas. KYNG-FM, KSNN-FM, Dallas, 1992—. Recipient award of excellence Am. Women in Radio and TV, 1994. Mem. Assn. Radio Mgrs. (pres. 1995). Office: Stas KYNG and KEWS-FM KSNN-FM 12201 Merit Dr Ste 930 Dallas TX 75251

SAVAGE, STEPHEN MICHAEL, lawyer; b. Norwich, Conn., Apr. 23, 1946; s. Alfred and Iva (Allen) S.; m. Lois Palestine, July 4, 1968; children: Meredith, William, Sam. BA, U. Pa., 1968; JD, Harvard U., 1973. Bar: Ariz. 1973, U.S. Dist. Ct. Ariz. 1973. With Fennemore Craig, Phoenix, 1973—, chmn. mgmt. com., 1988—. Bd. dirs. Ariz. Diabetes Assn., Phoenix, 1983-87, Ariz. Mus. Sci. and Tech., Phoenix, 1992—; chmn. bd. dirs. All Saints' Episcopal Day Sch., Phoenix, 1988; comdr., pres. Mounted Sheriff's Posse Maricopa County, Phoenix, 1992-93. Mem. ABA, State Bar Ariz. (chmn. sect. corp., banking and bus. law 1983-84), Maricopa County Bar Assn., Assn. Corp. Growth, Phoenix Country Club. Avocations: team roping, golf. Office: Fennemore Craig 2 N Central Ave Ste 2200 Phoenix AZ 85004-4406*

SAVAGE, THOMAS JOSEPH, college president, governance and planning consultant, educator, priest; b. Medford, Mass., Oct. 28, 1947; s. Frank James and Viola Augustine (Ballou) S. B.A. summa cum laude, Boston Coll., 1971; M. City Planning, U. Calif.-Berkeley, 1973; M. Pub. Policy, Harvard U., 1982, EdD, 1985. Assoc. Cheswick Ctr., Boston, 1973, dir., 1984—; assoc. Instl. Strategies Assocs., Cambridge, Mass., 1975-87; asst. acad. v.p. Fairfield (Conn.) Univ., 1986-88; pres. Rockhurst Coll., Kansas City, Mo., 1988—; adj. faculty Lesley Coll., Cambridge, 1982-85; cons. Lilly Endowment, Indpls., 1983-87; chmn. planning com. Jesuits New Eng. Province, Boston, 1985-88. Author: Seven Steps to a More Effective Board, 1994, The Goverance of Catholic Health Care Institutions, Catholic Health Assn., Spring, 1988; also articles. Del. Bridges for Peace, Soviet Union, 1985; Trustee Regis U., 1989—, U. Detroit Mercy, 1995—, St. Louis U., 1991—, Loyola Marymount, 1994—; bd. dirs. Valentine-Radford Comm., 1992—, Preferred Health Profls., 1992—, Kauffman Found., 1993—, Menninger Clinic, 1993—; co-chair FOCUS (Comprehensive Strategic Plan for Kansas City), 1992—; chmn. Brush Creek Ptnrs., 1994—. Mellon fellow, 1971-73. Mem. Am. Planning Assn., Nat. Planning Assn., AAAS, Assn. Jesuit Colls. and Univs. (bd. dirs. 1989—), World Future Soc., Bostonian Soc., Phi Beta Kappa. Roman Catholic. Club: Harvard. Address: Rockhurst Coll 1100 Rockhurst Rd Kansas City MO 64110-2561

SAVAGE, WALLACE HAMILTON, lawyer; b. Houston, Nov. 21, 1912; s. Homer H. and Mary (Wallace) S.; m. Dorothy Harris, Oct. 12, 1940; children—Virginia Wallace (Mrs. A. Lee McAlester), Dorothy Harris. B.S., U. Va., 1933; J.D., Harvard, 1936. Bar: Tex. 1937, Colo. 1937. Practiced in Dallas; Dallas County chmn., nat. vice chmn. Citizens Com. Hoover Report, 1952-54; mem., dir. Citizen's Com. for Reorgn. Exec. Branch of Govt., 1954-59. Author: A Bait of Perjury, 1970. Mayor pro tem City of Dallas, 1947-49, mayor, 1949-51; chmn. Dallas County Democratic Com., 1952-54, Tex. Dem. Com., 1952-54 . Served as comdr. USNR, 1941-45. Univ. fellow U. Colo., 1936- 37. Mem. Am., Dallas bar assns., State Bar Tex., Phi Delta Phi. Clubs: Dallas Country, Idlewild. Home: 5703 Swiss Ave Dallas TX 75214-4638

SAVAGE, WHITNEY LEE, artist, filmmaker; b. Charleston, W.Va., Dec. 17, 1928; s. Joseph Whitney and Janet (Kelly) S.; m. Sally Herbert, June 15, 1954 (div. Mar. 1966); children: Peter Lee, William Lon, Kate Abigail; m. Karen Haagensen, Mar. 2, 1966; children: Adam Whitney, Miranda Lee; 1 stepchild, Kristin Kearney. Student, W.Va. U., 1946-48, Pratt Inst., Bklyn., 1948-50, Art Students League, N.Y.C., 1950, New Sch. for Social Rsch., 1950-51. Art dir. N.W. Ayer Advt., N.Y.C., 1954-57, J. Walter Thompson, N.Y.C., 1957-59; owner, creative dir. Elektra Films, N.Y.C., 1960-64, Savage/Friedman, N.Y.C., 1964-70; cons. Bank St. Coll. Art mag. Three to Get Ready, 1978-80. Exhibited in one-man shows Chase Gallery, N.Y.C., 1956, Krasner Gallery, N.Y.C., 1961-66, 68-78, Beinville Gallery, New Orleans, 1980, Martin Molinary Gallery, N.Y.C., 1986, Sunrise Mus. Fine Arts, Charleston, W. Va., 1974, 87, Somers Gallery, N.Y., 1983, Century Assn., N.Y.C., 1990, O.K. Harris Gallery, N.Y.C., 1991, others; group shows include Silvermine Gallery, Norwalk, Conn., 1955, Mus. Modern Art, N.Y.C., 1961, Los Angeles County Mus., 1963, Rose Art Mus., Brandeis U., 1965, Huntington Hartford Mus., N.Y.C., 1965, Am. Acad. Arts and Letters, N.Y.C., 1975, Century Assn., N.Y.C., 1987-94, Nat. Acad. Design, N.Y.C., 1991-94; author, illustrator Aldo's Doghouse, 1978; writer, producer, dir.: Mickey Mouse in Vietnam (prize at Annecy, France Film Festival), 1966, more than 50 spots for Sesamest, 1971-89, Josefl Albers Color Theory, 1971, The End, a sinister day in the life of a president, 1982, The Hudson River and its Painters, 1986; animation of Aldo's Doghouse featured in PBS TV series Behind the Scenes, 1992. Trustee Riverkeeper, Garrison, N.Y., 1987—. Pvt. 1st class U.S. Army, 1950-52, Germany. Recipient Childe Hassam award for painting Am. Acad. Arts and Letters, 1975, Media Literary and Visual Arts Lifetime Achievement award State of W.Va., 1993; named John Simon Guggenheim fellow, Eng., 1961-62, gold medal Art Dirs. Club N.Y., 1964. Mem. Nat. Acad. Design (academician, Andrew Carnegie prize for painting 1991), Century Club of N.Y.C. (bd. mgmt. 1990-92, exhbn. com. 1992-93). Democrat. Home and Studio: 25 Millard Ave Tarrytown NY 10591-1439

SAVAGE, WILLIAM WOODROW, education educator; b. Onley, Va., Jan. 9, 1914; s. Frank Howard and Florence Elmira (Twyford) S.; m. Margaret Jane Clarke; children—Earl R., William W. A.B., Coll. William and Mary, 1937; M.A., U. Chgo., 1946, Ph.D., 1955; student, U. Va., summer 1951. Research editor, div. rural research Fed. Emergency Relief Adminstrn., Richmond, Va., 1935-36; div. mgr. Montgomery Ward & Co., Newport News, Va., 1937-38; statis. worker WPA, Richmond, 1938-39; counselor Va. Consultation Service, Richmond, 1939-42; acting dir. Va. Consultation Service, 1942-45; asst. state supr. guidance and consultation services Va. Dept. Edn., 1946-47; dean Longwood Coll., Farmville, Va., 1947-52; project coordinator, asso. dir. Midwest Adminstrn. Center, U. Chgo., 1952-56; dean Coll. Edn., U. S.C., 1956-65, prof. edn., 1956-79; curator U. S.C. Mus. Edn., 1973-85. Author: Interpersonal and Group Relations, 1968; Co-author: Readings in American Education, 1963; Editor: Work and Training, monthly Va. Bd. Edn, 1941-47, Administrator's Notebook, monthly Midwest Adminstrn. Center, 1954-56, U. S.C. Edn. Report, 1957-65, 67-85; adv. com.: Sch. Rev, 1954-56; Contbr. articles to jours. Mem. visitation and appraisal com. Nat. Coun. for Accreditation Tchr. Edn., 1964-67; bd. dirs. Friends of Libr., Va. Commonwealth U. Mem. S.C. Assn. Sch. Adminstrs., U. S.C. Soc., Wardlaw Club (pres. 1974-75), Order of White Jacket, Phi Delta Kappa. Methodist. Home: 1100 German School Rd Richmond VA 23225-4275

SAVAGEAU, MICHAEL ANTONIO, microbiology and immunology educator; b. Fargo, N.D., Dec. 3, 1940; s. Antonio Daniel and Jennie Ethelwin (Kaushagen) S.; m. Ann Elisa Birky, July 22, 1967; children—Mark Edward, Patrick Daniel, Elisa Marie. B.S., U. Minn., 1962; M.S., U. Iowa, 1963; Ph.D., Stanford U., 1967, postgrad., 1968-70; postgrad., UCLA, 1967-68. Research fellow UCLA, Los Angeles, 1967-68; lectr. Stanford U., Calif., 1968-69; from asst. to full prof. U. Mich., Ann Arbor, 1970—; sr. research fellow Max Planck Inst., Göttingen, Fed. Republic of Germany, 1976-77; fellow Australian Nat. U., Canberra, 1983-84; prof. microbiology and immunology U. Mich., Ann Arbor, 1978—, chmn. dept., 1982-85, 92—, prof. chem. engring., dir. cellular biotech. labs., 1988-91; dir. NIH trng. program in Cellular Biotechnology, 1991-92; cons. Upjohn Co., Kalamazoo, 1979-81, NIH, Bethesda, Md., 1981-82, 94-95, Synergen, Boulder, Colo., 1985-87, Found. for Microbiology lectr., 1993-95; vis. prof. dept. biochemistry U. Ariz., Tucson, 1994. Author: Biochemical Systems Analysis, 1976; mem. editl. bd. Math. Scis., 1976-95, editor, 1995—; mem. editl. bd. Jour. Theoretical Biology, 1989-96, mem. adv. bd., 1996—; mem. editl. bd. Nonlinear World, 1992—, Nonlinear Digest, 1992—; co-editor Math. Ecology, 1986—; contbr. articles to profl. jours. Australian Nat. U. fellow, 1983-84; Guggenheim Found., fellow N.Y.C., 1976-77; Fulbright Found., sr. research fellow, Washington, Fed. Republic of Germany, 1976-77; sr. fellow Mich. Soc. Fellows, 1990-94; grantee NIH, NSF, 1964—. Mem. AAAS, Am. Chem. Soc., Am. Soc. Microbiology, IEEE (sr.), Soc. Indsl. and Applied Math., Biophys. Soc., Soc. Gen. Physiologists, Soc. Math. Biology (bd. dirs. 1987-90). Office: U Mich Dept Microbiology and Immunology 5641 Med Sci II Ann Arbor MI 48109-0620

SAVARD, DENIS JOSEPH, professional hockey player; b. Pointe Gatineau, Que., Can., Feb. 4, 1961. With Chgo. Black Hawks, 1980-90, Montreal Canadiens, 1990-93, Tampa Bay Lightning, 1993—; mem. Stanley Cup championship team 1983; player NHL All-Star games, 1982-84, 86, 88, 91. Recipient Michel Briere trophy, 1979-80. Office: Chgo Blackhawks 1901 W Madison St Chicago IL 60612*

SAVARD, SERGE, professional hockey team executive; b. Montreal, Que., Can., Jan. 22, 1946. Hockey player Montreal Canadiens, 1966-81, mng. dir., 1983—; hockey player Winnipeg Jets, 1981-83; v.p. hockey, mng. dir. Montreal Canadiens. Winner Conn Symthe trophy, 1969, Bill Masterton Meml. trophy, 1979; named to Hockey Hall of Fame, 1986. Office: Montreal Canadiens, 2313 St Catherine St W, Montreal, PQ Canada H3H 1N2*

SAVARESE, RALPH J., lawyer; b. N.Y.C., Sept. 4, 1936. BBA, Iona Coll., 1958; LLB, Fordham U., 1961; postgrad., U. Mich., 1961-63. Bar: N.Y. 1962, D.C. 1963. Ptnr. Howrey & Simon, Washington. Grad. Law Study fellow U. Mich., 1961-63. Office: Howrey & Simon 1299 Pennsylvania Ave NW Washington DC 20004-2400*

SAVAS, EMANUEL S., public management educator; b. N.Y.C., June 8, 1931; s. John and Olga (Limbos) S.; m. Helen Andrew, Dec. 25, 1955; children: Jonathan, Stephen. BA, U. Chgo., 1951, BS, 1953; MA, Columbia U., 1956, PhD, 1960. Control systems cons. IBM, Yorktown Heights and White Plains, N.Y., 1959-65; urban systems mgr. N.Y.C., 1966-67; 1st dep. city adminstr. Office of Mayor of N.Y.C., 1967-72; chmn. Mayor's Urban Action Task Force, 1969-72; prof. pub. mgmt. Columbia U., N.Y.C., 1972-83; dir. Center for Govt. Studies Columbia U., 1973-83, assoc. dir. Center for Policy Rsch., 1973-81; asst. sec. for policy devel. and rsch. HUD, Washington, 1981-83; prof. mgmt. Baruch Coll., CUNY, 1981-94, prof. public policy, 1994—, dir. public policy program, 1994—, chm. dept. mgmt., 1986-93; dir. Privatization Rsch. Orgn., 1986—; cons. NSF, Nat. Bur. Standards, Am. Paper Inst., Nat. Endowment for Arts, HUD, Dept. Transp., World Bank, AID, U.S. Dept. State, President's Commn. on Privatization, UN, UN Devel. Program, ILO, UNIDO, USIA, also others; mem. voting bd. Blue Cross and Blue Shield Greater N.Y., 1976-79, bd. dirs., 1979-81; mem. Pres.-Elect's Urban Affairs Task Force, 1980, N.Y. State Senate Adv. Commn. on Privatization, 1990-95; mem. Gov. Pataki privatization coun., N.Y., 1995—; dir. U.S.-USSR Joint Project on Mgmt. Cities, 1973-81; advisor on privatization Govt. Poland, 1990-92, Govt. Lesotho, 1992, Govt. Ukraine, 1993, N.Y.C. mayor, 1994—. Author: Computer Control of Industrial Processes, 1965, Organization and Efficiency of Solid Waste Collection, 1977, Privatizing the Public Sector, 1982, Moscow's City Government, 1985, Privatization, 1987, 15 fgn. edits., others; editor: Alternatives for Delivering Public Services, 1977, Privatization for New York, 1992; mem. editorial bd. Urban Affairs Quar., Privatization Report, Privatization Watch, State and Local Govt. Rev.; contbr. 110 articles to profl. jours. Mem. N.Y.C. Mayor-elect Giuliani transition team, 1993, N.Y. Gov.-elect Pataki transition team, 1994. With U.S. Army, 1953-54, Korea. Recipient Systems Sci. and Cybernetics award IEEE, 1968, Louis Brownlow award Am. Soc. Public Adminstrn., 1970, Honor award Templeton Found., 1989, Leadership award Nat. Coun. Pub.-Private Partnerships, 1993. Mem. Sigma Xi, Psi Upsilon. Greek Orthodox. Club: City of N.Y. (trustee 1974-77, Richard Childs award 1979). Office: CUNY Baruch Coll Box F-1228 17 Lexington Ave New York NY 10010-5526

SAVCHENKO, ALLA, ballet mistress; arrived in Can., 1981; Diploma of excellence, Moscow Ballet Sch. Mem. Bolshoi Ballet, 1953-74; ballet mistress, choreographer Sovrenennik Theatre, Moscow, 1974-79; regisseur Royal Winnipeg Ballet, 1981-89, ballet mistress, 1989-90, sr. ballet mistress, 1989—. Leading roles include Humpbacked Horse, The Nutcracker, The Stone Flower, Fire of Paris, Cinderella, Swan Lake, The Sleeping Beauty. Office: Royal Winnipeg Ballet, 380 Graham Ave, Winnipeg, MB Canada R3C 4K2

SAVEKER, DAVID RICHARD, naval and marine architectural engineering executive; b. San Jose, Calif., Jan. 10, 1920; s. William Thomas and Bernice (Lloyd) S.; m. Jessie Mae Walters, June 19, 1941 (dec. 1995); m. Judy D. Saltzman, July 3, 1995; children: William, Linda, Richard (dec.), Jeffery Whittier. AA, San Jose State Coll., 1939; AB, Stanford U., 1941; cert. in naval architecture, U.S. Naval Acad., 1942; SM, MIT, 1946. Registered profl. engr., Calif. Commd. ensign USN, 1941, advanced through grades to capt., 1960, ret., 1968; assoc. prof. Calif. Poly. State U., San Luis Obispo, 1969-80; pres. D.R. Saveker Naval Architecture, Pismo Beach, Calif., 1980—; assoc. Mac Kinnon Searle Consortium, Alexandria, Va., 1991—. Inventor sinusoidal structure and applications. Research grantee NASA/Stanford Lab., 1973. Mem. Marine Tech. Soc., Soc. Naval Architects and Marine Engrs., Tau Beta Pi. Democrat. Methodist. Club: Cosmos (Washington). Avocations: history, music, water colors. Home: 711 Hanford St Pismo Beach CA 93449-2347

SAVELKOUL, DONALD CHARLES, lawyer; b. Mpls., July 29, 1917; s. Theodore Charles and Edith (Lindgren) S.; m. Mary Joan Holland, May 17, 1941; children: Jeffrey Charles, Jean Marie, Edward Joseph. BA magna cum laude, U. Minn., 1939; JD cum laude, William Mitchell Coll. Law, 1951. Bar: Minn. 1951, U.S. Dist. Ct. Minn. 1952, U.S. Ct. Appeals (8th cir.) 1960, U.S. Supreme Ct. 1971. Adminstrv. work various U.S. govt. depts., including Commerce, War, Labor, Wage Stblzn. Bd., 1940-51; mcpl. judge Fridley, Minn., 1952-53; pvt. practice law Mpls., St. Paul, Fridley, 1951—; chmn. bd. Fridley State Bank, 1962-95, Blaine State Bank, 1972—; pres. Bahrein, Inc., 1962-95, Blaine Bldg. Corp., 1972—, Babbscha Co., 1962-95; mem. faculty William Mitchell Coll. Law, 1952-59, corp. mem., 1956—; sec. Fridley Recreation and Svc. Co., 1955—; mem. Minn. Legislature, 1967-69. Mem. Gov.'s Com. Workers Compensation, 1965-67, Gov.'s Adv. Coun. on Employment Security, 1957-60; chmn. Fridley Police Civil Svc. Commn., 1962-63; gen. counsel Minn. AFL-CIO Fedn. Labor, 1952-71. 1st lt. AUS, 1943-46. Decorated Bronze Star; recipient Disting. Alumni award Coll. Liberal Arts U. Minn., 1995. Mem. ABA, Minn. Bar Assn. (chmn. 1957-58, bd. dirs. 1958-62, 68-69, labor law sect.), Hennepin County Bar Assn., Justice William Mitchell Soc., Am. Legion, U. Minn. Pres.'s Club, Phi Beta Kappa. Roman Catholic. Office: 916 Moore Lake Dr W Fridley MN 55432-5148

SAVELL, EDWARD LUPO, lawyer; b. Atlanta, Apr. 29, 1921; s. Leon M. and Lillian (Lupo) S.; m. Bettie Patterson Hoyt, Oct. 11, 1944; 1 dau., Mary Lillian Savell Clarke. B.B.A., Emory U., 1947, LL.B., 1949. Bar: Ga. 1948. Assoc. A.C. Latimer, Atlanta, 1948-53; ptnr. Carter, Latimer & Savell, Atlanta, 1953-56, Woodruff, Latimer & Savell (and successor firms), Atlanta, 1956-87; of counsel Savell & Williams, Atlanta, 1987—; instr. John Marshall Law Sch., 1951-55; dir. Legal Aid Soc., 1955-58; arbitrator Am. Arbitration Assn. and Fulton Superior Ct. Contbr. articles to legal jours. With USAF, 1942-45, CBI. Fellow Internat. Acad. Trial Lawyers (pres. 1978-79, Dean of Acad. 1976); mem. Atlanta Bar Assn. (sec.-treas. 1953-54), ABA, State Bar Ga., Ga. Def. Lawyers Assn. (founder, v.p.), Internat. Assn. Ins. Counsel, Atlanta Claims Assn., Lawyers Club Atlanta, Chi Phi, Phi Delta Phi. Presbyterian. Clubs: Cherokee Town and Country, Commerce, Univ. Yacht (past commodore). Office: Savell and Williams 2600 Marquis I Tower 245 Peachtree Center Ave NE Atlanta GA 30303-1222

SAVER, MARTIN, children's entertainer. Recipient Grammy award for Best Spoken Word Album for Children "Prokofiev: Peter and the Wolf" 1996. Office: Kelly Bush Pub Rels 7201 Melrose Ave Los Angeles CA 90046*

SAVETH, EDWARD NORMAN, history educator; b. N.Y.C., Feb. 16, 1915; s. Isidor and Eva (Vasa) S.; m. Harriet Obstler, June 22, 1975; 1 child by previous marriage, Henry. B.S.S., CCNY, 1935; M.A., Columbia U., 1937, Ph.D., 1946. Prof. history Grad. Faculty New Sch. for Social Research, N.Y.C., 1960-63; Fulbright prof. Kyoto U., Kyoto, Japan, 1964-65; prof. Dartmouth Coll., 1965-66; Disting. vis. prof. Tex. Lutheran Coll., Seguin, 1966-67; Disting. prof. SUNY-Fredonia, 1967-85; adj. prof. SUNY, Buffalo, 1987—; lectr. USIA, Nepal, 1965, Morocco, 1977; Fulbright prof. Hebrew U., Jerusalem, 1981; vis. prof. U. Rochester, 1972; lectr. Beijing Tchrs. Coll., 1989. Author: American historians and European Immigrants, 1947; author, editor: Understanding the American Past, 1954, Henry Adams, 1963, American History and the Social Sciences, 1964; revisions editor: Ency. Americana, 1962; contbr. numerous articles to mags. Mem. Am. Hist. Assn., Orgn. Am. Historians. Home: 11 High Ct Buffalo NY 14226-3527 Office: SUNY-Fredonia Dept History Buffalo NY 14260

SAVICH, RENÉ, broadway theater executive, producer; b. Chgo., Nov. 14, 1947; d. Nicholas and Elizabeth (Szakurski) S. BS, Northwestern U., 1969. Asst. house mgr. Minskoff Theatre, N.Y.C., 1973; mem. mgmt. staff The Shubert Orgn. Inc., N.Y.C., 1975-77, mgr. dept. maintenance, 1977-80; asst. house mgr. The Shubert Theatre, N.Y.C., 1975-77, Plymouth Theatre, N.Y.C., 1978; house mgr. Barrymore Theatre, N.Y.C., 1978-79; mgr. co. The Elephant Man, N.Y.C., 1980; house mgr. Playhouse Theatre, N.Y.C., 1980-81, Cort Theatre, N.Y.C., 1981-85, Golden Theatre, N.Y.C., 1985-86, Booth Theatre, N.Y.C., 1987—. Producer off-Broadway plays including Wine Untouched, 1979, Lou, 1981, Punchy, 1983. Mem. Assn. of Theatrical Press Agts. and Mgrs., Actors Equity Assn., Treas. and Ticket Sellers Union. Office: The Shubert Orgn Inc 234 W 44th St New York NY 10036-3909

SAVIKAS, VICTOR GEORGE, lawyer; b. Pitts., Mar. 13, 1941; s. Victor E. and Bertha (Takach) S.; m. Barbara Klabisch, Sept. 5, 1964 (div. Mar. 1989); children: Elizabeth, Adam, Andrew; m. Muriel Spencer Shankman, Apr. 21, 1990. BA, DePaul U., 1967, JD, 1968. Bar: Calif. 1989, Ill. 1968, D.C. 1971, U.S. Dist. Ct. (no. dist.) Ill. 1968, U.S. Dist. Ct. (cen. dist.) Calif. 1989. Atty., ptnr. Friedman & Koven, Chgo., 1968-75; ptnr. Karon, Savikas & Horn, Chgo., 1975-88, Keck, Mahin & Cate, Chgo., 1988-89; ptnr.-in-charge Keck, Mahin & Cate, L.A., 1989—; instr. DePaul U. Coll. Law, Chgo., 1976-78. Co-editor Ct. of Appeals for Fed. Cir. newsletter, 1983-87.

Mem. Spl. Commn. on Adminstrn. of Justice in Cook County, Chgo., 1984-87. Fellow Am. Coll. Trial Lawyers; mem. ABA, Assn. Bus. Trial Lawyers, L.A. County Bar Assn., Ill. State Bar Assn., Fed. Cir. Bar Assn. Office: Jones Day Reavis & Pogue 555 W 5th St Ste 4600 Los Angeles CA 90013-3002

SAVILLE, DUDLEY ALBERT, chemical engineering educator; b. Lincoln, Nebr., Feb. 25, 1933; s. George A. and Alta (Goddard) S.; m. Joy Wagner, Mar. 7, 1959; children: Alexander, Andrea. B.S., U. Nebr., 1954, M.S., 1959; Ph.D, U. Mich., 1966. Engr. Carbide & Carbon Chem. Co. (Institute), W. Va., 1954-55; research engr. Chevron Research Corp. (Richmond), Calif., 1959-61, Shell Devl. Co., Emeryville, Calif., 1966-68; asst. prof. Princeton U. (N.J.), 1968-71, assoc. prof., 1971-77, prof. dept. chem. engring., 1977. Assoc. editor Jour. Physico-Chem. Hydrodynamics, 1980-87; mem. adv. bd. Jour. Colloid Interface Sci., 1992-94; contbr. articles to profl. jours. Served to 1st lt. USAF, 1955-58. Mem. Am. Inst. Chem. Engrs., Am. Chem. Soc., Am. Phys. Soc. Office: Princeton U Dept Chem Engring Princeton NJ 08544

SAVILLE, THORNDIKE, JR., coastal engineer, consultant; b. Balt., Aug. 1, 1925; s. Thorndike and Edith Stedman (Wilson) S.; m. Janet Foster, Aug. 28, 1950; children: Sarah, Jennifer, Gordon. A.B., Harvard U., 1947; M.S., U. Calif.-Berkeley, 1949. Research asst. U. Calif., Berkeley, 1947-49; hydraulic engr. Beach Erosion Bd. and Coastal Engring. Research Center, Ft. Belvoir, Va., 1949-81; chief research div. Beach Erosion Bd. and Coastal Engring. Research Center, 1964-71, tech. dir., 1971-81. Contbr. over 75 articles to engring. and sci. publs. Served with USAAF, 1943-46. Recipient Meritorious Civilian Service award Dept. Army, 1981. Fellow AAAS, Wash. Acad. Scis., ASCE (Huber award 1963, Moffatt-Nichol award 1979, Internat. Coastal Engring. award 1991); mem. Am. Geophys. Union, Internat. Assn. for Hydraulic Rsch., Nat. Acad. Engring., Permanent Internat. Assn. Navigation Congresses (hon., U.S. commr. emeritus 1987—), Am. Shore and Beach Preservation Assn. (bd. dirs. 1976—, v.p. 1988-95), Cosmos Club (Washington). Home and Office: 5601 Albia Rd Bethesda MD 20816-3304 *A good leader takes the blame and gives the credit.*

SAVIN, RONALD RICHARD, chemical company executive, inventor; b. Cleve., Oct. 16, 1926; s. Samuel and Ada (Silver) S.; m. Gloria Ann Hopkins, Apr. 21, 1962; children: Danielle Elizabeth, Andrea Lianne. BA in Chemistry and Lit., U. Cin., 1944-46; BA in Chemistry and Literature, U. Mich., 1948; postgrad., Columbia U., 1948-49, Sorbonne, Paris, 1949-50; grad., Air War Coll., 1975, Indsl. Coll. Armed Forces, 1976. Pres., owner Premium Finishes, Inc., Cin., 1957-91; cons. aerospace and anti-corrosive coatings; inventor Hunting Indsl. Coatings. Contbr. articles on aerospace, marine industry and transp. to profl. jours.; holder 14 patents in field of aerospace and anti-corrosion coatings. With USAF, 1948-55, World War II and Korea, col. Res. 1979, ret. 1986. Mem. Steel Structures Painting Coun., Nat. Assn. Corrosion Engrs., Air Force Assn., Am. Internat. Club (Geneva), Res. Officers Assn., Army Navy Club. Avocations: scientific development, photography, tennis.

SAVINAR, TAD LEE, artist; b. Portland, Nov. 29, 1950; s. Norman David and Adele Frances (Silver) S.; m. Georgia Clark; 1 child. BA in Studio Art, The Colo. Coll., 1973. instr. art Marylhirst Coll., Portland, 1979-86; panel mem. NEA/Visual Arts Orgn. Panel, 1989, 95, chair, 1990; panel mem. NEA/Warhol Found., Rockefeller Found. Regional Initiative Funding, 1993, Oreg. Arts Commn., 1993. One-man shows include Portland Art Mus., 1980, Artist's Space, N.Y.C., 1982, L.A. Inst. Contemporary Art, 1983, Reed Coll., Portland, 1984, The Fabric Workshop, Phila., 1992, Savage Fine Art, Portland, 1994; exhibited in group shows at San Diego Art Mus., 1978, John Berggruen Gallery, San Francisco, 1978, Artist's Space, 1984, The New Mus. Contemporary Art, N.Y.C., 1985, Baskerville-Watson Gallery, N.Y.C., 1987, Portland Art Mus., 1991, 93; represented in permanent collections at Mus. Modern Art, N.Y.C., Nat. Archives, Smithsonian Inst., Washington, Portland Art Mus., U. Calif. Art Mus., Santa Barbara, Chase Manhattan Bank, N.Y.C., Aratex, Burbank, Calif., G. Stroemple, Portland, J. Schnitzer, Portland, Phillip Morris Collection, N.Y.C. Co-chair Autumn Harvest AIDS/Hospice Event, Portland, 1992. NEA grantee, 1984, 95, Portland Met. Arts Commn. Project grantee, 1984, 86, 87, travel grantee, 1991; Oreg. Arts Commn. fellow, 1983, NEA fellow, 1984, 95. Office: PO Box 10798 Portland OR 97210

SAVINELL, ROBERT FRANCIS, engineering educator; b. Cleve., May 26, 1950; s. Robert D. and Lotte R. Savinell; m. Coletta A. Savinell, Aug. 23, 1974; children: Teresa, Robert, Mark. BSChemE, Cleve. State U., 1973; MS, U. Pitts., 1974, PhD, 1977. Registered profl. engr., Ohio. Rsch. engr. Diamond Shamrock Corp., Painesville, Ohio, 1977-79; assoc. prof. U. Akron, Ohio, 1979-86; prof. Case Western Reserve U., Cleve., 1986—, dir. Ernest B. Yeager Ctr. for Electrochem. Scis., 1991—. Divsn. editor Jour. Electrochem. Soc., 1988-91; N.Am. editor Jour. Applied Electrochemistry, 1991—; contbr. articles to profl. jours. Named Presdl. Young Investigator, NSF, Washington, 1984-89, Outstanding Engring. Alumnus, Cleve. State U., 1984. Mem. AIChE (program chmn. 1986-92), Electrochem. Soc. (divsn. officer 1992—). Avocations: sailing, skiing. Office: Case Western Reserve U Dept Chem Engring AW Smith Bldg Cleveland OH 44106

SAVINI, TOM, make-up artist, actor, director; b. Pitts.; m. Nancy Hare, 1984. Film work includes Deathdream, 1972, Deranged, 1974, Martin, 1976, Dawn of the Dead, 1978, Effects, 1980, Eyes of a Stranger, 1980, Friday the 13th, 1980, Friday the 13th IV, The Burning, 1981, Maniac, 1981, The Prowler, 1981, Alone in the Dark, Creepshow, 1982, Midnight, 1983, Friday the 13th-The Final Chapter, 1984, Invasion U.S.A., 1985, Day of the Dead, 1985, The Texas Chainsaw Massacre, Part II, 1987, Monkey-Shines: An Experiment in Fear, 1988, Red Scorpion, 1989, Two Evileyes, 1990, Heartstopper, 1992, Trauma, 1993, H.P. Lovecrafts Necronomicon, 1994, Mr. Stitch, Ghostwriter, Killing Zoe; dir. Night of the Living Dead, 1990; actor appearences include Knightriders, 1981, The Ripper, 1986; dir. Night of the Living Dead, 1990, episodes Tales from The Darkside; writer: Grand Illusions, 1983, Grand Illusions Books II, 1988.

SAVITSKY, DANIEL, engineer, educator; b. N.Y.C., Sept. 26, 1921; s. Maxim and Anna (Oleksiw) S.; m. Mary Wysocki; children: Jean, James, Anne. BCE, CCNY, 1942; MSc, Stevens Inst. Tech., 1952; PhD, NYU, 1971. Registered profl. engr., N.Y. Structural engr. EDO Corp., College Point, N.Y., 1942-44; aero. rsch. scientist Nat. Adv. Com. for Aero., Langley Field, Va., 1944-47; prof. emeritus Stevens Inst. Tech., Hoboken, N.J., 1947—; chmn. high speed vehicle com. Internat. Towing Tank Conf., 1978-88; cons. Naval Studies Bd., Nat. Rsch. Coun. Author: (with others) Yearbook of Science and Technology, 1987; patentee hydrofoil controls. Mem. Soc. Naval Architects and Marine Engrs. (Adm. Cochrane award 1967), Am. Soc. Naval Engrs., Niantic Bay Yacht Club (Conn.), Sigma Xi. Roman Catholic. Avocations: sailing, skiing, tennis. Home: 597 Delcina Dr Westwood NJ 07675-6111 Office: Davidson Lab 711 Hudson St Hoboken NJ 07030-5953

SAVITSKY, THOMAS ROBERT, lawyer; b. Pa., Sept. 12, 1952; s. Stanley George and Adele (Kaleda) S.; m. Deborah Ann Sokirka, Jan. 13, 1973; children: Thomas Jason, Raina Alexandra. BS in Biology, Villanova U., 1974; MS in Microbiology, Temple U., 1978; JD, Widener U., 1983. Bar: U.S. Patent and Trademark Office, 1984, Mich. 1985, Tenn. 1988, U.S. Dist. Ct. (ea. dist.) Mich. 1985, U.S. Ct. Appeals (fed. cir.) 1991; cert. quality engr. Am. Soc. for Quality Control, 1981. Microbiologist Warner-Lambert Co., 1978-81; lab. supr. Betz Labs., Trevose, Pa., 1982-84; patent atty. The Dow Chem. Co., Midland, Mich., 1984-87, Eastman Chem. Co., Kingsport, Tenn., 1987-89; sr. patent atty. Eastman Chem. Co., Kingsport, 1989-91, licensing and bus. devel. mgr., 1991-92; asst. counsel Bristol-Myers Squibb Co., Princeton, N.J., 1992—. Mem. ABA, AAAS, Am. Intellectual Property Law Assn., Am. Soc. for Microbiology. Roman Catholic. Home: 26 Meadow Lane Pennington NJ 08534 Office: Bristol-Myers Squibb Co PO Box 4000 Princeton NJ 08543

SAVITT, STEVEN LEE, computer scientist; b. Mpls., May 25, 1949; s. Leonard Robert and Claire (Hurwitz) S.; m. Gloria Lynn Kumagai; children: Mariko, Leilani, Joshua. BSEE, U. Minn., 1971, PhD in Computer Sci., 1992. Founder, CEO Compmark I Corp., Mpls., 1972-83; rsch. sect. head Honeywell, Inc., Mpls., 1983-89; rsch. staff scientist Alliant Techsystems, Inc., Mpls., 1989—; co-chair database com. Automatic Target Recognizer Working Group, 1985-87. Mem. IEEE, Japanese-Am. Citizens League. Avocations: piano, classic car collecting, canoeing, tennis, swimming. Home: 332 Westwood Dr N Golden Valley MN 55422-5263

SAVITT, SUSAN SCHENKEL, lawyer; b. Bklyn., Aug. 21, 1943; d. Edward Charles and Sylvia (Dlugatch) S.; m. Harvey Savitt, July 2, 1969 (div. 1978); children: Andrew Todd, Daniel Cory. BA magna cum laude, Pa. State U., 1964; JD, Columbia U., 1968. Bar: N.Y. 1968, U.S. Dist. Ct. (so. and ea. dists.) N.Y. 1973, U.S. Tax Ct. 1973, U.S. Ct. Appeals (2d cir.) 1981, U.S. Supreme Ct. 1980. Atty. Nassau County Legal Svcs., Freeport, N.Y., 1973-74; asst. corp. counsel City of Yonkers, 1977-78; from assoc. to ptnr. Epstein, Becker & Green, P.C., N.Y.C., 1978-94; ptnr. Winston & Strawn, N.Y.C., 1994—; adj. prof. Elizabeth Seton Coll., Yonkers, 1982-83; mem. NYU exec. coun. Met. Ctr. for Ednl. Rsch. Devel. and Tng., 1987-90. Mem. Hastings-on-Hudson (N.Y.) Sch. Bd., 1984-93, v.p., 1986, 87-88, pres., 1989-90, 92-93; bd. dirs. Associated Blind, 1993-95, Search for Change, 1996—. Mem. ABA (internat. law sect., litigation and labor law sect.), N.Y. State Bar ASsn. (com. on women and the law, labor law sect. com. on individual rights and responsibilities), Women's Bar Assn. (litigation com.), N.Y. State Sch. Bd. Attys. Assn., Pa. State Alumni Club (v.p. Westchester County 1985-87), Phi Beta Kappa, Alpha Kappa Delta, Phi Gamma Mu, Pi Kappa Phi. Office: Winston & Strawn 175 Water St New York NY 10038

SAVITZ, MARTIN HAROLD, neurosurgeon; b. Boston, Jan. 20, 1942; s. Nathan and Bernice Beatrice (Segal) S.; m. Susan Rayna Gordon, June 23, 1968 (div. Sept. 1977); 1 child, Sean Isaac; m. Harmony Gwynne Keys, Oct. 28, 1979; 1 child, Ariel Austryn. AB, Harvard U., 1963; MD, Hahnemann, 1969. Diplomate Am. Bd. Neurol. Surgery, Am. Bd. Clin. Neurosurgery, Nat. Bd. Med. Examiners, Am. Bd. Forensic Medicine. Intern Boston City Hosp., 1969-70; resident Mount Sinai Hosp., N.Y.C., 1970-74; clin. instr. dept. neurosurgery Mt. Sinai Sch. Medicine, N.Y.C., 1974-82, asst. clin. prof., 1982-86, assoc. clin. prof., 1986-96; attending neurosurgeon Nyack (N.Y.) Hosp., Good Samaritan Hosp., Rockland County, N.Y., Cmty. Hosp., Dobbs Ferry, N.Y.; mem. pres.'s coun. Harvard Coll., 1991—, marshal of commencement, 1993—; mem. alumni bd. trustees Hahnemann U., 1991-94; 16 vis. lectureships in 8 different countries; head exam com. Am. Bd. Clin. Neurosurgery, 1995—. Contbg. editor Mt. Sinai Jour. Medicine, 1976-90, asst. editor, 1990—; mem. editl. bd. Jour. Orthopaedic Neurol. Medicine and Surgery, 1991—; contbr. 2 chpts. to textbooks, over 70 articles to profl. jours. Mem. pres.'s coun. Harvard Coll., 1991—, marshal of commencement, 1993—; mem. alumni bd. trustees Hahnemann U., 1991-94. Fellow ACS, Am. Biog. Assn., Internat. Coll. Surgeons (chmn.-elect U.S. sect. neurosurgery, 1992—, chmn., 1993, exec. com. 1994, chmn.-elect 1996), N.Y. Acad. Medicine, Phila. Coll. Physicians, Am. Acad. Neurol. Orthopaedic Surgery (bd. dirs. 1994—) Am. Forensic Examiners Coll. (ethics com. 1995—), Internat. Biog. Assn.; mem. AMA, AAAS, Am. Assn. Neurol. Surgeons, N.Y. Soc. Neurosurgery, Congress Neurol. Surgeons, N.Y. State Neurosurg. Soc., Internat. Fedn. of Surg. Colls., Internat. Soc. Minimal Intervention in Spinal Surgery, Hastings Ctr., N.Y. Acad. Scis., Alpha Omega Alpha. Jewish. Avocations: travel to all 7 continents, photography of rare fauna and flora, archeology. Home: Hobbit Holw New City NY 10956 Office: 55 Old Turnpike Rd Ste 101 Nanuet NY 10954-2449

SAVITZ, MAXINE LAZARUS, aerospace company executive; b. Balt., Feb. 13, 1937; d. Samuel and Harriette (Miller) Lazarus; m. Sumner Alan Savitz, Jan. 1, 1961; children: Adam Jonathan, Alison Carrie. BA in Chemistry magna cum laude, Bryn Mawr Coll., 1958; PhD in Organic Chemistry, MIT, 1961. Instr. chemistry Hunter Coll., N.Y.C., 1962-63; sr. electrochemist Mobility Equipment Rsch. and Devel. Ctr., Ft. Belvoir, Va., 1963-68; prof. chemistry Federal City Coll., Washington, 1968-72; program mgr. NSF, Washington, 1972-74; dir. FEA Office Bldgs. Policy Rshc. U.S. Dept. Energy, Washington, 1974-75, dir. div. indsl. conservation, 1975-76, from dir. div. bldgs. and community systems to dep asst sec., 1975-83; pres. Lighting Rsch. Inst., 1983-85; asst. to v.p. engring. Ceramic Components div. The Garrett Corp., 1985-87; gen. mgr. ceramic components divsn. AlliedSignal Inc., Torrance, Calif., 1987—; lectr. in field; bd. dirs. Am. Coun. for Energy Efficient Economy, 1984—, Internat. Inst. Energy Conservation, 1984-94, Energy Found., 1991—; cons. State Mich. Dept. Commerce, 1983, N.C. Alternative Energy Corp., 1983, Garrett Corp., 1983, Energy Engring. Bd., Nat. Rsch. Bd., 1986-93, Office Tech. Assessment, U.S. Congress Energy Demand Panel, 1987-91, nat. materials adv. bd. NRC, 1989-94; bd. dirs. U.S. Advanced Ceramic Assn., 1989—, chmn., 1992; adv. com. div. ceramics/materials ORNL, 1989-92, adv. com. dir., 1992—; adv. bd. Sec. Energy, 1992—; mem. Def. Sci. Bd., 1993-96; vis. com. adv. tech. Nat. Inst. Standards and Tech., 1993—. Editor Energy and Bldgs.; contbr. articles to profl. jours. Policy com. mem. NAE, 1994—. NSF postdoctoral fellow, 1961, 62, NIH predoctoral fellow, 1960, 61. Mem. Nat. Acad. Engring. Office: AlliedSignal Ceramic Components Divsn 2525 W 190th St Torrance CA 90504-6002

SAVITZ, SAMUEL J., actuarial consulting firm executive; b. Phila., Dec. 23, 1936; s. Paul and Ann (Gechman) S.; BS in Bus. Adminstrn., Temple U., 1958; postgrad. U. Pa., 1960-62, Temple U., 1965; m. Selma Goldberg, June 15, 1958; children: Jacqueline Beverly, Steven Leslie, Michelle Lynn. Pension analyst Provident Mut. Life Ins. Co., Phila., 1958-61; v.p. The Wirkman Co., Phila., 1961-64; pres. Samuel J. Savitz & Assoc., Inc., Phila., 1964-86; chmn. bd., cons. Exec. Compensation Plans, Inc., Phila., 1980-86; sr. prin. Laventhol & Horwath, Phila., 1986-90; pres., CEO Savitz Orgn., Inc., 1990—; vis. lectr. U. Pa., Phila., 1960, La. State U., 1972-74; faculty Villanova U., 1971-75; cons. in field. Mem. pension com. Fedn. Jewish Agys., Phila., 1960; bd. dirs. Am. com. Weizmann Inst. Sci., 1984-85, Phila. All-Star Forum, 1987-95, Mann Music Ctr., 1992—. With USAR, 1954-62. Mem. Am. Soc. Pension Actuaries (dir. 1969-75). Jewish. Club: Locust. Contbr. articles in field to profl. jours. Home: 470 Conshohocken State Rd Bala Cynwyd PA 19004-2639 Office: 1845 Walnut St Philadelphia PA 19103-4708

SAVOCA, ANTONIO LITTERIO, technology company executive; b. Cleve., Aug. 10, 1923; s. Peter Louis and Angelina Nancy (Ragonese) S.; m. Charlene Henson, Sept. 27, 1952; 1 child, Gina Savoca Rose. BBA, U. Okla., 1958. Mgr. dept. proposals Wasatch div. Thiokol Corp., Brigham City, Utah, 1963-66, asst. to gen. mgr., 1966-68, dir. fin. and adminstrn., 1968-74, sr. v.p., gen. mgr., 1974-83; pres., chief exec. officer Transpace Carriers, Inc., Greenbelt, Md., 1983-86; mgmt. cons. various cos., 1986-89; pres., chief exec. officer Atlantic Rsch. Corp. subs. Sequa Corp., Alexandria, Va., 1989—, also bd. dirs.; sr. v.p. Sequa Corp., N.Y.C., 1991—; chmn. bd. Kollsman Mfg. Inc. Co., 1991-96; bd. dirs. No. Va. Tech. Coun. Chmn. U.S. Savs. Bond Campaign, Alexandria, 1991. Lt. col. USAF, 1942-63; ETO; Korea. Mem. Nat. Assn. Mfrs., Air Force Assn., Assn. U.S. Army, Am. Def. Preparedness Assn., Italy-U.S. Bus. Conf. (bd. dirs.), Navy League, U.S. Space Found., Hon. Utah Cols., The Robert Trent Jones Golf Club, Ogden Golf and Country Club, Tower Club. Republican. Roman Catholic. Office: Atlantic Rsch Corp 1577 Spring Hill Rd Ste 600 Vienna VA 22182-2223

SAVOCCHIO, JOYCE A., mayor; b. Erie, Pa.; d. Daniel and Esther S. BA in History, Mercyhurst Coll., 1965; MEd, U. Pitts., 1969; cert. secondary sch. adminstrn., Edinboro U., 1975. Tchr. social studies Erie Sch. Dist., 1965-85, asst. prin. Strong Vincent High Sch., 1985-89, tchr. coord. high sch. task force, 1971-75; pres. Erie Edn. Assn., 1975-76; mem. coun. City of Erie, 1981-90, pres. coun., 1983, mayor, 1990—; bd. dirs., treas. Pa. League of Cities and Municipalities; mem. subcoms. on transp. and comms. U.S. Conf. of Mayors; bd. dirs. State Job Tng. Partnership Bd.; mem., sec. Electoral Coll. for Commonwealth of Pa.; mem. various comns. Erie Sch. Dist. Past pres. Erie Hist. Mus.; past mem. editl. bd. Erie Hist. Soc.; mem. Pa. Gov.'s Flagship Commn., Cmty. Task Force on Drug and Alcohol Abuse; bd. dirs. Pa. League Cities and Mcpls., co-chair legis. com. Named Woman of Yr., Dem. Women Erie, 1981, Italian Am. Women's Assn., 1987; recipient Disting. Alumna award Mercyhurst Coll., 1990, Community Svc. award Roosevelt Mid. Sch., 1990, Disting. Citizen award French Creek coun. Boy Scouts Am., 1991. Mem. Delta Kappa Gamma. Roman Catholic. Office: Office of Mayor Mcpl Bldg 626 State St Erie PA 16501-1128

SAVOIE, LEONARD NORMAN, transportation company executive; b. Manchester, N.H., Aug. 8, 1928; s. Joseph Peter and Angelina (Desmarais) S.; m. Elsie Anne Berscht, June 9, 1951; children: Deborah Anne, Judith Lynn, Andrew Peter. B.S., Queen's U., 1952; M.B.A., U. Detroit, 1955. Indsl. engr. Kelsey-Hayes Can. Ltd., Windsor, Ont., Can., 1952-60; mgmt. cons. P.S. Ross & Partners, Toronto, Ont., 1960-64; pres., gen. mgr. Kelsey-Hayes Can. Ltd., 1964-70; pres., chief exec. officer Algoma Central Ry., Sault Ste. Marie, Ont., 1970-93, vice-chmn., 1993—; bd. dirs. Can. Gen. Ins. Co., E-L Fin. Corp. Ltd., Empire Life Ins. Co., Newaygo Forest Products Ltd., Gt. Lakes Power Ltd. Bd. dirs. United Appeal. Mem. Profl. Engrs. Ont., Engring. Inst. Can., Canadian, Sault Ste. Marie chambers commerce. Clubs: Rotary, Toronto, Toronto Ry, Sault Ste. Marie Golf. Office: Algoma Cen Ry, 289 Bay St, Sault Sainte Marie, ON Canada P6A 4Z2

SAVONA, MICHAEL RICHARD, physician; b. N.Y.C., Oct. 21, 1947; s. Salvatore Joseph and Diana Grace (Menditto) S.; m. Dorothy O'Neill, Oct. 18, 1975. BS summa cum laude, Siena Coll., 1969; MD, SUNY, Buffalo, 1973. Diplomate Am. Bd. Internal Medicine. Intern in internal medicine Presbyn. Hosp. Columbia U., N.Y.C., 1973-74, resident in internal medicine 1974-76; vis. fellow internal medicine Delafield Hosp./Columbia U. Coll. Physicians and Surgeons, N.Y.C., 1974-76; practice medicine specializing in internal medicine Maui Med. Group, Wailuku, Hawaii, 1976-87, gen. practice medicine, 1987—; dir. ICU, Maui Meml. Hosp., also dir. respiratory therapy, CCU., chmn. dept. medicine, 1980—; clin. faculty John A. Burns Sch. Medicine, U. Hawaii, asst. prof. medicine, 1985—, asst. rsch. prof., 1989—. Bd. dirs. Maui Heart Assn.; dir. profl. edn. Maui chpt. Am. Cancer Soc.; mem. Maui County Hosp. Adv. Commn.; mem. coun. Community Cancer Program of Hawaii. Recipient James A. Gibson Wayne J. Atwell award, 1970, physiology award, 1970, Ernest Whitebsky award, 1971, Roche Lab. award, 1972, Pfiser Lab. award, 1973, Phillip Sang award, 1973, Hans Lowenstein M.D. Meml. award, 1973. Mem. AMA, Am. Thoracic Soc., Hawaii Thoracic Soc., Maui County Med. Assn. (past pres.), Hawaii Med. Assn., Hawaii Oncology Group, ACP, SW Oncology Coop. Group, Alpha Omega Alpha, Delta Epsilon Sigma. Office: 1830 Wells St Wailuku HI 96793-2365

SAVORY, MARK, management consultant, insurance company executive; b. Englewood, N.J., Oct. 5, 1943; s. William A. and Marion J. (Garland) S.; m. Rose Marie Proietti, Feb. 5, 1988. BA with honors, Rutgers U., Newark, 1965; MA, Columbia U., 1966; MBA, U. Conn., 1973. Sec.-dir. Hartford (Conn.) Ins. Group, 1971-81; ptnr. Coopers & Lybrand, N.Y.C., 1981-90; nat. dir. ins. cons. Ernst & Young, 1990—. Contbr. articles to profl. jours. V.p. Tallott Glen Assn., 1985. Capt. USAF, 1966-71. Mem. Internat. Ins. Soc. (bd. govs. 1988—), Heron Soc. (founding). Home: 26 Vom Eigen Dr Morristown NJ 07960-4747 Office: Ernst & Young 750 7th Ave New York NY 10019-6829

SAVOY, DOUGLAS EUGENE, bishop, religion educator, explorer, writer; b. Bellingham, Wash., May 11, 1927; s. Lewis Dell and Maymie (Janett) S.; m. Elvira Clarke, Dec. 5, 1957 (div.); 1 son, Jamil Sean (dec.); m. Sylvia Ontaneda, July 7, 1971; children: Douglas Eugene, Christopher Sean, Sylvia Jamila. Student, U. Portland, 1947-8; DST, D Canon and Sacred Law, Jamilian U. of the Ordained, 1980; PhD in Theology, DD (hon.), Tech. Inst. Bibl. Studies, Nev., 1990. Ordained to ministry Internat. Community of Christ Ch., 1962, bishop, 1971. Cardinal head bishop Internat. Community of Christ Ch., 1971—; lectr. in ministerial tng. studies, 1972—; pastor Univ. Chapel, Reno, 1979—; founder Jamilian Parochial Sch., 1976; chancellor, founder Sacred Coll. of Jamilian Theology; pres., founder Jamilian U. of the Ordained, 1980; pres. Advs. for Religious Rights and Freedoms; chmn. World Coun. for Human Spiritual Rights, 1984—; head Jamilian Order of Patriarchs, 1990—; engaged in newspaper pub. West Coast, 1949-56; began explorations in jungles east of Andes in Peru to prove his theory that high civilizations of Peru may have had their origin in jungles, 1967; pres., founder Andean Explorers Club, Found., Reno; pres., Advocates for Religious Rights and Freedoms; chmn., World Coun. for Human Spiritual Rights. Author: Antisuyo, The Search for Lost Cities of the High Amazon, 1970, Vilcabamba, Last City of the Incas, 1970, The Cosolargy Papers, vol. 1, 1970, vol. 2-3, 1972, The Child Christ, 1973, Arabic edit., 1976, Japanese edit., 1981, The Decoded New Testament, 1974, Arabic edit., 1981, The Millenium Edition of the Decoded New Testament, 1983, On The Trail of The Feathered Serpent, 1974, Code Book and Community Manual for Overseers, 1975, Prophecies of Jamil, First Prophecy to the Americas, Vol. 1, 1976, Second Prophecy to the Americas, 1976, The Secret Sayings of Jamil, The Image and the Word, Vol. 1, 1976, Vol. 2, 1977, Project X—The Search For the Secrets of Immortality, 1977, Prophecy to the Races of Man, Vol. 2, 1977, Solar Cultures of The Americas, 1977, Dream Analysis, 1977, Vision Analysis, 1977, Christoanalysis, 1978, The Essaei Document: Secrets of an Eternal Race, 1978, Millennium edit., 1983, The Lost Gospel of Jesus: Hidden Teachings of Christ, 1978, Millennium edit., 1983, Secret Sayings of Jamil, Vol. 3. 1978, Vol. 4, 1979, Prophecy to The Christian Churches, 1978, The Sayings, vol. 4, 1979, Solar Cultures of Oceania, 1979, Prophecy of The End Times, Vol. 4, 1980, The Holy Kabbalah and Secret Symbolism, Vols. 1 and 2, 1980, Solar Cultures of China, 1980, Christotherapy, 1980, Christophysics, 1980, Christodynamics, 1980, Code Book of Prophecy, 1980, The Sayings, vol. 5, 1980, vol. 6, 1981, Solar Cultures of India, 1981, Prophecy on the Golden Age of Light and the Nation of Nations, Vol. 5, 1981, Solar Cultures of Israel, vol. 3, 1981, The Counsels, 1982, Prophecy of the Universal Theocracy, vol. 6, 1982, Prophecy of the New Covenant, vol. 7, 1982, The Book of God's Revelation, 1983, Miracle of the Second Advent, 1984, Clerical Studies in Theology, Book I, Book II, Book III, Book IV, Transformative Theology: The School of Revelation, Transformative Theology: The School of Prophecy, Liturgical Theology: Preparation for Advanced Degrees, 1993; over 300 audio tape rec. lectures, 1974—, numerous others.; documentary film on Gran Vilaya, 1989; wrote, dir. videos Royal Roads to Discovery, Mystery of the Essenes of Old Israel, Secrets From the High Andes of Peru, 1993; contbr. articles on Peruvian cultures to mags., also articles on philosophy and religion; discoverer lost city of Incas at Vilcabamba Cuzco, numerous ancient cities in Amazonia including Gran Pajaten, Gran Vilaya, Monte Peruvia, Twelve Cities of the Condor. Trustee in Trust Episcopal Head Bishop Internat. Community of Christ. Served with AS USNR, 1944-46. Decorated officer Order of the Grand Cross (Republic of Peru), 1989; recipient numerous exploring awards including over 40 Flag awarndean Explorers Club, 1958-85 and Explorer of the Century trophy Andean Explorers Found., 1988, Silver Hummingbird award Ministry Industry and Tourism of Peru, 1987, medal of Merit Andres Reyes, 1989. Mem. Geog. Soc. Lima, Andean Explorers Found, Ocean Sailing Club, World Coun. for Human Spiritual Rights, Advs. for Religious Rights and Freedoms, Authors Guild. Clubs: Explorers (N.Y.C.); Andean Explorers Found. and Ocean Sailing. Home: 2025 La Fond Dr Reno NV 89509-3025 Office: 643 Ralston St Reno NV 89503-4436 *One who makes dreams come true is that person who gets an idea, figures out how to make it work and then throws all of his energy into the project, stopping at nothing.*

SAVOY, SUZANNE MARIE, critical care nurse; b. N.Y.C., Oct. 18, 1946; d. William Joseph and Mary Patricia (Moclair) S. BS, Columbia U., 1970; M in Nursing, UCLA, 1978. RN, CCRN, cert. CCRN, CS. Staff nurse MICU, transplant Jackson Meml. Hosp., Miami, Fla., 1970-72; staff nurse MICU Boston U. Hosp. (Mass.), 1972-74; staff nurse MICU VA Hosp., Long Beach, Calif., 1974-75; staff nurse MIRU Cedars-Sinai Med. Ctr., L.A., 1975-77; critical care clin. nursing specialist Anaheim (Calif.) Meml. Hosp., 1978-81; practitioner, instr. Rush-Presbyn.-St. Luke's Med. Ctr. Coll. Nursing, Chgo., 1982-88; rsch. assoc. dept. neurosurgery, Rush U., 1984-88; clin. rsch. assoc. Medtronic, Inc. Drug Adminstrn. Systems, Mpls., 1988-91; staff nurse critical care Harper Hosp., Detroit, 1992-93; clinical nurse specialist, surgical/trauma critical care, Detroit Recieving Hosp., 1993-95; critical care clin. nurse specialist Saginaw (Mich.) Gen. Hosp., 1996—; clin. instr. Wayne State U. Coll. of Nursing, Detroit, 1991-96; program coord. Critical Care ACNP-CC MSN, Wayne State U., 1993-96; critical care CNS Saginaw Gen. Hosp., 1996—; neurosci. clinician acute stroke unit Harper Hosp., Detroit, 1989; edn. cons. Critical Care Svcs., Inc., Orange, Calif., 1979-81. Co-author articles for profl. jours. Mem. Am. Assn. Neurosci. Nurses (treas. Ill. chpt. 1983-85, pres. 1986-87, SE Mich. chpt. 1992—, bd. dirs., treas., program chair), Am. Assn. Critical Care Nurses (bd. dirs. Long Beach chpt. 1981-82), Am. Assn. Sci. Nursing (mem. rsch. com. 1993-95), Lambda Gamma Phi (bd. dirs. 1994-96), Sigma Theta Tau. Roman Catholic. Office: Saginaw Gen Hosp 1447 N Harrison Saginaw MI 48602

SAVRANN, RICHARD ALLEN, lawyer; b. Boston, July 29, 1935; s. Abraham B. and Doris (Curhan) S.; m. Diane Barbara Kleven, Dec. 22,

1957; children: Stephen Keith, Russell Carl. BA, Harvard U., 1956, JD, 1959. Bar: Mass. 1959, U.S. Dist. Ct. Mass. 1963, U.S. Ct. Appeals (1st cir.) 1965. Exec. Klev Bro. Mfg., Derry, N.H., 1959-63; assoc. Law Office of Jerome Rappaport, Boston, 1963-68; asst. atty. gen. Commonwealth of Mass., Boston, 1968-70; ptnr. Newell, Savrann & Miller, Boston, 1970-75; sr. ptnr. Kunian, Savrann & Miller, Boston, 1976-81, Singer, Stoneman, Kunian & Kurland, P.C., Boston, 1981-88, Singer, Kunian * Kurland, P.C., Boston, 1988-90; sr. ptnr. Curhan, Kunian, Goshko, Berwick and Savrann, P.C., Boston, 1990-92; ptnr. Burns and Levinson, Boston, 1993—. Mem. Andover (Mass.) Housing Authority, 1972-90, chmn., 1984-90; pres. Hospice of Greater Lawrence, North Andover, Mass., 1984; bd. dirs. Boston Latin Sch. Found., 1987, clk., 1992—; bd. dirs. Comite Internat. de Sci. pour La Santè et l'Environ., Paris, 1993—. Mem. FBA, Am. Trial Lawyers Assn., Mass. Bar Assn., Indian Ridge Country Club, Eastpointe Golf and Racquet Club (Palm Beach Gardens, Fla.), Harvard Club (Andover) (pres. 1985—). Avocations: golf, opera. Home: 11 Sheridan Rd Andover MA 01810-5109 Office: Burns and Levinson 125 Summer St Boston MA 02110-1616

SAVRIN, LOUIS, lawyer; b. Phila., Jan. 20, 1927; s. William Philip and Anna (Sass) S.; m. Barbara J. Schwimmer, Jan. 16, 1954; children: Jonathan Eric, Philip Wade, Daniel Scott. B.S., N.Y. U., 1948; J.D., U. Pa., 1951. Bar: N.Y. 1952. Atty. tax dept. Arthur Young & Co. (C.P.A.'s), N.Y.C., 1951-55; pvt. practice N.Y.C., 1955—; gen. counsel, sec. Pickwick Internat., Inc., N.Y.C., 1965-77. Assoc. editor: U. Pa. Law Rev, 1949-51. Mem. sch. bd. Dist. 21, Bklyn., 1962-68. With AUS, 1945-46. Mem. N.Y. State Bar Assn., N.Y. County Lawyers Assn., Real Estate Tax Rev. Bar Assn.; mem. B'nai B'rith (pres. lodge 1957-59, named to lodge Hall of Fame 1967, Torch of Freedom award Anti-Defamation League 1982). Club: Mason. Home: 907 Lake Plymouth Dr Newton NJ 07860-8921 Office: 60 E 42nd St New York NY 10017-5003

SAWABINI, WADI ISSA, retired dentist; b. Jaffa, Palestine, Jan. 14, 1917; s. Issa J. and Julia C. (Malak) S.; m. Harriet Colgate Abbe Lack, Aug. 6, 1949; children—Wadi' Issa, Frederick Lack, Stuart John, Julia Malak. Student, College des Ecoles Chrétiennes, 1924-32; D.D.S., Am. U. Beirut, 1940. Grad. study Forsyth Dental Infirmary, 1940-41; intern Med. Center Hosp. Vt. (formerly DeGoesbriand Meml. Hosp.), Burlington, 1941-42; attending staff; assoc. pvt. practice Dr. Charles I. Taggart, 1942-51; pvt. practice Burlington, 1951-88, ret.; instr. oral pathology U. Vt., 1951-58; dir. U. Vt. (Sch. Dental Hygiene), 1953-72; asst. prof. oral hygiene U. Vt. (Coll. Medicine), 1958-72; chief dental staff Mary Fletcher Hosp., 1958-68, assoc. prof. dept. allied health scis., 1969-72. Mem. adv. bd. Vt. Pub. Health Dept.; mem. Vt. Bd. Health, 1980-86; v.p. bd. dirs. Overlake Day Sch., 1962-63; mem. Ethan Allen Homestead Fundraising Com., 1990—. Paul Harris fellow Burlington Rotary. Fellow Internat. Coll. Dentists (mem. exec. council 1950-54), Am. Coll. Dentists; mem. Vt. Dental Soc. (pres. 1956-57, mem. bd. rev., Disting. Service award 1972), New Eng. Dental Soc., Champlain Valley Dental Soc., C. of C., ADA, Fedn. Dentaire Internat. Republican. Episcopalian (vestryman). Clubs: Mason (Shriner), Rotary (dir. 1955-56, pres. 1961-62), Ethan Allen (Burlington). Home: Bldg O Apt 2 Gardenside Shelburne VT 05482-7316 *I attribute my life's happiness to my alma mater, The American Univeristy of Beirut. It gave me technical expertise and love to seek knowledge, international understandings, and service to fellowman without regard to color nationality or religion.*

SAWAKI, TSUKASA, optical engineer; b. Takaoka, Japan, June 17, 1925; s. Katsuyo Hirai and Toki Sawaki; m. Masako Iwata, Apr. 2, 1953. BE, U. Tokyo, 1948, D of Engring., 1961. Chief rschr. Govt. Indsl. Rsch. Inst., Osaka, Japan, 1952-60; group leader Rsch. Lab., sr. staff Semiconductor R&D Ctr. Matsushita Electronics Corp., Nagaokakyo, Japan, 1960-82; group mgr., exec. Vacuum Optics Corp. Japan, Gotemba, 1982—. Author: Vacuum Evaporation, 1965; co-author: Thin Film Handbook, 1983; co-inventor, 1963, Purple Ribbon medal, 1974. Mem. Phys. Soc. Japan. Avocations: reading, hiking, skiing, game of igo. Office: Vacuum Optics Corp Japan, 1413 Nakabata, Gotemba 412, Japan

SAWALLISCH, WOLFGANG, conductor; b. Munich, Germany, Aug. 26, 1923; s. Wilhelm and Maria (Obermeier) S.; ed. Wittelsbacher Gymnasium of Munich, Musikalische Ausbildung, pvt. music studies; m. S. Mechthild, 1952. Condr., Augsburg, 1947-53; musical dir. Aachen, 1953-58, Wiesbaden, 1958-60, Cologne Opera, 1960-63; condr. Hamburg Philharm. Orch., 1960-73, hon. mem., 1973—; prin. condr. Vienna Symphony Orch., 1960-70, hon. mem.; also prof. Staatliche Hochschule für Musik, Cologne, 1960-63; musical dir. Bayerische Staatsoper Munich, 1971-92, dir. Staatsoper Munich, 1982-92, hon. mem., 1992; permanent condr. Teatro alla Scala, Milan; condr. many festivals; rec. artist U.S. and Britain; hon. condr. NHK Symphony Orch., Tokyo, 1967; artistic dir. Suisse Romande Orch., Geneva, 1973-80; music dir. Phila. Orch., 1993—. Recipient Accademico Onorario Santa Cecilia, 1975; decorated Osterreichisches Ehrenkreuz für Kunst und Wissenschaft, Bundesverdienstkreuz, Bayerischer Verdienstorden, Grosses Bundesverdienstkreuz mit Stern (Fed. Republic Germany), Order of the Rising Sun Japan; recipient Bruckner-Ring, Vienna Symphony Orch., 1980; Bayerisches Maximilians-order für Wissenschaft and Kunst, 1984, Chevalier dans L'ordre National de la Légion d'Honneur de France, 1991. Mem. Richard Strauss Gesellschaft Munich (pres. 1976). Office: Phila Orch 1420 Locust St Philadelphia PA 19102-4223

SAWCHUK, RONALD JOHN, pharmaceutical sciences educator; came to U.S., 1966; m. Rosslyn Andrea Murison, July 8, 1967; children: David, Heather, Holly. BSc in Pharmacy, U. Toronto, Ont., Can., 1963, MSc in Pharmaceutics, 1966; PhD in Pharm. Chemistry, U. Calif., San Francisco, 1972. Tchg. asst. U. Toronto, 1963-65; pharmacist Toronto, 1966; tchg. asst. U. Calif., 1966-68; instr. pharmaceutics U. Minn., Mpls., 1971-72, asst. prof., 1972-77, assoc. prof., 1982-95, dir. bioanalytical and pharmacokinetic svcs., 1995—, assoc. dir. Clin. Pharmacokinetics Lab., Coll. Pharmacy, 1974-82, dir. Clin. Pharmacokinetics Lab., 1982-95; acting chmn. dep. pharms. U. Minn., 1983-86, dir. grad. studies in pharms., 1983-89, 92-94, dir. bioanalytic and pharmacokinetic svcs., 1995—; mem. organizing com. NATO Advanced Study Inst., Erice, Italy, 1994; cons. antiepileptic drug devel. program NIH/ Nat. Inst. of Neurol. Diseases and Stroke, 1991-93; mem. U.S. Pharmacopeia Com. of Revision, 1990-95. Editl. bd. Saudi Pharm. Jour., Jour. Pharm. Scis.; contbr. articles in pharmacokinetics and bioanalysis to sci. jours. Scholar Can. Found. for Advancement of Pharmacy, 1964, NRC Can., 1965-66; Warner-Lambert rsch. fellow, 1965; NIH tng. grantee, 1968-70; recipient Horace T. Morse-Amoco Found. award, 1986, Hallie Bruce Meml. Lectr. award, 1996. Fellow AAAS, Am. Assn. Pharm. Scientists. Achievements include research drug distribution and elimination studies utilizing microdialysis. Home: 1762 20th Ave NW New Brighton MN 55112 Office: U Minn Coll Pharmacy Dept Pharm Health Sci Unit F 308 Harvard St SE Minneapolis MN 55455

SAWDEI, MILAN A., lawyer; b. Bakersfield, Calif., Aug. 23, 1946. BA, U. Calif., Long Beach, 1969; JD, W.S.U., 1975. Bar: Calif. 1975, U.S. Dist. Ct. (ctrl. dist.) Calif. 1975. House counsel Sanyo Electric, Inc., 1975-77; assoc. counsel Brown Co. (Gulf & Western), 1978-80; divsn. counsel Petrolane, Inc., 1980-83; sr. counsel Bergen Brunswig Corp., Orange, Calif., 1983-90, v.p., chief legal officer, 1990-92, exec. v.p., chief legal officer, sec., 1992—. Mem. ABA, Am. Corp. Counsel Assn., Am. Soc. Corp. Secs., L.A. County Bar Assn. Office: Bergen Brunswig Corp 4000 W Metropolitan Dr Orange CA 92668-3502

SAWDEY, RICHARD MARSHALL, lawyer; b. Buffalo, Jan. 8, 1943; s. Marshall Douglas and Eleanor Katherine (Reichman) S.; m. Judith Hollister Helgeson, Aug. 12, 1967; children—David Marshall, Karin Elizabeth. B.S., Mich. State U., 1965; J.D., U. Mich., 1968. Bar: Ill. 1968. Assoc. McBride, Baker, Wienke & Schlosser, Chgo., 1968-73; atty. R.R. Donnelley & Sons, Chgo., 1974-75, asst. sec., 1975-83, sec., 1983-85; v.p., sec., 1985-88; 0f counsel Hoogendoorn, Talbot, Davids, Godfrey & Milligan, Chgo., 1988—. Mem. ABA, Chgo. Bar Assn. (chmn. fin. and investment svcs. com. 1994-95). Office: Hoogendoorn Talbot Davids Godfrey & Milligen 122 S Michigan Ave Ste 1220 Chicago IL 60603-6107

SAWHILL, ISABEL VAN DEVANTER, economist; b. Washington, Apr. 2, 1937; d. Winslow B. and Isabel E. Van Devanter; m. John C. Sawhill, Sept. 13, 1958; 1 son, James W. B.A., NYU, 1962, Ph.D., 1968. Policy analyst Office Sec. HEW, 1968-69, Office Mgmt. and Budget, 1969-70; asst. prof. econs. Goucher Coll., Balt., 1969-73; sr. research assoc. Urban Inst., 1973-77, program dir., 1975-77, program dir., sr. fellow, 1980-93; dir. Nat. Commn. Employment Policy, Washington, 1977-79; program assoc. dir. Office Mgmt. and Budget, 1993-95; sr. fellow and Arjay Miller chair in pub. policy Urban Inst., 1995—; vis. prof. Georgetown U. Law Ctr., 1990-91. Author: The Reagan Record, 1984, Challenge to Leadership, 1988. Past mem. Sec. of Labor's commn. on workforce quality and labor mkt. efficiency, Ctr. Strategic and Internat. Studies commn. on strenghtening of Am., NRC bd. on sci., tech., and econ. policy; bd. dirs. Assembly of Am., Manpower Demonstration Res. Corp., Resources of the Future, vice-chair; pres. Nat. Campaign Prevent Teen Pregnancy, 1996—. Mem. Am. Econ. Assn. (mem. exec. com.), Assn. Pub. Polit. Analysis and Mgmt. (pres. 1988), Phi Beta Kappa. Office: 2100 M St NW Washington DC 20037-1207

SAWHILL, JOHN CRITTENDEN, conservationist, economist, university president, government official; b. Cleve., June 12, 1936; s. James Mumford and Mary Munroe (Gipe) S.; AB, Princeton U., 1958; PhD, N.Y. U., 1963; m. Isabel Van Devanter, Sept. 13, 1958; 1 child, James W. With Merrill, Lynch, Pierce, Fenner & Smith, Washington, 1958-60; asst. dean, prof. NYU Sch. Bus. Adminstrn., 1960-63, pres. NYU Washington Sq., 1975-79; dir. credit rsch. and planning Comml. Credit Co., Balt., 1964-66, sr. v.p., 1968-73; sr. assoc. McKinsey & Co., Washington, 1966-68; assoc. dir. natural resources Office Mgmt. and Budget, Washington, 1973-74; adminstr. Fed. Energy Adminstrn., Washington, 1973-75; dep. sec. Dept. Energy, Washington, 1979-80; chmn. U.S. Synthetic Fuels Corp., Washington, 1980; bd. dirs. McKinsey & Co., Inc., Washington, 1980-90, Pacific Gas & Electric Co., NACCO Industries, Vanguard Group. Pres. The Nature Conservancy, Arlington, Va., 1990—; chmn. bd. trustees Whitehead Inst. Biomed. Rsch.; trustee Princeton U.; mem. Coun. on Fgn. Rels.; mem., dir. Trilateral Commn. Mem. AAAS (dir.), Met. Club (Washington), Chevy Chase Club (Md.), River Club (N.Y.C.). Office: The Nature Conservancy 1815 N Lynn St Arlington VA 22209-2003

SAWICKI, ZBIGNIEW PETER, lawyer; b. Hohenfels, Germany, Apr. 13, 1949; came to U.S., 1951; s. Witold and Marianna (Tukiendorf) S.; m. Katheryn Marie Loman, Aug. 19, 1972; children: James, Jeffrey, Jessica, Jason. BSChemE, Purdue U., 1972; MBA, Coll. St. Thomas, St. Paul, 1977; JD, Hamline U., 1980. Bar: Minn. 1980, U.S. Dist. Ct. Minn. 1981, U.S. Ct. Appeals (8th cir.) 1981, U.S. Patent and Trademark Office 1981, U.S. Ct. Appeals (fed. cir.) 1982, Can. Patent Office 1994, Can. Trademark Office 1995. Process engr. 3-M Co., St. Paul, 1973-75; process engring. supr. Conwed Corp., St. Paul, 1975-77; shareholder, bd. dirs. Kinney & Lange, Mpls., 1980—. Bd. dirs. Orono (Minn.) Hockey Boosters, 1992—. With USAF, 1970-72. Mem. ABA, Am. Intellectual Property Assn., Internat. Trademark Assn., Minn. Intellectual Property Assn. (past treas.), Am. Legion. Home: 4510 N Shore Dr Orono MN 55364 Office: Kinney & Lange 625 4th Ave S Minneapolis MN 55415-1624

SAWIN, NANCY CHURCHMAN, educator, artist, historian; b. Wilmington, Del., June 21, 1917; d. Sanford W. and Ellen (Quigley) S. BA, Principia Coll., 1938; MA, U. Del., 1940; D.Ed., U. Pa., 1962; PhD (hon.), Golden Beacom Coll., 1987. With Sanford Sch., Hockessin, Del., 1938-74; dean girls Sanford Sch., 1945-62, head sch., 1962-74; coordinator student services U. Del. Div. Continuing Edn., Newark, 1974-77; ednl. cons. DuPont Co., ICI Ams., 1976-80; chmn. Del. State Sci. Fair com., 1962; mem. com. Jr. Sci. and Humanities Symposium, 1962-76; mem. English, lang. arts adv. com. State Del., 1965-68; sec., dir. Recreation, Promotion and Service, Inc., 1963-74; mem. All-Am. Hockey Team, 1948-59. One-person shows include Ctr. for Creative Arts, 1993—, others; editor: The Eagle, 1961-62; co-pub., illustrator: Between the Bays, 1977, Delaware Sketchbook, 1976, Backroading Thruth Cecil County, 1977, Brick and Ballast, 1985; author, illustrator: Man-O-War My Island Home, 1978, Up the Spine and Down the Creek, 1982, Locks Traps and Corners, 1984, China Sketchbook, 1985, A Hockessin Diary, 1987, Privy to the Council, 1987, The Oulde King's Roade, 1989, North from Wilmington by Oulde Roads and Turnpikes, 1992, Once Upon a Time in the Country, 1994. Trustee Goldey Beacom Coll., pres., 1974-81, mem. safety coun., 1964-74; pres. Del. Sports Hall of Fame, 1982—; pres. bd. dirs. Del. Soc. for Preservation of Antiquities, 1986-88, chair, 1990—; chair fundraising com. Hockessin County Libr., 1989-94; bd. dirs. Preservation Del., 1996—. 2d lt. CAP, 1942-45. Recipient Medal of Merit, U. Del., 1989, DAR History medal, 1990, Hist. Preservation award New Castle County, 1996; named to Del. Sports Hall of Fame, 1977; charter mem. U.S. Field Hockey Hall of Fame, 1988; named to Hall of Fame of Del. Women, 1991, Wall of Fame, U. Del., 1991. Mem. Headmistress Assn. East, Del. Art Mus., Rehoboth Art League, Middle Atlantic States Assn. Colls. and Secondary Schs. (past pres.), Commn. on Secondary Schs., Red Clay Creek Assn., Internat. Fedn. Women's Hockey Assns. (past pres.), U.S. Field Hockey Assn. (past pres., named to Sports Hall of Fame 1987), Del. Field Hockey Assn. (past pres.), Nat. League Am. Pen Women, DAR (History medal), Daus. of Founders and Patriots, Nat. Soc. New Eng. Women, Daus. Colonial Wars, Del. Greenbank Questars (pres. 1993-94), Delta Kappa Gamma (past pres.), Pi Lambda Theta. Republican. Presbyterian (elder). Club: Quota (pres. Wilmington 1971-73, gov. 10th Dist. 1979-80). Address: North Light Studio 147 Sawin Ln Hockessin DE 19707-9713

SAWINSKI, VINCENT JOHN, chemistry educator; b. Chgo., Mar. 28, 1925; s. Stanley and Pearl (Gapinski) S.; m. Florence Whitman, Aug. 24, 1952; children—Christine Frances, Michael Patrick. B.S., Loyola U., 1948, M.A., 1950, Ph.D., 1962. Instr., asst. prof. chemistry, physiology and pharmacology Loyola U., Chgo., 1949-67; supervisory research chemist VA, Hines, Ill., 1961-66; assoc. prof. chemistry, phys. sci. City Colls. Chgo., 1967-71, prof., 1971-91, prof. emeritus, 1991—, chmn. phys. sci. dept. Wright campus, 1971-91. Contbr. articles to profl. jours. Served with U.S. Army, 1945-46. Fellow AAAS, Am. Inst. Chemists; mem. Am. Chem. Soc., Nat. Sci. Tchrs. Assn., Sigma Xi. Home: 1945 N 77th Ct Elmwood Park IL 60635-3623 Office: 4300 N Narragansett Ave Chicago IL 60634-1591

SAWIRIS, MILAD YOUSSEF, statistician, educator; b. Cairo, Jan. 11, 1922; came to U.S., 1966, naturalized, 1972; s. Youssef Sawiris and Faika Botros Samaan. B.Sc., Cairo U., 1942, diploma in edn., 1944, diploma higher edn., 1959; M.A., U. London, 1963, Ph.D., 1965; M.S., Stanford U., 1975. Tchr. math. Egyptian Govt. schs., 1944-48, 57-61, Sudan Govt. schs., 1948-57; mem. faculty Calif. State U., Sacramento, 1966-86, prof. emeritus, 1986—. Author research papers. Mem. Am. Statis. Assn. Mem. Coptic Orthodox Ch. Home: 8308 Caribbean Way Sacramento CA 95826-1657

SAWOROTNOW, PARFENY PAVLOVICH, mathematician, educator; b. Ust Medveditskaya, Russia, Feb. 20, 1924; came to U.S., 1949, naturalized, 1965; s. Pavel Ivanovich and Anna Davidovna (Soloview) S.; student U. Graz (Austria), 1946-49; MA (Peirce scholar), Harvard U., 1951, PhD (Shattuck fellow), 1955. Teaching fellow Harvard U., 1953-54; instr. math. Cath. U. Am., Washington, 1954-57, asst. prof., 1957-62, assoc. prof., 1962-67, prof., 1967—. NSF grantee, 1967, 70; with Georgetown U. and George Washington U., 1971-77. Mem. Am. Math. Soc., Math. Assn. Am., Calcutta Math. Soc., N.Y. Acad. Scis., AAUP, Sigma Xi. Mem. Eastern Orthodox Ch. Contbr. articles to and referred papers for math. rsch. jours. Home: 6 Avon Pl Hyattsville MD 20782-3328 Office: Cath U Am Dept Math 4th and Michigan Ave NE Washington DC 20064

SAWTELL, STEPHEN M., private investor, lawyer; b. St. Paul, Jan. 17, 1931; s. William Amos and Helen Mary (Fiegenbaum) S.; m. Helen Elizabeth Wencel, June 27, 1956; children: Stephen, Katherine H. Student, Northwestern U., 1948-50; BSc in Law, U. Nebr., 1956, JD, 1957; postgrad., Stanford U., 1974. Bar: Nebr. 1957. With No. Natural Gas Co. (now Enron, Inc.), Omaha, 1957-85, Dubuque Packing Co. of Omaha, 1987-88, CENI Corp., JinNeb Beef Ltd., Dalien, China, 1987-89; of counsel McMannama and Assocs., Inc., Omaha, 1988—. Pres. Omaha Symphony Assn., 1969-71, Jr. Achievement Omaha, 1975, Omaha Sister City Assn., 1974-83; chmn. Omaha Com. on Fgn. Rels., 1975-81; mem. bd. advisors Salvation Army, 1981—. With AUS, 1952-55. Named Omaha's Outstanding Young Man of Year Omaha Jr. C. of C., 1963. Mem. Masons, Rotary, Omaha Club, Omaha Country Club. Congregationalist. Home: 702 Ridgewood Ave Omaha NE 68114-5360

SAWTELLE, CARL S., psychiatric social worker; b. Boston, July 14, 1927; s. Carl Salvador and Martha (Bellamacina) S.; BA, Suffolk U., Boston, 1951; MSW, Simmons Sch. Social Work, 1953; m. Thelma Florence Ramsay, Aug. 20, 1950; children: Tracy Lynn, Lisa June. Social worker Tewksburry (Mass.) State Hosp., 1952; psychiat. social worker, head psychiat. social worker, dir. clin. social work Taunton (Mass.) State Hosp., 1953-74; 1st dir. clin. social work, Plymouth, Mass., 1974-78; co-founder, v.p. 1st legally established War On Poverty program Triumph, Inc., Taunton; co-founder 1st Greater Taunton Coun. on Alcoholism, 1972. With USCG, 1944-46. 1st lic. social worker in Mass., 1980. Mem. Nat. Assn. Social Workers (co-founder Southeast Mass. chpt. 1957, pres. 1957, Spl. Mass. Chpt. award 1978), Acad. Cert. Social Workers (chmn. 1962-72), Am. Legion, Mass. Mental Health Social Workers Assn. (co-founder, pres. 1972-74, other offices). Created innovated programs, resources, opportunities, svcs. to state mental hosp. patients and their families; mentor to young social workers; contbr. advancement of knowledge, practice quality and standards of psychiat. social work; father of licensing and registration of Social Workers in Mass. Home: 9 Tracywood Rd Canton MA 02021-3501

SAWYER, ANITA DAWN, special education educator; b. Harrison, Ark., July 8, 1963; d. Donnie Frank and Myrtle Darline (Curbow) Coxsey; m. Timothy Clarence Sawyer, Mar. 26, 1988; children: Benjamin Aram, Lukas Ryan, Lauren Nicole. AS, North Ark. Cmty. Tech. Coll., Harrison, 1984; BS in Edn., U. Ctrl. Ark., 1986. Cert. spl. edn.-mildy handicapped grades K-12. Jr. and sr. H.S. spl. educator Omaha (Ark.) Pub. Schs., 1986-91; extended yr. svcs. coord. Boone County Spl. Svcs., Harrison, summer 1987; tchr.-leader summer youth program Job Tng. Partnership Act, Harrison, summer 1991; jr. and sr. H.S. spl. educator Alpena (Ark.) Pub. Schs., 1991; indirect svcs. coord. Omaha (Ark.) H.S., 1986-91, Alpena (Ark.) H.S., 1991—, dist. spl. olympics coord., Omaha Pub. Schs., 1987-91, Alpena Pub. Schs., 1991—; adv. bd. mem. Omaha H.S. Future Bus. Leaders Am., 1990-91; coord. transitional svcs. Omaha, 1986-91, Alpena, 1991—; Pres., personnel policies committee, Alpena, 1995-96. Vol. internat. cert. Omaha (Ark.) and Ark. Spl. Olympics, 1986-91; fundraising and cmty. contact rep. United Way-Omaha (Ark.) H.S., 1989; spl. olympics coach in bowling, basketball, floor hockey and athletics Alpena (Ark.) and Ark. Spl. Olympics, 1991—. Mem. NEA, Ark. Edn. Assn. (bldg. rep., gen. assembly 1986-90), Omaha Edn. Assn. (v.p. 1986-87, pres. 1987-90, rep.), Coun. Exceptional Children, Omaha Booster Club (v.p. 1988-89), Omaha PTO, Alpena PTO. Baptist. Avocations: cooking, reading, crafts, playing piano, singing. Home: RR 4 Box 391C Harrison AR 72601-9155 Office: Alpena Pub Schs PO Box 270 300 S Denver Alpena AR 72611

SAWYER, CHARLES HENRY, anatomist, educator; b. Ludlow, Vt., Jan. 24, 1915; s. John Guy and Edith Mabel (Morgan) S.; m. Ruth Eleanor Schaeffer, Aug. 23, 1941; 1 dau., Joan Eleanor. BA, Middlebury Coll., 1937, DSc honoris causa, 1975; student, Cambridge U., Eng., 1937-38; Ph.D., Yale, 1941. Instr. anatomy Stanford, 1941-44; assoc., asst. prof., assoc. prof., prof. anatomy Duke U., 1944-51; prof. anatomy UCLA, Los Angeles, 1951-85; prof. emeritus UCLA, 1985—, chmn. dept., 1955-63, acting chmn., 1968-69, faculty research lectr., 1966-67. Editorial bd.: Endocrinology, 1955-59, Proc. Soc. Exptl. Biology and Medicine, 1959-63, Am. Jour. Physiology, 1972-75; Author papers on neuroendocrinology. Mem. Internat. Brain Research Orgn. (council 1964-68), AAAS, Am. Assn. Anatomists (v.p. 1969-70, Henry Gray award 1984), Am. Physiol. Soc., Am. Zool. Soc., Neurosci. Soc., Endocrine Soc. (council 1968-70, Koch award 1973), Am. Acad. Arts and Scis., Nat. Acad. Scis., Soc. Exptl. Biology and Medicine, Soc. Study Reprodn. (dir. 1969-71, Hartman award 1977), Internat. Neuroendocrine Soc. (council 1972-76), Hungarian Soc. Endocrinology and Metabolism (hon.), Japan Endocrin Soc. (hon.), Phi Beta Kappa, Sigma Xi. Home: 466 Tuallitan Rd Los Angeles CA 90049-1941 Office: U Calif Sch Medicine Dept Neurobiology Los Angeles CA 90024

SAWYER, CHARLES HENRY, educator, art museum director emeritus; b. Andover, Mass., Oct. 20, 1906; s. James Cowan and Mary Pepperrell (Frost) S.; m. Katharine Clay, June 28, 1934. BA, Yale U., 1929, MA, 1947; student, Harvard Law Sch., 1929-30; student of Fine Arts, Harvard U. Grad. Sch., 1930-32; LHD, Amherst Coll., 1950; DFA, U. New Hampshire, 1951; LHD, Clark U., 1953. Dir. Addison Gallery of Am. Art, art instr. Phillips Acad., Andover, Mass., 1930-40; dir. Worcester (Mass.) Art Mus., 1940-46; dir. divsn. of the arts, prof. history of art Yale U., New Haven, Conn., 1947-56; master Timothy Dwight Coll. Yale U., New Haven, 1947-53; dean Sch. of Architecture and Design, Yale U., New Haven, 1947-56; dir. mus. of art U. Mich., Ann Arbor, 1957-72, prof. history of art, 1957-76, dir. emeritus mus. of art, 1973—; mem. art adv. commn. Harvard U., 1940-58, Cambridge, , Amherst (Mass.) Coll., 1948-60, Smith Coll., Northampton, Mass. 1948-55, U. Notre Dame, Ind., 1973-82, Smithsonian Art Commn., Smithsonian Instn., Washington, 1953-80; trustee Corning (N.Y.) Mus. of Glass, 1950-75; prof. emeritus History of Art, U. Mich., 1977—. Author: (book) Art in English Public Schools, 1936; author various articles, exhibition catalogues etc., 1931—. Mem. Art Commn. State of Mass., Boston, 1940-44, Historic Sites Commn., State of New Hampshire, Concord, 1948-58, Arts Coun., State of Mich., Lansing, 1964-72. Named Hon. Mem. NMAA Commn. Washington, 1985—. Fellow Am. Acad. Arts and Scis.; mem. Assn. Art Mus. Dirs. (hon. mem. 1973—), Century Assn. N.Y., Am. Antiquarian Soc. Episcopalian. Avocations: hist. rsch., gardening. Home: 2 Highland Ln Ann Arbor MI 48104-1727

SAWYER, CHRISTOPHER GLENN, lawyer; b. Winston-Salem, N.C., Sept. 20, 1950; m. Julia Ann Fergerson; children: Frances Elizabeth, Christopher Glenn Jr. BA, U. N.C., 1972; MDiv, Yale U., 1975; JD, Duke U., 1978. Bar: Ga. 1978, N.C. 1978. Assoc. Alston & Bird, Atlanta, 1978-85, ptnr., 1985—; lectr. at profl. seminars. Bd. dirs. Lee Harper and Dancers, 1982-88, chmn., 1983-86; mem. exec. com. Atlanta Crime Corrdination Com., 1979-80; chmn. Ga. adv. bd. trustees The Trust for Pub. Land, 1990-94, bd. dirs., 1993—; clk. of sessions Trinity Presbyn. Ch., 1992-93. Mem. ABA, Ga. Bar Assn. (consumer rights and remedies com. 1980-81), N.C. Bar Assn., Nat. Conf. Bar Pres., The Nature Conservancy of Ga. (bd. dirs. 1990—, chmn., nat. real estate adv. bd., 1992—), Atlanta Bar Assn. (pres. 1989-90, bd. dirs. 1983—, exec. com. 1984-85, 87—), Atlanta Coun. Young Lawyers (bd. dirs. 1979-84), Atlanta Vol. Lawyers Found. (bd. dirs.), Atlanta Legal Aid Soc. (adv. bd. 1984-86), Lawyers Club of Atlanta, Atlanta Botan. Gardens, Atlanta Hist. Soc., Atlanta Music Festival Assn., Friends of Atlant Zoo, High Mus. Art, Yale Club of Ga. Presbyterian. Office: Alston & Bird 1 Atlantic Ctr 1201 W Peachtree St NW Atlanta GA 30309-3400*

SAWYER, (L.) DIANE, television journalist; b. Glasgow, Ky., Dec. 22, 1945; d. E.P. and Jean W. (Dunagan) S.; m. Mike Nichols, Apr. 29, 1988. BA, Wellesley Coll., 1967. Reporter Sta. WLKY-TV, Louisville, 1967-70; adminstr. press office White House, 1970-74; rschr. Richard Nixon's memoirs, 1974-78; gen. assignment reporter, then Dept. State corr. CBS News, 1978-81; co-anchor Morning News CBS, from 1981, co-anchor Early Morning News, 1982-84; corr., co-editor 60 Minutes CBS-TV, 1984-89; co-anchor Prime Time Live ABC News, 1989—; co-anchor Day One, 1995—, Turning Point. Recipient 2 Peabody awards for Pub. Svc., 1988, Robert F. Kennedy award 9 Emmy awrds, Spl. Dupont award, IRTS Lifetime Achievement award. Mem. Coun. Fgn. Rels. Office: PrimeTime Live 147 Columbus Ave Fl 3 New York NY 10023-5900

SAWYER, FORREST, newscaster; b. Lakeland, Fla.. BA, U. Fla., 1971, MA, 1976; student, U. Tex., Austin. Reporter, news dir. various radio stas., 1974-80; anchorman Sta. WAGA-TV (CBS affiliate), Atlanta, 1980-85; co-anchor Early Morning News CBS, N.Y.C.; now corr. Nightline ABC, N.Y.C., substitute anchor Nightline, anchor World News Sunday; anchor World News Sunday ABC News Day One, N.Y.C.; corr. covering Persian Gulf war for ABC-TV, 1991. Office: Day One 147 Columbus Ave Fl 8 New York NY 10023-5900

SAWYER, HOWARD JEROME, physician; b. Detroit, Nov. 17, 1929; s. Howard C. and Dorothy M. (Risley) S.; m. Janet Carol Hausen, July 24, 1954; children: Daniel William, Teresa Louise. BA in Philosophy, Wayne State U., 1952, MD, 1962, postdoctoral, 1969-72. Diplomate Am. Bd. Preventive Medicine in Occupational and Environ. Medicine. Intern William Beaumont Hosp., Royal Oak, Mich., 1962-63, resident in surgery, 1963-64; chief physician gen. parts div. Ford Motor Co., Rawsonville, Mich., 1964-66; med. dir. metall. products dept. Gen. Electric Co., Detroit, 1966-73; chem. and metal div. Gen. Electric Co., 1972-73; staff physician Detroit Indsl. Clinic, Inc., 1973-74; pres., med. dir. OccuMed Assocs., Inc., Farmington

Hills, Mich., 1974-84; dir. OccuMed div. Med. Service Corp. Am., Southfield, Mich., 1984-86; dir. occupational, environ. and preventive medicine Henry Ford Hosp., 1987-91; pres. Sawyer Med. Cons., P.C., 1991—; adj. asst. prof. occupational and environ. health scis. Wayne State U., 1974—; lectr. Sch. Pub. Health, U. Mich., Ann Arbor, 1977—; cons. med. dir. St. Joe Minerals Corp., 1976-87, Chesbrough Pond's Inc., 1979-83; cons. Anaconda, Bendix, Borg Warner Chems., Fed. Mogul, Gen. Electric, Gt. Lakes Chems., other corps. Contbr. articles to profl. jours., chpts. to textbooks. Fellow Am. Coll. Preventive Medicine, Am. Occupational and Environ. Med. Assn., Mich. Occupational and Environ. Med. Assn. (pres. 1986), Am. Acad. Occupational Medicine; mem. AMA, Detroit Occupational Physicians Assn. (pres. 1984), Mich. State Med. Soc., Oakland County Med. Soc., Am. Indsl. Hygiene Assn., Mich. Indsl. Hygiene Soc. Office: Sawyer Med Cons PC 7072 Edinborough Dr West Bloomfield MI 48322-4025

SAWYER, JOHN, professional football team executive; s. Charles S.; m. Ruth Sawyer; children: Anne, Elizabeth, Catherine, Mary. Pres., part owner Cin. Bengals, Nat. Football League; pres. J. Sawyer Co., Ohio, Miss., Mont., Wyo.; vice pres Cin. Bengals. Office: J Sawyer Co Provident Tower Cincinnati OH 45202 Office: Cin Bengals 200 Riverfront Stadium Cincinnati OH 45202-3500*

SAWYER, MARGO LUCY, artist, educator; b. Washington, May 6, 1958; d. Eugene Douglas and Joan Imogen (Alford) S.; m. Rosario Pizzi, June 20, 1992. BA hons., Chelsea Sch. Art, London, 1980; MFA, Yale U., 1982. Assoc. prof. U. Tex., Austin, 1988—; vis. artist Chelsea Sch. Art, London, 1982—, Sir J.J. Sch. Art, Bombay, India, 1982-83, Baroda Sch. Art, Gujarat, India, 1983, West Surrey Coll. Art & Design, Eng., 1983, Sch. Visual Arts, N.Y.C., 1983, 89, Yale U., New Haven, 1985, Tyler Sch. Art, Rome, 1987, RISD, Rome, 1987, U. Houston, 1994. One-person shows include Brit. Coun., Bombay, India, 1983, Barbara Toll Fine Arts, N.Y.C., 1989, 91, Sagacho Exhibit Space, Tokyo, 1996, others; group shows include Whitechapel Gallery, London, 1979, ICA, London, 1979, 80, Leo Castelli Gallery, N.Y.C., 1986, Portland (Maine) Mus. Art, 1987, U. Md. Art Gallery, Balt., 1988, Meyers/Bloom Gallery, Santa Monica, Calif., 1989, Archer M. Huntington Art Gallery, Austin, Tex., 1990, 91, 92, 93, 94, Harn Mus. Art, Gainesville, Fla., 1992, Laguna Gloria Art Mus., Austin, 1994, Abilene (Tex.) Outdoor Sculpture exhbn., 1995-96; permanent collections include Hyde Park, London, Cityarts Workshop, Paradise Restaurant, L.A., Portland Mus. Art, Samuel O. Harn Mus. Art, U. Fla., Prudential Ins., Chem. Bank, Champion Paper, and various pvt. collections. Am. Acad. Rome fellow, 1986-87, Japan Found. visual arts fellow, 1996; Travel grantee Ford Found., 1981, Fulbright grantee, 1982-83, 95-96, N.Y. State Coun. on Arts grantee, 1987, Travel grantee NEA, 1994. Office: U Tex at Austin Dept Art and Art History Austin TX 78712-1104 also: 516 Kamisatokatsuyama-cho, Oharano, Nishikyo-ku Kyoto-shi 610-11, Japan

SAWYER, NELSON BALDWIN, JR., credit union executive; b. Jacksonville, Fla., Nov. 11, 1948; s. Nelson Baldwin and Nancy (Watson) S.; m. Carla Lee Dowden, Aug. 9, 1986. BA, U. North Fla., 1974. Program cons. State of Fla., Jacksonville, 1974-81; product mgr. Qualified Plan Designs, Inc., Jacksonville, 1981-83, Associated Gen. Contractors, Jacksonville, 1983-86; membership mgr. Calif. Credit Union League, Pomona, 1986-87, comm. mgr., 1987-90; sr. v.p., COO Calif. League Svcs. Corp., Pomona, 1990-93; sr. v.p. Wescorp, San Dimas, Calif., 1994—; chmn. bd. dirs. Calif. Ctr. Credit Union, Product Rsch. Orgn. for Credit Unions. Bd. dirs. Jacksonville C. of C., 1984-85. Mem. U.S. Jaycees (pres. Jacksonville 1983-84, chmn. bd. '84-85, senator, U.S., 1984—, Outstanding Young Man Am. 1983), Am. Soc. Assn. Execs., Fla. Yacht Club. Republican. Episcopalian. Office: WesCorp 924 Overland Ct San Dimas CA 91773-1742

SAWYER, RAYMOND LEE, JR., motel chain executive; b. New Orleans, Oct. 7, 1935; s. Raymond Lee Sawyer and Eloise Falvy (Searcy) Easley; m. Dolores Jean Young, June 11, 1960; children: Lisa Kay, Linda Faye. BA, Northwestern State U., 1959. Art dir., advt. mgr. Natural Food and Farming Mag., Atlanta, Tex., 1959-66, editor, 1963-66; asst. editor, editor Tourist Court Jour./Southwest Water Works Jour., Temple, Tex., 1966-73; editor Tourist Court Jour./Southwest Water Works Jour., Temple, 1973-75; founding ptnr., sr. v.p. Budget Host Inns, Ft. Worth, 1975-83, pres., chief exec. officer, 1983—. Named Man of Yr. Motel Brokers Assn. Am., 1974; recipient Bob Gresham Meml. award Nat. Innkeeping Assn., 1975. Mem. Am. Automobile Assn. (mem. lodging adv. panel 1990—). Methodist. Avocations: photography, writing.

SAWYER, RAYMOND TERRY, lawyer; b. Cleve., Oct. 1, 1943; s. R. Terry and Fanny Katherine (Young) S.; m. Katherine Margaret Schneider, Aug. 5, 1972; children: Margaret Young, John Terry. BA, Yale U., 1965; LLB, Harvard U., 1968. Bar: Ohio 1969, U.S. Dist. Ct. (no. dist.) Ohio 1970. Assoc. Thompson, Hine and Flory, Cleve., 1968-76, ptnr., 1976-83, 86—; exec. dir. Ohio Housing Fin. Agy., Columbus, 1983-84; counsel to gov. State of Ohio, Columbus, 1984, chief of staff, 1985-86; chmn. Gov.'s commn. on housing, 1989-90; bd. dirs. Premix, Inc., North Kingsville, Ohio. Vol. VISTA, East Palo Alto, Calif., 1968-69; mem. Tech. Leadership Coun., Leadership Cleve., 1986-87, Cleve. Found. Study Commn. on Med. Rsch. Edn., 1991-92; mem. Ohio Bd. Regents, Columbus, 1987-96, chmn., 1992-93; trustee Cleve. Ballet, 1987—, Cleve. Orch., 1993—, Western Res. Hist. Soc.; bd. dirs. Premix, Inc., North Kingsville, Ohio; chmn. George W. Codrington Charitable Found. Named Man of Yr. Womanspace, 1982. Mem. ABA, Ohio State Bar Assn. (chair corp. law com. 1993-95), Clevel. Bar Assn., Yale U. Alumni Assn. (pres. Cleve. chpt. 1980-81). Democrat. Presbyterian. Office: Thompson Hine Flory PLL 3900 Society Ctr Cleveland OH 44114-1216

SAWYER, RICHARD, art director, production designer. Art dir.: (films) In Search of Noah's Ark, 1977, FM, 1978, Melvin and Howard, 1980, The Hand, 1981, The Border, 1982, Twilight Zone-The Movie ("Back There"), 1983, (TV movies) Rich Men, Single Women, 1990; prodn. designer: (films) Where the Buffalo Roam, 1980, Things Are Tough All Over, 1982, Off the Wall, 1983, Bachelor Party, 1984, Lost in America, 1985, Moving Violations, 1985, Three Amigos, 1986, Vibes, 1988, Big Man on Campus, 1989, (with Jeremy Railton) The Two Jakes, 1990, Innocent Blood, 1992, (TV movies) Mother and Daughter: The Loving War, 1980, Coward of the County, 1981, Lottery!, 1983, The Gambler, 1983, Shattered Vows, 1984, C.A.T. Squad, 1986. Office: The Lyons/Sheldon Agency 8344 Melrose Ave Ste 20 Los Angeles CA 90069-5496

SAWYER, ROBERT MCLARAN, history educator; b. St. Louis, Nov. 12, 1929; s. Lee McLaran and Harrie (Alcock) S.; m. Patricia Ann Covert, Nov. 23, 1955; children—Ann Marie, Lee McLaran, Gail Louise. B.S., S.E. Mo. State Coll., 1952; M.A., U. Ill., 1953; Ph.D., U. Mo., 1966. Tchr. Rolla (Mo.) Public Schs., 1955; asst. prof., then asso. prof. history U. Mo., Rolla., 1956-67; mem. faculty U. Nebr., Lincoln, 1967—; prof. history of edn. U. Nebr., 1969—, chmn. dept. history and philosophy of edn., 1975-81; mem. council U. Nebr. (Coll. Arts and Scis.), 1979—; vis. prof. Ark. State U., Jonesboro, summer 1966; proposal reviewer Nat. Endowment Humanities, 1979. Author: The History of the University of Nebraska, 1929-1969, 1973, The Many Faces of Teaching, 1987, The Art and Politics of College Teaching, 1992, The Black Student's Guide to College Success, 1993, The Handbook of College Teaching, 1994; also articles, revs. Served with AUS, 1953-55. Mem. Orgn. Am. Historians, History Edn. Soc., Am. Ednl. Studies Assn., Soc. Profs. Edn., Phi Alpha Theta, Phi Delta Kappa. Home: 2640 S 35th St Lincoln NE 68506-6623 Office: Univ Nebr 29 Henzlit Hall Lincoln NE 68588

SAWYER, THOMAS C., congressman; b. Akron, Ohio, Aug. 15, 1945; m. Joyce Handler, 1968; 1 child, Amanda. BA, U. Akron, 1968, MA, 1970. Pub. sch. tchr. Ohio; adminstr. state sch. for delinquent boys; legis. agt. Ohio Pub. Utilities Commn.; mem. Ohio House Reps., Columbus, 1977-83; mayor City of Akron, 1984-86; mem. 100th-104th Congresses from 14th Ohio dist., Washington, D.C., 1987—; mem. ec and ed opp com., subcom. employer-employee rels., mem. subcom. oversight and investigations com. stds. conduct, mem. transp. and infrastructure com., subcom. surf. transp.; mem. Transp. and Infrastructure com., subcom. surface transp. Democrat. Office: US Ho of Reps 1414 Longworth Bldg Washington DC 20515-3514

SAWYER, THOMAS EDGAR, management consultant; b. Homer, La., July 7, 1932; s. Sidney Edgar and Ruth (Bickham) S.; BS, UCLA, 1959; MA, Occidental Coll., 1969; PhD, Walden U., 1990; m. Joyce Mezzanatto, Aug. 22, 1954; children—Jeffrey T., Scott A., Robert J., Julie Anne. Project engr. Garrett Corp., L.A., 1954-60; mgr. devel. ops. TRW Systems, Redondo Beach, Calif., 1960-66; spl. asst. to gov. State of Calif., Sacramento, 1967-69; prin., gen. mgr. Planning Rsch. Corp., McLean, Va., 1969-72; dep. dir. OEO, Washington, 1972-74; assoc. prof. bus. mgmt. Brigham Young U., 1974-78; pres. Mesa Corp., Provo, 1978-82, chmn. bd., 1978-82; pres. and dir. Sage Inst. Internat., Inc., Provo, Utah, 1982-88; chmn. bd., CEO Pvt. Telecom Networks, Inc. (name changed to Nat. Applied Computer Techs., Inc.), Orem, Utah, 1988—; chief tech. officer GST Telecommunications (formerly Greenstar Telecomm., Inc.), San Francisco, 1993—; also bd. dirs., Vancouver, Wash., 1995—; dir. Intechna Corp., HighTech Corp., Indian Affiliates, Inc., Greenstar USA, Inc., San Francisco, 1994—. Chmn. Nat. Adv. Council Indian Affairs; chmn. Utah State Bd. Indian Affairs; mem. Utah Dist. Export Coun.; mem. Utah dist. SBA Council; chmn. So. Paiute Restoration Com.; mem. adv. coun. Nat. Bus. Assn.; mem. Utah Job Tng. Coordinating Coun. Served with USMC, 1950-53. Mem. Am. Mgmt. Assn., Am. Soc. Public Adminstrn., Utah Coun. Small Bus. (dir.), Utah State Hist. Soc. (bd. dirs. 1993—). Republican. Mormon. Club: Masons. Author: Assimilation Versus Self-Indentity: A Modern Native American Perspective, 1976, Computer Assisted Instruction: An Inevitable Breakthrough, Current Challenges of Welfare: A Review of Public Assistance As Distributive Justice, 1989, Impact of Failure By Senior Executives to Receive Accurate Critical Feedback on Pervasive Change, 1990, The Promise of Funding a New Educational Initiative Using the Microcomputer, 1988, New Software Models for training and Education delivery, 1989, New Organizations: How They Deviate from Classical Models, 1989, Increasing Productivity in Organizations: The Paradox, 1989, An Introduction and Assessment of Strategic Decision Making Paradigms in Complex Organizations, 1989, The Influence of Critical Feedback and Organizational Climate on Managerial Decision Making, 1990, Future of Technology in Education, 1989. Home: 548 W 630 S Orem UT 84058-6154 Office: Nat Applied Computer Techs Inc 744 S 400 E Orem UT 84058-6322

SAWYER, THOMAS WILLIAM, air force officer; b. Turlock, Calif., Nov. 19, 1933; s. Everett Edward and Marie Georgine (Gunderson) S.; m. Faith Barry Martin, Feb. 16, 1957; children: William Everet, John Martin, Susan Quincy. BS in Mil. Sci., U. Nebr., 1965; MS in Internat. Rels., George Washington U., 1974. Enlisted U.S. Air Force, 1952, commd. and advanced through grades to maj. gen., 1983; comdr. 57th Fighter Squadron, Keflavik, Iceland, 1971-73; chief internat. relations div. Hdqrs. U.S. Air Force, Washington, 1974-77; vice comdr. 20th Air Div., Fort Lee, Va., 1977-78; mil. asst. to Sec. Air Force, 1978-80; comdr. 26th Air Div., Luke AFB, Ariz., 1980-82; dep. ops. NORAD and Space Command, Colorado Springs, Colo., 1982-86; retired USAF, 1986; founder, pres. Aerospace Network Inc., 1986. Bd. dirs. Pikes Peak chpt. ARC, Colo./Wyo. chpt. Am. Def. Preparedness Assn. Decorated Disting. Service medal, Def. Disting. Service medal, Legion of Merit with 2 oak leaf clusters, Silver Star (2). Mem. Phoenix C. of C. (bd. dirs. 1980-82), Colorado Springs C. of C. Avocations: nat. security affairs, woodworking, automobile bldg. Home: 10 W Cheyenne Mountain Blvd Colorado Springs CO 80906-4335 Office: Aerospace Network Inc 10 W Cheyenne Mountain Blvd Colorado Springs CO 80906-4335

SAWYER, WILBUR HENDERSON, pharmacologist, educator; b. Brisbane, Australia, Mar. 23, 1921; s. Wilbur Augustus and Margaret Henderson S.; m. Marian Gholson Kittredge, Nov. 14, 1942 (dec. Mar. 1982); children: Wilbur Kittredge, Robert Kittredge, Thomas Kittredge, Richard Kittredge; m. Pomona Jean Mitchell, Aug. 28, 1982. A.B., Harvard U., 1942, M.D., 1945, PhD, 1950; DSc, Med. Coll. Ohio, Toledo, 1994. Instr. biology Harvard U., Cambridge, Mass., 1950-53; asst. prof. physiology NYU Med. Sch., N.Y.C., 1953-57; asso. prof. pharmacology Columbia U. Coll. Physicians and Surgeons, N.Y.C., 1957-64; prof. Columbia U. Coll. Physicians and Surgeons, 1964-78, Gustavus A. Pfeiffer prof., 1978-90, prof. emeritus, 1991—, spl. lectr., 1993—. Contbr. articles on exptl. endocrinology, physiology and pharmacology to profl. jours. Served to lt. (j.g.) M.C., USN, 1946-48. Recipient Lederle Med. Faculty award NYU, 1955-57; Fulbright-Hays Sr. scholar, 1974; Commonwealth Fund travelling fellow, 1965. Fellow AAAS; mem. Am. Soc. Zoologists, Am. Physiol. Soc., Soc. Gen. Physiologists, Soc. Exptl. Biology and Medicine, Endocrine Soc., Am. Soc.. Pharmacology and Exptl. Therapeutics, Harvey Soc., Soc. Endocrinology, Am. Peptide Soc., Alpha Omega Alpha. Home: 1490 Kings Ln Palo Alto CA 94303-2836

SAWYER, WILLIAM C., lawyer; b. Bangor, Maine, Aug. 26, 1929; s. Frank S. and Linda M. (Makanna) S.; m. Mary E. Eaton (dir.); m. Joan N. Gardner; children: William D., Constance, Faith. AB cum laude, Harvard Coll., 1951, JD, 1954. Bar: Mass., U.S. Dist. Ct. Mass., U.S. Dist. Ct. (so. dist.) Manhattan, U.S. Ct. Mil. Appeals, U.S. Supreme Ct. Assoc. Palmer & Dodge, Boston, 1958-61; ptnr. Sawyer, Burlingham, Tucker & Salloway, Boston, 1961-85, Dicara, Selig, Sawyer & Holt, Boston, 1985-90, Wood, Clarkin & Sawyer, Boston, 1990—; bd. dirs. Jones & Vining, Inc., Ayer Sales, Inc., Applied Geographics, Inc., Applied Tech., Inc., others. Contbr. articles to profl. jours. Bd. trustees Mass. Conv. Ctr. Authority, 1991—; pres., treas., chmn. Metro. Area Planning Coun., 1975-87; pres. Mass. Assn. Regional Planning Agys., 1980, 87; bd. dirs. Nat. Assn. Regional Couns., 1980-86; mem. Mass. Selectman's Assn., 1975—; bd. selectman Town of Action, 1967-75, chmn., 1969, 75; Rep. candidate Mass. Atty. Gen., 1990; pres. New Eng. Rep. Coun.; mem. Rep. State Com.; Rep. candidate Congress, 5th Congl. Dist., Mass., 1980. 1st lt. U.S. Army, 1955. Recipient Regional Leadership award Planning Commns. and Couns. New Eng., 1987, and others. Mem. ABA, Mass. Bar Assn., Boston Bar Assn. Avocations: tennis, painting, reading. Office: Wood Clarkin Sawyer 225 Franklin St Boston MA 02110

SAWYER, WILLIAM DALE, physician, educator, university dean, foundation administrator; b. Roodhouse, Ill., Dec. 28, 1929; s. Cloyd Howard and Eva Collier (Dale) S.; m. Jane Ann Stewart, Aug. 25, 1951; children—Dale Stewart, Carole Ann. Student, U. Ill., 1947-50; MD cum laude, Washington U., St. Louis, 1954; ScD (hon.), Mahidol U., Bangkok, 1988; DPH (hon.), Chiang Mai U., Thailand, 1993. Intern Washington U.-Barnes Hosp., 1954-55, resident, 1957-58, fellow, 1958-60; asst. prof. microbiology Johns Hopkins U., Balt., 1964-67; prof., chmn. dept. microbiology Rockefeller Found.-Mahidol U., Bangkok, 1967-73, Ind. U. Sch. Medicine, Indpls., 1973-80; prof. depts. medicine, microbiology and immunology Wright State U., Dayton, Ohio, 1981-87, dean Sch. Medicine,, 1981-87; pres. China Med. Bd. N.Y., Inc., 1987—; adj. prof. biology Ball State U., Muncie, Ind., 1978-80; hon. prof. microbiology Sun Yat Sen U. Med. Sci., 1987; hon. prof. Peking Union Med. Coll., 1989; hon. advisor Beijing Med. U.; cons. U.S. Army Med. R & D Command, WHO Immunology Ctr., Singapore, 1969-73; mem. bd. sci. advisers Armed Forces Inst. Pathology, 1975-80, chmn., 1979-80; adj. prof. medicine and microbiology and immunology N.Y. Med. Coll., Valhalla, 1990—; hon. prof. China Med. U., 1995, West China U. Med. Sci., 1995, Zhejiang Med. U., 1995, Jiujang Med. Coll., 1995. Contbr. numerous articles to profl. jours. Mem. Lobund adv. bd. U. Notre Dame. Served to maj. M.C., UAS, 1955-64. Recipient Gold medal of merit Airlangga U., Indonesia, 1992, Pub. Health Recognition award Asia-Pacific Acad. Consortium Pub. Health, 1993. Fellow ACP; mem. AAAS, Am. Soc. Microbiology (br. pres. 1976), Sci. Rsch. Soc. Am., Am. Fedn. Clin. Rsch., Ctrl. Soc. Clin. Rslch., Infectious Diseases Soc. Am., Soc. Exptl. Biology and Medicine, Am. Acad. Microbiology, Am. Assn. Pathologists, Assn. Am. Med. Colls. (coun. deans 1980-87), Phi Beta Kappa, Sigma Xi, Alpha Omega Alpha. Office: China Med Bd of NY Inc 750 3rd Ave New York NY 10017-2703

SAWYERS, ELIZABETH JOAN, librarian, administrator; b. San Diego, Dec. 2, 1936; d. William Henry and Elizabeth Georgiana (Price) S. A.A., Glendale Jr. Coll., 1957; B.A. in Bacteriology, UCLA, 1959, M.L.S., 1961. Asst. head acquisition sect. Nat. Library Medicine, Bethesda, Md., 1962-63, head acquisition sect., 1963-66, spl. asst. to chief tech. services div., 1966-69, spl. asst. to assoc. dir. for library ops., 1969-73; asst. dir. libraries for tech. services SUNY-Stony Brook, 1973-75; dir. Health Scis. Library Ohio State U., Columbus, 1975-90, spl. asst. to dir. Univ. librs., 1990—. Mem. Assn. Acad. Health Scis. Library Dirs. (sec./treas. 1981-83, pres. 1983-84), Med. Library Assn., Am. Soc. for Info. Sci., Spl. Libraries Assn., ALA. Office: Ohio State Univ Librs 1858 Neil Ave Columbus OH 43210-1225

SAWYERS, JOHN LAZELLE, surgeon; b. Centerville, Iowa, July 26, 1925; s. Francis Lazelle and Almira (Baker) S.; m. Julia Edwards, May 25, 1957; children: Charles Lazelle, Al Baker, Julia Edwards. A.B., U. Rochester, 1946; M.D., Johns Hopkins U., 1949. Diplomate: Am. Bd. Surgery (dir. 1981-87), Am. Bd. Thoracic Surgery. House officer surgery Johns Hopkins Hosp., Balt., 1949-50; asst. resident, resident in surgery Vanderbilt U. Hosp., Nashville, 1953-58; practice medicine specializing in surgery Nashville, 1958—; surgeon Edwards-Eve Clinic, 1958-60; chief surg. service Nashville Gen. Hosp., 1960-77; surgeon-in-chief St. Thomas Hosp., Nashville, 1977-82; prof. surgery Vanderbilt U., Nashville, chmn. dept. surgery, dir. sect. surg. scis., 1983-94. Bd. dirs. Davidson County unit Am. Cancer Soc. Served from lt. (j.g.) to lt. M.C. USNR, 1950-52. Fellow A.C.S. (gov. 1974-80, pres. Tenn. chpt. 1974); mem. Am. Surg. Assn. 1st v.p. 1994), Southeastern Surg. Congress (pres. 1980), So. Surg. Assn. (pres. 1987), Halsted Soc. (pres. 1981). Home: 403 Ellendale Ave Nashville TN 37205-3401 Office: Vanderbilt U Dept Surgery 1001 Oxford House Nashville TN 37232-4730

SAWYIER, CALVIN P., lawyer; b. Chgo., Oct. 7, 1921. AB, Chgo. U., 1942, MA, 1942; LLB, Harvard U., 1947. Bar: N.H. 1948, Ill. 1949. Ptnr. Winston & Strawn, Chgo. Mem. ABA, Ill. State Bar Assn., Chgo. Bar Assn., Chgo. Coun. Lawyers, Phi Beta Kappa. Office: Winston & Strawn 35 W Wacker Dr Chicago IL 60601-1614

SAWYIER, DAVID R., lawyer; b. Chgo., Feb. 2, 1951. BA, Harvard U., 1972, JD, 1977; MA, Oxford U., 1974; diploma law, Cambridge U., 1979. Bar: Ill. 1977, D.C. 1978. Law clerk U.S. Ct. Appeals D.C. cir., 1977-78; ptnr. Sidley & Austin, Chgo. Mem. ABA (bus. law sect.), Chgo. Bar Assn. (futures sect.). Office: Sidley & Austin 1 First Nat Plz Chicago IL 60603*

SAX, JOSEPH LAWRENCE, lawyer, educator; b. Chgo., Feb. 3, 1936; s. Benjamin Harry and Mary (Silverman) S.; m. Eleanor Charlotte Gettes, June 17, 1958; children—Katherine Elaine, Valerie Beth, Anne-Marie. AB, Harvard U., 1957; JD, U. Chgo., 1959; LLD (hon.), Ill. Inst. Tech., 1992. Bar: D.C. 1960, Mich., 1966, U.S. Supreme Ct. 1969. Atty. Dept. Justice, Washington, 1959-60; pvt. practice law Washington, 1960-62; prof. U. Colo., 1962-65, U. Mich., Ann Arbor, 1966-86; dep. asst. sec. and counselor U.S. Sec. Interior, Washington, 1994—; vis. prof. U. Calif. Law Sch., Berkeley, 1965-66, 86, U. Paris I, 1981, 82, Stanford Law Sch., 1985; fellow Ctr. Advanced Study in Behavioral Scis., 1977-78; cons. U.S. Senate Com. on Pub. Works, 1970-71; mem. cons. council Conservation Found., 1969-73; mem. legal adv. com. Pres.'s Council on Environ. Quality, 1970-72; mem. environ. studies bd. Nat. Acad. Sci., 1970-73; mem. Mich. Environ. Rev. Bd., 1973-74. Author: Waters and Water Rights, 1967, Water Law, Planning and Policy, 1968, Defending the Environment, 1971, Mountains Without Handrails, 1980, Legal Control of Water Resources, 1991. Bd. dirs. Environ. Law Inst., Washington, 1970-75; trustee Center for Law and Social Policy, 1970-76; regional gov. Internat. Coun. Environmental Law; gov.'s rep. Gt. Lakes Task Force, 1984-85. With USAF, 1960. Fellow AAAS; mem. University Club (San Francisco).

SAX, MARTIN, crystallographer; b. Wheeling, W.Va.. BS, U. Pitts., 1941, PhD in Phys. Chemistry, 1961. Rsch. chemist Trojan Powder Co., 1941-44, Glyco Products Co., 1951-59; asst. biochemist W. Pa. Hosp., 1946-57; postdoctoral crystallographer U. Pitts., 1961-63, asst. rsch. prof., 1963-66; rsch. chemist and dir. biocrystallography lab. Vets. Affairs Med. Ctr., Pitts., 1966—, assoc. chief staff R&D, 1972—; adj. prof. crystallographer U. Pitts., 1966-71, adj. prof., 1971—. Mem. AAAS, Am. Crystallography Assn., Am. Chem. Soc. Achievements include research in three dimensional structures and the functions of biological macromolecules as ascertained by x-ray diffractions from single crystals. Office: U Drive C Vets Adminstn Med Ctr Rsch Svc Pittsburgh PA 15240

SAX, STANLEY PAUL, manufacturing company executive; b. Cin., Sept. 1, 1925; s. Ben Philip and Goldie (Quitman) S.; children: Steven Jay, David Jay; m. Patricia Moran Leach, June 14, 1970; children: Cathy, Carolyn. A.B., U. Wis., 1948. Researcher Market Research Co. Am., Chgo., 1942; instr. U. Wis., 1948; v.p., dir. Am. Buff Co., Detroit, 1948-57; exec. v.p., dir. Am. Buff Co., Chgo., 1957—; pres. Speedway Buff Co.; pres., chmn. bd., dir. J.J. Siefen Co., 1961—; chmn. bd., pres. Sax Abrasive Corp., 1961—, Sax Cal. Corp., 1962—, Klem Chem. Corp., 1963—, Stan Sax Corp., Seco Chems., Inc., 1965—; chmn. bd. Buckingham Products Co., McAleer Mfg. Co., 1968—, Sax Realty Investment Corp., 1967—, Globe Compound Corp., 1971—, Goodison Mfg. Co., 1972—, Ana, Inc., 1974—; partner S & D Leasing Co. Contbr. articles to profl. jours. Trustee Sax Family Found.; nat. trustee Balt. Mus. Art; bd. dirs. Met. Soc. Crippled Children and Adults. Served to lt. AUS, 1943-46; to lt. col. Res. 1946—. Recipient Wis. scholar award. Mem. Mil. Order World Wars, Metal Finishing Suppliers Assn. (trustee), Detroit C. of C., Detroit Inst. Arts (patron), Friends of Am. Wing (Founders Soc.), Friends of Henry Ford Mus., Pres.'s Soc., Am. Electroplaters Soc., Am. Soc. for Abrasives, Soc. Mil. Engrs., Young President's Orgn., World Presidents Orgn., Chief Execs. Orgn., Amateur Athletic Union, Soc. Die Casting Engrs., Res. Officers Assn., V.F.W., Wis. Alumni Assn., Winterhur Collectors Circle Mt. Vernon 100, Phi Beta Kappa, Alpha Phi Omega, Phi Kappa Phi, Psi Chi, Phi Eta Sigma. Clubs: Elk (Detroit), Rotarian. (Detroit), Economic (Detroit), Renaissance (Detroit); Recess, Army-Navy. Lender furnishings to diplomatic reception rooms, Nat. Portrait Gallery, Smithsonian Inst.; benefactor fine arts com. Dept. State. Home: 1340 Pembroke Dr Bloomfield Hills MI 48304-2653 Office: 101 S Waterman St Detroit MI 48209-3065

SAXBE, WILLIAM BART, lawyer, former government official; b. Mechanicsburg, Ohio, June 24, 1916; s. Bart Rockwell and Faye Henry (Carey) S.; m. Ardath Louise Kleinhans, Sept. 14, 1940; children: William Bart, Juliet Louise Saxbe Blackburn, Charles Rockwell. A.B., Ohio State U., 1940; LL.B., 1948; hon. degrees, Central State U., Findlay Coll., Ohio Wesleyan U., Walsh Coll., Capital U., Wilmington Coll., Ohio State U., Bowling Green State U. Bar: Ohio 1948. Practiced in Mechanicsburg, 1948-55; partner Saxbe, Boyd & Prine, 1955-58; mem. Ohio Gen. Assembly, 1947-48, 49-50; majority leader Ho. Reps., 1951-52, speaker, 1953-54; atty. gen. Ohio, 1957-58, 63-68; partner Dargusch, Saxbe & Dargusch, 1960-63; mem. U.S. Senate from, Ohio, 1969-74; atty. gen. U.S., 1974; ambassador to India, 1975-77; partner firm Chester, Saxbe, Hoffman & Wilcox, Columbus, Ohio, 1977-81; of counsel firm Jones, Day, Reavis & Pogue, Cleve., 1981-84, Pearson, Ball & Dowd (merger Pearson, Ball & Dowd and Reed, Smith & McClay), Washington, 1984-93; ind. spl. counsel Central States Teamsters Pension Fund, 1982—; of counsel Chester Willcox & Saxbe, Columbus, Ohio, 1994—. Served with 107th Cav. AUS, 1940-42; Served with 107th Cav. USAAF, 1942-45; col. Res. Mem. Am., Ohio bar assns., Am. Judicature Soc., Chi Phi, Phi Delta Phi. Republican. Episcopalian. Clubs: Mason (33d degree) (Columbus), University (Columbus), Columbus Athletic (Columbus), Columbus (Columbus), Scioto Country (Columbus); Urbana (Ohio) Country; Burning Tree Country (Bethesda, Md.); Country of Fla. (Boynton Beach). Home: 1171 N Ocean Blvd Gulf Stream FL 33483-7273 Office: 4600 N Ocean Blvd Boynton Beach FL 33435-7312

SAXBERG, BORJE OSVALD, management educator; b. Helsinki, Finland, Jan. 25, 1928; came to U.S., 1950, naturalized, 1966; s. Oskar Valdemar and Martha (Granberg) S.; m. A. Margrete Haug; children: Bo Erland Haug, Bror Valdemar Haug. B.A., Swedish Sch. Bus. and Econs., 1950; B.S., Oreg. State U., 1952; M.S., U. Ill., 1953, Ph.D., 1958. Teaching asst., instr. U. Ill., 1953-57; prof. dept. mgmt. and orgn. U. Wash., 1957—; assoc. dean U. Wash. (Bus. Sch.), 1967-70, chmn. dept. mgmt. and orgn., 1972-76, chmn. faculty senate, 1980-81, chmn. dept. mgmt. and orgn., 1989-93; dir. program in entrepreneurship and innovation, 1993—; cons. in field. Author: (with R. Joseph Monsen) The Business World, 1967, (with H.P. Knowles) Personality and Leadership Behavior, 1971, (with R.A. Johnson) Management, Systems and Society, 1976, (with B. Mar) Managing High Technology, 1985. Ford Found. fellow, 1960-61. Mem. Am. Sociol. Assn., Rainier Club, Swedish Club (Seattle). Home: 7336 58th Ave NE Seattle WA 98115-6257 Office: Univ Wash Grad Sch Bus 353200 Seattle WA 98195-3200

SAXBY, LEWIS WEYBURN, JR., retired glass fiber manufacturing executive; b. Oak Park, Ill., Dec. 17, 1924; s. Lewis Weyburn Saxby and Dorothy (Porter) Willey; m. Kathryn Hutchinson, 1947 (dec. 1990); m. Kay Taylor, Jan. 23, 1993; children: Steven Jess, Ann, Jane Porter. BS, U. Calif.,

Berkeley, 1945; MBA, Stanford U., 1948. Prodn. trainee Owens-Corning Fiberglas Corp., Newark, Ohio, 1948-49; prodn. scheduler Santa Clara, Calif., 1949-51; estimator salesman San Francisco, 1951-52, dept. supr., 1952-56; br. mgr. Sacramento, Calif., 1956-58; br. mgr. Detroit, 1958-60, mgr. supply and contracting East, 1960-61; mgr. supply and contracting Toledo, 1961-66, v.p., mgr. supply and contracting, 1966-70, v.p. mech. products and constrn. services, 1971-74, v.p. mech. ops. div., 1974-78, sr. v.p., 1978-89; bd. dirs. Performance Contracting Group, Am. Borate Co. Bd. dirs., chmn. com. Toledo Conv. and Visitors Bur., 1986—. Served as ensign USNR, 1943-46. Recipient Gold Leadership award Jr. Achievemnt, Inc., 1981. Mem. Nat. Insulation Contractors (chmn. com. 1984—, Man of Yr. 1985), Inverness (Toledo) (bd. govs. 1976-80), Toledo Club. Republican. Presbyterian. Avocations: golf, tennis, travel, photography, snorkeling.

SAXE, DEBORAH CRANDALL, lawyer; b. Lima, Ohio, July 23, 1949; d. Robert Gordon and Lois Barker (Taylor) Crandall; m. Robert Saxe, June 3, 1989; children: Elizabeth Sara, Emily Jane. BA, Pa. State U., 1971; MA, UCLA, 1973, JD, 1978. Bar: Calif. 1978, D.C. 1979, U.S. Dist. Ct. D.C. 1979, U.S. Dist. Ct. (ea. dist.) Calif. 1981, , U.S. Dist. Ct. (ctrl. dist.) Calif. 1982, U.S. Dist. Ct. (no. and so. dists.) Calif. 1987, U.S. Ct. Appeals (4th and D.C. cirs.) 1979, U.S. Ct. Appeals (6th cir.) 1985, U.S. Ct. Appeals (8th and 9th cirs.) 1987, U.S. Ct. Appeals (2nd cir.) 1990, U.S. Supreme Ct. 1985. Assoc. Seyfarth, Shaw, Fairweather & Garaldson, Washington, 1978-83; assoc. Jones, Day, Reavis & Pogue, Washington, 1983-85; assoc. Jones, Day, Reavis & Pogue, L.A., 1985-87, ptnr., 1988—; judge pro tem, Small Claims Ct., L.A., 1985-88. Co-author: Advising California Employers, 1990, 2d edit., 1995; contbg. editor Employment Discrimination Law, 1989. Bd. dirs. Pediatric and Family Med. Ctr., L.A., 1990—. Mem. ABA (labor law sect. 1978—), Calif. Bar Assn. (labor law sect. 1985—), L.A. County Bar Assn. (labor law sect. 1985—, mem. exec. com. 1988—), Pi Lambda Theta, Phi Beta Kappa. Office: Jones Day Reavis & Pogue 555 W 5th St Ste 4600 Los Angeles CA 90013-3002

SAXE, EDWARD A., lawyer; b. Cambridge, Mass., July 5, 1933; s. Harry and Mildred (Pord) S.; m. Claire Sue Rosenthal, Dec. 23, 1956; children: James, Judith. AB, cum laude, Harvard U., 1954, LLB cum laude, 1957. Bar: Mass. 1957, U.S. Dist Ct. Mass. 1957, U.S. Tax Ct. 1957. Assoc. Sheridan & Randall, Framingham, Mass., 1957-58; exec. v.p. Eli Sandman Co., Worcester, Mass., 1958-59; mng. ptnr., chmn. Peabody & Brown, Boston, 1959-85; pres. Related Cos. Northeast, Inc., Boston, 1985-89; ptnr. Fine & Ambrogne, Boston, 1989-90, Bingham, Dana & Gould, Boston, 1990—. Trustee Beth Israel Hosp., Boston, 1980—, Combined Jewish Philathropies, Boston, 1970—; chmn. Town of Framingham (Mass.) Personnel Bd., 1963-66; adv. mem. Mayor's Office Cultural Affairs, Boston, 1975-78. With USAR, 1956-62. Mem. ABA, Mass. Bar Found. (life), Boston Bar Assn, Wightman Tennis Club (pres. 1975-76). Avocations: tennis, skiing, bicycling. Office: Bingham Dana & Gould 150 Federal St Boston MA 02110-1745

SAXE, LEONARD, social psychologist, educator; b. N.Y.C., June 12, 1947; s. Theodore and Majorie (Mayers) S.; m. Marion Gardner, Aug. 9, 1970; 1 child, Daniel. BS in Psychology, U. Pitts., 1969, MS in Psychology, 1972, PhD in Social Psychology, 1976. Asst. instr. U. Pitts., 1973-75; asst. then assoc. prof. psychology Boston U., 1976-88, assoc. dir. Ctr. Applied Social Sci., 1982-84, dir., 1984-87; rsch. prof. Heller Sch. Social Welfare Brandeis U., Waltham, Mass., 1988-90, adj. prof. psychology, adj. rsch. prof., 1990—; prof. psychology Grad. Ctr. CUNY, 1991—; head social-personality psychology, 1991-95; Fulbright sr. lectr. U. Haifa, Israel, 1981-82; mem. task force Children's Mental Health Rsch. Inst. Medicine-NAS, 1988-89; rev. coms. HHS-Healthcare Fin. Adminstr. NIMH, Nat. Inst. Drug Abuse, Dept. Edn.; cons., contractor Office Tech. Assessment, U.S. Congress, 1980-88. Author: (with others) Children's Mental Health: Problems and Treatment, 1987, (with M. Fine) Social Experiments: Methods for Design and Evaluation, 1981; editor: (with M.J. Saks) Advances in Applied Social Psychology, Vol. 3, 1986, (with D. Koretz) New Directions for Program Evaluation, 1982, (with D. Bar-Tal) The Social Psychology of Education: Theory and Research, 1978; contbr. chpts. to books, articles to profl. jours.; assoc. and mng. editor Personality and Social Psychology Bull., 1978-81; ad hoc reviewer various jours., book reviewer various pubs. Congl. fellow Office Tech. Assessment, 1979. Fellow APA (bd. dirs. sect. social and ethical responsibility 1985-88, Disting. Contbn. award 1989), AAAS, Soc. Psychol. Study Social Issues (coun. 1982-84, 87-89). Office: CUNY Grad Ctr 33 W 42nd St New York NY 10036-8003

SAXE, LINDA, psychiatric nurse, psychiatric social worker; b. San Antonio; d. Manuel and Beulah M. (Pope) Flores; m. Henry Irving Saxe, Feb. 22, 1961; 1 child, Susan. BSN, Tex. Women's U., 1988; MA in Social Work, U. Chgo., 1968. Cert. clin. nurse specialist, Va.; lic. prof. counselor, Tex.; adv. clin. practitioner, Tex.; lic. ind. clin. social worker, D.C. Forensic social worker Cook County Cts./Social Svcs., Chgo., 1969-74; clin. social worker Killgore Children's Psychiat. Hosp., Amarillo, Tex., 1975-77; cons. social worker Tex. Bd. Day Nurseries, Amarillo, Tex., 1975-77; program dir. Adolescent Ctr.-Houston Internat. Hosp., Houston, 1980-83, West Br. Ctr., Houston, 1984-86; psychiat. review specialist Am. Psychiat. Assn., Washington, 1987-90; intensive care mgmt. specialist Value Behavioral Health, Falls Church, Va., 1990—; clin. nurse specialist Multiple Personality Disorders Program, Psychiat. Inst. D.C., Washington, 1990—, Inpsych, Inc., 1994—. Mem. Sigma Theta Tau. Republican. Avocation: reading. Home: 1006 Salisbury Ct Sterling VA 20164-4807

SAXE, THELMA RICHARDS, secondary school educator, consultant; b. Ogdensburg, N.J., Apr. 21, 1941; d. George Francis and Evelyn May (Howell) Richards; m. Kenneth Elwood Meeker, Jr., June 22, 1957 (div. 1965); children: Sylvia Lorraine Meeker Hill, Michelle Louise Meeker Aromando, David Sean (dec.); m. Frederick Ely Saxe, Feb. 18, 1983; stepchildren: Jonathan Kent, Holly Harding Schenker. BA, William Paterson Coll., Wayne, N.J., 1972, MEd, 1975, postgrad., 1983-84; Dyslexia cert., Fairleigh Dickinson U., 1994. Cert. paralegal, dyslexia specialist Fairleigh Dickonson U. Tchr. handicapped Sussex (N.J.)-Wantage Regional Sch. Dist., 1972-75; resource rm. tchr. Sussex County Vo-Tech Sch., Sparta, N.J., 1975-77; learning cons. Sussex County Vo-Tech Sch., 1977-83; learning specialist Bennington-Rutland Supervisory Union, Manchester, Vt., 1986-87; learning cons. Stillwater (N.J.) Twp. Sch., 1987-88, Independence Twp. Cen. Sch., Great Meadows, N.J., 1989; learning cons., tutor in pvt. practice specializing dyslexia Sparta, 1986—; asst. prin. Harmony Twp. Sch., Harmony, N.J., 1989-92; learning cons. Montague (N.J.) Elem. Sch., 1996—; coord. gifted/talented Sussex Vo-Tech, 1980-83; coord. child study team Stillwater Twp. Sch., 1987-88, Montague Twp. Sch., 1996—. Mem. Coun. Exceptional Children, Learning Disabilities Assn., Orton Dyslexia Soc., N.J. Assn. Learning Cos., Kappa Delta Pi. Republican. Presbyterian. Avocations: music, singing, piano, autoharp, skiing, hiking, travel. Home: 17 Park Rd Sparta NJ 07871-2002 Office: Accent on Comm 350A Sparta Ave Sparta NJ 07871

SAXENA, AMOL, podiatrist, consultant; b. Palo Alto, Calif., June 5, 1962; s. Arjun Nath and Veera Saxena; m. Karen Ann Palermo, Aug. 11, 1985; children: Vijay, Tara Ann. Student, U. Calif., Davis, 1980-82; BA, Washington U., St. Louis, 1984; D in Podiatric Medicine, William Scholl Coll. Podiatric Medicine, 1988. Diplomate Am. Bd. Podiatric Surgery; lic. podiatrist, Calif., Ill. Resident in podiatric surgery VA Westside Br., Chgo., 1988-89; cons. Puma U.S.A., Inc., Framingham, Mass., 1986—; pvt. practice Mountain View, Calif., 1989-93; with dept. sports medicine Palo Alto Med. Found., 1993—; dir. Puma Sports Medicine, Framingham; mem. podiatry team St. Frances/Gunn Los Altos (Calif.) High Sch., Palo Alto, 1989—, Stanford (Calif.) U., 1989—; mem. med. staff El Camino Hosp., 1989—, team podiatrist Stanford U., 1989—. Guest editor Lower Extremity; mem. editl. bd. Jour. Foot and Ankle Surgery; contbr. articles to profl. jours. Vol. coach Gunn High Sch. Track and Cross County, Palo Alto, 1989—; podiatrist U.S. Olympic Track and Field Trials, New Orleans, 1992, 1993. Fellow Am. Acad. Podiatric Sports Medicine, Am. Coll. Foot and Ankle Surgeons; mem. Am. Podiatric Med. Assn., Calif. Podiatric Med. Assn., Am. Med. Soccer Assn., Aggie Running Club. Republican. Avocation: running. Office: 1197 E Arques Ave Sunnyvale CA 94086-3904 also: 913 Emerson St Palo Alto CA 94301-2415

SAXENA, ARJUN NATH, physicist; b. Lucknow, India, Apr. 1, 1932; s. Sheo and Mohan (Piyari) Shanker; came to U.S., 1956, naturalized, 1976; BSc, Lucknow U., 1950, MSc, 1952, profl. cert. in German, 1954; Post MS diploma, Inst. Nuclear Physics, Calcutta, India, 1955; PhD, Stanford U., 1963; m. Veera Saxena, Feb. 9, 1956; children: Rashmi, Amol, Varsha, Ashvin. Rsch. asst. Stanford U., 1956-60; mem. tech. staff Fairchild Semicondr. Co., Palo Alto, Calif., 1960-65; dept. head Sprague Electric Co., North Adams, Mass., 1965-69; mem. tech. staff RCA Labs., Princeton, N.J., 1969-71; pres., chmn. bd. Astro-Optics, Phila., 1972; pres. Internat. Sci. Co., Princeton Junction, N.J., 1973—; disting. vis. scientist Centre de Récherches Nucléaires, Strasbourg, France, 1973, 77; sr. staff scientist, mgr. engring. Data Gen. Corp., Sunnyvale, Calif., 1975-80; mgr. process tech. Signetics Corp., Sunnyvale, 1980-81; Gould AMI scientist, dir. advanced process devel. Gould AMI Semicondrs., Santa Clara, Calif., 1981-87; dir. Ctr. for Integrated Electronics, prof. dept. elec. and computer system engring. Rensselaer Poly. Inst., Troy, N.Y., 1987-96, emeritus prof., 1996—; disting. vis. scientist Inst. Microelectronics, Stuttgart, Germany, 1993-94. Treas. Pack 66, Boy Scouts Am., W. Windsor, N.J., 1970-74. Recipient Disting. Citizen award State of N.J., 1975. Mem. Am. Phys. Soc., IEEE, Electrochem. Soc., Stanford Alumni Assn. (life). Contbr. articles on semicondr. tech., optics, nuclear and high-energy physics to sci. jours., 1953—; patentee in field. Home: 4217 Pomona Ave Palo Alto CA 94306-4312

SAXENA, BRIJ B., biochemist, endocrinologist, educator. PhD, India; DSc, U. Muenster, W.Ger.; PhD, U. Wis., 1961. Asst. prof. biochemistry and endocrinology N.J. Coll. Medicine., 1966-74; assoc. prof. biochemistry Cornell U. Med. Coll., N.Y.C., 1974—; prof. biochemistry Cornell U. Med. Coll., 1974—, prof. endocrinology, 1981—, dir. div. reproductive endocrinology. Contbr. 200 articles to profl. jours. Recipient Career Scientist award N.Y.C. Health Research Council; Upjohn research award; Campoz da Paz award. Fellow Royal Soc. Medicine (London); mem. Am. Soc. Biol. Chemists, AAAS, Endocrine Soc., Harvey Soc., Am. Physiol. Soc., Am. Chem. Soc. Office: Cornell Univ Med Coll 1300 York Ave New York NY 10021-4805

SAXENA, NARENDRA K., marine research educator; b. Agra, India, Oct. 15, 1936; came to U.S., 1969; s. Brijbasi Lal and Sarbati Saxena; m. Cecilia H. Hsi, Mar. 21, 1970; Sarah Vasanti, Lorelle Sarita. Diploma Geodetic Engring., Tech. U., Hanover, Fed. Republic Germany, 1966; D in Tech Scis., Tech. U., Graz, Austria, 1972. Research assoc. geodetic sci. Ohio State U., Columbus, 1969-74; asst. prof. U. Ill., Urbana, 1974-78; asst. prof. U. Hawaii, Honolulu, 1978-81, assoc. prof., 1981-86, prof., 1986—, dept. chmn., 1994—; adj. research prof. Naval Postgrad. Sch., Monterey, Calif., 1984—; co-chmn. Pacific Congresses on Marine Tech., Honolulu, 1984, 86, 88; pres. Pacon Internat. Inc., 1987—. Editor Jour. Marine Geodesy, 1976—. Mem. Neighborhood Bd., Honolulu, 1984. Fellow Marine Tech. Soc. (various offices 1974—); mem. ASCE, Am. Geophys. Union, The Tsunami Soc. (sec. 1985—). Office: U Hawaii Dept Civil Engring Honolulu HI 96822

SAXER, RICHARD KARL, metallurgical engineer, retired air force officer; b. Toledo, Aug. 31, 1928; s. Alexander Albert and Gertrude Minnie (Kuebeler) S.; m. Marilyn Doris Mersereau, July 19, 1952; children—Jane Lynette, Robert Karl, Kris Renee, Ann Luette. Student, Bowling Green State U., 1946-48; BS, U. S. Naval Acad., 1952; MS in Aero. Mechanics Engring., Air Force Inst. Tech., 1957; PhD in Metall. Engring., Ohio State U., 1962; grad., Armed Forces Staff Coll., 1966, Indsl. Coll. Armed Forces, 1971. Commd. 2d lt. U.S. Air Force, 1952, advanced through grades to lt. gen., 1976; electronics officer, mech. officer (4th Tactical Support Sqadron, Tactical Air Command), Sandia Base, N.Mex., 1953-54; electronics and mech. officer, spl. weapons assembly sect. supr. (SAC 6th Aviation Depot Squadron), French Morocco, 1954-55; project engr. mech. equipment br. Air Force Spl. Weapon's Center, Kirtland AFB, N.Mex., 1957-59; project officer Nuclear Safety div., 1959-60; assoc. prof. dept. engring. mechanics Air Force Inst. Tech., 1962-66; asso. prof., dep. dept. head USAF Acad., 1966-70; comdr., dir. Air Force Materials Lab., Wright-Patterson AFB, Ohio, 1971-74; dep. for Reentry System Space and Missile Systems Orgn., 1974-77; dep. for aero equipment Aero. Systems Div., 1977-80, dep. for tactical systems, 1980, vice comdr., 1981-83; aero. systems div. dir. Def. Nuclear Agy., 1983-85, ret., 1985; pres. R.K. Saxer & Assocs., 1985-91; CEO Universal Tech. Corp., Dayton, Ohio, 1991—; research and tech. com. materials and structures NASA, 1973-74; chmn. planning group aerospace materials Interagy. Council Materials, 1973-74; mem. Nat. Mil. Adv. Bd., 1971-74, NATO adv. group for research and devel., 1973-74. Contbr. articles to profl. jours. Decorated Def. Disting. Svc. medal, Legion of Merit, Meritorious Service medal USAF, D.S.M., Joint Svc. Commendation medal, Air Force Commendation medal with 3 oak leaf clusters, Army Commendation medal U.S., Def. Superior Service medal, Cross of Gallantry with palm Vietnam, Def. Meritorious Service medal; recipient Disting. award for systems mgmt. Air Force Assn., 1979; Disting. Alumnus award Ohio State U., 1986. Mem. Air Force Assn., Am. Def. Preparedness Assn. (pres. Dayton 1977-78), Sigma Xi, Phi Lambda Epsilon, Alpha Sigma Mu, Masons, Shriners. Home: 215 Dalfaber Ln Springboro OH 45066

SAXL, JANE WILHELM, state legislator; b. N.Y.C., Aug. 26, 1939; d. Seymour F. and Doris (Fuld) Wilhelm; m. Joseph Saxl, Nov. 17, 1957; children: Susan S., Ruth L., Mary-Anne, Michael V. BA, Sangamon State U., 1973, MA, 1974. City councilor City of Bangor, Maine, 1987-93; mem. Maine Ho. Reps., Augusta, 1992—. sec./treas. Penobscot Valley Coun. Govts., 1988-91. Active Bangor Sch. Bd., 1984-87, Family Planning Maine, Natural Resources Coun., Penobscot Dem. Com.; bd. dirs. Bangor Beautiful, Bangor Conv. and Visitors Bur.; past chmn. Bangor Recycling. Mem. LWV (pres. Maine chpt. 1987-93), Nat. League State Legislators, Nat. Women's Polit. Caucus, Maine Women's Lobby, Friends of Bangor Pub. Libr., Spruce Run Assocs., Maine Audubon Soc., Tuesday Forum, Women's Legis. Lobby, N.Y. Pub. Libr. Democrat. Jewish. Avocations: bird watching, fly fishing. Home: 37 Pond St Bangor ME 04401-4641 Office: Maine Legislature State House Sta # 3 Augusta ME 04330

SAXON, DAVID STEPHEN, physics educator, university official; b. St. Paul, Feb. 8, 1920; s. Ivan and Rebecca (Moss) S.; m. Shirley Goodman, Jan. 6, 1940; children: Margaret Elizabeth, Barbara Susan, Linda Caroline, Catherine Louise, Victoria Jean, Charlotte Mala. BS, MIT, 1941, PhD, 1944; various hon. degrees. Research physicist Radiation Lab., Mass. Inst. Tech., 1943-46, Philips Labs., 1946-47; mem. faculty U. Calif., Los Angeles, 1947-75; prof. physics U. Calif., 1958-75, chmn. dept., 1963-66, dean phys. scis., 1966-68, vice chancellor, 1968-75, provost, 1974-75, pres., 1975-83, pres. emeritus, 1983—; mem. corp. MIT, 1977-90, life mem., 1990—, chmn. corp., 1983-90, hon. chmn., 1990-95; vis. scientist Centre d'Etudes Nucléaires, Saclay, France, 1968-69; vis. prof. faculty scis. U. Paris, Orsay, France, 1961-62; cons. to rsch. orgns., 1948—; mem. tech. adv. coun. Ford Motor Co., 1979-94. Author: Elementary Quantum Mechanics, 1968, (with A.E.S. Green and T. Sawada) The Nuclear Independent Particle Model, 1968, (with Julian Schwinger) Discontinuities in Wave Guides, 1968, (with William B. Fretter) Physics for the Liberal Arts Student, 1971. Mem. Mass. Ctr. Excellence, 1985-91; mem. com. to visit Med. Sch., Sch. Dental Medicine, Harvard U., 1985-90. Decorated Royal Order of No. Star; Guggenheim fellow Niels Bohr Inst. Theoretical Physics, Copenhagen, 1956-57, 61-62; Fulbright grantee, 1961-62. Fellow Am. Phys. Soc., Am. Acad. Arts and Scis., AAAS; mem. Am. Assn. Physics Tchrs., Am. Inst. Physics, Am. Philosophy Soc., Phi Beta Kappa, Sigma Xi, Sigma Pi Sigma. Spl. research theoretical physics, nuclear physics, quantum mechanics, electromagnetic theory, scattering theory. Home: 1008 Hilts Ave Los Angeles CA 90024-3215

SAXON, JOHN DAVID, lawyer, policy analyst, educator; b. Anniston, Ala., July 21, 1950; s. J.Z. and Sarah Elizabeth (Steadham) S.; m. Elizabeth Lord, Mar. 10, 1973. BA with honors, U. Ala., 1972, JD, 1977; grad. Exec. Program Stanford U., 1986; MA, U. N.C., 1973. Bar: Ala. 1977, U.S. Dist. Ct. (no. dist.) Ala. 1977, U.S. Supreme Ct. 1983, U.S. Dist. Ct. (mid. dist.) Ala. 1989, U.S. Dist. Ct. (so. dist.) Ala. 1990, U.S. Ct. Appeals (11th cir.) 1990, U.S. Ct. Appeals (5th cir.) 1992. Adminstrv. asst. to acting chief exec. officer U. Ala.-University, 1976-77; assoc. Sirote, Permutt, Friend, Friedman, Held & Apolinsky, P.A., Birmingham, Ala., 1977-78; spl. asst. to Vice Pres. U.S., Washington, 1978-79; counsel subcom. on jurisprudence and govt. rels. Com. on Judiciary, U.S. Senate, Washington, 1979-80, counsel Select Com. on Ethics, 1980-83; dir. corp. issues RCA, Washington, 1983-86; Washington rep., Gen. Electric Co., 1986-87; assoc. counsel U.S. Senate Select com. on secret mil. assistance to Iran and the Nicaraguan Opposition, 1987-88; spl. counsel U.S. Senate Armed Svcs. com., 1988; counsel, Johnston, Barton, Proctor, Swedlaw & Naff, Birmingham, 1988-90; atty. Gathings & Davis, Birmingham, 1990-92; ptnr. Cooper, Mitch, Crawford, Kuykendall & Whatley, 1992-95; pres. and prin. John D. Saxon, P.C., 1995—; adj. instr. polit. communication U. Md., 1982-83; instr. speech communication U. Ala.-University, 1973; instr. speech communication and mgmt. Brewer Jr. Coll., Tuscaloosa, 1975-77; adj. instr. civil litigation Samford U., Birmingham, 1977-78; adj. prof. Washington Coll. Law The Am. U., 1988; vis. scholar The Hastings Ctr., 1983; mem. Am. Observer Delegation, Kettering Found., U.S.-China Task Force, 1986; bd. dirs. White House Fellows Found., 1981-84 , pres., 1983-84; mem. bd. advisers Center for Publ. Law and Service, U. Ala. Sch. Law, 1976-83; bd. trustees Farrah Law Soc., 1988-94, vice-chmn., 1990-92, chmn., 1992-94; bd. dirs. exec. com. mem. U. Ala. Law Found.; mem. Pres.'s Commn. White House Fellowships, 1983-84, 93—; mem. Washington Local Devel. Corp, 1986-88; chmn. Ala. Clinton for Pres. Campaign, 1992, 96; mem. platform com. Dem. Nat. Conv., 1992; mem. policy adv. com. The Coalition for Excellence in Edn., chmn., 1991-92; dir. The A+ Rsch. Found.; mem. bd. advisors N.E. Ala. Devel. Forum, 1992—, Nat. Governing Bd. Common Cause, 1992-95, Leadership Birmingham Class of 1993-94; mem. pres. adv. coun. Birmingham So. Coll., 1993—; mem. adminstrv. bd. First United Meth. Ch., 1994—; co-pres. Birmingham Boys Choir Found., 1994—; asst. scoutmaster Troop 57 Boy Scouts of Am.; pres. Southside Baseball, 1995—; adv. com. The Blackburn Inst., U. Ala.; bd. dir. Miles Coll. Ctr. for Cmty. Econ. Devel., 1995—. Served to 2d lt. U.S. Army, 1974, capt. Res. White House Fellow, 1978-79; named Disting. Mil. Grad., U. Ala., 1972. Mem. ABA (spl. com. litigation sect.), Ala. Bar Assn., Birmingham Bar Assn. (chmn. profl. ethics com. 1991-92, mem. grievance com. 1992—, co-chmn. 1995—), Ala. Trial Lawyers Assn. (bd. govs. 1990-94, exec. com. 1994—), White House Fellows Assn. (pres. 1983-84), Kiwanis Club (Birmingham), Scabbard and Blade, The Order of Barristers, Bench and Bar (Outstanding Sr. award 1977), Downtown Dem. Club (pres. 1992-93), Omicron Delta Kappa, Omicron Delta Epsilon, Phi Alpha Theta, Pi Sigma Alpha. Methodist. Contbr. articles to newspapers and legal publs., chpts. to books.

SAXTON, H. JAMES, congressman; b. Scranton, Pa., Jan. 22, 1943; s. Hugh R. and Helen M. (Billings) S.; m. Helen Jean Gadomski, June 9, 1965; children—Jennifer, James Martin. B.A., East Stroudsburg State Coll., 1965; postgrad. in elem. edn., Temple U., 1967-68. Tchr. Bordentown Pub. Schs., Bordentown, N.J., 1965-68; realtor Jim Saxton Realty Co., Bordentown, N.J., 1968-85; assemblyman N.J. State Assembly, Trenton, 1975-81; state senator N.J. State Senate, Trenton, 1981-84; mem. 99th-104th Congresses from 13th (now 3rd) N.J. dist., Washington, D.C., 1984—; mem. nat. security com., chmn. resources subcom. on fisheries, wildlife & oceans, mem. joint econ. com.; mem. travel and tourism caucus, maritime caucus, congl. port caucus environ. and energy study conf., Rep. study com., Stripers Ltd. (99th Congress); sec. N.J. Congl. Del., Washington, 1985-89. Active Boy Scouts Am., Burlington Council. Bordentown C. of C. Club: Leadership Found. N.J. Lodge: Elks. Office: US Ho of Reps 339 Cannon House Office Bldg Washington DC 20515-3003*

SAXTON, JAMES, congressman; children: Martin, Jennifer. Tchr., small businessman; mem. U.S. Ho. of Reps., Washington, 1984—; vice-chmn. joint econ. com. U.S. Ho. of Reps., 104th Congress, Washington, chmn. Ho. subcom. Fisheries, Wildlife and Oceans; mem. Ho. Nat. Security Com. U.S. Ho. of Reps., Washington. Republican. Office: House Reps 339 Cannon House Office Bldg Washington DC 20515-3003 also: 7 Hadley Ave Toms River NJ 08753 also: 1 Maine Ave Cherry Hill NJ 08034*

SAXTON, RUTH OLSEN, educator, dean; b. Spokane, Wash., Apr. 18, 1941; d. O. Martin and Edith M. (Halsey) Olsen; m. Paul Malcom, Mar. 16, 1963; children: Kirsten Teresa, David Malcom, Katherine Blair. BA, Wheaton Coll., 1963; MA, Mills Coll., 1972; PhD, U. Calif., Berkeley, 1986. Calif. C.C. credential. Tchr. English Hyde Park H.S., Chgo., 1963-64; instr. English Coll. of Alameda, Calif., 1972-76, Mills Coll., Oakland, Calif., 1974-85; asst. prof. English Mills Coll., Oakland, 1985-90, assoc. prof. English, 1990—, dean of letters, 1993—; bd. mem. Calif. Writing Project Adv. Bd. Editor: Woolf & Lessing: Breaking the Mold, 1994; assoc. editor Woolf Studies Annual. Recipient Outstanding Tchr. award Sears Found., 1990. Mem. MLA, Va. Woolf Soc., Doris Lessing Soc. (newsletter editor 1991—). Democrat. Home: 800 Portal Ave Oakland CA 94610 Office: Mills College 5000 Macarthur Blvd Oakland CA 94613

SAXTON, WILLIAM MARVIN, lawyer; b. Joplin, Mo., Feb. 14, 1927; s. Clyde Marvin and Lea Ann (Farnan) S.; m. Helen Grace Klinefelter, June 1, 1974; children: Sherry Lynn, Patricia Ann Painter, William Daniel, Michael Lawrence. A.B., U. Mich., 1949, J.D., 1952. Bar: Mich. Mem. firm Love, Snyder & Lewis, Detroit, 1952-53; mem. firm Butzel, Long, Detroit, 1953—, dir., chmn., CEO, 1989-96; lectr. Inst. Continuing Legal Edn.; sec., bd. dirs. Fritz Broadcasting, Inc., 1983—; mem. mediation tribunal hearing panel for 3d Jud. Dist. Mich., 1989—, 6th Jud. Dist., 1994—. Trustee Detroit Music Hall Ctr. Soc. for the Performing Arts, 1984—; trustee Hist. Soc. U.S. Dist. Ct. (ea. dist.) Mich., 1992-95, pres., 1993-95. Recipient Distinguished award Mich. Road Builders Assn., 1987. Master of Bench Emeritus Am. Inn of Court; fellow Am. Coll. Trial Lawyers, Am. Bar Found., Mich. Bar Found.; mem. ABA, Detroit Bar Assn. (dir. 1974-79), Mich. Bar (mem. atty. discipline panel), Detroit Indsl. Rels. Rsch. Assn. (treas. 1980—, v.p. 1982, pres. 1984-85), Mich. Young Lawyers (pres. 1954-55), Am. Law Inst., Fed. Bar Assn., Indsl. Rels. Rsch. Assn. Am. Arbitration Assn., U.S. 6th Cir. Ct. Appeals (life, mem. jud. conf., mem. bicentennial com.), Am. Inn Ct., Cooley Club, Renaissance Club, Detroit Golf Club (dir. 1983-89), Detroit Athletic Club. Office: Butzel Long 150 W Jefferson Ave Ste 900 Detroit MI 48226-4415

SAY, ALLEN, children's writer, illustrator; b. Aug. 28, 1937; s. Masako Moriwaki; m. Deirdre Myles, Apr. 18, 1974; 1 child, Yuriko. Pub. EIZO Pr., Berkeley, 1968. Author, illustrator: Dr. Smith's Safari, 1972, Once Under the Cherry Blossom Tree: An Old Japanese Tale, 1974, The Feast of Lanterns, 1976, The Bicycle Man, 1982, A River Dream, 1988, The Lost Lake, 1989, Tree of Cranes, 1991, Grandfather's Journey, 1993 (Caldecott medal 1994, Boston Globe/Horn Book award 1994), The Stranger in the Mirror, 1995; author: The Innkeeper's Apprentice, 1989, El Chino, 1990; illustrator: A Canticle to the Waterbirds, 1968, Two Ways of Seeing, 1971, Magic and Night River, 1978, The Lucky Yak, 1980, The Secret Cross of Lorraine, 1981, How My Parents Learned to Eat, 1984 (Horn Book honor list 1984, Christopher award 1985), The Boy of the Three Year Nap, 1988 (Boston Globe/Horn Book award 1988, Caldecott honor book 1989). Office: care Houghton Mifflin 222 Berkeley St Boston MA 02116-3748*

SAYANO, REIZO RAY, electrochemical engineer; b. Los Angeles, Dec. 15, 1937; s. George Keiichiro and Miyo (Nakao) S.; m. Tamiko Shintani, May 28, 1967; children—Kiyomi Coleen, Naomi Jennifer. A.A., Los Angeles Community Coll., 1958; B.S., UCLA, 1960, M.S., 1962, Ph.D., 1967. Research asst. electrochem. and shock tube research dept. engring. UCLA, 1961-66; mem. staff TRW Systems, corrosion and advanced battery research and devel. Redondo Beach, Calif., 1966-78; dir. engring. Intermedics Intraocular Inc., Pasadena, Calif., 1978-80, dir. research and devel., 1980-82, v.p. engring. devel. and research, 1982-84; v.p. research and devel. Interpore Internat. Inc., 1984-85; dir. research and devel., product process devel. IOLAB Corp. subs. Johnson & Johnson Co., Claremont, Calif., 1985-87, dir. new tech., research and devel., 1987-88; v.p., gen. mgr. Nidek Techs., Inc., Pasadena, Calif., 1988—. NASA predoctoral trainee, 1964-65. Mem. Electrochem. Soc., Nat. Assn. Corrosion Engrs., AAAS, Am. Mgmt. Assn., Sigma Xi. Office: 675 S Arroyo Pky Ste 330 Pasadena CA 91105-3264

SAYATOVIC, WAYNE PETER, manufacturing company executive; b. Cleve., Feb. 8, 1946; s. Peter and Margaret Ann (Nestor) S.; m. Janice Elaine Zajac, July 27, 1968; children: Jason Scott, Jamie Elizabeth. BA in Econs., Syracuse U., 1967, MBA in Fin., 1969. Fin. mgmt. program Gen. Electric Co., Syracuse, N.Y., 1969-72; fin. and cost acctg. mgr. Lubriquip div. Houdaille Industries Inc., Solon, Ohio, 1972-75; contr. Hydraulics div. Houdaille Industries Inc., Buffalo, 1975-77, Strippit div Houdaille Industries Inc., Akron, N.Y., 1977-79; treas. Houdaille Industries Inc., Ft. Lauderdale, Fla., 1979-86; v.p., treas., sec. Houdaille Industries Inc., Northbrook, Ill.,

1986-88; v.p., treas., sec. IDEX Corp., Northbrook, 1988-91, v.p. fin., CFO, sec., 1992-94; sr. v.p. fin., CFO, sec., 1994—. Mem. Mfrs.' Alliance for Productivity & Innovation (fin. coun.). Office: IDEX Corp 630 Dundee Rd Northbrook IL 60062-2762

SAYER, JOHN SAMUEL, retired information systems consultant; b. St. Paul, July 27, 1917; s. Arthur Samuel and Genevieve (Ollis) S.; m. Elizabeth Hughes, June 9, 1940; children: Stephen, Susan, Kathryn, Nancy. BSME, U. Minn., 1940. Registered profl. engr., Del. Sect. mgr. E.I. Du Pont de Nemours & Co, Wilmington, Del., 1940-60; exec. v.p. Documentation, Inc., Washington, 1960-63; v.p. corp. devel. Aurbach Corp., Phila., 1963-65; exec. v.p. Leasco Systems & Rsch., Bethesda, Md., 1966-70, Leasco Info. Products, Silver Spring, Md., 1971-74; pres. Remac Info. Corp., Gaithersburg, Md., 1975-82; cons. John Sayer Assocs., Gaithersburg, 1983-94, ret., 1994; numerous presentations in field. Contbr. numerous articles to profl. jours. Recipient Info. Product of Yr. award Info. Industries Assn., 1973. Mem. ASME, Assn. Info. and Image Mgmt., Am. Inst. Info. Sci. Achievements include direction of work leading to critical path method of planning and scheduling, technical word thesarus, microfiche, data base publishing.

SAYER, MICHAEL, physics educator; b. Newport, Gwent, Wales, Nov. 6, 1935; emigrated to Can., 1960, naturalized, 1965; s. Charles Claude and Elizabeth Mary (Southcott) S.; m. Anne Moira Rogers, Aug. 27, 1960; children: Jane, Suzanne, Andrew, Christopher. BSc, U. Birmingham, Eng., 1957; PhD, U. Hull, Eng., 1961. Registered profl. engr. Postdoctoral fellow U. B.C., Vancouver, 1960-62; asst. prof. physics Queen's U., Kingston, Ont., 1962-67, assoc. prof., 1967-73, prof., 1973—, head dept. physics, 1977-82; assoc. dean for research Faculty Applied Sci. Queen's U., 1984-87; prof. materials and metallurgical enging. Queens U., Kingston, 1990—; sr. indsl. fellow, dir. research Almax Industries Ltd., 1987-88; vis. fellow Sheffield U., Eng., 1972-73; dir. Cansort Devices Ltd., Kingston, 1977—; vis. asst. prof. Trent U., Peterborough, Ont., 1965-66; mem. Can. Engring. Accreditation Bd., 1987-94. Contbr. articles to profl. jours.; patentee in field. Grantee Natural Sci. and Engring. Rsch. Coun. Can., 1962—; recipient Silver medal for Tech. Transfer Can. Award for Excellence, 1986, Bell Can. award Corp. Higher Edn. Forum, 1996. Fellow Royal Soc. Can., Can. Ceramic Soc. (pres. 1987-88, editor Can. Ceramic Quar. 1986—); mem. Am. Ceramic Soc., Materials Rsch. Soc., Assn. Profl. Engrs. Ont. Roman Catholic. Home: 97 Yonge St, Kingston, ON Canada K7M 1E4 Office: Queen's Univ, Dept Physics, Kingston, ON Canada K7L 3N6

SAYERS, KEN W(ILLIAM), writer and public relations executive; b. N.Y.C., July 31, 1942; s. William Verey and Doris Edith (Weale) S.; m. Rose Mary Beirao, Aug. 20, 1965; children: Wendy Elizabeth Sayers Rehnberg, Matthew Verey. BA in Journalism, CCNY, 1965; postgrad., Columbia U., 1970. Dep. chief book br. Office Asst. Sec. of Def. for Pub. Affairs, Washington, 1967-69; mgr. rsch. and analysis DMS, Inc., Greenwich, Conn., 1969-72; mgr. rsch. and publs. Lulejian & Assocs., Inc., Falls Church, Va., 1972-74; mgr. internat. pub. affairs Am. Cyanamid Co., Wayne, N.J., 1974-77; various positions IBM Corp., 1977—; pres. Halyard Ptnrs., Ridgefield, Conn., 1994—. Co-author: Anchors and Atoms, It Was a Very Good Year; author: Industrial Lasers; editor: Missiles and Spacecraft, World Aircraft Forecast; contbr. articles to profl. jours. Exec. officer Queens Nautical Cadets, Astoria, N.Y., 1963-65. Lt. USN, 1965-69. Decorated Joint Svc. Commendation medal. Home: 342 Limestone Rd Ridgefield CT 06877-2635 Office: IBM Corp Rt# 100 Somers NY 10589

SAYERS, MARTIN PETER, pediatric neurosurgeon; b. Big Stone Gap, Va., Jan. 2, 1922; s. Delbert Bancroft and Loula (Thompson) S.; m. Marjorie W. Garvin, May 8, 1943; children: Daniel Garvin Sayers, Stephen Putnam Sayers, Julia Hathaway Sayers Bolton, Elaine King Sayers Buck. B.A., Ohio State U., 1943, M.D., 1945; postgrad., U. Pa., 1948-51. Intern Phila. Gen. Hosp., 1945-46; resident in neurosurgery U. Pa. Hosps., Phila., 1948-51; practice medicine specializing in neurosurgery Columbus, Ohio, 1951—; mem. faculty Ohio State U., Columbus, 1951-87, clin. prof. neurosurgery, 1968-87, emeritus; chief dept. pediatric neurosurgery Ohio State U., 1960-87; cons. Bur. Crippled Children Services Ohio.; Neurosurgeon Project Hope, Ecuador, 1964, Ceylon, 1968, Cracow, Poland, 1979. Served as lt. M.C., USN, 1946-48. Mem. Am. Assn. Neurol. Surgeons (chmn. pediatric sect.), Congress Neurol. Surgeons (pres.), Neurosurg. Soc. Am. (pres.), Am. Soc. Pediatric Neurosurgery, Soc. Neurol. Surgeons. Office: 931 Chatham Ln Columbus OH 43221-2417

SAYERS, RICHARD JAMES, newspaper editor; b. Oil City, Pa., Mar. 16, 1947; s. Theodore Roosevelt and Ardella (Hanna) D.; m. Mary Catherine Smith, Nov. 22, 1974; children—Kelly Lyn, Rachel Richelle, Christopher Alan, Shannon Marie. Student, Albany Bus. Coll., Rochester Ins. Tech. Sports writer Rochester Times-Union, N.Y., 1969-74; sports editor Port Huron Times Herald, Mich., 1974-76; exec. sports editor Boston Herald Am., 1976-79; asst. mng. editor Detroit News, 1979-89; sr. editor THE NATIONAL Sports Daily, N.Y.C., 1989-91; editor Conn. Post, Bridgeport, 1991—. Grad. Multicultural Mgmt. Program fellow U. Mo., 1988. Presbyterian. Home: 98 Neponsit St Stamford CT 06902-4445

SAYERS, ROGER, academic administrator. Pres U. Ala., Tuscaloosa. Office: The U Ala Office of the Pres Tuscaloosa AL 35487

SAYES, JAMES OTTIS, religion educator, minister; b. Hudson, La., Nov. 16, 1922; s. Archie Lee and Alma Urania (Reid) S.; m. Delia Nell Melton, Oct. 29, 1944; children: James Melton, Deena Jan Sayes Thomas. BTh, So. Nazarene U., Bethany, Okla., 1944; postgrad., Cen. Bapt. Theol. Sem., Kansas City, Kans., 1944-45; BD, Nazarene Theol. Sem., Kansas City, Mo., 1947; MRE, DRE, So. Bapt. Theol. Sem., Ft. Worth, 1951, 55. Pastor Ch. of the Nazarene, Neosho, Mo., 1947-48, Maryville, Mo., 1948-50; pastor Arlington Heights Ch. of the Nazarene, Ft. Worth, 1951-54; assoc. pastor First Ch. Nazarene, Little Rock, 1954-56; prof. Olivet Nazarene U., Kankakee, Ill., 1956-94, prof. emeritus, 1994—; pastor Ch. of the Nazarene, Orland Park, Ill., 1985-88; pres. Ministerial Assn., Maryville, 1950. Mem. Am. Theol. Soc., Wesleyan Theol. Soc., Religious Educators Assn. Avocations: collecting dated R.R. nails, golf, horseback riding. Home: 480 S Bresee Ave Bourbonnais IL 60914-2265 Office: Olivet Nazarene U Dept of Religion Min Kankakee IL 60901

SAYETTA, THOMAS CHARLES, physics educator; b. Williamsport, Pa., Apr. 12, 1937; s. Morris and Gladys Pauline (Sunderland) S.; m. Patsy Anne Sherrill; 1 child, Susan Leigh. BS in Physics, U. S.C., 1959, PhD in Physics, 1964. Teaching asst. physics dept. U. S.C., Columbia, 1956-59; engr. RCA, Camden, N.J., 1959-60; teaching asst. physics dept. U. S.C., Columbia, 1960-63; rsch. asst. physics dept., 1963-64; prof. physics East Carolina U., Greenville, N.C., 1964—. Asst. editor Internat. Jour.. Math. and Math. Sci., 1979-83. Nat. treas. Chi Beta Phi, 1974-82. With USNR, 1954-62. Mem. Am. Assn. Physics Tchrs., Sigma Xi (pres. East Carolina U. chpt. 1970-71). Avocations: tennis, basketball. Home: 1117 Hillside Dr Greenville NC 27858-4522 Office: Physics Dept East Carolina U Greenville NC 27858

SAYKALLY, RICHARD JAMES, chemistry educator; b. Rhinelander, Wis., Sept. 10, 1947; s. Edwin L. and Helen M. S. BS, U. Wis., Eau Claire, 1970; PhD, U. Wis., Madison, 1977. Postdoctoral Nat. Bur. Standards, Boulder, Colo., 1977-79; asst. prof. U. Calif., Berkeley, 1979-83, assoc. prof., 1983-86, prof., 1986—, vice chmn. dept. chemistry, 1988-91; Bergman lectr. Yale U., 1987; Merck-Frost lectr. U. B.C., 1988; Bourke lectr. Royal Soc. Chemistry, 1992; Samuel M. McElvain lectr. U. Wis., Madison, 1995; Harry Emmett Gunning lectr. U. Alta., 1995; prin. investigator Lawrence Berkeley Lab., 1983-91; prin. investigator program Sci. for Sci., NSF; mem. Laser Sci. Topical Group Fellowship Com., 1993—; mem. internat. steering com. 12th Internat. Conf. on Laser Spectroscopy, 1995. Contbr. over 160 articles to profl. jours.; editl. rev. bd. Jour. Chem. Physics, 1993-95, Molecular Physics, 1983—, Chem. Physics Letters, 1987—, Spectroscopy Mag., 1986—, Rev. of Sci. Instruments, 1987-90. Recipient Disting. Alumnus award U. Wis., Eau Claire, 1987, Bomen Michelson prize for spectroscopy, 1989, E.K. Plyler prize for molecular spectroscopy, 1989, E.R. Lippincott medal OSA, SAS, 1992, Disting. Tchg. award U. Calif., 1992, Humboldt sr. scientist award, 1995; fellow Dreyfuss Found., 1979, Churchill fellow Cambridge U., 1995; presdl. investigator NSF, 1984-88. Fellow Am. Phys. Soc., Royal Soc. Chemistry, Am. Acad. Arts and Scis.; mem. AAAS, AAUP, Optical Soc. Am., Am. Chem. Soc. (Harrison Howe award 1992). Office: Univ California Dept of Chemistry 419 Latimer Hall # 1460 Berkeley CA 94720-1460

SAYLER, RICHARD H., lawyer; b. Rochester, N.Y., Jan. 24, 1945. AB, Dartmouth Coll., 1966; JD, U. Mich., 1969. Bar: N.Y. 1970, Ohio 1985. Law clk. to Hon. Lumbard U.S. Ct. Appeals (2nd cir.), 1969-70; law clk. to Hon. White U.S. Supreme Ct., 1970-71; spl. asst. to asst. atty. gen. Antitrust Divsn., U.S. Dept. Justice, Washington, 1972-74; ptnr. Jones, Day, Reavis & Pogue, Cleve. Office: Jones Day Reavis & Pogue N Point 901 Lakeside Ave E Cleveland OH 44114-1116

SAYLER, ROBERT NELSON, lawyer; b. Kansas City, Mo., June 1, 1940; s. John William and Roberta (Nelson) S.; m. Martha Leith, Aug. 1962; children: Christina, Bentley. BA, Stanford U., 1962; JD, Harvard U., 1965. Bar: U.S. Dist. Ct. D.C. 1966, U.S. Ct. Appeals (D.C. cir.) 1966, U.S. Supreme Ct. 1971, D.C. 1972, U.S. Ct. Appeals (2d cir.) 1977. From assoc. to ptnr. Covington & Burling, Washington, 1965—. V.p. Neighborhood Legal Services, Washington, 1980-82; pres. Legal Aid Soc., Washington, 1983-84. Fellow Am. Bar Found., Am. Coll. Trial Lawyers; mem. ABA (dir. programs, program chmn. 1981, 85, coun., chmn. litigation sect.). Democrat. Office: Covington & Burling PO Box 7566 1201 Pennsylvania Ave NW Washington DC 20004-2401

SAYLES, EDWARD THOMAS, theatrical producer; b. Auburn, N.Y., Feb. 19, 1952; s. Thomas Edward and Gilda Marie (Campolieto) S.; m. Sue Ann Kocks (div.); children: Austin, Celeste. BA, SUNY, Cortland, 1974; MA, Bowling Green (Ohio) State U., 1980. Producing dir. Uptown Stage, Cortland, 1975-76, Trotwood (Ohio) Circle Theatre, 1976-80, First St., Dayton, 1978-80, Merry-Go-Round Playhouse, Auburn, N.Y., 1980—; instr. SUNY, Cortland, 1975-76, guest prof., 1985-87; N.Y. State Coun. on the Arts, 1986—. Dir., collaborator original plays including Alice in Wonderland, 1985 (Nat. Showcase award 1988), Pictures at an American Exhibition, 1988; arranger A Modern Survey, 1985. Trustee Cayuga County United Way, Auburn, 1988—, Tomato Festival, 1987-89, Conf. Help for Alcohol and Drug Abuse, 1984-87. Recipient Creative Support award Nat. Endowment for the Arts, 1977-80, Ohio Arts Coun., 1977-80, Dayton (Ohio) Found., 1977-80, N.Y. State Coun. on the Arts, 1980-89. Mem. Owasco Country Club (bd. dirs.), Phi Alpha Theta (v.p. 1973), Alpha Psi Omega (v.p. 1974). Roman Catholic. Office: Merry Go Round Playhouse PO Box 506 Auburn NY 13021-0506

SAYLES, JOHN THOMAS, film director, writer, actor; b. Schenectady, Sept. 28, 1950; s. Donald John and Mary (Rausch) S. BS, Williams Coll., 1972. Author: Pride of the Bimbos, 1975, Union Dues, 1979, Thinking in Pictures: The Making of the Movie "Matewan," 1987, The Anarchists Convention, 1979, Los Gusanos, 1991; short stories I-80 Nebraska, M.490 - M.205, 1975 (O Henry award), Breed, Golden State, 1977 (O Henry award), Hoop; writer, dir. plays: New Hope for the Dead, 1981, Turnbuckle; screenwriter: Piranha, 1978, The Lady in Red, 1979, Battle Beyond the Stars, 1980, Alligator, 1981, The Challenge, 1982, Enormous Changes at the Last Minute, 1985, Wild Thing, 1987, The Clan of the Cave Bear, 1988, Breaking In, 1989; screenwriter, actor: The Howling, 1981; dir., screenwriter, actor: Return of the Secaucus Seven, 1980 (Los Angeles Film Critcs award, 1980), Lianna, 1983, The Brother From Another Planet, 1984, Matewan, 1987, Eight Men Out, 1988, City of Hope, 1991; dir., screenwriter: Baby, It's You, 1983, Passion Fish, 1992; actor: Hard Choices, 1986, Something Wild, 1986, Little Vegas, 1990, Straight Talk, 1992, Malcolm X, 1992, Matinee, 1993, My Life's in Turnaround, 1994; dir. Bruce Springsteen music videos Born in the U.S.A., I'm on Fire, Glory Days; TV work includes A Perfect Match, Unnatural Causes, Shannon's Deal, spl. Mountain View. MacArthur Found. grantee. Office: Paramount Pictures 5555 Melrose Ave Los Angeles CA 90038-3149 Office: Paradigm Ste 2600 10100 Santa Monica Blvd Los Angeles CA 90067

SAYLES, LEONARD ROBERT, management educator, consultant; b. Rochester, N.Y., Apr. 30, 1926; s. Robert and Rose (Sklof) S.; m. Kathy Ripin; children: Robert, Emily. BA with highest distinction, U. Rochester, 1946; PhD in Econs. and Social Sci, MIT, 1950. Asst. prof. Cornell U., 1950-53, U. Mich., 1953-56; prof. emeritus Grad. Sch. Bus. Adminstrn., Columbia U., 1956-91, prof. bus. adminstrn., 1962—, head div. indsl. relations and orgnl. behavior, 1960-72; adviser to adminstr. NASA, 1966-71; sr. rsch. scientist Ctr. for Creative Leadership, Greensboro, N.C., 1988-94; Disting. vis. lectr. McGill U., 1974; bd. govs. Center for Creative Leadership, 1984-88. Author: (with G. Strauss) The Local Union, 1953, Managerial Behavior, 1964, Human Behavior in Organizations, 1966, (with E. Chapple) Measure of Management, 1961, Behavior of Industrial Work Groups, 1958, Individualism and Big Business, 1963, (with W. Dowling) How Managers Motivate, 1971, (with M. Chandler) Managing Large Systems; Organizations for the Future, 1971, 2d edit., 1993, (with G. Strauss) Personnel, 4th edit. 1980, Managing Human Resources, 2d edit, 1981, Leadership, 1979, (with R. Burgelman) Inside Corporate Innovation, 1985, Managing in Real Organizations, 1989, The Working Leader, 1993; mem. editorial bd. Human Orgn., 1957-62. Fellow Am. Anthropol. Assn.; mem. Phi Beta Kappa.

SAYLES, THOMAS DYKE, JR., banker; b. Newton Center, Mass., Jan. 16, 1932; s. Thomas Dyke and Eleanor (Norton) S.; m. Patricia Blake, Dec. 11, 1954; children: Lynn Diane, Richard Norton, Stephen Dyke. A.B., Dartmouth, 1954; M.A., N.Y. U., 1961. With Mfrs. Hanover Trust Co., N.Y.C., 1958-70; v.p. Mfrs. Hanover Trust Co., 1966-70, sr. v.p., 1970; dir. Summit Trust Co., Summit, N.J., 1968—; exec. v.p., chief adminstrn. officer Summit Trust Co., 1970, pres., 1971-80, chmn., 1971-94; chmn., pres., chief exec. officer Summit Bancorp., 1974-87, chmn., chief exec. officer, 1987-94, chmn., 1994—; bd. dirs. Selective Ins. Group., Inc. Trustee Overlook Hosp., 1972-80, Drew U., 1984—, Papermill Playhouse, 1991—, NCCJ, 1991—, N.J. Israel Commn., 1991. With USAF, 1955-58. Mem. Chatham (N.J.) Jr. C. of C. (dir. 1965), N.J. State C. of C. (trustee 1992—). Clubs: Baltusrol (Springfield); Canoe Brook (Summit), Pine Valley. Home: 58 Lincoln Ave Chatham NJ 07928-2062 Office: Summit Bancorp One Main St Chatham NJ 07928*

SAYLOR, LARRY JAMES, lawyer; b. Biloxi, Miss., Nov. 7, 1948; s. Rufus Don and Alice Julia (Kidd) S.; m. Mary L. Mullendore, Dec. 27, 1975; children: David James, Stephen Michael. AB in Political Sci., Miami U., Oxford, Ohio, 1970; M in City and Regional Planning, Ohio State U., 1976; JD, U. Mich., 1976. Bar: D.C. 1976, Mich. 1977, U.S. Ct. Appeals (D.C. cir.) 1977, U.S. Ct. Appeals (6th cir.) 1978, U.S. Supreme Ct. 1981, U.S. Ct. Appeals (10th cir.) 1982. Law clk. to presiding judge U.S. Ct. Appeals (D.C. cir.), Washington, 1976-77; ptnr. Miller, Canfield, Paddock and Stone, Detroit, 1977—. Article editor Mich. Law Rev., 1975-76; contbr. articles to profl. jours. 1st lt. USAF, 1970-72. Mem. ABA (antitrust and litigation sects.), Mich. Bar Assn., (chair antitrust sect. 1994-95), D.C. Bar Assn., World Trade Club, Detroit Econ. Club. Avocations: skiing, woodworking. Home: 455 Lakeland St Grosse Pointe MI 48230-1654 Office: Miller Canfield Paddock & Stone 150 W Jefferson Ave Ste 2500 Detroit MI 48226-4415

SAYLOR, MARK JULIAN, editor; b. Wellsville, N.Y., Mar. 19, 1954; s. Richard Samuel and Naomi (Roth) S.; children: Samuel, Benjamin, Katie. BA cum laude, Harvard Coll., 1976. Staff writer Ark. Democrat, Little Rock, 1976-77; staff writer San Jose (Calif.) Mercury News, 1977-81, asst. met. editor, 1981-82, govt. and politics editor, 1982-85; asst. city editor San Diego County edit. LA Times, L.A., 1985-89, city editor San Diego edit., 1989-91, Calif. polit. editor, 1991-95; entertainment editor Business, 1995—. Avocation: chess master. Office: LA Times Times Mirror Sq Los Angeles CA 90053

SAYLOR, PETER M., architect; b. Phila., July 26, 1941; s. Harry T. and Dorothy (Johnson) S.; m. Caroline Metcalf, Apr. 4, 1970; children: Thomas S., Elizabeth B. B.Arch., U. Pa., 1963, M.Arch., 1965. Registered arch., Pa., N.J., Ind., Wis., Conn., Ohio, Minn. Architect Mitchell-Giurgola, Phila., 1967-70; ptnr. firm Dagit-Saylor Architects, Phila., 1970—; design critic, juror U. Pa., 1975—; bd. dirs. Found. for Architecture, Phila., 1980-90. V.p. Chestnut Hill Cmty. Assn., Phila., 1979, bd. dirs. 1976-79; bd. dirs. Saint's Hosp., Wyndmoor, Pa., 1981-86. Recipient various bldg. design award. Fellow AIA (bd. dirs. Phila. chpt. 1973-82, chpt. pres. 1981-82); mem. Pa. Soc. Archs., Chestnut Hill Hist. Soc. (bd. dirs. 1988-95, pres. 1989-92), Phila. Soc. Preservation of Landmarks (bd. dirs. 1989-96, pres. 1993-94), Phila. Mus. Art (friends bd. dirs. 1990-93), Phila. Cricket Club (bd. dirs. 1985-91), Mask and Wig Club (pres. 1980-81, bd. dirs. 1970-84). Republican. Episcopalian. Office: Dagit-Saylor Archs 100 S Broad St Philadelphia PA 19110-1023

SAYLOR, STEVEN WARREN, writer prose, fiction; b. Port Lavaca, Tex., Mar. 23, 1956; s. Lyman Harrison and Lucy Lee (Reeves) S. BA History, U. Tex., 1978. Author: Roman Blood, 1991, Arms of Nemesis, 1992, Catilina's Riddle, 1993 (Lambda Literary award 1994), The Venus Throw, 1995, A Murder on the Appian Way, 1996; contbr, short stories, essays to numerous mags. Mem. Mystery Writers of Am. (Robert L. Fish Meml. award 1993). Avocations: bicycling, furniture making, travel. Office: St Martins Press 175 5th Ave New York NY 10010-7703

SAYRE, DAVID, physicist; b. N.Y.C., Mar. 2, 1924; s. Ralph E. and Sylvia (Rosenbaum) S.; m. Anne Bowns, Dec. 26, 1947. BS, Yale U., 1944; MS, Auburn U., 1948; PhD, Oxford (Eng.) U., 1951. Staff mem. radiation lab. MIT, Cambridge, 1943-46; rsch. assoc. U. Pa., Phila., 1951-55; mathematician IBM Corp., N.Y.C., 1955-59, corp. dir. programming, 1959-62; mem. rsch. staff IBM T.J. Watson Rsch. Ctr., Yorktown Heights, N.Y., 1962-90, ret., 1990; cons. U.S. Office Naval Rsch., London, 1951; mem. U.S.A. Nat. Com. for Crystallography, 1952-55, 81-84, vice chmn., 1984-86; vis. fellow All Souls Coll., Oxford U., 1972-73; guest scientist dept. physics SUNY, Stony Brook, 1980—; guest rschr. Brookhaven Nat. Lab., Upton, N.Y., 1983—. Co-author: Waveforms, 1947; editor: Computational Crystallography, 1983; co-editor: Structural Studies on Molecules of Biological Interest, 1983, X-Ray Microscopy II, 1988; contbr. numerous articles to profl. jours. Trustee Village of Head-of-the-Harbor, L.I., N.Y., 1975-95. Mem. Am. Crystallographic Assn. (treas. 1952-55, pres. 1983, Fankuchen award 1989). Episcopalian. Achievements include devel. of atomicity-based direct phasing method for x-ray crystallography, (with others) of first FORTRAN compiler and first virtual computer system; contbns. to x-ray microscopy; observation (with others) of x-ray diffraction pattern from single biol. cell.

SAYRE, EDWARD VALE, chemist; b. Des Moines, Sept. 8, 1919; s. Edward Agnew and Audrey (Vale) S.; m. Virginia Nelle Rogers, Oct. 20, 1943. B.S., Iowa State U., 1941; A.M., Columbia U., 1943, Ph.D., 1949. Mgr. research sect. Manhattan Dist. project Columbia U., 1942-45; research chemist Eastman Kodak Research Labs., Rochester, N.Y., 1949-52; sr. chemist Brookhaven Nat. Lab., Upton, N.Y., 1952-84; research phys. scientist Smithsonian Instn., Washington, 1984—; dir. research Museum Fine Arts, Boston, 1975-80, sr. scientist, 1980-84; sr. scientist Alexander von Humboldt Found., 1980; vis. lectr. Stevens Inst. Tech., 1955-61; adj. prof. fine arts Inst. Fine Arts, N.Y. U., 1960-74; distinguished vis. prof. Am. U. Cairo, 1970; Regents prof. U. Calif., Irvine, 1972; mem. sci. advisory council Winterthur Mus. Contbr. numerous articles on research to profl. jours.; assoc. editor: Archaeometry, 1969-93, Art and Archaeology Tech. Abstracts, 1970-87, Jour. Archaeol. Sci., 1971-77. Guggenheim fellow, 1969; recipient U.S. sr. scientist award Alexander von Humboldt Found., 1980-81, George von Hevesy medal, 1984. Fellow Internat., Am. insts. for conservation hist. and artistic works; mem. Am. Chem. Soc. Club: Cosmos. Home: 2106 Wilkinson Pl Alexandria VA 22306-2540

SAYRE, E(NOCH) PHILLIP, political scientist, state official; b. Humboldt, Iowa, Apr. 19, 1926; s. Enoch Franklin and Grace Irene (Rusk) S.; m. Mary-Ellen Silverstone, May 25, 1957; children: Michael Franklin, Elisabeth Carol Sayre Lozinsky. BA, U. Wash., 1950; postgrad., Georgetown U., 1951-54. Campaign mgr. Congressman Henry M. Jackson and Senator W.G. Magnuson, Skagit County, Wash., 1950; mem. campaign staff Henry M. Jackson for U.S. Senate, Wash., 1953; adminstrv. asst. to Congressman John Lesinski, U.S. Ho. of Reps., Washington, 1954-56; ins. agt. State Mut. Life Assurance Co., Washington, 1956-62; staff assoc. J.D. Marsh & Assocs., Inc., Washington, 1962-64; dir. fin. planning, supr. ins. Capital Plans, Washington, 1964-68; v.p., registered prin. Diversified Planning Corp., Washington, 1968-70; adminstrv. analyst dept. fiscal svcs. Md. Gen. Assembly, Annapolis, 1970-80, sr. adminstrv. analyst, 1980—; staff dir. Md. Commn. on Intergovtl. Cooperation, 1974-78. Chmn. legis. com. Young Dems. D.C., 1954-56; co-founder Md. Com. for Fair Representation, 1960-62; chmn. issues com. We. Suburban Dem. Club Montgomery County, Md., 1962-64; mem. Md. Constl. Conv. Commn., 1965-67; co-chmn. Dem. Com. for Constn., Md., 1968; mem. steering com. Citizens for Proposed Constn. Md., 1968. Recipient resolution Md. Ho. of Dels., 1963, 65, Young Dem. of Yr. award Young Dems. Md., 1965, Outstanding Civic Achievement award Young Dems. Montgomery County, 1966. Mem. Am. Soc. for Pub. Adminstrn., World Future Soc., Bannockburn Civic Assn., Bannockburn Cmty. Club, Washington Ethical Soc. Avocations: reading, futurist interests, walking, outdoors, nature. Home: 6809 Laverock Ct Bethesda MD 20817-4912

SAYRE, JOHN MARSHALL, lawyer, former government official; b. Boulder, Colo., Nov. 9, 1921; s. Henry Marshall and Lulu M. (Cooper) S.; m. Jean Miller, Aug. 22, 1943; children: Henry M., Charles Franklin, John Marshall Jr., Ann Elizabeth Sayre Taggart (dec.). BA, U. Colo., 1943, JD, 1948. Bar: Colo. 1948, U.S. Dist. Ct. Colo. 1952, U.S. Ct. Appeals (10th cir.) 1964. Law clk. trust dept. Denver Nat. Bank, 1948-49; asst. cashier, trust officer Nat. State Bank of Boulder, 1949-50; ptnr. Ryan, Sayre, Martin, Brotzman, Boulder, 1950-66, Davis, Graham & Stubbs, Denver, 1966-89, of counsel, 1993—; asst. sec. of the Interior for Water and Sci., 1989-93. Bd. dirs. Boulder Sch. Dist. 3, 1951-57; city atty. City of Boulder, 1952-55; gen. counsel Colo. Mcpl. League, 1956-63; prin. counsel No. Colo. Water Conservancy Dist. and mcpl. subdist., 1964-87, spl. counsel, 1987, bd. dirs. dist., 1960-64; former legal counsel Colo. Assn. Commerce and Industry. Lt. (j.g.) USN, 1943-46, ret. Decorated Purple Heart. Fellow Am. Bar. Found. (life), Colo. Bar Found. (life); mem. ABA, Colo. Bar Assn., Boulder County Bar Assn. (pres. 1959), Denver Bar Assn., Nat. Water Resources Assn. (Colo. dir. 1980-89, 93-95, pres. 1984-86), Denver Country Club, Univ. Club, Mile High Club, Phi Gamma Delta, Phi Beta Kappa, Phi Delta Phi. Republican. Episcopalian. Office: Davis Graham & Stubbs PO Box 185 Denver CO 80201-0185 Home: 355 Ivanhoe St Denver CO 80220-5841

SAYRE, KENNETH MALCOLM, philosophy educator; b. Scottsbluff, Nebr., Aug. 13, 1928; s. Harry Malcolm and Mildred Florence (Potts) S.; m. Lucille Margaret Shea, Aug. 19, 1958 (dec. Apr. 1980); children: Gregory, Christopher, Jeffrey; m. Patricia Ann White, Apr. 4, 1983; 1 child, Michael. A.B., Grinnell Coll., Iowa, 1952; M.A., Harvard U., 1954, Ph.D., 1958. Asst. dean Grad. Sch. Arts and Letters Harvard U., Cambridge, Mass., 1953-56; systems analyst MIT, Cambridge, Mass., 1956-58; from instr. to prof. philosophy U. Notre Dame, Ind., 1958—, dir. Philosophic Inst., 1966—. Author: Recognition, 1965, Consciousness, 1969, Plato's Analytic Method, 1969, Cybernetics and the Philosophy of Mind, 1976, Moonflight, 1977, Starburst, 1977, Plato's Late Ontology, 1983, Plato's Literary Garden, 1995. Served with USN, 1946-48. NSF grantee, 1962-79. Mem. Am. Philos. Assn., Phi Beta Kappa. Home: 910 Weber Sq South Bend IN 46617-1850 Office: Univ Notre Dame Dept Philosophy Notre Dame IN 46556

SAYRE, LARRY D., religious organization executive. Dir. Am. Baptist Church Greater Indpls. Region. Office: American Baptist Churches of USA 1350 N Delaware St Indianapolis IN 46202-2415

SAYRE, RICHARD LAYTON, lawyer; b. Spokane, Wash., May 21, 1953; s. Charles Layton and Elizabeth Jane (Ward) S.; m. Karen Linda Sayre, Mar. 8, 1979; children: Wendi Sue Jackman, Tracey Lynn Turner. BA, U. Wash., 1976; JD, Gonzaga U., 1979. Bar: Wash. 1979, U.S. Dist. Ct. (ea. and we. dist.) Wash. 1979, U.S. Ct. Appeals (9th cir.) 1986; cert. elder law atty. Nat. Elder Law Found. Deputy prosecuting atty. Spokane County, Spokane, 1979-84; shareholder Underwood, Campbell, Brock & Cerutti, Spokane, 1984-92, Sayre & Sayre P.S., Spokane, 1992—; pres. Nat. Acad. Elder Law Attys., Washington, 1995—. Officer, trustee El Katif Shrine Temple, Spokane, 1988—; bd. govs. Shriner's Hosp. for Crippled Children, Spokane, 1994—; exec. officer Order of DeMolay, Washington, 1993—, active mem. internat. supreme coun. Recipient Pro Bono award Spokane County Bar Assn., 1991, Recognition of Achievement & Contribution award Lutheran Social Svcs. of Washington, Idaho, 1992. Mem. Spokane Estate Planning Coun. Democrat. Episcopal. Avocations: sailing, skiing. Office: Sayre & Sayre 111 W Cataldo Ste 210 Spokane WA 99201

SAYRE, ROBERT FREEMAN, English language educator; b. Columbus, Ohio, Nov. 6, 1933; s. Harrison M. and Mary (White) S.; (divorced); children—Gordon, Nathan, Laura; m. Hutha Refle, May 7, 1988. B.A., Wesleyan U., Middletown, Conn., 1955; Ph.D., Yale U., 1962. Instr. English U. Ill., Urbana, 1961-63; Fulbright lectr. Lund (Sweden) U., 1963-65; mem. faculty U. Iowa, 1965—, prof. English, 1972—; dir. inter-profl. seminars NEH, 1978, 79; Fulbright lectr. Montpellier, France, 1984; exch. prof. U. Copenhagen, 1988-89; mem. adv. bd. Leopold Ctr. for Sustainable Agr., 1994—. Author: The Examined Self: Benjamin Franklin, Henry Adams and Henry James, 1964, Adventures, Rhymes and Designs of Vachel Lindsay, 1968; Thoreau and the American Indians, 1977; editor: A Week on the Concord and Merrimac Rivers, Walden, The Maine Woods, Cape Cod (H.D. Thoreau), 1985, Take This Exit: Rediscovering the Iowa Landscape, 1989, New Essays on Walden, 1992, American Lives: An Anthology of Autobiographical Writing, 1994; contbr. articles and revs. to profl. jours. Guggenheim fellow, 1973-74. Mem. Am. Studies Assn., MLA. Office: U Iowa English Dept Iowa City IA 52242

SAYRE, ROBERT MARION, ambassador; b. Hillsboro, Oreg., Aug. 18, 1924; s. William Octavius and Mary (Brozka) S.; m. Elora Amanda Moyhihan, Dec. 29, 1951; children: Marian Amanda, Robert Marion, Daniel Humphrey. B.A. summa cum laude, Willamette U., 1949; J.D. cum laude (Alexander Welborn Weddell Peace prize 1956), George Washington U., 1956; M.A., Stanford U., 1960; LL.D., Willamette U., 1965. Bar: D.C. 1956, U.S. Ct. Appeals 1956, U.S. Supreme Ct. 1962. Joined U.S. Fgn. Service, 1949; econ. adviser on Latin Am., 1950-52, mil. adviser, 1952-57, officer charge inter-Am. security affairs, 1955-57; polit. counselor embassy Lima, Peru, 1958-59; fin. attache embassy Havana, Cuba, 1960; exec. sec. Task Force Latin Am., State Dept., 1961, officer charge Mexican affairs, 1961-63; dep. dir. Office Caribbean and Mexican Affairs, 1963-64; dir. Office Mexican Affairs, 1964; sr. staff mem. White House, 1964-65; sr. dep. asst. sec. Bur. Inter-Am. Affairs, Dept. State, 1965-68; acting asst. sec. Dept. State, 1967—; Am. ambassador to Uruguay, 1968-69, to Panama, 1969-74; sr. insp. Dept. State, 1974-75, insp. gen., 1975-78; ambassador to Brazil, 1978-81; chmn. U.S. Interdepartmental group on Terrorism, dir. Counter-terrorism and Emergency Planning Dept. State, 1981-84, sr. insp., 1985; ptnr. IRC Group, Inc., 1986-87; adv. to U.S. rep. OAS, 1985-87, under sec. for mgmt., 1987-94; sr. assoc. Global Bus. Access, Ltd., Washington, 1995—; chair Open Forum Working Group on Internat. Econs. U.S. Dept. State, 1995—. Sr. councilor Atlantic Coun. Washington Inst. Fgn. Affairs. Capt. AUS, WWII; col. REs., ret. Decorated Soc. Cross (Brazil); Cross of Balboa (Panama); recipient Outstanding Employee award Dept. State, 1952, Superior Honor awards, 1964, 75, Disting. Honor award, 1978, Outstanding Performance award, 1982, 83, 84, 85, Presdl. Meritorious award, 1986, Fgn. Svc. Cup award, 1990, Sec.'s Cert. of Appreciation, U.S. Dept. State, 1996. Mem. Blue Key, Phi Delta Theta, Phi Eta Sigma, Tau Kappa Alpha. Episcopalian. Club: Cosmos, Dacor. Home: 3714 Bent Branch Rd Falls Church VA 22041-1028 Office: Global Business Access Ltd 1825 I St NW Ste 400 Washington DC 20006-5403

SAYSETTE, JANICE ELAINE, vertebrate paleontologist, zoo archaeologist; b. San Francisco, Feb. 27, 1949; d. James Monroe and Isabel Christine (Saysette) Heffern; m. Thomas Arthur Haygood, Aug. 6, 1978 (div. June 1991); children: Grant Thomas, Ian James. AA in Nursing, Ohlone Coll., 1974; BSN, Metro State, 1981; MS in Nursing, U. Colo., 1982; MA in Anthropology, Colo. State U., 1990, postgrad., 1991—. Staff nurse Palo Alto (Calif.) VA Hosp., 1974-75, San Jose (Calif.) Hosp., 1975-78, O'Connor Hosp., San Jose, 1978-80; clin. nursing instr. U. No. Colo., Greeley, 1982-87; nursing supr. Poudre Valley Hosp., Ft. Collins, Colo., 1988-89; grad. teaching asst. Colo. State U., Ft. Collins, 1988-90, ind. contractor-zooarchaeology, 1990—; crew mem. U. Wyo. Lookingbill Archaeological Site, 1991; crew chief Denver Mus. Natural History Porqupine Cave Paleontological Site, 1993; lectr., presenter in field. Mem. Am. Soc. Mammalogists, Internat. Coun. Archaeozoology, Soc. Am. Archaeology, Soc. Vertebrate Paleontology. Democrat. Avocation: fly fishing, hiking. Office: Colo State U Dept of Biology Fort Collins CO 80523

SAYWELL, WILLIAM GEORGE GABRIEL, foundation administrator; b. Regina, Sask., Can., Dec. 1, 1936; s. John Ferdinand Tupper and Vera Marguerite S.; m. Helen Jane Larmer; children: Shelley Jayne, William James Tupper, Patricia Lynn. BA, U. Toronto, 1960, MA, 1961, PhD, 1968; LLD, U. B.C., 1994. Asst. prof. dept. East Asian studies U. Toronto, Ont., Ont., Can., 1963-69; asst. prof. U. Toronto, Ont., Can., 1969-71, assoc. prof., 1971-82, prof., 1982-83, chmn. dept., 1971-76; prof. dept. history, pres. Simon Fraser U., Burnaby, B.C., Can., 1983-93; pres., chief exec. officer Asia Pacific Found. of Can., Vancouver, B.C., 1993—; sinologist and 1st sec. Can. Embassy, Peking, 1972-73; dir. U. Toronto-York U. Ctr. Modern East Asia, 1974-75; prin. Innis Coll., 1976-79; vice provost U. Toronto, 1979-83; dir. Westcoast Energy, Spar Aerospace, Western Garnet. Author articles and revs. on Chinese affairs to profl. jours. Decorated Order B.C. Office: Asia Pacific Found Can, 666-999 Canada Pl, Vancouver, BC Canada V6C 3E1

SAZEGAR, MORTEZA, artist; b. Tehran, Iran, Nov. 11, 1933; s. Hassan Ali and Zahra (Frootan) S.; m. Patricia Jean Kaurich, July 13, 1959. B.A., U. Tex., El Paso, 1955, B.S., 1956; postgrad., Baylor U. Coll. Medicine, 1956-57, Cornell U., 1958-59. One man exhibitions include, Poindexter Gallery, N.Y.C., 1964, 67, 69, 71, 73, 75, 77, group exhibitions include, Detroit Inst. Arts, 1965, Chgo. Art Inst., 1965, Univ. Art Mus., U. Tex., Austin, 1965, 72, Whitney Mus. Am. Art, 1970, Cleve. Mus. Art, 1972, Corcoran Gallery Art, Washington, 1973, Tyler Sch. Art, Temple U., Phila., 1979; represented in permanent collections, Whitney Mus. Am. Art, N.Y.C., San Francisco Mus. Modern Art, Riverside Mus., N.Y.C., U. Mass., Amherst, Corcoran Gallery Art, Prudential Ins. Corp. Am., Mus. Contemporary Art, Tehran, Iran. Mem. Artists Equity Assn. Democrat. Address: RR# 1 Cochranville PA 19330

SAZIMA, HENRY JOHN, oral and maxillofacial surgery educator; b. Cleve., Dec. 25, 1927; s. Henry Charles and Frances (Masin) S.; m. Carol Ann Watson, Sept. 10, 1955; 1 child, Holly Ann Sazima Davani. BS, Case Western Res. U., 1948, DDS, 1953; grad. sch. medicine, U. Pa., 1956-57; grad. sch. edn., Chapman Coll., 1967-69. Diplomate Am. Bd. Oral and Maxillofacial Surgery. Chief maxillfacial div. Naval Support Act, Saigon, Republic of Viet Nam, 1969-70; chmn. dental dept. Naval Med. Ctr., Phila., 1971-73, San Diego, 1979-80; spl. asst. dentistry Sec. Def. Health Affairs, Washington, 1973-77; comdg. officer Naval Dental Ctr., Parris Island, S.C., 1977-79; dep. chief dental div. Bur. Medicine and Surgery, Washington, 1980-82; comdg. officer Nat. Naval Dental Ctr., Bethesda, Md., 1982-83; dir. resources div. Chief Naval Ops., Washington, 1983-84; dep. commdr. for readiness and logistics Naval Med. Command, Washington, 1984-87, ret. rear admiral, 1987; now clin. assoc. prof. oral and maxillofacial surgery Georgetown U. Med. Ctr.; exec. dir. Acad. Dentistry Internat., 1988—; emeritus, 1995; cons., lectr., researcher in field. Co-author: Management of War Injuries, 1977; contbr. articles to profl. jours. Recipient Residents award St. Vincent Charity Hosp., 1957. Fellow Am. Coll. Dentists, Assn. Oran and Maxillofacial Surgeons, Internat. Assn. Oral and Maxillofacial Surgeons, Acad. Dentistry Internat. (Blue Cloud award 1995); mem. Brit. Soc. Oral and Maxillofacial Surgeons, European Assn. Maxillofacial Surgery, Assn. Mil. Surgeons of U.S. (chmn. internat. com. 1984-86, Margetis award 1971), Internat. Coll. Dentists (dep. regent 1971-87), Omicron Kappa Upsilon, Delta Tau Delta, Psi Omega. Republican. Roman Catholic. Club: Mil. Order of CARABAO. Avocations: sports, tennis, music, travel. Home: 4924 Sentinel Dr Apt 105 Bethesda MD 20816-3506 Office: Acad Dentistry Internat Office of Exec Dir Ste 50 5125 Macarthur Blvd NW Washington DC 20016-3300

SBARBARO, ROBERT ARTHUR, banker; b. Bklyn., Jan. 24, 1933; s. John Vincent and Louise Olga (Perigone) S.; m. Kathleen Ann Noonan, Sept. 12, 1959; children—Robert, Paul, Nancy. B.A., Wagner Coll., 1954; grad., Stonier Sch. Banking, Rutgers U., 1977. CFP. Programming mgr. IBM, 1956-59; regional ops. mgr. Univac, 1959-65; asst. v.p., mgr. Computax Corp., N.Y.C., 1965-70; sr. v.p. Irving Trust Co., N.Y.C., 1970-89; pres. SPAR Cons., Montvale, N.J., 1989—. Mem. Montvale (N.J.) Recreation Commn., 1979-80; treas. Pascack Hills High Sch. Parents Assn., 1978-79; trustee Wagner Coll. Served with U.S. Navy, 1954-56. Recipient Alumni Achievement award Wagner Coll., 1987—. Mem. Data Processing Mgmt. Assn., Am. Banking Assn., Data Security Inst., Internat. Assn. for Fin. Planning. Republican. Roman Catholic. Avocation: sports. Home: 14 Sunrise Dr Montvale NJ 07645-1044 Office: SPAR Cons 14 Sunrise Dr Montvale NJ 07645-1044

SBORDON, WILLIAM G., publisher; b. Detroit, June 17, 1928; s. Victor George and Ernestine Marie (Schaible) S.; m. Edna Helen Nitkowski, June 18, 1949; children—Sharon A., William G., Carol M., David J., Edna J., James V. M.E., Wayne U., 1949. Dist. mgr. Plant Operation Mgmt., Detroit, 1965-69; dist. mgr. Design News, Detroit, 1969-76, Detroit mgr., 1972-76; nat. sales mgr. Modern Materials Handling, Boston, 1976-78, assoc. pub., 1978-80, v.p., pub., 1980—; v.p., pub. Cahners Pub. Co., Newton, Mass., 1980-93, v.p., pub. dir. OEM Group, 1993—. Mem. Bus. and Profl. Advt. Assn., Materials Handling Industry Am., Materials Handling Equipment Dist. Assn., Nat. Wooden Pallet and Container Assn., Inst. Caster Mfrs., Materials Handling Industry Am. (vice chmn.), Materials Handling Edn. Found., Inc. (pres.), Univ. Club. Roman Catholic. Avocations: gardening; woodworking; building. Office: Modern Materials Handling Cahners Publishing Co 275 Washington St Newton MA 02158-1646

SBUTTONI, KAREN RYAN, secondary school educator, reading specialist; b. Albany, N.Y., Sept. 9, 1953; d. Patrick Frederick and Virginia Mary (Moore) Ryan; m. Michael James Sbuttoni, Aug. 9, 1975; children: Michael Louis, Ashley Ryan. BS in Bus. Edn., Buffalo State Coll., 1979; MS in Bus. Edn., SUNY, Albany, 1983, MS in Reading, 1991, CAS in reading, 1994. Cert. reading specialist K-12 and bus. edn. 7-12, N.Y. Tchr. Williamsville East H.S., Buffalo, N.Y., spring 1979, East Irondequoit H.S., Rochester, N.Y., 1979-81; tchr., mem. admissions com. and outcomes com. The Albany Acad., 1992—; tchg. asst. SUNY, Albany, 1992. Religious edn. tchr. St. Pius X Ch., Loudonville, N.Y., 1982-84. Mem. Internat. Reading Assn., Nat. Coun. Tchrs. English. Avocations: skiing, biking, reading, cross-stitching. Office: The Albany Acad Academy Rd Albany NY 12208

SCAFE, LINCOLN ROBERT, JR., sales executive; b. Cleve., July 28, 1922; s. Lincoln Robert and Charlotte (Hawkins) S.; student Cornell U., 1940-41; m. Mary Anne Wilkinson, Nov. 14, 1945; children—Amanda Katharine, Lincoln Robert III. Service mgr. Avery Engring. Co., Cleve., 1946-51; nat. service mgr. Trane Co., LaCrosse, Wis., 1951-57; service and installation mgr. Mech. Equipment Supply Co., Honolulu, 1957-58; chief engr. Sam P. Wallace of Pacific, Honolulu, 1958-62; pres. Air Conditioning Service Co., Inc., Honolulu, 1962-84; sales engr. G.J. Campbell & Assocs., Seattle, 1984-89. Served with USNR, 1942-45; PTO. Mem. ASHRAE, Alpha Delta Phi. Clubs: Cornell Hawaii (past pres.); Outrigger Canoe. Republican. Author tech. service lit. and parts manuals; contbr. articles to trade publs. Home: 10721 SW 112th St Vashon WA 98070-3044 Office: GJ Campbell and Assocs 11613 Rainier Ave S Seattle WA 98178-3945

SCAFFIDI, JUDITH ANN, school volunteer program administrator; b. Bklyn., Aug. 2, 1950; d. Anthony William and Rose Virginia (Nocera) S. BA, SUNY, Plattsburg, 1972, MS, 1973; postgrad. Kennedy Learning Ctr., Einstein Coll. Medicine, 1983; PhD (hon.), Internat. U. Bombay, 1993; HHD (hon.), London Inst. Applied Rsch., 1993. Cert. secondary edn. English. VISTA mem. ACTION, N.Y.C., 1976-77; coord. cultural resources N.Y.C. Sch. Vol. Program, N.Y.C., 1977-80; dist. coord. in Bklyn. N.Y.C. Sch. Vol. Program, 1980—; field supr., adj. faculty Coll. for Human Svcs., N.Y.C., 1984-86; adv. coun. chairperson Ret. Sr. Vol. Program in Bklyn., 1983-86; adv. bd. Ret. Sr. Vol. Program in N.Y.C., 1983-86. Mem. Am. Friends Svc. Com., 1994—. Recipient award for svcs. in promotion literacy Internat. Reading Assn. and Bklyn. Reading Coun., 1986, award for outstanding leadership Ret. Sr. Vol. Program, 1986, cert. of appreciation Mayor City of N.Y., 1991,. Mem. NAFE, Nat. Sch. Vol. Program Ptnrs. in Edn., Cath. Tchrs. Assn. Bklyn. (del. sch. dist. 18, 1982-91), Am. Mus. Natural History, Internat. Platform Assn., World Found. Successful Women, Am. Biog. Inst. (rsch. bd. advisors 1992-93), Am. Biog. Inst. Rsch. Assn. (bd. govs. 1992—), Internat. Parliament for Safety and Peace (dep. mem. and diplomatic passport), Maisson Internat. de Intellectuels (Acad. MIDI), Cath. Alumni Club N.Y., Amnesty Internat. Roman Catholic. Avocations: foreign and domestic travel, reading, walking. Home: 2330 Ocean Ave Apt 3H Brooklyn NY 11229-3036 Office: NYC Sch Vol Program 352 Park Ave S 15th Fl New York NY 10010

SCAGLIONE, ALDO DOMENICO, literature educator; b. Turin, Italy, Jan. 10, 1925; came to U.S., 1951, naturalized, 1958; s. Teodoro and Angela (Grasso) S.; m. Jeanne M. Daman, June 28, 1952 (dec. June 1986); m. Marie M. Burns, Aug. 28, 1992. D.Modern Letters, U. Torino, 1948. Lectr. U. Toulouse, France, 1949-51; instr. Italian U. Chgo., 1951-52; mem. faculty U. Calif., Berkeley, 1952-68, prof. Italian and comparative lit., 1963-68, chmn. dept. Italian, 1963-65; W.R. Kenan prof. Romance langs., comparative lit. U. N.C., Chapel Hill, 1968-87; prof. Italian NYU, N.Y.C., 1987—, chmn. Italian dept., 1989-93, Erich Maria Remarque prof. lit., 1991—; vis. prof. Romance langs. Yale, 1965-66; vis. prof. comparative lit. Grad. Center, City U. N.Y., 1971-72; vis. prof. Italian, U. Va., fall, 1986; H.F. Johnson research prof. Inst. for Research in Humanities, Madison, Wis., 1981-82; Asso. Columbia U. Renaissance Seminar. Author: Nature and Love in the Late Middle Ages, 1963, Ars Grammatica, 1970, The Classical Theory of Composition, 1972, The Theory of German Word Order, 1981, Komponierte Prosa von der Antike bis zur Gegenwart, 2 vols., 1981, The Liberal Arts and the Jesuit College System, 1986, Knights at Court: Courtliness, Chivalry, and Courtesy from Ottonian Germany to the Italian Renaissance, 1991; also articles; editor: Orlando Innamorato, Amorum Libri, 2 vols., rev. edit., 1963, Francis Petrarch, Six Centuries Later: A Symposium, 1975, Ariosto 1974 in America, 1976, The Emergence of National Languages: A Symposium, 1984, The Divine Comedy and The Encyclopedia of Arts and Sciences, 1987, The Image of the Baroque, 1995, Series L'Interprete and Speculum Artium, Longo Editore, Ravenna, 1976—, (with Peter Lang) Series Studies in Italian Culture: Literature in History, 1989—; editor: Italian Culture, 1978-80; gen. editor: Romance Notes and N.C. Studies in Romance Langs. and Lits., 1971-75; assoc. editor: Romance Philology, 1963—, N.C. Studies in Comparative Literature, 1968-87, Studies in Philology, 1969-87, Amsterdam Studies in the History of Linguistics, 1977—, Annali d'Italianstica, 1983—, The Comparatist, 1983—, Differentia, 1984—, Italica, 1984—; U.S. corr.: Studi Francesi, 1961—. Chmn. Berkeley campus campaign Woodrow Wilson Nat. Found., 1964-65. Served with Italian Liberation Army, 1944-45. Decorated Knight Order of Merit (Italy); Fulbright fellow, 1951; Guggenheim fellow, 1958; Newberry Library sr. resident fellow Chgo., 1965; fellow Southeastern Inst. for Medieval and Renaissance Studies, 1968; fellow Cini Found. Program in Medieval and Renaissance Culture, 1973; fellow German Acad. Exchange, W.Ger., 1977, 80; fellow Rockefeller Found. Conf. and Study Center, Bellagio, Italy, 1978; dir. NEH Seminar for Coll. Tchrs., Chapel Hill, N.C., 1981. Mem. MLA (exec. coun. 1981-85), Internat. Linguistic Assn., N.Am. Assn. for History of Lang. Scis. (pres. 1989-92), Am. Boccaccio Assn. (pres. 1980-81), Am. Assn. Italian Studies (v.p. 1981-83, hon. pres. 1988-89), Renaissance Soc. Am., Dante Soc. Am. (coun. 1975-78, 81-83, 89-92), Am. Assn. Tchrs. Italian, Medieval Acad. Am., Am. Comparative Lit. Assn., Renaissance Soc. No. Calif. (pres. 1962-63). Home: 3 Reading Ave Frenchtown NJ 08825-1013 Office: 24 W 12th St New York NY 10011

SCALA, JAMES, health care industry consultant, author; b. Ramsey, N.J., Sept. 16, 1934; s. Luigi and Lorene (Hendrickson) S.; m. Nancy Peters, June 15, 1957; children: James, Gregory, Nancy, Kimberly. B.A., Columbia U., 1960; Ph.D., Cornell U., 1964; postgrad., Harvard U., 1968. Staff scientist Miami Valley Labs., Procter and Gamble Co., 1964-66; head life scis., dir. fundamental research Owens Ill. Corp., 1966-71; dir. nutrition T.J. Lipton Inc., 1971-75; dir. health scis. Gen. Foods Corp., 1975-78; v.p. sci. and tech. Shaklee Corp., San Francisco, 1978-85, sr. v.p. sci. affairs, 1986-87; lectr. Georgetown U. Med. Sch., U. Calif.-Berkeley extension. Author: Making the Vitamin Connection, 1985, The Arthritis Relief Diet, 1987, 89, Eating Right for a Bad Gut, 1990, 92, The High Blood Pressure Relief Diet, 1988, 90, Look 10 Years Younger, Feel 10 Years Better, 1991, 93, Prescription for Longevity, 1992, 94, If You Can't/Won't Stop Smoking, 1993; editor: Nutritional Determinants in Athletic Performance, 1981, New Protective Roles for Selected Nutrients, 1989; columnist Dance mag.; contbr. articles on nutrition and health scis. to profl. publs. With USAF, 1953-56. Disting. scholar U. Miami, Fla., 1977, Fla. Atlantic U., 1977. Mem. AAAS, Am. Inst. Nutrition, Am. Coll. Nutrition, Brit. Nutrition Soc., Sports Medicine Coun., Am. Soc. Cell Biology, Inst. Food Technologists, Astron. Soc. Pacific (bd. dirs., chmn. devel. coun.), Am. Dietetic Assn., Olympic Club (San Francisco), Oakland Yacht Club, Sigma Xi. Republican. *I am in awe of the incredible resiliency of living things, but most of all the human spirit.*

SCALA, JOHN CHARLES, secondary education educator, astronomer; b. Summit, N.J., Mar. 20, 1958; s. John Michael and Lola Ann (Bevilacque) S.; m. Virginia Anne Ronen, Oct. 11, 1980; children: Aubrey Lyn, Valerie Anne. BA in Astronomy, Lycoming Coll., 1980. Tchr. Stetson Mid. Sch., West Chester, Pa., 1980-82, Mendham (N.J.) H.S., 1982-83, Hopatcong (N.J.) Mid. Sch., 1983; shipment insp. Ciba-Geigy Pharms., Summit, 1983-87; tchr., dir. planetarium Lenape Valley H.S., Stanhope, N.J., 1987—; adj. prof. astronomy County Coll. Morris, Randolph, N.J., 1983-89, Sussex County C.C., Newton, N.J., 1989—; resource tchr. Am. Astron. Soc., Austin, Tex., 1994—. Merit badge counsellor Morris-Sussex coun. Boy Scouts Am., 1988—. Recipient Gov.'s Recognition award N.J. Dept. Edn., 1991, award A-Plus for Kids Network, 1993; named Tchr. of Yr., Lenape Valley H.S., 1995; Geraldine R. Dodge Found. grantee, summer 1993. Mem. NSTA, Internat. Planetarium Soc., Mid. Atlantic Planetarium Soc., Garden State Planetarium Resource Assn. Avocations: photography, reading, camping. Office: Lenape Valley HS Planetarium Sparta Rd Stanhope NJ 07874

SCALA, MARILYN CAMPBELL, special education educator, writer, consultant; b. Lansing, Mich., June 25, 1942; d. Coral Edward and Eloise (Doolittle) Campbell; children: Nicholas, Anne. BS Edn., U. Mich., 1964; MA Spl. Edn., Columbia U., 1967. Cert. elem. edn., spl. edn. tchr., N.Y. Tchr. physically handicapped Multi-Age, Port Chester, N.Y., 1964-66; tchr. spl. edn. PS 199, N.Y.C., 1966-69, Manhattan Sch. for Seriously Disturbed, N.Y.C., 1969-70; tchr. regular and spl. edn. Munsey Park Sch., Manhasset, N.Y., 1970—. Co-author: Three Voices: An Invitation to Poetry Across the Curriculum; contbr. articles to profl. jours. Recipient Disting. Svc. award Bd. Edn., Manhasset, 1989-90. Mem. Manhasset Edn. Assn. (corr. sec. 1992-95), Tchr. Resource Ctr. Bd., Dist. Shared Decision Making Team, Delta Kappa Gamma. Avocations: reading, writing, travel, museum visits. Office: Munsey Park Sch Hunt Lane Manhasset NY 11030

SCALA, SINCLAIRE MAXIMILIAN, retired aerospace engineer; b. Charleston, S.C., June 27, 1929; s. George and Goldie (Bocker) S.; m. Enid Joan Perlin, Mar. 25, 1951; children: Howard Alexander, Richard Perlin, Susanna Linda. BME cum laude, CCNY, 1950; postgrad., Columbia U., 1950, NYU, 1950-51; MME, U. Del., Newark, 1953; MA, Princeton U., 1955, PhD, 1957; MBA, U. Pa., 1978. Advanced devel. engr. Westinghouse Elec. Corp., Lester, Pa., 1951-53; rsch. fellow Princeton (N.J.) U. James Forrestal Rsch. Ctr., 1953-56; rsch. engr. GE, Phila., 1956-58, cons. high altitude gas dynamics, 1958-59, mgr. high altitude aerodynamics, 1959-64, mgr. theoretical fluid physics, 1964-68, mgr. fluid physics projects, 1968-69, mgr. environ. scis. lab., 1969-73, chief scientist, 1973-74, sr. cons. scientist, 1974-80, tech. dir. ind. R & D program, 1974-80, mgr. adv. weapons concepts, 1980-82, tech. dir. profl. devel. and edn. program, 1974-82, chmn. rsch. & engring. productivity coun., 1979-82; v.p. advanced engring. Fairchild Republic Co., Farmingdale, N.Y., 1982-83, v.p. advanced systems & tech. devel., 1983-84, v.p. strategic def., 1984-85, v.p. research, 1985-86, dir. rsch. and advanced product devel., 1986-87; dir. advanced programs Grumman Aircraft Systems, Bethpage, N.Y., 1987-91; dir. bus. planning Grumman Corp. Ops., Bethpage, 1991-94, ret., 1994; lectr. dept. physics Temple U., Phila, 1960-61; guest lectr. MIT, 1964-66; Colloquium lectr. various univs. to date; gen. chmn. AFOSR/GE Symposium on Dynamics of Manned Lifting Planetary Entry, Phila., 1962; mem. NASA Research & Tech. Adv. Subcom. on Fluid Mechanics, Washington, 1965-70; mem. indsl. and profl. adv. council dept. aerospace engring. Pa. State U., 1969-73; cons. Engring. & Tech. Socs. Council of Delaware Valley, Inc., Phila., 1980-82; active various symposiums. Contbr. articles to profl. jours.; patentee in field. Pres. Wyncote-West Elkins Park Community Council, Montgomery Co., Pa., 1963-65; v.p. Cheltenham Council Civic Assns., 1964-65; bd. dirs. Parents Assn. Syracuse U., 1969-73; panel mem. Continuing Edn. Com. Commonwealth of Pa., 1976-77. Recipient Alumni award in mech. engring. CCNY, 1950; NYU teaching fellow, 1950-51, Guggenheim fellow, 1953-55, Bakhmeteff fellow, 1955-56. Fellow AIAA (assoc.); mem. Air Force Assn., Am. Def. Preparedness Assn., Am. Soc. Engring. Edn., Assn. for Unmanned Vehicle Systems, Nat. Mgmt. Assn., N.Y. Acad. Sci., Tech. Mktg. Soc. Am., U.S. Space Found., Army Aviation Assn. of Am., World Future Soc., Elfun Soc., Sigma Xi, Tau Beta Pi, Pi Tau Sigma. Home: 2107 Alexis Ct Tarpon Springs FL 34689-2053

SCALAPINO, DOUGLAS JAMES, physics educator; b. San Francisco, Dec. 10, 1933; s. John and Marie Constance (Pederson) S.; m. Diane Holmes Lappe, June 19, 1955; children: Lisa, Leigh, Kenneth, Lynne, Anne. BS, Yale U., 1955; PhD, Stanford U., 1961. Rsch. assoc. Washington U., St. Louis, 1961-62; rsch. assoc. U. Pa., Phila., 1962-64, asst. prof., 1964-66, assoc. prof., 1966-68, prof., 1968-69; vis. prof. U. Calif., Santa Barbara, 1968-69, prof., 1969—; prin. investigator Inst. for Theoretical Physics, Santa Barbara, 1979—; cons. E.I. Du Pont De Nemours & Co. Inc., Wilmington, Del., 1963-88; Faculty Rsch. lectr., U. Calif., Santa Barbara, 1983; IBM Almaden Rsch. Ctr., San Jose, Calif., 1989—; mem. sci. adv. bd. Superconductor Techs.Inc., Santa Barbara, 1987—; fellow Los Alamos Nat. Lab., 1992—. Contbr. articles to profl. jours. Fellow Alfred P. Sloan Found., 1964-66, fellowship, Guggenheim Found., 1976-77.; grantee NSF, U.S. Dept. Energy, pvt. corps., 1965—. Mem. NAS, Am. Acad. Arts and Scis., Phi Beta Kappa, Sigma Xi. Office: U Calif Dept Physics Santa Barbara CA 93106

SCALAPINO, LESLIE, poet; b. Santa Barbara, Calif., July 25, 1947; d. Robert Anthony and Dee (Jessen) S.; m. Wesley St. John, 1968 (div.); m. Tom White, 1987. BA, Reed Coll.; MA, U. Calif., Berkeley. co-publisher O Books. Author: O and Other Poems, 1975, The Woman Who Could Read Poems, 1975, The Woman Who Could Read the Minds of Dogs, 1976, Instead of An Animal, 1978, This Eating and Walking at the Sale Time Is Associated All Right, 1979, Considering How Exaggerated Music Is, 1982, That They Were at the Beach, 1985, How Phenomena Appear to Unfold, 1990, The Return of Painting, the Pearl and Orion: A Trilogy, 1991, crowd and Not Evening of Light, 1992, Objects in the Terrifying Tense Longing from Taking place, 1994, Defoe, 1995, The Front Matter, Dead Souls, 1996, Selected Writings, 1996; editor: I One-An Anthology, 1988, O Two-An Anthology: What Is the Inside, What is the Outside?, 1991, War: O-Three, 1991, Subliminal Time-O Four, 1993. Nat. Endowment for Arts fellow, 1976, sr. fellow, 1986. Office: 5729 Clover Dr Oakland CA 94618-1622

SCALES, CLARENCE RAY, lawyer; b. Morton, Miss., Aug. 23, 1922; s. Felix Augustus and Zola (DuBose) S.; m. Lura Evelyn Lee, Aug. 20, 1948; children: Clarence Ray Jr., Linda Alcott, Philip Lee. LLB, U. Miss., 1949, JD, 1968. Miss. 1949. Ptnr. Scales & Scales, P.A., Jackson, Miss., 1949—. Democrat. Baptist. Home: 1022 Northpointe Dr Jackson MS 39211-2917 Office: 414 S State St Ste 201 Jackson MS 39201-5021

SCALES, DONALD KARL, dentist, military officer; b. Jacksonville, Fla., Apr. 7, 1960; s. Kenneth Ira and Marjorie Kathleen (Lahr) S. BS in Biology, The Citadel, 1982; DDS, Ind. U., 1989; postgrad., U. North Fla., 1982-85. Mem. affiliate faculty Ind. U. Dental Sch., Indpls., 1988-89; resident advanced edn. program in gen. dentistry MEDDAC student detachment U.S. Army, Ft. Carson, Colo., 1989-90; gen. dentistry officer 92d med. detachment, infection control officer U.S. Army, Hanau, Fed. Republic Germany, 1990-94; chief oral surgery Hanau Dental Clinic, 1990-91; dental surgeon 4th Brigade, 3d Infantry Divsn., 1991-92; clinic chief Aschaffenburg Dental Clinic, 1992; preventive dentistry officer/pub. health dentist 92d Med. Detachment, 1992-93; clinic chief U.S. Army Dental Clinic, Buedingen, 1993-94; dep. comdr. 92d Med. Detachment, 1994; dentist 86th Combat Support Hosp., Ft. Campbell, Ky., 1995—; dental cons. Westside Dental Care Ctr., Jacksonville, 1982—; lectr. and presenter in field; mem. exec. coun., mem. quality assurance com. 92nd Med. Detachment, 1991-92, Frankfurt (Germany) Dental Activity, 1993-94, Heidelburg (Germany) Dental Activity, 1994; rep. 7th Med. Command and U.S. European Command Dept. of Defense African Hosp. Project, 1993. Com. chmn. Panther edn. assistance program Hanau Am. H.S., 1990-94; CPR instr. Am. Heart Assn., Hanau, 1990-94; instr. dental asst. program ARC, Hanau, 1990-94. Mem. ADA, Acad. Gen. Dentistry, Assn. Mil. Surgeons of U.S., The Citadel Alumni Assn. (life), Ind. U. Alumni Assn. (life), Northeast Fla. Citadel Club, European Assn. Mil. Periodontist. Avocations: snow skiing, hiking, sailing, running, musical instruments. Home: USA DENTAC W2L8DC Fort Campbell KY 42223 Office: US Army Dentac Fort Campbell KY 42223

SCALES, JAMES RALPH, history educator, former university president; b. Jay, Okla., May 27, 1919; s. John Grover and Katie (Whitley) S.; m. Elizabeth Ann Randel, Aug. 4, 1944 (dec. Aug. 1992); children: Laura (dec.), Ann Catherine. B.A., Okla. Baptist U., 1939; M.A., U. Okla., 1941, Ph.D., 1949; postgrad., U. Chgo., 1941-42, 47-49, U. London, 1958; LL.D., Alderson Broaddus Coll., 1971, Duke U., 1976; Litt.D., No. Mich. U., 1972; L.H.D., Belmont Abbey Coll., 1981, Winston-Salem State U., 1984, William Jewell Coll., 1989. Reporter Miami (Okla.) News Record, 1934-35, Shawnee (Okla.) News-Star, 1935-36; instr. Okla. Baptist U., Shawnee, 1940-42, asst. prof., 1946-47, assoc. prof., 1947-51, prof. history, govt., 1951-61, v.p., 1950-53, exec. v.p., 1953-61, pres., 1961-65; dean arts and scis. Okla. State U., Stillwater, 1965-67; pres. Wake Forest U., Winston-Salem, N.C., 1967-83, Worrell prof. Anglo Am. studies, 1983—; founder Cimarron Rev., 1967—; Mem. Pres.'s Com. Edn. Beyond High Sch., 1957; mem. adv. com. U.S. Army Command and Gen. Staff Coll., Ft. Leavenworth, Kans., 1969-72, chmn., 1971-72; mem. U.S. del. UNESCO, 1978-81. Co-author: Oklahoma Politics: A History, 1983. Okla. del. Dem. Nat. Conv., 1956; bd. dirs. N.C. Civil Liberties Union; trustee Belmont Abbey Coll., 1977-80; mem. Bapt. Joint Com. on Pub. Affairs, 1990—. Signal officer USN, 1942-45. Named to Okla. Hall of Fame, 1983. Mem. Am. Hist. Assn., Am. Polit. Sci. Assn., AAUP, So. Assn. Bapt. Colls. (pres. 1969-70), Am. Guild Organists, N.C. Assn. Ind. Colls. (pres. 1969-71), Winston-Salem C. of C. (dir.), Nat. League for Nursing (hon.), Cherokee West, Phi Beta Kappa, Omicron Delta Kappa, Phi Eta Sigma. Baptist (deacon). Clubs: Rotary (Winston-Salem); University (N.Y.C.); Twin City (Winston-Salem); Bay Hill Golf and Country (Orlando, Fla.); Cape Fear (Wilmington, (N.C.); Miles Grant Country (Port Salerno, Fla.); Reform (London). Home: 5401 Indiana Ave A2 Winston Salem NC 27106-2809

SCALETTA, PHILLIP RALPH, III, lawyer; b. Iowa City, Iowa, Dec. 18, 1949; s. Phillip Jasper and Helen M. (Beedle) S.; m. Karen Lynn Scaletta, May 13, 1973; children: Phillip, Anthony, Alexander. BSIM, Purdue U., 1972, MS, 1972; JD, Ind. U., 1975. Bar: Ind. 1975, U.S. Dist. Ct. Ind. 1975, Ill. 1993. Assoc. Ice Miller Donadio & Ryan, Indpls., 1975-81, ptnr., 1981—. Contbr. articles to profl. jours. Chmn. Ind. Continuing Legal Edn. Found., Indpls., 1989; mem. Environ. Quality Control Water Com., 1988—. Mem. Ind. Bar Assn., Indpls. Bar Assn., Def. Rsch. Inst., Internat. Assn. Def. Counsel, Gyro Club Indpls. (v.p. 1992-93, pres. 1993-94, bd. dirs. 1990—). Avocations: golf, skiing, tennis. Home: 7256 Tuliptree Trl Indianapolis IN 46256-2136 Office: Ice Miller Donadio & Ryan 1 American Sq Indianapolis IN 46282-0001

SCALIA, ANTONIN, United States supreme court justice; b. Trenton, N.J., Mar. 11, 1936; s. S. Eugene and Catherine Louise (Panaro) S.; m. Maureen McCarthy, Sept. 10, 1960; children—Ann Forrest, Eugene, John Francis, Catherine Elisabeth, Mary Clare, Paul David, Matthew, Christopher James, Margaret Jane. A.B., Georgetown U., 1957; student, U. Fribourg, Switzerland, 1955-56; LL.B., Harvard, 1960. Bar: Ohio 1962, Va. 1970. Assoc. Jones Day Cockley & Reavis, Cleve., 1961-67; assoc. prof. U. Va. Law Sch., 1967-70; prof. law U. Va., 1970-74; gen. counsel Office Telecommunications Policy, Exec. Office of Pres., 1971-72; chmn. Adminstrv. Conf. U.S., Washington, 1972-74; asst. atty. gen. U.S. Office Legal Counsel, Justice Dept., 1974-77; vis. prof. Georgetown Law Center, 1977, Stanford Law Sch., 1980-81; vis. scholar Am. Enterprise Inst., 1977; prof. law U. Chgo., 1977-82; judge U.S. Ct. Appeals (D.C. cir.), 1982-86; justice U.S. Supreme Ct., Washington, 1986—. Editor: Regulation mag, 1979-82. Sheldon fellow Harvard U., 1960-61. Office: US Supreme Ct Supreme Ct Bldg 1 1st St NE Washington DC 20543-0002

SCALISE, CELESTE, lawyer; b. San Antonio, May 15, 1959; d. Robert and Edna (King) Scalise; m. James S. Boyd Jr., Oct. 6, 1984 (div. Dec. 1988); m. Marshall Bruce Lloyd, May 13, 1989 (div. July 1995). BA, U. Tex., San Antonio, 1979; JD, Tex. Tech U., 1983. Bar: Tex. 1984, U.S. Ct. Appeals (5th cir.) 1984, U.S. Dist. Ct. (so. dist.) Tex. 1985, U.S. Dist. Ct. (no. dist.) Tex. 1990, U.S. Dist. Ct. (we. dist.) Tex. 1991, U.S. Dist Ct. (ea. dist.) Tex. 1992. Field ops. asst. Bur. of Census U.S. Dept. of Commerce, San Antonio, 1980; title examiner, law clk. Lubbock (Tex.) Abstract & Title Co., 1982-83; assoc. Bonilla & Berlanga, Corpus Christi, Tex., 1983-89; sr. assoc. Heard, Goggan, Blair & Williams, San Antonio, 1989-90; assoc. Denton & McKamie, San Antonio, 1990, Joe Weiss and Assocs., San Antonio, 1990; assoc. field litigation office Cigna Law Offices of Sean P. Martinez, San Antonio, 1990—; mem. adv. group Camino Real Health Systems Agy., Inc., San Antonio, 1978-80. Mem. substance abuse adv. com. Planned Parenthood Bd., Corpus Christi, 1983-85; vice chair Nueces County Mental Health/Mental Retardation Substance Abuse Com., San Antonio, 1987-89. Mem. ABA (urban, state and local govt. sect., labor law sect.), Tex. Bar Assn., San Antonio Bar Assn., Bexar County Women's Bar Assn., U. Tex. at San Antonio Alumni Assn. (v.p.), Delta Theta Phi. Episcopalian. Avocations: photography, reading, gem and minerals collector. Home: 2130 W Gramercy Pl San Antonio TX 78201-4822 Office: Law Offices Sean P Martinez 300 Convent St San Antonio TX 78205-3701

SCALISH, FRANK ANTHONY, labor union administrator; b. Cleve., Nov. 5, 1940; s. John T. and Tillie M. (Rockman) S.; m. Carla Rita Cinti, 1960; children: John M., Frank A., Tina Marie. Grad. high sch., Cleve. Bus. agt. Local Union #1 Textile Processors Svc. Trades, Health Care Profl. and Tech. Employees Internat., Cleve., 1962—; sec., treas. Local Union #1, Cleve., 1978—; v.p. Internat. Union, Chgo., 1969-84, gen. pres., 1984—. Bd dirs. Cleve. Opera Theater, 1981-84. Recipient Israel Solidarity award Israeli Bonds, 1983. Roman Catholic. Avocations: hunting, fishing, golf, grandchildren. Office: Texile Processors Service Trades Health Care Prof Tech Employees 303 E Wacker Dr Ste 1109 Chicago IL 60601-5212

SCALLEN, THOMAS KAINE, broadcasting executive; b. Mpls., Aug. 14, 1925; s. Raymond A. and Lenore (Kaine) S.; m. Bille Jo Brice; children by previous marriage: Thomas, Sheila, Patrick, Eileen, Timothy and Maureen (twins). BA, St. Thomas Coll., 1949; JD, U. Denver, 1950. Bar: Minn. Asst. atty. gen. State of Minn., Mpls., 1950-55; sole practice Mpls., 1955-57; pres. Med. Investment Corp., Mpls., 1957—, Internat. Broadcasting Corp., Mpls., 1977—; owner Harlem Globetrotters; pres., exec. producer Ice Capades; chmn. bd. dirs. Century Park Pictures Corp., Los Angeles, chmn. bd. dirs. Blaine-Thompson Co., Inc., N.Y.C; chmn. Apache Plastics, Inc., Stockton, Calif. Served with AUS. Mem. World Pres. Orgn., Minn. Club, Calhoun Beach Club, L.A. Athletic Club. Clubs: University (St. Paul, Mpls.), Rochester (Minn.) Golf and Country, Edina (Minn.) Country, Athletic (Mpls.). Home: Heron Cove Windham NH 03087 Office: Internat Broadcasting Corp 80 S 8th St # 4701 Minneapolis MN 55402-2100

SCALZO, ROBERT EDWARD, middle school mathematics educator; b. Danbury, Conn., Aug. 13, 1941; s. John and Teresa (Falvo) S.; children by previous marriage: Laura L., William D., Robert M. BS, W.Va. State Coll., 1966; MA, Fairfield U., 1970, Cert. of Advanced Study, 1979. Cert. 7-12 history tchr., adminstr., supr. 4th-6th grade tchr. Mill Ridge Intermediate Sch., Danbury, 1966-79; 7th grade math. tchr. Rogers Park Mid. Sch., Danbury, 1980—. Vol. fireman Phoenix Hose Co. # 8, Danbury, 1960—, rec. sec., 1973—; usher St. Gregory The Great Ch., Danbury, 1980—. Recipient 25 Yr. Longevity award Phoenix Hose Co. # 8, 1985, Appreciation award Phoenix Hose Co. # 8, 1986, Appreciation award Danbury Vol. Firemen's Coun., 1987. Mem. NEA (Danbury grievance chairperson 1992—, Danbury bldg. chairperson 1986-90), Conn. Edn. Assn. (retirement commn. 1988—), Phi Delta Kappa (former rec. sec.). Democrat. Roman Catholic. Avocations: golf, biking, furniture refinishing, gardening. Home: 34 Ford Ln Danbury CT 06811

SCAMEHORN, JOHN FREDERICK, chemical engineer; b. York, Nebr., Oct. 26, 1953; s. Denver Alonzo and Mary Esther (Weber) S. BSChE, U. Nebr., 1973, MS, 1974; PhD, U. Tex., 1980. Registered profl. engr. Okla., Tex. Rsch. engr. Conoco, Ponca City, Okla., 1974-77; rsch. asst. U. Tex., Austin, 1977-80; rsch. engr. Shell Devel. Co., Houston, 1980-81; prof. U. Okla., Norman, Okla., 1981-92, Asahi glass chair, 1992—; v.p. Surfactant Assoc. Inc., Norman, 1987—; adv. bd. mem. EPA Hazardous Substance Rsch., Manhattan, Kans., 1989-90; organizer 65th Annual Colloid and Surface Sci. Symposium, Norman, 1991; assoc. editr. Jour Am. Oil Chemists Soc., 1986—; host radio show KGOU, Norman, 1984. Editor: Phenomena in Mixed Surfactant Systems, 1986, Surfactant Based Separation Processes, 1989, Solubilization in Surfactant Aggregates, 1995; contbr. articles to profl. jours. Bd. dirs. Opera Guild U. Okla., 1985-86. Recipient Cert. Appreciation ISEC Am. Chem. Soc., 1992. Mem. Am. Oil Chemists Soc. (mem. at large bd. 1990—), Am. Chemical Soc. (chair. elect. spearations subdivision 1994), Am. Inst. Chemical Engrs. Republican. Achievements include development of new techniques in surfactant-based separation processes, pioneering development of micellar-enhanced ultrafiltration for wastewater/groundwater, clean-up. Office: U Okla 100 E Boyd St Norman OK 73019-1000

SCAMMELL, MICHAEL, writer, translator; b. Lyndhurst, Hampshire, Eng., Jan. 16, 1935; s. Frederick George Talbot and Estelle Constance (Ayling) S.; m. Erika Roettges, Feb. 17, 1962 (div.); m. Rosemary Alise Nossiff, Aug. 11, 1990. BA with 1st Class Honours in Modern Langs., Nottingham (Eng.) U., 1958; PhD in Slavic Langs. and Lits., Columbia U., 1985. Lectr. in English Lang. and Lit. U. Ljubljana, Yugoslavia, 1958-59; instr. Russian Lang. and Lit. CCNY, 1961-63; dir. East European exchange program, N.Y. Inst. Humanities N.Y.U., N.Y.C., 1982-84; prof. dept. Russian Lit. Cornell U., Ithaca, N.Y., 1987-93, chair dept., 1987-92, dir. Soviet and East European Studies program, 1989-92; prof. writing and translation Sch. of the Arts, Columbia U., N.Y.C., 1994-96; bd. dirs. Internat. Ctr. Devel. Policy; freelance translator, N.Y.C. and London, 1962-65, London, 1967-71; lang. supr., programme asst. external svcs. East European divsn. BBC, London, 1965-67; founder, editor Index on Censorship, London, 1972-81; dir. Writers and Scholars Ednl. Trust, London, 1972-81; vis. prof. dept. Russian lit. Cornell U., 1986-87. Author: Blue Guide to Yugoslavia, the Adriatic Coast, 1969, Solzhenitsyn, a Biography, 1984, (L.A. Times Book prize 1984, Silver PEN award 1985); editor: Russia's Other Writers, 1970, La letteratura contemporanea nell'Europa dell'Est, 1977, Unofficial Art from the Soviet Union, 1977, The Solzhenitsyn Files, 1995; translator: Cities and Years (Konstantin Fedin) 1962, Crime and Punishment (Fyodor Dostoyevsky) 1963, The Gift (Vladimir Nabokov) 1963, The Defence (Vladimir Nabokov) 1964, Childhood, Boyhood & Youth (Leo Tolstoy) 1964, My Testimony (Anatoly Marchenko) 1969, To Build a Castle (Vladimir Bukovsky) 1978; author introduction Ressurection (Leo Tolstoy) 1963; contbg. translator various Slavic poetry anthologies; contbr. articles to profl. jours., reviews to newspapers. Internat. adv. com. Robert F. Kennedy Meml. Human Rights award, Washington, 1985-94. Cadet, Brit. Intelligence Corps., 1953-55. Post-grad. fellow Columbia U., 1959-61, sr. vis. fellow 1981-83, fellow, then assoc. fellow NYU, 1982-86, fellow Kennan Inst. Advanced Russian Studies, 1985, Post-doctoral fellow Harvard U., 1986; grantee Rockefeller Found., 1979, Ford Found., 1981-82, Leverhulme Trust, 1981-82, Nat. Endowment for the Humanities, 1993, Guggenheim Found., 1994; recipient Writers' bursary award Arts Coun. Gt. Britain, 1981, Humanities Divsn. award Ford Found., 1982-83. Mem. Internat. PEN (v.p. 1984—), PEN Am. Ctr. (v.p. 1995—), Internat. Acad. Scholarship and the Arts (bd. dirs. 1986—). Avocations: theatre, tennis, sailing. Office: Columbia Univ Writing divsn Sch Arts 412 Dodge Hall New York NY 10027

SCAMMON, RICHARD MONTGOMERY, political scientist; b. Mpls., July 17, 1915; s. Richard Everingham and Julia (Simms) S.; m. Mary Stark Allen., Feb. 20, 1952; 1 dau., Anne Valerie. A.B., U. Minn., 1935; A.M., U. Mich., 1938. Rsch. sec., radio office U. Chgo., 1939-41; with Office Mil. Govt. for Germany, U.S., 1945-48; chief, div. rsch. for Western Europe Dept. of State, 1948-55; dir. Elections Rsch. Center, 1955-61, 65-95; elections cons. NBC News, 1965-89; vis. fellow Am. Enterprise Inst.; mem. Israeli-Am. Electoral Conf., 1989; cons. to State Dept., 1979-80; dir. Bur. Census, Dept. Commerce, 1961-65. Co-author: The Real Majority; Editor: America Votes, America at the Polls. Chmn. U.S. delegation observe elections in, USSR, 1958; chmn. Pres.'s Commn. Registration and Voting Participation, 1963; mem. OAS electoral mission to, Dominican Republic, 1966; mem. Pres.'s Commn. to observe elections in Viet Nam, 1967; chmn. U.S. Select Commn. Western Hemisphere Immigration, 1966-68; pres. Nat. Council on Pub. Polls, 1969-70; mem. Pres.'s Commn. on Fed. Statistics, 1970-71, U.S. delegation Gen. Assembly UN, 1973, U.S. delegation observe elections in El Salvador, 1982; mem. Nat. Bipartisan Commn. on Central Am., 1983-84. Served with U.S. Army, 1941-46. Mem. Am. Polit. Sci. Assn., Am. Acad. Polit. and Social Sci., Acad. Polit. Sci. Club: Cosmos (Washington). Home: 5508 Greystone St Chevy Chase MD 20815-5534

SCANDALIOS, JOHN GEORGE, geneticist, educator; b. Nisyros Isle, Greece, Nov. 1, 1934; s. George John and Calliope (Broujos) S.; m. Penelope Anne Lawrence, Jan. 18, 1961; children: Artemis Christina, Melissa Joan, Nikki Eleni. B.A., U. Va., 1957; M.S., Adelphi U., 1960; Ph.D., U. Hawaii, 1965; D.Sc. (hon.), Aristotelian U. Thessaloniki, Greece, 1986. Assoc. in bacterial genetics Cold Spring Harbor Labs., 1960-62; NIH postdoctoral fellow U. Hawaii Med. Sch., 1965; asst. prof. Mich. State U., East Lansing, 1965-70; assoc. prof. Mich. State U., 1970-72; prof., head dept. biology U. S.C., Columbia, 1973-75; prof., head dept. genetics N.C. State U., Raleigh, 1975-85; disting. univ. research prof. N.C. State U., 1985—; mem. Inst. Molecular Biology and Biotechnology, Research. Ctr. Crete, Greece; vis. prof. genetics U. Calif., Davis, 1969; vis. prof. OAS, Argentina, Chile and Brazil, 1972; mem. recombinant DNA adv. com. NIH. Author: Physiological Genetics, 1979; editor: Developmental Genetics, Advances in Genetics, Current Topics in Medical and Biological Research; co-editor: Isozymes, 4 vols., 1975, Monographs in Developmental Biology, 1968-86; molecular biology editor Physiol. Plant, 1988—. Served with USAF, 1957. Alexander von Humboldt travel fellow, 1976; mem. exchange program NAS, U.S.-USSR. Fellow AAAS; mem. Genetics Soc. Am., Am. Soc. Biochemistry and Molecular Biology, Am. Genetic Assn. (pres.), Soc. Devel. Biology (dir.), Am. Inst. Biol. Scis., Am. Soc. Plant Physiologists, N.Y. Acad. Scis., Sigma Xi. Office: NC State U Dept Genetics PO Box 7614 Raleigh NC 27695

SCANDLING, WILLIAM FREDRIC, retired food service company executive; b. Rochester, N.Y., June 17, 1922; s. Fredric D. and Helen T. (Moran) S.; m. Margaret Warner, Apr. 19, 1949 (dec.); 1 child, Michael. A.B., Hobart Coll., 1949, LL.D. (hon.), 1967. Co-founding ptnr. ALS & Co., Geneva, N.Y., 1948, Saga Corp., Geneva, N.Y., 1949; co-founding ptnr. Saga Corp. (ALS and Saga Corp. merged), Menlo Park, Calif., 1962, dir., 1949-86, sec.-treas., 1949-68, pres., 1968-78, founder, dir., 1978-86; dir. Empire Broadcasting Corp., 1975-82; pres. Auburn Broadcasting Corp., Calif., 1975-82, dir., 1982-86. Trustee Hobart and William Smith Coll., Geneva, 1967—, chmn. 1971-82; trustee Deep Springs Coll., Calif., 1984-92, Nat. Council Salk Inst.; chmn., bd. dirs. Community Found. Santa Clara County, Calif., 1988-91. With USAAF, 1943-45. Mem. Kappa Alpha Soc., Menlo Country Club ((Woodside, Calif.), Seneca Yacht Club (Geneva), Genesee Valley Club (Rochester, N.Y.). Home: 134 Tuscaloosa Ave Atherton CA 94025

SCANDURA, JOSEPH MICHAEL, education researcher, software engineer; b. Bay Shore, N.Y., Apr. 29, 1932; s. Joseph and Lucy S.; m. Alice Baker, Aug. 13, 1960; children: Jeanne, Janette, Joseph, Julie. AB, U. Mich., 1953, MA, 1955; PhD, Syracuse U., 1962; postdoctoral, Stanford U., summer 1964, 68-69, U. Calif.-Berkeley, summer 1968, MIT, summer 1972; postgrad., U. Kiel, W.Ger., 1975, Inst. Ednl. Tech., Italy, summer 1978. Tchr. math., sci. White Plains, Bay Shore, 1953-56; instr. math., head wrestling coach Syracuse U., N.Y., 1956-63; asst. prof. edn., math. SUNY-Buffalo, 1963-64; research asst. prof. math. edn. Fla. State U., Tallahassee, 1964-66; dir. instructional systems, structural learning U. Pa., Phila., 1966—; founder, chmn. Intelligent Micro Systems, Narberth, Pa., 1978—; chmn. bd. sci. advisors MERGE Rsch. Inst., 1973; cons. jours., govt. agys., pub. cons., 1967—; cons. U.S. Office Edn., NSF, NAS, Tex. Instruments, Borg-Warner, U.S. Army; organizer, lectr., participant profl. confs., 1963—; dir. NATO Advanced Study Inst. on Structural Process Theories of Complex Human Behavior, 1977; coach undefeated Ea. Intercollegiate Wrestling Championship Team, 1963. Author: Mathematics - Concrete Behavioral Foundations, 1971, (with others) An Algorithmic Approach to Mathematics - Concrete Behavioral Foundations, 1971, Structural Learning I - Theory and Research, 1973, Problem Solving - A Structural Process Approach with Instructural Implications, 1977, (with A.B. Scandura) Structural Learning and Concrete Operations - An Approach to Piagetian Conservation, 1980, Cognitive Approach to Software Development, 1988, Prodoc (comprehensive suite of software devel. and maintenance tools), 1989, Cognitive Approach to Software Engineering and Re-engineering, 1991, Research on Program Modification under program control, 1992, NATO Advanced Study Inst., 1993, Automated Software Conversions and Re-engineering, 1993; contbr. over 170 articles to profl. jours.; editor: Research in Mathematics Education, 1967, Structural Learning II - Issues and Approaches, 1976, (with C.J. Brainerd) Structural Process Models of Complex Human Behavior, 1978; developer, producer numerous computer-based instructional systems and software devel. systems; patentee in field. Recipient Renssalaer award, 1949, Bausch and Lomb award, 1949, Nat. AAU Wrestling Champion and Outstanding Wrestler award, 1955; Fulbright scholar, 1975-76; U.S. Office Edn. fellow, 1978-79. Fellow APA (chmn. E.L. Thorndike award com. 1974-79); mem. AAUP, IEEE, Assn. Computing Machinery, Am. Ednl. Rsch. Assn. (past com. chmn.), Nat. Coun. Tchrs. Math. (past fed. funds com. chmn.), Math. Assn. Am., Psychonomic Soc., Structural Learning Soc. (chmn. 1969-80, 85-88, 95—, editor in chief Jour. Structural Learning 1976-90, Jour. Structural Learning and Intelligent Systems 1990—), Unif. Profs. for Acad. Order, Phi Kappa Phi, Phi Eta Sigma, Phi Delta Kappa. Home: 1249 Greentree Ln Narberth PA 19072-1219 Office: U Pa Instructional Systems Philadelphia PA 19104 *Accomodation to -- as well as leadership of -- groups, institutions and/or societies is an essential ingredient of success in most walks of life. There are circumstances, however, which require inner direction, whether developing a new scientific paradigm or standing firm against political pressures. Although vindication is rarely complete and often delayed, following one's best instincts yields its own rewards—perhaps the satisfaction of ultimately being proven right but more often simply knowing one did what had to be done.*

SCANES, COLIN GUY, animal sciences educator; b. London, July 11, 1947; s. Herbert Alfred and Marjorie Amy (Barltrop) S.; m. Carla Joy Turk, Apr. 25, 1976; children: Rosalind Amanda, Jaqueline Diana, Meredith Lyanne. BS, U. Hull, U.K., 1969; PhD, U. Wales, U.K., 1972; DSc, U. Hull, 1985. Lectr. U. Leeds, 1972-78; assoc. prof. Rutgrs U., New Brunswick, N.J., 1978-82; prof. animal sci. Rutgrs U., New Brunswick, 1982—, chmn. dept. animal sci., 1981—; mgr. USDA Competitive Grants Program, Washington, 1989-90; cons. in field. Editor 5 books; contbr. over 200 articles to profl. jours., numerous chpts. to books. NATO fellow, 1990-91; recipient Rutgers U. Trustees award for research, 1986. Mem. Am. Soc. Animal Sci., Am. Physiol. Soc., Poultry Sci. Assn., Endocrine Soc., Internat. Com. for Avian Endocrinology (pres. 1984-88), Animal Sci. Depts. Heads/Chairs Assn. (exec. com. chmn. 1990-91). Republican. Avocations: reading, running, family. Home: 1601 Van Buren Rd New Brunswick NJ 08902-3068 Office: Rutgers U Lipman Dr Cook Campus New Brunswick NJ 08903

SCANLAN, JAMES PATRICK, philosophy and Slavic studies educator; b. Chgo., Feb. 22, 1927; s. Gilbert Francis and Helen (Meyers) S.; m. Marilyn A. Morrison, June 12, 1948.;. BA, U. Chgo., 1948, MA, 1950, PhD, 1956. Research fellow Inst. Philos. Research, San Francisco, 1953-55; instr. Case Inst. Tech., Cleve., 1955-56; from instr. to assoc. prof. Goucher Coll., Balt., 1956-68; prof., dir. Slavic Ctr. U. Kans., Lawrence, 1968-70; prof. Ohio State U., Columbus, 1971-91, dir. Slavic Ctr., 1988-91, prof. emeritus, 1992—; vis. rsch. scholar Moscow State U., 1964-65, 69, Acad. Scis. USSR, Moscow, 1978, 93, Russian State U. for the Humanities, 1995; fgn. vis. fellow Slavic Rsch. Ctr., Hokkaido U., Sapporo, Japan, 1987-88. Author: Marxism in the USSR, 1985; editor: Historical Letters by Peter Lavrov, 1967, Soviet Studies in Philosophy, 1987-92, Russian Studies in Philosophy, 1992—, Technology, Culture and Development: The Experience of the Soviet Model, 1992, Russian Thought After Communism, 1994; co-editor: Russian Philosophy, 1965, Marxism and Religion in Eastern Europe, 1976. Served with USMC, 1945-46. Woodrow Wilson Internat. Ctr. fellow, 1982; recipient Translation award Nat. Translation Ctr., 1967, Faculty Research award Fulbright-Hays, 1982-83. Mem. Am. Philos. Assn., Am. Assn. Advancement Slavic Studies, Phi Beta Kappa. Home: 1000 Urlin Ave Apt 206 Columbus OH 43212-3324

SCANLAN, JOHN DOUGLAS, foreign service officer, former ambassador; b. Thief River Falls, Minn., Dec. 20, 1927; s. Paul Douglas and Ruby (Bennes) S.; m. Margaret Anne Calvi; children: Kathleen, Michael, Malia, John. B.A., U. Minn., 1952, M.A. in Russian Studies, 1955. Instr. U. Minn., 1955; Soviet research analyst U.S. Dept. State, Washington, 1956-58; third sec. Am. Embassy, Moscow, 1958-60; cultural attache Am. Embassy, Warsaw, 1961-65; second sec. Am. Embassy, Montevideo, 1966-67; prin. officer Am. Consulate, Poznan, Poland, 1967-69; sr. rep. to U.S. Dept. Defense, Washington, 1969-71; desk officer U.S.-Soviet bilateral relations, 1971-73; polit. counselor Am. Embassy, Warsaw, 1973-75; mem. state exec. seminar Washington, 1975-76; spl. asst. to Dir. Gen. of Fgn. Service, 1976-77; dep. dir. for Europe, USIA, 1977-79; dep. chief Mission in Belgrade, Yugoslavia, 1979-81; dep. asst. sec. of state for European affairs, 1981-82; fgn. affairs fellow Fletcher Sch. Law and Diplomacy, Tufts U., 1983-84; chmn. U.S. del. to Conf. on Security and Coop. in Europe, Cultural Forum Preparatory Conf., Budapest, 1984; amb. to Yugoslavia, Am. Embassy, Belgrade, 1985-89; dep. comdt. U.S. Army War Coll., Carlisle Barracks, Pa., 1989-91; v.p. East EUR, ICN Pharmaceutcals Inc.; mem. bd. Am. Drug Co., Project on Ethnic Rels.; mem. Kissinger-Sobchak St. Petersburg Commn., CSIS U.S.- European-Poland Action Commn.; adv. coun. ABA CEELI project. Mem. Planning Commn., Falls Church, Va., 1972-73, City Council, 1975-79. Recipient Presdl. Meritorious Service award for Diplomacy, 1984.

SCANLAN, JOHN JOSEPH, retired bishop; b. Ihiscarra, County Cork, Ireland, May 24, 1906; came to U.S., 1930; s. Peter Scanlan and Katherine Coleman. Student, Hallows Coll., Dublin, Ireland, 1923-30; LLD (hon.), Portland U., 1966; LHD (hon.), Chaminade U. Hawaii, 1980. Ordained priest Roman Cath. Ch., 1930. Asst. pastor Archiodese of San Francisco, 1930-50, pastor, 1950-54; aux. bishop Diocese of Honolulu, 1954-67, ordinary bishop, 1968-81, adminstr., 1981-82, ret., 1982; dir. archdiocesan coun. cath. men Archdiocese of San Francisco, 1952-54; mem. Cath. Philosophic Assn., San Francisco, 1940-50. Mem. Nat. Coun. Cath. Bishops. Home: Nazareth House 245 Nova Albion Way San Rafael CA 94903

SCANLAN, MICHAEL, priest, academic administrator; b. Far Rockaway, N.Y., Dec. 1, 1931; s. Vincent Michael and Marjorie (O'Keefe) S. BA, Williams Coll., 1953; JD, Harvard U., 1956; MDiv, St. Francis Sem., Loretto, Pa., 1975; LittD (hon.), Coll. Steubenville, 1972; LLD (hon.), Williams Coll., Williamstown, Mass., 1978; PdD (hon.), St. Francis Coll., Loretto, Pa., 1987. Ordained priest Roman Catholic Ch., 1964; Cross Pro Ecclesia et Pontifice, 1990. Acting dean Coll. Steubenville, Ohio, 1964-66, dean, 1966-69; rector pres. St. Francis Major Sem., Loretto, Pa., 1969-74; pres. Franciscan U. Steubenville, 1974—; mem. Pa. Fullbright Com., 1974; pres. FIRE Cath. Alliance for Faith, Intercession, Repentence and Evangelism, 1984—. Author: The Power in Penance, 1972, Inner Healing, 1974, A Portion of My Spirit, 1979, The San Damiano Cross, 1983, Turn to the Lord-A Call to Repentance, 1989, The Truth About Trouble, 1989, What Does God Want: A Practical Guide to Making Decisions, 1996; chmn. editl. bd. New Covenant mag., 1985-92. Mem. Diocese of Steubenville Ecumenical Commn., 1964-69; bd. dirs. Rumor Control Ctr., Steubenville, 1968-69, C. of C., Steubenville, 1976-79; bd. trustees St. Francis Prep. Sch., Spring Grove, Pa., 1969-74; vice-chmn., bd. trustees St. Francis Coll., Loretto, Pa., 1969-74; trustee United Way, Steubenville, 1975-80; chmn. nat. svc. com. Cath. Charismatic Renewal, 1975-78. Staff judge adv. USAF, 1956-57. Mem. Assn. Ind. Colls. and Univs. Ohio (sec. 1980-82), Nat. Cath. Edn. Assn. (vice-chmn. 1968-69), Cath. Edn. Assn. Pa. (chmn. sem. divsn. 1973), Ea. Major Sem.Rectors (sec. 1969), Fellowship of Cath. Scholars, Legatus. Roman Catholic. Avocations: tennis, golf. Office: Franciscan U Dept Academic Adminstr Franciscan Way Steubenville OH 43952 *If you are going to change something, you've got to live on vision, before you live on reality. You have to be so inspired by the vision, that you keep telling everybody until it gets in them, and they start living it with you.*

SCANLAN, RICHARD THOMAS, classics educator; b. St. Paul, May 30, 1928; s. Robert Lawrence and Catherine (Rockstroh) S.; m. Donna Mary Campion, Dec. 29, 1951; children: John, Susan, Catherine, Anne, Margaret. B.S., U. Minn., 1951, M.A., 1952. Tchr. Hastings High Sch., Minn., 1953-55, Edina High Sch., Minn., 1955-67; prof. classics U. Ill., Urbana, 1967—; ednl. cons., 1960-75. Author: Power in Words, 1983; computer courses, 1975, 77; Myths of Greece and Rome, 1986. Pres. bd. trustees Champaign Libr., 1980-92. With U.S. Army, 1946-48, Italy. Named Excellent Tchr. Am. Classical League, 1966; recipient Silver medal Nat. Coun. for Advancement of Edn., 1985. Mem. Am. Philol. Assn., Am. Classical League, Archaeol. Assn., Classical Assn. (Excellent Tchr.award 1974).

Roman Catholic. Home: 2103 Noel Dr Champaign IL 61821-6552 Office: Univ of Ill Dept of Classics Urbana IL 61801

SCANLAN, THOMAS CLEARY, publishing executive, editor; b. Birmingham, Mich., May 18, 1957; s. Thomas Matthew and Emily (Cleary) S.; m. Sally Sachs, June 20, 1981; children: Bridget C., Thomas M., Patrick J. BS, St. Louis U., 1979. Salesman Walter Heller Co., Chgo., 1979-82; pub., editor Surplus Record, Inc., Chgo., 1982—. Office: Surplus Record Inc 20 N Wacker Dr Chicago IL 60606-2806

SCANLAN, THOMAS JOSEPH, college president, educator; b. N.Y.C., Mar. 5, 1945; s. Thomas Joseph and Anna Marie (Schmitt) S. BA in Physics, Cath. U. Am., 1967; MA in Math., NYU, 1972; PhD in Bus. Adminstrn., Columbia U., 1978. Prin. Queen of Peace High Sch., North Arlington, N.J., 1972-75; dir. fin., edn. N.Y. Province, Bros. of Christian Schs., Lincroft, N.J., 1978-81; vice chancellor Bethlehem (Israel) U., 1981-87; pres. Manhattan Coll., Bronx, N.Y., 1987—; vice chmn. Commn. Ind. Colls. and Univs., 1996—, First Cova Life Ins. Co., 1993—. Trustee Lewis U., Romeoville, Ill., 1987—; bd. trustees Commn. on Ind. Colls. & Univs., 1994—, Assn. Cath. Colls. and Univs., 1994—. Recipient Pro Ecclesia et Pontifice medal, Pope John Paul II, Vatican City, 1986. Mem. Bros. of Christian Schs., Am. Coun. Edn., Assn. Cath. Colls. and Univs. (trustee 1994—), Assn. Am. Colls., Nat. Cath. Edn. Assn., Nat. Assns. Ind. Colls. and Univs., Nat. Collegiate Athletic Assn. (trustee Divsn. I), Metro Atlantic Athletic Assn., Equestrian Order of the Holy Sepulchre of Jerusalem, Phi Beta Kappa, Beta Gamma Sigma. Avocations: tennis, reading, movies. Office: Manhattan Coll Dept of Finance Manhattan Coll Pky Bronx NY 10471-3913

SCANLON, ANDREW, structural engineering educator; b. Bridge of Allan, Scotland, Apr. 16, 1944. BSc with honors, U. Glasgow, Scotland, 1966; PhD, U. Alta., Can., 1972. Civil engr. Pub. Works Can., Saint John, N.B., 1966-67; project engr. N.B. Devel. Corp., Fredericton, 1967-68; teaching asst. U. Alta., Edmonton, 1968-71; structural design engr. Duthie Newby and Assocs., Edmonton, 1971-73; structural divsn. head Reid, Crowther and Ptnrs. Ltd., Edmonton, 1973-78; sr. structural engr. structural evaluation sect. Constrn. Tech. Labs., Inc., 1978-80, mgr. analytical design sect., 1980-82; assoc. prof. civil engring. U. Alta., 1982-83, prof., 1983-87; prof. Pa. State U., University Park, 1987—, dir. transp. structures program. Pa. Transp. Inst., 1993—, acting head dept., 1991. Recipient Le Prix P.L. Pratley award Can. Soc. Civil Engring., 1990. Office: Pa State U 212 Sackett Bldg University Park PA 16802

SCANLON, CHARLES FRANCIS, army officer, retired, defense consultant; b. Nashville, Jan. 31, 1935; s. Francis James Gordon and Dorothy Rose (Compton) S.; m. Barbara Jean Schoen, Oct. 9, 1954; children: Teri, Brett, Ashlyn, Kellie. BA in Polit. Sci., U. Fla., 1960; grad., Command and Gen. Staff Coll., Ft. Leavenworth, Kans., 1970, Naval War Coll., Newport, R.I., 1977; MA in Am. Studies, U. Hawaii, 1974; postgrad., Pa. State U., 1982, Harvard U., 1984, 1992. Commd. 2d lt. U.S. Army, 1960, advanced through grades to maj. gen., 1988; chief collection U.S. Army Europe, Heidelberg, Germany, 1977-78; comdg. officer 66th Mil. Intelligence Brigade, Munich, 1978-80; chief ops. U.S. Army Intelligence and Security Command, Arlington, Va., 1980-82; exec. officer Dept. Army Asst. Chief Staff Intelligence, Washington, 1982-83; dep. commdr. gen. U.S. Army Intelligence and Security Command, Arlington, 1983-85; dir. estimates Def. Intelligence Agy., Washington, 1985-86, dir. attaches, 1986-90; comdg. gen. U.S. Army Intelligence and Security Command, Ft. Belvoir, Va., 1990-93; ret., 1993; pres. Def. and Internat. Consulting Svcs. Internat. Security, Counterintelligence Cons. Svcs., Fairfax Station, Va., 1993—. Decorated Def. D.S.M., Army D.S.M., Nat. Intelligence D.S.M., Legion of Merit with 3 oak leaf clusters, Bronze Star with 2 oak leaf clusters. Mem. Assn. U.S. Army, Nat. Mil. Intelligence Assn. (pres. 1974-76), Sigma Nu. Baptist. Avocations: boating, scuba diving, racquetball, soaring, reading. Home: 8036 Oak Hollow Ln Fairfax Station VA 22039-2627 Office: 8036 Oak Hollow Ln Fairfax VA 22039-2627 also: 435 Park Ave Satellite Beach FL 32937

SCANLON, DOROTHY THERESE, history educator; b. Bridgeport, Conn., Oct. 7, 1928; d. George F. and Mazie (Reardon) S.; AB, U. Pa., 1948, MA, 1949; MA, Boston Coll., 1953; PhD, Boston U., 1956; postdoctoral scholar Harvard U., 1962-64, 72. Tchr. history and Latin Marycliff Acad., Winchester, Mass., 1950-52; tchr. history Girls Latin Sch., Boston, 1952-57; prof. Boston State Coll., 1957-82, Mass. Coll. Art, 1982-95, prof. emerita, 1995—. Recipient Disting. Svc. award Boston State Coll., 1979, Faculty Award of Excellence, Mass. Coll. Art, 1985, Faculty Disting. Service award, Mass. Coll. Art, 1987. Mem. Pan-Am. Soc., Latin Am. Studies Assn., Am. Hist. Assn., Orgn. Am. Historians, Am. Studies Assn., Am. Assn. History of Medicine, History of Sci. Soc., AAUP, AAUW, Phi Alpha Theta, Delta Kappa Gamma. Author: Instructor's Manual to Accompany Lewis Hanke, Latin America: A Historical Reader, 1974; contbr. Biographical Dictionary of Social Welfare, 1986. Home: 23 Mooring Ln Dennis MA 02638 Office: Mass Coll Art Dept History 621 Huntington Ave Boston MA 02115-5801

SCANLON, EDWARD F., surgeon, educator; b. Waynesburg, Pa., Sept. 15, 1918; s. Hugh and Ellen S.; m. Virginia K. Scanlon, June 26, 1948; children: Cathy, Mary, Sally. B.S., Kenyon Coll., 1940, D.Sc. (hon.), 1983; M.D., Columbia U., 1943. Intern St. Luke's Presbyn. Hosp., Chgo., 1944; resident in surgery St. Luke's Presbyn. Hosp., 1946-50, Meml. Sloan Kettering, N.Y.C., 1950-53; fellow Meml. Sloan Kettering, 1953; mem. staff Evanston Hosp, Ill., 1953-89; chmn. dept. surgery Evanston Hosp, 1974-86; mem. faculty dept. surgery Northwestern U. Med. Sch., Chgo., 1953—, prof. surgery, 1971—, chief surg. oncology, 1974-86, emeritus prof., 1989—. Mem. editorial adv. bd. Cancer Treatment Reports, 1976-80, Jour. Surg. Oncology, 1982-93, Internat. Jour. Breast and Mammary Pathology, 1982-93, Seminars in Surg. Oncology, 1982-93; contbr. articles to med. jours. Bd. dirs. Evanston Hosp., 1977-86. Served with M.C., U.S. Army, 1944-46. Hayes Martin lectr., 1979, James Ewing lectr., 1984; recipient scholarship Shell Intercollegiate Aviation, 1940, Am. Cancer Soc. ann. divisional award, 1978. Fellow ACS (bd. govs. 1971-76); mem. Soc. Surg. Oncology (pres. 1974-75), Am. Cancer Soc. (pres. 1980-81), Internat. Union Against Cancer (com. internat. collaborative activities), Am. Surg. Assn., Soc. Head and Neck Surgeons (treas. 1974), Western Surg. Assn., Central Surg. Assn., Chgo. Surg. Soc., Phi Beta Kappa. Home: 1338 Edgewood Ln Northbrook IL 60062-4716

SCANLON, JANE CRONIN, mathematics educator; b. N.Y.C., July 17, 1922; d. John Timothy and Janet Smiley (Murphy) Cronin; m. Joseph C. Scanlon, Mar. 5, 1953 (div.); children: Justin, Mary, Anne, Edmund. Student, Highland Park Jr. Coll., 1939-41; BS, Wayne State U., 1943; MA, U. Mich., 1945, PhD, 1949. Mathematician Air Force Cambridge Research Center, 1951-54; instr. Wheaton Coll., Norton, Mass., 1954-55; asst. prof. Poly. Inst. Bklyn., 1957-58, asso. prof., 1958-60, prof., 1960-65; prof. math. Rutgers U., New Brunswick, N.J., 1965-91, prof. emerita, 1991—; cons. Singer-Kearfott Div., Naval Research Lab. Office Naval Research Fellow Princeton, 1948-49; Horace H. Rockham Postdoctoral fellow U. Mich., 1950-51, Rutgers Research Council fellow, 1968-69, 72-73; NSF vis. professorship for women Courant Inst., NYU, 1984-85. Author: Fixed Points and Topological Degree in Nonlinear Analysis, 1964, Advanced Calculus, 1967, Differential Equations: Introduction and Qualitative Theory, 1980, 2d edit., 1994, Mathematics of Cell Electrophysiology, 1980, Mathematical Aspects of Hodgkin-Huxley Neural Theory, 1987. Mem. Am. Math. Soc., Soc. for Indsl. and Applied Math., Math. Assn. Am., Internat. Soc. Chronobiology. Home: 110 Valentine St Highland Park NJ 08904-2106 Office: Rutgers U Dept Math New Brunswick NJ 08903

SCANLON, PATRICK MICHAEL, lawyer; b. Welch, W.Va., May 16, 1940; s. John Michael Scanlon and Jean Elizabeth (Hatfield) Irving; m. Joyce Janifer Haythorn, Feb. 27, 1965 (div. 1980); children: Alison Margaret, Janifer Colleen; m. Laura Reeves, Mar. 15, 1980; 1 child, Patrick Reeves. BA in Polit. Sci., U. Fla., 1965; JD, Stetson U., 1968. Bar: U.S. Dist. Ct. (no. dist.) Ga. 1969, U.S. Dist. Ct. (mid. dist.) Fla. 1971, U.S. Ct. Appeals (5th cir.) 1972, U.S. Supreme Ct. 1973, U.S. Ct. Appeals (6th cir.) 1975, Appeals (11th cir.) 1981, U.S. Dist. Ct. D.C. 1983. Assoc. Adair, Goldthwaite, Stanford, Atlanta, 1968-71, ptnr., 1971-76; v.p., treas. Adair, Goldthwaite & Daniel, P.C., Atlanta, 1976-80; exec. v.p. Adair & Goldthwaite, P.C., Washington, 1980-81; exec. v.p. Adair, Scanlon & McHugh, P.C., Washington, 1981-87, pres., 1987-88; gen. counsel Communications Workers of Am., Washington, 1988—; bd. dirs. AFL-CIO Lawyers Coordinating Com., Washington, 1988—, mem. Lawyers Adv. Panel, 1988—. Contbr. articles to profl. jours. With USNR, 1961-63. Mem. ABA (co-chair equal employment opportunity com. of labor and employment law sect. 1992-94). Democrat. Avocations: running, camping. Office: Communications Workers Am 501 3rd St NW Washington DC 20001-2760

SCANLON, PETER REDMOND, accountant; b. N.Y.C., Feb. 18, 1931; s. John Thomas and Loretta Dolores (Ryan) S.; m. Mary Jane E. Condon, Mar. 7, 1953; children: Peter, Barbara, Mark (dec.), Brian, Janet. BBA in Acctg., Iona Coll., 1952, LLD (hon.), 1992. CPA, N.Y. Mem. profl. staff Coopers & Lybrand, N.Y.C., 1956-66, ptnr., 1966-91, vice chmn., 1976-82, chmn., chief exec. officer, 1982-91, ret. chmn., 1991—; hon. ptnr. N.Y.C. Partnership, 1991. Lt. USN, 1952-56. Decorated Knight of Malta, Knight Holy Sepulchre; recipient Arthur A. Loftus award Iona Coll., 1974, Trustee award, 1990, Crain's N.Y. All Star award, 1990, Best in Class award Conf. Bd. Youth Edn., 1991. Mem. AICPA, N.Y. State Soc. CPAs, N.Y. Athletic Club. Roman Catholic. Office: Coopers & Lybrand 1251 Ave Of The Americas New York NY 10020-1104

SCANLON, ROSEMARY, economist; b. Inverness, N.S., Can., Dec. 25, 1939; d. Donald Angus and Mary Agnes (MacDonald) MacLellan; A.B., St. Francis Xavier U., N.S., 1959; M.A. (Ford Found. Scholar) U. New Brunswick, 1960; P.M.D., Harvard Bus. Sch., 1981; m. Michael Scanlon, Apr. 24, 1965 (div. 1979); children: Sean Donald, Jennifer; Instrn. econs. Coll. of William and Mary, Williamsburg, Va., 1960-63; asst. prof. Old Dominion U., Norfolk, Va., 1963-65; econ. analyst Port Authority of N.Y. and N.J., 1969-93; sr. economist for regional research, 1977-80, mgr. econ. devel. planning, N.Y.C., 1980-83, chief economist, 1983—; asst. dir. Planning and Devel. Dept., 1985; apptd. dep. state comtr., N.Y.C., 1993; bd. dirs. Nova Scotia Power, Inc. Bd. dirs. Rsch. Found. SUNY, 1987-93. Recipient Salute to Women in Business award YWCA of N.Y.C., 1980, Outstanding Achievement award, Exec. Dirs. award. Mem. Am. Econ. Assn., Nat. Council for Urban Econ. Devel. (bd. dirs. 1982-88). Author: The Arts as an Industry in N.Y.-N.J., 1983, The Arts as an Industry, 1993, The Regional Economy, 1993; (with others) Cities in a Global Soc., 1989; contbr. articles to profl. jours. Home: 10 Clinton St Apt 9T Brooklyn NY 11201-2710 Office: 270 Broadway New York NY 10007-2306

SCANLON, TERRENCE MAURICE, public policy foundation administrator; b. Milw., May 1, 1939; s. Maurice John and Anne (Hayes) S.; m. Judy Ball, June 14, 1969; children: Michael Mansfield, Justin Ball, Brendan Hayes. BS, Villanova U., 1961. Staff asst. The White House, Washington, 1963-67; with SBA, Washington, 1967-69; with Dept. of Commerce, Washington, 1969-83, mem. office Minority Bus. Enterprise, 1969-80, with Internat. Trade Adminstrn., 1980-81, with Minority Bus. Devel. Agy., 1981-83; mem. Consumer Product Safety Commn., Washington, 1983-89, vice chmn., 1983-84, chmn., 1985, 86-89; v.p., treas. The Heritage Found., Washington, 1989-91, v.p. corp. rels., 1991-94; chmn., pres. Capital Rsch. Ctr., Washington, 1994—. Am. Polit. Sci. Assn. Congl. fellow, 1967-68. Mem. Sovereign Mil. Order of Malta, University Club. Home: 4510 Dexter St NW Washington DC 20007-1115 Office: Capital Rsch Ctr Ste 800 727 15th St NW Washington DC 20005

SCANLON, THOMAS MICHAEL, lawyer; b. Indpls., Apr. 20, 1909; s. John H. and Anna C. (Ferriter) S.; m. Grace L. Barnett, July 10, 1937; children: Thomas M., Christopher G. A.B., Butler U., 1932; LL.B., Ind. U., 1935. Bar: Ind. 1935. Asso. Noel, Hickam, Boyd & Armstrong, Indpls., 1935-40; assoc. Barnes, Hickam, Pantzer & Boyd, 1940-43, ptnr., 1943-82; of counsel Barnes & Thornburg, 1982—; mem. Ind. Bd. Law Examiners, 1942-43, 47-52. Co-author: Preparation for Trial. Trustee emeritus Butler U. Served to lt. comdr. USNR, 1943-46. Fellow Am. Bar Found., Ind. Bar Found. (50-yr. award for disting. svc. 1986), Indpls. Bar Found.; mem. ABA (chmn. sect. antitrust law 1973-74), Ind. Bar Assn. (pres. 1955-56), Indpls. Bar Assn., Bar Assn. 7th Fed. Cir. (pres. 1956-57), Am. Law Inst. (life), Am. Coll. Trial Lawyers, Delta Tau Delta, Phi Delta Phi. Clubs: Lawyers of Indianapolis (Indpls.) (pres. 1964-65), Indpls. Literary (Indpls., pres. 1990-91), Woodstock (Indpls.), Players (Indpls., pres. 1962-63). Home: 9570 Copley Dr Indianapolis IN 46260-1430 Office: Merchants Bank Bldg Indianapolis IN 46204

SCANNELL, DALE PAUL, education educator; b. Iowa City, Mar. 3, 1929; s. Paul A. and Florence (Fieseler) S.; children—Steven, Jeffrey, Susan, Janet. B.A., U. Iowa, 1951, M.A., 1955, Ph.D., 1957. Tchr. Iowa City High Sch., 1950-51, 53-58; acting asst. prof. edn. U. Calif. at Berkeley, 1958-59; asst. prof. U. Kans., 1959-62, asso. prof., 1962-64, prof., 1964-67; assoc. dean U. Kans. (Grad. Sch.), 1963-67; prof. edn. U. Iowa, 1967-69; dean Sch. Edn. U. Kans., 1969-85; dean Coll. Edn. U. Md., College Park, 1985-91; prof. edn. Ind. U., Bloomington, 1994—; vis. prof., Lester prof. tchr. edn. U. S.C., 1993-94. Author: (with others) Tests of Academic Progress, 2d edit., 1971, Tests of Achievement and Proficiency, Form T, 1978, Form G, 1985, Form H, 1986, Form J, 1989, (with Oscar Haugh) Form K, 1993, Form L, 1993, Form M, 1995, Writing, Listening.Supplements, 1986, (with A.J. Edwards) Educational Psychology, 1968, (with V.H Noll and Robert Craig) Introduction to Educational Measurement, 4th edit., 1979, (with V.H. Holl and Rachel Noll) Introductory Readins in Educational Measurement, 1972, (with D.B. Tracy) Testing and Measurement in the Classroom, 1975. Served to lt. USAF, 1951-53. Mem. AAUP, Am. Ednl. Research Assn., Nat. Council Measurements in Edn., Phi Delta Kappa. Congregationalist. Club: Kiwanis. Home: 501 Copley Pl Indianapolis IN 46290-1050 Office: Ind Univ Dept of Ed Bloomington IN 47405 Office: IUPUI Indianapolis IN 46202

SCANNELL, WILLIAM EDWARD, aerospace company executive, consultant, psychologist; b. Muscatine, Iowa, Nov. 11, 1934; s. Mark Edward and Catharine Pearson (Fowler) S.; m. Barbara Ann Hoemann, Nov. 23, 1957; children: Cynthia Kay, Mark Edward, David Jerome, Terri Lynn, Stephen Patrick. BA in Gen. Edn., U. Nebr., 1961; BS in Engring., Ariz. State U., 1966; MS in Systems Engring., So. Meth. U., 1969; PhD, U.S. Internat. U., 1991. Commd. 2d lt. USAF, 1956, advanced through grades to lt. col., 1972; B-47 navigator-bombardier 98th Bomb Wing, Lincoln Air Force Base, Nebr., 1956-63; with Air Force Inst. of Tech., 1963-65, 68-69; chief mgmt. engring. team RAF Bentwaters, England, 1965-68; forward air contr. 20th Tactical Air Support Squadron USAF, Danang, Vietnam, 1970-71; program mgr. Hdqrs. USAF, Washington, 1971-74, staff asst. Office of Sec. Def., 1974-75, ret., 1975; account exec. Merrill Lynch, San Diego, 1975-77; program engring. chief Gen. Dynamics, San Diego, 1977-79, engring. chief, 1979-80, program mgr., 1980-83; mgr. integrated logistics support Northrop Corp., Hawthorne, Calif., 1984-88; mgr. B-2 program planning and scheduling Northrop Corp., Pico Rivera, Calif., 1988-91; pres. Scannell and Assocs., Borrego Springs, Calif., 1991—; mem. adj. faculty U.S. Internat. U., San Diego. Decorated DFC with three oak leaf clusters, Air medal with 11 oak leaf clusters. Mem. APA, Calif. Psychol. Assn., Soc. Indsl. and Orgnl. Psychology, Inst. Indsl. Engrs., Coronado Cays Yacht Club, Psi Chi. Republican. Roman Catholic. Home: 717 Anza Park Trail Borrego Springs CA 92004 Office: Scannell and Assocs PO Box 2392 Borrego Springs CA 92004-2392

SCARBOROUGH, CHARLES BISHOP, III, broadcast journalist, writer; b. Pitts., Nov. 4, 1943; s. Charles Bishop and Esther Francis (Campbell) S.; m. Linda Anne Gross, Dec. 14, 1972; children: Charles Bishop IV, Elizabeth Anne; m. Anne Ford Uzielli, Oct. 2, 1982; m. Ellen Carol Ward, Sept. 25, 1994. B.S., U. So. Miss., 1969. Prodn. mgr. Sta.-WLOX-TV, Biloxi, Miss., 1966-68; reporter, anchorman Sta.-WDAM-TV, Hattiesburg, Miss., 1968-69; reporter, anchorman, mng. editor Sta.-WAGA-TV, Atlanta, 1969-72; reporter, anchorman Sta.-WNAC-TV, Boston, 1972-74, NBC News, N.Y.C., 1974—. Author: (novels) Stryker, 1978, The Myrmidon Project, 1981, Aftershock, 1991. Served with USAF, 1961-65. Recipient awards for journalism AP (9), 1969-72, Emmy awards (22), 1974-94, award Aviation/Space Writers Assn., 1977, 78, 88, UPI award for journalism N.Y. Press Club award, 1988, 89, Sigma Delta Chi award, Deadline Club award, Terry Anderson Journalism award Working Press Assn. N.J., 1992. Mem. Phi Kappa Phi. Office: NBC News 30 Rockefeller Plz New York NY 10112

SCARBOROUGH, JOE, congressman; b. Atlanta, Apr. 9, 1963; m. Melanie Scarborough; Children: Joey, Andrew. BA, U. Ala., 1985; JD, U. Fla., 1990. Atty., 1990—; mem. 104th Congress from 1st Fla. dist., 1995—. Tchr. Sunday sch. 1st Bapt. Ch. Mem. Young Lawyer's Assn., Fellowship Christian Athletes. Republican. Office: US Ho of Reps 1523 Longworth Washington DC 20515

SCARBOROUGH, ROBERT HENRY, JR., coast guard officer; b. Hawkinsville, Ga., Mar. 12, 1923; s. Robert Henry and Janet Augusta (Burton) S.; m. Walterene Brant, July 1, 1946; children—Robert Henry, James Burton. BS, U.S. Mcht. Marine Acad., 1944; BBA, U. Hawaii, 1969, MBA, 1971; M.S., George Washington U., 1971, Armed Forces Staff Coll., 1963, Nat. War Coll., 1971. Commd. lt. (j.g.) USCG, 1949; advanced through grades to vice adm., 1978; chief Office of Ops. USCG, 1974-75, chief of staff, 1975-77, comdr. 9th Coast Guard Dist., 1977-78; vice comdt. USCG, Washington, 1978-82; ret. USCG, 1982; exec. dir. Navy League U.S., 1982-84; pres. Polaris Potomac Corp., 1985—. With USNR, 1942-49. Decorated Legion of Merit, D.S.M. Mem. Beta Gamma Sigma. Office: 5357 37th St N Arlington VA 22207-1312

SCARBROUGH, CLEVE KNOX, JR., museum director; b. Florence, Ala., July 17, 1939; s. Cleve Knox and Emma Lee (Matheny) S. B.S., U. No. Ala., 1962; M.A., U. Iowa, 1967. Asst. prof. art history U. Tenn., 1967-69; dir. Mint Mus. Art, Charlotte, N.C., 1969-76, Hunter Mus. Art, Chattanooga, 1976—; pres. N.C. Mus. Coun., 1976; bd. mem. adv. com. Tenn. Arts Commn., 1976-77, chmn. visual arts com., 1978—; mem. art selection com. TVA, 1983—, Provident Life Ins. Co., 1983—; cons. Mus. Assessment Program, 1984-94; grant evaluator Inst. Mus. Svcs., 1985-86; mem. art adv. com. First Tenn. Corp., 1991; lectr. Tenn. Gov.'s Conf. on the Arts, 1991. Compiler, editor: North Carolinians Collect, 1970, Pre Columbian Art of the Americas, 1971, Graphics by Four Modern Swiss Sculptors, 1972, British Paintings from the North Carolina Museum, 1973, Montain Landscapes by Swiss Artists, 1976. Mem. Chattanooga Landmark Com.; mem. City Planning Bd.; Bd. dirs. Chattanooga Conv. and Visitors Bur., 1977-79; advisor Chattanooga Cen. City Council, 1981-85, Tenn. State Mus., 1981, mem. Am. Federation of Arts Adv. Bd., 1987—. Served with USN, 1962-64. Mem. Am. Assn. Museums (accreditation vis. com. 1985-94), Southeastern Mus. Conf. (coun. 1976-80, 86-88, chmn. publs. com. 1979, rep. to Am. Assn. Mus.; bd. dirs. 1986-88), Rotary. Office: Hunter Mus Art 10 Bluff View St Chattanooga TN 37403-1111

SCARBROUGH, FRANK EDWARD, government official; b. Knoxville, Tenn., Sept. 27, 1942; s. James L. and Anna Dale (Edwards) S.; m. Deborah Griffin, Feb. 4, 1972; 1 child, Elizabeth Anne. BS, U. Tenn., 1964; AM, Harvard U., 1966, PhD, 1971. Rsch. assoc. U. Bern, Switzerland, 1971-73; instr. U. Pa., Phila., 1973-76; chemist food additive rev. FDA, Washington, 1977-80, chief regulatory affairs staff, 1980-86, dep. dir. Office Nutrition, 1986-89, dir. Office Nutrition, 1989-92, dir. Office Food Labeling, 1992—. Contbe. author: Food Labeling, 1994. Recipient award of merit FDA, 1985, Superior Svc. award USPHS, 1991, Disting. Svc. award HHS, 1993. Mem. Am. Chem. Soc., Am. Soc. Clin. Nutrition, Inst. Food Technologists. Office: FDA Office of Food Labeling 200 C St SW Washington DC 20204-0001

SCARBROUGH-LUTHER, PATSY WURTH, geographic information systems specialist; b. Paducah, Ky., Dec. 5, 1947; d. James Edward and Olean Barbara (Sietz) Wurth; m. Jerry Leon Scarbrough, Aug. 7, 1965 (div. 1985); children: Tracy Ann, Ashli Michele, Scott Jeremy; m. Robert W. Luther, Feb. 25, 1995. BS magna cum laude, Murray (Ky.) State U., 1988, MS, 1991. Cert. emergency med. technician. Instr. Ky. Cabinet for Human Resources, Frankfort, 1983-93, Vocat. Edn. Region I, Paducah, Ky., 1983-91, Murray State U., 1983-91, Calloway County Red Cross, Murray, 1985-89; exec. dir. Marshall County Red Cross, Benton, Ky., 1985-88; first aid attendant Ohio River Steel, Calvert City, Ky., 1985-86; profl. intern Johnson Controls, Cadiz, Ky., 1986; grad. asst. Murray State U., 1988-91; fellow U.S. Dept. Energy/Oak Ridge (Tenn.) Nat. Lab., 1989-90; postgrad. rsch. fellow U.S. Army Corps Engrs. Constrn. Engring. Rsch. Lab., Champaign, Ill., 1991-92, acting team leader spatial techs. support team, 1992-93; GIS facility mgr. environ. scis. divsn. Oak Ridge (Tenn.) Nat. Lab., 1993-95; mgr. GIS svcs. Solutions to Environ. Problems, Inc., Oak Ridge, 1995—. Troop leader Kentuckiana Girl Scouts, Benton, 1973-84, fund drive chmn., 1973-84. Mem. LWV, Am. Soc. Safety Engrs., Ky. EMT Instrs. Assn. (instr.), Western Ky. EMT Assn., Am. Soc. Photogrametry and Remote Sensing (Western Great Lake region sec., treas. 1992), Nat. Safety Coun. (cmty. health and emergency svcs. com.), Assn. Women in Sci., Tenn. Geog. Info. Coun., S.E. Regional ARC/INFO Users Group (chair 1995), Nat. Assn. Environ. Profls., Epsilon Pi Tau, Alpha Chi. Democrat. Roman Catholic. Home: 330 Melton Hill Dr Clinton TN 37716 Office: Solutions to Environ Problems Inc 1006 Culler Ct Oak Ridge TN 37830

SCARDINA, FRANK JOSEPH, real estate executive; b. Chgo., Feb. 18, 1948; s. Joseph Samuel and Marian Florence (Bogseth) S.; m. Diane Lynne Stern, Sept. 1, 1968; children: Brian Joseph, Kevin Stanley, Adam Charles, Todd Richard. BA in Econs, U. Denver, 1969; JD, U. Calif., Berkeley, 1972. Bar: Calif. 1972. Assoc. Mitchell, Silberberg & Knupp, L.A., 1975-77, Chickering and Gregory, San Francisco, 1972-75; corp. counsel Kaufman and Broad, Inc., L.A., 1978; v.p., gen. counsel Kaufman and Broad, Inc., 1979-80; pres. Kaufman and Broad Communities, Inc., 1981-89, Kaufman and Broad of So. Calif., 1985-90, Birtcher Homes, 1992-93; divsn. pres. Ryland Homes, 1993-94, regional pres. west region, 1994—; pres. M.J. Brock & Sons, Inc., 1994—; vis. lectr. Law Sch. U. So. Calif., 1987-92; mem. L.A. Blue Ribbon Com. for Affordable Housing, 1988. Pres. Bon Vivant Homeowners Assn., 1976-77; founding pres. Lindley Oaks Parents-Tchrs. Assn., 1979-80. Home: 6148 Edinburgh Ct Agoura Hills CA 91301-4141

SCARDINO, ALBERT JAMES, journalist; b. Balt., Sept. 22, 1948; s. Peter Lester and Mary Katherine (Mangelsdorf) S.; m. Marjorie Beth Morris, Apr. 19, 1974; children—Adelaide Katherine Morris, William Brown, Albert Henry Hugh. B.A., Columbia U., 1970; M.J., U. Calif.-Berkeley, 1976. Editor Ga. Gazette, Savannah, 1978-84; corr., editor N.Y. Times, N.Y.C., 1985-89; press sec. Mayor of N.Y.C., 1990-91; ind. journalist, 1991—. Editor, producer documentary film: Guale, 1976 (numerous awards 1976). Recipient Pulitzer Prize, 1984. Mem. Internat. Soc. Weekly Newspaper Editors (bd. dirs. 1983-86, Golden Quill award 1982), Columbia Coll. Alumni Assn. (sec. 1990-93). Home: 19 Empire House, Thurloe Pl, London SW7 2RU, England

SCARDINO, DON, artistic director. Artistic dir. Playwrights' Horizon; profl. musician. Director (plays) Godspell, A Few Good Men, Making Movies, I'm Getting My Act Together and Taking It On the Road, How I Got That Story, Later Life, A Cheever Evening (films) The People Next Door, Squirm, Cruising, He Knows You're Alone, Me and Veronica, (TV) 27 Wagons Full of Cotton, The Days and Nights of Molly Dodd, Law and Order, Tracey Ullman Takes on New York (Emmy nomination). Office: care Playwrights Horizons 416 W 42nd St New York NY 10036-6809

SCARDINO, MARJORIE MORRIS, publishing company executive; b. Flagstaff, Ariz., Jan. 25, 1947; d. Robert Weldon and Beth (Lamb) Morris; m. Albert James Scardino, Apr. 19, 1974; children: Adelaide Katherine Morris, William Brown, Albert Henry Hugh. BA, Baylor U.; JD, U. San Francisco. Ptnr. Brannen Wessels & Searcy, Savannah, Ga., 1976-85; pub. Ga. Gazette Pub. Co., Savannah, 1978-85; pres. The Economist Newspaper Group, Inc., N.Y.C., 1985-93; worldwide mng. dir. Economist Intelligence Unit, N.Y.C., 1992-93; chief exec. The Economist Group, London, 1993—; bd. dirs. The Economist Newspaper, Ltd., ConAgra, W.H. Smith; mem. vis. com. New Sch. for Social Rsch., N.Y.C., 1989—. Bd. dirs. Atlantic Coun., 1989, Pub. Radio Internat., 1993—. Office: The Economist Group, 25 St James's St, London SW1A 1HG, England also: The Economist 8th Fl 111 W 57th St Fl 8 New York NY 10019-2211

SCARF, HERBERT ELI, economics educator; b. Phila., July 25, 1930; s. Louis H. and Lena (Elkman) S.; m. Margaret Klein, June 28, 1953; children: Martha Anne Samuelson, Elizabeth Joan Stone, Susan Margaret Merrell. AB, Temple U., 1951; MA, Princeton U., 1952, PhD, 1954; LHD (hon.), U. Chgo., 1978. With RAND Corp., Santa Monica, Calif., 1954-57; asst. and assoc. prof. stats. Stanford U., Calif., 1957-63, fellow Ctr. for Advanced Study, 1962-63; vis. assoc. prof. Yale U., New Haven, 1959-60, prof. econs.,

1963-70, Stanley Resor prof. econs., 1970-78, Sterling prof. econs., 1979—; dir. Cowles Found. Research in Econs., Yale U., 1967-71, 1981-84, div. social sciences, 1971-72, 1973-74. Author: Studies in the Mathematical Theory of Inventory and Production, 1958, Computation of Economic Equilibria, 1973. Editor: Applied General Equilibrium Analysis, 1984. Recipient Lanchester prize Ops. Research Soc. of Am., 1974, Von Neumann medal, 1983; named Disting. fellow Am. Econ. Assn., 1991. Fellow Econometric Soc. (pres. 1983); mem. Am. Acad. Arts and Sciences, Nat. Acad. of Sciences, Am. Philos. Soc. Democrat. Jewish. Clubs: New Haven Lawn (Conn.), Yale (N.Y.C.). Office: Yale U Cowles Found Rsch Econs PO Box 208281 New Haven CT 06520-8281

SCARF, MARGARET (MAGGIE SCARF), author; b. Phila., May 13, 1932; d. Benjamin and Helen (Rotbin) Klein; m. Herbert Eli Scarf, June, 1953; children: Martha Samuelson, Elizabeth Stone, Susan Merrell. BA, South Conn. State U., 1989. Writer in residence Jonathan Edwards Coll., Yale U.; contbg. editor New Republic, Washington, DC, 1978—, Self Mag., N.Y.C., 1991—; writer-in-residence Jonathan Edwards Coll., 1995—; assoc. fellow Jonathan Edwards Coll. Yale U., New Haven, 1979, 81, 83; sr. fellow Bush Ctr. in Child Devel. and Social Policy, Yale U., 1991—; mem. adv. bd. Am. Psychiat. Press, Poynter Fellowship Journalism Yale U., 1995-96. Author: Meet Benjamin Franklin, 1968, Antarctica: Exploring the Frozen Continent, 1970, Body, Mind, Behavior, 1976 (Nat. Media award Am. Psychological Assn. 1977), Unfinished Business: Pressure Points in the Lives of Women, 1981, Intimate Partners: Patterns in Love and Marriage, 1987, Intimate Worlds: Life Inside the Family, 1996; contbr. numerous articles to jours. including N.Y. Times mag. and book rev., Psychology Today. Recipient Nat. Media award Am. Psychol. Found., 1971, 74, Conn. UN award Outstanding Conn. Women, 1987; grantee Smith Richardson Found., 1991-94; Ford Found. fellow, 1973-74, Neiman fellow Harvard U., 1975-76, Ctr. Advanced Study in Behavioral Scis. fellow, 1977-78, 85-86, Alicia Patterson Found. fellow, 1978-79. Mem. Conn. Soc. Psychoanalytic Psychologists, Am. Psychiat. Press (mem. adv. bd. 1992), Lawn Club, Elizabethans. Avocations: reading, hiking, swimming.

SCARFIOTTI, FERDINANDO, production designer. Prodn. designer: (films) The Conformist, 1971, Death in Venice, 1971, Avanti!, 1972, Last Tango in Paris, 1973, Daisy Miller, 1974, American Gigolo, 1980, Flash Gordon, 1980, Honky Tonk Freeway, 1981, Cat People, 1982, Bring on the Night, 1985, The Last Emperor, 1987 (Academy award best art direction 1987), Mamba, 1988, Toys, 1992 (Academy award nomination best art direction 1992). Office: care Art Directors Guild 11365 Ventura Blvd Ste 315 Studio City CA 91604-3148

SCARLATA, PAUL ANTHONY, oral surgeon; b. McKeesport, Pa., Apr. 3, 1935; s. Joseph Mario and Josephine Gloria (Battaglia) S.; B.S., U. Pitts., 1957, D.D.S., D.M.D., 1961; m. Mary Jane Parks, June 15, 1963 (dec. 1982); children: Stephanie, Anthony, Christopher, Matthew, Sarah; m. Darla K. Hosler, May 27, 1988 (div. 1994). Resident in oral surgery Western Pa. Hosp., Pitts., 1962-63, St. Luke's Hosp., N.Y.C., 1963-64; practice gen. dentistry and oral surgery, Chambersburg, Pa., 1967—; chief dental service Chambersburg Hosp., 1974-76, 82-84. Treas., Franklin County (Pa.) Heritage, 1971—, pres., 1977-78. Served with AUS, 1964-67. Recipient Buhl Planetarium Sci. award 1st prize Astronomy 6" Newtonian Reflector, 1952. Fellow Am. Assn. Oral and Maxillofacial Surgeons; mem. ADA, Pa., Western Pa., Gt. Lakes socs. oral surgeons, N.Y. Soc. Clin. Oral Pathologists, Am. Dental Soc. of Anesthetists, Cumberland Valley Dental Soc. (pres. 1982-83). Clubs: Chambersburg, South Penn Chess, Cumberland Valley Railroad Enthusiasts, Cumberland Valley Torch (Chambersburg), Antique Studebakers Club, Lions Greater Washington Mercedes Benz. Home: 444 Franklin Square Dr Chambersburg PA 17201-1465 Office: 556 E Queen St Chambersburg PA 17201-2942

SCARLETT, HAROLD O., retired retail executive, consultant; b. Detroit; s. Howard O. and Irene J. (LaSprance) S.; m. Helen L. Steigerwalt, Apr. 15, 1950. B.S. in Mech. Engring., Purdue U., 1949. Registered profl. engr., Mich. Design engr. Detroit Edison Co., 1949-52; air conditioning engr. S.S. Kresge Co., Detroit, 1952-55, chief mech. supt., 1955-65, asst. mgr. constrn. dept., 1965-69, gen. mgr., 1969-73; v.p. constrn. K mart Corp., Troy, Mich., 1973-87; pres. Huck Fixture Co. subs., Quincy, Ill, 1969-79; chmn. Huck Fixture Co. subs, Quincy, Ill, 1979-87;. Mem. corp. Merrill Palmer Inst., Detroit, 1980; corp. mem. Boys & Girls Clubs, 1983, Naples Bd. Appeals, 1990-96. With U.S. Army, 1942-45, PTO. Mem. Pi Tau Sigma, Tau Beta Pi. Home and Office: 626 Parkview Ln Naples FL 33940-3737

SCARMINACH, CHARLES ANTHONY, lawyer; b. Syracuse, N.Y., Feb. 19, 1944; s. John Louis and Lucy (Egnoto) S.; children: John, Catherine, Karen, Charles, Robert. MA, U. Buffalo, 1965; JD, Syracuse U., 1968. Bar: N.Y. 1968, S.C. 1974. Gen. counsel Sea Pines Co., Hilton Head Island, S.C., 1973-78; sole practice, Hilton Head Island, 1978-83; ptnr. Novit & Scarminach, P.A., Hilton Head Island, 1983-93; bd. dirs. Nations Bank, Hilton Head Island. Chmn. bd. Sea Pines Montessori Sch., Hilton Head Island, 1979-83; bd. dirs. Hilton Head Preparatory Sch., 1984-93, chmn. bd. trustees 1986-93. Maj. U.S. Army, 1968-73. Mem. ABA, S.C. Bar Assn., N.Y. State Bar Assn., Hilton Head Island C. of C. (bd. dirs. 1996—). Democrat. Roman Catholic. Club: Sea Pines. Home: 11 Governors Rd Hilton Head Island SC 29928-4153 Office: Novit & Scarminach PA PO Box 14 Hilton Head Island SC 29938-0014

SCARNE, JOHN, game company executive; b. Steubenville, Ohio, Mar. 4, 1903; s. Fiorangelo and Maria (Tamburro) S.; m. Steffi Kearney, 1956; 1 son, John Teeko. Student pub. schs., Guttenberg, N.J. Pres. John Scarne Games, Inc., North Bergen, N.J., 1950—; gaming cons. Hilton Hotels Internat. Magician stage, screen and television; Author: Scarne on Dice, 1945, Scarne on Cards, 1950, Scarne on Card Tricks, 1950, Scarne on Magic Tricks, 1952, Scarne's New Complete Guide to Gambling, 1962, The Odds Against Me, 1967, Scarne's Encyclopedia of Games, 1973, The Mafia Conspiracy, 1976, Scarne's Guide to Casino Gambling; Scarne's Guide to Modern Poker; Contbr. to: World Book Ency, 1970, Ency. Brit, 1975. Cons. to U.S. Armed Forces, 1941-45. Named Man of Year for Police Chiefs of U.S., 1960. Office: 8900 Boulevard E North Bergen NJ 07047-6055

SCARPA, ANTONIO, medicine educator, biomedical scientist; b. Padua, Italy, July 3, 1942; s. Angelo and Elena (DeRossi) S. MD cum laude, U. Padua, 1966, PhD in Pathology, 1970; MA (hon.), U. Pa., 1978. Asst. prof. biochemistry, biophysics U. Pa., Phila., 1973-76, assoc. prof., 1976-80, prof., 1980-86, dir. biomed. instrumentation group, 1983-86; prof. dept. pathology Jefferson U., Phila., 1986—; prof., chmn. dept. physiology Case Western Res. U., Cleve., 1986—, dir. tng. ctr., program project, 1983—, prof. medicine, 1989—; cons. study sect. NIH, Bethesda, 1984—, Am. Heart Assn., Dallas, 1986-91; pres., assoc. chair dept. phsiology, 1993-94. Editor (books): Frontiers of Biological Energetics, Calcium Transport and Cell Function, Transport ATPases, Membrane Pathology, Membrane and Cancer Cells; editor (jours.) Archives Biochemistry and Biophysics, Cell Calcium, Biochemistry Internat.; mem. editorial bd. Circulation Rsch., 1978-81, Biophys. Jour., 1979-82, Jour. Muscle Rsch., 1979—, Magnesium, 1982—, Physiol. Revs., 1982-90, FASEB Jour., 1987-92, Molecular Cellular Biochemistry, 1988—; contbr. numerous articles to profl. jours. Mem. Am. Soc. Physiologists, Am. Soc. Biol. Chemistry, Biophys. Soc. (exec. coun. 1980-83, 85-89, 94—), U.S. Bioenergetics Group (program chmn. 1974-75, 82, 83, exec. officer 1985—, assoc. chmn. dept. physiology, pres. 1993-95). Avocations: farming, sailing, painting. Office: Case Western Reserve Univ Dept Of Physiology Cleveland OH 44106

SCARPITTI, FRANK ROLAND, sociology educator; b. Butler, Pa., Nov. 12, 1936; s. Frank and Geneva (Costanza) S.; m. Ellen Louise Canfield, Sept. 5, 1959; children: Susan, Jeffrey. B.A., Cleve. State U., 1958; M.A., Ohio State U., 1959, Ph.D., 1962. Research asso. Ohio State U. Psychiat. Inst., Columbus, 1961-63; asst. prof. Rutgers U., 1963-67; asso. prof. sociology U. Del., 1967-69, prof., 1969—, chmn. dept., 1969-80, 88-94; cons. state and fed. govts.; Bd. dirs. Joint Commn. on Criminology and Criminal Justice Edn. and Standards, 1977-81. Author: Schizophrenics in the Community, 1967, Combatting Social Problems, 1967, Youth and Drugs, 1970, Group Interactions as Therapy, 1974, Social Problems, 1974, 77, 80, Deviance: Action, Reaction, Interaction, 1975, Women, Crime and Justice, 1980, The Young Drug User, 1980, Poisoning for Profit, 1985, Social Problems, 1989, 92, Social Problems: The Search for Solutions, 1994; contbr. articles to profl. jours. Recipient Hofheimer prize for research Am. Psychiat. Assn., 1967; mem. Danforth Found. asso. program. Mem. Am. Sociol. Assn., Am. Soc. Criminology (v.p. 1978-79, pres.-elect 1979-80, pres. 1980-81), AAUP, Alpha Kappa Delta, Phi Kappa Phi, Omicron Delta Kappa. Home: 104 Radcliffe Dr Newark DE 19711-3147

SCARR, SANDRA WOOD, psychology educator, researcher; b. Washington, Aug. 8, 1936; d. John Ruxton and Jane (Powell) Wood; m. Harry Alan Scarr, Dec. 26, 1961 (div. 1970); children: Phillip, Karen, Rebbecca, Stephanie; m. James Callan Walker, Aug. 9, 1982 (div. 1994). AB, Vassar Coll., 1958; AM, Harvard U., 1963, PhD, 1965. Asst. prof. psychology U. Md., College Park, 1964-67; assoc. prof. U. Pa., Phila., 1967-71; prof. U. Minn., Mpls., 1971-77, Yale U., New Haven, 1977-83; Commonwealth prof. U. Va., Charlottesville, 1983-95, chmn. dept. psychology, 1984-90; CEO, chmm. bd. dirs. KinderCare Learning Ctr., Inc., 1995—; mem. nat. adv. bd. Robert Wood Johnson Found., Princeton, N.J., 1985-91; coord. coun. psychology SUNY Bd. Regents, N.Y.C., 1984-92; prof. Kerstin Hesselgren, Sweden, 1993-94. Author: Race, Social Class and Individual Differences in IQ, 1981, Mother Care/Other Care, 1984 (Nat. Book award APA 1985), Caring for Children, 1989; editor Jour. Devel. Psychology, 1980-86, Current Directions in Psychol. Sci., 1991-95. Fellow Ctr. for Advanced Studies, Stanford U., Calif., 1976-77; grantee NIH, NSF, others, 1967—. Fellow AAAS, APA (chmn. com. on human rsch. 1980-83, coun. of reps. 1984—, bd. dirs. 1988—, pres.-elect 1995—, Award for Disting. Contbn. to Rsch. on Pub. Policy 1988), Am. Psychol. Soc. (bd. dirs. 1991—, James McKeen Cattell award 1993); mem. Am. Acad. Arts and Scis., Behavior Genetics Assn. (pres. 1985-86, mem. exec. coun. 1976-79, 84-87), Soc. for Rsch. in Child Devel. (governing coun. 1974-76, 87-93, chmn. fin. com. 1987-89, pres. 1989-91), Internat. Soc. for Study of Behavioral Devel. (exec. bd. 1987-94). Democrat. Avocations: dogs, gardening. Home: 1243 Maple View Dr Charlottesville VA 22902-8779 Office: U Va Dept Psychology Charlottesville VA 22903

SCARRITT, THOMAS VARNON, newspaper editor; b. Tuscaloosa, Ala., Jan. 28, 1953; s. Charles Wesley and Valerie (Varnon) S.; m. Kathryn Rush Hubbard, Dec. 28, 1973; children: Sara Kathryn, Thomas Varnon Jr. BA in Journalism, U. N.C., 1974; MBA, Samford U., 1995. Reporter The Birmingham (Ala.) News, 1975-79, Washington corr., 1979-83, news editor, 1983-85, editorial page editor, 1986-89, exec. editor, 1989—. Bd. dirs. Literacy Coun. Ctrl. Ala. mem. Am. Soc. Newspaper Editors, Soc. Profl. Journalists (pres. Ala. profl. chpt. 1988-89), Kiwanis (Birmingham), Phi Beta Kappa. Episcopal. Home: 4240 Clairmont Ave S Birmingham AL 35222-3724 Office: The Birmingham News 2200 4th Ave North Birmingham AL 35202

SCARROW, PAMELA KAY, health care manager; b. Washington, Nov. 4, 1949; d. Edward Charles and Elsie Lorine (Kay) Scarrow; m. Antonio Joseph Franz, Sept. 4, 1979; 1 child, Vanessa Motil Franz. AA, Navarro Coll., Tex., 1981; BS, Golden Gate U., 1983. Cert. med. staff coordinator, 1986, cert. profl. healthcare quality, 1996. Adminstrv. asst. Trust Ter. of the Pacific Islands, Saipan, Mariana Islands, 1976-79; adminstrv. asst. Navarro Coll., Corsicana, Tex., 1979-81; staff asst. San Francisco Symphony, 1981-82; med. staff liaison Calif. Med. Assn., San Francisco, 1982-87; provider, practitioner cons. Calif. Med. Rev., Inc., San Francisco, 1987-90; med. rev. specialist Am. Med. Peer Rev. Assn., Washington, 1990-93; adminstr. quality assessment Am. Coll. Ob-gyn., 1993—. Democrat. Roman Catholic. Office: Am Coll Ob-gyn 409 12th St SW Washington DC 20024-2125

SCARSE, OLIVIA MARIE, cardiologist, consultant; b. Chgo., Nov. 10, 1950; d. Oliver Marcus and Marjorie Ardis (Olsen) S. BS, North Park Coll., 1970; MD, Loyola U., Maywood, Ill., 1973. Diplomate Am. Bd. Internal Medicine, Am. Bd. Cardiovascular Diseases. Surg. intern Resurrection Hosp., Chgo., 1974; resident in internal medicine Northwestern U., Chgo., 1974-77; cardiovascular disease fellow U. Ill., Chgo., 1977-80; dir. cardiac catherization lab. Cook County Hosp., Chgo., 1981; dir. heart sta. MacNeal Hosp., Berwyn, Ill., 1983; dir. electrophysiology Hines VA Hosp., Maywood, Ill., 1984-85; dir. progressive care Columbus Hosp., Chgo., 1985-88, pvt. practice, 1984—; pvt. practice Ill. Masonic Hosp., Chgo., 1989—. Dir. continuous quality improvement Improvement Columbus, 1990-95. Pillsbury fellow Pillsbury Fund, 1980. Fellow Am. Coll. Cardiology; mem. AMA, ACP, Chgo. Med. Assn., Ill. State Med. Assn., Am. Heart Assn., Crescent Countries Found. for Med. Care, Cen. Ill. Med. Review Orgn. Avocations: musician, ballet and tap dancer, actress, model, singer. Home and Office: 2650 N Lakeview Ave Apt 4109 Chicago IL 60614-1833

SCASSA, EUGENE L., ambassador; b. Monaca, Pa., Feb. 6, 1939; married; 3 children. Student, Geneva Coll., 1957-58, 60-61, Fla. State U., 1963-64. With Fgn. Svc., 1962; comm. and records clk. U.S. Embassy, Panama, 1962-64; comm. officer U.S. Embassy, Quito, Ecuador, 1964-65; adminstrv. asst. U.S. Embassy, Libreville, Gabon, 1965-67; spl. asst. Bur. African Affairs, 1967-69; adminstrv. officer, consular officer U.S. Consulate, Mozambique, 1969-71; adminstrv. officer U.S. Embassy, Madagascar, 1971; adminstrv. and consular officer U.S. Consulate Gen., Monterrey, Mex., 1971-73; adminstrv. officer U.S. Embassy, Lusaka, Zambia, 1973-74, Reykjavik, Iceland, 1974-77; adminstrv. and conf. officer U.S. Mission, Geneva, 1978-80; adminstrv. counselor U.S. Embassy, Jidda, Saudi Arabia, 1980-82; with Nat. War Coll., 1982-83; divsn. chief bur. pers. Dept. of State, 1983-85, dep. exec. dir. bur. inter-Am. affairs, 1985-86, exec. dir., 1986-90, U.S. amb. to Belize, 1990—; diplomat in residence, vis. prof. internat. rels. St. Mary's U., San Antonio, Tex., 1994—. With U.S. Army, 1958-60. Office: Belize Amb to Belize Us Dept Of State Washington DC 20521

SCATURRO, PHILIP DAVID, investment banker; b. Newark, Dec. 8, 1938; s. Charles and Rose (Montino) S. BA, Williams Coll., 1960; JD, Columbia U., 1963, MBA, 1963. Analyst Ladenburg, Thalmann & Co., Inc., N.Y.C., 1964-67; v.p. Sellin, Forbes & Smith, N.Y.C., 1967; v.p. Allen & Co. Inc., N.Y.C., 1967-71, mng. dir., exec. v.p., 1977—; gen. ptnr. R&S Assocs., N.Y.C., 1972-76; pvt. investor, N.Y.C., 1976-77; bd. dirs., chmn. compensation com., mem. audit com. United Asset Mgmt. Co.; bd. dirs. Savoy Pictures Entertainment, Inc., N.Y.C., Asquith Ct. Ltd., London. Bd. dirs., exec. com., chmn. fin. com. N.Y.C. Opera; trustee, exec. com., chmn. audit com. New Sch. for Social Rsch.; mem. com. on alt. investments Williams Coll. Mem. Univ. Club (N.Y.C.). Avocations: Opera, music, theatre, wine, fly fishing. Office: Allen & Co 711 5th Ave New York NY 10022-3109

SCAVULLO, FRANCESCO, photographer; b. Staten Island, N.Y., Jan. 16, 1929; s. Angelo and Margaret (Pavis) S.; m. Carol McCallson, 1952. Student pub. schs., N.Y.C. Asst. photographer Horst at Vogue Studio, N.Y.C., 1946-48; photographer Seventeen mag., N.Y.C., 1948-50, Town and Country mag., 1950, Harper's Bazaar mag., 1960, Cosmopolitan mag., 1965—, Vogue mag., 1970; owner The Scavullo Gallery, 1988. Represented in permanent collection, Met. Mus. Art., Amon Carter Mus., Ft. Worth; author: Scavullo on Beauty, 1976, Scavullo Men, 1977, Scavullo Women, 1982, Scavullo, 1984. Recipient Photograph of Yr. award, 1977, numerous awards advt. art dirs. clubs. Mem. Dirs. Guild Am. Roman Catholic. Studio: 212 E 63rd St New York NY 10021-7604

SCEARSE, PATRICIA DOTSON, nurse educator, college dean; b. Wabash, Ind., Sept. 4, 1931; d. Claude Richard and Lilly Etta (Colvill) D.; m. Vernon Quinton Scearse, June 26, 1955 (dec. Mar. 1990); 1 child, Victoria Lynn Lenderman. BS, Earlham Coll., 1955; MS, U. Colo., 1968; D in Nursing Sci., U. Calif., San Francisco, 1974. RN. Staff nurse Reid Meml. Hosp., Richmond, Ind., 1954-55; head nurse, instr. Hillcrest Bapt. Hosp., Waco, Tex., 1955-56; instr. Sch. Nursing Candler Hosp., Savannah, Ga., 1956-60; adminstrv. asst., edn. cons. Wyo. State Bd. Nursing, Cheyenne, 1964-68; asst. prof. San Diego State U., 1969, Ball State U., Muncie, Ind., 1969-71; assoc. prof., area chairperson U. Mich., Ann Arbor, 1974-80; prof., dean Coll. Nursing Tex. Christian U., Ft. Worth, 1980-95, emeritus dean, prof., 1995—. Pub. policy editor Jour. Profl. Nursing, Phila., 1986-89; editorial cons. Jour. Pub. Health Nursing, New Haven, 1984-89; contbr. articles to profl. jours. Recipient Outstanding Nurse award Sigma Theat Tau, Beta Alpha, Ft. Worth, 1986; Kennedy Inst. Ethics postdoctoral fellow, Georgetown U., 1978. Mem. ANA, APHA (bd. govs. 1976), Am. Assn. Colls. of Nursing (bd. dirs. 1982-84, 85-87), Nat. League for Nursing, Coun. Baccalaureate and Higher Degree Programs (bd. rev.), Assn. Community Health Nurse Educators (named Great 100 Nurses 1992). Home: 5108 Ledgestone Dr Fort Worth TX 76132-2019

SCELSA, JOSEPH VINCENT, sociologist; b. N.Y.C., Dec. 7, 1945; s. Albert John and Katherine Mary S.; A.A., LIU, 1966, B.A., 1968; M.A., City U. N.Y., 1973, M.S.Ed., 1978; M.A., Columbia U., 1983, Ed.D., 1984; m. Joyce Ann Tisi, Nov. 13, 1981; 1 child, Jonathan. Counselor, tchr. N.Y.C. Bd. Edn., 1970-78, coord. career and occupational edn., 1979; coord. specialized counseling CUNY, 1979-81; pvt. practice counseling, N.Y.C., 1975—; lectr. grad. faculty Herbert H. Lehman Coll., 1980—; dir. Calandra Inst. CUNY, 1984—. Cert. sch. counselor, N.Y. Active Coun. of 1000 Nat. Italian-Am. Found; past vice chair multi cultural adv. bd. N.Y.C. Bd. Edn., 1990-91; N.Y. State Mentoring Program Adv. Bd., 1990—; bd. dirs. Nat. Ethnic Coalition Orgns., 1990—, Coalition Italo-Am. Assn., 1986—; Italian Apostalate, N.Y., 1993. Recipient Disting. Alumni award LIU, 1985, Organizational Leadership award Coalition Italo-Am. Assns., Inc., 1988, Americus award Bronx Community Coll., 1989, Role Model award Club DaVinci, 1990, Inte I-A Student Assn. award, CUNY, 1991, Intergroup Rels. Chancellor's award, 1994, FIERI Leadership award, 1993, Philip Mazzei award, 1993; named Cavaliere of Order of Merit Republic of Italy, 1992; Italian fellow John Jay Coll., 1993. Mem. Am. Counseling Assn., Am. Mental Health Counselors Assn. (cert. of recognition 1979, counselor of yr. 1983-84), Nat. Acad. Cert. Clin. Mental Health Counselors, Nat. Bd. for Cert. Counselers, Am.-Italian Hist. Assn., N.Y. State Mental Health Counselors Assn. (past pres., Outstanding Work award 1980), Ill. Club. Home: 41 Carwall Ave Mount Vernon NY 10552-1211 Office: CUNY Grad Ctr 33 W 42nd St New York NY 10036-8003

SCEPANSKI, JORDAN MICHAEL, librarian, administrator; b. Yonkers, N.Y., Nov. 21, 1942; s. Michael James and Margaret (Witko) S.; m. H. Lea Wells, Apr. 18, 1981; children—Kathryn Mary, Jordan Wells, Jennifer Elizabeth. BS, Manhattan Coll., 1964; MLn, Emory U., 1967; postgrad., U. N.C., Charlotte, 1976-77; M.B.A., U. Tenn., Nashville, 1982. Vol. Peace Corps, Turkey, 1964-66; adult services librarian Uniondale Pub. Library, N.Y., 1967-68; various profl. staff positions ALA, Chgo., 1970-73; asst. dir. library, asst. prof. U. N.C., Charlotte, 1974-78; dir. central library Vanderbilt U., Nashville, 1978-84; dir. univ. library and learning resources Calif. State U., Long Beach, 1984-96; exec. dir. Triangle Rsch. Librs. Network, Chapel Hill, N.C., 1996—; mgmt. intern Joint Univ. Librs., Nashville, 1977-78; cons./trainer Assn. Rsch. Librs., 1979-80; Fulbright lectr. Hacettepe U., Ankara, Turkey, 1981-82; cons. Coll. Charleston, S.C., No. Ky. U., Highlands Heights, Elon Coll., N.C., Calif. State U., L.A.; facilitator, trainer U. Notre Dame, South Bend, Ind., U. Nebr., Lincoln, U. Wyo.; founding mem. IBM Informa; bd. dirs. VTLS Inc. Contbr. articles to profl. jours. Served with U.S. Army, 1968-70. Recipient K.G. Saur award Coll. and Research Libraries publ., 1988; sr. fellow UCLA, 1983; faculty/librarian coop. research grantee Council on Library Resources, 1983. Mem. ALA (chair internat. rels. round table 1990-91), Western Assn. Schs. and Colls. (accreditation vis. team), Freedom to Read Found., Fulbright Alumni Assn., Jane Austen Soc. N.Am., Jane Austen Soc., S.W. Am.-Turkish Assn. So. Calif., Beta Phi Mu, Phi Beta Delta. Democrat. Roman Catholic. Office: Wilson Libr CB # 3940 Chapel Hill NC 27599-3940

SCHAAB, ARNOLD J., lawyer; b. Newark, Dec. 26, 1939; s. Robert George and Pauline (Levine) S.; m. Marcia Stecker, 1964 (div. 1978); children: Emily Diana, Genevieve; m. Patricia Caesar, Mar. 7, 1981 (div. 1996). BA, New Sch. for Social Rsch., 1962; LLB, Harvard U., 1965. Bar: N.Y. 1967, U.S. Dist. Ct. (so. and ea. dists.) N.Y. 1967. Assoc. Chadbourne & Parke, N.Y.C., 1966-69; ptnr. Anderson, Kill, Olick & Oshinsky, N.Y.C., 1969-78; sr. ptnr. Pryor, Cashman, Sherman & Flynn, N.Y.C., 1978—. Pres. Literacy Ptnrs., Inc.; mem. exec. com. Shaker Mus. and Libr., Old Chatham, N.Y.; mem. vis. com. Milano Grad. Sch. Mgmt. and Pub. Policy, New Sch. for Social Rsch. Fulbright scholar Law Faculty U. Paris, 1966. Fellow N.Y. Bar Found., Am. Bar Found.; mem. ABA (vice chair internat. fin. transactions com., forum com. on constrn. industry), N.Y. State Bar Assn. (chair internat. law and practice sect., chmn. spl. com. free trade in the Ams., ho. of dels., fin. com., long range planning com., by-laws com.), Assn. Bar City N.Y., Univ. Club (chmn. fin. com., chmn. audit com., mem. coun.), Doubles, The Netherland Club, Old Chatham Hunt Club. Office: Pryor Cashman Sherman & Flynn 410 Park Ave New York NY 10022-4407

SCHAACK, KARON L., state agency executive. BA in Mass Comm., U. S.D., 1964; tchg. cert., S.D. State U., 1966; grad. state execs. strategic leadership, Duke U., 1993. Tchr. Marshall (Minn.) H.S., 1971-73; coord. Comm. Libr., S.W. Minn. State Coll., Marshall, 1973-74; pub. info. cons. S.D. Edn. Assn., Pierre, 1977; publs. cons. S.D. State Planning Bur., Pierre, 1977, S.D. Right-To-Read, Pierre, 1977-78; edn. program specialist I, S.D. Dept. Edn. and Cultural Affairs, Pierre, 1978-80, edn. program specialist II, 1980-87, dir. instnl. svcs., 1987-91, dep. sec., 1991-95, acting sec., 1995—. Office: SD Dept Edn and Cultural Affairs 700 Governor's Dr Pierre SD 57501-2291

SCHAACK, PHILIP ANTHONY, retired beverage company executive; b. Evanston, Ill., June 6, 1921; s. Harry Charles and Lora Mary (Colford) S.; m. Elizabeth Eberhart, Mar. 27, 1943; children: Susan, Laura, Betsy. Student, Northwestern U., 1943; LLD (hon.), Ill. Benedictine Coll., 1977. Vice-pres. Joyce Beverages/Chgo., 1957-60; v.p. Joyce Beverages/Ill., Joliet, 1960-63, exec. v.p., 1963-65, pres., 1965-85; dir. Joyce Beverages/Ill. Retired ir. First Midwest Bank; past chmn., trustee Ill. Benedictine Coll.; vice-chmn. nat. devel. coun. Sisters of Providence. With USN, 1942-45. Mem. Chgo. Golf Club, Innisbrook Golf Club, Minocqua Country Club, Timber Ridge Country Club. Republican. Roman Catholic. Home: 1480 Aberdeen Ct Naperville IL 60564-9797

SCHAAF, MARTHA ECKERT, author, poet, library director, musician, composer, educator, lecturer; b. Madison, Ind., Sept. 21, 1911; d. Frederick William and Julia (Richert) Eckert; m. Clarence William Schaaf, Dec. 27, 1941 (dec. 1987); 1 child, Susan Elizabeth Lee. AB with distinction, Ind. U., 1933; MLS, Columbia U., 1945; postgrad., Butler U., Ind. U. Lic. tchr. English, French, Spanish, music. Libr. dir. Twp. System, Crothersville, Ind., 1936-38; libr. music instr. Angola, Ind., 1938-39, Howe High Sch., Indpls., 1939-42; libr. dir. Reitz High Sch., Evansville, Ind., 1942; county libr. organizer County Brs. Libr., Columbus, Ga., 1943; hosp. libr. dir. Camp Van Dorn, Woodville, Miss., 1943-44; organized libr. Bulova Sch. for Disabled Vets., L.I., N.Y., 1944-45; organized bus. rsch. libr. Eli Lilly & Co., Indpls., 1946-50; rsch. libr. Wallace Collection Ind. Hist. Soc. Libr., 1958-61; dir. Pub. Libr., Pompano Beach, Fla., 1967-72; pres. Ind. Spl. Libr. Assn., 1948. Author: Lew Wallace: Boy Writer, 1961, Duke Ellington: Music Master, 1975; contbg. author: War Paint and Wagon Wheels, 1968, Reading Incentive Series, 1969, The Nat. Library of Poetry; contbr. articles to profl. jours. Named Valedictorian, Madison (Ind.) H.S., 1929; recipient History award DAR, 1930, C. of C. award Pompano Beach, Fla., 1970, Editor's Choice award Nat. Libr. Poetry award, 1995, Disting. Alumni award Ind. U., 1983. Mem. Nat. League Am. Pen Women (Svc. award Boca Raton br. 1995), Internat. Soc. Poets, Acad. Am. Poets, Pen Women, Mortar Board, Ind. U. Alumni Assn., Columbia U. Alumni Assn., Boca Raton Music Guild, Phi Beta Kappa, Pi Lambda Theta, Chi Omega (Found. award Theta Beta chpt.). Avocations: piano, organ, choral direction, composing. Home: 51 SW 10th Ter Boca Raton FL 33432

SCHAAF, MIV, writer, graphic designer, composer; b. Oct. 3, 1920; m. Alfred Musso, 1959; 1 chld, Gia Musso. BA, Mich. State U., 1943; postgrad., Humboldt State U., 1988—. Owner Miv Schaaf Assocs., 1954—; seminar tchr. UCLA, U. Calif. Irvine, Scripps Coll., 1977—; del. White House Conf. Librs., 1979; judge Robert B. Campbell book collection UCLA, 1980; speaker in field. Author: Who Can Not Read About Crocodiles?, 1988; columnist L.A. Times, 1972-87, North Coast Jour., 1993—; writer 156 poems; composer more than 160 songs including Songs of Age and Songs of Rage. Pres. Archtl. Panel, L.A., 1954-72; founder Pasadena Cultural Heritage Commn., 1973. Recipient Premier award Pasadena Heritage, 1977, Met. Coop. Libr. System and Calif. Libr. Assn. award, 1982, Gold Crown award Pasadena Arts Coun., 1983. Avocation: playing cello. Home: 83 Wilson Ln Fieldbrook CA 95519 also: PO Box 707 Trinidad CA 95570

SCHAAP, RICHARD JAY, journalist; b. N.Y.C., Sept. 27, 1934; s. Maurice William and Leah (Lerner) S.; m. Barbara M. Barron, June 20, 1956 (div. 1967); children: Renee Beth, Michelle Anne; m. Madeleine Gottlieb, Aug. 29, 1967 (div. 1980); children: Jeremy Albert, Joanna Rose; m. Patricia Ann McLeod, May 17, 1981 ; children—Karen Joan, David Maurice. BS, Cornell U., 1955; MS, Columbia U., 1956. Sr. editor Newsweek, N.Y.C., 1956-63; city editor N.Y. Herald Tribune, 1964-66; correspondent NBC, N.Y.C., 1971-80, ABC, N.Y.C., 1980—; host of The Sports Reporters ESPN, 1990—. Author over 30 books including RFK, 1967, Turned On, 1967, (with Jerry Kramer) Instant Replay, 1968, (with Jimmy Breslin) 44, 1980, Steinbrenner!, 1982, The 1984 Olympic Games, 1984, (with Jerry Kramer) Distant Replay, 1985, (with Billy Crystal) Absolutely Mahvelous, 1986, (with Phil Simms and Phil McConkey) Simms to McConkey, 1987, (with Bo Jackson) Bo Knows Bo, 1990, (with Joe Montana) Montana, 1995, (with Tom Waddell) Gay Olympian, 1996, (with Nick Bollettierc) My Aces My Faults, 1996. Served to lt. U.S. Army, 1957-58. Recipient Emmy awards for Sid Caesar profile 1986, sports features 1986, Tom Waddell profile 1988, commentaries 1992, 94, 96, Columbia Sch. Journalism Alumni award, 1994, Cable Ace award, 1996. Office: ABC News 47 W 66th St New York NY 10023-6201

SCHABER, GORDON DUANE, law educator, former judge; b. Ashley, N.D., Nov. 22, 1927; s. Ronald and Esther (Schatz) S. A.B. with distinction, Sacramento State Coll., 1949; J.D. with honors, U. Calif. at San Francisco, 1952; LL.D., McGeorge Sch. Law, 1961, John Marshall Law Sch., 1983, Widener U., Del. Law Sch., 1984; LLD, Southwestern U., 1994. Bar: Calif. 1953. Pvt. practice Sacramento, 1953-65; ptnr. firm Schaber & Cecchettini, Sacramento, 1953-65; prof., asst. dean McGeorge Coll. of Law (now McGeorge Sch. Law of U. Pacific), Sacramento, 1953-56, asst. dean, 1956, acting dean, dean, prof. law, 1957-91, univ. counsellor, disting. prof. law, 1991—; presiding judge Superior Ct. Sacramento County, 1965-70; dir. Air Calif., 1974-81, Westgate Corp., 1979-82, Sacramento Cablevision, 1980-82, Capitol Bank of Commerce, vice chmn., 1987-90; chmn. bd. dirs. River City Cablevision Inc.; mem. Calif. Bd. Control, 1962-64; chmn. Greater Sacramento Plan Com., 1970; cons. on establishment Sch. Law at U. Puget Sound, 1970-71; cons. study on jud. workload Jud. Council Calif., 1971-72; mem. Adv. Com. to Chief Justice Calif. on Superior Ct. Mgmt., 1971; cons. vehicle theft study Calif. Hwy. Patrol, 1972; panelist Sacramento Bee Secret Witness Program, 1971-90; mem. adv. com. to Calif. Office Econ. Opportunity, Calif. Legal Services Expt., 1972; vice chmn. Calif. Ednl. Facilities Authority, 1978—; bd. dirs. Nat. Center Adminstrv. Justice, 1978; mem. President's Adminstrn. Justice Task Force, 1980; mem. Joint Task Force on Student Fin. Aid Com. and Govt. Rels., 1988-90, Com. to Study the Law Sch. Process, 1989-90, Ind. Law Sch. Com., 1989-90. Author: Contracts in a Nutshell, 1975, 3d rev. edit., 1990, Procedural Guide for the Evaluation and Accreditation of Court Facilities, 1977, (with others) The Twentieth Century and the Courthouse, 1977; contbr. articles to profl. jours., book reviewer. Mem. Telethon gift com. Sacramento-San Joaquin chpt. Muscular Dystrophy Assn., 1980; mem. Sierra Found. for Health (One Hundred Million Dollar Health Trust), 1987—; mem. adv. bd. Performing Arts Fund, Sacramento Bee, 1987—; mem. exec. com. Sacramento Area Commn. on Mather Conversion, 1989-90, Law Sch. Admission Coun., Fin. Aid Svcs. Com., 1989-90; past mem., bd. advisors Mental Health Soc. Sacramento, Better Bus. Bur., LWV; trustee Stanford Homes Found., 1980-87, Hon. Lorenzo Patino Scholarship Trust, 1984, Sierra Found. for Health, 1987—; bd. dirs. Sacramento Regional Found., 1982-87, Sutter Hosps. of Sacramento, 1978; mem. bd. advisors Coll. Pub. Interest Law, Pacific Legal Found., 1974—; vice chmn. Calif. Edn. Facilities Authority, 1978—; chmn. Sacramento County Dem. Ctrl. Com., 1960-64; mem. Dem. State Ctrl. Com., 1960-64, 74-82; founding chair Valley Vision, 1993-95; active numerous other civic coms. Named Sacramento County Young Man of Yr., 1962, Trial Judge of Yr. Calif. Trial Lawyers Assn., 1969, Humanitarian of Yr. Sacramento County Bar Assn., 1990, Sacramentan of Yr. Sacramento C. of C., 1994, Outstanding Alumnus Hastings Coll., 1994; recipient Legal Edn. and Jud. award Am. Trial Lawyers Assn., 1965, Order of Hornet Calif. State U., Sacramento, 1972, award Citizenship and Law Related Edn. Ctr., 1994, Silver Hope award Multiple Sclerosis Soc., 1994. Fellow Am. Bar Found.; mem. ABA (council sect. legal edn. and admissions to bar 1975, chmn. 1981, sec. 1982-92, adv. com. pres.-elect on competence of lawyers continuing edn. 1978, numerous other coms., Robert J. Kutak award 1991), Sacramento Bar Assn. (v.p. 1970), State Bar Calif. (mem. com. legislation 1969-89, spl. com. appellate cts. 1970-72, long range adv. planning com. 1972-89, vice chmn. com. law sch. edn. 1973, chmn. 1974, mem. commn. to study bar examination processes 1976-80, Merit Selection Com., others), Am. Judicature Soc., Order of Coif, Phi Delta Phi. Clubs: Commonwealth, Comstock, Sutter, Sacramento/Capitol, many others. Home: 937 Piedmont Dr Sacramento CA 95822-1701 Office: U Pacific McGeorge Sch La00 5th Ave Sacramento CA 95817-2705

SCHACHMAN, HOWARD KAPNEK, molecular biologist, educator; b. Phila., Dec. 5, 1918; s. Morris H. and Rose (Kapnek) S.; m. Ethel H. Lazarus, Oct. 20, 1945; children—Marc, David. BSChemE, Mass. Inst. Tech., 1939; PhD in Phys. Chemistry, Princeton, 1948; DSc (hon.), Northwestern U., 1974; MD (hon.), U. Naples, 1990. Fellow NIH, 1946-48; instr., asst. prof. U. Calif., Berkeley, 1948-54, assoc. prof. biochemistry, 1954-59, prof. biochemistry and molecular biology, 1959-91, chmn. dept. molecular biology, dir. virus lab., 1969-76; prof. emeritus, dept. molecular and cell biology U. Calif. at Berkeley, 1991-94; prof. grad. sch., 1994—, U. Calif. at Berkeley, 1994—; mem. sci. coun. and sci. adv. bd. Stazione Zoologica, Naples, Italy, 1988—; cons. bd. sci. Meml. Sloan-Kettering Cancer Ctr., 1988—; mem. sci. adv. com. Rsch. 1 Am., 1990—; William Lloyd Evans lectr. Ohio State U., 1988, Carl and Gerty Cori lectr., Washington U. Sch. Medicine, 1993; faculty rsch. lectr. U. Calif., Berkeley, 1994. Author: Ultracentrifugation in Biochemistry, 1959; developer of ultracentrifuge as a tool for studying macromolecules of biol. interest; condr. studies on structure and function of regulatory enzyme: aspartate transcrabamylase. Mem. bd. sci. counselors Cancer Biology and Diagnosis divsn. Nat. Cancer Inst., 1989-92; spl. advisor to dir. NIH, 1994—. Lt. USNR, 1945-47. Recipient John Scott award, 1964, Warren Triennial prize Mass. Gen. Hosp., 1965, Alexander von Humboldt award, 1990, Berkeley citation for disting. achievement and notable svc. U. Calif., 1993; Guggenheim Meml. fellow, 1956. Mem. AAAS, NAS (chmn. biochemistry sect. 1990-93, panelist sci. responsibility and conduct of rsch. 1990-92), Am. Chem. Soc. (award in chem. instrumentation 1962, Calif. sect. award 1958), Am. Soc. Biochemistry and Molecular Biology (pres. 1987-88, chmn. pub. affairs com. 1989—, Merck award 1986, Herbert A. Sober award 1994), Fedn. Am. Socs. for Exptl. Biology (pres. 1988-89, pub. affairs exec. com. 1989—, pub. svc. award 1994), Sigma Xi. Achievements include development of the ultracentrifuge as a tool for studying macromolecules of biological interest; studies on structure and function of a regulatory enzyme: Aspartate transcarbamylase. Office: U Calif Berkeley Dept Molecular and Cell Bio MCB Stanley 229 Stanley Hall #3206 Berkeley CA 94720-3206

SCHACHT, HENRY BREWER, manufacturing executive; b. Erie, Pa., Oct. 16, 1934; s. Henry Blass and Virginia (Brewer) S.; m. Nancy Godfrey, Aug. 27, 1960; children: James, Laura, Jane, Mary. BS, Yale U., 1956; MBA, Harvard U., 1962; DSc (hon.), DePauw U., 1982; MA (hon.), Yale U., 1988. Sales trainee Am. Brake Shoe Co., N.Y.C., 1956-57; investment mgr. Irwin Mgmt. Co., Columbus, Ind., 1962-64; v.p. fin. Cummins Engine Co., Inc., Columbus, 1964-66; v.p., cen. area mgr. internat. Cummins Engine Co., Inc., London, 1966-67; group v.p. internat. and subsidiaries Cummins Engine Co., Inc., 1967-69; pres. Cummins Engine Co., Inc., Columbus, 1969-77, CEO, 1977-94, chmn., 1977-95; chmn., CEO, Lucent Techs., Murray Hill, N.J., 1995—; bd. dirs. AT&T, Chase Manhattan Corp., Chase Manhattan Bank N.A., Alcoa. Trustee emeritus The Culver Ednl. Found.; active Bus. Coun., Coun. Fgn. Rels.; mem. The Assocs., Harvard Bus. Sch., The Bus. Enterprise Trust; hon. trustee Brookings Instn., Com. Econ. Devel., Yale Corp.; chmn. trustees Ford Found.; sr. mem. Conf. Bd. With USNR, 1957-60. Mem. Tau Beta Pi. Republican. Office: Lucent Techs 600 Mountain Ave New Providence NJ 07974

SCHACHT, HENRY MEVIS, writer, consultant; b. Pasadena, Calif., Feb. 28, 1916; s. Henry and Amelia (Claussen) S.; m. Mary Joan Turnbull, Dec. 30, 1937; children: Henry John, Linda Joan. BA, U. Calif., Berkeley, 1936. Info. specialist U. Calif., Berkeley, 1936-42; dir. agr. NBC, San Francisco, 1942-59, ABC, San Francisco, 1959-60; agrl. columnist San Francisco Chronicle, 1959-93; dir. agrl. info. U. Calif., 1961-65; v.p. corp. relations, corp. sec. Calif. Canners & Growers, San Francisco, 1965-81; freelance writer, 1936—; cons. radio-TV to FAO of UN, Cairo, 1963, Mexico City, 1965, Tokyo, 1966; dir. Calif. Co. for Internat. Trade; dir. Agrl. Issues Ctr., U. Calif. Pres. U.S. Fruit Export Coun., 1972-75; exec. sec. Commn. Calif. Agr. and Higher Edn., 1993-95; adv. bd. Agrl. Issues Ctr. U. Calif., 1990—. Mem. Pub. Relations Soc. Am., Pub. Relations Roundtable San Francisco, Nat. Assn. Farm Broadcasters, Agrl. Relations Council, Nat. Canners Assn. (dir. 1966-81). Home: 60 Hiller Dr Oakland CA 94618

SCHACHT, JOCHEN HEINRICH, biochemistry educator; b. Königsberg, Fed. Republic Germany, July 2, 1939; came to U.S., 1969; s. Heinz and Else (Sprenger) S.; m. Helga Hildegard Seidel, Jan. 27, 1967; children: Miriam Helga, Daniel Jochen. BS, U. Bonn, Fed. Republic Germany, 1962; MS in Chemistry, U. Heidelberg, Fed. Republic Germany, 1965, PhD in Biochemistry, 1968. Asst. research chemist, Mental Health Research Inst. U. Mich., Ann Arbor, 1969-72, from asst. prof. to assoc. prof. biochemistry, Dept. Biol. Chemistry & Otolaryngology, 1973-84, prof., 1984—, chmn. grad. program in physiol. acoustics, 1981—; vis. prof. Karolinska Inst., Stockholm, 1979-80; acting dir. Kresge Hearing Rsch. Inst., U. Mich., 1983-84, assoc. dir., 1989—; mem. hearing rsch. study sect. USPHS, NIH, Nat. Inst. Neurol. and Communicative Disorders and Stroke, 1986-89, Task Force Nat. Strategic Rsch. Plan, Nat. Insts. Deafness and Communication Disorders, USPHS, NIH. Mem. editl. bd. Hearing Rsch., 1990—; assoc. editor Audiology & Neuro-Otol., 1995—; contbr. more than 100 articles to profl. jours., book chpts., revs.; co-editor Neurochemistry of Cholinergic Receptors, 1974. Fogarty Sr. Internat. fellow NIH, 1979, Sen. J. Javitz Neurosci. investigator, 1984; recipient Chercheur Etranger rsch. award INSERM, Paris, 1986, 94, Animal Welfare award Erna-Graff Found., Berlin, 1987, Disting. Faculty Achievement award U. Mich., 1989, Employer of Yr. award Nat. Capital Assoc. Coop. Edn. and Gallaudet U., Washington. Mem. Deutsche Gesellschaft für Biologische Chemie, Am. Soc. Neurochemistry, Internat. Soc. Neurochemistry, Soc. for Neurosci., Assn. for Research in Otolaryngology, Am. Soc. Biol. Chemists. Avocations: photography, travel, birding. Office: U Mich Kresge Hearing Rsch Inst Ann Arbor MI 48109-0506

SCHACHT, LINDA JOAN, broadcast journalist; b. Berkeley, Calif., Sept. 11, 1944; d. Henry Mevis and Mary (Turnbull) S.; m. John Burdette Gage, May 1, 1976; children: Peter Turnbull, Katharine Burdette. BA, U. Calif., Berkeley, 1966, MJ, 1978. Reporter Sta. KQED-TV, San Francisco, 1974-76, Sta. KPIX-TV, San Francisco, 1976—; vis. faculty Grad. Sch. Journalism U. Calif., Berkeley, 1990—. Reporter Dem. conv., 1980 (Emmy award 1981), investigative article on second mortgage brokers, 1977 (Emmy award), on children as witnesses, 1984 (Calif. State Bar award 1985, ABA award 1986). Mem. Nat. Acad. TV Arts and Scis.

SCHACHT, RICHARD LAWRENCE, philosopher, educator; b. Racine, Wis., Dec. 19, 1941; s. Robert Hugo and Alice (Munger) S.; m. Judith Rowan; children: Eric Lawrence, Marshall Robert. B.A., Harvard U., 1963; M.A., Princeton U., 1965, Ph.D., 1967; postgrad. Tübingen U., Fed. Republic Germany, 1966-67. Asst. prof. U. Ill., Urbana-Champaign, 1967-71, assoc. prof., 1971-80, prof. philosophy, 1980—, Jubilee prof. of Liberal Arts and Scis., 1990—, chmn. dept., 1980-91, interim dean Coll. Liberal Arts and Scis., 1994; vis. prof. U. Oreg., 1969, U. Pitts., 1973, U. Mich., 1979; vis. scholar Tübingen U., 1975. Author: Alienation, 1970, Hegel and After, 1975, Nietzsche, 1983, Classical Modern Philosophers, 1984, The Future of Alienation, 1994, Making Sense of Nietzsche, 1995; editor: Nietzsche Selections, 1993, Nietzsche, Genealogy, Morality, 1994, Internat. Nietzsche Studies. Mem. Am. Philos. Assn. (chair com. on status and future of the profession), N.Am. Nietzsche Soc. (exec. dir.), Internat. Sociol. Assn. (v.p., research com. on alienation theory), AAUP. Office: U Ill Dept Philosophy 105 Gregory 810 S Wright St Urbana IL 61801

SCHACHT, RONALD STUART, lawyer; b. Stamford, Conn., Nov. 7, 1932; s. Saul Albert and Faye Dorothy (Gittleman) S.; m. Natalie Helene Goldman, June 17, 1956; children—Patti Ellen, Bonnie Anne, Cindy Joy. B.S., U. Conn., 1954; LL.B., NYU, 1957, LL.M., 1960. Bar: N.Y. 1957, D.C. 1980. Tax atty. IRS, N.Y.C., 1957-62; assoc. Proskauer Rose Goetz & Mendelsohn, N.Y.C., 1962-69, ptnr., 1969—, mng. ptnr., 1981-84, mem. exec. com., 1985-95; lectr. Practising Law Inst., NYU Inst. Fed. Taxation; adj. asst. prof. Sch. Continuing Edn. NYU, 1970-72. Bd. dirs. Congregation Agudath Shalom, Stamford, 1968-73; mem. com. Fedn. Jewish philanthropies, N.Y.C., 1972-80. Mem. N.Y. State Bar Assn., Assn. of Bar of City of N.Y., N.Y. County Lawyers Assn. (bd. dirs. 1977-83, chmn. ins. com. 1975-85), Newfield Swim Club (bd. dirs. 1967-70, pres. 1969), Phi Kappa Phi, Gamma Chi Epsilon. Democrat. Jewish. Home: 17280 Antigua Point Way Boca Raton FL 33487 Office: Proskauer Rose Goetz & Mendelsohn 1585 Broadway New York NY 10036-8200

SCHACHTER, BARRY, economist; b. Providence, R.I., Aug. 17, 1954; s. Hyman and Fannie (Dunder) S.; m. Joanne Fitzsimmons, Sept. 13, 1981; 1 child, Devra Fitzsimmons. BS in Econs., Bentley Coll., 1976, AS in Acctg., 1976; MA in Econs., Cornell U., 1979, PhD, 1982. From instr. to asst. prof. dept. Econs. Rutgers U., New Brunswick, N.J., 1980-82; from asst. prof., to assoc. prof. Simon Fraser U., Burnaby, B.C., 1982-88; assoc. prof. Tulane U., New Orleans, 1988-92; fin. economist divsn. econ. analysis Commodity Futures Trading Commn., Washington, 1990-94; fin. economist risk analysis divsn. Comptroller of the Currency, Washington, 1994—; lectr. U. Pa., 1994, Georgetown U., 1996; vis. asst. prof. U. Utah, Salt Lake City, 1987-88; vis. scholar rsch. dept. Internat. Monetary Fund, Washington, 1992-93; ad hoc referee Can. Coun. Killam Fellowship, 1988, Econ. Inquiry, 1983-84, Fin. Review, 1985, 89-90, Jour. Fin. Rsch. 1987-93, Fin. Mgmt., 1989-90, Jour. Bus. and Rsch., 1988, Jour. Fin., 1989, 91, Quarterly Jour. Econs., 1989, Jour. Money, Credit and Banking, 1989, Jour. Econ. Theory, 1990, Jour. Banking & Fin., 1990-93, Jour. Fin. Edn., 1990, Review of Quantatative Fin. and Acctg., 1991-92, Internat. Review Econs. and Fin., 1992, Soc. Scis. and Humanities Rsch. Coun. Can. 1993; speaker in field; presenter various confs. Contbr. articles to profl. jours., chpts. to books, annuals, proceedings; assoc. editor Internat. Rev. of Fin. Analysis, 1990—, Jour. Derivatives, 1993—, Fin. Mgmt., 1993—, Jour. Banking & Finance, 1995—, Jour. Fin. Engring., 1995—. Rsch. grantee Simon Fraser Univ., 1982, 84, 86, Inst. Quantitative Rsch. Fin., 1990; recipient Best Paper award Internat. Options Market, 1984. Mem. Am. Econs. Assn., Am. Fin. Assn., Fin. Mgmt. Assn., Internat. Assn. Fin. Engrs. (chair adv. bd. 1996), Western Fin. Assn. Office: Comptroller of the Currency Risk Analysis Divsn 250 E St SW Washington DC 20219

SCHACHTER, HARRY, biochemist, educator; b. Vienna, Austria, Feb. 25, 1933; came to Can., 1951; s. Asher and Miriam (Freund) S.; m. Judith Jakubovic, Dec. 23, 1958; children: Aviva, Asher. BA, U. Toronto, 1955, MD, 1959, PhD, 1964. From asst. prof. to assoc. prof. dept. biochemistry U. Toronto, 1964-72, prof., 1972—, chmn., 1984-89; sr. scientist Rsch. Inst. Hosp. for Sick Children, Toronto, 1976—; head biochemistry rsch. divsn. Rsch. Inst. Hosp. for Sick Children, 1976-89.

SCHACHTER, MAX, retired engineering services company executive; b. N.Y.C., Aug. 22, 1913; s. Morris and Rebecca (Sirota) S.; m. Ida Jensky, June 25, 1936; 1 son, Robert. Student, N.Y. U., 1932, CCNY, 1932-36, Cooper Union, 1942. Registered profl. engr., N.Y., N.J. Machine designer Torrington Mfg. Co., Conn., 1941-43, Machine & Tool Design Co., N.Y.C., 1943-48; chief engr. machine design div. Am. Machine & Foundry, Bklyn., 1949-51; chmn. Atlantic Design Co., Inc., Livingston, N.J., 1951-89, ret., 1989. Trustee, now pres. Ruth Gottscho Kidney Found., 1960—. Mem. ASME. Jewish.

SCHACHTER, MICHAEL BEN, psychiatrist; b. Bklyn., Jan. 15, 1941; s. Saul and Ann (Palestine) S.; m. Margaret Josephine Kavanagh, July 22, 1967 (div. Mar. 1979); children: Brian Joseph, Amy, Stefan James; m. Marlene Helen Brodsky, Aug. 22, 1982 (div. Mar. 1993); children: Adam Elliot, Jason Neil; m. Lisa Lackhai, July 19, 1993; 1 child, Seth Andrew. BA, Columbia U., 1961, MD, 1965. Diplomate Am. Bd. Psychiatry and Neurology in Psychiatry, Am. Bd. Chelation Therapy. Med., surg. and pediatric intern Hosp. for Joint Diseases and Med. Ctr., N.Y.C., 1965-66; resident psychiatry Downstate Med. Ctr., Kings County Hosp., Bklyn., 1966-69; staff psychiatrist Bklyn. Community Counseling Ctr., 1968-69; staff psychiatrist Rockland County Community Mental Health Ctr., Pomona, N.Y., 1971, dir. emergency and admissions, 1971-72, dir. outpatient clinic, 1972-74; founder, dir. Michael B. Schachter M.D., P.C. formerly Mountainview Med., Suffern, N.Y., 1974—; bd. dirs. Am. Bd. Chelation Therapy, 1983-88. Author: The Natural Way to a Healthy Prostate, 1995, (with David Sheinkin and Richard Hutton) The Food Connection, 1979, Food, Mind and Mood, 1980, 2d edit., 1987; contbr. articles to profl. jours. Maj. USAF, 1969-71. Recipient Appreciation award NHF, 1979, Carlos Lamar Pioneer Meml. award Am. Acad. Med. Preventics, 1979, Merit award Am. Acad. Craniomandibular Disorders, 1981, Physician's Recognition awards AMA. Fellow Am. Coll. for Advancement in Medicine (v.p. 1985-87, pres.-elect 1987-89, pres. 1989-91); mem. Am. Psychiat. Assn., Am. Acad. Environ. Medicine, Am. Coll. Nutrition, Found. for Advancement Innovative Medicine (v.p. 1986-94, pres. 1994—), Am. Preventive Med. Assn. (bd. dirs. 1993-95). Avocations: running, basketball, swimming, tennis, golf. Office: 2 Executive Blvd Ste 202 Suffern NY 10901-4164

SCHACHTER, OSCAR, lawyer, educator, arbitrator; b. N.Y.C., June 19, 1915; s. Max and Fannie (Javits) S.; m. Mollie Miller, Aug. 9, 1936 (dec. July 1980); children: Judith (Mrs. John Modell), Ellen (Mrs. John P. Leventhal); m. Muriel L. Sackler, June 14, 1982. BSS, Coll. City N.Y., 1936; JD, Columbia, 1939. Bar: N.Y. 1939. Editor-in-chief Columbia Law Rev., 1938-39; pvt. practice N.Y.C., 1939-40; atty. U.S. Dept. of Labor, Washington, 1940; chief nat. defense sect. in law dept. FCC, 1941; sect. of law com. and adviser on internat. communications Bd. of War Communications, 1941-42; prin., divisional asst., adviser on wartime econ. controls and on European liberated areas U.S. Dept. State, 1942-43; asst. gen. counsel UNRRA, 1944-46; drafting officer UNRRA council sessions, 1944-45; legal adv. UNRRA del. to USSR and Poland, 1945; legal counselor UN, 1946-52, dir. gen. legal div., 1952-66; dep. exec. dir., dir. studies UN Inst. for Tng. and Research, 1966-75; lectr. law Yale U. Law Sch., 1955-71; Carnegie lectr. Hague Acad. Internat. Law, 1963-82; Rosenthal lectr. Northwestern U. Law Sch., 1974; prof. Law Sch. and Faculty Internat. Affairs Columbia U., 1975—, Hamilton Fish prof. internat. law and diplomacy Law Sch. and Faculty Internat. Affairs, 1980-85, prof. emeritus Law Sch. and Faculty Internat. Affairs, 1985—; vis. prof Harvard Law Sch., 1982; chmn. legal com. UN Maritime Conf., 1948; legal cons. UNESCO, 1948; past dir. Gen. Legal Div. of UN; served as legal adviser various internat. confs. and UN couns. and coms.; sec. legal adv. com. UN Atomic Energy Commn., 1946-47; vice chmn. Internat. Investment Law Conf., 1958; exec. sec. Internat. Arbitration Conf., 1958; mem. panel arbitrators Internat. Ctr. for Settlement of Investment Disputes, 1980-87; judge Ct. Arbitration in Canada-France Maritime Boundary dispute, 1989-92; expert advisor UN com. on transnational sorps., 1990-93. Author: Relation of Law, Politics and Action in the U.N, 1964, Sharing the World's Resources, 1977, International Law in Theory and Practice, 1985, rev. edit., 1991; co-author: Across the Space Frontier, 1952, Toward Wider Acceptance of UN Treaties, 1971, International Law Cases and Materials, 1980, 3rd edit., 1993; contbr. articles and monographs on internat. law, internat. instns., legal philosophy, human rights, internat. peace and security, internat. resources to legal jours.; editor-in-chief Am. Jour. Internat. Law, 1978-84, hon. editor, 1985—; co-editor: Competition in International Business, 1981; editorial bd. Marine Policy. Bd. dirs. Internat. Peace Acad., 1970-82. Recipient Friedman award Columbia Law Sch., 1983, Carl Fulda award U. Tex. Law Sch., 1990, Columbia Law medal for excellence, 1991. Fellow Am. Acad. Arts and Scis., World Acad. Art and Sci.; mem. ABA, Am. Soc. Internat. Law (pres. 1968-70, hon. v.p., exec. coun., hon. pres. 1994—, Manley Hudson medal 1981, Cert. of Merit for creative scholarship 1992), Coun. on Fgn. Rels., Inst. de Droit Internat. (v.p. 1991—), Internat. Law Assn., Internat. Astronautical Acad., Phi Beta Kappa. Home: 11 E 86th St New York NY 10028-0548 Office: Columbia U Law Sch New York NY 10027

SCHACHTER, STEVEN CRAIG, neurologist; b. Cleve., Mar. 13, 1955; s. Robert and Diana (Marmorstein) S.; m. Susan Ginsberg, Aug. 14, 1977; children: Michael, David. BA, Western Res. Coll., 1976; MD, Case Western Res. U., 1980. Diplomate Am. Bd. Psychiatry and Neurology, Am. Bd. Clin. Neurophysiology, Nat. Bd. Med. Examiners; lic. physician, Mass. Intern N.C. Meml. Hosp., Chapel Hill, 1980-81; resident Longwood Area Neurology Program, Boston, 1981-84; teaching fellow in family medicine Case Western Res. Sch. Medicine, Cleve., 1977-78; fellow in electroencephalography and clin. epilepsy Beth Israel Hosp., Boston, 1984-86; clin. fellow in neurology Harvard U., Boston, 1981-84, instr. neurology, 1984-94, asst. prof., 1994—; from asst. in neurology to sr. assoc. neurology Beth Israel Hosp., Boston, 1985—; asst. in neurology Children's Hosp., Boston, 1988—; courtesy staff Deaconess Hosp., Faulkner Hosp., Boston. Contbr. numerous articles to profl. jours. Recipient Donald E. Minch Meml. award, 1980, Sandoz award, 1983, others; grantee NIH, Burroughs-Wellcome, Abbott Labs., Janssen Pharm., others. Mem. AAAS, AMA, Am. Acad. Neurology, Boston Soc. Psychiatry and Neurology, Mass. Med. Soc., Norfolk Dist. Med. Soc., Am. EEG Soc., N.Y. Acad. Scis., Mass. Neurol. Assn., Am. Acad. Clin. Neurophysiology, Am. Epilepsy Soc., Nat. Assn. Epilepsy Ctrs., Epilepsy Found. Am. (mem. profl. adv. bd.), Epilepsy Assn. Mass. (pres.), Soc. for Music Perception and Cognition, Rodin Remediation Acad., Alpha Omega Alpha. Home: 10 Pioneer Cir Sharon MA 02067-2744 Office: Beth Israel Hosp EEG Lab 330 Brookline Ave Boston MA 02215-5400

SCHACHTER, WILLIAM DAVID, sales and marketing executive; b. Bklyn., Apr. 7, 1942; s. Harold and Sadie (Holtzman) S.; m. Elaine T. Greenburg, Dec. 21, 1969; children—Mindy Beth, Randi Michelle. B.S., U.R.I., 1964; M.B.A., Pepperdine U., 1978. Salesman, Gt. Northern Investors, N.Y.C., 1968-70, Roerig div. Pfizer, N.Y.C., 1970-72; regional mgr. Crain Communications, Los Angeles, 1972-74; sales mgr. East/West Network, N.Y.C and Los Angeles, 1974-79; advt. dir. Mag. Div. OAG Inc., N.Y.C., 1979—; pres., CEO CSI Internat., N.Y.C., 1983—. Served to capt. Inf., U.S. Army, 1965-68; Vietnam. Republican. Jewish. Home: 1135 Park Ave New York NY 10017 Office: CSI Internat 800 2nd Ave New York NY 10017-4709

SCHACK, MARY LOU, clinical psychologist, educator; b. New Brunswick, N.J., June 28, 1941; d. John Alexander and Mary Grace (Rooney) S. BA, Trenton State Coll., 1963; MA, Temple U., 1969, PhD, 1972. Lic. psychologist, Pa. English tchr. Woodbridge (N.J.) Twp. Pub. Schs., 1963-67; teaching asst. psychology Temple U., Phila., 1968-72; postdoctoral intern Community Guidance Ctr., Trenton and Princeton, N.J., 1972-73; supervising psychologist Ill. Masonic Med. Ctr., Chgo., 1974-77; asst. clin. prof. Abraham Lincoln Med. U., Chgo., 1975-77; chief psychologist Phila. Psychol. Ctr., 1977-81; clin. asst. prof. psychology U. Pa., Phila., 1979-82; founder, dir. faculty Gestalt Therapy Inst. Phila., Bryn Mawr, 1982—; prs. PsychSolutions, Bala Cynwyd, Pa., 1992—. Dir. Eromin, Inc., Phila., 1978-82. Recipient scholarship N.J., 1959-63; fellow Temple U., 1969-72. Fellow Pa. Psychol. Assn., Phila. Soc. Clin. Psychologists (exec. bd. dirs. 1978-82); mem. APA, Assn. for Advancement of Gestalt Therapy. Avocations: gardening, collecting majolica. Home: 1315 Arrowmink Rd Villanova PA 19085-2147 Office: PsychSolutions 191 Presidential Blvd Ste # 113 Bala Cynwyd PA 19004-1004

SCHACTER, BRENT ALLAN, foundation administrator; b. Winnipeg, Man., Can., June 1, 1942; s. Irvin C. and Claire (Easton) S.; m. Sora Ludwig, Dec. 20, 1981; children: Isanne, Jennifer, Miriam. BSc, U. Man., 1965, MD with honors, 1965. Intern Winnipeg Gen. Hosp., 1965-66, jr. asst. resident, 1967-68; asst. resident internal medicine Barnes Hosp., St. Louis, 1968-69; clin. fellow hematology Barnes Hosp. and Washington U., St. Louis, 1969-70; rsch. fellow, asst. in medicine U. Tex. Southwestern Med. Sch., Dallas, 1970-72; asst. prof. internal medicine U. Man., Winnipeg, 1972-77, assoc. prof. medicine, 1977-87, prof., 1987—; Nat. Cancer Inst. of Can. Rsch. fellow Man. Cancer Treatment and Rsch. Found., Winnipeg, 1966-67, pres., CEO, 1993—; lectr. in field; sci. officer grant panel C, Nat. Cancer Inst. Can., 1978, mem., 1979-82; mem. Man. Health Rsch. Coun. grant panel, 1982-84, 89-91; adv. bd. Can. Porphyria Found., 1988—. Contbr. numerous articles and abstracts to profl. jours. Recipient Med. Rsch. Coun. Can. Vis. Scientist award, 1986; fellow Muscular Dystrophy Assn., 1964, John S. McEachern Meml. fellow Can. Cancer Soc., 1969-70, Med. Rsch. Coun. Can. fellow, 1970-72; Isbister scholar, Med. Rsch. Coun. Can. scholar, 1962, 75-80. Fellow Royal Coll. Physicians; mem. AAAS, Royal Coll. Physicians and Surgeons of Can. (specialty com. in med. oncology 1985—, bd. med. examiners in med. oncology 1987-90, specialty com. in hematology 1989-93, core com. mem. 1990—, chmn. bd. examiners med. oncology 1990-93, mem. regional adv. com. Sask./Man. dist. 1992—), Am. Fedn. for Clin. Rsch., Can. Soc. for Clin. Investigation (mem. awards com. 1980-82, chmn. 1981-82), Am. Assn. for Study of Liver Diseases, Am. Soc. Hematology, Can. Soc.

Hematology, Am. Soc. Clin. Oncology, Can. Bone Marrow Transplant Group, Can. Hemophilia Soc. (mem. clinic dirs. group 1990-93, sec-treas. 1991-93), Can. Liver Club. Avocations: cross-country skiing, scuba diving, model railroading. Home: 224 Lamont Blvd, Winnipeg, MB Canada R3P 0E9 Office: Manitoba Cancer Treatment and Research Foundation, 100 Olivia St, Winnipeg R3E 0V9

SCHAD, JAMES L., bishop; b. Phila., July 20, 1917. Grad. St. Mary's Sem., Balt. Ordained priest Roman Catholic Ch., 1943; ordained titular bishop of Panatoria and aux. bishop of Camden, 1966—; ret. Home: 1730 Kresson Rd Cherry Hill NJ 08003-2517

SCHAD, MIKE, professional football player; b. Trenton, ON, Canada, Oct. 2, 1963. BS, geography, physiology, Queens Coll., Canada, 1986. With L. A. Rams, 1986-89; guard Philadelphia Eagles, 1989-94, Cleveland Browns, 1994—. Dr. Z's All-Pro team, 1994.

SCHAD, THEODORE MACNEEVE, science research administrator, consultant; b. Balt., Aug. 25, 1918; s. William Henry and Emma Margaret (Scheldt) S.; m. Kathleen White, Nov. 5, 1944 (dec. Aug. 1989); children: Mary Jane, Rebecca Christina; m. Margot Cornwell, March 19, 1995. BSCE, Johns Hopkins U., 1939. Registered profl. engr., D.C. Various positions water resources engrng. U.S. Army C.E., U.S. Bur. Reclamation, Md., Colo., Oreg. Wash., 1939-54; prin. budget examiner water resources programs U.S. Bur. Budget, Exec. Office of Pres., 1954-58; sr. specialist engrng. and pub. works, dep. dir. Congl. Rsch. Svc., Libr. of Congress, 1958-68; staff dir. U.S. Senate Com. Nat. Water Resources, 1959-61; exec. dir. Nat. Water Commn., 1968-73; exec. sec. Environ. Studies Bd., 1973-77; dep. dir. Commn. Natural Resources, NAS, Washington, 1977-83; exec. dir. Nat. Ground Water Policy Forum, 1984-86; sr. fellow Conservation Found., Washington, 1986-; U.S. commr. Permanent Internat. Assn. Nav. Congresses, Brussels, 1963-70, commr. emeritus, 1987—; cons. U.S. Senate Com. Interior and Insular Affairs, 1963, U.S. Ho. of Reps. Com. Sci. and Tech., 1962-65, U.S. Office Saline Water, 1965-67, A.T. Kearney, Inc., Alexandria, Va., 1979-80, Chesapeake Rsch. Consortium, 1984, Ronco Cons. Corp., 1986—, Gambia River Basin Devel. Commn., Dakar, 1986-87, Apogee Rsch. Corp., 1987—, Office Tech. Assessment, U.S. Congress, 1992-95. Contbr. articles to Ency. Brit. and profl. jours. Treas. Nat. Speleol. Found., 1961-65, trustee, 1965—; bd. dirs. Vets. Coop. Housing Assn., Washington, 1958-81, v.p., 1960-72. Recipient Meritorious Svc. award U.S. Dept. Interior, 1950, Icko Iben award Am. Water Resources Assn., 1978, Henry P. Caulfield medal, 1990. Fellow ASCE (treas. Nat. Capital chpt. 1952-55, v.p. 1967, pres. 1968, Julian Hinds prize 1991); mem. AAAS, Nat. Speleol. Soc., Am. Water Works Assn. (hon.), Am. Geophys. Union, Am. Acad. Environ. Engrs., Nat. Acad. Pub. Adminstrn., Permanent Internat. Assn. Nav. Congresses, Internat. Commn. Irrigation and Drainage, Potomac Appalachian Trail Club, Cosmos Club, Colo. Mountain Club (Denver), Seattle Mountaineers Club. Home: 4540-25th Rd N Arlington VA 22207-4102 Office: The Conservation Found 1260-24th St NW Washington DC 20037

SCHADE, MALCOLM ROBERT, lawyer; b. Holyoke, Mass., Oct. 23, 1950; s. G. Malcolm and Dorothy Jean (Alderman) S.; m. Charlanne Reid Murray, June 26, 1971. BA magna cum laude, Windham Coll., 1971; JD, Columbia U., 1974, postgrad., 1975-76. Bar: N.Y. 1975, Mass. 1975, U.S. Dist. Ct. (so., ea., we. & no. dists.) N.Y. 1975, U.S. Ct. Appeals (2d cir.) 1975, U.S. Ct. Appeals (1st cir.) 1976, U.S. Supreme Ct. 1978, U.S. Dist. Ct. Vt. 1980, U.S. Ct. Appeals (6th cir.) 1985, U.S. Dist. Ct. (ea. dist.) Mich. 1988. Assoc. Kronish, Lieb, Shainswit, Weiner & Hellman, N.Y.C., 1977-79, Skadden Arps Slate Meagher & Flom, N.Y.C., 1980-83; ptnr. Alexander & Green, N.Y.C., 1984-86, Mudge Rose Guthrie Alexander & Ferdon, N.Y.C., 1987-95, Thacher, Proffit & Wood, N.Y.C., 1995—. Rapporteur (book) American Hostages in Iran, 1985. Trustee Windham Coll., Putney, Vt., 1970-71, 76-80, sec., 1977-80, chmn. bd., 1978-80. Mem. Assn. Bar of City of N.Y. (com. on internat. arms control & security affairs 1979-85), Mass. Bar Assn., Comml. Bar Assn. (London, overseas mem.), Down Town Assn., Larchmont Shore Club (bd. dirs. 1995—), Horseshoe Harbor Yacht Club. Congregationalist. Avocations: sailing, hunting, skiing. Home: 24 Beech Rd New Rochelle NY 10804-4304 Office: Thacher Proffitt & Wood Two World Trade Ctr New York NY 10048

SCHADE, STANLEY GREINERT, JR., hematologist, educator; b. Pitts., Dec. 21, 1933; s. Stanley G. and Charlotte (Marks) S.; m. Sylvia Zottu, Mar. 24, 1966; children: David Stanley, Robert Edward. BA in English, Hamilton Coll., 1955; MD, Yale U., 1961. Diplomate Am. Bd. Internal Medicine, Am. Bd. Hematology, Am. Bd. Oncology. Intern, resident, hematology fellow U. Wis., Madison, 1962-66; chief hematology Westside VA Hosp., Chgo., 1971-77; prof. medicine, chief hematology U. Ill., Chgo., 1978—. Contbr. articles to profl. jours. Served to maj. U.S. Army, 1967-69. Fulbright fellow Tubingen, Fed. Republic of Germany, 1956. Fellow Am. Coll. Physicians; mem. Am. Soc. Hematology. Presbyterian. Avocation: medical ethics. Home: 189 N Delaplaine Rd Riverside IL 60546-2060 Office: U Ill Health Scis Ctr Hematology Sect Dept Med 840 S Wood St Chicago IL 60612-7317

SCHADE, WILBERT CURTIS, educational administrator; b. St. Louis, Jan. 4, 1945; s. Wilbert Curtis and Florence Mary (Allen) S.; m. Jacqueline Siewert, May 14, 1977; children: Benjamin Allen Siewert, Timothy Knorr Siewert. BA, U. Pa., 1967; AM, Washington U., St. Louis, 1970; PhD, Ind. U., 1986. Teaching asst. dept. Romance Lang. Washington U., St. Louis, 1967-68; tchr. French St. Louis Priory Sch., 1970-71; assoc. instr. Dept. French and Italian, Ind. U., Bloomington, 1972-74, 76-80; tchr. French Webster Groves (Mo.) H.S., 1975-76; asst. dir. admissions Beloit (Wis.) Coll., 1980-83, assoc. dir. admissions, 1983-84; dir. coll. placement and dir. admissions Westover Sch., Middlebury, Conn., 1984-90; head upper sch. The Key Sch., Annapolis, Md., 1990-94, interim dir. devel., 1994-95; dir. coll. counseling, tchr. French, head lang. dept. Wasatch Acad., Mt. Pleasant, Utah, 1995-96, asst. headmaster for acad. affairs, dir. coll. counseling, 1996—; mem. Utah State Office Edn. Fgn. Lang. Instrl. Materials & Textbook Adv. Com., 1996—; lectr. in field. Co-editor: African Literature in its Social and Political Dimensions, 1983; contbr. articles to profl. jours. including World Lit. Written in English, Studies in 20th Century Lit. and articles in books. Mem. Anne Arundel County (Md.) Task Force on Year Round Edn., 1994-95. NEH Summer Inst. on African Am. Lit. and Film grantee, 1994. Mem. Nat. Assn. Coll. Admission Counselors (presenter nat. conf. 1985), African Lit. Assn. (exec. com. 1979), Phi Delta Kappa. Soc. of Friends. Avocation: tennis. Home: 47 S 100 W Mount Pleasant UT 84647 Office: Wasatch Acad 120 S 100 W Mount Pleasant UT 84647

SCHADT, JAMES P., publishing executive; s. Phillip Jr. and Jean D. (Cardy) S.; m. Barbara L. Soldmann, Aug. 16, 1959; children: Lauren C., Andrew F. BA, Northwestern U., 1960. With Procter & Gamble USA, 1960-73, Pepsi Inc., 1973-78, Consolidated Foods Corp., 1978-81; pres., CEO Cadbury Schweppes Inc., 1981-91; pres., COO Reader's Digest Assoc. Inc., Pleasantville, N.Y., 1991-94, pres., CEO, 1994—, chmn., pres., CEO, 1995—. Bd. dirs. DeWitt Wallace-Reader's Digest Fund, Lila Wallace-Reader's Digest Fund, DeWitt Wallace Fund for Meml. Sloan-Kettering Cancer Ctr., N.Y.C.; trustee Am. Enterprise Inst., Norwalk (Conn.) Hosp., Northwestern U. Mem. Am. Assn. Pubs., Bus. Roundtable, Mag. Pubs. Assn., Grocery Mfrs. Assn., Bling Brook Club, Purchase N.Y. Club, Chgo. Club, Fairfield County Hunt Club, Country Club of Fairfield, John's Island Club, Lotos Club. *

SCHADT, JAMES PHILLIP, consumer products executive; b. Saginaw, Mich., Aug. 7, 1938; s. Phillip, Jr., and Jean D. (Cardy) S.; BA, Northwestern U., 1960; m. Barbara L. Soldmann, Aug. 16, 1959; children: Lauren C., Andrew F. With Procter & Gamble, 1960-65, Glendinning Cos., 1965-70, Squibb Corp., 1970-73, PepsiCo, 1973-77, Sara Lee Corp., 1977-80; pres. Cadbury Schweppes plc, Stamford, Conn., 1981-91, also dir.; pres., COO, dir. Reader's Digest Assn., 1991-94, dir, pres., CEO, 1994-95, chmn., CEO 1995—; bd. dirs. DeWitt Wallace-Reader's Digest Fund, Lila Wallace-Reader's Digest Fund, DeWitt Wallace Fund Meml. Sloat-Kettering Cancer Ctr.; trustee Am. Enterprise Inst., Norwalk (Conn.) Hosp., Northwestern U. Mem. Am. Assn. Pubs., Bus. Roundtable, Conf. Bd., Mag. Pubs. Assn., Heritage Found, Grocery Manufacturers Assn., Blind Brook Club, Chgo. Club, Fairfield County Hunt Club, Country Club Fairfield, John's Island Club, Lotos Club. Home: 17 Owenoke Park Westport CT 06880-6834 Office: Reader's Digest Assn Reader's Digest Rd Pleasantville NY 10570-7000

SCHAECHTER, MOSELIO, microbiology educator; b. Milan, Italy, Apr. 26, 1928; children: Judy, John. Student Central U., Ecuador, 1947-49; MA, U. Kans., 1952; PhD, U. Pa., 1954. Postdoctoral fellow State Serum Inst., Copenhagen, 1956-58; instr., asst. prof., assoc. prof. U. Fla., Gainesville, 1958-62; from assoc. prof. to disting. prof. dept. microbiology Tufts U., Boston, 1962-95, prof. emeritus 1995—; adj. prof. San Diego State U., 1995—. Editor: Molecular Biology Bacterial Growth, 1985, Escherichia coli and Salmonella Typhimurium, 1987, 95, Mechanisms of Microbiol. Disease, 1989, 92. Mem. Am. Soc. Microbiology (pres. 1985-86, chmn. internat. activities), Am. Soc. Med. Sch. Microbiology Chmn. (pres. 1984-85, chair internat. activities 1986-94), Soc. Gen. Microbiology, Boston Mycol. Club, Sigma Xi. Avocations: field mycology; hiking. Office: San Diego State U Dept Biology San Diego CA 92182

SCHAEDLER, RUSSELL WILLIAM, microbiologist, physicians, educator; b. Hatfield, Pa., Dec. 17, 1927; s. Robert and Sophia Louise (Enz) S. B.S., Ursinus Coll., 1949; M.D., Jefferson Med. Coll., 1953. Intern Jefferson Med. Coll. Hosp., Thomas Jefferson U., Phila., 1953-54; prof., chmn. dept. microbiology Jefferson Med. Coll. Hosp., Thomas Jefferson U., 1968-91, Plimpton-Pugh prof., 1985—; asst. Rockefeller Inst. for Med. Research, asst. physician Hosp. of Rockefeller Inst., 1954-57; asst. prof. Rockefeller Inst., resident asso. physician, 1957-62, asso. prof., physician to Hosp., 1962-68; asso. mem. Armed Forces Epidemiology Bd., Enteric Commn., 1967-72; mem. bacteriology and mycology study sect. NIH, 1970-74, chmn., 1973-74; mem. and chmn. NIH bacteriology and mycology AHR study sect., 1978-82. Mem. editorial bd. Jour. Bacteriology, 1965-69, Jour. Infection and Immunity, 1970-72; contbr. articles to sci. jours. Bd. dirs. Cardeza Found. Served with U.S. Army, 1946-47. Mem. Am. Assn. Immunologists, Am. Soc. Microbiology, Am. Gastroent. Assn., Infectious Disease Soc. Am., Coll. Physicians Phila., Harvey Soc., AAAS, J. Aitken Meigs Med. Assn., N.Y. Tb and Health Assn. (bd. dirs. 1965-68), Sigma Xi, Alpha Omega Alpha. Clubs: Vesper, Sydenham Coterie. Research in anaerobes and microecology of the gut. Home: 320 Delancey St Philadelphia PA 19106-4209 Office: 1020 Locust St Philadelphia PA 19107-6731

SCHAEFER, ADOLPH OSCAR, JR., advertising agency executive; b. Phila., May 21, 1932; s. Adolph Oscar and Jessie Rae (Brooks) S.; m. Leslie C. Maurer, May 4, 1994; children by previous marriage: Jeffrey S., Andrew C.; adopted children: Deborah H., Scott S., Adrian L. Maurer, Senta G. Maurer. B.S. in Econs., Wharton Sch., U. Pa., 1954. With drug products div. Procter & Gamble, Cin., 1954-56; mfrs. rep. Towle & Son Co., Phila., 1956-61; ptnr. Rockett & Schaefer Advt., Phila., 1961-63; v.p. Eldridge Co., Phila., 1963-64; pres. Schaefer Advt. Inc., Valley Forge, Pa., 1964-87, chmn. bd. dirs., 1987-89; chmn. Direct Strategies, Inc., Devon, Pa., 1989-92. Mem. editorial adv. bd.: Pa. Gazette, U. Pa., 1970-72. Mem. alumni bd. mgrs. Episcopal Acad., 1969-73; pres. Valley Forge Gallery, Pa., 1992—, Corporate Insights, Wayne, Pa. Served with U.S. Army, 1954-56. Mem. Bus. and Profl. Advt. Assn. (Hall of Fame 1993), Pa. Soc. SAR, Union League Club, Phi Gamma Delta. Home: PO Box 752 Valley Forge PA 19482-0752

SCHAEFER, C. BARRY, railroad executive, lawyer, investment banker; b. Elizabeth, N.J., Feb. 23, 1939; s. Carl H. and Evelyn G. (Conk) S.; m. Carol Ann Craft, July 11, 1970; children: Sara Elizabeth, Susan Craft. BS in Engring., Princeton U., 1961; MS in Engring., U. Pa., 1962; LLB, Columbia U., 1965; MBA, NYU, 1970. Bar: N.Y. 1966, Nebr. 1972. With Kelley, Drye, Warren, N.Y.C., 1966-69; asst. gen. counsel Union Pacific Corp., N.Y.C., 1969-72; western gen. counsel Union Pacific R.R. Co., Omaha, 1972-74, v.p., western gen. counsel, 1974-77, v.p. law, 1977-82; sr. v.p. planning and corp. devel. Union Pacific Corp., N.Y.C., 1984-88; exec. v.p. Union Pacific Corp., Bethlehem, Pa., 1988; sr. advisor Dillon Read & Co. Inc., 1989-91; mng. dir. The Bridgeford Group, 1992—; dir. Ultramar Corp. Nat. bd. dirs. Jr. Achievement, Colorado Springs, Colo., 1986—. Mem. ABA, Nebr. Bar Assn., Racquet and Tennis Club (N.Y.C.), Round Hill Club (Greenwich, Conn.), Desert Mountain Club (Scottsdale, Ariz.).

SCHAEFER, CARL GEORGE LEWIS, writer, public relations and advertising executive; b. Cleve.; s. George S. and Margaret (Freyberg) S.; m. Virginia Clark, Sept. 2, 1938; 1 dau., Susan Diane Schaefer Francis. A.B., UCLA, 1931. Freelance mag. writer, 1931; pres. Pacific Intercollegiate Press Assn., 1931-32; reporter Hollywood (Calif.) Citizen-News, 1931-35; with Warner Bros.-Seven Arts, Burbank, Calif., 1935-71; dir. internat. relations Warner Bros.-Seven Arts, 1962-71; owner Carl Schaefer Enterprises, Hollywood, 1971—; bur. chief movie/TV mktg. Movie News, Singapore, Antena, B.A., 1975—; coord. internat. poster competition Hollywood Reporter, 1971-82, dir. spl. projects; exec. com. ShoWest, 1978—. Mem. internat. com. Acad. Motion Picture Arts and Scis., 1940—; chmn. internat. Hollywood Mus., 1964; vice chmn. Hollywood-Wilshire council Girl Scouts U.S., 1957-58; mem. Mayor Los Angeles Council Internat. Visitors, 1964—; mem. interview bd. Los Angeles Police Dept., 1965—; mem. adv. com. West Hollywood Hosp., 1983—; mng. dir. Internat. Festival Adv. Council, 1971—; nat. panel consumer arbitrators Better Bus. Bur. Los Angeles, 1984—; co-founder con. fgn. Oscars Acad. Motion Picture Arts & Scis. Served with OSS, World War II, ETO; ensign Calif. Naval Militia, 1935-36. Decorated Huesped de Honor Mexico; Legion of Honor France; Ordine al Merito Italy; l'Ordre de la Courrenne Belgium; recipient service plaque Acad. Motion Picture Arts and Scis., The Hollywood Reporter Spl. Key Art award, 1990. Mem. Am. Soc. French Legion of Honor, Assn. Motion Picture and TV Producers (chmn. internat. co. 1967-68, 69-70), Publicists Guild Am. (charter), Internat. Press Photo-Journalists (hon.), Fgn. Trade Assn. So. Calif. (past pres., chmn. bd.), Brit.-Am. (dir.), Los Angeles Chambers Commerce, Culver City C. of C., Western Pubs. Assn., Am. Bus. Press, Blue Key, Sigma Alpha Epsilon, Alpha Delta Sigma. Republican. Methodist. Clubs: Mason (Los Angeles) (Shriner), Press (Los Angeles), Brit. United Services (Los Angeles). Address: 3320 Bennett Dr Hollywood CA 90068-1704 *When I lose my imagination, I'll be more than happy to cash in the chips whatever—and slink off.*

SCHAEFER, CHARLES JAMES, III, advertising agency executive, consultant; b. Orange, N.J., Dec. 17, 1926; m. Eleanor Anne Montville, Apr. 8, 1961; 1 child, Charles James IV. A.B., Dartmouth Coll., 1948, M. Comml. Sci. Amos Tuck Sch., 1949. V.p. Dickie-Raymond, 1952-67; sr. v.p. Metromedia, 1968-69; exec. v.p., treas. The DR Group, Boston, 1969-76, pres., 1976-87; exec. v.p., dir. Needham Harper Worldwide Inc., N.Y.C., 1984-87; chmn. bd. Marcoa DR Group, Inc., N.Y.C., 1987-88; cons. Rapp Collins Marcoa, N.Y.C., 1989-92; advt. cons., 1992—. Trustee, mem. exec. com. Direct Mktg. Ednl. Found., 1983-89. With USN, 1945-46. Mem. Direct Mktg. Assn. (chmn. awards com. 1971-76, Hall of Fame com. 1978-81, ethics com. 1981-86), Assn. Direct Mktg. Agys. (pres. 1980-82, gen. chmn. Caples awards 1985, Direct Mktg. Day N.Y. 1988, N.Y. Direct Marketer of Yr. award 1987, Silver Apple award 1989, contbr. to jour.), Dartmouth Club of N.Y. (pres. 1968-70), Lotos Club (bd. dirs. 1985-88, treas. 1987-88), Canoe Brook Country Club (Summit, N.J.). Home and Office: 307 Hobart Ave Short Hills NJ 07078-2207

SCHAEFER, DAN L., congressman; b. Gutenberg, Iowa, Jan. 25, 1936; s. Alvin L. and Evelyn (Everson) S.; m. Mary Margaret Lenney, 1959; children: Danny, Darren, Joel, Jennifer. B.A., Niagara U., 1961, LLD (hon.), 1986; postgrad., Potsdam State U., 1961-64. Pub. relations cons., 1967-83; mem. Colo. Gen. Assembly, 1977-78; mem. Colo. Senate, 1979-83, pres. pro tem, 1981-82, majority whip, 1983; mem. 98th-103rd Congresses from 6th dist. Colo., Washington, 1983—; mem. house small bus. com., 1983, govt. ops. com., 1983, energy and commerce com., 1984-86 (subcoms. on fossil and synthetic fuels; commerce, transp. and tourism; oversight/investigations), environ. and energy study com., 1987— (subcoms. on Transp. and Hazardous materials, Telecom. and Fin.), Energy and Commerce ranking Rep Oversight and Investigations, 1993—, Rep. study com.; mem. house sci. and high tech. task force, mil. reforms caucus, congl. grace caucus; mem. adv. com., com. of concern for Soviet Jewry; mem. exec. bd. Environ. and Energy Study Com., 1995; chmn. Subcom. on Energy and Power House Commerce Com.; mem. Subcom. on Telecom. and Fin., House Vet. Affiars Com., Subcom. on Edn., Training, Employment and Housing, 1995—; co-chmn. The Mainstream Conservative Alliance. Co-chair Nat. Retail Sales Tax Caucus, Congl. Oil and Gas Forum; mem. Spkrs. Task Force on Environ.; founder House Renewable Energy Caucus; pres. Foothills Recreation Bd., 1973-76; sec. Jefferson County Rep. Party, Colo., 1975-76. With USMCR, 1955-57. Recipient Colo. Park and Recreation citation, 1976; named Elected Ofcl. of Yr., Lakewood/South Jeffco C. of C., 1986, 88, 90, Leadership award U.S. Congl. Adv. Bd., Am. Security Coun. Found., Taxpayers Friend award Nat. Taxpayer's Union, 1985-86, 88, 90, 91, 92, 93, 94, 95, Golden Bulldog award Watchdog of Treasury, 1985-86, 87-88, 88-89, 89-90, 91-92, 93-94, Spirit of Enterprise award U.S. C. of C., 1995, Nat. Health award Am. Assn. Nurse Anesthetists, 1996, Nat. Security Scorecare Perfect 100 award Ctr. for Security Policy, 1995. Mem. C. of C., Beta Theta Pi. Roman Catholic. Lodge: Rotary. Office: House of Representatives 2353 Rayburn House Office B Washington DC 20515

SCHAEFER, DAVID ARNOLD, lawyer; b. Cleve., May 3, 1948; s. Leonard and Maxine V. (Bassett) S.; m. Riki C. Freeman, Aug. 8, 1971; children—Kevin, Lindsey, Traci. BS, Miami U., Oxford, Ohio, 1970; MA, Northwestern, U., 1971; JD, Case Western Res. U., 1974. Bar: Ohio 1974, U.S. Dist. Ct. (no. dist.) Ohio 1974, U.S. Ct. Appeals (6th cir.) 1978, U.S. Supreme Ct. 1978. Ptnr. Guren, Merritt et al, 1980-84, Benesch, Friedlander et al, Cleve., 1984-93; McCarthy, Lebit, Crystal & Haiman, Cleve., 1993—; Author: Deposition Strategy, 1981, 2d edit., 1984; contbr. articles to profl. pubis. Soccer coach Ohio Amateur Youth Soccer League, Cleve., 1980-81, 84. Mem. ABA, Ohio State Bar Assn., Ohio Acad. Trial Lawyers (Disting. Svc. award 1980, seminar speaker 1982), Fed. Bar Assn. (pres. elect 1991-92, pres. 1992-93), Nat. Inst. Trial Advocacy (faculty), 8th Dist. Jud. Conf. (life). Office: McCarthy Lebit 1800 Midland Bldg 101 Prospect Ave W Cleveland OH 44115

SCHAEFER, GEORGE A., JR., bank executive. Chmn., pres., CEO Fifth Third Bancorp, Cin. Office: Fifth Third Bancorp 38 Fountain Square Plz Cincinnati OH 45263-0001*

SCHAEFER, GEORGE LOUIS, theatrical producer and director, educator; b. Wallingford, Conn., Dec. 16, 1920; s. Louis and Elsie (Otterbein) S.; m. Mildred Trares, Feb. 5, 1954. BA magna cum laude, Lafayette Coll., 1941, LittD, 1963; postgrad., Yale Drama Sch., 1942; LHD, Coker Coll., 1973. Producer, dir. TV series Hallmark Hall of Fame, 1955-68; freelance producer, dir., 1945—; assoc. dean sch. theater, film and TV UCLA, 1986-91; artistic dir. N.Y.C. Ctr. Theatre Co., 1949-52; dir. Dallas State Fair Musicals, 1952-58; pres. Compass Prodns., Inc., 1959-86. Dir. Broadway prodns. G.I. Hamlet, 1945, Man and Superman, 1947, The Linden Tree, 1948, The Heiress (revival), 1949, Idiot's Delight (revival), 1950, Southwest Corner, 1955, The Apple Cart, 1956, The Body Beautiful, 1958, Write Me a Murder, 1961, The Great Indoors, 1966, The Last of Mrs. Lincoln, 1972, Mixed Couples, 1980; co-prodr. Broadway and London prodns. The Teahouse of the August Moon, 1953; dir., co-prodr. Zenda for L.A. Civic Light Opera Co., 1963; prodr. To Broadway with Love for N.Y. World's Fair, 1964; prodr., dir. TV spls. Do Not Go Gentle Into That Good Night, 1967, A War of Children, Sandburg's Lincoln, 1974-76, In This House of Brede, 1975, Truman at Potsdam, Amelia Earhart, 1976, Our Town, 1977, First You Cry, Orchard Children, 1978, Blind Ambition, Mayflower, 1979, The Bunker, 1981, Jean Harris Trial, 1982, A Piano for Mrs. Cimino, 1982, Deadly Game, 1983, Answers, 1983, Right of Way, 1983, Children in the Crossfire, 1984, Stone Pillow, 1985, Mrs. Delafield Wants to Marry, 1986, Laura Lansing Slept Here, 1988, Let Me Hear You Whisper, 1990, The Man Upstairs, 1992, Harvey, 1996; dir. films An Enemy of the People, Generation, Doctor's Wives, Pendulum, Macbeth; dir. L.A. prodn. Leave It To Jane, 1987. Mem. Nat. Council on the Arts, 1983-88. Recipient Emmy awards, 1959, 60, 61, 68, 73, Dirs. Guild Am. TV awards, 1961, 64, 67, 68, Dinneen award Nat. Cath. Theatre Conf., 1964; named Dir. of Yr., Radio-TV Daily, 1957, 60, 63, 65; Am. Theatre fellow, 1995. Mem. Dirs. Guild Am. (v.p. 1961-79, pres. 1979-81), Phi Beta Kappa.

SCHAEFER, GORDON EMORY, food company executive; b. 1932; married. BS, Marquette U., 1956. With Peat, Marwick, Mitchell & Co., 1955-59; treas. Pabst Brewing Co., Milw., 1965-72, v.p. adminstrn., 1972-75, v.p. ops., 1975-76, exec. v.p. ops., 1976-89, cons., 1980—, dir.; pres., dir. Krier Foods Inc., Belgium, Wis., 1981-85, Corrs Beverages, Chgo., 1985-86; dir. bus. devel. Lakeside Packing Co., Manitowoc, Wis., 1989-92; mng. dir. Robertson Assocs., Mfg. Europe Ltd., Cardiff, Wales, U.K., 1993-94; bd. dirs. Fox Fin. Co., Grand Rapids, Mich., Melal Packaging Internat., Denver, Borg Industries, Inc., Marshfield, Wis.; fin. and ops. cons.; owner, operator Schaefer's Orchards. Home: 154 Granville Rd Cedarburg WI 53012-9509

SCHAEFER, HANS-ECKART, pathologist; b. Koblenz, Germany, Sept. 8, 1936; s. Hans and Mathilde (Sellerbeck) S.; m. Birgit Peters, Apr. 19, 1966. Degree in medicine, U. Mainz, Fed. Republic Germany, 1958; postgrad., U. Bonn, Fed. Republic Germany, 1962; MD, U. Bonn, 1963; PhD, U. Köln, Fed. Republic Germany, 1970. Med. diplomate. Resident Kantonales Hosp., Walenstadt, Switzerland, Städtisches Hosp., Pforzheim, Bollmanns Hosp., Nienburg, 1961-63; asst. physician Inst. Pathology U. Bonn, 1963-67; asst. physician Inst. Pathology U. Köln, 1967-73, head dept. ultrastructural pathology, 1973-83; mng. dir. Inst. Pathology U. Freiburg, Fed. Republic Germany, 1983—; also chair gen. and spl. pathology U. Freiburg. Author: Leukopoese and Myeloproliferative Erkrankungen, 1984; co-editor textbook Allgemeine und Spezielle Pathologie, 1989, 93, 95; exec. editor Pathology Rsch. and Practice. Fellow Heidelberg Acad. Wissenschaften; mem. Gesellschaft Histochemie (pres. 1983-84), Internat. Acad. Pathology, Internat. Soc. Hematology, Deutsche Gesellschaft Pathologie, Soc. Europaea Pneumologica, Deutsche Gesellschaft Säugetierforschung, Deutsche Gesellschaft Arteriosklerosefoschung (pres. 1989-92), Deutsche Gesellschaft Hämatologie Onkologie. Avocation: harpsichord playing. Home: Weinbergstrasse 15, D 79249 Merzhausen Federal Republic of Germany Office: Inst Pathology, Alberstrasse 19 PO Box 214, D 79002 Freiburg Germany

SCHAEFER, HENRY FREDERICK, III, chemistry educator; b. Grand Rapids, Mich., June 8, 1944; s. Henry Frederick Jr. and Janice Christine (Trost) S.; m. Karen Regine Rasmussen, Sept. 2, 1966; children: Charlotte, Pierre, Theodore, Rebecca, Caleb. BS in Chem. Physics, MIT, 1966; PhD in Chem. Physics, Stanford U., 1969. Asst. prof. chemistry U. Calif., Berkeley, 1969-74, assoc. prof., 1974-78, prof., 1978-87; Graham Perdue prof., dir. Ctr. for Computational Quantum Chemistry U. Ga., Athens, 1987—; Wilfred T. Doherty prof., dir. Inst. Theoretical Chemistry, U. Tex., Austin, 1979-80; endowed lectr. nat. U. Mex., 1979, Johns Hopkins U., 1982, Brown U., 1985, U. Canterbury, Christchurch, Ne Zealand, 1986, U. Kans., 1986, Vanderbilt U., 1988, U. Va., 1988, U. Alta, 1990, U. Guelph, Waterloo, Ont., 1991, Case Western Res. U., 1992, Kans. State U., 1993; Francis A. Schaeffer lectr. Covenant Sem., St. Louis, 1995; Mary E. Kapp lectr. Va. Commonwealth U., 1996. Author over 700 scientific puls. including: The Electronic Structure of Atoms and Molecules: A Survey of Rigorous Quantum Mechanical Results, 1972, Modern Theoretical Chemistry, 1977, Quantum Chemistry, 1983, A new Dimension to Quantum Chemistry, 1994; editor Jour. molecular Physics, 1991—. Recipient Pure Chemistry award Am. Chem. Soc., 1979, Leo Hendrik Baekeland award, 1983, Centenary medal Royal Soc. Chemistry, London, 1992; Sloan fellow, 1972, Guggenheim fellow, 1976-77; named one of 100 Outstanding Young Scientists in Am., Sci. Digest, 1984, named 3rd Most Highly cited chemist in world Science Watch, 1992. Fellow Am. Phys. Soc., Am. Sci. Affiliation; mem. Internat. Acad. Quantum Molecular Sci., Am. Chem. Soc. (chmn. divsn. phys. chemistry 1992). Presbyterian. Office: U Ga Ctr Computational Quantum Chemistry Athens GA 30602

SCHAEFER, J. SCOTT, religious organization administrator. Chief business officer San Francisco Theol. Sem. Presbyn. Ch., San Anselmo, Calif. Office: San Francisco Theol Sem 2 Kensington Rd San Anselmo CA 94960-2905

SCHAEFER, JACOB WERNLI, military systems consultant; b. Paullina, Iowa, June 27, 1919; s. Louis B. and Minnie (Wernli) S.; m. Mary Snow Carter, July 26, 1941; children: Joanna, James, Scott. B.M.E., Ohio State U., 1941, D.Sc. (hon.), 1976. Mem. staff Bell Labs., 1941-84; dir. Kwajalein (Marshall Islands) Field Sta., 1963-65; exec. dir. Holmdel, N.J., 1968-80, Murray Hill, N.J., 1980-81; exec. dir. Mil. Systems Div., Whippany, N.J., 1981-84, ret.; pvt. cons., 1984—. Contbr. articles to profl. jours. Pres.

Watchung (N.J.) Sch. Bd., 1954-63; trustee Bancroft Sch., Haddonfield, N.J., 1973—; chmn. Watchung Planning Bd., 1967-95; mem. Watchung Area coun. Boy Scouts Am., 1966-69. Capt. Ordnance Corps AUS, 1942-46. Recipient Disting. Alumnus award Ohio State U., 1966, 95, 2 Outstanding Civilian Svc. medals U.S. Army. Fellow IEEE; mem. Nat. Acad. Engring., ASME, Army Ordnance Assn. Republican. Patentee command guidance for anti-aircraft missiles, optical tracking systems for anti-aircraft fire control. Home: 115 Century Ln Watchung NJ 07060-6007

SCHAEFER, JIMMIE WAYNE, JR., agricultural company executive; b. Anna, Ill., Dec. 26, 1951; s. Jimmie Wayne and Wilma Jean (Kinder) S.; m. Melanie Kugel, Apr. 19, 1981; 1 child Jyoti. BS in Agronomy, So. Ill. U., 1974; MSCI, MERU, Switzerland, 1979. Br. mgr. World Plan Exec. Coun., Nashville, 1975-79; pres. Schaefer & Assoc., Inc., Fairfield, Iowa, 1979-82, J.W. Schaefer Mortgage Co., Fairfield, 1981-1982; chmn., chief exec. officer Soil Techs. Corp., Fairfield, 1982—; chmn. bd. Radiance Dairy Coop., Fairfield, 1980—; bd. dirs. FAE Credit Union, Fairfield, 1982-84; cons. BioField Rsch. Inc., Ottawa, Ont., Can., 1985—; lectr. microalgal applications in agr. to ednl. and rsch. instns. in numerous developing countries; mem. adv. bd. Inst. for Agr. and Environ. Studies, Maharishi Internat. U., Fairfield. Author: (with others) Turf Integrated Pest Management Systems, 1988; patentee in field. Mem. Am. Soc. Agronomy, Am. Soc. Agrl. Cons. Avocation: gentleman farmer. Home: RR 4 Box 134 Fairfield IA 52556-9204 Office: Soil Techs Corp RR# 4 Fairfield IA 52556-9804

SCHAEFER, JOHN PAUL, chemist, corporate executive; b. N.Y.C., Sept. 17, 1934; s. Conrad and Meta (Rekelkamm) S.; m. Helen Marie Schwarz, May 18, 1958; children—Ann Marie, Susan Margaret. B.S., Poly. Inst. Bklyn., 1955; Ph.D. in Chemistry, U. Ill., 1958; fellow, Calif. Inst. Tech., 1958-59. Asst. prof. U. Calif. at Berkeley, 1959-60; mem. faculty U. Ariz., 1960—, prof. chemistry, head dept., 1968-70; dean Coll. Liberal Arts U. Ariz., 1970-71, pres., 1971-82; pres. Rsch. Corp., 1982—, also bd. dirs.; chmn. bd. Rsch. Corp. Techs. Inc., 1988—; bd. dirs. Olin Corp., Rsch. Corp. Techs. Bd. dirs. Tucson Airport Authority; bd. govs. U.S.-Israel Binat. Sci. Found., 1972-77. Mem. AAAS, Nat. Audubon Soc., Tucson Audubon Soc. (pres. 1961-65), Am. Chem. Soc., Ariz. Acad., Nature Conservancy, Newcomen Soc., Sigma Xi, Phi Lambda Upsilon, Phi Kappa Phi. Office: Rsch Corp 101 N Wilmot Rd Ste 250 Tucson AZ 85711-3332

SCHAEFER, JON PATRICK, judge, lawyer; b. Fremont, Ohio, Nov. 20, 1948; s. Ellsworth Joseph and Lois Ann (Fought) S.; m. Kathryn Louise Koch, Aug. 21, 1971; children: Heather Marie, Matthew Thomas. BS, Bethel Coll., 1971; JD, Memphis State U., 1974. Bar: Ohio 1974, U.S. Dist. Ct. (no. dist.) Ohio 1977. Ptnr. McKown, Schaefer & McKown Co., L.P.A., Shelby, Ohio, 1974-84; pvt. practice Shelby, 1984-88; acting judge Shelby Mcpl. Ct., 1981-86, judge, 1986—; prosecutor, atty. City of Shelby, 1975-78. Mem. Richland County Dem. Exec. Com., 1975-76; bd. dirs. Shelby chpt. ARC, 1985—. Recipient Community Svc. award Richland County Sheriff's Dept., 1987. Mem. ABA, Ohio Bar Assn. (mem. unauthorized practice law com.), Richland County Bar Assn. Huron County Bar Assn., Ohio Trial Lawyers Assn., K.C. (grand knight Shelby chpt. 1979-83, Knight of the Yr. award 1984, Cath. Family of Yr. award 1986), Sertoma (pres. Shelby chpt. 1981-82, 90-91, dist. gov. 1985-86, Disting. Gov. award 1986), Shelby C. of C., Ohio Farm Bur., Catawba West Harbor Yacht Club. Avocations: boating, fishing, reading. Home: 65 Independence Dr Shelby OH 44875-1815 Office: Shelby Mcpl Ct 14 Church St Shelby OH 44875-1204

SCHAEFER, MARY ANN, health facility administrator, consultant; b. Chgo., May 18, 1942; d. Joseph and Mary A. (Kozyra) Strosnik; m. Robert Earl Schaefer, May 18, 1963; children: Debra Ann, Robert Joseph. Diploma in nursing, St. Francis Hosp. Sch. Nursing, Evanston, Ill., 1962; BA, Nat. Coll. Edn., Evanston, 1980; MBA in Health Svc. Mgmt., Webster U., 1990; MJ in Health Law, Loyola U., Chgo., 1993. Med. and surg. nurse Resurrection Med. Ctr., Chgo., 1962-79, charge nurse labor and delivery, 1978-79; coord. maternal child care Humana, Hoffman Estates, Ill., 1979-81; nurse mgr. labor and delivery Resurrection Med. Ctr., Chgo., 1981-91; mgr. Family Birthplace Resurrection Med. Ctr., Chgo., 1991—; cons., prin. M/B Assocs.-Consultants Perinatal Healthcare and Edn., Barrington, 1994—; seminar leader on childbirth edn., legal issues in nursing. Contbr. to Motor Facilitation Handbook; editorial bd. Essentials publ., Resurrection Med. Ctr. Mem. NAFE, NAACOG (cert. in inpatient obstetric nursing), Ill. Pub. Health Assn., Nat. Perinatal Assn., Perinatal Assn. Ill. (mem. exec. bd.), Am. Orgn. Nurse Execs. Home: 23370 N Juniper Ln Barrington IL 60010-2936

SCHAEFER, MICHAEL JUDE, industrial control systems engineer; b. Glen Ridge, N.J., Oct. 4, 1954; s. Hubert Emil and Agnes Alice (Boehmer) S.; m. Terry Lynn Vezerian, Jan. 28, 1988; m. Terri Lyn Armitage, July 10, 1993; children: Stephanie, Jessica, Nicole. Student, Grossmont C.C., 1976-78, U. Calif., San Diego, 1978-81; postgrad., U. Calif., San Diego, 1992. Gen. contractor Oakwood Constrn., San Diego, 1981-86; controls specialist Burke Engring., San Diego, 1986-90; control sys. engr. Omega Controls, San Diego, 1990-92, Centaurus Sys., San Diego, 1992-95, Medland Controls, Chula Vista, Calif., 1995—; cons. in field, 1995—. Mem. Instrument Soc. Am., Assn. Profl. Energy Mgrs. Achievements include being control system engineering project leader for seveal landmark highrises, prisons, military bases; performance of proof of concept engineering (hardware) for first bacnet type installation in the world. Home: 9375 E Heaney Cir Santee CA 92071 Office: 2363 Newton Ave # B San Diego CA 92116

SCHAEFER, ROBERT KARL, research scientist; b. Abington, Pa., Nov. 17, 1955; s. Frank Adolf and Dorothy Marie Schaefer; m. Katherine Marie Marvel, Dec. 7, 1991. BS in Physics cum laude, Wilkes Coll., 1977; MS in Physics, U. Del., 1980; PhD in Physics, Brandeis Univ., 1985. NRC rsch. fellow NASA/Goddard Space Flight Ctr., Greenbelt, Md., 1985-87; rsch. assoc. physics dept. Ohio State U., Columbus, 1987-89; rsch. scientist Bartol Rsch. Inst., Newark, Del., 1989—. Contbr. articles to profl. jours. Mem. Am. Phys. Soc. Achievements include pioneering work on the cold plus hot dark matter mode of galaxy formation; developed mathematical formalism for studying small density fluctuations in the early universe. Office: Univ Del Bartol Rsch Inst Newark DE 19716

SCHAEFER, ROBERT WAYNE, banker; b. Balt., Feb. 28, 1934; s. Roland Elmer and Lillian (Reid) S.; m. Elaine Lennon, May 18, 1963; children: Linda, Karen. Student, Balt. City Coll., 1949-51; BS in Acctg., U. Balt., 1955; MBA in Fin., Loyola Coll., 1971. C.P.A., Md. With First Nat. Bank of Md., Balt., 1951-55, 59—; comptroller First Nat. Bank of Md., 1961—, v.p., 1965-69, sr. v.p., 1969-73, exec. v.p., 1973—; instr. accounting N.C. State Coll., 1956-58; instr. accounting, econs., taxes, credit Balt. chpt. Am. Inst. Banking, 1960-66. Mem. Balt. City Sch. Bd., 1973-75, Balt. City Bd. Fin.; bd. dirs., treas. Balt. Area United Fund, 1964-79; past bd. dirs. Balt. coun. Boy Scouts Am., Balt. chpt. ARC, Boys Latin Sch.; trustee, pres. Wesley Home for Aged; bd. dirs. Balt. City Aquarium, Roland Park Country Sch., Md. Gen. Hosp., Western Md. Coll., 1981-92, Lyric Theatre, 1985—, Enoch Pratt Libr., 1986-93, Ind. Coll. Fund Md., 1990—, Coun. on Econ. Edn., YMCA Ctrl. Md., 1992, U. Balt. 1st lt. USMCR, 1956-58. Mem. Bank Adminstrn. Inst. (past pres., bd. dirs. Balt. chpt.), Md. CPA Assn., Fin. Execs. Inst., U. Balt. Alumni Assn. (bd. dirs. 1972—), U. Balt. Found., Valley Country Club. Republican. Methodist (bd. dirs., mem. finance com.). Home: 5903 Meadowood Rd Baltimore MD 21212-2436 Office: 1st Md Bancorp 1st Md Bldg 25 S Charles St Baltimore MD 21201-3330

SCHAEFER, SANDRA ELLEN, secondary education educator; b. Troy, Ohio, Oct. 19, 1945; d. Charles Donald and Maribelle (Morrin) Brown; m. James J. Wagner, Aug. 12, 1967 (div. 1975); m. Kenneth Lee Schaefer, Feb. 27, 1976; 1 child, Kenneth Charles. BS in Edn., Miami U., Oxford, Ohio, 1967, MEd in Ednl. Adminstrn., 1974, postgrad., 1974; postgrad., Wright State U., 1976-82. Cert. tchr., Ohio. Tchr. College Corner (Ohio) Schs., 1967-68, West Milton (Ohio) Pub. Schs., 1968-69, Smith Jr. High Sch., Vandalia, Ohio, 1969-73; math. coord. intermediate unit McGuffey Lab. Sch., Oxford, Ohio, 1973-74; math. coord. Vandalia-Butler City Schs., 1976-77; tchr. math., algebra Smith Jr. High Sch., Vandalia, Ohio, 1974-86; tchr. algebra and precalculus Butler High Sch., Vandalia, 1986—; participant profl. confs.; presenter workshops. Contbr. to profl. publs. Mem. fundraising com. Miami Montessori Sch., Troy, 1989-94; curriculum coordinating coun. Vandalia-Butler City Schs., 1985—; coach Mathcounts, 1983-87, Butler H.S. Acad. Challenge Team, 1990—; treas. GMVC Acad. Challenge League, 1992—. Mem. NEA, Am. Montessori Soc., Ohio Edn. Assn., Western Ohio Edn. Assn., Vandalia-Butler Edn. Assn., Assn. Supervision and Curriculum Devel., Sch. Sci. and Math. Assn., Nat. Coun. Tchrs. Math., Ohio Coun. Tchrs. Math. (Outstanding Math. Classroom Tchr. award 1986), Wright State U. Area Coun. Tchrs. Math. Avocations: swimming, travel. Home: 2610 Greenlawn Dr Troy OH 45373-4363 Office: Butler High Sch 600 S Dixie Dr Vandalia OH 45377-2550

SCHAEFER, THEODORE PETER, chemistry educator; b. Gnadenthal, Man., Can., July 22, 1933; s. Paul Jacob and Margarethe (Wiebe) S.; m. Nicola Caroline Sewell, Dec. 26, 1960; children: Catherine, Dominic, Benjamin. B.S. with Honors, U. Man., 1954, M.S., 1955; D.Phil. (Shell scholar), Oxford (Eng.) U., 1958; D.Sc. (hon. causa), U. Winnipeg, 1982. Prof. chemistry U. Man., Winnipeg, Can., 1958—, Univ. Disting. prof., 1982—; researcher NRC, Ottawa, Can., 1959, 62, Nat. Phys. Lab., Teddington, U.K., 1960, 65, Argonne Nat. Lab., Chgo., 1967, 68; sr. fellow, mem. grants com. NRC, Ottawa.; mem. council Nat. Scis. and Engring. Research Council, Ottawa., 1980-85. Contbr. articles on nuclear magnetic resonance to sci. jours. Recipient Herzberg award Spectroscopy Soc. Can., 1975. Fellow Chem. Inst. Can. (Noranda award 1973), Royal Soc. Can. Home: 210 Oak St, Winnipeg, MB Canada R3M 3R4 Office: Univ of Manitoba, Dept of Chemistry, Winnipeg, MB Canada R3T 2N2 *Persistence can sometimes emulate perspicacity.*

SCHAEFER, WILLIAM DAVID, English language educator; b. Dighton, Mass., May 11, 1928; s. Louis and Elsie K. (Otterbein) S.; m. Josephine R. Lamprecht, Aug. 8, 1958; 1 dau., Kimberly. B.A., NYU, 1957; M.S., U. Wis., 1958, Ph.D., 1962. Mem. faculty UCLA, 1962-90, prof. English, 1970-90, chmn. dept., 1969-71, exec. vice chancellor, 1978-87. Author: James (BV) Thomson: Beyond the City, 1965, Speedy Extinction of Evil and Misery, 1967, Education Without Compromise: From Chaos to Coherence in Higher Education, 1990; contbr. articles to profl. jours., short stories to literary mags. Served with AUS, 1954-56. Fulbright fellow Eng., 1961-62. Mem. MLA (exec. dir. 1971-78). Home: 164 Stagecoach Rd Bell Canyon CA 91307-1044 Office: UCLA 405 Hilgard Ave Los Angeles CA 90024-1301

SCHAEFER, WILLIAM G., lawyer; b. Kansas City, Mo., June 16, 1941; m. Sharon Saylor, Dec. 21, 1963; children: James, Kristen. BA, U. Kans., 1963; JD, Harvard U., 1966. Bar: Ill. 1966, D.C. 1978, Md. 1984. Ptnr. Sidley & Austin, Chgo. and Washington, 1966-74, 78-93; v.p., gen. counsel DeKalb Corp., Ill., 1974-77; spl. counsel Bechel Corp., Gaithersburg, Md., 1993—. Office: Bechtel Corp 9801 Washington Blvd Gaithersburg MD 20878

SCHAEFFER, BRENDA MAE, psychologist, author; b. Duluth, Minn.; d. Ralph J. Bernice M. (Johnson) Furtman; children: Heidi, Gordon III. BA in Sociology, Psychology and English cum laude, U. Minn., 1962; MA in Human Devel., St. Mary's Coll., Winona, Minn., 1976. Lic. psychologist, Minn.; cert. addictions specialist. Mem. faculty Coll. St. Scholastica, Duluth, 1976—; trainer, therapist, communications cons. Transactional Analysis Inst., Mpls., 1984-88; owner, clin. dir. Brenda M. Schaeffer and Assocs., Inc., Healthy Relationships, Inc.; vis. prof. U. Minn., Duluth, 1976—; guest lectr. dep. counseling U. Wis., Superior, 1980-81; nat. and internat. lectr. Author: Is It Love or Is It Addiction, 1987, Loving Me, Loving You, 1991, Signs of Healthy Love, Signs of Addictive Love, Power Plays, Addictive Love, Help Yourself Out; mem. editorial bd. Transactional Analysis Jour.; editor Healthy Relationships newsletter. Planner Lake Superior Task Force, Duluth, 1980-83; bd. dirs., sec. Nat. Coun. Sexual Addictions/Compulsions, 1992—, sec. 1994-95; v.p. H. Milton Erickson Inst. Minn., 1992-93. Mem. Internat. Transactional Analysis Assn. (1975), Transactional Anaylsis Inst. Minn. (founder, pres. 1984-86), U.S. Assn. Transactional Analysis, Northeast Minn. Transactional Analysis Seminar (founder and chairperson 1977-83). Office: 27306 County Road A Spooner WI 54801-9019

SCHAEFFER, EDWIN FRANK, JR., lawyer, finance company executive; b. N.Y.C., Nov. 29, 1930; s. Edwin Frank and Rachel Townsend (Bouchier) S.; m. Joan Cameron Sherwood, Apr. 7, 1956; children: Edwin Frank III, Cameron, Donald. AB, Washington and Lee U., 1952; JD, Harvard U., 1955. Bar: Ky, 1955, U.S. Dist. Ct. (ea. and we. dists.) Ky. 1957, U.S. Ct. Appeals (6th cir.) 1957. Assoc., Bullitt, Dawson & Tarrant, Louisville, 1955-60, ptnr., 1960-63; ptnr. Kincaid, Wilson, Schaeffer, Hembree & Kinser, P.S.C., Lexington, Ky., 1963-79, bd. dirs., chmn. bd. dirs., 1979-93; vice chmn., bd. dirs. Ky. Fin. Co., Inc., 1976-84, chmn., 1984-91; bd. dirs. Ky. Central Life Ins. Co., 1976-93, Central Bank & Trust Co., 1974-93, Bd. dirs. Lexington Philharm., 1970-80, United Way, 1976-80, 84-88, Lexington Ctr. Corp., 1982—, Hospice of Bluegrass, 1985-91. Served with JAGC, AUS, 1955-57. Fellow Am. Bar Found.; mem. ABA, Ky. State Bar Assn., Fayette County Bar Assn., Louisville Bar Assn., Greater Lexington C. of C. (bd. dirs. 1986-88). Democrat. Presbyterian. Club: Lexington Country. Address: 200 W Vine St Ste 810 Lexington KY 40507-1620

SCHAEFFER, GARY N., mayor; b. York, Pa., May 8, 1948; s. Calvin William and Jane Rae (Desenberg) R.; m. Katherine Lyn Dowler, June 22, 1968; children: Andrew, Ryan. BS, York Coll. of Pa., 1973. Tchr. Upper Adams Sch. Dist., Biglerville, Pa., 1974-75, Dallastown (Pa.) Area Schs., 1975-79, Laramie County Sch. Dist., Cheyenne, Wyo., 1982-89; owner Auto Hosp., Cheyenne, 1979-82; mayor City of Cheyenne, 1989—. Author: Eat your Heart Out, 1979. Sgt. USAF, 1967-71. Mem. Cheyenne C. of C. (bd. dirs. 1989—), Leads (bd. dirs. 1989—), VFW, Am. Legion, Amvets, U.S. Conf. of Mayors (chmn. subcom. on water 1990). Avocations: flying, skiing, horseback riding, auto repair. Home: 418 Lafayette Blvd Cheyenne WY 82009-2098 Office: City of Cheyenne 2101 Oneil Ave Cheyenne WY 82001-3512

SCHAEFFER, GLENN WILLIAM, casino corporate financial executive; b. Pomona, Calif., Oct. 11, 1953; s. William Donald and Mary Louise (Miller) S.; m. Deborah Lynn Helfer, Sept. 6, 1974 (div. Apr. 1981); m. Renee Sue Riebel, May 25, 1985. AB summa cum laude, U. Calif., Irvine, 1974, MA, 1975; MFA, U. Iowa, 1977. Fin. cons. Dean Witter, Los Angeles, 1977-78; assoc. Hill and Knowlton, Inc., Los Angeles, 1978-81; v.p. Ramada Inns, Inc., Phoenix, 1981-84; exec. v.p., chief fin. officer Circus Circus Enterprises, Inc., Las Vegas, Nev., 1984-91; pres. Circus Circus Enterprises, Inc., 1991-93; also bd. dirs. Circus Circus Enterprises, Inc., Las Vegas; ptnr. Gold Strike Resorts, Jean, Nev., 1993-95; pres. Circus Circus Enterprises, 1995—. Pres. Hitch fellow U. Calif.-Irvine, 1973-74. Mem. Phi Beta Kappa. Avocations: reading, bicycling. Office: Circus Circus Enterprises 2880 Las Vegas Blvd S Las Vegas NV 89019

SCHAEFFER, LEONARD DAVID, health care executive; b. Chgo., July 28, 1945; s. David and Sarah (Levin) S.; m. Pamela Lee Sidford, Aug. 11, 1968; children: David, Jacqueline. BA, Princeton U., 1969. Mgmt. cons. Arthur Andersen & Co., 1969-73; dep. dir. mgmt. Ill. Mental Health/Devel. Disability, Springfield, 1973-75; dir. Ill. Bur. of Budget, Springfield, 1975-76; v.p. Citibank, N.A., N.Y.C., 1976-78; asst. sec. mgmt. and budget HHS, Washington, 1978, adminstr. HCFA, 1978-80; exec. v.p., COO Student Loan Mktg. Assn., Washington, 1980-82; pres., CEO Group Health, Inc., Mpls., 1983-86; chmn., CEO Blue Cross of Calif., Woodland Hills, 1986—, WellPoint Health Networks Inc., 1993—; bd. dirs. Allergan, Inc., Irvine, Calif., Metra Biosystems; bd. councilors U. So. Calif. Sch. Pub. Adminstrn., 1988—; bd. dirs. exec com. Blue Cross-Blue Shield Assn., Chgo., 1986—; mem. Congl. Prospective Payment Assessment Commn., 1987-93; mem. Pew Health Professions Com., Phila., 1990-93; chmn. bd. trustees Nat. Health Found., L.A., 1992—; chmn. Nat. Inst. Health Care Mgmt., 1993—. Mem. editorial adv. bd. Managed Healthcare, 1989—. Bd. govs. Town Hall of Calif., L.A., 1989—. Kellogg Found. fellow, 1981-89, Internat. fellow King's Fund Coll., London, 1990—; recipient Citation-Outstanding Svc., Am. Acad. Pediats., 1981, Disting. Pub. Svc. award HEW, Washington, 1980, Leadership in Health Affairs award Hosp. Coun. So. Calif., 1992. Mem. Cosmos Club, Princeton Club, Regency Club. Office: Blue Cross of Calif 21555 Oxnard St Woodland Hills CA 91367-4943

SCHAEFFER, REINER HORST, air force officer, retired librarian, foreign language professional; b. Berlin, Lichterfelde, Fed. Republic Germany, Jan. 13, 1938; came to U.S., 1958; s. Immanuel Emil and Wilhelmine (Fahrni) Frei-S.; m. Cathy Anne Cormack, Apr. 6, 1966; 1 child, Brian Reiner. Nat. Cert., Bus. Sch., Thun, Switzerland, 1957; B.G.S. in Bus., U. Nebr., 1970; M.P.A. in Orgnl. Behavior, U. Mo., 1972; Ph.D. in Fgn. Lang. Edn., Ohio State U., 1979. Commd. officer USAF, 1958, advanced through grades to lt. col.; instr. German, French USAF Acad., Colorado Springs, Colo., 1975-77, assoc. prof., 1979-81, chmn. German, 1981, dir. librs., 1982-86, prof., 1986-92, dir. Acad. Librs., 1986—. Mem. People to People, Colorado Springs; bd. dirs. Friends of AF Acad. Librs. Named Disting. Grad. Air Force Inst. Tech, Wright-Patterson AFB, Ohio, 1979; recipient 5 Meritorious Service medals, 5 Air Force Commendation medals. Mem. Am. Assn. Tchrs. of German, Swiss Club (pres. Colorado Springs chpt. 1990-96, chmn.), Pi Alpha Alpha, Alpha Sigma Alpha. Republican. Avocations: skiing; golfing; hiking; soccer. Home: 515 Celtic Ct Colorado Springs CO 80921-1807 Office: Fgn Lang Ctr LLC 315 E Willamette Ave Colorado Springs CO 80903-1115

SCHAENGOLD, PHILLIP S., hospital adminstrator; b. Marseilles, France, Nov. 26, 1948; married;. BS, U. Cin., 1971, MBA, 1975; Doctorate, S.P. Chase Coll. Law, 1978. Dir. pharm. svcs. Providence Hosp., Cin., 1972-79, risk mgmt. coord., 1979-80; sr. sect. mgr. McDonnell Douglas Auto Co., St. Louis, 1980-82; asst. exec. dir. Menorah Med. Ctr., Kansas City, 1983-85, assoc. exec. dir., COO, 1985-86, pres., 1986-92; pres., CEO Sinai Hosp., Detroit, 1992—. Contrb. articles to profl. jours. Mem. Mich. Hosp. Assn. Home: 767 Fairfax Birmingham MI 48009 Office: Sinai Hosp 6767 W Outer Dr Detroit MI 48235-2893

SCHAER, WERNER, computer services executive; b. Olten, Switzerland, Sept. 23, 1940; came to U.S., 1966.; s. Friedrich and Erna Helen (Kreuzberger) S.; m. Marisa Casseres, Dec. 20, 1965; children: Sara Elaine, William Ernest. Diplom in Elec. Engring., Fed. Inst. Tech., Zurich, Switzerland, 1962; MBA, Pepperdine U., 1975. Systems analyst Sperry Rand, Zurich, Geneva, Phila., Washington, 1963-66; dir., v.p. devel. Computer Sci. Corp. Infonet, El Segundo, Calif., 1969-77; pres. Computer Scis. Corp. Europe, S.Am., Brussels, 1978-82; sr. v.p. Computer Scis. Corp. Systems Div., Falls Church, Va., 1983-86; pres. Computer Scis. Corp. Network Integration Div., Herndon, Va., 1987—. Mem. IEEE, Armed Forces Communications and Electronics Assn., Zofingia Club (Aarau, Switzerland, pres. 1958). Avocations: violin, tennis, skiing. Home: 12206 Thoroughbred Rd Herndon VA 22071-2007 Office: Computer Scis Corp 3190 Fairview Park Dr Falls Church VA 22042-4524

SCHAFER, ALICE TURNER, mathematics educator; b. Richmond, Va., June 18, 1915; d. John H. and Cleon (Dermott) Turner; m. Richard Donald Schafer, Sept. 8, 1942; children: John Dickerson, Richard Stone. AB, U. Richmond, 1936, DSc, 1964; MS, U. Chgo., 1940, PhD (fellow), 1942. Tchr. Glen Allen (Va.) High Sch., 1936-39; instr. math. Conn. Coll., New London, 1942-44; asst. prof. Conn. Coll., 1954-57, assoc. prof., 1957-61, prof., 1961-62; prof. math. Wellesley Coll., 1962-80, Helen Day Gould prof. math., 1969-80, Helen Day Gould prof. math. emerita, 1980—, affirmative action officer, 1980-82; prof. math. Marymount U., Arlington, Va., 1989-96; instr. U. Mich., Ann Arbor, 1945-46; lectr. Douglass Coll., New Brunswick, N.J., 1946-48; asst. prof. Swarthmore (Pa.) Coll., 1948-51, Drexel Inst. Tech., Phila., 1951-53; mathematician Johns Hopkins Applied Physics Lab., Silver Spring, Md., 1945; lectr. Simmons Coll., Boston, 1980-88, Radcliffe Coll. Seminars, Cambridge, Mass., 1980-85. Contbr. articles on women in math. and other articles to math. jours. Recipient Disting. Alumna award Westhampton Coll., U. Richmond, 1977; NSF sci. faculty fellow Inst. for Advanced Study, Princeton, N.J., 1958-59. Fellow AAAS (math. sect. A nominating com. 1979-83, mem.-at-large 1983-86, chair-elect sect. A 1991, chair 1992, retiring chair 1993, Assn. for Women in Math. rep., 1993—), AAUP (chmn. nat. com. W 1980-83, mem. nat. coun. 1984-87), Am. Math. Soc. (chmn. postdoctoral fellowship com. 1973-76, affirmative action procedures com. 1980-82, chair com. on Human Rights of Mathematicians 1988-94), Soc. Indsl. and Applied Math., Am. Statis. Assn., Inst. Math. Stats., Nat. Coun. Tchrs. of Math. (chair com. on women 1976-81), Math Assn. Am. (adv. com. for Women and Math. program 1987-89, dir. fund raising 1989-92, lectr. 1982—, chair devel. com. 1988-92), Internat. Congress Mathematicians (mem. fund raising com. 1986), Assn. for Women in Math. (pres. 1973-75, Alice T. Schafer Prize established 1989, chair fund raising com. 1992-94, leader math. del. women mathematicians to China 1990, U.S. chair postsecondary math. edn., U.S./China Joint Conf. on Edn. 1992, co-chair Citizen Amb. program People to People U.S. and China Joint Conf. on Women's Issues 1995, session women in sic. and math., rept. to sect. A, Disting. Svc. award 1996), Cosmos Club, Phi Beta Kappa, Sigma Xi, Sigma Delta Epsilon. Achievements include first study of singularities of space curves in projective differential geometry; research on undulation point of a space curve. Home: 2725 N Pollard St Arlington VA 22207-5038 Office: Marymount U Dept Math 2807 N Glebe Rd Arlington VA 22207-4299

SCHAFER, CARL WALTER, investment executive; b. Chgo., Jan. 16, 1936; s. MacHenry George and Gertrude (Herrick) S.; 1 child, MacHenry George II. BA with distinction, U. Rochester, 1958. Budget examiner Budget Bur., Exec. Office Pres., Washington, 1961-64, legis. analyst, 1964-66, dep. dir. budget preparation, 1966-68, dir. budget preparation, 1968-69; staff asst. U.S. Ho. of Reps. Appropriations Com., 1969; dir. budget Princeton (N.J.) U., 1969-72, treas., 1972-76, fin. v.p., treas., 1976-87, lectr. indsl. adminstrn., 1975; prin. Rockefeller & Co., Inc., 1987-90; pres. Atlantic Found., Princeton, N.J., 1990—; pres., CEO Palmer Square Inc., 1979-81; trustee, treas. McCarter Theatre Co. Inc., 1974-76; co-chmn. N.J. Gov.'s Task Force on Improving N.J. Econ. and Regulatory Climate, 1982-83; chmn. investment adv. com. Howard Hughes Med. Inst., 1985-92; trustee Am. Bible Soc., 1987-92; trustee, dir. Roadway Express, Inc., Wainoco Oil Corp., Nutraceutix Inc., Electronic Clearing House Inc., The Paine Webber and Guardian Groups of Mut. Funds, Evans Sys., Inc., Ardic Exploration and Devel. Ltd., Hidden Lake Gold Mines Ltd., U. Rochester Harbor Br. Inst. Inc., The Investment Fund for Founds., The Johnson Atelier and Sch. Sculpture, The Banbury Fund; mem. adv. coun. Domain Ptnrs.; mem. internat. adv. coun. Wm. Sword & Co., Inc.; trustee, chmn. fin. com. Chem. Heritage Found. Mem. Am. Coun. Learned Socs. (investment com.), Asset Mgmt. Advisors (investment com.), Rockefeller Ctr. Club (N.Y.C.), Phi Beta Kappa. Home and Office: PO Box 1164 Princeton NJ 08542-1164

SCHAFER, EDWARD T., governor; b. Bismarck, N.D., Aug. 8, 1946; s. Harold and Marian Schafer; m. Nancy Jones; children: Edward Thomas Jr., Ellie Sue, Eric Jones, Kari Jones. BSBA, U. N.D., 1969; MBA, Denver U., 1970. Quality control inspector Gold Seal, 1971-73, v.p., 1974, chmn. mgmt. com., 1975-78; owner/dir. H&S Distbn., 1976—; pres. Gold Seal, 1978-85, Dakota Classics, 1986—, TRIESCO Properties, 1986—, Fish 'N Dakota, 1990-94; gov. State of N.D., 1992—. Chmn. N.D. Micro Bus. Mktg. Alliance; pres. N.D. Heritage Group; adv. coun. Distributive Edn. Clubs of Am.; lectr. Hugh O'Brien Leadership Found.; counselor Junior Achievement; dir. Bismarck Recreation Coun.; trustee Missouri Valley Family YMCA; plankowner USS Theodore Roosevelt; ann. support com. Medcenter One Found.; mem. Bismarck State Coll. Found. Mem. NRA, Theodore Roosevelt Assn. (Theodore Roosevelt Medora Found., United Sportsman of N.D., U. N.D. Pres. Club, U. Mary Pres. Club, Bismarck-Mandan Rotary. Republican. Office: Office of the Governor 600 E Boulevard Ave Bismarck ND 58505-0001*

SCHAFER, JAMES HENRY, newspaper company executive; b. Seattle, Apr. 15, 1945; s. Henry and Fayette K. (Boasen) S.; m. Marcia W. Schafer, May 5, 1975; children—Christine Ann, Joel Henry. B.B.A., U. Wash., 1970. Dir labor relations The Bon, Seattle, 1967-79; dir. adminstrn. I.T.T. Rayonier, Seattle, 1979-83; v.p. indsl. relations Seattle Times, 1983—; dir. Health Care Purchasers, Seattle; mem. adv. council Seattle Pacific U., Seattle, 1984—. Bd. dirs. Wash. State Leukemia Soc., N.W. Kidney Found. Mem. C. of C. (leadership tomorrow 1984—). Clubs: Bellevue Athletic, Lakes, Rainier, City (Seattle). Office: Seattle Times PO Box 70 Seattle WA 98111-0070*

SCHAFER, JERRY SANFORD, film company executive, producer, writer, director; b. Los Angeles, July 4, 1934; s. Sidney S. and B. Schafer; children: Mark, Morgan, Martin, Aaron, Erik; m. Marianne Marks, Oct., 1979. Student, UCLA, 1951-54. Stuntman Hollywood (Calif.) studios, 1952-56; episodic TV writer, asst. to prodn. chief Four Star Prodns., North Hollywood, Calif., 1956-59; writer, producer, dir. The Legend of Billy the Kid Republic Studios, 1958; writer, producer, dir. worlds fair presentation

Am. Pavillion, The Quick Draw Theatre, Seattle and N.Y.C., 1962, 66; writer, producer, dir. musical comedies, wrote 30 original songs with music by Max Showalter Go For Your Gun, London, 1962; writer, producer, dir. mus. comedy shows, wrote 33 origianl songs with music by Shorty Rogers That Certain Girl, Las Vegas, 1967; writer, producer, dir. mus. shows Belle Starr, London, 1968; writer, producer, dir. mus. shows, wrote 30 original songs with music by Steve Allen The Piece-Full Palace, Las Vegas, 1969; writer, producer, dir. World's Fair presentation in American Pavillion Cowboys, Cowgirls & Kata, Osaka, Japan, 1970; pres. Sanford Internat. Entertainment, Inc., Las Vegas, 1978—; freelance writer, producer, dir., 1981—; entertainment dir. Del E. Webb Corp., Las Vegas, 1961-69; lectr., vis. prof. U. Nev., Las Vegas, 1985—. Writer, producer, dir.: (feature films) Tonight for Sure, 1959, The Little People, 1960, Along Came Jasper, 1961, Like It Is, 1972, Not My Daughter, 1972, The Low Price of Fame, 1973, wrote 8 original song lyrics, Shortcut to Terror, 1975, Horace & Fred, 1976, Fists of Steel, 1988 (mus. prodns.) On Stage with Judy Garland, An Evening with Pat Boone, Presenting Mr. Jack Benny!, Betty Grable/A Musical Musical!, Robert Goulet the Camelot Prince, The Polly Bergen Show, Brenda Lee on Stage!, Girls a la Carte, C'est la Femme, Speaking of Girls, 1964, Eddie Fisher/Almost Alive, (stage prodns.) The Blackhawk Gunfighters, 1963; producer, dir., 1962-69, Soul Follies, Flower Drum Song, Under the Yum Yum Tree, The Ziegfeld Follies, High Button Shoes, Anything Goes, over 100 TV spls., 1983-87, and over 25 TV shows in video with editing facility; writer numerous orignal songs with Shorty Rogers, Steve Allen and Max Showalter; creator interchangeable mobile video editing facility, 1989—. Apptd. comdr. Nat. Constable Assn., 1985. Named Producer of Yr. Am. Guild Variety Artists, 1964, 66; recipient PAVCA award Profl. Audio-Visual Communications Assn., 1985, Citizen of Yr. award Nev. Exec. Optimist Club, 1992, Appreciation award MADD, 1992, Nev. Gov.'s Proclamation, 1992, Citizen award Nev. Atty. Gen., 1993, R.A.I.D. award Nev. Hwy. Patrol, 1993, Nev. Gov.'s Industry award, 1993, Outstanding Contrbn. award Nev. Gov., 1993, Fighter Against Drug Abuse award Nat. Constables, 1994-95; holder world record for fastest draw, 1958-64. Mem. ASCAP, Nat. Counter Intelligence Assn. (invited), Nat. Orch. Leaders Assn., Ky. Cols. Assn. (invited), Nev. Motion Picture and TV Bd. (apptd. to adv. com. by Gov. Richard Bryan 1987), Dirs. Guild Am. Avocations: tennis, music, cooking.. Office: Internat Video Commn PO Box 15101 Las Vegas NV 89114-5101

SCHAFER, JOHN FRANCIS, plant pathologist; b. Pullman, Wash., Feb. 17, 1921; s. Edwin George and Ella Frances (Miles) S.; m. Joyce A. Marcks, Aug. 16, 1947; children—Patricia, Janice, James. B.S., Wash. State U., 1942; Ph.D., U. Wis., 1950. Asst. prof. to prof. plant pathology Purdue U., 1949-68; head dept. plant pathology Kans. State U., 1968-72; chmn. dept. plant pathology Wash. State U., Pullman, 1972-80; integrated pest mgmt. coordinator sci. and edn. USDA, 1980-81, acting nat. research program leader plant pathology Agrl. Research Service, 1981-82; dir. cereal rust lab. USDA, St. Paul, 1982-87, biol. sci. collaborator, 1987-95; vis. rsch. prof. Duquesne U., 1965-66; adj. prof. plant pathology U. Minn., 1982-92. Contbr. articles to profl. jours., chpts. to books. Served with AUS, 1942-46. Phi Sigma scholar, 1942. Fellow AAAS, Ind. Acad. Sci., Am. Phytopathol. Soc. (past pres.); mem. Am. Soc. Agronomy, Crop Sci. Soc. Am. Achievements include identification of increased resistance to wheat leaf rust by genetic recombination; demonstration of probabilities of virulence to genetic resistance combinations, of tolerance as a mechanism of disease control, of use of cultivaral diversity for disease protection; bred (with others) over 30 disease resistant cultivars of cereal crops, including Arthur wheat. Home: 1753 Lindig St Saint Paul MN 55113-5505 Office: Univ Minn Cereal Rust Lab Saint Paul MN 55108

SCHAFER, JOHN STEPHEN, foundation administrator; b. N.Y.C., Sept. 5, 1934; s. Stephen James and Siiri (Halmi) S.; m. Gertrud Rosa Fleischmann, June 14, 1958; children: Sylvia F., John Stephen, Karen D., Kristen H. B.A., Rutgers U., 1956, M.B.A., 1963. Advt. research mgr. Union Carbide Corp., N.Y.C., 1959-65; research mgr. Bus. Week, N.Y.C., 1965-66; v.p. Opinion Research Corp., Princeton, N.J., 1966-80; pres. Am. Econ. Found., Cleve., 1981—, trustee, 1975—; v.p., dir. Ams. for Competitive Enterprise System, Phila., 1970-82. Editor Linde Electric Welding Progress, 1959-62, ORC Pub. Opinion Index, 1966-72, AEF Straight Talk, 1981-82, Bellcore Exch., 1993-94. Polit. pollster Ed Clark for U.S. Pres., 1980; chmn. N.J. Libertarian party, 1983; nat. dir. U.S. Jaycees, 1965-66, v.p. N.J., 1964-65. Served to 1st lt. U.S. Army, 1957-59. Mem. Jr. Chamber Internat. (hon. life), Philosophan Soc., Scabbard and Blade, Delta Phi Alpha. Presbyterian. Home: 24 Fayson Lakes Rd Kinnelon NJ 07405-3137

SCHAFER, MICHAEL FREDERICK, orthopedic surgeon; b. Peoria, Ill., Aug. 17, 1942; s. Harold Martin and Frances May (Ward) S.; m. Eileen M. Briggs, Jan. 8, 1966; children—Steven, Brian, Kathy, David, Daniel. B.A., U. Iowa, 1964, M.D., 1967. Diplomate: Am. Bd. Orthopedic Surgery. Intern Chgo. Wesley Meml. Hosp., 1967-68; resident in orthopedic surgery Cook County Program, Northwestern U., Chgo., 1968-72; practice medicine specializing in orthopedic surgery Chgo., 1974—; asst. prof. orthopedic surgery Northwestern U., 1977—; Reyerson prof. and chmn. dept. orthopedic surgery; asso. attending orthopedic surgeon Northwestern Meml. Hosp., 1974—; adj. staff Children's Meml. Hosp., Chgo., 1974—; cons. VA Lakeside Hosp., 1974—; adv. bd. Center Sports Medicine, Northwestern U., 1976—; panelist Bur. Health Manpower, HEW, 1976; sec.-treas. Orthopedic Research and Edn. Found. Contbr. articles to med. jours. Served to maj. U.S. Army, 1973-74. Fellow Am. Orthopaedic Assn., Am. Acad. Orthopaedic Surgeons, Assn. Bone and Joint Surgeons; mem. AMA, Am. Orthopedic Soc. Sports Medicine, Ill. Med. Soc., Chgo. Med. Soc., Internat. Soc. Study of Pain, Scoliosis Rsch. Soc. Roman Catholic. Home: 1815 Ridgewood Ln W Glenview IL 60025-2205 Office: 303 E Chicago Ave Chicago IL 60611-3008

SCHAFER, RAYMOND MURRAY, composer, author; b. Sarnia, Ont., Can., July 18, 1933; s. Harold J. and Belle (Rose) S.; m. Jean C. Reed, Sept. 18, 1975. Studies with John Weinzweig, Royal Conservatory of Music, 1950-55; L.R.S.M., Royal Coll. and Royal Acad. Music, London, 1954. Artist in residence Meml. U. Nfld., 1963-65; prof. communications studies Simon Fraser U., Burnaby, B.C., Can., 1965-75; author, composer multimedia composition Ra, multimedia composition Princess of the Stars., 1985. Author: British Composers in Interview, 1963, The Composer in the Classroom, 1965, Ear Cleaning, 1967, The New Soundscape, 1969, The Book of Noise, 1970, When Words Sing, 1970, The Rhinoceros in the Classroom, 1974, E.T.A. Hoffmann and Music, 1975, Creative Music Education, 1976, The Tuning of the World, 1977, The Chaldean Inscription, 1978, The 16 Scribes, 1982, On Canadian Music, 1984, Dicamus et Labyrinthos, 1985, The Thinking Ear, 1986; novel Smoke, 1976; Composer: various works including Music for the Morning of the World, 1972, From the Tibetan Book of the Dead, 1968, String Quartet, 1970, Miniwanka, 1973, Son of Heldenleben, 1968. Recipient Arts award Can. Council, 1968-69, Fromm Music Found. award, 1969, Serge Koussevitzky Music Found. award, 1969, Can. Music Coun. medal, 1972, Leger prize, 1978, Priz Arthur Honegger, 1980, 1st Glenn Gould Prize, 1987, Banff Ctr. Sch. Fine Arts Nat. award, 1985; Guggenheim fellow, 1976. Mem. Can. League Composers. Can. Music Council, Sinfonia, Phi Mu Alpha.

SCHAFER, ROBERT LOUIS, agricultural engineer, researcher; b. Burlington, Iowa, Aug. 1, 1937; s. Marion Louis and Pansy (Head) S.; m. Carolyn Louise Henn, Aug. 1, 1959; 1 child, Elizabeth Diane. BS, Iowa State U., 1959, MS, 1961, PhD, 1965. Agrl. engr. Agrl. Rsch. Svc., USDA, Ames, Iowa, 1959-64, Auburn, Ala., 1964-95. Co-author: Advances in Soil Dynamics, 1994; contbr. articles to profl. jours. Fellow Am. Soc. Agrl. Engrs. Home: PO Box 188 Loachapoka AL 36865-0188

SCHAFER, RONALD WILLIAM, electrical engineering educator; b. Tecumseh, Nebr., Feb. 17, 1938; s. William Henry and Esther Sophia (Rinne) S.; m. Dorothy Margaret Hall, June 2, 1960; children: William R., John C. (dec.), Katherine L., Barbara Anne. Student, Doane Coll., Crete, Nebr., 1956-59; BEE, U. Nebr., 1961, MEE, 1962; PhD in Elec. Engring., MIT, 1968. Mem. tech. staff Bell Labs., Murray Hill, N.J., 1968-74; John O. McCarty prof. elec. engring. Ga. Inst. Tech., Atlanta, 1974—, Inst. prof., 1991—; chmn. bd. Atlanta Signal Processors Inc., 1983—. Co-author: Digital Signal Processing, 1974, Digital Processing of Speech Signals, 1979, Speech Analysis, 1979, Discrete-Time Signal Processing, 1989, Computer-Based Exercises for Signal Processing Using Matlab, 1995. Recipient Class of 34 Disting. Prof. award Ga. Inst. Tech., 1985. Fellow IEEE (Emanuel R. Piore award 1980, Edn. medal 1992), Acoustical Soc. Am.; mem. IEEE Acoustics Speech and Signal Processing Soc. (soc. award 1982), AAAS, Nat. Acad. Engring. Democrat. Methodist. Lodge: Kiwanis. Office: Ga Inst of Tech Dept of Elec Engring Atlanta GA 30332-0250

SCHAFER, SHARON MARIE, anesthesiologist; b. Detroit, Mar. 23, 1948; d. Charles Anthony and Dorothy Emma (Schweitzer) Pokriefka; m. Timothy John Schafer, Nov. 12, 1977; children: Patrick Christopher, Steven Michael. BS in Biology, Wayne State U., 1971, MD, 1975. Diplomate Am. Bd. Anesthesiology. Intern, resident Sinai Hosp. Detroit, 1975-78; pvt. practice anesthesiology Troy, Mich., 1988—. Mem. AMA, Am. Soc. Anesthesiologists. Roman Catholic. Home and Office: 5741 Folkstone Dr Troy MI 48098-3154

SCHAFER, THOMAS WILSON, advertising agency executive; b. Youngstown, Ohio, Sept. 12, 1939; s. Kenneth Charles and Clara Louise (Wilson) S.; m. Anne Kernwein, Jan. 22, 1972; children: Charles Kenneth, Bret Thomas. B.A., Colgate U., 1962. Salesman Gen. Foods Corp., 1962-65; sr. ptnr. Tatham EURO RSCG Advt., Chgo., 1965-93; chmn. Schafer Rsch., Inc., Savannah, Ga., 1993—. Past dir. Off the Street Club. Mem. Chgo. Advt. Fedn. (past exec. v.p.). Clubs: Bob O'Link Golf, Saddle and Cycle, Off The Street. Home: 5 Modena Rd Savannah GA 31411-2136 Office: Schafer Rsch Inc 5 Modena Rd Savannah GA 31411-2136

SCHAFER, WILLIAM HARRY, electric power industry administrator; b. South Portsmouth, Ky., Aug. 22, 1936; s. William Harry and Mary Minnie (Papillon) S. AS, Franklin U., 1980; BA, Capital U., 1987; MS, Greenwich U., 1992. Cert. fraud examiner; cert. protection profl.; cert. profl. mgr. With Columbus (Ohio) region Am. Electric Power (formerly Columbus So. Power), 1969—, risk mgmt. coord., 1989—; cons. in loss prevention field. First aid instr. Franklin County ARC, Columbus, 1965-93; mem. Simon Kenton coun. Boy Scouts Am., Columbus. Named Ky. Col., Gov. Ky., 1974, Ky. Adm., 1994, Hon. (Ohio) Lt. Gov., 1974; recupuent Columbus Mayor's award for Voluntary Svc., 1982, Outstanding Comty. Svc. award Ohio Senate, 1982, Humanitarian Achievement award Columbus Dispatch newspaper, 1983, Silver Beaver award Boy Scouts Am., 1979, 45 Yr. Vets award, 1992; James E. West fellow Boy Scouts Am., 1995. Mem. Am. Soc. Indsl. Security, Nat. Assn. Cert. Fraud Examiners, Acad. Security Educators and Trainers, Inst. Cert. Profl. Mgrs., Valley Forge Hist. Soc. (life), Ky. Hist. Soc. (life), U.S. Capitol Hist Soc. (supporting founding mem.), Nat. Safety Coun. (camping com. 1974-86), Nat. Fire Protection Assn. (edn. com. 1989-93), Children's Club-Children's Hosp. (charter), Masons, Shriners. Methodist. Avocations: back-packing, travel, humanities. Home: 60 Broadmeadows Blvd Apt 327 Columbus OH 43214-1152 Office: Am Electric Power Columbus Region 215 N Front St Columbus OH 43215-2255

SCHAFFER, DAVID IRVING, lawyer; b. N.Y.C., Oct. 17, 1935; s. Frank and Edith (Montlack) S.; m. Lois Ann Warshauer, June 16, 1957; children: Susan Edith Wenig, Eric Michael. B.A., U. Pa., 1956; LL.B., Harvard U., 1959. Bar: N.Y. 1960. Assoc. Shearman & Sterling, N.Y.C., 1960-65; sec., counsel Yale Express System, Inc., N.Y.C., 1965-66; sr. v.p., gen. counsel, sec. Avis, Inc., Garden City, N.Y., 1966-83; v.p., gen. counsel U.S. Surgical Corp., Norwalk, Conn., 1983-86; of counsel Meltzer, Lippe, Goldstein & Wolf, P.C., Mineola, N.Y., 1986-89, ptnr., 1989—; past pres. Nassau County Legal Aid Soc., 1984-86. Bd. dirs. United Community Fund, Great Neck, N.Y., 1980, L.I. Venture Group, 1988—. With USAR, 1960. Mem. ABA, N.Y. State Bar Assn., Nassau County Bar Assn., Harvard Club. Democrat. Home: 31 Amherst Rd Great Neck NY 11021-2910 Office: Meltzer Lippe Goldstein Wolf & Schlisser PC 190 Willis Ave Mineola NY 11501-2639

SCHAFFER, EDMUND JOHN, management consultant, retired engineering executive; b. N.Y.C., July 28, 1925; m. Muriel Spiro, Aug. 22, 1948; children: Diane Schaffer Garretson, Elaine Schaffer Luks. BS in Indsl. Engring., Syracuse U., 1950. Sr. staff indsl. engr. Carborundum Co., Niagara Falls, N.Y, 1952-60; mgr. mfg. Ford Motor Co., Detroit, 1952-60; sr. indsl. engr. ITT, N.Y.C., 1960-69, v.p., dir. worldwide indsl. engring. and mfg., 1969-82, ret., 1982; mgmt. cons. Short Hills, N.J., 1983—. With USN, 1943-47. Mem. Canoe Brook Country Club, Johns Island Country Club, Interlachen Country Club. Home: 63 Slope Dr Short Hills NJ 07078-1953

SCHAFFER, ROBERT WARREN, state senator; b. Cin., July 24, 1962; s. Robert James and Florence Ann (Bednar) S.; m. Maureen Elizabeth Menke, Feb. 8, 1986; children: Jennifer, Emily, Justin. BA in Polit. Sci., U. Dayton, 1984. Legis. asst. State of Ohio, Columbus, 1985; majority adminstrv. asst. Colo. Senate, Denver, 1985-87; Colo. senator representing Dist. 14 Ft. Collins, 1987—; chmn. state vets. and mil. affairs com. state affairs com., 1995—; commr. Colo. Advanced Tech. Inst., 1988—; proprietor No. Front Range Mktg. and Distbn., Inc. Mem. Mental Health Bd. Larimer County, 1986-87; mem. com. on human svcs. Nat. Conf. State Legislatures; campaing co-chair Arnold for Lt. Gov.; Republican candidate for Lt. Gov. of Colo., 1994. Named Nat. Legislator of Yr., Rep. Nat. Legislators Assn., 1995, Taxpayer Champion, Colo. Union of Taxpayers, 1995. Mem. Jaycees (Mover and Shaker award 1989), KC. Roman Catholic. Avocations: backpacking, skiing, baseball, painting, reading. Home: 3284 Silverthorne Dr Fort Collins CO 80526-2766 Office: The State Senate State Capitol Denver CO 80203

SCHAFFER, SETH ANDREW, lawyer; b. Bklyn., Jan. 7, 1942; m. Karen (Kiki) Cohn, Dec. 1, 1968; children: Amanda, Julia, James. BA in Econs. magna cum laude, Harvard U., 1963, LLB cum laude, 1967; postgrad., Cambridge (Eng.) U., 1964. Bar: N.Y. 1970, U.S. Dist. Ct. (so. dist.) N.Y. 1973, U.S. Ct. Appeals (2d cir.) 1973, U.S. Supreme Ct. 1980. Tchr. math. and econs. York (Pa.) Country Day Sch., 1967-68; assoc. dir. Vera Inst. Justice, 1969-72; asst. U.S. atty. U.S. Dist. Ct. (so. dist.) N.Y., 1972-75; chief counsel Moreland Act Commn. on Nursing Homes, N.Y.C., 1975-76; of counsel Stanley S. Arkin, P.C., Attys. at Law, 1976-77; v.p., gen. counsel, sec. of univ. NYU, N.Y.C., 1977-93, sr. v.p., gen. counsel, sec., 1993—; first v.p. Nat. Assn. Coll. and Univ., trustee Hosp. for Joint Diseases. Dir. Not for Profit Coordinating Com. N.Y. Henry fellow Cambridge U., Eng., 1964. Mem. Assn. Bar City N.Y., Phi Beta Kappa. Home: 14 Washington Mews New York NY 10003-6608 Office: NYU 70 Washington Sq S New York NY 10012-1091

SCHAFFNER, BERTRAM HENRY, psychiatrist; b. Erie, Pa., Nov. 12, 1912; s. Milton and Gerta (Herzog) S. Student, Harvard U., 1928-29, 32-33; AB, Swarthmore Coll., 1932; MD, Johns Hopkins U., 1937; diploma, William Alanson White Inst., 1953. Diplomate Am. Bd. Psychiatry, Am. Bd. Neurology. Intern Johns Hopkins Hosp., Balt., 1937-38; resident in neurology Mt. Sinai Hosp., N.Y.C., 1938-39; resident in psychiatry Bellevue Hosp., N.Y.C., 1939-40, N.Y. State Psychiat. Inst., N.Y.C., 1946-47; pvt. practice psychiatry and psychoanalysis N.Y.C., 1947—; lectr. Sch. Nursing Cornell U., N.Y.C., 1950-60; mem. faculty, clin. supr. in psychotherapy William Alanson White Inst. Psychoanalysis, 1960—, med. dir. HIV svc., clin. supr. psychoanalysis, 1993—; cons., editor confs. Josiah Macy Jr. Found., 1949, 50, 51; cons. U.S. Children's Bur., 1946-47, Bur. Mental Health, V.I., 1954-60, World Fedn. Mental Health, 1958-68, others; mem. N.Y. County dist. bd. Com. on Gay and Lesbian Issues; cons. WHO, 1960-67; founder, pres. U.S.-Caribbean Aid to Mental Health, Inc., 1960-69; organizer Biennial Caribbean Confs. for Mental Health, 1959-65; organizer, cons. Caribbean Fedn. for Mental Health, 1959-65; mem. rsch. study Pre-Soviet Russian Family and Culture, Columbia U., 1949-51. Mem. editl. bd. Jour. of Gay and Lesbian Psychotherapy, 1987—; author: Father Land: A Study of Authoritarianism in the German Family, 1948; contbr. numerous articles to profl. publs. Recipient Adolf Meyer award for Disting. Svc. in Behalf of Improved Care and Treatment of the Mentally Ill in the Caribbean, 1961. Fellow AMA (life), Am. Psychiat. Assn. (chmn. 1983-86, mem. com. on AIDS N.Y. County dist. br. 1989—, life), Am. Acad. Psychoanalysis (life), Caribbean Psychiat. Assn.; mem. Group for Advancement of Psychiatry (chair internat. rels. com. 1960-65, chair com. on human sexuality 1987—). Avocations: collecting Asian and Indian art. Home and Office: 220 Central Park S New York NY 10019

SCHAFFNER, CHARLES ETZEL, consulting engineering executive; b. N.Y.C., July 21, 1919; s. Louis C. and Christina (Etzel) S.; m. Olga T. Stroedecke, Feb. 13, 1943; children—Charles Etzel II, Linda Jean. B.C.E., Cooper Union, 1941, C.E., 1952; M.C.E., Bklyn. Poly. Inst., 1944; B.S.S.E., U. Ill., 1945, N.Y. U.; D.Sci (hon.), Iona Coll., 1983. Jr. engr. Moran Proctor, Freeman & Mueser, N.Y.C., 1941; instr. Cooper Union, 1941-44; mem. faculty Bklyn. Poly. Inst., 1946-70, prof. engring., 1957-70, adj. prof., 1970-72, asst. dean, 1954-57, assoc. dean, 1957-58, dean, dir. planning, 1958-62, v.p. adminstrn., 1962-70; v.p. Syska & Hennessy, Inc., 1970-73, sr. v.p., 1973-76, exec. v.p., 1976-85, vice chmn., 1985-86, cons., 1987—, also dir.; Chmn. nat. adv. bd. Summer Inst. Young Engring. Tchrs., 1959-63; mem. adv. panel NSF, 1960-70; chmn. exec. bd. N.Y.C. Bldg. Code Project, 1962-66; mem. panel 421.00 adv. to bldg. research div. Inst. Applied Tech., Nat. Bur. Standards, 1966-69; mem. bldg., constrn. adv. council Dept. Bldgs. City N.Y., 1966—; mem. bldg. research adv. bd. NRC, 1972-79, vice chmn., 1973-77; chmn., 1977-78, Mayor's Bldg. and Constrn. Adv. Council, 1971-73; exec. dir. Mayor's Fire Safety Com., 1971-73; mem. N.Y.C. Constrn. Industry Advisory Council, 1973—; v.p., bd. dirs. N.Y. Bldg. Congress, 1967-71, sec., 1971-75, chmn. govtl. affairs com., 1977-78, pres., 1979-83, chmn. council pres., 1983-87, chmn. council bus. and labor, 1987-88. Contbr. articles profl. jours. Commr. edn. dist., Locust Valley, N.Y., 1956-59, pres., 1958-59; commr. edn., pres. Central Dist. 3, Oyster Bay, N.Y., 1959-63; Trustee Cooper Union, 1975-78; trustee Cooper Union Research Found. Served with AUS, 1944-46. Named Outstanding Alumnus Cooper Union, 1966; Good Scout of Yr. Boy Scouts Am., 1979; recipient Disting. Alumnus award Poly. Alumni Assn., Alumnus of Year, 1972. Mem. Operation Democracy, ASCE (Civil Engr. of Year 1969), ASTM, Am. Arbitration Assn. (bd. arbitrators), Am. Soc. Engring. Edn. (v.p., gen. council 1965-67, v.p. fin. 1974-77, dir. 1965-67, 74-77, 78-81, pres. 1979-80), Nat. Inst. Bldg. Scis. (exec. com. consultative council 1978-82, dir. 1982-88), Engrs. Joint Council (dir. 1976-79), Am. Assn. Engring. Socs. (bd. govs. 1979-81, chmn. ednl. affairs council 1979-80), Am. Concrete Inst., N.Y. State Sch. Bds. Assn., N.Y. State Soc. Profl. Engrs. (dir. Nassau County chpt., Engr. of Year, Kings County chpt. 1968), Cooper Union Alumni Assn. (pres. 1973), Tau Beta Pi, Chi Epsilon, Omega Delta Phi. Clubs: Municipal, Nassau. Home and Office: Linden Farms Rd Locust Valley NY 11560

SCHAFFNER, ROBERTA IRENE, medical, surgical nurse; b. Vero Beach, Fla., Oct. 5, 1926; d. Robert Wesley and Harriett Louise (Davis) Routh; m. David Leonard Schaffner, Apr. 25, 1947 (div. July 1975); children: Penny Routh S., David Leonard II. Mem. cadet nurse corps, Charity Hosp., New Orleans, La., 1944-45; ADA, Montgomery County C.C., Blue Bell, Pa., 1978; BSN, Gwynedd (Pa.) Mercy Coll., 1982, MSN, 1984. RN Pa. Med.-surg. nurse Chestnut Hill Hosp., Phila., 1978—; mem. delegation to study health care delivery sys., Moscow, Tbillisi, Azerbeijan, Kiev, 1981, Shanghai, Beijing, Nanjing, Hong Kong, 1984, Milan, Pisa, Bologna, Florence, Rome, Sorento, Naples, 1985. Cadet U.S. Nurse Corps, 1945. Mem. Oncology Nursing Soc., Sigma Theta Tau. Republican. Home: 1600 Church Rd # A 214 Wyncote PA 19095-1926 Office: Chestnut Hill Hosp 8835 Germantown Ave Philadelphia PA 19118-2718

SCHAIE, K(LAUS) WARNER, human development and psychology educator, researcher; b. Stettin, Germany (now Poland), Feb. 1, 1928; came to U.S., 1947, naturalized, 1953; s. Sally and Lottie Louise (Gabriel) S.; m. Coloma J. Harrison, Aug. 9, 1953 (div. 1973); 1 child, Stephan; m. Sherry L. Willis, Nov. 20, 1981. A.A., City Coll. San Francisco, 1951; B.A., U. Calif.-Berkeley, 1952; M.S. U. Wash., 1953, Ph.D., 1956. Lic. psychologist, Calif., Pa. Postdoctoral fellow Washington U., St. Louis, 1956-57; asst. prof. psychology U. Nebr., Lincoln, 1957-1964, assoc. prof., 1964-68; prof., chmn. dept. psychology W.Va. U., Morgantown, 1964-73; prof. psychology, dir. Gerontology Research Inst., U. So. Calif., 1973-81; Evan Pugh prof. human devel. and psychology, dir. Gerontology Ctr., Pa. State U., University Park, 1981—; mem. devel. behavior study sect. NIH, Bethesda, Md., 1970-72, chmn., 1972-74, chmn. human devel. and aging study sect., 1979-84, mem. expert panel in comml. airline pilot retirement, 1981, data and safety bd. shep project, 1984-91. Author: Developmental Psychology; A Life Span Approach, 1981; Adult Development and Aging, 1982, 4th rev. edit., 1996, Intellectual Development in Adulthood: The Seattle Longitudinal Study, 1996; editor: Handbook of Psychology of Aging, 1977, 4th rev. edit., 1996, Longitudinal Studies of Adult Development, 1983, Cognitive Functioning and Social Structure over the Life Course, 1987, Methodological Issues in Research on Aging, 1988, Social Structure and Aging: Psychological Processes, 1989, Age Structuring in Comparative Perspective, 1989, The Course of Later Life, 1989, Self-Directedness: Cause and Effects Throughout the Life Course, 1990, Aging, Health Behaviors and Health Outcomes, 1992, Caregiving Systems: Formal and Informal Helpers, 1993, Societal Impact on Aging: Historical Perspectives, 1993, Adult Intergenerational Relations: Effects of Societal Change, 1995, Older Adults Decision Making and the Law, 1996; editor Ann. Rev. Gerontology and Geriatrics vol. 7, 1987, vol. 11, 1991; contbr. articles to profl. jours. Fellow APA (coun. reps. 1976-79, 83-86, Disting. Contbn. award 1982, Disting. Scientific Conbns. award, 1992), Gerontol. Soc. (Kleemeier award 1987), Am. Psychol. Soc.; mem. Psychometric Soc., Internat. Soc. Study Behavioral Devel. Unitarian. Avocations: hiking; stamps. Home: 425 Windmere Dr # 3A State College PA 16801 Office: Pa State U Dept Human Devel & Family Studies University Park PA 16802

SCHAIRER, GEORGE SWIFT, aeronautical engineer; b. Pitts., May 19, 1913; s. Otto Sorg and Elizabeth Blanche (Swift) S.; m. Mary Pauline Tarbox, June 20, 1935; children: Mary Elizabeth, George Edward, Sally Helen, John Otto. With Bendix Aviation Corp., South Bend, Ind., 1935-37, Consol. Vultee Aircraft Corp., San Diego, 1937-39; joined Boeing Airplane Co., Seattle, 1939, successively chief aerodynamist, staff engr. aerodynamics and powerplant, 1948-51, chief tech. staff, 1951-56, asst. chief engr., 1956-57, dir. research, 1957-59, v.p. research and devel., 1959-73, v.p. research, 1973-78, cons., 1978-88; mem. sci. adv. group USAAF, 1945-46; mem. com. on aerodynamics NACA; mem. tech. adv. panel on aeros. Dept. Def., 1954-61; sci. adv. bd. USAF, 1955-60; cons. ops. evaluation group USN, 1961; panel sci. and tech. manpower Pres.'s Sci. Adv. Com., 1962-64; sci. adv. com. Def. Intelligence Agy., 1966-70; mem. aeros. and space engring. bd. NRC, 1977-79. Contbr. articles to profl. jours. Trustee A Contemporary Theatre. Recipient Spirit of St. Louis award ASME, 1959, Guggenheim medal, 1967. Fellow AIAA (hon. fellow, Sylvanus Albert Reed award 1950, Wright Bros. lectr. 1964); mem. NAE, NAS, Internat. Acad. Astronautics, Am. Helicopter Soc., Soc. Naval Architects and Marine Engrs., Sigma Xi, Sigma Tau. Address: 4242 Hunts Point Rd Bellevue WA 98004-1106

SCHAKE, LOWELL MARTIN, animal science educator; b. Marthasville, Mo., June 6, 1938; s. Martin Charles and Flora Olinda (Rocklage) S.; m. Wendy Anne Walkinshaw, Sept. 11, 1959; children: Sheryl Anne, Lowell Scott. BS, U. Mo., 1960, MS, 1962; PhD, Tex. A&M U., 1967. Asst. prof. Tex. A&M U., College Station, 1965-67, assoc. prof., 1969-72, prof., 1972-84; asst. prof., area livestock specialist Tex. A&M U., Lubbock, 1967-69; prof., head animal sci. dept. U. Conn., Storrs, 1984-92; prof., chmn. animal sci. dept. Tex. Tech. U., Lubbock, 1992-95; developer applied animal ethology program Tex. A&M U., 1970, New Eng. Biotech Conf. series, 1990, S.W. Beef Forum, 1993; chmn. Am. Registry of Profl. Animal Scientist Com. on Profl. Stds., 1988; chmn. Nat. Com. Exec. Officers of Animal Vet., Dairy and Poultry Sci. Depts., 1992; cons. Alpart, Kingston, Jamaica, 1975, U.S. Feeds Grain Coun., 1970-73, A.O. Smith Products Inc., 1968-92, Humphrey Land & Cattle Co., Dallas, 1980-86; lectr. in field. Author: Growth and Finishing of Beef Cattle, A Class Handbook, 1982; contbr. articles to profl. jours. Recipient Innovative Teaching award Tex. A&M U., 1978. Mem. Am. Soc. Animal Sci., Plains Nutrition Coun. (adv. bd. 1967-80, sec.-treas. 1994-95, founder), Nat. Assn. Colls. and Tchrs. Agr., Am. Registry Profl. Animal Scientists (dir. for Northeast 1987-89), Coun. for Agr. Sci. and Tech. World Conf. on Animal Prodn., Am. Soc. Dairy Sci., Gamma Sigma Delta. Republican. Club: Tiger (College Station) (pres.). Avocations: fishing, gardening, outdoor work. Home: 13542 Carlos Fifth Ct Corpus Christi TX 78418

SCHALEBEN, ARVILLE, newspaper editor, writer, educator; b. Brown County, Minn., Jan. 25, 1907; s. Wilhelm and Ida (Helling) S.; m. Ida Androvandi, Sept. 14, 1935; children: Joy Schaleben Lewis, Susan Schaleben Wilson, Mary Schaleben Totero, Will. B.A., U. Minn., 1929. With Milw. Jour., 1929-72, reporter, asst. city editor, then city editor, 1936-46, asst. mng. editor, 1946-59, mng. editor, 1959-62, exec. editor, 1962-66, asso. editor, 1966-72; v.p. The Jour. Co., 1962-68, dir., 1960-72; editor-in-residence U. Wis., Madison, 1972—; also vis. prof. U. Wis.; vis. prof. Medill Sch.

Journalism, Northwestern U., 1972—; Riley prof. journalism Ind. U., Bloomington, 1972; lectr. U. Wis., Milw., 1976-77. Author: Your Future in Journalism; editorial bd. This Week mag.; contbr. anthologies: Folks Say of Will Rogers, The American Dream, Headlining America, News Stories of 1933, News Stories of 1934, Fifty and Feisty. Pres. Androvandi, Ltd., Milw. Dir. Fox Point (Wis.) Sch. Bd., 1942-48; mem. President's Com. for Handicapped, 1950-58; chmn. Nicolet High Sch. bldg. com., 1953. Named Wis. Journalist of Year, Soc. Profl. Journalists, 1975, 80; recipient Honor al Merito award N.Am. Assn. of Venezuela. Mem. Wis. AP Assn. (pres.), AP Mng. Editors Assn. (dir.; chmn. news research com. 1965, mem. media competition com., new methods com., com. future newspapers, co-editor 50-yr. associated press history, regent 1965—), Am. Newspaper Pubs. Assn. (mem. news research center steering com. 1964-72), Am. Soc. Newspaper Editors (co-chmn. edn. com., mem. research com., com. edn. for journalism, com. minorities), Internat. Press Inst., Soc. South Pole, Antarctican Soc., Sigma Delta Chi (chmn. Wis. 1958, mem. prof. goals com.). Congregationalist (past chmn. bldg. com.). Clubs: Milw. Press (pres. 1936-39, mem. Found.), Milw. Press (pres. Found. 1975-85, knight of Golden Quill, 1979), Ozaukee Country (Mequon, Wis.), Makai Golf and Tennis (Princeville, Hanalei, Hawaii). Home: 8254 N Gray Log Ln Milwaukee WI 53217-2862 Office: 333 W State St Milwaukee WI 53203-1305 also: U Wis-Madison Vilas Communications H Madison WI 53706 *In our good earth's eternity, not one among us is more enduring than the least among us unless he so lives to lengthen mankind's future.*

SCHALL, ALVIN ANTHONY, federal judge; b. N.Y.C., Apr. 4, 1944; s. Gordon William and Helen (Davis) S.; m. Sharon Frances LeBlanc, Apr. 25, 1970; children: Amanda Lanford, Anthony Davis. BA, Princeton U., 1966; JD, Tulane U., 1969. Bar: N.Y. 1970, U.S. Dist. Ct. (so. and ea. dists.) N.Y. 1973, U.S. Ct. Appeals (2d crct.) 1974, D.C. 1980, U.S. Dist. Ct. D.C. 1991, U.S. Ct. Appeals (D.C. crct.) 1991, U.S. Ct. Fed. Claims 1982, U.S. Ct. Appeals (fed. crct.) 1987, U.S. Supreme Ct. 1989. Assoc. Shearman & Sterling, N.Y.C., 1969-73; asst. U.S. atty. ea. dist. N.Y. Borough of Bklyn., 1973-78, chief appeals div., 1977-78; trial atty. civil div. U.S. Dept. Justice, Washington, 1978-87, sr. trial counsel, 1986-87, asst. to atty. gen., 1988-92; ptnr. Perlman & Ptnrs., Washington, 1987-88; judge U.S. Ct. Appeals (fed. crct.), Washington, 1992—. Office: 717 Madison Pl NW Washington DC 20439-0001

SCHALLENKAMP, KAY, academic administrator; b. Salem, S.D., Dec. 9, 1949; d. Arnold B. and Jennie M. (Koch) Krier; m. Ken Schallenkamp, Sept. 7, 1970; children: Heather, Jenni. BS, No. State Coll., 1972; MA, U. S.D., 1973; PhD, U. Colo., 1982. Prof. No. State Coll., Aberdeen, S.D., 1973-88, dept. chair, 1982-84, dean, 1984-88; provost Chadron (Nebr.) State Coll., 1988-92, U. Wis., Whitewater, 1992—; cons. North Ctrl. Assn., nursing homes, hosps. and ednl. instns. Contbr. articles to profl. jours. Commr. North Ctrl. Assn., 1995—. Bush fellow, 1980; named Outstanding Young Career Woman, Bus. and Profl. Women's Club, 1976. Mem. Am. Speech and Hearing Assn. (cert.), Rotary. Avocation: martial arts. Office: U Wis Whitewater 800 W Main St Whitewater WI 53190-1705

SCHALLER, GEORGE BEALS, zoologist; b. Berlin, May 26, 1933; s. Georg Ludwig S. and Bettina (Byrd) Iwersen; m. Kay Suzanne Morgan, Aug. 26, 1957; children: Eric, Mark. BS. in Zoology, BA in Anthropology, U. Alaska, 1955; Ph.D. in Zoology, U. Wis., 1962. Research assoc. Johns Hopkins U., Balt., 1963-66; research zoologist Wildlife Conservation Soc., Bronx, 1966—; adj. assoc. prof. Rockefeller U., N.Y.C., 1966—; research assoc. Am. Mus. Natural History. Author: The Mountain Gorilla, 1963 (Wildlife Soc. 1965), The Year of the Gorilla, 1964, The Deer and the Tiger, 1967, The Serengeti Lion, 1972 (Nat. Bookaward 1973), Golden Shadows, Flying Hooves, 1973, Mountain Monarchs, 1977, Stones of Silence, 1980, The Giant Pandas of Wolong, 1985, The Last Panda, 1993. Ctr. Advanced Study in Behavioral Scis. fellow, Standord U., 1962; fellow Guggenheim Found., 1971; decorated Order of Golden Ark (The Netherlands), Explorers medal, 1990; recipient gold medal World Wildlife Fund, 1980. Ctr. Advanced Study in Behavioral Scis. fellow, Stanford U., 1962; fellow Guggenheim Found., 1971; decorated Order of Golden Ark (The Netherlands), Explorers medal, 1990; recipient gold medal World Wildlife Fudn, 1980. Mem. Explorers Club (hon. dir. 1991). Office: Wildlife Conservation Soc Bronx Park Bronx NY 10462

SCHALLER, JANE GREEN, pediatrician; b. Cleve., June 26, 1934; d. George and May Alice (Wing) Green; children: Robert Thomas, George Charles, Margaret May. A.B., Hiram (Ohio) Coll., 1956; M.D. cum laude, Harvard U., 1960. Diplomate Am. Bd. Pediatrics, Am. Bd. Med. Examiners. Resident in pediatrics Children's Hosp.-U. Wash., Seattle, 1960-63; fellow immunology Children's Hosp. U. Wash., 1963-65; mem. faculty U. Wash. Med. Sch., 1965-83, prof. pediatrics, 1975-83; head div. rheumatic diseases Children's Hosp., Seattle, 1968-83; prof., chmn. dept. pediatrics Tufts U. Sch. Medicine/New Eng. Med. Ctr., 1983—; pediatrician-in-chief Boston Floating Hosp., 1983—; vis. physician Med. Rsch. Coun., Taplow, Eng., 1971-72; tech. advisor UN Study on the Impact of Armed Conflict on Children. Author articles in field.; Editorial bds. profl. jours. Bd. dirs. Seattle Chamber Music Festival, 1982-85; trustee Boston Chamber Music Soc., 1985—; mem. Boston adv. coun. UNICEF. Mem. Inst. Medicine of NAS, AAAS (sci. and human rights program), Soc. Pediatric Rsch., Am. Pediatric Soc., Am. Acad. Pediatrics (chmn. subcom. on children and human rights 1989—, com. on internat. child health 1990—), Am. Coll. Rheumatology, New Eng. Pediatric Soc. (pres. 1991-93), Assn. Med. Sch. Pediatric Chmn. (exec. com. 1986-89, rep. to coun. on govt. affairs and coun. of acad. socs.), Com. Health in So. Africa (exec. com. 1986—), Physicians for Human Rights (exec. com. 1986—, founding pres. 1986-89), Aesculapian Club (pres. 1988-89), Harvard U. Med. Sch. Alumni Coun. (v.p. 1977-80, pres. 1982-83), Internat. Rescue Com. (med. adv. com., women's commn. for refugee women and children), Mass. Women's Forum, Internat. Women's Forum, Tavern Club, Saturday Club. Office: Floating Hosp for Children 750 Washington St # 286 Boston MA 02111-1533

SCHALLER, JOANNE FRANCES, nursing consultant; b. Columbus, Ga., July 15, 1943; d. John Frank and Ethel Beatrice (Spring) Lanzendorfer; m. Robert Thomas Schaller, Jan. 22, 1977; 1 child, Amy. BS, Pacific Luth. U., 1969; M in Nursing, U. Wash., 1971. House supr. UCLA Hosp., 1971-72; outpatient supr. Harborview Hosp., Seattle, 1973-75; outpatient clinic and emergency room supr. U. Wash. Hosp., Seattle, 1975-77; co-author, researcher with Robert Schaller MD Seattle, 1977-87; prin. Nursing Expert-Standards of Care, Seattle, 1987—; cons. Wash. State Trial Lawyers, Wash. Assn. Criminal Def. Lawyers, 1989—; founder, CEO Present Perfect, Seattle, 1991—; appt. Breast Cancer cons. UWMC, 1995—. Contbr., editor articles to profl. jours. Bd. dirs. Pacific Arts Ctr., 1992—; vol. guardian ad litem King County Juvenile Ct., 1978—; vol. Make a Wish Found. U.S. Bank, 1984—, Multiple Sclerosis Assn., 1986—, Am. Heart Assn., 1986—, Internat. Children's Festival, 1987—, Seattle Children's Festival, 1987—, Seattle Dept. Parks and Recreation Open Space Com., 1990—, Pacific N.W. Athletic Congress, 1991—, Wash. Fed. Garden Clubs Jr. Advisor, 1992—, Fred Hutchison Cancer Rsch. Ctr., 1993—; mem. parent coun. Seattle Country Day Sch., 1986—; mem. Photo Coun. Seattle Art Mus., 1986—, Native Am. Coun., 1989—; mem. N.W. Coun. Seattle Art Mus., 1992—, mem. NAOO Coun. Seattle Art Mus., 1989—, Plestcheeff Inst. Decorative Arts, 1992—; mem. fundraiser Children's Hosp. Med. Ctr., 1977—, Breast Cancer Fund, 1994—, Susan G. Komen Breast Cancer Found., 1994—. Named 1st Migrant Health Care Nurse, State of Wash., 1969, 1st Am. nurse visiting China, 1974. Mem. AAUW, ANA, Wash. State Nurses Assn., U. Wash. Alumni Assn. Avocations: photography, writing, gardening, hiking, music. Home and Office: 914 Randolph Ave Seattle WA 98122-5267

SCHALLERT, EDWIN GLENN, lawyer; b. L.A., Aug. 7, 1952; s. William Joseph and Rosemarie Diane (Waggner) S. AB, Stanford U., 1974; JD, Harvard U., 1981, MPP, 1981. Bar: N.Y. 1974, U.S. Ct. Appeals (7th cir.) 1986, U.S. Ct. Appeals (2d cir.) 1989, U.S. Dist. Ct. (so. dist.) N.Y. 1975. Legis. aid to U.S. rep. Les Aspin Washington, 1975-78, law clk. to Hon. J. Skelly Wright, 1981-82, law clk. to Hon. Thurgood Marshall, 1982-83; assoc. Debevoise & Plimpton, N.Y.C., 1983-89, ptnr., 1989—. Mem. Internat. Inst. for Strategic Studies, Coun. Fgn. Rels. (term mem. 1983-88), Phi Beta Kappa. Democrat. Avocation: tennis. Office: Debevoise & Plimpton 875 3d Ave New York NY 10022-6225

SCHALLY, ANDREW VICTOR, endocrine oncologist, researcher; b. Poland, Nov. 30, 1926; came to U.S., 1957; s. Casimir Peter and Maria (Lacka) S.; m. Ana Maria Comaru, Aug., 1976; children: Karen, Gordon. B.Sc., McGill U., Can., 1955, Ph.D. in Biochemistry, 1957; 16 hon. doctorates. Research asst. biochemistry Nat. Inst. Med. Research, London, 1949-52; dept. psychiatry McGill U., Montreal, Que., 1952-57; research assoc., asst. prof. physiology and biochemistry Coll. Medicine, Baylor U., Houston, 1957-62; assoc. prof. Tulane U. Sch. Medicine, New Orleans, 1962-67, prof., 1967—; chief Endocrine Polypeptide and Cancer Inst. VA Med. Ctr., New Orleans; sr. med. investigator VA, 1973—. Author several books; contbr. articles to profl. jours. Recipient Van Meter prize Am. Thyroid Assn., 1969; Ayerst-Squibb award Endocrine Soc., 1970; William S. Middletown award VA, 1970; Ch. Mickle award U. Toronto, 1974; Gairdner Internat. award, 1974; Borden award Assn. Am. Med. Colls. and Borden Co. Found., 1975; Lasker Basic Research award, 1975; co-recipient Nobel prize for medicine, 1977; USPHS sr. research fellow, 1961-62. Mem. NAS, AAAS, Endocrine Soc., Am. Physiol. Soc., Soc. Biol. Chemists, Soc. Exptl. Biol. Medicine, Internat. Soc. Rsch. Biology Reprodn., Soc. Study Reprodn., Soc. Internat. Brain Rsch. Orgn., Mex. Acad. Medicine, Am. Soc. Animal Sci., Nat. Acad. Medicine Brazil, Acad. Medicine Venezuela, Acad. Sci. Hungary, Acad. Sci. Russia. Home: 5025 Kawanee Ave Metairie LA 70006-2547 Office: VA Hosp 1601 Perdido St New Orleans LA 70112-1207

SCHAMA, SIMON, historian, educator, author; b. London, England, Feb. 13, 1945; married; 2 children. BA, Cambridge (Eng.) U., 1966, MA in History, 1969. Prof. Humanities Old Dominion Found. Columbia U.; sr. assoc. Ctr. European Studies Harvard U., Cambridge, Mass., 1980-93. Author: Patriots and Liberators: Revolution in the Netherlands, 1780-1813, 1977 (Wolfson prize for history 1977, Leo Gershoy Meml. prize Am. Hist. Assn. 1978), Two Rothschilds and the Land of Israel, 1979, The Embarrassment of Riches: An Interpretation of Dutch Culture in the Golden Age, 1987, Citizens: A Chronicle of the French Revolution, 1989 (NCR prize for non-fiction), Dead Certainties, 1991, Landscape and Memory, 1995. Office: Columbia U Dept History New York NY 10027

SCHAMBRA, PHILIP ELLIS, federal agency administrator, radiobiologist; b. Saginaw, Mich., Nov. 8, 1934; s. William Philip and Gwendolyn Maude (Leister) S.; m. Uta Gertrude Bossel, Mar. 30, 1967 (div. Aug. 1981); children: Eric William Philip, Kirsten Uta, Heidi Maren; m. Donita Bartels Feldman, Aug. 15, 1990. BA, Rice U., 1956; PhD, Yale U., 1961. Examiner Office of Mgmt. and Budget Exec. Office of Pres., Washington, 1968-71, staff mem. Coun. on Environ. Quality, 1971-74; assoc. dir. Nat. Inst. Environ. Health Scis., Research Triangle Park, N.C., 1974-81; chief internat. coordination Fogarty Internat. Ctr. NIH, Bethesda, Md., 1981-84; sci. attache U.S. Embassy, New Delhi, 1984-88; dir. Fogarty Internat. Ctr. NIH, Bethesda, Md., 1988—. Contbr. articles on radiobiology to profl. jours. Recipient Superior Svc. award USPHS, 1989; Nat. Cancer Inst. fellow, 1958, Rsch. fellow NASA, 1964. Mem. AAAS. Avocations: sailing, racquetball. Home: 9104 Drumaldry Dr Bethesda MD 20817-3341

SCHANBERG, SAUL MURRAY, pharmacology educator; b. Clinton, Mass., Mar. 22, 1933; m. Rachel Weinbaum, Dec. 18, 1956; children: Laura E., Linda S. B.A., Clark U., 1954, M.A., 1956; Ph.D., Yale U., 1961, M.D., 1964. Cons. Calif. Dept. Mental Health, 1962-65; intern in pediatrics Albert Einstein Med. Ctr., N.Y.C., 1964-65; rsch. assoc. NIMH, 1965-67; asst. prof. Duke U. Med. Ctr., Durham, N.C., 1967-69, assoc. prof., 1969-73, prof. of pharmacology, 1973—; prof. psychiatry Duke U. Med. Ctr., 1983—; assoc. dean Duke U. Med. Ctr. Sch., 1987-93, chair phamacology, 1987-92. Cons. USPHS, Rockville, Md., 1983-84. NIMH grantee, 1968; NIH grantee, 1967. Fellow Am. Coll. Neuropsychopharmacology. Home: 1604 Pinecrest Rd Durham NC 27705-5832 Office: Duke U PO Box 3813 Durham NC 27710-3813

SCHANBERG, SYDNEY HILLEL, newspaper editor, columnist; b. Clinton, Mass., Jan. 17, 1934; s. Louis and Freda (Feinberg) S.; children—Jessica, Rebecca. B.A., Harvard U., 1955. Joined N.Y. Times, 1959, became reporter, 1960; bur. chief N.Y. Times, Albany, N.Y., 1967-69; chief bur. N.Y. Times, New Delhi, India, 1969-73; S.E. Asia corr. N.Y. Times, Singapore, 1973-75; met. editor N.Y. Times, 1977-80, columnist, 1981-85; assoc. editor, columnist Newsday, 1986—. Served with AUS, 1956-58. Recipient Page One award for fgn. reporting Newspaper Guild N.Y., 1972; George Polk Meml. award for fgn. reporting, 1972; spl. award for coverage fall of Phnom Penh, 1975; Overseas Press Club award for fgn. reporting, 1972; for fgn. photography, 1974; Bob Considine Meml. award, 1975; Pulitzer prize, 1975; Front Page award Newspaper Guild; Sigma Delta Chi award for disting. service in journalism. Office: Newsday Inc 2 Park Ave New York NY 10016-5603

SCHANDER, MARY LEA, police official; b. Bakersfield, Calif., June 11, 1947; d. Gerald John Lea and Marian Lea Coffman; BA (Augustana fellow) Calif. Luth. Coll., 1969; MA, UCLA, 1970; m. Edwin Schander, July 3, 1971. Staff aide City of Anaheim (Calif.) Police Dept., 1970-72, staff asst., 1972-78, sr. staff asst., 1978-80; with Resource Mgmt. Dept., City of Anaheim, 1980-82; asst. to dir. Pub. Safety Agy., City of Pasadena Police Dept., 1982-85, spl. asst. to police chief, 1985-88, adminstrv. comdr., 1988-92, police comdr., 1992—; freelance musician; publisher Australian Traditional Songs, 1985, Songs in the Air of Early California, 1994; lectr. Calif. Luth. Coll.; instr. Calif. State U., Northridge; cons. City of Lodz, Poland, Internat. Assn. Chiefs of Police; assessor Nat. Commn. on Accreditation for Law Enforcement Agencies; speaker, panelist League of Calif. Cities, Pasadena Commn. on Status of Women; mcpl. mgmt. asst. CLEARS; instr. Calif. State U., Northridge. Producer (cable TV program) Traditional Music Showcase. Contbr. articles in field to profl. jours. Bd. dirs. Women At Work. Recipient Police Chief's Spl. award City of Pasadena, 1987, Women at Work Medal of Excellence, 1988. Mem. Nat. Womens Political Caucus, Nat. Ctr. for Women in Policing, Pasadena Arts Coun., L.A. County Peace Officers, Internat. Assn. Chiefs of Police. Home: PO Box 50151 Pasadena CA 91115-0151 Office: Pasadena Police Dept 207 N Garfield Ave Pasadena CA 91101-1748

SCHANEY, DIANA L., accountant; b. Butler, Pa., July 31, 1947; d. Wayne Frederick and Helen Elaine (Horton) Herrit; m. C. Raymond Schaney, Feb. 8, 1969; children: Christopher Raymond, Nathan Frederick. RN, Lutheran Hosp. Sch. Nursing, 1968; BA in Acctg. magna cum laude, Edinboro U. of Pa., 1984. CPA. Oper. rm. nurse various hosps., 1968-81; staff acct. Local CPA Firm, Erie, Pa., 1984-87; ptnr. Local CPA Firm, Erie, 1988-89; sole pratitioner Diana L. Schaney, CPA, Erie, 1989-90; ptnr. Coleman Schaney & Co., Erie, 1990—. Mem. bd. dirs., treas. The Achievement Ctr., 1989—. Mem. AICPAs, Pa. Inst. CPAs (sec. Erie chpt.), Inst. Mgmt. Accts., Rotary Internat., Women's Roundtable of Erie. Republican. Episcopalian. Avocations: reading, golfing, walking, travelling. Home: 307 Rice Ave Girard PA 16417-1424 Office: Coleman Schaney & Co 1805 W 38th St Erie PA 16508-2168

SCHANFARBER, RICHARD CARL, real estate broker; b. Cleve., June 11, 1937; s. Edwin David and Helen (Newman) S.; m. Barbara A. Berger, Dec. 21, 1958 (div. Sept. 1981); children: Edwin Jeffrey, Lori Jo, Tammy Joy. Grad., NYU, 1959. Cert. profl. standards instr.; cert. energy instr.; cert. tchr. Ohio; lic. FCC broadcasters; lic. gun dealer. Pres. Erieview Realty Inc., Gates Mills, 1961—, Miller Warehouse, Gates Mills, 1968—, ERI Travel Co., Gates Mills, 1974—, ERI Sales Co., Gates Mills, 1979—; ptnr. Landwood Assocs. Ltd., Gates Mills, 1986—; pres. Eastgate Travel Svcs., Gates Mills, Ohio, 1987—. Pres. Shaker Hts. (Ohio) Alumni Assn., 1986—, Cleve. Area Bd. Realtors, 1981, Cleve. Warehouseman Assn., 1977-79; chmn. City of Cleve. Landmarks Commn., 1984—. Mem. NRA (life), Nat. Assn. Realtors, Ohio Assn. Realtors, Ohio Hist. Soc., Cleve. Growth Assn., Cleve. Area Bd. Realtors, Cleve. Zool. Soc., Cleve. Mus. Art, Mayfield Twp. Hist. Soc., Western Res. Hist. Soc. Republican. Jewish. Avocations: woodworking, gun collecting, coin collecting, antiques, travel. Home: 6719 Sandalwood Dr Gates Mills OH 44040-9619

SCHANFIELD, FANNIE SCHWARTZ, community volunteer; b. Mpls., Dec. 25, 1916; d. Simon Zouberman and Mary (Schmilovitz) Schwartz; m. Melvin M. Stock, Oct. 27, 1943 (dec. Apr. 1944); 1 child, Moses Samuel Schanfield; m. Abraham Schanfield, Aug. 28, 1947; children: David Colman, Miriam Schanfield Kieffer. Student, U. Minn., 1962-75. Author: My Thoughts, 1996. Bd. dirs. Jewish Cmty. Ctr., Mpls., 1975-96, chairperson older adult needs, 1982-88; past pres. Bnai Emet Women's League, Mpls., 1988-90; rschr., advocate Hunger Hennepin County, Mpls., 1969-75; sec. Joint Religious Legis. Coalition; v.p., bd. dirs. Cmty. Housing Svc., Mpls., 1971-85. Recipient Citation of Honor, Hennepin County Commn., 1989, Lifetime Achievement award Jewish Cmty. Ctr. Greater Mpls., 1995. Mem. NOW, Lupus Found. Minn., Internat. Soc. Poets, Hadassah (prs. 1967-69, Citation 1969). Jewish. Avocations: needlepoint, rug hooking, writing. Home: 3630 Phillips Pky Minneapolis MN 55426-3792

SCHANFIELD, MOSES SAMUEL, geneticist, educator; b. Mpls., Sept. 7, 1944; s. Abraham and Fanny (Schwartz) S. BA in Anthropology, U. Minn., 1966; AM in Anthropology, Harvard U., 1969; PhD in Human Genetics, U. Mich., 1971. Postdoctoral fellow in immunology U. Calif. Med. Ctr., San Francisco, 1971-74, rsch. geneticist, 1974-75; head of blood bank Milw. Blood Ctr., 1975-78; asst. dir. ARC, Washington, 1978-83; exec. dir. Genetic Testing Inst., Atlanta, 1983-85; lab. dir. Analytical Genetic Testing Ctr., Atlanta and Denver, 1985—; adj. asst. prof. Med. Coll. Wis., Milw., 1976-78; adj. assoc. prof. George Washington U., Washington, 1979-83, Emory U., Atlanta, 1984-89; adj. assoc. prof. Univ. Kans., 1992—; affiliated faculty Colo. State Univ., Fort Collins, 1992—. Author, editor: Immunobiology of the Erythrocyte, 1980; contbg. author: Immunogenetic Factors and Thalassaemia of Hepatitis, 1975; contbr. articles to profl. publs. Recipient Gold medal Latin Am. Congress Hemotherapy and Immunohematology, 1979, R&D 100 award, 1993. Fellow Am. Acad. Forensic Sci.; mem. Am. Soc. Crime Lab. Dirs., Am. Soc. Human Genetics, Human Biology Coun., Phi Kappa Phi. Achievements include discovery of the biological function of GC protein as vitamin D transport protein, of 2 sources of errors in DNA sizings. Office: Analytical Genetic Testing Ctr 7808 Cherry Crk South Dr # 201 Denver CO 80231-3218

SCHANK, ROGER CARL, computer science and psychology educator; b. N.Y.C., Mar. 12, 1946; s. Maxwell and Margaret (Rosenberg) S.; m. Diane Levine, Mar. 22, 1970; children: Hana, Joshua. B.S., Carnegie Inst. Tech., 1966; M.A., U. Tex., 1967, Ph.D., 1969; M.A. (hon.), Yale U., 1976. Asst. prof. linguistics and computer sci. Stanford (Calif.) U., 1968-74; rsch. fellow Inst. Semantics and Cognition, Castagnola, Switzerland, 1973-74; assoc. prof. computer sci. Yale U., New Haven, Conn., 1974-76, prof. computer sci. and psychology, 1976-89, chmn. dept. computer sci., 1980-85; John Evans prof. computer sci., psychology and edn., dir. Northwestern U., Evanston, Ill., 1989—; pres., chmn. bd. Cognitive Sys., Inc., New Haven, 1981-88; pres., chmn. Computeach, Inc., 1982-88; pres. Learning Scis. Corp., 1995—. Author: Conceptual Information Processing, 1975, Dynamic Memory, 1982, (with others) Scripts, Plans, Goals and Understanding, 1977, Cognitive Computer, 1984, Explanation Patterns, 1986, The Creative Attitude, 1988, Tell Me A Story, 1990, reprinted with new forward, 1995, The Connoisseur's Guide to the Mind, 1991, Engines for Education, 1995; editor Cognitive Sci. Jour.; inventor computer programs. Mem. Cognitive Sci. Soc. (founder). Office: Northwestern U Inst Learning Scis 1890 Maple Ave Evanston IL 60201-3155

SCHANNEP, JOHN DWIGHT, brokerage firm executive; b. Newport News, Va., May 23, 1934; s. Dwight Bahney and Harriet Louise (Quinn) S.; m. Helen Ann Harris, June 21, 1958; children: John Barton, Dwight David, Timothy Michael, Marie Louise. BS, U.S. Mil. Acad., 1956. Commd. 1st lt. U.S. Air Force, 1956; resigned, 1960; account exec. Dean Witter Reynolds, Phoenix, 1960-68, v.p., resident mgr., Tucson, 1968-83, sr. v.p., 1983-89, ret.; pres. Tucson Stock/Bond Club, 1971-72; bd. dirs. SNEDCO. Author, pub. Schannep Timing Indicator Quar. Letter, 1980—. Pres. Big Bros. Tucson, 1972-74. Mem. Nat. Assn. Security Dealers (Ariz. committeeman and chmn. 1971-73), Tucson C. of C. (v.p. 1971), Pinetop Lakes Golf and Country Club (treas. 1990-91, pres. 1991-93), West Point Soc. (pres. 1967), Lions (pres. Phoenix chpt. 1966). Republican. Episcopalian. Home: 5191 E Hill Place Dr Tucson AZ 85712-1346 Office: Dean Witter Reynolds 7070 N Oracle Rd Ste 100 Tucson AZ 85704-4338

SCHAPERY, RICHARD ALLAN, engineering educator; b. Duluth, Minn., Mar. 3, 1935; s. Aaron and Nellie (Slovut) S.; m. Mable Etta Burns, June 14, 1957; 1 child, Phillip Randal. BS in Mech. Engring. with high distinction, Wayne State U., 1957; MS, Calif. Inst. Tech., 1958, PhD in Aeros, 1962. Mem. faculty Purdue U., Lafayette, Ind., 1962-69; prof. civil and aerospace engring. Tex. A.&M. U., College Station, 1969-80, Disting. prof., 1980-90, Alumni prof., 1980-85, TEES chair, 1985-89, R.P. Gregory chair, 1989-90; dir. Mechanics and Materials Center, 1972-90; The Cockrell Family Regents chair in engring., prof. U. Tex., Austin, 1990—; Cons. industry, govt.; editor-in-chief Internat. Jour. of Fracture, 1996—. Contbr. to profl. jours. and books. Gen. Motors Corp. fellow, 1958, Woodrow Wilson fellow, 1960, Douglas Aircraft fellow, 1961; Purdue XL grantee, 1963; recipient machinery's award for design, 1957; Disting. Achievement award for rsch. Tex. A&M U., 1978, Disting. Engring. Alumni award Wayne State U., 1992. Fellow Soc. Engring. Science; mem. AIAA, Am. Ceramic Soc., Sigma Xi, Omicron Delta Kappa, Tau Beta Pi. Home: 7133 Valburn Dr Austin TX 78731-1812 Office: U Tex Dept Aerospace/Mechanics Engring Austin TX 78712

SCHAPIRO, DONALD, lawyer; b. N.Y.C., Aug. 8, 1925; s. John Max and Lydia (Chaitkin) S.; m. Ruth Ellen Goldman, June 29, 1952 (dec. Aug. 1991); m. Linda N. Solomon, Oct. 10, 1993; children: Jane G., Robert A. A.B., Yale U., 1944, LL.B., 1949. Bar: N.Y. 1949. Assoc. Paul, Weiss, Rifkind, Wharton & Garrison, N.Y.C., 1949-51; asst. chief counsel subcom. ways and means com. on adminstrn. revenue laws U.S. Ho. of Reps., Washington, 1951-52; assoc. Barrett, Smith, Schapiro, Simon & Armstrong, N.Y.C., 1952-55; partner Barrett, Smith, Schapiro, Simon & Armstrong, 1955-88; ptnr. Chadbourne & Parke, 1988—; vis. lectr. law Yale U. Law Sch., 1949-78, 94-95, instr. law and econs., 1945-49. Mem. Order of Coif, Phi Beta Kappa, Phi Delta Phi. Home: 1035 5th Ave New York NY 10028-0135 Office: Chadbourne & Parke 30 Rockefeller Plz New York NY 10112

SCHAPIRO, JEROME BENTLEY, chemical company executive; b. N.Y.C., Feb. 7, 1930; s. Sol and Claire (Rose) S.; B.Chem. Engring., Syracuse U., 1951; postgrad. Columbia U., 1951-52; m. Edith Irene Kravet, Dec. 27, 1953; children: Lois, Robert, Kenneth. Project engr. propellents br. U.S. Naval Air Rocket Test Sta., Lake Denmark, N.J., 1951-52; with Dixo Co., Inc., Rochelle Park, N.J., 1954—, pres., 1966—; lectr. detergent standards, drycleaning, care labeling, consumers standards, orgns., U.S., 1968—; U.S. del. spokesman on drycleaning Internat. Standards Orgn., Newton, Mass., 1971, Brussels, 1972, U.S. del. spokesman on dimensional stability of textiles, Paris, 1974, Ottawa, 1977, Copenhagen, 1981; chmn. U.S. del. com. on consumer affairs, Geneva, 1974, 75, 76, spokesman U.S. del. on textiles, Paris, 1974, mem. U.S. del. on care labeling of textiles, The Hague, Holland, 1974, U.S. del., chmn. del. council com. on consumer policy, Geneva, 1978, 79, 82, Israel, 1980, Paris, 1981; leader U.S. del. com. on dimensional stability of textiles, Manchester, Eng., 1984; fed. govtl. appointee to Industry Functional Adv. Com. on Standards, 1980-81; legal expert drycleaning techniques and procedures. Mem. Montclair (N.J.) Sch. Study Com., 1968-69; co-founder Jewish Focus, Inc., 1991, pub. Catskill/Hudson Jewish Star. 1st lt. USAF, 1952-53. Fellow ASTM (chmn. com. D-12 Soaps and Detergents 1974-79, mem. standing com. on internat. standards 1980-84, hon. mem. award com. D-13, textiles); mem. AIChE, Am. Nat. Standards Inst. (vice chmn. bd. dirs., 1983-85, exec. com. 1979-81, 83-85, bd. dir. 1979-85, fin. com. 1982-85, chmn. consumer council 1976, 79, 80, 81, mem. steering com. to advise Dept. Commerce on implementation GATT agreements 1976-77, mem. exec. standards coun., 1977-79), internat. standards coun., chmn. internat. consumer policy adv. com. 1978-86), Am. Assn. Textile Chemists and Colorists (mem. exec. com. on rsch. 1974-77, chmn. com. on dry cleaning 1976-88, vice chmn. internat. test methods com., 1982-86) Am. Chem. Soc., Standards Engring. Soc. (cert.), Internat. Standards Orgn. (mem. internat. standards steering com. for consumer affairs 1978-81), Nat. Small Bus. Assn. (assoc. trustee 1983-85). Jewish (v.p., treas. temple). Lodge: Masons. Home: PO Box 771 Wurtsboro NY 12790-0771 Office: 158 Central Ave PO Box 7038 Rochelle Park NJ 07662-4003

SCHAPIRO, MARY, federal agency administrator, lawyer; b. N.Y.C., June 19, 1955; d. Robert D. and Susan (Hall) S.; m. Charles A. Cadwell, Dec. 13, 1980. BA, Franklin and Marshall Coll., 1977; JD, George Washington U., 1980. Bar: D.C. 1980. Trial atty., 1980-81; counsel to chmn. Commodity

Futures Trading Commn., 1981-84; gen. counsel Futures Industry Assn., 1984-88; commr. SEC, Washington, 1988-94; chmn. Commodity Futures Trading Commn. (CFTC), Washington, 1994-96; pres. NASDR, Washington, 1996—. Office: NASDR 1735 K St NW Washington DC 20006

SCHAPIRO, MIRIAM, artist; b. Toronto, Ont., Can., Nov. 15, 1923; d. Theodore and Fannie (Cohen) S. BA, State U. Iowa, 1945, MA, 1946, MFA, 1949; hon. doctorate, Wooster Coll., 1983, Calif. Coll. Arts and Crafts, 1989, Mpls. Coll. Art and Design, 1994, Miami U., 1995, Moore Coll. Art, Phila., 1995. co-originator Womanhouse, Los Angeles, 1972, Heresies mag., N.Y.C., 1975; co-originator feminist art program Calif. Inst. Arts, Valencia, 1971; founding mem. Feminist Art Inst., N.Y.C.; mem. adv. bd. Women's Caucus for Art; assoc. mem. Heresies Collective; lectr. dept. art history U. Mich., 1987. Works in numerous books and catalogues; numerous one-woman shows including, Galerie Liatowitsch, Basel, Switzerland, 1979, Lerner Heller Gallery, N.Y.C., 1979, Barbara Gladstone Gallery, N.Y.C., 1980, Spencer Mus. Art, Lawrence, Kans., 1981, Everson Mus., Syracuse, N.Y., 1981, Galerie Rudolf Zwirner, Cologne, Fed. Republic Germany, 1981, Staatagalerie, Stuttgart, Fed. Republic Germany, 1983, Dart Gallery, Chgo, 1984, Bernice Steinbaum Gallery/Steinbaum Krauss Gallery, N.Y.C., 1986, 88, 90, 91, 94, Brevard Art Ctr. and Mus., Melbourne, Fla., 1991, Guild Hall Mus., East Hampton, N.Y., 1992, ARC Gallery, Chgo., 1993, James Madison U., Harrisburg, Va., 1994. others; retrospective exhbn., Wooster (Ohio) Coll. Art Mus., 1980; exhibited in numerous group shows, including, Palais de Beaux Arts, Brussels, 1979, Inst. Contemporary Art, Phila., 1979, Delahunty Gallery, Dallas, 1980, Indpls. Mus., 1980, Va. Mus., Richmond, 1980, Laguna Gloria Mus., Austin, Tex., 1980, R.O.S.C., Dublin, Ireland, 1980, Biennale of Sydney, Australia, 1982, Zurich, Switzerland, 1983, Sidney Janis Gallery, N.Y.C., 1984, Am. Acad. Arts and Letters, N.Y.C., 1985, Mus. Modern Art, N.Y.C., 1988, Whyte Mus. Can. Rockies, Banff, Alta., 1991, Nat. Mus. Women in Arts, Wash., 1993, Jane Voorhees Zimmerli art mus. Rutger's U., New Brunswick, N.J., 1994, Mus. of F.A. Boston, 1994, Santa Barbara Mus. of Art, 1994, Hudson River Mus. of Westchester, Yonkers, N.Y., 1995, Moca Los Angeles, Calif. Bronx Mus. of the Arts, N.Y., 1995; represented in permanent collections, Hirshhorn Mus., Washington, Bklyn. Mus., Met. Mus. Art, N.Y.C., Mus. Contemporary Art, San Diego, Mpls. Inst. Art, Mulvane Art Center, Topeka, Nat. Gallery Art, Washington, N.Y.U., Peter Ludwig Collection, Aachen, Germany, Stanford U., Palo Alto, Calif., Univ. Art Mus., Berkeley, Calif., Whitney Mus., N.Y.C., Worcester (Mass.) Art Mus., Santa Barbara (Calif.) Mus. Art, also others; author: (books) Women and the Creative Process, 1974, Rondo: An Artists Book, 1988; sculpture Anna and David, Rosslyn, Va., 1987. Guggenheim fellow, 1987, Nat. Endowment for Arts fellow; grantee Ford Found.; recipient numerous other grants and fellowships. Mem. Coll. Art Assn. (past dir.). Office: Steinbaum Krauss Gallery 132 Greene St New York NY 10012 *Process and ideology in an opulent, multilayered, eccentric and hopeful abstract art: 1. The need for order and stability. 2. The need to destroy order and stability in order to find something else. 3. Finding something else. Pattern, itself an architectural species, reflects order and stability. Then a need to create chaos as though life itself were taking place. Finally the bonding layer by layer, the interpenetration of paint, fabric, photograph, tea towel, ribbon, lace, and glue. A collage: a simultaneity; a visual dazzlement, a multi-layering, a final message for the senses. And the ideology which inspires the work itself? That is feminism, the wish to have the art speak as a woman speaks. To be sensitive to the material used as though there were a responsibility to history to repair the sense of omission and to have each substance in the collage be a reminder of a woman's dreams.*

SCHAPP, REBECCA MARIA, museum director; b. Stuttgart, Fed. Republic Germany, Dec. 12, 1956; came to U.S., 1957; d. Randall Todd and Elfriede Carolina (Scheppan) Spradlin; m. Thomas James Schapp, May 29, 1979. AA, DeAnza Coll., 1977; BA in Art, San Jose State U., 1979, MA in Art Adminstrn., 1985. Adminstrv. dir. Union Gallery, San Jose, Calif., 1979-82; mus. coordinator de Saisset Mus. Santa Clara (Calif.) U., 1982-86, asst. dir., 1984, acting dir., 1986-87, asst. dir., 1987-89, dep. dir., 1989-92, dir., 1993—. Mem. San Francisco Mus. Modern Art; bd. dirs. Works of San Jose, v.p. 1983-85. Mem. Non-Profit Gallery Assn. (bd. dirs.). Democrat. Avocations: racquetball, Jazzercise, bicycling, camping. Office: De Saisset Museum Santa Clara Univ 500 El Camino Real Santa Clara CA 95050-4345

SCHAPPELL, LOLA IRENE HILL, school system administrator; b. Rochester, N.Y., Feb. 17, 1940; d. Harrison Albert and Bertha May (McIntyle) Hill; m. Kerry W. Washburn, June 11, 1960 (div. Oct. 1968); children: Yvonne Marie Washburn White, Valerie Lee Washburn Anderson; m. Robert Nathaniel Schappell, Dec. 18, 1976. BS in Elem. Edn., SUNY, Brockport, 1962; MS in Edn., Purdue U., 1969; EdD, U. Mass., 1972. Cert. tchr., N.Y., N.C., curriculum specialist, adminstr., N.C. Ednl. psychologist Belchertown (Mass.) Sch. for Mentally Retarded, 1970-71; dir. reading Albion (N.Y.) Cen. Schs., 1972-73, Mexico (N.Y.) Cen. Schs., 1973-75; asst. prof. Fed. City Coll., Washington, 1975-76; curriculum specialist/reading Charlotte (N.C.)-Mecklenburg Schs., 1976-78, program specialist, 1978-81, asst. prin., 1981-84, elem. prin., 1984-88; elem. prin. Greensboro (N.C.) Pub. Schs., 1988-91, coord. spl. projects and grants, 1991-93; fgn. tchr. Guangzhou (China) Sr. Fin. Coll., 1995-96; mem. adv. bd. Gethsemane Enrichment Ctr., Charlotte, 1984-88; bd. dirs. Am. Field Svc., Attica, N.Y., 1964-67, N.Y. Baha'i Dist. Teaching Com., Mexico, 1973-75; exec. dir. GPS Excellence Fund, Greensboro, 1991-93; mem. Nat. Baha'i Edn. Task Force, 1995—; speaker in field. Prin. creator acceleration/enrichment program. Participant Guildord Women for Race Rels., Greensboro, 1991-92, Race Rels. Forum, Greensboro, 1992; resource developer Black Child Devel., Greensboro, 1992. Mem. AAUW, ASCD, Phi Delta Kappa. Mem. Baha'i Faith. Avocations: water skiing, swimming, walking, gardening, reading. Home: 701 Simpson St Greensboro NC 27401 Office: Guilford Co Pub Schs 701 N Eugene St Greensboro NC 27401-1621

SCHAR, DWIGHT C., construction company executive; b. 1942. With Ryan Homes, Washington, 1986-77, NVLand, 1977—, NVR L P, 1980-86; bd. dirs. NVCompanies Inc. Office: NVR L P 7601 Lewinsville Rd Ste 300 Mc Lean VA 22102-2815*

SCHARF, PETER MARK, Sanskrit and Indian studies educator; b. New Haven, Conn., June 14, 1958; s. Roy Herbert and Candida Maria (Boccuzzi) S. BA in Philosophy, Wesleyan U., 1981; postgrad., Brown U., 1982-83; PhD in Sanskrit, U. Pa., 1990. Computer analyst, programmer, 1981-83; teaching asst. U. Pa., 1985-86, postdoctoral fellow in linguistics, 1990-91, 93, 94; lectr. in classics Brown U., Providence, 1992—; vis. lectr. religious studies U. Va., 1992; presenter in field. Author: The Denotation of Generic Terms in Ancient Indian Philosophy: Gramma, Nyaya, and Mimamsa, 1996; contbr. articles to profl. jours. Outstanding High Sch. Sr.'s Semester scholar, 1976; Fgn. Lang. and Area Studies fellow, 1983-85, Jr. rsch. fellow Am. Inst. Indian Studies, 1986-88, Mellon grad. fellow, 1988-89, U. Pa. Dean's fellow, 1989-90. Mem. Am. Oriental Soc., Assn. for Asian Studies, Bhandarkar Oriental Rsch. Inst. (life). Avocations: chess, photography, transcendental meditation, mountain climbing. Office: Brown U Dept Classics PO Box 1856 Providence RI 02912-1856

SCHARF, WILLIAM, artist; b. Media, Pa., Feb. 22, 1927; s. Lester William and Ebba (Anderson) S.; m. Diana Denny, Mar. 11, 1947 (div. 1951); 1 child, William Denny; m. Sally Kravitch, Mar. 25, 1956; 1 child, Aaron Anderson. Student, Barnes Found., 1946-47; cert. in painting, Pa. Acad. of Fine Arts, 1947. Instr. Mus. Modern Art, N.Y.C., 1964, Sch. Visual Arts, N.Y.C., 1965-73, San Francisco Inst. Fine Arts, 1963, 66, 69, 74, 89. One-man shows include David Herbert Gallery, N.Y.C., 1960, 62, San Francisco Inst. Fine Arts, 1969, Neuberger Mus., Purchase, N.Y., 1976, High Mus., Atlanta, 1978, Armstrong Gallery, N.Y.C., 1987, U. Mich. Mus. Art, Ann Arbor, 1993; exhibited in group shows at Guggenheim Mus., N.Y.C., 1982, Hirschl-Adler Gallery, N.Y.C., 1980, Smith-Anderson Gallery, Palo Alto, Calif., Nat. Mus. Am. Art, Washington, 1987, 91, 92, Am. Acad. and Inst. Arts and Letters, N.Y.C., 1989, 91; represented in permanent collections Boston Inst. Contemporary Art, Bklyn Mus., Solomon r. Guggenheim Mus., N.Y.C., Newark Mus., Nat. Mus. Am. Art, Smith Coll. Mus., Northampton, Mass., Zimmerli Mus., Rutgers U., New Brunswick, N.J., U. Mich. Mus. art., Phillips Collection, Washington, The Neuroscis. Inst., San Diego. Trustee Rothko Found., N.Y.C., 1979-87; instr. Art Student's League, N.Y., 1987-94. With USAF, 1945-46. Emmlen Cresson fellow Pa. Acad. Fine Arts, 1948. Mem. Artist Equity Assn., Soc. of Illustrators.

SCHARFF, JOSEPH LAURENT, lawyer; b. New Orleans, Oct. 2, 1935; s. Joseph Roy and Celia Ray (Rosenhein) S.; m. Mary Susan Greulach, June 29, 1963; children: Catherine Elizabeth, Robert Laurent, Anne Victoria. BS in Journalism, Northwestern U., 1957; JD, Harvard U., 1964. Bar: D.C. 1965, U.S. Supreme Ct. 1970, U.S. Ct. Appeals (D.C. cir.) 1965, U.S. Ct. Appeals (2nd cir.) 1980, U.S. Ct. Appeals (5th cir.) 1973, U.S. Ct. Appeals (10th cir.); U.S. Ct. Claims 1965. From assoc. to ptnr. Pierson, Ball & Dowd, Washington, 1964-89; ptnr. Reed Smith Shaw & McClay, Washington, 1989-95, counsel, 1996—. Mem. ABA (fair trial-free press com. 1973-76, com. reps. media 1985-95, co-chmn. 1989-92), Fed. Comm. Bar Assn., Soc. Profl. Journalists, Radio-TV News Dirs. Assn. (counsel 1965-95, Disting. Svc. award 1987, Media Inst. First Amendment Adv. Coun.). Home: 12000 Turf Ln Reston VA 22091-2123 Office: Reed Smith Shaw and McClay Ste 1100 East Tower 1301 K St NW Washington DC 20005

SCHARFF, MATTHEW DANIEL, immunologist, cell biologist, educator; b. N.Y.C., Aug. 28, 1932; s. Harry and Constance S.; m. Carol Held, Dec. 19, 1954; children—Karen, Thomas, David. AB, Brown U., 1954, DrMedSci (hon.), 1994; MD, NYU, 1959. House officer II and IV med. service Boston City Hosp., 1959-61; research asso. NIH, 1961-63; asst. prof. Albert Einstein Coll. Medicine, Yeshiva U., Bronx, N.Y., 1963-67; asso. prof. Albert Einstein Coll. Medicine, Yeshiva U., 1967-71, prof. dept. cell biology, 1971—, chmn. dept., 1972-83, dir. div. biol. scis., 1975-81; asso. dir. Cancer Center, 1975-86, dir., 1986-95. Served with USPHS, 1961-63. Recipient Alumni Achievement award NYU Sch. Medicine, 1980, N.Y. Acad. Medicine medal, 1990, Commemorative award Albert Einstein Coll. Medicine, 1993, hon. Dr. Med. Sci., Brown U., 1994. Mem. Am. Assn. Immunologists, Am. Soc. Clin. Investigation, Nat. Acad. Scis., Am. Acad. Arts and Sci., Phi Beta Kappa, Sigma Xi, Alpha Omega Alpha. Office: Albert Einstein Coll Med Cancer Ctr 1300 Morris Pk Ave Bronx NY 10461-1926

SCHARLAU, CHARLES EDWARD, III, natural gas company executive; b. Chgo., Apr. 24, 1927; s. Charles Edward II and Esther (Powell) S.; m. Clydene Yvonne Sloop, Aug. 13, 1960; children: Caryn, Robin, Greg, Charles, Marti. LLB, U. Ark., 1951. Bar: Ark. 1951, U.S. Dist. Ct. (western dist.) Ark. 1951, U.S. Supreme Ct. 1958. Atty. Ark. Western Gas Co., Fayetteville, 1951-61, v.p., 1961-68, pres., 1968-78; pres., chmn. S.W. Energy Co., Fayetteville, 1978—; bd. dirs. C.H. Heist Co., Clearwater, Fla., McIlroy Bank and Trust Co., Fayetteville. Chmn. U. Ark. Devel. Coun., 1989—. With USMC, 1945-46. Mem. ABA, Ark. Bar Assn., So. Gas Assn., Nat. Assn. Mfrs. (bd. dirs. 1986-89), Am. Gas Assn. (bd. dirs. 1987-90), U. Ark. Alumni Assn. (pres. 1972-73), Ark. C. of C. (pres. 1977-79), Beta Gamma Sigma. Methodist. Avocations: reading, tennis, canoeing, sports. Home: 1506 Sunset Pl Fayetteville AR 72701-1627 Office: Ark Western Gas Co 1001 Sain St Fayetteville AR 72703-6206

SCHARLEMANN, ROBERT PAUL, religious studies educator, clergyman; b. Lake City, Minn., Apr. 4, 1929; s. Ernst Karl and Johanna Meta (Harre) S. Student, Northwestern Coll., Watertown, Wis., 1946-49; B.A., Concordia Coll. and Sem., St. Louis, 1952; B.D., Concordia Coll. and Sem., 1955; Dr. theol., U. Heidelberg (Germany), 1957. Ordained to ministry, Lutheran Ch., 1960. Instr. philosophy Valparaiso U., 1957-59; postdoctoral fellow Yale U., 1959-60; pastor Bethlehem Luth. Ch., Carlyle, Ill., 1960-62, Grace Luth. Ch., Durham, N.C., 1962-63; asst. prof. religion U. So. Calif., 1963-64, assoc. prof., 1964-66; assoc. prof. religion U. Iowa, Iowa City, 1966-68, prof., 1968-81; Commonwealth prof. religious studies U. Va., Charlottesville, 1981—; Fulbright-Hayes prof. U. Heidelberg, 1975-76. Author: Thomas Aquinas and John Gerhard, 1964, Reflection and Doubt in the Thought of Paul Tillich, 1969, The Being of God, 1981, Inscriptions and Reflections, 1989, The Reason of Following, 1991; editor Jour. of Am. Acad. Religion, 1980-85; contbr. articles to profl. jours. Mem. Am. Acad. Religion, Am. Theol. Soc., European Soc. Culture, Soc. for Philosophy of Religion. Office: U Va Dept Religious Studies Charlottesville VA 22903

SCHARP, ANDERS, manufacturing company executive; b. Stockholm, June 8, 1934; married. MEngring, Royal Inst. Tech., Stockholm, 1960. Head refrigeration lab. Elektro Helios, 1960-69; v.p. prodn. AB Electrolux, Stockholm, 1969-74, exec. v.p. prodn. and R&D, 1974-81; pres. AB Electrolux, Cleve., 1981-86; pres., CEO AB Electrolux, 1986-91, chmn., CEO, 1991—; chmn. Saab-Scania AB, Linkoping, Sweden, 1990—, AB SKF, Gothenburg, Sweden, 1992—, Incentive AB, Stockholm, 1992—; vice chmn. Investor AB, 1992—, Atlas Copco AB, 1992—; bd. dirs. Email Ltd., Australia. Mem. Royal Swedish Acad. Engring., Swedish Employers Confedn. (bd. dirs.), Assn. Swedish Engring. Industries (bd. dirs.), Fedn. Swedish Industries (bd. dirs.). Office: Electrolux AB, Lilla Essingen, S-105 45 Stockholm Sweden also: White Consol Industries Inc 11770 Berea Rd Cleveland OH 44111-1601*

SCHARP-RADOVIC, CAROL ANN, choreographer, classical ballet educator, artistic director; b. Ypsilanti, Mich., Aug. 9, 1940; d. John Lewis and Mary Vivien (Alther) Keeney; m. Jack Laurel Scharp, July 28, 1958 (div. July 1970); children: Kathryn E., Mark A.; m. Srecko Radovic, Nov. 15, 1989. Studied with Pereslavic, Danilova; student, Harkness Ballet, N.Y.C., Joffrey Ballet, N.Y.C., Eglevsky Ballet, N.Y.C., Briansky Ballet, Darvesh Ballet, N.Y.C.; studied with Jurgen Schneider, Am. Ballet Theatre, 1983-93; studied with Janina Cunova, Luba Gulyeava, Australian Ballet Co., 1983-93; studied with Ninel Kurgapkina, Ludmila Synelnikova, Genhrich Mayorov, Kirov Ballet, 1987-89; studied with Ludmila Sakharova, Perm Ballet, 1993; studied with Ludmila Synelnikova, Bolshoi Ballet Sch., Moscow, 1989; studied with Inna Zubkhovskaya, Alex. Stiopin, Lydia Goncharova, Valentina Chistova, Mararita Zagurskaya, Valentina Rumyantsema, Vaganova Ballet Acad., St. Petersburg, Russia, 1993. Ballet mistress Adrian (Mich.) Coll., 1982-84; founder, artistic dir. Ann Arbor (Mich.) Ballet Theatre, 1980—; studied with Janina Cunova; studied with Luba Gulyeava Kirov Ballet, 1984; former regional field judge Nat. Ballet Achievement Fund; dir. seminars Marygrove Coll., Detroit. Choreographer Cinderella, 1980, Nightingale, 1980, Nutcracker, 1984, Carnival of the Animals, 1981, Carmen, 1983, Midsummer Nights Dream, 1982, Vivaldi's Spring, 1990, Opulence, 1984, La Boutique Fantasque, 1995, Handel's Alcina, 1985, Gymnopedie, 1985, others. Ruth Mott grantee for choreography, 1982. Mem. Mich. Dance Assn. Avocations: gardening, reading, writing. Home: 6476 Huron River Dr Dexter MI 48130 Office: CAS Ballet Theatre Sch Ann Arbor Ballet Theatre 548 Church St Ann Arbor MI 48104-2514

SCHARRER, KARL KRISTOPHER, chemist, researcher; b. New Albany, Ind., Dec. 20, 1962; s. Alfred Keith and Nancy Sue (Kraus) S. BA, U. Louisville, 1993, postgrad., 1994—. Lab. technician Meth. Evang. Hosp., Louisville, 1986-88; gen. sci. instr. New Albany /Floyd County Schs., 1988-89; quality control chemist Am. Synthetic Rubber Corp., Louisville, 1989-91, rsch. chemist, 1991—. Mem. Floyd County Young Republicans, New Albany, 1988. Mem. AAAS, Am. Chem. Soc., Phi Kappa Alpha Alumni Assn., Sigma Xi. Republican. Roman Catholic. Home: 2823-1/2 Charlestown Rd New Albany IN 47150 Office: American Synthetic Rubber 4500 Camp Ground Rd Louisville KY 40216

SCHARUDA, VICTORIA, lawyer; b. Vineland, N.J., Aug. 3, 1967; d. Victor Scharuda and Elizabeth (Repin) Bennett. BA in History, Ursinus Coll., 1989; JD, Temple U., 1992. Bar: Ga. 1993. Corp. counsel Wells Fargo Armored Svc. Corp., Atlanta, 1993—. Active 1000 Lawyers for Justice, Atlanta, 1993. Recipient James D. Mandarino award Phila. Trial Lawyers Assn., 1992. Mem. NAFE. Avocations: painting, reading, crotcheting, football, softball. Office: Wells Fargo Armored Svc Corp 6165 Barfield Rd NE Ste 200 Atlanta GA 30328-4309

SCHATT, PAUL, newspaper editor; b. N.Y.C., Aug. 31, 1945; divorced; children: Suzannah, Andrew. BA with distinction Polit. Sci., English, Ariz. State U., 1967. Editor Ariz. Republic, 1964-66, reporter, 1965-74, urban affairs editor, 1974-75, asst. city editor, 1975-79, chief asst. city editor, 1979-82, asst. met. editor, 1985-86, met. editor, 1986-88, editor edit. pages, 1993—; asst. editor Ariz. Mag., 1981-82, editor, 1982-85; editor edit. pages Phoenix Gazette, 1988-93, The Ariz. Republic, 1993—; vis. lectr. Pub. Affairs Journalism, Ariz. State U., 1976—, instr. Mass. Comm. Dept., 1974-76; dir. Eugene C. Pulliam Fellowship. Phoenix program, 1990—; writing coach, 1989; del. Pre White House Conf. Librs., 1991. v.p. Crisis Nursery, 1984-87, bd. dirs. 1980-87; exec. bd. Hospice of the Valley, 1980-87; pres. Friends of Phoenix Pub. Libr., 1985-86, bd. dirs. 1986—; bd. trustees 1st Amendment Congress, 1989—; bd. dirs. Camelback Hosps. 1982-89, chmn. bd. dirs. 1986-87, Cactus Pine Coun. Girl Scouts Am., 1988-89, Sun Sounds Inc., 1982-89, Valley Leadership Inc., 1991—, alum. assn., 1985-89, Ariz. Zool. Soc., 1991—, Barrow Neurol. Found., 1991—, Kids Voting, 1991-93, Barry Goldwater Inst., 1991-93, Ariz. Club, 1991—. With Ariz. Nat. Guard, 1966-79. Recipient Montgomery award Outstanding Svc. to Community Friends of Phoenix Pub. Libr., 1989; profl. Journalism fellow Stanford U., 1970-71. Mem. Am. Soc. Newspaper Editors, Soc. Profl. Journalists (pres. Valley of Sun chpt. 1974-75, 83-84, exec. bd. 1988-92), Sigma Delta Chi (co-chair nat. convention 1974). Office: The Ariz Republic Editorial Dept 120 E Van Buren St Phoenix AZ 85004-2227

SCHATTEN, GERALD PHILLIP, cell biologist, reproductive biologist, educator; b. N.Y.C., Nov. 1, 1949; s. Frank and Sylvia Schatten; m. Heather Aronson, July 4, 1994; 1 child, Daniel. BS, U. Calif., Berkeley, 1971, PhD, 1975. Instr. U. Calif., Berkeley, 1975; postdoctoral fellow Rockefeller Found., 1976-77; successively asst. prof., assoc. prof., prof. Fla. State U., Tallahassee, 1979-86; prof. molecular biology, zoology and obstetrics gynecology U. Wis., Madison, 1986—, dir. integrated microscopy resource for biomed. rsch., 1986-92, dir. gamete and embryo biol. tng. program, 1989—; dir. gamete and embryo biol. tng. program U. Wis., Madison, 1988—; exec. bd. UNESCO Internat. Cell Rsch. Orgn., 1995—. Recipient Rsch. Career Devel. award NIH, 1981-86. Office: Univ Wis 1117 W Johnson St Madison WI 53706-1705

SCHATZ, IRWIN JACOB, cardiologist; b. St. Boniface, Man., Can., Oct. 16, 1931; came to U.S., 1956, naturalized, 1966; s. Jacob and Reva S.; m. Barbara Jane Binder, Nov. 12, 1967; children: Jacob, Edward, Stephen and Brian (twins). Student, U. Man., Can.), Winnipeg, 1951, M.D. with honors, 1956. Diplomate: Am. Bd. Internal Medicine. Intern Vancouver (B.C.) Gen. Hosp., 1955-56; resident Hammersmith Hosp., U. London, 1957, Mayo Clinic, Rochester, Minn., 1958-61; head sec. peripheral vascular disease Henry Ford Hosp., Detroit, 1961-68; asso. prof. medicine Wayne State U., 1968-71, chief sect. cardiovascular disease, 1969-71; assoc. prof., asso. dir. sect. cardiology U. Mich., 1972-73, prof. internal medicine, 1973-75; prof. medicine John A. Burns Sch. Medicine, U. Hawaii, 1975—, chmn. dept. medicine, 1975-90. Author: Orthostatic Hypotension, 1986; contbr. numerous articles to med. jours. Rockefeller Found. scholar, 1991. Master ACP (bd. govs. 1984-89, Laureate award Hawaii chpt. 1992); fellow Am. Coll. Cardiology (bd. govs. 1980-84); mem. Am. Heart Assn. (fellow couns. cardiology and circulation), Am. Fedn. Clin. Rsch., Asian-Pacific Soc. Cardiology (v.p. 1987-91), Accreditation Coun. for Grad. Med. Edn. (chmn. residence rev. com. internal medicine 1993-95), Hawaii Heart Assn. (pres.), Western Assn. Physicians, Am. Autonomic Soc. (chmn. bd. govs., pres.-elect), Pacific Interurban Club. Jewish. Home: 4983 Kolohala St Honolulu HI 96816-5126 Office: 1356 Lusitana St Honolulu HI 96813-2421

SCHATZ, MONA CLAIRE STRUHSAKER, social worker, educator; b. Phila., Jan. 4, 1950; d. Milton and Josephine (Kivo) S.; m. James Fredrick Struhsaker, Dec. 31, 1979 (div.); 1 child, Thain Mackenzie. BA, Metro State Coll., 1976; postgrad., U. Minn., 1976; MSW, U. Denver, 1979; D in Social Work/Social Welfare, U. Pa., 1986. Teaching fellow U. Pa., Phila., 1981-82; asst. prof. S.W. Mo. State U., Springfield, 1982-85; assoc. prof. Colo. State U., Ft. Collins, 1985—, field coord., 1986-88, dir. non-profit agy. adminstrn. program, 1995—, project dir. Edn. and Rsch. Inst. for Fostering Families, 1987—, dir. youth agy. adminstrn. program Am. Humanics, 1988-90; cons. Mgmt. and Behavioral Sci. Ctr., The Wharton Sch. U. Pa., 1981-82; resource specialist So. N.J. Health Sys. Agy., 1982; adj. faculty mem. U. Mo., Springfield, 1994; med. social worker Rehab. and Vis. Nurse Assn., 1985-90; mem. Colo. Child Welfare Adv. Com., Family Conservation Initiative; internat. cons. and trainer Inst. for Internat. Connections, Russia, Latvia, Albania, U.S., Hungary, Ukraine, Romania, 1992—. Contbr. articles to profl. jours. Cons., field rep. Big Bros./Big Sisters of Am., Phila., 1979-83; acting dir., asst. dir. Big Sisters of Colo., 1971-78; owner Polit. Cons. in Colo., Denver, 1978-79; active Food Co-op, Ft. Collins, Foster Parent, Denver, Capital Hill United Neighbors, Adams County (Denver) Social Planning Coun., Co., Colo. Justice Coun., Denver, Regional Girls Shelter, Springfield; bd. dirs. Crisis Helpline and Info. Svc. Scholar Lilly Endowment, Inc., 1976, Piton Found., 1978; recipient Spl. Recognition award Big Bros./Big Sisters of Am., 1983, Recognition award Am. Humanics Mgmt. Inst., 1990. Mem. Inst. Internat. Connections (bd. dirs.), Coun. Social Work Edn., Group for Study of Generalist Social Work, Social Welfare History Group, Nat. Assn. Social Workers (nominating com. Springfield chpt., state bd. dirs., No. Colo. rep.), Student Social Work Assn. Colo. State U. (adv. 1986-89), Permanency Planning Coun. for Children and Youth, NOW (treas. Springfield chpt. 1984-85), Student Nuclear Awareness Group (advisor), Student Social Work Assn. (advisor), Har Shalom, Alpha Delta Mu. Democrat. Avocations: cooking, traveling, reading, biking, sewing. Office: Colo State U Social Work Dept Fort Collins CO 80523

SCHATZ, PAUL FREDERICK, laboratory director; b. Cin., Aug. 24, 1944; s. Frederick Vincent and Nell (Sarles) S.; m. Eleanor Mae Smith, Aug. 19, 1967; children: Alexander, Christopher. BA, Colgate U., 1966; PhD in Chemistry, U. Wis., 1971. Lab. dir. U. Wis., Madison, 1971—. Author various computer programs. Mem. Am. Chem. Soc. Office: Univ Wis Dept Chemistry 1101 University Ave Madison WI 53706-1322

SCHATZ, S. MICHAEL, lawyer; b. Hartford, Conn., May 28, 1921; s. Nathan Arthur and Dora (Goldberg) S.; m. Norma Hirshon, Oct. 28, 1945; children—Andrew M., Debra J., Nathan A., Donald N. A.B., Cornell U., 1941, LL.B., 1942. Bar: Conn. bar, N.Y. bar also U.S. Fed. Cts. and U.S. Treasury Dept. Assoc., jr. ptnr., then sr. ptnr. Schatz & Schatz, Ribicoff & Kotkin, Hartford, 1946—; gen. counsel Conn. Vet. Assn., Tobacco Distbrs. Assn. Conn., Conn. State Dental Assn., Outdoor Advt. Assn. Conn.; Dir. Sage-Allen & Co., Inc., Edward Balf Co., Hartford, Dunham-Bush, Inc., West Hartford, Conn. Bank and Trust Co., West Hartford, Atlantic Carton Corp., Norwich, Ripley Co., Inc., Middletown, Conn., Griese Advt. Co., West Hartford; partner B.L. McTeague & Co., Hartford. Editor-in-chief: Cornell Law Quar. Mem. council Cornell U., exec. com. Law Sch.; bd. dirs. Hartford chpt. ARC, 1960-62, U. Conn. Found., St. Francis Hosp. Assn., Conn. Dental Service, Inc., Friends of Sch. Dental Medicine, U. Conn.; corporate mem. Saint Francis Hosp., Hartford Pub. Library, Mt. Sinai Hosp., Hartford. Served to lt. USNR, 1942-46; mem. adv. bd. Cornell Law Sch.; vice chmn. U. Conn. Found.; mem. Devel. Com. Hartford Jewish Endowment Found. Mem. Am., N.Y. State, Hartford County bar assns., State Bar Assn. Conn. (pres. jr. bar sect. 1951, exec. com., asst. sec.-treas. 1956-57, sec. 1957-59), Cornell Law Assn. (pres.) Order of Coif, Phi Beta Kappa, Phi Kappa Phi. Home: 4 Hampton Pl Avon CT 06001-4554 Office: Schatz & Schatz, Ribicoff & Kotkin 90 State House Sq Hartford CT 06103-3702

SCHATZBERG, ALAN FREDERIC, psychiatrist, researcher; b. N.Y.C., Oct. 17, 1944; s. Emanuel and Cila (Diamand) S.; m. Nancy R. Silverman, Aug. 27, 1972; children: Melissa Ann, Lindsey Diamand. BS, NYU, 1965, MD, 1968; MA (hon.), Harvard U., 1989. Diplomate Nat. Bd. Med. Examiners, Am. Bd. Psychiatry and Neurology. Intern Lenox Hill Hosp., N.Y.C., 1968-69; resident in psychiatry Mass. Mental Health Ctr., Boston, 1969-72; clin. fellow in psychiatry Harvard Med. Sch., Boston, 1969-72, asst. prof. psychiatry, 1977-82, assoc. prof., 1982-88, prof., 1988-91; interim psychiatrist-in-chief McLean Hosp., Belmont, Mass., 1984-86, dir. depression rsch. facility, 1985—, svc. chief, 1982-84, 86-88; psychiatrist adv. panel Eli Lilly & Co., Indpls., 1986-93; clin. dir. Mass. Mental Health Ctr., Boston, 1988-91; Kenneth T. Norris, Jr. prof. psychiatry and behavioral scis. Stanford U., 1991—, chmn. dept. psychiatry and behavioral scis. Sch. Medicine, 1991—; cons. AMA Videoclinics, Chgo., 1979-83; mem. AMA/FAA panel on health regulations, Chgo., 1984-86; mem. NIH Biol. Psychopathology and Clin. Neuroscis. Initial Rev. Group, 1991-95, chmn., 1993-94. Co-author: Manual of Clinical Psychopharmacology, 1986, 2d edit., 1991; contbr. more than 170 articles, book chpts. to profl. publs.; co-editor: Depression: Biology, Psychodynamics and Treatment, 1978, Hypothalamic-Pituitary-Adrenal Axis, 1988, Textbook of Psychopharmacology, 1995; mem. editl. bd. McLean Hosp. Jour., 1975-88, Jour. Psychiat. Rsch., 1986—, Integrative Psychiatry, 1990—, Harvard Rev. Psychiatry, 1993—, Archives of Gen. Psychiatry, 1995—, Psychoneuroendocrinology, 1995—, Annals Psychiatry, 1992—, Anxiety, 1993; assoc. editor-in-chief Depression, 1992—. Maj. USAF, 1972-74. Rsch. grantee NIMH, 1984-87, 94—, Poitras Charitable Found., 1985-93. Fellow Am. Psychiat. Assn., Am. Coll. Neuropsychopharmacology (coun. 1995—), Am. Psychopath. Assn.; mem. Am. Coll. Psychiatrists, Mass. Psychiat. Soc. (coun. 1987-90), No. Calif. Psychiat. Soc. Avocations: travel, theater, tennis, swimming, fine arts. Office: Stanford U Sch Medicine 401 Quarry Rd Rm 300 Stanford CA 94305-5548

SCHATZBERG, JERRY NED (JERROLD SCHATZBERG), film director; b. N.Y.C., June 26, 1927; s. Abraham and Lillian (Eiger) S.; children: Don S., Steven M. Student, U. Miami, 1947-48. Photography asst. to Bill Helburn, 1954-56; guest lectr. NYU Sch. Cinema Studies. Freelance still photographer and TV comml. dir., 1956-69; contbr. photographs to various mags. including Life; dir. feature films Puzzle of A Downfall Child, 1970, Panic In Needle Park, 1972, Scarecrow, 1973 (Cannes Film Festival Golden Palm), Sweet Revenge, 1977, The Seduction of Joe Tynan, 1979, Honeysuckle Rose, 1980, Misunderstood, 1984, No Small Affair, 1984, Street Smart, 1987, Reunion, 1991; films have appeared in various film festivals; TV Films include: Clinton and Nadine, 1988 (HBO). Served with USN, 1945-47. Mem. Acad. Motion Picture Arts and Scis., Dirs. Guild Am., Writers Guild Am.

SCHATZKI, GEORGE, law educator; b. 1933. A.B., Harvard U., 1955, LLB, 1958, LLM, 1965. Teaching fellow Harvard U., Cambridge, Mass., 1963-65; prof. law U. Tex.-Austin, 1965-79; dean U. Wash. Sch. Law, Seattle, 1979-82, prof., 1979-84; dean U. Conn. Sch. Law, Hartford, 1984-90, prof., 1984—; vis. prof. law U. Pa., Phila., 1973-74, Harvard U., Cambridge, Mass., 1977-78; vis. lectr. law Yale U., New Haven, 1993, 96. Co-author: Labor Relations and Social Problems: Collective Bargaining in Private Employment, 1978, Labor and Employment Law, 1988, 2d edit., 1995. Office: U Conn Law Sch 65 Elizabeth St Hartford CT 06105-2213

SCHAUB, HARRY CARL, lawyer; b. Hazleton, Pa., Feb. 3, 1929; s. Harry J. and Lida M. (Fisher) S.; m. Kathryn Klindt Deans, Aug. 14, 1982; children: Lisa A., Irene Cannon, Christian K. BA, U. Pa., 1950; JD, Yale U., 1955; postgrad., Columbia U., 1962. Bar: Pa. 1955. Assoc. Montgomery, McCracken, Walker & Rhoads, Phila., 1955-62; ptnr. Montgomery, McCracken, Walker & Rhoads, 1963—; consul Republic of Austria to State of Pa., 1978-84, consul gen., 1984—. Contbr. articles to profl. jours. V.p., bd. dirs. Luth. Ch. of Holy Communion, Phila., 1975-88; bd. dirs. YMCA Cen., Phila., 1986-91; chmn. bd. dirs. Consular Corps Coll., Richmond, Va., 1987—; mem. The Athenaeum of Phila., 1976—. Capt. U.S. Army, 1951-53. Decorated Golden Medal of Honor 1st class (Austria), 1992; recipient Johann Strauss award City of Vienna, 1979. Mem. ABA, Pa. Bar Assn., Phila. Bar Assn., Internat. Bar Assn., Am. Soc. Internat. Law, Am. Coun. on Germany, Austrian Soc. Pa. (v.p., bd. dirs. 1981—), John Peter Zenger Law Soc. (founder, bd. dirs., pres. 1994—), Union League of Phila., Rittenhouse Club, Mil. Order Fgn. Wars, The Franklin Inn, The Penn Club, Phi Beta Kappa, Pi Gamma Mu. Democrat. Lutheran. Home: 1420 Locust St Unit 7K Philadelphia PA 19102 Office: Montgomery McCracken 123 S Broad St Philadelphia PA 19109

SCHAUB, JAMES HAMILTON, engineering educator; b. Moundsville, W.Va., Jan. 27, 1925; s. Carroll Franklin and Lilian Hoyle (Hutchison) S.; m. Malinda Katherine Bailey, June 15, 1948. Student, George Washington U., 1942-43; B.S. in Civil Engring., Va. Poly. Inst., 1948; S.M. in Civil Engring., Harvard U., 1949; Ph.D., Purdue U., 1960. Registered profl. engr., Va. Soils engr. Ore. Hwy. Dept., 1949-50, 51-52; lab. dir. Palmer and Baker, Inc., Mobile, 1952-55; asst. prof. civil engring. Va. Poly. Inst., 1955-58; instr., research engr. Purdue U., 1958-60; prof. civil engring., chmn. dept. W.Va. U., 1960-67, assoc. dean engring., 1967-69; prof. civil engring., chmn. dept. U. Fla. at Gainesville, 1969-87, Disting. Service prof., 1984-92, NSF faculty fellow, 1975-76, affiliate prof. dept. history, 1977-92, Disting Svc. prof. emeritus, 1992—; acad. visitor dept. history of sci. and tech. Imperial Coll., U. London, 1975-76; Edwin P. Conquest chair humanities Va. Mil. Inst., 1986; vis. prof. Swarthmore Coll., spring 1988; cons. engr. to state, fed. and pvt. agys. and cos., 1960—. Co-author 2 books; author tech. papers. Served with inf. AUS, 1943-46; with C.E. 1950-51, ETO, Korea. Recipient Eminent Career award Coll. Engring, U. Fla., 1987. Mem. ASCE (named Engr. of Year, Fla. sect. 1974, William H. Wisely award 1986), Am. Pub. Works Assn. (pres. chpt. 1983-84, nat. dir.-at-large 1983-89), Order of Engr., Golden Key, Chi Epsilon, Phi Kappa Phi, Kappa Sigma, Sigma Xi, Tau Beta Pi. Episcopalian. Home: 4401 NW 15th Pl Gainesville FL 32605-4509

SCHAUB, MARILYN MCNAMARA, religion educator; b. Chgo., Mar. 24, 1928; d. Bernard Francis and Helen Katherine (Skehan) McNamara; m. R. Thomas Schaub, Oct. 25, 1969; 1 dau., Helen Ann. B.A., Rosary Coll., 1953; Ph.D., U. Fribourg, Switzerland, 1957; diploma, Ecole Biblique, Jerusalem, 1967. Asst. prof. classics and Bibl. studies Rosary Coll., River Forest, Ill., 1957-69; prof. Bibl. studies Duquesne U., Pitts., 1969-70, 73—; participant 8 archeol. excavations, Middle East; adminstrv. dir. expedition to the Southeast Dead Sea Plains, Jordan, 1989—; hon. assoc. Am. Schs. Oriental Rsch., 1966-67, trustee, 1986-89; Danforth assoc., 1972-80. Author: Friends and Friendship for St. Augustine, 1964; translator: (with H. Richter) Agape in the New Testament, 3 vols, 1963-65. Mem. Soc. Bibl. Lit., Catholic Bibl. Assn., Am. Acad. Religion. Democrat. Home: 25 Mckelvey Ave Pittsburgh PA 15218-1452 Office: Duquesne U Theology Dept Pittsburgh PA 15282

SCHAUB, SHERWOOD ANHDER, JR., management consultant; b. Rahway, N.J., Jan. 8, 1942; s. Sherwood Anhder Sr. and Doris (Beecher) S.; m. Diane Katherine Wells, July 29, 1967; children: Whitney, Kristen. BBA with honors, Nichols Coll., 1964; postgrad. in bus. adminstrn., Fairleigh Dickinson U., 1965-69. Cert. mgmt. cons. Dir. Gilbert Lane, N.Y.C., 1965-67; exec. v.p. Ward Clancy, N.Y.C., 1967-71; founder, chmn., CEO, sr. mng. ptnr. Goodrich & Sherwood Co., N.Y.C. 1971—; pres., chmn., CEO Reed, Cuff & Assocs., 1980-86; CEO Exec. Change, Inc., 1978; mem. adv. bd. Paine Webber; mem. Schwarzkopf Cup select com., 1992-95; pres. House of Hamilton, 1995, Trans Link Am., 1995; mem. bd. Restaurant Assocs. Author: Breakpoints, 1986; contbr. articles on mgmt. to mags. and profl. jours. Congl. advisor Pres. Ronald Reagan, 1986; head Bus. Task Force N.Y. for Reagan Adminstrn., 1987-89; bd. dirs. Conn. Pub. Broadcasting; trustee Nichols Coll., 1992-95, mem. exec. com., 1995, head presidl. search com. 1995. Decorated Knight Comanderie de Bordeaux 1993 (France); named Outstanding Alumnus, Nichols Coll., 1994; elected to U.S. 100 Top Recruiters, 1990-96. Mem. Nat. Assn. Corp. and Profl. Recruiters, Young Pres. Orgn. (bd. dirs. 1986-88, vice chmn. met. chpt. sounding bd., hospitality, edn. chmn., chpt. chmn. elect 1989), Pvt. Pilots Assn., World Pres. Orgn., Safari Club Internat. (bd. dirs., 1987-89, chpt. chmn. 1996), U.S. Equestrian Team. Congregationalist. Clubs: Chemists, University, Westfield Tennis, New Canaan Racquet, New Cannan Field, Am. Friends of Game Conservancy, Rolling Rock, Weston Gun Club, Mashomak Field and Game, Econ. of N.Y., Explorers (fellow), Madison Ave. Sports Car Driving & Chowder Society, Greenwich Polo, Ducks Unlimited (sponsor, co-chmn. So. Conn. 1994-96), Advt. Sportsmen of N.Y. (bd. dirs., treas.). Avocations: scuba diving, equestrian riding, big and small game hunting, antiques, sporting clays shooting. Office: Goodrich and Sherwood Co Hdqrs 521 5th Ave New York NY 10175

SCHAUBERT, DANIEL HAROLD, electrical engineering educator; b. Galesburg, Ill., Feb. 15, 1947; s. Robert Harold and Carolyn Virginia (Dunkle) S.; m. Joyce Marie Conard, June 15, 1968; 1 child, Karen Louise. BSEE, U. Ill., 1969, MS, 1970, PhD, 1974. Rsch. engr. U.S. Army Harry Diamond Labs., Adelphi, Md., 1977-80; rsch. engr., program mgr. U.S. Bur. Radiol. Health, Rockville, Md., 1980-82; prof. elec. engring. U. Mass., Amherst, 1982—; dept. head elec. and computer engring., 1994—. Patentee in field. 1st lt. U.S. Army, 1974-77. Fellow IEEE, IEEE Antennas and Propagation Soc. (membership chair 1980-82, editor newsletter 1982-84, sec.-treas. 1984-88). Office: U Mass Elec and Computer Engring Amherst MA 01003

SCHAUER, FREDERICK FRANKLIN, legal educator; b. Newark, Jan. 15, 1946; s. John Adolph and Clara (Balayti) S.; m. Margery Clare Stone, Aug. 25, 1968 (div. June, 1982); m. Virginia Jo Wise, May 25, 1985. AB, Dartmouth Coll., 1967, MBA, 1968; JD, Harvard U., 1972. Bar: Mass. 1972, U.S. Supreme Ct. 1976. Assoc. Fine & Ambrogne, Boston, 1972-74; asst. prof. law W.Va. U., Morgantown, 1974-76, assoc. prof., 1976-78; assoc. prof. Coll. William and Mary, Williamsburg, Va., 1978-80, Cutler prof., 1980-83; prof. of law U. Mich., Ann Arbor, 1983-90; Frank Stanton prof. of 1st Amendment Kennedy Sch. of Govt., Harvard U., Cambridge, Mass., 1990—; vis. scholar, mem. faculty law Wolfson Coll. Cambridge (Eng.) U., 1977-78; vis. prof. Law Sch., U. Chgo., 1990; vis. fellow Australian Nat. U., 1993; William Morton Disting. Sr. fellow in humanities Dartmouth Coll., 1991; vis. prof. law Harvard Law Sch., 1996; Ewald Disting. vis. prof. law U. Va., 1996. Author: The Law of Obscenity, 1976, Free Speech: A Philosophical Enquiry, 1982 (ABA cert. merit 1983), Supplements to Gunther Constitutional Law, 1983-95, Playing by the Rules: A Philosophical Examination of Rule Based Decision-Making in Law and Life, 1991, The First Amendment: A Reader, 1992, The Philosophy of Law, 1995; contbr. articles to profl. jours. Mem. Atty. Gen.'s Commn. on Pornography, 1985-86. Served with Mass. Army N.G., 1970-71. NEH fellow, summer 1980. Fellow Am. Acad. Arts and Scis.; mem. Am. Philos. Assn., Am. Soc. for Polit. and Legal Philosophy (v.p. 1996—), Assn. Am. Law Schs. (chmn. sect. constl. law 1984-86). Office: Kennedy Sch of Govt Harvard U Cambridge MA 02138

SCHAUER, LOUIS FRANK, lawyer; b. Chgo., Dec. 4, 1928; s. Frank William and Mary (Wittich) S.; m. Nancy Clair Wilson, Oct. 5, 1957; 1 son, Christopher. B.S., Northwestern U., 1949; LL.B., Harvard U., 1952. Bar: Ill. 1952. Assoc. law firm Lord, Bissell & Brook, Chgo., 1955-63, ptnr., 1963-92; sec. Arens Industries, Inc.; village atty. Western Springs, Ill., 1973-80. Author: (monograph) Indemnification and Insurance for Directors and Officers, 1989; contbr. articles to profl. jours. Pres. Village of Western Springs, 1981-85; chmn. West Suburban Mass Transit Dist., Western Chgo. Suburbs, 1971-73; trustee Chgo. Zool. Soc., Brookfield, 1979—, sec., 1993—; bd. dirs. Chgo. Opera Theater, 1988-90. Mem. ABA, Chgo. Bar Assn., Phi Beta Kappa. Clubs: Legal (Chgo.), Law (Chgo.), Union League (Chgo.); LaGrange Country. Home: 178 Maplewood Rd Riverside IL 60546-1844 Office: Lord Bissell & Brook 115 S La Salle St Fl 3200 Chicago IL 60603-3902

SCHAUER, RALPH FLOYD, microelectronics company executive; b. Waterloo, Iowa, May 31, 1930; s. Herman Carl and Louise Emma (Mixdorf) S.; m. Gwen Elaine Maurer, Mar. 31, 1961; children: Wren, Heidi, Rebecca. BSEE, Iowa State U., 1952, MS, 1957, PhD, 1960. Mgr. design, test and research IBM, Fishkill, N.Y., 1960-80; dir. corp. tech. ctr. Wang Labs. Inc., Lowell, Mass., 1980-82; v.p. computer aided design Ford Microelectronics Inc., Colorado Springs, Colo., 1982—. Patentee in field. Pres. Lakeland Sch. Bd., Shrub Oak, N.Y., 1974, Putnam Valley (N.Y.) Free Library, 1968-78. Served to lt. USN, 1952-55. Mem. IEEE. Democrat. Lutheran. Avocations: collecting Am. antique furniture, metal ware, pewter and art. Office: Ford Microelectronics Inc 9965 Fedro Drive Colorado Springs CO 80921*

SCHAUER, WILBERT EDWARD, JR., lawyer, manufacturing company executive; b. Milw., Oct. 28, 1926; s. Wilbert Edward and Gertrude (Nickel) S.; m. Genevieve Stone, June 23, 1951; children—Jeffrey Edward, Constance Emily, Gregory Wilbert, Martha Ann, Jennifer Caroline. B.B.A., U. Wis., 1949, M.B.A., 1950, J.D., 1950. Bar: Wis. 1950. Accountant Pub. Service Commn. Wis., 1950-52; with Rexnord, Inc., Milw., 1952-87; v.p. finance, treas. Rexnord, Inc., 1968-76, v.p. fin. and law, 1977-78, exec. v.p. fin. and adminstrn., 1978-86, vice chmn., 1986-87. Alderman, Brookfield, Wis., 1958-68; pres. Common Council, 1966-68. Mem. Milw. Club, Westmoor Country Club (Brookfield, Wis.), Bluemound Golf and Country Club. Moorings Country Club. Home: 3215 Gulf Shore Blvd N # PH4 Naples FL 33940-3947

SCHAUF, VICTORIA, pediatrician, educator, infectious diseases consultant; b. N.Y.C., Feb. 17, 1943; d. Maurice J. and Ruth H. (Baker) Bisson; m. Michael Delaney; 2 children. BS with honors in Microbiology, U. Chgo., 1965, MD with honors, 1969. Intern pediatrics U. Chgo. Hosp., 1969-70; resident pediatrics Sinai Hosp. of Balt., 1970-71; chief resident pediatrics Children's Hosp. Nat. Med. Ctr., Washington, 1971-72; rsch. trainee NIH, Bethesda, Md., 1972; asst. prof. microbiology Rush Med. Coll., Chgo., 1972-74; prof. pediatrics, head pediatric infectious diseases U. Ill., Chgo., 1974-84; med. officer FDA, Rockville, Md., 1984-86; chmn. dept. pediatrics Nassau County Med. Ctr., East Meadow, N.Y., 1986-90; prof. pediatrics SUNY, Stony Brook, 1987-94; vis. prof. Rockefeller U., 1990-92; mem. vis. faculty Chiang Mai (Thailand) U., 1978; mem. ad hoc com. study sects. NIH, Bethesda, 1981-82; bd. dirs. Pearl Stetler Rsch. Fond., Chgo., 1982-84; cons. FDA, 1987-88, 93-95, Can. Bur. Human Prescription Drugs, Ottawa, 1990—, biotech. investors, 1993—; course dir. pediatric infectious diseases rev. course Cornell U. Med. Coll., N.Y.C., 1994, faculty, 1995. Producer TV programs in field; contbr. articles to profl. jours., chpts. to books. Vol. physician Cook County Hosp., Chgo., 1974-84; mem. adv. com. Nat. Hansen's Disease Ctr., La., 1986, Nassau County Day Care Coun., N.Y., 1988-90; mem. adv. bd. Surg. Aid to Children of World, N.Y., 1986-90. Am. Lung Assn. grantee U. Ill., 1977; recipient contract NIH, U. Ill., 1978-81, grantee, 1979-84. Fellow Infectious Diseases Soc. Am.; mem. Pediatric Infectious Diseases Soc. (exec. bd.), Soc. Pediatric Rsch., Am. Pediatric Soc., AAAS, Am. Soc. Microbiology, Am. Acad. Pediatrics, NOW, Phi Beta Kappa, Alpha Omega Alpha. Avocations: organic gardening, walking.

SCHAUFUSS, PETER, dancer, producer, choreographer, ballet director; b. Copenhagen, Denmark, Apr. 26, 1950; s. Frank Schaufuss and Mona Vangsaae S. Student, Royal Danish Ballet Sch. Apprentice with Royal Danish Ballet, 1965; soloist Nat. Ballet Can., 1967-68, Royal Danish Ballet, 1969-70; prin. with LFB, 1970-74, N.Y.C. Ballet, 1974-77, Nat. Ballet Can., 1977-83; artistic dir. London Festival Ballet (now English Nat. Ballet), 1984-90; ballet dir. Deutsche Oper Berlin, 1990-93, Royal Danish Ballet, 1994-95; guest appearances in Can., Denmark, France, Germany, Italy, Japan, U.K., U.S.A., USSR, Austria, S.Am.; presented BBC TV series Dancer, 1984; numerous other TV appearances; created roles include Rhapsodie Espagnole, The Steadfast Tin Soldier (Balanchine), Phantom of the Opera (Petit), Verdi Variations, Orpheus (MacMillan); ballets produced include La Sylphide (London Festival Ballet, Stuttgart Ballet, Roland Petit's Ballet de Marseille, Deutsche Oper Berlin, Teatro Comunale Firenze, Vienna State Opera, Opernhaus Zurich, Teatro dell'Opera di Roma, Hessisches Staatstheater Wiesbaden, Ballet Du Rhin, Royal Danish Ballet), Napoli (Nat. Ballet Can., Teatro San Carlo, Naples, English Nat. Ballet, formerly London Festival Ballet), Folktale (Deutsche Oper Berlin), Dances from Napoli (London Festival Ballet), Bournonville (Aterballetto), The Nutcracker (London Festival Ballet, Deutsche Oper Berlin), Giselle (Deutsche Oper Berlin), Tchiakovsky Trilogy (Deutsche Oper Berlin), Sleeping Beauty (Deutsche Oper Berlin), Swan Lake (Deutsche Oper Berlin); staging of Romeo and Juliet (Royal Danish Ballet). Decorated Officier de l'Ordre de la Couronne, Royaume de Belgique, 1995; recipient Solo award 2d Internat. Ballet Competition, Moscow, 1973, Star of the Yr. award Abendzeitung, Munich, 1978, Evening Std. award, 1979, Soc. of West End Theatres Ballet award (now Oliver), 1979, Manchester Evening News Theatre awards-dance, 1986, Laker Olprisen, Copenhagen, 1988, Berlin Co. award for best ballet prodn. Berlinerzeitung, 1991, Edinburgh Festival Critics prize, 1991, Critics prize Edinburgh Festival, 1991; named Knight of the Dannebrog, 1988. Office: care Papoutsis Rep Ltd, 18 Sundial Ave, London SE25 4BX, England

SCHAUMBURG, HERBERT HOWARD, neurology educator; b. Houston, Tex., Nov. 6, 1932; m. Joanna Jane Austin; children: Barnabas Paul, Kristin Elizabeth. AB cum laude, Harvard Coll., 1956; MD, Washington U., 1960. Instr. in neurology Albert Einstein Coll. of Medicine, N.Y.C., 1964-67, asst. prof. neurology, 1967-69, assoc. prof. neurology, 1972-76, prof., 1976—, vice chmn., 1977-84, acting chmn., 1984-86, chmn., 1986—; instr. pathology Harvard Med. Sch., Boston, 1969-71. Mem. Am. Acad. Neurology, Am. Assn. Neuropathologists, Am. Neurol. Assn., Soc. Toxicology, Soc. Neurosci. Home: 616 King Ave City Island Bronx NY 10464 Office: Albert Einstein Coll Medicine 1300 Morris Park Ave Bronx NY 10461-1926

SCHAUT, JOSEPH WILLIAM, banker; b. Cleve., May 30, 1928; s. Francis Xavier and Emma Gertrude (Urmann) S.; m. Susan Stiver, Apr. 23, 1955; children: Deborah Anne Schaut Payne, Gregory F., Mary Theresa Schaut Bentley, Michael J. B in Social Sci. in Econs., Georgetown U., 1950, JD, 1953. Bar: D.C. 1953, U.S. Mil. Ct. Appeals 1953, U.S. Dist. Ct. D.C. 1953, U.S. Ct. Appeals (D.C. cir.) 1953, Ohio 1954. Tax analyst Republic Steel Corp., Cleve., 1953-60, asst. to sec., 1960-67, asst. sec., 1967-81; dir. corp. properties Republic Steel Corp., 1976-84; corp. sec. Republic Steel Corp., Cleve., 1981-84; bus. cons., 1984-85; sr. trust officer AmeriTrust Co. Nat. Assn., 1986-92; sr. trust officer Soc. Nat. Bank, Cleve., 1992-93, v.p., 1993-96; v.p. Mellon Bank F.S.B., 1996—. Served to col. USAR, 1950-78. Recipient award Silver Beaver Greater Cleve. council Boy Scouts Am., 1975. Mem. Am. Soc. Corp. Secs. (dir. 1976-79), Ohio State Bar Assn., Greater Cleve. Growth Assn., Delta Theta Phi, Pi Gamma Mu. Roman Catholic. Office: Skylight Office Tower Ste 920 1660 W Second St Cleveland OH 44113

SCHAWLOW, ARTHUR LEONARD, physicist, educator; b. Mt. Vernon, N.Y., May 5, 1921; s. Arthur and Helen (Mason) S.; m. Aurelia Keith Townes, May 19, 1951; children: Arthur Keith, Helen Aurelia, Edith Ellen. BA, U. Toronto, Ont., Can., 1941, MA, 1942, PhD, 1949, LLD (hon.), 1970; DSc (hon.), U. Ghent, Belgium, 1968, U. Bradford, Eng., 1970, U. Ala., 1984, Trinity Coll., Dublin, Ireland, 1986; DTech (hon.), U. Lund, Sweden, 1987; DSL (hon.), Victoria U., Toronto, 1993. Postdoctoral fellow, research asso. Columbia, 1949-51; vis. assoc. prof. Columbia U., 1960; research physicist Bell Telephone Labs., 1951-61, cons., 1961-62; prof. physics Stanford U., 1961-91, also J.G. Jackson-C.J. Wood prof. physics, 1978, prof. emeritus, 1991—, exec. head dept. physics, 1966-70, acting chmn. dept., 1973-74. Author: (with C.H. Townes) Microwave Spectroscopy, 1955; Co-inventor (with C.H. Townes), optical maser or laser, 1958. Recipient Ballantine medal Franklin Inst., 1962, Thomas Young medal and prize Inst. Physics and Phys. Soc., London, 1963, Schawlow medal Laser Inst. Am., 1982, Nobel prize in physics, 1981, Nat. Medal of Sci., NSF, 1991, Arata award High Temperature Soc. Japan, 1994; named Calif. Scientist of Yr., 1973, Marconi Internat. fellow, 1977. Fellow Am. Acad. Arts and Scis., Am. Phys. Soc. (coun. 1966-70, chmn. div. electron and atomic physics 1974, pres. 1981), Optical Soc. Am. (hon. mem. 1983, dir.-at-large 1966-68, pres. 1975, Frederick Ives medal 1976); mem. NAS, IEEE (Liebmann prize 1964), AAAS (chmn. physics sect. 1979), Am. Philos. Soc., Royal Irish Acad. (hon.). Office: Stanford U Dept Physics Stanford CA 94305

SCHECHNER, RICHARD, theater director, author, educator; b. Newark, Aug. 23, 1934; s. Sheridan and Selma Sophia (Schwarz) S.; m. Carol Martin; children: Samuel MacIntosh, Sophia Martin. BA, Cornell U., 1956; postgrad., Johns Hopkins U., 1957; MA, State U. Iowa, 1958; PhD, Tulane U., 1962. Asst. prof. theatre Tulane U., 1962-66, assoc. prof., 1966-67; prof. performance studies NYU, 1967-91, Univ. prof., 1991—; co-founder, co-dir. New Orleans Group, 1965-67; founder, dir. Performance Group, N.Y.C., 1967-80; founder, artistic dir. East Coast Artists, 1991—; bd. dirs. Theatre Comms. Group, 1977-78; advisor Internat. Theatre Inst., 1975-77, Ctr. Performance Rsch., Cardiff, 1993—; pres. Bunch of Exptl. Theatres, 1975, 77, Fulbright Theatre Discipline Com., 1988-91. Author: Public Domain, 1968, Environmental Theater, 1973 (with others) Theatres, Spaces, Environments, 1975, Essays on Performance Theory, 1977, 2d edit. 1988, (with others) Makbeth, 1977, The End of Humanism, 1982, Performative Circumstances, 1983, Betweeen Theater and Anthropology, 1985, (with Samuel MacIntosh-Schechner) The Engleburt Stories: North to the Tropics, 1987, The Future of Ritual, 1993; editor: Dionysus in 69, 1970; co-editor: Free Southern Theater, 1968, Ritual, Play, and Performance, 1976, By Means of Performance, 1990; gen. editor: (serieis) Worlds of Performance, 1993—; editor: The Drama Rev., 1962-69, 85—, contbg. editor, 1971-85; adv. editor Jour. Ritual Studies, 1987—; adv. editor Text and Performance Quar., 1988—; dir. Dionysus in 69, 1968, Macbeth, 1969, Commune, 1970, The Toothe of Crime, 1972, Mother Courage, 1975, The Marilyn Project, 1975, Oedipus, 1977, Cops, 1978, The Balcony, 1979, The Red Snake, 1981, Richard's Lear, 1981, The Cherry Orchard, 1983, Prometheus Project, 1985, Don Juan, 1987, Tomorrow He'll Be Out of the Mountains, 1989, Ma Rainey's Black Botton, 1992, Faust/Gastronome, 1993, Three Sisters, 1995, The Oresteia, 1995. Served with AUS, 1958-60. Recipient Modello prize, 1985, Contbns. to Theatre Spl. award New England Theatre Conf., 1991, Work in Theatre award Towson State U., 1991; grantee John D. Rockefeller 3d Fund, 1971-72, 76, Asian Cultural Coun., 1988; Guggenheim fellow, 1976, Fulbright fellow, 1976, 83, N.Y. Inst. Humanities fellow, 1987-94, NEH sr. rsch. fellow, 1988. Office: NYU 721 Broadway 6th Fl Washington Sq New York NY 10003

SCHECHTER, ARTHUR LOUIS, lawyer; b. Rosenberg, Tex., Dec. 6, 1939; s. Morris and Helen (Brilling) S.; m. Joyce Proler, Aug. 26, 1965; children: Leslie Schechter Karpas, Jennifer Schechter Rosen. BA, U. Tex., 1962, JD, 1964; postgrad. U. Houston, 1964-65. Bar: Tex. 1964, U.S. Dist. Ct. (ea. and so. dists.) Tex. 1966, U.S. Ct. Appeals (5th cir.), U.S. Supreme Ct. 1976, cert. Tex. Bd. Legal Specialization to Personal Injury Trial Law, 1964-94. Pres. Arthur L. Schechter & Assocs., 1992-94, Schechter & Marshall, L.L.P., 1994—; spkr. Marine Law Seminar, 1983; spkr. in field. Contbr. to Law Rev., 1984. Bd. dirs. Theatre Under the Stars, Houston, 1972-78, Congregation Beth Israel, Houston, 1972-84, pres., 1982-84; pres. Am. Jewish Com., Houston, 1982-84, chmn. fgn. rels. com., chmn. United Jewish Campaign exec. com., chmn. 1993-94; pres. Jewish Fedn. Gtr. Houston, 1994—; mem. fin. coun. Nat. Dem. Orgn., 1979; mng. trustee, mem. fin. com. Dem. Nat. Com., 1992—, fin. chmn. Tex. Clinton/Gore '96; v.p., exec. com. Nat. Jewish Dem. Coun., 1992—; mem. Leadership Cir., Dem. Senatorial Campaign Com.; mem. Deans Council, U. Tex. Law Sch. Found., Austin, 1981-84, U.S. Holocaust Coun., 1994—; pres. Beth Israel Congregation, 1988-90; bd. trustees Schlenker Sch. Coun. Recipient Svc. award Congregation Beth Israel, 1976, Pres. award NAACP, 1992, Love award Child Advocate Houston, Benefactor award Jewish Chautauqua Soc., 1995, Nat. Am. Jewish Com. Human Rels. award, 1996. Mem. ATLA, Tex. Trial Lawyers Assn. (chmn. admiralty sect., presenter 1985-87), Jewish Fedn. Houston (bd. mem., v.p., pres. 1994—), Houston Trial Lawyers Assn., Houston Bar Assn. Democrat. Jewish. Clubs: Westwood Country (bd. dirs., sec.). Home: 19A Westlane Houston TX 77019

SCHECHTER, AUDREY, medical, surgical nurse; b. N.Y.C., July 6, 1934; d. Abraham and Ruth (Greenwald) Levine; m. Edwin Schechter, Sept. 1, 1957; children: Laurie, Michael. Diploma, Bellevue Sch. of Nursing, 1957; BSN, SUNY, Albany, 1987; MSN, Coll. Of New Rochelle, 1991. CCRN, TNCC. Crit. care nurse The Stamford (Conn.) Hosp., 1970-90, clin. nurse specialist, 1991-94; pacemaker testing nurse Cardiol. Assocs., Darien, Conn., 1974-87; preceptor/mentor for master's students Pace U., Purchase, N.Y., 1991-93; nurse Lyme Vaccine Investigation Study, Stamford, 1995—; asst. dir. of nursing Mediplex of Stamford, 1995—; leader for arthritis self-help classes, Arthritis Found., 1994-95; chart rev. Malpractice Legal Cons., Conn., 1994; mem. speaker's bur., Arthritis Found., 1994-95. Devel.: (in-house manual) Orthopedic Learning Manual, Bony Fragments - Orthopedic Bits and Pieces, 1990-94. Mem. AACN (treas. Fairfield County chpt. 1982-90). Avocations: reading, walking, theater, exercise workshops. Home: 158 Four Brooks Rd Stamford CT 06903

SCHECHTER, DANIEL PHILIP, lawyer; b. N.Y.C., Nov. 29, 1942; s. Isadore and Jenny (Waldman) S.; m. Sara P. Howell (div. 1977); children: Matthew, Ellen; m. Elizabeth L. Cooke, Oct. 1, 1983. BA, Columbia U., 1964, LLB, 1967. Bar: N.Y. 1968. Law clk. to judge U.S. Dist. Ct. (so. dist.) N.Y., N.Y.C., 1967-68; assoc. Fried, Frank, Harris, Shriver & Jacobson, N.Y.C., 1968-75, ptnr., 1975—. Mem. ABA, N.Y. City Bar Assn. Club: India House (N.Y.C.). Office: Fried Frank Harris Shriver & Jacobson 1 New York Plz New York NY 10004*

SCHECHTER, GERALDINE POPPA, hematologist; b. N.Y.C., Jan. 16, 1938; d. Josif and Victoria (Nosi) P.; m. Alan Neil Schechter, Feb. 6, 1965; children: Daniele Malka, Andrew M.R. AB, Vassar Coll., Poughkeepsie, N.Y., 1959; MD, Columbia U., 1963. Diplomate Am. Bd. Internal Medicine, Am. Bd. Hematology. Intern, resident Presbyn. Hosp., N.Y.C., 1963-65; resident, fellow, rsch. assoc. VA Med. Ctr., Washington, 1965-70, staff physician, 1970-74, chief hematology, 1974—; asst., assoc. prof. medicine George Washington U., Washington, 1971-81, prof. medicine, 1981—; mem. hematology com. Am. Bd. Internal Medicine, Phila., 1985-91, bd. dirs., 1990-95, residency review com. internal medicine, 1996—. Mem. editl. bd. Blood, 1985-89; contbr. articles to hematologic jours. Office: VA Med Ctr Hematology Sect 50 Irving St NW Washington DC 20422-0001

SCHECHTER, SOL, clothes company executive; b. 1916; married. With Shirt Mfrs., N.Y., 1936-40, Overndorfer-Marcus Inc., 1940-41; br. owner Atlas Shirt Co. Inc.; prin. Lenoir Shirt Co.; pres. Hampton Industries Inc., 1946—. Office: Hampton Industries Inc PO Box 614 2000 Greenville Hwy Kinston NC 28501-1845*

SCHECHTER, STEPHEN L., political scientist; b. Washington, Nov. 28, 1945; s. William J. and Blossom (Rapaport) S.; m. Stephanie A. Thompson, Feb. 16, 1993; 1 child, Sarah J.; 1 stepdaughter: Kelly Anne Thompson. BA, Syracuse U., 1967; PhD, U. Pitts., 1972. Acting dir. Ctr. for Study of Federalism/Temple U., 1973-76; asst. to full prof. polit. sci. Russell Sage Coll., Troy, N.Y., 1977—; exec. dir. N.Y. State Commn. on Bicentennial of U.S. Constitution, 1986-90; dir. Coun. for Citizenship Edn. Russell Sage Coll., N.Y., 1990—; coord. We The People, 1992—; pres. N.Y. State Coun. on Social Edn., 1992-93; presenter workshops in field; sr. rsch. advisor N.Y. State Commn. on the Capital Region, 1995-96. Co-editor: World of the Founders: New York Communities in the Federal Period, 1990, Contexts of the Bill of Rights, 1990, New York and the Union, New York and the Bicentennial, 1990; editor: Roots of the Republic: American Founding Documents Interpreted, 1990, others; contbr. articles to profl. jours., chpts. to books in field; editor: Social Sci. Record, 1993-96. Chmn. Rensselaer County Bicentennial Commn., 1991. Mem. Nat. Coun. Social Studies (state del. 1991), Internat. Assn. Ctrs. for Fed. Studies (co-founder 1976), Am. Polit. Sci. Assn., N.Y. State Acad. Pub. Adminstrn., others. Office: Russell Sage Coll 45 Ferry St Troy NY 12180-4115

SCHECKNER, SY, former greeting card company executive; b. N.Y.C., Aug. 8, 1924; s. Morris and Bella S.; m. Georgene W. Carrigan, Aug. 17, 1974; children: Barry David, Michael Matthew, Jeri Bella,. Student, CCNY, U. Pitts., U. Ill. Sr. v.p., dir. Papercraft Corp., Pitts, 1956-75, Am. Greetings Corp., Cleve., 1975-85; pres. Knomark, Inc., Plus Mark, Inc.; gen. ptnr. Doubletree Investments. Vice chmn. bd. trustees Tusculum Coll., Greeneville, Tenn. Served with U.S. Army, 1942-45. Decorated Purple Heart. Office: 1480 S Military Trl West Palm Beach FL 33415-9176

SCHECTER, M., book publishing executive. With Educatinal Reading Service Inc., Mahwah, N.J., 1961-89; pres. Troll Assoc., Mahwah, N.J., 1968—. Office: Troll Associates 100 Corporate Dr Mahwah NJ 07430-2041

SCHECTMAN, HERBERT A., lawyer, corporate executive; b. N.Y.C., Aug. 8, 1930; s. Leon and Ethel (Brown) S.; m. Evelyn P. DePalma, Apr. 15, 1956 (div. 1974); children: Bart T., Robert; m. Lois Regent Driscoll, Apr. 11, 1974. AB, Syracuse U., 1952; MA, Columbia U., 1958, JD, 1958. Bar: N.Y. 1959. Atty. U.S. Govt., Bklyn., 1958-60, The Lummus Co., N.Y.C., 1960-62; assoc. gen. counsel GE Credit Corp., N.Y.C. and Chgo., 1962-67; div. counsel GE, N.Y.C., 1967-69; ptnr. Belfer, Bogart & Schectman, N.Y.C., 1969-74; sr. v.p. ops. and adminstrn., gen. counsel Chrysler Capital Corp. (formerly E.F. Hutton Credit Corp.), Greenwich, Conn., 1974-87, sr. v.p., group exec. mergers, acquisitions and corp. fin. group, 1988-89, exec. v.p., sector exec. merchant banking svcs., 1989-91; sr. v.p. credit and ops. Chrysler Capital Corp. (formerly E.F. Hutton Credit Corp.), Greenwich, 1991-96; also bd. dirs. Chrysler Capital Corp. (formerly E.F. Hutton Credit Corp.), Greenwich, Conn.; arbitrator N.Y.C. Civil Ct. Small Claims, N.Y.C., 1974—; with Herbert A Schectman, Greenwich, Conn., 1996—. Served with USAF, 1951-54; ETO. Mem. N.Y. State Bar Assn., Am. Judges Assn. Office: Herbert A Schectman Law Firm 2 Greenwich PlazaSte 100 Greenwich CT 06830*

SCHEEDER, LOUIS, theater producer, director, educator; b. N.Y.C., Dec. 26, 1946; s. Louis W. and Julia H. (Callery) S. BA in English Lit., Georgetown U., 1968; postgrad., Sch. of Arts, Columbia U., 1968-69; MA in Performance Studies, NYU, 1995. Founder, dir. The Classical Studio NYU, 1991—; dir. NYU Tisch Sch. of the Arts, Shakespeare Ensemble, 1989-90; mem. adv. council Nat. Com. on Arts and Edn., 1977-82; mem. D.C. Commn. on Arts and Humanities, 1976-80; bd. advs. New Playwrights' Theatre of Washington, 1975-82; asst. stage mgr. Arena Stage, Washington, 1969-70; dir., producer Folger Theatre Group, Washington, 1973-81; cons. Ctr. for Renaissance and Baroque Studies U. Md., 1984-91; asst. dir. Royal Shakespeare Co. Stratford-Upon-Avon, Eng., 1988. Dir., producer plays including Creeps (Am. premiere), 1973, The Farm (Am. premiere), 1974, The Collected Works of Billy the Kid (Am. premiere), 1975, Henry V, 1976, The Fool (Am. premiere), 1976, Mummer's End (world premiere), 1977, Teeth 'n' Smiles (Am. premiere), 1977, Two Gentlemen of Verona, 1977, Mackerel (world premiere), 1978, Black Elk Speaks (tour), 1978, Richard III, 1978, Whose Life Is It Anyway? (Am. premiere), 1978, Richard II, 1978, As You Like It, 1979, Custer (Kennedy Center), 1979, Charlie and Algernon (Kennedy Center), 1980, Crossing Niagara (Am. premiere), 1981, Love's Labour's Lost, 1981; also dir. Broadway, Off Broadway, regional prodns. including (Broadway) Charlie and Algernon, 1980, (off-Broadway) Creeps, 1973, Passover, 1986, (off-off-Broadway) The Gettysburg Sound Bite, 1989, Brunch At Trudy And Paul's, 1990, The Christmas Rules, 1991, The Monkey Business, 1992; dir. All's Well That Ends Well, 1990; dance: dir. Near Ruins, N.Y.; producer How I Got that Story (off-Broadway), 1982, Diamonds (off-Broadway), 1984, Today, I Am A Fountain Pen (off-Broadway), 1986; dir. Man. Theatre Centre, 1982, 83, 84, Nat. Arts Centre, Ottawa, Ont., Can., 1984, Hedda Gabler, Centre Stage, Toronto, 1985, Reg: Life in the Trees, GeVa Theatre, 1991; asst. dir. Broadway prodn. Carrie, 1988. Recipient Dixon award Georgetown U., 1968, Alumni Achievement award Georgetown U. Alumni Club Met. Washiington, 1981, Mayors Arts award, D.C., 1982, Acad. Excellence award NYU, 1995. Mem. Soc. Stage Dirs. and Choreographers, Episc. Actors Guild (mem. council). Home: 7 Stuyvesant Oval New York NY 10009-1901

SCHEEL, NELS EARL, financial executive, accountant; b. Spencer, Wis., Sept. 25, 1925; s. Roland Edward and Louise Ernestine (Hake) S.; m. Elaine Marie Carlisle, Aug. 28, 1949; children: Thomas W., John E., Martha L., Mark A., Mary E. BS, Youngstown Coll., 1949; MBA, U. Pa., 1950. CPA, Ohio. Staff acct. Lybrand Ross Bros., Cleve., 1950-54; asst. controller Century Foods, Youngstown, Ohio, 1954-62; treas., controller The Bailey Co., Cleve., 1962-63, Golden Dawn Foods, Sharon, Pa., 1963-82; v.p., chief fin. officer Peter J. Schmitt Co., Sharon, 1982-89; cons. to industry Columbiana, 1989—; part-time faculty Youngstown (Ohio) State U., 1954-94; bd. mem. Sovereign Cirs., Inc., North Jackson, Ohio, 1992—, bd. chmn., 1995—. Pres. Crestview Bd. Edn., Columbiana, Ohio, 1970-81. Staff sgt. AUS, 1943-46, PTO, hon. discharge. Mem. Am. Inst. CPA's, Ohio Soc. CPA's.

SCHEELE, PAUL DRAKE, former hospital supply corporate executive; b. Elgin, Ill., Aug. 6, 1922; s. Arthur R. and Helen M. (Christiansen) S. B.A., Coe Coll., 1944; M.B.A., Harvard, 1947. With Am. Hosp. Supply Corp., 1947—; pres. Harleco div., Phila., 1966-68; group v.p. Am. Hosp. Supply Corp., 1968-70; exec. v.p., also pres. internat. group Am. Hosp. Supply Corp., Evanston, Ill., 1970-74, v.p., asst. to chmn. bd., 1974-81. Chmn. bd. trustees Coe Coll. Served to 1st lt., inf. AUS, 1943-46. Mem. Harvard Bus. Sch. Club, Harvard Club Fla., Econ. Club (Chgo.), Tau Kappa Epsilon, Pi Delta Epsilon.

SCHEELER, CHARLES, construction company executive; b. Balt., June 20, 1925; s. George F. and Catherine Louise (Seward) S.; m. Mary Katherine Scarborough, Aug. 22, 1953; children—Charles P., George D., Donald C. B.S., U. Md., 1948, LL.B., 1952. Bar: Md. 1952; CPA, Md. With C. J. Langenfelder & Son, Inc., Balt., 1949—; exec. v.p., treas. C. J. Langenfelder & Son., Inc., 1974-77, pres., chief exec. officer, 1977-95; chmn. bd. Rosedale Fed. Savs. & Loan Assn. Served with USN, 1943-46, PTO. Mem. AICPA, Md. Assn. CPAs. Office: 8427 Pulaski Hwy Baltimore MD 21237-3022

SCHEELER, JAMES ARTHUR, architect; b. Pontiac, Ill., Dec. 20, 1927; s. Aman B. and Jane (Steele) S.; m. Barbara Jean Lloyd, Sept. 2, 1950; children: James Erich, Carl Aman, Orissa Jane Elizabeth. B.S. with highest honors, U. Ill., 1951, M.S., 1952; postgrad., U. Liverpool, 1952-53. Grad. asst. U. Ill., Urbana, 1950-52; draftsman-designer Lundeen & Hilfinger, Bloomington, Ill., 1952-53; designer Skidmore, Owings & Merrill, Chgo., 1955-59; partner Richardson, Severns, Scheeler & Assos., Inc., Champaign, Ill., 1959-65; v.p., treas. Richardson, Severns, Scheeler & Assos., Inc., 1965-71; vice chmn. bd., dir. Prodn. Systems for Architects and Engrs., Inc., 1973-81; vis. critic U. Ill., 1959-60. Mem. Plan Commn., Champaign, 1966—, chmn., 1969-71; mem. Champaign County Regional Planning Commn., 1967-71; bd. dirs. Nat. Center for a Barrier-Free Environment, 1978—, pres., 1981. Served with USN, 1946-47. Recipient various archtl. awards.; Francis J. Plym fellow, 1953-54; Fulbright fellow, 1953. Fellow AIA (treas. Ctrl. Ill. chpt. 1967-68, sec. 1968-69, pres. 1970-71, nat. dep. exec. v.p. 1971-76, pres. corp. 1974-78, exec. v.p. 1971-76, pres. corp. 1974-78, exec. v.p. 1977-78, program devel. group exec. 1976-85, sr. exec. 1985-88, v.p. design practice group 1989, resident fellow 1990—), Internat. Union of Archs. Profl. Practice Commn. (sec. 1994—), Fedn. Colls. Archs. Republic Mex. (hon.); mem. Ill. Arts Coun. (archtl. adv. bd. 1966-71), Montessori Soc. Champaign-Urbana (dir. 1964-66), Gargoyle, Scarab, Phi Kappa Phi, Lambda Chi Alpha, Lambda Alpha. Episcopalian. Address: 11179 Saffold Way Reston VA 22090-3824

SCHEER, JULIAN WEISEL, business executive, author; b. Richmond, Va., Feb. 20, 1926; s. George Fabian and Hilda (Knopf) S.; m. Suzanne Fugler Huggan, Oct. 9, 1965; 1 child, Hilary Susannah; children by previous marriage: Susan, David Scott, George Grey. AB, U. N.C., 1950. Reporter Mid-Va. Publs., Richmond, 1939-43; asst. dir. Sports Info, UNC, 1947-53; pres. Scheer Syndicate, Chapel Hill, N.C., 1947-53; columnist, reporter Charlotte (N.C.) News, 1953-62; asst. adminstr. pub. affairs NASA, 1962-71; ptnr. Sullivan, Murray & Scheer, Washington, 1971-76; sr. v.p. corp. affairs LTV Corp., Dallas, 1976-93; ptnr. Murray, Scheer, Tapia and Montgomery, Washington, 1993—; bd. dirs. several corps.; mem. adv. coun. NASA. Freelance writer, author. Bd. dirs. Sch. Journalism, U. N.C. With U.S. Mcht. Marine, 1943-46; with USNR, 1946-53. Mem. Algonquin Soc., City Tavern Club, Sigma Delta Chi, Pi Lambda Phi. Home: 8303 Old Dumfries Rd Catlett VA 22019-1940

SCHEER, MILTON DAVID, chemical physicist; b. N.Y.C., Dec. 22, 1922; s. Abraham and Lena (Brauner) S.; m. Emily Hirsch, June 23, 1945; children—Jessica, Richard Mark, Julia Rachel. B.S., CCNY, 1943; M.S., N.Y. U., 1947, Ph.D., 1951. Chemist Bd. Econ. Warfare, Guatemala, C. Am., 1943-44; research asst. N.Y. U., 1947-50; combustion scientist U.S. Naval Air Rocket Test Sta., Dover, N.J., 1950-52; phys. chemist U.S. Bur. Mines, Pitts., 1952-55; research scientist Gen. Electric Co., Cin., 1955-58; phys. chemist Nat. Bur. Standards, Washington, 1958-68; chief photochemistry sect. Nat. Bur. Standards, 1968-70, chief phys. chemistry div., 1970-77; dir. Center for Thermodynamics and Molecular Sci., Nat. Measurement Lab., 1977-80; research scientist chem. kinetics div. Ctr. for Chem. Physics, Nat. Measurement Lab., 1981-85; ptnr. McNesby & Scheer Research Assocs., 1985-89; rsch. cons. U.S. Dept. Energy, Germantown, Md., 1990-94; vis. prof. U. Md., 1980-81; Fulbright scholar U. Rome, 1982-83. Contbr. numerous articles to profl. jours. Served with USN, 1944-46. Fellow Am. Inst. Chemists, AAAS; mem. Am. Chem. Soc., Am. Phys. Soc. Home: 15100 Interlachen Dr Apt 512 Silver Spring MD 20906-5605

SCHEER, TERRI LYNN, special education educator; b. St. Charles, Mo., Oct. 1, 1961; d. Michael Vincent Sr. and Christine May (Stepp) Brush. Student, U. Mo., 1984. Mental retardation profl. Community Living for Handicap, St. Charles, 1984-85; tchr. adult spl. edn. St. Louis Assn. for Retarded Citizens, 1985-86; tchr. spl. edn. Fransic Howell Sch. Dist., St. Charles, 1986-89; tchr. vocat. spl. edn. Spl. Sch. Dist., St. Louis, 1989—; mem. adv. bd. Lewis and Clark Tech. Sch., St. Charles, 1987-88; student coun. advisor West County Tech. Sch., St. Louis, 1989—, sr. class advisor, 1991—, mem. adv. bd. Vocat. Indsl. Clubs Am., 1991—. Explorer leader Boy Scouts Am., St. Louis, 1991-91. Mem. Mo. Vocat. Assn., Nat. Assn. Vocat. Edn. Spl. Needs Personnel.

SCHEERER, ERNEST WILLIAM, dentist; b. Wabash, Ind., May 18, 1932; s. Ernest William and Anna Lucille (Bahler) S.; m. Ingrid Elvy Yvonne, Sept. 28, 1973. BS, Purdue U., 1954; DDS, Ind. U., 1961. Intern The Queen's Hosp., Honolulu, 1961-62; assoc. Pvt. Dental Practice, Honolulu, 1963-65; owner Pvt. Solo Dental Practice, Honolulu, 1965-75; ptnr. Dental Adminstrn., Honolulu, 1975-78; pres. Scheerer & West Dental Corp., Honolulu, 1978—; chief Dept. Dentistry Queen's Hosp., Honolulu. Contbr. various clin. articles to profl. jours. Mem. Big Bros., Hawaii, 1968-74. Mem. Master Acad. Gen. Dentistry, Hawaii Acad. Gen. Dentistry (past pres.), Am. Coll. Dentists, ADA, Hawaii Dental Assn. (treas.), Internat. Acad. Gnathology, Pierre Fauchard Soc., Fedn. Dental Internat., Am. Equilibration Soc., Acad. of Osseointegration, Am. Acad. Esthetic Dentistry, Am. Coll. Dentists O.K.U., Hawaii Med. Libr. (sec.), Elks. Mem. United Ch. of Christ. Club: Pacific. Avocations: tennis, travel, Hawaiian music. Office: Scheerer & West Inc 735 Bishop St Ste 211 Honolulu HI 96813-4816

SCHEERER, PAUL J., lawyer; b. Sturgeon Bay, Wis., 1945. BA, U. Mich., 1967; JD magna cum laude, U. Minn., 1970. Bar: Minn. 1970. Assoc. prof. William Mitchell Coll. Law, 1972-74; ptnr. Dorsey & Whitney, Mpls. Office: Dorsey & Whitney 220 S 6th St Minneapolis MN 55402-4502*

SCHEETZ, SISTER MARY JOELLEN, English language educator; b. Lafayette, Ind., May 20, 1926; d. Joseph Albert and Ellen Isabelle (Fitzgerald) S. A.B., St. Francis Coll., 1956; M.A., U. Notre Dame, 1964; Ph.D., U. Mich., 1970. Tchr. English, Bishop Luers High Sch., Fort Wayne, Ind., 1965-67; acad. dean St. Francis Coll., Fort Wayne, 1967-68; pres. St. Francis Coll., Ft. Wayne, Ind., 1970-93; pres. emeritus; English lang. prof. St. Francis Coll., Ft. Wayne, Ind., 1993—. Mem. Nat. Coun. Tchrs. English, Delta Epsilon Sigma. Office: St Francis Coll 2701 Spring St Fort Wayne IN 46808-3939

SCHEFFER, LUDO CAREL PETER, educational administrator, researcher, consultant; b. Bussum, The Netherlands, Sept. 3, 1960; s. Lukas Albert and Alida Johanna Theodora (Kassenaar) S.; m. Gwynne Rochelle Smith, oct. 1, 1994; 1 child, William Alexander. PhD, Free U., Amsterdam, The Netherlands, 1987, U. Pa., 1995. Cons., trainer Shell Netherlands, Rotterdam, 1987-88; cons. trainee Hollandse Beton Groep, The Hague, The Netherlands, 1988; rsch. asst. lit. rsch. ctr. U. Pa., Phila., 1988-90; rsch. asst. Nat. Ctr. on Adult Lit., Phila., 1990-91, lit. fellow, 1991-93, project dir., 1993—. Co-author: Students At Risk: Pitfalls and Promising Plans, 1993; (newsletter) NCAL Connections, 1994. Bd. dirs. CHAMP, Phila., 1991, Shelter Lit. Network, Pila., 1992; exec. dir., chair Shelnet, Phila., 1993. Recipient Cmty. Leadership award Internat. Ho. of Phila., 1991; named Phi Beta Delta scholar, 1992. Mem. APA (assoc.), Am. Ednl. Rsch. Assn., New Eng. Ednl. Rsch. Assn., Jean Piaget Soc., Amnesty Internat., Habitat for Humanity, So. Poverty Law Ctr., Phila. Concerned About Housing. Avocations: reading, arts, sports. Home: 325 Spruce St Philadelphia PA 19106-3818

SCHEFFLER, ECKART ARTHUR, publisher; b. Glauchau, Germany, June 8, 1941; came to U.S., 1963; s. Arthur Ernst and Marianne (Baltzer) S.; m. Hannelore Baustian, July 29, 1966; children: Thomas, Daniel. Bookseller Buchhändlerschule, Leipzig, Germany, 1955-58; bookstore mgr. Bücher-Binder, Stuttgart, Germany, 1959-62; v.p. Adler's Fgn. Books Inc., N.Y.C., 1963-72, Walter de Gruyter Inc., Hawthorne, N.Y., 1972—. Served with USAR, 1964-69. Mem. Am. Assn. Pubs., Internat. Group of Sci., Tech. and Med. Pubs., Scholarly Pubs. Assn. Lutheran. Lodge: Rotary. Home: RR #1 Mount Kisco NY 10549-9801 Office: Walter de Gruyter 200 Saw Mill River Rd Hawthorne NY 10532-1525

SCHEFFLER, ISRAEL, philosopher, educator; b. N.Y.C., Nov. 25, 1923; s. Leon and Ethel (Grünberg) S.; m. Rosalind Zuckerbrod, June 26, 1949; children: Samuel, Laurie. B.A., Bklyn. Coll., 1945, M.A., 1948; M.H.L., Jewish Theol. Sem., 1949; Ph.D. (Ford fellow 1951), U. Pa., 1952; A.M. (hon.), Harvard U., 1959; D.H.L. (hon.), Jewish Theol. Sem., 1993. Mem. faculty Harvard U., 1952-92, prof. edn., 1961-62, prof. edn. and philosophy, 1962-64, Victor S. Thomas prof. edn. and philosophy, 1964-92, professor emeritus, 1992—, hon. research fellow in cognitive studies, 1965-66, co-dir. Research Ctr. for Philosophy of Edn., 1983—; Fellow Center for Advanced Study in Behavioral Scis., 1972-73. Author: The Language of Education, 1960, The Anatomy of Inquiry, 1963, Conditions of Knowledge, 1965, Science and Subjectivity, 1967, Reason and Teaching, 1973, Four Pragmatists, 1974, Beyond the Letter, 1979, Of Human Potential, 1985, Inquiries, 1986, In Praise of the Cognitive Emotions, 1991, Teachers of My Youth, 1995; co-author: Work, Education and Leadership, 1995; editor: Philosophy and Education, 1958, 66; co-editor: Logic and Art, 1972; contbr. articles to profl. jours. Recipient Alumni award of merit Bklyn. Coll., 1967, Disting. Svc. medal Tchrs. Coll., Columbia, 1980, Benjamin Shevach award Boston Hebrew Coll., 1995; Guggenheim fellow, 1958-59, 72-73; NSF grantee, 1962, 65. Mem. Am. Acad. Arts and Scis., Am. Philos. Assn., Philosophy Edn. Soc., Nat. Acad. Edn. (charter), Philosophy of Sci. Assn. (prs. 1973-75). Office: Harvard U Larsen Hall Cambridge MA 02138

SCHEFFLER, LEWIS FRANCIS, pastor, educator, research scientist; b. Springfield, Ohio, Oct. 13, 1928; s. Lewis Francis and Emily Louise (Kloker) S.; m. Willa Pauline Cole, Aug. 9, 1949 (div. 1978); children: Lewis F. Fischer, Richard Thomas, Gary Arlen, Tonni Kay; m. Mary Lee Smith, Apr. 18, 1978; stepchildren: Kimberly McCollum, Jeffrey McIlroy, Kerry Buell. BA in Liberal Arts, Cin. Bible Seminary, 1950; AA in Bus., Jefferson Coll., 1989; MAT, Webster U., 1989. Quality assurance Tectum Corp., Newark, 1954-57; rsch. group leader Owens-Corning Fiberglas, Granville, Ohio, 1957-64; tech. asst. to v.p. R&D and Engring., 1960-63; rsch. adminstr. Modiglas Fibers Corp., Bremen, Ohio, 1965-68; dir. R & D Flex-O-Lite Corp., St. Louis, 1968-71; pastor Christian Ch., St. Louis, 1972-75; police commns. Brentwood (Mo.) Police Dept., 1975-87; pastor Christian Ch., Potosi, Mo., 1988-89, Slater (Mo.) Christian Ch., 1989-93, Laddonia Christian Ch., 1994—; asst. prof. English lang. and lit. Mo. Valley Coll., Marshall, 1989-93; adj. prof. theology Mo. Sch. Religion, 1993—; organizing co-chmn. aerospace composite materials com. ASTM, 1961; mem. exec. bd. Northwest Area Christian Ch., 1989-93; mem. Coun. of Areas of Mid-Am. Region Christian Ch., 1990-93; cons. in field. Contbr. articles to profl. jours. Patentee in field. Money raiser United Appeal, chaplaincy Blessing Hosp., Quincy, Ill., 1974; vol. Ill. Divsn. Children and Family Svcs., 1972-75; sec. exec. com. N.W. Area Christian Ch. (Disciples of Christ). Mem. Medieval Acad. Am., Mo. Philol. Assn. Avocations: philosophy and pomology. Home: RR 1 Box 32A Laddonia MO 63352-9710 *Now and then, God has so touched people in such a way that, recognizing it, we think "So that's what God must be like!" and our ethical and moral sensitivities are heightened.*

SCHEFFMAN, DAVID THEODORE, economist, management educator, consultant; b. Milaca, Minn., Dec. 1, 1943; s. David Theodore and Fern Virginia (Maas) S.; m. Cathy Schutz, May 11, 1989. BA, U. Minn., 1967; PhD, MIT, 1971. Lectr. Boston Coll., 1970-71; from asst. prof. to assoc. prof. Univ. Western Ont., London, Can., 1971-81; sr. economist FTC, Washington, 1979-82, dep. dir., 1983-86, dir., bur. econs., 1985-88; Justin Potter prof., prof. bus. strategy and mktg. Vanderbilt U., Nashville, 1989—; prof., dir. Inst. Applied Econs. Concordia U., Montreal, Que., Can., 1982-83; adj. prof. Georgetown U. Law Ctr., Washington, 1986; cons. Ont. Econ. Coun., Toronto, 1973-81, GM, 1977, Ctrl. Oil Inquiry, Ottawa, Ont., 1982-84, Ctrl. Govt., Ottawa, 1979—, Can. Competition Tribunal, 1987-89, Can. Bur. Competition Policy, 1988-91, U.S. Sentencing Commn., 1988-89, PepsiCo, 1989-93, Kraft Gen. Food, 1989-92, PacifiCorp, 1989-93, NERA, 1991-93, Boeing, 1992—, LECG, 1993—, Berwind Industries, Inc., 1993-95, Comm. Ctrl., Inc., Applied Innovation, Inc., TEC, 1995—, Norlel, 1995. Author: Speculation and Monopoly in Urban Development: Analytical Foundations, 1977, An Economic Analysis of Provincial Land Use Policies in Ontario, 1980, Social Regulation in Markets for Consumer Goods and Services, 1982, An Economic Analysis of the Impact of Rising Oil Prices on Urban Structure, 1983, Strategy, Structure, and Antitrust in the Carbonated Soft Drink Industry, 1992. Recipient Dissertation Fellowship award NSF, 1967-68; vis. scholar U. Minn., 1978. Mem. Am. Econ. Assn., Strategic Mgmt. Soc., Am. Mgmt. Assn., Am. Mktg. Assn. Office: Owen Grad Sch Mgmt Vanderbilt U Nashville TN 37203

SCHEFTNER, GEROLD, marketing executive; b. Milw., June 1, 1937; s. Arthur Joseph and Alice Agnes (Gregory) S.; m. Chantal Scheftner; children: Mark A., Mary L., Michael D. Student, Milw. Bus. Inst., 1953, Great Lakes Naval Acad. Sch. Dental-Med. Surgery, USAF, 1955-56, USAF Inst., 1959, Marquette U., 1959-60. Territorial rep. Mossey-Otto Co., Milw., 1960-63; with Den-Tal-Ez Mfg. Co., Des Moines, 1963—; dir. fgn. affairs Den-Tal-Ez Mfg. Co., 1969-71; dir. Far Ea. affairs, 1971-72, exec. dir. internat. sales/mktg., 1973, v.p., gen. mgr. internat. ops., 1974—, also corp. dir., 1969—; chmn. bd. Den-Tal-Ez Ltd., Gt. Britain, 1974—; prs., mktg. specialist Pennwalt/Jelenko; pres. S&S Scheftner, Ltd., Biel/Bienne, Mainz, Germany, Switzerland subs.; adviser Kuwait M.O.H., Saudi Arabia; pres., mktg. specialist Productivity Tng. Corp., Calif., Tek-Scan Inc. subs. GE, Boston, Swift Instruments, Boston, LMT Laser, San Clemente, Calif.; researcher dental therapy equipment and apparatus Relaxodont (dental patient anxiety relaxer), Temple U., 21st Century Group, Jacksonville, Fla., OralSafe, Inc., Temecula, Calif.; mfr. disposable dental surgery instruments for WHO, Geneva. Pub. Zahn Dental Co. Catalog. Bd. dirs. Dist. Export Coun. Iowa, 1976-77; mem. Lake Panorama (Iowa) Devel. Assn., 1972-73; chmn. World Trade Coun. Iowa, 1976-77; adv. bd. bldg. program St. Charles Boys Home, Milw., 1963. With USAF, 1955-59. Recipient Presdl. Mgr. of Yr. award Den-Tal-Ez Co., 1967, Lectr. award Faculdade de Odontologia, U. Ribeirao Preto, Brazil, 1974. Mem. Am. Dental Trade Assn., Am. Dental Mfrs. Assn., Hong Kong Dental Trade Assn. (hon.), Saudi Dental Soc. (advisor sci. dental products, concepts), Internat. Platform Assn., Greater Des Moines C. of C. (dir. 1976-77), Lions. Republican. Office: Silbergasse 6, CH-2502 Biel Switzerland *Live enthusiastically, expand your natural attributes, be truthful and sincere, assume responsibility, avoid prejudice of the innocent, respect authority, live for today, but improve tomorrow-pray consistently and confidently, love and be loved, be proud of your noble heritage of being an American.*

SCHEIB, GERALD PAUL, fine art educator, jeweler, metalsmith; b. L.A., Dec. 26, 1937; s. Harry William and Olive Bauer (Cartwright) S.; m. Elizabeth Ann Galligan, Dec. 27, 1965 (div. 1978); children: Gregory Paul, Geoffrey Paul; m. Dedra Lynn True, Oct. 1, 1983; 1 child, Adam True. AA, East L.A. Jr. Coll., 1959; BA, Calif. State U., L.A., 1962, MFA, 1968. Cert. life teaching credential in fine arts, secondary and coll. tchr., Calif. Secondary tchr. art L.A. Unified Sch. Dist., 1963-77; prof. fine art L.A. Community Coll. Dist., 1977—; pres. faculty senate L.A. Mission Coll., San Fernando, Calif., 1983-84; bargaining unit rep., AFT Coll. Guild Local 1521; elected Arts and Letters chair L.A. Mission Coll., 1993; owner, mgr. Artificers Bench, Sylmar, Calif., 1976—. With USNR, 1955—. Recipient of tribute City of L.A., 1983, Citizen of Month award, Los Angeles County, 1983. Mem. Calif. Art Edn. Assn. (membership chmn. 1985-87, pres.-elect 1989-91, pres. 1991-93, Calif.'s Outstanding Art Educator in Higher Edn. 1994-95), San Fernando Active 20-30 Club (pres. 1981-82), Nat. Assn. Scholars, Sons of Union Vets of Civil War. Republican. Avocations: collecting antiques, creating custom jewelry. Office: 13356 Eldridge Ave Sylmar CA 91342-3200

SCHEIBE, KARL EDWARD, psychology educator; b. Belleville, Ill., Mar. 5, 1937; s. John Henry and Esther Julia (Friesen) S.; m. Elizabeth Wentworth Mixter, Sept. 10, 1961; children: David Sawyer, Robert Daniel. B.S., Trinity Coll., 1959; Ph.D., U. Calif.-Berkeley, 1963; M.A. (hon.), Wesleyan U., 1973. Faculty mem. Wesleyan U., Middletown, Conn., 1963—, prof. psychology, 1973—, chmn. dept., 1973-76, 79-81, 86-88; v.p. Stonington Inst., 1984-91; dir. Saybrook Counseling Ctr., 1990—; vis. prof. U. So. Calif., 1974; dir. rev. panels NSF Sci. Profl. Devel. Program, 1975-81; cons. Am. Council Edn., 1975-81. Author: Beliefs and Values, 1970, Mirror, Masks, Lies and Secrets, 1979, Studies in Social Identity, 1983, Self Studies: The Psychology of Self and Identity, 1995. Trustee Trinity Coll., Hartford, Conn., 1977-83; moderator congregation First Ch. of Christ, Middletown, 1981-82. Woodrow Wilson fellow, 1959; NSF fellow, 1961; NIMH research grantee, 1964-68; Fulbright fellow Cath. U. Sao Paulo, Brazil, 1972-73, 84. Mem. Am. Psychol. Assn., New Eng. Psychol. Assn., Eastern Psychol. Assn., Conn. Acad. Arts and Scis., Phi Beta Kappa. Congregationalist. Home: 11 Long Ln Middletown CT 06457-4046 Office: Wesleyan U Dept Psychology Middletown CT 06457

SCHEIBEL, ARNOLD BERNARD, psychiatrist, educator, research director; b. N.Y.C., Jan. 18, 1923; s. William and Ethel (Greenberg) S.; m. Madge Mila Ragland, Mar. 3, 1950 (dec. Jan. 1977); m. Marian Diamond, Sept. 1982. B.A., Columbia U., 1944, M.D., 1946; M.S., U. Ill., 1952. Intern Mt. Sinai Hosp., N.Y.C., 1946-47; resident psychiatry Barnes and McMillan Hosp., St. Louis, 1947-48, Ill. Neuropsychiat. Inst., Chgo., 1950-52; asst. prof. psychiatry and anatomy U. Tenn. Med. Sch., 1952-53, assoc. prof., 1953-55; assoc. prof. UCLA Med. Center, 1955-67, prof. psychiatry and anatomy, 1967—, mem. Brain Rsch. Inst., 1960—, acting dir. Brain Rsch. Inst., 1987-90, dir., 1990-95; cons. VA hosps., Los Angeles, 1956—. Contbr. numerous articles to tech. jours, chpts. to books.; editorial bd.: Brain

Research, 1967-77, Developmental Psychobiology, 1968—, Internat. Jour. Neurosci., 1969—, Jour. Biol. Psychiatry, 1968—, Jour. Theoretical Biology, 1980—. Mem. Pres.'s Commn. on Aging, Nat. Inst. Aging, 1980—. Served with AUS, 1943-46; from lt. to capt. M.C. AUS, 1948-50. Guggenheim fellow (with wife), 1953-54, 59. Fellow Am. Acad. Arts and Scis., Norwegian Acad. Scis., Am. Psychiat. Assn. (lifetime); mem. AAAS, Am. Neurol. Assn., Soc. Neuorosci., Pyschiat. Rsch. Assn. Am. Assn. Anatomists, Soc. Biol. Psychiatry, So. Calif. Psychiat. Assn. Home: 16231 Morrison St Encino CA 91436-1331 Office: Dept of Med Research UCLA Los Angeles CA 90024 *Intense personal tragedy can embitter life and choke off further personal creativity. It may also offer the opportunity to open new doors in the discovery of self. I am more aware than ever of my good fortune in having the opportunity to teach, to continue investigative work in the structure and function of the brain, and to give love and care to those who need it. I am more than ever convinced that loving and being loved is the greatest good that we can know, the state in which we most nearly fulfill our roles as human beings.*

SCHEIBEL, JAMES ALLEN, volunteer service executive; b. St. Paul, Aug. 30, 1947; s. Donald Louis and Beverly Wanda (Call) Urista; m. Mary Pat Lee, July 10, 1987.. AA, Nazareth Hall, 1967; BA, St. John's U., 1969; Hon. Doctorate, Coll. St. Catherine, 1993. City coun. aide to Joanne Showalter St. Paul, 1978-79; vol. 15th anniversary VISTA, 1979-80; v.p. Mondale's Youth Employment Task Force, Washington, 1980-81; assoc. dir. Citizen Heritage Ctr., St. Paul, 1981-82; city coun. mem. City of St. Paul, 1982-89, mayor, 1990-94; v.p., dir. domestic vol. svc. programs Corp. Nat. Svc., Washington, 1994—; mem. nat. adv. coun. Ctr. for Global Orgn., 1990—; chmn. U.S. Conf. of Mayors Task Force on Hunger, 1990-94; mem. Lifelong Literacy Project, St. Paul, 1990-94; mem., bd. dirs. Nat. Law Ctr. on Homelessness and Poverty. Mem. Partnership for Democracy, Washington, 1988-91. Recipient Spurgeon award, 1985, Am. Jewish Com. Humanitarian award, 1990, Chip Fricke award Nagasaki Sister City Com., 1993, Bravo award St. Paul C. of C., 1993. Office: Corp for Nat Svc Office of CEO Domestic Volunteer Svc Program 1201 New York Ave NW Washington DC 20525-3917*

SCHEIBEL, KENNETH MAYNARD, journalist; b. Campbell, Nebr., May 17, 1920; s. G. Alfred and Rachel Christine (Koch) S.; m. Helen Schmitt, May 14, 1955 (div. Sept. 1977); children: Victor Warren Schmitt, William Becker Schmitt, Kenneth Jr., Sally. Student, George Washington U., 1938-41; BA, U. Va., 1947, MA, 1949. Mag. salesman Periodical Pubs. Service Bur., Inc., 1935-38; reporter Internat. News Service, Washington, 1940-41, Wall St. Jour., Washington, 1949-51; Washington corr. Gannett Newspapers, 1951-63; syndicated columnist N.Am. Newspaper Alliance, 1963-64; chief Washington bur. Donrey Media Group, 1964-67; founder, bur. chief Washington Bur. News, 1967—; founder nat. syndicated column Washington Farm Beat, 1970-85; Washington corr. Wis. State Jour., 1963-66, LaCrosse (Wis.) Tribune, 1963-66, Billings (Mont.) Gazette, 1964-71, V.I. Network, 1966-67, Moline (Ill.) Daily Dispatch, 1967-68, Drovers' Jour., 1967-68, Newport News (Va.) Daily Press & Times Herald, 1969-71, Packer Pub. Co., 1964-74, Gasoline Retailer, 1966-67, Okla., Farmer Stockman; congl. corr. F-D-C Reports, 1975-77; Washington columnist Farm Jour., 1960-75; covered nat. polit. convs., campaigns; v.p. Fraser Assos. (public relations), Washington, 1976-79; Congl. broadcast interviewer. Contbr. nat. mags., newspaper syndicates. Incorporator War Meml. of Korea, Washington, 1981; editor Nat. Ctr. Fin. and Econ. Info., U.S.-Saudi Arabian Joint Econ. Commn., Riyadh, 1985-86. Capt. AUS, 1941-46, 755th Tank Bn., 1942-45, Europe, North Africa, Italy. Decorated Bronze star, U.S. Army Occupation medal, Combat Infantryman badge; co-recipient Croix De Guerre (France), Thoth award for excellence in pub. rels., 1980. Mem. Izaak Walton League Am., White House Corrs. Assn., Overseas Press Club of Am., Am. Radio Relay League, Sigma Chi. Presbyn. Clubs: Nat. Press (Washington) (financial sec., gov. 1969-73, vice chmn. bd. 1971), dir. Nat. Press Bldg. Corp. (Washington) (1973, v.p., pres. club and bldg. corp. 1974). Home: 1325 18th St NW Apt 302 Washington DC 20036-6505 *The greatest sins are timidity and self indulgence, the greatest virtue is to love. Live each day, don't fret about yesterday or tomorrow. Enjoy the senses, learn from others, and never forget that both love and hate are returned.*

SCHEIBER, HARRY N., law educator; b. N.Y.C., 1935. BA, Columbia U., 1955; MA, Cornell U., 1957, PhD, 1961; MA (hon.), Dartmouth Coll., 1965. instr. to assoc. prof. history Dartmouth Coll., 1960-68, prof., 1968-71; prof. Am. history U. Calif., San Diego, 1971-80; prof. law Boalt Hall, U. Calif., Berkeley, 1980—, chmn. jurisprudence and social policy program, 1982-84, 90-93, assoc. dean, 1990-93, 95—; The Stefan Riesenfeld Prof., 1991—; vice chair Univ. Academic Senate, 1993-94. chair, 1994-95; Fulbright disting. sr. lectr., Australia, 1983, marine affairs coord. Calif. Sea Grant Coll. Program, 1989—; vis. rsch. prof. Law Inst. U. Uppsala, Sweden, 1995. Chmn. Littleton Griswold Prize Legal History, 1985-88; pres. N.H. Civil Liberties Union, 1969-70; chmn. Project '87 Task Force on Pub. Programs, Washington, 1982-85; dir. Berkeley Seminar on Federalism, 1986—; cons. judiciary study U.S. Adv. Commn. Intergovernmental Rels., 1985-88; dir. NEH Inst. on Constitutionalism, U. Calif., Berkeley, 1986-87, 88-91. Recipient Sea Grant Colls. award, 1981-83, 84-85, 86-96; fellow Ctr. Advanced Study in Behavioral Scis., Stanford Calif., 1967, 71; Guggenheim fellow, 1971, 88; Rockefeller Found. humanities fellow, 1979, NEH fellow, 1985-86; NSF grantee, 1979, 80, 88-89; Fellow U. Calif. Humanities Rsch. Inst., 1989. Mem. Am. Hist. Assn., Orgn. Am. Historians, Am. Soc. Intl. Law, Agrl. History Soc. (pres. 1978), Econ. History Assn. (trustee 1978-80), Law and Soc. Assn. (trustee 1979-81), Am. Soc. Legal History (dir. 1982-86, 90—), Nat. Assessment History and Citizenship Edn. (chmn. nat. acad. bd. 1986-87), Marine Affairs and Policy Assn. (bd. dirs. 1991—), Ocean Governance Study Group (steering com. 1991—), Internat. Coun. Environ. Law. Author numerous books including: (with L. Friedman) American Law and the Constitutional Order, 1978, 2d edit. 1988; contbr. articles to law revs.and social sci. jours., 1963—. Office: U Calif Berkeley Law Sch Boalt Hall Berkeley CA 94720-2150

SCHEIBER, STEPHEN CARL, psychiatrist; b. N.Y.C., May 2, 1938; s. Irving Martin and Frieda Olga (Schor) S.; m. Mary Ann McDonnell, Sept. 14, 1965; children: Lisa Susan, Martin Irving, Laura Ann. BA, Columbia Coll., 1960; MD, SUNY, Buffalo, 1964. Diplomate Am. Bd. Psychiatry and Neurology. Intern Mary Fletcher Hosp., Burlington, Vt., 1964-65; resident in psychiatry Strong Meml. Hosp., Rochester, N.Y., 1967-70; asst. prof. U. Ariz., Tucson, 1970-76, assoc. prof., 1976-81, prof., 1981-86; exec. sec. Am. Bd. Psychiatry and Neurology, Inc., Deerfield, Ill., 1986-89; exec. v.p. Am. Bd. Psychiatry and Neurology, Inc., 1989—; adj. prof. psychiatry Northwestern U., Chgo. and Evanston, 1986—, Med. Coll. Wis., Milw., 1986—. Co-editor: The Impaired Physician, 1983, Certification, Recertification and Lifetime Learning in Psychiatry, 1994; contbr. articles to profl. jours. Mem. med. adv. com. Casas de los Ninos, Tucson, 1974-86; mem. mental health adv. com. Tucson Health Planning Coun., 1974-75; med. student interviewer Office of Med. Edn., 1975; mem. Glenbrook (Ill.) Norht H.S. Boosters Club, 1988-91; treas. Robert E. Jones Found., 1988-96. Surgeon USPHS, 1965-67. Grantee Group Therapy Outcome Studies on Inpatient Service, 1980, Dialysis and Schizophrenia Pilot Project NIH, 1978; recipient Outstanding Tchr. award U. Ariz., 1986. Fellow Am. Psychiat. Assn. (chmn. imparied physician com. 1985-88, cons. 1988-92), Am. Coll. Psychiatrists (bd. regents 1992—, treas. 1995—), Am. Assn. Dirs. Psychiat. Residency Tng. (pres. 1981-82), Assn. Acad. Psychiatry (Parliamentary sec. 1979*84, treas. 1984-88, pres.-elect 1988-89, pres. 1989-90), Group for Advancement of Psychiatry (invited mem., chmn. mem. edn. com. 1987-91, bd. dirs., sec. 1993—), Oracle Heights Club (pres. 1983-84). Democrat. Jewish. Office: Am Bd Psychiatry & Neurology 500 Lake Cook Rd Ste 335 Deerfield IL 60015-4939

SCHEICH, JOHN F., lawyer; b. Bklyn., Aug. 6, 1942; s. Frank A. and Dorothy (O'Hara) S. BA, St. John's U., N.Y.C., 1963, JD, 1966; postgrad., John Marshall Law Sch., Chgo., 1968. Bar: N.Y. 1967, U.S. Ct. Internat. Trade Admission 1969, U.S. Dist. Ct. (ea. and so. dists.) N.Y. 1971, U.S. Ct. Appeals (2d cir.) 1971, U.S. Supreme Ct. 1975, Pa. 1980. Spl. agt. FBI U.S. Dept. Justice, Washington, 1966-69; asst. dist. atty. Queens County, Kew Gardens, N.Y., 1969-72; pvt. practice John F. Scheich, P.C., Richmond Hill, N.Y., 1970-76, 79-91; ptnr. Raia & Scheich, P.C., Richmond Hill, N.Y., 1976-79; sr. ptnr. Scheich & Goldsmith, P.C., Richmond Hill, N.Y., 1991-95, Scheich, Goldsmith & Dreishpoon, P.C., Richmond Hill and Hicksville, N.Y., 1996—; lectr. estate planning Nat. Bus. Inst., 1994; mem. assigned counsel panel for indigent defendants in major felony and murder cases 9th and 11th jud. dists. N.Y. State Supreme Ct., Queens County, 1972-94; lectr. Lawyers in the Classroom, 1979-91; chmn. arbitration panel Civil Ct. City of N.Y., 1981-90; bd. dirs. Ra-Li Brokerage Corp., v.p., 1975—; mem. adv. bd. 1st Am. Title Ins. Co. Am., 1995—. Editor: Conashaugh Courier, 1989-92; mem. editorial bd., 1988-92; contbg. columnist, 1981-89. Mem. Com. for Beautification of East Norwich, N.Y., 1983—, bd. dirs., 1993—; pres. local chpt. Holy Name Soc., 1971-73; bd. dirs. Conashaugh Lakes Cmty. Assn., Milford, Pa., 1981-90, organizing mem. Conashaugh Lakes owners interim com., 1977-81, sec. 1981-82, v.p. 1982-84, pres. 1984-86, past pres. 1986-88; mem. St. Edward's Syosset, N.Y. Sch. Bd., 1986-90; mem. parish coun. Our Lady of Perpetual Help, 1976-82, pres. 1978-80, mem. fin. com., adv. to pastor, 1970-82, chmn. fin. com., 1979-82; bd. dirs. Northslope II Homeowners Assn., Shawnee-on-Delaware, Pa., 1988-90, 92-94; mem. East Norwich Rep. Club, 1982—, bd. dirs. 1984-87, 93—, v.p. 1987-89, pres. 1989-93; nat. trust and estate assoc. Meml. Sloane Kettering Cancer Ctr., 1994—; active Internat. Wine Ctr., 1985—, St. Edward the Confessor Ch., Syosset, N.Y., 1982—, St. Vincent Ch., Dingman Hills, Pa., 1977—, St. Dominic's Ch., Oyster Bay, N.Y., 1982—, Lincoln Ctr. Performing Arts, Inc., 1985—, Nat. Rep. Senatorial Com., 1988—, Bravo Soc., 1994—, Concern for Dying, 1984—, Sea Cliff Chamber Players, 1992—; mem. Nassau County Rep. Com., 1993—, St. John Vianney Roman Catholic Ch., St. Pete Beach, Fla., 1994—, Performing Arts Ctr. Pinellas County, St. Petersburg, Fla., 1994—. Recipient J. Edgar Hoover award, 1967, award of appreciation, Civil Trial Inst., St. John's U. Sch. of Law, 1991, 95, Disting. Svc. award, 1992, cert. of appreciaiton Conashaugh Lakes Cmty. Assn., 1990, Dist. Svc. award Kiwanis Club, 1992, Cert. of Merit for Disting. Svc. award Nassau County Exec. Hon. Thomas Gulotta, 1989, Presdl. Order of Merit award Pres. George Bush, 1991, Order of Merit award Nat. Rep. Senatorial Com., 1994; named one of Best Trial Lawyers in the U.S., Town and Country mag., 1985. Mem. ABA (cert. of appreciation Am. Bar Endowment 1992), ATLA, Pa. State Bar Assn., N.Y. State Bar Assn., Queens County Bar Assn., Nassau County Bar Assn., N.Y. State Trial Lawyers Assn., Ciminal Cts. Bar Assn., Internat. Platform Assn., John Marshall Lawyers Assn. (bd. dirs., pres. 1992—), Soc. Former Spl. Agts. of FBI, N.Y. State Assn. Criminal Def. Lawyers, St. John's Coll. Alumni Assn., Asst. Dist. Attys. Assn. Queens County, St. John's U. Sch. of Law Alumni Assn., St. John's Prep. Sch. Alumni Assn., Friends of the Arts of Nassau County, Inc., Cath. Lawyers Guild of Queens County, N.Y., KC, Phi Alpha Delta. Avocation: collecting fine wines. Home: 170 Sugar Toms Ln East Norwich NY 11732-1153 Office: Scheich Goldsmith & Dreishpoon PC 103-42 Lefferts Blvd Richmond Hill NY 11419-2012 also: 109 Newbridge Rd Hicksville NY 11801-3908 also: 3901 Conashaugh Trl Box 4042, Conashaugh Lakes Milford PA 18337

SCHEIDERER, PHYLLIS JACKSON, nursing administrator; b. Columbus, Ohio, Jan. 4, 1935; d. Ped Wilbur and Clara Maxine (Shopshear) Jackson; m. Reinhard C. Scheiderer, Nov. 27, 1955; children: John P., George C. Diploma in nursing tech., Marion (Ohio) Tech. Coll., 1984; student, Capitol U. RN, Ohio; cert. correctional health profl. Nursing supr. Ohio Reformatory for Women, Marysville; adminstr. health care, dir. nursing Franklin Pre-Release Ctr., Columbus; mem. nurses edn. com. Ohio Dept. Rehab. and Corrections; cert. AIDS counselor Franklin Pre-Release Ctr. Vol. Health Check, Delaware, Ohio, Columbus, 1988, 89, 90, Teddy Bear Day, Columbus Zoo; mem. Women's Health Network, Columbus. Recipient Dorothy Cornealous award Mid Ohio Dist. Nurses Assn., 1995. Mem. ANA (continuing edn. ind. rev. panelist), Ohio Nurses Assn. (legis. liaison), Mid.-Ohio Nurses Assn. (membership and media rels. com.), Am. Correctional Assn., Am. Correctional Health Svcs. Assn., Aids Svc. Connection, Take it to the Streets Found.

SCHEIDT, W. ROBERT, chemistry educator, researcher; b. Richmond Heights, Mo., Nov. 13, 1942; s. Walter Martin and Martha (Videtich) S.; m. Kathryn Sue Barnes, Aug. 9, 1964; children: Karl Andrew, David Martin. BS, U. Mo., 1964; MS, U. Mich., 1965, PhD, 1968; postdoctoral studies, Cornell U., 1970. Asst. prof. U. Notre Dame, Ind., 1970-76, assoc. prof., 1976-80, prof., 1980—; vis. prof. U. Wash., Seattle, 1980, U. Paris (Orsay), France, 1991; mem. review sect. Metallobiochemistry NIH, Bethesda, 1991—. Contbr. articles to profl. jours. Fellow AAAS; mem. Am. Chem. Soc. (assoc. editor Chem. Revs. jour. 1980-85), Am. Crystallographic Assn., Sigma X. Democrat. Office: U Notre Dame Dept Chemisty Notre Dame IN 46556

SCHEIE, PAUL OLAF, physics educator; b. Marietta, Minn., June 24, 1933; s. Olaf Johan and Selma Pricilla (Varhus) S.; m. Mary Anna Harrison, May 18, 1963; children—Eric, Maren. B.A., St. Olaf Coll., Northfield, Minn., 1955; M.S., U. N.Mex., 1957; Ph.D., Pa. State U., 1965. Asst. prof. physics Oklahoma City U., 1958-63; asst. prof. biophysics Pa. State U., State Coll., 1965-73; prof. physics Tex. Luth. Coll., Seguin, 1973—, interim acad. dean, 1976. Contbr. articles to profl. publs. Recipient Faculty Alumni award, Tex. Luth. Coll., 1985. Mem. Biophys. Soc., AAAS, Am. Assn. Physics Tchrs., Royal Micros. Soc., Sigma Xi. Lutheran. Lodge: Lions. Avocations: woodworking, gardening. Home: 207 Leonard Seguin TX 78155-5110 Office: Tex Luth Coll 1000 W Court St Seguin TX 78155-5978

SCHEIFLY, JOHN EDWARD, retired lawyer; b. Mexico, Mo., Aug. 25, 1925; s. Luke Clauser and Isabella (Sprankle) S.; m. Patricia Ann Lenhart, Dec. 27, 1947; children: John Edward, Jan Ellen. Sc.B., Brown U., 1945; J.D., Washington and Lee U., 1948. Bar: W.Va. 1948, Calif. 1954. Practice law L.A., 1953—; mem. firm Baker, Scheifly & Porter, Huntington, W.Va., 1949-53, McClean, Salisbury, Petty & McClean, L.A., 1953-57, Willis, Butler, Scheifly, Leydorf & Grant (and predecessors), L.A., 1958-81, Bryan, Cave, McPheeters & McRoberts, L.A., 1981-84; mem. firm Morgan, Lewis & Bockius, L.A., 1984-90, counsel, 1990—; lectr. tax law U. So. Calif., 1960-74. Author lectr. fed. tax matters profl. publs., insts. Dir. Presbyn. Intercommunity Hosp., Whittier, Calif., 1994—. Lt. USNR, 1943-46, 51-53. Mem. ABA (mem. coun. sect. taxation 1974-77), State Bar Calif., Los Angeles County Bar Assn. (chmn. tax sect. 1965-66), Jonathan Club (L.A.), Hacienda Golf Club (LaHabra, Calif.), Monterey Country Club (Palm Desert, Calif.). Home: 9441 Friendly Woods Ln Whittier CA 90605-1658 Office: Morgan Lewis & Bockius 801 S Grand Ave Los Angeles CA 90017-4613

SCHEIMAN, EUGENE R., lawyer; b. Bklyn., July 15, 1943. BA, L.I. U., 1966; JD cum laude, Bklyn. Law Sch., 1969. Bar: N.Y. 1970, U.S. Dist. Ct. (so. and ea. dists.) N.Y. 1971, U.S. Ct. Appeals (1st cir.) 1972, U.S. Ct. Appeals (5th cir.) 1973, U.S. Ct. Appeals (4th cir.) 1974, U.S. Supreme Ct. 1976, U.S. Ct. Appeals (2nd cir.) 1977, U.S. Ct. Appeals (fed. cir.), U.S. Ct. Appeals (11th cir.) 1989, U.S. Ct. Appeals (3rd cir.) 1990. Mem. Baer Marks & Upham, N.Y.C. Rsch. editor Bklyn. Law Rev., 1968, editor-in-chief, 1969. Mem. ABA (sect. on individual rights and responsibilities), N.Y. State Bar Assn., Assn. Bar. City of N.Y. (mem. com. comm. and media law), Philonomic Honor Soc. Office: Baer Marks & Upham 805 3rd Ave New York NY 10022-7513

SCHEIMER, LOUIS, film and television producer; b. Pitts., Oct. 19, 1928; s. Sam and Lena (Kessler) S.; m. Jay Wucher, Dec. 29, 1953; children—Lane, Erika. BFA, Carnegie Inst. Tech., 1952. With various animation studios, 1955-62; founder, pres. Filmation Studios, Woodland Hills, Calif., 1962-89; pres. Lou Scheimer Prodns., Woodland Hills, Calif., 1989—. Producer: (animated TV programs) Archie, 1968, Fat Albert, 1972 (Wilbur award, Scott Newman Drug Abuse Prevention award 1985), Star Trek, 1973 (Emmy award 1974), Isis, 1975, Tarzan, 1976, Space Academy, 1977, He-Man and Masters of the Universe, 1983, She-Ra Princess of Power, 1985, Ghostbusters, 1986, BraveStarr, 1987, Arch Angels, 1995 (feature film) Pinocchio and the Emperor of the Night, 1987, Happily Ever After, 1989. Recipient Christopher award, 1972, Emmy award, 1979. Mem. Nat. Acad. TV Arts and Scis., Motion Picture Acad. Jewish. Office: Lou Scheimer Prodns 20300 Ventura Blvd Ste 145 Woodland Hills CA 91364

SCHEIN, EDGAR HENRY, management educator; b. Zurich, Switzerland, Mar. 5, 1928; came to U.S., 1939, naturalized, 1944; s. Marcel and Hilde (Schoenbeck) S.; m. Mary Louise Lodmell, July 28, 1956; children—Louisa, Elizabeth, Peter. Ph.B., U. Chgo., 1946, B.A., 1947; B.A., Stanford U., 1948, M.A., 1949; Ph.D., Harvard U., 1953. Teaching asst. statistics Stanford U., 1947-49; teaching asst. social psychology Harvard U., 1949-52; research psychologist, neuropsychiatry div. Walter Reed Army Inst. Research, also chief social psychology sect., 1952-56; mem. faculty MIT, 1956—, prof. orgnl. psychology and mgmt., 1964—, chmn. orgn. studies group Sloan Sch. Mgmt., 1972-81, Sloan Fellows prof. mgmt., 1978—; mem. bd., exec. com. Nat. Tng. Labs., 1962-64; cons. to govt. and industry, 1956—. Author books and articles in field. Served to capt. AUS, 1950-56. Recipient Aux. Research award Social Sci. Research Council, 1958. Mem. Am. Psychol. Assn., Am. Sociol. Assn., Phi Beta Kappa, Sigma Xi. Office: MIT Sloan Sch Mgmt Cambridge MA 02139

SCHEIN, HARVEY L., communications executive; b. N.Y.C., Sept. 15, 1927; s. Morris and Matilda (Feld) S.; m. Joy Carol Gitlin, Dec. 11, 1963; children: Mark David, Justin Harris. A.B., NYU, 1949; LL.B., Harvard U., 1952. Bar: N.Y. 1953. Asso. Rosenman, Colin, Kaye, Petschek & Freund, N.Y.C., 1952-58; gen. atty. Columbia Records div. CBS, also asst. sec. CBS, 1958-60, div. v.p. internat., 1961-67; pres. CBS Internat. div., 1968-71, CBS Columbia Group, 1971-72; pres., chief exec. officer Sony Corp. Am., 1972-77, chmn., 1977-78; exec. v.p. Warner Communications Inc., 1978-80; pres. Warner Plays, Inc., 1978-80; pres., chief exec. officer Polygram Corp., 1980-83; exec. v.p., dir. News America Pub. Inc., 1983-88; pres., chief exec. officer Skyband Inc., 1983-88; v.p., bd. dirs. Internat. Fedn. Phonographic Industries, 1969-73; mem. Marconi Internat. Fellowship Council; mem. adv. council Partners of the Americas; asst. sec. Franklin D. Roosevelt Found., 1952-58. Editor: Harvard Law Rev., 1951-52. Served with USNR, 1945. Mem. Phi Beta Kappa.

SCHEIN, PHILIP SAMUEL, physician, educator, pharmaceutical executive; b. Asbury Park, N.J., May 10, 1939; s. Irving and Henrietta (Setzer) S.; m. Dorothy Rosenfeld, May 28, 1967; children: Deborah, Andrew. A.B., Rutgers U., 1961; M.D., SUNY, Syracuse, 1965. Diplomate Am. Bd. Internal Medicine (chmn. med. oncology com. 1980-83). Intern Beth Israel Hosp., Boston, 1966-68, resident, 1968-69, 70-71; sr. house officer Radcliffe Infirmary, Oxford, Eng., 1969-70; instr. medicine Harvard U., 1970-71; sr. investigator Nat. Cancer Inst., Bethesda, Md., 1971-74, head clin. pharm. sect., 1973-74; dir. div. med. oncology Georgetown U. Hosp., 1974-83; sci. dir. Georgetown U. Cancer Ctr., 1974-83; v.p. clin. R & D worldwide Smith Kline and French Labs., Phila., 1983-86; chmn., CEO U.S. Biosci., 1987—; cons. oncology Walter Reed Gen. Hosp., Washington, 1971-84, Clin. Ctr., NIH, 1971-84; assoc. prof. medicine and pharmacology Georgetown U., 1974-77, prof., 1977—; adj. prof. medicine Brown U., 1983—, medicine and pharmacology U. Penn., 1983-, pharmacology Temple U., 1984—; mem. Nat. Pancreatic Cancer Project, 1974-79; chmn. Gastrointestinal Tumor Study Group, 1974-83; FDA adv. com. on oncology drugs, 1979-81, Mid-Atlantic Oncology Program; mem. Nat. Cancer Adv. Bd., 1994—. Fellow Royal Soc. Medicine, ACP, Royal Coll. Physicians London, Royal Coll. Physicians Glasgow; mem. Am. Soc. Clin. Oncology (bd. dirs. 1979-83, pres. 1983), Am. Assn. Cancer Research, Am. Soc. Clin. Investigation, Am. Soc. Hematology, Assn. Am. Physicians, Am. Soc. Clin. Pharmacology Therapeutics, Sigma Xi, Alpha Omega Alpha. Club: Union League. Research on mechanisms of action of cancer chemotherapy drugs, prediction and prevention drug toxicity, treatment malignant and hematologic diseases. Office: US Bioscience 100 Front St West Conshohocken PA 19428-2800

SCHEIN, VIRGINIA ELLEN, psychologist; b. Rahway, N.J., June 23, 1943; d. Jacob Charles and Anne S.; m. Rupert F. Chisholm. BA cum laude, Cornell U., 1965; PhD, N.Y.U., 1969. Lic. psychologist, Pa. 1 child, Alexander Nikos. Sr. research assoc. Am. Mgmt. Assn., N.Y.C., 1969-70; mgr. personnel research Life Office Mgmt. Assn., N.Y.C., 1970-72; dir. personnel research Met. Life Ins. Co. N.Y.C., 1972-75; asso. prof. Sch. Mgmt. Case Western Res. U., Cleve., 1975-76; vis. asso. prof. Sch. Orgn. and Mgmt., Yale U., New Haven, 1976-77; assoc. prof. mgmt. Wharton Sch. U. Pa., Phila., 1977-80; mgmt. cons. Virginia E. Schein, PhD, P.C., 1975—; assoc. prof. psychology Bernard M. Baruch Coll., City U. N.Y., 1982-85; prof. mgmt. Gettysburg Coll., Pa., 1986—, chair mgmt. dept., 1993-95. Co-author: Power and Organization Development, 1988; Author: Working from the Margins, 1995; mem. editorial rev. bds. Women Mgmt. Rev., Acad. Mgmt. Execs.; contbr. articles to profl. jours. Bd. dirs. Keystone Rsch. Ctr., Family Planning Ctr., Survivors, Inc., past pres. bd.; bd. dirs. Pvt. Industry Coun. Mem. Am. Psychol. Assn. (council reps. 1978-80, com. on women 1980-83), Met. Assn. Applied Psychology (pres. 1973-74), Acad. Mgmt., (rep. orgn. devel. div. 1979-81, mem. exec. com. women mgmt. divsn.), Internat. Assn. Applied Psychology, Am. Psychol. Soc., Psi Chi. Office: Gettysburg Coll Dept Mgmt Gettysburg PA 17325

SCHEINBAUM, DAVID, photography educator; b. Bklyn., Apr. 14, 1951; s. Louis and Rhoda (Feerman) S.; m. Vicki Golden, May 30, 1973 (div. 1975); m. Janet Ann Goldberg-Russek, Mar. 21, 1982; stepchildren: Jonathan Russek, Andra Russek; 1 child, Zachary. BA, CUNY, 1973. Instr. photography Pace U., N.Y.C., 1974-75, LaGuardia (N.Y.) Community Coll., 1975-78; assoc. prof. art Coll. Santa Fe, 1979-81, 82—, assoc. prof. of art photography, 1981—; full prof., 1996—; printer, asst. to Beaumont Newhall, Santa Fe, 1980-93; printer to Eliot Porter, Santa Fe, 1980-90; co-dir. Scheinbaum & Russek, Ltd., Santa Fe, 1979—. Author: (photographs) Bisti, 1987, Miami Beach: Photographs of an American Dream, 1990; photography exhbns. include Pace U., 1974, Midtown Y Gallery, N.Y., 1977, Santa Fe Gallery for Photography, 1979, 81, The Armory for the Arts, Santa Fe, 1980, 1981, Sea Breeze Gallery, Block Island, R.I., 1982, Highlands U., Las Vegas, N.Mex., 1982, Gov's. Gallery, Santa Fe, 1982, Santa Fe Festival for the Arts, 1982, Coll. Santa Fe, 1983, Dem. Conv., San Francisco, 1984, Mus. Natural History, Albuquerque, Bisti/Miami Beach Photogroup Coral Gables, Fla., 1990, Ctr. Met. Studies U. Mo., St. Louis, 1988, Earthscope Expo '90 Photo Mus., Osaka, Japan, 1990, Jamestown C.C., N.Y., 1990, Neikrug Photo Gallery Internat., Tokyo, 1987; in permanent collections Norton Gallery Mus., West Palm Beach, Fla, Amon Carter Mus., Ft. Worth, N.Mex. State U., Las Cruces, Ctr. Creative Photography, Tucson, Ariz., Mus. Fine Arts, Santa Fe, Bklyn. Mus., U. Okla., Norman, Bibliothèque Nationale France, Paris, Gernsheim Collection. U. Tex., Austin, Albuquerque Mus., Rockwell Mus., Corning, N.Y., Chase Manhattan Bank, N.Y. Pub. Libr., Fogg Art Mus., Harvard U., Met. Mus. Art, N.Y.C., Frito-Lay Collection, Kans. City, Expo 90 Photo Mus., Osaka, Coll. Art Gallery, SUNY, New Paltz, N.Y., Univ. Art Mus., U. N.Mex. Inducted Wall of Fame Kingsborough C.C., N.Y., 1994. Mem. N.Mex. Coun. on Photography (founder, v.p., bd. dirs.), Santa Fe Ctr. Photography (bd. dirs. 1978-85). Jewish. Home: 369 Montezuma Ave # 345 Santa Fe NM 87501-2626 Office: Coll Santa Fe Saint Michaels Dr Santa Fe NM 87501

SCHEINBERG, LABE CHARLES, physician, educator; b. Memphis, Dec. 11, 1925; m. Louise Goldman, Jan. 6, 1952: children: Susan, David, Ellen, Amy. A.B., U. N.C., 1945; M.D., U. Tenn., 1948. Intern Wesley Meml. Hosp., Chgo., 1949; resident psychiatry Elgin (Ill.) State Hosp., 1950; resident, asst. neurology Neurol. Inst., N.Y., 1952-56; mem. faculty Albert Einstein Coll. Medicine, 1956-93, prof. neurology, asst. dean, 1968-69, assoc. dean, 1969-70, prof. rehab. medicine and psychiatry, dean, 1970-72; dir. neurology Hosp., 1966-73; dir. dept. neurology and psychiatry St. Barnabas Hosp., Bronx, N.Y., 1974-79; prof. neurology Mt. Sinai Med. ctr., N.Y.C., 1993—. Cons. editor: N.Y. Acad. Scis., 1964, 84; founding editor-in-chief Jour. Neurologic Rehab., Rehab. Reports, Multiple Sclerosis Rsch. Reports. Served as capt. M.C. USAF, 1951-52. Fellow Am. Acad. Neurology; mem. Am. Neurol. Assn., Am. Assn. Neuro-pathology, Am. Soc. Exptl. Pathology, Phi Beta Kappa, Alpha Omega Alpha. Home: 9 Oak Ln Scarsdale NY 10583-1621 Office: Mt Sinai Med Ctr 5 E 98th St New York NY 10029-6501

SCHEINBERG, PERITZ, neurologist; b. Miami, Fla., Dec. 21, 1920; s. Mendel and Esther Dobrisch (Asch) S.; m. Chantal D'Adesky, Mar. 12, 1971; children: Philip Asch, Richard David, Marissa. A.B. in Chemistry, Emory U., 1941, M.D., 1944. Diplomate: Am. Bd. Internal Medicine, Am. Bd. Psychiatry and Neurology. Intern Grady Hosp., Atlanta, 1944-45; resident in internal medicine and neurology Grady Hosp. and Duke U. Hosp., 1946-50; research asst. prof. physiology U. Miami Med. Research Unit, Miami, Fla., 1950-53; asso. prof. neurology U. Miami Med. Research Unit, 1955-57, prof. neurology, 1957—; chmn. dept. neurology U. Miami Sch. Medicine, 1961—. Author, editor books in field.; contbr. articles to profl. jours. Served with M.C. USNR, 1945-46, 53-55. Fellow ACP, Am. Acad. Neurology; mem. Am. Neurol. Assn. (pres. 1981), Assn. Univ. Profs. Neurology (pres. 1977-78), Am. Heart Assn., Nat. Multiple Sclerosis Soc.

(mem. med. adv. bd.). Democrat. Jewish. Office: U Miami Jackson Meml Med Ctr 1611 NW 12th Ave Miami FL 33136-1005

SCHEINBERG, STEVEN ELIOT, investment banker; b. N.Y.C., Mar. 2, 1952; s. Arnold Lewis and Mildred (Schapira) S.; m. Robin Scheinberg; children: Michael Aaron and Andrew Ross (twins), Rachel Lillian. BA in Econs., U. Conn., 1973, MA in Econs., 1976; cert. in real estate, NYU, 1980. Economist Conn. Gen. Assembly, Hartford, 1975-77; dir. mcpl. bond research Shearson Hayden Stone, N.Y.C., 1977-79; sr. assoc. Matthews and Wright Inc., N.Y.C., 1979-80; v.p., dir. mcpl. bond rsch. Shearson/Am. Express, N.Y.C., 1980-82; v.p., dir. equity rsch. S.D. Cohn and Co., N.Y.C., 1982-83; v.p., chief fin. officer Audre Inc., San Diego, 1983-85, also bd. dirs.; mng. dir., bd. dirs. RGS Capital Mgmt. Inc., N.Y.C., 1985-89; v.p., ltd. ptnr. Robert Sheridan and Ptnrs., Miami, Fla., 1989-92; cons. Miami, 1992—; sr. ptnr. Cambridge Capital Holdings. Adminstrv. chmn. bd. govs. U. Conn., 1971-72. Mass. Audubon Soc. fellow, 1974. Mem. Nat. Assn. Bus. Economists. Office: 801 Brickell Ave Ste 944 Miami FL 33131-2900

SCHEINDLIN, RAYMOND PAUL, Hebrew literature educator, translator; b. Phila., May 13, 1940; s. Irving and Betty (Bernstein) S.; m. Shira Ann Joffe, Mar. 1969 (div. 1981); children—Dov Baer, Dahlia Rachel; m. Janice Clair Meyerson, 1986. B.A., U. Pa., 1961; M.H.L., Jewish Theol. Sem., N.Y.C., 1963; Ph.D., Columbia U., N.Y.C., 1971. Ordained rabbi, 1965. Asst. prof. McGill U., Montreal, Que., Can., 1969-72; asst. prof. Cornell U., Ithaca, N.Y., 1972-74; assoc. prof. Jewish Theol. Sem. of Am., N.Y.C., 1974-85, prof. Hebrew lit., 1985—, provost, 1984-90; dir. Shalom Spiegel Inst. of Medieval Hebrew Lit., 1996—; rabbi Congregation Baith Israel Anshei Emes, Bklyn., 1979-82; mem. publ. com. Jewish Publ. Soc., Phila., 1985-90; mem. internat. adv. com. Ctr. for Judaic Studies U. Pa., 1995—; mem. bd. acad. advisors Catalan Mus. Jewish Culture, Gerona, Spain, 1993—; mem. editl. com. Jewish Quar. Rev., 1995—. Translator: (novella) Of Bygone Days by Mendele Mokher Seforim, 1973, Jewish Liturgy: A Comprehensive History by Ismar Elbogen, 1993; author: Form & Structure in the Poetry of Al-Mu'tamid Ibn 'Abbad, 1974, 201 Arabic Verbs, 1978, Wine, Women, and Death: Medieval Hebrew Poems on the Good Life, 1986, The Gazelle: Medieval Hebrew Poems on God, Israel and the Soul, 1991, (libretto) Miriam and the Angel of Death, 1984; mem. editorial com. Prooftexts, 1988—, Edebiyat, 1992—, Studies in Muslim-Jewish Relations, 1992—. Guggenheim fellow, 1988, Annenberg Inst. fellow, 1993; sr. assoc. fellow Oxford Centre for Postgrad. Hebrew Studies. Mem. Soc. for Judeo-Arabic Studies (exec. com.), World Union for Jewish Studies , Assn. Jewish Studies, Jewish Publ. Soc. (bd. dirs. 1987-93). Home: 420 Riverside Dr New York NY 10025-7773 Office: Jewish Theol Sem Am 3080 Broadway New York NY 10027-4650

SCHEINDLIN, SHIRA A., federal judge; b. Washington, Aug. 16, 1946; d. Boris and Miriam (Shapiro) Joffe; m. Stanley Friedman, May 22, 1982; 2 children. BA cum laude, U. Mich., 1967; MA in Far Ea. Studies, Columbia U., 1969; JD cum laude, Cornell U., 1975. Bar: N.Y. 1976. With Stroock, Stroock & Lavan, 1975-76; law clerk to Hon. Charles L. Brieant, Jr. U.S. Dist. Ct. (so. dist.) N.Y., 1976-77; asst. U.S. atty. Ea. Dist. N.Y., 1977-81; gen. counsel N.Y.C. Dept. of Investigation, 1981-82; U.S. magistrate U.S. Dist. Ct. (ea. dist.) N.Y., 1982-86; with Budd, Larner, Gross, Rosenbaum, Greenberg & Sade, Short Hills, N.J., 1986-90, ptnr., 1990; ptnr. Herzfeld & Rubin, N.Y.C., 1990-94; endispute mem. Judicial Panel, 1992-94; judge U.S. Dist. Ct. (so. dist.) N.Y., 1994—; adj. prof. law Bklyn. Law Sch., 1983—; mem. 2d Cir. Conf. Planning Com., So. Dist. Adv. Com., 1991-94. Recipient Spl. Achievement award Dept. of Justice, 1980. Mem. Fedn. Bar Coun. (trustee 1986-88, 90—, v.p. 1988-90), N.Y. State Bar Assn. (chair comml. and fed. litigation sect. 1991-92), N.Y. County Lawyers Assn. (bd. dirs. 1992-95, chair tort sect. 1992-94), Assn. of Bar of City of N.Y. Office: US Courthouse 500 Pearl St Rm 1050 New York NY 10007

SCHEINER, JAMES IRA, engineering company executive; b. Mpls., May 7, 1944; s. Samuel L. and Sally Scheiner; m. Kristin Scofield; children: Alec, Zachary, Meredith. BS in Civil Engring., U.S. Mil. Acad., 1965; MPA, MCE, Princeton U., 1967. Registered profl. engr., Pa. Cons., prin. transp. consulting divsn. Booz-Allen and Hamilton, 1971-79; dep. sec. adminstrn. Pa. Dept. Transp., 1979-83; sec. revenue Commonwealth of Pa., 1983-87; v.p. Huth Engrs., Inc., 1987-88; pres. Stoner Assocs., Inc., 1988-91; pres., COO Benatec Assocs., Inc., 1991—. Contbr. articles to profl. jours. Vice chair area bd. Leadership Harrisburg; group chair 1993 campaign cabinet capital region United Way; mem. Pa. Chamber Bus. and Industry Bd.; mem. Harsco Bd.; trustee Harrisburg Area C.C. Capt. CE, U.S. Army, Vietnam, 1967-71. Decorated Bronze Star, Purple Heart; recipient Disting. Svc. award Nat. Gov.'s Assn., 1986. Office: Benatec Assocs 101 Erford Rd Camp Hill PA 17011-1808

SCHEINFELD, JAMES DAVID, travel agency executive; b. Milw., Nov. 11, 1926; s. Aaron and Sylvia (Rosenberg) S.; children from previous marriage: John Stephen, Nancy Ellen, Robert Alan; m. Elna Magnusson, 1994. BA in Econs. magna cum laude, U. Wis., 1949. With Manpower, Inc., 1948-78, salesman, Chgo., 1949-51, br. mgr., 1951-53, nat. sales mgr., Milw., 1953-56, dir. sales, corp. sec., 1956-59, v.p. sales, 1959-62, exec. v.p. mktg., 1962-65, exec. v.p. (sr.), chief ops. officer, 1965-76, v.p. spl. projects, 1976-78, mem. exec. com., bd. dirs., 1959-76, cons., 1978-84; exec. v.p., chief exec. officer, bd. dirs. Transpersonal, Inc., Any Task Inc., Manpower Argentina, Manpower Europe, Manpower Ltd. (U.K.), Manpower Australia, Manpower Japan, Manpower Germany GmbH, Manpower Norway, Manpower Denmark, Manpower Venezuela, 1966-76; pres. Travway Internat. Inc. - Funway Holidays, Funjet, 1976-81, Aide Svcs., Inc., Tampa, Fla., 1976-81; pres., chief exec. officer Travelpower Inc., 1976-84; sr. v.p. Carlson Travel Network, 1984—; mem. Hickory Travel Systems Inc., 1977-85, bd. dirs., 1978-85, pres., 1980-82, pres. emeritus, 1982—. Contbr. articles to profl. jours. Chmn. Cancer Crusade Milw. County, 1970; bd. dirs. Sinai-Samaritan Med. Ctr., Better Bus. Bur. Milw., 1979-90, Found. for Santa Barbara City Coll., 1989—; trustee Santa Barbara Med. Found. Clinic, 1990—, U. Wis.-Milw. Found., 1981-91; mem. bus. adv. bd. U. Wis.-Milw., 1987—; mem. adv. bd. Sch. Fine Arts, U. Wis.-Milw., 1986-93; chmn. bus. adv. bd. Santa Barbara City Coll., 1988-92; mem. Greater Milw. Com., 1984—. With USNR, 1944-46. Mem. Nat. Assn. Temporary Svcs. (pres. 1975-76, bd. dirs. 1969-77), Univ. Milw. Club, La Cumbre Country Club (Santa Barbara), Rotary Club of Montecito Calif. Home: 129 Rametto Rd Santa Barbara CA 93108 Office: 9076 N Deerbrook Trail Milwaukee WI 53223-2474 *I do not often walk or look back where my footprints are. I prefer to walk that part of the beach I have never walked before. I am a person who thinks more about tomorrow than yesterday . . . more about what can be done than what has been done . . . more about challenges than accomplishments. Looking back is helpful only if I can find a sign to help me in my future.*

SCHEINHOLTZ, LEONARD LOUIS, lawyer; b. Pitts., June 2, 1927; s. Bernard A. and Marie (Getzel) S.; m. Joan R. Libenson, Aug. 16, 1953; children: Stuart, Nancy, Barry. B.A., U. Pa., 1948, M.A., 1949; LL.B., Columbia U., 1953. Bar: Pa. 1954, U.S. Ct. Appeals (3d cir.) 1959, U.S. Ct. Appeals (6th cir.) 1968, U.S. Supreme Ct. 1972, U.S. Ct. Appeals (4th cir.) 1973, U.S. Ct. Appeals (5th cir.) 1981, U.S. Ct. Appeals (11th cir.) 1991, U.S. Ct. Appeals (2d cir.) 1993. Assoc. Reed, Smith, Shaw & McClay, Pitts., 1953-62, spl. ptnr., 1962-64, gen. ptnr., 1964—, head labor dept., 1980-86; dir. Am. Arbitration Assn., N.Y.C., 1980-96. Author: Exemption Under the Anti-Trust Laws for Joint Employer Activity, 1982, The Arbitrator as Judge and Jury: Another Look at Statutory Law in Arbitration, 1985. Vice chmn. Pa. AAA Fedn., Harrisburg, 1982-85 ; chmn. W. Pa. AAA Motor Club, 1979-82; trustee Montefiore Hosp., Pitts., 1976-79. Served with USN, 1945-46. Mem. ABA, Pa. Bar Assn., Allegheny County Bar Assn. Republican. Jewish. Home: 746 Pinoak Rd Pittsburgh PA 15243-1153 Office: Reed Smith Shaw & McClay Mellon Sq 435 6th Ave Pittsburgh PA 15219-1809

SCHEINKMAN, JOSÉ ALEXANDRE, economics educator; b. Rio de Janeiro, Brazil, Jan. 11, 1948; s. Samuel and Sara (Lerner) S.; m. Michele Zitrin, Dec. 14, 1969; 1 child, Andrei Zitrin. B.A., U. Fed. Rio de Janeiro, 1969; M.S., Instituto de Matematica Pura e Aplicado, Brazil, 1970; M.A., U. Rochester, 1972, Ph.D., 1973. Asst. prof. econs. U. Chgo., 1973-76, assoc. prof., 1976-81, prof., 1981-86, Alvin H. Baum prof. economics, 1987—, chmn. econs. dept.; v.p. Goldman, Sachs & Co., 1987-89; vis. prof. Instituto de Matematica Pura e Aplicado Brazil, 1979-80, Fundação Getulio Vargas, Brazil, 1979-80, U. Paris, 1985-94; external Prof. Sante Fe Inst., 1989—; Harry Johnson lectr. Royal Econ. Soc./Assn. Univ. Tchrs. in Econs., 1989; cons. Ministry of Planning, Brazil, 1981. Editor: General Equilibrium Growth and Trade, 1975, Jour. Polit. Economy, Chgo., 1983-94; contbr. articles to profl. jours. NSF grantee. Fellow AAAS, Econometric Soc. Home: 5719 S Kenwood Ave Chicago IL 60637-1743 Office: Univ Chicago 1126 E 59th St Chicago IL 60637-1580

SCHEINMAN, STANLEY BRUCE, venture capital executive, lawyer; b. N.Y.C., Nov. 13, 1933; s. Samuel and Sadie (Seiffer) S.; m. Susan L. Elstein (dec.); m. Janet L. Donnely, Dec. 30, 1975 (dec.); children: Catherine Amy, Anthony Paul, Sarah, Jean, Norah Jane. AB, Cornell U., 1954; MBA, CCNY, 1957; JD (Harlan Fisk Stone scholar), Columbia U., 1960. Bar: N.Y. 1960. Assoc. firm Cravath, Swaine & Moore, N.Y.C., 1960-62; capital projects officer, legis. programs staff coord. AID, Washington, 1962-64; sr. exec. officer Bur. Pvt. Enterprise AID, 1982-83; v.p. fin. and adminstrn. svcs. industries div., also v.p., counsel internat. div. PepsiCo, Inc., 1965-70; v.p. fin. and adminstrn. pharm. div. Revlon, Inc., 1970-72; sr. v.p. MCI Communications, 1972-76; pres., chief oper. officer FSC Corp., Pitts., 1976-81; pres. New Venture Capital Corp., Washington, 1984-85; prin. Re Venture Assocs., Salisbury, Conn., 1985-86; chmn., chief exec. officer Internat. 800 Telcom Corp., Geneva, 1987-88; pres., chief exec. officer Zurich Depository Corp., Manhasset, N.Y., 1988-89; exec. v.p. AMIF&S Ltd., N.Y.C., 1989-91; pres. IT Svc. Corp., Westport, Conn., 1991-92; v.p. ops. and bus. devel. EQ Corp., Westport, 1992-95. Mem. Assn. of Bar of City of N.Y., Fin. Execs. Inst., Internat. Execs. Assn., Paris-Am. Club, Fgn. Svc. Club, Cornell Club. Home: PO Box 3355 Westport CT 06880-8355 Office: 206 Danbury Rd Wilton CT 06897

SCHEINMAN, STEVEN JAY, medical educator; b. Monticello, N.Y., Oct. 22, 1951; married; 2 children. AB summa cum laude, Amherst Coll., 1973; MD cum laude, Yale U., 1977. Diplomate Am. Bd. Internal Medicine in nephrology; lic. physician, N.Y., Conn. Resident internal medicine Yale-New Haven Hosp., 1977-80; chief resident internal medicine Upstate Med. Ctr., Syracuse, N.Y., 1980-81, fellow nephrology, 1981-83; fellow nephrology Yale-New Haven Hosp., 1983-84; asst. prof. medicine SUNY Health Sci. Ctr., Syracuse, 1984-90, asst. prof. pharmacology, 1988-90, assoc. prof. medicine and pharmacology, 1990-94, prof. medicine, prof. pharmacology, 1994—, chief nephrology sect. dept. medicine, 1994—; vis. scientist MRC Molecular Medicine Group, Royal Postgrad. Med. Sch., Hammersmith Hosp., London, 1992, 95; vis. scholar dept. biochemistry U. Oxford, 1985; attending physician U. Hosp., Syracuse, Crouse-Irving Meml. Hosp., Syracuse, VA Med. Ctr., Syracuse; dir. Nephrology Fellowship Program, 1993—; spkr. seminars, confs., orgns. Mem. editl. bd. Yale Jour. Biology and Medicine, 1975-77; contbr. articles to profl. jours. Recipient Lange award Yale U. Sch. Medicine, 1976, Resident Merit award Conn. chpt. ACP, 1980, NIH Nat. Rsch. Svc. award, 1981-83, NIH clin. investigator award, 1985-90, Charles R. Ross Rsch. award SUNY-Health Sci. Ctr., 1992; grantee Nat. Inst. Arthritis Diabetes Digestive and Kidney Diseases, 1981-83, 85-90, 95—, Am. Heart Assn., 1985, 88-90, 90-91, 92-95, 95—, NATO, 1995—. Mem. Am. Soc. Clin. Investigation, Am. Fedn. Clin. Rsch., Am. Soc. Nephrology, Internat. Soc. Nephrology, Am. Physiol. Soc., Am. Soc. Bone and Mineral Rsch., Am. Heart Assn. Coun. on Kidney, Assn. Subspecialty Profs., Phi Beta Kappa. Home: 24 University Ave Hamilton NY 13346 Office: SUNY Health Sci Ctr 750 E Adams St Syracuse NY 13210

SCHELBERT, HEINRICH RUEDIGER, nuclear medicine physician; b. Wuerzberg, Germany, Nov. 5, 1939. MD, J. Maximillian U., Wuerzburg, Germany, 1964. Diplomate Am. Bd. Nuclear Medicine. Intern Mercy Med. Ctr., Phila., 1966-67; resident Mercy Med. Ctr., 1967-68, 70-71; resident cardiology U. Dusseldorf, Germany, 1971-72; fellow cardiology, resident nuclear medicine U. Calif., San Diego, 1968-69, 72-73; hosp. assoc. UCLA Med. Ctr., 1977—; prof. radiol. scis. UCLA Sch. Medicine, L.A., 1980-93, prof. pharmacol. and radiol. scis., 1993—. Recipient Georg von Hevesy prize 2d Internat. Congress World Fedn. Nuclear Medicine and Radiation Biology, 1978, 3d Internat. Congress World Fedn. Nuclear Medicine and Radiation Biology, 1982. Fellow Am. Coll. Cardiology; mem. Am. Heart Assn. (disting. scientific achievement award 1989), Soc. Nuclear Medicine (Herrman L. Blumgart pioneer lectr. award 1989). Office: UCLA Sch Medicine Dept Molecular & Med Pharm 23-148 CHS Los Angeles CA 90024-1735

SCHELER, BRAD ERIC, lawyer; b. Bklyn., Oct. 11, 1953; s. Bernard and Rita Regina (Miller) S.; m. Amy Ruth Frolick, Mar. 30, 1980; children: Ali M., Maddie H., Zoey B. BA magna cum laude, Lehigh U., 1974; JD, Hofstra U., 1977. Bar: N.Y. 1978, U.S. Dist. Ct. (so. and ea. dists.) N.Y. 1978. Assoc. Weil, Gotshal & Manges, N.Y.C., 1977-81; sr. ptnr., chmn. bankruptcy and restructuring practice Fried, Frank, Harris, Shriver & Jacobson, N.Y.C., 1981—. Rsch. editor Hofstra U. Law Rev., 1975-77. Treas., bus. mgr. Trustees of Gramercy Park, N.Y.C., 1979-87. Mem. ABA (bus. bankruptcy com. corp. banking and bus. law sect., creditors' rights com. litig. sect.), N.Y. State Bar Assn., Assn. Bar City of N.Y. (com. on bankruptcy and corp. reorgn. 1991-94), Sigma Alpha Mu (v.p. 1973). Jewish. Home: 32 Maple Hill Dr Larchmont NY 10538-1614 Office: Fried Frank Harris 1 New York Plz New York NY 10004

SCHELL, ALLAN CARTER, retired electrical engineer; b. New Bedford, Mass., Apr. 14, 1934; s. Charles Carter and Elizabeth (Moore) S.; m. Shirley T. Sardineer; children: Alice Rosalind, Cynthia Anne. B.S., MIT, 1956, M.S.E.E., 1956, Sc.D., 1961; student, Tech. U. Delft, Netherlands, 1956-57. Research physicist Air Force Cambridge Research Labs., Bedford, Mass., 1956-76; Guenter Loeser Meml. lectr. Air Force Cambridge Research Labs., 1965; dir. electromagnetics directorate Rome Air Devel. Ctr., Bedford, 1976-87; chief scientist Hdqrs. USAF Systems Command, 1987-92; chief scientist, dep. dir. sci. and tech. Hdqrs. USAF Materiel Command, 1992-94; dir. Electro; vis. assoc. prof. MIT, 1974; chair dept. of elec. engring. adv. coun. U. Pa., 1992-94. Contbr. articles to profl. jours.; patentee in field (9). Served as lt. USAF, 1958-60. Recipient Fulbright award, 1956-57, Meritorious Exec. award U.S. Govt., 1989; NSF fellow, 1955-56, 60-61. Fellow IEEE (bd. dirs. 1981-82, editor IEEE Press 1976-79, Procs. of IEEE 1990-92), Antennas and Propagation Soc. of IEEE (pres. 1978, editor tran. 1969-71, John T. Bolljahn award 1966), Internat. Sic. Radio Union (U.S. nat. com.), Air Force Assn., Sigma Xi, Tau Beta Pi.

SCHELL, BRAXTON, lawyer; b. Raleigh, N.C., Feb. 24, 1924; s. Marshall H. and Margaret (Newsom) S.; m. Ann Cooper Knight, Mar. 30, 1951 (div. 1982); children: Braxton, Richard Knight, James Gray.; m. Mary Rehill, Apr. 16, 1983. Student, N.C. State Coll., 1942-43; B.S., U. N.C., 1948, J.D. with honors, 1951. Bar: N.C. 1951. Since practiced in Greensboro; assoc. Smith, Moore, Smith, Schell & Hunter, Greensboro, 1951-56; ptnr. Smith, Moore, Smith, Schell & Hunter, 1956-85, Smith, Helms, Mullis, and Moore, 1986-87, Schell, Bray, Aycock, Abel & Livingston, 1987—; gen. counsel, dir. Texfi Industries, Inc. Flagler Sys. and The Breakers Palm Beach, Inc.; bd. dirs. Kenan Transport Co. Assoc. editor: N.C. Law Rev. 1950-51. Chmn. Special Liason Tax Com. Southeastern Region, 1960-61; bd. dirs. N.C. Outward Bound Sch., 1975-88, chmn., 1977-80; trustee Outward Bound, Inc., 1978-81; bd. dirs. William R. Kenan Fund for Pvt. Enterprise, Arts and Engring., Tech. and Sci. Served with USAAF, 1942-45. Fellow Am. Bar Found.; mem. Am., N.C. bar assns., Order of Coif, Phi Beta Kappa. Presbyn. Clubs: Greensboro Country (pres. 1971-72), Greensboro City (dir. 1980—). Home: 422B Fisher Park Cir Greensboro NC 27401-1615 Office: Schell Bray Aycock Abel & Livingston 1500 Renaissance Pla Greensboro NC 27420

SCHELL, JAMES MUNSON, financial executive; b. Kalamazoo, Mich., Mar. 25, 1944; s. Frank John and Shirley I. S.; m. Susan O'Laughlin, Aug. 6, 1966; children: Karen, Michael, Ryan. B.A., Vanderbilt U., 1966; M.B.A., Washington U., 1968. Dir. term and internat. financing Chrysler Fin. Corp., Troy, Mich., 1976-79, v.p., treas., 1980-81; v.p. domestic treasury Am. Express Co., N.Y.C., 1981-82; v.p. fin. resources Hertz Corp., N.Y.C., 1982-83; v.p., chief fin. officer Clabir Corp., Greenwich, Conn., 1983-84; v.p., treas. Fairchild Industries, 1985-87; ind. fin. cons., 1987—; bd. dirs. Jackson-Jordan Corp., CTI Industries. Republican. Roman Catholic. Home: 40 Stony Brook Rd Darien CT 06820-4326

SCHELL, JOAN BRUNING, information specialist, business science librarian; b. N.Y.C., June 9, 1932; d. Walter Henry and Gertrude Emily (Goossen) Bruning; m. Harold Benton Schell, Aug. 27, 1955 (div. 1978); children: Jeffrey Mark, Sue Lynne. AB, Wittenberg U., 1954; postgrad., Syracuse U., 1963, U. Md., 1965-66; MLS, U. Pitts., 1968. Actuarial, claims asst. Nationwide Ins., Columbus, Ohio, 1954-57; tech. report typist Cornell U., Ithaca, N.Y., 1957; bus. libr. asst. U. Pitts., 1969; bus. reference libr. Dallas Pub. Libr., 1971-73, Pub. Libr. Cin. and Hamilton County, Cin., 1973-79; book selection coord. Pub. Libr. Cin. & Hamilton County, Cin., 1979-83, asst. to main libr., 1983-85; literacy tutor Cin. LEARN, 1985-89; recorder feminist lit. Womyn's Braille Press, Mpls., 1985-89; wellness program asst. Times Pub. Co., St. Petersburg, Fla., 1989-96, Taoist Tai Chi Soc., 1995—; dir. Wittenberg U., Springfield, Ohio, 1988—; bd. dirs. Crazy Ladies Ctr. Inc., Cin., 1989-93; coord. Fla. west coast Old Lesbians Organizing for Change, 1993-95; sec., trustee Clio Found., Inc., 1995—; docent Fla. Internat. Mus., 1994—. Compiler: (reference source) Greater Cincinnati Business Index, 1975-79; editor: New Reference Materials, 1983, 84. Mem. Tampa Bay YWCA Women's Guild, St. Petersburg, 1991-95; vol. NOW Elect Women Campaign, St. Petersburg, 1990-92, Senator Helen G. Davis Reelection, St. Petersburg, 1992. Mem. ALA, Spl. Librs. Assn. (treas., archivist 1974-83), Am. Assn. Individual Investors, Laubach Literary Action, Taoist Tai Chi Soc., Beta Phi Mu Libr. Sci. Hon., Phi Delta Gamma Grad. Women Hon. Avocations: travel, reading, figure skating fan, yoga, swimming. Address: PO Box 7472 Saint Petersburg FL 33734-7472

SCHELL, MAXIMILIAN, actor, director; b. Vienna, Austria, Dec. 8, 1930; s. Hermann Ferdinand and Margarethe (Noé von Nordberg) S. Student, Humanistisches Gymnasium, Basel, Switzerland, Freies Gymnasium, Zürich, Switzerland, also univs., Zürich, Basel and Munich. Various appearances on stage in Switzerland and Germany, 1952-55; German film debut in Children, Mothers and a General, 1955; Am. film debut in Young Lions, 1958; on Broadway stage in Interlock, 1958; prin. roles in films Judgment at Nuremberg, 1961 (Acad. award Best Actor), Five Finger Exercise, 1961, Reluctant Saint, 1962, Condemned of Altona, 1962, Topkapi, 1963, Return from the Ashes, 1965, The Deadly Affair, 1966, Counterpoint, 1967, The Castle, 1968, Simon Bolivar, 1969, First Love, 1970, Pope Joan, 1971, Paulina 1880, 1972, The Man in the Glass Booth, 1974, The Odessa File, 1974, Assassination in Sarajevo, 1975, Cross of Iron, 1976, A Bridge Too Far, 1976, Julia, 1976, The Black Hole, 1979, Players, 1978, Avalanche Express, 1978, The Chosen, 1980, Les Iles, 1981, Man Under Suspicion, 1983, The Assisi Underground, 1984, The Rosegarden, 1989, The Freshman, 1989, Labyrinth, 1990, A Far Off Place, 1993, Little Odessa, 1995; various appearances in stage roles Hamlet, Prince of Homburg, Mannerhouse, Don Carlos, Durell's Sappho, A Patriot for Me, London, 1965, Broadway, 1969, Old Times Vienna, 1972, Everyman, Salzburg Festival, 1978-82, Poor Murderer, Berlin, 1982, Der Seidene Schuh, Salzburg Festival, 1985; producer, dir. films include The Pedestrian, 1973, End of the Game, 1975, Tales from the Vienna Woods, 1978; producer film Ansichten eines Clowns, 1975; dir., co-author screenplay, actor in film First Love, 1969, Marlene, 1983; stage dir. plays include All For the Best, Vienna, 1966, Hamlet, Munich, 1968, Pygmalion, Dusseldorf, 1970; (opera) La Traviata, 1975, Tales from the Vienna Woods, London, 1977, The Undiscovered Country, Salzburg Festival, 1979, 80, opera Cornet, Deutsche Opera, Berlin, 1985, Glaube Liebe Hoffnung, Moscow, 1989; prin. TV film appearances include Heidi, 1968, The Diary of Anne Frank, 1980, Phantom of the Opera, 1983, miniseries Peter the Great, 1984-85, Young Catherine, 1990, Wiseguy, 1990, Miss Rose White, 1991, Stalin, HBO, 1992 (Emmy nomination, Supporting Actor - Miniseries or Special, Cable Ace award, Best Supporting actor). Corporal Swiss Army, 1948-49. Recipient N.Y. Critics Circle award, 1961, 78, 86, Acad. award, 1961, Golden Globe award, 1962, 74, Silver Shell award, 1970, 75, German Fed. award, 1971, 79, 80, 84, Chgo. Film Critics award, 1973, Golden Cup award, Germany, 1974, Gold Hugo award, 1979, Nat. Soc. Film Critics award, 1986; nominated Critics award (Broadway), 1961, Academy award, 1970, 74, 75, 78, 85. Home: Culmannstr 49, CH-8006 Zurich Switzerland Office: Innovative Artists 1999 Ave of the Stars Ste 2850 Los Angeles CA 90067 also: Mgmt Erna Baumbauer, Keplerstr 2, 8000 Munich 90, Germany*

SCHELL, MERRY L., critical care and oncological nurse; b. Seminole, Tex., Sept. 16, 1946; d. Tiny Hollis and Mary Elizabeth (Yates) Odom; m. Thomas E. Schell, Jan. 17, 1965; children: Carrie Elizabeth, Thomas Wade. AS, Bakersfield Community Coll., 1977; BSBA, U. San Francisco, 1984. Cert. oncology nurse specialist. Dir. nursing Med. Pers. Pool, Bakersfield, Calif.; head nurse in oncology and hematology San Joaquin Community Hosp., Bakersfield; clin. dir. critical cre Delano (Calif.) Regional Med. Ctr. Mem. Oncology Nursing Soc.

SCHELL, PAUL E.S., dean. Dean Architecture and Urban Planning U. Wash. Office: U Wash Sch of Architecture Seattle WA 98195*

SCHELL, RICHARD A., federal judge; b. 1950. BA, So. Meth. U., 1972, JD, 1975. Bar: Tex. 1975. Asst. dist. atty. Collin County, Tex., 1976; mem. firm Boyd, Veigel & Gay, 1977-81; judge County Ct. Law Collin County, 1982-86, 219th Jud. Dist. Ct. Tex., 1986-88, U.S. Dist Ct. (ea. dist.) Tex., Beaumont, 1988—; instr. rsch. methods and legal writing So. Meth. U., 1975-76. Mem. State Bar Tex. Office: US Dist Ct PO Box 1470 Beaumont TX 77704-1470*

SCHELLEN, NANDO, opera director; b. The Hague, The Netherlands, Oct. 11, 1934; came to U.S., 1993; m. Deborah Raymond, June 19, 1991; 4 children. Mng. dir. Netherlands Opera, 1969-79, assoc. gen. dir., 1979-87; gen. artistic dir. Sweelinck Conservatory of Music, Amsterdam, 1990-93; gen. dir. Indpls. Opera, 1993-96; freelance stage dir., 1982—. Home: 209 E 45th St Indianapolis IN 46205

SCHELLENBERG, KARL ABRAHAM, biochemist; b. Hillsboro, Kans., July 13, 1931; s. Theodore R. and Alma Alice (Groening) S.; m. Elizabeth Joan Booker, Aug. 20, 1955; children: Robert, Elizabeth, Richard, Margaret. BS, Coll. William and Mary, 1953; MD, Johns Hopkins U., 1957; PhD, Harvard U., 1964. Asst. prof. Johns Hopkins U., Balt., 1963-68; assoc. prof. physiol. chemistry Johns Hopkins U., 1968-73; prof., chmn. dept. biochemistry Eastern Va. Med. Sch., Norfolk, 1973—; mem. adv. bd. NSF Middle Atlantic Mass Spectrometry Lab.; mem. adv. com. dept. chem. scis. Old Dominion U.; mem. adv. com. dept. chemistry Coll. William and Mary. Contbr. articles to profl. jours. John and Mary R. Markle Found. scholar, 1965-70; NIH grantee. Mem. Nat. Bd. Med. Examiners (biochemistry test com. 1989-92), Assn. Am. Med. Schs. (panel on the gen. profl. edn. of the physician 1982-84), Assn. Med. Sch. Depts. Biochemistry (sec. 1987-91), Am. Soc. Biol. Chemists, Am. Chem. Soc., N.Y. Acad. Scis., Va. Acad. Scis., Oxygen Soc., Phi Beta Kappa, Sigma Xi (Tidewater, Va. chpt. sec. 1990-91, pres. 1992-93, pres. 1995-96). Club: Pithotomy. Patentee in field. Home: 1332 Lakeview Dr Virginia Beach VA 23455-4130 Office: Eastern Va Med Sch PO Box 1980 Norfolk VA 23501-1980

SCHELLENBERGER, ROBERT EARL, management educator and department chairman; b. Janesville, Wis., July 25, 1932; s. Ervin William and Adelaide Louise (Keller) S.; m. Linda Eula Todd, Dec. 30, 1961; children: Brian T., Keith W., Heidi L. BSBA, U. Wis., 1958, MBA, 1959; PhD, U. N.C., 1963. Personnel supr. Libby McNeill and Libby, Janesville, Wis., 1957-58; from asst. prof. to assoc. prof. chmn. div. stats. dept. bus U. Md., College Park, 1963-68; chair dept. mgmt. So. Ill. U., Carbondale, Ill., 1968-70; dir. planning Sch. Human Resources Devel. So. Ill. U., Carbondale, 1970-71, prof. mgmt., 1968-71; vis. prof., dir. program evaluation Babcock Grad. Sch. Mgmt., Wake Forest U., Winston-Salem, N.C., 1971-73; prof. dept. mgmt. Temple U., Phila., 1973-81, from chmn. dept. mgmt. to asst. to acad. vice chancellor, 1975-77; prof. decision scis. dept. East Carolina U., Greenville, N.C., 1981—, chmn. decision scis. dept., 1989-95; pres. Md. Rsch. and Cons., Hyattsville, 1964-67; v.p. Ea. Acad. Mgmt., 1967; cons. Comml. Credit Corp., Balt., 1966. Author: Managerial Analysis, 1967, Policy Formulation, 1978, 2d edit., 1982; co-editor Jour. of Econs. and Bus., 1976; developer (software package) MANYSYM, 1965, 68, 78, 82, 86. Chmn. Utilities Com., Carbondale, 1970-72. Title IV NDEA fellow U. N.C., 1960-62, Earhart Jr. fellow U. Wis. Mem. Assn. for Bus. Simulation, SE Decision Scis. Inst., Decision Scis. Inst. (bd. dirs. 1974-77), Beta Gamma Sigma. Office: East Carolina U Decision Scis Dept Greenville NC 27858

SCHELLER, SANFORD GREGORY, printing company executive; b. Newark, July 7, 1931; s. John Arthur Scheller and Harriet (Gregory) Tate; m. Marjory Meyer, Dec. 31, 1950; children: Sanford Gregory Jr., Douglas Meyer, Bradford John, Frances Scheller Lavin, Eric Bruce. BBA, Westminster Coll., New Wilmington, Pa., 1953. V.p., gen. mgr. St. Regis Corp., N.Y.C., 1978-84, Champion Internat., Stamford, Conn., 1984-85; pres., chief exec. officer Treasure Chest Advt., Glendora, Calif., 1986-95; vice chmn. Big Flower Press Holdings, Inc., N.Y.C., 1995—. Republican. Office: Big Flower Press Holdings Ste 28 13000 Sawgrass Village Cir Ponte Vedra Beach FL 32082

SCHELLING, JOHN PAUL, lawyer, consultant; b. Chgo., Aug. 24, 1924; s. Lawrence C. and Hattie (La Bonte) S.; m. V. Jacqueline Davis, Aug. 27, 1945; children: Lawrence, Donna Schelling Scheer, Gloria Schelling Boughers. Student, St. Mary's Coll., Winona, Minn., 1942-43, U. Ill., 1946-47; J.D., Loyola U., Chgo., 1950; postgrad., U. Chgo., 1954-55. Bar: Ill. 1950, Va. 1986. Assoc. McMahon & Plunkett, Chgo., 1950-51; mem. indsl. relations staff Union Asbestos & Rubber Co., Chgo., 1951-56; fin. mgr. Land-Air, Inc. subs. Dynalectron Corp., Chgo., 1956-60; sec. Dynalectron Corp., McLean, Va., 1960-65; v.p. Dynalectron Corp., McLean, 1962-71, v.p., gen. counsel, 1972-76, sr. v.p. fin. and adminstrn. group, 1977-78, sr. v.p. adminstrn. group, 1979-84, sr. v.p. adminstrn. group, gen. counsel, 1984-86, ret., 1986; chmn. Esop com. DynCorp, 1987—. Bd. dirs., v.p. Potomac Hills Citizens Assn., McLean, 1963-64; organizer, bd. dirs., v.p. Highland Swim Club, McLean, 1964-67; bd. dirs. McLean Orch., 1984-86; trustee Fairfax Couty Pub. Schs. Edn. Fund., 1984-86; bd. dirs. Shorewood Property Owners Assn., 1990—, sec.-treas., 1990-92, pres., 1992-95, v.p., 1995—. With USNR, 1943-46. Mem. D.C. Bar Assn., Va. Bar Assn., Delta Theta Phi. Home: 167 Laurelwood Dr Mineral VA 23117 Office: Dyncorp 2000 Edmund Halley Dr Reston VA 22091-3468

SCHELLING, THOMAS CROMBIE, economist, educator; b. Oakland, Calif., Apr. 14, 1921; s. John M. and Zelda M. (Ayres) S.; m. Corinne T. Saposs, Sept. 13, 1947 (div. 1991); children: Andrew, Thomas, Daniel, Robert; m. Alice M. Coleman, Nov. 8, 1991. AB, U. Calif., Berkeley, 1943; PhD, Harvard U., 1951. U.S. govt. economist Copenhagen, Paris, Washington, 1948-53; prof. econs. Yale U., 1953-58, Harvard U., Cambridge, Mass., 1958—; prof. econs. and pub. affairs U. Md., College Park, 1990—; sr. staff mem. RAND Corp., 1958-59; chmn. rsch. adv. bd. Com. Econ. Devel., 1978-81, 84-85; mem. sci. adv. bd. USAF, 1960-64, def. sci. bd., 1966-70; mem. mil. econ. adv. panel CIA, 1980-85; trustee Aerospace Corp., 1984-93. Author: National Income Behavior, 1951, International Economics, 1958, The Strategy of Conflict, 1960, Arms and Influence, 1966, Micromotives and Macrobehavior, 1978, Choice and Consequence, 1984; co-author: Strategy and Arms Control, 1961. Recipient Frank E. Seidman Disting. award in polit. economy, 1977. Fellow Am. Acad. Arts and Scis., AAAS, Assn. for Pub. Policy Analysis and Mgmt., Am. Econ. Assn. (pres. 1991, Disting. mem. award); mem. NAS (rsch. award, 1993), Inst. Medicine, Ea. Econ. Assn. (pres. 1996). Office: Univ Md Sch Pub Affairs College Park MD 20742

SCHELLMAN, JOHN A., chemistry educator; b. Phila., Oct. 24, 1924; s. John and Mary (Mason) S.; m. Charlotte Green, Feb. 10, 1954; children: Heidi M., Lise C. AB, Temple U., 1948; MS, Princeton U., 1949, PhD, 1951; PhD (hon.), Chalmers U., Sweden, 1983, U. Padua, Italy, 1990. USPHS postdoctoral fellow U. Utah, 1951-52, Carlsberg Lab., Copenhagen, 1953-55; DuPont fellow U. Minn., Mpls., 1955-56; asst. prof. chemistry U. Minn., 1956-58; assoc. prof. chemistry Inst. Molecular Biology, U. Oreg., Eugene, 1958-63; prof. chemistry, rsch. assoc. Inst. Molecular Biology, U. Oreg., 1963—; vis. Lab. Chem. Physics, Nat. Inst. Arthritis and Metabolic Diseases, NIH, Bethesda, Md., 1980; vis. prof. Chalmers U., Sweden, 1986, U. Padua, Italy, 1987. Contbr. articles to profl. jours. Served with U.S. Army, 1943-46. Fellow Rask-Oersted Found., 1954, Sloan Found., 1959-63, Guggenheim Found., 1969-70. Fellow Am. Phys. Soc.; mem. NAS, Am. Chem. Soc., Am. Soc. Biochemistry and Molecular Biology, Am. Acad. Arts and Scis., Biophys. Soc., Phi Beta Kappa, Sigma Xi. Democrat. Home: 780 Lorane Hwy Eugene OR 97405-2340 Office: Univ Oreg Inst Molecular Biology Eugene OR 97403

SCHELM, ROGER LEONARD, information systems specialist; b. Kingston, N.Y., July 29, 1936; s. Frederick G. and Elizabeth M. (Wojciehowski) S.; m. Gloria Mae Dutterer, June 13, 1958; children: Sandra Lee Kern, Theresa Jean Sollitto, Ginger Lisa Teesdale. B.A. in Polit. Sci., Western Md. Coll., 1958; M.A. in Pub. Adminstrn., Am. U., 1970; postgrad., U. Md., 1960-62. Analytic equipment programmer Nat. Security Agy., Ft. Meade, Md., 1958-60; computer cons. various cons. firms Balt. and Washington, 1960-68; mgr. army plans and programs Informatics Inc., Bethesda, Md., 1968; mgr. def. programs Automation Tech. Inc., Wheaton, Md., 1968-69; dir. advanced planning Genasys Corp., Washington, 1969-71; mgr. info. systems Ins. Co. North Am., Phila., 1971-72, sect. mgr. computing ops., 1972-74; mgr. tech. services INA Corp., Phila., 1974-75; mem. spl. tech. projects INA Corp. merger with Conn. Gen. Ins. Co. to form CIGNA Corp. 1982, Phila., 1975-76, asst. dir. tech. services, 1977, asst. dir. spl. tech. projects, 1977-78, asst. dir. adminstrn., 1978-79, asst. dir. resource mgmt., data ctr. design, contingency planning, 1979-80; dir. corp. info. tech. now CIGNA Corp., Phila., 1981-82, dir. planning and control ops. div., 1982-83, v.p. strategic planning, systems div., 1983-84, v.p. applied research/expert systems, systems div., 1984-92; co-founder, pres. Schelm Internat., Inc., Cherry Hill, N.J., 1992—; mem. adj. faculty Camden Coll., N.J., 1978-82; mem. Camden County EDP Adv. Com., 1980-82; mem. faculty Drexel U., Phila., 1983-95. Author: Ednl. Computer mag., 1982; mem. editl. adv. bd., author Small Sys. World mag., 1982-84; mem. editl. adv. bd. Spang-Robinson Report, 1986-87, Machine Intelligence News, 1987-93, AI Expert mag., 1985-88; cons. editor Expert Sys. Jour., 1987-91. Tech. advisor various sch. bds., colls., univs. and non-profit orgns. Served to capt. U.S. Army, 1959. Mem. Am. Assn. Artificial Intelligence, Assn. Computing Machinery (founder Delaware Valley chpt. vice. chmn., program chmn. 1983-84, chmn. 1984-85, founder Del. Valley Spl. Interest Group in Artificial Intelligence, 1985, vice chmn. 1985-87), World Future Soc. Home: 506 Balsam Rd Cherry Hill NJ 08003-3202 Office: Schelm Internat Inc PO Box 172 Cherry Hill NJ 08003-0172

SCHENCK, BENJAMIN ROBINSON, insurance consultant; b. N.Y.C., July 21, 1938; s. John T. and Harriet Buffum (Hall) S.; m. Sally V. Sullivan, Aug. 27, 1960; children: Steven T., Elizabeth F., Timothy S. B.A., William Coll., Williamstown, Mass, 1960; LL.B., Harvard U., 1963. Bar: N.Y. 1964, Mass. 1978. Asst. counsel to gov. State of N.Y., Albany, 1963-66; assoc. Bond, Schoeneck & King, Syracuse, N.Y., 1966-68; dep. supt., 1st dep. sup. and supt. State of N.Y. Dept. Ins., N.Y.C., 1968-75; sr. v.p. Shearson Hayden Stone Inc., N.Y.C., 1975-77; sr. v.p. State Mut. Life Assurance Co. Am., 1977-86, exec. v.p., 1986-89; pres. Worcester Mut. Ins. Co., 1979-83, Cen. Mass. Health Care, Inc., Worcester, 1989-93. Home: 85 Stockbridge Rd Lee MA 01238-9308 Office: 63 State Rd Great Barrington MA 01230-1223

SCHENCK, FREDERICK A., business executive; b. Trenton, May 12, 1928; s. Frederick A. and Alwilda M. (McLain) S.; m. Quinta Chapman, Jan. 25, 1974. Student, Howard U., 1948-50; B.S., Rider Coll., 1958, M.A., 1976. With N.J. Dept. Community Affairs, 1967-72; dir. youth and family services div. N.J. Dept. Instns. and Agys., 1972-74; dep. dir. adminstrn. purchase and property div. N.J. Treasury Dept., 1974-77; secretarial rep. Fed. Region II, Dept. Commerce, 1977-78; dep. under sec. Dept. Commerce, 1978-79; sr. v.p. adminstrn. Resorts Internat. Hotel Casino, Atlantic City, 1979-88; v.p. personnel Cunard Lines Ltd., N.Y.C., 1988-93; self employed mgmt. cons. Secaucus, N.J., 1995—; bd. dirs. Bur. Nat. Affairs Inc.; mem. adv. com. on judicial conduct N.J. Supreme Ct. With USNR, 1946-48. Mem. N.J. Gov.'s Commn. on Disabled; bd. dirs. Bur. Nat. Affairs Inc. With USNR, 1946-48. Mem. Am. Soc. Public Adminstrn., N.J. C. of C. Presbyterian. Club: Sundowners, Nat. Guardsmen, Inc. Home: 569 Sanderling Ct Secaucus NJ 07094-2220

SCHENCK, JACK LEE, retired electric utility executive; b. Morgantown, W.Va., Aug. 2, 1938; s. Ernest Jacob and Virginia Belle (Kelley) S.; m. Rita Elizabeth Pietschmann, June 7, 1979; 1 son, Erik. B.S.E.E., B.A. in Social Sci., Mich. State U., 1961; M.B.A., NYU, 1975. Engr. AID, Tunis, Tunisia, 1961, Detroit Edison Co., 1962-63; engr., economist OECD, Paris, 1963-70; v.p. econ. policy analysis Edison Electric Inst., N.Y.C. and Washington, 1970-81; v.p., treas. Gulf States Utilities Co., Beaumont, Tex., 1981-92, sr. v.p., CFO, 1992-94; cons. on electric utility restructuring and privatization in the former Soviet Union, 1994—. Mem. Internat. Assn. Energy Econs., Triangle Club, Eta Kappa Nu. Republican.

SCHENCK, JOHN FREDERIC, physician; b. Decatur, Ind., June 7, 1939; s. John C. Schenck and Mildred Blosser; m. Jane Stark, Oct. 12, 1962 (div. 1982); children: Brooke, Kimberly, David; m. Susan J. Kalia, Oct. 8, 1994; 1 stepchild, Tania. BS in Physics, Rensselaer Poly. Inst., 1961, PhD in Physics, 1965; MD, Albany Med. Coll., 1977. Intern Albany (N.Y.) Med. Ctr. Hosp., 1977-78; staff scientist electronics lab GE, Syracuse, N.Y., 1965-73; staff mem., sr. scientist corp. R & D ctr. GE, Schenectady, N.Y., 1973—; assoc. prof. electrical engring. Syracuse U., 1970-73; mem. med. staff Ellis Hosp., Schenectady, 1981—; adj. asst. prof. dept. radiology U. Pa., 1983—. Contbr. articles to profl. jours; 12 patents in field of magnetic resonance imaging. Recipient S.S. Greenfield award Am. Assn. Physicists in Medicine, 1993; NSF fellow, 1962-63; Nat. Merit Scholar, 1957-61. Mem. IEEE, AAAS, Internat. Soc. Magnetic Resonance in Medicine, Am. Phys. Soc., N.Y. Acad. Sci., Sigma Xi. Home: 17 Carrie Ct Niskayuna NY 12309-2223 Office: GE Corp Rsch Devel Bldg K1 NMR Schenectady NY 12309 also: 4914 Ravine Ct Ann Arbor MI 48105

SCHENDEL, DAN ELDON, management consultant, business educator; b. Norwalk, Wis., Mar. 29, 1934; s. Leonard A. and Marian T. (Koch) S.; B.S. in Metall.Engring., U. Wis., 1956; M.B.A., Ohio State U., 1959; Ph.D. (Ford Found. fellow), Stanford U., 1963; m. Mary Lou Sigler, Sept. 1, 1956; children: Suzanne, Pamela, Sharon. With ALCOA, 1956, U.S. Civil Service, 1959-60, SRI, 1963-65; prof. mgmt., dir. exec. edn. programs Purdue U., 1965—; vis. prof. U. Mich., 1988-89, U. Chgo., 1990-91; pres. Strategic Mgmt. Assocs., Inc. Served with USAF, 1956-59. Fellow Acad. Mgmt.; mem. Strategic Mgmt. Soc. (founding pres., exec. dir.), The Planning Forum. Club: Lafayette Country. Author: (with others) Strategy Formulation: Analytical Concepts, 1978, Divided Loyalties, 1980, Fundamental Issues in Strategy, 1994; editor: (with others) Strategic Management: A New View of Business Policy and Planning, 1979; founding editor Strategic Mgmt. Jour., 1980—. Home: 1327 N Grant St West Lafayette IN 47906-2463 Office: Krannert Grad Sch Mgmt Purdue U West Lafayette IN 47907

SCHENDEL, STEPHEN ALFRED, plastic surgery educator, oral surgeon; b. Mpls., Oct. 10, 1947; s. Alfred Reck and Jeanne Shirley (Hagquist) S.; m. Susan Elizabeth Brown, Aug. 15, 1969; children: Elliott, Mélisande. BA, St. Olaf Coll., Northfield, Minn., 1969; BS with high distinction, U. Minn., 1971, DDS, 1973; diplome asst. etranger with high honors, U. Nantes, France, 1980; MD, U. Hawaii, 1983. Diplomate Am. Bd. Plastic Surgery, Nat. Bd. Med. Examiners, Nat. Bd. Dental Examienrs, Am. Bd. Oral and Maxillofacial Surgery (adv. com., bd. examiner 1991-95). Fellow in oral pathology U. Minn. Sch. Dentistry, Mpls., 1972; pvt. practice gen. dentistry, then oral-maxillofac. surgery, Honolulu, 1974-75, 80-83; resident in gen. dentistry Queen's Med. Ctr., Honolulu, 1973-74; intern, then resident in oral and maxillofacial surgery Parkland Meml. Hosp., Dallas, 1975-79; resident in gen. surgery Baylor U. Med. Ctr., Dallas, 1983-84; resident in gen. surgery Stanford (Calif.) U. Med. Ctr., 1984-86, resident in plastic surgery, 1986-89, acting assoc. prof. surgery, 1989-91, assoc. prof., 1991-95, head div. plastic and reconstructive surgery, 1992—, dir. residency tng., 1992—, chmn. dept. functional restoration, 1994, chmn., 1994—, prof., 1995—; head plastic surgery, dir. Craniofacial Ctr. Lucile Salter Packard Children's Hosp., Stanford; asst. to Dr. Paul Tessier, Paris, 1987-88; asst. dept. stomatology and maxillofacial surgery Centre Hospitalier Regional Nantes, 1979-80; referee Annals Plastic Surgery, 1989—, Am. Jour. Orthodontics and Dentofacial Orthopedics, 1990—; presenter in field; mem. staff John Peter Smith Hosp., Ft. Worth, 1979; asst. clin. prof. surgery U. Hawaii John A Burns Sch. Medicine, Honolulu, 1980-84; chief plastic surgery svc., mem. med. bd. Lucile Salter Packard Children's Hosp. at Stanford, 1991—; mem. organizing com. 1st Hawaii-Pacific Cleft Palate Program, 1983; mem. in-svc. exam. com. Plastic Surgery Ednl. Found., 1992-93. Assoc. editor Selected Readings in Oral and Maxillofacial Surgery, 1989—; contbr. articles and abstracts to med. and dental jours., chpts. to books. Recipient Disting. Alumnus award St. Olaf Coll., 1993; Fulbright fellow, Nantes, 1979-80, Chateaubriand fellow Govt. of France, 1987-88. Fellow ACS, Am. Acad. Pediat.; mem. European Assn. Cranio-Maxillofacial Surgeons (mem. craniofacial com. 1989-91), Am. Soc. Pediat., Soc. Baylor Surgeons (founding), French Assn. Maxillofacial Surgeons (fgn.), Am. Cleft Palate-Craniofacial Assn., Am. Soc. Plastic and Reconstructive Surgeons (mem. sci. program com. 1992—), Am. Soc. Maxillofacial Surgeons (mem. basic course syllabus com. 1991-93, mem. membership com. 1991—, mem. sci. program com. 1991—, mem. Best Paper award com. 1991—, mem. craniofacial and maxillofacial com. 1993—, bd. dirs.-at-large 1993—, mem. Calif. carriers adv. com. 1993—, liaison to Am. Assn. Orthodontics 1994), Assn. Acad. Chairmen Plastic Surgery, Zedplast (bd. dirs., mem. surgery com. 1993—), Calif. Med. Assn. (mem. sci. adv. panel on plastic surgery 1992—), Omicron Kappa Upsilon. Avocation: fly fishing. Office: Stanford U Med Ctr NC-104 Div Plastic-Reconstr Surg Stanford CA 94305

SCHENEWERK, SHARON KAY, counselor; b. Jefferson City, Mo., Oct. 31, 1960; d. John T. and Arah Eloise (Wood) Martin; m. Dale Robert Schenewerk Sr., May 19, 1984; children: Dale Robert Jr., Angela Louise. BA, N.E. Mo. State U., 1983, MA, 1993. Nat. cert. counselor. Dir. careers unltd. Linn (Mo.) Tech. Coll., 1983-84; admissions counselor Wichita (Kans.) State U., 1985-87; counselor intern N.E. Mo. State U., Kirksville, 1992, asst. to dean, 1992—; supr. Kelly Svcs., Columbia, Mo., 1985, Syracuse N.Y., 1988. Mem. Big Bros./Big Sisters, Sedgwick County, Wichita, 1985-87; vol. Willard Sch. Dist., Kirksville, Mo., 1993. Named Outstanding Young Women in Am., 1983; Pershing Leadership scholar, 1979-83. Mem. ACA, Nat. Career Devel. Assn., Nat. Assn. Student Pers. Admisntrs., Assn. for Humanistic Edn. and Devel. Democrat. Baptist. Avocations: aerobics, piano, international cooking. Home: 2407 N Oak Ln Kirksville MO 63501-2171 Office: NE Mo State U Missouri Hall # 120 Kirksville MO 63501-4993

SCHENK, DEBORAH HUFFMAN, law educator; b. 1947. BA, Cornell U., 1969; JD, Columbia U., 1972; LLM, NYU, 1976. Bar: N.Y. 1973. From asst. prof. to prof. law Bklyn. Law Sch., 1974-85; prof. law NYU, N.Y.C., 1985—; vis. prof. Harvard U., spring 1982, NYU, 1983-85, Yale U., 1989. Author: Federal Taxation of S Corporation, 1986, supp., 1995; (with M. Graetz) Federal Income Taxation, 1995; (with B. Wolfman & J. Holden) Ethical Problems in Federal Tax Practice, 1995; editor-in-chief Tax Law Rev. Mem. ABA (tax sect.), ALI, Am. Coll. Tax Counsel, N.Y. State Bar Assn. Home: 219 Kane St Brooklyn NY 11231-4437 Office: NYU Sch Law 40 Washington Sq S New York NY 10012-1005

SCHENK, JOHN ERWIN, environmental engineer; b. Ann Arbor, Mich., Nov. 16, 1940; s. Erwin Karl and Erma Ida (Burkhardt) S.; m. Nancy Ann Klabunde, Feb. 27, 1965; children: Timothy John, Laura Ann. BS, U. Mich., 1963, MS, 1964, PhD, 1969. Cert. profl. engr., Mich. Exec. v.p. Environ. Control Tech., Ann Arbor, Mich., 1969-86; from v.p. to pres. ENCOTEC, Inc., Ann Arbor, 1986—. Mem. Water Environment Fedn., Mich. Water Pollution Control Assn. (com. 1978-85). Avocations: gardening, fishing. Office: ENCOTEC Inc 3985 Research Park Dr Ann Arbor MI 48108

SCHENK, JOSEPH BERNARD, museum director; b. Glendale, Ariz., Mar. 28, 1953; m. Jacqueline Van Lienop; children: Brian, Stuart. BA in Mus. Staff Preparation, Huntingdon Coll., 1974; MA in Art Edn., Ball State U., 1979; postgrad., U. Calif., Berkeley, 1986. Exhibits asst. Hunter Mus. of Art, Chattanooga, 1974-75; asst. dir. Alford House/Anderson Fine Arts Ctr., Anderson, Ind., 1976, exec. dir., 1976-79; exec. dir. Okefenokee Heritage Ctr., Waycross, Ga., 1979-83; dir. So. Forest World, Waycross, 1979-83, Chattahoochee Valley Art Mus., LaGrange, Ga., 1983-88, Mobile (Ala.) Mus. of Art, 1988—; bd. dirs. U.S. Sports Acad. Art Mus.; v.p. Ala. Mus. Assn., 1994-96, pres., 1996—; adv. panelist Visual Arts Fellowships, Ala. State Coun. on the Arts, 1994-95, Profl. Touring Panel Ga. Coun. for Arts, 1983-84, PRACSO Panel Ga. Coun. for Arts, 1984-86, Arch. & Environ. Arts Ind. Arts Commn., 1978-79, Mus. Ind. Arts Commn., 1977-79; Ind. rep. Small Mus. Com. Midwest Mus. Conf., 1978-79. Pub. numerous art catalogs; editor newsletter Ga. Assembly of Community Arts Agys., 1987-88. Art juror at numerous pub. and pvt. art shows; bd. dirs. Ga. Alliance for Arts Edn., 1982-84, Assn. Ind. Mus., 1979, Mobile Arts Coun., 1989-90, Ga. Assembly Community Arts Agys., 1986-88; commr. Madison County Hist. Home, Anderson, 1977-79; mem. dedication com., cons. Krannert Fine Arts Ctr., Anderson Coll., 1979; mem. com. forest festival tourism and conventions Waycross/Ware County C. of C., 1979-83; bd. dirs. Southeastern Ga. Travel and Tourism Assn., 1981-83, sec., 1981-82, pres., 1982-83. Grantee Nat. Endowment for Arts, Ala. State Coun. on Arts, Mobile Arts Coun., Ga. Endowment for Humanities, Ga. Coun. Arts, Ala. Arts Found., Inst. Mus. Svcs., Ga. Gov.'s Intern Program, others; recipient Spark Plug of Yr. award Waycross Jaycees, 1981; Mus. Mgmt. Inst. scholar, 1986. Mem. Am. Assn. Mus., Southeastern Mus. Conf., Ala. Mus. Assn. (v.p. 1994—), Rotary, Mobile United. Home: 6401 Sugar Creek Dr S Mobile AL 36695 Office: Mobile Museum of Art PO Box 8426 4850 Museum Dr Mobile AL 36689

SCHENK, QUENTIN FREDERICK, retired social work educator, mayor; b. Fort Madison, Iowa, Aug. 25, 1922; s. Fred Edward John and Ida (Sabrowsky) S.; m. Patricia J. Kelley, Aug. 6, 1946 (div. Apr. 1970); children: Fred W. (dec. 1972), Patricia, Karl, Martha; m. Emmy Lou Willson, May 23, 1970. B.A., Willamette U., 1948; M.S., U. Wis., 1950, M.S. in Social Work, 1953, Ph.D., 1953. Asst. prof. social work U. Wis.-Madison, 1953-55, prof., chmn. extension social work, 1961-63; prof., former dean Sch. Social Welfare, Milw., 1962-68, prof. emeritus, 1990—; assoc. prof. U. Mo., 1955-61; project specialist Ford Found., 1968-71; Spl. cons. on urban mission in Africa United Presbyn. Ch., 1971—, World Council Chs., 1971—; adviser to Haile Sellassie I U., Addis Ababa, Ethiopia, 1968-71; Alderman City of Cedarburg (Wis.), 1974-82, mayor, 1982-86. Author: (with Emmy Lou Schenk) Pulling Up Roots, 1978, Welfare Society and the Helping Professions, 1981; author sect. on Ethiopia, Welfare in Africa, 1987; contbr. articles, bulls., reports to profl. lit. Mem. Nat. Trust for Hist. Preservation, Wis. Hist. Preservation Negotiating Bd.; chmn. bd. Guest House, Milw., 1987-89; mem. Sierra Club, Planned Parenthood, Unitarian Fellowship Eau Claire, ACLU, Dem. Party of Wis. Pilot USNR, 1942-46. Decorated Air medal with 3 gold stars, DFC; recipient Presdl. citation Pres. Harry Truman, 1948. Mem. AAUP, Am. Sociol. Assn., Am. Assn. Ret. Persons, Coun. on Social Work Edn., Aircraft Owners and Pilots Assn. Home: # 409 550 Graham Ave Eau Claire WI 54701

SCHENK, SUSAN KIRKPATRICK, geriatric psychiatry nurse; b. New Richmond, Ind., Nov. 29, 1938; d. William Marcius and Frances (Kirkpatrick) Gaither; m. Richard Dee Brown, Aug. 13, 1960 (div. Feb. 1972); children: Christopher, David, Lisa; m. John Francis Schenk, July 24, 1975 (widowed Apr. 1995). BSN, Ind. U., 1962; postgrad., U. Del., 1973-75. RN, PHN, BCLS; cert. community coll. tchr., Calif. Staff nurse, then asst. dir. nursing Bloomington (Ind.) Hosp., 1962-66; charge nurse Newark (Del.) Manor, 1967-69; charge nurse GU Union Hosp., Terre Haute, Ind., 1971-72; clin. instr. nursing Ind. State U., Terre Haute, 1972-73; clin. instr. psychiatric nursing U. Del., Newark, 1974-75; psychiatric nursing care coord. VA Med. Ctr., Perry Point, Md., 1975-78; nurse educator Grossmont Hosp., La Mesa, Calif., 1978-90, cmty. rels. coord., 1990-91; dir. psychiat. svcs. Scripps Hosp. East County, El Cajon, Calif., 1991—; tech. advisor San Diego County Bd. Supervisors, 1987; tech. cons. Remedy Home and Health Care, San Diego, 1988; expert panelist Srs. Speak Out, KPBS-TV, San Diego, 1988; guest lectr. San Diego State U., 1987. Editor: Teaching Basic Caregiver Skills, 1988; author, performer tng. videotape Basic Caregiver Skills, 1988. Mem. patient svcs. com. Nat. Multiple Sclerosis Soc., San Diego, 1986-89; bd. dirs. Assn. for Quality and Participation, 1989. Adminstrn. on Aging/DHHS grantee, 1988. Mem. Am. Psychiat. Nurses Assn., Ind. U. Alumni Assn. (life), Mensa, Sigma Theta Tau. Avocations: bluegrass banjo, piano, gardening, reading. Home: 9435 Carlton Oaks Dr # D Santee CA 92071-2588 Office: Scripps Hosp East County 1688 E Main St El Cajon CA 92021-5204

SCHENK, WORTHINGTON GEORGE, JR., surgeon, educator; b. Buffalo, Feb. 10, 1922; s. Worthington George and Edna (Klein) S.; m. Jean L.K. Lyon, Mar. 9, 1946; children: Martha, Lura, Worthington George III, Elsa, Gregory, Molly, Andrew. B.A., Williams Coll., 1942; M.D., Harvard U., 1945. Diplomate: Am. Bd. Surgery. With U. Buffalo, 1948-66, assoc. prof. surgery, 1959-66; prof. surgery SUNY, Buffalo, 1966-85; acting chmn. dept. surgery SUNY, 1969-72, chmn., 1972-85; dir. surgery Erie County Med. Ctr., Buffalo, 1966-85; ret., 1985. Editorial bd. Current Surgery; contbr. articles to profl. jours. Mem. AMA, Am. So. surg. assns., Am. Assn. Surgery Trauma, Soc. Univ. Surgeons, Soc. Vascular Surgery (past treas., pres. 1976), Soc. Clin. Surgery (sec. 1966-72), Internat. Cardiovascular Soc., ACS, Soc. for Surgery of Alimentary Tract, Surg. Biology Club, Phi Beta Kappa. Home: 38 Front Ave Hanford Bay Silver Creek NY 14136 *It has been a great pleasure to have been involved in the development of vascular surgery from its inception. Retrospectively, my basic laboratory type research contributions now give me the greatest satisfaction, far more than any number of surgical operations. Next in importance is the satisfaction of having turned out more than 25 research fellows.*

SCHENKEL, PETER, food company executive. CEO So. Foods Group, Dallas. Office: Southern Foods Group PO Box 279000 Dallas TX 75227

SCHENKEL, SUZANNE CHANCE, natural resource specialist; b. Phila., Mar. 12, 1940; d. Henry Martyn Chance II and Suzanne (Sharpless) Jameson; m. John Lackland Hardinge Schenkel, June 15, 1963; children: John Jr., Andrew Chance. BS in Edn., Tufts U., 1962. Tchr. Roland Pk. Country Sch., Balt., 1962-65; exec. dir. Mass. Citizens' Com. for Dental Health, Springfield, 1981-83; pub., editor Women's Investment Newsletter, Longmeadow, Mass., 1985-89; pub. affairs officer USDA's Soil Conservation Svc., Amherst, Mass., 1990-93; program mgr. conservation & ecosys. assistance divsn. USDA's Natural Resources Conservation Svc., Washington, 1993—; staff Merchant Marine and Fisheries com. U.S. Ho. of Reps., Washington, 1993. Author Wetlands Protection and Management Act. Chmn. Longmeadow (Mass.) Conservation Commn., 1984-90; supr. Hampden County (Mass.) Conservation Dist., 1985-90; bd. dirs., v.p. League of Women Voters of Mass., Boston, 1974-85; exec. com. Water Supply Citizens' Adv. Com., Water Resources Authority, Mass., 1979-90. Mem. Soil and Water Conservation Soc., Nat. Assn. Conservation Dists. Episcopalian. Avocations: golf, tennis, sailing. Home: 1052 Carriage Hill Pky Annapolis MD 21401-6505 Office: USDA Natural Resources Conservation Svc/Ecosystem Asst Divsn/PO Box 2890 Washington DC 20013

SCHENKENBERG, MARY MARTIN, principal; b. Oakland, Calif., Nov. 29, 1944; d. Leo Patrick and Florence Kathryn (Brinkoetter) Martin; m. Philip Rawson Schenkenberg III, Aug. 20, 1966; children: Philip Rawson IV, Amy Lynn, Stephen Patrick. BA in English, Fontbonne Coll., 1966; MA Teaching in English, St. Louis U., 1975, PhD in English, 1991. Cert. tchr., Mo. Asst. prof. Fontbonne Coll., St. Louis, 1978-85; English dept. chair Nerinx Hall High Sch., St. Louis, 1979-89; asst. prof. Webster U., St. Louis, 1986-89; co-prin. Nerinx Hall High Sch., St. Louis, 1989-92, prin., 1992—; adj. prof. St. Louis U., 1985-89; advanced placement reader Ednl. Testing Svc., Princeton, N.J., 1986-89. Author: (with others) The English Classroom in the Computer Age, 1991. Bd. pres. Mary, Queen of Peace Sch., St. Louis, 1977. Mem. ASCD, Nat. Coun. Tchrs. English, Greater St. Louis Tchrs. English (bd. dirs. 1989—). Roman Catholic. Avocations: tennis, theater, travel. Office: Nerinx Hall High Sch 530 E Lockwood Ave Webster Groves MO 63119

SCHENKER, ALEXANDER MARIAN, Slavic linguistics educator; b. Cracow, Poland, Dec. 20, 1924; came to U.S., 1946, naturalized, 1952; s. Oskar and Gizela (Szaminski) S.; m. Krystyna Czajka, Oct. 15, 1970; children: Alfred R., Michael J., Catherine I. Student, Stalinabad Pedagogical Inst., 1943-46, U. Paris, 1947-48; M.A., Yale U., 1950, Ph.D., 1953. Asst. in instrn. Yale U., New Haven, 1950-52; instr. Yale U., 1952-56, asst. prof., 1956-63, asso. prof., 1963-67, prof. Slavic linguistics, 1967—; vis. prof. Slavic linguistics U. Calif., Berkeley, 1969-70. Author: Polish Declension, 1964, Beginning Polish, 2 vols., rev. edit., 1973, The Dawn of Slavic: Introduction to Slavic Philology, 1996; editor: Fifteen Modern Polish Short Stories, 1970, American Contributions to the 10th Internat., Congress of Slavists Linguistics, 1988; co-editor: For Wiktor Weintraub, 1975, The Slavic Literary Languages, 1980, Studies in Slavic Linguistics and Poetics, 1982. Mem. Conn. Acad. Arts and Scis., Polish Inst. Arts/Scis., Am. Assn. Tchrs. Slavic and E. European Langs., Am. Assn. Advancement Slavic Studies. Home:

145 Deepwood Dr Hamden CT 06517 Office: Yale U Dept Slavic Langs and Lits PO Box 208236 New Haven CT 06520-8236

SCHENKER, CARL RICHARD, JR., lawyer; b. Portland, Oreg., Feb. 28, 1949; s. Carl Richard and Frances Emily (Cole) S.; m. Susan Sherman Richardson, Mar. 29, 1986. BA, Stanford U., 1971, JD, 1974. Bar: Calif. 1974, D.C. 1977, U.S. Dist. Ct. (so. dist.) Calif. 1977, U.S. Supreme Ct. 1978, U.S. Dist. Ct. D.C. 1980, U.S. Ct. Appeals (5th and 11th cirs.) 1981, U.S. Ct. Appeals (D.C. cir.) 1983, U.S. Ct. Appeals (2d cir.) 1992. Law clk. to Hon. Shirley M. Hufstedler U.S. Ct. Appeals (9th cir.), L.A., 1974-75; law clk. to Hon. Lewis F. Powell, Jr. U.S. Supreme Ct., Washington, 1975-76; assoc. O'Melveny & Myers, Washington, 1976-82, ptnr., 1982—. Pres. Stanford Law Review, 1973-74; contbr. articles to profl. jours. Mem. ABA, Fed. Bar Assn., D.C. Bar Assn., Phi Beta Kappa. Office: O'Melveny & Myers 555 13th St NW Washington DC 20004-1109

SCHENKER, ERIC, university dean, economist; b. Vienna, Austria, Feb. 24, 1931; came to U.S., 1939, naturalized, 1945; s. Adolph and Olga (Strauss) S.; m. Virginia Martha Wick, Apr. 14, 1963; children: David, Richard, Robert. B.B.A., CCNY, 1952; M.S., U. Tenn., 1955; Ph.D., U. Fla., 1957. Asst. prof. Mich. State U., 1957-59; mem. faculty U. Wis.-Milw., 1959—, prof. econs., 1965—; dean U. Wis.-Milw. (Sch. Bus. Adminstrn.), 1976—; dir. Urban Research Center, 1974-76; asso. dir. Center Great Lakes Studies, 1967-74, sr. scientist, 1974—; asso. dean Coll. Letters and Scis., 1963-69; bd. dirs. Am. Med. Bldgs., Ampco Metal; cons. in field. Author: The Port of Milwaukee: An Economic Review, 1967; co-author: Port Planning and Development as Related to Problems of U.S. Ports and the U.S. Coastal Environment, 1974, The Great Lakes Transportation System, 1976, Port Development in the United States, 1976, Maritime Labor Organizations on the Great Lakes-St. Lawrence Seaway System, 1978, Great Lakes Transportation System in the 80s, 1986; also monographs and articles. Sr. mem. Milw. Bd. Harbor Commrs., 1960-72, chmn., 1965-68; chmn. panel on future port requirements of U.S., Maritime Transp. Research Bd., Nat. Acad. Scis., 1973-76, chmn. panel on reducing tankbarge pollution, 1980-81; mem. pilotage adv. bd. to U.S. sec. transp., 1972-75; trustee Mt. Sinai Med. Ctr, 1984-88; mem. Econ. Progress Authority of Milw. Met. Sewerage Dist., 1983-88, Marine Bd., NAS, 1982-83, Gov.'s Coun. on Econ. Issues, 1983—. Served with AUS, 1952-54. Mem. Am. Econs. Assn., So. Econs. Assn., Phi Kappa Phi, Alpha Kappa Psi, Beta Gamma Sigma, Beta Alpha Psi. Home: 2254 W Dunwood Rd Milwaukee WI 53209-1818

SCHENKER, LEO, retired utility company executive; b. Vienna, Austria, Jan. 3, 1922; came to U.S., 1952, naturalized, 1959; s. Max and Selda Lea (Podhorcer) S.; m. Alda R. Tinson, Jan. 20, 1949; children: Michael Gregory, Deborah Anne. B.S. with first class honors, U. London, 1942; M.A. in Sci. (Can. Inst. Steel Constrn. fellow), U. Toronto, 1950; Ph.D., U. Mich., 1954. Mng. dir. METAG Ltd., London, 1945-48; asst. rsch. engr. Hydro-Electric Power Commn. of Ont. (Can.), Toronto, 1948-52; rsch. assoc. U. Mich., Ann Arbor, 1952-54; with Bell Telephone Labs., 1954-87, various positions, dir. mil. electronic tech., 1968-71; dir. Loop Maintenance Systems Lab., 1971-80, exec. dir. Central Office Ops. div., 1980-83, exec. dir. network system planning div., 1983-84, exec. dir. tech. info. div., 1984-87; adj. prof. electrical enging. Cooper Union, N.Y.C. Served with RAF, 1942-45. Recipient Duggan medal Can. Inst. Steel Constrn., 1950. Fellow IEEE, Sigma Xi, Phi Kappa Phi. Patentee communications tech. field.

SCHENKER, MARC BENET, preventive medicine educator; b. L.A., Aug. 25, 1947; s. Steve and Dosella Schenker; m. Heath Massey, Oct. 8; children: Yael, Phoebe, Hilary. BA, U. Calif., Berkeley, 1969; MD, U. Calif., San Francisco, 1973; MPH, Harvard U., Boston, 1980. Instr. medicine Harvard U., Boston, 1980-82; asst. prof. medicine U. Calif., Davis, 1982-86, assoc. prof., 1986-92, prof., 1992—, chmn. dept. cmty. and internat. health, 1995—. Fellow ACP; mem. Am. Coll. Occupl. Medicine, Am. Thoracic Soc., Am. Pub. Health Assn., Soc. Epidemiologic Rsch., Am. Coll. Epidemiology, Soc. Occupl. Environ. Health, Internat. Commn. Occupl. Health, Phi Beta Kappa, Alpha Omega Alpha. Office: Dept Cmty and Intl Hlth TB 168 Davis CA 95616-8638

SCHENKER, STEVEN, physician, educator; b. Poland, Oct. 5, 1929; came to U.S., 1943, naturalized, 1946; s. Alfred and Ernestyna S.; m. Sally Ann Wood, May 11, 1956; children: Julie C. Schenker Burn, Steven A., David S., Andrew G., Jennifer E.; m. Jo Ann Neumann, Nov. 24, 1985. B.A., Cornell U., 1951, M.D., 1955. Intern Harvard Service-Boston City Hosp., 1955-56, resident in medicine, 1956-58; asst. prof. medicine U. Cin. Sch. Medicine, 1961-63; asst. prof. U. Tex., Southwestern Sch. Medicine, 1963-67, assoc. prof. medicine, 1967-70; prof. medicine, biochemistry, dir. div. gastroenterology Vanderbilt U. Sch. Medicine, Nashville VA Hosp., 1970-82; prof. medicine and pharmacology, dir. div. gastroenterology U. Tex. Sch. Medicine, San Antonio, 1982—; chmn. study sect. Nat. Inst. on Alcohol Abuse and Addiction, 1980-83; chmn. study sects. VA, 1985-88. Editor: Hepatology, 1985-90. Contbr. numerous articles in field to profl. jours. Recipient Markle award, 1963; Career Devel. award NIH, 1968; Jurzykowski Found. for Research in Medicine award, 1979, Alcoholism Research Soc. award 1987. Mem. Am. Assn. for Study Study of Liver Diseases (pres. 1980), Am. Soc. Clin. Investigation, Assn. Am. Physicians, Am. Gastroent. Soc., Am. Soc. Pharm. and Exptl. Therapeutics, Am. Soc. Clin. Nutrition, Internat. Soc. for Study of Liver Diseases, Alpha Omega Alpha. Home: 26025 Mesa Oak Dr San Antonio TX 78255-3533 Office: U Tex Med Sch San Antonio TX 78284

SCHENKKAN, ROBERT FREDERIC, writer, actor; b. Chapel Hill, N.C., Mar. 19, 1953; s. Robert Frederic Sr. and Jean (McKenzie) S.; m. Mary Anne Dorward, Dec. 1, 1984; children: Sarah Victoria, Joshua McHenry. BA in Theatre Arts, U. Tex., 1975; MFA in Acting, Cornell U., 1977. Author: (plays) Final Passages, 1981, The Survivalist, 1982 (best of the fringe award Edinburgh Festival 1984), Tachinoki, 1987, Tall Tales, 1988 (Playwrights Forum award 1988, Best One Act Plays 1993), Heaven on Earth, 1989 (Julie Harris Playwright award Beverly Hills Theatre Guild 1989), The Kentucky Cycle, 1991 (Pulitzer prize for drama 1992, L.A. Drama Critics Circle Best Play award 1992, Penn Ctr. West award 1993, Best Play Tony award nominee 1993, Best Play Drama Desk award nominee 1993), Conversations with the Spanish Lady and Other One-Act Plays, 1993, (films) Crazy Horse, 1996, Magic, 1996, The Long Ride Home, 1995. Grantee Vogelstein Found., 1982, Arthur Found., 1988, Fund for New Am. Plays grantee 1990, Calif. Arts Coun. grantee, 1991. Mem. Writers Guild, Dramatists Guild, Actors Equity, SAG, Ensemble Studio Theatre.

SCHENKMAN, JOHN BORIS, pharmacologist, educator; b. N.Y.C., Feb. 10, 1936; s. Abraham and Theresa (Moses) S.; m. Deanna Owen, June 5, 1960; children: Jeffrey Alan, Laura Ruth. BA in Chemistry, Bklyn. Coll., 1960; PhD in Biochemistry, SUNY Upstate Med. Ctr., Syracuse, 1964. Postdoctoral fellow U. Pa. Johnson Found., Phila., 1964-67, Inst. Protein Research Osaka U., Japan, 1967-68, Inst. Toxicology Tübingen U., Fed. Republic Germany, 1968; asst. prof. Yale U. Sch. Medicine, New Haven, 1968-71, assoc. prof., 1971-78; prof., dept. head. U. Conn. Health Ctr., Farmington, 1978-87; prof. U. Conn., Farmington, 1987—. Contbr. articles to profl. jours. Served as sgt. U.S. Army, 1953-55. Research grantee NIH, NSF; recipient Research Career Devel award NIH, 1971-76. Mem. Am. Soc. Biochemists and Molecular Biologists, AM. Soc. Pharmacology Exptl. Therapeutics, Brit. Biochemistry Soc., Soc. Toxicology, Am. Med. Sch. Pharmacologists (councilor 1987-88). Jewish. Avocations: fishing, botany, wine making. Office: U Conn Sch Medicine Dept Phamacology Farmington CT 06030-1505

SCHENTAG, JEROME JOHN, pharmacy educator; b. St. Clair, Mich., Jan. 25, 1950; s. John and Rose (Petracek) S.; m. Rita R. Sloan, June 26, 1976; 1 child, Annie Sloan. BS in Pharmacy, U. Nebr., 1973; D. Pharmacy, Phila. Coll. Pharmacy, 1975. Postdoctoral fellow SUNY, Buffalo, 1975-76, asst. prof. of pharmacy, 1976-81, assoc. prof., 1981-86, prof., 1986—; dir. Clin. Pharmacokinetics Lab., Millard Fillmore Hosp., Buffalo. Editor: Applied Pharmacokinetics, 1981, 2d edit., 1985; contbr. over 175 articles to profl. publs. Am. Coll. Clin. Pharmacy fellow, 1985; recipient Disting. Young Alumni award Phila. Coll. of Pharmacy, 1989. Fellow Am. Assn. Pharm. Scientists; mem. Am. Soc. Microbiology. Office: Millard Fillmore Hosp Clin Pharmacokinetics Buffalo NY 14209

SCHEPISI, FRED, producer, director, screenwriter; b. Melbourne, Australia, Dec. 26, 1939. Student, Assumption Coll., Marcellin Coll. assessor student films Swinburne Inst. Tech., Melbourne; with govt. sponsored exptl. Film Fund; founder prodn. co. The Film Ho. Dir. films including Libido, 1973, Barbarosa, 1982, Iceman, 1984, Plenty, 1985, Roxanne, 1987; prodr., dir. The Russia House, 1990, Mr. Baseball, 1992, Six Degrees of Separation, 1993, I.Q., 1994; screenwriter, dir., prodr. The Devil's Playground, 1976 (Best Film award Australian Film Inst.), The Chant of Jimmie Blacksmith, 1978, A Cry in the Dark, 1988 (Best Screenplay award Australian Film Inst.). Address: ICM 8942 Wilshire Blvd Los Angeles CA 90211

SCHEPPACH, RAYMOND CARL, JR., association executive, economist; b. Hamden, Conn., Mar. 28, 1940; s. Raymond Carl and Margret (Barrie) S.; m. Anna Roberts, July 14, 1962 (div. Nov. 1978); children: Kristine, Raymond Scott; m. Trevia Dean, Apr. 28, 1985. B.A., U. Maine, 1962; M.A., U. Conn., 1965, Ph.D., 1970. Vice pres., sr. cons. Jack Faucett Assocs., Chevy Chase, Md., 1969-75; asst. dir. natural resources and commerce Congl. Budget Office, Washington, 1976-80, dep. dir. office, 1980-82; exec. dir. Nat. Govs. Assn., Washington, 1982—. Author: State Projections of the Gross national Product, 1970 and 1980, Transportation Productivity: Measurement and Policy Applications, 1975, Energy Policy Analysis and Congressional Action, 1982, New Directions in Economic Policy: An Agenda for the 1980's, 1984. Served to capt. U.S. Army, 1962-64. Mem. Am. Econ. Assn. Home: 4078 Rosamora Ct Mc Lean VA 22101-5807 Office: Nat Govs Assn 444 N Capitol St NW Washington DC 20001-1512*

SCHER, HOWARD DENNIS, lawyer; b. Ft. Monmouth, N.J., Apr. 23, 1945; s. George Scher and Rita (Eitches) Zar; children: Seth Micah, Eli David. BA, Brandeis U., 1967; JD, Rutgers U., 1971. Bar: Pa. 1971, U.S. Dist. Ct. (ea. dist.) Pa. 1971, U.S. Ct. Appeals (3rd cir.) 1971, U.S. Supreme Ct. 1975. Asst. city solicitor City of Phila., 1971-73; assoc. Goodis, Greenfield, Henry & Edelstein, Phila., 1973-77; assoc. Montgomery, McCracken, Walker & Rhoads, Phila., 1977-80, ptnr., 1980—. V.p. Jewish Employment Vocat. Svcs., Phila., 1988—; trustee Fedn. of Jewish Agys. of Greater Phila.; dir. Akiba Hebrew Acad., Merion, Pa.; mem. pres.'s coun. Brandeis U. Fellow Am. Coll. Trial Lawyers; mem. ABA, Pa. Bar Assn., Phila. Bar Assn., Brandeis U. Alumni Assn. (v.p. 1983-87). Home: 2222 Locust St Philadelphia PA 19103-5511 Office: Montgomery McCracken Walker & Rhoads 123 S Broad St Philadelphia PA 19109

SCHER, IRVING, lawyer; b. N.Y.C., July 22, 1933; s. Charles and Tillie (Ballenberg) S.; m. Amy Lynn Katz, June 8, 1985; 1 child, Sara Katz-Scher. BA, City Coll. N.Y., 1955; JD, Columbia U., 1962. Bar: N.Y. 1963. Assoc. Weil, Gotshal & Manges, N.Y.C., 1962-69, ptnr., 1969—; adj. prof. NYU Sch. Law, 1972—; co-chmn. ann. anti-trust law inst. Practicing Law Inst., N.Y.C., 1976—; adv. bd. Antitrust and Trade Regulation Reports, 1980—. Editor Columbia Law Rev., 1960-61, revs. editor, 1961-62; editor, co-author: Antitrust Advisor, 4th edit., 1995; contbr. articles to profl. jours. Served as lt. USNR, 1955-59. Recipient Harlan Fiske Stone scholarship Columbia Law Sch., 1960-62, Nat. Scholarship award Columbia Law Sch., 1961-62, Gluck scholarship Columbia Law Sch., 1960-61. Mem. ABA (chmn. antitrust law section 1988-89), N.Y. State Bar Assn. (chmn. antitrust law section 1980-81). Jewish. Avocations: skiing, theater. Office: Weil Gotshal & Manges 767 5th Ave New York NY 10153

SCHER, ROBERT SANDER, instrument design company executive; b. Cin., May 24, 1934; s. Stanford Samuel and Eva (Ordan) S.; m. Audrey Erna Gordon, Oct. 21, 1961; children: Sarahh, Alexander, Aaron. SB, MIT, 1956, SM, 1958, Diploma in Mech. Enging., 1960, ScD, 1963. Rsch. and teaching asst. MIT, Cambridge, Mass., 1957-62; control system engr. RCA, Hightstown, N.J., 1963-65; enging. mgr. Sequential Info. System, Elmsford, N.Y., 1965-71; tech. dir. Teledyne Gurley, Troy, N.Y., 1971-78, v.p. enging., 1978-86, pres., 1986-92; pres. Encoder Design Assocs., Clifton Park, N.Y., 1993—. Co-author patent Linear Digital Readout, 1975. Mem. ASME, Optical Soc. Am. Jewish. Avocation: chamber music. Home: 2 Laurel Oak Ln Clifton Park NY 12065-4712

SCHER, STEVEN PAUL, literature educator; b. Budapest, Hungary, Mar. 2, 1936; came to U.S., 1957, naturalized, 1963; Diploma in piano, Bela Bartok Conservatory of Music, Budapest, 1955; B.A. cum laude, Yale U., 1960, M.A., 1963, Ph.D., 1966. Instr. German, Columbia U., N.Y.C., 1965-67; asst. prof. German, Yale U., New Haven, 1967-70; assoc. prof. Yale U., 1970-74; prof. German and comparative lit. Dartmouth Coll., Hanover, N.H., 1974—; chmn. dept. Dartmouth Coll., 1974-80, acting chmn. dept., 1982-83, Ted and Helen Geisel 3d Century prof. humanities, 1984-89; vis. prof. U. Paderborn, Fed. Republic Germany, summer 1980, Karl-Franzens-U. Graz, Austria, summer 1984; grant reviewer Guggenheim Found., NEH, Am. Council Learned Socs., others; cons. univ. presses and scholarly jours.; lectr. throughout world. Author: Verbal Music in German Literature, 1968; editor: (with Charles McClelland) Postwar German Culture: An Anthology, 1974, 2d edit., 1980, Interpretationen: Zu E.T.A. Hoffmann, 1981, (with Ulrich Weisstein) Literature and the Other Arts. Proc. of IXth Congress of Internat. Comparative Lit. Assn., Innsbruck, vol. 3, 1981, Literatur und Musik. Ein Handbuch zur Theorie und Praxis eines komparatistischen Grenzgebietes, 1984, Music and Text: Critical Inquiries, 1992; contbr. articles and essays to scholarly jours. Morse fellow, 1969-70; Humboldt fellow, 1972-73; Yale Coll. scholar, 1957-60, grad. fellow, 1960-62; DAAD grantee U. Munich, 1964-65. Mem. MLA (chmn. bibliography com. of div. lit. 1972-86), Am. Comparative Lit. Assn., Internat. Comparative Lit. Assn., Internat. P.E.N. Club. Home: 102 S Main St Hanover NH 03755-2040 Office: Dartmouth College Dept German Dartmouth Hall Hanover NH 03755

SCHER, VALERIE JEAN, music critic; b. Chgo., Jan. 31, 1952; d. Jacob and Klema (Seider) S.; m. David Clark Elliott, Sept. 6, 1980; children: Sabrina, Travis. B in Performance Piano, Northwestern U., Evanston, Ill., 1974, M in Music History, 1976, postgrad., 1978. Asst. music critic Chgo. Daily News, 1975-78; asst. music and dance critic Chgo. Sun-Times, 1978-82; dance critic, asst. music critic Phila. Inquirer, 1982-83; music and dance critic San Diego Tribune, 1984-91, music, dance and theater critic, 1991-92; music critic San Diego Union-Tribune, 1992—. Mem. Music Critics Assn. Avocations: horseback riding, gardening, cooking. Office: San Diego Union-Tribune 350 Camino De La Reina San Diego CA 92108-3003

SCHERAGA, HAROLD ABRAHAM, physical chemistry educator; b. Bklyn., Oct. 18, 1921; s. Samuel and Etta (Goldberg) S.; m. Miriam Kurnow, June 20, 1943; children: Judith Anne, Deborah Ruth, Daniel Michael. B.S., CCNY, 1941; A.M., Duke U., 1942, Ph.D., 1946, Sc.D. (hon.), 1961; Sc.D. (hon.), U. Rochester, 1988, U. San Luis, 1992, Technion, 1993. Teaching, research asst. Duke U., 1941-46; fellow Harvard Med. Sch., 1946-47; instr. chemistry Cornell U., 1947-50, asst. prof., 1950-53, assoc. prof., 1953-58, prof., 1958-65, Todd prof. chemistry, 1965-92, Todd prof. chemistry emeritus, 1992—, chmn. dept., 1960-67; vis. assoc. biochemist Brookhaven Nat. Lab., summers 1950, 51, cons. biology dept., 1950-56; vis. lectr. div. protein chemistry Wool Research Labs., Melbourne, Australia, 1959; vis. prof. Soc. for Promotion Sci., Japan, Aug. 1977; mem. tech. adv. panel Xerox Corp., 1969-71, 74-79; Mem. biochemistry tng. com. NIH, 1963-65; mem. research career award com. NIGMS, 1967-71; commn. molecular biophysics Internat. Union for Pure and Applied Biophysics, 1965-69, mem. commn. macromolecular biophysics, 1969-75, pres., 1972-75, mem. commn. subcellular and macromolecular biophysics, 1975-81; adv. panel molecular biology NSF, 1960-62; Welch Found. lectr., 1962, Harvey lectr., 1968, Gallagher lectr., 1968, Lemieux lectr., 1973, Hill lectr., 1976, Venable lectr., 1981; co-chmn. Gordon Conf. on Proteins, 1963; mem. council Gordon Research Confs., 1969-71. Author: Protein Structure, Theory of Helix-Coil Transitions in Biopolymers; co-editor Molecular Biology, 1961-86; mem. editl. bd. Physiol. Chemistry and Physics, 1969-75, Mechanochemistry and Motility, 1970-71, Thrombosis Rsch., 1972-76, Biophys. Jour., 1973-75, Macromolecules, 1973-84, Computers and Chemistry, 1974-84, Internat. Jour. Peptide and Protein Chemistry, 1982—; corr. PAABS Revista, 1971-73; mem. editl. adv. bd. Biopolymers, 1963—, Biochemistry, 1969-74, 85—, Structural Chemistry, 1989-93, Jour. Computational Polymer Sci., 1991—, Jour. Biomolecular NMR, 1991—, Jour. Biomed. Sci., 1994—, Jour. Am. Chem. Soc., 1995—. Mem. Ithaca Bd. Edn., 1958-59; Bd. govs. Weizmann Inst., Israel, 1970—; mem. staff Naval Research Lab. Project, Air Force OSRD Project, World War II. Fulbright, Guggenheim fellow Carlsberg Lab., Copenhagen, 1956-57, Weizmann Inst., Israel, 1963; NIH Spl. fellow Weizmann Inst., 1970; Fogarty scholar NIH, 1984, 86, 88-91; recipient Townsend Harris medal CCNY, 1970, Chemistry Alumni Sci. Achievements award, 1977, Kowalski medal Internat. Soc. Thrombosis and Haemostatis, 1983, Linderstrøm-Lang medal Carlsberg Lab., 1983, Internat. Soc. of Quantum Chemistry and Quantum Pharmacology award in Theoretical Biology, 1993, Stein & Moore award Protein Soc., 1995; named Hon. mem. Soc. Polymer Sci. Japan, 1995. Fellow AAAS; mem. NAS, Am. Chem. Soc. (chmn. Cornell sect. 1955-56, mem. exec. com. div. biol. chemistry 1966-69, vice chmn. divsn. biol. chemistry 1970, chmn. divsn. biol. chemistry 1971, Eli Lilly award 1957, Nichols medal 1974, Kendall award 1978, Pauling award 1985, Mobil award 1990, Repligen award 1990), Am. Soc. Biol. Chemists, Biophys. Soc. (coun. 1967-70), Am. Acad. Arts and Scis., N.Y. Acad. Scis. (hon. life), Hungarian Biophys. Soc. (hon.), Soc. Polymer Sci. (Japan, hon mem.), Phi Beta Kappa, Sigma Xi, Phi Lambda Upsilon. Home: 212 Homestead Ter Ithaca NY 14850-6220

SCHERER, FREDERIC MICHAEL, economics educator; b. Ottawa, Ill., Aug. 1, 1932; s. Walter King and Margaret (Lucey) S.; m. Barbara A. Silbermann, Aug. 17, 1957; children: Thomas, Karen S. Main, Christina. AB with honors, U. Mich., 1954; MBA with high distinction, Harvard U., 1958, PhD, 1963. Asst. prof. Princeton (N.J.) U., 1963-66; prof. econs. U. Mich., Ann Arbor, 1966-72; chief economist FTC, Washington, 1974-76; prof. econs. Northwestern U., Evanston, Ill., 1976-82; Joseph Wharton prof. polit. economy Swarthmore (Pa.) Coll., 1982-89; Larsen prof. pub. policy and mgmt. Harvard U., Cambridge, Mass., 1989—; vis. prof. Ctrl. European U., Prague, 1993-94. Author: The Weapons Acquisition Process, 1964 (Lancaster prize 1964), Industrial Market Structure and Economic Performance, 1970, 3d rev. edit., 1990, The Economics of Multi-Plant Operation, 1975, Innovation and Growth, 1984, International High-Technology Competition, 1992, Competition Policies for an Integrated World Economy, 1994, Industry Structure, Strategy and Punblic Policy, 1996; co-author: Mergers, Sell-Offs and Economic Efficiency, 1987; mem. editl. bd. Jour. Indsl. Econs., 1982-89, Jour. Econ. Lit., 1989—; assoc. editor Ency. Econs., 1983—. Mem. adv. panel NSF, Washington, 1980-83, U.S. Office Tech. Assessment, 1989-93. Sr. research fellow Internat. Inst. Mgmt., 1972-74, Am. Stats. Assn. Census fellow, 1989-90; Baker scholar Harvard U., 1957; grantee NSF, 1970, 79, 82; O'Melveny & Myers Centennial Rsch. grantee, 1989. Mem. European Assn. for Rsch. in Indsl. Econs. (co-founder 1974), Internat. J.A. Schumpeter Assn. (pres. 1988-90), Brit-N.Am. Com., Am. Econ. Assn. (v.p. 1988), Indsl. Orgn. Soc. (pres. 1992), So. Econ. Assn. (v.p. 1990). Democrat. Roman Catholic. Avocations: listening to music, musicology. Home: 48 Pier 7 Charlestown MA 02129 Office: Harvard U John F Kennedy Sch Govt Cambridge MA 02138

SCHERER, GEORGE W., materials scientist. With Dupont, Inc., Wilmington, Del. Recipient Ralph K. Iler award in the Chemistry of Colloidal Materials Am. Chem. Soc., 1995. Office: DuPont Co Exptl Sta 356/384 Wilmington DE 19880

SCHERER, HAROLD NICHOLAS, JR., electric utility company executive, engineer; b. Plainfield, N.J., Apr. 5, 1929; s. Harold Nicholas and Nora (McDonough) S.; m. Jane Neely, Sept. 6, 1952 (div.); children—Anne Scherer McConnell, Peter; m. Patricia Condon, May 4, 1974; stepchildren: James, John, Joseph, Jeffery Ludwig, Jean Ludwig Ransdell. B.E., Yale U., 1951; M.B.A., Rutgers U., 1955. Registered profl. engr., N.J., Mass. Various enging. positions Pub. Service Electric and Gas Co., Newark, 1951-63; various enging. positions Am. Electric Power Service Corp., N.Y.C., 1963-68, asst. chief. elec. engr., 1968-69, chief elec. engr., 1969-73, v.p. elec. engr., 1973-82; sr. v.p. elec. enging. Am. Electric Power Service Corp., Columbus, Ohio, 1982-90; also dir. Am. Electric Power Service Corp., until 1990; pres. Commonwealth Electric Co., Wareham, Mass., 1990-93, Cambridge Electric Light Co., Canal Electric Co., Com/Steam Co., 1990-93; bd. dirs. Commonwealth Electric Co., Cambridge Electric Light Co., Com/Steam Co., Commonwealth Svcs. Co., Canal Electric Co.; cons. utility mgmt. and enging., 1993—; mem. joint U.S.-USSR working group on power transmission, 1975-81, joint U.S.-Italy working group on power transmission, 1979-88; vice-chmn. Am. Nat. Stds., N.Y.C., 1985-87; v.p. U.S. Nat. Com., 1985-93, pres., 1993—, chmn. U.S. tech. com. Internat. Conf. on Large High Voltage Electric Sys., 1985-91, internat. adminstrv. coun., 1988—, internat. exec. com., 1993—; mem. enging. rev. bd. Bonneville Power Adminstrn., 1984-94; chmn. elec. sys. and equipment com. Edison Electric Inst., 1989-90, pres. power enging. edn. found., 1992—. Contbr. articles to profl. jours. Pres. N.J. Jr. C. of C., 1960-61; councilman City of Plainfield, 1963-65; mem. Watchung (N.J.) Hills Regional H.S. Bd. Edn., 1970-72; pres. Woods at Josephinum Civic Assn., Worthington, Ohio, 1983-84. Recipient Clayton Frost award U.S. Jaycees, 1961, Young Man of Yr. award Plainfield Jaycees, 1963, Lifetime Achievement award T&D Mag., 1990. Fellow IEEE (v.p. power enging. soc. 1988-89, pres. 1990-91, William Habirshaw award for transmission and distbn. enging. 1986); mem. NAE, Tau Beta Pi, Beta Gamma Sigma. Republican. Home and Office: 467 Bay Ln Centerville MA 02632-3352

SCHERER, KARLA, foundation executive, venture capitalist; b. Detroit, Jan. 13, 1937; d. Robert Pauli and Margaret (Lindsey) S.; m. Peter R. Fink, Sept. 14, 1957 (div. July 1989); children: Christina Lammert, Hadley McKenzie Tolliver, Allison Augusta Scherer; m. Theodore Souris, Sept. 5, 1992. Student, Wellesley Coll., 1954-55; BA, U. Mich., 1957. Chmn. Karla Scherer Found., Detroit, 1989—; advisor on shareholders' rights; speaker on corp. governance to various univs. and profl. assns.; condr. workshops in field; leader only successful proxy contest of maj. U.S. publicly held corp., 1988. Trustee Eton Acad., Birmingham, Mich., 1989—; mem. vis. com. Fordham U. Grad. Sch. Bus. Adminstrn.; former mem. bd. dirs. Cottage Hosp., Univ. Liggett Sch., Music Hall, Detroit League for Handicapped; former mem. adv. bd. Wellesley Coll; former mem. Rep. Dennis M. Hertel's Candidate Selection Com. for Armed Svcs. Acads.; mem. U. Mich. Ctr. for the Edn. of Women Leadership Coun. Named Outstanding Woman Leader of Yr. Oakland U., 1990, one of Metro Detroit's Dynamic Women Women's Econ. Club, 1992, Entrepreneur of Yr. Finalist, 1993. Mem. Women's Forum Mich., Econ. Club Detroit (bd. dirs. 1991—), Women's Econ. Club Detroit, Detroit Club, Detroit Athletic Club, Country Club Detroit, Grosse Pointe Club, Renaissance Club (bd. dirs. 1995—). Office: 100 Renaissance Ctr Ste 1680 Detroit MI 48243-1009

SCHERER, RONALD CALLAWAY, voice scientist, educator; b. Akron, Ohio, Sept. 11, 1945; s. Belden Davis and Lois Ramona (Callaway) S.; children: Christopher, Maria. BS, Kent State U., 1968; MA, Ind. U., 1972; PhD, U. Iowa, 1981. Research asst. U. Iowa, Iowa City, 1979-81, asst. research scientist, 1981-83, adj. asst. prof., 1983-88, adj. assoc. prof., 1988—; adj. asst. prof. U. Denver, 1984-86; asst. adj. prof. U. Colo., Boulder, 1984-93, adj. assoc. prof., 1993—; research scientist The Denver Ctr. for the Performing Arts, 1983-88, sr. scientist, 1988—; lectr. voice and speech sci. Nat. Theatre Conservatory, Denver, 1990-94; asst. clin. prof. Sch. Medicine U. Colo., Denver, 1988—; adj. assoc. prof. U. Okla., 1992—; affiliate clin. prof. U. No. Colo., 1993—; mem. exec. and legis. bd. Nat. Ctr. for Voice and Speech, 1990—. Author: (with Dr. I. Titze) Vocal Fold Physiology: Biomechanics, Acoustics and Phonatory Control, 1983; contbr. articles to profl. jours. Nat. Inst. Dental Research fellow, 1972-76. Fellow Internat. Soc. Phonetic Scis. (auditor 1988-91); mem. Internat. Arts Medicine Assn., Am. Speech-Lang.-Hearing Assn., Acoustical Soc. Am., Internat. Assn. Logopedics and Phoniatrics, Am. Assn. Phonetic Scis. (nominating com. 1985-87), Collegium Medicorum Theatri, Sigma Xi, Pi Mu Epsilon. Office: Denver Ctr for Performing Arts 1245 Champa St Denver CO 80204-2104

SCHERF, CHRISTOPHER N., foundation administrator; b. N.Y.C., Aug. 8, 1950; s. Richard Edward and Doris Margaret (Farley) S.; m. Diane Frances Koenig, Nov. 13, 1981; children: Casey Lyn, Donna Streit, Donald Makofske. BA, U. Md., 1972. Sports writer Hagerstown (Md.) Morning Herald, 1973, UPI, N.Y.C., 1973-77, The Courier-Jour., Louisville, 1977-78; mgr. media rels. N.Y. Racing Assn., Jamaica, 1978-82; dir. svc. bur. Thoroughbred Racing Assns. of N.Am., 1982-88, exec. v.p., 1988—; also bd. dirs. Thoroughbred Racing Assns. of N.Am., Elkton, Md.; bd. dirs. TRA Ins. Co., TRA Enterprises, Inc.; trustees adv. comm. Am. Horse Coun., 1988—. Co-author: Pro Basketball'76-'77, 1976, Pro Basketball '77-'78, 1977. Mem. Turf Publicists Am., Nat. Turf Writers Assn., Am. Soc. Assn.

Execs. Office: Thoroughbred Racing Assn(TRA) 420 Fair Hill Dr Elkton MD 21921-2573

SCHERF, JOHN GEORGE, IV, lawyer; b. Tuscaloosa, Ala., Oct. 12, 1962; s. John G. III and Roberta Cannon (Timmons) S.; m. Lorie Lankford, Feb. 12, 1994; 1 child, Austin Tyler. AA, Okaloosa Walton Jr. Coll., Niceville, Fla., 1983; BA in Psychology, U. West Fla., 1987; JD, Samford U., 1991. Bar: Ala. 1992, U.S. Dist. Ct. (no. dist.) Ala., 1994. Clk., assoc. Taylor & Robinson, Birmingham, Ala., 1992-93; assoc. Frank S. Buck, P.C., Birmingham, Ala., 1993-95; pvt. practice Birmingham, Ala., 1995—. Mem. Assn. Trial Lawyers Am., Ala. Bar Assn., Ala. Trial Lawyers Assn., Birmingham Bar Assn. Democrat. Methodist. Home: 611 Springs Ave Birmingham AL 35242 Office: Scherf Griffin & Davis LLC 2122 First Ave N Birmingham AL 35203

SCHERGER, JOSEPH E., family physician, educator; b. Delphos, Ohio, Aug. 29, 1950; m. Carol M. Wintermute, Aug. 7, 1973; children: Adrian, Gabriel. BS summa cum laude, U. Dayton, 1971; MD, UCLA, 1975. Family practice residency U. Wash., Seattle, 1975-78; clin. instr. U. Calif. Sch. Medicine, Davis, 1978-80, asst. clin. prof., 1980-84, assoc. clin. prof., 1984-90, clin. prof., 1990—, dir. predoctoral program, 1991-92; med. dir. family practice and community medicine Sharp Healthcare, San Diego, 1992—. Recipeient Hippocratic Oath award UCLA, Calif. Physician of Yr. award Am. Acad. Family Physicians. Mem. Inst. Medicine of NAS, Am. Acad. Family Physicians, Soc. Tchrs. Family Medicine. Home: 3205 Rim Rock Cir Encinitas CA 92024-5718 Office: UC Davis Dept Family Practice TB 152 Davis CA 95616

SCHERICH, EDWARD BAPTISTE, retired diversified company executive; b. Inland, Nebr., Dec. 3, 1923; s. Clarence H. and Clara E. (Baptiste) S.; m. Hyacinth Rau, Aug. 11, 1945 (div. 1980); children: Carol, Eileen, John.; m. Antoinette Currera, 1981; 1 stepdau., Sylvia McNamara. B.B.A., Tulane U., 1948. Acct. Colo. Milling & Elevator Co., Denver, 1948-50; accountant, office mgr. Southdown, Inc., New Orleans, 1950-55; controller Southdown, Inc., 1955-69; v.p. finance, sec., treas. Southdown Sugars Inc., New Orleans, 1970-73; v.p., sec., treas. Southdown Land Co., New Orleans, 1971-75; sec.-treas. Southdown, Inc., Houston, 1975-78; v.p., sec. Southdown, Inc., 1979-84, treas., 1980-83; ind. fin. cons., 1984—; pres. Valmax Inc., 1989—. Served in USNR, 1943-45. Mem. Beta Gamma Sigma. Home: 633 Brouilly Dr Kenner LA 70065-1101 Office: PO Box 641307 Kenner LA 70064-1307

SCHERICH, ERWIN THOMAS, civil engineer, consultant; b. Inland, Nebr., Dec. 6, 1918; s. Harry Erwin and Ella (Peterson) S.; student Hastings Coll., 1937-39, N.C. State Coll., 1943-44; B.S., U. Nebr., 1946-48; M.S., U. Colo., 1948-51; m. Jessie Mae Funk, Jan. 1, 1947; children—Janna Rae Scherich Thornton, Jerilyn Mae Scherich Dobson, Mark Thomas. Civil and design engr. U.S. Bur. Reclamation, Denver, 1948-84, chief spillways and outlets sect., 1974-75, chief dams br., div. design, 1975-78, chief tech. rev. staff, 1978-79, chief div. tech. rev. Office of Asst. Commr. Engring. and Rsch. Ctr., 1980-84; cons. civil engr., 1984—. Mem. U.S. Com. Internat. Commn. on Large Dams. Served with AUS, 1941-45. Registered profl. engr., Colo. Fellow ASCE; mem. NSPE (nat. dir. 1981-87, v.p. southwestern region 1991-93), Profl. Engrs. Colo. (pres. 1977-78), Jefferson County West C. of C. Republican. Methodist. Home and Office: 3915 Balsam St Wheat Ridge CO 80033

SCHERMER, JUDITH KAHN, lawyer; b. N.Y.C., Feb. 28, 1949; d. Robert and Barbara Kahn; m. Daniel Woodrough Schermer; 1 child, Sarah Nicole. BA, U. Chgo., 1971; JD, William Mitchell Coll. Law, 1987. Bar: Minn. 1987, U.S. Dist. Ct. Minn. 1987. Advt. and promotion specialist U. Chgo. Press, 1971-75; systems analyst Allstate Ins. Co., Northbrook, Ill., 1975-78, Lutheran Brotherhood, Mpls., 1980-83; polit. aide Mpls. City Coun., 1986-87; ptnr. Schermer & Schermer, Mpls., 1987—. Pres., feminist caucus Dem. Farm Labor Party; bd. dirs. Women Candidates Devel. coalition. Mem. ATLA, Minn. Trial Lawyers Assn. (bd. govs., chair employment law sect.), Minn. State Bar Assn., Minn. Women Lawyers, Nat. Employment Law Assn. Home: 4624 Washburn Ave S Minneapolis MN 55410-1846 Office: Schermer and Schermer Lumber Exch Bldg 10 S 5th St Ste 700 Minneapolis MN 55402-1033

SCHERR, ALLAN LEE, computer scientist, executive; b. Balt., Nov. 18, 1940; s. Morris and Sarah (Kratzmar) S.; m. Marsha Kahn, Sept. 2, 1962 (div. 1974); children: Elise A., Stephanie L.; m. Linda Martin, June 8, 1980; 1 child, Katherine M. B.E.E., MIT, 1962, M.E.E., 1962, Ph.D.E.E., 1965. Mgr. time sharing option design System Devel. div. IBM, Poughkeepsie, N.Y., 1967-70; mgr. multiple virtual storage (MVS) project IBM, 1971-74; mgr. distributed systems programming System Communications div. IBM, Kingston, N.Y., 1977-80; dir. communications programming IBM, 1980-81; dir. communications and applications systems corp. staff IBM, Armonk, N.Y., 1981-83; dir. engring. and programming systems products div. IBM, White Plains, N.Y., 1983-86; dir. integrated applications info. systems div. IBM, Milford, Conn., 1986-88, v.p. devel. and integration application systems div., 1988-89, application solutions dir. architecture and devel., Application Solutions Line Bus., 1990-91; v.p. tech. World Wide Cons. Practices IBM Cons. Group, Milford, Conn., 1991-93; ind. cons. bus. process engring., info. tech., tech. mgmt. Weston, Conn., 1993-94; sr. v.p. software engring. EMC Corp., Hopkinton, Mass., 1994—; seminar leader Werner Erhard & Assocs., N.Y.C., 1982-90. Author: An Analysis of Time-Shared Computer Systems, 1966 (Grace Murray Hopper award Assn. Computing Machinery 1975); patentee in field. Mem. The Hunger Project, San Francisco, 1977—. IBM fellow, 1984. Fellow IEEE; mem. Sigma Xi, Tau Beta Pi, Eta Kappa Nu. Democrat. Home: 12 Doeskin Dr Framingham MA 01701-3067

SCHERR, BARRY PAUL, foreign language educator; b. Hartford, Conn., May 20, 1945; s. Joseph and Helen Lillian (Shapiro) S.; m. Sylvia Egelman, Sept. 8, 1974; children: Sonia, David. AB magna cum laude, Harvard U., 1966; AM, U. Chgo., 1967, PhD, 1973. From acting asst. prof. to asst. prof. U. Washington, Seattle, 1970-74; from asst. prof. to prof. Russian Dartmouth Coll., Hanover, N.H., 1974—, chair dept. Russian, 1981-90, chair program Linguistics, Cognitive Sci., 1989—; ad hoc svc. Bd. Examiners State N.H. Teacher Certification; co-dir. seminar Soviet Union for Secondary Sch. Tchrs., 1984; co-organizer Internat. Conf. Russian Verse Theory, 1987, Internat. Conf. Anna Akhmatova and the Poets of Tsarskoe Selo, 1989. Author: Russian Poetry: Meter, Rhythm and Rhyme, 1986, Maxim Gorky, 1988; co-trans. The Seeker of Adventure, Alexander Grin, 1989; mem. editorial bd. Slavic and East European Jour., 1978-88; co-editor: Russian Verse Theory: Procs. of the 1987 Conference at UCLA, 1987, ORUS! Studia litteraria Slavica in honorem Hugh McLean, 1995, A Sense of Place: Tsarskoe Selo and Its Poets, 1993; contbr. articles to profl. jours. Scholar Harvard Coll., 1963-66; fellow NDEA, 1966-69; grantee Internat. Rsch. and Exchange Bd., 1969-70, NEH, 1987, 89, U.S. Dept. Edn., 1987-89, Dartmouth Coll. Sr. Faculty, 1988; summer rsch. grantee Grad. Sch., Inst. Comparative and Fgn. Area Studies U. Wash., 1973. Mem. MLA (exec. com. assoc. dept. fgn. langs. 1983-85, del. assembly 1986-88), Am. Assn. Advancement Slavic Studies, Am. Assn. Tchrs. Slavic and East European Langs. (pres. 1987-88, founder, past pres. No. New England chpt., numerous coms.). Office: Dartmouth Coll Russian Dept 44 N College St Hanover NH 03755-1801

SCHERR, LAWRENCE, physician, educator; b. N.Y.C., Nov. 6, 1928; s. Harry and Sophia (Schwartz) S.; m. Peggy L. Binenkorb, June 13, 1954; children: Cynthia E., Robert W. AB, Cornell U., 1950, MD, 1957. Diplomate Am. Bd. Internal Medicine (bd. dirs., sec.-treas. 1979-86). Intern Cornell Med. divsn. Bellevue Hosp. and Meml. Ctr., 1957-58, asst. resident, 1958-59, rsch. fellow cardiorenal lab., 1959-60, chief resident, 1960-61, co-dir. cardiorenal lab., 1961-62, asst. vis. physician, 1961-63, assoc. vis. physician, 1963-65, dir. cardiology and renal unit, 1963-67, assoc. dir., 1964-67, vis. physician, 1966-68; physician to out-patients N.Y. Hosp., 1961-63, asst. attending physician, 1963-66, assoc. attending physician, 1966-71, attending physician, 1971—; asst. attending physician Sloan-Kettering Cancer Ctr., 1962-71, cons., 1971—; chmn. dept. medicine North Shore Univ. Hosp., 1967—, dir. acad. affairs, 1969-93, sr. v.p. med. affairs, 1993—; asst. in medicine Med. Coll. Cornell U., 1958-59; rsch. fellow N.Y. Heart Assn., 1959-60, instr. medicine, 1960-63, asst. prof., 1963-66, assoc. prof., 1966-71, David J. Greene Disting. prof., 1971—, assoc. dean, 1969—; career scientist Health Rsch. Coun., N.Y.C., 1962-66; tchg. scholar Am. Heart Assn., 1966-67; pres. N.Y. State Bd. Medicine, 1974-75; bd. dirs. Nat. Bd. Med. Examiners, 1976-80; chmn. Accreditation Coun. for Grad. Med. Edn., 1988, N.Y. State Coun. on Grad. Edn., 1987-92. Contbr. articles to profl. jours. Lt. USNR, 1950-53. Fellow N.Y. Acad. Medicine, Am. Heart Assn. (coun. on clin. cardiology); mem. ACP (master, chmn. and gov. Downstate N.Y. region II 1975-80, regent 1980-86, chmn. bd. regents 1985-86; nat. pres.-elect 1986-87, pres. 1987-88, pres. emeritus), AMA, Am. Fedn. Clin. Rsch., Harvey Soc., N.Y. Med. Soc., Nassau County Med. Soc., Assn. Am. Med. Colls., Am. Clin. and Climatologic Assn. Home: 19 Doral Dr Manhasset NY 11030-3907 Office: No Shore Univ Hosp Manhasset NY 11030

SCHERSTEN, H. DONALD, management consultant, realtor, mortgage broker; b. Titusville, Pa., Nov. 6, 1919; s. H.J. and Clara (Brown) S.; m. Katherine Conley; 1 dau. by previous marriage, Sandra S. Hotard. B.S., Temple U., 1941; postgrad., Tulsa U., 1946-48, Columbia U., 1955. With Creole Petroleum Corp. (affiliate Exxon Corp.), 1948-69, successively dist. field chief accountant Cabimas, Venezuela, coordinator procedures, fin. statements and audits, asst. controller, 1951-62; controller Creole Petroleum Corp. (affiliate Exxon Corp.), Caracas, 1962-69; gen. auditor Exxon Corp., N.Y.C., 1969-74; coordinator math., computers, systems Exxon Corp., 1975-76; pres. H. Donald Schersten & Assocs. (Mgmt. Cons.), 1977—, R.J. Reynolds Nabisco, 1977-78; realtor, 1985—; lic. mortgage broker, 1986—. Pres. council Am. Ch. Caracas, 1960. Served to 1st lt. AUS, 1942-45. Named to Acct. Alumni Hall of Fame, Temple U., 1985. Mem. Am. Petroleum Inst. (chmn. audit com. 1974-76), Inst. Internal Auditors (cert.), U.S. Power Squadrons, USCG Aux. (comdr. 1984). Clubs: Internat, Safari, Toastmasters (past pres. Caracas chpt.), Los Rancheros Deep Sea Fishing. Home: 4683 Gleve Farm Rd Sarasota FL 34235-1806

SCHETKY, LAURENCE MCDONALD, metallurgist, researcher; b. Baguio, The Philippines, July 15, 1922; s. Gerald Laurence and Ethyl Jane (McDonald) S.; m. Diane Heiskell, Dec. 12, 1977 (div. Feb. 1986); mem. Karen Searles, July 12, 1986 (div. Oct. 1994); 1 child, Mark Christian. B-SChemE, Rensselaer Poly Inst., Troy, N.Y., 1943, MMetE, 1948, PhD, 1953. Registered profl. engr., Mass. Rsch. fellow MIT, Cambridge, 1953-59; v.p. rsch. Alloyd Electronics, Inc., Cambridge, 1959-63; dir. R & D Internat. Copper Rsch. Assn., Inc., N.Y.C., 1963-83; pres. Memory Metals, Inc., Stamford, Conn., 1983-86; v.p., chief scientist Memry Corp., Brookfield, Conn., 1987—; dir. Photoetching Engring., Inc., Milford, Mass., 1985—. Editor: Beryllium Technology, 2 vol., 1966, The Metallurgy of Copper, 13 vols., 1966-83; author: (with others) Copper in Iron and Steel, 1982; contbr. over 100 articles to physics and metallurgy jours. With USN, 1944-46, PTO. Rsch. fellow Alcoa Corp., 1948-53. Fellow Am. Soc. Metals Internat. (life), Brit. Inst. Metals; mem. AIME (life). Republican. Episcopalian. Achievements include 5 patents in Electron Beam Technology, Vapor Phase Deposition, Shape Memory Actuators. Home: 77 Rock House Rd Easton CT 06612-1003 Office: Memry Corp 57 Commerce Dr Brookfield CT 06804-3405

SCHEU, DAVID ROBERT, SR., historic site director; b. Milw., Feb. 8, 1944; s. Oscar Charles Jr. and Dorothy Marie (Schmitz) S.; m. Deborah Singleton Hill, Feb. 3, 1968; children: David R. Jr., Stephanie Ann Scheu Aman. BS in Engring., U.S. Naval Acad., 1967; MBA, U. So. Ill., Edwardsville, 1980. Commd. ensign USN, 1967, advanced through grades to capt., 1988; served on USS Sterett, 1967-69, USS Buchanan, 1970-71; stationed at US Naval Acad., 1971-74; served on USS Berkeley, 1975-77; stationed at Fleet Combat Tng. Ctr. Pacific, 1977-80; served on USS Hepburn, 1980-81, USS New Jersey, 1981-83, USS Edson, 1984-86; stationed at Comcargru Seven, 1986-89, Mil. Sealift Command, 1989-91; dir. Battleship N.C. Meml., Wilmington, N.C., 1991—. Bd. dirs. Travel Coun. N.C., Raleigh, 1991—, N.C. Maritime History Coun., Beaufort, 1991—, Cape Fear Coast Conv. and Visitors Bur., Wilmington, 1992—, Hist. Naval Ships Assn., 1994—. Mem. U.S. Naval Inst., Navy League U.S., S.E. Tourism Soc., Ret. Officers Assn. Roman Catholic. Avocations: sailing, jogging. Office: USS NC Battleship Meml PO Box 480 Wilmington NC 28402-0480

SCHEU, LYNN MCLAUGHLIN, scientific publication editor; b. Lancaster, Ohio, July 9, 1942; d. Franklin Neil and Carol Lois (Bigham) McLaughlin; m. Richard V. Scheu, Apr. 16, 1966; children: David Edward, Michael Patrick. BS, Auburn U., 1964; postgrad., Ohio State U., 1964-66. English, French tchr. Reynoldsburg (Ohio) H.S., 1966-70; adj. curator mollusks Mus. History & Sci., Louisville, 1978-85; editor Am. Conchologist, Saddlebrook, N.J., 1987—; chairperson Lambis Group, 1996—; mem. adv. editl. bd. Bailey Matthews Shell Mus. and Ednl. Found., Sanibel, Fla., 1988—. Mem. exec. bd. Friends of Libr., Louisville, 1989-95; mem. Mayor's Task Force on Librs., Louisville, 1988-89. Mem. Conchologists Am. (bd. dirs. 1987—). Avocations: shell collecting, fossils, landscape gardening. Home and Office: 1222 Holsworth Ln Louisville KY 40222

SCHEUER, PAUL JOSEF, chemistry educator; b. Heilbronn, Germany, May 25, 1915; came to U.S., 1938; s. Albert and Emma (Neu) S.; m. Alice Elizabeth Dash, Sept. 5, 1950; children: Elizabeth E., Deborah A., David A., Jonathan L.L. BS with high honors, Northeastern U., Boston, 1943; MA, Harvard U., 1947, PhD, 1950. Asst. prof. chemistry U. Hawaii, Honolulu, 1950-55, assoc. prof. chemistry, 1956-61, prof. chemistry, 1961-85, prof. chemistry emeritus, 1985—; vis. prof. Orsted Inst., U. Copenhagen, 1977, 89; Toyo Suisan vis. prof. U. Tokyo, 1992. Author: Chemistry of Marine Natural Products, 1973, editor 12 series, 1978-93; contbr. over 250 articles to profl. jours. Spl. agt. U.S. Army, 1944-46, ETO. Recipient Rsch. Achievement award Am. Soc. Pharmacognosy, 1994; named P.J. Scheuer award Marine Chemists, 1992; NATO fellow, 1975. Fellow AAAS, Royal Soc. Chemistry; mem. Am. Chem. Soc. (sect. chair 1956, 87, Ernest Guenther award 1994), Northeastern U. Alumni Assn. (Disting. Alumni award 1984). Office: U Hawaii Chemistry Dept 2545 The Mall Honolulu HI 96822-2275

SCHEUERMAN, ELEANOR JOYCE MILLER, medical association administrator; b. Jersey City, N.J., July 7, 1937; d. Lawrence Houseman and Bridie E.J. (Moran) M.; m. William Henry Scheuerman, Jr., Sept. 5, 1969; 1 child, Sheila Brigid. BS in Nursing, Seton Hall, 1959; MA in Pub. Health, N.Y.U., 1964. RN, N.J., Mass. Pvt. duty nurse Jersey City Med. Ctr., 1959-60; pub. health nurse Pub. Health Nursing Svc. of Jersey City, 1959-63, 66; health educator Acad. St. Aloysius, Jersey City, 1962-64; instr. sch. nursing Seton Hall Univ., South Orange, N.J., 1964-67; dir. Pub. Health Nursing Agy., Washington, N.J., 1967-93; head nurse Hunterdon Devel. Ctr., Clinton, N.J., 1989-93; bd. dirs. Warren County Office on Aging, 1974-93, Legal Svc. of Warren County, 1976-77; med. and health staff chief Warren County Civil Def. and Disaster Control, 1979; info. and referral svc. area com. Warren County Human Svcs., 1985-91, adv. coun., 1983-91, chair protective svcs. com., 1984-91. Chair suprs.' workshop com. Home Health Assembly of N.J., 1974-75; adv. coun. for practical nursing Warren County Vocat. Tech. Sch., 1986-93. Mem. Nat. League for Nursing (bd. dirs. 1977-78), APHA, Am. Sch. Health Assn. (fellow 1965), Am. Nursing Assn. (pub. health sect., membership chair 1960, v.p. dist. 2 1962), N.J. State Nurses Assn. (membership chair 1965), Sigma Theta Tau.

SCHEUFFELE, TRACY LYNNE, accountant; b. Battle Creek, Mich., Feb. 7, 1968; d. Kent Allan Schwartz and Marie Elaine (Decker) Dowd; m. Scott Dwight Scheuffele, Sept. 21, 1990 (div.). BA, Western Mich. U., 1990; postgrad., Ind. U. Acctg. assoc. James River Corp., Kalamazoo, Mich., 1990-91, cost acct., 1991-92; contr. James River Corp., Kendallville, Ind., 1992-96, contr. Sys. Implementation Project, 1995—. Mem. Inst. Mgmt. Accts. (sec. 1990-91, treas. 1991-92, v.p. membership 1992-93, v.p. fin. and adminstrn. 1993-94), Internat. Mgmt. Coun. Republican. Roman Catholic. Avocations: aerobics, hiking, computers, travel, reading. Home: 57 F Adams Cir Fairfield OH 45014 Office: James River Corp One Better Way Rd Milford OH 45150-3266

SCHEUPELEIN, ROBERT JOHN, government official; b. Brookhaven, N.Y., May 9, 1932; s. Ernest and Mary (Leonowitz) S.; m. Kathleen Ehrenberger (div. 1980). BA in Chemistry, U. Miami, 1955, MS in Phys. Chemistry, 1956; PhD in Phys. Chemistry, U. Utah, 1961; postgrad., Harvard U., 1982. Rsch. assoc. dermatology Harvard Med. Sch., Cambridge, Mass., 1962-68, assoc. in biophysics and dermatology, 1968-70, prin. assoc. in biophysics, 1970-77; chief dermal and ocular toxicology br. Bur. Foods, FDA, Washington, 1977-79, dir. div. food animal additives, 1979-82; dep. dir. Office Toxicological Scis., Ctr. for Food Safety and Applied Nutrition, Washington, 1983-88, dir. Office Toxicological Scis., 1988-92, dir. Office Rsch. Skills, 1992-94; prin. The Weinberg Group Inc, Washington, 1994—; course dir. skin biology and physiology Harvard-MIT Program in Health Sci., 1971-76; mem. White House USTP Task Force on Chem. Carcinogens, Washington, 1983-85; mem. task force on risk assessment and risk mgmt. HHS, Washington, 1984-85; mem. risk assessment subcom. Nat. Sci. and Tech. Coun., 1994—. Editor: Biological Basis for Risk Assessment of Dioxins, 1991; contbr. articles to sci. jours., chpts. to books. Capt. USAR, 1961-62. Recipient sci. lit. award Soc. Cosmetic Chemists, 1968, citation Bur. Roods, FDA, 1980, award of merit FDA, 1987; sr. exec. fellow Harvard U. John F. Kennedy Sch. Govt., 1982. Mem. AAAS; mem. Soc. for Risk Analysis. Avocations: tennis, woodworking, ballroom dancing, writing. Home: 5140 Maris Ave Alexandria VA 22304-1963

SCHEURING, GARRY JOSEPH, banker; b. 1939; married. BS, U. Notre Dame, 1961; MBA, U. Chgo., 1964. With Booz, Allen & Hamilton, Inc., 1961-62; with Continental Bank Corp., 1964-91, sr. v.p., then exec. v.p., then sector exec., then vice chmn., also bd. dirs.; with Midlantic Corp, Edison, N.J., 1991-95; vice chmn. PNC Bank Corp, East Brunswick, N.J., 1996—; also bd. dirs. Midlantic Corp., Edison, N.J. Office: PNC Bank Corp Two Tower Ctr East Brunswick NJ 08816-1100

SCHEVILL, JAMES ERWIN, poet, playwright; b. Berkeley, Calif., June 10, 1920; s. Rudolph and Margaret (Erwin) S.; m. Margot Helmuth, Aug. 2, 1966; children (by previous marriage): Deborah, Susanna. BS, Harvard U., 1942; MA (ad eundem), Brown U.; LHD (hon.), R.I. Coll., 1986. Mem. faculty San Francisco State Coll., 1959-68, prof. English, 1968, dir. Poetry Center, 1961-68; prof. Brown U., 1969-85, prof. emeritus, 1985—; reader various univs., insts., and orgns. Author: (poems) Tensions, 1947, The American Fantasies, 1951, The Right to Greet, 1955, Selected Poems 1945-59, 1959, Private Dooms & Public Destinations: Poems 1945-62, 1962, The Stalingrad Elegies, 1964, Release, 1968, Violence & Glory: Poems 1962-68, 1969, The Buddhist Car & Other Characters, 1973, Pursuing Elegy: A Poem About Haiti, 1974, The Mayan Poems, 1978, Fire of Eyes: A Guatemalan Sequence, 1979, The American Fantasies: Collected Poems 1945-81, 1983, The Invisible Volcano, 1985, Ghost Names/Ghost Numbers, 1986, Ambiguous Dancers of Fame: Collected Poems 1945-86 Vol. II, 1987, Winter Channels, 1994, The Complete American Fantasies, 1996; (biographies) Sherwood Anderson: His Life and Work, 1951, The Roaring Market and the Silent Tomb, 1956, Bern Porter: A Personal Biography, 1993; (plays) High Sinners, Low Angels, 1953, The Bloody Tenet, 1957, Voices of Mass. and Capital A, 1958, The Black President and Other Plays, 1965, Lovecraft's Follies, 1971, Breakout: In Search of New Theatrical Environments, 1973, Cathedral of Ice, 1975, reprinted in internat. anthology Plays of the Holocaust, 1988, Oppenheimer's Chair, 1985, Collected Short Plays, 1986, Monologue on S.J. Perelman, 1986, Time of the Hand and Eye, 1986, Mother O Or The Last American Mother, 1990, (with Mary Gail) The Garden on F Street, 1992, The Phantom of Life: A Melville Play, 1993, Five Plays, 1993; (novel) The Arena of Ants, 1977; (rec.) Performance Poems, 1984; (translation) The Cid, 1961; editor: Six Historians (by F. Schevill), 1956, (with others) Wastepaper Theatre Anthology, 1978; plays produced in various theaters in U.S. including Guthrie Theatre, Mpls., Magic Theatre, San Francisco, La Mama, N.Y.C., Trinity Repertory Co., Providence, Goodman Theatre, Chgo., Berkeley Repertory Theatre, R.I. Playwrights Theatre, Volkstheater, Rostock, German Dem. Republic, others. Served to capt. AUS, 1942-46. Ford Found. grantee, 1954, 60-61, R.I. Com. on Humanities grantee, 1975; Fund Advancement Edn., 1953-54, Office for Advanced Drama Research fellow, 1957, Rockefeller fellow, 1964, Guggenheim fellow, 1981, McKnight fellow, 1984; recipient Performance prize Nat. Theatre Competition, 1945, 2d prize Phelan Biography Competition, 1954, 2d prize Phelan Drama Competition, 1958, William Carlos Williams award, 1965, Roadsted Found. award, 1966, Gov.'s award R.I., 1975, Best Story of Yr. award Ariz. Quart., 1977; story selected for O. Henry Awards Prize Stories, 1978; award in lit. Am. Acad. and Inst. Arts and Letters, 1991; work commd. by Nat. Council Chs., 1956-61, Fromm Found., 1959, Trinity Repertory Co., R.I. Hosp., 1986, Providence Coll., 1986, Magdalena Group, 1992. Home: 1309 Oxford St Berkeley CA 94709-1424 Office: Brown U Dept English Providence RI 02912

SCHEVING, LAWRENCE EINAR, anatomy educator, scientist; b. Hensel, N.D., Oct. 20, 1920; s. Einar L. and Mary (Brown) S.; m. Virginia M. Krumdick, Aug. 6, 1949; children: Lawrence, Mary, John, Jennifer, Patricia (dec.). BS in Biology, DePaul U., 1949, MS in Zoology, 1950; PhD, Loyola U., Chgo., 1957. Mem. faculty Lewis Coll., Lockport, Ill.; successively instr., asst. prof., asso. prof. and head dept. biol. sci. Lewis Coll., 1950-57; prof. anatomy Chgo. Med. Sch., 1957-67, La. State U. Med. Sch., New Orleans, 1967-70, U. Ark. Coll. Med., Little Rock, 1970-74; Rebsamen prof. anat. sci. U. Ark. Coll. Med., 1974-91, Rebsamen prof. emeritus, 1991—; vis. prof. U. Bergen, Norway, 1952, The Med. Sch. Hanover, Fed. Republic Germany, 1973; dir. chronobiology course Chautauqua series NSF, 1979; dir. NATO Advanced Study Insts., 1979, Workshop on chronobiotech. and chronobiol. engring., 1985; dir. Fedn. Am. Socs. Exptl. Biology summer research conf., Copper Mountain, Colo., 1988; mem. breast cancer task force Nat. Cancer Inst.; mem. U.S. Army med. research and devel. adv. com., 1982—; cons. to VA. Author: Biological Rhythms in Structure and Function, 1981; editor: Chronobiology, 1974, Chronobiotech. and Chronobiol. Engring. 1986, Research Advance in Chronobiology, 1987 (2 vols.); numerous chpts. to books, over 270 articles in field of chronobiology and other biol. areas to profl. jours.; mem. editorial bd.: Chronobiologia, Chronobiology Internat., Am. Jour. Anatomy. Served to capt. AUS, 1940-45; col. Res. Decorated Bronze Star, Disting. Svc. medal, others; recipient Research award Chgo. Med. Sch. Bd. Dirs., 1962, Most Helpful Prof. award La. State U., 1968, award for Excellence in Nat. Leadership and Lifes Work, Gov. N.D., 1992; named Prof. Year Student Council Chgo. Med. Sch., 1964; recipient Golden Apple award student body U. Ark. Med. Sch., 1972; Alexander von Humboldt Sr. Scientist prize German govt., 1973, Highest Faculty award U. Ark. Med. Soc., 1987, others. Mem. AAAS, Am. Soc. Anatomists, Am. Assn. Cancer Research, Am. Soc. Zoologists, Am. Soc. Photobiology, Internat. Soc. Chronobiology (hon. mem., sec.-treas. 1971-83, pres.-elect 1983-85, pres. 1985-89), So. Assn. Anatomists (past councillor), Am. Indsl. Hygiene Assn. (traditional workshifts com. 1983-89), Sigma Xi (chpt. pres. 1964-65). Roman Catholic. Home: 10200 W Bluemound Rd Apt 329 Wauwatosa WI 53226

SCHEWE, DONALD BRUCE, archivist, library director; b. Cleve., Oct. 28, 1943; s. Norman Edward and Theodora (Robinson) S.; m. Charlene R. Wenz, June 10, 1965; children: Amanda Marie, Ann Elizabeth. BA, U. Nebr., 1964, MA, 1968; PhD, Ohio State U., 1971. Archivist Franklin D. Roosevelt Library, Hyde Park, N.Y., 1972-77, supervisory archivist, 1977-79, asst. dir., 1979-81; dir. Carter Presdl. Materials Project, Atlanta, 1981-86, Jimmy Carter Library, Atlanta, 1986—. Editor: Franklin D. Roosevelt and Foreign Affairs, 1981. With U.S. Army, 1964-66, Vietnam, ret. lt. col. Mem. Assn. Records Mgrs. and Adminstrs., Soc. Ga. Archivists, Orgn. Am. Historians. Episcopalian. Lodge: Rotary. Office: Jimmy Carter Libr 441 Freedom Pky Atlanta GA 30307-1498

SCHEWEL, ELLIOT SIDNEY, state senator, furniture company executive; b. Lynchburg, Va., June 20, 1924; m. Rosel H. Hoffberger. B.S. in Econs., Washington and Lee U. Former pres. Schewel Furniture Co.; mem. Va. Senate, 1976—, chmn. edn. and health com. . Served with U.S. Army, World War II. Democrat. Office: Va Senate Gen Assembly Bldg 9th & Broad Sts Richmond VA 23219

SCHEXNAYDER, BRIAN EDWARD, opera singer; b. Port Arthur, Tex., Sept. 18, 1953; s. Leonard and Dorothy (Carrier) S.; m. Sherri Scallan, Oct. 2, 1976. BA in Music, U. Southwestern La., 1976; postgrad., Juilliard Sch. Music, 1976-80. Performances with Met. Opera, N.Y.C., Paris Opera Co., Edmonton (Alta., Can.) Opera Co., New Orleans Opera Co., Santiago (Chile) Opera, Winnipeg (Man., Can.) Opera, St. Petersburg (Fla.) Opera, Jackson (Miss.) Opera Co., San Francisco Opera, Frankfurt Opera, Hamburg Staatsoper Opera, Oper der Studt Bonn, Spoleto (Italy) Festival of Two Worlds, Cin. Opera, Fla. Grand Opera. Mem. Am. Guild Musicians. Avocations: computers, billiards, remote control airplanes.

SCHEXNAYDER, CHARLOTTE TILLAR, state legislator; b. Tillar, Ark., Dec. 25, 1923; d. Jewell Stephen and Bertha (Terry) Tillar; m. Melvin John Schexnayder Sr., Aug. 18, 1946; children: M. John Jr., Sarah Holden, Stephen. BA, La. State U., 1944, postgrad., 1947-48. Asst. editor La. Agrl. Extension, Baton Rouge, 1944; editor The McGehee (Ark.) Times, 1945-46, 48-53; editor, co-publisher The Dumas (Ark.) Clarion, 1954-85, publisher, 1985—; mem. Ark. Ho. of Reps., Little Rock, 1985—, asst. speaker pro tem, 1995—; pres. Ark. Assn. Women, 1955, Nat. Newspaper Assn., Washington, 1991-92, Ark. Press. Assn., Little Rock, 1982, Nat. Fedn. Press Women, Blue Springs, Mo., 1977-78, Litte Rock chpt. Soc. Profl. Journalists, 1973; mem. pres.'s coun. Winrock Internat., 1990—. Editor: Images of the Past, 1991. 1st woman mem. Ark. Bd. Pardons and Parole, 1975-80; mem. Ark. Legis. Coun., 1985-92; v.p. Desha County Mus., 1989—; dir. Dumas Indsl. Found., 1986—; mem. exec. com. Ark. Ctrl. Radiation Therapy Inst., 1991-92; mem. adv. bd. Ark. Profl. Women Achievement, 1992—; vice chair Ark. Rural Devel. Commn., 1991-96; mem. Winrock Internat. Adv. Coun., 1991—. Named Disting. Alumnus Ark. A&M Coll., 1971, Woman of Achievement Nat. Fedn. Press Women, 1970, Outstanding Arkansan C. of C., 1986; recipient Ark. Profl. Women of Distinction award No. Bank, Little Rock, 1990, Emma McKinnery award Nation's Top Cmty. Newspaper Woman, 1980, Journalist award Nat. Conf. of Christians and Jews, 1989, Lifetime Achievement award Nat. Fedn. Press Women, 1992, Outstanding Svc. award Ark. Assn. Elem. Prins., Disting. Svc. award Ark. Press Assn., 1993; named to La. State U. Alumni Hall of Distinction, 1994; named one Top 100 Ark. Women, Ark. Bus., 1995, 96. Mem. Pi Beta Phi (Crest award 1992), Ark. Delta Coun. (chmn. of bd. dirs. 1989—). Democrat. Roman Catholic. Home: 322 Court St Dumas AR 71639-2718 Office: Clarion Publishing Co Inc 136 E Waterman St Dumas AR 71639-2227

SCHEY, JOHN ANTHONY, metallurgical engineering educator; b. Sopron, Hungary, Dec. 19, 1922; came to U.S., 1962; s. Mihaly and Hedvig Terez (Topfl) S.; m. Margit Maria Sule, Sept. 13, 1926; 1 child, John Francis. Diplome metall. engring., Tech. U., Sopron, 1946; candidate tech. scis., Acad. Scis., Budapest, Hungary, 1953; D of Engring. (hon.), U. Stuttgart, 1987, U. Heavy Industry, Miskolc, Hungary, 1989. Cert. mfg. engr.; registered profl. engr. Chief technologist Iron and Metal Works, Csepel, Hungary, 1947-51; reader Tech. U., Miskolc, Hungary, 1951-56; dept. head Brit. Aluminium Co. Research Labs., 1957-62; metall. advisor Ill. Inst. Tech. Research Inst., Chgo., 1962-68; prof. U. Ill., Chgo., 1968-74; prof. U. Waterloo, Ont., Can., 1974-88, disting. prof. emeritus, 1988; resource person Niagara Inst., Ontario, 1980; course dir. Forging Industry Assn., Cleve., 1978; cons. to various corps. in U.S. and Can. Author: Tribology in Metalworking, 1983, Introduction to Manufacturing Processes, 2d edit., 1987; patentee in field. Recipient W.H.A. Robertson award Inst. Metals, 1966. Fellow Am. Soc. Metals, Soc. Mfg. Engrs. (Gold Medal award 1974); mem. Nat. Acad. Engring., Can. Inst. Mining and Metallurgy (Dofasco award 1984); fgn. mem. Hungarian Acad. Scis. Avocations: music, history, impact of technology on soc.

SCHIAFFINO, S(ILVIO) STEPHEN, retired medical society executive, consultant; b. Bklyn., Nov. 1, 1927; s. Stephen Anthony and Jane (DiDonato) S.; m. Josephine Rose Bovello, Apr. 25, 1954; children—Susan, Stephen. BS, Georgetown U., 1946, MS, 1948, Ph.D. in Biochemistry, 1956. Research biochemist div. nutrition FDA, Washington, 1948-50; asst. br. chief div. FDA, 1954-60; mgr. chemistry dept. Hazelton Labs., Vienna, Va., 1960-61; with NIH, 1961—; scientist adminstr. NIH (Nat. Cancer Inst.), 1961-64, asst. chief research grants rev. br., 1964-69, chief., 1969-72, asso. dir. for sci. rev., 1972-78, dep. dir. div. research grants, 1978-86; sr. sci. advisor office of extramural research and tng., office of dir. NIH, 1986-87; exec. officer, sci. officer Am. Soc. for Clin. Nutrition, Bethesda, Md., 1987-93; cons., 1993—; cons. in field. Served with AUS, 1950-53. Recipient Superior Service award FDA, 1960, Superior Service award NIH, 1969. Mem. AAAS, Am. Soc. for Clin. Nutrition., Am. Inst. Nutrition.

SCHIAVELLI, MELVYN DAVID, academic administrator, chemistry educator, researcher; b. Chgo., Aug. 8, 1942; s. Gene James and Frances Elizabeth (Giacomo) S.; m. Virginia Farrell, Sept. 10, 1966; children—Timothy, Karen. BS in Chemistry, DePaul U., 1964; PhD in Chemistry, U. Calif., Berkeley, 1967. Rsch. assoc. Mich. State U., East Lansing, 1967-68; from asst. prof. to assoc. prof. chemistry Coll. William and Mary, Williamsburg, Va., 1968-80; prof. chemistry Coll. William and Mary, Williamsburg, 1980-94, chmn. dept. chemistry, 1978-84, dean Faculty Arts and Scis., 1984-86; provost Coll. William and Mary, 1986-93, acting pres., 1992; prof. chem. and biochem., provost U. Del., Newark, 1994—. Contbr. articles to profl. jours., 1969—. Grantee NSF Petroleum Rsch. Fund, 1969-90. Mem. Am. Chem. Soc., Royal Inst. Chemists, Sigma Xi. Roman Catholic. Office: U Del Office Univ Provost 129 Hullihen Hall Newark DE 19711-3649

SCHIAVELLO, BRUNO, mechanical engineer; b. Gerocarne, Italy, July 12, 1945; came to the U.S., 1982; s. Francesco and Marianna (Sirgiovanni) S. BS in Mech. Engring., U. Rome, 1974; MS in Fluid Dynamics, Von Karman Inst., 1975. Registered profl. engr., Italy. Hydraulic rschr. Worthington SpA, Desio, Italy, 1975-79, product engr., 1979-82; assoc. dir. hydraulics McGraw Edison-Worthington, Mountainside, N.J., 1982-83, dir. hydraulics, 1983-85; mgr. fluid dynamics Dresser Pump Divsn., Harrison, N.J., 1985-93; dir. fluid dynamics Ingersoll Dresser Pumps, Phillipsburg, N.J., 1993—; mem. adv. com. pump symposium Tex. A&M U., College Station, 1984—; lectr. Von Karman Inst., 1978, Conf. Norwegian Chartered Engrs., 1986, 88; contbr. articles to profl. jours. Mem. Am. Assn. Mech. Engrs., Soc. Hydrotechnique de France, Internat. Assn. Hydraulic Rsch., AIAA. Achievements include development of computer prediction methods for pump performance, advanced designs of pump leading to performance improvement and/or cost reduction of centrifugal and mixed flow pumps, single and multistage; designed two-phase flow pumps. Home: 246 Millburn Ave Apt C Millburn NJ 07041-1724

SCHIAVI, RAUL CONSTANTE, psychiatrist, educator, researcher; b. Buenos Aires, Argentina, Jan. 7, 1930; came to U.S. 1956; s. Constantino and Maria (Acquier) S.; m. Michelle deMiniac, Aug. 26, 1960; children; Isabelle, Nadine, Viviane. MD, U. Buenos Aires, 1953. Diplomate Am. Bd. Psychiatry and Neurology. Fgn. asst. psychiatry U. Paris, 1955-56; resident in psychiatry U. Pa., Phila., 1956-59; instr. psychiatry U. Pa., 1959-61; assoc. College de France, Paris, 1961-63; asst. prof. psychiatry Cornell U., N.Y.C., 1963-66; assoc. prof. psychiatry SUNY, Downstate Med. Ctr., Bklyn., 1966-71, Mt. Sinai Sch. Medicine, N.Y.C., 1971-78; prof. psychiatry Mt. Sinai Sch. Medicine, 1978-96, emeritus prof. psychiatry, 1996—; fellow Found. Fund for Rsch. in Psychiatry, 1958-63; cons. NIMH, 1966-70, 77-81 (Rsch. Sci. Devel. award 1966, grantee 1976-95)); dir. human sexuality program Mt. Sinai Sch. Medicine, 1973-96; advisor WHO, 1989. Contbr. articles to profl. jours., chpts. to books; co-editor Jour. Sex and Marital Therapy; mem. editl. bd. Archives of Sexual Behavior, Hormones and Behavior, Psychosomatic Medicine, Revista Latinoamericana de Sexologia, Quaderni de Sessuologia Clinica, Revista Argentina de Sexualidad Humana, Annual Rev. Sex Rsch. Recipient Masters and Johnson award Soc. for Sex Therapy and Rsch., 1991; grantee NIH, 1977-80, 87-95, others. Fellow Am. Psychopathol. Assn., Psychiat. Rsch. Soc., Am. Psychiat. Assn. (life fellow, cons. 1989, Excellence in Edn. award 1992); mem. AAAS, Am. Psychosomatic Soc. (coun. 1985-88), Internat. Acad. Sex Rsch. (pres. 1995-96), Soc. Sex Therapy and Rsch. (pres. 1984-86), Sex Info and Edn. Coun. of U.S. (bd. dirs. 1979-83), Internat. Soc. Psychoneuroendocrinology, Sigma Xi. Office: Mt Sinai Sch Medicine 1 Gustave L Levy Pl New York NY 10029-6504

SCHIAVINA, LAURA MARGARET, artist; b. Springfield, Mass., Nov. 27, 1917; d. Joseph A. and Egidia (Bernini) Schiavina; student Traphagen Sch. of Fashion, 1944-46, U. R.I., 1967, Cornell U., 1968, Art Students League, 1973-74. With Eastern States Farmers Exchange, Springfield, 1935-44; with Marsh & McLennan, 1944-75, adminstrv. asst., 1971-75, librarian Wm. M. Mercer, Inc. subs., 1975-80; represented by Z Gallery, N.Y.C. One-woman shows at Little Gallery, Barbizon Hotel, N.Y.C., 1968, Galerie Internat., N.Y.C., 1969, Z Gallery, N.Y.C., 1993, 94; exhibited in group shows at Westfield (Mass.) Coll., 1968, Nat. Acad., N.Y.C., 1969, Bergen Mus. of Art and Sci., Paramus, N.J., 1991, Stuhr Mus. of the Prairie Pioneer, Grand Isle, Nebr., 1990, Nat. Soc. of Painters in Casein and Acrylic, 1992, 94, Washington & Lee U., Lexington, Va., 1993, Darke County Ctr. for Arts, Greenville, Ohio, 1993, NLAPW 1992 Biennial Sumner Mus., Washington, 1992, 1994 Biennial Cork Gallery, N.Y.C.; Lever House, N.Y.C., 1973, 74, 83, 84, 85, 86, 87, 95, Queensboro C.C. Gallery, 1984, 94, Cork Gallery, N.Y.C., 1984, 93, 94, Westbeth Gallery, N.Y.C., 1985, 88, Nat. Arts Club, 1986, 88—, Isis Gallery, 1986, Morin-Miller Galleries, 1988; also various exhbns. with Wall St. Art Assn., Nat. Art. League and Jackson Heights Art Club, Audubon Artists, 1969, 86, 88—, Salmagundi Club, 1996—, Nat. Assn. Women Artists travel show centennial exhibits at 5 art ctrs. and mus., 1989, and ann. exhbns., 1989—; represented in pvt. collections. Recipient numerous prizes, awards. Mem. Wall St. Art Assn. (v.p. 1972-76), Audubon Artists, Inc., Nat. Art League, Burr Artists Inc., Nat. Assn. Women Artists, N.Y. Artists Equity, Nat. League Am. Pen Women, Jackson Heights Art Club (pres. 1970-71), The Catholic Fine Arts Soc., Salmagundi Club. Home: 35-25 78th St Jackson Heights NY 11372 Studio: 41 Union Sq W # 406 New York NY 10003-3208

SCHIAVO, A. MARY FACKLER, federal official, lawyer; b. Pioneer, Ohio, Sept. 4, 1955. AB cum laude, Harvard U., 1976; MA, Ohio State U., 1977; JD, NYU, 1980. Bar: Mo. 1980, U.S. Dist. Ct. (we. dist.) Mo. 1980, U.S. Ct. Appeals (8th cir.) 1983, U.S. Ct. Appeals (10th cir.) 1985, U.S. Supreme Ct. 1990, D.C. 1993, Md. 1994. Assoc. law firm, Kansas City, Mo., 1980-82; asst. U.S. atty. we. dist. Mo. U.S. Dept. Justice, Kansas City, 1982-85, fed. prosecutor organized crime and racketeering strike force, 1985-86; White House fellow, spl. asst. to U.S. Atty. Gen. U.S. Dept. Justice, Washington, 1987-88; exec. dir. Bush/Quayle '88 Campaign, State of Mo., 1988; atty. law firm, Kansas City, 1989; asst. sec. labor-mgmt. standards U.S. Dept. Labor, Washington, 1989-90; insp. gen. U.S. Dept. Transp., Washington, 1990—; instr. U.S. Atty. Gen.'s Adv. Inst., Washington, 1986, 88, FBI Acad., Quantico, Va., 1988; guest lectr. NYU Sch. Law, 1986, 88, 91; bd. dirs. Dept. Labor Acad., 1989-90; bd. dirs. White House Fellows Assn. and Found., 1992-96, 2d v.p., 1992-93, chair ann. meeting, 1993, 1st v.p., 1993-94, pres. 1994-95; mem. Pres.'s Coun. on Integrity and Efficiency, 1990—, Pres.'s Commn. on White House Fellowships, 1994-95. Bd. dirs. Root-Tilden Scholarship program NYU, 1982-89. Recipient Thompson award Ohio State U. Alumni, 1988, Aviation Laurel citation Aviation Week and Space Tech. mag., 1992, Aviation Laurel award Aviation Week and Space Tech. mag., 1995; named one of Top Ten Coll. Women in U.S., 1975, one of ten Outstanding Young Working Women in Am., 1987, Kansas City Career Woman of Yr., 1988; Ohio State U. fellow, 1976-77; U.S.-Japan Leadership fellow, 1995; Root-Tilden legal scholar NYU, 1977-79. Mem. ABA (ho. of dels. 1986-89, assembly del. 1986-89, litigation sect. complex crimes com.), Mo. Bar Assn. (bd. govs. 1986-89, chmn. pro bono task force 1984-86, young lawyers coun. 1983-86, Outstanding Svc. award 1986), Exec. Women in Govt., Harvard Club of Washington, Charter 100, Women's Fgn. Policy Group. Avocations: pilot, ventriloquist. Office: US Dept Transp Office of Insp Gen 400 7th St SW Ste 9210 Washington DC 20590-0001

SCHIAVONE, LOUIS, III, advertising executive; b. Boston, June 19, 1954; s. Louis II and Louise Margaret (Palmieri) S. BA in English magna cum laude, St. Michael's Coll., Colchester, Vt., 1976; MA in English, Columbia U., 1978. Copywriter Naftzger & Kuhe, Farmington, Conn., 1979-84; v.p., sr. copywriter Ogilvy & Mather, N.Y.C., 1986-87, McCann-Erickson, N.Y.C., 1987-88; sr. v.p., creative dir. W. B. Doner & Co., Southfield, Mich., 1988—. Vol., cons. Motown Mus., Detroit; Haven group facilitator Haven Ctr. for Battered Women and Children, Pontiac, Mich.; bd. dirs. Founders Jr. Coun. Detroit (Mich.) Inst. Arts, 1994—. Democrat. Office: WB Doner & Co 25900 Northwestern Hwy Southfield MI 48075

SCHIAVONI, THOMAS JOHN, social studies educator; b. Sag Harbor, N.Y., July 7, 1993; s. Francis G. and Ann M. (O'Rourke) S. BA, SUNY, Cortland, 1986; MA in Liberal Arts, SUNY, Stony Brook, 1993. Social studies tchr. The Desisto Sch., Stockbridge, Mass., 1986-87, Bd. Coop. Ednl. Svcs. 1, Southampton, N.Y., 1987-90, Center Moriches (N.Y.) Union Free Sch. Dist., 1988—; adj. instr. sociology Syracuse U.; com. mem. The Social Studies K-12 Curriculum com., Center Moriches UFSD, 1991, com. chmn. com. on middle sch. reform. Office: Center Moriches UFSD 311 Frowein Rd Center Moriches NY 11934-2217

SCHIAZZA, GUIDO DOMENIC (GUY SCHIAZZA), educational association administrator; b. Phila., May 17, 1930; s. Guido and Claudina (DiPrinzio) S.; m. Irmgard Heidi Reissmueller, May 15, 1954. BA, Pa. State U., 1952; postgrad., St. Joseph's U., 1954-55, Villanova U., 1954-55, Temple U., 1955-58. Cert. tchr., Pa.; cert. clinician, ednl. specialist, instructional specialist, sch. psychologist, guidance counselor, reading specialist. Speech therapist, lang. arts instr. Commonwealth of Pa., Dept. Edn., 1956-59; founder, clinician, instr., dir., bd. pres. Communicative Arts Ctr., Inc., Drexel Hill, Pa., 1958, Communication Skills Community Resources Ctr., Inc., Drexel Hill, Pa., 1958, 1964—; charter mem. exec. bd., bd. pres. United Pvt. Acad. Schs., Assn. of Pa., Drexel Hill, 1966—; exec. bd. govs., bd. chmn. The Accrediting Commn., Drexel Hill, 1971—; charter mem. Pa. State Univ. Radio and TV Guild, University Park, Pa., 1951—; mem. legis. action com., Pa. State U., Univ. Park, 1988—; cons. communications skills, The Accrediting Commn., 1971—, United Pvt. Acad. Schs. Assn., Pa., 1966—. Founder, chmn., CEO Am. Ednl. Group, 1991—; chmn. CEO Internat. Ednl. Group, 1991—; CEO Cmty. Resources Ctr., Drexel Hill, 1991—, project coord. Energy Quest, 1992—; active Nat. Com. to Preserve Social Security and Medicare, Washington, 1986—, Am. Imigration Control Found., Monterey, Va., 1987—, English First, Springfield, Va., 1988—; mem. pres.'s coun. Rep. Nat. Comm., 1989—, Nat. Rep. Senatorial Com., 1989—, Rep. Presdl. Task Force, 1989—. 1st Lt. Signal Corps, U.S. Army, 1952-54. Recipient Svc. award United Pvt. Acad. Sch. Assn. Pa., Monroeville, Pa., 1978, Disting. Achievement and Svc. award Bd. Govs. of the Accrediting Commn., Downington, Pa., 1980, Dr. Charles Boehm Edn. of Yr. award University Park, Pa., 1990, Loyal and Dedicated Svc. award The Accrediting Commn., 1974. Mem. NEA, Libr. Congress (chartered), Internat. Platform Assn., Pa. Edn. Assn., Jefferson Ednl. Found., World Affairs Coun. Phila., Heritage Found., Nat. Trust for Hist. Preservation, Phila. Nat. Congl. Club, Pa. State U. Nittany Lions Club, Pa. State U. Alumni Assn., Pa. State U. Football Lettermen's Club. Republican. Roman Catholic. Avocations: music, home and garden design, automotive design, reading, golf. Office: The Accrediting Commn 436 Burmont Rd Drexel Hill PA 19026-3630

SCHICHLER, ROBERT LAWRENCE, English language educator; b. Rochester, N.Y., May 16, 1951; s. Alfred James and Elizabeth Johanna (Flugel) S. BA in English, SUNY, Geneseo, 1974, MA in English, 1978; PhD of English, Binghamton U., 1987. Writer, asst. administr. Artists-in-Residence Program, Rochester, N.Y., 1978-79; substitute tchr. City Sch. Dist., Rochester, 1980-82; instr. English Talmudical Inst. Upstate N.Y., Rochester, 1981-82, Binghamton (N.Y.) U., 1983-84; rsch. asst. Medieval and Renaissance Texts and Studies, Binghamton, 1985-86; adj. asst. prof. Rochester Inst. Tech., 1987-89; assoc. prof. English Ark. State U., State University, 1989—; adj. asst. prof. Monroe C.C., Rochester, 1987-89. Author: King of the Once Wild Frontier: Reflections of a Canal Walker, 1993; editor: Lady in Waiting: Poems in English and Spanish, 1994, Abstracts of Papers in Anglo-Saxon Studies, 1988—, Ctr. for Medieval and Early Renaissance Studies, Binghamton, 1986-94, Spillway Publs., Rochester, 1992—; asst. editor: Old English Newsletter, 1986-87, Mediaevalia, Binghamton, 1988-89; contbr. articles to profl. jours. Active Pres's. Nat. Steering Com., 1995—. Mem. Internat. Soc. Anglo-Saxonists, Internat. Ctr. Medieval Art, Medieval Acad. Am., Modern Lang. Assn. Am., South Cen. Modern Lang. Assn., Ark. Philol. Assn. Home: 726 Southwest Dr Apt K-2 Jonesboro AR 72401-7074 Office: Dept English and Philosophy Ark State U State University AR 72467-1890

SCHICK, BRIAN KEITH, middle school educator; b. St. Louis, Aug. 21, 1968; s. Dennis Alexander and Joan Frances (Jedlink) S.; m. Patricia Ann McNutt, Aug. 16, 1991. BS in Edn., U. Mo., 1989; MA in Teaching, Webster U., 1991. Lang. arts/social studies tchr. Mehlville Sch. Dist., St. Louis, 1989-94; reading tchr. Rockwood Sch. Dist., Eureka, Mo., 1994—; presenter workshop Critical Thinking-Mehlville Staff Devel., 1991; com. mem. Mehlville Strategic Planning Facilities Com., St. Louis, 1991-94; ex-officio exec. mem. Mehlville-Oakville Sch. Dist. Found., St. Louis, 1993-94; com. mem. Mehlville Strategic Planning Mid. Sch. Com., St. Louis, 1993-94; core team leader Oakville Jr. Sch. Improvement Leadership Team, St. Louis, 1993-94. Author: (song lyrics) Constitution Rap, 1990. Com. mem., advisor March of Dimes-Walk Am., St. Louis, 1994. Grantee Mehlville-Oakville Found., 1994; Personal Responsibility Edn. Program grantee, 1995; Rockwood Profl. Devel. grantee, 1995. Mem. ASCD, NEA, Nat. Coun. Social Studies, Mehlville Community Tchrs. Assn. (bldg rep. 1989-94). Roman Catholic. Avocations: music, pets, reading, Hallmark ornament collecting, travel. Home: 2707 Kenny Dr Saint Louis MO 63125-3725 Office: LaSalle Springs Mid Sch 3300 Highway 109 Glencoe MO 63038-2201

SCHICK, EDGAR BREHOB, German literature educator; b. Phila., June 28, 1934; s. Claude Ernest and Martha Henrietta (Brehob) S.; m. Margaret Barbara Buehl, Feb. 12, 1938; children: Susanne, Christina. AB magna cum laude, Muhlenberg Coll., 1955; MA, Rutgers U., 1962, PhD, 1965. Asst. prof. German SUNY, Binghamton, 1963-68; asst. to pres. SUNY, Albany, 1968-72, asst. prof., 1968-72; v.p. acad. affairs St. John Fisher Coll., Rochester, N.Y., 1972-78, exec. v.p., 1978-80, assoc. prof., 1972-80; pres. Nasson Coll., Springvale, Maine, 1980-83; provost, v.p. acad. affairs, prof. Eastern Ill. U., Charleston, 1984-87; exec. dir. Bd. Trustees, Md. State Univs. & Colls., Annapolis, 1987-88; vice chancellor for policy and planning U. Md. System, Adelphi, 1988-91; sr. fellow Am. Assn. State Colls. and Univs., 1991-94; cons. Assn. Governing Bds., 1993-95; chmn. visitation team Mid. States Assn. Colls. and Schs., Phila., 1975-79; cons. IBM, Yorkville, N.Y., 1968, Nat. Luth. Campus Ministry, 1968-85, USAID, 1992-95. Author: Metaphorical Organicism in the Early Herder, 1971, Shared Visions of Public Higher Education Governance: Structures and Leadership Styles That Work, 1992, The "Local Board" in Multi-Campus Public Universities, 1994; contbr. articles on German lit. and higher edn. to profl. jours. Bd. dirs. United Way, 1981-82, Maine Ind. Colls. Assn., 1981-93, Deaton Hosp., Balt.; mem. Accreditation Bd. for Engring. Tech.; pres. Oakleigh Forest Civic Assn. Univ. fellow, Rutgers U., New Brunswick, N.Y., 1962-63; grantee Carnegie Found., Dept. HEW. Mem. Am. Assn. Higher Edn., Am. Assn. Univ. Adminstrs., Am. Assn. Tchrs. German, Assn. for Instl. Rsch., Soc. for Coll. and Univ. Planning, Thomas Mann Soc., Nat. Soc. Fund-Raising Execs. Lutheran. Home: 106 Quinn Rd Severna Park MD 21146-3015

SCHICK, HARRY LEON, investment company executive; b. N.Y.C., Oct. 24, 1927; s. Martin and Sadie (Spitz) S.; m. Eleanor Alter, Oct. 16, 1982; m. Inge Nussbaum, Oct. 12, 1964 (div. Nov. 1971); 1 child, Susan. A.B. magna cum laude, Bklyn. Coll., 1947; M.S., Columbia U., 1948; postgrad., NYU, 1948-52. Securities analyst Sutro Bros., N.Y.C., 1948-52; asst. to pres. Clairdale Enterprises, Inc., N.Y.C., 1953-66; mgr. arbitrage dept. First Manhattan Co., N.Y.C., 1966-69, gen. ptnr., 1969-91, ltd. ptnr., 1992—; lectr. Donaldson Sch. Orgn. and Mgmt., Yale U., New Haven, 1978-88, NYU Grad. Sch. Bus. Adminstrn., N.Y.C., 1977; lectr. in field. Bd. dirs. Overseers Libr. of Jewish Theol. Sem.; trustee Washington Inst. for Near East Policy. Mem. Inst. Chartered Fin. Analysts, Am. Fin. Assn., Am. Econ. Assn., N.Y. Soc. Security Analysts (bd. dirs. 1975-76), Beta Gamma Sigma. Jewish. Home: 215 E 68th St Apt 15Y New York NY 10021-5726 Office: First Manhattan Co 437 Madison Ave New York NY 10022-7001

SCHICK, IRVIN HENRY, academic administrator, educator; b. Wilkes-Barre, Pa., Aug. 10, 1924; s. Irvin and Elizabeth (Valentine) S.; diploma Bliss Elec. Sch., 1947; B.E.E. with distinction, George WashingtonU., 1958; M.S. in Elec. Engring. (NSF fellow), U. Md., 1961; m. Marilyn Freeman, July 17, 1954 (dec. Aug. 1961); m. Marjorie Bletch Beach, Dec. 23, 1967; 1dau., Carolyn Patricia. Engring. asst. Jeddo-Highland Coal Co. (Pa.), 1942-43; instr. Bliss Elec. Sch., Washington, 1947-50; prof. math. and elec. engring., dept. head Montgomery Coll., Rockville, Md., 1950-65, dir. extension, 1965-67, dean adminstrn., 1967-75, adminstrv. v.p., 1975-78, prof. emeritus, adminstrv. v.p. emeritus, 1978—. Tchr., tutor, cons. indsl. cos. 1949—. Served with USAAF, 1943-46. Mem. AAUP, Montgomery County Edn. Assn., Md. State Tchrs. Assn., IEEE, Am. Assn. Sch. Adminstrs., Internat. Platform Assn., Bliss Elec. Soc. (bd. govs.,past pres., Trout Troupe Theatrical Organ. (bd. govs.), Theta Tau, Sigma Tau (past pres.), Sigma Pi Sigma, Tau Beta Pi. Home: 105 Fleetwood Ter Silver Spring MD 20910-5512

SCHICK, JANELLE KEYSAR, interior designer; b. Camden, Ark., Mar. 19, 1946; d. Wayne Clyde Keysar and Mary Frances (Stansel) Ernst; m. Richard Henry Schick, July 24, 1976; children: Sheri L., Zachary R. AA in Interior Design, Scottsdale (Ariz.) C.C., 1980. Cert. Nat. Coun. for Interior Design Qualification. Asst. designer Don Beams & Assocs., Phoenix, 1980-81; interior designer Peter Lendrum & Assocs., Phoenix, 1981-82, Tulliani Interiors, Scottsdale, 1982-83; assoc. Design Concepts, Scottsdale, 1983-86, Lara & Rowlands, Scottsdale, 1986-90, Pat Bacon & Assocs., Scottsdale, 1990-91; dir. mktg. and residential design Hart Interiors, Tempe, Ariz., 1991; jr. ptnr. Inter Plan Design Group, Scottsdale, 1991—; vis. faculty Scottsdale C.C., 1985-86. Dir. Scottsdale chpt. Am. Field Svc. Internat., 1980-87, host parent students from Belgium, 1984-85, students from New Zealand, 1994. Mem. Am. Soc. Interior Designers (profl., chmn. mktg. com. Ariz. chpt. 1992-95, allied mem. rep. bd. dirs. Ariz. North chpt. 1992-94, Presdl. citation 1989, 93, 94), Homebuilders Assn. Ctrl. Ariz. (assoc., mem. allied com. 1993-95). Avocations: sewing, snow skiing, scuba diving, golf. Office: Inter Plan Design Group 7373 N Scottsdale Rd Ste A17B Scottsdale AZ 85253

SCHICK, MICHAEL WILLIAM, public relations executive; b. San Antonio, July 17, 1956; s. Lawrence Martin and Jeanne Frances (McCuen) S.; m. Diana Lynn McGinty, Mar. 14, 1988; 1 child, Tiffany Michele. B in Media Arts with honors, U. S.C., 1979. Dir. prodns., asst. v.p. S.C. Savs. & Loan League, Columbia, 1978-81; dep. press sec. to U.S. Sen. Strom Thurmond Washington, 1981-85; sr. assoc. Civic Svc. Inc., Washington, 1985—. Co-founder, chmn. First Monday Night, McLean, Va., 1981-94; active Young Reps., Reston, Va., 1990-92, Fourth Presbyn. Ch., Bethesda, Md., 1988—; chmn. Creative Living Internat., Reston, 1988—. Mem. Am. Assn. Polit. Conss. Republican. Avocations: golf, tennis, soccer, sailing, guitar. Home: 11560 Brass Lantern Ct Reston VA 22094-1221 Office: Civic Svc Inc 1050 Connecticut Ave NW Ste 870 Washington DC 20036-5303

SCHICK, SETH HARVEY, land resource economist; b. Kaysville, Utah, June 8, 1936; s. George and Ruth (Harvey) S.; m. Karren Hodgson, Sept. 2, 1960; children: Jeffery, Scott, Daranee, Alison. BS in Econs., Utah State U., 1962; MS in Econs., N.C. State at Raleigh, Utah State U., 1964; postgrad., U. Ariz., 1967-68. Mktg. rep. Proctor and Gamble, Salt Lake City, 1962; economist Fed. Milk Mktg., Denver, 1964; land resource economist Harza Engring. Co., Chgo., 1965-70; land resource economist Schick Internat., Salt Lake City, 1970-74, pres., land resource economist, 1974—; project economist Tipton Kalmback Co., Denver, 1976, Electro Watt Engring. Co., Zurich, Switzerland, 1984-85; spl. assignment resource economist on irrigation systems mgmt. USAID, Sri Lanka, 1987-88; resource economist on irrigation system improvement project Asian Devel. Bank, Leyte Island, Philippines, 1993-94; resource economist pricing culinary water Utah Municipalities, 1994-96, Schick Internat., Inc. Served with USAF, 1954-58. Democrat. Mormon. Office: Schick Internat Inc 3010 First Commerce Ctr 175 W 200 S Salt Lake City UT 84101-1413

SCHICKEL, RICHARD, writer, film critic; b. Milw., Feb. 10, 1933; s. Edward J. and Helen (Hendricks) S.; children: Erika Tracy, Jessica Avery. BS, U. Wis., 1955. Sr. editor Look mag., 1957-60, Show mag., 1960-63; freelance writer, 1963—; film critic Life mag., 1965-72, Time mag., 1973—; cons. Rockefeller Bros. Fund, 1964, Rockefeller Found., 1965; lectr. in history art Yale, 1972, 76; adj. prof. film, U. S. Calif., 1989; pres. Lorac Prodns., 1986—. Author: The World of Carnegie Hall, 1960, The Stars, 1962, Movies: The History of an Art and an Institution, 1964, The Gentle Knight, 1964, The Disney Version, 1968, The World of Goya, 1968, Second Sight: Notes on Some Movies, 1972, His Picture in the Papers, 1974, Harold Lloyd: The Shape of Laughter, 1974, The Men Who Made the Movies, 1975, The World of Tennis, 1975, The Fairbanks Album, 1975, Singled Out, 1981, Cary Grant, A Celebration, 1984, D.W. Griffith: An American Life, 1984, James Cagney, A Celebration, 1985, Intimate Strangers: The Culture of Celebrity, 1985, Striking Poses, 1987, Schickel on Film, 1989, Brando: A Life In Our Times, 1991, Double Indemnity, 1992; co-author: Lena, 1965, The Platinum Years, 1974, Hollywood at Home, 1990 (novel) Another I, Another You, 1978; co-editor: Film 67-68, 1968; producer, dir., writer (TV series) The Men Who Made the Movies, 1973; producer, writer: (TV spls.) Life Goes to the Movies, 1976, SPFX, 1980, Cary Grant, A Celebration, 1989; producer, wirter, dir.: (TV spls.) Funny Business, 1978, Into the Morning: Willa Cather's America, 1978, The Horror Show, 1979, James Cagney: That Yankee Doodle Dandy, 1981, From Star Wars to Jedi: The Making of a

Saga, 1983, Minnelli on Minnelli; Liza Remebers Vincent, 1987, Gary Cooper: American Life, American Legend, 1989, Myrna Loy : So Nice to Come Home To, 1990, Barbara Stanwyck: Fire and Desire, 1991, Eastwood & Co.; Making Unforgiven, 1992, Hollywood on Hollywood, 1993, Elia Kazan: A Director's Journey, 1995. Recipient Book prize Brit. Film Inst., 1985; Guggenheim fellow, 1964. Mem. Nat. Soc. Film Critics, N.Y. Film Critics, Dirs. Guild Am., Writers Guild Am.

SCHICKELE, PETER, composer; b. Ames, Iowa, July 17, 1935; s. Rainer Wolfgang and Elizabeth (Wilcox) S.; m. Susan Sindall, Oct. 27, 1962; children: Karla, Matthew. B.A., Swarthmore Coll., 1957; M.S., Julliard Sch. Music, 1960; PhD (hon.), Swarthmore, 1980. Composer-in-residence Los Angeles High Sch., 1960-61; faculty Swarthmore Coll., 1961-62, Juilliard Sch. Music, 1961-65, Aspen Festival Music, Colo., 1963. Composer: scores for films The Crazy Quilt, 1965, Funny Man, 1967, Silent Running, 1972, several non-theatrical and TV films; arranger for: Joan Baez albums Noel, 1966, Joan, 1967, Baptism, 1968; composer mus. score for film at Tex. pavilion of Hemisfair, San Antonio, 1968; TV appearances include: Profile on the Arts, Camera Three, Bach 'N' Roll, 13 Stars for 13, Dick Cavett Show, Mike Douglas Show, David Frost Show, ABC Comedy News, Tonight Show with Johnny Carson; comedian, recorded: An Evening with P.D.Q. Bach, 1968, P.D.Q. Bach: 1712 Overture and Other Musical Assaults, 1989, Oedipus Tex and Other Choral Calamities, 1990, WTWP-Classical Talkity-Talk Radio, 1991, Music for an Awful Lot of Winds and Percussion, 1992, other comedy albums; mem., The Open Window, chamber-rock trio, 1967-71; composer and lyricist: Oh Calcutta; composer String Quartet No. 1, American Dreams and numerous works for orch., chorus, piano, chamber music, band, organ, voice and instruments, 1953—; creator, host Schickele Mix, Pub. Radio Internat., family concerts with Am. Symphony Orch., 1994—; author: The Definitive Biography of P.D.Q. Bach. Recipient Gershwin Meml. award, 1959, Elizabeth Tow Newman Contemporary Music award, 1964, Grammy awards, 1990-93, Deems Taylor award; Ford Found. grantee. Mem. ASCAP, Am. Music Ctr., Assn. Classical Music, Am. Fedn. Musicians. Avocation: crossword puzzles. Office: ICM Artists care Stewart Warkow 40 W 57th St New York NY 10019-4001

SCHIDLOW, DANIEL, pediatrician, medical association administrator; b. Santiago, Chile, Oct. 23, 1947; m. Sally Rosen; children: David, Michael, Jessica. Grad., U. Chile, 1972. Diplomate Am. Bd. Pediatrics, Am. Bd. Pediatric Pulmonology; lic. in D.C., Pa., N.J. Rotating intern U. Chile Hosp., U. Chile Sch. Medicine, 1971-72, resident in internal medicine, instr. phys. diagnosis, 1972-73; resident, emergency rm. physician in pediatrics E.G. Cortes Hosp. Children, U. Chile, 1973-74; resident in pediatrics Albert Einstein Coll. Medicine Bronx (N.Y.)-Lebanon Hosp. Ctr., 1974-76; fellow pediatric pulmonary medicine St. Christopher's Hosp. Children, Phila., 1976-78; chief sect. pediatric pulmonology dept. pediatrics St. Christopher's Hosp. Children, 1983-94, sr. v.p. clin. affairs, 1994—; from asst. to assoc. prof. pediatrics sch. medicine Temple U., Phila., 1978-90, prof., 1990-94, dep. chmn. dept. pediatrics, 1991-94; prof., sr. vice chmn. dept. pediatrics Med. Coll. Pa./Hahnemann U. Med. Sch., Phila., 1994—; attending physician St. Christopher's Hosp. Children, 1978—, dir. fellowship tng. and edn. program sect. pediatric pulmonology, 1979-91, assoc. dir. pediatric pulmonary and cystic fibrosis ctr., 1981-83, med. dir. dept. respiratory therapy, 1982-88, project dir. Phila. pediatric pulmonary ctr., 1983-86, dir. cystic fibrosis ctr., 1983—, chair capital campaign com. dept. pediatrics, 1987, mem. exec. com. med. staff, 1988—, mem. various coms.; courtesy staff Lancaster (Pa.) Gen. Hosp., 1980-82; cons. divsn. rehab. Pa. Dept. Health, 1983—; mem. promotions com. dept. pediatrics sch. medicine Temple U., 1986—, chmn. com. appointments clin.-educator track 1991—; attending staff no. divsn. Albert Einstein Med. Ctr., 1987—; cons. Nat. Ctr. Youth Disabilities, 1987—; mem. med. adv. coun. Cystic Fibrosis Found., Bethesda, Md., 1987—, trustee, 1990—, med. dir. home care svcs., 1991—, various other positons; consulting staff Temple U. Hosp., 1988—; mem. organizing com. N.Am. Cystic Fibrosis Conf., 1990-93, co-chmn., 1992—; co-chmn. Nat. Concensus Conf. Pulmonary Complications Cystic Fibrosis, McLean, Va., 1992; mem. adv. bd. Phila. Parenting Assocs., 1992—. Reviewer Jour. Pediatrics, Am. Jour. Diseases Children, others. Named Illustrious Guest, City of LaPlata, Argentina, 1992. Fellow Am. Acad. Pediatrics (Pa. chpt., sect. diseases chest), Am. Coll. Chest Physicians (sect. cardiopulmonary diseases children); mem. AAAS, Am. Thoracic Soc. (mem. nominating com. 1993—), Am. Fedn. Clin. Rsch., Chilean Pediatric Soc. (hon.), Pa. Thoracic Soc., Ea. Soc. Pediatric Rsch., Phila. Pediatric Soc. Home: 315 N Bowman Ave Merion Station PA 19066-1523 Office: St Christopher's Hosp Chldn Office Med and Acad Affairs Erie Ave at Front St Philadelphia PA 19134

SCHIEBLER, GEROLD LUDWIG, physician, educator; b. Hamburg, Pa., June 20, 1928; s. Alwin Robert and Charlotte Elizabeth (Schmoele) S.; m. Audrey Jean Lincourt, Jan. 8, 1954; children: Mark, Marcella, Kristen, Bettina, Wanda, Michele. BS, Franklin and Marshall Coll., 1950; MD, Harvard U., 1954. Intern pediatrics and internal medicine Mass. Gen. Hosp., Boston, 1954-55, resident, 1955-56; resident pediatrics U. Minn. Hosp., Mpls., 1956-57, fellow pediatric cardiology, 1957-58, rsch. fellow, 1958-59; rsch. fellow sect. physiology Mayo Clinic and Mayo Found., 1959-60; asst. prof. pediatric cardiology U. Fla., 1960-63, assoc. prof., 1963-66, prof., 1966-92, Disting. Svc. prof., 1992—, chmn. dept. pediatrics, 1968-85, assoc. v.p. for health affairs for external rels., 1985—; dir. div. Children's Med. Svcs., State of Fla., 1973-74. Author: (with L.P. Elliott) The X-ray Diagnosis of Congenital Cardiac Disease in Infants, Children and Adults, 1968, 2d edit., 1979, (with L.J. Krovetz and I.H. Gessner) Pediatric Cardiology, 2d edit., 1979. Mem. AAAS, Inst. Medicine NAS, Am. Acad. Pediatrics (Abraham Jacobi award 1993), AMA (Benjamin Rush award 1993), Am. Coll. Cardiology, Soc. Pediatric Rsch. (emeritus), Fla. Pediatric Soc. (exec. com.), Fla. Heart Assn. (past pres.), Fla. Med. Assn. (past v.p., bd. govs., pres. 1991-92), Phi Beta Kappa, Alpha Omega Alpha. Home: 2115 NW 15th Ave Gainesville FL 32605-5216

SCHIEDER, JOSEPH EUGENE, clergyman; b. Buffalo, Sept. 23, 1908; s. Robert and Mary Loretta (Quinn) S. B.A., Niagara U., 1931; M.A., St. Bonaventure U., 1935; Ph.D., U. Ottawa, Ont., Can., 1943; LL.D., St. Vincent's Coll., 1951; Litt.D. (hon.), Seaton Hall U., 1954; L.H.D. (hon.), LaSalle Coll., 1956, Canisius Coll., 1986; D. in Pedagogy, Niagara U., 1987, Doctor (hon.). Ordained priest Roman Catholic Ch., 1935; dir. Youth Retreats Diocese of Buffalo, 1939-48; diocesan dir. Confraternity of Christian Doctrine, Buffalo, 1941-48; dir. youth bur. Buffalo Police Dept., 1942-48; nat. dir. Cath. Youth Am., Washington, 1948-61; also dir. youth dept. Nat. Cath. Welfare Conf., Washington; apptd. Papal Chamberlain, 1950, Domestic Prelate, 1953, Prothonatary Apostolic, 1968; pastor St. Andrew's Ch., Buffalo, 1963-76; founder, 1st dir. St. Andrew's Montessori Sch., 1973; mem. Mental Health Bd., 1968—; dean theology Marymount Coll., Arlington, Va., 1961-63; diocesan consultor, 1969—; regional coordinator Diocese of Buffalo, procurator diocesan properties, 1977—; founder Nat. Cath. Youth Week; chmn. Permanent Com. Pub. Decency, Buffalo, 1941-48; diocesan dir. financial drive Diocese of Buffalo, 1971; mem. White House Conf. Children and Youth, 1950; adviser on Youth Spl. Mission to Germany USAF, 1952; Spl. Mission to Tokyo, Japan for UNESCO, 1953; adviser on youth U.S. Sec. Labor, 1951-60; adviser on fitness of youth to Pres. Eisenhower, 1955-60; chmn. task force founding Stella Niagara Ednl. Parks, Niagara Falls, N.Y.; mem. exec. bd. Cantalician Center, Buffalo; mem. adv. bd. ARC, Kenmore Mercy Hosp. Author: Talks to Parents, 1954, Spiritual Lifts for Youth, 1956; Editor of: Youth mag, 1949-61. Mem. ho. of dels. United Way, 1973—, vice chmn., 1975; bd. dirs. Oral Sch., Ft. Lauderdale, Fla., 1977; vice chmn. Bicentennial Celebration; bd. trustees Erie County Library Assn., 1979—; bd. fin. Diocese of Buffalo, 1979—; chmn. Buffalo div. Christian Bros. Tricentennial World Anniversary, 1981; Founder, past bd. dirs. various Cath. youth assns.; bd. founders St. Andrew's Country Day Sch.; chmn. Drug Abuse Program, Ft. Lauderdale, Fla., 1981—; mem. adv. bd. Project Korle Bu Accra Ghana, West Africa, 1983. Served as adviser to Cath. chief chaplain USAF, 1953; chief chaplain AUS, 1954. Recipient award Christian Bros., 1947, award Mayor of Rome, Italy, 1950, Archdiocese award Hartford, Conn., 1954, De la Salle medal Manhattan Coll., 1958, Padre Youth award for U.S., 1961, Star Solidarity from Pres. Italy, 1969, Bishop McNulty Meml. award, 1973, Pres.'s medal St. John's Coll., Washington, 1973; also awards dioceses Charleston, S.C.; also awards dioceses Wichita, Kans.; Man of Yr. award Town of Tonawanda, 1977; award for prestigious service Buffalo Fire Dept., 1980; 1st recipient Signum Fidei Outstanding Alumni award St. Joseph's Collegiate Inst., 1984; Spl. Gift award for outstanding service to Diocese of Buffalo, 1986; Outstanding Service to Diocese of Buffalo citation Office Bishop of Buffalo, Oustanding Assistance and Help citation United Cerebral Palsy Assn., 1987; named Man of Yr., Marian Guild St. Andrew's Ch., Kenmore, N.Y. Clubs: University (Washington); Niagara Falls Country; Park Country (Buffalo), Saturn (Buffalo); Amherst (N.Y.) Country; Tower (Ft. Lauderdale, Fla.). Lodge: K.C. (4th deg.). Address: 72 Somersby Ct Buffalo NY 14221-4949 *Zeal for my position and my vocation, accompanied by hard labor, has contributed much to whatever success I have attained. Love of people and sincerity and the spirit of sacrifice where others are concerned has added to my happiness in life. My faith in God has made difficult undertakings much easier.*

SCHIEFELBUSCH, RICHARD L., research administrator; b. Osawatomie, Kans., July 23, 1918; s. Edward Francis and Emma (Martie) S.; m. Ruth Lenore Magee, Sept. 20, 1942; children—Lary, Carol, Jean. B.S., Kans. State Tchrs. Coll., 1940; M.A. in Speech Pathology and Psychology, U. Kans., 1947; Ph.D. in Speech Pathology, Northwestern U., 1951. Mem. faculty U. Kans., Lawrence, 1946-89, prof. speech pathology and audiology, 1959-69; dir. Speech and Hearing Clinic Schiefelbusch Speech and Hearing Clinic, Lawrence, 1949-56; dir. Bur. Child Research U. Kans., Lawrence, 1955-90, Univ. Disting. prof., 1969-89; Univ. Disting. prof. emeritus, 1989—; chmn. child lang. grad. degree program U. Kans., Lawrence, 1983-89, interim dir. Gerontology Ctr., 1989-91; interim dir. Inst. for Life Span Studies Schiefelbusch Inst. for Life Span Studies, Lawrence, 1989-90; dir. Kans. Center Mental Retardation and Human Devel., Lawrence, 1969-89; co-dir. Kans. Research Inst. Learning Disabilities, Lawrence, 1977-81; sr. scientist VA Hosp., Topeka, 1991-93; cons. in field, dir. research grants. Author book series Language Intervention; also numerous articles in field; mem. editorial bds. profl. jours. Served with USAAF, 1941-46. Recipient Disting. Service award Nat. Assn. for Retarded Citizens, 1983; Disting. Achievement award Pittsburg State U., 1985, Disting. Accomplishment award Am. Assn. Univ. Affiliated Programs, 1987; Fulbright scholar, Australia, 1986. Fellow Am. Assn. Mental Deficiency (Spl. award 1975, Edn. award 1986), Am. Speech and Hearing Assn. (assn. honoree 1976, v.p. edn. and sci. affairs 1980-82); mem. Council Exceptional Children. Home: 3113 Campfire Dr Lawrence KS 66049-2012 Office: U Kans Bur Child Rsch Lawrence KS 66045

SCHIEFFER, BOB, broadcast journalist; b. Austin, Tex.; m. Patricia Penrose; children: Susan, Sharon. B.A. in Journalism, Tex. Christian U. Reporter Ft. Worth Star-Telegram; news anchorman Sta. WBAP-TV, Dallas-Ft. Worth; with CBS News, 1969—, Pentagon corr., 1970-74, White House corr., 1974-79, chief Washington corr., 1982—; anchorman CBS Sunday Night News, 1973-74, Sunday edit. CBS Evening News, 1976—, Monday-through-Friday edits. Morning, 1979-80; co-anchorman CBS Morning News, from 1985; also participant CBS news spls. and spl. reports, including Peace and the Pentagon, 1974, Watergate-The White House Transcripts, 1974, The Mysterious Alert, 1974, 1976, Ground Zero, 1981; Democratic Nat. Conv., 1976, Republican Nat. Conv., Campaign '72; and mem. Emmy award-winning team CBS Evening News with Walter Cronkite, 1971; currently moderator Face the Nation CBS News, chief Washington corr.; co-anchor CBS Weekend News/Sunday News, N.Y.C. Author: (with Gary Paul Gates) The Acting President, 1989. Recipient various awards Sigma Delta Chi, various awards Tex. Associated Broadcasters, various awards AP Mng. Editors; co-recipient Emmy awards. Office: care CBS News Weekend/Sunday News 524 W 57th St New York NY 10019-2902

SCHIEFFER, J. THOMAS, professional baseball team executive. Pres. Texas Rangers. Office: Texas Rangers 1000 Ballpark Way Arlington TX 76011-5168

SCHIELE, PAUL ELLSWORTH, JR., educational business owner, writer; b. Phila., Nov. 20, 1924; s. Paul Ellsworth Sr. and Maud (Barclay) S.; m. Sarah Irene Knauss, Aug. 20, 1946; children: Patricia Schiele Tiemann, Sandra Schiele Kicklighter, Deborah Schiele Hartigan. AT, Temple U., 1949; BA, LaVerne U., 1955; MA, Claremont Associated Colls., 1961; PhD, U.S. Internat. U., San Diego, 1970. Cert. sec. tchr., Calif. 1961. Tchr. sci. and math. Lincoln High Sch., Phila., 1956-57, Ontario (Calif.) Sch. Dist., 1957-65; math. and sci. cons. Hacienda La Puente U. Sch. Dist., Calif., 1965-75; asst. prof. Calif. State U., Fullerton, 1975-83; pres., owner Creative Learning Environments and Resources, Glendora, Calif., 1983—, cons. sci. curriculum, 1985—; dir. title III project ESEA, 1974-75, cons. for project, 1975-77; cons. in field. Author: Primary Science, 1972, 2d edit., 1976, (novel) Under Cover of Night, 1995; editor: A Living World, 1974, 2d edit., 1986; writer 9 sound filmstrips, model units for sci. and math. activity books, 10 sci. activities for L.A. Outdoor Edn. Program, 1980; editor 21 sci. and math. activity books; writer, co-dir. (TV) Marine Biology Series, 1970-71; contbr. munerous articles to profl. mags., 1960-85; writer and designer of 2 sci. ednl. games; designer in field. Apptd. adv. com. Sci. and Humanities Symposium Calif. Mus. Sci. and Industry, 1974; mem. State Sci. Permit Com., Tide Pools of Calif. Coast, 1974-75; active Playhouse 90, Pasadena (Calif.) Playhouse; mem. Friends of Libr., Friends Libr. Found. Mem. Internat. Platform Assn., ABI Rsch. Assn. (bd. govs.), Calif. Elem. Edn. Assn. (hon.), Nat. PTA (hon.), Calif. Inter-Sci. Coun. (pres., chmn. 1971, 72), Elem Sch. Scis. Assn. (past pres., bd. dirs.), Phi Delta Kappa (chartered). Republican. Lutheran. Avocations: travel, etchings, art collecting, fencing. Home: 231 Catherine Park Dr Glendora CA 91741-3018

SCHIER, DONALD STEPHEN, language educator; b. Ft. Madison, Iowa, Sept. 10, 1914; s. Francis and Marcella (Kenny) S. B.A., State U. Iowa, 1936; M.A., Columbia U., 1937, Ph.D., 1941. Mem. faculty State Tchrs. Coll., Bemidji, Minn., 1939-41, 41-42, Ill. Inst. Tech., 1946; mem. faculty Carleton Coll., Northfield, Minn., 1946-80; prof. French Carleton Coll., 1953-80; vis. prof. U. Wis., 1964-65; Brown tutor in French U. of South, Sewanee, Tenn., 1980-81. Author: Louis-Bertrand Castel, 1942; editor: (with Scott Elledge) The Continental Model, 1960, 2d edit., 1970; (Bertrand de Fontenelle), Nouveaux Dialogues des morts, 1965, rev. edit., 1974; translator: Letter on Italian Music (Charles de Brosses), 1978. Mem. selection com. Young Scholar Program, Nat. Found. Arts and Humanities, 1966-67. Served to capt. AUS, 1942-46. Mem. MLA, Am. Assn. Tchrs. French, Am. Soc. Eighteenth-Century Studies. Home: 750 Weaver Dairy Rd Apt 1106 Chapel Hill NC 27514-1441

SCHIER, MARY JANE, science writer; b. Houston, Mar. 10, 1939; d. James F. and Jerry Mae (Crisp) McDonald; B.S. in Journalism, Tex. Woman's U., 1961; m. John Christian Schier, Aug. 26, 1961; children—John Christian, II, Mark Edward. Reporter, San Antonio Express and News, 1962-64; med. writer Daily Oklahoman, also Oklahoma City Times, 1965-66; reporter, med. writer Houston Post, 1966-84; sci. writer, univ. editor U. Tex. M.D. Anderson Cancer Ctr., 1984—. Recipient award Tex. Headliners Club, 1969, Tex. Med. Assn., 1972-74, 76, 78, 79, 80, 82 Tex. Hosp. Assn., 1974, 82, Tex. Public Health Assn., 1976, 77, 78, others. Mem. Houston Press Club Ednl. Found. (pres 1992—). Lutheran. Home: 9742 Tappenbeck Dr Houston TX 77055-4102 Office: 1515 Holcombe Blvd Houston TX 77030-4009

SCHIESER, HANS ALOIS, education educator; b. Ulm, Germany, July 15, 1931; came to U.S., 1965; s. Alois and Anna (Stegmann) S.; m. Margret H. Schröer, June 6, 1962; children: Peter, Elisabeth. BA, Kepler Gymnasium, Ulm, 1952; MA in Philosophy, Passau, Fed. Republic Germany, 1959; EdM, Pedagogic Acad., Weingarten, Fed. Republic Germany, 1962; PhD, Loyola U., 1970. Head tchr. Pestalozzischule, Ulm, 1964-65; learning disabilities tchr. Jeanine Schultz Meml. Sch., Skokie, Ill., 1966-67; co-dir. Oak Therapeutic Sch., Evanston, Ill., 1967-70; assoc. prof. to prof. edn. DePaul U., Chgo., 1969-91, prof. emeritus, 1991—; cons. various indsl. and bus. tng. programs, 1978-91; program cons. Delphian Soc., L.A., 1977-90; rschr., tchr. in Germany, 1991—; active in tchrs. edn. Midwest Montessori Tchr. Tng. Ctr., Evanston, Ill.; mem. adv. bd. Verein Psychol.; founding dean Acad. Culture, History and Religion, Chelyabinsk, Russia, 1995. Author chpts. in books; contbr. numerous articles U.S. and German publs.; adv. bd. Ann. Edits. Sociology, Dushkin Pub. Group, 1985-91. Pres. N.Am. Family Svc. Found., Oak Lawn, Ill., 1974-91; bd. dirs. S.O.S. Children's Villages USA, Washington, 1986-94; pres. emeritus S.O.S. Children's Village Ill., Inc., Chgo.; pub. policy expert Domestic Issues Heritage Found., 1991—; bd. govs. Invest-in-Am. Nat. Found., Phila., 1988-90. Rsch. grantee DePaul U., 1985-86, Rsch. sabbatical, 1989. Mem. Am. Ednl. Studies Assn., Nat. Soc. for Study of Edn., Philosophy of Edn. Soc. U.S.A., Soc. Educators and Scholars (bd. dirs. 1984-90), Am. Montessori Soc., Thomas More Gesellschaft/Amici Mori Europe, Phi Delta Kappa (pres. Zeta chpt., Chgo. 1973-75). Home: 136 Dodge Ave Evanston IL 60202-3661 Home: Veilchenweg 9, D-89134 Bermaringen Germany Office: DePaul U 2320 N Kenmore Ave Chicago IL 60614-3298

SCHIESS, BETTY BONE, priest; b. Cin., Apr. 2, 1923; d. Evan Paul and Leah (Mitchell) Bone; m. William A. Schiess, Aug. 28, 1947; children: William A. (dec.), Richard Corwine, Sarah. BA, U. Cin., 1945; MA, Syracuse U., 1947; MDiv, Rochester Ctr. for Theol. Studies, 1972. Ordained priest Episcopal Ch., 1974; priest assoc. Grace Episc. Ch., Syracuse, N.Y., 1975; mem. N.Y. Task Force on Life and Law (apptd. by gov.) 1985—; chaplain Syracuse U., 1976-78, Cornell U., Ithaca, N.Y., 1978-79; rector Grace Episc. Ch., Mexico, N.Y., 1984-89; cons. Women's Issues Network Episc. Ch. in U.S., 1987—; writer, lectr., cons. religion and feminism, 1979—. Author: Take Back the Church, Indeed The Witness, 1982, Creativity and Procreativity: Some Thoughts on Eve and the Opposition and How Episcopalians Make Ethical Decisions, Plumline, 1988, Send in the Clowns, Chrysalis, Journal of the Swedenborg Foundation, 1994; contbr. forward to book. Bd. dirs. People for Pub. TV in N.Y., 1978, Religious Coalition for Abortion Rights; trustee Elizabeth Cady Stanton Found., 1979; mem. policy com. Coun. Adolescent Pregnancy; mem. N.Y. State Task Force Life and the Law, 1983—. Recipient Gov.'s award Women of Merit in Religion, 1984, Ralph E. Kharas award ACLU Cen. N.Y., 1986 Goodall disting. alumna award & Hills Sch., 1988, Human Rightes award Human Rights Commn. of Syracuse and Onondaga County, N.Y., 1989; inducted into Nat. Women's Hall of Fame, 1994. Mem. NOW (Syracuse), Internat. Assn. Women Ministers (dir. 1978, pres. 1984-87), Na'amat U.S. (hon. life), Mortar Bd., Theta Chi Beta. Democrat. Home and Office: 107 Bradford Ln Syracuse NY 13224-1901 Office: Grace Episcopal Ch Main St Mexico NY 13114

SCHIESSLER, ROBERT WALTER, retired chemical and oil company executive; b. Honesdale, Pa., Oct. 2, 1918; s. Walter A. and Josephine (Herzog) S.; m. Betty Hartman, June 5, 1939; children—Lynn Alice, Dale Ann; m. Florence Cutler, Aug. 16, 1968. B.S., Pa. State U., 1939, Ph.D., 1944; M.S., McGill U., 1941. Research chemist Gen. Electric Co., Schenectady, 1941; from instr. to asso. Prof. chemistry and dir. Am. Petroleum Inst. Research Pa. State U., 1942-55; chemistry and physics cons., 1946-55; tech. dir. Central Research div. Mobil Oil Co., Paulsboro and Princeton, N.J., 1950-60; mgr. central research div., asst. gen. mgr. research dept. Central Research div. Mobil Oil Co., 1960-62, gen. mgr. research dept., 1962-67; v.p. research Mobil Research & Devel. Corp., 1967-68; chmn., pres. Indsl. Reactor Labs., Inc., 1966-67; mgr. long-range planning Mobil Oil Corp., 1968-72, gen. mgr. real estate and land devel., 1972-83; chmn. Mobil Land Devel. Corp., 1972-83; pres. Sandvik, Inc., 1983-84; chmn. bd. trustees Gordon Rsch. Conf., Inc., 1957; mem. bd. Am. Chem. Soc. Peroleum Rsch. Fund, 1955-59, 60-63; Rsch. chemist Can. govt., 1940-41. Co-Author: Chemistry of Petroleum Hydrocarbons, 1954, Discoverer method for prodn. super-explosive used by U.S. and Can., World War II. Recipient award in petroleum chemistry Am. Chem. Soc., 1953; named outstanding young man State Coll. of Pa., outstanding young man Jr. C. of C., 1952; recipient Wisdom award, 1970. Fellow Am. Inst. Chemists, AAAS (v.p. for chemistry, chmn. chemistry sect. 1960); mem. Am. Chem. Soc., AAUP, Sigma Xi, Phi Lambda Upsilon, Phi Eta Sigma. Home: 1500 Palisade Ave Fort Lee NJ 07024

SCHIFF, CRAIG MITCHELL, computer company executive; b. N.Y.C., June 11, 1955; s. Stanley and Bernice Mary (Kostman) S.; m. LuAnn Bellantoni, June 26, 1982; 1 child, Holly Ann. BS in Biology, SUNY, New Paltz, 1977; MBA in Fin., Fordham U., 1987. Programmer NPD Rsch., Floral Park, N.Y., 1977-79; fin. programmer Gulf & Western, N.Y.C., 1979-80; project mgr. GE, N.Y.C., 1980-83; v.p. Hyperion Software (formerly IMRS, Inc.), Stamford, Conn., 1983—. Pres. Majestic Tenants Corp., Forest Hills, 1982—. Democrat. Jewish. Avocations: traveling, videos, reading. Home: 11020 71st Ave Apt 432 Forest Hills NY 11375-4572 Office: Hyperion Software 900 Long Ridge Rd Stamford CT 06902-1247*

SCHIFF, DAVID TEVELE, investment banker; b. N.Y.C., Sept. 3, 1936; s. John Mortimer and Edith Brevoort (Baker) S.; m. Martha Elisabeth Lawler, May 11, 1963; children: Andrew Newman, David Baker, Ashley Reynolds. B.Engring., Yale U., 1958. Trainee Chem. Bank N.Y. Trust, N.Y.C., 1959-62; analyst Madison Fund, N.Y.C., 1962; assoc., then partner Kuhn, Loeb & Co., N.Y.C., 1963-77; vice chmn. Kuhn Loeb & Co. Inc., 1977; mng. dir. Lehman Bros. Kuhn Loeb Inc., N.Y.C., 1977-83; also dir. Lehman Bros. Kuhn Loeb Inc.; mng. ptnr. Kuhn, Loeb & Co. (formerly KLS Enterprises), 1984—; chmn. Touchwood Records, LLC, 1995—; dir., vice chmn. Am. Crown Life Ins. Co., N.Y.C., 1981-95; bd. dirs. Crown Life Ins. Co., Toronto, 1971-92; mem. lower Manhattan adv. bd. Chem. Bank, 1977-85; chmn. Touchwood Records, LLC, 1995—. Trustee Met. Mus. Art, Citizens Budget Commn., N.Y.C., Greater N.Y. coun. Boy Scouts Am.; trustee, chmn. bd. Wildlife Conservation Soc.; trustee Beekman Downtown Hosp., 1966-82, chmn., 1975-79; trustee Brooks Sch., North Andover, Mass., 1972-90, treas., 1987-90; bd. govs. Yale U. Art Galleries, Fed. Hall Meml. Assn.; adv. bd. dirs. Outward Bound, Inc.; mem. Provident Loan Soc. N.Y.; bd. dirs. Am. Hosp. of Paris Found., N.Y.C., 1987. With AUS, 1959. Mem. Econ. Club N.Y.C., Pilgrims U.S., Brook Club, Century Assn., River Club, Maroon Creek Club (Aspen, Colo.), Mill Reef Club (Antigua), Yale Club N.Y.C., Am. Bugatti Club, Vintage Sports Car Club Am. Republican. Episcopalian. Home: 770 Park Ave New York NY 10021-4153 Office: 485 Madison Ave 20th Fl New York NY 10022

SCHIFF, DONALD WILFRED, pediatrician, educator; b. Detroit, Sept. 11, 1925; s. Henry and Kate (Boesky) S.; m. Rosalie Pergament; children: Stephen, Jeffrey, Susan, Douglas. Student, Wayne State U., 1943-44, Oberlin Coll., 1944-45; MD, Wayne State U., 1949. Diplomate Am. Bd. Pediatrics. Intern Detroit Receiving Hosp., 1949-50; resident in pediatrics U. Colo., 1954-55, chief resident in pediatrics, 1955-56; instr. U. Colo. Health Scis. Ctr., Denver, 1956-59, asst. clin. prof., 1959-69, assoc. clin. prof., 1969-78, clin. prof., 1978-87, prof., 1987—; pvt. practice Littleton (Colo.) Clinic, 1956-86, chmn. bd., 1973-79; med. dir. HMO Colo., Denver, 1980-86; med. dir. Child Health Clinic The Children's Hosp., Denver. Contbr. articles to profl. jours. Bd. dirs. Sch. Dist. VI, Colo., 1962; pres. Arapahoe Mental Health Clinic, Denver, 1966-70, bd. dirs., 1964-70; adv. coun. State of Colo. Medicaid, Denver, 1981—. With USN, 1944-46, USPHS, 1952-54, Turtle Mountain Indian Reservation, N.D. Recipient 25 Yrs. Teaching award U. Colo. Sch. Medicine, 1981. Mem. Am. Acad. Pediatrics (chmn. Colo. chpt. 1973-79, alternate dist. chmn. 1977-81, chmn. dist. 8 1981-86, nat. pres. 1988-89), Rocky Mountain Pediatric Soc., Colo. Med. Soc. Home: 600 Front Range Rd Littleton CO 80120-4052 Office: The Children's Hosp Child Health Clinic Box BO32 1056 E 19th Ave Denver CO 80218-1007

SCHIFF, EUGENE ROGER, medical educator, hepatologist; b. Cin., Jan. 3, 1937; s. Leon and Augusta (Miller) S.; m. Dana Kendall, Dec. 27, 1965; children: David, Lisa. BA, U. Mich., 1958; MD, Columbia U., 1962. Diplomate Am. Bd. Internal Medicine, Am. Bd. Gastroenterology, Nat. Bd. Med. Examiners. Intern and med. resident Cin. Gen. Hosp., 1962-64; med. resident Parkland Meml. Hosp., Dallas, 1966-67; USPHS postdoctoral fellow in gastroenterology Southwestern Med. Sch., U. Tex., Dallas, 1967-69; asst. prof. medicine U. Miami (Fla.) Sch. Medicine, 1969-74, assoc. prof., 1974-78, prof., 1978—, chief div. hepatology, 1971—, dir. Ctr. for Liver Diseases, 1982—; chief hepatology sect. VA Med. Ctr., Miami, 1971—; chmn. adv. com. on gastrointestinal drugs FDA, Rockville, Md., 1983-85, 88-92. Co-editor: Diseases of the Liver, 5th edit., 1982, 6th edit., 1987, 7th edit. 1993. Lt. comdr. USPHS, 1964-66. Master Am. Coll. Gastroenterology; fellow ACP (gov. Fla. chpt. 1984-88); mem. AMA, Am. Assn. for Study of Liver Diseases (sec.-treas. 1991—), Am. Bd. Internal Medicine (subspecialty bd. gastroenterology), Internat. Assn. for Study of Liver Diseases, Am. Gastroenterology Assn. (chmn. Biliary Disorders sect. 1993-95), Argentine Soc. Gastroenterology (hon.). Jewish. Home: 10445 SW 109th St Miami FL 33176-3455 Office: U Miami 1500 NW 12th Ave Ste 1101 Miami FL 33136-1038

SCHIFF, GARY STUART, academic administrator, educator; b. Bklyn., Mar. 27, 1947; s. Jacob and Lillian (Grumet) S.; divorced; children: Jeremy Jay, Rina Joy. BA, Bin Hebrew Lit., Yeshiva U., 1968; MA, Columbia U., 1970, Cert. in Middle East Studies, 1973, PhD, 1973. Asst. prof. Jewish studies and polit. sci. CUNY, 1973-76; dir. Mid. East affairs Nat. Jewish Community Rels. Coun., N.Y.C., 1976-78; exec. asst. to pres. Acad. for Ednl. Devel., N.Y.C., 1978-83; pres. Gratz Coll., Melrose Park, Pa., 1983—. Author: Tradition and Politics: The Religious Parties of Israel, 1977, The Energy Education Catalog, 1981; contbr. articles to profl. jours. Grantee NEH, Ford Found., Danforth Found., Woodrow Wilson Found., William Penn Found., Pew Charitable Trusts. Mem. Assn. of Colls. of Jewish Studies (bd. dirs.), Assn. for Israel Studies (v.p.), Coun. for Jewish Edn. (bd. dirs.), Assn. for Jewish Studies, World Jewish Congress (governing bd.), Am. Jewish Com. (N.Y. chpt. bd. dirs., Phila. chpt. communal affairs commn.). Avocations: liturgical music, boating, cats. Home: 130 Spruce St Philadelphia PA 19106-4319 Office: Gratz Coll Old York Rd & Melrose Ave Melrose Park PA 19027

SCHIFF, JOHN JEFFERSON, insurance company executive; b. Cin., Apr. 19, 1916; s. John Jefferson and Marguerite (Cleveland) S.; m. Mary Reid, July 26, 1941; children: John Jefferson, Suzanne, Thomas R. BSc in Commerce, Ohio State U., 1938. Vice chmn. Cin. Ins. Co., 1979—; pres. Cin. Fin. Corp., 1979-91, chief exec. officer, 1987-91; chmn., exec. com. Cin Fin Corp., 1991—; v.p. Deaconess Hosp. of Cin., Griffith Found. for Ins. Chmn. Cin. Art Mus.; trustee Am. Inst. for Property and Liability Underwriters; chmn. investment com. Navy League of the U.S. Served to lt. comdr. Supply Corps, USN, 1942-46. Named Ins. Man of Yr. in Cin., Cin. Ins. Bd., 1977. Mem. Cin. C. of C. (v.p. 1972). Republican. Methodist. Clubs: Queen City, Western Hills Country, Cin. Country, Royal Poinciana Golf. Home: 1926 Beech Grove Dr Cincinnati OH 45233-4912 Office: Cin Fin Corp PO Box 145496 Cincinnati OH 45250-5496

SCHIFF, MARGARET SCOTT, newspaper publishing executive. V.p. controller and personnel adminstr. Washington Post. Office: Washington Post Co 1150 15th St NW Washington DC 20071-0001

SCHIFF, MARTIN, physician, surgeon; b. Phila., July 16, 1922; s. Isidore and Cecelia (Miller) S.; m. Mildred Tepley, Jan. 5, 1946; children: Denise Schiff Simon, Michael, David. BS, Pa. State U., 1943; MD, U. Calif.-Irvine, 1951. Intern L.A. County Gen. Hosp., 1950-51; gen. practice medicine specializing in bariatrics L.A., 1951—; mem. staff Brotman Meml. Hosp.; lectr. L.A. area community colls. Author: Eat & Stay Slim, 1972, Miracle Weight-Loss Guide, 1976, One-Day-At-A-Time Weight Loss Plan, 1980, (5 tapes) Weight Loss Plan for Health, Happiness & A Longer Life Span, 1982, The Thin Connection, 1986. Lt. USN, 1943-45, PTO. Mem. AMA, Calif. Med. Assn., L.A. Med. Assn., Am. Soc. Weight Control Specialists. Home: 1220 Corsica Dr Pacific Palisades CA 90272-4016 Office: 12900 Venice Blvd Los Angeles CA 90066-3543

SCHIFF, ROBERT, health care consultancy company executive; b. N.Y.C., Jan. 7, 1942; s. Henry and Jeanette (Levine) S.; m. Adrianne Bendich, Aug. 16, 1964 (div. July 1979); children: Jorden, Debra; m. Joann McTaggart, Aug. 24, 1986. BS, CCNY, 1964; MS, Iowa State U., 1966; PhD, U. Calif., Davis, 1968. Asst. prof. anatomy Tufts U. Sch. Medicine, Boston, 1969-72; mgr. serology rsch. Hyland divsn. Baxter Labs., Costa Mesa, Calif., 1972-74; dir. R & D J.T. Baker Diagnostics, Bethlehem, Pa., 1974-77; dir. diagnostic R & D Hoffmann-LaRoche, Nutley, N.J., 1977-80; group v.p. Warner Lambert Co., Morris Plains, N.J., 1980-82; pres., CEO Schiff & Co., Inc., West Caldwell, N.J., 1982—; Del. Nat. Commn. for Clin. Lab. Stds., 1979-80; vice chmn. R & D Coun. N.J., 1980-82; bd. dirs. E.P.I. subs. E-Z-EM, Westbury, N.Y., 1991—. Contbr. numerous articles to profl. jours.; patentee in field. Aid to Cancer Rsch. grantee, Mass., 1970. Mem. N.Y. Acad. Sci., Regulatory Affairs Profl. Soc. (cert.), Am. Soc. Quality Control (cert. quality auditor), Am. Assn. Clin. Chemistry, Sigma Xi. Avocation: licensed pilot. Office: Schiff & Co 1129 Bloomfield Ave West Caldwell NJ 07006-7123

SCHIFF, STEFAN OTTO, zoologist, educator; b. Braunschweig, Germany, July 22, 1930; came to U.S., 1941, naturalized, 1943; s. Walther and Johanne Ilse (Muller) S.; m. Laura Frances Ward, June 6, 1957; children—Sena, Stefanie. B.S., Roanoke Coll., 1952; Ph.D., U. Tenn., 1964. USPHS trainee, 1961-63; mem. faculty George Washington U., Washington, 1964—, prof. zoology, 1976-95, prof. emeritus, 1995, chmn. dept. biol. scis., 1977-87, dir. grad. genetics program, 1971-95. Author: Twenty-One Afternoons of Biology, 3d edit., 1986, Buttons: Art in Miniature, 1980. Mem. Radiation Rsch. Soc., Sigma Xi. Lutheran. Home: 10710 Howerton Ave Fairfax VA 22030-2917 Office: George Washington U Bell Hall 302 B Washington DC 20052

SCHIFF, STEVEN HARVEY, congressman, lawyer; b. Chicago, Ill., Mar. 18, 1947; s. Alan Jerome and Helen M. (Ripper) S.; m. Marcia Lewis, Nov. 8, 1968; children: Jaimi, Daniel. BA, U. Ill., Chgo., 1968; JD, U. N.Mex., 1972. Bar: N.Mex. 1972, U.S. Dist. Ct. N.Mex. 1972, U.S. Ct. Appeals (10th cir.) 1980. Asst. dist. atty. Dist. Atty.'s Office, Albuquerque, 1972-77, sole practice, 1977-79; asst. city atty. City of Albuquerque, 1979-81; dist. atty. State of N.Mex., Albuquerque, 1981-89; mem. 101st-104th Congresses from 1st N.Mex. dist., Washington, D.C., 1989—; mem. govt. reform & oversight com. U.S. House of Reps., mem. judiciary com. and standards of ofcl. conduct com., chmn. sci. subcom. on basic rsch.; lectr. U. N.Mex., Albuquerque, 1981—. Chmn. Bernalillo County Rep. Party Conv., Albuquerque, 1984, 87, staff judge adv. N.Mex. Air N.G. Col. JAGC, USAFR. Recipient Law Enforcement Commendation medal SR, 1984. Mem. ABA, Albuquerque Bar Assn., N.Mex. Bar Assn. Republican. Jewish. Club: Civitan. Lodge: B'nai Brith (pres. 1976-78). Home: 804 Summit Ave NE Albuquerque NM 87106-2045 Office: House of Reps 2404 Rayburn Washington DC 20515-3101 also: 625 Silver Ave SW Ste 140 Albuquerque NM 87102*

SCHIFFER, CLAUDIA, model. Model Guess? jeans, 1989—, Revlon cosmetics, Chanel. Runway debut in Chanel fashion show, 1990; appeared on covers of Mademoiselle, Cosmopolitan, Vogue, and over 100 others. Office: Met Model Agy USA 5 Union Sq W New York NY 10003-3306

SCHIFFER, DANIEL L., gas company executive; m. Sheila Schiffer; children: Michael, Eric. AB, Bklyn. Coll., 1964; JD, Cornell U., 1967. Law clk. U.S. Ct. Appeals (2d cir.); pvt. practice N.Y.C.; spl. asst. N.Y. Pub. Svc. Commn., N.Y.C.; now sr. v.p., gen. counsel, sec. MCN Corp., 1989—. Trustee Batsford Gen. Hosp. Mem. ABA, Mich. State Bar Assn., Detroit Bar Assn., Fed. Energy Bar Assn. Avocations: sports, reading, bridge. Office: MCN Corp 500 Griswold St Detroit MI 48226-3700

SCHIFFER, JOHN PAUL, physicist; b. Budapest, Hungary, Nov. 22, 1930; came to U.S., 1947, naturalized, 1953; s. Ernest and Elisabeth (Tornai) S.; m. Marianne Tsuk, June 28, 1960; children: Celia Anne, Peter Ernest. AB, Oberlin Coll., 1951; MS, Yale U., 1952, PhD, 1954. Research asso. Rice Inst., Houston, 1954-56; asst. physicist Argonne (Ill.) Nat. Lab., 1956-59, asso. physicist, 1960-63, sr. physicist, 1964—, assoc. dir. physics div., 1964-79, 83—, dir. physics div., 1979-82; prof. physics U. Chgo., 1968—; vis. asso. prof. Princeton, 1964; vis. prof. U. Rochester, N.Y., 1967-68; mem. adv. coms. nuclear physics Nat. Acad. Scis.; mem. program adv. or rev. coms. Los Alamos Meson Physics Facility, 1971-73, Ind. U. Cylotron Facility, 1974-77, Lab. for Nuclear Sci., M.I.T., 1975-79, Lawrence Berkeley Lab, Bevalac, 1978-80, Swiss Inst. Nuclear Research, 1981-85, Max Planck Inst. Nuclear Physics, 1982-85; mem. physics adv. panel NSF, 1971-73; mem. Nuclear Sci. Adv. Com. Dept. Energy/NSF, 1981-85, chmn., 1983-85; chmn. program adv. com. CEBAF, 1986-91; mem. subcom. Implementation of 1989 Long Range Plan for Nuclear Sci. Editor: Comments on Nuclear and Particle Physics, 1971-75; assoc. editor Revs. Modern Physics, 1972-77; mem. editorial bd. Phys. Rev. C, 1983-85; editor: Physics Letters, 1978—; mem. editorial com. ann. revs. of nuclear and particle sci., 1987-91; contbr. articles on nuclear structure physics and nuclear reactions to phys. jours. and books. Mem. cold fusion panel Dept. Energy, 1989. Recipient Alexander V. Humboldt Found. sr. U.S. scientist award, 1973-74; Wilbur Cross medal Yale U., 1985; Guggenheim fellow, 1959-60. Fellow AAAS (mem. coun., chair physics sect. 1992-93), Am. Phys. Soc. (chmn. div. nuclear physics 1975-76, Tom W. Bonner prize 1976); mem. NAS, Danish Acad. Arts and Letters. Research on nuclear structure, Mössbauer effect, heavy-ion reactions, pion interactions in nuclei, quark searches, condensation in confined cold plasmas. Office: Physics Division Argonne Nat Lab Argonne IL 60439

SCHIFFER, LOIS JANE, lawyer; b. Washington, Feb. 22, 1945; d. Benjamin and Clara (Goldberg) S. BA, Radcliffe Coll., 1966; JD, Harvard U., 1969. Bar: Mass. 1969, D.C. 1971, U.S. Supreme Ct. 1973. Legal svcs. lawyer Boston Legal Assistance Project, 1969-70; ct. law clk. D.C. Circuit Ct., Washington, 1970-71; assoc. Leva, Hawes, Symington, Martin, Oppenheimer, Washington, 1971-74; lawyer Ctr. for Law and Social Policy, Washington, 1974-78; chief gen. litigation sect. Land and Natural Resources div. U.S. Dept. Justice, Washington, 1978-81, spl. litigation counsel, 1981-84; gen. counsel Nat. Pub. Radio, Washington, 1984-89; ptnr. Nussbaum & Wald, Washington, 1989-93; acting asst. atty. gen. environ. and natural resources divsn. U.S. Dept. Justice, Washington, 1993-94, asst. atty. gen. environ. and natural resources divsn., 1994—; adj. prof. environ. law Georgetown U. Law Ctr., Washington, 1986—. Bd. dirs. Women's Legal Def. Fund, 1975-86, Am. Rivers, 1989-93; bd. dirs. ACLU/NCA, 1982-93, pres., 1988-90. Fellow Am. Bar Found.; mem. Phi Beta Kappa. Democrat. Jewish. Avocations: reading, movies, hiking. Home: 4640 Brandywine St NW Washington DC 20016-4449

SCHIFFMAN, DAVID M., lawyer; b. Chgo., June 8, 1953. AB magna cum laude, Harvard U., 1974, JD cum laude, 1977. Bar: Ill. 1977. Ptnr. Sidley & Austin, Chgo. Mem. ABA (antitrust law sect., bus. law sect. litigation sect.), Chgo. Bar Assn., Chgo. Coun. Lawyers, Phi Beta Kappa. Office: Sidley & Austin 1 First Nat Plz Chicago IL 60603*

SCHIFFMAN, GERALD, microbiologist, educator; b. N.Y.C., May 22, 1926; s. Samuel and Mollie (Brookner) S.; m. Lillian Ebert, July 12, 1951; children: Stewart, Howard. B.A. cum laude, NYU, 1948, Ph.D., 1954. Asst. prof. and disting. prof. microbiology Coll. Physicians and Surgeons, Columbia U., N.Y.C., 1960-63; asso. prof. dept. research medicine and microbiology U. Pa., Phila., 1963-70; prof. SUNY Health Sci. Ctr., Bklyn., 1970—, disting. svc. prof., 1995—; cons. Contbr. articles to profl. jours. Served in U.S. Army, 1943-45, ETO. Decorated Bronze Star; recipient Nichols award, 1947; Atomic Energy fellow, 1948-52; NIH grantee, 1974-94. Mem. Am. Assn. Immunologists, Am. Chem. Soc., Am. Soc. Microbiology, AAAS, Harvey Soc., Soc. Complex Carbohydrates, Sigma Xi, Phi Beta Kappa, Mu Chi Sigma, Pi Mu Epsilon. Jewish. Office: 450 Clarkson Ave Brooklyn NY 11203-2012

SCHIFFMAN, HAROLD FOSDICK, Asian language educator; b. Buffalo, Feb. 19, 1938; s. Merl and Mathilda (Keller) S.; m. Marilyn Gail Hornberg, June 10, 1978; 1 son, Timothy Marc Rajendran. B.A., Antioch Coll., 1960; M.A., U. Chgo., 1966, Ph.D., 1969. Lectr. anthropology U. Calif.-Davis, 1966-67; asst. prof. U. Wash., Seattle, 1967-73, assoc. prof., 1973-78, prof., 1978-95, chmn. dept. Asian langs., 1982-87; prof. South Asian studies U. Pa., Phila., 1995—, acad. dir. Penn Lang. Ctr., Luce prof. lang. learning, 1995—; Trustee Am. Inst. Indian Studies, Chgo., 1979-82; lang. dir. Southeast Asian Summer Studies Inst., 1992-93, mem. lang. adv. com., 1993-94. Author: A Grammar of Spoken Tamil, 1979, A Reference Grammar of Spoken Kannada, 1983, Linguistic Culture and Language Policy, 1996; co-editor: Dravidian Phonological Systems, 1975; co-author: Language and Society in South Asia, 1981. Pres. bd. dirs. Seattle Pro Musica (choral group), 1976-78; mem. Pacific Northwest Chamber Chorus, Seattle, 1983-87. Sr. fellow Am. Inst. Indian Studies, 1976, 78; grantee U.S. Office Edn., 1971, 74, 78, NEH, 1984-87, Smithsonian Inst., 1984-87, Fulbright Rsch., 1993-94. Mem. Assn. Asian Studies (S. Asia council 1982-85), Am. Inst. Indian Studies (trustee 1979-82), Soc. S. Indian Studies (sec.-treas. 1973-75), Internat. Assn. Tamil Research (v.p. 1987-89). Quaker. Office: U Pa Dept South Asian Studies 820 Williams Hall Philadelphia PA 19104-6305

SCHIFFMAN, JOSEPH HARRIS, literary historian, educator; b. N.Y.C., June 13, 1914; s. Samuel and Norma Minnie (Berger) S.; m. Elizabeth Selsbee, Nov. 29, 1941; children: Jessica, Joshua. BA, L.I. U., 1937; MA, Columbia U., 1947; PhD, NYU, 1951. Instr. dept. English, L.I. U., 1945-49, asst. prof., 1949-51, assoc. prof., 1951-58, coord. grad. program Am. studies, 1956-58; prof. English Dickinson Coll., Carlisle, Pa., 1958-79, James Hope Caldwell prof. Am. studies, 1968-79, emeritus prof., 1979—, prof. continuing edn., 1979-86, 90-94, chmn. dept. English, 1959-69; sr. Fulbright vis. prof., India, 1964, U. Bordeaux (France), 1965-66, U. Indonesia, 1981-82; vis. prof. Grad. Sch. U. Pa., 1960, 67, New Coll., U. South Fla., spring 1981; lectr. U. P.R., 1984, Lifetime Learning, Sarasota, 1984-88, Elderhostel U., Del., 1995; fgn. expert vis. prof. East China Normal U., Shanghai, 1985; founding dir. Am. Studies Rsch. Centre, India, 1964, Am. adv. com., 1990—; lectr. French Ednl. Radio System, 1966, acad. specialist program, Malaysia, Internat. Communication Agy., 1982; PhD theses examiner various univs., India, 1970—; mem. faculty Internat. Am. Studies & Lang. Seminar, Salzburg, Austria; lectr. numerous orgns. including Mark Twain Assn. N.Y., Walt Whitman Birthplace Assn., MLA, Am. Studies Assn., Rotary, Pa. Writers Group, Jewish Community Ctr., Bosler Free Libr., AAUW, YWCA, Bethany Retirement Community, U.S.-China Peoples Friendship Assn., Sr. Action Ctr., Pa. Poets Soc., Harrisburg Manuscript Club, Golden Age Club, Encore Books and Music, Cumberland County Med. Soc. Alliance. With U.S. Army, 1942-45, ETO. Recipient Lindback Found. Disting. Teaching award, 1962, Fulbright-Hays award U.S. State Dept., 1964, 65, 81, Alumni award L.I. U., 1976. Mem. Am. Studies Assn. (pres. Met. N.Y. chpt. 1958-59), MLA (head Am. lit. internat. bibliography com. 1961-64), Nat. Council Tchrs. English. Author: (with Lewis Leary) American Literature: A Critical History from Its Beginning to the Present, Ency. World Lit., 1973, William Faulkner, A Dramatic Evocation, 1981; contbr. articles on Am. writers to lit. jours.; contbr. introductions to Looking Backward (Edward Bellamy), 1959, Brook Farm (Lindsay Swift), 1961, Three Shorter Novels of Herman Melville, 1962; editor: Edward Bellamy, Selected Writings on Religion and Society, 1955, Edward Bellamy, The Duke of Stockbridge, 1962; recs. including Idealist, Activist, The Haunted Chamber, The World a Ship, In Search of America, The Roaring Twenties, A Utopian Dream, also revs. to scholarly jours. Home: 551 S Hanover St Carlisle PA 17013-3919 Office: Dickinson Coll Carlisle PA 17013

SCHIFFMAN, ROBERT STANLEY, environmental test equipment manufacturing executive; b. Passaic, N.J., Jan. 25, 1944; s. Saul and Lillian (Gold) S.; m. Anita Joyce Sikeman, Aug. 15, 1965; children: Caren L., Glenn H., Robyn L. BSBA in Mgmt., Clark U., 1965; MBA in Mktg., Seton Hall U., 1970. Chmn., pres., CEO, bd. dirs. Tenney Engring. Inc., Union, N.J., 1977—. Mem. Inst. Environ. Sci. (sr.), Aircraft Owners and Pilots Assn. Office: Tenney Engring Inc 1090 Springfield Rd Union NJ 07083-8197

SCHIFFMAN, STEPHAN, management consultant; b. N.Y.C., June 14, 1946; s. Walter and Martha S.; B.S., Ithaca Coll., 1968; MSW, Cornell U., 1969; postgrad U. Md., 1971-72, Detroit U., 1971-73; m. Anne Feinglass, Aug. 25, 1974; children: Daniele Megan, Jennifer Ruth. Prin. Stephan Schiffman Assocs., N.Y.C., 1972—; dir. tng. United Jewish Appeal, N.Y.C., 1975—; practice psychotherapy, N.Y.C., 1976—; speaker on motivation and success, power sales, 1989; dir. D.E.I. Mgmt. Group, N.Y.C., 1979—; prin. Stephan Schiffman Telemarketing, 1992; mem. faculty Adelphi U., Garden City, N.Y., 1976-80; lectr. N.Y. U., 1977-80, New Sch. Social Rsch., 1978—, Queen's Coll., 1985—, Norwalk C.C., 1989;. Author: Cold Calling Techniques that Work, 1991, 3d edit., 1979, cassette edit. 1991, The Consultant's Handbook, 1988, 25 Sales Mistakes, 1990, Power Sales Presentations, 1989, Sales Habits of Highly Successful People, 1991; contbr. articles to profl. jours. Mem. Inst. Mgmt. Cons., Nat. Soc. Fund Raisers (dir.), Am. Mgmt. Assn., TC Acad. Arts and Scis., Soc. Profl. Mgmt. Cons., Am. Soc. Tng. and Devel., N.Y.C. Chamber Commerce and Industry (edn. chair, speaker), N.Y. Athletic Club. Jewish. Home: 235 E 87th St New York NY 10128-3225 Office: 888 7th Ave 9th Flr New York NY 10106-5230

SCHIFFMAN, SUSAN STOLTE, medical psychologist, educator; b. Chgo., Aug. 24, 1940; d. Paul R. and Mildred (Glicksman) Stolte; m. Harold Schiffman (div.); 1 child, Amy Lise; m. H. Troy Nagle, July 22, 1989. BA, Syracuse U., 1965; PhD, Duke U., 1970. Lic. psychologist, N.C. Postdoctoral fellow Duke U., Durham, N.C., 1970-72, asst. prof., 1972-77, assoc. prof., 1978-83, full prof., 1983—; cons., mem. adv. bd. Nutrasweet, Chgo., 1978—, Nestle, Vevey, Switzerland, 1990, Fragrance Rsch. Fund, N.Y.C., 1986—, and others. Author: Introduction to Multidimensional Scaling: Theory, Methods and Applications, 1981, Flavor Set-Point Weight Loss Cookbook, 1990. Nat. Inst. Aging grantee, 1972—. Mem. Assn. Chemoreception Scis., European Chemoreception Rsch. Orgn., Soc. for Neurosci. Office: Duke U Med Sch Dept Psychiatry Box 3259 Durham NC 27708-0086

SCHIFFNER, CHARLES ROBERT, architect; b. Reno, Sept. 2, 1948; Robert Charles and Evelyn (Keck) S.; m. Iovanna Lloyd Wright, Nov. 1971 (div. Sept. 1981); m. Adrienne Anita McAndrews, Jan. 22, 1983. Student, Sacramento Jr. Coll., 1967-68, Frank Lloyd Wright Sch. Architecture, 1968-77. Registered architect, Ariz., Nev., Wis. Architect Taliesin Associated Architects, Scottsdale, Ariz., 1977-83; pvt. practice architecture Phoenix, 1983—; lectr. The Frank Lloyd Wright Sch. of Architecture, 1994, 95. Named one of 25 Most Promising Young Americans Under 35, U.S. mag., 1979; recipient AIA Honor award Western Mountain Region, 1993, Western Home awards Sunset Mag., 1989, 91, AIA Ariz. Merit award, 1993 and numerous others. Home: 5202 E Osborn Rd Phoenix AZ 85018-6137 Office: Camelhead Office Ctr 2600 N 44th St # 208 Phoenix AZ 85008-1521

SCHIFFNER, JOAN LESSING, consultant; b. Hollywood, Calif., Nov. 26, 1944; d. Lessing Robert and Ruth Isabel (Chamberlain) Sattler; children: Robert Garrett, Gregory Garrett, Laura Garrett. BA, San Jose State U., 1970, postgrad.; postgrad., U. Calif. Cert. in non-profit orgn.mgmt. Cons. to health and human svc. govtl. and non-profit orgns. Civilian Pers. Office, Fort Ord, Calif., 1993—; ptnr. Millson, Schiffner and Assocs.; bd. dirs. Growth and Opportunity, Inc. Am. Red Cross, 1990—; cons. Saving Our Libr.'s Excellence Com. 1992-93. Pub. info. officer San Benito County (Calif.) United Way, bd. dirs., 1988-90; founding mem. San Benito County Vol. Ctr. Task Force, San Benito County Cable Access Commn., 1987-90; co-founder San Benito County Action Team; vice chair San Benito County Voluntary Orgns. Active in Disasters, 1990-91; appointed to cen. com. ARC No. Calif. Earthquake Relief and Preparedness Project, 1991; pres. Network of San Benito, 1988-90; mem. San Benito County Econ. Group, Mex. Am. Com. on Edn., 1970—, Hollister Sister Cities Assn., 1989—; sec. bd. dirs. Econ. Devel. Corp.; exec. dir. San Benito County Interfaith, 1990-91; mem. adv. bd. San Benito Health Found., 1991—; pub. rels. chair San Benito County AIDS Project, 1992-94; active numerous non-profit and civic orgns.; bd. dirs ARC. Mem. AAUW, San Benito County C. of C., Phi Alpha Theta, Psi Chi, Alpha Kappa Delta. Democrat. Roman Catholic. Avocations: dancing, piano, swimming, hiking. Home: 845 Helen Dr Hollister CA 95023-6613

SCHIFFRIN, ANDRE, publisher; b. Paris, June 12, 1935; came to U.S., 1941; s. Jacques and Simone (Heymann) S.; m. Maria Elena de la Iglesia, June 14, 1961; children—Anya, Natalia. B.A. summa cum laude, Yale U., 1957; M.A. with 1st class honors, Cambridge U., Eng., 1959. With New Am. Library, 1959-63; with Pantheon Books, Inc., N.Y.C., 1962-90, editor, then editor in chief, mng. dir., 1969-90; pub. Schocken Books subs. Pantheon Books Inc., 1987-90; pres. Fund for Ind. Pub., N.Y.C., 1990—; dir., editor in chief The New Press, N.Y.C., 1990—; mem. spl. com. Am. Ctr., Paris, 1994—; vis. fellow Davenport Coll., 1977-79; vis. lectr. Yale U., 1977, 79; bd. dirs. The New Press, N.Y.C. Contbr. articles to profl. jours., N.Y. Times Book Rev., Nation, New Republic. Mem. coun. Smithsonian Instn., 1969—; bd. dirs. N.Y. Coun. for Humanities, 1978—, mem. exec. com., 1979-80; bd. dirs. N.Y. Civil Liberties Union; mem. freedom to pub. com. Assn. Am. Pubs., 1976-78; mem. vis. com. history dept. Princeton U., 1978—; mem. freedom to read com. AAUP, 1985—; mem. U.S. cultural del. to Peoples Republic China, 1983, 87; mem. vis. com. grad. faculty The New Sch., 1995—. Mellon fellow Clare Coll., 1957, hon. scholar, 1959; hon. fellow Trumbull Coll., Yale U., 1979—; Fulbright travel grantee, 1958-59. Fellow N.Y. Inst. for the Humanities. Home: 250 W 94th St New York NY 10025-6954 Office: The New Press 450 W 41st St New York NY 10036-6807

SCHIFRIN, LALO, composer; b. Buenos Aires, June 21, 1932. Student, Juan Carlos Paz and Olivier Messiaen.; PhD (hon.), RISD, 1989. Tchr. composition UCLA, 1970-71; guest condr. Israel Philharm, L.A. Philharm, L.A. Chamber Orch., Indpls. Symphony, Atlanta Symphony. Argentinian rep., Internat. Jazz Festival, Paris, 1955, formed own jazz group; composer for stage, modern dance, TV; with Dizzy Gillespie's band, 1962; film and TV composer, Hollywood, Calif., 1964—; compositions: (for ballet) Jazz Faust, 1963, (for orch.) Piano Concerto # 1, 1986, Cantos Aztecas, 1989, Concerto for guitar and orch., 1986, Concerto for double bass and orch., 1987, Three tangos for flute, harp and strings, 1987, Dance concertantes for clarinet and orch., 1990, Impressions for trumpet and orch., 1990, La Nouvelle Orleans Woodwind Quitet, 1991, Concerto # 2, 1992, Cantares Argentinos, 1992, Symphony # 1 for orch., 1993 (opera) The Trial of Louis XVI, 1988; theme for TV series Mission: Impossible (2 Grammy awards); film scores include The Cincinnati Kid, 1965, Cool Hand Luke, 1967, The Fox, 1968; film scores include Kelly's Heroes, 1970, W.U.S.A., 1970, Pussycat, Pussycat, I Love You, 1970, Bullit, 1970, Dirty Harry, 1971, THX-1138, 1971, The Beguiled, 1971, Magnum Force, 1973, The Four Musketeers, 1975, The Eagle Has Landed, 1977, Voyage of the Damned, 1976, Rollercoaster, 1977, Telefon, 1977, Boulevard Nights, 1979, The Concorde-Airport '79, 1979, Competition, 1981, Sudden Impact, 1984, The Sting II, 1985, The Fourth Protocol, 1987, The Fourth Protocol, 1987; TV series The Young-Lawyers, Mannix, 'Mission Impossible', Starsky and Hutch; writer orchestration for Grand Finale medley for Carreras, Domingo and Pavarotti, Rome, 1991; commd. Steinway Found piano concerto The Americas, selected by Nat. Symphony Orch., 1992. Recipient 4 Grammy awards, 1967, 1969, 1986, 6 Acad. award nominations Acad. Motion Picture Arts and Scis., 1966, 67, 75, 77, 80, 82, Walk of Fame award Hollywood C. of C.; chevalier de l'Ordre des Arts et des Lettres French gov. Office: CAA 9830 Wilshire Blvd Beverly Hills CA 90212

SCHIFSKY, CHARLES MARK, magazine editor; b. St. Paul, May 19, 1962; s. William Charles and Kathleen Jeanne (Lau) S.; m. Gina Maria Gelsomino, Oct. 8, 1994; 1 child, Amanda Jeanne. BA in Journalism and Pub. Rels., U. St. Thomas, St. Paul, 1987. With Bill Schifsky Enterprises, St. Paul, 1977-87; pub. rels. rep. Ramsey County Info. Office, St. Paul, 1987; clutch specialist Gary Ormsby Racing, Auburn, Calif., 1988-90; co-crew chief Jack Clark Racing, Indpls., 1990-91; assoc. editor Car Craft mag. Peterson Pub. Co., L.A., 1992-93, editor, 1993—. Mem. Motor Press Guild, Nat. Hot Rod Assn. (mem. top fuel world championship team 1989). Avocations: travel, photography, golf, motorsports. Office: Petersen Pub/Car Craft Mag 6420 Wilshire Blvd Los Angeles CA 90048-5502

SCHIFTER, RICHARD, lawyer, government official; b. Vienna, Austria, July 31, 1923; came to U.S., 1938; s. Paul and Balbina (Blass) S.; m. Lilo Krueger, July 3, 1948; children: Judith, Deborah, Richard P., Barbara, Karen. BS in Social Sci. summa cum laude, CCNY, 1943; LLB, Yale U., 1951; DHL (hon.), Hebrew Union Coll., 1992. Bar: Conn. 1951, D.C. 1952, U.S. Supreme Ct. 1954, Md., 1958. Assoc. Fried, Frank, Harris, Shriver & Jacobson, Washington, 1951-57, ptnr., 1957-84; dep. U.S. rep. with rank of ambassador UN Security Council, N.Y.C., 1984-85; asst. sec. of state for human rights and humanitarian affairs Dept. State, Washington, 1985-92; U.S. rep. UN Human Rights Commn., Geneva, 1983-86, 93; spl. asst. to pres., counselor Nat. Security Coun., Washington, 1993—; head U.S. del. Conf. on Security and Cooperation in Europe Experts Meeting on Human Rights, Ottawa, Ont., Can., 1985, Dem. Insts., Oslo, 1991; bd. dirs. U.S. Inst. Peace, 1986-92; mem. Congl. Commn. on Security and Cooperation in Europe, 1986-92. V.p., pres. Md. Bd. Edn., Balt., 1959-79; chmn. Md. Gov.'s Commn. on Funding Edn. of Handicapped Children, 1975-77, Md. Values Edn. Commn., 1979-83, Montgomery County Dem. Cen. Com., Md., 1966-70; del. Dem. Nat. Conv., 1968; bd. govs., chmn. Nat. Adv. Com., Am. Jewish Com., 1992-93. With U.S. Army, 1943-46, ETO. Recipient Disting. Svc. award Sec. of State, 1992. Mem. Phi Beta Kappa. Democrat. Jewish. Home: 6907 Crail Dr Bethesda MD 20817-4723 Office: Nat Security Coun Washington DC 20506

SCHILD, RAYMOND DOUGLAS, lawyer; b. Chgo., Dec. 20, 1952; s. Stanley Martin and Cassoundra Lee (McArdle) S.; m. Ellen Arthea Carstensen, Oct. 24, 1987; children: Brian Christopher, Melissa Nicole. Student, U.S. Mil. Acad., 1970; BA summa cum laude, De Paul U., 1974, JD magna cum laude, 1982; M in Life Scis., Order of Essenes, 1996. Bar: Ill. 1982, U.S. Dist. Ct. (no. dist.) Ill. 1982, U.S. Ct. Appeals (7th cir.) 1982, Idaho 1989, U.S. Dist. Ct. Idaho 1989, U.S. Ct. Appeals (9th cir.) 1989, U.S. Supreme Ct. 1990. Assoc. Clausen, Miller, Gorman, Caffrey & Witous, Chgo., 1982-84; law clk. to chief judge law divsn. Cir. Ct. Cook County, Chgo., 1984-85; assoc. John G. Phillips & Assocs., Chgo., 1985-87, Martin, Chapman, Park

& Burkett, Boise, Idaho, 1988-89; pvt. practice Boise, 1989-90; pres. and mng. ptnr. Martin, Chapman, Schild & Lassaw, Chartered, Boise, 1990—; bd. dirs. Image Concepts Internat., Inc., Boise; lectr. on legal edn. ICLE and NBI, 1993—. Co-host legal radio talk show KFXD, 1994; legal columnist Idaho Bus. Rev., 1988—. Mem. adv. bd. Alliance for the Mentally Ill, Boise, 1991—, Parents and Youth Against Drug Abuse, Boise, 1991-92; fair housing adminstr. Sauk Village (Ill.) Govt., 1987-88; instr. Ada County Youth Ct., Boise, 1992—. Schmitt fellow DePaul U., 1974; recipient award of merit Chgo. Law Coalition, 1987. Mem. ATLA, Idaho Trial Lawyers' Assn., Ill. State Bar Assn., Idaho State Bar Assn., Boise Estate Planning Counsel, Shriners (temple atty. 1994—), Masons (jr. steward 1992—). Avocations: tennis, trombone, writing, music. Office: Martin Chapman Schild & Lassaw Chartered 216 W Jefferson St Boise ID 83702

SCHILD, RUDOLPH ERNST, astronomer, educator; b. Chgo., Jan. 10, 1940; s. Kasimir A. and Anneliese (Schuricht) S.; m. Jane H. Struss, July 28, 1982. BS, U. Chgo., 1962, MS, 1963, PhD, 1966. Rsch. fellow Calif. Inst. Tech., Pasadena, 1966-69; scientific dir., 1.5m Telescope Program Smithsonian Astrophysical Obs., Amado, Ariz., 1969-74; astronomer Harvard-Smithsonian Ctr. for Astrophysics, Cambridge, Mass., 1974--; lectr. Harvard U., 1975-83. Author: (slide set) The Electronic Sky: Digital Images of the Cosmos, 1985, (CD-ROM) Voyage to the Stars: The Rudy Schild Collection; contbr. over 100 articles to scholarly and profl. jours. Mem. Am. Astronomical Soc., Internat. Astronomical Union. Achievements include 2 patents; discovery of gravitational microlensing. Office: Ctr for Astrophysics 60 Garden St Cambridge MA 02138-1516

SCHILDHAUSE, SOL, lawyer; b. N.Y.C., Sept. 5, 1917; s. Jacob and Fannie (Gerber) S.; m. Phyllis Sydell, May 23, 1943 (divorced); children: Susan Schildhause Tash, Peter, Richard. BS, CUNY, 1937; JD, Harvard U., 1940. Bar: N.Y. 1941, D.C. 1972, U.S. Ct. Claims 1975, U.S. Supreme Ct. 1978. Mng. ptnr. Sta. KOMA-AM, Oklahoma City, 1956-57; adminstrv. law judge FCC, Washington, 1963-66, chief cable TV bur., 1966-73; ptnr. D.C. office Farrow, Schildhause & Wilson, 1973-93; chmn. bd., gen. counsel The Media Inst., Washington; lectr. Practicing Law Inst., 1985. Mem. ABA (asst. chmn. cable TV com. 1986), FCC Bar Assn. Democrat. Jewish. Club: Harvard (Washington).

SCHILLER, ALFRED GEORGE, veterinarian, educator; b. Irma, Wis., Dec. 5, 1918; s. Adam and Bertha Schiller; m. Carolyn Capps, Apr. 14, 1944; children: James, Charles. DVM, Mich. State U., 1943; MS, U. Ill., 1956. Bd. cert. vet. surgery. Gen. practice vet. medicine Mpls., 1947-52; from instr. to prof. U. Ill., Urbana, 1952-87, head small animal clinic, 1954-74, asst. head dept. vet. medicine, 1974-76, acting dept. head vet. medicine, 1976-78, acting assoc. dean acad. affairs, 1978-79, acting dir. lab. animal care, 1979-80, asst. dept. head vet. clin. medicine, from 1980, prof. emeritus, 1987—. Contbr. articles to profl. jours. Served to capt. U.S. Army, 1944-47. Recipient Alumni award Mich. State U., 1978. Mem. Am. Vet. Medicine Assn. (various coms.), Ill. State Vet. Medicine Assn. (various coms., Meritorious Svc. award 1972), Am. Coll. Vet. Surgeons (recorder 1968-69, v.p. 1970-71, pres.-elect 1971-72, pres. 1972-73, chmn. 1973-74, exec. sec. 1975-90, Disting. Svc. award 1985).

SCHILLER, ARTHUR A., architect, educator; b. N.Y.C., July 23, 1910; s. Valentine and Rose (Bayer) S.; m. Anne O'Donnell, June 12, 1937; children: Valerie Schiller Schaefer, Virginia Schiller Waicul, Eileen Schiller Toomey. BArch, NYU, 1933; diploma, Beaux Arts Inst. Design, N.Y.C., 1935; MArch, MIT, 1939. Registered profl. architect, N.Y. Architect U.S. Govt., Washington, 1936-38, N.Y.C. Dept. Parks, 1938-47; chief architect Bd. Higher Edn., N.Y.C., 1947-51, dir. architecture and engring., 1951-67; coord. campus planning Queens Coll., N.Y.C., 1967-73; adj. prof. N.Y. Inst. Technology, Old Westbury, 1973-91; cons. Triboro Bridge Authority, N.Y.C., 1946; lectr. CCNY, 1957-67. Mayor Village of Plandome Manor, N.Y., 1965-87, trustee, 1960-65; trustee Sci. Mus. L.I. 1986—. Named Man of Yr. AARP, 1990, Sr. Citizen of Yr. Nassau County, State of N.Y., 1992 . Fellow AIA (pres. Queens chpt. 1957-58); mem. N.Y. State Assn. Architects (dir. 1959-60), Assn. Univ. Architects (emeritus), U.S. Power Squadron (comdr. 1961-62, budget dir. 1988-91), Elks (life). Avocations: boating, gardening, conducting defensive driving courses for older citizens. Home: 15 Luquer Rd Manhasset NY 11030-1015

SCHILLER, DONALD CHARLES, lawyer; b. Chgo., Dec. 8, 1942; s. Sidney S. and Edith (Lastick) S.; m. Eileen Fagin, June 14, 1964; children—Eric, Jonathan. Student, Lake Forest Coll., 1960-63; J.D., DePaul U., 1966. Bar: Ill. 1966, U.S. Dist. Ct. (no. dist.) Ill. 1966, U.S. Supreme Ct. 1972. Ptnr. Schiller, DuCanto & Fleck (formerly Schiller & Schiller and Schiller & DuCanto), Chgo., 1966—; chair domestic rels. adv. com. Cir. Ct. Cook County, 1993—, exec. com., 1986-93; speaker profl. confs. Contbr. chpts. and articles to profl. publs. Mem. steering com. on juvenile ct. watching, LWV, 1980-81. Recipient Maurice Weigle award Chgo. Bar Found., 1978, Disting. Alumni award, DePaul U., 1988, various certs. of appreciation profl. groups: named One of Am.'s Best Divorce Lawyers, Town and Country, 1985, The Nat. Law Jour., 1987, The Best Lawyers in Am., 1987, 89, 91, 93, One of Chgo's. Best Div. Lawyers, Crain's Chgo. Bus., 1981, Today Chgo. Woman, 1985, Inside Chgo. mag., 1988. Fellow Am. Bar Found., Am. Acad. Matrimonial Lawyers (chair continuing legal edn. 1993-94); mem. ABA (bd. govs. 1994—, chmn. family law sect. 1985-86, Ill. State del. 1980-84, mem. Ho. of Dels. 1984, editor-in-chief Family Law Newsletter 1977-79; mem. editorial bd., assoc. editor Family Adv. Mag. 1979-84, speaker at confs. and meetings), Ill. Bar Assn. (chmn. family law sect. 1976-77, editor Family Law Bull. 1976-77, bd. govs. 1977-83, treas. 1981-84, v.p. 1984-86, pres. 1987-88, chmn. various coms., lectr., incorporator Ill. State Bar Assn. Risk Retention Group, Inc. 1988, pres. 1988-89), Chgo. Bar Assn., Am. Coll. Family Law Trial Lawyers (diplomate). Office: Schiller DuCanto & Fleck 200 N La Salle St Ste 2700 Chicago IL 60601-1014

SCHILLER, ERIC M., lawyer; b. Detroit, Mar. 19, 1946; s. Stanley Schiller and Sara (Barliant) Benson; m. Jill E. Friedman, Aug. 16, 1970; children: Colin, Daniel, Jonathan. BA, Ind. U., 1968; JD, Northwestern U., 1971. Bar: Ill. 1971. Assoc. Sonnenschein Nath & Rosenthal, Chgo., 1971-78, ptnr., 1978—; mem. exec. com. Sonnenschein, Nath & Rosenthal, 1971—; lectr. ALI-ABA. Exec. bd. dirs. Anti-Defamation League of Chgo., 1989-92. Mem. ABA, Chgo. Bar Assn., Chgo. Coun. Lawyers, The Law Club of Chgo., John Henry Wigmore Club of Northwestern U. Law Sch. (exec. com. 1990-93), The Met. Club, Lake Shore Country Club. Home: 7 Rockgate Ln Glencoe IL 60022-1250 Office: Sonnenschein Nath & Rosenthal 8000 Sears Towers Chicago IL 60606

SCHILLER, FRANCIS, neurologist, medical historian; b. Prague, Czechoslovakia, Jan. 23, 1909; came to U.S., 1950; s. Friedrich and Luise (Mannheimer) S. MD, German U., Prague, 1933. Diplomate Am. Bd. Psychiatry and Neurology. With U. Calif. Med. Sch., San Francisco, 1951-79, clin. prof. neurology, 1972, emeritus prof, neurology, 1979; neurologist Kaiser Permanente Med. Group, San Francisco, 1953-78; cons. neurology Pub. Health Svc., San Francisco, 1978-81, VA Compensation & Pension, San Francisco, 1984—; sr. lectr. history and health sci. U. Calif., San Francisco, 1962—. Author: Paul Broca, 1824-80, 1979, A Möbius Strip, 1981; contbr. articles to profl. jours. Fellow Am. Acad. Neurology, San Francisco Neurology Soc.; mem. Internat. Acad. History of Medicine, Bay Area History of Medicine Club (pres. San Francisco cht. 1975-76). Avocations: gardening, piano. Home: 2730 Wawona St San Francisco CA 94116-2866 Office: U Calif Dept History of Health Scis Box 0726 Parnassus Ave 458 San Francisco CA 94122-2721

SCHILLER, HERBERT IRVING, social scientist, author; b. N.Y.C., Nov. 5, 1919; s. Benjamin Franklin and Gertrude (Perner) S.; m. Anita Rosenbaum, Nov. 5, 1946; children: Daniel T., P. Zachary. B in Social Sci., CCNY, 1940; MA, Columbia U., 1941; PhD, NYU, 1960. Teaching fellow CCNY, 1940-41, lectr. econs., 1949-59; economist U.S. Govt., 1941-42, 46-48; mem. faculty Pratt Inst., Bklyn., 1950-63; prof. econs., chmn. dept. social studies Pratt Inst., 1962-63; research assoc. prof. Bur. Econ. and Bus. Research, U. Ill. at Urbana, 1963-65, research prof., 1965-70; prof. communication U. Calif., San Diego, 1970-90, prof. emeritus, 1990—; lectr. Bklyn. Acad. Music, 1961-66; vis. fellow Inst. Policy Studies, Wash., 1968; vis. prof. U. Amsterdam, 1972-74; Thord-Gray vis. lectr. U. Stockholm, 1978; vis. prof. comms. Hunter Coll., CUNY, 1978-79, Am. U., 1991-93, NYU, 1993—. Author: Mass Communications and American Empire, 1969, rev. edit., 1992, Superstate: Readings in the Military-Industrial Complex, 1970, The Mind Managers, 1973, Communication and Cultural Domination, 1976, Who Knows: Information in the Age of the Fortune 500, 1981, Information and the Crisis Economy, 1984, Culture Inc.: The Corporate Takeover of Public Expression, 1989, Information Inequality, 1996, (with others) Hope and Folly: The U.S. and UNESCO, 1945-85, 1989; editor Quar. Rev. Econs. and Bus., 1963-70; co-editor: Triumph of the Image: The Media's War in the Persian Gulf, 1992, Beyond National Sovereignty: International Communication in the 1990s, 1993. Served with AUS, 1942-45, MTO. Mem. AAAS, Internat. Assn. Mass Communication Research (v.p.), Internat. Inst. Communications (trustee 1978-84), AAUP (sec. Ill. U.), Phi Beta Kappa. Home: 7109 Monte Vista Ave La Jolla CA 92037-5326 Office: U Calif San Diego La Jolla CA 92093

SCHILLER, JAMES JOSEPH, lawyer; b. Cleve., July 1, 1933; s. Jacob Peter and Helen Elizabeth (Tosh) S.; m. Sara Brooke Wilson, Oct. 24, 1964; children: Charles A., Brooke V.G., Kristan W. BS, Case Inst. Tech., 1955; JD, U. Mich., 1961. Bar: Ohio 1962. Assoc. Marshman, Hornbeck & Hollington, Cleve., 1961-68; ptnr. Marshman, Snyder & Seeley, Cleve., 1968-73, Zellmer & Gruber, Cleve., 1973-80, Weston, Hurd, Fallon, Paisley & Howley, Cleve., 1980-88, Porter, Wright, Morris & Arthur, Cleve., 1989-95, Schiller & Ryan, Cleve., 1995—. Campaign mgr. John J. Gilligan for Gov. of Ohio, Cuyahoga County, 1970; campaign dir. U.S. Senator Howard M. Metzenbaum, Cleve., 1973; mem. Ohio Dem. Com., 1970-73; dep. registrar motor vehicles Dept. Hwy. Safety, Cuyahoga County, 1971-74; trustee Greater Cleve. Regional Transit Authority, 1985-87; vestryman Christ Episcopal Ch., Shaker Heights, Ohio, 1974-76, 90-93, clk., 1974-76, sr. warden, 1992-93; chmn. bd. suprs. ChristCh. Found., 1995—. Recipient Cert. Commendation Bd. County Commrs., 1987. Mem. ABA, Ohio State Bar Assn. (ethics com. 1986-88), Cleve. Bar Assn., Rowfant Club (fin. com. 1988, coun. Fellowes 1990-91, 95—, advocate 1992-95), Union Club, Cleve. Skating Club. Avocations: sailing, skiing, restoring furniture. Home: 3311 Maynard Rd Cleveland OH 44122-3437 Office: Schiller & Ryan The Arcade 401 Euclid Ave Ste 332 Cleveland OH 44114

SCHILLER, JERRY A., retired manufacturing company executive; b. Moline, Ill., Sept. 2, 1932; s. Walter A. and Mae (Sears) S.; m. Betty Fuller; children: Michele Schiller Smead, Susan Schiller Fortune, Richard, Lisa Schiller Swank, Sandra Schiller Rogers, Sara Schiller Siefleff. BA in Bus. Adminstrn. and Acctg., Augustana Coll., 1954. CPA, Iowa. Mgr. internal auditing Maytag Co., Newton, Iowa, 1962-75, asst. controller, 1975-84, asst. v.p., controller, 1984-85; v.p., chief fin. officer Maytag Corp., Newton, Iowa, 1985-86, sr. v.p., chief fin. officer, 1986-89, exec. v.p., chief fin. officer, 1989—, also trustee, 1989-93; ret., 1994; bd. dirs. Amerivend, AMAC Ins. Co., treas; mem. various coms. Maytag Mgmt. Club, Newton. Chmn. Newton Community Childrens Day Care Ctr., 1967; pres. Newton YMCA, 1970; auditor Newton Community Ctr. Fund Dr., 1973; various offices Our Savior Luth. Ch., Citizens Com. for Schs.; bd. dirs. Des Moines Ballet, 1986. Recipient Outstanding Religious Leader award Newton Jaycees, 1968, Outstanding Alumni award Augustana Coll.,1990. Mem. Fin. Execs. Inst., Iowa Soc. CPAs, Am. Inst. CPAs. Home: PO Box 515 Newton IA 50208-0515 Office: Maytag Corp 403 W 4th St N Newton IA 50208-3026

SCHILLER, LAWRENCE JULIAN, motion picture producer, director; b. N.Y.C., Dec. 28, 1936; s. Isidore and Jean (Liebowitz) S.; children: Suzanne, Marc, Howard, Anthony, Cameron. B.A., Pepperdine Coll., 1958. Photojournalist Life mag., 1959-69, Paris Match, 1960-69, London Sun. Times, 1960-69. Producer, dir.; (films) Hey, I'm Alive, The Winds of Kitty Hawk, Marilyn, Raid on Short Creek, An Act of Love, The Executioner's Song (Emmy award), Peter the Great (Emmy award), By Reason of Insanity, Margret Brourke-White Story, Plot to Killl Hitler, Double Jeopardy; author: Sunshine, Marilyn; collaborator: (with Albert Goldman) Lenny Bruce (with Eugene Smith) Minamata, (with Norman Mailer) The Executioner's Song (Pulitzer prize 1980), Oswald's Tale; (with O.J. Simpson) I Want To Tell You. Chmn. bd. dirs. Am.-Soviet Film Initiative, 1988; Am. del. Moscow Internat. Forum on Peace, 1987; mem. USSR-USA Bi-Lateral Talks, 1988. Recipient numerous awards in photojournalism Nat. Press Photographers Assn., Acad. award for The Man Who Skied Down Everest, 1975. Mem. Nat. Press Photographers Assn., Calif. Press Photographers Assn., Dirs. Guild of Am., Acad. of Motion Picture Arts and Scis. Democrat. Jewish.

SCHILLER, PIETER JON, venture capital executive; b. Orange, N.J., Jan. 14, 1938; s. John Fasel and Helen Roff (Roberts) S.; m. Elizabeth Ann Williams, Nov. 20, 1965; children—Cathryn Ann, Suzanne Elizabeth. B.A. in Econs. with honors, Middlebury (Vt.) Coll., 1960; M.B.A., N.Y. U., 1966. Fin. analyst Merck & Co., Inc., N.Y.C., 1960-61; fin. analyst, asst. div. controller, dir. auditing, then asst. controller Allied Chem. Corp., N.Y.C. and Morristown, N.J., 1961-75; treas. Allied Chem. Corp., 1975-79, v.p. planning and devel., 1979-83; Allied Corp. exec. v.p. diagnostic ops. Allied Health & Sci. Products Co., 1983-86; pres. subs. Instrumentation Lab., Lexington, Mass., 1983-86; gen. ptnr. Advanced Tech. Ventures, Boston, 1986—; bd. dirs. Anthra Pharms., Inc., Princeton, N.J., Afferon Corp., Phoenix, HealthShare Tech., Acton, Mass., Avicenna Sys. Corp., Cambridge, Mass., CollaGenex Pharms., Inc., Newtown, Pa., Novoste Corp., Norcross, Ga. Chmn. bd. trustees Newark Boys Chorus Sch., 1976-78, pres. bd., 1974-76; trustee Colonial Symphony Soc., 1978-85, v.p., 1980-82, pres. 1982-83, Morris Mus., Morristown, Concord (Mass.) Mus., 1994-96, v.p. 1996—; bd. dirs. New Eng. Coun., Boston, 1983-86, Middlebury Coll. Alumni Assn., 1989—, v.p. 1992-94, pres. 1994-96; chmn. allocations com. United Way of Morris County, 1974-79, v.p. bd. dirs., mem. exec. com., 1979-80; trustee Morris Mus. Arts and Scis., 1980-83. Mem. Fin. Execs. Inst. Republican. Episcopalian. Avocations: skiing, photography. Home: 1373 Monument St Concord MA 01742-5328

SCHILLER, WILLIAM RICHARD, surgeon; b. Bennett, Colo., Jan. 14, 1937; s. Francis T. and Frances M. (Finks) S.; m. Beverlee Schiller; children from previous marriage: Julie, Lisa. B.S., Drury Coll., Springfield, Mo., 1958; M.D., Northwestern U., 1962. Diplomate Am. Bd. Surgery; cert. of added qualifications in surg. critical care, 1987, recertified in surg. critical care, 1994. Intern Passavant Meml. Hosp., Chgo., 1962-63; resident Northwestern U. Clin. Tng. Program, Chgo., 1963-68; assoc. prof. surgery Med. Coll Ohio, Toledo, 1970-78; prof. surgery U. N.Mex, Albuquerque, 1978-83; dir. Trauma Ctr. St. Joseph's Hosp., Phoenix, 1983-89; dir. burn and trauma ctr. Maricopa Med. Ctr., Phoenix, 1989—; clin. prof. surgery U. Ariz. Health Sci. Ctr.; prof. surgery Mayo Grad. Sch. Medicine, Rochester, Minn. Contbr. chpts. to books, articles to profl. jours. Served as maj. M.C. U.S. Army, 1968-70, Vietnam. Fellow ACS; mem. Am. Assn. Surgery of Trauma, Cen. Surg. Assn., Western Surg. Assn., Soc. Surgery of Alimentary Tract, Am. Burn Assn., Internat. Soc. of Surgery. Republican. Home: 8226 E Via De La Escuela Scottsdale AZ 85258-3054 Office: Burn and Trauma Ctr Maricopa Med Ctr 2601 E Roosevelt St Phoenix AZ 85008-4973

SCHILLING, ARLO LEONARD, bank executive; b. Huntington, Ind., Oct. 13, 1924; s. Jacob Howard and Nova Elnora (Rusher) S.; m. Gloria Ann Wygant, Oct. 20, 1946; children: Nancy, Emily, Janey. BS in Edn., Huntington Coll., 1948; MS in Edn., Ind. U., 1950; PhD in Econ., Edn., Psychology, Purdue U., 1958. Tchr. Avilla Pub. Schs., Ind., 1948-52; prin. Coesse Pub. Schs., Ind., 1952-55, Montpelier Pub. Schs., Ind., 1955-56; instr. Purdue U., West Lafayette, Ind., 1956-58; asst. supt. Elkhart Pub. Schs., Ind., 1958-60; pres. North Cen. Coll., Naperville, Ill., 1960-75; chmn., dir., vice chair chmn. Harris Bank Naperville, 1975-94; ret.; vice chmn. Paramount Arts Centre Endowment, Aurora, Ill., 1983—; interim pres. Bank Fox Valley, Westmont, 1975-80. Life trustee North Ctrl. Coll., Naperville, 1960—; mem. pres.'s adv. coun. Sch. Edn., Purdue U., West Lafayette, Ind. With U.S. Army, 1943-45, ETO. Mem. NEA, Rotary (pres. 1968), Phi Delta Kappa, Kappa Delta Pi. Republican. Methodist. Avocations: gardening, reading, public speaking, fund raising. Home: 38 W 55 Deerpath Rd Batavia IL 60510

SCHILLING, DAVID AUGUST, management educator; b. Camden, N.J., Feb. 2, 1951; s. Spencer August and Ruth Elaine (Halvorsen) S.; m. Catherine Petersen. BS in Physics with honors, Miami U., 1972; PhD, Johns Hopkins U., 1976. Asst. prof. mgmt. scis. Am. U., Washington, 1976-78; asst. prof. mgmt. scis. Ohio State U., Columbus, 1978-83, assoc. prof. mgmt. scis., 1983-87, assoc. prof., dir. MBA program prof. mgmt. scis., 1987-88, assoc. prof., chmn. mgmt. scis., 1988-89, prof., chmn. mgmt. scis., 1989—. Contbr. articles to profl. jours. Mem. Phi Beta Kappa. Home: 2226 Picket Post Ln Columbus OH 43220 Office: Ohio State U Columbus OH 43210-1399

SCHILLING, EMILY BORN, editor, association executive; b. Lawton, Okla., Oct. 2, 1959; d. George Arthur and Sumiko (Nagamine) Born; m. Mark David Schilling, June 26, 1995. BS, Ball State U., 1981. Cert. rural electric communicator Nat. Rural Electric Coop. Assn. Feature writer The News-Sentinel, Fort Wayne, Ind., 1981-83; wire editor The Noblesville (Ind.) Daily Ledger, 1983; staff writer Ind. Statewide Assn. Rural Electric Coops., Indpls., 1983-84, mng. editor, 1984-85, editor, 1985—. Author: Power to the People, 1985. Mem. Coop. Communicators Assn. (Michael Graznak award 1990), Internat. Assn. Bus. Communicators (award of excellence dist. 7 1985), Elec. Women's Round Table Inc. (Power award 1994), Electric Inst. Ind., Nat. Electric Cooperatives Statewide Editors Assn. Office: Ind Statewide Assn RECs 720 N High School Rd Indianapolis IN 46214-3756

SCHILLING, FREDERICK AUGUSTUS, JR., geologist, consultant; b. Phila., Apr. 12, 1931; s. Frederick Augustus and Emma Hope (Christoffer) S.; m. Ardis Ione Dovre, June 12, 1957 (div. 1987); children: Frederick Christopher, Jennifer Dovre. BS in Geology, Wash. State U., 1953; PhD in Geology, Stanford U., 1962. Computer geophysicist United Geophys. Corp., Pasadena, Calif., 1955-56; geologist various orgns., 1956-61, U.S. Geol. Survey, 1961-64; underground engr. Climax (Colo.) Molybdenum Co., 1966-68; geologist Keradamex Inc., Anaconda Co., M.P. Grace, Ranchers Exploration & Devel. Corp., Albuquerque and Grants, N.Mex., 1968-84, Hecla Mining Co., Coeur d'Alene, Idaho, 1984-86, various engring. and environ. firms, Calif., 1986-91; prin. F. Schilling Cons., Canyon Lake, Calif., 1991—. Author: Bibliography of Uranium, 1976. Del. citizen amb. program People to People Internat., USSR, 1990-91. With U.S. Army, 1953-55. Fellow Explorers Club; mem. Geol. Soc. Am., Am. Assn. Petroleum Geologists, Soc. Mining Engrs., Internat. Platform Assn., Adventurers' Club Inc. L.A., Masons, Kiwanis, Sigma Xi, Sigma Gamma Epsilon. Republican. Presbyterian. Avocation: track and field. Office: F Schilling Cons 30037 Steel Head Dr Canyon Lake CA 92587-7460

SCHILLING, JOHN ALBERT, surgeon; b. Kansas City, Mo., Nov. 5, 1917; s. Carl Fielding and Lottie Lee (Henderson) S.; m. Lucy West, June 8, 1957 (dec.); children: Christine Henderson, Katharine Ann, Jolyon David, John Jay; m. Helen R. Spelbrink, May 28, 1979. A.B. with honors, Dartmouth Coll., 1937; M.D., Harvard U., 1941. Diplomate Am. Bd. Surgery (chmn. 1969). Intern, then resident in surgery Roosevelt Hosp., N.Y.C., 1941-44; mem. faculty U. Rochester (N.Y.) Med. Sch., 1945-53, asst. prof. surgery, 1955-56; prof. surgery, head dept. U. Okla. Med. Sch., 1956-74; prof. surgery U. Wash. Med. Sch., Seattle, 1974—; chmn. dept. U. Wash. Med. Sch., 1975-83, prof. emeritus, 1988—; mem. bd. sci. counselors Nat. Cancer Inst., chmn., 1969; also mem. diagnosis subcom. breast cancer task force; chmn. adv. com. to surgeon gen. on metabolism of trauma Army Med. Research and Devel. Command; mem. surgery study sect., div. research grants NIH; chief surgery USAF Sch. Aviation Medicine, 1953-55; cons. Surgeon Gen. USAF, 1959-75. Author articles, chpts. in books, abstracts, reports.; editorial bd. Am. Jour. Surgery, Annals of Surgery. Served to maj. M.C. USAF, 1953-55. Grantee Army Office Surgeon Gen., 1956-80. Mem. ACS (bd. govs., chmn. com. surg. edn. in med. schs., 1st v.p. 1977-78), Am. S., Western, Pan-Pacific, N. Pacific, Pacific Coast surg. assns., Soc. Univ. Surgeons, Southwestern Surg. Soc., Central Surg. Soc., Southwestern Surg. Congress (hon. mem. 1978), Okla. Surg. Assn. (pres. 1970-71, hon. mem. 1974) Am. Assn. Surgery Trauma, Surg. Biology Club, Am. Physiol. Soc., Soc. Surg. Chmn., Am. Trauma Soc., Seattle Surg. Soc., Soc. Exptl. Pathology, Soc. Surgery Alimentary Tract, Explorers Club, Alpha Omega Alpha. Clubs: Yacht (Seattle), University (Seattle). Home: 9807 Lake Washington Blvd NE Bellevue WA 98004-5431 Office: Dept Surgery (RF-25) Univ Wash Medical Sch Seattle WA 98195

SCHILLING, JOHN MICHAEL, golf course executive; b. Hiawatha, Kans., Nov. 23, 1951; s. George H. and Darlene J. (Wachter) S.; m. Pamela S. Hischke, Sept. 5, 1969; children: John II, James. Student Highland Coll., 1971-72; BS in Journalism, U. Kans., 1974. Assoc. editor Kans. Electric Coops., Topeka, 1975-76, editor, 1976-79; editor Golf Course Supts. Assn. Am., Lawrence, Kans., 1978-79, mktg. dir., 1979-83, exec. dir., 1983-93; pres. St. Andrews Corp., Lawrence, 1994—. Contbr. articles to profl. jours. Mem. Am. Soc. Assn. Execs., Nat. Assn. Expn. Mgrs., Am. Advt. Fedn., U.S. Golf Assn., Nat. Golf Found. (bd. dirs.), Internat. Assn. Golf Adminstrs. Republican. Lutheran. Club: Alvamar Country (Lawrence). Avocations: golf, boating, coaching, breeding dogs, reading, computers. Home: 854 E 1259 Rd Lawrence KS 66042-9460 Office: St Andrews Corp PO Box 3407 Lawrence KS 66046

SCHILLING, WARNER ROLLER, political scientist, educator; b. Glendale, Calif., May 23, 1925; s. Jule Frederick and Pauline Frances de Berri (Warner) S.; m. Jane Pierce Metzger, Jan. 27, 1951 (dec. Nov. 1983); children: Jonathan, Frederick. A.B., Yale U., 1949, M.A., 1951, Ph.D., 1954. Research fellow Center Internat. Studies, Princeton U., 1953-54; asst. prof. internat. relations Mass. Inst. Tech., 1957-58; mem. faculty Columbia, 1954—, prof. govt., 1967-73, James T. Shotwell prof. internat. relations, 1973—; dir. Inst. War and Peace Studies, 1976-86; cons., occasional lectr. in field. Co-author: Strategy, Politics and Defense Budgets, 1962, European Security and the Atlantic System, 1973, American Arms and a Changing Europe, 1973; Contbr. numerous articles to jours. Served with USAAF, 1944-46. Guggenheim fellow, 1964-65; resident fellow Bellagio Study and Conf. Center, 1975. Mem. Internat. Inst. Strategic Studies, Council Fgn. Relations. Club: Leonia Democratic. Home: 496 Park Ave Leonia NJ 07605-1243 Office: 420 W 118th St New York NY 10027-7213

SCHILLING, WILLIAM RICHARD, aerospace engineer, research and development company executive; b. Manheim, Pa., Jan. 12, 1933; s. William Thomas and Ora Lee (Worley) S.; m. Patricia Elise Brigman, June 8, 1957; 1 child, Duane Thomas. BCE, Va. Poly. Inst., 1956; MS in Structural Engring., Pa. State U., 1959; MS in Aero. Engring., U. So. Calif., 1961, Engrs. Degree in Aerospace Engring., 1966. Aerodynamist Douglas Aircraft Co., Santa Monica, Calif., 1956-64; study chmn. Research Analysis Corp., McLean, Va., 1964-72; div. mgr. Sci. Applications, Inc., McLean, 1972-78; pres., chief exec. officer McLean Rsch. Ctr., Inc., 1978-89; exec. v.p. Wackenhut Applied Techs. Ctr., Fairfax, Va., 1989-91; dir. bus. devel., dir. sys. rsch. divsn., bd. dirs. Internat. Devel. and Resources, Inc., Falls Church, Va., 1991—; pres. Systems Rsch. Corp., Falls Church, 1991—; pres., bd. dirs. LaMancha Co., Santa Fe, 1985-89. Contbr. numerous articles to profl. jours. Chmn. com. Boy Scouts Am., McLean, 1968-78; vol. Am. Heart Assn., McLean, 1984-89; bd. dirs., chief exec. officer Internat. Housing Devel., McLean, 1986—. Mem. Assn. U.S. Army, Am. Def. Preparedness, Va. C. of C. Baptist. Avocations: classical lit., art, music, travel. Home: 6523 Old Dominion Dr Mc Lean VA 22101-4613 Office: Internat Devel & Resources 3900 Jermantown Rd Ste 450 Fairfax VA 22030-4900

SCHILLINGER, EDWIN JOSEPH, physics educator; b. Chgo., July 14, 1923; s. Edwin Joseph and Marie (Wolf) S.; m. Carmelita Larocco, Aug. 27, 1949; children—Rosemarie, Mary, Ann, Edwin, Jerome, Elizabeth. B.S., DePaul U., 1944; M.S., U. Notre Dame, 1948, Ph.D., 1950. Mem. faculty DePaul U., Chgo., 1950—, prof. physics, 1963-88, prof. emeritus, 1988—, chmn. dept., 1952-68, 76-79, dean Coll. Liberal Arts and Scis., 1966-70, acting dean, 1980-81; ednl. cons. Served with AUS, 1944-46. Decorated Purple Heart; recipient merit award Chgo. Tech. Socs., 1976; AEC fellow, 1948-50. Fellow Am. Phys. Soc.; mem. Am. Assn. Physics Tchrs., AAAS, Ill. Acad. Sci., Chgo. Acad. Tech. (charter mem.), Sigma Xi. Roman Catholic. Home: 7724 W Peterson Ave Chicago IL 60631-2246

SCHILLING-NORDAL, GERALDINE ANN, secondary school educator; b. Springfield, Mass., Feb. 4, 1935; d. Robert Milton and Helen Veronica (Ewald) Schilling; m. Reidar Johannes Nordal. BS, Boston U., 1956, MEd, 1957; postgrad., Springfield Coll. Tchr. art Agawam (Mass.) Jr. H.S., 1957-58; tchr. art Agawam H.S., 1958—, K-12 art acad. coord., 1995-96, 1995-96; instr. oil painting univ. ext. course Agawam Night Sch., 1957-58; instr. creative arts Agawam Evening Sch., 1973-80. Active Agawam Town Report Com., 1967-77, Agawam Hist. Commn., 1979-87, Agawam Arts and

Humanities Com., 1979-85, Agawam Minerva Davis Libr. Study Com., 1987—, Agawam Cultural Coun., 1994—; sec. Agawam Town Beautification Com., 1974-87; mem. town tchrs. rep. Agawam Bicentennial Com., 1975-77; chmn. 40th anniversary St. John the Evangelist Ch., Agawam, 1986, co-chmn. 50th anniversary com., 1996, mem. renovation com., 1983; decoration chmn. town-wide Halloween parties, Agawam, 1971-93; recruiter Miss Agawam Pageant. Mem. NEA, ASCD, Agawam Edn. Assn. (sec. 1970-74, 76-77), Hampden County Tchrs. Assn., Mass. Tchrs. Assn., Mass. Art Edn. Assn., Nat. Art Edn. Assn., New Eng. Art Edn. Assn., Mass. Alliance for Art Edn., Am. Assn. Ret. Persons, Mass. Cath. Order Foresters, West Springfield Neighborhood House Alumni Assn. (pres. 1966, advisor 1968), West Springfield H.S. Alumni Assn. (3d v.p. 1968-70, 1st v.p. 1970-71, pres. 1972-74), Boston U. Alumni Club Springfield Area (organizer area giving campaigns 1957-62, class agt. 1985—, mem. area scholarship com. 1995—), Am. Legion (life), Zeta Chi Delta (pres. 1955-56), Delta Kappa Gamma (Alpha chpt., art chairperson, reservation chmn. art work and hist. archives). Office: Agawam Sr High Sch 760 Cooper St Agawam MA 01001-2177

SCHILLINGS, DENNY LYNN, history educator; b. Mt. Carmel, Ill., June 28, 1947; s. Grady Lynn and Mary Lucille (Walters) S.; m. Karen Krek; children: Denise, Corinne. AA, Wabash Valley Coll., 1967; BEd, Ea. Ill. U., 1969, MA in History, 1972; postgrad., Chgo. State U., Govs. State U., Ill. State U., No. Ill. U. Grad. asst. dept. history Ea. Ill. U., Charleston, 1969; tchr. Edwards County High Sch., Albion, Ill., 1969-70, Sheldon (Ill.) High Sch., 1971-73, Homewood-Flossmoor (Ill.) High Sch., 1973—; participant, con. Atlantic Coun. U.S. and NATO, Washington, 1986, Internat. Soviet-U.S. Textbook Project Conf., Racine, Wis., 1987; moderator Soviet-U.S. Textbook Study: Final Report, Dallas, 1987; chair history content adv. com. Ill. Tchr. Certification Requirements Com. 1986—; mem. Ill. State Bd. Edn., Com. to Establish Learner Outcomes, 1984—, Joint Task Force on Admission Requirements Ill. State Bd. on Higher Edn., 1986—; mem. adv. com. for Jefferson Found. Sch. Programs, 1987—, Ill. State Bd. Edn.'s Goals Assessment Adv. Com., 1987—. Author: (with others) Economics, 1986, The Examination in Social Studies, 1989, Links Across Time and Place: A World History, 1990, Illinois Government Text, 1990, Challenge of Freedom, 1990; author: The Living Constitution, 1991; co-editor: Teaching the Constition, 1987; reviewer, cons. for ednl. instns. and organizations; chair editorial bd. Social Edn., 1983; contbg. editor Social Studies Tchr., 1987-88. Mem. steering com. Homewood-Floosmoor High Sch. Found., 1983-84. Mem. NEA, Am. Hist. Assn. (James Harvey Robinson prize com. 1990-91), Ill. Assn. Advancement History, Ill. Coun. Social Studies (v.p. 1981, editor newsletter 1979-84, pres. 1983), Ill. Edn. Assn. (Gt. Lakes coord. com. 1982-83), Nat. Coun. Social Studies (publs. bd. 1983-86, bd. dirs. 1987-90, 94-96, exec. com. 1989-90, chair conf. com. 1989-90, pres. 1993-94, program planning com. 1989, 91), World History Assn., Phi Alpha Theta. Avocations: computers, reading. Home: 18447 Aberdeen St Homewood IL 60430-3525 Office: Homewood-Flossmoor High Sch 999 Kedzie Ave Flossmoor IL 60422-2248

SCHILSKY, RICHARD LEWIS, oncologist, researcher; b. N.Y.C., June 6, 1950; s. Murray and Shirley (Cohen) S.; m. Cynthia Schum, Sept. 24, 1977; children: Allison, Meredith. BA cum laude, U. Pa., Phila., 1971; MD with honors, U. Chgo., 1975. Diplomate Nat. Bd. Med. Examiners, Am. Bd. Internal Medicine (subspecialty med. oncology); lic. physician, Mo., Ill. Intern, resident medicine Parkland Meml. Hosp., Southwestern Med. Sch., Dallas, 1975-77; clin. assoc. medicine br. and clin. pharmacology br. Div. Cancer Treatment, Nat. Cancer Inst., Bethesda, Md., 1977-80, cancer expert clin. pharmacology br., 1980-81; asst. prof. dept. internal medicine U. Mo.-Columbia Sch. Medicine, 1981-84; asst. prof. dept. medicine U. Chgo. Pritzker Sch. Medicine and Michael Reese Med. Ctrs., 1984-86, assoc. prof. dept. medicine, 1986-89; assoc. dir. joint sect. hematology and med. oncology U. Chgo. and Michael Reese Med. Ctrs., 1986-89; assoc. prof. dept. medicine, assoc. dir. sect. U. Chgo. Pritzker Sch. Medicine, 1989-91, prof. dept. medicine sect. hematology-oncology, 1991—; dir. U. Chgo. Cancer Rsch. Ctr., 1991—; chmn. Cancer and Leukemia Group B, Chgo., 1995—; Vivian Saykaly vis. prof. oncology McGill U., 1962; mem. sci. com. 5th Internat. Congress on Anti-Cancer Chemotherapy, 1995; mem. adv. panel on hematologic and neoplastic disease U.S. Pharmacopeial Conv., 1991-95; bd. dirs. Assn. Am. Cancer Insts., 1995—; mem. cancer ctr. support grant rev. com. Nat. Cancer Inst., NIH, 1992-95; mem. expert panel on advances in cancer treatment, 1992-93; mem. Cancer Ctrs. Working Group, 1996—. Mem. editl. bd. Investigational New Drugs, 1988-95, Jour. Clin. Oncology, 1990-93, Contemporary Oncology, 1991-95, Jour. Cancer Rsch. and Clin. Oncology, 1991—; assoc. editor Clin. Cancer Rsch., 1994—; contbr. articles to profl. jours., chpts. to books. With USPHS, 1977-80. Recipient Spl. Advancement for Performance award VA, 1983, Fletcher Scholar award Cancer Rsch. Found., 1989; grantee VA, 1981-87, Am. Cancer Soc., 1983-86, 92-95, Ill. Cancer Coun., 1985-86, Michael Reese Inst. Coun., 1985-86, Nat. Cancer Inst., 1987, 88-90, Burroughs-Wellcome Co., 1987-88, NIH/Nat. Cancer Inst., 1988—. Fellow ACP; mem. AAAS, Am. Soc. Clin. Oncology (chmn. pub. rels. com. 1994—), Am. Assn. Cancer Rsch. (chmn. Ill. state legis. com. 1992—), Am. Fedn. Clin. Rsch. (senator Midwest sect. 1983-84, councilor 1983-86, chmn.-elect 1987-88, chmn. 1988-89), Am. Assn. Cancer Edn., Am. Soc. Clin. Pharmacology and Therapeutics, Ctrl. Soc. Clin. Rsch., N.Y. Acad. Scis., Assn. Am. Cancer Insts. (bd. dirs. 1995—), Chgo. Soc. Internal Medicine, Sigma Xi, Alpha Epsilon Delta, Alpha Omega Alpha. Office: U Chgo Cancer Rsch Ctr 5841 S Maryland Ave Chicago IL 60637-1470

SCHILZ, JOHN J., communications educator. BA in Journalism, U. Mont., 1962; MPhil, Oxford U., 1979, DPhil, 1981. Newswriter, reporter Voice of Am. News, Washington, 1971-72; bur. chief Voice of Am. News, Tokyo, 1974-77; commentator, think tank cons. BBS, London, 1977-79; coverage editor Voice of Am., 1979-82; deputy dir. Voice of Am. News Divsn., 1982-84; South Asia corr. Voice of Am. News, Islamabad, Afghanistan, 1987-89; analyst Oxford Analutica, 1984-88; prof. Nat. War Coll., Washington, 1989-91; sr. corr. Voice of Am. News, 1984-87, 91-92; assoc. dir. publs. The Arms Control Assn., 1992-95; prof. internat. communications Boston U. Coll. Communication, 1995—; presenter in field. Editor Arms Control Today mag., 1992—; contbr. articles to profl. jours. With USAF, 1963-71. Office: Coll Communications 640 Commonwealth Ave Boston MA 02215

SCHIMBERG, A(RMAND) BRUCE, retired lawyer; b. Chgo., Aug. 26, 1927; s. Archie and Helen (Isay) S.; m. Barbara Zisook; children: Geoffrey, Kate. Ph.B., U. Chgo., 1949, J.D., 1952. Bar: Ohio 1952, Ill. 1955, U.S. Supreme Ct. 1987. Assoc. Paxton & Seasongood, Cin., 1952-55; ptnr. Schimberg, Greenberger, Kraus & Jacobs, Chgo., 1955-65, Leibman, Williams, Bennett, Baird & Minow, Chgo., 1965-72; ptnr. Sidley & Austin, Chgo., 1972-92, counsel, 1993-94, ret., 1994; lectr. U. Chgo., 1993-94; ret., 1994; gen. counsel Comml. Fin. Assn., 1978-94; past mem. editorial bd. Lender Liability News. Mng. and assoc. editor U. Chgo. Law Rev., 1951-52; contbr. articles to legal jours. Bd. dirs. U. Chgo. Law Sch. Alumni Assn., 1969-72; dir. vis. com. U. Chgo. Law Sch., 1980-83. Mem. ABA (chmn. subcom. and charter mem. comml. fin. svcs. com.), Am. Coll. Comml. Fin. Lawyers (pres. 1994-95, bd. regents), Ill. Bar Assn. (chair comml. banking, bankruptcy sect. 1972-73), Chgo. Bar Assn. (chair ucc com., 1966, bd. mgrs. 1968-70, chair judiciary com. 1971-72), Law Club Chgo., Mid-Day Club, Lake Shore Country Club. Home: 132 E Delaware Pl Apt 5002 Chicago IL 60611-1442

SCHIMBERG, BARBARA HODES, organizational development consultant; b. Chgo., Nov. 30, 1941; d. David and Tybe Zisook; children from previous marriage: Brian, Valery; m. A. Bruce Schimberg, Dec. 29, 1984. BS, Northwestern U., 1962. Ptnr. Just Causes, cons. not-for-profit orgns., Chgo., 1978-86; cons. in philanthropy, community involvement, and organizational devel., 1987—; Chgo. cons. Population Resource Ctr., 1978-82. Woman's bd. dirs. Mus. Contemporary Art; bd. dirs., vice chmn. Med. Rsch. Inst. Coun., Michael Reese Med. Ctr.; bd. dirs., chmn. Midwest Women's Ctr.; trustee Francis W. Parker Sch.; bd. dirs. Women's Issues Network, 1991—, pres., 1993-94; mem. honorary bd. Med. Rsch. Inst. Coun., Children's Meml. Hosp. Mem. ACLU (adv. com.). Office: 132 E Delaware Pl Apt 5002 Chicago IL 60611-1442

SCHIMBERG, HENRY AARON, soft drink company executive; b. Chgo., Mar. 3, 1933; s. Arnold and Judith (Aaron) S.; m. Linda Waxberg, June 21, 1975; children: Aaron David, Alexis Leigh. BA, Beloit Coll., 1954. Exec. v.p. Nehi Royal Crown Corp., Chgo., 1970-76; pres. Royal Crown Bottling Co., Los Angeles, 1976-79; pres. bottling ops. Royal Crown Cola Co., Rolling Meadows, Ill., 1979-82; pres., CEO, bd. dirs. Coca-Cola Bottling Midwest, Mpls., 1982-91, Cen. States Coca-Cola Bottling Co., Springfield, Ill., 1985-91, Coca-Cola Bottling Co. of St. Louis, 1986-91, Cin. Coca-Cola Bottling Co., 1986-91, Mid-States Coca-Cola Bottling Co., Paducah, Ky., 1986-91; pres., COO, bd. dirs. Johnston Coca-Cola Bottling Group, Chattanooga, Tenn., 1986-91, Coca-Cola Enterprises Inc., Atlanta, 1991—, Pacific Coca-Cola Bottling Co., Bellevue, Wash., 1992—, Austin Coca-Cola Bottling Co., Dallas; bd. dirs. Johnston So. Co., Chattanooga. Cpl. U.S. Army, 1954-56. Mem. Minn. Soft Drink Assn. (bd. dirs. 1983—), Wis. Soft Drink Assn., Ill. Soft Drink Assn. (pres. 1974-76), Nat. Soft Drink Assn. (exec. bd. 1986—, chmn. 1994—), Coca-Cola Bottlers Assn. (bd. govs. 1986—). Jewish. Avocations: tennis, skiing. Office: Coca-Cola Enterprises Inc 2500 Windy Ridge Pkwy Atlanta GA 30339

SCHIMEK, DIANNA RUTH REBMAN, state legislator; b. Holdrege, Nebr., Mar. 21, 1940; d. Ralph William and Elizabeth Julia (Wilmot) Rebman; m. Herbert Henry Schimek, 1963; children: Samuel Wolfgang, Saul William. AA, Colo. Women's Coll., 1960; student, U. Nebr., Lincoln, 1960-61; BA magna cum laude, U. Nebr., Kearney, 1963. Former tchr. and realtor; mem. Nebr. Legislature, Lincoln, 1989—, chmn. govt., mil. and vets. affairs com., 1993-94, vice chair urban affairs com., 1995—. Chmn. Nebr. Dem. Com., 1984-88, mem. exec. com., 1987-88; past pres., sec. bd. dirs. Downtown Sr. Ctr. Found.; mem. exec. bd. Midwest Conf. of State Govts., co-chair health and human svcs. com. Mem. Nat. Conf. State Legislators Women's Network (bd. dirs.), P.E.O., Soroptomists. Democrat. Unitarian. Home: 2321 Camelot Ct Lincoln NE 68512-1457 Office: Dist # 27 State Capital Lincoln NE 68509

SCHIMELPFENIG, C(LARENCE) W(ILLIAM), JR., chemistry educator; b. Dallas, Apr. 8, 1930; s. Clarence William and Hulda Anna Louise (Borchardt) S.; m. Dorothy Marie Massey, Apr. 28, 1956; children: Laurel Ann, Gretchen Marie, Michael William. BS, North Tex. State U., 1953, MS, 1954; PhD, U. Ill., 1957. Asst. prof. George Washington U., Washington, 1957-59, U. North Tex., Denton, 1959-62; rsch. chemist E.I. du Pont de Nemours and Co., Wilmington, Del., 1962-72; asst. prof. SUNY, Buffalo, 1973-75, Erskine Coll., Due West, S.C., 1975-76; assoc. prof. Tex. Wesleyan Coll., Ft. Worth, 1976-81, U. North Tex., Denton, 1981-82; prof. chemistry Dallas Bapt. U., 1982-91; adj. prof. chemistry U. Tex., Arlington, 1991—; curator (part-time vol.) Libr. Spl. Collections, U. Tex., Dallas, 1995—. Patentee chlorination method, moistenable hot melt adhesive; contbr. articles to profl. jours. Dist. commr. Boy Scouts of Am., Wilmington, Del., 1972; mem. Crime Watch Bd., Pantego, Tex., 1987-91; mem. Planning and Zoning Commn., Pantego, 1991—; elder Hanover Presbyn. Ch., Wilmington. Recipient grants Robert A. Welch Found., Houston, 1960-62, '78-81, Silver Beaver award, Boy Scouts of Am., 1973. Mem. Am. Chem. Soc. (program dir. meeting-in-miniature, Dallas-Ft. Worth 1981), Sigma Xi, Alpha Chi Sigma, Phi Lambda Upsilon. Republican. Presbyterian. Avocations: gardening, nature study. Office: U Tex Arlington Dept Chemistry Box 19065 Arlington TX 76019-0065

SCHIMKE, KAREN, public health officer. BA in Social Welfare, U. Nebr., 1963; MSW, Western Res. U., Cleve., 1967; student, Juran Inst., Washington, 1993; student program for sr. execs., Harvard U., 1994. Cert. social worker, N.Y. Child welfare worker Rosebud Indian Reservation S.D. Dept. Welfare, Pierre, 1964-67; supr., caseworker child protection dept. Children's Aid Soc. and SPCC, Buffalo, 1967-68, dir. child protection dept., 1968-70; tchg. asst. SUNY, Buffalo, 1971-72; pvt. counselor, 1972-78, 80-82; tchg. asst., trainer social work program State U. Coll., Buffalo, 1974-75; evaluator Empire State Coll., SUNY, Buffalo, 1976-81; asst. prof. social work program Daemen Coll., Snyder, N.Y., 1977-78; asst. dep. commr. Erie County Dept. Social Svcs., Buffalo, 1978-80; cons. Child and Family Svcs., Buffalo, 1981-82; regional dir. divsn. family & children svcs. N.Y. State Dept. Social Svcs., Buffalo, 1982-88; commr. Erie County Dept. Social Svcs., 1988-93; exec. dep. commr. N.Y. State Dept. Social Svcs., Buffalo, 1993-95, N.Y. State Dept. Health, Albany, 1995—; cons. The Permanent Planning Project, Regional Rsch. Inst. Human Svcs., Portland (Oreg.) State U., 1980, N.Y. State Dept. Social Svcs., Albany, 1981; mem. cmty. adv. com. SUNY-Buffalo Sch. Social Work, 1983-88; mem. Home Energy Assistance Program Block Grant Adv. Coun. N.Y. State, 1991-93; mem. N.Y. State Adv. Com. on Legal Advocacy, 1991-93; mem. adv. com. to N.Y. State Permanent Interagy. Com. on Early Childhood Programs, 1991-93; mem. reorgn. task force on quality N.Y. State Dept. Social Svcs., 1992; mem. child care adv. com. Erie C.C. Bd. dirs. Coordinated Care Mgmt. Corp., 1988-93, Buffalo Urban League, 1988-93, Pvt. Industry Coun., 1988-93; cmty. advisor Jr. League Buffalo, 1984-93; bd. dirs. Parents Anonymous State Resource Office, Rochester, N.Y., 1982-84; bd. dirs. Parents Anonymous of Buffalo and Erie County, 1979-86, pres., 1981-84; bd. trustees Buffalo Gen. Hosp., 1979-80; mem. Erie County Child Abuse Task Force, 1978-80; bd. dirs. Ctrl Erie Cmty. Mental Health Ctr., Inc., 1977-80, pres., 1977-80; bd. dirs. Child and Adolescent Psychiat. Clinic, Inc., 1977-78, Buffalo Gen. Hosp. Cmty. Mental Health Ctr., 1974-80, Citizens Com. for Children of Western N.Y., 1972-78. Recipient Cmty. U. Citation, State U. Buffalo, Cmty. Adv. Coun., 1986, Cmty. Svc. award Coordinated Care Mgmt. Corp., 1989, Leadership and Support award Employees of the Erie County Home & Infirmary, 1989, Civic Leadership award Benedict House, 1989, Cmty. Mental Health award Cmty. Bd. of Buffalo Gen. Hosp. and Cmty. Mental Health Ctr., 1990, award of excellence Everywoman Opportunity Ctr., Inc., 1990, Friend award Ednl. Opportunity Ctr., Divsn. Student Affairs, 1990, Friend of Children award Gateway Children's Home, 1991, Cmty. Recognition award Parents Anonymous, 1991, Disting. Svc. award SUNY-Albany, Rockefeller Coll. Sch. Social Work, 1992, Cmty. Recognition award Ctrl. Referral Svc., 1992, Brotherhood/Sisterhood award in social svcs. NCCJ, 1993, William B. Hoyt Advocacy award Child & Family Svcs., 1993, Humanitarian award Luth. Ch. Home, 1994. Mem. NASW (mem. western divsn. bd. 1982-84, 86-88, Social Worker of Yr. 1979, Nat. Child Labor Com. Lewis Hine award 1985), Acad. Cert. Social Workers, N.Y. Pub. Welfare Assn. (bd. dirs. 1988—), Am. Pub. Welfare Assn., Nat. Assn. Pub. Child Welfare Adminstrs. Home: 230 Oakgrove Dr Buffalo NY 14221 Office: NY Health Dept Corning Tower Empire State Plz Albany NY 12237-0001

SCHIMMEL, PAUL REINHARD, biochemist, biophysicist, educator; b. Hartford, Conn., Aug. 4, 1940; s. Alfred E. and Doris (Hudson) S.; m. Judith F. Ritz, Dec. 30, 1961; children: Kirsten, Katherine. A.B., Ohio Wesleyan U., 1962; postgrad., Tufts U. Sch. Medicine, 1962-63, Mass. Inst. Tech., 1963-65, Cornell U., 1965-66, Stanford U., 1966-67, U. Calif., Santa Barbara, 1975-76; Ph.D., Mass. Inst. Tech., 1966; DSc (hon.), Ohio Wesleyan U., 1996. Asst. prof. biology and chemistry MIT, 1967-71, assoc. prof., 1971-76, prof. biochemistry and biophysics, 1976-92, John D. and Catherine T. MacArthur prof. biochemistry and biophysics, 1992—; mem. NIH Study Sect. Physiol. Chemistry, 1975-79; indsl. cons. on enzymes and recombinant DNA. Author: (with C. Cantor) Biophysical Chemistry, 3 vols., 1980; mem. editl. bd. Archives Biochemistry, Biophysics, 1976-80, Nucleic Acids Rsch., 1976-80, Jour. Biol. Chemistry, 1977-82, Biopolymers, 1979-88, Internat. Jour. Biol. Macromolecules, 1983-89, Trends in Biochem. Scis., 1984—, Biochemistry, 1989—, Accounts of Chem. Rsch., 1989-94, European Jour. Biochemistry, 1991—, Protein Sci., 1991-94, Proc. Nat. Acad. Scis., 1993—. Alfred P. Sloan fellow, 1970-72. Fellow AAAS (chmn. Amory prize com. 1995-96); mem. NAS (class II chemistry sect. rep. 1995-96), Am. Chem. Soc. (Pfizer award 1978, chmn. divsn. biol. chemistry 1984-85) Am. Soc. for Biochemistry and Molecular Biology (chmn. nominating com. 1990, awards com. 1995), RNA Soc. Office: MIT Dept Biology Cambridge MA 02139

SCHIMMINGER, ROBIN, state legislator; b. Tonawanda, N.Y., Sept. 17, 1947; s. Linus Joseph and Doris Wilson S.; m. Melinda Downey, Apr. 21, 1978. BA, Canisius Coll., 1969; JD, NYU, 1972. Bar: N.Y. Legislator Erie County Legislature, Buffalo, N.Y., 1974-76, N.Y. State Assembly, Buffalo, 1977—; chmn. N.Y. State Assembly Sml. Bus. Com., Albany, 1985—; mem. Coun. State Govts., Nat. Conf. of State Legislatures. Author: (legislation) N.Y. State Audit and Internal Control Act, 1987, N.Y. State Toxic Torts Law, 1986, N.Y. State Equal Access to Justice Act, 1989, Omnibus Procurement Act, 1992, Excelsior Linked Deposit Act, 1993, Self-Employment Assistance Act, 1994. Bd. dirs. Buffalo Hearing and Speech Ctr., Better Bus. Bur. of Buffalo, Jr. Achievement of Western N.Y., Cardinal O'Hara High Sch., Tonawanda; bd. regents Canisius Coll. Recipient award for contbns. to small business U.S. Small Bus. Adminstrn., guardian of sm. bus. award Nat. Fedn. Ind. Bus., citation for disting. svc. Disabled Am. Vets., pres.'s citation N.Y. State Osteopathic Med. Soc., advocacy award Alzheimer's Disease and Related Disorders Assn. Western N.Y., 1987. Mem. Bar Assn. of Erie County, Buffalo C. of C. Democrat. Roman Catholic. Avocations: tennis, hiking, reading. Office: 3514 Delaware Ave Kenmore NY 14217-1235

SCHIMPF, JOHN JOSEPH, real estate developer; b. Paterson, N.J., May 19, 1949; s. Joseph Stephen and Veronica Barbara (Blad) S.; m. Barbara Ann Reid, June 3, 1972; children: Laryn Michelle, Brian Scott, Alysson Marie. BA magna cum laude in Spanish Lit., Seton Hall U., 1971; MA in Comparative Lit., U. Wis., 1974, MA in Spanish Lit., 1975; MBA in Fin. and Mktg., Columbia U., 1977. Corp. loan officer petroleum div. Chase Manhattan Bank, N.Y.C., 1977-79; mgr. treasury ops. Marsh & McLennan Cos., Inc., N.Y.C., 1980-81; exec. v.p., dir. Hovnanian Enterprises, Inc., Red Bank, N.J., 1981—; bd. dirs. Hovnanian Enterprises, Inc., Red Bank, N.J., New Fortis Corp., King, N.C. Trustee Brookdale C.C. Found., Lincroft, N.J., Emmanuel Cancer Found., Iselin, N.J.; mem. adv. bd. to chancellor Seton Hall U. Served to 1st lt. U.S. Army, 1971-73. Mem. Nat. Assn. Indsl. and Office Parks, Nat. Assn. Sr. Living Industries. Roman Catholic. Avocations: reading, art, racquetball, traveling. Office: Hovnanian Enterprises Inc 10 Hwy 35 PO Box 500 Red Bank NJ 07701

SCHIMPFF, STEPHEN CALLENDER, internist, oncologist; b. Cleve., Nov. 23, 1941; s. Leo Donald and Lorraine (McClintock) S.; m. Carol Rawstrom, Sept. 2, 1963; 1 child, Elizabeth Callender. BA, Rutgers U., 1963; MD, Yale U., 1967. Diplomate Am. Bd. Internal Medicine, Am. Bd. Med. Examiners. Intern Yale-New Haven Hosp., 1967-68, resident, 1968-69; acting head med. svc. Balt. Cancer Rsch. Program, 1970-71, sr. investigator, 1973-76, head. infection rsch. sect., 1976-81; head infectious diseases and microbiology sect. U. Md., Balt., 1981-83, prof. medicine, 1979, prof. oncology, head divsn. infectious disease, 1979-85, Am. Cancer Soc. prof. oncology, 1985-89, dir. Cancer Ctr., 1982-85; exec. v.p. U. Md. Med. System, 1985—; Co-founder Multinat. Assn. for Supportive Care in Cancer, 1988—. Editor: Comprehensive Textbook Oncology, 1986, 91, Recent Results in Cancer Research—Infectious Complications in Bone Marrow Transplantation, 1993; contbr. articles to profl. jours. Bd. dirs. Md. Hosp. Edn. Inst., 1987—, vice chmn. 1992—, sec. 1991-92; bd. dirs. Md. Cancer Consortium, 1990—; bd. dirs. Md. Easter Seal Soc., 1989-92, vice chmn., 1990-92; leader Girl Scouts U.S., 1982. Fellow ACP, Infectious Diseases Soc. Am.; mem. Am. Soc. Clin. Oncology (sec., treas. 1985-88), Am. Assn. Cancer Rsch., Md. Assn. Nonprofit Orgns. (bd. dirs. 1991—, vice chmn. 1991-94, chmn. 1994—), Alpha Omega Alpha. Home: 10129 Pasture Gate Ln Columbia MD 21044-1735 Office: U Md Med System 22 S Greene St Baltimore MD 21201-1544

SCHINDEL, DONALD MARVIN, lawyer; b. Chgo., Jan. 5, 1932; s. Harry L. and Ann (Schiff) S.; m. Alice Martha Andrews, Apr. 24, 1960; children—Susan, Judith, Andrea. B.S. in Acctg., U. Ill., 1953; J.D., U. Chgo., 1956. Bar: Ill. 1956. Ptnr. Sonnenschein, Nath & Rosenthal, Chgo., 1956—. Author: Estate Administration and Tax Planning for Survivors, 1987, supplements, 1988—. Pres. Congregation Beth Or, Deerfield, Ill., 1983-85. Fellow Am. Coll. Trust and Estate Counsel; mem. Chgo. Estate Planning Council, ABA, Ill. Bar Assn., Chgo. Bar Assn. (chmn. probate practice com. 1981-82). Clubs: Metropolitan, East Bank (Chgo.). Avocations: tennis, photography, carpentry, running, juggling. Home: 636 Rice St Highland Park IL 60035-5012 Office: Sonnenschein Nath & Rosenthal 8000 Sears Tower 233 S Wacker Dr Chicago IL 60606-6306

SCHINDERLE, ROBERT FRANK, retired hospital administrator; b. Mayville, Wis., Aug. 3, 1923; m. Elizabeth, June 23, 1949; children—David, Gary, Mary, Brian. B.S., Marquette U., 1949; M.S., Northwestern U., 1959. Asst. office mgr. Western Leather Co., Milw., 1949-51; mgr. bus. office St. Francis Hosp., Peoria, Ill., 1951-55; credit mgr. Mercy Hosp., Chgo., 1955-59, asst. to adminstr., 1957-58, controller, 1958-59, asst. adminstr., 1959-65; asst. adminstr. St. Joseph Hosp., Joliet, Ill., 1965-70, assoc. adminstr., 1970-71, adminstr., 1971-76, exec. dir., 1976-86; dir. corp. legis. affairs and devel. Franciscan Sisters Health Care Corp., Mokena, Ill., 1986-89, ret.; chmn. Areawide Hosp. Emergency Services Council. Bd. dirs. Region IX Health Systems Agy., Our Lady of Angels Retirement Home, Joliet, Joliet YMCA, St. Joseph Coll. Nursing, Joliet. Fellow Am. Coll. Hosp. Adminstrs.; mem. Am. Hosp. Assn., Ill. Hosp. Assn. (chmn. 1975-76), Catholic Hosp. Assn. (dir.), Ill. Cath. Hosp. Assn. (chmn. 1972-73). Roman Catholic. Lodges: Rotary, Elks, KC. Home: 408 W Newkirk Dr Plainfield IL 60544-1838

SCHINDLER, ALBERT ISADORE, physicist, educator; b. Pitts., June 24, 1927; s. Jonas and Esther (Nass) S.; m. Phyllis Irene Liberman, June 17, 1951; children—Janet Mae, Jerald Scott, Ellen Susan. B.S., Carnegie Inst. Tech., 1947, M.S., 1948, D.Sc., 1950. Research asst. Carnegie Inst. Tech., Pitts., 1947-50, research physicist, 1950-51; supervisory rsch. physicist Naval Rsch. Lab., Washington, 1951-75; assoc. dir. research for material sci. and component tech. Naval Research Lab., 1975-85; prof. materials engring. and physics Purdue U., West Lafayette, Ind., 1985-92, cons., 1992—, dir. Ind. Ctr. for Innovative Superconductor Tech., 1988-91, dir. Midwest Superconductivity Consortium, 1990-91; dir. div. materials rsch. NSF, Washington, 1988-90; cons. Recipient E.O. Hulburt award Naval Research Lab., 1956, Nat. Capitol award for applied sci., 1962, Pure Sci. award Naval Research Lab.-Sci. Research Soc. Am., 1965, award Washington Acad. Scis., 1965, USN Disting. Achievement in Sci. award, 1975, Alumni Merit award Carngie Mellon U., 1976, Sr. Exec. Service award Dept. Navy, 1983. Fellow Am. Phys. Soc.; mem. Sigma Xi. (dir.). Home: 6615 Sulky Ln Rockville MD 20852-4344

SCHINDLER, ALEXANDER MOSHE, rabbi, organization executive; b. Munich, Germany, Oct. 4, 1925; s. Eliezer and Sali (Hoyda) S.; m. Rhea Rosenblum, Sept. 29, 1956; children—Elisa Ruth, Debra Lee, Joshua Michael, Judith Rachel, Jonathan David. B in Social Sci., CCNY, 1950; B in Hebrew Letters, Hebrew Union Coll., 1951, M in Hebrew Letters, 1953, DD (hon.), 1977; DHL (hon.), U. S.C., 1987, Lafayette U., 1988; DD (hon.), Hamilton Coll., 1990; LLD (hon.), Coll. of Holy Cross, 1994, Wittenberg U., 1995; DHL (hon.), Hebrew Union Coll., 1996. Ordained rabbi, 1953. Asst. rabbi Temple Emanuel, Worcester, Mass., 1953-56; assoc., rabbi Temple Emanuel, 1956-59; dir. New Eng. council Union Am. Hebrew Congregations, 1959-63, nat. dir. edn., 1963-67, v.p., 1967-72; pres.-elect, 1972, pres., 1973—; mem. exec. bd. Conf. Pres. Major Am. Jewish Orgns., 1967—, chmn., 1976-78; mem. exec. bd. Hebrew Union Coll./Jewish Inst. Religion, 1967-96; v.p. Meml. Found. for Jewish Culture, 1967—, chmn. exec. com., 1994—; v.p. World Jewish Congress; mem. exec. com. World Zionist Orgn., 1973—; mem. exec. com. Joint Distbn. Com., 1987—, sec., 1992-94; bd. govs. Hebrew Union Coll., 1973-96; v.p. World Union for Progressive Judaism. Author: From Discrimination to Extermination, 1950; lit. editor: CCAR Jour., 1959-63; founding editor: Dimensions, Reform Judaism's quar. religious thought, 1966—; editor: Reform Judaism's graded text book series, 1963-67. Served with AUS, 1943-46. Decorated Bronze Star, Purple Heart; recipient Solomon Bublick prize Hebrew U. Jerusalem, 1978; Townsend Harris medal CCNY, 1979. Mem. Am. Assn. Jewish Edn. (exec. bd. 1963-67), Ctrl. Conf. Am. Rabbis (exec. bd. 1967-96). Home: 6 River Ln Westport CT 06800 Office: Union Am Hebrew Congregations 838 5th Ave New York NY 10021 *To live life fully, clinging to its many gifts with all my might—and then, paradoxically, to let go when life compels us to surrender what it gave.*

SCHINDLER, CHARLES ALVIN, microbiologist, educator; b. Boston, Dec. 27, 1924; s. Edward Esau and Esther Marian (Weisman) S.; m. Barbara Jean Francois, Jan. 14, 1955; children: Marian Giffin, Susan, Neal. BS in Biology, Rensselaer Poly. Inst., 1950; MS, U. Tex., 1956, PhD, 1961. Commd. officer USAF, 1951, advanced through grades to maj., 1965; asst. dir. for biology and medicine at atomic weapons tests Armed Forces Spl. Weapons Project, Camp Mercury, Nev., 1953; rsch. scientist USAF, 1954-68; tchr. Norman (Okla.) Pub. Schs., 1968-86; asst. prof. U. Okla., Flagler Coll., 1968-86; cons., sci. supr. Oklahoma City (Okla.) Sch. Dist., 1989-93; cons. Mead Johnson Rsch. Ctr., Evansville, Ind., 1962-72. Contbr. articles to profl. jours. Coun. mem. Norman (Okla.) City Coun., 1967-81, 83-85. Fellow Charles E. Lewis Fellowship Com., Austin, Tex., 1958; rsch. grantee

NSF, Norman, 1972. Mem. Soc. Gen. Microbiology, Sigma Xi. Achievements include U.S. and foreign patents on the bacteriolytic agent Lysost aphin. Avocations: electronics, photography, bridge. Home: 2000 Morgan Dr Norman OK 73069

SCHINDLER, DONALD WARREN, biopharmaceutical engineer, consultant; b. Westfield, N.J., Apr. 2, 1925; s. Wilbur Vincent and Francis Lillian (Hollberg) S.; m. Scot N. Stahl, Sept. 7, 1947 (div. Aug. 1971); children: Leslie, Mark; m. Dorothy Jean Martin, July 1, 1980; children: William, Bruce, Judy, Patricia, Donna, Holly, Larry. AB in Biol. Scis., Marietta (Ohio) Coll.; postgrad., Rutgers U. Dir. biol. mfg. Ortho Pharm. Corp., Raritan, N.J., 1951-59; mgr. biol. mfg. Warner-Lambert Pharm. Co., Morris Plains, N.J., 1959-74; gen. mgr. Fisher Sci. Diagnostics Div., Orangeburg, N.Y., 1978-82; pres. SRC Assocs., Park Ridge, N.J., 1982-94, Schindler Assocs., Montvale, N.J., 1994—; mem. adv. bd. Okla. Immunological Labs., Oklahoma City, 1972-78; cons. Serono Labs., Inc., Boston, 1982-91, U. Minn., Mpls., 1984-91, Ares Applied Rsch. N.V. Gen., 1982-90. Pres. Passaic Twp. Sch. Bd., Stirling, N.J., 1964-70; trustee 1st Congl. Ch., Park Ridge, N.J., 1987-90; deacon 1st Presbyn. Ch., Montvale, N.J., 1968-71; regional dir. tng. Boy Scouts Am. Watchung Area coun., Plainfield, N.J., 1968-71. With USNR, 1942-46, PTO. Mem. VFW, Am. Chem. Soc., Am. Inst. Chemists, Am. Legion, N.Y. Acad. Scis., Newcomen Soc., Parenteral Drug Assn., Internat. Soc. Pharm. Engrs., Beta Beta Beta, Alpha Sigma Phi. Republican. Office: Schindler Assocs Ste 101 150 Upper Saddle River Rd Montvale NJ 07645-1027

SCHINDLER, JUDI(TH KAY), public relations executive, marketing consultant; b. Chgo., Nov. 23, 1941; d. Gilbert G. and Rosalie (Karlin) Cone; m. Jack Joel Schindler, Nov. 1, 1964; 1 child, Adam Jason. BS in Journalism, U. Ill., 1964. Assoc. editor Irving Cloud Publs., Lincolnwood, Ill., 1963-64; asst. dir. publicity Israel Bond Campaign, Chgo., 1965-69; v.p. pub. relations Realty Co. of Am., Chgo., 1969-70; dir. pub. relations Pvt. Telecommunications, Chgo., 1970-78; pres. Schindler Communications, Chgo., 1978—; del. White House Conf. on Small Bus., Washington, 1980, 86; mem. adv. bd. Entrepreneurship Inst., Chgo., 1988-92. Bd. dirs. Family Matters Comty. Ctr.; mem. Chgo. bd. Roosevelt U.; leader luncheon coun. YWCA, Chgo., 1987, 89-90, 92; appointee small bus. com. Ill. Devel. Bd., 1988-89. Named Nat. Women in Bus. Adv. SBA, 1986, Chgo. Woman Bus. Owner of Yr., Continential Bank and Nat. Assn. Women Bus. Owners, 1989, Ill. Finalist Entrepreneur of Yr. award, 1991, 92. Mem. Nat. Assn. Women Bus. Owners (pres. Chgo. chpt. 1980-81, nat. v.p. membership 1988-89), Small Bus. United of Ill., Ill. Coun. Growing Cos. (vice chair 1993-94), Publicity Club Chgo., Alpha Epsilon Phi. Office: Schindler Comm 500 N Clark St Chicago IL 60610-4202

SCHINDLER, MARVIN SAMUEL, foreign language educator; b. Boston, Jan. 2, 1932; s. Edward Esau and Esther Marian (Wiseman) S.; m. Roslyn Frances Abt, Aug. 11, 1974; children: Daniel Mark, Lore Elaine, Inge-Marie, Neal Elliott. B.A., U. Mass., 1953; M.A., Ohio State U., 1955, Ph.D., 1965. Instr. German Pa. State U., Pottsville, 1955-59; asst. prof. Ohio State U., 1965-67; asso. prof. German, asso. dean Grad. Sch. Arts and Scis., U. Va., Charlottesville, 1967-71; prof. German, chmn. dept. fgn. langs. No. Ill. U., DeKalb, 1971-74; prof. German, chmn. dept. Romance and Germanic langs. and lits. Wayne State U., Detroit, 1974-83; dir. Jr. Yr. in Germany Programs Wayne State U., 1975—. Author: The Sonnets of Andreas Gryphius, 1971; asso. editor: German Quar, 1971-78. Fulbright fellow, 1961-62; ehrensenator Albert-Ludwigs Universität, Freiburg;Bundesverdienstkreuz, 1. Klasse, Fed. Republic of Germany. Mem. Am. Assn. Tchrs. German (exec. council), MLA, Assn. Depts. Fgn. Langs. (exec. com., pres. 1981), Midwest Modern Lang. Assn. Home: 10075 Lincoln Dr Huntington Wd MI 48070-1507 Office: 487 Manoogian Hall Wayne State Univ Detroit MI 48202

SCHINDLER, PESACH, rabbi, educator, author; b. Munich, Germany, Apr. 11, 1931; came to U.S., 1940; s. Alexander Moshe and Esther (Zwickler) S.; m. Shulamith Feldman, June 30, 1954; children: Chaya, Gita, Meyer, Nechama, Avi. BA, CCNY Bklyn. Coll., 1953; MS, Yeshiva U., 1964; PhD, NYU, 1972; D Pedagogy (hon.), Jewish Theol. Sem., N.Y.C., 1987. Ordained rabbi, 1956. Dir. edn. Congregation Adath Israel, Toronto, Ont., Can., 1959-65; asst. dir. edn. United Synagogue of Am., N.Y.C., 1965-72; dir. Ctr. for Conservative Judaism United Synagogue of Am., Jerusalem, 1972—; asst. prof. Hebrew U., Jerusalem, 1975—; faculty U. Toronto Sch. Theology Jewish Studies Program in Jerusalem, 1986—, Sem. Jewish Studies, Jerusalem, 1988—; mem. internat. bd. Yad Vashem, Jerusalem, 1980—. Author: Hasidic Responses to the Holocaust in the Light of Hasidic Thought, 1990; contbr. numerous articles to profl. jours. Founding mem. Hebrew U. Orch., Jerusalem, 1988. Mem. Rabbinical Assembly (rabbinic ct. on conversion 1988—, com. on Jewish law 1990—), Educators Assembly, Jerusalem Long Distance Running Club (chmn. 1984-87). Office: United Synagogue Conservative Judaism, PO Box 7456, Jerusalem 94205, Israel *Therfore faith is confrontation with the incredulous and with doubt. The struggle for redemption is therefore confrontation with the non-redemptive. Both represent a form of creation ex-nihilo—a marvelous gift from the Almighty to even the humblest human being, His partner in the constant drama in the response to life.*

SCHINDLER, PETER DAVID, child and adolescent psychiatrist; b. Berlin, Germany, Jan. 12, 1931; came to U.S. 1936; s. George David and Elizabeth (Sonntag) S.; m. Marianne Gertrude Leber; children: Thomas Kevin, Claudia Elizabeth. BA, Lafayette Coll., 1952; MD, U. Basel, Switzerland, 1960. Diplomate Am. Bd. Psychiatry and Neurology, Am. Bd. Child Psychiatry. Intern Stamford (Conn.) Hosp., 1960-61; resident adult psychiatry Temple U. Med. Sch. and Hosp., Phila., 1962-63; resident child psychiatry St. Christopher's Hosp. for Children, Temple U. Med. Sch., 1963-65; resident psychoanalytic, adult, adolescent and child tng. Phila. Psychoanalytic Inst., 1963-76; pvt. practice West Chester, Pa., 1965—; mem. staff adolescent psychiatry Chester County Mental Health Ctr. (now Family Svc.-Mental Health Ctrs. Chester County), West Chester, Pa., 1965-66; med. dir. Chester County Mental Health Ctr. (now Family Svc.-Mental Health Ctrs. Chester County), Pa., 1966-74; cons. Chester County Mental Health Ctr. (now Family Svc.-Mental Health Ctrs. Chester County), West Chester, Pa., 1974—; dir. child/adolescent psychiatry div. A.I. duPont Inst., Wilmington, Del., 1990-96; cons. Child Diagnostic and Devel. Clinic, Dept. Devel. Medicine, Alfred I. duPont Inst., Wilmington, 1965-79, dir. dept. psychol. medicine, 1979-83; cons. Vis. Nurse Assn. Del., Sch. Wellness Ctrs. Del., 1994—; chief psychiat. cons. A.I. duPont Sch. Dist., Wilmington, 1966-78; vol. faculty assoc. clin. prof. Thomas Jefferson U., Phila., 1980-92; mem. staff Chester County Hosp., 1971—; cons. Presbyn. Children's Sch., Rosemont, Pa., 1965-77, Paoli (Pa.) Meml. Hosp., 1966—, Chester County Sch. Dist., 1968-69, West Chester U., 1972-75, lectr. 1969-70; cons. St. Mary's Providence Sch., Elverson, Pa., 1972-76, Westtown (Pa.) Sch., 1977—; mem. ad hoc ethics com. Med. Ctr. Del., Wilmington, 1984-87, profl. entries com. dept. psychiatry, 1989; cons. child/adolescent psychiatry div. child mental health, State of Del., Wilmington, 1985—; cons. in field The Melmark Home, Berwyn, Pa., 1984—; speaker in field. With U.S. Army, 1953-54. Fellow Am. Acad. Child and Adolescent Psychiatry (mental retardation com. 1987—), Am. Acad. Pediatrics (assoc. 1982—); mem. AMA (Pysician's Recognition award), Am. Psychiat. Assn., Chester County Med. Soc., Del. Psychiat. Assn., Med. Soc. Del. (physicians health com. 1979—), New Castle County Med. Soc., Pa. Med. Soc., Pa. Psychiat. Assn., Phila. Psychoanalytic Soc., Soc. Liaison Psychiatry, Sigma Xi. Avocation: sailing. Home and Office: 816 Denton Hollow Rd West Chester PA 19382-7023

SCHINDLER, WILLIAM STANLEY, retired public relations executive; b. Detroit, Jan. 4, 1933; s. William Henry and Katherine (Schilling) S. Student, Wayne State U., 1950-53. Sr. v.p. Campbell-Ewald Co., Warren, Mich., 1968-85; v.p. pub. rels. Detroit Med. Ctr., 1985-92; interim v.p. Wayne State U., Detroit, 1993; cons. to bus., univs., and founds.; v.p. Sandusky Pub. Co., Mich. Editor: Progress Report-New Detroit, Inc, 1969. Past mem. Detroit Hist. Commn., Detroit Fire Commn.; chmn. Detroit CSC; past pres. Detroit Hist. Soc., Hist. Soc. Mich.; mem. Gov's. Sesquicentennial Commn.; bd. dirs. Adult Well-Being Svcs., Sacred Heart Rehab. Ctr., Brush Park Devel. Authority, Harper Hosp. Aux. With U.S. Army, 1954-56. Decorated Commendation Medal with pendant. Mem. Pub. Rels. Soc. Am., Adcraft Club Detroit, Detroit Press Club, Soms Whiskey Rebellion, Recess Club, Univ. Club, Detroit Athletic Club, Prismatic Club, Box 12 Club. Home: 8741 W Wescott Dr Peoria AZ 85382-3694

SCHINK, FRANK EDWARD, electrical engineer; b. N.Y.C., May 14, 1922; s. Frank and Elizabeth (Kreps) S.; m. Barbara Jean McCally, Oct. 26, 1946; children: Stephen Frank, Thomas Ross. BEE, Bklyn. Poly. (now Poly. U. N.Y.), 1952, MEE, 1955. Registered profl. engr., N.Y., N.J. Elec. engr. George G. Sharp, Naval Architect, N.Y.C., 1940-43, 45, Anaconda Co., N.Y.C., 1946-59, Anaconda-Jurden Assocs., N.Y.C., 1959-61; sr. engr. M.W. Kellogg Co., N.Y.C., 1961-62; sr. engr. Port Authority of N.Y. & N.J., N.Y.C., 1962-77, cons. engr., 1977-84, chief elec. engr., 1984-89; pvt. practice elec. cons. Cranford, N.J., 1989—; mem. various comms. ELECTRO Confs., 1976—, past bd. dirs.; mem. adv. coun. N.J. Union County Transp., Westfield, 1977-79; mem. Port Authority Maintenance Improvement coun., N.Y.C., 1979-80; mem. com. IEEE Vehicular Tech. Conf., 1993; lectr. seminars Internat. Elec. Exposition and Congress, 1986, 87. Author/editor: Environmental Impact Assessment, 1977; contbr. articles to profl. jours. Pres. Brookside Civic Assn., Cranford, 1960-62; chmn. Cub Scout and Boy Scouts Troops, Cranford, 1960-65; capt. United Fund, Cranford, 1962; tchr. Am. Coun. for Emigres, N.Y.C., 1975. With U.S. Army, 1943-45, ETO. Fellow IEEE (vice chmn. region I 1986-87; chmn. N.Y. sect. 1984-85, vice chmn. 1982-84, treas. 1981-82, editor N.Y. sect. Monitor 1989-90, life mem. com. 1994—; also various coms.); mem. IEEE Power Engring Soc. (ad com. 1978-87, exec. com. 1983-87, chpts. rep. 1976-80, chmn. Winter Power Cponf., N.Y. 1990—), IEEE Industry Applications Soc. (coun. mem. 1977-90), Tau Beta Pi, Eta Kappa Nu. Republican. Methodist. Home and Office: 14 Middlebury Ln Cranford NJ 07016-1622

SCHINK, JAMES HARVEY, lawyer; b. Oak Park, Ill., Oct. 2, 1943; s. Norbert F. and Gwendolyn H. (Hummel) S.; m. Lisa Wilder Haskell, Jan. 1, 1972 (div. 1980); children—David, Caroline, Elizabeth; m. April Townley, Aug. 14, 1982. BA, Yale U., 1965, JD, 1968. Bar: Ill. 1968, Colo. 1982. Assoc. Sidley & Austin, Chgo., 1968; law clk. to judge U.S. Ct. Appeals, Chgo., 1968-69; assoc. Kirkland & Ellis, Chgo., 1969-72, ptnr., 1972—. Sustaining fellow Art Inst. Chgo. Mem. ABA, Ill. Bar Assn., Chgo. Bar Assn., Chgo. Club, Univ. Club, Saddle and Cycle Club, Mid-Am. Club, Econ. Club of Chgo., Chgo. Yacht Club, Denver Athletic Club, Vail Racquet Club, Yale Club of N.Y.C., Point O' Woods Golf and Tennis Club (Benton Harbor, Mich.). Republican. Presbyterian. Home: 1530 N State Pky Chicago IL 60610-1614 Office: Kirkland & Ellis 200 E Randolph St Ste 6100 Chicago IL 60601-6436

SCHINKEL, CLAUS, chemical company executive; b. Mexico City, July 27, 1925; s. Claus and Erna (Gautier) S.; m. Helga Elisabeth Dobler, Dec. 10, 1949 (div. July 1965); children: Susana, Hildegard, Ingrid, Claus-Werner; m. Dulce Maria Garcia-de-Presno, Oct. 28, 1977. Degree in chem. engring., U. Nacional Autonoma Mex., 1948. Mgr. Schinkel, S.A., Mexico City, 1949-57; CEO, dir. Consultores Industriales, S.A., Mexico City, 1957-77, Depositos Unidos, S.A. de C.V., Mexico City, 1957-92, Tecnica Quimica, S.a. de C.V., Mexico City, 1957—, Grupo T.Q. Asesores, S.A. de C.V., Mexico City, 1988—. Mem. Soc. Exalumnos de Facultad de Quimica, Colegio Aleman Alexander von Humboldt, A.C., Rotary Club (pres. Ajusco Pedregal Club 1989-90). Lutheran. Avocations: tennis, archeology. Home: Fuego 31, 01900 Mexico City Mexico Office: Tecnica Quimica SA de CV, Calle Diez # 123, 09070 Mexico City Mexico

SCHIPPER, MERLE, art historian and critic, exhibition curator; b. Toronto, Ont., Can.; came to U.S., 1943; d. Leon J. and Libby (Genesove) Solway; m. Bernard Schipper, May 22, 1943 (div. Jan. 1980); children: Lee, Amy Schipper Howe. BA, U. Toronto, 1943; MA, UCLA, 1970, PhD, 1974. Instr. extension UCLA, 1974-78, 83-84, lectr. summer session, 1977-79, 84; vis. artist grad. sch. Claremont (Calif.) U., 1979; lectr. U. So. Calif., L.A., 1985; corr. L.A. ARTNews, N.Y.C., 1985-87; columnist ARTScene, L.A., 1987—; project dir. Santa Monica (Calif.) Arts Found., 1987-89; art book reviewer L.A. Daily News, 1990-91; organizer Congress Internat. Assn. Art Critics, 1991; mem. pub. art panel Santa Monica Arts Commn., 1993—; mem. artist selection panel Met. Transp. Assn., Chinatown Sta., 1993. Panelist, mem. grants com. Art Orgn. Dept. Cultural Affairs, L.A., 1984-85; mem. selection com. of sculpture installation Calif. Med. Ctr., L.A., 1986; mem. Rev. Com. Hist. Resources Survey Project, L.A., 1978-85, So. Calif. Com. for Contemporary Art Documentation, L.A., 1985-89. Rsch. fellow Indo-U.S. Subcommn., 1988; travel grantee Ptnrs. of Ams., 1989. Mem. Coll. Art Assn., Internat. Assn. Art Critics. Home and Office: 835 Grant St Apt 3 Santa Monica CA 90405-1328

SCHIPPERS, DAVID PHILIP, lawyer; b. Chgo., Nov. 4, 1929; s. David Philip and Angela Marie (Lyons) S.; m. Jacquelin Joyce Liautaud, Apr. 19, 1952; children: David P. III, Kathleen M., Antoinette M., Ann L., Colleen M., Thomas M., Kevin D., Mary A., Patrick F., Peter A. BA, Loyola U., Chgo., 1955, JD, 1959. Bar: Ill. 1959, U.S. Dist. Ct. (no. dist.) Ill. 1959, U.S. Ct. Appeals (7th cir.) 1962, U.S. Supreme Ct., 1966, U.S. Dist. Ct. (so. dist.) Ill. 1973, U.S. Ct. Appeals (9th cir.) 1976, U.S. Ct. Claims 1979, U.S. Ct. Appeals (3d, 4th, 6th, 8th cirs.) 1981, U.S. Ct. Appeals (fed. cir.) 1983, Wis. 1985, U.S. Ct. Mil. Appeals 1987. Service rep. Ill. Bell Telephone Co., Chgo., 1950-59; assoc. Pope, Ballard, Uriell, Kennedy, Shepard & Fowle, Chgo., 1959-62; asst. atty. U.S. Dept. Justice, Chgo., 1962-63, spl. asst. atty. gen., 1963-64, chief organized crime and racketeering sec., 1964-67; ptnr. Schippers & Bailey, Chgo., 1967—; adj. prof. Willamette U., Salem, Oreg., 1972—, Loyola U. Sch. Law, Chgo., 1972—; lectr. J.A.G. Sch., Maxwell AFB, Ala., 1988, 89. Active Cath. League Religious Freedom, Chgo., 1986—; Ill. Dept. Law Enforcement Merit Bd., Springfield, 1987-93; Ill. Crime Investigating Com., Chgo., 1969. Decorated knight Equestrian Order of the Holy Sepulchre, 1995—; recipient Alumni medal of Excellence, Loyola U., 1967, citation Loyola U. Alumni Assn., 1970. Mem. ABA, Fed. Bar Assn., Ill. Bar Assn., Chgo. Bar Assn., Am. Arbitration Assn., Am. Trial Lawyers Assn., Ill. Trial Lawyers Assn., Appellate Lawyers Assn., Nat. Assn. Criminal Def. Lawyers, Chgo. Crime Commn., Fed. Criminal Investigators Assn., Markey Inn of Ct. Club. Office: Schippers & Bailey 36th Fl 20 N Clark St Chicago IL 60602

SCHIRMEISTER, CHARLES F., lawyer; b. Jersey City, June 18, 1929; s. Charles F. and Louise P. (Schneider) S.; m. Barbara Jean Fredericks, Feb. 9, 1952; children—Pamela, Charles Bradford. B.A., U. Mich., 1951; LL.B., Fordham U., 1956. Bar: N.Y. 1956, U.S. Dist. Ct. (so. dist) N.Y., U.S. Ct. Appeals (2d cir.), U.S. Supreme Ct. 1961. Asst. dist. atty. N.Y. County (N.Y.), 1956-61; assoc. Reid & Priest, N.Y.C., 1961-71, ptnr., 1971—. Trustee, deacon, Community Congregational Ch., Short Hills, N.J.; trustee Ocean Grove (N.J.) Camp Meeting Assn. Served to capt. USMC, 1951-53. Mem. ABA, N.Y. County Lawyers Assn., Fed. Bar Coun., Sigma Alpha Epsilon. Republican. Clubs: University (N.Y.C.), Canoe Brook Country Club (Summit, N.J.). Avocations: tennis, oenology, golf. Home: 15 Beechcroft Rd Short Hills NJ 07078-1648 Office: Reid & Priest 40 W 57th St New York NY 10019-4001

SCHIRMER, HENRY WILLIAM, architect; b. St. Joseph, Mo., Dec. 8, 1922; s. Henry William and Asta (Hansen) S.; m. Jane Irene Krueger; children: Andrew Lewis, Monica Sue, Daniel F. Carr. AS, St. Joseph Jr. Coll., 1942; BArch Design, U. Mich., 1949. Staff architect Eugene Meier, Architect, St. Joseph, 1939, Neville, Sharp & Simon, Kansas City, Mo., 1946, 49, Ramey & Himes, Wichita, Kans., 1950-57; ptnr. Schaefer & Schirmer, Wichita, 1957-60, Schaefer, Schirmer & Eflin, Wichita, 1960-72, Schaefer, Schirmer & Assocs. P.A., Wichita, 1972-76; prin. Henry W. Schirmer, Topeka, 1976-92, Green Valley, 1993—. Editor: Profile Ofcl. Directory of AIA, 1978, 80, 83, 85, 87, 89-90, 91-92, pub., 1985-92; contbr. AIA Handbook; works include Burn Ctr. U. Kans. Med. Ctr., Allen County Community Jr. Coll., Iola, Kans., Rainbow Mental Health Ctr., Kansas City, Kans., Capitol Area Plaza Project, Topeka. Pres. East Br. YMCA, 1954—; bd. dirs. Wichita YMCA, 1956-73, San Ignacio Heights Home Owners Assn., 1995—. With C.E. U.S. Army, ETO. Decorated Purple Heart. Fellow AIA (past pres. Kans. chpt., seminar leader, chmn. nat. com. office mgmt.1976, nat. bd. dirs. 1979-81, treas. 1982-86, fin. com. 1988, nat. documents com. 1978, chmn. nat. com. on project mgmt. 1977, Edward C. Kemper medal 1990); mem. Kans. Bd. Tech. Professions (chmn. bd. 1985, 87), Nat. Coun. Architl. Registration Bds. (profl. conduct com. 1986-89, procedures and documents com. 1990), Tau Sigma Delta. Lutheran. Home: 4191 S Emelita Dr Green Valley AZ 85614-5614

SCHIRN, JANET SUGERMAN, interior designer; b. Jersey City, N.Y.; d. Oscar H. and Mary (Lustig) S.; 1 child, Martha. BFA, Pratt Inst.; MFA, Columbia U.; postgrad. in Architecture, U. Ill. Tchr. N.Y.C. Bd. Edn.; dir. N.Y.C. Bd. Adult Edn.; pres. Janet Schirn Design Group, Chgo., N.Y.C., 1950—; prin. The J S Collection, N.Y.C., 1978—; adj. prof. So. Ill. U., 1991-92; mem. adv. bd. Du Pont Co., Monsanto, 1981—, So. Ill. U., 1990—. Contbr. articles to interior design mag. Bd. dirs. Washington Archtl. Forum, 1992—, Chgo. Archtl. Assistance Ctr., 1975, pres., 1982; adv. bd. mem. Mundelein Coll. dept. interior architecture, 1978; mem. Met. Planning Coun., Chgo., 1980—, Art Resources Teaching, 1984—; mem. aux. bd. Sch. of Art Ins., Ill. Arts Alliance, 1992—. Recipient award Chgo. Lighting Inst., 1989, 92, 93, 95, Villeroy and Boch gold award, 1990, Designer mag. residential award, 1990, Edward Fields 1st prize Rug Design, 1991, 1st prize project awards ASID, 1993, 95. Mem. UNESCO (steering com. tall bldgs. and urban habitat coun.), Am. Soc. Interior Designers (nat. pres. 1986, nat. treas. 1984, regional v.p. 1981, pres. Ill. chpt. 1977-78, nat. dir. 1979-83, chmn. pub. affairs 1989), Illuminating Engring. Soc., Am. Inst. Architects (nat. urban planning and design com. 1981-85), Chgo. Network, Internat. Fedn. Interior Designers (exec. bd. dirs. 1992-96). Home: 220 E Walton St Chicago IL 60611-1534 Office: Janet Schirn Design Group 401 N Franklin St Chicago IL 60610-4400 also: 521 5th Ave New York NY 10175 also: 821 Delaware Ave SW Washington DC 20024-4207

SCHIRO, JAMES J., brokerage house executive; m. Tomasina Schiro; 2 children. Grad., St. John's U., D of Comml. Sci. (hon.), 1995; grad., Amos Tuck Sch. Exec. Program. With Price Waterhouse, 1967—, ptnr., 1979, chmn. mining spl. svcs. group, 1979-88, nat. dir. merger and acquisitions svcs., vice chmn., mng. ptnr. N.Y. met. region, mng. ptnr. N.Y. office; chmn., sr. ptnr. Price Waterhouse LLP; mem. U.S. Firm's Mgmt. com., World Firm's Gen. Coun.; bd. govs. World Econ. Forum; treas., exec. com. U.S. Coun. for Internat. Bus.; chairperson Bus. Improvement Dist. task force N.Y.C. Partnership/C. of C. econ. devel. com.; mem. leadership com. Lincoln Ctr. Consolidated Corp. Fund. Mem. leadership com. Lincoln Ctr. Consolidated Corp. Fund; mem. N.Y. steering com. Accts. Coalition on Liability Refor; chairperson fin. com., bd. trustees McCarter Theatre, Princeton, N.J. Recipient Ellis Island Medal of Honor, 1994, St. John's U. Alumni Pietas medal, 1992, Avenue of the Americas Assn.'s Gold Key award, 1992. Mem. AICPA, N.Y. State Soc. of Pub. Accts., Regional Plan Assn. (bd. dirs.). Office: 1177 Avenue of the Americas New York NY 10036

SCHIRRA, WALTER MARTY, JR., business consultant, former astronaut; b. Hackensack, N.J., Mar. 12, 1923; s. Walter Marty and Florence (Leach) S.; m. Josephine Cook Fraser, Feb. 23, 1946; children: Walter Marty III, Suzanne Karen. Student, Newark Coll. Engring., 1940-42; B.S., U.S. Naval Acad., 1945; D. Astronautics (hon.), Lafayette Coll., U. So. Calif., N.J. Inst. Tech. Commd. ensign U.S. Navy, 1945, advanced through grades to capt., 1965; designated naval aviator, 1948; service aboard battle cruiser Alaska, 1945-46; service with 7th Fleet, 1946; assigned Fighter Squadron 71, 1948-51; exchange pilot 154th USAF Fighter Bomber Squadron, 1951; engaged in devel. Sidewinder missile China Lake, Calif., 1952-54; project pilot F7U-3 Cutlass; also instr. pilot F7U-3 Cutlass and FJ3 Fury, 1954-56; ops. officer Fighter Squadron 124, U.S.S. Lexington, 1956-57; assigned Naval Air Safety Officer Sch., 1957, Naval Air Test Ctr., 1958-59; engaged in suitability devel. work F4H, 1958-59; joined Project Mercury, man-in-space, NASA, 1959; pilot spacecraft Sigma 7 in 6 orbital flight, Oct. 1962; in charge operations and tng. Astronaut Office, 1964-69; command pilot Gemini 6 which made rendezvous with target, Gemini 7, Dec. 1965; comdr. 11 day flight Apollo 7, 1968; ret., 1969; pres. Regency Investors, Inc., Denver, 1969-70; chmn., chief exec. officer ECCO Corp., Englewood, Colo., 1970-73; chmn. Sernco, Inc., 1973-74; with Johns-Manville Corp., Denver, 1974-77; v.p. devel. Goodwin Cos., Inc., Littleton, Colo., 1978-79; ind. cons., 1979-80; dir. Kimberly Clark, 1983-91. Decorated D.F.C.(3), Air medal (2), Navy D.S.M.; recipient Distinguished Service medal (2) NASA, Exceptional Service medal. Fellow Am. Astronautical Soc., Soc. Exptl. Test Pilots. Home and Office: PO Box 73 Rancho Santa Fe CA 92067-0073

SCHISGAL, MURRAY JOSEPH, playwright; b. N.Y.C., Nov. 25, 1926; s. Abraham and Irene (Sperling) S.; m. Reene Schapiro, June 29, 1958; children: Jane, Zachary. Student, Bklyn. Conservatory of Music, 1948, L.I. U., 1950; LLB, Bklyn. Law Sch., 1953; BA, New Sch. Social Research, 1959. Author: The Typists and The Tiger, London, 1960, N.Y.C., 1963, Ducks and Lovers, London, 1961, Knit One, Purl Two, Boston, 1963, Luv (One of the Best Plays of 1964-65), London, 1963, N.Y.C., 1964, Fragments, Windows and other plays, 1965, Best Short Plays, 1981, 83, 85; contbr. to Best Short American Plays 1994-1995; original TV plays The Love Song of Barney Kempinski, 1966, Natasha Kovolina Pipishinski, 1976; off-Broadway Fragments, 1967, The Basement, 1967; Jimmy Shine, 1968, 69; Broadway The Chinese, N.Y.C., 1970 (pub. in Best Short Plays of the World Theatre 1973), Dr. Fish, 1970, An American Millionaire, 1974, All Over Town, 1974 (pub. Best Plays 1974-75); screenplay The Tiger Makes Out, 1967, The Pushcart Peddlers, prod. off-off-Broadway, 1979; novel Days and Nights of a French Horn Player, 1980, Walter and the Flatulist; prod. off-Broadway The Downstairs Boys, 1980, The Songs of War, 1989; prod. regional theatre A Need for Brussels Sprouts, 1981, Play Time, Denver Ctr. Theatre, 1991, The Japanese Foreign Trade Minister, Cleve. Playhouse, 1992, 74 Georgia Ave., 1992, Circus Life, 1992; prod. Broadway Twice Around the Park, 1982; Other Plays, 1983, Closet Madness and Other Plays, 1984, Popkins, Paris, 1990, Play Time, 1991, The Songs of War, 1989; prod. Off Broadway The New Yorkers, 1984, Circus Life, 1995; prodr. Extensions, 1994; co-author: screenplay Tootsie (Winner Los Angeles Film Critics, N.Y. Film Critics, Nat. Soc. Film Critics, Writers Guild Am. award for best comedy); author Luv and Other Plays, 1983, The Rabbi and the Toyota Dealer, 1985, Jealousy, There are No Sacher Tortes in Our Society, 1985, Old Wine in a New Bottle, 1987, Road Show, 1987, Man Dangling, 1988, Oatmeal and Kisses, 1990, (with others) Best Short American Plays of 1991, 92-93, Sexaholics and Other Plays, 1995, Extensions, 1994. Recipient Vernon Rice award otustanding achievement off-Broadway Theatre, 1963; Outer Circle award Outstanding Theatre, 1963; named Outstanding Playwright, 1963. Office: care Arthur B Greene Internat Creative Mgmt 101 Park Ave 43d Fl New York NY 10178-9999

SCHIZER, ZEVIE BARUCH, lawyer; b. Bklyn., Dec. 19, 1928; s. David and Bertha (Rudavsky) S.; m. Hazel Gerber, Aug. 23, 1962; children: Deborah Gail, Miriam Anne, David Michael. BA magna cum laude, NYU, 1950; JD, Yale U., 1953. Bar: N.Y. 1954, U.S. Dist. Ct. (so. and ea. dist.) N.Y. 1959, U.S. Ct. Appeals (2d cir.) 1959, U.S. Supreme Ct. 1959. Assoc. Guzik & Boukstein, N.Y.C., 1953-54; teaching fellow NYU, 1954-55; assoc. Philips, Nizer, Benjamin & Krim, N.Y.C., 1955-56, Aranow, Brodsky, Einhorn & Dann, N.Y.C., 1956-57; asst. counsel jud. inquiry Appellate Divsn. 2nd Dept., Bklyn., 1957-62; assoc. Hays, Porter, Spanier & Curtis, N.Y.C., 1963-68, ptnr., 1968-85; sec. United Aircraft Products, Inc., Dayton, Ohio, 1970-83; ptnr. Schizer & Schizer, N.Y.C., 1985—. Trustee Bklyn. Pub. Libr., 1966—, pres. 1985-88, N.Y. Young Dem. Club, N.Y.C., 1960-61; trustee East Midwood Jewish Ctr., Bklyn., 1991—. Mem. N.Y. County Lawyers Assn. (mem. profl. ethics com., mem. com. on profl. discipline), Phi Beta Kappa. Democrat. Jewish. Home: 1134 E 23rd St Brooklyn NY 11210-4519 Office: Schizer & Schizer 3 New York Plz New York NY 10004-2442

SCHLACHTER, DEBORAH BRISTOW, special education educator, consultant; b. Ajo, Ariz., Dec. 21, 1957; d. John Edward Jr. and Anne Elizabeth (Butler) Bristow; m. James Martin Schlachter Jr., July 25, 1981; children: James Martin, Katie Elizabeth, Joshua Timothy, Jacob Leslie, Jean Nicole. BE, Stephen F. Austin, 1981; MEd, U. N. Tex., 1991. Cert. tchr., Tex. Pvt. practice spl. needs tutor Dallas/Ft. Worth, 1981-91; pvt. practice family in home child care Lancaster, Tex., 1982-89; instr.-coord. Cedar Valley Coll., Lancaster, 1989—; tchr. DeSoto (Tex.) Ind. Sch. Dist., 1990-91; kindergarten tchr. Dallas Ind. Sch. Dist., 1991-92, ESL tchr. 1st grade, 1992-93; 4-6th grade Montessori tchr. Dallas Pub. Sch., 1993-95; co-leader strategic planning Lancaster Ind. Sch. Dist., 1992-93. Co-editor: Resource Handbook for Educators on American Indians, 1993-94. Vol. tutor Women's Halfway House, Nacogdoches, Tex., 1980-81; trainer in spl. needs children PTA, Dallas-Ft. Worth, 1990—, active Dallas-Lancaster, 1984—; voting mem. Dallas Native Am. Parent Adv. Com., 1992-94; vol. Harry Stone Montessori Acad. PTA, v.p., 1995-96, 96-97. Mem. ASCD, AAUW, Nat. Assn. Edn. Young Children, Nat. Indian Edn. Assn., Nat. Mus. Am. Indian, Am. Montessori Soc., So. Assn. Children Under Six, Dallas Assn. Edn. Young Children, Native Am. Rights Funds, Am. Indian Resource and

Edn. Coalition. Episcopalian. Avocations: reading, horseback riding, swimming, cooking, travel. Home: 532 Laurel St Lancaster TX 75134-3220

SCHLAFER, DONALD HUGHES, veterinary pathologist; b. Sidney, N.Y., July 15, 1948; s. Donald Hughes and Mildred (Gamewell) S., Jr.; m. Judith Ann Appleton, Aug. 2, 1980; children: Nathan James, Russell Matthew. BS, Cornell U., 1971, MS, 1975; DVM, N.Y. State Coll. Vet. Medicine, Ithaca, 1974; PhD, Coll. Vet. Medicine, Athens, Ga., 1982. Diplomate Am. Coll. Vet. Pathologists, Am. Coll. Theriogenologists (exec. com. 1993—), Am. Coll. Vet. Microbiologists. Gen. practice vet. medicine Guilderland Animal Hosp., Altamont, N.Y., 1975-77; resident dept. vet. pathology U. Ga., Athens, 1977-79; research pathologist USDA Plum Island Animal Disease Ctr., Greenport, N.Y., 1975-82; asst. prof. dept. vet. pathology Cornell U., Ithaca, 1982-88, assoc. prof., 1988—, dir. Bovine Research Ctr., 1982-91;, 1982-91; cons. in field, 1983—. Contbr. articles to profl. publs. Mem. AVMA, Soc. for Study of Reprodn., Soc. for Theriogenology (exec. com. 1993-96), U.S. Animal Health Assn. Office: NY State Coll Vet Medicine Cornell U Ithaca NY 14853

SCHLAFLY, HUBERT JOSEPH, JR., communications executive; b. St. Louis, Aug. 14, 1919; s. Hubert J. and Mary Ross (Parker) S.; m. Leona Martin, June 12, 1944. B.S. in Elec. Engring, U. Notre Dame, 1941; post-grad., Syracuse U. extension, 1946-47. Electronics engr. Gen. Electric Co., Schenectady, 1941-44, Syracuse, 1946-47; project engr. Radiation Lab., Mass., Inst. Tech., 1944-45; dir. TV research 20th Century-Fox Film Corp., N.Y.C., 1947-51; a founder Teleprompter Corp., N.Y.C., 1951, v.p., 1951-74, pres., 1971-72, exec. v.p. tech. devel., 1972-74; pres. Transponder Corp., Greenwich, 1977-86; chmn., chief exec. officer Portel Services Corp., 1984-86; chmn., pres. Portel Services Network, Inc., 1987-91, chmn. bd., 1991—; cons. in field; industry coord., chmn. exec. com., cable tech. adv. com. FCC, 1972-75; adviser com. telecom. Nat. Acad. Engring.; advisor Sloan Commn. Cable Comms.; mem. engring. adv. coun. U. Notre Dame, 1977—, vice chmn., 1983, chmn., 1984; lectr. in field; dir., sec. Milbrook Corp., 1994—. Author: Computer in the Living Room. Bd. govs. Milbrook Club, 1993—. Recipient Engring. Honor award U. Notre Dame, 1976, Nat. Acad. T.V. Arts and Scis. Emmy award, 1992. Fellow Soc. Motion Picture and TV Engrs.; mem. IEEE (Delmer Ports award 1979, life), Nat. Cable TV Assn. (chmn. standards com. 1965-69, chmn. domestic satellite com. 1971-73, chmn. future svcs. com. 1972, assns. com. 1981, Outstanding Tech. Achievements award 1974), Cable TV Pioneers, Electronic Industries Assn. (chmn. broadband cable sect. 1971-73, founding chmn. broadband communications com.), Soc. Cable TV Engrs. (sr.), Fairfield Found. (hon.); named Notre Dame alumni Man of Yr., 1992. Roman Catholic. Clubs: Milbrook Country, Rotary (pres. Greenwich club 1991-92), Knights of Malta, Knight St. Gregory the Great. Patentee in field. Home and Office: 27 Orchard Dr Greenwich CT 06830-6711

SCHLAFLY, PHYLLIS STEWART, author; b. St. Louis, Aug. 15, 1924; d. John Bruce and Odile (Dodge) Stewart; m. Fred Schlafly, Oct. 20, 1949; children: John F., Bruce S., Roger S., Phyllis Liza Forshaw, Andrew L., Anne V. BA, Washington U., St. Louis, 1944, JD, 1978; MA, Harvard U., 1945; LLD, Niagara U., 1976. Bar: Ill. 1979, D.C. 1984, Mo. 1985, U.S. Supreme Ct. 1987. Syndicated columnist Copley News Svc., 1976—; pres. Eagle Forum, 1975—; broadcaster Spectrum, CBS Radio Network, 1973-78; commentator Cable TV News Network, 1980-83, Matters of Opinion sta. WBBM-AM, Chgo., 1973-75. Author, pub.: Phyllis Schlafly Report, 1967—; author: A Choice Not an Echo, 1964, The Gravediggers, 1964, Strike From Space, 1965, Safe Not Sorry, 1967, The Betrayers, 1968, Mindszenty The Man, 1972, Kissinger on the Couch, 1975, Ambush at Vladivostok, 1976, The Power of the Positive Woman, 1977, First Reader, 1994; editor: Child Abuse in the Classroom, 1984, Pornography's Victims, 1987, Equal Pay for Unequal Work, 1984, Who Will Rock the Cradle, 1989, Stronger Families or Bigger Government, 1990, Meddlesome Mandate: Rethinking Family Leave, 1991. Del. Rep. Nat. Conv., 1956, 64, 68, 84, 88, 92, 96, alt., 1960, 80; pres. Ill. Fedn. Rep. Women, 1960-64; 1st v.p. Nat. Fedn. Rep. Women, 1964-67; mem. Ill. Commn. on Status of Women, 1975-85; nat. chmn. Stop ERA, 1972—; mem. Ronald Reagan's Def. Policy Adv. Group, 1980; mem. Commn. on Bicentennial of U.S. Constn., 1985-91; mem. Adminstrv. Conf. U.S., 1983-86. Recipient 10 Honor awards Freedoms Found., Brotherhood award NCCJ, 1975; named Woman of Achievement in Pub. Affairs St. Louis Globe-Democrat, 1963, one of 10 most admired women in world Good Housekeeping poll, 1977-90. Mem. ABA, DAR (nat. chmn. Am. history 1965-68, nat. chmn. bicentennial com. 1967-70, nat. chmn. nat. def. 1977-80, 83-95), Ill. Bar Assn., Phi Beta Kappa, Pi Sigma Alpha. Office: Eagle Forum 7800 Bonhomme Ave Saint Louis MO 63105-1906

SCHLAGEL, RICHARD H., philosophy educator; b. Springfield, Mass., Nov. 22, 1925. BS in Pre-Med cum laude, Springfield Coll., 1949; MA in Philosophy, Boston U., 1952, PhD, 1955. Instr. philosophy Coll. of Wooster, 1954-55; instr. Clark U., 1955-56; asst. prof. George Washington U., 1956-62, assoc. prof., 1962-68, prof., 1968—, chmn. dept., 1965-69, 70-71, 77-83, named Elton prof. philosophy, 1986; sabbatical, Paris, with travel throughout Europe, 1962-63, 69-70, 76-77, 83-84, 90-91. Author: From Myth to Modern Mind: A Study of the Origins and Growth of Scientific Thought, vol. 1, Theology through Ptolemy, vol. 2, 1995, Copernicus through Quantum Mechanics, 1996, Contextual Realism: A Metaphysical Framework for Modern Science, 1986; contbr. articles and reviews to profl. jours. Borden Parker Browne fellow, 1953-54. Mem. AAUP, Am. Philos. Assn., Washington Philosophy Club (v.p. 1964-65, pres. 1965-66). Office: George Washington U Dept Philosophy Washington DC 20052

SCHLAGER, KEN, journalist, media strategist; b. Queens, N.Y., Sept. 28, 1951; s. Morris D. and Sylvia Schlager; m. Robin Solomon, Sept. 25, 1983; children: Steven, Hanna. BA, SUNY, Buffalo, 1972; MA, U. Mo., Columbia, 1977. Copy editor, reporter Ft. Lauderdale (Fla.) News, 1977-80, Gannett Newspapers, Westchester, N.Y., 1981-83; assoc. editor N.Y. Post, N.Y.C., 1983-85; mng. editor Billboard mag., N.Y.C., 1985-95, dir., strategic devel., 1995—.

SCHLAGETER, ROBERT WILLIAM, museum administrator; b. Streator, Ill., May 10, 1925; s. Herman Pete and Ida (Ladtkow) S.; divorced; children—David Michael, Robert William. Diploma, Karl Ruprecht Univ., Heidelberg, Fed. Republic Germany, 1950; BA, U. Ill., 1950, MFA, 1957. Asst. prof. U. Tenn., Knoxville, 1952-58; dir. Mint Mus. Art, Charlotte, N.C., 1958-66; assoc. dir. Downtown Gallery, N.Y.C., 1966, Ackland Art Ctr., U. N.C., Chapel Hill, 1967-76; dir. Cummer Gallery Art, Jacksonville, Fla., 1976-92, dir. emeritus, 1992—; fine arts cons. corp. and pvt. collecting, 1993—. Author: (exhbn. catalogue) Winslow Homer's Florida, George Inness' Florida, Martin Johnson Heade Florida, Robert Henri-George Bellows. Served with U.S. Army, 1943-45, ETO. Home: 5201 Atlantic Blvd Apt 2 Jacksonville FL 32207-2473

SCHLAIFER, CHARLES, advertising executive; b. Omaha, July 1, 1909; s. Abraham Schlaifer; m. Evelyn Chaikin, June 10, 1934 (dec. Oct. 1978); children: Arlene Lois Silk, Roberta Semer; m. Ann Mesavage, July 31, 1980. Privately ed.; Litt.D. (hon.), John F. Kennedy Coll., 1969. Newspaper reporter Omaha, 1926-29; advt. dir. Publix Tri-States Theatres, Nebr., Iowa, 1929-37; mng. dir. United Artists Theatres, San Francisco, 1937-42; nat. advt. cons. United Artists Producers, 1937-42; nat. advt. mgr. 20th Century-Fox Film Corp., N.Y.C., 1942-45; v.p. charge advt. and pub. relations 20th Century-Fox Film Corp., 1945-49; pres. Charles Schlaifer & Co., Inc., N.Y.C., 1949—; vis. prof. New Sch. Social Research; expert witness U.S. Congl. and Senatorial coms. on mental health, 1949—. Author: Advertising Code, Motion Picture Assn., 1948; co-author: Action for Mental Health, 1961, Heart's Work, 1991; contbr. articles to psychiat. jours. Mem. Pres.'s Com. Employment Handicapped, 1960—; founder, co-chmn. Nat. Mental Health Com., 1949-57; mem. nat. mental health adv. council Surgeon Gen. U.S., 1950-54; sec.-treas. Joint Commn. Mental Illness and Health, 1955-61; vice chmn. Found. Child Mental Welfare, 1963; mem. Gov.'s Youth Council State N.Y.; chmn. N.Y. State Mental Hygiene Facilities Improvement Corp., 1963—, White House Conf. Children, 1970; sec.-treas., bd. dirs. Joint Commn. Mental Health Children; chmn. N.Y. State Facilities Devel. Corp., 1963-78; mem. adv. council NIMH, 1976—; bd. dirs. Hillside Hosp., League Sch. For Seriously Disturbed Children, Menninger Found., Nat. Mental Hygiene Com. Recipient Social Conscience award Karen Horney Clinic, 1972; Hon. fellow Postgrad. Center Mental Health. Fellow Am. Psychiat. Assn. (hon.), Brit. Royal Soc. Health (hon.), Am. Orthopsychiat. Assn. (hon.); Mem. Nat. Assn. Mental Health (founder), Acad. for Motion Picture Arts and Scis., Harmonie Club. Home and Office: 150 E 69th St New York NY 10021-5704

SCHLAIN, BARBARA ELLEN, lawyer; b. N.Y.C., May 28, 1948; d. William and Evelyn (Youdelman) S.; B.A., Wellesley Coll., 1969; M.A., Columbia U., 1970; J.D., Yale U., 1973. Bar: N.Y. 1974, U.S. Dist. Ct. (so. dist.) N.Y. 1974, U.S. Ct. Appeals (2d cir.) 1975, U.S. Dist. Ct. (ea. dist.) N.Y. 1977. Assoc. firm Donovan Leisure Newton & Irvine, N.Y.C., 1973-76, Graubard Moskovitz McGoldrick Dannett & Horowitz, N.Y.C., 1976-79; atty. McGraw-Hill, Inc., N.Y.C., 1979-80, asst. gen. counsel, 1980-86, v.p., assoc. gen. counsel, asst. sec., 1986—. sec. proprietary rights com. Info. Industry Assn., 1982-83. Author outlines Practicing Law Inst., 1983, 84, 85, 86, 88; contbr. numerous articles to profl. jours. Bd. dirs., v.p., sec. Dance Research Found., N.Y.C., 1983-86, chmn. 1986—. Phi Beta Kappa scholar, Durant scholar Wellesley Coll., 1967-69. Mem. ABA, Assn. Am. Pubs. (lawyers com. 1979—), Assn. Bar City N.Y. (communications law com. 1985-88). Office: The McGraw-Hill Companies 1221 Ave Of The Americas New York NY 10020-1001

SCHLARMAN, STANLEY GERARD, bishop; b. Belleville, Ill., July 27, 1933. Student, St. Henry Prep. Sem., Belleville, Gregorian U., Rome, St. Louis U. Ordained priest Roman Catholic Ch., 1958, consecrated bishop, 1979. Titular bishop of Capri and aux. bishop of Belleville, 1979-83; bishop of Dodge City Kans., 1983—. Office: Diocese of Dodge City PO Box 137 910 Central Ave Dodge City KS 67801-4513*

SCHLATTER, GEORGE H., producer, director, writer; b. Birmingham; m. Jolene Brand; two children. Student, Pepperdine U. Producer numerous shows including (TV series) Dinah Shore Shows, 1957-62, 60-62, Judy Garland Show, 1963, Steve Lawrence Show, 1965, Colgate Comedy Hour, 1967, Laugh-In, 1967-73, 76-77, Bill Cosby Series, 1972-73, Cher, 1975, Real People, 1979; (TV spls.) Grammy Awards 1965, 68, 69, 70, Jonathan Winters, 1964, Meredith Willson, 1964, Danny Thomas, 1964, 65, Ernie Ford, 1967, Laugh-In, 1967, Dinah Shore, 1969, Doris Day, 1974, Cher, 1975, Diana Ross, 1975, Goldie Hawn, 1975, Goldie & Liza Together, 1980, Joe Piscopo, 1986, George Schlatter's Comedy Club Spl., 1988, Beverly Hills 75th Anniversary, 1989, Sammy Davis Jr. 60th Anniversary Celebration, 1989, 25th Anniversary of the Jerry Lewis Labor Day Telethon, 1990, Sinatra 75th: The Best is Yet to Come, 1990, Soc. of Singers Salute to Frank Sinatra, 1990, Real People Reunion Spl., 1991, A Party for Richard Pryor, 1991, (charitable events) Thalians Tribute to Marianne and Kenny Rogers, 1981, Sun Valley Ski Tournament, 1985, 86, Am. Cinematheque Tribute to Eddie Murphy, 1986, to Bette Midler, 1987, to Robin Williams, 1988, Tel Aviv Found. Cinematheque Tribute to Goldie Hawn and Stan Kamen, 1987, AIDS Project Los Angeles Benefit, 1987, Big Sisters Benefit, 1988, Beverly Hills 75th Anniversary Honoring Frank Sinatra, 1989, Paul Newman/Joanne Woodward Event for the Scott Newman Found., 1990, Carousel of Hope Ball (Barbara/Marvin Davis Diabetes Found., 1990. Recipient 5 Emmys, 22 Emmy nominations, Golden Globe awards, Image awards, Monitor awards, Dirs. Guild award, Producers Guild award, Writer's Guild award ; named Internat. Radio and TV Man of Yr.; awarded a star on Hollywood Blvd.'s Walk of Fame. Avocations: skiing, horseback riding, sailing, scuba diving. Office: William Morris Agy 151 S El Camino Dr Beverly Hills CA 90212-2704

SCHLATTER, KONRAD, corporate executive; b. Zurich, Switzerland, Nov. 6, 1935; came to U.S., 1981; m. Janet Dodd; children: Benedict, Katherine, Frederick. BBA, Bus. Sch. Commerce Assn. Coll., Zurich, Switzerland, 1955. With affiliates of CPC Internat., France, Switzerland, England, 1956-67; comptroller CPC Europe div. CPC Internat., Brussels, 1967-70; dir. fin. CPC Asia div. CPC Internat., Hong Kong, 1970-71, v.p. fin., 1971-76, sr. v.p. fin., 1976-79; chmn. CPC Japan div. CPC Internat., Tokyo, 1979-81; comptroller CPC Internat. Inc., Englewood Cliffs, N.J., 1981-87, v.p. fin. planning, reporting, control, 1987—, alsp sr. v.p. and CFO. Trustee Elisabeth Morrow Sch., Englewood Cliffs, mem. fin. com.; bd. dirs. Englewood Hosp. Mem. Fin. Execs. Inst., N.J. Hist. Soc. (bd. dirs.), Japan Soc., N.Y.C. Office: CPC Internat Inc Box 8000 International Plz Englewood Cliffs NJ 07632*

SCHLECK, THOMAS TODD, financial executive; b. Dodgeville, Wis., June 2, 1947; s. Clarence Carl and Helen Gertrude (Zwettler) S.; m. Carol A. Amos, Dec. 1, 1973; children: Erin, Heather, Alexandra, Gregory. BBA in Fin., U. Wis., 1970. V.p. Banl of Am. NT & SA, L.A., 1970-82; v.p., treas. Am. Med. Internat., Beverly Hills, Calif., 1982-88; CFO, treas., dir. EPIC Holdings, Inc., Dallas, 1988-95; CEO, CFO Am. Health Properties, Englewood, Col., 1995—; mem. southwestern adv. bd. Arkwright Mut. Ins. Co.; bd. dirs. EPIC Holdings, Inc. Bd. dirs. Dallas Adult Literacy Coun., 1993-94. Mem. Leading Chief Fin. Officers, Los Cabarellos. *

SCHLECKSER, JAMES HENRY, sales and engineering executive; b. Rahway, N.J., Sept. 16, 1962; s. Henry and Mary Ellen (Counihan) S.; m. Denise Priscille Bergeron, July 2, 1988. B of Chem. Engring., U. Del., 1984; MBA, U. Conn., 1988. Cert. engr.-in-tng., Del. Product engr. Rogers Corp., Manchester, Conn., 1984-86; asst. corp. sec. R/MAT Inc., Manchester, 1986-88; product supr. Rogers Corp., Manchester, 1986-88; product mgr. J.M. Ney Electronics, Bloomfield, Conn., 1988-90; sales mgr. Ney Ultrasonics, Bloomfield, 1990-92; dir. sales and engring. NEY Ultrasonics, Bloomfield, 1992-95; v.p. sales and mktg. General Eastern, Woburn, Mass., 1995—; chmn. Ultrasonic Industry Standards, Dayton, Ohio, 1994. Author: (book chpt.) Modern Plastics Ency., 1988; contbr. articles to profl. jours. including Soc. Vacuum Coaters, Circuits Assembly, Plastics Engring. Chmn. Internat. Spl. Olympics, Bolton, Conn., 1995; exec. com. Canon Greater Hartford Open, Cromwell, Conn., 1988-94; dir. Hartford Jaycees, 1990-92. Recipient Brownfield award Jaycees, 1989, State Champion Pub. Speaking, 1990. Mem. Soc. Automotive Engrs. (bd. dirs. local chpt. 1989). Home: 64 Shoddy Mill Rd Bolton CT 06043

SCHLEEDE, GLENN ROY, energy market and policy consultant; b. Lyons, N.Y., June 12, 1933; m. Sandra Christine Klafehn, Dec. 27, 1958; children: Kristen M., Kimberly J., Kendall E. BA, Gustavus Adolphus Coll., 1960; MA, U. Minn., 1968; advanced mgmt. program, Harvard U., 1987. Research asst. Indsl. Relations Ctr., U. Minn., Mpls., 1960-61; mgmt. intern, then contractor personnel specialist AEC, Argonne, Ill. and Germantown, Md., 1961-65; asst. chief div. natural resources U.S. Office Mgmt. and Budget, Exec. Office of Pres., Washington, 1965-72, exec. assoc. dir., 1981; dep. assoc. dir. Office of Policy Analysis, AEC, Germantown, 1972-73; assoc. dir. energy and sci. Domestic Council, The White House, Washington, 1973-77; sr. v.p. Nat. Coal Assn., Washington, 1977-81; pres. New Eng. Energy Inc., Westborough, Mass., 1982-92, also bd. dirs.; v.p. New Eng. Power Service Co., Westborough, 1982-92, also bd. dirs.; v.p. New Eng. Electric System, Westborough, 1986-92; pres., CEO, dir. Energy Market and Policy Analysis, Inc., Reston, Va., 1992—. Author numerous speeches, papers and congl. testimony on various nat. energy policy issues. Recipient Disting. Alumni in Bus. award Gustavus Adolphus Coll. Alumni Assn., St. Peter, Minn., 1987. Republican. Lutheran. Avocations: reading, travel, carpentry. Home: 1414 Hemingway Ct Reston VA 22094-1241 Office: Energy Market and Policy Analysis Inc PO Box 3875 Reston VA 22090-1875

SCHLEGEL, FRED EUGENE, lawyer; b. Indpls., July 24, 1941; s. Fred George and Dorothy (Bruce) S.; m. Jane Wessels, Aug. 14, 1965; children: Julia, Charles, Alexandra. BA, Northwestern U., 1963; JD with distinction, U. Mich., 1966. Bar: Ind. 1966. Assoc. lawyer Baker & Daniels, Indpls., 1966-72, ptnr., 1972—; vice chmn. Meridian St. Preservation Commn., Indpls., 1975-90; bd. dirs. Indpls. Water Co., IWC Resources Corp. Contbr. articles to profl. jours. Chmn. Indpls. Pub. Schs. Edn. Found., 1988-90; pres. Festival Music Soc., 1974-75, 79, 86-87; bd. dirs. Indpls. Symphony Orch., 1991—, Arts Coun. Indpls. Mem. ABA, Ind. Bar Assn., Fed. Energy Bar Assn., Northwestern U. Alumni Club Indpls. (pres. 1992-94). Republican. Presbyterian. Office: Baker and Daniels 300 N Meridian St Ste 2700 Indianapolis IN 46204-1755

SCHLEGEL, JOHN FREDERICK, management consultant, speaker, trainer; b. Ogden, Utah, Dec. 18, 1944; s. Max Joseph and Mary Georgia (Whittaker) S.; m. Priscilla Mary Hecht, Sept. 8, 1967. BS in Pharmacy, U. Pacific, 1967; D of Pharmacy, U. So. Calif., 1972, postdoctoral fellow, 1972-73, MS in Edn., 1980; ScD in Pharmacy (hon.), Mass. Coll. Pharmacy, 1984, L.I. U., 1985. Lic. pharmacist, Calif., Nev.; cert. assoc. exec. Chief pharmacist U. So. Calif. Sch. Pharmacy, Los Angeles, 1967-73, dir. pharmacy admissions, 1973-75; dir. office student affairs Am. Assn. Colls. Pharmacy, Alexandria, Va., 1975-77, asst. exec. dir., 1977-81, exec. dir., 1981-84; chief exec. officer Am. Pharm. Assn., Washington, 1984-89; exec. v.p., chief exec. officer Am. Acad. Facial Plastic and Reconstructive Surgery, Washington, 1989-92; pres. Schlegel & Assocs., Chevy Chase, Md., 1992—; cons. U.S. Govt., VA, HHS, various pharm. cos., assns. and schs. pharmacy. Contbr. over 60 articles on pharmacy, health care and assn. mgmt.; presenter in field. Nat. del. White House Conf. on Aging, Washington, 1981. Disting. alumnus U. So. Calif. Sch. Pharmacy, 1985, U. the Pacific Sch. Pharmacy, 1987. Fellow Am. Soc. Assn. Execs.; mem. Am. Soc. Assn. Execs., Am. Pharm. Assn., Am. Assn. Med. Soc. Execs., Group Health Assn. (trustee, officer), Greater Washington Soc. Assn. Execs., Phi Delta Chi (charter, bd. counsellors). Avocations: tennis, classical music, gardening. Office: 7423 Lynnhurst St Chevy Chase MD 20815-3101

SCHLEGEL, JOHN PETER, academic administrator; b. Dubuque, Iowa, July 31, 1943; s. Aaron Joseph and Irma Joan (Hingtgen) S. BA, St. Louis U., 1969, MA, 1970; BDiv, U. London, 1973; DPhil, Oxford U., 1977. Joined Soc. of Jesus, 1963, ordained priest Roman Cath. Ch., 1973. From asst. prof. to assoc. prof. Creighton U., Omaha, 1976-79, asst. acad. v.p., 1978-82; dean Coll. Arts and Scis. Rockhurst Coll., Kansas City, Mo., 1982-84, Marquette U., Milw., 1984-88; exec. and acad. v.p. John Carroll U., Cleve., 1988-91; pres. U. San Francisco, 1991—; cons. Orgn. for Econ. Devel. and Cooperation, Paris, 1975-76. Author: Bilingualism and Canadian Policy in Africa, 1979; editor: Towards a Redefinition of Development, 1976; contbr. articles to profl. jours. Mem. Milwaukee County Arts Coun., 1986-88, Mo. Coun. on Humanities, Kansas City, 1984; trustee St. Louis U., 1985-91, Loyola U. Chgo., 1988-95, Loyola U. New Orleans, 1995—, St. Ignatius H.S., Cleve., 1990-91, Loyola Coll. in Md., 1992—; bd. dirs. San Francisco ARC, 1991-94, Coro Found., Commonwealth Club Calif. Oxford U. grantee, 1974-76; Govt. of Can. grantee, 1977-78. Mem. Am. Coun. on Edn., Can. Studies in U.S., Olympic Club, Univ. Club, Bohemian Club. Avocations: racquet sports, classical music, cooking, hiking. Office: U San Francisco Office of Pres 2130 Fulton St San Francisco CA 94117-1080

SCHLEIFER, THOMAS C., management consultant, author, lecturer. BS in Constrn. Mgmt., E. Carolina U., 1989, MS in Constrn. Mgmt., 1990; PhD, Herriot-Watt U., 1994. Owner Schleifer Bros., Inc., Hanover, N.J., 1964-75; owner, founder, pres., internat. cons. firm CMA Cons. Group, Morristown, N.J., 1976-86; dir. appropriate tech., vol. Habitat for Humanity, Americus, Ga., 1987-88; assoc. prof. Ariz. State U., Tempe, 1990-92; eminent scholar Del E. Webb Sch. Constrn., Ariz. State U., 1993-94; vis. prof. East Carolina U., 1989-90; former chmn. continuing edn. com. Associated Gen. Contractors Am.; lectr. and presenter in field. Author: Construction Contractors' Survival Guide, 1990, Glossary of Suretyship and Related Terms, 1981; contbr. articles to profl. jours. Bd. advisors Habitat for Humanity Internat., 1989—. Mem. Am. Inst. Constructors (bd. dirs. 1990-93), Am. Arbitration Assn. (N.J. adv. coun. 1968-75), Am. Concrete Inst. (edn. com. 1972-76), Associated Gen. Contractors Am. (chmn. continuing edn. com. 1970-76), Assn. Advancement 3d World (internat. adv. coun. 1988-91). Home and Office: 5625 N 75th Pl Scottsdale AZ 85250-6471

SCHLENDER, WILLIAM ELMER, management sciences educator; b. Sawyer, Mich., Oct. 28, 1920; s. Gustav A. and Marie (Zindler) S.; m. Lela R. Pullen, June 9, 1956 (dec. June 1983); m. Margaret C. Krahn, Mar. 3, 1987. A.B., Valparaiso U., 1941; M.B.A., U. Denver, 1947; Ph.D., Ohio State U., 1955. With U.S. Rubber Co., 1941-43, 46; asst. prof. bus. adminstrn. Bowling Green State U., 1947-53; asst. prof. bus. orgn., prof. Ohio State U., 1954-65, asst. dean, 1959-62; assoc. dean Ohio State U. (Coll. Commerce and Adminstrn.), 1962-63; prof. mgmt. U. Tex., 1965-68, chmn. dept., 1966-68; dean Cleve. State U. Coll. Bus. Adminstrn., 1968-75, prof. mgmt., 1975-76; Internat. Luth. Laymen's League prof. bus. ethics Valparaiso (Ind.) U., 1976-79, Richard E. Meier prof. mgmt., 1983-86, Richard E. Meier prof. emeritus, 1986—; vis. assoc. prof. mgmt. Columbia U., 1957-58; vis. prof. mgmt. U. Tex., Arlington, 1981-82; cons. in field; bd. govs. Internat. Ins. Soc., 1972-90; bd. dirs. Carrier Enterprises. Author: (with M.J. Jucius) Elements of Managerial Action, 3d edit, 1973, (with others) Management in Perspective: Selected Readings, 1965; Editor: (with others) Management in a Dynamic Society, 1965; Contbr. (with others) articles to profl. jours. Served with AUS, 1943-45. Decorated Bronze Star. Fellow Acad. Mgmt.; mem. Indsl. Rels. Rsch. Assn. (pres. N.E. Ohio chpt. 1971-72), Internat. Coun. Small Bus., Am. Legion (exec. order Ohio comdr.), Tau Kappa Epsilon, Soc. for Case Rsch., Beta Gamma Sigma, Sigma Iota Epsilon, Pi Sigma Epsilon, Alpha Kappa Psi, Phi Kappa Phi, Rotary. Home: PO Box 446 Sawyer MI 49125-0446 Office: Coll Bus Adminstrn Valparaiso U Valparaiso IN 46383 *I resolved long ago that where I worked and what I did would be guided not by prestige considerations, but by the answers to three questions: (1) Will my work allow me to grow by discovering and developing my capabilities? (2) Will it make a significant contribution to my profession and to the community? (3) Will I enjoy doing it? My career, and my personal philosophy, have these underlying guidelines.*

SCHLENNER, DIANE MARIE, elementary school educator; b. Phila., Aug. 31, 1971; d. Robert Joseph and Donna Catherine (Janthor) S. BEd, Bloomsburg U., 1993. Sales clk. Party Parrot, Chester, N.J., 1987-88; dietary aide Heath Village Retirement Home, Hackettstown, N.J., 1988-89; aide Campus Child Ctr., Bloomsburg, Pa., 1990; sec. First Gen. Svcs., Flanders, N.J., 1990; clk. typist Picatinny Arsenal, Rockaway, N.J., 1990-91; clk. typist, sec. sociology dept. Bloomsburg (Pa.) U., 1992. Mem. Assn. Childhood Edn. Iternat., Pa. State Edn. Assn., Psychology Assn., Kappa Delta Pi, Phi Iota Chi. Roman Catholic. Home: 21 Nestlingwood Dr Long Valley NJ 07853-3526

SCHLENSKER, GARY CHRIS, landscaping company executive; b. Indpls., Nov. 12, 1950; s. Christian Frederick and Doris Jean (Shannon) S.; m. Ann Marie Tobin, Oct. 27, 1979; children: Laura Patricia, Christian Frederick II. Student, Purdue U., 1969-71, 73; A Bus. Adminstrn., Clark Coll., 1979; cert. emergency med. technician, Ind. Vocat. Tech. Inst., Lafayette, 1974. Salesman Modern Reference, Indpls., 1971; orthopaedic technician St. Elizabeth Hosp., Lafayette, 1973-75, asst. mgr. ambulance service, 1975; sales asst. Merck, Sharpe & Dohme, Oakbrook, Ill., 1975-77; v.p. Turfco, Inc., Zionsville, Ind., 1977-84; pres. Turfscape, Inc., Zionsville, 1984—; speaker Midwest Turf Conf., 1991. With U.S. Army, 1971-73. Mem. Nat. Fedn. Ind. Bus., Midwest Turf Found., Better Bus. Bur., Ohio Turf Found., Internat. Erosion Control Assn., Ind. C. of C., Zionsville C. of C., Indpls. Landscape Assn., Phi Kappa Psi. Presbyterian. Avocations: woodworking, golf.

SCHLENTZ, ROBERT JOSEPH, reliability engineer; b. Chgo., Dec. 9, 1940; s. Harold Joseph and Katherine (Dufalo) S.; m. Eileen Ellen Pride, May 10, 1969; children: Julie Joann, Karen Katherine. BS in Physics, DePaul U., 1963, MS in Physics, 1965. Registered profl. engr., Minn. Assoc. rsch. scientist U. Notre Dame, Ind., 1966-68; dept. mgr. electro magnetic compatibility, staff engr. Medtronic, Fridley, Minn., 1968-77; project engr. Maico Hearing Instruments, Edina, Minn., 1977-83; sr. specialist reliability engring. 3M (Minn. Mining & Mfg.), St. Paul, 1983—. Treas. Mpls. Dem. Farmer-Labor Com., Mpls., 1985-88. Mem. IEEE (sr., twin cities sect. chair), Minn. Soc. Profl. Engrs. (bd. dirs.). Roman Catholic. Avocations: music, science fiction, politics. Home: 3040 Buchanan St NE Minneapolis MN 55418 Office: 3M 3M Ctr Saint Paul MN 55144

SCHLESINGER, ARTHUR (MEIER), JR., writer, educator; b. Columbus, Ohio, Oct. 15, 1917; s. Arthur M. and Elizabeth (Bancroft) S.; m. Marian Cannon, 1940 (div. 1970); children: Stephen Cannon, Katharine Kinderman, Christina, Andrew Bancroft; m. Alexandra Emmet, July 9, 1971; 1 son, Robert Emmet Kennedy. AB summa cum laude, Harvard U., 1938, mem. Soc. of Fellows, 1939-42; postgrad. (Henry fellow), Cambridge (Eng.) U., 1938-39; hon. degrees, Muhlenberg Coll., 1950, Bethany Coll., 1956, U. N.B., 1966, New Sch. Social Rsch., 1966, Tusculum Coll., 1966, R.I. Coll.,

1969, Aquinas Coll., 1971, Western New Eng. Coll., 1974, Ripon Coll., 1976, Iona Coll., 1977, Utah State U., 1978, U. Louisville, 1978, Northeastern U., 1981, Rutgers U., 1982, SUNY-Albany, 1984, U. N.H., 1985, U. Oxford, 1987, Akron U., 1987, Brandeis U., 1988, U. Mass., Boston, 1990, Hofstra U., 1991, Adelphi U., 1992, Dominican Coll., 1992, Mt. Ida Coll., 1993, Middlebury Coll., 1994, Roosevelt U., 1995, Lynn U., 1996. With OWI, 1942-43, OSS, 1943-45; assoc. prof. history Harvard U., 1946-54, prof., 1954-62; vis. fellow Inst. Advanced Study, Princeton, N.J., 1966; Schweitzer prof. humanities CUNY, 1966-95; cons. Econ. Cooperation Adminstrn., 1948, Mutual Security Adminstrn., 1951-52; spl. asst. to Pres. of U.S., 1961-64; mem. jury Cannes Film Festival, 1964; mem. Adlai E. Stevenson campaign staff, 1952, 56; chmn. Franklin Delano Roosevelt Four Freedoms Found., 1983—; trustee Robert F. Kennedy Meml., Twentieth Century Fund.; adv. Arthur and Elizabeth Schlesinger Library. Author: Orestes A. Brownson, 1939, The Age of Jackson, 1945 (Pulitzer prize for history 1946), The Vital Center, 1949, (with R.H. Rovere) The General and the President, 1951, The Age of Roosevelt Vol. I: The Crisis of the Old Order 1919-1933, 1957 (Francis Parkman prize Soc. Am. Historians 1957, Frederic Bancroft prize Columbia U. 1958), The Age of Roosevelt Vol. II: The Coming of the New Deal, 1958, The Age of Roosevelt Vol. III: The Politics of Upheaval, 1960, Kennedy or Nixon: Does It Make Any Difference?, 1960, The Politics of Hope, 1963, (with John Blum) The National Experience, 1963, A Thousand Days, 1965 (Pulitzer prize for biography 1966, Nat. Book award 1966), The Bitter Heritage, 1967, The Crisis of Confidence, 1969, The Imperial Presidency, 1973 (Sidney Hillman Found. award 1973), Robert Kennedy and His Times, 1978 (Nat. Book award 1979), The Cycles of American History, 1986, The Disuniting of America, 1991; contbr. articles to mags. and newspapers; film reviewer: Show mag, 1962-64, Vogue, 1967-72, Saturday Rev., 1977-80, Am. Heritage, 1981-82; editor: Harvard Guide to American History, 1954, Guide to Politics, 1954, Paths to American Thought, 1963, The Promise of American Life, 1967, The Best and the Last of Edwin O'Connor, 1970, History of American Presidential Elections 1789-1972, 1971, 1972-1984, 1986, The Coming to Power, 1972, The Dynamics of World Power: A Documentary History of United States Foreign Policy 1945-1973, 1973, History of U.S. Political Parties, 1973, Congress Investigates, 1975, The American Statesman, 1982, The Almanac of American History, 1983, Running for President, 1994; screenwriter: (teleplay) The Journey of Robert F. Kennedy. Served with AUS, 1945. Decorated comdr. Order of Orange-Nassau (The Netherlands), Ordem del Libertador (Venezuela); recipient Nat. Inst. and Am. Acad. Arts and Letters gold medal in history and biography, 1967, Ohio Gov.'s award for history, 1973, Eugene V. Debs award in edn., 1974, Fregene prize for lit. (Italy), 1983; Guggenheim fellow, 1946; Am. Acad. Arts and Letters grantee, 1946. Mem. Am. Hist. Assn., Orgn. Am. Historians, Soc. Am. Historians (pres. 1989-92), Am. Acad. and Inst. Arts and Letters (pres. 1981-84, chancellor 1984-87), Am. Philos. Soc., Mass. Hist. Soc., Colonial Soc. Mass., Russian Acad. Scis., Franklin and Eleanor Roosevelt Inst. (co-chmn. 1983—), ACLU, Coun. Fgn. Rels., Ams. for Dem. Action (nat. chmn. 1952-54), Century Assn., Phi Beta Kappa. Democt. Unitarian. Home: 455 E 51st St New York NY 10022-6474 Office: CUNY 33 W 42nd St New York NY 10036-8003

SCHLESINGER, B. FRANK, architect, educator; b. N.Y.C., Sept. 17, 1925; s. Augustus and Ethel (Brower) S.; m. Draga A. Christy; children: Jeff, Nike, Katherine, Daniel, Christy Anna; 1 stepson, Frances L. Haley Jr. Student, Middlebury Coll., 1946-48; BS, U. Ill., 1950; MArch, Harvard U., 1954. Draftsman Hugh Stubbins Assocs., 1953-55, Marcel Breuer, 1955-56; practice architecture Princeton, N.J., 1956-59, Doylestown, Pa., 1959-69, Phila., 1969-71, Washington, 1971—; instr. archtl. design U. Pa., 1957-60; vis. critic Columbia Sch. Architecture, 1962-63, U. Pa., 1965; KEA disting. prof. Sch. Architecture, U. Md., 1971, prof. architecture, 1971—. With USNR, 1943-46. Recipient design awards Pa. Soc. Archs., 1960-65, 69, 84, Bronze medal, 1965, Silver medal, 1973, Design awards Progressive Arch., 1966, 67, 69, 72, 74, awards Interfaith Forum on Religion, Art and Arch., 1987, 92. Fellow AIA (design awards Phila. chpt. 1960, 61, 63-65, 68, 69, No. Va. chpt. 1975, Washington chpt. 1990, 92); mem. Harvard Grad. Sch. Design Alumni Assn. (pres. 1971-73), Associated Harvard Alumni (dir. 1972). Address: 5053 Massachusetts Ave NW Washington DC 20016-4312

SCHLESINGER, CAROLE LYNN, elementary education educator; b. Detroit, May 13, 1961; d. Robert Schlesinger and Regenia Compere. Student, Kalamazoo Coll., 1981-84; BA, U. Mich., 1986; teaching cert., Eastern Mich. U., 1992. Cert. elem. tchr., Mich. Bank teller U. Mich. Credit Union, Ann Arbor, 1987; rsch. asst. dept. postgrad. medicine U. Mich., Ann Arbor, 1987; fin. planner IDS Fin. Svcs., Ann Arbor, 1988-89; telemarketer U. Mich. Telefund, Ann Arbor, 1989-90; enumerator U.S. Bur. Census, Ann Arbor, 1990; reading and math. tutor Reading and Learning Skills Ctr., Ann Arbor, 1991-92; interpreter Living Sci. Found., Wixom, Mich., 1992-94; intern planning and mgmt. info. div. Peace Corps., Washington, 1985; intern Com. for Econ. Devel., Washington, 1985. Elder 1st Presbyn. Ch., Ann Arbor, 1992-94; canvasser, vol. Pub. Interest Rsch. group in Mich., Ann Arbor, 1986-87; trainee Groundwater Edn., Esatern Mich. U., Ypsilanti, 1991, mem. dean's adv. com., 1992; mem., group leader Ann Arbor Dems., 1984-87. Mem. ASCD, Mich. Reading Assn., Washtenaw Reading Coun., Mich. Coun. Tchrs. Math., Nat. Coun. Tchrs. Math., Mich. Sci. Tchrs. Assn., Kappa Delta Pi.

SCHLESINGER, DAVID HARVEY, medical educator, researcher; b. N.Y.C., Apr. 28, 1939; s. Philip T. and Fay (Margolis) S.; m. Joan M. Aurelia; children: Sarah Jane, Karen Louise. BA, Columbia U., 1962; MS, Albany Med. Coll., 1965; PhD, Mt. Sinai Med. and Grad. Sch., 1972. Research fellow in medicine Mass. Gen. Hosp., Harvard Med. Sch., Boston, 1972-75, instr., 1975-77; asst. in biochemistry Mass. Gen. Hosp., Harvard Med. Sch., 1975-77; rsch. assoc. prof. U. Ill. Med. Ctr., Chgo., 1977-81; rsch. prof. exptl. medicine NYU Med. Ctr., N.Y.C., 1981-95, co-dir. neuroscis. sect. mental health clin. rsch. ctr., 1981-90; dir. microsequency and sythesis facility Kaplan Cancer Ctr., 1983-91; co-dir. neuroscis. sect. mental health clin. rsch. ctr., dir. microsequencing and synthesis faculty Kaplan Cancer Ctr., N.Y. med. Ctr., 1983-92; cons. Ortho Pharm. Co., 1977-91, Armour Pharm., 1971-81, Emisphere Techs., Inc., 1987-93; cons. in drug delivery systems. Editor: monograph Neurobyphysical Peptide Hormones and Other Biological Active Peptides, 1981; editor and contbg. author: Macromolecular Sequencing and Synthesis: Selected Methods and Application, 1988. Recipient Lectureship award Fundacion Gen. Mediterranean, Madrid, 1975. Mem. N.Y. Acad. Scis., Am. Physiol. Soc., Am. Soc. Biol. Chemists, Am. Chem. Soc. Office: NYU Med Ctr 550 1st Ave New York NY 10016-6481

SCHLESINGER, EDWARD BRUCE, neurological surgeon; b. Pitts., Sept. 6, 1913; s. Samuel B. and Sara Marie (Schlesinger) S.; m. Mary Eddy, Nov. 1941; children—Jane, Mary, Ralph, Prudence. B.A., U. Pa., 1934, M.D., 1938. Diplomate Am. Bd. Neurosurgery. Mem. faculty Columbia Coll. Phys. and Surg., N.Y.C., 1946—; prof. clin. neurol. surgery Columbia Coll. Phys. and Surg., 1964—, Byron Stookey prof., chmn. dept. neurol. surgery, 1973-80, Byron Stookey prof. emeritus, 1980—; dir. neurol. surgery Columbia Presbyn. Hosp., 1973-80, pres. med. bd., 1976-79; cons. in neurosurgery Presbyn. Hosp., 1980-87, cons. emeritus, 1987—. Author rsch. publs. on uses, effects of curare in disease, lesions of central nervous system, localization of brain tumors using radioactive tagged isotopes, genetic problems in neurosurgery and spinal disorders. Trustee Matheson Found., chmn. Elsberg fellowship com.; trustee Sharon (Conn.) Hosp. Recipient emeritus rsch. award Presbyn. Hosp. Fellow N.Y. Acad. Scis., N.Y. Acad. Medicine; mem. AAAS, AMA, Am. Assn. Neurol. Surgeons, Harvey Soc., Neurosurg Soc. Am. (pres. 1970-71), Soc. Neurol. Surgeons, Am. Assn. Surgery of Trauma, Am. Rheumatism Soc., Am. Coll. Clin. Pharmacology and Chemotherapy, Ea. Assn. Electroencephalographers, Sigma Xi. Achievements include investigation of clinical pathological markers of genetic disorders and the syndromes created. Home: PO Box 3239 Fort Lee NJ 07024-9239 Office: 710 W 168th St New York NY 10032-2603

SCHLESINGER, HARVEY ERWIN, judge; b. N.Y.C., June 4, 1940. BA, The Citadel, 1962; JD, U. Richmond, 1965. Bar: Va. 1965, Fla. 1965, U.S. Supreme Ct. 1968. Corp. counsel Seaboard Coast Line R.R. Co., Jacksonville, Fla., 1968-70; chief asst. U.S. atty. Middle Dist. Fla., Jacksonville, 1970-75, U.S. magistrate judge, 1975-91, U.S. Dist. judge, 1991—; adj. prof. U. N. Fla., 1984-91; mem. adv. com. on Fed. Rules of Criminal Procedure to U.S. Supreme Ct., 1986-93; chmn. U.S. Dist. Ct. Forms Task Force, Washington, 1983—. Served to capt. JAGC U.S. Army, 1965-68. Bd. dirs. Pine Castle Ctr. for Mentally Retarded, Jacksonville, 1970-87 , pres., 1972-74, chmn. bd. dirs., 1973-74, 76, trustee Pine Castle Found., 1972-76; trustee Congregation Ahavath Chesed, Jacksonville, 1970—, v.p., 1975-80, pres., 1980-82; v.p. S.E. council Union Am. Hebrew Congregations, 1984-88; asst. commissioner for exploring N. Fla. council Boy Scouts Am., 1983-86, exec. com., 1986—; mem. Boy Scouts Am. Nat. Jewish com. on Scouting, Irving, Tex., 1986-93, recipient Silver Beaver award Boy Scouts Am., 1986; trustee River Garden Home for Aged, 1982—, sec., 1985; co-chmn. bd. govs. Jacksonville chpt. NCCJ, 1983—, presiding co-chmn. 1984-89, nat. bd. trustees, N.Y.C., 1986-93. Recipient George Washington Medal Honor, Freedoms Found, Valley Forge, Pa, 1987, Silver Medallion Humanitarian award Nat. COnf. Christians and Jews, 1992. Mem. ABA (fed. rules of evidence and criminal procedure com. 1979—, Flascher award 1989), Va. Bar Assn., Fla. Bar Assn., Fed. Judges Assn., Nat. Council U.S. Magistrates (pres. 1987, v.p. 1985, pres. elect 1986, sec. 1983, treas. 1984), Jacksonville Bar Assn., Fed. Bar Assn. (pres. Jacksonville chpt. 1974, 75, 81-82), Am. Judicature Soc., Chester Bedell Am. Inns of Ct. (pres. 1992—. Lodge: Rotary (Paul Harris fellow, pres. S. Jacksonville club), Mason (past master, past venerable master, knights commander of Ct. Honour, Scottish rite bodies), Shriner. Office: 311 W Monroe St PO Box 1740 Jacksonville FL 32201

SCHLESINGER, JAMES RODNEY, economist; b. N.Y.C., Feb. 15, 1929; s. Julius and Rhea (Rogen) S.; m. Rachel Mellinger, June 19, 1954; children: Cora K., Charles L., Ann R., William F., Emily, Thomas S., Clara, James Rodney. A.B. summa cum laude, Harvard U., 1950, A.M., 1952, Ph.D., 1956. Asst. prof., then assoc. prof. U. Va., 1955-63; sr. staff mem. RAND Corp., 1963-67; dir. strategic studies, 1967-69; asst. dir. Bur. Budget, 1969, acting dep. dir., 1969-70; asst. dir. Office Mgmt. and Budget, 1970-71; chmn. AEC, 1971-73; dir. CIA, Feb.-July 1973; U.S. sec. def., 1973-75; vis. scholar Johns Hopkins Sch. Advanced Internat. Studies, 1976-77; asst. to Pres., 1977; sec. Dept. Energy, 1977-79; counselor Ctr. for Strategic and Internat. Studies, Georgetown U., 1979—; sr. adv. Lehman Bros., 1979—; cons. in field. Author: The Political Economy of National Security, 1960, America at Century's End, 1989; co-author: Issues in Defense Economics, 1967. Frederick Sheldon prize fellow Harvard U., 1950-51. Mem. Phi Beta Kappa. Republican. Presbyterian. Office: Lehman Bros 800 Connecticut Ave NW Washington DC 20006-2709

SCHLESINGER, JOHN RICHARD, film, opera and theater director; b. London, Feb. 16, 1926; s. Bernard Edward and Winifred Henrietta (Regensburg) S. B.A., Balliol Coll., Oxford U., 1950. Dir. BBC TV, 1958-60. Dir. feature films including Terminus, 1961 (Golden Lion award Venice Film Festival, Brit. Acad. award), A Kind of Loving, 1962 (Golden Bear award Berlin Film Festival), Billy Liar, 1963, Darling, 1965 (N.Y. Critics award, Acad. nomination), Far From the Madding Crowd, 1966, Midnight Cowboy, 1968 (Acad. award best dir., best film, Brit. Acad. award best dir., best film), Sunday Bloody Sunday, 1970 (David di Donatello award, Brit. Acad. award best dir., best film), Day of the Locust, 1974, Marathon Man, 1976, Yanks, 1979 (Nat. Bd. Rev. award, New Std. award), Honky Tonk Freeway, 1980, Separate Tables, 1982, An Englishman Abroad, 1983 (Brit. Acad. award best single drama, Broadcasting Press Guild award best single drama, Barcelona Film Festival award best fiction film), The Falcon and the Snowman, 1983, The Believers, 1986, Madame Sousatzka, 1988, Pacific Heights, 1991, The Innocent, 1993, Eye for an Eye, 1995, Bafta Fellowship, 1996, TV films including An Englishman Abroad (BBC), 1983 (David Wark Griffith award for best TV film), A Question of Attribution (PBS), 1992 (Brit. Acad. award best single drama), Cold Comfort Farm (BBC), 1994, plays including Days in the Trees, 1966, I and Albert, 1972, Heartbreak House, 1974, Julius Caesar, 1977, True West, 1981, Les Contes d'Hoffmann, 1980-81 (Soc. West End Theatre award), Der Rosenkavalier, 1984-85, Un Ballo in Maschera, 1989; assoc. dir. Nat. Theatre, London, 1973—. Served with Royal Engrs., 1944-48. Recipient David di Donatello Spl. Dir. award, 1980, Shakespeare prize, 1981, The Hamptons Internat. Film Festival Disting. Achievement award, 1995. Address: 6 Cranley Mansion, 160 Gloucester Rd, London SW7 4QF, England

SCHLESINGER, JOSEPH ABRAHAM, political scientist; b. Boston, Jan. 4, 1922; s. Monroe Jacob and Millie (Romansky) S.; m. Mildred Saks, Sept. 9, 1951; children: Elizabeth Hannah, Jacob Monroe. Student, Hobart Coll., 1938-40; A.B., U. Chgo., 1942; A.M., Harvard U., 1947; Ph.D., Yale U., 1955. Instr. Boston U., 1947-49; teaching fellow Wesleyan U., Middletown, Conn., 1952-53; mem. faculty Mich. State U., East Lansing, 1953—; prof. polit. sci. Mich. State U., 1963—; vis. prof. U. Calif., Berkeley, 1964-65. Author: How They Became Governor, 1957, Ambition and Politics: Political Careers in the United States, 1966, Political Parties and the Winning of Office, 1991, also articles. Del. Ingham County (Mich.) Democratic Conv., 1966-68. Served with AUS, 1943-45. Cowles fellow, 1950-51; Block fellow, 1951-52; grantee Social Sci. Research Council, 1955-57, 68-69; recipient Distinguished Faculty award Mich. State U., 1976, Sr. Fulbright award for Rsch. Western Europe, 1990—. Mem. Am. Polit. Sci. Assn. (coun. 1981-83, 1st ann. award for outstanding pub. paper 1986, Samuel Eldersveld award for lifetime achievement 1993), Midwest Polit. Sci. Assn. (v.p. 1969-70), So. Polit. Sci. Assn., Mich. Conf. Polit. Scientists, Acad. Polit. Sci. Democrat. Jewish. Home: 930 Roxburgh Ave East Lansing MI 48823-3131 Office: Dept Polit Sci Mich State Univ East Lansing MI 48824

SCHLESINGER, MILTON JOSEPH, virology educator, researcher; b. Wheeling, W.Va., Nov. 26, 1927; s. Milton J. and Caroline (Oppenheimer) S.; m. Sondra Orenstein, Jan. 30, 1955. BS, Yale U., 1951; MS, U. Rochester, 1953; PhD, U. Mich., 1959. Rsch. assoc. U. Mich., Ann Arbor, 1953-56, 59-60; guest rsch. investigator Inst. Superiore di Sanita, Rome, 1960-61; rsch. assoc. MIT, Cambridge, 1961-64; asst. prof. virology Washington U. Sch. Medicine, St. Louis, 1964-67, assoc. prof., 1967-72, prof., 1972—; chmn. exec. coun. divsn. biol. and biomed. scis., 1992-94; vis. scientist Imperial Cancer Rsch. Fund, London, 1974-75; vis. scholar Harvard U., Cambridge, 1989-90, 95-96; mem. adv. panels Am. Heart Assn., Dallas, 1975-78, NSF, Washington, 1978-82; mem. sci. adv. bd. Friedrich Miescher Inst., Basel, Switzerland, 1988—, chmn., 1992—; nat. lectr. Sigma Xi, 1991-93. Editor: Heat Shock, 1982, Togaviridae of Flaviviridae, 1986, Lipid Modification of Proteins, 1992, (monographs) The Ubiquitin System, 1988, Stress Oriteins, 1990; mem. editl. bd. virology, 1975-92, Jour. Biol. Chemistry, 1982-87, Molecular and Cellular Biology, 1983-92. Bd. dirs. ACLU, St. Louis, 1966-72, Coalition for Environ., St. Louis, 1989-92. Mem. AAAS, Am. Biol. Chemistry and Molecular Biology, Am. Soc. Microbiology, Am. Soc. Virologists, Am. Chem. Soc., Protein Soc. Office: Dept Molecular Micro 8230 Washington U Med Sch 660 S Euclid Ave Saint Louis MO 63110-1010

SCHLESINGER, ROBERT WALTER, microbiologist, microbiology educator emeritus; b. Hamburg, Germany, Mar. 27, 1913; came to U.S., 1938, naturalized, 1943; s. Emil and Flora (Strelitz) S.; m. Adeline P. Sacks, Jan. 7, 1942; children: Robert, Ann. Student, U. Hamburg Med. Sch., 1931-34; M.D., U. Basel, Switzerland, 1937. Guest investigator Inst. Bacteriology and Hygiene, U. Basel, 1937-38; intern Beekman Hosp., N.Y.C., Stamford (Conn.) Hosp., 1938-40; fellow, asst. pathology and bacteriology Rockefeller Inst., N.Y.C., 1940-46; assoc. research prof. pathology, head virus research lab. U. Pitts. Sch. Medicine, 1946-47; assoc. mem., div. infectious diseases Pub. Health Research Inst., City of N.Y., Inc., 1947-55; prof., chmn. dept. microbiology St. Louis U. Sch. Medicine, 1955-63; prof. dept. microbiology U. Medicine and Dentistry N.J.-Robt. Wood Johnson Med. Sch., Piscataway, 1963-83, emeritus disting. prof., 1984—, chmn., 1963-80, also acting dean.; cons. Sec. War, 1946; mem., chmn. virology study sect. NIH; mem., chmn. microbiology and infectious disease adv. com. Nat. Inst. Allergy and Infectious Disease, NIH; mem. adv. com. Nat. Cancer Inst.; mem. cell biology and virology adv. com. Am. Cancer Soc. Editor: Virology; contbr. articles to sci. jours., chpts. to books. Served as capt. M.C. AUS, 1944-46. Recipient Humboldt award Fed. Republic Germany, 1981; Guggenheim fellow, 1972-73. Mem. Am. Acad. Microbiology, Am. Assn. Immunologists, Am. Soc. Microbiology, Am. Soc. Cancer Rsch., AAAS, Am. Soc. Virology, N.Y. Acad. Scis., Sigma Xi, Alpha Omega Alpha. Home and Office: 7 Langley Rd Falmouth MA 02540

SCHLESINGER, RUDOLF BERTHOLD, lawyer, educator; b. Munich, Germany, Oct. 11, 1909; s. Morris and Emma (Aufhauser) S.; m. Ruth Hirschland, Sept. 4, 1942; children: Steven, June, Fay. Dr. Jur., U. Munich, 1933; LLB, Columbia U., 1942; Dr. Jur. (hon.), U. Trento, 1994. Bar: N.Y. 1942, U.S. Supreme Ct. 1946. Law sec. to Chief Judge Irving Lehman, N.Y. Ct. Appeals, 1942-43; confidential law sec. Judges N.Y. Ct. Appeals, 1943-44; asso. Milbank, Tweed, Hope & Hadley, N.Y.C., 1944-48; asso. prof. Cornell U., 1948-51, prof., 1951-75, William N. Cromwell prof. internat. and comparative law, 1956-75; prof. Hastings Coll. Law, U. Calif., 1975—, vis. prof., 1974; Cons. N.Y. State Law Rev. Commn., 1949—; mem. adv. com. internat. rules of jud. procedure, 1959-66; vis. prof. Columbia, 1952, Salzburg Seminar, 1964; Charles Inglis Thomson disting. vis. prof. U. Colo., summer 1976. Author: Cases, Text and Materials on Comparative Law, 4th edit., 1980, (with Baade, Damaska and Herzog) 5th edit., 1988, (with Baade, Herzog and Wise) Supplement to 5th edit., 1994; Formation of Contracts: A Study of the Common Core of Legal Systems, 2 vols., 1968, others; editor-in-chief Columbia Law Rev., 1941-42; bd. editors Am. Jour. Comparative Law; author articles on legal topics. Trustee Cornell U., 1961-66. Carnegie Corp. Reflective year fellowship, 1962-63. Mem. Am. Law Inst. (life), Am. Bar Assn., Internat. Acad. Comparative Law, Phi Beta Kappa, Order of Coif. Home: 1333 Jones St San Francisco CA 94109-4112 Office: U Calif Hastings Coll of Law 200 Mcallister St San Francisco CA 94102-4978

SCHLESINGER, RUTH HIRSCHLAND, art curator, consultant; b. Essen, Germany, Mar. 11, 1920; came to U.S., 1936; d. Kurt M. and Henriette (Simons) Hirschland; m. Rudolf B. Schlesinger, Sept. 4, 1942; children: Steven, June, Fay. BA cum laude, Wheaton Coll., Norton, Mass., 1942; intern, Met. Mus. of Art, N.Y.C., 1941. Dir. Upstairs Gallery, Ithaca, N.Y., 1960-67; curatorial asst. Andrew D. White Mus. Cornell U., Ithaca, N.Y., 1967-70; curator of prints Herbert F. Johnson Mus. Cornell U., 1970-75; art curator Hastings Coll. of the Law U. Calif., San Francisco, 1978—. Author: (mus. catalog) 15th and 16th Century Prints of No. Europe from the Nat. Gallery of Art-Rosenwald Collection, 1973, other catalogs. Mem. UN World Centre founding com., 1979-84; mem. art adv. com. N.Y. State Fair, Syracuse, 1973; cons. Gallery Assn., State of N.Y., 1972-74. Recipient History of Art prizes Wheaton Coll., 1941, 42. Home: 1333 Jones St Apt 810 San Francisco CA 94109-4112 Office: U Calif Hastings Coll of Law 200 McAllister San Francisco CA 94102

SCHLESINGER, SANFORD JOEL, lawyer; b. N.Y.C., Feb. 8, 1943; s. Irving and Ruth (Rubin) S.; children: Merideth, Jarrod, Alexandra; m. Suzanne Beth Mangold, 1994; 1 stepchild, Mariel Mangold. BS in Govt. with hons., Columbia U., 1963; JD, Fordham U., 1966. Bar: N.Y. 1966, U.S. Dist. Ct. (so. and ea. dists.) N.Y. 1967, U.S. Ct. Appeals (2d cir.) 1968, U.S. Ct. Internat. Trade 1969, U.S. Tax Ct. 1993, U.S. Supreme Ct. 1978. Assoc. Frankenthaler & Kohn, N.Y.C., 1966-67; asst. atty. gen. trusts and estates bur. charitable found. div. State of N.Y., N.Y.C., 1967-69; ptnr. Rose & Schlesinger, N.Y.C., 1969-81, Goldshmidt, Oshatz, Powsner & Saft, N.Y.C., 1981-85; ptnr., head trusts and estates dept. Shea & Gould, N.Y.C., 1985-93; ptnr., head wills and estates dept. Kaye, Scholer, Fierman, Hays & Handler, N.Y.C., 1993—; adj. faculty Columbia U. Sch. Law, 1989-94; adj. prof. N.Y. Law Sch., 1978—; adj. prof. grad. program in estate planning U. Miami Sch. Law, 1995—; mem. estate planning adv. com. Practising Law Inst., 1990—; bd. advisors and contbrs. Jour. of S Corp. Taxation, 1989-96; lectr. in field; condr. workshops in field. Author: Estate Planning for the Elderly Client, 1984, Planning for the Elderly or Incapacitated Client, 1993; columnist, mem. editl. bd. Estate Planning mag., 1995—; contbr. articles to profl. jours. Mem. adv. bd. Inst. Fed. Taxation NYU, 1988-96, chmn., 1993-94; mem. legis adv. com. Scarsdale (N.Y.) Sch. Bd., 1981-83, mem. nominating com., 1979-82; pres. dist. 17 N.Y.C. Cmty. Sch. Bd., 1970-71; mem. fin. and estate planning adv. bd. Commerce Clearing House, 1988—. Fellow Am. Coll. Trust and Estate Counsel; mem. ABA (chmn. social security and other govt. entitlements com. 1990-91, chmn. probate and trust com.-estate planning, drafting charitable giving coms., 1992-94), Internat. Acad. Estate & Trust Law (Academician 1992—), Nat. Acad. Elder Law Attys., Bklyn. Bar Assn., Assn. of Bar of City of N.Y., Consular Law Soc., N.Y. State Bar Assn. (treas. trusts and estates sect. 1991-92, sec. trusts and estates sect. 1992-93, chmn. trusts and estates sect. 1994-95, chmn. exec. com. 1st jud. dist. 1987-91, jour. bd. editors 1995—). Avocations: baseball, writing. Office: Kaye Scholer Fierman Hays & Handler 425 Park Ave New York NY 10022-3506

SCHLESINGER, STEPHEN LYONS, horticulturist; b. N.Y.C., July 24, 1940; s. Nathan and Gertrude (Lyons) S.; m. Barbara Bernthal, Feb. 17, 1963; children—Adam Lyons, Lauren Elizabeth. B.A., Williams Coll., 1962; student, U. Paris, 1960-61; M.A. in French, Columbia U., 1964. Lectr. in French Hunter Coll., 1963-64; lectr. in French Columbia U., summers 1963-64; adminstrv. asst. John Simon Guggenheim Meml. Found., N.Y.C., 1965-67, asst. sec., 1967-70, assoc. sec., 1970-73, sec., 1973-88, spl. cons., 1988-89; ind. cons., 1989-90; assoc. dir., dir. maj. gifts The Corella and Bertram F. Bonner Found., Princeton, N.J., 1990-91; nurseryman Dubrow's Nurseries, Livingston, N.J., 1990-95; garden ctr. horticulturist, 1995—. Woodrow Wilson fellow, 1962-63. Home: 17 Prospect Ter Montclair NJ 07042-3204 Office: DuBrow's Nurseries 251 W Northfield Rd Livingston NJ 07039

SCHLESINGER, VIOLET MURRAY, biomedical consultant; b. Denver, June 14, 1929; d. Robert Robertson Ferguson and Virginia Lee (Murray) Corbin; m. Robert Alexander Schlesinger, June 14, 1953; children: Roberta Diane, William Alexander. BA, U. Colo., 1952; MA, Goddard Coll., 1967; mins. license, Bethesda Sch. Ministry, 1990; PhD, Columbia Pacific, 1993. Prof. Ecole Normale, Tours, France, 1952-53; tchr. Denver and L.A. Pub. Schs., 1953-56; exec. dir. Wilde Woode Children's Ctr., Palm Springs, Calif., 1980-87; trustee Anderson Children's Found., Palm Springs, 1987-90; pastor Candle Cross Chapel, Palm Springs, 1990-95; exec. dir. Prevention Pays, Palm Springs, 1990-95. Author: Spiritual, Mental and Physical, 1967, A Wholistic Approach to Wellness A Needed Answer to American Healthcare Crises, 1993. Pastor Candle Cross Chapel, 1990-94. Republican. Avocation: hiking. Home: 380 Pablo Dr Palm Springs CA 92262

SCHLESS, PHYLLIS ROSS, investment banker; d. Lewis H. and Doris G. Ross; m. Aaron Backer Schless, July 7, 1970; 1 son, Daniel Lewis Ross. Cert., N.Y. Playhouse Sch. of Theatre, 1962, N.Y. Sch. Interior Design, 1964; B.A. in Econs., Wellesley Coll., 1964; M.B.A., Stanford U., 1966. Assoc. internat. fin. Kuhn Loeb & Co., N.Y.C., 1966-70; fin. cons., 1971-73; sr. fin. analyst Trans World Airlines, N.Y.C., 1974-75; corp. fin., mergers and acquisitions Lazard Freres & Co., 1976-79; dir. mergers and acquisitions Am. Can Co., Greenwich, Conn., 1979-82; v.p. mergers and acquisitions Bear, Stearns & Co., N.Y.C., 1982-84; sr. v.p. corp. acquisitions Integrated Resources, 1984-85; chmn., chief exec. officer Ross Fin. Svcs. Group Inc., 1985—; supervisory dir. Merrill Lynch HYTS Funds, 1991—; bd. dirs. Calvery Hosp. Fund Bd., chair investment coun., 1995—; trustee A.E. Tinker Fund, 1993—; trustee Nat. Child Labor Com., 1981-95, chmn., 1992-94; trustee New World Found., 1986-92, chair fin. com., treas. 1988-92; bd. dirs. Stanford Bus. Sch. Club, N.Y., 1994—. Pres. Greater Bridgeport nat. Coun. Jewish Women, 1971-73, bd. dirs., 1974-75; bd. dirs. Girls Clubs Am., 1975-78, mem. exec. com., 1982-89, pres., 1984-86; bd. dirs. Pulaine Koner Dance Co., 1979-81, So. Conn. Child Guidance Clinic, 1981-83, New Canaan United Way, 1981-83, treas. Wellesley Class '64, 1984-89. Mem. Univ. Club. Home: 12 E 86th St New York NY 10028 Office: Ross Fin Svcs Group Inc 122 E 42nd St Ste 4005 New York NY 10168-4099

SCHLESSINGER, BERNARD S., retired university dean; b. Toronto, Ont., Can., Mar. 19, 1930; came to U.S., 1938, naturalized, 1948; s. Morris and Eleanor Schlessinger; m. June Hirsch, Dec. 21, 1952; chldren: Rashelle, Jill, Joel. B.S., Roosevelt U., 1950; M.S., Miami U., Oxford, Ohio, 1952; Ph.D., U. Wis., 1955; M.L.S., U. R.I., 1975. Research chemist Am. Can Co., Barrington, Ill, 1955-56; dept. head Chem. Abstracts, Columbus, Ohio, 1958-66; info. researcher Olin Corp., New Haven, 1966-68; asst. dir. Library Sch., So. Conn. State Coll., New Haven, 1968-74; prof. library sci. U. S.C., 1975-77; dean Library Sch. U. R.I., Kingston, 1977-82; prof. Sch. Libr. Sci. Tex. Woman's U., Denton, 1982-92; ret., 1992. Contbr. articles to profl. jours. Served with USAF, 1956-58. Named Outstanding Alumnus U. R.I. Grad. Library Sch., 1978. Mem. ALA, Tex. Library Assn., Sigma Xi, Phi Lambda Upsilon, Beta Phi Mu. Home: 15707 Hamilton St Omaha NE 68118-2339

SCHLESSINGER, JOSEPH, pharmacology educator. BSc in Chemistry/Physics magna cum laude, The Hebrew U., Jerusalem, 1968, MSC in Chemistry magna cum laude, 1969; PhD, The Weizmann Inst. Sci., Rehovot, Israel, 1974. Postdoctoral assoc. dept. chemistry Sch. Applied Physics, Cornell U., 1974-76; vis. scientist immunology br. Nat. Cancer Inst., NIH, Bethesda, Md., 1977-78; sr. scientist dept. chem. immunology The Weizmann Inst. Sci., Rehovot, 1978-80, assoc. prof. dept. chem. immunology, 1980-84, prof. dept. chem. immunology, Ruth & Leonard Simon prof., 1984-91; dir. div. molecular biology Biotech. Rsch. Ctr. Meloy Labs., Inc., Rockville, Md., 1985-86, dir. Biotech. Rsch. Ctr., 1986-88; rsch. dir. Rorer Biotech., Inc., King of Prussia, Pa., 1988-90; prof., chmn. dept. pharmcology NYU Med. Ctr., N.Y.C., 1990—. Mem. editorial bds. European Molecular Biology Orgn. Jour., Jour. Cell Biology, Cell Regulation, Cancer Rsch., Receptors, Growth Factors, Cell Crowth & Differentiation, Protein Engineering, Oncogenes and Growth Factor Abstracts; contbr. articles to profl. jours. Recipient Sara Leedy Prize, Weizmann Inst. Sci., 1980, Levinson Prize, 1984; Hestrin Prize, Biochem. Soc. Israel, 1983. Mem. European Molecular Biology Orgn. Office: NYU Med Ctr Dept Pharmacology 550 1st Ave New York NY 10016-6481*

SCHLEUNING, ALEXANDER J., II, otolaryngologist; b. Portland, Oreg., 1934. MD, U. Oreg., 1960. Intern Oreg. Hosps., Portland, 1960-61, resident in otolaryngology, 1961-65; mem. staff Oreg. Health Sci. U., Portland; prof. otolaryngology Oreg. Health Sci. U. Fellow AAOHNS; mem. AMA, ABO, AADO-HNS. Office: 3181 SW Sam Jackson Park Rd Portland OR 97201-3011

SCHLEUSENER, RICHARD AUGUST, college president; b. Oxford, Nebr., May 6, 1926; s. August William and Katherine Charlotte (Albrecht) S.; m. Elaine Emma Wilhelm, June 12, 1949; children: Kathryn Jeanne Schleusener Miller, Richard Dennis, Rand Lee, Debra Sue, Jeffrey Thomas. B.S., U. Nebr., 1949; M.S., Kans. State U., 1956; Ph.D., Colo. State U., 1958; postgrad., MIT, 1951-52; D.Sc. (hon.), U. Nebr., 1984. Research engr. Colo. State U., 1958-64, dir. Inst. Atmospheric Sci.; prof., head dept. meteorology S.D. Sch. Mines and Tech., Rapid City, 1965-74, v.p., dean engring., 1974-75, acting pres., 1975-76, pres., 1976-86; pres. Black Hills Regional Eye Inst. Found., 1987—; Cons. weather modification Interior Dept., 1964—, U.S. Forest Service, 1966—, UNESCO, 1971—, also pvt. firms. Contbr. articles to tech. jours. Served with USAF, 1950-55. Mem. Am. Meteorol. Soc., Am. Geophys. Union, Rotary, Sigma Xi, Beta Sigma Psi. Lutheran. Home: 315 S Berry Pine Rd Rapid City SD 57702-1923

SCHLEY, ARLENE DORIS, retired federal agency administrator; b. Aberdeen, S.D., May 17, 1937; d. Armund Theodore and Alvina Emily (erdman) S. BS, Northern State U., 1958; MBA, Rockhurst Coll., 1981. Tchr. music Sioux Falls Schs., 1958-59; edn. dir. S.D. Farmers Union, Huron, 1959-66; tng. officer, intern U.S. GSA, Kansas City, 1966-71; regional personnel officer U.S. GSA, Chgo., 1971-74; dir. personnel mgmt. staff U.S. GSA, Washington, 1974-77, regional controller, 1977-82, dep. regional adminstr. nat. capitol reg., 1982-83; deputy regional adminstr. U.S. GSA, Ft. Worth, 1987-95; dir. ctrl. adminstrv. ctr. Dept. of Commerce, Kansas City, 1983-87; ret., 1995. Combined fed. campaign chmn. Tarrant County Combined Fed. Campaign and United Way, Ft. Worth, 1989-91; chair fine arts commn. Rural Cultural Ctr.; bd. dirs. Aberdeen Area Arts Coun. Recipient Presdl. Meritorious Rank award, Washington, 1989; named Disting. Alumnus Northern State U., 1987. Mem. Am. Soc. Pub. Adminstrs. (nat. coun. 1990-93, chpt. pres. 1990-91, mem. exec. com. sect. for women 1992-95, Pub. Adminstr. of Yr. 1993), Fed. Exec. Inst. Alumni Assn., Federally Employed Women. Lutheran. Avocations: piano, singing, opera, symphony. Home: 510 22nd Ave NE Aberdeen SD 57401

SCHLEY, REEVE, III, artist; b. N.Y.C., Mar. 11, 1936; s. Reeve and Elizabeth (Boies) S.; m. Georgia Terry, Oct. 5, 1968; children: Marie B., Reeve T. B.A., Yale U., 1959; M.F.A., U. Pa., 1962; studied with, Josef Buchty, Munich, 1954-55. Instr. watercolor NAD, N.Y.C., 1981—. Exhibited in group shows including Spook Farm Gallery, Farm Hills, N.J., 1958, Hunterdon County Art Ctr. Ann., 1959, Pa. Acad., 1966, N.J. State Mus., Trenton, 1967, Tenn. Fine Arts Ctr., Nashville, 1973, Okla. Art Ctr., Oklahoma City, 1974, Butler Inst. Am. Art, Youngstown, Ohio, 1974, Drew U., 1975, Silvermine Guild Artists, 1975, NAD, 1977-78, Bklyn. Mus., 1984; one-man shows Vendo Nubes Gallery, Chestnut Hill, Pa., 1967, 71, Phila. Art Alliance, 1969, Spook Farm Gallery, 1970, Saratoga (N.Y.) Gallery, 1972-75, Graham Gallery, N.Y., 1973-94, N.J. State Mus., 1978, Hull Gallery, Washington, 1978, 80, Byck Gallery, Louisville, 1979, Peale House Gallery, Pa. Acad. Fine Arts, 1980, Gallerie Arnoldi-Livie, Munich, 1985, New Orleans Acad. Fine Arts, 1985; represented in permanent collections N.J. State Mus., Trenton, NAD, Newark Mus., Bklyn. Mus., Yale U. Art Gallery, Heublein Collection, Somerset County Coll., Tenneco Chems. Recipient Ranger Fund purchase prize NAD, 1981, 85, cert. of merit, 1978, 95; Best in Show award Hunterdon County Art Ctr., 1974, Laura M. Gross Meml. award Silvermine Guild Artists, 1975, purchase prize Somerset County Coll. Tri-State Exhbn., 1975, 2d prize for watercolor Sumerset Art Assn., 1975; Cresson travel scholar Pa. Acad. Fine Arts, 1962; fellow N.J. Coun. Arts, 1979.

SCHLEY, WAYNE A., political consultant; b. Hamilton, Mont., May 22, 1940. AA, Shasta Coll., 1960; BS, Sacramento State U., 1963; MS, Am. U., 1974; postgrad., U. Alaska, 1970, Harvard U. Cert. high sch. teaching (lifetime) Calif. Dept. Edn. Tchr., admin. Placer High Sch., Auburn, Calif., 1963-70; spl. asst. to Sen. Ted Stevens, Washington, 1971-77; staff dir. minority and majority subcom. civil svc. Post Office and Gen. Svcs., Washington, 1977-86; minroity staff dir. Senate Com. on Rules and Adminstrn., Washington, 1987-92; commr. U.S. Postal Rate Commn., Washington, 1992-95; cons. on legis. and postal issues Washington, 1995—. Chmn. Calif. Teenage Reps., 1963-64; regional v.p. Calif. Young Reps., 1964-66, state sgt. at arms, 1966-67; mem. Placer County Rep. Ctrl. Com., 1965-70. Recipient Cert. Achievement JFK Sch. Govt. Harvard U., 1982. Home and Office: 614 Massachusetts Ave NE Washington DC 20002-6006

SCHLEY, WILLIAM SHAIN, otorhinolaryngologist; b. Columbus, Ga., Sept. 21, 1940; s. Frances Brooking Schley and Susie (Smith) Mathews. BA, Emory U., 1962, MD, 1966. Intern mixed surg. The Roosevelt Hosp., N.Y.C., 1966-67, resident in surgery, 1967-68; resident in otorhinolaryngology N.Y. Hosp.-Cornell Med. Ctr., N.Y.C., 1970-73; clin. instr. otorhinolaryngology Cornell U. Med. Coll., 1972-75, clin. asst. prof., 1975-81, assoc. prof., 1982—, acting chmn. dept. otorhinolaryngology, 1988-94, chmn. dept. otorhinolarygology, 1994—; Otorhinolaryngologist to putpatients with pvt. patient privileges N.Y. Hosp., 1973-75, asst. attending otorhinolaryngologist with pvt. patient privileges, 1975-81, assoc. attending, 1992—, acting otorhinolaryngologist-in-chief, 1988-94, otorhinolaryngologist-in-chief, 1994—; assoc. asst. surgeon otolaryngology Manhattan Eye, Ear, Nose and Throat Hosp., 1988—; sec. med. bd. N.Y. Hosp., 1994—; mem. co-chmn. vis. day com. The N.Y. Hosp.-Cornell Med. Ctr., 1996—. Author: (with others) Pulmonary Diseases of the Fetus Newborn and Child, 1978; contbr. numerous articles to profl. pubs. Vestry St. James Ch., N.Y.C., 1994—; mem. ad hoc bd. visitors Emory U., 1994-95. Lt. comdr. USNR. Recipient Eagle Scout Boy Scouts Am., 1954. Fellow ACS (Manhattan dist. #2 com. on applicants 1991—); mem. Am. Acad. Otolaryngology-Head and Neck Surgery, Med. Soc. State of N.Y., N.Y. State Soc. Otolaryngology-Head and Neck Surgery (exec. coun. 1974-80, dist. dir. 1980), County Med. Soc. N.Y., N.Y. Laryngol. Soc. (sec.-treas. 1981-84, v.p. 1984-85, pres. 1985-86), N.Y. Bronchoscopic Soc. (v.p. 1986-94, pres. 1994—), Assn. Emory Alumni (bd. govs. 1990—, pres.-elect 1993-94, pres. 1994-95), Omicron Delta Kappa. Episcopalian. Avocations: astronomy, ornithology. Home: 320 E 72nd St New York NY 10021-4769 Office: NY Hosp Starr 541 525 E 68th St New York NY 10021-4873

SCHLICHTEMEIER-NUTZMAN, SUE EVELYN, training consultant; b. Omaha, May 30, 1950; d. StuarTaylor and LaVera YVaughn (Conn) S.; m. Ronald E. Sorensen, Dec. 2, 1972 (div. Aug., 1984); m. Wade Edwin Nutzman, Aug. 27, 1988. BA in Journalism, U. Nebr., 1972, MA in Tng. and Devel., 1988, postgrad., 1989—. Advt. mgr. Burton Harpsichord Co., Lincoln, 1970-71; editorial asst. Nebr. Natural Resources Commn., Lincoln, 1971-72; editor Nebr. Personnel Dept., Lincoln, 1972-73; public info. specialist Governor's Budget Office, Lincoln, 1973-74; mental health cons. Mentl Health Ctr., Lincoln, 1974-81; tng. cons., keynote speaker Lincoln, 1977—; adj. advt. instr. U. Nebr., Lincoln, 1977-81, diversity instr., 1992—, orgn. cons., 1990—, dir. math camp, 1993—, team bldg. tnr. 1993—, motivational spkr. Author: Seeds of Change, 1985, Assertiveness Training, 1990, Help in the Aftermath, 1995; contbr. feature articles and reviews to newspapers and other pubs. Organist, youth music dir., trustee, historian, Nehawka (Nebr.) United Meth. Ch., 1985-93; dir. Community Youth Music Program, Nehawka, 1988-93; sec. Conestoga Found Bd., Murray, Nebr. 1988-92; treas. Conestoga Bd. Edn., Murray, 1988-92; project leader 4-H, 1993—; dir. Math Camp, 1993—; mem. steering com. Conestoga, 1994—; mem. Eastern Nebr. Regional Math Sci. Coalition, 1995—; many other civic and charitable roles as vol. Recipient fellowship U. Nebr., Lincoln, 1991-92. Mem. ASTD, Bus. and Profl. Women (keynote spkr. 1991-92), , Lincoln Music Tchrs. Assn., Missouri Valley Adult Edn. Assn., Adult and Continuing Edn. Assn. Nebr., Internat. Platform Speakers Assn., Am. Bus. Women's Assn. (keynote speaker 1993), U. Nebr. Alumni Assn. (life). Democrat. Avocations: flower gardening, piano, art, reading, writing. Home and Office: Tng Cons 3412 Mount Pleasant Dr Nehawka NE 68413-2424

SCHLICHTING, NANCY MARGARET, hospital administrator; b. N.Y.C., Nov. 21, 1954. B, Duke U., 1976; M, Cornell U., 1979. Adminstrv. resident Meml. Hosp. Cancer, N.Y.C., 1978; fellow Blue Cross-Blue Shield Assn., Chgo., 1979-80; asst. dirs. ops. Akron (Ohio) City Hosp., 1980-81, assoc. dir. planning, 1981-83, exec. v.p., 1983-88; exec. v.p. Riverside Meth. Hosps., Columbus, Ohio, 1988-92, pres., COO, 1992-93; pres., CEO, 1993-95; pres. Catholic Health Initiatives, eastern region, 1995—. Home: 887 Neil Ave Columbus OH 43215-1334 Office: Catholic Health Initiatives 1 McIntire Dr Chester PA 19014-1196*

SCHLICKAU, GEORGE HANS, cattle breeder, professional association executive; b. Haven, Kans., Nov. 2, 1922; s. Albert Rudulph and Florence Elsabe (Wittorff) S.; m. Lois Marie Ritthaler, Apr. 26, 1955; children: Bruce Alan, Susan Marie, James Darwin, Nancy Ann. Grad. high sch. Breeder registered Schlickau Hereford cattle, Haven, 1943—; pres. Reno County (Kans.) Hereford Assn., 1947-56, treas., 1956-58; dir. Reno County Cattleman's Assn., 1970-74, sec., 1970-71, treas., 1974; dir. Kans. Hereford Assn., 1955-71, 84-90, v.p., 1959, pres., 1960, 61; mem. organizing bd. Kans. Bull Test Sta., county committeeman Kans. Livestock Assn., 1960-75, bd. dirs., 1976-80, v.p. purebred coun., 1990-91, pres. purebred coun., 1992-93; bd. dirs. Am. Hereford Assn., 1969-75, v.p., 1973-74, pres., 1974-75; bd. dirs. Am. Nat. Cattleman's Assn., 1974-76; mem. fgn. trade com. Nat. Cattlemsn's Assn., 1990-93. Contbr. articles in field to profl. jours.; exhibitor, also winner numerous awards at major cattle shows across country; guest speaker, judge at numerous Hereford cattle events across country. Host ann. judging sch. and contest for Future Farmers Am. and 4-H youth, 1940-84; dir. Kans. Nat. Jr. Livestock Show, 1973—, sec., 1982-83, chmn., 1984-85, bd. govs., 1988—; bd. dirs. Haven State Bank, 1962—, Equus Beds Groundwater Mgmt. Dist. 2, 1975-79, Beef leader Haven 4-H Club, 1947-67; mem. Haven H.S. Bd., 1962-65, clk., 1964-65; mem. agrl. adv. com. Hutchinson (Kans.) Cmty. Jr. Coll., Kans., 1974-82; adv. Am. Jr. Hereford Assn., 1977-82; pres. Parent-Tchr. League Luth. Sch., 1979-80, 83-84; mem. zoning bd. City of Haven, 1985-88; bd. dirs. Ark Valley Electric Coop Assn., 1984-96, v.p., 1986-90, pres. 1990-93, Dist. IV Kans. Electric Coop., 1986-96, chmmn., 1992; bd. dirs. Kans. Coop. Coun., 1994-96; vice chmn. KACRE, 1992, chmn. 1993; adv. coun. mem. Arthur Capper Coop. Ctr., 1994-96. Recipient Am. Farmer Degree award Future Farmers Am., 1942, Reno County Outstanding Young Farmer award Hutchinson Jaycees, 1959, Kans. Hereford Herdsman of the Year award High Plains Jour., 1960, Soil Conservation award Kans. Bankers Assn., 1968, Hon. State Farmer Degree award Future Farmers Am., 1972, Kans. Hereford Breeder of Yr., 1976, Portrait Gallery Outstanding Livestock Breeder award Kans. State U. Block and Bridle Club, 1978, Reno County 4-H Family of Yr. award, 1987, Reno County Farm Focus Family award Hutchinson C. of C., 1989, Stockman of Yr. award Kansas Livestock and Meat Industry Coun., 1994; named Kans. Seedstock Producer of Yr. BIF, 1988; Kans Jr. Livestock Show dedicatory, 1991, Master Farmer, Master Farm Homemaker, 1991. Mem. Kans. Wheat Growers Assn., Kans. Farm Bur., Haven Industries, Inc., Kansas City (Kans.) Hereford Club, Kans. State U. Block and Bridle Club (hon. mem.), Haven Booster Club (sec. 1952-53, pres. 1954-56), Future Farmers Am. (mem. adv. com. Haven chpt. 1971—). Lutheran (mem. sch. bd. 1967-70, chmn. 1969-70; chmn. ch. bd. 8 yrs., chmn. congregation 1984-88, elder 1977-79). Home: 11701 E K96 Hwy Haven KS 67543

SCHLICKE, CARL PAUL, retired surgeon; b. Bklyn., Mar. 16, 1910; s. Carl Paul and Eunice Gertrude (Hope) S.; m. Hilda Meek Hinckley, Aug. 30, 1937; children: Paul Van Waters, Suzanne Parker. AB, UCLA, 1931; MD, Johns Hopkins Med. Sch., 1935; MS in Surgery, U. Minn., 1940. Diplomate Am. Bd. Surgery. Intern John Hopkins Hosp., Balt., 1935; asst. resident in surgery L.I. (N.Y.) Coll. Hosp., 1936-37; chmn. surg. dept. Sacred Heart Med. Ctr., Rochester, Minn., 1958-75; surgeon Rockwood Clinic, 1946-79, sr. surgeon, 1951-75; clin. assoc. prof. surgery U. Wash., Seattle, 1969-75, clin. prof., 1975-82; retired Rockwood Clinic, 1979; clin. prof. emeritus U. Wash., Seattle, 1982—; staff St. Lukes Hosp., 1946-51, Sacred Heart Hosp., 1950-79; cons Spokane (Wash.) Vets. Hosp., Fairchild AFB Hosp. Author: Working Together: A History of a Medical Group Practice, 1980, General George Wright, Guardian of the Pacific Coast, 1988, Spokane and Inland Empire Blood Bank, 1990; contbr. over 70 articles to profl. jours., 16 articles to hist. jours. Fellow ACS (gov., regent, 1st v.p.), mem. AMA, Spokane County Med. Soc., Washington State Med. Assn. (pres. 1965-66), Am. Surg. Assn. (2d v.p. 1976), Spokane Surg. Soc. (pres. 1960), North Pacific Surg. Assn. (pres. 1964), Western Surg. Assn. (pres. 1972), Pacific Coast Surg. Assn. (pres. 1972), Pacific Coast Surg. Assn. (pres. 1976-77), Internat. Soc. Surgery, Soc. Surgery Alimentary Tract, Surgeon's Travel Club, Mayo Clinic Alumni Assn. (pres. 1968), Barber Surgeons Pacific NW, Alpha Omega Alpha, Sigma Pi. Republican. Avocations: swimming, canoeing, listening to jazz music. Home: E 826 Overbluff Rd Spokane WA 99203

SCHLICKEISEN, RODGER OSCAR, non-profit environmental organization executive; b. Houston, Jan. 24, 1941; s. Oscar and Elvene Alice (Rennemo) S.; m. Susan Jane Culver, May 23, 1970; 1 child, Derek. BA, U. Wash., 1963; MBA, Harvard U., 1965; DBA, George Washington U., 1978. Loan officer Export-Import Bank of U.S., Washington, 1968-70; pres. Gryphon, Inc., Washington, 1970-74; group dir. com. on budget U.S. Senate, Washington, 1974-79; assoc. dir. econs. and govt. U.S. Office of Mgmt. and Budget, Washington, 1979-80; v.p. Craver, Mathews, Smith & Co., Falls Church, Va., 1980-81, CEO, 1981-87; chief of staff Office of U.S. Senator Max Baucus, Washington, 1987-91; pres., CEO Defenders of Wildlife, Washington, 1991—; bd. dirs. Island Resources Found., St. Thomas, V.I., Ctr. for Policy Alternatives, Washington; bd. advisors Environ. Comms. Orgn., L.A., 1992—, Environ. Media Assn., L.A., 1992—. Contbr. articles to profl. pubs. Va. state chmn. Common Cause, 1971-74. Mem. Soc. for Conservation Biology. Office: Defenders of Wildlife 1101 14th St NW Washington DC 20005-5601*

SCHLICKMAN, J. ANDREW, lawyer; b. Washington, Mar. 28, 1952. AB, Georgetown U., 1974; JD, U. Chgo., 1978. Bar: Ill. 1978, U.S. Supreme Ct. 1987. Ptnr. Sidley & Austin, Chgo. Coord. author: International Environmental Law and Regulation, 1991, 2d edit., 1994. Mem. ABA, Ill State Bar Assn.. Chgo. Bar Assn., Internat. Bar Assn. Office: Sidley & Austin 1 First Nat Plz Chicago IL 60603

SCHLIEBS, CHARLES ALLAN, lawyer; b. Kansas City, Mo., Dec. 3, 1950; s. Edgar Emil and Elsie Elizabeth (Rosher) S.; m. Melanie Emily Schuldis, Nov. 15, 1981. BA, BS in Econ., U. Pa., 1972; JD, Vanderbilt U., 1975. Bar: Mo. 1975, U.S. Supreme Ct. 1979, Pa. 1984. Assoc. Blackwell Sanders Matheny Weary & Lombardi, Kansas City, 1975-79, ptnr., 1980-82, various corp. positons, 1982-88; ptnr. Jones, Day, Reavis & Pogue, Pitts., 1988-89, adminstv. ptnr., 1989—; mem. adv. bd. U. Pitts. Sch. Law Ctr. Internat. Legal Edn., 1995—, mem. internat. adv. bd. U. Pitts. Grad. Sch. Pub. and Internat. Affairs, 1990—, Duquesne U., Palumbo Sch. Bus. Adminstrn., Pitts., 1990—. Mem. ABA, Internat. Bar Assn., Pa. Bar Assn., Duquesne Club. Home: 10 Myrtle Hill Rd Sewickley PA 15143-8700 Office: Jones Day Reavis & Pogue 1 Mellon Bank Ctr Pittsburgh PA 15258-0001

SCHLIEVE, HY C. J., principal; b. Mandan, N.D., Apr. 4, 1952; s. Calvin L. and Loretta L. (Johnson) S.; m. Terri Ann Hansen, Dec. 30, 1977; children: Derek, Aaron, Jessica. BA, N.D. State U., 1974, MS, 1984; EdD, Calif. Coast U., 1994. Tchr., coach Halliday (N.D.) Pub. Sch., 1974-75, Drake (N.D.) Pub. Sch., 1975-76, Montpelier (N.D.) Pub. Sch., 1976-81; prin. Unity Pub. Sch., Petersburg, N.D., 1981-83, Page (N.D.) Pub. Sch., 1983-85; supt. Wolford (N.D.) Pub. Sch., 1985-87, Garrison (N.D.) Pub. Schs., 1987-93; prin. Buhl Joint Sch. Dist. 412, Idaho, 1993-95, Oconto Falls Area Sch. Dist., Wis., 1995—; com. mem. NDASA Rsch. and Evaluation, Garrison, 1988-93; fiscal agt. Mo. Hills Consortium, McLean County, N.D., 1989-93; cons. asbestos Garrison Pub. Sch. Dist., 1987-93. Sec. Govtl. Affairs Com., Garrison, 1987-93; mem. Tourism Com., Garrison, 1988-92, Econ. Devel. Com., 1988-89. Recipient Nat. Superintendent of the Yr. awd., North Dakota, Am. Assn. of School Administrators, 1992. Mem. Nat. Assn. Secondary Sch. Prins. (prin. assessor tng. 1990), NSBA Fed. Policy Coords. Network. Avocations: golf, hunting, fishing, bowling, outdoor activities. Home: 175 N Farm Rd Oconto Falls WI 54154 Office: Oconto Falls High Sch 408 Cedar Oconto Falls WI 54154

SCHLINGER, WARREN GLEASON, retired chemical engineer; b. Los Angeles, May 29, 1923; s. William McKinley and Esther (Gleason) S.; m. Katharine S. Stewart, June 29, 1947; children: Michael S., Norman W., Sarah Lynne. BS, Calif. Inst. Tech., 1944, MS, 1946, PhD, 1949. Registered profl. engr., Calif. Instr. Calif. Inst. Tech., Pasadena, 1949-53; chem. engr. Texaco Inc., Montebello, Calif., 1953-61, supr. research, 1961-69, mgr., 1969-81, assoc. dir., 1981-87, ret. 1987; cons. 1987—. Contbr. numerous articles to profl. publs. Patentee in field. Fellow Am. Inst. Chem. Engrs. (Chem. Engring. Practice award 1981, So. Calif. sect. Tech. Achievement award 1976; Electric Power Research Inst. Achievement award 1985); mem. NAE, Am. Chem. Soc., Sigma Xi, Tau Beta Pi. Clubs: Jonathan (Los Angeles); Calif. Country (Whittier). Home: 3835 Shadow Grove Rd Pasadena CA 91107-2241

SCHLITT, WILLIAM JOSEPH, III, metallurgical engineer; b. Columbus, Ohio, June 12, 1942; s. William Joseph Jr. and Florence (McCall) S.; m. Anne Marie Ritchie, Apr. 1, 1994. BS in Metall. Engring., Carnegie Inst. Tech., 1964; PhD in Metallurgy, Pa. State U., 1968. Registered profl. engr., Tex. Scientist Kennecott Minerals Co., Salt Lake City, 1968-75, sr. scientist, 1975-76, mgr. hydrometallurgy dept., 1977-81, prin. program mgr., 1981-82; process staff mgr. Brown & Root, Inc., Houston, 1982-83, mgr. tech., 1983-93, product line mgr. chems., 1993-94; mgr. process tech. Davy Internat., San Ramon, Calif., 1994—; mem. oversight com. soln. mining NSF, Socoro, N.Mex., 1977-79; mem. oversight com. smelter flue dust Environ. Prot. Agy., Butte, Mont., 1978-79; mem. internat. adv. bd. In Situ jour., N.Y.C., 1988—. Editor: In Situ Uranium Leaching and Ground Water Restoration, 1979, Leaching and Recovering Copper from As-Mined Materials, 1980 (Publ. Bd. Commendation 1981), Gold and Silver--Leaching, Recovery and Economics, 1981, Interfacing Technologies in Solution Mining, 1982 (Publ. Bd. Commendation 1983), Salts and Brines '85, 1985; assoc. editor: (handbook) SME Mining Engineering Handbook, 1992; contbr. more than 30 tech. articles to profl. jours., trade publs., and proc. volumes including Metall. Transactions B, AIME Transactions, In Situ, Minerals and Metall. Processing. Pres. Ft. Bend County Kennel Club, Richmond, Tex., 1988-90. Trainee NSF, 1984-88. Mem. Soc. Mining Engrs. (bd. dirs. 1984-95, chmn. mining and exploration divsn. 1986-87), The Metall. Soc. (bd. dirs. 1982-83), Can. Inst. Mining and Metallurgy, Sigma Xi, Tau Beta Pi, Phi Kappa Phi. Achievements include patents in field. Avocation: licensed dog show judge. Office: Davy Internat 2440 Camino Ramon #100 San Ramon CA 94583

SCHLITTER, STANLEY ALLEN, lawyer; b. Decorah, Iowa, Jan. 27, 1950; s. Joseph Everett and Lillian Helena (Helgerson) S.; m. Sheila Lynn Edwards, Sept. 24, 1977; children: Stephanie Anne, Joseph Allen, John Edward. BS, Iowa State U., 1972; JD, U. Iowa, 1977. Bar: Ill. 1977, U.S. Dist. Ct. (no. dist.) Ill. 1977, U.S. Ct. Appeals (7th cir.) 1981, U.S. Ct. Appeals (Fed. cir.) 1982, D.C. 1989. Assoc. Kirkland & Ellis, Chgo., 1977-84, ptnr., 1984-88; ptnr. Kirkland & Ellis, Washington, 1988-91, Jenner & Block, Chgo., 1991—. Mem. ABA, IEEE, Am. Intellectual Property Law Assn. Office: Jenner & Block One IBM Plaza Chicago IL 60611-3608

SCHLOEGEL, GEORGE ANTHONY, banker; b. Gulfport, Miss., June 17, 1940; s. Joseph A. and Nancy (Bertucci) S.; m. Peggy Jay Harry, Mar. 14, 1959; children: Matthew, Melissa, Mark, Michael. B.S., La. State U., 1962; grad. various bank mgmt. courses. With Hancock Bank, Gulfport, 1956-59, 62—; pres. Hancock Bank, 1990—; with Whitney Nat. Bank, New Orleans, 1960-62; bd. dirs. BIPEC of Miss., Miss. Power Co., Inc. Pres. Gulfport Mcpl. Separate Sch. Dist., 1971-80, St. James Roman Cath. Ch. Parish Coun., Gulfport, 1972-74, Miss. Gulf Coast Jr. Coll. Found., 1978-85; mem. adv. bd. Gulfport Salvation Army, 1963-76; commr. Boy Scouts Am., 1970-74; chmn. Miss USA Pageant, 1979-81; mem. Miss. Bd. Econ. Devel., 1980-85; pres. Grad. Sch. Banking, South La. State U., 1990-92. With USNG, 1954-62. Recipient Pine Burr Dist. Scouting award, 1974. Mem. Am. Bankers Assn., Am. Inst. Banking, Bank Mktg. Assn., Miss. Bankers Assn. (v.p.), U.S. Jaycees (v.p. 1969-70, Clayton Frost Meml. award 1969), Miss. Jaycees (pres. 1968-69, Outstanding Young Man award 1965), Gulfport Jaycees (pres. 1965, Disting. Svc. award 1965), Miss. Gulf Coast C. of C. (pres. 1994), Gulfport Yacht Club (commodore 1982-83). Office: Hancock Bank 1 Hancock Plz Gulfport MS 39501-1948

SCHLOEMANN, ERNST FRITZ (RUDOLF AUGUST), physicist, engineer; b. Borgholzhausen, Germany, Dec. 13, 1926; came to U.S., 1954, naturalized, 1965; s. Hermann Wilhelm and Auguste Wilhelmine (Koch) S.; m. Gisela Mattiat, June 19, 1955 (dec. 1990); children: Susan C., Sonia G., Barbara I.; m. Sally (Duren) Heatter, Nov. 5, 1994. BS, U. Göttingen, Fed. Republic of Germany, 1951, MS, 1953, PhD, 1954. With rsch. div. Raytheon Co., Lexington, Mass., 1955-94, electronics sys. divsn., 1994-95; ind. cons. Weston, Mass., 1995—; cons. scientist, 1964-95; vis. assoc. prof. Stanford U., 1961-62; vis. prof. U. Hamburg, Germany, 1966. Assoc. editor: Jour. Applied Physics, 1974-76; contbr. numerous articles to profl. jours. Recipient T.L. Phillips award for Excellence in Tech., 1990. Fellow IEEE, Am. Phys. Soc., Sigma Xi. Democrat. Unitarian. Achievements include patents in field of magnetic materials and their application to microwave technology. Home & Office: 38 Brook Rd Weston MA 02193-1797

SCHLOERB, PAUL RICHARD, surgeon, educator; b. Buffalo, Oct. 22, 1919; s. Herman George and Vera (Gross) S.; m. Louise M. Grimmer, Feb. 25, 1950; children: Ronald G., Patricia Johnson, Marilyn A. Hock, Dorothy E. Schloerb Hoban, Paul Richard. A.B., Harvard U., 1941; M.D., U. Rochester, 1944. Intern U. Rochester Med. Sch., 1944-45, asst. resident, 1947-48, instr. surgery, 1952; research fellow, resident Peter Bent Brigham Hosp., Boston, 1948-52; mem. faculty U. Kans. Med. Ctr., Kansas City, 1952-79, prof. surgery, 1964-79, 88—, dean for research, 1972-79, dir. nutritional support svc., 1993—; prof. surgery U. Rochester (N.Y.) Med Ctr., 1979-88, adj. prof. surgery, 1988-90; surgeon Strong Meml. Hosp., 1979-88, dir. Surg. ICU, 1979-85, dir. surg. nutritional support service. Contbr. over 100 articles to profl. jours. Served to lt. (j.g.), M.C. USNR, 1944-45; to lt. 1953-55. Mem. AMA, ACS, AAAS, Am. Surg. Assn., Soc. U. Surgeons, Am. Physiol. Soc., Internat. Soc. Surgery, Ctrl. Surg. Assn., Am. Assn. for Surgery of Trauma, Am. Assn. Cancer Rsch., Biomed. Engring. Soc., Am. Inst. Nurition, Am. Soc. Clin. Nutrition, Sigma Xi. Office: Dept Surgery U Kansas Med Ctr Kansas City KS 66160

SCHLOM, JEFFREY BERT, research scientist; b. N.Y.C., June 22, 1942; s. David and Anna (Klein) S.; children: Amy Melissa, Steven Michael. BS (Pres.'s scholar), Ohio State U., 1964; MS, Adelphi U., 1966; Ph.D., Rutgers U., 1969. Instr. Columbia Coll. Phys. and Surg., 1969-71, asst. prof., 1971-73; chmn. breast cancer virus segment Nat Cancer Inst., NIH, Bethesda, Md., 1973-76; chief lab. tumor immunology and biology Nat Cancer Inst., NIH, 1983—, head exptl. oncology sect., 1976-83; prof. George Washington U., Washington, 1975—; disting. lectr. Can. Cancer Soc., 1985. Mem. numerous editorial bds.; contbr. numerous articles to profl. jours. Recipient Dir.'s award NIH, 1977, 89. Mem. Am. Assn. Cancer Rsch. (Rosenthal award 1985), Am. Soc. Cytology (Basic Rsch. award 1987). Office: Insts of Health Bldg 10 Rm 8B07 Bethesda MD 20892

SCHLOSS, HOWARD M., federal agency administrator; b. New Orleans, Jan. 30, 1960; m. Debbi Schloss; 1 child, Michael Austin. BFA in Journalism, So. Meth. U., 1982. Copy editor Fort Worth Star-Telegram; writer, editor United Press Internat., Dallas, 1982; asst. to the op-ed page editor Fort Worth Star-Telegram, 1983-87; dep. commn. dir., comm. dir. Dem. Congl. Campaign Com., 1987-91; with Treasury Dept., 1993—, dep. asst. sec. for pub. affairs, 1994—; asst. sec. of the treasury for pub. affairs, 1995—. office: Dept of Treasury Public Affairs 1500 Pennsylvania Ave NW Washington DC 20220*

SCHLOSS, MARTIN, educational administrator; b. Bklyn., May 18, 1947; s. Albert and Marian Lois (Finkelstein) S.; m. Caroline B. Adler, Mar. 8, 1970; children: Zev, Shani, Naomi. BA in Sociology, Yeshiva U., 1969, ABD in Adminstrn. and Supervision, 1990; MS in Spl. Edn., Bklyn. Coll., 1975. Ordained rabbi, Yeshiva Chaim Avraham, 1971; cert. tchr., N.Y. Coord. religious edn. Maimonides Inst., Queens, N.Y., 1969-77, coord. religious activities, 1975-77, tchr. spl. edn., 1977-78; tchr. spl. edn. P.S. 205 M., Bklyn., 1978-79; instr. Stern Coll., Yeshiva U., N.Y.C., 1980; dir. spl. edn. ctr. Bd. Jewish Edn., N.Y.C., 1980—, dir. divsn. sch. svcs., 1992—; adj. undergrad. instr. Coll. of S.I., N.Y.C., 1982, grad. instr., 1992; co-founder Consortium of Spl. Edn., N.Y.C. and Washington, 1986—; co-chair Task Force on Spl. Edn., N.Y.; chair subcom. Task Force-Handicapped, N.Y.; supr. Vols. in Spl. Edn., 1989—; supr. BJE/Scheuer Family Found. Resource Rm. Program, 1987—, Three R's Program, 1981—, Vocat. Prep. Program, 1983—, Jewish Heritage Program, 1980—, Substance Abuse Prevention Program, 1985—; numerous presentations in field. Exec. editor jour. The Jewish Special Educator, 1992; contbr. articles to profl. publs.; author curriculum in field; co-editor Learning Disabilities - A Handbook for Jewish Educators, 1985, Resource Room Programming - A Handbook for Educators in Jewish Schools, 1988; contbr. articles to profl. publs.; editor Purim Kit. Mem. adv. com. N.Y. State Edn. Dept., Albany, 1988, mem. nonpub. sch. office, 1986; mem. nat. leadership commn. U.S. Dept. Edn., Washington, 1988. Recipient award of distinction Worcester (Mass.) Jewish Cmty., 1973, Ednl. Leadership award OTSAR, 1982, Sam and Rose Hurrowitz award Fedn. of Jewish Philanthropies, 1983. Mem. Coun. for Exceptional Children, Inst. for Spl. Edn. Enrichment (founder, coord. 1989—), Assn. Jewish Spl. Educators (founder, mem. editl. bd. spl. edit. 1988-92), Am. Assn. for Mentally Retarded. Democrat. Avocations: sports, computers. Home: 1831 53rd St Brooklyn NY 11204-1526 Office: Bd Jewish Edn 426 W 58th St New York NY 10019-1102

SCHLOSS, NATHAN, economist; b. Balt., Jan. 14, 1927; s. Howard L. and Louise (Levi) S.; BS in Bus., Johns Hopkins U., 1950; m. Rosa Montalvo, Mar. 1, 1958; children: Nina L., Carolyn D. Buyer, Pacific Coast gen. merchandise office Sears Roebuck & Co., Los Angeles, 1955-60, staff asst. econ. research dept., Chgo., 1960-63; sr. market analyst corp. rsch. dept. Montgomery Ward & Co., Chgo., 1963-65; rsch. mgr. real estate dept. Walgreen Co., Chgo., 1970-72; v.p. rsch. and planning Maron Properties Ltd., Montreal, Que., Can., 1972-74; corp. economist, fin. analyst Real Estate Rsch. Corp., Chgo., 1974-88, sr. v.p., 1986-88, treas., chief fin. analyst, 1982-88; economist Office of Ill. Atty. Gen., Chgo., 1988—; cons. economist, since 1965—; mem. com. on price indexes and productivity fgn. labor Bus. Research Adv. Council of Bur. Labor Stats., Dept. Labor, 1979-88, also chairperson (1985-86), com. on employment and unemployment. Recipient Commendable Svc. award Dept. Labor, 1987. Mem. Plan Commn., Village of Wilmette, Ill., 1975-77, mem. tech. adv. com. on employment and tng. data Ill. Employment and Tng. Coun., 1979-82; mem. tech. adv. com. Ill. Job Tng. Coordinating Council, 1983-87. Mem. Am. Mktg. Assn., Nat. Assn. Bus. Economists, Lambda Alpha. Contbr. articles on fin. and market analysis of real estate to profl. jours. Home: 115 Hollywood Ct Wilmette IL 60091-3122 Office: 100 W Randolph St Chicago IL 60601-3218

SCHLOSS, SAMUEL LEOPOLD, JR., retired food service executive, consultant; b. Montgomery, Ala., Mar. 30, 1926; s. Samuel Leopold and Amelia (Strauss) S.; m. Burke Hart Klein; children: Stephen, Alyce, Adam. BS in Indsl. Engring., Ga. Inst. Tech., 1947; MS in Indsl. Engring., Columbia U., 1948. Sec. Schloss and Kahn Inc., Montgomery, 1948-56, pres., 1956-86, chmn., 1986-94. Pres. Montgomery Acad., 1979-80, bd. dirs. emeritus, 1982; control bd. Montgomery Com. of One Hundred, 1984-86; bd. dirs. YMCA Metro Bd. Capt. USAFR, 1960. Mem. Montgomery C. of C. (pres. 1983), Standard Club (pres. 1964), Capital City Club (bd. govs. 1977-80), Rotary (pres. 1972-73), Montgomery Country Club. Republican. Office: Union Bank Tower 60 Commerce St Ste 1210 Montgomery AL 36104-3563

SCHLOSSBERG, FRED PAUL, elementary education educator; b. N.Y.C., May 30, 1944; s. Alexander and Mae S.; divorced; 1 child, Elan. BSBA, Boston U., 1966; M of Phys. Edn., NYU, 1983. Tchr. elem. sch. N.Y.C. Bd. Edn., 1966—; coach local basketball team, North Bellmore, N.Y., 1988—, local baseball team, North Bellmore, 1988-92. Vol. Alcoholics Anonymous, West Hempstead, N.Y., 1987-93; tutor Literacy Vols. Am. Democrat. Avocations: physical fitness, collecting sports and non-sports cards, comic books and memorabilia, music, travel. Home: 2392 Bedford Ave # A Bellmore NY 11710-3619

SCHLOSSBERG, STEPHEN I., management consultant; b. Roanoke, Va., May 18, 1921; s. Morris Joseph and Jennie (Weinstein) S.; m. Mary Coleman Bazelon, 1953 (div. 1958); m. Nancy Kamin, June 6, 1963; children: Mark Jay, Karen Jean. BS in Commerce, U. Va., 1956, LLB, 1957. Asst. mgr. Kanns, Inc., Roanoke, Va., 1945-49; mem. labor organ. staff Internat. Ladies Garment Workers Union, N.Y.C., 1949-54; assoc., ptnr. Van Arkel & Kaiser, Washington, 1957-61; spl. asst. to dir. Fed. Mediation and Conciliation Service, Washington, 1961-63; gen. counsel, dir. govt. relations Internat. Union UAW, Detroit, 1963-81; ptnr. Zwerdling, Schlossberg, Leibig & Kahn, Washington, 1981-85; dep. under sec. for labor-mgmt. relations and coop. programs U.S. Dept. Labor, Washington, 1985-87; spl. advisor to dir. gen. and dir. Washington br. ILO, 1987-94; with The Kamber Group, Washington, 1995—; cons., advisor in field; former mem. Presdl. Adv. Bd. on Ambassadorial Appointments, Presdl. Commn. on Indsl. Competiveness; adj. prof. law Georgetown U. Law Ctr., 1962-63, 84-85. Author: Organizing and the Law, 1967, 2d edit. (with Frederick Sherman), 1971, 3d edit. (with Judith Scott), 1983, 4th edit., 1991. Served to staff sgt. U.S. Army, 1941-45, ETO. Mem. ABA (commn. on nat. inst. justice, former co-chmn. internat. labor law com., sect. on labor law, former mem. consortium on legal services, former mem. spl. com. on election law), Order of Coif, Raven Soc., Omicron Delta Kappa. Home: 2801 New Mexico NW # PH17 Washington DC 20007 Office: The Kamber Group 1920 L St NW Washington DC 20036

SCHLOSSER, ANNE GRIFFIN, librarian; b. N.Y.C., Dec. 28, 1939; d. C. Russell and Gertrude (Taylor) Griffin; m. Gary J. Schlosser, Dec. 28, 1965. BA in History, Wheaton Coll., Norton, Mass., 1962; MLS, Simmons Coll., 1964; cert. archives adminstrn. Nat. Archives and Records Service, Am. U., 1970. Head UCLA Theater Arts Library, 1964-69; dir. Louis B. Mayer Libr., Am. Film Inst., L.A., 1969-88, dir. film/TV documentation workshop, 1977-87; head Cinema-TV Libr. and Archives of the Performing Arts, U. So. Calif., L.A., 1988-91; dir. Entertainment Resources Seminar, 1990; dir. rsch. libr. Warner Bros., 1991—. Project dir.: Motion Pictures, Television, Radio: A Union Catalogue of Manuscript and Special Collections in the Western U.S., 1977. Active Hollywood Dog Obedience Club, Calif. Numerous grants for script indexing, manuscript cataloging, library automation. Mem. Soc. Am. Archivists, Soc. Calif. Archivists (pres. 1982-83), Theater Library Assn. (exec. bd. 1983-86), Women in Film, Spl. Librs. Assn.. Democrat. Episcopalian. Avocations: running, swimming, reading, dog obedience training. Office: Warner Bros Rsch Libr 5200 Lankershim Blvd Ste 100 North Hollywood CA 91601-3100

SCHLOSSER, HERBERT S., broadcasting company executive; b. Atlantic City, Apr. 21, 1926; s. Abraham and Anna (Olesker) S.; m. Judith P. Gassner, July 8, 1951; children: Lynn C., Eric M. A.B. summa cum laude, Princeton, 1948; LL.B., Yale, 1951. Bar: N.Y. 1952. Assoc. firm Wickes, Riddell, Bloomer, Jacobi & McGuire, N.Y.C., 1951-54, Phillips, Nizer, Benjamin, Krim & Ballon, N.Y.C., 1954-57; with NBC, 1957-78; v.p., gen. mgr. subsidiary Calif. Nat. Prodns., Inc., 1960-61, dir. talent and program adminstrn., 1961-62, v.p. talent and program adminstrn., 1962-66; v.p. programs West Coast NBC, 1966-72; exec. v.p. NBC-TV Network, 1972-73, pres., 1973-74, mem. bd. dirs., 1973-78; pres. NBC, Inc., 1974-78, chief exec. officer, 1977-78; exec. v.p. RCA, 1978-85; sr. advisor broadcasting and entertainment Wertheim Schroder & Co., Inc., N.Y.C., 1986—; bd. dirs. Am. TV and Communications Corp. Trustee Internat. Radio and TV Found., 1972-74; former mem. govs. Ford's Theatre Soc.; former trustee Nat. Urban League; chmn. bd. Am. Mus. of the Moving Image. With USNR, 1944-46. Recipient Humanitarian award NCCJ, 1974, Gold Brotherhood award, 1978. Mem. Assn. of Bar of City of N.Y., Am., N.Y. State bar assns., Council on Fgn. Relations, Acad. TV Arts and Scis., Advt. Council (past dir.), Yale Law Sch. Assn., Internat. Radio and TV Soc. (trustee 1973-74), Hollywood Radio and TV Soc. (trustee 1970-72), Phi Beta Kappa (pres. alumni assn. So. Calif. 1970-72, mem. Phi Betta Kappa assocs.). Club: Princeton (N.Y.). Office: Am Mus of the Moving Image 36-01 35th Ave Long Island City NY 11106

SCHLOSSER, SONDRA JEAN, school and community health nurse; b. Falls City, Nebr., Sept. 15, 1942; d. Wirsell Hanes and Colleen Elizabeth (Young) Witler; m. Gary Lynn Schlosser, Aug. 10, 1963 (dec. July 1985); children: Rebecca Lynn, Lenora Rae, Lance Reed. Profl. Registered Nurse, Immanuel Hosp., Omaha, 1963; BA, U. Nebr., 1983, postgrad., 1990-94. RN. Sch.-community health nurse DuPage Pub. Health Social Svc., Wheaton, Ill., 1965-68; occupational health nurse Goodyear Tire & Rubber, Lincoln, Nebr., 1976-80, Brunswick Corp., Lincoln, 1982-83; with juvenile diversion program Merrick County Atty., Central City, Nebr., 1983-85; sch.-community health nurse U. Nebr., Lincoln, 1986-88, Pub. Sch. Dist. 1, Ashland, Nebr., 1988—; educator Drug Free Nebr. Cadre, Ashland, 1987-91; trainer comprehensive health State Dept. Edn., Lincoln, 1991-94; cons. spl. needs children State Dept. Health, Lincoln, 1993-94. Mem. parish nurse adv. bd. 1st United Meth. Ch., Lincoln, 1988-93, tchr. Sunday sch., chair various coms.; mem. parish nurse adv. bd. St. Elizabeth's Community Hosp., Lincoln, 1992-93; mem. health welfare bd. Interchurch Ministries Nebr., Lincoln, 1993-94. Mem. Nat. Assn. Sch. Nurses, Nebr. Edn. Assn., Nebr. Sch. Nurses Assn. Avocations: quilting, birding, walking. Home: 1720 Surfside Dr Lincoln NE 68528-1746

SCHLOSSER, THEA SUSSANNE, advocate administrator executive; b. Hasenfeld, Germany, June 1, 1937; d. Theodor and Anna (Poppe) Hermesmeyer; divorced; children: Ingrid, Evelyn. Ed. in home econs., Austria; attended, N.Y. Inst. Photography, Modern Sch. Photography; postgrad., Am. Coll. Nutrition. Prin. World Wide Slides, Santa Barbara; founder Chronic Fatigue and Immune Dysfunction Media Awareness Assn., Santa Barbara; assoc. TV show Growing Younger; promotional dir. Kuhnan MD Xenotransplant Ctr.; advt. and bus. cons.; speaker, lectr. on chronic fatigue immune dysfunction of TV, radio, others. Author, publisher: Beyond the Dark Cloud, Road to Recovery from Chronic Fatigue and Immune Dysfunction after 25 Years, 1996; founder-pres., publisher-editor CFID Health Update Internat. Newsletter; inventor game show Challenge Your IQ. Recipient numerous gold medals in photography; swimming champion Austria, 1950. Mem. AMa, Internat. Platform Assn. Avocation: collecting art. Office: Chronic Fatigue Media Awareness Assn 14 Camino Verde Santa Barbara CA 93103-2144

SCHLOSSMAN, JOHN ISAAC, architect; b. Chgo., Aug. 21, 1931; s. Norman Joseph and Carol (Rosenfeld) S.; m. Shirley Goulding Rhodes, Feb. 8, 1959; children: Marc N., Gail S. Mewhort, Peter C. Student, Grinnell Coll., 1949-50; BA, U. Minn., 1953, BArch, 1955; MArch, MIT, 1956. Registered architect, Ill., Fla. Archtl. designer The Architects Collaborative, Cambridge, Mass., 1956-57; architect Loebl Schlossman & Hackl and predecessors, Chgo., 1959-65, assoc., 1965-70, prin., 1970—; bd. overseers Coll. Arch. Illinois Inst. Tech., Chgo.; founding bd. dirs. Chgo. Archtl. Assistance Ctr., 1974-79. Chmn. Glencoe Plan Commn., Ill., 1977-82; trustee Com. for Green Bay Trail, Glencoe, 1970-77, Chgo. Arch. Found., 1971-75, Graham Found. for Advanced Studies in Fine Arts, 1995—; bd. dirs. Merit Music Program, Chgo., 1983-93, pres., 1988-90. Named dir. for life Young Men's Jewish Council, Chgo., 1971; Rotch travelling scholar, 1957. Fellow AIA (trustee ins. trust 1971-76, chmn. ins. com. 1974-75, v.p. Chgo. chpt. 1975, chmn. architects liability com. 1976, 80-82, hon. found. trustee 1995—), Archtl. Soc. of Art Inst. Chgo., Tavern Club (gov. 1986-88, v.p. 1990), The Arts Club, Alpha Rho Chi,. Office: Loebl Schlossman & Hackl 130 E Randolph St Ste 3400 Chicago IL 60601-6313

SCHLOSSMAN, STUART FRANKLIN, physician, educator, researcher; b. N.Y.C., Apr. 18, 1935; s. Abe and Pearl (Susser) S.; m. Judith Seryl Rubin, May 25, 1958; children: Robert, Peter. BA magna cum laude, NYU, 1955, MD, 1958; MA, Harvard U., 1975. Intern in medicine med. divsn. III Bellevue Hosp., N.Y.C., 1958-59, asst. resident in medicine med. divsn. III, 1959-60; Nat. Found. fellow dept. microbiology Coll. Physicians Columbia U., N.Y.C., 1960-62; asst. physician med. svc. Vanderbilt Clinic, Coll. Physician USPHS, Washington, 1960-62; Ward hematology fellow dept. internal medicine Sch. Washington U., St. Louis, 1962-63; rsch. assoc. lab. biochemistry Nat. Cancer Inst. USPHS, Washington, 1963-65; clin. instr. in medicine Sch. of Medicine George Washington U., 1964-65; assoc. in medicine, dir. blood bank Beth Israel Hosp., Boston, 1965-66; instr. Med. Sch. Harvard U., Boston, 1966-68, asst. physician, 1967-68, chief clin. immunology, 1971-73; physician Beth Israel Hosp., Boston, 1968—; from asst. to assoc. prof. medicine Harvard Med. Sch., Boston, 1968-77, prof., 1977—, Baruj Benacerraf prof. medicine, 1990—, chief divsn. tumor immunology and immunotherapy, 1973—; sr. physician Brigham and Women's Hosp., Boston, 1976—. Mem. editorial bd. Jour. of Immunology, 1969-74, Cellular Immunology, 1970—, Human Immunology, 1979-84, Clin. Immunology and Immunopathology, 1979—, Hybridoma, 1980—, Cancer Investigation, 1981, Stem Cells, 1981, Cancer Revs., 1984—, Internat. Jour. of Cell Cloning, 1983-86; mem. adv. bd. Cancer Treatment Reports, 1976-80; assoc. editor Human Lymphocyte Differentation, 1980-82; contbr. numerous articles to profl. jours. Recipient Solomon Berson Achievement award, 1984, Robert Koch prize and medal, 1984. Fellow AAAS; mem. NAS, Am. Soc. Hematology, Am. Soc. Immunologists, Am. Soc. Clin. Investigation, Assn. Am. Physicians, Inst. of Medicine, Alpha Omega Alpha. Office: Dana-Farber Cancer Inst 44 Binney St Boston MA 02215-9999

SCHLOTFELDT, ROZELLA MAY, nursing educator; b. DeWitt, Iowa, June 29, 1914; d. John W. and Clara C. (Doering) S. BS, State U. Iowa, 1935; MS, U. Chgo., 1947, PhD, 1956; DSc (hon.), Georgetown U., 1972, Adelphi U., 1979, Wayne State U., 1983, U. Ill., Chgo., 1985, Kent State U., 1987, U. Cin., 1989; LHD (hon.), Med. U. S.C., 1976. Staff nurse State U. Iowa, VA Hosp., 1935-39; instr., supr. maternity nursing (State U. Iowa), 1939-44; asst. prof. U. Colo. Sch. Nursing, 1947-48; assoc., then asso. prof. Wayne State U. Coll. Nursing, 1948-55; prof., asso. dean Wayne State U. Coll. Nursing (Coll. Nursing), 1957-60; dean Frances Payne Bolton Sch. Nursing, Case Western Res. U., 1960-72, prof., 1960-82, prof., dean emeritus, 1982—; vis. prof. Rutgers U., 1984-89, 90—, U. Pa., 1985-86; spl. cons. Surgeon Gen.'s Adv. Group on Nursing, 1961-63; mem. nursing research study sect. USPHS, 1962-66; mem. Nat. League for Nursing-USPHS Com. on Nursing Edn. Facilities, 1962-64; mem. com. on health goals Cleve. Health Council, 1961-66; mem. Cleve. Health Planning and Devel. Commn., 1969-72; adv. com. div. nursing W.K. Kellog Found., 1959-67; v.p. Ohio Bd. Nursing Edn. and Nurse Registration, 1970-71, pres., 1971-72; mem. Nat. Health Services Research Tng. Com., 1970-71; mem. supply and edn. panel Health Manpower Com., 1966-67; rev. com. Nurse Tng. Act, 1967-68; bd. visitors Duke U. Med. Center, 1968-70; mem. council, exec. com. Inst. Medicine of Nat. Acad. Scis., 1971-75; mem. nat. adv. health services council Health Services and Mental Health Adminstrn., 1971-75; mem. def. adv. com. on women in services Dept. Def., 1972-75; bd. mem., treas. Nursing Home Adv. and Research Council, 1975—; mem. adv. panel Health Services Research Commn. on Human Resources, Nat. Acad. Sci., 1977-85; cons. Walter Reed Army Inst.; adv. council on nursing, U.S. VA, 1965-69, chmn., 1966-69; mem. Yale U.; Council Com. on Med. Affairs, 1981-86; mem. adv. bd. Scholarly Inquiry for Nursing Practice, 1987—. Mem. editorial bd.: Advances in Nursing Sci, Inquiry, 1982-85, Jour. Nursing Edn., 1982-91; contbr. numerous articles to profl. jours. Bd. vis. Syracuse U., 1990—. Served to 1st lt. Army Nurse Corps, 1944-46. Recipient Disting. Svc. award U. Iowa, 1973, Case Western Res. U., 1991, N. Watts Lifetime Achievement award, 1995; named Living Legend, Am. Acad. Nursing, 1995. Fellow Am. Acad. Nursing (v.p. 1975-77, Living Legend award 1995), Nat. League Nursing; mem. ANA (chmn. commn. on nurse edn. 1967-70, mem. com. for studying credentialling 1976-79, adv. com. W.K. Kellogg Nat. Fellowship program 1981-85), Pi Lambda Theta, Sigma Theta Tau (nat. v.p. 1948-50, selection com., disting. lectr. program 1986-87, Founders award for creativity 1985). Home: 1111 Carver Rd Cleveland OH 44112-3635 Office: 2121 Abington Rd Cleveland OH 44106-2333

SCHLOTTERBECK, WALTER ALBERT, manufacturing company executive, lawyer; b. N.Y.C., Dec. 22, 1926; s. Albert Gottlob and Maria Louise (Fritz) S.; m. Pauline Elizabeth Hoerz, Sept. 2, 1951; children—Susan, Thomas, Paul. A.B., Columbia U., 1949, LL.B., 1952. Bar: N.Y. 1953. Counsel Gen. Electric Co. (various locations), 1952-87; v.p., corp. counsel Gen. Electric Co. (various locations), N.Y.C., 1970-77; sec. Gen. Electric Co. (various locations), 1975-76, gen. counsel, 1976-87, sr. v.p., 1977-87. Served with USNR, 1944-46. Home: 201 Overlake Dr E Medina WA 98004-5331

SCHLOTZHAUER, VIRGINIA HUGHES, parliamentarian; b. Washington, July 24, 1913; d. William and Secy Alice (Royston) Hughes; m. Elbert O. Schlotzhauer, May 16, 1936; children: Carol Schlotzhauer Hinds, Jean Schlotzhauer Sumner, Jude Schlotzhauer Wilson. AB in LS, George Washington U., 1934. Mem. libr. staff George Washington U., Washington, 1934; various clerical positions U.S. Govt., ARC, Washington, Phoenix, mid-1930s, Washington and Phoenix ARC, mid. 1930s; cons. parliamentarian Washington, 1967—; cons. Nat. Parliamentarian Edn. Project for Colls. and Univs. sponsored by Am. Inst. Parliamentarians funded by William Randolph Hearst Found., 1993-95; presenter seminars. Author: A Parliamentarian's Book of Limericks, 1984; (with others) Parliamentary Opinions, 1982, Parliamentary Opinions II, 1992; primary contbr./cons. column Parliamentary Jour.; contbr. articles to profl. publs. Mem. steering and bylaws coms., sec. Nominating Conv. for Endorsement of Candidates for Bd. Edn., Montgomery County, Md., 1966; election reporter ABC-LWV, Prince George's County, Md., 1970s; v.p., bylaws com. Planned Parenthood Am., Prince George's County, late 1960s and 70s; group leader, bd. dirs., sec., trustee Potomac Area coun. Camp Fire Girls, Md. and D.C. area, 1940s and 50s; participant nonpartisan and Dem. polit. campaigns; judge various contests Future Bus. Leaders Am., Washington, 1970s. Mem. AAUW (life, named gift Bethesda-Chevy Chase br. 1962, named gift Md. divsn. 1972), Am. Inst. Parliamentarians (cert. profl. parliamentarian, mem. adv. coun. or bd. dirs. 1966—, pres. D.C. chpt. 1966-68, opinions com. 1974—, chmn. 1974-78, cons., named changed to Virginia Schlotzhauer D.C. chpt. 1984), Nat. Assn. Parliamentarians (profl. registered parliamentarian, mem. coms.), D.C. Assn. Parliamentarians (founding pres., 1st hon. pres., Achievement award 1976), Westerners. Avocations: travel, writing, poetry, gardening, Spanish language and culture. Home and Office: 9819 Indian Queen Point Rd Fort Washington MD 20744-6904

SCHLUB, TERESA RAE, minister; b. Oak Park, Ill., July 11, 1946; d. Robert Carl and Shirley Rae (Listhartke) Grupe; m. George Jonas Schlub, Aug. 29, 1981; stepchildren: Kathy Bruns, Gary, Greg, Dean. BA, Westmar Teikyo U., 1971; MDiv, Garrett Evangel. Seminary, Evanston, Ill., 1974. Ordained deacon United Meth. Ch., 1973, elder, 1978. Asst. minister First United Meth. Ch., Morris, Ill., 1974-76; minister Leaf River (Ill.) German Valley United Meth. Ch., 1976-82, East Jordan United Meth. Ch., Sterling, Ill., 1982-86, Paw Paw (Ill.) United Meth. Ch., 1986-89, Community United Meth. Ch., LaMoille, Ill., 1989-95, Capron (Ill.) United Meth. Ch., 1995—; mem. alumni coun., sec. Garrett Evangel. Theol. Seminary, Evanston, 1974-76; mem. Conf. Bd. of Evangelism, 1974-76. Bd. dirs. Green Hills coun. Girls Scouts U.S., Freeport, Ill., 1986-88, Lee County Red Cross, Dixon, Ill., 1986-89, Crossroads Counseling Ctr., Mendota, 1989-91; bd. dirs. Quad County Counseling Ctr., Princeton, 1991—, treas., 1993-94; mem. Ill. Home Extension Assn., Grundy, Ogle, Whiteside and Lee Counties, 1974-89; sec. DeKalb Dist. Com. Ordained Ministry. Home: 339 W North PO Box 322 Capron IL 61012 Office: Capron United Meth Ch 345 67th St Capron IL 61012 *Life becomes meaningful when one is able to become vulnerable and be willing to take risks. This becomes possible when one has faith in God and confidence in the self. It also helps to know and experience the love of others.*

SCHLUETER, DAVID ARNOLD, law educator; b. Sioux City, Iowa, Apr. 29, 1946; s. Arnold E. and Helen A. (Dettmann) S.; m. Linda L. Boston, Apr. 22, 1972; children: Jennifer, Jonathan. BA, Tex. A&M U., 1969; JD, Baylor U., 1971, LLM, U. Va., 1981. Bar: Tex. 1971, D.C. 1973, U.S. Ct. Mil. Appeals 1972, U.S. Supreme Ct. 1976. Legal counsel U.S. Supreme Ct., Washington, 1981-83; assoc. dean St. Mary's U., San Antonio, 1984-89, prof. law, 1986—; reporter Fed. Adv. Com. on Criminal Rules, 1988—; chmn. JAG adv. coun., 1974-75. Author: Military Criminal Justice: Practice and Procedure, 1982, 3d edit., 1992; (with others) Military Rules of Evidence Manual, 1981, 3d edit., 1991, Texas Rules of Evidence Manual, 1983, 4th edit., 1995, Texas Evidentiary Foundations, 1992, Military Evidentiary Foundations, 1994; contbr. articles to legal publs. Maj. JAGC, U.S. Army, 1972-81. Fellow Am. Law Inst., Tex. Bar Found. (life), Am. Bar Found. (life); mem. ABA (vice chmn. criminal justice sect. coun. 1991-94, vice chmn. com. on criminal justice and mil. 1983-84, chmn. standing com. on mil. law 1991-92, chmn. editl. adv. bd., Criminal Justice Mag., 1989-91), Tex. Bar Assn. Republican. Lutheran. Office: St Marys U Sch Law 1 Camino Santa Maria St San Antonio TX 78228-8603

SCHLUETER, ERIKA MANRIQUEZ, civil engineer research scientist; b. Santiago, Chile; came to U.S., 1980; d. Javier Bustos Manriquez and Constantina Vilos Anso; m. Ross Donald Schlueter, May, 1981; children: Dietrich, Kurt. B of Civil Constrn., Cath. U., Santiago, 1980; postgrad., MIT, 1980-81, San Jose State U., 1983; MS in Civil Engring., U. Wash., 1986; PhD in Engring. Sci., U. Calif., Berkeley, 1995. Instr. continuing edn. Cath. U., Santiago, 1975-77, tchg. asst., 1976-77; hydrogeologist Celzac Co., Santiago, 1978; med. asst. Stanford (Calif.) U. Med. Ctr., 1981, fin. aids analyst, 1981-82; homemaker Pleasanton, 1986-88; rsch. asst. Lawrence Berkeley Nat. Lab. U. Calif., Berkeley, 1988-95; rsch. scientist Lawrence Berkeley Nat. Lab. U. Calif., Berkeley, 1995—. Contbr. numerous articles to profl. jours. Fulbright fellow, 1980-81, Janes Lewis fellow, 1990-91. Mem. ASCE, Soc. Petroleum Engrs., Am. Geophys. Union, Soc. Exploration Geophysicists (Award of Merit 1994-95). Republican. Roman Catholic. Home: 780 Cragmont Ave Berkeley CA 94708 Office: Lawrence Berkley Nat Lab MS 90-1116 1 Cyclotron Rd Berkeley CA 94720

SCHLUSSER, ROBERT ELMER, lawyer; b. Harrisburg, Pa., Aug. 24, 1942; s. Elmer Charles and Mildred Gladys (Brown) S.; m. Margaret Murray Steiniger, June 10, 1966 (div. Dec. 1980); children: Adam, Jason, Hannah; m. Joanna Reiver, Jul. 16, 1982; children: Amelia, Daniel. BA in econs. cum laude, Dickinson Coll., 1964; JD, Dickinson Sch. Law, 1967; LLM in taxation, George Washington U., 1969. Bar: Pa. 1967, Del. 1971, N.Mex. 1993, U.S. Dist. Ct. (mid. dist.) Pa. 1968, U.S. Dist. Ct. Del. 1972, U.S. Ct. Appeals (3rd cir.) 1973, U.S. Ct. Appeals, 1991, U.S. Supreme Ct. 1973. U.S. Ct. Fed. Claims, 1970. Dir. Murdoch & Walsh P.A., Wilmington, Del., 1969-82; ptnr. Schlusser & Reiver, Wilmington, Del., 1982-87, Schlusser, Reiver, Hughes & Sisk, Wilmington, Del., 1988-94; dir. Schlusser & Reiver P.A., Wilmington, 1995—; speaker at numerous confs., seminars. Contbr. articles to profl. jours. Office: Schlusser & Reiver 1700 W 14th St Wilmington DE 19806

SCHLUTER, PETER MUELLER, electronics company executive; b. Greenwich, Conn., May 24, 1933; s. Fredric Edward and Charlotte (Mueller) S.; m. Jaquelin Ambler Lamond, Apr. 18, 1970 (div. June 1990); children: Jane Randolph, Charlotte Mueller, Anne Ambler. BME, Cornell U., 1956; postgrad. Harvard U. Grad. Sch. Bus. Adminstrn., 1982. Sr. engr. Thiokol Chem. Corp., Brigham City, Utah, 1958-59; asso. Porter Internat. Co., Washington, 1960-65, v.p., 1965-66, pres., treas., dir., 1966-70; pres., treas. dir. Zito Co., Derry, N.H., 1970-72; internat. bus. cons., Washington, 1972-74; v.p., dir. Buck Engring. Co. Inc., Farmingdale, N.J., 1975, pres., CEO, dir., 1975—; hon. mem. City and Guilds of London Inst. Mem. Republican Inaugural Book and Program Com., 1969; mem. cmty. adv. bd. Monmouth coun. Girl Scouts U.S.; mem. adv. council Monmouth (N.J.) Coll. Sch. Bus. Admin.; bd. dirs. United Way of Monmouth County.; trustee Monmouth Med. Ctr.; N.Am. rep., mem. presidium WORLDDIDAC, Bern, Switzerland, v.p., 1996—. Recipient Golden Osprey award So. Monmouth County C. of C., 1995. Fellow City and Guilds of London Inst. (hon.); mem. World Assn. Mfrs. and Distributors of Ednl. Materials (N.Am. rep.), Metropolitan Club Washington, Rumson Country Club, Pi Tau Sigma. Home: 4 Quaker Ln Little Silver NJ 07739-1806 Office: PO Box 686 Farmingdale NJ 07727-0686

SCHLUTH, MICHAEL VERNON, advertising agency executive; b. Phila., Aug. 8, 1944; s. Frank Charles and Charlotte Laurel (Hanwell) S.; A.S. in Mktg., La Salle Coll., 1968; m. Nancy Jane Weller, Jan. 14, 1967; children—Lori Ann, Donna Jean, Michael Philip; m. Susan Katherine Nice, Sept. 10, 1988; 1 child, Brendan Hunter. Advt. sales rep. Phila. Newspapers, Inc., 1968-75; pres. Alstin Advt., Inc., Phila., 1975—; owner, pres. Lordon-Michaelson Assocs., 1984—. Bd. dirs. Phila affiliate Nat. Human Resources Assn., 1995. Served with U.S. Army, 1963-65. Office: 1435 Walnut St Philadelphia PA 19102-3219

SCHMALBECK, RICHARD LOUIS, university dean, lawyer; b. Chgo., Dec. 31, 1947; s. George Louis and Betty Jeanne (Strecker) S.; m. Linda Michaels; children: Suzanne, Sabine. AB in Econs. with honors, U. Chgo., 1970, JD, 1975. Bar: Ohio 1975, D.C. 1977. Asst. to dir. and economist Ill. Housing Devel. Authority, Chgo., 1971-73; assoc. Vorys, Sater, Seymour & Pease, Columbus, Ohio, 1975-76; spl. asst. to assoc. dir. for econs. and govt. Office of Mgmt. and Budget, Washington, 1976-77; assoc. Caplin & Drysdale, Washington, 1977-80; assoc. prof. law Duke U., Durham, N.C., 1980-84, prof. law, 1984-90, 93—, vice chmn. acad. coun., 1984-85; dean U. Ill. Coll. Law, Champaign, 1990-93. Assoc. editor U. Chgo. Law Rev., 1974-75; contbr. articles to profl. jours. Mem. ABA (articles editor jour. 1977-80), Am. Law Inst., Phi Beta Kappa. Office: Duke University Sch of Law PO Box 90360 Durham NC 27708-0360

SCHMALE, ALLEN LEE, financial services company executive; b. Addieville, Ill., Feb. 12, 1933; s. Arnold August and Leona Karoline (Becker) S.; m. Lorraine Marie Loyet, July 19, 1952; children: Judith Ann, Arnold August II, Michelle Lee, René Cerise, Allen Kent. CLU, ChFC. Salesman Western & So. Life Ins. Co., St. Louis, 1955-56, Monarch Life Ins. Co., St. Louis, 1956-58, Mass. Indemnity & Life Ins., St. Louis, 1958-65; pres. Schmale Fin. Svcs., Inc., Okawville, Ill., 1965-88, chmn., 1988—, also bd. dirs. Trustee Village of Okawville, 1976-80, mem. bus. devel. com.; vice chmn. Washington County (Ill.) Rep. Com.; coord. Edgar for Gov., Ill., 1990, 94; pres. St. Peters Ch., 1975-77; br. officer Walnut St. Securities Inc. Recipient Contbns. to Growth award Belleville (Ill.) Area Coll., 1977. Mem. Am. Soc. CLU and ChFC, East Side Life Underwriters (pres. 1971-72), Million Dollar Roundtable, Ill. Life Underwriters (bd. dirs. 1975-78), Nat. Assn. Life Underwriters (del. 1971), Estate Planning Coun. St. Louis, Okawville Comty. Club (pres. 1974-76). Republican. Avocation: golf. Home: 5304 County Highway 6 Okawville IL 62271-2530 Office: Schmale Fin Svcs Inc 611 S Front St Okawville IL 62271-2121

SCHMALENBERGER, JERRY LEW, pastor, seminary administrator; b. Greenville, Ohio, Jan. 23, 1934; s. Harry Henry and Lima Marie (Hormel) S.; m. Carol Ann Walthall, June 8, 1956; children: Stephen, Bethany Allison, Sarah Layton. BA, Wittenberg U., 1956, DDiv (hon.), 1984; MDiv, Hamma Sch. Theology, Springfield, Ohio, 1959, D of Ministry, 1976. Ordained to ministry Luth. Ch., 1959. Dir. Camp Mowana, Mansfield, Ohio, 1958-59; pastor 3d Luth. Ch., Springfield, 1959-61, 1st Luth. Ch., Bellefontaine, Ohio, 1961-66; sr. pastor 1st Luth. Ch., Tiffin, Ohio, 1966-70, Mansfield, 1970-79; sr. pastor St. John's Luth. Ch., Des Moines, 1979-88; pres., prof. parish ministry Pacific Luth. Theol. Sem., Berkeley, Calif., 1988-96; co-dir. Iowa Luth. Hosp. Min. of Health Program, Des Moines, 1986-88; Roland Payne lectr. Gbarnga (Liberia) Sch. Theology, 1987; lectr. Luth. Theol. Sem., Hong Kong, 1994, The United Theol. Coll., Kingston, Jamaica, 1994. Author: Lutheran Christians' Beliefs Book One, 1984, Book Two, 1987, Iowa Parables and Iowa Psalms, 1984, Saints Who Shaped the Church, 1986, Stewards of Creation, 1987, Nights Worth Remembering, 1989, The Vine and the Branches, 1992, Call to Witness, 1993, Plane Thoughts on Parish Ministry, 1994, Invitation to Discipleship, 1995, The Preacher's Edge, 1996; columnist Rite Ideas, 1987-88. Bd. dirs. Grand View Coll., Des Moines, 1980-88, Wittenberg U., Springfield, Ohio, 1974-87, Luth. Social Services of Iowa, 1980-87, chmn. pre fund drive, 1988; bd. dirs. Planned Parenthood of Mid-Iowa, Des Moines, 1987-88; dir. Evang. Outreach/Luth. Ch. Am., 1983-85; mem. Iowa Luth. Hosp. Charitable Trust, 1986-88; chair Com. for Homeless Fund, Des Moines, 1986. Named Outstanding Alumni Wittenberg U., 1965, Young Man of Yr. Tiffin Jaycees, 1965, Man of Yr. Bellefontaine Jaycees, Disting. Alumni award Trinty Sem., Columbus, 1989. Mem. NAACP, Acad. Preachers, Acad. Evangelists (organizer 1986—), Kiwanis, Rotary. Avocations: historical research and writing, travel, boating. Home & Office: 2770 Marin Ave Berkeley CA 94708-1530 *Personal philosophy: Not perfect, but forgiven, we find real life in living ours for others.*

SCHMALENSEE, RICHARD LEE, economist, government official, educator; b. Belleville, Ill., Feb. 16, 1944; s. Fred and Marjorie June (Veigel) S.; SB, MIT, 1965, PhD, 1970; m. Edeth Diane Hawk, Aug. 19, 1967; children: Alexander Clayton, Nicholas Hawk. Asst. prof., assoc. prof. econs. U. Calif., San Diego, 1970-77; assoc. prof. applied econs. Sloan Sch. Mgmt. MIT, Cambridge, Mass., 1977-79, prof., 1979-86, prof. econs. and mgmt., 1986-89, Gordon Y Billard prof., 1988—, dir. MIT Ctr. for Energy and Environ. Policy Rsch., 1991—; dir. L.I. Lighting, Co.; mem. Pres.'s Coun. Econ. Advisors, 1989-91; NSF grantee, 1975-77, 81-83; research fellow U. Louvain (Belgium), 1973-74, 85. Fellow AAAS, Econometric Soc.; mem. Am. Econ. Assn. (nominating com. 1987, exec. com. 1993-95). Author: The Economics of Advertising, 1972; The Control of Natural Monopoly, 1979; co-author: Markets for Power, 1983, Economics, 1988; co-editor: Handbook of Industrial Organization, 1989; mem. editorial bd. Jour. Indsl. Econs., 1981-89, Am. Econ. Rev., 1982-86, Internat. Jour. Indsl. Orgns., 1982-89, Jour. Econs. & Mgmt. Strategy, 1993—, Jour. Econ. Perspectives, 1993—. Home: 20 Malia Ter Chestnut Hill MA 02167-1326 Office: MIT 50 Memorial Dr Rm E52-456 Cambridge MA 02142-1347

SCHMALSTIEG, WILLIAM RIEGEL, Slavic languages educator; b. Sayre, Pa., Oct. 3, 1929; s. John William and Dorothy Augusta (Riegel) S.; m. Emily Lou Botdorf, Mar. 28, 1952; children: Linda, Roxanne. BA, U. Minn., 1950; postgrad., Columbia U., 1952; MA, U. Pa., 1951, PhD, 1956; PhD (hon.), Vilnius U., 1994. Instr. U. Ky., Lexington, 1956-59; asst. prof. Lafayette Coll., Easton, Pa., 1959-63; assoc. prof. U. Minn., Mpls., 1963-64; prof. Pa. State U., University Park, 1964—, head dept. Slavic langs., 1969-91; mem. Internat. Commn. Balto-Slavic Linguistics, 1973—; appointed Edwin Erle Sparks prof. Slavic Lang., 1990. Author: (with L. Dambriunas and A. Klimas) An Introduction to Modern Lithuanian, 1966, 4th edit., 1990, 5th edit., 1993, An Old Prussian Grammar, 1974, Studies in Old Prussian, 1976, Indo-European Linguistics, 1980, An Introduction to Old Church Slavic, 1976, 2d edit., 1983, A Lithuanian Historical Syntax, 1988; (with Warren Held and Janet Gertz) Beginning Hittite, 1988, A Student Guide to the Genitive of Agent in the Indo-European Languages, 1995, An Introduction to Old Russian, 1995; editor Gen. Linguistics, 1971-82. Served to 1st lt. U.S. Army, 1952-54. NEH grantee, 1978-79, Fulbright grantee and exch. scholar Acad. Scis., Vilnius, USSR, 1986; recipient Humanities medal Pa. State U., 1983, Friend of Lithuania award Knights of Lithuania, 1990; named Disting. Alumnus Breck Sch., 1990. Mem. Assn. Advancement Baltic Studies (pres. 1982-84), Am. Assn. Tchrs. of Slavic and East European Langs. Episcopalian. Home: 814 Cornwall Rd State College PA 16803-1430 Office: Dept Slavic Langs Pa State U University Park PA 16802

SCHMALTZ, ROY EDGAR, JR., artist, art educator; b. Belfield, N.D., Feb. 23, 1937; s. Roy and Mercedes (Martin) S.; m. Julia Mabel Swan, Feb. 1, 1958; children: Liese Marlene, Jennifer Lynn, Gregory Jason. Student Otis Art Inst., Los Angeles, 1959-60, U. Wash., 1960-61, Akademie der Bildenden Kunste, Munich, W. Ger., 1965-66; B.F.A., San Francisco Art Inst., 1963, M.F.A., 1965. Lectr. art coll. of Notre Dame, Belmont, Calif., 1968-70, M. H. De Young Meml. Art Mus., San Francisco, 1968-70; prof. art St. Mary's Coll. of Calif., Moraga, 1969—, chmn. dept. art; mem. artists' bd. San Francisco Art Inst., 1989-92; exhbns. include: Seattle Art Mus., 1959, M. H. De Young Meml. Art Mus., 1969, Frye Art Mus., Seattle, 1957, San Francisco Mus. Modern Art, 1971, U. Calif.-Santa Cruz, 1977, Fine Arts Mus. of San Francisco, 1978, Oakland Art Mus., 1979, Rutgers U., Camden, N.J., 1979, Springfield (Mo.) Art Mus., 1980, Butler Inst. Am. Art, Youngstown, Ohio, 1981, Huntsville (Ala.) Mus. Art, 1982, Haggin Mus., Stockton, Calif., 1982, U. Hawaii-Hilo, 1983, Alaska State Mus., Juneau, 1981, Tex. State U., San Marcos, 1980, Crocker Art Mus., Sacramento, 1982, Hearst Art Gallery, 1986; group exhbns. include San Francisco Internat. Airport Gallery, 1987, Solano Coll., Fairfield, Calif., 1988, U. Del., Newark, 1988, San Francisco Art Inst., 1989, Natsoulas Gallery, Davis, Calif., 1989, Bedford Regional Ctr. Arts, Walnut Creek, Calif., 1989, Contemporary Realist Gallery, San Francisco, 1994, Hearst Art Gallery, Moraba, Calif., 1995; represented in permanent collections: Richmond Art Ctr. (Calif.), U. Hawaii-Hilo, Las Vegas Art Mus. (Nev.), Hoyt Mus. and Inst. Fine Arts, New Castle, Pa., Frye Art Mus., San Francisco Art Inst., M. H. De Young Meml. Art Mus., Mills Coll., Oakland, Amerika-Haus, Munich, Contra Costa County Art Collection, Walnut Creek, Calif., Western Wash. U., Bellingham, Clemson U., S.C.; dir. Hearst Art Gallery, St. Mary's Coll.; vis. artist lectr. Academie Art Coll., San Francisco, 1971, grad. program Lone Mountain Coll., San Francisco, 1973-74. Coach Little League Baseball Team, Concord, Calif., 1982, mem. artist's bd. San Francisco Art Inst., 1989-93. Fulbright fellow, 1965-66; Frye Art Mus. traveling fellow, 1957; recipient Painting award All Calif. Ann., 1965; Nat. Watercolor award Chautauqua Inst., 1980; Seattle Art Assn. Painting award, 1957; San Francisco Art Inst. award, 1961; Otis Art Inst. award, 1959; Walnut Creek Civic Art Ctr. award, 1982, San Francisco Art Commn. award, 1985, Calif. State Fair Art award, 1985, Sears award for excellence in leadership, 1989-90. Mem. Coll. Art Assn., Fine Arts Mus. of San Francisco, AAUP, San Francisco Art Inst. Alumni Assn. Home: 1020 Whistler Dr Suisun City CA 94585-2929 Office: Saint Marys Coll Dept Art Moraga CA 94575

SCHMALZ, CARL NELSON, JR., artist, educator, printmaker; b. Ann Arbor, Mich., Dec. 26, 1926; s. Carl Nelson and Esther Dorothy (Fowler) S.; m. Dolores Irene Tourangeau, Dec. 2, 1950; children: Stephen Theodore (dec.), Mathew Nelson, Julia Irene. A.B., Harvard U., 1948, M.A., 1949, Ph.D., 1958; M.A. (hon.), Amherst Coll., 1969. Teaching fellow in fine arts Harvard U., Cambridge, Mass., 1950-52; asst. prof. Bowdoin Coll., Brunswick, Maine, 1953-62; curator, asst. dir. Walker Art Mus., 1953-62; asst. prof. Harvard U., 1960; prof. Amherst Coll., 1962-95, prof. emeritus, 1995—; lectr. in field. Author: Watercolor Lessons from Eliot O'Hara, 1974, Watercolor Your Way, 1978, Finding and Improving Your Painting Style, 1986, paperback, 1992; exhibited in one-man shows including Cambridge (Mass.) Art Assn., 1948, Laing Gallery, Portland, Maine, 1955, Amherst (Mass.) Coll., 1963, U. Mass., 1965, W.C. Rawls Mus., Va., 1972, Concord (Mass.) Art Assn., 1974, Govt. House, Hamilton, Bermuda, 1979, Jones Library, Amherst, Mass., 1979, The Arlington, Kennebunkport, Maine, 1980, Harmon-Meek Gallery, Naples, Fla., 1987, 91, 92, Gallery at 6 Deering St., Portland, Maine, 1987, 91, Fretz Gallery, Portland, 1987-88; exhibited in group shows including Jordan Marsh Co., 1947, 48, 50, 71-73, Colby Coll., 1958, Carnegie Inst., Pitts., 1963, FAR Gallery, N.Y.C., 1964-68, Am. Watercolor Soc., 1966, 68, 70, Bowdoin Coll. Mus., 1973, Balt. Watercolor Soc., 1976, Boston Atheneum, 1979, Watercolor U.S.A. Honor Soc., 1989, 91, Maine Art Gallery, 1991, Rolly-Michaux Gallery, Boston, 1995; represented in permanent collections: Walker Art Mus., Brunswick, Maine, Jones & Laughlin Steel Corp., Diners Club Am., Kalamazoo Art Center, Hampshire Coll., Zanesville Art Inst., Blue Cross/Blue Shield, Philharmonic Ctr. for the Arts, Naples, Fla.; work published in various pubs. including The Artist's Guide for Using Color, 1992, The Artist's Mag., 1994, Splash 3: Ideas and Inspirations, 1994. Mem. exec. bd. Interfaith Housing Corp., Amherst, 1966-76; pres. bd. trustees Amherst Day Sch., 1966-69; mem. Pelham Arts Lottery Coun., 1984-90; v.p. bd. dirs. Portland Mus. Art, 1957-62. Bacon fellow, 1951; recipient 1st prize watercolor Cambridge Art Assn. Ann., 1947; 1st prize for traditional watercolor Virginia Beach Boardwalk Show, 1965; South Mo. Trust purchase award Watercolor U.S.A., 1970; 1st prize watercolor 30th Ann. Kennebunk River Club Show, 1985. Mem. Coll. Art Assn., Watercolor U.S.A. Honor Soc. Democrat.

SCHMALZRIED, MARVIN EUGENE, financial consultant; b. Dighton, Kans., Nov. 11, 1924; s. Carl D. and Marie M. (Bahm) S.; m. Jean Landino, Nov. 27, 1946; children—Darlene, Candace, Cynthia, Derek, Valerie, Rebecca. B.B.A., Northwestern U., 1949; LL.B., U. Conn., 1955. Bar: Conn. bar 1955; C.P.A., Conn. Acct. Webster, Blanchard & Willard, CPA's (named changed to Price Waterhouse & Co.), Hartford, Conn., 1950-55; contr., asst. treas. J.B. Williams Co., Glastonbury, Conn., 1955-57; treas., sec. Curtis 1000, Inc. (name changed to Am Bus. Products, Inc.), Atlanta, 1957-61; asst. to pres. Am. Home Products Corp., N.Y.C., 1961-63, comptroller, 1964-67, v.p., 1967-72, sr. v.p., 1972-84; pres. Venda Vid, Inc., N.Y.C., 1986-90; sr. v.p. View-Master Ideal Group, Inc., N.Y.C., 1987-90; exec. v.p. Strategics Inc., 1993-95; bd. dirs. Am. Bus. Products, Inc., Atlanta. Recipient Gold medal Conn. Soc. C.P.A.'s, 1953. Mem. AICPA, ABA, Old Greenwich Friday Evening Reading Soc. (pres.). Club: Darien Country. Home and Office: 26 Cove Ave Norwalk CT 06855-2400

SCHMANDT-BESSERAT, DENISE, archaeologist, educator; b. Ay, France, Aug. 10, 1933; came to U.S., 1965, naturalized, 1970; d. Victor and Jeanne (Crabit) Besserat; m. Jurgen Schmandt, Dec. 27, 1956; children: Alexander, Christopher, Phillip. Ed., Ecole du Louvre, 1965. Research fellow in Near Eastern Archaeology Peabody Mus. Harvard U., Cambridge, Mass., 1969-71; fellow Radcliffe Inst., Cambridge, 1969-71; asst. prof. Middle Eastern studies U. Tex., Austin, 1972-81, assoc. prof., 1981-88, prof., 1988—; acting chief curator U. Tex. Art Mus., 1978-79; vis. assoc. prof. U. Calif., Berkeley, 1987-88. Author: Before Writing, 1992; adv. editor Tech. and Culture, 1978-92; mem. editl. bd. Written Communication, 1993-95, Visible Lang., 1985—; contbr. articles to profl. jours. Recipient Kayden Nat. U. Press Book award, 1992; Wenner-Gren Foun. grantee, 1970-71, NEA grantee, 1974-75, 77-78, ACLS grantee, 1984, Deutscher Akademischer Austauschdienst grantee, 1986, NEH grantee, 1992; NEH fellow, 1979-80, U. Wis. Inst. for Rsch. in Humanities fellow,, 1984-85, USIA, Am. Ctr. Oriental Rsch. fellow, 1994-95. Mem. Am. Oriental Soc., Archeol. Inst. Am. (governing bd. 1983-89), Am. Anthropol. Assn., Am. Schs. of Oriental Rsch., Centro Internationale Ricerche Archeologiche Anthropologiche e Storiche (Rome). Office: U of Tex Austin TX 78712

SCHMANKE, KYLE LYNDON, radiological physicist; b. Fort Worth, Aug. 11, 1958; s. Don Arther and Linda Kay (Farmer) S.; m. Charice Renel, Nov. 5, 1964. BS in Physics, U. Tex., Arlington, 1988; MS in Radiol. Physics, U. Tex.-Arlington & U Tex., Dallas, 1994. Lic. med. physicist, Tex. Med. physicist Moncrief Radiation Ctr., Ft. Worth, 1989, Parkland Meml. Hosp., Dallas, 1990-91; radiological physicist Presbyn. Hosp. Dallas, 1992-93, Med. Physics Cons., 1989—; med. physics computer cons. IMPAC Med. Sys., Mountain View, Calif., 1993—. 2nd class petty officer USN, 1976-82. Mem. Am. Assn. Physicists in Medicine, Sigma Pi Sigma, Alpha Chi. Avocations: black belt competitor in Am. karate, weightlifting. Home: 5110 Winterberry Ct Arlington TX 76018-1441 Office: Med Physics Cons PO Box 180396 Arlington TX 76096-0396

SCHMAUSS, STEPHEN ANTHONY, retired computer programmer; b. L.A., June 1, 1940; s. Kenneth and Doris (Armstrong) S. Student, UCLA, 1975, Mt. San Antonio Coll., 1989. Programmer Centaur Computer Sys., Glendale, Calif., 1970-75, Kaynar Industries, Fullerton, Calif., 1975-82; sr. systems programmer Shiley Inc., Irvine, Calif., 1982-94; ret., 1994; cons. J.P.L., Pasadena, Calif., 1975, FiServ, Spokane, Wash., 1994. With USN, 1958-63. Democrat. Avocations: boating, fishing, astronomy.

SCHMEER, ARLINE CATHERINE, cancer research development chemotherapy scientist; b. Rochester, N.Y., Nov. 14, 1929; d. Edward Jacob and Madeline Margaret (Haines) S. BA, Coll. St. Mary of the Springs, Columbus, Ohio, 1951; MS in Biology, Notre Dame U., 1961; PhD in Biomedicine, U. Colo., 1969; DSc (hon.), Albertus Magnus Coll., New Haven, Conn., 1974, SUNY, Potsdam, 1990. Chmn. sci. dept. Watterson High Sch./Diocese of Columbus, 1954-59, St. Vincent Ferrer High Sch./ Archdiocese of N.Y., N.Y.C., 1959-62; chmn. dept. biology Ohio Dominican Coll., Columbus, 1963-72; chmn. dept. anti-cancer agents of marine origin Am. Cancer Rsch. Ctr., Denver, 1972-82; dir. Mercenene Cancer Rsch. Inst., New Haven, 1982-93; sr. prin. investigator Marine Biol. Lab., Woods Hole, Mass., 1962-72, corp. mem., mem. libr. com., 1964—; rsch. prof. Med. Sch., U. Wüzburg, Germany, 1969-70; pres., chief exec. officer Med. Rsch. Found., 1972—; participant, contbr. Internat. Cancer Congress, 1966—. Contbr. articles to biol. pubs. Grantee Am. Cancer Soc., 1965; NSF fellow, 1957-62, NIH fellow, 1966-69; recipient numerous teaching awards, Ohi Acad. Scis. and others. Fellow Royal Microscopical Soc. Eng. (life); mem. N.Y. Acad. Sci. (life), Am. Soc. Cell Biology, Internat. Cancer Congresses. Roman Catholic. Avocations: photography, fishing. Office: Mercenene Cancer Rsch Inst 790 Prospect St New Haven CT 06511-1224

SCHMELING, GARETH, classics educator; b. Algoma, Wis., May 28, 1940; married. B.A., Northwestern Coll., 1963; M.A. (Knapp fellow), U. Wis., 1964, Ph.D. (Knapp travelling grantee 1965-66, Univ. fellow 1967-68), 1968. Asst. prof. classics U. Va., 1968-70; assoc. prof. U. Fla., 1970-74, prof., 1974—, chmn. classics, 1974—, chmn. humanities, 1974-76, dir. Center for Studies in Humanities, 1978-87, prin. investigator Humanities Perspectives on Professions, 1975-87, acting chmn. dept. philosophy, 1986-88; vis. prof. U. Colo., Boulder, 1992; panelist, research div. Nat. Endowment for Humanities, also mem. nat. bd. consultants. Translator and author Introduction: Cornelius Nepos: Lives of Famous Men, 1971; author: Petronius' Satyricon, 1971, Ovid's the Art of Love, 1972, Chariton and the Rise of Ancient Fiction, 1974, Homer's the Odyssey, 1974, A Bibliography of Petronius, 1977, Xenophon of Ephesus, 1980, Historia Apollonii Regis Tyri, 1988, The Novel in the Ancient World, 1996; contbr. numerous articles, revs. to profl. jours.; editor: Newsletter Petronian Soc. 1970—; editorial com.: U. Fla. Press Humanities Monographs, 1978—. Named 1 of 5 Tchrs. of Yr. for Arts and Scis. U. Fla., 1973; recipient Rome prize Am. Acad., 1977-78; U. Va. faculty fellow, summer 1969, summer 1970; U. Fla. fellow, summer 1971, summer 1974; Nat. Endowment for Humanities fellow, 1973-74; Am. Council Learned Socs. summer fellow, 1974; Am. Philos. Soc. grantee, 1970, 71, 72, 77-78, 84-85; U. Fla. grantee, 1977-78. Fellow Am. Acad. in Rome; mem. Am. Philol. Assn., Am. Classical League, Vergilian Soc., Classical Assn. of Middle West and South (sec.-treas. 1975-82, pres. 1985-86). Home: 320 NW 30th St Gainesville FL 32607-2524 Office: Dept Classics U Fla Gainesville FL 32611

SCHMELTZER, DAVID, lawyer; b. N.Y.C., Mar. 8, 1930; s. Harry Schmeltzer and Julia Hoffman Liebman; m. Louise Rose Levy, June 10, 1962; 1 child, Daniel Havram. BA, L.I. U., 1957; LLB, Bklyn. Law Sch., 1960. Bar: N.Y. 1961. Assoc. Charles Struckler Law Office, N.Y.C., 1960-61; mng. atty. Otterbourg, Steindler, Houston & Rosen, N.Y.C., 1961-62; pub. counsel U.S. Maritime Adminstrn., Washington, 1962-66; atty. Dept. Commerce, Washington, 1966; asst. chief counsel Nat. Hwy. Traffic and Safety Ad, Washington, 1967-73; asst. gen. counsel Consumer Product Safety Commn., Washington, 1973-75, dep. gen. counsel, 1975-77, acting gen. counsel, 1976-77, dir. compliance, 1977—; instr. U. Md. Univ Coll., College Park, 1979-90; mng. dir. Inst. Safety Analysis, Rockville, Md., 1981. Avocation: tennis. Home: 9424 Garden Ct Potomac MD 20854-3964 Office: US Cons Prod Safety Commn Compliance Office 4330 E West Hwy Bethesda MD 20814-4408

SCHMELTZER, EDWARD, lawyer; b. N.Y.C., Aug. 22, 1923; s. Harry A. and Julia (Hoffman) S.; m. Elizabeth Ann Cooper, June 19, 1949; children: Henry Cooper, Elizabeth Sabine. B.A., Hunter Coll., 1950; M.A., Columbia U., 1951; J.D., George Washington U., 1954. Bar: D.C. 1954, U.S. Supreme Ct 1958. Economist PHA, 1951-53; econ. cons., 1953-54; trial atty. Fed. Maritime Bd. Maritime Adminstrn., 1955-60; dir. bur. domestic regulation Fed. Maritime Commn., 1961-66, mng. dir., 1966-69; ptnr. Morgan, Lewis & Bockius, 1969-76, Schmeltzer, Aptaker & Shepard, 1976—; U.S. rep. 12th Diplomatic Conf. on Internat. Maritime Law, Brussels, 1967, 13th Diplomatic Conf., Brussels, 1968. Mem. bd. editors: Jour. Maritime Law and Commerce; Contbr. articles to profl. jours. Served with USAAF, 1943-46. Recipient Fed. Maritime Commn.; Distinguished Service award, 1969. Mem. Maritime Adminstrv. Bar Assn. (pres. 1971-73). Club: Cosmos (Washington). Home: 10412 Buckboard Pl Rockville MD 20854-3805 Office: The Watergate 2600 Virginia Ave NW Washington DC 20037-1905

SCHMELZER, HENRY LOUIS PHILLIP, lawyer, financial company executive; b. Concord, Mass., Aug. 10, 1943; s. Frank Elden and Carroll (Blanning) S.; m. Cynthia E. Livingston, Sept. 28, 1978. B.A., U. Maine, 1965; J.D., George Washington U., 1968. Bar: Mass. 1971. Atty. State Mut. Life Assurance Co., Worcester, Mass., 1970-72; various positions New Eng. Securities Corp., Boston, 1972-90, pres., dir., 1991-92; v.p. New Eng. Mut. Life Ins. Co., 1983-87; pres., trustee New Eng. Funds, 1992—. pres., trustee New Eng. Funds, 1992—; bd. dirs. Back Bay Advisors, Maine Bank & Trust Co. Bd. overseers U.S.S. Constitution Mus. Capt. M.I., U.S. Army, 1968-70, Vietnam. Decorated Bronze Star with oak leaf cluster. Mem. Investment Co. Inst. (legis. com.), Boston Com. on Fgn. Rels., Portland (Maine) Yacht Club. Unitarian. Office: New Eng Funds LP 399 Boylston St Ste 10 Boston MA 02116-3305

SCHMEMANN, SERGE, journalist; b. Paris, Apr. 12, 1945; arrived in U.S., 1951; s. Rev Alexander and Juliana (Ossorguine) S.; m. Mary Schidlovsky, Sept. 13, 1970; children: Anne, Alexander, Nathalie. BA cum laude, Harvard U., 1967; MA, Columbia U., 1971; LittD (hon.), Middlebury Coll., 1995. Desk editor AP, N.Y.C., 1972-75, UN corr., 1975-77, South Africa corr., 1977-79, Moscow corr., 1979-80; Moscow bur. chief N.Y. Times, 1980-87, 91-95, Bonn bur. chief, 1987-90, Jerusalem bur. chief, 1995—. Contbr. articles to profl. publs. With US Army, 1968-70, Vietnam. Recipient Hal Boyle award, Overseas Press Club, 1986, Pulitzer Prize for Coverage of German Reunification, 1991. Mem. Phi Beta Kappa. Avocations: piano, carpentry. Office: NY Times 229 W 43rd St New York NY 10036-3913

SCHMERGEL, GABRIEL, pharmaceutical company executive; b. Budapest, Hungary, May 14, 1940; came to U.S., 1956, naturalized, 1962; s. Geza and Elizabeth (Kovacs) S. BSME, Rensselaer Poly. Inst., 1962; MBA (Baker scholar), Harvard U., 1967; PhD (hon.), Worcester Poly. Tech. Inst., 1988. With Baxter Travenol Labs., Inc., 1967-81; gen. mgr. Baxter Travenol Labs., Gmbh, München, Fed. Republic Germany, 1969-71, Baxter Belgium, Brussels, 1971-74; area dir. Baxter Travenol Labs., Inc., Deerfield, Ill., 1974-75; v.p. Baxter Travenol Labs., Inc., Europe, Brussels, 1975-79; pres. internat. Baxter Travenol Labs., Inc., Deerfield, Ill., 1979-81; pres., chief exec. officer Genetics Inst., Cambridge, Mass., 1981—. Bd. govs. New Eng. Med. Ctr.; trustee Mass. Biotech. Rsch. Inst. Served to 1st lt. Ordnance Corps U.S. Army, 1963-65. Mem. ASME, Pharm. Mfrs. Assn., Indsl. Biotech. Assn. (past pres. 1986).

SCHMERLING, ERWIN ROBERT, counselor, retired physicist; b. Vienna, Austria, July 28, 1929; came to U.S., 1955, naturalized, 1962; s. Heinrich H. and Lily (Goldsmith) S.; m. Esther M. Schmerling, Apr. 5, 1957; children: Susan D., Elaine M. BA, Cambridge U., 1950, MA, 1954, PhD in Radio Physics, 1958; grad., Advanced Mgmt. Program, Harvard, 1969, Fed. Exec. Inst., 1975. Asst. prof. elec. engring. Pa. State U., University Park, 1955-60, assoc. prof., 1960-62, 63-64; staff scientist NASA-Hdqrs., Washington, 1962-63, program chief ionospheric physics, magnetospheric physics, space plasma physics, 1964-82; asst. dir. space and earth scis. Goddard Space Flight Ctr., NASA, Greenbelt, Md., 1984-86; chief data system scientist Office Space Science and Applications NASA Hdqrs., Washington, 1986-88; SAIS program scientist NASA, Washington, 1988-89; data system scientist solar system exploration div. NASA Hdqrs., Washington, 1989-90, program mgr. astrophysics data systems, 1991-94; counselor Svc. Corps of Retired Execs. (SCORE); mem. U.S. coms. III and IV Internat. Sci. Radio Union, 1985—, sec. U.S. Com. III, 1966-69, chmn., 1969-72; chmn. subcom. C1 Com. Space Rsch. (COSPAR), 1984-88; mem. Adv. Group Aerospace Research and Devel.; vis. scholar Stanford U., 1983; cons. RCA, Gen. Electric, 1959-62. Contbr. papers to profl. jours. Recipient medal for contbns. to internat. geophys. programs Soviet Geophys. Soc., 1985. Fellow IEEE (mem. wave propagation standards com.); mem. Am. Geophys. Union, AAAS, Sigma Xi. Home: 9917 La Duke Dr Kensington MD 20895-3140

SCHMEROLD, WILFRIED LOTHAR, dermatologist; b. Munich, Germany, Dec. 30, 1919; came to U.S., 1956; s. Wilhelm and Frieda (Hinterwinkler) S.; m. Perlette J. Joers, 1962 (div. Apr. 1974); children: Klaus, John, Will, James, Susan, Paul, Carl, Mike, Tom, Marianne. Abiturient, Altes Realgymnasium, 1938; MD, U. Munich, 1945. Bd. cert. dermatologist, dermatopathologist. Intern U Munich Med. Faculty, 1945-46; asst. UN Hosp., Munich, 1946-50, Max Planck Inst., Munich, 1951-52, U. Erlangen, Germany, 1952-53, U. Munich, 1953-56; intern Fairview Park Hosp., Cleve., 1956-57; asst. U. Ill., Chgo., 1957-60, instr., 1960-75, clin. asst. prof., 1975—; dermatologist pvt. practice, Carol Stream, Ill., 1959—, dermatopathologist, 1978—. Contbr. articles to profl. jours. Charter mem. founders club Ctrl. DuPage Hosp., Winfield, Ill., 1963. Fellow AMA, Am. Acad. Dermatology (life), German Dermatological Soc. (life), Am. Soc. Dermatopathology, Ill. Dermatological Soc., Ill. State Med. Soc., Chgo. Dermatological Soc. Roman Catholic. Avocations: opera, travel, anthropology, archaeology, history. Office: Mona Kea Med Park 507 Thornhill Dr # B Carol Stream IL 60188-2703

SCHMERTMANN, JOHN HENRY, civil engineer, educator, consultant; b. N.Y.C., Dec. 2, 1928; s. Johannes Conrad Schmertmann and Margarete Anna-Marie (Carstens) Schmertmann Ottesen; m. Pauline Anne Grange, Aug. 11, 1956; children: Carl, Gary, Neil, Joy. B.S.C.E., MIT, 1950; M.S.C.E., Northwestern U., 1954, Ph.D. in Civil Engring., 1962. Registered profl. engr., Fla. Soils engr. Mueser Rutledge Cons. Engrs., N.Y.C., 1951-54; soils engr. C.E., U.S. Army, Wilmette, Ill., 1954-56; asst. prof. civil engring. U. Fla., Gainesville, 1956-62; assoc. prof. U. Fla., 1962-65, prof., 1965-79, adj. prof., prof. emeritus; prin. Schmertmann & Crapps, Inc., Gainesville, 1979—; postdoctoral fellow Norwegian Geotech. Inst., Oslo,

1962-63; vis. scientist div. bldg. research NRC Can., Ottawa Ont., 1971-72. Author numerous profl. papers. Fellow ASCE (br. pres. 1972, Collingwood prize 1956, Norman medal 1971, State of the Art award 1977, Middlebrooks award 1981, Terzaghi lectr. 1989), Fla. Engring. Soc.; mem. Nat. Acad. Engring., ASTM (subcom. chmn. 1974—). Republican. Lutheran. Avocation: sport fishing. Office: Schmertmann & Crapps Inc 4509 NW 23rd Ave Ste 19 Gainesville FL 32606

SCHMERTZ, ERIC JOSEPH, lawyer, educator; b. N.Y.C., Dec. 24, 1925; married; 4 children. A.B., Union Coll., 1948, LL.D. (hon.), 1978; cert., Alliance Francaise, Paris, 1948; J.D., NYU, 1954. Bar: N.Y. 1955. Internat. rep. Am. Fedn. State, County and Mcpl. Employees, AFL-CIO, N.Y.C., 1950-52; asst. v.p., dir. labor tribunals Am. Arbitration Assn., N.Y.C., 1952-57, 59-60; indsl. relations dir. Metal Textile Corp. subs. Gen. Cable Corp., Roselle, N.J., 1957-59; exec. dir. N.Y. State Bd. Mediation, 1960-62, corp. dir., 1962-68; labor-mgmt. arbitrator N.Y.C., 1962—; mem. faculty Hofstra U. Sch. Bus., 1962-70; prof. Hofstra U. Sch. Law, 1970—, Edward F. Carlough disting. prof. labor law, 1981—, dean Sch. Law, 1982-89; of counsel Rivkin, Radler, Kremer, 1989—; commr. labor rels. City of N.Y., 1990-91; 1st Beckley lectr. in bus. U. Vt., 1981; bd. dirs. Wilshire Oil Co.; mem. N.Y. State Pub. Employment Rels. Bd., 1991—; cons. and lectr. in field. Co-author: (with R.L. Greenman) Personnel Administration and the Law, 1978; contbr. chpts. to books, articles to profl. jours., to profl. law confs., seminars and workshops. Mem. numerous civic orgns. Served to lt. USN, 1943-46. Recipient Testimonial award Southeast Republican Club, 1969; Alexander Hamilton award Rep. Law Students Assn.; Eric J. Schmertz Disting. Professorship Pub. Law and Pub. Svc. established Hofstra Law Sch., 1993. Mem. Nat. Acad. Arbitrators, Am. Arbitration Assn. (law com., Whitney North Seymour Sr. medal 1984), Fed. Mediation and Conciliation Svc., N.Y. Mediation Bd., N.J. Mediation Bd., N.J. Pub. Employment Rels. Bd., Hofstra U. Club, Princeton Club. Office: 275 Madison Ave New York NY 10016-1101

SCHMERTZ, HERBERT, public relations and advertising executive; b. Yonkers, N.Y., Mar. 22, 1930; s. Max and Hetty (Frank) S.; children: Anthony, Lexy, Nicole, Thomas, Conor. AB, Union Coll., 1952, LLD (hon.), 1977; LLB, Columbia U., 1955. Bar: N.Y. State 1958. With Am. Arbitration Assn., N.Y.C., 1955-61; gen. counsel, asst. to dir. Fedn. Mediation and Conciliation Svc., N.Y.C., 1961-66; with Mobil Oil Corp., N.Y.C., 1966—; pres. Mobil Shipping and Transp. Co., 1973-74; v.p. pub. affairs Mobil Oil Corp., 1974-88; pres. The Schmertz Co., Inc., N.Y.C., 1988—, Washington, 1990—. Author: Good-bye to the Low Profile, 1986; co-author Takeover, 1980. Appointee Pres.'s Commn. on Broadcasting to Cuba, U.S. Adv. Commn. on Pub. Diplomacy; mem. adv. coun. NYU Sch. Arts; bd. dirs. USO Met. N.Y.C.; trustee Media Inst.; bd. govs. Media and Society Seminars Columbia U. Grad. Sch. Journalism. Served with CIC U.S. Army, 1955-57. Mem. Coun. Fgn. Rels., N.Y. Athletic Club. Democrat. Jewish. Office: Schmertz Co Inc 1185 Ave of the Americas 8th FL New York NY 10036-2601 also: Schmertz Co Washington 555 13th St Ste 1300 E Washington DC 20004-1109

SCHMERTZ, MILDRED FLOYD, editor, writer; b. Pitts., Mar. 29, 1925; d. Robert Watson and Mildred Patricia (Floyd) S. B.Arch., Carnegie Mellon U., 1947; M.F.A., Yale U., 1957. Archtl. designer John Schurko, Architect, Pitts., 1947-55; assoc. editor Archtl. Record, N.Y.C., 1957-65; sr. editor Archtl. Record, 1965-80, exec. editor, 1980-85, editor-in-chief, 1985-90; vis. lectr. Yale Sch. Architecture, 1979—. Editor, contbr.: New Life for Old Buildings; other books on architecture and planning. Bd. mgrs. Jr. League, City of N.Y., 1964-65; commr. N.Y. Landmarks Preservation Commn., 1988-91. Fellow AIA; mem. Archtl. League N.Y., Mcpl. Art Soc. N.Y., Century Assn. (N.Y.C.). Home and Office: 310 E 46th St New York NY 10017-3002

SCHMETTERER, ROBERT ALLEN, advertising executive; b. N.Y.C., Nov. 23, 1943; s. Robert Mayer and Rosalie (Fernandez) S.; children: Adam, Tyler; m. Stacy Lynn Chiarello, Sept. 26, 1987. B.S., Fairleigh Dickinson U., 1967, M.B.A., 1970. Sales promotion mgr. Brit. Motor Corp., Leonia, N.J., 1963-68; market research dir. Volvo, Rockleigh, N.J., 1968-71; v.p. market rsch. Scali, McCabe, Sloves Inc., N.Y.C., 1971-73, sr. v.p. dir. account service, 1974-79, exec. v.p., chief oper. officer, mng. dir., 1979-84; pres., chief exec. officer/worldwide HCM, N.Y.C. and Paris, 1984-87; pres., ptnr. Messner, Vetere, Berger, Carey, Schmetterer, N.Y.C., 1987—; bd. dirs. N.Y.C. Partnership, 1987—. Mem. Advt. Club N.Y. (dir. 1983). Home: Snedens Landing Palisades NY 10964 Office: Messner Vetere Berger McNamee Schmetterer 350 Hudson St New York NY 10014-4504*

SCHMID, HARALD HEINRICH OTTO, biochemistry educator, academic director; b. Graz, Styria, Austria, Dec. 10, 1935; Came to U.S., 1962; s. Engelbert and Annemarie (Kletetschka) S.; m. Patricia Caroline Igou, May 21, 1977. MS, U. Graz, 1957, LLD, 1962, PhD, 1964. Rsch. fellow Hormel inst. U. Minn., Austin, 1962-65, rsch. assoc., 1965-66, asst. prof., 1966-70, assoc. prof., 1970-74, prof., 1974—; cons. NIH, Bethesda, Md., 1977—; acting dir. Hormel inst. U. Minn., 1985-87, exec. dir., 1987—; lectr. Mayo Med. Sch., Rochester, Minn., 1990—. Mng. editor Chemistry and Physics of Lipids, Elsevier Sci. Publs., Amsterdam, The Netherlands, 1984—; contbr. numerous articles to profl. jours. Rsch. grantee NIH, 1967—. Mem. AAAS, Am. Soc. Biochemistry and Molecular Biology, Am. Chem. Soc., The Oxygen Soc. Avocations: yacht racing, downhill skiing, tennis, classical music. Home: 2701 2d Ave NW Austin MN 55912-9541 Office: U Minn Hormel Inst 801 16th Ave NE Austin MN 55912-3679

SCHMID, LYNETTE SUE, child and adolescent psychiatrist; b. Tecumseh, Nebr., May 28, 1958; d. Mel Vern John and Janice Wilda (Bohling) S.; m. Vijendra Sundar, June 13, 1987; children: Jesse Christopher Mikaéle, Eric Lynn Kalani, Christina Elizabeth Ululani. BS, U. Nebr., 1979; MD, U. Nebr., Omaha, 1984; postgrad., U. Mo., 1984-89. Diplomate Am. Bd. Med. Examiners, Am. Bd. Psychiatry and Neurology. Child and adolescent psychiatrist Fulton (Mo.) State Hosp., 1990-91, Mid-Mo. Mental Health Ctr., Columbia, Mo., 1991—; clin. asst. prof. psychiatry U. Mo., Columbia, 1990—. Contbr. articles to profl. jours. Mem. Am. Psychiat. Assn., Am. Acad. Child and Adolescent Psychiatry, Ctrl. Mo. Psychiat. Assn. (sec.-treas. 1992-93, pres.- elect 1993-94, pres. 1994-95), U. Nebr. Alumni Assn., Phi Beta Kappa, Alpha Omega Alpha. Republican. Baptist. Avocations: walking, reading, studying scripture.

SCHMID, RUDI (RUDOLF SCHMID), internist, educator, university official; b. Switzerland, May 2, 1922; came to U.S., 1948, naturalized, 1954; s. Rudolf and Bertha (Schiesser) S.; m. Sonja D. Wild, Sept. 17, 1949; children: Isabelle S., Peter R. BS, Gymnasium Zurich, 1941; MD, U. Zurich, 1947; PhD, U. Minn., 1954. Intern U. Calif. Med. Center, San Francisco, 1948-49; resident medicine U. Minn., 1949-52, instr., 1952-54; research fellow biochemistry Columbia U., 1954-55; investigator NIH, Bethesda, Md., 1955-57; assoc. medicine Harvard U., 1957-59, asst. prof., 1959-62; prof. medicine U. Chgo., 1962-66; prof. medicine U. Calif., San Francisco, 1966-91, prof. emeritus, 1991—, dean Sch. Medicine, 1983-89, assoc. dean internat. rels., 1989-95; Cons. U.S. Army Surgeon Gen., USPHS, VA. Mem. editorial bd. Jour. Clin. Investigation, 1965-70, Blood, 1962-75, Gastroenterology, 1965-70, Jour. Investigative Dermatology, 1968-72, Annals Internal Medicine, 1975-79, Proceedings Soc. Exptl. Biology and Medicine, 1974-84, Chinese Jour. Clin. Scis., Jour. Lab. Clin. Medicine, 1991—, Hepatology Comm. Internat. (Japan), 1993—; cons. editor Gastroenterology, 1981-86. Served with Swiss Army, 1943-48. Master ACP; fellow AAAS, N.Y. Acad. Scis., Royal Coll. Physicians; mem. NAS, Am. Acad. Arts and Scis., Assn. Am. Physicians (pres. 1986), Am. Soc. Clin. Investigation, Am. Soc. Biol. Chemistry and Molecular Biology, Am. Soc. Hematology, Am. Gastroenterol. Assn., Am. Assn. Study Liver Disease (pres. 1965), Internat. Assn. Study Liver (pres. 1980), Swiss Acad. Med. Scis. (mem. senate), Leopoldina, German-Am. Acad. Coun. Research in metabolism of hemoglobin, heme, prophyrins, bile pigments, liver and muscle. Home: 211 Woodland Rd Kentfield CA 94904-2631 Office: U Calif Med Sch Office of Dean PO Box 0410 San Francisco CA 94143-0410

SCHMID, WILFRIED, mathematician; b. Hamburg, Germany, May 28, 1943; came to U.S., 1960; s. Wolfgang and Kathe (Erfling) S. BA, Princeton U., 1964; MA, U. Calif., Berkeley, 1966, PhD, 1967. Asst. prof. math. U. Calif., Berkeley, 1967-70; prof. math. Columbia U., 1970-78, Harvard U., 1978—; vis. mem. Inst. for Advanced Study, Princeton, 1969-70, 75-76; vis. prof. U. Bonn, 1973-74. Editor Springer Ergebnisse der Mathematik; contbr. articles to profl. jours. Sloan fellow, 1968-70, Guggenheim fellow, 1975-76, 88-89. Home: Silver Hill Rd Lincoln MA 01773 Office: Harvard U Dept Mathematics Cambridge MA 02138

SCHMIDHAUSER, JOHN RICHARD, political science educator; b. N.Y.C., Jan. 3, 1922; s. Richard J. and Gertrude (Grabinger) S.; m. Thelma Lorraine Ficker, June 9, 1952; children: Steven, Paul, Thomas, John C., Martha, Sarah, Susan. B.A. with honors, U. Del., 1949; M.A., U. Va., 1952, Ph.D., 1954. Instr. U. Va., 1952-54; prof. constl. law U. Iowa, 1954-64, prof. polit. sci., 1967-73; prof. polit. sci. U. So. Calif., 1973-92, prof. emeritus, 1993—; mem. 89th Congress 1st dist. Iowa.; research fellow Research Inst. on Jud. Process, Social Sci. Research Council, 1958; sr. fellow law and behavorial scis. U. Chgo., 1959-60; Talbot vis. prof. govt. U. Va., 1982-83. Author: The Role of Supreme Court as Final Arbiter in Federal-State Relations, 1789-1957, 1958, The Supreme Court; Its Politics, Personalities and Procedures, 1960, Constitutional Law in the Political Process, 1963, (with Berg) The Supreme Court and Congress, 1972, (with Berg and Hahn) American Political Institutions and Corruption, 1976, (with Totten) Whaling in Japan-U.S. Relations, 1978, Judges and Justices, 1979, Constitutional Law in American Politics, 1984, Comparative Judicial Politics, 1987; also numerous articles in jours. Chmn. Citizens Action Com. for Fair Representation in Iowa Legislature, 1961; dist. chmn. Operation Support Pres. Kennedy and Johnson, 1961—; chmn. Johnson County Dem. Ctrl. Com., 1961-64; del. Iowa Dem. Convs., 1956, 58, 60, 62; mem. Dem. Nat. Com. Alumni Coun., 1986—; chmn. Santa Barbara, Calif. Dem. Ctrl. Com., 1991-92; mem. exec. com. Los Padres chpt. of the Sierra Club, 1992—; sec. Santa Barbara Dem. League, 1993—. With USNR, 1941-45, PTO. Recipient Raubenheimer award U. So. Calif., 1991, Golden Key award for Comparative Rsch, 1991. Mem. Iowa City Mgr. Assn. (bd. reps. 1956-59, chmn. handbook revision 1958), Internat. Polit. Sci. Assn. (chmn. research com. for comparative jud. studies 1980-88), Am. Polit. Sci. Assn., Midwestern Polit. Sci. Assn., Western Polit. Sci. Assn. (v.p., program chmn. 1980-81, pres.-elect 1981-82), AAUP (sec.-treas. State U. Iowa 1958-59, mem. com. on relationship fed. and state govt. to higher edn., mem. exec. com. U. So. Calif. chpt. 1983-92), Humanities Soc., Raven Soc., Phi Beta Kappa, Phi Kappa Phi. Unitarian (chmn. Iowa City Soc. Men's Club 1960-61). Home: 726 Arbol Verde St Carpinteria CA 93013-2508 *For the young today the opportunity for a good education puts them at the threshold of great opportunities. I encourage them to enjoy that with the same spirit that my generation experienced.*

SCHMIDLY, DAVID J., academic administrator, dean; b. Levelland, Tex., Dec. 20, 1943; m. Janet Elaine Knox, June 2, 1966; children: Katherine Elaine, Brian James. BS in Biology, Tex. Tech U., 1966, MS in Zoology, 1968; PhD in Zoology, U. Ill., 1971. From asst. prof. to prof. dept. wildlife fisheries scis. Tex. A&M U., College Station, 1971-82, prof., 1982—, head dept. wildlife, 1986-92; CEO, campus dean Tex. A&M U., Galveston, 1992—; chief curator Tex. Coop. Wildlife Coll., College Station, 1983-86; v.p. Tex. Inst. Oceanography, 1992—; cons. Nat. Park Svc., Wildlife Assocs., Walton and Assocs., Continental Shelf Assn., LGL; press adv. com. Tex. A&M U., 1983—; charter mem. Tex. A&M U. Faculty Senate, 1983-85; chmn. Scholarship Com., 1978-82; lectr. various workshops and seminars. Author: The Mammals of Trans-Pecos Texas including Big Bend National Park and Guadalupe Mountains National Park, 1977, Texas Mammals East of the Balcones Fault Zone, 1983, The Bats of Texas, 1991, The Mammals of Texas, 1994; contbr. articles to profl. jours. Trustee Tex. Nature Conservancy, 1991—. Recipient Dist. Prof. award Assn. Grad. Wildlife and Fisheries Scis., 1985, Donald W. Tinkle Rsch. Excellence award Southwestern Assn. Naturalists, 1988, Diploma Recognition La Universidad Autonoma de Guadalajara, 1989, La Universidad Autonoma de Tamaulipas, 1990. Fellow Tex. Soc. Sci. (bd. dirs. 1979-81); mem. AAAS, Am. Soc. Mammalogists (life, editor Jour. Mammalogy 1975-78), Am. Inst. Biol. Scis. (bd. dirs. 1993—, coun. affiliate socs. 1989—), Am. Naturalist, Soc. Marine Mammalogy (charter mem.), Soc. Systematic Zoology, The Wildlife Soc. Soc. Conservation Biology, Nat. Geog. Sci. Soc., S.W. Assn. Naturalists (life mem., bd. govs. 1980-86, 91—, pres. 1981, trustee 1986—), Tex. Mammal Soc. (pres. 1985-86), Assn. Systematic Collections (bd. dirs.), Chihuahuan Desert Rsch. Inst. (v.p. bd. scientists 1982—, bd. dirs. 1991), Mexican Soc. Mammalogists, Sigma Xi (v.p. 1986-87, pres. 1987-88), Disting. Scientist award 1991), Beta Beta Beta. Phi Sigma, Phi Kapa Phi. Home: 54 Adler Cir Galveston TX 77551-5828 Office: Tex A&M U at Galveston Office of Dean PO Box 1675 Galveston TX 77553-1675

SCHMIDMAN, JO ANN, artistic director. BFA, Boston U., 1970. Performer Joseph Chaikin's Open Theatre, N.Y.C.; artistic dir., writer, actor, prodr., light and concept designer Omaha Magic Theatre, 1968—; project dir., fiscal agt. for more than 90 found., corp., govt. grants; lectr. internationally; condr. workshops in ensemble acting, directing, collaborative theatre, performance art and storytelling; tchr. playwriting and poetry at various univs.; reporter Theatre Program, NEA, 1980—, mem. artistic advancement com., 1987-89, 92, chmn., 1988-89, mem. theatre overview panel, 1988; mem. Japanese-Am. Fellowship Com., 1987. Contbg. writer: 100,001 Horror Stores of the Plains, 1976, This Sleep Among Women, 1978, Running Gag, 1980 (commd. perfs. 1980 Winter Olympics); dir., performer: (with Sora Kimberlain) Yellow Strapping, 1980, (with Kimberlain) Blue Tube, 1980, (with Kimberlain) White Out, 1980, (with Kimberlain) Reflected Light, 1980, Change Yer Image, 1981, Aliens Under Glass, 1982, Velveeta Meltdown, 1982, Watch Where We Walk, 1983, (with Megan Terry) X-Rayed-Iate: E-Motion in Action, 1984, Astro*Bride, 1984, (with Terry) Sea of Forms, 1986, (with Terry) Walking Through Walls, 1987, (with Terry) Babes Unchained, (with Terry and Kimberlain) Body Leaks, 1990, Belches on Couches, 1993; dir.: (with Terry, Kimberlain, and Calif. State students) Cancel That Last Thought or See the 270 Foot Woman in Spandex, 1989, (with Terry and Kimberlain) Sound Fields, 1991, (with Terry) Remote Control, 1994, (with Terry and Kimberlain) Star Path Moon Stop, 1995; editor (with Terry and Kimberlain) Right Brain Vacation Photos, 1972-92; performer: Terminal, Open Theatre, 1971-73; contbg. writer, performer: Mutation Show and Nightwalk, Open Theatre, 1970-73 (Obie award); prodr., dir., performer numerous plays. Artist-in-the-Schs. in Performing Arts grantee Nebr. Arts Coun. Home: 2309 Hanscom Blvd Omaha NE 68105-3143 Office: Omaha Magic Theatre 325 S 16th St Omaha NE 68102

SCHMID-SCHOENBEIN, GEERT WILFRIED, biomedical engineer, educator; b. Albstadt, Baden-Wurttemberg, Germany, Jan. 1, 1948; came to U.S., 1971; s. Ernst and Ursula Schmid; m. Renate Schmid-Schoenbein, July 3, 1976; children: Philip, Mark, Peter. Vordiplom, Liebig U., Giessen, Germany, 1971; PhD in Bioengring., U. Calif., San Diego, 1976. Staff assoc. dept. physiology Columbia U., N.Y.C., 1976-77, sr. assoc., 1977-79; asst. prof. dept. applied mechs. & engring. scis. U. Calif., San Diego, 1979-84, assoc. prof., 1984-89, prof., 1989—. Editor: Frontiers in Biomechanics, 1986, Physiology and Pathophysiology of Leukocyte Adhesion, 1994. Recipient Melville medal ASME, 1990. Fellow Am. Inst. for Med. & Biol. Engring., Am. Heart Assn.; mem. Biomed. Engring. Soc. (pres. 1991-92), Am. Microcirculatory Soc., European Microciculatory Soc., Am. Physiol. Soc. Achievements include bioengineering research of cardiovascular disease. Office: U Calif San Diego Dept Bioengineering La Jolla CA 92093-0412

SCHMIDT, ADOLPH WILLIAM, retired ambassador; b. McKeesport, Pa., Sept. 13, 1904; s. Adolph and Louise (Schmidt) S.; m. Helen Sedgley Mellon, June 27, 1936; children—Helen Schmidt Claire, Thomas M. A.B., Princeton U., 1926, LL.D. (hon.), 1977; M.B.A., Harvard U., 1929; certificates, U. Dijon, U. Berlin and U. Paris, Sorbonne, 1926-27; LL.D. (hon.), U. Pitts, 1954, U. N.B., 1973; L.H.D., Chatham Coll., 1965, Carnegie-Mellon U., 1981. Officer Mellon Nat. Bank and affiliated orgns., Pitts., 1929-42; chmn. bd., dir. Columbia Radiator Co., McKeesport, 1939-42; mem. exec. com., dir. Pitts. Coal Co., 1940-42; v.p., gov. T. Mellon & Sons, Pitts., 1946-69; trustee A.W. Mellon Ednl. and Charitable Trust, pres., 1954-65; trustee Old Dominion Found., 1941-69, Carnegie Inst., 1965-92; ambassador to Can. Ottawa, Ont., 1969-74; U.S. del. Conf. on North Atlantic Community, Bruges, Belgium, 1957, Atlantic Congress, London, Eng., 1959, Atlantic Conv. NATO Nations, Paris, France, 1962; adviser to U.S. delegation Econ. Commn. for, Europe, Geneva, Switzerland, 1967; bd. govs. Atlantic Inst., Paris; bd. dirs. Atlantic Council U.S., Washington. Co-founder Pitts. Playhouse, 1934, Pitts. Symphony, 1937; pres. Presbyn.-Univ. Hosp., 1946-47; 1st chmn. Three Rivers Arts Festival, 1960; pres., chmn. Allegheny Conf. on Community Devel., Pitts., 1956-61; vice chmn. Urban Redevel. Authority, 1954-59; 1st chmn. Southwestern Pa. Regional Planning Commn., 1960; mem. bus. and internat. coms. Nat. Planning Assn., 1955-69; mem. Can.-Am. Com., 1974-80; chmn. Pa. State Planning Bd., 1955-68; dir. Population Crisis Com., Washington, 1965-69, Population-Environment Balance, Inc., 1973-89; mem. bd. visitors and govs. St. Johns Coll., Annapolis, Md. and Santa Fe, N.Mex., also chmn., 1956, 62; mem. grad. council Princeton U. Served from capt. to lt. col. U.S. Army, 1942-46; with OSS in Africa and Europe; Allied Control Commn. Berlin. Awarded Bronze Star, Two Battle Stars; Benjamin Rush award Allegheny Co. Med. Soc., 1950; David Glick award World Affairs Council, 1965. Mem. Coun. Fgn. Rels., Mil. Order World Wars, Coun. Am. Ambs. Republican. Presbyterian. Clubs: Links, Anglers (N.Y.C.); Duquesne (Pitts.), Pitts. Golf; Laurel Valley Golf, Rolling Rock (Ligonier, Pa.); Metropolitan (Washington). Home: RR 4 Ligonier PA 15658-9804

SCHMIDT, ALLEN EDWARD, religious foundation administrator; b. Barriere, B.C., Can., Oct. 30, 1932; s. Ernst Waldemar and Agda Elvira (Rosen) S.; m. Catherine Edith Lee, June 19, 1954; children: Rebecca Lee Wade, Leanne Ruth Birdwell, Joseph Allen. BA with honors, Hardin-Simmons U., 1957; MDiv, Golden Gate Bapt. Sem., 1962. Owner, operator trucking co. Barriere, 1949-52; founding pastor Temple Bapt. Ch., Fairfield, Calif., 1960-61, Pike Rd. Bapt. Ch., Surrey, B.C., 1961-66, Royal Heights Bapt. Ch., Delta, B.C., 1966-81; Can. ch. coord. N.W. Bapt. Conv., Portland, Oreg., 1981; exec. dir., treas. Can. Conv. of So. Baptists, Cochrane, Alta., Can., 1985—. Pres. PTA, Surrey, 1977-79, Surrey Ministerial, 1975-77, N.W. Bapt. Conv., Portland, 1976-78, exec. bd. dirs., chmn., 1971-75. Home: 128 Riverview Cir, Cochrane, AB Canada T0L 0W4 Office: Can Conv So Baptists, Bag 300, Cochrane, AB Canada T0L 0W0

SCHMIDT, ARTHUR, film editor. Editor: (films) (with Jim Clark) The Last Remake of Beau Geste, 1977, Coal Miner's Daughter, 1980 (Academy award nomination best film editing 1980), The Escape Artist, 1982, Firstborn, 1984, The Buddy System, 1984, (with Harry Keramidas) Back to the Future, 1985, Fandango, 1985, (with Gib Jaffe) Ruthless People, 1986, Who Framed Roger Rabbit?, 1988 (Academy award best film editing 1988), (with Keramidas) Back to the Future II, 1989, (with Keramidas) Back to the Future III, 1990, (with Dov Hoenig) The Last of the Mohicans, 1992, Death Becomes Her, 1992, (with Jim Miller) Addams Family Values, 1993, Forrest Gump, 1994 (Academy award best film editing 1994), The Birdcage, 1996. Office: care Motion Picture Editors 7715 W Sunset Blvd Ste 220 Los Angeles CA 90046-3912

SCHMIDT, ARTHUR LOUIS, retired state senator, businessman; b. Cold Spring, Ky., May 1, 1927; s. Joseph E. and Elizabeth (Bertsch) S.; m. Marian Seibert, Apr. 28, 1951; children: Karen, Marianne. Mgr. mktg. Cin. Bell, 1946-83; dir. Provident Bank of Ky., 1964-93. Mem. City Council, Cold Spring, Ky., 1962-63; mem. Ky. Ho. of Reps., 1963-83; mem. Ky. Senate, 1983-92.

SCHMIDT, BARNET MICHAEL, communications and electronic engineer; b. New Milford, N.J., June 30, 1958; s. Frank Lowell and Lee (Fishkin) S. BSEE, Stevens Inst. Tech., 1980, BS Computer Sci., 1980, MSEE, 1985. Comml. pilot/instrument. Electronic engr. Cessna Aircraft Co., Boonton, N.J., 1980-81; sr. systems engr. Timeplex Corp., Unisys Co., Woodcliff Lake, N.J., 1981-85; mem. tech. staff, cons. AT&T Bell Labs., Holmdel, N.J., 1985-90; mem. tech. staff Bell Comms. Rsch., Piscataway, N.J., 1990-95, AT&T Bell Labs., Holmdel, N.J., 1995—; cons. engr. Computer Scis. Corp., El Segundo, Calif., 1986-90. Patentee in field. Mem. IEEE. Achievements include inventing neural-network based intelligent systems for isolating hidden troubles in telecomms. networks; inventing of novel adaptive filter synthesis techniques. Office: AT&T Bell Labs Bell Comms Rsch Inc Crawfords Corner Rd Holmdel NJ 07733-1988

SCHMIDT, BENNO CHARLES, investment company executive; b. Abilene, Tex., 1913; m. Nancy Montgomery Fleischmann; children: Benno, Ralph, Thomas (dec.), John and William (twins). BA, LLB, U. Tex., 1936; LLD (honoris causa), Columbia U.; LHD (hon.), N.Y. Med. Coll. Mem. law faculty U. Tex., 1936-40; Thayer teaching fellow Harvard U. Sch. Law, Cambridge, 1940-41; with Office Gen. Counsel, War Prodn. Bd., Washington, 1941-42; gen. counsel Office Fgn. Liquidation Commn., Dept. State, Washington, 1945-46; mng. ptnr. J.H. Whitney & Co., N.Y.C., 1946-92, sr. ptnr., 1993—; chmn.-emeritus Freeport-McMoRan Copper & Gold; dir.-emeritus Freeport-McMoRan Inc., McMoRan Oil & Gas Co.; past dir., officer numerous bus. enterprises with holdings in U.S., Australia and Western Europe including Schlumberger Ltd., CBS, Inc., Memorex Corp., Gen. Signal Corp., Transco Energy Co., San Jacinto Petroleum, Global Marine, Inc., others. Chmn. Pres.'s Cancer Panel, 1971-80; mem. Pres.'s Biomed. Rsch. Panel, 1975-76; chmn. Bedford-Stuyvesant Devel. & Svcs. Corp., 1969-84, Fund for City N.Y., 1968-77, Roosevelt Island Devel. Corp., 1969-76; pres. Am. Australian Assn., 1971-86, Thomas Payne Schmidt Found., 1972-86; chmn. bd. Meml. Sloan-Kettering Cancer Ctr., 1982-90, hon. co-chmn., 1990—; trustee Gen. Motors Cancer Rsch. Found., Whitney Mus. Am. Art, 1965-84, Carnegie Found. for Internat. Peace, 1977-81; mem. chancellor's coun., devel bd. U. Tex.; mem. centennial commn., Rockefeller U. Coun., U. Tex. Served to col. AUS, 1942-45. Decorated Legion of Merit, Bronze Star; Legion d'Honneur, Croix de Guerre with palms, French medal of Merit; named Disting. Alumnus U. Tex., 1969, Outstanding Alumnus Law Sch., 1981; recipient cert. of award Am. Assn. Cancer Research, 1971, Clement Cleveland award for disting. service in crusade to control cancer N.Y.C. div. Am. Cancer Soc., 1972, Nat. award for disting. service, 1974, Papanicolaou award for disting. service to cancer control, 1974, James Ewing Soc. Ann. award for outstanding contbns. in fight against cancer, 1975, Alfred P. Sloan, Jr. Meml. award N.Y.C. div. Am. Cancer Soc., 1977, Stanley P. Reimann medal The Fox Chase Cancer Center, Phila., 1977, medal City of Rotterdam, 1977; NIH Dir.'s award, 1978, Bristol-Myers award for disting. service in cancer research, 1979. Mem. Am. Australian Assn., Alpha Omega Alpha (hon.).

SCHMIDT, BERLIE LOUIS, agricultural research administrator; b. Treynor, Iowa, Oct. 2, 1932; s. Hans Frederick and Louisa Amalie (Guttau) S.; m. Joanne Doris Bruning, Sept. 4, 1954 (dec. Apr. 1982); children: Brian, Luanne Schmidt Code, Kevin, Kimberly Schmidt Nelson, Christy Schmidt Mash; m. Bonnijane G. Mehlhop, June 14, 1986. B.S., Iowa State U., 1954, M.S., 1959, Ph.D., 1962. Soil scientist Soil Conservation Svc. USDA, Council Bluffs, Iowa, 1954-57; grad. rsch. assoc. Iowa State U., Ames, 1957-62; asst. prof. agronomy Ohio State U., Wooster, 1962-65, assoc. prof., 1965-69; prof., assoc. chmn. dept. agronomy Ohio State U., Columbus, 1969-75, prof., chmn. dept. agronomy, 1975-86, prof., coord. Conservation Tillage Systems Program, 1986-87; soil scientist, program mgr. water quality program Coop. State Rsch., Edn. and Extension Svc., USDA, Washington, 1987—; program dir. Nat. Rsch. Initiative Competitive Rsch. Grants Program, 1994—. Editor: Determinants of Soil Loss Tolerance, 1982; contbr. articles to sci. jours. Elder Worthington United Presbyterian Ch., 1983. With U.S. Army, 1954-56, PTO. Fellow Am. Soc. Agronomy, Ohio Acad. Sci., Soil Sci. Soc. Am.; mem. Soil and Water Conservation Soc. Am. (Outstanding Mem. award All-Ohio chpt. 1977), Internat. Soc. Soil Sci., Coun. Agrl. Sci. and Tech. Republican. Home: 2103 Kedge Dr Vienna VA 22181-3211 Office: USDA CSREES 329 Aerospace Bldg Washington DC 20250-2210

SCHMIDT, BRUCE RANDOLPH, science administrator, researcher; b. N.Y.C., June 19, 1948; s. Charles Henry and Beverly (Quinby) S.; m. Jackie Gillmor, Aug. 14, 1971; children: Valerie, Michael. BS in Fisheries Mgmt., Utah State U., 1970; MS in Wildlife and Fisheries Sci., S.D. State U., 1975. Fisheries technician Alaska Dept. Fish & Game, King Salmon, summer 1969, fisheries technician, crew leader, summer 1970; biol. aide, temporary Utah Divsn. Wildlife Resources, Dutch John, summer 1971; fisheries rsch. biologist Utah Divsn. Wildlife Resources, Lake Powell, 1971-72; rsch. project leader Utah Divsn. Wildlife Resources, Flaming Gorge, 1977-83; fisheries sect. planner Utah Divsn. Wildlife Resources, Salt Lake City, 1983-84, chief of fisheries, 1984-94; rsch. asst. S.D. State U., Brookings, 1973-74; fisheries rsch. biologist S.D. Dept. Game & Fish, Webster, 1975-77; rsch. sect. supr. Oreg. Dept. Fish & Wildlife, Corvallis, 1994—; chair N.Am. Fisheries Leadership Workshop, Snowbird, Utah, 1990. Lead author: (statewide mgmt. plan) A Conceptual Management Plan for Cutthroat Trout in Utah, 1995. Valedictorian Utah State U., 1970. Mem. Am. Fisheries Soc. (pres.

adminstr.'s sect. 1990). Home: 3146 NW Greenbriar Pl Corvallis OR 97330 Office: Oregon Dept Fish & Wildlife 850 SW 15th St Corvallis OR 97333*

SCHMIDT, CAROLYN LEA, elementary school educator; b. Waterloo, Iowa, Apr. 5, 1949; d. Carl George and Leola Marie (Flater) S. Student, Wartburg Coll., 1967-69; BS, Iowa State U., 1971; MA, U. Iowa, 1980. Cert. elem., learning disabilities, chpt. I reading tchr., Iowa. 5th grade tchr. Midland Cmty. Schs., Wyoming, Iowa, 1971-78; 4th grade tchr. Walnut Ridge Acad., Waterloo, Iowa, 1978-79; learning disabilities tchr. Ft. Dodge (Iowa) Cmty. Schs., 1980-82, chpt. I reading tchr., 1982—; active dist. in-svcs. and confs. in field. Active First Evang. Free Ch., Ft. Dodge, 1980-89. Mem. Internat. Reading Assn. Avocations: Macintosh computers, classical guitars, reading, sports.

SCHMIDT, CHARLES J., library administrator. Office: Mid Ga Regional Libr 1180 Washington Ave Macon GA 31201-1790

SCHMIDT, CHARLES T., JR., labor and industrial relations educator. Prof., dir. labor and indsl. rels. rsch., labor arbitrator. Office: University of Rhode Island Labor Research Ctr Adams House Kingston RI 02881*

SCHMIDT, CHAUNCEY EVERETT, banker; b. Oxford, Ia., June 7, 1931; s. Walter Frederick and Vilda (Saxton) S.; m. Anne Garrett McWilliams, Mar. 3, 1954; children: Carla, Julia, Chauncey Everett. B.S., U.S. Naval Acad., 1953; M.B.A., Harvard U., 1959. With First Nat. Bank, Chgo., 1959-76; v.p., gen. mgr. br. First Nat. Bank, London, Eng., 1965-68; v.p. for First Nat. Bank, Europe, Middle East, Africa, 1968-69; sr. v.p. First Nat. Bank, Chgo., 1969-72; exec. v.p. First Nat. Bank, 1972, vice chmn. bd., 1973, pres., 1974-76; chmn. bd., chief exec. officer, dir. Bank of Calif. N.A., San Francisco, 1976—; chmn. bd., pres., chief exec. officer, dir. BanCal Tri-State Corp., 1976—; dir. Amfac, Inc., Honolulu; mem. Adv. Council Japan-U.S. Econ. Relations; adv. bd. Pacific Rim Bankers Program. Exec. bd. and pres. San Francisco Bay Area council Boy Scouts Am.; council SRI Internat.; bd. dirs. Bay Area Council; bd. govs. San Francisco Symphony; trustee U.S. Naval War Coll. Fedn., Newport, R.I. Served with USAF, 1953-56. Mem. Assn. Res. City Bankers, Am. Bankers Assn., Internat. Monetary Conf., Calif. Bankers Clearing House Assn. (dir.), Calif. Roundtable (dir.), Japan-Calif. Assn. Clubs: Comml. (Chgo.); Bankers (San Francisco), Bohemian (San Francisco). Home: 40 Why Worry Farm Woodside CA 94062-3602 Office: One Bush St San Francisco CA 94104-1300

SCHMIDT, CHUCK, professional football team executive; b. Detroit, Jan. 22, 1947; m. Sharon Schmidt; children: Scott, Krista, Matthew. Degree in bus., U. Mich.; grad. degree in fin., Wayne State U. Formerly with Ernst and Whinney; CPA Detroit Lions, from 1976, also contr., then v.p. fin., until 1987, exec. v.p., chief oper. officer, 1989—. Bd. dirs., sec., treas. Detroit Lions Charities; bd. dirs. CATCH, Pontiac (Mich.) Devel. Found. Office: Detroit Lions 1200 Featherstone Rd Pontiac MI 48342-1938*

SCHMIDT, CLARENCE ANTON, financial consultant; b. Chgo., Nov. 28, 1935; s. Clarence Lawrence and Anna Elizabeth (Leske) S.; m. Anne Louise Wolfer, Feb. 28, 1959; children: J. Paul, Carolyn Anne Schmidt Noll. BS in Indsl. Mgmt., Carnegie-Mellon U., 1957, MS in Indsl. Adminstrn., 1958. ChFC; CLU. Cost engr. Eastman Kodak Co., Rochester, N.Y., 1958-65; supr. cost engring. Eastman Kodak Co., Rochester, 1965-67; corp. mgr. fin. plans Litton Industries, Beverly Hills, Calif., 1967-69; v.p. fin. machine tool group Litton Industries, Hartford, Conn., 1969-72; v.p. fin., CFO, Hillenbrand Industries, Batesville, Ind., 1972-76, Consol. Aluminum Corp., St. Louis, 1976-79; spl. agt. Northwestern Mut. Life, St. Louis, 1979-85; fin. counselor Cigna Fin. Advisors, St. Louis, 1985-93; fin. cons. Clarence A. Schmidt, ChFC, St. Louis, 1994—. Bd. dirs. Luth. Ministries Assn., St. Louis, 1983-91, pres., 1988-90. Mem. Am. Soc. CLU's and ChFC's (instr. wealth accumulation 1994), Internat. Assn. for Fin. Planning, Nat. Assn. Life Underwriters, Estate Planning Coun. St. Louis. Republican. Avocations: tennis, bridge. Office: 139 Ladue Oaks Dr Saint Louis MO 63141-8129

SCHMIDT, CLAUDE HENRI, retired research administrator; b. Geneva, Switzerland, May 6, 1924; came to U.S., 1935; s. Roger Auguste Schmidt and Lucette (Henriette) Wuhrman; m. Melicent Esther Hane, June 25, 1953; children—Valerie Lynn, Jeffrey Allan. A.B., Stanford U., 1948, M.A., 1950; Ph.D., Iowa State U., 1956. With Agrl. Rsch. Svc., USDA, 1956-88; rsch. entomologist Orlando, Fla., 1956-62; project leader Fargo, N.D., 1964-67; br. chief Beltsville, Md., 1967-72; area dir. N. Cen. region Fargo, 1972-82, lab. dir., 1982-88, acting dir. Red River Valley Agrl. Rsch. Ctr., 1988; collaborator, 1988—; entomologist IAEA, Vienna, Austria, 1962-64; sec. Nat. Mosquito Fish and Wildlife Commn., Washington, 1968-72. Editor Leafy Spurge News, 1994—; contbr. articles to profl. jours. Served with AUS, Signal Corps 1942-46, to 1st lt. Med. Service Corps, 1950-53. Fellow Washington Acad. Sci., AAAS; mem. Am. Mosquito Control Assn. (pres. 1981-82), Am. Chem. Soc., Entomol. Soc. Am. Republican. Lodge: Elks. Home: 1827 3rd St N Fargo ND 58102-2335

SCHMIDT, CYRIL JAMES, librarian; b. Flint, Mich., June 27, 1939; s. Cyril August and Elizabeth Josephine S.; m. Martha Joe Meadows, May 22, 1965; children: Susan, Emily. BA, Cath. U. Am., 1962; MSLS, Columbia U., 1963; Ph.D., Fla. State U., 1974. Asst. bus. and industry dept. Flint Pub. Library, 1963-65; reference librarian Gen. Motors Inst., Flint, 1965; asso. librarian S.W. Tex. State U., San Marcos, 1965-67; head undergrad. libraries, asst. prof. Ohio State U., 1967-70; dir. libraries SUNY, Albany, 1972-79; also mem. faculty SUNY (Sch. Library and Info. Sci.); univ. librarian Brown U., Providence, 1979-81; exec. v.p. Rsch. Libraries Group, Stanford, Calif., 1981-89; prin. cons. Schmidt & Assocs., Palo Alto, Calif., 1989—; univ. prof., libr. San Jose (Calif.) State U., 1992—. Author papers in field. Libr. Svcs. Act fellow, 1962-63, Higher Edn. Act fellow, 1970-72. Mem. ALA, ACLU, Pi Sigma Alpha, Beta Phi Mu. Home: 244 Forest Ave Palo Alto CA 94301-2510 Office: San Jose State U 1 Washington Sq San Jose CA 95112-3613

SCHMIDT, EDWARD CRAIG, lawyer; b. Pitts., Nov. 26, 1947; s. Harold Robert and Bernice (Williams) S.; m. Elizabeth Lowry Rial, Aug. 18, 1973; children: Harold Robert II, Robert Rial. BA, U. Mich., 1969; JD, U. Pitts., 1972. Bar: Pa. 1972, U.S. Dist. Ct. (we. dist.) Pa. 1972, U.S. Ct. Appeals (3d. cir.) 1972, U.S. Ct. Appeals (D.C. cir.) 1975, U.S. Supreme Ct. 1981, U.S. Ct. Appeals (9th cir.) 1982, U.S. Ct. Appeals (4th cir.) 1982, U.S. Ct. Appeals (6th cir.) 1987, U.S. Ct. Appeals (11th cir.) 1990, U.S. Ct. Appeals (2d cir.) 1992, U.S. Ct. Appeals (4th cir.) 1994. Assoc. Rose, Schmidt, Hasley & Di Salle, Pitts., 1972-77, ptnr., 1977-90, Jones, Day Reavis & Pogue, Pitts.; mem. adv. com. Superior Ct. Pa., 1978-80. Co-editor; Antitrust Discovery Handbook-Supplement, 1982; asst. editor: Antitrust Discovery Handbook, 1980; contbr. articles to profl. jours. Bd. dirs. Urban League, Pitts., 1974-77. Mem. Supreme Ct. Hist. Soc., Pa. Bar Assn., D.C. Bar Assn., Allegheny County Bar Assn. (pub. rels. com. coun. civil litigation sect. 1977-80), Internat. Acad. Trial Laywers, Acad. Trial Lawyers Allegheny County (bd. govs. 1985-87), Assn. Def. Trial Attys., U. Pitts. Law Alumni Assn. (bd. govs. 1980). Clubs: Rolling Rock (Ligonier, Pa.), Duquesne (Pitts.), Longue Vue (Pitts.). Republican. Home: 159 Washington St Pittsburgh PA 15218-1351 Office: Jones Day Reavis & Pogue One Mellon Bank Ctr 31st Fl 500 Grant St Pittsburgh PA 15219-2502

SCHMIDT, FRANK BROAKER, executive recruiter; b. Shamokin, Pa., Aug. 8, 1939; s. Frank Wilhelm and Doris (Maurer) S.; children by previous marrage: Susan E., Tracie A.; m. Elizabeth Mallen, Mar. 18, 1989; children: Alexandra M., Frank W.M. BS, U. Pa., 1962; MBA, Case Western Res. U., 1969; cert. brewmaster, Siebel Inst. Brewing Tech., Chgo., 1964. With Carling Brewing Co., Cleve., 1964-69, mgr. sales and advt. div., brand mgr., 1969-70; advt. and merchandising mgr. The Pepsi-Cola Co., Purchase, N.Y., 1970-73, dir. mktg. programs, then dir. mgmt. devel., 1973-74; mgr. sales and mktg. The Olga Co., Van Nuys, Calif., 1974-75; pres. F.B. Schmidt, Internat., L.A., 1975—; chmn. Mediterranean Properties, 1994—. Author: Draft Beer Manual, 1967, Assn. Nat. Advertisers Computerized Media System, 1970. Chmn. Morrison Ranch Estates Homeowners Assn., 1993—. Mem. Calif. Exec. Recruiters Assn., Wharton Alumni Assn., Personnel Cons. Am. (region chmn. 1981-83, chmn. 92-95), Am. Mktg. Assn. Republican. Avocations: automobile racing, flying, marathon bicycling. Office: 30423 Canwood St Ste 239 Agoura Hills CA 91301-4318

SCHMIDT, FRED (ORVAL FREDERICK SCHMIDT), editor; b. Lone Wolf, Okla., Sept. 17, 1922; s. Otto Frederick and Mabel Marie (Johnson) S.; m. Eleanor Minerva Austin, Jan. 15, 1949; 1 son, Frederick Curtis. Student, U. Okla., 1941-42, Chgo. Sch. Photography, 1947-48. Photographer, color technician James Israel Studio, Mt. Vernon, Ohio, 1949-55; from adminstrv. asst. to mng. editor Profl. Photographers Am., Inc., 1955-74; editorial dir. Photomethods, N.Y.C., 1974-85, Internat. TV, 1983-85, Photo/Design, 1984-85; exec. editor Video Mgr., 1985-88; cons. editor Tape/Disc Bus., 1987-89; tchr. photojournalism Milw. Area Tech. Coll., 1965-66, mem. adv. bd., 1972-74; lectr. No. Ill. U., 1968-73; sec. Profl. Photographers, Ohio, 1954-55. Co-author: Opportunities in Photography, 1978. Bd. advisers Chgo. Internat. Film Festival, 1967-75. Served with USCGR, 1942-46. Recipient Nat. award Profl. Photographers Am., 1964, award of Nikola Tesla medal World Coun. Profl. Photographers, 1995. Mem. Am. Soc. Photographers (hon. assco.), Yugoslavia Fedn. Profl. Photographers (hon.), Profl. Photographers of Israel, Internat. TV Assn. (Svc. award). Home and Office: 138 Joralemon St Brooklyn NY 11201-4714

SCHMIDT, GENE EARL, hospital administrator; b. Goessel, Kans., Aug. 5, 1942; s. Arthur K. and Hedwig (Neufeld) S.; m. Marcia K. Hiebert, June 24, 1966; 1 child, William. BA in Social Scis., Bethel Coll., 1964; MHA, U. Minn., 1970. Adminstr. Brook Lane Psychiat. Ctr., Hagerstown, Md., 1966-68; exec. dir. Community Mental Health Ctr., Indpls., 1970; asst. adminstr. Children's Hosp., Columbus, Ohio, 1970-73; exec. v.p. St. Francis Hosp., Miami Beach, Fla., 1973-86; pres. Hutchinson (Kans.) Hosp. Corp., 1986—. Pres. Am. Cancer Soc., Hutchinson, 1990-92; bd. dirs. Tng. and Evaluation Ctr. for Handicapped, ARC, Hutchinson, 1988—, chmn., 1993; mem. advance gifts chmn. United Way, Hutchinson, 1992. Fellow Am. Coll. Healthcare Execs.; mem. Kans. Hosp. Assn. (bd. dirs. 1989-94), Greater Hutchinson C. of C. (chmn. 1992), Rotary. Republican. Presbyterian. Home: 2503 Briarwood Ln Hutchinson KS 67502-1803 Office: Hutchinson Hosp 1701 E 23rd Ave Hutchinson KS 67502-1105

SCHMIDT, GEORGE, physicist; b. Budapest, Hungary, Aug. 1, 1926; s. Laszlo Schmidt and Katalin Wellisch; m. Katalin Varkonyi, June 26, 1955; children: Franklin R., Ronald W. Diploma in Elec. Engring., Tech. U., Budapest, 1950; PhD in Physics, Hungarian Acad. Scis., Budapest, 1956; M in Engring., Stevens Inst. Tech., 1961. Sr. lectr. Israel Inst. Tech., Haifa, Israel, 1957-58; asst. prof. Stevens Inst. Tech., Hoboken, N.J., 1959-61, assoc. prof., 1961-63, prof. physics, 1963-83, George Meade Bond prof. physics and engring. physics, 1983—; vis. prof. U. Wis., 1965, UCLA, 1972-73; vis. scientist Culham Labs., Culham, Eng., 1965, Ecole Polytechnique, Paris, 1979-80; cons. Sci. Applications Inc., Washington, 1981—, Poly. U. of N.Y., 1984—, Berkeley Assocs., Washington, 1985. Author: Physics of High Temperature Plasmas, 1966, 2nd rev. edit., 1979; contbr. sci. articles to profl. jours. Recipient Research award Stevens Inst. Tech., 1961. Fellow Am. Phys. Soc.; mem. N.Y. Acad. Scis. Office: Stevens Inst of Tech Dept Of Physics Hoboken NJ 07030

SCHMIDT, HAROLD EUGENE, real estate company executive; b. Cedar Rapids, Iowa, Oct. 12, 1925; s. Alfons W. and Lillie (Schlegel) S.; m. Lucy Hermann, Apr. 13, 1957; children: Harold, Sandra. B.S. in Civil Engring, U. Iowa, 1949; M.S. in San. Engring, MIT, 1953. Research and devel. engr. Chgo. Pump Co., 1949-51; engr. A.B. Kononoff, Miami, Fla., 1956-58; with Gen. Devel. Corp., Miami, 1958-82; v.p. utilities, asst. v.p. ops. Gen. Devel. Corp., 1967-72, v.p., 1972-81, v.p. community div., 1973-81, sr. v.p., 1981-82; pres. Gen. Devel. Utilities Inc., 1972-82, Kingsway Properties, Inc., 1982—; dir. Port Charllote Bank, Fla. Served to capt. USAF, 1951-56. Mem. Am. Water Works Assn., Water Pollution Control Fedn., Sigma Xi, Chi Epsilon. Home and Office: 12313 Kingsway Cir Arcadia FL 33821

SCHMIDT, HERMAN J., former oil company executive; b. Davenport, Iowa, Feb. 26, 1917; s. Herman and Lillian (Beard) S.; m. Eileen Carpenter, Dec. 20, 1967; children: Paul David, Sarah Louise. AB, U. Iowa, 1938; JD, Harvard U., 1941. Bar: N.Y. 1943. With Cravath, Swaine & Moore, 1941-44, 47-51; tax counsel Socony Mobil Oil Co. Inc. (now Mobil Corp.), N.Y.C., 1951-55, adminstrv. asst. to gen. counsel, 1955, assoc. gen. counsel, 1955-56, gen. counsel, 1956-59, exec. v.p., 1959-74, vice chmn., 1974-78, dir., 1957-78; pres. Mobil Internat. Oil Co., 1959-63; bd. dirs. H.J. Heinz Co., MAPCO, Inc., Hon Industries, Inc. Former chmn. bd. trustees Am. Enterprise Inst.; hon. life trustee U. Iowa Found. Served to 1st lt. M.I. Corps, AUS, 1944-47. Mem. Harvard Law Rev. Assn., Blind Brook Club (Ryebrook, N.Y.), Phi Beta Kappa, Phi Gamma Delta. Home: 15 Oakley Ln Greenwich CT 06830-3025

SCHMIDT, JAKOB EDWARD, medical and medicolegal lexicographer, physician, author, inventor; b. Riga, Livonia, Latvia, June 16, 1906; came to U.S., 1924, naturalized, 1929; s. Michael E. and Rachel I. (Goldman) S. Grad., Balt. City Coll., 1929; Ph.G., U. Md., 1932, BS in Pharmacy, 1935, MD, 1937, postgrad., 1939. Intern Sinai Hosp., Balt.; gen. practice medicine Balt., 1940-53; resident Charlestown, Ind., 1953—; indsl. physician Ind. Ordnance Works, 1953-54; med. and medicolegal lexicographer, 1950—; pres. Sculptural Med. Jewelers, 1973-76; mem. revision com. U.S. Pharmacopeia XI. Columnist What's the Good Word, Balt. Sun; Sharpen Your Tongue, Am. Mercury; The Medical Lexicographer, Modern Medicine; Medical Semantics, Medical Science; Underworld English, Police; Medical Vocabulary Builder, Trauma; English Word Power and Culture, Charlestown Courier, Understanding Med. Talk; assoc. med. editor, Trauma, 1959-88; editor: Medical Dictionary, 1959—; compiler: 50,000-word vocabulary test, 1956; contbr. numerous articles to med. jours., lay press, including Esquire, Playboy, also to press svcs., including UPI, NANA, others; cons. JAMA on med. terminology, also cons. med. terminology to legal profession and cts., to mfrs. on med. tradenames and trademarks; author: Terminology of Sensual Emotions, 1954, Medical Terms Defined for the Layman, 1957, REVERSICON, A Physician's Medical Word Finder, 1958, Medical Discoveries, Who and When, 1959, Dictionary of Medical Slang and Related Expressions, 1959, Narcotics, Lingo and Lore, 1959, The Libido, Its Scientific, Lay, and Slang Terminology, 1960, Baby Name Finder—The Source and Romance of Names, 1961, Schmidt's Illustrated Attorneys' Dictionary of Medicine and Word Finder, 1962, One Thousand Elegant Phrases, 1965, Medical Lexicographer, A Study of Medical Terminology, 1966, The Cyclopedic Lexicon of Sex Terminology, 1967, Police Medical Dictionary, 1968, Practical Nurses' Medical Dictionary, 1968, A Paramedical Dictionary, 1969, 2d edit., 1973, Structural Units of Medical and Biological Terms, 1969, English Word Power for Physicians and other Professionals, 1971, English Idioms and Americanisms, 1972, English Speech for Foreign Students, 1973, Textbook of Medical Terminology, 1973, Visual Aids for Paramedical Vocabulary, 1973, Analyzer of Medical-Paramedical Vocabulary, 1973, Index of Medical-Paramedical Vocabulary, 1974, Schmidt Diccionario para Auxiliares de la Medicina, 1976, Literary Foreplay, 1983, Romantic's Lexicon, 1987, Schmidt's Illustrated Attorneys' Dictionary of Medicine and Word Finder, 18th edit., 4 vols., 1981, 28th edit., 5 vols., 1995. Recipient Owl gold medal Balt. City Coll., 1929; Rho Chi gold medal U. Md. Sch. Pharmacy, 1932; gold medal for excellence in all subjects, 1932; cert. of honor U. Md. Sch. Medicine, 1937; award and citation N.Y. met. chpt. Am. Med. Writers' Assn., 1959. Mem. Am. Dialect Soc., Natural History Soc., Am. Name Soc., Am. Med. Writers' Assn., Internat. Soc. Gen. Semantics, AMA, Med. and Chirurgical Faculty of Md., Balt. City Med. Soc., Nat. Assn. Standard Med. Vocabulary, Nat. Soc. Lit. and Arts, Authors' Guild, Authors' League, Am. Mus. Natural History, Cousteau Soc., Smithsonian Instn., Planetary Soc., Nat. Writers' Club, Rho Chi, others. Achievemants include invention of iodine-pentoxide-shunt method and apparatus for detection of carbon monoxide in oxygen, atmosphere, and medicinal gases; shock-proof electric fuse; magnetic needle finger ring; prosthetic mammary papilla; discovered effect of cesium and related metals on oxidation of organic matter in lakes, ponds and drinking water, the TV eye phenomenon, others. Home: 934 Monroe St Charlestown IN 47111-1557

SCHMIDT, JAMES CRAIG, retired bank executive, bankruptcy examiner; b. Peoria, Ill., Sept. 27, 1927; s. Walter Henry and Clara (Wolfenbarger) S.; m. Jerrie Louise Bond, Dec. 6, 1958; children: Julie, Sandra, Suzanne. Student, Ill. Wesleyan U., 1945, 48-50, Ph.B. in Bus. Adminstrn, 1952; postgrad., U. Ill. Coll. Law, 1950-52; J.D., DePaul U., 1953. Spl. agt. Fidelity & Deposit Co., Chgo., 1956-58; with Home Fed. Savs. & Loan Assn., San Diego, 1958-67; asst. sec. bus. and transp. State of Calif., 1967-69; vice-chmn., pres. Gt. Am. Bank, San Diego, 1969-88; pres. Conf. Fed. Savs. and Loans of Calif., 1974-75; mem. Calif. Toll Bridge Authority, 1969-74; mem. Calif. State Transp. Bd., 1972-78; past chmn. San Diego Bal. Commn. Task Force. Pres. San Diego Holiday Bowl Football Game, 1986; dir. Friends of Legal Aid; bd. dirs. Greater San Diego Sports Assn., Californians for Better Transp. Served with USN, 1945-48. Mem. Calif. Bar Assn., Ill. Bar Assn., Calif. League Savs. Instns. (chmn. 1986-87), Calif. C. of C. (bd. dirs. 1987-90), U.S. Savs. Instn. League (exec. com. 1983-86), San Diego Country Club, univ Club, Sigma Chi, Phi Delta Phi. Office: Ste 0-2 8380 Hercules St La Mesa CA 91942-2922

SCHMIDT, JANIS ILENE, elementary education education; b. Wyandot County, Ohio., Feb. 4, 1930; d. Floyd Dale and Edith June (Clark) Herbert; m. William Frederick Schmidt, Aug. 27, 1950; children: Lon William, Randy Floyd. BS, Findlay Coll., 1968; MEd, Ashland Coll., 1986. Cert. elem. tchr., Ohio. Elem. tchr. Wharton (Ohio) Elem., 1950-52, Upper Sandusky (Ohio) Schs., 1967—. Author: Improvement of Retention, 1986. Officer Beta Usando Literary Club, Upper Sandusky, 1993; mem. Wyandot Meml. Hosp. Guild, 1980-95, North Salem Luth. Ch. Tchr., officer, 1950—, Tri-G Mothers League, 1953-80. Jennings scholar The Martha Holden Jennings Found., Ohio, 1969-73. Mem. Internat. Reading Assn. (com. chmn. 1990). Republican. Lutheran. Avocations: golf, boating, bicycling, gardening, sewing. Home: 569 N Warpole St Upper Sandusky OH 43351-9332 Office: East Sch 401 3rd St Upper Sandusky OH 43351-1105

SCHMIDT, JEAN MARIE, microbiology educator; b. Waterloo, Iowa, June 5, 1938; d. John Frederick and Opal Marie (Lowe) S. BA, U. Iowa, 1959, MS, 1961; PhD, U. Calif., Berkeley, 1965. NIH postdoctoral fellow U. Edinburgh, Scotland, 1965-66; asst. prof. Ariz. State U., Tempe, 1966-71, assoc. prof., 1971-79, prof. microbiology, 1979—, assoc. dir. for biology Cancer Rsch. Inst., 1982—, acting chair dept. microbiology, 1988-89. Author: (with others) Bergey's Manual of Systematic Bacteriology, 1989; contbr. articles to jours. NSF grantee, 1981. Fellow AAAS; mem. Am. Soc. Microbiology (divsn. chmn. 1979-80), Phi Beta Kappa, Sigma Xi. Democrat. Methodist. Avocations: backpacking, photography, piano.

SCHMIDT, JOHN RICHARD, agricultural economics educator; b. Madison, Wis., July 3, 1929; s. Oscar John and Alma Theodora (Ula) S.; m. Rosemary Pigorsch, Oct. 7, 1951; children: Janet, Deborah, Allen. B.S., U. Wis., 1951, M.S., 1953; Ph.D., U. Minn., 1960. Asst. prof. agr. econs. U. Wis., Madison, 1956-61, assoc. prof., 1961-65, prof., 1965-95, prof. emeritus, 1995—, chmn. dept., 1966-70; owner, mgr. JRS Computing Svcs., Madison, 1995—; farm mgmt. cons. Am. Farm Bur. Fedn., Chgo., 1962; cons. Banco de Mexico, 1972-84, IBRD (World Bank), 1973—; Agrl. Devel. Bank Iran, 1974-76; mem. adv. bd. Internat. Devel. Inst., 1983. Contbr. articles to tech. jours., also monographs, bulls. Bd. dirs. U. Wis. Credit Union, 1968-77, pres., 1969-75; mem. com. Wis.-Upper Mich. Synod Sem., 1972-75, mem. ch. coun. 1967-69, 72-75, pres. 1974-75. Mem. Am. Agrl. Econs. Assn., Western Farm Econs. Assn., Rotary, Delta Theta Sigma (nat. sec. 1962-64), Gamma Sigma Delta (pres. Wis. chpt. 1975). Lutheran. Home: 106 Frigate Dr Madison WI 53705-4426 Office: JRS Computing Svcs 6601 Grand Teton Plz Ste 4 Madison WI 53719-1049

SCHMIDT, JOHN THOMAS, neurobiologist; b. Louisville, Sept. 25, 1949; s. Adolph William and Olivia Ann (Hohl) S.; m. Marilyn Joan Gough, Jan. 6, 1979; children: Sarah, Benjamin. BS in Physics, U. Detroit, 1971; PhD in Biophysics, U. Mich., 1976. Postdoctoral assoc. Nat. Inst. for Med. Rsch., London, 1976-77, Vanderbilt U. Med. Sch., Nashville, 1977-80; asst. prof. biol. scis. SUNY, Albany, 1980-85, assoc. prof. biol. scis., 1985-94, prof. biog. scis., 1994, dir. Neurobiology Rsch. Ctr., 1988—. Editor: Activity-Driven CNS Changes, 1991. Mem. Soc. for Neuroscis. (treas. Hudson Berkshire chpt. 1981-83, pres. 1987-89), N.Y. Acad. Scis. Office: SUNY Neurobiology Rsch Ctr 1400 Washington Ave Albany NY 12222-0100

SCHMIDT, JOSEPH DAVID, urologist; b. Chgo., July 29, 1937; s. Louis and Marian (Fleigel) S.; m. Andrea Maxine Herman, Oct. 28, 1962. BS in Medicine, U. Ill., 1959, MD, 1961. Diplomate Am. Bd. Urology. Rotating intern Presbyn. St. Luke's Hosp., Chgo., 1961-62, resident in surgery, 1962-63; resident in urology The Johns Hopkins Hosp., Balt., 1963-67; faculty U. Iowa Coll. Medicine, Iowa City, 1969-76; faculty U. Calif., San Diego, 1976—, prof., head div. urology, 1976—, vice-chmn. dept. surgery, 1985—; cons. U.S. Dept. Navy, San Diego, 1976—; attending urologist Vets. Affairs Dept., San Diego, 1976—. Author, editor: Gynecological and Obstetric Urology, 1978, 82, 93. Capt. USAF, 1967-69. Recipient Francis Senear award. U. Ill., 1961. Fellow Am. Coll. of Surgeons; mem. AMA, Am. Urol. Assn. Inc., Alpha Omega Alpha. Avocations: collecting antique medical books, manuscripts. Office: U Calif Med Ctr Divsn Urology 200 W Arbor Dr San Diego CA 92103-8897

SCHMIDT, JULIUS, sculptor; b. Stamford, Conn., June 2, 1923; s. Louis Frank and Susie (Koment) S.; m. Carolyn Marsha Wolf (div.); children: Ania J., Ianos; m. Mary Katherine Powers, 1981 (div.); 1 child, Araan J. Student, Okla. A&M U., 1950-51; B.F.A., Cranbrook Acad. Art, 1952, M.F.A., 1955; student, Ossip Zadkine, Paris, 1953, Accademia di Belle Arti, Florence, Italy, 1954. Chmn. sculpture dept. Kansas City Art Inst., 1954-59, R.I. Sch. Design, 1959-60, U. Calif.-Berkeley, 1961-62, Cranbrook Acad. Art, 1962-70, U. Iowa, Iowa City, 1970-93; ret., 1993. 34 one-man shows 1953—; exhibited in group shows Allen Meml. Art Mus., Oberlin, Ohio, 1958, Arts Club of Chgo. and Milw. Art Center, 1958, Art Inst. Chgo., Mus. Modern Art, N.Y.C., 1960, Whitney Mus., 1960-63, Gallerie Claude Bernard, Paris, 1960, Guggenheim Mus., 1962, San Francisco Mus. Art, 1962, Phila. Art Alliance, 1963, Battersea Park, London, 1963, Sao Paolo Bienal, Brazil, 1963, White House Festival of Arts, Washington, 1965, Bienale Middleheim, Belgium, 1971; represented in permanent collections Nelson Gallery-Atkins Mus., Kansas City, Mo., Art Inst., Chgo., Mus. Modern Art, N.Y.C., Mus. U. Nebr., Whitney Mus. Am. Art, N.Y.C., Krannert Art Mus., Urbana, Ill., Washington, U., Walker Art Center, Mpls., Albright-Knox Mus., Buffalo, Detroit Inst. Art, U. Calif. Art Mus., Cranbrook Acad. Art, Mich., Princeton Mus. Art, Hirshhorn Mus., Washington, numerous others. Served with USNR, World War II. Guggenheim fellow, 1963-64. Address: 5 Highview Knls NE Iowa City IA 52240-9149

SCHMIDT, KLAUS DIETER, management consultant, university administrator, marketing and management educator; b. Eisenach, Germany, May 8, 1930; came to U.S., 1949, naturalized, 1952; s. Kurt Heinrich and Luise (Kruger) S.; B.A. in Econs., U. Calif., Berkeley, 1951; M.B.A., Stanford U., 1953; Ph.D. in Bus. Adminstrn., Golden Gate U., 1978; m. Lynda Hollister Wheelwright, June 29, 1950; children: Karen, Claudia. Buyer, jr. mdse. mgr. Broadway Hale, 1952-54; sales mgr. Ames Harris Neville Co., 1954-56, ops. mgr., 1956-57; gen. mgr. Boise Cascade Corp., 1957-60; pres., chmn. bd. Kimball-Schmidt Inc., San Rafael, Calif., 1960-73, chmn. subs. Kalwall Pacific, 1962-67, chmn. subs. AFGOA Corp., 1966-69; asst. prof. mgmt. and mktg. San Francisco State U., 1970-75, assoc. prof. mgmt., 1975-80, prof. mgmt. and mktg., 1980-85, chmn. dept. mgmt. and mktg., 1979-85, prof. emeritus, 1989—, assoc. dean sch. bus. emeritus, 1985-88; chmn. Schmidt Cons. Group, 1988—; dir. Ctr. for World Bus., 1976-88, dir. U.S.-Japan Inst., 1981-88, editor-in-chief Sch. Bus. Jours., 1980-88; U.S. negotiator on Afghanistan issue, 1980-88; mem. Dept. Commerce Dist. Export Council, 1982-88; research cons. SRI Internat. Republican. Mem. Alpha Deta Phi, Beta Gamma Sigma. Club: University (San Francisco). Author 20-booklet series Doing Business In ..., 1978-80. Office: PO Box 269 Brooklin ME 04616-0269

SCHMIDT, KLAUS FRANZ, advertising executive; b. Dessau, Germany, May 25, 1928; came to U.S., 1951; naturalized, 1957; s. Franz and Elfriede (Klamroth) S.; m. Gisela Garbrecht, June 19, 1954; children: Dagmar Schmidt Etkin, Ena Schmidt. Student, Coll. of Journalism, Aachen, Germany, 1947-48, Sch. of Design and Printing, Bochum, Germany, 1948-50; BA, Wayne State U., 1956. Printer, compositor, 1948-56; type dir. Mogul Williams & Saylor, N.Y.C., 1956-59, Doyle, Dane, Bernbach, N.Y.C., 1959-61; type dir. Young & Rubicam, N.Y.C., 1961-68, v.p., dir. print ops., 1968-75, v.p., dir. creative support, 1975-85, sr. v.p., mgr. prodn. svcs., 1985-91; advt./graphic arts cons., 1991—; co-organizer Vision Congress Internat. Ctr. for Communications Arts & Scis., N.Y.C., 1965, 67, 69, 77; chmn., bd.

trustees Internat. Ctr. Typographic Arts, N.Y.C. 1969-70. Am. editor Der Druckspiegel, 1957-64; contbg. editor Print Mag., 1968—, The Dunn Report, 1991-95. Recipient Typomundus award, 1964, Internat. Book Exhbn. award, Leipzig, Germany, 1965. Mem. Print Advt. Assn. (chmn. N.Y. chpt. 1969-71, nat. sr. v.p. 1971-75), Am. Assn. Advt. Agys. (chmn. subcom. on phototypography 1969-75), Digital Distbn. of Advt. to Publ. Assn. (vice chmn. 1991-95), N.Y. Type Dirs. Club (pres. 1984-86, awards 1962, 64-66, 68, 69), N.Y. Art Dirs. Club (v.p. 1984-86), Advt. Prodn. Club (pres. 1982-84), Gravure Advt. Coun. (chmn. 1970-72). Home and office: 549 Munroe Ave Tarrytown NY 10591

SCHMIDT, L. LEE, JR., university official; b. Mullinville, Kans., Oct. 2, 1937; s. Lester Lee and Mary (Gilliam) S.; m. Sarah Sue Lookingbill, Aug. 12, 1961; children: Suzanne, Jon. B.S. in Bus. Adminstrn., U. Ark., 1962, Ph.D., 1971; M.B.A., Tex. Tech U., 1963. CPA, Colo. Audit sr. Ernst & Young, Fort Worth, 1963-66; mgr. acctg. The Western Co., Fort Worth, 1966-67; asst. prof. U. Tex.-Arlington, 1967-68; instr. U. Ark., Fayetteville, 1968-71; prof. acctg., chmn. dept. Colo. State U., Ft. Collins, 1971-87, assoc. dean Coll. Bus., 1988-92; assoc. dean Coll. Bus. Adminstrn., U. Tex., El Paso, 1992—; speaker in field. Contbr. articles to profl. jours. Served with USN, 1955-58. Earhart Found. fellow, 1968-69. Mem. AICPA, Am. Acctg. Assn., Fin. Execs. Inst., Beta Gamma Sigma, Beta Alpha Psi. Office: U Tex Coll Bus Adminstrn El Paso TX 79968

SCHMIDT, L(AIL) WILLIAM, JR., lawyer; b. Thomas, Okla., Nov. 22, 1936; s. Lail William and Violet Kathleen (Kuper) S.; m. Diana Gail (div. May 1986); children: Kimberly Ann, Andrea Michelle; m. Marilyn Sue, Aug. 11, 1990. BA in Psychology, U. Colo., 1959; JD, U. Mich., 1962. Bar: Colo. 1962, U.S. Dist. Ct. Colo. 1964, U.S. Tax Ct. 1971, U.S. Ct. Appeals (10th cir.) 1964. Ptnr. Holland & Hart, Denver, 1962-77, Schmidt, Elrod & Wills, Denver, 1977-85, Moye, Giles, O'Keefe, Vermeire & Gorrell, Denver, 1985-90; of counsel Hill, Held, Metzger, Lofgren & Peele, Dallas, 1989—; pvt. practive law Denver, 1990—; lectr. profl. orgns. Author: How To Live-and Die-with Colorado Probate, 1985, A Practical Guide to the Revocable Living Trust, 1990; contbr. articles to legal jours. Pres. Luth. Med. Ctr. Found., Wheat Ridge, Colo., 1985-89; pres. Rocky Mountain Prison and Drug Found., Denver, 1986—; bd. dirs. Luth. Hosp., Wheat Ridge, 1988-92; bd. dirs. Denver Planned Giving Roundtable, Bonfils Blood Ctr. Found. Fellow Am. Coll. Trust and Estate Counsel (Colo. chmn. 1981-86); mem. ABA, Am. Judicature Soc., Rocky Mtn. Estate Planning Coun. (founder, pres. 1970-71), Greater Denver Tax Counsel Assn., Am. Soc. Magicians, Denver Athletic Club, Phi Delta Phi. Republican. Baptist. Avocation: magic. Office: 1050 17th St Ste 1700 Denver CO 80265 also: Law Offices of Gregory J Morris 300 S 4th St Las Vegas NV 89101-6014

SCHMIDT, LAURA LEE, elementary and middle school gifted and talented educator, special education educator; b. South Bend, Ind., Sept. 6, 1960; d. Max A. and Sandra Lee (Engmark) Tudor; m. William Michael Schmidt, Aug. 7, 1982; children: Sandra Lorena, Charlotte Lee. BA, U. Ky., 1982; postgrad., Augustana Coll., Sioux Falls, S.D., U. S.D.; MEd, S.D. State U., 1991. Cert. elem. K-8, spl. edn. K-12, mid./jr. h.s., gifted edn. K-12, S.D. Spl. edn. tchr. Owen County Sch. Dist., Owenton, Ky.; elem. sch. tchr. White River (S.D.) Sch. Dist.; elem. and music tchr. St. Liborius Sch., Orient, S.D.; spl. edn. and chpt. I tchr. Cresbard (S.D.) Sch.; gifted edn. tchr. Douglas Mid. Sch., Douglas Sch. Dist., Box Elder, S.D. Easter seals camp counselor; vol. Spl. Olympics; accompianist high sch. choir. Mem. Dir. Spl. Edn., Mortar Board, Lambda Sigma. Home: 614 Bluebird Dr Box Elder SD 57719-9509

SCHMIDT, MAARTEN, astronomy educator; b. Groningen, Netherlands, Dec. 28, 1929; came to U.S., 1959; s. Wilhelm and Antje (Haringhuizen) S.; m. Cornelia Johanna Tom, Sept. 16, 1955; children: Elizabeth Tjimkje, Maryke Antje, Anne Wilhelmina. BSc, U. Groningen, 1949; PhD, Leiden U., Netherlands, 1956; ScD, Yale U., 1966. Sci. officer Leiden Obs., The Netherlands, 1953-59; postdoctoral fellow Mt. Wilson Obs., Pasadena, Calif., 1956-58; mem. faculty Calif. Inst. Tech., 1959-95, prof. astronomy, 1964-95, exec. officer for astronomy, 1972-75, chmn. div. physics, math. and astronomy, 1975-78; mem. staff Hale Obs., 1959-80, dir., 1978-80. Co-winner Calif. Scientist of Yr. award, 1964. Fellow Am. Acad. Arts and Scis. (Rumford award 1968); mem. Am. Astron. Soc. (Helen B. Warner prize 1964, Russell lecture award 1978), NAS (fgn. assoc., recip. James Craig Watson Medal, 1991), Internat. Astron. Union, Royal Astron. Soc. (assoc., Gold medal 1980). Office: Calif Inst Tech 105 24 Robinson Lab 1201 E California Blvd Pasadena CA 91125-0001

SCHMIDT, MARY BERRY, educational administrator; b. Roswell, N.Mex., Feb. 9, 1956; d. Philip Leslie and Carmen Estella (Colon) Berry; 1 child, Jennifer Marie Schmidt. BS, U. Tex. at El Paso, 1983; MEd, 1985. Cert. mid-mgmt., provisional generic spl. edn., provisional early childhood edn. handicapped child, provisional elem., profl. reading specialist, provisional kindergarten, computer literacy. Tchr. 3rd grade El Paso ISD Burnet Elem., 1983-85, tchr. 1st grade, 1985-87; gifted and talented tchr. 6th grade El Paso ISD Edgar Park Elem., 1987-88; gifted and talented tchr. 5th grade El Paso ISD Omar Bradley Elem., 1988-89; gifted and talented, computer lit. tchr. 5th grade El Paso Coldwell Elem. Intermediate, 1989-92; asst. prin. El Paso ISD Mesita Elem., 1992—; bd. mem. Nat. Cmty. for Prevention of Child Abuse, 1985-91, Our Lady of Assumption Sch. Bd., 1986-90, El Paso; fashion show coord. Loretto Acad., El Paso, 1993-94; presenter in field. Sec. Monterey Park Assn., El Paso, 1986-90; leader Girl Scouts Am., El Paso, 1987-90, Leadership El Paso, 1993-94. Named Top 10 Tchrs. El Paso ISD, 1988. Mem. PTA, Tex. Elem. Prin. Assn., Paso del Norte Assn. Supervision and Curriculum, Tex. Assn. Gifted and Talented, Internat. Reading Assn., Assn. Childhood Edn., El Paso Techs. Assn., Delta Kappa Gamma. Roman Catholic. Avocations: snowmobiling, reading, crafts, shopping. Home: 3432 Clearview Ln El Paso TX 79904-4528

SCHMIDT, SISTER MARY SYLVIA (PATRICIA ELLA NORA SCHMIDT), nun; b. Devine, Tex., Feb. 8, 1937; d. George Martin and Ella Mary (Brieden) S. BS in Edn., Our Lady of the Lake Coll., 1956; postgrad., St. Mary's U., San Antonio, summers 1962-63, 83-86. Joined Sisters of Divine Providence, Roman Cath. Ch., 1950, Sisters for Christian Community, 1970. Tchr. St. Joseph's Elem. Sch., Shreveport, La., 1956-61, Bishop Forest High Sch., Schulenburg, Tex., 1961-62, St. Mary's High Sch., Fredericksburg, Tex., 1962-66, St. Louis High Sch., Castroville, Tex., 1966-67; tchr., head dept. religion Bishop Kelly High Sch., Tulsa, 1967-70; coord. youth program Tulsa, 1970-72; resource worker office of edn. Diocese of Tulsa, 1971-73; pastoral asst. St. Thomas More Cath. Ch., Tulsa, 1973-82; assoc. dir. Tulsa Met. Ministry, 1982-88, exec. dir., 1988—; exec. sec. pastoral coun. Diocese of Tulsa, 1981—; chmn. high challenge sch. bd. Tulsa Pub. Schs. Chair Tulsa Fire and Police Chaplaincy Bd., 1983-85, Tulsa Human Rights Commn., 1984-91; bd. dirs. Family and Children Svcs., Tulsa, 1986-90. Recipient Pinnacle award Tulsa Commn. on Status of Women, 1989, City of Faith award Cascia Hall High Sch., 1990, Samaritan of Yr. award Kairas Ctr., 1992, Humanitarian award St. Paul African-Meth.-Episcopal Ch., 1993, Outstanding Christian Woman award, 1993. Mem. Nat. Assn. Ecumenical Staff (chair 1989-90), LWV (bd. dirs. local chpt.). Democrat. Office: Tulsa Met Ministry 221 S Nogales Ave Tulsa OK 74127-8721

SCHMIDT, MICHAEL JACK, former professional baseball player; b. Dayton, Ohio, Sept. 27, 1949; m. Donna Wightman; children: Jessica Roe, Jonathan Michael. BBA, Ohio U., Athens. With Phila. Phillies, 1972-89. Nat. League Player in All-Star Game, 1974, 76, 77, 79-84, 86, 87; named Most Valuable player, National League, 1980,1981, 1986., Most Valuable Player 1980 World Series; recipient 10 Golden Glove awards; inducted into Baseball Hall of Fame, 1995.

SCHMIDT, NANCY CHARLENE LINDER, English and journalism educator; b. Canton, Ohio, May 10, 1940; d. Charles William Masters and Mona Louise (Branch) Masters Swindell; m. Walter C. Linder, Sept. 6, 1958 (div. 1974); children: Karen Linder Heard, Cynthia Linder Webb, Walter Charles Jr.; m. Charles Mathew Schmidt, Aug. 19, 1978; children: John, Michael, Greta Schmidt Wacker. BS in Edn., Kent State U., 1974, BS in English, 1979, BS in Journalism, 1985. Cert. elem. tchr., English tchr., journalism tchr. Jr. high sch. reading tchr. New Philadelphia (Ohio) City Schs., 1974-77; jr. high sch. tchr. Plain Local Schs., Canton, 1977-78; high sch. tchr., advisor yearbook, newspaper Nordonia Hills City Schs., Macedonia, Ohio, 1979—. Coun. pres. Village of Boston Heights, Ohio, 1983-86; leader Girl Scouts USA, 1965-73; children's choir dir. Broadway United Meth. Ch., 1965-74, Sun. sch. supt., 1965-73; pres. New Phila. Welcome Wagon Club, 1964-66. Mem. ASCD, Nat. Coun. English Tchrs., Nordonia Hills Educators Assn. (pres. 1989-91, v.p. 1991-93, bd. dir. 1993—). Republican. Avocations: boating, fishing, ceramics, reading. Home: 630 Fairfield Ln Aurora OH 44202-7836 Office: Nordonia High Sch 8006 S Bedford Rd Macedonia OH 44056-2025

SCHMIDT, NANCY J., anthropologist, educator; b. Cin., May 17, 1936; d. Leon Herbert and Ida (Genther) S. B.A., Oberlin Coll., 1958; M.A., U. Minn., 1961; Ph.D., Northwestern U., 1965; M.L.S., Ind. U., 1971. Asst. prof. anthropology St. Lawrence U., Canton, N.Y., 1966-68; asst. prof. anthropology Stanislaus State Coll., Turlock, Calif., 1968-70; assoc. prof. anthropology Rockford Coll., Ill., 1971-74; vis. assoc. prof. anthropology and African Studies U. Ill., Urbana, 1974-77; librarian Harvard U. Tozzer Library, Cambridge, Mass., 1977-84; African studies area specialist, adj. prof. anthropology Ind. U., Bloomington, 1984—; with cooperative Curriculum Devel. Ctr., Manitowoc, Wis., summer 1967, African Outreach Workshop U. Ill., spring-summer 1974, Twentieth Century Children's Writers St. James Press, London, 1977, 82, 89, NSF, Chautauqua course Visual Evidence and Women's Roles, Nov. 1976, Apr. 1977. Author: Children's Fiction about Africa in English N.Y., 1981, Subsaharan African Films and Filmmakers: A Preliminary Bibliography, 1986, Subsaharan African Films and Filmmakers: An Annotated Bibliography, 1988; Supplement to Children's Books on Africa and their Authors, N.Y., 1979; Children's Books on Africa and Their Authors N.Y., 1975, Reports on AIDS in the African Press: An Annotated Bibliography, 1988, Supplement, 1990, Subsaharan African Films and Filmmakers 1987-92: An Annotated Bibliography, 1994; founder, editor: Anthropological Lit. Jour., 1978-84; editor Africana Libraries Newsletter, 1986-91; contbr. articles to profl. jours. Founding mem. Sinnissippi chpt. Nat. Audubon Soc., Rockford, Ill., 1972. Mem. ALA, African Lit. Assn. (exec. coun. 1983-85), African Studies Assn. (bd. dirs. 1994-96), Africana Librs. Coun. (chmn. 1992-93, editor newsletter), Internat. Union Anthrop. and Ethnol. Scis. (commn. on documentation 1973—), Soc. for Humanistic Anthropology (book rev. editor 1982-85, editl. bd. 1990-93), Am. Anthrop. Assn. (anthropology curriculum study project Chgo. 1963-65), Assn. for Study African Lit., Soc. Visual Anthropology (bd. dirs. 1986-91). Office: Ind U Main Library E660 Bloomington IN 47405

SCHMIDT, PATRICIA FAIN, nurse educator; b. Chgo., June 17, 1941; d. Lawrence D. and Catherine B. (Schira) Fain; m. Donald W. Schmidt, July 16, 1966; children: Kathryn, Kristine, Michael. BSN, Coll. of St. Teresa, 1963; MSN, Marquette U., 1965; EdD, U.S. Internat. U., 1981. Instr. Coll. of St. Teresa, Winona, Minn.; asst. prof. San Diego State U.; interim dean for mathematics and natural and health scis. Palomar Coll., San Marcos, Calif. Mem. Sigma Theta Tau. Home: 12573 Utopia Way San Diego CA 92128-2229

SCHMIDT, PATRICIA RUGGIANO, education educator; b. Ft. Bragg, N.C., Jan. 13, 1944; d. Samuel and Elva (Beckmann) Ruggiano; m. Thomas Jay Schmidt, Nov. 11, 1967; children: Thomas Jay Jr., Anthony Charles. BA cum laude, Potsdam (N.Y.) Coll., 1965; MEd, U. Mass., 1966; EdD, Syracuse U., 1993. Cert. tchr. elem. tchr. (nursery sch. to grade 6), N.Y. State, K-12 reading tchr., N.Y. State. Elem. tchr. Liverpool (N.Y.) Pub. Schs., 1966-68; reading specialist Fayetteville-Manlius (N.Y.) Schs., 1973-91; grad. asst. Syracuse U., 1991-92, adj. instr., 1992-93; adj. instr. Oswego (N.Y.) Coll., 1992-93, Le Moyne Coll., Syracuse, 1992-93; asst. prof. edn. LeMoyne Coll., Syracuse, 1993—; treas./negotiator for N.Y. State United Tchrs., Fayetteville-Manlius Tchrs. Assn., 1984-91; N.Am. del. to Eastern Europe for rsch. exchange and study People to People, Budapest, St. Petersburg, Moscow, 1993; presenter in field. Contbr. article to profl. jour. William Sheldon fellow, 1992-93. Mem. Internat. Reading Assn., Am. Ednl. Rsch. Assn., Nat. Reading Conf., N.Y. State Reading Assn., Kappa Delta Pi, Phi Delta Kappa. Avocations: skiing, golf, gardening, hiking, travel. Home: RD 3 Ray Rd Canastota NY 13032 Office: Le Moyne Coll 212 Reilly Hall Syracuse NY 13214

SCHMIDT, PAUL JOSEPH, physician, educator; b. N.Y.C., Oct. 22, 1925; s. Joseph and Anna (Schwanzl) S.; BS Fordham U., 1948; MS, St. Louis U., 1952; MD, NYU, 1953; m. Louise Kern Fredericks, June 18, 1953; children: Damien, Matthew, Thomas, Maria. Intern, St. Elizabeth's Hosp., Boston, 1953-54; staff assoc. Nat. Microbiol. Inst., Bethesda, Md., 1954-55; chief blood bank dept. NIH, Bethesda, Md., 1955-74, asst. chief clin. pathology dept., 1963-65; sr. asst. surgeon, USPHS, 1954, advanced through grades to med. dir., 1964-74; assoc. clin. prof. pathology, then clin. prof. Georgetown U., Washington, 1965-75; dir. S.W. Fla. Blood Bank, Inc., Tampa, 1975-90, pres. 1987-90; head transfusion medicine, Transfusion Medicine Acad. Ctr., 1991—; prof. pathology U. So. Fla., Tampa, 1975—; cons. com. on Blood, AMA, 1964-69; tech. adv. Blood Transfusion Rsch. div. US Army, 1966-74; res. adv. com. Blood Program, ARC, 1967-73; com. Human Rsch., ARC, 1968-74; council on Immunohematology, Am. Soc. Clin. Pathologists, 1968-74; com. Anticoagulant Solutions, NRC-Nat. Acad. Sci., 1968-70; com. Plasmapheresis, NRC-Nat. Acad. Sci., 1969-70; com. Blood Bank Programs, N.Y.C., 1969-70; com. Component Therapy, NRC-Nat. Acad. Sci., 1969; com. standards, Am. Assn. Blood Banks, 1970-85 (chmn. 1981-85); Task Force on Blood Banking, dept. HEW, 1972-73; adv. com. Blood Diseases and Resources, Nat. Heart Lung Blood Inst., 1975-79; cons. to surgeon gen. U.S. Navy, 1976; dir. clin. svcs. ARC Blood Svcs., San Juan, P.R., 1993-95; clin. prof. pathology U. P.R., 1993—, Koppisch lectr., 1994; Molthan Meml. lectr. Pa. Assn. Blood Banks, 1995. Mem. svc. and rehab. com. Fla. div. Am. Cancer Soc., 1976-84; bd. dirs. ARC, Tampa 1978-83 (v.p. 1980); com. Transfusion Transmitted Viruses, Coll. Am. Pathologists 1981-91; com. Transfusion Medicine, Coll. Am. Pathologists, 1981-92; bd. dirs. Am. Blood Commn., 1985-87. Served with U.S. Army, 1944-46. Recipient Jour. Club Rsch. award, NYU, 1952, Silver medal Spanish Red Cross, 1960; Emily Cooley award Am. Assn. Blood Banks, 1974, John Elliott award, 1993. Diplomate Am. Bd. Pathology, Nat. Bd. Med. Examiners. Fellow Coll. Am. Pathologists (emeritus); mem. Am. Assn. Blood Banks (pres. 1987-88), Internat. Assn. History Medicine, Internat. Soc. Blood Transfusion, Fla. Assn. Blood Banks (pres. 1980-81), Cosmos, Rotary. Roman Catholic. Contbr. articles to profl. jours., editorial bd. Transfusion, 1968—, Annals Clinical Lab. Sci., 1971-74, Blood, 1976-77; editor: Progress in Transfusion and Transplantation, 1972; described etiology of renal failure after hemolytic blood transfusion reactions, 1967, Rh null disease, 1967. Office: PO Box 2125 Tampa FL 33601-2125

SCHMIDT, PAUL WICKHAM, lawyer; b. Milw., June 25, 1948; s. Edmund Julian and Barbara (Wickham) S.; m. Cathryn Ann Piehl, June 27, 1970; children: Thomas Wickham, William Piehl, Anna Patchin. BA cum laude, Lawrence U., 1970; JD cum laude, U. Wis., 1973. Bar: Wis. 1973, U.S. Dist. Ct. (we. dist.) Wis. 1973, U.S. Supreme Ct. 1982, D.C. 1988. Atty. advisor Bd. Immigration Appeals, Washington, 1973-76; gen. atty. office of gen. counsel Immigration and Naturalization Service, Washington, 1976-78, acting gen. counsel, 1979-81, 86-87, dep. gen. counsel, 1978-87; assoc. Jones, Day, Reavis & Pogue, Washington, 1987-89, ptnr., 1990-92; mng. ptnr. Fragomen, Del Ray & Bernsen, P.C., Washington, 1993-95; chmn. Bd. of Immigration Appeals, Falls Church, Va., 1995—. Mem. ABA, D.C. Bar Assn., Wis. Bar Assn., Fed. Bar Assn. (immigration sect.). Avocations: crew volunteer, gardening, camping, history. Home: 711 S View Ter Alexandria VA 22314-4923 Office: Bd Immigration Appeals Skyline Tower 5107 Leesburg Pike Ste 2400 Falls Church VA 22041

SCHMIDT, PETER GUSTAV, shipbuilding industry executive; b. Tumwater, Wash., Dec. 3, 1921; s. Peter G. and Clara Louise (Muench) S.; m. Elva Mary Ingalls, Dec. 3, 1945; children: Mimi Schmidt Fielding, Jill Schmidt Crowson, Janet Schmidt Mano, Hans. BSME, U. Wash., 1948; MS in Naval Architecture and Marine Engring., U. Mich., 1950. Naval architect Nat. Steel Shipbldg. Corp., San Diego, 1950-52, Carl J. Nordstrom/P. Spaulding, Seattle, 1952-53; pres. Marine Constrn. & Design Co., Seattle, 1953—, Astilleros Marco Chilena Ltd., Santiago, Chile, 1960—, Marco Peruana S.A., Lima, Peru, 1965—, Campbell Industries, San Diego, 1979—. Author papers on fishing gear and vessels. Served to lt (j.g.) USN, 1942-45, PTO. Recipient Puget Sound's Maritime Man of Yr. award Puget Sound Press Assn., 1975. Mem. Soc. Naval Architects and Marine Engrs., Wash. State Boatbuilders Assn. (pres. 1956-58), Alpha Delta Phi. Avocations: competitive sailing, classical music. Office: Marine Constrn & Design 2300 W Commodore Way Seattle WA 98199-1226

SCHMIDT, RICHARD MARTEN, JR., lawyer; b. Winfield, Kans., Aug. 2, 1924; s. Richard M. and Ida (Marten) S.; m. Ann Downing, Jan. 2, 1948; children—Eric, Gregory, Rolf (dec.), Heidi. A.B., U. Denver, 1945, J.D., 1948. Bar: Colo. bar 1948, D.C. bar 1968. Dep. dist. atty. City and County of Denver, 1949-50; mem. firm McComb, Zarlengo, Mott & Schmidt, Denver, 1950-54; ptnr. Schmidt & Van Cise (and predecessor), Denver, 1954-65; 65; gen. counsel USIA, 1965-68; ptnr. Cohn and Marks, Washington, 1969—; counsel spl. agrl. investigating subcom. Counsel Am. Soc. Newspaper Editors, 1968—; mem. Gov.'s Coun. Local Govt., Colo., 1963-64; chmn. Mayor's Jud. Adv. Com., Denver, 1963-64, Gov.'s Supreme Ct. Nominating Com., 1964-65; mem. Gov.'s Oil Shale Adv. Com., 1963-65, Colo. Commn. on Higher Edn., 1965; mem. bd. Nat. Press Found., 1993—. Trustee U. Denver. Mem. ABA (chmn. standing com. on assn. comms. 1969-73, chmn. forum com. on comms. 1979-81, co-chmn. nat. conf. lawyers and reps. of media 1984—, mem. commn. on lawyer advt. 1964—), Colo. Bar Assn. (gov.), Denver Bar Assn. (pres. 1963-64), D.C. Bar Assn., Cosmos Club (Washington). Episcopalian. Home: 115 5th St SE Washington DC 20003-1123 Office: Cohn and Marks 1333 New Hampshire Ave NW Washington DC 20036-1511

SCHMIDT, ROBERT CHARLES, JR., finance executive; b. Oklahoma City, Apr. 2, 1942; s. Robert Charles and Francis Laura (Schiele) S.; m. Susan G. Dietz-Felbinger, Nov. 8, 1974; children: Laura Stewart, Elizabeth Berry. B.A., Westminster Coll., Fulton, Mo., 1964; postgrad., U. Okla., 1972, London Grad. Sch. Bus. Studies, 1974-76. Exec. trainee First Nat. Bank in St. Louis, 1967-68, comml. banker, 1968-74, v.p., mgr. client services div., 1974-76; v.p. treasury ops. Am. Express Co., N.Y.C., 1976-81, dep. treas., 1981-86; chmn. bd. Am. Express Export Credit Corp., 1982-86; group v.p., gen. mgr. Nat. Data Corp., Atlanta, 1986-88, exec. v.p., 1988-89; exec. v.p. Capital Guaranty Corp., San Francisco, 1989-91; pres. Tampsco Enterprises, Inc., St. Louis, 1993; ptnr. The Whitelaw Group, St. Louis, 1994-96; pres. SCM Group, Inc., St. Louis, 1996—; cons. City of N.Y., 1977. Loaned exec. United Fund, St. Louis, 1973; trustee Congl. Summer Assembly Edn. Fund, 1993—, Anglican Inst., 1996. Served with U.S. Army, 1965-67. Decorated Army Commendation medal; recipient cert. of merit USO, 1966, Alumni Achievement award Westminster Coll., 1977. Mem. Treas. Group (chmn. 1982-83), Noonday Club (St. Louis), Crystal Downs Country Club (Frankfort, Mich.), Beta Theta Pi. Republican. Episcopalian. Office: 625 S Skinker Blvd Saint Louis MO 63105

SCHMIDT, ROBERT MILTON, physician, scientist, educator; b. Milw., May 7, 1944; s. Milton W. and Edith J. (Martinek) S.; children Eric Whitney, Edward Huntington. AB, Northwestern U., 1966; MD, Columbia U., 1970; MPH, Harvard U., 1975; PhD in Law, Medicine and Pub. Policy, Emory U., 1982. Diplomate Am. Bd. Preventive Medicine. Resident in internal medicine Univ. Hosp. U. Calif.-San Diego, 1970-71; resident in preventive medicine Ctrs. Disease Control, Atlanta, 1971-74; commd. med. officer USPHS, 1971; advanced through grades to comdr., 1973; dir. hematology div. Nat. Ctr. for Disease Control, Atlanta, 1971-78, spl. asst. to dir., 1978-79, inactive res., 1979—; clin. asst. prof. pediatrics Tufts U. Med. Sch., 1974-86; clin. asst. prof. medicine Emory U. Med. Sch., 1971-81, clin. asst. prof. community health, 1976-86; clin. assoc. prof. humanities in medicine Morehouse Med. Sch., 1977-79; attending physician dept. medicine Wilcox Meml. Hosp., Lihue, Hawaii, 1979-82, Calif. Pacific Med. Ctr., San Francisco, 1983—; dir. Ctr. Preventive Medicine and Health Research, 1983—, dir. Health Watch, 1983—; sr. scientist Inst. Epidemiology and Behavioral Medicine, Inst. Cancer Research, Calif. Pacific Med. Ctr., San Francisco, 1983-88; prof. hematology and gerontology, dir. Ctr. Preventive Medicine and Health Rsch., chair health professions program San Francisco State U., 1983—; cons. WHO, FDA, Washington, NIH, Bethesda, Md., Govt. of China, Mayo Clinic, Rochester, Minn., Northwestern U., Evanston, Ill., U. R.I., Kingston, Pan Am. Health Orgn., Inst. Pub. Health, Italy, Nat. Inst. Aging Rsch. Ctr., Balt., U. Calif., San Diego, U. Ill., Chgo., Columbia U., N.Y.C., Brown U., Providence, U. Calif., L.A., Harvard U., Boston, U. Chgo., Emory U., Atlanta, Duke U., N.C., U. Tex., Houston, Ariz. State U., U. Hawaii, Honolulu, U. Paris, U. Geneva, U. Munich, Heidelberg U., U. Frankfurt, U. Berlin, Cambridge (Eng.) U., U. Singapore, others; vis. rsch. prof. gerontology Ariz. State U., 1989-90; mem. numerous sci. and profl. adv. bds., panels, coms. Mem. editorial bd. Am. Jour. Clin. Pathology, 1976-82, The Advisor, 1988—, Generations, 1989—, Alternative Therapies in Health and Medicine; book and film reviewer Sci. Books and Films, 1988—; author: 17 books and manuals including Hematology Laboratory Series, 4 vols., 1979-86, CRC Handbook Series in Clinical Laboratory Science, 1976—; assoc. editor: Contemporary Gerontology, 1993—; contbr. over 270 articles to sci. jours. Alumni regent Columbia U. Coll. Physicians and Surgeons, 1980—. Northwestern U. scholar, 1964-66; NSF fellow, 1964-66; Health Professions scholar, 1966-70; USPHS fellow, 1967-70; Microbiology, Urology, Upjohn Achievement, Borden Rsch. and Virginia Kneeland Frantz scholar awards Columbia U., 1970; recipient Am. Soc. Pharmacol. and Exptl. Therapy award in pharmacology, 1970, Commendation medal USPHS, 1973, Leadership Recognition awards San Francisco State U., 1984-89, 91-94, Meritorious Performance and Profl. Promise award, 1989, Meritorious Svc. award, San Francisco State U., 1992, Student Disting. Teaching and Svc. award Pre-Health Professions Student Alliance, 1992. Fellow ACP (commentator ACP Jour. Club/Annals of Internal Medicine 1993—), AAAS (med. scis. sect.), Royal Soc. Medicine (London), Gerontol. Soc. Am., Am. Geriatrics Soc., Am. Coll. Preventive Medicine (sci. com.), Am. Soc. Clin. Pathology, Internat. Soc. Hematology; mem. AMA, APHA, Am. Med. Informatics, Internat. Commn. for Standardization in Hematology, Am. Soc. Hematology, Internat. Soc. Thrombosis and Hemostasis, Acad. Clin. Lab. Physicians and Scientists, Am. Assn. Blood Banks, Nat. Assn. Advisors for Health Professions (bd. dirs.), Am. Assn. Med. Informatics (chair prevention and health evaluation informatics WG), Calif. Coun. Gerontology and Geriatrics, Am. Coll. Occupl. and Environ. Medicine, Assn. Tchrs. Preventive Medicine (edn. com., rsch. com.), Am. Soc. Microbiology, Am. Soc. Aging (editl. bd. 1990—, Dychtwald Pub. Spng award 1991), N.Y. Acad. Scis., Internat. Health Evaluation Assn. (v.p. for Ams. 1992—, bd. dirs., pres. 1994—), Cosmos Club, Golden Key (hon. faculty mem.), Army and Navy Club (Washington), Harvard Club (N.Y.), Sigma Xi, others. Home: 25 Hinckley Walk San Francisco CA 94111-2303 Office: Health Watch Ctr 2100 Webster St Ste 508 San Francisco CA 94115-2381

SCHMIDT, RONALD HANS, architect; b. Hoboken, N.J., Sept. 9, 1938. BArch., Syracuse U., 1961. Sr. designer Skidmore, Owings & Merrill, N.Y.C., 1963-68; ptnr., dir. archtl. design Grad. Partnership, Newark, 1968-81; pres., chief exec. officer Ronald Schmidt & Assocs., P.A., Hackensack, N.J., 1981—. Recipient numerous awards. Office: 222 Grand Ave Englewood NJ 07631-4352

SCHMIDT, RONALD R., academic administrator. BA, Point Loma Nazarene Coll.; MA, U. So. Calif.; EdD, Brigham Young U. Rsch. asst. office of lt. gov. State of Calif., Sacramento, 1966; faculty dept. sociology and polit. sci. Am. River Coll., Sacramento, 1966-69, chmn. divsn. behavioral scis., 1970-77; assoc. dir. master planning Los Rios C.C. Dist., Sacramento, 1977, devel. officer, 1977-80; exec. dir., sec. Los Rios Found., Sacramento, 1978-80; dir. devel. Friends U., Wichita, Kans., 1980-82; v.p. instnl. advancement So. Nazarene U., Bethany, Okla., 1982-86; exec. v.p., chief ops. officer Young Life Found., Colorado Springs, Colo., 1986-91; exec. v.p., chief ops. officer Colo. Christian U., Lakewood, Colo., 1992-93, pres., 1993—; cons. Statewide Vocat. Ednl. Needs Assessment Project, Calif. C.C., The Gallup Orgn., Johns Hopkins U., So. Regional Edn. Bd.; v.p. Assn. Nazarene Bldg. Profls., chmn. State Liaison Com., Pub. Svc./Social Work Edn.; co-dir. Human Svcs. Career Devel. Project, Intergovtl. Personnel Act Grant Project; pres. Los Rios C.C. Dist. Divsn. Chmn.'s Assn. State rep. Calif. C.C. Assn. Home: 8063 S Zephyr St Littleton CO 80123-5536

SCHMIDT, RUTH ANN, college president emerita; b. Mountain Lake, Minn., Sept. 16, 1930; d. Jacob A. and Anna A. (Ewert) S. B.A., Augsburg Coll., Mpls., 1952; M.A., U. Mo., 1955; Ph.D., U. Ill., 1962; LLD, Gordon Coll., 1987. Asst. prof. Spanish Mary Baldwin Coll., Staunton, Va., 1955-58; asst. prof. Spanish SUNY-Albany, 1962-67, assoc. prof., 1967-78, dean of humanities, 1971-76; prof. and provost Wheaton Coll., Norton, Mass., 1978-

82; pres. Agnes Scott Coll., Decatur, Ga., 1982-94; pres. emerita Agnes Scott Coll., Decatur, Ga., 1994—; chair Women's Coll. Coalition, 1986-88. Author: Ortega Munilla y sus novelas, 1973, Cartas entre dos amigos del teatro, 1969. Trustee Gordon Coll., Wenham, Mass., 1980-86, Lyon Coll., 1993—; bd. dirs. DeKalb C. of C., 1982-85, Atlanta Coll. Art, 1984-94; mem. exec. com. Women's Coll. Coalition, 1983-88; v.p. So. Univ. Conf., 1993. Named Disting. Alumna Augsburg Coll., 1973. Mem. Assn. Am. Colls. (dir. 1979-82, treas. 1982-83), So. Values in Higher Edn., Am. Coun. Edn. (commn. on women in higher edn. 1985-88), AAUW, Assn. Pvt. Colls. and Univs. Ga. (pres. 1987-89), Internat. Women's Forum, Young Women's Christian Assn. Acad. Women Achievers. Democrat. Presbyterian.

SCHMIDT, SANDRA JEAN, financial analyst; b. Limestone, Maine, Mar. 21, 1955; d. Dale Laban and Marie Audrey (Bailey) Winters; m. Lee Lloyd Schmidt, Oct. 20, 1973; children: Colby Lee, Katrina Leesa. AA summa cum laude, Anne Arundel Community Coll., 1987; BS summa cum laude, U. Balt., 1990. CPA, Md. Enlisted U.S. Army, 1973, traffic analyst, 1973-85, resigned, 1985; auditor Md. State Office of Legislative Audits, Balt., 1990-93; fin. analyst Md. Ins. Adminstrn., Balt., 1993—. Tutor Anne Arundel County Literacy Coun., Pasadena, Md., 1990—; mentor U. Balt., 1991; host family Am. Intercultural Student Exchange, 1992—. Mem. AICPA, Am. Soc. Women Accts., Md. Assn. CPAs, Soc. Fin. Examiners, U. Balt. Alumni Assn., Alpha Chi, Beta Gamma Sigma, Phi Theta Kappa. Republican. Baptist. Home: 7716 Pinyon Rd Hanover MD 21076-1585

SCHMIDT, STANLEY ALBERT, editor, writer; b. Cin., Mar. 7, 1944; s. Otto Elliott William and Georgia (Metcalf) S.; m. Joyce Mary Tokarz, June 9, 1979. BS, U. Cin., 1966; MA, Case Western Res. U., 1968, PhD, 1969. Asst. prof. physics Heidelberg Coll., Tiffin, Ohio, 1969-78; free-lance writer Lake Peekskill, N.Y., 1968—; editor Analog Sci. Fiction and Fact Dell Mags., N.Y.C., 1978—; mem. bd. advisors Nat. Space Soc., Washington, 1982—. Author: Newton and the Quasi-Apple, 1975, The Sins of the Fathers, 1976, Lifeboat Earth, 1978, Analog Yearbook II, 1981, Analog's Golden Anniversary Anthology, 1980, Analog: Readers' Choice, 1981, Analog's Children of the Future, 1982, Analog's Lighter Side, 1982, Analog: Writers' Choice, 1983, War and Peace: Possible Futures from Analog, 1983, Aliens from Analog, 1983, Writer's Choice, Vol. II, 1984, From Mind to Mind, 1984, Analog's Expanding Universe, 1986, Tweedlioop, 1986, Unknown, 1988, Unknown Worlds, 1989, Analog Essays in Science, 1990, Writing Science Fiction and Fantasy, 1991, Aliens and Alien Societies, 1995; contbr. stories to science fiction mags., articles to mags., chpts. to books. Mem. Sci. Fiction and Fantasy Writers Am., Am. Assn. Physics Tchrs., Am. Fedn. Musicians. Avocations: photography, hiking, linguistics, cooking, flying. Office: Analog Sci Fiction 1540 Broadway New York NY 10036-4039

SCHMIDT, STANLEY EUGENE, retired speech educator; b. Harrington, Wash., Dec. 14, 1927; s. Otto Jacob and Ella Genevieve (Wilson) S.; m. Randall Lee, Stephen Douglas. BS in Edn., U. Idaho, 1956; MEd in Adminstrn., U. Oreg., 1958; MA in Speech, Wash. State U., 1975. Supt., tchr., coach Rose Lake (Idaho) Sch. Dist. # 35, 1949-55; forensics coach, speech tchr. Jefferson H.S., Portland, Oreg., 1955-65; dir. forensics Portland C.C., 1965-93, lead speech instr., 1979-82, subject area chmn., 1986-90; adj. prof. speech U. Portland, 1987-93; subject-area chmn., 1986-90, parliamentarian faculty senate, 1975-80. Co-author anthology: The Literature of the Oral Tradition, 1963. Chmn., precinct committeeman Rep. Party, Kootenai County, Idaho, 1951-53; mem. Easter Seal Soc., Portland, 1980—; pres. Kootenai County Tchrs. Assn., 1953-54, North Idaho Edn. Assn., 1954-55, Oreg. Speech Assn., 1960-61, Oreg. C.C. Speech Assn., 1971-72. Recipient Excellence award U.S. Bank, Portland, 1993, Merit award N.W. Forensic Assn., 1992. Mem. Portland Rose Soc., Royal Rosarian, Masons (jr. grand deacon 1990-91, jr. grand steward 1991-92, grand orator, 1992-93, dist. dep. 1986-90, 32d deg. Scottish Rite, comdr. 1989-90), Cryptic Masons of Oreg. (grand orator 1994-95), Tualitin Valley Shrine Club, Shriners (pres. 1991, bd. dirs. 1989—), Red Cross of Constantine (St. Laurence Conclave, recorder 1993—, dir. of the work 1989—). Baptist. Avocations: rose gardening, stamps, coins, fishing, sports. Home: 5460 SW Palatine St Portland OR 97219-7259 Office: Portland CC Speech Dept PO Box 19000 Portland OR 97219

SCHMIDT, STEPHEN CHRISTOPHER, agricultural economist, educator; b. Isztimer, Hungary, Dec. 20, 1920; came to U.S., 1949, naturalized, 1965; s. Francis Michael and Anne Marie (Angeli) S.; m. Susan M. Varszegi, Dec. 20, 1945; children—Stephen Peter, David William. Dr.Sc., U. Budapest, Hungary, 1945; Ph.D., McGill U., Montreal, Que., Can., 1958. Asst. head dept. Hungary Ministry Commerce, Budapest, 1947-48; asst. prof. U. Ky., Lexington, 1955-57, Mont. State U., Bozeman, 1957-59; asst. prof. U. Ill., Urbana-Champaign, 1959-63, assoc. prof., 1963-70, prof. agrl. mktg. and policy, 1970-91, prof. emeritus, 1991—. Fulbright grantee Bulgaria, 1992-93; Ford Found. fellow, 1959; Agrl. Devel. Coun. grantee, 1966, U. Man. Rsch. fellow, 1968-69, Ford Found. rsch. grantee, 1973, 74, Whitehall found. grantee, 1979, Internat. Inst. Applied Systems Analyses (Laxenburg, Austria) rsch. scholar, 1976-77, USDA Intergovtl. Personnel Act grantee, 1983-84. Mem. Am. Agrl. Econs. Assn. (award 1979), Internat. Assn. Agrl. Economists, Am. Assn. Advancement Slavic Studies, Ea. Econ. Assn., Sigma Xi, Gamma Sigma Delta. Office: 1301 W Gregory Dr Urbana IL 61801-3608

SCHMIDT, STEPHEN ROBERT, lawyer; b. Louisville, Jan. 29, 1948; s. Adolph William and Olivia Ann (Hohl) S.; m. Wanda Jean Owen, Aug. 17, 1974; children: Johannes, Kathryn. AB, St. Louis U., 1969; Fulbright fellow, Universität Hamburg, 1969-70; MA, Ohio State U., 1971, JD, 1974. Assoc. Brown, Todd & Heyburn PLLC, Louisville, 1974-79, mem. 1980—. Co-author: Bad Faith Litigation in Kentucky, 1992, Insurance Coverage Law in Kentucky, 1994, Insurance Law in Kentucky, 1995, Insurance Law: Third Party Coverage in Kentucky, 1996; editor Ohio State Law Jour., 1973-74; contbr. articles to profl. jours. Named one of Outstanding Young Men of Am. Jaycees, 1983. Mem. ABA (chair comml. torts com., torts and ins. practice sect. 1995-96, speaker ann. meeting 1993, 94), Ohio State U. Alumni Club (pres. Louisville 1983, 86, 93, treas. 1987—), Fulbright Assn., Order of the Coif, Phi Beta Kappa. Avocations: photography, computers, playing cards, golf. Office: Brown Todd & Heyburn PLLC 3200 Providian Ctr 400 W Market St Louisville KY 40202-3346

SCHMIDT, TERRY LANE, health care executive; b. Chgo., Nov. 28, 1943; s. LeRoy C. and Eunic P. S.; children: Christie Anne, Terry Lane II. B.S., Bowling Green State U., 1965; M.B.A. in Health Care Adminstrn, George Washington U., 1971. Resident in hosp. adminstrn. U. Pitts. Med. Center, VA Hosp., Pitts., 1968-69; adminstrv. asst. Mt. Sinai Med. Center, N.Y.C., 1969-70; asst. dir. Health Facilities Planning Council of Met. Washington, 1970-71; asst. dir. dept. govtl. relations A.M.A., Washington, 1971-74; pres. Terry L. Schmidt Inc. Physician Svcs. Group, San Diego, 1974—; exec. dir., chief operating officer Emergency Health Assocs. P.C., Phoenix, 1989-91, Charleston Emergency Physicians, S.C., S.C., 1990-95, Joplin Emergency Physican Assocs., 1991-92, Big Valley Med. Group, 1991-92, Blue Ridge Emergency Physicians, P.C., 1992-93, Berkeley Emergency Physicians, P.C., 1992-93; pres. Med. Cons. Inc., 1983-84; v.p. Crisis Communications Corp. Ltd., 1982-90; pres. Washington Actions on Health, 1975-78; partner Washington counsel Medicine and Health, 1979-81; pres. Ambulance Corp. Am., La Jolla, Calif., 1984-87; chmn., pres. Univ. Inst., 1992—; lectr., part-time faculty dept. health care adminstrn. George Washington U., 1969-84, preceptor, 1971-84; adj. prof. grad. sch. Pub. Health San Diego State U., 1989—, preceptor, 1989—, clin. prof., 1995—; asst. prof. Nat. Naval Sch. Health Care Adminstrn., 1971-73; faculty CSC Legis. Insts., 1972-76, Am. Assn. State Colls. and U. Health Tng. Insts.; mem. adv. com. ambulatory care standards Joint Commn. Accreditation of Hosps., 1971-72; guest lectr. health care adminstrn. Nat. U., San Diego, 1992—; adj. prof. Bus. Adminstrn. U.S. Internat. U., San Diego, 1994-95. Author: Congress and Health: An Introduction to the Legislative Process and the Key Participants, 1976, A Directory of Federal Health Resources and Services for the Disadvantaged, 1976, Health Care Reimbursement: A Glossary, 1983; mem. editl. adv. bd. Nation's Health, 1971-73; contbr. articles to profl. jours. Bd. dirs. Nat. Eye Found., 1976-78. Mem. Am. Hosp. Assn., Med. Group Mgmt. Assn., Hosp. Fin. Mgmt. Assn., Med. Group Mgrs., Assn. Venture Capital Groups (bd. dirs. 1984-89), Med. Adminstrs. of Calif., San Diego Venture Group (chair 1984-87), U. Calif. San Diego Venture Group (chair 1984-87), U. Calif. San Diego Faculty Club, University Club (life), Nat. Dem. Club (life), Nat. Rep. Club (life), Capitol Hill Club (life), Alpha Phi Omega (pres. Bowling Green alumni chpt. 1967-70, sec.-treas. alumni assn. 1968-71). Office: 9191 Towne Center Dr Ste 360 San Diego CA 92122

SCHMIDT, THOMAS CARSON, international development banker; b. York, Pa., Oct. 15, 1930; s. George Small and Josephine Foot (Reifsnider) S.; m. Lucy Carter Searby, Aug. 21, 1954 (div. May 1980); children: Peter, Lucy, Thomas.; m. Robin G. Berry, Nov. 26, 1983; 1 stepdau., Julia Barclay. A.B., Princeton U., 1952; M.Div., Va. Sem., 1955; Ph.D. in Policy Scis., SUNY, 1971. Ordained priest Episcopal Ch., 1955; rector St. Alban's Ch., Bogota, Colombia, 1955-58; asst. St. James, New London, Conn., 1958-61; rector St. Andrew's, Longmeadow, Mass., 1961-68; on leave serving Diocese Zululand-Swaziland, South Africa, 1965-66; mgmt. cons., 1968-71, asst. commr. edn. State of R.I., 1971-73; mem. R.I. Gov.'s Policy and Program Rev. Staff Providence, 1973-75; commr. edn. State of R.I., 1975-80; v.p. Partners of the Americas, 1980-81; mgmt. cons. nat. and fgn. firms, 1981-83, 94—; pub. adminstrn. specialist Internat. Bank Reconstrn. and Devel. (World Bank), 1983-89, sr. gen. educator, 1989-94. Chmn. manpower task force R.I. Health Sci. Edn. Coun., 1973-75, mem. exec. bd., 1973-75; mem. edn. com. Maine Coun. Chs.; bd. dirs. Comty. Bldg. Trust. Mem. Internat. Soc. Ednl. Planners (treas. 1973), Internat. Assn. Applied Social Scientists, Council Chief State Sch. Officers (bd. dirs. 1976-80), State Higher Edn. Exec. Officers Assn. (legis. com.), Am. Assn. State Colls. and Univs. (legis. com.), SUNY Buffalo Alumni Assn. (dir.). Home: HC 61 Box 63 Bristol ME 04539-8803

SCHMIDT, THOMAS JOSEPH, JR., lawyer; b. New Haven, Jan. 16, 1945; s. Thomas Joseph and Rosemary (O'Shaughnessy) S.; m. Linda Diane Crider, Nov. 16, 1974; children: Elizabeth Anne, Thomas Joseph III, Karen Diana. AB, Xavier U., 1967; JD, U. Cin., 1970. Bar: Ohio 1970, U.S. Ct. Mil. Appeals 1970. Commd. 2d lt. U.S. Army, 1967, advanced through grades to capt., 1969-75; legal officer U.S. Army Corps Engrs., Ft. Hayes, Ohio, 1967-68, Ft. Knox, Ky., 1969-70; atty. U.S. Army JAGC, Ft. Benning, Ga., 1971-75; asst. counsel Midland Enterprises Inc., Cin., 1975-77, assoc. gen. counsel, 1977-83, gen. counsel, 1983-87, gen. counsel, sec., 1987-95, v.p., gen. counsel and sec., 1995—. Republican. Roman Catholic. Office: Midland Enterprises Inc 300 Pike St Cincinnati OH 45202

SCHMIDT, WILLIAM ARTHUR, JR., lawyer; b. Cleve., Oct. 2, 1939; s. William Arthur and Caroline (Jäger) S.; m. Gerilyn Pearl Smith, Sept. 30, 1967; children: Deborah, Dawn, Jennifer. BSBA, Kent State U., 1962; JD, Cleve. State U., 1968. Bar: Ohio 1968, Ill. 1990. Contract specialist NASA-Lewis Rsch. Ctr., Cleve., 1962-66, procurement analyst, 1967-68; atty. Def. Logistics Agy., Alexandria, Va., 1968-73; assoc. counsel Naval Sea Sys. Command, Arlington, Va., 1973-75; procurement policy analyst Energy R & D Agy., Germantown, Md., 1975-76; sr. atty. U.S. Dept. Energy, Germantown, Md., 1976-78; counsel spl. projects U.S. Dept. Energy, Oak Ridge, Tenn., 1978-83; adminstrv. judge Agr. Bd. Contract Appeals, Washington, 1983-87, HUD, Washington, 1987; chief legal counsel Fermilab, Batavia, Ill., 1987-92; gen. counsel Univ. Rsch. Assn., Inc., Washington, 1992—. Co-author: (NASA handbook) R & D Business Practices, 1968. Mem. Fed. Bar Assn. (past pres. East Tenn. 1978-83, 25 Yr. Svc. award 1994), Ill. Bar Assn., Bd. Contract Appeals Judges Assn. (dir.-sec. 1986-88), Sr. Execs. Assn., Delta Theta Phi (dist. chancellor 1978-83), Sigma Chi. Republican. Lutheran. Avocations: antiques, boating, choir, civil war history. Home: 7209 Bloomsbury Ln Spotsylvania VA 22553-1944 Office: Univ Rsch Assn Inc 1111 19th St NW Ste 400 Washington DC 20036-3603

SCHMIDT, WILLIAM C., chemical company executive; b. Niles, Mich., Sept. 27, 1938; s. Felix A. and Anna (Reifschneider) S.; m. Bethany Ann Boyd, Dec. 17, 1966; 1 child, Craig W. B.B.A., U. Mich., 1960, M.B.A., 1961. Cert. Mgmt. Acct. Various acctg. positions Dow Chem. Co., Midland, Mich., 1961-73; controller Dow Chem. Pacific Ltd., Hong Kong, 1973-78; area controller Dow Chem. Co., Midland, Mich., 1978-82, asst. corp. controller, 1982—; v.p., chief fin. officer DowElanco, Indpls., 1989—; bd. dirs. Noble Ctrs. Chmn. bd. dirs. Midland Hosp. Ctr., 1986-89; bd. dirs. Mid-Mich. Health Care Corp., 1983-89, chmn. bd., 1986-88; treas., bd. dirs. Indpls. Symphony Orch., 1992—. Cpl. U.S. Army, 1962-64. Mem. Inst. Mgmt. Accts., Inst. Cert. Mgmt. Accts. (regent 1985-89), Am. Indsl. Health Coun. (treas. 1986-87), Fin. Execs. Inst. Ind. C. of C. (bd. dirs. 1992—). Methodist. Home: 4958 St Charles Pl Carmel IN 46033-5936 Office: DowElanco 9330 Zionsville Rd Indianapolis IN 46268-1053

SCHMIDT-NIELSEN, BODIL MIMI (MRS. ROGER G. CHAGNON), physiologist; b. Copenhagen, Denmark, Nov. 3, 1918; came to U.S., 1946, naturalized, 1952; d. August and Marie (Jorgensen) Krogh; m. Knut Schmidt-Nielsen, Sept. 20, 1939 (div. Feb. 1966); children: Astrid, Bent, Bodil; m. Roger G. Chagnon, Oct. 1968. D.D.S., U. Copenhagen, 1941, D.Odont., 1946, DPhil., 1955; D.Sc. (hon.), Bates Coll., 1983. Faculty Duke, Durham, N.C., 1952-64; prof. biology Case Western Res. U., Cleve., 1964-71, chmn. dept., 1970-71, adj. prof., 1971-74; trustee Mt. Desert Island Biol. Lab., Maine, research scientist, 1971-86, exec. com., 1978-85, v.p., 1979-81, pres., 1981-85; adj. prof. Brown U., Providence, 1972-78, dept. physiol. U. Fla., Gainesville, 1987—; Mem. tng. grant com. NIGMS, 1967-71. Author: August and Marie Krogh, Lives in Science, 1995; editor: Urea and the Kidney, 1970; assoc. editor Am. Jour. Physiology: Regulatory, Integrative and Comparative Physiology, 1978-81. Trustee Coll. of Atlantic, Bar Harbor, Maine, 1972-92. Recipient Career award NIH, 1962-64, John Simon Guggenheim Meml. fellow, 1952-53; Bowditch lectr., 1958, Jacobaeus lectr., 1974. Fellow AAAS (de. coun. 1977-79), N.Y. Acad. Scis., Am. Acad. Arts and Scis.; mem. Am. Physiol. Soc. (coun. 1971-77, pres. 1975-76, Ray G. Daggs award 1989, Orr Reynolds award 1994, August Knogh lectr. 1994), Soc. Exptl. Biology and Medicine (coun. 1969-71). Research, publs. on biochemistry of saliva, water metabolism of desert animals, urea excretion, peristalsis of renal pelvis and concentrating mechanism, comparative kedney physiology, comparative physiology of excretory organs. Home: 4426 SW 103rd Ct Gainesville FL 32608-7146 Office: U Fla Dept Physiology Gainesville FL 32605

SCHMIDT-NIELSEN, KNUT, physiologist, educator; b. Norway, Sept. 24, 1915; came to U.S., 1946, naturalized, 1952; s. Sigval and Signe Torborg (Sturzen-Becker) Schmidt-N. Mag. Scient., U. Copenhagen, 1941, Dr. Phil., 1946; Dr. Med. (hon.), U. Lund, Sweden, 1985; D in Philosophy (hon.), U. Tondheim, Norway, 1993. Research fellow Carlsberg Labs., Copenhagen, 1941-44, Carlsberg Labs. (U. Copenhagen), 1944-46; research assoc. zoology Swarthmore (Pa.) Coll., 1946-48; docent U. Oslo, Norway, 1947-49; research assoc. physiology Stanford U., 1948-49; asst. prof. Coll. Medicine, U. Cin., 1949-52; prof. physiology Duke U., Durham, N.C., 1952—; James B. Duke prof. physiology Duke U., 1963—; Harvey Soc. lectr., 1962; Regents' lectr. U. Calif. at Davis, 1963; Brody Meml. lectr. U. Mo., 1962; Hans Gadow lectr. Cambridge (Eng.) U., 1971; vis. Agassiz prof. Harvard, 1972; Wellcome vis. prof. U. S.D., 1988; mem. panel environmental biology NSF, 1957-61; mem. sci. adv. com. New Eng. Regional Primate Center, 1962-66; mem. nat. adv. bd. physiol. research lab. Scripps Instn. Oceanography, U. Calif. at San Diego, 1963-69, chmn., 1968-69; organizing com. 1st Internat. Conf. on Comparative Physiology, 1972-80; pres. Internat. Union Physiol. Scis., 1980-86, mem. U.S. nat. com. 1966-78, vice chmn. U.S. nat. com., 1969-78; mem. subcom. on environmental physiology U.S. nat. com. Internat. Biol. Programme, 1965-67; mem. com. on research utilization uncommon animals, div. biology and agr. Nat. Acad. Scis., 1966-68; mem. animal resources adv. com. NIH, 1968; mem. adv. bd. Bio-Med. Scis., Inc., 1973-74; chief scientist Scripps Instn. Amazon expdn., 1967. Author: Animal Physiology, 3d. edit, 1970, The Physiology of Desert Animals; Physiological Problems of Heat and Water, 1964, How Animals Work, 1972, Animal Physiology; Adaptation and Environment, 1975, 2d edit., 1979, 3d edit., 1983, Scaling: Why is Animal Size So Important?, 1984; sect. editor Am. Jour. Physiology, 1961-64, 70-76; editor Jour. Applied Physiology, 1961-64, 70-76; mem. editorial bd. Jour. Cellular and Comparative Physiology, 1961-66, Physiol. Zoology, 1959-70, Am. Jour. Physiology, 1971-76, Jour. Applied Physiology, 1971-76, Jour. Exptl. Biology, 1975-79, 83-86; cons. editor: Annals of Arid Zone, 1962—; hon. editorial adv. bd. Comparative Biochemistry and Physiology, 1962-63; chief editor News in Physiol Scis., 1985-88, cons. editor, 1988—; contbr. articles to sci. publs. Guggenheim fellow, 1953-54; grantee Office Naval Rsch., 1952-54, 58-61, UNESCO, 1953-54, Office Q.M. Gen., 1953-54, Office Surgeon Gen., 1953-54, NIH, 1955-86, NSF, 1957-61, 59-60, 60-61, 61-63; recipient Rsch. Career award USPHS, 1964-85, Internat. prize for biology Japan Soc. for the Promotion of Sci., 1992. Fellow AAAS, N.Y. Acad. Sci., Am. Acad. Arts and Scis.; mem. NAS, N.C. Acad. Sci. (Poteat award 1957), Am. Physiol. Soc., Am. Soc. Zoologists (chmn. div. comparative physiology 1964), Soc. Exptl. Biology, Royal Danish Acad., Acad. Scis. (France) (fgn. assoc.), Royal Norwegian Soc. Arts. and Sci., Norwegian Acad. Scis. and Letters, Physiol. Soc. London (assoc.), Royal Soc. London (fgn.); hon. mem. Am. Soc. Zoologists, Harvey Soc., Zool. Soc. London, Deutsche Ornitologengesellshaft. Office: Duke Univ Dept Zoology Box 90325 Durham NC 27708-0325

SCHMIEDER, CARL, jeweler; b. Phoenix, Apr. 27, 1938; s. Otto and Ruby Mable (Harkey) S.; m. Carole Ann Roberts, June 13, 1959; children: Gail, Susan, Nancy, Amy. Student Bradley Horological Sch., Peoria, Ill., 1959-61; BA, Pomona Coll., 1961; Owner timepiece repair svc., Peoria, 1959-61; clock repairman Otto Schmieder & Son, Phoenix, 1961-65, v.p., 1965-70, pres., 1970—, chief exec. officer, 1970—. Mem. subcom. Leap Commn., 1966; area rep. Pomona Coll., 1972-76. Cert. jeweler; cert. gemologist, gemologist appraiser; recipient Design award Diamonds Internat., 1965, Cultured Pearl Design award, 1967, 68, Diamonds for Christmas award, 1970; winner Am. Diamond Jewelry Competition, 1973; bd. dirs. Lincoln Hosp., 1983—, Ariz. Mus., 1984-88; delegate White House Conf. on Small Bus., 1986, 95; chmn. Gov.'s Conf. on Small Bus., 1988-91; col. Confederate Air Force. Mem. Am. Gem. Soc. (dir. 1973-86, nat. chmn. nomenclature com. 1975-77, chmn. membership com. 1977-81, officer 1981-86), Ariz. Jewelers Assn. (Man of Yr. 1974), Jewelers Security Alliance (dir. 1974-78), Jewelers Vigilance Com. (dir. 1981-87), Jewelry Industry Council (dir. 1982-88), 24 Karat Club So. Calif., Exptl. Aircraft Assn., Warbirds of Am. (dir. 1990—), Deer Valley (Ariz.) Airport Tenants Assn. (dir. 1980-90, pres. 1983-90), Ariz. C. of C. (bd. dirs. 1985-89), Small Bus. Council (bd. dirs. 1985-89, chmn. 1988, del. to White House Conf., 1986, 95, chmn. Govs. Conf. on small bus. 1988-89), Nat. Small Bus. United (bd. dirs. 1990-94), Kiwanis (pres. Valley of Sun chpt. 1975-76), Friends of Iberia, Rotary. Republican. Methodist. Home: 537 W Kaler Dr Phoenix AZ 85021-7244 Office: Park Ctrl Phoenix AZ 85013

SCHMIEL, DAVID GERHARD, clergyman, religious education administrator; b. Cedarburg, Wis., Dec. 10, 1931; s. Gerhard August and Frieda Helena (Labrenz) S.; m. Shirley Ann Friede, July 6, 1957; children: Mark, Peter, Steven, Daniel, Julia. BA, Northwestern Coll., 1953; ThD, Concordia Sem., 1967. Pastor St. Paul's Luth. Ch., Gresham, Nebr., 1958-60, Onalaska, Wis., 1960-62; prof. St. Paul's Coll., Concordia, Mo., 1962-70; prof., dean Concordia Coll., St. Paul, 1970-81; dir. instrn. Concordia Sem., St. Louis, 1981-82; pres. Concordia Coll., Ann Arbor, Mich., 1983-91; dir. theol. edn. svc. Luth. Ch.-Mo. Synod, St. Louis, 1991-93; pres. Concordia Theol. Sem., Ft. Wayne, Ind., 1993-95. Author: Via Propria and Via Mystica...Gerson, 1969. Found. for Reformation Rsch. Jr. fellow, Southeastern Inst. for Medieval and Renaissance Studies, Jr. fellow, 1965, 66, 68.

SCHMIT, LUCIEN ANDRÉ, JR., structural engineer; b. N.Y.C., May 5, 1928; s. Lucien Alexander and Eleanor Jessie (Donley) S.; m. Eleanor Constance Trabish, June 24, 1951; 1 son, Lucien Alexander, III. B.S., MIT, 1949, M.S., 1950. Structures engr. Grumman Aircraft Co., Bethpage, N.Y., 1951-53; research engr., aeroelastic and structures lab. MIT, 1954-58; asst. prof. engring. (Case Inst. Tech.), 1958-60, assoc. prof., 1961-63, prof., 1964-70; prof. engring. and applied sci. UCLA, 1970-91, Rockwell prof. aerospace engring. emeritus, 1991—; mem. sci. adv. bd. USAF, 1977-84. Contbr. numerous articles on analysis and synthesis of structural systems, finite elements methods, design of fiber composite components and multidisciplinary design optimization to profl. jours. Fellow AIAA (Design Lecture award 1977, Structures, Structural Dynamics and Materials award 1979, Multidisciplinary Design Optimization award 1994), ASCE, Am. Acad. Mechanics; mem. NAE. Home: 545 3rd Ave S Edmonds WA 98020-4103

SCHMITT, BERNARD W., bishop. Ordained priest Roman Cath. Ch., 1955, ordained to episcopacy, 1988. Titular bishop Walla Walla, Wash., 1988-89; bishop Diocese of Wheeling-Charleston, W.Va., 1989—. Office: Chancery Office Box 230 1300 Byron St Wheeling WV 26003-3315*

SCHMITT, GARY A., energy company director; b. Idaho Falls, May 29, 1952; s. Bernard Frank and Betty Fay (Brown) S.; m. Nancy Panos, June 15, 1974; 1 child, Kyle Christopher. BS, U. Utah, 1974; MS, Va. Tech., 1976. Registered profl. engr., Utah. Indsl. engr. Mountain Fuel Supply, Salt Lake City, 1976-80, ops. mgr., 1980-85, sales mgr., 1985-90; dir. Questar Corp., Salt Lake City, 1990—; adj. prof. Westminster Coll., Salt Lake City, 1980-84; cons. Mktg./Mgmt. Inc., Salt Lake City, 1984-88; pres. Inst. Indsl. Engring., Salt Lake City, 1980-81. Contbr. articles to profl. jours. Participant Gov.'s Clean Air Task Force, Salt Lake City, 1991. Recipient Gold medal Pacific Coast Gas Assn., 1984, Silver medal 1982, Bronze medal, 1988, Mktg. Program award Am. Gass Assn., 1989. Mem. Assn. Energy Engrs., Rotary. Democrat. Episcopalian. Avocations: tennis, golf, hiking, basketball. Home: 1428 Canterbury Dr Salt Lake City UT 84108-2831 Office: Questar Corp 180 1st Ave Salt Lake City UT 84103-2301

SCHMITT, GEORGE FREDERICK, JR., materials engineer; b. Louisville, Nov. 3, 1939; s. George Frederick and Jane Limbird (Hurst) S.; m. Ann Cheatham, July 31, 1965; 2 children. BS, U. Louisville, 1962, MS, 1963; MBA, Ohio State U., 1966. Asst. dir. nonmetallic materials divsn. USAF Materials Directorate, Wright Lab., Wright Patterson AFB, Ohio, 1966—; advanced engring devel. mgr. USAF Materials Lab., Wright Patterson AFB, Ohio, 1986-90; chief plans and programs br. USAF Materials Lab., Wright AFB, Ohio, 1989-90; guest lectr. U. Dayton, 1970, 95, Cath. U., 1973, U. Mich., 1975. Contbr. articles profl. jours. Mem. Kettering (Ohio) Civic Band, 1965—, Affiliate Socs. Council of Dayton, 1972-81. Served to 1st lt. USAF, 1963-66. Named Fed. Profl. Employee of Yr. Dayton, 1972, One of Ten Outstanding Engrs., Engrs. Week, 1975, Air Force Meritorious Civilian Svc. award, 1994. Fellow Soc. for Advancement Materials and Process Engrs. (Best Paper award 1973, nat. sec. 1975-76, nat. membership chmn. 1977-79, nat. v.p. 1979-81, nat pres. 1981-82, chmn. long-range planning com. 1983-87, trustee 1991—, chmn. Internat. SAMPE Symposium 1996), AIAA (assoc.)(materials tech. com.); mem. ASTM (rec. sec. 72-75, chmn. com. on erosion and wear 1976-79, chmn. liaison subcom. 1979-83, award of merit 1981), Am. Chem. Soc., Affiliate Socs. Coun. Dayton (chmn. 1978-79). Republican. Lutheran. Home: 1500 Wardmier Dr Dayton OH 45459-3354 Office: WL Materials Directorate MLB Wright-Patterson AFB 2941 P St Bldg 654 Dayton OH 45433-7750

SCHMITT, GEORGE JOSEPH, chemist; b. Farmingdale, N.Y., June 21, 1928; s. Joseph Frank and Carolyn (Henych) S.; m. E. Christine Schneider, Feb. 10, 1952; children: Paul, Carol, Mark, David. BS in Chemistry, Bklyn. Poly. Inst., 1950; PhD in Chemistry, SUNY, Syracuse, 1960. Chemist Am. Cyanamid, Bound Brook, N.J., 1953-57; chemist Allied Chem., Morristown, N.J., 1960-61, group leader, 1961-63, assoc. dir. rsch., 1963-69, mgr. rsch., 1969-80, dir. Polymer Lab., 1980-89, dir. Structural Polymers Lab., 1989-94; ret.; adv. bd. N.J. R & D Coun., 1982-85. 1st lt. U.S. Army, 1950-53. Named NSF fellow, 1957-60. Mem. Am. Chem. Soc., Soc. for Advancement Materials and Processing Engring., Sigma Xi. Achievments include research on polymer synthesis, structure/property relationships, bipolar membranes, advanced composites, bioresorbble polymers, electrically conducting polymers, composite armor.

SCHMITT, HARRISON HAGAN, former senator, geologist, astronaut, consultant; b. Santa Rita, N.Mex., July 3, 1935; s. Harrison A. and Ethel (Hagan) S. BA, Calif. Inst. Tech., 1957; postgrad. (Fulbright fellow), U. Oslo, 1957-58; PhD (NSF fellow), Harvard U., 1964; hon. degree, Franklin and Marshall Coll., 1977, Colo Sch. Mines, 1971, Rensselaer Poly Inst., 1973. Geologist U.S Geol. Survey, 1964-65; astronaut NASA, 1965; lunar module pilot Apollo 17, 1972, spl. asst. to adminstr., 1974; asst. adminstr. Office Energy Programs, 1974; mem. U.S. Senate, N.Mex., 1977-83; cons., 1983—; mem. Pres.' Fgn. Intelligence Adv. Bd., 1984-85, Army Sci. Bd., 1985-90, Pres.' Ethics Commn., 1989; chmn. tech. adv. bd. Army Rsch. Lab.; adj. prof. U. Wis., 1995—; chair, pres. Annapolis Ctr., 1994—; bd. dirs. Orbital Scis. Corp. Trustee The Lovelace Insts. Recipient MSC Superior Achievement award, 1970, Disting. Svc. medal NASA, 1973, Lovelace award NASA, 1989, Gilbert award GSA, 1989. Mem. AIAA, AAAS, Geol. Soc. Am., Am. Geophys. Union, Am. Assn. Petroleum Geologists. Home: PO Box 14338 Albuquerque NM 87191-4338

SCHMITT, HOWARD STANLEY, minister; b. Waterloo, Ont., Can., Oct. 19, 1933; came to U.S., 1971; s. Delton Howard and Beulah (Weber) S.; m. Dorothy Jean West, May 20, 1960; children: Valerie Jean Schmitt Jones, Jeffrey Howard. B Theology, Toronto Bible Coll., Ont., Can., 1963. Ordained to ministry Mennonite Ch., 1963. Pastor Wanner Mennonite Ch., Cambridge, Ont., 1960-71, Calvary Mennonite Ch., Ayr, Ont., 1964-69, S. Union Mennonite Ch., West Liberty, Ohio, 1971-83; hosp. chaplain Mary Rutan Hosp., Bellefontaine, Ohio, 1983-85; dir. devel. Adriel Sch., West Liberty, Ohio, 1985-86; pastor Bay Shore Mennonite Ch., Sarasota, Fla., 1986-95, Sharon Mennonite Ch., Plain City, Ohio, 1995—; sec. Mennonite Conf. Ont., Cambridge, 1970-71; overseer Ohio Conf. Mennonites, West Liberty, 1972-78, 84-86; moderator Southeast Mennonite Conf., Sarasota, 1989-92; mem. Mennonite Ch. Gen. Bd., 1991-95. Vice chair Mary Rutan Hosp. Bd., 1978-83. Recipient 13 Yrs. Svc. award Vol. Chaplains Group, Mary Rutan Hosp., 1985. Mem. Sarasota Mennonite Mins. Fellowship (past, sec., chmn.).

SCHMITT, JOHANNA MARIE, plant population biologist, educator; b. Phila., Mar. 12, 1953; d. William Francis and Laura Belle (Wear) S.; m. Darrell Marion West, Aug. 6, 1983. BA, Swarthmore (Pa.) Coll., 1974; PhD, Stanford U., 1981. Postdoctoral rsch. assoc. Duke U., Durham, N.C., 1981-82; asst. prof. Brown U., Providence, 1982-87, assoc. prof. biology, 1987-94, prof., 1994—; mem. adv. panel NSF on population biology, 1989; mem. R.I. Task Force, New Eng. Plant Conservation program, 1991—. Assoc. editor Evolution, 1990-92; contbr. articles to profl. jours. including Evolution, Ecology, Am. Naturalist, Jour. Ecology, Nature. Bd. dirs. Sojourner House, Providence, 1989-92. NSF grad. fellow, 1974, mid. career fellow, 1992-93; rsch. grantee, 1984—; recipient faculty award for women, 1991—. Mem. Soc. for Study of Evolution (coun. mem. 1990-92, exec. v.p. 1994-95), Bot. Soc. Am., Ecol. Soc. Am., Am. Soc. Naturalists (v.p. elect 1996). Achievements include research on ecological genetics of natural plant populations: density-dependent phenomena, gene flow and population structure, inbreeding depression, the evolution of sex, maternal effects, seed ecology, natural selection, evolution of plasticity, adaptive significance of phytochrome, ecological risks of transgenic plants. Office: Brown Univ Dept Ecology & Evolutionary Sci Providence RI 02912

SCHMITT, KARL MICHAEL, retired political scientist; b. Louisville, Ky., July 22, 1922; s. Edward Peter and Mary Ann (Iula) S.; m. Grace Bernadette Leary, June 18, 1949; children: Karl, Edward, Barbara, William, Michael. B.A., Cath. U. Am., 1947, M.A., 1949; Ph.D., U. Pa., 1954. Teaching asst. U. Pa., 1948-50; instr. history Niagara U., 1950-54, asst. prof., 1954-55; research analyst U.S. Dept. State, 1955-58; asst. prof. dept. govt. U. Tex., 1958-63, assoc. prof., 1963-66, prof., 1966-91, prof. emeritus, 1991—, chmn., 1975-80; vis. prof. U. Calif., Los Angeles, summer 1959, Nat. War Coll., 1970-71; vis. sr. fellow U. Manchester, Eng., 1988-89; cons. Dept. of State, 1962-70. Author: Communism in Mexico; A Study in Political Frustration, 1965, Mexico and the United States, 1821-1973: Conflict and Coexistence, 1974, others. Contbr. articles to profl. jours. Served with U.S. Army, 1943-45. Decorated Purple Heart. Mem. Tex. Cath. Hist. Assn. (pres. 1976-77). Roman Catholic. Home: 2603 Pinewood Ter Austin TX 78757-2136 Office: Dept Govt U Tex Austin TX 78712

SCHMITT, MARY ELIZABETH, postal supervisor; b. Detroit, Sept. 16, 1948; d. Jerome Ferdinand and Margaret Ellen (Beauregard) S. BS, Ea. Mich. U., 1979. Waitress, hostess Mr. Steak, Westland, Mich., 1969-70; mgr. housewares K-Mart, Ypsilanti, Mich., 1971, asst. mgr., jewelry, 1972; postal clk. U.S. Postal Svc., Ann Arbor, Mich., 1972-88, postal supr., 1988—. Crisis intervention counselor Ozone House, Ann Arbor, 1978; convenor Gray Panthers of Huron Valley, Ann Arbor, 1979-80; active Greenpeace. Mem. LWV, Nat. Assn. Postal Suprs., Ann Arbor Postal Fed. Credit Union (v.p. 1987—), Sierra Club, Ancestry Club. Roman Catholic. Avocations: travel, reading, hiking, canoeing, genealogy. Home: PO Box 1833 Ann Arbor MI 48106-1833 Office: US Postal Svc 2075 W Stadium Blvd Ann Arbor MI 48103-7011

SCHMITT, NANCY CAIN, public and corporate relations executive, writer; b. Fayetteville, N.C., June 12, 1942; d. Carlton White and Cleo Margaret (Parnell) Cain; m. Louis Dennis Schmitt, July 13, 1974 (div.). BA, Wake Forest U., 1960-64. Intern Winston-Salem (N.C.) Jour.-Sentinel, 1963-64; reporter Gastonia (N.C.) Gazette, 1964-66; copy editor, reporter Twin City Sentinel, Winston-Salem, 1966-67; entertainment editor Fayetteville Observer, 1967-78; lifestyle editor Anchorage Times, 1978-83; pub. rels. specialist Multivisions Cable TV Co., Anchorage, 1983-84; editor Alaska Jour. of Commerce, Anchorage, 1984-85; sr. comms. specialist U.S. Postal Svc., 1985—. Author: How to Care for Your Car: A Women's Guide to Car Care in Alaska, 1978 (award 1979); mem. editorial bd. Episc. Diocean of Alaska, Fairbanks, 1983-86; contbr. articles to profl. jours. and nat. publs. Recipient Asst. Postmaster Gen.'s award for excellence, USPS Corp. Rel. VP Opportunity award. Mem. Nat. Fedn. Press Women (bd. mem. 1990-91), Pub. Rels. Soc. Am., Alaska Press Women (pres. treas., sec., communicator of achievement, recipient numerous awards), Alaska Press Club (recipient 3 awards), Rotary Internat. (bd. dirs. 1991-92). Home: 6716 E 16th Ave Apt A Anchorage AK 99504-2513 Office: U S Postal Svc Corp Rels 3720 Barrow St Anchorage AK 99599-0041

SCHMITT, PAUL JOHN, history educator; b. Pitts., Jan. 25, 1951; s. Phillip John and Adeline Marie (Barnhart) S.; m. Ruth Margaret Glass, June 20, 1987. BS, Ariz. State U., 1976, BA in Edn., 1978; MA, U. Nev., Las Vegas, 1994. Registration clk. Hermosa Inn Resort, Scottsdale, Ariz., 1978-79, asst. mgr., 1979-82; convention svc. mgr. Carefree (Ariz.) Inn Resort, 1982-84; tchr. Tonopah (Nev.) High Sch., 1984-85; reservation clk. Desert Inn Country Club and Spa, Las Vegas, Nev., 1985-92; prof. history C.C. of So. Nev., Las Vegas, 1992—. Mem. Assn. Am. Geographers, Orgn. Am. Historians, Am. Western History Assn., Orgn. Am. Historians, Phi Alpha Theta, Gamma Theta Upsilon. Avocations: reading, photography, horseback riding. Office: CC So Nev Cheyenne Campus Dept Regional Studies 3200 E Cheyenne Ave S2C North Las Vegas NV 89030

SCHMITT, PAUL JOSEPH, biomedical research executive; b. York, Pa., May 16, 1951; s. Paul Joseph and Helen Therese (Stapleton) S.; m. Sharon Zavaglia, July 27, 1994; children: Tara, Cari, Paul, Michael. BS in Fin., Lehigh U., 1974; MBA, Rutgers U., 1979. Fin. analyst Nabisco, East Hanover, N.J., 1974-77, contr. FSD divsn., 1977-79; group mgr. fin. BOC Group, Montvale, N.J., 1979-80, dir. strategic planning, 1980-81; v.p., gen. mgr. Ohmeda (subs. BOC Group), Orchard Park, N.Y., 1981-86; pres., COO Brolectron, Hackensack, N.J., 1986-88; pres., CEO DNX Corp., Princeton, N.J., 1988-94, chmn., pres., CEO, 1994—; bd. dirs. Biotech Coun. N.J., Princeton, Nextran, Inc., Princeton. Home: 15 Bonnie Way Allendale NJ 07401 Office: DNX Corp 575 Rte 28 Raritan NJ 08869

SCHMITT, ROLAND WALTER, retired academic administrator; b. Seguin, Tex., July 24, 1923; s. Walter L. and Myrtle F. (Caldwell) S.; m. Claire Freeman Kunz, Sept. 19, 1957; children: Lorenz Allen, Brian Walter, Alice Elizabeth, Henry Caldwell. BA in Math, U. Tex., 1947, BS in Physics, 1947, MA in Physics, 1948; PhD, Rice U., 1951; DSc (hon.), Worcester Poly. Inst., 1985, U. Pa., 1985; DCL (hon.), Union Coll., 1985; DL (hon.), Lehigh U., 1986; DSc (hon.), U. S.C., 1988, Universite De Technologie De Compiegne, 1991; DL (hon.), Coll. St. Rose, 1992, Russell Sage, 1993, Hartford Grad. Ctr., 1995. With GE, 1951-88; R & D mgr. phys. sci. and engring. GE, Schenectady, 1967-74; mgr. energy sci. and engring. R & D GE, 1974-78, v.p. corp. R & D, 1978-82, sr. v.p. corp. R & D, 1982-86, sr. v.p. sci. and tech., 1986-88, ret., 1988; pres. Rensselaer Poly. Inst., Troy, N.Y., 1988-93; bd. dirs. Gen. Signal Corp.; mem. tech. adv. bd. Chrysler Corp.; 1990-93; past pres. Indsl. Rsch. Inst.; mem. energy rsch. adv. bd. U.S. Dept. Energy, 1977-83; chmn. CORETECH, 1988-93; mem. Com. on Japan, NRC, 1988-90, Comml. Devel. Ind. Adv. Group, NASA, 1988-90; exec. com. Coun. on Competitiveness, 1988-93; chmn. NRC Panel on Export Controls, 1989-91; mem. Dept. Commerce Adv. Commn. on Patent Law Reform, 1990-92; mem. adv. bd. Oak Ridge Nat. Lab., 1993—; chmn. Motorola's Sci. Adv. Bd., 1995—; chmn. rsch. priority panel for NRC Future of Space Sci., 1994-95. Trustee N.E. Savs. Bank, 1978-84; bd. advisors Union Coll., Schenectady, 1981-84, Argonne Univs. Assn., 1979-82, RPI, 1982-88; bd. govs. Albany Med. Ctr. Hosp., 1979-82, 88-90; bd. dirs. Sunnyview Hosp. and Rehab. Ctr., 1978-86, Coun. on Superconductivity for Am. Competitiveness, 1987-89; mem. exec. com. N.Y. State Ctr. for Hazardous Waste Mgmt., 1988-89; chmn. Office of Tech. Assessment adv. panel on industry and environment; mem. Nat. Commn. Ill. Inst. Tech., 1993-94. With USAAF, 1943-46. Recipient RPI Community Svc. award, 1982, award for disting. contbns. Stony Brook Found., 1985, Rice U. Disting. Alumni award, 1985, IRI Medalist award, 1989, Royal Swedish Acad. of Engring. Sci., 1990, Arthur M. Bueche award Nat. Acad. of Engring.,1995; named Fgn. Assn. of Engring. Acad. of Japan. Fellow AAAS, IEEE (Centennial medal 1984, Engring. Leadership award 1989, Founders medal 1992, Hoover medal 1993), Am. Phys. Soc. (Pake award 1993), Am. Acad. Arts and Scis.; mem. NAE (coun., Beuche award 1995), Am. Inst. Physics (chmn. 1993—), Coun. Sci. Soc. (pres. exec. bd. 1993—), N.Y. Acad. Scis. (pres. coun. 1993—), Nat. Sci. Bd. (chmn. 1982), Dirs. Indsl. rsch., Rensselaer Alumni Assn. (Disting. alumni award 1993). Office: Ste 459 400 Clifton Corporate Pky Clifton Park NY 12065-3829

SCHMITT, WOLFGANG RUDOLF, consumer products executive; b. Koblenz, Germany, Mar. 12, 1944; s. Josef H. and M.H. (Baldus) S.; m. Toni A. Yoder, June 30, 1974; children: Christopher, Corey, Clayton. BA, Otterbein Coll., 1966; AMP, Harvard U. Bus. Sch., 1986. With Rubbermaid Inc., Wooster, Ohio, 1966—, pres., gen. mgr. housewares products div., 1984-91, exec. v.p., bd. dirs., 1987-91, pres., chief operating officer, 1991—; chmn., CEO, 1993—; bd. dirs. Parker Hannifin Corp., Kimberly-Clark Corp. Bd. dirs. Otterbein Coll., 1992—. Avocations: horticulture, tennis, sailing. Office: Rubbermaid Inc 1147 Akron Rd Wooster OH 44691-6000

SCHMITTER, CHARLES HARRY, electronics manufacturing company executive, lawyer; b. Paterson, N.J., Feb. 4, 1928; s. Charles and Jennie (Schoe) S.; m. Margaret Ann Roose, Oct. 24, 1964 (dec. Dec. 1989). A.B. magna cum laude, Rutgers U., 1948; J.D., Columbia, 1953. Bar: N.Y. bar 1956, Mich. bar 1960. Asso. atty. firm Cravath, Swaine & Moore, N.Y.C., 1955-59; asst. sec. Ford Motor Co., 1959-64; corp. sec. Sperry Rand Corp. (now Unisys Corp.), N.Y.C., 1964-87, ret., 1987. Served with AUS, 1953-55. Mem. Am. Bar Assn., Am. Soc. Corp. Secretaries, Phi Alpha Delta, Theta Chi. Club: Rockefeller Center Luncheon (N.Y.C.). Home: 420 E 51st St New York NY 10022-8014

SCHMITZ, CHARLES EDISON, evangelist; b. Mendota, Ill., July 18, 1919; s. Charles Francis Schmitz and Lucetta Margaret (Foulk) Schmitz Kaufmann; m. Eunice Magdalene Ewy, June 1, 1942; children: Charles Elwood, Jon Lee. Student, Wheaton Coll., 1936-37, 38, 39; BA, Wartburg Coll., Waverly, Iowa, 1940; BD, Wartburg Theol. Sem., Dubuque, Iowa, 1942, MDiv, 1977. Ordained to ministry Luth. Ch., 1942. Founding pastor Ascension Luth. Ch., L.A., 1942-48, Am. Evang. Luth. Ch., Phoenix, 1948-65; dir. intermountain missions, founding pastor 14 Evang. Luth. Parishes, Calif., Ariz., N.Mex., Fla., 1948-65; evangelist Am. Luth. Ch., Mpls., 1965-73; sr. pastor Peace Luth. Ch., Palm Bay, Fla., 1973-89; pastor-at-large Am. Evang. Luth. Ch., Phoenix, 1989—; charter mem. Navajo Luth. Mission, Rock Point, Ariz., 1960—; pastoral advisor Ariz. Luth. Outdoor Ministry Assn., Prescott, 1958-65, 89—; Kogudus Internat. Retreat master and chaplain, Fla., Berlin and Marbach, Germany, 1990; mem. transition team Fla. Synod Evang. Luth. Ch. Am., 1985-89. Author: Evangelism for the Seventies, 1970; co-author: ABC's of Life, 1968; assoc. editor Good News mag., 1965-71. Founder, chmn. Ariz. Ch. Conf. on Adult and Youth Problems, 1956-65; vice chmn. synod worship & ch. music com. Am. Luth. Ch., Mpls., 1960-66; chmn. Space Coast Luth. Retirement Ctr., Palm Bay, Fla., 1985-89; chaplain Ariz. chpt. Luth. Brotherhood, 1991—. Named Citizen of Yr., Palm Bay C. of C., 1979. Mem. Nat. Assn. Evangelicals, German Am. Nat. Congress (nat. chaplain), Lions (officer Phoenix and Palm Bay clubs 1952—, Ariz. Dist. 21A chaplain 1994—), Kiwanis (bd. dirs. L.A. chpt. 1942-48). Republican. Home: 12444 W Toreador Dr Sun City West AZ 85375-1926 *The truly modern person today who, like the scribes of old, would aspire to fulfillment in leadership would do well to remember Jesus' words: "Therefore every scribe who has been trained for the Kingdom of Heaven is like the master of a household who brings out of his treasure what is new and what is old." (Matt. 13:52).*

SCHMITZ, DANIEL DEAN, mechanical engineer; b. Moorhead, Minn., Apr. 8, 1964; s. Thomas Oswin and Diane Marie (Bruski) S. Student, Bismarck State Coll., 1983-85; BS, N.D. State U., 1987. Registered profl. engr. N.D., Minn., N.Y., Pa., Ga., Va. Mech. engr. Crisafulli Pump Co., Glendive, Mont., 1988-90, Beazely Engring., PC, Bismarck, N.D., 1990-93; mech. engr., dir. design and product prodn., project mgr. Henning, Metz, Hartford & Assocs., Inc., Fargo, N.D., 1993-95; chief mech. engr. SSR Engr., Inc., East Grand Forks, Minn., 1995—. Mem. ASHRAE, NSPE, Am. Soc. Plumbing Engrs. Avocations: boating, waterskiing, restoring vehicles, bicycling. Office: SSR Engrs Inc PO Box 471 East Grand Forks MN 56721

SCHMITZ, DENNIS MATHEW, English language educator; b. Dubuque, Iowa, Aug. 11, 1937; s. Anthony Peter and Roselyn S.; m. Loretta D'Agostino, Aug. 20, 1960; children—Anne, Sara, Martha, Paul, Matthew. B.A., Loras Coll., 1959; M.A., U. Chgo., 1961. Instr. English Ill. Inst. Tech., Chgo., 1961-62, U. Wis., Milw., 1962-66; asst. prof. Calif. State U., Sacramento, 1966-69, assoc. prof., 1969-74, prof., 1974—; poet-in-residence, 1966—. Author: We Weep for Our Strangeness, 1969, Double Exposures, 1971, Goodwill, Inc., 1976, String, 1980, Singing, 1985, Eden, 1989, About Night: Selected and New Poems, 1993. Recipient Discovery award Poetry Center, N.Y.C., 1968; winner First Book Competition Follett Pub. Co., 1969; di Castagnola award Poetry Soc. Am., 1986; Shelley Meml. award Poetry Soc. Am., 1987; NEA fellow, 1976-77, 85-86, 92-93, Guggenheim fellow, 1978-79. Mem. PEN, Assoc. Writing Programs. Roman Catholic. Office: Calif State U Dept English 6000 J St Sacramento CA 95819-2605

SCHMITZ, DOLORES JEAN, primary education educator; b. River Falls, Wis., Dec. 27, 1931; d. Otto and Helen Olive (Webster) Kreuziger; m. Karl Matthias Schmitz Jr., Aug. 18, 1956; children: Victoria Jane, Karl III. BS, U. Wis., River Falls, 1953; MS, Nat. Coll. Edn., 1982; postgrad., U. Minn., Mankato, 1969, U. Melbourne, Australia, 1989, U. Wis., Milw., 1989, Carroll Coll., 1990, Cardinal Stritch, 1990. Cert. tchr., Wis. Tchr. Manitowoc (Wis.) Pub. Schs., 1953-56, West Allis (Wis.) Pub. Schs., 1956-59, Lowell Sch., Milw., 1960-63, Victory Sch., Milw., 1964; tchr. Palmer Sch., Milw., 1966-84, 86-94, unit leader, 1984-86; ret., 1994; co-organizer Headstart Tchg. Staff Assn., Milw., 1968; insvc. organizer Headstart and Early Childhood, Milw., 1969-92; pilot tchr. for Whole Lang., Hi-Scope and Math. Their Way, 1988-93; bd. dirs. Cuurriculum Devel. Ctr. of Milw. Edn. Ctr., 1993-94. Author: (curriculum) Writing to Read, 1987, Cooperation and Young Children (ERIC award 1982), Kindergarten Curriculum, 1953. Former supporter Milw. Art Mus., Milw. Pub. Mus., Milw. County Zoo, Whitefish Bay Pub. Libr., Earthwatch Riveredge Nature Ctr.; vol. fgn. visitor program Milw. Internat. Inst., 1966-94, holiday folk fair, 1976-94, Earthwatch, 1989; lobbyist Milw. Pub. Sch. Bd. and State of Wis., 1986-93; coord. comty. vols., 1990-94. Grantee Greater Milw. Edn. Trust, 1989. Mem. NEA (life), ASCD, Milw. Kindergarten Assn. (rec. sec. 1986-93), Nat. Assn. for Edn. of Young Children, Tchrs. Applying Whole Lang., Wis. Early Childhood Assn., Milw. Tchrs. Ednl. Assn. (co-chmn. com. early childhood 1984-86), Assn. for Childhood Edn. Internat. (charter pres. Manitowoc chpt. 1955-56), Milw. Educating Computer Assn., Alpha Psi Omega. Roman Catholic. Avocations: bicycling, nature. Home: 312 8th Ave Apt 1 Tierra Verde FL 33715-1801 *Like a very old song said-Accentuate the POSITIVE, eliminate the negative,and don't mess with Mr. In-Between. Life is better for you and everyone around you if these "rules" are followed. Success=If it is to be, it is up to me. I can.*

SCHMITZ, FRANCIS DAVID, lawyer; b. Milw., July 13, 1950; s. Joseph Francis and Helen Julia (Rudzik) S.; m. Elizabeth Ann Brinker, Dec. 12, 1975; children: Sarah, Catherine. BA, St. Norbert Coll., 1972; MBA, So. Ill. U., 1975; JD, Marquette U., 1983. Bar: Wis. 1983, U.S. Dist. Ct. (ea. and we. dists.) Wis. 1983, U.S. Ct. Appeals (7th cir.) 1985. Law clk. to judge U.S. Ct. Appeals (7th cir.), Chgo., 1983-84; asst. U.S. atty. for ea. dist. Wis. U.S. Dept. Justice, Milw., 1984—. Capt. U.S. Army, 1973-80, lt. col. USAR, 1980—. Mem. State Bar Wis., Assn. U.S. Army, Res. Officer Assn. U.S. Roman Catholic. Avocations: flyfishing, jogging. Office: Office US Atty 517 E Wisconsin Ave Milwaukee WI 53202

SCHMITZ, JOHN ALBERT, veterinary pathologist; b. Silverton, Oreg., Oct. 21, 1940; s. John J. and Ann G. (Wavra) S.; m. M. Charlene Busch, Aug. 7, 1971. D.V.M., Colo. State U., 1964; Ph.D., U. Mo., 1971. Asst. prof. vet. sci. dept. U. Nebr., Lincoln, 1971-72, prof., head vet., biomed. sci. dept. 1984—; assoc. prof., asst. dean Coll. Vet. Medicine, Oreg. State U., Corvallis, 1972-78, prof., dir. Vet. Diagnostic Lab., 1978-84. Contbr. articles to profl. jours. Mem. AVMA (rsch. coun.), Am. Assn. Vet. Lab. Diagnosticians (bd. govs.), Nebr. Vet. Med. Assn. (bd. dirs.), Am. Coll. Vet. Pathologists, Internat. Acad. Pathologists. Office: U Nebr Dept Vet & Biomed Sci Fair St At E Campus Loop Lincoln NE 68583-0905

SCHMITZ, ROBERT ALLEN, publishing executive, investor; b. Chgo., Jan. 19, 1941; s. John and Lee (Zeal) S.; m. Jenny Ann Quest, Aug. 23, 1969 (div.); children: Alexander, Nicholas, Lara, Maximilian. BA with distinction, U. Mich., 1963; MBA, MIT, 1965. Asst. to pres. Lima (Peru) Light and Power Co., 1965-67; acquisition analyst W.R. Grace Co., N.Y.C., 1967-69; asst. to chmn. N.W. Industries, N.Y.C., 1969-70; prin. McKinsey & Co., Inc., N.Y.C., 1970-82; v.p. books Dow Jones & Co., N.Y.C., 1982-88; chmn., pres., chief exec. officer Richard D. Irwin, Inc., Homewood, Ill., 1983-89; pres., founder Quest Capital Ltd., 1989—; investment cons. Soros Fund Mgmt., 1990-92; mgn. dir., sr. ptnr. Trust Co. of the West, 1993—; mem. adv. bd. Coll. Commerce De Paul U., Chgo., 1985—; bd. dirs. Nilfisk PLC, Copenhagen, Adams Rite Sabre, Inc., Glendale, Calif., Superior Fireplace Co., Fullerton, Calif., Houston Foods Co., Chgo., Archibald Candy Co., Chgo., US Media Group, Inc., Crystal City, Mo., Ctrl. Valley Publ., Merced, Hobby Products Co., Inc., Penrose, Colo., Automated Bar Controls, Vacaville, Calif. Pres. Cultural Arts Ctr. Found., Homewood, Ill. Mem. Assn. Am. Pubs. (chmn. higher edn. divsn. 1989), Nature Conservancy (trustee N.Y. state chpt.). Office: Trust Co of the West 200 Park Ave Ste 2200 New York NY 10166-0005

SCHMITZ, ROGER ANTHONY, chemical engineering educator, academic administrator; b. Carlyle, Ill., Oct. 22, 1934; s. Alfred Bernard and Wilma Afra (Aarns) S.; m. Ruth Mary Kuhl, Aug. 31, 1957; children—Jan, Joy, Joni. B.S. in Chem. Engring., U. Ill., 1959; Ph.D. in Chem. Engring., U. Minn., 1962. Prof. chem. engring. U. Ill., Urbana, 1962-79; Keating-Crawford prof. chem. engring. U. Notre Dame, Ind., 1979—, chmn. dept. chem. engring., 1979-81, dean engring., 1981-87; v.p., assoc. provost U. Notre Dame, 1987-95; cons. Amoco Chems., Naperville, Ill., 1966-77; vis. prof. Calif. Inst. Tech., Los Angeles, 1968-69, U. So. Calif., Los Angeles, 1968-69. Contbr. articles to profl. jours. Served with U.S. Army, 1953-55. Guggenheim found. fellow, 1968. Mem. Nat. Acad. Engring., Am. Inst. Chem. Engrs. (A.P. Colburn award 1970, R.H. Wilhelm award 1981), Am. Chem. Soc., Am. Soc. for Engring. Edn. (George Westinghouse award 1977). Roman Catholic. Home: 16865 Londonberry Ln South Bend IN 46635-1444 Office: U Notre Dame 301 Cushing Hall Notre Dame IN 46556

SCHMITZ, SHIRLEY GERTRUDE, marketing and sales executive; b. Brackenridge, Pa., Dec. 19, 1927; d. Wienand Gerard and Florence Marie (Grimm) S. BA, Ariz. State U., 1949. Tchr., guidance counselor Mesa High Sch., Ariz., 1949-51; area mgr. Field Enterprises Ednl. Corp., Phoenix, 1951-52, dist. mgr., 1952, regional mgr., 1953-55, br. mgr., Montreal, Que., Can., 1955-61, nat. supr., Chgo., 1961-63, asst. sales mgr., 1963-65, nat. sales mgr., 1965-70; v.p., gen. sales mgr. F.E. Compton Co. div. Ency. Brit., Chgo., 1970-71, exec. v.p., dir. sales, 1971-73; pres. CHB Port-A-Book Store, Inc., 1973-76; gen. mgr. Bobbs-Merrill Co., Inc., Indpls., 1976-82; v.p. sales U.S. Telephone Communications of Midwest, Inc., Chgo., 1982-83; exec. v.p. sales and market devel. Entertainment Publs., Corp., Birmingham, Mich., 1983-89, sr. v.p. mktg. and sales, Troy, Mich., 1989-92; prin. S.G. Schmitz and Assocs., Chgo., 1992—; bd. dirs. Ariz. Tech. Incubator; bd. advisors Ctr. Advancement of Small Bus., Ariz. State U. Sch. Bus; bd. dirs. Spectral, Inc., Colourtech, Inc. Recipient Twin award Nat. Bd. YWCA, 1987. Recipient Honors award Beta Gamma Sigma, 1995, Disting. Achievement award Sch. Bus. Ariz. State U., 1995; Angel award Nat. Assn. Women Bus. Owners, 1996. Mem. USGA (assoc.), Internat. Platform Assn., Am. Mgmt. Assn., Nat. Bus. Incubation Assn., Nat. Geographic Soc., Nat. Space Soc., World Future Soc., Ariz. State U. Alumni Assn. Republican. Roman Catholic. Home: 93 Miller Rd Lake Zurich IL 60047-1395

SCHMOEKER, PETER FRANK, secondary school educator; b. St. Louis, Oct. 1, 1957; s. Ernst Alfred and Annemarie Dora (Kawohl) S.; m. Maggy Noelle Taunay, Sept. 29, 1979; children: Adrienne Nepenthe, Camille Aureli, Genevieve Helena. BA in Biology and German, Washington U., St. Louis, 1980; MEd, U. Mo., St. Louis, 1990. Cert. tchr. German, biology, gen. sci., Mo. Med. rsch. tech. II Washington U., 1979-85; sci. and German tchr. Pattonville Sch. Dist., St. Louis, 1985—; math. and sci. tutor Loretto Learning Ctr., Webster Groves, Mo., 1986—. Leader Boy Scouts Am., 1990—; del. leader People to People Amb. Program, 1994. Mem. NEA, PTA, Eagle Scout Assn., CIM Floaters (pres. 1990—), Goethe Inst. Lutheran. Avocations: sailing, climbing, hiking, caving, camping. Home: 6907 Mitchell Ave Saint Louis MO 63139-3650 Office: Pattonville Heights Mid Sch 195 Fee Fee Rd Maryland Heights MO 63043-2709

SCHMOKE, KURT L., mayor; b. Balt., Dec. 1, 1949; m. Patricia Schmoke; children: Katherine, Gregory. BA, Yale U., 1971; JD, Harvard U., 1976. Former assoc. Piper & Marbury; former pvt. practice; asst. U.S. atty Balt.; state's atty. Maryland, 1982-87; mayor Baltimore, 1987—; apptd. mem. White House Domestice Policy Staff, 1977-78; former mem. Gov.'s Commn. on Prison Overcrowding; former mem. Md. Criminal justice Coord. Coun. & Task Force to Reform Insanity Def.; founder Balt. Community Devel. Financing Corp., 1988—. Rhodes Scholar Yale U. Office: Office of the Mayor 100 Holliday St Baltimore MD 21202-3417*

SCHMOLDER, EULALIA LEFFERS, food and nutrition educator; b. Omaha, July 4, 1919; d. Fred John and Ida Martha (Meyer) Leffers; m. Carl James Schmolder, Sept. 15, 1950. BS, Ohio State U., 1943; MS, Tex. Woman's U., 1967, PhD, 1969. Registered and lic. dietitian, Tex. Dietitian dormitory food svc. Ohio State U., Columbus, 1944-49; dir. food svc. Deshler Walleck Hotel, Columbus, 1949-50; dietitian Dallas Ind. Sch. Dist., 1951-58, 59-60, 1965-66; grad. asst. food preparation labs. Tex. Woman's U., Denton, 1967-68, from asst. to assoc. prof., 1969-70, 78; dir. dietetics Baylor U. Med. Ctr., Dallas, 1970-73; asst. prof. home econs. Sam Houston State U., Huntsville, Tex., 1975-81; ret., 1981, presenter in field food and nutrition, , 1981—; with food svc. mgmt. dept. Parkland Meml. Hosp., Dallas, part-time 1950, 51-53. Author: Organization and Management of a Hospital Department of Dietetics, 1985. Vol. Sr. Citizens Cmty. Ctr., Ferris, Tex., 1992, Ellis county and nat. polit. candidates, 1992—, Nursing Home, Ferris, 1992-93; tchr. Bible studies, 1992; sec. United Meth. Women, 1992—. Faculty grantee Sam Houston State U. Mem. Am. Dietetic Assn., Am. Home Econ. Assn., Tex. Dietetic Assn., Tex. Nutrition Coun., Dallas Dietetic Assn., Dallas Dietetic Assn. Cons. Interest Group, Soc. Nutrition Edn., Nutrition Today Soc., Ea. Star (officer 1992-93), 3 Garden Club (v.p. 1992-93), Book Rev. Club (pres. 1993—). Methodist. Avocations: gardening, politics, opera and symphonies, entertaining, playing bridge. Home and Office: 1200 S Interstate Highway 45 Ferris TX 75125-8106

SCHMOLKA, LEO LOUIS, law educator; b. Paris, Apr. 25, 1939; came to U.S., 1944; s. Francis and Irene S.; m. Lucille J. Schoenbaum, July 29, 1965; children—Andrew, Gregory. A.B., Dartmouth Coll., 1960; LL.B., Harvard U., 1963; LL.M., NYU, 1971. Bar: N.Y. 1964. Assoc. Weil, Gotshal and Manges, N.Y.C., 1964-71; ptnr. Weil, Gotshal and Manges, 1971-81, of counsel, 1981—; adj. asst. prof. law NYU Sch. of Law, 1971-75; adj. assoc. prof. law NYU Law Sch., 1975-76, adj. prof., 1977-80, assoc. prof., 1981-84, prof., 1985—, mem. faculty, dir. IRS/NYU continuing profl. edn. program, 1987—; cons. U.S. Treasury Dept. Office Tax Policy, Washington, 1994-95, Am. Law Inst., 1979-86, U. Miami (Fla.) Estate Planning Inst., 1976-80; vis. adj. prof. law U. Miami Sch. Law, 1977, 80; vis. lectr. continuing legal edn. various univs. and tax insts., 1973—. Contbr. articles to legal jours. Fellow Am. Coll. Trust and Estate Counsel; mem. ABA, N.Y. State Bar Assn. (chmn. com. on income taxation estates and trusts 1973-75, estate and gift tax 1976-77, mem. exec. com. tax sect. 1978), Internat. Acad. Estate and Trust Law (academician). Office: NYU Sch Law 40 Washington Sq S Rm 430 New York NY 10012-1005

SCHMOLL, HANS JOACHIM, medical educator; b. Hannover, Germany, June 21, 1946; s. Johannes and Edeltraut (Schneider) S. MD, Med. U. Hannover, 1970, PhD, 1982. Rsch. assoc. Med. U., Hannover, 1971-84, prof. medicine and hematology-oncology, 1984-95; prof. medicine and hematology dept. hematology and oncology Martin Luther U., Halle-Wittenberg, Germany, 1996—. Author: Kompendium Intern Onkologie, 1986. Home: Ludwig Barnay Strasse 9, D-30175 Hannover Germany Office: Martin Luther Univ, Dept Hematology/Oncology, D-06120 Halle-Saale Germany

SCHMOLL, HARRY F., JR., lawyer, educator; b. Somers Point, N.J., Jan. 20, 1939; s. Harry F. Sr and Margaret E. Schmoll; m. Rita L. Miescier, Aug. 29, 1977. BS, Rider Coll., 1960; JD, Temple U., 1967. Bar: Pa., D.C. 1969, N.J. 1975. With claims dept. Social Security Adminstrn., Phila., 1960-67; staff atty. Pa. State U., State College, 1968-69; regional dir. Pa. Crime Commn., State College, 1969-70; campaign aide U.S. Senator Hugh Scott, Harrisburg, Pa., 1970; pvt. practice law, State College, 1970-74, Manahawkin, N.J., 1975—; instr. criminal justice Pa. State U., University Park, 1969-74, assoc. prof. criminal justice, bus. law Burlington County Coll., Pemberton, N.J., 1974-92, prof., 1992—, pres. elect edn. assn., 1992-93, pres. edn. assn., 1993-94; judge mcpl. ct., Stafford Twp., 1982-85. Gen. counsel German Heritage Coun. of N.J., Inc.; active Barnegat Twp. Rent Control Bd., 1991, Barnegat Twp. Zoning Bd., 1994. Author: New Jersey Criminal Law Workbook, 1976, 2nd edit. 1979. Mem. Stafford Twp. Com., 1979-81, dep. mayor, 1979. Trustee Pheasant Run Homeowners Assn., Barnegat, N.J., 1992-95. Mem. Pa. Bar Assn., N.J. Bar Assn., Ocean County Bar Assn., German-Am. Club of So. Ocean County (past pres.). Office: 6 Citrus Ct Barnegat NJ 08005-3126

SCHMULTS, EDWARD CHARLES, lawyer, corporate and philanthropic administrator; b. Paterson, N.J., Feb. 6, 1931; s. Edward M. and Mildred (Moore) S.; m. Diane E. Beers, Apr. 23, 1960; children: Alison C., Edward M., Robert C. B.S., Yale U., 1953; J.D., Harvard U., 1958. Bar: N.Y. 1959, D.C. 1974. Assoc. White & Case, N.Y.C., 1958-65; ptnr. White & Case, 1965-73, 77-81; gen. counsel Treasury Dept., Washington, 1973-74; undersec. Treasury Dept., 1974-75; dep. counsel to Pres. U.S., 1975-76; dep. atty. gen. of U.S. Dept. Justice, Washington, 1981-84; sr. v.p. external rels., gen. counsel GTE Corp., Stamford, Conn., 1984-94; lectr. securities laws. Bd. dirs. Greenpoint Fin. Corp., Germany Fund, Ctrl. European Equity Fund; trustee Edna McConnell Clark Found.; chmn. bd. trustees Refugee Policy Group. With USMC, 1953-55. Mem. Am. Bar Assn., Assn. Bar City N.Y., Adminstrv. Conf. U.S. (council 1977-84). Clubs: Sakonnet Golf (Little Compton, R.I.); Metropolitan (Washington).

SCHMUTZ, ARTHUR WALTER, lawyer; b. Akron, Ohio, Aug. 2, 1921; s. Paul Edward and Elizabeth (Williams) S.; m. Elizabeth Moore, June 17, 1951; children: David H., Stuart R., Jonathan M., Anne Marie. AB summa cum laude, Johns Hopkins U., 1949; LLB cum laude, Harvard U., 1952. Bar: Calif. 1953. Assoc. Gibson, Dunn & Crutcher, L.A., 1952-59, ptnr., 1960-69, sr. ptnr., 1969-86, adv. ptnr., 1987-90, adv. counsel, 1991—; bd. dirs. H.F. Ahmanson & Co. Home Savs. Am., L.A., Ducommun Inc., L.A. Trustee Orthopaedic Hosp., L.A. With USAAF, 1942-45. Decorated Bronze Star. Fellow Am. Bar Found.; mem. Calif. Club, La Jolla Beach and Tennis Club, Lakeside Golf Club, Phi Beta Kappa. Office: 333 S Grand Ave Los Angeles CA 90071-1504

SCHMUTZ, CHARLES REID, university foundation executive; b. Youngstown, Ohio, Jan. 26, 1942; s. Charles Edward and Alice Mae (Bliss) S.; m. Judith Rhodes Seiple, June 19, 1965; children: Charles Reid Jr., Andrew Edward, Jill Caroline. AB in Econs., Brown U., 1964. Lab. technician The Standard Slag Co., Youngstown, 1964-65; direct salesman The Standard Slag Co., Cleve., 1965-69; mktg. and prodn. scheduler The Standard Slag Co., Youngstown, 1969-73, mktg. and indsl. engr., 1973-85, gen. mgr., v.p. ops., 1985-89; pres. Youngstown State U. Found., 1989—; bd. dirs. StanCorp., Youngstown. Bd. dirs. Youngstown Playhouse, Jr. Achievement Mahoning Valley. Named to Hall of Fame, Ohio Aggregates Assn., 1990. Mem. Rotary. Methodist. Avocations: golf, tennis.

SCHMUTZHART, BERTHOLD JOSEF, sculptor, educator, art and education consultant; b. Salzburg, Austria, Aug. 17, 1928; came to U.S., 1958, naturalized, 1963; s. Berthold Josef and Anna (Valaschek) S. Student, Acad. for Applied Art, Vienna, Austria, 1956. Cert. fed. tchr., Austria. Prof. Wekschulheim Felbertal, Salzburg, 1951-58; sculptor Washington, 1959-60; tchr. Longfellow Sch., Bethesda, Md., 1960-63; prof., chmn. dept. sculpture Corcoran Sch. Art, Washington, 1963-94, prof. emeritus, 1994—; lectr. Smithsonian Instn., Washington, 1968-84. One-man shows include Fredericksburg Gallery Fine Art, Va., 1967-73, Franz Bader Gallery, Washington, 1978, 81, 83, 86, 88; group shows include Nat. Collection Fine Arts, Washington, 1961-70, High Mus. Art, Atlanta, 1965, Ark. Art Ctr., Little Rock, 1966, Birmingham Mus. Art, Ala., 1967, Hirschhorn Mus. and Sculpture Garden, Washington, 1981, Nat. Gallery Modern Art, New Delhi, 1990; represented in permanent collections Hirschhorn Collection; designer fountain, Gallery of Modern Art, Fredericksburg, 1967; author: The Handmade Furniture Book, 1981; contbr. articles to profl. jours. Fine arts panelist D.C. Commn. for Arts, 1973-79; chmn. bd. Market Five Gallery, Washington, 1978-82; bd. dirs. Franz Bader Gallery, Washington, 1981-86; trustee Arts for the Aging, Inc., Washington, 1990—. Recipient 1st prize Washington Religious Arts Council, 1960, for sculpture, Little Rock, 1966, Louisville, 1968, Silver medal Audubon Soc., Washington, 1971. Mem. Guild for Religious Architects, Artists Equity Assn. (pres. D.C. chpt. 1973-75), AAUP, Am. Austrian Soc. (pres. 1968-70, exec. com.), Soaring Soc. Am. Home: 32 Layline Ln Fredericksburg VA 22406-4061

SCHNABEL, JOHN HENRY, retired music educator; b. Evansville, Ind., Mar. 15, 1915; s. Arthur John and Myrtle L. (Walters) S.; m. Emily H. Wepfer, June 28, 1938; children: Jack D. (dec.), Julia Belle Schnabel Klinke, Diane Schnabel Williams Clayton (dec.), Kathlee Mae Schnabel Wong. B.S., Evansville Coll., 1939; Mus.M., Northwestern U., 1947; Ed.D., Ind. U., 1954; B. A. in Fine Arts, So. Ill. U.-Edwardsville, 1975. Dir. bands Evansville Coll., 1937-39; supr. music Carlisle-Haddon Twp. schs., Carlisle, Ind., 1939-42; supr. music, dir. bands Jasper (Ind.) High Sch., 1942-49; asso. prof. music, dir. bands Panhandle A. and M. Coll., Goodwell, Okla., 1949-52; prin. Stratford (Tex.) Ind. Sch., 1952-53; grad. asst. Ind. U., 1953-54; vis. prof. Miami U., Oxford, Ohio, 1954-55; dir. admissions Park Coll., Parkville, Mo., 1955-57; registrar, dir. admissions So. Ill. U., Edwardsville, 1957-67, mem. faculty, 1957-80, prof. edn., 1973-80, prof. emeritus, 1980—, head fine arts div., 1961-62, dir. teaching learning centers, 1972-75, coordinator computer based instrn. lab., 1977-80; cons. computer assisted instrn., 1980-90, mgmt. cons., 1980—, ret., 1996; chmn. bd., chief exec. officer George G. Fetter Co., Louisville, 1970—. Author: An Evaluation of Extra-Class Activities, 1966, Ten Years of University Progres, 1967; others; condr. workshops in oboe and watercolor. Oboist, mem. bd. dirs. Alton (Ill.) Civic Symphony, 1957-61; oboist other orchs., 1929—; adv. council Ednl. Resources Info. Center Ednl. Facilities, U. Wis., Madison, 1965-67; Bd. dirs. Alton Meml. Hosp., 1967—. Served with AUS, 1945. Mem. Assn. Collegiate Registrars (chmn. facilities com. 1965-67), Am. Assn. Collegiate Registrars and Admissions Officers, Am. Assn. Sch. Adminstrs., Council Ednl. Facilities Planning, Am. Assn. Higher Edn., Assn. Ednl. Data Systems, Assn. Devel. Computer Based Instrnl. Systems, Internat. Double Reed Soc. (patron), Phi Delta Kappa, Phi Mu Alpha, Kappa Kappa Psi. Methodist. Club: Rotary. Home and Office: 2305 Fairview Dr Alton IL 62002-5627

SCHNABEL, ROBERT VICTOR, retired academic administrator; b. Scarsdale, N.Y., Sept. 28, 1922; s. Frederick Victor and Louise Elizabeth (Frick) S.; m. Ellen Edyth Foelber, June 7, 1946; children: Mark F., Philip P. Student, Concordia Sem., St. Louis, 1943-45; AB, Bowdoin Coll., 1944; MS, Fordham U., 1951, PhD, 1955; LLD (hon.), Concordia Coll., 1988. Tchr. St. Paul's Sch., Ft. Wayne, Ind., 1945-49; prin. St. Matthew's Sch., N.Y.C., 1949-52; assoc. supt. edn. Central Dist., Luth. Ch.-Mo. Synod, 1952-56; asst. prof. philosophy Concordia Sr. Coll., Ft. Wayne, 1956-60, assoc. prof., 1960-65, prof., acad. dean, 1966-71; pres. Concordia Coll., Bronxville, N.Y., 1971-76; acad. v.p., dean Wartburg Coll., Waverly, Iowa, 1976-78; pres. Valparaiso (Ind.) U., 1978-88; cons. Luth. Edn. Conf. N.Am., 1977-88. Contbr. articles to profl. jours. Mem. AAUP, Luth. Acad. Scholarship, Assoc. Colls. Ind., Nat. Assn. Ind. Colls. and Univs., Rotary, Phi Delta Kappa. Office: Valparaiso Univ 23 Huegli Hall Valparaiso IN 46383

SCHNABEL, ROCKWELL ANTHONY, ambassador; b. Amsterdam, Holland, Dec. 30, 1936; came to U.S., 1957; s. Hans and Wilhelmina S.; m. Marna Belle Del Mar, 1964; children: Mary Darrin, Christy Ann, Everton Anthony. Student, Trinity Coll., Haarlem, Netherlands, 1951-56. Pres. Unilife Assurance Group S.H. Luxembourg, 1974-78; dir. Bateman Eichler, Hill Richards, Los Angeles, 1967-82, sr. v.p., 1969-82, vice chmn. bd., chmn. exec. com., 1978-82; pres. Bateman Eichler Hill Richard Group, Los Angeles, 1981-83; amb. to Finland U.S. Dept. State; under sec. for travel and tourism U.S. Dept. Commerce, Washington, 1989-91, dep. sec., 1991-92, acting sec. of commerce, 1992-93; ptnr. Trident Capital LLP Inc., L.A., 1992—; bd. dirs. Internat. Game Tech., Amax Gold Inc., Cyprus Amax Minerals Inc., CSG Systems Inc. Past pres. L.A. Pension Bd., Calif., 1982; mem. L.A. Olympic Organizing Com., 1983-84. With Air N.G., 1958-64. Decorated comdr. Order of Good Hope, South Africa, Grand Cross of Lion of Finland; recipient Gold medal Dutch Govt., U.S. Dept. Commerce, medal of honor the Netherlands Olympic Com. Mem. L.A. Beach Club, Calif. Club, L.A. Country Club. Office: Trident Capital Inc Ste 2020 11100 Santa Monica Blvd Los Angeles CA 90025

SCHNABLE, GEORGE LUTHER, chemist; b. Reading, Pa., Nov. 26, 1927; s. L. Irvin and Laura C. (Albright) S.; m. Peggy Jane Butera, May 4, 1957; children: Lee Ann, Joseph G. BS, Albright Coll., 1950; MS, U. Pa., 1951, PhD, 1953. Project engr. Lansdale (Pa.) Tube Co., 1953-58; engring. specialist Philco Corp., Lansdale, 1958-61; mgr. materials and processes Philco-Ford Corp., Blue Bell, Pa., 1961-71; head process rsch. RCA Labs., Princeton, N.J., 1971-80, head device physics and reliability, 1980-87; head device physics and reliability David Sarnoff Rsch. Ctr., Princeton, 1987-91; ind. tech. cons. Schnable Assocs., Lansdale, 1991—. Author: (with others) Advances in Electronics and Electron Physics, 1971, The Chemistry of the Semiconductor Industry, 1987, Microelectronics Reliability, 1989, Microelectronics Manufacturing Diagnostics Handbook, 1993; editor spl. issue RCA Rev., 1984; divsn. editor Jour. of Electrochem. Soc., 1978-90; contbr. 80 articles to profl. publs. With U.S. Army, 1946-47. Fellow AAAS, Am. Inst. Chemists, Electrochem. Soc. (chm. Phila. sect. 1969-71); mem. IEEE (sr.) (assoc. guest editor Proceedings 1974), Alpha Chi Sigma, Phi Lambda Upsilon, Sigma Xi. Achievements include 39 patents (several with others); contributions to semiconductor device fabrication technology and reliability. Home and Office: Schnable Assocs 619 Knoll Dr Lansdale PA 19446-2925

SCHNACK, GAYLE HEMINGWAY JEPSON (MRS. HAROLD CLIFFORD SCHNACK), corporate executive; b. Mpls., Aug. 14, 1926; d. Jasper Jay and Ursula (Hemingway) Jepson; student U. Hawaii, 1946; m. Harold Clifford Schnack, Mar. 22, 1947; children: Jerrald Jay, Georgina, Roberta, Michael Clifford. Skater, Shipstad & Johnson Ice Follies, 1944-46; v.p. Harcliff Corp., Honolulu, 1964—, Schnack Indsl. Corp., Honolulu, 1969—, Nutmeg Corp., Cedar Corp.; ltd. ptnr. Koa Corp. Mem. Internat. Platform Assn., Beta Sigma Phi (chpt. pres. 1955-56, pres. city council 1956-57). Established Ursula Hemingway Jepson art award, Carlton Coll., Ernest Hemingway creative writing award, U. Hawaii. Office: PO Box 3077 Honolulu HI 96802-3077 also: 1200 Riverside Dr Reno NV 89503

SCHNACK, HAROLD CLIFFORD, lawyer; b. Honolulu, Sept. 27, 1918; s. Ferdinand J. H. and Mary (Pearson) S.; m. Gayle Hemingway Jepson, Mar. 22, 1947; children: Jerrald Jay, Georgina Schnack Hankinson, Roberta Schnack Poulin, Michael Clifford. BA, Stanford, 1940, LLB, 1947. Bar: Hawaii, 1947. Dep. prosecutor City and County Honolulu, 1947-48; gen. practice with father F. Schnack, 1948-60; pvt. practice, Honolulu, 1960-86; pres. Harcliff Corp., 1961—, Schnack Indsl. Corp., 1969-73, Instant Printers, Inc., 1971-81, Koa Corp., 1964—, Nutmeg Corp., 1963-89, Global Answer System, Inc., 1972-78. Pres. Goodwill Industries of Honolulu, 1971-72. Mem. ABA, Hawaii Bar Assn., Internat. Platform Soc., Nat. Fedn. Ind. Bus. Com. of 100, Outrigger Canoe Club, Phi Alpha Delta, Alpha Sigma Phi. Office: 817 A Cedar St PO Box 3077 Honolulu HI 96802

SCHNACK, LARRY GENE, university chancellor; b. Harlan, Iowa, Mar. 19, 1937; s. Alvin and Twyla (Kulbom) S.; m. Carol Jean Hansen, Sept. 1, 1955; children—Lorrie, Kevin, Mark, Rachelle. B.S. in Gen. Sci., Iowa State U., 1958, Ph.D. in Organic Chemistry, 1965. Tchr. Emmons High Sch., Minn., 1958-61; mem. faculty, adminstr. U. Wis.-Eau Claire, 1965—, prof. chemistry, 1981—, chancellor, 1985—; bd. dirs. Firstar Bank, No. States Power Co. Mem. Eau Claire Area Indsl. Devel. Corp., Momentum Chippewa Valley. Recipient DuPont Teaching award Iowa State U., 1965, Disting. Service award Nat. Residence Hall Hon., Eau Claire, Wis., 1984. Mem. Eau Claire Country Club, Rotary (past pres. local club), Eau Claire C. of C. Office: U Wis Office of Chancellor Eau Claire WI 54702-4004

SCHNACKENBERG, ROY LEE, artist; b. Chgo., Jan. 14, 1934; s. Elmer J. and Hazel (Bard) S.; children: Marke, Douglas; m. Shirley Goldman, 1986. B.F.A., Miami U., Oxford, Ohio, 1956. One-man shows include, Joachim Gallery, Chgo., 1962, Main St. Galleries, Chgo., 1963, 64, 66, 68-69, Michael Wyman Gallery, Chgo., 1972, Esther Robles Gallery, Los Angeles, 1973; group exhbns. include print and drawing biennial, Art Inst. Chgo., 1961, Chgo. and Vicinity Show Art Inst. Chgo., 1961, 62, 64, 66-69, 73, 78, Soc. Contemporary Art, Art Inst. Chgo., 1962, 70, New Horizons in Sculpture, Chgo., 1962, 2d ann. art dealers show, N.Y.C., 1963, Ill. Biennial Show, Champaign, 1965, 67, Twelve Chgo. Artists, Walker Mus., Mpls., 1965, also, , Mulvane Art Center, Topeka, 1965, 50 States of Art Exhibit, Burpee Mus., Rockford, Ill.; Recent Aquisitions Exhbn., Whitney Mus., 1967, also, ann. exhbn. painting and sculpture, 1967, 68-69, 69-70, No. Ill. U. group exhbn., Normal, 1968-69, Western Ill. U. show, Macomb, 1968-69, Ill. Arts Council traveling Sculpture exhbn., 1968-69, Des Moines Art Center exhbn., New Am. Realists, Konsthallen, Gotenborg, Sweden, 1970, The Art of Playboy World Tour, Milan, 1971,, Dept. Interior Bicentennial Exhbn., Corcoran Gallery, Washington, 1976,; nat. tour 200 Years of Illustration, N.Y. Hist. Soc.; Zriny-Hayes Gallery, Chgo., 1978, Mitchell Mus., Champaign, Ill., 1980, Continuity and Change, Chgo. Artists, 1983, Snead Gallery, Rockford, Ill., 1985, 89, 91, 93, 94, Chgo. Arts Club; executed mural Crucible, South Chgo. Savs. Bank, 1977; 2d ann. art dealers executed mural, S.E. Savs. & Loan, 1979; represented in permanent collections, Whitney Mus. Am. Art, N.Y.C., Art Inst. Chgo., Mus. Contemporary Art, Chgo., Burpee Art Mus., Rockford, Ill., others. Served with AUS, 1956-58. Recipient Joseph R. Shapiro award New Horizons in Sculpture, Chgo., 1962; Slobe award, 1964; Viehler award, 1965; Logan medal, 1973; Municipal award, 1974; all Art Inst. Chgo.; recipient purchase prize Burpee Mus., 1965, Copley Found. award N.Y.C., 1967. Mem. Arts Club of Chgo., Chgo. Yacht Club.

SCHNAIBERG, ALLAN, sociology educator; b. Montreal, Que., Can., Aug. 20, 1939; came to U.S., 1964; s. Harry and Belle (Katzoff) S.; m. Edith L. Harshbarger, Sept. 1, 1981; children by previous marriage: Lynn Renee, Jill Ann. B.S., McGill U., 1960; M.A., U. Mich., 1964, Ph.D., 1968. Analytical chemist Can. Nat. Rys., Montreal, 1960-61; materials and process engr. Canadair, Ltd., Montreal, 1961-63; asso. dir. West Malaysian Family Survey, Kuala Lumpur, 1966-67; prof. sociology Northwestern U., Evanston, Ill., 1969—, chmn. dept. sociology Northwestern U., 1976-79; cons. Wissenschaftszentrun, Berlin. Author: The Environment: From Surplus to Scarcity, 1992; co-author: Environment and Society: The Enduring Conflict, 1994, Local Environmental Struggles: Citizen Activism in the Treadmill of Production, 1996; co-editor: Distributional Conflicts in Environmental Resource Policy, 1986. Population Council fellow, 1967-68; Nat. Inst. Child Health and Human Devel. research grantee, 1970-72. Mem. Am. Sociol. Assn. (Disting. Contbn. award environ. sociology sect. 1984, chmn. environ. and tech. div. 1991-93), Soc. for Study Social Problems (chmn. environ. problems divsn. 1978-80, mem. C. Wright Mills com. 1979). Home: 6615 N Fairfield Ave Chicago IL 60645-4405 Office: 1810 Chicago Ave Evanston IL 60208-0812 *Learn conventional wisdom, but be prepared to challenge it at all times. What most people agree upon is often wrong, though they won't welcome you bringing this to their attention.*

SCHNAITMAN, WILLIAM KENNETH, finance company executive; b. Talbot County, Md., May 12, 1926; s. William and Catherine Almeda (Cheezum) S.; m. Beverly June Marshall, July 13, 1963. Student, Strayer Bus. Sch., Balt., 1943. Clk. Comml. Credit Co., Balt., 1946-70; asst. sec. Comml. Credit Co., 1970-72, treas., 1972-75, dir. cash mgmt., 1976-87, ret., 1987. With AUS, 1944-46, ETO. Home: 12520 Wye Ln Wye Mills MD 21679-2050

SCHNALL, DAVID JAY, management and administration educator; b. Bklyn., Mar. 20, 1948; married; 3 children. BA in polit. sci., Yeshiva U., 1969, MS in Jewish studies, 1972; MA in polit. sci., Fordham U., 1971, PhD, 1974. Ordained min. Yeshiva U., 1972. Adj. prof. dept. polit. sci. Fordham U., 1971-73; adj. prof. dept. social sci. Rockland Cmty. Coll. SUNY, 1972-73; adj. prof. dept. Judaic studies Bklyn. Coll. CUNY, 1974-76; assoc. prof. dept. polit. sci. Coll. S.I. CUNY, 1972-79; prof. dept. pub. adminstrn. L.I. U., 1979-91; Herbert Schiff prof. mgmt. and adminstrn. Yeshiva U., 1991—; cons. Hadassah Women's Zionist Orgn., 1979-80, Jewish Cmty. Rels. Coun. N.Y., 1985-86, Ctr. Mgmt. Analysis, 1981—, Health Exec. Assistance League, 1985—, United Jewish Appeal, Fedn. of Jewish Philanthropies, Jewish Bd. Family Svcs., N.Y. Gov.'s Office of Employee Rels. Author: The Jewish Agenda: Essays in Contemporary Jewish Life, 1987, Beyond the Green Line: Israeli Settlements West of the Jordan, 1984, Radical Dissent in Contemporary Israeli Politics: Cracks in the Wall, 1979, Ethnicity and Suburban Local Politics, 1975; co-editor: Crisis and Challenge: The Jewish Family in the 21st Century, 1995, Contemporary Issues in Health Care, 1984; contbr. articles to profl. jours. Mem. Orthodox Caucus, N.Y., 1991—, Nat. Orthodox Leadership Conf., N.Y., 1993-95; mem. Coun. on Social Work Edn.; mem. Rabbinical Coun. of Am. Grantee Lucius Littauer Found., CUNY Rsch. Found., Sigma Xi, Meml. Foun. Jewish Culture, L.I. U. Rsch. Coun.; fellow Nat. Def. Edn. Program, N.Y. State Pub. Adminstrn. Program, Fordham U. Grad. Coun. Mem. Phi Beta Kappa, Pi Sigma Alpha, Pi Alpha Alpha. Democrat. Jewish. Avocations: writing, traveling. Office: Yeshiva Univ B1205 500 W 185th St New York NY 10033

SCHNALL, EDITH LEA (MRS. HERBERT SCHNALL), microbiologist, educator; b. N.Y.C., Apr. 11, 1922; d. Irving and Sadie (Raab) Spitzer; AB, Hunter Coll., 1942; AM, Columbia U., 1947, PhD, 1967; m. Herbert Schnall, Aug. 21, 1949; children: Neil David, Carolyn Beth. Clin. pathologist Roosevelt Hosp., N.Y.C., 1942-44; instr. Adelphi Coll., Garden City, N.Y., 1944-46; asst. med. mycologist Columbia Coll. Physicians and Surgeons, N.Y.C., 1946-47, 49-50; instr. Bklyn. Coll., 1947; mem. faculty Sarah Lawrence Coll., Bronxville, N.Y., 1947-48; lectr. Hunter Coll., N.Y.C., 1947-67; adj. assoc. prof. Lehman Coll., City U. N.Y., 1968; asst. prof. Queensborough Community Coll., City U. N.Y., 1967, assoc. prof. microbiology, 1968-75, prof., 1975—, adminstr. Med. Lab. Tech. Program, 1985—; vis. prof. Coll. Physicians and Surgeons, Columbia U., N.Y.C., 1974; advanced biology examiner U. London, 1970—. Mem. Alley Restoration Com., N.Y.C., 1971—; mem. legis. adv. com. Assembly of the State of N.Y., 1972. Mem. Community Bd. 11, Queens, N.Y., 1974—, 3d vice-chmn., 1987-92, 2nd vice chmn., 1992—; public dir. of bd. dirs. Inst. Continuing Dental Edn. Queens County, Dental Soc. N.Y. State and ADA, 1973—. Rsch. fellow NIH, 1948-49; faculty rsch. fellow, grantee-in-aid Rsch. Found. of SUNY, 1968-70; faculty rsch. grant Rsch. Found. City U. N.Y., 1971-74. Mem. Internat. Soc. Human and Animal Mycology, AAAS, Am. Soc. Microbiology (coun., N.Y.C. br. 1981—, co-chairperson ann. meeting com. 1981-82, chair program com. 1982-83, v.p. 1984-86, pres. 1986-88), Med. Mycology Soc. N.Y. (sec.-treas. 1967-68, v.p. 1968-69, 78-79, archivist 1974—, fin. advisor 1983—, pres. 1969-70, 79-80, 81-82), Bot. Soc. Am., Med. Mycology Soc. Americas, Mycology Soc. Am., N.Y. Acad. Scis., Sigma Xi, Phi Sigma. Clubs: Torrey Botanical (N.Y. State); Queensborough Community Coll. Women's (pres. 1971-73) (N.Y.C.). Editor: Newsletter of Med. Mycology Soc. N.Y., 1969-85; founder, editor Female Perspective newsletter of Queensborough Community Coll. Women's Club, 1971-73. Home: 21406 29th Ave Flushing NY 11360-2622

SCHNAPF, ABRAHAM, aerospace engineer, consultant; b. N.Y.C., Aug. 1, 1921; s. Meyer and Gussie (Schaeffler) S.; m. Edna Wilensky, Oct. 24, 1943; children: Donald J., Bruce M. BSME, CCNY, 1948; MSME, Drexel Inst. Tech., 1953. Registered profl. engr., N.J. Devel. engr. on lighter-than-air aircraft Goodyear Aircraft Corp., Akron, Ohio, 1948-50; mgr. fire control system def. electronics RCA, Camden, N.Y., 1950-55, mgr. airbourne navigation system, aerospace weapon system, 1955-58; program mgr. TIROS/TOS weather satellite systems RCA Astro-Electronics, Princeton, N.J., 1958-70, mgr. satellite programs, 1970-79, prin. scientist, 1979-82; cons. Aerospace Systems Engring., Willingboro, N.J., 1982—; lectr., presenter on meteor. satellites, space tech., communication satellites. Sgt. USAF, 1943-46. Recipient award Nat. Press Club Washington, 1975, award Am. Soc. Quality Control-NASA, 1968, Pub. Svc. award NASA, 1969, cert. of appreciation U.S. Dept. Commerce, 1984, RCA David Sarnoff award; inducted into Space Tech. Hall of Fame, 1992; named to 5000 Personalities of the World, named Internat. Man. of Yr. 1992-93. Fellow AIAA; mem. Am. Astro. Soc., Am. Meterol. Soc., Space Pioneers, N.Y. Acad. Scis. (mem. think tank week sessions 1980's), N.J. Arbitration Soc. Home and Office: 41 Pond Ln # 160 Willingboro NJ 08046-2756

SCHNAPP, ROGER HERBERT, lawyer; b. N.Y.C., Mar. 17, 1946; s. Michael Jay and Beatrice Joan (Becker) S.; m. Candice Jacqueline Larson, Sept. 15, 1979; 1 child, Monica Alexis. BS, Cornell U., 1966; JD, Harvard U., 1969; postgrad. Pub. Utility Mgmt. Program, U. Mich., 1978. Bar: N.Y. 1970,, U.S. Ct. Appeals (2d cir.) 1970, U.S. Supreme, 1974, U.S. Dist. Ct. (so. dist.) N.Y. 1975, U.S. Ct. Appeals (4th and 6th cirs.) 1976, U.S. Ct. Appeals (7th cir.) 1977, U.S. Dist. Ct. (so. dist.) N.Y. 1975, U.S. Dist. Ct. (no. dist.) Calif. 1980, U.S. Ct. Appeals (8th cir.) 1980, Calif., 1982, U.S. Dist. Ct. (cen. dist.) Calif. 1982, U.S. Ct. Dist. (ea. dist.) Calif., 1984. Atty. CAB, Washington, 1969-70; labor atty. Western Electric Co., N.Y.C., 1970-71; mgr. employee rels. Am. Airlines, N.Y.C., 1971-74; labor counsel Am. Electric Power Svc. Corp., N.Y.C., 1974-78, sr. labor counsel, 1978-80; indsl. rels. counsel Trans World Airlines, N.Y.C., 1980-81; sr. assoc. Parker, Milliken, Clark & O'Hara, L.A., 1981-82; ptnr. Rutan & Tucker, Costa Mesa, Calif., 1983-84, Memel, Jacobs, Pierno, Gersh & Ellsworth, Newport Beach, Calif., 1985-86, Memel, Jacobs & Ellsworth, Newport Beach, 1986-87; pvt. practice, Newport Beach, 1987—; bd. dirs. Dynamic Constrn., Inc., Laguna Hills, Calif., 1986—; commentator labor rels. Fin. News Network; commentator Sta. KOCN Radio, 1990-91; lectr. Calif. Western Law Sch., Calif. State U.-Fullerton, Calif. State Conf. Small Bus.; lectr. collective bargaining Pace U., N.Y.C.; lectr. on labor law Coun. on Edn. in Mgmt.; N.E. regional coord. Pressler for Pres., 1979-80. Mem. bus. rsch. adv. coun. U.S. Dept. Labor; trustee Chapman U., 1991-95. Mem. Calif. Bar Assn., Am. Arbitration Assn. (adv. com. Orange County area, cons. collective bargaining com.), Conf. R.R. and Airline Labor Lawyers, Orange County Bar Assn., Balboa Bay Club, The Ctr. Club. Republican. Jewish. Author: Arbitration Issues for the 1980s, 1981, A Look at Three Companies, 1982; editor-in-chief Indsl. and Labor Rels. Forum, 1964-66; columnist Orange County Bus. Jour., 1989-91; contbr. articles to profl. publs. Office: PO Box 9049 Newport Beach CA 92658-1049

SCHNARE, ROBERT EDEY, JR., library director; b. Morristown, N.J., Dec. 31, 1944; s. Robert Edey and Olive Margaret (Flatt) S.; m. MaryKay Wise, Aug. 29, 1970; 1 child, Katharine Grace. BA, William Paterson Coll., 1967; MLS, U. Pitts., 1968; MA, U. Conn., 1971. Reference libr. history dept. Conn. State Libr., Hartford, 1968-73; head spl. collections U.S. Mil. Acad. Libr., West Point, N.Y., 1973-86; libr. dir. U.S. Naval War Coll., Newport, R.I., 1986—; chmn. Consortium of R.I. Acad. and Rsch. Librs., Providence, 1991-93; bd. dirs. Coalition of Libr. Advocates, Providence, 1991—; chmn. edn. and tng. com. R.I. Preservation Planning Grant, 1991-92; del. White House Conf. on Libr. and Info. Svcs., 1990—; chmn. preservation working group New England Libr. Network, Newton, Mass., 1992—; mem. com. on mgmt. Anne S.K. Brown Mil. Collection, 1987—; mem. Mid-Atlantic Archivist Conf., 1973—; mem. preservation working group Fed. Libr. Info. Ctr. Com., 1991—. Publ. editor Conservation Adminstrn. News, 1979-87, mem. editl. bd., 1987-94; contbr. articles to profl. jours., chpt. to book; compiler Union List of Mil. Edn. Coordinating Com. Library Resources, 1994. Chmn. gifted adv. coun. Providence Bd. Edn., 1990-92; chmn. stewardship St. Martin's Episcopal Ch., Providence, 1990; vol. Providence schs., 1992—. Named Disting. Grad., William Paterson Coll., 1985; recipient Disting. Svc. award Conservation Adminstrn. News, 1987, 94, Dept. of the Army's Comdr.'s award for civilian svc. U.S. Mil. Acad., 1987, Navy Dept.'s Meritorious Civilian Svc. award Naval War Coll., 1995. Mem. ALA, Spl. Librs. Assn., Assn. for Study Conn. History, New Eng. Archivists. Office: US Naval War Coll Libr 686 Cushing Rd Newport RI 02841-1201

SCHNECK, JEROME M., psychiatrist, medical historian, educator; b. N.Y.C., Jan. 2, 1920; s. Maurice and Rose (Weiss) S.; m. Shirley R. Kaufman, July 24, 1943. AB, Cornell U., 1939; MD, SUNY-Bklyn., 1943. Diplomate Am. Bd. Psychiatry and Neurology. Intern Interfaith Med. Ctr., 1943; mem. psychiat. staff Menninger Clinic, Topeka, 1944-45; chief psychiatry and sociology dept. Fort Missoula, Mont., 1946, Camp Cooke, Calif., 1947; mem. psychiat. staff L.I. Coll. Hosp., 1947-48, Kings County Hosp., 1948-70, SUNY Hosp., Bklyn., 1955-70; assoc. vis. psychiatrist Kings County Hosp., 1949-70; mem. psychiat. staff State U. Hosp., Bklyn., 1955-70; pvt. practice N.Y.C., 1947—; attending psychiatrist St. Vincent's Hosp. and Med. Ctr. N.Y., 1970—, hon. sr. psychiatrist, 1990—; psychiat. cons. VA Regional Office, 1947-48, N.Y. State Dept. Social Svcs., 1977-83, N.Y. State Dept. Civil Svc., 1978-84, N.Y. State Office Ct. Adminstrn., 1978-85, N.Y. State Dept. Edn., 1981-83; dir. Mt. Vernon Mental Hygiene Clinic, 1947-52; assoc. chief psychiatrist Westchester County Dept. Health, 1949-50, cons., 1951-52; clin. instr. L.I. Coll. Medicine, 1947-50; clin. assoc. SUNY Coll. Medicine, Bklyn., 1950-53, asst. prof., 1955-58, assoc. prof., 1958-70; supervising psychiatrist Community Guidance Svcs., 1955-70; cons. coun. on mental health AMA, 1956-58; cons. NBC, 1962, Ctr. Rsch. in Hypnotherapy, 1964-70; vis. lectr. N.Y. Med. Coll.-Met. Hosp., 1965; faculty Am. Inst. Psychotherapy and Psychoanalysis, 1970-85. Author: Hypnosis in Modern Medicine, 1953, 2d edit., 1959, Spanish lang. edit., 1962, 3rd edit., 1963, Studies in Scientific Hypnosis, 1954, A History of Psychiatry, 1960, The Principles and Practice of Hypnoanalysis, 1965 (Best Book award Soc. For Clin. and Exptl. Hypnosis 1965); editor: Hypnotherapy, Hypnosis and Personality, 1951; author over 400 med. and sci. publs., book chpts., articles; mem. bd. editors: Personality: Symposia on Topical Issues, 1960-61, Jour. Integrative and Eclectic Psychotherapy, 1986-89; contbg. editor Psychosomatics, 1961-75; mem. editorial bd. Voices—The Art and Science of Psychotherapy, 1965; features editor The Interne, 1942, co-editor, 1943. Capt. AUS, 1945-47. Recipient Clarence B. Farrar award Clarke Inst. of Psychiatry, U. Toronto, 1976. Fellow AAAS, APA, Am. Med. Authors, Acad. Psychosomatic Medicine, Am. Psychiat. Assn. (life), Soc. for Clin. and Exptl. Hypnosis (life, founder, founding pres. 1949-56, exec. coun. 1949—, assoc. editor jour. 1953—, Award of Merit 1955, Gold medal 1958, Bernard B. Raginsky award 1966, Shirley Schneck award 1970, Roy M. Dorcus award 1980, Spl. Presdl. award 1986), Am. Acad. Psychotherapists (co-founder, v.p. 1956-58), Am. Med. Writers Assn., Am. Soc. Psychoanalytic Physicians (founding fellow, bd. dirs. 1958-62), Am. Soc. Clin. Hypnosis (life mem.), Internat. Soc. Clin. and Exptl. Hypnosis (co-founder, bd. dirs. 1958-68, founding fellow), Internat. Acad. Eclectic Psychotherapists (charter fellow); mem. AMA, Soc. Acad. Achievement (charter), Soc. Apothecaries London, Inst. Practicing Psychotherapists, Pan Am. Med. Assn. (v.p. sect. clin. hypnosis 1960-65, N.Am. v.p. 1966), N.Y. Soc. Med. History (exec. com. 1956-62), Am. Bd. Med. Hypnosis (founder, pres. 1958-60, life bd. dirs.), Inst. Rsch. in Hypnosis Inc. (bd. dirs., bd. editors 1957-70), Am. Assn. History Medicine, History of Sci. Soc., Assn. Advancement Psychotherapy (charter) Can. Med. History Assn., N.Y. Soc. for Clin. Psychiatry (chmn. com. on history of psychiatry), Charles F. Menninger Soc., Sigma Xi. Address: 26 W 9th St New York NY 10011-8971

SCHNECK, PAUL BENNETT, computer scientist; b. N.Y.C., Aug. 15, 1945; s. Irving and Doris (Grossman) S.; m. Marjorie Ann Axelrod, Feb. 5, 1967; children: Phyllis Adele, Melanie Jane. BS, Columbia U., 1965, MS, 1966; PhD, NYU Courant Inst. Math. Scis., 1979. Computer scientist Inst. for Space Studies, N.Y.C., 1970-76; program mgr. Goddard Space Flight Ctr., Greenbelt, Md., 1976-79; asst. to dir. Goddard Space Flight Ctr., Greenbelt, 1979-80, chief info. extraction div., 1980-81, asst. dir., 1981-83; head info. sci. div. Office of Naval Rsch., Arlington, Va., 1983-85; dir. Supercomputing Rsch. Ctr., Bowie, Md., 1985-93; chief scientist Inst. Defense Analyses, 1993; fellow Mitre Corp., McLean, Va., 1993-96, dir. info. sys. and fellow, 1994-96; dir. info. sys. and fellow Mitretek Systems, Inc., McLean, Va., 1996—; vice chmn. bd. Nat. Info. Tech. Ctr., 1993, chmn. bd., CEO, 1994, exec. com., 1994—; mem. adv. bd. Inst. Computational Sci. and Informatics, George Mason U., 1995—; mem. adv. bd. computer scis. U. Md., College Park, 1989—; tchr. Columbia U., Johns Hopkins U., U. Md. Author: Supercomputer Architecture, 1987; contbr. articles to Ency. of Computer Sci. and Tech., Ann. Rev. of Computer Sci., Ency. Phys. Sci. and Tech. Yearbook. Fellow IEEE; mem. Assn. for Computing Machinery, Brit. Computer Soc., Engring. Coun. (chartered engr., Eng.). Achievements include design and implementation of the science supervisory system in use at NASA from 1968-83, on the IBM 360/95 and 370/165, and the Amdahl 470/V6, V7; and of the vector/parallel compiler. Office: Mitretek Systems Inc 7525 Colshire Dr Mc Lean VA 22102-7500

SCHNECK, STUART AUSTIN, retired neurologist, educator; b. N.Y.C., Apr. 1, 1929; s. Maurice and Sara Ruth (Knapp) S.; m. Ida I. Nakashima, Mar. 2, 1956; children—Lisa, Christopher. B.S. magna cum laude, Franklin and Marshall Coll., 1949; M.D., U. Pa., 1953. Diplomate Am. Bd. Psychiatry and Neurology (bd. dirs., sec. 1990-91, v.p. 1991-92, pres. 1992-93). Intern Hosp. U. Pa., Phila., 1953-54; resident in medicine U. Colo. Med. Center, Denver, 1954-55, 57-58, resident in neurology, 1958-61; instr. neurology U. Colo. Sch. Medicine, 1959-61; instr. neuropathology Columbia U., N.Y.C., 1961-63; vis. fellow in neurology Vanderbilt Clinic, Columbia-Presbyn. Med. Center, N.Y.C., 1961-63; asst. prof. neurology and pathology U. Colo., 1963-67, assoc. prof., 1967-70, prof., 1970-95, assoc. dean clin. affairs Sch. Medicine, 1984-89, emeritus prof., 1996—; cons. Fitzsimons Army Hosp., VA, Nat. Jewish Hosp.; pres. med. bd. Univ. Hosp., Denver, 1983-89, bd. dirs., 1989-90. Contbr. articles to profl. jours. Served with USAF, 1955-57. USPHS fellow, 1961-63. Mem. AAAS, Am. Acad. Neurology, Am. Assn. Neuropathologists, Am. Neurol. Assn., Alpha Omega Alpha (bd. dirs. 1979-89, treas., pres. 1990-93).

SCHNEEMAN, BARBARA OLDS, agricultural studies educator; b. Seattle, Oct. 3, 1948; d. William Arthur and Rose (Antush) Olds; m. Paul Schneeman, Mar. 23, 1974; 1 child, Eric. BS in Food Sci. and Tech., U. Calif., Davis, 1970; PhD in Nutrition, U. Calif., Berkeley, 1974. NIH postdoctoral fellow gastrointestinal physiology Children's Hosp., Oakland, Calif., 1974-76; asst. prof. nutrition dept. nutrition and food sci. & tech. U. Calif., Davis, 1976-82, asst. nutritionist, 1976-82, assoc. prof. nutrition, assoc. nutritionist, 1982-86, acting chmn. dept. nutrition, 1984-85, prof. nutrition, nutritionist, 1986—, prof. dept. internal medicine divsn. clin. nutrition, 1986—, assoc. dean Coll. Agrl. and Environ. Scis., 1985-88, dean Coll. Agrl. and Environ. Scis., 1993—, dir. programs. divsn. agr. and natural resources, 1993—; vis. scientist Cardiovascular Rsch. Inst., U. Calif., San Francisco, 1991-92; lectr. women in sci. series Coll. St. Catherine, St. Paul, 1987; adv. dir. Blud Cross Calif., 1992-95; mem. dietary guidelines for Ams. adv. com. to Secs. of Agr., Health and Human Svcs., 1989-90, 94-95; mem. expert panel on food safety and nutrition Inst. Food Technologists, 1985-91; mem. external adv. bd. Post Ctr. for Nutrition and Health, 1989-90; counsilor Soc. for Exptl. Biology and Medicine, 1988-91. Assoc. editor Jour. Nutrition, 1991-94; contbg. editor Nutrition Revs., 1982-90; editl. bd. Jour. Nutrition, 1982-87, Procs. for Soc. Exptl. Biology and Medicine, 1985-91, Acad. Press: Food Sci. and Nutrition, 1988—. Fellow arteriosclerosis coun. Am. Heart Assn. Fellow NDEA, U. Calif., Berkeley; food sci. scholar; recipient Outstanding Cmty. Svc. award Tierra del Oro coun. Girl Scouts U.S., 1995, Future Leaders award for rsch. Nutrition Found., 1978-80, Samuel Cate Prescott award for rsch. Inst. Food Tech., 1985, Farma Food Internat. Fibre prize, Copenhagen, 1989. Mem. AAAS, Inst. Food Technologists (sec.-treas. nutrition divsn. 1988-89), Am. Physiol. Soc., Am. Inst. Nutrition (treas. 1989-92), Am. Heart Assn. (fellow arteriosclerosis coun.). Office: U Calif Davis Coll Agriculture/Envir Sci Coll Agrl and Environ Scis Davis CA 95616

SCHNEEMANN, CAROLEE, painter, performing artist, filmmaker, writer; b. Pa., Oct. 12, 1939. B.A., Bard Coll., 1960; M.F.A., U. Ill., 1961. Originated Kinetic Theater, 1962; with Judson Dance Theater, 1962-66; performance works, film showings throughout U.S. and Europe; (erotic film) Fuses, 1964-68 (Spl. Jury Selection Cannes 1968); (most recent film) Kitch's Last Meal, 1973-78; (video tapes) Up To and Including Her Limits, 1974-77, Interior Scroll—The Cave, 1995, ABC-We Print Anything—In the Cards, 1976-77, Homerunmuse, 1977; performance installations include Palazzo Reale, Milan, Italy, Art Inst. Chgo., 1980; performance tour Fresh Blood—A Dream Morphology, France, Belgium, Holland, 1981; (books) Parts of a Body House Book, 1972, Cezanne, She Was A Great Painter, 1974, ABC—We Print Anything—In the Cards, 1979, More than Meat Joy, Complete Performance Works and Selected Writings, 1979; exhbns. Whitney Mus., 1984, 85, 93, 95, Mus. Modern Art, N.Y.C., 1992, 95, 96, Ctr. Georges Pompidou, Paris, 1995, New Mus., N.Y.C., 1992, 95, 96. Guggenheim fellow 1993; recipient grants N.Y. State Coun. on Arts, 1968, NEA, 1974, 77-78, 83, Gottlieb Found., 1987. Office: 437 Springtown Rd New Paltz NY 12561-3027

SCHNEEWIND, JEROME BORGES, philosophy educator; b. Mt. Vernon, N.Y., May 17, 1930; s. Jerome John and Charlotte (Borges) S.; m. Elizabeth G.R. Hughes, Feb. 23, 1963; children: Sarah, Rachel, Hannah. B.A., Cornell U., 1951; M.A., Princeton U., 1953, Ph.D., 1957. Instr. philosophy U. Chgo., 1957-60, Princeton U., 1960-61; asst. prof. Yale U., 1961-63; asso. prof. philosophy U. Pitts., 1964-68, prof., 1968-75, dean Coll. Arts and Scis., 1969-73; v.p., provost Hunter Coll., CUNY, 1975-81; prof. philosophy Johns Hopkins U., Balt., 1981—, chmn. dept., 1981-91; philosophy adviser Ency. Americana, 1967—; mem. adv. bd. sci. tech. and values program NEH, 1975-78; mem. Coun. for Phil. Studies, 1975-80. Author: Backgrounds of English Victorian Literature, 1970, Sidgwick's Ethics and Victorian Moral Philosophy, 1977; editor: Moral Philosophy From Montaigne to Kant, 1990; editorial bd. Victorian Studies, 1968-75, The Monist, 1969-76, Am. Philosophy Quar., 1975-77, Philos. Studies, 1975-78, Jour. of History Ideas, 1985—, pres. bd. dirs., 1988—; contbr. articles on ethics and history of ethics to publs. Served with Signal Corps, AUS, 1954-56. Mellon postdoctoral fellow, 1963-64; Guggenheim fellow, 1967-68; Am. Council Learned Socs. grantee, 1973; NEH sr. fellow, 1974, Ctr. for Advanced Study in the Behavioral Scis., 1992-93. Fellow AAAS; mem. Am. Philos. Assn. (exec. com. Ea. divsn. 1964-67, chmn. com. on teaching philosophy 1973-78, nominating com. 1986-88, v.p. Ea. divsn. 1994-95, pres. 1995-96). Office: Philosophy Dept Johns Hopkins U Baltimore MD 21218

SCHNEIDER, ADELE SANDRA, clinical geneticist; b. Johannesburg, South Africa, Mar. 21, 1949; came to U.S., 1976, naturalized, 1981; d. Michael and Annette (Sive) S.; m. Gordon Mark Cohen, July 2, 1978; children: Jeffrey, Brian, Adrienne. MB, BChir, Witwatersrand U., Johannesburg, South Africa, 1973. Intern in internal medicine Baragwanath Hosp., Johannesburg, 1974, intern in gen. surgery, 1974; sr. house officer in pediatrics Coronation Hosp., Johannesburg, 1975; sr. house officer in radiation therapy Johannesburg Gen. Hosp., 1975-76; resident in pediatrics Wilmington (Del.) Med. Ctr., 1976-78; fellow in clin. genetics and metabolic diseases Children's Hosp. of Phila., 1978-81, staff physician Cystic Fibrosis Clinic, 1987-88; staff pediatrician Children's Rehab. Hosp., Phila., 1981-82, dir. pediatrics, 1982-87, acting med. dir., 1984-85; clin. instr. dept. pediatrics Jefferson Med. Coll., Phila., 1982-84, clin. asst. prof. dept. pediatrics, 1984—; clin. geneticist Hahnemann Univ. Hosp., Phila., 1987-90, asst. clin. prof. dept. pediatrics and neoplastic diseases, 1987-90; clin. geneticist Albert Einstein Med. Ctr., Phila., 1990-92, acting dir. med. genetics, 1992-93, dir. clin. genetics program, 1993—; mem. courtesy faculty Sch. Medicine Temple U., Phila., 1987; clin. geneticist St. Christopher's Hosp. for Children, Phila., 1987; genetics cons. dept. pediatrics Bryn Mawr (Pa.) Hosp.; presenter, lectr. in field. Contbr. articles to profl. jours. Bd. dirs. Phila. Parenting Associates, 1986-93. Fellow Am. Coll. Med. Genetics; mem. Am. Soc. Human Genetics, Am. Chem. Soc. Office: Albert Einstein Med Ctr Dept Pediatrics 5501 Old York Rd Philadelphia PA 19141-3001

SCHNEIDER, ALLAN STANFORD, biochemistry neuroscience and pharmacology educator, biomedical research scientist; b. N.Y.C., Sept. 26, 1940; s. Harry and Edith (Gonsky) S.; m. Mary-Jane Beekman Tunis, Dec. 14, 1968; children: Henry Seth, Joseph Benjamin. B.Chem. Engring., Rensselaer Poly. Inst., 1961; M.S., Pa. State U., 1963; Ph.D., U. Calif.-Berkeley, 1968. Chem. engr. E.I. du Pont de Nemours & Co. Exptl. Sta., Wilmington, Del., 1963-64; postdoctoral fellow Weizmann Inst. Sci., Rehovot, Israel, 1969-71; staff fellow NIH, Bethesda, Md., 1971-73; assoc. Sloan-Kettering Inst. Cancer Research, N.Y.C., 1974-80, assoc. mem., 1980-85; asst. prof. Cornell U. Grad. Sch. Med. Scis., N.Y.C., 1974-80, assoc. prof. biochemistry, 1981-83, assoc. prof. cell biology and genetic, 1983-85, chmn. biochemistry unit Sloan-Kettering div., 1982-83; assoc. prof. pharmacology and toxicology Albany (N.Y.) Med. Coll., N.Y., 1985-86, prof. pharmacology and toxicology, 1986-94; prof. pharmacology and neurosci. Albany (N.Y.) Med. Coll., 1995—; dir. grad. studies Albany (N.Y.) Med. Coll., N.Y., 1987-91; vis. prof. Weizmann Inst. Sci., Rehovot, Israel, 1987; vis. rsch. scholar U. Bergen, Norway, 1989, 95. Contbr. chpts to books, sci. articles to profl. jours. Rsch. grantee Am. Cancer Soc., 1980-83, Am. Heart Assn., 1977-82, 90-93, NIH, 1982—, NSF, 1977-79, Cystic Fibrosis Found., 1980-82; established investigator Am. Heart Assn., 1977-82. Mem. Am. Soc. Biochemistry and Molecular Biology, Biophys. Soc., Soc. Neurosci., Am. Heart Assn. (coun. on basic sci. 1977-95), Phi Lambda Upsilon, Tau Beta Pi (internat. sci. adv. com. for chromaffin cell biology 1987-93). Achievements include first isolation and characterization of chromaffin cells of the adrenal gland now widely used as a model neuronal cell culture system; determination of the relation between cytosolic calcium signals and neurohormone (adrenaline) secretion, relevant to cellular mechanism of hormone and neurotransmitter release; spectroscopic characterization of protein structure in situ in biomembranes and cells; theoretical and experimental analysis of optical activity spectra of turbid biological suspensions; research on neurochemistry of adrenal chromaffin cells, regulation of hormone and neurotransmitter release and mechanisms of nicotine dependence. Office: Dept Pharmacology & Neurosci Albany Med Coll A 136 Albany NY 12208

SCHNEIDER, ARTHUR PAUL, retired videotape and film editor, author; b. Rochester, N.Y., Jan. 26, 1930; s. Mendell Phillip and Frieda (Bl) S.; m. Helen Deloise Thompson, June 5, 1954; children: Robert Paul, Lori Ann. Student, U. So. Calif., 1953. With NBC, 1951-68, film and videotape editor, 1953-60, developer double system method of editing video tape, 1958; pres. Burbank (Calif.) Film Editing, Inc., 1968-72, Electronic Video Industries Inc., 1977-79; supr. video tape editing Consol. Film Industries Inc., Hollywood, Calif., 1972-76, editorial supr., 1980-83; pvt. practice editing, 1983-88; cons., lectr., author. Film and tape editor all: Bob Hope shows, 1960-67; supr. NBC kinescope and video tape editors (1966-67); video tape editor: Laugh-In Series, 1967-68; video tape editor: Comedy Shop Series, 1977-80; post-prodn. cons. to Video Systems and Broadcast Engring. mag.; video tape editor: TV series Sonny & Cher, 1973, Sonny Comedy Revue, 1974, Tony Orlando and Dawn, 1974, Hudson Bros., summer, 1974, Dean Martin Series, 1975-76, Mickey Mouse Club Series, Walt Disney Prodns., 1976, Redd Foxx Series, 1977; (author: Electronic Post Production and Videotape Editing, 1989 (pub. in Chinese 1995), Electronic Post Production Terms and Concepts, 1990; contbg. author: Association of Cinema and Video Laboratores (ACVL) Handbook, 5th edit., 1995, Focal Guide to Electronic Media CDRom Version, 1996, Jump Cut: Memoirs of a Pioneer Television Editor, 1996; contbr. articles to publs. in field. Recipient Broadcast Preceptor award San Francisco State U., 1975; named hon. Ky. Col. Mem. Acad. Television Arts and Scis. (Emmy nominations and Emmy award for video tape editing 1966, 68, 73, 84, gov. 1977-80, sec. 1980-81), Am. Cinema Editors (life), Soc. Motion Picture and TV Engrs., Delta Kappa Alpha (life). Home: PO Box 156 Fish Camp CA 93623-0156

SCHNEIDER, ARTHUR SANFORD, physician, educator; b. Los Angeles, Mar. 24, 1929; s. Max and Fannie (Ragin) S.; m. Edith Kadison, Aug. 20, 1950; children: Jo Ann Schneider Farris, William Scott, Lynnellen. B.S., UCLA, 1951; M.D., Chgo. Med. Sch., 1955. Diplomate Am. Bd. Internal Medicine, Am. Bd. Pathology. Intern, Wadsworth VA Hosp., Los Angeles, 1955-56; resident Wadsworth VA Hosp., 1956-59, chief clin. pathology sect., 1962-68; mem. faculty UCLA, 1961-75, clin. assoc. prof., 1971-75; chmn. dept. clin. pathology City of Hope Med. Ctr., Duarte, Calif., 1968-75; prof., chmn. dept. clin. pathology Whittier Coll., 1974-75; prof., chmn. dept. pathology Chgo. Med. Sch., 1975—; chief lab. service VA Med. Ctr., North Chicago, Ill., 1975-86, chief lab. hematology, 1986-94. Contbr. numerous chpts. to books and articles to med. jours. Served to capt. M.C., USAF, 1959-61. Fellow ACP, Coll. Am. Pathologists, Am. Soc. Clin. Pathologists; mem. AAUP, AMA, Internat. Acad. Pathology, Am. Assn. for Investigative Pathology, Assn. Pathology Chairmen, Acad. Clin. Lab. Physicians and Scientists, Am. Soc. Hematology, Am. Assn. Blood Banks, Am. Soc. Clin. Rsch., Ill. Med. Soc., Lake County Med. Soc., Sigma Xi, Alpha Omega Alpha, Phi Delta Epsilon. Office: Chgo Med Sch 3333 Green Bay Rd North Chicago IL 60064-3037

SCHNEIDER, BENJAMIN, psychology educator; b. N.Y.C., Aug. 11, 1938; s. Leo and Rose (Cohen) S.; m. H. Brenda Jacobson, Jan. 29, 1961; children: Lee Andrew, Rhody Yve. BA, Alfred U., 1960; MBA, CUNY, 1962; PhD, U. Md., 1967. Lic. psychologist, Md. Asst. prof. adminstrv. scis. and psychology Yale U., New Haven, 1967-71; prof. psychology-mgmt. U. Md., College Park, 1971-79, prof. psychology and mgmt., 1982—; John A. Hannah prof. orgnl. behavior Mich. State U., East Lansing, 1979-82; v.p. Orgnl. and Pers. Rsch., Inc. Author: (with D.T. Hall) Organizational Climates and Careers, 1973, Staffing Organizations, 1976, 2d edit. (with N. Schmitt), 1986; (with F.D. Schoorman) Facilitating Work Effectiveness, 1988, Organizational Climate and Culture, 1990, (with D.E. Bowen) Winning the Service Game, 1995; mem. editl. rev. bd. Acad. Mgmt. Jour., 1971-86, Adminstrv. Sci. Quar., 1976-82, Jour. Applied Psychology, 1988—, Brit. Mgmt. Jour., 1989—, Internat. Jour. Svc. Industry Mgmt., 1989—, Pers. Psychology, 1994—. Fulbright grantee, 1973-74. Fellow APA, Am. Psychol. Soc., Soc. for Indsl. and Orgnl. Psychology (pres. 1984-85), Acad. Mgmt. (pres. orgnl. behavior div. 1982-83). Home: 8122 Thoreau Dr Bethesda MD 20817-3105 Office: U Maryland Dept Psychology College Park MD 20742

SCHNEIDER, CALVIN, physician; b. N.Y.C., Oct. 23, 1924; s. Harry and Bertha (Green) S.; A.B., U. So. Calif., 1951, M.D., 1955; J.D., LaVerne (Calif.) Coll., 1973; m. Elizabeth Gayle Thomas, Dec. 27, 1967. Intern Los Angeles County Gen. Hosp., 1955-56, staff physician, 1956-57; practice medicine West Covina, Calif., 1957—; staff Inter-Community Med. Ctr., Covina, Calif. Cons. physician Charter Oak Hosp., Covina, 1960—. With USNR, 1943-47. Mem. AMA, Calif., L.A. County med. assns. Republican. Lutheran. Office: 224 W College St Covina CA 91723-1902

SCHNEIDER, CARL EDWARD, law educator; b. Exeter, N.H., Feb. 23, 1948; s. Carl Jacob and Mabel Dot (Jones) S.; m. Joan L. Wagner, Jan. 6, 1976. BA, Harvard Coll., 1972; JD, U. Mich., 1979. Curriculum specialist Mass. Tchrs. Assn., Boston, 1972-75; law clk. to judge U.S. Ct. Appeals (D.C. cir.), Washington, 1979-80; law clk. Potter Stewart U.S. Supreme Ct., Washington, 1980-81; asst. prof. law U. Mich., Ann Arbor, 1981-84, assoc. prof. law, 1984-86, prof. law, 1986—. Author: (with Margaret F. Brinig) An Invitation to Family Law, 1996; editor: (book) The Law and Politics of Abortion, 1980; contbr. articles to profl. jours. Fellow Am. Council of Learned Socs., Ford Found., 1985; life fellow Clare Coll., Cambridge. Mem. Order of Coif. Office: U Mich Law Sch 625 S State St Ann Arbor MI 48109-1215

SCHNEIDER, CARL WILLIAM, lawyer; b. Phila., Apr. 27, 1932; s. Nathan J. and Eleanor M. (Milgram) S.; m. Mary Ellen Baylinson; children—Eric, Mark, Adam, Cara. B.A., Cornell U., 1953; LL.B. magna cum laude, U. Pa., 1956. Bar: Pa. 1957. Law clk. U.S. Ct. Appeals (3d cir.), Phila., 1956-57; sr. law clk. U.S. Supreme Ct., Phila., 1957-58; assoc. Wolf, Block, Schorr and Solis-Cohen, Phila., 1958-65; ptnr. Wolf, Block, Schorr and Solis-Cohen, 1965—; spl. advisor divsn. corp. fin. SEC, Washington, 1964; lectr. securities law U. Pa., 1968-70, vis. assoc. prof., 1978-81, acting dir. Ctr. for Study Fin. Instns.; bd. editors and advisors Rev. Securities and Commodities Regulations. Author: SEC Consequences of Corporate Acquisitions, 1971; also numerous articles; mem. editorial adv. bd. Securities Regulation Law Jour. Pres. Found. of Jewish Families and Children's Svc., Phila.; bd. dirs. Phila. Geriatric Ctr. Mem. ABA, Fed. Bar Assn., Pa. Bar Assn., Phila. Bar Assn. (chmn. sect. corp. banking and bus. law 1972). Home: 235 Linden Dr Elkins Park PA 19027-1341 Office: Wolf Block Schorr Packard Bldg 12th Fl SE Corner 15 Chestnut St Philadelphia PA 19102

SCHNEIDER, CHARLES I., newspaper executive; b. Chgo., Apr. 6, 1923; s. Samuel Hiram and Eva (Smith) S.; m. Barbara Anne Krause, Oct. 27, 1963; children: Susan, Charles I. Jr., Kim, Karen, Traci. BS, Northwestern U., 1944. Indsl. engr., sales mgr., v.p. mktg. Curtis-Electro Lighting Corp., Chgo., 1945-54, pres., 1954-62; pres. Jefferson Electronics, Inc., Santa Barbara, Calif., 1962-64; pres. 3 sub., v.p., asst. to pres. Am. Bldg. Maintenance Industries, Los Angeles, 1964-66; group v.p. Times Mirror Co., Los Angeles, 1966-88; ret. Times Mirror Co.; pvt. investor and cons., 1988—; bd. dirs. Jeppesen Sanderson, Inc., Denver, Graphic Controls Corp., Buffalo, Regional Airports Improvement Corp. Bd. regents Northwestern U., Evanston, Ill.; trustee, past pres. Reiss-Davis Child Study Center, L.A.; bd. govs., past pres. The Music Ctr.; trustee the Menninger Found.; pres. St. John's Hosp. and Health Ctr. Found., Santa Monica, Calif. Served with AUS, 1942-44. Mem. Chief Execs. Orgn. (past pres., bd. dirs.). Clubs: Standard (Chgo.); Beverly Hills Tennis (Calif.); Big. Ten of So. Calif. Avocations: tennis, squash, music, reading. Home: 522 N Beverly Dr Beverly Hills CA 90210-3318 *An individual's growth and success as a manager are in direct proportion to his or her ability to develop, motivate and lead able, capable people.*

SCHNEIDER, CRAIG WILLIAM, biology educator, research botanist; b. Manchester, N.H., Oct. 23, 1948; married, 1972; 3 children. BA, Gettysburg Coll., 1970; PhD in Botany, Duke U., 1975. From asst. to assoc. prof. Trinity Coll., Hartford, Conn., 1975-87, prof. biology, 1987—, Charles A. Dana rsch. prof., 1995-97. Recipient Gerald W. Prescott award Phycological Society of Am., 1993. Mem. Phycological Soc. Am. (Gerald W. Prescott award 1993), Internat. Phycological Soc., Brit. Phycological Soc., Am. Inst. Biol. Scis., N.E. Algal Soc. Achievements include research in Benthic algal studies on the Southeastern United States continental shelf and in Bermuda, benthic algal ecology in Connecticut, life-history cultural studies, red-algal morphological studies. Office: Trinity Coll Dept Biology 300 Summit St Hartford CT 06106-3100

SCHNEIDER, DAN W., lawyer, consultant; b. Salem, Oreg., Apr. 28, 1947; s. Harold Otto and Frances Louise (Warner) S.; m. Nancy Merle Schmalzbauer, Mar. 29, 1945; children: Mark Warner, Edward Michael. BA cum laude, St. Olaf Coll., 1969; JD, Willamette U., 1974; LLM, Columbia U., 1975. Bar: Oreg. 1974, D.C. 1978, Ill. 1987. Trial atty. U.S. Dept. Justice Antitrust, Washington, 1975-79; dep. assoc. dir. U.S. SEC, Washington, 1979-86; gen. ptnr. Schiff Hardin & Waite, Chgo., 1986-95; name ptnr. Smith Lodge & Schneider, Chgo., 1995—; bd. dirs. NygaarArt, Northfield, Minn. Contbr. articles to profl. jours. Trustee, sec. Ill. Acad. Fine Arts, Chgo., 1990—; mem. adv. bd. Steensland Art Mus., Northfield, 1990—. Recipient 1st prize Nathan Burkan Law Essay Competition ASCAP, N.Y., 1974, Christie award Securities Transfer Assn., 1987. Mem. Met. Club. Chgo., Monroe Club. Avocations: art collecting, art writing, music composition. Office: Smith Lodge & Schneider 55 W Monroe Chicago IL 60603

SCHNEIDER, DAVID J., psychology educator, academic administrator; b. Indpls., July 24, 1940; s. Joseph C. and Ruby Marie (Disque) S.; m. Doris Elizabeth Lieben, Dec. 21, 1962; children: Kristen Lynn, Caitlin Ann. BA, Wabash Coll., 1962; PhD, Stanford U., 1966. Asst. prof. Amherst (Mass.) Coll., 1966-71; assoc. prof. Brandeis U., Waltham, Mass., 1971-75; assoc. prof. U. Tex. San Antonio, 1975-78, prof., 1978-88; prof. Rice U., Houston, 1989—; vis. asst. prof. Stanford (Calif.) U., 1970-71; vis. prof. Ind. U., Bloomington, 1987-88; chmn. psychology Rice U., 1990—. Author: Person Perception, 1979, Introduction to Social Psychology, 1988; editor (periodical) Social Cognition, 1980-92. Home: 2107 Southgate Blvd Houston TX 77030-2111 Office: Rice Univ PO Box 1892 Psychology Dept 6100 S Main Houston TX 77251

SCHNEIDER, DAVID MILLER, lawyer; b. Cleve., July 27, 1937; s. Earl Philip and Margaret (Miller) S.; children: Philip M., Elizabeth Dale. B.A., Yale U., 1959; LL.B., Harvard U., 1962. Assoc. Baker & Hostetler, Cleve., 1962-72, ptnr., 1972-89; sr. v.p., chief legal officer Progressive Casualty Ins. Co., Cleve., 1989—; sec. The Progressive Corp., Cleve., 1989—. Trustee Alcoholism Svcs. of Cleve., 1977—, pres., 1980-82, chmn., 1982-84; v.p. Ctr. for Human Svcs., Cleve., 1980-83; trustee Cleve. chpt. NCCJ, 1986—. Mem. ABA, Ohio Bar Assn., Bar Assn. Cleve., Union Club, Tavern Club, Hunt Club, Town Club (Jamestown, N.Y.), Ojibway Club (Pointe au Baril, Ont., Can.). Republican. Episcopalian. Home: 2767 Belgrave Rd Cleveland OH 44124-4601 Office: The Progressive Corp 6300 Wilson Mills Rd Cleveland OH 44143-2109

SCHNEIDER, DONALD FREDERIC, banker; b. N.Y.C., Nov. 12, 1939; s. Charles and Lillian (Anton) S.; m. Mary Patricia McCafferty, Sept. 7, 1963; children—Laurie, John. B.S., Lehigh U., 1961; M.B.A., N.Y. U., 1968. Mgmt. trainee Marine Midland Bank, N.Y.C., 1961-65, asst. sec., 1965-68, asst. v.p., 1968-69, v.p., 1969-79; v.p. 1st Nat. Bank Chgo., 1979-87; fin. cons. Cigna Individual Fin. Svcs. Co., Chgo., 1987; v.p. Irving Trust Co./Bank of N.Y., 1987-90, Citibank N.A., N.Y.C., 1990—; mem. corp. trust activities com. Am. Bankers Assn., fiduciary and securities ops. exec. com. Mem. Am. Soc. Corporate Secs. (pres. Chgo. region 1987), Securities Transfer Assn. Home: 88 Penwood Rd Basking Ridge NJ 07920-2240 Office: Citibank NA 111 Wall St New York NY 10043-1000

SCHNEIDER, DONALD J., trucking company executive; b. 1935. BA, St. Norbert Coll., 1957; MBA, U. Pa. CEO Schneider Transport Inc., Green Bay, Wis., 1957—, Schneider National. Office: Schneider National PO Box 2545 Green Bay WI 54306*

SCHNEIDER, DUANE BERNARD, English literature educator, publisher; b. South Bend, Ind., Nov. 15, 1937; s. William H. and Lillian L. (Pitchford) S.; children: Jeffrey, Eric, Lisa, Emily. B.A., Miami U., Oxford, Ohio, 1958; M.A., Kent State U., 1960; Ph.D., U. Colo., 1965. Instr. engring. English U. Colo., 1960-65; asst. prof. English Ohio U., Athens, 1965-70, assoc. prof., 1970-75, prof., 1975—, chmn. Faculty Senate, 1981-83, chmn. dept. English, 1983-86; dir. Ohio U. Press, 1986-95; editor, pub. Croissant & Co., 1968—. Author: (with others) Anais Nin: An Introduction, 1979. Mem. Thomas Wolfe Soc. (trustee, pres. 1979-81). Home: PO Box 282 Athens OH 45701-0282

SCHNEIDER, EDWARD LEE, botanic garden administrator; b. Portland, Oreg., Sept. 14, 1947; s. Edward John and Elizabeth (Mathews) S.; m. Sandra Lee Alfarone, Aug. 2, 1968; children: Kenneth L., Cassandra L. BA, Cen. Wash. U., 1969, MS, 1971; PhD, U. Calif., Santa Barbara, 1974. From asst. to assoc. prof. botany S.W. Tex. State U., San Marcos, 1974-84, prof., 1984-94, chmn. biology dept., 1984-89, dean sci., 1989-92; exec. dir. Santa Barbara (Calif.) Botanic Garden, 1992—. Author: The Botanical World; contbr. articles to profl. jours. NSF grantee, 1980, 90; recipient Presdl. Rsch. award S.W. Tex. State U., 1985. Fellow Tex. Acad. Sci. (pres. 1992-93); mem. Internat. Water Lily Soc. (bd. dirs., sec. 1989—, inducted into Hall of Fame), Internat. Pollination Congress, Nat. Coun. Deans, Tex. Assn. Deans. Home: 1140 Tunnel Rd Santa Barbara CA 93105-2134 Office: Santa Barbara Botanic Garden 1212 Mission Canyon Rd Santa Barbara CA 93105-2126

SCHNEIDER, EDWARD LEWIS, medicine educator, research administrator; b. N.Y.C., June 22, 1940; s. Samuel and Ann (Soskin) S. BS, Rensselaer Poly. Inst., 1961; MD, Boston U., 1966. Intern and resident N.Y. Hosp.-Cornell U., N.Y.C., 1966-68; staff fellow Nat. Inst. Allergy and Infectious Diseases, Bethesda, Md., 1968-70; research fellow U. Calif., San Francisco, 1970-73; chief, sect. on cell aging Nat. Inst. Aging, Balt., 1973-79, assoc. dir., 1980-84, dep. dir., 1984-87; prof. medicine, dir. Davis Inst. on Aging U. Colo., Denver, 1979-80; dean Leonard Davis Sch. Gerontology U. So. Calif., L.A., 1986—, exec. dir. Ethel Percy Andrus Gerontology Ctr., 1986—, prof. medicine, 1987—, William and Sylvia Kugel prof. gerontology, 1989—; sci. dir. Buck Ctr. for Rsch. in Aging, 1989—; cons. MacArthur Found., Chgo., 1985-93, R.W. Johnson Found., Princeton, N.J., 1982-87, Brookdale Found., N.Y.C., 1985-89. Editor: The Genetics of Aging, 1978, The Aging Reproductive System, 1978, Biological Markers of Aging, 1982, Handbook of the Biology of Aging, 1985, 95, Interrelationship Among Aging Cancer and Differentiation, 1985, Teaching Nursing Home, 1985, Modern Biological Theories of Aging, 1987, The Black American Elderly, 1988, Elder Care and the Work Force, 1990. Med. dir. USPHS, 1968—. Recipient Roche award, 1964. Fellow Gerontology Soc., Am. Soc. Clin. Investigation; mem. Am. Assn. Retired Persons, U.S. Naval Acad. Sailing Squadron (coach 1980-86). Office: U So Calif Andrus Gerontology Ctr Los Angeles CA 90089-0191

SCHNEIDER, ELAINE FOGEL, special education educator, consultant; b. Bklyn., Mar. 6, 1947; d. Maurice Seymour and Lillian (Marowitz) F.; m. Jack Schneider, June 12, 1977; 1 child, Karli. BA, Hunter Coll., 1967; MA, Queens Coll., 1969, NYU, 1977; PhD, Calif. Coast U., 1985. Cert. tchr.; registered dance/movement therapist. Speech-lang. pathologist N.Y. Dept. Edn., 1969-72; dir. Dance Theatre, Coconut Grove, Fla., 1972-75; chairperson Lancaster (Calif.) Sch. Dist., 1978-81; exec. dir. Antelope Valley Lang. Movement Therapy, Lancaster, 1981—, Antelope Valley Infant Devel., Lancaster, 1983—. Author: Pictures Please! Adult Language Supplement, 1990, The Power of Touch: Infant Message, 1995, In Infants and Young Children, 1996; contbr. articles to profl. jours.. Bd. dirs. Families for Families Resource Ctr., Lancaster, 1993—, United Way, Lancaster, 1988—; mem. adv. bd. L.A. County Child Care, 1991—; mem. L.A. County teen pregnancy program State of Calif. Interagy. Coord. Coun., 1988—, state coun. appointee, 1988—; mem. Assistance League of Antelope Valley, 1992-94. Recipient L.A. County award Bd. Suprs., 1993, People Who Make a Difference award Antelope Valley Press, 1994; grantee March of Dimes, 1993. Mem. Am. Speech-Lang.-Hearing Assn.cert. infant massage instr., dir.-elect dist. 7), Am. Dancer therapy assn., Am. Speech-Lang. Pathologists in Pvt. Practice, Infant Devel. Assn., Nat. Assn. for Edn. Young Children, So. Calif. Assn. Edn. of Young Children, Rotary. Avocations: yoga, skiing, dancing. Office: Antelope Valley Infant Dev 1051 W Avenue M Ste 205 Lancaster CA 93534-8156

SCHNEIDER, GENE W., cable television company executive, movie theater executive; b. Enid, Okla., Sept. 8, 1926; s. Harry W. and Gladys C. (Campbell) S.; m. Phyllis Gertrude Stelter, Jan. 23, 1954 (dec. 1975); children: Mark Lyle, Marta Gene Schneider Randell, Tina Michele, Carla Gene; m. Louise Huguette Rouillier, June 21, 1977; children: Michele Marie Seiver, Kim Marie Crosby, Carter John Price. BS in Engring., U. Tex., 1949. Registered profl. engr. With Continental Oil Co., 1949-51, Kwik Kafe Koffee Service, 1951-52, United Artists Entertainment Co. (and predecessors), 1952—; chmn. United Artists Entertainment Co. (and predecessors), Denver; bd. dirs. Turner Broadcasting, Atlanta, C-SPAN. Washington, Blockbuster Entertainment Corp., Ft. Lauderdale, Think Entertainment, Studio City, Calif.; chmn. United Internat. Holdings Inc., 1989—. Active Hope for the Children, St. Joseph's Hosp. Assn. Bd., others. Served with USN, 1944-46. Mem. Nat. Cable TV Assn. (bd. dirs.), Econ. Club Colo. (founding mem.). Republican. Clubs: Vintage (Indian Wells, Calif.); Cherry Hills Country (Englewood, Colo.), Glenmoor Country. Avocations: golf, tennis, hunting, fishing. Home: 6 Sunrise Dr Englewood CO 80110-4107 Office: United Artists PO Box 5227 Englewood CO 80155-5227

SCHNEIDER, GEORGE T., obstetrician-gynecologist; b. New Orleans; s. George Edmond Schneider and Erna Marie Kraft; 1 child, Lynne Schneider Cantrell. Diploma, U. Heidelberg, Fed. Republic Germany, 1938; BS, Tulane U., 1941, MD, 1944. Intern Touro Infirmary, New Orleans, 1944-45, resident ob-gyn, 1945-47; resident ob-gyn U.S. Naval Hosp., Creat Lakes, Ill., 1947-48; vice chmn. Ochsner Med. Instns., New Orleans, 1960-86, cons., 1986—; prof. ob-gyn Sch. Medicine, La. State U., New Orleans, 1965—. Contbr. numerous articles to profl. jours. Bd. dirs. Assn. Internat. Edn., Houston, 1984—, YMCA New Orleans, 1985—, Am. Cancer Soc. La. Lt. USNR, 1945. Recipient Cert. of Merit Cancer Soc. El Salvador, 1980; named hon. counsul Honduras, 1988. Fellow ACS, Am. Coll. Ob-Gyn; mem. Ob-Gyn Soc. New Orleans (past pres.), Internat. Soc. Reproductive Medicine (past pres.), Hospitaliers Order St. Lazarus. Presbyterian. Office: Ochsner Med Instns 1514 Jefferson Hwy New Orleans LA 70121-2429

SCHNEIDER, GEORGE WILLIAM, horticulturist, educator, researcher; b. East Canton, Ohio, Apr. 4, 1916; s. John W. and Cleta (Harter) S.; m. Bernice M. Youtz; children: William Wayne, George Russell. BS, Ohio State U., 1938, MS, 1939; PhD, Rutgers U., 1950. Grad. instr. Ohio State U., Columbus, 1939; instr. N.Mex. State Coll., Las Cruces, 1939-46; asst. prof. Rutgers U., New Brunswick, N.J., 1946-50; from assoc. prof. to prof. horticulture N.C. State U., Raleigh, 1950-58; head dept. horticulture U. Ky., Lexington, 1958-60, assoc. dir. extension, 1960-69, prof. hort., 1969—; chmn. extension bd. U. Wis., Madison, 1966, ECOP Com. on Devel., Washington, 1968-69. Author: Fruit Growing, 1963; contbr. articles to profl. jours. Chmn. First Meth. Ch., Lexington, 1965. Lt. (j.g.) USN, 1943-46, ATO. Fellow AAAS, Am. Soc. Hort. Sci. (pomology chmn.). Home: 249 Greenbriar Rd Lexington KY 40503-2633

SCHNEIDER, HAROLD JOEL, radiologist; b. Cin., Aug. 9, 1923; s. Henry W. and Sarah Miriam (Hauser) S.; m. Mary Zipperstein, Dec. 23, 1945; children—Jill, Elizabeth, Ann, Jane. M.D., U. Cin., 1947. Diplomate: Am. Bd. Radiology. Intern Cin. Gen. Hosp., 1947-48, resident in radiology, 1953-56; resident in surgery Holzer Hosp. and Clinic, Gallipolis, Ohio, 1948-49; gen. practice medicine Dayton, Ohio, 1949-50; asst. prof. radiology U. Ala. Med. Sch., Birmingham, 1956-59; asso. prof. radiology U. Cin. Med. Center, 1959-69, prof. radiology, 1969-91, prof. emeritus, 1991—; dir. diagnostic radiology Christian R. Holmes Hosp., 1959-91; former cons. Cin. VA Hosp. Contbr. articles to profl. jours. Served to lt. USNR, 1950-52. Fellow Am. Coll. Radiology; mem. Radiol. Soc. N.Am., Am. Roentgen Ray Soc., Ohio Radiol. Soc., Ohio Med. Soc., Greater Cin. Radiol. Soc., Cin. Acad. Medicine. Home: 7290 Elbrook Ave Cincinnati OH 45237-2946

SCHNEIDER, HOWARD, lawyer; b. N.Y.C., Mar. 21, 1935; s. Abraham and Lena (Pincus) S.; m. Anne Evelyn Gorfinkle; children—Andrea Rose, Jeffrey Winston. AB, Cornell U., 1956, JD with distinction, 1959. Bar: N.Y. 1959, D.C. 1976. Assoc., then ptnr. Stroock & Stroock, N.Y.C., 1959-75; gen. counsel Commodity Futures Trading Commn., Washington, 1975-77, Rosenman & Colin, N.Y.C., 1977—. Contbr. articles to profl. jours. Served to capt. USAR, 1956-66. Mem. Assn. Bar of City of N.Y. (chmn. com. 1982—), Harmonie Club (N.Y.C.). Republican. Jewish. Home: 830 Park Ave New York NY 10021 Office: Rosenman & Colin 575 Madison Ave New York NY 10022-2511

SCHNEIDER, JAMES JOSEPH, military theory educator, consultant; b. Oshkosh, Wis., June 18, 1947; s. Joseph Edward and Virginia Gertrude Schneider; m. Peggy L. Spees, July 28, 1973 (dec. May 1976); m. Claretta Virginia Burton, Nov. 11, 1984; children: Kevin, Jason, Jenifer, Julie. BA, U. Wis., Oshkosh, 1973, MA, 1974; PhD, U. Kans., 1992. Planning evaluator Winnegago County, Oshkosh, 1978-80; ops. rsch. analyst Tng. and Doctrine Command Analysis Ctr., Ft. Leavenworth, Kans., 1980-84; prof. mil. theory Sch. Advanced Mil. Studies U.S. Army Command and Gen. Staff Coll., Ft. Leavenworth, 1984—; adj. assoc. prof. history Russian and East European Studies Ctr., U. Kans., 1994—. Author: (monograph) Exponential Decay of Armies in Battle, 1985, The Structure of Strategic Revolution, 1994; also numerous articles. With U.S. Army, 1965-68, Vietnam. Recipient medal for civilian achievement Dept. Army, 1989, Bronze Order of St. George, U.S. Cav. Assn., 1990. Mem. Am. Hist. Assn., Mil. Ops. Rsch. Soc. Office: U S Army Command/Gen Staff Coll Sch Advanced Mil Studies Fort Leavenworth KS 66027

SCHNEIDER, JAN, obstetrics and gynecology educator; b. Prague, Czechoslovakia, Dec. 10, 1933; came to U.S., 1963, naturalized, 1967; s. Evzen and Erika S.; m. Sandra Wilson, May 20, 1961; children—Hana, Donald, Kathryn, Jonathan. M.B., U. London, 1957; M.P.H., U. Mich., 1967. Prof. ob-gyn, chief obstetric service dept. ob-gyn U. Mich. Med. Sch., Ann Arbor, 1963-77; prof., chmn. ob-gyn Med. Coll. Pa. and Hahnemann U., Phila., 1978—. Editor: (with R. J. Bolognese and R. H. Schwarz) Perinatal Medicine, 2d edit, 1981. Fellow Am. Coll. Obstetricians and Gynecologists, Soc. Perinatal Obstetricians, Am. Gynecol. and Obstet. Soc., Phila. Obstet. Soc. Presbyterian. Office: Med Coll Pa 3300 Henry Ave Philadelphia PA 19129-1121

SCHNEIDER, JANE HARRIS, sculptor; b. Trenton, N.J., Jan. 2, 1932; d. Leon Harris and Dorothy (Perlman) Rosenthal; m. Alfred R. Schneider, July 25, 1953; children: Lee, Jeffry, Elizabeth. BA, Wellesley Coll. Exhibited work in numerous group and one-person shows including June Kelly Gallery, 1988, 90, 93, 95, Nassau County Mus. Fine Art, Roslyn, n.Y., 1988, Alternative Mus., N.Y.C., 1985, Phila. Art Alliance, 1984, Atrium Gallery, St. Louis, 1993, 96, Bill Bace Gallery, 1992, Triplex Gallery, N.Y.C., 1991, Rockland Ctr. for Arts, West Nyack, N.Y., 1990, Hudson River Mus., Yonkers, N.Y., 1989, Sculpture Ctr., N.Y.C., 1988, many others; sculpture represented in numerous pub. and pvt. collections. Avocations: swimming, gardening. Office/Studio: 75 Grand St New York NY 10013-2219

SCHNEIDER, JANET M., arts administrator, curator, painter; b. N.Y.C., June 6, 1950. d. August Arthur and Joan (Battaglia) S.; m. Michael Francis Sperendi, Sept. 21, 1985. BA summa cum laude, Queens Coll., CUNY, 1972; spl. study fine arts Boston U. Tanglewood Inst., 1971. With Queens Mus., Flushing, N.Y.C., 1973-89, curator, 1973-75, program dir., 1975-77, exec. dir., 1977-89. Collections arranged include: Sons and others, Women Artists See Men (author catalog), 1975, Urban Aesthetics (author catalog), 1976, Masters of the Brush, Chinese Painting and Calligraphy from the Sixteenth to the Nineteenth Century (co-author catalog), 1977, Symcho Moszkowicz: Portrait of the Artist in Postwar Europe (author catalog), 1978, Shipwrecked 1622, The Lost Treasure of Philip IV (author catalog), 1981, Michaelangelo: A Sculptor's World (author catalog), 1983, Joseph Cornell: Revisited (author catalog), 1992, Blueprint for Change: The Life and Times of Lewis H. Latimer (co-author catalog), 1995. Chmn. Cultural Instns. Group, N.Y.C., 1986-87; mem. N.Y.C. Commn. for Cultural Affairs, 1991-93; bd. dirs. N.Y.C. Partnership, 1987-88, Gallery Assn. N.Y. State 1979-81. Mem. Artists Choice Mus. (trustee 1979-82), Am. Assn. Mus., Phi Beta Kappa.

SCHNEIDER, JOANNE, artist; b. Lima, Ohio, Dec. 4, 1919; d. Joseph and Laura (Office) Federman; m. Norman Schneider, May 15, 1941; children—Melanie Schneider Tucker, Lois Schneider Oppenheim. B.F.A., Syracuse U., 1941. One-man shows John Heller Gallery, N.Y.C., 1954, 55, 57, 58, Tirca Karlis Gallery, Provincetown, Mass., 1963, Frank Rehn Gallery, N.Y.C., 1965, 66, 69, 72, 75, Elaine Benson Gallery, Bridgehamton, N.Y., 1972, 74, 79, 85, St. Mary's Coll., St. Mary's City, Md., 1978, Alonzo Gallery, N.Y.C., 1978, Discovery Art Gallery, Clifton, N.J., 1978; group shows include Whitney Mus., N.Y.C., Pa. Acad. Arts, Corcoran Galleries, Washington, Toledo Mus., U. Nebr., Everson Mus., Syracuse, N.Y.; represented in permanent collections Met. Mus. Art, N.Y.C., Colby Coll., Syracuse U., Butler Inst., St. Mary's Coll., U. Notre Dame, Guild Hall, East Hampton, N.Y. Recipient Audubon Artists Stanley Grumbacher Meml. award, 1972. Address: 35 E 75th St New York NY 10021-2761 *A life spent in pursuit of creative expression is a fuller, more satisfying life.*

SCHNEIDER, JOHN ARNOLD, business investor; b. Chgo., Dec. 4, 1926; s. Arnold George and Anna (Wagner) S.; m. Elizabeth C. Simpson, Oct. 20, 1951; children: Richard Ward, William Arnold, Elizabeth Anne. B.S., U. Notre Dame, 1948. Exec. assignments with CBS-TV in Chgo. and N.Y.C., 1950-58; v.p., gen. mgr. sta. WCAU-TV, Phila., 1958-64; sta. WCBS-TV, N.Y.C., 1964-65; pres. CBS TV Network, 1965-66, CBS/Broadcast Group, 1966-69, 71-77; exec. v.p. CBS, Inc., 1969-71, sr. v.p., from, 1977; pres., chief exec. officer Warner Amex Satellite Entertainment Corp., 1979-84. Trustee, mem. exec. com. U. Notre Dame; trustee Com. for Econ. Devel. Served with USNR, 1943-46. Roman Catholic. Club: Indian Harbor Yacht. Home: 155 Clapboard Ridge Rd Greenwich CT 06831

SCHNEIDER, JOHN DAVID, theatre director, playwright, actor, jazz singer; b. Fond du Lac, Wis., June 7, 1948; s. David Elmer and Bernice Catherine (Pable) S. BA, St. Norbert Coll., 1970. Mem. Theatre X, Milw., 1971—; also artistic dir., 1978—, profl. playwright, 1973—; vocalist, leader John Schneider Orch., Milw., 1988—. Author: (plays) Scenarios For the Living/For the Dead, 1983; author numerous plays. Recipient New Works award Wis. Arts Bd., 1990; NEA fellow, 1988, Milwaukee County fellow, 1991, Program Devel. grantee Theatre Comms. Group-Pew Charitable Trust, 1992. Office: Theatre X 158 N Broadway St Milwaukee WI 53202

SCHNEIDER, JOHN HOKE, health science administrator; b. Eau Claire, Wis., Sept. 29, 1931; div.; 2 children. B.S. in Chemistry, U. Wis., Madison, 1953, M.S. in Exptl. Oncology, 1955, Ph.D., 1958. Rsch. asst. McArdle Meml. Lab., U. Wis., 1953-58; asst. prof. biochemistry Am. U. Beirut, 1958-61, Vanderbilt U. Med. Sch., 1961-62; editor in chief Biol. Abstracts, Phila., 1962-63; grants assoc. tng. program NIH, Bethesda, Md., 1963-64; sci. and tech. info. specialist, office program planning and analysis Nat. Cancer Inst., 1964-74, dir. internat. cancer rsch. data bank program, 1974-84, sci. rev. adminstr., grants rev. br., 1984-89, program dir. cancer tng. br., 1989-96 retired, ret., 1996. Author numerous papers on nucleic acid rsch. and info. sci. Recipient numerous achievement awards. Mem. AAAS, Phi Beta Kappa, Sigma Xi. Home: 8414 Downybrook Dr Chevy Chase MD 20815

SCHNEIDER, KEITH HILARY, news correspondent, journalist; b. White Plains, N.Y., Apr. 19, 1956; s. Martin Herbert and Jo-Anne Rosalyn (Spitzer) S.; m. Florence Marianne Barone, Oct. 20, 1984. BA, Haverford Coll., 1978. Reporter Wilkes-Barre (Pa.) Times Leader, 1978-80, The News and Courier, Charleston, S.C., 1980-81; editor S.C. Featured, Charleston, 1981-83, News West, Sacramento, Calif., 1983-85; corr. Washington Bur. N.Y. Times, 1985-87, nat. corr., 1987—. Recipient Judson Chapman award for pub. svc., 1980 and Feature Writing award, 1981 S.C. Press Assn., Columbia, George Polk Meml. award for environ. reporting, 1984, George Polk Meml. award for nat. reporting, 1989 L.I. Univ., N.Y. Jewish. Avocations: hiking, climbing, running, weight lifting, writing. Home: 12178 Nurnberger Rd Thompsonville MI 49683-9511 Office: New York Times Washington Bur 1627 I St NW Fl 7 Washington DC 20006-4007

SCHNEIDER, MAHLON C., lawyer; b. 1939. BA, U. Minn., 1962, law degree, 1964. Bar: Minn. 1965. Atty. Green Giant Co., 1980; atty. Pillsbury, 1980-84, v.p., gen. counsel foods divsn., 1984-89; corp. atty. Geo. A. Hormel & Co., Austin, Minn., 1989-90, v.p., gen. counsel, 1990—. Office: Hormel & Co PO Box 800 Austin MN 55912-0800

SCHNEIDER, MARK, political science educator; b. N.Y.C., Oct. 28, 1946; s. Irving and Ida (Schwartz) S.; m. Susan Roth, June 27, 1986; children: Johanna, Elizabeth. BA, Bklyn. Coll., 1967; PhD, U. N.C., 1974. Asst. prof. polit. sci. U. Mich., Ann Arbor, 1973-74; asst. prof. polit. sci. SUNY, Stony Brook, 1974-78, assoc. prof., 1978-85, prof., 1985—, chmn. dept., 1986—; Fulbright sr. lectr., India, 1980-81. Author: The Competitive City, 1989, Public Entrepreneurs, 1995; contbr. articles to profl. jours. Mem. Am. Polit. Sci. Assn., Midwest Polit. Sci. Assn. Office: SUNY Dept Polit Sci Stony Brook NY 11794

SCHNEIDER, MARK LEWIS, government official; b. Newark, Dec. 31, 1941; s. Benjamin and Ruth (Kobran) S.; m. Susan Gilbert, June 20, 1965; children: Aaron Mitchell, Miriam Beth. A.B. in Journalism with honors, U. Calif., Berkeley, 1963; M.A. in Polit. Sci., San Jose State Coll., 1965. Reporter UPI, San Francisco, 1963-64, San Francisco Call Bull., 1965; vol. Peace Corps, El Salvador, 1966-68; reporter Washington News Call Bull., 1969-70; mem. staff U.S. Senate Judiciary Subcom., 1970-71; legis. asst. to Sen. Edward M. Kennedy, 1971-77, 80-81; mem. U.S. Senate del. North Atlantic Assembly, 1971-73; dep. asst. sec. for human rights Dept. State, Washington, 1977-79; mem. del. UN Gen. Assembly, 1978, UN Human Rights Commn., 1979; coordinator policy planning, sr. advisor Pan Am. Health Orgn., 1981-93; adminstr. for Latin Am. and Caribbean USAID, 1993—; lectr. Kennedy Inst. Politics, Harvard U., 1976. Bd. dirs. Internat. Human Rights Law Group. Fulbright fellow, 1976; Recipient F.W. Richardson award Calif. Press Assn., 1963. Mem. Am. Polit. Sci. Assn., Latin Am. Studies Assn. Democrat. Jewish. Home: 3517 Tilden St NW Washington DC 20008-3122

SCHNEIDER, MARTIN AARON, photojournalist, ecologist, engineer, writer, artist, television director, public intervenor, educator, university instructor, lecturer; b. N.Y.C., Sept. 23, 1926; s. Morris and Florence (Frohlich) S. Stuyvesant Science, 1941-44, CUNY, 1947-52. Editor in chief Nocturne; freelance artist, 1941—, freelance photographer, 1954—; photojournalist Life, Time, Newsweek, Sports Illustrated, N.Y. Times, NBC-TV, Ency. Britannica, Mpls. Tribune, Handball Illustrated, Time Annual Year in Review, Grolier Ency., Crowell-Collier Ency., NBC Startime, Variety, Time-Life: Ecology, Saturday Review of Literature, 1960—; ecologist, USPHS, U.S. Senate, U.S. EPA, N.Y.C.EPA, N.Y. State Dept. Environ. Conservation, N.Y.C. Dept. Air Pollution, 1964—; product safety engineer, designer, builder, crash-safety, pollution and radiation monitoring, multi-alternate fuel, laboratory vehicle, 1967—, instr., lectr. NYU, Cornell U., Ithaca, NY, New Sch. Social Rsch., N.Y.C., SUNY, Albany, Cooper Union, N.Y.C., CUNY, Iowa U., lectr. in field, 1969—; pub. intervenor, N.Y.C. Health Dept., N.Y. State Health Dept., N.Y. State Dept. Environ. Conservation, Gov. Rockefeller's State Study Commission for N.Y.C. (Scott Commission), U.S. District Ct., N.Y. Supreme Ct.; People of N.Y.C., N.Y.C. Council, N.Y. Attorney General, 1970—. TV news guest NBC Today, CBS, ABC, 1970—; radio news guest, TV and radio commentator, 1970—; author: Breath of Death, 1972, Consumer Genocide, 1992; The Schneider Tapes, 1996, War Against War, ed. 1996, Crash Genocide: Millions Killed by Suppressed Safety, 1996; co-author: America-Photographic Statements, 1972, Eye of Conscience, 1974; dir., prodr., writer, cinematographer (TV documentaries) Environment Crusade, CBS, 1970, The Poisoned Air, CBS, 1970, Killers of the Environment, NBC, 1971, Censorship of Pollution Solutions by Media and Government, PBS, 1974, No Justice for Victims-Criminals Only, 1992; contbr. N.Y. Times, Ency. Britannica, Macmillan Ency. of Photographic Artists, N.Y. Village Voice "Whole Earth Ranger: Ecology's Batman", New World Or No World (Frank Herbert) 1970—; photography exhibited at Mus. Modern Art, N.Y.C., 1958—, George Eastman House Mus., Rochester, N.Y., 1963, 64—, Libr. Congress, 1970, Smithsonian Instn., 1972—, Art Inst. Chgo., 1973—, Whitney Mus., N.Y.C., 1978—; painting exhibited at Guggenheim Mus., N.Y.C., 1943; film exhibited at Am. Mus. Natural History, N.Y.C., 1969-72. Served with U.S. Army Paratroopers, 1944-46, PTO. Fellowship grantee Creative Artists Pub. Svc., 1977, 78; recipient TV Franny Consumer Advocacy award, 1974, for work that was a basis for the first Clean Air Act of 1970. Jewish. Office: 1501 Broadway Ste 2907 New York NY 10036-5601 *Where millions are endangered where my work makes a difference--despite gunfire, vehicle sabotage, seizure of home and all possessions, censorship--there is no dream for me in moving mere mountains, but only in moving man to move himself.*

SCHNEIDER, MATTHEW ROGER, lawyer; b. N.Y.C., Nov. 7, 1948; s. Theodore David Schneider and Rosalind (Schwartz) Werner; m. Marjorie Ann Friedlander, Mar. 6, 1976; children: Adam Benjamin, Emily Beth. BA, Cornell U., 1970; student, Georgetown U., 1971; JD, Cath. U., Washington, 1974. Bar: D.C. 1976, U.S. Dist. Ct. D.C., 1994. Staff asst. U.S. Senate Jud. Com., Washington, 1973-74; counsel U.S. Senate Govt. Ops. Com., Washington, 1974-77; spl. asst. Office of Sec. Def., Washington, 1977-79; dir. legis. affairs SEC, Washington, 1979-81, sr. counsel, divsn. corp. fin., 1981-82; chief of staff U.S. Senator Jeff Bingaman, Washington, 1983-85; prin. Law Office Matthew Schneider, Washington, 1985-87; ptnr. Willkie, Farr & Gallagher, Washington, 1987-95, Garvy, Schubert & Barer, 1996—. Bd. dirs. Capitol Hill Hosp., Washington, 1981-87, Epilepsy Found. for Nat. Capital Area. Avocations: biking, singing, guitar. Office: Garvy Schubert & Barer 5th Fl 1000 Potomac St NW Washington DC 20007

SCHNEIDER, MICHAEL JOSEPH, biologist; b. Saginaw, Mich., Apr. 21, 1938; s. Michael Elias and Jane (Moffitt) S.; m. Janet Marie Potter, Nov. 24, 1967. B.S., U. Mich., 1960; M.S., U. Tenn., 1962; Ph.D. (Hutchinson Meml. fellow 1963-64, John M. Coulter research fellow 1964-65), U. Chgo., 1965. Resident research assoc. Nat. Acad. Scis., Beltsville, Md., 1965-67; USPHS fellow U. Wis., Madison, 1967-68; asst. prof. biology Columbia U., 1968-73; mem. faculty U. Mich., Dearborn, 1973—, prof. biology, 1975—, chmn. dept. natural scis., 1975-80, 83-89, assoc. provost for acad. affairs, 1990, interim provost, vice chancellor for acad. affairs, 1991; vis. prof. Plant Research Lab., Mich. State U., East Lansing, 1980-81. Contbr. articles profl. jours. Mem. AAAS, Am. Soc. Plant Physiologists, Am. Soc. Photobiology, Sigma Xi. Home: 4654 Mulberry Woods Cir Ann Arbor MI 48105 Office: U Mich-Dearborn Dept Nat Scis Dearborn MI 48128-1491

SCHNEIDER, NORMAN M., food manufacturing company executive; b. N.Y.C., Feb. 5, 1911; s. David and Edith S.; m. JoAnne Federman, May 15, 1940; children: Melanie Schneider Tucker, Lois Schneider Oppenheim. B.A., U. Scranton, 1932. Partner Norsid Co., N.Y.C., 1932-46; founder, pres. Allison Mfg. Co., N.Y.C., 1946-70; pres. and chmn. leisure products div. Beatrice Co. Inc., Chgo., 1970-81; mgmt. cons. Beatrice Co. Inc., 1981-86; pres. Schneider Assocs., N.Y.C., 1987—; former mem. N.Y. Bd. Trade; bd. dirs. Park Electrochem. Corp., Toys R Us, Datascope Corp. Recipient Man of Yr. award Boy Scouts Am. Mem. Explorers Club, Harmonie Club. Office: 46 E 70th St New York NY 10021-4928

SCHNEIDER, PAM HORVITZ, lawyer; b. Cleve., Nov. 29, 1951; m. Milton S. Schneider, June 30, 1973; 1 child, Sarah Anne. BA, U. Pa., 1973; JD, Columbia U., 1976. Bar: N.Y. 1977, Pa. 1979. Assoc. White & Case, N.Y.C., 1976-78; assoc. Drinker Biddle & Reath, Phila., 1978-84, ptnr., 1984—. Contbr. articles to profl. jours. Mem. ABA (vice chair real property probate and trust law sect.), Internat. Acad. Estate and Trust Law (academician). Office: Drinker Biddle & Reath 1345 Chestnut St Philadelphia PA 19107-3426

SCHNEIDER, PETER RAYMOND, political scientist; b. Muskogee, Okla., Aug. 8, 1939; s. Leo Frederick and Tillie Oleta (Cannon) S.; m. Anne Larason, Jan. 22, 1964 (div. 1983); children: Christopher, Geoffrey; m. Adrienne Armstrong, Dec. 19, 1986; 1 child, Robbie. BS, Okla. State U., 1966, MS, 1968; PhD, Ind. U., 1974. News editor No. Va. Sun, Arlington, 1961-62; news writer AP, Balt., 1962, Balt. News-Am., 1962-65; asst. prof. U.

Oreg., Eugene, 1974-76; pres. Inst. of Policy Analysis, Eugene, 1976-83; v.p. Am. Justice Inst., Sacramento, 1983; dir. Ctr. for Assessment of The Juvenile Justice Ctr., Sacramento, 1983; v.p. Nat. Partnership, Washington, 1985; sr. rsch. scientist Pacific Inst. for Rsch. and Evaluation, Bethesda, Md., 1984-92, dir. justice div., 1986-89; pres. Inst. of Policy Analysis, Vienna, Va., 1992-95; CEO IPA Internat., Inc., Vienna, 1995—. Contbr. numerous articles to profl. jours., chpts. to books. Recipient Julia Lathrop award Am. Criminal Justice Assn., 1985. Mem. Am. Polit. Sci. Assn., Am. Restitution Assn., Pi Sigma Alpha, Sigma Delta Chi, Phi Kappa Phi, Omicron Delta Kappa, Phi Kappa Theta. Avocations: flying, tennis, selling wine. Home: 9025 Streamview Ln Vienna VA 22182-1726 Office: IPA Internat Inc 8133 Leesburg Pike Ste 260 Vienna VA 22182-2706 *In a career devoted to the pursuit of knowledge, I have learned that nothing - absolutely nothing - is worth more than lessons learned from painful personal experience. To my regret, I usually learned such lessons after the opportunities toprofit from them had already passed. If I could do it over again I would be more daring and venturesome and make my mistakes early, while there was still plenty of time to invest the information.*

SCHNEIDER, PHYLLIS LEAH, writer, editor; b. Seattle, Apr. 19, 1947; d. Edward Lee Booth and Harriet Phyllis (Ebbinghaus) Russell; m. Clifford Donald Schneider, June 14, 1969; 1 child, Pearl Brooke. B.A., Pacific Luth. U., 1969; M.A., U. Wash., 1972. Fiction, features editor Seventeen Mag., N.Y.C., 1975-80; mng. editor Weight Watchers Mag., N.Y.C., 1980-81; editor YM mag., N.Y.C., 1981-86. Author: Parents Book of Infant Colic, 1990, Kids Who Make a Difference, 1993, Straight Talk on Women's Health: How to Get the Health Care You Deserve, 1993, Hot Health Care Careers, 1993, What Kids Like To Do, 1993. Recipient Centennial Recognition award Pacific Luth. U., 1990. Democrat. Episcopalian.

SCHNEIDER, RAYMOND CLINTON, architect, educator; b. Smyrna, N.Y., Dec. 10, 1920; s. George William and Helen (Carey) S.; m. Margaret Maude Pearce, Sept. 16, 1943 (dec. Aug. 1982); children: Stephen Eric, Martha Anne (dec.), Pearce Clinton; m. Ruth Brown Martsolf, Jan. 2, 1983 (div. Jan. 1986); m. Gertraude R. McMullen, May 28, 1986 (div. Sept. 1988); life ptnr. M. Maxine La Shell (dec. Jan. 1996). B.S. in Architecture, Kans. State U., 1949, M.S. in Edn, 1952; Ed.D., Stanford U., 1955. Registered architect, Kans. Architect firms in Salina and Manhattan, Kans., 1947-51; assoc. dir. sch. planning lab., asso. dir. W. Regional Center Ednl. Facilities Lab., also research asso., lectr. edn. Stanford U., Palo Alto, 1955-62; head personnel subsystems sect., systems tech. lab. Sylvania Corp., Mountain View, Calif., 1962-63; dir. research and planning Porter, Gogerty, Meston, San Jose, Calif., 1963-64; assoc. prof. edn. and architecture U. Wash., Seattle, 1964-78; prof. architecture and edn. U. Wash., 1978-82, prof. emeritus, 1983—; asst. to dean, 1964-73, dir. grad. program architecture, 1976-83, exhibiting artist and sculptor, 1946—, cons. in field. Author articles in field, chpts. in books. Served with AUS, 1942-46. Kellogg fellow, 1953-54; Masonite Co. fellow, 1954-55; Borg-Warner Co. fellow, 1954-55. Mem. VFW (life), Am. Legion. Address: 4406 SW 29th Ter Topeka KS 66614-3102

SCHNEIDER, RICHARD GRAHAM, lawyer; b. Bryn Mawr, Pa., Aug. 2, 1930; s. Vincent Bernard and Marion Scott (Graham) S.; m. Margaret Peter Fritz, Feb. 15, 1958; children: Margaret W., Richard Graham, John F. BA, Yale U., 1952; JD, U. Pa., 1957. Bar: Pa. 1958. Assoc. Dechert Price & Rhoads, Phila., 1957-66; ptnr. Dechert Price & Rhoads, 1966—. Case editor U. Pa. Law Rev., 1956-57. Trustee Baldwin Sch., Bryn Mawr, 1971-79; trustee Episcopal Acad., Merion, Pa., 1976-83. 1st lt. USAF, 1952-54, PTO. Mem. ABA, Pa. Bar Assn., Phila. Bar Assn., Order of Coif, Merion Cricket Club, Merion Golf Club, Yale Club (pres. 1966-68). Republican. Presbyterian. Office: Dechert Price & Rhoads 4000 Bell Atlantic Tower 1717 Arch St Philadelphia PA 19103-2713

SCHNEIDER, RICHARD T(HEODORE), optics research executive, engineer; b. Munich, July 29, 1927; came to U.S., 1961; s. Wilhelm and Martha E. (Hofmann) S.; m. Lore M. Reinhard, May 16, 1950; children: Ursula M. Schneider Long, Richard W. Diploma in physics, U. Stuttgart, Fed. Republic of Germany, 1958, PhD, 1961. Registered profl. engr. Calif. Teaching asst. U. Stuttgart, 1958-61; sect. chief Allison div. Gen. Motors Corp., Indpls., 1961-65; assoc. prof. U. Fla., Gainesville, 1965-68, prof., 1968-88, prof. emeritus, 1988-90; pres. Eye Rsch. Lab., Inc., Alachua, Fla., 1984-90; chief scientist RTS Labs., Inc., Alachua, 1984-92; cons. Allison div. Gen. Motors Corp., Indpls., 1965-67; IPA assignment Eglin AFB, Ft. Walton Beach, Fla., 1983; liaison scientist USN Office Naval Rsch., London, 1975. Editor: Uranium Plasmas, 1971; patentee in field; contbr. articles to profl. jours. Recipient Medal for Exceptional Sci. Achievement, NASA, 1975, Outstanding Tech. Achievement award, Fla. Engrng. Soc., 1978. Mem. Optical Soc. Am., Am. Phys. Soc., Internat. Soc. for Optical Engrng., Sigms Xi, Tau Beta Pi (Eminent Engr. 1970). Avocation: flying airplanes. Home: 12903 NW 112th Ave Alachua FL 32615 Office: Eye Rsch Lab 1663 Technology Ave Alachua FL 32615-9499

SCHNEIDER, ROBERT EDWARD, insurance company executive, actuary; b. Hartford, Conn., June 3, 1950; s. F. Russell and Barbara (Carey) S.; m. Catherine Genetti, Sept. 9, 1978; children: Christopher Michael, Andrew Robert. AB, Middlebury Coll., 1972. Asst. actuary Nat. Life Ins. Co., Montpelier, Vt., 1972-75; asst. actuary New Eng. Mut. Life Ins. Co., Boston, 1975-77, assoc. actuary, 1977-81, 2d v.p. then v.p., actuary, 1981-84, sr. v.p., actuary, 1984-91, exec. v.p., CFO, 1991—; bd. dirs. New Eng. Variable Life Ins. Co., Wilmington, Del., New England Mutual Life Ins. Co., Boston, New Eng. Securities Corp., Boston. Mem. editorial bd. Actuarial Digest, Atlanta, 1986-88. Bd. dirs. Exec. Service Corps of New Eng., Boston, 1987-93. Fellow Soc. of Actuaries, Can. Inst. Actuaries; mem. Am. Acad. Actuaries. Roman Catholic. Home: 52 Westminster Rd Newton MA 02159-2355 Office: New England Mut Life Ins Co 501 Boylston St Boston MA 02116-3706

SCHNEIDER, ROBERT JAY, oncologist; b. Miami, Fla., May 31, 1949; s. Irving and Ethel (Pack) S.; m. Barbara Cunningham, June 1, 1974; children: Matthew, Kirsten. Student, Washington U., 1967-69; BA cum laude, Boston U., 1971; MD, Albert Einstein Coll. Medicine, N.Y.C., 1975. Diplomate Am. Bd. Internal Medicine, Am. Bd. Oncology; lic. physician, N.Y. Intern, jr. and sr. resident internal medicine Bronx Mcpl. Hosp., N.Y.C., 1975-78; fellow med. oncology Meml. Sloan-Kettering Cancer Ctr., N.Y.C., 1978-80, adj. attending physician/cons. dept. medicine, 1981—; asst. prof. medicine N.Y. Med. Coll., Valhalla, 1980-81; clin. instr. medicine Cornell U. Med. Coll., 1978-80; jr. clin. faculty fellow Am. Cancer Soc., 1980-81; mem. N.Y. Met. Breast Cancer Group, 1990—; cons. cancer program No. Westchester Hosp. Ctr., Mt. Kisco, N.Y., 1981-82; mem. staff Westchester County Med. Ctr., Valhalla, N.Y., No. Westchester Hosp. Ctr., Mt. Kisco, Meml. Sloan-Kettering Cancer Ctr., N.Y.C. Contbr. articles to profl. jours. Recipient Clin. Fellowship award Am. Cancer Soc., 1978-79. Mem. Am. Soc. Clin. Oncology, Westchester County Med. Soc., N.Y. State Med. Soc., Woodway Country Club. Republican. Presbyterian. Achievements include research in detection and treatment of early breast cancer, the human spirit in the fight against cancer, salvage chemotherapy with etoposide, ifosfamide and cisplatin in refractory germ cell tumors. Office: 439 E Main St Mount Kisco NY 10549-3404

SCHNEIDER, ROBERT JEROME, lawyer; b. Cin., June 22, 1947; s. Jerome William and Agnes (Moehringer) S.; m. Janice Loraine Eckhoff, Dec. 13, 1968; children: Aaron Haisley, Jared Alan, Margot Laraine. BS in Mech. Engrng., U. Cin., 1970, JD, 1973. Bar: Ill. 1973, U.S. Dist. Ct. (no. dist.) Ill. 1973, U.S. Ct. Appeals (7th cir.) 1973, U.S. Ct. Appeals (fed. cir.) 1973-82. Ptnr. Mason, Kolehmainen, Rathburn & Wyss, Chgo., 1973-82; ptnr., asst. chmn. patents, chmn. intellectual property dept. McDermott, Will & Emery, Chgo., 1982-94; ptnr. intellectual property and tech. svcs. group Keck Mahin & Cate, Chgo., 1994—. Mem. ABA, ASME, Ill. Bar Assn., Chgo. Bar Assn., Licensing Execs. Soc., Intellectual Property Law Assn. Chgo. (sec. 1981-83), Fedn. Internat. des Conseils en Proriete Industrielle, Assn. Internationale Pour la Protection de la Propriété Industrielle, Internat. Trademark Assn., Am. Intellectual Property Law Assn., Inter-Pacific Bar Assn., Tower Club (bd. govs. 1988—, v.p. 1994-95, pres. 1995—). Republican. Roman Catholic. Home: 1609 Asbury Ave Winnetka IL 60093-1303 Office: Keck Mahin & Cate 77 W Wacker Dr Chicago IL 60601-1629

SCHNEIDER, ROY, U.S. Virgin Island government official. Gov. Govt. of U.S. V.I., St. Thomas. Office: Office of Gov Kogens Glade Saint Thomas VI 00802

SCHNEIDER, SAMUEL JAMES, JR., ceramic engineer; b. St. Louis, Sept. 11, 1930; s. Samuel and Dorothy Helen (Pins) S.; m. Joan Carolyn McMahon, Aug. 6, 1955; children: Steven, Michael, Sandra. BS in Ceramic Engrng., U. Mo., Rolla, 1952, Profl. Ceramic Engr., 1975. Ceramic engr. Laclede Refractory Co., St. Louis, 1952-53; phys. scientist ceramics Nat. Bur. Stds., Gaithersburg, Md., 1955-74, asst. to dir. Inst. Materials Rsch., 1974-81, dep. chief. cermics divsn., 1981-84; sci. advisor to dir. Materials Sci. and Engrng. Lab. Nat. Inst. Stds. & Tech., Gaithersburg, 1984—; bd. trustees Orton Found., Columbus, Ohio, 1986—; chmn. TC 206 Interant. Stds. Orgn., Geneva, 1994—; exec. sec. materials tech. subcom. Office Sci. and Tech. Policy, Washington, 1991—. Editor: Handbook on Advanced Ceramics, ASM Engineering Series, 1993; contbr. articles to profl. jours. Elder Rockville (Md.) United Ch. With CIC, U.S. Army, 1953-55. Recipient silver medal/Rosa award Dept. Commerce, Washington, 1970, 88, internat. prize Japan Ceramic Assn., 1994; named Academian Internat. Acad. Ceramics, Italy, 1994. Fellow ASTM (award of merit 1984), Am. Ceramic Soc. (Refractories award 1985); mem. Nat. Inst. Ceramic Engrs., Lakewood Country Club. Republican. Presbyterian. Achievements include research on phase equilibria-high temperature techniques, energy, materials, issues R&D policy; coordination of interagency materials R&D program among 10 federal agencies-materials standard; instrumental in the development of international standard for ceramics. Avocations: golf, skiing. Home: 5 Marlin Ct Rockville MD 20853-3611 Office: Nat Inst Stds & Tech Gaithersburg MD 20899

SCHNEIDER, SOL, electronic engineer, consultant, researcher; b. N.Y.C., Feb. 24, 1924; s. David and Naomi F. Schneider; m. Rhoda B. Schneider, Apr. 16, 1950; children: Sandra E., Barry. BA, CUNY Bklyn. Coll., 1946; MS, NYU, 1949. Supervisory physicist U.S. Army Electronics Tech. and Devices Lab., Ft. Monmouth, N.J., 1948-80, chief pulse power and plasma devices, 1956-80; cons. Rockwell Internat., Canoga Park, Calif., 1980-81, U.S. Army Pulse Power Ctr., Ft. Monmouth, 1982—, SRI, Internat., Menlo Park, Calif., 1983-91, Vitronics, Inc., Eatontown, N.J., 1987-96, Berkeley Rsch. Assocs., Springfield, Va., 1996—; adj. prof. Southwestern Ctr. for Elec. Engrng. Edn., St. Cloud, Fla., 1980-86; cons. Los Alamos (N.Mex.) Nat. Lab., 1980-81; mem. USN Pulsed Power Tech. Adv. Group, Washington, 1978-80, SDIO Pulsed Power Tech. Adv. Group, 1983-93; assoc. mem. Adv. Group on Electronic Devices, Dept. Def., Washington, 1970-80. Contbr. articles to profl. jours.; holder 14 patents. With U.S. Army, 1943-46, ETO. Recipient Spl. Act award Sec. Army, 1963, U.S. Army R&D Achievement award Dept. Army, 1963, 78, Army Sci. award, 1978. Fellow IEEE (life; chmn./editor symposium proc. 1957-80, chmn. emeritus power modulator symposium 1981—, co-chmn. high voltage workshop 1989-90, exec. com. 1991—, High Voltage award 1991, Germeshausen award 1992); mem. Am. Phys. Soc. (exec. com. gaseous electronics conf. 1961-66, sec. 1964, exec. com. electron and atomic physics divsn. 1965-66). Home: 100 Arrowwood Ct Red Bank NJ 07701-6717

SCHNEIDER, STEPHEN HENRY, climatologist, environmental policy analyst, researcher; b. N.Y.C., Feb. 11, 1945; s. Samuel and Doris C. (Swarte) S.; married, 1995; 2 children from previous marriage. BS, Columbia U., 1966, MS, 1967, PhD in Mechanical Engring., 1971; DSc (hon.), N.J. Inst. Tech., 1990, Monmouth Coll., 1991. NAS, NRC postdoctoral research assoc. Goddard Inst. Space Studies NASA, N.Y.C., 1971-72; fellow advanced study program Nat. Ctr. Atmospheric Research, Boulder, Colo., 1972-73, scientist, dep. head climate project, 1973-78, acting leader climate sensitivity group, 1978-80, head visitors program and dep. dir. advanced study program, 1980-87; sr. scientist Nat. Ctr. Atmospheric Research, Boulder, 1980-96; head interdisciplinary climate systems sect. Nat. Ctr. Atmospheric Research, Boulder, Colo., 1987-92; prof. dept. biol. scis. and sr. fellow Inst. Internat. Study Stanford (Calif.) U., 1992—; affil. prof. U. Corp. Atmospheric Rsch. Lamont-Doherty Geol. Obs., Columbia, U., 1976-83; mem. Carter-Mondale Sci. Policy Task Force, 1976; sci. adviser Clinton-Gore, 1992; sci. adviser, interviewee Nova, Sta. WGBH-TV, Planet Earth, Sta. WQED-TV; mem. internat. sci. coms. climatic change, ecology, energy, environ. edn., food and pub. policy; expert witness congl. coms.; mem. Def. Sci. Bd. Task Force on Atmospheric Obscuration; lead author Intergovtl. Panel on Climate Change, Working Group I, 1994-95. Author: (with Lynne E. Mesirow) The Genesis Strategy: Climate and Global Survival, 1976, (with Lynne Morton) The Primordial Bond: Exploring Connections Between Man and Nature Through Humanities and Science, 1981, (with Randi S. Londer) The Co-evolution of Climate and Life, 1984, Global Warming: Are We Entering the Greenhouse Century?, 1989, (with W. Bach) Interactions of Food and Climate, 1981, (with R.S. Chen and E. Boulding) Social Science Research and Climate Change: An Interdisciplinary Appraisal, 1983, (with K.C. Land) Forecasting in the Social and Natural Sciences, 1987; (with P. Baston) Scientists on Gaia, 1990; editor-in-chief: The Ency. of Weather and Climate, 1996, Laboratory Earth, 1996; editor: Climatic Change, 1976—; contbr. sci. and popular articles on theory of climate, influence of climate on world, relation of dvelopment change to world food, population, energy and environ. policy issues, environ. aftereffects of nuclear war, carbon dioxiede greenhouse effect, pub. understanding sci., environ. edn. Recipient Louis J. Battan Author's award Am. Meteorol. Soc., 1990; named one of 100 Outstanding Young Scientists in Am. by Sci. Digest, 1984; MacArthur Found. Prize fellow John D. and Catherine T. MacArthur Found., 1992. Fellow AAAS (Westinghouse award 1991), Scientists Inst. for Pub. Info.; mem. U.S. Assn. Club Rome, Am. Meteorological Soc., Am. Geophysical Union, Nat. Fedn. Am. Scientists. Office: Stanford U Dept Biological Scis Stanford CA 94305-5020

SCHNEIDER, THOMAS AQUINAS, surgeon, educator; b. St. Charles, Mo., Dec. 22, 1934; s. Vincent Augustine and Anna Maria (Marheineke) S.; m. Joyce Elaine Diehr, June 7, 1958; children: Lisa, Thomas, Dawn, Tracy. BS, Loras Coll., 1954; MD, St. Louis U., 1958. Diplomate Am. Bd. Surgery. Resident surgery St. Louis City Hosp., 1958-63; pvt. practice St. Charles, 1963—; clin. instr., St. Louis U., 1966-91, asst. clin. prof. 1991—; med. dir. vascular lab. St. Joseph Health Ctr., St. Charles, 1991—, dir. trauma svc. 1981-91. Fellow ACS; mem. Mo. Com. on Trauma, St. Louis Surg. Soc. (councilor 1988-91, v.p. 1996—), St. Louis Vascular Soc. (pres. 1993-95), Hodgen Club (pres. 1988), Alpha Omega Alpha. Roman Catholic. Avocations: golf, music, history. Office: 2850 W Clay St Saint Charles MO 63301-2536

SCHNEIDER, THOMAS PATRICK, financial planner; b. St. Louis, July 14, 1948; s. Maurice Jacob and Josephine C. (Flynn) S.; m. Rachel Marie Samel, June 27, 1969; children: Jacob, Zachary, Marc, Claire, Julie, Paul. BS in Civil Engring., U. Mo., Rolla, 1975. Cert. fin. planner. City engr. Florissant, Mo., 1975-78; mfg. rep. Sprayial Sys., St. Louis, 1978-81; fin. planner First Fin. Group, Clayton, Mo., 1982-86, Wamhoff Fin. Planning Co., Florissant, 1987—. Coun. rep. City of Florissant, Mo., 1979—. Petty officer 2nd class USN, 1967-72, Viet Nam; lt. (j.g.) USNR, 1976-79. Mem. Internat. Assn. Fin. Planners, NALU, Inst. CFP, Florissant C. of C., Rotary Internat. (sgt.-at-arms 1992), VFW, Optimist Internat. Roman Catholic. Avocations: tournament golf, soccer, history, family activities. Office: Wamhoff Fin Planning Co 3224 N Us Highway 67 Florissant MO 63033-1646

SCHNEIDER, THOMAS RICHARD, hospital administrator; b. Cin., July 16, 1944; s. Richard Arthur and Janet (Tingley) S.; m. Judith Ann Johnson, June 10, 1967; children: Gregory Thomas, Marcia Kay, Jill Elise. BS in Bus. Adminstrn., Miami U., Oxford, Ohio, 1966; MHA, U. Minn., 1968. Asst. adminstr. Meml. Hosp. of South Bend, Ind., 1971-77, Ft. Hamilton-Hughes Meml. Hosp., Hamilton, Ohio, 1977-82; assoc. adminstr. Ft. Hamilton-Hughes Meml. Hosp., 5, Ohio, 1982-84, assoc. adminstr., chief oper. officer, 1984-85, v.p. ops. and profl. svcs., 1985-91; adminstr. Shriners Hosp. for Crippled Children, Shreveport, La., 1992—; chmn. health careers Greater Cin. Hosp. Coun., 1983-90; mem. adv. bd. Xavier U. Ctr. for Health Mgmt. Edn., Cin., 1985-91; trustee Cmty. Blood Ctr., Dayton, Ohio, 1985-91. Trustee, 1st v.p. YMCA of Hamilton-Fairfield, 1990; chmn. city charter comms. com. City of Hamilton, 1990; chmn. pub. svc. div. United Way of Hamilton-Fairfield, 1988-90. Mem. Med. Svc. Corps. USN, 1968-71. Recipient disting. svc. award YMCA, 1982, great American family award of honor, 1990, proclamation Mayor and City Coun. of Hamilton, 1992. Fellow Am. Coll. Healthcare Execs.; mem. Rotary Internat., Masons, Shriner. Republican. Methodist. Avocations: fishing, golf, boating, reading, clowning. Home: 535 Northpark Dr Bossier City LA 71111 Office: Shriners Hosp 3100 Samford Ave Shreveport LA 71103-4239

SCHNEIDER, VALERIE LOIS, speech educator; b. Chgo., Feb. 12, 1941; d. Ralph Joseph and Gertrude Blanche (Gaffron) S. BA, Carroll Coll., 1963; MA, U. Wis., 1966; PhD, U. Fla., 1969; cert. advanced study Appalachian State U., 1981. Tchr. English and history Montello High Sch. (Wis.), 1963-64; dir. forensics and drama Montello High Sch., 1963-64; instr. speech U. Fla., Gainesville, 1966-68, asst. prof. speech, 1969-70; asst. prof. speech Edinboro (Pa.) State Coll., 1970-71; assoc. prof. speech East Tenn. State U., Johnson City, 1971-76, prof. speech, 1976—; instr. newspaper course Johnson City Press Chronicle, 1979, Elizabethton Star, Erwin Record, Mountain City Tomahawk, Jonesboro Herald and Tribune, 1980; mem. investor panel USA Today, 1991-92. Editor East Tenn. State U. evening and off-campus newsletter, 1984-91; assoc. editor: Homiletic, 1974-76; columnist Video Visions, Kingsport Times-News (Tenn.), 1984-86; book reviewer Pulpit Digest, 1986-90; contbr. articles on speech to profl. jours. Chmn. AAUW Mass Media Study Group Com., Johnson City, 1973-74. Recipient Creative Writing award Va. Highlands Arts Festival, 1973; award Kingsport (Tenn.) Times News, 1984, 85, Tri-Cities Met. Advt. Fedn., 1983, 84; Danforth assoc., 1977; finalist Money mag. contest 'Best Personal Fin. Mgrs.', 1994. Mem. Speech Communication Assn. (Tenn. rep. to states adv. council 1974-75), So., Tenn. (exec. bd. 1974-77, publs. bd. 1974-78, pres. 1977-78), Religious Speech Communication Assn. (Best article award 1976), Tenn. Basic Skills Council (exec. bd. 1979-80, v.p. 1980-81, pres. 1981-82), AAUW (v.p. chpt. 1974-75, pres. 1975-76, corp. rep. for East Tenn. State U. 1974-76), Am. Assn. Continuing Higher Edn., Bus. and Profl. Women's Club (chpt. exec. bd. 1972-73, v.p. 1976-77), Mensa, Delta Sigma Rho-Tau Kappa Alpha, Phi Delta Kappa, Delta Kappa Gamma, Pi Gamma Mu. Presbyterian. Home: 3201 Buckingham Rd Johnson City TN 37604-2715 Office: East Tenn State U PO Box 23098 Johnson City TN 37614-0124

SCHNEIDER, WILLIAM CHARLES, aerospace consultant; b. N.Y.C., Dec. 24, 1923; s. Charles J. and Margaret (Stoeffler) S.; m. Roseann Vasco, Oct. 6, 1964; children: Catherine M., Jeanne M., Robert J., Robert Sherer. BS, MIT, 1949; MS, U. Va., 1952; D in Engring., Cath. U. Am., 1976. Rsch. scientist NACA Langley Rsch. Ctr., Hampton, Va., 1949-55; asst. br. head Air-to-Air Missiles Bur. Aeros., Washington, 1955-60; dir. space vehicles USN Bur. Weapons, Washington, 1960-61; dir. space systems Internat. Tel. & Tel., Nutley, N.J., 1961-63; dep. dir. Gemini program Office Manned Space Flight NASA Hdqrs., Washington, 1963-65; dir., dep. dir. operations, mission dir. Office Manned Space Flight NASA Hdqrs. (Gemini program), 1965-66; dir. Apollo Applications Missions, 1966-67, Apollo Mission dir., 1967-68, dir. Skylab program, 1968-74, dep. assoc. adminstr. for space transp. systems, 1974-78, assoc. adminstr. for space tracking and data systems, 1979-80; v.p. mgmt. and product assurance Systems Group Computer Scis. Corp., Falls Church, Va., 1980-83; v.p. control systems Computer Scis. Corp., Falls Church, 1983-85, v.p. devel., 1985-90; cons., 1990—; mem. life scis. strategic planning bd. NASA, life scis. div. working group, aerospace medicine adv. com. NASA, mem. space sta. adv. com.; mem. adv. space tech. com. NRC; bd. dirs. Spacetech Inc. Mem. bd. visitors Cath. U. Served with USNR, 1942-46. Recipient Exceptional Service medal NASA, 1965, Distinguished Service medal, 1968-73, Outstanding Leadership medal, 1980; Apollo Group Achievement award, 1969; Astronautics Engr. award, 1974; Robert J. Collier trophy, 1974; Am. Astronautical Soc. Space Flight award, 1974. Fellow AIAA, Internat. Acad. Astronautics, Planetary Soc., Am. Astron. Soc. (v.p.); mem. VFW, Armed Forces Comm. and Electronics Assn., Energy Mgmt. and Control Soc., NASA Alumni League (treas.), Brit. Interplanetary Soc. Home and Office: 11801 Clintwood Pl Silver Spring MD 20902-1707

SCHNEIDER, WILLIAM GEORGE, former life insurance company executive; b. Shenandoah, Iowa, Jan. 18, 1919; s. Fred M. and Abba F. (Ferguson) S.; m. Phyllis Welch, Mar. 28, 1943; children—Stephen F., Richard W. B.A., State U. Iowa, 1940; postgrad., N.Y. U. With Met. Life Ins. Co., 1940-41, 45-46; with Bankers Life Co. (now named Prin. Fin. Group), Des Moines, 1946-84; sr. v.p. Bankers Life Co., 1970-82, exec. v.p., 1982-84, ret., 1984. Served with AUS, 1941-45. Fellow Soc. Actuaries; mem. Am. Acad. Actuaries, Phi Beta Kappa. Republican. Clubs: Des Moines, Des Moines Golf and Country. Home: 3662 Ingersoll Ave Apt 414 Des Moines IA 50312-3422

SCHNEIDER, WILLIAM GEORGE, chemist, research consultant; b. Wolseley, Sask., Can., June 1, 1915; s. Michael and Phillipina (Krauschaar) S.; m. Jean Purves, Sept. 2, 1940; children: Judith Schneider Saunders, Joanne Schneider Spurrier. B.Sc., U. Sask., 1937, M.Sc., 1939, D.Sc., 1969; Ph.D., McGill U., 1941, D.Sc., 1970; D.Sc. (hon.), York U., 1966, Meml. U., 1968, McMaster U., 1969, Laval U., 1969, Moncton U., 1969, U. N.B., 1970, U. Montreal, 1970, Acadia U., 1976, U. Regina, 1976, Ottawa U., 1978; LL.D., U. Alta., 1968, Laurentian U., 1968. Head phys. chemistry sect., div. chemistry NRC Can., Ottawa, Ont., 1946-63; dir. div. pure chemistry NRC Can., 1963-65, v.p., 1965-67, pres., 1967-80; research cons., 1980—. Author: (with J.A. Pople, H.J. Bernstein) High Resolution Nuclear Magnetic Resonance, 1959; contbr. articles to profl. jours. Decorated Order of Can., 1977. Fellow Royal Soc. Can. (Henry Marshall Tory medal), Royal Soc. London, Chem. Inst. Can. (medal 1969, Montreal medal 1973); mem. Internat. Union Pure and Applied Chemistry (pres. 1983-85). Office: Unit # 2, 65 Whitemarl Dr, Ottawa, ON Canada K1L 8J9

SCHNEIDER, WILLYS HOPE, lawyer; b. N.Y.C., Sept. 27, 1952; d. Leon and Lillian (Friedman) S.; m. Stephen Andrew Kals, Jan. 21, 1979; children: Peter, Josefine. AB, Princeton U., 1974; JD, Columbia U., 1977. Bar: N.Y. 1978, U.S. Dist. Ct. (ea. and so. dists.) N.Y. 1978, U.S. Tax Ct. 1979. Law clk. to hon. Jack B. Weinstein U.S. Dist. Ct. (ea. dist.) N.Y., Bklyn., 1977-78; assoc. Paul, Weiss, Rifkind, Wharton & Garrison, N.Y.C., 1978-83; ptnr. Kaye, Scholer, Fierman, Hays & Handler, N.Y.C., 1983—. Contbr. articles to profl. jours. Mem. ABA, N.Y. State Bar Assn., Assn. of Bar of City of N.Y. Home: 320 W End Ave New York NY 10023-8110 Office: Kaye Scholer Fierman Hays & Handler 425 Park Ave New York NY 10022-3506

SCHNEIDER, WOLF, magazine editor, writer; b. N.Y.C., Mar. 5, 1953; d. Mortimer Stanley and Helene Carol (Werner) S. BA, CCNY, 1975; MA, U. So. Calif., 1976. Disc jockey Sta. KNCN-FM, Corpus Christi, Tex., 1977-78; producer Sta. KMET-FM, L.A., 1980-85; editor Videopreview mag., L.A., 1986; film reporter The Hollywood Reporter, L.A., 1987-88; dir. pub. rels. Showtime Networks, L.A., 1989-90; editor Am. Film Mag., L.A., 1990-92; film columnist L.A. Weekly, 1995—; panel moderator NCTA Conv., 1985, panel moderator Billboard Am. Film Inst. Video Conf., L.A., 1987; guest lectr. Assn. of Film Commrs. Cineposium, L.A.1988; awards judge Nat. Cable Forum Ace awards, L.A., 1986, 88; course instr. Am. Film Inst., L.A., 1991, 92. Contbr. articles to profl. jours., popular mags. Mem. publicity com. IFP West, L.A., 1989-90. Mem. PEN/West, 1990—, AFI, 1989—. Avocation: horseback riding. Office: LA Weekly 6715 W Sunset Blvd Los Angeles CA 90028-7107

SCHNEIDERMAN, DAVID ABBOTT, publisher, journalist; b. N.Y.C., Apr. 14, 1947; s. Robert D. and Mary (Torres) S.; m. Peggy Rosenthal, Sept. 19, 1981. BA, Johns Hopkins U., 1969, MA, 1970. Asst. to the editor oped page N.Y. Times, 1970-74, dep. editor, 1974-78; editor in chief Village Voice, N.Y.C., 1979-87, pub., 1985-88, 91—, pres., 1985—; publ. 7 Days, N.Y.C., 1988-90; pres. Stern Pub., 1995—; chmn. L.A. (Calif.) Weekly Inc., 1995—; mem. libr. coun. Johns Hopkins U. Office: Village Voice 36 Cooper Sq New York NY 10003-7118 also: LA Weekly 6715 Sunset Blvd Los Angeles CA 90028-7107

SCHNEIDERMAN, IRWIN, lawyer; b. N.Y.C., May 28, 1923; s. Meyer and Bessie (Klein) S.; m. Roberta Haig, Nov. 28, 1966; 1 child, Eric T. BA, Bklyn. Coll., 1943; LLB cum laude, Harvard U., 1948. Bar: N.Y. 1949, D.C. 1952. Assoc. Cahill Gordon & Reindel, N.Y.C., 1948-59, ptnr., 1959-89, sr. counsel, 1990—; spl. cons. to chmn. SEC, 1981-82, mem. adv. com. on tender offers, 1983. Trustee Bklyn. Coll. Found., 1983—; co-chmn. N.Y.C. Opera, 1993—; bd. dirs. WNYC Found., 1989—, City Ctr. Music and Drama, Inc., 1990—, N.Y.C. NARAL, 1990—, Lincoln Ctr. for

Performing Arts, Inc., 1994—. Lt. (j.g.) USNR, 1943-46. Mem. Harvard Club. Home: 203 E 72nd St New York NY 10021-4568 Office: Cahill Gordon & Reindel 80 Pine St New York NY 10005-1702

SCHNEIER, HARVEY ALLEN, physician, pharmaceutical researcher; b. Rochester, N.Y., Jan. 5, 1942; s. Jacob G. and Rose (Ergort) S.; m. Lynn C. Teitelbaum, Aug. 9, 1964 (div. Dec. 1981); m. Barrie Mandel; children: Matthew, Margo, Jonathan. AB, Columbia U., 1963, MD, 1967. Diplomate Am. Bd. Internal Medicine. Asst. chief gen. med. svc. Walter Reed Army Med. Ctr., Washington, 1971-72; assoc. in medicine Columbia-Presbyn. Med. Ctr., N.Y.C., 1973-75, asst. attending physician, 1975-89, assoc. attending physician, 1989—; assoc. med. dir. Forest Labs., Inc., N.Y.C., 1993—; asst. prof. clin. medicine Columbia P&S, 1975-89, assoc. clin. prof., 1989—; corp. med. cons. United Brands Co., N.Y.C., 1980-92; cons. Am. Bd. Internal Medicine, Phila., 1991—; assoc. med. dir. Forest Labs., Inc., 1993—. Served to maj. M.C. U.S. Army, 1969-73. Decorated Meritorious Svc. medal. Mem. ACP, AMA, Alpha Omega Alpha. Avocations: theater, folk art collecting. Home: 25 Harrison St New York NY 10013-2705 Office: Forest Labs Inc 909 3rd Ave New York NY 10022-4731

SCHNEITER, GEORGE, government executive; b. Louisville, Oct. 30, 1937. BSME, Purdue U., 1959, MSME, 196, PhD in Mech. Engring., 1966. Rsch. asst., instr. rocket propulsion Purdue U., 1960-65; dir. Advanced Ballistic Reentry Sys. program Aerospace Corp., 1965-73; dep. dir. Dept. of Def. SALT Task Force Office of Sec. of Def., 1973-81, sr. advisor to Sec. of Def.'s Rep. to SALT del., 1973-81; team leader for study on Advanced Tactical Aircraft Ctr. for Naval Analyses, 1981-86; dir. strategic aeronautical and theater nuclear sys. Office of Dir. Def. Rsch. & Engring., Office of Sec. of Def., 1986-88; dir. strategic and space sys. Office of Under Sec. of Def., Office of Sec. of Def., 1988-94, dir. strategic and tactical sys., 1994—. Recipient Meritorious Exec. Presdl. award, 1980, 89. Mem. AIAA. Office: Dept of Defense Strategic & Theater Nuclear Forces The Pentagon Washington DC 20301

SCHNELL, CARLTON BRYCE, lawyer; b. Youngstown, Ohio, Jan. 1, 1932; s. Carlton Wilhelm and Helen Jean (Alexander) S.; m. Dorothy Stewart Apple, Aug. 15, 1953; children—Laura, Margaret, Heidi. B.A., Yale U., 1953, LL.B., 1956. Bar: Ohio 1956. Assoc. Arter & Hadden, Cleve., 1956-65, ptnr., 1966—, mng. ptnr., 1977-82; mng. ptnr. Arter & Hadden, Washington, 1982-84. Exec. comm. mem. Greater Cleve. Growth Assn., Cleve., 1983—; chmn. Build Up Cleve., 1981-89; profl. chmn. United Way, Cleve., 1983; co-chmn. Charter Rev. Commn., Cleve., 1983-84; pres. Citizen's League Rsch. Inst., 1992-95. Named Vol. of Yr., Leadership Cleve., 1985. Mem. Tex. Club Cleve. (pres. 1972-73), Cleve. Tax Inst. (chmn. 1978), Ohio C. of C. (trustee 1977-80). Republican. Presbyterian. Clubs: Union, Pepper Pike. Avocations: golf; tennis. Home: 31450 Shaker Blvd Cleveland OH 44124-5153 Office: Arter & Hadden 1100 Huntington Blvd Cleveland OH 44115

SCHNELL, GEORGE ADAM, geographer, educator; b. Phila., July 13, 1931; s. Earl Blackwood and Emily (Bernheimer) S.; m. Mary Lou Williams, June 21, 1958; children: David Adam, Douglas Powell, Thomas Earl. BS, West Chester U., 1958; MS, Pa. State U., 1960, PhD, 1965; postdoctoral study, Ohio State U., 1965. Asst. prof. Coll. SUNY, New Paltz, 1962-65, assoc. prof., 1965-68, prof. geography, 1968—, founding chmn. dept., 1968-94; vis. assoc. prof. U. Hawaii, summer, 1966; cons. cmty. action programming, 1965; manuscript reader, cons. to several pubs., 1967—; founder, founding bd. dirs. Inst. for Devel., Planning and Land Use Studies, 1986—; cons. Mid-Hudson Pattern for Progress, 1986, Open Space Inst., 1987, Mid-Hudson Regional Econ. Devel. Coun., 1989, Urban Devel. Corp., 1989-90, 93, Tech. Devel. Ctr., 1991, Catskill Ctr., 1991, Ednl. Testing Svc., 1993; consulting editor Exams Unltd., Albany, N.Y., 1995—; mem. exec. bd. dirs. Hudson Valley Study Ctr.; cons. depts. of geography, 1988—. Author: (with others) The Local Community: A Handbook for Teachers, 1971, The World's Population, Problems of Growth, 1972, Pennsylvania Coal: Resources, Technology, Utilization, 1983, West Virginia and Appalachia: Selected Readings, 1977, Hazardous and Toxic Wastes: Technology, Management and Health Effects, 1984, Environmental Radon: Occurrence, Control and Health Hazards, 1990, Natural and Technological Disasters: Causes, Effects and Preventive Measures, 1992, Conservation and Resource Management, 1993; co-author: (with M.S. Monmonier) The Study of Population: Elements, Patterns, Processes, 1983, Map Appreciation, 1988, Medicine and Health Care into the 21st Century, 1995; editor: (with G.J. Demko and H.M. Rose) Population Geography: A Reader, 1970; contbr. articles to profl. jours.; presenter papers to more than 60 ann. meetings of scholarly and profl. socs. Appt. mem. local bds. and coms. Town and Village of New Paltz, and New Paltz Ctrl. Sch. Dist., 1965—; elder Reformed Ch. of New Paltz. With AUS, 1952-54. Recipient Excellence award N.Y. State/United Univ. Professions, 1990; Disting. Alumnus award West Chester U., 1994. Mem. Assn. Am. Geographers, Pa. Geog. Soc. (mem. editl. bd. Pa. Geographer, Disting. Geographer award 1994), Pa. Acad. Sci. (assoc. editor jour. 1988—). Home: 29 River Park Dr New Paltz NY 12561-2636 Office: SUNY at New Paltz Dept Geography 75 S Manheim Blvd New Paltz NY 12561-2499

SCHNELL, JOSEPH, dancer; b. Marin County, Calif.. Student, Sch. Am. Ballet, 1983; scholarship student, The Joffrey Ballet Sch., 1984-85. Dancer Joffrey II Dancers, N.Y.C., 1984, The Joffrey Ballet, N.Y.C., 1987—. Office: The Joffrey Ballet 130 W 56th St New York NY 10019-3818

SCHNELL, ROBERT LEE, JR., lawyer; b. Mpls., Sept. 20, 1948; s. Robert Lee and Dorothy Mae (Buran) S.; m. Jacqueline Irene Husak, Dec. 19, 1969 (div. Aug. 1988); children: Robert Lee III, Elizabeth Anne, Jennifer Irene; m. Julie Ann Bemlott, Sept. 29, 1989; children: Helen Bridget, Michael Henry. BA cum laude, Princeton U., 1970; JD magna cum laude, Harvard U., 1974. Bar: Minn. 1974, U.S. Dist. Ct. Minn. 1974, U.S. Ct. Appeals (8th cir.) 1975, U.S. Supreme Ct. 1990. Assoc. Faegre & Benson, Mpls., 1974-81, ptnr., 1982—. Bd. dirs. United Way of Mpls., 1992-93. Office: Faegre & Benson 2200 Norwest Ctr 90 S 7th St Minneapolis MN 55402-3903

SCHNELL, ROGER THOMAS, retired military officer, state official; b. Wabasha, Minn., Dec. 11, 1936; s. Donald William and Eva Louise (Barton) S.; m. Barbara Ann McDonald, Dec. 18, 1959 (div. Mar. 1968); children: Thomas Allen, Scott Douglas. A in Mil. Sci., Command and Gen. Staff Coll., 1975; A in Bus. Administn., Wayland Bapt. U., 1987. Commd. 2d lt. Alaska N.G., 1959, advanced through grades to col., 1975; shop supt. Alaska N.G., Anchorage, 1965-71, personnel mgr., 1972-74, chief of staff, 1974-87, dir. logistics, 1987; electrician Alaska R.R., Anchorage, 1955-61, elec. foreman, 1962-64; dir. support personnel mgmt. Joint Staff Alaska N.G., 1988-92, ret.; personnel mgr. State of Alaska, 1992; asst. commr. dept. mil. and vets. affairs State of Alaska, Ft. Richardson, 1992-95, dep. commr. dept. mil. and vets. affairs, 1995—. Bd. dirs. Meth. Trust Fund. Mem. Fed. Profl. Labor Relations Execs. (sec. 1974-75), Alaska N.G. Officers Assn. (pres. 1976-78, bd. dirs. 1988—), Am. Legion, Amvets. Republican. Methodist. Lodge: Elks. Avocations: traveling, photography. Home: 6911 Hunt Ave Anchorage AK 99504-1891 Office: Dept Mil and Vets Affairs State of Alaska PO Box 5800 Camp Denali Bldg # 4900 Anchorage AK 99505-5800 *Personal philosophy: Success is built on honesty, hard work, determination, committment and the ability to make personal sacrifices to strive for high professional goals. Always keep a positive attitude and treat each person as you would like to be treated.*

SCHNELLE, KARL BENJAMIN, JR., chemical engineering educator, consultant, researcher; b. Canton, Ohio, Dec. 8, 1930; s. Karl Benjamin and Kathryn Emily (Hollingsworth) S.; m. Mary Margaret Dabney, Sept. 8, 1954; children: Karl Dabney, Kathryn Chappell. BS, Carnegie Mellon U., 1952, MS, 1957, PhD, 1959. Registered profl. engr., Tenn. Chem. engr., shift foreman Organics area Pitts. Plate Glass Co., New Martinsville, W.Va., 1952-54; asst. prof. chem. engring. Vanderbilt U., 1958-61, assoc. prof., 1961-64, assoc. prof. environ. and air resources engring., 1967-70, prof., 1970-80, chmn. div. socio-technol. systems, 1972-75, chmn. environ. and water resources engring., 1975-76, chmn. environ. engring. and policy mgmt. dept., 1976-80, chmn. chem. engring. dept., 1980-88, prof. chem. and environ. engring., 1980—; Alexander Heard disting. svc. prof., 1995-96; v.p. ECCE, Nashville, 1983-88, pres., 1989—; mem. Air Pollution Control Bd., State Tenn., 1978-82, 82-87; Fulbright prof. U. Liege, Belgium, 1977; invited prof. Universite Catholique de Louvain, Belgium, 1982; vis. prof. chem. engring. Danish Tech. Inst., Lyngby, Denmark, 1988-89. Fellow AICE; mem. Air and Waste Mgmt. Assn., Instrument Soc. Am., Am. Soc. Engring. Edn., Am. Soc. Environ. Engrs., Sigma Xi, Phi Kappa Phi, Tau Beta Pi. Office: Vanderbilt U PO Box 1683 Station B Nashville TN 37235

SCHNELLER, JOHN, IV, lawyer; b. Metairie, La., June 26, 1966; s. John III and Sylvia Marie (Johns) S.; m. Patricia Lee Richard, Sept. 30, 1995. BS in Econs., U. Pa., 1988; JD, U. Ill., 1991; LLM in Taxation, NYU, 1992. Bar: La. 1992, Tex. 1993, U.S. Tax Ct. 1993. Assoc. Guarisco, Weiler & Cordes, New Orleans, 1992-93, Schlanger, Mills, Mayer & Grossberg, LLP, Houston, 1993-95, Chamberlian, Hrdlicka, White, Williams & Martin, 1995—. Mem. ABA, Tex. Bar Assn., La. State Bar Assn., Houston Bar Assn., Houston Young Lawyers Assn. Avocations: golf, fishing, reading, computers, travel. Office: Chamberlain Hrdlicka et al 1200 Smith St Ste 1400 Houston TX 77002

SCHNEPF, CARRIE BIGGS, sales and marketing professional; b. Mesa, Ariz., Sept. 3, 1960; d. Robert Darrel and Carolyn Sarah (Cox) Biggs; m. Mark Edward Schnepf, Apr. 13, 1991. Degree in Comm., Brigham Young U., 1979-85. Anchor Sta. KIVI-TV, Boise, Idaho, 1985-87; reporter, anchor Sta. KPHO-TV, Phoenix, 1987-89; sales and mktg. profl. Ariz. Escrowq & Title, Phoenix, 1989-91; mktg. dir. country store, festival site, tours Schnepf Farms, Queen Creek, AZ, 1995—; comml. spokesperson Robert Black Agy., Phoenix, 1989—; with promotions dept. Country Thunder USA, Queen Creek, 1993—; pres. The Regal Group, Phoenix, 1992—. Chmn. spl. event Ariz. Spl. Olympics, Phoenix, 1991—; bd. dirs. Am. Heart Assn., Phoenix, 1993—, chmn. spl. event, 1993—; mem. fundraising com. PreHab of Ariz., Mesa, 1991—; founding mem., chmn. Project B.E.S.T., Queen Creek. Recipient chmn.'s award Ariz. Spl. Olympics, 1993. Mem. Desert Club (publicity com. 1992—). Republican. Avocations: musical theatre, piano playing, travel, all outdoor sports, cooking. Home and Office: 22601 E Cloud Rd Queen Creek AZ 85242-9556

SCHNEPS, JACK, physics educator; b. N.Y.C., Aug. 18, 1929; s. Elias and Rose (Rephen) S.; m. Lucia DeMarchi, Mar. 11, 1960; children: Loredana, Melissa, Leila. B.A., N.Y. U., 1951; M.S., U. Wis., 1953, Ph.D., 1956. Asst. prof. physics Tufts U., 1956-60, asso. prof., 1960-63, prof., 1963—, chmn. dept. physics, 1980-89, Vannevar Bush chair, 1995—; vis. scientist European Orgn. Nuclear Research, Geneva, Switzerland, 1965-66; lectr. Internat. Sch. Elementary Particle Physics, Yugoslavia, 1968; vis. research fellow Univ. Coll., London, Eng., 1973-74; vis. prof. Ecole Polytechnique, Palaiseau, France, 1982-83, The Technion, Haifa, Israel, 1989-90. Contbg. author: Methods in Subnuclear Physics, Vol. IV, 1970; editor Proc. of Neutrino 88, 1989; contbr. articles to profl. jours. NSF postdoctoral fellow U. Padua, Italy, 1958-59. Fellow Am. Phys. Soc.; mem. European Phys. Soc., AAUP, Phi Beta Kappa, Sigma Xi. Home: 3 Foxcroft Rd Winchester MA 01890-2407 Office: Dept Physics Tufts U Medford MA 02155

SCHNERING, PHILIP BLESSED, investment banker; b. Detroit, Dec. 26, 1917; s. Otto Young and Dorothy (Russell) S.; m. Ruth Scott, June 10, 1940; children: Sally, Sandra, Philip S., Judith, Wendy. BA, U. Chgo., 1939. Salesman, retail crew worker, factory trainee Curtiss Candy Co., Chgo., 1938-40, salesman supr., 1940, dist. field mgr., 1941-43, asst. to pres., 1943-48, v.p., div. sales mgr., 1948-53, exec. v.p., 1953-58; dir. comml. devel. McCormick & Co., Inc., Balt., 1958-64; exec. v.p. Farboil Co., Balt., 1965-66; pres. Bowen Co., Balt., 1966-72; investment banker, 1973—; chmn. bd. Curtiss Breeding Svc., Cary, Ill. Vice pres. Balt. Boy Scouts Am.; past pres., dir. Balt. coun. Camp Fire Girls; chmn. nat. bd., dir. fin. com. Nat. Camp Fire Girls; trustee Nat. Coun. Crime and Delinquency; chmn. Md. Commn. Crime and Delinquency; assoc. trustee Northwestern U. Mem. Am. Mgmt. Assn., Soc. Am. Archaeology, Antique Auto Club, Balt. Yacht Club, Green Spring Valley Hunt Club. Home: 13801 York Rd N-10 Cockeysville MD 21030

SCHNITZER, ARLENE DIRECTOR, art dealer; b. Salem, Oreg., Jan. 10, 1929; d. Simon M. and Helen (Holtzman) Director; m. Harold J. Schnitzer, Sept. 11, 1949; 1 child, Jordan. Student U. Wash., 1947-48; BFA (hon.) Pacific NW Coll. Art., 1988. Founder, pres. Fountain Gallery of Art, Portland, Oreg., 1951-86; exec. v.p. Harsch Investment Corp., 1951—. Apptd. to Oreg. State Bd. Higher Edn., 1987-88; former bd. dirs. Oreg. Symphony Assn., v.p. Oreg. Symphony; former bd. dirs. U.S. Dist. Ct. Hist. Soc.; former bd. dirs. Boys and Girls Club, 1988—; mem. Gov.'s Expo '86 Commn., Oreg.; mem. exec. com., former bd. dirs. Artquake; former mem. adv. bd. Our New Beginnings; past bd. dirs. Artists Initiative for a Contemporary Art Collection; former trustee Reed Coll., 1982-88; mem. exec. com. bd. dirs. N.W. Bus. Com. for Arts.; trustee, mem. exec. com. Oreg. Health Scis. Univ. Found.; mem. arts acquisition and collections com. Portland Art Mus.; mem. Nat. Com. for the Performing Arts, Kennedy Ctr., 1995—, Nat. Coun. of the Fine Arts of San Francisco; adv. bd. Svcs. to Children and Families, Orgn.; bd. trustees Oreg. Jewish Cmty. Found., 1996—; mem. Nat. Coun. Fine Arts Mus. San Francisco, 1995—. Recipient Aubrey Watzek award Lewis and Clark Coll., 1981, Pioneer award U. Oreg., 1985, Met. Arts Commn. award, 1985, White Rose award March of Dimes, 1987, Disting. Svc. award Western Oreg. State Coll. 1988, Oreg. Urban League Equal Opportunity award 1988, Gov's. award for Arts, 1987, Woman of Achievement award YWCA, 1987, Disting. Svc. award U. Oreg., 1991, SAFECO Art Leadership award ArtFair/Seattle, 1994, Portland First Citizen award Portland Met. Assn. Realtors, 1995; honored by Portland Art Assn., 1979. Mem. Univ. Club, Multnomah Athletic Club, Portland Golf Club. Office: Harsch Investment Corp 1121 SW Salmon St Portland OR 97205-2000

SCHNITZER, JAN EUGENIUSZ, medical educator, scientist; b. Pitts., June 24, 1957. BSChemE, Princeton U., 1980, MD, U. Pitts., 1985. Assoc. rsch. scientist Sch. Medicine Yale U., New Haven, Conn., 1985-90; asst. prof. San Diego Sch. Medicine U. Calif., La Jolla, 1990-93; asst. prof. Harvard Med. Sch., Boston, 1994-95, assoc. prof., 1995—. Mem. editl. bd. Am. Jour. Physiology-Heart, 1993—. Recipient Investigator award Am. Heart Assn. and Genentech, 1993—; grantee NIH, 1989—. Office: Harvard Med Sch Beth Israel Hosp Path 330 Brookline Ave Rsch N Boston MA 02215

SCHNITZER, ROBERT C., theater administrator; b. N.Y.C., Sept. 8, 1906; s. Louis and Clara (diBilliani) S.; m. Marcella Abels Cisney, June 7, 1953. Grad., Horace Mann Sch. for Boys, 1923; A.B., Columbia U., 1927. State dir. Del., asst. dep. nat. dir. Fed. Theatre Project, 1936-39; exec. dir. Civic Theatre, Kalamazoo, Mich., 1939-40; faculty Vassar Coll., 1941-42, Smith Coll., 1942-43, Columbia U. Sch. Dramatic Arts, 1948-54; cons. Martha Graham Sch. Dance, Rollins Sch. Theatre, Randall Sch. Theatre, Dramatic Workshop of New Sch., Denver Red Rocks Theatre, Utah Centennial, 1945-49; vets. counselor Nat. Theater Conf., 1945-46; gen. mgr. ANTA Exptl. Theatre, 1946-47, Cheryl Crawford Prodns., 1952-53, Gilbert Miller Prodns., 1953-54, Am. Nat. Theatre and Acad. Internat. Cultural Exch.; profl. agt. for 3500 Am. performers to over 100 fgn. countries Dept. State, 1954-60; gen. mgr. overseas tour Theatre Guild Am. Repertory Co. under auspices of Dept. State, 1960-61; exec. dir. Profl. Theatre Program U. Mich., Ann Arbor, prof. theatre arts, 1961-73, prof. emeritus and exec. dir. emeritus, 1974—; co-founder, exec. dir. Univ. Resident Theatre Assn., 1969-74; cons., 1974—; del. U.S. Nat. Conf. on UNESCO, 1953-57, 1st Inter-Am. Conf. Exch. Persons, 1958; vis. theatre expert German Fgn. Office Cultural Exch. Program, 1965; cons. to pres. U. Bridgeport for Coll. Fine Arts, 1975-87; disting. vis. prof. U. Miami, Fla., 1980, U. Bridgeport, Conn., 1981; co-founder Westport Arts Ctr., 1984, interim pres.,1 985, v.p., 1986, chmn. bd., 1987-89, chmn. emeritus, 1989—; mem. Fulbright selection com. theatre arts, 1955-59, Mich. Coun. Arts, 1961-73; hon. bd. dirs. Westport/Weston Arts Coun., 1969-84. Stage mgr., actor, Theatre Guild, Walter Hampden, Katherine Cornell, other Broadway cos., 1927-36; owner, dir., Robin Hood Summer Theatre, Arden, Del., 1933-40; gen. mgr. U.S. participation, Denmark Hamlet Festival, Elsinore, 1949, 1st Am. Ballet Theatre tour, Europe, 1950, U.S. ofcl. participation, Berlin Festivals, 1951-53, U.S. participation, Congress Cultural Freedom Festival, Paris, 1952, U.S. Salute to France, Paris, 1955; arranged visits to U.S., Greek Nat. Theatre, 1952, Yugoslav Nat. Folk Ballet, 1956, Shanta Rao East Indian Dance Co., 1957; Contbr. articles in field to various publs. Mem. Weston (Conn.) Cultural Events Com., 1995—. Served with ARC, 1943-45, CBI. Recipient Pres.'s Citation U. Mich., 1971, Arts Mgmt. Career award for svcs. to Am. theater, 1971, Sidney Howard award, 1951; Rockefeller Found. grantee, 1948; grad. fellow in theater adminstrn. named in his honor U. Mich., 1974; Robert C. Schnitzer theater memorabilia collection established at George Mason U. Mem. Coll. Fellows of Am. Theatre (life), Actors Equity Assn., Am. Nat. Theatre and Acad., Assn. Theatrical Press Agts. and Mgrs., Nat. Coun. Arts and Govt., Nat. Theatre Conf., Theatre Libr. Assn., U.S Inst. Theatre Technicians, The Players Club, The Century Club. Home: 9 Riverbank Rd Weston CT 06883-2316

SCHNITZLEIN, HAROLD NORMAN, anatomy educator; b. Hannibal, Mo., Aug. 29, 1927; s. Harold Daniel and Martha Anna (Wilhelm) S.; m. Harriett Elizabeth Scheidker, June 2, 1949; children: Jan Elizabeth, Paul Norman, Daniel Richard, Thomas Harry. AB, Westminster Coll., Fulton, Mo., 1950; MS, St. Louis U., 1952, PhD, 1954. USPHS fellow Dept. Anatomy St. Louis U., 1951-54; instr. anatomy U. Ala., Birmingham, 1954-57, asst. prof., 1957-62, assoc. prof., 1962-70, prof., 1970-73; chmn., prof. anatomy U. S. Fla. Coll. Medicine, Tampa, 1973-78, prof., 1978-85, prof. anatomy and radiology, 1985-93, prof. anatomy, radiology, neurology, 1985-93; clin. prof. radiology U Diagnostic Inst., Tampa, 1993-94, prof. emeritus anatomy, 1995—. Coeditor: Correlative Comparative Anatomy Vertebrate Tel., 1982, Imaging Anatomy: Head and Spine, 2d edit., 1990. Sgt. USAAF, 1946-47. Office: U Diagnostic Inst Tampa FL 33612

SCHNOBRICH, ROGER WILLIAM, lawyer; b. New Ulm, Minn., Dec. 21, 1929; s. Arthur George and Amanda (Reinhart) S.; m. Angeline Ann Schmitz, Jan. 21, 1961; children: Julie A. Johnson, Jennifer L. Holmers, Kathryn M. Kubinski, Karen L. Holetz. BBA, U. Minn., 1952, JD, 1954. Bar: Minn. 1954. Assoc. Fredrikson and Byron, Mpls., 1956-58; pvt. practice Mpls., 1958-60; ptnr. Popham Haik, Schnobrich & Kaufman, Mpls., 1960—; bd. dirs. numerous corps., Mpls. With U.S. Army, 1954-56. Mem. ABA, Minn. Bar Assn., Hennepin County Bar Assn., Order of Coif, Law Rev. Roman Catholic. Avocations: family, jogging, reading, golf. Home: 530 Waycliff Dr N Wayzata MN 55391-1385 Office: Popham Haik Schnobrich & Kaufman 3300 Piper Jaffray Tower 22 S 9th St Minneapolis MN 55402-3389

SCHNUCK, CRAIG D., grocery stores company executive; b. 1948. MBA, Cornell U., 1971. With Schnuck Markets, Inc., Hazelwood, Mo., 1971—, v.p., 1975-76, exec. v.p., sec., 1976-83, pres., chief exec. officer, 1983—, also bd. dirs. Office: Schnuck Markets Inc 11420 Lackland Rd Saint Louis MO 63146-6928*

SCHNUCKER, ROBERT VICTOR, history and religion educator; b. Waterloo, Iowa, Sept. 30, 1932; s. Felix Victor and Josephine (Maasdam) S.; m. Anna Mae Engelkes, Sept. 18, 1955; children: Sarai Ann, Sar Victor, Christjahn Dietrich. AB, NE Mo. State U., 1953; BD, U. Dubuque, 1956; MA, U. Iowa, 1960, PhD, 1969. Ordained to ministry Presbyn. Ch., 1956/. Pastor United Presbyn. Ch. USA, Springville, Iowa, 1956-63, Meth.-Presbyn. Ch., Labelle, Mo., 1976—; asst. prof. N.E. Mo. State U., Kirksville, 1963-65, assoc. prof., 1963-65, prof., 1969—; dir. Thomas Jefferson U. Press; supr. Bible exam. Presbyn. Ch. USA, Louisville, 1977-89; bd. dirs. Ctr. for Reformation Rsch., St. Louis, 1984—; pres. Conf. of Hist. Jours., 1993. Author: A Glossary of Terms for Western Civilization, 1975, Helping Humanities Journal Survive, 1985, History Assessment Test, 1990; editor: Calviniana, 1989, Historians of Early Modern Europe, 1976-93, Network News Exch., 1978-88; pres. 1st and 2d Editing History, Conf. for Hist. Jour., 1985—; book rev. editor, mng. editor 16th Century Jour., 1972—; pub. 16th Century Essays and Studies, 1980—; contbr. articles to profl. jours. Fellow Soc. Sci. Study of Religion, 1988; NEH grantee for jour. pubs., 1980. Mem. AAUP, Am. Acad. Religion, Renaissance Soc. Am., Am. History Assn. (chmn. Robinson prize com. 1987), Am. Soc. Ch. History, Soc. History of Edn., Soc. Bibl. Lit., Soc. for Reformation Rsch., Soc. Scholarly Pubs., Soc. for Values in Higher Edn., Conf. for Hist. Jour., Am. Coun. Learned Soc. (exec. bd. conf. adminstr. officers 1993-96, sec. 1994, chmn. 1995-96), Conf. Faith and History, 16th Century Studies Cons. (exec. sec. 1972—).

SCHNUR, ROBERT ARNOLD, lawyer; b. White Plains, N.Y., Oct. 25, 1938; s. Conrad Edward and Ruth (Mehr) S.; children: Daniel, Jonathan. BA, Cornell U., 1960; JD, Harvard U., 1963. Bar: Wis. 1965, Ill. 1966. Assoc. Michael, Best & Friedrich, Milw., 1966-73, ptnr., 1973—; chmn. Wis. Tax News, 1983-90; adj. prof. tax law U. Wis. Law Sch., 1988—. Capt. U.S. Army, 1963-65. Mem. ABA, Wis. Bar Assn. (chmn. tax sect. 1986-88), Milw. Bar Assn. Home: 929 N Astor St Milwaukee WI 53202-3454 Office: Michael Best Friedrich 100 E Wisconsin Ave Milwaukee WI 53202-4107

SCHOBEL, GEORGE, insurance company executive. With Blue Cross Blue Shield of R.I., Providence, 1959—, now sr. v.p. Office: Blue Cross Blue Shield of RI 444 Westminster St Providence RI 02903-3254*

SCHOBER, CHARLES COLEMAN, III, psychiatrist, psychoanalyst; b. Shreveport, La., Nov. 30, 1924; s. Charles Coleman and Mabel Lee (Welsh) S.; B.S., La. State U., 1946, M.D., 1949; m. Martha Elizabeth Welsh, Dec. 27, 1947 (dec.); children—Irene Lee, Ann Welsh; m. 2d, Agerene Maburl Stiles, Feb. 4, 1972; 1 son, Charles Coleman. Intern, Phila. Gen. Hosp., 1949-51; resident in psychiatry Norristown (Pa.) State Hosp., 1953-57; practice medicine specializing in psychiatry and psychoanalysis, Phila., 1957-71; asso. clin. dir. Inst. Pa. Hosp., Phila., 1957-60, clin. dir., 1960-64, attending psychiatrist, 1960-68, sr. attending psychiatrist, 1968-71; mem. faculty Phila. Psychoanalytic Inst., 1966-71; clin. instr. U. Pa. Sch. Medicine, 1957-62, clin. asso., 1962-68, clin. asst. prof., 1968-71; prof., chmn. dept. psychiatry La. State U. Med. Center, Shreveport, 1971-73, chief psychiatry service, 1971-73; chief psychiatry service VA Hosp., Shreveport, 1971-73; faculty New Orleans Psychoanalytic Inst., 1972-73; mem. faculty St. Louis Psychoanalytic Inst., 1973-78; clin. prof. psychiatry St. Louis U. Med. Sch., 1973-78; clin. prof. psychiatry St. Louis U. Med. Sch., 1973-78; active med. staff psychiatry St. Louis U. Hosp., 1973-78; cons. psychiatry Jefferson Barracks VA Hosp., St. Louis, 1973-78; pvt. practice medicine, specializing in psychiatry and psychoanalysis, Shreveport, 1978-93; clin. prof. psychiatry, mem. med. staff psychiatry La. State U. Med. Center Hosp., Shreveport, 1978—; chief psychiatry service Schumpert Med. Center, 1982-84; med. and clin. dir. psychiatry Willis Knighton Med. Ctr., 1986-89; dir. adult psychiatric treatment program Charter Forest Hosp., Shreveport, 1989—, prof. psychiat. La. State U. Med. Ctr., Shreveport, 1992—; dir. in-patient svc. psychiat., psychoanalysis out patient clinic, 1992—. Served to capt. M.C., USAF, 1951-53. Diplomate Am. Bd. Psychiatry and Neurology (examiner). Fellow Am. Coll. Psychiatrists, Am. Psychiat. Assn.; mem. Am. Psychoanalytic Assn., AMA, La. Psychiat. Soc., La. Med. Soc., New Orleans Psychoanalytic Soc., Phila. Psychoanalytic Soc. Club: Rotary. Contbr. articles to profl. and med. jours. Home: 626 Wilder Pl Shreveport LA 71104-4326

SCHOBER, ROBERT CHARLES, electrical engineer; b. Phila., Sept. 20, 1940; s. Rudolph Ernst and Kathryn Elizabeth (Ehrisman) S.; m. Mary Eve Kanuika, Jan. 14, 1961; children: Robert Charles, Stephen Scott, Susan Marya. BS in Engring. (Scott Award scholar), Widner U., 1965; postgrad., Bklyn. Poly. Extension at Gen. Electric Co., Valley Forge, Pa., 1965-67, U. Colo., 1968-69, Calif. State U.-Long Beach, 1969-75, U. So. Calif., 1983-84. Engr. Gen. Electric Co., Valley Forge, 1965-68, Martin Marietta Corp., Denver, 1968-69; sr. engr. Jet Propulsion Lab., Pasadena, Calif., 1969-73, sr. staff, 1986—; mem. tech. staff Hughes Semiconductor Co., Newport Beach, Calif., 1973-75; prin. engr. Am. Hosp. Supply Corp., Irvine, Calif., 1975-83; sr. staff engr. TRW Systems, Redondo Beach, Calif., 1983-84; cons. Biomed. LSI, Huntington Beach, Calif. Mem. IEEE (student br. pres. 1963-65), Soc. for Indsl. and Applied Math., Assn. for computing Machinery, Tau Bea Pi. Republican. Patentee cardiac pacemakers. Current Work: Develop large scale integrated circuits for computer, spacecraft, and military, as well as commercial applications; design high speed signal processing integrated circuits; instrumental in starting the quest for low power integrated circuits; actively persuing the advancment of ultra low power technology; provides dissemination through public domain distribution of a low power MOSIS cell library, workshops and publications. Subspecialties: application specific microprocessor architecture design; ultra low power analog and digital systems and integrated circuits; integrated circuit design; focal plane electronic signal processing arrays, neural networks; synchro converter electronics; sigma-delta analog to digital converters and signal processing electronics;

implantable medical devices including cardiac pacemakers, defibulators and hearing aids. Office: Jet Propulsion Lab 4800 Oak Grove Dr Pasadena CA 91109-8001

SCHOCHOR, JONATHAN, lawyer; b. Suffern, N.Y., Sept. 9, 1946; s. Abraham and Betty (Hechtor) S.; m. Joan Elaine Brown, May 31, 1970; children: Lauren Aimee, Daniel Ross. BA, Pa. State U., 1968; JD, Am. U., 1971. Bar: D.C. 1971, U.S. Dist. Ct. D.C. 1971, U.S. Ct. Appeals (D.C. cir.) 1971, Md. 1974, U.S. Dist. Ct. Md. 1974, U.S. Ct. Appeals (4th cir.) 1974, U.S. Supreme Ct. 1986. Assoc., McKenna, Wilkinson & Kittner, Washington, 1970-74; assoc. Ellin & Baker, Balt., 1974-84; ptnr. Schochor, Federico & Staton, Balt., 1984—; lectr. in law; expert witness to state legis. Assoc. editor-in-chief American U. Law Rev., 1970-71. Mem. ABA, Assn. Trial Lawyers Am. (state del. 1991, state gov. 1992-95), Am. Bd. Trial Advocates (membership com. 1994—), Am. Bd. Trial Advocates, Am. Judicature Soc., Md. State Bar Assn. (spl. com. on health claims arbitration 1983), Md. Trial Lawyers Assn. (bd. govs. 1986-87, mem. legis. com., 1985-88, chmn. legis. com. 1986-87, sec. 1987-88, exec. com. 1987-92, v.p. 1987-88, pres.-elect 1989, pres. 1990-91), Balt. City Bar Assn. (legis. com. 1986-87, spl. com. on tort reform 1986, medicolegal com. 1989-90, circuit ct. for Balt. City task force-civil document mgmt. system 1994—), Bar Assn. D.C., Internat. Platform Assn., Phi Alpha Delta. Office: Schochor Federico & Staton PA 1211 Saint Paul St Baltimore MD 21202-2705

SCHOCK, FRANKLIN H., clergy member, church administrator. Supt. Evangelical Congregational Church Retirement Village, Myerstown, Pa. Office: Evang Congl Ch PO Box 186 100 W Park Ave Myerstown PA 17067

SCHOCK, ROBERT NORMAN, geophysicist; b. Monticello, N.Y., May 25, 1939; s. Carl Louis and Norma Elizabeth (Greenfield) S.; m. Susan Esther Benton, Nov. 28, 1959; children: Pamela Ann, Patricia Elizabeth, Christina Benton. B.S., Colo. Coll., 1961; M.S., Rensselaer Poly. Inst., 1963, Ph.D., 1966; postgrad., Northwestern U., 1963-64. Cert. Calif. state wine judge. Jr. geophys. trainee Continental Oil Co., Sheridan, Wyo., 1960; jr. geologist Texaco In., Billings, Mont., 1961; teaching asst. Rensselaer Poly. Inst., Troy, N.Y., 1961-63, research asst., 1964-66; research assoc. U. Chgo., 1966-68; sr. research scientist Lawrence Livermore Nat. Lab., U. Calif., 1968—, group leader high pressure physics, 1972-74, sect. leader geoscis. and engring., 1974-76, div. leader earth scis., 1976-81, head dept. earth scis., 1981-87, energy program leader, 1987-92, dep. assoc. dir. for energy, 1992—; pres. Pressure Sys. Rsch. Inc.; mem. faculty Chabot Coll., 1969-71; dir. Alameda County Flood Control and Water Conservation Dist., 1984-86; mem. adv. panel on geoscis. U.S. Energy, 1985-87; chair adv. com. U. Calif. Energy Inst., 1992—; mem. rsch. adv. com. Gas Rsch. Inst., Chgo., 1995—. Mem. editl. bd. Rev. Sci. Instruments, 1975-77; assoc. editor Jour. Geophys. Rsch., 1978-80; bd. assoc. editors 11th Lunar and Planetary Sci. Conf., 1980; mem. adv. bd. Physics ans Chemistry of Minerals, 1983—; rsch. and publs. on high pressure physics, solid state physics, physics of earth interior, rock deformation, energy R&D and energy policy. Fulbright sr. fellow U. Bonn (Germany), 1973; vis. research fellow Australian Nat. U. Canberra, 1980-81. Mem. AAAS, Am. Geophys. Union, Sigma Xi, Commonwealth of Calif. Club, Cosmos Club (Washington). Office: Lawrence Livermore Nat Lab PO Box 808 Livermore CA 94551-0808

SCHOECK, RICHARD JOSEPH, English and humanities scholar; b. N.Y.C., Oct. 10, 1920; s. Gustav J. and Frances M. (Kuntz) S.; m. Reta R. Haberer, 1945 (div. 1976); children: Eric R., Christine C., Jennifer A.; m. Megan S. Lloyd, Feb. 19, 1977. M.A., Princeton U., 1949, Ph.D., 1949. Instr. English Cornell U., 1949-55; asst. prof., then assoc. prof. U. Notre Dame, 1955-61; prof. English U. Toronto, 1961-71; head dept. English St. Michael's Coll., 1965-70; prof. vernacular lit. Pontifical Inst. Mediaeval Studies, Toronto, 1964-71; dir. rsch. activities Folger Shakespeare Libr., also dir. Folger Inst. Renaissance and 18th Century Studies, 1970-74; adj. prof. English Cath. U. Am., 1972; prof. English, medieval and renaissance studies U. Md., 1974-75; prof. English and humanities U. Colo., Boulder, 1975-89, prof. emeritus, 1987—; chmn. dept. integrated studies U. Colo., 1976-79; chmn. comparative lit., 1983-84; prof. Anglistik Universität Trier, 1987-90, head dept., 1988-89; adj. prof. English U. Kans., Lawrence, 1990—; Vincent J. Flynn prof. letters Coll. St. Thomas, 1969; vis. prof. Princeton U., 1964, U. Dallas, 1985; vis. fellow Inst. Advanced Studies in Humanities, Edinburgh, 1984-85; vis. scholar Corpus Christi Coll., Oxford, 1994; fellow in the Ctr. for the Book, Brit. Libr., 1995-96; cons. NEH; bd. dirs. Natural Law Inst. U. Notre Dame; advisor Italian Acad. for Advanced Studies in Am., 1993—; fellow Assn. Advancement Edn., 1952-53, Yale U., 1959-60, Can. Coun. 1967-68. Author: The Achievement of Thomas More, 1976, Intertextuality and Renaissance Texts, 1984, Erasmus Grandescens, 1988, (poems) A Raging Agains Chaos, 1989, Erasmus of Europe, Vol I, 1991, Vol. II, 1993, (poems) The Eye of a Traveller, 1992, The Knights Book (1993); author also numerous articles, papers, revs.; editor: Delehaye's Legends of the Saints, 1961, Editing 16th Century Texts, 1966 (Roger Ascham), The Scholemaster, 1966, Shakespeare Quar., 1972-74, Acta Conventus Neo-Latini Bononiensis, 1985; gen. editor: The Confutation of Tyndale, 3 vols., 1973; co-editor: Voices of Literature, 2 vols, 1964, 66, Chaucer Criticism, 2 vols, 1960, 61, Style, Rhetoric and Rhythm: Essays by M.W. Croll, 1966, Acta Conventus Neo-Latini Torontonensis, 1991; former gen. editor: Patterns of Literary Criticism; spl. editor Canada vol. Rev. Nat. Literatures, 1977, Sir Thomas Browne and the Republic of Letters, 1982, A Special Number of English Language Notes, 1982; gen. editor (series) Renaissance Masters 1992—; mem. editorial bds. profl. jours. Served with U.S. Army, 1940-46. Guggenheim Found. fellow, 1968-69, Fulbright fellow, 1983; recipient Centennial medal U. Colo., 1976; grantee: Can. Coun., UNESCO, Am. Coun. Learned Socs., U. Toronto, U. Colo. Fellow Royal Soc. Can., Royal Hist. Soc.; mem. Internat. Assn. Neo-Latin Studies (pres. 1976-79), MLA, Renaissance Soc. Am., PEN (N.Y.), Can. Humanities Assn., Internat. Assn. U. Profs. English, Assn. Can. Studies in U.S. Home: 232 Dakota St Lawrence KS 66046-4710 *More than a thousand years ago Bede summed up what are for me the principles of my professional career: I have always thought it fitting to learn and to teach and to write.*

SCHOEFFMANN, RUDOLF, consulting engineer; b. Linz, Austria, May 25, 1926; s. Rudolf and Anna (Hartl) S.; m. Herta Buttinger, Apr. 20, 1954; children: Monka M.B., Margit M.A., Rudolf M.G. Ing., Engring. Sch. Linz, 1944; Dipl.Ing., Tech. U. Vienna, Austria, 1951. Constructor Vôest, Linz, 1951-55, constrn. group leader, 1955-65, mgr., 1959-65, divsn. mgr., 1965-72; cons. Allis Chalmers Corp., Milw., 1972-81; dir. and cons. Rokop-Davy, Stockton, Eng., 1980-82; pvt. cons. engr. Linz, 1973—. Contbr. articles to profl. jours. Recipient Silver Cross of Merit, Pres. of Austria, 1969. Mem. Club of Engrs. and Architects, Chamber of Cons. Engrs., Golf Club of Linz. Roman Catholic. Achievements include 18 patents. Avocations: golf, skiing, swimming, chess.

SCHOELLER, DALE ALAN, nutrition research educator; b. Milw., June 8, 1948; s. Arthur B. and Anne Clare (Maas) S.; m. Madeline Mary Juresh, Aug. 22, 1970; children: Nicholas Paul, Gregory Scott, Erica Lee. BS with honors, U. Wis., Milw., 1970; PhD, Ind. U., 1974. Postdoctoral fellow Argonne (Ill.) Nat. Lab., 1974-76; from asst. prof. to prof., also rsch. assoc. U. Chgo., 1976-91, assoc. prof., 1991—, prof., 1996; chmn. com. on human nutrition and nutritional biology U. Chgo., 1991—. Author: (book chpt.) Obesity, 1992; co-author: (book chpt.) Annual Review of Nutrition, 1991. Achievements include development of stable isotope methods for the study of human energy metabolism including first human use of doubly labeled water for measurement of free-living total energy expenditure. Avocations: coaching youth sports including basketball, baseball and hockey. Mem. Am. Inst. Nutrition (Mead Johnson award 1987), Am. Soc. for Clin. Nutrition, Am. Soc. for Mass Spectrometry, N.Am. Soc. for Study of Obesity. Office: U of Chgo Pritzker Sch of Medicine 5841 S Maryland Ave Chicago IL 60637-1463

SCHOEN, ALVIN E., JR., environmental engineer; b. Milford, Conn., Jan. 3, 1945; s. Alvin E. and Thelma (Terrace) S.; m. Mary Ann Kosik; 1 child, Matthew S. BA in Math., U. Conn., 1968, BS in Engring., 1971; MSCE, Polytechnic Inst. of N.Y., 1977; PhD in Environ. Engring., U. Okla., 1994. Registered profl. engr., Ohio, Maine, N.Y., Conn., Mass., N.H., Va., Okla., N.J.; Diplomate Am. Acad. Environ. Engrs. Field engr. Mobil Oil Corp., Scarsdale, N.Y., 1973-76, engring. supr., 1976-80; project engr. Mobil Oil Corp., Fairfax, Va., 1980-82; group leader, process engr. Mobil Oil Corp., Oklahoma City, 1985-89; environ. engr. rsch. and devel. Mobil Oil Corp., Princeton, N.J., 1989—; project engr. Arabian Am. Oil, Dhahran, Saudi Arabia, 1982-85; commr. Inland Wetlands Commn., Brookfield, Conn., 1978-80, Environ. Commn., Montgomery Twsp, N.J., 1992-93. 1st lt. C.E., U.S. Army, 1968-70, Vietnam. Fellow ASCE; mem. Am. Petroleum Inst. (mktg. terminal effluent task force, liner work group), Nat. Soc. Profl. Engrs., Water Environ. Fedn., Lions Clubs Internat. Office: Mobil Rsch and Devel Corp PO Box 1026 Princeton NJ 08543

SCHOEN, LAURA FEIO, public relations executive, consultant; b. São Paulo, Brazil, Feb. 29, 1956; came to U.S., 1981; d. Luciano and Eny Dora (Feio) S.; m. Robert R. Kaufman, Oct. 29, 1983. BA in Journalist, Faculdade da Cidade, Rio de Janeiro, 1977; MA in Internat. Rels., U. Pa., 1983. Account exec. Denison/Ted Bates, Rio de Janeiro, 1974-75; mgr. pub. rels. and spl. events Estrutural Agy., Rio de Janeiro, 1975-81; internat. coord. mgr. Burson-Marsteller, N.Y.C., 1984-88, v.p., 1988-91, sr. v.p., 1991; sr. v.p. Creamer Dickson Basford, N.Y.C., 1991—, exec. v.p., 1994. Exec. producer (documentary) Winners, 1988-89. Recipient scholarship Rotary, 1981-82. Mem. Pub. Rels. Soc. Am., Fgn. Press Assn. Avocations: reading, arts, photography, jogging, travel. Office: Creamer Dickson Basford 1633 Broadway New York NY 10019-6708

SCHOEN, STEVAN JAY, lawyer; b. N.Y.C., May 19, 1944; s. Al and Ann (Spevack) S.; m. Cynthia Lukens; children: Andrew Adams, Anna Kim. BS, U. Pa., 1966; JD, Cornell U., 1969; MPhil in Internat. Law, Cambridge U. (Eng.), 1979. Bar: N.Mex. 1970, N.Y. 1970, U.S. Supreme Ct. 1976, U.S. Tax Ct. 1973, U.S. Ct. Internat. Trade 1982. Nat. dir. Vista law recruitment U.S. OEO, Washington, 1970-71; atty. Legal Aid Soc. of Albuquerque, 1971-73; chief atty., spl. asst. atty. gen. N.Mex. Dept. Health and Social Svcs., Albuquerque, 1973-77; ptnr. Brennan, Schoen & Eisenstadt, 1979-88, Messersmith, McNeill & Schoen, 1989—; probate judge, Sandoval County, 1990—; arbitrator, NYSE. mem. N.Mex. Supreme Ct. Appellate Rules Com., 1982-92; chmn. rules com. Com. on Fgn. Legal Cons., 1993, Jud. Edn. Planning Com.; mem. Children's Code Rules Com., 1976-78. Bd. dirs., officer, Placitas Vol Fire Brigade, 1973-86; mem. Albequerque Adv. Com. on Fgn. Trade Zone. Recipient Cert. for Outstanding Svc. to Judiciary N.Mex. Supreme Ct., 1982, cert. of Appreciation, N.Mex. Supreme Ct., 1992, Cert. of Appreciation, N.Mex. Sec. of State, 1980, Cert. of Appreciation, U.S. OEO, 1971, Pro Bono Pub. Svc. award 1989, cert. Recognition Legal Aid, 1994, award Las Placitas Assn., 1996. Mem. Am. Judges Assn., Nat. Coll. Probate Judges, State Bar N.Mex. (past chmn. real property, probate and trust sect. 1989, Outstanding Contbn. award 1989, task force on regulation of advt. 1990-91, past chmn. appellate practice sect. 1991, past chmn. internat. law sect. 1991-92, commn. on professionalism 1992-95, organizing com. U.S.-Mex. law inst. 1992), N.Mex. Probate Judges Assn. (chmn. 1993-96), Oxford-Cambridge Soc. N.Mex. (sec.), N.Mex. Assn. Counties (adv. bd.). Home: 14 Rainbow Valley Rd Placitas NM 87043-8801 Office: 5700 Harper Dr NE Ste 430 Albuquerque NM 87109-3573

SCHOEN, WILLIAM JACK, financier; b. Los Angeles, Aug. 2, 1935; s. Jack Conrad and Kathryn Mabel (Stegmayer) S.; m. Sharon Ann Barto, Oct. 1, 1966; children: Kathryn Lynn, Karen Anne, Kristine Lea, William Jack. BS in Fin. magna cum laude, U. So. Calif., 1960, MBA, 1963. Mktg. mgr. Anchor Hocking Glass Co., 1964-68; v.p. sales and mktg. Obear-Nester Glass Co., 1968-71; pres. Pierce Glass Co., Port Allegheny, Pa., 1971-73; pres., chief exec. officer, dir. F.&M. Schaefer Brewing Co., N.Y.C., 1973-81; now chmn., pres. Wilshar Mgmt. Co. Inc., Naples, Fla., 1981—; chmn., pres. Health Mgmt. Assocs. Inc., Naples, 1983—; also bd. dirs. Health Mgmt. Assocs. Inc.; bd. dirs. 1st Union Nat. Bank Fla. Contbr. to indsl. publns. Served with USMC, 1953-56, Korea. Mem. Phi Kappa Phi. Republican. Episcopalian. Clubs: Port Royal, Quail Creek Country.

SCHOENBAUM, DAVID LEON, historian; b. Milw., Mar. 26, 1935; s. Milton Lionel and Leah (Hertz) S.; m. Tamara Holtermann, June 6, 1963; children—Michael, Miriam. B.A., U. Wis.-Madison, 1955, M.A., 1958; D.Phil., St. Antony's Coll., Oxford U., 1965. Reporter Waterloo Courier, Iowa, 1957-58; copy editor Mpls. Tribune, 1958-59; asst. prof. Kent State U., Ohio, 1966-67; from asst. prof. to prof. history U. Iowa, Iowa City, 1967—; guest prof. U. Freiburg, Fed. Republic Germany, 1974-75, U. Bonn, Fed. Republic Germany, 1989; prof. U.S. Naval War Coll., Newport, R.I., 1976-77, Johns Hopkins Univ. Sch. of Advanced Internat. Studies, Bologna Ctr., Bologna, Italy, 1991-93; occasional free-lance journalist. Author: Hitler's Social Revolution, 1966, The Spiegel Affair, 1968, Zabern 1913, 1983, The United States and The State of Israel, 1993; co-author: (with Elizabeth Pond) The German Question and Other German Questions, 1996. Fulbright grantee, Bonn. Fed. Republic Germany, 1959, sr. scholar, 1973-74, 88-89; Guggenheim grantee, 1975, German Marshall Fund U.S. grantee, 1986—; sr. scholar Truman Presdl. Library, Independence, Mo., 1982-83; fellow Woodrow Wilson Ctr. , 1984-85, German Soc. Fgn. Affairs, Bonn, 1988-89. Jewish. Avocation: chamber music (violin and viola). Home: 617 Holt Ave Iowa City IA 52246-2917 Office: U Iowa Dept History Iowa City IA 52242

SCHOENBERG, LAWRENCE JOSEPH, computer services company executive; b. N.Y.C., July 4, 1932; s. Samuel and Selma (Shapiro) S.; m. Barbara Brizdle, Sept. 15, 1990; children: Douglas, Eric, Julie. A.B., U. Pa., 1953, M.B.A., 1956. Sr. systems analyst IBM, N.Y.C., 1956-59; asst. mgr. systems Litton, Orange, N.J., 1959-61; sr. cons. Computer Scis., N.Y.C., 1961-63; exec. v.p. Automation Scis., N.Y.C., 1963-65; chmn., chief exec. officer AGS Computers, Mountainside, N.J., 1966-91; chmn. ITAA (formerly ADAPSO), Arlington, Va., 1983; bd. dirs. Penn-Am. Group, Inc., Marisel Inc., Sungard Inc.; chmn. Gov. Tech. Svcs., Inc. Contbr. articles to profl. jours. Trustee Charles Babbage Inst., Dickinson Coll., N.J. Comty. Found.; assoc. trustee U. Pa. Cpl. U.S. army, 1953-55. Mem. Software Industry Assn. (dir. 1976-91), Orange Lawn Tennis Club, Germantown Cricket Club, Longboat Key Club, Racquet Club of East Hampton. Office: GTSI Inc PO Box 8460 Longboat Key FL 34228-8460

SCHOENBERG, MARK GEORGE, government agency administrator; b. Bklyn., Nov. 22, 1947; s. Abraham Arthur and Ruth Millie (Dunn) S. BA, Columbia U., 1971, postgrad., 1972-73; postgrad., N.C. State U., 1971-72. Research asst. NIMH-sponsored project at N.C. State U., Raleigh, 1971-72; asst. to pres. Key Electric Ltd., Glen Oaks, N.Y., 1973-76; gen. mgr. Key Electric Ltd., Los Angeles, 1976; asst. to pres. Kalsan Electric, Hempstead, N.Y., 1977; asst. mgr. Lincoln Inn, Rockville Ctr., N.Y., 1978; expert, cons. EPA, Washington, 1978; assoc. dir. U.S. Regulatory Council, Washington, 1979-82; exec. dir. Regulatory Info. Service Ctr., Washington, 1982—. Mem. Sr. Exec. Assn., Train Collectors Assn., Lionel Collectors Club Am. Avocations: healthy gourmet cooking, model railroading, early music, wine collecting. Office: Regulatory Info Svc Ctr Exec Office of Pres 750 17th St NW Ste 500 Washington DC 20006-4606

SCHOENBERGER, JAMES EDWIN, federal agency administrator; b. Dayton, Ohio, Sept. 7, 1947; s. Harry Robert and Elizabeth Jane (Hollenkamp) S.; m. Aura Victoria Montana, June 24, 1977; children: David, Eric. BS in Civil Engring., Purdue U., 1969; MBA, Harvard U., 1971. V.p. ops. for midwestern housing developer Herman Devel. Group, Indpls., 1971-74; various positions New Communities Adminstrn. and with sec. HUD, Washington, 1974-77, assoc. dep. asst. sec., 1981-83; dir. land utilization Peabody Coal Co., St. Louis, 1977-81; sr. v.p. ops. The Investment Group, Washington, 1983-86; gen. dep. asst. fed. housing commr. U.S. HUD, Washington, 1987-89, assoc. gen., dep. asst. sec., 1990—. Roman Catholic. Avocation: computers. Office: HUD 451 7th St SW Rm 9106 Washington DC 20410-0001

SCHOENBERGER, STEVEN HARRIS, physician, research consultant; b. Cleve., Nov. 26, 1950; s. Stanford L. and Irene (Gold) S. BA, Tulane U., 1972; MD, U. Autonoma Guadalajara, Mex., 1976. Diplomate Am. Bd. of Urology. Asst. prof. Tulane U. Sch. Medicine, New Orleans, 1983—; rsch. assoc. Delta Regional Primate Rsch. Ctr., Covington, La., 1983-85; chmn. laser com., Lawrence and Meml. Hosp., New London, Conn., 1989—, rsch. cons. Pfizer Med. Group, Groton, Conn., 1989—. Fellow ACS, Am. Soc. Laser Medicine and Surgery; mem. Soc. Univ. Urologists, N.Y. Acad. Scis., New Eng. Escadrille. Office: 3 Shaw's Cove Ste 206 New London CT 06320

SCHOENBRUN, LARRY LYNN, lawyer; b. Tyler, Tex., Mar. 10, 1940; s. Mano and Elsie (Lefkovitz) S.; m. Celia Roosth, June 30, 1963; children: Benjamin C., Michael E., Kathryn L. AB, U. Tex., 1962, LLB, 1965. Ptnr. Gardere & Wynne, L.L.P., and predecessor firms, Dallas, 1965—. Pres., bd. dirs. Comty. Homes for Adults, Inc., Dallas, 1986-87; bd. dirs. Jewish Fedn. Greater Dallas, 1987—; treas., 1989-91, v.p., 1991-95; vice chmn. Found. Jewish Fedn. Greater Dallas, 1988-91, chmn., 1991-95; v.p. Jewish Comty. Ctr., Dallas; bd. dirs. United Way of Dallas, 1992-95. Recipient Jurisprudence award Anti-Defamation League, 1989. Mem. ABA, Tex. State Bar Assn. (securities com. 1970—, vice chmn. 1974-75, chmn. 1975-77, coun. bus. law sect. 1975-83, vice chmn. 1980-81, chmn. 1981-82), Dallas Bar Assn., Tex. Bus. Law Found. (bd. dirs. 1988—, exec. com. 1988—, chmn. 1989-91). Office: Gardere & Wynne LLP 3000 Thanksgiving Tower 1601 Elm St Dallas TX 75201-7254

SCHOENBUCHER, BRUCE, health physicist; b. Dec. 15, 1943; s. Albert King and Alice Elizabeth (Thomson) S.; m. Patty Jo Parry, Feb. 3, 1965 (div. Feb. 1980); children: Teresa Marie, Bonnie Lynn Schoenbucher Mendoza; m. Nancy Lippincott, Jan. 3, 1987; 1 child, Carly Cramer Cutler. BS in Radiation Protection Engring., Tex. A&M U., 1977, MS in Nuclear Engring., 1982. Lic. med. physicist, Tex.; cert. healthcare safety profl. Health physicist nuclear sci. ctr. Tex. A&M U., College Station, 1971-75, health physicist Coll. Vet. Medicine, 1977-79; mgr. radiation safety programs U. Tex. Med. Br., Galveston, 1980-88, asst. dir. environ. health and safety, 1984-88, radiation safety officer, dir. environ. health and safety, 1988—; radiation safety officer Burn Inst Shriners Hosp. for Crippled Children, Galveston, 1991—; presenter in field. Contbr. articles to profl. publs. With USN, 1962-71. Mem. APHA, Health Physics Soc. (med. sect. exec. bd. 1993-96, mem. pub. info. com. 1981-84, chmn. 1982-84), South Tex. Chpt. Health Physics Soc. (chmn. ad hoc com. on licensure of med. physicists, chmn. fin. com. 1986-88, treas. 1980-85, pres-elect 1985-86, pres. 1986-87), Am. Assn. Physicists in Medicine, Am. Biol. Safety Assn., Am. Soc. Safety Engrs., Laser Inst. Am., Nat. Fire Protection Assn., Tex. Safety Assn., Galveston C. of C., U.S. Coast Guard Auxiliary, Phi Kappa Phi, Sigma Nu Epsilon, Tau Beta Pi. Office: U Tex Med Br 301 Univ Blvd Galveston TX 77555-0633

SCHOENDIENST, ALBERT FRED (RED SCHOENDIENST), professional baseball coach, former baseball player; b. Germantown, Ill., Feb. 2, 1923; m. Mary Eileen O'Reilly; children: Colleen, Cathleen, Eileen, Kevin. Infielder St. Louis Cardinals, 1945-56, 61-63, N.Y. Giants, 1956-57, Milw. Braves, 1957-61; coach St. Louis Cardinals, 1961-64, 1979—, now special assistant to gen. mgr., mgr., 1964-77; coach Oakland Athletics, Calif., 1977-78. Mem. Nat. League All-Star team, 10 times, player in 9 games; mem. World Series Championship team, 1946, 57; managed team to World Series Championship, 1967; inducted into Major League Baseball Hall of Fame, 1989. Office: Saint Louis Cardinals 250 Stadium Plz Saint Louis MO 63102-1722*

SCHOENE, KATHLEEN SNYDER, lawyer; b. Glen Ridge, N.J., July 24, 1953; d. John Kent and Margaret Ann (Bronder) Snyder. BA, Grinnell Coll., 1974; MS, So. Conn. State Coll., 1976; JD, Washington U., St. Louis, 1982. Bar: Mo. 1982, U.S. Dist. Ct. (we. and ea. dists.) Mo. 1982, Ill. 1983. Head libr. Mo. Hist. Soc., St. Louis, 1976-79; assoc. Peper, Martin, Jensen, Maichel & Hetlage, St. Louis, 1982-88, ptnr., 1989—; bd. dirs. Legal Svcs. of Eastern Mo. Author: (with others) Missouri Corporation Law and Practice, 1985; contbr. articles to profl. jours. Trustee Grinnell (Iowa) Coll., ex officio voting mem., 1991-93; bd. dirs. Jr. League St. Louis, 1995-96, Leadership Ctr. Greater St. Louis, 1995—. Mem. ABA, Nat. Health Lawyers Assn., Nat. Assn. Bond Lawyers, The Mo. Bar, Ill. State Bar Assn., Bar Assn. Met. St. Louis (treas. 1991-92, sec. 1992-93, v.p. 1993-94, pres.-elect 1994-95, pres. 1995-96, chairperson small bus. com. 1987-88, mem. exec. com. 1988-96, chairperson bus. law sect. 1988-89, mem. exec. com. young lawyers sect. 1988-90), St. Louis Bar Found. (bd. dirs. 1994—, v.p. 1995-96, pres. 1996—). Home: 7824 Cornell Ave Saint Louis MO 63130-3701 Office: Peper Martin Jensen Maichel & Hetlage 720 Olive St Fl 24 Saint Louis MO 63101-2338

SCHOENER, THOMAS WILLIAM, zoology educator, researcher; b. Lancaster, Pa., Aug. 9, 1943; s. Harold Cloyd and Alta Marjorie (Hewitt) S.; m. Susan L. Keen, 1985. BA, Harvard Coll., 1965, PhD, 1969. Asst. prof. Harvard Coll., Cambridge, Mass., 1972-73, assoc. prof., 1973-75; assoc. prof. U. Wash., Seattle, 1975-76, prof., 1976-80; prof. U. Calif., Davis, 1980—, chairperson sect. evolution and ecology divsn. biol. scis., 1993—. Mem. editorial bd. dirs. Oecologia, 1984-93, Acta Oecologia, 1989—; past mem. editorial bd. Evolution, Am. Naturalist, Sci.; contbr. chpts. to books, articles to profl. jours. Recipient MacArthur prize Ecol. Soc. Am., 1987; grantee NSF, 1975—, Nat. Geog. Soc.; jr. fellow Harvard U., 1969-72; Guggenheim fellow, 1992-93. Mem. NAS, AAAS, Am. Acad. Arts and Scis., Am. Ornithologists Union (elective), Am. Soc. Naturalists, Ecol. Soc. Am., Am. Soc. Ichthyologists and Nerpetologists, Cooper Ornithol. Soc., Wilson Ornithol. Soc., Am. Arachnological Soc., Bahamas Nat. Trust. Avocations: weight lifting; reading. Office: U Calif Sect Evolution and Ecology Davis CA 95616

SCHOENFELD, HANNS-MARTIN WALTER, accounting educator; b. Leipzig, Germany, July 12, 1928; came to U.S., 1962, naturalized, 1968; s. Alwin and Lisbeth (Kirbach) S.; m. Margit Frese, Aug. 10, 1956; 1 child, Gabriele. MBA, U. Hamburg, Fed. Republic Germany, 1952, DBA, 1954; PhD, U. Braunschweig, Fed. Republic Germany, 1966. Pvt. practice acctg. Hamburg, 1948-54; bus. cons. Europe, 1958-62; faculty accountancy U. Ill., Urbana, 1962—, prof. acctg., bus. adminstrn., 1967—, Weldon Powell prof. acctg., 1976, 80-81, H. T. Scovill prof. acctg., 1985-94; prof. emeritus, 1994—, Office of West European Studies, 1994—; lectr., cons. in bus. and acctg., Eng., Belgium, Austria, Denmark, Brazil, Fed. Republic of Germany, Poland, Japan, Switzerland, Hungary, Czechoslovakia, German Dem. Republic, 1962—; vis. prof. ECON U. Vienna, Austria, 1984—, Handelshochschule, Leipzig, Germany, 1996—. Author: numerous books including Management Dictionary 2 vols., 4th edit, 1971, Cost Accounting, 8th edit, 1974-95, Management Development, 1967, Cost Terminology and Cost Theory, 1974, (with J. Sheth) Export Marketing: Lessons from Europe, 1981, (with H.P. Holzer) Managerial Accounting and Analysis in Multinational Enterprises, 1986, (with L. Noerreklit) Resources of the Firm, 1996. With German Army, 1944-45. Mem. Am. Acctg. Assn. (chmn. internat. sect. 1976-77), Acad. Acctg. Historians (v.p. 1976-77, pres. 1978-79), Acad. Internat. Bus., German Profs. Bus. Adminstrn., German Assn. Indsl. Engring., European Acctg. Assn., Council of European Studies, Internat. Assn. for Acctg. Edn. and Rsch., Beta Gamma Sigma, Beta Alpha Psi. Home: 1014 Devonshire Dr Champaign IL 61821-6620 Office: U Ill 398 Commerce Bldg W 1206 S 6th St Champaign IL 61820-6915

SCHOENFELD, JIM, professional hockey coach. Head coach Washington Capitols, 1994—. Office: Washington Capitols USAIR Arena Landover MD 20785*

SCHOENFELD, MICHAEL P., lawyer; b. Bronx, N.Y., Oct. 17, 1935; s. Jack and Anne S.; B.S. in Acctg., N.Y.U., 1955; LL.B., LL.D., Fordham U., 1958; m. Helen Schorr, Apr. 3, 1960; children—Daniel, Steven, Tracy. Admitted to N.Y. bar, 1959, U.S. Supreme Ct., 1963; atty. Am. Home Assurance Co., N.Y.C., 1958-62; ptnr. firm Schoenfeld & Schoenfeld, Melville, 1959—; v.p. Interstate Brokerage Corp., 1965-84, pres., 1984—; ptnr. Melville Realty Co., 1977—; legal adv. various bus. orgns. Vice pres., trustee Temple Beth David, Commack, N.Y., 1972-75; chmn. Community Action Com. of Dix Hills and Commack, 1970-72, Dix Hills Planning Bd., 1972-74; treas. Dix Hills Republican Club, 1976-80; mem. Huntington (N.Y.) Zoning Bd. Appeals, 1980-91, chmn., 1986-89. Recipient United Jerusalem award Israel Bond Drive, 1977; City of Hope Service award; George Bacon award Fordham Law Sch. Mem. N.Y. State Bar Assn., Suffolk County Bar Assn. Home: 14 Clayton Dr Dix Hills NY 11746-5517 Office: 999 Walt Whitman Rd Huntington Station NY 11747-3007

SCHOENFELD, THEODORE MARK, industrial engineer; b. N.Y.C., July 10, 1907; s. Emil and Serena (Kertesz) S.; widowed; 1 child, Edward Lawrence. BS, CCNY, 1930; Grad. Cert. Pub. Adminstrn., NYU, 1938; Grad. Cert. Indsl. Engring., Stevens Inst. Tech., 1945. Profl. engr., Calif. Newspaperman Daily News Record, Christian Sci. Monitor, N.Y.C., 1930-33; asst. dir. methods and systems City of New York, 1934-41; adminstrv. officer U.S. Dept. of State, N.Y.C., 1944-45; chief indsl. engr. MGM Internat. Films Corp., N.Y.C., 1945-48; indsl. engr. and mgmt. cons. George S.

May Co., N.Y.C., Park Ridge, Ill., 1949-73; exec. v.p. Ramco Mfg. Co., Roselle Park, N.J., 1974-91; vol. medicare counselor, chmn. outreach com., cert. lectr. Chime, Princeton, N.J., 1992—. Author: The Safety Shield Story, 1984; contbg. author: Worldwide Multi-National Symposium, 1976. Dir. U.S. Peace Corps Aux., N.Y.C. and L.I., 1968-69; v.p. Bklyn. Soc. for Ethical Culture, N.Y.C., 1964-79, pres., 1980-85. With field artillery U.S. Army, 1943-44. Recipient Legis. commendation N.J. Senate, 1982, Nat. Chem. award with honors Chem. Processing Mag., 1980, with highest honors, 1982; named Disting. Engr. of U.S., Engring. Joint Coun., 1983; named to Cambridge/Oxford list of persons who in the course of history have contributed to the advancement of sci., 1985. Fellow Am. Inst. Chemists, N.J. Inst. Chemists (mem. gov. coun. 1988—); mem. Am. Inst. Indsl. Engrs. (nat. divs. dir. 1974-75), Princeton Ethical Humanist Fellowship (pres., 1986-87, founder). Democrat. Achievements include inventing the Spra-Gard - most widely used safety device against hazardous chemical fluids used by chemical plants throughout the world; inventing the first safety shield to protect against hydrofluoric acid, first effective safety shield for expansion joints, "Gain Sharing Plan" used by automobile dealer service departments throughout the U.S.; creating secondary distribution pattern for flowers resulting in sales of flowers by supermarkets and green grocers throughout the U.S. Home: 86 C Empress Plaza Cranbury NJ 08512

SCHOENFELD, WALTER EDWIN, manufacturing company executive; b. Seattle, Nov. 6, 1930; s. Max and Edna Lucille (Reinhardt) S.; m. Esther Behar, Nov. 27, 1955; children—Lea Anne, Jeffrey, Gary. B.B.A., U. Wash., 1952. Vice pres., dir. Sunshine Mining Co., Kellogg, Idaho, 1964-69, First N.W. Industries, Inc. (Seattle Super Sonics), 1968-79; chmn. bd., pres. Schoenfeld Industries, Inc. (diversified holding co.), 1968-93; vice chmn., acting pres., CEO, Vans, Inc., 1993—; ptnr. Seattle Mariners Baseball Club, 1977-81, Seattle Sounds Soccer Club, 1974-79; v.p., dir. Chief Execs. Orgn., 1987—; bd. dirs. Hazel Bishop Cosmetics; bd. dirs., vice chmn. Vans Shoes, 1993—; pres., CEO Van's Inc., 1993—; chmn. Schoenfeld Neckwear Corp., Seattle, 1983-87, Taylor & Burke Ltd., U.K., 1987-88, Schoenfeld Group, Seattle, 1987-88; trustee Seattle Found., 1987—, N.W. Artificial Kidney Ctr., Seattle, 1967-88. Bd. dirs. Wash. China Rels. Coun., 1980—, Sterling Recreation Orgn., 1985—; chmn. Access Long Distance of Washington; bd. govs. Weizmann Inst. Sci., Rehovot, Israel, 1980—; trustee Barbara Sinatra Children's Ctr., Eisenhower Hosp., Rancho Mirage, Calif., 1990—. With AUS, 1952-55, Korea. Recipient various service awards. Mem. Chief Execs. Orgn., Seattle C. of C., Ranier Club, Seattle Yacht Club, Mercer Island Country Club, Tamarisk Country Club (Rancho Mirage, Calif.), Mission Hills Country Club (Bellevue, Wash.), Alpha Kappa Psi. Office: 2001 6th Ave Ste 2550 Seattle WA 98121-2522

SCHOENHARD, WILLIAM CHARLES, JR., health care executive; b. Kansas City, Mo., Sept. 26, 1949; s. William Charles S. and Joyce Evans (Thornsberry) Bell; m. Kathleen Ann Klosterman, June 3, 1972; children: Sarah Elizabeth, Thomas William. BS in Pub. Adminstrn., U. Mo., 1971; M of Health Adminstrn. with honors, Washington U., St. Louis, 1975. V.p., dir. gen. svcs. Deaconess Hosp., St. Louis, 1975-78; assoc. exec. dir. St. Mary's Health Ctr., St. Louis, 1978-81; exec. dir. Arcadia Valley Hosp., Pilot Knob, Mo., 1981-82, St. Joseph Health Ctr., St. Charles, Mo., 1982-86; exec. v.p., COO SSM Health Care Sys., St. Louis, 1986—; bd. dirs. Mark Twain Bank, 1986—. Contbr. articles to profl. jours. Pres. Shaw Neighborhood Improvement Assn., St. Louis, 1979-80; mem. adv. bd. St. Louis chpt. Lifeseekers, 1985-94; mem. bd. mgrs. Kirkwood-Webster (Mo.) YMCA, 1990—, sec., 1996—; mem. bd. mgrs. Nat. Affairs Round Table Sen. Christopher Bond, St. Louis, 1990; mem. nat. adv. coun. Healthcare Forum, 1992—; mem. healthcare adv. bd. Sanford Brown Colls., 1992-94; mem. leadership excellence com. Cath. Health Assn. U.S., 1993—; mem. steering com. Greater St. Louis Healthcare Alliance, 1994-95; bd. dirs. St. Andrews Mgmt. Svcs., Inc., 1994-95. With USN, 1971-72, Vietnam. Fellow Am. Coll. Health Care Execs.; mem. Mid-Am. Transplant Assn. (bd. dirs. 1995—), Am. Legion, Navy League U.S., Univ. Club St. Louis, Phi Eta Sigma, Pi Omicron Sigma, Delta Upsilon, Delta Sigma Pi. Roman Catholic. Avocations: reading, walking. Home: 420 Fairwood Ln Saint Louis MO 63122-4429 Office: SSM Health Care System 477 N Lindbergh Blvd Saint Louis MO 63141-7813

SCHOENHERR, JOHN (CARL), artist, illustrator; b. N.Y.C., July 5, 1935; s. John Ferdinand and Frances (Braun) S.; m. Judith Gray; children: Jennifer L., Ian G. BFA, Pratt Inst., 1956. Painter/illustrator book: Owl Moon, 1987 (Caldecott medal 1988). Recipient World Sci. Fiction award World Sci. Fiction Conv., London, 1965, silver medal Phila. Acad. Natural Sci., 1984, purchase award Hiram Blauvelt Art Mus., 1994. Mem. Am. Soc. Mammalogists, Soc. Illustrators, Soc. Animal Artists (medal 1979, 85). Home and Office: 135 Upper Creek Rd Stockton NJ 08559-1209

SCHOENRICH, EDYTH HULL, academic administrator, physician; b. Cleve., Sept. 9, 1919; d. Edwin John and Maud Mabel (Kelly) Hull; m. Carlos Schoenrich, Aug. 9, 1942; children: Lola, Olaf. AB, Duke U., 1941; MD, U. Chgo., 1947; MPH, John Hopkins U., 1971. Diplomate Am. Bd. Internal Medicine, Am. Bd. Preventive Medicine. Intern John Hopkins Hosp., Balt., 1948-49, asst. resident medicine, 1949-50, postdoctoral fellow medicine, 1950-51, chief resident, pvt. wards, 1951-52; asst. chief, acting chief dept. chronic and cmty. medicine Balt. City Hosp., Balt., 1963-66; dir. svc. to chronically ill and aging Md. State Dept. Health, Balt., 1966-74; dir. divsn. pub. health adminstrn. Sch. Pub. Health, John Hopkins U., Balt., 1974-77, assoc. dean academic affairs, 1977-86, dir. part time profl. programs and dep. dir. MPH program, 1986—, prof. dept. health policy and mgmt., 1974—, joint appointment medicine, 1978—. Contbd. articles to profl. jours. Bd. trustees Friends Life Care Cmty., 1984—; Kennedy-Krieger Inst., Balt., 1985—, Vis. Nurses Assn., 1990—. Recipient Stebbins medal John Hopkins U., 1989. Fellow Am. Col. Physicians, Am. Coll. Preventive Medicine; mem. Assn. Tchrs. Preventive Medicine, Am. Pub. Health Assn., Med. Chirurg. Soc. Md., Balt. City Med. Soc., Phi Beta Kappa, Alpha Omega Alpha, Delta Omega. Avocations: gardening, music, theater, swimming. Home: 1402 Boyce Ave Baltimore MD 21204-6512 Office: Johns Hopkins Univ Sch Pub Health 615 N Wolfe St Baltimore MD 21205-2103

SCHOENROCK, JAMES V., religious organization administrator. Pres. Bapt. Missionary Assoc. of Am. Office: Baptist Missionary Assoc of Am 611 Butler St Springhill LA 71075-2519

SCHOEPPEL, JOHN FREDERICK, mechanical and electrical engineer, consultant; b. South Bend, Ind., Oct. 25, 1917; s. Frederick Otto and Helen Irene (Johnson) S.; m. Jacqueline Mae Gall, Apr. 17, 1949; children: Pamela Jo, Sonja Lou. BSc, Northwestern U., Evanston, Ill., 1939. Devel. engr. Honeywell, Inc., Mpls., 1939-47; mgr. flight references Lear, Inc., Grand Rapids, Mich., 1947-60; gen. mgr. instrn. and control divsn. Pneumo, Grand Rapids, Mich., 1960-66; dir. new products NWL Corp., Kalamazoo, 1966-71; v.p., gen. mgr. Sundstrand Data Control, Redmond, Wash., 1971-73; exec.. v.p. Veriflo Corp., Richmond, Calif., 1974-90, cons. R & D, 1990—. Contbr. articles to profl. jours. Mem. ASTM, Semiconductor Equipment Mfrs. Inst. (com. 1990-92), SEMATECH Standards (com. 1991-93). Republican. Achievements include patents for Autopilots, Gyros, Flight Reference Display, Equipment for Semiconductor Production, Automatic Autopilot; development of two gyro stable platforms for aircraft outpilot, modern all-attitude flight displays for Airforce and Navy. Avocations: advanced woodworking, photography, sound systems.

SCHOESLER, MARK GERALD, state legislator, farmer; b. Ritzville, Wash., Feb. 16, 1957; s. Gerald E. and Dorothy (Heinemann) S.; m. Ginger J. Van Aelst, Apr. 8, 1978; children: Veronica, Cody. AA, Spokane (Wash.) C.C., 1977. Mem. Wash. Ho. of Reps., Olympia, 1992—; asst. majority floor leader, mem. rules, agr. and ecology, fin., and corrections coms. Pres. Wash. Friends Farms and Forests, 1991-92; mem. Cmty. Econ. Revitalization Bd. Mem. Wash. Assn. Wheat Growers (dir. 1990-92). Republican. Mem. United. Ch. Christ. Home: Rte 1 Box 151 Ritzville WA 99169

SCHOETTGER, THEODORE LEO, city official; b. Burton, Nebr., Sept. 2, 1920; s. Frederick and Louise Cecelia (Gierau) S.; m. Kathlyn Marguerite Hughey, June 3, 1943; children—Gregory Paul, Julie Anne. B.S. in Bus. Adminstrn. with Distinction, U. Nebr., 1948. C.P.A., Calif. Sr. acct. Haskins & Sells, Los Angeles, 1948-55; controller Beckman Instruments, Inc., Fullerton, Calif., 1955-58; corp. chief acct. Beckman Instruments, Inc., 1958-60; treas. Docummun Inc., Los Angeles, 1960-77; fin. dir. City of Orange, Calif., 1977-93. Mem. fin. com., treas., bd. dirs. Childrens Hosp. Served to lt. USNR, 1942-45. Mem. Calif. Soc. CPA's (nat. dir., v.p., past pres. Los Angeles chpt.), Fin. Execs. Inst., Mcpl. Fin. Officers Assn., Beta Gamma Sigma, Alpha Kappa Psi. Methodist. Clubs: Jonathan, Town Hall. Home: 9626 Shellyfield Rd Downey CA 90240-3418

SCHOETTLE, FERDINAND P., legal educator; b. Phila., Aug. 17, 1933; s. Ferdinand P. and Helen Louise (White) S.; m. E. Bok, Feb. 13, 1965 (div. 1976); m. D. Jean Thomson, Nov. 24, 1979 (div. 1982); children—Michael, Derek. B.A. in History, Princeton U., 1955; LL.D., Harvard U., 1960, M.A. in Econs., 1978, Ph.D., 1983. Bar: Pa. 1961, Minn. 1968. Asst., U.S. Senator J.S. Clark, Washington, 1961-62; assoc. Morgan, Lewis & Bockius, Phila., 1963-67; prof. law U. Minn. Law Sch., Mpls., 1967—; vis. prof. Harvard U., 1972-74, Uppsala U., Sweden, 1984; guest scholar Brookings Inst., Washington, 1992-93. Co-author: State and Local Taxes, 1974; editor: Tax Policy Notes, 1993—; contbr. articles to profl. jours. Served to lt. USN, 1955-57. Mem. sailing U.S. Olympic Team, 1956, 60. Mem. ABA (chmn. taxes and revenue com. 1979-82), Am. Law Inst. Home: 15B3 Spa Creek Landing Annapolis MD 21403 Office: U Minn Sch Law Minneapolis MN 55455

SCHOETTLER, GAIL SINTON, state official; b. Los Angeles, Oct. 21, 1943; d. James and Norma (McLellan) Sinton; children: Lee, Thomas, James; m. Donald L. Stevens, June 23, 1990. BA in Econs., Stanford U., 1965; MA in History, U. Calif., Santa Barbara, 1969, PhD in History, 1975. Businesswoman Denver, 1975-83; exec. dir. Colo. Dept. of Personnel, Denver, 1983-86; treas. State of Colo., Denver, 1987-94, lt. govern., 1995—; bd. dirs. Nat. Jewish Hosp., Nat. Taxpayers' Union, Douglas County Edn. Found.; past bd. dirs. Pub. Employees Retirement Assn., Mi Casa Resource Ctr., Women's Bank, Denver, Equitable Bankshares of Colo., Equitable Bank, Littleton; chair Colo. Commn. Indian Affairs, Aerospace States Assn.; mem. adv. com. on external regulation of nuclear safety U.S. Dept. Energy, 1995—; mem. bd. trustees U. No. Colo., 1981-87. Mem. Douglas County Bd. Edn., Colo., 1979-87, pres., 1983-87; trustee U. No. Colo., Greeley, 1981-87; pres. Denver Children's Mus., 1975-85. Recipient Disting. Alumna award U. Calif. at Santa Barbara, 1987. Mem. Nat. Women's Forum (bd. dirs. 1981-89, pres. 1983-85), Internat. Women's Forum (mem. bd. dirs. 1981-89, pres. 83-85), Women Execs. in State Govt. (bd. dirs. 1981-87, chmn. 1988), Leadership Denver Assn. (bd. dirs. 1987, named Outstanding Alumna 1985), Nat. Assn. State Treas., Stanford Alumni Assn., Denver Rotary. Democrat.

SCHOETZ, DAVID JOHN, JR., colon and rectal surgeon; b. Milw., Oct. 29, 1948; s. David John and Beverly (Rogers) S.; m. Ruthanne Brennan, Mar. 25, 1972; children: Elizabeth Anne, David John III. BA, Coll. of Holy Cross, 1970; MD, Med. Coll. Wis., Milw., 1974. Resident in surgery Boston U. Med. Ctr., 1974-81; resident in colon/rectal surgery Lahey Clinic Med. Ctr., Burlington, Mass., 1981-82, staff colon-rectal surgeon, 1982—, chmn. dept. colon-rectal surgery, 1987—. Fellow ACS, Am. Soc. Colon and Rectal Surgeons; mem. Am. Bd. Colon-Rectal Surgery (pres. 1994-95). Office: Lahey Clinic Med Ctr 41 Mall Rd Burlington MA 01803-4136

SCHOFIELD, ANTHONY WAYNE, judge; b. Farmington, N.Mex., Mar. 5, 1949; s. Aldred Edward and Marguerite (Knudsen) S.; m. Rebecca Ann Rosecrans, May 11, 1971; children: Josie, Matthew Paul, Peter Christian, Addie, Joshua James, M. Thomas, Jacob L., Daniel Z. BA, Brigham Young U., 1973, JD, 1976. Bar: Utah 1976, U.S. Dist. Ct. Utah 1976, U.S. Ct. Appeals (7th and 10th cirs.) 1977. Law clk. to hon. judge A. Sherman Christansen U.S. Dist. Ct. Utah, Salt Lake City, 1976-77; assoc. Ferenz, Bramhall, Williams & Gruskin, Agana, Guam, 1977-79; pvt. practice American Fork, Utah, 1979-80; assoc. Jardine, Linebaugh, Brown & Dunn, Salt Lake City, 1980-81; mem., dir. Ray, Quinney & Nebeker, Provo, Utah; judge 4th Jud. Dist. Ct., Provo, Utah, 1993—. Bishop Mormon Ch., American Fork, 1985-88; commr. American Fork City Planning Commn., 1980-85; trustee American Fork Hosp., 1984-93. Mem. Cen. Utah Bar Assn. (pres. 1987, 91—). Avocations: photography, music. Home: 338 Storrs Ave American Fork UT 84003-2635 Office: 125 N 100 West Provo UT 84601

SCHOFIELD, CALVIN ONDERDONK, JR., bishop; b. Delhi, N.Y., Jan. 6, 1933; s. Calvin O. and Mabel (Lenton) S.; m. Elaine Marie Fullerton, Aug. 3, 1963; children: Susan Elaine, Robert Lenton. B.A., Hobart Coll., 1959, S.T.D. (Hon.), 1980; M.Div., Berkeley Div. Sch., 1959, D.D. (hon.), 1979; D.D. (hon.), U. of the South, 1981. Ordained priest Episcopal Ch., 1962; curate St. Peter's Episcopal Ch., St. Petersburg, Fla., 1962-64; vicar St. Andrew's Episcopal Ch., Miami, Fla., 1964-70; rector St. Andrew's Episcopal Ch., 1970-78; bishop coadjutor Diocese S.E. Fla., Miami, 1978-79, bishop, 1980—; exec. bd. Presiding Bishops Fund for World Relief; exec. coun. Episcopal Ch., 1991—. Regent U. of the South, Sewanee, Tenn., 1988—. Capt. chaplain corps USNR, 1960-85; ret., 1985. Mem. Naval Res. Assn., Naval Inst. Republican. Office: 525 NE 15th St Miami FL 33132-1411

SCHOFIELD, DONALD STEWART, real estate investment trust executive; b. Stoneham, Mass., Dec. 5, 1928; s. Roland Walter and Ida Louise (Smith) S.; m. Marion Gertrude Caulk, Dec. 10, 1950; children: Diane Schofield Garretson, Linda Schofield MacAyeal, Lora Schofield Ilhardt. BSBA summa cum laude, Boston U., 1956, MBA, 1957. CPA, Mass. Sr. mgr. Price Waterhouse & Co., Boston, 1956-66; v.p., treas. Wolf Rsch. & Devel. Co., Boston, 1966-68; exec. v.p. Gen. Investment & Devel. Co., Boston, 1969-76; pres. Windsor Investment Co., Boston, 1976-78; pres., chief exec. officer First Union Real Estate Investments, Cleve., 1978-85, chmn., pres., CEO, 1985-93, trustee, 1985-93; chmn., CEO, trustee, 1993, ind. cons., 1994—; dir. Nat. City Bank, Cleve.; trustee Univ. Circle Inc., Cleve. Served with Signal Corps. U.S. Army, 1951-52, Korea. Mem. Nat. Assn. Real Estate Investment Trusts (govt. rels. com.), Union Club, The Club at Soc. Ctr.

SCHOFIELD, JOHN TREVOR, environmental management company executive; b. Manchester, Eng., Mar. 1, 1938; s. John and Hilda May (Mumford) S.; m. Jennifer Ann Wood, June 4, 1960 (div. Aug. 1980); children: Karen Jane, Alistair John; m. Susan B. West, July 24, 1982; 1 child, Kimberly. BS, U. Manchester, 1959. Dir. European ops. Borg-Warner Chem. Corp., Amsterdam, The Netherlands, 1964-70; mng. dir. Tunnel Holdings PLC, London, 1970-78; chief exec. officer, pres. Stablex Corp., Radnor, Pa., 1978-81; sr. v.p. Internat. Tech. Corp., Torrance, Calif., 1981-91; pres., CEO, chmn. Thermatrix Inc., San Jose, Calif., 1992—; mem. adv. bd. Cupertino Nat. Bank; bd. dirs. Spectrum Diagnostics, Phys. Scis., Inc.; sec.-treas. Environ. Export Coun. U.S.A. Mem. Bd. Calif. Environ. Bus. Coun. (co-chmn.), Environ. Tech. Adv. Coun. for Calif. Avocation: public speaking, gourmet cooking. Office: Thermatrix Inc Ste 248 101 Metro Dr San Jose CA 95110

SCHOFIELD, JOHN-DAVID MERCER, bishop; b. Somerville, Mass., Oct. 6, 1938; s. William David and Edith Putnam (Stockman) S. BA, Dartmouth Coll., 1960; MDiv, Gen. Theol. Sem., N.Y.C., 1963, DD (hon.), 1989. Joined Monks of Mt. Tabor, Byzantine Cath. Ch., 1978; ordained priest Episcopal Ch. Asst. priest Ch. of St. Mary the Virgin, San Francisco, 1963-65, Our Most Holy Redeemer Ch., London, 1965-69; rector, retreat master St. Columba's Ch. and Retreat House, Inverness, Calif., 1969-88; bishop Episcopal Diocese of San Joaquin, Fresno, Calif., 1988—; aggregate Holy Transfiguration Monastery, 1984—; bishop protector Order Agape and Reconciliation, Chemainus, B.C., Can., 1990—. Episcopal visitor to Community of Christian Family Ministry, Vista, Calif., 1991—; trustee Nashotah House Sem., Wis., 1991—. Mem. Episcopal Synod of Am. (founder 1989), Episcopalians United (bd. dirs. 1987—). Republican. Office: Diocese of San Joaquin 4159 E Dakota Ave Fresno CA 93726-5227

SCHOFIELD, PAUL MICHAEL, finance company executive; b. Wilmington, Del., Mar. 30, 1937; s. John Edward and Sabina A. (Clarke) S.; m. Carol Ann Hane, July 11, 1964; children—Paul Michael, Andrew Clarke, Dennis Charles. B.A., LaSalle U., Phila., 1960; postgrad., U. Del., 1963. Asst. treas. Sears Roebuck Acceptance Corp., Wilmington, Del., 1971-73, asst. v.p., 1973-74, treas., 1974-83, v.p., treas., 1983-87; pres., treas. Discover Credit Corp., Wilmington, 1987—. Campaign capt. United Way of Del., 1978; campaign capt. Boys Club Del., 1979. Mem. Del. Fin. Assn. (treas.), Phila. Treas. Club. Democrat. Roman Catholic. Club: Irish Culture of Del. (treas. 1980). Avocations: reading; golf; woodworking. Home: 2014 Delaware Ave Wilmington DE 19806-2208 Office: Discover Credit Corp 3711 Kennett Pike Wilmington DE 19807-2102

SCHOFIELD, ROBERT E(DWIN), history educator, academic administrator; b. Milford, Neb., June 1, 1923; s. Charles Edwin and Nora May (Fullerton) S.; m. Mary-Peale Smith, June 20, 1959; 1 son, Charles Stockton Peale. A.B., Princeton, 1944; M.S., U. Minn., 1948; Ph.D., Harvard, 1955. Research asst. Fercleve Corp. and Clinton Labs., Oak Ridge, 1944-46; research assoc. Knolls Atomic Power Lab., Gen. Electric Co., 1948-51; asst. prof., then assoc. prof. history U. Kans., Lawrence, 1955-60; mem. faculty Case Western Res. U., Cleve., 1960-79, prof. history of sci., 1963-72, Lynn Thorndike prof. history of sci., 1972-79; prof. history Iowa State U., Ames, 1979-93, prof. emeritus, 1993—, dir. grad. program history tech. and sci., 1979-92; mem. Inst. Advanced Study, 1967-68, 74-75; Sigma Xi nat. lectr., 1978-80. Author: The Lunar Society of Birmingham, 1963, Scientific Autobiography of Joseph Priestley: Selected Scientific Correspondence, 1966, Mechanism and Materialism: British Natural Philosophy in an Age of Reason, 1970, (with D.G.C. Allan) Stephen Hales: Scientist and Philanthropist, 1980. Served with AUS, 1945-46. Fulbright fellow, 1953-54; Guggenheim fellow, 1959-60, 67-68. Fellow Am. Phys. Soc., Royal Soc. Arts; mem. History of Sci. Soc., Soc. History Tech., Midwest Junto History of Sci., Am. Soc. 18th Century Studies, Acad. Internat. d'Histoire des Scis. (corr.). Home: 44 Sycamore Rd Princeton NJ 08540-5323

SCHOFIELD, WILLIAM, psychologist, educator; b. Springfield, Mass., Apr. 19, 1921; s. William and Angie Mae (St. John) S.; m. Geraldine Bryan, Jan. 11, 1946; children: Bryan St. John, Gwen Star. BS, Springfield Coll., 1942; MA, U. Minn., 1946, PhD, 1948. Diplomate Am. Bd. Profl. Psychology. Instr. U. Minn., Mpls., 1947-48; asst. prof. U. Minn., 1948-51, assoc. prof., 1951-59, prof. psychology, 1959-88, prof. emeritus, 1988—; vis. prof. U. Wash., 1960, U. Colo., 1965; Cons. VA Hosp., Mpls.; examiner, instr. USCG Aux., 1968—; mem. adv. council VA, 1970-75; Mem. med. policy adv. com. Dept. Pub. Welfare Minn., 1960-68; mem. mental health services research rev. com. NIMH, 1969-73; bd. dirs. Profl. Exam. Service, 1976-81; mem. editorial bd. Roche Psychiat. Service Inst.; mem. Minn. State Bd. Psychology, 1983-86. Author: Psychotherapy: The Purchase of Friendship, 1964, 2d edit., 1986, Pragmatics of Psychotherapy, 1988; contbr. articles to profl. jours. Served with USAAF, 1943-46. Fellow Am. Psychol. Assn. (com. on health ins. 1968-71, membership com. 1968-71, sec.-treas. clin. div. 1969-72, chmn. task force on health research 1973-75, chmn. sect. health research div. psychologists in pub. service 1977, mem. com. profl. standards 1982-85, chair com. 1984-85); mem. Midwestern Psychol. Assn., Minn. Psychol. Assn. (exec. sec. 1954-59), AAAS, AAUP, Assn. Am. Med. Colls. (chmn. com. on measurement of personality 1970-74), Sigma Xi, Pi Gamma Mu. Home: 4300 W River Pky Minneapolis MN 55406-3681 Home (winter): 1500 Beach Rd # 202 Tequesta FL 33469-2826 Office: U Minn Hosp 420 Delaware St SE Minneapolis MN 55455-0374

SCHOGGEN, PHIL H(OWARD), psychologist, educator; b. Tulsa, Aug. 28, 1923; s. Walter B. and Emma F. (Alexander) S.; m. Maxine F. Spoor, June 28, 1944; children: Leida, Christopher, Ann, Susan. AB in Psychology, Park Coll., 1946; MS, U. Kans., Lawrence, 1951, Ph.D. in Psychology, 1954. Asst. prof. psychology U. Oreg., 1957-62, assoc. prof., 1962-66; prof., chmn. dept. psychology George Peabody Coll., 1966-75; prof. York U., Toronto, Ont., Can., 1975-77; prof. human devel. and family studies N.Y. State Coll. Human Ecology, Cornell U., 1977-90, prof. emeritus, 1990—, chmn. dept., 1977-82. Author: (with R. G. Barker) Qualities of Community Life, 1973; Behavior Settings: A Revision and Extension of Roger G. Barker's Ecological Psychology, 1989. Served with USNR, 1944-46, 50-51. Mem. APA. Home: 121 Vossland Dr Nashville TN 37205-3617

SCHOGT, HENRY GILIUS, foreign language educator; b. Amsterdam, May 24, 1927; s. Johannes Herman and Ida Jacoba (Van Rijn) S.; m. Corrie Frenkel, Apr. 2, 1955; children—Barbara, Philibert Johannes, Elida. B.A. in French, U. Amsterdam, 1947, B.A. in Russian, 1948, M.A. in Russian, 1951, M.A. cum laude in French, 1952; Ph.D. in French, U. Utrecht, 1960. Docent Russian U. Groningen, The Netherlands, 1953-63; sr. lectr. French U. Utrecht, The Netherlands, 1954-63; master asst. gen. linguistics U. Paris, 1963-64; vis. lectr. Russian and French Princeton (N.J.) U., 1964-66; prof. French and linguistics U. Toronto, Ont., Can., 1966-92. Author: books including Les causes de la double issue de e fermé tonique libre en français, 1960, Le système verbal du français contemporain, 1968, Sémantique synchronique, synonymie, homonymie, polysémie, 1976, (with Pierre Léon and Edward Burstynsky) La phonologie, 1977, Linguistics, Literary Analysis and Literary Translation, 1988. Fellow Royal Soc. Can.; mem. Société de linguistique de Paris, Can. Linguistic Assn. Home: 47 Turner Rd, Toronto, ON Canada M6G 3H7 Office: Dept French, Univ Toronto, Toronto, ON Canada M5S 1A1 *My ideas and goals in life are closely connected with the ideals of a socialist system of distribution of wealth and of individual responsibility towards one's fellow human beings and towards society.*

SCHOLDER, FRITZ, artist; b. Breckenridge, Minn., Oct. 6, 1937; ž. Student, Wis. State Coll., 1956-57; AA, Sacramento City Coll., 1958; BA, Sacramento State Coll., 1960; MFA, U. Ariz., 1963, DFA (hon.), 1985; DFA (hon.), Ripon Coll., Wis., 1984, Concordia Coll., Minn., 1986; HHD (hon.), Coll. Sante Fe; DFA (hon.), U. Wis., Superior, 1993. Teaching asst. art Univ. Ariz., 1962-64; instr. art history, advanced painting Inst. Am. Indian Arts, 1964-69; artist in residence Dartmouth Coll., 1973; guest artist Santa Fe Art Inst., 1987, Okla. Art Inst., 1980-81, 88, Am. U., Washington, 1990. One-man shows: Crocker Art Gallery, Sacramento, 1959, Coll. Santa Fe, 1967, Roswell (N.Mex.) Art Center, 1969, Tally Richards Gallery Contemporary Art, Taos, N.Mex., 1971, 73, 75, 78, 79, St. John's Coll., Santa Fe, 1972, Cordier & Ekstrom, N.Y.C., 1972, 74, 76, 78, 90, Gimpel & Weitzenhoffer, N.Y.C., 1977, Graphics 1 and 2, Boston, 1977, Smith Andersen Gallery, Palo Alto, Calif., 1979, Plains Mus., Moorhead, Minn., 1980, 1981-89, Scottsdale Center for Arts, 1981, Tucson Mus. Art, 1981, Weintraub Gallery, N.Y.C., 1981, ACA Galleries, N.Y.C., 1984, 86, Sena Galleries West, Santa Fe, N.Mex., 1986, 87, Louis Newman Galleries, L.A., 1985, 87, 90-94, Schneider Mus. Art, Ashland, Oreg., 1990, Alexander Gallery, N.Y., 1991, Riva Yares Gallery, Scottsdale, Ariz., 1992, 94; exhibited group shows: Carnegie Art Inst., Butler Inst. Am. Art, Calif. Palace of Legion of Honor, Houston Mus. Fine Arts, Dallas Mus. Fine Arts, San Francisco Mus. Art, Denver Art Mus., Ft. Worth Art Center, Basel Art 5, Linden Mus., Stuttgart, Philbrook Art Center, Oakland Art Mus., Tucson Art Center, N.Mex. Art Mus., Edinburgh Art Festival, Museo de Bellas Artes, Buenos Aires, Biblioteca Nacional, Santiago, Chile, Mus. voor Landen-Volkenkunder, Rotterdam, Amerika Haus, Berlin Festival, Center for Arts of Indian Am., Washington, Yellowstone Art Center, Nat. Mus. Modern Art, Tokyo, Kyoto, Japan, also other fgn. and Am. shows, Smithsonian tour, Bucharest, Berlin, London, Ankara, Madrid, Belgrade, Athens, 1972-73; represented in permanent collections: Mus. Modern Art, N.Y.C., Art Inst. Chgo., Center Culturel Americain, Paris, Art Gallery Toronto, NEA, Houston Mus. Fine Arts, Boston Fine Arts Mus., Milw. Art Mus., Portland (Oreg.) Art Mus., Dallas Mus. Fine Arts, Bur. Indian Affairs, Mus. N.Mex., Smithsonian Instn., Bklyn. Mus., Phoenix Art Mus., San Diego Fine Arts Gallery, Okla. Art Center, Brigham Young U., Heard Mus., Phoenix, Bibliotheque Nat., Paris, San Francisco Mus. Art, Hermitage Mus., Leningrad, others; Included in: American Prints and Printmakers; Subject of: PBS film Fritz Scholder, 1976, PBS film Fritz Scholder, An American Portrait, 1983; author: Fritz Scholder Lithograph, 1975, 1983, Scholder/Indians, Fritz Scholder, Rizzoli, Fritz Scholder, Paintings and Monotypes, Afternoon Nap, 1991, Live Dog/Evil God, 1992, Fritz Scholder, A Survey of Paintings, 1993, Remnants of Memory, 1993, Fritz Scholder's Book of Symbols for Children, 1994, Fritz Scholder, Thirty Years of Sculpture, 1994; guest artist Santa Fe Art Inst., 1987, Taos Inst. Art, 1990, Am. U., Washington, 1990. Recipient Ford Found. purchase award, 1962, 1st prize W.Va. Centennial Exhbn., 1973, purchase prize 13th S.W. Print Drawing Show, 1963, Hallmark purchase award, 1965, 1st prize Scottsdale Indian Nat., 1966, Grand prize Washington Biennial Indian Show, 1967, Grand prize Scottsdale Indian Nat., 1969, jurors award S.W. Fine Arts Biennial, 1970, 71, 72, prize in painting Am. Acad. and Inst. Arts and Letters, 1977, award in painting AAAL, 1977, internat. prize in lithography Intergrafiks, Berlin, 1980, 90, N.D. Gov.'s award in arts, 1981, N.Mex. Gov.'s award, 1983, Societaire Salon d'Automne, Paris, 1983, Golden Plate award Am. Acad. Achievement, 1985, Third prize Intergrafiks, 1990, Laird Leadership award in the arts U. Wis.,

Stevens point, 1995; John Jay Whitney fellow, 1962-63. Address: 118 Cattletrack Rd Scottsdale AZ 85251 *I Believe in Art, Love, and Magick.*

SCHOLEFIELD, ADELINE PEGGY, therapist; b. Bklyn., Nov. 23, 1932; d. C. Joseph and Connie (Campbell) Taylor; m. Paul Robert Scholefield, June 26, 1954; children: Debra, Robert, Scott, Colin, Colleen, Heidi, Alan, Gene, Timothy, Christina, Holly, Shawn. Cert. radiol. technician, NYU, 1953; BS, N.H. Coll., 1989; MS in Human Svc., Springfield Coll., 1991. Registered radiol. technician, N.Y.; lic. mental health therapist. X-ray technician St. Elizabeth's Hosp., N.Y.C., 1951-53, St. Joseph' Hosp., Lowell, Mass., 1954-67; owner, operator Maplewood Farm Family Care, Peperell, Mass., 1968—, Lauranne Village, Laconia, N.H., 1979-81; issues aide Offices of Senator Edward M. Kennedy, Boston, 1984-85, health and human svc. rep., 1985-87; liaison Dept. Social Svcs., Boston, Fitchbourg, Mass., 1988—, mem. steering com. of adv. coun.; sec. Statewide Adv. Coun., 1992. Foster parent Maplewood Farm, Pepperell, 1956—; staff Dem. State Com., Boston, 1987; sec. pers. bd. Town of Pepperell, 1989-90; vol. support/group loss and bereavement therapist, Naukeag Hosp., Ashbourham, Mass., 1993—, vol. therapist, 1991—; mem. adv. com. Coun. of Aging Commn.; mem. St. Josph's Parish Coun., Pepperell; ad hoc com. VA Hosp. Named Foster Parent of Yr. State of Mass., Boston, 1985; recipient commendation for family care VA, Bedford, Mass., 1971-73, 76, 81; Goldie Rogers award Dept. Social Svcs., 1994, Commr. award, 1996. Mem. Mass. Assn. Profl. Foster Care, Lioness Club (charter). Roman Catholic. Avocations: music, reading. Home and Office: 1 Chestnut St # 183 Pepperell MA 01463-1013

SCHOLEFIELD, PETER GORDON, health agency executive; b. Newport, Wales, June 26, 1925; emigrated to Can., 1947, naturalized, 1952; s. Tom and Margaret (Bithell) S.; m. Erna Mary Cooper, Sept. 29, 1951; children—David, John, Paul. B.Sc., U. Wales, 1944, M.Sc., 1946, D.Sc., 1960; Ph.D., McGill U., Montreal, Que., Can., 1949. From research fellow to prof. biochemistry McGill U., 1949-65, dir. cancer research unit, 1965-69; asst. exec. dir. Nat. Cancer Inst. Can., Toronto, 1969-80; exec. dir. Nat. Cancer Inst. Can., 1980-91, spl. adviser to chief exec. officer, 1991-92; dir. grants and awards Alta. Heritage Found. for Med. Rsch., Edmonton, 1992-94; coord. acad. affairs Samuel Lunenfeld Rsch. Inst. Mt. Sinai Hosp., Toronto, 1994—; chair rsch. policy com., bd. dirs. Alxheimer Soc. of Can., 1994—. Home: 161 Allanhurst Dr, Islington, ON Canada M9A 4K5 Office: Mt Sinai Hosp, Samuel Lunenfeld Rsch Inst, 600 University Ave, Toronto, ON Canada M5G 1X5

SCHOLER, SUE WYANT, state legislator; b. Topeka, Oct. 20, 1936; d. Zint Elwin and Virginia Louise (Achenbach) Wyant; m. Charles Frey Scholer, Jan. 27, 1957; children: Elizabeth Scholer Truelove, Charles W., Virginia M. Scholer McCal. Student, Kans. State U., 1954-56. Draftsman The Farm Clinic, West Lafayette, Ind., 1978-79; assessor Wabash Twp., West Lafayette, 1979-84; commr. Tippecanoe County, Lafayette, Ind., 1984-90; state rep. Dist. 26 Ind. Statehouse, Indpls., 1990—; asst. minority whip, 1992-94, majority whip, 1994—; mem. Tippecanoe County Area Plan Commn., 1984-90. Bd. dirs. Crisis Ctr., Lafayette, 1984-89, Tippecanoe Arts Fedn., 1990—, United Way, Lafayette, 1990-93; mem. Lafayette Conv. and Visitors Bur., 1988-90. Recipient Salute to Women Govt. and Politics award, 1986, United Sr. Action award, Outstanding Legislator award, 1993, Small Bus. Champion award, 1995, Ind. Libr. Fedn. Legislator award, 1995. Mem. Ind. Assn. County Commrs. (treas. 1990), Assn. Ind. Counties (legis. com. 1988-90), Greater Lafayette C. of C. (ex-officio bd. 1984-90), Sagamore Bus. and Profl. Women, LWV, P.E.O., Purdue Women's Club (past treas.), Kappa Kappa Kappa (past pres. Epsilon chpt.), Delta Delta Delta (past pres. alumnae, house corp. treas.). Republican. Presbyterian. Avocations: golf, needlework, reading. Home: 807 Essex St West Lafayette IN 47906-1534 Office: Indiana Statehouse Rm 3A-4 Indianapolis IN 46204

SCHOLES, EDISON EARL, army officer; b. McCaysville, Ga., Aug. 16, 1939; s. Alvin L. and Marie (Plemmons) S.; m. Elva E. Bussey, June 4, 1961; children: Juana Kimberly Scholes Scherer, Tracy Michele Scholes Heller, Michael Lee. BS in Physics cum laude, No. Ga. Coll., 1961; MS in Ops. Rsch., Naval Postgrad. Sch., 1970; postgrad., Army War Coll., 1980, Harvard Def. Policy Seminar, 1991. Commd. 2d lt. U.S. Army, 1961, advanced through grades to maj. gen., 1991; comdr. A Detachment, 10th Spl. Forces Group, 1st Spl. Forces U.S. ArmyEurope, 1963-66; comdr. Co. D, 2d Bn.(Abn.), 8th Cav., 1st Cav. Div. U.S. Army, Republic of Vietnam, 1967-68; comdr. 1st Bn., 23d Inf., 2d Inf. Div. U.S. Army, Republic of Korea, 1976-77; comdr. 2d Tng. Bn., Sch. Brigade, U.S. Army Inf. Sch. U.S. Army, Ft. Benning, Ga., 1978-79, comdr. 1st Inf. Tng. Brigade, U.S. Army Infantry Tng. Ctr., 1983-85; dep. commanding gen. chief of staff 3d U.S. Army/U.S. Army Cen. Command U.S. Army, Ft. McPherson, Ga., 1986-88; asst. div. comdr. 82d Airborne Div. U.S. Army, Ft. Bragg, N.C., 1988-89, chief of staff XVIII Airborne Corps, 1989-90; chief of staff joint task force-south, Op. Just Cause U.S. Army, 1989-90; dep. commanding gen. XVIII Airborne Corps, Operation Desert Shield/Desert Storm U.S. Army, Saudi Arabia, Iraq, 1990-91; dep. commanding gen. XVIII Airborne Corps U.S. Army, Ft. Bragg, 1991-93; dep. comdr. Allied Land Forces, S.E. Europe NATO, 1993—; postgrad. Harvard Def. Policy Seminar, 1991; program gen. mgr. Saudi Arabia N.G. Modernization Program, Vinnell Arabia, 1995—. Decorated Disting. Svc. medal, Silver Star, Legion of Merit with oak leaf cluster, Bronze Star with V device and 4 oak leaf clusters, Purple Heart with oak leaf cluster, 6 Air medals, Army Commendation medal with V device and oak leaf cluster, Armed Forces Expeditionary medal, Vietnam Svc. medal with 6 campaign stars, Southwest Asia Svc. medal with 3 campaign stars, Combat Infantry badge, Expert Infantry badge, Army Gen. Staff badge, Meritorious Svc. medal, Nat. Def. Svc. medal with oak leaf cluster, Kuwait Liberation medal; Cross of Gallantry with Silver and Bronze Stars and Palm (Republic of Vietnam), S.W. Asia Svc. medal with 3 stars; numerous other domestic and foreign awards and skill badges. Mem. 82d Airborne Divsn. Assn., Spl. Forces Assn. (chpt. XXXIV), U.S. Army Ranger Assn., Assn. of U.S. Army, VFW, Officers' Club. Baptist. Avocations: running, reading, camping, fishing. Office: Vinnell Corp Unit 61322 Box A2-R APO AE 09803

SCHOLES, MYRON S., law and finance educator; b. 1941. BA, McMaster U., 1962, MBA, 1964; PhD, U. Chgo., 1969. Instr. U. Chgo. Bus. Sch., 1967-68; prof. U. Chgo., 1976-83; asst. prof. MIT Mgmt. Sch., Cambridge, 1968-72, assoc. prof., 1972-73; assoc. prof. U. Chgo., 1973-75, prof., 1975-79, Edward Eagle Brown prof. fin., 1979-82; dir. Ctr. for Rsch. in Security Prices U. Chgo., 1975-81; prof. law Stanford (Calif.) U., 1983—, Frank E. Buck prof. fin.; sr. rsch. fellow Hoover Instn. Stanford U., 1988—; mng. dir. Salomon Bros., 1991-93, prin. long-term capital mgmt., 1994—. Office: Stanford U Grad Sch Bus Stanford CA 94305

SCHOLL, ALLAN HENRY, retired school system administrator, education consultant; b. Bklyn., May 6, 1935; s. Joseph Arnold and Edith (Epstein) S.; m. Marina Alexandra Mihailovich, July 3, 1960. BA, UCLA, 1957; MA, U. So. Calif., 1959, PhD in History, 1973. Lic. gen. secondary tchr. (life), administrv. svcs. (life), jr. coll. tchr. (life) Calif. Tchr. social studies L.A. Unified Sch. Dist., 1960-82, adviser social studies sr. high schs. div., 1982-84, dir. secondary social scis. Office Instrn., 1984-91; instr. history L.A. City Coll., 1966-69, U. So. Calif., L.A., 1968-69, Community Coll., Rio Hondo, Calif., 1972-74, Cerritos (Calif.) Coll., 1973-74; dir. Almar Ednl. Cons., Pasadena, Calif., 1991—; curriculum developer, writer history tchg. and resource guides; cons. Pasadena Unified Sch. Dist., 1987-88, Coll. Bd., 1980-88, Autry Mus. Western Heritage, 1992—, L.A. Unified Sch. Dist. Office Gifted Programs, 1995—; edn. cons. Am. Odyssey, 1991; cons. H.S. govt. and U.S. history textbooks, 1987. Author: United States History and Art, 1992; co-author: 20th Century World History: The Modern Era, 1993, History of the World: The Modern Era, 1994, History of the World, 1995; co-developer, contbr.: The Treatment of People of African Descent in Nazi Occupied Europe, 1995, The Holocaust Timeline, 1995, Those Who Dared: Rescuers and Rescued, 1995; cons. Anne Frank in Historical Perspective, 1995; contbr. articles to profl. jours. Bd. dirs. Pasadena Chamber Orch., 1977-78, Pasadena Symphony Orch., 1984-85, Pasadena Centennial Com., 1985; mem. exec. bd., chmn. edn. com. Martyrs Meml. and Mus. of Holocaust of L.A., 1992—; mem. Ednl. adv. bd. Autry Mus. of Western Heritage, 1992—. With U.S. Army, 1958-59. NDEA fellow Russian lang. studies, 1962; Chouinard Art Inst. scholar, 1952. Mem. Am. Hist. Assn., Nat. Coun. Social Studies, Calif. Coun. Social Studies, Soc. Calif. Social Studies Assn. (bd. dirs. 1982-84), Assoc. Adminstrs. L.A. (legis. coun. 1983-85), Crohn's and Colitis Found. Am., Phi Alpha Theta. Avocations: reading, hiking, travel, painting, tennis. *Personal philosophy: I have always believed that to achieve in life one should work hard and never give up. That is the only way we can ever hope to make a lasting contribution to society.*

SCHOLL, DAVID ALLEN, federal judge; b. Bethlehem, Pa., Aug. 20, 1944; s. George Raymond and Beatrice Roberta (Weaver) S.; m. Cynthia Ann Schuler Vetere, June, 1966 (div. 1972); m. Portia Elizabeth White, May 26, 1973; children: Tracy, Xavier; 1 stepchild, Sierra Milan. AB, Franklin & Marshall Coll., 1966; JD, Villanova U., 1969. Bar: Pa. 1969, U.S. Dist. Ct. (ea. dist.) 1970, U.S. Ct. Appeals (3d cir.) 1971, U.S. Tax Ct. 1975, U.S. Supreme Ct. 1975. Staff atty. Community Legal Services, Inc., Phila., 1969-73, 77-80; exec. dir. Delaware County Legal Assistance Assn., Chester, Pa., 1973-76; mng. atty. Lehigh Valley Legal Services, Bethelehem, Allentown, Pa., 1980-86; judge U.S. Bankruptcy Ct., Phila., 1986-94, chief judge, 1994—. Bd. dirs. Phila. Vols. for Indigent Program, 1988-94, Consumer Bankruptcy Assistance Project, 1992—. Recipient Joseph Harris award Ba'Hais of Lehigh Valley, Bethelehem, 1984. Mem. Pa. Bar Assn. (chairperson consumer law commn., 1983-86), Northampton County Bar Assn. Avocations: baseball, rock music. Home: 118 N Highland Ave Bala Cynwyd PA 19004-3027 Office: US Bankruptcy Ct 3118 US Courthouse 601 Market St Philadelphia PA 19106-1510

SCHOLL, GLEN, principal; b. Newhall, Calif., Nov. 5, 1946; s. Thomas and Charlotte Avis (Levey) S.; m. Judith Anne Jones, Sept. 10, 1965; children: Marilee, Glena, Douglas, Arlen, Wesley, Laura, Keith. BS, U. Utah, 1969; MA in Edn., No. Ariz. U., 1972. specialist in ednl. adminstrn. Tchr. Fredonia (Ariz.) Pub. Schs., 1969-72; acting prin. Bullhead City (Ariz.) Sch. #15, 1974-75; prin. Bullhead Primary Sch., 1975-78, Bullhead City Intermediate Sch., 1978-89, Copper Rim Elem. Sch., Globe, Ariz., 1989—; pres., v.p. Bullhead City PTA, 1975-76; pres. Bullhead City Roadrunner Bobbysox, 1976-77, Mohave County Sch. Adminstrn., Kingman, Ariz., 1979-80. Dist. commr. Gila Dist. Boy Scouts Am., Globe, 1994 (Silver Beaver award 1987), dist. River Valley Dist., Bullhead City, 1979 (Dist. award Merit 1980). Mem. Nat. Assn. Elem. Sch. Prins., Ariz. Sch. Adminstrs. Assn., Rotary (pres. 1994). Republican. Mem. LDS Ch. Avocations: family history research, woodworking, camping. Home: 185 Amarillo Dr Globe AZ 85501-1501 Office: Copper Rim Elem Sch 501 E Ash St Globe AZ 85501-2206

SCHOLLANDER, WENDELL LESLIE, JR., lawyer; b. Ocala, Fla., May 17, 1943; s. Wendell Leslie and Martha Dent (Perry) S.; m. Jayn Mary Cochran, Aug. 22, 1970; 1 son, Wendell Leslie III. BS, U. Pa., 1966, MBA, 1968; student law, Stetson U., 1969-70; JD, Duke U., 1972. Bar: N.C. 1977, Tenn. 1972, Fla. 1987. With Container Corp. Am., Fernandina, Fla., 1968-69; assoc. firm Miller, Martin, Chattanooga, 1972-75; asst. counsel R.J. Reynolds Industries, Inc., 1975-78, assoc. counsel, 1978-79, sr. assoc. counsel, 1979-82, sr. counsel, 1982-85; gen. counsel RJR Archer, Inc., Winston-Salem, N.C., 1979-85, of counsel, 1978-85; Finger, Parker & Avram, Winston-Salem, 1985-87; ptnr. Schollander, Winston-Salem, 1987—; gen. counsel Splty. Tobacco Council, 1985-87. Mem. ABA, N.C. Bar Assn., Forsyth County Bar Assn., Mensa, SAR, Phi Delta Phi, Kappa Sigma. Presbyterian. Home: 2011 Georgia Ave Winston Salem NC 27104 Office: 2000 W 1st St Ste 509 Winston Salem NC 27104

SCHOLLE, ROGER HAL, dentist; b. Cleve., Oct. 31, 1936; s. Martin Henry Edward and Irene Frances (Lawrence) S. B.A., Northwestern U., 1958, D.D.S., 1962; M.S., U. Chgo., 1968. Diplomate: Am. Bd. Oral Pathology. Resident trainee in oral pathology U. Chgo. Hosp. and Clinics, 1965-67; asst. sec. Council on Dental Therapeutics, 1968-77; pvt. practice dentistry Chgo., 1970—. Editor: Am. Dental Assn. Jour., Chgo., 1978-86, Ill. State Dental Jour., 1987-93, Chgo. Dental Soc. Rev., 1993—. Bd. dirs. Ill. div. Am. Cancer Soc., 1979-83. Served to capt. M.C. USAF, 1962-64. Fellow Am. Coll. Dentists, Internat. Coll. Dentists, Ondontgraphic Soc. Chgo., Pierre Fouchard Soc.; mem. Omicron Kappa Upsilon, Delta Sigma Delta. Address: 166 E Superior St Chicago IL 60611-2928

SCHOLLMAIER, EDGAR H., pharmaceutical products company executive; b. 1933; married. BA, U. Cin., 1956; MBA, Harvard U., 1958. With Alcon Labs., Inc., Ft. Worth, 1958—, dist. mgr., 1959-61, div. mgr., 1961-62, mgr. program planning, 1962-63, dir. mktg., 1963-64, v.p., gen. mgr. mktg., 1964-71, exec. v.p., 1971-72, chief operating officer, from 1972, pres., 1972—, chmn., chief exec. officer, 1977—, also bd. dirs. Office: Alcon Surgical Inc 6201 South Fwy Fort Worth TX 76134-2001*

SCHOLNICK, ROBERT J., college dean, English language educator; b. Boston, June 22, 1941; s. I. Allen and Ruth (Kleiman) S.; m. Sylvia Bette Huberman, June 21, 1964; children: Joshua David, Jonathan Ben. BA, U. Pa., 1962; MA, Brandeis U., 1964, PhD, 1969. Asst. prof. English Coll. William and Mary, Williamsburg, Va., 1967-74, assoc. prof., 1974-80, prof., 1980—, dean grad. studies, 1986—, founding dir. Am. studies program, 1981; chair applied sci. Coll. William and Mary, Williamsburg, 1986-88; bd. dirs. Univ. Press of Va., Charlottesville, 1988-92; mem. adv. bd. Am. Periodicals. Author: Edmund Clarence Stedman, 1977; editor Am. Lit. and Sci., 1992; contbr. articles to profl. jours. NEH fellow Coll. Tchrs., 1986-87. Mem. MLA, Rsch. Soc. for Am. Periodicals (founding pres.), Am. Studies Assn., Soc. for Sci., Va. Consortium Sci. and Engring. Univs. (bd. dirs. 1992—), B'nai B'rith Va. (Hillel svc. award 1986), Phi Beta Kappa. Avocations: distance running, arts. Home: 149 Indian Springs Rd Williamsburg VA 23185-3938 Office: Coll of William and Mary Williamsburg VA 23185

SCHOLSKY, MARTIN JOSEPH, priest; b. Stafford Spring, Conn., Jan. 16, 1930; s. Sigmund Felix and Mary Magdalen (Wysocki) S. BA, St. John's Sem., 1952, MA in History, 1956; MA in Classical Greek, Cath. U. of Am., 1966. Ordained priest Roman Cath. Ch., 1956. Asst. pastor St. Peter's Ch., Hartford, Conn., 1956-61; prin. St. Peter's Sch., Hartford, 1956-58; instr. St. Thomas Sem., Bloomfield, Conn., 1961-67; admissions dir. St. Thomas Sem., Bloomfield, 1965-67; vocations dir. Archdiocese of Hartford, 1967-78; chaplain Newington (Conn.) Children's Hosp., 1961-78; weekend asst. St. Mary's Ch., Newington, 1961-78; pastor St. Bartholomew Ch., Manchester, Conn., 1978-90; dean Manchester Deanery, 1989-91; spiritual dir. St. Thomas Aquinas High Sch., New Britain, Conn., 1991-92; weekend asst. St. Francis of Assis Ch., South Windsor, Conn., 1991-92; instr. Holy Apostle's Sem. & Coll., Cromwell, Conn., 1988-94; pastor St. Mary's Ch., East Hartford, Conn., 1992—. Contbr. articles to profl. jours. Home: 36 Griswold St Manchester CT 06040-3928 Office: St Marys Ch East East Hartford CT 06108 *Conscience is not our own personal feelings about things; rather, it is our innate awareness of the rightness and wrongness of our deeds as God sees them, an awareness, often denied, that still remains the measure by which God will ultimately judge us all.*

SCHOLTEN, MENNO NICO, mortgage banker; b. Assen, Drenthe, Netherlands, June 18, 1943; came to U.S., 1949; s. Nico Menno and Hennie (Nienhuis) S.; m. Susan Sumnar, Aug. 11, 1973; 1 child, Paul Menno. BArch., U. Calif., Berkeley, 1967; MBA, DePaul U., 1980. Registered architect. Architect various, including Skidmore, Owings & Merrill, others, Chgo., 1968-78, Knight Architects, Engrs. and Planners, Chgo., 1978-81, 1989-92; asst. v.p. constrn. lending adminstr. First Nat. Bank of Chgo., 1981-85; v.p. real estate group First Tex. Savs., Dallas, 1985-87; mgr. constrn. lending Household Internat. (Household Bank), Prospect Heights, Ill., 1992—. Patentee chair design, 1979. Recipient award of merit Chgo. Assn. of Commerce and Industry and Internat. Trade Club of Chgo., 1979. Mem. AIA (Chgo. chpt.), Homebuilders Assn. of Greater Chgo., Am. Guild Organists (bd. dirs., treas. 1991-94), Calif. Scholarship Fedn. (life mem.), Delta Mu Delta.. Avocations: tennis, skiing. Home: 3521 Central St Evanston IL 60201

SCHOLTZ, ROBERT ARNO, electrical engineering educator; b. Lebanon, Ohio, Jan. 26, 1936; s. William Paul and Erna Johanna (Weigel) S.; m. Laura Elizabeth McKeon, June 16, 1962; children: Michael William, Paul Andrew. BSEE, U. Cin., 1958; MSEE, U. So. Calif., 1960; PhD, Stanford U., 1964. Co-op student Sheffield Corp., Dayton, Ohio, 1953-58; MS and PhD fellow Hughes Aircraft Co., Culver City, Calif., 1958-63, sr. staff engr., 1963-78; prof. U. So. Calif., L.A., 1963—; vis. prof. U. Hawaii, 1969, 78; cons. LinCom Corp., L.A., 1975-81, Axiomatix Inc., L.A., 1980-86, JPL, Pasadena, 1985, Tech. Group, 1987-89, TRW, 1989, Pulson Comm., 1992-93, Colley-Godward, Palo Alto, 1994. Co-author: Spread Spectrum Comm., 3 vols., 1984, Spread Spectrum Communications Handbook, 1994, Basic Concepts in Information Theory and Coding, 1994; contbr. numerous articles to profl. jours. (recipient Leonard G. Abraham Prize Paper award 1983, Donald G. Fink Prize award 1984, Signal Processing Soc. Sr. Paper award 1992). Pres., South Bay Community Concert Orgn., Redondo Beach, Calif., 1975-79. Fellow IEEE (bd. govs. info. theory group 1981-86, bd. govs. communication soc. 1981-83, chmn. fin. com. NTC 1977, program chmn. ISIT 1981). Office: U So Calif Comm Scis Inst Dept Elec Engring Los Angeles CA 90089-2565

SCHOLZ, CHRISTOPHER HENRY, geophysicist; b. Pasadena, Calif., Feb. 25, 1943; s. Joseph George and Elizabeth (Ochsner) S.; m. Paula Hanna, May 19, 1962 (div. 1978); children: Erich Fredericj, Adirenne Louise; m. Yoshiko Yanagisawa, Feb. 8, 1986; 1 child, Morika Tsujimura. BS, U. Nev., 1964; PhD, MIT, 1967. Rsch. fellow Calif. Inst. Tech., Pasadena, 1967-68; rsch. assoc. Lamont-Doherty Geol. Obs., Columbia U., N.Y.C., 1968-70; sr. rsch. assoc. Lamont-Doherty Geol. Obs., Columbia U., 1970—, assoc. prof. geology, 1971-75, prof., 1975—. Author: The Mechanics of Earthquakes and Faulting, 1990; contbr. articles on earthquakes, deformation of the earth, mech. properties of rock to profl. jours. A.P. Sloan fellow, 1975-77; C.I. Green fellow, 1980-81. Fellow Am. Geophys. Union; mem. Seismol. Soc. Am., Médaille du Collége de France. Office: Lamont-Doherty Earth Obs Palisades NY 10964

SCHOMAKER, VERNER, chemist, educator; b. Nehawka, Nebr., June 22, 1914; s. Edwin Henry and Anna (Heesch) S.; m. Judith Rooke, Sept. 9, 1944; children: David Rooke, Eric Alan, Peter Edwin. B.S., U. Nebr., 1934, M.S., 1935; Ph.D., Calif. Inst. Tech., 1938. With Union Carbide Research Inst., 1958-65, asst. dir., 1959-63, assoc. dir., 1963-65; prof. chemistry U. Wash., Seattle, 1965-84; prof. emeritus U. Wash., 1984—, chmn. dept., 1965-70; vis. assoc. Calif. Inst. Tech., 1984-92, faculty assoc., 1992—. Contbr. articles on molecular structure to chem. jours. John Simon Guggenheim Meml. Found. fellow, 1947-48; Recipient Am. Chem. Soc. award in pure chemistry, 1950. Fellow AAAS, N.Y. Acad. Scis.; mem. Am. Chem. Soc., Am. Crystallographic Assn. (pres. 1961-62), Sigma Xi. Home: 12506 26th Ave NE Apt 103 Seattle WA 98125-4300

SCHOMER, HOWARD, retired clergyman, educator, social policy consultant; b. Chgo., June 9, 1915; s. Frank Michael and Daisy (Aline) S.; m. Elsie Pauline Swenson, Mar. 23, 1942; children: Karine, Mark, Paul, Ellen. B.S. summa cum laude, Harvard U., 1937, postgrad., 1939-40; student, Chgo. Theol. Sem., 1938-39, 40-41, D.D., 1954; LL.D., Olivet Coll., 1966. Ordained to ministry Congl. Ch., 1941. Student pastor Fitzwilliam, N.H., Oak Park, Ill.; asst. dean U. Chgo. Chapel., 1940-41; counsellor Am. history Harvard U., 1939-40; civilian pub. service Am. Friends Service Com., 1941-45; Am. Bd. Mission fellow to chs. of Europe Chambon-sur-Lignon, France, 1946-55; history tchr., work camp dir. Coll. Cevenol; founder internat. conf. center Accueil Fraternel, Permanent Conf. Protestant Chs. in Latin Countries of Europe; asst. to rapporteur UN Commn. on Human Rights, UN Econ. and Social Council, 1947-48; inter-church aid sec. for Europe World Council Chs., Geneva, 1955-58; pres., prof. ch. history Chgo. Theol. Sem., 1959-66; exec. dir. dept. specialized ministries Div. Overseas Ministries, Nat. Council Chs., N.Y.C., 1967-70; participant integration demonstrations in Ala., Ga., Washington, Chgo., SCLC, 1960-66; world issues sec. United Ch. Bd. World Ministries, 1971-80; Indochina liaison officer World Council of Chs., 1970-71; United Ch. of Christ officer for social responsibility in investments, 1972-81; founder, dir. Corp. Adv. Services, 1980-90; founder, mem. United Ch. Christ Working Group with United Ch. in German Democratic Rep. and Fed. Rep. of Germany, 1977-86; vis. prof. religion and society Andover Newton Theol. Sch., 1981; vis. lectr. Manchester Coll.; St. John's U.; Woodrow Wilson vis. fellow Drew U., 1981; pres. Internat. Fellowship of Reconciliation, 1959-63, v.p., 1963-65; participant 1st-3d assemblies World Council Chs., Amsterdam, 1948, Evanston, 1954, New Delhi, 1961; rep. UN non-govt. orgn. UNIAPAC, 1979-85; pastoral assoc. First Congl. Ch. (United Ch. Christ), Montclair, N.J., 1983-89; delegated observer Vatican Council II, 1963; v.p. Am. Friends Coll. Cevenol., 1981-89; bd. dirs. Interfaith Center for Corp. Responsibility, 1973-81; chmn. exec. com. Freedom of Faith - A Christian Com. for Religious Rights, 1978-81; mem. nat. adv. bd. N.Y. State Martin Luther King Jr. Inst. for Nonviolence, 1989-92. Translator: The Prayer of the Church Universal (Marc Boegner), 1954; editor: The Oppression of Protestants in Spain, 1955, the Role of Transnational Business in Mass Economic Development, 1975; editor-at-large Christian Century, 1959-70; contbr.; Business, Religion and Ethics-Inquiry and Encounter, 1982, Aspects of Hope, 1993; articles to religious and interdisciplinary publs.; corr. in U.S. for Évangile et Liberté, 1988—. Past co-chmn. Chgo. Com. for Sane Nuclear Policy; bd. dirs. World Conf. on Religion and Peace, 1974-84, sec. for Kampuchea issues, 1979-81; former trustee Am. Waldensian Aid Soc.; mem. internat. council Internat. Ctr. Integrative Studies, 1984-91, bd. dirs., 1987-91; trustee Internat. Inst. for Effective Communication, 1987-93; bd. dirs. Alternative Lifelong Learning, 1992—, Cambodian Found. for Justice, Peace and Devel., 1993—. Mem. ACLU, Wider Quaker Fellowship, Fellowship Reconciliation, Ctr. for Theology and the Natural Scis., Outlook Club (Berkeley), Harvard Club San Francisco, Phi Beta Kappa. Home: 110 41st St Apt 512 Oakland CA 94611 *The human capacity to hope and the power of hope to achieve either good or evil are astonishing. Reasonable hope for the better calls simply for dedicated effort. Mystical hope for the perfect demands consecrated surrender.*

SCHOMMER, CAROL MARIE, principal. Prin. Madonna High Sch. Recipient Blue Ribbon, 1990-91. Office: Madonna High Sch 4055 W Belmont Ave Chicago IL 60641-4700

SCHONBERG, ALAN ROBERT, management recruiting executive; b. N.Y.C., Oct. 23, 1928; s. Julius and Evelyn (Guzik) S.; m. Carole May Kreisman, Dec. 27, 1975; children: William, Evelyn, David, Jeffrey. Nat. sales mgr. Majestic Specialties, Inc., Cleve., 1953-63; pres. Internat. Personnel, Inc., Cleve., 1963-65, Mgmt. Recruiters Internat., Inc., Cleve., 1965—. V.p., bd. dirs. Jewish Vocat. Service, Cleve., 1983—; bd. dirs. Mt. Sinai Hosp., Cleve. Served to sgt. U.S. Army, Germany. Named one of Cleve.'s 86 Most Interesting People, Cleve. Mag., 1986. Mem. Internat. Franchise Assn., Internat. Confederation Pvt. Employment Agys. Assns., Am. Mgmt. Assn., Assn. Human Resource Cons. (chmn. 1980—), Org. for Rehab. and Training (ORT). Avocation: world travel. Office: Mgmt Recruiters Internat Inc 200 Public Sq 31st Floor Cleveland OH 44114*

SCHÖNBERG, BESSIE, dance educator; b. Hanover, Germany, Dec. 27, 1906; m. Dimitry Varley Jan. 6, 1934. Student, U. Oreg., 2 yrs.; studied with Martha Hill, Martha Graham; BA, Bennington Coll., 1936. Dancer Martha Graham Dance Co., N.Y.C., 1931; asst. to Martha Hill Bennington Coll. and/or Bennington Sch. of the Dance, 1933-35, 34-41; dance instr. Sarah Lawrence Coll., Bronxville, N.Y., 1936-41, head dance dept., 1941-75, 1941, prof. emerita, 1975—; tchr. dance dept. Juilliard, N.Y.C., 1993—; guest tchr. Ohio State U., Wesleyan U., U. N.H., George Mason U., The Art of Movement Ctr., London, Contemporary Dance Ctr., London, Dance Theatre Workshop, N.Y.C., Dance Theatre Harlem, N.Y.C.; dance cons. Hunter Coll., N.Y.C., Oberlin (Ohio) Coll., Dennison U., Wesleyan U.; mem. appeals bd. N.Y. State Coun. on Arts; mem. adv. panel NEA Dance Program; chmn., bd. dirs. Dance Theatre Workshop. Appeared in Martha Graham's dances including Primitive Mysteries, Ceremonials, Heretic, Project in Movement for a Divine Comedy. Mentor fellow NEA, 1994; recipient citation Assn. Am. Dance Cos., 1975, Lifetime Achievement in Dance Bessie award, 1987-88, Gov. Arts award N.Y. State, 1989, Ernie award Dance/USA, 1994; The N.Y. Dance and Performance Awards are named in her honor as The BESSIES. Office: Sarah Lawrence Coll Dept Dance 1 Meadway Bronxville NY 10708-5931

SCHONBERG, HAROLD CHARLES, music critic, columnist; b. N.Y.C., Nov. 29, 1915; s. David and Minnie (Kirsch) S.; m. Rosalyn Krokover, Nov. 28, 1942; m. Helene Cornell, May 10, 1975. BA cum laude, Bklyn. Coll., 1937; MA, NYU, 1938; LittD, Temple U., 1964; LHD, Grinnell Coll., 1967. Assoc. editor Am. Music Lover, 1939-41; contbr. editor Mus. Digest, 1946-48; music critic N.Y. Sun, 1946-50; contbg. editor, record columnist Mus. Courier, 1948-52; music and record critic N.Y. Times, 1950-60, sr. music critic, 1960-80, cultural corr., 1980-85; columnist on The Gramophone of London, 1948-60; judge many internat. piano competitions. Author: The

Guide to Long-Playing Records, Chamber and Solo Instrumental Music, 1955, The Collector's Chopin and Schumann, 1959, The Great Pianists, 1963, The Great Conductors, 1967, Lives of the Great Composers, 1970, Grandmasters of Chess, 1973, Facing the Music, 1981, The Glorious Ones--Classical Music's Legendary Performers, 1985, Horowitz: His Life and Music, 1992; illustrated own articles with caricatures; contbg. editor Internat. Ency. Music and Musicians. Served as 1st lt. Airborne Signal Corps AUS, 1942-46. Recipient Pulitzer prize for criticism, 1971. Clubs: Manhattan Chess, Century Assn., Army and Navy. Home: 160 Riverside Dr New York NY 10024-2106

SCHONBERG, WILLIAM PETER, aerospace, mechanical, civil engineering educator; b. N.Y.C., Mar. 25, 1960; s. Christian and Tamara (Kalnev) S.; m. Jane Heminover, Sept. 7, 1986; children: Christina Carol, Richard William. BSCE cum laude, Princeton U., 1981; MS in Engring., Northwestern U., 1983, PhD, 1986. Asst. prof. civil engring. U. Ala., Huntsville, 1986-91, assoc. prof., 1991-94, prof., 1994—, chair civil and environ. engring. dept., 1995—; mem. working group NASA Boeing Space Sta., 1987-90. Contbr. articles to profl. publs. Recipient rsch. and creative works award U. Ala.-Huntsville Found., 1992; Walter P. Murphy fellow, 1981-82, summer faculty fellow NASA, 1987, 88, 94, 95, Air Force Office Sci. Rsch., 1992, 93; grantee U. Ala.-Huntsville Rsch. Inst., 1987-92. Mem. AIAA (sr., Young Engr. of Yr. award 1990, Lawrence Sperry award 1995), ASME, ASCE, Am. Acad. Mechanics, Tau Beta Pi. Avocations: astronomy, stamps, mystery novels, rock & roll music, travel. Office: U Ala Huntsville 4701 University Dr NW Huntsville AL 35899-0100

SCHÖNEMANN, PETER HANS, psychology educator; b. Pethau, Fed. Republic Germany, July 15, 1929; came to U.S., 1960, naturalized, 1965; s. Max Paul Franz and Hertha Anna (Kahle) S.; m. Roberta Dianne Federbush, Jan. 29, 1962; children: Raoul Dieter, Nicole Deborah. Vordiplom in Psychologie, U. Munich, 1956; Hauptdiplom in Psychologie, U. Goettingen, 1959; Ph.D., U. Ill., 1964. Thurstone postdoctoral fellow U. N.C., 1965-66; asst. prof., then assoc. prof. Ohio State U., 1966-69; postdoctoral fellow Ednl. Testing Service, Princeton, N.J., 1967-68; vis. prof. Technische Hochschule, Aachen, Fed. Republic Germany, 1981; mem. faculty Purdue U., 1969—, prof. psychology, 1971—; vis. prof. Univs. Munich, Bielefeld and Braunschweig, 1984-85, Nat. Taiwan U., 1992. Author papers in field. Mem. Psychonomic Soc., Soc. Multivariate Exptl. Psychology. Office: Dept Psychol Scis Purdue U Lafayette IN 47907

SCHONFELD, GUSTAV, medical educator, researcher; b. Mukacevo, Ukraine, May 8, 1934; came to U.S., 1946; s. Alexander Schonfeld and Helena Gottesmann; m. Miriam Steinberg, May 28, 1961; children: Joshua Lawrence, Julia Elizabeth, Jeremy David. BA, Washington U., St. Louis, 1956, MD, 1960. Diplomate Am. Bd. Internal Medicine. Intern. Bellevue Med. Ctr. NYU, 1960-61, resident in internal medicine, 1961-63; chief resident in internal medicine Jewish Hosp., St. Louis, 1963-64; NIH trainee in endocrinology and metabolism Washington U., St. Louis, 1964-66, instr. medicine, 1965-66, asst. prof. medicine, 1968-70, assoc. prof. preventive medicine and medicine, 1972-77, prof. preventive medicine and prof. internal medicine, 1977-86, William B. Kountz prof. medicine, 1987—, dir. atherosclerosis and lipid rsch. ctr,, 1972—, acting head dept. preventive medicine, 1983-86, mem. exec. faculty Sch. Medicine, 1983-86, chmn. whole univ. faculty senate coun., 1995—; rsch. assoc. Cochran VA Hosp., St. Louis, 1965-66, clin. investigator, 1968-70, cons. in internal medicine, 1972—; rsch. flight med. officer USAF Sch. Aerospace Medicine, Brooks AFB, Tex., 1966-68; asst. physician Barnes Hosp., St. Louis, 1972-86; assoc. physician Barnes Hosp., 1986—; clin. instr. medicine Harvard U. Med. Sch., Boston, 1970-72; assoc. prof. metabolism and human nutrition, asst. dir. Clin. Rsch. Ctr. MIT, Boston, 1970-72; mem. rsch. com. Mo. Heart Assn., 1978-80; expert witness working group on atherosclerosis Nat. Heart, Lung and Blood Inst., 1979, Nat. Diabetes Adv. Bd., 1979; mem. endocrinologic and metabolic drugs adv. com. USPHS, FDA, 1982-86; mem. nutritional study sect. NIH, 19844-88, spl. reviewer metabolism study sect.; mem. adult treatment guidelines panel Nat. Cholesterol Edn. Program, 1986—; mem. Consenseus Devel. Conf. on Triglyceride, High Density Lipoprotein and Coronary Heart Disease, 1992—; cons. Am. Egg Bd., Am. Dairy Bd., Inst. Shortening and Edible Oils, Ciba-Geigy, Sandoz, Fournier, Parke-Davis, Bristol-Meyers Squibb, Monsanto/Searle. Editor: Atherosclerosis; past mem. editorial bd. Jour. Clin. Endocrinology and Metabolism, Jour. Clin. Investigation; mem. editorial bd. Jour. Lipid Rsch. Recipient Berg Prize in Microbiology, 1957, 58, Faculty/Alumni award Washington U., 1995; named Physician honoree Am. Heart Assn. Mo. Affiliate, 1995; grantee merit status NIH. Fellow ACP; mem. Assn. Am. Physicians, Am. Soc. for Clin. Investigation, Am. Physiol. Soc., Am. Soc. Biol. Chemists, Am. Inst. Nutrition, Am. Diabetes Assn., Am. Heart Assn. (program com. coun. on atherosclerosis 1977-80, 86-88, nat. com. 1980-84, pathology rsch. com. 1980-83, budget com. 1991, awards com. 1992), Endocrine Soc., Alpha Omega Alpha. Office: Washington U Sch Medicine Box 8046 660 S Euclid Saint Louis MO 63110

SCHONFELD, WILLIAM ROST, political science educator, researcher; b. N.Y.C., Aug. 28, 1942; s. William A. and Louise R. (Rost) S.; m. Elena Beortegui, Jan. 23, 1964; children: Natalie Beortegui, Elizabeth Lynn Beortegui. Student, Cornell U., 1960-61; B.A. cum laude with honors, NYU, 1964; M.A., Princeton U., 1968, Ph.D., 1970. Research asst. Princeton U., 1966-69, research assoc., 1969-70, vis. lectr., 1970; asst. prof. polit. sci. U. Calif.-Irvine, 1970-75, assoc. prof., 1975-81, prof., 1981—, dean Sch. Social Scis., 1982—; sr. lectr. Fond. Nat. de Sci. Politique, Paris, 1973-74; researcher Centre de Sociologie des Organisations, Paris, 1976-78. Author: Youth and Authority in France, 1971, Obedience and Revolt, 1976, Ethnographie du PS et du RPR, 1985. Recipient Disting. Teaching award U. Calif.-Irvine, 1984; Fulbright fellow Bordeaux, France, 1964-65; Danforth grad. fellow, 1964-69; Fulbright sr. lectr. Paris, 1973-74; NSF-CNRS Exchange of Scientists fellow Paris, 1976-78; Ford Found. grantee France, Spain, 1978-79; finalist Prof. Yr. Council for Advancement and Support of Edn., 1984. Mem. Am. Polit. Sci. Assn., Assoc. Francaise de Sci. Pol., Phi Beta Kappa. Office: U Calif Sch Social Scis Irvine CA 92717

SCHONHOLTZ, JOAN SONDRA HIRSCH, banker, civic worker; b. N.Y.C., Sept. 8, 1933; d. Joseph G. and Mildred (Klebanoff) Hirsch; m. George J. Schonholtz, Aug. 21, 1951; children: Margot Beth, Steven Robert, Barbara Ellen. Student, Vassar Coll., 1950-52; B.A., Barnard Coll., 1954; postgrad., Am. U., 1963. Chmn. bd. dirs., founding mem. Ist Women's Bank of Md., Rockville, 1976—; chmn. FWB Bancorp., Rockville, 1982—. Pres. Ft. Benning Med. Wives, Ga., 1962-63; sec. Montgomery County Women's Med. Aux., Md., 1968; bd. dirs. Svc. Guild of Washington, 1968-77, sec., 1969-70, pres., 1975-77; bd. dirs. Pilot Sch. for Blind Multiple Handicapped Children, Washington, 1968-77; bd. dirs. Strathmore Hall Arts Ctr., N. Bethesda, Md., 1992—; spl. gifts chmn. Cancer Soc. Montgomery County, 1968, 69; mem. Washington Adv. Coun. on Deaf-Blind Children, 1972-74; chmn. Friends of Wash. Adventist Hosp., Takoma Park, Md., 1993-94. Recipient Outstanding Service award Service Guild of Washington, 1969. Republican. Jewish. Clubs: Vassar, Barnard. Home: 10839 Lockland Rd Potomac MD 20854-1855

SCHONHORN, HAROLD, chemist, researcher; b. N.Y.C., Apr. 2, 1928; s. Benjamin and Dorothy (Gitlin) S.; m. Esther Matesky, Jan. 17, 1954; children: Deborah, Jeremy. BS, Bklyn. Coll., 1950; PhD, N.Y. Polytech. U., 1959. Mem. tech. staff Bell Labs., Murray Hill, N.J., 1961-84; v.p. R & D Polyken Tech. div. Kendall Co., Lexington, Mass., 1984-93; pres. Schonhorn Consultants, 1993—. Contbr. over 100 articles to profl. jours. Pres. B'nai B'rith Lodge, Summit, N.J., 1970. With U.S. Army, 1953-55, Korea. Mem. Am. Chem. Soc. Achievements include 15 patents.

SCHONWETTER, RONALD SCOTT, physician, educator; b. Miami Beach, Fla., Apr. 24, 1958; s. Morris Jack and Joyce (Trager) S.; m. Rita A. Nemitoff, Mar. 2, 1986; children: Sara Wendi, Rachel Elana, Jonathan Harris. BA in Chemistry and Psychology with high honors, Emory U., 1979; MD, U. South Fla., 1984. Diplomate Am. Bd. Internal Medicine, Nat. Bd. Med. Examiners. Intern in primary care internal medicine Baylor Coll. Medicine, Houston, 1984-85, resident in primary care internal medicine, 1985-87; fellow in geriatric medicine Baylor Coll. Medicine and VA Med. Ctr., Houston, 1987-89; asst. prof. medicine divsn. geriatric medicine, dept. internal medicine, coll. medicine U. South Fla., Tampa, 1989-94, assoc. prof. medicine, div. geriatric medicine, 1994—; assoc. med. dir. Hospice Hillsborough, Inc., Tampa, 1989-92, med. dir., 1992—, med. dir. palliative care clinic, 1993—; med. dir. Univ. Village Nursing Ctr., Tampa, 1989-94; staff physician Tampa Gen. Hosp. Skilled Nursing Facility, 1989—; cons. internist suncoast gerontology memory disorder clinic Coll. Medicine, U. South Fla., 1989-93; mem. hospice steering com., 1993—; vice chmn. Am. Bd. Hospice and Palliative Medicine, 1996—; presenter in field. Contbr. articles to profl. jours. Recipient New Investigator award Am. Geriatric Soc. and Merck U.S. Human Health, 1994. Fellow ACP, Am. Geriatrics Soc. (mem. ethics com. 1992—); mem. Am. Med. Dirs. Assn. (cert. med. dir.), Nat. Hospice Orgn. (mem. coun. hospice profls. 1994—), Gerontol. Soc. Am., Acad. Hospice Physicians (mem. rsch. com. 1993—). Jewish. Office: U South Fla Coll Medicine Dept Internal Medicine Divsn Geriatric Medicine 12901 Bruce B Downs Blvd Tampa FL 33612-4742

SCHOOLAR, JOSEPH CLAYTON, psychiatrist, pharmacologist, educator; b. Marks, Miss., Feb. 28, 1928; s. Adrian Taylor and Leah (Covington) S.; m. Betty Jane Peck, Nov. 2, 1960; children—Jonathan Covington, Cynthia Jane, Geoffrey Michael, Catherine Elizabeth, Adrian Carson. A.B., U. Tenn., Memphis, 1950, M.S., 1952; Ph.D., U. Chgo., 1957, M.D., 1960. Diplomate Am. Bd. Psychiatry and Neurology. Chief drug abuse research TRIMS, Houston, 1966-72; assoc. prof. U. Tex. Grad. Sch. Biomed. Scis., Houston, 1968—; prof. psychiatry Baylor Coll. Medicine, Houston, 1975—, prof. pharmacology, 1974—, chief div. psychopharmacology, 1973—; dir. Tex. Research Inst. Mental Scis., Houston, 1972-85; mem. Nat. Bd. Med. Examiners' Task Force on Drug Abuse and Alcoholism, 1982—; mem. Drug Abuse Adv. Com., FDA, Washington, 1983-85, chmn., 1984; chmn. profl. needs planning task force Nat. Inst. Drug Abuse, Washington, 1977—. Editor: Current Issues in Adolescent Psychiatry, 1973, Research and the Psychiatric Patient, 1975, The Kinetics of Psychiatric Drugs, 1979, Serotonin in Biological Psychiatry - Advanced in Biochemical Psychopharmacology, 1982. Cons. Parents' League Houston, 1972-74; mem. coordinating com. Citizens Mental Health Service, Houston, 1976; mem. acad. com. for study of violence Houston Police Dept., 1979; bd. dirs. Can-Do-It, Houston, 1982—. Served to 1st lt. U.S. Army, 1945-47. Recipient Eugen Kahn award Baylor Coll. Medicine, Houston, 1964. Fellow Am. Psychiat. Assn., Am. Coll. Psychiatrists; mem. Am. Coll. Neuropsychopharmacology, Collegium Internationale NeuroPsychopharmacologicum, Am. Soc. Pharmacology and Exptl. Therapeutics. Episcopalian. Home: 2222 Sunset Blvd Houston TX 77005-1530 Office: Baylor Coll Medicine One Baylor Pla Houston TX 77030

SCHOOLEY, CHARLES EARL, electrical engineer, consultant; b. Archie, Mo., Sept. 18, 1905; s. Charles Elias and Virginia Maria (Bone) S.; m. Dorothy S. Alexander, Apr. 29, 1934 (dec. 1965); 1 dau., Dorothy Virginia; m. Dolores Harter, Apr. 1966 (dec. 1993). B.S. in Elec. Engring, U. Mo., 1928. Registered profl. engr., Ga. With Ozark Utilities Co., Bolivar Telephone Co., Mo. Pacific R.R.; transmission engr. Long Lines dept. Am. Tel. & Tel. Co., St. Louis, Kansas City, N.Y.C., 1927-44; co-axial carrier engr., elec. coordination engr. Am. Tel. & Tel. Co., N.Y.C., 1944-48; div. engr. Am. Tel. & Tel. Co., Washington, 1948-49; facility engr., engr. transmission, comml. devel. engr. Am. Tel. & Tel. Co., 1949-51, toll dialing engr., plant extension engr., system planning engr., operating and engring. dep., 1951-53, asst. chief engr., dir. customer products planning, 1956-57; chief engr. So. Bell Tel. & Tel. Co., Atlanta, 1953-55; v.p. operations, dir. Ind. Bell Telephone Co., Indpls., 1957-59; dir. operations, mem. bd. long lines dept. Am. Tel. & Tel. Co., N.Y., 1959-66; dir., v.p. Transpacific Communications Co., Transocean Cable Ship Co., Eastern Tel. & Tel. Co., 1960-66, 9 other Am. Tel. & Tel. subs; v.p., treas., dir. Eds, Inc., Sharon, Conn., 1970-85. Vice pres. Berkshire Hills (Conn.) Music and Dance Assn., 1970-78; v.p., treas. Wingspread Found., 1977—; trustee Brevard (N.C.) Music Ctr., 1994—. Recipient Disting. Service to Engring. medal U. Mo., 1960. Fellow IEEE; mem. Ga. Engring. Soc., Met. Club (N.Y.C.), Hendersonville (N.C.) Country Club, QEBH U. Mo., Delta Upsilon (bd. dirs. 1962-70), Eta Kappa Nu. Address: PO Box 746 Hendersonville NC 28793-0746 also: PO Box 633 Winter Haven FL 33882-0633 also: 210 Crooked Creek Rd Hendersonville NC 28739-6822

SCHOOLEY, DOLORES HARTER, entertainment administrator; b. Nora Springs, Iowa, May 2, 1905; d. Amil A. and Elizabeth (Sefert) Zemke; m. Leslie J. Harter, June 5, 1934 (dec. 1963); m. Charles Earl Schooley, Apr. 1, 1966. BE, BA, U. Colo., 1927; MA, Northwestern U., 1931. Tchr. high sch. Consol. Schs., Johnstown, Colo., 1927-28, Byers, Colo., 1928-29, Clayton, Mo., 1931-34; theatrical makeup artist, 1937-86; instr. theatrical makeup dramatic clubs, N.J. Theatre League; lectr., demonstrator theatrical makeup, dramatic and women's clubs, high schs., N.J. and N.Y. area, 1937-53; nat. officer, entertainer, dir. internat. entertainment project for mil. posts Phi Beta Nat. Profl. Fraternity for Creative & Performing Arts, 1951-61; cons. radio broadcast series Sta. WNYC, N.Y., 1962-65; dir. community rels. Wingspread Summer Theatre, Colon, Mich., 1955; co-chmn. Valley Shore Community Concerts, Conn., 1958-61, artist mgr., 1959—; founder, pres. Berkshire Hills Music and Dance Assn., Conn., 1970-78; mem. Music Mountain Corp., Falls Village, Conn., 1975-81. Trustee Sharon (Conn.) Creative Arts Found., 1970-73; hon. trustee Bar Harbor Maine Festival, 1968-80; founder, pres. Wingspread Found., Conn. 1977—; mem. adv. bd. Community Found. of Henderson County, N.C., 1990-93; trustee Brevard (N.C.) Music Ctr., 1990-93. Mem. Montclair (N.J.) Dramatic Club (chmn. and instr. makeup), Rehearsal Club (program chmn.), Montclair (N.J.) Women's Club (dir. plays, chmn. drama dept.), Sharon (Conn.) Women's Club, Sharon Rep. Women's Club (pres. 1982-85), Sharon Country Club, Hendersonville (N.C.) Country Club, Alpha Omicron Pi., Phi Beta (nat. profl. fraternity for peforming arts). Congregationalist. Address: PO Box 746 Hendersonville NC 28793-0746

SCHOOLMAN, ARNOLD, neurological surgeon; b. Worcester, Mass., Oct. 31, 1927; s. Samuel and Sarah (Koffman) Schulman; m. Gloria June Feder, Nov. 10, 1963; children: Hugh Sinclair, (Jill) Annette. Student, U. Mass., 1945-46; BA, Emory U., 1950; PhD, Yale U., 1954, MD, 1957. Diplomate Am. Bd Neurol. Surgery, Nat. Bd. Med. Examiners. Intern U. Calif. Hosp., San Francisco, 1957-58; resident in neurol. surgery Columbia-Presbyn. Med. Ctr., Neurol. Inst. N.Y., N.Y.C., 1958-62; instr. neurol. surgery U. Kans. Sch. Medicine, Kansas City, 1962, asst. prof. surgery, 1964; assoc. prof. U. Mo. Sch. Medicine, Kansas City, 1976; chief sect. neurosurgery Research Med. Ctr., Kansas City, 1982; dir. Midwest Neurol. Inst., 1982-83. Patentee in field. Served with USN, 1946-48. Fellow ACS (mem. Mo. chpt.); mem. AMA, Mo. State Med. Assn., Kansas City Med. Soc., Kansas City Neurosurg. Soc. (pres. 1984-85), Kansas City Neurol. Soc., Rocky Mountain Neurosurg. Soc., Am. Assn. Neurol. Surgeons, AAAS, Mo. Neurol. Soc., Internat. Coll. Surgeons, Congress Neurol. Surgeons, Brit. Royal Soc. Medicine, Phi Beta Kappa, Sigma Xi. Avocation: pilot. Home: 8705 Catalina St Shawnee Mission KS 66207-2351 Office: 1000 E 50th St Ste 310 Kansas City MO 64110-2215

SCHOOLS, CHARLES HUGHLETTE, banker, lawyer; b. Lansing, Mich., May 24, 1929; s. Robert Thomas and Lillian Pearl (Lawson) S.; B.S., Am. U., 1952, M.A., 1958; J.D., Washington Coll. of Law, 1963; LL.D., Bethune-Cookman U., 1973; m. Rosemarie Sanchez, Nov. 22, 1952; children—Charles, Michael. Dir. phys. plant Am. U., 1952-66; owner, 1957—, Gen. Security Co., Washington, 1969—; chmn., pres. Consol. Ventures Ltd.; pres., chmn. bd. McLean Bank (Va.), 1974—, Instl. Environ. Mgmt. Services; chmn. bd. Harper & Co.; chmn., pres. Community Assos. of Va., Associated Real Estate Mgmt. Services; dir. Computer Data Systems Inc., DAC Devel. Ltd., Am. Indsl. Devel. Corp., Intercoastal of Iran; mem. Met. Bd. Trades. Pres., McLean Boys' Club; bd. dirs. D.C. Spl. Olympics, Nat. Kidney Found.; trustee Bethune Cookman Coll., Western Md. Coll., Randolph Macon Acad. Served with USAAF, 1946-47, USAF, 1947-48. Mem. Va. C. of C., Profl. Businessman's Orgn., Alpha Tau Omega. Democrat. Clubs: Georgetown of Washington, Touchdown of Washington, Univ. of Washington, Washington Golf and Country, Pisces (Washington); Halifax (Daytona Beach, Fla.); Masons. Home: 1320 Darnall Dr Mc Lean VA 22101-3006 Office: 1313 Dolley Madison Blvd Mc Lean VA 22101-3926

SCHOONHOVEN, RAY JAMES, retired lawyer; b. Elgin, Ill., May 24, 1921; s. Ray Covey and Rosina Madeline (Schram) (White) S.; m. Marie Theresa Dunn, Dec. 11, 1943; children: Marie Kathleen, Ray James, Jr., Pamela Suzanne, John Philip, Rose Lynne. B.S.C., U. Notre Dame, 1943; J.D., Northwestern U., 1948. Bar: Ill. 1949, U.S. Supreme Ct. 1954, D.C. 1973, U.S. Ct. Mil. Appeals 1954. Assoc. Seyfarth, Shaw Fairweather & Geraldson, Chgo., 1949-57, ptnr., 1957-92; ret.; chief rulings and ops. br. Wage Stabilization Bd. Region VII, Chgo., 1951-52. Book rev. editor: Ill. Law Rev., 1948. Served to lt.comdr. USNR, 1942-62. Mem. ABA, Ill. State Bar Assn., Chgo. Bar Assn., D.C. Bar Assn., Chgo. Athletic Assn., Univ. Club. Chgo., Order of Coif. Republican. Roman Catholic. Home: 6636 N Ponchartrain Blvd Chicago IL 60646-1428 Office: Seyfarth Shaw Fairweather & Geraldson 55 E Monroe St Ste 4200 Chicago IL 60603-5803 *I work hard to preserve our free enterprise system and, hopefully, to make such contribution to our society that it is better for my having been a part of it.*

SCHOONMAKER, SAMUEL VAIL, III, lawyer; b. Newburgh, N.Y., Sept. 1, 1935; s. Samuel V. Jr. and Catherine (Wilson) S.; m. Carolyn Peters, Sept. 18, 1965; children: Samuel V. IV, Frederick P. BA magna cum laude, Yale U., 1958, JD, 1961. Bar: Conn. 1961, U.S. Dist. Ct. Conn. 1961, U.S. Dist. Ct. (so. and ea. dist.) N.Y. 1964, U.S. Ct. Appeals (2d cir.) 1964, U.S. Supreme Ct. 1965. Assoc. Cummings & Lockwood, Stamford, Conn., 1961-70, ptnr., 1970—, co-mng. ptnr., 1987-90, mng. ptnr., 1990—, chmn. exec. com., 1987—; founder Schoonmaker & George, PC, Greenwich, Conn., 1996—; state trial referee Conn. Superior Ct., 1989; pres. Schoonmaker Family Assn., New Paltz, N.Y., 1975-77. Sr. topical editor Conn. Bar Jour., 1977-81; mem. bd. editors Fairshare and America Jour., 1992; contbr. articles to profl. jours. Chmn. Conn. Child Support Commn., 1984-86; mem. Conn. Family Support Com., 1986-90; mem. Darien (Conn.) Rep. Town Com., 1974-76, town meeting, 1990—; pres. Youth Tennis Found. New Eng., Needham, Mass., 1975-77; pres. New Eng. Lawn Tennis Assn., 1977-79 (Man of Yr. award 1979). Fellow Am. Acad. Matrimonial Lawyers Conn. (bd. mgrs., Disting. Svc. award 1988), Internat. Acad. Matrimonial Lawyers, Am. Bar Found.; mem. ABA (chmn. family law sect. 1982-83), Conn. Bar Assn. (chmn. family law sect. 1971-74), Conn. Bus. and Industry Assn. (bd. dirs. 1993—), S.W. Conn. Bus. and Industry Assn. (bd. dirs. 1990—), Pub. Defenders Assn. (chmn.), Wee Burn Country Club (Darien, Conn., asst. sec.), Yale Club (N.Y.C.), Phi Beta Kappa. Avocation: tennis, platform tennis. Home: 231 Old Kings Hwy Darien CT 06820 Office: Schoonmaker & George PO Box 5059 5 Edgewood Ave Greenwich CT 06931-5059

SCHOONMAKER POWELL, THELMA, film editor; b. 1940; m. Michael Powell, 1984 (dec. 1990). Editor: (films) Who's That Knocking at My Door, 1968, Woodstock, 1970 (Academy award nomination best film editing 1970), Raging Bull, 1980 (Academy award best film editing 1980), The King of Comedy, 1983, After Hours, 1985, The Color of Money, 1986, The Last Temptation of Christ, 1988, New York Stories ("Life Lessons"), 1989, GoodFellas, 1990 (Academy award nomination best film editing 1990), Cape Fear, 1992, The Age of Innocence, 1993, A Personal Journey with Martin Scorsese Through American Movies, 1995, Casino, 1995. Office: Cappa Prodns 445 Park Ave 7th Fl New York NY 10022

SCHOONOVER, JACK RONALD, judge; b. Winona, Minn., July 23, 1934; s. Richard M. and Elizabeth A. (Hargeisheimer) S.; student Winona State Coll., 1956-58; LLB, U. Fla., 1962; m. Ann Marie Kroez, June 18, 1965; children: Jack Ronald, Wayne J. Bar: Fla. 1962. Atty. Wotitzky, Wotitzky & Schoonover, 1962-69, Schoonover, Olmsted & Schwarz, 1969-75; spl. asst. state's atty., State of Fla., 1969-72; city atty. City of Punta Gorda, Fla., city judge, 1973-74; judge 20th Jud. Cir. Ct., Ft. Myers, Fla., 1975-81, 2d Dist. Ct. Appeal, 1981—, chief judge, 1990-92; atty. Charlotte County Sch. Bd., 1969-75, Charlotte County Zoning Bd., Charlotte County Devel. Authority; mem. unauthorized practice law com. 12th Jud. Cir., mem. grievance com. 20th Jud. Cir.; adj. prof. Edison C.C. Tchr. Charlotte County Adult Edn. Assn. Served with USAF, 1952-56. Mem. Am. Legion. Home: 1224 Stratton Ct W Lakeland FL 33813-2348 Office: PO Box 327 Lakeland FL 33802-0327

SCHOONOVER, JEAN WAY, public relations consultant; b. Richfield Springs, N.Y.. AB, Cornell U., 1941. With D-A-Y Pub. Rels., Ogilvy & Mather Co., N.Y.C., 1949-91, D-A-Y Pub. Rels. Inc. and predecessor, N.Y.C., 1949—; owner, pres. Dudley-Anderson-Yutzy Pub. Rels. Inc. and predecessor, N.Y.C., 1970—; chmn. Dudley-Anderson-Yutzy Pub. Relations Inc. and predecessor, 1984-88; merger with Ogilvy & Mather, 1983; sr. v.p. Ogilvy & Mather U.S., 1984-91; vice chmn. Ogilvy Pub. Relations Group, 1986-91; ind. cons., 1992—; pres. YWCA of the City of N.Y., 1994—; mem., historian, Pub. Relations Seminar; mem. U.S. Dept. Agriculture Agribusiness Promotion Council, 1985—. Trustee Cornell U., 1975-80; mem. Def. Adv. Com. on Women in Svcs., 1987-89. Named Advt. Woman of Yr. Am. Advt. Fedn., 1972, one of Outstanding Women in Bus. & Labor, Women's Equity Action League, 1985; recipient Matrix award, 1976, Nat. Headliner award, 1984, N.Y. Women in Comm., 1976, Leadership award Internat. Orgn. Women Bus. Owners, 1980, Entrepreneurial Woman award Women Bus. Owners N.Y., 1981, Women of Distinction award Soroptimists Internat. N.Y., 1995. Mem. Women Execs. in Pub. Rels. N.Y.C. (pres. 1979-80), Pub. Rels. Soc. Am., Pub. Rels. Soc. N.Y. (pres. 1979), Womens Forum, Women's City Club. Home: 25 Stuyvesant St New York NY 10003-7505

SCHOPLER, JOHN HENRY, psychologist, educator; b. Fuerth, Fed. Republic Germany, Nov. 5, 1930; came to U.S., 1938, naturalized, 1943; s. Ernest H. and Erna (Oppenheimer) S.; m. Janice E. Hough, Dec. 12, 1969; children: Kari, Lisa, Andrew, David. B.A., U. Rochester, 1952; M.A., U. N.Mex., 1953; Ph.D., U. Colo., 1958. Mem. faculty U. N.C., Chapel Hill, 1957—; asso. prof. psychology U. N.C., 1964-69, prof., 1969—, chmn. dept., 1976-83; NSF sr. postdoctoral fellow London Sch. Econs. and Polit. Sci., 1966-67, Kenan prof., 1983-84. Author: (with Chester Insko) Experimental Social Psychology, 1972; co-founder, asso. editor: (with John Thibaut) Jour. Exptl. Social Psychology, 1964-69; contbr. (with Chester Insko) articles to profl. jours. Fulbright scholar, 1974-75. Fellow Am. Psychol. Assn., Soc. Psychol. Study Social Issues, N.C. Psychol. Assn.; mem. Soc. Explt. Social Psychology. Office: U NC Dept Psychology Chapel Hill NC 27514

SCHOPPER, SUE FRANKS, maternal, women's health and medical/surgical nurse; b. Stigler, Okla., Mar. 25, 1938; d. Everett and Ruby (McCaslin) F.; m. Jared B. Schopper, Jan. 27, 1978; children: Robert, Jenny, Melody. Assoc. Diploma Nursing, Bacone Coll., Muskogee, Okla., 1973; BSN, Northeastern State U., Tahlequah, Okla., 1991. RN, Okla. Supr. VA Med. Ctr., Muskogee, 1973-78; charge nurse obstetrics-labor-delivery room, newborn nursery Hastings Hosp., Tahlequah, 1979; charge nurse surg. floor Tahlequah City Hosp., 1983-90; pediatric nurse Pediatric Clinic, Tahlequah, 1990—; RN cons. Green Acres Retirement Ctr., Tahlequah, 1989—. Home: 402 Wheeler St Tahlequah OK 74464-6301 Office: Pediatric Clinic 1607 S Muskogee Ave Tahlequah OK 74464-5430

SCHOPPMANN, MICHAEL JOSEPH, lawyer; b. N.Y.C., May 17, 1960; s. Fred Richard and Dorothy Ann (Wood) S.; m. Marlene Elizabeth Macbeth, Nov. 21, 1987; children: Michael, Steven. BS, St. John's U., 1982; JD, Seton Hall U., 1985. Bar: N.J. 1985, U.S. Dist. Ct. N.J. 1986, U.S. Supreme Ct. 1992, D.C. 1993, N.Y. 1994. Assoc. Baker Garber Duffy & Baker, Hoboken, N.J., 1985-87; counsel Johnstone Skok Loughlin & Lane, Westfield, N.J., 1987-90; prin. Kern Augustine Conroy & Schoppmann, Bridgewater, N.J., 1990—. Author, editor: (text) Basic Health Law, 1993. Mem. ABA, Assn. Trial Lawyers Am., N.J. Bar Assn. (chair adminstrv. law sect. 1994—), N.Y. Bar Assn., Somerset County Bar Assn. Office: Kern Augustine Conroy & Schoppmann 1120 Rte 22 Bridgewater NJ 08807

SCHOPPMEYER, MARTIN WILLIAM, education educator; b. Weehawken, N.J., Sept. 15, 1929; s. William G. and Madeleine M. (Haas) S.; m. Marilyn M. Myers, Aug. 9, 1958; children: Susan Ann, Martin William. B.S., Fordham U., 1950; Ed.M., U. Fla., 1955, Ed.D., 1962. Tchr. Fla. pub. schs., 1955-59; instr., then asst. prof. U. Fla., 1960-63; assoc. prof., then prof. edn. Fla. Atlantic U., Boca Raton, 1963-68; dir. continuing edn. Fla. Atlantic U., 1965-67; mem. faculty U. Ark., Fayetteville, 1968—; prof. edn. U. Ark., 1971-93; univ. prof. U. Ark., Fayetteville, 1993—; program coord. for ednl. adminstrn. U. Ark., 1983-90; mem. Nat. Adv. Coun. Edn. Professions Devel., 1973-76; exec. sec. Ark. Sch. Study Coun., 1976—; evaluator instructional tng. program Nat. Tng. Fund, 1978; bd. dirs. Women's Ednl. and Devel. Inst., 1977-80, Nat. Sch. Devel. Coun., sec., 1989-90, v.p. 1990, pres., 1990-92; mem. oversight com. South Conway (Ark.) County Sch. Dist.; mem. state commn. to study effect of Amendment 59 to Ark. Constn. Author books, monographs, articles in field. Mem. president's coun. Subiaco Acad., 1984-90; chmn. Subiaco Sch. Bd., 1990-93, mem.,

1993—. With U.S. Army, 1951-53, Korea. Recipient numerous fed. grants. Mem. NEA, Ark. Edn. Assn. (past chpt. pres.), Ark. Assn. Ednl. Adminstrs., KC, Rotary, Kappa Delta Pi, Phi Delta Kappa, Delta Tau Kappa. Roman Catholic. Home: 2950 Sheryl Ave Fayetteville AR 72703-3542 Office: U Ark 231 Grad Edn Bldg Fayetteville AR 72701 *The only really sound investment for a family, a community, or a society is that money spent for the education of its youth.*

SCHOR, JOSEPH MARTIN, pharmaceutical executive, biochemist; b. Bklyn., Jan. 10, 1929; s. Aaron Jacob and Rhea Iress (Kay) S.; children: Esther Helen, Joshua David, Gideon Alexander; m. Laura Sharon Strumingher, June 14, 1992. B.S. magna cum laude, CCNY, 1951; Ph.D., Fla. State U., 1957. Sr. research chemist Armour Pharm. Co., Kankakee, Ill., 1957-59, Lederle Labs., Pearl River, N.Y., 1959-64; dir. biochemistry Endo Labs., Garden City, N.Y., 1964-76; v.p. sci. affairs Forest Labs., N.Y.C., 1977-94, sr. v.p. scientific affairs emeritus, Forest Labs, 1995—. Editor, contbr.: Chemical Control of Fibrinolysis-Thrombolysis, 1970. Contbr. articles to profl. jours. Patentee in field. USPHS fellow, 1955-57. Fellow Am. Inst. Chemists (cert. profl. chemist); mem. Am. Chem. Soc. (chmn. Nassau County subsect. 1971-72), Internat. Soc. on Thrombosis and Hemostasis, N.Y. Acad. Scis., AAAS, Phi Beta Kappa, Sigma Xi. Home: 28 Meleny Rd Locust Valley NY 11560-1221

SCHOR, LAURA STRUMINGHER, academic administrator, historian; b. N.Y.C., June 24, 1945; d. David Charles and Esther Rachel (Pearl) Gross; children: Eric Alain, Neil Remy; m. Joseph Martin Schor, June 14, 1992. BA, Queens Coll., CUNY, 1967; MA, U. Rochester, 1970, PhD, 1974. Asst. prof. SUNY, Fredonia, 1973-79; assoc. prof., dir. women's studies U. Cin., 1979-85, prof., vice provost, 1985-89; prof., provost, v.p. acad. affairs Hunter Coll., CUNY, N.Y.C., 1989—. Author: Women and the Making of the Working Class, 1979, What Were Little Boys and Girls Made Of?, 1984, The Odyssey of Flora Tristan, 1988, Les Jolies Femmes d'Edouard de Beaumont, 1994. Mem. Internat. Soc. for Study European Ideas, Am. Hist. Assn., French Hist. Assn., Phi Beta Kappa. Office: CUNY-Hunter Coll Office of Provost 695 Park Ave New York NY 10021-5024

SCHOR, OLGA SEEMANN, mental health counselor, real estate broker; b. Havana, Cuba, Mar. 2, 1951; came to U.S., 1961; d. Olga del Carmen (Hernandez) S.; m. David Michael Schor, Apr. 22, 1979; 1 child, Andrew. A.A., Miami Dade Community Coll., 1971; B.A., U. Fla.-Gainesville, 1973; M.Edn., U. Miami, Fla., 1976; Psy.D., Nova U., 1981; cert. Bert Rodgers Sch. Real Estate, Miami, 1981, Gold Coast Sch. Real Estate, 1988; lic. real estate broker. Teaching asst. U. Fla., Gainesville, 1972-73; counselor U. Miami, Fla., 1974-79; assoc. psychotherapist Linda H. Jamrozy & Assocs., Miami, 1976-78, Interactive Systems, Miami, 1978-79; psychometrist Jackson Meml. Hosp., Miami, 1978-79; assoc. psychotherapist Behavioral Medicine Inst., Miami, 1979-85, Tony Ciminero & Assocs., Miami, 1985-86; lectr. U. Miami, 1976-78, Jackson Meml. Hosp. Sch. Nursing, Miami, 1976; real estate broker The Keyes Co. Realtor, Coral Gables, 1981-88, Keyes Asset Mgmt., Miami, 1988—; sec./treas. bd. dirs. BODS Inc., Miami. Recipient Assoc. of Quarter award Keyes Co. Realtors, 1986. Mem. Am. Psychol. and Guidance Assn., Keyes Comml. Roundtable, Keyes Inner Circle, Coral Gables Bd. Realtors, Gulliver Acad.'s Parents Bd., Dade County Mental Health Assn., Million Dollar Sales Club. Club: South Fla. Sailing Assn. (Miami). Avocations: sailing; diving; reading; running; theater; acting; tennis. Office: Keyes Asset Mgmt Inc 1 SE 3rd Ave Fl 11 Miami FL 33131-1704

SCHOR, STANLEY SIDNEY, mathematical sciences educator; b. Phila., Mar. 3, 1922; s. Joseph and Dorothy (Abrams) S.; m. Irene Sternberg, June 19, 1949; children—Mark, Robin, Randi. A.B., U. Pa., 1943, A.M., 1950, Ph.D., 1952; certificate, U. Cin., 1944. Instr. U. Pa., Phila., 1950-53, asst. prof. stats., 1953-58, assoc. prof., 1958-64, dir. Nat. Periodic Health Exam. Research Group, 1958-64; dir. biostats. AMA, Chgo., 1964-66; prof. biostats. Chgo. Med. Sch., 1964-66; prof., chmn. dept. biometrics Temple U. Med. Sch., 1966-75, adj. prof., 1975-85; vis. prof. Tel Aviv U., 1973-74, Med. Coll. Pa., 1979; exec. dir. Cbards, Merck Sharp & Dohme, West Point, Pa., 1975-91; clin. prof. Hahnemann Med. Sch., 1975-85; cons. in field. Author: Fundamentals of Biostatistics, 1968; mem. editorial staff Jour. Trauma, 1955-91, Jour. AMA, 1964-91, Chest, 1966-91; contbr. articles to profl. jours. Served with AUS, 1943-46. Fellow Am. Public Health Assn., Am. Statis. Assn., Phila. Coll. Physicians; mem. Biometric Soc., AAUP, Royal Soc. Health, Pi Gamma Mu. Home: 3912 S Ocean Blvd Apt 1105 Highland Beach FL 33487

SCHOR, SUZI, lawyer; b. Chgo., Feb. 1, 1947; d. Samuel S. and Dorothy Helen (Hineline); 1 child, Kate. BABA, Ind. U., 1964; MBA Mktg., Northwestern U., 1967, JD, 1970; PhD in Fine Arts (hon.), U. Nev., PhD in Clin. Psychology, 1989. Bar: Ill., 1971. Pvt. practice L.A., 1971-80; v.p. legal affairs Little Gypzy Mgmt., Inc., Beverly Hills, Calif., 1980—. Contbr. articles to profl. jours. Bd. dirs. Nat. Ctr. for Hyperactive Children, L.A., 1989-91, sec. Rainbow Guild Cancer Charity, L.A., 1985-89, ind. cons. Jewish Legal Aid, L.A., 1988—; campaign coord. advisor Dem. Nat. Campaign, L.A., 1990, 94. Mem. ABA (criminal justice com. 1994), AAUW, NAADAC, CAADAC, L.A. Breakfast Club (chmn. entertainment 1988-90), Rotary. Jewish. Avocations: singing, skiing, writing.

SCHORE, ROBERT, social worker, educator; b. N.Y.C., July 29, 1934; s. David and Helen S.; married, three children. Student, Mesivta Tifereth Jerusalem, N.Y.C., 1947-48; BA, CCNY, 1955; MS, Columbia U., 1959; cert. advanced study, SUNY, New Paltz, 1985; postgrad., Postgrad. Ctr. for Mental, Health, 1967, Inst. for Rational-Emotive, Therapy, Bank St. Coll., 1984, Rockland Conservatory Music, 1992—. Diplomate Clin. Social Work, NASW; cert. social worker, impartial hearing officer, sch. dist. adminstr., supr. sch. social workers, N.Y. Social worker Dept. Social Svcs./Child Placement Svcs., N.Y.C., 1956-58, Edwin Gould Found., N.Y.C., 1959-63; supr. with NIMH dem. project Shield Inst., Bronx, N.Y., 1963-65; sch. social worker N.Y.C. Bd. Edn. Bur. Child Guidance, Bronx, 1965-80; sch. social worker Com. on Spl. Edn., Bronx, 1980-85, High Sch. Clin. Svcs., Bronx, 1986-91; pvt. practice West Nyack, N.Y., 1992-95; psychotherapist Ind. Consultation Ctr., Bronx, 1967, Rockland County Mental Health Ctr., Monsey, N.Y., 1968-69; rsch. assoc., editor/NIMH demo project Nathan Kline Inst., Orangeburg, N.Y., 1968-85; instr. CCNY, 1966; field instr. NYU, 1970-73; adj. prof. Rockland C.C., Suffern, N.Y., 1993—; fair hearing officer N.Y. State Edn. Dept., 1992—; adminstrv. intern Clarkstown Sch. Dist., West Nyack, 1984-85; workshop leader in field. Editor: Orb Mag., 1950-51; contb. chpts. to books, articles to profl. jours. Supr., cons. Vol. Counseling Svc., New City, N.Y., 1992-94; bd. dirs. Rockland Hebrew Day Sch., 1986; violinist Riverdale Orchestra, Suburban Symphony of Rockland, Ramapo Orchestral Soc., N.Y. With USAR, 1957-63. Mem. Am. Fedn. Tchrs., N.Y. State United Tchrs., United Fedn. Tchrs., Acad. Cert. Social Workers. Jewish. Avocations: photography, music, violin, piano, amateur radio. Office: PO Box 276 Monsey NY 10952-0276

SCHORER, JOSEPH U., lawyer; b. Baraboo, Wis., June 15, 1953. BA, Northwestern U., 1975; JD, Harvard U., 1978. Bar: Calif. 1978, U.S. Dist. Ct. (so. dist.) Calif. 1978, Ill. 1981, U.S. Dist. Ct. (no. dist.) Ill. 1981, U.S. Ct. Appeals (7th cir.) 1982, U.S. Ct. Appeals (5th cir.) 1987, U.S. Ct. Appeals (10th cir.) 1988. Ptnr. Mayer, Brown & Platt, Chgo. Office: Mayer Brown & Platt 190 S La Salle St Chicago IL 60603-3410*

SCHORER, SUKI, ballet teacher; b. Boston; d. Mark and Ruth (Page) S.; 1 child, Nicole. Studied with, George Balanchine. Dancer San Francisco Ballet, 1956-59, N.Y.C. Ballet, 1959-72; prin. dancer N.Y.C. Ballet Co., 1968-72, artistic assoc. lecture demonstration program, 1972-95; mem. faculty Sch. Am. Ballet, 1972—; internat. guest tchr. and lectr. specializing in Balanchine tng. and technique; artist dir., tchr. on Balanchine Essays (videos). Author (monograph) Balanchine Pointework, 1995; created roles in Balanchine's Harlequinade, Don Quixote, Midsummer Night's Dream, Jewels, La Source, Raymonda Variations; repertory included prin. roles in Apollo, Serenade, Concerto Barocco Symphony in C, La Somnambula, Stars and Stripes, Tarantella, Valse Fantaisie, The Nutcracker, Brahams Schoenberg, La Valse, Western Symphony, Ivesiana, Divertimento # 15, Ballet Imperial, others. Office: Sch of Am Ballet 70 Lincoln Center Plz New York NY 10023

SCHORGL, THOMAS BARRY, arts administrator; b. St. Louis, Mar. 1, 1950; s. Francis William and Janet Sarah (Peterson) S.; m. Elizabeth Ann Eades, Aug. 6, 1977; children: Matthew, Ann, Joseph. BFA, U. Iowa, 1973, MA in Drawing, 1974; MFA in Printmaking, Miami U., Oxford, Ohio, 1976; apprenticeship, Atelier, Garrigue, France, 1976; postgrad., U. Notre Dame, 1979. Comml. artist R.H. Donnelly, Chgo., 1977; curator Art Ctr. Inc., South Bend, Ind., 1977-78, dir. acting, 1978, exec. dir., 1978-81; account exec. James P. Carroll & Assocs., South Bend, 1981-83; exec. dir Ind. Arts. Commn., Indpls., 1983-94; pres., CEO Culture Works, Dayton, Ohio, 1994—; cons. in field. Chmn. Arts Midwest, 1989-91, treas., 1987, 88; panelist Nat. Endowment for Arts, 1985-90, chmn. grants panel Art is Basic to Edn., 1986-89. Mem. Great Lakes Arts Alliance (sec., treas. 1983-85, merger com.), Affiliated State Arts Agys. Upper Midwest (chmn. program com. 1985—), Arts Midwest (chmn. 1989-91), Nat. Assembly of State Arts Agys. (bd. dirs. 1991—). Avocations: visual arts, antiques, endurance sports. Office: Culture Works 126 N Main St Ste 100 Dayton OH 45402-1766

SCHORLING, WILLIAM HARRISON, lawyer; b. Ann Arbor, Mich., Jan. 7, 1949; s. Otis William Schorling and Ruthann (Bales) Schorling Moorehead; m. Lynne Ann Newcomb, June 1, 1974; children: Katherine Pearce, Ann Oury, John Roberts. BA cum laude, Denison U., 1971; JD cum laude, U. Mich., 1975. Bar: Pa. 1975, U.S. Ct. Appeals (3d cir.) 1977. Ptnr. Eckert, Seamans, Cherin & Mellott, Pitts., 1984-89, Klett Lieber Rooney & Schorling, Pitts., 1989—; lectr. Pa. Bar Inst., Harrisburg, 1983—, Comml. Law League, N.Y.C., 1984—, Profl. Edn. Systems, Inc., Eau Claire, Wis., 1986—, Southwest Legal Found., Dallas, 1994—; gov. bd. Comml. Fin. Assn. Edn. Found., 1991—; bd. dirs. Consumer Bankruptcy Assistance Project, 1995—. Contbr. articles to profl. jours. Fellow Am. Bar Found.; mem. ABA (chmn. bus. bankruptcy com., lectr. 1988—), Am. Banker Inst. (lectr. 1994—), Phila. Bar Assn., E. Dist. Bankruptcy Assn., Pa. Bar Assn. (lectr. 1983—), Allegheny County Bar Assn. (chmn. bankruptcy and comml. law sect. 1991), Longue Vue Club, Duquesne Club, Rivers Club, Pa. Soc. Presbyterian. Home: 5600 Northumberland St Pittsburgh PA 15217-1238 Office: Klett Lieber Rooney & Schorling 1 Logan Sq 28th Fl Philadelphia PA 19103

SCHORNACK, JOHN JAMES, accountant; b. Chgo., Nov. 22, 1930; s. John Joseph and Helen Patricia (Patrickus) S.; m. Barbara Anne Lelli, June 5, 1965; children: Mark Boyd, Anne Marguerite Trueman, Erin Keeley Schornack Dickes, Tracy Bevan. BS, Loyola U., 1951; MBA, Northwestern U., 1956; grad., Advanced Mgmt. Program, Harvard Bus. Sch., 1969. With Ernst & Young (formerly Arthur Young & Co.), 1955-91, partner, 1964-91; firm dir. personnel Ernst & Young (formerly Arthur Young & Co.), N.Y.C., 1966-71; asst. mng. ptnr. N.Y.C. office Ernst & Young (formerly Arthur Young & Co.), 1971-72, mng. ptnr., 1972-74, mng. ptnr. Chgo. office, 1976-85, mng. ptnr. Midwest region, vice chmn., 1985-91; mem. mgmt. com. Arthur Young & Co.; mgmt. com. Arthur Young & Co.; vice chmn., mng. ptnr. Midwest region Ernst & Young, 1989-91; bd. dirs., chmn. Ernst & Young Found., 1981-91; chmn., bd. dirs., CEO Kraft Seal Corp.; bd. dirs. Binks Mfg. Co., Franklin Park, Ill., North Shore Bancorp, Inc., Sally Berger Comm. Co. Exec. bd. Chgo. Youth Ctrs., 1979-95, pres., 1984-86; bd. govs. Chgo. Symphony, 1979-85, trustee, 1985—; vol. United Way, 1975-92, dir., 1989-92; vis. adv. com. sch. accountancy DePaul U., 1980-83; mem. Loyola U. Citizens Bd., 1977-94, chmn., 1993-94; mem. adv. com. Northwestern U. Grad. Sch. Mgmt., 1967-91; coun. U. Chgo. Grad. Sch. Bus., 1982-91; bd. dirs. Met. Planning Coun., 1992-95; trustee Kohl Children's Mus., 1994—, Lyric Opera, 1984-92, Cath. Theol. Union, 1992—, Graham Found., 1992—; trustee Barat Coll., 1983—, vice chmn., 1985-90, chmn., 1990—; trustee St. Francis Hosp., 1986—, vice chmn., 1991-94. Mem. AICPA, Am. Acctg. Assn., Ill. Soc. CPA's, Midwest-Japan Assn. (chmn. 1983—), Japan Am. Soc., 410 Club, Economic Club, Tavern Club, Chgo. Club, Glen View Club, Ocean Club. Home: 314 Regent Wood Northfield IL 60093-2762 Office: Ernst & Young LLP Midwest Regional Office 233 S Wacker Dr Chicago IL 60606-6306 also: Kraft Seal Corp 13777 W Laurel Dr Lake Forest IL 60045-4530

SCHORR, ALAN EDWARD, librarian, publisher; b. N.Y.C., Jan. 7, 1945; s. Herbert and Regina (Fingerman) S.; m. Debra Genner, June 11, 1967; 1 son, Zebediah. BA, CUNY, 1966; MA, Syracuse U., 1967; postgrad., U. Iowa, 1967-71; MLS, U. Tex., 1973. Tchr., rsch. asst. dept. history U. Iowa, 1967-70; govt. publs. and map libr., asst. prof. Elmer E. Rasmuson Libr., U. Alaska, 1973-78; assoc. prof., dir. libr. U. Alaska, Juneau, 1978-84; prof., dean univ. libr. Calif. State U., Fullerton, 1984-86; pres. The Denali Press, Juneau, 1986—; freelance indexer and bibliographer; vis. lectr. Birmingham (Eng.) Poly., 1981; mem. Alaska Ednl. Del. to China, 1975. Author: Alaska Place Names, 1974, 4th edit., 1991, Directory of Special Libraries in Alaska, 1975, Government Reference Books, 1974-75, 1976, 1976-77, 1978, Government Documents in the Library Literature 1909-1974, 1976, ALA RSBRC Manual, 1979, Federal Documents Librarianship 1879-1987, 1988, Hispanic Resource Directory, 1988, 3d edit., 1996, Refugee and Immigrant Resource Directory, 1990, 92, 94; editor: The Sourdough, 1974-75, Directory of Services for Refugees and Immigrants, 1987, 3d edit., 1993, Guide to Smithsonian serial publs., 1987 ; book reviewer, columnist: S.E. Alaska Empire, 1979—, L.A. Times; contbr. articles to profl. jours. Mem. Auke Bay (Alaska) Vol. Fire Dept.; mem. Juneau Borough Cemetery Adv. Com., 1980-81, Juneau Borough Libr. Adv. Com., 1981-82, Am. Book Awards Com., 1980; mem. strategic com. Juneau Sch. Bd., Juneau Bd. Edn., 1991—, chmn. facilities com., 1994—. Mem. ALA (reference and subscription books rev. com. 1975-86, reference and adult services div. publs. com. 1975-77, Nat. Assn. Hispanic Publications, Mudge citation commn. 1977-79, 84-86, Dartmouth Coll. Medal Commn., Governing Council 1977-84, Dewey medal com. 1984-85, Denali Press award), Alaska Library Assn. (exec. bd. 1974-75, nominating com. 1977-79), Pacific N.W. Library Assn. (rep. publs. com. 1973-75), Assn. Coll. and Research Libraries (publ. com. 1976-80), Spl. Libraries Assn. (assoc. editor geography and map div. bull. 1975-76), Soc. for Scholarly Pub., Internat. Assn. Ind. Pubs (bd. dirs. 1990-92, 95—), Pub. Mktg. Assn., PEN Ctr. USA West, Amnesty Internat., Explorers Club N.Y., No. Pub. Consortium (regional rep. 1993—). Office: PO Box 1535 Juneau AK 99802

SCHORR, ALVIN LOUIS, social worker, educator; b. N.Y.C., Apr. 13, 1921; s. Louis and Tillie (Godiner) S.; m. Ann Girson, Aug. 21, 1948; children—Jessica Lee, Kenneth L., Wendy Lauren. B.S.S., CCNY, 1941; M.S.W., Washington U., St. Louis, 1943; D.H.L., Adelphi U., 1975. With Family Service No. Va., 1956-58; family life specialist Office Commr. Social Security, 1958-62; vis. prof. London (Eng.) Sch. Econs., 1962-63; acting chief long range research Social Security Adminstrn., 1963-64; dir. research and planning Office Econ. Opportunity, 1965-66; dep. asst. sec. Dept. Health, Edn. and Welfare, 1967-69; prof. social policy, dir. income maintenance project Brandeis U., 1969-70; dean Grad. Sch. Social Work, N.Y.U., 1970-73; gen. dir. Community Service Soc. N.Y., 1973-77; vis. prof. Cath. U. Am., 1977-79; Leonard W. Mayo prof. Case Western Res. U., 1979-92, Leonard W. Mayo prof. emeritus, 1992—; Fulbright sr. rsch. scholar, 1962-63; vist. prof. Hebrew U., Jerusalem, 1986, Fla. Internat. U., 1995, N.Mex. State U., 1996; vis. scholar London Sch. Econs., 1991-92. Author: Filial Responsibility in the Modern American Family, 1961, Slums and Social Insecurity, 1963, Social Services and Social Security in France, 1964, Poor Kids, 1966, Explorations in Social Policy, 1968, Children and Decent People, 1974, Jubilee for Our Times, 1977, Thy Father and Thy Mother, 1980, Common Decency: Domestic Policies After Reagan, 1986, Economic Development in Cleveland: A Dissenting View, 1991; The British Personal Social Services: An Outside View, 1992. Recipient Disting. Service in Social Welfare award Washington U. Alumni Assn., 1969; recipient Michael Schwerner award, 1972. Fellow Nat. Acad. Social Ins.; mem. Phi Beta Kappa. Home: 1701 E 12th St Apt 14tw Cleveland OH 44114-3207 Office: Case Western Res U Mandel Sch Appl Social Sci Cleveland OH 44106

SCHORR, BRIAN LEWIS, lawyer, business executive; b. N.Y.C., Oct. 5, 1958; s. Phillip I. and Hannah Schorr; m. Amy B. Horowitz, Aug. 19, 1984; 2 children. BA magna cum laude, MA, Wesleyan U., Middletown, Conn., 1979; JD, NYU, 1982. Bar: N.Y. 1983, D.C. 1985, U.S. Supreme Ct. 1988. Assoc. Paul, Weiss, Rifkind, Wharton & Garrison, N.Y.C., 1982-90, ptnr., 1991-94; exec. v.p., gen. counsel Triarc Cos., Inc., N.Y.C., 1994—; mem. bd. advisors Jour. Ltd. Liability Cos.; lectr. CLE programs. Author: Schorr on New York Limited Liability Companies Partnerships, 1994; contbr. articles to legal jours. Vice pres. Bronx (N.Y.) H.S. Sci. Endowment Fund, Inc. Mem. ABA, N.Y. State Bar Assn., Assn. Bar City N.Y. (chmn. com. on corp. law 1993-96, co-chmn. joint drafting com. N.Y. ltd. liability co. law), Tri Bar Opinion Com., Bronx H.S. Sci. Alumni Assn. (trustee). Office: Triarc Cos Inc 900 3d Ave New York NY 10022

SCHORR, DANIEL LOUIS, broadcast journalist, author, lecturer; b. N.Y.C., Aug. 31, 1916; s. Louis and Tillie (Godiner) S.; m. Lisbeth Bamberger, 1967; children: Jonathan, Lisa. B.S.S., CCNY, 1939; hon. doctorate, Kalamazoo Coll., Columbia Coll., Chgo., Wilkes U., Nebr. Wesleyan U., L.I. U., Brandeis U., Spartus Coll. Asst. editor Jewish Telegraphic Agy., 1934-41; news editor ANETA (Netherlands) News Agy. in N.Y., 1941-48; free-lance corr. N.Y. Times, Christian Sci. Monitor, London Daily Mail, 1948-53; Washington corr. CBS News; also spl. assignments CBS News, Latin Am. and Europe, 1953-55; reopened CBS Moscow Bur., 1955; roving assignments U.S. and Europe, 1958-60; chief CBS News Bur., Germany, Central Europe, 1960-66; Washington corr. CBS, 1966-76; Regents prof. U. Calif., Berkeley, 1977; columnist Des Moines Register-Tribune Syndicate, 1977-80; sr. Washington corr. Cable News Network, 1980-85; sr. analyst Nat. Public Radio, 1985—. Author: Don't Get Sick in America!, 1971, Clearing the Air, 1977. Decorated officer Orange Nassau (The Netherlands), Grand Cross of Merit (Germany); recipient citations of excellence for radio-TV reporting Soviet Union Overseas Press CLub, 1956, Best TV Interpretation of Fgn. News award 1963, ACLU and others awards for pub. suppressed White House intelligence report, Emmy awards for coverage of Watergate, 1972, 73, 74, Peabody award for lifetime of uncompromising reporting of highest integrity, 1992, George Polk award for radio commentary L.I. U., 1994, Disting. Svc. award Am. Soc. Journalism and Mass Comm., 1994, Golden Baton award for lifetime achievement A.I. Du-Pont Columbia U., 1996; inducted in Hall of Fame Soc. Profl. Journalistsm 1991. Mem. Am. Fedn. Radio-TV Artists, Council on Fgn. Relations N.Y.C. *Journalism, for more than a half century, has been both profession and outlook on life. I have always felt myself the observer and nonparticipant, the quintessential outsider. I have pursued the sense of things behind the appearance of things, the meaning behind the manipulation. I have fought, with dubious success, against the blurring of the media line between reality and fantasy.*

SCHORR, LISBETH BAMBERGER, child and family policy analyst, author, educator; b. Munich, Jan. 20, 1931; d. Fred S. and Lotte (Krafft) Bamberger; m. Daniel L. Schorr, Jan. 8, 1967; children—Jonathan, Lisa. BA with highest honors, U. Calif., Berkeley, 1952; LHD (hon.), Wilkes U., 1991, U. Md., 1994. Med. care cons. U.A.W. and Community Health Assn., Detroit, 1956-58; asst. dir. Dept. Social Security AFL-CIO, Washington, 1958-65; acting chief CAP Health Svcs., OEO, 1965-66; chief program planning Office for Health Affairs, OEO, Washington, 1967; cons. Children's Def. Fund, Washington, 1973-79; scholar-in-residence Inst. of Medicine, 1979-80; chmn. Select Panel on Promotion Child Health, 1979-80; adj. prof. maternal and child health U. N.C., Chapel Hill, 1981-85; lectr. social medicine Harvard U. Med. Sch., 1984—; dir. project on effective interventions Harvard U., 1988—; nat. coun. Alan Gutmacher Inst., 1974-79, 82-85; pub. mem. Am. Bd. Pediatrics, 1978-84; vice chmn. Found. for Child Devel., 1978-84, bd. dirs., 1976-84, 86-94; mem. coun. Nat. Ctr. for Children in Poverty, 1987-96; mem. children's program adv. com. Edna McConnell Clark Found., 1987—; bd. dirs. Pub. Edn. Fund Network, 1991-93; co-chair Roundtable on Comprehensive Cmty. Inititatives spen Inst., 1992—, chair roundtable steering com. on evaluation, 1994—; mem. bd. on children and families NAS, 1993-95; mem. nat. Commn. State and Local Pub. Svcs., 1992-94; mem. task force on young children Carnegie Corp., 19-94; mem. sec.'s adv. com. Head Start quality and expansion, 1993-94; trustee City Yr., 1994—; mem. exec. com. Harvard Project on Schooling and Children. Author: Within Our Reach: Breaking the Cycle of Disadvantage, 1988. Recipient Dale Richmond Meml. award Am. Acad. Pediatrics, 1977, 9th Ann. Robert F. Kennedy Book award, 1989, Nelson Cruikshank award nat. Coun. Sr. Citizens, 1990, Porter prize, 1993. Mem. Inst. Medicine, NAS, Nat. Acad. on Social Ins., Phi Beta Kappa. Home: 3113 Woodley Rd NW Washington DC 20008-3449

SCHORR, MARTIN MARK, forensic psychologist, educator, writer; b. Sept. 16, 1923; m. Dolores Gene Tyson, June 14, 1952; 1 child, Jeanne Ann. Student Balliol Coll., Oxford (Eng.) U., 1945-46; AB cum laude, Adelphi U., 1949; postgrad., U. Tex., 1949-50; MS, Purdue U., 1953; PhD, U. Denver, 1960; postgrad., U. Tex. Diplomate in psychology; diplomate Am. Bd. Profl. Disability Cons., Am. Bd. Forensic Examiners, Am. Bd. Forensic Medicine; lic. clin. psychologist. Chief clin. psychol. svcs. San Diego County Mental Hosp., 1963-67; clin. dir. human services San Diego County, 1963-76; pvt. practice, forensic specialist San Diego, 1962—; forensic examiner superior, fed. and mil. cts., San Diego, 1962—; prof. abnormal psychology San Diego State U., 1965-68; chief dept. psychology Center City (Calif.) Hosp., 1976-79; cons. Dept. Corrections State of Calif., Minnewawa, 1970-73, Disability Evaluation Dept. Health, 1972-75, Calif. State Indsl. Accident Commn., 1972-78, Calif. Criminal Justice Adminstrn., 1975-77, Vista Hill Found., Mercy Hosp. Mental Health, Foodmaker Corp., Convent Sacred Heart, El Cajon, FAA Examiner. Author: Death by Prescription, 1988; dir.: Alpha Centauri Prodns. Recipient award for aid in developing Whistle Blower Law Calif. Assembly, 1986. Fellow Internat. Assn. Social Psychiatry, Internat. Biog. Assn. (life: Great Britain), Am. Coll. Forensic Examiners (life), Am. Bd. Forensic Med.; mem. AAAS, PEN, APA, Am. Acad. Forensic Scis. (qualified med. evaluator), Internat. Platform Assn., World Mental Health Assn., Mystery Writers Am., Nat. Writers Club, Mensa. Home: University City 2970 Arnoldson Ave San Diego CA 92122-2114 Office: 275 F St Chula Vista CA 91910-2820 *Personal philosophy: Some wag once said that the hardest thing one learns in life is which bridge to cross and which to burn!.*

SCHORR, MARVIN G., technology company executive; b. N.Y.C., Mar. 10, 1925; s. Samuel and Fannie (Smolen) S.; m. Rosalie Yorshis, Dec. 22, 1957; children: Eric Douglas, Susan Ellen. BS, Yale U., 1944, MS, 1947, PhD, 1949. Research asst., instr. Yale U., New Haven, 1946-47; project dir. physics and electronics div. Tracerlab, Inc., 1940-51; exec. v.p., treas. Tech/Ops., Inc., Boston, 1951-62, pres., chief exec. officer, 1962-88, chmn. 1988—; spl. cons. USAF, 1951-52; dir. Mass. Tech. Devel. Corp., 1973-76, chmn. bd., 1976-83; dir. Ealing Corp., 1965-76, Hysil Mfg. Co., 1965-78, Dynamics Research Corp., 1978-85, Helix Tech. Corp., Costar Corp. Mem. nuclear engrng. adv. com. Lowell Inst. Tech., 1958-68; trustee Park Sch., 1974-80; trustee Am. Coll. Greece, 1970-82, chmn. exec. com., 1980-82, hon. trustee, 1982—; trustee New Eng. Deaconess Hosp., 1972—, vice chmn. bd., 1978-81, chmn., 1981-86. Served with U.S. Army, 1944-46. Fellow AAAS; mem. IEEE, Ops. Research Soc. Am., Am. Phys. Soc., Young Pres. Orgn. (chmn. New Eng. chpt. 1967-68), Boston Com. Fgn. Relations, The Forty-Niners, World Bus. Council, Chief Execs. Orgn., Internat. Bus. Ctr.-Chief Exec. Officers Round Table, Explorers Club. Clubs: Cosmos (Washington); Harvard, St. Botolph, Union (Boston); Yale (Boston and N.Y.C.); Longwood Cricket (Brookline, Mass.). Home: 330 Beacon St Boston MA 02116 Office: Tech/Ops Corp 1 Beacon St Boston MA 02108

SCHORR, S. L., lawyer; b. N.Y.C., Feb. 19, 1930; s. Charles and Clara (Lerech) S.; m. Eleanor Daru, Mar. 23, 1956; children: Lewis, Andrew, Emily, Roberta. Student, L.I. U., 1948-50; LLB, Bklyn. Law Sch., 1953. Bar: N.Y. 1955, Ariz. 1962, U.S. Dist. Ct. Ariz. 1962, U.S. Supreme Ct. 1979. Planning commr. Pima County, Tucson, 1959-62; asst. city mgr. Tucson, 1962-63; ptnr. Lewis and Roca, Tucson, 1988—; co-chair Continuing Legal Edn. Seminar on Ballot Box Zoning, U. Ariz., 1991, Ariz. State Bar Continuing Legal Edn. Seminar on Land Use Regulation and Litigation, 1977, 86, 89, 95. Bd. dirs. Pima Coll., 1966-67; mem. Commn. on Improved Govtl. Mgmt., Tucson, 1974-77, Gov.'s Econ. Planning and Devel. Adv. Bd., Phoenix, 1983-85; chmn. Gov.'s Task Force on Seriously Mentally Ill, Phoenix, 1989-91. Mem. Ariz. Bar Assn., Pima County Bar Assn. Democrat. Office: Lewis and Roca 1 S Church Ave Ste 700 Tucson AZ 85701-1620

SCHORRE, LOUIS CHARLES, JR., artist; b. Cuero, Tex., Mar. 9, 1925; s. Louis Charles and Anna (Barthlome) S.; m. Margaret Phipps Storm, July 17, 1948; children—Alice Ann Schorre Stultz, Martha Schorre Jackson, Robin Elisabeth Schorre Glover. B.F.A., U. Tex., 1948. Instr. art Mus. Fine Arts, Houston, 1950-55; prof. Sch. Architecture, Rice U., 1962-72. One-man shows: Tex. Gallery, Meredith Long Gallery, Contemporary Arts Mus.; paintings and drawings in numerous publs. also pvt. and corp. collections throughout U.S.; Author, editor, art dir.: Life Class, 1968 (gold medals in N.Y.C. and abroad); author: Drawings and Notes, 1975, Drawing and Notes II, 1983. Served with USMCR, 1943-46. Studio: 2406 Tangley St Houston TX 77005-2514 *I am influenced by everything that is happening . . . therefore I am touched by the romance of history, the excitement and depression of now and the anticipation of what is to be. I am motivated by love received and given . . . hopefully I am still a child.*

SCHORSCH, ISMAR, clergyman, Jewish history educator; b. Hannover, Germany, Nov. 3, 1935; m. Sally Korn; children: Jonathan, Rebecca, Naomi. BA, Ursinus Coll., 1957; MA, Columbia U., 1961, PhD, 1969; MHL, Jewish Theol. Sem. Am., 1962; LittD (hon.), Wittenberg U., 1989, Ursinus Coll., 1990, Gratz Coll., 1995. Ordained rabbi, 1962. Instr. Jewish Theol. Sem., N.Y.C., 1964-68; asst. prof. Jewish Theol. Sem. Am., N.Y.C., 1970-72, assoc. prof., 1972-76, prof., 1976—, dean Grad. Sch., 1975-79, provost, 1980-84; asst. prof. Jewish history Columbia U., N.Y.C., 1968-70; bd. dirs. Leo Baeck Inst., 1976, mem. exec. com., 1980, pres., 1985-86, 90—, mem. editorial bd. of yearbook, 1987. Author: From Text to Context: The Turn to History in Modern Judaism, 1994; contbr. articles to Judaism, also other profl. publs. Chancellor Jewish Theol. Sem., 1986—. Chaplain U.S. Army, 1962-64. Recipient Clark F. Ansley award Columbia U. Press, 1969; NEH fellow, 1979-80. Fellow Am. Acad. Jewish Rsch. Office: Jewish Theol Sem 3080 Broadway New York NY 10027-4650

SCHORSKE, CARL EMIL, historian, educator; b. N.Y.C., Mar. 15, 1915; s. Theodore A. and Gertrude (Goldschmidt) S.; m. Elizabeth Gilbert Rorke, June 14, 1941; children: Carl Theodore, Anne (Mrs. J. L. Edwards), Stephen James, John Simon, Richard Robert. AB, Columbia U., 1936; MA, Harvard U., 1937, PhD, 1950; DLitt (hon.), Wesleyan U., 1967, Bard Coll., 1982, Clark U., 1983, New Sch. Social Rsch., 1986, Miami U., 1987, SUNY, Stony Brook, 1988, Monmouth Coll., 1994; DPhil (hon.), U. Salzburg, 1986. Prof. history Wesleyan U., Middletown, Conn., 1946-60; prof. history U. Calif.-Berkeley, 1960-69; prof. history Princeton U., 1969-80, emeritus, 1980—; DLitt (hon.) U. Graz, 1996. Author: (with Hoyt Price) The Problem of Germany, 1947, German Social Democracy 1905-17, 1955, Fin-de-Siècle Vienna, 1980. Served to lt. (j.g.) USNR, 1943-46; with OSS, 1941-46. Recipient Austrian Cross of Honor for arts and scis., 1979, Pulitzer prize for gen. nonfiction, 1981, Grand prize for cultural edn. City of Vienna, 1985; named Officer, French Order Arts and Letters, 1987, Great Silver medal of Honor, Austria, 1996; MacArthur fellow, 1981-86. Fellow Royal Acad. Fine Arts Netherlands (hon.); mem. Am. Acad. Arts and Scis., Austrian Acad. Scis. (corr.), Am. Hist. Assn. (council 1964-68, Disting. Scholar award 1992), Ctr. Advanced Study Behavioral Sci., Inst. Advanced Study., Getty Ctr. Home: 106 Winant Rd Princeton NJ 08540-6738

SCHORZMAN, CLARICE B., principal. Prin. Jemtegaard Mid. Sch. Recipient Blue Ribbon Sch. award 1990-91. Office: Jemtegaard Mid Sch 35300 SE Evergreen Blvd Washougal WA 98671-9753

SCHOTLAND, DONALD LEWIS, neurologist, educator; b. Orange, N.J., Sept. 21, 1930; s. Joseph Henry and Elsie (Block) S.; m. Estherina Shems, Jan. 11, 1976; children: John, Thomas, Peter. AB, Harvard U., 1952, MD, 1957; spl. student, MIT, 1955-56; MA (hon.), U. Pa., 1973. Diplomate: Am. Bd. Psychiatry and Neurology. Intern U. Ill. Research and Edn. Hosp., 1957-58; asst. resident in neurology Columbia Presbyn. Med. Center, N.Y.C., 1958-61; asst. neurologist Columbia Presbyn. Med. Center, 1961-65, asst. attending neurologist, 1965-66; asst. in neurology Coll. Physicians and Surgeons, Columbia U., N.Y.C., 1960-61; vis. fellow in neurology Coll. Physicians and Surgeons, Columbia U., 1961-64, assoc. in neurology, 1964-66, asst. prof. neurology, 1966-67; assoc. prof. Sch. Medicine U. Pa., Phila., 1967-72, prof. Sch. Medicine, 1972—; prof. Sch. Medicine, 1972—; speaker profl. confs., U.S., Can., Italy, Japan, China, France, Israel, Finland; dir. Henry M. Watts, Jr. Neuromuscular Disease Rsch. Ctr., 1974-90. Editor: Diseases of the Motor Unit, 1982; contbr. articles, papers to profl. publs. Served to 1st lt. USAR, 1958-65. NIH postdoctoral fellow, 1961-64; recipient Research Career Devel. award, 1966-67, various grants NIH and Muscular Dystrophy Assn. Fellow Coll. of Physicians of Phila.; mem. Am. Acad. Neurology, Am. Neurol. Assn., Phila. Neurol. Soc., Muscular Dystrophy Assn. (sci. adv. com. 1974-86, chmn. fellowship com. 1974-86, chmn. 6th Internat. Conf. 1980). Home: 1310 Wyngate Rd Wynnewood PA 19096-2455 Office: Hosp of Univ Pa 3400 Spruce St Philadelphia PA 19104

SCHOTLAND, SARA DEUTCH, lawyer; b. Washington, May 2, 1948; d. Michael Joseph and Rachel (Fischer) Deutch; m. Roy Arnold Schotland; children: Rebecca, Joseph. AB magna cum laude, Harvard U., 1968; JD, Georgetown U., 1971. Law clk. to Hon. Oscar Davis U.S. Ct. Appeals Fed. Cir., Washington, 1971-72; ptnr. Cleary Gottlieb Steen & Hamilton, Washington, 1972—; adj. prof. George Washington U. Law Ctr., 1995—. Office: 1752 N St NW Washington DC 20036-2806

SCHOTT, JOHN (ROBERT), international consultant, educator; b. Rochester, N.Y., Jan. 30, 1936; s. John and Ellen (Waite) S.; m. Diane Elizabeth Dempsey, June 19, 1963; children: Elizabeth Anne (dec.), Jennifer, Jared Reed, George Kermit Alexander. BA magna cum laude, Haverford Coll., 1957; postgrad., Oxford U., 1957-59; PhD, Harvard U., 1964. Resident tutor in govt. Eliot House, Harvard Coll., Cambridge, Mass., 1960-64; inst. polit. sci. Wellesley (Mass.) Coll., 1964-66; policy planning specialist AID, Washington, 1966-67; chief Title IX div. AID, Washington, 1967-68; vis. prof. polit. devel. Fletcher Sch. Law & Diplomacy, Tufts U., Medford, Mass., 1968-70; sr. v.p. Thunderbird Grad. Sch. Internat. Mgmt., Phoenix, 1970-71; cons. internat. affairs Francestown, N.H., 1971-74; pres. Schott & Assocs., Inc., Jaffrey Center, N.H., 1974-93; mem. U.S. Del. World Assembly Internat. Secretariat for Voluntary Service, New Delhi, 1967; advisor Office Prime Minister Royal Thai Govt., Bangkok, 1978-80, Minister Cooperatives Govt. of Indonesia, Jakarta, 1983-84; research asst. spl. appointment The Brookings Inst., Washington, 1960-61;. Author: Kenya Tragedy: European Colonization in East Africa, 1964, Frances' Town: History of Francestown, N.H., 1972, A Five-Year Comprehensive Plan for Development of Agricultural Cooperatives in Thailand, 1979, Recana-Komprehensip Pengembangan Kud, Jakarta, Indonesia, 1985, also various govt. reports and articles in profl. jours. and regional publs.; editor: An Experiment in Integrated Rural Development, 1978. Bd. of Selectmen, Francestown, N.H., 1975-78; trustee Spaulding Youth Ctr., Tilton, N.H., 1971-82, 85-89, pres. bd. trustees, 1972-75; trustee Internat. Inst. Rural Reconstrn., N.Y.C., 1979-89, mem. exec. con., 1985-89, bd. trustees N.H. Pub. Radio, 1990—, chmn., 1993-95; mem. spl. study commn. Coop. Extension Svc. State of N.H., 1980-81, also mem. scenic and cultural by-ways com., 1993-96; forestry rep. County Extension Coun., Hillsboro County, N.H., 1979-82; pres. N.H. Timberland Owner's Assn., 1989-90, bd. dirs., 1988-91; chmn. N.H. chpt. The Nature Conservancy, 1990-93, hon. trustee, 1993—, chmn. N.H. Timber-Tourism Coalition, 1990-94; vice-chmn, Foresters Lic. Bd. State of N.H., 1990-95; bd. trustees Cheshire Med. Ctr., 1992-94, RiverMead Retirement Cmty., Peterborough, N.H., 1993—, exec. com., 1994—. Rotary Found. fellow, 1957-58, Coslett Found. fellow, 1958-59, Harvard Arts & Scis. fellow, 1959-60, Fulbright scholar, 1962-63. Mem. Am. Forestry Inst. (cert. tree farmer). Home and Office: Schott & Assocs Inc PO Box 660 Jaffrey NH 03452-0660

SCHOTT, MARGE, professional baseball team executive; b. 1928; d. Edward and Charlotte Unnewehr; m. Charles J. Schott, 1952 (dec. 1968). Owner Schottco, Cin.; ltd. ptnr. Cin. Reds, 1981-84, gen. ptnr., 1984-85, owner, pres., 1985—, chief exec. officer. Office: Cin Reds 100 Riverfront Stadium Cincinnati OH 45202*

SCHOTTA, CHARLES, economist, government official; b. Kansas City, Mo., Feb. 27, 1935; s. Charles and Katherine (Boyer) S.; m. Sarita Gattis, Sept. 9, 1960. B.A., Tex. Christian U., 1957; M.A., Brown U., 1959, postgrad., 1962-65. Assoc. prof. econ. Va. Tech. Inst. and State U., Blacksburg, 1967-71; dir. econometrics staff U.S. Treasury, Washington, 1971-74, dir. office internat. fin. analysis, 1974-77, dir. office internat. energy policy, 1977-79, dep. asst. sec. commodities and natural resources, 1979-83, dep. asst. sec. Arabian Peninsula affairs, 1983-90; dep. asst. sec. Ea. Europe, Soviet and Mid. Ea. policy, 1990-92; dep. asst. sec. Mid. Ea. and energy policy Dept. Treasury, 1992-96, counselor Middle East affairs, 1996—; pres. Tech. Assocs., Inc., Blacksburg, Va., 1969-71. Author: Property and Casualty Insurance Ratemaking, 1971; contbr. articles to profl. jours. H.B. Earhart Found. fellow, 1963; Richard D. Irwin Found. fellow, 1964. Presbyterian. Clubs: Cosmos (Washington). Home: 104 Prince St Alexandria VA 22314-3312 Office: US Dept of the Treasury 15th Pennsylvania Ave NW Washington DC 20220

SCHOTTELKOTTE, ALBERT JOSEPH, broadcasting executive; b. Cheviot, Ohio, Mar. 19, 1927; s. Albert William and Venetta (Mentrup) S.; m. Elaine Green, Jan 2, 1988; children: Paul J., Carol A., Matthew J., Joseph G., Louis A., Mary J., Ellen E. Noble, William E., Michael H., Linda Brewer, Martha Schottelkotte, Amy Wholeber. Student pub. and parochial schs. With Cin. Enquirer, 1943-61, successively copy boy, city-wide reporter, columnist, 1953-61; news broadcaster Sta. WSAI, Cin., 1953-59; news broadcaster Sta. WCPO-TV, 1959-94, dir. news-spl. events, 1961-83, sta. dir., 1983-88; gen. mgr. news div. Scripps-Howard Broadcasting Co., 1969-81, v.p. for news, 1971-81, sr. v.p., 1981-93; pres., chief exec. officer, trustee Scripps Howard Found., 1986—. Served with AUS, 1950-52. Recipient Nat. CD award for reporting on subject, 1958, Disting. Broadcaster award Alpha Epsilon Ro, 1990, Carr Van Anda award E.W. Scripps Sch. Journalism Ohio U., 1996—; charter inductee Cin. Journalism Hall of Fame Soc. Profl. Journalists, 1990; inducted into Cin. Broadcasting Hall of Fame, 1992. Mem. Bankers Club, Maketewah Country Club (Cin.), Sea Pines Country Club (Hilton Head, S.C.), Hidden Valley Golf Club. Roman Catholic. Home: 1032 St Moritz Ct Lawrenceburg IN 47025 Office: Scripps Howard 312 Walnut St Cincinnati OH 45202-4024

SCHOTTENFELD, DAVID, epidemiologist, educator; b. N.Y.C., Mar. 25, 1931; m. Rosalie C. Schaeffer; children: Jacqueline, Stephen. AB, Hamilton Coll., 1952; MD, Cornell U., 1956; MS in Pub. Health, Harvard U., 1963. Diplomate Am. Bd. Internal Medicine, Am. Bd. Preventive Medicine. Intern in internal medicine Duke U., Durham, N.C., 1956-57; resident in internal medicine Meml. Sloan-Kettering Cancer Ctr., Cornell U. Med. Coll., N.Y.C., 1957-59; Craver fellow med. oncology Meml. Sloan-Kettering Cancer Ctr., 1961-62; clin. instr. dept. pub. health Cornell U., N.Y.C., 1963-67, asst. prof. dept. pub. health, 1965-70, assoc. prof. dept. pub. health, 1970-73, prof. dept. pub. health, 1973-86; John G. Searle prof., chmn. epidemiology sch. pub. health U. Mich., Ann Arbor, 1986—, prof. internal medicine, 1986—; vis. prof. epidemiology U. Minn., Mpls., 1968, 71, 74, 82, 86; W.G. Cosbie lectr. Can. Oncology Soc., 1987. Editor: Cancer Epidemiology and Prevention, 1982; author 9 books; contbr. more than 160 articles to profl. jours. Served with USPHS, 1959-61. Recipient Acad. Career award in Preventive Oncology, Nat. Cancer Inst., 1980-85. Fellow AAAS, ACP, Am. Coll. Preventive Medicine, Am. Coll. Epidemiology, Armed Forces Epidemiology Bd.; mem. Phi Beta Kappa. Office: U of Mich Sch Pub Health Dept Epidemiology 109 Observatory St Ann Arbor MI 48109-2029

SCHOTTENHEIMER, MARTIN EDWARD, professional football coach; b. Canonsburg, Pa., Sept. 23, 1943; m. Patricia Schottenheimer; children—Kristen, Brian. B.A., U. Pitts., 1964. Football player Buffalo Bills, NFL, 1965-68, Boston Patriots, 1969-70; real estate developer Miami and Denver, 1971-74; asst. coach World Football League, Portland, 1974, N.Y. Giants, 1975-77, Detroit Lions, 1978-79; asst. coach Cleve. Browns, 1980-84, head coach, 1985-88; head coach Kansas City Chiefs, 1989—. Office: Kansas City Chiefs 1 Arrowhead Dr Kansas City MO 64129-1651*

SCHOTTENSTEIN, JAY L., retail executive; b. 1954. Grad., Ind. U. With Schottenstein Stores, Columbus, Ohio, vice chmn., exec. v.p., CEO, 1992—. Office: Schottenstein Stores 1800 Moler Rd Columbus OH 43207*

SCHOTTENSTEIN, SAUL, retail company executive; b. 1924; married. Pres., dir. Schottenstein Stores, Columbus, Ohio, 1972—. Office: Schottenstein Stores Corp 3241 Westville Rd Columbus OH 43224 also: Schottenstein Stores Corp 1800 Moler Rd Columbus OH 43207-1680*

SCHOTTER, ANDREW ROYE, economics educator, consultant; b. N.Y.C., June 6, 1947; s. I. Harvey and Sara (Rothstein) S.; m. Anne Howland, June 7, 1970; children: Geoffrey, Elizabeth. BS, Cornell U., 1969; MA, PhD, NYU, 1974. Asst. prof. Syracuse (N.Y.) U., 1974-75; asst. prof. NYU, 1975-81, assoc. prof., 1981-86; prof., chmn. econs. dept. NYU, N.Y.C., 1989—, chmn. C.V. Starr Ctr. for Applied Econs., 1986-89; vis. asst. prof. Cornell U., Ithaca, 1974-75; vis. prof. U. Venice, 1993; cons. Gulf & Western Corp., N.Y. 1987, Pegalis & Wachsman, Great Neck, N.Y., 1987-88, Nat. Econ. Rsch. Assocs., White Plains, N.Y., 1989—. Author: Economic Theory of Social Institutions, 1981, Free Market Economics: A Critical Appraisal, 1985, 2d edit., 1990, Microeconomics: A Modern Approach, 1993; mem. editl. bd.: Am. Econ. Rev., 1995—. Grantee Office of Naval Rsch., 1980-85, NSF, 1988-90; recipient Kenan Enterprise award, 1993. Mem. Am. Econ. Assn., Econometric Soc. Office: NYU Dept Econs 269 Mercer St New York NY 10003-6633

SCHOTTLAND, EDWARD MORROW, hospital administrator; b. N.Y.C., Aug. 5, 1946; s. Leo Edward and Harriet (Morrow) S.; m. Nancy Resnick, June 25, 1977; 1 child, David. BA, Queens Coll., CUNY, 1968; MPS, Cornell U., 1973. Asst. adminstr. Mercy Hosp., Rockville Centre, N.Y., 1973-75, asst. adminstr. and dir. planning, 1975-79; pres. Kosair Crippled Children's Hosp., Louisville, 1979-81, sr. v.p., chief adminstrv. officer Kosair Children's Hosp., Louisville, 1983-89; v.p. NKC, Inc., Louisville, 1981-83, sr. v.p., 1983-89; exec. v.p. The Miriam Hosp., Providence, R.I., 1989—; sr. v.p. Lifespan, Providence, R.I., 1995—; mem. Gov.'s Adv. Council on Med. Assistance. Chmn. Jefferson County Child Abuse Authority, Louisville, 1981-83, dir., 1979-86; bd. dirs. Suicide Prevention and Edn. Ctr., Louisville, 1982-86, HARI, 1990—, Interfaith Health Coun., v.p., 1994—, RIMRI, Inc., 1994—; bd. trustee Barrington (R.I.) Pub. Libr.; chmn. bd. Beavertail Prodns., 1995—; Fellow Am. Coll. Health Execs. (regent 1994—); mem. Nat. Assn. Children's Hosps. and Related Institutions (bd. dirs.). Home: 3 Stratford Rd Barrington RI 02806-3617 Office: The Miriam Hosp 164 Summit Ave Providence RI 02906-2800

SCHOULTZ, LARS, political scientist, educator; b. San Gabriel, Calif., Aug. 23, 1942; s. Ture Wilhelm and Bernice (Bowie) S.; m. Jane Volland, Jan. 18, 1969; children: Nils Gibson, Karina Anne. BA, Stanford U., 1964, MA, 1966; PhD, U. N.C., 1973. Prof. Miami U., Oxford, Ohio, 1973-77, U. Fla., Gainesville, 1977-79; William Rand Kenan Jr. prof. polit. sci. U. N.C., Chapel Hill, 1979—. Author: Human Rights and U.S. Policy Toward Latin America, 1981, National Security and U.S. Policy Toward Latin America, 1987, The Populist Challenge, 1983. Sgt. U.S. Army, 1966-67. MacArthur fellow in internat. peace and security MacArthur Found., 1990-91, Fulbright fellow, Rockefeller Found. fellow, Ford Found. fellow, Social Sci. Rsch. Coun., Woodrow Wilson fellow, 1994-95. Mem. Latin Am. Studies Assn. (pres. 1991-92, v.p. 1990-91). Democrat. Home: 250 Glandon Dr Chapel Hill NC 27514-3816 Office: U NC Inst Latin Am Studies Chapel Hill NC 27599

SCHOUMACHER, BRUCE HERBERT, lawyer; b. Chgo., May 23, 1940; s. Herbert Edward and Mildred Helen (Wagner) S.; m. Alicia Wesley Sanchez, Nov. 4, 1967; children: Liana Cristina, Janina Maria. BS, Northwestern U., 1961; MBA, U. Chgo., 1963, JD, 1966. Bar: Nebr. 1966, U.S. Dist. Ct. Nebr. 1966, Ill. 1971, U.S. Dist. Ct. (no. dist.) Ill. 1971, U.S. Ct. Appeals (7th cir.) 1979, U.S. Supreme Ct. 1982, U.S. Ct. Fed. Claims 1986. Assoc. Luebs, Tracy & Huebner, Grand Island, Nebr., 1966-67; assoc. McDermott, Will & Emery, Chgo., 1971-76, ptnr., 1976-89; ptnr. Querrey & Harrow, Ltd., Chgo., 1989—; instr. bus. adminstrn. Bellevue Coll., Nebr., 1967-70; lectr. U. Md., Overseas Program, 1970. Author: Engineers and the Law: An Overview, 1986; contbg. author: Construction Law, 1986; co-author: Successful Business Plans for Architects, 1992; contbr. articles to profl. jours. Served to capt. USAF, 1967-71, Vietnam. Decorated Bronze Star, 1971. Fellow Am. Coll. Constrn. Lawyers; mem. ABA, AIA (profl. affiliate), Nebr. Bar Assn., Ill. State Bar Assn. (ad hoc com. large law firms 1992-94, chmn. membership and bar activities com. 1988-89, coun. ins. law sect. 1986-91, mem. spl. com. on computerized legal rsch. 1986-87), Chgo. Bar Assn. (chmn. fed. civil procedure com. 1982-83), Def. Rsch. Inst., Ill. Assn. Def. Trial Counsel, Chgo. Bldg. Congress (bd. dirs. 1985—, sec. 1987-89, 95—, v.p. 1989-91), Western Soc. Engrs. (assoc.), The Legal Club, The Law Club, Tower Club (Chgo.), Univ. Club Chgo., Pi Kappa Alpha, Phi Delta Phi. Republican. Methodist. Office: Querrey & Harrow Ltd 180 N Stetson Ave Chicago IL 60601-6710

SCHOW, TERRY D., state official; b. Ogden, Utah, Dec. 14, 1948; s. Hugh Stuart Sloan and Minnie Aurelia (Ellis) Mohler; m. June Hansen, Feb. 14, 1973; children: Amy, Jason. AD, Honolulu C.C., 1975; BA, Chaminade U., 1975. Cert. in mgmt., Utah. Spl. and criminal investigator State of Utah, Ogden, 1976-83, lead investigator, 1984-92; investigator Fed. Govt., Salt Lake City, Denver, 1983-84; mgr. State of Utah, Ogden, 1992—. Mem. Gov.'s Coun. on Vets. Issues, 1989—, chmn., 1990—; mem. State of Utah Privatization Policy Bd., 1989-92; chmn. 1st Congressional Dist. Utah Rep. Party, 1982-83, mem. state exec. com., 1982-83; chmn. legis. dist. Weber County Rep. Party, Ogden, 1987-91, 93—; trustee Utah's Vietnam Meml., Salt Lake City, 1988—; leader Boy Scouts Am., Ogden, 1985—. Sgt. U.S. Army, 1967-70, 72-76; Vietnam. Decorated Bronze Star, 1970, Combat Inf. Badge, 1970; recipient Championship Team Trophy Pistol U.S. Army, 1975. Mem. DAV (life Weber chpt. 4, comdr. 1993—, state 3d jr. vice comdr. 1992, state 2d jr. vice comdr. 1993—, state sr. vice comdr. 1994, state comdr. 1995—), NRA (life), VFW, AL, Utah Peace Officers Assn., Utah Pub. Employees Assn. (bd. dirs. 1988-89, v.p. 1989-92, pres. 1992-93, chmn. Ogden Valley dist.), Kiwanis (Ogden chpt. pres. 1992-93, pres. Layton chpt. 1985-86, named Kiwanian of Yr. 1982-83, lt. gov. divsn. 3 ut/ld dist. Kiwanis internat. bd. dirs., 1995—, homeless vets. fellow Ogden 1992—, Weber County vets. meml. com. 1994—). Republican. Mormon. Avocations: woodworking, photography, scouting. Home: 4045 Bona Villa Dr Ogden UT 84403-3203 Office: State of Utah Office Recoveries 2540 Washington Blvd Fl 4 Ogden UT 84401-3112

SCHOWALTER, JOHN ERWIN, child and adolescent psychiatry educator; b. Milw., Mar. 15, 1936; s. Raymond Phillip and Martha (Kowalke) S.; m. Ellen Virginia Lefferts, June 11, 1960; children: Jay, Bethany. BS, U. Wis.-Madison, 1957, MD, 1960. Diplomate Am. Bd. Psychiatry and Neurology (com. on cert. in child psychiatry 1983-85, chmn. 1986-87, bd. dirs. 1993—); cert. in adult and child psychiatry also psychoanalysis. Intern in pediatrics Yale-New Haven Hosp., 1960-61; asst. resident in psychiatry Cin. Gen. Hosp., 1961-63; fellow in child psychiatry Yale Child Study Ctr., 1963-65; psychiatrist Mental Hygiene Clinic U.S. Army, Ft. Ord, Calif., 1965-67; asst. prof. Yale U. Child Study Ctr., New Haven, 1967-70, assoc. prof. Sch. Medicine, 1970-75, dir. tng., 1971-96, prof. pediatrics and psychiatry, 1975—, chief child psychiatry, 1982-90, dir. child psychiatry clin. svcs., 1990—, Albert J. Solnit prof. child psychiatry and pediatrics, 1989—; mem. publ. com. Yale U. Press, 1992—; mem. sci. adv. bd. Sophia Found. Med. Rsch., Rotterdam, The Netherlands, 1984-89; dir. mental health and substance abuse Yale Preferred Health Plan, 1995—. Co-author: The Family Handbook of Adolescence, 1979; contbr. numerous articles, book revs.; mem. editorial bd. Pediatrics, 1976-81, Children's Health Care, 1977—, Jour. Am. Psychoanalytic Assn., 1978, Pediatrics in Rev., 1978-85; asst. editor Jour. Am. Acad. Child and Adolescent Psychiatry, 1988—; co-editor Yearbook Psychiatry and Applied Mental Health, 1988—. Capt. U.S. Army, 1965-67. Fellow Am. Acad. Child and Adolescent Psychiatry (sec. 1985-87, pres. 1989-91), Am. Coll. Psychiatrists, Am. Acad. Pediatrics (affiliate); mem. Am. Pediatric Soc., Am. Psychoanalytic Assn. (cert. adult and child), Group for Advancement Psychiatry (com. on child psychiatry 1981, bd. dirs. 1989-91, pres. 1993-95), Assn. for Care of Children's Health (pres. 1984-86), AMA (residency rev. com. for psychiatry 1983-87, 89-94), Soc. Profs. Child Psychiatry (pres. 1984-86), We. New Eng. Inst. Psychoanalysis (mem. faculty in child psychoanalysis 1980—, supervisor child psychoanalysis 1984—, pres. 1986-88), Conn. and New Haven med. socs., Conn. Coun. Child Psychiatrists (pres. 1979-81), Benjamin Rush Soc., DARE Am. (mem. sci. adv. panel), others, Sigma Xi. Lutheran. Home: 606 Ellsworth Ave New Haven CT 06511-1636 Office: Yale U Child Study Ctr PO Box 207900 230 S Frontage Rd New Haven CT 06520-7900

SCHOWALTER, WILLIAM RAYMOND, college dean, educator; b. Milw., Dec. 15, 1929; s. Raymond Philip and Martha (Kowalke) S.; m. Jane Ruth Gregg, Aug. 22, 1953; children: Katherine Ruth, Mary Patricia, David Gregg. BS, U. Wis., 1951; postgrad., Inst. Paper Chemistry, 1951-52; MS, U. Ill., 1953, PhD, 1957; PhD (hon.), Inst. Nat. Poly. Lorraine, France, 1996. Asst. prof. dept. chem. engring. Princeton U., 1957-63, assoc. prof., 1963-66, prof., 1966-86, Class of 1950 prof. engring. and applied sci., 1986-89, acting chmn. dept. chem. engring., 1971, chmn. dept. chem. engring., 1978-87, assoc. dean Sch. Engring. and Applied Sci., 1971-77; dean Coll. Engring. U. Ill., Urbana, 1989—; Sherman Fairchild disting. scholar Calif. Inst. Tech., 1977-78; vis. fellow U. Salford, Eng., 1974; vis. sr. fellow Sci. Rsch. Coun., U. Cambridge, Eng., 1970; cons. to chem. and petroleum cos.; editl. adv. bd. McGraw-Hill Pub. Co., 1964-92; co-chmn. Internat. Seminar for Heat and Mass Transfer, 1970; vis. com. for chem. engring. MIT, 1979-87, Lehigh U., 1980-87, Stanford U., 1990—; evaluation panelist Ctr. Chem. Engring. Nat. Bur. Standards, 1982-88, chmn., 1986-88; mem. commn. engring. and tech. sys. NRC, 1983-88; engring. rsch. bd., 1984-86, com. on chem. engring. frontiers; adv. coun. chem. engring. Cornell U., 1983-91; adv. coun. Sch. Engring., Rice U., 1986-92; adv. com. Ill. Inst. Tech., 1992—; acad. adv. bd. Sematech Corp., 1992—; Reilly lectr. in chem. engring. U. Notre Dame, 1985, Van Winkle lectr. in chem. engring. U. Tex., Austin, 1986, David M. Mason lectr. in chem. engring. Stanford U., 1987; bd. dirs. BankIllinois Trust Co. Author: Mechanics of Non-Newtonian Fluids, 1978; co-author: Colloidal Dispersions, 1989; mem. editl. com. Ann. Rev. Fluid Mechanics, 1974-80, Internat. Jour. Chem. Engring., 1974-94, Indsl. and Engring. Chemistry Fundamentals, 1975-78, Jour. Non-Newtonian Fluid Mechanics, 1976—, AIChE Jour., 1979-83; contbr. articles to profl. jours. Mem. State of Ill. Gov.'s Sci. Adv. Com., 1989—. Served with AUS, 1953-55. Recipient Lectureship award Chem. Engring. div. Am. Soc. Engring. Edn., 1971, Disting. Service citation Coll. Engring., U. Wis.-Madison, 1983; Guggenheim fellow, 1987-88. Fellow AIChE (William H. Walker award 1982, bd. dirs. 1992-94), Am. Acad. Arts and Scis.; mem. ASEE (mem. exec. com. engr. deans coun. 1992—), NAE (awards com. 1986-88, chmn. 1987, acad. adv. bd. 1991—, chmn. 1992—, coun. 1994—), Am. Chem. Soc., Soc. Rheology (exec. com. 1977-79, v.p. 1981-83, pres. 1983-85, Bingham medal 1988), Sigma Xi, Tau Beta Pi, Phi Lambda Upsilon, Phi Eta Sigma. Home: 1846 Maynard Dr Champaign IL 61821-5268

SCHOWE, SHERAL LEE SPEAKS, special education educator; b. San Francisco, June 14, 1953; d. Veral John and Myrtle Lee (Hunter) Speaks; m. Derryll Boyd Schowe, Aug. 7, 1982; 1 child, Devin. B degree, Brigham Young U., 1977, M degree, 1979; AA, Ricks Coll., Rexburg, Idaho, 1974; fellow, Gallaudet Coll., 1978. Lic. therapeutic recreation specialist; cert. spl. edn. instr.; cert. edn. adminstrn. Asst. Calif. Jud. Edn. and Rsch., Berkeley; coord. Cottonwood Elem. Community Sch., Holladay, Utah; founder, coord. handicap svcs. Granite Dist. Community Edn., Salt Lake City; founder, coord. ind. living skills program Hartvigsen Community Sch., Salt Lake City; area dir., exec. dir. Utah Spl. Olympics, Sandy, Utah; fund raising cons. non-profit orgns.; spl. edn. instr. Granite Sch. Dist, Salt Lake City; developer, instr. Transition Intervention program for Behaviorally Disordered Elem. Students, 1994—; owner, dir. Wasatch Acad. Wine. Contbr. numerous articles to profl. jours. Mem. archtl. barriers com. Salt Lake 504 Coun., 1978-80; mem. Salt Lake County Cmty. Devel. Citizens Adv. Coun., 1981, vice chair, 1982, chair, 1983; mem. panel Salt Lake County Title XX Adv. Coun., 1984-87; pres., moderator Presbyn. Women United Cottonwood Presbyn. Ch., 1992, 93, deacon, 1992, 93, 94; v.p. PTA Truman Elem. Sch., 1991, 92, 93, PTA rep. 1992, 93, tchr. v.p., mem. Granite Dist. Coun.; rep. Granite Edn. Assn., 1992, 93. Named Edn. of Handicapped of Yr. Mental Retardation Assn., 1982, Woman of Yr. Salt Lake City JayCees, 1982; recipient Outstanding Contribution to Fitness award Utah Gov's. Coun. on Health & Physical Fitness, 1990. Mem. Utah Community Edn. Assn. (Profl. Community Educator of Yr. 1987), Nat. Assn. Spl. Olympics Profls. (bd. dirs. 1990), Coun. Exceptional Children, Zonta (svc. com. chair 1987, bd. dirs. 1988, pub. rels. chair 1990, '91, Soviet Art Exch.chair 1991, '92, '93), Exec. Women's Svc. Orgn., Russian Cultural Exch. Program (chair 1992, 93), Presbyn. Women's Assn. Democrat. Presbyterian. Home: 11454 High Mountain Dr Sandy UT 84092-5661 Office: Granite Sch Dist Dept Spl Edn 340 E 3545 S Salt Lake City UT 84115-4697

SCHRADER, ESTHER, journalist; b. N.Y.C., Aug. 10, 1965; d. Martin H. and Cecelia (Sofer) S. BA, Dartmouth Coll., 1987. Reporter Albany N.Y. Times-Union, 1985-86, L.A. Times, 1987-89; freelance corr. various newspapers and mags., 1989-90; polit. reporter San Jose (Calif.) Mercury News, 1990-93; Mex. and Ctrl. Am. bur. chief Knight-Ridder Newspapers, Miami, Fla., 1993—. Contbr. articles to profl. jours. Recipient Best Consumer Journalism award Nat. Press Club, 1986, Best Investigative Story award No. Calif. Press Club, 1991, Fgn. Reporting award, 1992. Mem. Corrs. Assn.

Mex. Office: Knight-Ridder Newspapers, Presidente Carpanzasz Casa 4, CP04000 Mexico City Mexico

SCHRADER, HARRY CHRISTIAN, JR., retired naval officer; b. Sheboygan, Wis., Aug. 4, 1932; s. Harry Christian and Edna Flora (Stubbe) S.; m. Carol Joan Gossman, June 23, 1956; 1 child, Mary Clare. BS, U.S. Naval Acad., 1955; MS, U.S. Naval Postgrad. Sch., 1963. Commd. ensign USN, 1955, advanced through grades to vice adm., 1982; comdr. U.S.S. Tawasa, 1963-64, U.S.S. A. Hamilton, 1970-72, U.S.S. Jackson, 1972-73, U.S.S. Gilmore, 1973-75, U.S.S. Long Beach, 1975-78; dir. MLSF Amphibious, Mine Warfare and Advanced Vehicles div. Office Naval Ops., Washington, 1978-80; comdr. Cruiser Destroyer Group One, San Diego, 1980-82, Naval Surface Forces, U.S. Pacific Fleet, San Diego, 1982-85; ret. USN, 1985; mgr. Middle East/NATO programs, autonetics div. Rockwell Internat., Anaheim, Calif., 1985-87; pres. Coronado (Calif.) Tech. Internat., 1987; bd. dirs. Continental Maritime Industries, Inc. Mem. Am. Def. Preparedness Assn., San Diego Oceans Found. (mem. adv. bd.), Sigma Xi.

SCHRADER, HELEN MAYE, retired municipal worker; b. Akron, Ohio, June 8, 1920; d. Simon P. and Helen Cecelia (Fennessy) Eberz; widowed; children: Alfred E., Kathleen Therese Schrader Wein. Notary pub. Insp., clk. Fed. Govt. agys., 1940; stenographer Chem. Warfare divsn. USAF, Akron, 1954; clk., stenographer VA; elected clk./treas. of twp. Springfield (Ohio) Twp., 1956-92. Sec. Springfield Dem. Club, Akron, 1957—; sec., treas. Springfield Twp. Civic Club, 1980—. Mem. Summit County Assn. of Trustees and Clks. (sec. 1959-78, 83-92, Svc. plaque 1979, 92). Roman Catholic. Avocations: needlework, flower arranging, crossword puzzles. Home: 693 Neal Rd Akron OH 44312-3709

SCHRADER, HENRY CARL, civil engineer, consultant; b. Chgo., Jan. 5, 1918; s. Henry Fred and Helene (Arkenberg) S.; m. Marium Warner, Aug. 22, 1942; children: Henry Carl, Gary Warner. BS in Civil Engring., U. Ill., 1940, MS in Civil Engring., 1959; diploma Indsl. Coll. Armed Forces, Ft. McNair, D.C., 1962. Registered profl. engr., Ill., Va., Md., D.C., Pa., Mass., N.C. Commd. 2nd lt., U.S. Army, 1940; advanced through grades to maj. gen., 1971; dist. engr. Corps of Engrs., Okinawa, Ryukus Island, 1962-64; chief systems analysis Office Chief Staff Dept Army, Washington, 1966-67, dir. mgmt. info. systems, 1967-70; comdr. 18th Engr. Brigade, Vietnam, 1970-71, comdr. Computer Systems Command, Ft. Belvior, Va., 1971-73; ret., 1973; prin. mktg. Dalton Dalton Newport, Washington, 1973-84; v.p. URS Dalton, 1984-86; v.p. URS Cons., 1986—; specialist high speed ground transp. systems, 1978—. Decorated Air Medal with 2 clusters, Disting. Svc. medal with cluster, Legion of Merit with 3 clusters; Engr. Yr. award Dept. Civil Engring. U. Ill., 1971. Fellow Am. Soc. Civil Engrs., Soc. Am. Mil. Engrs. (dir. 1979-86); mem. Nat. Soc. Profl. Engrs., Am. Rd. and Transportation Bldrs. Assn. (bd. dirs. 1982-95, pres. planning and design div. 1988-90, pres. pub./pvt. ventures div. 1990-92, railroads adv. coun. 1977—), Am. Railway Engring. Assn., HighSpeed Rail Assn. (bd. dirs. 1982—, vice chmn. 1990-92, chmn. membership com. 1985—), Army and Navy Club, Bethesda Country Club (dir. 1983-86), Farmington Country Club. Republican. Episcopalian.

SCHRADER, KEITH WILLIAM, mathematician; b. Neligh, Nebr., Apr. 22, 1938; s. William Charles and Gail (Hughes) S.; m. Carol Jean Taylor, Dec. 26, 1960; children: Jeffrey, Melinda. B.S., U. Nebr., 1959, M.S., 1961, Ph.D., 1966; postgrad., Stanford U., 1961-63. Engr. Sylvania Co., Mountain View, Calif., 1962-63; asst. prof. dept. math U. Mo.-Columbia, 1966-69, assoc. prof., 1969-78, prof., 1978-79, chmn. dept. math. prof., 1979-82, 85-88, prof. dept. math., 1988—. Bd. dirs. Schrader Inst. Early Learning, Columbia, 1970-83; mem. Planning And Zoning Commn., 1980-90. NASA grantee, 1967-68; NSF grantee, 1969-70. Mem. Am. Math. Soc., Sigma Xi, Sigma Phi Epsilon. Office: Dept Math U Mo Columbia MO 65211-0001

SCHRADER, LAWRENCE EDWIN, plant physiologist, educator; b. Atchison, Kans., Oct. 22, 1941; s. Edwin Carl and Jenna Kathryn (Tobiason) S.; m. Elfriede J. Massier, Mar. 14, 1981. BS, Kans. State U., 1963; PhD, U. Ill., 1967; grad., Inst. Ednl. Mgmt., Harvard U., 1991. Asst. prof. dept. agronomy U. Wis., Madison, 1969-72; assoc. prof. U. Wis., 1972-76, prof., 1976-84; prof., head dept. agronomy U. Ill., Urbana, 1985-89; dean Coll. Agr. and Home Econs. Wash. State U., Pullman, 1989-94, prof. dept. horticulture, 1994—; chief competitive rsch. grants office Dept. Agr., Washington, 1980-81; trustee, treas. Agrl. Satellite Corp., 1991-94. Contbr. chpts. to books, articles to profl. jours. Active Consortium for Internat. Devel., 1989-94, chair fin. com., vice chair exec. com., 1990-92, trustee 1989-94; mem. exec. com. Coun. Agrl. Heads of Agr., 1992-94. Capt. U.S. Army, 1967-69. Recipient Soybean Researchers Recognition award 1983, Disting. Service award in Agriculture Kansas State U., 1987; Romnes Faculty fellow U. Wis., 1979. Fellow AAAS (mem. steering group, sect. agr. 1991-95, chair-elect sect. on agr., food and renewable resources 1995—, chair 1996—), Am. Soc. Agronomy, Crop Sci. Soc. Am.; mem. Am. Soc. Plant Physiologists (sec. 1983-85, pres.-elect 1986, pres. 1987), Am. Chem. Soc., Sigma Xi, Gamma Sigma Delta, Phi Kappa Phi, Phi Eta Sigma, Blue Key, Alpha Zeta. Methodist. Home: 3504 Crestview Rd Wenatchee WA 98801-9668 Office: Wash State U Tree Fruit Rsch & Extension Ctr 1100 N Western Ave Wenatchee WA 98801-1230

SCHRADER, LEE FREDERICK, agricultural economist; b. Okawville, Ill., Mar. 11, 1933; s. Fred and Alma (Koenemann) S.; m. Martha Ellen Kohl, Dec. 27, 1958; children—Mark, Katherine, Amanda. B.S., U. Ill., 1955; M.S., Mich. State U., 1958; Ph.D., U. Calif., Berkeley, 1961. Buyer Lever Bros. Co., N.Y.C., 1961-64; economist Armour & Co., Chgo., 1965-66; mem. faculty Sch. Agr. Purdue U., West Lafayette, Ind., 1966—; prof. agrl. econs. Sch. Agr. Purdue U., 1971—. Author: (with R.A. Goldberg) Farmers' Cooperatives and Federal Income Taxes, 1975; contbr. articles to profl. jours. Served with U.S. Army, 1955-57. Mem. Am. Agrl. Econs. Assn. Home: 128 Seneca Ln West Lafayette IN 47906-2041 Office: Purdue U Dept Agrl Econs West Lafayette IN 47907

SCHRADER, MARTIN HARRY, retired publisher; b. Queens, N.Y., Nov. 26, 1924; s. Harry F. and Ida (Spiess) S.; m. Cecelia Sofer, July 7, 1957; children: Howard, Daniel, Esther. B.A., Queens Coll., 1946. Vice pres. Alfred Auerbach & Co., 1950-60; dir. mktg. House Beautiful mag., N.Y.C., 1960-65; pub. spl. publs. div. House Beautiful mag., 1965-69; pub. Town and Country mag., N.Y.C., 1969-77, Harpers Bazaar, 1977-91; retired, 1991—; v.p. Hearst Mags., 1983-91; lectr. merchandising Fairleigh Dickenson U., 1958-61, Parson Sch. Design, 1976—, Merchandising New Sch. Grad. Ctr., 1984; advt. Cosmetics Plus, N.Y.C.; cons. Columbia Journalism Rev., Sports Traveler Mag., Reed Reference Pub. Pro-bono pub. Westchester Arts News/Westchester Arts Coun.; author bi-weekly column Gannett Suburban Newspapers, quarterly column Westchester 60 Plus Mag. Former nat. adv. bd. Salk Inst., La Jolla, Calif.; bd. govs. Coty Fashion Critics Awards.; bd. dirs. Mother's Day Found., Ednl. Found. Fashion Industries. Recipient Human Relations award Am. Jewish Com., 1979. Mem. U.S. Lawn Tennis Assn. (umpire's com. 1961-94). Jewish (trustee temple 1965-94).

SCHRADER, MICHAEL EUGENE, trade journal columnist, editor; b. Jersey City, Apr. 3, 1938; s. Eugene Charles and Anne Veronica (Kane) S. BA, NYU, 1961, MA, 1963; postgrad., UCLA, 1965-67, 68-69, Trinity Coll., Dublin, 1967-68, U. Copenhagen, Denmark, 1970. Asst. editor Macmillan Co., N.Y.C., 1962-64; teaching asst. U. Ill., Urbana, 1964-65; teaching asst., rsch. asst. UCLA, 1965-67, 68-69; sr. copy editor Dell Pub. Co., N.Y.C., 1971-72; copy chief Sat. Rev. mag., N.Y.C., 1972-76, Penthouse mag., N.Y.C., 1976-82; assoc. editor Med. Econs. mag., Oradell, N.J., 1982; sr. copy editor Woman's World mag., Englewood, N.J., 1983-84; book reviewer, sr. copy editor Nation's Restaurant News, N.Y.C., 1985—. Columnist: From the Bookshelf, in Nation's Restaurant News, 1988—. Friend of Bobst Libr., NYU, 1994—, established Anne Kane Schrader Cookbook and Nutrition Collection. Recipient Danish Marshall award U. Copenhagen, 1970; Fulbright scholar, 1967-68. Mem. Internat. Assn. Culinary Profls., James Beard Found. (assoc., judge food and beverage book awards 1991-94). Democrat. Roman Catholic. Avocations: reading fiction and poetry, growing house plants, cooking, watching television, taking long walks. Home: 10 Waterside Plz Apt 4 H New York NY 10010-2610 Office: Lebhar-Friedman Inc Nation's Restaurant News 425 Park Ave New York NY 10022-3506

SCHRADER, PAUL JOSEPH, film writer, director; b. Grand Rapids, Mich., July 22, 1946; s. Charles A. and Joan (Fisher) S.; m. Jeannine Oppewall (div.); m. Mary Beth Hurt, Aug. 6, 1983. B.A., Calvin Coll., 1968; M.A., UCLA., 1970. Film critic Los Angeles Free Press, Coast mag., 1970-71; editor Cinema mag., 1970. Author: Transcendental Style in Film: Ozu, Bresson, Dreyer, 1972, Schrader on Schrader, 1989; screenwriter: The Yakuza, 1975, Taxi Driver, 1976, Obsession, 1976, Rolling Thunder, 1978, Raging Bull, 1980, The Mosquito Coast, 1986, The Last Temptation of Christ, 1988; screenwriter, prodr.: Old Boyfriends, 1978; screenwriter, dir.: Blue Collar, 1977, Hardcore, 1978, American Gigolo, 1979, Mishima: A Life in Four Chapters, 1985, Light of Day, 1987, Light Sleeper, 1992; dir.: Cat People, 1982, Patty Hearst, 1988, The Comfort of Strangers, 1990. Address: 9696 Culver Blvd Ste 203 Culver City CA 90232-2753 also: care Jeff Berg ICM 8942 Wilshire Blvd Beverly Hills CA 90211-1934

SCHRADER, THOMAS F., utilities executive; b. Indpls., 1950. Grad., Princeton U., 1972, 78. Pres., chief exec. officer Wis. Gas Co., Milw. Office: Wis Gas Co 626 E Wisconsin Ave Milwaukee WI 53202-4603

SCHRADER, WILLIAM JOSEPH, accountant, educator; b. Leroy, Tex., Sept. 21, 1929; s. Rudolph L. and Lela V. (Gaylor) S.; m. Nancy L. Etnier, Mar. 22, 1953 (dec. 1974); children: Diana, Dale (dec. 1974), Frank; m. Mary Kuhns Maserick, Mar. 6, 1976. BBA, Baylor U., 1950; MBA, Ind. U., 1951; PhD, U. Wash., 1959. CPA, Tex. Acct. Texaco, New Orleans, 1949, A.C. Upleger & Co. (C.P.A.'s), Waco, Tex., 1949-50; instr. U. Wash., Seattle, 1952-54; asst. prof. to prof. accounting Pa. State U., University Park, 1954-91; head dept. accounting and mgmt. info. systems Pa. State U., 1976-86; prof. emeritus, 1992—; bd. dirs. various firms including Ceramic Finishing Co., Ultran Labs., Inc., Applied Sci. Labs., Inc., Cenco Assocs. Inc., 1968—; gen. ptnr. investment partnerships; Fulbright prof. U. Dar es Salaam, 1973-75; vis. prof. U. Zimbabwe, 1987; dir. linkage project with U. Zimbabwe, 1982-87; resident advisor mgmt. tng. project U. West Indies, 1989-90; mem. bd. advs. Inst. of Chartered Accts. of The Caribbean, 1988—; trustee Alpha Real Estate and Mortgage Trust. Author: Income Measurement by Products and Periods, 1959, (with Malcom & Willingham) Financial Accounting: An Events Approach, 1981; contbr. articles to profl. publs. including Jour. of Risk and Ins., Acctg. Rev., Abacus, Fin. Exec., Acctg. Horizons, Acctg. Historians Jour. Active Centre County (Pa.) Task Force on Housing, 1969-70; trustee Fair Housing Inc. Liquidating Trust. Mem. AICPA, AAUP, Am. Acctg. Assn., Acad. Acctg. Historians. Baptist. Clubs: Am. Philatelic Soc, Am. Philatelic Research Library. Home: 305 Adams Ave State College PA 16803-3606 Office: 240 Beam Bus Adminstrn Bldg University Park PA 16802

SCHRADY, DAVID ALAN, operations research educator; b. Akron, Ohio, Nov. 11, 1939; s. Marvin G. and Sheila A. (O'Neill) S.; m. Mary E. Hilt, Sept. 1, 1962; children: Peter, Patrick, Matthew. BS, Case Inst. Tech., 1961, MS, 1963, PhD, 1965. Prof., chmn. Naval Postgrad. Sch., Monterey, Calif., 1974-76, dean acad. planning, 1976-80, provost and acad. dean, 1980-87, prof. ops. rsch., 1988—; Disting. prof. Naval Postgrad. Sch., Monterey, 1995—; vis. prof. Cranfield Inst. Tech./Royal Mil. Coll. of Sci., Shrivenham, Eng., fall 1987-spring 88. Contbr. articles to profl. jours. Recipient Goodeve medal Ops. Rsch. Soc., U.K., 1992. Mem. Ops. Rsch. Soc. Am. (pres. 1983-84, Kimball medal 1994), Mil. Ops. Rsch. Soc. (pres. 1978-79, Wanner Meml. award 1984), Internat. Fedn. Ops. Rsch. Socs. (hon. treas. 1988—), Inst. Mgmt. Scis. Avocation: guitar, motor sports. Office: Naval Postgrad Sch Dept Ops Rsch Monterey CA 93943-5000

SCHRAG, ADELE FRISBIE, business education educator; b. Cynthiana, Ky., May 7, 1921; d. Shirley Ledyard and Edna Kate (Ford) S.; m. William Albert Schrag, Apr. 6, 1963; 1 stepchild, Marie Carol. B.S., Temple U., 1942; M.A., N.Y. U., 1944, Ph.D., 1961. Tchr. Manor Twp. High Sch., Millersville, Pa., 1942-43, Downingtown (Pa.) Sr. High Sch., 1943-50; instr., asst. prof. Temple U. Sch. Bus. and Pub. Administrn., 1950-60; prof. bus. edn. and vocat. edn. Coll. Edn., 1960-85, sr. prof. edn., 1985-88, prof. emeritus, 1988—; vis. lectr. N.Y. U.; cons. Phila. Community Coll., 1967-82. Editor: Business Education for the Automated Office, 1964; author: (with Estelle L. Popham and Wanda Blockhus) A Teaching-Learning System for Business Education, 1975, How to Dictate, 1981, Office Procedures Update, 1982, (with Robert Poland) A Teaching System for Business Subjects, 1988; contbr. articles to profl. jours., chpts. to books. Trustee Meth. Hosp., 1981-85, Sun Cities Symphony Assn., 1988-93, Maricopa Habitat for Humanity, 1994—. Recipient Profl. Panhellenic award, 1963; Kensington High Sch. Alumnae award, 1972. Mem. Soc. Automation in Bus. Edn. (pres. 1969-73, dir. 1974), Nat. Assn. Bus. Tchr. Edn. (pres. 1983-84), Bus. Edn. Certification Council, Phi Gamma Nu (nat. treas. 1952-54, nat. sec. 1954-56), Delta Pi Epsilon (policy commn. for bus. and econ. edn. 1975-78, dir. research found. 1978-83, pres. research found. 1983). Home: 17838 N Conquistador Dr Sun City West AZ 85375-5118

SCHRAG, EDWARD A., JR., lawyer; b. Milw., Mar. 27, 1932; s. Edward A. and Mabel Lena (Baumbach) S.; m. Leslie Jean Israel, June 19, 1954; children: Amelia Marie Schrag Prack, Katherine Allison Schrag Roberts, Edward A. III (dec.). B.S. in Econs, U. Pa., 1954; J.D., Harvard, 1960. Bar: Ohio 1961. Assoc., then firm partner, now of counsel Vorys, Sater, Seymour and Pease, Columbus, 1960—; sec. Ranco Inc., 1972-87; trustee Lake of Woods Water Co., 1972-91; mem. Ohio div. Securities Adv. Com. Mem. Downtown Area Com., 1970-74. Served to lt. (j.g.) USNR, 1954-57. Mem. ABA, Ohio Bar Assn. (chmn. corp. law com. 1986-88, chmn. securities regulation subcom., spl. com. bus. cts., bd. govs., corp. counsel sect., chmn. 1991-93), Columbus Bar Assn., Columbus Area C. of C., Navy League, Alpha Tau Omega, Beta Gamma Sigma, Phi Sigma Alpha, Pi Gamma Mu. Episcopalian. Clubs: Kiwanis, Capital, Crichton, Ohio State U. Pres.'s, University. Home: 9400 White Oak Ln Westerville OH 43082-9606 Office: Vorys Sater Seymour & Pease PO Box 1008 52 E Gay St Columbus OH 43216-1008

SCHRAG, PETER, editor, writer; b. Karlsruhe, Germany, July 24, 1931; came to U.S., 1941, naturalized, 1953; s. Otto and Judith (Haas) S.; m. Melissa Jane Mowrer, June 9, 1953 (div. 1969); children: Mitzi, Erin Andrew; m. Diane Divoky, May 24, 1969 (div. 1981); children: David Divoky, Benaiah Divoky; m. Patricia Ternahan, Jan. 1, 1988. A.B. cum laude, Amherst Coll., 1953. Reporter El Paso (Tex.) Herald Post, 1953-55; asst. sec., asst. dir. publs. Amherst Coll., 1955-66, instr. Am. Studies, 1960-64; asso. edn. editor Sat. Rev., 1966-68, exec. editor, 1968-69; editor Change mag., 1969-70; editor at large Saturday Rev., 1969-72; contbg. editor Saturday Review/Education, 1972-73; editorial adv. bd. The Columbia Forum, 1972-75; editorial bd. Social Policy, 1971—; contbg. editor More, 1974-78, Inquiry, 1977-80, The Am. Prospect, 1995—; editorial page editor Sacramento Bee and McClatchy Newspapers, 1978—; vis. lectr. U. Mass. Sch. Edn., 1970-72; fellow in profl. journalism Stanford U., Palo Alto, Calif., 1973-74; lectr. U. Calif. at Berkeley, 1974-78, 90—; Pulitzer Prize juror, 1988-89. Author: Voices in the Classroom, 1965, Village School Downtown, 1967, Out of Place in America, 1971, The Decline of the Wasp, 1972, The End of the American Future, 1973, Test of Loyalty, 1974, (with Diane Divoky) The Myth of the Hyperactive Child, 1975, Mind Control, 1978; contbr. articles. Mem. adv. com. Student Rights Project, N.Y. Civil Liberties Union, 1970-72; mem. Com. Study History, 1958-72; trustee Emma Willard Sch., 1967-69; bd. dirs. Park Sch., Oakland, Calif., 1976-77, Ctr. for Investigative Reporting, 1979-81; bd. visitors Claremont Grad. Sch.; mem. bd. advisors Pub. Policy Inst. Calif. Guggenheim fellow, 1971-72; Nat. Endowment for Arts fellow, 1976-77. Office: Sacramento Bee 21st & Q St Sacramento CA 95852

SCHRAGE, ROSE, educational administrator; b. Montelimar, France, Apr. 15, 1942; came to U.S., 1947; d. Abraham and Celia (Silbiger) Levine; m. Samuel Schrage, Dec. 12, 1935 (dec. 1976); children: Abraham, Leon. BRE, Beth Rivkah Tchrs. Sem., Bklyn., 1968; Paralegal, Manpower Career Devel. Agy., Bklyn., 1973; MS, L.I. U., 1975; Advanced Cert. Ednl. Adminstrn., Bklyn. Coll., 1983. Cert. sch. dist. adminstr., guidance counselor, tchr., asst. prin. Sec. N.Y.C., 1964-68; police adminstrv. aide N.Y.C. Police Dept., 1974-75; coordinator state reading aid program Sch. Dist. 14, Bklyn., 1977-78, project dir. Title VII, 1978-81, asst. dir. reimbursable fed. and state programs, 1981-85, dist. bus. mgr., 1985-94, asst. prin., 1994—; chmn. N.Y.C. Bd. Edn. IMPACT Com., Bklyn., 1986—. Author (poem): Never Again, 1983; contbg. editor Chai Today; contbr. articles on current affairs and concerns to profl. jours. Del. Republican. Jud. Conf., 1968; founder, pres Concerned Parents, Bklyn., 1977; radio co-host Israeli War Heroes Fund-Radiothon, Bklyn.; family counselor local social agys., Bklyn. Recipient Cert. of Appreciation as vol. regional coord. N.Y. State Mentoring Program N.Y. Gov. Cuomo, 1991. Mem. Am. Assn. Sch. Adminstrs., Assn. Orthodox Jewish Tchrs. (v.p. exec. bd.), N.Y. State Assn. Sch. Bus. Ofcls., N.Y.C. Assn. Sch. Bus. Ofcls., Coun. Suprs. and Adminstrs. Avocations: tennis, needlepoint, piano, reading, communal activities.

SCHRAGER, JAMES E., financial company executive, educator; b. South Bend, Ind., Apr. 5, 1950; s. Howard W. and Eleanor (Kahn) Schrager; m. Teresa Plank, Feb. 21, 1987; children: Max Plank, Michael Elliot. BA Econs., Oakland U., 1971; MBA Acctg., U. Colo., 1975; JD, DePaul U., 1979; PhD, U. Chgo., 1993. CPA, Ill. Acct. Fleetwood Enterprises, Vacaville, Calif., 1973-74; controller Moduline Inds., Colorado Springs, Colo., 1974-75; acct. Haskins & Sells CPAs, Chgo., 1975-77; ptnr. Schrager Stearns & Co., Chgo., 1978-82; gen. mgr. Colson Equipment, Caruthersville, Mo., 1982-84; v.p., CFO Gatz Bros. & Co., San Francisco, 1984-88, exec. v.p., 1989; pres. Gt. Lakes Group, Inc., South Bend, 1989—; sr. lectr. U. Chgo., 1982—; adj. instr. Notre Dame U., South Bend, 1992-93. Inventor patent for shock-absorbent stretcher chassis, 1984; contbr. articles to profl. jours. Mem. AICPA, Ill. Inst. Cert. Pub. Accts. Avocations: sailboat racing, automobile restoration, skiing.

SCHRAGIS, STEVEN M., publisher, lawyer; b. N.Y.C., Oct. 25, 1956; s. Alvin I. and Carole (Kaskel) S.; m. Donna Reservitz. BS in Econs., Tufts U., 1978; JD, Am. U., 1981. Atty. Finley Kemble Wagner, N.Y.C., 1981-84; real estate developer Carol Mgmt./Doral, N.Y.C., 1984-89; pub. Carol Pub. Group, N.Y.C., 1989—. Office: Carol Pub Group 600 Madison Ave New York NY 10022

SCHRAM, MARTIN JAY, journalist; b. Chgo., Sept. 15, 1942; s. Marlo Joseph and Charleene Janice (Fidler) S.; m. Patricia Stewart Morgan, May 23, 1964; children—Kenneth Marlo, David Morgan. B.A., U. Fla., 1964. Reporter The Miami (Fla.) News, 1964-65; reporter Newsday, Garden City, N.Y., 1965-67; mem. Washington bur. Newsday, 1967-69, White House corr., 1969-73, chief Washington bur., sr. editor paper, 1973-79; writer on the presidency Washington Post, 1979-81, nat. affairs writer, 1981-86; assoc. editor, editor Sunday edits. Chgo. Sun-Times, 1986-87; asst. mng. editor, editor Sunday edits. Rocky Mountain News, Denver, 1987-88; polit. columnist United Feature Syndicate, Newspaper Enterprise Assn., 1989-94, Scripps Howard News Svc., Washington, 1994—; commentator Cable News Network, 1988—; nat. editor Washingtonian Mag., 1988-90; fellow Gannett Ctr. for Media Studies, Columbia U., 1985-86; guest scholar Woodrow Wilson Internat. Ctr., 1990-91. Author: Running for President, A Journal of the Carter Campaign, 1976, Running for President: 1976, The Carter Campaign, 1977; (with others) The Pursuit of the Presidency, 1980, The Great American Video Game: Presidential Politics in the Television Age, 1987, Speaking Freely, 1995; co-editor: Mandate for Change, 1993. Recipient James Wright Brown Meml. award Sigma Delta Chi, 1965, Lowell Mellet award Pa. State U., 1988. Office: 1090 Vermont Ave NW Ste 1000 Washington DC 20005-4905

SCHRAM, RONALD BYARD, lawyer; b. Detroit, Sept. 7, 1942; s. Byron Canby and Mary Louise (Byard) S.; m. Carol Lorraine Anderson, July 19, 1969; children: Laura Mary, Alison Leigh. BA, Dartmouth Coll., 1964; MA in Econs., Cambridge U., England, 1966; JD, U. Mich., 1969, LLM, 1970, SJD, 1971. Bar: Mass. 1970. Assoc. Ropes & Gray, Boston, 1970-78, ptnr., 1978—. Trustee Dartmouth Coll., Hanover, N.H., 1981-92, Dartmouth-Hitchcock Med. Ctr., Lebanon, N.H., 1983-93, New Eng. Sports Mus., Cambridge, Mass., 1984—, Derby Acad., Hingham, Mass., 1982-89. Keasbey Found. fellow, Phila., 1964-66; George M. Humphrey fellow in law econ. policy, U. Mich. Law Sch., Ann Arbor, 1969-70. Mem. Boston Bar Assn., Am. Acad. Hosp. Attys., Phi Beta Kappa. Office: Ropes & Gray 1 International Pl Boston MA 02110-2600

SCHRAM, STEPHEN C., professional basketball team executive; m. Patricia Wilcox; children: Parker, Caitlin. Diploma, U. Wyo.; MBA, MAAP, Duke U., 1984. Legis. asst. U.S. Sen. Malcolm Wallop, Washington; assoc. Morgan Stanley, 1984, v.p. fixed income securities divsn.; exec. Brookwood Investments, 1991—; vice chmn. bd. dirs. Boston Celtics; pres. Boston Celtics Ltd. Partnership, Boston Celtics Comm. Ltd. Partnership; bd. dirs. Aexco Petroleum, MPO Videotronics. Office: Celtics Ltd Partnership 151 Merrimac St Boston MA 02111

SCHRAMEK, TOMAS, ballet dancer; b. Bratislava, Czechoslovakia, Sept. 11, 1944; emigrated to Can., 1968, naturalized, 1973; s. Hans and Valeria (Neudorfer) S. BA in Fine Arts, Acad. Mus. and Theatre Arts, Bratislava, 1968. Mem. Sluk, Slovakia folk dance ensemble, 1959-68, prin. dancer, 1964-68; dancer Nat. Ballet Can., 1969-71, soloist, 1971-73, prin. dancer, 1973-91, prin. character artist, tchr., coach, 1991—. Mem. Actors Equity Assn., Assn. Can. TV and Radio Artists. Home: 117 Welland Ave, 205 Belsize Dr, Toronto, ON Canada M4S 1M3 Office: Nat Ballet Canada, 157 King St E, Toronto, ON Canada M5C 1G9

SCHRAMM, BERNARD CHARLES, JR., advertising agency executive; b. Balt., Jan. 23, 1928; s. Bernard C. and Juliet Marie (Barranger) S.; m. Florence Mae Fangman, 1950; children: Stephanie Schramm McDaniel, Carol Schramm Molander, Bernard Charles III, Claudia Schramm Chitwood. Student, Balt. Poly. Inst., 1942-46. Prodn. mgr. Van Sant, Dugdale & Co., Balt., 1946-52; media dir. AWL Advt., Balt., 1952-55; dir. prodn. Henry J. Kaufman Assocs., Washington, 1955-58; exec. v.p. Avalon Hill Co., Balt., 1958-64; v.p. Cargill, Wilson & Acree Advt., Richmond, Va., 1964-68; pres. William Cook Advt. Inc. (now The William Cook Agy. Inc.), Jacksonville, Fla., 1968-89; chmn. bd. William Cook Advt. Inc. (now The William Cook Agy. Inc.), Jacksonville, 1989—; bd. dirs. Otis F. Smith Found., chmn., 1991-93. Mem. exec. com., v.p. United Way N.E. Fla., 1982-87, bd. dirs., 1982-93; bd. dirs. N.E. Fla. chpt. ARC, 1976-89, chmn., 1980-81; bd. dirs. Fla. C.C. Found., 1976-89; chmn. bd. dirs. Otis F. Smith Found., 1991-93. Mem. Am. Assn. Advt. Agys. (chmn. Fla. coun., 1984-85, elected vice-chmn. So. Region Bd. of Govs., 1988—, chmn., 1989, nat. bd. dirs., mem. agy. mgmt. com., elected chmn. So. Region Bd. Govs. 1989), Jacksonville area C. of C., San Jose Club, River Club (Jacksonville), Ponte Vedra Club. Republican. Roman Catholic. Avocations: golf, reading, spectator sports. Home: 1220 Journeys End Ln Jacksonville FL 32223-1753 Office: William Cook Agy Inc 225 Water St Ste 1600 Jacksonville FL 32202-5149

SCHRAUT, KENNETH CHARLES, mathematician, educator; b. Hillsboro, Ill., May 19, 1913; s. Charles Frederick and Theresa (Panska) S.; m. Virginia Haury, Feb. 5, 1952; 1 dau., Marilyn Szorc. A.B. with honors, U. Ill., 1936; M.A., U. Cin., 1938, Ph.D., 1940. Vis. instr. U. Notre Dame, summer 1940; instr. dept. math. U. Dayton, (Ohio), 1940-41; asst. prof. U. Dayton, 1941-44, assoc. prof., 1944-48, prof., 1948-72, chmn. dept. math., 1954-72, Disting. Service prof., 1972—, project dir. Research Ctr., 1951-54; vis. lectr. Ohio State U. Grad. Sch., 1946-49; acting prof. U. Cin. Grad. Sch., 1958-60; dir. NSF Math. Inst., Cath. U., Ponce, P.R., summer 1959, U. Dayton, 1961-69, 72; chmn., bd. dirs. Honor Seminars of Met. Dayton, 1987-93. Recipient Lackner award, 1987. Mem. Am. Math. Soc., Math. Assn. Am., Am. Soc. Engring. Edn. (chmn. math. sect. 1967-68, 78-79, mem. exec. com. 1969-73, 76, program chmn. 1977-78), Sigma Xi, Pi Mu Epsilon. Home: 448 Mirage Dr Kokomo IN 46901-7037

SCHRAUTH, WILLIAM LAWRENCE, banker, lawyer; b. Bklyn., Apr. 25, 1935; s. William L. and Louise (Rowland) S.; m. Nancy T. Tollner, Dec. 26, 1959; children—Christopher W., Anne, Michael J., Catherine A. B.A., St. Bonaventure U., Olean, N.Y., 1956; J.D., Fordham U., 1960. Bar: N.Y. 1960. Ptnr., Evans, Severn, Bankert & Peet and predecessor firms, Utica, N.Y., 1962-73; v.p. The Savs. Bank of Utica, 1973-74, exec. v.p., 1974-77, pres., 1977—; trustee RSI Retirement Trust. Bd. dirs. Oneida County Indsl. Devel. Corp. (pres. Utica Found.), Utica. Mem. C. of C. Greater Utica Area. Republican. Office: The Savs Bank of Utica 233 Genesee St Utica NY 13501-2811

SCHREADLEY, RICHARD LEE, writer, retired newspaper editor; b. Harrisburg, Pa., Jan. 3, 1931; s. Harry Leroy and Flora Rebecca (McQuilken) S.; m. Doris Arlene Sheaffer, Dec. 18, 1952; 1 child, Rhys Leroy. B.A., Dickinson Coll., 1952; M.A., Tufts U., 1968, M.A.L.D., 1969, Ph.D., 1972. Reporter The News and Courier, Charleston, S.C., 1975; asso. editor The Evening Post, Charleston, 1975-76; editorial page editor The Evening Post, 1976-77, editor, 1977-81; exec. editor The Evening Post and The News and Courier, 1981-88; assoc. editor and sr. writer mil. and polit. affairs The News and Courier, 1989. Author: From the Rivers to the Sea, The United States Navy in Vietnam, 1992, Virtue and Valor, The Washington Light Infantry in Peace and in War, 1996. Chmn. Fgn. Affairs Forum of Charleston, 1987-88, mem. steering com., 1989. Served to comdr. USN, 1949-52, 56-73. Mem. Navy League, Ret. Officer Assn., Washington Light Infantry, Army-Navy Club of Washington, Country Club of Charleston. Home: 812 Clearview Dr Charleston SC 29412-4511

SCHRECK, ROBERT A., JR., lawyer; b. Buffalo, July 22, 1952. BS in Bus. Adminstrn., Georgetown U., 1974; MBA, Northwestern U., 1975, JD, 1978. Bar: Ill. 1978. Ptnr. McDermott, Will & Emery, Chgo., 1978—. Mem. ABA, Chgo. Bar Asns., Chgo. Soc. Clubs. Office: McDermott Will & Emery 227 W Monroe St Chicago IL 60606-5016

SCHRECKINGER, SY EDWARD, advertising executive, consultant; b. Bklyn., Jan. 10, 1937; s. Robert and Bessie (Gable) S.; m. Linda Fiarman, Mar. 4, 1962; children: Jamie Fran, Jon Gary. B.F.A., Pratt Inst., 1958. Art dir. Sudler and Hennesey, N.Y.C., 1958-61; sr. art dir. Marschalk Co., N.Y.C., 1961-63; group supr. Grey Advt., N.Y.C., 1963-66; v.p., assoc. creative dir. Hicks & Greist, N.Y.C., 1966-69; sr. v.p., assoc. creative dir. Young & Rubicam Inc., N.Y.C., 1969-88; advert. and mktg. cons. Oceanside, N.Y., 1988—. Recipient Lion Venice Internat. Film Festival, 1972, Andy Ad Club, N.Y., 1965, 86, award Internat. Bus. Assn., Best award Hollywood Radio & TV Soc., 1971, Clio Am. TV Comml. Festival, 1967, 72, 82, 85, Effy, 1985. Jewish.

SCHREIBER, ALAN HICKMAN, lawyer; b. Muncie, Ind., Apr. 4, 1944; s. Ephriam and Clarrisa (Hickman) S.; m. Phyllis Jean Chamberlain, Dec. 22, 1972; children—Jennifer Aline, Brett Justin. Student DePauw U., 1962-64; B.S. in Bus., Ind. U., 1966, J.D., 1969. Bar: Fla. 1971, U.S. Dist. Ct. (so. dist.) Fla. Asst., State Atty.'s Office, Ft. Lauderdale, Fla., 1971-76; pub. defender 17th Jud. Circuit, Ft. Lauderdale, 1976—; cons. Fla. Bar News on Criminal Law, 1982; lobbyist for indigent funding, Fla., 1980—; apptd. to Supreme Ct. Com. on Racial and Ethic Bias; co-chair Chiles-MacKay task force on criminal justice. Contbr. articles to profl. jours. Mem. Dem. Exec. Com., Ft. Lauderdale, 1980; mem. Plantation Dem. Club, 1983; campaign chmn. Goldstein for Atty. Gen. Fla., 1982. Named Young Dem. of Yr., Broward County Young Dems., 1980; Man of Yr., Jewish War Vets., 1982; recipient B'nai B'rith Pub. Servant award, 1990. Mem. Fla. Bar Assn., Broward County Bar Assn., ABA, Nat. Legal Aid Defenders Assn., Phi Alpha Delta. Home: 885 Orchid Dr Fort Lauderdale FL 33317-1221 Office: 201 SE 6th St 3rd Fl North Wing Fort Lauderdale FL 33301-3302

SCHREIBER, BERTRAM MANUEL, mathematics educator; b. Seattle, Nov. 4, 1940; s. Isador and Amy (Hurwitz) S.; m. Rita Ruth Stusser, June 30, 1963; children: Susannah M. Schreiber Bechhofer, Deborah H. Schreiber Shapiro, Abraham D., Elisabeth T. BA, Yeshiva U., 1962; MS, U. Wash., 1966, PhD, 1968. Asst. prof. Wayne State U., Detroit, 1968-71, assoc. prof., 1971-78, prof., 1978—, chair dept. math., 1987-90; vis. prof. Hebrew U., Jerusalem, 1975, Mich. State U., East Lansing, 1982-83, Nat. U. Singapore, 1992, U. New South Wales, Australia, 1992, Indian Statis. Inst., 1993, Tata Inst. Fund Res., Bombay, 1993, Bar Ilan U., 1993, Tel Aviv U., 1993, U. Utrecht, The Netherlands, 1993, U. Wroclaw, Poland, 1993. Contbr. articles to profl. jours. NSF grantee, 1968-87; Sci. and Engring. Rsch. Coun. Gt. Britain fellow U. Edinburgh, Scotland, 1976. Mem. Am. Math. Soc., Math. Assn. Am., Israel Math. Union, Edinburgh Math. Soc. Achievements include research in the fields of harmonic analysis, topological groups, and probability theory. Office: Wayne State U Dept Math Detroit MI 48202

SCHREIBER, EILEEN SHER, artist; b. Denver; d. Michael Herschel and Sarah Deborah (Tannenbaum) Sher; student U. Utah, 1942-45, N.Y.U. extension, 1966-68, Montclair (N.J.) State Coll., 1975-79; also pvt. art study; m. Jonas Schreiber, Mar. 27, 1945; children—Jeffrey, Barbara, Michael. Exhibited Morris Mus. Arts and Scis., Morristown, N.J., 1965-73, N.J. State Mus., 1969, Lever House, N.Y.C., 1971, Paramus (N.J.) Mus., 1973, Newark Mus., 1978, Am. Water Color Soc., Audubon Artists, N.A.D. Gallery, N.Y.C., Pallazzo Vecchio Florence (Italy), Art Expo 1987, 1988, Newark Mus., 1991-92; represented in permanent collections Tex. A&M U., Sunbelt Computers, Phoenix, Ariz., State of N.J., Morris Mus., Seton Hall U., Bloomfield (N.J.) Coll., Barclay Bank of Eng., N.J., Somerset Coll., NYU, Morris County State Coll., Broad Nat. Bank, Newark, IBM, Am. Telephone Co., RCA, Johnson & Johnson, Champion Internat. Paper Co., SONY, Mitsubishi, Celanese Co., Squibb Corp., Nabisco, Nat. Bank Phila., NYU, Data Control, Sperry Univac, Ga. Pacific Co., Pub. Svc. Co. N.J., Forms Galleries, Delray Beach, Fla., Robin Hutchins Galleries, Maplewood, N.J., others; also pvt. collections. Recipient awards N.J. Watercolor Soc., 1969, 72, Marian E. Halpern Memorial award Nat. Assn. Women Artists, 1970; 1st award in watercolor Hunterdon Art Center, 1972, Best in Show award Short Hills State Show, 1976, Tri-State Purchase award Somerset Coll., 1977, Art Expo, N.Y.C. 1987, 88, ; numerous others. Mem. Nat. Assn. Women Artists (chmn. watercolor jury; Collage award 1983, Marian Halpren meml. award 1995), Nat., N.J. Artists Equity, Printmaker Coun. Visual Artists (1st award in printmaking 1996). Home: 22 Powell Dr West Orange NJ 07052-1337

SCHREIBER, GEORGE RICHARD, association executive, writer; b. Ironton, Ohio, July 4, 1922; s. George Joseph and Marie Frances (Heitzman) S.; m. Veva Jeanette Hopkins, May 14, 1945; children—Susan (Mrs. Arlan Shorey), George, Ellen (Mrs. Norman Hodge). A.B., St. Joseph's Coll., Rensselaer, Ind., 1943, L.H.D., 1974; M.A., U. Chgo., 1944. Exec. editor Billboard mag., 1945-60; editor, pub. Vend mag., 1946-66; editorial dir. Billboard Publs., 1966-70; pres., chief exec. officer Nat. Automatic Mdsg. Assn., Chgo., 1970-88, pres. emeritus, 1988—; mem. staff and faculty U. Chgo., 1944-46. Author: Verses from the River Country, 1941, What Makes News, 1943, Automatic Selling, 1954, A Concise History of Vending in the U.S.A, 1965, revised 2d edit., 1990, The Bobby Baker Affair—How to Make Millions in Washington, 1964; contbg. author: Handbook of Modern Marketing, 1986, Vending For Investors-How to Spot Phony Deals, 1994. Chmn. Glenview (Ill.) Plan Commn., 1962-64, mayor, 1964-67; chmn. Region 1, Chgo. Area Transp. Study Group, 1962-63; bd. dirs. Rockefeller Meml. Chapel, U. Chgo., 1944-45; trustee St. Joseph's Coll., 1964—, chmn., 1970-76, life trustee, 1978—. Recipient Jesse H. Neal award for editorial achievement, 1964; dedication of St. Joseph's Coll. (Ind.) G. Richard Schreiber Dept. Humanities, 1987. Mem. The Authors Guild Inc., Am. Bus. Press (editorial bd.), Assn. Econs. Council, Am. Soc. Assn. Execs., Tavern Club, Internat. Club, Tower Club. Home: 735 Ravine Ave Lake Bluff IL 60044-2625

SCHREIBER, HARRY, JR., management consultant; b. Columbus, Ohio, Apr. 1, 1934; s. C. Harry and Audrey (Sard) S.; BS, Mass. Inst. Tech., 1955; MBA, Boston U., 1958; m. Margaret Ruth Heinzman, June 12, 1955; children: Margaret Elizabeth, Thomas Edward, Amy Katherine Schreiber Garcia. CPA, N.Y. Accountant truck and coach div. Gen. Motors Corp., Pontiac, Mich., 1955; instr. Mass. Inst. Tech., 1958-62; pres. Data-Service, Inc., Boston, 1961-65; pres. Harry Schreiber Assos., Wellesley, Mass., 1965; mgr., nat. dir. merchandising consulting Peat, Marwick, Mitchell & Co., N.Y.C., 1966-70, partner, Chgo., 1970-75; chmn. bd. Close, Martin, Schreiber & Co., 1975-82; partner Deloitte Haskins & Sells, 1983-85; chmn. bd. Harry Schreiber & Assocs., Ltd., 1985—. Pub. Retail Working Papers, 1991—. Staff, Work Simplification Conf. Lake Placid, N.Y., 1960-61; Tobe retailing lectr. Harvard Bus. Sch., 1964. Served to 1st lt. AUS, 1956-58. Mem. Am. Inst. Indsl. Engrs. (chmn. data-processing div. 1964-66, chpt. v.p. 1961, 65, chmn. retail industries div. 1976-78), Com. Internat. Congress Transp. Confs., Assn. for Computing Machinery, Assn. for Systems Mgmt., Inst. Mgmt. Scis., Retail Rsch. Soc., Retail Fin. Execs., Nat. Retail Mchts. Assn. (retail systems specifications com., acctg. stds. com.), Food Distbn. Research Soc. (dir. 1972-78, pres. 1974), Japan-Am. Soc. Chgo. Republican. Methodist. Clubs: MIT Faculty; Hidden Creek Country (Reston, Va.), Chester River Yacht and Country Club (Chestertown, Md.); Army and Navy (Washington); Plaza (Chgo.).

SCHREIBER, JAMES RALPH, obstetrics-gynecology researcher; b. Rosebud, Tex., May 29, 1946; m. Lester B. and Jane Elinore (Hodges) S.; m. Mary Celia Schmitt, Aug. 16, 1968; children: Lisa, Joseph, Laura, Cynthia. BA, Rice U., 1968; MD, Johns Hopkins U., 1972. Cert. Am. Coll. Ob-Gyn, Am. Bd. Reproductive Endocrinology. Intern. ob-gyn. U. So. Calif. Los Angeles County Hosp., 1972-73, resident ob-gyn., 1973-74, 76-78; fellow reproductive endocrinology NIH, Bethesda, Md., 1974-76; asst. prof. ob-gyn U. Calif., San Diego, 1978-82; assoc. prof. U. Chgo., 1982-87, prof., 1988-91; prof., chmn. dept. Washington U., St. Louis, 1991—. Contbr. articles to profl. jours. Grantee NIH, 1978—. Mem. Endocrine Soc., Soc. Gynecologic Investigation. Home: 22 Frontenac Estates Saint Louis MO 63131-2600 Office: Washington U Sch Medicine Dept Ob-Gyn 4911 Barnes Hospital Plz Saint Louis MO 63110-1003

SCHREIBER, JOHN T., lawyer; b. N.Y.C., Mar. 30, 1960; s. Toby Schreiber and Morley Ann (Perrish) Clark; m. Theresa Ann Sawyer, Aug. 11, 1984; children: Zoe Cassandra Bloch Schreiber, Alana Nichole Perrish Schreiber. BA Politics, Brandeis U., 1982; JD, Santa Clara U., 1986. Bar: Calif. 1987; U.S. Dist. Ct. (no. dist.) Calif. 1987; U.S. Dist. Ct. (ea. dist.) Calif. 1990; U.S. Ct. Appeals (9th cir.) 1989. Assoc. Law Offices of Wm. D. McHugh, San Jose, Calif., 1987-88, Hallgrimson, McNichols, McCann & Inderbitzen, Pleasanton, Calif., 1989-92; pvt. practice Walnut Creek, Calif., 1993—; bd. dirs. East Bay Depot for Creative Re-use, Oakland. Field coord. Cen. Contra Costa County, Tom Bradley Campaign for Govs., Concord, Calif., 1982, Clinton-Gore Campaign, Walnut Creek, Calif., 1992; mem. Ask-A-Lawyer Program Contra Costa Legal Svcs. Found., Richmond, Calif., 1992—; co-chair Clinton-Gore Contra Costa County, 1996. Mem. ABA, Contra Costa Bar Assn. (program dir. appellate sect. 1993-95, pres. appellate sect. 1995-96), MCLE com. 1995—), Bar Assn. San Francisco (appellate sect. 1993—), Santa Clara Bar Assn., Am. Israeli Polit. Action Com. Avocations: reading, golf, softball, movies, exercising. Office: 961 Ygnacio Valley Rd Walnut Creek CA 94596

SCHREIBER, MARVIN MANDEL, agronomist, educator; b. Springfield, Mass., Oct. 17, 1925; s. William and Florence Schreiber; m. Phyllis E. Altman, Dec. 18, 1949; 1 child, Michelle. BS, U. Mass., 1950; MS, U. Ariz., 1951; PhD, Cornell U., 1954. Asst. prof. dept. agronomy Cornell U., Ithaca, N.Y., 1954-59; assoc. prof. dept. botany and plant pathology Purdue U., West Lafayette, Ind., 1959-73—, prof., 1973—; rsch. agronomist Agrl. Rsch. Svc. USDA, West Lafayette, 1959—. Fellow AAAS, Am. Soc. Agronomy, Weed Sci. Soc. Am.; mem. Internat. Weed Sci. Soc. (pres. 1979-81), Controlled Release Soc., Coun. Agrl. Sci. and Tech., Sigma Xi. Avocations: golf, gardening. Office: Dept Botany & Plant Pathology Purdue U Lilly Hall Life Scis West Lafayette IN 47907

SCHREIBER, MELVYN HIRSH, radiologist; b. Galveston, Tex., May 28, 1931; s. Edward and Sue Schreiber; m. Laurentina; children—William, Diane, Karen, Lori. M.D., U. Tex. Med. Br., Galveston, 1955. Diplomate: Am. Bd. Radiology (trustee 1987—). Intern U. Tex. Med. Br., Galveston, 1955-56; resident U. Tex. Med. Br., 1956-59, asst. prof. radiology, 1961-64, asso. prof., 1964-67, prof., 1967—, chmn. dept. radiology, 1976-91. Author: Old Dog, New Tricks, A Collection of Essays, 1995. Served as capt. M.C. U.S. Army, 1959-61. Markle Found. scholar, 1963-68. Fellow Am. Coll. Radiology; mem. Assn. Univ. Radiologists (pres. 1974-75). Office: U Tex Med Br Dept Radiology Galveston TX 77555

SCHREIBER, PAUL SOLOMON, lawyer; b. Krakow, Poland, Mar. 29, 1941; came to U.S., 1949; s. John and Betty (Silber) S.; m. Joan A. Perlmutter, Mar. 20, 1971; children: Douglas Arun, Stacey Lauren. BS, CCNY, 1963; LLB, NYU, 1966, LLM, 1967; postgrad., U. Paris, 1967-68. Bar: N.Y. 1966. Assoc. Marshal, Bratter, Greene, Allison & Tucker, N.Y.C., 1969-76, ptnr., 1976-82; ptnr. Kramer, Levin, Naftalis, Nessen, Kamin & Frankel, N.Y.C., 1982-94, Shearman & Sterling, N.Y.C., 1994—; bd. dirs. Harbor Trust Co., Hoboken, N.J., 1985-92. Editor: Annual Survey Am. Law; co-author articles, papers and revs. Trustee, v.p. Park Ave. Synagogue, N.Y.C., 1985—; bd. dirs. Am. Friends of the Rambam Med. Ctr., N.Y.C., 1989—, N.Y.C. chpt. of Nat. Multiple Sclerosis Soc., 1991—, Sch. for Strings, 1994—; bd. overseers Rabbinical Sch. Jewish Theol. Sem., 1995—. Arthur Garfield Hayes fellow; Ford Found. fellow. Democrat. Jewish. Office: Shearman & Sterling 599 Lexington Ave New York NY 10022-6030

SCHREIBER, SALLY ANN, lawyer; b. El Paso, Tex., July 23, 1951; d. Warren Thomas and Joyce (Honey) S.; children: Amanda Honey, Ryan Thorp Luther. BBA, U. N.Mex., 1973; JD, Stanford U., 1976. Bar: Calif. 1976, Tex. 1977. Assoc. Johnson & Swanson, Dallas, 1976-81, ptnr., 1981-89; mem. firm Johnson & Gibbs, P.C., Dallas, 1989-93; of counsel Cox & Smith, Inc., Dallas, 1993-94; shareholder Munsch Hardt Kopf Harr & Dinan, P.C., Dallas, 1994—; spkr. Advanced Mgmt. Rsch. Internat., Dallas, 1984, U. Tex., Austin, 1984, 89, 91, 93, Houston, 1994, Dallas, 1995, State Bar of Tex., Dallas, 1989, Lubbock, Arlington, San Antonio, 1990, Houston, 1994, South Tex. Coll. Law, Houston, 1990, 94. Editor Stanford U. Law Rev., 1975-76; co-author paper Internat. Bar Assn., 1986. Bd. dirs. The Lyric Opera of Dallas, 1982-86, bd. trustees, 1986-90; mem. law sch. bd. vis. Stanford (Calif.) U., 1981-84; dir. Tex. Bus. Law Found., 1989—, treas. 1994-96, sec. 1996—. Mem. ABA, Tex. Bar Assn. (revision corp. law com. 1981—, vice chair 1993—, ptnrship. law com. 1985—, ltd. liability company com. 1992—, opinion com. 1989—), Calif. Bar Assn., Dallas Bar Assn. Home: 2737 Purdue Ave Dallas TX 75225-7910 Office: Munsch Hardt Kopf Harr & Dinan PC 4000 Fountain Pl 1445 Ross Ave Dallas TX 75202-2812

SCHREIBER, WILLIAM FRANCIS, electrical engineer; b. N.Y.C., Sept. 18, 1925. BS, Columbia U., 1945, MS, 1947; PhD, Harvard U., 1953. Jr. engr. Sylvania Elec. Products, Inc., 1947-49; rsch. assoc. Harvard U., Cambridge, Mass., 1953; rsch. physicist Technicolor Corp., 1953-59; prof. elec. engring. Mass. Inst. Tech., Cambridge, 1959-83, dir. advanced tv rsch. program, 1983-89. Fellow IEEE; mem. Nat. Acad. Engring., Sigma Xi. Office: MIT M/S 36-545 Cambridge MA 02139

SCHREIER, PETER, tenor; b. Meissen, Germany, July 29, 1935. Ed., Dresden Hochschule für Musik, Germany. With Dresden State Opera, Germany, 1959-63, Berlin Staatsoper, Germany, 1963. Appearances include Vienna State Opera, Salzburg Festival, La Scala, Milan, Sadler's Wells, London, Met. Opera, N.Y.C., Teatro Colon, Buenos Aires; recital debut London, 1978; debut as conductor, 1969; has conducted recordings of several choral works by J.S. Bach and Mozart. Office: Kammersänger, Calberlastr 13, D-01326 Dresden Germany

SCHREINER, ALBERT WILLIAM, physician, educator; b. Cin., Feb. 15, 1926; s. Albert William and Ruth Mary (Neuer) S.; m. Jean Tellstrom, Dec. 12, 1953; 1 child, David William. BS, U. Cin., 1947, MD, 1949. Diplomate: Am. Bd. Internal Medicine. Clin. investigator VA Hosp., Cin., 1957-59, chief med. service, 1959-68, dir. dept. internal medicine, 1968-93; dir. resident program internal medicine Christ Hosp., Cin., 1978-87; mem. faculty U. Cin. Coll. Medicine, 1955—, assoc. prof. medicine, 1962-67, prof. internal medicine, 1967—; attending physician Cin. Gen. Hosp., 1957—; cons. to med. dir. Gen. Electric, 1987—; med. dirs. United Home Care Hospice, 1993—, United Home Care Agy. Contbr. articles to tech. jours. Bd. dirs., chmn. health com. Community Action Commn., 1968-701 trustee Drake Meml. Hosp., 1975-78, Leukemia Found. Southwest Ohio, Cancer Control, Am. Cancer Soc., bd. dirs. Hamilton County unit, 1990; bd. dirs. Gamble Inst. Med. Rsch., Cin., 1991—. Fellow ACP; mem. N.Y. Acad. Scis., Am. Fedn. Clin. Rsch., Ohio Med. Assn., Ohio Soc. Internal Medicine (trustee 1978, sec.-treas. 1981-85, v.p. 1982-83, pres. 1984-85), Clin. Soc. Internal Medicine (pres. 1979-80), Assn. Program Dirs. Internal Medicine, Am. Soc. Clin. Rsch. Program Dirs. Internal Medicine, Am. Leukemia Soc. (med. adv. exec. bd.), Am. Cancer Soc. (bd. dirs. Hamilton County unit 1990), Phi Beta Kappa, Sigma Xi. Episcopalian. Home: 8040 S Clippinger Dr Cincinnati OH 45243-3248 Office: 2139 Auburn Ave Cincinnati OH 45219-2906

SCHREINER, GEORGE E., nephrologist, educator, writer; b. Buffalo, Apr. 26, 1922; s. George Frederick and Eleanor (Kreig) S.; m. Joanne Baker, Apr. 3, 1948; children: George F., Mary E., Meredith Schreiner Maclay, William P., Sara B. Schreiner Kendall, Lise Schreiner Salmon, Peter K., Robert P. (dec.). AB magna cum laude, Canisius Coll., 1943, HLD (hon.), 1973; MD cum laude, Georgetown U., 1946, HLD, 1973, ScD (hon.), 1987. Intern Boston City Hosp., 1946-47; fellow in nephrology N.Y. U., 1947-50; resident in medicine Washington VA Hosp., 1950-51; dir. renal clinic Georgetown U. Hosp., 1951-52, 55-61, instr. medicine, 1955-58, asst. prof. medicine, 1958-61, asso. prof. medicine, dir. renal and electrolyte div., 1961-70, prof. medicine, dir. nephrology div., 1970-87, Disting. prof. medicine, 1987—; mem. staff Arlington Hosp., D.C. Gen. Hosp.; cons. VA Hosp., Walter Reed Army Hosp., Speakers Bur., Merck, Hoechst-Roussel, Baxter, George E. Schreiner Premed. Ctr., Canisius Coll. Editor in chief Am. Soc. Artificial Internal Organs, 1957-86, editor emeritus, 1986—; editor in chief: Procs. of Clin. Dialysis, Transplant Forum and Controveries in Nephrology, 1979-84; co-editor: 20 Years Nephrology at Grosshadern; contbr. chpts. to books, articles to profl. jours. Bd. dirs. Washington Heart Assn.; bd. trustees Internat. Soc. for Art Orgns., 1986—; bd. sponsors Nat. Kidney Found.; governing bd. Ctr. for Crisis Counseling, Washington; mem. com. academics, com. devel., bd. trustees Canisius Coll., Buffalo, 1988-94. Recipient Davidson award Med. Soc. D.C., Pres.'s award, 1979, David Hume award Nat. Kidney Found., 1980, Pub. Svc. award NASA, Nettuno d'Argento award U. Bologna, 1988, Achievement award Am. Assn. Kidney Patients, Laureate award Am. Coll. Physicians, Washington; guest of honor Greece Soc. Nephrology-Internat. Congress on Acute Renal Failure. Fellow ACP, Royal Soc. Physicians and Surgeons (Glasgow, Walton lectr.); mem. Soc. Exptl. Biology, Nat. Drug Rsch. Bd., Am. Soc. Physiology, Am. Soc. Pharmacology and Clin. Therapeutics, So. Salt, Water and Kidney Club, Am. Soc. Artificial Internal Organs (past pres.), Internat. Soc. Artificial Organs (life trustee), Nat. Kidney Found. (past pres.), Internat. Soc. Nephrology (pres. 1978-81, past pres., mem. exec. com. 1981-84), Am. Soc. Nephrology (past pres., John Peters award 1989), Assn. Am. Physicians, Am. Soc. Clin. Investigation, Am. Fedn. for Clin. Rsch. (past pres., past treas.), D.C. Med. Soc., Washington Heart Assn. (past pres.), Renal Transplant Physicians, Coun. Transplantation, Am. Soc. Hypertension, Am. Clin. and Climatologic Assn., Wash. Acad. Medicine (admission com. 1987-90, chmn. 1990), Cosmos Club (Washington), Duckwoods Country Club (Kitty Hawk, N.C.), Tralee Golf Club (Kerry, Ireland). Roman Catholic. Home: PO Box 199 Great Falls VA 22066-0199 Office: Georgetown U Hosp 3800 Reservoir Rd NW Washington DC 20007-2196

SCHREINER, JOHN CHRISTIAN, economics consultant, software publisher; b. Los Angeles, Nov. 2, 1933; s. Alexander and Margaret S.; m. Marie Nielsen, June 19, 1967; children: Christian Alexander, Carl Arthur, Elizabeth, Nathan Alexander. B.S.M.E., U. Utah, 1958; M.B.A., Harvard U., 1960; Ph.D., UCLA, 1970. Chartered fin. analyst. Design engr. Eimco Corp., Salt Lake City and N.Y.C., 1957-59; credit exec. James Talcott, Inc., N.Y.C. and Boston, 1960-65; lectr. mgmt. U. Utah, 1965-66; mem. faculty Grad. Sch. Mgmt., U. Minn., Mpls., 1969-84; chmn. dept. fin. and ins. Grad. Sch. Mgmt., U. Minn., 1973-74, 76-81; pres. The Sebastian Group, Inc., 1984—; dir. Deluxe Corp.; cons. to corps. and govt. agys. Co-author: Executive Recruiting: How Companies Obtain Management Talent, 1960; contbr. articles to profl. jours. Mem. Fin. Execs. Inst., Fin. Analysts Fedn., Tau Beta Pi, Phi Kappa Phi. Republican. Mem. Ch. Jesus Christ of Latter-day Saints (missionary, Ger. 1953-56). Club: Harvard Bus. Sch. Minn. Office: The Sebastian Group Inc 5730 Duluth St Minneapolis MN 55422

SCHREMPF, DETLEF, professional basketball player; b. Leverkusen, Germany, Jan. 21, 1963. Student, U. Washington. Forward Dallas Mavericks, 1985-89, Indiana Pacers, 1989-93, Seattle Supersonics, 1993—; player West German Olympic Team, 1984, 92. Recipient Sixth Man award NBA, 1991, 92; mem. NBA All-Star team, 1993. *

SCHRENK, W(ILLI) JUERGEN, health care company executive; b. Dachau, Germany, June 19, 1945; came to U.S., 1972; s. Willi Schrenk and Irmgard (Urbanek) Meinhardt; m. Ruth Halfenberg, Nov. 10, 1971; 1 child, Ralph Michael. PhD, U. Cologne, Germany, 1972. Rsch. fellow Harvard Med. Sch., Boston, 1972-73; guest scientist Nat. Cancer Inst., Bethesda, Md., 1972-73; asst. rsch. prof. U. Calif., Santa Barbara, 1974-77; sr. scientist Abbott Labs., North Chicago, Ill., 1977-79; sci. dir. Boehringer Mannheim GmbH, Tutzing, Germany, 1979-85; sr. dir. R & D Boehringer Mannheim Corp., Indpls., 1986-89; sr. v.p. R & D Gen-Probe, San Diego, 1989-90; v.p. R & D Wampole Labs., Cranbury, N.J., 1990-94; v.p. tech. mgmt. Corange Internat. Ltd., Bermuda, 1994-95; sr. v.p. tech. mgmt. Boehringer Mannheim Group, Gaithersburg, Md., 1996—. Contbr. articles to profl. jours; patentee in field. Established nature preserves in U.S. and Fed. Republic of Germany, 1975-85. Fellow Fed. Republic of Germany, 1964-70, Deutsche Forschungs-Gemeinschaft, 1972-74. Mem. Nature Conservancy, World Wildlife Fund. Avocations: nature photography, skiing, hiking, traveling. Home: 1 Stream Valley Ct Laytonsville MD 20882-1273 Office: Boehringer Mannheim Tech Off 101 Orchard Ridge Dr Gaithersburg MD 20878-1952

SCHREYER, LESLIE JOHN, lawyer; b. N.Y.C., Apr. 11, 1946; s. Oscar and Greta (Loebl) S.; m. Judith Camps, Sept. 25, 1994; 1 child, Gabrielle. BA, Columbia U., 1967; LLB, Yale U., 1970; LLM in Taxation, N.Y.U., 1977. Bar: N.Y. 1971. Assoc. Chadbourne & Parke, N.Y.C., 1970-78, ptnr., 1978-81, 83—; dep. internat. tax counsel U.S. Treasury Dept., 1981-83; adj. assoc. prof. law NYU, 1990—; cons. Am. Law Inst., Fed. Income Tax Project on Internat. Aspects of U.S. Income Taxation, 1983-91. Author: (with others) Foreign Tax Credit, 1980; contbr. numerous articles to profl. jours. Bd. dirs. The Poster Soc., N.Y.C., 1985-93, 910 Park Ave Corp., 1993-94. Mem. ABA, Internat. Bar Assn., Internat. Fiscal Assn., N.Y. State Bar Assn., Assn. of Bar of City of N.Y., Phi Beta Kappa. Republican. Home: 60 E End Ave New York NY 10028 Office: Chadbourne & Parke 30 Rockefeller Plz New York NY 10112

SCHREYER, WILLIAM ALLEN, retired investment firm executive; b. Williamsport, Pa., Jan. 13, 1928; s. William L. and Elizabeth (Engel) S.; m. Joan Legg, Oct. 17, 1953; 1 child, DrueAnne Frazier. BA, Pa. State U., 1948. With Merrill Lynch, Inc. and predecessors, N.Y.C., 1948-93; CEO Merrill Lynch & Co., N.Y.C., 1984-92, chmn., 1985-93; chmn. emeritus, 1993—; bd. dirs. Schering-Plough Corp., Callaway Golf Co., Deere & Co., True North Comm. Inc., Willis Corroon Group. Trustee Ctr. for Strategic and Internat. Studies, Pa. State U., chmn. bd. trustees. With USAF, 1955-56. Mem. Econ. Club N.Y., River Club, Links Club, Saturn Club, Springdale Golf Club, Bedens Brook Club, Eldorado Country Club, Georgetown Club, Met. Club, Old Baldy Club, Tournament Players Club, Nassau Club, Knights of Malta. Roman Catholic. Office: Merrill Lynch & Co Inc 800 Scudders Mill Rd Plainsboro NJ 08536-1606

SCHRICKER, ETHEL KILLINGSWORTH, business management, public relations, and marketing consultant, public speaker; b. Hagerstown, Md., July 22, 1937; d. Lloyd Granville and Ethel Mull; children: Jeanne, Lori, Jerri; m. Robert Lee Schricker, June 6, 1993. BA in Mgmt., Hood Coll., 1994; postgrad. in Psychology, Hood Coll, 1994—. Vol. Literacy Coun., Frederick, 1976-84, Dept. Social Svcs., Frederick, 1984; bd. ruling elders Frederick Presbyn. Ch., 1989-92. Named Bus. Woman of Yr. Frederick Bus. and Profl. Women, 1992. Mem. Assn. Sch. Bus. Ofcls. (chairperson seminar devel. com. 1990-94), Frederick County Assn. Adminstrv. and Supervisory Pers., Frederick County C. of C., Frederick County Advt. Fedn., Carroll Creek Rotary Club, Toastmasters Internat. (area gov. 1991-92, pub. rels. 1991-93, v.p. pub. rels. 1995—). Avocations: photography, bicycling. Home: PO Box 15 Frederick MO 21705-0015

SCHRIEFFER, JOHN ROBERT, physics educator, science administrator; b. Oak Park, Ill., May 31, 1931; s. John Henry and Louise (Anderson) S.; m. Anne Grete Thomsen, Dec. 30, 1960; children: Anne Bolette, Paul Karsten, Anne Regina. BS, MIT, 1953; MS, U. Ill., 1954, PhD, 1957, ScD, 1974; ScD (hon.), Tech. U., Munich, Germany, 1968, U. Geneva, 1968, U. Pa., 1973, U. Cin., 1977, U. Tel Aviv, 1987, U. Ala., 1990. NSF postdoctoral fellow U. Birmingham, Eng., also; Niels Bohr Inst., Copenhagen, 1957-58; asst. prof. U. Chgo., 1958-59; asst. prof., then assoc. prof. U. Ill., 1959-62; prof. U. Pa., Phila., 1962-79; Mary Amanda Wood prof. physics U. Pa., 1964-79; Andrew D. White prof. at large Cornell U., 1969-75; prof. U. Calif., Santa Barbara, 1980-91, Chancellor's prof., 1984-91, dir. Inst. for Theoretical Physics, 1984-89; Univ. prof. Fla. State U., Tallahassee, 1992—, Univ. Eminent Scholar prof., 1995—, chief scientist Nat. High Magnetic Field

Lab., 1992—. Author: Theory of Superconductivity, 1964. Guggenheim fellow Copenhagen, 1967; Los Alamos Nat. Lab. fellow; Recipient Comstock prize Nat. Acad. Sci.; Nobel Prize for Physics, 1972; John Ericsson medal Am. Soc. Swedish Engrs., 1976; Alumni Achievement award U. Ill., 1979; recipient Nat. Medal of Sci., 1984; Exxon faculty fellow, 1979-89. Fellow Am. Phys. Soc. (v.p. 1994, pres.-elect 1995, pres. 1996, Oliver E. Buckley solid state physics prize 1986); mem. NAS (coun. 1990—), Am. Acad. Arts and Scis., Coun. Nat. Acad. Sci., Royal Danish Acad. Scis. and Letters, Acad. Sci. USSR. Office: Fla State UNHMFL 1800 E Paul Dirac Dr Tallahassee FL 32306-4005

SCHRIER, ARNOLD, historian, educator; b. N.Y.C., May 30, 1925; s. Samuel and Yetta (Levine) S.; m. Sondra Weinshelbaum, June 12, 1949; children—Susan Lynn, Jay Alan, Linda Lee, Paula Kay. Student, Bethany Coll., W.Va., 1943-44, Ohio Wesleyan U., 1944-45; B.S., Northwestern U., 1949, M.A., 1950, Ph.D. (Social Sci. Research Council fellow, Univ. fellow), 1956. Asst. prof. history U. Cin., 1956-61, assoc. prof., 1961-66, prof., 1966-95, dir. grad. studies history, 1969-78, Walter C. Langsam prof. modern European history, 1972-95; Walter C. Langsam prof. history emeritus, 1995—; vis. asst. prof. history Northwestern U., Evanston, Ill., 1960; vis. assoc. prof. history Ind. U., Bloomington, 1965-66; vis. lectr. Russian history Duke U., 1966; disting. vis. prof. U.S. Air Force Acad., 1983-84; dir. NDEA Inst. World History for Secondary Sch. Tchrs., U. Cin., 1965; Am. del. Joint U.S.-USSR Textbook Study Commn., 1989. Author: Ireland and the American Emigration, 1958, reissued, 1970, The Development of Civilization, 1961-62, Modern European Civilization, 1963, Living World History, 1964, rev., 1993, Twentieth Century World, 1974, History and Life: the World and Its People, 1977, rev., 1993, A Russian Looks at America, 1979. Pres. Ohio Acad. History, 1973-74, Midwest Slavic Conf., 1980. Served with USNR, 1943-46, 52-54. Recipient Disting. Svc. award Ohio Acad. History, 1992; Am. Council Learned Socs. fgn. area fellow, 1963-64. Mem. World History Assn. (v.p. 1986-88, pres. 1988-90). Home: 10 Diplomat Dr Cincinnati OH 45215-2073 Office: Univ Cincinnati Dept History Mail Location 373 Cincinnati OH 45221

SCHRIER, ROBERT WILLIAM, physician, educator; b. Indpls., Feb. 19, 1936; s. Arthur E. and Helen M. Schrier; m. Barbara Lindley, June 14, 1959; children: David, Debbie, Douglas, Derek, Denise. BA, Depauw U., 1957; MD, Ind. U., 1962. Intern Marion County (Ind.) Hosp., 1962; resident U. Wash., Seattle, 1963-65; pvt. practice specializing in nephrology Denver, 1972—; asst. prof. U. Calif. Med. Ctr., San Francisco, 1969-72, assoc. mem., 1970-72, assoc. dir. renal div., 1971-72, assoc. prof., 1972; prof., head renal disease U. Colo. Sch. Med., Denver, 1972—, prof., chmn. Dept.of Medicine, 1976—. Pres. Nat. Kidney Found., 1984-86. With U.S. Army, 1966-69. Mem. ACP (master), Am. Soc. Nephrology (treas. 1979-81, pres. 1983), Internat. Soc. Nephrology (treas. 1981-90, v.p. 1990-95, pres. 1995—), Am. Clin. and Climatol. Assn. (v.p. 1986), Assn. Am. Physicians (pres. 1994-95), Western Assn. Physicians (pres. 1982), Alpha Omega Alpha. Office: U Colo Health Scis Ctr Dept Medicine 4200 E 9th Ave Denver CO 80220-3706

SCHRIER, STANLEY LEONARD, physician, educator; b. N.Y.C., Jan. 2, 1929; s. Harry and Nettie (Schwartz) S.; m. Peggy Helen Pepper, June 6, 1953; children: Rachel, Leslie, David. A.B., U. Colo., 1949; M.D., Johns Hopkins U., 1954. Diplomate Am. Bd. Internal Medicine (chmn. subsplty. bd. hematology). Intern Oster Med. Service, Johns Hopkins Hosp., 1954-55; resident U. Mich., Ann Arbor, 1955-56, U. Chgo. Hosp., 1958-59; sr. asst. surgeon USPHS, 1956-58; instr. medicine Stanford Sch. Medicine, Calif., 1959-60; asst. prof. medicine Stanford Sch. Medicine, 1960-63, assoc. prof., 1963-72, prof. medicine, 1972-95, chief divsn. hematology, 1968-94; vis. scientist Weizmann Inst., Rehovot, Israel, 1967-68; vis. prof. Oxford U., Eng., 1975-76, Hebrew U., Jerusalem, 1982-83. John and Mary Markle scholar, 1961; recipient Kaiser award Stanford U., 1972, Kaiser award Stanford U., 1974, 75, David Rytand award, 1982, Eleanor Roosevelt Union Internationale Contre le Cancer award, 1975-76. Mem. Am. Soc. Hematology (exec. com.), Am. Physiol. Soc., Soc. Exptl. Biology and Medicine, Am. Soc. Clin. Investigation, Western Assn. Physicians. Democrat. Jewish. Office: Stanford U Sch Medicine 300 Pasteur Dr Palo Alto CA 94304-2203

SCHRIESHEIM, ALAN, research administrator; b. N.Y.C., Mar. 8, 1930; s. Morton and Frances (Greenberg) S.; m. Beatrice D. Brand, June 28, 1953; children: Laura Lynn, Robert Alan. BS in Chemistry, Poly. Inst. Bklyn., 1951; PhD in Phys. Organic Chemistry, Pa. State U., 1954; DSc (hon.), No. Ill. U., 1991; PhD (hon.), Ill. Inst. Tech., Chgo., 1992; Laureate, Lincoln Acad., 1996. Chemist Nat. Bur. Standards, 1954-56; with Exxon Research & Engring. Co., 1956-83, dir. corp. research, 1975-79; gen. mgr. Exxon Engring., 1979-83; sr. dep. lab. dir., chief operating officer Argonne Nat. Lab., 1983-84, lab. dir., CEO, 1984—; prof. chemistry dept. U. Chgo., 1984—; Karcher lectr. U. Okla., 1977; Hurd lectr. Northwestern U., 1980; Rosenstiel lectr. Brandeis U., 1982; Welch Found. lectr., 1987; com. svc. NRC, 1980—; vis. com. chemistry dept. MIT, 1977-82; mem. vis. com. mech. engring. and aerospace dept. Princeton (N.J.) U., 1983-87, mem. vis. com. chemistry dept., 1983-87; mem. Pure and Applied Chemistry Com.; del. to People's Republic of China, 1978; mem. Presdl. Nat. Commn. on Superconductivity, 1989-91, U.S.-USSR Joint Commn. on Basic Sci. Rsch, 1990—; mem. U.S. nat com. Internat. Union Pure and Applied Chemistry, 1982-85; mem. magnetic fusion adv. com. Div. Phys. Scis. U. Chgo. Magnetic Fusion adv. com. to U.S. DOE, 1983-86; mem. Dept. Energy Rsch. Adv. Bd., 1983-85, Congl. Adv. Com. on Sci. and Tech., 1985—; mem. vis. coms. Stanford (Calif.) U., U. Utah, Tex. A&M U., Lehigh U.; bd. govs. Argonne Nat. Lab.; mem. adv. com. on space systems and tech. NASA, 1987—; mem. nuclear engring. and engring. physics vis. com. U. Wis., Madison; mem. Coun. Gt. Lakes Govs. Regional Econ. Devel. Commn. 1987—, rev. bd. Compact Ignition Tomamak Princeton U., 1988-91; advisor Sears Investment Mgmt. Co., 1988-89; bd. dirs. Petroleum Rsch. Fund, ARCH Devel. Corp., HEICO, Valley Indsl. Assn., Coun. on Superconductivity for Am. Competitiveness; mem. State of Ill. Commn. on the Future of Pub. Svc., 1990-92; co-chair Indsl. Rsch. Inst. Nat. Labs./Industry Panel, 1984-87; mem. Nat Acad. Engring. Adv. Commn. on Tech. and Soc., 1991-92, Sun Electric Corp. Bd., 1991-92, U.S. House of Reps. subcom. on Sci.-Adv. Group on Renewing U.S. Sci. Policy, 1992—; mem. Chgo. Acad. of Scis. acad. coun., 1994—; mem. adv. bd. Chemtech; mem. sr. action group on R&D investment strategies Ctr. for Strategic & Internat. Studies; bd. vis. Astronomy and Astrophysics Pa. State U., 1995—. Adv. bd. Chemtech, 1970-85; editl. bd. Rsch. & Devel., 1988-92, Superconductor Industry, 1988—; patentee in field. Mem. spl. vis. com. Field Mus. of Natural History, Chgo., 1987-88; bd. dirs. LaRabida Children's Hosp. and Rsch. Ctr., Children's Meml. Hosp., Children's Meml. Inst. for Edn. and Rsch.; trustee The Latin Sch. of Chgo., 1990-92; adv. bd. WBEZ Chicagland Pub. Radio Cmty., 1990—; mem. Conservation Found. DuPage County, 1983—, Econ. Devel. Adv. Commn. of DuPage County, 1984-88, State of Ill. Gov.'s Commn. on Sci. and Tech., 1986-90, Inst. for Ill. Council Advisors, 1988—, Ill. Coalition Bd. Dirs., 1989—, Inst. for Ill. Adv. Rev. Panel, 1986-88, NASA Sci. Tech. Adv. Com. Manpower Requirements Ad Hoc Rev. Team, 1988-91, State of Ill. Gov. Sci. and Exec. com., 1989—, U. Ill. Engring. Vis. com., Urbana-Champaign, 1986—; trustee Tchrs. Acad. for Math. and Sci. Tchrs. in Chgo., 1990—; bd. visitors astronomy & astrophysics Pa. State U., 1995—. Recipient Outstanding Alumni Fellow award Pa. State U., 1985; laureate Lincoln Acad. Ill., 1996; Disting. fellow Poly. U., 1989. Fellow AAAS (coun. del. chem. sect. 1986-92, bd. dirs. 1992—, sci. engring. and pub. policy com. 1992, standing com. audit 1992, selection com. to bring FSU scientists to ann. mtg. 1995—), N.Y. Acad. Scis.; mem. NAE (adv. com. tech. and soc. 1991-92, chair study fgn. participation in U.S. R&D 1993—, mem. program adv. com. 1992—), AIChE (AIChE award com. 1992—), Am. Chem. Soc. (petroleum chemistry award 1969, chmn. petroleum di chemistry and pub. affairs 1983-91, joint bd. coun. com. on sci. 1983-87, award in petroleum chemistry com. 1995—), Am. Mgmt. Assn. (R&D con. 1988—), Nat. Conf. Advancement Rsch. (conf. com. 1985—, site selection com. 1994, conf. com. 50th ann. 1996), Am. Petroleum Inst. (rsch. coord. coun.), Am. Nuclear Soc., Rohm and Haas (bd. dirs.), Indsl. Rsch. Inst. (fed. adv. com. to Fed. Sci. and Tech. Com. 1992—, co-chmn. Nat. Labs. Indsl. Panel 1984-87, sr. action group on R&D Investment Strategies), Ctr. Strategic and Internat. Studies (sr. action group 1995—), Carlton Club (bd. govs. 1992—), Cosmos Club, Chgo. Club, Econ. Club, Comml. Club, Sigma Xi, Phi Lambda Upsilon. Home: 1440 N Lake Shore Dr Apt 31ac Chicago IL 60610-1686 Office: Argonne Nat Lab 9700 S Cass Ave Argonne IL 60439-4803

SCHRIEVER, BERNARD ADOLPH, management consultant; b. Bremen, Germany, Sept. 14, 1910; came to U.S., 1917, naturalized, 1923; s. Adolph Niholaus and Elizabeth (Milch) S.; m. Dora Brett, Jan. 3, 1938; children: Brett Arnold, Dodie Elizabeth Schriever Moeller, Barbara Alice Schriever Allan. B.S., Tex. A&M U., 1931; M.S.M.E., Stanford U., 1942; D.Sc. (hon.), Creighton U., 1958, Rider Coll., 1958, Adelphia Coll., 1959, Rollins Coll., 1959; D.Aero. Sci. (hon.), U. Mich., 1961; D.Eng. (hon.), Bklyn. Poly. Inst., 1961; LL.D. (hon.), Loyola U., Los Angeles, 1960. Commd. 2d lt. U.S. Army Air Force, 1938; advanced through grades to gen. U.S. Air Force, 1961; comdr. ICBM Program, 1954-59, AFSC, 1959-66; ret., 1966; chmn. bd. Schriever & McKee, Washington, 1971-87; cons. B.A. Schriever, 1987—. Decorated D.S.M., D.S.M. with oak leaf cluster, Legion of Merit, Air medal, Purple Heart; named to Aviation Hall of Fame, 1980; recipient Forrestal award, 1987. Hon. fellow AIAA; mem. NAE, Am. Astron. Soc., Air Force Assn. Club: Burning Tree. Home: 4501 Dexter St NW Washington DC 20007-1116 Office: 2300 M St NW Ste 900 Washington DC 20037-1434

SCHRIEVER, FRED MARTIN, energy, environmental and information technology executive; b. N.Y.C.; s. Samuel and Sara S.; m. Cheri G. Spatt; children: Melissa Ann, Elizabeth Ellen. BME, Poly. U. N.Y., 1956, MME, 1958. Registered profl. engr., N.Y., Wash. cert. mgmt. cons. Chief engr. div. Sperry Corp., N.Y.C., 1956-64; ptnr. Booz, Allen and Hamilton, N.Y.C. and Washington, 1964-71; sr. v.p. Reliance Group Holdings, Inc., N.Y.C., 1971—; chmn., pres. RCG Internat. Inc., N.Y.C., 1971—; chmn. Werner Mgmt. Consultants Inc., RCG Info. Tech., Inc., RCG Moody Ltd.; bd. dirs. RCG Hagler Bailly Inc. Fellow Inst. of Dirs., Inst. Mgmt. Consultants U.K.; mem. ASME, Inst. Mgmt. Consultants. Club: Metropolitan. Home: PO Box 32 Westport CT 06881-0032

SCHRIVER, JOHN T., III, lawyer; b. Evanston, Ill., May 18, 1945. AB, Coll. of Holy Cross, 1967; JD, Georgetown U., 1971. Bar: Ill. 1971, Fla. 1972. Ptnr. McDermott, Will & Emery, Chgo. Mem. ABA, Chgo. Bar Assn., Fla. Bar. Office: McDermott Will & Emery 227 W Monroe St Chicago IL 60606-5016*

SCHROCK, BARBARA JEAN, clinical neuropsychologist; b. Odessa, Tex., July 16, 1952; d. Clarence and Lillian Bernice (Howard) S.; m. Kevin David Gerhart, Aug. 20, 1977; children: David Adam Gerhart, Kathryn Margaret Gerhart. BA, U. Redlands, 1975; MA, U. Houston, 1983, PhD, 1985. Cert. clin. neuropsychologist. Clin. co-dir. Transitional Learning Community, Galveston, Tex., 1982-84; assoc. dir. U. Houston Neuropsychology Cons., 1984-86; staff neuropsychologist Santa Clara Valley Med Ctr., San Jose, Calif., 1986-89; pvt. practice, consultation San Jose, 1989-90; pvt. practice San Diego, 1990—; head dept. rehab. psychology svcs. Sharp Rehab. Ctr., San Diego, 1991—, clin. dir. disability assessment program, 1992—; asst. clin. prof. dept. psychiatry U. Calif., San Diego, 1993—; rehab. cons. Stepping Stones, San Jose, 1988-90; neuropsychology cons. Saratoga (Calif.) Sub-Acute, 1989-90. Mem. APA, Internat. Neuropsychol. Soc., Calif. Psychol. Assn. Office: Sharp Rehab Ctr 2999 Health Center Dr San Diego CA 92123-2762

SCHROCK, HAROLD ARTHUR, manufacturing company executive; b. Goshen, Ind., Apr. 10, 1915; s. Arthur E. and Anna (Shaner) S.; m. Thelma A. Hostetler, Sept. 3, 1938; children—Sara (Mrs. William Barrett), Susan (Mrs. John Graff), Cinda (Mrs. Stephen McKinney), Douglas. B.A, Goshen Coll., 1937. Chmn. bd. dirs. Starcraft Co., Goshen, 1967-71; pres. Goshen Sash & Door Co., Smoker-Craft, Inc., New Paris, Earthway Products, Bristol, Inc., Goshen Iron & Metal Co.; chmn. 1st Nat. Bank of Goshen; v.p. Ind. Capital Co., Ft. Wayne; pres. Ivy Terrace, Inc., Goshen, Marque, Inc., Goshen. Past pres. Greater Goshen Assn., Jr. Achievement, Goshen Gen. Hosp., Goshen Pub. Library; pres. Goshen Hosp. Found. Mem. Goshen C. of C. (pres. 1952). Republican. Lutheran (v.p. vestry). Clubs: Elcona Country (Goshen), Maplecrest Country (Goshen); John's Island (Vero Beach, Fla.); Rotary (past pres.). Home: 510 Carter Rd Goshen IN 46526-5210 Office: US 33 E Goshen IN 46526 Also: Goshen Sash & Door Co Inc 603-13 E Purl St Goshen IN 46526

SCHROCK, SIMON, retail executive; b. Oakland, Md., Dec. 28, 1936; s. Noah and Cora (Burkholder) S.; m. Eva Lena Yoder, June 7, 1959 (dec. Apr. 1962); m. Pauline Yoder, Sept. 29, 1963; children: Janice Yvonne, Eldon Laverne, Ivan Dale. With Eastern States Farm Supply Co., Oakland, Md., 1957-59, Children's Hosp., Washington, 1959-61, Copp Properties, 1961-75; pres. Choice Books of No. Va., Fairfax, 1975—; chmn. Lighthouse Lit., 1976—. Author: Get on With Living, 1976, Price of Missing Life, 1981, One-Anothering, 1986, Vow-Keepers Vow-Breakers, A Smoother Journey, 1994. Contbr. articles to ch. jours. Chmn. Faith Christian Sch. Bd., 1977-95; bishop Faith Christian Fellowship, Catlett, Va., 1981—. Avocations: traveling; camping; biking. Office: 11923 Lee Hwy Fairfax VA 22030-6708

SCHROCK, VIRGIL EDWIN, mechanical and nuclear engineer; b. San Diego, Jan. 22, 1926; s. Melvin J. and Madge (Ellis) S.; m. Virginia Lee Whorton, July 27, 1946; children: Douglas Richard, Nancy Grace. B.S., U. Wis., Madison, 1946, M.S., 1948; M.E., U. Calif., Berkeley, 1952. Registered profl. engr., Calif. Instr. U. Wis., 1946-48; mem. faculty U. Calif., Berkeley, 1948—; prof. nuclear engring. U. Calif., 1968—, asst. dean, 1968-74; prof. emeritus, 1991-94; prof. Grad. Sch. U. Calif., 1994—; cons. to govt. and industry. Contbr. articles to profl. jours. Served with USNR, 1943-46, 52-53. Grantee C.I.S.E., Milan, Italy, 1962-63, 74-75, also USAF, USN, AEC, NSF, NRC, Dept. Energy, Electric Power Research Inst.; recipient Glenn Murphy award Am. Soc. Engring. Edn., 1983; Japan Soc. Promotion Sci. research fellow, 1984. Fellow ASME (life, chmn. heat transfer divsn. 1976-77, tech. editor Jour Heat Transfer 1977-83, Heat Transfer Meml. award 1985, Heat Transfer Divsn. 50th Anniversary award 1988, Best Paper award 1991), Am. Nuclear Soc. (chmn. thermal hydraulics divsn. 1980-81, Best Paper award 1985, Best Paper award Internat. Conf. Nuclear Reactor Thermal Hydraulics 1993, Technical Achievement award 1995), Am. Soc. for Engring. Edn. Home: 258 Orchard Rd Orinda CA 94563-3532 Office: U Calif Dept Nuclear Engring Berkeley CA 94720-1730

SCHRODER, DIETER KARL, electrical engineering educator; b. Lübeck, Germany, June 18, 1935; came to U.S., 1964; s. Wilhelm and Martha (Werner) S.; m. Beverley Claire Parchment, Aug. 4, 1961; children: Mark, Derek. BSc, McGill U., Montreal, Que., Can., 1962, MSc, 1964; PhD, U. Ill., 1968. Sr. engr. research and devel. sect. Westinghouse Electric Corp., Pitts., 1968-73, fellow engr., 1973-77, adv. engr., 1977-79, mgr., 1979-81; prof. elec. engring. Ariz. State U., Tempe, 1981—; researcher Inst. Solid-State Physics, Freiburg, Fed. Republic Germany, 1978-79. Author: Advanced MOS Devices, 1987, Semiconductor Material and Device Characterization, 1990; patentee in field; contbr. articles to profl. jours. Fellow IEEE (disting. nat. lectr. 1993-94); mem. Electrochem. Soc., Sigma Xi, Eta Kappa Nu. Mem. Baha'i Faith. Home: 1927 E Bendix Dr Tempe AZ 85283-4203 Office: Ariz State U Dept Elec Engring Tempe AZ 85287-5706

SCHRÖDER, HARALD BERTEL, aerospace industry executive; b. Stockholm, Dec. 31, 1924; s. Bertel and Selma Katarina (Kraepelien) S.; m. Kjerstin Sjögren, Mar. 17, 1949; children: Göran, Hans, Henrik. M in Aeronautics Engring., Swedish Royal Inst. Tech., Stockholm, 1948. Developmental engr. SAAB-Scania AB, Linköping, Sweden, 1957-62, program mgr. SAAB Viggen Fighter Program, 1962-68, v.p. aircraft sector, 1971-83; sr. v.p. SAAB aircraft div., gen. mgr. SAAB-Aircraft div., 1983-87; exec. v.p. SAAB-Scania AB, Linköping, Sweden, 1987-91; pres. Industry Group JAS AB, 1980-91; adviser to pres. Saab Mil. Aircraft, 1991-95. Mem. Royal Swedish Acad. War Scis., Swedish Assn. Def. Industries (pres. 1987-89, bd. dirs. 1989-92), Swedish Aerospace Industries Assn. (pres. 1991-94), European Aerospace Industries Assn. (v.p. 1992-94). Home: Banergatan 53, 11522S Stockholm Sweden

SCHRODER, JACK SPALDING, JR., lawyer; b. Atlanta, July 10, 1948; s. Jack Spalding Sr. and Van (Spalding) S.; m. Karen Keyworth, Sept. 1, 1973; children: Jack Spalding III, James Edward. BA, Emory U., 1970; JD, U. Ga., 1973. Bar: Ga. 1973, U.S. Dist. Ct. (no. dist.) Ga. 1973, U.S. Ct. Appeals (5th cir.) 1973, U.S. Ct. Appeals (11th cir.) 1982. Assoc. Alston & Bird, Atlanta, 1973-78, ptnr., 1978—. Co-editor, contbr. author: Georgia Hospital Law Manual, 1979, 84, 92, Credentialing: Strategies for a Changing Environment/BNa's Health Law and Business Series, 1996. Participant Leadership Ga., Atlanta, 1986, United Way (chmn. legal div.), Atlanta, 1980. Mem. ABA (vice chmn. medicine and law com. 1989-90), Am. Acad. Healthcare Attys. (bd. dirs. 1994—, chmn. med. staff and physician rels. com. 1991-94), Ga. Acad. Hosp. Attys. (pres. 1981-82), State Bar Ga. (bd. govs. 1987-89), Atlanta Coun. Younger Lawyers (pres. 1977-78), Atlanta Bar Assn. (pres. 1982-83), Atlanta Bar Found. (pres. 1991-95). Office: Alston & Bird 1 Atlantic Ctr 1201 W Peachtree St NW Atlanta GA 30309-3400

SCHRODER, JOHN L., JR., retired mining engineer; b. Martinsburg, W.Va.. BS in Mining Engring., W.Va. Sch. Mines, MS, 1941. Registered profl. engr., W.Va., Ky. Jr. engr. H.C. Frick Coke Co. U.S. Steel, Uniontown, Pa., 1941-44; prodn., safety engr. Gay Coal and Coke Gay Mining Cos., 1946-49.; asst. engr. mine planning U.S. Steel, Gary, W.Va., 1949-51, asst. chief engr., 1951-1953; chief engr. U.S. Steel, Lynch, Gary, Ky., 1953-1958; gen. supt. U.S. Steel, Lynch, 1958-70; gen. mgr. coal ops. U.S. Steel, Pitts., 1970-79, v.p. coal ops. resource devel., 1979-81, pres. subsidiary U.S. Steel Mining Co., Inc., 1981-83, ret., 1983; spl. asst. to the pres. Am. Mining Congress, 1983-84; dean Coll. Mineral and Engry Resources W.Va. U., 1984-91, ret., 1991; chmn. Mine Insps. Exam. Bd.; mem Govs. Moore's Energy Task Force. Lt. j.g. USN, 1944-46. Recipient Howard N. Evanson award Soc. Mining, Metallurgy and Exploration, 1991. Mem. AIME (Erskine Ramsay medal 1992), Nat. Mine Rescue Assn., W.Va. Coal Mining Inst., Old Timers Club, King Coal Club. Office: 228 Maple Ave Morgantown WV 26505-6666

SCHROEDER, AARON HAROLD, songwriter; b. Bklyn., Sept. 7, 1926; s. Max and Pearl (Miller) S. m. Abby Steinberg, Oct. 31, 1967; 1 child, Rachel Amy. Student, music and art high schs., N.Y.C. Contact man Warner Bros. Music, Mills Music; profl. mgr. Charley Barnett; owner A. Schroeder Internat., Ltd. and subs. cos., N.Y.C., 1960-77; founder, pres. Musicor Records, N.Y.C., 1960-65. Mus. dir. film The Four Musketeers; producer TV spl. country music, 1979; composer songs for Fund Drives Berkshire United Way, 1986-87, N.Y. State Dept. Agr., Fairview Hosp., 1988, Operation Earth, 1990; composer songs Not as a Stranger, I Got Stung, Mandolins in the Moonlight, Stuck on You, Twixt Twelve and Twenty, Fools Hall of Fame, Because They're Young, French Foreign Legion, Time and the River, I'm Gonna Knock on Your Door, Rubber Ball, It's Now or Never, Big Hunk of Love, Today's Teardrops, Good Luck Charm, Once She Was Mine; film theme Four Musketeers, She Can Put Her Shoes Under My Bed Anytime, If I Could Only Touch Your Life, We're All In the Same Boat; score for motion picture and TV series Lucky Luke including original songs The Lonesomest Cowboy In the West, Lopin' Along, Lotta Legs' Hotel, Put Your Pistol Back in Your Holster, Cowboy's Lament, numerous others; composer for PBS Pilot "Grover's Corner", 1990, PBS spl. Chanukah at Grover's Corner, 1992; sponsored and pub. numerous award-winning songwriters. Mem. ASCAP (elections bd.), NARAS (gov. 1962). Home: RR 2 Box 118 Great Barrington MA 01230-9808 Office: 200 W 51st St Ste 706 New York NY 10019-6202

SCHROEDER, ALFRED CHRISTIAN, electronics research engineer; b. West New Brighton, N.Y., Feb. 28, 1915; s. Alfred and Chryssa (Weishaar) S.; m. Janet Ellis, Sept. 26, 1936 (dec.); 1 dau., Carol Ann Schroeder Castle.; m. Dorothy Holloway, Nov. 21, 1981. BS, MIT, 1937, MS, 1937. Mem. tech. staff David Sarnoff Rsch. Ctr. RCA, Princeton, N.J., 1937—. Contbr. articles to profl. jours. Recipient RCA Lab. awards, 1947, 50, 51, 52, 57, 70. Fellow IEEE (Vladimir Zworykin award 1971); mem. AAAS, Optical Soc. Am., Soc. Motion Picture and TV Engrs. (David Sarnoff Gold medal 1965), Soc. Info. Display (Karl Ferdinand Braun prize 1989), Sigma Xi. Quaker. Achievements include 75 patents for color TV products including shadow mask tube. Home: Pennswood Village Apt I-114 Newtown PA 18940 Office: SRI Internat David Sarnoff Rsch Ctr Princeton NJ 08540

SCHROEDER, ARNOLD LEON, mathematics educator; b. Honolulu, May 27, 1935; s. Arnold Leon and Wynelle (Russell) S.; BS in Math., Oreg. State U., 1960, MS in Stats., 1962; NSF Insts. at UCLA, 1964, U. So. Calif., 1965; m. Maybelle Ruth Walker, Nov. 9, 1956; children: Steven, Michael, Wendy. Assoc. prof. math. Long Beach (Calif.) C.C., 1962—; computer cons. McDonnell-Douglas Corp., 1966-74, statis. researcher in med. and social sci., 1976-80; cons. statis. software including SPSS, BMDP, and Fortran, 1980—; dir. Schroeder's Statis. Svcs. Author: Statistics/Math Note's for Colleges, 1986—. Chmn. bd. elders Grace Bible Ch., South Gate, Calif., 1985-92. Served with USAF, 1953-57. Mem. Faculty Assn. Calif. C.C., C.C. Assn., Am. Bowlers Tour (life). Home: 5481 E Hill St Long Beach CA 90815-1923 Office: 4901 E Carson St Long Beach CA 90808-1706

SCHROEDER, BARBET G., director; b. Teheran, Iran, Apr. 26, 1941. Film critic Cahiers du Cinema, L'air de Paris, 1958-63; owner, prin. Films du Losange, 1963—. Film dir.: More, 1969, The Valley, 1972, General Idi Amin Dada, 1974, Maitress, 1975, Koko, Talking Gorilla, 1978, Cheaters, 1983, The Charles Bukowski Tapes, 1985, Barfly, 1987, Reversal of Fortune, 1990 (Acad. award nominee best dir. 1990, Golden Globe award nominee best dir. film 1990), Single White Female, 1992, Kiss of Death, 1995, Before and After, 1996; film prodr.: La Boulangerene de Monceau, 1962, La Carriere de Suzanne, 1963, Mediterrannee, 1964, Six in Paris, 1968, My Night at Maud's, 1968, The Collector, 1966, Claire's Knee, 1971, Chloe in the Afternoon, 1972, (with Tchalgadjieff), Out One, 1972, (with Pierre Cottrell) The Mother and the Whore, 1973, Celine and Julie Go Boating, 1974, Flocons d'or, 1975, Perceval, 1978, Improper Conduct, 1983, La Carriere de Suzanne, Mediterrannee, Tu Imagines Robinson, (with Stephane Tchalga Djieff) Out One, The Marquise of O, 1975, Le Passe-Montagne, 1977, The Rites of Death, Le Navire Night, Le Pont du Nord; asst. to dir. Jean-Luc Goddard for The Soldiers, 1968; co-prodr.: Chinese Roulette, 1977, La Boulangere de Monceau, 1962, The American Friend, 1977; appeared in films The Soldiers, 1960, Six in Paris, 1965, The Mother and the Whore, 1973, Celine and Julie Go Boating, 1974, L'amour Par Terre, Roberte, 1978, The Golden Boat, 1990, Beverly Hills Cop III, 1994, La Reine Margot, 1994; screenwriter: (with Paul Gegauff) More, 1969, (with Gegauff) The Valley, 1972, Maitress, 1975, Cheaters, 1983. Office: CAA 9830 Wilshire Blvd Beverly Hills CA 90212-1804

SCHROEDER, BILL E., lawyer; b. Long Beach, Calif., Jan. 16, 1942. BA, Stanford U., 1963; LLB, U. Calif., 1966. Bar: Calif. 1967. Ptnr. Baker & Hostetler, L.A. Mem. ABA, State Bar Calif., L.A. County Bar Assn. Office: Baker & Hostetler 600 Wilshire Blvd Los Angeles CA 90017-3212*

SCHROEDER, CHARLES EDGAR, banker, investment management executive; b. Chgo., Nov. 17, 1935; s. William Edward and Lelia Lorraine (Anderson) S.; m. Martha Elizabeth Runnette, Dec. 30, 1958; children: Charles Edgar, Timothy Creighton, Elizabeth Linton. BA in Econs., Dartmouth Coll., 1957; MBA, Amos Tuck Sch., 1958. Treas. Miami Corp., Chgo., 1969-78, pres., 1978—; chmn., bd. dirs Blvd. Bank of Chgo., 1981-91; chmn. Blvd. Bancorp., Inc., 1991-94; bd. dirs. Nat.-Standard Co., Niles, Mich. Trustee Northwestern Meml. Hosp., 1985-93, Northwestern U., 1989—. Lt. (j.g.) USN, 1958-60. Mem. Fin. Analysts Soc. of Chgo., Chgo. Club, Glen View Club, Michigan Shores Club, Comml. Club. Office: Miami Corp 410 N Michigan Ave Chicago IL 60611-4211

SCHROEDER, CHARLES HENRY, corporate treasurer; b. Akron, Ohio, May 25, 1942; s. Charles Henry Sr. and Marion Belle (Buzenberg) S.; m. Marilyn Sue Patterson, Aug. 28, 1965; children—Rebecca Lynn, William Charles. B.A., Ohio Wesleyan U., 1964; M.B.A., Case Western Res. U., 1968, Stanford U., 1986. Treas. Ford Corp. subs. Ford Motor Co., South Africa, 1972-75; treas. Ford Microelectronics, Inc., 1980-82, Ford Aerospace Corp., 1978-90; v.p., treas. Loral Aerospace Corp. and Space Systems/Loral, Newport Beach, Calif., 1990—. Mem. Stanford U. Alumni Cons. Team for Orange County non-profit orgns., 1993. Recipient Fin. award for outstanding research Cleve. Soc. Security Analysts, 1967. Mem. L.A. Treas.' Club (pres. 1991—), Case-Western Res. U. Orange County Alumni Assn. (pres. 1990). Republican. Episcopalian. Home: 26336 Golada Mission Viejo CA 92692-3285 Office: Loral Aerospace Corp 3501 Jamboree Rd Ste 500 Newport Beach CA 92660-2944

SCHROEDER, DAVID HAROLD, health care facility executive; b. Chgo., Oct. 22, 1940; s. Harry T. and Clara D. (Dexter) S.; m. Clara Doorn, Dec. 27, 1964; children: Gregory D., Elizabeth M. BBA, Kans. State Coll., 1965; MBA, Wichita State U., 1968; postgrad., U. Ill., 1968-69. CPA, Ill. Supt. cost acctg. Boeing Co., Wichita, Kans., 1965-68; sr. v.p., treas. Riverside

Med. Ctr., Kankakee, Ill., 1971—; treas. Riverside Health System, 1982—, Kankakee Valley Health Inc., 1985—, Health Info. Systems Coop., 1991—; v.p., treas. Oakside Corp., Kankakee, 1982—; bd. dirs. Harmony Home Health Svc., Inc., Naperville, Ill.; mem. faculty various profl. orgns.; adj. prof. econs. divsn. health adminstrn. Gov.'s State U., University Park, Ill., 1990-95; trustee Riverside Found. Trust, 1989—, RMC Found., 1989—, Sr. Living Ctr., 1989—. Contbg. author: Cost Containment in Hospitals, 1980; contbr. articles to profl. jours. Trustee Riverside Found. Trust, 1989—, RMC Found., 1989—, Sr. Living Ctr., 1989—; pres. Riverside Employees Credit Union, 1976-79; founder Kankakee Trinity Acad., 1980, Riverview Hist. Dist., Kankakee, 1982; pres. Kankakee County Mental Health Ctr., 1982-84, United Way Kankakee County, 1984-85; chmn. Ill. Provider Trust, Naperville, 1983-85; mem. adv. bd. Students in Free Enterprise, Olivet Nazarene U., Kankakee, 1989—; pres. adv. coun. divsn. health adminstrn., preceptor Gov.'s State U., 1987—; trustee, treas. Am. Luth. Ch.; wish granter Make a Wish Found., 1994—; dir. Kankakee County Hist. Soc., 1995. Capt. U.S. Army, 1969-71. Fellow Am. Coll. Healthcare Execs., Halthcare Fin. Mgmt. Assn. (pres. 1975-76, cert. mgr. patient accounts 1981), Fin. Analysts Fedn.; mem. AICPA, Ill. Hosp. Assn. (chmn. coun. health fin. 1982-85), Inst. Chartered Fin. Analysts, Nat. Assn. Accts., Fin. Exec. Inst., Ill. CPA Soc., Healthcare Fin. Mgmt. Assn. (William G. Follmer award 1977, Robert H. Reeves award 1981, Muncie Gold award 1987, Founders medal of honor 1990), Investment Analysts Soc. Chgo., Inc., Kankakee County Hist. Soc. (dir. 1995—), Classic Car Club Am., Packard Club, Kiwanis (pres.), Masons, Alpha Kappa Psi, Sigma Chi. Avocations: classical automobile restoration, architectural preservation, computers. Home: 901 S Chicago Ave Kankakee IL 60901-5236 Office: Riverside Med Ctr 350 N Wall St Kankakee IL 60901-2901 *Life's four important questions: Why? Why not? Why not you? Why not now?.*

SCHROEDER, DONALD PERRY, retired food products company executive; b. Danville, Ill., Nov. 2, 1930; s. Donald Joseph and Pauline Hannah (Critchfield) S.; m. Barbara Ann Engle, Jan. 6, 1951; children: Patricia Ann Schroeder Capizzi, Helen Schroeder Marrano, Jeffrey Joseph. Student, Purdue U., 1949, Stanford U., 1982. Mgr. Schroeders I.G.A. Supermarket, Danville, 1950-57; specialist retail meat J.M. Jones Co., Champaign, Ill., 1957-59, mgr. retail zone, 1959-62, dir. meat ops., 1962-67; dir. customer services Olean (N.Y.) Wholesale Grocery Co., 1967-70; nat. dir. meat Ind. Grocers Alliance, Chgo., 1970-74; dir. meat ops. Fleming Cos., Inc., Topeka, 1974-83; v.p. meat., produce ops. Fleming Cos., Inc., Oklahoma City, 1983-88, v.p. meat ops., 1988-89, ret., 1989; chmn. meat council Ind. Grocers Alliance, Chgo., 1962-87. Bd. dirs. Big Bros./Sisters Greater Oklahoma City, 1984-87, North Side YMCA, Oklahoma City, 1988-90. Mem. Nat. Livestock and Meat Bd. (universal meat cut identity com. 1970-73), United Fresh Fruit and Vegetable (bd. dirs. 1984-87). Republican. Roman Catholic. Avocations: yard and garden work, golf, fishing. Home: 5 Charnela Ln Hot Springs Village AR 71909-3030

SCHROEDER, DOUGLAS FREDRICK, architect; b. Omaha, June 12, 1935; s. Walter Elmer and Ellen Ruth (Niles) S.; m. Joanne Vlecides, July 5, 1980. B.Arch., U. Mich., 1959. Registered Architect, Ill., N.C., Mich. Designer, draftsman C.F. Murphy Assocs., Chgo., 1959-63; architect, sr. architect Skidmore, Owings & Merrill, Chgo., 1964-67; architect, ptnr. Schroeder, Yamamoto & Schreiber, Chgo., 1968-69; ptnr. Hinds & Schroeder, Ltd., Chgo., 1972-74; propr. Douglas Schroeder Assocs., Chgo., 1974-83, 93—; ptnr. Siegel & Schroeder, P.C., Chgo., 1983-91; dir. SGA Planning and Constrn. Cons. Co. div. Goforth Group, Chgo., 1991-93; v.p. Yacht Harbor Mgmt. Co., South Haven, Mich., 1983-88; dir. Inland Architect Mag. Contbr. articles to profl. jours. Bd. dirs. Chgo. Archtl. Assistance Ctr., 1982-84; chmn. Mass. Transp. Crisis Com., Chgo., 1973, Ill. Futures Forum, 1976-77; pres. Ill. Planning and Conservation League, Chgo., 1971-74. Named Outstanding Alumnus Lake Superior State U., 1971. Fellow AIA; mem. Am. Arbitration Assn. (arbitrator). Unitarian. Club: Cliff Dwellers (dir. 1971-74). Home: 700 W Irving Park Rd Apt 4A Chicago IL 60613-3133 Office: Douglas Schroeder Assocs Arch & Planners 625 N Michigan Ave Ste 1600 Chicago IL 60611-3109

SCHROEDER, DOUGLAS JAY, lawyer; b. Detroit, Apr. 19, 1947; s. Oliver and Jean Schroeder; m. Stephanie Schroeder; children: Alex, Nicholas. BA in Bus., Mich. State U., 1971; JD, U. Detroit, 1975. Bar: Mich. 1975. Law clk. to Hon. Norman R. Barnard Oakland County Probate Ct., Pontiac, Mich., 1971-73; law clk. to Hon. Farrell E. Roberts Oakland County Cir. Ct., Pontiac, 1973-75; ptnr. Dean & Fulkerson, Troy, Mich., 1975-81, 81-87; atty. Gase, Williams & Schroeder, Troy, 1987—. Mem. South Oakland County Bar Assn., Troy Rotary Club (pres. 1985). Avocations: golf, sailing. Office: Gase Williams & Schroeder 290 Town Center Dr Troy MI 48084-1774

SCHROEDER, EDMUND R., lawyer; b. N.Y.C., Feb. 6, 1933; s. Robert C. and Rose A. (Garramone) S.; m. Elaine P. Diserio, Jan. 21, 1961; children: Edmund Jr., Christopher, Elizabeth. AB cum laude, Harvard U., 1953, LLB, 1958. Assoc. Archibald R. Graustein, N.Y.C., 1958-61, Root, Barrett, Cohen, Knapp & Smith, N.Y.C., 1961-67; ptnr. Barrett Knapp Smith & Schapiro, N.Y.C., 1967-88, Lord Day & Lord/Barrett Smith, N.Y.C., 1988-94, Cadwalader, Wickersham & Taft, N.Y.C., 1994—; mem. adv. com. Commodity Futures Trading Commn. on Definition and Regulation of Market Instruments, 1975-76. Contbr. articles to profl. jours. Bd. dirs. Orch. St. Luke's N.Y.C., 1987—, chmn. exec. com., 1993—; bd. trustees The United Way of Scarsdale-Edgemont, 1990-92; mem. Scarsdale Bd. Edn., 1976-79; co-founder, 1st chmn. Edn. Through Music, Inc., N.Y.C., 1991—; bd. trustees Hoff-Barthelson Music Sch., Scarsdale, 1974—, chmn. bd., 1986-90, hon. chmn., 1990—; bd. trustees The Nat. Guild Comty. Schs. Arts, Englewood, N.J., 1992—; bd. advisors Sacred Heart/Mt. Carmel Sch. for Arts, Mt. Vernon, 1995—; arbitrator Am. Arbitration Assn., Nat. Futures Assn. Mem. ABA (chmn. com. futures regulation 1981-85), Bar Assn. City of N.Y. (founder, 1st chmn. com. futures regulation 1976-81), N.Y. State Bar Assn. (com. comty. and future law and regulation 1996—), Scarsdale Golf Club. Office: Cadwalader Wickersham & Taft 100 Maiden Ln New York NY 10038

SCHROEDER, EDWIN MAHER, law educator, law library administrator, university dean; b. New Orleans, June 25, 1937; s. Edwin Charles and Lucille Mary (Maher) S.; m. Marietta Louise DeFazio, Aug. 1, 1936; children—Edwin Charles II, Jonathan David, Margaret Louise. A.A., St. Joseph Sem., St. Benedict, La., 1957; Ph.B., Gregorian U., Rome, 1959; J.D., Tulane U., 1964; M.S., Fla. State U., 1970. Bar: Mass. 1964. Teaching fellow Boston Coll. Law Sch., 1964-65; asst. prof. law U. Conn., 1965-68; asst. prof., asst. law librarian U. Tex., 1968-69; asst. prof. Fla. State U., 1969-71, assoc. prof., 1971-75, prof., 1975—, dir. Law Library, 1969—, asst. dean Coll. Law, 1979-83, assoc. dean Coll. Law, 1983-93. Mem. ABA, Am. Assn. Law Libraries (v.p. Southeastern chpt. 1983-84, pres. 1984-85), Order of Coif, Beta Phi Mu. Roman Catholic. Home: 806 Middlebrooks Cir Tallahassee FL 32312-2439 Office: Law Libr Fla State U Coll Law Tallahassee FL 32306

SCHROEDER, FRED ERICH HARALD, humanities educator; b. Manitowoc, Wis., June 3, 1932; s. Alfred William and Sissel Marie (Lovell) S.; m. Janet June Knope, Aug. 21, 1954; 1 child, Erich Karl. BS, U. Wis., 1960; MA, U. Minn., 1963, PhD, 1968. Elementary sch. tchr. various locations, Wis., 1952-60; asst. prof. English U. Minn., Duluth, 1968-71, assoc. prof. English, 1971-74, prof. behavioral sci., 1977-82, prof. humanities, 1974—, dir. Ctr. for Am. Studies, 1986-87, dir. Inst. Interdisciplinary Studies, 1987-90, dir. dept. humanities and classics, 1989-90, dir. grad. liberal studies, 1992-95. Author: Joining the Human Race: How To Teach Humanities, 1972, Outlaw Aesthetics: Arts and the Public Mind, 1977; editor Interdisciplinary Humanities (formerly Humanities Edn. jour.), 1983-95, 5000 Years of Popular Culture, 1980, 20th Century Popular Culture in Museums and Libraries, 1981, Front Yard America: The Evolution and Meanings of a Domestic Vernacular Landscape, 1993; lectr., writer Nat. Humanities Series, 1969-71. Mem. Minn. Humanities Commn., 1985-90. Woodrow Wilson Nat. Found. fellow, 1960-61, dissertation fellow 1963; NEH scholar, 1969-70; Inst. for Human Values in Medicine fellow, 1976. Mem. Am. Culture Assn. (pres. 1984-87), Nat. Assn. Humanities Edn. (pres. 1987-89, exec. sec.-treas. 1989-96), Am. Assn. for State and Local History (seminar instr. 1978-82), Popular Culture Assn. Avocations: collecting art, woodworking, gardening. Home: 5756 N Shore Dr Duluth MN 55804-9660

SCHROEDER, FREDRIC KAUFFMANN, federal commissioner; b. Lima, Peru, May 6, 1957; s. Florence Schroeder; m. Cathlene Ann Nusser, Jan. 3, 1981; children: Carrie Ann, Matthew Stephen. BA in Psychology, San Fransisco State U., 1977, MA in Spl. Edn., 1978, postgrad., 1980; PhD in Ednl. Adminstrn., U. N. Mex. Cert. elem. and secondary adminstrn.; spl. edn., N. Mex. Tchr., coord. Albuquerque Pub. Schs., 1980-86; exec. dir. N. Mex. Commn. for the Blind, 1986-94; commr. Rehab. Svcs. Adminstrn. U.S. Dept. Edn., 1994—; cons. City of Albuquerque, 1985, Minn. Acads. for Deaf and Blind, 1985, Gulf South Rsch. Inst., New Orleans, 1986, Metro. Ctr. for Ind. Living, 1988. Contbr. articles to profl. jours. Office: US Dept Edn Mary Switzer Bldg Rm 3028 330 C St SW Washington DC 20202

SCHROEDER, HAROLD KENNETH, JR., lawyer; b. Buffalo, Aug. 6, 1936; s. Harold Kenneth and Margaret Mary (Mescall) S.; m. Jean Louise Benbenek, Aug. 20, 1958; children: Mary Margaret, Mark, Keith, Kurt, Jennifer. BS, Canisius Coll., 1958; JD, U. Buffalo, 1961; ML, Georgetown U., 1962. Bar: N.Y. 1961, D.C. 1961, Fla. 1979, U.S. Dist. Ct. (we. dist.) N.Y. 1961, U.S. Ct. Appeals (2d cir.) 1981. Trial atty. U.S. Dept. Justice, Washington, 1962-63; spl. asst. U.S. Atty. D.C. Washington, 1962-63; U.S. Atty. Western Dist. N.Y. U.S. Dept. Justice, Buffalo, 1969-72; ptnr. Hodgson, Russ, Andrews, Woods & Goodyear, Buffalo, 1963-69, sr. ptnr., 1972—; chmn. fed. merit selection panel U.S. Magistrate Judge We. Dist. N.Y., 1989, 92, 94; merit selection panel Fed. Pub. Defender We. Dist. N.Y., 1991, 95; mem. U.S. Civil Justice Reform Act, N.Y. Author: (with others) Law and Tactics in Federal Criminal Cases, 1964. V.p. Orchard Park, N.Y. Cen. Sch. Dist., 1972-76, Buffalo Sem., 1972-88. E. Barrett Prettyman fellow Georgetown U., 1961; recipient Disting. Alumnus award U. Buffalo Law Sch., 1996. Mem. Erie County Bar Assn. Avocation: tennis. Home: 3872 Baker Rd Orchard Park NY 14127 Office: Hodgson Russ Andrews Woods & Goodyear 1800 One M&T Plaza Buffalo NY 14203

SCHROEDER, HENRY J., health science organization administrator. Dir. Inst. for the Study of Devel. Disablities, Ind. U., Bloomington, Ind. Office: Ind U Inst Study Devel Disabilities 2853 E 10th St Bloomington IN 47408-2601*

SCHROEDER, HENRY WILLIAM, publisher; b. Cleve., Wis., Sept. 7, 1928; s. Henry and Esther Julia (Kammann) S. ; m. Dorothy Hildebrand, Aug. 18, 1956 (div.); children: Susan Schroeder Smith, Katherine Jean Duhamel; m. Elizabeth Churbuck, Aug. 15, 1977 (dec.); children: Joy, Bill, Stephen; m. Mary Vae Legler, Feb. 15, 1992; 1 child, Derek Legler. BS, U. Wis., 1957, MS, 1959. Info. dir. Wis. Farm Bur., Madison, 1960-63; asst. dir. pub. rels. Credit Union Internat., Madison, 1963-65; editor, co-pub. Verona Press (Wis.), Oreg. Observer (Wis.), 1966—, also v.p. Southwest Suburban Publs., Inc., 1966-80; co-pub. Fitchburg Star, 1974—, also pres. Southwest Suburban Publs. and Schroeder Publs., Inc., 1980—; pub. Blade-Atlas, Blanchardville, Wis., 1977-83; pres., pub. Leader Publ. Corp., Evansville, Wis., 1981-88; pub. Cmty. Herald Newspapers Corp., 1988—, Monona Herald and McFarland Life newspapers, Clinton (Wis.) Topper, 1994—; pub. Country Courier, Hinckley, Ill. Mem. Gov.'s UN Commn., 1974. Served with USNR, 1949-53. Mem. Wis. Newspaper Assn. (pres. 1983-84), Wis. Newspaper Assn. (bd. dir. 1973-86, 94—), WNA Found. (pres. 1990-91), Madison Press Club, Madison Advt. Fedn., Nat. Newspaper Assn. (govt. affairs conf., chmn. services com., state chmn., Better Newspaper Contest), Suburban Newspapers Am., Verona C. of C. (pres. 1970, 91), Madison Club, East Madison Optimists (bd. dirs. 1993—, pres. 1995-96), Masons (master 1970, bd. dirs. jour. 1990-93, pres. jour., bd. dirs. 1993—), Shriners, Royal Order Jesters. Republican. Office: Verona Press 120 W Verona Ave Verona WI 53593-1315

SCHROEDER, HERMAN ELBERT, scientific consultant; b. Bklyn., July 6, 1915; s. Henry W. and Caroline (Schmidt) S.; m. Elizabeth Barnes, June 13, 1938; children: Nancy Schroeder Tarczy, Edward L., Peter H., Martha L. Schroeder Lewis. A.B. summa cum laude, Harvard, 1936, A.M., 1937, Ph.D., 1939. With E.I. du Pont de Nemours & Co., Wilmington, Del., 1938-80; asst. dir. R&D E.I. du Pont de Nemours & Co., 1957-63, dir. R&D, 1963-80; pres. Schroeder Sci. Svcs., Inc., 1980—; sci. cons. Met. Mus. Art, N.Y.C., Smithsonian Instn., Winterthur Mus. Mem. Chester County Sch. Bd., Unionville, Pa., 1950-56; pres. Assn. Harvard Chemists, 1955-56; mem. vis. com. Harvard Chemistry Dept., 1960-72; mem. sci. adv. com. Winterthur Mus.; trustee, chmn. research com. U. Del. Research Found., 1976-84, former v.p. Recipient award Internat. Inst. Synthetic Rubber Producers, 1979, Lavoisier medal DuPont, 1992. Mem. AAAS, Am. Chem. Soc. (Charles Goodyear medal 1984), N.Y. Acad. Scis., Phi Beta Kappa, Alpha Chi Sigma. Home and Office: 74 Stonegates 4031 Kennett Pike Greenville DE 19807-2037 *A life in industrial research has been for me both challenging and rewarding. Forces which impel me are largely the compulsion to look for the new, to change for the better, be it by finding better ways to do things or by inventing products to make the world function better. Gratifyingly, these often make the world aesthetically more pleasant and sometimes cleaner. I am concerned by the growing hostility of society to science and to developments that ensure a more comfortable life and safer food and energy than would otherwise be possible.*

SCHROEDER, JOHN H., university chancellor; b. Twin Falls, Idaho, Sept. 13, 1943; s. Herman John and Azalia (Kimes) S.; m. Sandra Barrow; children: John K., Andrew Barrow. BA, Lewis and Clark Coll., Portland, Oreg., 1965; MA, U. Va., 1967, PhD, 1971. Instr. history U. Wis., Milw., 1970-71, asst. prof., 1971-76, assoc. prof., 1976-86, prof., 1986—, Am. Coun. on Edn. fellow, 1982-83, assoc. dean, 1976-82, asst. to vice chancellor, 1982-85, acting vice chancellor, 1985-87, vice chancellor, 1987-90, chancellor, 1990—; Louis M. Sears Meml. lectr. Purdue U., 1978; bd. dirs. Columbia Health Sys., Inc. Author: Mr. Polk's War: American Opposition and Dissent, 1973, The Commercial and Diplomatic Role of the American Navy 1829-1861, 1985. Bd. dirs. Greater Milw. Com., Milw. Boys and Girls Club, Milw. Pub. Policy Forum, Greater Milw. Edn. Trust, Wis. Jr. Achievement, Commn. on Urban Agenda; mem. Milw. Conf. on Employment, Edn. and Race, Milw. Quality Edn. Commn. Recipient Edward and Rosa Uhrig award U. Wis.-Milw., 1974, Disting. Teaching award AMOCO/U. Wis.-Milw., 1975. Mem. Orgn. Am. Historians, Soc. for History of Early Republic, Soc. for History Am. Fgn. Rels., Nat. Assn. State Univs. and Land Grant Colls. (bd. dirs.), Rotary. Office: U Wis 2310 E Hartford Ave Milwaukee WI 53211-3165

SCHROEDER, JOYCE KATHERINE, research analyst; b. Moline, Ill., Apr. 1, 1951; d. Reinhold J. and Miriam-May Schroeder. BS in Math., U. Ill., 1973, MA in Ops. Rsch., 1978. Underwriter/programmer Springfield, Ill., 1973-76; ops. rsch. analyst Ill. Dept. Transp., Springfield, 1976-78, data analyst, 1978-80, team leader, fatal accident reporting sys., 1980-83, mgr. safety project evaluation, 1983-92, mgr. accident studies and investigation, 1992—; sys. engring. del. to China China Assn. for Sci. and Tech., 1986; mem. staff Driving While Intoxicated Adv. Coun. and Task Force, State of Ill., 1983-86, 89-92, Gov. Task Force on Occupant Protection, 1988-90; active Ill. Traffic Safety Info. Sys. Coun., 1993—. Vol. Animal Protective League, Springfield; leaderbd. co-chairperson LPGA Rail Classic, Springfield, 1983-87; amb. of goodwill Lions of Ill. Found., 1993, trustee, 1995—. Lions Clubs Internat. Melvin Jones fellow, 1993, Lions of Ill. Found. fellow, 1995. Mem. Lions of Ill. Found. (amb. of goodwill 1993, trustee 1995—), Springfield Lincoln Land Lions Club (charter pres. 1988-90, treas. 1993-95, news editor 1995—), Lions Club (dist. gov. Ill. 1992-93, state membership coord. 1994—, Melvin Jones fellow 1993), Past. Dist. Gov. Assn. (sec.-treas. 1993—, Phi Kappa Phi, Kappa Delta Pi. Avocations: dogs, travel, music, sports, humanitarian svc. Office: Ill Dept Transp 3215 Executive Park Dr Springfield IL 62703-4509

SCHROEDER, MARY MURPHY, federal judge; b. Boulder, Colo., Dec. 4, 1940; d. Richard and Theresa (Kahn) Murphy; m. Milton R. Schroeder, Oct. 15, 1965; children: Caroline Theresa, Katherine Emily. B.A., Swarthmore Coll., 1962; J.D., U. Chgo., 1965. Bar: Ill. 1966, D.C. 1966, Ariz. 1970. Trial atty. Dept. Justice, Washington, 1965-69; law clk. Hon. Jesse Udall, Ariz. Supreme Ct., 1970; mem. firm Lewis and Roca, Phoenix, 1971-75; judge Ariz. Ct. Appeals, Phoenix, 1975-79, U.S. Ct. Appeals (9th cir.), Phoenix, 1979—; vis. instr. Ariz. State U. Coll. Law, 1976, 77, 78. Contbr. articles to profl. jours. Mem. ABA, Ariz. Bar Assn., Fed. Bar Assn., Am. Law Inst. (coun. mem.), Am. Judicature Soc., Soroptimists. Democrat. Office: US Ct Appeals 9th Cir 6421 Courthouse & Fed Bldg 230 N 1st Ave Phoenix AZ 85025-0230

SCHROEDER, MERRIE JO, law librarian; b. Detroit, Dec. 4, 1950; d. Albert Elmer Warren and Betty Jane (Kyser) Warren-Smith; m. Patrick Paul McNally, June 15, 1974 (div. June 30, 1990); 1 child, Sean Paul; m. Theodore Robert Schroeder, Jan. 2, 1996. BA in Elem. Edn., Mich. State U., 1972; MA in Libr. Media, U. Colo., Denver, 1990. Elem. sch. tchr. Fraser (Mich.) Pub. Schs., 1972-75; circulation clk. Adams County (Colo.) Libr., 1975-76; sub. tchr. Jefferson County Sch. Dist., Lakewood, Colo., 1976-77; health scis. libr. tech. St. Anthony Hosps., Denver, 1977-84; tech. svcs. libr. Holland & Hart, Denver, 1984-88, mgr. libr. and file svc., 1988—; mem. adv. bd. West Pub. Co., Eagan, Minn., 1995—. Author: (chpt.) Winning with Computers, 1991. Recipient Excellence in Pvt. Law Librarianship award West Pub. Co., 1996. Mem. Am. Assn. Law Librs., Colo. Assn. Law Librs. (editor jour./newsletter 1992-95). Home: 2576 Vivian Lakewood CO 80215 Office: Holland and Hart 555 17th St # 2900 Denver CO 80202

SCHROEDER, PATRICIA SCOTT (MRS. JAMES WHITE SCHROEDER), congresswoman; b. Portland, Oreg., July 30, 1940; d. Lee Combs and Bernice (Lemoin) Scott; m. James White Schroeder, Aug. 18, 1962; children: Scott William, Jamie Christine. B.A. magna cum laude, U. Minn., 1961; J.D., Harvard U., 1964. Bar: Colo. 1964. Field atty. NLRB, Denver, 1964-66; practiced in Denver, 1966-72; hearing officer Colo. Dept. Personnel, 1971-72; mem. faculty U. Colo., 1969-72, Community Coll., Denver, 1969-70, Regis Coll., Denver, 1970-72; mem. 93d-104th Congresses from 1st Colo. dist., 1973-96; co-chmn. Congl. Caucus for Women's Issues, 1976-96; mem. Ho. of Reps., ranking minority mem. judiciary subcom. on the Constitution, mem. Nat. Security Com. Congregationalist. Office: US Ho of Reps 2307 Rayburn House Office Washington DC 20515

SCHROEDER, PAUL HERMAN, entomologist; b. Elmer, N.J., Sept. 26, 1930; s. Harry and Emily (Blumke) S.; m. Janet Elma Wiedrich, Feb. 8, 1964; children: Paula, Jama, David, Krista. BS, Rutgers U., 1952, MS, 1960, PhD, 1963. County agrl. agt. Passaic County N.J., Paterson, 1952-57; rsch. asst. Rutgers U., New Brunswick, N.J., 1957-63; biologist entomology and nematology Niagara Chem. Divsn. FMC, Middleport, N.Y., 1963-64; nematologist Niagara Chem. Divsn. FMC, Middleport, 1964-66, mgr. field rsch., 1966-70; mgr. Gasport (N.Y.) Rsch. Field Sta. Niagara Chem. Divsn. FMC, 1970-71; nematologist Castle & Cook Corp., Dole Divsn., Honolulu and Lanai City, Hawaii, 1971-76; product devel. mgr. Union Carbide Corp., Agrl. Products Divsn., Salinas and Jacksonville, 1976-80; registration specialist US EPA, Washington, 1980-92, efficacy reviewer and registration mgr., 1992—. Mem. Entomol. Soc. Am., Soc. Nematologists, Sigma Xi. Home: 14626 Batavia Dr Centreville VA 22020 Office: US EPA 401 M St Washington DC

SCHROEDER, ROBERT J., veterinarian, association executive; b. Fort Collins, Colo., Nov. 19, 1921; s. John Henry and Mildred Margaret (McElravy) S.; m. Janice Lorraine Dringman, Aug. 24, 1947; children: Jeri Lee, Craig Reed, Curtis John. DVM, Colo. State U., 1947; postgrad., Army Med. Svc. Meat and Dairy Hygiene Sch., 1951, L.A. County Civil Svc. Commn., 1960. Diplomate Am. Coll. Vet. Preventative Medicine; cert. vet. Calif. 1949. Vet. Food and Mouth Disease Control U.S. Dept. Agrl., Mex., 1947-48; vet. Food and Mouth Disease Control L.A. County Livestock Dept., 1947-50, 52-53, sr. vet., 1953-57, dir., 1957-65; county vet. L.A. Dept. Vets., 1965-72; clin. prof. pathology U. So. Calif., L.A., 1968-79, clin. prof. community medicine and pub. health, 1971-78, prof. emeritus, 1979—; dep. dir. L.A. County Dept. Health Svcs., 1972-78; mem. policy staff L.A. County Dept. Health Svcs., 1972-78, mem. exec. staff, 1972-78, chmn. programs and priorities task force, 1972-78; cons. N.Am. Rockwell Corp. Life Scis. Opers. of Autonetics, 1968-69, Santa Cruz Island Co., 1953-92; nat. civilian cons. Surgeon Gen. USAF, 1969-71. Ecology and pub. health editor Animal Cavalcade, 1970-72; guest editor: AVMA Jour., 1985-87. Active Citizens Com. for Vet. Med. Sch., 1965-70; chmn. steering com. So. Calif. Sch. Vet. Medicine, 1964-68. 1st lt. U.S. Army, 1943-46, 50-52. Recipient Disting. Svc. award Colo. State U. So. Calif. Alumni Assn., 1967, Disting. Vet. Leadership award So. Calif. Vet. Med. Assn., 1969, Honor Alumnus Achievement award Colo. State U., 1969. Mem. AVMA (Pub. Svc. award 1991, pres. 1967-68, pres.-elect. 1967-68, mem. exec. bd. 1961-66, mem. coun. edn. 1969-74, chmn. com. accreditation on tng. for animal technicians 1972—, mem. AVMA-Am. Assn. Vet. Med. Colls. Liaison com., 1969—), U.S. Animal Health Assn. (mem. exec. com. 1957, chmn. pub. health com. 1958-65, mem. mastitis com. 1965—), Med. Rsch. Assn. Calif. (bd. dirs. 1967—), Calif. Regional Med. Programs Adv. Coun. (mem. area V. adv. coun. 1970-73, chmn. 1973, mem. program evaluation com. 1973—), L.A. Area C. of C. (mem. farm/food/fiber com. 1957—). Home: 9738 Tecum Rd Downey CA 90240-3148

SCHROEDER, STEPHEN ROBERT, psychology researcher; b. Leipsic, Ohio, Oct. 28, 1936. BA, Josephinum Coll., 1958; MA, U. Toledo, 1964; PhD, U. Pitts., 1967. Lic. psychologist, Ohio, N.C. Postdoctoral rsch. assoc. Learning Rsch. and Devel. Ctr., U. Pitts., 1967-68; clin. asst. prof. dept. psychology U. N.C., Chapel Hill, 1968-73, clin. assoc. prof. depts. psychology and psychiatry, 1973-77, rsch. assoc. prof. dept. psychology, 1977-87, rsch. sci. Biol. Scis. Rsch. Ctr., 1973-87, assoc. prof. dept. psychiatry, 1977-86, prof. dept. psychiatry, 1986-87; dir. psychology Murdoch Ctr., Butner, N.C., 1973-75, dir. rsch. and devel., 1975-77; prof. dept. psychology and psychiatry Ohio State U., Columbus, 1987-90, dir. The Nisonger Ctr., 1987-90; prof. dept. human devel. and family life U. Kans., Lawrence, 1990—, prof. dept. pharmacology and toxicology, 1990—, dir. Bur. Child Rsch., 1990—, dir. Schiefelbusch Inst. for Life Span Studies, 1990—; mem. program com. Gatlinburg Conf. on Mental Retardation and Devel. Disabilities, 1977-92, program chmn., 1992—; mem. N.C. divsn. Mental Health and Mental Retardation Rsch. Grants Rev. Bd., 1977-86; mem. statewide lead screening com. N.C. Dept. Meternal and Child Health, 1979-86; founding chmn. Annie Sullivan Enterprises, Inc., 1982-89, active, 1989-92, chmn., 1992—; mem. rsch. grant rev. bd. Ont. Mental Health Found., 1984—; mem. internat. rsch. exch. subcom. for Rsch. in Ednl. Rehab. in U.S. and German Dem. Republic, 1984-90; gen. ad hoc mem. grant rev. bd. NIMH, 1984; mem. mental retardation study com. NICHD, 1989-90; rsch. cons. Am. Occupational Therapy Found., Inc.; cons. pediats. ward N.C. Meml. Hosp., 1977-86; cons. civil rights divsn. U.S. Dept. Justice, 1987—; cons. No. Va. Tng. Ctr., 1983-85, 91, Murdoch Ctr., Western Carolina Ctr., Caswell Ctr., 1977-89; bd. dirs. Corp. of Guardianship; active Ohio Devel. Disabilities Planning Coun., 1987-90, Kans. Planning Coun. on Devel. Disabilities Svcs., 1990—, Kans. Prevention Task Force, 1991—, Gov. Task Force on Respite Care, 1991—. Author, editor chpts. to books; editor Am. Jour. Mental Retardation, 1987—; co-editor Jour. Applied Rsch. in Mental Retardation, 1980-86, Rsch. in Devel. Disabilities, 1987—; mem. editl. bd. Jour. Applied Behaviour Analysis, 1973-74, Mental Retardation, 1977-93, Analysis and Intervention in Devel. Disabilities, 1981-82; guest reviewer Jour. Applied Behaviour Analysis, Pediat. Psychology, Am. Jour. Psychiatry, Jour. Autism and Childhood Scizophrenia, Child Devel., Sci., Perceptual and Motor Skills, Pediatrics, Neurotoxicology; contbr. articles, papers to profl. jours. Mem. adv. bd. Ohio United Cerebral Palsy, 1988-90; active Ohio Prevention Coalition, 1987-90. Recipient Karl Heinz Renker medallion for interdisciplinary sci. collaboration German Dem. Republic, 1989. Fellow APA (pres. divsn. 33 mental retardation 1986-87, Nicholas Hobbs award 1989); mem. AAAS, Am. Assn. Mental Retardation, Am. Acad. Mental Retardation, Assn. Advancement Behavior Therapy (task force on self-injurious behavior 1981-82), Assn. Behavior Analysis, N.Y. Acad. Scis., Sertoma Club. Office: U Kansas KS Ctr Rsch Mental Retardation 1052 Dole Human Devel Ctr Lawrence KS 66045

SCHROEDER, STEVEN ALFRED, medical educator, researcher, foundation executive; b. N.Y.C., July 26, 1939; s. Arthur Edward and Norma (Scheinberg) S.; m. Sally B. Ross, Oct. 21, 1967; children: David Arthur, Alan Ross. BA, Stanford U., 1960; MD, Harvard U., 1964; LHD (hon.), Boston U., 1996, Rush-Presbyn.-St. Luke's Med., Chgo., 1996. Am. Bd. Internal Medicine. Intern and resident in internal medicine Harvard Med. Service, Boston City Hosp., 1964-66, 68-70; asst. prof., then assoc. prof. George Washington Med. Ctr., Washington, 1971-76; vis. prof. St. Thomas' Hosp. Med. Sch., London, 1982-83; prof. medicine, chief div. gen. internal medicine, mem. Inst. Health Policy Studies U. Calif., San Francisco, 1976-90; pres. Robert Wood Johnson Found., Princeton, N.J., 1990—; cons. various govtl. and philanthropic health orgns.; chair internat. adv. com. faculty medicine Ben Gurion U., Israel. Sr. editor Current Medical Diagnosis and Treatment, 1987-93; mem. editorial bd. New Eng. Mag.; contbr. numerous articles to profl. jours. Mem. U.S. Prospective Payment Assessment Commn., 1983-88. With USPHS, 1966-68. Master ACP; mem. Physicians for Social Responsibility, Am. Pub. Health Assn., Assn. Am. Physicians, Inst. Medicine, Soc. Gen. Internal Medicine (past pres.), Phi Beta Kappa, Alpha Omega Alpha. Home: 49 W Shore Dr Pennington NJ 08534-2006 Office: Robert Wood Johnson Found PO Box 2316 Princeton NJ 08543-2316

SCHROEDER, WILLIAM JOHN, electronics executive; b. Havre de Grace, Md., June 9, 1944; s. William Martin and Dorothy Jeanne (McLaughlin) S.; m. Marilee Jane Alne, May 28, 1966; children: Kristen, Kari Britt, Kimberley. BSEE, Marquette U., 1967, MSEE, 1968; MBA, Harvard U., 1972. Devel. engr. Honeywell Inc., Mpls., 1968-70; mgmt. cons. McKinsey & Co., Los Angeles, 1972-76; mgr. product planning Memorex Corp., Santa Clara, Calif., 1976-78; pres. Priam Corp., San Jose, Calif., 1978-85, chmn., 1985-86; pres. Conner Peripherals, Inc., San Jose, 1986-89, vice chmn., 1989-94; CEO Arcada Software Inc., a Conner Co., 1993-94; pres., CEO Diamond Multimedia Systems, Inc., San Jose, Calif., 1994—; bd. dirs. Xircom Corp., Thousand Oaks, Calif., MetaTools Inc., Carpenteria, Calif. Office: Diamond Multimedia Systems Inc 2880 Junction Ave San Jose CA 95134-1922

SCHROEDER, W(ILLIAM) WIDICK, religion educator; b. Newton, Kans., Nov. 12, 1928; s. William Fredric and Irene (Widick) S.; m. Gayle Eadie, Sept. 1, 1956; children: Scott David, Carla Gayle. BA, Bethel Coll., 1949; MA, Mich. State U., East Lansing, 1952; BDiv, Chgo. Theol. Sem., 1955; PhD, U. Chgo., 1960; DD (hon.), Chgo. Theol. Seminary, 1995. Ordained to ministry Congl. Christian Ch., 1955. Instr. Mich. State U., East Lansing, 1953-54, U. Chgo., 1958-60; from asst. prof. to prof. religion and society Chgo. Theol. Sem., 1960-94, prof. emeritus, 1994—; vis. fellow Mansfield Coll., Oxford, Eng., 1966; vis. scholar Ctr. for Process Studies, Claremont, Calif., 1976; vis. lectr. in ethics and soc. Divinity Sch. U. Chgo., 1967-71, 76; editor Rev. of Religious Rsch., 1964-69. Author: (with Victor Obenhaus) Religion in American Culture: Unity and Diversity in a Midwestern County, 1964; Cognitive Structures and Religious Research, 1970; (with Victor Obenhaus, Larry A. Jones and Thomas P. Sweetser) Suburban Religion: Churches and Synagogues in the American Experience, 1974; (with Keith A. Davis) Where Do I Stand? Living Theological Options for Contemporary Christians, 1973, rev. edit., 1975, 3d edit., 1978; Flawed Process and Sectarian Substance: Analytic and Critical Perspectives on the United Church of Christ General Synod Pronouncement, Christian Faith: Economic Life and Justice, 1990, Toward Belief: Essays in the Human Sciences, Social Ethics, and Philosophical Theology, 1996; co-editor: (with Philip Hefner) Belonging and Alienation: Religious Foundations for the Human Future, 1976; (with Gibson Winter) Belief and Ethics: Essays in Ethics, the Human Sciences and Ministry in Honor of W. Alvin Pitcher, 1978; (with John B. Cobb, Jr.) Process Philosophy and Social Thought, 1981; (with Perry LeFevre) Spiritual Nurture, Congregational Development, 1984, Pastoral Care and Liberation Praxis: Essays in Personal and Social Transformation, 1986, Creative Ministries in Contemporary Christianity, 1991; (with Franklin I. Gamwell) Economic Life: Process Interpretations and Critical Responses, 1988. Mem. Am. Acad. Religion, Am. Sociol. Assn., Soc. for the Sci. Study of Religion, Religious Rsch. Assn., Ctr. for Process Studies, Soc. Christian Ethics. Home: 2738 Virginia Pl Homewood IL 60430-1135 Office: Chgo Theol Sem 5757 S University Ave Chicago IL 60637-1507 *The aims of existence are aesthetic satisfaction and intensity of feeling. In facilitating these aims, the Divine Reality is the locus of potentiality, the mediator of experience, the evoker of feeling and the ultimate recipient of all that has become.*

SCHROEPFER, GEORGE JOHN, JR., biochemistry educator; b. St. Paul, June 15, 1932; s. George John and Catherine Rita (Callaghan) S.; children: Lisa Marie Schoepfer Schwartz, Cynthia Marie Schoepfer Winzenried, Stephanie Marie, Jeanine Marie Schroepfer Smith, Dana Marie Schroepfer Rethwisch. BS, U. Minn., 1955, MD, 1957, Phd, 1961. Intern U. Minn. Hosps., 1957-58; rsch. fellow depts. biochemistry and internal medicine U. Minn., 1958-61, asst. prof. biochemistry, 1963-64; rsch. fellow chemistry dept. Harvard U., Cambridge, Mass., 1962-63; asst. prof. biochemistry U. Ill., 1964-67, assoc. prof., 1967-70; dir. Sch. Basic Med. Scis. U. Ill., Urbana, 1968-1970; prof. U. Ill., 1970-72; prof. biochemistry and chemistry Rice U., Houston, 1972-83, Ralph and Dorothy Looney prof. biochemistry, prof. chemistry, 1983—, dir. lab. basic med. sci., 1987—, chmn. biochemistry dept., 1972-84, sci. dir. Inst. Biosci. and Bioengring., 1987—; vis. scientist Med. Rsch. Coun. Unit Hammersmith Hosp., London, 1961-62; mem. subcom. on biochem. nomenclature NAS, 1965-68; mem. biochemistry, tng. com. Nat. Inst. Gen. Med. Scis. NIH, 1970-73, ad-hoc com. tng. in biochemistry, 1974; cons. Am. Cyanamid Co., 1984-90, undergrad. biol. scis. edn. panel Howard Hughes Med. Inst., 1988; vis. prof. Sci. and Tech. Agy. Japan, 1993. Assoc. editor Lipids, 1969-76; mem. editl. bd. Jour. Biol. Chemistry, 1974-79, Jour. Lipid Rsch., 1983-88, Current Pharm. Design, 1995—. Fellow AAAS, Arteriosclerosis Coun. of Am. Heart Assn.; mem. Am. Chem. Soc., Am. Soc. Biochemistry and Molecular Biology, Am. Soc. Mass Spectrom, Sigma Xi, Alpha Omega Alpha. Office: Rice U Dept Biochem PO Box 1892 Houston TX 77251-1892

SCHROER, BERNARD JON, industrial engineering educator; b. Seymour, Ind., Oct. 11, 1941; s. Alvin J. and Selma A. (Mellencamp) S.; m. Kathleen Dittman, July 5, 1963; children: Shannon, Bradley. BSE, Western Mich. U., 1964; MSE, U. Ala., 1967; PhD, Okla. State U., 1972. Registered profl. engr., Ala. Mech. designer Sandia Labs., Albuquerque, 1962-63; engr. Teledyne Co., Huntsville, Ala., 1964-67, Boeing Co., Huntsville, 1967-70, Computer Sci. Corp., Huntsville, 1970-72; dir. Johnson Ctr. U. Ala., 1972-91, prof., 1991-94, chmn. dept. indsl. and systems engring., 1994—, assoc. v.p. rsch., 1994—; mem. adv. coun. Energy Dept., Montgomery, Ala., 1980-86; bd. dirs So. Solar Energy Ctr., Atlanta, 1980-83; mem. gov.'s cabinet State of Ala., Montgomery, 1982. Author: Modern Apparel Manufacturing Systems and Simulation, 1991; contbr. articles to profl. jours. Named Outstanding Engr., Robotics Internat., 1986, Outstanding Engr., Ala. Soc. Profl. Engrs., 1987; recipient summer traineeship NSF, 1971. Fellow Inst. Indsl. Engr. (pres. 1972, 86, Outstanding Engr. 1973, 77); mem. NSPE, Soc. Computer Simulation, Tech. Transfer Soc., Huntsville Rotary. Lutheran. Home: 716 Owens Dr SE Huntsville AL 35801-2034 Office: U Ala Coll Engring Huntsville AL 35899

SCHROER, EDMUND ARMIN, utility company executive; b. Hammond, Ind., Feb. 14, 1928; s. Edmund Henry and Florence Evelyn (Schmidt) S.; m. Lisa V. Strope; children: James, Fredrik, Amy, Lisa, Timothy, Suzanne. BA, Valparaiso U., 1949; JD, Northwestern U., 1952. Bar: Ind. 1952. Pvt. practice law Hammond, 1952—; assoc. Crumpacker & Friedrich, 1952; ptnr. Crumpacker & Schroer, 1954-56; assoc., then ptnr. Lawyer, Friedrich, Petrie & Tweedle, 1957-62; ptnr. Lawyer, Schroer & Eichhorn, 1963-66; sr. ptnr. Schroer, Eichhorn & Morrow, Hammond, 1967-77; pres., chief exec. officer No. Ind. Pub. Svc. Co., Inc., Hammond, 1977-93; chmn. No. Ind. Pub. Svc. Co., Hammond, 1978-93, chmn., chief exec. officer, 1989-93, also bd. dirs.; chmn., pres., chief exec. officer NIPSCO Industries, Inc., 1987-93; cons. NIPSCO Industries Inc., Hammond, 1993-96; also bd. dirs.; asst. dist. atty., No. Ind., 1954-56; trustee Ill. Ins. Exch., 1993-95. Trustee Sch. Bd., Munster, Ind., 1969-71, pres., 1971; fin. chmn. Rep. Party, Hammond, 1958-62; del. Ind. Rep. Conv., 1958, 60, 64, 66, 68. Mem. Fed. Bar Assn., Am. Gas Assn. (chmn. 1986), Rotary (pres. Hammond club 1968). Lutheran. Home and Office: No Ind Pub Svc Co 5265 Hohman Ave Hammond IN 46320-1722

SCHROLL, EDWIN JOHN, theater educator, stage director; b. Watertown, N.Y., Feb. 14, 1941; s. Clarence Edwin and Frances Lucille (Snyder) S. BS, Lyndon State Coll., 1966; MS, Oswego State U., 1971. Cert. tchr. N.Y. English tchr. jr. high sch. Watertown (N.Y.) Sch. System, 1966-67; English tchr. high sch. Belleville (N.Y.) Cen. Sch., 1967-71; English tchr. high sch. Massena (N.Y.) Cen. Sch., 1971-76, drama and speech tchr., 1988—, drama coach, 1975—, forensics coach; engr., announcer, programmer Pathways to Peace program Sta. WNCQ, Watertown, 1967-92. Cinematographer, writer, narrator, prodr. (documentaries) The United States: A Bicentennial Tour, 1976, Europe on $100 a Day, 1986; cinematographer (TV film) Partying, 1989; dir. various high sch. prodns.; actor various community prodns. Bd. dirs. Youth in Action, 1993-94; active Nat. Family Opinion, 1991—; state advocate Ednl. Theatre Assn., 1996—. Mem. Nat. Geog. Soc., Ednl. Theatre Assn., Archaeology Inst. Am. Republican. Mem. LDS Ch. Avocations: stamp and coin collecting, gardening, historical research, genealogy, travel. Home: PO Box 216 143 S Murray St Cape Vincent NY 13618 Office: Massena Sch System 290 Main St Massena NY 13662-1901

SCHROPP, JAMES HOWARD, lawyer; b. Lebanon, Pa., June 20, 1943; s. Howard J. and Maud E. (Parker) S.; m. Jo Ann Simpson, Sept. 4, 1965; children: James A., John C., Jeffrey M., Jeremy M. BA, U. Richmond, 1965; JD, Georgetown U., 1973. Bar: D.C. 1973, U.S. Supreme Ct. 1980. Asst. gen. counsel SEC, Washington, 1973-79; ptnr. Fried, Frank, Harris, Shriver & Jacobson, Washington, 1979—; adj. prof. Georgetown U., Washington, 1982-86; mem. faculty Na.t Inst. for Trial Advocacy. Mem. ABA (discovery com. litigation sect. 1984-86, tender offer litigation subcom. corp. banking and bus. law sect. 1985-86, task force on broker-dealer compliance supervisory procedures 1987-89). Office: Fried Frank Harris Shriver & Jacobson 1001 Pennsylvania Ave NW Washington DC 20004-2505

SCHROTE, JOHN ELLIS, retired government executive; b. Findlay, Ohio, May 6, 1936; s. Millard L. and Alberta (Ellis) S.; m. Rachel Daly, Mar. 2, 1957; children: James D., Gretchen Schrote Kent. BS in Agriculture, Ohio State U., 1958; MBA, Xavier U., 1964. Buyer-expediter McGraw Constrn. Co., Middletown, Ohio, 1958-59; buyer Armco Corp., Middletown, 1959-66; adminstrv. asst. Congressman D.E. Lukens, Washington, 1967-71; prin. asst. dir. OEO, Washington, 1971-72; spl. asst. sec. USDA, Washington, 1972-76, nat. rep. congl. com., 1976-79, acting asst. sec., 1981-82; adminstrv. asst. Congressman F.J. Sensenbrenner, Jr., Washington, 1979-81, 1984-89; dep. dir. presdl. pers. office The White House, 1982-83; exec. v.p. Bishop Bryant & Assocs., Washington, 1983-84; asst. to sec. and dir. congl. affairs Dept. Interior, Washington, 1989, dep. asst. sec. policy mgmt. and budget, 1989-91, asst. sec. policy mgmt. and budget, 1991-93; retired, 1993. Mem. Nat. Policy Forum/The Environ. Policy Coun., 1994, N.C. Seafood Indsl. Park Authority, Currituck County Econ. Devel. Bd., Currituck County Rep. Exec. Com., 3d Dist. Rep. Exec. Com., N.C. State Rep. Exec. Com.; chmn. Currituck County Ext. Svc. Adv. Leadership Coun.; chmn., bd. dirs. Currituck County 4-H Found.; v.p. Ocean Hills Property Owners Assn.; sec./treas. bd. dirs. 60 Found. Mem. Carolla Bus. Assn. Episcopalian. Home: PO Box 209 Corolla NC 27927

SCHROTH, PETER W(ILLIAM), lawyer, management and law educator; b. Camden, N.J., July 24, 1946; s. Walter and Patricia Anne (Page) S.; children: Laura Salome Erickson-Schroth, Julia James. AB, Shimer Coll., 1966; JD, U. Chgo., 1969; M in Comparative Law, U.Chgo., 1971; SJD, U. Mich., 1979; postgrad., U. Freiburg, Fed. Republic Germany, Faculté Internationale pour l'Enseignement de Droit Comparé; MBA, Rensselaer Poly. Inst., 1988. Bar: Ill. 1969, N.Y. 1979, Conn. 1985, Mass. 1990; solicitor Supreme Ct. England and Wales 1995. Asst. prof. So. Meth. U., 1973-77; fellow in law and humanities Harvard U., 1976-77, vis. scholar, 1980-81; assoc. prof. N.Y. Law Sch., 1977-81; prof. law Hamline U., St. Paul, 1981-83; faculté Internationale pour l'Enseignement De Droit Comparé; dep. gen. counsel Equator Bank Ltd., 1984-87; v.p., dep. gen. counsel Equator Holdings Ltd., 1987-94, v.p., gen. counsel, 1994—; adj. prof. law U. Conn., 1985-86, Western New Eng. Coll., 1988—, adj. prof. of mgmt. Hartford Grad. Ctr., 1988—. Author: Foreign Investment in the United States, 2d edit., 1977; (with Stiefel) Products Liability: European Proposals and American Experience, 1981, Doing Business in Sub-Saharan Africa, 1991; bd. editors Am. Jour. Comparative Law, 1981-84, 91—, Conn. Bar Jour., N.Y. Internat. Law Rev.; contbr. articles to profl. jours. Mem. ABA (editor in chief ABA Environ. Law Symposium 1980-82), Am. Soc. Comparative Law (bd. dirs. 1978-84, 91—), Am. Fgn. Law Assn., Internat. Bar Assn., Internat. Law Assn. (com. multinat. banking), Acad. Internat. Bus., Conn. Civil Liberties Union (bd. dirs. 1985-92), Environ. Law Inst. (assoc.), Columbia U. Peace Seminar (assoc.), Hartford Club (bd. govs. 1995—). Office: Equator House 45 Glastonbury Blvd Glastonbury CT 06033-4411

SCHROTH, THOMAS NOLAN, editor; b. Trenton, N.J., Dec. 21, 1920; s. Frank David and Loretta (Nolan) S.; m. Colette Streit, May 1, 1948 (div. 1958); 1 child, Valerie; m. Patricia Wiggins, Sept. 27, 1958; children: Jennifer, Amy, Anne. Student, Tuck Sch. Bus. Adminstrn., 1942; AB, Dartmouth Coll., 1943. Reporter Time, Washington, 1946-47, UPI, Boston, 1947-48; reporter, news editor Bklyn. Eagle, 1948-51, mng. editor, 1951-55; editorial adviser Magnum Photos, Inc., N.Y.C., 1955; exec. editor, pub. Congl. Quar. Inc. and Editorial Research Reports, Washington, 1955-68; founder, editor Nat. Jour. Ctr. Polit. Rsch., Washington, 1969-70; communications adviser Pub. Broadcasting Environment Ctr., Washington, 1970-71; asst. dir. pub. affairs for communications EPA, Washington, 1970-71, cons., 1972; exec. editor The Ellsworth (Maine) American, 1972-77; co-pub.-editor (with Patricia Schroth) Maine Life Mag., Sedgwick, 1977-81; editorial cons. U. Maine, Bangor, 1976-90; mng. editor South-North News Svc., Hanover, N.H., 1987-91; co-pub. New Leaf Pubs., Sedgwick, Maine, 1990—; mem. Am. Press Inst. Seminar for Mng. Editors, 1953. Editor: Congress and the Nation, 1946-64--A Review of Government and Politics in the Postwar Years; editor Improving the U. of Maine trustee's pamphlet. Elected selectman Town of Sedgwick, 1987, 89, 90; bd. dirs. Blue Hill (Maine) Meml. Hosp., 1978-93, Bangor Symphony Orch., 1981-87; bd. dirs., v.p. Island Nursing Home, Deer Isle, Maine, 1985—; mem. Maine State Dem. Com., Augusta, 1985-92; bd. dirs. Downeast Transp., Inc., 1993—. 1st lt. Army Airways Comm. Sys., USAAF, WWII. Mem. Sigma Delta Chi. Avocations: gardening, walking, music. Home and Office: 50 Benjamin River Rd Sedgwick ME 04676-9729

SCHRUM, ED P., manufacturing company executive; b. 1927. Grad., N.C. State U., 1951. With Carolina Mills, Inc., Maiden, N.C., 1951—, pres., 1976-86, pres., chief exec. officer, treas., 1986—, also bd. dirs. Office: Carolina Mills Inc 618 Carolina Ave Maiden NC 28650-1100*

SCHRUM, JAKE BENNETT, university administrator; b. Greenville, Tex., Feb. 9, 1946; s. Jake M. and Julia (Bennett) S.; m. Alice Woodman, Dec. 28, 1968; children: Julia Elizabeth, Emily Katharine. B.A., Southwestern U., 1968; M.Div., Yale U., 1973; postgrad. Harvard U., 1983. Ordained to ministry Methodist Ch., 1969. Devel. officer Yale U., New Haven, 1973-77; dir. devel. Muhlenberg Coll., Allentown, Pa., 1977-78; v.p. Tex. Wesleyan Coll., Fort Worth, 1978-82; v.p. univ. rels. Southwestern U., Georgetown, Tex., 1982-85; v.p. Emory U., Atlanta, 1985-91; pres. Tex. Wesleyan U., 1991-96; chmn. CASE; bd. dirs. Bd. Ind. Colls. & Univs. Tex., 1994-95, Bd. Tex. Ind. Coll. Found., Found. Ind. Higher Educators, 1995—; trustee United Way; adv. bd. Fort Worth Habitat for Humanity. Named Man of Yr., Bnai Brith North Tex., 1995. Mem. Coun. Advancement and Support Edn., Nat. Assn. Ind. Colls. and Univs. (bd. dirs. 1995—), Rotary. Avocations: golf, public speaking, tennis. Office: Texas Wesleyan University 1201 Wesleyan Fort Worth TX 76105

SCHRUMPF, ROBYN LYNN, dentist; b. San Francisco, July 15, 1959; d. Walter Fred and Donna De Ella (Rogelstad) S. BS, U. Calif., Davis, 1981; DDS, Creighton U., 1985; cert. gen. practice residency, VA Med. Ctr., Palo Alto, Calif., 1986. With dental staff VA Med. Ctr., Palo Alto, 1985-86; with dental staff VA Med. Ctr., Menlo Park, Calif., 1985-86, respite team cons. dentist, 1986; assoc. Milpitas (Calif.) Dental Ctr., 1987—, Sunnyvale (Calif.) Dental Group, 1987-89; pvt. practice Sunnyvale, 1989—; dir. dentistry Idylwood Care Ctr., Sunnyvale, Calif., 1991—; dentist Macy (Nebr.) Indian Reservation, 1984, Spinal Cord Injury Ctr., Palo Alto, 1985-86, Blind Rehab. Ctr., Palo Alto, 1985-86; instr. preventive dental care Girl Scouts U.S., Sunnyvale, 1987. Regents scholar U. Calif., Davis, 1977-78, Albert Bijou Meml. scholar U. Calif., Davis, 1978-79; Lonney White scholar Creighton U., 1984. Mem. ADA, Am. Soc. Dentistry for Children (pres. Creighton U. chpt. 1982-85, merit award 1985), Calif. Dental Assn., Calif. Soc. Dentistry for Children, Calif. Scholarship Fedn. (pres. 1977), U.S. Gymnastics Fedn., Omicron Kappa Upsilon. Lutheran. Avocations: dance, singing, community theater, swimming, aerobics.

SCHRUTT, NORMAN, broadcast company executive; b. Buffalo; m. Lynda Schrutt; 2 children. Attended, U. Buffalo. Acct. exec. Sta. WKBW-AM Radio, Buffalo, 1963-70, sales mgr., 1970-77, v.p., gen. mgr., 1977-80; v.p., gen. mgr. Sta. KZLA-AM/FM Radio, L.A., 1980-81; pres., gen. mgr. WKHX-AM/FM, Atlanta, 1981-87; pres. Capital Cities/ABC Radio Networks- Group II, N.Y.C., 1987—; responsible daily ops. of ten stas. including WLS-AM/FM, Chgo., WAML-AM/WRQX-FM, Washington, WBAP-AM/KSCS-FM, Dallas, Fort Worth, WKHX-AM/FM, Atlanta, KQRS-AM/FM, Mpls.; bd. dirs. Better Bus. Bur., Atlanta. Recipient Gabriel award, 1980, Clio award, 1981 for writing and producing pub. svc. Mem. Assn. Country Music Stas., Ga. Assn. Broadcasters, Cobb C. of C. (bd. dirs.), Georgian Club. Office: Capital Cities/ABC Broadcast Group 77 W 66th St New York NY 10023-6201

SCHTEINGART, DAVID EDUARDO, internist; b. Buenos Aires, Oct. 17, 1930; came to U.S., 1957; s. Mario and Flora (Garfunkel) S.; m. Monica Naomi Starkman, July 3, 1960; children: Miriam, Judith, M. Daniel. MD, U. Buenos Aires, 1955. Diplomate Am. Bd. Internal Medicine. Fellow Mt. Sinai Hosp., N.Y.C., 1957-58, Maimonides Hosp., Bklyn., 1958-59; fellow U. Mich., Ann Arbor, 1959-62, instr., 1962-63, asst. prof., 1963-68, assoc. prof., 1968-72, prof., 1972—. Contbr. articles to profl. jours., books. Pres. Beth Israel Congregation, Ann Arbor, 1974-79, Hebrew Day Sch., Ann Arbor, 1984-86, Jewish Fedn. Washtenaw County, Ann Arbor. Recipient rsch. grants NIH, Bethesda, Md., 1985—. Fellow Am. Coll. Physicians; mem. Endocrine Soc., N.Y. Acad. Scis., Am. Soc. Clin. Nutrition, Cen. Soc. Clin. Rsch., Am. Fedn. Clin. Rsch. Jewish. Avocations: tennis, running, community activities. Office: U Mich Med Sch 1150 W Medical Center Dr Ann Arbor MI 48109-0726

SCHUBART, MARK ALLEN, arts and education executive; b. N.Y.C., May 24, 1918; s. Henry Allen and Pauline (Werner) S. Student pvt. schs., U.S. and France; studied, piano with Celia Wolberg, theory with Marion Nugent, flute with Ruth Freeman, composition with Roger Sessions. Assoc. editor Eton Pub. Corp., 1937-40; asst. music editor newspaper PM, 1940-44; music editor N.Y. Times, 1944-46; dir. pub. activities Juilliard Sch. Music, 1946-49, dean, v.p., 1949-62; exec. dir. The Lincoln Center Fund, Lincoln Center Performing Arts, Inc., N.Y.C., 1963-66; dir. edn. Lincoln Center Performing Arts, Inc., 1966-75; dir. Lincoln Center Inst., 1975-90, pres., 1990-95, chmn., 1995—. Composer two song cycles, opera, concert overture, songs.; Author: Performing Arts Institutions and Young People; Contbr. articles profl. jour. Home: 30 Park Ave New York NY 10016-3894 Office: 70 Lincoln Center Plz New York NY 10023-6548

SCHUBART, RICHARD DOUGLAS, academic director; b. Pitts., May 9, 1945; m. Caren Elizabeth Nelson; children: Darcy, Lindsey, Nelson. BA in History, Kenyon Coll., 1967; MA in History, SUNY, Binghamton, 1970, PhD in History, 1984. Instr. Am. studies SUNY, Binghamton, 1971-73; instr. history Phillips Exeter (N.H.) Acad., 1973, dir. humanities, 1978-88, dir. admissions and fin. aid, 1988—; presenter symposia and confs.; lectr. comparative Can.-Am. studies Concordia U. Montreal, 1973-74; vis. scholar U. N.H., 1980; cons. NEH, 1983, 84, 86, N.H. Humanities Coun., 1982-89, Nat. Trust Hist. Preservation, 1988-89. Author: Ralph Borsodi: A Biography of A Uptopian Decentralist, 1986-1977, 1984, New Hampshire, The State That Made Us A Nation, 1989, New Hampshire Legislative Leaders, Biographical Profiles, 1991; editor: (with Henry F. Bedford) Documents on Early Industrialization, 1977, (with Henry G. Bragdon) History of A Free People, 9th edit., 1979; editorial bd. Phillips Exeter Alumni Bull., 1980—, adv. bd. Jour. Teaching History, 1981-85; contbr. articles to profl. jours. Bd. dirs. Exeter-Can. Found., 1990—, Assn. Boarding Schs., 1992—, Secondary Sch. Admission Test Bd., 1992—; pres. Fedn. Am. and Internat. Schs., 1993—. Recipient Stanford U. award for Secondary Sch. Teaching, 1980, Faculty Humanist award N.H. Humanities Coun., 1981, John F. Scott award for Svc. to Students, 1983, OAH-Rockefeller Scholar award Am. History, 1984; James Madison fellow, 1987-89, Boston U. fellow Nat. Ctr. Am.'s Founding Documents, 1991-92; grantee Phillips Exeter Acad., 1982, 85, NEH, 1982;. Mem. Am. Assn. State and Local History, Orgn. Am. Historians, Am. Studies Assn., N.H. State Hist. Soc., Exeter Hist. Soc. (officer, trustee 1983—). Office: Phillips Exeter Acad 60 Front St Exeter NH 03833-2734

SCHUBEL, JERRY ROBERT, marine science educator, scientist, university dean; b. Bad Axe, Mich., Jan. 26, 1936; s. Theodore Howard and Laura Alberta (Gobel) S.; m. Margaret Ann Hostetler, June 14, 1958; children: Susan Elizabeth, Kathryn Ann. BS, Alma Coll., 1957; MA in Teaching, Harvard U., 1959; PhD, Johns Hopkins U., 1968. Rsch. assoc. Chesapeake Bay Inst., Johns Hopkins U., Balt., 1968-69, rsch. scientist, 1969-74, adj. rsch. prof., assoc. dir., 1973-74; dir. Marine Sci. Rsch. Ctr., SUNY, Stony Brook, 1974-83; dean, leading prof. SUNY, Stony Brook, 1983-94; acting dir. Waste Mgmt. Inst., SUNY, Stony Brook, 1985-87; provost SUNY, Stony Brook, 1986-89; dir. COAST Inst., SUNY, Stony Brook, 1989; Disting. Svc. prof. SUNY, Stony Brook, 1994-95, prof. emeritus, 1995—; pres., CEO The New Eng. Aquarium, Boston, 1994—; hon. prof. East China Normal U., Shanghai, 1985—; sec. exec. com. Commn. on Food, Environment and Renewable Resources, 1993, chair steering com., 1994; mem. governing bd. Regional Marine Rsch. Program, Greater N.Y. Bight, 1993-94. Author: The Living Chesapeake, 1981, The Life and Death of the Chesapeake Bay, 1986; (with H.A. Neal) Solid Waste Management and the Environment, 1987, Garbage and Trash: Can We Convert Mountains Into Molehills?, 1992; editor: (with B. C. Marcy Jr.) Power Plant Entrainment, 1978; (with others) The Great South Bay, 1991; sr. editor Coastal Ocean Pollution Assement News, 1981-86; co-editor in chief Estuaries, 1986-88; editorial bd. CRC Revs. in Aquatic Scis.; contbr. articles to profl. jours. Mem. adv. bd. Environ. Sci. Com. Outer Continental Shelf, Minerals Mgmt. Scs., 1984-86, chmn., 1986; bd. dirs. N.E. Area Remote Sensing Sys., 1983-85, L.I. Incubator Corp.; v.p. L.I. Forum for Tech., 1989-92; chair Mass. Outfall Monitoring Task Force, 1995—; mem. sci. adv. bd. EPA, 1996—. Recipient L.I. Sound Am. Environment Edn. award, 1987, Stony Brook U. medal, 1989, Matthew Fontaine Maury award, 1990, Ben Gurion U. medal, 1993; Alfred P. Sloan fellow, 1959. Mem. Nat. Acad. Sci. (marine bd. 1989-94, exec. com. 1990, vice chair 1991-94, chair 1992-94, com. on Coastal Ocean 1989-93), Nat. Assn. State Univ. and Land Grant Colls. (bd. dirs. marine divsn., chmn. 1986-88), L.I. Environ. Coun., L.I. Marine Resources Adv. Coun. (chair 1990-94), L.I. Rsch. Inst. (bd. dirs. 1992-94), L.I. Environ.-Econ. Roundtable (co-chair 1991-92), Suffolk County Recycling Commn., (chmn. 1987-88), Estuarine Rsch. Fedn. (v.p. 1982-83, pres. 1985-87), N.Y. Sea Grant Inst. (chmn. governing bd. 1988-90, gov.'s task force on coastal resources 1990-91), The Nature Conservancy (trustee L.I. chpt. 1991-94), Franklin Electronic Pubs. (bd. dirs. 1991—), Taproot (bd. dirs. 1988-93, vice chair 1990-93), Sigma Xi, Phi Sigma Pi. Avocation: photography. Home: 10 Thacher St Apt 115 Boston MA 02113-1753 Office: New England Aquarium Central Wharf Boston MA 02110-3399

SCHUBERT, BARBARA SCHUELE, performing company executive; b. Cleve., Feb. 21, 1939; d. William Edward and Mildred Marianne (Matousek) Schuele; m. John Dwan Schubert, June 15, 1963; children: William Edward, Christopher John, David Matthew. BS in Social Scis., John Carroll U, 1962, MA in English, 1967; MEd, 1980. Cert. secondary tchr., elem. remedial reading tchr., Ohio. Tchr. Sch. on Magnolia, Cleve., 1980-82, Ruffing Montessori, Cleve., 1982-83; tchr. English U. Sch., Chagrin Falls, Ohio, 1983-86; gen. mgr. Ohio Ballet, Akron, 1987-90, assoc. dir., 1990—; bd. trustees Ohio Ballet, 1974-87. Bd. dirs. John Carroll U., 1990—; active Beaumont Sch., Ballet Guilds Internat. Roman Catholic. Club: Cleve. Skating. Office: Ohio Ballet 354 W Market St Akron OH 44303-2027

SCHUBERT, E. FRED, electrical engineer; b. Stuttgart, Germany, Feb. 8, 1956; came to U.S., 1985; s. Konrad and Martha Ruth (Reichert) S.; m. Jutta Maria Lukai, Feb. 22, 1980; children: Anne F., Martin F., Ursula V. Diploma in Engring., U. Stuttgart, 1981, D in Engring., 1986. Rsch. assoc. Max Planck Inst., Stuttgart, 1981-85; mem. tech. staff, prin. investigator AT&T Bell Labs., Murray Hill, N.J., 1985-95; prof. dept. elec. and computer engring. Ctr. for Photonics Rsch., Boston U., 1995—. Author: Doping in III-V Semiconductors, 1993; editor: Delta Doping of Semiconductors, 1996. Mem. IEEE (sr.), Am. Phys. Soc., Optical Soc. Am., Verein Deutscher Elektrotechniker. Roman Catholic. Home: 49 Angela St Canton MA 02021 Office: Boston U Dept Elec and Computer Engring 44 Cummington St Boston MA 02215

SCHUBERT, GLENDON, political scientist, educator; b. Oneida, N.Y., June 7, 1918; s. Glendon Austin and Agnes (Rogers) S.; m. Elizabeth Josephine Neal (dec. 1949); children: Frank, James; m. Elizabeth Harris; children: Susan, Kathleen, Robin. A.B., Syracuse U., 1940, Ph.D., 1948.

Mem. faculties Syracuse U., 1946-48, UCLA, 1948-49, Howard U., 1949-50, Rutgers U., 1950-51, Franklin and Marshall Coll., 1951-52, Mich. State U., 1952-67, U. Minn., 1955; William Rand Kenan Jr. prof. polit. sci. U. N.C. at Chapel Hill, 1967-68; u. prof. York U., 1968-70; u. prof. polit. sci. U. Hawaii, 1970—; rsch. prof. polit. sci. So. Ill. U. at Carbondale, 1986-91; Fulbright lectr. U. Oslo, Norway, 1959-60; fellow Center for Advanced Study in Behavioral Scis., 1960-61; sr. scholar in residence Center for Cultural and Tech. Interchange Between East and West, U. Hawaii, 1963-64, 65; Fulbright-Hays research scholar, Netherlands, 1977; NSF faculty fellow U. Groningen, Netherlands, 1977-78; NATO sr. fellow, U.K.; fellow Netherlands Inst. Advanced Study Humanities and Social Sci., Wassenaar, Netherlands, 1978-79. Author over 25 books; assoc. editor for biosocial behavior The Behavioral and Brain Sci.; adv. editor Jour. Social and Evolutionary Systems, Politics and the Life Scis., 1980-90; contbr. articles to profl. jours. in biobehavioral and polit. sci., and pub. policy. Served with Signal Intelligence U.S. Army, 1942-46. Decorated Bronze Star; recipient Regents' medal and award for excellence in research U. Hawaii, 1975. Mem. Am. Polit. Sci. Assn. (past mem. exec. coun.), Assn. Polit. Life Scis. (past pres.), Internat. Soc. Human Ethology, Phi Beta Kappa. Office: Univ Hawaii Dept Polit Sci 2424 Maile Way Honolulu HI 96822-2223

SCHUBERT, GUENTHER ERICH, pathologist; b. Mosul, Iraq, Aug. 17, 1930; s. Erich Waldemar and Martha Camilla (Zschitzschmann) S.; m. Gisela Schultz, June 13, 1959; children: Frank, Marion, Dirk. MD, University, Heidelberg, Germany, 1957; pvt. docent in pathology, University, Tuebingen, Germany, 1966. Asst. med. dir. University Tuebingen, Fed. Republic of Germany, 1966-76; head Inst. Pathology, Wuppertal, Fed. Republic of Germany, 1976—; chair of pathology U. Witten-Herdecke, Fed. Republic of Germany, 1985—. Co-author: Coloratlas of Cytodiagnosis of the Prostate, 1975, Endoscopy of the Urinary Bladder, 1989; author: Textbook of Pathology, 1981, 87. Mem. Wissenschaftlicher Beirat, Bundesarztekammer, Bonn, Germany, 1976-85; pres. Medizinisch Naturwissenschaftliche Gesellschaft, Wuppertal, 1984-85, Onkologischer Schwerpunkt, Wuppertal, 1985-93, OSP Bergisch-Land, 1992-95, Bergische Arbeitsgemeinschaft fur Gastroenterologie, Wuppertal, 1987-88, 90-91, 94-95. Mem. Deutsche Gesellschaft fur Pathologie, Deutsche Gesellschaft fur Nephrologie, Deutsche Gesellschaft fur Urologie, Internat. Acad. of Pathology, Lions. Avocations: music, diving, photography. Home: Am Anschlag 71, D-42ii3 Wuppertal 1, Germany Office: Inst of Pathology, Heusner Strasse 40, 42 283 Wuppertal 2, Germany

SCHUBERT, JOHN EDWARD, former banker; b. Rochester, N.Y., Jan. 22, 1912; s. Charles A. and Matilda M. (von Rohr) S.; m. Margaret Cecelia la Plante, Nov. 11, 1939 (dec. Jan. 1977); children: Susan R. (Mrs. Dennis E. Coyne), Patricia S. (Mrs. Daniel L. Starks); m. Florence Margaret Moran, Nov. 14, 1977 (dec. Dec. 1978); m. Rita H. Strowe, Mar. 27, 1993. Student, Syracuse U., 1929-30; grad., Rochester Bus. Inst., 1932; hon. degree accounting, 1955; grad., Rutgers U. Grad. Sch. Banking, 1950. With Security Trust Co., Rochester, 1930-44; with Community Savs. Bank, Rochester, 1944-77; pres., chief exec. officer Community Savs. Bank, 1965-73, chmn., chief exec. officer, 1973-75, chmn., 1976-77; dir. Seneca Towers, Inc., Rochester Mgmt. Inc.; realtor Real Estate Bd. Rochester; assoc. Red Barn Properties, Inc. Bd. dirs. Met. Rochester Found., Inc., Sr. Citizens Homes, Inc.; bd. dirs. Automobile Club Rochester, pres., 1977; trustee emeritus Rochester Inst. Tech. Mem. Oak Hill Country Club (v.p. 1964-67, bd. govs. 1962-68, 78-81), Beta Gamma Sigma (hon. U. Rochester chpt.). Home: 18 Winding Brook Dr Fairport NY 14450-2541 Office: 6 Schoen Pl Pittsford NY 14534-2026

SCHUBERT, RICHARD FRANCIS, consultant; b. Trenton, N.J., Nov. 2, 1936; s. Yaro and Frances Mary (Hustak) S.; m. Sarah Jane Lockington, Aug. 24, 1957; children: Robyn, David. BA cum laude, Eastern Nazarene Coll., 1958; LLB, Yale U., 1961. Bar: Pa. 1962, U.S. Supreme Ct 1972. Arbitration atty. Bethlehem Steel Corp., Pa., 1961-66; asst. mgr. labor relations Bethlehem Steel Corp., 1966-70; exec. asst. to undersec. labor Washington, 1970; gen. counsel labor, 1971-73, dep. sec. labor, 1973-75; asst. to v.p. indsl. relations Bethlehem Steel Corp., 1973, asst. v.p. public affairs, 1975-77, v.p. public affairs, 1977-79, pres., 1979-80, vice chmn., 1980-82; pres. ARC, 1982-89; pres., CEO Points of Light Found., 1990-95; bd. dirs. Weirton Steel, Mgmt. Tng. Corp. Bd. dirs. Nat. Alliance Bus., Inst. Ethics, Cmty. Hope, Inc.; chmn. Internat. Youth Found., Biorelease Inc., Nazarene Compassionate Ministries; chmn. Peter F. Drucker Found. Mem. Pa. Bar Assn., Northampton County Bar Assn., Coun. on Fgn. Rels., Am. Iron and Steel Inst. (past chmn. com. on internat. trade), Ctr. Excellence Govt., Ea. Nazarene Alumni Assn. (pres. 1969-73), Phi Alpha Delta. Mem. Ch. of Nazarene. Home: 7811 Old Dominion Dr Mc Lean VA 22102-2425 Office: Ste 416 1155 Connecticut Ave NW Washington DC 20036

SCHUBERT, RONALD HAYWARD, retired aerospace engineer; b. Bklyn., Aug. 25, 1932; s. John and Joan Sarah (Hayward) S.; m. Dorothy May Smith, Mar. 5, 1953 (div. 1961); children: Marcus H., Malcolm F., Ronald J. (dec.), Ann E.; m. Linda Jane van der Ploeg, Mar. 6, 1961 (div. 1988). BA cum laude, Ohio State U., 1956. Assoc. engr. Hughes Aircraft Co., Fullerton, Calif., 1957-61; physicist Nat. Cash Register Co., Dayton, Ohio, 1962-63; sr. research engr. Lockheed Missiles and Space Co., Sunnyvale, Calif., 1963-90. Served as staff sgt. USMC, 1951-54. Recipient Hon. mention Woodrow Wilson Fellowship Com. Mem. Phi Beta Kappa. Democrat. Roman Catholic. Achievements include pioneering work in reconnaissance satellite orbit concealment; devel. of digital computer simulations for all aspects of the diversified aerospace mission and its environment; guidance system and autopilot specialist. Home: 201 W California Ave Apt 1023 Sunnyvale CA 94086-5035

SCHUBERT, WILLIAM HENRY, curriculum studies educator; b. Garrett, Ind., July 6, 1944; s. Walter William and Mary Madeline (Grube) S.; children by previous marriage: Ellen Elaine, Karen Margaret; m. Ann Lynn Lopez, Dec. 3, 1977; children: Heidi Ann, Henry William. BS, Manchester Coll., 1966; MS, Ind. U., 1967; PhD, U. Ill., 1975. Tchr., Fairmount, El Sierra and Herrick Schs., Downers Grove, Ill., 1967-75; clin. instr. U. Wis., Madison, 1969-73; teaching asst., univ. fellow U. Ill., Urbana, 1973-75; asst. prof. U. Ill., Chgo., 1975-80, assoc. prof., 1981-85, prof., 1985—, coord. secondary edn., 1979-82; coord. instrl. leadership, 1979-85, dir. grad. studies Coll. Edn., 1983-85, coord. grad. curriculum studies, 1985—, coord. edn. studies, 1990-94, chair area curriculum and instruction, 1990-94; vis. assoc. prof. U. Victoria (B.C., Can.), 1981; disting. vis. prof. U. S.C., 1986. Mem. Profs. of Curriculum (factotum 1984-85), Soc. for Study of Curriculum History (founding mem., sec.-treas. 1981-82, pres. 1982-83), Am. Ednl. Rsch. Assn. (chmn. creation and utilization of curriculum knowledge 1980-82, program chmn. curriculum studies div. 1982-83, sec. Div. B 1989-91), Am. Assn. Colls. for Tchr. Edn., John Dewey Soc. (bd. dirs. 1986-95, chair awards com., 1988-90, co-chair lectures commn., 1989-91, pres. elect, 1990-91, pres. 1992-93), ASCD (steering com. of curriculum com. 1980-83, pubs. com. 1987-90, internat. polling panel 1990—), Am. Ednl. Studies Assn., World Coun. for Curriculum and Instrn., Soc. for Profs. of Edn., Nat. Soc. for Study of Edn., Inst. Dem. in Edn., Masons, Scottish Rite, Phi Delta Kappa, Phi Kappa Phi (pres. U. Ill.-Chgo. chpt. 1981-82). Author: (with Ann Lopez) Curriculum Books: The First Eighty Years, 1980; author: Curriculum: Perspective, Paradigm, and Possibility, 1986; (with Edmund C. Short and George Willis) Toward Excellence in Curriculum Inquiry, 1985; editor: (with Ann Lopez) Conceptions of Curriculum Knowledge: Focus on Students and Teachers, 1982, (with George Willis) Reflections from The Heart of Ednl. Inquiry: Understanding Curriculum and Teaching Through the Arts, 1991, (with William Ayers) Teacher Lore: Learning From Our Own Experience, 1992, (with George Willis, R. Bullough, C. Kridel, J. Holton) The American Curriculum: A Documentary History, 1993; assoc. editor: Ednl. Theory; former mem. editl. bd. Ednl. Studies; cons. editor Phenomenology Pedagogy; adv. bd. Teaching Edn., Pi Lamda Theta Pubs., 1995—; mem. editl. bd. Ednl. Theory; cons. editor Jour. Curriculum and Supervision; editorial bd. Curriculum and Teaching; reviewing editor Jour. Gang Behaviour; editor: book series Student Lore, SUNY Press, 1990—; cons. editor Jour. Curriculum Discourse and Dialogue; contbr. over 150 articles to profl. publs. Home: 727 S Ashland Ave Chicago IL 60607-3165 Office: U Ill Coll Edn M/C 147 1040 W Harrison St Chicago IL 60607-7129

SCHUBERT, WILLIAM KUENNETH, hospital medical center executive; b. Cin., July 12, 1926; s. Wilfred Schubert and Amanda Kuenneth; m. Mary Jane Pamperin, June 5, 1948; children: Carol, Joanne, Barbara, Nancy. BS, U. Cin., 1949, MD, 1952. Diplomate Am. Bd. Pediatrics. Pvt. practice specializing in pediatrics Cin., 1956-63; dir. clin. research ctr. Children's Hosp. Med. Ctr., Cin., 1963-76; dir. div. gastroenterology Children's Hosp., Cin., 1968-79; prof. pediatrics U. Cin., 1969—, assoc. sr. v.p. for children's hosp. affairs Coll. Medicine, 1993—; chief of staff Children's Hosp. Med. Ctr., Cin., 1972-88; chmn. dept. pediatrics U. Cin., 1979-93; dir. Children's Hosp. Rsch. Found., Cin., 1979-93; pres., CEO Children's Hosp. Med. Ctr., Cin., 1983—; v.p. Ohio Solid Organ Transplant Consortium, Columbus, 1986-87, pres., 1987-88, alt. trustee, 1988—; regional bd. dirs. Ameritrust Corp., 1988-91; trustee med. rsch. James N. Gamble Inst., Cin., 1989-95. Contbr. over 100 articles to profl. jours. Trustee Greater Cin. Hosp. Coun., 1986—, Assn. of Ohio Children's Hosp., Columbus, 1986—, The Springer Sch., Cin., 1994—; chmn. Greater Cin. Hosp. Coun., 1989; co-chmn. Citizen's Com. for Med. Ctr., Cin., 1980-81; chmn. Hosp. Divsn. 1988 Fine Arts Fund, Cin., 1987; hon. trustee Babies' Milk Fund, Children's and Prenatal Clinics, Cin., 1994—. Fellow Am. Acad. Pediatrics; mem. Am. Pediatric Soc. (councillor 1986-93), Soc. Pediatric Research, Assn. Med. Sch. Pediatric Dept. Chmn., Cin. Acad. Medicine, AMA, Midwestern Soc. for Pediatric Research, Am. Assn. for Study of Liver Diseases, Central Soc. Clin. Research, Am. Gastroenterological Assn., N.Am. Soc. Pediatric Gastroenterology, Nat. Reye's Syndrome Found. (med. dir. 1976-87), Internat. Assn. Study Liver Diseases. Club: Queen City (Cin.). Office: Children's Hosp Med Ctr 3333 Burnet Ave Cincinnati OH 45229-3026

SCHUCHART, JOHN ALBERT, JR., utility company executive; b. Omaha, Nov. 13, 1929; s. John A. and Mildred Vera (Kessler) S.; m. Ruth Joyce Schock, Dec. 2, 1950; children: Deborah J. Kelley, Susan K. Felton. BS in Bus, U. Nebr., 1950; grad., Stanford U. Exec. Program, 1968. With No. Natural Gas Co., Omaha, 1950-71, asst. sec., 1958-60, mgr. acctg., 1960-66, adminstrv. mgr., 1966-71; v.p., treas. Intermountain Gas Co., Boise, Idaho, 1972-75, chief fin. officer, 1973-75; fin. v.p. and treas., chief fin. officer Mont.-Dakota Utilities Co. (now MDU Resources Group, Inc.), Bismarck, N.D., 1976-77, pres., chief oper. officer, 1978-80, pres., 1980-92, CEO, 1980-94, chmn. bd., 1983—, also dir. Contbr. articles to profl. jours. Trustee Bismarck YMCA, N.D. chpt. Nature Conservancy; mem. bd. regents U. Mary, Bismarck; vice chair bus. adv. bd. Coll. Bus., Mont. State U., Billings. With AUS, 1951-53. Recipient Am. Gas Assn. Order of Acctg. Merit award, 1968, 78, Scroll and Merit award Adminstrv. Mgmt. Soc., 1972, U. Nebr. at Omaha citation of Alumnus Achievement, 1987, Coll. of Bus. Disting. Achievement award, 1989, CEO of Yr. award Fin. World Mag., 1993, Commn. and Leadership award Dist. 20 Toastmasters Internat., 1994. Mem. Apple Creek Country Club, Mpls. Athletic Club, Elks, Delta Sigma Pi. Republican. Methodist. Home: 1014 Cottage Dr Bismarck ND 58501-2458 Office: MDU Resources Group Inc 400 N 4th St Bismarck ND 58501-4022

SCHUCHERT, JOSEPH, light manufacturing executive. Ceo Kelso & Co. Inc., N.Y.C., 1980—. Office: Kelso Asi Partners 320 Park Ave Fl 24 New York NY 10022-6022*

SCHUCK, CARL JOSEPH, lawyer; b. Phila., Nov. 21, 1915; s. Joseph and Christina (Schadl) S.; m. Mary Elizabeth Box, June 7, 1941; children: Mary Ann (dec.), John, James, Catherine, Christopher. BS, St. Mary's Coll., 1937; postgrad., U. So. Calif., 1937-38; JD, Georgetown U., 1941. Bar: D.C. 1940, Calif. 1943, U.S. Supreme Ct. 1952. Atty. Dept. Justice, Washington, 1940-42, Alien Property Custodian, San Francisco, 1942-44; mem. firm Overton, Lyman & Prince, L.A., 1947-79, profl. corp. mem. firm, 1979-85; lectr. Practising Law Inst., 1973; Del. 9th Cir. Jud. Conf., 1963-80, chmn. lawyer-dels. com., 1972, mem. exec. com., 1976-80, chmn. exec. com., 1977-78, mem. sr. adv. bd., 1989-95; mem. disciplinary bd. State Bar Calif., 1970-71. Fellow Am. Coll. Trial Lawyers (chmn. com. on complex litigation 1979-81, regent 1981-85), L.A. County Bar Assn. (trustee 1974-76), Phi Alpha Delta. Club: Chancery (pres. 1984-85). Home and Office: 16916 Hierba Dr Apt 157 San Diego CA 92128

SCHUCK, JOYCE HABER, author; b. N.Y.C., Dec. 9, 1937; d. Frank F. and Florence (Smith) H.; m. Stephen Martin Schuck, June 15, 1958; children: William David, Thomas Allen, Ann Elizabeth. BA in Human Svcs. and Counseling, Loretto Hts. Coll., Denver, 1982. Counselor, tchr. Vision Quest, Colorado Springs, 1979-82; cons., program designer for govt. agys. Colorado Springs, 1982-85; author, 1987—; asst. to cons. Volusia County Dept. Corrections, Daytona Beach, Fla., 1982; cons. student svcs. program Pikes Peak C.C., Colorado Springs, 1982; cons., designer Juvenile Probation of El Paso County, Colorado Springs, 1982, 4th Jud. Dist./Dist. Atty.'s Office, Colorado Springs, 1984. Author: Political Wives, Veiled Lives, 1991. Co-founder Community Transitions, Colorado Springs, 1984; coord. El. Paso County Shape Up Program, 1982; v.p. Community Coun. of Pikes Peak Region, Colorado Springs, 1983, Women's Found. of Colo., Denver, 1987. Recipient Mayor's award for civic leadership City of Colorado Springs, 1983. Mem. Jr. League of Colorado Springs (sustaining), Salon de Femme (founding). Avocations: tennis, skiing, hiking.

SCHUCK, MARJORIE MASSEY, publisher, editor, authors' consultant; b. Winchester, Va., Oct. 9, 1921; d. Carl Frederick and Margaret Harriet (Parmelee) Massey; student U. Minn., 1941-43, New Sch., N.Y.C., 1948, N.Y. U., 1952, 54-55; m. Ernest George Metcalfe, Dec. 2, 1943 (div. Oct. 1949); m. 2d, Franz Schuck, Nov. 11, 1953 (dec. Jan. 1958). Mem. editorial bd. St. Petersburg Poetry Assn., 1967-68; co-editor, pub. poetry Venture Mag., St. Petersburg, Fla., 1968-69, editor, pub., 1969-79; co-editor, pub. Poetry Venture Quar. Essays, Vol. I, 1968-69, Vol. 2, 1970-71; pub., editor poetry anthologies, 1972—; founder, owner, pres. Valkyrie Press, Inc. (name changed to Valkyrie Pub. House 1980), 1972—; cons. designs and formats, trade publs. and ann. reports, lit. books and pamphlets, 1973—; founder Valkyrie Press Roundtable Workshop and Forum for Writers, 1975-79; established Valkyrie Press Reference Libr., 1976-80; pub., editor The Valkyrie Internat. Newsletter, 1986—; exec. dir. Inter-Cultural Forum Villanor Ctr., Tampa, Fla., 1987-94; dir. edn. The Villanor Mus. Fine and Decorative Arts, Tampa, 1994, St. Petersburg, 1994—; pres. Found. for Human Potentials, Inc., Tampa, 1988-94; representative distbr. Marg Art Publs. of India (Bombay), 1992—; mem. pres. coun. U. South Fla., 1993—; lectr. in field. Judge poetry and speech contests Gulf Beach Women's Club, 1970, Fine Arts Festival dist. 14. Am. Fedn. Women's Clubs, 1970, South and West, Inc., 1972, The Sunstone Rev., 1973, Internat. Toastmistress Clubs, 1974, 78, Beaux Arts Poetry Festival, 1983, 89, 92, 93, 94, 95, 96; judge poetry contest Fla. State conf. Nat. League Am. Pen Women, 1989; judge Fla. Gov.'s Screenwriters Competition, 1984—. Corr.-rec. sec. Women's Aux. Hosp. for Spl. Surgery, N.Y.C., 1947-59; active St. Petersburg Mus. Fine Arts (charter), St. Petersburg Sister City Com., St. Petersburg Arts Ctr. Assn.; mem. Orange Belt express com. 1988 Centennial Celebration for St. Petersburg; mem. Com. of 100 of Pinellas County, Inc., exec. bd., 1975-77, membership chmn., 1975-77; pub. rels. chmn. Soc. for prevention Cruelty to Animals, 1968-71, bd. dirs., 1968-71, 75-77; founder, mem. Pinellas County Arts Coun., 1976-79, chmn., 1977-78; mem. grant rev. panel for lit. Fine Arts Coun. of Fla., 1979; mem. pres.'s coun. U. South Fla., 1994—. Named One of 76 Fla. Patriots, Fla. Bicentennial Commn., 1976; a recipient 1st ann. People of Dedication award Salvation Army, Tampa, 1984; named to Poetica Hall of Fame, Tampa Bay Poetry Coun., 1994. Mem. Am. Assn. Museums, Acad. Am. Poets, Fla. Suncoast Writers' Confs. (founder, co-dir., lectr. 1973-83, adv. bd. 1984—), Coordinating Council Lit. Mags., Friends of Libr. of St. Petersburg, Suncoast Mgmt. Inst. (exec. bd.; chmn. Women in Mgmt. 1977-78), Pi Beta Phi. Republican. Episcopalian. Author: Speeches and Writings for Cause of Freedom, 1973. Contbr. poetry to profl. jours. Home and Office: 8245 26th Ave N Saint Petersburg FL 33710-2857 *To live and work for the sharing ofieads and feelings while helping to create atmospheres of mutuality and understanding can lead to genuine communication. One hopes such efforts will enhance harmony between people everywhere.*

SCHUCK, PETER HORNER, lawyer, educator; b. N.Y.C., Apr. 26, 1940; s. Samuel H. and Lucille (Horner) S.; m. Marcy Cantor, June 26, 1966; children: Christopher, Julie. BA with honors, Cornell U., 1962; JD cum laude, Harvard U., 1965, MA, 1969; LLM, NYU, 1966; MA (hon.), Yale U., 1982. Bar: N.Y. State 1966, D.C. 1972. Practiced law N.Y.C., 1965-68; teaching fellow in govt. Harvard U., 1969-71; cons. (Center for Study of Responsive Law), Washington, 1971-72; dir. Washington office Consumers Union, 1972-77; dep. asst. sec. for planning and evaluation HEW, Washington, 1977-79; vis. scholar Am. Enterprise Inst. for Public Policy Research, Washington, 1979; assoc. prof. law Yale U., 1979-81, prof., 1981-86, Simeon E. Baldwin prof. law, 1986—, dep. dean, 1993-94; vis. prof. Georgetown U. Law Ctr., 1986-87, NYU Law Sch., fall 1994; lectr. profl., acad., bus., univ., govt. and citizen groups. Author: The Judiciary Committees, 1975, Suing Government, 1983, Citizenship without Consent, 1985, Agent Orange on Trial, 1986, enlarged edit., 1987; editor: Tort Law and the Public Interest, 1991, Foundations of Administrative Law, 1994; contbr. articles and revs. to profl. and popular publs. Guggenheim fellow, 1984-85; recipient Silver Gavel award ABA, 1987. Jewish.

SCHUCK, THOMAS ROBERT, lawyer; b. Findlay, Ohio, Feb. 7, 1950; s. Robert Damon and Katherine Margaretta (Beynon) S.; m. Pamela Lee Bakan, Sept. 2, 1979. BA, DePauw U., 1972; MA, U. Kent, U.K., 1974; JD, Harvard U., 1976. Bar: Ohio 1976, U.S. Dist. Ct. (no. dist.) Ohio 1977, U.S. Dist. Ct. (so. dist.) Ohio 1979, Ariz. 1990, U.S. Ct. Appeals (6th cir.) 1978, U.S. Ct. Appeals (9th cir.) 1991. Law clk. U.S. Dist. Ct., Cleve., 1976-79; assoc. Taft, Stettinius & Hollister, Cin., 1979-87, ptnr., 1987—; participant Ohio Bench Bar Conf., Columbus, 1990, 91; barrister Am. Inn of Ct., 1986-87. Contbg. author: Aids and the Law, 2d edit. 1992; contbr. articles to profl. jours. Trustee Mental Health Svcs. East, Inc., Cin., 1985-91; mem. Clermont County Mental Health Bd., Batavia, Ohio, 1992—; mem. May Festival Assocs., Cin., 1984-86; spl. gifts com. Cin. Art Acad., 1987; mem. WGUC Radio Community Bd., 1984-86. Rotary Internat. Found. grad. fellow, 1972. Mem. FBA (pres. Cin. chpt. 1994-95), Ohio Bar Assn., Cin. Bar Assn., Potter Stewart Am. Inn of Ct. (barrister 1986-87), U.S. Rowing Assn. (asst. referee), Harvard Club Cin. (pres. 1995-96), Camargo Hunt Club, Masons, Phi Beta Kappa, Delta Chi, Phi Eta Sigma, Sigma Delta Chi. Republican. Methodist. Avocations: reading, photography. Home: 189 State Route 133 Felicity OH 45120-9706 Office: 1800 Star Bank Ctr 425 Walnut St Cincinnati OH 45202-3904

SCHUDEL, HANSJOERG, international business consultant; b. Wald, Switzerland, Sept. 27, 1937; s. Rene and Alice S. Ed., Coll. Bus. Adminstrn., Zurich, Switzerland. With Byk-Gulden, Konstanz, Germany and Sao Paulo, Brazil, 1962-69, Hicksville, N.Y., 1964-69; pres., chief exec. officer, dir. Stinnes Corp., N.Y.C., 1971-83; exec. officer Stinnes A.G., Muelheim, Fed. Republic of Germany, 1978-83; rep. for the Americas First Arab Pacific Corp. Ltd., Chappaqua, N.Y., 1984—. Mem. German-Am. C. of C. (bd. dirs. 1976-83), Internat. World Travelers Club, Swiss Soc., Confrerie de la Chaine des Rotisseurs, Order des Coteaux de Champagne, Foothills Assn. (bd. dirs.). Office: First Arab Pacific Corp Ltd 1275 4th St Ste 307 Santa Rosa CA 95404-4049

SCHUDER, RAYMOND FRANCIS, lawyer; b. Wickford, R.I., Dec. 27, 1926; s. Rollie Milton and Selma (Ball) S.; AB, Emory U., 1949, JD, 1951; m. Betty Jo Williams, Mar. 14, 1948; children: Gregg Williams, Glen Arva. Bar: Ga. 1951. With Trust Co., Ga., Atlanta, 1951-54; assoc. firm Wheeler, Robinson & Thurmond, Gainesville, Ga., 1954-59; pvt. practice law, Gainesville, 1959-70, 76—; ptnr. Schuder & Brown, Gainesville, 1971-76; Mcpl. ct. judge, Gainesville, 1956-60, 73-75, Magistrate ct. judge, 1985—; bd. dirs. Lanier Securities, Inc. Supr. Upper Chattahoochee Soil and Water Conservation Dist., 1971-74; chief exec. officer, bd. dirs. Charles Thompson Estes Found., Inc., Gainesville. Cpl. USMCR, 1944-50; 1st lt. USAR, ret. Mem. State Bar Ga. (gov. 1966-70), Gainesville-Northeastern (pres. 1969-70) Bar Assn., Am. Legion, V.F.W., Elks. Methodist. Home: 2224 Riverside Dr Gainesville GA 30501-1232 Office: 500 Spring St E Gainesville GA 30501-3792

SCHUELE, DONALD EDWARD, physics educator; b. Cleve., June 16, 1934; s. Edward and Mildred (Matousek) S.; m. Clare Ann Kirchner, Sept. 5, 1956; children: Donna, Karen, Melanie, Judy, Rachel, Ruth. BS, John Carroll U., Cleve., 1956, MS, 1957; PhD, Case Inst. Tech., 1962. Instr. physics and math. John Carroll U., 1956-59; part-time instr. physics Case Inst. Tech., 1959-62, instr., asst. prof., assoc. prof., 1962-70; mem. tech. staff Bell Telephone Labs., 1970-72; assoc. prof. physics Case Western Res. U., 1972-74, prof., 1974—, dean undergrad. coll., 1973-76, chmn. dept. physics, 1976-78; vice dean Case Inst. Tech., 1978-83, v.p. for undergrad. and grad. studies, 1983-84, dean, 1984-86, prof. physics, 1986-88, dean math. and natural sci., 1988-89, Albert A. Michaelson prof. physics, 1989—, acting chmn. elec. engring. and applied physics, 1992-93; cons. in field. Co-editor: Critical Revs. in Solid State Scis, 1969-84; contbr. articles to profl. jours.; patentee in field. Mem. adv. bd. St. Charles Borromeo Sch., 1970-72; pres. Seed Found., 1986-89; trustee St. Mary's Sem., 1980-93; mem. Olympic Sports Equipment and Tech. Com., 1982-93; trustee Newman Found., 1983—, Northeastern Ohio Sci. Fair, 1983—; mem. Diocesan Pastoral Coun., 1992-94; active Rep. Presdl. task force. NSF Faculty fellow, 1961-63; recipient Disting. Physics Alumnus award John Carroll U., 1983. Mem. Am. Phys. Soc. (vice chair Ohio sect. 1995-96, chair 1996—), Am. Assn. Physics Tchrs., North Coast Thermal Analysis Soc., Newman Apostolate, Case Alumni Coun. (life, treas. 1992—), Sigma Xi, Alpha Sigma Nu, Tau Beta Pi. Republican. Roman Catholic. Achievements include patents fluid pressure device, impact wrench torque calibrator. Home: 4892 Countryside Rd Cleveland OH 44124-2513 Office: Case Western Res U 10900 Euclid Ave Cleveland OH 44106-1712

SCHUELER, JAN FRANCES MENIER, early childhood special education administrator; b. Port Clinton, Ohio, July 3, 1955; d. Vito Joseph and Isabelle Mae (Robron) Menier; m. Jerold Douglas Schueler, Mar. 18, 1977; children: Ryan, Blair, Chase. BEd in Spl. Edn., Bowling Green State U., 1977; MEd in Early Childhood, U. Toledo, Ohio, 1991. Cert. spl. edn. tchr., elem. prin., supr., pre-sch. and K-8 tchr., Ohio. Kindergarten tchr. Sandusky County (Ohio) Ednl. Svc. Ctr., 1977-80; kindergarten tchr. Huron (Ohio) City Schs., 1986-89, pre-sch. tchr., 1989-90, pre-sch. spl. edn. tchr., 1989-90; early childhood svcs. coord. No. Ohio Spl. Edn. Regional Resource Ctr., Oberlin, Ohio, 1991-94; early childhood spl. edn. dir. Sandusky County Office of Ednl. Svcs., Fremont, Ohio, 1994—; developer Huron City Schs. Pre-sch. Program, 1989-91; cons. No. Ohio SERRC, Oberlin, 1991-94, Early Childhood divsn. Ohio Dept. Edn., Columbus, 1991-94; mem. adv. bd. Berlin-Milan (Ohio) Schs. Pre-sch., 1992-94, Lorain County Office of Edn. Pre-schs., Elyria, Ohio, 1992-94. Supr. Middleground Family Reunification Program, Norwalk, Ohio, 1993-95; mem. com. Huron Athletic Boosters, Inc., 1992—, sec. 1995—; concession co-chair Huron Baseball Program, Inc., 1993-95. Mem. ASCD, Nat. Assn. for Edn. of Young Children, Coun. for Exceptional Children, Assn. for Early Childhood Edn. Internat., Children and Adults with Attention Deficit Disorder (chpt. coord. 1993-95), Phi Delta Kappa (v.p. membership Firelands chpt. 1996—), Pi Lambda Theta. Home: 307 Wexford Dr Huron OH 44839-1459 Office: Sandusky County Ednl Svc Ctr 602 W State St Fremont OH 43420-2534

SCHUELKE, JOHN PAUL, religious organization administrator; b. Benton Harbor, Mich., Nov. 5, 1934; s. Alwin E. and Martha M. (Schoeneberg) S.; m. Noreta H. Petersen, Sept. 9, 1956; children: Alvin, Mary, Sheryl, Brian. BS in Acctg., U. Wyo., 1957; LLD (hon.), Concordia U., Irvine, Calif., 1983. CPA. From acct. to sr. acct. Colo. Interstate Gas Co., Colorado Springs, 1957-63; staff acct. Arthur Anderson & Co., Denver, 1963-64; mgr. fin. control Colo. Interstate Corp., Colorado Springs., 1964-67, dir. fin. control, 1967-71; adminstrv. v.p. mfg. divsn. Marsh Instrument Co. subs. Colo. Mfg. Corp., Skokie, Ill., 1971-72; exec. dir. bd. dirs., COO Luth. Ch.-Mo. Synod, St. Louis, 1972—; Lectr. in field. Asst. scoutmaster Boy Scouts Am., Colorado Springs; governing bd. Com. Luth. Cooperation; former mem. governing bd. Luth. Coun.-USA; mem. St. Matthew Luth. Ch., St. Louis. Recipient God and Country award Eagle Scouts. Mem. Alpha Kappa Psi, Gamma Delta (former pres.). Avocations: traveling, fishing, reading.

SCHUELLER, THOMAS GEORGE, lawyer; b. Budapest, Hungary, Oct. 4, 1936; came to U.S., 1938; s. Herbert H. and Edith (Geiringer) S.; m. Sandra Burke, Sept. 3, 1960 (div. Apr. 1982); children: Katherine, Matthew, John. AB cum laude, Amherst Coll., 1958; LLB, Harvard U., 1962. Bar: N.Y. 1963. Salesman Gen. Mills. Inc., Utica, N.Y., 1958-59; assoc. Hughes Hubbard & Reed, N.Y.C., 1962-69, ptnr., 1969—. Bd. dirs., sec. Ballet Hispanico, N.Y.C., 1987—. Mem. ABA, Assn. of Bar of City of N.Y., Phi Beta Kappa. Home: 169 E 78th St New York NY 10021-0405 Office: Hughes Hubbard & Reed 1 Battery Park Plz New York NY 10004-1405

SCHUELLER, WOLFGANG AUGUSTUS, architectural educator, writer; b. Aachen, Germany, Sept. 10, 1934; came to U.S., 1964; s. Sepp and Mathilde (Kallff) S.; m. Ria Herpers, Apr. 22, 1960; 1 child, Uschi. Diploma in Engring. in Civil Engring., FH Aachen, Germany, 1960; BS in Archtl. Engring. with honors, N.D. State U., 1966; MSCE in Structural Engring., Lehigh U., 1968; BArch, Syracuse U., 1971. Registered profl. engr., N.Y., Pa. Supr. constrn., structural engr. Hochtief A.G., Munich and Essen, Fed. Republic of Germany, 1960-63; structural designer Green Blanksteen Russel Assocs., Winnipeg, Man., Can., 1963-64; structural engr. Pioneer Svc. and Engring. Co., Chgo., 1966-67, Richardson, Gordon Assocs., Pitts., 1968-69; prof. architecture Syracuse U (N.Y.), 1971-82, Va. Poly. Inst., Blacksburg, 1982-94, U. Fla., Gainesville, 1994—. Author: Highrise Building Structures, 1977, Horizontal-Span Building Structures, 1983, The Vertical Building Structure, 1990, The Design of Building Structures, 1996. Mem. ASCE, Nat. Soc. Archtl.Engrs., Soc. for History of Tech., Coun. on Tall Bldgs. and Urban Habitat, Sigma Xi, Phi Kappa Phi, Tau Beta Pi. Achievements include rsch. and pubs. on relationship between bldg. sci., structures in particular, and architecture. Avocations: classical music (opera), jazz, history of art, jogging. Office: U Fla Coll Arch Gainesville FL 32611-5702

SCHUEPPERT, GEORGE LOUIS, financial executive; b. Merrill, Wis., July 1, 1938; s. George Henry and Eleanor Natalie (Pautz) S.; m. Kathleen Kay Carpenter, May 6, 1967; children—Steven Andrew, Stephanie Roanne, Stenning Karl. B.B.A., U. Wis., Madison, 1961; M.B.A., U. Chgo., 1969. Treas., controller Steiger-Rathke Devel. Co., Phoenix, 1964-65; various positions Continental Ill. Nat., Chgo., 1965-76, 1981-86; mng. dir. Continental Ill. Ltd., London, 1977-81; sr. v.p. Continental Ill. Nat. Bank, Chgo., 1982-86; ptnr. Coopers & Lybrand, Chgo., 1986-87; exec. v.p. fin. CBI Industries Inc, Oak Brook, Ill., 1987-95; also bd. dirs. CBI Industries Inc, Oak Brook, 1987-95; exec. v.p., CFO Outboard Marine Corp., Waukegan, Ill., 1996—; bd. dirs. Wells Mfg. Co. Bd. dirs., chmn. fin. com. Gt. Books Found.; bd. advisors CPA's for Pub. Interest; vice chmn., bd. dirs. De Paul U. Gov. Asst. Project. Lt. (j.g.) USN, 1961-64. Recipient Herfurth award U. Wis., 1960. Mem. Econ. Club Chgo. (bd. dirs., chmn. membership com.). Republican. Avocations: history; civic affairs; architecture; travel; golf. Home: 97 Otis Rd Barrington IL 60010-5129 Office: Outboard Marine Corp 100 Sea Horse Dr Waukegan IL 60085

SCHUERMAN, JOHN RICHARD, social work educator; b. Scotts Bluff, Nebr., Feb. 27, 1938; s. Lawrence and Mildred Jeanette (France) S.; m. Charlotte Kavaloski, Sept. 12, 1964; children: Gabrielle Ann, Matthew Lawrence. B.S., U. Chgo., 1960, M.A., 1963, Ph.D., 1970. Social worker Ill. Dept. Mental Health, Chgo., 1963-65; mem. faculty Sch. Social Service Adminstrn., U. Chgo., 1968—, prof. social work, 1978—, asso. dean, 1970-79; mem. Ill. Mental Health Planning Bd., 1971-73; cons. in field. Author: Research and Evaluation in the Human Services, 1983, Multivariate Analysis in the Human Services, 1983, Putting Families First: An Experiment in Family Preservation, 1994. Editor jour. Social Service Rev.; research on child welfare, use of artificial intelligence in social welfare. Home: 1229 E 50th St Chicago IL 60615-2908 Office: 969 E 60th St Chicago IL 60637-2640

SCHUERMAN, NORBERT JOEL, school superintendent; b. DeWitt, Nebr., Dec. 26, 1934; s. Edwin J. and Martha (Finkbeiner) S.; m. Charlette Ann Detling, Aug. 6, 1960; children: Robert, Brenda, Todd. B of Music Edn., U. Nebr., 1957, MEd, 1959, EdS in Ednl. Mgmt. and Supervision, 1964, EdD, 1967. Cert. profl. tchr. (life), Nebr. Tchr. Clatonia-Bennet (Nebr.) Pub. Sch., 1954-58; tchr., prin. Mullen (Nebr.) Pub. Sch., 1958-61; prin. Ainsworth (Nebr.) Pub. Sch., 1961-63; sr. high sch. vice prin. Lincoln (Nebr.) Pub. Sch., 1963-66, 67-69; sr. high sch. prin. Arapahoe County Sch. Dist. 6, Littleton, Colo., 1969-74; from asst. supt. to assoc. supt. to supt. Omaha Pub. Schs., 1974—; trustee, mem. exec. com. Nebr. Coun. Econ. Edn., 1985—; bd. dirs. Nat. Study Sch. Evaluation, 1986-90, Charles Drew Health Ctr., 1985-95, Fontenelle Forest, 1987-92, 95—; bd. trustees Western Heritage Mus., 1994—; mem. exec. com. Coun. Gt. City Schs., 1988—; mem. Nat. Urban Edn. Task Force, 1990—; mem. Nat. Adv. Bd. for Active Citizenship Today, 1992—; mem. bd. advisors Close Up Found., 1992—; mem. adminstrs. adv. com. U. Nebr.-Lincoln Tchrs. Coll. Mem. adv. com. Mid-Am. coun. Boy Scouts Am., 1984—; coun. regents Big Bros./Big Sisters of Midlands, Omaha, 1986—; bd. dirs. United Way of Midlands, 1985—; adv. bd. Omaha Children's Mus., 1988—. Named Nebr. Supt. of Yr., 1991; recipient Disting. Svc. award Nebr. Coun. Sch. Adminstrs., 1988, awards of honor Nat. Sch. Pub. Rels. Assn., 1991, Nebr. PTA Outstanding PTA Advocate award; named to Exec. Educator mag.'s Top 100 Sch. Execs., 1993. Mem. Am. Assn. Sch. Adminstrs. (urban schs. com. 1992—), Nebr. Coun. Sch. Adminstrs., Omaha Sch. Adminstrs. Assn., North Ctrl. Assn. (bd. dirs. 1983-89, chmn. 1987-88), Large City Schs. Supts. (pres. 1992-93), NCCJ (bd. dirs. 1990—), Nebr. Schoolmasters Club, Urban League of Nebr., Nat. Congress Parents and Tchrs. (hon. life), Nebr. Congress Parents and Tchrs. (hon. life), Phi Delta Kappa, Omicron Delta Kappa. Home: 4007 N 94th St Omaha NE 68134-3927 Office: Omaha Sch Dist 3215 Cuming St Omaha NE 68131-2000

SCHUESSLER, ANNEMARIE, pianist, educator; b. Wheaton, Ill., Apr. 20, 1951; d. Joseph John and Maureen Eileen (Harrington) S. MusB, Manhattanville Coll., 1973; MusM, Northwestern U., 1980, MusD, 1987; artists diploma with honors, Hochschule für Musik, Wurzburg, Germany, 1982. Music dir. Am. Mil. Community of Kitzingen, Germany, 1976-78; tchr. Music Arts Sch., Highland Park, Ill., 1978-82, Jack Benny Fine Arts Ctr., Waukegan, Ill., 1982-88; lectr. DePaul U. Sch. Music, Chgo., 1984-88; asst. prof. La. State U. Sch. Music, Baton Rouge, 1988-89, Ithaca (N.Y.) Coll. Sch. Music, 1989-92; asst. prof., piano Ball State U. Sch. Music, Muncie, Ind., 1992—; adj. prof. Suzuki program Wheaton (Ill.) Coll., 1982-88, Triton Coll., River Grove, Ill., 1980-82; adjudicator nat. competitions; vis. asst. prof. Eastman Sch. Music, Rochester, N.Y., 1990-91; adj. instr. Northwestern U., Evanston, Ill., 1980-81; lectr. Kang Reung, South Korea, 1990, Teagu, Korea, 1993; lectr., performer European Piano Tchrs. Assn., Eng., 1991; performer Maly Hall, St. Petersburg, Russia, 1993—. Contbr. articles to profl. jours. Eckstein scholar Northwestern U., 1978—. Mem. ISSTIP, EPTA, Nat. Conf. on Piano Pedagogy, Coll. Music Soc. (Sec. N.E. chpt. 1992-94), Ind. Music Tchrs. Assn. (bd. dirs.), Music Tchrs. Nat. Assn., Pi Kappa Lambda. Avocations: swimming, travel, cooking. Office: Ball State U Sch Music Muncie IN 47305

SCHUESSLER, KARL FREDERICK, sociologist, educator; b. Quincy, Ill., Feb. 15, 1915; s. Hugo and Elsa (Westerbeck) S.; m. Lucille Smith, June 27, 1946; children—Thomas Brian. B.A., Evansville (Ind.) Coll., 1936; M.A., U. Chgo., 1939; Ph.D., Ind. U., 1947. Sociologist Ill. State Prison, 1938; tchr. Highland Park (Ill). High Sch., 1939-40; instr. Vanderbilt U., 1946-47; mem. faculty Ind. U., 1947—, prof. sociology, 1960-76, Distinguished prof. sociology, 1976—, chmn. dept., 1961-69; rsch. cons. Thammasat U., Bangkok, Thailand, 1963; vis. prof. UCLA, 1957, U. Calif.-Berkeley, 1965-66, U. Wash., 1967; guest scholar Ctr. for Survey Rsch., Mannheim (Germany) U., 1979-80, vis. prof., 1980-81; fellow Inst. Sociology, U. Hamburg, Germany, summer 1983; mem. adv. panel sociology NSF, 1962-63; mem. behavioral sect. NIH, 1964-68; mem. social sci. rsch. study sect. NIMH, 1968-69, social sci. tng. study sect., 1969-73; mem. NRC, 1970-75. Author: (with J.H. Mueller) Statistical Reasoning in Sociology, 1961; Social Research Methods; Analyzing Social Data, 1971; (with H. Costner) Statistical Reasoning in Sociology, 3d edit, 1977; (with Dagmar Krebs) Soziale Empfindungen: Ein Interkultureller Skalenvergelich bei Deutschen und Amerikanern, 1987; also numerous articles.; editor: (with Cohen and Lindesmith) The Sutherland Papers, 1956, (with E.H. Sutherland) On Analyzing Crime, 1972, (with Demerath and Larsen) Public Policy and Sociology, 1975, Am. Sociol. Rev., 1969-71, Sociol. Methodology, 1977-79, Musical Taste and Social Background, 1980, Measuring Social Life Feelings, 1982. Served to lt. USNR, 1942-46. Fellow AAAS; mem. Am. Sociol. Assn., Am. Statis. Assn. Home: 1820 E Hunter Ave Bloomington IN 47401-5284

SCHUESSLER FIORENZA, ELISABETH, theology educator; b. Tschanad, Romania, Apr. 17, 1938; parents German citizens; d. Peter and Magdalena Schuessler; m. Francis Fiorenza, Dec. 17, 1967; 1 child, Chris. MDiv, U. Wuerzburg, Federal Republic of Germany, 1962; Dr of Theology, U. Muenster, Federal Republic of Germany, 1970; Lic. Theol, U. Wuerzburg, 1963. Asst. prof. theology U. Notre Dame, South Bend, Ind., 1970-75, assoc. prof., 1975-80, prof., 1980-84; instr. U. Muenster, 1966-67; Talbot prof. New Testament Episcopal Div. Sch., Cambridge, Mass., 1984-88; Krister Stendahl prof. div. in scripture and interpretation Harvard U., Cambridge, Mass., 1988—; Harry Emerson Fosdick vis. prof. Union Theol. Sem., N.Y.C., 1974-75; guest prof. U. Tuebingen, Federal Republic of Germany, 1987, Cath. Theol. faculty Luzern, Switzerland, 1990. Author: Der Vergessene Partner, 1964, Priester für Gott, 1972, The Apocalypse, 1976, Invitation to the Book of Revelation, 1981, In Memory of Her, 1983, Bread not Stone, 1984, Judgement or Justice, 1985, Revelation: Vision of a Just World, 1991, But She Said - Feminist Practices of Biblical Interpretation, 1992, Discipleship of Equals: A Critical Feminist Ekklesiology of Liberation, 1993, Jesus: Miriam's Child and Sophia's Prophet, Critical Issues in Feminist Christology, 1994; editor: Searching the Scriptures, 2 vols, 1993, 94; founding co-editor Jour. Feminist Studies in Religion; also editor other works. Mem. Am. Acad. Religion, Soc. Bibl. Lit. (past pres.). Office: Harvard Div Sch 45 Francis Ave Cambridge MA 02138-1911

SCHUETTE, MICHAEL, lawyer; b. Manitowoc, Wis., Apr. 19, 1937; s. Elmer A. and Mary Irene (Hart) S.; m. Mary Dare Whiteside, Oct. 28, 1961; 1 child, Sharon Mary. B.S., Northwestern U., 1959, J.D., 1962. Bar: Ill. 1962, U.S. Dist. Ct. (no. dist.) Ill. 1962. With Lord, Bissell & Brook, Chgo., 1961—, ptnr, 1971—; dir. Corralitos Astron. Research Assn., Horizons for Blind. Mem. ABA (past chmn. coal com. natural resources sect.), Chgo. Bar Assn. Club: Law (Chgo.). Office: Lord Bissell & Brook 115 S La Salle St Chicago IL 60603-3801

SCHUETZENDUEBEL, WOLFRAM GERHARD, engineering executive; b. Germany, Feb. 17, 1932; came to U.S., 1958; s. Gerhard Egon and Kaethe (Warmbier) S.; m. Ingeborg Jutta Lesch, Dec.15, 1960. BME, Tech. U. Berlin, 1956, MME, MS in Power Engring., 1958; DSc in Nuclear Engring., U. Beverly Hills, L.A., 1979. Registered profl. engr., Calif. Asst. mgr. boiler engring. dept. Riley Stoker Corp., Worcester, Mass., 1958-61; sect. mgr. systems devel. Combustion Engring., Inc., Windsor, Conn., 1961-68; various tech. mgmt. positions Gen. Atomic Co. (subs. Gulf Oil Corp.), San Diego, 1968-79; dir. utilities Solvent Refined Coal Internat., Inc. (subs. Gulf Oil Corp.), Denver, 1979-81, Gulf Oil Corp., Houston, 1981-82; pres. Endyne Internat., Inc., Houston, 1982-84; v.p. engring. and technology, sr. v.p. ops. Blount Energy Resource Corp., Montgomery, Ala., 1984-91; v.p. Birwelco-Montenay Inc., Miami, Fla., 1991—; fgn. corr. Resch Verlag, Munich, 1975—; bd.dirs. W&E Umwelttechnik A.G., A Previous Blount Co., Zurich, Switzerland, 1986-89. Patentee in field; author, co-author, translator tech. and sci. works. Fellow ASME (past chmn. nuclear heat exchanger com.); mem. Nat. Assn. Corrosion Engrs. (cert. corrosion specialist), Assn. German Profl. Engrs., Assn. Energy Engrs. (sr. mem.), Cogeneration Inst., Integrated Waste Svcs. Assn., Solid Waste Assn. N.Am. Home: 801 Timberlane Rd Pike Road AL 36064-2208 Office: Birwelco-Montenay Inc 3225 Aviation Ave Miami FL 33133-4741

SCHUG, KENNETH ROBERT, chemistry educator; b. Easton, Pa., Aug. 27, 1924; s. Howard Lester and Marion Henry (Hulbert) S.; m. Miyoko Ishiyama, June 13, 1948; children: Carey Tyler, Carson Blake, Reed Porter. Student, Johns Hopkins U., 1942-43; B.A., Stanford U., 1945; Ph.D., U. So. Calif., 1955. Instr. Seton Hall Coll., South Orange, N.J., 1948-50; research assoc. U. Wis.-Madison, 1954-56; instr. Ill. Inst. Tech., Chgo., 1956-59, asst. prof., 1959-65, assoc. prof., 1965-75, prof. chemistry, 1975—, chmn. dept. chemistry, 1976-82, 85-87, 89-90; project dir. Chgo. Area Health and Med. Careers Program, 1979—; project co-dir. Sci. and Math. Initiative for Learning Enhancement, 1985—; project dir. Howard Hughes Med. Inst. Undergrad. Biol. Scis. Program, 1992—; cons. Argonne (Ill.) Nat. Lab., 1960-62. Co-author: Eigo Kagoku Ronbun no Kakikata, 1979; contbr. articles to profl. jours. Trustee Michael Reese Health Plan, Chgo., 1976-91, Michael Reese Found., 1991—; bd. dirs. Hyde Park Consumers Coop. Soc., 1982-94. Fulbright scholar, 1964-65; grantee in field. Mem. Am. Chem. Soc. (dir., officer Chgo. sect. 1978-84). Home: 1466 E Park Pl Chicago IL 60637-1836 Office: Ill Inst Tech Dv Chemistry IIT Ctr Chicago IL 60616

SCHUH, FRANK JOSEPH, drilling engineering company executive, consultant; b. Columbus, Ohio, Feb. 3, 1935; s. Sebastian and Elizabeth (Zorn) S.; m. Alice Virgene Kasler, June 16, 1956; children: Dwain Joseph, Michael James, Barbara Ann. BS in Petroleum Engring., Ohio State U., 1956, MS in Petroleum Engring., 1956. Registered profl. engr., Ohio. Drilling and rsch. engr. Atlantic Refining Co., Tex., La., 1956-62; mem. drilling engring. staff, dir. engring. Atlantic Richfield Co., Dallas, 1962-82; mgr. drilling rsch., sr. advisor Atlantic Richfield Co., Plano, Tex., 1982-86; v.p. Enertech Engring. & Tech., Dallas, 1986-87; pres. Drilling Tech., Inc., Plano, 1987—; v.p. Supreme Resources Corp., Dallas, 1988-92; founder, 1st pres. Drilling Engring. Assn., Dallas, 1983-85. Author: Drilling Equations, 1975; patentee horizontal drilling, high frequency measurement system; 26 other patents. Precinct, region chmn. Rep. Party, Dallas, 1964-74; vol. bldg. com. Mary Immaculate Ch., Dallas, 1965-66; mem. tech. engring. and devel. com. Ocean Drilling Program, Bryan, Tex., 1980—. Recipient outstanding achievement in field of engring. award Nat. Engrs. Coun., 1980, Robert Earl McConnell award Am. Inst. Mining Engrs., 1994, Ohio State Univ. Coll. of Engring. Benjamin G. Lamme Meritorious Achievement medel, 1995. Mem. NAE, Soc. Petroleum Engrs. (nat. bd. dirs. 1983-86, Drilling Engring. award 1986, Disting. Mem. award 1989), Am. Petroleum Inst. (chmn. com. 6, 1985-88, svc. citation 1986), Am. Assn. Drilling Engrs., Soc. Ind. Profl. Earth Scientists, Petroleum Engrs. Club (pres. 1974-75), Ohio State U. Alumni Club (pres. 1968-69), Dallas-Ft. Worth Oilman's Club (handicapper 1973-86). Avocations: golf, sailing. Office: Drilling Tech Inc 5808 Wavertree Ln Ste 1000 Plano TX 75093-4513

SCHUH, G(EORGE) EDWARD, university dean, agricultural economist; b. Indpls., Sept. 13, 1930; s. George Edward and Viola (Lentz) S.; m. Maria Ignez, May 23, 1965; children: Audrey, Susan, Tanya. BS in Agrl. Edn, Purdue U., 1952, DAgr (hon.), 1992; MS in Agrl. Econs., Mich. State U., 1954; MA in Econs, U. Chgo., 1958, PhD, 1961; prof. (hon.), Fed. U. Vicosa, Brazil, 1965; hon. doctorate, Purdue U., 1992. From instr. to prof. agrl. econs. Purdue U., 1959-79; dir. Center for Public Policy and Public Affairs, 1977-78; dep. undersec. for internat. affairs and commodity programs Dept. Agr., Washington, 1978-79, chair bd. for internat. food and agrl. devel., 1995—; prof. agrl. and applied econs., head dept. U. Minn., 1979-84; dir. agr. and rural devel. World Bank, Washington, 1984-87; dean Humphrey Inst. for Pub. Affairs, U. Minn., 1987—; program advisor Ford Found., 1966-72; sr. staff economist Pres.'s Coun. Econ. Advisors, 1974-75. Author, editor profl. books; contbr. numerous articles to profl. publs. Served with U.S. Army, 1954-56. Fellow AAAS, Am. Acad. Arts and Scis., Am. Agrl. Econs. Assn. (Thesis award 1962, Pub. Rsch. award 1971, Article award 1975, Policy award 1979, Publ. of Lasting Value award 1988, bd. dirs. 1977-80, pres.-elect 1980-81, pres. 1981-82); mem. Internat. Assn. Agrl. Econs., Am. Econ. Assn., Brazilian Soc. Agrl. Economists. Office: Humphrey Ctr U Minn 301 19th Ave S Minneapolis MN 55455-0429

SCHUHMANN, REINHARDT, JR., metallurgical engineering educator, consultant; b. Corpus Christi, Tex., Dec. 16, 1914; s. Reinhardt and Alice (Shuford) S.; m. Betsy Jane Hancock, Aug. 29, 1937; children—Martha Schuh, Alice Bishop. Student, Calif. Inst. Tech., 1929-31; B.S. in Metall. Engring., Mo. Sch. Mines, 1933; M.S. in Metall. Engring., Mont. Sch. Mines, 1935; Sc.D. in Metallurgy, MIT, 1938; DEng (hon.), Purdue U., 1993. Instr. to assoc. prof. MIT, Cambridge, 1938-54; prof. metall. engring. Purdue U., West Lafayette, Ind., 1954-64, head Sch. Metall. Engring., 1959-64, Ross prof. engring., 1964-81, Ross prof. engring. emeritus, 1981—; Battelle vis. prof. Ohio State U., Columbus, 1966-67; Kroll vis. prof. Colo. Sch. Mines, Golden, 1977; metall. engring. cons., 1946—. Author: Metallurgical Engineering, 1952; contbr. articles to profl. jours.; co-inventor Q-S oxygen process, oxygen sprinkle smelting. Fellow Metall. Soc. of AIME (charter; James Douglas Gold medal 1970, Mineral Industry Edn. award 1975, Extractive metallurgy lectr. 1965, Extractive metallurgy Sci. awards 1959, 77), Am. Soc. for Metals, AAAS; mem. Nat. Acad. Engring., Am. Chem. Soc. Democrat. Episcopalian. Club: Parlor (pres. 1963-64)(Lafayette). Lodge: Rotary. Avocations: classical music; hiking. Home: 1206 Hayes St West Lafayette IN 47906-2318 Office: Purdue U Sch Materials Engring West Lafayette IN 47907

SCHUILING, WILLIAM E., automotive executive; b. 1941. BS, Mich. State U., 1963; postgrad., Wayne State U., 1967-69; BA in Fin. Acctg., U. Mich. With mktg. divsn. Cadillac Corp., Detroit, 1969-71; CEO Brown Automotive Group, 1971—. With U.S. Army, 1964-67. Office: Brown Automotive Group 10287 Lee Hwy Fairfax VA 22030-2202 Office: 10287 Lee Hwy Fairfax VA 22030*

SCHUKER, STEPHEN ALAN, historian, educator; b. N.Y.C., Feb. 16, 1939; s. Louis A. and Millicent (Milchman) S. AB summa cum laude, Cornell U., 1959; AM, Harvard U., 1962, PhD, 1969; divorced; children: Lauren, Daniel. Asst. head hist. rsch. naval history div. Office Chief Naval Ops., 1959-61; instr. history Harvard U., Cambridge, Mass., 1968-69, asst. prof., 1969-74, lectr., 1974-75; vis. assoc. prof. European studies Sch. Advanced Internat. Studies, Johns Hopkins U., Washington, 1977, adj. prof., 1978-83; assoc. prof. history Brandeis U., Waltham, Mass., 1977-82, prof., 1982-91; Commonwealth prof. history U. Va., Charlottesville, 1991-92, William W. Corcoran prof., 1992—; syndic U. Press New Eng., 1979-81; cons. Nat. Commn. Documents and Records Federal Ofcls., 1976, Rockefeller Found., 1981. Lt. USNR, 1959-61. Nat. Endowment Humanities fellow, 1972-73; Am. Council Learned Socs. fellow, 1976-77, 85; sr. fellow USIA-Fulbright Commn., 1984, fellow internat. security John D. and Catherine T. MacArthur Found., 1987-89, fellow Historisches Kolleg, Bayerische Akademie der Wissenschaften, 1996—. Mem. Am. Hist. Assn., Soc. Historians Am. Fgn. Relations. Author: The End of French Predominance in Europe (George Louis Beer prize, Gilbert Chinard prize), 1976, American "Reparations" to Germany, 1919-1933: Implications for the Third World Debt Crisis, 1988; contbr. articles to profl. jours. Office: U Va Corcoran Dept History University Station Charlottesville VA 22906

SCHUKNECHT, HAROLD FREDERICK, physician, educator; b. Chancellor, S.D., Feb. 10, 1917; s. J.G. and Dena (Weeldreyer) S.; m. Anne Bodle, June 30, 1941; children—Judith, James. Student, U. S.D., 1934-36; B.S., S.D. Sch. Med. Scis., 1938; M.D., Rush Med. Coll., 1940; M.S. (hon.), Harvard, 1961; D.Sc. (hon.), U. S.D., 1972. Diplomate: Am. Bd. Otolaryngology. Intern Mercy Hosp., Des Moines, 1940-41; resident U. Chgo. Clinics, 1946-49; asst. prof. otolaryngology U. Chgo., 1949-53; assoc. surgeon Henry Ford Hosp., Detroit, 1953-61; Walter A. Le Compte prof. otology, prof. laryngology Harvard Med. Sch., Boston, 1961-87, prof. emeritus otology, 1987—; chief otolaryngology Mass. Eye and Ear Infirmary, 1961-84, emeritus chief otolaryngology, 1984—. Author nearly 300 jour. articles, more than 70 revs., chpts., editorials, 7 books on anatomy, surgery, pathology of the ear. Recipient Achievement award Deafness Rsch. Found., N.Y.C., Beltone award, Shambaugh prize Collegium ORL, Disting. Alumnus award Rush Med. Coll.; named to S.D. Hall of Fame. Fellow Acoustical Soc. Am., Royal Coll. Surgeons (Glasgow) (hon.), Royal Coll. Surgeons (Edinburgh) (hon.); mem. AMA, Am. Acad. Ophthalmology and Otolaryngology(Disting. award contbns. clin. otology), Am. Triological Soc., Am. Otol. Soc. (award merit), Mass., Suffolk County med. socs., New Eng. Otolaryn. Soc., Soc. Univ. Otolaryngologists, Collegium ORL Amicitiae Sacrum, Deutsche Akademie der Naturforscher Leopoldina, Am. Neurotology Soc., Assn. for Research in Otolaryngology(Award of Merit), Phila. Laryngol. Soc., Sigma Xi; hon. mem. S.D. Acad. Ophthalmology and Otolaryngology, Royal Soc. Medicine (London) (hon.), also otolaryn. socs. in South Africa, Panama, Australia, Nicaragua, Colombia, Japan, Egypt, Austria, Germany. Spl. research pathology ear and physiology hearing. Home: 263 Highland St Weston MA 02193-1111 Office: 243 Charles St Boston MA 02114-3002

SCHULBERG, BUDD, author; b. N.Y.C., Mar. 27, 1914; s. Benjamin P. and Adeline (Jaffe) S.; m. Virginia Ray, July 23, 1936 (div. 1942); 1 dau., Victoria; m. Victoria Anderson, Feb. 17, 1943 (div. 1964); children: Stephen, David; m. Geraldine Brooks, July 12, 1964 (dec. 1977); m. Betsy Anne Langman, June 9, 1979; children: Benn Stuart, Jessica A. Student, Deerfield Acad., 1931-32; AB cum laude, Dartmouth Coll., 1936, LLD, 1960; LittD, Long Island U., 1983; DHL, Hofstra U., 1987. Boxing editor Sports Illustrated; pres., prodr. Schulberg Prodns.; founder, dir. Watts Writers Workshop, L.A., 1965—; founder, chmn. Frederick Douglass Creative Arts Ctr., N.Y.C., 1971—. Screenwriter, Hollywood, 1936-39; writer "The Schulberg Report", Newsday Syndicate; author: What Makes Sammy Run?, 1941, The Harder They Fall, 1947, The Disenchanted, 1950, Some Faces in the Crowd, 1953, Waterfront, 1955 (Christopher award 1955), Sanctuary V, 1969, The Four Seasons of Success, 1972, Loser and Still Champion: Muhammad Ali, 1972, Swan Watch, 1975, Everything that Moves, 1980, Moving Pictures: Memories of a Hollywood Prince, 1981, Love, Action, Laughter and Other Sad Tales, 1990, Sparring with Hemingway: And Other Stories of the Fight Game, 1995; editor: From the Ashes: Voices of Watts, 1967; screenwriter: (films) (with Samuel Ornitz) Little Orphan Annie, 1938, (with F. Scott Fitzgerald) Winter Carnival, 1939, Weekend for Three, 1941, (with Martin Berkeley) City without Men, 1943, Government Girl, 1943, On the Waterfront, 1954 (Academy award best original story and screenplay 1954, N.Y. Critics award 1954, Fgn. Corrs. award 1954, Screen Writers Guild award 1954, Venice Festival award 1954), A Face in the Crowd, 1957 (German Film Critics award 1957), Wind across the Everglades, 1958, (teleplays) The Pharmacist's Mate, 1951; playwright: The Disenchanted: A Play in Three Acts, 1958, What Make's Sammy Run?, 1959, (musical) Senor Discretion Himself, 1985; contbr. to Sports Illustrated, Life, N.Y. Times Book Rev., Esquire, Newsday Syndicate, Los Angeles Times Book Rev., N.Y. Times Sunday Mag., Playboy. Bd. dirs. Westminster Neighborhood Assn., L.A., 1965-68, Inner City Cultural Ctr., L.A., 1965-68; mem. nat. adv. commn. on black participation John F. Kennedy Ctr. for Performing Arts; trustee Humanitas Prize. Lt. (j.g.) USNR, 1943-46, assigned to OSS. Awarded Army Commendation Ribbon for gathering photog. evidence of war crimes for Nuremberg Trial, 1945-46; recipient Susie Humanitarian award B'nai B'rith, Image award NAACP, Journalism award Dartmouth Coll., Merit award Lotos Club., L.A. Community Svc. award, 1966, B'hai Human Rights award, 1968, spl. award for Watts Writers Workshop, New Eng. Theater Conf., 1969, Amistad award, award for work with black writers Howard U., Prix Literaire, Deauville Festival 1989, World Boxing Assn. Living Legend award, 1990, Westhampton Writers Lifetime Achievement award, 1989, Southampton Cultural Ctr. 1st Annual Literature award, 1992, Heritage award Deerfield Acad., 1986. Mem. Dramatists Guild, ASCAP, Authors Guild N.Y.C. (mem. council), ACLU, Writers Guild East (mem. coun.), P.E.N., Sphinx (Dartmouth), Phi Beta Kappa. Office: Miriam Altshuler Lit Agy RR # 1 Box 5 Old Post Rd Red Hook NY 12571 Also: The Artists Agy care Mickey Freiberg 10000 Santa Monica Blvd Ste 300 Los Angeles CA 90067-7007

SCHULBERG, JAY WILLIAM, advertising agency executive; b. N.Y.C., July 17, 1939; s. Perry and Esther (Eagle) S.; m. Kathryn Carmel Nicholson, Sept. 18, 1968. BS (Founder's Day award 1961), NYU, 1961. With Seagram's Inc., 1962, Grumman Aircraft Co., 1963-66; With Foote, Cone & Belding Inc., 1967-68; with Ogilvy & Mather, Inc., N.Y.C., 1968-87; exec. v.p., head creative dept. Ogilvy & Mather, Inc., 1985-87, also mem. U.S. coun. dirs., 1988—; vice chmn., chief creative officer, bd. dirs. Bozell Worldwide, N.Y.C., 1987—; also bd. dirs. Bozell, N.Y.C., operating bd.; bd. dirs. Ogilvy & Mather Worldwide. Creator advt. campaigns for Am. Express, Bahamas, TWA, Maxwell House Coffee, Country Time, Gen. Foods, Duracell, Hardees, Brit. Tourism, Hershey's, Huggies, Merrill Lynch, N.Y. Times, Excedrin, Milk "Mustache", Tyco, USAF, Mass. Mut., Vanity Fair, Vassrette, others. Developed Big Apple campaign, N.Y.C. With AUS, 1962. Recipient Art Dirs. Club awards, One Show awards, Andy awards, Addy awards, Cannes, Hollywood Festival awards, 6 David Ogilvy awards; named Creative Dir. of Yr. Adweek Mag., 1986. Mem. The One Club, Internat. Rescue Com. (bd. dirs.).

SCHULER, JAMES JOSEPH, vascular surgeon; b. Aurora, Ill., Feb. 12, 1946; s. Ella Schuler; m. Catherine Weller, 1969; children: James Jr., Matthew. BS, St. John's U., 1968; MD, U. Ill., 1972, MS, 1975. Diplomate Am. Bd. Surgery, Am. Bd. Vascular Surgery. Intern U. Ill., Chgo., 1972-73, resident, 1973-78, chief resident, 1978-79, instr., 1975-79, asst. prof., 1980-85, assoc. prof., 1985-92, prof. surgery, 1992—, chief divsn. vascular surgery, 1988—; lectr. Cook County Grad. Sch., Chgo., 1991—; attending surgeon Cook County Hosp., Chgo., 1992—, West Side Vets. Hosp., Chgo., 1979—. Assoc. editor: Civilian Vascular Trauma, 1992; co-author numerous book chpts.; contbr. articles to profl. jours. Vascular Surgery fellow U. Ill., 1979-80; rsch. grantee numerous granting bodies, 1980—. Fellow ACS; mem. Am. Venous Forum, Soc. for Vascular Surgery, Western Surg. Assn., Internat. Soc. for Cardiovascular Surgery, Midwestern Vascular Surg. Soc., Alpha Omega Alpha. Republican. Roman Catholic. Avocations: hunting, fishing. Office: U Ill Hosp 1740 W Taylor St Ste 2200 Chicago IL 60612-7232

SCHULER, ROBERT HUGO, chemist, educator; b. Buffalo, Jan. 4, 1926; s. Robert H. and Mary J. (Mayer) S.; m. Florence J. Forrest, June 18, 1952; children: Mary A., Margaret A., Carol A., Robert E., Thomas C. BS, Canisius Coll., Buffalo, 1946; PhD, U. Notre Dame, 1949. Asst. prof. chemistry Canisius Coll., 1949-53; asso. chemist, then chemist Brookhaven Nat. Lab., 1953-56; staff fellow, dir. radiation research lab. Mellon Inst., 1956-76, mem. adv. bd., 1962-76; prof. chemistry, dir. radiation research lab. Carnegie-Mellon U., 1967-76; prof. chemistry U. Notre Dame, Ind., 1976—; dir. radiation lab. U. Notre Dame, Ind., 1976-95, dir. emeritus, 1995—; John A. Zahm prof. radiation chemistry U. Notre Dame, 1986—; Raman prof. U. Madras, India, 1985-86; vis. prof. Hebrew U., Israel, 1980. Author articles in field. Recipient Curie medal Poland, 1992. Fellow AAAS; mem. Am. Chem. Soc., Am. Phys. Soc., Chem. Soc., Radiation Research Soc. (pres. 1975-76), Sigma Xi. Club: Cosmos. Office: U Notre Dame Radiation Lab Notre Dame IN 46556

SCHULER, ROBERT LEO, appraiser, consultant; b. Cin., June 15, 1943; s. Del D. and Virginia D. (Heyl) S.; m. Shelagh J. Moritz, Aug. 11, 1962; children: Robert C., Sherry L. V.p. Comprehensive Appraisal Service, Inc., Cin., 1977—; bd. dirs. Hamilton County Regional Planning Commn., Cin., 1987-88; mem. exec. com., past pres. OKI Regional Coun. Govts., Cin., 1981-92. Councilman City of Deer Park, Ohio, 1979-86; trustee Sycamore Twp., 1988-92; Ohio state rep. 36th dist. Mem. Am. Assn. Cert. Appraiser (sr.), Cin. Bd. Realtors, Ohio Assn. Realtors, Jaycees (v.p.). Republican. Roman Catholic. Home: 3648 Jeffrey Ct Cincinnati OH 45236-1544 Office: PO Box 36442 Cincinnati OH 45236-0442

SCHULER, THEODORE ANTHONY, civil engineer, city official; b. Louisville, July 1, 1934; s. Henry R. and Virginia (Meisner) S.; m. Jane A. Bandy, July 29, 1979; children: Marc, Elizabeth, Eric, Ellen. BCE, U. Louisville, 1957, M.Engring., 1973. Registered profl. engr., Tenn., Ky.; registered land surveyor. Design, constrn. engr. Brighton Engring. Co., Frankfort, Ky., 1960-65; design engr. Hensley-Schmidt Inc., Chattanooga, 1965-68, assoc. mem., 1969-73, sr. assoc. mem., 1973-75, prin., asst. v.p., head Knoxville office, 1975-81; chief planning engr. engring. dept. City of Knoxville, 1981—. Served to lt. (j.g.) USNR, 1957-60. Fellow ASCE. Home: 5907 Adelia Dr Knoxville TN 37920-5801 Office: Dept Engring City County-Bldg Rm 483 Knoxville TN 37901

SCHULHOF, MICHAEL PETER, entertainment, electronics company executive; b. N.Y.C., Nov. 30, 1942; s. Rudolph B. and Hannelore (Buck) S.; m. Paola Nissim, Apr. 17, 1969; children: David Kenneth, Jonathan Nissim. BA, Grinnell Coll., 1964, DSc (hon.), 1990; MS, Cornell U., 1967; PhD (NSF fellow), Brandeis U., 1970. Lic. comml. pilot. Am. research fellow Brookhaven Nat. Lab., Uptown, N.Y., 1969-71; asst. to v.p. mfg. CBS Records, Inc., N.Y.C., 1971-73, mem. exec. com., bd. dirs., 1987—; gen. mgr. bus. products div. Sony Corp., N.Y.C., 1973-77, v.p., 1977-78, sr. v.p., 1978-86; pres. Sony Industries, N.Y.C., 1978-86; chmn. Digital Audio Disc Corp., Terre Haute, Ind., 1986-96; pres. Sony Software Corp., 1991-96; pres., CEO Sony Corp. Am., 1993-95; chmn. bd. dirs. Quadriga Art Inc., 1980—; bd. dirs. Sony Corp., Japan, Sony Corp. Am., Sony Pictures Entertainment, Materials Rsch. Corp.; chmn. Sony Music Entertainment. Contbr. articles to profl. jours. Patentee audio disc apparatus, 1986. Trustee Brandeis U., 1990—, Mus. TV and Radio, N.Y.C., Lincoln Ctr. for Performing Arts, Inc., N.Y.C., The Brookings Instn., Washington; bd. dirs. Ctr. on Addiction and Substance Abuse at Columbia U., N.Y.C.; mem. investment and svcs. policy adv. com. to U.S. Trade Rep.; active Com. Fgn. Rels. NSF fellw Brandeis U. Mem. Am. Phys. Soc. (dir. 1978), Computer and Bus. Equipment Mfrs. Assn. (dir.), Am. Radio Relay League, Aircraft Owners and Pilots Assn., Guggenhiem Mus., Whitney Mus., Harmony Club, Gipsy Trail Club, East Hampton Tennis Club, Profile Club, Fenway Golf Club, Atlantic Golf Club. Office: 375 Park Ave New York NY 10152

SCHULHOFER, STEPHEN JOSEPH, law educator, consultant; b. N.Y.C., Aug. 20, 1942; s. Joseph and Myrelle S.; m. Laurie Wohl, May 28, 1975; children: Samuel, Jonah. AB, Princeton U., 1964; LLB, Harvard U., 1967. Bar: D.C. 1968, U.S. Dist. Ct. (ea. dist.) Pa. 1973, U.S. Supreme Ct. 1973. Law clk. U.S. Supreme Ct., Washington, 1967-69; assoc. Coudert Freres, Paris, 1969-72; prof. law U. Pa., Phila., 1972-86; prof. U. Chgo., 1986—. speedy trial reporter U.S. Dist. Ct., Wilmington, Del., 1975-80; cons. U.S. EPA, Washington, 1977-78, U.S. Sentencing Commn., Washington, 1987-94. Author: Prosecutorial Discretion and Federal Sentencing Reform, 1979. Editor: Criminal Law and its Processes, 1983, 89, 95; contbr. articles to profl. jours. Trustee, Community Legal Services, Inc., Phila., 1981-86. Walter Meyer grantee Am. Bar Found., 1984. Mem. ACLU (Ill. bd. dirs. 1993—), Law and Soc. Assn. Office: U Chgo Law Sch 1111 E 60th St Chicago IL 60637-2702

SCHULIAN, JOHN (NIELSEN SCHULIAN), screenwriter, author; b. L.A., Jan. 31, 1945; s. John and Estella Katherine (Nielsen) S.; m. Paula Lynn Ellis, Aug. 20, 1977 (div. Oct. 1984). BA, U. Utah, 1967; MS, Northwestern U., 1968. Copy editor Salt Lake City Tribune, 1968; reporter Balt. Evening Sun, 1970-75; sportswriter Washington Post, 1975-77; sports columnist Chgo. Daily News, 1977-78, Chgo. Sun-Times, 1978-84, Phila. Daily News, 1984-86; staff writer Miami Vice, Universal City, Calif., 1986-87, story editor, 1987; story editor The Slap Maxwell Story, North Hollywood, Calif., 1987-88; exec. story editor TV series Wiseguy, Hollywood, 1988-89; co-producer TV series Midnight Caller, Burbank, Calif., 1989-90; supervising producer Midnight Caller, 1990-91; co-exec. producer TV series Reasonable Doubts, Burbank, Calif., 1991-92; creative cons. TV series The Untouchables, L.A., 1992-93; co-exec. producer TV series Hercules, Universal City, Calif., 1994—; co-creator Xena: Warrior Princess, Universal City, Calif., 1995. Author: Writers' Fighters and Other Sweet Scientists, 1983; contbg. editor Panorama mag., 1980-81; syndicated columnist UP Syndicate; commentator Nat. Pub. Radio, 1985-86; cons. The Reader's Catalog, 1989; contbr. articles to Playboy, Gentlemen's Quar., Sports Illustrated, The National, L.A. Times; included in The Best Am. Sports Writing, 1994. Mem. Pacific Coast League Hist. Soc. With U.S. Army, 1968-70. Recipient Nat. Headliners Club award, 1980, Column Writing award AP Sports Editors, 1979, 82, Best Sports Stories award, 1983, 84, Nat Fleischer Excellence in Boxing Journalism award Boxing Writers Assn. Am., 1985. Mem. Writers Guild Am., Phi Beta Kappa. Office: Peter Benedek United Talent Agy 9560 Wilshire Blvd Beverly Hills CA 90212

SCHULKIN, JAY, neuroscientist, educator; b. N.Y.C., Dec. 29, 1952; s. Stanley and Rosalind (Linder) S.; m. April A. Oliver, Mar. 1990; 1 child, Danielle Ann. BA in Philosophy, SUNY, Purchase, 1977; MA in Philosophy, U. Pa., 1980, PhD in Behavorial Sci., 1983. Rsch. assoc. dept. psychology NYU, N.Y.C., 1981-83; rsch. prof. dept. anatomy U. Pa., Phila., 1987-92; rsch. prof. dept. neuroendocrinology Rockefeller U., N.Y.C., 1992—; chief behavioral neurosci. unit, neuroendocrinology br. NIMH, Washington, 1992—; coord. program project grant NIMH, 1988-92. Author: Sodium Hunger, 1991, Pursuit of Inquiry, 1992; author: editor: Preoperative Events: Effects of Behavior Following Brain Damage, 1989, Hormonally Induced Changes in Mind & Brain, 1993; mem. editorial bd. mag. Behavioral Neurosci., 1992-94. Tchr. Summer Sci. Acad., U. Pa., Phila., 1989—. MacArthur Found. fellow, 1983; NATO grantee, 1988-90. Mem. APA, Inst. for Neurol. Scis., Soc. for Neurosci., Am. Philos. Soc. Office: NIMH Neuroendocrine Br Behavioral Neurosci Unit 6000 Rockville Pike Bethesda MD 10892

SCHULL, MYRA EDNA, librarian; b. Vienna, Austria, May 3, 1951; came to U.S., 1952; d. Verlin Watson and Wiltraud Ingeborg (Oftner) Miller; m. Terence William Schull, May 26, 1972; 1 child, Michael William. AB, Ball State U., 1973, MA, 1977; MLS, Ind. U., 1992. Tchr. English, German Shenandoah Sch. Corp., Middletown, Ind., 1973-84; head audio visual Muncie (Ind.) Pub. Libr., 1985-86; media specialist Delaware Cmty. Sch. Corp., Muncie, 1988—. Mem. libr. adv. bd. High St. Meth. Ch., Muncie, 1991—. Tchr. Creativity grantee Lilly Endowment Inc., Indpls., 1993. Mem. Assn. Ind. Media Educators, Job's Daus. (life, honored queen), Internat. Assn. Sch. Librs., Internat. Reading Assn., Coun. for Basic Edn. Avocations: travel, reading, dog obedience training. Home: 218 N Riley Rd Muncie IN 47304-3946 Office: Delaware Cmty Sch Corp 7821 State Rd 3 N Muncie IN 47303

SCHULLER, DAVID EDWARD, cancer center administrator, otolaryngology; b. Cleve., Oct. 20, 1944; m. Carole Ann Hauss, June 24, 1967; children: Rebecca, Michael. BA, Rutgers U., 1966; MD cum laude, Ohio State U., 1970. Diplomate Am. Bd. Otolaryngology 1975. Intern dept. surgery U. Hosps. Cleve., 1970-71; resident dept. otolaryngology Ohio State U., Columbus, 1971-72; resident dept. surgery U. Hosps. Cleve., 1972-73; fellow head and neck surgery Pack Med. Found. with John Conley, N.Y.C., 1973; resident dept. otolaryngology Ohio State U. Hosps., Columbus, 1973-75; fellow head and neck oncology and facial plastic and reconstructive surgery U. Iowa, Iowa City, 1975-76; from clin. instr. to prof. and chmn. dept. otolaryngology The Ohio State U., Columbus, 1971—; dir. Compehensive Cancer Ctr. & Arthur G. James Cancer Hosp. and Rsch. Inst., Columbus, 1988—; prof. Sch. Allied Med. Professions The Ohio State U., 1990—; mem., chmn. various coms. Ohio State U. Hosps. and Coll. Medicine, 1976—; dir. CCC head and neck oncology program Ohio State U., 1977—, hosps. physician flr. coord. 10th flr., 1977-82, dir. laser-microsurgery teaching and rsch. lab., 1987-88; mem. various coms. Grant Hosp., 1980-84; mem. Accreditation Coun. for the Grad. Med. Edn. Residency Review Com. for Otolaryngology, 1985—, chmn., 1988—; vis. prof., lectr. numerous instns. Author: (books) (with others) Otolaryngology-Head and Neck Surgery-4 Vols., 1986, Textbook of Otolaryngology-7th Edit., 1988, Otolaryngology-Head and Neck Surgery-Update I, 1988, Musculocutaneous Flaps in Head and Neck Reconstructive Surgery, 1989, Otolaryngology-Head and Neck Surgery Update II, 1990, Otorinolaringologia-Cirugia de Cabeza y Culleo, 1991, Otolaryngology-Head and Neck Surgery-4 Vols., 1992; contbr. chpts. to books and articles to profl. jours.; mem. editorial bd. New Horizons in Otolaryngology/Head and Neck Surgery, 1982-87, The Laryngoscope, 1986—, Am. Jour. Otolaryngology, 1988—, Facial Plastic Surgery Internat. Quar. Monographs, 1992—; mem. rev. bd. Jour. Head and Neck Surgery, 1985—; mem. editorial rev. bd. Otolaryngology-Head and Neck Surgery, 1990—; reviewer New Eng. Jour Medicine, 1992—. Trustee Ohio Cancer Found., 1988—; dir. Am. Bd. Otolaryngology, 1988—. Recipient Cert. of Appreciation, Scioto Meml. Hosp., 1982, Edmund Prince Fowler award Triological Soc., 1984; Henry Rutgers scholar Rutgers U., 1965-66; grantee Nat. Cancer Inst., 1980-88, 90—, Bremer Found., 1982-83, 87-88, Photomedica Inc., 1986-89, Upjohn Co., 1986-90, others. Mem. AMA (mem. rev. panel Archives of Otolaryngology-Head and Neck Surgery 1984—), Am. Cancer Soc. (mem. instl. grant rev. com. 1980—, chmn. rehab. com. Franklin County unit 1981-82, mem. profl. edn. com. 1981—, chmn. 1982-85, v.p. 1982-83, pres. 1986, 87, trustee Ohio divsn. 1988—), Am. Assn. Cosmetic Surgeons, Am. Acad. Facial Plastic and Reconstructive Surgery (mem. rsch. com. 1977-82, chmn. residency rels. com. 1982-85, mem. program com. 1982-85, v.p. mid. sect. 1983-87, chmn. by-laws com. 1988—, treas. 1988—, Honor award 1989), Am. Coll. Surgeons, Am. Cleft Palate Assn., Assn. Am. Cancer Insts., Am. Soc. Head and Neck Injury, Am. Acad. Otolaryngology Head and Neck Surgery (mem. editorial bd. self-instructional package program 1982—, del. bd. govs. 1982-87, Honor award 1983), Am. Soc. Laser Medicine and Surgery, Am. Laryngological, Rhinological, Otological Soc., Inc., Am. Laryngological Assn., Am. Soc. Clin. Oncology (mem. program com. 1989—), Am. Assn. Cancer Researchers, Am. Soc. Head and Neck Surgery (mem. coun. 1983-86, chmn. scholastic and fellowship award com. 1984-86, mem. profl. rels. and pub. edn. com. 1989—), Southwest Oncology Group (chmn. head and neck com. 1983—), Collegium ORLAS, Ohio State Med. Assn. (pres. sect. otolaryngology 1987—), Ohio Soc. Otolaryngology (pres. 1985, 86, 87), Acad. Medicine of Columbus and Franklin County, Columbus E.E.N.T. Soc., Franklin County Acad. Medicine (mem. profl. rels. com. 1982—), Head an. 1984-86, chmn. 1986-89), Assn. Rsch. Otolaryngology, Ohio State U. Med. Alumni Soc. (class rep. 1980—, v.p. 1987-88, pres. 1989-90), Med. Forum, Med. Review Club, Order of Hippocrates (charter), Alpha Omega Alpha. Office: 456 W 10th Ave Columbus OH 43210-1240 also: Ohio State Univ Comp Cancer Ctr 300 W 10th Ave Columbus OH 43210-1240

SCHULLER, DIANE ETHEL, allergist, immunologist, educator; b. Bklyn., Nov. 27, 1943; d. Charles William and Dorothy Schuller. AB cum laude with honors in Biology, Bryn Mawr Coll., 1965. Diplomate Am. Bd. Allergy and Immunology, Am. Bd. Pediatrics, Nat. Bd. Med. Examiniers. M.D., SUNY Downstate Med. Sch., Bklyn., 1970. Intern, then resident in pediatrics Roosevelt Hosp., N.Y.C., 1970-72, resident in allergy Cooke Inst. Allergy, 1972-74; assoc. in pediatrics Geisinger Med. Center, Danville, Pa., 1974-95, dir. dept. pediatric allergy, immunology and pulmonary diseases 1978-95; asst. clin. prof. pediatrics Hershey Med. Coll., Pa. State U., 1974-79, assoc. clin. prof., 1979-88; clin. prof. Jefferson Med. Coll., Phila., 1989-95; dir. pediatric allergy, immunology, pulmonology Pa. State U., Milton S. Hershey Med. Ctr., 1995—, prof. pediatrics, 1995—. Bd. dirs. Central Pa. Lung and Health Assn.; bd. dirs., exec. com. Am. Lung Assn. of Pa., sec., 1992— ; chmn. Susquehanna Valley Lung Assn., 1983—; mem. scholarship com. Bryn Mawr Club, N.Y., 1970-75; mem. Columbia-Montour Home Health Svcs. Adv. Group of Profl. Personnel, 1975-95. Editl. bd. Annals of Allergy. Recipient Physicians Recognition award AMA, 1973-76, 74-76, 75-78, 79-82, 83-86, 1987-90, 91-94, 95—. Fellow Am. Acad. Pediatrics, Am. Coll. Allergy Asthma and Immunology (2d v.p. 1988, bd. regents 1989-92, exec. com. 1990-93, v.p. 1992-93, pres.-elect 1993-94, pres. 1994-95), Am. Assn. Clin. Immunology and Allergy (regional dir., exec. com.), Joint Coun. Allergy and Immunology (bd. dirs. 1986-95; treas. of joint coun. 1991-93), Am. Acad. Allergy and Immunology; mem. Am. Assn. Cert. Allergists, Pa., N.Y. State allergy socs., N.Y. State, N.Y. County med. socs. Office: Milton S Hershey Med Ctr Pa State U Hershey PA 17033 also: 11 Brandywine Hershey PA 17033

SCHULLER, GUNTHER ALEXANDER, composer; b. N.Y.C., Nov. 22, 1925; s. Arthur E. and Elsie (Bernartz) S.; m. Marjorie Black, June 8, 1948; children: Edwin Gunther, George Alexander. Student, St. Thomas Choir Sch., N.Y.C.; MusD (hon.), Manhattan Sch. Music, 1987, Northeastern U., 1967, U. Ill., 1968, Colby Coll., 1969, Williams Coll., 1975, Cleve. Inst. Music, 1977, New Eng. Conservatory Music, 1978, Rutgers U., 1980, Manhattan Sch. Music, 1987, Oberlin Coll., 1989. tchr. Manhattan Sch. Music, 1950-63; head composition dept. Tanglewood, 1963-84; pres. New Eng. Conservatory of Music, 1967-77; artistic dir. Berkshire Music Center, Tanglewood, 1969-84, Festival at Sandpoint, 1985—; founder, pres. Margun Music Inc., 1975, GM Recs., 1980. French horn player, Ballet Theatre, then prin. horn player, Cin. Symphony Orch., 1943-45, prin. French horn, Met. Opera Orch., 1945-59, Concerto #1 for Horn, 1945; composer: Quartet for Four Double Basses, 1947, Fantasy for Unaccompanied Cello, 1951, Recitative and Rondo for Violin and Piano, 1953, Music for Violin, Piano and Percussion, 1957, Contours, 1958, Woodwind Quintet, 1958, Seven Studies on Themes of Paul Klee, 1959, Spectra, 1960, Six Renaissance Lyrics, 1962, String Quartet No. 2, 1965, Symphony, 1965, opera The Visitation 1966, opera Fisherman and His Wife, 1970, Capriccio Stravagante, 1972, The Power Within Us, 1972, Tre Invenzioni, 1972, Three Nocturnes, 1973, Four Soundscapes, 1974, Concerto No. 2 for Orch., 1975, Triplum II, 1975, Horn Concerto No. 2, 1976, Violin Concerto, 1976, Diptych for organ, 1976, Sonata Serenata, 1978, Contrabassoon Concerto, 1978, Deaï for 3 orchs., 1978, Trumpet Concerto, 1979, Octet, 1979, Eine Kleine Posaunenmusik, 1980, In Praise of Winds (Symphony for Large Wind Orch.), 1981, Symphony for Organ, 1982, Concerto Quaternio, 1983, Concerto for Bassoon and Orch., 1984, Farbenspiel (Concerto No. 3 for Orch.), 1985, On Light Wings (piano quartet), 1984; author: Horn Technique, 1962, Early Jazz: Its Roots and Development, 1968, Musings: The Musical Worlds of Gunther Schuller, 1985, The Swing Era, 1989; premiere of Symphony for Brass and Percussion, Cin., 1950, Salzburg Festival, 1957, Dramatic Overture, N.Y. Philharm., 1956, String Quartet, Number 1 Contemporary Arts Festival, U. Ill., 1957, String Quartet Number 3, 1986, Concertino for Jazz Quartet and Orch, Balt. Symphony Orch., 1959, Seven Studies on Themes of Paul Klee, Ford Found., commn., Minn. Symphony, 1959, Spectra, N.Y. Philharm. 1960, Music for Brass Quintet, Coolidge Found., Library of Congress, 1961, Concerto No. 1 for Orch, Chgo. Symphony Orch., 1966, Triplum, N.Y. Philharm. commd. Lincoln Center, 1967, Aphorisms for Flute and String Trio commd, Carlton Coll. Centennial, 1967, Eine Kleine Posaunenmusik, 1980, In Praise of Winds, 1983, Concerto Quaternio, N.Y. Philharm., 1983, Duologue for Violin and Piano, Library of Congress, 1984, Farbenspiel, Berlin Philharm., 1985, Concerto for Viola and Orch., 1985, String Quartet No. 3, 1986, Chimeric Images, 1988, Concerto for String Quartet and Orchestra, 1988, Concerto for Flute and Orchestra, 1988, On Winged Flight: A Divertimento for Band, 1989, Chamber Concerto, 1989, Concerto for Piano Three Hands, 1989, Phantasmata for Violin and Marinba, 1989, 5 Impromptus Eng. Horn and String Quartet, 1989, Impromptus and Cadenzas, 1990, Hommage à Rayechla for 8 cellos/or multiples thereof, 1990, A Trio Setting for clarinet, violin, piano, 1990, Violin Concert No. 2, 1991, Sonata Fantasia for piano, 1992, Ritmica Melodia Armonia for orchestra, 1992, Of Reminiscences and Reflections for orchestra, 1993 (Pulitzer Prize for music 1994), Brass Quintet No. 2, 1993, The Past is in the Present for orchestra, 1994, Sextet for left hand piano and woodwind quintet, 1994, Concerto for organ and orchestra, 1994, Mondrian's Vision, 1994. Guggenheim fellow, 1962, 63, MacArthur fellow, 1991; recipient Creative Arts award Brandeis U., 1960, Deems Taylor award ASCAP, 1970, Alice M. Ditson Conducting award, 1970, Rodgers and Hammerstein award, 1971, Friedheim award, 1988, William Schuman award Columbia U., 1989, Down Beat Lifetime Achievement award, 1993, Pulitzer prize in music, 1994, BMI Lifetime Achievement award, 1994; named Composer of Yr., Mus. Am., 1995. Mem. Nat. Inst. Arts and Letters, Am. Acad. Arts and Scis. Address: care Margun Music Inc 167 Dudley Rd Newton Center MA 02159-2830 also: care Festival at Sandpoint PO Box 695 Sandpoint ID 83864-0695

SCHULLER, ROBERT HAROLD, clergyman, author; b. Alton, Iowa, Sept. 16, 1926; s. Anthony and Jennie (Beltman) S.; m. Arvella DeHaan, June 15, 1950; children: Sheila, Robert, Jeanne, Carol, Gretchen. B.A., Hope Coll., 1947; B.D., Western Theol. Sem., 1950; D.D., Hope Coll., 1973; LL.D., Azusa Pacific Coll., 1970, Pepperdine U., 1976; Litt.D., Barrington Coll., 1977. Ordained to ministry Reformed Ch. in Am., 1950; pastor Ivanhoe Ref. Ch., Chgo., 1950-55; founder, sr. pastor Garden Grove (Calif.) Community Ch., 1955—; founder, pres. Hour of Power TV Ministry, Garden Grove, 1970—; founder, dir. Robert H. Schuller Inst. for Successful Ch. Leadership, Garden Grove, 1970—; chmn. nat. religious sponsor program Religion in Am. Life, N.Y.C., 1975—; bd. dirs. Freedom Found. Author: God's Way to the Good Life, 1963, Your Future Is Your Friend, 1964, Move Ahead with Possibility Thinking, 1967, Self Love, the Dynamic Force of Success, 1969, Power Ideas for a Happy Family, 1972, The Greatest Possibility Thinker That Ever Lived, 1973, Turn Your Scars into Stars, 1973, You Can Become the Person You Want To Be, 1973, Your Church Has Real Possibilities, 1974, Love or Loneliness— You Decide, 1974, Positive Prayers for Power-Filled Living, 1976, Keep on Believing, 1976, Reach Out for New Life, 1977, Peace of Mind Through Possibility Thinking, 1977, Turning Your Stress Into Strength, 1978, Daily Power Thoughts, 1978, The Peak to Peek Principle, 1981, Living Positively One Day at a Time, 1981, Self Esteem: The New Reformation, 1982, Tough Times Never Last, But, Tough People Do!, 1983, Tough Minded Faith for Tender hearted People, 1984, The Be-Happy Attitudes, 1985, Be Happy You Are Loved, 1986, Success is Never Ending, Failure is Never Final, 1988, Believe in the God Who Believes in You, 1989; co-author: The Courage of Carol, 1978. Bd. dirs. Religion in Am. Life; pres. bd. dirs. Christian Counseling Service; founder Robert H. Schuller Corr. Center for Possibility Thinkers, 1976. Recipient Disting. Alumnus award Hope Coll., 1970, Prin. award Freedoms Found., 1974; named Headliner of Year in Religion, Orange County, 1977, Clergyman of Year, Religious Heritage Am., 1977. Mem. Religious Guild Architects (hon.), AIA (bd. dirs. 1986—). Club: Rotary. Office: Religion in Am Life 12141 Lewis St Garden Grove CA 92640-4627

SCHULMAN, EVELINE DOLIN, psychologist, author, consultant; b. N.Y.C.; d. George and Fannie (Simon) Dolin; m. Sol Schulman, June 3, 1941; children: Mark H., Ken S. BS, CCNY, 1939, postgrad., 1940-42; postgrad., State U. Iowa, 1939-40, Am. U., 1947; MEd, U. Md., 1954, EdD, 1957, postgrad., 1979-81. Tchr. Children's Colony, N.Y.C., 1941-42; registrar-tchr. Rockwood Nursery Sch., N.Y.C., 1942-43; asst. dir. Settlement House, Juanita Kauman Nye Council House; dir./tchr. nursery sch., Washington, 1947-48; dir.-tchr. Greenway Co-op. Nursery Sch., Washington, 1947-48, Fairfax Co-op. Nursery Sch., Washington, 1948-50, Community Nursery Sch., Silver Spring, Md., 1952-54; grad. asst. U. Md., 1954-55; psychologist, cons. Prince Georges County Council of Kindergarten and Nursery Schs., 1955-57; psychologist, lectr. Am. U., Washington, 1957; instr. psychology Community Coll. Balt., 1958-62, chmn. dept., 1962-73, prof. psychology, 1964-73, dir. mental health tech. program, 1967-73; lectr. human devel. Inst. for Child Study, U. Md., 1967-68, 69-71; prof. mental health Morgan State Coll., Towson, 1971-77; dir. evaluation and tng. Md. Mental Retardation Adminstrn., Balt., 1974-76, asst. dir. adminstrn., 1976-77; dir., cons. human services Ctr. for Devel. Inter-Personal Skills, Silver Spring, 1977—; cons. Nat. Disabilities Assn., 1980. Author: Intervention in Human Services—A Guide to Skills and Knowledge, 1974, 4th edit., 1991, Focus on the Retarded Adult, 1980; contbr. articles in field to profl. jours. Active Montgomery County Com. for Cmty. Edn., about Mentally Ill, 1982-86, Clifton T. Perkins Adv. Bd., 1972-80, chmn., 1974-80; chmn. Montgomery County Coun. Adult Pub. Guardianship Rev. Bds. Md., 1986—, Wheaton Cmty. Mental Health Adv. Com., 1978—. Fellow, U. Md., 1954-55. Mem. ACA, Am. Psychol. Assn., Am. Assn. Mental Health Counselors Assn., Gerontol. Soc., Nat. Coun. on Aging, Md. Assn. Jr. Colls. (pres. 1967-69). Office: Ctr for Devel Inter-Personal Skills 1103 Caddington Ave Silver Spring MD 20901-1114

SCHULMAN, GRACE, poet, English language educator; b. N.Y.C.; d. Bernard and Marcella (Freiberger) Waldman, m. Jerome L. Schulman, Sept. 6, 1959. Student, Bard Coll., Johns Hopkins U.; BS, Am. U., 1955; MA, NYU, 1960, PhD, 1971. Prof. Baruch Coll., N.Y.C., 1971—; poetry editor The Nation, N.Y.C., 1971—; mem. Brandeis Commn. Author: (poetry) Burn Down the Icons, 1976, Hemispheres, 1984, For That Day Only, 1994, (critical study) Marianne Moore: The Poetry of Engagement; translator (postry) At the Stone of Losses, Carmi/Present Tense Award. Fellow Yaddo, 1973, 75, 77, 79, 81, 93, MacDowell Colony, 1973, 75, 77, Rockefeller Inst., 1986, fellow in poetry N.Y. Found. for Arts, 1995; recipient Delmore Schwartz Meml. award for poetry, 1996. Mem. PEN (past v.p.), Poetry Soc. Am., Nat. Book Critics Cir., Authors Guild. Home: 1 University Pl Apt 14F New York NY 10003-4519

SCHULMAN, HAROLD, obstetrician, gynecologist, perinatologist; b. Newark, Oct. 26, 1930; m. Rosemarie Vincenti; childrne: Stanley H., Sandra C., Gina M. B.S., U. Fla., 1951; M.D., Emory U., 1955. Diplomate Am. Bd. Ob-Gyn., Am. Bd. Maternal and Fetal Medicine; registered diagnostic med. sonographer. Intern Jackson Meml. Hosp., Miami, Fla., 1955-56; resident Jackson Meml. Hosp., 1958-61; instr. dept. ob-gyn. U. Miami (Fla.) Sch. Medicine, 1961; instr., asst. prof. dept. ob-gyn. Temple U. Sch. Medicine, Phila., 1961-65; asst. prof. dept. ob-gyn. Albert Einstein Coll. Medicine, Bronx, 1965-67; assoc. prof. Albert Einstein Coll. Medicine, 1968-71, prof., 1971—, acting dept. chmn., 1972-73, chmn., 1973-80; assoc. dir. dept. ob-gyn Bronx Mcpl. Hosp. Ctr., 1967-70, dep. dir., 1970-72; chmn. dept. ob-gyn. Winthrop U. Hosp., Mineola, N.Y., 1984-93; prof. ob-gyn SUNY, Stony Brook, 1984-93; chmn. dept. ob-gyn. Lawnwood Regional Med. Ctr., Ft. Pierce, FL, 1995—. Contbr. articles to profl. pubs. Served to capt. U.S. Army, 1956-58. Am. Cancer Soc. fellow, 1959-60; USPHS trainee, 1965-66. Fellow Am. Coll. Obstetricians and Gynecologists (vice chmn. Dist. II 1972-75); mem. Bronx County Obstet. Soc. (pres. 1974), Soc. for Gynecologic Investigation, AAAS, Assn. Profs. of Ob-Gyn., Obstet. Soc. (sec. 1978-80, pres. 1982-83), N.Y. Obstetrical Soc., Soc. Perinatal Physicians, Am. Gynecologic and Obstetric Soc., Am. Gynecol. Obstetrics, N.Y. Obstetics Soc. (pres. 1982), Phi Beta Kappa, Alpha Omega Alpha; hon. mem. Miami Ob-Gyn. Soc., South Atlantic Obstetricians and Gynecologists Soc., Buffalo Gynecologic and Obstetric Soc. (E.G. Winkler meml. lectr.), Croatian Ultrasound Soc. (hon.). Democrat. Jewish. Office: 4605 N A1A Vero Beach FL 32963-1345

SCHULMAN, JOSEPH DANIEL, physician, medical geneticist, executive, reproductive biologist, educator; b. Bklyn., Dec. 20, 1941; s. Max and Miriam (Grossman) S.; m. Dixie A. King; children: Erica N., Julie K. B.A., Bklyn. Coll., 1961; M.D., Harvard U., 1966. Diplomate Am. Bd. Pediatrics, Am. Bd. Ob-Gyn, Am. Bd. Med. Genetics. Intern, resident in pediatrics Mass. Gen. Hosp., Boston, 1966-68; clin. assoc. Nat. Inst. Arthritis and Metabolic Diseases, 1968-70; resident in obstetrics and gynecology and fellow in pediatrics N.Y. Hosp.-Cornell Med. Center, 1970-73; Gilbert and Nat. Found. fellow Cambridge (Eng.) U., 1973-74; head sect. human biochem. genetics Nat. Inst. Child Health and Human Devel., NIH, Bethesda, Md., 1974-83; dir. med. genetics program NIH, Bethesda, Md., 1979-1983; prof. ob/gyn, pediatrics, and genetics George Washington U., 1983-84; dir., CEO Genetics & IVF Inst., Fairfax, Va., 1984—; chmn. Genetics & IVF,

Inc., Bethesda, Md., 1988—; prof. human genetics, pediatrics, obstetrics and gynecology Med. Coll. Va., 1984—; with dept. ob-gyn Fairfax Hosp., 1984—; advisor to numerous govt. and private agys. Author 3 books; contbr. numerous articles to med. jours.; editorial bd. Molecular Human Reproduction, 1995—. Served with USPHS, 1968-70, 74-83. Fellow Am. Coll. Obstetricians and Gynecologists; mem. Soc. Pediatric Research, Soc. Gynecologic Investigation, Am. Soc. Clin. Investigation, Am. Soc. Human Genetics, Am. Fertility Soc., Phi Beta Kappa, Sigma Xi. Clubs: Harvard, Cosmos. Office: 3020 Javier Rd Fairfax VA 22031-4627

SCHULMAN, MARK ALLEN, market research company executive; b. Phila., Nov. 15, 1945; s. Morris and Ida (Dunn) S. AB, Washington Coll., Chestertown, Md., 1967; MA, U. Wis., 1968; PhD, Rutgers U., 1979. Dir., div. experimental studies U. Md. Ea. Shore, Princess Anne, Md., 1972-75; sr. project dir. Eagleton Inst. Poll Rutgers U., New Brunswick, N.J., 1975-77; sr. v.p. Louis Harris and Assocs., Inc., N.Y.C., 1977-81; pres. Schulman, Ronca & Bucuvalas, Inc., N.Y.C., 1981—. Bd. visitors and govs. Washington Coll., 1990—. Mem. Am. Assn. Pub. Opinion Rsch. (pres. N.Y. chpt. 1994-95, sec./treas. 1996-97). Office: Schulman Ronca & Bucuvalas Inc 145 E 32d St New York NY 10016

SCHULMAN, MICHAEL ROBERT, lawyer; b. Washington, Sept. 10, 1946; s. James H. and Doris (Greenfield) S.; m. Joan M. Camperlino, Feb. 18, 1978; children: Douglas James, Jacie Lauren. BA, Carnegie-Mellon U., 1968; MA in Teaching, Duquesne U., 1971, JD cum laude, 1977. Bar: Pa. 1977, Tex. 1980. Math. tchr. Allderdice High Sch., Pitts., 1968-76; legal asst. Wheeling-Pittsburgh Steel Corp., Pitts., 1976-77; law clk. to judge U.S. Dist. Ct. (we. dist.) Pa., Pitts., 1977-79; assoc. Vinson & Elkins, Houston, 1980-83, Johnson & Wortley, P.C., Dallas, 1983-84; ptnr. Johnson & Swanson, Dallas, 1984-95; sr. shareholder Locke Purnell Rain Harrell, P.C., Dallas, 1995—. Mem. Nat. Assn. Bond Lawyers (panelist 1985), Tex. Bar Assn. Avocations: tennis, karate, skiing, running. Office: Locke Purnell Rain Harrell 2200 Ross Ave Ste 2200 Dallas TX 75201-6776

SCHULMAN, ROBERT S., lawyer; b. N.Y.C., July 9, 1941; s. Donald Benedict and Edythe (Smythe) S.; m. Susan Jan Von Helbig, Sept. 18, 1974; children: Elizabeth Jane, Jennifer Lynn. BA, Rutgers Univ, New Brunswick, 1963; JD cum laude, Rutgers Univ, Newark, 1966. Bar: N.J. 1967, Calif. 1976, U.S. Dist. Ct. N.J. 1967, U.S. Supreme Ct. 1970, U.S. Dist. Cts. (ctrl., no., so., ea., dists.) Calif. 1976, U.S. Ct. Appeals (9th cir.) Calif. 1976. With Pitney, Hardin & Kipp, Newark, N.J., 1966-74; dept. atty. gen. Office of N.J. Atty. Gen., Trenton, N.J., 1974-75; assoc. Cox, Castle & Nicholson, L.A., 1976-80; ptnr. Zobrist, Garner & Garrett, L.A., 1980-83, Stephens, Berg, Lasater & Schulman, L.A., 1984-91, Crosby, Heafey, Roach & May, L.A., 1991—; atty. Bd. of Edn., Fairview, N.J., 1972, Bd. of Adjustment, Fairview, N.J., 1971-73. Contbr. articles to profl. jours. dir. Deafwest Theatre, L.A., Calif., 1991—. Mem. State Bar of Calif., San Gabriel Country Club, La Canada Country Club (pres.1987). Republican. Congregationalist. Home: 4229 Mesa Vista Dr La Canada Flintridge CA 91011-3825 Office: Crosby Heafey Roach & May 700 S Flower St Los Angeles CA 90017-4101

SCHULMAN, SIDNEY, neurologist, educator; b. Chgo., Mar. 1, 1923; s. Samuel E. and Ethel (Miller) S.; m. Mary Jean Diamond, June 17, 1945; children—Samuel E., Patricia, Daniel. B.S., U. Chgo., 1944, M.D., 1946. Asst. prof. neurology U. Chgo., 1952-57, asso. prof., 1957-65, prof., 1965-75, Ellen C. Manning prof., div. biol. scis., 1975—. Served with M.C. AUS, 1947-49. Mem. Am. Neurol. Assn., U. Chgo. Med. Alumni Assn. (pres. 1968-69), Chgo. Neurol. Soc. (pres. 1964-65). Home: 5000 S East End Ave Chicago IL 60615-3140 Office: U Chgo Culver Hall 1025 E 57th St Chicago IL 60637-1508

SCHULMAN, TOM, screenwriter. BA, Vanderbilt Univ. Writer: (films) Dead Poets Society, 1989 (Academy award best original screenplay 1989), What About Bob?, 1991; co-writer: (films) Honey, I Shrunk the Kids, 1989, Second Sight, 1989, Medicine Man, 1992; exec. prodr.: (films) Indecent Proposal, 1993. Office: care CAA 9830 Wilshire Blvd Beverly Hills CA 90212-1804

SCHULTE, BRUCE JOHN, lawyer; b. Burlington, Iowa, June 27, 1953; s. James Andrew and Julia Germaine (Van Dale) S.; m. Mary E. Guest, July 1984 (div. Feb. 1995); children: James, John. BA in Am. Studies, U. Notre Dame, 1975; JD, U. Iowa, 1978. Bar: Iowa 1978, U.S. Dist. Ct. (so. dist.) Iowa 1979, U.S. Ct. Appeals (8th cir.) 1982, Minn. 1988, U.S. Dist. Ct. Minn. 1988, Ill. 1989. Law clk. Justice K. David Harris Supreme Ct. Iowa, Des Moines, 1978-79; ptnr. Dailey, Rutwer, Bawer, Schultz & Hahn, Burlington, Iowa, 1979-87; atty. Bennett, Inqvaldson & McInerny, Mpls., 1988; gen. counsel Blackwood Corp., St. Paul, 1988-89; publs. editor Nat. Inst. for Trial Advocacy-U. Notre Dame, Ind., 1989-91; asst. dean pub. affairs Chgo. (Ill.) Kent Coll. Law, 1991-94; dep. dir. assoc. rels. West Pub., Eagan, Minn., 1995—; key person com. ATLA, 1984-88; mem. commn. on jud. dists. Supreme Ct. Iowa, 1987-88; publs. com. Nat. Law Firm Mktg. Assn., 1993-94. Author: Persuasive Expert Testimony, 1990, Lasser Disc Technology in the Courtroom, 1990; editor: Cases and Materials on Evidence, 1991, Modern State and Federal Evidence, 1991, Problems and Cases for Legal Writing, 1991. Mem. state ctrl. com. Iowa Dem. party, 1984-88; devel. com. Frances Xavier Ward Sch., Chgo., 1993—; mem. cmty. task force Chgo. (Ill.) Downtown Circulater Project, 1994—; v.p. pub. affairs U. Notre Dame Alumni Class of 1975. Notre Dame scholar U. Notre Dame, Ind., 1971-72; recipient Spectra award Internat. Assn. Bus. Communicators, 1993, Silver Trumpet, Publicity Club Chgo., 1994. Mem. ABA (mem. tech. com. lawyers conf. jud. adminstrn. divsn. 1995—), Ill. Bar Assn. (standing com. legal edn. and admission to bar 1993—), Chgo. Bar Assn., Assn. Am. Law Schs., Chgo. Pub. Rels. Forum, Notre Dame Club Chgo. (co-chair Hesburgh forum com. 1993—, trustee 1995—). Avocations: sailing, choir, gardening. Home and Office: 10312 S Prospect Ave Chicago IL 60643

SCHULTE, DAVID MICHAEL, investment banker; b. N.Y.C., Nov. 12, 1946; s. Irving and Ruth (Stein) S.; m. Nancy Fisher, June 30, 1968; children: Michael B., Katherine F. BA, Williams Coll., 1968; postgrad., Exeter Coll., Oxford (Eng.) U., 1968-69; JD, Yale U., 1972. Bar: D.C. 1973. Law clk. to Mr. Justice Stewart, U.S. Supreme Ct., 1972-73; spl. asst. to pres. N.W. Industries, Inc., Chgo., 1973-75; v.p. corp. devel. N.W. Industries, Inc., 1975-79, exec. v.p., 1979-80; sr. v.p. Salomon Bros., Chgo., 1980-84; mng. ptnr. Chilmark Ptnrs., Chgo., 1984—. Editor-in-chief: Yale Law Jour, 1971-72. John E. Moody scholar Exeter Coll., Oxford U., 1968-69. Mem. Washington Bar Assn., Chgo. Club, Racquet Club, Bryn Mawr Country Club. Office: Chilmark Ptnrs 2 N Riverside Plz Ste 1500 Chicago IL 60606-2608

SCHULTE, FRANCIS B., archbishop; b. Philadelphia, PA, Dec. 23, 1926. Grad., St. Charles Borromeo Sem. Ordained priest Roman Catholic Ch., 1952. Apptd. titular bishop of Afufenia and aux. bishop of Phila., 1981-85; bishop Wheeling-Charleston, W.Va., 1985-89; archbishop New Orleans, 1989—. Office: 7887 Walmsley Ave New Orleans LA 70125-3431

SCHULTE, FREDERICK JAMES, newpaper editor; b. Mpls., June 6, 1952; s. Philip William and Katherine Louise (Regan) S. BA, U. Va., 1974. Contbg. editor, feature writer Washington Times, 1974-75; news reporter Internat. Med. News Group, Washington, 1976-78; med. writer, gen. assignment reporter Sun-Sentinel, Ft. Lauderdale, Fla., 1978-83, investigative team leader, 1983-88, asst. regional editor, 1988-90, investigations editor, 1990—. Author: Fleeced! Telemarketing Rip-Offs and How to Avoid Them., 1995. Recipient Excellence in Med. Journalism award Fla. Med. Assn., 1983, 1st Pl. Investigative Reporting award Fla. Press Club, 1983, 1st Pl. Sustained Coverage award Inland Daily Press Assn., 1983, Non-deadlin Reporting prize Sigma Delta Chi, 1983, Green Eyeshade award Sigma Delta Chi, 1983, 1st Pl. Pub. Svc. award Fla. Press Club, 1986, 87, 89, 90, Media Merit award Assn. Trial Lawyers Am., 1986, 1st Pl. award Big Bros./Big Sisters Am., 1987, 1st Pl. Pub. Svc. award Fla. Soc. Newspaper Editors, 1987, Children's Express Jounalism award, 1987, 1st Pl. Investigative Reporting award Unity Awards in Media, 1987, Pulitzer Prize finalist, 1987, Worth Bingham Meml. Fund prize, 1989, Cert. of Merit, So. Journalism awards, 1990, Freedom of Info. award AP Mng. Editors Assn., 1990, Lowell Thomas award, 1992, John Hancock award, 1992, Silver Gavel award ABA, 1992, Depth Reporting award Fla. Soc. Newpaper Editors, 1993, Pub. Affairs/Social Issues Reporting award Unity Awards in Media, 1993, George Polk award L.I. U., 1993, Gerald Loeb award U. Calif., 1994. Mem. Investigative Reporters and Editors (S.E. regional coord., Disting. Investigative Reporting award 1985). Office: Sun-Sentinel 200 E Las Olas Blvd Fort Lauderdale FL 33301-2248

SCHULTE, HENRY FRANK, journalism educator; b. Lincoln, Nebr., Sept. 24, 1924; s. Henry F. and Neva Irene (Arnold) S.; m. Irene Nef, May 12, 1951; children: Nancy, Susanne; m. Ann M. Raleigh, Dec. 4, 1993. AB, McGill U., 1951; MS, Columbia, 1952; PhD, U. Ill., 1966. Editor-corr. U.P.I., London, 1954-56; mgr. U.P.I., Spain, 1956-62; assoc. prof. journalism Pa. State U., 1965-69; chmn. newspaper dept. Syracuse (N.Y.) U., 1969-72, prof. journalism, 1980-94; dean Newhouse Sch. Pub. Communications, 1972-80; cons. Nat. Endowment for Arts; dir. WCNY-TV/FM; external examiner U. W.I., 1975-78; cons. external degree program U. State of N.Y. Author: The Spanish Press, 1470-1966: Print, Power and Politics, 1968; Editor, pub.: Mingote's World, 1957. Chmn. Jesse H. Neal awards judging Assn. Bus. Pubs. Served with AUS, 1945-46. Mem. Internat. Press Inst., Inter-Am. Press Assn., Soc. Profl. Journalists, Women in Communications, Assn. for Edn. in Journalism, N.Y. State Soc. Newspaper Editors (exec. sec. 1969-73), Assn. Edn. in Journalism/Am. Newspaper Publishers Assn. (regional liaison officer 1976-81), Overseas Press Club. Club: Hillsboro (Hillsboro Beach, Fla.). Home: 89 Mccoy Rd Jaffrey NH 03452-1662

SCHULTE, HENRY GUSTAVE, college administrator; b. Seattle, Oct. 14, 1920; s. John Henry and Alma (Winter) S.; m. Joan Noel Burton, Aug. 20, 1949; children—Steven Craig, Scott John, Jane Martha. B.A. in Econs. and Bus., U. Wash., 1948. With D.K. MacDonald & Co., Seattle, 1952-67, asst. treas., 1957-60, treas., 1960-67; bus. mgr. legal firm Bogle, Gates, Dobrin, Wakefield & Long, Seattle, 1967; adminstr. Child Devel. and Mental Retardation Ctr. U. Wash., Seattle, 1968-86; mem. steering com. mental retardation research ctrs. group Nat. Inst. Child Health and Human Devel., 1971-85. Mem. exec. bd., treas. Assn. Univ. Affiliated Facilities, 1974-77. Served with AUS, 1940-45. Mem. Soc. Research Adminstrs. (mem. exec. com. 1971-72), Am. Assn. Mental Deficiency. Office: U Wash WJ-10 Seattle WA 98195

SCHULTE, JEFFREY LEWIS, lawyer; b. N.Y.C., July 24, 1949; s. Irving and Ruth (Stein) S.; m. Elizabeth Ewan Kaiser, Aug. 13, 1977; children: Andrew Riggs, Ian Garretson, Elizabeth Alexandra. BA, Williams Coll., 1971; postgrad., Harvard U., 1971-72; JD, Yale U., 1976. Bar: Pa. 1978, Ga. 1993. Law clk. to hon. John J. Gibbons U.S. Ct. Appeals (3d cir.), Newark, 1976-77; assoc. Schnader, Harrison, Segal & Lewis, Phila., 1977-84, ptnr., 1985-92; founding ptnr. Schnader, Harrison, Segal & Lewis, Atlanta, 1992—. Contbr. articles to profl. jours. Bd. dirs. North Ardmore (Pa.) Civic Assn., pres., 1990; bd. dirs. Main Line YMCA, chmn., 1989-91; active Ardmore (Pa.) Alliance Project. Mem. ABA, Pa. Bar Assn., State Bar Ga., Phila. Bar Assn., Atlanta Bar Assn. (chmn. comm. and media rels. com.), World Trade Ctr. Atlanta, Atlanta Venture Forum, Bus. and Tech. Alliance, Yale Club of Ga., Williams Club Atlanta, Merion Cricket Club, Weekapaug Yacht Club (R.I.), Weekapaug Tennis Club, Phi Beta Kappa. Office: Schnader Harrison Segal & Lewis Ste 2800 303 Peachtree St NE Atlanta GA 30308-3252

SCHULTE, JOSEPHINE HELEN, historian, educator; b. Foley, Ala., May 9, 1929; d. Mathias and Theresia (Honner) S. AA, Sacred Heart Jr. Coll., Cullman, Ala., 1949; BS in History, Spring Hill Coll., 1957; MA in History, U. So. Miss., 1961; MA in German, Trinity U., San Antonio, 1976; PhD in History, Loyola U., Chgo., 1969. Steamship agt. Gulf Steamship Agy., Mobile, Ala., 1949-58; translator banks in Mobile, 1949-62; German tchr. Brookley Field AFB, Mobile, 1951-62; adminstrv. asst., rsch. assoc. So. Inst. Mgmt., Louisville, 1959-60; spl. lectr. Spring Hill Coll., Mobile, 1960-63; teaching fellow Loyola U., Chgo., 1962-66; asst. prof. Latin Am. history U. of Americas, Mexico City, 1967-70; from assoc. prof. to prof. St. Mary's U., San Antonio, 1970—, coord. Latin Am. studies program, 1972-90, grad. advisor in history, 1973-94; invited to read a paper Internat. Coloquy, U. Lima, Peru, 1991, U. Yucatan, Mex., 1992, U. Maritima, Valparaiso, Chile, 1993; book reviewer. Author: (with Raymond Schmandt) Civil War Chaplains--A Document From A Jesuit Community, 1962, The Spring Hill College Diary, 1861-65, Gabino Barreda y su mision diplomatica en Alemania, 1878-79 Historia Mexicana, 1974; translator: El Positivismo en Mexico, 1974. Grantee OAS, 1966-67, Newberry Library, 1978, Spanish Govt. and OAS, 1981-82; Fulbright grantee, 1983. Mem. Southwestern Conf. L.Am. Studies, German Geneal. Soc., Cath. Hist. Assn., Gottscheer Rsch. Assn. (bd. dirs.). Roman Catholic. Avocations: photography, genealogy, crocheting, collecting postcards and slides, travel. Home: 1415 Babcock Rd San Antonio TX 78201-6640

SCHULTE, STEPHEN CHARLES, lawyer; b. Evanston, Ill., June 26, 1952; s. George John and Mary Ruth (Lamping) S.; m. Kathleen Ann O'Donnell, Sept. 4, 1982; children: Kate, Maureen, John. BA magna cum laude, St. Louis U., 1973, JD, 1976. Bar: Ill. 1976, U.S. Dist. Ct. (no. dist.) Ill. 1976, U.S. Ct. Appeals (7th cir.) 1991. Atty. Perz & McGuire, Chgo., 1976-83; ptnr. Winston & Strawn, Chgo., 1983—. Founder, bd. dirs. Greater Orgn. for Less Fortunate (GOLF), Chgo., 1982—; fundraiser for Maryville Acad.; mem. Glenview Park Dist. Commn., 1989—, v.p., 1991-92, pres., 1992-93. Mem. ABA, Ill. State Bar Assn., Chgo. Bar Assn., Ill. Trial Lawyers Assn., Ill. Assn. Def. Trial Counsel, Chgo. Vol. Legal Svcs., Nat. Legal Aid Defender Assn., Phi Beta Kappa. Avocations: basketball, baseball, golf, music, travel. Home: 1222 Pine St Glenview IL 60025-2918 Office: Winston & Strawn 35 W Wacker Dr Chicago IL 60601-1614

SCHULTE, STEPHEN JOHN, lawyer, educator; b. N.Y.C., July 7, 1938; s. John and Marjorie (Fried) S.; m. Patricia Walker, June 6, 1962 (div.); children: Susan Jean, Jeffrey David, Elizabeth Ann; m. Margaret Van Doren Cook, Mar. 12, 1975. BA, Brown U., 1960; JD, Columbia U., 1963. Bar: N.Y. 1964. Assoc. Lowenstein, Pitcher, Hochkiss & Parr, N.Y.C., 1963-66, Fried, Frank, Harris, Shriver & Jacobson, N.Y.C., 1966-69; founding ptnr. Schulte Roth & Zabel, N.Y.C., 1969—; also chmn. corp. dept. Schulte, Roth & Zabel, N.Y.C.; adj. prof. law Benjamin N. Cardozo Law Sch., Yeshiva U., 1992—, bd. dirs., 1995—; adj. prof. law Fordham U., 1992—; lectr. securities law field; panelist various forums. Trustee Choate Rosemary Hall Sch., Wallingford, Conn., 1982—, chmn. investment and fin. com., 1984-85, chmn. devel. com., 1985-86, chmn. nominating com., 1986-89, chmn. bd. trustees, 1990-95. Mem. ABA, N.Y. State Bar Assn. (com. on securities regulation), Assn. Bar City N.Y. (com. on securities regulation, chmn. subcom. on disclosure policy and tender offers), Norfolk Country Club. Office: Schulte Roth & Zabel 900 3rd Ave New York NY 10022-4728

SCHULTES, RICHARD EVANS, retired botanist, biology educator; b. Boston, Jan. 12, 1915; s. Otto Richard and Maude Beatrice (Bagley) S.; m. Dorothy Crawford McNeil, Mar. 26, 1959; children: Richard Evans II, Neil Parker and Alexandra Ames (twins). AB cum laude, Harvard U., 1937, AM, 1938, PhD, 1941; MH (hon.), Universidad Nacional de Colombia, Bogotá, 1953; DSci (hon.), Mass. Coll. Pharmacy, 1987. Plant explorer, NRC rsch. fellow Harvard Bot. Mus., Cambridge, Mass., 1941-42; research asso. Harvard Bot. Mus., 1942-53; curator Orchid Herbarium of Oakes Ames, 1953-58, curator econ. botany, 1958-85, exec. dir., 1967-70, dir., 1970-85; Guggenheim Found. fellow, collaborator U.S. Dept. Agr., Amazon of Colombia, 1942-43; plant explorer in S.Am., Bur. Plant Industry, 1944-54; prof. biology Harvard U., 1970-72, Paul C. Mangelsdorf prof. natural scis., 1973-81, Edward C. Jeffrey prof. biology, 1981-85, emeritus prof., 1985—; adj. prof. pharmacognosy U. Ill., Chgo., 1975—; Hubert Humphrey vis. prof. Macalaster Coll., 1979; field agt. Rubber Devel. Corp. of U.S. Govt., in S.Am., 1943-44; collaborator Instituto Agronômico Norte, Belém, Brazil, 1948-50; hon. prof. Universidad Nacional de Colombia, 1953—, prof. econ. botany, 1963; bot. cons. Smith, Kline & French Co., Phila., 1957-67; mem. NIH Adv. Panel, 1964; mem. selection com. for Latin Am. Guggenheim Found., 1964-85; mem. sci. adv. bd. Palm Oil Rsch. Inst., Malaysia, 1980-89; mem. sci. adv. bd. Shaman Pharmaceuticals, 1988—; chmn. Ethnobotany Specialist Group, Internat. Union Nature, Switzerland; chmn. on-site visit U. Hawaii Natural Products Grant NIH, 1966, Deutche Gesellschaft für Arzneiphanzenforchung, Berlin, 1967, III Internat. Pharm. Congress, São Paulo, I Amazonian Biol. Symposium, Belém, Brazil, Symposium Ethnpharmacologic Search for Psychoactive drugs, San Francisco, others; Laura L. Barnes Annual lectr. Morris Arboretum, Phila., 1969; Koch lectr. Rho Chi Soc., Pitts., 33d Internat. Congress Pharm. Sci., Stockholm, 1971; vis. prof. econ. botany, plants in relation to man's progress Jardín Botánico, Medellín, Colombia, 1973; Cecil and Ida H. Green vis. lectr. U. B.C., Vancouver, Can., 1974; co-organizer Internat. Symposium Erythdroxylon, Equador, 1979, co-dir. phase VII Alpha Helix Rsch. plant medicines Witoto, Bora Indianas, Peru, 1977, 2d Philip Morris Symposium, Richmond, Va., 1975, I Solanacese Conf., U. Birmingham, Eng., 1977, Soc. of Americanists, Manchester, Eng., 1982, Salah Workshop for Conservation of Wildlands, Sultanate of Oman, 1983, Symposium of Environ. Protection, 1992, Etnobotanica-92, Córdoba, Spain, 1992, Spruce Meml. Symposium, Castle Howard, Yorkshire, Eng., 1993, INDERENA Bogotá, 1988, others; organizer Internat. Symposium Erythroxylon, Equador, 1979; vis. scholar Rockefeller Study Conf. Centre, Bellagio, Italy, 1980, 88; cons. Rubber Rsch. Inst., Malaysia, 1988—. Author: (with P. A. Vestal) Economic Botany of the Kiowa Indians, 1941, Native Orchids of Trinidad and Tobago, 1960, (with A. F. Hill) Plants and Human Affairs, 1960, rev. edit., 1968, (with A. S. Pease) Generic Names of Orchids—their Origin and Meaning, 1963, (with A. Hofmann) The Botany and Chemistry of Hallucinogens, 1973, rev. edit., 1980, Hallucinogenic Plants, 1976, Plants of the Gods, 1979, Plant Hallucinogens, 1976, (with W.A. Davis) The Glass Flowers at Harvard, 1982, Where the Gods Reign, 1987, El Reino de los Dioses, 1988, (with R.F. Raffauf) The Healing Forest, 1990, Vine of the Soul: Medicine Men of the Colombian Amazon—Their Plants and Rituals, 1992; contbg. author: Ency. Biol. Scis, 1961, Ency. Brit, 1966, 83, Ency. Biochemistry, 1967, McGraw-Hill Yearbook Sci., Tech, 1937-85, New Royal Horticulture Dictionary (ethnobotany chpt., 1992); author numerous Harvard Bot. Mus. Leaflets.; Asst. editor: Chronica Botanica, 1947-52; editor: Bot. Mus. Leaflets, 1957-85, Econ. Botany, 1962-79; mem. editorial bd. Lloydia, 1965-76, Altered States of Consciousness, 1973—, Jour. Psychedelic Drugs, 1974—; co-editor: series Psychoactive Plants of the World, Yale U. Press, 1987—; mem. adv. bd.: Horticulture, 1976-78, Jour. Ethnopharmacology, 1978—, Soc. Pharmacology, 1976—, Elaeis, 1988—, Flora of Ecuador, 1976—, Jour. Latin Am. Folklore, Ethnobotany (India) (also founding mem.), 1989—, Environ. Awareness (India) 1988—, Bol. Mus. Goeldi (Brazil), 1987—, Environ. Conservation (Geneva), 1987—; contbr. numerous articles to profl. jours. Mem. governing bd. Amazonas 2000, Bogotá; assoc. in ethnobotany Museo del Oro, Bogotá, 1974—; chmn. NRC panels, 1974, 75; mem. NRC Workshops on Natural Products, Sri Lanka, 1975, participant numerous sems., congresses, meetings; mem. adv. bd. Fitzhugh Ludlow Libr., Native Land Found., 1980, Morgan Meml. Archives Chadron State Coll., 1987—, Albert Hofmann Found.; v.p. Margeret Mee Amazon Trust, Royal Bot. Gardens. Decorated Orden de Victoria Regia, Cruz de Boyacá (Colombia); recipient award, 1981, gold medal for conservation presented by Duke of Edinburgh, 1984, Tyler prize for environ. achievement, 1984, Mass. Gov.'s recognition award Nat. Sci. Week, 1985, cert. of merit Bot. Soc. Am., 1991, Jannaki-Ammal medal, 1992, Linnean medal, 1992, medal Harvard U., 1992, Martín de la Cruz medal, 1992, George Sobert Unite Medal of Honor, Mass. Hortucultural Soc., 1995; grantee Rockefeller Found., 1982. Fellow Am. Acad. Arts and Scis., Am. Coll. Neuropsychopharmacology (sci. spkr. San Juan, P.R. 1984), Third World Acad. Scis., Acad. Scis. India, Internat. Soc. Naturalists; mem. NAS, Linnean Soc. (London), Academia Colombiana Ciéncias Exactas, Fisico-Quimicas y Naturales, Inst. Ecuatoriano Ciéncias Naturales, Soc. Sci. Antonio Alzate (Mexico), Argentine Acad. Scis., Am. Orchid Soc. (life hon.), Pan Am. Soc. New Eng., Soc. Mexicana Micologie (hon.), Assn. Amigos Jardines Botánicos (life), Soc. Econ. Botany (organizer ann. meeting 1961, Disting. Botanist of Yr. 1979), New Eng. Bot. Club (pres. 1954-60), Internat. Assn. Plant Taxonomy, Am. Acad. Achievement, Am. Soc. Pharmacognosy, Phytochem. Soc. N.Am., Soc. Colombiana Orquideologia, Soc. Ethnobot. India, Assn. Tropical Biology, Internat. Soc. Ethnobiology, Soc. Cubana Botánica, Sigam Xi (pres. Harvard chpt. 1971-72, medal 1985), Phi Beta Kappa, Beta Nu chpt. Phi Sigma (first hon.). Unitarian (vestryman Kings Chapel, Boston 1974-76, 82-85). Home: 78 Larchmont Rd Melrose MA 02176-2906 Office: Bot Museum Harvard U Cambridge MA 02138

SCHULTESS, LEROY KENNETH, lawyer, consultant; b. Garrett, Ind., May 7, 1907; s. George Mathias and Elizabeth (Lehmbeck) S.; m. Sarah Mildred Atwater, Apr. 28, 1942. AB, Mich. U., 1929; JD, Northwestern U., 1932. Bar: Ind. 1933. Practice law, LaGrange, Ind.; pres. Creek Chub Bait Co., Garrett, Lure, Inc., Garrett; hon. dir. Farmers State Bank, LaGrange. Recipient Meritorious awards Farmers State Bank, VFW, Boy Scouts Am., Am. Lung Assn. Mem. U. Mich. Alumni Assn., LaGrange C. of C., ABA, Ind. Bar Assn. (Golden Anniversary award), LaGrange County Bar Assn. (Outstanding and Dedicated Svc. awards), Sigma Chi, Phi Delta Phi. Clubs: Rotary (LaGrange) (pres. 1956-7), LaGrange Country. Lodges: Shriners, Masons. Home: 414 W Michigan St Lagrange IN 46761-1710 Office: Farmers State Bank Bldg 220 S Detroit St Lagrange IN 46761-1808

SCHULTHEIS, EDWIN MILFORD, dean, business educator; b. N.Y.C., Apr. 15, 1928; s. Milford Theodore and Lillian May (Hill) S.; BS, Hofstra Coll., 1950; MBA, N.Y. U. Grad. Sch. Bus. Adminstrn., 1958, EdD, Sch. Edn., 1972; m. Joan Edna Bruckner, June 23, 1956. Officer mgr., sales rep. Topton Rug Mfg. Co., N.Y.C., 1950-54; area mgr., trainer Mobil Oil Co., N.Y.C., 1954-62; coord. distributive edn. North Babylon (N.Y.) Pub. Schs., 1962-88; prof. bus. adminstrn. SUNY, Farmingdale, 1970-91; asst. prof. edn. NYU, 1973—; dir. edn. Syracuse (N.Y.) U., 1973-78; chmn. bus. mktg. and indsl. edn. depts. North Babylon (N.Y.) Pub. Schs., 1988-91, chmn. dept. bus. adminstrn. Five Towns Coll., Seaford, N.Y., 1991-92; divsn. chmn. bus. and tech. Five Towns Coll., Dix Hills, N.Y., 1992—, dean instrn., 1993—, dep. dean of faculty, 1993—; test writer, cons. N.Y. State Dept. Edn., Albany, 1965—; textbook reviewer McGraw-Hill Book Co., N.Y.C., 1967-69; cons. Cornell U., 1975; dist. adviser Distributive Edn. Clubs N.Y., 1970, bd. govs. , trustee, 1975-78; mem. curriculum adv. council Suffolk County (N.Y.) Distributive Edn. Assn., 1967—. Author: Content and Structure of Belief-Disbelief Systems, 1972. Elder Presbyn. Ch., U.S.A. Named N.Y. State Tchr. of Yr., 1976; Outstanding Tchr. in N.Y. State, 1978; recipient Outstanding Svc. award Distributive Edn. Clubs. N.Y., Suffolk County Distributive Edn. Assn., Tchr. Excellence award N.Y. State, 1980, Citation for Excellence in Edn. Gov. Mario Cuomo N.Y., 1991, Citation Excellence in Teaching Babylon Twp., 1991. Mem. Acad. Mgmt., Am. Petroleum Inst., Am. Security Coun., Suffolk County Assn. Distributive Edn. Tchrs. (mem. exec. bd. 1962-74), N.Y. State (pres. 1975-78), L.I. Distributive Edn. Assns. (hon. life, exec. bd. 1972-75), N.Y. State Occupational Edn. Assn. (v.p. 1975-78), L.I. Bus. Edn. Chmns. Assn. (hon. life), Distributive Edn. Clubs Am. (regional leader 1972-75, hon. life 1991), Phi Delta Kappa, Kappa Delta Pi, Sigma Alpha Lambda. Presbyterian (ordained ruling elder). Club: Bellport (N.Y.) Golf. Author: Modern Petroleum Marketing, 1971. Home: 14 Thorn Hedge Rd Bellport NY 11713-2616 Office: Five Towns Coll Dix Hills NY 11746-6055

SCHULTZ, ALBERT BARRY, engineering educator; b. Phila., Oct. 10, 1933; s. George D. and Belle (Seidman) S.; m. Susan Resnikov, Aug. 25, 1955; children—Carl, Adam, Robin. B.S., U. Rochester, 1955; M.Engring., Yale U., 1959, Ph.D., 1962. Asst. prof. U. Del., Newark, 1962-65; asst. prof. U. Ill., Chgo., 1965-66, assoc. prof., 1966-71, prof., 1971-83; Vennema prof. U. Mich., Ann Arbor, 1983—. Contbr. numerous articles to profl. jours. Served to lt. USN, 1955-58. Rsch. Career award NIH, 1975-80; Javits Neurosci. Investigator award NIH, 1985-92. Mem. NAE, Internat. Soc. for Study of Lumbar Spine (pres. 1981-82), ASME (chmn. bioengring. div. 1981-82, H.R. Lissner award 1990), Am. Soc. of Biomechanics (pres. 1982-83), U.S. Nat. Com. on Biomechanics (chmn. 1982-85), Phi Beta Kappa. Office: U Mich 3112 GG Brown Lab Ann Arbor MI 48109-2125

SCHULTZ, ANDREW SCHULTZ, JR., industrial engineering educator; b. Harrisburg, Pa., Aug. 14, 1913; s. Andrew S. and Ada (DeHaven) S.; m. Mary S. Mory, Sept. 2, 1939; children: Susan Tapscott, Andrew M. Student, Phillips (Andover) Acad., 1928-32; B.S., Cornell U., 1936, Ph.D., 1941. Installer N.J. Bell Telephone Co., 1936-37; instr. Sibley Sch. Mech. Engring., Coll. Engring. Cornell U., 1937-41, asst. prof., 1941-46, asso. prof., 1946-50, prof., head dept. indsl. and engring. adminstrn., 1950-62; dean Coll. Engring. Cornell U., 1963-72, acting dean, 1978, Spencer T. Olin prof. engring., 1973-80, emeritus, 1980—; v.p. Logistics Mgmt. Inst., Wash., 1962-63; chmn. bd. trustees Logistics Mgmt. Inst., 1972-84, trustee, 1985-89. Bd. dirs. Engring. Council Profl. Devel., 1968-73. Served as lt. col. AUS, 1941-46; indsl. service ammunition div. Office Chief Ordnance. Fellow Am. Inst. Indsl. Engrs. (dir. research 1955-62); mem. Am. Soc. Engring. Edn., Triangle, Tau Beta Pi, Pi Tau Sigma, Phi Gamma Delta. Home: 100 Vicars Landing Way PH 1 Ponte Vedra Beach FL 32082-3127

SCHULTZ, ARTHUR JOSEPH, JR., retired trade association executive; b. Detroit, June 20, 1918; s. Arthur Joseph and Olive U. (Beauchesne) S.; m. Barbara Farnan, Aug. 20, 1942; children: Arthur, Robert, William, Barbara, John, Karen. Student, Naval War Coll., 1956-57, Brookings Inst., 1962, Naval Line Sch., 1947-48, U. Detroit, 1937-39. Joined U.S. Navy, 1940, commd. ensign, 1940, advanced through grades to capt., 1950; comdg. officer Com. Strike/S. NATO, Verona, Italy, 1959-61, Naval Air Sta., Grosse Ile, Mich., 1961-63, ret., 1963; pres. Chrysler Corp. subs., Highland Park, Mich., 1971-75; dep. adminstr. VA, Washington, 1975-77; pres. Steel Shipping Container Inst., Union, N.J., 1977-89; ret., 1989. Vice pres. Detroit Aviation Commn., 1968-77; bd. dirs. United Way Union County, Elizabeth, N.J., 1981-85, sec./treas., 1983-85; chmn. Hazardous Materials Adv. Com., Washington, 1984-85. Decorated Navy Cross; recipient Meritorious Service award VA, 1977. Mem. Am. Soc. Assn. Execs., Soc. Automotive Engrs., Mil. Order World Wars, Boca Royale Golf and Country Club (Fla.). Republican. Roman Catholic. Home: 55 Cayman Isles Blvd Englewood FL 34223-1832

SCHULTZ, ARTHUR LEROY, clergyman, educator; b. Johnstown, Pa., June 14, 1928; s. Elmer Albert Robert and Alice Lizetta (Flegal) S.; m. Mildred Louise Stouffer, Nov. 29, 1948; children: Thomas Arthur, Rebecca Louise. BA, Otterbein Coll., 1949; MDiv, United Theol. Sem., 1952; MEd, U. Pitts., 1955, PhD, 1963. Sr. min. Albright United Meth. Ch., Pitts., 1952-56; dir. pub. rels. Otterbein Coll., Westerville, Ohio, 1956-65, adj. prof. religion and philosophy, 1990--; pres. Albright Coll., Reading, Pa., 1965-77, Ashland (Ohio) Coll., 1977-80; exec. dir. Cen. Ohio Radio Reading Svc., Columbus, 1980-84; parish min. Ch. Master United Meth., Westerville, 1984-89; min. of visitation Ch. Messiah United Meth., Westerville, 1991—; pres. Pa. Assn. Colls. & Univs., Harrisburg, 1974-75. Trustee Reading Hosp., 1967-77, Wyoming Sem., Kingston, Pa., 1971-80; v.p. Found. for Ind. Colls. Pa., Harrisburg, 1972-73; pres. Pa. Coun. on Alcohol Problems, Harrisburg, 1968-76; pres. Westerville (Ohio) Hist. Soc., 1986-89, Westerville Area Ministerial Assn., 1992-93. Named Outstanding Young Man of the Year Jr. C. of C., Westerville, Ohio, 1960. Mem. Brookstone Cmty. Assn. (sec. bd. trustees 1994—), Rotary (charter pres. 1959, dist. gov. 1965-66, dist. sec.-treas. 1982-93), Masons, Shriners, Torch Club. Republican. Methodist. Avocations: collecting post cards, golf, tennis, travel. Home: 151 Sandstone Loop Westerville OH 43081-4579

SCHULTZ, ARTHUR WARREN, communications company executive; b. N.Y.C., Jan. 13, 1922; s. Milton Warren and Genevieve (Dann) S.; grad. U. Chgo.; D.Letters (hon.), Rosary Coll.; m. Elizabeth Carroll Mahan, 1949 (div. 1987); children—Arthur Warren, John Carroll (dec.), Julia Hollingsworth; m. Susan Keefe, 1988. With Foote, Cone & Belding Communications, Chgo., 1948-82, v.p., 1957-63, sr. v.p., dir., 1963-69, exec. v.p., 1969, chmn. bd., CEO, 1970-81, chmn. exec. com., CEO, 1981-82; dir. Chgo. Sun-Times Co., Folger Adams Co.; vice chmn. Chgo. Sun-Times Newspaper Co., 1989-94. Pres. Cook County Sch. Nursing, 1963-64, Welfare Council Met. Chgo., 1965-67; mem. bus. adv. council Urban League Chgo., 1971-82; chmn. Nat. Com. to Save Am.'s Cultural Collections, 1990-94; mem. Pres.'s Com. on Arts and Humanities, 1984-93; bd. dirs. Chgo. Crime Commn., 1965-71, Community Fund Chgo., 1966-67, Better Bus. Bur., 1970-78, Lyric Opera Chgo., 1967-77, Chgo. Council Fgn. Relations, 1977-86, Chgo. Public TV, 1978-82, Chgo. Central Area Com., 1978-82; trustee YWCA, 1962-74, Calif. Coll. Arts and Crafts, 1985-87; trustee Art Inst. Chgo., 1975—, chmn. bd., 1981-84; trustee U. Chgo., 1977—, Santa Barbara Mus. Art, 1988—, pres., 1989-92. Editor Caring for Your Collections. Served to 1st lt. USAAF, 1943-45. Recipient Alumni Service award U. Chgo., 1986. Mem. Am. Assn. Advt. Agys. (dir. 1968-71, 74-76, chmn. Chgo. council 1964-65, chmn. Central region 1970-71), Delta Kappa Epsilon. Episcopalian. Clubs: Commercial, Old Elm, Valley (Montecito, Calif.), Birnam Wood. Home and Office: 2072 China Flat Rd Santa Barbara CA 93108-2211

SCHULTZ, BRYAN CHRISTOPHER, dermatologist, educator; b. Evergreen Park, Ill., June 29, 1949; s. Warren H. and Norinne A. (McNamara) S.; m. Cathleen T. Fitzgerald, May 14, 1977; children: Carrie T., Megan C., Erin L. B.S., Loyola U., Chgo., 1971; M.D., Loyola Stritch Sch. Medicine, 1974. Diplomate Am. Bd. Dermatology. Intern St. Joseph's Hosp., Chgo., 1975; resident Northwestern U., Chgo., 1976-79; assoc. clin. prof. Loyola U., Maywood, Ill., 1979—; practice medicine specializing in dermatology, Oak Park, Ill., 1979—; cons. dermatologist West Suburban Hosp., Oak Park Hosp., Gottlieb Hosp., Westlake Hosp., MacNeal Hosp., 1979—. Author: Office Practice of Skin Surgery, 1985. Patentee surgical instrument. Contbr. articles to sci. publs. Supr., founder pub. awareness program for skin cancer Loyola U. Stritch Sch. Medicine, 1983—; operator Ultraviolet-Ozone meter, Ill., 1983—. Mem. Am. Acad. Dermatology, Am. Soc. Dermatologic Surgery, Internat. Soc. Dermatologic Surgery, Soc. Investigative Dermatology, Chgo. Dermatologic Soc., AMA (del. intern and resident sect. 1975), Ill. Dermatologic Soc. (exec. com. 1981, chmn. membership com. 1983-84), Soc. Cosmetic Chemists, Royal Soc. Medicine, Alpha Sigma Nu. Office: Affil in Dis & Skin Surg SC 159 Westgate Oak Park IL 60301

SCHULTZ, CARL HERBERT, real estate management and development company executive; b. Chgo., Jan. 9, 1925; s. Herbert V. and Olga (Swanson) S.; m. Helen Ann Stevesson, June 6, 1948; children: Mark Carl, Julia Ann. B.S. in Gen. Engring., Iowa State U., 1948. With Schultz Bros. Co., 1948—; mdse. mgr. and store planner Schultz Bros. Co., Chgo., 1962-70; v.p. Schultz Bros. Co., Lake Zurich, Ill., 1968-72; pres. Schultz Bros. Co., 1972—, Ill. Schultz Bros. Co., Ind. Schultz Bros. Co., Iowa Schultz Bros. Co., Wis. Schultz Bros. Co. Mem. Lake Bluff (Ill.) Zoning Bd. Appeals, 1976-85, chmn., 1978-85. Served with U.S. Army, 1944-46. Mem. Lake Zurich Indsl. Coun. (sec. 1976), Assn. Gen. Mdse. Chains (dir. 1975-86, exec. com. 1983-86, chmn. nat. conv. 1982), Ill. Retail Mchts. Assn. (dir. 1984-89), Wis. Retail Fedn. (dir. 1981-89). Presbyterian. Club: Bath and Tennis (Lake Bluff). Home: 701 E Center Ave Lake Bluff IL 60044-2607 Office: 785 Oakwood Rd Ste 102S Lake Zurich IL 60047-1549

SCHULTZ, CARMEN HELEN, copywriter, translator; b. Caracas, Venezuela, Jan. 22, 1962; came to U.S., 1975; d. Arthur Henry and Alicia M. (Mercedes) S. BA in Fgn. Langs. cum laude, So. Meth. U., 1984; postgrad., U. Tex., Dallas, 1987—, Monterey Inst. Internat. Study, 1987-94; Bus. Cert., U. Tex., Austin, 1995. Tech. translator Mobil Oil Exploration & Producing Svcs., Dallas, 1984-85; freelance translator/interpreter Dallas, 1985-87; abstractor/rsch. asst. Rand Corp., Santa Monica, Calif., 1987; Hispanic comm. coord. Mary Kay Cosmetics, Inc., Dallas, 1987-93; bilingual copywriter Rapp Collins Worldwide, Irving, Tex., 1993-94; translator/copy editor Ornelas & Assocs., Dallas, 1994-95; translator/writer Assocs. Corp. of N.Am., Irving, 1995—. Editor/translator: Belleza Total, 1992 (Internat. Mercury award); founder, editor (newsletter) Entérate, 1988 (Hispanic 100 1990, 91); contbg. writer Applause, 1992 (Award of Merit IPBC). So. Meth. U. scholar, 1980-84. Mem. Am. Translators Assn., Am. Lit. Translators Assn., Metroplex Interpreters and Translators Assn., Dallas Hispanic C. of C., Pi Delta Phi, Sigma Delta Pi. Roman Catholic. Home: 7008 Town Bluff Dr Dallas TX 75248-5524 Office: Assocs Corp NAm 250 Carpenter Freeway Irving TX 75062

SCHULTZ, CLARENCE CARVEN, JR., sociology educator; b. Temple, Tex., Oct. 31, 1924; s. Clarence Carven Sr. and Bea Alice (Newton) S.; m. Margie Frances Beran, Oct. 29, 1943; children: Timothy Wayne, Theresa Bea. BS, SW Tex. State U., 1948, MA, 1949; PhD, U. Tex., 1970; AA (hon.), Lee Coll., 1989. Adminstrv. asst. Interstate Theatres, Temple, 1941-42; advt. sales rep. Temple Daily Telegram, 1942-43; asst. mgr. McClellan Stores, Tex., 1946-47; history and sociology instr. S.W. Tex. State U., San Marcos, 1949-52, from asst. prof. to prof., 1965-90, prof. emeritus, 1991; chmn. dept. sociology and anthropology SW Tex. State U., San Marcos, 1971-76, dean Sch. Liberal Arts, 1977-78; teaching fellow U. Tex., Austin, 1952-53; mem. faculty Lee Coll., Baytown, Tex., 1953-65, chmn. div. social scis., 1961-65; curriculum cons. to various pub. schs.; presenter workshops in field. Author: Practical Probation: Handbook, 1972; editor: Family Perspectives, 1975; contbr. articles to prof. jours., chpt. to book. Ens. USNR, 1943-46. Recipient S.W. Tex. Pedogog Teaching Excellence award, 1973, 74, Disting. Tchr. award S.W. Tex. State U. Alumni Assn., 1976, S.W. Tex. Presdl. award for excellence in teaching, 1985, Award of Honor, S.W. Tex. State U. Alumni Assn., 1991; named Piper Prof., Minnie Stevens Piper Found., 1976, Outstanding Former Instr., Lee Coll. Former Students' Assn., 1988; appointed Adm. in Tex. Navy by State Gov., 1969. Mem. NEA-Ret., Tex. Ret. Tchrs. Assn., Tex. State Tchrs. Assn., San Marcos Area Ret. Tchrs., Alpha Chi, Alpha Kappa Delta. Methodist. Home: 604 Franklin Dr San Marcos TX 78666-2426 Office: SW Tex State U Dept Sociology Anthrop San Marcos TX 78666

SCHULTZ, CLARENCE JOHN, minister; b. Morris Twp., Wis., Aug. 4, 1937; s. Clarence John Sr. and Ella Mae (Feavel) S.; m. Doroland Kay King, Aug. 24, 1957 (dec. Jan. 1974); children: Sharon Kay, Susan May Schultz Rogers; m. Martha Ann Aylor, Apr. 5, 1975. BS, Bryan Coll., 1960. Ordained to ministry Conservative Congl. Ch., 1961. Min. 1st Congl. Ch., Herreid, S.D., 1961-66, Immanuel Evang. Congl. Ch., Sheboygan, Wis., 1966-77, Hope Congl. Ch., Superior, Wis., 1977-83, Zion Evang. Ch., Scottsbluff, Nebr., 1983-89; min. 1st Congl. Ch., Buffalo Center, Iowa, 1989-92, Kenosha, Wis., 1992—. Mem. Conservative Congl. Christian Conf. (rec. sec. 1973-82, v.p. 1994-96, Rocky Mountain area rep. 1987-89, endorser of chaplains 1988—, mem. credentials com. 1988—), Rotary (mem. ch. chaplain com. 1993-95). Avocations: amateur radio, golf. Home: 7023 Pershing Blvd Kenosha WI 53142 Office: First Congl Ch 5934 8th Ave Kenosha WI 53140

SCHULTZ, DEAN M., finance company executive; b. 1947. AB, Colgate U., 1969; JD, Georgetown U., 1972. Ptnr. Robinson, Williams & Angeloff Law Firm, Rochester, N.Y., 1973-80; with First Fed. Savings & Loan Assn., Rochester, 1980-84; sr. v.p., gen. counsel FHLB, N.Y.C., 1984-86, exec. v.p., 1986-91; pres., CEO Fed. Home Loan Bank, San Francisco, 1991—. Office: Fed Home Loan Bank 600 California St San Francisco CA 94108-2704*

SCHULTZ, DENNIS BERNARD, lawyer; b. Detroit, Oct. 15, 1946; s. Bernard George and Madeline Laverne (Riffenberg) S.; m. Andi Lynn Leslie, Apr. 18, 1967; 1 child, Karanne Anne. BS, Wayne State U., 1970; JD, Detroit Coll. Law, 1977. Bar: Mich. 1977, U.S. Dist. Ct. (ea. dist.) Mich., U.S. Ct. Appeals (6th cir.), U.S. Dist. Ct. (we. dist.) Pa. V.p. Barkay Bldg. Co., Ferndale, Mich., to 1976; law clk. Hon. George N. Bashara, Mich. Ct. Appeals, Detroit, 1977; shareholder Butzel Long, Detroit, 1978—. Editor Detroit Coll. Law Rev., 1977. Detroit Coll. Law Alumni Assn. scholar, 1976, Mich. Consolidated Gas Co. scholar, 1977. Mem. Detroit Bar Assn., Mich. Bar Assn. Republican. Roman Catholic. Avocations: boating, biking, golf. Office: Butzel Long 150 W Jefferson Ave Ste 900 Detroit MI 48226-4415

SCHULTZ, DOUGLAS GEORGE, art museum director; b. Oakland, Calif., Oct. 3, 1947; s. Leon H. and Teresa (deMonte) S. A.B., U. Calif., Berkeley, 1969, M.A. in History of Art, 1972; grad., Inst. Arts Adminstrn., Harvard U., 1971. Summer intern Nat. Gallery of Art, Washington, 1970; curatorial intern Albright-Knox Art Gallery, Buffalo, 1972; asst. curator Albright-Knox Art Gallery, 1973-75, asso. curator, 1975-76, curator, 1977-79, chief curator, 1980-83, dir., 1983—; adj. prof. art history SUNY, Buffalo, 1975-79; mem. adv. bd. Arts Council of Buffalo and Erie County 1975—. Office: Albright-Knox Art Gallery 1285 Elmwood Ave Buffalo NY 14222-1003

SCHULTZ, EILEEN HEDY, graphic designer; b. Yonkers, N.Y.; d. Harry Arthur and Hedy Evelyn (Morchel) S. B.F.A., Sch. Visual Arts, 1955. Staff artist C.A. Parshall Studios, N.Y.C., 1955-57; editorial art dir. Paradise of the Pacific, Honolulu, 1957-58; graphic designer Adler Advt. Agy., N.Y.C., 1958-59; art dir. Good Housekeeping Mag., N.Y.C., 1959-82; creative dir. advt. and sales promotion Good Housekeeping Mag., 1982-86; creative dir. Hearst Promo, 1986-87; pres. Design Internat., N.Y.C., 1987—; creative dir. The Depository Trust Co., 1987—. Art dir., editor, designer, 50th Art Directors Club Annual, 1973; columnist: Art Direction, 1969—. Dir. Sch. Visual Arts, N.Y.C., 1978—; trustee Sch. Art League, 1978—; advisor Fashion Inst. Tech., 1979—; mem. adv. commn. N.Y.C. Community Colls., 1979—. Named Yonkers Ambassador of Good Will to Netherlands, 1955; recipient Outstanding Achievement Sch. Visual Arts Alumni Soc., 1976, Sch. Art League Youth award, 1976. Mem. Art Dirs. Club (pres. 1975-77), Soc. Illustrators (pres. 1991-93), Joint Ethics Com. (chmn. 1978-80), Am. Inst. Graphic Arts, Soc. Publ. Designers, Type Dirs. Club.

SCHULTZ, FRANKLIN M., retired lawyer; b. Cin., June 16, 1917; s. Max and Goldie (Wise) S.; m. Jean Carol Barnett, Apr. 5, 1946 (dec. 1981); children: William B., John M., Katherine, Caroline; m. Virginia B. Henderson, Sept. 4, 1983. BA, Yale U., 1939, LLB, 1942. Bar: Ohio 1947, D.C. 1954, Mass. 1985, U.S. Supreme Ct. 1954. Atty. Fed. Power Commn., 1946-47; assoc. prof. Sch. Law, Ind. U., Bloomington, 1947-53; with firm Purcell & Nelson, Washington, 1953-80; ptnr. Purcell & Nelson, 1957-80, Reavis & McGrath, Washington, 1980-85; lawyer-in-residence Sch. Law, Washington and Lee U., 1985, vis. prof., 1991-94, ret., 1994; vis. prof. Sch. Law, U. Iowa, 1986-90; lectr. Sch. Law, George Washington U., 1958-59; vis. prof. Sch. Law, U. Va., 1975; mem. ednl. appeal bd. U.S. Dept. Edn., 1974-82. Contbr. articles to profl. jours. Trustee Nantucket Land Coun., 1992—. Served to capt. AUS, 1942-46. Decorated Bronze stars. Mem. ABA (mem. council adminstrv. law sect. 1966-69, chmn. 1970-71, del. ho. of dels. 1972-74), D.C. Bar (gen. counsel 1977-79, mem. legal ethics com. 1976-81), Am. Law Inst., Am. Bar Found., Adminstrv. Conf. U.S. (council 1980-82). Home: 1953 Marthas Rd Alexandria VA 22307-1966

SCHULTZ, FREDERICK HENRY, investor, former government official; b. Jacksonville, Fla., Jan. 16, 1929; s. Clifford G. and Mae (Wangler) S.; m. Nancy Reilly, Aug., 1951; children: Catherine G., Frederick H., Clifford G., John R. B.A., Princeton U., 1951; postgrad., U. Fla. Sch. Law, 1954-56. With Barnett Nat. Bank, Jacksonville, 1956-57; owner, operator investment firm, from 1957; mem. Fla. Ho. of Reps., 1963-70, speaker of the house, 1968-70; chmn. bd. Barnett Investment Svcs., Inc.; dir. Barnett Banks Inc., to 1979; vice chmn. bd. govs. Fed. Res. System, Washington, 1979-82; bd. dirs. Barnett Banks, Inc., Am. Heritage Life Ins. Co., S.E. Atlantic Inc., Riverside Group, Inc., Wickes Lumber Co. Served to lt. U.S. Army, 1952-54, Korea. Decorated Bronze Star. Roman Catholic. Office: PO Box 1200 Jacksonville FL 32201-1200

SCHULTZ, HARRY, health science organization administrator. Dir. St. Boniface Gen. Hosp. Rsch. Ctr., Winnipeg, MB, Canada. Office: U Manitoba St Boniface Gen Hosp, 351 Tache Ave, Winnipeg, MB Canada R2H 2A6*

SCHULTZ, JEROLD MARVIN, materials scientist, educator; b. San Francisco, June 21, 1935; s. Ernst and Florence (Rubin) S.; m. Peggy June Ostrom, July 30, 1960; children: Carrie, Timothy, Peter, Anna. BS, U. Calif., Berkeley, 1957, MS, 1958; PhD, Carnegie-Mellon U., 1965. Intermediate engr. Westinghouse Rsch. Labs., Pitts., 1959-61; mem. faculty U. Del., Newark, 1964—. Author: Polymer Materials Science, 1974, Diffraction for Materials Scientists, 1982; editor: Properties of Solid Polymeric Materials, 1977, Solid State Behavior of Linear Polyesters and Polyamides, 1990; contbr. over 150 articles to profl. jours. Flutist Newark Symphony Orch., 1966—. Recipient Sr. Am. Scientist award Alexander von Humboldt Stiftung, Germany, 1977, 82, Kliment Ohridzki medal Peoples Republic of Bulgaria, 1986. Mem. Am. Phys. Soc., Polymer Processing Soc. Democrat. Episcopalian. Achievements include 8 patents on polymer processing and materials. Office: U Del Materials Sci Program Newark DE 19716

SCHULTZ, JEROME SAMSON, biochemical engineer, educator; b. Bklyn., June 25, 1933; s. Henry Herman and Sally (Warburg) S.; m. Jane Paula Schwartz, Sept. 1, 1955; children: Daniel Stuart, Judith Susan, Kathryn Ann. BS in Chem. Engring., Columbia U., 1954, MS, 1956; PhD in Biochemistry, U. Wis., 1958. Group leader biochem. rsch. Lederle Labs., N.Y., 1958-64; asst. prof. dept. chem. engring. U. Mich., Ann Arbor, 1964-67, assoc. prof., 1967-70, prof., 1970-77, chmn., 1977-85; sect. head, emerging engring. techs. NSF, Washington, 1985-86, dep. dir. cross-disciplinary rsch., 1986-87; dir. Ctr. for Biotech. and Bioengring. U. Pitts., 1987—, prof. chem. engring., 1987—, prof. medicine, 1990—, dir. bioengring. program, 1991—. Editor Biotechnology Progress, 1988—; contbr. articles to profl. jours.; patentee in field. NIH rsch. career devel. awardee, 1970-75. Fellow Am. Inst. for Med. and Biol. Engring. (pres. 1995); mem. AAAS, Nat. Acad. Engring., Am. Chem. Soc. (past chmn. biochem. tech. divsn.), AIChE (past chmn. food and bioengring. divsn., Bioengring. award 1984), Am. Soc. Artificial Internal Organs, Nat. Acad. Engring., Sigma Xi, Phi Lambda Upsilon, Tau Beta Pi. Home: 111 Bentley Dr Pittsburgh PA 15238-2501 Office: U Pitts Ctr Biotechnol & Bioengring 300 Technology Dr Pittsburgh PA 15219

SCHULTZ, KAREN ROSE, clinical social worker, author, publisher, speaker; b. Huntington, N.Y., June 16, 1958; d. Eugene Alfred and Laura Rose (Palazzolo) Squeri; m. Richard S. Schultz, Apr. 8, 1989. BA with honors, SUNY, Binghamton, 1980; MA, U. Chgo., 1982. Lic. clin. social worker, Ill. Unit dir., adminstr. Camp Algonquin, Ill., 1981; clin. social worker United Charities Chgo., 1982-86; social worker Hartgrove Hosp., Chgo., 1986-87; pvt. practice, Oak Brook, Ill., 1987—; trainer, speaker various groups, schs. and orgns., DuPage County, Ill., 1988-89; group leader Optifast Program, Oak Park and Aurora, Ill., 1989-90; instr. social work Morraine Valley C.C., Palos Hills, Ill., 1989-90; instr. eating disorders Coll. of Dupage, Glen Ellyn, Ill., 1990-92, mem. eating disorder com., 1989—, tchr. intuition and counseling, 1995—. Editor, contbg. author The River Within newsletter, 1989—. Com. mem. DuPage Consortium, 1987-89. Mem. NASW (registerd, diplomate), acad. Cert. Social Workers, Nat. Speakers Assn., Profl. Speakers Ill., Toastmasters Interant., Women Entrepreneurs DuPage. Avocations: creative writing, aerobics, yoga, personal growth. Office: 900 Jorie Blvd Ste 234 Oak Brook IL 60521-2230

SCHULTZ, KURT LEE, lawyer; b. Chgo., Feb. 13, 1946; s. William Ernst Schultz and Patricia Marie (Chelminski) Facchine; m. Jane Marmet Lerro, Sept. 9, 1972; children: Jane, Melissa, Katherine, Laura. BA, U. Pa., 1967; JD, Ohio State U., 1972. Bar: Ill. 1972. Law clk. to Judge Richard B. Austin U.S. Dist. Ct. (no. dist.) Ill., Chgo., 1972-73; assoc. Winston & Strawn, Chgo., 1972-78, ptnr., 1978—. Trustee Ravinia Festival, Highland Park, Ill., 1990—; bd. dirs. Youth Guidance, Chgo., 1984—. 1st lt. U.S. Army, 1967-69. Mem. Order of Coif. Office: Winston & Strawn 35 W Wacker Dr Chicago IL 60601-1614

SCHULTZ, LOUIS EDWIN, management consultant; b. Foster, Nebr., Aug. 8, 1931; s. Louis Albert and Lula Pusey (Cox) S.; m. Mary Kathleen Peck, Mar. 3, 1962; children: Kurt Michael, Kristen Leigh. BSEE, U. Nebr., 1959; MBA, Pepperdine U., 1974. Mktg. mgr. Bell & Howell, Pasadena, Calif., 1962-70; dir. mktg. Cogar Corp., Utica, N.Y., 1970-71; product mgr. Pertec Corp., L.A., 1971-73; gen. mgr. Control Data Corp., Mpls., 1973-84; founder, CEO Process Mgmt. Inst. Inc., Mpls., Minn., 1984—; adv. bd. Inst. for Productivity Through Quality, U. Tenn., Knoxville, 1982-84. Author: Managing in the Worldwide Competitive Society, 1984, Quality Management Philosophies, 1985, Profiles in Quality, 1994; co-author: Quality Handbook for Small Business, 1994, Deming, The Way We Knew Him, 1995. Mem. Gov.'s Commn. on Productivity, St. Paul, 1986; chmn. Wirth Park Tree Restoration Com., Mpls., 1983; mem. Productivity Planning Com., St. Paul, 1985—. Staff sgt. USMC, 1952-54; advisor to Deming Forum, 1985—; judge Minn. Quality award, 1992. Recipient Profl. Partnership award U. Minn., 1987. Mem. Am. Soc. Performance Improvement (bd. dirs. 1984-89, outstanding svc. award), Minn. Coun. for Quality (bd. dirs. 1987—), Human Sys. Mgmt. (edtl. bd.), Asia-Pacific Orgn. Quality Control, Toastmasters Internat. Republican. Methodist. Office: Process Mgmt Inst 7801 E Bush Lake Rd Ste 360 Minneapolis MN 55439-3113

SCHULTZ, LOUIS MICHAEL, advertising agency executive; b. Detroit, Aug. 24, 1944; s. Henry Richard and Genevieve (Jankowski) S.; children: Christian David, Kimberly Ann. B.A., Mich. State U., 1967; M.B.A., Wayne State U., 1970. Staff Campbell-Ewald, Warren, Mich., 1967-74; v.p. group dir. Campbell-Ewald, 1975-77, sr. v.p., assoc. dir., 1977-82, group sr. v.p., 1982-83, exec. v.p., 1984-87; exec. v.p. Lintas: USA, 1987—; chmn. Lintas: WW Media Coun., 1991; mem. devel. council IPG, N.Y.C., 1984—; pres., COO CE Comm., 1994—; bd. dirs. Campbell-Ewald. Advisor, Detroit Renaissance Com., 1981-84. With USAR, 1967-73. Mem. Nat. Acad. TV Arts and Scis., Am. Women in Radio and TV, Am. Mktg. Assn., Detroit Advt. Assn., Ad. Club N.Y. (bd. dirs.), Great Oaks Country Club, Adcraft Club, Marco Polo Club, Old Club, Hidden Valley Club, Longboat Key Club. Republican. Roman Catholic. Avocations: golf; tennis; travel. Home: 1435 Kirts # 204 Troy MI 48084-9999 Office: CE Comms 30400 Van Dyke Warren MI 48093

SCHULTZ, LOUIS WILLIAM, judge; b. Deep River, Iowa, Mar. 24, 1927; s. M. Louis and Esther Louise (Behrens) S.; m. D. Jean Stephen, Nov. 6, 1949; children: Marcia, Mark, Paul. Student, Central Coll., Pella, Iowa, 1944-45, 46-47; LL.B., Drake U., Des Moines, 1949. Bar: Iowa. Claims supr. Iowa Farm Mut. Ins. Co., Des Moines, 1949-55; partner firm Harned, Schultz & McMeen, Marengo, Iowa, 1955-71; judge Iowa Dist. Ct. (6th dist.), 1971-80; justice Iowa Supreme Ct., 1980-93; county atty. Iowa County, 1960-68; ret., 1993. Served with USNR, 1945-46. Mem. Am. Bar Assn., Iowa Bar Assn. (bd. govs.), Iowa Judges Assn. (pres.). Office: U Iowa Coll Law # 1488 Iowa City IA 52242

SCHULTZ, MADELYN CAHN, health educator; b. Pitts., June 2, 1929; d. Abraham Cahn and Leah (Wenkert) Cahn-Katz; m. Harold Schultz, Aug. 12, 1956 (dec. Oct. 1971); 1 child, Robert Alan. BS, U. Pitts., 1950, MEd, 1956; PhD, U. Md., 1994. Cert. elem. tchr., spl. edn. tchr., Pa. Tchr. Pitts. Bd. Edn., 1950-60; spl. edn. tchr. Friendship House, Scranton, Pa., 1965-67, Lackawanna County, Scranton, 1970-71; ednl. coord. Pa. Dept. Welfare, Scranton and Harrisburg, Pa., 1971-72; devel. disabilities program specialist U.S. Dept. HHS/Adminstrv. Devel. Disabilities, Phila., 1972-78, Atlanta, 1978-81, Washington, 1981-85; desk officer U.S. Dept. HHS/Adminstrn. Children, Youth & Families, Washington, 1985-87, head start program specialist, 1987—; cons. on infant and toddler programs Head Start Bur., Washington, 1982-92. Author regulation proposals in field. Mem. AAUW, Nat. Assn. Edn. of Young Child, Soc. for Rsch. in Child Devel., Am. Cancer Soc. Avocations: folk dancing, folk singing, amateur theater. Office: US Dept HHS Head Start Bur 330 C St SW Washington DC 20201-0001

SCHULTZ, MICHAEL, stage and film director, film producer; b. Milw., Nov. 10, 1938; s. Leo Schultz and Katherine (Frances) Leslie; m. Gloria Jean Jones. Ed., U. Wis., Marquette U. Dir. stage plays Waiting for Godot, 1966, Song of the Lusitanian Bogey, Negro Ensemble Co., N.Y.C., 1968, and London, 1968, Kongi's Harvest, God Is a (Guess What), Does A Tiger Wear a Necktie, 1969; Broadway debut The Reckoning, 1969, Eugene O'Neill Meml. Theatre, 1969; Operation Sidewinder, Dream on Monkey Mountain, 1970, What the Winesellers Buy, 1974, Mulebone, Lincoln Ctr., 1991; dir. films including To Be Young, Gifted and Black, 1971, Together for Days, 1973, Cooley High, 1975, Car Wash, 1976, Greased Lightning, 1977, Which Way Is Up?, 1977, Sgt. Pepper's Lonely Hearts Club Band, 1978, Scavenger Hunt, 1979, Carbon Copy, 1981, Bustin Loose, 1983, The Last Dragon, 1985, Krush Groove, 1985, Disorderlies, 1987, Livin' Large, 1991, Ceremonies in Dark Old Men; dir. TV films Benny's Place, 1982, For Us The Living, 1983, The Jerk, Too, 1984, Timestalkers, 1986, Rock n' Roll Mom, 1988, Jury Duty, 1989, Hammer and Slammer, 1990, Dayo, 1992, Picket Fences, 1993-94, Young Indiana Jones, 1994. Office: PO Box 1940 Santa Monica CA 90406-1940

SCHULTZ, PETER G., chemistry educator. PhD, Calif. Inst. Tech., 1984. Mem. faculty chemistry dept. U. Calif., Berkeley, 1985—, now prof.; founding scientist Affymax Rsch. Inst., 1988; investigator Howard Hughes Med. Inst., 1994—; founder Symyx Techs., 1995—. NIH Postdoctoral fellow, MIT; recipient Nobel Laureate Signature award for Grad. Edn. in Chemistry, Pure Chemistry award, Arthur C. Cope award, Am. Chem. Soc., 1990, Alan T. Waterman award NSF, 1988, Ernest Orlando Lawrence Meml. award U.S. Dept. Energy, 1991, Wolf Prize in Chemistry, 1994, Eli Lilly award Am. Chem. Soc., 1991, DuPont Merck Young Investigator award, 1992, Humboldt Rsch. award for Sr. U.S. Scientist, 1992, Calif. Scientist of Yr. award, 1995. Mem. NAS, Am. Acad. Arts and Scis. Office: U Calif Dept Chemistry Berkeley CA 94720

SCHULTZ, PHILIP, poet, novelist, educator; b. Rochester, N.Y., Jan. 6, 1945; s. Samuel B. and Lillian (Bernstein) S. Student, U. Louisville, 1963-65, San Francisco State U., 1965-67; BA in English Lit, U. Iowa, 1968, MFA in Poetry, 1971. Various clerical positions Dept. Social Services, San Francisco, 1969-70; writer-in-residence Kalamazoo Coll., 1971-72; lectr. in poetry Newton (Mass.) Coll. of Sacred Heart, 1973-74; lectr. in writing U. Mass., Boston, 1973-75; tchr. poetry elem. schs. in Mich., 1971-72, Mass., 1974-75, N.Y., 1977-80; dir., founder Writers Studio (pvt. sch.), 1984—; lectr. in creative writing NYU, N.Y.C., 1978-88; dir. grad. creative writing program NYU, 1984-88; mem. faculty Columbia U., 1981-82. Author: (poems) Like Wings (Am. Acad.-Inst. of Arts and Letters award 1979), 1978 (Nat. Book Award nomination 1979), Deep Within the Ravine (Lamont poetry selection Acad. Am. Poets 1984), 1985, (chapbook) My Guardian Angel Stein, 1986; contbr. numerous poems to lit. jours. and mags. including Poetry, also short stories to lit. jours. (Kansas City Star Poetry award 1971, Discovery-Nation Poetry award 1976); featured in anthology 100 Years of American Poetry, 1996. N.Y. State Council for the Arts fellow, 1976, 80; Nat. Endowment Arts fellow, 1980-81; Fulbright grantee, 1983; N.Y. Found. for Arts fellow, 1985. Mem. PEN, Poetry Soc. Am. (governing bd. 1984-88), Modern Poetry Assn., Authors Guild Inc. Democrat. Jewish. Address: 88 Osburne Ln East Hampton NY 11937-2207 *I place clarity and precision above all else in my work, and if these are the modes of expression, honesty of feeling provides the substance as well as the goal. I believe the art of good writing takes place in the art of revision, which, if taxing, often enough gives me the time to get to the heart of the matter. I choose to write about only those things which I feel most passionate about: the particular circumstances of my life.*

SCHULTZ, RICHARD CARLTON, plastic surgeon; b. Grosse Pointe, Mich., Nov. 19, 1927; s. Herbert H. and Carmen (Huebner) S.; m. Pauline Zimmermann, Oct. 8, 1955; children: Richard, Lisa, Alexandra, Jennifer. McGregor scholar, U. Mich., 1946-49; M.D., Wayne State U., 1953. Diplomate Am. Bd. Plastic Surgery. Intern Harper Hosp., Detroit, 1953-54; resident in gen. surgery Harper Hosp., 1954-55, U.S. Army Hosp., Fort Carson, Colo., 1955-57; resident in plastic surgery St. Luke's Hosp., Chgo., 1957-58, U. Ill. Hosp., Chgo., 1958-59, VA Hosp., Hines, Ill., 1959-60; practice medicine specializing in plastic surgery Park Ridge, Ill., 1961—; clin. asst. prof. surgery U. Ill. Coll. Medicine, 1966-70, assoc. prof. surgery, 1970-76, prof., 1976—, head div. plastic surgery, 1970-87; pres. med. staff Lutheran Gen. Hosp., Park Ridge, 1977-79; vis. prof. U. Pitts., 1972, U. Miss., 1973, U. Pisa, Italy, 1974, Jikei U. Coll. Medicine, Tokyo, 1976, Ind. U., 1977, U. Helsinki, 1977, U. N.Mex., 1978, U. Milan, 1981, So. Ill. Sch. Medicine, 1982, Tulane U. Med. Sch., 1983, Shanghai 2d Med. Coll., 1984, U. Guadalajara (Mex.), 1986, Gazi U., Turkey, 1988, U. Coll. Medicine Tsuksba, Japan, 1996; participant, guest surgeon Physicians for Peace, Turkey and Greece, 1988, Israel and Occupied Ters., 1990, Egypt, 1991, Luthuania, Estonia, 1993 (team leader); leader citizen amb. People to People Internat. Del. Plastic Surgeons to Albania & Russia, 1994. Author: Facial Injuries, 1970, 3d edit., 1988, Maxillo-Facial Injuries from Vehicle Accidents, 1975, Outpatient Surgery, 1979. Mem. sch. bd., Lake Zurich, Ill., 1966-72, pres., 1968-72; pres. Chgo. Found. for Plastic Surgery, 1966—. Served to capt. M.C., AUS, 1955-57. Recipient research award Ednl. Found. Am. Soc. Plastic and Reconstructive Surgery, 1964-65, Med. Tribune Auto Safety award, 1967, Robert H. Ivy award, 1969, Disting. Sci. Achievement award Wayne U. Coll. Medicine Alumni, 1975; Sanvenero-Rosselli award, 1981; Fulbright scholar U. Uppsala, Sweden, 1960-61. Fellow ACS (pres. local commn. on trauma 1985-87); mem. Am. Assn. Plastic Surgeons (trustee 1990-91), Am. Soc. Plastic and Reconstructive Surgeons, Midwestern Assn. Plastic Surgeons (pres. 1978-79), Chgo. Soc. Plastic Surgeons (pres. 1970-72), Midwestern Assn. Plastic Surgeons (pres. 1978-79), Am. Soc. Maxillofacial Surgeons (pres. 1988-89, award of honor 1986), Am. Assn. Automotive Medicine (pres. 1970-71, A. Merkin award 1982), Am. Cleft Palate Assn., Am. Soc. Aesthetic Plastic Surgery, Tord Skoog Soc. Plastic Surgeons (pres. 1971-75), Can. Soc. Plastic Surgery, Chilean Soc. Plastic Surgery (corr.), Japanese Soc. Plastic Surgery (corr.), Cuban Soc. Maxillofacial Surgery (corr.). Home: 21150 N Middleton Dr Kildeer IL 60047-8503 Office: 1875 Dempster St Park Ridge IL 60068-1163

SCHULTZ, RICHARD DALE, national athletic organizations executive; b. Grinnell, Iowa, Sept. 5, 1929; s. August Henry and Marjorie Ruth (Turner) S.; m. Jacquilyn Lu Duistermars, June 26, 1949; children: Robert Dale, William Joel, Kim Marie. BS, Cen. Coll., Pella, Iowa, 1950; EdD Honoris Causa, Cen. Coll., 1987; LLD (hon.), Wartburg Coll., 1988, Alma Coll., 1989, Luther Coll., 1991; Phd, U.S. Sports Acad., 1993. Head basketball coach, athletic dir. Humboldt (Iowa) High Sch., 1950-60; freshman basketball coach U. Iowa, Iowa City, 1960-62; head baseball coach, assoc. basketball coach U. Iowa, 1962-70, head basketball coach, 1970-74, asst. v.p., 1974-76; dir. athletics and phys. edn. Cornell U., Ithaca, N.Y., 1976-81; dir. athletics U. Va., Charlottesville, 1981-87; exec. dir. NCAA, Mission, Kans., 1987-94; pres. Global Sports Enterprises, 1994-95; exec. dir. U.S. Olympic Com., Colorado Springs, Colo., 1995—; mem. honors ct. Nat. Football Found. and Hall of Fame, Nat. Basketball Hall of Fame, 1992; chmn. bd. NCAA Found., 1989; organizer Iowa Steel Mill, Inc. Author: A Course of Study for the Coaching of Baseball, 1964, The Theory and Techniques of Coaching Basketball, 1970; Contbr. articles to mags. Bd. dirs. Fellowship of Christian Athletes, 1986, chmn., 1990; chmn. Multiple Sclerosis, 1974-75; mem. Knight Found. Commn. on Intercollegiate Athletics, 1990—; mem. adv. com. on svc. acad. athletic programs Def. Dept. Recipient Disting. Alumni award Ctrl. Coll., Pella, 1970, Lifetime Svc. award U. Iowa, 1994, Corbett award NCADA, 1994; mem. Basketball Hall of Fame Honor Ct., 1992; inducted into Iowa Baseball Hall of Fame, 1993. Mem. Nat. Assn. Coll. Basketball Coaches, Ea. Coll. Athletic Assn. (mem. exec. com. 1980-81), Am. Basketball Coaches Assn. (Award of Honor 1994), Am. Football Coaches Assn. (lifetime membership award 1995). Home: 3670 Twisted Oak Cir Colorado Springs CO 80904-2138 Office: US Olympic Com One Olympic Plz Colorado Springs CO 80909

SCHULTZ, RICHARD MARTIN, electronics application engineering executive; b. Chgo., June 6, 1954; s. Richard J. and Rose Mary (Bianchi) S.; m. Gina Marie Ehlers, June 19, 1976; children: Erin Michelle, Nicole Kathryn. BSEE, Rose-Hulman, 1976. Engring. technician Honeywell Comml. Div., Arlington Heights, Ill., 1972-76, design engr., 1976-77; sr. design engr. Honeywell Comml. Div., Arlington Heights, 1978-79, Honeywell Bldg. Svcs. Div., Arlington Heights, 1979-80, Tex. Instruments Inc., Arlington Heights, 1980-81; dir. engring. URL Inc. OEM Group, Elk Grove, Ill., 1981, 82; pres. R.M. Schultz & Assocs. Inc., Crystal Lake, Ill., 1981—, McHenry, Ill., 1988—; pres. Enclave Corp., McHenry, 1988—. Inventor, patentee in field. Mem. McHenry County Solid Waste Com., McHenry, 1990, McHenry County Indsl. Coun., McHenry, 1988—, Corp. Presidents Roundtable, Schaumburg, Ill., 1986-88. Named to Virgil Order of the Arrow, 1970. Mem. McHenry C. of C. Republican. Avocations: hunting, fishing, reading, racquetball. Home: 3370 Executive Dr Marengo IL 60152-9180 Office: R M Schultz & Assocs Inc 1809 S State Route 31 Mc Henry IL 60050-8292

SCHULTZ, RICHARD OTTO, ophthalmologist, educator; b. Racine, Wis., Mar. 19, 1930; s. Henry Arthur and Josephine (Wagoner) S.; m. Diane Haldane, Sept. 29, 1990; children: Henry Reid, Richard Paul, Karen Jo. B.A., U. Wis., 1950, M.S., 1954; M.D., Albany Med. Coll., 1956; M.Sc., U. Iowa, 1960. Diplomate: Am. Bd. Ophthalmology. Intern, Univ. Hosps., Iowa City, 1956-57; resident in opthalmology Univ. Hosps., 1957-60; chief ophthalmology sect. div. Indian health USPHS, Phoenix, 1960-63; practice medicine specializing in ophthalmology Phoenix, 1963; NIH spl. fellow in ophthalmic microbiology U. Calif., San Francisco, 1963-64; clin. assoc. U. Calif., 1963-64, research assoc., 1963-64; assoc. prof., chmn. dept. ophthalmology Marquette U. Sch. Medicine (now Med. Coll. Wis.), Milw., 1964-68; prof., chmn. Marquette U. Sch. Medicine (now Med. Coll. Wis.), 1968—; dir. Eye Inst.; dir. ophthalmology Milw. Regional Med. Ctr.; mem. nat. adv. eye coun. NIH, 1984-88; cons. VA regional ctr. Milw. Children's, Columbia, Luth. and St. Mary's hosps., Milw. Contbr. articles to profl. jours. Served with USPHS, 1960-63. Fellow Am. Acad. Ophthalmology, ACS, Am. Ophthal. Soc.; mem. Assn. Univ. Profs. Ophthalmology (trustee, pres. 1978), AMA, Am., Milw. ophthalmol. socs., Assn. Research Vision and Ophthalmology, N.Y. Acad. Scis., Research to Prevent Blindness, Oxford Ophthalmol. Congress (Eng.), State Med. Soc. Wis., Wis. Soc. Prevention Blindness, Med. Soc. Milw. County, Milw. Acad. Medicine. Home: 12500 W Grove Ter Elm Grove WI 53122-1973 Office: 8700 W Wisconsin Ave Milwaukee WI 53226-3512

SCHULTZ, SAMUEL JACOB, clergyman, educator; b. Mountain Lake, Minn., June 9, 1914; s. David D. and Anna (Eitzen) S.; m. Eyla June Tolliver, June 17, 1943; children: Linda Sue, David Carl. AA, Bethel Coll., 1938; BA, John Fletcher Coll., 1940; BD, Faith Theol. Sem., 1944; MST, Harvard U., 1945, ThD, 1949. Ordained to ministry Christian and Missionary Alliance Ch., 1944; pastor First Meth. Ch., Pine River, Minn., 1940-41, Waldo Congl. Ch., Brockton, Mass., 1944-45, Evang. Bapt. Ch., Belmont, Mass., 1945-47; prof. Gordon Coll., Boston, 1946-47, Bethel Coll. and Sem., St. Paul, 1947-49, St. Paul Bible Inst., 1948-49; prof. Wheaton (Ill.) Coll., 1949-80, prof. emeritus, 1980—, Samuel Robinson prof. Bible and theology, 1955-80, chmn. Bible and philosophy dept., 1957-63, chmn. div. Bibl. edn. and philosophy, 1963-67, chmn. div. Bibl. studies, 1972-79; prof. Old Testament and Bible Exposition Trinity Coll. Grad. Sch. (name now Tampa Bay Theol. Sem.), Dunedin (now Holiday), Fla., 1987-93; prof. Old Testament St. Petersburg (Fla.) Theol. Sem., adj. prof. St. Petersburg Jr. Coll., 1995—; interim supply pastor Bible Ch. Winnetka, Ill., 1951, 60; resident supply pastor South Shore Bapt. Ch., Hingham, Mass., 1958-59. Author: The Old Testament Speaks, 1960, 3d edit., 1980, 4th edit., 1990, Law and History, 1964, The Prophets Speak, 1968, Deuteronomy-Gospel of Love, 1971, The Gospel of Moses, 1974, 79, Interpreting the Word of God, 1976, Leviticus-God Dwelling Among His People, 1983, The Message of the Old Testament, 1986; contbr. Deuteronomy commentary to The Complete Biblical Libr., 1996. Mem. bd. edn. Bethel Coll. and Sem., 1960-65; historian Conservative Congregation Christian Conf., 1980-86; bd. dirs. Inst. in Basic Youth Conflicts, 1965-80, Congl. Christian Hist. Soc., 1984—, Brookwoods Christian Camps and Confs., Inc., Alton, N.H., 1978—; trustee Gordon-Conwell Sem., South Hamilton, Mass., 1980—, Lexington (Mass.) Christian Acad., 1987—. NYU study grantee Israel, 1966, Wheaton Coll. Alumni research grantee, 1958. Mem. Soc. Bibl. Lit., Evang. Theol. Soc. (editor Jour. 1962-75), Near East Archaeol. Soc. (sec., bd. dir.), Wheaton Coll. Scholastic Honors Soc., Phi Sigma Tau. Book the Living and Active Word of God dedicated in his honor, 1983. Home: 143 East St Lexington MA 02173-1913 *Love the Lord your God with all your heart and with all your soul and with all your strength and your neighbor as yourself.*

SCHULTZ, STANLEY GEORGE, physiologist, educator; b. Bayonne, N.J., Oct. 26, 1931; s. Aaron and Sylvia (Kaplan) S.; m. Harriet Taran, Dec. 25, 1960; children: Jeffrey, Kenneth. A.B. summa cum laude, Columbia U., 1952; M.D., N.Y. U., 1956. Intern Bellevue Hosp., N.Y.C., 1956-57; resident Bellevue Hosp., 1957-59; research assoc. in biophysics Harvard U., 1959-62, instr. biophysics, 1964-67; assoc. prof. physiology U. Pitts., 1967-70, prof. physiology, 1970-79; prof., chmn. dept. physiology U. Tex. Med. Sch., Houston, 1979—, prof. dept. internal medicine, 1979—; cons. USPHS, NIH, 1970—; mem. physiology test com. Nat. Bd. Med. Examiners, 1974-79, chmn., 1976-79. Editor Am. Jour. Physiology, Jour. Applied Physiology, 1971-75, Physiol. Revs., 1979-85, Handbook of Physiology: The Gastrointestinal Tract, 1989-91—; mem. editl. bd. Jour. Gen. Physiology, 1969-88, Ann. Revs. Physiology, 1974-81, Current Topics in Membranes and Transport, 1975-81, Jour. Membrane Biology, 1977—, Biochim. Biophys. Acta, 1987-89; assoc. editor Ann. Revs. Physiology, 1977-81; assoc. editor News in Physiol. Scis., 1989-94, editor, 1994—; contbr. articles to profl. jours. Served to capt. M.C. USAF, 1962-64. Recipient Research Career award NIH, 1969-74; overseas fellow Churchill Coll., Cambridge U., 1975-76. Mem. AAAS, Am. Heart Assn. (estab. investigator 1964-68), Am. Physiol. Soc. (councillor 1989-91, pres.-elect 1991-92, pres. 1992-93, past pres. 1993-94), Fed. Am. Soc. Exptl. Biology (exec. bd. 1992-95), Biophys. Soc., Soc. Gen. Physiologists, Internat. Cell Rsch. Orgn., Internat. Union Physiol. Scis. (chmn. internat. com. gastrointestinal physiology 1977-80, chmn. U.S. nat. com. 1992—), Assn. Am. Physicians, Am. Assn. Ob-Gyn. (hon. fellow), Assn. Chmn. Depts. Physiology (pres. 1985-86), Sigma Xi, Phi Beta Kappa. Home: 4955 Heatherglen Dr Houston TX 77096-4213

SCHULTZ, T. PAUL, economics educator; b. Ames, Iowa, May 24, 1940; s. Theodore W. and Esther (Werth) S.; m. Judith Hoenack, Sept. 16, 1967; children: Lara, Joel, Rebecca. BA, Swarthmore Coll., 1961; PhD, MIT, 1966; MA (hon.), Yale U., 1974. Cons. Joint Econ. Com., Washington, 1964; researcher econs. dept. Rand Corp., Santa Monica, Calif., 1965-72, dir. population research, 1968-72; prof. econs. U. Minn., Mpls., 1972-75; prof. econs. Yale U., New Haven, 1974—, dir. Econ. Growth Ctr., 1983—; cons. World Bank, Rockefeller Found.; mem. com. on population NAS, Washington, 1987-89, 90-93. Author: Structural Change in a Developing Country, 1971, Economics of Population, 1981; editor: (books) The State of Development Economics, 1988, Investment In Women's Human Capital, 1995, (periodical) Research in Population Economics, 1985, 88, 91, 96; assoc. editor Jour. Population Econs., 1991—, Econ. of Edn. Rev., 1993—, China Econ. Rev., 1994—. Fellow AAAS (population resources environ. com. 1985-89, nomination com. 1987-90); mem. Am. Econ. Assn., Econometrics Soc., Population Assn. Am. (bd. dirs. 1979-81), Internat. Union for Sci. Study Population, Soc. for Study Social Biology (bd. dirs. 1986-89), European Soc. for Population Econs. (bd. dirs. 1992—, pres. elect 1996), Econ. Rsch. Forum for Arab Countries. Office: Yale U Econ Growth Ctr PO Box 208269 27 Hillhouse Ave New Haven CT 06520-8269

SCHULTZ, THEODORE WILLIAM, retired economist, educator; b. Arlington, S.D., Apr. 30, 1902; s. Henry Edward and Anna Elizabeth (Weiss) S.; m. Esther Florence Werth; children: Elaine, Margaret, T. Paul. Grad., Sch. Agr., Brookings, S.D., 1924; B.S., S.D. State Coll., 1927, D.Sc. (hon.), 1959; M.S., U. Wis., 1928, Ph.D., 1930; LL.D. (hon.), Grinnell Coll., 1949, Mich. State U., in 1962, U. Ill., 1968, U. Wis., 1968, Cath. U. Chile, 1979, U. Dijon, France, 1981; LL.D., N.C. State U., 1984. Mem. faculty Iowa State Coll., Ames, 1930-43; prof., head dept. econs. and sociology Iowa State Coll., 1934-43; prof. econs. U. Chgo., 1943-72, chmn. dept. econs., 1946-61, Charles L. Hutchinson Disting. Service prof., 1952-72, prof. emeritus, 1972—; econ. adviser, occasional cons. Com. Econ. Devel., U.S. Dept. Agr., Dept. State, Fed. Res. Bd., various congl. coms., U.S. Dept. Commerce, FAO, U.S. Dept. Def., Germany, 1948, Fgn. Econ. Adminstrn., U.K. and Germany, 1945, IBRD, Resources for the Future, Twentieth Century Fund, Nat. Farm Inst., others.; dir. Nat. Bur. Econ. Research, 1949-67; research dir. Studies of Tech. Assistance in Latin Am.; bd. mem. Nat. Planning Assn.; chmn. Am. Famine Mission to India, 1946; studies of agrl. developments, central Europe and Russia, 1929, Scandinavian countries and Scotland, 1936, Brazil, Uruguay and Argentina, 1941, Western Europe, 1955. Author: Redirecting Farm Policy, 1943, Food for the World, 1945, Agriculture in an Unstable Economy, 1945, Production and Welfare in Agriculture, 1950, The Economic Organization of Agriculture, 1953, Economic Test in Latin America, 1956, Transforming Traditional Agriculture, 1964, The Economic Value of Education, 1963, Economic Crises in World Agriculture, 1965, Economic Growth and Agriculture, 1968, Investment in Human Capital: The Role of Education And of Research, 1971, Human Resources, 1972, Economics of the Family: Marriage, Children, and Human Capital, 1974, Distortions of Agricultural Incentives, 1978, Investing in People: The Economics of Population Quality, 1981, Restoring Economic Equilibrium: Human Capital in the Modernizing Economy, 1990, The Economics of Being Poor, 1993, Origins of Increasing Returns, 1993; co-author: Measures for Economic Development of Under-Developed Countries, 1951; editor: Jour. Farm Econs., 1939-42; contbr. articles to profl. jours. Research fellow Center Advanced Study in Behavioral Sci., 1956-57; recipient Nobel prize in Econs., 1979. Fellow Am. Acad. Arts and Scis., Am. Farm Econs. Assn., Nat. Acad. Scis.; mem. Am. Agrl. Econ. Assn., Am. Econ. Assn. (pres. 1960, Walker medal 1972), Am. Philos. Soc., Royal Econ. Soc., Nat. Acad. Edn., others. Home: 5620 S Kimbark Ave Chicago IL 60637-1606 Office: U Chgo Dept Econs 1126 E 59th St Chicago IL 60637-1580*

SCHULTZ, WILLIAM E., management consultant. V.p. fin. Kearney Internat., Chgo. Office: Kearney Internat 222 W Adams St Ste 2500 Chicago IL 60606

SCHULTZ-DROUIN, JUDITH, educational administrator, consultant; b. Boston, Oct. 2, 1960; d. William Leonard and Jeanne Anne (Parker) Schultz; m. Thomas Richard Drouin, Oct. 26, 1991. BA in Psychology, Plymouth (N.H.) State Coll., 1982; MA in Counseling Psychology, Antioch New Eng. Grad. Sch., Keene, N.H., 1989. Recreation therapist Laconia (N.H.) Devel. Svcs., 1982-85, program dir. recreation dept., 1985-86, behavior specialist vocat. svcs., 1986-87, tng. and devel. therapist, psychology dept., 1987-89, psychologist for the state, 1989-90; program supr. Spaulding Youth Ctr., Tilton, N.H., 1990-92, program dir., 1992—; adv. bd. N.H. Vocat. Tech. Inst., Laconia, 1993—, assoc. prof., 1991; cons. in field. Song writer, profl. musician, 1977—. A founder youth sailing program Winnipesaukee Sailing Assn., Gilford, N.H., 1988. Mem. Winnipesaukee Yacht Club. Avocations: yacht racing, skiing, hiking, travel. Home: 52 Roberts Rd PO Box 7171 Gilford NH 03247 Office: Spaulding Youth Ctr PO Box 189 Tilton NH 03276-0189

SCHULTZE, CHARLES LOUIS, economist, educator; b. Alexandria, Va., Dec. 12, 1924; s. Richard Lee and Nora Woolls (Baggett) S.; m. Rita Irene Hertzog, Sept. 6, 1947; children: Karen M., Kevin C., Helen L., Kathleen, Carol, Mary. A.B., Georgetown U., 1948, M.A., 1950; Ph.D., U. Md., 1960. Mem. staff Pres.'s Council Econ. Advisers, 1952, 54-58; chmn. Pres.'s Council Econ. Advisors, 1977-81; assoc. prof. econs. Ind. U., 1959-61; prof. econs. U. Md., 1961-87; asst. dir. U.S. Bur. of Budget, 1962-64, dir., 1965-67; sr. fellow Brookings Instn., Washington, 1968-76, 81—. Author: (with others) Setting National Priorities, 6 vols., 1970, 71, 72, 73, 83, 90, The Public Use of Private Interest, 1977, Other Times, Other Places, 1986, (with others) Barriers to European Growth, 1987, (with others) An American Trade Strategy, 1990, Memos to the President, 1992. Served with AUS, 1943-46. Decorated Purple Heart, Bronze Star. Mem. Am. Econ. Assn. (pres. 1984). Office: Brookings Instn 1775 Massachusetts Ave NW Washington DC 20036-2188

SCHULZ, CHARLES MONROE, cartoonist; b. Mpls., Nov. 26, 1922; s. Carl and Dena (Halverson) S.; m. Joyce Halverson, Apr. 18, 1949 (div. 1972); children: Meredith, Charles Monroe, Craig, Amy, Jill; m. Jean Clyde, 1973. LHD (hon.), Anderson Coll., 1963; DHL (hon.), St. Mary's Coll. of CA, 1969. Cartoonist St. Paul Pioneer Press, Sat. Eve. Post, 1948-49. Created syndicated comic strip Peanuts, 1950—; author of many collections of Peanuts strips and cartoons; screenwriter of several teleplays and feature films based on the Peanuts strip; exhbns. include Around the World and Home Again: A Tribute to the Art of Charles M. Schulz, 1994—, Around the Moon and Home Again: A Tribute to the Art of Charles M. Schulz, 1995—. With U.S. Army, 1943-45. Recipient Outstanding Cartoonist award Nat. Cartoonist Soc., 1955, 1964; Yale Humor award, 1956; School Bell award, Nat. Edn. Assn., 1960; Peabody award and Emmy award for CBS cartoon special "A Charlie Brown Christmas", 1966; Charles M. Schulz award for contribution to the field of cartooning, United Feature Syndicate, 1980; inducted into Cartoonists Hall of Fame. Mem. Nat. Cartoonists Soc. Office: Number One Snoopy Place Santa Rosa CA 95401 also: United Feature Syndicate 200 Park Ave New York NY 10166-0005*

SCHULZ, JUERGEN, art history educator; b. Kiel, Germany, Aug. 18, 1927; came to U.S., 1938; s. Johannes Martin Askan Schulz and Ilse (Lebenbaum) Hiller; m. Justine Hume, Sept. 1951 (div. 1968); children: Christoph (dec.), Ursula, Catherine; m. Anne Markham, May 19, 1969; 1 child, Jeremy. BA, U. Calif., Berkeley, 1950; PhD in History of Art, U. London, 1958. Reporter San Francisco Chronicle, 1950-51; copy editor UPI, London, 1952-53; from instr. to prof. history of art U. Calif., 1958-68; prof. Brown, Providence, 1968-90, Andrea V. Rosenthal prof. history art and architecture, 1990-95; mem. Inst. for Advanced Study, Princeton, N.J., 1971-72. Author: Venetian Painted Ceilings of the Renaissance, 1968, Printed Plans and...Views of Venice, 1971, La cartografia tra scienza e arte, 1990; also articles. Staff sgt. U.S. Army, 1945-48. Decorated grande ufficiale Ordine della Stella della Solidarieta della Repubblica Italiana; Guggenheim fellow, 1966-67. Mem. Ateneo Veneto. Office: Brown U Dept History Art and Architecture PO Box 1855 Providence RI 02912-1855

SCHULZ, MARIANNE, accountant; b. East Orange, N.J.; d. Clifford W. Schulz; m. James A. Willits, Dec. 29, 1991; 1 child, Lukas James. BA in Bus., U. Wash., 1979. Cert. mgmt. acct. Contr. Farwest Spl. Products, Bellevue, Wash., 1974-88; acct. Lakeside Industries, Bellevue, Wash., 1988—. Mem. Inst. Mgmt. Accts. (bd. dirs. 1990-92, v.p. 1992-93).

SCHULZ, MARY ELIZABETH, lawyer; b. New Ulm, Minn., Oct. 6, 1950; d. Paul F. and Elizabeth B. (Wichtel) S. BA cum laude, Mankato State U., 1972; JD, So. Meth. U., 1976. Bar: Tex., 1976, Ky., 1992, Ohio, 1993. Atty. Kagay, Turner, Eyres & Robertson, Dallas, 1976-78; asst. regional counsel U.S. EPA, Dallas, 1978-86; atty. Gardere & Wynne, Dallas, 1986-89, Valvoline, Inc., Lexington, Ky., 1989-90; counsel Olin Corp., E. Alton, Ill., 1990-92; sr. environ. counsel B.F. Goodrich Co., Akron, Ohio, 1992—. Mem. ABA. Office: B F Goodrich Co 3925 Embassy Pky Akron OH 44333-1763

SCHULZ, MICHAEL JOHN, fire and explosion analyst, consultant; b. Milw., Oct. 7, 1958; s. John F. and JoAnn E. (Carlson) S.; m. Donna M. Guzman; children: Kari L., Brian M. BS in Fire and Safety Engring. Tech., U. Cin., 1996; grad., U.S. Fire Adminstrn. Acad. Cert. fire and explosion investigator; cert. fire protection specialist; cert. fire investigation instr.; cert. fire svc. instr. II. Fire investigator Cedarburg (Wis.) Police Dept., 1979-90; capt., fire investigator Cedarburg (Wis.) Fire Dept., 1981-90; sr. staff expert John A. Kennedy & Assoc., Hoffman Estates, Ill., 1990—; cons. U.S. Fire Adminstrn.; instr. fire tech. and police sci. depts. Milw. (Wis.) Area Tech. Coll.; instr. fire sci. tech. dept. William Rainey Harper C.C.; lectr. in field. Author: Manual for the Determination of Electrical Fire Causes, 1988, Guide for Fire and Explosion Investigations, 1992. Recipient Common Coun. Commendation, City of Cedarburg, Wis., 1986; named Firefighter of Yr., Ozaukee County Assn. Fire Depts., 1985. Mem. ASTM, Nat. Assn. Fire Investigators (bd. dirs. 1987—, nat. cert. bd. 1987—, chmn. edn. com., editor The Nat. Fire Investigator, Man of Yr. 1991), Nat. Fire Protection Assn. (tech. com. on fire investigations 1985—, fire svc. sect., sect. rep. tech. com. on fire investigations 1985-92, sec. rep. nat. conf. on fire investigation instrn., mem. bd. dirs. fire sci. and tech. educators sect.), Fire Marshal's Assn. N.Am. (assoc.), Nat. Inst. Bldg. Scis. (reviewing mem. fire rsch. sub-com.), Bldg. Ofcls. and Code Adminstrs. Internat., So. Bldg. Code Congress Internat., Internat. Bldg. Code Ofcls., Internat. Assn. Arson Investigators (John Charles Wilson scholarship award 1982), Ill. Chpt. Internat. Assn. Arson Investigators, Internat. Soc. Fire Svc. Instrs., Nat. Conf. Fire Investigation Instrn. (bd. dirs.), Wis. Soc. Fire Svc. Instrs., Ky. Cols. Republican. Lutheran. Avocation: amateur radio. Office: John A Kennedy & Assocs 2155 Stonington Ave Ste 118 Hoffman Estates IL 60195

SCHULZ, RALPH RICHARD, publishing consultant; b. N.Y.C., June 5, 1928; s. Harry and Margaret (Faecher) S.; m. Joyce S. Woolf, Sept. 9, 1951; children: Laura Stern, Barbara Tejerina, Susan. BS in Chemistry, CCNY, 1950. Asst. editor McLean-Hunter Pub. Co., Toronto, Can., 1950; assoc. editor McGraw-Hill Pub. Co., N.Y.C., 1951-60, mng. editor, 1960-68, editor-in-chief, 1968-73; dir. McGraw-Hill World News, N.Y.C., 1973-76; v.p. editorial dept. McGraw-Hill Pubs. Co., N.Y.C., 1976-84; sr. v.p. editorial dept. McGraw-Hill, Inc., N.Y.C., 1985-92; pub. cons., 1992—; v.p. DeSilva & Phillips Inc., N.Y.C.; adj. prof. Grad. Sch. Bus. Adminstrn., Fordham U., 1990—. Author to numerous mag. on bus. and sci. Trustee Correspondents Fund, N.Y.C., 1979—; bd. dirs. Bus. Press Ednl. Found., N.Y.C., 1986—, McGraw-Hill Found., N.Y.C., 1987-92, Copyright Clearence Ctr., N.Y.C., 1983-92. Petty officer USN, 1946-48. Recipient Honor award for disting. svc. in journalism Ohio U., 1972, Jesse H. Neal Editorial Achievement award Am. Bus. Press, 1972. Mem. Am. Soc. Mag. editors (exec. com. 1984-88), Overseas Press Club Am. (bd. dirs. 1969-73), Nat. Press Club, Players Club (bd. dirs. 1974-78), Silurians, Sigma Delta Chi. Office: DeSilva & Phillips Inc 444 Park Ave S New York NY 10016

SCHULZ, RAYMOND ALEXANDER, medical marketing professional, consultant; b. Paris, June 2, 1946; s. Helmut W. and Colette (Prieur) S.; m. Dixie Lee Suzanne Specht, Apr. 9, 1977 (div. Dec. 1990); children: Christopher, William. BA in Physics, W.Va. U., 1970; MS in Computer Sci., Columbia U., N.Y.C., 1975. Sr. programmer Meml. Sloan Kettering Cancer Ctr., N.Y.C., 1972-74; program coord. Neurol. Inst. Columbia Presbyn. Hosp., N.Y.C., 1974-76; engring. mgr. EMI Med. Systems, Northbrook, Ill., 1976-78; product mgr. Johnson & Johnson (Technicare), Solon, Ohio, 1978-80; group product mgr. Siemens Corp., Iselin, N.J., 1980-82; mktg. mgr. Toshiba Am. Med. Systems (formerly Diasonics MRI), South San Francisco, 1983-92; dir. mktg. Voxel, Laguna Hills, Calif., 1992—. Contbr. over 70 papers on the application of holography to a variety of med. specialties to profl. publs. Recipient first prize Roentgen Centenary Congress, 1995. Mem. Am. Assn. Physicists in Medicine, N.Y. Acad. Scis., Internat. Soc. Magnetic Rsch. in Medicine, Larchmont Yacht Club, Commonwealth Club Calif., Eta Kappa Nu. Avocations: skiing, running, hiking, swimming, mountainbiking. Office: Voxel 26081 Merit Circle Ste 117 Laguna Hills CA 92653

SCHULZ, RICHARD BURKART, electrical engineer, consultant; b. Phila., May 21, 1920; s. Herman G. Schulz and Laura (Burkart) Luckenbill; m. Jeannette Charlotte Vollmer, Nov. 22, 1958; 1 child, Steven Edward. BSEE, U. Pa., 1942, MSEE, 1951. Rsch. assoc. U. Pa., Phila., 1942-46; owner Electro-Search, Phila., 1947-55; program devel. coord. Armour Rsch. Found., Chgo., 1955-61; chief electro-interference United Control Corp.,

Redmond, Wash., 1961-62; chief electro-compatibility Boeing Co., Seattle, 1962-70; staff engr. S.W. Rsch. Inst., San Antonio, 1970-74; sci. advisor IIT Rsch. Inst., Annapolis, Md., 1974-83; mgr. EMC and TEMPEST Xerox Corp., Lewisville, Tex., 1983-87; EMC cons. Carrollton, Tex., 1987—. Contbr. 4 chpts. to Handbook on EMC, 1995, also numerous tech. papers to profl. publs. Named Life Master Am. Contract Bridge League. Fellow IEEE (life; Centennial medal 1984, Standards plaque 1991); mem. IEEE Soc. on Electromagnetic Compatibility (life; treas. 1966-67, pres. 1968, bd. dirs. 1961-89, chmn. internat. conf. 1968, tech. program chmn. internat. conf. 1993, L.G. Cumming plaque 1980, Richard R. Stoddart award 1988), Toastmasters Club. Republican. Lutheran. Home and Office: 2030 Cologne Dr Carrollton TX 75007-2334

SCHULZ, ROCKWELL IRWIN, health administration educator; b. Milw., June 30, 1929; s. Irwin W.P. and Ruth Mary (Rockwell) S.; m. Susan Clare Marriott Learmonth; children from previous marriage: Rockwell A., Michael T., Kerry G., David T. BS, Lawrence U., Appleton, Wis., 1951; MHA, U. Minn., 1955; PhD (spl. rsch. fellow HEW 1969-72), U. Wis., 1972. Asst. adminstr. Charles T. Miller Hosp., St. Paul, 1955-56; adminstr. Pember Nuzum Clinic, Janesville, Wis., 1956-61, Meml. Hosp., Manitowoc, Wis., 1961-63; cons. Booz, Allen & Hamilton, Chgo., 1963-66; asst. dean Tulane U. Med. Sch., 1966-67; asso. dean U. Tex. Southwestern Med. Sch., Dallas, 1967-69; mem. faculty U. Wis. Med. Sch., Madison, 1969—, prof. preventive medicine, dir. Internat. Ctr. for Health Services Studies,, 1979—; cons. in field. Author: Management of Hospitals, 1976, 2d edit., 1983, Teams and Top Management in British National Health Services, 1984, Management of Hospitals and Health Services: Strategic Issues and Performance, 1990; also articles. Served with USCG, 1951-53. WHO fellow, 1981, Fulbright sr. rsch. fellow, 1985-86; recipient Hubert H. Humphrey award for best articles Jour. Health and Human Resources Adminstr., 1981, Vernon E. Weekworth award for best rsch. paper U. Minn. Hosp. & Health Svcs. Adminstrn., 1992, best paper award health sect. Acad. of Mgmt., 1992. Mem. Am. Acad. Mgmt., Am. Hosp. Assn., Am. Pub. Health Assn., Assn. for Health Svcs. Rsch. Home: 1 Langdon St Madison WI 53703 Address: U Wis Med Scis Ctr 1300 University Ave Madison WI 53706-1510

SCHULZ, RUDOLPH WALTER, university dean emeritus; b. Chgo., Aug. 10, 1930; s. Walter Adolph and Minna Louise (Burmeister) S.; m. Charlotte Helen Adams, Sept. 8, 1956; children: Stephanie Sue, Kyle Scott. B.S., Northwestern U., 1954, Ph.D., 1958; M.A., Stanford, 1955. Lectr., research asso. Northwestern U., 1956-58, instr., 1958-59; asst. prof. psychology Carnegie-Mellon U., 1959-60; asst. prof. U. Iowa, 1960-64, asso. prof., 1964-66, prof., 1966-95, prof., chmn. dept., 1970-73, dean for advanced studies, 1976-91; cons. in field, mem. NSF fellowship selection panel, 1962-68; NSF vis. scientist, 1962-76; bd. dirs. Midwest Univs. Consortium for Internat. Activities, Inc., 1977-91. Cons. editor: Jour. Exptl. Psychology, 1962-74, Jour. Verbal Learning and Verbal Behavior, 1964-74, Contemporary Psychology, 1970-81; editor: Psychonomic Science, 1971-72, Memory and Cognition, 1972-76; Contbr. articles to profl. jours. Served with USNR, 1950-52. Decorated Air medal.; Old Gold research fellow U. Iowa, 1963; NSF research grantee, 1964-76. Fellow Am. Psychol. Assn., AAAS (mem. council 1974-75), Am. Psychol. Soc. (charter); mem. Psychnomic Soc., Midwestern Psychol. Assn. (sec.-treas. 1973-76, pres. 1978), Sigma Xi. Home: 8 Fairview Knls NE Iowa City IA 52240-9147

SCHULZ, WILLIAM FREDERICK, human rights association executive; b. Pitts., Nov. 14, 1949; s. William F. and Jean Smith; m. Beth Graham, 1993. AB, Oberlin Coll., 1971; MA, Meadville/Lombard Theol. Sch., 1973, DMin, 1975, DDiv, 1987; MA, U. Chgo., 1974; DHL, Nova Southea. U., 1995. Minister First Parish Unitarian Universalist, Bedford, Mass., 1975-78; dir. social responsibility Unitarian Universalist Assn., Boston, 1978-79, exec. v.p., 1979-85, pres., 1985-93; exec. dir. Amnesty Internat. USA, 1994—. Author: Finding Time and Other Delicacies, 1992; editor, contbr. Transforming Words: Six Essays on Preaching, 1984, 2d edit., 1996. Recipient Albert Francis Christie prize, 1973, 75. Mem. ACLU, Unitarian Universalist Mins. Assn. Democrat. Home: 10 Castle Harbor Rd Huntington NY 11743-1209

SCHULZE, ERIC WILLIAM, lawyer, legal publications editor, publisher; b. Libertyville, Ill., July 8, 1952; s. Robert Carl and Barbara (Mayo) S. BA, U. Tex., 1973, JD, 1977. Bar: Tex. 1977, U.S. Dist. Ct. (we. dist.) Tex. 1987, U.S. Ct. Appeals (5th cir.) 1987, U.S. Dist. Ct. (ea. and so. dists.) Tex. 1988, U.S. Dist. Ct. (no. dist.) Tex. 1989, U.S. Supreme Ct. 1989; bd. cert. civil appellate law Tex. Bd. Legal Specialization, 1990—. Rsch. asst. U. Tex., Austin, 1978; legis. aide Tex. Ho. of Reps., Austin, 1979-81; editor Tex. Sch. Law News, Austin, 1982-85; assoc. Hairston, Walsh & Anderson, Austin, 1986-87; ptnr. Walsh, Anderson, Underwood, Schulze & Aldridge, Austin, 1988—, mng. ptnr., 1993—; editor Tex. Sch. Adminstrs. Legal Digest, Austin, 1986-92, co-pub., 1991—, mng. editor, 1992—. Editor: (legal reference books) Texas Education Code Annotated, 1982-85. Del. Tex. State Democratic Conv., 1982, Travis County Dem. Conv., 1982, 84, 86. Recipient Merit award for pubs. Internat. Assn. Bus. Communicators-Austin br., 1983, Merit award for authorship Coll. of State Bar Tex., 1992. Mem. Fed. Bar Assn., Am. Bar Assn., Tex. Bar Assn., Travis County Bar Assn., Bar Assn. of 5th Cir., Defense Rsch. Inst., Nat. Council Sch. Attys., Tex. Council Sch. Attys., Nat. Orgn. Legal Problems in Edn., Toastmasters (pres. Capital City chpt. 1995). Home: 3905 Idlewild Rd Austin TX 78731-6144 Office: Walsh Anderson Underwood Schulze & Aldridge PO Box 2156 Austin TX 78768-2156

SCHULZE, FRANZ, JR., art critic, educator; b. Uniontown, Pa., Jan. 30, 1927; s. Franz and Anna E. (Krimmel) S.; m. Marianne Gaw, June 24, 1961 (div. 1975); children: F. C. Matthew, Lukas; m. Stephanie Mora, 1992. Student, Northwestern U., 1943; Ph.B., U. Chgo., 1945; B.F.A., Sch. Art Inst. Chgo., 1949, M.F.A., 1950; postgrad., Acad. Fine Arts, Munich, Germany, 1956-57. Instr. art Purdue U., 1950-52; chmn. dept. art Lake Forest (Ill.) Coll., 1952-58, artist-in-residence, 1958-61, prof. art, 1961—, Hollender prof. art, 1974-91; art critic Chgo. Daily News, 1962-78, Chgo. Sun-Times, 1978-85; adj. prof. U. Ill., Chgo., 1996; Chgo. corr. in art Christian Sci. Monitor, 1958-62; art and arch. critic The Chicagoan, 1973-74; mem. vis. com. dept. art U. Chgo., 1974—. Author: Art, Architecture and Civilization, 1969, Fantastic Images: Chicago Art Since 1945, 1972, 100 Years of Chicago Architecture, 1976, Stealing Is My Game, 1976, Mies van der Rohe: A Critical Biography, 1985, The University Club of Chicago: A Heritage, 1987, Mariotti, 1988; editor: Mies van der Rohe: Critical Essays, 1989, Mies van der Rohe Archive, 1993; co-editor Chicago's Famous Buildings, 1993, Philip Johnson: Life and Work, 1994; contbg. editor Art News, 1973—, Inland Architect, 1975-94. Trustee Ragdale Found., Lake Forest, 1981—. Recipient Harbison award for tchg. Danforth Found. of St. Louis, 1971; Adenauer fellow, 1956-57; Ford Found. fellow, 1964-65; Graham Found. for Advanced Studies in the Fine Arts fellow, 1971, 81, 93; NEH fellow, 1982, 88; Skidmore Owings & Merrill Found. fellow, 1983; recipient Disting. Svc. award Chgo. Phi Beta Kappa Soc., 1972; Hon. Mention Hitchcock Book award Soc. Archtl. Historians, 1987. Mem. AAUP, Coll. Art Assn. (bd. dirs. 1983-86), Archives Am. Art (adv. com.), Soc. Archtl. Historians. Office: Lake Forest Coll Dept Art Lake Forest IL 60045

SCHULZE, HORST H., hotel company executive. Pres., COO The Ritz Carlton Hotel Co., Atlanta. Office: The Ritz-Carlton Hotel Co 3414 Peachtree Rd NE Ste 300 Atlanta GA 30326-1164*

SCHULZE, RICHARD HANS, engineering executive, environmental engineer; b. Buffalo, May 28, 1933; s. Hans Joachim and Lucy (Kawczynska) S.; m. Jacqueline Van Luppen, Nov. 2, 1967 (div. Aug. 1979); children: Richard Hans Jr., Linda Schulze Keefer, John; m. Enika Grooters, Aug. 29, 1987. BSME, Princeton U., 1954; MBA, Northwestern U., 1958. Registered profl. engr., Tex. Rsch. analyst U.S. Steel Corp., Pitts., 1958-60; chief engr. G&H Rsch. and Devel., McKeesport, Pa., 1960-62; cons. Mgmt. and Mktg. Inst., N.Y.C., 1962-63, IITRI mgmt. consulting div., N.Y.C., 1963-64; market analyst plastics div. Mobil Chem. Co., N.Y.C., 1964-66; market devel. mgr. Mobil Chem. Co., Jacksonville, Ill., 1966-68; dist. sales mgr. Mobil Chem. Co., Dallas, 1967-71; pres. Ecology Audits, Inc. (Core Labs.), Dallas, 1971-74, Trinity Cons,, Inc., Dallas, 1974—; instr. over 200 short courses on dispersion moedling of air pollutants throughout world. Contbr. articles to Jour. of Air and Waste Mgmt. Assn., Atmospheric Environ., others; presented papers at sci. symposiums, seminars, confs. Mem. Dallas Symphony Assn., Mus. of Art; bd. dirs. Dallas Opera, 1993—; elder Preston Hollow Presbyn. Ch., 1996—; commr. to Grace Presbytery, 1996. Lt. (j.g.) USNR, 1954-56. Mem. ASME, TAPPI (air quality com.), Am. Acad. Environ. Engrs. (diplomate), Am. Chem. Soc., Am. Meteorol. Soc., Air and Waste Mgmt. Assn. (bd. dirs. 1986-89, 90-93, v.p. 1988-89, 1st v.p. 1990-91, pres. 1991-92, past pres. 1992-93), Nat. Soc. for Clear Air (U.K.), Soc. Petroleum Engrs. (chmn. environ. health and safety award com.), Soc. for Risk Analysis, Semi-Condr. Safety Assn., Verein Deutscher Ingenieure, Assn. Francaise des Ingénieurs et Techniciens Environ., Dallas Bar Assn., Inst. Profl. Environ. Practice (qualified environ. profl., trustee 1993-95). Home: 7619 Marquette St Dallas TX 75225-4412 Office: Trinity Cons Inc 12801 N Central Expy Ste 1200 Dallas TX 75243-1716

SCHULZE, RICHARD M., consumer products executive; b. 1941. With No. States Sales Co., 1962—; now chmn., CEO, dir. Besy Buy Co., Inc., Eden Prairie, Minn. Office: Best Buy Co 7075 Flying Cloud Dr Eden Prairie MN 55344*

SCHULZ-WIDMAR, RUSSELL EUGENE, musician, educator, composer; b. Harvard, Ill., July 29, 1944; s. Friederich Wilhelm and Helen (DeVries) Schulz; m. Suzanne Widmar, Aug. 26, 1967 (div. Sept. 1995); children: John Frederick, Karl Andrew. MusB, Valparaiso U., 1966; SMM, Union Theol. Sem., N.Y.C., 1968; DMA, U. Tex., 1974; postgrad., Royal Sch. Ch. Music, London, summer 1976. Dir. music Univ. United Meth. Ch., Austin, 1971-93, Good Shepherd Episcopal Ch., Austin, 1993—; lectr. Austin (Tex.) Presbyn. Theol. Sem., 1975-91; prof. Episcopal Theol. Sem. S.W., Austin, 1974—; dean Evergreen Music Conf., 1981-87; mem. Standing Commn. on Ch. Music, Episcopal Ch., 1978-85. Editor: (hymnal) Songs of Thanks and Praise, 1980; co-editor: New Hymnal for Colleges and Schools, 1992; chmn. The Hymnal 1982, 1985. Recipient Disting. Alumnus award Valparaiso U., 1988. Mem. Hymn Soc. U.S. and Can. (pres. 1988-90), Order of St. John of Jerusalem. Office: PO Box 2247 Austin TX 78768-2247

SCHUMACHER, ELIZABETH SWISHER, garden ornaments shop owner; b. Webster City, Iowa, Apr. 1, 1940; d. Andrew Dale and Harriet Elizabeth (Hudson) Swisher; m. H. Ralph Schumacher Jr., July 13, 1963; children: Heidi Ruth, Kaethe Beth. BS, U. Colo., 1961; student, Barnes Found. Sch Horticulture, 1976. Owner Garden Accents, West Conshohocken, Pa., 1979—; lectr. on garden ornaments, hillside gradening, water in the garden, 1979—; exhibitor designer show house Vassar Coll., Phila. area sites, 1984—, Phila. Flower Show, 1996—. Contbr. articles to Fine Gardening, Green Scene, Gardens and Landscapes. Recipient Outstanding Landscaping award Pa. Nurserymen's Assn., 1972, Residential Beautification award Upper Merion Twp., 1974, 76, 86, Exhibit of Distinction award Phila. Flower Show, 1989, 1st prize Comml. Exhibit, 1996. Mem. Pa. Hort. Soc. (hotline vol. 1987—), Rhododendron Soc. Am. Office: Garden Accents 4 Union Hill Rd W Conshohocken PA 19428-2719

SCHUMACHER, GEBHARD FRIEDERICH BERNHARD, obstetrician-gynecologist; b. Osnabrueck, Fed. Republic Germany, June 13, 1924; came to U.S., 1962; s. Kaspar and Magarete (Pommer) S.; m. Anne Rose Zanker, Oct. 24, 1958; children: Michael A., Marc M. M.D., U. Goettingen and Tuebingen, 1951; Sc.D. equivalent in obstetrics and gynecology, U. Tuebingen, 1962. Intern U. Tuebingen Med. Sch., 1951-52; tng. biochemistry Max Planck Inst. Biochemistry, Tuebingen, 1952-53; tng. biochemistry and immunology Max Planck Inst. Virus Research, 1953-54; resident in ob-gyn U. Tuebingen, 1954-59, tng. internal medicine, 1959, asst. scientist in ob-gyn and biochem. research, 1959-62, dozent in ob-gyn, 1964-65; Research assoc. in immunology Inst. Tb Research, U. Ill. Coll. Medicine, 1962-63; research assoc., asst. prof. ob-gyn U. Chgo., 1963-64; assoc. prof. ob-gyn asst. prof. biochemistry Albany Med. Coll. of Union U., 1965-67; research physician, div. labs. and research N.Y. State Dept. Health, Albany, 1965-67; assoc. prof. ob-gyn U. Chgo.-Chgo. Lying-In Hosp., 1967-73, chief sect. reproductive biology, 1971-91, prof. Immunology, 1974-91; prof. Biol. Sci. Collegiate Divsn. U. Chgo., 1982—; prof. emeritus U. Chgo., 1991—; cons. WHO, NIH, other nat. and internat. orgns.; mem. tech. and sci. adv. bds. Family Health Internat., Cistron Tech. Inc. Author: (with Beller) The Biology of the Fluids of the Female Genital Tract, 1979; (with Dhindsa) Immunological Aspects of Infertility and Fertility Regulation, 1980; (with Kaiser) Human Reproduction, Fertility, Sterility, Contraception, German edit., 1981, Spanish edit., 1986; contbr. articles to profl. jours. Fellow Am. Coll. Obstetricians and Gynecologists; mem. Soc. Gynecologic Investigation, Am. Soc. Reproductive Medicine, Soc. Study of Reprodn., Am. Acad. Reproductive Medicine, Am. Soc. Cytology, Am. Soc. Investigative Pathology, Am. Soc. Andrology, Chgo. Assn. Reproductive Endocrinologists (pres. 1985-86), N.Y. Acad. Scis., Deutsche Gesellschaft für Gynakologie und Gebrutshilfe, Gesellschaft für Biologische Chemie, Deutsche Gesellschaft für Immunologie, Deutsche Gesellschaft für Bluttransfusion, Gesellschaft Deutscher Naturforscher und Aerzte. Home and Office: 557 Hamilton Wood Rd Homewood IL 60430-4403

SCHUMACHER, HANS H., steel company executive; b. Bad Polzin, Prussia, Germany, Nov. 20, 1933; came to U.S., 1960; s. Karl Heinrich and Helene Erna Martha (Droese) S.; m. Anke Margarethe Johannssen, July 10, 1963 (div. Apr. 1964). BSME, Engring. Acad., Wismar, Germany, 1954; MSc in Mech. Engring, Germany, 1993. Engr. shop and prodn. Mathias Thesen Werft, Wismar, Fed. Republic Germany, 1954-55; project engr. Hauni Maschinenfabrik, Hamburg, Fed. Republic Germany, 1955-56; marine engr. Schlieker Werft, Hamburg, 1956-60; liaison engr. Schlieker Werft, N.Y.C., 1960-62; asst. supr. Hudson Engring. Co., Hoboken, N.J., 1960; marine engr. J.J. Henry Co., Inc., N.Y.C., 1962-63; resident engr. Voest-Alpine Internat. Corp., N.Y.C., 1963-65, pres., dir., 1965—; chmn. Voest-Alpine Can. Corp., Vancouver, B.C., 1987; bd. dirs. Va. Crews Coal Co., Welch, W.Va., Third Colony Corp., N.Y.C.; chmn. Vaico, Inc., N.Y.C.; vice chmn. Voest Alpine Internat. Corp., through 1993. Mem. U.S.-Austrian C. of C. (dir. N.Y.C.). Clubs: Sixty East (N.Y.C.), Southampton (N.Y.) Beach and Tennis. Avocations: swimming, antiques. Address: 180 E 79th St Ph A New York NY 10021-0437

SCHUMACHER, H(ARRY) RALPH, internist, researcher, medical educator; b. Montreal, Feb. 14, 1933; s. H. Ralph and Dorothy (Shreiner) S.; m. Elizabeth Jean Swisher, July 13, 1963; children: Heidi Ruth, Kaethe Beth. B.S., Ursinus Coll., 1955; M.D., U. Pa., 1959. Intern Denver Gen. Hosp., 1959-60; resident in medicine Wadsworth VA Hosp., L.A., 1960-62, fellow in rheumatology, 1962-63; fellow in rheumatology Robert B. Brigham Hosp. and Harvard U. Med. Sch., Boston, 1965-67; chief arthritis-immunology ctr. VA Med. Ctr., Phila., 1967—; faculty mem. U. Pa. Sch. Medicine, Phila., 1967—, prof. medicine, 1979—, acting arthritis div. chief, 1978-80, 91-95; vis. scholar NIH, 1994—. Author: Gout and Pseudogout, 1978, Essentials of a Differential Diagnosis of Rhematoid Arthritis, 1981, Rheumatoid Arthritis, 1988, Case Studies in Rheumatology for the House Officer, 1989, Atlas of Synovial Fluid and Crystal Identification, 1991, A Practical Guide to Synovial Fluid Analysis, 1991; editor: Primer on Rheumatic Diseases, 1981—, Jour. Clin. Rheumatology, 1994—; mem. editorial bd. Jour. Rheumatology, 1973—, Arthritis and Rheumatism, 1981-88, Revue du Rhumatisme, 1992—, Brit. Jour. Clin. Practice, 1992—, New European Rheumatology, 1993—, Japanese Jour. Rheumatology, 1993—; contbr. articles to profl. jours.; lectr., author gardening. Pres. Eastern Pa. chpt. Arthritis Found., 1980-82; chmn., founder Phila. Garden Tours, 1987—; bd. dirs. Hemochromatosis Research Found., 1984—, Am. Bd. Med. Advancement China, 1983—. Served with M.C. USAF, 1963-65. Recipient Van-Breeman award The Netherland Rheumatism Soc., 1988; Deposition VA grantee, 1967—, NIH grantee, 1981. Fellow ACP; mem. Am. Coll. Rheumatology (pres. Southeastern region 1981-82), Phila. Rheumatism Soc. (pres. 1980), Phila. Electron Microscopy Soc. (chmn. 1975-76), Rheumatism Soc. Mex., Rheumatism Soc. Australia, Rheumatism Soc. Colombia, Rheumatism Soc. Chile, Rheumatism Soc. Republic of China, Rheumatism Soc. Argentina, Med. Soc. Argentina, Assn. Mil. Surgeons (Philip Hench award 1986), Fedn. Clin. Rsch., AAAS. Office: Hosp U Pa Ste G, 3d fl Ravdin Bldg 3400 Spruce St Philadelphia PA 19104 *I try to teach meticulous observation and questioning of dogma both in daily care of patients and in laboratory investigation of the poorly understood rheumatic diseases.*

SCHUMACHER, HENRY JEROLD, former career officer, business executive; b. Torrance, Calif., June 17, 1934; s. Henry John and Rene (Wilcox) S.; m. Barbara Howell, Aug. 24, 1958; children: Sheri Lynn, Henry Jerold II. Student, Stanford U., 1953; B.S., U.S. Mil. Acad., 1957; M.S., Northeastern U., Boston, 1965; M.B.A., Auburn U., 1977. Commd. lt. U.S. Army, 1958, advanced through grades to maj. gen., 1982; army attaché Moscow, 1969-71; chief communications ops. Vietnam, 1971-72; exec. officer Office Chief of Staff, 1972-75; comdr. U.S. Army Communications Command, Panama, 1977-79; dir. network integration, Office Asst. Chief of Staff Automation and Communications, Dept. Army, 1979-81; comdr. The White House Communications Agy., Washington, 1981-82; chief U.S. Army Signal Corps, 1981-83; ret., 1983; sr. v.p. Visa Internat., 1983-86; chief oper. officer Fuel Tech., Inc., Stamford, Conn., 1986-87; pres. IMM Systems, Phila., 1987-89; exec. v.p. Cylink Corp., Sunnyvale, Calif., 1990-95; exec. dir. Hiller Mus. of No. Calif. Aviation History, Redwood City, 1995—. Decorated Def. D.S.M., D.S.M., Legion of Merit. Home: 156 Normandy Ct San Carlos CA 94070-1519 Office: Hiller Mus No Calif Aviation History 1300 Hancock St Redwood City CA 94063

SCHUMACHER, JEFFREY DAVID, principal; b. Peoria, Ill., Oct. 29, 1962; s. Harold and Verlene (Baute) S.; m. Carla Jane Sturdevant, Oct. 10, 1989. BS in Elem. Edn. and Spl. Edn., Drake U., Des Moines, 1985; MS in Elem. and Secondary Adminstrn., U. Iowa, 1991. Cert. tchr. K-9, spl. edn. tchr. K-9, adminstr. pre K-12. Spl. edn. tchr. grades 6-8 Des Moines Pub. Schs., 1985-86; spl. edn. sci. tchr. grades 5-9 Orchard Place Campus Sch., Des Moines, 1986-89; tchr. sci. Vinton Shellsburg (Iowa) Sch. Dist., 1989-91; system-wide prin. Nishna Valley Cmty. Schs., Hastings, Iowa, 1991—. Founding mem. Nishna Valley Am. Field Svc., Hastings, 1992; bd. dirs. S.W. Iowa Prins. Acad., Council Bluffs, 1993—; advisor spl. edn. Area Edn. Agy., Council Bluffs, 1992—; pres. Corner Conf. Prins., 1993-94. Des Moines Ind. Schs. grantee, 1988-89. Mem. Nat. Assn. Sch. Prins., Am. Assn. Sch. Prins., Nat. Middle Sch. Assn., Sch. Adminstrs. of Iowa, Nat. Assn. Elem. Sch. Prins., Phi Delta Kappa. Avocations: reading, outdoor activities, travel. Home: 1109 Valleyway Dr Glenwood IA 51534-1238 Office: Nishna Valley Cmty Sch Dist RR 1 Box 80B Hastings IA 51540-9763

SCHUMACHER, JOEL, film writer, director; b. N.Y.C., Aug. 29, 1939; s. Francis and Marian (Kantor) S. BA, Parsons U., 1965. Costume designer: (stage) The Time of the Cuckoo, 1974, (films) Play It As It Lays, 1972, The Last of Sheila, 1972, Blume In Love, 1973, Sleeper, 1973, The Prisoner of Second Avenue, 1975, Interiors, 1978; screenwriter: Car Wash, 1976, Sparkle, 1976, The Wiz, 1978; screenwriter, dir.: (films) D.C. Cab, 1983, St. Elmo's Fire, 1985, (TV movies) The Virginia Hill Story, 1974, Amateur Night at the Dixie Bar and Grill, 1979; dir.: The Incredible Shrinking Woman, 1981, The Lost Boys, 1987, Cousins, 1989, Flatliners, 1990, Dying Young, 1991, Falling Down, 1993, The Client, 1994, Batman Forever, 1995, A Time to Kill, 1996; exec. prodr.: Foxfire, 1985, Slow Burn, 1986; writer, exec. prodr.: (TV pilot) Now We're Cookin', 1983; prodn. designer: Killer Bees, 1974. Office: CAA 9830 Wilshire Blvd Beverly Hills CA 90212-1804*

SCHUMACHER, JOHN CHRISTIAN, semiconductor materials and air pollution control equipment manufacturing company executive; b. Spring Valley, Ill., Feb. 8, 1935; s. Joseph Charles and Theresa Isobel (Flynn) S.; children: Jennifer Lea, Jesse Colin, Jacqueline Chanel. B.S., Stanford U., 1956; M.S., M.I.T., 1958; Ph.D., Stanford U., 1973. Research engr. Calif. Inst. Tech., 1958-60; research and teaching asst. M.I.T., 1960-62; dept. mgr. Lockheed Missile & Space Co., Sunnyvale, Calif., 1962-64, program mgr., Lockheed Research, Palo Alto, Calif., 1964-69; research asso., thesis dir. Stanford U., 1969-73; v.p. J. C. Schumacher Co., Oceanside, Calif., 1973-74, pres., 1974-76, pres., chief exec. officer, 1976-86, Diamond Cubic Corp., 1986-87; founder, pres., chief exec. officer, Custom Engineered Materials, Inc., 1987-92; founder J.C. Schumacher Assocs., Carlsbad, Calif., 1992—. Chmn. Oceanside New Bus. and Industry Commn., 1976-78. Mem. Oceanside C. of C. (dir. 1974-78), Electrochem. Soc., Newcomen Soc., IEEE, AAAS, Phys. Soc. Am., Am. Inst. Chem. Engrs. Republican. Club: La Jolla Country. Patentee improved semicondr. device processing materials and equipment; low cost silicon; energy efficient photovoltaic solar cell mfg., air pollution control equipment.

SCHUMACHER, JON LEE, lawyer; b. Rochester, N.Y., Feb. 28, 1937; s. Howard Alexander and Ruth (Simmons) S.; m. Katherine Truesdell, Apr. 22, 1967; children: Sara Truesdell, Howard Alexander II. AB, Princeton U., 1959; JD, U. Va., 1964. Bar: N.Y. 1964. With Nixon Hargrave Devans & Doyle L.L.P., Rochester, 1964—; mem. mgmt. com. Nixon, Hargrave, Devans & Doyle, Rochester, 1986-90, mng. ptnr., 1988-90. Co-author Charitable Giving and Solicitation. Bd. dirs., officer Rochester Area Found., Inc., 1987-94, United Way, 1986—; pres. estate planning Coun. Rochester, 1986-87. Fellow Am. Coll. Trusts and Estate Counsel; mem. ABA, N.Y. State Bar Assn. (exec. com. trusts and estates law sect. 1985, 88, 94—, chmn. estate planning com. 1992-94, chmn.-elect 1996), Monroe County Bar Assn. (found. pres. 1995-96), Country Club of Rochester, Genesee Valley Club. Republican. Presbyterian. Avocations: jogging, music. Home: 550 Allens Creek Rd Rochester NY 14618-3406 Office: Nixon Hargrave Devans & Doyle Clinton Sq PO Box 1051 Rochester NY 14603-1051

SCHUMACHER, JOSEPH CHARLES, chemical engineer; b. Peru, Ill., Sept. 15, 1911; s. Joseph F. and Josephine (Mattes) S.; m. Theresa Flynn, Jan. 28, 1933; children—John Christian, Kathleen Schumacher Hoffman, Stephen Joseph, Paul; m. Mary Margaret Maher, Jan. 5, 1985. Student, U. Ill., 1928-30; A.B., U. So. Calif., 1946. Research chemist, prodn. supr. Carus Chem. Co., LaSalle, Ill., 1931-40; research and devel. chem. engr. Fine Chems., Inc., Los Angeles, 1940-41; co-founder Western Electro-chem. Co., Los Angeles, 1941, v.p., dir. research, 1941-54, dir.; dir. research Am. Potash & Chem. Corp., 1954-56, v.p. research, 1956-67; v.p. AFN Inc., 1956-67, Kerr-McGee Chem. Corp., 1967-69; founder J.C. Schumacher Co., Oceanside, Calif., 1971, pres., 1971-74, chmn. bd., 1974-86. Regional editor Electrochem. Soc. Jour., 1953-59; co-author, editor Perchlorates; mem. editorial adv. bd. Research Mgmt., 1963-69; contbr. articles to profl. jours.; patentee in chem. products, processes and apparatus. Trustee Whittier Coll., 1968-77. Recipient Honors award U. So. Calif. Chemistry Alumni Soc., 1962. Mem. Electrochem. Soc. (Vittorio de Nora Diamond Shamrock Engring. and Tech. gold medal 1982), Am. Chem. Soc., Planetary Soc., Sigma Xi, Phi Kappa Theta. Roman Catholic. Clubs: Los Angeles Country, Jonathan. Home and Office: 2220 Ave of Stars West Tower # 704 Los Angeles CA 90067

SCHUMACHER, LARRY P., health facility administrator; b. Waseca, Minn., Apr. 26, 1959; s. James H. and Judith A. (Voight) S.; m. Casey A. Hager, June 26, 1982; children: Matthew, Nicholas, Nathan, Mark. Diploma, Burge Sch. Nursing, 1980; BSN, S.W. Mo. State U., 1983; MS in Nursing, Ind. U., 1985. RN, Iowa; cert. nursing adminstr. advanced, 1989. Dir. critical care and med. nursing Rsch. Med. Ctr., Kansas City, Mo.; v.p. nursing and anesthesia St. Joseph Mercy Hosp., Mason City, Iowa; v.p. patient care svcs. Mercy Hosp., Mason City, Iowa; v.p. patient svcs., chief nursing officer North Iowa Mercy Health Ctr., Mason City; sr. vp. clin. integration, chief nursing officer North Iowa Mercy Health Network. Mem. ACHE, ANA, Nat. League Nursing, Am. Orgn. Nurse Execs. Home: 115 10th St NW Mason City IA 50401-2016

SCHUMACHER, ROBERT DENISON, banker; b. Evanston, Ill., Dec. 16, 1933; s. Frank Ade and Dorothy Ormonde (Hilton) S.; m. Mary Ann Montgomery, Aug. 25, 1956; children—Stephen Michael, Jeffrey Hilton. B.A., Williams Coll., 1956; postgrad., Grad. Bus. Sch. N.Y. U., 1957-59; P.M.D., Harvard Bus. Sch., 1966. With Irving Trust Co., N.Y.C., 1956-89, sr. v.p., 1977-89, mgr. adminstrv. services, 1987-89, ret., 1989. Treas. Calvary, Holy Communion and St. George's Episcopal Ch., 1976-79, warden, 1980-86, 89-93; trustee The Church Club, 1993—, treas., 1994—. Mem. The Church Club. Republican. Home: 431 E 20th St New York NY 10010-7502

SCHUMACHER, ROBERT JOSEPH, petroleum company executive; b. Independence, Kans., Mar. 7, 1929; s. Arthur V. and Margaret F. (Templeman) S.; m. Edith Katherine Kelly, Sept. 30, 1950; children: Mary Beth Schumacher Millett, Kathy, Kyle, William. BS in Commerce, Tex. Christian U., 1950; M Profl. Acctg., U. Tex., 1951. CPA, Tex. Staff acct. Sproles & Woodard, CPA's, Ft. Worth, 1950-52; sec., treas. Sojourner Drilling Corp., Abilene, Tex., 1952-68; ind. oil and gas operator, Ft. Worth, 1967-73; pres., chief exec. officer Texland Petroleum, Inc., Ft. Worth, 1973—; chmn., chief exec. officer Pride Refining, Inc., Abilene, 1989-93; pres., CEO Texland

Petroleum Inc., Ft. Worth, Tex., 1973—; bd. dirs. Aztec Mfg. Co., Ft. Worth. Staff sgt. U.S. Army, 1946-48. Republican. Roman Catholic.

SCHUMACHER, THERESA ROSE, singer, musician; b. Muskegon, Mich.; d. Boles and Marguerite (Lassard) Pietkiewicz; m. Glenn O. Schumacher, 1968 (div. 1988); children: Pamela Harrington Boller, Daniel Mark Harrington. BS in Sociology, Fairmont State Coll., 1975. Active W.Va. U. Symphony Choir, 1988—, 93 Fairmont State Coll. Choir; musician with spl. knowledge of music from 1735-1850, Nat. Park Svcs., 1989—. Mem. AAUW, W.Va. Poetry Soc., Morgantown, W.Va. Poetry Soc. Avocations: special knowledge of cacti and succlents, storytelling, writing poetry, country and folk music. Home: PO Box 162 Mannington WV 26582-0162

SCHUMACHER, WILLIAM JACOB, retired army officer; b. Scranton, Pa., Apr. 15, 1938; s. Jacob and Kathryn Isabel (Williams) S.; m. Sandra Dee Caryl, July 23, 1960; children: Caryl Lee, Leslie Karen. BSEE, Lafayette Coll., 1960; MS in Aerospace Engrng., Pa. State U., 1970. Commd. 2d lt. U.S. Army, 1960, advanced through grades to brig. gen., 1989; asst. prof. dept. engrng. U.S. Mil. Acad., West Point, N.Y., 1970-73; student Def. Systems Mgmt. Coll., Ft. Belvoir, Va., 1975; asst. project mgr. Office of Project Mgr., Rock Island (Ill.) Arsenal, 1976-78; asst. mgr. conventional ammunition and guided missiles div. Cannon Arty. Weapons System, Picatinny (N.J.) Arsenal, 1978-81; comdg. officer Iowa Army Ammunition Plant, Burlington, 1981-83; student U.S. Army War Coll., Carlisle, Pa., 1983-84; project mgr. for Hellfire U.S. Army Missile Command, Huntsville, Ala., 1984-87; program exec. officer Close Combat Missiles, Huntsville, 1987-88, Fire Support, Huntsville, 1988-90; dep. ammunition, asst. sec. army rsch., devel., acquisition Hdqrs. Army Materiel Command, Washington, 1990-92; dep. comdg. officer Strategic Def. Command, Huntsville, 1992; retired, tech. cons. Garber Internat. Assocs., Inc., Arlington, Va., 1992; gen. mgr. strategic systems Martin Marietta, Arlington, Va., 1992-95; v.p. Bunyard Enterprises, Inc., Alexandria, Va. Mem. Assn. U.S. Army, Am. Def. Preparedness Assn., Phi Kappa Phi. Avocations: swimming, gardening, book collecting.

SCHUMACKER, RANDALL ERNEST, educational psychologist; b. Oakes, N.D., May 26, 1951; s. Ernest and Helen (Jackson) S.; m. Joanne Cummins, July 24, 1952; children: Rachel Ann, Jamie Maureen. AA, William Rainey Harper Jr. Coll, 1970; BS, Western Ill. U., 1972; MS, So. Ill. U., 1978, PhD, 1984. Rsch. asst. So. Ill. U., Carbondale, 1980-84, assoc. dir. computing, 1984-87; asst. prof. U. North Tex., Denton, 1988-90, assoc. prof., 1991—; vis. prof. So. Ill. U., 1980-84; vis. scholar U. Chgo.; cons. Tex. Acad. Math. & Sci., Denton, 1993, Carrollton-Farmers Branch (Tex.), 1991-94, Profl. Devel., 1989-92; presenter in field. Contbr. articles to profl. jours. Mem. Am. Psychol. Assn., Am. Ednl. Rsch. Assn., Southwest Ednl. Rsch. Assn., Am. Statis. Assn., Midwestern Ednl. Rsch. Assn., Nat. Coun. Measurement Edn., Phi Delta Kappa. Republican. Lutheran. Avocations: sailing, golf, gardening. Office: U North Tex Coll Edn Denton TX 76203

SCHUMAKER, DALE H., paper manufacturing company executive; b. 1933. BS, U. Wis., 1955. Engr. Am. Can Co., Neenah, Wis., 1955-65; with Appleton (Wis.) Papers, Inc., 1965—, v.p. mfg., 1965-79, 1979-84, sr. v.p. mfg., 1984-85, exec. v.p., 1985-86, pres., chief operating officer, 1986—, now chmn. Office: Appleton Papers Inc 825 E Wisconsin Ave Appleton WI 54911-3873*

SCHUMAKER, LARRY LEE, mathematics educator; b. Aberdeen, S.D., Nov. 5, 1939; s. Lee B. and Irene Elizabeth (Kelly) S.; m. Gerda Ingeborg Boguszewski, June 10, 1963; 1 child, Annabel Louise. BS in Math., S.D. Sch. of Mines, 1961; MS in Math., Stanford U., 1962, PhD in Math., 1966. Staff mathematician Hughes Aircraft Co., Culver City, Calif., 1961-63; research asst. Stanford U., 1964-65, instr. computer sci. dept., 1966; research mem. Math. Research Ctr., U. Wis., Madison, 1966-68; asst. prof. to assoc. prof. U. Tex., 1968-74, prof. of math., 1974-79; prof. math. Tex. A&M U., 1981-88; dir. Ctr. for Approximation Theory Texas A&M U., 1981-88; prof. of math. Vanderbilt U., Nashville, 1988—; visiting prof. and researcher in field. Author: Approximation Functions, 1967, Approximation Theory I, 1973, Approximation Theory II, 1976, Spline Functions: Basic Theory, 1980, Approximation Theory IV, 1983, Approximation Theory V, 1986, Topics in Multivariate Approximation, 1987, Mathematical Methods in Computer-aided Geometric Design, 1989, Approximation Theory VI, 1989, Approximation Theory VI, Part II, 1989, Approximation Theory VII, 1992, Curves and Surfaces, 1991, Mathematical Methods in Computer-aided Geometric Design II, 1992, Numerical Methods of Approximation Theory, Vol. 9, 1992, Recent Advances in Wavelets, 1993, Curves and Surfaces in Geometric Design, 1994, Wavelets, Images, and Surface Fitting, 1994, Mathematical Methods for Curves and Surfaces, 1995, Approximation Theory VIII, Vol. 1, 1995, Vol. 2, 1995. Recipient Humboldt Prize Humboldt Found., 1989, Centennial Outstanding Grad. award S.D. Sch. Mines and Tech., 1985, Student Coun. Tchg. Excellence award Tex. A&M U., 1981; named Humboldt fellow, 1978-79. Mem. Soc. for Indsl. & Applied Math., Am. Math. Soc., The Math. Assn. Am.. Office: Vanderbilt U Dept Of Math Nashville TN 37240

SCHUMAN, ALLAN L., chemical company executive; b. 1937. BS, NYU, 1955. With Ecolab Inc., St. Paul, 1957—, v.p. mktg. and nat. acctg., 1972-78, v.p. mktg. devel., 1978-79, now pres., CEO. Office: Ecolab Inc Ecolab Ctr Saint Paul MN 55102

SCHUMAN, GERALD EUGENE, soil scientist; b. Sheridan, Wyo., July 5, 1944; s. George and Mollie (Michael) S.; m. Mabel F. Kaisler, Mar. 27, 1965; children: William G., Kara L. BS in Soil Sci., U. Wyo., 1966; MS in Soil Sci., U. Nev., 1969; PhD in Agronomy, U. Nebr., 1974. Cert. profl. soil scientist. Soil scientist USDA Agrl. Rsch. Svc., Reno, 1966-69, Lincoln, Nebr., 1969-75; soil scientist USDA Agrl. Rsch. Svc., Cheyenne, Wyo., 1975-77, soil scientist, rsch. leader, 1977—; reclamation cons. HKM Assocs., Billings, Mont., 1986-88. Co-editor: Reclaiming Mine Soils, 1987, symposium proc. Soil and Overburgen in Reclamation, 1983; contbr. articles to profl. jours., book chpts. Mem., pres., elder, trustee Our Savior Luth. Ch., Cheyenne, 1975—. Recipient Profl. of Yr. award Orgn. Profl. Employees of USDA, 1988. Fellow Soil Sci. Soc. Am., Am. Soc. Agronomy (cert.), Soil and Water Conservation Soc. (bd. dirs. 1986-89, commendation 1980), Soil Sci. Soc. Am.; mem. Am. Soc. Surface Mining and Reclamation (nat. exec. com. 1991-93, pres. 1992-93, Reclamation Rsch. award 1991), Soc. for Range Mgmt. (Man of the Range award Wyo. sect. 1993, Outstanding Achievement award 1995), Internat. Soil Sci. Soc. Avocations: fishing, hunting, traveling. Office: High Plains Grasslands Rsch Sta 8408 Hildreth Rd Cheyenne WY 82009-8809

SCHUMAN, HOWARD, sociologist, educator; b. Cin., Mar. 16, 1928; s. Robert A. and Esther (Bohn) S.; m. Josephine Miles, Sept. 1, 1951; children—Marc, Elisabeth, David. Student, U. Chgo., 1947-48; A.B., Antioch Coll., 1953; M.S. in Psychology, Trinity U., 1956; Ph.D. in Sociology, Harvard, 1961. Research asso. Harvard, 1961-64; asst. prof. U. Mich., Ann Arbor, 1964-67; asso. prof. U. Mich., 1967-71, prof. sociology, 1971—, chmn. dept., 1970-73, dir. Detroit Area Study, 1965-71, program dir. Survey Research Ctr., 1974—, dir. Survey Research Ctr., 1982-90, prof. emeritus, rsch. scientific emeritus, 1996—. Author: (with others) Economic Development and Individual Change, Racial Attitudes in Fifteen American Cities, Conversations at Random, Black Racial Attitudes, Questions and Answers in Attitude Surveys, Racial Attitudes in America. Served with AUS, 1954-56. Fellow Am. Acad. Arts and Scis.; mem. Am. Sociol. Soc., Am. Assn. for Pub. Opinion Rsch. (pres. 1985-86). Home: HC 31 Box 477 Phippsburg ME 04562-9708

SCHUMAN, NANCY KATHLEEN, secondary education educator; b. Cleve., May 26, 1946; d. Ralph Henry and Eola Kathleen (Land) S. BA, Wellesley Coll., 1968; M Accountancy and Fin. Info. Sys., Cleve. State U., 1988. Cert. tchr., Ohio. Clk. Warner & Swasey Co., Solon, Ohio, 1968-70; bookkeeper J.H. Hinz Co., Cleve., 1970-73; tchr. music Bedford (Ohio) City Schs., 1973—; dir. handbell choirs St. Andrew Episcopal Ch., Mentor, Ohio, 1980—; singer Cleve. Orch. Chorus, 1973-89. Mem. Am. Guild English Handbell Ringers, Mensa, Christian Coalition, Phi Beta (chpt. treas. 1990-95, nat. treas. 1992-95, spl. recognition award 1994). Republican. Episcopalian. Avocations: reading, horseback riding, travel. Home: 5481 Millwood Ln # D Willoughby OH 44094-3263 Office: Aurora Upper Intermediate Sch 24200 Aurora Rd Bedford Heights OH 44146

SCHUMANN, ALICE MELCHER, medical technologist, educator, sheep farmer; b. Cleve., Sept. 1, 1931; d. John Henry and Marian Louise (Clark) M.; m. Stuart McKee Struever, Aug. 21, 1956 (div. June 1983); children: Nathan Chester, Hanna Russell; m. John Otto Schumann, July 3, 1985. BS, Colby Coll., New London, N.H., 1953. Cert. tchr.; cert. med. technologist. Rschr. Lakeside Hosp., Cleve., 1953-54, Bambridge (Ohio) Schs., 1954-55, Shalersville (Ohio) Schs., 1955-56, Richtnior Sch., Overland, Mo., 1956-57; sci. tchr. Tonica (Ill.) High Sch., 1956-58, Morton Grove (Ill.) High Sch., 1958-60, Univ. Chgo. Lab Sch., 1960-65; co-founder Ctr. for Am. Archeology, dir. flotation rsch. U. Chgo. Campus, Kampsville, Ill., 1957-71, head of supplies distbn., dir. food svcs. dept.; head mailing dept. Found. for Ill. Archeology, Evanston and Kampsville, Ill., 1971-83; sheep farmer, wool processor Gravel Hill Farm, Kampsville, 1983—. Vol. Mt. Sinai Hosp., Cleve., 1948-49; tchr. Title I Dist. 40, Kampsville, 1970-71. Recipient Beverly Booth award Colby Coll., 1953, 1st prize for hand spun yarn DeKalb County Fair, Sandwich, Ill., 1987, 88. Mem. Precious Fibers Found., Natural Colored Wool Growers Assn., Farm Bur. of Calhoun County. Avocations: wool growing, spinning wool and cotton, knitting, raising Great Pyrenees guard dogs for sheep, gardening. Home and Office: Gravel Hill Farm RR 1 Box 121A Kampsville IL 62053-9720

SCHUMANN, WILLIAM HENRY, III, financial executive; b. Iowa City, Aug. 28, 1950; s. William Henry Jr. and Eunice Vere (Doak) S.; m. Denise Suzane Hargrove, Sept. 29, 1979; children: Stefanie Lynn, John William, Kimberly Ann, Robert William. BS, UCLA, 1972; MS, U. So. Calif., 1973. Program mgmt. analyst Hughes Helicopters, Culver City, Calif., 1973-75; mgr. fin. planning Sunkist Growers, Sherman Oaks, Calif., 1975-81; dir. North Am. Ops. Agrl. Chem. Group, FMC Corp., Chgo., 1981—; bd. dirs. Gt. Lakes Advisors; v.p., gen. mgr. Agrl. Products Group, Phila., 1995—. Republican. Office: FMC Corp Agrl Chem Group 1735 Market St Philadelphia PA 19103-7501

SCHUMER, CHARLES ELLIS, congressman; b. Brooklyn, N.Y., Nov. 23, 1950; s. Abraham and Selma (Rosen) S.; m. Iris Weinshall, 1980; 1 child, Jessica Emily. BA magna cum laude, Harvard U., 1971, J.D. with honors, 1974. Bar: N.Y. 1975. Mem. staff U.S. Senator Claiborne Pell, 1973; assoc. Paul, Weiss, Rifking, Wharton and Garrison, 1974; mem. N.Y. State Assembly, 1975-80, chmn. subcom. on city mgmt. and governance, 1977, chmn. com. on oversight and investigation, 1979; mem. 97th-98th Congresses from 16th N.Y. Dist., 99th-104th Congresses from 10th (now 9th) N.Y. dist., Washington, D.C., 1985—; mem. Banking & Fin. Svcs. Com., ranking minority mem. jud. subcom. on crime. Mem. B'nai Brith, Phi Beta Kappa. Democrat. Jewish. Office: US House of Reps Rayburn House Office Bldg Rm 2211 Washington DC 20515*

SCHUMER, WILLIAM, surgeon, educator; b. Chgo., June 29, 1926; s. Solomon and Gussie (Gross) S.; children—Scott, Fern. M.B., Chgo. Med. Sch., 1949, M.D., 1950; M.S., U. Ill., 1966. Diplomate: Am. Bd. Surgery. Intern Mt. Sinai Hosp. Med. Center, Chgo., 1949-50; resident Mt. Sinai Hosp. Med. Center, 1950-54; asst. prof. surgery Chgo. Med. Sch., 1959-65, asst. prof. cardiovascular research, 1964-65; attending surgeon, then asst. chief surgery Mt. Sinai Hosp., Chgo., 1962-65; attending surgeon Hines (Ill.) VA Hosp., 1960-63, VA West Side Hosp., Chgo., 1963-64; dir. surg. service U. Calif. at Davis, Sacramento County Med. Center, 1965-67; chief surg. service VA West Side Hosp., 1967-75; assoc. prof. surgery faculty Abraham Lincoln Sch. Medicine, U. Ill., Chgo., 1967-69; prof. surgery Abraham Lincoln Sch. Medicine, U. Ill., 1969-75; prof. biol. chemistry Grad. Coll., U. Ill. Med. Center, Chgo., 1974-75; mem. staff U. Ill. Hosp., 1967-75; surgery, chmn. dept. U. HEalth Scis./Chgo. Med. Sch., North Chicago, Ill., 1975-90, disting. prof., 1990—; chief surg. service North Chicago VA Med. Center, 1975-79, attending surgeon, 1979-80, chief gen. surg. sect., 1980-82, attending surg. sect., 1983—; chmn. dept. surgery Mt. Sinai Med. Center, Chgo., 1990—; prof. biochemistry U. Health Scis. Chgo. Med. Sch., 1977—, also prof. critical care medicine, disting. prof., 1990—; Mem. numerous coms. VA. Co-editor: Corticosteroids in the Treatment of Shock: Principles and Practice, 1974, Advances in Shock Research, Vol. 2, 1979, Vol. 4, 1980, Vol. 6, 1981, Molecular and Cellular Aspects of Shock and Trauma, Vol. 3, 1983-88; assoc. editor: Circulatory Shock, 1976-79, editor, 1979-88, cons. editor, 1988—; contbr. numerous articles to profl. jours, chpts. to books. Recipient Disting. Alumnus award, 1974, Honors Achievement award Angiology Research Found., 1965, Morris L. Parker award for meritorious research Chgo. Med. Sch., 1976; also numerous awards for sci. exhibits and films. Mem. AAAS, AAUP, ACS, AMA, Am. Assn. Surgery of Trauma, Am. Physiol. Soc., Am. Surg. Assn., Assn. Am. Med. Colls., Assn. VA Surgeons (pres. 1976), Ctrl. Soc. Clin. Rsch., Ctrl. Surg. Soc., Midwest Surg. Soc., Ill. Surg. Soc., Chgo. Shock Soc. (pres. 1978-79), Collegium Internat. Chirurgiae Digestivae, Digestive Disease Found., Inst. Medicine Chgo., N.Y. Acad. Scis., Reticuloendothelial Soc., Soc. Internat. de Chirurgie, Soc. Surgery Alimentary Tract, Soc. Critical Care Medicine, Internat. Fedn. Surg. Colls., Soc. Univ. Surgeons, Surg. Infection Soc., Warren H. Cole Soc., Alumni Assn. U. Ill., Alumni Assn. Chgo. Med. Sch. (prees. Chgo. chpt.), Minn. Surg. Soc. (hon.), Sigma Xi, Alpha Omega Alpha. Office: Mt Sinai Hosp Med Ctr U Health Scis Chgo Med Sch California Ave at 15th St Chicago IL 60608

SCHUMM, STANLEY ALFRED, geologist, educator; b. Kearny, N.J., Feb. 22, 1927; s. Alfred Henry and Mary Elizabeth (Murdock) S.; m. Ethel Patricia Radli, Sept. 3, 1950; children: Brian Murdock, Mary Theresa, Christine Ann. BA, Upsala Coll., 1950; PhD, Columbia U., 1955. Research geologist U.S. Geol. Survey, Denver, 1955-67; prof. geology Colo. State U., Ft. Collins, 1967-86, Univ. disting. prof., 1986—, acting asso. dean, 1973-74; vis. prof. U. Calif., Berkeley, 1959-60, U. Witwatersrand, South Africa, 1975; fellow U. Sydney, Australia, 1964-65, U. New South Wales, 1988; vice chmn. U.S. Nat. Com. Quaternary Rsch., 1967-70, 75-82; dist. vis. scientist U. tex., 1970; vis. lectr. numerous univs. in U.S., vis. scientist N.Z., Europe, Can., Venezuela, Brazil; vis. scientist Polish Acad. Sci., 1969; cons. to govt. agys., engrng. firms; prin. geomorphologist, dir. Water Engring. Tech., Davis, Calif., and Ft. Collins, Colo., 1980-81; sr. assoc. Ayres Assocs., Ft. Collins; prin. investigator rsch. projects NSF, 1969-92, Colo. Agrl. Expt. Sta., 1970-75, Army Rsch. Office, 1970-80, 82-93, Office Water Rsch. and Tech., 1974-83, Nat. Park Svc., 1975-77, Fed. Hwy. Adminstrn., 1978-80, Soil Conservation Svc., 1980-85, NASA, 1984-88, Smithsonian Inst., 1986-87, Can. Internat. Devel. Agy., 1991-92. Author: The Fluvial System, 1977, To Interpret the Earth, 1991; co-author: Incised Channels, 1984, Geomorphology, 1985, Experimental Fluvial Geomorphology, 1987; editor: United States Contribution to Quaternary Research, 1969, River Morphology, 1972, Slope Morphology, 1973, Drainage Basin Morphology, 1977, Physical Geography of W.M. Davis, 1980, The Variability of Large Alluvial Rivers, 1994; contbr. chpts. to sci. books, articles to profl. jours. Served with USNR, 1944-45. Recipient Disting. Alumnus award Upsala Coll., 1980, L.W. Durrell award Colo. State U., 1980, Linton award Brit. Geomorphology Rsch. Group, 1981, Warren prize Nat. Acad. Sci., 1986, Best Paper award Soc. Sedimentary Geology, 1996; Harkness fellow U. Canterbury, N.Z., 1983; fellow Japanese Soc. for Advancement of Sci., 1983, Dept. Agr., Republic of South Africa, 1984, Australian Nat. U., 1988; named honor scientist Colo. State U. chpt. Sigma Xi, 1986. Fellow AAAS, Geol. Soc. Am. (asso. editor 1973-75, vice chmn. geomorphology div. 1978-79, chmn. 1979-80, Kirk Bryan award 1979); mem. Am. Geophys. Union (Horton award 1958, assoc. editor 1973-75), ASCE, Internat. Geog. Union, Assn. Am. Geographers, Internat. Assn. Quaternary Research, Am. Quaternary Assn. (councillor), Sigma Xi (pres. Colo. State U. chpt. 1987-88, honor scientist 1987). Home: 1308 Rollingwood Ln Fort Collins CO 80525-1946 Office: Colo State U Dept Earth Resources Fort Collins CO 80525 also: Ayres Assocs 3665 John F Kennedy Pky Fort Collins CO 80525-3152

SCHUNK, ROBERT WALTER, astrophysics research administrator; b. N.Y.C.. BS, NYU, 1965; PhD in Phys. Fluids, Yale U., 1970. Fellow space physics Inst. Sci. and Tech., U. Mich., 1970-71; rsch. assoc. geophysicist Yale U., 1971-73; rsch. assoc. space physics U. Calif., San Diego, 1973-76; assoc. prof. Utah State U., Logan, 1976-79, prof. physics, 1979—; mem. Com. Solar Terrestrial Rsch., Geophys. Rsch. Bd., Nat. Acad. Sci., 1979-82, Nat. Ctr. Atmospheric Rsch. Computer Divsns. Adv. Panel, 1980-83; prin. invester Solar Terrestrial Theory Program, 1980—. Assoc. editor Jour. Geophys. Rsch., 1977-80. Recipient Gov.'s Medal Sci. & Tech., Utah, 1988. Mem. AAAS, Am. Geophys. Union. Home: Utah State U Ctr Atmospheric Space Logan UT 84322-0001

SCHUNKE, HILDEGARD HEIDEL, accountant; b. Indpls., Nov. 24, 1948; d. Edwin Carl and Hildegard Adelheid (Baumbach) S. BA, Ball State U., Muncie, Ind., 1971, MA in German/English, 1973, MA in Acctg., 1975. CPA, Ind., Calif. Exch. teaching grad. asst. Padagogische Hochschule, Germany, 1971-72; teaching grad. asst. German/acctg. Ball State U., Muncie, 1972, 74-75, asst. prof. acctg., 1975-78; investing rschr. Family Partnership, Muncie, 1977-83; staff acct. Am. Lawn Mower Co., Muncie, 1984-88, G&J Seiberlich, CPAs, St. Helena, Calif., 1988-89, R.A. Gullotta, MBA, CPA, Sonoma, Calif., 1989-90; plant acct. Napa Pipe Corp., Napa, Calif., 1990—; continuing edn. instr. Calif. Soc. CPAs, Redwood City, 1990. ESOL instr. Napa County Project Upgrade, 1988-92; ticketing and refreshments com. North Ba Philharmonic Orch., Napa, 1988—, North Bay Wind Ensemble, Napa, 1988—. Mem. AICPAs, Calif. Soc. CPAs, Ind. Soc. CPAs, Inst. Internal Auditors, Environ. Auditing Roundtable, Am. Soc. Quality Control. Avocations: gardening, transcribing, translating and reading German. Home: 1117 Devonshire Ct Suisun City CA 94585-3343 Office: Napa Pipe Corp 1025 Kaiser Rd Napa CA 94558-6257

SCHUPAK, LESLIE ALLEN, public relations company executive; b. Spokane, Wash., Apr. 5, 1945; s. Leo and Henrietta (Neumann) S.; m. Dianne Barbara Goldin, June 23, 1968; 1 child, Adam J. BS, Boston U., 1967, MS, 1971. Asst. to pres., account exec. Sperber Assocs., Inc., Boston, 1968-69; account supr. Wilcox & Williams, N.Y.C., 1969-70; v.p., mgr. Daniel J. Edelman, Inc., N.Y.C., 1970-72; mng. ptnr. Kanan, Corbin, Schupak & Aronow, Inc., N.Y.C., 1972—. Pres. Whippoorwill Lake Property Owners Assn., Chappaqua, N.Y., 1984-88; mem. exec. com. Coll. Comm., Boston U. With U.S. Army, 1968-73. Mem. Nat. Investor Rels. Inst., Donald Ross Soc., Metropolis Country Club (White Plains, N.Y.), Desert Mountain Club (Scottsdale, Ariz.), Met. Golf Assn. Avocations: golf; tennis; fly fishing. Home: 2 Whippoorwill Close Chappaqua NY 10514-2330 Office: KCS&A Pub Rels 820 2nd Ave New York NY 10017-4504

SCHUPP, ANASTASIA LUKA, lawyer; b. Chgo.; d. Joseph Anthony and Anastasia Maria (Romel) Luka; m. William Schupp, Apr. 20, 1968 (div. June 1994); 1 child, William Joseph. BS in Social Sci., Loyola U., 1966, JD, 1977; MA, U. Mich., 1968. Bar: Ill. 1982, U.S. Supreme Ct. 1994. Law libr. Seyfarth, Shaw, Fairweather & Geraldson, Chgo., 1979-82; ptnr. Flader & Haces, Chgo., 1982-85; assocl. Hyatt Legal Svcs., Chgo., 1985-86; pvt. practice Chgo., 1986—; lectr. Chgo. Bd. Realtors, 1988-89, Robert Morris Coll., Orland Park, Ill., 1993, East West U., Chgo., 1993, Montay Coll., Chgo., 1994—, academic coun., 1994—. Editor: An Ethnic Christmas, 1982; (newsletter) The Overture, 1980-81; contbr. articles to profl. jours. Vol. Chgo. Vol. Legal Svcs., 1991—; arbitrator Chgo. Archdiocese, 1994—; atty. coord. Com. to Elect Richard J. Owens for Judge, Chgo., 1993-94. Mem. Womens Bar aSsn. Ill. (chair com. 1984, 94), Chgo. Bar Assn., Advs. Soc. (historian 1985-87). Democrat. Roman Catholic. Avocations: art, writing, gardening. Home and Office: 5425 S Richmond St Chicago IL 60632

SCHUR, JEFFREY, advertising executive; b. Capetown, Cape of Good Hope, Union of South Africa, May 3, 1946; Canadian citizen; came to U.S., 1992; s. Lionel Harry and Dorothy (Siman) S.; m. Lucille Stella Breakey, Nov. 30, 1965; children: David Leon, Cynthia-Jean. Diploma in Mktg., Cape Coll. for Advanced Tech. Edn., Capetown, 1970. Account exec. J. Walter Thompson, Capetown and Johannesburg, Republic of South Africa, 1969-71; account dir. Ogilvy & Mather, Johannesburg, 1971-76; internat. vp. Latin Am. base Ogilvy & Mather, N.Y.C., 1976-78; account dir. Ogilvy & Mather, Toronto, Ont., Can., 1978-80; sp. gen. mgr., pres. Saatchi & Saatchi, Toronto, 1980-84; pres., chief exec. officer Needham Harper Can., Toronto, 1985-86, Schur Peppler & Assocs., Toronto, 1986-89, Doner Schur Peppler, Toronto, 1989-92; exec. v.p. Earle Palmer Brown, N.Y.C., 1992-94; ptnr. Doig, Elliott, Schur Inc., N.Y.C., 1994—. Dir. Outward Bound, Toronto, 1980-83, Can. Liver Found., Toronto, 1984-86, Toronto Family Svc. Assn., 1985, York Mills Valley Assn., Toronto, 1990-92, Children's Aid, Toronto, 1991-92, S.A. Defence Forces 1st Parachute Bn., 1964-73. Mem. Chartered Inst. Mktg. (lectr. 1971-73, examiner 1973-74, edn. chmn. 1974-75, rsch. award 1970), Devil's Glen Club, Royal Marsh Harbour Yacht Club. Avocations: skiing, scuba, literature, gardening. Home: 55 Shore Rd Old Greenwich CT 06870-0249 Office: Doig Elliott Schur Inc 58A W 15th St New York NY 10011-6835

SCHUR, LEON MILTON, economist, educator; b. Milw., Jan. 11, 1923; s. Ben and Bertha (Stein) S.; m. Edith Laiken, Sept. 4, 1949; children—Julie Miriam, Claudia Laiken, Amy Ruth. Student, U. Wis., 1941-43, Dartmouth, 1943-44; B.A., U. Wis., 1946, Ph.D., 1955. From instr. to prof. econs. La. State U., 1954-64; prof. econs., dir. Ctr. Econ. Edn. U. Wis., Milw., 1964—, acting chancellor, 1979-80, chmn. dept. econs., 1987—; vis. prof. Tulane U., 1961, U. Wis., 1962; dir. Univ. Nat. Bank., Wis. Coun. Econ. Edn., 1964—. Contbr. articles to profl. jours. Bernard F. Sliger chair econ. edn. Fla. State U., 1989—; dir. Discovery World Mus. Sci., Econs. and Tech., 1978—. From seaman to lt. (j.g.) USNR, 1943-46. Mem. Am. Econ. Assn., Am. Finance Assn., Am. Assn. U. Profs., Wis. Econ. Assn. (pres. 1975-77), Phi Eta Sigma, Beta Gamma Sigma. Jewish. Home: 173 W Suburban Dr Milwaukee WI 53217-2336

SCHUR, SUSAN DORFMAN, public affairs consultant; b. Newark, Feb. 27, 1940; d. Norman and Jeanette (Handelman) Dorfman; children: Diana Elisabeth, Erica Marlene. BA, Goucher Coll., 1961. Adminstr. fed. housing, fgn. aid, anti-poverty programs, 1961-67; mem. Mass. Housing Appeals Com., 1977-86; mem., v.p. Bd. of Alderman, Newton, Mass., 1974-81; mem. Mass. Ho. of Reps., 1981-94; pvt. pub. affairs cons., Newton, Mass., 1995—. Mem. Newton Dem. City Com., 1970—.

SCHURE, ALEXANDER, university chancellor; b. Can., Aug. 4, 1920; s. Harry Joshua and Bessie (Ginsberg) S.; m. Dorothy Rubin, Dec. 8, 1943 (dec. June 1981); children: Barbara, Matthew, Louis, Jonathan; m. Gail Doris Strollo, Sept. 12, 1984. A.S.T. in Elec. Engring, Pratt Inst., 1943; B.S., CCNY, 1947; M.A., N.Y. U., 1948, Ph.D., 1950, Ed.D., 1953; D.Engring. Sci., Nova U., 1975; DSc, N.Y. Inst. Tech., 1976; LL.D., Boca Raton Coll., 1976, L.I. U., 1983; L.H.D., Columbia Coll., 1983; D of Pedagogy, N.Y. Chiropractic Coll., 1985. Asst. dir. Melville Radio Insts., N.Y.C., 1945-48; pres. Crescent Sch. Radio and Televison, Bklyn., 1948-55, Crescent Electronics Corp., N.Y.C., 1951-55, N.Y. Tech. Inst., Bklyn., 1953-55; pres., chancellor N.Y. Inst. Tech., 1955-91, chancellor emeritus, 1991—; pres., CEO, chancellor The Univ. Fedn., Inc., 1995—; founder Computer Graphics Lab NY Inst. Tech., 1985-91; chancellor, CEO, Nova U., 1970-85; mem. Fla. State Bd. Ind. Colls. and Univs., 1991—; pres. Vidbits, Inc.; dir. Seversky Electronatom Corp., Executone Inc; cons. N.Y. State Dept. Edn., U.S. Office Edn., UNESCO; mem. Regents Regional Coordinating Council for Post-Secondary Edn. in N.Y.C., 1973—, Nassau County Consortia on Higher Edn., L.I., 1971—, Alfred P. Sloan Found. adv. com. for expanding minority opportunities in engring., 1974; rep. to Nat. Assn. State Adv. Council, 1975—; chmn. N.Y. Title IV Adv. Council, 1975-77; mem. steering com. L.I. Regional Adv. Council, 1974—; chair Regents Adv. Council on Learning Techs., 1986-88; mem., trustee exec. com. Commn. Ind. Colls. and Univs.; mem. adv. council learning technologies N.Y. State Dept. Edn., 1982—; mem. Accreditation Task Force for Council on Postsecondary Accreditation/SHEEBO Project on Assessing Long Distance Learning Via Telecommunications (Project ALLTEL), 1982—; mem. N.Y. State Motion Picture and TV adv. bd., chairperson tech. com.; dir. numerous research projects; expert witness Ho. Reps. com. of Commn. on Sci. and Astronautics; mem. Fla. State Bd. Ind. Colls. and Univs. Author and/or edited textbooks, film producer; designer automatic teaching machine; built one of first computer-controlled anthropomorphic speech devices, 1959; patentee in field. Pres. bd. dirs., trustee L.I. Ednl. TV Coun., Garden City; bd. dirs. Coun. Higher Ednl. Instns., N.Y.C., 1973-83. Served with Signal Corps AUS, 1942-45. 1st inductee Fine Arts Mus. of Long Island's Computer Hall of Fame, 1986. Mem. IEEE (L.I. sect. Gruenwald award 1988), N.Y. Acad. Sci., Am. Inst. Engring. Edn., N.E.A., Electronic Industries Assn. (chmn. task force curriculum devel.), Phi Delta Kappa, Delta Mu Delta, Eta Kappa Nu. Office: NY Inst Tech Office Chancellor Emeritus Old Westbury NY 11568 *The world is an ever changing, ever challenging reality, filled with opportunities for individual fulfillment and success. A positive philosophy* *toward life does much to make the realization of individual potential an actuality.*

SCHURE, MATTHEW, college president; b. N.Y.C., May 26, 1948; s. Alexander and Dorothy (Rubin) S.; m. Judith Z. Birchman, Aug. 12, 1973; children: Jared, Deborah. BA magna cum laude with high honors in Psychology, Queens Coll., 1969; MA, Columbia U., 1970, MPH, 1976, PhD, 1976. Lic. psychologist, N.Y. Mem. faculty N.Y. Inst. Tech., Old Westbury, 1969—, research assoc., instr., asst. prof., assoc. prof. behavioral scis., 1969-70, counselor, 1970-72, assoc. dir. Human Resources Devel. Ctr., 1973-77, assoc. dean acad. assessment, 1977-78, dir. Human Resources Devel. Ctr., 1978-81, pres., 1982—; dep. provost, chmn. dept. community medicine N.Y. Coll. Osteo. Medicine, 1981-91. Author: Hannah's Trial: Our Triumph Over Infertility, 1981; contbr. articles and papers in field to profl. pubs. Trustee Commn. on Ind. Colls. and Univs., 1983-86, St. Barnabas Hosp., L.I. Regional Adv. Coun. on Higher Edn.; chmn. bd. trustees N.Y. State Higher Edn. Svcs. Corp., 1993—; mem. N.Y. State Coun. on Problem Gambling, 1995; chmn. program com. Pvt. Industry Coun., Town of Oyster Bay. Mem. APA, Nassau County Psychol. Assn., Am. Assn. Colls. of Osteo. Medicine (trustee), Phi Beta Kappa. Office: NY Inst Tech PO Box 8000 Old Westbury NY 11568-8000

SCHURE, TERI, publishing executive. Pub. World Press Rev., N.Y.C. Office: World Press Rev 200 Madison Ave New York NY 10016-3903

SCHURENBERG, ERIC, magazine editor; b. Cin., Aug. 23, 1953; s. Carl Joseph and Lorraine Claire (Willows) S.; m. Judith Margaret Dowd, Apr. 30, 1983; 1 child, Emilie. AB, Brown U., 1975. Sr. editor Money Mag., N.Y.C., 1990-95, asst. mng. editor, 1995—; commentator Nightly Bus. Report, 1990—; pers. fin. reporter WCBS News, 1994—. Pers. fin. editor Marketplace Radio, 1993—, Mut. Broadcasting Sys., 1988-96. Recipient Nat. Mag. award Am. Soc. Mag. Editors, 1988, Page One award Newspaper Guild of N.Y., 1989, Gerald Loeb award Anderson Sch., UCLA, 1989.

SCHURMAN, DAVID JAY, orthopedic surgeon, educator; b. Chgo., Apr. 25, 1940; s. Shepherd P. and Dorothy (Laskey) S.; m. Martha Ellen Rocker, Mar. 8, 1967; children: Hilary Sue, Theodore Shepherd. BA, Yale U., 1961; MD, Columbia U., 1965. Intern Baylor U., Houston, 1965-67; resident in gen. surgery Mt. Sinai Hosp., N.Y.C., 1966-67; resident in orthop. surgery UCLA, 1969-72; asst. rsch. surgeon UCLA Med. Sch., 1972-73; asst. prof. orthopedic surgery Stanford Med. Sch., 1973-79, assoc. prof., 1979-87, prof., 1987—. Capt. USAF, 1967-69. Fellow NIH, 1972-73; grantee NIH, 1976—. Mem. Am. Orthopaedic Assn. (bd. dirs. 1994-95), Clin. Orthopaedics and Related Rsch. (bd. dirs. 1994—). Office: Stanford U Sch of Medicine R146 Divsn Orthop Surgery 300 Pasteur Dr Stanford CA 94305

SCHURZ, FRANKLIN DUNN, JR., media executive; b. South Bend, Ind., May 22, 1931; s. Franklin Dunn and Martha (Montgomery) S.; m. Robin Rowan Tullis, Nov. 22, 1975 (div. 1985). A.B., Harvard U., 1952, M.B.A., 1956, A.M.P., 1984. Exec. asst. South Bend Tribune, 1956-60, dir., 1961-76, sec., 1970-75, assoc. pub., 1971-72, editor, pub., 1972-82, exec. v.p., 1975-76, pres., 1976-82; asst. pub. Morning Herald and Daily Mail, Hagerstown, Md., 1960-62; pub. Morning Herald and Daily Mail, 1962-70, editor, 1966-70; pres. Schurz Communications, Inc., 1982—, treas., 1983-89. Chmn. Ind. Arts Commn., 1979-81; bd. regents St. Marys Coll., Notre Dame, Ind., 1977-83; chmn. adv. coun. Coll. Arts and Letters Notre Dame U., 1980-82; bd. dirs. Ind. Endowment Ednl. Excellence Inc., Indpls., 1987-90; mem. pres.'s coun. Ind. U., Bloomington, 1988—. 2d lt. U.S. Army, 1952-54. Recipient Presdl. Award of Merit Nat. Newspaper Assn., 1965, Frank Rogers award Rotary, South Bend, 1980. Mem. Am. Press Inst. (bd. dirs. 1985-94), AP (chmn. audit com. 1979-84), Chesapeake AP Assn. (past pres.), Md.-Del.-D.C. Press Assn. (past pres.), The Press-Enterprise (bd. dirs. 1992—), Hoosier State Press Assn. (past pres.), Newspaper Advt. Bur. (past bd. dirs.), South Bend Mishawaka Area C. of C. (pres. 1980-82), Am. Soc. Newspaper Editors, Inst. Newspaper Fin. Execs. (past pres.), South Bend Country Club, Nat. Press Club, Soc. Profl. Journalists. Presbyterian. Home: 1329 E Erskine Manor Hl South Bend IN 46614-2186 Office: Schurz Communications Inc 225 W Colfax Ave South Bend IN 46626-1000

SCHURZ, SCOTT CLARK, journalist, publisher; b. South Bend, Ind., Feb. 23, 1936; s. Franklin Dunn and Martha (Montgomery) S.; m. Kathryn Joan Foley, Aug. 5, 1967; children: Scott Clark, Alexandra Carol, John Danforth. B.A., Denison U., 1957. Asst. instr. U. Md., 1957-58; adminstrv. asst. South Bend Tribune, 1960-66; circulation cons. Imperial Valley Press, El Centro, Calif., 1966; asst. to pub. Bloomington (Ind.) Herald-Times/Bedford Times-Mail, 1966-70, pub., 1970—; personnel mgr. Bloomington Herald-Times, 1969-72, promotion mgr., 1969-81, dir. promotions, 1981-86, editor-in-chief, 1977—; editorial chmn. Bedford Times-Mail, 1972-81, editor-in-chief, 1981—; pub., editor-in-chief Sunday Herald Times; pres. Herald-Times, Inc., dir., v.p.; dir. Schurz Communications, Inc. Pres., Bloomington Boys' Club, 19701, Jr. Achievement Monroe County, 1971-73; bd. dirs. United Way Monroe County, 1979-81. Served with U.S. Army, 1958-60. Mem. Internat. Newspaper Mktg. Assn. (pres. 1986), Inland Daily Press Assn. (pres. 1989), Newspaper Assn. Am. (bd. dirs. 1992-95), Inter-Am. Press Assn. (bd. dirs. 1995—), Hoosier State Press Assn. (pres. 1989), Newspaper Advt. Bur. (bd. dirs. 1987-92). Republican. Presbyterian. Office: Herald Times Inc 1900 S Walnut St Bloomington IN 47401-7720

SCHUSSLER, THEODORE, lawyer, physician, educator, consultant; b. N.Y.C., July 27, 1934; s. Jack and Fannie (Blank) S.; m. Barbara Ann Gordon, June 18, 1961; children: Deborah, Jonathan, Rebecca. B.A. in Polit. Sci., Bklyn. Coll., 1955; LL.B., Bklyn. Law Sch., 1958; J.D., Bklyn. Law Sch., 1967; M.D., U. Lausanne (Switzerland), 1974. Bar: N.Y. 1959, U.S. Dist. Ct. (so. and ea. dists.) N.Y. 1975, U.S. Tax Ct. 1961, U.S. Ct. Appeals (2d cir.) 1962, U.S. Supreme Ct. 1975. Clerkship and practice, N.Y.C., 1956, 58-59; legal editor tax div. Prentice-Hall, Inc., Englewood Cliffs, N.J., 1956; vol. criminal law div. Legal Aid Soc., N.Y.C., 1959; atty. legal dept. N.Y.C. Dept. Welfare, 1959-60; sole practice, N.Y.C., 1960—; sr. staff asst. IBM-Indsl. Medicine Program, 1969-70, 74-76; intern in medicine St. Vincent's Med. Center of Richmond, S.I., N.Y., 1976-77, resident emergency medicine, 1977-79; resident in gerontology, chief house physician Carmel Richmond Nursing Home, S.I., 1978-80; surg. rotation emergency dept. Met. Hosp. Ctr., 1979; house physician dept. medicine Richmond Meml. Hosp. and Health Ctr., 1979-80; gen. practice medicine, 1980—; attending physician, former chief dept. family practice, former chmn. med. care evaluation, med. records and by-laws coms., former physician, advisor emergency dept., former mem. blood transfusion, credential's, emergency dept. coms., former mem. exec. com., mem. med. staff Community Hosp. of Bklyn., 1980-94; attending physician Meth. Hosp., Bklyn., 1984-92; supervising emergency dept. physician, dept. ambulatory care Meth. Hosp., Bklyn., 1980-83; attending physician Kings Hwy. Hosp., 1981-88, coord. emergency dept., 1981; clin. instr. dept. preventive medicine and community health, Downstate Med. Ctr. SUNY, Bklyn., 1981-88, clin. asst. prof., 1988—, SUNY Health Science Ctr., med. dir. divsn. devel. disabilities Mishkon-Jewish Bd. Family & Children's Svc., Bklyn., 1982—; primary care physician Jewish Home and Hosp. for Aged, N.Y.C., 1993-94; cons. in gerontology Palm Beach Home for Adults, Bklyn., 1980-92; cons. indsl. medicine IBM, 1990-92; tchr., instr., lectr., prof., 1954—; med.-legal cons. to professions of medicine and law. Dem. County Committeeman, 44th Assembly Dist., Bklyn., del. to judicial conv.; mem. exec. bd. United Ind. Dems. Bklyn. Capt. (med. corp.) USAR. Recipient Pub. and Community Svc. award United Ind. Dems. 44th assembly dist., Bklyn. Fellow Am. Coll. Legal Medicine; mem. Am. Coll. Emergency Physicians (past bd. dir. N.Y. chpt., past chmn. medico-legal com. N.Y. chpt.), Assn. Arbitrators of Civil Ct. of N.Y. (small claims divsn., arbitrator), United Univ. Professions, Bklyn. Law Sch. Alumni Assn. (bd. dirs.), Delta Sigma Rho. Author: Torts; Jurisdiction and Practice in Federal Courts; Constitutional Law; Conflict of Laws; contbr. articles to profl. jours. Home and Office: 760 E 10th St Apt 6H Brooklyn NY 11230-2352

SCHUSTER, CHARLES ROBERTS, federal government scientist; b. Woodbury, N.J., Jan. 24, 1930; s. Charles Roberts and Ruth E. S.; m. Chris-Ellyn Johanson, Nov. 1972. AB, Gettysburg Coll., 1951; MS, U. N.Mex., 1953; PhD, U. Md., 1962. Prof. psychiatry and behavioral scis. U. Chgo., 1972—, dir. rsch ctr. drug abuse, 1973-86, acting chmn. dept. psychiatry, 1985-86; dir. Nat. Inst. on Drug Abuse, Rockville, Md., 1986-92; sr. rsch. scientist, 1992—; mem. Dept. Health Human Svcs. Commn. on Orphan Diseases, 1987-89, Com. on Problems Drug Dependence, Inc., 1978—; chmn. expert com. WHO, 1975, expert adv. panel on drug dependence. Author: Behavioral Pharmacology, 1968, Drug Dependence, 1970; contbr. over 150 articles to profl. jours. Fellow AAAS, Am. Psychol. Assn. (pres. div. 28 1977-78), Am. Coll. Neuropsychopharmacology; mem. Behavioral Pharmacology Soc. (pres. 1976-78), Inst. Medicine. Office: Nat Inst on Drug Abuse Addiction Rsch Ctr 4940 Eastern Ave Bldg C Baltimore MD 21224-2735

SCHUSTER, ELAINE, civil rights professional, state official; b. Detroit, Sept. 26, 1947; d. William Alfred and Aimee Isabelle (Cote) LeBlanc; m. James William Schuster, Sept. 6, 1969; 1 child, Cambrian James. BA, Wayne State U., 1972, postgrad., 1974-75, paralegal cert., 1991. Asst. payments Mich. Dept. Social Svcs., Detroit, 1972-73; rights rep. Mich. Dept. Civil Rights, Detroit, 1973-80, 82-87, 90, asst. dir. div., 1987-90, supr., 1993—; court adminstr. Chippewa-Ottawa Conservation Ct., Bay Mills, Mich., 1980-82; quality assurance coord. State Mental Health Facility, Southgate, Mich., 1991-93; acting interim dir. Mich. Indian Commn., Detroit, 1995. Author: Critique, An Indian Tours Michilimackinac, 1981; contbr. articles and poems to mags. and profl. jours. Bd. dirs. Tri-County Native Ams., Warren, Mich., 1982-89, sec. Native Am. Sesquicentennial subcom., Mich., 1987; mem. Linking Lifetimes, mentor program for Native Am. youth, 1992-93; sec., newsletter editor various civic orgns.; also other polit. and civic activities. Native Am. fellow Mich. State U., 1989. Mem. ACLU (bd. dirs. Union-Oakland county 1987-88). Democrat. Avocations: exploring local historical and natural places of interest, research, fitness. Office: Mich Dept Civil Rights 1200 6th St Detroit MI 48226-2424

SCHUSTER, GARY FRANCIS, public relations executive; b. Detroit, Jan. 26, 1942; s. Dwayne Alger and Mary Elizabeth (Cullen) S.; m. Barbara Anne Leopold, Aug. 30, 1968; children—Rory Anne, Reid Patrick. B.S. in Journalism/Psychology, Wayne State U., 1966. Gen. assignment reporter Royal Oak (Mich.) Tribune, 1966-68; gen. assignment reporter Detroit News, 1968-70, state capital corr., 1970-74; bur. chief Detroit News, Lansing, 1974-75; chief asst. city editor Detroit News, Detroit, 1975-76; city editor Detroit News, 1976-77, news editor, 1977-78, Washington Bur. chief, 1978-85, White House corr., 1978-85; White House corr. CBS News, 1985-86; pvt. practice media cons., 1986-87; v.p. corp. relations Union Pacific Corp., 1987—. Mem. White House Corrs. Assn. (pres. 1985-86), Saucon Valley Country Club (Bethlehem, Pa.). Roman Catholic.

SCHUSTER, KAREN SUTTON, administrator; b. New Brunswick, N.J., Aug. 26, 1952; d. Alfred Michael and Carmen (Collado) Sutton; m. Derek Vance Schuster, May 31, 1976; children: Sloane, Brooke, Devon, Megan, Christopher. BA, Hofstra U., 1974; postgrad., NYU, 1987-89. Asst. to dir. Mus. Am. Folk Art, N.Y.C., 1975-76, acting dir., 1976-77, bd. dirs., exec. com. officer, 1980-88, gallery dir., 1989-92, dir. ops., 1992-94, dep. dir. planning and adminstrn., 1994-95; v.p. Sotheby's, N.Y.C., 1995—. Bd. dirs. Family Dynamics, N.Y.C., 1976-80. Mem. Cosmopolitan Club (younger members chmn.), Maidstone Club, Coral Beach Club. Democrat. Episcopalian. Home: 79 E 79th St Apt 9 New York NY 10021-0202 Office: Sotheby's 1334 York Ave New York NY 10021

SCHUSTER, MARVIN MEIER, physician, educator; b. Danville, Va., Aug. 30, 1929; s. Isaac and Rosel (Katzenstein) S.; m. Lois R. Bernstein, Feb. 19, 1961; children: Roberta, Nancy, Cathy. BA, BS, U. Chgo., 1951; MD, 1955. Diplomate Am. Bd. Internal Medicine. Intern Kings County Hosp., Bklyn., 1955-56; resident Balt. City Hosp., 1956-58, chief digestive disease div., resident Johns Hopkins Bayview Med. Ctr., 1961—; Johns Hopkins Hosp., Balt., 1958-61; prof. medicine and psychiatry Johns Hopkins U. Sch. Medicine, Balt., 1976—. Author: Gastrointestinal Disorders: Behavioral and Physiological Basis for Treatment; Keeping Control: Understanding and Managing Fecal Incontinence; editor: Gastrointestinal Motility Disorders, 1981, Atlas of Gastrointestinal Motility, 1994; contbr. chpts. to textbooks, articles to profl. jours.; mem. editorial bd.: Gastroenterology, 1978-81, Gastrointestinal Endoscopy, 1979-81, Psychosomatics, 1979—. Bd. dirs. Am. Cancer Soc., 1975—, pres., 1984-86; chmn. med. adv. bd. Balt. Ostomy Assn., 1966—. Recipient St. George Disting. Service award Am. Cancer Soc., 1979. Fellow ACP, Am. Psychiat. Assn.; mem. Am. Gastroent. Assn. (chmn. audiovisual com. 1975-78), Am. Soc. Gastrointestinal Endoscopy (governing bd. 1975-78), Am. Coll. Gastroenterology (pres. 1996) Am. Physiol. Soc., AAUP. Democrat. Jewish. Research on gastroenterology and application of biofeedback to gastrointestinal control. Home: 10 Red Cedar Ct Baltimore MD 21208-6305 Office: Johns Hopkins Bayview Med Ctr 4940 Eastern Ave Baltimore MD 21224-2735

SCHUSTER, PHILIP FREDERICK, II, lawyer, writer; b. Denver, Aug. 26, 1945; s. Philip Frederick and Ruth Elizabeth (Robar) S.; m. Barbara Lynn Nordquist, June 7, 1975; children: Philip Christian, Matthew Dale. BA, U. Wash., 1967; JD, Willamette U., 1972. Bar: Oreg. 1972, U.S. Dist. Ct. Oreg. 1974, U.S. Ct. Appeals (9th cir.) 1986, U.S. Supreme Ct. 1986. Dep. dist. atty. Multnomah County, Portland, Oreg., 1972; title examiner Pioneer Nat. Title Co., Portland, 1973-74; assoc. Buss, Leichner et al, Portland, 1975-76; from assoc. to ptnr. Kitson & Bond, Portland, 1976-77; pvt. practice Portland, 1977-95; ptnr. Dierking and Schuster, Portland, 1996—; arbitrator Multnomah County Arbitration Program, 1985—. Contbr. articles to profl. jours. Organizer Legal Aid Svcs. for Community Clinics, Salem, Oreg. and Seattle, 1969-73; Dem. committeeman, Seattle, 1965-70. Mem. ABA, ATLA, NAACP (exec. bd. Portland, Oreg. chpt. 1979—), ACLU, Multnomah Bar Assn. (Vol. Lawyers Project), Internat. Platform Assn., Alpha Phi Alpha. Avocations: river drifting, camping, swimming, jogging, karate, writing. Office: 1500 NE Irving St Ste 540 Portland OR 97232-4209 *Hard work and perseverance are the keys to accomplishing any goal. Protecting and nurturing our children and our environment are life's most noble goals. Success is the pursuit of these goals.*

SCHUSTER, ROBERT PARKS, lawyer; b. St. Louis, Oct. 25, 1945; s. William Thomas Schuster and Carolyn Cornforth (Daugherty) Hathaway; 1 child, Susan Michele. AB, Yale U., 1967; JD with honors, U. of Wyo., 1970; LLM, Harvard U., 1971. Bar: Wyo. 1971, U.S. Ct. Appeals (10th cir.) 1979, U.S. Supreme Ct. 1984, Utah 1990. Dep. county atty. County of Natrona, Casper, Wyo., 1971-73; pvt. practice law, Casper, 1973-76; assoc. Spence & Moriarity, Casper, 1976-78; ptnr. Spence, Moriarity & Schuster, Jackson, Wyo., 1978—. Trustee U. Wyo., 1985-89; Wyo. Dem. nominee for U.S. House of Reps., 1994; polit. columnist Casper Star Tribune, 1987-94. Ford Found. Urban Law fellow, 1970-71; pres. United Way of Natrona County, 1974; bd. dirs. Dancers Workshop, 1981-83; chair Wyo. selection com. Rhodes Scholarship, 1989—; mem. bd. visitors Coll. Arts and Scis., U. Wyo., 1991—; mem. platform com. Dem. Nat. Conv. 1992—; mem. Dem. Nat. Com., 1992; mem. Wyo. Public Policy Forum, 1992—; bd. dirs. Cmty. Visual Art Assn.. Mem. ABA, ATLA, Wyo. Trial Lawyers Assn. Home: PO Box 548 Jackson WY 83001-0548 Office: Spence Moriarity & Schuster 15 S Jackson St Jackson WY 83001

SCHUSTER, SEYMOUR, mathematician, educator; b. Bronx, N.Y., July 31, 1926; s. Oscar and Goldie (Smilowitz) S.; m. Marilyn Weinberg, May 2, 1954; children: Paul Samuel, Eve Elizabeth. B.A., Pa. State U., 1947; A.M., Columbia U., 1948; Ph.D., Pa. State U., 1953; postgrad. (fellow), U. Toronto, 1952-53. Instr. Pa. State U., 1950-52; instr. Poly. Inst. N.Y., 1953-54, asst. prof., 1954-56, assoc. prof., 1956-58; vis. assoc. prof. Carleton Coll., Northfield, Minn., 1958-59, assoc. prof., 1959-63, prof. math., 1968—, chmn. dept., 1973-76, William H. Laird prof. math. and liberal arts, 1992-94, William H. Laird prof. emeritus, 1994—; vis. assoc. prof. U. N.C., Chapel Hill, 1961; research assoc. math. dept. U. Minn., Mpls., 1962-63, assoc. prof., 1963-65; assoc. prof. Minn. Math Center, 1965-68, dir. coll. geometry project, 1964-74; dir. Acad. Year Inst. for Coll. Tchrs., 1966-67, NSF Faculty fellow, 1970-71; vis. scholar U. Calif., Santa Barbara, 1970-71, U. Ariz., 1990; guest scholar Western Mich. U., 1976, 81; vis. prof. Western Wash. U., 1983, U. Oreg., 1986. Author: (with K. O. May) Undergraduate Research in Mathematics, 1961, Elementary Vector Geometry, 1962, (with P.C. Rosenbloom) Prelude to Analysis, 1966; also research articles on geometry, graph theory, and analysis.; cons. editor Xerox Pub. Co., 1962-71; assoc. editor, editorial bd.: Am. Math. Monthly, 1969-86; assoc. editor: Indian Jour. Math. Edn, 1976-86; co-producer 12 films on geometry. Served with USNR, 1944-46. Recipient Honor award Am. Film Festival, 1967, Golden Eagle award Cine Film Festival, 1967, 68; named found. fellow Inst. for Combinatorics and Applications. Mem. Math. Assn. Am., Am. Math. Soc., Sigma Xi, Pi Mu Epsilon. Home: 316 Sumner St E Northfield MN 55057-2843

SCHUSTER, TODD MERVYN, biophysics educator, biotechnology company executive; b. Mpls., June 27, 1933; s. David Theodore and Ann (Kaluser) S.; m. Nancy Joanne Barnes, Jan. 25, 1958; 1 child, Lela Alexa. B.A., Wayne State U., 1958, M.S., 1960; Ph.D., Washington U., 1963. Research assoc. Max Planck Inst. Phys. Chemistry, Goettingen, W.Ger., 1963-66; asst. prof. SUNY-Buffalo, 1966-70; assoc. prof. U. Conn., Storrs, 1970-75, prof. biochemistry, biophysics, 1975—, dept. head, 1977-81, dir. Biotech. Ctr., 1986-90; pres., founder Xenogen Inc., 1986-90; vis. prof. Ind. U., Bloomington, 1975, U. Peking, People's Republic of China, 1987; McCollum-Pratt vis. prof. Johns Hopkins U., Balt., 1979-80; mem. NIH grant rev. panels, biophysics and biophys. chemistry panel, 1971-75, biomed. scis. postdoctoral fellowship panel, 1976, Sickle Cell Disease Adv. Panel, 1977; mem. biol. instrumentation rev panel NSF, 1984-90, biol. facilities, 1987-90, sci. and tech. ctrs., 1988-90; mem. BBS adv. coun. NSF, 1989-92; chmn. adv. com. Nat. Cell Culture Ctr., 1990—; program dir. Nat. Analytical Untracentri Fugation Facility, 1987-94. Contbr. research articles on rapid reaction kinetics, biopolymers, hemeprotein structure and function, virus structure and assembly to profl. jours. USPHS fellow, 1959-63, 63-66. Mem. AAAS, Am. Chem. Soc., Conn. Acad. Sci. and Engring., Biophys. Soc., Protein Soc., Am. Soc. Biol. Chemists, Am. Soc. Virology. Home: 556 Wormwood Hill Rd Mansfield CT 06250-1040 Office: U Conn Dept Molecular and Cell Biology PO Box 125 Storrs Mansfield CT 06268-0125 also: Xenogen Inc 321 Fisher Bldg Detroit CT 06269-3125

SCHUT, DONNA SUE, elementary education educator; b. Sioux Center, Iowa, Mar. 23, 1961; d. James Martin and Gertrude (Buyert) Intveld; m. Eric Peter Schut, July 21, 1958; 1 child, Alyssa Nichole. BA, Northwestern Coll., Orange City, Iowa, 1983, MA, 1990. Lic. tchr., Iowa. Tchr. Sioux Center Community Schs., 1983—, dept. head social studies dept., 1989-91, 4th grade team leader, 1994—; supr. student tchrs. Northwestern Coll., Orange City, 1986-87, 88-89, 90-91, 92-93, 94-95. Mem. N.W. Iowa Reading Assn. (bldg. rep. 1983—), Sioux Center Edn. Assn., Nat. Coun. for Tchrs. Math., Iowa Coun. for Social Studies, Geographic Alliance Iowa, Assn. Supervision and Curriculum Devel., Internat. Reading Assn. Avocations: reading, baking, collecting cats, spending time with family. Office: Kinsey Elem Sioux Center Community Schs 397 10th St SE Sioux Center IA 51250

SCHUTT, WALTER EUGENE, lawyer; b. Cleve., July 27, 1917; s. Erle Minchin and Elizabeth (Eastman) S.; A.B., Miami U., Oxford, Ohio, 1939; J.D., U. Cin., 1948; m. Dorothy Louise Gilbert, Apr. 18, 1942; children: Gretchen Sue, Stephen David, Elizabeth Ann, Robert Barclay. Admitted to Ohio bar, 1948, U.S. Dist. Ct. (so. dist.) Ohio 1953, U.S. Supreme Ct. bar, 1962, U.S. Tax Ct. 1983, U.S. Ct. Appeals (6th cir.) 1986. Practiced in Wilmington, Ohio, 1948—; city solicitor, Wilmington, 1950-53. Mem. Wilmington Bd. Edn., 1958-65; chmn. Clinton County chpt. ARC, 1951-53; Wilmington chmn. Cin. Symphony Orch. Area Artists Series, 1969-71; trustee Wilmington Coll., 1962-74, sec., 1966-74; trustee Quaker Hill Found., Richmond, Ind., 1970-75, Friends Fellowship Community, Inc., 1986-93; rep. U.S. preparations com. 6th Internat. Assembly World Council of Chs., 1982. Served to 1st lt. USAAF, 1943-46. Decorated D.F.C.; recipient Disting. Service award Wilmington Jr. C. of C., 1953. Mem. Am. Bar Assn. (arms control and disarmament com. 1977-80), Ohio State Bar Assn., Clinton County Bar Assn. (past pres.), World Peace Through Law Ctr. Mem. Soc. of Friends (presiding clk. Friends United Meeting 1978-81, rep. to bd. Nat. Council Chs. of Christ 1985—; presiding clk. Friends com. on. nat. legis. 1984-87). Club: Rotary. Home: 81 Columbus St Wilmington OH 45177-1801 Office: Thorne Bldg 36 1/2 N South St Wilmington OH 45177-2254

SCHUTTA, HENRY SZCZESNY, neurologist, educator; b. Gdansk, Poland, Sept. 15, 1928; came to U.S., 1962, naturalized, 1967; s. Jakub and Janina (Zerbst) S.; m. Henryka Kosmal, Apr. 29, 1950; children—Katharine, Mark, Caroline. M.B., B.S., U. Sydney, Australia, 1955, M.D., 1968. Jr. resident, then sr. resident St. Vincent's Hosp., Sydney, 1956-58; acad. registrar, house physician Nat. Hosp. Nervous Diseases, London, 1958-62; neurologist Pa. Hosp., Phila., 1962-73; asso. prof. neurology U. Pa. Med. Sch., 1963-73; prof. neurology, chmn. dept. SUNY Downstate Med. Center, Bklyn., 1973-80; prof. U. Wis. Med. Sch., 1980-95, chmn. dept. neurology, 1980-95. Research on bilirubin encephalopathy, cerebral edema, degeneration and regeneration of muscle. Home: 3510 Blackhawk Dr Madison WI 53705-1406 Office: U Hosp 600 Highland Ave Madison WI 53792-0001

SCHUTTE, ANNE JACOBSON, historian, educator; b. Palo Alto, Calif., Apr. 24, 1940; d. David Samuel and Mildred Rose (Ashworth) J.; m. William Metcalf Schutte, Dec. 21, 1967 (div. Jan. 1990). BA in History magna cum laude, Brown U., 1962; AM in History, Stanford U., 1963, PhD in History and Humanities, 1969. Instr. Lawrence U., 1966-69, asst. prof., 1971-77, assoc. prof., 1977-85, prof., 1985-91; prof. U. Va., Charlottesville, 1992—; bd. dirs. Ctr. for Reformation Rsch., 1980-83; mem. exec. com. Newberry Libr. program Assoc. Colls. Midwest, 1981-83, 86-88, 90-91; mem. steering com. Com. Women's Concerns, 1984-85. Author: Pier Paolo Vergerio: The Making of an Italian Reformer, 1977, Printed Italian Vernacular Religious Books, 1465-1550: A Finding List, 1983, Pier Paolo Vergerio e la Riforma a Venezia, 1489-1549, 1988 (trans. Virginia Cappelletti, Anna Maria Fabbrini); editor: Cecilia Ferrazzi, Autobiografia de una santa mancata, 1990, English edit., 1996; translator: Heavenly Supper: The Story of Maria Janis (Fulvio Tomizza), 1991, Verieties of Italian Anticlericalism (Silvana Seidel Menchi), 1993; also articles and numerous revs. We. Regional Alumnae scholar Brown U., 1957-59, 60-62, Stanford U., 1963-65, Stanford U./Italian Govt., 1965-66, Newberry Libr., 1978, S.E. Inst. Medieval and Renaissance Studies, 1979, NEH, 1979-80, 88-89, Gladys Krieble Delmas, 1985, 96; scholar Inst. Reformation Rsch., 1965; Grantee Fulbright Found., 1965-66, Pro Helvetia Found., 1966, Am. Philos. Soc., 1971, NEH 1979-80, 88-89, 95. Mem. Am. Hist. Soc., Am. Soc. Ch. History (coun.), Coordinating Com. for Women in Hist. Profession, Renaissance Soc. Am., 16th Century Studies Conf. (editorial bd. jour. 1972—, v.p. 1973-74, 79-80, pres. 1980-81), Soc. Italian Hist. Socs., Soc. Reformation Rsch. (nominating com. 1981-83, exec. coun. 1987-90, program sec. 1992-95). Office: U Va Dept History Charlottesville VA 22903

SCHUTZ, DONALD FRANK, geochemist, corporate executive; b. Orange, Tex., Sept. 22, 1934; s. Theodore J. and Mildred Irene (Chandler) S.; m. Beatriz Valera, May 18, 1958; children: Delfino, Celita. BS in Geology cum laude, Yale U., 1956, PhD in Geology, 1964; MA in Geology, Rice U., 1958. Research staff geologist Yale U., New Haven, 1963-64; mgr. nuclear geochemistry dept. Teledyne Isotopes, Westwood, N.J., 1968-70, v.p., 1970-75, pres., 1975-93; engring. group exec. Teledyne, Inc., Westwood, 1989-92; chief scientist Teledyne Environ. Systems, 1992-93; gen. mgr. Teledyne Brown Engring. Environ. Svcs., 1993—; v.p. Teledyne Environ., Inc.; mem. low level waste adv. com. N.J. Dept. Environ. Protection, Trenton, 1988-90; chmn. com. on radioactive materials N.J. BIA, Trenton, 1980-88. Pres. Children's Aid and Adoption Soc. N.J. Inc., Bogota, 1976-95, Am. Amateur Judo Found., River Vale, N.J., 1979-89; bd. dirs. Yale U. Alumni Fund, 1989-94; co-chmn. Children's Aid and Family Svcs. Inc., 1995—. Recipient Antarctic Service medal U.S. Congress, 1964. Mem. Geochem. Soc., Am. Nuclear Soc. (chmn. no. N.J. sect. 1988-89, environ. scis. divsn., bd. dirs., chair 1995—, pub. policy com. 1991—), Am. Assn. Engring. Soc. Internat. Affairs (standing com. sustainable devel. 1995—), Geol. Soc. Am., Soc. Petroleum Engrs., Am. Assn. Radon Sci. and Tech. (pres. 1986-89, treas. 1990-95), Am. Assn. Petroleum Geologists, Yale Alumni Assn. (bd. dirs. Bergen County and vicinity chpt. 1989—), Sigma Xi. Office: Teledyne Brown Engring Environ Svcs 50 Van Buren Ave Westwood NJ 07675-3242

SCHUTZ, HERBERT DIETRICH, publishing executive; b. Munich, Germany, July 16, 1922; came to U.S., 1924; naturalized, 1930; s. Anton Friedrich and Maria Hedwig (Gross) S.; m. Suzanne Cameron, Mar. 22, 1971; children: Leslie, Suzanne; children by previous marriage: Prescott (dec.), Peter, Jeffrey, Elizabeth. BS, Harvard Coll., 1944. Ptnr. N.Y. Graphic Soc. Ltd., Greenwich, Conn., 1946-66, pres., editor in chief, 1966-81, chmn. bd., 1982-84; v.p. Time Inc., N.Y.C., 1966-81; chmn., pres. Schutz and Co., Fine Arts, Greenwich, 1982—. Served to 1st lt. USMC, 1943-46.

Mem. Harvard Club (N.Y.C.), Belle Haven Club, Field Club. Home and Office: The Barn Dewart Rd Greenwich CT 06830-3417

SCHUTZ, JOHN ADOLPH, historian, educator, former university dean; b. L.A., Apr. 10, 1919; s. Adolph J. and Augusta K. (Gluecker) S. AA, Bakersfield Coll., 1940; BA, UCLA, 1942, MA, 1943, PhD, 1945. Asst. prof. history Calif. Inst. Tech., Pasadena, 1945-53; assoc. prof. history Whittier (Calif.) Coll., 1953-56, prof., 1956-65; prof. Am. history U. So. Calif., L.A., 1965-91; chmn. dept. history U. So. Calif., 1974-76, dean social scis. and communication, 1976-82. Author: William Shirley: King's Governor of Massachusetts, 1961, Peter Oliver's Origin and Progress of the American Rebellion, 1967, The Promise of America, 1970, The American Republic, 1978, Dawning of America, 1981, Spur of Fame: Dialogues of John Adams and Benjamin Rush, 1980, A Noble Pursuit: A Sesquicentennial History of the New England Historic Genealogical Society, 1995; joint editor: Golden State Series; contbg. author: Spain's Colonial Outpost, 1985, Generations and Change: Genealogical Perspectives in Social History, 1986, Making of America: Society and Culture of the United States, 1990, rev. edit., 1992. Trustee Citizens Rsch. Found., 1985—. NEH grantee, 1971; Sr. Faculty grantee, 1971-74. Mem. Am. Hist. Assn. (pres. Pacific Coast br. 1972-73, sec.-treas. 1995—), Am. Studies Assn. (pres. 1974-75), Mass. Hist. Soc. (corr.), New Eng. Hist. Geneal. Soc. (trustee 1988—, editor, author intro. book Boston Merchant Census of 1789, 1989, rec. sec. 1995—), Colonial Soc. Mass. (corr.). Home and Office: 1100 White Knoll Dr Los Angeles CA 90012-1353 *The excitement of collegiate activities makes each year an adventure in learning and a renewal of one's youth.*

SCHUTZE, CHARLES R(OBERT), lawyer; b. Osaka, Japan, Oct. 19, 1950; s. Alexander J. and Chieko (Teranishi) S.; m. Marsha Lynn Gutweiler, Sept. 25, 1992. BS, Fordham U., 1972; MBA, Iona Coll., 1980; JD, Pace U., 1987. Bar: Wis. 1990, Conn. 1988, U.S. Dist. Ct. (we. and ea. dists.) Wis. 1990, U.S. Ct. Appeals (7th cir.) 1991, U.S. Tax Ct. 1991, U.S. Dist. Ct. Conn. 1988, U.S. Supreme Ct. 1995. Staff acct. Peat, Marwick, Mitchell, White Plains, N.Y., 1972-73; acct. supervisor Dorr-Oliver Inc., Stamford, Conn., 1973-77; acctg. mgr. Arnold Bakers, Greenwich, Conn., 1977-79; dir. acctg. & taxes Howmet Turbin & Components, Greenwich, 1979-87; pvt. practice law Greenwich, Madison, 1987-90, 92—; atty. Stolper Koritzinsky Brewster, Madison, Wis., 1990-92. Mem. AICPAs, ATLA, Nat. Assn. Accts. Avocation: computer programming. Office: 306 E Wilson St Madison WI 53703-3427

SCHUUR, DIANE JOAN, vocalist; b. Tacoma, Dec. 10, 1953; d. David Schuur. Ed. high sch., Vancouver, Wash. Albums include Pilot of My Destiny, 1983, Deedles, Schuur Thing, 1986, Timeless (Grammy award for female jazz vocal 1986), Diane Schuur and the Count Basie Orchestra (Grammy award for female jazz vocal 1987), Talkin' 'Bout You, 1988, Pure Schuur, 1991 (reached #1 on Billboard contemporary jazz chart, nominated for Grammy award 1991), In Tribute, 1992, Love Songs, 1993 (Grammy nomination, Best Traditional Vocal), 1993 (Grammy nomination, The Christmas Song), (with B.B. King) Heart to Heart, 1994 (entered at #1 on Billboard contemporary jazz chart), Love Walked In, 1996; performed at the White House, Monterey Jazz Festival, Hollywood Bowl; toured Japan, Far East, South Am., Europe. *"There is no plateau that can't be reached, no obstacle that can't be overcome if you believe in yourself and your higher power".*

SCHUUR, ROBERT GEORGE, lawyer; b. Kalamazoo, Dec. 5, 1931; s. George Garrett and Louise Margaret (DeVries) S.; m. Susan Elizabeth White, Sept. 28, 1968; children—Arah Louise Adele, Jeremiah Donald Garrett. A.B., U. Mich., 1953, LL.B., 1955. Bar: Mich. 1955, N.Y. 1956. Assoc. Reid & Priest, N.Y.C., 1955-65, ptnr., 1966—. Served with USN, 1956-58. Mem. ABA, N.Y. State Bar Assn., Assn. of Bar of City of N.Y., Phi Beta Kappa. Club: University (N.Y.C.). Home: 163 E 82nd St New York NY 10028-1856 Office: Reid & Priest 40 W 57th St New York NY 10019-4001

SCHUYLER, DANIEL MERRICK, lawyer, educator; b. Oconomowoc, Wis., July 26, 1912; s. Daniel J. and Fannie Sybil (Moorhouse) S.; m. Claribel Seaman, June 15, 1935; children: Daniel M., Sheila Gordon. AB summa cum laude, Dartmouth Coll., 1934; JD, Northwestern U., 1937. Bar: Ill. 1937, U.S. Supreme Ct. 1942, Wis. 1943. Tchr. constl. history Chgo. Latin Sch., 1935-37; assoc. Schuyler & Hennessy (attys.), 1937-42, ptnr., 1946-48; ptnr. Schuyler, Richert & Stough, 1948-58, Schuyler, Stough & Morris, Chgo., 1958-76, Schuyler, Ballard & Cowen, 1976-83, Schuyler, Roche & Zwirner, P.C., 1983—; treas., sec. and controller B-W Superchargers, Inc. div. Borg-Warner Corp., Milw., 1942-46; lectr. trusts, real property, future interests Northwestern U. Sch. Law, 1946-50, asso. prof. law, 1950-52, prof., 1952-80, prof. emeritus, 1980—. Author: (with Homer F. Carey) Illinois Law of Future Interests, 1941; supplements, 1947, 54; (with William M. McGovern, Jr.) Illinois Trust and Will Manual, 1970; supplements, 1972, 74, 76, 77, 79, 80, 81, 82, 83, 84; contbr. to profl. jours. Rep. nominee for judge Cook County Cir. Ct., 1958; bd. dirs., life mem. United Cerebral Palsy Greater Chgo., Lawrence Hall Youth Svcs. Fellow Am. Bar Found.; mem. ABA (past mem. ho. of dels., past chmn. sect. real property, probate and trust law), Chgo. Estate Planning Coun. (past pres., Dist. Svc. award 1977), Am. Coll. Trust and Estate Counsel (past pres.), Chgo. Bar Assn. (past chmn. coms. on trust law and post-admission edn., past bd. mgrs.), Ill. Bar Assn. (past chmn. real estate and legal edn. sects., past bd. govs.), Wis. Bar Assn., Legal Club, Law Club, Univ. Club, Order of Coif, Phi Beta Kappa, Phi Kappa Psi. Home: 909 W Foster Ave Apt 403 Chicago IL 60640-2510 Office: Schuyler Roche & Zwirner PC Ste 3800 130 E Randolph St Chicago IL 60601-6342

SCHUYLER, JANE, fine arts educator; b. Flushing, N.Y., Nov. 2, 1943; d. Frank James and Helen (Oberhofer) S. BA, Queens Coll., 1965; MA, Hunter Coll., 1967; PhD, Columbia U., 1972. Asst. prof. art history Montclair State Coll., Upper Montclair, N.J., 1970; assoc. prof. C.W. Post Coll., L.I. Univ., Greenvale, N.Y., 1971-73, adj. assoc. profl, 1977-78; coord. fine arts, asst. prof. York Coll., CUNY, Jamaica, 1973-77, 78-87, assoc. prof., 1988-92, prof. 1993-96, prof. emerita, 1996—. Home: 35-37 78th St Jackson Heights NY 11372

SCHUYLER, ROBERT LEN, investment company executive; b. Burwell, Nebr., Mar. 4, 1936; s. Norman S. and Ilva M. (Hoppes) S.; m. Mary Carol Huston, June 13, 1958; children: Kylie Anne, Nina Leigh, Melynn Kae, Gwyer Lenn. BS, U. Nebr., 1958; MBA, Harvard U., 1960. Asst. to treas. Potlatch Forests, Inc., Lewiston, Idaho, 1962-64; dir. corp. planning Potlatch Forests, Inc., San Francisco, 1964-66; mgr. fin. analysis Weyerhaeuser Co., Tacoma, 1966-68; mgr. investment evaluation dept. Weyerhaeuser Co., 1968-70, v.p. fin. and planning, 1970-72, sr. v.p. fin. and planning, 1972-85, exec. v.p., chief fin. officer, 1985-91; mng. ptnr. Nisqually Ptnrs., Tacoma, 1991—; chief exec. officer Grande Alberta Paper, Ltd., 1992—; past mem. nat. adv. bd. Chem. Bank, U. Wash. MBA program, coun. fin. exec. Conf. Bd., Pvt. Sector Coun., exec. com. Am. Paper Inst.; bd. dirs. Multicare Health Sys., Paragon Trade Brands Inc., One Sport, Inc. Bd. dirs. Tacoma-Pierce County YMCA. Mem. Anglers Club. Home: 12101 Gravelly Lake Dr SW Tacoma WA 98499-1415

SCHWAAB, RICHARD LEWIS, lawyer, educator; b. Oconomowoc, Wis., Nov. 15, 1945. s. Thomas L. and Phyllis N. (Lord) S.; m. Lynn Louise Howie; children: Amy, William, Andrew, Matthew. BSChemE, U. Wis., 1967; JD with honors, George Washington U., 1971, LLM in Internat. Law with highest honors, 1979. Bar: Va. 1971, U.S. Dist. Ct. (ea. dist.) Va. 1979, U.S. Supreme Ct. 1980, U.S. Ct. Appeals (fed. cir.) 1982. Ptnr., Stepno, Schwaab & Linn, Arlington, 1972-74, Bacon & Thomas, Arlington, 1974-78, Schwartz, Jeffery, Schwaab, Mack, Blumenthal & Evans, P.C., Alexandria, 1978-88; ptnr. in charge, chair dept. intellectual property Foley & Lardner, Washington, 1988—; lectr. law George Washington U., 1978-88, George Mason U., 1989—. Max Planck Inst. Fgn. and Internat. Patent, Copyright and Competition Law fellow, 1971-72. Mem. ABA, Am. Intellectual Property Law Assn., Va. State Bar (gov. 1974-78), Am. Soc. Internat. Law, Internat. Patent and Trademark Assn., Internat. Fedn. Indsl. Property Attys., Christian Legal Soc., Phi Kappa Phi, Tau Beta Pi. Co-author Patent Practice, 6 vols., 1976-95; International Patent Law: EPC & PCT, 3 vols., 1978; Intellectual Property Protection for Biotechnology Worldwide, 1987; contbr. articles to profl. jours. Home: 6326 Karmich St Fairfax VA 22039-1621 Office: Foley & Lardner 3000 K St NW Ste 500 Washington DC 20007-5109

SCHWAB, ARTHUR JAMES, lawyer; b. Pitts., Dec. 7, 1946; s. Earl Walter and Helen Alice (Gascoine) S.; m. Karen Jenny, Sept. 2, 1967; children: John Arthur, Ellen Katherine, David Earl. Student, Muskingum Coll., 1964-65; AB, Grove City Coll., 1968; JD, U. Va., 1972. Bar: Pa. 1972, N.J. 1985, U.S. Dist. Ct. (we. dist.) Pa. 1972, U.S. Dist. Ct. (ea dist.) Pa. 1978, U.S. Dist. Ct. (no. dist.) Ohio 1979, U.S. Dist. Ct. S.C. 1980, U.S. Dist. Ct. N.Mex. 1981, U.S. Dist. Ct. Mass. 1984, U.S. Dist. Ct. N.J. 1984, U.S. Ct. Appeals (3d cir.) 1972, U.S. Ct. Appeals (11th cir.) 1982, U.S. Ct. Appeals (4th cir.) 1982, U.S. Ct. Appeals (8th cir.) 1991, U.S. Ct. Appeals (9th cir.) 1995, U.S. Supreme Ct. 1975. Ptnr. Reed, Smith, Shaw and McClay, Pitts., 1973-90; ptnr., chair of litigation Buchanan Ingersoll, Pitts., 1990—. Mem. editorial bd. Va. Law Rev., Sch. Law U. Va., Charlottesville, 1972. Bd. dirs. Grove City (Pa.) Coll. Mem. Acad. Trial Lawyers Allegheny County (bd. dirs.), Allegheny County Bar Assn., (past pres. civil litigation sect.), Duquesne Club, Rivers Club. Republican. Presbyterian. Home: 3000 Old Orchard Ct Gibsonia PA 15044 Office: Buchanan Ingersoll One Oxford Ctr 301 Grant St 20th Fl Pittsburgh PA 15219-1410

SCHWAB, CHARLES R., brokerage house executive; b. Sacramento, 1937; m. Helen O'Neill; 5 children. Stanford U., 1959, Postgrad., 1961. Formerly mut. fund mgr. Marin County, Calif.; founder brokerage San Francisco, 1971; now chmn., CEO Charles Schwab & Co., Inc. Author: How to be Your Own Stockbroker, 1984. Republican. Office: Charles Schwab & Co Inc 101 Montgomery St San Francisco CA 94104-4122

SCHWAB, EILEEN CAULFIELD, lawyer, educator; b. N.Y.C., Feb. 11, 1944; d. James Francis and Mary Alice (Fay) Caulfield; m. Terrance W. Schwab, Jan. 4, 1969; children: Matthew Caulfield, Catherine Grimley, Claire Gillespie. BA, Hunter Coll., 1965; JD, Columbia U., 1971; BA magna cum laude. Bar: N.Y. 1972, U.S. Dist. Ct. (so. and ea. dists.) N.Y. 1975, U.S. Ct. Appeals (2d cir.) 1975, U.S. Tax Ct. 1980, U.S. Ct. Appeals (10th cir.) 1993. Assoc. Poletti Friedin, N.Y.C., 1971-72, Hughes Hubbard & Reed, N.Y.C., 1972-75, Davis Polk & Wardwell, N.Y.C., 1975-81; dep. bur. chief Charities Bu., Atty. Gen. of N.Y., 1981-82; counsel Brown & Wood, N.Y.C., 1983—, ptnr., 1984; adj. prof. N.Y. Law Sch.; mediator atty. disciplinary com. first dept., N.Y. Co-chmn. gift planning adv. com. Archdiocese of N.Y.C.; dir. Cath. Found. for the Future, Cath. Communal Fund. Fellow Am. Coll. Trust and Estate Counsel; mem. N.Y. State Bar Assn. (exec. com. trust and estate sect.), Assn. Bar City N.Y., Phi Beta Kappa. Democrat. Roman Catholic.

SCHWAB, FRANK, JR., management consultant; b. Brookline, Mass., Dec. 19, 1932; s. Frank Sr. and Phyllis (Robinson) F. BA, Rutgers U., 1952; MBA, Harvard Bus. Sch., 1956. Cert. mgmt. cons. Internal auditor Champion Paper, Inc., Hamilton, Ohio, 1956-57; mgmt. engr. Champion Paper, Inc., Pasadena, Tex., 1957-58; cons., assoc. Booz Allen & Hamilton, N.Y.C., 1958-65; dir. trans. planning Planning Rsch. Corp., L.A., 1965; pres., CEO F.R. Schwab & Assocs., N.Y.C., 1965-82; pres., co-CEO Fenvessy & Schwab, N.Y.C., 1982-87; pres., CEO Anderson & Schwab, N.Y.C., 1987—; bd. dirs. Sugarland Oil Corp., N.Y.C., mfrs. and svcs. divsn. nat. mining assn., Washington, Infosafe Corp., N.Y.C. With Nat. Mining Hall of Fame & Mus., Leadville, Colo., 1992—, mem. nominating com. 1st lt. U.S. Army, 1952-54, Korea. Decorated Nat. Def. Svc. medal, Korean Svc. medal with bronze star, Commendation ribbon with medal pendant, UN Svc. medal. Mem. Inst. Mgmt. Cons. (pres. N.Y. chpt. 1975-77), Am. Arbitration Assn. (panel arbitrator), Mil. Order Fgn. Wars (vet. companion), Maidstone Club, Union Club, River Club, King Coal Club. Republican. Avocation: tennis. Office: Anderson & Schwab Inc 444 Madison Ave New York NY 10022-6903

SCHWAB, GEORGE DAVID, social science educator, author; b. Nov. 25, 1931; s. Arkady and Klara (Jacobson) S.; BA, City Coll. N.Y., 1954; MA, Columbia, 1955, PhD, 1968; m. Eleonora Storch, Feb. 27, 1965; children: Clarence Boris, Claude Arkady, Solan Bernhard. Lectr., Columbia Coll., N.Y.C., 1959; lectr. CUNY, 1960-68, asst. prof. history, 1968-72, assoc. prof. history, 1973-79, prof., 1980—. Mem. Columbia U. Seminar on the History of Legal and Polit. Thought and Institutions; dir. Conf. History and Politics, CUNY. Trustee, pres., mem. exec. com. Nat. Com. Am. Fgn. Policy. Mem. Am. Hist. Assn., Am. Polit. Sci. Assn. Author: Dayez: Beyond Abstract Art, 1967; Enemy oder Foe, 1968; Switzerland's Tactical Nuclear Weapons Policy, 1969; The Challenge of the Exception: An Introduction to the Political Ideas of Carl Schmitt, 1970, 2d edit., 89; Appeasement and Detente, 1975, 81; Carl Schmitt: Political Opportunist?, 1975; translator: The Concept of the Political with Comments by Leo Strauss (Carl Schmitt), 1976, 96; Legality and Illegality as Instruments of Revolutionaries in their Quest for Power: Remarks Occasioned by the Outlook of Herbert Marcuse, 1978; The German State in Historical Perspective, 1978; Ideology: Reality or Rhetoric?, 1978; Ideology and Foreign Policy, 1978, 81; The Decision: Is the American Sovereign at Bay?, 1978; State and Nation: Toward a Further Clarification, 1980; American Foreign Politics at the Crossroads, 1980; Carl Schmitt: Through a Glass Darkly, 1980; From Quantity and Heterogeneity to Quality and Homogeneity: Toward a New Foreign Policy, 1980; Toward an Open-Society Bloc, 1980; Eurocommunism: The Ideological and Political Theoretical Foundations, 1981; American Foreign Policy at the Crossroads, 1982; A Decade of the National Committee on American Foreign Policy, 1984; trans. Political Theology: Four Chapters on the Concept of Sovereignty (Carl Schmitt), 1985, 88; The Destruction of a Family, 1987; Elie Wiesel: Between Jerusalem and New York, 1990; The Broken Vow, the Good Obtained, 1991; Thoughts of a Collector, 1991; Carl Schmitt Hysteria in the United States, 1992; Contextualizing Carl Schmitt's Concept of Grossraum, 1994, The Leviathan in the State Theory of Thomas Hobbes (Carl Schmitt), 1996; editor Am. Fgn. Policy Interests; series Global Perspectives in History and Politics. Home: 140 Riverside Dr New York NY 10024-2605 Office: CUNY New York NY 10036

SCHWAB, GLENN ORVILLE, retired agricultural engineering educator, consultant; b. Gridley, Kans., Dec. 30, 1919; s. Edward and Lizzie (Sauder) S.; married; children: Richard, Lawrence,Mary Kay. BS, Kans. State. U., 1942; MS, Iowa State U., 1947, PhD, 1951; postdoctoral, Utah State U., 1966. Registered profl. engr., Ohio. Instr. to prof. agrl. engring. Iowa State U., Ames, 1947-56; prof. agrl. engring. Ohio State U., Columbus, 1956-85, prof. emeritus, 1985—; cons. Powell, Ohio, 1985—; bd. dirs. Internat. Water Mgmt. Program, Columbus. Co-author: Soil and Water Conservation Engineering, 4th edit., 1993, Agricultural and Forest Hydrology, 1986, Soil and Water Management Systems, 4th edit., 1996; contbr. articles to profl. jours. Served to capt. U.S. Army, 1942-46. Fellow Am. Soc. Agrl. Engrs. (bd. dirs. soil and water div. 1976-78, Hancock Brick and Tile Drainage Engr. 1968, John Deere medal 1987), Am. Soc. Engrs. Edn., Am. Soc. Testing Materials, Soil and Water Conservation Soc. Am., Am. Geophysical Union, Internat. Commn. Irrigation and Drainage. Avocations: rock polishing, wood working, photography, traveling. Home: 2637 Summit View Rd Powell OH 43065-8879 Office: Ohio State U 590 Woody Hayes Dr Columbus OH 43210-1058

SCHWAB, HAROLD LEE, lawyer; b. N.Y.C., Feb. 5, 1932; s. Harold Walter and Beatrice (Braverman) S.; m. Rowena Vivian Strauss, June 12, 1953; children: Andrew, Lisa, James. B.A., Harvard Coll., 1953; LL.B., Boston Coll., 1956. Bar: N.Y. 1957, U.S. Ct. Mil. Appeals 1958, U.S. Dist. Cts. (so. and ea. dist.) N.Y. 1967, U.S. Ct. Appeals (2d cir.) 1971, U.S. Supreme Ct. 1971, U.S. Dist. Ct. (no. dist.) N.Y. 1974, U.S. Ct. Appeals (D.C. cir.) 1986, U.S. Dist. Ct. (we. dist.) N.Y. 1988, U.S. Ct. Appeals (11th cir.) 1988, U.S. Ct. Appeals (5th cir.) 1991. Vice pres. H.W. Schwab Textile Corp., N.Y.C., 1959-60; assoc. Emile Z. Berman & A. Harold Frost, N.Y.C., 1960-67, ptnr., 1967-74; sr. ptnr. Lester Schwab Katz & Dwyer, N.Y.C., 1974—; lectr. N.Y. State Bar Assn., N.Y. County Lawyers Assn. Served to lt. col. USAFR. Mem. ABA, ASTM, Soc. Automotive Engrs., Assn. for Advancement of Automotive Medicine, Product Liability Adv. Council, N.Y. State Bar Assn. (chmn. trial lawyers sect. 1980-81), Am. Bd. Trial Advs. (pres. N.Y. chpt. 1982-83), Fedn. Ins. and Corp. Counsel (v.p. 1979-80), Assn. of Bar of City of N.Y. N.Y. County Lawyers Assn., N.Y. State Trial Lawyers Assn., Def. Assn. N.Y. Clubs: Harvard of N.Y., Governors Island Officers, Drug and Chem., Mason. Contbr. articles to legal jours.; editor Trial Lawyers Sect. Newsletter-N.Y. State Bar Assn., 1981-84; mem. editorial bd. Jour. Products and Toxics Libility, 1976—. Home: 205 Beach # 142D St Neponsit NY 11694 Office: Lester Schwab Katz & Dwyer 120 Broadway New York NY 10271

SCHWAB, HERMANN CASPAR, banker; b. N.Y.C., Jan. 8, 1920; s. Hermann Caspar and Ruth (Bliss) S.; m. C. Meteer Shanks, July 5, 1955; children: Henry R., Lesley Schwab Forman, Margery Schwab Weekes, Stuart Taylor, George Bliss, Katharine Lambard Schwab Kimmick. Grad., St. Marks Sch., 1937, Yale U., 1941. With Hanover Bank, 1941-44, 46-55, asst. sec., 1949-53, asst. v.p., 1953-55; ptnr. Dick & Merle Smith, 1956; v.p. Empire Trust Co., 1957-66, sr. v.p., 1965-66; with Bank N.Y., 1966-67; sr. v.p. Schroder Trust Co., N.Y.C., 1967-73, dir., 1970-73; pres., dir. Cheapside Dollar Fund Ltd., N.Y.C., 1970-88; sr. v.p. Schroder Capital Mgmt. Inc., N.Y.C., 1973-84, cons., 1984-88; chmn., dir. Schroder Capitol Funds Inc., 1988—. Mayor Oyster Bay Cove, N.Y., 1973-85, trustee, 1965—; trustee St. Lukes-Roosevelt Hosp. Ctr. 2d lt. inf., AUS, 1943-46. Mem. Piping Rock Club (Locust Valley, N.Y.). Home: 34 Northern Blvd Oyster Bay NY 11771-4105

SCHWAB, HOWARD JOEL, judge; b. Charleston, W.Va., Feb. 13, 1943; s. Joseph Simon and Gertrude (Hadas) S.; m. Michelle Roberts, July 4, 1970; children: Joshua Raphael, Bethany Alexis. BA in History with honors, UCLA, 1964, JD, 1967. Bar: Calif. 1968, U.S. Dist. Ct. (cen. dist.) Calif. 1968, U.S. Ct. Appeals (9th cir.) 1970, U.S. Supreme Ct. 1972. Clk. legal adminstrn. Litton Industries, L.A., 1967-68; dep. city atty. L.A., 1968-69; dep. atty. gen. State of Calif., L.A., 1969-84; judge Mcpl. Ct. L.A. Jud. Dist., 1984-85; judge Superior Ct. Superior Ct. L.A. County, L.A., 1985—; mem. faculty Berkeley (Calif.) Judicial Coll., 1987—. Contbr. articles to profl. jours. Recipient CDAA William E. James award Calif. Dist. Atty.'s Assn., 1981. Mem. San Fernando Valley Bar Assn., Inn. of Ct., Phi Alpha Delta. Democrat. Jewish. Avocations: history, book collecting. Office: LA Superior Ct 6230 Sylmar Ave Van Nuys CA 91401-2712

SCHWAB, JOHN HARRIS, microbiology and immunology educator; b. St. Cloud, Minn., Nov. 20, 1927; s. John David and Katherine (Harris) S.; m. Ruth Ann Graves, Sept. 1, 1951; children: Stewart, Thomas, Anna, Kellogg. BS, U. Minn., 1949, MS, 1950, PhD, 1953. Asst. prof. U. N.C., Chapel Hill, 1953-67, prof., 1967—; Cary C. Boshamer prof., 1982—; scientist Lister Inst. Preventive Medicine, London, 1960, MRC Rheumatism Rsch. Unit, Taplow, England, 1968, Radiobiol. Inst., Rijswijk, The Netherlands, 1975, Pasteur Inst., Paris, 1985. Contbr. articles to profl. jours. and chpts. to books. Recipient Faculty Scholar award Josiah Macy Jr. Found., 1975; NIH Spl. fellow, 1960, 68; Fogarty Internat. fellow NIH, Paris, 1985. Mem. Am. Soc. Mibrobiology (editor Infection and Immunity jour. 1980-85), Am. Assn. Immunologists, AAAS.

SCHWAB, JOHN JOSEPH, psychiatrist, educator; b. Cumberland, Md., Feb. 10, 1923; s. Joseph L. and Eleanor (Cadden) S.; m. Ruby Baxter, Aug. 4, 1945; 1 dau., Mary Eleanor. BS, U. Ky., 1946; MD, U. Louisville, 1946; MS in Physiology (Med. fellow), U. Ill., 1949; postgrad., Duke U., 1951-52, U. Fla., 1959-61. Diplomate: Nat. Bd. Med. Examiners. Intern Phila. Gen. Hosp., 1947-48; resident medicine Louisville Gen. Hosp., 1949-50; edn. officer med. coll. U. Yokohama, 1952-54; internist, psychosomaticist Holzer Clinic, Gallipolis, Ohio, 1954-59; resident psychiatry U. Fla. Hosp., 1959-61; NIMH Career tchr. U. Fla., Gainesville, 1962-64, mem. faculty, 1961-73, prof. psychiatry and medicine, 1967-73, dir. cons. liaison program, 1964-67, resident tng. dir., 1965-71; prin. investigator Fla. Health Study, 1969-74; prof., chmn. dept. psychiatry and behavioral scis. Sch. Medicine U. Louisville, 1973-91, prof. psychiatry, 1991-93, prof. emeritus, 1993—, assoc. dir. clin. psychopharm. rsch., 1991—; chmn. epidemiologic studies rev. com. Ctr. for Epidemiologic Studies, NIMH, 1973-75, cons. psychiatry br., 1975-92; cons. Old Order Amish Study of Depression, 1978—; vol. vis. lectr. Howard U., 1992; ann. vis. lectr. U. Wurzburg, Germany; vis. prof. El-Azar U., Cairo, 1991; prin. investigator LSVL Family Health Study, 1982—. Author: Handbook of Psychiatric Consultation, 1968; also articles; co-author: Sociocultural Roots of Mental Illness: An Epidemiologic Survey, 1978, Social Order and Mental Health, 1979; first author: Family Mental Health, 1993; assoc. editor Psychosomatics, 1965-86; co-editor: Man for Humanity: On Concordance V. Discord in Human Behavior, 1972, Social Psychiatry, vol. 1, 1974, The Psychiatric Examination, 1974. Capt. USAMC, 1949-54. Fellow Am. Coll. Psychiatrists (regent 1977-79), Collegium Internat. Neuro-Psychopharmacologicum, Internat. Assn. Social Psychiatry, AAAS, Am. Psychiat. Assn. (chmn. council research and devel. 1974-75); mem. AMA, Acad. Psychosomatic Medicine (exec. 1965-72, pres. 1970-71), Group for Advancement Psychiatry (bd. dirs. 1985-87), So. Med. Assn., Jefferson County Med. Soc., Ky. Psychiat. Assn., Am. Assn. Social Psychiatry (pres. 1971-73), Alpha Omega Alpha (Outstanding Performance award for Affirmative Action U. Louisville 1986), World Assn. Soc. Psychology (internat. adv. com., Rome, 1991), Psychiatrists for Better Psychiat. (pres. 1992—), U. of the World (co-chair health, edn. com. 1992—). Research on applicability of psychiatric concepts to general medicine, sociocultural aspects of mental illness; establishing guidelines for identification and management of medical patients whose illnesses are complicated by emotional stress; epidemiology of mental illness; depression and the family; clinical psychopharmacology, historical and epidemiologic perspectives on the family. Home: 6217 Innes Trace Rd Louisville KY 40222-6008

SCHWAB, KENNETH LYNN, college president; b. Wolcott, Ind., Feb. 5, 1947; m. Patrician N. Schwab; children: Kempten, Carlton, Christopher. BS, Purdue U., 1969; MEd, U. N.C., 1972; EdD, Ind. U., 1978. Spl. edn. tchr. Defiance (Ohio) City Schs., 1969-70; asst. dean students Guilford Coll., Greensboro, N.C., 1970-74, dean of students, 1974-86, asst. to pres. for instnl. planning, 1980-86; sr. v.p. for instnl. planning, 1986-88; exec. v.p. for adminstrn. U. S.C., Columbia, 1988-91; pres., CEO Centenary Coll. La., Shreveport, 1991—. Fellow Am. Coun. on Edn. Office: Centenary College of La PO Box 41188 Shreveport LA 71134-1188

SCHWAB, PAUL JOSIAH, psychiatrist, educator; b. Waxahachie, Tex., Jan. 14, 1932; s. Paul Josiah and Anna Marie (Baeuerle) S.; m. Martha Anne Beed, June 8, 1953; children: Paul Josiah III, John Conrad, Mark Whitney. BA, N. Cen. Coll., 1953; MD, Baylor U., 1957. Diplomate Am. Bd. Psychiatry and Neurology. Intern Phila. Gen. Hosp., 1957-58; clin. assoc. Nat. Cancer Inst., Bethesda, Md., 1958-60; resident in internal medicine U. Chgo., 1960-62, resident psychiatry, 1962-65, chief resident and instr. psychiatry, 1965; pvt. practice Naperville, Ill., 1965—; lectr. psychiatry U. Chgo., 1968-74, assoc. prof., 1974-79; clin. assoc., 1979-86, clin. assoc. prof., 1986—; dir. residency tng. U. Chgo., 1976-79, dir. in-patient unit and day treatment program, 1975-79. Contbr. articles to profl. jours. Bd. trustees North Ctrl. Coll., chair liaison com., 1983—, vice-chmn. acad. and student affairs com., 1983-92, vice chair admissions, fin. aid and student devel., 1992-95. Fellow Am. Psychiat. Assn. (Nancy C.A. Roeske award 1991); mem. AMA, Am. Soc. Clin. Psychopharmacology, Acad. Clin. Psychiatrists, Alpha Omega Alpha. Republican. Methodist. Office: 1200 Tall Oaks Ct Naperville IL 60540-9494

SCHWAB, SUSAN CAROL, university dean. BA in Polit. Economy, Williams Coll., 1976; MA in Applied Econs., Stanford U., 1977; PhD in Pub. Adminstrn., George Washington U., 1993. U.S. trade negotiator Office of Pres.'s Spl. Trade Rep., Washington, 1977-79; trade policy officer U.S. Embassy, Tokyo, 1980-81; chief economist, legis. asst. for internat. trade for Senator John C. Danforth, 1981-86, legis. dir., until 1989; asst. sec. commerce, dir. gen. U.S. and Fgn. Comml. Svc. Dept. Commerce, 1989-93; with corp. strategy office Motorola, Inc., Schaumburg, Ill., 1993-95; dean U. Md. Sch. Pub. Affairs, College Park, 1995—. Office: U Md Sch Pub Affairs College Park MD 20742

SCHWAB, TERRANCE WALTER, lawyer; b. Pitts., May 19, 1940; m. Eileen Caulfield, Jan. 4, 1969; children: Matthew Caulfield, Catherine Grimley, Claire Gillespie. BA magna cum laude, Harvard U., 1962; LLB cum laude, Columbia U., 1966. Assoc. Milbank, Tweed, Hadley & McCloy, N.Y.C., 1966-70; assoc. Kelley, Drye & Warren, N.Y.C., 1970-74, ptnr., 1975-96; sr. v.p., gen. counsel internat. dept. The Sanwa Bank Ltd., N.Y.C., 1996—; lectr. various profl. orgns. Assoc. editor: Law Practice of Alexander Hamilton, 1964-1980; contbr. articles to profl. jours. Active Am. Coun. on Germany, N.Y.C., 1987—; trustee, chmn. St. Luke's Chamber Ensemble, N.Y.C., 1980-82; trustee, sec. Caramoor Ctr. for Music and Arts, Katonah,

N.Y., 1971—; trustee Sch. of Convent of Sacred Heart, N.Y.C., 1987—, chmn., 1990-93. Mem. ABA, N.Y. State Bar Assn., Assn. of Bar of City of N.Y., German Am. C. of C., Harvard Club, Deutscher Verein, Swiss Soc. N.Y. Office: The Sanwa Bank Ltd 55 E 52d St New York NY 10055

SCHWABE, ARTHUR DAVID, physician, educator; b. Varel, Germany, Feb. 1, 1924; came to U.S., 1938, naturalized, 1943; s. Curt and Frieda (Roseno) S. M.D., U. Chgo., 1956. Intern UCLA Med. Center, 1956-57, asst. resident, then assoc. resident medicine, 1957-59, chief resident medicine, 1960-61, USPHS fellow gastroenterology, 1959-60; now mem. staff; chief gastroenterology Harbor Gen. Hosp., Torrance, Calif., 1962-67; cons. Wadsworth VA Center, Los Angeles; mem. faculty UCLA Med. Sch., 1961—, asst. prof. medicine, 1962-67, assoc. prof., 1967-71, prof., 1971-89, chief div. gastroenterology, 1967-88, vice chmn. dept. medicine, 1971-74, emeritus prof., 1989—. Contbr. articles to profl. jours. Served with AUS, 1943-46. Recipient UCLA Golden Apple award sr. class UCLA, 1967, 70, Outstanding Tchr. award UCLA Med. House Staff, 1968, 78, Disting. Teaching award UCLA, 1971, S.M. Mellinkoff Faculty award, 1983; Edward F. Kraft scholar, 1951; Ambrose and Gladys Bowyer fellow medicine, 1958-59. Fellow ACP; mem. Am. Gastroenterol. Assn., N.Y. Acad. Sci., So. Calif. Soc. Gastroenterology (pres. 1969), Western Assn. Physicians, Western Soc. Clin. Investigation, Western Gut Club (chmn. 1969-70), Alpha Omega Alpha. Office: 10833 Le Conte Ave Los Angeles CA 90024

SCHWABE, CALVIN WALTER, veterinarian, medical historian, medical educator; b. Newark, Mar. 15, 1927; s. Calvin Walter and Marie Catherine (Hassfeld) S.; m. Gwendolyn Joyce Thompson, June 7, 1951; children: Catherine Marie, Christopher Lawrence. BS, Va. Poly. Inst., 1948; MS, U. Hawaii, 1950; DVM, Auburn U., 1954; MPH, Harvard U., 1955, ScD, 1956. Diplomate Am. Coll. Vet. Preventive Medicine. From assoc. prof. to prof. parasitology and epidemiology, chmn. dept. tropical health, and asst. dir. Sch. Pub. Health, Am. U. Beirut, 1956-66; mem. Secretariat of WHO, Geneva, 1964-66; prof. epidemiology Sch. Vet. Medicine, also Sch. Medicine, U. Calif., Davis, 1966-91, chmn. dept. epidemiology and preventive medicine, 1966-70; assoc. dean Sch. Vet. Medicine, U. Calif., Davis, 1970-71, adj. prof. Agrl. History Ctr., 1984-91, prof. emeritus, 1991—; cons. Futurevet Assocs., Davis and Pedreguer,, Spain, 1991—; cons. WHO, UN Environ. Program, FAO, NIH, Pan Am. Health Orgn., UNICEF, Nat. Rsch. Coun.; univ. lectr. U. Sask.; Fulbright vis. prof. Univ. Coll. East Africa, Cambridge (Eng.) U., U. Khartoum; Srinivasan Meml. lectr. U. Madras; Spink lectr. comparative medicine U. Minn.; Franklin lectr. scis. and humanities Auburn U.; Entwhistle lectr. Cambridge U.; Schofield lectr. U. Guelph; mem. Am. Rsch. Ctr. Egypt. Author: Veterinary Medicine and Human Health, 1969, 84, What Should a Veterinarian Do?, 1972, Epidemiology in Veterinary Practice, 1977, Cattle, Priests and Progress in Medicine, 1978, Unmentionable Cuisine, 1980, Development Among Africa's Migratory Pastoralists, 1996; also articles. Recipient Karl F. Meyer Gold Headed Cane award Am. Vet. Epidemiology Assn., 1985, Disting. Alumnus award Auburn U., 1992. Fellow Am. Pub. Health Assn. (governing coun. 1974-76); mem. AVMA, Am. Soc. Tropical Medicine and Hygiene, History of Sci. Soc., Sudan Studies Assn. Democrat. Mem. Soc. of Friends. Avocations: collecting musical instruments, cooking, raising bamboos. Home (winter): 849 A St Davis CA 95616-1916 Home (summer): Apartado 90, Pedreguer Alicante 03750, Spain

SCHWABE, PETER ALEXANDER, JR., judge; b. Portland, Oreg., July 23, 1935; s. Peter Alexander and Evelyn (Zingleman) S.; A.B., Stanford, 1958; J.D., Willamette U., 1960; m. Bonnie Jean LeBaron, June 21, 1958; children: Mark, Karen, Diane, Patricia, Kurt. Admitted to Oreg. bar, 1960; pvt. practice, Portland, 1960-76; fed. adminstrv. law judge, 1976—. Mem. ABA, Oreg. State Bar Assn., Beta Theta Pi, Phi Delta Phi. Home: 4366 Dorking Ct Sacramento CA 95864-6150 Office: 2031 Howe Ave Sacramento CA 95825-0176

SCHWALM, FRITZ EKKEHARDT, biology educator; b. Arolsen, Hesse, Germany, Feb. 17, 1936; came to U.S., 1968; s. Fritz Heinrich and Elisabeth Agnes (Wirth) S.; m. Renate Gertrud Streichhahn, Feb. 10, 1962; children—Anneliese, Fritz-Uwe, Karen. PhD, Philipps U., Germany, 1964; Staatsexamen, Philipps U., 1965. Educator boarding sch., Kiel, Fed. Republic Germany, 1956-57; lectr. Folk Universitetet, Stockholm, Sweden, 1959-60; research assoc. U. Witwatersrand, Johannesburg, South Africa, 1966-67, U. Notre Dame, South Bend, Ind., 1968-70; asst. prof., then assoc. prof. Ill. State U., Normal, Ill., 1970-82; assoc. prof. biology, then prof., chair dept. Tex. Woman's U., Denton, 1982—, dir. Animal Care Facility, 1990—, chmn. pro tem grad. coun., 1991-92; coord., chmn. S.W. Conf. for Devel. Biology, Denton, 1985, 90, 96. Author: (monograph) Insect Morphogenesis, 1988; mem. editl. bd. Palmer Jour. Rsch.; contbr. articles to profl. jours. Vice pres. PTA, Normal, 1975. Fellow Anglo-Am. Corp. South Africa, 1966, 67; NATO advanced research fellow, Freiburg, Fed. Republic Germany 1977. Mem. AAAS, Soc. for Integrative and Comparative Biology, Deutsche Zoologische Gesellschaft, Soc. for Devel. Biology, Phi Kappa Phi (chpt. pres. 1993-96). Home: 1116 Linden Dr Denton TX 76201-2721 Office: Tex Woman's U Biology Sci Rsch Lab Denton TX 76204

SCHWAM, MARVIN ALBERT, graphic design company executive; b. Newark, Apr. 18, 1942; s. Meyer and Fannie (Lerman) S.; m. Jeanette Fein, June 13, 1964; children: Frederic, Matthew. BFA, Cooper Union, 1964. Staff artist Doremus & Co., 1964-66; mgr. Flowerental Corp., N.Y.C., 1966-68; pres. M. Schwam Floralart, N.Y.C., 1968-75; exec. v.p., bd. chmn. Florenco Foliage Systems Corp., N.Y.C., 1975-88; pres. Am. Christmas Decorating Service Inc., N.Y.C.; chmn. bd. Am. Christmas Decorations, Ltd., 1989—; pres. Marc Shaw Graphics, Inc., N.Y.C., Florenco Graphics Systems, Inc.; exec. v.p. Display Arts Worldwide, 1975-88; pres. Creative Animations, Inc., 1988-90; creative dir., v.p. Rennoc Animations, Inc., 1988-90; pres. Almar Communications, Ltd., 1990—, Sayso Communications, Ltd., 1990—, Gay Entertainment TV, Inc., 1992—. Industry chmn. March of Dimes, 1975-78, pres. bd. dirs. Happi Found. for Autistic People, N.Y.C.; trustee Nat. Found. Jewish Genetic Diseases; patron Young Adult Inst. and Workshop, Inc.; co-chmn. restaurant, hotel and entertainment industry luncheon Boy Scouts Am., 1988—; chmn. benefit com. Plan Internat. USA, 1991-92. Recipient award of merit for service to Gen. Motors Corp., 1978, award for Highlight of Christmas, Citibank/Citicorp Center, 1978, Disting. Service award Coler Hosp., 1982-86, Sr. Citizens of Roosevelt Island. Mem. Mcpl. Art Soc. N.Y., Am. Mus. Natural History, Alumni Assn. Cooper Union (2d Century Soc. fellow), Internat. Platform Assn. Designer largest artificial Christmas tree in U.S., Radio City Music Hall, N.Y.C., 1979; decorator Pulitzer Fountain, N.Y.C., 1979-80 Christmas season; chief designer Town Sq., New Orleans, Christmas, 1981, Albany (N.Y.) Tricentennial, 1986; interior landscape designer La. State Pavillion World's Fair, New Orleans, 1984; co-chmn. Nat. Restaurant, Hotel and Entertainment Industry Luncheon, N.Y.C., 1988—. Home: 7 E 17th St New York NY 10003-1913 Office: Am Christmas Decorations Inc 280 E 134th St Bronx NY 10454-4407

SCHWAN, ALFRED, food products executive. Pres., CEO Schwan Sales Enterprises, Inc., Marshall, Minn., 1965—. Office: Schwan Sales Enterprises 115 W College Dr Marshall MN 56258-1747*

SCHWAN, HERMAN PAUL, electrical engineering and physical science educator, research scientist; b. Aachen, Germany, Aug. 7, 1915; came to U.S., 1947, naturalized, 1952; s. Wilhelm and Meta (Pattberg) S.; m. Anne Marie DelBorello, June 15, 1949; children: Barbara, Margaret, Steven, Carol, Cathryn. Student, U. Goettingen, 1934-37; Ph.D., U. Frankfurt, 1940; Doctor habil. in physics and biophysics, 1946; D.Sc. (hon.), U. Pa., 1986. Research scientist, prof. Kaiser Wilhelm Inst. Biophysics, 1937-47, asst. dir., 1945-47; research sci. USN, 1947-50; prof. elec. engring., prof. elec. engring. in phys. medicine, assoc. prof. phys. medicine U. Pa., Phila., 1950-83, Alfed F. Moore prof. emeritus, 1983—; dir. electromed. div. U. Pa., 1952-73, chmn. biomed. engring., 1961-73, program dir. biomed. engr. tng. program, 1960-77; vis. prof. U. Calif.-Berkeley, 1956, U. Frankfurt Fed. Republic Germany, 1962, U. Würzburg, Fed. Republic Germany, 1986-87; lectr. Johns Hopkins U., 1962-67, Drexel U., Phila., 1983-90; W.W. Clyde vis. prof. U. Utah, Salt Lake City, 1980; 10th Lauristan Taylor lectr. Nat. Council Radiation Protection and Measurements, 1986; Fgn. sci. mem. Max Planck Inst. Biophysics, Germany, 1962—; cons. NIH, 1962-90; chmn. nat. and internat. meetings biomed. engring. and biophysics, 1959, 61, 65; mem. nat. adv. council environ. health HEW, 1969-71; mem. Nat. Acad. Scis.-NRC coms., 1968-87, Nat. Acad. Engring., 1975—. Co-author: Advances in Medical and Biological Physics, 1957, Therapeutic Heat, 1958, Physical Techniques in Medicine and Biology, 1963; editor: Biol. Engring, 1969; co-editor: Interactions Between Electromagnetic Fields and Cells, 1985; mem. editorial bd. Environ. Biophysics, IEEE Transactions Med. Biol. Engring., Jour. Phys. Med. Biol., Nonionizing Radiation, Bioelectromagnetics; contbr. articles to profl. jours. Recipient Citizenship award Phila., 1952, 1st prize AIEE, 1953, Achievement award Phila. Inst. Radio Engring., 1963, Rajewsky prize for biophysics, 1974, U.S. sr. scientist award Alexander von Humboldt Found., 1980-81, Biomed. Engring. Edn. award Am. Soc. Engring. Edn., 1983, d'Arsonval award Bioelectromagnetics Soc., 1985. Fellow IEEE (Morlock award 1967, Edison medal 1983, Centennial award 1984, Phila. Sect. award 1991, chmn. and vice chmn. nat. profl. group biomed. engring. 1955, 62-68), AAAS, Am. Inst. Med. and Biol. Engring.; mem. Am. Standards Assn. (chmn. 1961-65), Biophys. Soc. (publicity com., council, constn. com.), German Biophys. Soc. (hon.), Soc. for Cryobiology, Internat. Fedn. Med., and Biol. Engring., Bioelectromagnetics Soc., Biomed. Engring. Soc. (founder, dir. 1968-71), Sigma Xi, Eta Kappa Nu. Achievements include discovery of counterion relaxation; dielectric spectroscopy of cells and tissues; nonlinearity law of electrode polarization; research on nonionizing radiation biophysics; fundamentals electromagnetic bioengineering; first standard for safe exposure to electrical fields; development of biomedical engineering and education. Home: 99 Kynlyn Rd Wayne PA 19087-2849 also: 162 59th St Avalon NJ 08202-1207 Office: U Pa Dept Bioengring D2 Hayden Hall Philadelphia PA 19104

SCHWAN, LEROY BERNARD, artist, retired educator; b. Somerset, Wis., Dec. 8, 1932; s. Joseph L. and Dorothy (Papenfuss) S.; student Wis. State U., River Falls, 1951-53, Southeastern Signal Sch., Ga., 1954; children from previous marriage: David A., Mark J., William R., Catherine L., Maria E. BS, U. Minn., 1958, MEd, 1960, postgrad., 1961-64; postgrad. No. Mich. U., 1965, Tex. Tech. U., 1970, So. Ill. U., 1978, U. Iowa, 1980, EdD (hon.), 1988. Head art dept. Unity Pub. Schs., Milltown, Wis., 1958-61; instr. art Fridley Pub. Schs., Mpls., 1961-64; asst. prof. art No. Mich. U., Marquette, 1964-66; asst. prof. art Mankato (Minn.) State Coll., 1966-71, assoc. prof., 1971-74, tchr. off-campus grad. classes Northeast Mo. State U., John Wood Community Coll.; dir. Art Workshop Educultural Center, 1968; dir. art edn. Quincy (Ill.) Pub. Schs., 1974-78, art tchr., 1978-88, ret. 1988; tchr. art to mentally retarded children, Faribault, Minn., Owatonna, Minn., Mankato, Lake Owasso Children's Home, St. Paul; dir. art workshops, Mankato, 1970, St. Paul, 1972, 73, 74, 75; dir. workshops tchrs. mentally retarded Mankato, 1971, Faribault, 1972, Omaha, 1972-73, Quincy, 1974, 79, 82, 84-86, asst. adj. Ill. VA Home, 1980—; one-man shows: Estherville Jr. Coll., 1968, Mankato State Coll., 1968, 71, 73, Farmington, Wis., 1970, 71, 91, Good Thunder, Minn., 1972, Quincy, 1975, 77, 84, Mankato, Minn., 1975, Western Ill. U., 1979, St. Croix River Valley Arts Coun. Gallery, Osceola, Wis., 1993, 94, 95, The Northern Ctr. for the Arts, Amery, Wis., 1994; exhibited in group shows: Pentagon, Washington, 1955, U. Minn., 1958, No. Mich. U., 1965, St. Cloud State Coll., 1967, Moorhead State Coll., 1967, Bemidji (Minn.) State Coll., 1967, MacNider Mus., Mason City, Iowa, 1969, 72, 73, 74, Gallery 500, Mankato, Minn., 1970, Rochester, Minn., 1972, Minn. Mus., St. Paul, 1973, Hannibal, Mo., 1976, 77-78, Quincy, Ill., 1976, 77, 85, Ill. Art Educators Show, 1984-85, Tchrs. Retirement Art Show, Springfield, Ill., 1987; producer ednl. TV series, 1964-65, also 2 shows Kids Komments, Sta. WGEM, Quincy; mural commd. Gem City Coll., 1977. Webelos leader Twin Valley council Boy Scouts Am., 1968-69. Served with Signal Corps, AUS, 1954-56. Recipient cert. of accomplishment Sec. Army, 1955, Golden Poet award, 1985, 86, 88, 90, 91, Silver Poet award 1989. Mem. Nat. Art Edn. Assn., Ill. Art Edn. Assn., Cath. Order Foresters, Am. Legion, Phi Delta Kappa. Author: Art Curriculum Guide Unity Public Schs., 1961; Portrait of Jean, 1974; Schwan's Art Activities, 1984, Poems of Life, 1995; co-author: Bryant-Schwan Design Test, 1971, Bryant-Schwan Art Guide, 1973; contbr. articles to profl. jours., poems to Am. Poetry Assn. publs., 1984-94. Home: 849 County Road H New Richmond WI 54017-6209

SCHWANAUER, FRANCIS, philosopher, educator; b. Zsámbék, Hungary, Jan. 20, 1933; came to U.S., 1959; s. Georg and Maria (Keller) S.; m. Johanna Maria Koelln, Sept. 29, 1957; children: Stephan Michael, Miriam Frances. Maturum, Ulrich von Hutten Gymnasium, Korntal, Germany, 1954; PhD, U. Stuttgart, Germany, 1959. Asst. prof. Lebanon Valley Coll., Annville, Pa., 1960-62, U. Maine, Orono, 1962-65; asst. prof. U. So. Maine, Portland Gorham, 1965-67, assoc. prof., 1967-72, prof., 1972—. Author: Truth is a Neighborhood with Nothing in Between, 1977, Those Fallacies by Slight of Reason, 1978, No Many is not a One (For the Case is Comparison), 1981, The Flesh of Thought is Pleasure or Pain, 1982, To Make Sure is to Cohere, 1982, Philosophical Fact and Paradox, 1987, Fables from the Fox, 1991. Grantee John Anson Kittredge Ednl. Fund, 1991, 93. Mem. New England Philos. Assn., Internat. Platform Assn. Democrat. Roman Catholic. Avocation: fishing. Home: 4 Woodmont St Portland ME 04102-2709

SCHWANBECK, VICTOR RAYMOND, lawyer, civilian military employee; b. Roswell, N.Mex., Jan. 23, 1944; s. Raymond Victor and Melouise (Johnson) S.; m. Betty Gale Wilcox, Sept. 14, 1979; children: Tracy, Kimberly. BA, Ariz. State U., 1966; JD, U. Ariz., 1969. Bar: Ariz. 1969, U.S. Ct. Appeals (fed. cir.) 1984, U.S. Ct. Mil. Appeals 1971, U.S. Supreme Ct. 1974. Commd. 2d lt. USAF, 1966, advanced through grades to brigadier gen., 1993; lawyer Pima County Pub. Def., Tucson, 1972; assoc. Miller Pitt & Feldman, Tucson, 1972-74; ptnr. Cannon & Schwanbeck, Tucson, 1974-78, Schwanbeck & Present, Tucson, 1978—. Asst. adjutant gen. Ariz. Nat. Guard. Decorated Meritorious Svc. medal, Legion of Merit, Air Force Commendation medal with 1 oak leaf cluster, Air Force Achievement medal. Mem. Ariz. Bar Assn., Ariz. Trial Lawyers, Pima County Bar Assn., Rotary, Elks, Sertoma (pres. 1976-77). Office: Schwanbeck & Present 627 N Swan Rd Tucson AZ 85711-2101

SCHWANDA, TOM, religious studies educator; b. E. Stroudsburg, Pa., Oct. 23, 1950; s. Theodore Frank and Madlyn Betty (Backensto) S.; m. Grace Elaine Dunning, July 30, 1977; children: Rebecca Joy, Stephen Andrew. Student, Worcester Polytechnic Inst., 1968-69; BA in Econ., Moravian Coll., 1969-72; student, Gordon-Conwell Sem., 1972-74; MDiv, New Brunswick Sem., 1975; DMin, Fuller Theol. Sem., 1992. Ordained to ministry Reformed Ch. in Am., 1975. Pastor Wanaque (N.J.) Reformed Ch., 1975-87; pastor congl. care Immanuel Reformed Ch., Grand Rapids, Mich., 1987-92; interim sr. pastor Remembrance Reformed Ch., Grand Rapids, 1992-93; rsch. fellow H. Henry Meeter Ctr. for Calvin Studies Calvin Coll., Grand Rapids, 1993-95; instr. spirituality and worship Bethlehem Ctr. for Spirituality, Grand Rapids, 1993—; dir. Reformed Spirituality Network, Grand Rapids, 1992—; assoc. for family ministry and spiritual formation Reformed Ch. in Am., 1995—; organizer, convener Gathering Reformed Spirituality, 1993, 94, 95; chair spirituality com. Synod of Great Lakes, 1989—, mem. Christian discipleship com., 1988-94; mem. ch. life, evangelism, missions com. South Grand Rapids Classics, chair, 1992; mem. commn. on worship Reformed Ch. in Am., 1978-94; mem. care of students com. Passaic Classis, 1975, 87, chair, 1978, 83-86, pres., 1979. Contbr. articles to religious jours.; author poetry; manuscript reader, evaluator religious pub. co. Established, managed Wanaque Cmty. Food Pantry, 1977-87; vol. Domestic Crisis Ctr., Grand Rapids, 1988—; bd. dirs. Nat. Inst. Rehabilitation Engring., Hewitt, N.J., 1984—, pres. bd. dirs., 1986—. Recipient Barnabas award Iglesia Cristiana Ebenezer, 1987. Mem. Czechoslovak Soc. Arts and Sci., Czechoslovak Hist. Conf., Soc. for Study of Christian Spirituality. Avocations: running, landscaping, genealogy/family history. Home and Office: 6125 Capitan Dr SE Grand Rapids MI 49546-6721

SCHWANN, WILLIAM JOSEPH, publisher, musician, discographer; b. Salem, Ill., May 13, 1913; s. Henry W. and Effie A. (Garthwait) Schwan; m. Aire-Maija Kutvonen, June 1, 1959. Student, Louisville Conservatory Music, 1930-31; A.B., U. Louisville, 1935, D.Mus. (hon.), 1969; D.Mus. (hon.), New Eng. Conservatory Music, 1982; postgrad., Boston U. Sch. Music, 1935-36, Harvard U., 1937-38. Organist, music dir. various chs. Louisville, 1930-35; organ concerts, broadcasts, 1930-40; tchr. organ, piano, organist, music dir. Boston area, 1935-50; music revs. Boston Herald, Boston Transcript, others, 1937-39; owner Record Shop, Cambridge, Mass., 1939-53; mem. staff Radiation Lab., MIT, 1942-45; compiler, pub. 1st Long Playing Record Catalog now known as monthly Schwann-1 Record and Tape Guide, 1949, Artist Listing LP Catalog, semi-ann. Schwann-2 Record and Tape Guide, Schwann Children's Rec. Catalog, Basic Rec. Library, Basic Jazz Record Library, 1953-83, Schwann Record Catalog (now known as quarterly Schwann and Schwann Spectrum Catalogs, ann. Schwann Artist Listing Catalog), 1984—; pres., treas. W. Schwann, Inc., 1957-77; pres., pub., chief exec. officer ABC Schwann Publications, Inc., 1976-83. Editor: White House Record Library Catalog (listing 2,000 RIAA LP record collection presented to White House), Vol. I, 1973, Vol. II, 1981. Trustee Marlboro Sch. Music, Boston Ballet Co.; bd. dirs. Greater Boston Youth Symphony Orch., Longy Sch. Music, Cambridge Soc. Early Music. Recipient Disting. alumnus award U. Louisville, 1980, 1st Alumni Fellows award, 1990, Citation for Disting. Svcs., Music Libr. Assn. Am., 1983, George Peabody medal for outstanding contbns. to music in Am. Peabody Inst., Johns Hopkins U., 1984; Hon. Gold Record award for 35 yrs. of svc. to music industry and pub. Recording Industry Assn. Am., 1984; Disting. Pub. Svc. to Profession Silver medal Boston U., 1985, Disting. Alumni award, 1994; Arion award Cambridge Soc. Early Music, 1991. Mem. Nat. Audubon Soc. (life), Nat. Parks and Conservation Assn. (life), New Eng. Wild Flower Preservation Soc.(life), Save-the-Redwoods League (life), Soc. for Protection N.H. Forests (life), Am. Forestry Assn. (life), Trustees of Reservations (life), Wilderness Soc. (life), Izaak Walton League (life), Nature Conservancy (life), Appalachian Mountain Club (life), Sierra Club (life), Sigma Alpha Iota (hon.). Clubs: St. Botolph, Harvard of Boston, Harvard Mus. Assn. Home and Office: 26 Old Winter St Lincoln MA 01773-3406

SCHWANTNER, JOSEPH, composer, educator; b. Chgo., Mar. 22, 1943; m. Janet Elaine Rossate; 2 children. B.Mus., Chgo. Conservatory Coll.; M.Mus., Northwestern U., 1966, D.Mus., 1968. Teaching fellow Northwestern U., 1966-68; mem. faculty Chgo. Conservatory Coll., 1967-68; asst. prof. Pacific Lutheran U., 1968-69, Ball State U., 1969-70; successively asst. prof., assoc. prof., prof. Eastman Sch. Music, U. Rochester, 1970—; composer-in-residence St. Louis Symphony Orch., 1982-84. Compositions include Aftertones of Infinity (Pulitzer prize for music 1979), Diaphonia Intervallum, Chronicon, Autumn Canticle, Consortium, In Aeternum, Modis Caelestis, Canticle for the Evening Bells, Elixir, Wild Angels of the Open Hills, And the Mountains Rising Nowhere, Sparrows. Recipient Faricy award, 1965, BMI Student award, 1965, 66, 67, Bearns prize Columbia U., 1967; Nat. Inst. Arts and Letters Charles Ives scholar, 1970; N.Y. State Council on Arts Creative Arts Public Service grantee, 1973; NEA grantee; Guggenheim fellow, 1978-79. Office: Eastman Sch Music 26 Gibbs St Rochester NY 14604-2505

SCHWANZ, DEBORAH ANN, psychiatric nurse; b. South Bend, Ind., Jan. 1, 1952; d. Ned Christian and Rita Jane (Witucki) S. Diploma in nursing, Meml. Hosp. Sch. Nursing, South Bend, 1973; BS in Health Arts, Coll. of St. Francis, Joliet, Ill., 1991. RN, Fla.; cert. psychiat. and mental health nurse ANCC. House float nurse Meml. Hosp., 1973; psychiat. team leader St. Anthony's Hosp., St. Petersburg, Fla., 1974-81, asst. head nurse, 1981-84, clin. mgr. psychiatry, instr. aggression control techniques, 1984-89; weekend nursing supr. Boley, Inc., St. Petersburg, 1989-92; nurse therapist various nursing homes, St. Petersburg, 1992-93, Physicians' Cmty. Hosp., St. Petersburg, 1993-94; contract psychiat. nurse St. Anthony's Home Health Care, St. Petersburg, 1986-94; psychiat. home health nurse Shands Home Care, Largo, Fla., 1995—; presenter on psychiat. nursing at seminars and workshops, St. Petersburg and Clearwater, Fla., 1984-88. Mem. St. Petersburg Dem. Club. Mem. NOW (past sec. Pinellas chpt.), Mental Health Assn., Meml. Hosp. Sch. Nursing Alumni Assn., Sierra Club. Avocations: collecting old political buttons, pets, watching sports, playing trivia games. Office: 7249 Bryan Dairy Rd Largo FL 34647-1540

SCHWANZ, H(ERMAN) LEE, publishing company executive; b. Lorimor, Iowa, Apr. 29, 1923; s. Arthur I. and Elva Rae (Caffery) S.; m. Kathleen J. Boland, Sept. 1, 1947; children: Michael L., Leslie Anne Schwanz Satran, Stephen E., Susan E. Schwanz Pigorsch. B.S. in Agrl. Journalism, Iowa State U., 1947. Farm editor Cedar Rapids (Iowa) Gazette, 1947-50; asso. editor Country Gentleman mag. Curtis Pub. Co., Phila., 1950-55; editor, pub. Agrl. Pubs., Milw., 1955-70; pres., pub. Market Communications, Milw., 1970-81, Elmbrook Publishing Co., Brookfield, Wis., 1981-90, H. Lee Schwanz & Assocs., Brookfield, 1990—. Editor Farmer's Digest, 1970-88, Buying for the Farm. 1981-87. Served with 90th inf. div. AUS, 1943-46. Decorated Silver Star. Mem. Westmoor Country Club, Soc. Profl. Journalists. Republican. Methodist. Home and Office: 2645 Maple Hill Ln Brookfield WI 53045-4356

SCHWARCZ, HENRY PHILIP, geologist, educator; b. Chgo., July 22, 1933; s. Arthur and Zita Elizabeth (Strauss) S.; m. Molly Ann Robinson, Dec. 20, 1964; 1 child, Joshua Arthur. A.B., U. Chgo., 1952; M.Sc. in Geochemistry, Calif. Inst. Tech., 1955, Ph.D. in Geology, 1960. Rsch. assoc. E. Fermi Inst., U. Chgo., 1960-62; prof. geology McMaster U., Hamilton, Ont., Can., 1962—, chmn., assoc. mem. dept. anthropology, 1988-91; mem. assoc. com. on meteorites NRC of Can., 1978-86; vis. fellow Clare Hall Coll. Cambridge U., 1991-92, Australian Nat. U., 1995; vis. prof. Hebrew U., Jerusalem, 1992; assoc. mem. dept. anthropology U. Toronto, 1993—; mem. panel refs. Rivista di Antropologia (Roma). Assoc. editor Geochimica et Cosmochimica Acta, 1984-96, Jour. Human Evolution, 1994—, Geoarchaeology, 1994—; mem. editorial bd. Jour. Archaeol. Sci., 1986—; contbr. articles to profl. jours., chpts. to books. Fulbright fellow, Pisa, Italy, 1968-69, Killam fellow Can. Coun., 1993—. Fellow Royal Soc. Can., Geol. Soc. Am. (Archeol. Geol. Div. award 1991); mem. Geochem. Soc., Lithoprobe NSERC 1991—), Am. Quaternary Assn., Acad. III Sci. (mem. coun.), Geol. Soc. Am. (chmn. archeol. geol. divsn.). Avocations: playing violin, drawing. Office: McMaster Univ, Dept Geology, Hamilton, ON Canada L8S 4M1

SCHWARCZ, STEVEN LANCE, law educator, lawyer; b. N.Y.C., Nov. 10, 1949; s. Charles and Elinor Schwarcz; m. Susan Beth Kolodny, Aug. 24, 1975; children: Daniel Benjamin, Rebekah Mara. BS summa cum laude, in Aero. Engring., New York U., 1971; JD, Columbia U., 1974. Bar: N.Y. 1975, U.S. Dist. Ct. (so. dist.) N.Y. 1975. Assoc. Shearman & Sterling, N.Y.C., 1974-82, ptnr., 1983-89; ptnr, chmn. structured fin. practice group Kaye, Scholer, Fierman, Hays & Handler, 1989-96; adj. prof. law Yeshiva U., Benjamin N. Cardozo Sch. Law, N.Y.C., 1983-92; vis. lectr. Yale Law Sch., 1992-96; lectr. in law Columbia Law Sch., 1992-96; prof. law Duke U. Sch. Law, 1996—. Contbr. articles to profl. jours. Chmn. Friends of the Eldridge St. Synagogue, N.Y.C., 1979—, Legis. Drafting Rsch. Fund. Recipient First Prize award Pub. Speaking Contest, NYU, 1971; George Granger Brown scholar, 1971; NSF grantee in Math., 1969. Fellow Am. Coll. Commercial Fin. Lawyers; mem. Am. Law Inst., Assn. of Bar of City of N.Y. (environ. law com. 1975-78, nuclear tech. com. 1979-81, sci. and law com. 1985—, chmn. 1987—). Tau Beta Pi. Jewish. Office: Duke U Sch Law Box 90362 Science Dr & Towerview Rd Durham NC 27708

SCHWARCZ, VERA, East Asian studies educator, history educator; b. May 8, 1947; came to U.S. in 1961; BA in French Lit. and Oriental Religions, Vassar Coll., 1969; MA in East Asian Studies, Yale U., 1971; PhD in Chinese History, Stanford U., 1977. Instr. history Stanford U., 1973; lectr. Chinese history Wesleyan U., Middletown, Conn., 1975-77, asst. prof. Chinese history, 1975-83, chair East Asian studies, 1982-84, 85-88, prof. history, 1988—, Mansfield Freeman prof. East Asian studies, 1988—; dir. Mansfield Freeman Ctr. East Asian Studies, 1987-88; bd. dirs. Sino-Judaic Inst.; vis. scholar Beijing U., China, 1983, 86, 89, exchange scholar, 1979-80; vis. scholar Centre de documentation sur la Chine Contemporaine, Paris, 1985, Mishkenot Sha'ananim, Jerusalem, 1991, Chinese Acad. Social Sci., Internat. Inst. Chinese Culture, Beijing, 1989; guest lectr. DAO Assn., Cluj, Romania, 1993; other study trips to Taiwan, Hong Kong, Beijing, Tibet. Author: China: Inside the People's Republic, 1972, Long Road Home: A China Journal, 1984, The Chinese Enlightenment: The Legacy of the May Fourth Movement in Modern China, 1986, Zhongguo de qimeng yundong (China's Enlightenment), 1989, Time for Telling Truth is Running Out: Conversations with Zhang Shenfu, 1992; editorial bd. China Rev. Internat., Bulletin Concerned Asian Scholars, 1979—, History and Theory, 1981-84; contbr. articles to profl. jours.; contbr. poems, fiction to mags.; speaker in field. Guggenheim fellow 1989-90, Founders fellow AAUQ, 1988-89, Faculty fellow Ctr. Humanities Wesleyan U., 1981, Rsch. fellow Social Sci. Rsch. Coun., 1982-83, Advanced Trainee fellow NAS, 1979-80, NDFL fellow 1973-74, Kent fellow Danforth Found., 1971-73, AAUW grantee, 1974-75, Am. Coun. Learned Societies grantee, 1978, Am. Philosophical Soc. grantee, 1981, 85. Mem. AAUP, Assn. Asian Studies (Levenson prize com. 1991-92, chair, 1992-93, coun. confs. 1989—, com. women 1977-78), New

Eng. Assn. Asian Studies (pres. 1988-89), Am. Hist. Assn., New Eng. China Faculty Seminar (Harvard), Modern China Faculty Seminar (Columbia), Soc. Values Higher Edn., China Inst. (N.Y.). Office: Wesleyan U Wesleyan Sta Middletown CT 06459

SCHWARK, HOWARD EDWARD, civil engineer; b. Bonfield, Ill., Aug. 31, 1917; s. Edward F. and Florence M. (Schultz) S.; m. Arlene M. Highbarger, Sept. 28, 1940 (dec. May 1990); m. Carol D. Kehoe, June 1, 1991; children: Timothy Kehoe, Maureen Kehoe, Colleen Corbin. Student St. Viators Coll., Bourbonnias, Ill., 1935-37; BS, U. Ill., 1942. Asst. to county supt. hwys. Ford County (Ill.), 1941-43; engr. E. I. DuPont de Nemours Co., 1942; asst. county supt. hwys. Kankakee County (Ill.), 1946-52, county supt. hwys., 1952-82; bd. dirs. First Am. Bank, Kankakee Devel. Corp.; adviser county rds. FHWA, 1973-82; spl. cons. ESCA Consultants, Urbana, Ill., 1982—, v.p., 1988—. Co-chmn., Rep. Finance Com., 1962-66; pres. Kankakee Pk. Dist., 1959-70; mem. tech. adv. com. to Ill. Transp. Study Commn., 1975-82; trustee, pres. Azariah Buck Old People's Home, ret.; mem. exec. bd. Rainbow coun. Boy Scouts Am.; bd. dirs. Soil and Water Conservation Svc., 1967-74. Served with AUS, 1943-46. Recipient Disting. Alumnus award Civil Engring. Alumni Assn. U. Ill., 1975; Disting. Svc. award U.S. Dept. Transp., 1982; Spl. Achievement award as road adv. for Region 5, FHWA, 1982. Mem. Nat. Soc. Profl. Engrs. (life), Nat. Assn. County Engrs. (life mem., v.p. North Central region 1979-81, Urban County Engr. of Yr. award 1982), Ill. Soc. Profl. Engrs. (life), Ill. Assn. County Supts. Hwys. (life mem., pres. 1970), Ill. Engring. Coun. (pres. 1971-72), Am. Road and Transp. Builders Assn. (life mem., dir. county div. 1969-75, dir. 1975-81, pres. county div. 1975; Outstanding Service award transp. ofcls. div. 1981, Ralph R. Bartelsmeyer award 1983), Kankakee Area C. of C. (dir. 1960-74), Am. Soc. Profl. Engrs., Western Soc. Engrs., Twp. Ofcls. Ill., Freelance Photographers Assn., Ill. Wildlife Fedn. Lutheran. Lodges: Rotary, South Wilmington Sportsman. Home: 319 Berkshire Ct Bourbonnais IL 60914-1552

SCHWARTING, ARTHUR ERNEST, retired pharmacognosy educator and university dean; b. Waubay, S.D., June 8, 1917; s. John Ernest and Johanna Martha (Boelte) S.; m. Roberta L. Mitchell, June 14, 1941; children: Jon Michael, Stephen Arthur (dec.), Gerald Allen. B.S., S.D. State U., 1940; Ph.D., Ohio State U., 1943. Instr. U. Nebr., 1943-45, asst. prof., 1945-49; assoc. prof. U. Conn., Storrs, 1949-53, prof. pharmacognosy, 1953-81, prof. emeritus, 1981—, dean Sch. Pharmacy, 1970-80; vis. prof. U. Munich, 1968-69. Author: (with others) Introduction to Chromatography, 1968, 2d edit., 1985; editor: Jour. Natural Products, 1960-76. Mem. Mansfield Bd. Edn., Conn., 1965-70; bd. dirs. Am. Found. Pharm. Edn., 1974-80. Recipient Research Achievement award Am. Pharm. Assn. Found., 1964; U. Conn. Alumni Assn. award for faculty excellence, 1965, Centennial Achievement award Ohio State U., 1970, Disting. Alumnus award S.D. State U., 1986. Fellow AAAS; mem. Am. Assn. Colls. Pharmacy (pres. 1971-72, pres. council deans 1977-78), Am. Pharm. Assn., Am. Soc. Pharmacognosy (hon. mem. 1981), Sigma Xi, Phi Lambda Upsilon, Phi Kappa Phi, Rho Chi. Lutheran. Research and publs. on chemistry and biochemistry of natural drug products. Home: 529 Village Pl Longwood FL 32779-6042

SCHWARTZ, AARON ROBERT, lawyer, former state legislator; b. Galveston, Tex., July 17, 1926; s. Joseph and Clara (Bulbe) S.; m. Marilyn Cohn, July 14, 1951; children: Richard Austin, Robert Allen, John Reed, Thomas Lee. Pre-law student, Tex. A&M U., 1948; J.D., U. Tex., 1951. Bar: Tex. 1951. Mem. Tex. Ho. of Reps., 1955-59; Mem. Tex. Senate, 1960-81, past chmn. rules, jurisprudence and natural resources coms.; chmn. Tex. Coastal & Marine Coun., U.S. Coastal States Orgn.; adj. legis. prof. Bates Law Sch., U. Houston. Contbr. articles to profl. jours. Mem. exec. com. Galveston Bay Fond.; apptd. to Tex. Oil Spill Oversight Commn., 1993. Served with USN, 944-46, to 2d lt. USAFR, 1948-53. Recipient conservation and legis. awards, Outstanding Citizen award Galveston Jr. C. of C., 1981, Man of Yr., People of Vision award Galveston chpt. Soc. for Prevention of Blindness, 1986, Disting. Service award Nat. Hurricane Conf., Tex. Coastal Mgmt. Adv. Com., 1987. Mem. Tex. State Bar Assn., Galveston County Bar Assn. Democrat. Jewish. Home: PO Box 3398 Galveston TX 77552-0398

SCHWARTZ, ALAN E., lawyer; b. Detroit, Dec. 21, 1925; s. Maurice H. and Sophia (Welkowitz) S.; m. Marianne Shapero, Aug. 24, 1950; children: Marc Alan, Kurt Nathan, Ruth Anne. Student, Western Mich. Coll., 1944-45; BA with distinction, U. Mich., 1947; LLB magna cum laude, Harvard U., 1950; LLD (hon.), Wayne State U., 1983, U. Detroit, 1985. Bar: N.Y. 1951, Mich. 1952. Assoc. Kelley, Drye & Warren, N.Y.C., 1950-52; mem. Honigman, Miller, Schwartz & Cohn, Detroit, 1952—; now sr. mem. Honigman, Miller, Schwartz & Cohn; spl. asst. counsel N.Y. State Crime Commn., 1951; dir. Unisys Corp., Detroit Edison Co., Core Industries Inc., Handleman Co., Howell Industries, Inc., Pulte Corp., Comerica Inc. Editor: Harvard Law Rev., 1950. Vice pres., mem. exec. com. Detroit Symphony Orch.; v.p., bd. dirs. United Found.; bd. dirs. Detroit Renaissance, Detroit Econ. Growth Corp., New Detroit, Met. Affairs Corp., Jewish Welfare Fedn. Detroit; trustee Community Found. for Southeastern Mich., Harper-Grace Hosp., Interlochen Arts Acad., Skillman Found.; adv. mem. Arts Commn., City of Detroit. Served as ensign Supply Corps, USNR, 1945-46. Recipient Mich. Heritage Hall of Fame award, 1984, George W. Romney award for lifetime achievement in volunteerism, 1994. Mem. Mich. Bar Assns. Clubs: Franklin Hills Country; Detroit, Economic (dir.). Home: 4120 Echo Rd Bloomfield Hills MI 48302-1941 Office: Honigman Miller Schwartz & Cohn 2290 1st National Bldg Detroit MI 48226

SCHWARTZ, ALAN GIFFORD, sport company executive; b. N.Y.C., Nov. 7, 1931; s. Kevie Waldemar and Vera (Isaacs) S.; m. Roslyn Smulian, Sept. 6, 1958; children: Steven, Andrew, Sally, Elizabeth. BS, Yale U., 1952; MBA, Harvard U., 1954. Ptnr. Gifford Investment Co., Chgo., 1954—; CEO Tennis Corp. of Am., Chgo., 1969—, chmn. bd., 1974—; chmn. exec. com. First Colonia Bankshares, Chgo., 1984—; dir. Mich. Ave. Nat. Bank, Chgo., Comtrex Systems, Inc., Mt. Laurel, N.J.; trustee Roosevelt U., 1994—; mem. bd. dirs. Inst. European & Asian Studies, 1993—, U.S. Tennis Assn., 1994—. Contbr. articles to profl. jours.; editorial cons. Club Industry mag., 1985—. Bd. dirs. Grad. Sch. of Bus., Duke U., Durham, N.C., 1977—, McCormick Boys and Girls Club, 1989—. Elected to Club Industry Hall of Fame, 1987. Mem. Standard Club of Chgo. Jewish. Avocations: travel, tennis. Office: Tennis Corp of Am 2020 W Fullerton Ave Chicago IL 60647-3351*

SCHWARTZ, ALAN LEIGH, pediatrician, educator; b. N.Y.C., Apr. 25, 1948; s. Robert and Joyce (Goldner) S.; m. Judith Child, June 22, 1974; 1 child, Timothy Child. BA, Case Western Res. U., 1974, PHD in Pharmacology, 1974, MD, 1976. Diplomate Am. Bd. Pediatrics. Intern Children's Hosp., Boston, 1976-77, resident, 1976-78, fellow Dana Farber Cancer Inst., 1978-80; instr. Harvard Med. Sch., Boston, 1980-81, asst. prof., 1981-83, assoc. prof., 1983-86; prof. pediatrics, molecular biology and pharmacology Washington U. Sch. Medicine, St. Louis, 1986—, chmn. dept. pediatrics, 1995—; vis. scientist MIT, Boston, 1979-82; mem. sci. adv. bd. Nat. Inst. Child Health and Human Devel., NIH, Bethesda, Md., 1988-94; investigator Am. Heart Assn. Alumni Endowed Prof. Pediatrics, Wash. U. Sch. Medicine, 1987—. Office: Washington U Sch Medicine Dept Pediatrics Box 8116 One Children's Pl Saint Louis MO 63110-1093

SCHWARTZ, ALAN VICTOR, advertising agency executive; b. Detroit, July 12, 1948; s. Seymour and Adeline (Goldstein) S.; m. Linda Toba Dershowitz, Aug. 20, 1981; children: Stacy Ilana, Andrew Robert. B.S. with honors, Lehigh U., 1970; M.B.A. with highest honors, Cornell U., 1972. C.P.A., N.Y. Mgr. Price Waterhouse, Huntington, N.Y., 1972-79; v.p. dir. fin. control Doyle Dane Bernbach, N.Y.C., 1979-81; v.p. chief fin. officer Bernard Hodes Advt., N.Y.C., 1981-84, sr. v.p., chief operating and fin. officer, 1984-87, exec. v.p., chief operating and fin. officer, 1987—. bd. mgrs. Evans Tower, treas. 1991-92, pres. 1991-92; Vice campaign chmn. United Way, L.I., 1978. Mem. Nat. Assn. Accts. (various directorships and treas.), N.Y. State Soc. C.P.A.s, Lehigh Alumni Assn. (pres. L.I. chpt. 1977-79, treas. 1975-77). Office: Bernard Hodes Advt 555 Madison Ave New York NY 10022-3301

SCHWARTZ, ALFRED, university dean; b. Chgo., Jan. 8, 1922; s. Isadore and Lena (Ziff) S.; m. Delle Weiss, Aug. 26, 1945; children: Reid Mitchell, Karen Ruth. B.Ed., Chgo. Tchrs. Coll., 1944; M.A. in Polit. Sci., U. Chgo., 1946, Ph.D. in Ednl. Adminstrn., 1949. Tchr. Chgo. pub. schs., 1944-45; contact officer VA, 1946; instr. U. Chgo. Lab. Sch., 1946-50; assoc. prof. edn. Drake U., 1950-56, U. Del.; also exec. sec. Del. Sch. Study Council, 1956-58; dean (Univ. Coll.); prof. Coll. Edn., Drake U., 1958-85, dean, 1964-79, 80-84, dean emeritus, 1985; acting v.p. acad. adminstrn. Coll. Edn., Coll. Edn., 1979-80; cons., 1985—; adviser Iowa Dept. Pub. Instrn.; mem. coordinating bd. Nat. Council Accreditation for Tchr. Edn.; chmn. tchr. edn. and adv. com. Iowa Dept. Pub. Instrn. Author: (with Harlan L. Hagman) Administration in Profile for School Executives, 1954, (with Stuart Tiedeman) Evaluating Student Progress, 1957, (with Willard Fox) Managerial Guide for School Principals, 1965. Mem. Gov.'s Commn. State-Local Relations. Mem. World Council on Curriculum and Instrn., Iowa Assn. Colls. for Tchr. Edn. (pres., exec. sec.), Am. Profs. for Peace in Middle East, Am. Ednl. Research Assn., Iowa Edn. Assn., NEA, Phi Delta Kappa, Kappa Delta Pi. Home: 3450 3rd Ave Apt 511 San Diego CA 92103-4939

SCHWARTZ, ALLEN G., federal judge; b. Bklyn., Aug. 23, 1934; s. Herbert and Florence (Safier) S.; m. Joan Ruth Teitel, Jan. 17, 1965; children: David Aaron, Rachel Ann, Deborah Eve. BBA, CCNY, 1955; LLB, U. Pa., 1958. Bar: N.Y. 1958. Asst. dist. atty. Office of Dist. Atty., N.Y. County, 1959-62; assoc. firm Paskus Gordon & Hyman, N.Y.C., 1962-65; ptnr. firm Koch Lankenau Schwartz & Kovner, N.Y.C., 1965-69, Dornbush Mensch Mandelstam & Schwartz, N.Y.C., 1969-75; mem. Schwartz & Schreiber, P.C., N.Y.C., 1975-77; corp. counsel City of N.Y., 1978-81; mem. Schwartz Klink & Schreiber, P.C., 1982-87; ptnr. Proskauer Rose Goetz & Mendelsohn, N.Y.C., 1987-94; judge U.S. Dist. Ct. (so. dist.) N.Y., N.Y.C., 1994—; mem. ex officio N.Y.C. Bd. Ethics, 1978-81; pro bono sports commr. City of N.Y., 1982-83. Research editor: U. Pa. Law Rev, 1957-58. Office: US Courthouse 500 Pearl St Rm 1350 New York NY 10007

SCHWARTZ, ALLYSON Y., state senator; b. N.Y.C., Oct. 3, 1948; d. Everett and Renee Perl Young; m. David Schwartz, 1970; children: Daniel, Jordan. BA, Simmons Coll., 1970; MSS, Bryn Mawr Coll., 1972. Founder, exec. dir. Elizabeth Blackwell Health Ctr. for Women, 1975-88; acting commr., 1st dep. commr. Dept. Human Svcs., 1988-90; mem. Pa. State Senate 4th dist., 1990—; minority chmn. Edn. Com., 1994—; mem. Aging and Youth Com., Pub. Health and Welfare Com., Comty. and Econ. Devel. Com. Policy. Mem. State Bd. Edn., 1995—; mem. Pa. Coun. on Higher Edn., Pa. 2000, 1990—, Pa. Hist. and Mus. Commn.; vice chair assembly on fed. issues Nat. Coun. State Legislators, 1994; v.p. Women's Network; bd. dirs. Ctr. for Policy Alternatives, 1992—. Named Social Worker of Yr. Nat. Assn. Social Workers, 1990. Mem. Child Welfare League. Office: Senate State Capital Harrisburg PA 17101

SCHWARTZ, AMY ELIZABETH, editorial writer, columnist; b. N.Y.C., July 26, 1962; d. Stuart Grad and Doris (Greenburg) S. BA, Harvard U., 1984. Rschr. Harper's mag., N.Y.C., 1984; reporter, rschr. The New Republic, Washington, 1985; rschr., writer The Washington Post, 1985-89, editorial writer, 1989—, columnist, 1993—. Vol. tchr. Jewish Study Ctr., Washington, 1993-94. Recipient Bernie Harrison Meml. award for commentary Washington-Balt. Newspaper Guild, 1992, 94, 95; Humboldt Found. Chancellor scholar, Bonn, Germany, 1990-91. Mem. Newspaper Guild. Jewish. Office: Washington Post Editorial Page 1150 15th St NW Washington DC 20071-0001

SCHWARTZ, AMY MARGARET, children's book author, illustrator; b. San Diego, Apr. 2, 1954; d. Isador Henry and Eva (Herzberg) S.; m. Leonard Seth Marcus, May 20, 1990; 1 child, Jacob Henry. Student, Antioch Coll., 1972-73; BFA, Calif. Coll. Arts and Crafts, 1975. Author, illustrator: Bea and Mr. Jones, 1982, Begin at the Beginning, 1983, Her Majesty, Aunt Essie, 1984, Mrs. Moskowitz and the Sabbath Candlesticks, 1984, Yossel Zissel and the Wisdom of Chelm, 1986, Oma and Bobo, 1987, Annabelle Swift, Kindergartner, 1988, (with Leonard S. Marcus) Mother Goose's Little Misfortunes, 1991, Camper of the Week, 1991, A Teeny-Tiny Baby, 1994, (with Henry Schwartz) Make A Face, 1994; illustrator numerous others, including The Purple Coat, 1986, How I Captured a Dinosaur, 1989. Recipient numerous award Parents Choice, 1982, 88; feature book award Parents Choice, 1982, rev. book, 1983; One of Best Books award Sch. Libr. Jour., 1982, 87, 88, starred rev. book, 1984, 93, 94; One of 100 Best Children's Books award N.Y. Pub. Libr., 1983, 88, 90, 94, Children's Choice award Internat. Reading Assn.-CBS, 1984, Nat. Jewish Book award, 1984, award Assn. Jewish Librs., 1984, Christopher award, 1989, Notable Book award ALA, 1987, 88, award Libr. of Congress, 1988, Parents mag., 1988, N.Y. Times Book Review Best Illus. Childrens Book, 1994, N.Y. Times Book Review Notable Childrens Book, 1994. Office: care Jane Feder 305 E 24th St New York NY 10010-4011

SCHWARTZ, ANNA JACOBSON, economic historian; b. N.Y.C., Nov. 11, 1915; married; four children. BA, Barnard Coll., 1934; MA, Columbia U., 1935, PhD, 1964; LittD (hon.), U. Fla., 1987; ArtsD (hon.), Stonehill Coll., 1989; LLD (hon.), Iona Coll., 1992. Researcher USDA, 1936, Columbia U. Social Sci. Research Council, 1936-41; mem. sr. research staff Nat. Bur. Econ. Research Inc., N.Y.C., 1941—; instr. Bklyn. Coll., 1952, Baruch Coll., 1959-60; adj. prof. econs. grad. CCNY, 1967-69, grad. sch. CUNY, 1986—, NYU Grad. Sch. Arts and Sci., 1969-70; hon. vis. prof. City U. Bus. Sch., London, 1984—. Mem. editorial bd. Am. Econ. Rev., 1972-78, Jour. Money, Credit and Banking, 1974-75, 84—, Jour. Monetary Econs., 1975—, Jour. Fin. Svcs. Rsch., 1993—; contbr. numerous articles to profl. jours. Disting. fellow Am. Econ. Assn., 1993. Mem. Western Econ. Assn. (pres. 1987-88). Office: Nat Bur Econ Research 269 Mercer St Fl 8 New York NY 10003-6633

SCHWARTZ, ANTHONY, veterinary surgeon, educator; b. Bklyn., July 30, 1940; s. Murray and Miriam Sarah (Wittes) S.; m. Claudia Rosenberg, July 21, 1963; children: Thomas Frederick, Eric Leigh. Student, Mich. State U., 1957-58; DVM, Cornell U., 1963; PhD, Ohio State U., 1972. Diplomate Am. Coll. Vet. Surgeons (bd. of regents 1989-92). Gen. practice vet. medicine Huntington, N.Y., 1963-66; resident in surgery Animal Med. Ctr., N.Y.C., 1968-69; resident in surgery Ohio State U., Columbus, 1969-70, asst. prof., head sect. small animal surgery, 1973; asst. prof. then assoc. prof. comparative medicine Yale U. Sch. Medicine, New Haven, 1973-79; assoc. prof. then prof., chmn. dept. surgery, assoc. dean Tufts U. Sch. Vet. Medicine, Boston, 1979-89; assoc. dean clin. edn. Tufts U. Sch. Vet. Medicine, 1989-93, prof., chmn. dept. surgery, assoc. dean academic affairs, 1993—; cons. U.S. Surg. Corp., Norwalk, Conn., 1975—. Author: (with others) Small Animal Surgery, 1989, Complications in Small Animal Surgery, 1996; edit. bd. Vet. Surgery, 1987-90, Jour. Investigative Surgery, 1987—; assoc. editor: Textbook of Small Animal Surgery, 1985; contbr. articles to profl. jours. Capt. U.S. Army Vet Corps., 1966-68. Recipient 1st prize N.Y. State Vet. Med. Soc., 1963; Robert Wood Johnson Health Policy fellow, Washington, 1988-89; NIH grantee, 1975-84. Mem. AVMA (legis. planning com. 1989-92, coun. on govt. affairs 1992-97), AAAS, Am. Assn. Immunologists, Am. Assn. Vet. Clinicians, Assn. Am. Vet. Med. Colls. (Washington, exec. dir., treas. 1992-93), Nat. Acads. of Practice, Mass. Vet. Medicine Assn. (animal welfare com. 1990—, chmn. 1990-91), Sigma Xi, Phi Kappa Phi. Democrat. Jewish. Office: Tufts U Sch Vet Medicine 200 Westboro Rd North Grafton MA 01536-1828

SCHWARTZ, ARNOLD (ARNIE SHAYNE), pharmacologist, biophysicist, biochemist, educator, actor, director, producer; b. Bronx, N.Y., Mar. 1, 1929; s. Saul and Ray S.; m. Ina Price, Dec. 23, 1956; children: Tracy, Stacy. BSc in Pharmacy cum laude, LIU, 1951, DSc (hon.), 1988; MSc, Ohio State U., Columbus, 1957; PhD, SUNY, Bklyn., 1960. Mem. faculty Baylor Coll. Medicine, 1962-77, prof. pharmacology, 1968-72, head div. myocardial biology, chmn. dept. cell biophysics, 1972-77, Disting. Univ. prof., 1989; Edward Wendland prof. materia medica and therapeutics U. Cin. Med. Ctr., 1977-89, chmn. dept. pharmacology and cell biophysics, 1977-94; dir. Inst. Molecular Pharmacology and Biophysics, 1994—; mem. rev. panels Nat. Heart, Lung and Blood Inst. and Am. Heart Assn., 1970-89; pres. Am. sect. Internat. Soc. for Heart Research, 1976-77; pres. drug cons. co. CVR, Inc. Mem. editorial bds. profl. jours.; editor: Methods in Pharmacology Series; contbr. over 400 articles on cardiovascular pharmacology and biochemistry, mechanisms of digitalis and calcium antagonist action, role of calcium in cardiac function, molecular biology of ion channesl and receptors to profl. jours. Actor, dir. profl. theatre, TV, cinema, med. and health TV. Served with USAF, 1952-56. Recipient Rsch. Career Devel. award, 1965-72, Samuel Kaplan, M.D. Visionary award S.W. Ohio affiliate Am. Heart Assn., 1992, Rsch. Merit award, 1992, Otto Krayer award in pharmacology Am. Soc. Pharmacology and Exptl. Therapy, 1993, Ariens award in molecular pharmacology Dutch. Pharmacol. Soc., 1993; Josiah Macy scholar Oxford U., 1979-80; NIH fellow, 1960-62; NIH grantee, 1989. Fellow Am. Coll. Cardiology; mem. N.Y. Acad. Sci. Office: Univ Cin Med Ctr 231 Bethesda Ave Cincinnati OH 45229-2827 *The need to discover is of paramount importance.*

SCHWARTZ, ARTHUR ROBERT, food writer, critic, consultant; b. N.Y.C., Mar. 24, 1947; s. Lawrence and Sydell Bedona (Sonkin) S.; m. Elaine Billie Rothseid, Aug. 16, 1969 (div. 1982). BS in Bus. and Journalism, U. Md., 1968; MA, CUNY, Bklyn., 1970. Editor Bklyn. Graphic, 1968-69; food and wine writer Newsday, L.I., N.Y., 1969-79; exec. food editor N.Y. Daily News, 1979-89, restaurant critic, 1979—; lectr. New Sch. for Social Rsch., N.Y.C., 1987—; TV reporter Sta. WNYW-TV Fox-5, N.Y.C., 1989; talk show host Sta. WOR Radio, 1992—; syndicated food critic. Author: Cooking in a Small Kitchen, 1979, What To Cook When You Think There's Nothing in the House to Eat, 1992, Soup Suppers, 1994; contbr. author: Better Times; also numerous mag. articles. Home and Office: 320 E 42nd St New York NY 10017-5900

SCHWARTZ, AUBREY EARL, artist; b. N.Y.C., Jan. 13, 1928; s. Louis and Clara S. Student, Art Students League, Bklyn. Mus. Art Sch., 1969-94; Prof. emeritus Harpur Coll., SUNY, Binghamton, 1994—; prof. art Harpur Coll., SUNY, Binghamton, 1969—. One-man shows Grippi Gallery, N.Y.C., 1958, Art U.S.A., N.Y. Coliseum, N.Y.C., 1959, Contemporary Graphic Art, U.S. State Dept., 1959, group shows include Whitney Mus. Am. Art, N.Y.C., 1957; represented in permanent collections Nat. Gallery Art, Washington, Bklyn. Mus. Art, Phila. Mus. Art, Library Congress, Washington, Art Inst. Chgo. Recipient 1st prize for graphic art Boston Arts Festival 1960; Guggenheim fellow, 1958-60; Tamarind fellow, 1960; N.Y. State CAPS fellow, 1973-74. Home: 104 Main St Afton NY 13730

SCHWARTZ, BARRY FREDRIC, lawyer, diversified holding company executive; b. Phila., Apr. 16, 1949; s. Albert and Evelyn (Strauss) S.; m. Sherry L. Handsman, Mar. 21, 1985; children: Fanny Rose, Abraham David. AB cum laude, Kenyon Coll., 1970; JD, Georgetown U., 1974. Bar: Pa. 1974, Ill. 1974, U.S. Ct. Appeals (7th cir.) 1975, U.S. Ct. Appeals (3d cir.) 1978, U.S. Ct. Appeals (4th cir.) 1979, U.S. Ct. Appeals (6th cir.) 1981, U.S. Supreme Ct. 1981, N.Y. 1992. Assoc. Sachnoff, Schrager, Jones & Weaver, Chgo., 1974-76; ptnr. Wolf, Block, Schorr & Solis-Cohen, Phila., 1976-89; exec. v.p. gen. counsel MacAndrews & Forbes Holdings, Inc., N.Y.C., 1989—; dir. Mut. Series Fund Inc., 1994. Mem. alumni coun. Kenyon Coll., Gambier, Ohio, 1985; chmn., bd. dirs. Pub. Interest Law Ctr. Phila., 1989, Greenwich (Conn.) Jewish Fedn.; trustee Temple Sholom, Greenwich; dir. Westchester Holocaust Commn. Mem. ABA, Pa. Bar Assn., Phila. Bar Assn. Avocations: tennis, golf, jogging, sea kayaking. Home: 143 Park Ave Greenwich CT 06830-4849 Office: MacAndrews & Forbes Holdings Inc 35 E 62nd St New York NY 10021-8016

SCHWARTZ, BARRY STEVEN, lawyer; b. Bklyn., Mar. 12, 1950; s. Joseph and Helen (Lipkin) S.; m. Sherry Licht Cooper, Feb. 18, 1984; 1 child, Jennifer. BA, NYU, 1972; JD, Cath. U. Am., 1975. Bar: N.Y. 1976, U.S. Dist. Ct. (so. dist.) 1976, N.J. 1979, U.S. Ct. Appeals (2d cir.) 1988. Assoc. Seavey, Fingerit & Vogel, N.Y.C., 1976-81; pvt. practice law N.Y.C., 1980—; of counsel Seavey, Fingerit, Vogel, Oziel & Skoller, N.Y.C.; atty. West New York (N.J.) Rent Control Board, 1984-86. Assoc. editor Cath. U. Law Rev., 1974-75. Mem. ABA, N.Y. State Bar Assn., Masons (master Audubon-Gotham club 1986). Avocations: music, reading, travel. Home: 6 Corn Mill Ct Saddle River NJ 07458-1232 Office: Seavey Fingerit Vogel Oziel 60 E 86th St New York NY 10028-1009

SCHWARTZ, BERNARD, lawyer, educator; b. N.Y.C., Aug. 25, 1923; s. Isidore and Ethel (Levenson) S.; m. Aileen Haas, Apr. 18, 1950; 1 child, Brian Michael. BSS, CCNY, 1944; LLB, NYU, 1944; LLM, Harvard U., 1945; PhD, Cambridge (Eng.) U., 1947, LLD, 1956; Doctorat d'Universite, U. Paris, 1963. Bar: N.Y. 1945. Mem. law faculty NYU, 1947-92, Edwin D. Webb prof. law, 1963-92; Chapman Disting. prof. law U. of Tulsa, 1992—; cons. Hoover Commn., 1955; chief counsel, staff dir. spl. subcom. legislative oversight U.S. Ho. Reps., 1957-58; Tagore Law lectr., Calcutta, India, 1984; corr. mem. Nat. Acad. Law and Social Scis., Argentina, 1986—. Author: French Administrative Law and the Common Law World, 1954, The Supreme Court, 1957, The Professor and the Commissions, 1959, Introduction to American Administrative Law, 1962, The Reins of Power, 1963, Commentary on the Constitution of the U.S., 5 vols., 1963-68, The Roots of Freedom, 1967, Legal Control of Government, 1972, Constitutional Law: A Textbook, 1972, 2d edit., 1979, The Law in America, 1974, Administrative Law, 1976, 3d edit., 1991, The Great Rights of Mankind, 1977, expanded edit., 1992, Administrative Law: A Casebook, 1977, 4th edit., 1994, Super Chief: Earl Warren and His Supreme Court, 1983, Inside the Warren Court, 1983, The Unpublished Opinions of the Warren Court, 1985, Some Makers of American Law, 1985, Swann's Way: The School Busing Case and the Supreme Court, 1986, Behind Bakke: The Supreme Court and Affirmative Action, 1988, The Unpublished Opinions of the Burger Court, 1988, The Ascent of Pragmatism: The Burger Court in Action, 1990, The New Right and the Constitution, 1990, Constitutional Issues: Freedom of the Press, 1992, Main Currents in American Legal Thought, 1993, A History of the Supreme Court, 1993, The Unpublished Opinions of the Rehnquist Court, 1996, Decision: How The Supreme Court Decides Cases, 1996. Ann. Survey Am. Law dedicated in his name, 1988. Mem. ABA. Office: U Tulsa Coll Of Law Tulsa OK 74104

SCHWARTZ, BERNARD, physician; b. Toronto, Can., Nov. 12, 1927; s. Samuel and Gertrude (Levinsky) S.; children: Lawrence Frederick, Karen Lynne, Jennifer Carla, Ariane Samara. M.D., U. Toronto, 1951; M.S., State U. Iowa, 1953, Ph.D., 1959. Intern U. Iowa Hosps., State U. Iowa, 1951-52, resident ophthalmology, 1951-54; research fellow U. Iowa, 1954-58; asst. prof. to assoc. prof. Downstate Med. Center fo State U. N.Y., 1958-68; prof. ophthalmology Tufts U., 1968-93, chmn. dept., 1968-90, prof. emeritus ophthalmology, 1993—. Author: Syphilis and the Eye; Editor in chief of: Survey of Ophthalmology, 1968—; Contbr. articles to profl. jours. Dir. Mass. Soc. Prevention of Blindness. Fellow Am. Acad. Ophthalmology, ACS; mem. Assn. Rsch. in Ophthalmology, New Eng. Ophthalmol. Soc., N.Y. Acad. Medicine, N.Y. Acad. Scis., Soc. Française D'Ophthalmologie, Sigma Xi. Home: 180 Beacon St Boston MA 02116-1401 Office: 20 Park Plz Ste 535 Boston MA 02116-4303

SCHWARTZ, BERNARD See CURTIS, TONY

SCHWARTZ, BERNARD L., electronics company executive; b. 1925. BBA, CCNY, 1948. Ptnr. Schnee, Hover & Schwartz, 1948-62; sr. v.p. APL Corp., Fla., 1962-68; with Leasco Corp., 1969-72; chmn. bd., chief exec. officer Leasco Corp., Miami Beach, 1969-72; with Loral Corp., N.Y.C., 1972—, former pres., 1973-81, chmn., chief exec. officer, 1972—, also dir.; chmn., chief executive officer, K&F Industries, Inc. With U.S. Army, 1943-45. *

SCHWARTZ, CARL EDWARD, artist, printmaker; b. Detroit, Sept. 20, 1935; s. Carl and Verna (Steiner) S.; m. Kay Joyce Hofmann, June 18, 1955 (div.); children: Dawn Ellen, Cari Leigh; m. Frieda Nelson, Oct. 17, 1982 (div.); m. Dinah Lee Wilson, Jan. 20, 1996. BFA, Art Inst. Chgo. Sch.-U. Chgo., 1957. tchr. art , Chgo., N. Shore Art League, Suburban Fine Arts Center, Deerpath Art League. One-man shows include, South Bend (Ind.) Art Center, Feingarten Gallery, Chgo., 1960, Bernard Horwich Center, Chgo., Covenant Club, Chgo., Barat Coll., Chgo. Pub. Library, Alverno Coll., 1020 Art Center, Rosenberg Gallery, Peoria (Ill.) Art Guild, 1977, Ill. State Mus., 1977 Ill. Inst. Tech., 1978, Miller Gallery, Chgo., 1979, Union League Club, Chgo., 1982, Art Inst. Rental and Sale Gallery, Chgo., 1982, Horwich Gallery, Chgo., 1983, Lake Forest (Ill.) Coll., 1983, Campanile-Capponi Contemporary Gallery, Chgo., 1987, Nagata Gallery, Ft. Myers, Fla., 1988, Jan Cicero Gallery, Chgo., 1990; numerous group shows include 9th Ann. Michigana Exhbt, Detroit (Cloetingh and Deman award 1959), Hyde Park Art Center, Chgo., 1960 (5th Ann. Jury Exhbn. prize), Spectrum Exhbn. '63, Chgo. (1st prize), New Horizons Exhbt, Chgo., 1960 (Joseph Shapiro award), Nat. Design Center, Chgo., 1965 (New Horizons in Painting

1st prize), 3d Ann. Chgo. Arts Competition, 1962 (1st prize), Union League Club, Chgo., 1967 (2d prize), N. Shore Art League Ann. Drawing and Print Show, Chgo., 1965 (1st prize), Artists Guild Chgo., 1965 (prize), McCormack Pl., Chgo., 1965 (1st prize), Detroit Art Inst., 1965 (Commonwealth prize), Park Forest (Ill.) Art Exhbn. 1969 (Best of Show), 14th Ann. Virginia Beach (Va.) Show, 1969 (Best of Show), Suburban Fine Arts Center, Highland Park, Ill., 1970 (prize), 15th Ann. Virginia Beach Show, 1970 (prize), 32d Ann. Artists Guild, Chgo., 1970 (2d prize), N. Shore Art League Print and Drawing Show, 1970 (prize), 16th Ann. Virginia Beach Show, 1971 (2d prize), Ill. State Fair, 1972 (prize), Artists Guild Chgo., 1972 (1st prize), 17th Ann. Virginia Beach Exhbt, 1972 (1st prize), Artists Guild 50th Fine Art Exhbn., Chgo., 1973 (prize), Dickinson State U., 1973 (prize), N. Shore Art League Print Exhbn, 1973 (prize), Lakehurst Exhbt, 1974 (prize), Union League Art Exhbt, 1974 (1st prize), Artists Guild Fine Arts Exhbn., 1974 (best of Show), Bluegrass Painting Exhbn, Louisville, 1975 (award), Union League Art Exhbn, 1976 (prize); represented in permanent collections, Brit. Mus., London, Smithsonian Inst., Washington, Art Inst. Chgo., Jan Cicero Gallery, Chgo., Foster Harmon Gallery, Sarasota, Fla. Home: 13872 Pine Villa Ln Fort Myers FL 33912-1620 *I am a painter of light. I'm intrigued and fascinated with form. To me, there are two worlds- the one we all live in, and the one that I create. Painting is the discipline by which I constantly rediscover both of these worlds.*

SCHWARTZ, CARL ROBERT EMDEN, psychiatrist and educator; b. N.Y.C., Feb. 23, 1955. AB magna cum laude, Harvard U., 1976, MD, 1981. Intern in pediatrics Children's Hosp. Med. Ctr., Boston, 1981-82; resident in psychiatry Mass. Gen. Hosp., Boston, 1982-84, chief resident, acute psychiatry svc., 1984-85, postgrad. fellow in psychoanalytic psychotherapy, 1985-86; Ethel DuPont-Warren rsch. fellow Harvard Med. Sch., Boston, 1985-86; postdoctoral rsch. fellow clin. rsch. tng. program Mass. Mental Health Ctr., Boston, 1986-88; Warren-Whitman-Richardson fellow Harvard Med. Sch., 1988-90, instr. psychiatry, 1988—. Fiske fellow Harvard Coll./Trinity Coll. England, 1976-77; Recipient Scientist Devel. award NIH, 1990—. Mem. APA, Soc. Rsch. in Child Devel., Soc. Rsch. Child and Adolescent Psychopathology, Phi Beta Kappa. Office: Harvard Med Sch 74 Fenwood Rd Boston MA 02115-6113

SCHWARTZ, CAROL LEVITT, former government official; b. Greenville, Miss., Jan. 20, 1944; d. Stanley and Hilda (Simmons) Levitt; m. David H. Schwartz (dec.); children: Stephanie, Hilary, Douglas. BS in Spl. and Elem. Edn., U. Tex., 1965. Mem. transiton team Office of Pres. Elect, 1980-81; con. office presdl. personnel The White House, Washington, 1981; cons. U.S. Dept. Edn., Washington, 1982; pres. sec. U.S. Ho. Reps., Washington, 1982-83; mem. at large Coun. of D.C., Washington, 1985-89; candidate for mayor, Washington, 1986, 94; vice chmn. Nat. Edn. Commn. on Time and Leaarning, 1992-94, Nat. Adv. Coun. on Disadvantaged Children, 1974-79; lectr. in field; radio commentator, 1990-91. Regional columnist Washington Jewish Week, 1995—. Mem. D.C. Bd. Edn., 1974-82, v.p., 1977-80; bd. dirs. Met. Police Boys and Girls Club, 1st v.p., 1989-93, pres., 1994—, chmn. membership com., 1984-93; mem. adv. com. Am. Coun. Young Polit. Leaders, 1982-90; mem. Nat. Coun. Friends Kennedy Ctr., 1984-91; bd. dirs. Whitman-Walker Clinic, 1988—, v.p., 1995—; bd. dirs. St. John's Child Devel. Ctr., 1989-91; trustee Kennedy Ctr. Cmty. and Friends Bd., 1991—, chmn. ednl. task force, 1993—; trustee Jewish Coun. on Aging, 1991-93; v.p. adv. bd. Am. Automobile Assn., 1988—; bd. dirs. Washington Hebrew Congregation, 1995—. Mem. Cosmos Club. Republican. Jewish.

SCHWARTZ, CHARLES, JR., federal judge; b. New Orleans, Aug. 20, 1922; s. Charles and Sophie (Hess) S.; m. Patricia May, Aug. 31, 1950; children—Priscilla May, John Putney. BA, Tulane U., 1943, JD, 1947. Bar: La. 1947. Ptnr. Guste, Barnett & Little, 1947-70; practiced in New Orleans, until 1976; ptnr. firm Little, Schwartz & Dussom, 1970-76; dist. counsel Gulf Coast dist. U.S. Maritime Adminstrn., 1953-62; judge U.S. Dist. Ct. (ea. dist.) La., New Orleans, 1976—; mem. Fgn. Itelligence Surveillance Ct., 1992—; prof. Tulane U. Law Sch.; lectr. continuing law insts.; mem. Jud. Conf. Com. U.S. on implementation of jury system, 1981-85; mem. permanent adv. bd. Tulane Admiralty Law Inst., 1984—. Bd. editors Tulane Law Rev. Pres. New Orleans unit Am. Cancer Soc., 1956-57; v.p., chmn. budget com. United Fund Greater New Orleans Area, 1959-61, trustee, 1953-65; bd. dirs. Cancer Assn. Greater New Orleans, 1958—, pres., 1958-59, 72-73; bd. dirs. United Cancer Council, 1963-85, pres., 1971-73; mem. com. on grants to agencies Community Chest, 1965-87; men's adv. com. League Women Voters, 1966-68; chmn. com. admissions of program devel. and coordination com. United Way Greater New Orleans, 1974-77; mem. comml. panel Am. Arbitration Assn., 1974-76; bd. dirs. Willow Wood Home, 1979-85, 1989-92; bd. mgrs. Touro Infirmary, 1992—; trustee Metairie Park Country Day Sch., 1977-83; mem. La. Republican Central Com., 1961-76; mem. Orleans Parish Rep. Exec. Com., 1960-75, chmn., 1964-75; mem. Jefferson Parish Rep. Exec. Com., 1975-76; del. Rep. Nat. Conv., 1960, 64, 68; mem. nat. budget and consultation com. United Community Funds and Coun. of Am., 1961; bd. dirs. Community Svcs. Coun., 1971-73. Served to 2d lt. AUS, 1943-46; maj. U.S. Army Res.; ret. Mem. La. Bar Assn. New Orleans Bar Assn. (legis. com. 1970-75), Fed. Bar Assn., Fgn. Rels. Assn. New Orleans (bd. dirs. 1957-61), 5th Cir. Dist. Judges Assn. (pres. 1984-85), Lakewood Country Club (bd. dirs. 1967-68, pres. 1975-77). Office: US Dist Ct C-317 US Courthouse 500 Camp St New Orleans LA 70130-3313

SCHWARTZ, CHARLES D., broadcast executive; b. Phila., Sept. 6, 1948; s. Howard I. and Jane (Cohen) S.; m. Susan Greenspan, June 28, 1970; children: Daniel, Michael, Amy. BFA, U. Cin., 1970. Media planner, buyer Grey Advt., Inc., N.Y.C., 1970-71; account exec. CBS Radio Spot Sales, CBS, Inc., N.Y.C., 1971-74; retail sales mgr. Sta. WCBS-AM, CBS, Inc., N.Y.C., 1974-75; sales mgr. CBS Radio Spot Sales, CBS, Inc., N.Y.C., 1975-76; gen. sales mgr. Sta. WBBM-AM, CBS, Inc., Chgo., 1976-79; v.p., gen. mgr. Sta. WCAU-AM, CBS, Inc., Phila., 1979-80; pres., chief operating officer Newsystems Group, Inc., Phila., 1980-87; pres., chief executive officer, chmn. Panache Broadcasting, Phila., 1987—. Bd. govs. Likoff Cardiovasc. Inst., Hahneman U., Phila., 1988—, mem. exec. com., 1988—. Avocations: writing, travel. Office: Sta WWDB-FM 166 E Levering Mill Rd Bala Cynwyd PA 19004-2664

SCHWARTZ, CHARLES FREDERICK, retired economist, consultant; b. Balt., May 2, 1916; s. Charles Herzog and Cora (Miller) S.; m. Marika Rupis, June 7, 1941; children: Mary Louise Schwartz Solomon, Charles Anthony. BA, U. Va., 1936, MA, 1937, PhD, 1939; postgrad., Va. Poly. Inst., 1937-38, Georgetown U., 1941-42. Instr. rural econs. U. Va., 1939-41; economist nat. income div. Office Bus. Econs., U.S. Dept. Commerce, 1941-51, asst. chief, 1951-56, asst. dir. Office Bus. Econs., 1956-59; chief N.Am. div. Western Hemisphere Dept., IMF, 1959-62, asst. dir. Western Hemisphere Dept., 1962-66, dep. dir. rsch. dept., 1966-79, dir. adjustment studies, 1979-83; chmn. investment com. Staff Retirement Plan, IMF, 1979-85, spl. cons., office mng. dir., 1983-86; cons., 1987—; cons. Exec. Office of Pres., mem. adv. coms. on balance of payments stats., 1963-65, 75-76. Author publs. on nat. income, the world economy. Recipient gold medal for exceptional svc. Dept. Commerce, 1951. Mem. Internat. Assn. Rsch. in Income and Wealth, Conf. on Rsch. in Income and Wealth (chmn., exec. com. 1961-62), Am. Econ. Assn., Am. Statis. Assn., Phi Beta Kappa, Theta Delta Chi. Home: 7504 Honeywell Ln Bethesda MD 20814-1028

SCHWARTZ, CHARLES PHINEAS, JR., replacement auto parts company executive, lawyer; b. Chgo., Apr. 23, 1927; s. Charles Phineas and Lavinia Duffy (Schulman) S.; m. Joan Straus, Aug. 12, 1954 (div. 1971); children: Alex, Ned, Debra, Emily; m. Susan Lamm Hirsch, Dec. 18, 1976. A.B., U. Chgo., 1945; LL.B., Harvard U., 1950. Bar: Ill. 1950, N.Y. 1951, U.S. Supreme Ct. 1955. Assoc. Szold & Brandwen, N.Y.C., 1950-52; rsch. assoc., teaching fellow Harvard U. Law Sch., Cambridge, Mass., 1952-56; pvt. practice Chgo., 1956-61; ptnr. Straus, Blosser & McDowell, Chgo., 1961-67; fin. and bus. cons. Chgo., 1967-75, 93—; pres., chief exec. officer Champion Parts Inc., Oak Brook, Ill., 1975-86, chmn. bd., chief exec. officer, 1986-92; chmn. emeritus Champion Parts Inc., Oak Brook, 1992—; dir. Supercrete Ltd., Winnipeg, Man., Can., 1964-80, Athey Products Corp., Raleigh, N.C., 1967-86. Trustee, officer Hull House Assn., Chgo., 1958-70; dir., officer Chgo. Fedn. Settlements, 1972-79; dir., officer, pres. Friends of the Parks, Chgo., 1982—; dir., officer, pres. Hyde Park Coop. Soc., 1962-68; pres. U. Cho. Lab. Schs. Parents Assn., 1970-72, 75-77; trustee KAM Isaiah Isrel Congregation, 1975-85; bd. dirs. Chgo. Hearing Soc., 1996—. Served with USNR, 1945-46. Recipient Boulton Meml. award for disting. bus. statesmanship and dedicated service rendered to the entire auto parts rebuilding industry Automotive Parts Rebuilders Assn., 1987. Mem. ABA, Motor Equipment and Mfrs. Assn. (dir. 1977-81), Automotive Pres. Coun., Heavy Duty Bus. Forum, Automotive Sales Coun., Soc. Automotive Engrs., Automotive Parts Rebuilders Assn. (dir., officer, chmn. 1988—), Chgo. Coun. Lawyers, Heavy Vehicle Maintenance Group (officer 1994—), Chgo. Hearing Soc. (dir. 1996—), Quadrangle Club (Chgo.), Harvard Club (N.Y.C.). Jewish. Clubs: Quadrangle (Chgo.); Harvard (N.Y.C.). Office: 230 E Ohio St Ste 120 Chicago IL 60611-3201

SCHWARTZ, CHARLES WALTER, lawyer; b. Brenham, Tex., Dec. 27, 1953; s. Walter C. and Annie (Kuehn) S. BS, U. Tex., Austin, 1975, MA, 1980, JD, 1977; LLM, Harvard U., 1980. Bar: Tex. 1977; bd. cert. civil appellate law Tex. Bd. Legal Specialization. Law clk. to judge U.S. Ct. Appeals (5th cir.), Austin, Tex., 1977-79; assoc. Vinson & Elkins L.L.P., Houston, 1980-86, ptnr., 1986—. Contbr. articles to law revs. Mem. ABA, Tex. Bar Assn., Tex. Bar Found., Houston Bar Found., Houston Bar Assn., Am. Law Inst., Tex. Law Rev. Assn., Bar Assn. of 5th Cir. Home: 2825 Albans Rd Houston TX 77005-2309 Office: Vinson & Elkins LLP 2300 First City Tower 1001 Fannin St Houston TX 77002

SCHWARTZ, DANIEL BENNETT, artist; b. N.Y.C., Feb. 16, 1929; s. Bennett Henry and Lillian (Blumenthal) S.; m. Judith Nancy Kass, June 12, 1955 (div. 1980); 1 child, Claudia Bennet. Grad., High Sch. of Music and Art, N.Y.C., 1946; student, Art Students League, 1946, Y. Kuniyoshi; BFA, R.I. Sch. Design, 1949. Instr. pvt. painting class, 1965-81, 90-95, Parsons Sch. Design, 1983. One man shows include Davis Galleries, N.Y.C., 1955, 56, 58, 60, Hirschl & Adler Galleries, N.Y.C., 1963, Maxwell Galleries, San Francisco, 1964, Babcock Galleries, N.Y.C., 1967, F.A.R. Galleries, N.Y.C., 1970, Armstrong Galleries, N.Y.C., 1985, 87, Hammer Galleries, N.Y.C., 1994; exhibited in group shows at Albany Inst. History and Art, Am. Fedn. Arts, Butler Inst. Am. Art, Libr. of Congress, Nat. Acad. Design, Pa. Acad. Fine Art, Whitney Mus. Art, Collection Nat. Portrait Gallery, others; subject of various articles. Louis C. Tiffany Found. grantee, 1956, 60; recipient Purchase prize Am. Acad. Arts and letters, 1964, 84, 11 Gold medals Soc. Illustrators, N.Y.C., 1960-85, Obrig prize for painting Nat. Acad. Design, 1990, winner 1st Benjamin Altman Figure prize, 1992. Mem. Century Assn. Avocation: jazz piano. Home and Office: 48 E 13th St New York NY 10003-4631

SCHWARTZ, DANIEL C., lawyer; b. Pa., 1943. AB, Stanford U., 1965; JD, George Washington U., 1969. Bar: D.C. 1969. Asst. to dir. Bur. Competition, FTC, Washington, 1973-75, asst. dir. evaluation, 1975-77, dep. dir., 1977-79; gen. counsel Nat. Security Agy., Washington, 1979-81; ptnr. Bryan Cave LLP, Washington. Mem. ABA. Office: Bryan Cave LLP 700 13th St NW Washington DC 20005-3960

SCHWARTZ, DAVID, retail executive; b. 1945. With Skaggs Drug Stores, 1965-77; v.p. rocky mtns. divsn. Albertsons Inc., 1977-86; v.p. drug and mdse. The Kroger Co., 1986-87; pres., COO Perry Drug Stores, Inc., 1987-91; pres., CEO Smitty's Super Value, Inc., 1991-93; pres., COO Phar-Mor Inc, Youngstown, Ohio, 1993—. Office: Phar-Mor Inc 20 Federal Plz W Youngstown OH 44503-1423*

SCHWARTZ, DONALD, chemistry educator; b. Scarsdale, N.Y., Dec. 27, 1927; s. Harry A. and Ethel S.; m. Lois Schwartz, Sept. 8, 1948; children: Leanne, Mark W., Scott B., Bradley F. BS., U. Mo., 1949; M.S., Mont. State U., 1951; Ph.D., Pa. State U., 1955. Program dir. NSF, 1966-68; asso. dean Grad. Sch., Memphis State U., 1968-70; dean advanced studies Fla. Atlantic U., Boca Raton, 1970-71; v.p., acting pres. State U. N.Y., Buffalo, 1971-74; chancellor Ind. U.-Purdue U., Ft. Wayne, Ind., 1974-78; chancellor, prof. U. Colo., Colorado Springs, 1978-83, prof., 1983-93, prof. emeritus, 1993—; cons. in field. Author papers structure of coal and organo-titanium compounds, also on higher edn. Bd. dirs. Colorado Springs Osteo. Found., 1985—. Served with USCG, 1945. Research fellow AEC, 1953-55; N.Y. State fellow, 1947-48. Mem. Am. Chem. Soc., AAAS, Sigma Xi, Phi Lambda Upsilon, Phi Delta Kappa. Clubs: Rotary, Country of Colo, Shriners. Home: 21 Sanford Rd Colorado Springs CO 80906-4219 Office: U of Colo Cragmor Rd Colorado Springs CO 80907 *Each can become all that he or she is capable of being through education, hard work and compassion for other human beings. This I believe.*

SCHWARTZ, DONALD FRANKLIN, communication educator; b. Jamestown, N.D., Feb. 20, 1935; s. Frank William and Mabel Esther (Williams) S.; m. Lois Carolyn Bonnema, June 26, 1965; children: Daria, Karin, Marc. B.S., N.D. State U., 1957, M.S., 1961; Ph.D., Mich. State U., 1968. Asst. dir. pub. rels. N.D. State U., Fargo, 1959-66, chmn. social scis., 1969-71, chmn. communication, 1967-79; instr. communication Mich. State U., East Lansing, 1966-67; vis. scientist U.S. Dept. Agr., Washington, 1979-80; prof. communication Cornell U., Ithaca, N.Y., 1980—, chmn. dept., 1980-85; vis. scholar U. N.Mex., 1994. Contbr. articles to profl. jours. Recipient Outstanding Svc. award Future Farmers Am., 1976, Svc. award USDA, 1980, A.D. White Prof. of Yr. award, 1993. Mem. AAUP, Internat. Comm. Assn. (sec., pub. rels. interest group 1992-93), Am. Acad. Mgmt., Am. Soc. Pers. Adminstrn. (chpt. pres. 1976-77), Pub. Rels. Soc. Am. (nat. faculty advisor student assn. 1989-90, vice-chair educators sect. 1992, Pres.'s Citation for Leadership 1990, nat. ednl. affairs com. 1993-96). Roman Catholic. Office: Cornell U Dept Communication 311 Kennedy Hall Ithaca NY 14853-4203

SCHWARTZ, DONALD LEE, lawyer; b. Milw., Dec. 8, 1948; s. Bernard L. and Ruth M. (Marshall) S.; m. Susan J. Dunst, June 5, 1971; children: Stephanie Jane, Cheryl Ruth. BA, Macalester Coll., 1971; JD, U. Chgo., 1974. Bar: Ill. 1974. Assoc. Sidley & Austin, Chgo., 1974-80, ptnr., 1980-88; ptnr. Latham & Watkins, Chgo., 1988—. Chmn. Ill. Conservative Union, 1979-81, bd. dirs. 1977-85. Served with U.S. Army, 1971-77. Mem. ABA (uniform comml. code com., comml. fin. svcs. commn.), Ill. Bar Assn. (sec. coun. banking and bankuprtcy sect. 1982-83), Chgo. Bar Assn. (chmn. comml. law com. 1980-81, fin. insts. com. 1982-83), Ivanhoe Country Club, Monroe Club, Met. Club. Republican. Episcopalian. Avocation: golf. Home: 191 Park Ave Glencoe IL 60022-1351 Office: Latham & Watkins Ste 5800 Sears Tower Chicago IL 60606

SCHWARTZ, DORIS RUHBEL, nursing educator, consultant; b. Bklyn., May 30, 1915; d. Henry and Florence Marie (Shuttleworth) S. BS, NYU, 1953, MS, 1958. RN, N.Y. Staff nurse Meth. Hosp., Bklyn., 1942-43; pub. health nurse Vis. Nurse Assn., Bklyn., 1947-51; pub. health nurse Cornell U. Med. Coll., Cornell-N.Y. Hosp. Sch. Nursing, N.Y.C., 1951-61, tchr. pub. health nursing, geriatric nursing, 1961-80; ret., 1990; sr. fellow U. Pa. Sch. Nursing, Phila., 1981-90, mem. bd. dirs. Elders With Adult Dependants. Author: Give Us to Go Blithely, 1990 (Book of Yr. award Am. Jour. Nursing 1991); sr. author: The Elderly Chronically Ill Patient: Nursing and Psychosocial Needs, 1963; co-author: Geriatrics and Geriatric Nursing, 1983 (Book of Yr. award Am. Jour. Nursing 1984); contbr. articles to profl. jours. Mem. adv. com. nursing WHO, Geneva, 1971-79; adv. com. Robert Wood Johnson Found., Teaching Nursing Home Project, Princeton, N.J., U. Pa. Wharton Sch. Study of Continuing Care Retirement Communities, 1981-83; vol. Foulkeways Continuing Care Retirement Cmty., Gwynedd, Pa. Served to capt. N.C., U.S. Army, 1943-47, PTO. Rockefeller fellow U. Toronto, 1950-51, Mary Roberts fellow Am. Jour. Nursing, 1955, Fogarty fellow NIH, 1975-76; recipient Diamond Jubilee Nursing award N.Y. County RNs Assn., 1979. Fellow Inst. Medicine of NAS, APHA (Disting. Career award nursing sect. 1979), Am. Acad. Nursing (charter, coun. 1973-74); mem. ANA (Pearl McIver award 1979), Soroptimist (v.p. N.Y.C. club 1974-75), Sigma Theta Tau (Founders award 1979, Mentor award Alpha Upsilon chpt. 1992). Democrat. Mem. Soc. of Friends. Avocations: travel; writing; people.

SCHWARTZ, EDWARD ARTHUR, lawyer, foundation executive; b. Boston, Sept. 27, 1937; s. Abe and Sophie (Gottheim) S.; children: Eric Allen, Jeffrey Michael. AB, Oberlin Coll., 1959; LLB, Boston Coll., 1962; postgrad., Am. U., 1958-59, Northeastern U., 1970; postgrad. exec. program, Stanford U., 1979. Bar: Conn. 1962, Mass. 1965. Legal intern Office Atty. Gen. Commonwealth of Mass., 1961; assoc. Schatz & Schatz, Hartford, Conn., 1962-65, Cohn, Reimer & Pollack, Boston, 1965-67; v.p., gen. coun. sec. Digital Equipment Corp., Maynard, Mass., 1967-88; pres. New Eng. Legal Found., Boston, 1990—, also bd. dirs.; vis. prof. law Boston Coll., 1986, adj. prof., 1987-89; also bd. dirs.; bd. dirs. The Computer Mus. Editor Boston Coll. Indsl. and Comml. Law Rev, 1960-62, Ann. Survey Mass. Law, 1960-62. Mem. ABA, Mass. Bar Assn.,Boston Bar Assn. Home: 62 Todd Pond Rd Lincoln MA 01773-3808

SCHWARTZ, EDWARD J., federal judge; b. 1912. Judge Mcpl. Ct. and Superior Ct., San Diego; judge U.S. Dist. Ct. for So. Dist. Calif., former chief judge, now sr. judge. Office: US Dist Ct Courtroom 1 940 Front St San Diego CA 92189-8994*

SCHWARTZ, ELEANOR BRANTLEY, academic administrator; b. Kite, Ga., Jan. 1, 1937; d. Jesse Melvin and Hazel (Hill) Brantley; children: John, Cynthia. Student Mercer U., Ga., 1954-55; student U. Va., 1955, Ga. Southern Coll., 1956-57, BBA, Ga. State U., 1962, MBA, 1963, DBA, 1969. Adminstrv. asst. Fin. Agy., 1954, Fed. Govt., Va., Pa., Ga., 1956-59; asst. dean admissions Ga. State U., Atlanta, 1961-66, asst. prof., 1966-70; assoc. prof. Cleve. State U., 1970-75, prof. and assoc. dean, 1975-80; dean, Harzfeld prof. U. Mo., Kansas City, 1980-87, vice chancellor acad. affairs, 1987-91, interim chancellor, 1991-92, chancellor, 1992—; disting. vis. prof. Berry Coll., Rome, Ga., N.Y. State U. Coll., Fredonia, Mons U., Belgium; cons. pvt. industry, U.S., Europe, Can.; bd. dirs. ANUHCO, Rsch. Med. Ctr., United Group of Mutual Funds, Waddell & Reed Funds, Inc., Torchmark/ United Funds, Toy and Miniature Mus., Menorah Med. Ctr. Found., NCCJ, Econ. Devel. Corp. of Kansas City, Midwest Grain Products, Silicon Prairie Tech. Assn., Mo. Planning Coun. for Devel. Disabilities, 1995—, Am. Coun. Edn. Commn. on Minorities in Higher Edn., 1995—, Assn. Gov. Bds. Univs. and Colls., 1995—. Author: Sex Barriers in Business, 1971, Contemporary Readings in Marketing, 1974; (with Muczyk and Smith) Principles of Supervision, 1984. Chmn., Mayor's Task Force in Govt. Efficiency, Kansas City, Mo., 1984; mem. community planning and research council United Way Kansas City, 1983-85; bd. dirs. Jr. Achievement, 1982-86; Mo. Planning Coun. Devel. Disabilities, 1995—. Recipient Disting. Faculty award Cleve. State U., 1974, Cleve., 60 Women of Achievement Girls Scouts Council Mid Continent, 1983; named Career Woman of Yr. Kansas City, Mo., 1989; recipient disting. svc. award Kansas State U., 1992. Mem. Am. Mktg. Assn., Acad. Internat. Bus., Am. Mgmt. Assn., Am. Case Research Assn., Internat. Soc. Study Behavioral Devel., Greater Kansas City C. of C. (ex. officio, bd. dirs.), Phi Kappa Phi, Golden Key, Alpha Iota Delta.

SCHWARTZ, ELI, economics educator, writer; b. N.Y.C., Apr. 2, 1921; s. Israel and Tillie (Shapiro) S.; m. Renee S. Kartiganer, Aug. 29, 1948; children: Pamela F., Alan G. B.S., Denver U., 1943; M.A., U. Conn., 1948; Ph.D., Brown U., 1952. Instr. U. R.I., Kingston, 1947-48; asst. instr. Brown U., Providence, 1948-51; chief regional economist Office Price Stblzn., Boston, 1951-53; lectr. Mich. State U., East Lansing, 1953-54; asst. prof. econs. Lehigh U., Bethlehem, Pa., 1954-58, assoc. prof., 1958-62, prof., 1962-91, Charles Macfarlane prof. econs., 1978-91, chmn. dept. econs., 1978-84, ret., 1991; cons. econs. and fin., expert witness Schwartz-Aronson Assocs., Bethlehem, 1965—. Author: Corporate Finance, 1962, Trouble in Eden, 1980; editor: Managing Municipal Finance, 1980, 83, 87, Restructuring the Thrift Industry, 1989, Theory and Application of the Interest Rate, 1993. With U.S. Army, 1943-46, ETO. Recipient sr. teaching Lehigh U., 1972; Earhart Found. grantee, 1978. Mem. Am. Econs. Assn., Am. Fin. Assn., Nat. Assn. Forensic Econs. (founding mem.). Jewish. Home: 3185 W Cedar St Allentown PA 18104 Office: Lehigh U Dept Econs Rauch Ctr 37 Bethlehem PA 18015 *If I have achieved any success it is because I am interested in the subject matter of my field. I am fortunate to enjoy reading, teaching, consulting and writing.*

SCHWARTZ, ELIAS, pediatrician; b. N.Y.C., Aug. 30, 1935; s. Rubin and Dusha (Premysler) S.; m. Esta Rosenberg, June 12, 1960; children: Samuel, Robert. AB, Columbia Coll., 1956; MD, Columbia U., 1960; MA (hon.), U. Pa., 1972. From asst. prof. to assoc. prof. pediatrics Jefferson Med. Coll., Phila., 1967-72; prof. pediatrics Sch. Medicine U. Pa., Phila., 1972—, prof. pediatrics and human genetics Sch. Medicine, 1979—, chmn. dept. pediatrics Sch. Medicine, 1990—; physician-in-chief Children's Hosp. Phila., 1990—; mem. adv. bd. Cooley's Anemia Found., N.Y.C., 1976—; policy bd. sickle cell program NIH, Bethesda, Md., 1987-95, reviewer's res., 1991—; sci. adv. bd. Enzon, Inc., Piscataway, N.J., 1992—. Editor Hemoglobinopathies in Children, 1980; contbr. over 200 articles to med. and sci. jours. With Phila. Healthcare Congress, 1991-94. Capt. USAF, 1963-65. Grantee NIH, 1968—. Mem. Am. Soc. Pediatric Hematology/Oncology (pres. 1989-91), Am. Soc. Clin. Investigation, Assn. Am. Physicians, Am. Pediatric Soc., Soc. for Pediatric Rsch. Achievements include rsch. in transfusion treatment of strokes in sickle cell disease, comprehensive program for removal of excess iron in chronically transfused patients, delineation of abnormalities of globin synthesis in several inherited hemoglobin disorders, discovery of genetic defects in several types of thalassemia, cloning and analysis of several human megakaryocyte genes. Office: Children's Hosp Phila 34th St Civic Center Blvd Philadelphia PA 19104

SCHWARTZ, ELIEZER LAZAR, psychologist, educator; b. Arad, Romania, Dec. 14, 1947; came to U.S., 1974; s. George and Elka (Rothchild) S.; m. Susan Ellen Lorge; children: Dafna, Michal, Amitai. BA in Psychology, Hebrew U., Jerusalem, Israel, 1973; MS in Psychology, Ill. Inst. Tech., 1975, PhD in Psychology, 1977. Cert. clin. psychologist, Ill. Psychologist, chief svc. Chgo.-Read Mental Health Ctr., 1979-80; core faculty Ill. Sch. Profl. Psychology, Chgo., 1981—; clin. psychologist Ray Graham Assn. for Handicapped, Elmhurst, Ill., 1981-89; dir. clin. svcs. Michael Solomon Psychology Ctr., Chgo., 1989-91; instr. Northwestern U., Evanston, Ill., summers 1988—; dir. neuropsychology Brownstone Ctr., Chgo., 1991-92; cons. Jewish Vocat. Svcs., Chgo., 1983-84, 91-92, North Suburban Spl. Edn. Orgn., Arlington Heights, Ill., 1985-91, Grant Hosp., Chgo., 1991-95; dir. clin. tng. Ill. Sch. Profl. Psychology. Author: (with others) Severe Developmental Disabilities, 1987, The Mental Status Exam, 1989; contbr. articles to profl. jours. Mem. APA, ASCD, Ill. Psych. Assn., Coun. for Exceptional Children. Jewish. Avocations: reading, listening to classical music. Office: 20 S Clark St Chicago IL 60603

SCHWARTZ, ELLIOTT SHELLING, composer, author, music educator; b. Bklyn, Jan. 19, 1936; s. Nathan and Rose (Shelling) S.; m. Dorothy Rose Feldman, June 26, 1960; children: Nina, Jonathan. A.B., Columbia U., 1957, M.A., 1958, Ed. D., 1962. Instr. music U. Mass., Amherst, 1960-64; asst. prof. music Bowdoin Coll., Brunswick, Maine, 1964-70, assoc. prof., 1970-75, prof. music, 1975—; vis. prof. music Ohio State U., Columbus, 1988-92; vis. composer Trinity Coll. Music, London, 1967, U. Calif. Coll. Creative Studies, Santa Barbara, 1970, 73, 74; composer, pianist, commentator British Broadcast Corp, London, 1972, 74, 78, 83; vis. research musician Center Music Expt., La Jolla, Calif., 1978-79; disting. vis. prof. Ohio State U., 1985-86; music cons. Holt, Rinehart & Winston, Random House, Schirmer Books, N.Y.C., 1977—; vis. fellow Robinson Coll., Cambridge U., U.K., 1993-94. Composer: Island, 1970 (Internat. Gaudeamus prize 1970), Chamber Concertos I-IV, 1977-81, Extended Piano, 1980, Dream Music With Variations, 1983, Four Ohio Portraits, 1986, Memorial in Two Parts, 1989, Elan, 1990, Rows Garden, 1993, Equinox, 1994, Timepiece, 1994, Chiaroscuro, 1995, Reflections, 1995; author: Electronic Music: A Listener's Guide, 1973, Music: Ways of Listening, 1982, (with Daniel Godfrey) Music Since 1945: Issues, Materials and Literature, 1993; editor: (with Barney Childs) Contemporary Composers on Contemporary Music, 1967; contbr. articles to mus. jours. Nat. Endowment for Arts composition grantee, 1974, 76, 82; Rockefeller Found. residence fellow Bellagio, Italy, 1980, 89; MacDowell Colony resident fellow, 1965, 66; Yaddo residence fellow, 1977; recipient Maine State award Maine Commn. Arts and Humanities, 1970, McKim Commn., 1986. Mem. Am. Music Ctr. (v.p. 1981-87), Coll. Music Soc. (nat. coun. 1982-88, pres. 1988-90), Am. Soc. Univ. Composers (nat. coun. 1968-72, nat. chmn. 1983-88), Am. Composers Alliance (governing bd. 1994—). Home: Po Box 451 South Freeport ME 04078 Office: Bowdoin Coll Dept Music Brunswick ME 04011

SCHWARTZ, ESTAR ALMA, lawyer; b. Bklyn., June 29, 1950; d. Henry Israel and Elaine Florence (Scheiner) Sutel; m. Lawrence Gerald Schwartz, June 28, 1976 (div. Dec. 1977); 1 child, Joshua (dec.). JD, N.Y.U., 1980. owner Estaris Paralegal Svc., Flushing, N.Y., 1992—. Mgr., ptnr. Scheiner,

Scheiner, DeVito & Wytte, N.Y.C., 1966-81; fed. govt., social security fraud specialist DHHS, OI, OIG, SSFIS, N.Y.C., 1982-83; pensions Todtman, Epstein, et al, N.Y.C., 1983-85; office mgr., sec. Sills, Beck, Cummis, N.Y.C., 1985-86; office mgr., bookkeeper Philip, Birnbaum & Assocs., N.Y.C., 1986-87; office mgr., sec. Stanley Posses, Esq., Queens, N.Y., 1989-90. Democrat. Jewish. Avocations: needlepoint, horseback riding, tennis, bowling, writing children's stories. Home and Office: 67-20 Parsons Blvd Apt 2A Flushing NY 11365-2960

SCHWARTZ, GORDON FRANCIS, surgeon, educator; b. Plainfield, N.J., Apr. 29, 1935; s. Samuel H. and Mary (Adelman) S.; m. Rochelle DeG. Krantz, Sept. 5, 1959; children—Amory Blair, Susan Leslie. A.B., Princeton U., 1956; M.D., Harvard U., 1960; MBA, U. Pa., 1990. Intern N.Y. Hosp.-Cornell Med. Ctr., N.Y.C., 1960-61; resident in surgery Columbia-Presbyterian Med. Ctr., N.Y.C., 1963-68; instr. surgery Columbia U., N.Y.C., 1966-68; assoc. in surgery U. Pa., Phila., 1968-70; dir. clin. services Breast Diagnostic Ctr. Jefferson Med. Coll., 1973-78, asst. prof. surgery, 1970-71, assoc. prof., 1971-78, prof., 1978—; practice medicine specializing in surgery and diseases of breast, Phila., 1968—; founder, chmn. acad. com. Breast Health Inst., 1990—; edtl. bd. The Breast Jour., 1994—. Author: (with R.H. Guthrie, Jr.) Reconstructive and Aesthetic Mammoplasty, 1980, Atlas of Breast Surgery, 1996. Mem. Pa. Gov.'s Task Force on Cancer, 1976-82; mem. breast cancer task force Phila. chpt. Am. Cancer Soc.; mem. clin. investigation rev. com. Nat. Cancer Inst., 1992-95. Served to capt. AUS, 1961-63. NIH Cancer Control fellow, 1968-69. Mem. ACS, AMA, AAUP, Assn. for Acad. Surgery, Allen O. Whipple Surg. Assn., Soc. Surg. Oncology, Internat. Cardiovasc. Soc., Soc. for Surgery Alimentary Tract, Am. Soc. Clin. Oncology, Soc. for Study Breast Diseases (pres. 1981-83), Soc. Internat. Senologie (treas. 1982-90, v.p. 1990-92, sci. com. 1992—), Pa. Med. Soc., Am. Soc. Transplant Surgeons, N.Y. Acad. Scis., Am. Soc. Artificial Internal Organs, Am. Radium Soc., Philadelphia County Med. Soc., Italian Soc. Senology (hon.), Greek Surg. Soc. (hon.), Union League, Locust Club, Princeton Club (pres. Phila. 1989-91), Princeton Club (N.Y.C.), Princeton Terrace Club, Nassau Club, Phi Beta Kappa, Sigma Xi, Alpha Omega Alpha, Nu Sigma Nu. Republican. Jewish. Home: 1805 Delancey Pl Philadelphia PA 19103-6606 Office: 1015 Chestnut St Fl 510 Philadelphia PA 19107-4305

SCHWARTZ, HARRY, journalist; b. N.Y.C., Sept. 10, 1919; s. Sam and Rose (Schnell) S.; m. Ruth E. Blumner, June 8, 1941; children: William Daniel (dec.), John Leonard, Robert Steven. BA, Columbia U., 1940, MA, 1941, PhD, 1943. Economist War Prodn. Bd., 1942-43; economist OSS, 1944-46; asst. prof. econs. Syracuse U., 1946-48, assoc. prof., 1948-51, prof., 1951-53; mem. editorial bd. N.Y. Times, N.Y.C., 1951-79; disting. prof. SUNY, New Paltz, 1967-79; vis. prof. med. econs. Coll. Physicians and Surgeons, Columbia U., 1974, 78-79, writer in residence dept. surgery, 1979-87; columnist Pharm. Exec. mag., 1981—, Scrip mag., 1984—, Am. Med. News, 1989-91; Backman lectr. med. ethics Hebrew Union Coll., 1981; mem. Nat. Bd. Med. Examiners, 1979-83; Mem. exec. com. N.Y. Blood Center, 1973-87. Author: Russia's Soviet Economy, 1949, China, 1966, Prague's 200 Days, 1968, The Case for American Medicine, 1972, Breakthrough: The Discovery of Modern Medicines at Janssen, 1990; columnist Pvt. Practice mag., 1979-91, editor, 1980-84; mem. editl. bd. Psychiat. Times, 1985-94; contbr. numerous articles to profl. jours., newspapers, including Wall St. Jour., N.Y. Times, USA Today. With U.S. Army, 1943-45. Jewish. Home: PO Box 1169 Scarsdale NY 10583-9169

SCHWARTZ, HARRY KANE, lawyer; b. Phila., Apr. 20, 1934; s. M. Murray and Minne G. (Schoenfeld) S.; m. Marinda Kelley, June 20, 1961; children: Anthony Clark, Amanda Lyle. B.A. summa cum laude, Harvard Coll., 1955; Fulbright fellow, Worcester Coll., Oxford U., 1955-56; LL.B. magna cum laude, U. Pa., 1959. Bar: Pa. 1960, D.C. 1961, U.S. Supreme Ct. 1965. Law clk. U.S. Ct. of Appeals, Washington, 1960-61; asst. U.S. atty., 1961-62; atty. SEC, 1962-63; legis. asst. U.S. Sen. Joseph S. Clark, 1963-66; counsel U.S. Senate Subcom. on Employment, Manpower and Poverty, 1966-68; ptnr. Dechert Price & Rhoads, 1969-76; asst. sec. for legislation and intergovtl. relations HUD, Washington, 1977-78; staff adv. domestic policy staff White House, 1978-79; ptnr. Lane & Edson (P.C.), 1979-88, Dewey, Ballantine, Bushby, Palmer & Wood, Washington, 1988-92; dir. Ctr. Preservation Policy Studies, Nat. Trust for Hist. Preservation, 1992-93; spl. projects advisor Office of Cultural Resources, Nat. Park Svc., 1994-95; of counsel Shulman, Rogers, Gandal, Pordy & Ecker, P.A., 1995—; dir. Phila. Urban Coalition, 1974-76; nat. task force dir. Carter-Mondale Campaign, 1976. Served with Army N.G., 1961-65. Fellow Salzburg Seminar in Am. Studies, 1964. Mem. Am., Pa., Phila. bar assns., Order of Coif, Phi Beta Kappa. Democrat. Jewish. Club: Cosmos. Office: 11921 Rockville Pike 3d Fl Rockville MD 20852-2743

SCHWARTZ, HENRY GERARD, surgeon, educator; b. N.Y.C., Mar. 11, 1909; s. Nathan Theodore and Marie (Zagat) S.; m. Edith Courtenay Robinson, Sept. 13, 1934; children: Henry G., Michael R., Richard H. A.B., Princeton, 1928; M.D., Johns Hopkins, 1932. Diplomate: Am. Bd. Neurol. Surgery (chmn. 1968-70). Denison fellow with Prof. O. Foerster, Breslau, Germany, 1931; surg. house officer Johns Hopkins Hosp., 1932-33; NRC fellow Harvard Med. Sch., 1933-35, instr. anatomy, 1935-36; fellow neurol. surgery Washington U. Med. Sch., St. Louis, 1936-37; instr., asst. prof., assoc. prof. neurol. surgery Washington U. Med. Sch., 1937-46, prof., 1946-88, August Busch prof. emeritus, 1988—; acting surgeon-in-chief Barnes and Allied hosps., 1965-67; chief neurosurgeon Barnes, St. Louis Children's hosps., 1946-74; cons. neurosurgeon St. Louis City, Jewish, Los Alamos (N.M.) hosps.; cons. to surgeon gen. USPHS. to surgeon gen. U.S. Army.; Mem. subcom. neurosurgery NRC; del. World Fedn. Neurosurgery. Mem. editorial bd. Jour. Neurosurgery, chmn. 1967-69, editor, 1975-84. Served with AUS, 1942-45. Decorated Legion of Merit; recipient ofcl. citation and commendation Brit. Army, Harvey Cushing medal, 1979. Fellow ACS (adv. council on neurosurgery 1950, 60, v.p. 1972-73); mem. Soc. Neurol. Surgeons (pres. 1968-69), Am. Acad. Neurol. Surgery (pres. 1951-52), Harvey Cushing Soc. (pres. 1967-68), Am. Neurol. Assn. (hon.), Assn. Research Nervous and Mental Disease, Central Neuropsychiat. Assn. Am., Assn. Anatomists, So. Neurosurg. Soc. (pres. 1953-54), Soc. Med. Cons. to Armed Forces, Am. Surg. Assn. (v.p. 1975-76), Soc. de Neuro-Chirurgie de Langue Francaise, Excelsior Surg. Soc., Johns Hopkins Soc. Scholars, Soc. Internat. de Chirugie (Alpha Omega Alpha leader Am. medicine 1978), World Fedn. Neurosurg. Socs. (hon. pres.), Sigma Xi, Alpha Omega Alpha. Home: 2 Briar Oak Saint Louis MO 63132-4204 Office: Barnes Hosp Pl Saint Louis MO 63110

SCHWARTZ, HERBERT FREDERICK, lawyer; b. Bklyn., Aug. 23, 1935; s. Henry and Blanche Theodora (goldberg) S.; m. Gail Lubets, Jan. 23, 1960; children: Wendy Helene, Karen Anne, Peter Andrew; m. Nan Budde Chequer, Mar. 13, 1987; stepchildren: Elizabeth, Anne, Laura. BSEE, MIT, 1957; MA in Applied Econs., U. Pa., 1964, LLB, 1964. Assoc. Fish & Neave, N.Y.C., 1964-70; jr. ptnr. Fish & Neave, 1970-71, ptnr., 1972—, mng. ptnr., 1985-91; lectr. law U. Pa., Phila., 1980-89, adj. prof., 1990—. Mem. adv. bd. PTC Jour., Washington, 1983; author: "Patent Law and Practice," Federal Judicial Center, 1988, 2d. edition, 1995; contbr. articles to profl. jours. Vice-chmn. Jr. Yacht Racing Assn. of L.I. Sound, 1985-88. Fist lt UAS, Signal Corps, 1957-59. Mem. U.S. Trademark Assn., Assn. of Bar of City of N.Y., Am. Intellectual Property Lawyers Assn., N.Y. Intellectual Property Lawyers Assn., Am. Law Inst., Order of Coif, N.Y. Yacht Club, Riverside Yacht Club (bd. govs.). Avocation: racing sailboats. Home: 24 Cherry Tree Ln Riverside CT 06878-2629 Office: Fish & Neave 1251 Avenue Of The Americas New York NY 10020-1104

SCHWARTZ, HILDA G., retired judge; b. N.Y.C.; d. Solomon and Anna Leah (Rubin) Ginsburg; m. Herman N. Schwartz, Feb. 21, 1930; 1 child, John Michael. BS, Washington Sq. Coll. of NYU; LLB, NYU, 1929. Bar: N.Y. 1930. Pvt. practice, 1930-46; sec., bur. head, trial commr. Bd. Estimate, N.Y.C., 1946-51; city magistrate City of N.Y., 1951-58, city treas., head dept. finance, 1958-62, dir. finance, 1962-64, judge civil ct., 1965-71; justice state supreme ct. State of N.Y., 1972-83; ret., 1983; counsel to law firm, 1984; chmn. law com. Bd. Magistrates, 1953-58; chmn. home term panel judges, 1954-56; judge adolescent ct., 1953-58. Mem. welfare adv. bd. N.Y. Jr. League, 1953-56; bd. mgrs. Greenwich House, 1946-48; v.p. Young Dem. club 1935-37; trustee Village Temple, 1956-61, chair dedication com., 1957; chair exec. bd. Coun. Org. Am. Jewish Congress, 1958; hon. chair, bd. dirs. Women's League for Histadrut, 1959; vice-chair Greenwich Village Fresh Air Fund, 1962; co-chair community breakfast State of Israel Bonds, 1956; bd. dirs. Washington Sq. Outdoor Art Exhibit, 1950-58, Washington Sq. Coll. Alumni Assn., 1967. Recipient Citation by Women for Achievement, 1951, Award of Merit Women Lawyers Assn. State of N.Y., 1957, Scroll of Key award Key Women, 1959, Honor award Am. Jewish Congress Coun. of Orgns., 1959, Honor award Greenwich Village Community for State of Israel Bonds, 1960, Mother of Yr. award Justice Lodge Masons, 1960, First Egalitarian award Aegis Soc., Fed. Negro Civil Svc. Orgns., 1961, Honor award B'nai B'rith, 1963, Interfaith award, 1963, Alumni Achievement award NYU Washington Sq. Coll. Alumni Assn., 1968; named Woman of Achievement Fedn. Jewish Women Orgns., 1959, Patron ann. bridge, Cath. Ctr. NYU, 1960. Mem. ABA, Assn. of Bar of City of N.Y. (mem. lectr., legal aid, matrimonial law, profl. and jud. ethics coms.), N.Y. State Assn. Women Judges (hon. mem., bd. dirs., Outstanding Jud. Achievement award 1983), Supreme Ct. Justices Assn. of City of N.Y. (bd. dirs. 1976-89), Ins. Arbitrator Forums (arbitrator), N.Y. County Lawyers Assn. (profl. ethics com.), N.Y. State Bar Assn. (jud. sabbaticals com.), N.Y. Women's Bar Assn. (past pres., founder, mem. adv. bd., scroll of honor 1958, Disting. Svc. award 1977, Lifetime Contbn. to Justice award 1984), Nat. Assn. Women Judges, Assn. Supreme Ct. Justices State of N.Y. (community rels., retirement and pensions, jud. sabbatical coms.), Hadassah (hon. mem. N.Y. chpt. 1961), United HIAS Women's Div. (life), Emerald Soc. (hon. mem. 1961), Histadrut (hon. mem. 1960), Iota Tau Tau (hon.). Office: 43 5th Ave New York NY 10003-4368

SCHWARTZ, IRVING DONN, architect; b. Chgo., June 11, 1927; s. Simon S. and Rose P. (Pilot) S.; children: Charles, Linda. B.S., U. Ill., 1949, B.S. in Architecture, 1965, M.S. in Architecture, 1972. Registered architect, Ill., Ind., Fla., D.C., Ohio, Ga., Ala., Calif., N.H., Va., Md., Pa. Chief standard cost and indsl. engring. Lanzit Corrugated Box Co., Chgo., 1950-53; pres. Kaufman, Inc., Champaign, Ill., 1953-60; v.p. Hart Mirror Plate Co., Grand Rapids, Mich., 1953-60; asso. Richardson, Severns, Scheeler & Assos., Inc., Champaign, 1960-71; pres. IDS, Inc., Champaign, 1971-83, ADI, Dallas, 1983-86, IDS/B, Inc., Dallas, 1986—; prof. architecture Grad. Sch. Architecture, U. Ill., 1976-83; assoc. prof. design U. North Tex.; cons. in field. Mem. Champaign County Devel. Council; mem. Model Community Coordinating Council, Champaign; co-chmn. bldg. com. Mercy Hosp.; bd. frat. affairs U. Ill.; bd. dirs. United Fund. Served to 2d lt. U.S. Army, 1945-47. Recipient archtl. design research award, graphic design citation Progressive Architecture mag., 1974, Gold Key Design award Hospitality Mag., 1994. Fellow Am. Soc. Interior Designers (treas. 1976, nat. pres. 1978, Louis Tregre award 1992, Nat. design award 1983); mem. AIA (Design award 1983), Nat. Council Archtl. Registration Bds., Nat. Council Interior Design Qualifications (bd. dirs., pres. 1980), Tex. Assn. Interior Design (pres. 1993). Club: Standard (Chgo.). Home: 4443 Westway Ave Dallas TX 75205-3630 Office: IDS/B Inc 2777 N Stemmons Fwy Ste 1650 Dallas TX 75207-2229

SCHWARTZ, IRVING LEON, physician, scientist, educator; b. Cedarhurst, N.Y., Dec. 25, 1918; s. Abraham and Rose (Doniger) S.; m. Felice T. Nierenberg, Jan. 12, 1946; children: Cornelia Ann, Albert Anthony, James Oliver. AB, Columbia U., 1939; MD, NYU, 1943. Diplomate: Am. Bd. Internal Medicine. Intern, then asst. resident Bellevue Hosp., N.Y.C., 1943-44, 46-47; NIH fellow physiology NYU Coll. Medicine, N.Y.C., 1947-50; Am. Physiol. Soc. Porter fellow, also Gibbs meml. fellow in clin. sci. Rockefeller Inst., N.Y.C., 1950-51, Am. Heart Assn. fellow, 1951-52, asst., then assoc., 1952-58; asst. physician, then assoc. physician Rockefeller Inst. Hosp., 1950-58; sr. scientist Brookhaven Nat. Lab., Upton, N.Y., 1958-61, research collaborator, 1961—; attending physician Brookhaven Nat. Lab. Hosp., 1958—; Joseph Eichberg prof. physiology, dir. dept. U. Cin. Coll. Medicine, 1961-65; dean grad. faculties Mt. Sinai Med. and Grad. Schs., CUNY, 1965-80, prof. physiology and biophysics, chmn. dept., 1968-79, exec. officer biomed. scis. doctoral program, 1969-72, Dr. Harold and Golden Lamport disting. prof., 1979—; dir. Ctr. Peptide and Membrane Research Mt. Sinai Med. Ctr., 1979-87; dean emeritus Mt. Sinai Grad. Sch. Biol. Scis., 1980—. Contbr. articles to sci. publs. Pres. Life Scis. Found., 1962—. Served from 1st lt. to capt., M.C. AUS, 1944-46. Recipient Solomon A. Berson Med. Alumni Achievement award NYU Sch. Medicine, 1973. Fellow A.C.P.; mem. Am. Physiol. Soc., Soc. Exptl. Biology and Medicine, Am. Soc. Clin. Investigation, Am. Fedn. Clin. Research, Biophys. Soc., Endocrine Soc., Harvey Soc., Soc. for Neurosci., Am. Heart Assn., John Jay Assos. Columbia Coll., AAAS, N.Y. Acad. Sci., Sigma Xi, Alpha Omega Alpha. Home: 1120 5th Ave New York NY 10128-0144 also: 9 Thorn Hedge Rd Bellport NY 11713-2615 Office: Mt Sinai Med Ctr Box 1022 Mt Sinai Med Ctr Box 932 100th St and Fifth Ave New York NY 10029 also: Med Research Center Brookhaven Nat Lab Upton NY 11973 *The excitement and stimulation that comes from a productive collaboration with other people has been a major source of satisfaction in my life. I feel privileged to have had the opportunity to interact with a wide range of imaginative and inspiring colleagues, students and friends, including my wife of 50 years, whose extraordinary career emphasized the importance of idealism, commitment, persistence and a felicitous blending of focus and flexibility.*

SCHWARTZ, JEROME MERRILL, lawyer; b. Pittsfield, Mass., Oct. 3, 1952; s. Harry and Pauline (Bricker) S.; m. Gail Eileen Schulman, May 29, 1977; children: Karen Beth, Steven Robert. BSEE magna cum laude, U. Mich., 1974, JD magna cum laude, 1977. Bar: Mich. 1977, U.S. Ct. Appeals (6th cir.) 1979, U.S. Supreme Ct. 1990. Assoc. Dickinson, Wright, Moon, Van Dusen & Freeman, Detroit, 1977-83, ptnr., 1984—. Bd. dirs., chmn. Am. Heart Assn. Mich.; mem. regional adv. bd. Anti-Defamation League. Mem. Detroit Bar Assn., Assn. for Corp. Growth Inc., Comml. Fin. Assn. Edn. Found. (adv. bd.), Nat. Assn. Securities Dealers (panel of arbitrators). Office: 500 Woodward Ave Ste 4000 Detroit MI 48226-3423

SCHWARTZ, JERROLD BENNETT, school system administrator; b. Pitts., Jan. 19, 1942; s. Norman D. and Selma (Bass) S.; m. Nancy Feldman, Dec. 29, 1963; children: Mindy Cohen, Cathy Backal, Michael. EdB, U. Miami, 1963; MEd, U. Ga., 1969, specialist in adminstrn. and supervision, 1974; PhD, Ga. State U., 1983. Tchr. Dade County Sch. System, Miami, Fla., 1963-64; tchr. DeKalb County Sch. System, Decatur, Ga., 1966-70, prin., 1970-84, instructional coord., 1984-85, coord. staff devel., 1985-86, asst. dir. staff devel., 1986-94, dir. staff devel., 1994—; adj. asst. prof. Ga. State U., Atlanta, 1986—. 1st Lt. U.S. Army, 1964-66. Named Outstanding Young Educator, DeKalb County Jaycees, Decatur, 1970, Hon. Llife Mem., Ga. PTA, 1976; recipient Cert. Appreciation, Alliance for Arts Edn., Washington, 1980, Assn. Children With Learning Disabilities, Decatur, 1982. Mem. ASCD. Nat. Staff Devel. Coun., Ga. Staff. Devel. Coun. (Disting. Staff Developer award 1995), DeKalb Assn. Educators (newsletter editor, 25 Yr. Svc. award 1991), Met. Atlanta Tchrs. Edn. Group (pres. 1994). Jewish. Avocations: basketball, aerobics, collecting inspirationals, poetry. Office: DeKalb County Sch System 3770 N Decatur Rd Decatur GA 30032-1005

SCHWARTZ, JOHN JAMES, association executive, consultant; b. New Rochelle, N.Y., Aug. 28, 1919; s. Edwin Benner and Marjorie Helen (James) S.; m. Katharine S. Sprackling, Jan. 6, 1942; children: Christopher Louis. Grad. high sch., New Rochelle; student, Mercersburg Acad., 1938. Campaign dir. John Price Jones Inc., N.Y.C., 1946-50; dir. pub. relations and fund raising Travelers Aid Soc. N.Y., N.Y.C., 1950-55; dir. devel. Community Service Soc., N.Y.C., 1955-57, Near East Found., N.Y.C., 1957-60; v.p. G.A. Brakeley & Co. Inc., N.Y.C., 1960-61; dir. devel. Fgn. Policy Assn., N.Y.C., 1962-64; founding pres. Greater N.Y. Nat. Soc. of Fund Raising Execs., 1964; asst. v.p. for crusade Am. Cancer Soc., N.Y.C., 1964-66; exec. dir. Am. Assn. Fund Raising Counsel, N.Y.C., 1966-68, exec. v.p., 1968-72, pres., 1972-87; founding bd. mem. Ind. Sector, Washington, 1980-85, mem. com. to measurably increase giving; mem., former pres. Com. on Nat. Ctr. for Charitable Stats.; spl. cons. to Com. on Pvt. Philanthropy and Pub. Needs., 1973; chair pvt. adv. group Nat. Assn. Attys. Gen. Model Law Project. Author: Modern American Philanthropy; A Personal Account, 1994. Mem. adv. bd. mgmt. fund-raising NYU Cert. Program; mem. adv. coun. Grad. Sch. Mgmt. and Urban Professions, New Sch. Social Rsch.; active formation of 5 borough coalitions Daring Coals for Caring Soc., N.Y.C., 1987; cons. Ind. U. Ctr. on Philanthropy, 1988-91, Cmty. Counselling Svc. Co., Inc., 1988-91; pres. Nat. Philanthropy Day, 1988-90, mem. hon. com., 1981; bd. dirs.-at-large USA World Fund Raising Coun., 1993; pres. Friends of the Westport Libr., 1995-96. Capt. USAAF, 1941-46; PTO. Recipient Disting. Profl. Service to Philanthropy award Am. Assn. Fund-Raising Counsel, N.Y., 1976, Outstanding Agy. Profl. award United Way Am., Alexandria, 1982. Mem. Nat. Charities Info. Bur. (bd. dirs. 1978-94), Nat. Soc. Fund-Raising Execs. (bd. dirs. 1964-90, past pres.), Fairfield County Nat. Soc. Fund-Raising Dirs. (bd. dirs. 1992—), Am. Assn. Ret. Persons (bd. dirs. Andrus Found. 1983-90), 501C-3 Soc., Princeton Club (N.Y.C.). Democrat. Unitarian. Avocations: writing history, ship models.

SCHWARTZ, JOHN NORMAN, health care executive; b. Watertown, Minn., Dec. 13, 1945; s. Norman O. and Marion G. (Tesch) S. BA, Augsburg Coll., Mpls., 1967; MHA, U. Minn., 1969. Adminstrv. resident Luth. Hosp. and Med. Ctr., Wheat Ridge, Colo., 1968-69; asst. adminstr. St. Luke's Hosp., Milw., 1969-73, med. adminstr., 1973-75, v.p., 1975-84; sr. v.p. and chief oper. officer Good Samaritan Med. Ctr., Milw., 1984-85, pres. and chief exec. officer, 1985-88; exec. v.p. Aurora Health Care Inc., Milw., 1988-89; gen. mgr. SmithKline Beecham Clin. Labs., Schaumburg, Ill., 1989-90; chief exec. Trinity Hosp. of Advocate Health Care, Chgo., 1991—; bd. dirs. Samaritan Health Plan, Milw., 1984-89. Bd. dirs. Gt. Lakes Hemophilia Found., Milw., 1975-89, Gov.'s appointee to Coun. on Hemophilia and Related Blood Disorders, Madison, 1978, Sullivan Chamber Ensemble, Milw., 1975-84, S. Chgo. YMCA, 1993—. Recipient First Place award Color Photography, Milw. Jour. Co., 1983. Fellow Am. Coll. Healthcare Execs. (regent 1993—). Lutheran. Avocations: jogging, photography, music, choral singing. Office: Trinity Hosp 2320 E 93rd St Chicago IL 60617-3909

SCHWARTZ, JOSEPH, retired container company executive; b. N.Y.C., Apr. 22, 1911; s. Nathan and Ida (Estrich) S.; m. Hazel Shapiro, Dec. 25, 1932; children—Arlene Schwartz Bornstein, Linda Schwartz Rosenbaum. Grad., high sch. Ptnr. Mut. Paper Co., Lynn, Mass., 1928-38; treas. Allied Container Corp., Hyde Park, Mass., 1938-56; pres., treas. Allied Container Corp., Dedham, Hyde Park, 1956-84; chmn. bd. Cargal, Ltd., Lod Israel; ret. v.p. Union Camp Corp., Wayne, N.J. Fellow Brandeis U. Home: #307 3960 Oaks Clubhouse Dr Apt 307 Pompano Beach FL 33069-3645

SCHWARTZ, JOSEPH, English language educator; b. Milw., Apr. 9, 1925; s. Alfred George and Mary (Brandt) S.; m. Joan Jackson, Aug. 28, 1954; 1 son, Adam. B.A., Marquette U., 1946, M.A., 1947; Ph.D., U. Wis., 1952. Teaching asst. Marquette U., Milw., 1946-47; instr. Marquette U., 1947-48, 50-54, asst. prof., 1954-59, assoc. prof., 1959-64, prof., 1964-90, chmn. dept. English, 1963-75, prof. emeritus, 1990—; teaching fellow U. Wis., 1948-50; Chmn. region X Woodrow Wilson Nat. Fellowship Found., 1967-73; pres. bd. edn. Archdiocese of Milw., 1977-79. Author: A Reader for Writers, 3d edit., 1971, Perspectives on Language, 1963, Province of Rhetoric, 1965, Poetry: Meaning and Form, 1969, Hart Crane: A Critical Bibliography, 1970, Hart Crane: A Descriptive Bibliography, 1972, Exposition, 2d edit., 1971, Hart Crane: A Reference Guide, 1983; sr. editor: Renascence Mag., 1978-95. Recipient Distinguished Alumni award Marquette U. Sch. Speech, 1967, Outstanding Tchr. award Marquette U., 1974; Ford Found. grantee, 1956; Am. Council Learned Socs. grantee, 1972, 89; HEW grantee, 1966, 67. Mem. Nat. Coun. Tchrs. English (nat. dir. 1965-68), Modern Lang. Assn., Midwest Modern Lang Assn. (exec. com. 1973-76), Fellowship of Cath. Scholars (bd. dirs. 1987-90), Conf. on Christianity and Lit. (bd. dirs. 1987-90), Phi Beta Kappa, Alpha Sigma Nu (hon.). Republican. Roman Catholic. Home: 8516 W Mequon Rd # 112 Thiensville WI 53097-3100 Office: Marquette U PO Box 1888 Renascence Brooks Hall Milwaukee WI 53201-1888

SCHWARTZ, KESSEL, modern language educator; b. Kansas City, Mo., Mar. 19, 1920; s. Henry and Dora (Tanenbaum) S.; m. Barbara Lewin, Apr. 3, 1947; children: Joseph David, Deborah, Edward, Michael. B.A., U. Mo., 1940, M.A., 1941; Ph.D., Columbia U., 1953. Asst. instr. U. Mo., 1940-42; dir. cultural ctrs. in Nicaragua, Ecuador, cultural observer in Costa Rica State Dept., 1946-48; instr. Hofstra, Hamilton, Colby colls., 1948-53; asst. prof. U. Vt., 1953-57; assoc. prof., then prof. modern langs., chmn. dept. U. Ark., 1957-62; prof. modern langs. U. Miami, Fla., 1962-90; chmn. dept. U. Miami, 1962-64, 74-83, dir. grad. studies, 1964-65, 83-90, now emeritus prof.; vis. prof. U. N.C., Chapel Hill, 1966-67. Author: The Ecuadorian Novel, 1953, An Introduction to Modern Spanish Literature, 1967, The Meaning of Existence in Contemporary Hispanic Literature, 1969, Vicente Aleixandre, 1970, Juan Goytisolo, 1970, A New History of Spanish American Fiction, 1972 (named Outstanding Acad. Book of Year, Am. Assn. Coll. and Research Librarians), Studies on Twentieth Century Spanish and Spanish American Literature, 1983; co-author: A New History of Spanish Literature, 1961, rev. edit., 1991, A New Anthology of Spanish Literature, 1968; assoc. editor Hispania, 1965-84; editorial adv. bd.: Anales de Literatura Española Contemporánea Folio; Fiestas (Goytisolo), notes and introduction, 1964; contbr. numerous articles to profl. jours., chpts. to books, ency. Nat. patronato Letras de Oro Spanish Literary Prizes. Served with AUS, 1942-46. July 14, 1989 declared Kessel Schwartz Day in Coral Gables, Miami and Dade County by mayors' proclamation. Mem. MLA (group sec. 1964, group chmn. 1965, chmn. nominating com. for modern Spanish lit. 1966-68), Am. Assn. Tchrs. Spanish and Portuguese (chmn. Peninsular lit. sect. 1972), Internat. Assn. Hispanists, Phi Beta Kappa (pres. So. Fla. chpt. 1977), Phi Sigma Iota, Sigma Delta Pi (nat. Order of Don Quijote award 1984, Order of Discoverers award 1989), Pi Delta Phi, Delta Phi Alpha, Omicron Delta Kappa. Home: 6400 Maynada St Miami FL 33146-3318 *If men loved one another sufficiently, we might not need our legal systems. Given our imperfect nature as human beings, we must believe in some higher goals to give meaning to our lives but be ever vigilant that in the pursuit of success we do not infringe upon the happiness of others or confuse the means with the end.*

SCHWARTZ, LEON, foreign language educator; b. Boston, Aug. 22, 1922; s. Charles and Celia (Emer) S.; m. Jeanne Gurtat, Mar. 31, 1949; children—Eric Alan, Claire Marie. Student, Providence Coll., 1939-41; B.A., U. Calif. at Los Angeles, 1948; certificat de phonetique, U. Paris, 1949; M.A, U. So. Cal., 1950, Ph.D., 1962. Tchr. English, Spanish and Latin Redlands (Calif.) Jr. High Sch., 1951-54; high sch. tchr. Spanish and French, 1954-59; prof. French Calif. State U., Los Angeles, 1959-87, emeritus, 1987—, chmn. dept. fgn. langs. and lit., 1970-73. Author: Diderot and the Jews, 1981. Served as 2d lt. USAAF, 1942-45. Decorated Air medal with 5 oak leaf clusters; recipient Outstanding Prof. award Calif. State U. at Los Angeles, 1976. Mem. Am. Assn. Tchrs. French, Modern and Classical Lang. Assn. So. Calif., Western Soc. 18th Century Studies, Am. Soc. 18th Century Studies, Société Diderot, Phi Beta Kappa, Phi Kappa Phi, Pi Delta Phi, Sigma Delta Pi, Alpha Mu Gamma. Office: Calif State U Dept Modern Langs and Lit Los Angeles CA 90032

SCHWARTZ, LEONARD, lawyer; b. Bklyn., May 12, 1954; s. Harry and Betty (Krull) S.; m. Barbara Greenberg, Oct. 22, 1977; children: Jason, Rebecca, Ariele. BA magna cum laude, Bklyn. Coll., 1974, JD, 1977. Bar: N.Y. 1978, U.S. Dist. Ct. (so. and ea. dists.) N.Y. 1978, U.S. Supreme Ct. 1991. Assoc. John Anthony Bonina & Assocs., Bklyn., 1977-80, Law Firm John J. Feeley, N.Y.C., 1980, Fuchsberg & Fuchsberg, N.Y.C., 1980-83; ptnr. Oliveri & Schwartz P.C., N.Y.C., 1983—; panelist Med. Malpractice Mediation Panel N.Y., Kings, Richmond Counties, 1985—. Mem. Assn. Trial Lawyers Am., Am. Arbitration Assn. (panelist 1985—), N.Y. State Bar Assn., N.Y. State Trial Lawyers Assn (bd. dirs. 1993—), N.Y. County Lawyers Assn. (com. mcpl. liability 1992—). Office: Oliveri & Schwartz PC 30 Vesey St Ste 1000 New York NY 10007

SCHWARTZ, LILLIAN FELDMAN, artist, filmaker, art analyst, author, nurse; b. Cin., July 13, 1927; d. Jacob and Katie (Green) Feldman; m. Jack James Schwartz, Dec. 22, 1946; children: Jeffrey Hugh, Laurens Robert. RN, U. Cin., 1947; Dr. honoris causa, Kean Coll., 1988. Nurse Cin. Gen. Hosp., 1947; head supr. premature nursery St. Louis Maternity Hosp., 1947-48; cons. AT&T Bell Labs., Murray Hill, N.J., 1968—; pres. Computer Creations Corp., Watchung, N.J., 1989—; cons. Bell Communications Research, Morristown, N.J., 1984-92; artist-in-residence Sta. WNET, N.Y.C., 1972-74; cons. T.J. Watson Rsch. Lab. IBM Corp., Yorktown, N.Y., 1975, 82-84; vis. mem. computer sci. dept. U.. Md., College Park, 1974-80; adj. prof. fine arts Kean Coll., Union, N.J., 1980-82, Rutgers U., New Brunswick, N.J., 1982-83; adj. prof. dept. psychology NYU, N.Y.C., 1985-86, assoc. prof. computer sci.; guest lectr. Princeton U., Columbia U., Yale U., Rockefeller U.; mem. grad. faculty Sch. Visual Arts, N.Y.C., 1990—. Co-author: The Computer Artist's Handbook; contbd. articles to profl. jours including Scientific Am., 1995; contbr. chpts. to books, also

Trans. Am. Philos. Soc., vol. 75, Part 6, 1985; one-woman shows of sculpture and paintings include Columbia U., 1967, 68, Rabin and Krueger Gallery, Newark, 1968; films shown at Met. Mus., N.Y.C., Franklin Inst., Phila., 1972, U. Toronto, 1972, am. Embassy, London, 1972, L.A. County Mus., Corcoran Gallery, Washington, 1972, Whitney Mus., N.Y.C., 1973, Grand Palais, Paris, Musee Nat. d'Art Moderne, Paris, IBM, and others. Recipient numerous art and film awards, Emmy award Mus. Modern Art, 1984, Computer Graphics World Smithsonian awards for virtual reality, art analysis, inventing computer medium for art and animation, 1993; named Outstanding Alumnus, U. Cin., 1987; grantee Nat. Endowment for Arts, 1977, 81, Corp. Pub. Broadcasting, 1979, Nat. Endowment Composers and Librettists, 1981. Fellow World Acad. of Art and Sci.; mem. NATAS, Am. Film Inst., Info. Film Prodrs. Am., Soc. Motion Picture and TV Engrs., Internat. Sculptors Assn., Centro Studi Pierfrancescani (Sansepolcro, Italy, founding mem.). Pioneer in use of computers as art media; commd. to create computer poster and TV comml. for opening New Mus. Modern Art, 1984; discovered identities of the Mona Lisa, hidden and surface, 1987, and identified steps DaVinci made in transforming Isabella, Duchess of Aragon, into the Mona Lisa using his own features as the model, 1993; discovered perspective used by DaVinci in The Last Supper, 1988; identified time of day and tree of thorns in Piero della Francesca's Resurrection; discovered Elizabeth I is model for Martin Droeshout engraving of Shakespeare, 1991; performed first transmission of computer drawing between U.S. and Germany, 1990; used morphing algorithms to determine Leonardo's creative decision-making steps in transforming the Duchess of Aragon into the Mona Lisa using his own features to segue; discovered metnod Leonardo used to create his Grotesques, 1994. *I have always been provoked by and concerned with the mechanical and technological world around me. I enjoy experimenting with traditional media and combining them with technology today. For example, I used computers as an art medium when computers were solely programmed for scientific purposes. By using the computer to understand the creative process I have made clear the intent of the great masters and applied their decision-making steps to my own work. The excitement in creating is to discover and to make a new world. My present success was achieved in part by being able to make new rules and not be hindered by old or obvious solutions.*

SCHWARTZ, LLOYD, music critic, poet; b. N.Y.C., Nov. 29, 1941; s. Sam and Ida (Singer) S. BA, Queens Coll., N.Y.C., 1962; MA, Harvard U., 1963, PhD, 1976. Classical music editor Boston Phoenix, 1977—; dir. creative writing U. Mass., Boston, 1982-84, 86-88, 1990—; classical music critic Fresh Air Nat. Pub. Radio, Phila., 1987—; prof. English U. Mass., Boston, 1986—. Author: (poems) These People, 1981, (play) These People: Voices for the Stage, 1990, Goodnight, Gracie, 1992; editor: Ploughshares, 1979, Elizabeth Bishop and Her Art, 1983; actor The Spider's Web, 1975-82; dir. These People: Voices for the Stage, 1990, (operas) L'Heure Espagnol (Ravel), 1972, Mavra (Stravinsky), 1973. Recipient Pulitzer prize for criticism, 1994; NEA creative writing fellow in poetry, 1990. Mem. PEN (exec. com. New Eng. chpt. 1983—) PEN Am., Poetry Soc. Am., MLA, New Eng. Poetry Club. Avocations: collecting old recordings, books. Home: 27 Pennsylvania Ave Somerville MA 02145-2217 Office: Boston Phoenix 126 Brookline Ave Boston MA 02215-3920

SCHWARTZ, LLOYD MARVIN, newspaper and magazine correspondent, broadcaster; b. Bklyn., Mar. 6, 1923; s. Philip and Celia W. Schwartz; m. Doris Grossman, May 19, 1946; children: Ellen, Philip, Laura. BA, NYU, 1944. NYU corr. N.Y. Times, 1942-44; news editor, writer Trade Union Courier, 1943-44; reporter Lima (Ohio) News, 1945; reporter, The White House corr. Fairchild Publs., Washington, 1945-65; Washington bur. chief Fairchild Publs., 1965-88; Congl. corr. Fairchild News Service, 1977-88; panelist, news broadcaster Voice of Am., AFL-CIO, Fairchild Broadcast News and WJR-Detroit; Congl. corr. Van Dahl Publs., Albany, Oreg., 1980-90, mem. Senate and Ho. of Reps. Periodical Press Galleries, 1946-93; Congl. corr. Linn's Stamp News, Sidney, Ohio, 1990-92; cons. Rsch. Inst. of Am. Democrat. Jewish.

SCHWARTZ, LOUIS BROWN, legal educator; b. Phila., Feb. 22, 1913; s. Samuel and Rose (Brown) S.; m. Berta Wilson, Mar. 29, 1937 (div. 1954); children: Johanna, Victoria; m. Miriam Robbins Humboldt, Sept. 16, 1964. B.S. in Econs, U. Pa., 1932, J.D., 1935. Bar: Pa. 1935, U.S. Supreme Ct. 1942. Atty. SEC, Washington, 1935-39; chief gen. crimes and spl. projects sect. Dept. Justice, 1939-43, chief judgment and enforcement sect. antitrust div., 1945-46; also mem. inter-departmental coms. on war crimes and status-of-forces treaties; prof. law U. Pa. Law Sch., 1946-83, Benjamin Franklin prof., 1964-83; prof. law Hastings Coll. Law, U. Calif., 1983—; vis. prof. Harvard U., Columbia U., U. Calif. at Berkeley, Cambridge (Eng.) U.; Ford vis. Am. prof. Inst. Advanced Legal Studies, U. London (Eng.), 1974; vis. disting. prof. Ariz. State U., 1980; mem. Atty. Gen.'s Nat. Com. Study Antitrust Laws, 1954-55, Pa. Gov.'s Commn. on Penal and Correctional Affairs, 1956-60; adv. commn. Revision Pa. Penal Code, 1963-68; nat. adv. council Nat. Defender Project, 1964-69; dir. Nat. Commn. on Reform of Fed. Criminal Laws, 1968-71; co-reporter Model Penal Code Am. Law Inst., 1962; cons. FTC, Dept. Justice, other agencies. Author: Free Enterprise and Economic Organization, 1959, 6th edit. (with John J. Flynn, Harry First) titled Antitrust and Government Regulation, 1983-85 (2 vols.), Le Système Pénal des Etats-Unis, 1964, Law Enforcement Handbook for Police, 1970, 2d edit., 1979, Proposed Federal Criminal Code, (with Comments and Working Papers), 1971; contbr. numerous articles to profl. jours. Served as lt. (j.g.) USNR, 1944-45. Mem. Ams. Democratic Action (nat. bd.), Am. Law Inst. (adv. com. pre-arraignment code), Order of Coif. Home: 2955 Pierce St San Francisco CA 94123-3824 Office: U Calif Hastings Coll Law 200 Mcallister St San Francisco CA 94102-4707

SCHWARTZ, LYLE H., materials scientist, government official; b. Chgo., Aug. 2, 1936; s. Joseph K. Schwartz and Helen (Shefsky) Bernards; divorced; children—Ara, Justin; m. Celesta Sue Jurkovich, Sept. 1, 1973. B.S. in Sci. Engring., Northwestern U., 1959, Ph.D. in Materials Sci., 1964. Prof. materials sci. Northwestern U., Evanston, Ill., 1964-84, dir. Materials Research Ctr., 1979-84; dir. materials sci. and engr. lab. Nat. Inst. Standards and Tech., Dept. Commerce, Gaithersburg, Md., 1984—; cons. Argonne Nat. Labs., Ill., 1965-79; vis. scientist Bell Telephone Labs., Murray Hill, N.J., 1971-73. Author: (with J.B. Cohen) Diffraction From Materials, 1977, 2d edit., 1987; also numerous articles and papers. NSF fellow, 1962-63; recipient Presdl. Rank Award of Meritorious Exec. for outstanding govt. svc., 1990. Fellow Am. Soc. for Metals; mem. AAAS, AIME, Nat. Acad. Engring., Am. Phys. Soc., Am. Crystallography Assn., Materials Rsch. Soc., Sigma Xi.

SCHWARTZ, MARILYN, columnist. Columnist Dallas Morning News. Office: The Dallas Morning News Communications News PO Box 655237 Dallas TX 75265

SCHWARTZ, MARSHALL ZANE, pediatric surgeon; b. Mpls., Sept. 1, 1945; s. Sidney Shay and Peggy Belle (Lieberman) S.; m. Michele Carroll Walker, Oct. 16, 1971; children: Lisa, Jeffrey. BS, U. Minn., 1968, MD, 1970. Diplomate Am. Bd. Surgery, Am. Bd. Pediatric Surgery,. Intern N.Y. Hosp., N.Y.C., 1970-71; resident in gen. surgery U. Minn., Mpls., 1971-73, 75-76, rsch. fellow, 1974-75; jr. resident in pediatric surgery Children's Hosp. Med. Ctr., Harvard Med. Sch., 1973-74, sr. resident in pediatric surgery, 1976-77, chief resident in pediatric surgery, 1977-78; instr. Med. Sch. Harvard U., Boston, 1978-79; asst. in surgery Childrens Hosp. Med. Ctr., Boston, 1978-79; asst. prof. Med. Br. U. Tex., Galveston, 1979-81, assoc. prof. Med. Br., 1981-83, chief. pediatric surgery Med. Br., 1980-83; assoc. prof. U. Calif., Davis, 1983-86, prof., 1986-92, chief pediatric surgery, 1983-92, chmn. helicopter svcs., programmatic subcom., 1984-86, vice chmn. faculty Sch. Medicine, 1990-91, chmn. faculty Sch. Medicine, 1991-92; prof. surgery and pediatrics George Washington Sch. Medicine, 1992—; surgeon-in-chief, chmn. dept. pediatric surgery Children's Nat. Med. Ctr., Washington, 1992—. Editorial bd. Journal of Pediatric Surgery, 1988—. Pres. bd. dirs. Sacramento Children's Hosp. Found., 1990-92; vice chmn. Bd. of Childrens Faculty Assocs., Childrens Nat. Med. Ctr. Recipient Basil O'Connor Rsch. award March of Dimes Found., 1981, Young Investigator award NIH, 1982, Found. for Children Rsch. award, 1982, James W. McLaughlin award U. Tex., 1983. Fellow ACS; mem. Am. Surg. Assn., Soc. Univ. Surgeon, Am. Pediatric Surg. Assn., Soc. Surgery of the Alimentary Tract, Pacific Assn. of Pediatric Surgeons (pres., pres.-elect). Jewish. Avocations: skiing, fishing, wood working. Office: Children's Nat Med Ctr Dept Pediatric Surgery 111 Michigan Ave NW Washington DC 20010-2970

SCHWARTZ, MARVIN, lawyer; b. Phila., Nov. 3, 1922; s. Abe and Freda (Newman) S.; m. Joyce Ellen Sidner, Sept. 7, 1947; children: John Burkhart, Daniel Bruce, Pamela Louise Pier. LL.B., U. Pa., 1949. Bar: Pa. 1950, N.Y. 1951, D.C. 1955. Law sec. to judge U.S. Ct. Appeals, 3d Circuit, Phila., 1949-50; law sec. to Justice Burton U.S. Supreme Ct., Washington, 1950-51; assoc. Sullivan & Cromwell, N.Y.C., 1951-60; ptnr. Sullivan & Cromwell, 1960-92; mediator U.S. Dist. (so. dist.) N.Y., N.Y. Supreme Ct. Comml. Divsn.; arbitrator Am. Arbitration Assn., N.Y. Stock Exch., Nat. Assn. Securities Dealers. Spl. master appellate divsn. 1st dept. Supreme Ct. N.Y.; chmn. Zoning Bd. of Adjustment, Alpine, N.J., 1966-74; mem. Planning Bd., Alpine, 1966-67; bd. overseers emeritus U. Pa. Law Sch. With Signal Corps U.S. Army, 1943-46. Mem. ABA, N.Y. Bar Assn., D.C. Bar Assn., Am. Coll. Trial Lawyers (sec. 1986-88, bd. regents 1981-86, chmn. Downstate N.Y. com. 1976-78), Am. Law Inst. (adviser complex litigation project), Univ. Club (N.Y.C.), Litchfield (Conn.) Country Club. Democrat. Jewish. Office: Sullivan & Cromwell 125 Broad St New York NY 10004-2400

SCHWARTZ, MELVIN, physics educator, laboratory administrator; b. N.Y.C., Nov. 2, 1932; s. Harry and Hannah (Shulman) S.; m. Marilyn Fenster, Nov. 25, 1953; children: David N., Diane R., Betty Lynn. A.B., Columbia U., 1953, Ph.D., 1958, DSc honoris causa, 1991. Assoc. physicist Brookhaven Nat. Lab., 1956-58; mem. faculty Columbia U., N.Y.C., 1958-66; prof. physics Columbia U., 1963-66, Stanford U., Calif., 1966-83; cons. prof. Stanford U., 1983-91; chmn. Digital Pathways, Inc., Mountain View, Calif., 1970-91; assoc. dir. high energy and nuclear physics Brookhaven Nat. Lab., Upton, N.Y., 1991-94; prof. physics Columbia U., N.Y.C., 1991-94, I.I. Rabi prof. physics, 1994—. Co-discoverer muon neutrino, 1962. Bd. govs. Weizmann Inst. Sci. Recipient Nobel prize in physics, 1988, John Jay award Columbia Coll., 1989, Alexander Hamilton medal Columbia U.; Guggenheim fellow, 1968. Fellow Am. Phys. Soc. (Hughes award 1964); mem. NAS. Home: 61 S Howells Point Rd Bellport NY 11713-2621 Office: Columbia U Dept Physics New York NY 10027

SCHWARTZ, MICHAEL, university president, sociology educator; b. Chgo., July 29, 1937; s. Norman and Lillian (Ruthenberg) S.; m. Ettabelle Slutsky, Aug. 23, 1959; children: Monica, Kenneth, Rachel. BS in Psychology, U. Ill., 1958, MA in Indsl. Relations, 1959, PhD in Sociology, 1962; LLD (hon.), Youngstown State U., 1990. Asst. prof. sociology and psychology Wayne State U., Detroit, 1962-64; asst. prof. sociology Ind. U., Bloomington, 1964, assoc. prof. sociology, 1966-70; prof., chmn. dept. sociology Fla. Atlantic U., Boca Raton, 1970-72, dean Coll. Social Sci., 1972-76; v.p. grad. studies and research Kent (Ohio) State U., 1976-78, interim pres., 1977, acting v.p. acad. affairs, 1977-78, v.p. acad. and student affairs, 1978-80, provost, v.p. acad. and student affairs, 1980-82, pres., 1982-91; pres. emeritus and trustee's prof. Kent State U., 1991—; acting dir. Inst. for Social Rsch., Ind. U., 1966-67; tng. cons. Operation Head Start in Ind., 1964-70; cons. Office of Manpower, Automation and Tng., U.S. Dept. Labor, 1964-65. Cons. editor, Sociometry, 1966-70, assoc. editor, 1970; reader Am. Sociol. Rev. papers; author: (with Elton F. Jackson) Study Guide to the Study of Sociology, 1968; contbr. articles to profl. jours., chpts. to books. Chmn. Mid-Am. Conf. Coun. Pres.; rep. Nat. Coll. Athletic Assn. Pres.'s Commn.; corps evaluators North Ctrl. Assn. Colls. and Schs.; mem. bd. visitors Air U., USAF; mem. Akron (Ohio) Regional Devel. Bd., N.E. Ednl. TV of Ohio, Inc., N.E. Ohio Univs. Coll. Medicine; trustee Akron Symphony Orch. Assn.; mem. State of Ohio Post-Secondary Rev. Entity, 1995; mem. Assn. of Governing Bds. Commn. on Strengthening the Presidency. Recipient Disting. Tchr. award Fla. Atlantic U., 1970-71, Meritorious Svc. award Am. Assn. State Colls. and Univs., 1990; Michael Schwartz Ctr., Kent State U., named in his honor, 1991. Mem. Ohio Tchr. Edn. and Cert. Adv. Commn., Akron Press Club, Cleve. Press Club, Pine Lake Trout Club. Office: Kent State U 405 White Hall Kent OH 44242

SCHWARTZ, MICHAEL ALAN, physician; b. N.Y.C., Dec. 13, 1944; s. David Henry and Ray Schwartz; m. Joan Kay Clayton, Jan. 12, 1979; children: Dana, David, Elizabeth. AB, Princeton, 1965; MD, Cornell U., 1969. Intern, medicine N.Y. Hosp., Cornell, 1969-70; resident, psychiatry N.Y. Hosp., Cornell, Westchester, 1970-74; clin. assoc. NIMH, Washington, 1972-74; asst. prof. psychiatry Cornell Med. Coll., N.Y.C., 1974-76; assoc. to prof. of psychiatry N.Y. Med. Coll., 1976-92; prof. and vice chmn. dept. psychiatry Case Western Res. U., Cleve., 1992—. Editor: (with Manfred Spitzer, Christoph Mundt, Friedrick Uehlein) Phenomenology, Language, and Schizophrenia, 1992, (with John Sadler and Osborn Wiggins) Psychiatric Diagnostic Classification, 1994; asst. editor Integrative Psychiatry, 1990—; mem. editl. bd. Comprehensive Psychiatry, 1991—, Jour. of Personality Disorders, 1992—; assoc. editor Philosophy, Psychiatry, Psychology, 1993—; contbr. articles to numerous sci. jours. Fellow Am. Psychiat. Assn., Assn. for Advancement of Philosophy and Psychiatry (pres. 1991-94, founding pres. 1994—).

SCHWARTZ, MICHAEL ROBINSON, health administrator; b. St. Louis, Mar. 18, 1940; s. Henry G. and Edith C. (Robinson) S.; children: Christine, Richard; m. Kathleen Nowicki, Dec., 9, 1989. AB, Dartmouth Coll., 1962; MHA, U. Minn., 1964. Asst. in adminstrn. Shands Teaching Hosp., Gainesville, Fla., 1966-67; asst. dir. Shands Teaching Hosp., Gainesville, 1967-68, assoc. dir., 1968-73; assoc. adminstr. St. Joseph Mercy Hosp., Pontiac, Mich., 1973-76; pres. St. Joseph Mercy Hosp., 1976-85; exec. v.p. Mercy Health Svcs., Farmington Hills, Mich., 1985—; chief oper. officer Mercy Health Svcs., Farmington Hills, 1988—; exec. v.p. Ea. Mich. region Sisters of Mercy Health Corp., 1991-92; non-resident lectr. U. Mich., 1982—; cons. prof. Oakland U., 1980-88; asst. prof. hosp. adminstrn. U. Fla., 1967-73; pres. Eastern Mich. Regional Bd. Sisters of Mercy Health Corp., 1976-79; bd. dirs. Lourdes Nursing Home, 1973-83, v.p., 1974, pres., 1975; bd. dirs. Oakland Livingston Human Svc. Agy., 1977-81; bd. dirs. Mercy Sch. Nursing, 1976-84, v.p., 1981-84; bd. dirs. United Way-Pontiac/North Oakland, 1976-85, v.p., 1982-84; bd. dirs. Oakland Health Edn. Program, 1977-85, treas., 1978-79; bd. dirs. Blue Cross/Blue Shield of Mich. 1982-86, coms. 1978-86, chair hosp. contingent to participating hosp. agreement adv. com., 1989—; bd. dirs. Greater Detroit Area Health Coun., 1983-88, 93—; chmn. bd. dirs., pres. Accord Ins. Co. Ltd., 1983-88; chmn. bd. dirs. Mercy Alternative, 1986-92, 93—; chmn. bd. dirs. Venzke Svc. Co., 1983-88, pres., 1983-84; chmn., bd. dirs., pres. Venzke Ins. Co. Ltd., 1988—; bd. dirs. Mercy Info. Systems, 1986-92, Pontiac Devel. Found., 1984-86; mem. audit and fin. com. Am. Healthcare Systems, 1988-92; mem. S.E. Mich. Hosp. Coun., chmn. pub. rels. com., 1983-85, bd. dirs. Hosp. Fund 1986—; trustee Sisters of Mercy Health Corp., 1991-93, sec. bd. trustees, 1993. With U.S. Army, 1964-66. Fellow Am. Coll. Healthcare Execs. (mem. exec. com. on higher edn. 1990-93, Mich Regent's award 1992); mem. Mich. Hosp. Assn. (at-large rep. corp. bd. 1990—, exec. com. 1992—), Am. Healthcare Systems Risk Retention Group (bd. dirs. 1990-91), Pontiac Urban League (pers. com. 1979), Comprehensive Health Planning Coun. (com. mem. 1976-81). Office: Mercy Health Svcs 34605 W 12 Mile Rd Farmington MI 48331-3263

SCHWARTZ, MILTON LEWIS, federal judge; b. Oakland, Calif., Jan. 20, 1920; s. Colman and Selma (Lavenson) S.; m. Barbara Ann Moore, May 15, 1942; children: Dirk L., Tracy Ann, Damon M., Brooke. A.B., U. Calif. at Berkeley, 1941, J.D., 1948. Bar: Calif. bar 1949. Research asst. 3d Dist. Ct. Appeal, Sacramento, 1948; dep. dist. atty., 1949-51; practice in Sacramento, 1951-79; partner McDonough, Holland, Schwartz & Allen, 1953-79; U.S. dist. judge Eastern Dist. Calif., U.S. Dist. Ct., Calif., 1979—; prof. law McGeorge Coll. Law, Sacramento, 1952-55; mem. Com. Bar Examiners Calif., 1971-75. Pres. Bd. Edn. Sacramento City Sch. Dist., 1961; v.p. Calif. Bd. Edn., 1967-68; trustee Sutterville Heights Sch. Dist. Served to maj. 40th Inf. Divsn. AUS, 1942-46, PTO. Named Sacramento County Judge of Yr., 1990; Milton L. Schwartz Am. Inn of Court named in his honor, Davis, Calif. Fellow Am. Coll. Trial Lawyers; mem. State Bar Calif., Am. Bar Assn., Am. Bd. Trial Advocates, Anthony M. Kennedy Am. Inn of Ct. (pres. 1988-90, pres. emeritus 1990—). Office: US Dist Ct 1060 US Courthouse 650 Capitol Mall Sacramento CA 95814-4708

SCHWARTZ, MIRIAM CATHERINE, biology educator; b. Tarlac, Luzon, Philippines, Mar. 9, 1964; came to U.S., 1980; d. Conrado Palarca and Elena Obcena (Domingo) Estanislao; m. Jason Jay Schwartz, July 20, 1987. BS in Biology, Calif. State U., L.A., 1985; PhD, Purdue U., 1992. Rsch. asst., rsch. assoc. dept. biol. sci. Purdue U., West Lafayette, Ind., 1988-93, teaching asst., instr., 1988-93; postdoctoral fellow sch. med. divsn. Emory U., Atlanta, 1993-94; biology lectr. Spelman Coll., Atlanta, 1994—. Contbr. articles to profl. jours. Aux. vol. Emory Univ. Hosp., Atlanta, 1993—. Mem. Phi Kappa Phi, Golden Key Nat. Honor Soc. Avocations: playing piano, reading business history and political science, hiking, cooking. Office: Spelman Coll Atlanta GA 30314

SCHWARTZ, MISCHA, electrical engineering educator; b. N.Y.C., Sept. 21, 1926; s. Isaiah and Bessie (Weinstein) S.; m. Lillian Mitchnick, June 23, 1957 (div.); 1 son, David; m. Charlotte F. Berney, July 12, 1970. B.E.E., Cooper Union, 1947; M.E.E., Poly. Inst. Bklyn., 1949; Ph.D. in Applied Physics (Sperry Gyroscope grad. scholar), Harvard U., 1951. Project engr. Sperry Gyroscope Co., 1947-52; mem. faculty Poly. Inst. Bklyn., 1952-74, prof. elec. engring., 1959-74, head dept., 1961-65; prof. elec. engring. and computer sci. Columbia U., N.Y.C., 1974-88, Charles Batchelor prof. elec. engring., 1988—, dir. Ctr. for Telecommunications Research, 1985-88; part-time tchr. Adelphi Coll., 1951-52, CCNY, 1952; cons. radiation physicist Montefiore Hosp., N.Y.C., 1954-56; vis. prof. sys. sci. dept. UCLA, 1964; vis. prof. dept. elec. engring. and computer sci. Columbia U., 1973-74; vis. prof. dept. electronic and elec. engring. U. Coll., London, 1995; chmn. Commn. C, U.S. Nat. Com. Internat. Union Radio Sci., 1977-80; vis. scientist IBM Rsch., 1980, 94, NYMEX Sci. and Tech., 1986; vis. mem. tech. staff AT&T Bell Labs., 1995; cons. in field. Author: Information Transmission, Modulation and Noise, 4th edit., 1990, (with L. Shaw) Signal Processing, 1975, Computer Communication Network Design and Analysis, 1977, Telecommunications Networks, 1987, Broadband Integrated Networks, 1996; editor, contbr.: Communication Systems and Techniques, 1966. Served with AUS, 1944-46. NSF sci. faculty fellow, 1965-66; recipient Disting. Vis. award Australian-Am. Ednl. Found., 1975, Vis. Scientist award Nippon Tel. & Tel., 1981, Tchg. award Columbia U., 1984, Gano Dunn award Cooper Union, 1986, Mayor's award for excellence in tech., City of N.Y., 1995; finalist Mayor's Awards for Excellence in Sci. & Tech., City of N.Y., 1992. Fellow AAAS, IEEE (chmn. adminstrv. com. profl. group info. theory 1964-65, bd. dirs. 1978-79, bd. govs. Comm. Soc. 1973-79, v.p. 1982-83, pres. 1984-85, Edn. medal 1983, IEEE Centennial Hall of Fame 1984, Region 1 award for leadership in mgmt. Ctr. for Telecom. Rsch. 1990, Edwin Armstrong award for contbns. to telecomm. 1994); mem. NAE, AAUP (chpt. pres. 1970-72), Assn. for Computing Machinery, Sigma Xi, Tau Beta Pi, Eta Kappa Nu. Home: 66 Maple Dr Great Neck NY 11021-1928 Office: Columbia U Schapiro CEPSR Rm 806 New York NY 10027

SCHWARTZ, MURRAY LOUIS, lawyer, educator, academic administrator; b. Phila., Oct. 27, 1920; s. Harry and Isabelle (Friedman) S.; m. Audrey James, Feb. 12, 1950; children: Deborah, Jonathan, Daniel. BS, Pa. State U., 1942; LLB, U. Pa., 1949; LLD (hon.), Lewis and Clark Coll., 1977. Bar: Pa. 1950, U.S. Ct. Appeals (D.C. cir.) 1950, U.S. Supreme Ct. 1954. Chemist Standard Oil Ind., Whiting, 1942-44; law clk. Fred M. Vinson, Chief Justice U.S, 1949-51; assoc. firm Shea, Greenman, Gardner & McConnaughey, Washington, 1951-53; spl. asst. to U.S. atty. gen. Office Solicitor Gen., 1953-54; 1st dept. city solicitor City Phila., 1954-56; assoc. firm Dilworth, Paxson, Kalish & Green, Phila., 1956-58; prof. law Law Sch., UCLA, 1958-91, dean, 1969-75; David G. Price and Dallas P. Price prof. of law UCLA, 1988-89, exec. vice chancellor, 1988-91; vice chancellor academic affairs U. Calif., Santa Barbara, 1991-92, interim sr. v.p. acad. affairs, 1992-93; chmn. exec. com., bd. dirs. Social Sci. Rsch. Coun., 1981-85; bd. dirs. Mattel, Inc. Author: (with K.L. Karst and A.J. Schwartz) The Evolution of Law in the Barrios of Caracas, 1973, Law and the American Future, 1976, Lawyers and the Legal Profession, 2d edit. 1985; contbr. articles to profl. jours. Served to lt. (j.g.) USNR, 1944-46. Home: 1339 Marinette Rd Pacific Palisades CA 90272-2626

SCHWARTZ, MURRAY MERLE, federal judge; b. 1931. BS, Wharton Sch. U. Pa., 1952; LLB, U. Pa., 1955; LLM, U. Va., 1982. Part-time referee in bankruptcy Dist. of Del., 1969-74; judge U.S. Dist. Ct. Del., 1974—, chief judge, 1985-89. Author: The Exercise of Supervisory Power by the Third Circuit Court of Appeals, 1982. Mem. ABA, Del. State Bar Assn., Am. Judicature Soc. Office: US Dist Ct 844 N King St Wilmington DE 19801-3519

SCHWARTZ, NEENA BETTY, endocrinologist, educator; b. Balt., Dec. 10, 1926; d. Paul Howard and Pauline (Shulman) S. A.B., Goucher Coll., 1948, D.Sc. (hon.), 1982; M.S., Northwestern U., 1950, Ph.D., 1953. From instr. to prof. U. Ill. Coll. Medicine, Chgo., 1953-72; asst. dean for faculty U. Ill. Coll. Medicine, 1968-70; prof. physiology Northwestern U. Med. Sch., Chgo., 1973-74; Deering prof. Northwestern U., Evanston, Ill., 1974—, chmn. dept. biol. scis., 1974-78, acting dean, Coll. Arts and Scis., 1996—. Contbr. chpts. to books, articles to profl. jours. NIH research grantee, 1955—. Fellow AAAS; mem. Am. Acad. Arts Scis., Endocrine Soc. (v.p. 1970-71, mem. coun. 1979-83, pres. 1982-83, Williams award 1985), Soc. for Study of Reprodn. (dir. 1975-77, exec. v.p. 1976-77, pres. 1977-78, Carl Hartman award 1992), Am. Physio. Soc., Soc. for Neurosci., Phi Beta Kappa. Home: 1511 Lincoln St Evanston IL 60201-2338

SCHWARTZ, NORMAN L., lawyer; b. N.Y.C., Nov. 2, 1935; s. Louis and Rose (Tendlar) S.; m. Sandra Jean Coffae, Nov. 20, 1960; children: Debra, Cathy. BBA cum laude, Ohio State U., 1957, JD summa cum laude, 1960; LLM in Taxation, Georgetown U., 1968. Bar: Ohio 1960, D.C. 1968, Fla. 1991, U.S. Ct. Claims 1986, U.S. Tax Ct. 1961, U.S. Supreme Ct. 1967. Pvt. practice Columbus, Ohio, 1960-61, Dayton, Ohio, 1962-64; atty. IRS, Washington, 1964-68; ptnr. Cohen and Uretz, Washington, 1969-85, Morgan, Lewis & Bockius, Washington, 1985-88; atty. Arthur Andersen LLP, Sarasota, Fla., 1988—. Served with USAF, 1961-62; capt. Ohio Air NG 1960-64. Mem. ABA (chmn. com. on S corps. 1973-74 tax sect.). Democrat. Jewish. Avocations: reading, jogging. Home: 4761 Pine Harrier Dr Sarasota FL 34231-3360 Office: Arthur Andersen LLP 2803 Fruitville Rd Sarasota FL 34237-5323

SCHWARTZ, PERRY LESTER, information systems engineer, consultant; b. Bklyn., July 29, 1939; s. Max David and Sylvia (Weinberger) S.; m. Arlene Metz, Jan. 24, 1960; 3 children. BEE, CUNY, 1957-62; MS in Indsl. Engring. and Computer Sci., NYU, 1967. Registered profl. engr., N.J.; registered profl. planner, N.J.; cert. mediator and arbitrator, expert witness communicator. Microwave engr. Airbourne Inst. Lab., Deer Park, N.Y., 1962-63, ITT Fed. Labs., Nutley, N.J., 1963-64; program mgr. Western Electric Co., N.Y.C., 1964-69; dept. head RCA, Princeton, N.J., 1970-71; dir. engring. Warner Communications Inc., N.Y.C., 1972-74; cons. engr. Intertech Assocs., Marlboro, N.J., 1974—; adj. faculty CCNY, 1962-71, Ocean County Coll., Toms River, N.J., 1981-83, Rutgers U., New Brunswick, N.J., 1984-87; lectr. N.J. Dept. EnergyEdn., 1994, 95. Mem. Am. Cons. Engrs. Coun., Nat. Assn. Radio and Telecom. Engrs. (sr. mem., charter mem., cert. master engr. in wire and RF, Cert. of Distinction 1994-95), IEEE (sr.), Intelligent Bldgs. Inst. Found. (steering com., trustee 1982-89), Nat. Soc. Profl. Engrs., Cons. Engrs. Coun. N.J., Am. Arbitration Assn., N.Y. Acad. Sci., Zeta Beta Tau (chpt. founder 1958), K.P. Office: Intertech Assoc Pla 79 Marlboro NJ 07746

SCHWARTZ, PETER EDWARD, physician, gynecologic oncology educator; b. N.Y.C., Mar. 28, 1941; s. Bernard and Marcia (Firkser) S.; m. Arlene Harriet Eigen, Aug. 18, 1966; children: Bruce, Andrew, Kenneth. BS, Union Coll., Schenectady, N.Y., 1962; MD, Yeshiva U., N.Y.C., 1966; MA (hon.), Yale U., 1985. Diplomate Am. Bd. Ob-Gyn., Am. Bd. Gynecol. Oncology. Surg. intern U. Ky. Med. Ctr., Lexington, 1966-67; resident in ob-gyn. Yale-New Haven Hosp., 1967-71; fellow in gynecol. oncology U. Tex. M.D. Anderson Hosp., Houston, 1973-75; asst. prof. Yale U. Sch. Medicine, New Haven, 1975-80, assoc. prof., 1980-85, prof., 1985—, now vice chmn. dept. ob-gyn., 1992—. Maj. USAF, 1971-73. John Slade Ely Prof. of obstetrics and gynecology at Yale U. (hon. chair). Office: Yale U Sch Medicine Dept Ob-Gyn 333 Cedar St New Haven CT 06510-3206

SCHWARTZ, RENEE GERSTLER, lawyer; b. Bklyn., June 18, 1933; d. Samuel and Lillian (Neulander) Gerstler; m. Alfred L. Schwartz, July 30, 1955; children—Carolyn Susan, Deborah Jane. A.B., Bklyn, Coll., 1953; LL.B., Columbia U., 1955. Bar: N.Y. 1956, U.S. Dist. Ct. (so. and ea. dists.) N.Y. 1956, U.S. Ct. Appeals (2d cir.) 1956, U.S. Dist. Ct. D.C. 1983, U.S. Supreme Ct. 1986. Ptnr., Botein, Hays & Sklar, N.Y.C., 1955-89, Kronish,

Lieb, Weiner & Hellman, N.Y.C., 1990—. Bd. dirs. New Land Found., N.Y.C., 1965—. Mem. Bar Assn. City N.Y. Home: 115 Central Park W New York NY 10023-4153 Office: Kronish Lieb Weiner & Hellman 1114 Avenue Of The Americas New York NY 10036-7703

SCHWARTZ, RICHARD BRENTON, English language educator, university dean, writer; b. Cin., Oct. 5, 1941; s. Jack Jay and Marie Mildred (Schnelle) S.; m. Judith Mary Alexis Lang, Sept. 7, 1963; 1 son, Jonathan Francis. AB cum laude, U. Notre Dame, 1963; AM, U. Ill., 1964, PhD, 1967. Instr. English U.S. Mil. Acad., 1967-69; asst. prof. U. Wis.-Madison, 1969-72, assoc. prof., 1972-78, prof., 1978-81; assoc. dean U. Wis.-Madison (Grad. Sch.), 1977, 79-81; prof. English, dean Grad. Sch., Georgetown U., Washington, 1981—, interim exec. v.p. for main campus academic affairs, 1991-92; interim exec. v.p. for the main campus Georgetown U., Washington, 1995-96; mem. exec. bd. Ctr. Strategic and Internat. Studies, 1981-87. Author: Samuel Johnson and the New Science, 1971 (runner-up Gustave O. Arlt prize), Samuel Johnson and the Problem of Evil, 1975, Boswell's Johnson: A Preface to the Life, 1978, Daily Life in Johnson's London, 1983, Japanese edit., 1990, (novel) Frozen Stare, 1989; editor: The Plays of Arthur Murphy, 4 vols., 1979, Theory and Tradition in Eighteenth-Century Studies, 1990; contbr. articles to profl. jours. Served to capt. U.S. Army, 1967-69. Nat. Endowment Humanities grantee, 1970, 87; Inst. for Research in Humanities fellow, 1976; Am. Council Learned Socs. fellow, 1978-79; H.I. Romnes fellow, 1978-81. Mem. Mystery Writers Am., Johnson Soc. So. Calif., Am. Soc. Eighteenth-Century Studies, Coun. Grad. Schs., N.E. Assn. Grad. Schs. (exec. com. 1986-88), Assn. Grad. Schs. in Cath. Univs. (exec. com. 1984-87), Assn. Literary Scholars and Critics, N. Am. Conf. Brit. Studies, George Town Club, Alpha Sigma Nu, Alpha Sigma Lambda. Roman Catholic. Home: 4132 41st St N Arlington VA 22207-4802 Office: Georgetown Univ Grad Sch Dept of English Washington DC 20057

SCHWARTZ, RICHARD DERECKTOR, sociologist, educator; b. Newark, Apr. 26, 1925; s. Selig and Tillie (Derecktor) S.; m. Emilie Zane Rosenbaum, June 30, 1946; children: David, Margaret Jane, Deborah. B.A., Yale U., 1947, Ph.D. in Sociology, 1952; LL.D. (hon.), Am. Internat. Coll., 1977. Research fellow Inst. Human Relations, Yale, 1951-54, instr., asst. prof. sociology and law, 1953-61; faculty Northwestern U., Evanston, 1961-71; prof. sociology Northwestern U., 1964-71, prof. sociology and law, 1966-71; dir. Council Intersocietal Studies, 1965-70, co-dir. law and social sci. program, 1967-70; dean, provost Faculty of Law and Jurisprudence, State U. N.Y. at Buffalo, 1971-76; Ernest I. White rsch. prof. law Syracuse U., 1977—; rsch. cons. Nat. Coun. Juvenile Ct. Judges, 1961-68; lecture tour for U.S. Embassy, India, 1968; adviser U.S. Dept. Justice, 1977-80; cons. U.S. Dept. Transp., 1968-69, Nat. Conf. Commrs. on Uniform State Laws, 1968-70, ABA, 1979-83; mem. com. law enforcement and adminstrn. of justice NAS, 1975-85; fellowship referee Russell Sage Found., 1970-77, NEH, 1972-77, NSF, 1978-81; mem. bd. edn., Orange, Conn., 1954-61; mem. exec. com. Am. Friends Svc. Com., Middle Atlantic Region, 1987-92; chmn. Am. Coalition for Middle East Dialogue, 1990-93. Author: (with others) Society and the Legal Order, 1970, Criminal Law, 1974, Nonreactive Measures in the Social Sciences, 1980, Handbook of Regulation and Administrative Law, 1994; founding editor: Law and Soc. Rev., 1966-69. Served with USNR, 1943-45. Ctr. for Advanced Study in Behavioral Scis. fellow, 1989-90. Fellow AAAS; mem. ABA (nonprofl. legal edn. com. 1986-89), Am. Sociol. Assn., Law and Soc. Assn. (pres. 1972-75). Jewish. Home: 15 Clarmar Rd Fayetteville NY 13066-1603 Office: Syracuse U Coll Law Syracuse NY 13244-1030 *I believe that we could create a better way of life if we structured society to encourage-rather than to penalize-altruism. Although I have not yet contributed much toward achieving such a society, the effort to do so has been satisfying.*

SCHWARTZ, RICHARD FREDERICK, electrical engineering educator; b. Albany, N.Y., May 31, 1922; s. Frederick William and Mary Hoyle (Holland) S.; m. Ruth Louise Feldman, Oct. 25, 1945 (div. Oct. 1977); children: Kathryn Gail, Frederick Earl, Karl Edward, Eric Christian, Frieda Diane; m. Margaret Camp Boes, May 29, 1982. BEE, Rensselaer Poly. Inst., Troy, N.Y., 1943, MEE, 1948; PhD, U. Pa., 1959. Registered profl. engr., Pa., Mich. Instr. Rensselaer Poly. Inst., Troy, 1947-48; engr. Radio Corp. Am., Camden, N.J., 1948-51; instr. U. Pa., Phila., 1951-53, rsch. assoc., 1953-59, asst. prof. electrical engring., 1959-62, assoc. prof. electrical engring., 1962-73; prof. elec. engring. Mich. Tech. U., Houghton, 1973-85; prof. elec. engring. SUNY, Binghamton, 1985-95, prof. emeritus, 1995—; vis. asst. prof. U. Mich., Ann Arbor, 1960; cons. Pa. Bar Assn. Endowment, Armstrong Cork Co., Am. Electronics Labs., Inc., IBM, RCA, City of Phila., GE. Co-author: The Eavesdroppers, 1959. Active Delaware County Symphony, Pa., 1967-72, Keeweehaw Symphony Orch., Houghton, 1973-85, Endicott Tech. Ctr., 1995—. With U.S. Army, 1942-46. Mem. IEEE (sr., life), AAAS, NSPE, Am. Soc. Engring. Edn., N.Y. Soc. Profl. Engrs. (Engr. of Yr. 1995, edn. award 1996), Acoustical Soc. Am., Audio Engring. Soc., Catgut Acoustical Soc., Order of the Engr., Sigma Xi, Eta Kappa Nu, Tau Beta Tau. Democrat. Unitarian. Achievements include patents for tuning sys., 1954, oscillator frequency control, 1954, transistor amplifier with high undistorted output, 1954. Home: 2624 Bornt Hill Rd Endicott NY 13760 Office: SUNY Dept Electrical Engring PO Box 6000 Binghamton NY 13902-6000

SCHWARTZ, RICHARD JOHN, electrical engineering educator, researcher; b. Waukesha, Wis., Aug. 12, 1935; s. Sylvester John and LaVerne Mary (Lepien) S.; m. Mary Jo Collins, June 29, 1957; children: Richard, Stephan, Susan, Elizabeth, Barbara, Peter, Christopher, Margarett. BSEE, U. Wis., 1957; SM, MIT, 1959, ScD, 1962. Mem. tech. staff Sarnoff Rsch. Labs. RCA, Princeton, N.J., 1957-58; instr. MIT, Cambridge, 1961-62; v.p. Energy Conversions, Inc., Cambridge, 1962-64; assoc. prof. Purdue U., West Lafayette, Ind., 1964-71, prof., 1972—, head dept., 1985-95, dean engring., 1995—, dir. Optoelectronic Ctr., 1986-89; bd. dir. Nat. Elec. Engring. Dept. Heads Assn.; solar cells cons., 1965—. Contbr. chpts. to books, articles to profl. jours. Served to 2nd lt. U.S. Army, 1957-58. Recipient Disting. Svc. medal U. Wis., 1989, Centennial medal, 1991. Fellow IEEE. Achievements include development of high intensity solar cells, of surface charge transfer device, and of numerical models for solar cells. Office: Purdue U 1285 Elec Engring Elec Engring Rsch Lab West Lafayette IN 47907

SCHWARTZ, ROBERT, automotive manufacturing company executive, marketing executive; b. Atlantic City, N.J., Mar. 9, 1939; s. Robert A. and Irene (Davis) S.; m. Judith H. Amole, Apr. 30, 1961. B.S., Drexel U., 1961; M.B.A., Wash. State U., 1962. With Ford Motor Co., 1964-70; dist. mgr. Simplicity Mfg., Port Washington, Wis., 1970-71; zone mgr. Am. Motors Corp., Boston, 1971-72, N.Y.C., 1972-74; dir. sales ops. Am. Motors Corp., Detroit, 1975; regional mgr. Am. Motors Corp., 1975-76; gen. mgr. Am. Motors Corp. (U.S. sales), 1976-80; mng. dir. Am. Motors Corp. (N.Am. sales and distbn.), 1981-83; pres. Am. Motors Sales Corp., Detroit, 1978-81, v.p. N.Am. sales, 1981-83; v.p. sales and mktg. Rolls-Royce Motors Inc., Lyndhurst, N.J., 1983-85, pres., chief exec. officer, 1986-89; pres. Motors Mgmt., Neptune, N.J., 1989-93; pres., CEO Automotive Ventures, Inc., Wayne, N.J., 1993—. Mem. Metropolitan Club (N.Y.C.).

SCHWARTZ, ROBERT GEORGE, retired insurance company executive; b. Czechoslovakia, Mar. 27, 1928; came to U.S., 1929, naturalized, 1935; s. George and Frances (Antoni) S.; m. Caroline Bachurski, Oct. 12, 1952; children: Joanne, Tracy, Robert G. BA, Pa. State U., 1949; MBA, NYU, 1956. With Met. Life Ins. Co., N.Y.C., 1949-93, v.p. securities, 1962-70, v.p., 1970-75, sr. v.p., 1975-78, exec. v.p., 1979-80, vice chmn. bd., 1980-83, chmn. investment com., 1980-93, chmn. bd., 1983-93, chmn. bd., pres., chief exec. officer, 1989-93; bd. dirs. Met. Life Ins. Co., Potlatch Corp., San Francisco, Lowe's Cos., Inc., North Wilkesboro, N.C., COMSAT Corp., Bethesda, Md., Mobil Corp., Fairfax, Va., Reader's Digest Assn., Inc., Consol. Edison Co. of N.Y., CS First Boston, Inc., Lone Star Industries, Inc., Stamford, Conn., Ascent Entertainment Group, Inc., Denver, Horatio Alger Assn. Trustee Com. for Econ. Devel.; bd. visitors Smeal Coll., Pa. State U., mem. nat. devel. coun. With AUS, 1950-52. Mem. Bus. Coun., Sky Club, Blind Brook Country Club, Alpha Chi Rho. Office: MetLife Bldg 200 Park Ave Ste 5700 New York NY 10166-0005

SCHWARTZ, ROBERT M., lawyer; b. Phila., Aug. 6, 1940; s. Nathan and Miriam (Albus) S.; m. Karen Leaf, Feb. 11, 1966; children: Eric, Lauren. BS, Pa. State U., 1962; JD, Villanova U., 1965. Bar: Pa. 1965, U.S. Ct. Appeals (3rd cir.) 1965. Law clk. to presiding justice Common Pleas Ct. Montgomery County, Norristown, Pa., 1965; v.p., assoc. counsel Commonwealth Land Title Ins. Co., Phila., 1969-73; ptnr. in charge real estate group and bus. dept. White and Williams, Phila., 1973—. Speaker numerous lectures and seminars in field. Mem. regional civil rights com. and regional bd. trustees Anti-Defamation League. Capt. JAGC, U.S. Army, 1966-69. Mem. Phila. Bar Assn. (chmn. real property com. 1981, exec. bd. real property sect. 1983-89, 91, chmn. real property sect. 1986), Am. Coll. Real Estate Lawyers (best lawyers in Am. award 1989—), Am. Land Title Assn. (leader's counsel group 1993—, Order of Coif. Republican. Jewish. Avocations: bridge, tennis. Office: White and Williams 1650 Market St Philadelphia PA 19103-7301

SCHWARTZ, ROBERT S., lawyer; b. Bklyn., Jan. 7, 1949. BA cum laude, Cornell U., 1971; JD cum laude, U. Pa., 1974. Bar: Pa. 1974, D.C. 1979. Law clerk to sr. judge U.S. Dist. Ct. dist. Del., 1974-75; trial atty. intellectual property sect. antitrust divsn. U.S. Dept. Justice, 1975-79; ptnr. McDermott, Will & Emery, Washington. Mem. ABA, D.C. Bar. Office: McDermott Will & Emery 1850 K St NW Washington DC 20006-2213*

SCHWARTZ, ROBERT TERRY, professional association executive; b. Irvington, N.J., Sept. 29, 1950; s. Edward Herman and Harriet Selma (Rosenstein) S.; m. Carol Fawn Mullenix, July 27, 1975; children: Zachary Jacob, Allison Lizabeth. BFA, Kansas City Art Inst., 1973; M of Indsl. Design, R.I. Sch. Design, 1975. Red Cross project dir. R.I. Sch. Design, Providence, 1975-76; head indsl. design/architecture ARC Nat. Hdqrs., Washington, 1976-88; dir. sci. and tech. Health Industry Mfrs. Assn., Washington, 1988-90; exec. dir., COO Worldesign Found., Great Falls, Va., 1990—, Indsl. Designers Soc. Am., Great Falls, 1990—; provider expert testimony before Congress, 1994, commencement address, Kansas City Art Inst., 1995. Contbr. chpts. to books, articles to profl. jours.; presenter in field; holder 5 patents, 1 trademark. Recipient Project of Merit award Indsl. Design Mag., 1985, Cert. of Achievement, ARC, 1988, Louis B. Tiffany award ARC, 1987, numerous others; Nat. Endowment for the Arts grantee, 1984, 92, 94; EPA grantee, 1992. Mem. Am. Soc. Assn. Execs., Greater Washington Soc. Assn. Execs., Am. Design Coun. (ofcl. rep.). Avocations: Edison antiquities collecting, sailing. Office: Indsl Designers Soc Am 1142 Walker Rd Great Falls VA 22066-1836

SCHWARTZ, ROSELIND SHIRLEY GRANT, podiatrist; b. N.Y.C., Apr. 23, 1922; d. Joseph and Amy (Jacobs) Grant; m. Herman Schwartz, Dec. 19, 1943 (dec. Sept., 1980); children: Arthur Zachary, Raymond Dana. BA, NYU, 1943; D Podiatry cum laude, L.I. U., 1947, DPM, 1970; postgrad., L.A. Trade Tech. Coll., 1973-75. Notary pub., Calif. Pvt. practice Podiatry N.Y.C., 1947-73; cons. L.A., 1973-76, travel cons., 1974—; owner, mgr. Ros Travel, N.Y.C., 1995—. Bd. dirs. Welfare League for Retarded Children, 1955-73, chmn. Annual Souvenir Jour., 1955-65, Annual Luncheon, 25th anniversary, 1968, pres., 1969-70; pres. Sisterhood of Community Ctr. of Israel, N.Y., 1966-67; Cub den mother Boy Scouts Am., N.Y., 1960-63; class mother Pub. Schs., N.Y., 1960-66, pres. Parents' Assn. Jr. High Sch., N.Y., 1966-69; bd. dirs., pres. Barrington-Terryhill Condominium Assn., 1981—; vol. UCLA, 1981—; mem. Adv. Coms., Nurse Anesthesists, Infant & Child Care, 1981—. Recipient testimonial Community Ctr. Israel, Bronx, N.Y., 1971, award for devoted leadership Welfare League, 1963, 65. Mem. ARC, IATA, Assn. Wives of Physicians, Podiatry Soc. N.Y. State, Bus. and Profl. Women. Avocations: collecting stamps and coins, travel. Home and Office: Ros Travel 269 W 11th St Ste 3C New York NY 10014-2493

SCHWARTZ, ROY RICHARD, holding company executive; b. N.Y.C., Mar. 27, 1943; s. Julius and Mildred (Friedman) S.; m. Sharon Massler, June 3, 1965; children: Lisa Beth, Meridith Sara, Greg Mathew. AB, Washington Coll., Chestertown, Md., 1964; JD, Columbia U., 1967. Asst. counsel N.Y.C., 1967-68; assoc. Blumberg, Singer, N.Y.C., 1968-72, Kelly, Drye, N.Y.C., 1969-72; U.S. counsel U.S. Imasco Ltd., N.J., 1972-74; sr. U.S. counsel Imasco Ltd., N.J., 1974-78; pres. Imasco Holdings, N.J., 1978-82; v.p. Imasco Resources, Montreal, 1983; v.p. corp. devel. Imasco Ltd., Montreal, 1984-89, sr. v.p., 1989—; bd. dirs. Ulster Petroleums Ltd. Mem. Montreal Bd. of Trade, Univ. Club. Office: Imasco Ltd, 600 de Maisonneuve Blvd W, Montreal, PQ Canada H3A 3K7

SCHWARTZ, SAMUEL, business consultant, retired chemical company executive; b. Moose Jaw, Sask., Can., Nov. 12, 1927; came to U.S., 1951, naturalized, 1965; s. Benjamin and Rose (Becker) S.; m. Margaret Patterson, Feb. 20, 1956; children: Michael R., Thomas R., David C., Janet C. BA, U. Sask., 1948, B in Commerce, 1950; MBA, Harvard U., 1953. Research assoc. Harvard Bus. Sch., Boston, 1953-57; with Conoco Inc., 1957-83; sr. v.p. coordinating and planning Conoco Inc., Stamford, Conn., 1974-75; sr. v.p. corp. planning Conoco Inc., 1975-78, sr. v.p. adminstrv., 1978-80, group sr. v.p. adminstrv., 1980-83; sr. v.p. adminstrv. E.I. duPont de Nemours & Co., Wilmington, Del., 1983-87, sr. v.p., corp. plans dept., 1987-88; dir. Conoco Inc. Consol. Coal Co., 1981-88. Trustee Inst. for the Future, Menlo Park, Calif., 1975-92, Henry du Pont Winterthur Mus., Winterthur, Del., trustee, 1984—, chmn., 1994—.

SCHWARTZ, SEYMOUR IRA, surgeon, educator; b. N.Y.C., Jan. 22, 1928; s. Samuel and Martha (Paul) S.; m. Ruth Elaine Wainer, June 18, 1949; children: Richard, Kenneth, David. BA, U. Wis., 1947; MD, NYU, 1950; PhD (hon.), U. Lund, Sweden, 1989; FRCS (hon.), y. Intern Strong Meml. Hosp., Rochester, N.Y., 1950-51, resident, 1951-52, 54-57; asst. prof. surgery U. Rochester, N.Y., 1959-63, assoc. prof, 1963-67, prof., 1967—, chmn. dept., 1987—, dir. surg. rsch., 1962-82; nat. cons. USAF, 1968-77; mem. surgery study sect. A, NIH, 1974-78. Co-author: Mapping of America, 1980, Surgical Reflections, 1991, Mapping of the French and Indian War, 1994; co-editor: Maingot's Abdominal Operations, 2 edits.; editor-in-chief: Year Book of Surgery, 6 edits., 1969—. Bd. mgrs. Strong Meml. Hosp., Rochester. Lt. (j.g.) USN, 1952-54. Recipient Sesquicentennial medal U. S.C., 1974, Acrel medal Swedish Surg. Assn., 1974, Yandell medal U. Louisville (Ky.), 1978, Roswell Park medal, 1989, Albert Kaiser medal, 1992; John and Mary R. Markle scholar in acad. medicine, 1960. Fellow ACS (regent 1988, chmn. bd. regents 1994—, programs and ethics com. 1989—, Disting. Svc. award 1986), Royal Coll. Surgeons Edinburgh (hon.), Ctrl. Surg. Soc. (pres. 1981-82), So. Surg. Soc., Soc. Univ. Surgeons, Soc. Clin. Surgery (pres. 1985), Am. Surg. Assn. (pres. 1993-94), Am. Antiquarian Soc., Grolier Club (N.Y.C.), Cosmos Club (Washington), Genesee Valley Club, Phi Beta Kappa, Alpha Omega Alpha. Avocation: collecting antique maps. Office: U Rochester Med Ctr 601 Elmwood Ave Rochester NY 14642-0001

SCHWARTZ, SHARON GELTNER, communications executive; b. Lakeland, Fla., Dec. 10, 1958; d. Bernard Benjamin and Gail (Bergad) G.; m. Eric Michael Schwartz, Dec. 30, 1995. AA, Wm. Rainey Harper Coll., 1978; BJ, U. Ill., 1980. Editor White House Weekly Feistritzer Publs., Washington, 1980, Instl. Investor, Washington, 1981-83; freelance writer Alexandria, Va., 1984-90; feature writer, investigative reporter, fgn. corr. Knight Ridder Newspapers, Boca Raton, Fla., 1990-92; book editor Weiss Rsch., Palm Beach Gardens, Fla., 1994-95; comm. mgr. Achievers Unltd., West Palm Beach, Fla., 1995—; writer, researcher The Naisbitt Group, Washington, 1985-86; legal researcher David James Ltd., Bethesda, Md., 1986-87; invited panelist The Poynter Inst. Media Studies, 1992. Author: (with others) Weekends Away from Washington, D.C., 1989, Fodor's Wall Street Journal Guide to Business Travel, 1991; contbr. articles to Quill, Washington Journalism Rev., Media Bus. Quar., Am. Writer. Participant Women's March on Washington, 1986; fundraiser United Jewish Appeal, Washington, 1986-88.; rep. D.C. writers in Bangkok Royal Thai Embassy, Washington, 1986, Palm Beach County, Fla., Yellow Feathers gridiron, 1990-91. Recipient Nat. Headliner award for outstanding news reporting Press Club of Atlantic City, 1993. Mem. NOW, Washington Ind. Writers (Michael Halberstam award 1983), House and Senate Periodical Corrs., Amnesty Internat., Fla. Press Assn., Nat. Writers Union (del. nat. conv. 1994), Regional Reporters Assn., Nat. Women's Art Mus. (charter), U. Ill. Alumni Assn. Investigative Reporters and Editors. Home: 1441 Brandywine Rd Apt 500 I West Palm Beach FL 33409-2049 Office: Achievers Unltd West Tower 9th Fl 777 S Flagler Dr West Palm Beach FL 33401

SCHWARTZ, SHIRLEY E., chemist; b. Detroit, Aug. 26, 1935; d. Emil Victor and Jessie Grace (Galbraith) Eckwall; m. Ronald Elmer Schwartz, Aug. 25, 1957; children: Steven Dennis, Bradley Allen, George Byron. BS, U. Mich., 1957, Detroit Inst. Tech., 1978; MS, Wayne State U., 1962, PhD, 1970. Asst. prof. Detroit Inst. Tech., 1973-78, head divsn. math. sci., 1976-78; mem. rsch. staff BASF Wyandotte (Mich.) Corp., 1978-81, head sect. functional fluids, 1981; sr. staff rsch. scientist GM, Warren, Mich., 1981—. Contbr. articles to profl. jours.; patentee in field. Recipient Gold award Engring. Soc. Detroit, 1989. Fellow Soc. Tribologists and Lubrication Engrs. (treas. Detroit sect. 1981, vice chmn. 1982, chmn. 1982-83, chmn. wear tech. com. 1987-88, bd. dirs. 1985-91, assoc. editor 1989-90, contbg. editor 1989—, Wilbur Deutsch award 1987, P.M. Ku award 1994); mem. Am. Chem. Soc., Soc. In Vitro Biology, Soc. Automotive Engrs. (Excellence in Oral Presentation award 1986, 91, 94, Arch T. Colwell Merit award 1991, Lloyd L. Withrow Disting. Spkr. award 1995), Mensa, Classic Guitar Soc. Mich., U.S. Power Squadrons, Detroit Navigators, Sigma Xi. Lutheran. Office: GM NAO Rsch & Devel Ctr 30500 Mound Rd Warren MI 48092-2031 *I've spent a number of very pleasant hours trying to make water behave like oil and alcohol behave like gasoline—a quest not much different from that of the ancient alchemists, who also spent their time trying to convert one substance to another.*

SCHWARTZ, STEPHEN BLAIR, retired information industry executive; b. Chgo., Oct. 19, 1934; s. Herbert S. and Gertrude (Weinstein) S.; m. Nancy Jean Astrof, Dec. 18, 1955; children: Debra Lee Schwartz Zaret, Susan Beth Schwartz Derene. B.S. in Indsl. Engring., Northwestern U., 1957. With IBM Corp., 1957-92; various mgmt. positions, dir. product programs Harrison, N.Y., to 1977, v.p. Systems Communications div., 1977-81; v.p. Armonk, N.Y., 1982-90; v.p. Am. Far East Corp. subs. IBM Corp. Tokyo, 1982-84; pres., CEO Satellite Bus. Systems, McLean, Va., 1984; v.p., asst. group exec. Telecommunications, 1985-86, v.p., pres. Systems Products Div., 1986-88, v.p., gen. mgr. Application Bus. Systems, 1988-90; sr. v.p. market driven quality Stamford, Conn., 1990-92; bd. dirs. Niagara Mohawk Power Corp., MFRI, Inc. Mem. PGA Nat. Golf Club (Palm Beach Gardens, Fla.). Republican. Jewish.

SCHWARTZ, STEPHEN JAY, lawyer; b. Portland, Maine, Sept. 6, 1960; s. Jack Leonard and Sara Belle (Modes) S.; m. Susan Greenspun, Oct. 25, 1987; children: Leonard Samuel, Andrew Joseph. BA with distinction, U. Maine, 1982; JD, Santa Clara U., 1985. Bar: Maine 1985, U.S. Dist. Ct. Maine 1985. Asst. dist. atty. Prosecutorial Dist. No. 1 York County, Alfred, Maine, 1986-87; ptnr. Schwartz & Schwartz, P.A., Portland, Maine, 1987—; mem. criminal rules adv. com. Maine Supreme Jud. Ct., 1991—. Comments editor Santa Clara Law Rev., 1985; editor Maine Defender, 1992—; mem. editl. adv. com. Maine Bar Jour., 1990—. Pres. Jewish Fedn. and Cmty. of So. Maine, Portland, 1994-96. Recipient Richard D. Aronson Young Leadership award Jewish Fedn. and Cmty. of So. Maine, 1994. Mem. ABA, ATLA, Maine State Bar Assn. (chmn. criminal law sect. 1991-92), Cumberland Bar Assn., Maine Trial Lawyers Assn., Nat. Assn. Criminal Def. Lawyers, Maine Assn. Criminal Def. Lawyers (founder, 1st pres. 1992-93), Pi Sigma Alpha, Sigma Phi Epsilon. Office: Schwartz & Schwartz PA 482 Congress St PO Box 15337 Portland ME 04112-5337

SCHWARTZ, STEPHEN LAWRENCE, composer, lyricist; b. N.Y.C., Mar. 6, 1948; s. Stanley Leonard and Sheila Lorna (Siegel) S.; m. Carole Ann Piasecki, June 6, 1969; children—Scott Lawrence, Jessica Lauren. Student, Juilliard Sch. Music, 1960-64; B.F.A., Carnegie-Mellon U., 1968. Works include: title song for film Butterflies Are Free, 1969; (theatre) music and new lyrics Godspell, 1971, four songs, adaptation and direction Working, 1978, music for 3 songs Personals, 1985, (with Leonard Bernstein) English texts for Leonard Bernstein's Mass, 1971, music and lyrics Pippin, 1972, The Magic Show, 1974, The Baker's Wife, 1976, Children of Eden, 1991; (films) lyrics Rags, 1986, Life with Mikey, 1993, Pocahontas, 1995 (Acad. award nominee for best original score 1996, Acad. award for best original song 1996), The Hunchback of Notre Dame, 1996; (juvenile) The Perfect Peach, 1977, The Trip, 1983. Recipient Drama Desk awards, 1971, 78, Grammy awards, 1971. Mem. ASCAP, Nat. Acad. Rec. Arts and Scis. Address: 33 Red Oak Ln Ridgefield CT 06877

SCHWARTZ, STEVEN JAY, food science educator; b. Bklyn., Dec. 30, 1953; s. Maurice and Helen (Granitz) S.; m. Elizabeth Strahlman, Aug. 19; children: Brian David, Eric Brandon. BS in Organic Chemistry, SUNY, Stony Brook, 1976; MS in Food Chemistry, U. Wis., 1979, PhD in Environ. Toxicology and Food Sci., 1982. Rsch. and undergrad. teaching asst. SUNY, Stony Brook, 1975-76, lectr. dept. chemistry, 1976-77; teaching asst. U. Wis., Madison, 1977, rsch. asst. dept. food sci. and environ. toxicology, 1978-82; asst. prof. dept. food sci. N.C. State U., Raleigh, 1983-88, assoc. prof. dept. food sci., 1988-93, asst. dir. Ctr. Aseptic Processing and Packaging Studies, 1990-93, prof. dept. food sci., 1993-95; site dir. NSF Ctr. Aseptic Processing and Packaging Studies, Raleigh, 1993—; Karl Haas endowed chair in food industries dept. food sci. and tech. Ohio State U.; vis. scholar Bogor Agrl. U., Indonesia, 1991; lectr. in field. Mem. editorial bd., assoc. editor Jour. Food Quality, 1990—; contbr. numerous articles, abstracts to profl. jours. Recipient award Audits Internat. Tech. Writing Competition, Spring, 1990, Best Paper award Triangle Chromatography Symposium, 1993. Mem. Am. Chem. Soc., Am. Assn. Cereal Chemists, Inst. Food Technologists (grad. fellow, chmn. symposia com. 1993-94, program com. 1986-93, vice chmn., chmn. and past chmn. 1990-93, expert panel Food Safety and Nutrition 1987-90, Food Sci. Writing Award jury 1990), Inst. Nutrition, Fedn. of Am. Soc. Exptl. Biologists, Am. Inst. Nutrition, Phi Beta Kappa, Phi Tau Sigma, Sigma Xi (Outstanding Young Investigator Rsch. award 1989-90). Office: Ohio State U 122 Vivian Hall 2121 Fyffe Rd Columbus OH 43210

SCHWARTZ, THEODORE B., physician, educator; b. Phila., Feb. 14, 1918; s. William F. and Fanny (Farkas) S.; m. Genevieve Etta Bangs, Jan. 9, 1948; children: Richard, Steven, Michael, David, Jonathan, Thomas. B.S., Franklin and Marshall Coll., 1939; M.D., Johns Hopkins U., 1943. Diplomate Am. Bd. Internal Medicine (bd. govs., 1970-78, sec.-treas., 1976-78). Intern Osler Clinic, Johns Hopkins Hosp., 1943-44; asst. resident medicine Salt Lake City Gen. Hosp., 1946-47, resident medicine, 1947-48; fellow medicine Duke U. Med. Sch., 1948-50, assoc. medicine, asst. prof. medicine, 1950-55; dir. sect. endocrinology and metabolism Rush-Presbyn.-St. Luke's Med. Center, Chgo., 1955-82; attending physician Rush-Presbyn.-St. Luke's Med. Center, 1960—; chmn. dept. medicine Rush-Presbyn.-St. Lukes's Med. Center, 1970-82; cons. endocrinology Hines (Ill.) VA Hosp., 1956-71, Great Lakes Naval Hosp., 1960-74; prof. medicine U. Ill. Coll. Medicine, 1960-71; prof., chmn. dept. medicine Rush Med. Coll., 1971-82; prof. medicine U. Wash., Seattle, 1982-96; chief med. services VA Med. Ctr., Boise, 1982-86; mem. Am. Bd. Med. Spltys., 1972-79. Editor: Yearbook of Endocrinology, 1964-86, endocrinology article Ency. Brit., 1985—; contbr. articles to profl. jours. Bd. dirs. Boise Art Mus., 1984-92. Served with M.C. AUS, 1944-46. Decorated Bronze Star. Fellow ACP (publs. com. 1973-78, chmn. subcom. on aging 1982-85, mem. health and pub. policy com.), Am. Assn. Clin. Endocrinology (hon.), Am. Coll. Endocrinology (hon.); mem. Assn. Program Dirs. Internal Medicine (councilor 1978-80), Am. Fedn. Clin. Rsch., Am. Diabetes Assn., Diabetes Assn. Greater Chgo. (bd. dirs.), Am. Soc. Clin. Investigation, Am. Clin. and Climatol. Assn., Am. Thyroid Assn., Endocrine Soc., Ctrl. Clin. Rsch. Club, Ctrl. Soc. Clin. Rsch., Chgo. Soc. Internal Medicine (pres. 1966-67), Phi Beta Kappa, Alpha Omega Alpha. Address: 200 Lee St Evanston IL 60202

SCHWARTZ, VALERIE BREUER, interior designer; b. Senica, Czechoslovakia, May 13, 1912; came to U.S., 1928, naturalized, 1928; d. Jacob and Ethel (Weiss) Breuer; m. Leo Schwartz, Feb. 5, 1939; children—Catherine, Robert, William. Student State Real Gymnazium, Prague, 1925-28; Parsons N.Y. Sch. of Fine and Applied Arts, 1930-32. Cert. Am. Soc. Interior Designers. Self-employed interior designer, N.J., 1932—. Contbr. to various mags. including N.Y. Times, House & Garden, Cue Mag., Confort, Argentina; guest radio talk shows. Mem. Hadassah (life). Designed Holocaust Room, Kean Coll., N.J.

SCHWARTZ, VICTOR ELLIOT, lawyer; b. N.Y.C., July 3, 1940. AB summa cum laude, Boston U., 1962; JD magna cum laude, Columbia U., 1965. Bar: N.Y. 1965, Ohio 1974. Law clk. to judge So. Dist. N.Y., 1965-67; from asst. to assoc. prof. law U. Cin., 1967-72, prof., 1972-79, acting dean, 1973-74; vis. prof. U. Va. Law Sch., 1970-71; adj. prof. law U. Cin., 1985—; ptnr. firm Crowell & Moring, Washington; sr. ptnr. firm Fed. Interagy. task Force on Products Liability, 1976; bd. dirs. Am. Tort Reform

Assn.; chmn. Civil Justice Task Force, Am. Legis. Exch. Coun.; adj. prof. law Georgetown U., 1987—; chmn. Dept. of Commerce Task Force on Product Liability and Accident Compensation, 1977-80. Author: Comparative Negligence, 1974, 3d edit., 1994; (with Prosser and Wade) Cases and Materials on Torts, 1976, 9th edit., 1994, How to Prepare for the Multi-State Bar Examination, 1977, Products Liability: Cases and Trends, 1987, Products Liability: Asset Trends, 1988, (with Lee and Kelly) Multistate Legislation, 1985; editor: Columbia Law Rev., 1965; prin. draftsman: Model Uniform Product Liability Act. Recipient Sec. of Commerce award for disting. svc.; named One of 100 Most Influential Attys. in U.S., Nat. Law 3, 1994. Mem. Am. Bar Assn. (chmn. products liability com. 1979, uniform laws com. 1981, torts and ins. practice sect.), Am. Law Inst. (adv. com. Restatement Third of Torts), Phi Beta Kappa. Office: Crowell & Moring 1001 Pennsylvania Ave NW Washington DC 20004-2505 *The greatest joys in life are found in one's relationships, be it business, romance or friendship, with other people.*

SCHWARTZ, WILLIAM, lawyer, educator; b. Providence, May 6, 1933; s. Morris Victor and Martha (Glassman) S.; m. Bernice Konigsberg, Jan. 13, 1957; children: Alan Gershon, Robin Libby. A.A., Boston U., 1952, J.D. magna cum laude, 1955, M.A., 1960; postgrad., Harvard Law Sch., 1955-56. Bar: D.C. 1956, Mass. 1962, N.Y. 1989. Prof. law Boston U., 1955-91, Fletcher prof. law, 1968-70, Roscoe Pound prof. law, 1970-73, dean Sch. of Law, 1980-88, dir. Ctr. for Estate Planning, 1988-91; univ. prof. Yeshiva U., N.Y.C., 1991—; of counsel Swartz & Swartz; v.p. for acad. affairs, chief acad. officer Yeshiva U., N.Y.C., 1993—; counsel Cadwalader, Wickersham and Taft, N.Y.C., Washington, L.A., 1988—; mem. faculty Frances Glessner Lee Inst., Harvard Med. Sch., Nat. Coll. Probate Judges, 1970, 77, 78, 79, 88; gen. dir. Assn. Trial Lawyers Am., 1968-73; reporter New Eng. Trial Judges Conf., 1965-67; participant Nat. Met. Cts. Conf., 1968; dir. Mass. Probate Study, 1976—; chmn. spl. com. on police procedures City of Boston, 1989, 91; vice chmn. bd. UST Corp., chmn., 1993-94; bd. dirs. Viacom Inc., Viacom Internat. Inc., UST Corp., WCI Steel, Inc.; mem. legal adv. com. N.Y. Stock Exch. Author: Future Interests and Estate Planning, 1965, 77, 81, 86, Comparative Negligence, 1970, A Products Liability Primer, 1970, Civil Trial Practice Manual, 1972, New Vistas in Litigation, 1973, Massachusetts Pleading and Practice, 7 vols., 1974-80, Estate Planning and Living Trusts, 1990, The Convention Method: The Unused Amending Superhighway, 1995, others; note editor: Boston U. Law Rev., 1954-55; property editor: Annual Survey of Mass. Law, 1960—; contbr. articles to legal jours. Bd. dirs. Kerry Found.; trustee Hebrew Coll., 1975—, Salve Regina Univ.; rep. Office Public Info., UN, 1968-73; chmn. legal adv. panel Nat. Commn. Med. Malpractice, 1972-73; examiner of titles Commonwealth of Mass., 1964—; spl. counsel Mass. Bay Transp. Authority, 1979; trustee Yeshiva U. Recipient Homer Albers award Boston U., 1955, John Ordronaux prize, 1955; Disting. Service award Religious Zionists Am., 1977; William W. Treat award; William O. Douglas award. Fellow Am. Coll. Probate Counsel; mem. ABA, Am. Law Inst., Mass. Bar Assn. (chmn. task force tort liability), Nat. Coll. Probate Judges (hon. mem.), Phi Beta Kappa. Office: 500 W 185th St New York NY 10033-3201 *I have been guided by the maxim: "Ideals are like stars. You cannot touch them with your hands, but like the seafaring man, if you choose them as your guide and follow them, you will reach your destiny."*

SCHWARTZ, WILLIAM A(LLEN), broadcasting and cable executive; b. Detroit, Nov. 29, 1938; m. Marlene J. Cohen; children: Jonathan, Cynthia, Michael. BA in Mktg. and Broadcasting, Wayne State U., 1961; postgrad. Bernard Baruch Grad. Sch. Bus.Mgr. research projects NBC, 1963-66; asst. dir. research Columbia Pictures, 1966; v.p., gen. mgr. Sta. WUAB-TV, Cleve., 1968-73; v.p. ops. Telerep, Inc., N.Y.C., 1973-74; v.p., gen. mgr. Sta. KTVU-TV, Oakland, Calif., 1974-79; pres. Cox Broadcasting div., Atlanta, 1979-81; pres. Cox Communications, Inc., Atlanta, 1981-87, chief exec. officer, 1983-87; pres., chief operating officer Cox Enterprises, Inc., Atlanta, 1985-87; chmn., chief exec. officer Capital Cable, 1988—; pres., chief exec. officer Cannell Communications, L.P., 1989-95, First Media Television, L.P., 1995—. Office: 400 Perimeter Center Ter NE Atlanta GA 30346-1227

SCHWARTZ, WILLIAM B., JR., ambassador; b. Atlanta, Nov. 14, 1921; s. William B. and Ruth (Kuhn) S.; m. Sonia Weinberg, Dec. 3, 1942; children—William B., Arthur Jay, Robert C. B.S., U. N.C., 1942. Various positions, then v.p. Nat. Service Industries, Atlanta, 1945-68; pres. Weine Investment Corp., Atlanta, 1969-77; amb. to Bahamas, 1977-81; bd. dirs. Weine Investment Corp., Balco Energy, Phenix Supply, Artex Internat. Mem. pres.'s council Brandeis U., 1966—, chancellor's club U. N.C., Bd. Councillors Carter Ctr., Emory U.; trustee, past chmn. Atlanta chapt. Am. Jewish Com.; chmn. Chatham Valley Found.; bd. dirs. Met. Atlanta Rapid Transit Authority, 1969-76, vice chmn., 1971-73; bd. dirs. Big Bros. Atlanta, Atlanta Jewish Welfare Fedn.; former mem. Pres.'s Council Oglethorp U.; former mem. bd. dirs. Jewish Home for the Aged; chmn. bd. visitors Emory U., 1966-74. Served with USN, 1942-45. Recipient Man of Yr. award Am. Jewish Com., 1972. Mem. Coun. Am. Ambs. Clubs: Standard (Atlanta), Commerce (Atlanta); East Hill (Nassau), Lyford Cay (Nassau); Longboat Key (Fla.); City (Sarasota). Lodges: B'nai Brith, Masons, Shriners. Home: 2724 Peachtree Rd Atlanta GA 30305 also: 1211 Gulf Of Mexico Dr Longboat Key FL 34228

SCHWARTZ, WILLIAM BENJAMIN, educator, physician; b. Montgomery, Ala., May 16, 1922; s. William Benjamin and Molly (Vendruff) S.; children: Eric A., Kenneth B., Laurie A. M.D., Duke U., 1945. Diplomate: Am. Bd. Internal Medicine (mem. test com. nephrology). Intern, then asst. resident medicine U. Chgo. Clinics, 1945-46; asst. medicine Peter Bent Brigham Hosp., Boston; also research fellow medicine Harvard Med. Sch., 1948-50; fellow medicine Children's Hosp., Boston, 1949-50; mem. faculty Tufts U. Sch. Medicine, 1950-96, prof. medicine, 1958-96, Endicott prof., 1975-76, Vannevar Bush Univ. prof., 1976-96, chmn. dept. medicine, 1971-76; mem. staff New Eng. Center Hosps., 1950—, sr. physician, chief renal service, 1959-71, physician-in-chief, 1971-76; prof. medicine U. So. Calif., L.A., 1996—; Established investigator Am. Heart Assn., 1956-61; chmn. gen. medicine study sect. NIH, 1965-69; mem. sci. adv. bd. USAF, 1965-68, Nat. Kidney Found., 1968—, chmn., 1970—; mem. tng. com. Nat. Heart Inst., 1969-70; prin. adviser health scis. program, Rand Corp., 1977-88. Author numerous articles in field. Markle scholar med. scis., 1950-55. Mem. Inst. Medicine NAS, Am. Soc. Nephrology (pres. 1974-75), Acad. Arts and Scis., ACP, Am. Fedn. Clin. Research, Am. Physiol. Soc., Am. Soc. Clin. Investigation, Assn. Am. Physicians, Phi Beta Kappa, Sigma Xi, Alpha Omega Alpha. Office: U So Calif 1355 San Pablo St Ste 143 Los Angeles CA 90033

SCHWARTZBAUER, ROBERT ALAN, lawyer; b. St. Paul, July 5, 1944; s. Bernard S. and Helen B. (Ringus) S.; m. Karen S. Carlson, Sept. 10, 1965; children: Christopher, Jessica, Peter. BA, U. Minn., 1966, JD, 1969. Bar: Minn. 1969. Atty. Dorsey & Whitney, Mpls., 1969-75, ptnr., 1975—. Mem. ABA, Minn. State Bar Assn., Phi Beta Kappa. Avocations: hunting, photography. Office: Dorsey & Whitney 220 S 6th St Minneapolis MN 55402-4502*

SCHWARTZBERG, ALLAN ZELIG, psychiatrist, educator; b. Cleve., Dec. 5, 1930; s. Joseph and Jeanette (Eisenman) S.; m. Katherine Weiss, June 19, 1955; children: Shana, Robert. BS cum laude, Case Western Res. U., 1951; MD, Ohio State U., 1955. Diplomate Am. Bd. Psychiatry and Neurology. Intern, resident in psychiatry Johns Hopkins Hosp., Balt., 1955-59; pvt. practice, Gaithersburg, Md.; asst. prof. psychiatry Georgetown U. Sch. Medicine, Washington, 1964-66, asst. clin. prof., 1966-79, assoc. clin. prof., 1979-89, clin. prof., 1989—; vis. prof. faculty seminar in community psychiatry Harvard U. Med. Sch., Boston, 1965-67; cons. Walt Whitman High Sch., Bethesda, Md., 1980—, Passage Crisis Ctr., Montgomery County Health Dept., 1974-82, psychiat. tng. br. NIMH, 1971-74. Editor-in-chief Internat. Annals Adolescent Psychiatry, 1988—; co-editor Adolescent Psychiatry, Vols. 8-19; contbr. articles to med. jours. Recipient Vicennial medal Georgetown U., 1984. Fellow Am. Psychiat. Assn., Am. Soc. for Adolescent Psychiatry, Am. Soc. Psychoanalytic Physicians (pres. 1986-87); mem. AMA, Am. Group Psychotherapy Assn., Am. Coll. Psychiatrists, B'nai B'rith, Phi Beta Kappa. Republican. Jewish. Home: 6616 Kenhill Rd Bethesda MD 20817-6014 Office: Suburban Psychiat Assocs 8943 Shady Grove Ct Gaithersburg MD 20877-1308

SCHWARTZBERG, MARTIN M., chemical company executive; b. N.Y.C., Dec. 10, 1935; s. Morris H. and Anne C. (Steskanin) S.; m. Florence M. Bloom, Sept. 22, 1957; children: Steven E., Michael C., Scott A. B ChemE, NYU, 1956; MBA, Wayne State U., 1965. Asst. to div. mgr. Pennwalt Corp., Phila., 1969-72, mgr. mktg. service, 1972-74, asst. to chief exec. officer, 1974-76, mng. dir. chems. Europe, 1976-78, mng. dir. splt. chems., 1978-80, pres. agrichems. div., 1980-85, pres. inorganic chems. div., 1985, v.p. chems., 1985-87, sr. v.p. chems., 1987-89; group pres. Elf Atochem N.Am., Inc. (formerly Pennwalt Corp.), Phila., 1990-94, ret., 1995. Bd. dirs. Camden County chpt. ARC. Served with U.S. Army, 1959. Mem. Sigma Iota Epsilon. Avocations: volleyball, golf.

SCHWARTZEL, CHARLES BOONE, lawyer; b. Louisville, Jan. 4, 1950; s. Charles Joseph and Rosemary Jane (Redens) S.; m. Rose Marie Carlisi, June 20, 1980; children: Sally Ann, Charles Gerard. BA, Vanderbilt U., 1972; JD, U. Tex., 1975. Bar: Tex. 1975. Atty. Vinson & Elkins L.L.P., Houston, 1975—, ptnr., 1983—. Contbr. articles to profl. jours. Councilman City of West University Place, Tex., 1985-89; vol. Trees For Houston, 1985—. Fellow Am. Coll. Trust and Estate Counsel; mem. ABA (chmn. real property, probate and trust law sect. com. on creditors' rights in estates and trusts 1989-93), Tex. Bar Assn., Houston Bar Assn. Roman Catholic. Office: Vinson & Elkins LLP 1001 Fannin Ste 1935 Houston TX 77002-6760

SCHWARTZHOFF, JAMES PAUL, foundation executive; b. Waukon, Iowa, June 24, 1937; s. Harold J. and Mary (Regan) Schwartzhoff; m. Mary Lou Hess, Apr. 23, 1960; children: Tammara, Eric, Stephanie, Mark, Laurie, Michelle, Steven. B, U. Iowa, 1962. Asst. chief auditor Wis. Dept. Tax, Madison, 1962-67; mgr. treas. dept. Mead Johnson and Co., Evansville, Ind., 1967-69; v.p., treas. Kettering Found., Dayton, Ohio, 1969—; chmn., treas. bd. Pastoral Counseling Ctr., Dayton, 1975-81; treas. Ohio River Rd. Runners, Dayton, 1986-87. Treas. Nat. Issues Forums Inst., Coun. Pub. Policy Edn., Ctr. for Community and Ednl. Devel.; mem. Donor's Forum Ohio Fin. Com., 1990-92; mem. investment com. U. Dayton; adv. com. JMB Endowment and Found. Realty Funds, 1991-94. Cpl. U.S. Army, 1957-59. Mem. AICPA, Found. Fin. Officers Group, Southern Ohio Pension Fund Group. Avocations: bicycling, backpacking, photography, woodworking. Office: Kettering Found 200 Commons Rd Dayton OH 45459-2788

SCHWARTZMAN, DAVID, economist, educator; b. Montreal, Que., Can., Apr. 22, 1924; came to U.S., 1954, naturalized, 1964; s. Joseph and Jeannette (Zurick) S.; m. Gertrude Schneiderman, June 17, 1951; children—Michael, Jason, Paul. B.A., McGill U., 1945; postgrad., U. Minn., 1945-46; Ph.D., U. Calif. at Berkeley, 1953. Lectr. McGill U., 1948-51; economist Dominion Bur. Statistics, 1951-53, United 5to $1.00 Stores, Can., 1953-54; instr. Columbia, 1954-58; asst. prof. N.Y. U., 1958-60; assoc. prof. New Sch. for Social Research, N.Y.C., 1960-64; prof. New Sch. for Social Rsch., 1964—, chmn. dept. econs., 1966-69, 76, 83-84; mem. staff Nat. Bur. Econ. Research, 1963-69; prof. environ. medicine and community health state U. N.Y. Downstate Med. Center, part-time, 1969-70; Cons. Royal Commn. on Farm Machinery, Ottawa, Can., 1968-70, U.S. Bur. Census, 1973, anti-trust div. U.S. Dept. Justice, 1973, U.S. Council on Wage and Price Stability, Exec. Office of Pres., 1975-76; adj. mem. Com. on Trade Regulation, N.Y. County Lawyers' Assn., 1976-85; Bd. advisors Inst. Health Economics and Social Studies, 1976-80. Author: Oligopoly in the Farm Machine Industry, 1970, Decline of Service in Retail Trade, 1971, The Expected Return from Pharmaceutical Research, 1975, Innovation in the Pharmaceutical Industry, 1976, Games of Chicken: Four Decades of Nuclear Policy, 1988, Economic Policy: An Agenda for the Nineties, 1989, The Japanese Television Cartel: A Study Based on Matsushita v. Zenith, 1993; contbr. articles to profl. jours. Mem. Am. Econ. Assn. Home: 285 Central Park W New York NY 10024-3006 Office: New Sch for Social Rsch Dept Econs 65 5th Ave New York NY 10003-3003

SCHWARTZMAN, GLENDA JOY, artist; b. L.A., Dec. 24, 1939; d. Morton and Thelma Lorrain (Bryer) S.; m. Leonard I. Schwartzman, June 21, 1961 (div. Sept. 1973); children: James Elliot, Eric Bennett. Student, Otis Art Inst., Calif., 1958, Chouinard Art Inst., Calif., 1959-60. One-woman shows include: Angeles Press, L.A., 1990, Boringer Gallery, Dallas, 1988, Krieger Gallery, Santa Barbara, Calif., 1987, SOMA Exhbns., Denver, 1986, De Vorsan Gallery, 1987, Inamori, Beverly Hills, Calif., 1982, Lelia Ivy Gallery, Santa Monica, Calif., 1982, others; group shows include TransAmerica Bldg., San Francisco, 1990, Wells Fargo Bank, L.A., 1990, La Jolla (Calif.) Mus., 1990, 1989, Col.-Jems Studios, others; work in pub. and pvt. collections; author: (book) Art in California, 1990. Mem. Dems., Calif., Benedict Canyon. Recipient fine art scholarship Otist Art Inst. Mem. Calif. Yacht Club, So. Calif. Women's Caucas for Art. Jewish. Avocations: chess, bridge, boating. Office: Glenda Schwartzman Studio 807 Hampton Dr Venice CA 90291-3020

SCHWARTZMAN, JAMES CHARLES, lawyer; b. Kearney, Nebr., Apr. 17, 1945; s. Bernard and Estelle (Lubin) S.; m. Nancy Miriam Hankin, June 26, 1967; children: Kimberly Hankin, Kamian Hankin. B.A., Washington U., St. Louis, 1967; J.D. cum laude, Villanova U., 1972. Bar: Pa. 1972, U.S. Dist. Ct. (ea. dist.) Pa. 1973, U.S. Ct. Appeals (3d cir.) 1973, U.S. Supreme Ct. 1979, U.S. Tax Ct. 1979, U.S. Ct. Claims 1979. Law clk. U.S. Dist. Ct. (ea. dist.) Pa., Phila., 1972-73, U.S. Supreme Ct. Pa.; asst. U.S. atty. U.S. Dept. Justice, Phila., 1973-77; sr. ptnr. Schwartzman & Hepps, P.C., Phila., 1977-92; Schwartzman & Assocs., 1993—; mem. Disciplinary Bd., Supreme Ct. Pa., 1983-89, vice chmn., 1985-86, chmn., 1986-88; dir. Bank & Trust Co. of Old York Rd., Willow Grove, Pa., 1983-92; bd. dirs. Southeastern Pa. Trans. Authorty, 1992—, Blue Cross of Phila., 1993—; mem. Phila. Spl. Trial Ct. Nominating Commn., 1987-95. Contbr. article to Villanova Law Rev., 1972, mem. editorial staff, 1971-72. Mem. Pa. Bar Assn., Phila. Bar Assn., Pa. Trial Lawyers Assn., Phila. Trial Lawyers Assn., Continuing Legal Edn. Bd. (vice chmn. 1992-95, chmn. 1996—), Order of Coif. Office: Schwartzman & Assocs 17th Fl 1337 Chestnut St Fl 17 Philadelphia PA 19107-3317

SCHWARY, RONALD LOUIS, motion picture producer; b. The Dalles, Oreg., May 23, 1944; s. Mitchell Louis and Lorraine (Ablan) S.; children: Brian L., Neil L. BS, U. So. Calif., 1967. Pres. Schwary Enterprises, L.A., 1985—. Prodr. (motion pictures) Ordinary People, 1980 (Golden Globe award 1981, Acad. award 1981), Absence of Malice, 1981, Tootsie, 1982, A Soldier's Story, 1984, Batteries Not Included, 1987, Havana, 1990, Scent of a Woman, 1992, Cops and Robbersons, 1994, SAbrina, 1995; (TV series) Tour of Duty, 1987. Mem. Dirs. Guild Am. Republican. Roman Catholic.

SCHWARZ, CARL W., lawyer; b. Milw., Jan. 28, 1936. BCE, Cornell U., 1958; JD with honors, George Washington U., 1962, LLM, 1966. Bar: Wis. 1962. D.C. 1969. Trial atty. Antitrust divsn., U.S. Dept. Justice, 1962-64, Fgn. Commerce Sect., 1964-69; ptnr. McDermott, Will & Emory, Washington. Mem. ABA, Internat. Bar Assn., D.C. Bar, State Bar Wis. Office: McDermott Will & Emery 1850 K St NW Washington DC 20006-2213*

SCHWARZ, EGON, humanities and German language educator, author, literary critic; b. Vienna, Austria, Aug. 8, 1922; came to U.S., 1949, naturalized, 1956; s. Oscar and Erna S.; m. Dorothea K. Klockenbusch, June 8, 1950; children—Rudolf Joachim, Caroline Elisabeth, Gabriela Barbara. Ph.D., U. Wash., 1954. Mem. faculty Harvard U., 1954-61; mem. faculty dept. Germanic langs. and lit. Washington U., St. Louis, 1961—, prof. German, 1963—, Rosa May Disting. Univ. prof. in the Humanities, 1975-93, prof. emeritus, 1993—; vis. prof. U. Hamburg, Fed. Republic Germany, 1962-63, U. Calif., Berkeley, 1963-65, Middlebury Coll., 1969, U. Calif.-Irvine, 1977, U. Tübingen, 1986; William Evans prof. U. Otago, Dunedin, N.Z., 1984; Disting. scholar Ohio State U., Columbus, 1987, U. Graz, Austria, 1989, 93, U. Siegen, 1993-94. Author: Hofmannsthal und Calderon, 1962, Joseph von Eichendorff, 1972, Das verschluckte Schluchzen-Poesie und Politik bei Rainer Maria Rilke, 1972, Keine Zeit für Eichendorff: Chronik unfreiwilliger Wanderjahre; an autobiography, 1979, revised and expanded, 1992, Dichtung, Kritik, Geschichte: Essays zur Literatur 1900-1930, 1983, Literatur aus vier Kulturen: Essays und Besprechungen, 1987, also numerous other books. Recipient Joseph von Eichendorff medal, 1986, Austrian Medal of Honor for Arts and Scis., 1991, Alexander von Humboldt prize for fgn. scholars, 1995; Guggenheim fellow, 1957-58, Fulbright fellow, 1962-63, sr. fellow NEH, 1970-71, fellow Ctr. for Interdisciplinary Studies, Bielefeld, Germany, 1980-81; grantee Am. Coun. Learned Socs., 1962-63. Mem. MLA (hon.), Am. Assn. Tchrs. German, German Acad. Lang. and Lit. Home: 1036 Oakland Ave Saint Louis MO 63122-6565 Office: Washington U German Dept Saint Louis MO 63130 *When I was young, heroic phantasies were closer to my heart than ethical ones, desires of self-fulfillment stronger than the hopes for an equitable world. Today my horizon is broader in that I wish for a society where personal satisfactions are not achieved at the expense of others, where the earth which one generation inherits is not left more depleted to the next, a society which does not coerce other societies.*

SCHWARZ, GERARD, conductor, musician; b. Weehawken, N.J., Aug. 19, 1947; s. John and Gerta (Weiss) S.; m. Jody Greitzer, June 23, 1984; children: Alysandra, Daniel, Gabriella, Julian. BS, Juilliard Sch., 1972, MA, 1972; DFA (hon.), Fairleigh Dickinson U., Seattle U.; DMus (hon.), U. Puget Sound. Trumpet player Am. Symphony Orch., 1965-72, Am. Brass Quintet, 1965-73, N.Y. Philharm., 1973-77; trumpet player, guest condr. Aspen Music Festival, 1969-75, bd. dirs., 1973-75; music dir. Erick Hawkins Dance Co., 1967-72, SoHo Ensemble, 1969-75, Eliot Feld Ballet Co., N.Y.C., 1972-78; prin. condr. Waterloo Festival, 1975-93, Music Sch. Princeton (N.J.) U.; music dir. N.Y. Chamber Symphony, 1977—, L.A. Chamber Orch., 1978-86, White Mountains (N.H.) Music Festival, 1978-80, Music Today at Merkin Concert Hall, N.Y.C., 1988-89; music advisor Mostly Mozart Festival, Lincoln Ctr., N.Y.C., 1982-84, music dir., 1984—; music advisor Seattle Symphony, 1983-84, prin. condr., 1984-85, music dir., 1985—; artistic advisor Tokyu Bunkamura's Orchard Hall, Japan, 1994—; mem. faculty Juilliard Sch., N.Y.C., 1975-83, Mannes Coll. Music, 1973-79, Montclair (N.J.) State Coll., 1975-80; guest condr. various orchs. including Phila. Orch., L.A. Philharmonic, St. Louis, Buffalo, Detroit, San Francisco, Atlanta, Houston, Pitts., Minn., Jerusalem Symphony, Israel Chamber Orch., Moscow Philharmonic, Moscow Radio Orch., Orch. Nat. de France, Paris, London Symphony Orch., Frankfurt Radio, Stockholm Radio, Helsinki Philharm., Ensemble InterContemporain, Monte Carlo Philharm., Nat. Orch. Spain, English Chamber Orch., London Symphony, Scottish Chamber Orch., City of Birmingham (Eng.) Symphony, Nouvel Orchestre Philharmonique, Sydney (Australia) Symphony, Melbourne (Australia) Symphony, Orchestre National de Lyon, France, Orchestre Philharm. de Montpellier, France, Washington Opera, Da Capo Chamber Players, 20th Century Chamber Orch., Chamber Music Soc. Lincoln Ctr., San Francisco Opera, Seattle Opera, Tokyu Bunkamura, Japan, Residentie Orch. of The Hague, The Netherlands, St. Louis Symphony, London Mozart Players, Kirov Orch., St. Petersburg, Russia, Tokyo Philharm., Royal Liverpool (Eng.) Philharm., Vancouver (Can.) Symphony Orch., City of London Symphonia, Evian Festival in France, 1994; also numerous appearances on TV; rec. artist Columbia, Nonesuch, Vox, MMO, Desto, Angel, Delos records; record: Seattle Symphony 1994-95 Season, 1995. Bd. dirs. Naumburg Found., 1975—. Recipient award for concert artists Ford Found., 1973, Grammy award nominee, Mumms Ovation award, Record of Yr. awards, Ditson Condrs. award Columbia U., 1989; named Condr. of Yr., Musical Am. Internat. Directory of Performing Arts, 1994. Office: NY Chamber Symphony 1395 Lexington Ave New York NY 10128-1647

SCHWARZ, GLENN VERNON, editor; b. Chgo., Nov. 24, 1947; s. Vernon Edward and LaVerne Louise (Schuster) S.; m. Cynthia Frances Meisenhoelder, June 17, 1984; 1 child, Chloe. BA, San Francisco State U., 1970. Sports writer San Francisco Examiner, 1970-87, sports editor, 1988—. Fundraiser San Francisco Zoological Soc., 1987—. Mem. AP Sports Editors, Baseball Writers Assn. Am. (bd. dirs. 1986-87). Avocation: nature travel. Office: San Francisco Examiner 110 5th St San Francisco CA 94103-2918

SCHWARZ, H. MARSHALL, trust company executive; b. 1936; married. BA, Harvard U., 1958, MBA, 1961. With U.S. Trust Co., N.Y.C., 1967—, chmn, chief exec. officer, 1990—; bd. dirs. Bowne & Co., Inc., Atlantic Mut. Co. Bd. dirs. United Way, N.Y.C.; chmn. ARC in Greater N.Y.C.; trustee Columbia U. Tchrs. Coll., Milton Acad., Camille and Henry Dreyfus Found. Office: US Trust Co NY 114 W 47th St New York NY 10036-1510

SCHWARZ, J(AMES) CONRAD, psychology educator; b. Hartford, Conn., Sept. 19, 1936; s. William Merlin and Violet May (List) S.; m. Lois J. Stonebraker, 1956 (div. 1981); m. Carolina A.B. Herfkens, Oct. 12, 1984. BS, Pa. State U., 1958; MA, Ohio State U., 1961, PhD, 1963. Lic. clin. psychologist, Conn.; cert. psychologist, N.Y. Rsch. asst. Pa. State U., 1957-58; psychol. trainee Chillicothe (Ohio) VA N.P. Hosp., 1958-60; psychol. intern Columbus (Ohio) VA Out-Patient Clinic, 1960-61; instr. psychology Bowling Green (Ohio) State U., 1962-64, asst. prof., 1964-65; asst. prof., mem. teaching faculty grad. tng. Syracuse U, 1965-70, assoc. prof., 1970-72; assoc. prof., mem. teaching faculty grad. tng. program U. Conn., Storrs, 1972-75, prof., mem. teaching faculty grad. tng. program, 1975—; pvt. practice clin. psychology North Windham, Conn., 1973-94, 1995—; asst. field assessment officer Peace Corps Tng. Programs, 1967-68; clin. psychology cons. VA Out-Patient Clinic, Syracuse, 1968-72, Onodaga Co. Mental Health Clinic, Syracuse, 1969-72; with Windham Pub. Schs.-Project Self-Search, 1974-76; cons. Ea. Conn. Mental Health Group, 1974-83, Bermuda Govt., Child Devel. Project, 1979-82, Optimum Resource, Inc., Software for Learning Disabled Children. Author: Deck-a-Dot Manual: An Educational Card Game Program to Develop Arithmetic Readiness, 1970; If This Is Love, Why Do I Feel So Insecure?, 1989, 90, Teacher's Manual for Optimum Resource Reading Program, 1991; cons. editor Devel. Psychology, 1981-84; co-developer The Optimum Resource Reading Program, 1991; contbr. articles to profl. jours. USPHS fellow, 1958-59, 61-62; grantee Nat. Lab. Early Childhood Edn. Ctr. Syracuse U., 1968-71, NIMH, 1978-83, 84-85, Nat. Inst. Alcohol Abuse and Addiction, 1986-89, U. Conn. Rsch. Found., 1985-87. Mem. APA (div. clin., family psychology), Soc. Rsch. in Child Devel., Sigma Xi, Phi Beta Kappa, Psi Chi, Phi Eta Sigma, Phi Kappa Phi. Avocations: tennis, landscape gardening. Office: U Conn Dept Psychology 406 Babbidge Rd Storrs Mansfield CT 06269-1020

SCHWARZ, JOHN J.H., state senator, surgeon; b. Chgo., Nov. 15, 1937; s. Frank William and Helen Veronica (Brennan) S.; m. Anne Louise Ennia, Jan. 16, 1971 (dec. Feb. 1990); 1 child, Brennan Louise. BA, U. Mich., 1959; MD, Wayne State U., 1964. Physician, surgeon Battle Creek, Mich., 1974—; mayor City of Battle Creek, 1985-87; senator State of Mich., 1987—, pres. pro tempore, 1994—. Trustee Olivet Coll., 1991—, Wayland Acad., 1992—. Lt. comdr. USN, 1965-67. Mem. AMA, Am. Coll. Surgeons, Am. Soc. for Head & Neck Surgery. Republican. Roman Catholic. Office: State Senate State Capital Lansing MI 48909

SCHWARZ, JOSEPH EDMUND, artist; b. Hartford, Conn., May 13, 1929; s. Jules and Dora (Sklarinsky) S.; m. Jean Bunker Chalmers, Jan. 29, 1951; children: David Bunker, Dina Ruth, Jonathan Chalmers, Adam Jules; m. Sarah Rollings, Oct. 21, 1971. B.F.A., Ohio Wesleyan U., 1950; M.F.A., U. Ill., 1952; Ph.D., Ohio State U., 1957. instr. Ohio State U., 1952-57; assoc. prof. U. Ga., 1957-68; prof., dir. grad. studies Va. Commonwealth U., 1968-73; prof. U. Maine- Machias, 1973-74, Auburn U., Montgomery, Ala., 1977—, head dept. fine arts, 1977—. Exhibited group shows, Butler Art Inst. Ann., 1949-55, Southeastern Ann., Atlanta, 1957, 59-61, 66-67, Chrysler Show, Provincetown, Mass., 1958, Hunter Gallery Ann., Chattanooga, 1960-62, 67, Whitney Ann., N.Y.C., 1958, Montgomery Mus.; represented pub. art collections, Butler Art Inst., Atlanta High Mus., Ball State U., Temple Beth Israel, Hartford, LaGrange Coll. U. Ga. Sch. Law. Home: 165 Vivian Ln Wetumpka AL 36092-4480 Office: Dept Fine Arts Auburn U Montgomery AL 36177 *As a humanist and as a painter, my life's goal is to be actually what I hope I am, that is to realize myself, to develop fully whatever it is that makes my life unique. I want my paintings to be records of my ideas and values, and if it should be that my being and my work have specialty, then I would hope that others would find there compassion and passion, a witnessing of human joy and pain and, finally, affirmation of the beauty of man and of human life.*

SCHWARZ, JOSEPHINE LINDEMAN, retired ballet company director, choreographer; b. Dayton, Ohio, Apr. 8, 1908; d. Joseph and Hannah (Lindeman) S. D.F.A. (hon.), U. Dayton, 1974; H.H.D. (hon.), Wright State U., 1983. Founder, dir. Schwarz Sch. Dance, Dayton, 1927-84, Exptl. Group for Young Dancers (now Dayton Ballet), 1937-79; mem. Weidman Theatre Dance Co., 1934-37; guest tchr., lectr., choreographer Hunter Coll., N.Y.C.,

YM-YWHA, N.Y.C., also regional dance companies in, Cleve., Phila., Indpls., Houston; pres. N.E. Regional Ballet Assn., 1961; chmn. dance adv. panel Ohio Arts Council, 1967-70; founder, program dir. Nat. Craft Choreography Confs., 1968-70; dance advisory panels Nat. Endowment for Arts, 1975-78; also Ohio Arts Council, 1975-78. Profl. dancer Adolph Bolm's Ballet Intime, Ravinia Opera Ballet, Chgo., 1925-27; European study and performances, 1929-30; author articles. Recipient award Ohio Arts Council, 1977, Spl. Achievement award YWCA, 1982, Brotherhood award Dayton chpt. NCCJ, 1984, Pegasus award Ohioana Library Assn., 1987, Northeast award Regional Dance Am., 1990; inducted into Ohio Women's Hall of Fame, 1991. Mem. Nat. Assn. Regional Ballet (bd. dirs. 1970-75), Am. Dance Guild (award 1985), Friends Dayton Ballet, Dayton Art Inst. Jewish. Home: 350 Ponca Pl # 122 Boulder CO 80303-3802 *There are no short cuts.*

SCHWARZ, MELVIN A., lawyer; b. Cin., Feb. 20, 1950; s. John. H. and Ann (Gruenebaum) S.; m. Roberta M. Edge, July 14, 1979; children: Emily, Julia. BA, Johns Hopkins U., 1972; JD, U. Chgo., 1975. Bar: Pa., N.Y., U.S. Dist. Ct. (ea. & mid. dists.) Pa., U.S. Dist. Ct. (ea., so. & no. dists.) N.Y., U.S. Ct. Appeals (1st, 2d & 3d cirs.), U.S. Supreme Ct. Assoc. Dechert Price & Rhoads, Phila., 1975-83; ptnr. Dechert Price & Rhoads, N.Y.C., 1983—. Mem. Phila. Bar Assn., Assn. of Bar of City of N.Y., Order of Coif, Phi Beta Kappa. Office: Dechert Price & Rhoads 477 Madison Ave New York NY 10022-5802

SCHWARZ, MICHAEL, lawyer; b. Brookline, Mass., Oct. 19, 1952; s. Jules Lewis and Estelle (Kosberg) S. BA magna cum laude, U. No. Colo., 1975; postgrad. U. N.Mex., 1977, JD, 1980; Rsch. reader in Negligence Law, Oxford U., 1978; diploma in Legal Studies, Cambridge U., 1981. Bar: N.Mex. 1980, U.S. Dist. Ct. N.Mex. 1980, U.S. Ct. Appeals (10th, D.C., and Fed. cirs.) 1982, U.S. Ct. Internat. Trade, 1982, U.S. Tax Ct. 1982, U.S. Supreme Ct. 1983, N.Y. 1987. VISTA vol., Albuquerque, 1975-77; rsch. fellow N.Mex. Legal Support Project, Albuquerque, 1978-79; supr. law Cambridge (Eng.) U., 1980-81; law clk. to chief justice Supreme Ct. N.Mex., Santa Fe, 1981-82; pvt. practice law, Santa Fe, 1982—; spl. prosecutor City of Santa Fe, 1985; spl. asst. atty. gen., 1986-88; mem. editorial adv. com. Social Security Reporting Svc., 1983-95. Author: New Mexico Appellate Manual, 1990, 2nd. edit., 1994; contbr. articles to profl. jours. Vice dir. Colo. Pub. Interest Rsch. Group, 1974; scoutmaster Great S.W. Area coun. Boy Scouts Am., 1977-79; mem. N.Mex. Acupuncture Licensing Bd., 1983. Recipient Cert. of Appreciation Cambridge U., 1981, Nathan Burkan Meml. award, 1980, N.Mex. Supreme Ct. Cert. Recognition, 1992, 93, 95. Mem. ABA (litigation com. on profl. responsibility, litigation com. on pretrial practice and discovery), ATLA, Am. Arbit. Assn., State Bar N.Y., N.Mex. State Bar (bd. dirs. employment law sect. 1990-96, chair employment law sect. 1991-92), N.Y. Bar Assn., First Jud. Dist. Bar Assn. (treas. 1987-88, sec. 1988-89, v.p. 1989-1990, pres. 1990-91, local rules com. mem. 1989-92), N.Mex. Supreme Ct. (standing com. on profl. conduct 1990—, hearing officer, reviewing officer disciplinary com. 1993—), Am. Inns. of Ct. N.Mex. (barrister), Nat. Employment Lawyers Assn. (Nat. chpt., N.Mex. chpt.), Sierra Club, Amnesty Internat., Nat. Audubon Soc. Home and Office: PO Box 1656 Santa Fe NM 87504-1656

SCHWARZ, PAUL WINSTON, lawyer, business company executive, judge; b. Sacramento, Sept. 24, 1948; s. Egon Ferdinand and Louise (Fulcher) S.; m. Virginia Adams, July 12, 1987; children: Austin Winston, Julie Adams. BA in Philosophy, Calif. State U., San Jose, 1971; JD, Santa Clara U., 1974. Bar: Pa. 1975, U.S. Supreme Ct. 1978, U.S. Ct. Appeals (D.C. cir.) 1987, Va. 1992. Commd. 2d. lt. U.S. Army, 1971, advanced through grades to lt. col., 1992; corp. counsel, v.p. Oracle Corp., Bethesda, Md., 1992-93; sec., corp. counsel Oracle Complex Systems Corp., Arlington, Va., 1992-93; counsel McAleese & Associates, P.C., Washington, DC, 1993-94; apptd. U.S. adminstrv. law judge, 1994. Author: A Roadmap into the World of Federal Contracts, 1989. Decorated Legion of Merit, U.S. Army Gen. Staff Badge award. Mem. ABA (chmn. com. on pub. contract law gen. practice sect. 1991, vice-chmn. judiciary com. 1995), Army and Navy Country Club, Army and Navy Club Washington D.C., Nat. Soc. SAR. Episcopalian. Avocations: swimming, pistol. Home: 5336 Sugar Hill Dr Houston TX 77056-2028

SCHWARZ, RALPH JACQUES, engineering educator; b. Hamburg, Germany, June 13, 1922; naturalized, 1944; s. Simon J. and Anna (Schoendorff) S.; m. Irene Lassally, Sept. 9, 1951; children: Ronald Paul, Sylvia Anne. B.S., Columbia U., 1943, M.S., 1944, Ph.D., 1949; postgrad., Poly. Inst. Bklyn., 1944-45, N.Y. U., 1946-47. Registered profl. engr., N.Y. Mem. faculty Columbia U., 1943-92, prof. elec. engring., 1958-92, chmn. dept., 1958-65, 71-72, assoc. dean acad. affairs Faculty Engring. and Applied Sci., 1972-75, acting dean, 1975-76, 80-81, vice dean, Thayer Lindsley prof., 1976-92, Thayer Lindsley prof. emeritus, 1992—; cons. systems analysis, communications and noise theory, 1945—; vis. assoc. prof. UCLA, 1956; adviser Inst. Internat. Edn., 1952-65; vis. scientist IBM Research Center, 1969-70. Author: (with M.G. Salvadori) Differential Equations in Engineering Problems, 1954, (with B. Friedland) Linear Systems, 1965. Bd. dirs. Armstrong Meml. Research Found.; trustee Associated Univs., Inc., 1980-92. Fellow IEEE (chmn. circuit theory group 1963-65, Centennial medal 1984); mem. Communications Soc. (bd. govs.), Am. Soc. Engring. Edn., AAAS, Sigma Xi, Tau Beta Pi, Pi Mu Epsilon, Eta Kappa Nu. Home: 33 Wood Ln New Rochelle NY 10804-3709 Office: Columbia U Engring Dept 116th St And Broadway New York NY 10027

SCHWARZ, RICHARD HOWARD, obstetrician, gynecologist, educator; b. Easton, Pa., Jan. 10, 1931; s. Howard Eugene and Blanche Elizabeth (Smith) S.; m. Patricia Marie Lewis, Mar. 11, 1978; children by previous marriage: Martha L., Nancy Schwarz Tedesco, Paul H., Mary Katherine Schwarz Murray. MD, Jefferson Med. Coll., 1955; MA (hon.), U. Pa., Phila., 1971. Diplomate Am. Bd. Ob-Gyn. (examiner 1977—). Intern, then resident Phila. Gen. Hosp., 1955-59; prof. U. Pa., Phila., 1963-78; prof., chmn. Downstate Med. Ctr., Bklyn., 1978-90, dean, v.p. acad. affairs, 1983-89, provost, v.p. clin. affairs, 1988-93, interim pres., 1993-94, prof. ob-gyn., 1990-96, Disting. Svc. prof. ob-gyn., 1996—; obstetrical cons. March of Dimes Birth Defects Found., 1995—. Author: Septic Abortion, 1968. Editor: Handbook of Obstetric Emergencies, 1984, mem. editorial bd. jour. Ob-Gyn., Milw., 1983-87; contbr. articles to profl. jours. Bd. dirs. March of Dimes, N.Y.C., 1985-95. Capt. USAF, 1959-63. Mem. Am. Coll. Obstetricians and Gynecologists (chmn. dist. 2 1984-87, v.p. 1989-90, pres. elect 1990-91, pres. 1991-92). Republican. Presbyterian. Office: SUNY Health Sci Ctr 450 Clarkon Ave Dept ObG Brooklyn NY 11203-2012

SCHWARZ, RICHARD WILLIAM, historian, educator; b. Wataga, Ill., Sept. 11, 1925; s. George William and Mildred (Imschweiler) S.; m. Joyce Frances Anderson, June 11, 1950; children: Constance Kay, Richard Paul, Dwight Luther. BA, Andrews U., 1949; MS, U. Ill., 1953; MA, U. Mich., 1959, PhD, 1964. Tchr.-librarian Broadview Acad., La Grange, Ill., 1949-53, Adelphian Acad., Holly, Mich., 1953-55; instr. history Andrews U., 1955-58, asst. librarian, 1955-56, acting librarian, 1956-58, asst. prof., 1958-63, assoc. prof., 1963-68, prof., 1968-89, acting chmn. dept. history and polit. sci., 1964-66, prof. emeritus, 1989—, chmn., 1966-77, v.p. acad. adminstrn., 1977-87; reference libr. Berrien Springs Community Libr., 1990-93; vis. instr. Mich. State U., 1967; book reviewer Library Jour., 1957-77. Author: John Harvey Kellogg, M.D, 1970, Lightbearers to the Remnant, 1979; bd. editors: Studies in Adventist History, 1971-83. Del. Berrien County Republican Conv., 1966, 68, 74. Served with USNR, 1944-46. Mem. Assn. 7th-Day Adventists Historians (pres. 1987), Phi Beta Kappa, Phi Alpha Theta, Phi Kappa Phi. Home: 113 Oakwood Pl Hendersonville NC 28792-9521

SCHWARZ, ROBERT DEVLIN, art dealer; b. Atlantic City, N.J., July 11, 1942; s. Frank Samuel and Marie (Devlin) S.; m. Pamela Pillion; children: Robert, Jr., Elizabeth, Jonathan. BS, Dickinson Coll., 1964. Curator Stephen Girard Collection, Phila., 1970-80; pres., curator The Schwarz Gallery, Phila., 1981—; pres., owner. Author: Catalogue of the Stephen Girard Collection, 1980, A Gallery Collects Peale, 1987. Mem. bd. dirs. Conservation Ctr., 1995. Mem. Art Dealers Assn. Am., Art and Antiques Deales League Am. Republican. Presbyterian. Office: The Schwarz Gallery 1806 Chestnut St Philadelphia PA 19103-4902

SCHWARZ, STEVEN E., electrical engineering educator, administrator; b. L.A., Jan. 29, 1939; s. Carl and Lillian Schwarz; m. Janet Lee Paschal, July 27, 1963. BS, Cal Tech, 1959, MS, 1961, PhD, 1964; AM, Harvard U., 1962. From asst. prof. to prof. elec. engring. U. Calif., Berkeley, 1964—, assoc. dean Coll. Engring., 1991—. Author: Electromagnetics for Engineers, 1990; co-author: Electrical Engineering, An Introduction, 1984, 93; contbr. articles to profl. jours. Guggenheim fellow, 1971-72. Fellow IEEE. Office: U Calif Berkeley Electrical Engring Dept 231 Cory Hall Berkeley CA 94720-1770

SCHWARZ, WOLFGANG, psychologist; b. Stuttgart, Ger., Oct. 30, 1926; s. Mole and Edith (Gutstein) S.; brought to U.S., 1934, naturalized, 1940; A.B., N.Y. U., 1948, A.M., 1949, Ph.D., 1956; m. Cynthia Mae Johnson, Sept. 12, 1949 (div.); children—Amy Maria, Casey Andrew, Darcy Lynn, Priscilla Anne, Lydia Beth, Emily Jane; m. Susan Decker, 1976; children—Jaime Bartholomew, Noah. Intern, Bellevue Med. Center, N.Y., 1949-51; chief psychology Rip Van Winkle Med. Found., Hudson, N.Y., 1951-53; dir. psychology Hillcrest Med. Center, Tulsa, 1953-56, Hollywood Presbyn. Hosp., Los Angeles, 1956-58; cons. psychology Cedars Lebanon Hosp., Los Angeles, 1956-58; spl. cons. to D.C. Govt., 1959-61, NIH, Bethesda, Md., 1962-64; dir. psychol. research Mass. Dept. Mental Health, Boston and Malden, 1965-68; individual practice clin. psychology, Tulsa, 1953-56, Beverly Hills, Calif., 1956-59, Washington, 1959-63, Concord and Malden, Mass., 1963-73, Mt. Kisco, N.Y., 1973—; lectr. U. Tulsa, 1953-54, Hillcrest Med. Center, Tulsa, 1953-56, Los Angeles State Coll., 1956-57; asst. prof. Howard U., 1961; asso. prof. George Washington U., 1961-62; vis. research asst. Harvard Psychiatry, Lab., 1966-68; prof. Malden Hosp., 1968-71; cons. No. Westchester Hosp., 1974—, United Hosp., 1975—, Four Winds Hosp., 1975-80; cons. psychology Peace Corps, Mass., 1969—. Mem. exec. com. Mayor's Model City Program, Malden, 1967-68. Served with USNR, 1945-46. Recipient Founder's Day award N.Y. U., 1956, Individual award USPHS/NIH, 1960-64. Diplomate Am. Bd. Profl. Psychology. Mem. Am., N.Y., Mass. psychol. assns., Washington Soc. History of Medicine (exec. com. 1963-64), N.Y. Acad. Scis., Psi Chi, Beta Lambda Sigma. Author: A Survey of the Mental Health Facilities in the District of Columbia, 1961; also articles. Home: 81 Paulding Dr Chappaqua NY 10514-2818 Office: 121 Smith Ave Mount Kisco NY 10549-2815

SCHWARZENEGGER, ARNOLD ALOIS, actor, author; b. Graz, Austria, July 30, 1947; came to U.S., 1968, naturalized, 1983; s. Karl and Aurelia (Jedrny) S.; m. Maria Owings Shriver, Apr. 26, 1986; children: Katherine Eunice, Christina Aurelia, Patrick. BA in Bus. and Internat. Econs., U. Wis., Superior. Owner prodn. co. and real estate. Actor: (films) Stay Hungry, 1976 (Golden Globe award 1976), Pumping Iron, 1977, The Villain, 1979, Conan, The Barbarian, 1982, Conan, The Destroyer, 1983, The Terminator, 1984, Commando, 1985, Red Sonja, 1985, Raw Deal, 1986, Predator, 1987, Running Man, 1987, Red Heat, 1988, Twins, 1988, Total Recall, 1990, Kindergarten Cop, 1990, Terminator 2: Judgement Day, 1991, The Last Action Hero, 1993, True Lies, 1994, Junior, 1994, Terminator 2: 3-D, 1996, Jingle All the Way, 1996, Eraser, 1996, Crusade, 1996; (TV spl.) Sinatra: 80 Years My Way, 1995; (TV movies) The Jayne Mansfield Story, 1980; dir. TV movie Christmas in Connecticut, 1992; host A Very Special Christmas Story; dir. The Switch, Tales from the Crypt, HBO, 1990; author: Arnold: The Education of a Bodybuilder, 1977, Arnold's Bodyshaping for Women, 1979, Arnold's Bodybuilding for Men, 1981, Arnold's Encyclopedia of Modern Bodybuilding, 1985; prodr. bodybuilding video tape. Nat. weight tng. coach Spl. Olympics; vol. prison rehab. programs; chmn. Pres.'s Coun. on Phys. Fitness and Sports, 1990. Bodybldg. champion, 1965-80; named Jr. Mr. Europe, 1965, Best Built Man of Europe, 1966, Mr. Europe, 1966; Internat. Powerlifting Championship, 1966, German Powerlifting Championship, 1968; IFFB (Internat. Fedn. Body Builders) Mr. Internat., 1968, IFFB Mr. Universe (amateur), 1969; NABBA (Nat. Assn. Body Builders) Mr. Universe (amateur), 1967, NABBA Mr. Universe (profl.), 1968, 69, 70; Mr. World, 1970; IFFB Mr. Olympia, 1970, 71, 72, 73, 74, 75, 80; recipient Golden Globe award for Best Newcomer in Films, 1976, Timmie Award The Touchdown Club, 1990; named Video Star Yr. VSDA, 1990; voted Internat. Star of 1984, ShoWest. Office: care ICM 8942 Wilshire Blvd Beverly Hills CA 90211*

SCHWARZER, WILLIAM W., federal judge; b. Berlin, Apr. 30, 1925; came to U.S., 1938, naturalized, 1944; s. John F. and Edith M. (Daniel) S.; m. Anne Halbersleben, Feb. 2, 1951; children: Jane Elizabeth, Andrew William. AB cum laude, U. So. Calif., 1948; LLB cum laude, Harvard U., 1951. Bar: Calif. 1953, U.S. Supreme Ct. 1967. Teaching fellow Harvard U. Law Sch., 1951-52; asso. firm McCutchen, Doyle, Brown & Enersen, San Francisco, 1952-60; ptnr. McCutchen, Doyle, Brown & Enersen, 1960-76; judge U.S. Dist. Ct (no. dist.) Calif., San Francisco, 1976—; dir. Fed. Jud. Ctr., Washington, 1990-95; sr. counsel Pres.'s Commn. on CIA Activities Within the U.S., 1975; chmn. U.S. Jud. Conf. Com. Fed.-State Jurisdiction, 1987-90; mem. faculty Nat. Inst. Trial Advocacy, Fed. Jud. Ctr., All-ABA, U.S.-Can. Legal Exch., 1987, Anglo-U.S. Jud. Exch., 1994-95, Salzburg Seminar on Am. Studies; disting. prof. Hastings Coll. Law U. Calif. Author: Managing Antitrust and Other Complex Litigation, 1982, Civil Discovery and Manadatory Disclosure, 1994, Federal Civil Procedure Before Trial, 1994; contbr. articles to legal pubs., aviation jours. Trustee World Affairs Coun. No. Calif., 1961-88; chmn. bd. trustees Marin Country Day Sch., 1963-66; chmn. Marin County Aviation Commn., 1969-76; mem. vis. com. Harvard Law Sch., 1981-86. Served with Intelligence, U.S. Army, 1943-46. Fellow Am. Coll. Trial Lawyers (S. Gates award 1992), Am. Bar Found.; mem. ABA (Meador Rosenberg award 1995), Am. Law Inst., San Francisco Bar Assn., State Bar Calif., Coun. Fgn. Rels. Office: 450 Golden Gate Ave San Francisco CA 94102

SCHWARZKOPF, GLORIA A., education educator, psychotherapist; b. Chgo., Apr. 20, 1926; m. Alfred E. Grossenbacher. BE, Chgo. State U., 1949, MEd in Libr. Sci., 1956. Cert. nat. recovery specialist, reality therapist; libr. sci. endorsement; cert. hypnotherapist; nat. forensic counselor. Tchr. Chgo. Bd. Edn., 1949-91, inservice trainer in substance abuse, 1990, 91; co-therapist ATC outpatient unit Ingalls Meml. Hosp., Chgo., 1981-86; recovery specialist Interaction Inst., Evergreen Park, Ill., 1993-95; instr. Govs. State U., University Park, Ill., 1987, 91, South Suburban Coll., South Holland, Ill., 1991, Prairie State Coll., Chicago Heights, Ill., 1993, 96. columnist Peoples Choice Weekly, 1991-93. Citizens Amb. Program del. to Russia and Czechoslovakia, 1996. Recipient Sci. Tchr. of Yr. award, 1976, Svc. Recognition award, 1985, IMSA Recognition award, 1988; grantee Chgo. Pub. Sch., 1981. Mem. NEA, Nat. Assn. Forensic Counselors, Sci. Tchrs. Assn., Ill. Alcoholism Counselors Alliance, Nat. Alcoholism Coun., Am. Assn. Hypnotherapists, Am. Assn. Behavioral Therapists, Soc. of Am. for Recovery (nat. cert. recovery specialist). Home: 2216 W 91st St Chicago IL 60620-6238

SCHWARZLOSE, RICHARD ALLEN, journalism educator; b. Chgo., Mar. 18, 1937; s. Paul Fowler and Muriel Beth (Kingsley) S.; m. Sally Jean Frye, July 27, 1963; children: Daniel Frye, Rebecca Frye. BS in Journalism, U. Ill., 1959, MA in Polit. Sci., 1960, PhD in Communications, 1965. Reporter, telegraph editor News-Gazette, Champaign, Ill., 1955-62; asst. prof. journalism Purdue U., West Lafayette, Ind., 1965-68; from asst. prof. to prof. journalism Northwestern U., Evanston, Ill., 1968—, assoc. dean Sch. Journalism, 1989-93. Author: Newspapers: A Reference Guide, 1987, Nation's Newsbrokers, 2 vols., 1989-90; author monograph; contbr. numerous articles to profl. jours. Peterson rsch. grantee Am. Antiquarian Soc., Worcester, Mass., 1984. Mem. Assn. for Edn. in Journalism and Mass Communications, Soc. Profl. Journalists. Unitarian. Avocations: biking, conducting seminars with adult groups. Home: 2712 Payne St Evanston IL 60201-2028 Office: Northwestern U Medill Sch Journalism Evanston IL 60208

SCHWARZROCK, SHIRLEY PRATT, author, lecturer, educator; b. Mpls., Feb. 27, 1914; d. Theodore Ray and Myrtle Pearl (Westphal) Pratt; m. Loren H. Schwarzrock, Oct. 19, 1945 (dec. 1966); children: Kay Linda, Ted Kenneth, Lorraine V. BS, U. Minn., 1935, MA, 1942, PhD, 1974. Sec. to chmn. speech dept., U. Minn., Mpls., 1935, instr. in speech, 1946, team tchr. in creative arts workshops for tchrs., 1955-56, guest lectr. Dental Sch., 1967-72, asst. prof. (part-time) of practice adminstrn. Sch. Dentistry, 1972-80; tchr. speech, drama and English, Preston (Minn.) H.S., 1935-37; tchr. speech, drama and English, Owatonna (Minn.) H.S., 1937-39, also dir. dramatics, 1937-39; tchr. creative dramatics and English, tchr.-counselor Webster Groves (Mo.) Jr. H.S., 1939-40; dir. dramatics and tchr.-counselor Webster Groves Sr. H.S., 1940-43; exec. sec. bus. and profl. dept. YWCA, Mpls., 1943-45; tchr. speech and drama Covent of the Visitation, St. Paul, 1958; editor pro-tem Am. Acad. Dental Practice Adminstrn., 1966-68; guest tchr. Coll. St. Catherine, St. Paul, 1969; vol. mgr. Gift Shop, Eitel Hosp., Mpls., 1981-83, Edina Cmty. Resource Pool, 1992-95; cmty. citizen mem. planning, evaluating, reporting com. Edina Pub. Sch. System, 1993-96; tutor for reading, writing, and speaking, 1993-96; cons. for dental med. programs Normandale C.C., Bloomington, Minn., 1968, vol. tutor, 1996—; cons. on pub. rels. to dentists, 1954-96; guest lectr. to various dental groups, 1966-95; lectr. Internat. Congress on Arts and Communication, 1980, Am. Inst. Banking, 1981; condr. tutorials in speaking and profl. office mgmt., 1985-96; owner Shirley Schwarzrock's Exec. Support Svc., 1989—; cons. to mktg. communications mgr. Ergodyne Corp., St. Paul, 1991-92; freelance editor med. support bus., 1992. Author books (series): Coping with Personal Identity, Coping with Human Relationships, Coping with Facts and Fantasies, Coping with Teenage Problems, 1984; individual book titles include: Do I Know the "Me" Others See?, My Life-What Shall I Do With It?, Living with Loneliness, Learning to Make Better Decisions, Grades, What's So Important About Them, Anyway?, Facts and Fantasies About Alcohol, Facts and Fantasies About Drugs, Facts and Fantasies About Smoking, Food as a Crutch, Facts and Fantasies About the Roles of Men and Women, You Always Communicate Something, Appreciating People-Their Likenesses and Differences, Fitting In, To Like and Be Liked, Can You Talk With Someone Else? Coping with Emotional Pain, Some Common Crutches, Parents Can Be a Problem, Coping with Cliques, Crises Youth Face Today, Effective Dental Assisting, (with L.H. Schwarzrock) 1954, 59, 67, (with J.R. Jensen) 1973, 78, 82, (with J.R. Jensen, Kay Schwarzrock, Lorraine Schwarzrock) 1990, Workbook for Effective Dental Assisting, 1960, 68, 73, (with Lorraine Schwarzrock), 1978, 82, 90, Manual for Effective Dental Assisting, 1968, 73, 78, 82, 90; (with Donovan F. Ward), Effective Medical Assisting, 1969, 76; Workbook for Effective Medical Assisting, 1969, 76, Manual for Effective Medical Assisting, 1969, 76; (with C.G. Wrenn) The Coping With Series of Books for High School Students, 1970, 73; The Coping With Manual, 1973, Contemporary Concerns, of Youth, 1980. Pres. University Elem. Sch. PTA, 1955-56. Fellow Internat. Biog. Assn.; mem. Minn. Acad. Dental Practice Adminstrn. (hon.), Minn. Historical Soc., 1992—, Minn. Geneaolgical Soc., 1992—, Zeta Phi Eta (pres. 1948-49), Eta Sigma Upsilon. Home: 7448 W Shore Dr Edina MN 55435-4022 *Growing up as a latch key child, challenged to accomplish adult tasks accompanied by "You can do it Kid," provided me with the ability to face challenges from scrubbing floors to delving deeply into research. Assured that there is a solution to every problem, I absorbed the knowledge and skills my professors taught, developed my creativity and spiritual awareness, and learned to listen sensitively and compassionately. This training enabled me to draw forth creative expression from adolescents, respond to their many needs, and to develop adults' communication skills in numerous settings.*

SCHWARZSCHILD, MARTIN, astronomer, educator; b. Potsdam, Germany, May 31, 1912; came to U.S., 1937, naturalized, 1942; s. Karl and Else (Rosenbach) S.; m. Barbara Cherry, Aug. 24, 1945. Ph.D., U. Goettingen, 1935; D.Sc. (hon.), Swarthmore Coll., 1960, Columbia U., 1973; DSc, Princeton U., 1992. Research fellow Inst. Astrophysics, Oslo (Norway) U., 1936-37, Harvard U. Obs., 1937-40; lectr., later asst. prof. Rutherfurd Obs., Columbia U., 1940-47; prof. Princeton U., 1947-50, Higgins prof. astronomy, 1950-79. Author: Structure and Evolution of the Stars. Served to 1st lt. AUS, 1942-45. Recipient Dannie Heineman prize Akademie der Wissenschaften zu Goettingen, Germany, 1967, Albert A. Michelson award Case Western Res. U., 1967, Newcomb Cleveland Prize AAAS, 1987, Rittenhouse Silver medal, 1966, Prix Janssen Société astronomique de France, 1970, Medal from l'Assn. Pour le Developpement Internat. de l'Observatoire de Nice, 1986, Gerlach-Adolph von Muenchausen Medaille Goettingen U., 1987, Dirk Brouwer award Am. Astron. Soc., 1991, Balzan prize, 1994. Fellow Am. Acad. Arts and Scis.; mem. Internat. Astron. Union (v.p. 1964-70), Akademie der Naturforscher Leopoldina, Royal Astron. Soc. (asso., Gold medal 1969, Eddington medal 1963), Royal Astron. Soc. Can. (hon.), Am. Astron. Soc. (pres. 1970-72), Nat. Acad. Scis. (Henry Draper medal 1961), Soc. Royale des Sciences de Liege (corr.), Royal Netherlands Acad. Sci. and Letters (fgn.), Royal Danish Acad. Sci. and Letters (fgn.), Norwegian Acad. Sci. and Letters, Astron. Soc. Pacific (Bruce medal 1965), Am. Philos. Soc., Sigma Xi.

SCHWARZSCHILD, PATRICIA MICHAELSON, lawyer; b. Washington, Jan. 15, 1950; d. Louis LeRoy and Katherine Ann (Elmore) Michaelson; m. William Harry Schwarzschild, June 9, 1973 (div.); children—W.H., Michael Todd. B.S., Va. Tech. U., 1972; J.D., Vanderbilt U., 1975. Bar: Va. 1975, U.S. Dist. Ct. (ea. dist.) Va. 1975, U.S. Ct. Appeals (4th cir.) 1981. Staff atty. Va. State Corp. Commn., Richmond, 1975-77; assoc. McGuire, Woods & Battle, Richmond, 1977-81; ptnr. Hunton & Williams, Richmond, 1981—. mem. exec. com., bd. dirs. Va. Capital Representation Resouce Ctr. Bd. dirs. YMCA, Richmond, 1977-83, Richmond Children's Mus., 1980-81, Va. Fedn. Planned Parenthood, Richmond, 1983-86. Fellow Va. Law Found. (exec. coun.); mem. ABA (council on issues affecting legal profession), Va. Bar Assn. (chmn. membership com. 1982-84, bd. govs. litigation section), Va. Bar (fellow young lawyers sect.), Am. Judicature Soc. Club: Westwood Racquet. Office: Hunton & Williams E Tower Riverfront Plz 951 E Byrd St Richmond VA 23219-4040*

SCHWEBACH, GERHARD HERMANN, microbiologist; b. Asch, Czechoslovakia, Feb. 27, 1944; came to U.S., 1957; s. Leonard Valentine and Gertrude Margareta (Rogler) S.; m. Janet Elaine Peterson, June 1, 1966; children: Derek, Heidi, Daniel, Adam, Nathan, Elisabeth. MS, Brigham Young U., Provo, Utah, 1967; Cert. in Med. Tech., Malcolm grow Med. Ctr., Andrews AFB, Md., 1976. Cert. med. technologist. Honorarium prof. U. Colo., Colorado Springs, 1976-82; sci. instr. Pikes Peak C.C., Colorado Springs, 1988-92, Nat. Coll., Colorado Springs, 1992—; sr. microbiologist Water Resources divsn. City of Colorado Springs, 1982—; cons./rschs. Schwebach Environ. and Pub. Health Svcs., Colorado Springs, 1994—. Author: Practical Guide to Microbial and Parasitic Diseases, 1980; contbr. articles to profl. jours. Cub master Boy Scouts Am., Colo., 1977-79, explorer advisor, Utah, 1972-74; cmty. soccer coach Parks and Recreation, Colorado Springs, 1986-88. Capt. USAF, 1969-79. Decorated Air Force commendation medal with oak leaf cluster, meritorious svc. medal. Mem. Coll. Allied Health Profls. of Am. (pres. 1979—), Am. Soc. Microbiology, Am. Soc. Clin. Pathologists, Am. Pub. Health Assn. Republican. LDS. Achievements include development of appropriate fecal coliform, total coliform and fecal streptococcus indicator levels for certain water reuse applications. Avocations: camping, soccer. Home: 3160 Meander Cir Colorado Springs CO 80917 Office: City of Colorado Springs PO Box 1103 Colorado Springs CO 80947

SCHWEBACH, MARTHA KEENE, nurse practitioner; b. Pratt, Kans., Feb. 3, 1939; d. Samuel Sidney and Alice Katherine (Sanko) Keene; m. Donald E. Schwebach, Sept. 3, 1960; children: Douglas, Cynthia, Daryl, Dean. Dominican Sch. of Nursing, 1960, U. N.Mex., 1968; Fellow, U. N.Mex., 1968-69. Cert. family nurse practitioner, 1977. Lectr., co-author, fellow dept. epidemiology, cmty. medicine U. N.Mex. Sch. of Medicine, Albuquerque, 1968-72; pilot project U. N.Mex., 1969-72; adminstr. Hope Med. Ctr., Inc., Estancia, N.Mex., 1970-77, Moriarty (N.Mex.) Med. Clinic, 1977-82, Ctrl. N.Mex. Med. Ctr., Inc., Moriarty, 1982-91; family nurse practitioner Family Health Clinic, Moriarty, 1992—; established not-for-profit med. organ. with later expansion to urgent care ctr.; cons. for establishment of rural clinics; grant writer in field. Contbr. numerous publs. to profl. jours. Guest lectr. for AMA, Am. Hosp. Assn., Josiah Macy Jr. Found., Dept. Health, Edn. and Welfare. Recipient formal recognition for nurses where practice reflects high profl. stds.; honored by Pres. Gerald R. Ford at Oval Office of White House, 1974; named N.Mex. Outstanding Young Woman of Yr., 1974, 90, one of Outstanding Young Women of Am., 1974; first family nurse practitioner in U.S. Mem. ANA, Am. Nurses Credentialing Ctr., ANA Coun. on Advanced Practice, N. Mex. Nurses Assn., N. Mex. Nurse Practitioner Council. Avocations: art, photography, gardening. Home: PO Box 327 901 Martinez Rd Moriarty NM 87035 Office: Family Health Clinic 1108 Rt 66 SW Moriarty NM 87035

SCHWEBEL, ANDREW I., psychology educator; b. N.Y.C., Feb. 5, 1943; s. Milton and Bernice Lois (Davison) S.; m. Carol Rose Lubinsky, May 25, 1969; children—David, Sara. B.A., Antioch Coll., 1965; M.S., Yale U., 1967; Ph.D., 1969. Lic. psychologist, Ohio; cert. family therapist, Ohio.

Asst. prof. psychology Ohio State U., Columbus, 1969-73; assoc. prof. Ohio State U., 1973-79, prof., 1979—; pvt. practice clin. psychology Columbus, 1977—; psychol. cons. SE Ohio Comprehensive Planning Agy., Cambridge, Ohio, 1970-73; adj. prof. Union for Experimenting Colls. and Univs., Yellow Springs, Ohio, 1971—; cons. Social Ecology Equity Change Quest, Baton Rouge, 1973-75; host Let's Talk It Over, WBNS-AM Radio, Columbus, 1980-81; v.p for human relations New Communities Corp., Columbus; columnist Suburban News Press. Author: Student Teacher's Handbook, 1979, 3rd rev., 1996, Personal Adjustment and Growth: A Life-Span Approach, 1983, 2d rev. edit., 1990, A Guide to a Happier Family: Overcoming the Anger, Frustration and Boredom that Destroy Family Life, 1989; co-author: Understanding and Helping Families: A Cognitive-Behavioral Approach; co-editor: Mental Health of Ethnic Minorities, 1991; assoc. editor Family Rels., 1993—, Jour. Personal and Interpersonal Loss, 1995—. Bd. dirs. Urban Alternatives, 1976-87, Columbus Fathers, 1977-89, New Communities, 1981—; edn. com. The Wellington Sch.; mem. profl. adv. bd. Peers Unlimited, 1993—; chmn. Gov.'s Com. on Child Support. Recipient award City of Columbus Dept. Devel., 1979, Ohio Dept. Mental Health, 1980-82. Fellow APA; mem. Cmty. Devel. Soc., Internat. Personal Rels. Network, Nat. Coun. for Therapy and Rehab. through Horticulture, Authors Guild, N.Y. Acad. Scis., Nat. Acad. for Cert. Family Therapists (adv. bd. 1995—), Sigma Xi. Office: Ohio State U Dept Psychology 1885 Neil Ave Mall Columbus OH 43210-1222

SCHWEBEL, MILTON, psychologist, educator; b. Troy, N.Y., May 11, 1914; s. Frank and Sarah (Oxenhandler) S.; m. Bernice Lois Davison, Sept. 3, 1939; children: Andrew I., Robert S. AB, Union Coll., 1934; MA, SUNY, Albany, 1936; PhD, Columbia U., 1949; certificate in psychotherapy, Postgrad. Ctr. Mental Health, 1958. Lic. psychologist, N.Y., N.J.; diplomate Am. Bd. Examiners Profl. Psychology. Asst. prof. psychology Mohawk Champlain Coll., 1946-49; asst. to prof. edn., dept. chmn., assoc. dean NYU, 1949-67; dean, prof. Grad. Sch. Edn., Rutgers U., New Brunswick, N.J., 1967-77; prof. Grad. Sch. Applied and Profl. Psychology, 1977-85, prof. emeritus, 1985—; vis. prof. U. So. Calif., U. Hawaii; postdoctoral fellow Postgrad. Ctr. Mental Health, 1954-56, lectr. psychology; cons. NIMH, U.S., state and city depts. edn., ednl. ministries in Europe, Asia, univs. and pub. schs.; pvt. cons. psychologist and psychotherapist, 1953—. Author: A Guide to a Happier Family, 1989, Personal Adjustment and Growth, 1990, Student Teachers Handbook, 3rd edit., 1996, Interests of Pharmacists, Health Counseling, Who Can Be Educated?; editor: Mental Health Implications of Life in the Nuclear Age, 1986, Facilitating Cognitive Development, 1986, Promoting Cognitive Growth Over the Life Span, 1990, Behavioral Science and Human Survival, The Impact of Ideology on the I.Q. Controversy; editor Peace & Conflict: Jour. Peace Psychology, 1993—; co-editor Bull. Peace Psychology, 1991-94; mem. editl. bd. Am. Jour. Orthopsychiatry, Readings in Mental Health, Jour. Contemporary Psychotherapy, Jour. Counseling Psychology, Jour. Social Issues, others. Mem. sci. adv. bd. Internat. Ctr. for Enhancement of Learning Potential, 1988—; trustee Edn. Law Ctr., 1973-81, Nat. Com. Employment Youth, Nat. Child Labor Com., 1967-75, Union Exptl. Colls. and Univs., 1976-78; pres. Nat. Orgn. for Migrant Children, 1980-85; pres. Inst. of Arts and Humanities, 1984-95. Served with AUS, 1943-46, ETO. Met. Applied Rsch. Coun. fellow, 1970-71. Fellow APA, Am. Psychol. Soc., Am. Orthopsychiatry Assn., Soc. Psychol. Study Social Issues, Jean Piaget Soc. (trustee), Am. Ednl. Rsch. Assn., N.Y. Acad. Scis., Psychologists for Social Responsibility (pres.), Inst. Arts and Humanities Edn. (pres.), Sigma Xi. Home: 1050 George St Apt 17L New Brunswick NJ 08901-1025 Office: Rutgers U Grad Sch Applied and Profl Psychology Piscataway NJ 08854

SCHWEBEL, RENATA MANASSE, sculptor; b. Zwickau, Germany, Mar. 6, 1930; d. George and Anne Marie (Simon) Manasse; came to U.S., 1940, naturalized, 1946; m. Jack P. Schwebel, May 10, 1955; children: Judith, Barbara, Diane. BA, Antioch Coll., 1953; MFA, Columbia U., 1961; student Art Students League, 1967-69. Cartographer, Ecostate, Inc., Ridgewood, N.J., 1949; display artist Silvestri, Inc., Chgo., 1950-51; asst. Mazzolini Art Found., Yellow Springs, Ohio, 1952; one-person show Columbia U., 1961, Greenwich Art Barn, Conn., 1975, Sculpture Ctr., N.Y.C., 1979, Pelham Art Ctr., N.Y., 1981, New Rochelle Libr. Gallery, N.Y., 1980, outdoor installation Alfresco, Katonah Gallery, 1989, Berman/Daferner Gallery, N.Y.C., 1992-93; exhibited in group shows Stamford Mus., Conn., 1967, 96, Hudson River Mus., Yonkers, N.Y., 1972, 74, Wadsworth Atheneum, Hartford, 1975, Silvermine New Eng. Anns., 1972, 76, 80, 95, Silvermine Gallery, 1991, New Britain Mus. Am. Art, Conn., 1974, Sculptors Guild Anns., 1974—, Imprimatur Gallery, St. Paul, 1985, Bergen County Mus., N.J., 1983, Sculpture Ctr., N.Y.C., 1978-88, Katonah Gallery, N.Y., 1986-90, Cast Iron Gallery, N.Y.C., 1991, 93, Kyoto (Japan) Gallery, 1993; traveling show exhibited in Am. cultural ctrs. in Egypt and Israel, 1981, FFS Gallery, N.Y.C., 1994, 95, N.Y. Design Ctr., N.Y.C., 1996; represented in permanent collection S.W. Bell, Columbia U., Colt Industries, Am. Airlines, ComCraft Industries, Nairobi, Grüber Haus, Berlin, Mus. Fgn. Art, Sofia, Bulgaria. Bd. dirs. Fine Arts Fedn., N.Y., 1985-87; trustee Sculpture Ctr., 1980-88, chmn. exhbn. com., 1986-88; mem. adv. bd. Pehlham Art Ctr., 1982. Mem. Sculptors Guild (bd. dirs., pres. 1980-83), Antioch Coll. Assn. (bd. dirs. 1971-77), Ams. for Peace Now (bd. dirs. 1991—), Nat. Assn. Women Artists (Willis Meml. prize 1974, Medal of Honor 1981, Paley Meml. award 1979), Audubon Artists (Chaim Gross award 1980, medal of honor 1982, Rennick award 1986, 90, 92, 95), Conn. Acad. Fine Arts, N.Y. Soc. Women Artists, Artists Equity N.Y., Katonah Gallery (artist mem. 1986-90). Home: 10 Dogwood Hills Pound Ridge NY 10576-1508

SCHWEBEL, STEPHEN MYRON, judge, arbitrator; b. N.Y.C., Mar. 10, 1929; s. Victor and Pauline (Pfeffer) S.; m. Louise Ingrid Nancy Killander, Aug. 2, 1972; children: Jennifer, Anna. BA in Govt. magna cum laude with highest honors in govt., Harvard U., 1950; postgrad., Cambridge (Eng.) U., 1950-51; LLB, Yale U., 1954; LLD, Bhopal (India) U., 1983. Bar: N.Y. 1955, U.S. Supreme Ct. 1965, D.C. 1976. Dir. UN hdqrs. office World Fedn. UN Assns., 1950-53; lectr. Am. fgn. policy various univs. U.S. State Dept., India, 1952; research, drafting asst. to Trygve Lie for writing of In the Cause of Peace, 1953; assoc. White & Case, N.Y.C., 1954-59; asst. prof. law Harvard U., Cambridge, Mass., 1959-61; asst. legal advisor U.S. Dept. State, Washington, 1961-66, dep. legal advisor, 1973-81; exec. dir. Am. Soc. Internat. Law, Washington, 1967-72; Burling prof. internat. law Sch. of Advanced Internat. Studies, Johns Hopkins U., Washington, 1967-81; judge Internat. Ct. Justice, The Hague, The Netherlands, 1981—; v.p. Internat. Ct. Justice, The Hague, 1994—; spl. rep. Micronesian claims U.S. Dept. State, 1966-71; legal adviser U.S. del. 16th-20th and 4th Spl. Gen. Assemblies UN; U.S. assoc. rep. Internat. Ct. Justice, 1962, U.S. dep. agt., 1979-80, U.S. counsel, 1980; U.S. rep., chmn. U.S. del. to 1st session UN Spl. Com on Principles Internat. Law concerning friendly relations and cooperation among states, Mexico City, 1964; U.S. rep. on adv. com. UN Program Assistance in Teaching, Study, Dissemination and Wider Appreciation Internat. Law, 1966-74; U.S. counsel Franco-Am. Air Arbitration, 1978; legal adv. U.S. del. to 32d and 33d WHO Assemblies, Geneva, 1979-80; vis. prof. internat. law Australian Nat. U., Canberra, 1969; U.S. rep., chmn. del. 3d session UN Spl. Com. on Question Defining Aggression, Geneva, 1970; counselor internat. law U.S. Dept. State, 1973; U.S. rep., chmn. del. 2d and 4th sessions UNCTAD Working Group on Charter Econ. Rights and Duties of States, Geneva, 1973, Mexico City, 1974; U.S. alt. rep. UN Econ. and Social Council, Geneva, 1974; legal adviser U.S. del. Conf. Internat. Econ. Coop., Paris, 1975; mem. U.S. Tripartite Adv. Com. on Internat. Labor Standards, 1980, Internat. Law Commn., UN, Geneva, 1977-81; spl. rapporteur internat. watercourses Internat. Law Commn., UN, 1977-81, chmn. drafting com., 1978; mem. bd. arbitration Brit. Petroleum v. Iran and Nat. Iranian Oil Co., Paris, 1982-85; pres. arbitration tribunal Marine Dr. Ltd. v. Ghana Investments Ctr. and Govt. of Ghana, 1988-90; chmn. or party-apptd. arbitrator internat. comml. arbitration tribunals, 1988—; mem. exec. com. Commn. Study Orgn. Peace, 1948-61; adv. joint com. law internat. transactions Am. Law Inst. and Am. Bar Assn., 1959-61; nat. chmn. Collegiate Council for UN, 1948-50; pres. Internat. Student Movement for UN, 1950-51; undergrad. orator Harvard U. Commencement, 1950; mem. adv. bd. Ctr. Oceans Law and Policy U. Va., 1975-81; vice chmn. Sec. State's Adv. Com. Pvt. Internat. Law, 1978-79, chmn., 1979-81; mem. internat. adv. bd. Cambridge U. Ctr. for Rsch. in Internat. Law, 1983—, mem. bd. electors Whewell Professorship in Internat. Law U. Cambridge, 1983—; mem. overseers' com. to visit Harvard U. Law Sch., 1991—; cons. Ford. Found., 1990; chmn. supervisory bd. Telders Internat. Law Moot Court Competition, The Hague, Netherlands, 1993—, vis. lect. Cambridge U., 1957, Inst. Universitaire de Hautes Etudes Internationales, Geneva, 1980; Carnegie lectr. Hague Acad. Internat. Law, 1972; Brown lectr. Cath. U., 1983; Lauterpacht. lectr., Cambridge U., 1983; jurisprudential lectr. U. Wash., 1985; Otto Walter Internat. Fellow, N.Y. Law Sch., 1987; Sherrill lectr. Yale U., 1988; Centennial Morris vis. prof. Chgo.-Kent Coll. of Law, 1988; Page Disting. vis. jurist U. Kans., 1988; Allison lectr. Suffolk Law Sch., 1989; Regents' lectr. U. Calif. Berkeley, 1990; Wing-Tat Lee lectr. Loyola U., 1990; Ford Found. lectr. U. N.Mex., U. Wash., U. Ind., Vanderbilt U., U. Minn., 1991, U. Ca.A., U. Houston, U. Miami, Emory U., Notre Dame U., 1992, U. Iowa, U. Pitts., 1993; Ben C. Green lectr. Case Western Res. U., 1992; Blaine Sloan lectr. Pace U., 1993; Hauser lectr. NYU Law Sch., 1994; Goff lectr., Hong Kong Polytechnic Law Faculty, 1994; pres. Adminstrv. Tribunal Internat. Monetary Fund, 1994—. Author: The Secretary-General of the United Nations, 1952, International Arbitration: Three Salient Problems, 1987, Justice in International Law, 1994; editor: The Effectiveness of International Decisions, 1971; mem. editorial bd. Am. Jour. Internat. Law, 1967-81; chmn. editorial adv. com. Internat. Legal Materials, 1967-73. Frank Knox fellow Harvard U., 1950-51; recipient Gherini prize Yale Law Sch., 1954, Pres. medal Johns Hopkins U., 1992, Harold Weill medal NYU, 1992. Mem. ABA, Am. Soc. Internat. Law (exec. v.p. 1967-73, hon. v.p. 1982-95, hon. pres. 1996—), Internat. Law Assn., Inst. Droit Internat., Coun. Fgn. Rels., Acad. of Experts (v.p. 1995—), Harvard Club (N.Y.C.), Athenaeum (London), Haagsche Club (The Hague), Cosmos Club (Washington), Phi Beta Kappa. Avocations: music, cycling.

SCHWED, PETER, author, retired editor and publisher; b. N.Y.C., Jan. 18, 1911; s. Frederick and Bertie (Stiefel) S.; m. Antonia Sanxay Holding, Mar. 6, 1947; children: Katharine Holding (Mrs. Eric F. Wood), Peter Gregory, Laura Sanxay (Mrs. Michael Sirico), Roger Eaton. Grad., Lawrenceville (N.J.) Sch., 1928; student, Princeton, 1929-32. Asst. v.p. Provident Loan Soc. N.Y., 1932-42; with Simon & Schuster, Inc., N.Y.C., 1946-84; v.p., exec. editor Simon & Schuster, Inc., 1957-62, exec. v.p., 1962-66, pub. trade books, 1966-72, chmn. editorial bd., 1972-82, editorial chmn. emeritus, 1982-84, dir., 1966-72. Author: Sinister Tennis, 1975, God Bless Pawnbrokers, 1975, The Serve and the Overhead Smash, 1976, Hanging in There, 1977; (with Nancy Lopez) The Education of a Woman Golfer, 1979, Test Your Tennis IQ, 1981, Turning the Pages, 1984, Overtime: A 20th Century Sports Odyssey, 1987, How to Talk Tennis, 1988, Quality Tennis after 50...Or 60...Or 70...Or..., 1990, The Common Cold Crusade: A Novel Not to be Sneezed At, 1994, Plum to Peter: Letters of P.G. Wodehoue to his Editor, 1996; compiler: The Cook Charts, 1994; editor: (with H.W. Wind) Great Stories From the World of Sports, 1958; (with Allison Danzig) The Fireside Book of Tennis, 1972; contbr. articles to jours. Trustee Lawrenceville Sch., 1968-72. Capt. F.A. AUS, World War II. Decorated Bronze Star, Purple Heart. Mem. Authors Guild, P.E.N., Century Assn. Democrat. Home: 151 W 86th St New York NY 10024-3401 *I suppose my guiding principle has been to face up to problems and difficult situations as immediately as I can, even if taking more time to think about them might have resulted in better ideas and actions. But an honest, un-Machiavellian handling of matters, without putting them off while brooding about them, has always struck me as effective when I do it, and appealing when others do. I try to carry this principle through with everyone, from my wife and children, through my office associates, to community affairs. It gives me a reputation ranging from bluntness to rudeness with those whose favorite I may not be, but I would hope one of respect and admiration with those about whom I care.*

SCHWEGMAN, MONICA JOAN, artist; b. Hamilton, OH, Apr. 19, 1958; d. David Michael and LaVerne Henrietta (Mergy) Kiley; m. Craig Alfred Schwegman, Oct. 6, 1978; children: Craig, Sarah. Student, U. Cin., 1976-78; AAS, Brookdale C.C., 1978; postgrad., Kansas City Art Inst., 1990. Mgmt. trainee coll. coop. Marshall Fields, Chgo., 1977-78; decorator, cons. Sears, Toms River, N.J., 1985-88; artist, owner studio and gallery Lampasas, Tex., 1990-94; chmn. Keystone Art Alliance, Lampasas, 1991-94; art dir. Theatre for Lampasas, 1993-94. Exhibited in group shows at Gallery One, Marble Falls, Tex., Found Art, Lampasas, KBVO TV Set Design, Austin, Tex., Breckenrdige Fine Arts Ctr., Pasillo De Artes Gallery, Austin, Contemporary Art Exhibit, Lampasas, Gannon U., Erie, Pa., Glass Growers Gallery, Erie. Instr. art City of Lampasas/Sparts, 1993. Mem. Tex. Fine Artist Assn., Lampasas C. of C. (mem. tourism com. 1993). Republican. Roman Catholic. Avocations: reading, aerobics, volleyball.

SCHWEGMANN, JOHN F., consumer products company executive. Ceo, gen. manager, partner Schwegmann Giant Super Markets, New Orleans, La., 1967—. Office: Schwegmann Giant Super Markets 5300 Old Gentilly Rd New Orleans LA 70126-5007*

SCHWEGMANN, MELINDA, former state official; b. Austin, Tex., Oct. 25, 1946; m. John F. Schwegmann; 3 children. Student, La. State U.; grad. in Edn., U. New Orleans, 1968. Former pub. sch. tchr.; past pres. La. Soc. for Prevention of Cruelty to Animals; lt. gov. La., 1991-95; now dir. Schwegmann's Giant Supermarkets. Mem. bd. Schwegmann Giant Super Markets; chmn. bd. Goodwill Industries; bd. dirs. Met. Area Com. New Orleans; sec. bd. dir.s Jr. Achievement; former mem. Jefferson Beautification Com. Office: PO Box 26099 New Orleans LA 70186

SCHWEICHLER, MARY ELLEN, childhood education educator, consultant; b. Buffalo, N.Y., Oct. 19, 1931; d. Joseph John and Teresa Mary (McVey) Carter; (div. May 1973); children: Michele, Richard, Maria Regina, Beth, David. Cert. Indsl. and Labor Rels., Cornell U., 1983; BS magna cum laude, SUNY, Buffalo, 1986, postgrad. studies, 1986—. Cert. early childhood edn. Postulant and tchr. Missionary Servants Blessed Trinity Pre-Sch., Phila., 1950-51; tchr., adminstr., founder Southtowns Pre-Sch. Devel., Blasdell, N.Y., 1975-82; asst. coor. dept. surgery 3d yr. student program sch. medicine SUNY, Buffalo, 1982-84, asst. to chair Health and Behavioral Scis., 1984-88; lectr. early childhood edn. Orchard Pk. (N.Y.) Sch. Dist., 1975-82, SUNY Buffalo, 1975-82; cons. early childhood edn. Day Care Assn. Resource Ctr., Buffalo, 1987—. Contbr. articles profl. publs.; author numerous poems. Vol. Head Start, Lackawanna, N.Y., 1970-75, P.R. Teen Ctr., Lackawanna, 1970-72; mem. Orchard Pk. Enrollment and Bldg. Utilization Com., 1982, Orchard Pk. Edn. Adv. Bd., 1988, Nat. Multiple Sclerosis Soc., 1990—, Found. for Internat. Cooperation, 1965-69, Christian Family Movement, 1962-70, U-U Task Force on Domestic Violence, 1993—; founding mem. West N.Y. chpt. Reyes Syndrome Found., 1979-83; ombudsman ARC, Buffalo, 1989—; workshop leader Career Devel. Ctr. for Women in Govt., Albany, N.Y., 1982-84; trainer Smoking Cessation Am. Lung Assn., Buffalo, 1984-86. Recipient Appreciation award, Orchard Park Sch. Bd., 1988. Mem. Women's Auxiliary Am. Physical Therapy Assn. (founder, pres. 1965-72), Nardin Acad. Alumni (bd. dirs. 1965-70), Alpha Sigma Lambda (sec. 1987—). Unitarian. Avocation: reading. Home: 36 Arthur Ave 318 Blasdell NY 14219

SCHWEICKART, JIM, advertising executive, broadcast consultant; b. Toledo, June 25, 1950; s. Norman Marvin and Anne Belle (Cress) S.; m. Deborah J., Aug. 14, 1971; children: Jennifer, Kimberly, Stephen. BA in Polit. Sci, Taylor U., Upland, Ind., 1972. News anchor, announcer Sta. WCMR, Elkhart, Ind., 1967-71; news anchor, disc jockey Sta. WWHC, Hartford City, Ind., 1971-72; gen. mgr. Sta. WTUC, Taylor U., 1971; news dir. Sta. WCMR, Elkhart, 1972-74; news anchor Sta. WOWO, Fort Wayne, Ind., 1974-78, Sta. KDKA, Pitts., 1978-79; gen. mgr. Sta. WBCL-FM, Fort Wayne, 1979-85; owner advt. agy., broadcast cons. Fort Wayne, 1984—. Bd. dirs. Christians for Polit. Alternatives; elder bd. Blackhawk Bapt. Ch. Republican. Baptist.

SCHWEICKART, RUSSELL LOUIS, communications executive, astronaut; b. Neptune, N.J., Oct. 25, 1935; s. George L. Schweickart; children: Vicki Louise, Russell and Randolph (twins), Elin Ashley, Diana Croom; m. Nancy Kudriavetz Ramsey; step-children: Matthew Forbes Ramsey, David Scot Ramsey. B.S. in Aero. Engring, Mass. Inst. Tech., 1956, M.S. in Aeros. and Astronautics, 1963. Former research scientist Mass. Inst. Tech. Exptl. Astronomy Lab.; astronaut Johnson Manned Spacecraft Center, Houston, lunar module pilot (Apollo 9, 1969); dir. user affairs Office of Applications, NASA; sci. adv. to Gov. Edmund G. Brown, Jr. State of Calif., 1977-79; chmn. Calif. Energy Commn., 1979-83, commr., 1979-85; pres., founder Assn. Space Explorers, 1985—; pres. NRS Communications, San Francisco, 1991-94; exec. v.p. CTA Comml. Systems, Rockville, Md., 1994—; cons. and lectr. in field. Trustee Calif. Acad. Sci. Served as pilot USAF, 1956-60, 61; Capt. Mass. Air N.G. Recipient Distinguished Service medal NASA, 1970, Exceptional Service medal NASA, 1974, De La Vaulx medal FAI, 1970, Spl. Trustees award Nat. Acad. TV Arts and Scis., 1969. Fellow Am. Astronautical Soc.; mem. Soc. Exptl. Test Pilots, AIAA, Sigma Xi. Club: Explorers. Office: CTA Comml Systems 6116 Executive Blvd Ste 800 Rockville MD 20852-4920

SCHWEIG, MARGARET BERRIS, meeting and special events consultant; b. Detroit, Mar. 23, 1928; d. Jacob Meyer and Anne Lucille (Schiller) Berris; m. Eugene Schweig Jr., Nov. 24, 1951 (dec.); children: Eugene III, John A., Suzanne. Student, U. Mich., 1945-47. Founder, pres. St. Louis Scene, Inc., 1975-94. Mem. St. Louis Conv. and Visitors Commn., St. Louis Forum. Mem. Meeting Planners Internat., Am. Soc. Assn. Execs., Profl. Conv. Mgmt. Assn., Nat. Assn. Exposition Mgrs., Internat. Spl. Events Soc., Hotel Sales Mgmt. Assn. (bd. dirs. 1977-80), Regional Commerce and Growth Assn., The Network (pres. 1980-81).

SCHWEIKER, MARK S., lieutenant governor; b. Bucks County, Pa., 1953; s. John and Mary S.; m. Katherine Schweiker; children: Brett, Eric, Kara. BS, Bloomsburg U., 1975; MA in Adminstrn., Rider U., 1983. Merrill Lynch, McGraw Hill; Supr. Middletown Twp., 1979; commr. Bucks County, Pa., 1987-94; lt. gov., pres. of the senate, chmn. of the bd. of pardons State of Pa., 1995—; former chmn. Dela. Valley Regional Fin. Authority. Former bd. dirs. Bucks County United Way. Recipient Alumnus of Yr. Bloomsburg U., 1990, Outstanding Svc. to Conservation award Nature Conservancy Pa. Branch. Office: 200 Main Capitol Harrisburg PA 17120-0002

SCHWEIKER, RICHARD SCHULTZ, trade association executive, former senator, former cabinet secretary; b. Norristown, Pa., June 1, 1926; s. Malcolm Alderfer and Blanche (Schultz) S.; m. Claire Joan Coleman, Sept. 10, 1955; children: Malcolm C., Lani, Kyle, Richard S. Jr., Lara Kristi. BA, Pa. State U., 1950; D of Pub. Svcs. (hon.), Temple U., 1970; D.Sc. (hon.), Georgetown U., 1981. Bus. exec., 1950-60; mem. 87th-90th congresses from 13th Dist. Pa., mem. house armed services and govt. ops. coms.; U.S. senator from Pa., 1969-80; mem. appropriations com., ranking mem. Labor-HEW subcom., ranking mem. health and human resources com., ranking mem. health subcom.; sec. HHS, 1981-83; pres. Am. Council Life Ins., Washington, 1983-94; bd. dirs. Tenet Healthcare Corp., LabOne Inc.; chmn. Partnership for Prevention, 1991—. Alt. del. Nat. Rep. Conv., 1952, 56, del., 1972, 80; designated v.p. candidate with Reagan for Pres. of U.S., 1976. Served with USNR, World War II. Recipient Disting. Alumnus award Pa. State U., 1970, Dr. Charles H. Best award Am. Diabetes Assn., 1974, Outstanding Alumnus of Yr. award Phi Kappa Sigma, 1982, Gold medal Pa. Assn. Broadcasters, 1982, Nat. Outstanding Svc. award Headstart, 1983, Pub. Svc. Gold medal Surgeon Gen. U.S., 1988, Govt. Achievement award Juvenile Diabetes Found., 1990, Disting. Achievement award Nat. Coun. on Aging, 1991, John Newton Russell award Nat. Assn. Life Underwriters, 1992; named Outstanding Young Man of Yr., Jr. C. of C., 1960. Mem. Phi Beta Kappa. Address: 904 Lynton Pl Mc Lean VA 22102-2113

SCHWEIKERT, NORMAN CARL, musician; b. Los Angeles, Oct. 8, 1937; s. Carl Albert and Hilda (Meade) S.; m. Sally Hardin Haizlip, July 22, 1961; 1 son, Eric Carl. Mus.B. performer's certificate in horn, Eastman Sch. Music, 1961. teaching assoc. Northwestern U., 1973-75, assoc. prof. (part-time), 1975—; horn instr. Nat. Music Camp, Interlochen, 1967; curator Leland B. Greenleaf Collection Mus. Instruments, Interlochen, 1970-71. Successively 4th, 2d and 3d horn with, Rochester Philharmonic, Civic and Eastman-Rochester symphonies, 1955-62, 64-66, instr. horn, mem., Interlochen (Mich.) Arts Quintet, Interlochen Arts Acad., 1966-71, 1st horn, Rochester Chamber Orch., 1965-66, Midland (Mich.) Symphony Orch., 1969-71, 1st horn, soloist, Northwestern Mich. Symphony Orch., 1966-71, Chgo. Little Symphony, tours, 1967, 68, asst. 1st horn, soloist, Chgo. Symphony Orch., 1971-75, 2d horn, Chgo. Symphony Orch., 1975—; appearances with, Eastman Chamber Orch., Rochester Bach Festival, Aspen Festival Orch., Moravian Music Festival, Alaska Festival, Peninsula Music Festival, Rochester Brass Quintet, Canterbury Wind Quintet, Westchester Brass Quintet, Eastman Wind Ensemble, Chgo. Symphony Winds, Quadrangle Chamber Players; soloist, New Japan Philharmonic, rec. artist for, Mercury, Columbia, Everest, C.R.I., Capitol. Mark Ednl., London-Decca, DGG, RCA Victor records, Sheffield Lab, Koch; recitals, also lecture demonstrations.; Contbr. articles to profl. jours. Served with AUS, 1962-64. Recipient certificate of merit City Chgo., 1971. Mem. Internat. Horn Soc. (chmn. organizing com., sec.-treas. 1970-72, adv. coun. 1972-76), Am. Mus. Instrument Soc., Phi Mu Alpha Sinfonia (life alumni mem.), Pi Kappa Lambda. Home: 1491 Edgewood Rd Lake Forest IL 60045-1314 Office: care Chgo Symphony Orch 220 S Michigan Ave Chicago IL 60604-2508

SCHWEINHART, RICHARD ALEXANDER, health care company executive; b. Louisville, Sept. 19, 1949; s. John Lawrence and A. Alicia (Kotheimer) S.; m. Margaret Loraine Hobbs, July 17, 1971; children: John Edward, Jennifer Lynn. AB in Acctg., Bellarmine Coll., 1971. CPA, Ky. Staff Coopers & Lybrand, Louisville, 1971-75; asst. contr. Humana Inc., Louisville, 1975-82, dir. acctg., 1982-83, contr., 1983-85, v.p., contr., 1985-88, v.p. fin., 1988-91, sr. v.p. fin., 1991-93; sr. v.p. fin. Galen Health Care, Inc., Louisville, 1993, Columbia/HCA Healthcare Corp., Louisville, 1993-95; sr. v.p. new bus. and network devel. Columbia/HCA Healthcare Corp., Nashville, 1995—. Bd. dirs. Goodwill Industries Ky., 1988-94, treas., 1989-90, vice chmn., 1991-92, chmn., 1992-93; mem. Leadership Louisville, 1987-88. Mem. AICPA, Ky. Soc. CPAs. Democrat. Roman Catholic. Avocations: golf, genealogy. Office: Columbia/HCA Healthcare 1 Park Plaza Nashville TN 37203-0550

SCHWEITZER, GEORGE, communications executive; b. N.Y.C., 1951. BS in Broadcasting and Film, Boston U., 1972. Prodn. supr. CBS-TV, N.Y.C., 1972-76; dir. comms. Sta. CBS-TV, N.Y.C., 1979, v.p. comms. and ops., 1980-82, v.p. comms. and info., 1982-87, v.p. comms., 1988-91, sr. v.p. mktg. and comms., 1991-94, exec. v.p. mktg. and comms., 1994—; v.p., dir. copr. rels. Young & Rubicam, 1987-88. Office: Sta CBS-TV 51 W 52d St New York NY 10019

SCHWEITZER, GEORGE KEENE, chemistry educator; b. Poplar Bluff, Mo., Dec. 5, 1924; s. Francis John and Ruth Elizabeth (Keene) S.; m. Verna Lee Pratt, June 4, 1948; children: Ruth Anne, Deborah Keene, Eric George. BA, Central Coll., 1945, ScD in Philosophy, 1964; MS, U. Ill., 1946, PhD in Chemistry, 1948; MA, Columbia U., 1959; PhD in History, NYU, 1964. Asst. Central Coll., 1943-45; fellow U. Ill., 1946-48; asst. prof. chemistry U. Tenn., 1948-52, assoc. prof., 1952-58, prof., 1960-69, Alumni Distinguished prof., 1970—; cons. to Monsanto Co., Proctor & Gamble, Internat. Tech., Am. Cyanamid Co., AEC, U.S. Army, Massengill; lectr. colls. and univs. Adv. bd. Va. Intermont Coll. Author: Radioactive Tracer Techniques, 1950, The Doctorate, 1966, Genealogical Source Handbook, 1979, Civil War Genealogy, 1980, Tennessee Genealogical Research, 1981, Kentucky Genealogical Research, 1981, Revolutionary War Genealogy, 1982, Virginia Genealogical Research, 1982, War of 1812 Genealogy, 1983, North Carolina Genealogical Research, 1983, South Carolina Genealogical Research, 1984, Pennsylvania Genealogical Research, 1985, Georgia Genealogical Research, 1987, New York Genealogical Research, 1988, Massachusetts Genealogical Research, 1989, Maryland Genealogical Research, 1991, German Genealogical Research, 1992, Ohio Genealogical Research, 1994, Indiana Genealogical Research, 1996; also 155 articles. Faculty fellow Columbia U., 1958-60. Mem. Am. Chem. Soc., Am. Philos. Assn., History Sci. Soc., Soc. Genealogists, Phi Beta Kappa, Sigma Xi. Home: 407 Ascot Ct Knoxville TN 37923-5807

SCHWEITZER, MELVIN L., commissioner, lawyer; b. N.Y.C., Oct. 27, 1944. BA, NYU, 1966; JD, Fordham U., 1969. Bar: N.Y. 1969. Atty. Rogers & Wells, N.Y.C.; commr. The Port Authority of N.Y. and N.J., 1993—; assoc. Rogers & Wells, N.Y.C., 1969-74, ptnr., 1975—; mem. Gov. Commn. on N.Y. Fin. Svcs.Industry, 1989—. Counsel, law chmn. N.Y. State Dem. Com., 1974-85. Mem. Assn. Bar City N.Y., Phi Sigma Alpha. Office: Rogers & Wells 200 Park Ave New York NY 10166-0005

SCHWEITZER, N. TINA, photojournalist, television producer, director, writer, international consultant public relations, media relations, government relations; b. Hartford, Conn., Apr. 7, 1941; d. Abraham Aaron Morris and

Ruth Blanche (Shifreen) S. BS, Emerson Coll., 1964. Freelance writer Boston and Washington, 1965-67; editor, chief prodn. maj. feature publ., mem. press-info. staff Embassy of Republic of Indonesia, Washington, 1967-68; researcher, writer Congl. Quar., Inc., Washington, 1969-70; owner Schweitzer Assocs., Hartford, Conn. and Washington, 1970-78, 79—; dir. comty. rels., media rels. and govt. rels. Advocacy Svcs. for the Deaf, West Hartford, Conn., 1978-79; del. White House Conf. Small Bus., 1986; mem. faculty Conn. Re-employment Workshop Middlesex Comty. Tech. Coll.; profl. model. Corr. The Farmington (Conn.) Valley Herald, 1984; first bus. columnist Hartford Woman newspaper, 1984; contbr. articles to numerous govtl. and comml. publs.; author: Media Kit, 1978, Women's Job Hunting Guide, 1983, You Can Do It! A Practical Guide for Job Hunting and Career-Changing, 1987, Men On the Tor (Violet Hunter), 1990; writer, designer, producer series of TV videotape pub. svc. announcements on employment deaf or hard-of-hearing, 1983-84; contbr. editorials to TV Stas. WFSB, 1977, 84, 86, WVIT, 1983; writer, ind. producer, dir., talk-show host Sta. WVIT-TV, 1987. Mem. State-wide Health Coordinating Coun., a U.S. Govt./Conn. Health Dept. project, 1978-80; adviser Conn. Office Advocacy to Handicapped; mem. legis. task force State of Conn., 1978-80, 1978-79; del. first Conn. Gov.'s Conf. on Libr. and Info. Svcs., 1978; candidate Conn. Ho. of Reps., 1982; aux. police officer Hartford Police Dept., 1976-77; acting chmn. Comm. Com. Unitarian Meeting House, West Hartford; dir. pub. rels. Greater Hartford Com. UNICEF, 1984-86; affiliated Rep. Town Com., Hartford., 1989; apptd. to Nat. Pub. Rels./Advt. Adv. Coun. Am. Mensa Ltd., 1989; press rep. Mensa Internat. 1st Joint Conf. Am. Coun. Edn. and Conf. European Rectors, 1989. Recipient Presdl. Sports award Pres.'s Coun. on Phys. Fitness and Sports, 1992, 93,94; hon. fellow John F. Kennedy Presdl. Libr. Mus. Found. Mem. Nat. Writers Union, Nat. Press Photographers Assn., Inter-Am. Press Assn., Mensa, Sherlock Holmes Soc. London, Sigma Delta Chi. Address: 2350 Commonwealth Ave Apt 2-1 Auburndale MA 02166-1779

SCHWEITZER, PETER, advertising agency executive; b. Chgo., Aug. 31, 1939; children: Mark, Cynthia, Jenifer, Samantha; m. Elaine Elkin, 1986; children: Dana, Taylor. B.A., U. of Mich., 1961; MBA, W. Mich. U., 1967. With Post div. Gen. Foods, 1961-69; v.p. Grey Advt., 1969-76; sr. v.p. J. Walter Thompson, 1976-79; sr. v.p. mktg. Burger King Corp.; sr. v.p., gen. mgr., then exec. v.p., gen. mgr. J. Walter Thompson USA, Inc.-Detroit; v. chmn. of agency ops. J. Walter Thompson Co., Detroit, 1988-95, pres., 1995—. also: J Walter Thompson Co 466 Lexington Ave New York NY 10017-3140*

SCHWEITZER, THEODORE GOTTLIEB, III, United Nations administrator; b. Hannibal, Mo., Aug. 28, 1942; s. Theodore Gottlieb Jr. and Dorothy Lois (Burnett) S. Cert. in French Lang., U. Paris, 1968; BA, U. Iowa, 1970, MA, 1974. Cert. Thai Lang. Am. Univ. Alumnae Assn., Bangkok, 1976, profl. tchr., Iowa. Tchr., librarian Lewis County Schs., Ewing, Mo., 1971-73; head librarian Internat. Sch., Bangkok, 1974-76; info. officer U.S. Army, Udorn, Thailand, 1974-76; dir. media services Am. Sch., Teheran, 1976-77; dir. media svcs. Am. Sch., Isfahan, Iran, 1977-78; refugee officer UN HCR, Geneva and Bangkok, 1979—; founder S.E. Asia Rescue Found., Ft. Walton Beach, Fla., 1981—, Hanoi Fgn. Langs. U., 1992-94. Author: Ted Schweitzer Story, 1985, (with Malcolm McConnell) Inside Hanoi's Secret Archives-Solving the MIA Mystery, 1995. Spl. rep. to Vietnam, Office of the Sec. of Def., Washington, 1992-94. With USAF, 1959-62. Recipient Award of merit SOS Boat people Com., San Diego, 1982, replica of Nobel Peace Prize, UN High Commr. for Refugees, 1981. Mem. Mensa. Republican. Baptist. Avocations: writing, reading, scuba diving, photography, private pilot. Home: 762 Sailfish Dr Fort Walton Beach FL 32548-6041 Office: UN High Commr for Refuges, Palais Des Nations, Geneva Switzerland

SCHWEITZER, WILLIAM H., lawyer; b. Cleve., June 6, 1944. BA, Trinity Coll., 1966; JD, Georgetown U., 1969. Bar: D.C. 1970. Asst. U.S. atty. U.S. Attys. Office, Washington, 1970-73; mng. ptnr. Baker & Hostetler, Washington. Mem. ABA, D.C. Bar. Office: Baker & Hostetler Washington Sq 1050 Connecticut Ave NW Ste 1100 Washington DC 20036-5303*

SCHWEIZER, KARL WOLFGANG, historian, writer; b. Mannheim, Fed. Republic Germany, June 30, 1946; came to U.S., 1988; s. Ernest Schweizer; m. Elizabeth Wild, 1969; 1 child, Paul. BA in History, Wilfrid Laurier U., Can., 1969; MA, U. Waterloo, Can., 1970; PhD, Cambridge U., 1976. Prof. history Bishop's U., Lenoxville, Que., Can., 1976-88; chmn. dept. Bishop's U., Can., 1978-79, 82-84, 86; prof., chmn. humanities dept. N.J. Inst. Tech., Newark, 1988-93, prof. history dept. social sci. and policy studies, 1993—; grad. faculty Rutgers U., 1993—; vis. lectr. U. Guelph, Can., 1978-80; rsch. assoc. Russian Rsch. Ctr., Ill., 1979-80; acad. visitor London Sch. Econs., 1986, 94, vis. scholar, 1986-87, Queens U., Ont., Can., 1986-87; vis. fellow Darwin Coll., Cambridge, 1987, 94, Princeton U., 1994, Yale U., 1994. Author: Francois de Callieres: The Art of Diplomacy, 1983, Lord Bute: Essays in Reinterpretation, 1988, England, Prussia and the Seven Years War, 1989, Frederick the Great, William Pitt and Lord Bute, 1991, (with J. Osborne) Cobbett in His Times, 1990, Lord Chatham, 1993, Francois de Callieres: Diplomat of the Sun King, 1995; co-author: The Origins of War in Early Modern Europe, 1987; editor: The Devonshire Political Diary, 1757-1762, 1982, Diplomatic Thought 1648-1815, 1982, Warfare and Tactics in the 18th Century, 1984; co-editor: (with J. Black) Essays in European History 1648-1815 in Honour of Ragnhild Hatton, 1985, Politics and the Press in Hanoverian Britain, 1989, Herbert Butterfield: Essays on the History of Science, 1996; contbr. numerous articles to profl. jours. and mags. Mem. N.J. Gov.'s Adv. Panel on Higher Edn. Restructuring, 1994. Recipient thesis defence award Can. Coun., 1976, travel awards Peterhouse Coll., 1971-73, Adelle Mellen prize for outstanding contbn. to scholarship Edwin Mellen Press, 1989, Citation award N.J. Writer's Conf., 1993; fellow U. Waterloo, 1969-70, Province of Ont., 1969-70, Can. Coun., 1970-75; named Wilfred Laurier Proficiency scholar, 1966-69; rsch. grantee Bishop's U., 1977, 78, 80, 82, 83, postdoctoral rsch. grantee Can. Coun., 1977-78, 82-83, grantee Inter-Univ. Ctr. for European Studies, 1978, 81, conf. grantee S.S.H.R.C., 1985; travel grantee NEH, 1991, N.J. Com. for Humanities. Fellow Royal Hist. Soc.; mem. Internat. Commn. on History of Internat. Rels., Cambridge Hist. Soc., North American Conf. on Brit. Studies, Can. Assn. Scottish Studies, Can. Assn. 18th Century Studies, Inst. Hist. Rsch. Avocations: travel, writing, reading. Home: 37 Lenape Trl Chatham NJ 07928-1812 Office: Dept Social Scis and Policy Studies NJ Inst Tech Newark NJ 07102

SCHWEIZER, KENNETH STEVEN, physics educator; b. Phila., Jan. 20, 1953; s. Kenneth Paul and Grace Norma (Fischer) S.; m. Janis Eve Pelletier, Oct. 18, 1986; children: Gregory Michael, Daniel Patrick. BS, Drexel U., 1975; MS, U. Ill., 1976, PhD, 1981. Postdoctoral rsch. assoc. AT&T Bell Labs., Murray Hill, N.J., 1981-83; sr. mem. tech. staff Sandia Nat. Labs., Albuquerque, 1983-91; prof. materials sci. engrng. and chemistry U. Ill., Urbana, 1991—; chmn. polymers divsn., 1994—. Contbr. articles to profl. jours. Recipient Sandia award for Excellence, 1990, R&D 100 award, 1992. Mem. Am. Phys. Soc. (John H. Dillon medal 1991), Am. Chem. Soc., Sigma Xi, Pi Mu Epsilon. Office: U Ill Dept Materials Sci Engring 1304 W Green St Urbana IL 61801-2920

SCHWEIZER, PAUL DOUGLAS, museum director; b. Bklyn., Nov. 26, 1946; s. Alvin Charles and Marie Gertrude (Scholtz) S.; m. Jane Kulczycki, June 10, 1978. BA, Marietta Coll., Ohio, 1968; MA, U. Del., 1975, PhD, 1979; postgrad. Mus. Mgmt. Inst., U. Calif., Berkeley, 1990. Instr. art history St Lawrence U., Canton, N.Y., 1977-78; asst. prof. St. Lawrence U., Canton, N.Y., 1978-80; curator St. Lawrence U. (Brush Gallery), Canton, N.Y., 1977-78; dir. St. Lawrence U., Canton, N.Y., 1979-80, Munson-Williams-Proctor Inst. Mus. Art, Utica, N.Y., 1980—. Author exhbn. catalog; contbr. articles to profl. jours. Bd. dirs. Remington Art Mus., Ogdensburg, N.Y., 1979-80; bd. dirs. Williamstown (Mass.) Regional Art Conservation Lab., 1981-92, pres., 1988-92. Rsch. grantee Nat. Endowment for Arts, 1978. Mem. Coll. Art Assn., Assn. Art Mus. Dirs., N.Y. State Assn. Art Mus. (trustee 1993-95), Mus. Assn. N.Y. (councilor 1995—), Gallery Allocation of N.Y., Otsego Sailing Club, Alpha Sigma Phi, Omicron Delta Kappa. Office: Munson-Williams-Proctor Inst Mus Art 310 Genesee St Utica NY 13502-4764

SCHWEMM, JOHN BUTLER, printing company executive, lawyer; b. Barrington, Ill., May 18, 1934; s. Earl M. and Eunice (Butler) S.; m. Nancy Lea Prickett, Sept. 7, 1956; children: Catherine Ann, Karen Elizabeth. AB, Amherst Coll., 1956; JD, U. Mich., 1959. Bar: Ill. 1959. With Sidley & Austin, Chgo., 1959-65; with legal dept. R.R. Donnelley & Sons Co., Chgo., 1965-69; gen. counsel R.R. Donnelley & Sons Co., 1969-75, v.p., 1971-75, pres., 1981-87, chmn., 1983-89, dir., 1980-92; bd. dirs. William Blair Mut. Funds, Inc., Walgreen Co., USG Corp. Life trustee Northwestern U., Chgo. Mem. Law Club Chgo., Order of Coif, Phi Beta Kappa. Clubs: Chgo., Univ., Mid-Am., Comml., Hinsdale (Ill.) Golf, Old Elm. Home and Office: 2 Turvey Ct Downers Grove IL 60515-4530

SCHWENDEMAN, PAUL WILLIAM, lawyer; b. Chgo., Apr. 7, 1945; s. Oscar and Edna Dorothy (Ellis) S.; m. Shirley Anne Starke; children: Paul A., John E., Thomas D. BA in Econs., Carleton Coll.; MSJ, Northwestern U.; JD, Duquesne U. Bar: Pa. 1978. Mgr. divsn. ops. Greater Waterbury (Conn.) C. of C., 1971-75; v.p. Greater Pitts. C. of C., 1975-78; assoc. Kirkpatrick & Lockhart, Pitts., 1978-84, ptnr., 1984—. Lt. USNR, 1971. Office: Kirkpatrick & Lockhart 1500 Oliver Building Bldg Pittsburgh PA 15222-2312

SCHWENDIMAN, GARY, business administration educator; b. Colfax, Wash., Aug. 1, 1940; s. John L. and Naomi (Garner) S.; m. Jill Bateman, June 3, 1966; children: Todd, Heidi, Lisa, Wendy, Julie. B.S. with honors, Wash. State U., 1962; M.S., Brigham Young U., 1968, Ph.D., 1971. Prof. Marshall U., W. Va., 1969-72, Gen. Motors Inst., Flint, Mich., 1972-73; prof., assoc. dean Coll. Bus. Adminstrn. U. Nebr., Lincoln, 1973-77, dean, prof. Coll. Bus. Adminstrn., 1977—; bd. dirs. InaCom, Inc., Nebr. Human Resources Inst., Midwest Conf. on Bus.; bd. dirs. Gallup, Inc.; ind. adv. com. Savings Assn. Ins. Fund House and Senate Com. on Banking, Housing, and Urban Affairs; chmn. Schwendiman Funds; gen. ptnr. World Mkts. Fund L.P., Cash Alternative Fund L.P., Equity Fund L.P., Banc Fund L.P., Internat. Fund L.P., Global High Performance Fund L.P.; trustee N.R., Inc., Employees Pension Trust. Editor: (with S. M. Lee) Japanese Management, 1982, Management by Japanese Systems, 1982. Bd. dirs. St. Elizabeth Community Health Ctr., Lincoln, Nebr., 1976-78, United Way Lincoln, 1978-80, area council Boy Scouts Am., Lincoln, 1976-80, Gupta Charitable Found.; trustee Jr. Achievement. Mem. Am. Assembly of Collegiate Schs. Bus. (investment com.), Lincoln C. of C. and Industry (edn. com.), Nebr. Coun. Econ. Edn. (exec. com.), Newcomen Soc., Round Table, Polemic Club, Beta Gamma Sigma (bd. govs., chair Investment and Fin. Com.). Office: Univ Nebraska Lincoln Dept Mgmt 256 CBA Lincoln NE 68588-0491*

SCHWENDINGER, CHARLES JOSEPH, public administration educator, researcher; b. Dubuque, Iowa, July 2, 1931; s. Leo James and Loretta Lucille (Meyers) S.; m. Marion Jean Blain, June 11, 1957 (div. 1981); 1 child, Julieanne Schwendinger Wattles; m. Chieko Ikeda, Oct. 13, 1982. BA in History, Va. Mil. Inst., 1957; MPA, U. Okla., 1980, D Pub. Adminstrn., 1991. Commd. 2d lt. U.S. Army, 1957, advanced through grades to lt. col., 1971, served in various locations including Vietnam, 1957-78, ret., 1978; asst. prof. pub. adminstrn. Troy (Ala.) State U., 1986-88, assoc. prof., 1989, 91—; lectr. in field. Contbr. to profl. publs. Sgt. U.S. Army, 1949-53. Decorated Bronze Star medal with 2 oak leaf clusters, Air medal. Fellow Pi Alpha Alpha (chpt. pres. 1980-86, 89-90), Pi Sigma Alpha; mem. DAV, VFW, NRA, Am. Soc. Pub. Adminstrn. (coun. mem. Okla. chpt. 1989-90), Internat. City Mgmt. Assn., Am. Legion, Ret. Officers Assn. Roman Catholic. Home: PO Box 6378 Tampa FL 33608-0378 Office: Troy State U Fla Region PO Box 6472 Mac Dill AFB FL 33608

SCHWENGER, FRANCES, library director; b. Hamilton, Ont., Can., Oct. 20, 1936. BA in Psychology and English, U. Western Ont., 1970; MLS, U. Toronto, 1972. Head cataloguing health scis. libr. McMaster U., 1972-74; with Hamilton Pub. Libr., 1974-82, head ctrl. libr., 1980-82; asst. dir. Met. Toronto Ref. Libr., 1982-86, CEO, 1986—. Mem. ALA, Can. Libr. Assn., Ont. Libr. Assn., Internat. Assn. Met. City Librs., Internat. Fedn. Libr. Assns. and Instns. (mem. standing com. pub. librs. 1993—). Office: Met Toronto Libr Bd, Reference Libr 789 Yonge St, Toronto, ON Canada M4W 2G8

SCHWENKE, ROGER DEAN, lawyer; b. Washington, Oct. 18, 1944; s. Clarence Raymond and Virginia Ruth (Gould) S.; m. Carol Lynne Flenniken, Nov. 29, 1980; 1 son, Matthew Robert; stepchildren: Tracy L. Wolf Dickey, Mary M. Wolf. BA, Ohio State U., 1966; JD with honors, U. Fla., 1969. Bar: Fla. 1970. Instr. Coll. Law, U. Fla., Gainesville, 1969-70; assoc. Carlton, Fields, Ward, Emmanuel, Smith & Cutler, P.A., Tampa, Fla., 1970-74, ptnr., 1975—, adminstr., dept. head Real Estate, Environ. and Land Use Dept., 1978—; adj. prof. Coll. Law, Stetson U., St. Petersburg, Fla., 1979-80. Author chpt. in Environmental Regulation and Litigation in Florida, 1987; contbr. articles to profl. jours. Mem. diocesan coun. Episc. Diocese SW Fla., 1978-86, mem. standing com., 1990-93. Recipient Gertrude Brick Law Rev. prize U. Fla., 1969. Fellow Am. Coll. Real Estate Lawyers (bd. govs. 1985-88), Am. Law Inst.; mem. ABA (standing com. on environ. law, coun. real property sect. 1981—), Fla. Bar Assn., Air & Waste Mgmt. Assn., Order of Coif, Greater Tampa C. of C. (chmn. environ. coun. 1980-81), Tampa Club. Democrat. Office: Carlton Fields PO Box 3239 Tampa FL 33601-3239

SCHWENN, LEE WILLIAM, retired medical center executive; b. Morrisonville, Wis., Dec. 23, 1925; s. LeRoy William and Vivian Mae (Kramer) S.; m. Glenna Edith Mehne, Jan. 16, 1947; 1 son, William Lee. B.S., U. Wis., 1948; M.P.H., U. N.C., 1956. Tchr. pub. schs. Appleton, Wis., 1948-52; teaching cons. Wis. Health Dept., 1952-53; adminstrv. asst. Madison (Wis.) Health Dept., 1953-57; adminstrv. cons. U.S. Children's Bur., Atlanta Regional Office, 1957-58; adminstr. USPHS, Washington, 1958-66; assoc. dir. D.C. Dept. Health, 1966-70, D.C. Dept. Human Resources, 1970-71; exec. v.p. Maimonides Med. Center, Bklyn., 1971-88, pres., 1988-89, spl. cons. Bd. Trustees, 1989—. Recipient Distinguished Pub. Service award D.C. Govt., 1970. Mem. Am. Pub. Health Assn., Am. Acad. Health Adminstrs., Delta Omega. Home: 1007 Westminster Dr Greensboro NC 27410-4551

SCHWERDT, LISA MARY, English language educator; b. Coral Gables, Fla., Feb. 7, 1953; d. Henry G. and Dilys Doris (Bandurske) S. BS, Fla. Internat. U., 1973, BA, 1977; MA, Purdue U., 1979, PhD, 1984. Cert. secondary educator English, spl. edn., Fla. English instr. Green Sch. of English, Tokyo, Japan, 1973-75; spl. edn. tchr. Carol City (Fla.) Elem. Sch., 1975-77; grad. instr. Purdue U., West Lafayette, Ind., 1977-85; asst. prof. U. North Ala., Florence, 1985-89; adj. lectr. U. Cen. Fla., Orlando, 1989-90, Rollins Coll., Winter Pk., Fla., 1989-90; assoc. prof. English Calif. U. of Pa., 1990—, interim assoc. dean, 1995—. Author: Isherwood's Fiction, 1989; contbr. articles and book revs. to profl. jours. Mem. Sierra Club, Pitts., 1990—, Planned Parenthood, Pitts., 1986—. Grantee Purdue Found., 1982; recipient Excellence in Teaching award Purdue U., 1979, 81. Mem. MLA, Coll. English Assn., Nat. Coun. Tchrs. English, N.E. MLA, Pa. Coll. English Assn., Soc. for the Study of Narrative Lit., Soc. for Health and Human Values. Unitarian. Home: 5337 California Ave Bethel Park PA 15102-3821 Office: Calif U of Pa Dept English California PA 15419

SCHWERIN, HORACE S., marketing research executive; b. N.Y.C., Jan. 18, 1914; s. Paul and Rose (Lewis) S.; m. Lorraine Roth, June 14, 1941 (div. Dec. 1969); children—Barbara, Bruce; m. Enid May Highton, Apr. 28, 1973. B.S., Lafayette Coll., 1935; M.A., Kings Coll., London (Eng.) U., 1936; M.S., U. Paris, France, 1937. Gen. mgr., research dir., cons. N.Y. advt. agys., 1936-41; pres. Research Analysts, Inc., 1946; chmn. bd. Schwerin Research Corp., N.Y.C., Toronto, London, Hamburg, to 1968; chmn., pres. Horace Schwerin & Assos., Englewood Cliffs, N.J., 1968-72; dir. marketing devel. Campbell Soup Co., Camden, N.J., 1972—, v.p. market planning Canned Food div., 1977-82, mktg. strategy cons., 1982—; CEO, chmn. Schwerin Murphy, Inc., 1991—. Author: (with Henry H. Newell) Persuasion in Marketing, 1981; also articles on market research, nutrition, use of govt. data bases. Served as capt. U.S. Army, 1946. Decorated Legion of Merit with oak leaf cluster; inducted into Market Rsch. Coun. Hall of Fame, 1992. Mem. Am. Mktg. Assn., Market Rsch. Coun., Can. Club (N.Y.C.), Princeton Club (N.Y.C.). Methodist. Home: 5D Toll Gate Of Moorestown Moorestown NJ 08057 Office: 633 E Main St Moorestown NJ 08057-3059

SCHWERIN, KARL HENRY, anthropology educator, researcher; b. Bertha, Minn., Feb. 21, 1936; s. Henry William and Audrey Merle (Jahn) S.; m. Judith Drewanne Altermatt, Sept. 1, 1958 (div. May 1975); children: Karl Frederic, Marguerite DelValle; m. Partha Louise Hake Buell, Jan. 25, 1979; stepchildren: Tamara, Brent, Taryn. BA, U. Calif., Berkeley, 1958; PhD, UCLA, 1965. Instr. Los Angeles State Coll., 1963; asst. prof. anthropology U. N.Mex., Albuquerque, 1963-68, assoc. prof., 1968-72, prof., 1972—, asst. chmn. dept. anthropology, 1983-85, chmn. dept. anthropology, 1987-93; prof. invitado Inst. Venezolano de Investigaciones Cientificas, Caracas, 1979. Author: Oil and Steel Processes of Karinya Culture Change, 1966, Antropologia Social, 1969, Winds Across the Atlantic, 1970; editor: Food Energy in Tropical Ecosystems, 1985; contbr. articles to profl. jours. V.p. Parents without Ptnr., Albuquerque, 1976-77. Grantee Cordell Hull Found., Venezuela, 1961-62, N.Y. Zool. Soc., Honduras, 1981; Fulbright scholar Cañar, Ecuador, 1969-70, Paris, 1986. Fellow Am. Anthropol. Assn.; mem. Am. Ethnol. Soc., Am. Soc. Ethnohistory (pres. 1975), Southwestern Anthropol. Assn. (co-editor Southwestern Jour. Anthropology 1972-75), N.Mex. Cactus and Succulent Soc. (v.p. 1970-71), Maxwell Mus. Assn. (bd. dirs. 1984-85), Internat. Congress of Americanists (35th-40th, 43d, 46th, 48th), Sigma Xi (chpt. pres. 1980-81). Avocations: photography, gardening, hiking, camping, cycling. Office: U NMex Dept Anthropology Albuquerque NM 87131

SCHWERIN, WARREN LYONS, real estate developer; b. N.Y.C., Sept. 1, 1938; s. Clarence M. III and Helena (Lyons) S.; children: Kathryn Amy, James Warren. BA, Trinity Coll., 1960. Founding ptnr. Omega Properties, N.Y., 1961-70; pres. Arlen Shopping Ctrs., N.Y., 1970-73; pres., co-founder Related Properties, Inc., N.Y.C., 1973—. Past pres. Long Island Hearing and Speech Soc., past treas., trustee Buckley Country Day Sch.; mem. bd. overseers Southampton Coll.; bd. dirs. League for the Hard of Hearing, Indian River Land Trust, Marine Bank, Vero Beach, Fla. Mem. Internat. Council of Shopping Ctrs., Urban Land Inst. Office: Related Properties 625 Madison Ave New York NY 10022-1801

SCHWERING, FELIX KARL, electronics engineer, researcher; b. Cologne, Nordrhein-Westfalen, Federal Republic of Germany, June 4, 1930; came to U.S., 1964; s. Felix Bernhard and Maria (Heinrichs) S. BS, U. Aachen, Federal Republic of Germany, 1951, Diplom-Ingenieur, 1954, PhD, 1957. Asst. prof. U. Aachen, Federal Republic of Germany, 1956-58; electronic scientist U.S. Army R & D Labs., Fort Monmouth, N.J., 1958-61; project leader AEG-Telefunken, Ulm, Federal Republic of Germany, 1961-64; rsch. scientist U.S. Army Communication Electronics Command, Fort Monmouth, N.J., 1964—; vis. lab. assoc. U.S. Army Rsch. Office, Rsch. Triangle, N.C., 1984-85; vis. prof. N.J. Inst. Tech., Newark, 1986—, Rutgers U., New Brunswick, N.J., 1973-87. Author: (with others) Millimeter Wave Antennas, 1988; author and editor (with others) Microwave Antennas, 1989; mem. editorial bd. Microwave and Optical Tech. Letters, 1988—; contbr. over 30 articles to profl. jours.; patentee in field. Fellow IEEE (Best Paper award Antennas and Propagation Soc. 1961, 82), Internat. Sci. Radio Union, Am. Geophys. Union, Armed Forces Comm. Electronics Assn., Sigma Xi. Roman Catholic. Office: US Army Comm Elec Command Amsel Rd St # C Fort Monmouth NJ 07703

SCHWETZ, BERNARD ANTHONY, toxicologist; b. Cadott, Wis., Nov. 27, 1940; married; 4 children. BS in Biology, U. Wis., Stevens Point, 1962; DVM, U. Minn., 1967; MS in Pharmacology, U. Iowa, 1968, PhD in Pharmacology, 1970. Diplomate Am. Bd. Toxicology. USPHS trainee dept. vet. physiology and pharmacology U. Minn., 1964-66; USPHS trainee dept. pharmacology U. Iowa, 1966-70; toxicologist Dow Chem. U.S.A., Midland, Mich., 1970-78, dir. toxicology rsch. lab., 1978-82; chief sys. toxicity br. divsn. toxicology rsch. and testing NIEHS, Research Triangle Park, N.C., 1982-92, acting dir. environ. toxicology program, 1993; dir. Nat. Ctr. for Toxicol. Rsch., Jefferson, Ark., 1993—; assoc. commr. for sci. FDA, Rockville, Md., 1994—; adj. prof. U. Ark. for Med. Scis., 1993—, Mich. State U., East Lansing, 1973-82, N.C. State U., Raleigh, 1985-93. Assoc. editor Fundamental and Applied Toxicology, 1983-86, editor, 1986-92; editl. adv. bd. Environ. Health Perspectives and Critical Revs. in Toxicology, 1984—; contbr. numerous articles to profl. pubs. Recipient Arnold J. Lehman award Soc. of Toxicology, 1991, Dir.'s award NIH, 1991, Founders award Chem. Industry Inst. of Toxicology, 1994, FDA Commr.'s Spl. citation, 1995. Mem. AVMA, Soc. Toxicology (charter mem. Mich. chpt., councilor 1984-86, pres. N.C. chpt. 1987, pres. reproductive toxicology speciality sect. 1986, south ctrl. chpt.), Teratology Soc. (treas. 1978-82), Behavioral Teratology Soc., Phi Zeta. Avocations: fishing, photography. Office: Nat Ctr Toxicol Rsch HFT-1 3900 Nctr Rd Jefferson AR 72079-9501

SCHWICHTENBERG, DARYL ROBERT, drilling engineer; b. nr. Tulare, S.D., Nov. 8, 1929; s. Robert Carl and Lillian Rose (Hardie) S.; m. Helen M. Spencer, 1955 (div. Jan. 1971); children: Helayne, Randall, Hyalyn, Halcyon, Rustan; m. Helen Elizabeth Doehring, Nov. 11, 1971 (div. May 1982); 1 child, Suzanne. Student, U. Wyo., 1954-55; BSME, S.D. Sch. Mines and Tech., 1957; postgrad., Alexander Hamilton Inst., N.Y.C., 1962-63. Lic. pilot, rated AMEL. Office engr. Ingersoll-Rand Co., Mpls., 1957-58; sub br. mgr. Ingersoll-Rand Co., Duluth, Minn., 1959-60; product engr. Ingersoll-Rand Co., N.Y.C., 1960-63, devel. engr., 1964; sales mgr. Ingersoll-Rand Co., Phillipsburg, N.J., 1965; pres., founder Daryl Drilling Co., Inc., Flagstaff, Ariz., 1965-82; pres. Silent Rose Mining Co., Fallon, Nev., 1982-85; sr. design engr. Nev. Test Site Fenix & Scisson, 1985-90; prin. project engr. Raytheon Svcs. Nev., 1990-95; project mgr. Raytheon Svcs. Nev., Nev. Test Site, 1995—; co-owner, mgr. Dead Shot Ranch, Bondurant, Wyo., 1977-82. Inventor electronic subtitling for opera patrons. 1st lt. U.S. Army, 1950-54, Korea. Decorated Bronze Star. Mem. ASME, NRA, VFW, Inst. Shaft Drilling Tech. (speaker, instr. 1986—), Am. Legion, Mensa. Republican. Avocations: hunting, raising and training horses, flying, prospecting. Office: Raytheon Svcs Nev PO Box 328 Mercury NV 89023-0328

SCHWIER, PRISCILLA LAMB GUYTON, television broadcasting company executive; b. Toledo, Ohio, May 8, 1939; d. Edward Oliver and Prudence (Hutchinson) L.; m. Robert T. Guyton, June 21, 1963 (dec. Sept. 1976); children—Melissa, Margaret, Robert; m. Frederick W. Schwier, May 11, 1984. B.A., Smith Coll., 1961; M.A., U. Toledo, 1972. Pres. Gt. Lakes Communications, Inc., 1982—; vice chmn. Seilon, Inc., Toledo, 1981-83, also dir. Contbr. articles to profl. jours. Trustee Wilberforce U., Ohio, 1983—, Planned Parenthood, Toledo, 1979-83, Maumee Valley Country Day Sch., Toledo; bd. dirs. N.W. Ohio Hospice, 1991—. Episcopal Ch., Maumee, Ohio, 1983—; bd. trustees Toledo Hosp., Maumee Country Day Sch., 1986-92; pres. Edward Lamb Found., 1987—. Democrat. Episcopalian. Home: 345 E Front St Perrysburg OH 43551-2131 Office: 129 W Wayne St Ste 100 Maumee OH 43537-2150

SCHWIETZ, ROGER L., bishop. Ordained priest Roman Cath. Ch., 1967, consecrated bishop, 1990. Bishop Diocese of Duluth, Minn., 1989—. Home: 2803 E 4th St Duluth MN 55812-1501 Office: Diocese of Duluth 2803 E 4th St Duluth MN 55812-1501*

SCHWIMMER, DAVID, actor; b. Queens, N.Y.. BS in Speech/Theater, Northwestern U., 1988. Co-founder The Lookingglass Theater Co., Chgo., 1988; actor Friends, 1994—. Stage appearances include West, The Odyssey, Of One Blood, In the Eye of the Beholder, The Master and Margarita; dir. The Jungle, The Serpent, Alice in Wonderland; TV appearances include Monty NYPD Blue, L.A. Law, The Wonder Years; film appearances include Flight of the Invader, 1991, Crossing the Bridge, 1993, Twenty Bucks, 1993, The Pallbearer, 1995. Office: The Gersh Agy 232 N Canon Dr Beverly Hills CA 90210*

SCHWIND, MICHAEL ANGELO, law educator; b. Vienna, Austria, July 2, 1924; came to U.S., 1951; s. Siegfried and Sali (Salner) S. J.D., U. Central, Ecuador, 1949; LL.M. in Internat. Law, NYU, 1953, LL.B., 1957. Bar: Ecuador 1949, N.Y. 1957, U.S. Supreme Ct. 1967. Pvt. practice N.Y.C., 1957-69; Lectr. law NYU Sch. Law, 1959-63, adj. asst. prof., 1963-64, assoc. prof., 1964-67, prof., 1967-94, prof. emeritus, 1994—; dir. Inter-Am. Law Inst., Inst. Comparative Law, NYU Sch. Law, 1967-71. Bd. editors Am. Jour. Comparative Law. Mem. Am. Assn. Comparative Study Law (bd. dirs.), Am. Fgn. Law Assn. (bd. dirs. 1980-83, 84-87, 88-91, 93-96, v.p. 1983-84, 91-93, 96—), Am. Soc. Internat. Law. Office: NYU Sch Law 40 Washington Sq S Rm 321 New York NY 10012-1005

SCHWING, CHARLES E., architect; b. Plaquemine, La., Nov. 21, 1929; s. Calvin Kendrick and Mary Howard (Slack) S.; m. Cynthia Benjamin, June 14, 1952 (div. 1967); children—Calvin Kendick III, Therra Cynthia; m. Geraldine Fleniken Hofmann, Dec. 27, 1969; 1 stepson, Steven Blake. Student, La. State U., 1947-51; B.S., Ga. Inst. Tech., 1953, B.Architecture, 1954; 3e Assessit de'Architecture, Ecole Des Beaux-Arts. Field insp. Bodman, Murrell and Smith, Baton Rouge, 1954-55; assoc. architect Post & Harelson, Baton Rouge, 1955-59; partner Hughes and Schwing, Baton Rouge, 1959-61; owner Charles E. Schwing, Baton Rouge, 1961-69, Charles E. Schwing & Assos., Baton Rouge, 1969—; v.p. Schwing Inc., Baton Rouge, 1979-89; pres. Schwing Inc., Plaquemine, La., 1989; mem. La. State Bd. Archtl. Examiners, 1983-95 (pres. 1988-89), Nat. Coun. Archtl. Registration Bds. (chmn. Region III 1988-89, bd. dirs. 1990-93), adv. bd. Architects Nat. Employers Trust. Bd. dirs. Baton Rouge Area Found., 1986-92, treas. 1987-89; bd. dirs. Womens Hosp., 1993-94. Fellow AIA (treas., exec. com., dir., planning com., chmn. finance com. 1976-77, treas., exec. com., dir., fin. com. rsch. corp. 1976-77, treas., dir. found. 1976-77, v.p. 1978, pres.-elect 1979, pres. 1980), Royal Architecture Inst. Can. (hon.); mem. La. Architects Assn. (sec.-treas. 1971, v.p. 1972, pres. 1973), Venezuelan Soc. Architects (hon.), Bolivian Inst. Architects (hon.), C. of C., La. State U. Alumni Fedn., Ga. Tech. Alumni Club, Sigma Alpha Epsilon. Episcopalian. Clubs: Baton Rouge Country, City. Home: Stone's Throw 8655 Jefferson Hwy Apt 12 Baton Rouge LA 70809-2244 Office: 721 Government St Ste 101 Baton Rouge LA 70802-6029

SCHWINKENDORF, KEVIN NEIL, nuclear engineer; b. Newberg, Oreg., Mar. 11, 1959; s. Waldemar Adolf and Hattie Bertha (Baumgarten) S. BS, Oreg. State U., 1981, MS, 1983; postgrad., U. Wash. Reg. profl. engr., Wash. Advanced engr. UNC Nuclear Industries, Richland, Wash., 1983-84, engr., 1986-87; sr. engr. Westinghouse Hanford Co., Richland, 1987—; v.p. numerical methods, Analyst Devel. Corp., Scappoose, Oreg., 1990—. Designer: (ballistics software) PC-Bullet-ADCs, 1990 (Best Paper award 1992); author tech. publ. in field. Participant March of Dimes Walk-a-Thon, Richland, 1989, 90. Mem. Am. Nuclear Soc., NSPE, NRA, Soc. Computer Simulation, Safari Club Internat., Tau Beta Pi. Republican. Avocations: hunting, target shooting, personal computing, model building, bicycling. Home: 1121 Pine St Richland WA 99352-2135 Office: Nuc Analysis and Characterization Devel Dept WHC PO Box 1970 MSIN HO-38 Richland WA 99352

SCHWINN-JORDAN, BARBARA (BARBARA SCHWINN), painter; b. Glen Ridge, N.J.; d. Carl Wilhelm Ludwig and Helen Louise (Jordan) Schwinn; m. Frank Bertram Jordan, Jr.; children: Janine Jordan, Frank Bertram III. Grad. N.Y. Sch. Fine and Applied Art (Parsons), N.Y. and Paris; student Grand Cen. Art Sch., Art Students League, Grand Chaumiere, Academie Julien-Paris, Columbia U., NAD. Illustrator mags. including Vogue, 1930's, Ladies Home Jour., Saturday Evening Post, Colliers, Good Housekeeping, Cosmopolitan, McCall's, American, Town and Country, 1940's-60's. Women's Jour., Eng., Hors Zu, Fed. Republic Germany, Marie Claire, France, other fgn. publs., 1950's-60's. Portrait painter, including Queen Sirikit, Princess Margaret, Princess Grace; freelance painter, 1970—; one-man shows include Soc. of Illustrators, 1940, 50, Barry Stephens Gallery, 1950, Bodley Gallery, N.Y.C., 1971, 80, C.C., West Mifflin, Pa., 1973, Duquesne U., 1973, Mus. Am. Illustration, N.Y.C., 1991, Illustration House, N.Y.C., 1991, Giraffics Gallery, East Hampton, N.Y., 1991-95 (also rep.); exhibited in group shows including NAD, 1955, Royal Acad., London, Guild Hall, N.Y., 1981, Summit N.J. Art Ctr., 1981, Meredith Long Gallery, Houston, 1983, Mus. Soc. Illustrators, N.Y., 1985, The Marcus Gallery, Sante Fe, 1985, 86, The Gerald Peters Gallery, Santa Fe, 1985, 86, Brandywine Mus., Pa., 1986, New Britain (Conn.) Mus. Am. Art, 1986, Armory Show, N.Y.C., 1992-94, The Women's Ctr., Chapel Hill, N.C., 1993-94, Greenville County Mus. Art, S.C., 1995, The Soc. of the Four Arts, Palm Beach, Fla., 1995, The Hyde Collection, Glens Falls, N.Y., 1995, Ga. Mus. Art, 1995, Heckscher Mus., L.I., N.Y., 1995; works represented Holbrook Collection, Ga. Mus. Art, Eureka Coll., Ill., New Britain Mus. Am. Art, Mus. of Soc. of Illustrators, N.Y.C., Brandywine Mus., Pa., Sanford Low Meml. Collection, Del. Art Mus., Wilmington, Mus. Am. Illustration, N.Y.C., Glenbow Mus., Calgary, Alberta, Can.; represented in traveling show Del. Art Mus. 1994-95; various pvt. and gallery collections; work featured in America's Great Women Illustrators 1850-1950, 1985; lectr., instr. illustration Parsons Sch., 1952-54; founder adv. coun. Art Instrn. Sch., 1956-70. Chmn. art com. UNICEF greeting cards, 1950-61 mem. com. Spence Chapin Sch., Philharm. Soc., 1950's-60's. Winner prizes Art Dirs. Club, 1950, Guild Hall, 1969. Assoc. mem. Guggenheim Mus. Mem. Cosmopolitan Club N.Y. Author: Technique of Barbara Schwinn, 1956; World of Fashion Art, 1968. Home and Studio: 579 Fearrington Post Pittsboro NC 27312

SCHWITTERS, ROY FREDERICK, physicist, educator; b. Seattle, Wash., June 20, 1944; s. Walter Frederick and Margaret Lois (Boyer) S.; m. Karen Elizabeth Chrystal, June 18, 1965; children: Marc Frederick, Anne Elizabeth, Adam Thomas. S.B., MIT, 1966, Ph.D., 1971. Research asso. Stanford U. Linear Accelerator Center, 1971-74, asst. prof., then asso. prof., 1974-79; prof. physics Harvard U., 1979-90; scientist Fermi Nat. Accelerator Lab., Batavia, Ill., 1980-88; dir. superconducting supercollider Fermi Nat. Accelerator Lab., 1989-93; prof. physics U. Tex., Austin, 1994—. Author papers on high energy physics; asso. editor: Ann. Rev. Nuclear and Particle Sci; div. asso. editor: Phys. Rev. Letters. Recipient Alan T. Waterman award NSF, 1980. W.K.H. Panofsky Prize, Am Physical Soc., 1996. Fellow AAAS, Am. Phys. Soc. (W. K. H. Panofsky Prize, 1996), Am. Acad. Arts and Scis. Home: 1718 Cromwell Hill Austin TX 78703 Office: U Tex Dept Physics Austin TX 78712-1081

SCHWOLSKY, PETER M., gas industry executive, lawyer, partner; b. Apr. 29, 1946. BA cum laude, U. Pa., 1968; JD, U. Mich., 1971. Pvt. practice, 1971-73; asst. to gen. counsel N.Y. Stock Exch., 1973-75; gen. counsel Conn. Gen. Life Ins. Co., 1975-77; legis. asst. Sen. Lowell P. Weicker, Conn., 1977-79; counsel Electric Power Rsch. Inst., Washington, 1979-86; ptnr. Steptoe & Johnson, Washington, 1986-91; exec. v.p. N.J. Resources Corp., Princeton, 1991-95; sr. v.p., chief legal officer Columbia Gas Sys. Inc., Wilmington, Del., 1995—. Contbr. articles to profl. jours. Mem. ABA, D.C. Bar Assn., Conn. Bar Assn. Office: 20 Montchanin Rd Wilmington DE 19807

SCHWYN, CHARLES EDWARD, accountant; b. Muncie, Ind., Oct. 12, 1932; s. John and Lela Mae (Oliver) S.; m. Mary Helen Nickey, May 25, 1952 (dec.); children: Douglas, Craig, Beth; m. Madelyn Steinmetz. BS, Ball State U., 1957. CPA, Calif., D.C. With Haskins, Sells & Orlando, Chgo., Orlando, Fla., 1958-67; mgr. Deloitte, Haskins & Sells, Milan, Italy, 1967-70, San Francisco, 1970-80; with Deloitte, Haskins & Sells (now Deloitte & Touche), Oakland, Calif., ptnr. in charge, 1980-92, ret., 1992. Bd. dirs. Jr. Ctr. Art and Sci., 1982-89, pres., 1987-88; bd. dirs., trustee Oakland Symphony, 1982-86, 89-91; bd. dirs. Oakland Met. YMCA, 1984-89, Oakland Police Activities League, 1981-91, Joe Morgan Youth Found., 1982-91, Summit Med. Ctr., 1989-94; bd. dirs. Marcus A. Foster Ednl. Inst., 1986-95, pres., 1991-93; mem. adv. bd. Festival of Lake, 1984-89, U. Oakland Met. Forum, 1992—; co-chmn. Commn. for Positive Change in Oakland Pub. Schs.; mem. campaign cabinet United Way Bay Area, 1989; bd. regents Samuel Merritt Coll., 1994—. With USN, 1952-56. Recipient Cert. Recognition Calif. Legis. Assembly, 1988, Ctr. for Ind. Living award, Oakland Bus. Arts award for outstanding bus. leader Oakland C. of C., 1992; date of job retirement honored in his name by Oakland mayor. Mem. AICPA (coun. 1987-90), Oakland C. of C. (chmn. bd. dirs. 1987-88, exec. com. 1982-89), Oakland Met. C. of C., pres., 1996, Calif. Soc. CPAs (bd. dirs. 1979-81, 83-84, 85-87, pres. San Francisco chpt. 1983-84), Nat. Assn. Accts. (pres. Fla. chpt. 1967), Claremont Country Club (treas., bd. dirs. 1989—), Lakeview Club (bd. govs. 1987-92), Oakland 100 Club (pres. 1994), Rotary (bd. dirs. Oakland club 1986-88, 91-92, treas. 1984-86, pres. 1991-92). Office: Deloitte & Touche 2101 Webster St Fl 20 Oakland CA 94612-3027

SCIAME, JOSEPH, university administrator; b. Bklyn., Sept. 9, 1941; s. Joseph and Sophie (Pintacuda) S. EdB, St. John's U., 1971. Fin. aid officer, asst. to dean of admissions St. John's U., Jamaica, N.Y., 1967-71, dir. fin. aid, 1971-82, dean fin. aid, 1982, v.p. fin. aid and student svcs., 1982-94, v.p. for govt. and community rels., 1994—; mem. Gov. Commn. on Sch. Achievement, 1971—, chairperson, 1993—; pres. N.Y. Assn. Student Fin. Aid Adminstrn., 1980-82, Ea. Assn. Student Fin. Aid Adminstrn., 1986-87. Chmn. bd. ethics Town of North Hempstead, N.Y., 1984—; nat. chmn., bd. dirs. Garibaldi-Meucci Mus., N.Y., 1987-93. Decorated cavaliere del Merito della Repubblica Italiana; recipient Lifetime Membership award Ea. Assn., 1995, Achievement award N.Y. State Fin. Aid Adminstrs., 1982, Congl. Record award, 1979, 91, 93, 94, 95. Mem. Nat. Assn. Student Fin. Aid Adminstrs. (chmn. 1987-88, Disting. Svc. award 1988, Leadership award 1994), Assn. Equestrian Order Holy Sepulchre (knight grand cross 1991, knight invested 1980), Order Sons of Italy in Am. (lodge pres. 1974-78, state pres. 1993—), Futures in Edn. Found. (vice chair 1991-93, chair 1994—) . Roman Catholic. Avocations: walking, cooking, gardening, reading, lecturing. Home: 6 Jones St New Hyde Park NY 11040-1616 also: Trout Ln Southampton NY 11968 Office: St John's Univ Off VP Govt & Community Rels Jamaica NY 11439

SCIANCE, CARROLL THOMAS, chemical engineer; b. Okemah, Okla., Feb. 16, 1939; s. Carroll Elmer and Winifred (Black) S.; BS in Chem. Engring., U. Okla., 1960, M in Chem. Engring., 1964, PhD, 1966; m. Anita Ruth Fischer, Jan. 30, 1960; children: Steven, Frederick, Thomas, Erica. With E.I. duPont de Nemours & Co., Inc., 1966-95, planning mgr. nylon intermediates div., petrochem. dept., Wilmington, Del., 1978-80, tech. mgr., 1980-83, dir. engring. research, engring. dept., 1983-87, prin. cons. corp. research and devel. planning div., 1987-89; mgr. petroleum products R&D div., Conoco, Inc., 1989-93; dir. Environ. Tech. Partnerships, ctrl. R & D dept. DuPont, 1993-95; pres. Sci. Consulting Svcs., Inc., 1995—; guest lectr. U. Tex., Austin, 1996—. Mem. math. scis. and edn. bd. Nat. Rsch. Coun., 1987-89, adv. bd. NIST for Chem. Sci. & Tech., 1988-94. Served as officer USAR, 1961-63. Fellow Am. Inst. Chem. Engrs. (bd. dirs. materials engring. and scis. div. 1986-92, chmn. new tech. com. 1990-92, govt. rels. com. 1993-96); mem. Fedn. Materials Socs. (v.p. 1988-92, pres. 1993-94), Am. Chem. Soc. (mem. environ. R & D com. 1995—), N.Y. Acad. Scis., Sigma Xi. Home: 9 Aston Cir Hockessin DE 19707-2500

SCIANNA, RUSSELL WILLIAM, lawyer, educator; b. Reading, Pa., Sept. 26, 1956; s. Russell Joseph and Marjorie Louise (Wilson) S.; m. Joanne Frances Melcher, June 24, 1978; children: Russell Jr., Christopher, Elizabeth, Nicholas. BS in Fgn. Service, Georgetown U., 1978; JD, Boston U., 1981; MBA, Kutztown U., 1991. Bar: Pa. 1981, U.S. Dist. Ct. (ea. dist.) Pa. 1985. Tax acct. Ernst & Whinney, Reading, 1981-82; sole practice Reading, 1982-87; pres. Bulldog Assocs., Inc., 1987-92; assoc. atty. Forry, Ullman, Ullman, & Ferry, PC, 1992-94; pvt. practice, 1994—; lectr. bus. law and acctg. Penn State U., Reading, 1982-85; lectr. bus. Reading Area C.C., 1990-93; solicitor Reading Zoning Hearing Bd. and Civil Svc. Bds., 1994—; pres. Reading Optical Co., Inc., 1982-84; asst. pub. defender, asst. dist. atty. Berks County, Reading, 1985. Mem. Reading Zoning Hearing Bd., 1982-86; trustee Reading Area Community Coll., 1985-86; bd. dirs. Reading Cen. Br. YMCA, 1982-85. Mem. Pa. Bar Assn., Berks County Bar Assn., Rotary-West Reading/Wyomissing. Avocations: golf, backgammon. Office: PO Box 7622 225 Kenhorst Blvd Reading PA 19603-7622

SCIARRA, JOHN J., physician, educator; b. West Haven, Conn., Mar. 4, 1932; s. John and Mary Grace (Sanzone) S.; m. Barbara Crafts Patton, Jan. 9, 1960; children: Vanessa Patton, John Crafts, Leonard Chapman. BS, Yale U., 1953; MD, Columbia U., N.Y.C., 1957, PhD, 1963. Asst. prof. Columbia U., N.Y.C., 1964-68; prof., dept. head U. Minn. Med. Sch., Mpls., 1968-74; prof. Northwestern U. Med. Sch., Chgo., 1974—; chmn. ob-gyn Northwestern Meml. Hosp., Chgo., 1974—. Editor Gyn-Ob Reference Series, 1973—, Internat. Jour. Gyn-Ob, 1985—. V.p. med. affairs Chgo. Maternity Ctr., Chgo., 1974—. Fellow Am. Coll. Ob-Gyn. (chmn. internal affairs com. 1985-89); mem. Internat. Fedn. Ob-Gyn. (pres. elect 1988-91), Assn. Profs. Ob-Gyn. (sec. 1976-79, pres. 1980), Am. Assn. Maternal and Neonatal Health (pres. 1980-89, coun. resident edn. in ob-gyn. 1988—), Gyn-Ob. Found., Am. Fertility Soc. (Hartman award 1965, bd. dirs. 1971-73), Assn. Profs. Ob-Gyn. (sec.-treas. 1987—), Cen. Assn. Ob-Gyn. (trustees 1986—), Yale Club N.Y.C., Carleton Club Chgo. Club: Yale (N.Y.C.); Carleton (Chgo.). Avocation: photography, food, wine. Office: Northwestern U Med Sch 333 E Superior St Chicago IL 60611-3015

SCIFRES, CHARLES JOEL, agricultural educator; b. Foster, Okla., June 1, 1941; married, 1961; 2 children. BS, Okla. State U., 1963, MS, 1965; PhD in Agronomy, Botany, U. Nebr., 1968. Asst. rsch. agronomist range ecology Agrl. Rsch. Svc. USDA, 1965-68; asst. prof. range mgmt. Tex. A&M U., 1968-69, assoc. prof. range ecology and improvements, 1969-76, prof. range sci., prof. range ecology and devel. range sci., 1976-87; prof. dept. agr. U. Ark., Fayetteville, 1987—. Mem. Weed Sci. Soc. Am., Soc. Range Mgmt., Sigma Xi. Achievements include research in development of vegetation manipulation systems for rangeland resources; management for maximum productivity of usable products from the resource while maintaining its ecological integrity; persistence and modes of dissipation of herbicides from the range ecosystem; life history of key range species and community dynamics following manipulation. Office: U Ark Rm 203 Dept Agr Fayetteville AR 72701*

SCIFRES, DONALD R., semiconductor laser, fiber optics and electronics company executive; b. Lafayette, Ind.; m. Carol Scifres. B.S., Purdue U., 1968; M.S., U. Ill., 1970, Ph.D., 1972. Research and teaching asst. U. Ill., Urbana, 1968-72; research fellow, area mgr. Xerox Corp., Palo Alto, Calif., 1972-83; founder, pres., CEO SDL, Inc., San Jose, Calif., 1983—, dir., 1983—, chmn., 1992—; nat. lectr. IEEE Quantum Electronics Soc., 1979. Bd. editors Jour. Fiber and Integrated Optics, 1978; mem. editorial adv. bd. Photonics Spectra, 1992—; contbr. articles to tech. jours.; patentee in field. Recipient Disting. Engring. Alumni award Purdue U., 1990, Outstanding Elec. Engr. award, 1992; recipient Engring. Alumni award U. Ill., 1991, Alumni Honor award, 1993; U. Ill. fellow, 1968; Gen. Telephone and Electronics fellow, 1970-72. Fellow IEEE (Jack Morton award 1985), IEEE Lasers and Electro-Optics Soc. (pres. 1992, Engrign. Achievement award 1994), Optical Soc. Am. (Edward H. Land medal 1996); mem. Am. Phys. Soc., Lasers and Electro-Optics Mfg. Assn. (bd. dirs. 1992—, sec. 1994, pres. 1996), Tau Beta Pi, Eta Kappa Nu, Phi Eta Sigma. Office: SDL Inc 80 Rose Orchard Way San Jose CA 95134-1365

SCIPIO, L(OUIS) ALBERT, II, aerospace science engineering educator, architect, military historian; b. Juarez, Mex., Aug. 22, 1922; s. Louis Albert and Marie Leona (Richardson) S.; m. Katherine Ruth Jones, Aug. 15, 1942; children: Louis Albert, Karen R. B.S., Tuskegee Inst., 1943; B.Civil Engring., U. Minn., 1948, M.S., 1950, Ph.D., 1958. Archtl. draftsman McKissack & McKissack, Tuskegee, Ala., 1943; instr. Tuskegee Inst., 1946; designer Long & Thorshov, Mpls., 1948-50; lectr. U. Minn., Mpls., 1950-59; research physicist Hughes Aircraft Co., Culver City, Calif., 1954; Fulbright prof. Cairo U., Giza, Egypt, 1955-56; assoc. prof. mechanics Howard U., Washington, 1959-61; Fulbright prof. Cairo U., Giza, Egypt, 1955-56; dir. grad. studies for engring. and architecture, prof. aerospace engring. Howard U., Washington, 1967-70, Univ. prof. space scis., 1970-87, Disting. Univ. prof. emeritus, 1987—; prof. phys. scis. U. P.R., Mayaguez, 1961-63; prof. aerospace engring. U. Pitts., 1963-67; pub. Roman Publs., Silver Springs, Md., 1981—; cons. in field; author Compendium of Aircraft Stress Analysis and Design, 1956. Author: Principles on Continua with Applications, 1966, Structural Design Concepts, 1967, E.M. Collar Insignia, 1907-1926, 1981, Last of the Black Regulars, 1983, With the Red Hand Division, 1985, The 24th Infantry at Fort Benning, 1986, Pre-War Days at Tuskegee, 1987. Bd. visitors Air Force Inst. Tech., 1979-83. Served with AUS, 1943-46. Mem. N.Y. Acad. Scis., Internat. Assn. Bridge and Structural Engrs., Soc. Natural Philosophy, AIAA, AAAS; mem. Am. Phys. Soc.; mem. NSPE, Co. of Mil. Historians, Coun. on Am. Mil. Past, Phi Beta Kappa, Sigma Xi, Alpha Kappa Mu, Pi Mu Epsilon, Sigma Pi Sigma, Sigma Gamma Tau, Pi Tau Sigma. Home: 12511 Montclair Dr Silver Spring MD 20904-2053

SCIPIONE, RICHARD STEPHEN, insurance company executive, lawyer; b. Newton, Mass., Aug. 27, 1937; s. Charles John and Alice (Scotto) S.; m. Lois Mugford, Aug. 29, 1964; children: Jeffrey Charles, Douglas Loring. BA, Harvard U., 1959; LLB, Boston U., 1962. Bar: Mass. 1962. Atty. John Hancock Mut. Life Ins. Co., Boston, 1965-69, asst. counsel, 1969-74, assoc. counsel, 1975-79, sr. assoc. counsel, 1980-82, 2d v.p., counsel, 1982-84, v.p., gen. solicitor, 1984-85, sr. v.p. and gen. solicitor, 1986-87, gen. counsel, 1987—; chmn. bd. dirs. New England Legal Found.; bd. dirs. John Hancock Advisers/Distbrs.; trustee John Hancock Mutual Funds. Served to capt. U.S. Army, 1962-65. Mem. ABA (dir. New Eng. Coun.), Assn. Life Ins. Counsel (gov. 1994—), Chatham Yacht Club. Office: John Hancock Mut Life Ins Co Box 111 John Hancock Pl Boston MA 02117

SCIRE, FRANK JACKSON, retired radar scientist; b. Bklyn., July 15, 1928; s. Marco and Marianna (Bianco) S.; m. Jacqueline Deleranko, June 21, 1958; children: Marianne, Mark, Paul. BS in EE, Pratt Inst., 1952; MS in EE, NYU, 1958; PhD in EE, Poytech. Inst. Bklyn., 1967. Mem. tech. staff Bell Telephone Labs., N.Y.C., 1952-54; mgr. missile electronics Maxson Electronics, N.Y.C., Great River, N.Y., 1954-63; dept. head advanced radar systems Sperry, Unisys, Paramax, Great Neck, N.Y., 1963-93; radar scientist rep. U.S. on NATO Adv. Bd. for NIAG-16, Washington and N.Y.C. at NATO Countries, 1985-86; advanced radar tech. coord. Unisys Tech. Transfer Team, Great Neck, N.Y., 1990-92; radar cons. for defense and air traffic, Unisys and Alcott, N.Y., 1993-94. Contbr. articles to profl. jours., papers to sci. confs. Tutor calculus and stats., for referred coll. students, Melville, N.Y., 1970-80; asst. soccer coach St Elizabeth Parish, Melville, N.Y., 1979; asst. baseball coach Little League, Huntington, N.Y., 1981. Mem. IEEE, Mus. Natural History, Sigma Xi, Tau Beta Pi. Republican. Roman Catholic. Achievements include patents on missile guidance, hi-radar visibility in the presence of clutter and jamming, electronic scanning; provided radar solution to USAF for the DEW line detection, tracking, identification of low-flying hostile aircraft by incorporating simultaneously hi data rates with long dwell times; designed and developed a mobile solid state radar capable of extracting aircraft space, time data over land or sea in a sustainable severe clutter-jamming environment. Home and Office: Advanced Radar Consulting 19 Saxon St Melville NY 11747

SCIRICA, ANTHONY JOSEPH, federal judge; b. Norristown, Pa., Dec. 16, 1940; s. A. Benjamin and Anna (Sclafani) S.; m. Susan Morgan, May 6, 1966; children—Benjamin, Sara. B.A., Wesleyan U., 1962; J.D., U. Mich., 1965; postgrad., Central U., Caracas, Venezuela, 1966. Bar: Pa., 1966, U.S. Dist. Ct. (ea. dist.) Pa., 1984, U.S. Ct. Appeals (3d cir.), 1987. Ptnr. McGrory, Scirica, Wentz & Fernandez, Norristown, Pa., 1966-80; asst. dist. atty. Montgomery County, Pa., 1967-69; mem. Pa. Ho. of Reps, Harrisburg, 1971-79; judge Montgomery County Ct. Common Pleas, Pa., 1980-84, U.S. Dist. Ct. (ea. dist.) Pa., Phila., 1984-87, U.S. Ct. Appeals (3d cir.), 1987—; chmn. Pa. Sentencing Commn., 1980-85. Fulbright scholar Central U., Caracas, Venezuela, 1966. Mem. Montgomery Bar Assn., Pa. Bar Assn., ABA. Roman Catholic. Office: US Courthouse Independence Mall W #22614 601 Market St Philadelphia PA 19106-1510

SCISM, DANIEL REED, lawyer; b. Evansville, Ind., Aug. 27, 1936; s. Daniel William and Ardath Josephine (Gibbs) S.; m. Paula Anne Sedgwick, June 21, 1958; children: Darby Claire, Joshua Reed. BA, DePauw U., 1958; JD, Ind. U., 1965. Bar: Ind. 1965, U.S. Dist. Ct. (so. dist.) Ind. 1965, U.S. Ct. Appeals (7th cir.) 1967, U.S. Supreme Ct. 1976. Reporter Dayton (Ohio) Jour.-Herald, 1958-59; editor Mead Johnson & Co., Evansville, 1962; first assoc., then ptnr. Roberts, Ryder, Rogers & Scism and predecessor firms, Indpls., 1965-86; ptnr. Barnes & Thornburg, Indpls., 1987—; cons. Ind. Personnel Assn., 1984—. Treas. Marion County chpt. Myasthenia Gravis Found., Indpls., 1970; v.p. Marion County Mental Health Assn., Indpls., 1970-71; pres. The Suemma Coleman Agy., Indpls., 1973-74; bd. dirs. Ind. Humanities Coun., 1995—. Edwards fellow Ind. U., 1964. Mem. ABA, Ind. Bar Assn., Indpls. Bar Assn., Ind. State C. of C. (social legis. com. 1970-80). Methodist. Clubs: Indpls. Athletic; Woodland Country (bd. dirs. 1984-88) (Carmel, Ind.). Home: 11070 Winding Brook Ln Indianapolis IN 46280-1258 Office: Barnes & Thornburg 1313 Mchts Bank Bldg 11 S Meridian St Indianapolis IN 46204-3506

SCITOVSKY, ANNE AICKELIN, economist; b. Ludwigshafen, Germany, Apr. 17, 1915; came to U.S., 1931, naturalized, 1938; d. Hans W. and Gertrude Margarete Aickelin; 1 dau., Catherine Margaret. Student, Smith Coll., 1933-35; B.A., Barnard Coll., 1937; postgrad., London Sch. Econs., 1937-39; M.A. in Econs., Columbia U., 1941. Mem. staff legis. reference svc. Libr. of Congress, 1941-44; mem. staff Social Security Bd., 1944-46; with Palo Alto (Calif.) Med. Rsch. Found., 1963—, chief health econs. div., 1973-91, sr. staff scientist, 1992—; lectr. Inst. Health Policy Studies, U. Calif., San Francisco, 1975—; mem. Inst. Medicine of NAS, Nat. Acad. Social Ins., Pres.'s Commn. for Study of Ethical Problems in Medicine and Biomed. and Behavioral Rsch., 1979-82, U.S. Nat. Com. on Vital and Health Stats., 1975-78, Health Resources and Svcs. Adminstrn., AIDS adv. com., 1990-94; cons. HHS, Inst. Medicine Coun. on Health Care Tech. Assessment, 1986-90. Mem. Am. Assn. for Health Svc. Rsch., Am. Pub. Health Assn. Home: 161 Erica Way Menlo Park CA 94028-7439 Office: Palo Alto Med Found Rsch Inst 860 Bryant St Palo Alto CA 94301-2707

SCIULLA, MICHAEL GARRI, foundation administrator; b. Bklyn., Dec. 31, 1950; s. Frank and Dolores (Delind) S.; m. Carol Goff, Sept. 4, 1988; 1 child, Logan Michael. BA, Eisenhower Coll., 1973; postgrad., Carleton U., 1973-75. Registered lobbyist U.S. Congress. Reporter Geneva (N.Y.) Times, 1975; legis. asst. U.S. Ho. Reps., Washington, 1975-76, 77-78; reporter V.I. Post, St. Thomas, 1979; v.p., dir. BOAT/U.S., Alexandria, Va., 1980—; bd. dirs. Recreational Boaters Calif., Sacramento. Contbr. articles to profl. jours. Mem. Am. League Anglers and Boaters (bd. dirs., former pres.), Boating Writers Internat., Sport Fishing and Boating Partnership Coun. Office: BOAT/US 880 S Pickett St Alexandria VA 22304

SCLAR, CHARLES BERTRAM, geology educator, researcher; b. Newark, Mar. 16, 1925; s. Norman and Dorothy (Botvinick) S.; m. Ruth E. Choyke, Feb. 10, 1946; children: David A., Philip J. BS, CCNY, 1946; MS, Yale U., 1948, PhD, 1951. Instr. dept. geology Ohio State U., 1949-51; research petrographer Battelle Meml. Inst. (Minerals Processing div.), Columbus, Ohio, 1951-53, prin. research geologist, 1953-57, asst. tech. cons., 1957-59, asst. tech. cons. chem. physics div., 1959-62, research fellow, 1962-65, assoc. chief, dir. high pressure lab., 1965-68; prof., dept. geol. scis. Lehigh U., Bethlehem, Pa., 1968-90; prof. emeritus Lehigh U., Bethlehem, 1990—; chmn. dept. geol. scis. Lehigh U., Bethlehem, Pa., 1976-85; prin. investigator Apollo program NASA, 1968-78. Contbr. articles to profl. jours.; patentee in field. William E. Ford scholar Yale U., 1947-48, James Dwight Dana fellow, 1948-49. Fellow Mineralogical Soc. Am., Geol. Soc. Am., Soc. Econ. Geol. Home: 2075 Pleasant Dr Bethlehem PA 18015-5134 Office: Lehigh U Dept Earth and Environ Scis 31 Williams Dr Bethlehem PA 18015-3126

SCOFIELD, GORDON LLOYD, mechanical engineer, educator; b. Huron, S.D., Sept. 29, 1925; s. Perry Lee and Zella (Reese) S.; m. Nancy Lou Cooney, Dec. 27, 1947; children: Cathy Lynn, Terrence Lee. B.M.E., Purdue U., 1946; M.M.E., U. Mo., Rolla, 1949; Ph.D. in M.E, U. Okla., 1968. Instr. mech. engring. S.D. State Coll., Brookings, 1946-47; successively grad. asst., instr., asst. prof., asso. prof., prof. U. Mo., Rolla, 1947-69; prof., head mech. engring.-engring. mechs. dept. Mich. Technol. U., Houghton, 1969-81; disting. prof. mech. engring. S.D. Sch. Mines and Tech., Rapid City, 1981-88; asst. v.p. for acad. affairs S.D. Sch. Mines and Tech., 1981-83, v.p., dean engring., 1984-86; pres. S.D. Sch. Mines and Tech. Found., 1982-90; cons. U.S. Naval Ordnance Test Sta., China Lake, Calif., 1956-71; bd. dirs. Accreditation Bd. for Engring. and Tech., 1994—; cons. to industry. Served with USNR, 1943-46. NSF sci. faculty fellow, 1966-67; recipient alumni achievement award U. Mo., Rolla, 1975. Mem. Soc. Automotive Engrs. (pres. 1977), ASME, Am. Soc. Engring. Edn., AIAA, Sigma Xi, Tau Beta Pi, Pi Tau Sigma, Phi Kappa Phi. Home: PO Box 1085 Rapid City SD 57709-1085 *Satisfaction comes from sharing achievements. By acknowledging and sharing the importance of others in our success it is possible to accomplish more that is worth remembering.*

SCOFIELD, JOHN, jazz guitarist; b. Wilton, Conn., Dec. 26, 1951; s. Leavitt and Anne Fay S.; m. Susan Scofield, 1978; children: Jean, Evan. Student, Berklee Sch. Music, 1970-73. Profl. musician, 1974—; with Billy Cobham George Duke Band, 1974-77; with Dave Liebman quintet, 1978-82; with Miles Davis Band, 1983-85, soloist, collaborating musician, group leader, 1986—; with Enja/rec. artist, 1977-82; Grammavision rec. artist, 1984-89, Blue note rec. artist, 1990—; adv. bd. Guitar Player Mag. Albums include Live, 1977, Rough House, 1978, Shinola, 1982, Still Warm, 1985, Blue Matter, 1986, Loud Jazz, 1987, Pick Hits, 1987, Flat Out, 1989, Slo Sco, 1990, Time on My Hands, 1990, Meant to Be, 1991, Grace Under Pressure, 1992, What We Do, 1993, (with Pat Metheney) I Can See Your

House From Here, 1994, Hand Jive, 1994. Recipient numerous Down Beat Mag. Internat. Critic/ Reader Polls.

SCOFIELD, LOUIS M., JR., lawyer; b. Brownsville, Tex., Jan. 14, 1952; s. Louis M. and Betsy Lee (Aiken) S.; children: Christopher, Nicholas. BS in Geology with highest honors with highest distinction, U. Mich., 1974; JD with honors, U. Tex., 1977. Bar: Tex. 1977, U.S. Dist. Ct. (ea. and so. dists.) Tex., U.S. Ct. Appeals (5th cir.) 1981, U.S. Supreme Ct. 1984. spkr. Jefferson County Ins. Adjusters, S.E. Tex. Ind. Ins. Agts., Gulf Ins. Co., Dallas, Employers Casualty Co., Beaumont, Tex. Employment Commn., Jefferson County Young Lawyers Assn., Jefferson County Bar Assn., South Tex. Coll. of Law, John Gray Inst., Lamar U., 1991, Tex. Assn. Def. Counsel, 1991; cert. arbitrator Nat. Panel of Consumer Arbitrators; arbitrator BBB; presenter Forest Park H.S., Martin Elem. Sch., St. Anne's Sch. Contbr. articles to profl. jours.; columnist Jefferson County Bar Jour. Patron Beaumont Heritage Soc., John J. French Mus.; bd. dirs. Beaumont Heritage Soc., 1983-84, mem. endowment fund com., 1988; chmn. lawyers divsn. United Appeals Campaign, 1984; grand patron Jr. League of Beaumont, 1989, 90. Fellow Tex. Bar Found., State Bar of Tex. (mentors com. 1995); mem. ABA, Tex. Assn. Def. Counsel (dir. at large 1986-87, v.p. 1987-89, adminstrv. v.p. 1989-90, program chmn. San Diego 1989), Assn. Def. Trial Attys., Am. Judicature Soc., Jefferson County Bar Assn. (disaster relief project 1979, outstanding young lawyer's com. 1980), Beaumont Country Club, Tower Club of Beaumont, Phi Beta Kappa. Democrat. Episcopalian. Avocations: golf, reading, fishing. Home: 4790 Littlefield Beaumont TX 77706 Office: Mehaffy & Weber PO Box 16 Beaumont TX 77704

SCOFIELD, PAUL, actor; b. Jan. 21, 1922; m. Joy Parker; 2 children. Trained London Mask Theatre Drama Sch., Birmingham Repertory Theatre 1941, 43-46; Stratford-on-Avon Shakespeare Meml. Theatre, 1946-48, Arts Theatre, 1946, Phoenix Theatre, 1947. With H.M. Tennent, 1949-56; assoc. dir. Nat. Theatre, 1970-71; has appeared in Adventure Story, Chekhov's Seagull, Anouilh's Ring Round the Moon, Gielgud's prodn. Much Ado About Nothing, Charles Morgan's The River Line, Richard II, The Way of the World, Venice Preserved, Time Remembered, A Question of Fact, Hamlet, Power and the Glory, Family Reunion, A Dead Secret, Expresso Bongo, The Complaisant Lover, A Man for All Seasons, Stratford Festival, Ont., Can., 1961, Coriolanus, Don Armado, New York, 1961-62, A Man for All Seasons, London, 1962-63, King Lear, N.Y.C, Moscow and Ea. Europe, 1964, Timon, 1965, Staircase, 1966, The Government Inspector, 1967, Macbeth, 1968, The Hotel in Amsterdam, 1968, Uncle Vanya, 1970, The Captain of Kopenik, 1971, Rules of the Game, 1971, Savages 1973, The Tempest, 1974, 75, Dimetos, 1976, Volpone, 1977, The Madras House, 1977, The Family, 1978, Amadeus 1979, Othello, 1980, Don Quixote, 1982, A Midsummer Night's Dream, 1982, I'm Not Rappaport, 1986-87, Heartbreak House, 1992; films: The Train, 1963, A Man for All Seasons (Oscar and N.Y. Film Critics award Moscow Film Festival and Brit. Film Acad. awards), King Lear, 1970, Scorpio, 1972, Bartleby, 1980, A Delicate Balance, A Potting Shed, 1981, If Winter Comes, 1981, Song at Twilight 1982, Come into the Garden Maud, 1982, 1919, 1985, Anna Karenina, 1984, Mr. Corbett's Ghost, 1986, The Attic, 1987, Why The Whales Came, 1989, Henry V, 1990, Hamlet, 1990, UTZ, 1991, Quiz Show, 1994, The Little Riders, 1995, The Crucible, 1995; appeared TV Martin Chuzzlewit, 1994. Decorated comdr. Brit. Empire. Address: The Gables, Balcombe Sussex RH17 6ND, England

SCOFIELD, RICHARD MELBOURNE, career officer; b. Hartford, Conn., Apr. 6, 1938; s. Melbourne Frank and Evelyn (Moors) S.; m. Cornelia Ellen Love, Dec. 27, 1961; children: Catherine Scofield Easley, Karen Elizabeth, Elizabeth Ann. BBA, U. Mass., 1960; MBA, Okla. U., 1970; MSSM, U. So. Calif., L.A., 1973. Commd. 2d lt. USAF, 1961, advanced through grades to lt. gen., 1994; student pilot 3500th Flying Tng. Wing, Reese AFB, Tex., 1961-62; pilot C-130 6550th Ops. Group, Patrick AFB, Fla., 1962-64; pilot C-123 315th Air Div., Danang Air Base, Republic of Vietnam, 1964-65; aerial recovery pilot C-130 6594th Test Squadron, Hickam AFB, Hawaii, 1965-69; grad. student Okla. U., Norman, 1969-70; aerial recovery pilot C-130 OL-1 Satellite Control Facility, Edwards AFB, Calif., 1970-73; student Armed Forces Staff Coll., Norfolk, Va., 1973; chief program evaluation div. E-3A System Program Office, Hanscom AFB, Mass., 1973-76; student Def. Systems Mgmt. Coll., Ft. Belvoir, Va., 1976; asst. dep. chief of staff, systems Hdqrs. Air Force Systems Command, Andrews AFB, Md., 1976-81; program dir. F-117 System Program Office Aero. Systems Div., Wright-Patterson AFB, Ohio, 1981-83, program dir. B-2 System Program Office, 1983-91; program exec. officer for Bombers, Missiles and Trainers Office of Asst. Sec. of Air Force, Acquisition, Pentagon, Washington, 1991-94; comdr. Aero. Systems Ctr., Wright-Patterson AFB, Ohio, 1994—; ad. prof. Golden Gate U., San Francisco, 1970-76. Decorated DSM, Legion of Merit, DFC, Air medal with ten oak leaf clusters, Meritorious Svc. medal Air Force Commendation medal, Nat. Def. medal. Mem. Air Force Assn. (Ira Eaker fellow 1990), Am. Def. Preparedness Assn. Roman Catholic. Avocation: golf. Home: 29 Westover Ave 265 Rebel Ct Beavercreek OH 45434

SCOGIN, TROY POPE, publishing company executive, accounts executive; b. Manchester, Ala., Oct. 31, 1932; s. James David and Thelma Katie (Helton) S.; m. Katie Elizabeth Bates, May 26, 1956; children: Norma Kay, Joyce Marie. BA, Howard Coll., 1955; MDiv, So. Baptist Theol. Seminary, Louisville, 1959; MA, Samford U., 1972. Ordained to ministry Baptist Ch., 1956. Pastor West Port (Ky.) Baptist Ch., 1956-58, Providence Baptist Ch., Bellevue, Ohio, 1958-61; chaplain/capt. USAF, Lincoln, Nebr., 1961-64; pastor Sycamore (Ala.) Baptist Ch., 1964-65; sales rep. Houghton Mifflin Co., Boston, 1965-74, regional mgr., 1974-89, spl. asst. to exec. v.p. coll. div., 1989-90, v.p., 1984—, nat. accounts exec., 1990-92; pastor Ross Ave. Bapt. Ch. Intercity Mission, Dallas, 1993—; faculty Eastfield Coll., 1992—. Chmn. bd. deacons Ross Avenue Bapt. Ch., Dallas, 1991; mem. adv. bd. Ross Avenue Ctr. Mem. Am. Mgmt. Assn., Am. Soc. Tng. Devel., Nat. Coun. Tchrs. English, Tex. Jr. Coll. Tchrs. Assn., Phi Kappa Phi, Omicron Delta Kappa (nat. leadership fraternity pres. 1954), Alpha Phi Omega (nat. svc. fraternity pres. 1952). Democrat. Avocations: bowling, swimming, fishing, tennis, golf. Home: 15742 Havenrock Cir Dallas TX 75248-4219 *Accomplishment of goals requires setting priorities. Anything worth doing is worth doing well. To determine what is worthwhile decide if it is right, if it is needed, and if it is worth the cost.*

SCOGLAND, WILLIAM LEE, lawyer; b. Moline, Ill., Apr. 2, 1949; s. Maurice William and Harriet Rebecca (Lee) S.; m. Victoria Lynn Whitham, Oct. 9, 1976; 1 child, Thomas. BA magna cum laude, Augustana Coll., 1971; JD cum laude, Harvard U., 1975. Bar: Ill. 1975, U.S. Dist. Ct. (no. dist.) Ill. 1975. Assoc. Wildman, Harrold, Allen & Dixon, Chgo., 1975-77, Hughes Hubbard & Reed, Milw., 1977-81; from assoc. to ptnr. Jenner & Block, Chgo., 1981—. Author: Fiduciary Duty: What Does It Mean?, 1989; co-author Employee Benefits Law, 1987. Mem. Phi Beta Kappa, Omicron Delta Kappa. Republican. Office: Jenner & Block 1 E Ibm Plz Chicago IL 60611

SCOLES, CLYDE SHELDON, library director; b. Columbus, Ohio, Apr. 14, 1949; s. Edward L. and Edna M. (Ruddock) S.; m. Diane Francis, July 14, 1976; children: David, Kevin, Karen, Stephen. BS, Ohio State U., 1971; MLS, U. Mich., 1972. Librarian Columbus Pub. Library, 1972-74; library dir. Zanesville (Ohio) Pub. Library, 1974-78; asst. dir. Toledo-Lucas County Pub. Library, 1978-85, dir., 1985—; adj. lectr., libr. bldg. cons. U. Mich.; v.p. bd. dirs. Read for Literacy. Mem. ALA, Ohio Libr. Assn., Ohio Libr. Coun., Toledo C. of C., Com. of 100, Maumee Hist. Soc. Club: Torch (Toledo). Lodge: Rotary.

SCOLES, EUGENE FRANCIS, law educator, lawyer; b. Shelby, Iowa, June 12, 1921; s. Sam and Nola E. (Leslie) S.; m. R. Helen Glawson, Sept. 6, 1942; children—Kathleen Elizabeth, Janene Helen. A.B., U. Iowa, 1943, J.D., 1945; LL.M., Harvard U., 1949; J.S.D., Columbia U., 1955. Bar: Iowa 1945, Ill. 1946. Assoc. Seyfarth-Shaw & Fairweather, Chgo., 1945-46; asst. prof. law Northeastern U., 1946-48, assoc. prof., 1948-49; assoc. prof. U. Fla., 1949-51, prof., 1951-56; prof. U. Ill., Champaign, 1956-68; Max Rowe prof. law U. Ill., 1982-89, prof. emeritus, 1989—; vis. prof. McGeorge Law Sch. U. Pacific, Sacramento, 1989-92; prof. U. Oreg., 1968-82, dean Sch. Law, 1968-74, disting. prof. emeritus, 1982—; vis. prof. Khartoum U., Sudan, 1964-65. Author: (with H.F. Goodrich) Conflict of Laws, 4th edit., 1964, (with R.J. Weintraub) Cases and Materials on Conflict of Laws, 2d edit., 1972, (with E.C. Halbach, Jr.) Problems and Materials on Decedents' Estates and Trusts, 5th edit., 1993, Problems and Materials on Future Interests, 1977, (with P. Hay) Conflict of Laws, 2d edit., 1992; contbr. articles to profl. jours.; notes and legislation editor Iowa Law Rev., 1945; reporter Uniform Probate Code Project, 1966-70; mem. joint editorial bd. Uniform Probate Code, 1972—. Mem. ABA, Soc. Pub. Tchrs. Law, Am. Law Inst., Ill. Bar Assn., Assn. Am. Law Schs. (pres. 1978), Order of Coif. Home: 1931 Kimberly Dr Eugene OR 97405-5849 Office: U Oreg Sch of Law 11th And Kincaid Eugene OR 97403-1221

SCOLLARD, PATRICK JOHN, hospital executive; b. Chgo., Apr. 20, 1937; s. Patrick J. and Kathleen (Cooney) S.; m. Gloria Ann Carroll, July 1, 1961; children: Kevin, Maureen, Daniel, Thomas, Brian. B.S. in Econs., Marquette U., 1959; grad. sr. exec. devel. program, MIT, 1976. With Equitable Life Assurance Soc. U.S., N.Y.C., 1962-79, asst. v.p., 1969-71, v.p., personnel dir., 1971-75, v.p. corp. adminstrv. svcs., 1975-79; sr. v.p. Chem. Bank, N.Y.C., 1979-80, exec. v.p., 1980-87, chief adminstrv. officer, 1987-92; pres., CEO St. Francis Hosp., Roslyn, N.Y., 1992—; bd. dirs. Work in Am.; met. regional adv. bd. Chase Manhattan Corp. Mem. bd. Cath. Charities; former chmn. Woodstock Theol. Ctr.; bd. dirs. St. Francis Hosp. Office: St Francis Hosp 100 Port Washington Blvd Roslyn NY 11576-1353

SCOLNICK, EDWARD MARK, science administrator; b. Boston, Aug. 9, 1940; s. Barbara (Chasen) Scolnick; m. Barbara Bachrach; children: Laura, Jason, Daniel. AB, Harvard U., 1961; MD, Harvard U. Med. Sch., 1965. Intern Mass. Gen. Hosp., 1965-66, asst. resident internal medicine, 1966-67; research assoc. USPHS, 1967-69; sr. staff fellow lab. biochem. genetics NIH, 1969-70; instr. NIH Sem., 1970; sr. staff fellow viral leukemia and lymphoma br. Nat. Cancer Inst., 1970-71, spl. advisor to spl. virus cancer program, 1973-78, mem. coordinating com. for virus cancer program, 1975-78, chief. lab. tumor virus genetics, head. molecular virology sect., 1975-82; exec. dir. basic research virus and cell biology research Merck Sharp & Dohme Rsch. Labs., West Point, Pa., 1982-83, v.p. virus and cell biology research, 1983-84, sr. v.p., 1984, pres., 1985-93; sr. v.p. Merck & Co., Inc., 1991-93, exec. v.p., pres. rsch., 1993—; adj. prof. microbiology Sch. Medicine U. Pa., 1983-86. Editor-in-chief Jour. Virology; mem. editorial bd. Virology; contbr. numerous articles to profl. jours.;. Served with USPHS, 1965-67. Recipient Arthur S. Fleming award, 1976, PHS Superior Svc. award, 1978, Eli Lilly award, 1980, Indsl. Rsch. Inst. medal, 1990. Mem. NAS, Am. Soc. Biol. Chemists, Am. Soc. Microbiologists. Home: 811 Wickfield Rd Wynnewood PA 19096-1610 Office: Merck Rsch Labs PO Box 2000 Rahway NJ 07065-0900

SCOMMEGNA, ANTONIO, physician, educator; b. Barletta, Italy, Aug. 26, 1931; came to U.S., 1954, naturalized, 1960; s. Francesco Paola and Antonietta (Maresca) S.; m. Lillian F. Sinkiewicz, May 3, 1958; children: Paola, Frank, Roger. B.A., State Lyceum A. Casardi, Barletta, 1947; M.D., U. Bari (Italy), 1953. Diplomate: Am. Bd. Obstetrics and Gynecology, also sub-bd. endocrinology and reprodn. Rotating intern New Eng. Hosp., Boston, 1954-55; resident obstetrics and gynecology Michael Reese Hosp. and Med. Center, Chgo., 1956-59; fellow dept. research human reprodn. Michael Reese Hosp. and Med. Center, 1960-61, research assoc., 1961; fellow steroid tng. program Worcester Found. Exptl. Biology, also Clark U., Shrewsbury, Mass., 1964-65; asso. prof. obstetrics and gynecology Chgo. Med. Sch., 1965-69; mem. staff Michael Reese Hosp. and Med. Center, 1961—, attending physician obstetrics and gynecology, 1961—, dir. sect. gynecologic endocrinology, 1965-81; dir. ambulatory care obstetrics and gynecology Mandel Clinic, 1968-69, chmn. dept., 1969—, trustee, 1977-80; prof. dept. obstetrics and gynecology Pritzker Sch. Medicine, U. Chgo., 1969—. Author numerous articles in field. Fulbright fellow, 1954-55. Fellow Am. Coll. Obstetricians and Gynecologists, Endocrine Soc., Chgo. Inst. Medicine, Am. Gynecol. and Obstet. Soc.; mem. AMA, Ill., Chgo. med. socs., Am. Fertility Soc., Chgo. Gynecol. Soc. (sec. 1976-79, pres. 1981-82), Soc. Study Reprodn., AAAS, Soc. for Gynecologic Investigation. Home: 1023E W Vernon Park Pl Chicago IL 60607-3400 Office: Michael Reese Hosp Lake Shore Dr At 31st St Chicago IL 60613

SCONIERS, M. L., bishop. Bishop of Western Fla., Ch. of God in Christ, Orlando. Office: Ch of God in Christ PO Box 5472 Orlando FL 32805

SCOPAZ, JOHN MATTHEW, banker; b. N.Y.C., June 24, 1948; s. John J. and Alice L. (Zustovich) S.; m. Linda N. Nelson, Mar. 17, 1973; children: Jennifer, Lauren, Kristen. BSChemE, Manhattan Coll., 1970; MBA, NYU, 1973. Plant engr. Colgate Palmolive, N.Y.C., 1970-72; systems analyst Colgate Palmolive, N.Y.C., 1973-74; mng. dir., v.p. Citicorp (BHC Resources), N.Y.C., 1975-81; exec. v.p. Republic Nat. Bank, N.Y.C., 1981—; chmn., bd. dirs. Republic Info. & Communications Svcs., N.Y.C. Coach Pelham (N.Y.) Little League; bd. dirs., pres. N.Y. League Hard of Hearing. Mem. Am. Mgmt. Assn., N.Y. Clearing House (mem. steering com.). Republican. Roman Catholic. Avocations: family, skiing, tennis. Office: Republic Nat Bank 452 5th Ave New York NY 10018-2706

SCOPES, GARY MARTIN, professional association executive; b. St. Petersburg, Fla., July 16, 1947; s. Louis Martin and Eleanor Beebe (Kurkjian) S.; m. Connie Joy Kowalski, Sept. 16, 1967; children: Darryl, Sandra, Adrian. BA in Rhetoric, U. South Fla., 1971. Cert. assn. exec. (nationally). Lobbyist La. Mcpl. Assn., Baton Rouge, 1972-74; exec. dir. Soc. La. CPAs, Metairie, 1974-84, Tex. Soc. CPAs, Dallas, 1984-87, Inst. Mgmt. Accts. (formerly Nat. Assn. Accts.), Montvale, N.J., 1987—; pres. La. Soc. Assn. Execs., 1980-81, CPA Soc. Execs. Assn., 1982-83, Kaypro Computer Users Group, 1979. 1st lt. U.S. Army, 1966-69. Mem. N.J. Soc. Assn. Execs. (pres. 1995). Avocations: tennis, skiing, golf, fishing, guitar. Home: 1 Van Wyck St Montvale NJ 07645-1025 Office: Institute of Mngmt Accountants 10 Paragon Dr Montvale NJ 07645-1718

SCORDELIS, ALEXANDER COSTICAS, civil engineering educator; b. San Francisco, Sept. 27, 1923; s. Philip Kostas and Vasilica (Zois) S.; m. Georgia Gumas, May 9, 1948; children: Byron, Karen. B.S., U. Calif., Berkeley, 1948; M.S., M.I.T., 1949. Registered profl. engr., Calif. Structural designer Pacific Gas & Electric Co., San Francisco, 1948; engr. Bechtel Corp., San Francisco, summer 1951, 52, 53, 54; instr. civil engring. U. Calif., Berkeley, 1949-50; asst. prof. U. Calif., 1951-56, asso. prof., 1957-61, prof., 1962-89; asst. dean U. Calif. (Coll. Engring.), 1962-65, vice chmn. div. structural engring, structural mechanics, 1970-73, Nishkian prof. emeritus, 1990—; cons. engring. firms, govt. agys. Contbr. articles on analysis and design of complex structural systems, reinforced and prestressed concrete shell and bridge structures to profl. jours. Served to capt., C.E. U.S. Army, 1943-46, ETO. Decorated Bronze star, Purple Heart; recipient Western Electric award Am. Soc. Engring. Edn., 1978; Axion award Hellenic Am. Profl. Soc., 1979; Best paper award Canadian Soc. Civil Engring., 1982, K.B. Woods award NAS Transp. Rsch. Bd., 1983, Citation U. Calif. Berkeley, 1989, Disting. Engring. Alumnus award Berkeley Engring. ALumni Soc., 1993, Leadership award Am. Segmental Bridge Inst., 1993, Freyssinet medal Internat. Fedn. for Prestressed Concrete, 1994. Fellow ASCE (hon. mem. 1989, Moisseiff award 1976, 81, 92, Howard award 1989), Am. Concrete Inst.; mem. Internat. Assn. Shell and Spatial Structures (hon., Torroja medal 1994), Internat. Assn. Bridge and Structural Engring., Structural Engrs. Assn. Calif., Nat. Acad. Engring. Home: 724 Gelston Pl El Cerrito CA 94530-3045 Office: 729 Davis Hall # U Calif Berkeley CA 94720

SCORGIE, GLEN G., religious organization leader; b. Mar. 29, 1952; married; 3 children. BTh, Can. Bible Coll., 1973; MA, Wheaton Grad. Sch., 1974; MS, Regent Coll., 1982; postgrad., Cambridge U., 1983; PhD, U. St. Andrews, 1986. Data-processing mktg. asst. IBm Can., Toronto, 1974-76; dir. admissions Can Bible Coll., Regina, 1976-79, asst. prof. theology, 1984-88, acting dean faculty, 1989, assoc. prof. theology, 1988-91; dean, v.p. N.Am. Bapt. Coll., 1991—; adj. prof. theology Can. Theol. Sem., 1984-91; speaker in field. Author: A Call for Continuity: The Theological Contribution of James Orr, 1988; contbr. articles to profl. jours. British Govt. Overseas Rsch. scholar, 1981-84, Ont. scholar, 1969; recipient Regent Coll. Ch. History prize, 1981. Mem. Can. Theol. Soc., Can. Soc. Ch. History, Can. Evang. Theol. Assn., Conf. Faith and History, Delta Epsilon Chi. Office: Am Bapt Coll, 11525 23d Ave, Edmonton, Canada T6J 4T3

SCORSESE, MARTIN, film director, writer; b. Flushing, N.Y., Nov. 17, 1942; s. Charles and Catherine (Cappa) S.; m. Laraine Marie Brennan, May 15, 1965 (div.), 1 daughter: Catherine Terese Glinora Sophia; m. Julia Cameron, 1975 (div.), 1 daughter: Dominica Elizabeth; m. Isabella Rosellini, Sept. 29, 1979 (div. 1983); m. Barbara DeFina, Feb. 9, 1985. BS in Film Communications, NYU, 1964, MA in Film Communications, 1966. Faculty asst., then instr. film NYU, N.Y.C., 1963-70. films include: (dir.): The Big Shave, 1968 (also writer), Who's That Knocking at My Door?, 1968 (also writer, assoc. prodr., actor), Boxcar Bertha, 1972 (also actor), Mean Streets, 1973 (also co-writer, actor), Alice Doesn't Live Here Anymore, 1975, Taxi Driver, 1976 (also actor, Palme d'Or Cannes Internat. Film Festival), New York, New York, 1977, The Last Waltz, 1978, Raging Bull, 1980, The King of Comedy, 1983 (also actor), After Hours, 1985, The Color of Money, 1986, The Last Temptation of Christ, 1988, New York Stories (Life Lessons), 1989, GoodFellas, 1990 (also co-writer), Cape Fear, 1991, The Age of Innocence, 1993 (also co-writer), Casino, 1995 (also writer); (prodr.): The Grifters, 1990, Mad Dog and Glory, 1993, Clockers, 1995; (exec. prodr.): Naked in New York, 1994; documentaries include: (editor): Woodstock, 1970 (also asst. dir.), Elvis on Tour, 1973; (assoc. prodr.): Medicine Ball Caravan, 1971; (dir.): Street Scenes 1970, 1970, Italianamerican, 1974, American Boy: A Profile of Steven Price, 1979, Man in Milan, 1990; other film appearances include: Cannonball, 1976, Pavlova: A Woman for All Seasons, 1983, 'Round Midnight, 1986, Akira Kurosawa's Dreams, 1990, Guilty by Suspicion, 1991, Quiz Show, 1994, Search and Destroy, 1995 (also prodr.), (TV film) La Memoire retrouvee, 1996. Recipient Edward L. Kingsley Found. award, 1963-64, 1st prize Rosenthal Found. awards Soc. Cinemetologists, 1964, 1st prize Screen Producer's Guild, 1965, 1st prize Brown U. Film Festival, 1965, also others; named Best Dir. Cannes Film Festival, 1986. Office: Barbara Moskowitz Yohalem Gillman Co 477 Madison Ave Fl 9 New York NY 10022-5802 also: care CAA 9830 Wilshire Blvd Beverly Hills CA 90212-1804*

SCORZA, SYLVIO JOSEPH, religion educator; b. Zürich, Switzerland, Mar. 21, 1923; came to U.S., 1929; s. Joseph Peter and Helena Christina (Kopp) S.; m. Phyllis Joan VanSetters, June 6, 1952; children: Christine Marie, Philip Joseph, John Forrest. AA, Woodrow Wilson Jr. Coll., 1942; AB, Hope Coll., 1945; BD, Western Theol. Sem., Holland, Mich., 1953; ThD, Princeton Theol. Sem., 1956; PhD, U. Ill., 1972. Ordained to ministry Ref. Ch. in Am., 1955. Stated supply pastor Hickory Bottom Charge, Loysburg, Pa., 1957-58; prof. religion Northwestern Coll., Orange City, Iowa, 1959-90, prof. emeritus, 1990—; vis. prof. Lancaster (Pa.) Theol. Sem., 1956-57, Western Theol. Sem., Holland, Mich., 1958-59; v.p. Ref. Ch. in Am., N.Y.C., 1988-89, pres., 1989-90, moderator, exec. com., 1990-91. Co-editor: Concordance to the Greek and Hebrew Text of Ruth, The Computer Bible, Septuagint series, Vols. XXX, XXX-B, 1988-89; contbr. articles to profl. jours. County del. Iowa Dems., Ft. Dodge, 1984. Recipient Disting. Alumnus award Hope Coll., 1989, Homecoming Honors award Northwestern Coll. N Club, 1990, Handicapped Person of Siouxland award Siouxland Com. for the Handicapped, 1990, Gov.'s award Iowa Commn. of Persons with Disabilities, 1990, Victory award Nat. Rehab. Hosp., 1991. Mem. Internat. Orgn. for Septuagint and Cognate Studies, Smithsonian Instsn., Nat. Geog. Soc., Iowa State Chess Assn. (v.p. 1984-85, dir. postal tournament 1987—). Avocations: chess, bridge. Home: 520 2nd St SW Orange City IA 51041-1728 Office: Northwestern Coll Orange City IA 51041

SCOTT, A. HUGH, lawyer; b. Auckland, New Zealand, Jan. 10, 1947; came to U.S., 1957; s. John E. and Leona (Lacey) S.; m. Susan Campbell, Dec. 3, 1946; 1 child, Matthew Campbell. BA, Williams Coll., 1968; JD, Columbia U., 1974. Bar: Mass. 1974, U.S. Dist. Ct. Mass 1975, U.S. Ct. Appeals (1st cir.) 1975, U.S. Supreme Ct. 1982. Asst. U.S. atty. U.S. Atty.'s Office, Boston, 1978-83; assoc. Choate, Hall & Stewart, Boston, 1975-78, 83-85, ptnr., 1986—. Lt. (j.g.) USNR, 1968-71. Democrat. Unitarian. Home: 10 Cazenove St Boston MA 02116-6205 Office: Exchange Pl 53 State St Boston MA 02109-2804

SCOTT, A. TIMOTHY, lawyer; b. Natchez, Miss., Feb. 16, 1952; s. John William and Patricia (O'Reilly) S.; m. Nancy E. Howard, June 7, 1976; children: Kevin Howard, Brian Howard. BA in Psychology, Stanford U., 1974, JD, 1977. Bar: Calif. 1977, U.S. Tax Ct. 1978. Assoc. then ptnr. Agnew, Miller & Carlson, L.A., 1977-83; assoc. Greenberg, Glusker, Fields, Claman & Machtinger, L.A., 1983; ptnr. Sachs & Phelps, L.A., 1983-91; mem. Heller, Ehrman White & McAuliffe, L.A., 1991—; speaker in field. Note editor Stanford Law Rev., 1976-77; contbr. article to profl. publs., chpt. to book. Mem. ABA, L.A. County Bar Assn. (chmn. real estate taxation com. 1988-91, exec. com., taxation sect. 1989-91), Order of Coif. Democrat. Avocations: volleyball, gardening, Calif. wine, contemporary art. Office: Heller Ehrman White & McAuliffe 601 S Figueroa St Fl 40 Los Angeles CA 90017-5704

SCOTT, ADRIENNE, social worker, psychotherapist; b. N.Y.C.; d. William and Anne Scott; m. Ross F. Grumet, Nov. 10, 1957 (div. Aug. 1969). BA, Finch Coll., 1957; postgrad., NYU, 1958-62, MA in English, 1958; MSW, Adelphi U., 1988. Mem. English faculty Fordham U., N.Y.C., 1966-68; editor Blueboy Mag., Miami, Fla., 1974, "M" Mag., N.Y.C., 1976; freelance writer N.Y.C., 1958—; mem. English faculty NYU, 1958-65; pres. Googolplex Video, N.Y.C., 1981-86; clin. social worker Mt. Sinai Hosp., N.Y.C., 1988-93, Stuyvesant Polyclinic, N.Y.C., 1993—; presenter Nat. Methadone Conf., 1992. Author: Film as Film, 1970; contbg. editor Menstyle Mag., 1995; contbr. articles to numerous mags., including Vogue, Interview, N.Y. mag.; pioneer in fashion video; videographer documentaries; performance artist in Robert Wilson's King of Spain, 1973. Mem. exec. com. Adopt-An-AIDS Rschr. Program Rockefeller U.; nat. co-chairperson Gay Rights Nat. Lobby, 1976. Mem. NASW (cert.), AAUW, Assn. for Psychoanalytic Self Psychology. Home: 165 E 66th St New York NY 10021-6132 Office: 7 Patchin Pl New York NY 10011-8341

SCOTT, ALASTAIR IAN, chemistry educator; b. Glasgow, Scotland, Apr. 10, 1928; came to U.S., 1968; s. William and Nell (Newton) S.; m. Elizabeth Wilson Walters, Mar. 4, 1950; children: William Stewart, Ann Walker. B.Sc., Glasgow U., 1949, Ph.D., 1952, D.Sc., 1964; M.A. (hon.), Yale U., 1968; D.Sc. (hon.), U. Coimbra, Portugal, 1990, U. Pierre & Marie Curie, Paris, 1992. Lectr. organic chemistry Glasgow U., 1957-62; prof. U. B.C., Vancouver, 1962-65, Sussex (Eng.) U., 1965-68, Yale U., 1968-77; disting. prof. Tex. A&M U., 1977-80, Davidson prof. sci., 1982—; prof. dept. chemistry U. Edinburgh, Scotland, 1980-82; cons. in field. Author: Interpretations of Ultraviolet Spectra of Natural Products, 1964; contbr. articles to profl. jours. Recipient rsch. achievement award Am. Soc. Pharmacognosy, 1993. Fellow Royal Soc., Royal Soc. Edinburght; mem. Am. Chem. Soc. (Ernest Guenther award 1976, A.C. Cope scholar 1992), Chem. Soc. (Corday-Morgan medal 1964, Centenary lectr. 1994, Tetrahedron prize for creativity in organic chemistry 1995), Biochem. Soc., Japan Pharm. Soc. (hon.). Office: Tex A&M U Chemistry Dept College Station TX 77843

SCOTT, ALEXANDER ROBINSON, engineering association executive; b. Elizabeth, N.J., June 15, 1941; s. Marvin Chester and Jane (Robinson) S.; m. Angela Jean Kendall, July 17, 1971; children: Alexander Robinson, Jennifer Angela, Ashley Kendall. B.A. in History, Va. Mil. Inst., 1963; M.A. in Personnel and Counseling Psychology, Rutgers U., 1965. Sales mgr. Hilton Hotels, 1967-70; meetings mgr. Am. Inst. Mining Engrs., N.Y.C., 1971-73; exec. dir. Minerals, Metals and Materials Soc., 1973—. Served with U.S. Army, 1965-67. Decorated Bronze Star. Mem. Am. Soc. Assn. Execs. Republican. Baptist. Home: 107 Staghorn Dr Sewickley PA 15143-9506 Office: TMS 420 Commonwealth Dr Warrendale PA 15086-7511

SCOTT, ALICE H., librarian; b. Jefferson, Ga.; d. Frank D. and Annie D. (Colbert) Holly; m. Alphonso Scott, Mar. 1, 1959; children—Christopher, Alison. A.B., Spelman Coll., Atlanta, 1957; M.L.S., Atlanta U., 1958; Ph.D., U. Chgo., 1983. Librarian Bklyn. Pub. Library, 1958-59; br. librarian Chgo. Pub. Library, 1959-72, dir. Woodson Regional Library, 1974-77, dir. community relations, 1977-82, dep. commr., 1982-87, asst. commr., 1987—. Doctoral fellow, 1973. Mem. ALA (councilor 1982-85), Ill. Library Assn., Chgo. Spelman Club, DuSable Mus., Chgo. Urban League. Democrat. Baptist. Office: Chgo Pub Library 400 S State St Chicago IL 60605-1203

SCOTT, ALLEN JOHN, geography educator; b. Liverpool, England, Dec. 23, 1938; came to U.S., 1980; s. William Rule and Nella Maria (Pieri) S.; m.

Nga Thuy Nguyen, Jan. 19, 1979. BA, Oxford (Eng.) U., 1961; PhD, Northwestern U., 1965. Research assoc. dept. town planning U. Coll. London, 1967-69; prof. geography UCLA, 1980—; prof. geography and urgan planning U. Toronto, Ont., Can., 1969-80; dir. Lewis Ctr. for Regional Policy Studies UCLA, 1990-94, assoc. dean Sch. Pub. Policy and Social Rsch., 1994—; Professeur associé U. Paris, 1974. Author: Combinatorial Programming, 1971, Urban Land Nexus, 1980, Metropolis, 1988, New Industrial Spaces, 1988, Technopolis, 1993. Fellow Com. on Scholarly Communication with People's Republic China, 1986. Croucher fellow U. Hong Kong, 1984; Guggenheim fellow, 1986-87. Office: UCLA Sch Pub Policy/ Social Rsch Los Angeles CA 90095

SCOTT, AMY ANNETTE HOLLOWAY, nursing educator; b. St. Albans, W.Va., Apr. 10, 1916; d. Oliver and Mary (Lee) Holloway; m. William M. Jefferson, June 22, 1932, (div. Oct. 1933); 1 child, William M. Jefferson, m. Vann Hyland Scott, Mar. 15, 1952, (dec. Dec. 1972). BS in Nursing Edn., Cath. U., Washington, 1948; cert. in psychiat. nursing, U. Paris, Paris, 1959. Indsl. nurse Curtiss Wright Air Plane Co., Lambert Field, St. Louis, 1941-44; faculty St. Thomas U., Manila, Philippines Island, 1948-50; pub. health nurse St. Louis Health Dept., 1951-56; capt. USAF Nursing Corps, Paris, 1956-60; resigned as maj. USAF (Nurse Corps), 1960, 1960; faculty St. Louis State Hosp., 1960-67; dept. head St. Vincents Hosp., St. Louis, 1967-68; faculty RN, creator psychiat. program Sch. of Nursing Jewish Hosp., 1968-72; adminstrv. nurse St. Louis State Hosp., 1972-84; initiated first psychiatric program sch. nursing, Jewish Hosp. Author: (short story) Two Letters, 1962, (novel) Storms, 1987, Life's Journey, 1993. Past bd. dirs. county bd. Mo. U., 1984-88; hon. citizen Colonial Williamsburg, Va.; mem. Rep. Presdl. Task Force; mem. Women in the Arts '94. Recipient Key to Colonial Williamsburg, Va., Medal of Merit, Rep. Presdl. Task Force, 1992; named to Rep. Presdl. Task Force Honor Roll, 1993, Nat. Women's Hall of Fame, 1995, Women's Hall of Fame, 1996. Mem. AAUW, NAFE, Internat. Fedn. Univ. Women, Internat. Soc. Quality Assurance in Health Care, N.Y. Acad. Scis., Am. Biog. Inst. (life, governing bd.), Women in the Arts, Cambridge Centre Engring., Internat. Platform Assn. Roman Catholic. Avocations: music, boating, horseback riding, dog sled riding, travel.

SCOTT, ANDREW, corporate executive; b. St. Paul, Apr. 5, 1928; s. Ulric and Annamay (Gorry) S.; m. Kathleen Kennedy, May 7, 1960; children: Andrea Kennedy Scott, Lucia Scott Duff. BS, U. Minn., 1950, LLB, 1952. Bar: Minn. 1952. Ptnr. Doherty, Rumble & Butler, Mpls. and St. Paul, 1952-77; chmn. Andrew Scott Ltd., Mpls., 1978-81; founder, vice chmn. Cray Rsch. Inc., Mpls., 1972-95, also bd. dirs. Bd. dirs. Minn. Orchestral Assn., Mpls., 1961-78, First Trust Co., Inc., St. Paul, 1981-90; trustee Mpls. Soc. Fine Arts, 1966-78, Twin City Area Pub. TV Corp., St. Paul, 1967-74, St. Paul Acad./Summit Sch., 1972-75. Mem. ABA, Computer Law Assn. Roman Catholic. Avocations: gardening, tai chi, megalithic cave art, skiing, zazen. Home: 1941 Penn Ave S Minneapolis MN 55405-2210 Office: Cray Rsch Inc 655A Lone Oak Dr Eagan MN 55121-1560

SCOTT, ANN, professional society administrator; b. St. Anthony, Idaho, Feb. 1, 1941; d. Thomas Myrthen and Henrietta (Minson) B.; m. Kenneth Wayne Scott, Nov. 20, 1961; children: Shannon, Catherine, Andrew, Lorraine, Kimberly, Carolyn. Student in human devel. and family rels., Brigham Young U., 1959-61. V.p. Am. Family Soc., Washington, 1975—; pres. Lamorah stake primary children's program LDS Ch., Rochester, N.Y., 1963-66, Washington stake mother edn. leader Rockville, Md., 1994—. Co-author: Family Tree, 1965, The Great Am. Family Builder, 1992. Helped organize the Great Am. Family award program, Washington. Avocation: writing. OFfice: Am Family Society 5013 Russett Rd Rockville MD 20853-2966

SCOTT, ANNA MARIE PORTER WALL, sociology educator; b. South Fulton, Tenn.; d. Thomas Madison and Jevvie Roggie (Patton) P.; m. John T. Scott Sr. (dec.); 1 child, Harvey G. BA, U. Ill., MEd, MSW. Cert. tchr. and social worker, Ill. Caseworker Dept. Pub. Aid, Champaign, Ill.; psychiat. social worker Vets. Hosp., Danville, Ill.; prof. sociology Parkland Coll., Champaign, Ill. Mem. Dem. Ctrl. Com., 1974-78; head Dem. 21st Congl. Dist., 1974-78; del. Nominating Conv./Mini Conv., 1975, 76; vol. Nominating Com., 1988; commr. Ill. Banking Bd.; mem. AME Ch., Hadassah; mem. Vet. of Armed Svcs. Named Outstanding Black Alumni, U. Ill., Urbana, 1977. Mem. LWV, NAACP, Nat. Coun. Negro Women (past pres.), Am. Legion, AMVETS, Champaign-Urbana Symphony Guild, Order Ea. Star (grand organist Eureka Grand chpt.). Avocations: pub. speaking, piano, baking, gardening, politics. Home: 309 W Michigan Ave Urbana IL 61801-4945 Office: Parkland Coll 2400 W Bradley Ave Champaign IL 61821-1806

SCOTT, ANNE BYRD FIROR, history educator; b. Montezuma, Ga., Apr. 24, 1921; d. John William and Mary Valentine (Moss) Firor; m. Andrew Mackay Scott, June 2, 1947; children: Rebecca, David MacKay, Donald MacKay. AB, U. Ga., 1941; MA, Northwestern U., 1944; PhD, Radcliffe Coll., 1958; LHD (hon.), Lindenwood Coll., 1968, Queens Coll., 1985, Northwestern U., 1989, Radcliffe Coll., 1990, U. of the South, 1990, Cornell Coll., 1991. Congressional rep., editor LWV of U.S., 1944-53; lectr. history Haverford Coll., 1957-58, U. N.C., Chapel Hill, 1959-60; asst. prof. history Duke U., Durham, N.C., 1961-67; assoc. prof. Duke U., 1968-70, prof., 1971-80, W.K. Boyd prof., 1980-91, W.K. Boyd prof. emerita, 1992—, chmn. dept., 1981-85; Gastprofessor Universität, Bonn, Germany, 1992-93; vis. prof. Johns Hopkins U., 1972-73, Stanford U., 1974, Harvard U., 1984, Cornell U., 1993, Williams Coll., 1994; Times-Mirror scholar Huntington Libr., 1995; vice chmn. Nat. Humanities Ctr., 1991—; mem. adv. com. Schlesinger Libr.; Fulbright lectr., 1984, 92-93. Author: The Southern Lady, 1970, 25th anniversary edit., 1995, (with Andrew MacKay Scott) One Half the People, 1974, Making the Invisible Woman Visible, 1984, Natural Allies, 1991; editor: Jane Addams, Democracy and Social Ethics, 1964, The American woman, 1970, Women in American Life, 1970, Women and Men in American Life, 1976, Unheard Voices, 1993; mem. editl. bd. Revs. in Am. History, 1976-81, Am. Quar., 1974-78, Jour. So. History, 1978-84; contbr. articles to profl. jours. Chmn. Gov.'s Commn. on Status of Women, 1963-64; mem. Citizens Adv. Council on Status of Women U.S., 1964-68. AAUW fellow, 1956-57; grantee NEH, 1967-68, 76-77, Nat. Humanities Ctr., 1980-81; grad. medal Radcliffe Coll., 1986, Duke U. medal, 1991, John Caldwell medal N.C. Humanities Coun., 1994; fellow Ctrl. Advanced Study in Behavioral Sci., 1986-87; Fulbright scholar, 1984, 92-93. Mem. Am. Antiquarian Soc., Orgn. Am. Historians (exec. bd. 1973-76, pres. 1983), So. Hist. Assn. (exec. bd. 1976-79, pres. 1989), Soc. Am. Historians, Phi Beta Kappa. Democrat. Office: Duke U Dept History Durham NC 27708

SCOTT, BILL, advertising agency executive; b. Phila., Sept. 1, 1949; s. Norris A. and Jean (Satterthwaite) S. BA in Writing, West Chester U., 1971; BS in Radio-TV-Film, Temple U., Phila., 1974. Advt. coord. S.M.S., Malvern, Pa., 1978-81; dir. pub. rels. Thomas R. Sundheim Inc., Jenkintown, Pa., 1981-88; v.p., creative dir. Kingswood Advt., Inc., Ardmore, Pa., 1988—; cons. Yonex USA, Torrance, Calif., 1989—, Nat. Trust for Historic Preservation, Washington, 1994—. Author: Chinese Kung-Fu, 1976; creator, writer comic strip Latchkids, 1995—. Republican. Episcopalian. Avocations: tennis, running, weightlifting, writing. Home: 77 Croton Rd Strafford PA 19087-2663 Office: Kingswood Advt Inc Cricket Ter Ardmore PA 19003

SCOTT, BRADWELL DAVIDSON, educational administrator, writer, consultant; b. L.A., Sept. 12, 1949; s. Clifford Norton and Florence Marguerite (Jafraty) S.; m. Darian Jeanne Garritson, June 30, 1974; children: Nathan Hunter, Jamieson Fair. BFA, Calif. Inst. Arts, 1971; MA, Pacific Sch. Religion, 1978. Dir. Sherwood Oaks H.S., Van Nuys, Calif., 1971-73; sr. editl. assoc. U. and Coll. Orgn. Activities, Boston, 1979-89; headmaster Chgo. Jr. Sch., Elgin, Ill., 1989-92; ednl. affairs dir. Kumon Ednl. Inst., Boston, 1992—; adv. grad. study Pacific Sch. Religion/U. Calif., Berkeley, 1978-84; introducer, accreditation evaluator Ind. Schs. Assn. of the Ctrl. States, 1989—; co-founder, publicist Fox Valley Ill. Phi Delta Kappa Edl. Fraternity, Elgin, 1990-92; prin.'s mentor Raymond (Wash.) Pub. Schs. Dist., 1992-94; ednl. writer cons., sr. assoc. Diversified Creative Svcs., Boston, 1992—. Editor, author (ednl. newsletter) Approaching Thunder: Developments on the American Educational Horizon, 1993—; author Regional Lab., Edn. Devel. Ctr., and Inst. for Responsive Edn. Mem. ASCD, Ednl. Press Assn., Internat. Assn. Bus. Communicators. Avocations: video prodn., writing poetry. Home: 96 Wash Pond Rd Hampstead NH 03841-2108 Office: Kumon Ednl Inst 699 Boylston St Ste 2 Boston MA 02116-2836

SCOTT, CAMPBELL, artist; b. Milngavie, Scotland, Oct. 5, 1930; s. Robert and Catherine S. Apprentice woodcarver, Glasgow, Scotland, 1946-51; student, Royal Acad. Art, Copenhagen, 1965-66; studies with, S.W. Hayter, Paris, 1966. Exhbns. include 1st Biennial Internat. Graphics, Krakow, Poland, 1966, 1st Brit. Internat. Prin Biennale, Eng., 1969, traveling exhbn., Nat. Gallery Can., Ottawa, 1969, 4th Am. Biennial Engraving, Santiago, Chile, Can. Embassy, Washington, 1971, Pratt Inst., N.Y.C., 1971; represented in permanent collections, Brit. Mus., Bibliotheque Nat., Paris, Scottish Nat. Gallery Modern Art, Montreal Mus. Art, Victoria and Albert Mus., London, Art Gallery of Ont., Toronto, Can., Hart House Collection, U. Toronto; commd. works include: bronze sculpture, Pub. Libr. Niagara Falls, Can., wood sculpture, Pub. Libr., St. Catharines, Can.; mural, The Pumphouse Art Ctr. Niagara on the Lake, Can. Mem. Print and Drawing Council Can. Address: 89 Byron, Niagara on the Lake, ON Canada L0S 1J0

SCOTT, CAMPBELL, actor; b. N.Y.C., July 19, 1962; s. George C. Scott and Colleen Dewhurst. Appearences include (theatre) The Queen and the Rebels, 1982, The Real Thing, 1984, Our Town, 1984, Hay Fever, 1985, A Man For All Seasons, 1986, Dalliance, 1986, Copperhead, 1987, Ah, Wilderness!, 1987-88, Long Day's Journey Into Night, 1987-88, (TV movies) The Kennedys of Massachusetts, 1990, The Perfect Tribute, 1991, (films) Five Corners, 1987, From Hollywood to Deadwood, 1988, Longtime Companion, 1989, Ain't No Way Back, 1990, The Sheltering Sky, 1990, Dying Young, 1991, Dead Again, 1991, Singles, 1992, Mrs. Parker and the Vicious Circle, 1994, The Innocent, 1994. Office: Paradigm Talent Agency 10100 Santa Monica Blvd Fl 25 Los Angeles CA 90067-4003*

SCOTT, CAROL LEE, child care educator; b. Monte Vista, Colo., Jan. 10, 1944; d. Robert A. and Thelma G. (Allen) Jay; m. Bates E. Shaw, June 4, 1966 (dec. Feb. 1976); children: Crystal A., Sharon L.; m. James W. Scott, July 23, 1977. BA in Home Econs., Friends U., 1965; MS, Okla. State U., 1973. Cert. in family and consumer scis., child and parenting specialist; lic. profl. counselor. Receptionist Cen. Assembly of God Ch., Wichita, Kans., summer 1965; office worker Henry's Inc., Wichita, 1965-66; tchr. home econs. Wichita High Sch. South, 1966, Cir. High Sch., Towanda, Kans., 1966-68, Fairfax (Okla.) High Sch., 1968-74; tchr. vocat. home econs. Derby (Kans.) High Sch., 1974-75; child devel. specialist Bi-State Mental Health Found., Ponca City, Okla., 1975-87; instr. child care Pioneer Tech. Ctr., Ponca City, 1987—, dir., 1987-89, 93—; cons. Phil Fitzgerald Assocs. Archs., Ponca City, 1980, Head Start Okla., 1981-86; trainer, paraprofl. Child Care Careers, 1980—; validator Nat. Assn. Edn. Young Children 1992—. Contbg. author Child Abuse Prevention Mini Curriculum. Mem. sch. bd. Ponca City Schs., 1982-85, title IV-A parent com., 1985-89; area chmn. Heart Fund, 1985; chmn. edn. com. Dist. XVII Child Abuse Prevention Task Force, Okla., 1985—, treas., 1989—; mem. cultural affairs com. Ponca City Adv. Bd., 1986-89; co-chair Week of the Young Child Com. for Kay County, 1991—. Mem. NEA, Am. Vocat. Assn., Am. Assn. Family and Consumer Scis., Okla. Vocat. Assn., Okla. Assn. Vocat. Home Econs. Tchrs., Okla. Edn. Assn., Okla. Assn. for Edn. Young Children, Okla. Early Childhood Assn., So. Early Childhood Assn. (chmn. 1992-93, past chmn. 1993-94, exec. coun. at-large 1994-96), Nat. Assn. Vocat. Home Econs. Tchrs., Nat. Assn. for Edn. Young Children (validator for early childhood programs seeking accreditation by divsn. Nat. Acad. Early Childhood Programs 1992—), Friends of Day Care. Republican. Methodist. Home: 414 Virginia Ave Ponca City OK 74601-3436

SCOTT, CATHERINE DOROTHY, librarian, information consultant; b. Washington, June 21, 1927; d. Leroy Stearns Scott and Agnes Frances (Meade) Scott Schellenberg. AB in English, Cath. U. Am., 1950, MS in Library Sci., 1955. Asst. Librarian Export-Import Bank U.S.A., Washington, 1951-55; asst. librarian Nat. Assn. Home Builders, 1955-62, reference librarian, 1956-62; founder, chief tech. librarian, Bellcomm, Inc., subs. AT&T, Washington, 1962-72; chief librarian Nat. Air and Space Mus., Smithsonian Instn., Washington, 1972-82, chief librarian Mus. Reference Ctr., 1982-88, sr. reference librarian, 1989-95; info. cons., 1995—; bd. visitors Cath. U. Am. Library Sci. Sch. and Libraries, 1984-93; apptd. by Pres., mem. Nat. Commn. Libraries and Info. Sci., 1971-76. Editor International Handbook of Aerospace Awards and Trophies, 1980, 81; guest editor Aeronautics and Space Flight Collections, 1985, in Spl. Collections, 1984. Vice-chmn. D.C. Rep. Com., 1960-68; mem. platform com. Rep. Nat. Com., 1964, sec., 1968; del. Rep. Nat. Conv., San Francisco, 1964, Miami, Fla., 1968. Recipient Sec.'s Disting. Service award Smithsonian Instn., 1976, Alumni Achievement award Cath. U. Am., 1977, Disting. Fed. Svc. Nat. Commn. Libr. and Info. Sci. medal, 1985. Mem. Spl. Librs. Assn. (pres. Washington chpt. 1973-74, cons. 1976-89, chmn. cons. com. 1994—, chmn. aerospace div. 1980-81, aerospace divsn. 30th anniversary com. 1995, Disting. Svc. award 1982, nat. dir. 1986-89, bd. dirs. 1986-89, 91-94, Washington chpt. awards com. 1990-91, assn. pres.-elect 1991-92, pres. 1992-93, immediate past pres. 1993-94, chair assn. awards and honors 1994-95), Am. Soc. Assn. Execs. (internat. roundtable), Am. Soc. Info. Scis. (com. chmn.), Internat. Fedn. Library Assns. (del. 1976, 83, 85, 88, 89), Friends of Cath. U. Libraries (founder, pres. 1984-88, exec. coun. 1984—), Nat. Fedn. Rep. Women, Rep. Women's Fed. Forum, League Rep. Women D.C. (dir. mem. 1995—, mem. nominating com. 1996—), Capital Yacht Club (Washington). Roman Catholic.

SCOTT, CHARLES DAVID, chemical engineer, consultant; b. Chaffee, Mo., Oct. 24, 1929; s. Charles Perry and Alma Gertrude (Kendall) S.; m. Alice Reba Bardill, Feb. 11, 1956; children—Timothy Charles, Mary Alice, Lisa Ann. B.S. in Chem. Engring., U. Mo., 1951; M.S. in Chem. Engring., U. Tenn., 1961, Ph.D., 1966. Registered profl. engr., Tenn. Devel. engr. Union Carbide Corp., Oak Ridge, 1953-57; research engr. Oak Ridge Nat. Lab., 1957-73, sect. chief, 1973-76, assoc. div. dir., 1976-83, research fellow, 1983-86, sr. research fellow, 1987-94; dir. bioprocessing rsch. and devel. ctr., 1991-94; engring. R & D cons., Oak Ridge, 1994—; adj. prof. chem. engring. U. Tenn., Knoxville. Served to 1st lt. AUS, 1951-53. Recipient U.S. Dept. Energy E.O. Lawrence award, 1980, U. Tenn. Nathan W. Doughtery award, 1987, U. Mo. Honor award, 1988, David Perlman award Am. Chem. Soc., 1994; Union Carbide Corp. fellow, 1983; Martin Marietta Sr. Corp. fellow, 1987. Mem. AAAS, Am. Chem. Soc. (chmn. separation sci. subdiv.), Am. Assn. Clin. Chemistry (chmn. com. advanced analytical concepts, nat. award 1980), Am. Inst. Chem. Engrs. (bd. dirs.), Nat. Acad. Engring., Sigma Xi, Alpha Chi Sigma. Lutheran. Contbr. articles to profl. jours.; patentee in field.

SCOTT, CHARLES FRANCIS, health facility administrator; b. Phila., Mar. 21, 1950; married. BS, Princeton U., 1972; M in Health Adminstrn., U. Chgo., 1975. Diplomate Am. Coll. Health Care Execs. Adminstrv. intern Med. Coll. Pa. and Hosp., Phila., 1974; adminstrv. asst. Reading (Pa.) Hosp. & Med. Ctr., 1975-78; asst. adminstr. ops. Mercy Hosp., Council Bluffs, Iowa, 1979-82; assoc. exec. dir. ops. Tampa (Fla.) Gen. Hosp., 1982-84; v.p. St. Joseph's Hosp., Tampa, 1984-88, COO, adminstr., 1988-93, pres. hosp. ops., 1993—. Office: St Josephs Hosp 3001 W Martin King Luther Tampa FL 33677-4227

SCOTT, CHARLES LEWIS, photojournalist; b. Grayville, Ill., Aug. 18, 1924; s. Marvin Joseph and Prudence (Blood) S.; m. Jane Turner, Jan. 14, 1945 (dec. 1983); children—Lyntha Ann, Thomas Marvin; m. Martha McDonald, Aug. 23, 1986. B.S. in Journalism, U. Ill., 1948; M.S., Ohio U., 1970. Photographer Champaign-Urbana (Ill.) Courier, 1946-50, chief photographer, 1953-56; photographer Ill. Natural History Survey, 1946-51, Binghamton (N.Y.) Press, 1951-53; asst. picture editor Milw. Jour., 1956-58; picture editor, 1958-66; graphics dir. Chgo. Daily News, 1966-69; instr. Sch. Journalism, Ohio U., Athens, 1969-70; asst. prof. Sch. Journalism, Ohio U., 1971-72, asso. prof., 1972-74, 76-77, prof., 1977—; dir. Sch. Visual Communication, 1978-95; picture editor Chgo. Tribune, 1974-76; dir. photography Rocky Mountain News, Denver, 1987-88; ret., 1995. Served with U.S. Navy, 1942-45. Decorated D.F.C., Air medal (3); recipient numerous awards in regional and nat. news photo contests. Mem. Nat. Press Photographers Assn. (charter mem., Newspaper Photographer of Yr. 1952, Editor of Yr. 1966, Joseph Sprague Meml. award 1975, Robin F. Garland Educator award 1979), Soc. Profl. Journalists, Ohio News Photographers Assn. (Lifetime Achievement award 1995). Presbyterian. Home: 8559 Lavelle Rd Athens OH 45701-9190

SCOTT, CHARLOTTE H., business educator; b. Yonkers, N.Y., Mar. 18, 1925; d. Edgar B. and Charlotte Agnes (Palmer) Hanley; m. Nathan Alexander Scott, Jr., Dec. 21, 1946; children: Nathan Alexander Scott, Leslie Kristin Scott Ashamu. A.B., Barnard Coll., 1947; postgrad., Am. U., 1949-53; M.B.A., U. Chgo., 1964; LL.D., Allegheny Coll., 1981. Research asso. Nat. Bur. Econ. Research, N.Y.C., 1947-48; economist R.W. Goldsmith Assos., Washington, 1948-55, U. Chgo., 1955-56, Fed. Res. Bank, Chgo., 1956-71; asst. v.p. Fed. Res. Bank, 1971-76; prof. bus. adminstrn. and commerce, sr. fellow Tayloe Murphy Inst., U. Va., Charlottesville, 1976-86; prof. commerce and edn. U. Va., Charlottesville, 1986—; bd. dirs. Atlantic Rural Expn., Inc.; mem. adv. bd. NationsBank Charlottesville, 1991-93; mem. nat. adv. bd. coun. SBA, 1979-82; mem. consumer adv. coun. bd. govs. FRS, 1979-82, vice chmn., 1980-81, chmn., 1981-82. Mem. editorial bd. Jour. Retail Banking, 1978-85, Jour. Internat. Assn. Personnel Women, 1981-85; contbr. articles to profl. jours. Pres. women's bd. Chgo. Urban League, 1967-69; mem. Va. Commn. on Status of Women, 1982-85, Gov.'s Commn. on Va.'s Future, 1982-85, Gov.'s Commn. on Efficiency in Govt., 1985-87; treas. Va. Women's Cultural History Project, 1982-85; bd. dirs. Boys and Girls Club of Charlottesville/Albemarle; governing bd. Charlottesville/Albemarle Found., 1993—; mem. adv. bd. Ash Lawn-Highland Mus. Mem. Internat. Assn. Personnel Women (v.p. mems.-at-large 1980-82), Am. Edn. Fin. Assn., Va. Assn. Econs., Acad. Mgmt., Barnard Coll./Columbia U. Alumnae Assn. (bd. dirs. 1977-81, trustee 1977-81). Episcopalian. Home: 1419 Hilltop Rd Charlottesville VA 22903-1226 Office: U Va McIntire Sch Commerce Monroe Hall Charlottesville VA 22903

SCOTT, DALE ALLAN, major league umpire; b. Springfield, Oreg., Aug. 14, 1959; s. Jesse Lee and Betty Ann (Potts) S. AS, Lane C.C., 1979. Radio disc jockey Sta. KBDF, Eugene, Oreg., 1976-81; minor league umpire various orgns., 1981-85; umpire Am. League, 1986—; ofcl. h.s. basketball Portland Basketball Ofcls. Assn., 1986—; ofcl. h.s. football Portland Football Ofcls. Assn., 1989—. Democrat. Office: Am League Profl Baseball 350 Park Ave New York NY 10022-6022

SCOTT, DARREL JOSEPH, healthcare executive; b. Indpls., Sept. 12, 1947; s. Hubert Norris and Beverly June (Hiatt) S.; m. Janice L. Meredith, June 21, 1969; children: Andrew, Brennan. BA, Ind. U., 1969, MHA with high honors, 1971; JD, U. Louisville, 1990. Planning assoc. Ind. Hosp. Assn., Indpls., 1970-72; asst. dir. Welborn Bapt. Hosp., Evansville, Ind., 1972-77, AMA, Chgo., 1977-78; pres., chief exec. officer King's Daus. Hosp., Madison, Ind., 1978-90; v.p. legal svcs. Sisters St. Francis Health Svcs., Mishawaka, Ind., 1990-94, sr. v.p. corp. affairs, 1994—; mem. Ind. Emergency Med. Services Commn., 1974-75. Bd. dirs. Jefferson County United Way, 1979-85; chair coms. Trinity United Methodist Ch., Madison, 1982, Clay United Meth. Ch., 1992-95. Fellow Am. Coll. Healthcare Execs. Republican. Home: 51563 Fox Pointe Ln Granger IN 46530-8473 Office: Srs of St Francis Hlth Servs PO Box 1290 Mishawaka IN 46546-1290

SCOTT, DAVID BYTOVETZSKI, dental research and forensic odontology consultant; b. Providence, May 8, 1919; 4 children. A.B., Brown U., 1939; D.D.S., U. Md., 1943; M.S., U. Rochester, 1944; Sc.D. (hon.), Med. and Dental Coll. N.J., 1979, U. Louis Pasteur, Strasbourg, France, 1981. Commd. officer thru grades to asst. surgeon gen. (rear adm.) USPHS, 1944-65, 75-81; mem. staff Nat. Inst. Dental Rsch., NIH, Bethesda, Md., 1944-56, chief lab. histology and pathology, 1956-65, dir., 1976-82; mem. faculty Case Western Res. U., Cleve., 1965-76, Thomas J. Hill disting. prof. phys. biology Sch. Dentistry,, 1965-76, dean Sch. Dentistry, 1969-76; ind. cons. dental rsch. and forensic odontology, 1982—. Recipient Arthur S. Flemming award U.S. Jr. C. of C., 1955, Rsch. Achievement award, Mass. Dental Soc., 1978, Fred Birnberg Dental Rsch. medal, Columbia U., 1978, Callahan Meml. award Ohio Dental Assn., 1985; named to Hall of Fame, Sch. of Dentistry, U. Md., 1990; decorated Order of Rising Sun, Govt. of Japan, 1983. Mem. ADA, Am. Acad. Forensic Sci. (Forensic Odontology award 1981), Electron Micros. Soc. Am., Internat. Coll. Dentists, Am. Coll. Dentists, Internat. Assn. Dental Rsch. (award for Rsch. in Mineralization 1968), Royal Soc. Medicine (hon.), Am. Bd. Forensic Odontology (cert.). Home and Office: 9100 Belvoir Woods Pky Apt 209 Fort Belvoir VA 22060-2713

SCOTT, DAVID J., beverage executive. With Davidson & Omara, N.Y.C., 1981-86, RGR Nabisco, Winston-Salem, N.C., 1981-86; sr. v.p., sec. Heublein Inc., Farmington, Conn., 1986—. Office: Heublein Inc PO Box 778 450 Columbus Blvd Hartford CT 06142-0778*

SCOTT, DAVID KNIGHT, physicist, university administrator; b. North Ronaldsay, Scotland, Mar. 2, 1940; married, 1966; 3 children. BSc, Edinburgh U., 1962; DPhil in Nuclear Physics, Oxford U., 1967. Rsch. officer nuclear physics lab. Oxford U., 1970-73; rsch. fellow nuclear physics Balliol Coll., 1967-70, sr. rsch. fellow, 1970-73; physicist Lawrence Berkeley Lab. U. Calif., 1973-75, sr. scientist nuclear sci., 1975-79; prof. physics, astronomy and chemistry Nat. Superconducting Cyclotron Lab. Mich. State U., East Lansing, 1979-93; Hannah disting. prof. physics, astronomy and chemistry Mich. State U., East Lansing, 1979-86, assoc. provost, 1983-86, provost, v.p. acad. affairs, 1986-92; Hannah Disting. prof. learning, sci. and soc. Nat. Superconducting Cyclotron Lab. Mich. State U., East Lansing, 1992-93; chancellor U. Mass., Amherst, 1993—. Fellow Am. Phys. Soc. Office: U Mass Office of Chancellor 374 Whitmore Adminstrn Bldg Amherst MA 01003

SCOTT, DAVID MICHAEL, pharmacy educator; b. St. Paul, July 5, 1949; s. David Marvin and Cecelia (Ventura) S.; m. Patti L. Anderson, May 1, 1976; children: Michael, Justin, Nathan. BS, U. Minn., 1972, MPH, 1982, PhD, 1987. Lic. pharmacist, Minn. Pharmacy intern United Hosps., St. Paul, 1972-73, staff pharmacist, 1973-75; pharmacy dir. Cmty.-Univ. Health Care Ctr., Mpls., 1975-84; clin. instr. pharmacy U. Minn., Mpls., 1975-86; assoc. dir. orthop. rsch. St. Paul Ramsey Med. Ctr., 1984-86; assoc. prof. U. Nebr. Med. Ctr., Omaha, 1986—; project epidemiologist Toward a Drug-Free Nebr., Nebr. Dept. Edn., Lincoln, 1989—; mem. Springville Elem. Sch. Drug Abuse, Omaha, 1988—; faculty advisor Acad. Student Pharmacists, Omaha, 1994—. Contbr. articles to sci. jours. Coach Keystone Little League, Omaha, 1991-94; bd. dirs. Butler-Gast YMCA, Omaha, 1992—; vice chmn. bd. dirs., 1994-95; chmn. Nebr. PACT (Pulling Ams. Cmtys. Together) Sch. Truancy Task Force, Lincoln, 1994—. Grantee NARD Rsch. Found., Alexandria, Va., 1991-94. Mem. APHA (mem. program com. 1991-93), Am. Ednl. Rsch. Assn., Nat. Assn. Retail Pharmacists (faculty liaison 1987—), Am. Assn. Colls. of Pharmacy (mem. program com. 1990-92, grant 1995—), Internat. Soc. Pharmacoepidemiology (mem. program com. 1992-94). Avocations: jogging, softball, golf, reading, children's sports. Home: 5305 Raven Oaks Dr Omaha NE 68152-1750 Office: U Nebr Med Ctr Coll Pharmcy 600 S 42nd St Omaha NE 68105-1002

SCOTT, DAVID WARREN, statistics educator; b. Oak Park, Ill., July 16, 1950; s. John V. and Nancy (Mellers) S.; m. Jean Charlotte Madera, June 15, 1974; children: Hilary Kathryn, Elizabeth Alison, Warren Robert. BA, Rice U., 1972, MA, 1976, PhD, 1976. Asst. prof. Baylor Coll. Medicine, Houston, 1976-79; asst. prof. Rice U., Houston, 1979-80, assoc. prof., 1980-85, chmn. statistics dept., 1990-93; vis. prof. Stanford U., Palo Alto, Calif., 1985-86; vis. prof. Dept. Def., Ft. Meade, Md., 1993-94. Co-editor: jour. Computational Stats. and jour. Stat. Scis.; contbr. articles to profl. publs.; author: Multivariate Density Estimation, 1992. Grantee NASA, 1982-84, Office Naval Rsch., 1985-93, NSF, 1993—. Fellow Internat. Stats. Inst., Inst. Math. Stats., Am. Statis. Assn.; mem. Am. Status Soc. (assoc. editor jour. 1983-94), Inst. Math. Statis. (cons.). Avocations: woodworking, hiking, family. Home: 4143 Marlowe St Houston TX 77005-1953 Office: Rice U Dept Stats PO Box 1892 Houston TX 77251

SCOTT, DEBORAH EMONT, curator; b. Passaic, N.J.; d. Rhoda (Baumgarten) Emont; m. George Andrew Scott, June 4, 1983; children: Meredith Suzanne, Diana Faith. BA, Rutgers U., 1973; MA, Oberlin Coll., 1979. Asst. curator Allen Meml. Art Mus., Oberlin, Ohio, 1977-79; curator collections Memphis Brooks Mus. Art, 1979-83; curator The Nelson-Atkins Mus. Art, Kansas City, 1983—; project dir. Henry Moore Sculpture Garden, 1986—. Author: (catalogue) Alan Shields, 1983, (essay) Jonathan Borofsky, 1988, (essay) Judith Shea, 1989, (interview) John Ahearn, 1990, (essay)

Gerhard Richter, 1990, (essay) Kathy Muehlemann, 1991, (essay) Nate Fors, 1991, (essay) Julian Schnabel, 1991, (essay) Louise Bourgeois, 1994, (essay) Joel Shapiro, 1995. Office: Nelson-Atkins Mus Art 4525 Oak St Kansas City MO 64111-1818

SCOTT, DONALD ALLISON, lawyer; b. Phila., Oct. 7, 1929; s. Garfield and Grace Louise (Nevin) S.; m. Jeanne Marie Cooper, June 25, 1955; children: Allison Cooper, Andrew Garfield, John Wallace, Lindsay Nevin. A.B., Princeton U., 1951; J.D., Harvard U., 1956. Bar: Pa. 1958. Law clk. Judge Learned Hand, U.S. Ct. Appeals, 2d Circuit, 1956-57; assoc. Morgan, Lewis & Bockius, LLP, Phila., 1957-64, ptnr., 1964—. Served with USNR, 1951-53. Mem. ABA, Pa. Bar Assn., Phila. Bar Assn., Am. Law Inst., Merion Cricket Club, Paupack Hills Golf Club. Presbyterian. Home: 714 W Mt Airy Ave Philadelphia PA 19119-3326 Office: Morgan Lewis & Bockius LLP 2000 One Logan Sq Philadelphia PA 19103

SCOTT, DONALD MICHAEL, educational association administrator, educator; b. L.A., Sept. 26, 1943; s. Bernard Hendry and Barbara (Lannin) S.; m. Patricia Ilene Pancoast, Oct. 24, 1964 (div. June 1971); children: William Bernard, Kenneth George. BA, San Francisco State U., 1965, MA, 1986. Cert. tchr. Calif. Tchr. Mercy High Sch., San Francisco, 1968-71; park ranger Calif. State Park System, Half Moon Bay, 1968-77; tchr. adult div. Jefferson Union High Sch. Dist., Daly City, Calif., 1973-87; dir. NASA-NPS Project Wider Focus, Daly City, 1983-90; dir. Geo.S. Spl. Projects Wider Focus, San Francisco, 1990—; also bd. dirs. Wider Focus, Daly City; nat. park ranger/naturalist Grant-Kohrs Ranch Nat. Hist. Site, Deer Lodge, Mont., 1987-88; nat. park ranger pub. affairs fire team Yellowstone Nat. Park, 1988; nat. park ranger Golden Gate Recreation Area, 1988-92; rsch. subject NASA, Mountain View, Calif., 1986-90; guest artist Yosemite (Calif.) Nat. Park, 1986; nat. park ranger Golden Gate Nat. Recreation Area, Nat. Park Svc., San Francisco, 1986, nat. park svc. history cons. to Bay Dist., 1988-94; adj. asst. prof. Skyline Coll., 1989-94, Coll. San Mateo, 1992-94; aerospace edn. specialist NASA/OSU/AESP, 1994—. Contbr. articles, photographs to profl. jours., mags. Pres. Youth for Kennedy, Lafayette, calif., 1960; panelist Community Bds. of San Francisco, 1978-87; city chair Yes on A com., So. San Francisco, San Mateo County, Calif., 1986; active CONTACT Orgn., 1991—, bd. dirs. 1995—. Mem. Yosemite Assn. (life), Wider Focus, Friends of George R. Stewart, Nat. Sci. Tchrs. Assn., Nat. Coun. of Tchrs. of Math., Internat. Tech. Edn. Assn., Smithsonian Air and Space (charter mem.), Planetary Soc. (charter mem.). Democrat. Avocations: photography, hiking, camping, travel. Home and Office: MST12A NASA Ames Rsch Ctr Moffett Field CA 94035-1000

SCOTT, EDWARD PHILIP, lawyer; b. Somers Point, N.J., Dec. 17, 1937; s. Harry Edward and Gladys Louise (Atkinson) s.; m. Jane Anne Wilby, June 6, 1961; children: Young-Joon, Edward P. Jr., Lauren, Tracey. BA, Rutgers U., 1959; JD, U. Pa., 1963. Bar: N.J. 1963, D.C. 1968. Assoc. Arnold & Porter, Washington, 1967-68; atty./advisor Peace Corps, Washington, 1968-69, dep. gen. counsel, 1970; dep. dir. Peace Corps, Seoul, Korea, 1971-72; dir. Peace Corps, Korea, 1972-73; staff atty. Mental Health Law Project, Washington, 1973-77; minority gen. counsel U.S. Senate Com Vets. Affairs, Washington, 1981-86, gen. counsel, 1977-80, 87-90; chief counsel, staff dir. U.S. Senate on Com. Vets. Affairs, Washington, 1990-93; asst. sec. for Congressional affairs Dept. Vets. Affairs, Washington, 1993—; legis. asst. Sen. Alan Cranston, D.C. 1981-88. Author: Mental Health Issues in State Law, 1976. Capt. USAF, 1964-67. Mem. ABA, D.C. Bar Assn., Audubon Naturalist Soc., Montgomery County Road Runners. Democrat. Avocations: running, birding, scuba diving. Home: 3703 Inverness Dr Chevy Chase MD 20815-5660 Office: Dept Vets Affairs Asst Sec Congl Affairs 810 Vermont Ave NW Washington DC 20420

SCOTT, EDWARD WILLIAM, JR., computer software company executive; b. Panama City, Panama, May 25, 1938; s. Edward William and Janice Gertrude (Grimison) S.; m. Cheryl S. Gilliland, apr. 23, 1988; children: Edward William, Heather Yolanda Deirdre, Reece Donald. BA, Mich. State U., 1959, MA, 1963; BA, Oxford (Eng.) U., 1962. Personnel specialist Panama Canal Co., 1962-64, staff asst. to dir. personnel, 1964-66; personnel officer IRS, Detroit, 1966-68; staff personnel mgmt. specialist U.S. Dept. Justice, Washington, 1968-69; chief personnel systems and evaluation sect. U.S. Dept. Justice, 1970-72; dir. U.S. Dept. Justice (Office Mgmt. Programs), 1972-74; asso. dep. commr. planning and evaluation U.S. Dept. Justice (U.S. Immigration and Naturalization Service), 1974-75, dep. asst. atty. gen. adminstrn., 1972-75; asst. sec. for adminstrn. (Transp. Dept.), 1977-80; pres. Office Power, Inc., Washington, 1980-81; dir. mktg. Computer Consoles, Inc., 1981-84; v.p. mktg. Dest Systems, 1984-85; dir. govt. mktg. Sun Microsystems, Mountain View, Calif., 1985-88; exec. v.p. Pyramid Tech., Mountain View, 1988-95; founder, exec. v.p. worldwide ops. BEA Sys., Inc., Sunnyvale, Calif., 1995—; pres. U.S. Dept. Justice Fed. Credit Union, 1970-73. Recipient Presdl. Mgmt. Improvement certificate, 1971; Spl. Commendation award Dept. Justice, 1973; also Spl. Achievement award, 1976; William A. Jump Meml. award, 1974; presdl. sr. exec. service rank of Disting. Exec., 1980; Mich. State U. scholar, 1957-60. Mem. Phi Eta Sigma, Phi Kappa Phi. Democrat. Office: BEA Sys Inc 385 Moffett Park Dr Sunnyvale CA 94089

SCOTT, ELIZABETH, social service administrator; b. Aberdeen, Md., Sept. 28, 1954; d. Thomas and Mary Alberta (Adams) S.; 1 child, Cha Rae L'Nise. Student, Md. Inst. Coll. Art, Balt., 1972-75, U. Balt., 1977-79. Employment counselor City of Balt., 1976-78; supr. U.S. Postal Svc., Balt., 1978-83; work study counselor Westside Skill Ctr., Balt., 1984-85; gen. mgr. 32d St. Pla., Balt., 1985-87; office mgr. Md. Citizen Action Coalition, Balt., 1988-89; exec. dir. Coalition of Peninsula Orgns., Balt., 1989-93, Heart, Body and Soul, Inc., Balt., 1993; legis. coord. Planned Parenthood of Md., Balt., 1993-94; exec. dir. Balt. Housing Roundtable, 1994—; faculty assoc. Johns Hopkins U., Balt., 1993—, cons. Sch. Pub. Health, 1991—; mem. exec. com. Inner City Cmty. Devel. Corp., 1990-92. Bd. dirs. Light St. Housing Corp., Balt., Balt. Cable Access Corp., Md. Citizen Action Coalition, Md. Low Income Housing Info. Svc., 1989-91, Jobs with Peace, 1989-91, Women's Housing Coalition; bd. dirs. South Balt. Youth Ctr., pres., 1992-93; mem. gubernatorial transition subcom. on neighborhood revitalization and cmty. devel. Md. Forward, 1994; media rep. Save Our Cities March on Washington, 1991-92; mem. jazz com. Md. Mus. African Art, Columbia, 1994—; mem. Walters Art Gallery, Washington; mem. Gov.'s Task Force on Home Ownership; adv. coun. Empower Balt. Mgmt. Corp. Adv. Coun., 1996—; mem. women's caucus U.S. Network for Habitat II, 1995—; mem. gov.'s task force for homeownership; rep. UN preparatory com. Habitat II, N.Y.C., 1996; rep. UN mega conf. on human settlements Habitat II, Istanbul, Turkey, 1996. Recipient Contbn. award Balt. Commonwealth, 1992, Balt. City Pub. Schs., 1990, Community Svc. award State of md., 1990, 91, 92, Svc. award United Way of Cen. Md., 1991, Svc. award U.S. Postal Svc., 1983. Mem. Smithsonian Instns., Md. Assn. Housing Redevel. (bd. dirs. 1995—). Home: 3609 Kimble Rd Baltimore MD 21218-2027

SCOTT, ELLIOT, production designer. Prodn. designer: (films) The Americanization of Emily, 1964, The Incredible Sarah, 1976 (Academy award nomination best art direction 1976), Warlords of Atlantis, 1978, The Fifth Musketeer, 1979, Arabian Adventure, 1979, The Watcher in the Woods, 1980, Dragonslayer, 1981, Evil Under the Sun, 1982, The Pirates of Penzance, 1983, Labyrinth, 1985, (with Roger Cain) Who Framed Roger Rabbit?, 1988 (Academy award nomination best art direction 1988), Indiana Jones and the Last Crusade, 1989. Office: care Art Directors Guild 11365 Ventura Blvd Ste 315 Studio City CA 91604-3148

SCOTT, EUGENIE CAROL, science foundation director, anthropologist; b. LaCrosse, Wis., Oct. 24, 1945; d. Allen K. and Virginia Meliss (Derr) S.; m. Robert Abner Black, Oct. 18, 1965 (div. 1970); m. Thomas Charles Sager, Dec. 30, 1971; 1 child, Carrie Ellen Sager. BS, U. Wis., Milw., 1967, MS, 1968; PhD, U. Mo., 1974. Asst. prof. anthropology U. Ky., Lexington, 1974-82; postdoctoral fellow U. Calif., San Francisco, 1983-84; asst. prof. U. Colo., Boulder, 1984-86; exec. dir., pub. newsletter NCSE Reports, Nat. Ctr. Sci. Edn., Berkeley, Calif., 1987—; bd. dirs. Nat. Pub. Edn. and Religious Liberty, Washington; pub. Bookwatch Revs., 1988-92. Author, editor: Biology Textbooks, The New Generation, 1990; prodr. videotape series How Scientists Know About...; featured guest as sci. authority on creationism and/or pseudosci. Recipient Disting. Alumnus award U. Mo. Arts & Scis., 1993. Fellow Com. for Sci. Investigation Claims of Paranormal (Sci. and Edn. award 1991), Calif. Acad. Scis. (elected 1994); mem. Am. Assn. Phys. Anthropology (bd. dirs., exec. com. 1988-93, sec.-treas. 1993—). Office: Nat Ctr Sci Edn PO Box 9477 Berkeley CA 94709-0477

SCOTT, FREDERICK ISADORE, JR., editor, business executive; b. Balt., Oct. 27, 1927; s. Frederick Isadore and Rebecca Esther (Waller) S.; m. Viola Fowlkes, Feb. 4, 1949. B.E. in Chem. Engring, Johns Hopkins, 1950; M.S. in Mgmt. Engring, Newark Coll. Engring., 1956. Chem. process engr. in research and devel. RCA, Harrison, N.J., 1951-59; with Kearfott div. Gen. Precision Aerospace, Little Falls, N.J., 1960-62; asst. sales mgr. Isotopes, Inc., Westwood, N.J., 1964-66; mgr. capacitor sect. Wellington Electronics, Inc., Englewood, N.J., 1967-68; owner F.I. Scott & Assos. (med. equipment), Montclair, N.J., 1968-80; tech. product mktg. and editorial svcs. F.I. scott & Assocs., Check, Va., 1980-86; editor instrumentation publ. Am. Lab. and Internat. Lab., Fairfield, Conn., 1968-80, cons. editor, 1980—; pres. Group Tech., Ltd., 1979—; editor Am. Clin. Lab., 1990—. Served with AUS, 1946-47. Mem. Am. Chem. Soc. (sr.), AAAS, N.Y. Acad. Sci., IEEE (editor newsletter No. N.J. sect. 1957-58, chmn. publs. com. 1958-59), N.Y. Micros. Soc. Home and Office: 1 E Chase St Apt 410 Baltimore MD 21202-2557 *Perhaps the most significant aspect of my life is a long-felt realization that each person is ultimately responsible for his or her condition in life. Application of this principle continually requires that the individual assess a failure in such a way as to determine how his or her actions might have avoided it or, if unavoidable, how its recurrence can be obviated. Accepting responsibility in this manner can, I believe, lead the way toward a society based on a federation of autonomous individuals delegating authority to units of government when appropriate but clearly retaining the capability to recall that delegated authority should it be abused.*

SCOTT, FREDRIC WINTHROP, veterinarian; b. Greenfield, Mass., Nov. 22, 1935; s. Clifton William and Mildred E. (Bradford) S.; m. Lois Ellen Williams, May 26, 1957; children: Duane Douglas, John Gardner, Raymond Clifton. BS in Chemistry, U. Mass., 1958; DVM, Cornell U., 1962, PhD in Virology, 1968. Veterinarian Rutland (Vt.) Vet. Clinic, 1962-64; rsch. veterinarian USDA, Plum Island Animal Disease Ctr., Greenport, N.Y., 1964-65; NIH postdoctoral fellow Cornell U., Ithaca, N.Y., 1965-68, asst. prof. vet. microbiology, 1968-73, assoc. prof. vet. microbiology, 1973-79, prof. microbiology and immunology, 1979—; dir. Cronell Feline Health Ctr., 1974—; mem. bd. comparative virology WHO/FAO; mem. vet. med. adv. com. Ctr. for Vet. Medicine, FDA, Rockville, Md., 1984-86; mem. vet. sci. tech. adv. coun. Agrl. and Tech. Coll., SUNY, Delhi, 1972-75; cons., rschr. in field. Editor-in-chief Feline Practice Jour.; co-author: Infectious Diseases Domestic Animals, 1988, Infectious Diseases, 1986; contbr. articles to profl. pubs.; inventor vaccines. Bd. elders Bethel Grove Bible Ch., 1979-91, 93—; faculty advisor Christian Vet. Fellowship; coach youth baseball and hockey; mem. Town of Ithaca Planning Bd.; mem. troop com. Boy Scouts Am., Ellis Hollow. Nat. Acads. Practice disting. scholar in vet. medicine, 1991—; NIH grantee, 1970-83. Fellow Acad. Feline Practice (bd. dirs. 1991—); mem. AVMA (sci. program com. 1973-81, coun. on biologic and therapeutic agts. 1986-92, chmn. 1987-89), Am. Coll. Vet. Microbiologists (diplomate, examinations com. 1975-79), Am. Soc. Virology, N.Y. State Vet. Med. Soc. (com. on small animal practice 1985-90), So. Tier Vet. Med. Assn., Am. Assn. Feline Practitioners (pres. 1976-78, adv. bd. past pres. 1990—, rsch. award 1975), Am. Animal Hosp. Assn. (Carnation award 1990), Conf. Rsch. Workers on Animal Diseases. Republican. Mem. Evangelical Ch. Avocations: golf, archery, gardening, basketball. Office: Cornell U Coll Vet Medicine Feline Health Ctr Ithaca NY 14853

SCOTT, GARY KUPER, retired academic administrator; b. Jefferson City, Mo., Jan. 3, 1933; s. Ralph Elmer and Lillian Rachel (Kuper) S.; children—Tina Marie, Lisa René , Corey Kuper. A.A., Jefferson City Jr. Coll., 1953; B.Ed., Western Wash. State Coll., 1960, M.Ed., 1962; Ph.D., U. Minn., 1965. Dir. student counseling center Minot (N.D.) State Coll., 1965-67; faculty, head dept. psychology Lincoln U., Jefferson City, 1967-77, chmn. dept. edn. and psychology, 1979-83, dean Sch. Edn. and Grad. Studies, 1983-85, dir. grad. and continuing edn., 1985-88, dean grad. and continuing edn., 1988-95; ret., 1995. Pres. Cole County Mental Health Assn., 1969-70; Bd. dirs. YMCA.; mem. Jefferson City Sch. Bd., 1985-87; mem. Cole County Democratic Com., 1968-70. Mem. Am., Mo. psychol. assns. Club: Rotary. Home: 1002 Roseridge Cir Jefferson City MO 65101-3640

SCOTT, GEORGE CAMPBELL, actor, director; b. Wise, Va., Oct. 18, 1927; s. George C. and Helena S.; m. Carolyn Hughs (div.); m. Patricia Reed (div.); m. Colleen Dewhurst, 1960 (div.); m. Trish Van Devere, Feb. 2, 1972; 6 children from previous marriages. Student, U. Mo., 1950. Actor stock cos., 1950-57; N.Y.C. debut as Richard III, Shakespeare Festival, 1957; stage appearances include As You Like It, 1958, Children of Darkness, 1958, Antony and Cleopatra, 1959, Merchant of Venice, 1960, 62, The Wall, 1960, Desire Under the Elms, 1963, Plaza Suite, 1968, Uncle Vanya, 1974, Andersonville Trial, 1959, Comes a Day, 1959, Present Laughter, 1982, Design for Living, 1984, The Boys of Summer, 1986, On Borrowed Time, 1991, Wrongturn at Lungfish, 1993; co-founder, Theatre of Mich. Co., Inc., 1961; produced: stage appearances include Great Day in the Morning, 1962; dir., played: title role General Seeger, 1962; dir.: title role All God's Chillun Got Wings, 1975; actor, dir.: title role Death of a Salesman, 1975, Sly Fox, 1976; films include The Hanging Tree, 1959, Anatomy of a Murder, 1959, The Hustler, 1961, The List of Adrian Messenger, 1963, Dr. Strangelove (Or How I Learned To Stop Worrying And Love The Bomb), 1964, The Bible, 1966, Flim-Flam Man, 1967, Patton, 1970, The Hospital, 1971, The Last Run, 1971, They Might Be Giants, 1971, The New Centurions, 1972, Rage (also dir.), 1972, The Day of the Dolphin, 1973, Oklahoma Crude, 1973, The Savage is Loose (also prodr. and dir.), 1974, The Hindenburg, 1975, Beauty and the Beast, 1976, Islands in the Stream, 1977, Crossed Swords, 1978, Movie, Movie, 1978, Hardcore, 1979, The Changeling, 1980, The Formula, 1980, Taps, 1981, Firestarter, The Exorcist III, 1990, The Rescuers Down Under (voice) 1990, Malice, 1993; TV plays include Kraft Mystery Theatre, Omnibus, Playhouse 90, Play of Week, Hallmark Hall of Fame, The Price; others; dir.: The Andersonville Trial (Emmy award for prodn.); TV movies: Jane Eyre, 1971, Fear on Trial, 1975, Oliver Twist, 1982, China Rose, 1983, A Christmas Carol, 1984, Mussolini: The Untold Story, 1985, Choices, 1986, The Last Days of Patton, 1986, The Murders in the Rue Morgue, 1986, Pals, 1987, The Ryan White Story, 1989, Descending Angel, 1990, Finding the Way Home, 1991; TV series East Side/ West Side, 1963, Mr. President, 1986, Traps, 1994. Recipient Clarence Derwent award 1958, Vernon Rice award 1958, Theatre World award 1958, Obie award Village Voice 1958, 63, Golden Globe 1970, refused Oscar for film Patton 1971, Emmy for The Price, 1971; Genie (Can.) 1980. Served with USMC, 1945-49. Mem. Actors Equity Assn., Screen Actors Guild, AFTRA, Dirs. Guild Am., Soc. Stage Dirs. and Choreographers. Office: Charles H Stern Agency Inc 11766 Wilshire Blvd Ste 760 Los Angeles CA 90025-1530*

SCOTT, GEORGE ERNEST, publisher, writer; b. Detroit, Sept. 12, 1924; s. George Ernest and Ruth Janet (Moffett) S.; m. Lois Aurlie Brown, Mar. 28, 1953; m. Elaine Lorraine Phillips, Feb. 14, 1982. Student, U. Detroit, 1946-47, Woodbury Coll., Los Angeles, 1947-48. With advt. prodn. dept. D.P. Brother Advt., Detroit, 1947-49, Ruthrauff & Ryan Advt., Detroit, 1950-51; advt. account exec. Betteridge & Co. Advt., Detroit, 1951-53; founder, 1954; pub., pres. Scott Advt. & Pub. Co., Livonia, Mich.; owner, pub. Ceramic Arts & Crafts mag., 1955—. Ceramic Teaching Projects and Trade News, quar., 1965—. Songwriter: (words and music) I Want A Lovin' Man, Tropic Memories, A Second Chance at Love, I Think I'm Falling in Love With You, Sing, Sing, Sing at Christmas, Boomerang Lovin' You's the Best Thing Tthat I Do and Over 100 More. With USNR, 1942-46. Mem. Nat. Ceramic Mfrs. Assn. (past dir.), Mich. Ceramic Dealers Assn. (past pres.). Home: 574 Herald St Plymouth MI 48170-1537

SCOTT, GWENDOLYN HARRISON, educator, consultant; b. Sheridan, Wyo., Mar. 11, 1927; d. Leonard Elliott and Danora (Smith) Harrison; m. Harold R. Scott Sr., Jan. 22, 1951 (div. Apr. 15, 1978); children: Victoria Vitatoe, Claudia Hinds, Harold Roy Jr. BFA, U. Denver, 1948, MA, 1968. Cert. secondary tchr., Colo. Elem. tchr. Kansas City Pub. Schs., Kans., 1948-50; art tchr. Children's Mus., Denver, 1953-58; elem. tchr. Denver Pub. Schs., 1964-69; social sci. instr. Loretto Heights Coll., 1969-70; high sch. social sci. tchr. Denver Pub. Schs., 1970-86; free-lance lectr. Blacks in the west, 1986—; cons., facilitator Anti-Defamation League, Denver, 1989—; adj. instr. C.C. of Aurora (Colo.), 1990—. Author: (curriculum) Comparative Study of Am. and Kenyan Women, 1985; co-author: A World of Difference Colorado Guide, 1989, Teaching the Film Schindler's List, 1994. Coun. bd. mem. Colo. Com. for Women's History, 1993—; bd. dirs. Denver Sister Cities Interant., 1992—; congl. dist. rep. Colo. Coun. for Libr. Devel., Colo. State Libr. Dept., 1990—, exec. bd. mem., 1992—. Fulbright scholar Washington, 1980, India, 1980, Kenya, 1985; women's studies grantee Southwest Inst. for Women's Rsch., Ariz. U., 1983-84; NEH grantee Kansas State U., 1977; recipient Altera M. Bryant award Women United the World, Denver, 1992. Mem. Nat. League Am. Pen Women (treas. Denver br. 1989—, svc. award 1994), Colo. Coun. for Social Studies (urban reg. dir. 1982-84, svc. award 1984), Black Educator United (outstanding sec. tchr. award 1977), Delta Kappa Gamma (v.p. 1988-92, rose award 1994). Democrat. Avocations: reading, writing, traveling, drawing and painting. Home: 6632 E Asbury Ave Denver CO 80224-2314

SCOTT, HAL S., law educator; b. 1943. AB, Princeton U., 1965; MA, Stanford U., 1967; JD, U. Chgo., 1972. Law clk. to judge U.S. Ct. Appeals D.C. Cir., Washington, 1972-73, to assoc. justice White, U.S. Supreme Ct., Washington, 1973-74; acting prof. law U. Calif.-Berkeley, 1974-75; asst. prof. law Harvard U. Sch. Law, Cambridge, Mass., 1975-79, prof., 1980-90, Nomura prof. internat. fin. systems, 1990—; cons. IBM, N.Y.C., 1977. Contbr. articles to legal jours. Dir. Program on Internat. Fin. Systems. Mem. Internat. Acad. of Consumer and Comml. Law (past pres.). Office: Law Sch Harvard U Cambridge MA 02138

SCOTT, HANSON L., airport executive; m. Laraine Newman; children: Craig, Randy. Student, N.Mex. State U.; BS in Engring. Scis., USAF Acad., 1961; MBA, Auburn U.; grad., Air Force Air Command and Staff Coll., Dept. Def. Indsl. Coll. of the Armed Forces; postgrad., St. Louis U. Commd. 2d lt. USAF, advanced through grades to brigadier gen.; vice-comdr., dir. ops. 314th Tactical Airlift Wing, Little Rock AFB, 1982-85; comdr. 463rd Tactical Airlift Wing, Dyess AFB, Abilene, Tex., 1985-86; comdr., installation comdr. 1st Spl. Ops. Wing, Hurlburt Field, Fla., 1986-87, vice-comdr. spl. ops. command, 1987-89; comdr. spl. ops. command Pacific Camp H. M. Smith, Hawaii, 1989-91; prin., sr. mktg. dir. Quatro Corp., Albuquerque, 1992-93; dir. aviation Albuquerque Internat. Airport, 1994—, Albuquerque's Double Eagle II Airport, 1994—. Decorated Def. Disting. Svc. medal, Legion of Merit with oak leaf cluster, Disting. Flying Cross, Meritorious Svc. medal with 3 oak leaf clusters, Air medal with 8 oak leaf clusters. Mem. Am. Assn. Airport Execs. Office: Albuquerque Internat Airport 2200 Sunport Blvd PO Box 9022 Albuquerque NM 87106

SCOTT, HELEN CECILE, critical care nurse; b. Paragould, Ark., Apr. 30, 1929; d. Cecil Lloyd and Ora Elvie (Gatlin) Cox; m. Benjamin J. Scott, Dec. 19, 1948; children: Sharon J. Yarbrough, Susan Cecile. ADN, So. State Coll., Magnolia, Ark., 1970; BSN, Graceland Coll., Lamoni, Iowa, 1986. Staff nurse Independence (Mo.) Regional Hosp., clin. care coord.; short-course instr. Jennie Lund Sch. Nursing, Independence; CVI specialist Wellness div. Independence Regional Health Ctr.; part-time critical care staff nurse. Mem. AACN. Home: 808 N Cherokee St Independence MO 64056-1959

SCOTT, HENRY LAWRENCE, concert pianist, humorist; b. Tivoli on Hudson, N.Y., Jan. 20, 1908; s. Walter and Mary Wigram (Keeney) S.; m. Mary Bell Bard, Aug. 28, 1938; children: Barbara Bell, Henry Lawrence. Student, Syracuse (N.Y.) U., class 1930; L.H.D., Bard Coll., Annandale, N.Y., 1964. head Henry Scott Sch. Modern Piano, N.Y.C.; mem. faculty Champlin Sch., 1940-42; pres., chmn. bd. Solo Theater of Am. Corp., 1948; asst. to pres. Bard Coll., Annandale-on-Hudson, 1966; investment adviser Johnson Lane Space and Smith, 1978-89, Interstate Johnson Lane, 1989—. Teaching and radio, screen, stage and TV work, 1931-41; concert work, throughout U.S., 1939—, debut, Town Hall, 1941, Carnegie Hall, 1945-46, 27 transcontinental concert tours, Carnegie Hall, N.Y.C. (2), Town Hall, N.Y.C. (2), Detroit Town Hall, Kansas City Town Hall, West Point Mil. Academy (12), Akron Concert Course, Fine Arts Series, Worcester, U. Minn. (8), U. Tex. (3), U. Notre Dame (2), Miss Porters Sch., Conn. (2), St. Mark's Sch., Southborough, Mass. (5), So. Ill. U. (10), USAF Acad., 1960, Mt. Mary Coll., Milw., Emanuel Missionary Coll., Mich., Pacific Union Coll., Calif., U. So. Calif., Amherst (Mass.) U., Dartmouth Coll., Purdue U., U. N.C., U. Oreg., Med. Coll. Va., Union Coll., Lincoln, Nebr., U. N.Mex., Teaching and radio, screen, stage and TV work, Woman's Inst., Knoxville Friday Morning Musicales, Syracuse, Meml. Auditorium, Lowell, Mass., Eaton Auditorium, Toronto, Met. Opera House, N.Y.C., U. Wash., U. Utah, U. Fla. (3), U. Ga., Artists Series, San Diego, U. N.C. (3), North-Western State Coll. (7), 6th tour, Can., 1966-67, Hawaiian Islands, Saudi Arabia, 1963; guest artist various orchs. and symphonies; indsl. concerts for, General Electric Co., Eastman Kodak, IBM Corp., others, 1958-61; pioneer concert humor; now presenting humorous and ednl. lecture recitals in schs., colls., univs. and concert halls; producer, star: Concerto for Fun, 1949; introduced: Fun at the Philharmonic, 1952; guest appearance: TV show Be Our Guest, 1960; Composer: Clavichord Joe; inventor Technic Mittens for piano practice. Trustee Bard Coll., Annandale, N.Y., 1969-70, Charleston Symphony Orch., 1971-75, Charleston Concert Assn., 1971-78, pres., 1979-84; trustee, 2d v.p. Dock St. Theater, Charleston, 1981-83; founder, chmn. Stockholder Adv. Found., 1975-83, Stockholder Adv. Assn., Inc., 1976-79; bd. visitors Kanuga Episcopal Conf. Ctr., Henderson, N.C., 1985-88; trustee, treas. Dockside Assn., Charleston, 1986-87, pres., 1989-91; life mem. Dutchess County (N.Y.) Hist. Soc. Mem. Carolina Yacht Club (Charleston), Old Town Club (Charleston, pres. 1981-82). Republican. Episcopalian. Address: Dockside Charleston SC 29401 *Fulfillment in life comes from serving and giving. My most frequent prayer is "Lord help me to be a better husband, father and friend".*

SCOTT, H(ERBERT) ANDREW, retired chemical engineer; b. Marion, Va., Mar. 29, 1924; s. Charles Wassum and Carolyn Enyde (Snider) S.; widowed; children: Mark Andrew, Paul Ethan; m. Helen R. LaFollette, July 21, 1984. BSChemE, Va. Tech. Inst. and State U., 1944, MSChemE, 1947. Registered profl. engr., Tenn. Chem. engr. Tenn. Eastman Co., Kingsport, 1947-55, asst. to works mgr., 1955-60, supt. glycol dept., 1960-64, supt. polymers dept., 1964-67, dir. engring. div., 1970-87; plant mgr. Holston Def. Corp., Kingsport, 1967-70, dir. systems devel., 1970-73, dir. engring. dvsn., 1974-87; vis. prof. U. Alaska, Fairbanks, 1988-89; mem. standards com. Eastman Kodak Co., Rochester, N.Y., 1982-87. Mem. mayor's adv. com. City of Kingsport, 1971-76; chmn. Kingsport Park Commn., 1976-80. Sgt. AUS, 1944-46. Named Engr. of yr., Tenn. Soc. Profl. Engrs., 1984. Fellow AIChE (mem. Inst. Chem. Process Safety 1984-87, vocat. guidance com. 1960-64, chmn. local sect. 1956); mem. Am. Soc. Engring. Edn., Am. Soc. Engring. Mgmt., Kiwanis. Republican. Presbyterian. Achievements include patent in process for manufacture of acetic anhydride, implement pioneering quality management for knowledge workers, design for manufacturing chemicals from coal. Home: 4512 Chickasaw Rd Kingsport TN 37664-2110 *Being born of honest, ambitious and loving religious parants in a small town in the mountains of the USA was a great start. Work was a virtue, wages in a depression a life saver! Successfully practicing chemical enginerring in one of America's great companies complete the image.*

SCOTT, HOWARD WINFIELD, JR., temporary help services company executive; b. Greenwich, Conn., Feb. 24, 1935; s. Howard Winfield and Janet (Lewis) S.; B.S., Northwestern U., 1957; m. Joan Ann MacDonald, Aug. 12, 1961; children: Howard Winfield III, Thomas MacDonald, Ann Elizabeth. With R.H. Donnelly Corp., Chgo., 1958-59; sales rep. Masonite Corp., Chgo. also Madison, Wis., 1959-61; sales rep. Manpower Inc., Chgo., 1961-63, br. mgr., Kansas City, Mo., 1963-65, area mgr., Mo. and Kans., 1964-65, regional mgr. Salespower div., Phila., 1965-66; asst. advt. mgr. soups Campbell Soup Co., Camden, N.J., 1966-68; pres. PARTIME, Inc., Paoli, Pa., 1968-74; dir. marketing Kelly Services Inc., Southfield, Mich., 1974-78; pres. CDI Temporary Services, Inc., 1978-91; pres. Dunhill Pers. System, Inc., Woodbury, N.Y., 1991-94; v.p. SOS Temporary Svcs., Salt Lake City, 1994; pres., chief operating officer SOS Staffing Svcs., Salt Lake City, 1995—. Served with AUS, 1957-58. Mem. Nat. Assn. Temporary Services (sec. 1970-71, pres. 1971-73, bd. dirs. 1982-91), Kappa Sigma. Republican. Home: 4030 Saddleback Rd Park City UT 84098-4809 also: 1204 Annapolis Sea Colony E Bethany Beach DE 19930 Office: SOS Staffing Svcs 1415 S Main Salt Lake City UT 84115

SCOTT, HUGH PATRICK, physician, naval officer; b. Phila., Feb. 12, 1938; s. Hugh Patrick and Martha (Papiana) S.; m. Diane Marie Lopatzie, July 1, 1961; children: Karen, Brendan, Catherine. BA, LaSalle Coll., 1960; DO, Phila. Coll. Osteo. Medicine, 1964, LLD (hon.), 1991. Diplomate Am. Osteo. Bd. Ophthalmology and Otolaryngology. Intern Detroit Osteo. Hosp., Highland Park, Mich., 1964-65, resident otorhinolatyngology, 1965-68; lt. med. corps USNR, 1967, advanced through grades to rear adm., 1991; naval med. officer U.S. Naval Dispensary N.O.B., Norfolk, Va., 1968-70, Submarine Squadron 10, Groton, Conn.; Submarine Group 2; naval med. officer Naval Submarine Med. Ctr., New London, Conn., 1975-83; dir. undersea medicine and radiation health Naval Med. Command, Washington, 1983-86; comdg. officer Naval Hosp., Groton, 1986-88, Camp Lejeune, N.C., 1988-90; fleet surgeon Comdr. in Chief, U.S. Pacific Fleet, Pearl Harbor, Hawaii, 1990-91; asst. chief for operational medicine and fleet support Bur. Medicine and Surgery, Washington, 1991-92; dir. med. resources, plans and policy Office Chief of Naval Ops., Washington, 1992-94; asst. clin. prof. medicine Mich. State U., Lansing, Mich., 1970-75; pvt. practice, Madison Heights, Mich., 1970-75; cons. Am. Coll. Undersea and Hyperbaric Medicine, Washington, 1985-86. Decorated Legion of Merit, Gold Star (3). Fellow Osteo. Coll. Ophthalmology and Otolaryngology, Am. Acad. Otolaryngology and Head and Neck Surgery; mem. Am. Osteo. Coll. Otolaryngology--Head and Neck Surgery (pres., chmn. bd. govs.). Republican. Roman Catholic. Home: 3707 Merlin Way Annandale VA 22003-1326

SCOTT, IRENE FEAGIN, federal judge; b. Union Springs, Ala., Oct. 6, 1912; d. Arthur H. and Irene (Peach) Feagin; m. Thomas Jefferson Scott, Dec. 27, 1939 (dec.); children: Thomas Jefferson, Irene Scott Carroll. A.B., U. Ala., 1932, LL.B., 1936, LL.D., 1978; LL.M., Catholic U. Am., 1939. Bar: Ala. 1936. Law libr. U. Ala. Law Sch., 1932-34; atty. Office Chief Counsel IRS, 1937-50, mem. excess profits tax coun., 1950-52, spl. asst. to head appeals div., 1952-59, staff asst. to chief counsel, 1959-60; judge U.S. Tax Ct., 1960-82, sr. judge serving on recall, 1982—. Contbr. articles to Women Lawyers Jour. Bd. dirs. Mt. Olivet Found., Arlington. Mem. ABA (taxation sect.), Ala. Bar Assn., Fed. Bar Assn., D.C. Bar Assn. (hon.), Nat. Assn. Women Lawyers, Nat. Assn. Women Judges, Kappa Delta, Kappa Beta Pi. Office: US Tax Ct 400 2nd St NW Washington DC 20217-0001

SCOTT, ISADORE MEYER, former energy company executive; b. Wilcoe, W.Va., Nov. 21, 1912; s. David and Libby (Roston) S.; m. Joan Rosenwald, Feb. 14, 1943; children: Betsy Scott Kleeblatt, Peggy, Jonathan D. A.B., W.Va. U., 1934, M.A., 1938; J.D., Washington and Lee U., 1937; LLD, West Va. U., 1983. Bar: Va. 1937. Practiced law Richmond, Va., 1937-38; v.p. Lee I. Robinson Hosiery Mills., Phila., 1938-42; with Winner Mfg. Co., Inc., Trenton, 1947-61, v.p., 1947-51, pres., 1951-61; chmn. bd. Tri-Instl. Facilities, Inc., Phila., 1962-78; chmn. bd. TOSCO Corp., Los Angeles, 1976-83, vice-chmn. bd., 1983-87; bd. dirs., chmn. Univ. City Assocs., Inc.; founder, mem. U.S. Adv. Bd. Brit.-Am. Project. Bd. dirs. S.E. Pa. chpt. ARC, Internat. Rescue Com., Univ. City Sci. Ctr., Phila.; mem. adv. com. Urban Affair Partnership; bd. dirs. emeritus, former mem. exec. com., vice-chmn. Phila. Mus. Art; former chmn. World Affairs Council Phila.; mem. Phila. Com. Fgn. Rels.; trustee emeritus Washington and Lee U.; emeritus trustee George C. Marshall Found. With inf. U.S. Army, 1942-46, NATOUSA, ETO. Decorated Legion of Merit, Silver Star, Purple Heart, Bronze Star (U.S.); Crown of Italy; medal of merit Czechoslovakia; Mentioned-in-dispatches, Eng.; fellow Mus. Am. Jewish History. Mem. Va. State Bar, Phila. Club, Gulph Mills Golf, Anglers of Phila., Masons, Phi Beta Kappa, Omicron Delta Kappa, Order of Coif. (hon.). Republican. Jewish. Clubs: Phila.; Gulph Mills Golf, Anglers of Phila. Lodge: Masons.

SCOTT, J. DON, religious organization adminstrator. Pres. World Vision Can. Office: World Vision Can, 6630 Turner Valley Rd, Mississauga, ON Canada LSN 2S4*

SCOTT, JACQUELINE DELMAR PARKER, educational association administrator, business administrator, consultant, fundraiser; b. L.A., May 18, 1947; d. Thomas Aubrey and Daisy Beatrice (Singleton) Parker (div.); children: Tres Mali, Olympia Ranee, Stephen Thomas. AA in Theatre Arts, L.A. City Coll., 1970; BA in Econs., Calif. State U., Dominquez Hills, Carson, 1973; MBA, Golden Gate U., 1979. Cert. parenting instr. 1994. Sales clk. Newberry's Dept. Store, L.A., 1963-65; long distance operator Pacific Telephone Co., L.A., 1965-66; PBX operator Sears, Roebuck & Co., L.A., 1966-68; retail clk. Otey's Grocery Store, Nashville, 1968-69; collector N.Am. Credit, L.A., 1970-71; office mgr. Dr. S. Edward Tucker, L.A., 1972-74; staff coord. sch. edn. dept. Calif. State U., 1973-74; bank auditor Security Pacific Bank, L.A., 1974-76, corp. loan asst., 1976-77; dist. credit analyst Crocker Nat. Bank, L.A., 1977-78, asst. v.p., 1978-80; capital planning adminstr. TRW, Inc., Redondo Beach, Calif., 1980-82, ops. bus. adminstr., 1982-84, lab. sr. bus. adminstr., 1984-86, project bus. mgr., 1986-87, div. sr. bus. adminstr., 1987-92; ptnr., co-author, co-facilitator, cons. Diversified Event Planners, Inc., L.A., 1990-93; asst. area devel. dir. United Negro Coll. Fund, L.A., 1993—. Co-founder career growth awareness com. TRW Employees Bootstrap, Redondo Beach, Calif., 1980, pres., 1983-84; role model Inglewood High Sch., TRW Youth Motivation Task Force, Redondo Beach, 1981-83, Crozier Jr. High Sch., 1981-83, Monroe Jr. High Sch., Redondo Beach, 1981-83, Frank D. Parent Career Day, TRW Affirmative Action Com., Redondo Beach, 1987, St. Bernard's Career Day, 1991; chairperson community involvement com., 1981, chairperson disaster com., 1989-90; chairperson gen. and local welfare com. TRW Employees Charitable Orgn., 1989-90, disaster com. chair, 1988-89, bd. dirs. 1987-89; pres. Mgmt. Effectiveness Program Alumnae, L.A., 1982-83, TRW Employees Bootstrap Program Alumnae, 1983-84; group leader Jack & Jill of Am., Inc., South L.A., 1980-81, parliamentarian, 1986-87, v.p., 1981-82, chpt. pres., 1984-86, regional dir., 1987-89, nat. program dir., 1992—, liaison to Young Black Scholars Program, 1986—; bd. dirs. Adolescent Pregnancy Child Watch, 1993—, Jack & Jill Am. Found., 1992—; L.A. mem. Nat. Black Child Devel. Inst., 1994—; vol. ARC, 1994—; parenting instr. Am. Red Cross, 1994—. Recipient commendation NAACP, 1985, United Negro Coll. Fund, 1986, United Way, 1988, Austistic Children's Telephon, 1980, Inglewood Sch. Dist., 1981, Pres. award Harbor Area Chpt. Links, Inc., 1985, Women of Achievement award City of L.A., Black Pers. Assn., 1994. Mem. Black Women's Forum (sponsor), Delta Sigma Theta. Avocations: reading, dancing.

SCOTT, JAMES J., retired mining engineer; b. Wiota, Wis., Apr. 22, 1928; m. Edna M. Kettler, 1947; 5 children. BS, Mo. Sch. of Mines, 1950; MS, U. Wis., 1959, PhD in Mining Engring., 1962. Mine engr. Bethlehem (Pa.) Steel Co., 1950-53, mine foreman, 1953-57; from instr. to asst. prof. mining U. Wis., 1957-63; assoc. prof. U. Mo., Rolla, 1963-65, prof. mining, 1965-80, chmn. depts. mining & petroleum, 1970-76; gen. mgr. Black River Mine, Marble Cliff Quarries Co., 1967; asst. dir. mining rsch. US Bur. Mines, 1970—; adj. prof. mining engring. U. Mo., Rolla, 1980—; pres. Scott Mine Tech. Svc. Inc. Recipient Rock Mechanics award Soc. Mining Engrs. Mem. Am. Inst. Mining, Metall. and Petroleum Engrs. (Daniel C. Jackling award 1990), Can. Inst. Mining and Metallurgy. Achievements include research in field rock mechanics, mine operational problems, experimental stress analysis, photoelasticity, model studies, stress distribution problems, mine and research management; patentee in field. Home: 16720 State Rt O Rolla MO 65401 Office: Scott MTS Inc 16720 State Rt 0 Rolla MO 65401

SCOTT, JAMES MARTIN, state legislator, healthcare system executive; b. Fairfax County, Va., June 11, 1938; s. Fred Sharp and Mary Ruth (Bishop) S.; m. Nancy Virginia Cromwell, Nov. 27, 1976; children: Catherine Virginia, Mary Alice. BA in English, U. N.C., 1960, MA in English, 1965; MPA, George Mason U., 1982. Tchr. Edison High Sch., Fairfax, Va., 1963-64; exec. dir. Fairfax Community Action Program, 1966-69, Washington Suburban Inst., Fairfax, 1969-72; bd. suprs. Fairfax County, 1972-86; dir. comminuty affairs Inova Health System, Springfield, Va., 1986-90, asst. v.p., 1990—; mem. Va. Ho. Dels., Richmond, 1992—; pres. Va. Assn. Counties, Richmond, 1978-79; chair No. Va. Transp. Commn., Arlington, 1982. Pres. Fairfax Fair, 1988-90; bd. dirs. Washington Area Housing Partnership, 1990—, Washington Met. Coun. Govts., 1993—. Recipient David and Betty Scull Pub. Svc. award Washington Met. Coun. Govts., 1983; named Fairfax County Citizen of Yr., Washington Post, 1991. Democrat. Methodist. Avocation: sports. Office: PO Box 359 Merrifield VA 22116-0359

SCOTT, JAMES MICHAEL, environmental research administrator; b. San Diego, Sept. 20, 1941; m. 1966; 2 children. BS, San Diego State U., 1966, MA, 1970; PhD in Zoology, Oreg. State U., 1973. Biol. aide U.S. Bur. Comml. Fisheries, 1966-68; asst. curator vertebrates Nat. Hist. Mus., Oreg. State U., 1969-73; rschr. Dept. Fisheries & Wildlife, 1973-74; biologist in charge Mauna Loa Field Sta. U.S. Fish & Wildlife Svc., 1974-84, dir. Condor Field Sta., 1984-86; instr. ornithology Malheur Environ. Field Sta., Pacific U., 1972, 73; leader Fish & Wildlife Rsch. Unit U. Idaho, Moscow, 1986—; leader Maui Forest Bird Recovery Team, 1975-79, Hawaii Forest Bird Recovery Team, 1975; mem. Am. Ornithologists Union Conservatory, 1974-75, 75-76, sci. adv. bd. Nature Conservatory Hawaii Forest Bird Project, 1981; Richard M. Nixon scholar Whittier Coll.; mem. Palila Recovery Team, 1975. Mem. Nature Conservancy, Elective Am. Ornithologists Union, Ecol. Soc. Am., The Wildlife Soc., Soc. Conservation Biology, Inst. Biol. Sci. Office: U Idaho Fish & Wildlife Rsch Unit 1130 Kamiaken Moscow ID 83843*

SCOTT, JAMES WHITE, newspaper editor; b. Lebanon, Kans., Feb. 22, 1926; s. James Malcolm and Bernice (White) S.; m. Sammy Peete, June 9, 1950; children: James Peete, Thomas Whiteford, Edward English. B.J., U. Kans., 1950. Reporter Kansas City (Mo.) Times, 1950-54; editorial writer Kansas City (Mo.) Star, 1954-93, nat. affairs writer, arts and entertainment assoc. editor, 1968-77, v.p., 1987-93; editor editorial pages Star and Times, 1977-93, sr. editor, 1993-96. Served with AUS, 1944-46, ETO. Mem. Delta Upsilon. Episcopalian. Home: 3204 W 83rd Ter Leawood KS 66206-1304 Office: Kansas City Star 1729 Grand Blvd Kansas City MO 64108-1413

SCOTT, JIM, sound recording engineer. Recipient Grammy award for Best Engineered Album, Non Classical ("Wildflowers" by Tom Petty), 1996. Office: East End Mgmt 8209 Melrose Ave 2nd Fl Los Angeles CA 90046*

SCOTT, JOANNA JEANNE, writer, English language educator; b. Rochester, N.Y., June 22, 1960; d. Walter Lee and Yvonne (de Potter) S.; m. James Burton Longenbach; 1 child, Kathryn Scott Longenbach. BA, Trinity Coll., Hartford, 1982; MA, Brown U., 1985. Asst. prof. English U. Md., College Park, 1987-88; from asst. to assoc. prof. U. Rochester, N.Y., 1988-95, prof., 1995—. Author: (novels) Fading, My Parmacheese Belle, 1987, The Closest Possible Union, 1988, Arrogance, 1990, (collection of stories) Various Antidotes, 1994 (PEN/Faulkner award nomination 1995), The Manikin, 1996. Recipient Richard and Hinde Rosenthal award Am. Acad.-Inst. Arts and Letters, 1991; fellow Guggenheim Found., 1988, MacArthur Found., 1992—; PEN fellow nomination, 1991, 95. Mem. PEN, Writers of Books (bd. dirs. 1993—). Office: U of Rochester Dept of English Rochester NY 14627*

SCOTT, JOHN BROOKS, research institute executive; b. Morenci, Ariz., Aug. 8, 1931; s. Brooks and Lucile (Slagle) S.; m. Jo Ann Rohrbach, June 5, 1987; children from previous marriage: Janice, Steven, Sarah. B.S., U. Ariz., 1957, M.A., 1959. Asst. prof. systems engring. U. Ariz., Tucson, 1959-61; mgr. Bell Aerosystems Co., Tucson, 1961-62; sr. v.p. IIT Research Inst., Annapolis, Md., 1962-90; pres. IIT Research Inst., Chgo., 1990—. Author papers on computer software, electromagnetic compatibility. Past pres. bd. dirs. Md. Hall for Creative Arts, Inc.; past chmn. Md. Hall Found.; mem. bd. govs. IIT Rsch. Inst.; trustee Ill. Inst. Tech. Sr. mem. IEEE, Greater Annapolis C. of C. (pres. 1987); mem. University Club Chgo., Phi Kappa Phi, Sigma Pi Sigma, Pi Mu Epsilon. Home: 215 Cinnamon Ln Edgewater MD 21037-1144 Office: 10 W 35th St Chicago IL 60616-3703

SCOTT, JOHN BURT, life insurance executive; b. St. Louis, July 25, 1944; s. Conley J. and Margaret (Dowdy) S.; m. Darlene Kuhnen Lady, Nov. 18, 1967; children: Kristen, Kathryn. BA in English, U. of South, 1966; MBA in Fin., Loyola U., 1971. Fin. analyst Kemper Nat. Property and Casualty Cos., Chgo., 1967-73; fin. officer Kemper Life, Long Grove, Ill., 1973-77, v.p. ops., 1977-86, pres., chief exec. officer, 1986-87, chmn., pres., chief exec. officer, 1987—; bd. dirs. Fed. Kemper Life Long Grove, Fidelity Life Assn., Long Grove, Kemper Investors Life, Long Grove, Kemper Fin. Cos., Chgo., Am. Coun. Life Insurers, Washington, Ill. Life Ins. Coun., Springfield, Nat. Orgn. Life and Health Guaranty Assn. Bd. dirs., exec. com. Omni Youth Svcs., Buffalo Grove, Ill., 1989—; bd. dirs. Lake County United Way, Life & Health Med. Rsch. Fund. Fellow Life Mgmt. Inst. Episcopalian. Avocations: golf, tennis. *

SCOTT, JOHN CARLYLE, gynecologist, oncologist; b. Mpls., Sept. 24, 1933; s. Horace Golden and Grace (Melges) S.; m. Beth Krause, 1958 (div. 1977); m. Paola Maria Martini, Feb. 8, 1986; children: Jeff, David, Suzanne, Danielle. AB, Princeton U., 1956; BS, MD, U. Minn., 1961. Diplomate Am. Coll. Ob-gyn., Pan Am. Ob-gyn. Soc. Intern Sch. Medicine Marquette U., Milw., 1961-62, resident Sch. Medicine, 1962-66; resident Harvard Med. Sch., Boston, 1965; Am. Cancer fellow Marquette Med. Sch., Milw., 1966-67, instr. ob-gyn., 1966-67; clin. instr. ob-gyn. U. Wash. Med. Sch., Seattle, 1968-75, clin. asst. prof., 1975-85, clin. assoc. prof., 1985—; mem. faculty adv. com. dept. ob-gyn. U. Wash., Seattle, 1973—. Author: First Aid for N.W. Boaters, 1977; author Am. Jour. Ob-Gyn., 1970, 75, 77. Bd. dirs. Renton (Wash.) Handicapped Ctr., 1968-70, March of Dimes, 1974-79; bd. dirs. enabling sys. U. Hawaii, Honolulu, 1977-80. Capt. U.S. Army, 1950-52, Korea. Decorated U.S. Senate Medal of Freedom, Bronze and Silver Stars, Pres. Ronald Reagan's Task Force Medal of Merit and Eternal Flame of Freedom. Fellow Royal Soc. Medicine (gynecology and oncology sects.), Am. Coll. Ob-Gyn, Internat. Coll. Surgeons (sec. U.S. sect. 1994, v.p. worldwide); mem. Pan Am. Ob-Gyn Soc., S.W. Oncology Group, N.W. Oncology Group, Puget Sound Oncology Group, Seattle Gynecol. Soc. (pres. 1978), Baker Channing Soc., Sigma Xi. Avocations: photography, constrn., ornithology, sailing, skiing. Home: 726 16th Ave E Seattle WA 98112 Office: 9730 4th Ave NE Ste 202 Seattle WA 98115

SCOTT, JOHN CONSTANTE, marketing company executive; b. Charleston, S.C., Jan. 31, 1941; s. John C. and Annabelle (Holmes) S.; m. Mary Frances Turner. BS in Psychology, St. Joseph's U., Phila., 1975; JD, Temple U., 1979. Commd. USAF, 1962, advanced through grades to lt. col.; served in Vietnam; resigned, 1972; personnel mgr. Campbell Soup Co., Camden, N.J., 1972-79, corp. mgr. employee relations, 1980-84; v.p. ops. Insilco Corp., Meriden, Conn., 1984-89; v.p. human resources Howmet Corp., Greenwich, Conn., 1989-92; pres. StarMedia, Inc., Greenwich, 1992—. Mem. pres.'s coun. St. Joseph's U., 1985-90. Mem. ABA, N.J. Bar Assn., Pa. Bar Assn., Res. Officers Assn. (life), Greater Meriden C. of C. (bd. dirs. 1986-89). Roman Catholic. Avocations: mountain hiking, flying. Office: 15 E Putnam Ave Ste 320 Greenwich CT 06830-5424 *Peace: The product of justice; politics: the major subset of religion; law (human) rules that institutionalize political power (often as not related to justice).*

SCOTT, JOHN EDWARD, librarian; b. Washington, Ga., Aug. 12, 1920; s. John Edward and Martha Heard (Williams) S.; m. Dorris Louise Webb, Jan 28, 1948; children—Patricia Louise, Clifford Allen, Martha Ellen. A.B., Morehouse Coll., 1948; B.L.S., Atlanta U., 1949; M.L.S., U. Ill., 1955. Librarian Kans. Tech. Inst., Topeka, 1949-55; circulation librarian Va. State Coll., Petersburg, 1955-56; asst. reference librarian U. Kans., 1956-57; dir. library resources W. Va. State Coll., 1957—. Served with USNR, 1942-46. Mem. AAUP, ALA (councilor 1964—, chmn. coll. libraries sect. 1969-70), Southeastern Library Assn. (treas. 1979—), W.Va. Library Assn. (chmn coll. library sect. 1958-60, pres. 1961-62), Tri-State Assn. Coll. and Research Libraries, Middle Atlantic Regional Library Fedn. (exec. bd.), Kappa Delta Pi, Beta Phi Mu, Alpha Phi Alpha. Home: PO Box 303 Institute WV 25112-0303

SCOTT, JOHN EDWARD SMITH, lawyer; b. St. Louis, Aug. 6, 1936; s. Gordon Hatler and Luella Margarite (Smith) S.; m. Beverly Joan Phillips, Dec. 17, 1960; 1 dau., Pamela Anne. AB, Albion Coll., 1958; JD, Wayne State U., 1961. Bar: Mich. 1961, U.S. Dist. Ct. (ea. dist.) Mich. 1962, U.S. Dist. Ct. (we. dist.) Mich. 1970, U.S. Tax. Ct. 1979, U.S. Ct. Appeals (6th cir.) 1964, U.S. Supreme Ct. 1966. Law clk. Supreme Ct. Mich., Lansing, 1961-62; assoc. Dickinson, Wright, Moon, Van Dusen & Freeman, Detroit, 1962-69, ptnr., 1970—; adj. prof. U. Detroit Law Sch., 1967-71. Supreme Ct. appointee State Bar Rep. Assembly, Detroit, 1972-77; mayor City of Pleasant Ridge, Mich., 1973-81; commr. Mich. Appellate Defender Commn., Detroit, 1979—, chmn., 1992—; hearing referee Mich. Civil Rights Commn., Detroit, 1974-80; chmn. Detroit Legal Aid & Defender Commn., 1972-77; chmn. case flow mgmt. com. Mich. Supreme Ct., 1989-90. Fellow Am. Coll. Trial Lawyers, Internat. Soc. Barristers; mem. ABA (chmn. trial evidence com. sect. litigation 1988-91), Am. Bd. Advs., Internat. Assn. Def. Counsel, Am. Bar Found., Mich. Bar Found., Detroit Golf Club. Office: Dickinson Wright Moon Van Dusen & Freeman Ste 4000 500 Woodward Ave Detroit MI 48226

SCOTT, JOHN PAUL, psychologist, educator, author; b. Kansas City, Mo., Dec. 17, 1909; s. John William and Vivian (Armstrong) S.; m. Sarah Fisher, June 18, 1933 (dec. Sept. 1978); children: Jean Scott Franck, Vivian Scott Hixson, John, David; m. Mary-Vesta Marston, June 30, 1979. BA, U. Wyo., 1930; postgrad., Lincoln Coll., U. Oxford, Eng., 1930-32; PhD, U. Chgo., 1935. Asst. in zoology U. Chgo., 1932-35, prof. biopsychology, 1958; mem. faculty Wabash Coll., Crawfordsville, Ind., 1935-45, prof. zoology, 1942-45, chmn. dept., 1935-45; chmn. div. behavior studies Roscoe B. Jackson Meml. Lab., Bar Harbor, Maine, 1945-58, trustee, 1946-49, sr. staff scientist, 1958-65; rsch. prof. psychology Bowling Green (Ohio) U., 1965-80, Ohio Regents prof., 1968-80, prof. emeritus, 1980—; dir. Ctr. for Rsch. on Social Behavior, 1966-80; rsch. prof. psychology Tufts U., Medford, Mass., 1982-83; mem. Maine Bd. Psychol. Examiners, 1956-59. Author: Animal Behavior, 1958, 72, Aggression, 1958, 75, (with John L. Fuller) Genetics and the Social Behavior of the Dog, 1965, Early Experience and the Organization of Behavior, 1968, (with C.J. Pfaffenberger) Guide Dogs for the Blind, 1976, The Evolution of Social Systems, 1989; also sci. articles, chpts in books; editor: (with Sarah F. Scott) Social Control and Social Change, 1971, (with Basil Eleftheriou) The Physiology of Aggression and Defeat, 1971, (with Edward Senay) Separation and Depression, 1972, Critical Periods, 1978. Rhodes scholar, U. Oxford, 1930-32; recipient Jordan prize Ind. Acad. Sci., 1947, Disting. Alumnus award U. Wyo., 1976, Dobzhansky award for eminent rsch. Behavior Genetics Assn., 1987, Outstanding Achievement award U. Wyo., 1990; Ctr. Advanced Study in Behavioral Scis. fellow, 1963-64. Fellow AAAS, Am. Psychol. Assn., Animal Behavior Soc. (Disting. Animal Behaviorist award 1990), N.Y. Zool. Soc.; mem. Maine Psychol. Assn. (pres. 1953-54), Am. Soc. Zoologists, Am. Eugenics Soc. (v.p. 1963), Ecol. Soc. Am. (chmn. sect. animal behavior and sociobiology 1957-58), Internat. Soc. for Devel. Psychobiology (pres. 1972-78), Internat. Soc. for Rsch. on Aggression (pres. 1973-74), Behavior Genetics Assn. (pres. 1975-76), Phi Beta Kappa, Sigma Xi. Office: Bowling Green State U Bowling Green OH 43403

SCOTT, JOHN ROLAND, lawyer, oil company executive; b. Wichita Falls, Tex., May 13, 1937; s. John Robert and Margaret Willena (Rouse) S.; m. Joan Carol Redding, Sept. 5, 1959; 1 child, John Howard. LLB, Baylor Sch. Law, Waco, Tex., 1962. Bar: Tex. 1962, Alaska 1970, U.S. Dist. Ct. (we. dist.) Tex. 1965, U.S. Dist. Ct. Alaska 1975. Assoc. litigation sect Lynch & Chappell, Midland, Tex., 1962-65; regional atty. Atlantic Richfield Co., Midland, 1965-79; sr. atty., Anchorage, 1969-77, sr. atty., Dallas, 1977-80; v.p., assoc. gen. counsel Mitchell Energy & Devel. Corp., Houston, 1980-82; asst. gen. counsel Hunt Oil Co., Dallas., 1982-84, v.p., chief counsel, 1984-91; v.p. gen. counsel, 1991—; bar examiner in Alaska, 1974-77. Mem. State Bar Tex. (lectr.), Dallas Bar Assn., ABA, Phi Alpha Delta. Republican. Clubs: Petroleum (Dallas). Office: Hunt Oil Co 1445 Ross Ave Dallas TX 75202-2812

SCOTT, JOHN WALTER, chemical engineer, research management executive; b. Berkeley, Calif., May 27, 1919; s. John Walter and Cora Viola (Wampfler) S.; m. Jane Ellen Newman, June 27, 1942; children—Nancy, Barbara, Charles, James, Richard. B.S. in Chemistry, U. Calif.-Berkeley, 1941, M.S. in Chem. Engring., 1951. Registered profl. chem. engr., Calif. Process and catalyst research and devel. Chevron Research, Richmond, Calif., 1946-67, v.p., 1967-84, cons., 1985—. Contbr. articles to profl. jours.; patentee in field. Trustee U. Calif.-Berkeley Found., 1985-91; adv. coun. Lawrence Hall of Sci., 1990—; mem. coun. Town of Ross, Calif., 1992—. Capt. U.S. Army, 1941-46. Fellow Am. Inst. Chem. Engrs. (awards com. 1979-84, award 1978), AAAS; mem. Nat. Acad. Engring., Am. Chem. Soc., Am. Petroleum Inst. (chmn. research data info. services 1971-73, 77-80, cert. of appreciation 1983). Avocations: history; travel. Home: PO Box 2004 Ross CA 94957-2004

SCOTT, JOHN WILLIAM, food processing executive; b. Okamoto, Hyogo-Ken, Japan, July 12, 1935; s. John William and Alice Cunningham (Harrison) S.; m. Marilyn Merrill Ackland, July 20, 1962; children: John William, Matthew Thompson, Julia Leigh Harrison, Robert Augustine Thornton. AB, Princeton U., 1958. With CPC, Chgo. and Mexico, 1957-63; ops. mgr. Maizena (CPC), Cali, Colombia, 1964-65; mng. dir. PROMASA (CPC), Guatemala City, Guatemala, 1965-69, IMSA (CPC), Montevideo, Uruguay, 1969-70, Productos Knorr (CPC), Caracas, Venezuela, 1971-75; v.p. consumer div. Refinacoes de Milho (CPC), Sao Paulo, Brazil, 1975-79; mng. dir. Refinerias de Maiz (CPC), Buenos Aires, Argentina, 1979-83; asst. to pres. CPC Internat., Englewood Cliffs, N.J., 1983-84, v.p., 1985—. Bd. dirs. ACCION Internat., Boston, 1986—; bd. dirs. Dwight Englewood (N.J.) Sch., 1990—, pres. bd. trustees, 1992-95; pres. Englewood Cmty. Chest, 1988. With AUS, 1954-56. Mem. Princeton Club (N.Y.C.), Englewood Field Club. Democrat. Episcopalian. Avocation: squash, sailing. Home: 40 Lydecker St Englewood NJ 07631-3005 Office: CPC Internat Inc International Plaza PO Box 8000 Englewood Cliffs NJ 07632-9976

SCOTT, JOSEPH C., professional hockey team executive; m. Pat Scott; children: Joe Jr., Greg, Jeff, Trent, Linda. Owner Phila. Flyers, now chmn. emeritus; lifetime mem. NHL Bd. Govs., 1985—. Bd. dirs. Jr. Baseball Fedn., Big Bros Am., Police Athletic League, Little Quakers, Pop Warner Little Scholars, Inc., Pa. Sports Hall of Fame, Maxwell Club, IVB Golf Classic; mem. John Wanamaker awards com. and boys work com. Union League of Phila. Named to Pa. Sports Hall of Fame, 1974; co-recipient Pop Warner award for youth activities, 1960. Office: Phila Flyers Core States Spectrum 3601 S Broad St Philadelphia PA 19148

SCOTT, JOYCE ALAINE, university official; b. Long Beach, Calif., May 21, 1943; d. Emmett Emery Scott and Grace (Evans) Wedum. B.A., U. Conn., 1964; M.A., U. Va., 1966; Ph.D., Duke U., 1973. From instr. to assoc. prof. U. Wyo., Laramie, 1971-74, asst. dean, 1974-78, asst. v.p. acad. affairs, 1976-81, assoc. v.p. acad. affairs, 1981-84; provost, v.p. SUNY-Potsdam, 1984-86; exec. v.p. Wichita State U., Kans., 1986-90, v.p. on spl. assignment, 1990-91; sr. cons. Am. Assn. State Colls. and Univs., 1991-92, v.p. acad. and internat. programs, 1992—; mem. Commn. on Ednl. Credit and Credentials of Am. Council on Edn., Washington, 1982-87; cons. faculty Am. Open U., Lincoln, Nebr., 1981-82. Contbr. articles to profl. jours. Mem. MLA, AAUW, AAHE, Am. Assn. Tchrs. French, Phi Beta Kappa, Phi Sigma Iota. Republican. Presbyterian. Office: AASCU 1 Dupont Cir NW Ste 700 Washington DC 20036-1110

SCOTT, KELLY, newspaper editor. Mng. editor sunday calendar The L.A. Times. Office: LA Times Times Mirror Sq Los Angeles CA 90012-3816

SCOTT, KENNETH ELSNER, mechanical engineering educator; b. Webster, Mass., May 18, 1926; s. Henry Anderson and Amanda (Elsner) S.; m. Elizabeth Ann Oldham, June 21, 1952; children—Kenneth Elsner, Cynthia Lynne, Jeffrey Alan, Donald Leighton. B.S. in Mech. Engring, Worcester Poly. Inst., 1948, M.S., 1954. Registered profl. engr., Mass. Mem. faculty Worcester Poly. Inst., 1948-91, prof. mech. engring., 1966-91, prof. emeritus, 1991—, George I. Alden prof. engring., 1971-75, inst. dir. audio-visual devel., 1971-74, dir. instructional TV, 1974-90, dir. CAD Lab., 1981-93, acting head dept. mech. engring., 1988-89. Mem. bd. health, Holden, Mass., 1963-70. Served with AUS, 1944-46. Recipient Trustees' award for Outstanding Tchr. of Year, 1971, Western Electric Fund award for excellence in instrn. New Eng. sect. Am. Soc. Engring. Edn., 1972, Teaching Excellence and Campus Leadership award Sears-Roebuck Found., 1990-91. Fellow ASME (exec. com. Worcester sect. 1952-57, sec.-treas. 1955-56, chmn. 1956-57, region I chmn. profl. divs. com. 1957-59, chmn. agenda, audit, budget and nominating com. Worcester 1957-58, chmn. symposium lubrication Worcester sect. 1957-58, chmn. Adm. Earle award com. 1958-59, chmn. devel. com. 1960-61); mem. Am. Soc. Engring. Edn. (sec.-treas. New Eng.), Sigma Xi, Pi Tau Sigma, Tau Beta Pi. Home: 9750 Cypress Lake Dr Fort Myers FL 33919-6064

SCOTT, KENNETH EUGENE, lawyer, educator; b. Western Springs, Ill., Nov. 21, 1928; s. Kenneth L. and Bernice (Albright) S.; m. Viviane H. May, Sept. 22, 1956 (dec. Feb. 1982); children: Clifton, Jeffrey, Linda; m. Priscilla Gay, July 30, 1989. BA in Econs., Coll. William and Mary, 1949; MA in Polit. Sci., Princeton U., 1953; LLB, Stanford U., 1956. Bar: N.Y. 1957, Calif. 1957, D.C. 1967. Assoc. Sullivan & Cromwell, N.Y.C., 1956-59, Musick, Peeler & Garrett, L.A., 1959-61; chief dep. savs. and loan commr. State of Calif., L.A., 1961-63; gen. counsel Fed. Home Loan Bank Bd., Washington, 1963-67; Parsons prof. law and bus. Stanford (Calif.) Law Sch., 1968-95; sr. rsch. fellow Hoover Instn., 1978-95; mem. Shadow Fin. Regulatory Com., 1986—; bd. dirs. Benham Capital Mgmt. Mut. Fund, Mountain View, Calif., RCM Capital Funds, San Francisco. Author: (with others) Retail Banking in the Electronic Age, 1977; co-editor: The Economics of Corporation Law and Securities Regulation, 1980. Mem. ABA, Calif. Bar Assn., Phi Beta Kappa, Order of Coif, Pi Kappa Alpha, Omicron Delta Kappa. Home: 610 Gerona Rd Stanford CA 94305-8453 Office: Crown Quadrangle Stanford Law Sch Stanford CA 94305-8610

SCOTT, KENNETH R., transportation executive; b. Iowa City. BCE, U. Iowa, 1960; MCE, U. Mo., Rolla, 1966. Commd. U.S. Army, 1961, advanced through grades, 1970; airport project engr. Norfolk (Va.) Airport Authority, 1970-72, asst. airport mgr., 1971-72, exec. dir., 1972—; adj. prof. Embry-Riddle Aero. U. at Norfolk Naval Air Sta. and Langley AFB. Bd. dirs. Norfolk Cmty. Promotion Corp., Va. Aviation and Space Edn. Forum. Mem. Am. Assn. Airport Execs., Va. Airport Operators Coun. Office: Norfolk Airport Authority Norfolk Intl Airport Norfolk VA 23518-5897

SCOTT, KENNETH WAYNE, social services administrator; b. Washington, Nov. 6, 1936; s. Kenneth LeRoy and Mary Eliza (Whittle) S.; m. Ann Bassett; children: Shannon, Catherine, Andrew, Lorraine, Kimberly. BA in Indsl. Design, U. Kans., 1961; MS in Edn., SUNY, Brockport, 1970. Product designer Eastman Kodak Co., Rochester, N.Y., 1961-66; corp. tng. staff Eastman Kodak Co., Rochester, 1966-67, spl. liaison coord. joint rsch. with SUNY, 1967-69; v.p. Leadership Sys., Inc., Silver Spring, Md., 1970-75; pres., founder Am. Family Soc., Washington, 1975—; cons. Million Dollar Round Table Family Time Project, DesPlaines, Ill., 1975-80, Nat. Assn. Life Underwriters, Washington, 1976-80; guest spkr. Co-author (family tree genealogy game) Family Tree, 1965. Dist. vice chmn. Boy Scouts Nat. Capitol Area Coun., Rockvill, 1972-73; dir. pub. affairs The Ch. of Jesus Christ of LDS-Washington (D.C.) Multiregion, 1994—. Recipent Merit award Boy Scouts Am., Rockville, 1972. Office: Am Family Soc 5013 Russett Rd Rockville MD 20853

SCOTT, LARRY MARCUS, aerospace engineer, mathematician; b. Bingham Canyon, Utah, June 14, 1945; s. Wright Marcus Scott and Margaret Ruth (Jackson) Sturzenegger; m. Paula Inger Elisabeth Kjellman, Aug. 21, 1972; children: Paul Marcus, Laura Elizabeth. BS, Brigham Young U., 1971; MS, Boston U., 1983. Engr. lifting body re-entry mechs. Douglas Missile and Space Systems, Sant Monica, Calif., 1965-66; missionary and dist. leader Ch. of Jesus Christ of Latterday Saints, Finland, 1966-69; researcher Math. Dept. Brigham Young U. for Air Force, Provo, Utah, 1969-71; researcher Russian Translation Linguistics Brigham Young U. for Nat. Security Agy., Provo, 1971-72; internship in Plasma Physics, Physics Dept. Brigham Young U., Provo, 1972-73; sci. programmer Lockheed Elect. Co., Edwards AFB, Calif., 1973-75; mathematician 6521 Range Squadron, 6250 Test Wing, Edwards AFB, 1976-80 1982-85; exchange sci. Inst. for Flight Dynamics, DFVLR, Federal Republic Germany, 1980-82; mathematician A.F. Logistics Command, Hill AFB, Utah, 1985-87; software engineer Ball Systems Engring. Div., Edwards AFB, 1987-89; nav. engr. Short Range Attack Missile, 1989-91; avionics engr. F-15E, Edwards AFB, Calif., 1992—. Co-author: Invention disclosure on laser nozzle, 1976, Evaluation of F-15E Operational Flight Program, AF Tech. Report TR 92-021, AFFTC-TR-94-08; author: report for DFVLR in Germany, 1982, USAF Disclosure, 1984; Russian translator Sister Base Program, 1994. Quorum Pres. Ch. of Latter Day Saints, Palmdale, Calif. 1973-74, Lancaster, Calif. 1984-85, Quorum Counselor, Lancaster 1988-90, high counselor, 1994—; asst. varsity scout, Bountiful, Utah 1985-86. Recipient Bank of Am. Language Award, Hawthorne, Calif. 1963, Scholarship to Brigham Young U. 1963, Hon. Cert. Defense Language Inst., Monterey, Calif. 1980. Republican. Avocations: computers, classical music, playing baroque music, musical improvisation, mathematics, genealogy.

SCOTT, LAWRENCE VERNON, microbiology educator; b. Anthony, Kans., Jan. 28, 1917; s. Lawrence Garfield and Mable Grace (Madden) S.; m. Elizabeth Buchanan Rowe, Jan. 28, 1945; children: James Robert, Jean Elizabeth, Lawrence Rowe. B.A., Phillips U., 1940; M.S., U. Okla., Norman, 1947; Sc.D., Johns Hopkins U., 1950. Asst. prof. bacteriology, asso. prof., 1950-58; prof. microbiology and immunology Sch. Medicine, U. Okla. Health Sci. Center, Oklahoma City, 1958-83, prof. emeritus, 1983—; chmn. dept. microbiology and immunology Sch. Medicine, U. Okla. Health Sci. Center, 1961-83; fellow in tropical medicine La. State U., 1967; cons. microbiologist St. Anthony and VA Hosps., 1957—; vis. prof. U. Otago, Dunedin, N.Z.; condr. microbiol. rsch. South Pole Sta., Antarctica, 1974, 75; participant People to People program to China, 1983, med. missions to Jamaica, 1988-93; invited participant reconciliation trip to Vietnam, 1993. Contbr. writings to profl. publs.; author: Medical Microbiology, 1982. Served to lt. USNR, 1942-46. Recipient Disting. Alumnus award Phillips U., 1968, Superior and Profl. Univ. Svc. award U. Okla., 1984. Mem. Am. Soc. Microbiology, Am. Acad. Microbiology, Assn. Med. Sch. Microbiologists (chmn.), N.Y. Acad. Scis., Okla. Acad. Scis., Am. Soc. Tropical Medicine and Hygiene, Sigma Xi. Democrat. Mem. Christian Church (Disciples of Christ). Condr. research. Home: 4125 NW 61st Ter Oklahoma City OK 73112-1346 Office: PO Box 26901 Oklahoma City OK 73126 *Through hard work and education, my goal was to repay society. Thus, it has been important to make a contribution. In all activities, honesty and integrity are central.*

SCOTT, LEE HANSEN, retired holding company executive; b. Atlanta, Sept. 25, 1926; s. Elbert Lee and Auguste Lillian (Hansen) S.; m. Margaret Lee Smith, July 20, 1951; children: Bradley Hansen, Randall Lee. B.E.E., U. Fla., 1949. With Fla. Power Corp., St. Petersburg, 1949-94; dir. constrn., maintenance and operating Fla. Power Corp., 1968-71, v.p. customer ops., 1971-77, sr. v.p. ops., 1977-83, pres., 1983-88, chmn. bd., 1988-90, also bd. dirs.; also bd. dirs. Fla. Progress Corp.; retired, 1994; bd. dirs. Sun Banks; cons. in field. Pres. St. Petersburg chpt. ARC, 1977, Pinellas Com. of 100, 1980, Community Services Council, 1970, St. Petersburg Progress, 1983, Bus. and Industry Employment Devel. Council, 1983; chmn. bd. United Way. Served with USAF, 1944-46. Named Mr. Sun of St. Petersburg, 1990. Mem. Fla. Engring. Soc., IEEE, Elec. Council Fla. (pres. 1979), St. Petersburg C. of C. (v.p. 1980), Fla. C. of C. (pres. 1987-88), Pinellas Suncoast C. of C. (past chmn., chmn. bd. trustees). Presbyterian. Home: 601 Apalachee Dr NE Saint Petersburg FL 33702-2766

SCOTT, LEONARD LEWY, JR., mathematician, educator; b. Little Rock, Oct. 17, 1942; s. Leonard Lewy and Mary Ella (Simcoe) S.; m. Mary Ellena Broach; children: Mary Lisette, Walter Lewy. BA, Vanderbilt U., 1964; PhD, Yale U., 1968. Instr. U. Chgo., 1968-70; asst. prof. Yale U., New Haven, 1970-71; from assoc. prof. to prof. U. Va., Charlottesville, 1971-87, McConnell/Bernard prof., 1987—; vis. fellow All Souls Coll., Oxford U., 1992. Mem. editorial bd. Jour. Algebra, 1990—; contbr. articles to profl. jours. including Annals Math., Inventionés, Publ. Math IHES. Rsch. grantee NSF, 1972—, Sci. and Engring. Rsch. Coun. (Eng.), 1983, 92. Mem. Am. Math. Soc. (chmn. S.E. speaker sect. 1985-86, nat. nominating com. 1988-89, editorial bd. Univ. Lectr. Series 1987—, chmn. 1993—). Achievements include origination of maximal subgroups program in finite group theory; development of isomorphism problem for group rings; invention of quasi-hereditary algebras; proof of Carlson's conjecture on group cohomology; demonstration of generic cohomology for finite and algebraic groups. Home: 3250 Tearose Ln Charlottesville VA 22903-9361 Office: U Va Dept Math New Cabell Dr Charlottesville VA 22903

SCOTT, LORRAINE ANN, fraternal organization executive; b. Cleve., Dec. 14, 1947; d. Harry F. and Ann Mae (Dolecek) Dufek; m. John William Scott, Jan. 4, 1969; 1 son, Bruce. BBA, Dyke Coll., Cleve., 1967. Acct., Fulton, Reid & Staples, Cleve., 1967-69; acct., data control Nat. City Bank, Cleve., 1969-70; asst. treas. Independence (Ohio) Bd. of Edn. 1978-80; exec. dir. Nat. Frat. of Phi Gamma Nu, Cleve., 1980—; owner, pres. L.A. Comics and Collectibles, Inc., 1988—. Mem. Am. Soc. Assn. Execs., Coll. Fraternities Editors Assn. Republican. Lutheran. Editor Phi Gamma Nu mag., 1980—.

SCOTT, LOUIS EDWARD, advertising agency executive; b. Waterbury, Conn., June 17, 1923; s. Louis Arthur and Ellen (Eckert) S.; m. Phyllis Corrine Denker, Jan. 27, 1942; children: Susan Louise, Eric Richard, Jane Lynn. BS, U. Calif., Berkeley, 1944. Sr. account exec. McCarty Co., L.A., 1946-50; with Foote, Cone & Belding, L.A., 1950-87; v.p. Foote, Cone & Belding, 1956, gen. mgr., 1959, became sr. v.p., 1963, dir., 1961—, chmn. exec. com., 1970-82; chmn. ops. com., pres. Foote, Cone & Belding/Honig, 1975-82; bd. dirs. Smart and Final Corp., Casino Internat., True North Comm.. Chmn. publicity com. Los Angeles Community Chest, 1960; patron mem. Los Angeles YMCA; mem. Freedoms Found.; chmn. So. Calif. advisory bd. Advt. Council; mem. exec. advisory bd. Art Center Coll. Design. Served with U.S. Maritime Service, also USNR, World War II. Named Western Advt. Man of Year, 1972. Mem. Am. Assn. Advt. Agys. (dir., past chmn. Western region), L.A. Advt. Club (dir.), L.A. C. of C., L.A. World Affairs Coun., Town Hall Club, Rio Verde Country Club, Seattle Yacht Club, Cruising Club Am. Home: PO Box 65079 Port Ludlow WA 98365-0079 Office: 101 E Erie St Chicago IL 60611-2811

SCOTT, MANUEL, church administrator. Officer Bd. of Evangelism of the Nat. Baptist Conv. USA, Dallas. Office: Natl. Baptist Conv. USA 2600 S Marsalis Ave Dallas TX 75216-3021

SCOTT, MARIANNE FLORENCE, librarian, educator; b. Toronto, Dec. 4, 1928; d. Merle Redvers and Florence Ethel (Hutton) S. BA, McGill U., Montreal, Que., Can., 1949, BLS, 1952; LLD (hon.), York U., 1985, Dalhousie U., 1989; DLitt (hon.), Laurentian U., 1990. Asst. librarian Bank of Montreal, 1952-55; law librarian McGill U., 1955-73, law area librarian, 1973-75, dir. libraries, 1975-84, lectr. legal bibliography faculty of law, 1964-75; nat. librarian Nat. Library of Can., Ottawa, Ont., 1984—. Co-founder, editor: Index to Can. Legal Periodical Lit, 1963—; contbr. articles to profl. jours. Decorated Officer of the Order of Can., 1995. Mem. Internat. Assn. Law Libraries (dir. 1974-77), Am. Assn. Law Libraries, Can. Assn. Law Libraries (pres. 1963-69, exec. bd. 1973-75, honored mem. 1980—), Can. Library Assn. (council and dir. 1980-82, 1st v.p. 1980-81, pres. 1981-82), Corp. Profl. Librarians of Que. (v.p. 1975-76), Can. Assn. Research Libraries (pres. 1978-79, past pres. 1979-80, exec. com. 1980-81, sec.-treas. 1983-84), Ctr. for Research Libraries (dir. 1980-83), Internat. Fedn. Library Assns. (honor com. for 1982 conf. 1979-82), Conf. of Dirs. of Nat. Libraries (chmn. 1988-92). Home: 119 Dorothea Dr, Ottawa, ON Canada K1V 7C6 Office: Nat Libr Can, 395 Wellington St, Ottawa, ON Canada K1A 0N4

SCOTT, MARK W., editor; b. Dearborn, Mich., Apr. 5, 1954; s. Walter Joseph and Audrey Elizabeth (Van Kirk) S. BA, Western Mich. U., 1977; MA, Ctrl. Mich. U., 1982. Asst. editor Gale Rsch. Inc., Detroit, 1981-82, assoc. editor, 1982-85, editor, 1985-88, sr. editor, 1988-91; sr. editor The Taft Group, Rockville, Md., 1991-94, exec. editor, 1994—. Office: The Taft Group 12300 Twinbrook Pky Ste 520 Rockville MD 20852-1606

SCOTT, MELLOUISE JACQUELINE, educational media specialist, master storyteller; b. Sanford, Fla., Mar. 1, 1943; d. Herbert and Mattye (Williams) Cherry; m. Robert Edward Scott, Jr., July 1, 1972; 1 child, Nolan Edward. B.A., Talladega Coll., 1965; M.L.S., Rutgers U., 1974, Ed.M., 1976, Ed.S., 1982. Media specialist Seminole County Bd. Edn., Sanford, 1965-72, Edison Bd. Edn. (N.J.), 1972—. Mem. ALA, N.J. Edn. Assn., NEA, Ednl. Media Assn. N.J. Baptist. Home: PO Box 8 Fords NJ 08863-0008 Office: Edison Bd Edn Mcpl Complex Edison NJ 08817

SCOTT, MICHAEL, lawyer; b. N.Y.C., Oct. 11, 1930; s. Irvin Leslie and Dorothy (Chandler) S.; m. Cynthia Ann Meredith, July 17, 1954; children: Elizabeth, Gregory, Andrew. BA, Cornell U., 1952; JD, U. Mich., 1958; diploma, Grad. Inst. of Internat. Studies, Geneva, 1959. Bar: Ohio 1959, D.C. 1971, Calif. 1981. Assoc. Squire, Sanders & Dempsey, Cleve., 1959-67, ptnr., 1967-71; ptnr. Squire, Sanders & Dempsey, Washington, 1971-1994; lawyer Amer Soc of Anesthesiologists, Washigton D.C., 1994; pres. Ohio State Legal Services Assn., Columbus, 1969-70, Nat. Capital Area Health Care Coalition, Washington, 1985—. Served to lt. (j.g.) USN, 1952-55. Mem. ABA, Ohio Bar Assn., D.C. Bar Assn., Calif. Bar Assn. Clubs: Met. (Washington), Union (Cleve.). Home: 7133 Deepwood Dr Chagrin Falls OH 44022-2646 Office: Amer Soc of Anesthesiologists 1101 Vermont Ave NW Washington DC 20005*

SCOTT, MICHAEL DENNIS, lawyer; b. Mpls., Nov. 6, 1945; s. Frank Walton and Donna Julia (Howard) S.; m. Blanca Josefina Palacios, Dec. 12, 1981; children: Michael Dennis, Cindal Marie, Derek Walton. B.S., MIT, 1967; J.D., UCLA, 1974. Bar: Calif. 1974, U.S. Dist. Ct. (no., so. and cen. dists.) Calif. 1974, U.S. Patent Office 1974, U.S. Ct. Appeals (9th cir.) 1974, U.S. Supreme Ct. 1978, U.S. Ct. Appeals (fed. cir.) 1989. Systems programmer NASA Electronics Research Lab., Cambridge, Mass., 1967-69, Computer Sciences Corp., El Segundo, Calif., 1969-71, Univac, Valencia, Calif., 1971; from assoc. to ptnr. Smaltz & Neelley, Los Angeles, 1974-81; exec. dir. Ctr. for Computer/Law, Los Angeles, 1977-94; sole practice Los Angeles, 1981-86, 88-89; pres. Law and Tech. Press, 1981-94; ptnr. Scott & Roxborough, Los Angeles, 1986-88, Graham & James, 1989-93; v.p., gen. counsel Sanctuary Woods Multimedia, Inc., San Mateo, Calif., 1993-94; pres., CEO Wildwood Interactive, Inc., Manhattan Beach, Calif., 1994—; of counsel Steinhart & Falconer, San Francisco, 1995—; adj. assoc. prof. law Southwestern U., L.A., 1975-80; chmn. World Computer Law Congress, L.A., 1991, 93. Author: (with David S. Yen) Computer Law Bibliography, 1979, The Scott Report, 1981-86, Computer Law, 1984, Scott on Computer Law, 1991, Law of Online Commerce, 1996, Scott on Multimedia Law, 1996, Multimedia: Law and Practice, 1993; editor in chief: Computer/Law Jour., 1978-94, Software Protection, 1982-92, Software Law Jour., 1985-94, Internat. Computer Law Adviser, 1986-92, The Cyberspace Lawyer, 1996—. Mem. Computer Law Assn. (bd. dirs. 1994—), Calif. State Bar Assn. Office: Steinhart & Falconer 32nd Fl 333 Market St San Francisco CA 94105

SCOTT, MICHAEL LESTER, artist, educator; b. Lawrence, Kans., Sept. 24, 1952; s. Lester F. and Robbie (Guthrie) S.; m. Cheryl Ann Scott, May 24, 1982 (div.); children: Erik, Maxfield. BFA, Kans. City Art Inst., 1976; MFA, U. Cin., 1978. instr. Baker Hunt Found., Covington, Ky., 1986-93, Art Acad. of Cin. Work represented in pub. collections Butler Mus. Art, Youngstown, Ohio, New Orleans Mus. Art, Cin. Art Mus., Mus. Acquisitions of Chgo., J.B. Speed Mus., Bronnin-Foreman, Louisville, Owensboro (Ky.) Mus. Art, Hunter Mus. Art, Chattanooga, Phila. Mus. Art, Manhattan Life, N.Y.C. Mem. Sierra Club, Wilderness Soc., Green Peace, Nature Conservancy, Redwood League, Oxbow Found. Avocation: canoeist. Home and Studio: 2477 Country Pl New Richmond OH 45157-9511

SCOTT, MICHAEL TIMOTHY, lawyer; b. Scranton, Pa., Jan. 12, 1951; s. Thomas F. and Elizabeth (Moran) S.; m. Karen Marian Scott, July 8, 1972; children: Jeffrey, Abigail, Zachary. BS, Pa. State U., 1972; JD magna cum laude, U. Pa., 1976. Bar: Pa. 1976, D.C. 1977. Assoc. Pepper, Hamilton & Scheetz, Phila., 1976-77, ptnr., 1981-87; assoc. Arnold & Porter, Washington, 1977-79; atty. Dept. Justice, Washington, 1979-81; ptnr. Reed, Smith, Shaw & McClay, Phila., 1987—. Contbr. articles to profl. jours. Mem. ABA. Office: Reed Smith Shaw & McClay 2500 One Liberty Pl Philadelphia PA 19103

SCOTT, MIMI KOBLENZ, actress, publicist, journalist, psychotherapist; b. Albany, N.Y., Dec. 15, 1940; d. Edmund Akiba and Tillie (Paul) Koblenz; m. Barry Stuart Scott, Aug. 13, 1961 (dec. Nov. 1991); children: Karen Scott Zantay, Jeffrey B. BA in Speech, English Edn., Russell Sage Coll., 1962; MA in Speech Edn., SUNY, Albany, 1968; M in Social Welfare, SUNY, 1985; PhD in Psychology, Pacific Western U., Encino, Calif., 1985. Cert. tchr., social worker. Tchr. English, speech Albany Pub. Schs., 1961-63; hostess, producer talkshow Sta. WAST-TV 13, Albany, 1973-75; freelance actress N.Y.C., 1975-77; producer, actress Four Seasons Dinner Theater, Albany, 1978-82; instr. of theatre Albany Jr. Coll., 1981-83; pvt. practice psychotherapy Albany, N.Y., 1985-92; exec. producer City of Albany Park Playhouse, 1989-92; actor self-employed N.Y.C., 1992—; guest psychotherapist Sally Jessy Raphael Show, 1992, 93, Jane Whitney Show, 1994, A Current Affair, 1995, News Talk TV, 1995. Scriptwriter, dir., actress TV movie, 1995; feature writer Backstage, 1995-96; (off-Broadway) Grandma Sylvia's Funeral. Event organizer AmFar, 1985; co-chmn. March of Dimes Telethon, 1985-86; fundraiser Leukemia Found., 1987, Aids Benefit, N. Miami Beach, Fla., 1988; elected to SUNY Albany U. Found., 1990. Recipient FDR Nat. Achievement award March of Dimes, 1985, Recognition Cert. Capital Dist. Psychiat. Ctr., 1983, 84, 85; named Woman of Yr. YWCA, 1986, Commr. Albany Tricentennial Celebration, 1986; Mimi Scott Day proclaimed by Mayor of Albany, 1989. Mem. AEA, SAG, AFTRA, NASW. Jewish. Avocations: horseback riding, boating, golf, tennis. Home and Office: 211 West 71st # 6C New York NY 10023

SCOTT, NATHAN ALEXANDER, JR., minister, literary critic, religion educator; b. Cleve., Apr. 24, 1925; s. Nathan Alexander and Maggie (Martin) S.; m. Charlotte Hanley, Dec. 21, 1946; children: Nathan Alexander III, Leslie K. AB, U. Mich., 1944; BD, Union Theol. Sem., 1946; PhD, Columbia U., 1949; LittD, Ripon Coll., 1965, St. Mary's Coll., Notre Dame, Ind., 1969, Denison U., 1976, Brown U., 1981, Northwestern U., 1982, Elizabethtown Coll., 1989; LHD, Wittenberg U., 1965; DD, Phila. Div. Sch., 1967; STD, Gen. Theol. Sem., 1968; LHD, U. D.C., 1976; DD, The Protestant Episcopal Theological Seminary in Va., 1985; HumD, U. Mich., 1988; LHD, Wesleyan U., 1989, Bates Coll., 1990; STD, Univ of the South, 1992; DD, Kenyon Coll., 1993; Ordained priest Episcopal Ch., 1960; canon theologian Cathedral St. James, Chgo., 1967-76. dean of chapel, Va. Union U., 1946-47; instr. humanities, Howard U., 1948-51, asst. prof., 1951-53, assoc. prof., 1953-55; asst. prof. theology and literature, U. Chgo., 1955-58, assoc. prof., 1958-64, prof., 1964-72, Shailer Mathews prof. of theology and lit., 1972-76, prof. English, 1967-76; Commonwealth prof. religious studies, U. Va., 1976-81, William R. Kenan prof. religious studies, 1981-90, prof. English, 1976-90, prof. emeritus, 1990—. Author: Rehearsals of Discomposure: Alienation and Reconciliation in Modern Literature, 1952, The Tragic Vision and the Christian Faith, 1957, Modern Literature and the Religious Frontier, 1958, Albert Camus, 1962, Reinhold Niebuhr, 1963, The New Orpheus: Essays toward a Christian Poetic, 1964, The Climate of Faith in Modern Literature, 1965, The Broken Center: Studies in the Theological Horizon of Modern Literature, 1966, Ernest Hemingway, 1966, The Modern Vision of Death, 1967, Adversity and Grace: Studies in Recent American Literature, 1968, Negative Capability: Studies in the New Literature and the Religious Situation, 1969, The Unquiet Vision: Mirrors of Man in Existentialism, 1969, The Wild Prayer of Longing: Poetry and the Sacred, 1971, Nathanael West, 1971, Three American Moralists: Mailer, Bellow, Trilling, 1973, The Poetry of Civic Virtue: Eliot, Malraux, Auden, 1976, Mirrors of Man in Existentialism, 1978, The Poetics of Belief: Studies in Coleridge, Arnold, Pater, Santayana, Stevens and Heidegger, 1985, Visions of Presence in Modern American Poetry, 1993; co-editor Jour. Religion, 1963-77, (with Ronald Sharp) Reading George Steiner, 1994; adv. editor Religion and Lit., Literature and Theology, Callaloo. Fellow Am. Acad. of Arts and Scis.; mem. Soc. Arts, Religion and Contemporary Culture, Soc. for Values in Higher Edn. (Kent fellow), MLA., Am. Acad. Religion (pres. 1986), Century Assn. (N.Y.C.), Quadrangle Club, Arts Club (Chgo.), Greencroft Club (Charlottesville, Va.). Office: U Va Dept Religious Studies Charlottesville VA 22903

SCOTT, NAUMAN S., federal judge; b. New Roads, La., June 15, 1916; s. Nauman Steele and Sidonie (Provosty) S.; m. Blanche Hammond, Jan. 8, 1942; children: A shley, Nauman S. III, John W., Arthur Hammond. A.B., Amherst Coll., 1938; LL.B., Tulane U., 1941. Bar: La. 1942. Practiced in Alexandria; judge U.S. Dist. Ct. for La., Western dist., Alexandria, 1970—, former chief judge; mem. jud. council La. Supreme Ct., 1961-70. Chmn. local United Fund, local unit ARC; bd. dirs. La. Assn. for Mental Health, Vocat. and Rehab. Center. Served to 1st lt. 1942-45. Mem. ABA, La. Bar Assn. (nominating com.), Alexandria Bar Assn. (pres. 1965-66), Alexandria C. of C., Young Men's Bus. Assn. Republican. Roman Catholic. Club: Kiwanis. Office: US Dist Ct PO Box 312 Alexandria LA 71309-0312

SCOTT, NORMAN LAURENCE, engineering consultant; b. Meadow Grove, Nebr., Oct. 17, 1931; s. Laurence Ray Scott and Ruth Louise Braun; m. Joan Culbertson, Jan. 21, 1956; 1 child, Douglas Jay. BS in Civil Engring., U. Nebr., 1954. Registered profl. engr., Ill., Fla., Md., Minn., Va., Tex.; registered structural engr., Ill. Sales engr. R.H. Wright & Son, Ft. Lauderdale, Fla., 1956-58; mgr. Wright of Palm Beach, West Palm Beach, Fla., 1958-59; exec. sec. Prestressed Concrete Inst., Chgo., 1959-63; gen. mgr. Wiss, Janney, Elstner & Assoc., Northbrook, Ill., 1963-66; pres., chmn. The Consulting Engrs. Group Inc., Mt. Prospect, Ill., 1966—. 1st lt. USAF, 1954-56. Mem. ASCE (life), Am. Concrete Inst. (hon., pres. 1983-84, Henry C. Turner medal 1993), Ill. Soc. Profl. Engrs. (pres. North Shore chpt. 1962). Republican. Home: 701 Chatham Dr Glenview IL 60025-4403 Office: The Consulting Engrs Group 55 E Euclid Ave Mount Prospect IL 60056-1287

SCOTT, NORMAN ROY, academic administrator, agricultural engineering educator; b. Spokane, Wash., Sept. 6, 1936; s. Roy Samuel and Agnes Sarafia (Lilljegren) S.; m. Sharon R. Cogley, June 17, 1961; children: Robin, Nanette, Shirlene. BS in Agrl. Engring., Wash. State U., 1958; PhD, Cornell U., 1962. Mem. faculty agrl. engring dept. Cornell U., Ithaca, N.Y., 1962—, chmn. agrl. engring. dept., 1978-84, dir. office for rsch. agrl. experimentation sta., 1984-89, v.p. rsch. and advanced studies, 1989—; mem. bd. on agriculture NRC, Nat. Acad. Scis., 1993—. Contbr. articles to profl. jours.; patentee in field. Recipient Alumni Achievement award Wash. State U., 1995. Fellow Am. Inst. for Med. and Biol. Engring. (founding 1991), Am. Soc. Agrl. Engrs. (tech. v.p. 1989-92, pres. elect 1992-93, pres. 1993-94, Henry Glese award 1989); mem. AAAS, N.Y. Acad. Scis., Nat. Acad. Engring., Am. Soc. for Engring. Edn., Instrument Soc. Am. (sr.). Democrat. Methodist. Avocations: sailing, golf. Home: 1662 Taughannock Blvd Trumansburg NY 14886-9120 Office: Cornell U Rsch and Advanced Studies 314 Day Hall Ithaca NY 14853-2801

SCOTT, OLOF HENDERSON, JR., priest; b. Phila., May 13, 1942; s. Olof Henderson and Julia Irene (Rutroff) S.; m. Eva Jakowenko, Sept. 13, 1969; children: Lisa Ann, Christopher Olof, Timothy Nicholas. BA in Physics, Franklin and Marshall Coll., 1964; MS in Nuclear Engring., Pa. State U., 1966; postgrad., St. Vladimir's Orthodox Theol. Sem., 1975-76. Ordained deacon Antiochian Orthodox Christian Ch., 1975, priest, 1976, archpriest, 1988. Ops. engr. S3G ops. Knolls Atomic Power Lab., GE Co., Schenectady, N.Y., 1966-68; project engr. S3G ops. Knolls Atomic Power Lab., GE Co., 1968-69; lead nuclear engr. Seabrook Nuclear project Pub. Svc. Co. of N.H., Manchester, 1969-70; project engr. VEPCO projects Nuclear Energy Sys. divsn. Westinghouse Elec. Co., Monroeville, Pa., 1970-72; project mgr. VEPCO projects Nuclear Energy Sys. divsn. Westinghouse Elec. Co., 1972-74, regional sales mgr. mktg., 1974-75; pastor St. George Orthodox Ch., Charleston, W.Va., 1976—; dean of clergy Appalachian-Ohio Valley Deanery, 1976—; spiritual advisor NAC-SOYO of Archdiocese, 1977-82, vice-chmn. inter-orthodox and inter-faith rels., 1987—; mem. exec. bd. W.Va. Coun. Chs., 1977—; bd. govs. Nat. Coun. Chs., 1977—, mem. nominating com., 1979-81, exec. com., 1985—, membership com., 1988-91, unity and rels., 1989-92; mem. West Va. Ecumenical Coalition on Infant Mortality, 1992—. Contbr. articles to profl. jours. Bd. dirs. Religious Coalition for Cmty. Renewal in Charleston, 1987-95; bd. dirs. Kanawha Home for Children, 1986-89, pres., 1989; long-range planning com. W.Va. State Rep. Exec. Com., 1985-87. Mem. Acad. Parish Clergy (pres. W.Va. chpt. 1983-85), Am. Nuclear Soc., St. Vladimir's Theol. Found., Charleston Ministerial Assn., Order of St. John of Jerusalem-Knights Hospitellers (chaplain 1985—), Soc. for Preservation and Encouragement Barbershop Quartet Singing in Am. Inc. (v.p. 1984-85), Pa. State Club W.Va. (pres. 1984-88), Alden Kindred of Am., Sigma Pi Sigma, Delta Sigma Phi. Avocations: camping, barbershop quartet, motorcycling. Home: 4409 Staunton Ave SE Charleston WV 25304-1743 Office: St George Orthodox Ch PO Box 2044 Charleston WV 25327-2044 *My thoughts on life are but mere recitations of the Holy Scripture and my feeble attempts at making Those words and Thoughts my own.*

SCOTT, OTTO, writer; b. N.Y.C., May 26, 1918; s. Otto Felix and Katherine (McGivney) S.; m. Rose Massing (div. 1952); 1 child, Katherine; m. Nellie Mouradian (div. 1963); children: Mary, Philipa; m. Anna Barney Scott, Apr. 29, 1963; 1 child, Ann Elizabeth. MA in Polit. Sci., Valley Christian U., Fresno, Calif., 1985. Mem. staff United Features Syndicate, N.Y.C., 1939-40; v.p. Globaltronix de Venezuela, Caracas, 1954-56, Mohr Assocs., N.Y.C., 1957-59, Becker, Scott & Assocs., N.Y.C., 1960-63; editor

Bill Bros., N.Y.C., 1964-67; asst. to chmn. Ashland (Ky.) Oil, Inc., 1968, 69; edn. writer, reviewer San Diego Union Tribune, 1970; sr. writer Chalcedon Found., Vallecito, Calif., 1982-94; cons. Ashland Oil, Inc., 1972—; editor, pub. Otto Scott's Compass, Seattle, 1990—. Author: History Ashland Oil (The Exception) 1968, Robespierre: Voice of Virtue (History French Revolution), 1974, The Professional: Biography of J.B. Saunders, 1976, The Creative Ordeal: History of Raytheon Corporation, 1976, James I: The Fool as King, 1976, 86, Other End of the Lifeboat (History of South Africa), 1985, Buried Treasure: The Story of Arch Mineral, 1987, The Secret Six: The Fool as Martyr, 1987, The Great Christian Revolution, 1991, The Powered Hand, History of Black and Decker, 1994. With U.S. Merchant Marine, 1941-47. Mem. Author's Guild, Overseas Press Club, Com. for Nat. Policy, Com. for Monetary Rsch. and Edn. Presbyterian. Office: Otto Scotts Compass Uncommon Books 828 S 299th Pl Federal Way WA 98003-3749

SCOTT, RALPH C., physician, educator; b. Bethel, Ohio, June 7, 1921; s. John Carey and Leona (Laycock) S.; m. Rosemary Ann Schultz, June 26, 1945; children: Susan Ann, Barbara Lynne, Marianne Elizabeth. BS, U. Cin., 1943, MD, 1945. Diplomate: Am. Bd. Internal Medicine (subspecialty cardiovascular disease). InternUniv. Hosps. U. Iowa, 1945-46; resident, asst. dept. pathology Coll. Medicine U. Cin., 1948-49, fellow internal medicine Coll. Medicine, 1949-53, fellow cardiology Coll. Medicine, 1953-57, mem. faculty Coll. Medicine, 1950—, prof. medicine Coll. Medicine, 1968—; staff clinics Cin. Gen. Hosp., 1950-75, clinician in internal medicine, 1952-75, dir. cardiac clinics, 1965-75, attending physician med. service, 1958—; staff VA Hosp., Cin. 1954-86, 1992—, cons., 1961-86, 92—; attending physician Med. Svc., Christian R. Holmes Hosp., Cin., 1957-86; attending staff USAF Hosp., Wright Patterson AFB, 1960—; staff Good Samaritan Hosp., Cin., 1961—, cons., 1967—; staff Jewish Hosp., Cin., 1957—, cons., 1968—; cons. Children's Hosp., Cin., 1968—; attending physician Providence Hosp., Cin., 1971—, dir. cardiology, 1971-94. Contbr. articles to med. jours.; editorial bd. Am. Heart Jour, 1967-79, Jour. Electrocardiology, 1967—; editor: Electro-Cardiographic-Pathologic Conf., Jour. Electrocardiology, 1967—, Clin. Cardiology and Diabetes, 5 vols, 1981. Capt. AUS, 1946-48. Nat. Heart Inst. grantee, 1964-68, 67-74, 76-82, 1985-90. Fellow ACP, Am. Coll. Cardiology, Am. Coll. Chest Physicians, Coun. Clin. Cardiology, Coun. Clin. Epidemiology and Prevention; mem. Ohio State Med. Assn., Cin. Acad. Medicine, Cen. Soc. Clin. Rsch., Am. Heart Assn., Cin. Soc. Internal Medicine, Heart Assn. Southwestern Ohio, Am. Fedn. for Clin. Rsch., Internat. Cardiovascular Soc., Am. Soc. Preventive Cardiology, Sigma Xi, Alpha Omega Alpha, Phi Eta Sigma, Phi Chi. Home: 2955 Alpine Ter Cincinnati OH 45208-3407 Office: U Cin Med Ctr 231 Bethesda Ave Cincinnati OH 45229-2827

SCOTT, RALPH MASON, physician, radiation oncology educator; b. Leemont, Va., Nov. 23, 1921; s. Benjamin Thomas and Marion Hazel (Mason) S.; m. Alice Latine Francisco, Dec. 21, 1946; children: Susan Taylor, Ralph Mason, John Thomas. BA, U. Va., 1947; MD, Med. Coll. Va., 1950. Diplomate Am. Bd. Radiology (trustee 1965-76, treas. 1969-70, v.p. 1970-72, pres. 1972-74). Intern Robert Packer Hosp., Sayre, Pa., 1953-54, resident, 1954-57, dir. radiation therapy and nuclear medicine sect., 1957-59; with Christie Hosp. and Holt Radium Inst., Manchester, England, 1956-57; asst. prof. radiology U. Chgo. Med. Sch., 1959-60; assoc. prof. radiology, dir. radiation therapy and radioisotopes U. Louisville Med. Sch., 1960-64, prof., dir. radiation therapy, 1964-77, prof. radiation therapy, 1981-82; prof. emeritus U. Louisville, 1995; dir. J. Graham Brown Regional Cancer Ctr., Health Scis. Ctr. U. Louisville Med. Sch., 1981-82; dir. dept. radiation medicine Christ Hosp., Cin., 1982-93; ret.; clin. prof. radiology U. Cin. Coll. Medicine, 1982-93; prof., chmn. dept. therapeutic radiology U. Md. Sch. Med., 1977-80; dir. radiation therapy program div. cancer rsch. resources and ctrs., Nat. Cancer Inst. (on leave from U. Louisville), 1976-77. Pres. Ky. divsn. Am. Cancer Soc., 1972-73; bd. dirs. LADD, 1993-95, NKAR, 1993-95, Day Spring Inc., 1993—, United Health Care, 1994-95. Served to lt. (j.g.) USNR, 1943-45. Fellow Christie Hosp. and Holt Radium Inst., Manchester, Eng., 1956-57. Mem. Am. Roentgen-Ray Soc. (exec. coun. 1968—, chmn. exec. coun. 1972-73), AMA, Am. Coll. Radiology (vice chmn. commn. on cancer 1968-69), Am. Radium Soc., Am. Soc. Therapeutic Radiologists, Assn. U. Radiologists, Radiol. Soc. N.Am., Pi Kappa Alpha, Phi Chi. Home: 5516 Tecumseh Cir Louisville KY 40207-1692

SCOTT, RAYMOND PETER WILLIAM, chemistry research educator, writer; b. Erith, Eng., June 20, 1924; came to U.S., 1969; s. Ronald and Annie (Hoadley) S.; m. Barbara Winifred Doreen Strange, Apr. 20, 1946; children: Kerry Raymond, Kevin Francis. B.Sc., U. London, 1946, D.Sc., 1958. Lab. leader Burroughs Welcome, Dartford, Eng., 1946-48; chief chemist APCM, 1948-52; research mgr. Benzole Producers, Watford, Eng., 1952-60; divisional mgr. Unilever, Sharnbrook and Bedfordshire, Eng., 1960-69; dir. phys. chemistry Hoffamn La Roche, Nutley, N.J., 1969-80; dir. applied rsch. Perkin-Elmer, Norwalk, Conn., 1980-86; research prof. dept. chemistry Georgetown U., Washington, 1986—; rsch. prof. dept. chemistry Birkbeck Coll., London. Author: Liquid Chromatography Detectors, 1977, 3d edit., 1987, Contemporary Liquid Chromatography, 1976, Liquid Chromatography Column Theory, 1991, Silica Gel and Bonded Phases, 1993, Liquid Chromatography for the Analyst, 1994, Chromatography Techniques, 1995, Chromatography Detectors, 1996; editor: Gas Chromatography, 1960, Small Bore Columns in Liquid Chromatography, 1983. Recipient Tswett medal Am. Internat. Symposia on Chromatography, 1978; recipient Tswett award USSR Tech. Inst. Moscow, 1978, Martin medal in chromatography Chromatography Group Gt. Britain, 1982. Fellow Royal Soc. Chemistry (chartered, Analysis and Instrumentation award 1988), Am. Inst. Chemists (cert.), Am. Chem. Soc. (Chromatography award 1977). Office: Chemistry Dept Georgetown U Washington DC 20057 also: Birkbeck Coll, Chemistry Dept, London England

SCOTT, REBECCA ANDREWS, biology educator; b. Sunny Hill, La., June 4, 1939; d. Hayward and Dorothy (Nicholson) Andrews; m. Earl P. Scott, June 8, 1957; children: Stephanie Scott Dilworth, Cheryl L. BS, So. U., 1962; MS, Eastern Mich. U., 1969. Biology tchr., Detroit, 1966-68; sci. tchr. Ann Arbor (Mich.) Pub. Schs., 1968-69; biology tchr. North High Sch., Mpls., 1972—, coord. math., sci. tech. magnet, 1986—, advisor Jets Sci. Club. Mem. LVW (pres. 1981-83, 87-89, treas. 1989-94), Nat. Sci. Tchrs. Assn., Minn. Sci. Tchrs. Assn., Minn. Acad. Sci., Nat. Assn. Biology Tchrs., Iota Phi Lambda (pres. 1995—). Democrat. Presbyterian. Home: 3112 Wendhurst Ave Minneapolis MN 55418-1726 Office: 1500 James Ave N Minneapolis MN 55411-3161

SCOTT, RICHARD G., church official; b. Pocatello, Idaho, Nov. 7, 1928; s. Kenneth Leroy and Mary Whittle S.; m. Jeanen Watkins, July 16, 1953; 7 children. Degree in mech. engring., George Washington U.; postgrad. in nuclear engring. Mem. staff naval and land based power plants, 1953-65; head North Mission LDS Ch., Cordoba, Argentina, 1965-69; regional rep. in Uruguay, Paraguay, N.C., S.C., Va., Washington LDS Ch., 1969-77, mem. 1st Quorum of Seventy, 1977-83, mem. presidency of 1st Quorum of Seventy, 1983-88, apostle, 1988—. Avocations: jazz and classical music, hiking, birding, painting. Office: LDS Ch 50 E North Temple Salt Lake City UT 84150-0002

SCOTT, RICHARD L., health and medical products company executive; b. Kansas City, Mo., 1953. BSBA, U. Mo.; JD, So. Meth. U. Bar: Tex. Pvt. practice, until 1987; pres., CEO, Columbia/HCA Healthcare Corp., Nashville, 1987—; bd. dirs. Banc One Corp. Recipient silver award as CEO of Yr. Fin. World mag.; named One of Top 25 Performers, U.S. News & World Report, 1995. Mem. Healthcare Leadership Coun., Bus. Roundtable, Bus. Coun. Office: Basic Am Med Inc 201 W Main St Louisville KY 40202-1366

SCOTT, RICHARD THURSTON, publishing executive; b. Glens Falls, N.Y., Apr. 28, 1936; s. Richard T. and Yvonne M. (Roulier) S.; m. Jeanne M. DeFilippo, Sept. 27, 1959; children: Kimberly Ann, Debra Lynne. BA, Colgate U., 1958; MS, Coll. St. Rose, Albany, N.Y., 1962. Supr., tchr. Glens Falls City Schs., 1962-66; reading coordinator pub. schs. Kingston, N.Y., 1966-68; div. mgr. Reader's Digest, Pleasantville, N.Y., 1968-84; pres., pub. David McKay Co., Inc., N.Y.C., 1985-86; pres. pub. Fodor's Travel Guides, N.Y.C., 1986-87; pub. Bantam Travel Books Bantam, Doubleday Dell Pub. Group, N.Y.C., 1987—. Author short stories, 1972; contbr. articles to profl. jours. pres. Mahopac (N.Y.) Pub. Library, 1975-80. Home: Mekeel St Katonah NY 10536 Office: Am Bookseller Mag 828 S Broadway Tarrytown NY 10591

SCOTT, RICHARD WALDO, lawyer; b. N.Y.C., July 8, 1953; s. Walter Vanderbilt Jr. and Ella Louise (Becker) S.; m. Karen Trussell, May 25, 1974 (div. Oct. 1984); children: Richard Jr., Amanda, Margaret; m. Laure Ellen Copland, Mar. 9, 1986. AB, Duke U., 1974, JD, 1977. Bar: N.Y. 1978, Tex. 1980. Assoc. Sullivan & Cromwell, N.Y.C., 1977-79; assoc. Vinson & Elkins, Houston, 1979-84, ptnr., 1984—. Mem. ABA, Tex. Bar Assn., Order of Coif, Phi Beta Kappa. Republican. Presbyterian. Avocations: golf, music, sailing. Home: 122 Paul Revere Dr Houston TX 77024-6107 Office: Vinson & Elkins 3300 First City Tower 1001 Fannin St Houston TX 77002

SCOTT, RIDLEY, film director; b. South Shields, Northumberland, Eng., Nov. 30, 1939. Ed., Royal Coll. Art, London. Dir.: (films) Boy on Bicycle, The Duellists, 1978, Allen, 1978, Blade Runner, 1982, Legend, 1986, Someone to Watch Over Me (also exec. prodr.), 1987, Black Rain, 1989, Thelma & Louise (also co-prodr.), 1991, 1492: Conquest of Paradise (also co-prodr.); co-prodr.: The Browning Version, 1994, White Squall, 1996; exec. prodr.: Monkey Trouble, 1994; dir. more than 3,000 TV commls.; set designer Z-Cars, The Informers series (BBC, London). Winner Design scholarship, N.Y. Office: CAA 9830 Wilshire Blvd Beverly Hills CA 90212

SCOTT, ROBERT ALLYN, academic administrator; b. Englewood, N.J., Apr. 16, 1939; s. William D. and Ann. F. (Waterman) S.; m. Phyllis Virginia Brice, Mar. 23, 1963; children: Ryan Keith, Kira Elizabeth. BA, Bucknell U., 1961; PhD, Cornell U., 1975. Mgmt. trainee Procter & Gamble Co., Phila., 1961-63; asst. dir. admissions Bucknell U., Lewisburg, Pa., 1965-67; asst. dean Coll. Arts and Scis. Cornell U., Ithaca, 1967-69, assoc. dean, 1969-79, anthropology faculty, 1978-79; dir. acad. affairs Ind. Commn. for Higher Edn., Indpls., 1979-84, asst. commr., 1984-85; pres. Ramapo (N.J.) Coll., 1985—; cons. Sta. WSKG Pub. TV and Radio, 1977-79, also to various colls. and univs., pubs., 1966—; mem. curriculum adv. com. Ind. Bd. Edn., 1984-87, Lilly Endowment Think Tank, 1984-86; mem. nat. adv. panel Ind. 21st Century Schooling Project, 1990-92; sr. cons., chair N.J. Higher Edn. Restructuring Team, 1994; bd. dirs. World Trade Coun., Hackensack Med. Ctr., NCO Investors II, L.P., Proteus Assocs., Inc.; chmn. bd. Am. Ednl. Products, Inc., 1995. Author books and monographs; editorial bd. Cornell Rev., 1976-79; book rev. editor Coll. and Univ., 1974-78; cons. editor Change mag., 1979—; cons. editor Jour. Higher Edn., 1985—; exec. editor Saturday Evening Post book div. Curtis Pub. Co., 1982-85; contbr. articles to sociols., ednl. and popular publs. Trustee Bucknell U., 1976-78, First Unitarian Ch., Ithaca, 1970-73, 78-79, chmn., 1971-73, Unitarian Universalist Ch. of Indpls., 1980-85. With USNR, 1963-65. Spencer Found. rsch. grantee, 1977; recipient Sagamore of the Wabash award, 1986, Prudential Found. Leader of Yr. award, 1987, Disting. Svc. award West Bergen Mental Health Ctr., 1991, NYU Presdl. medal, 1994. Fellow Am. Anthrop. Assn.; mem. Assn. Study Higher Edn., Am. Sociol. Assn., Am. Assn. Higher Edn., Am. Assn. State Colls. & Univs. (Coll. and Univ. Satellite Ednl. Sys. chair, coun. on Liberal Arts and Scis., chair 1990-93), O.E.C.D. (higher edn. program Paris), Am. Coun. on Edn. Commn. On Internat. Edn. (chair), Am. Forum, Higher Edn. Colloqiuium (chmn. 1982-84), N.J. Assn. of Coll. and Univs. (chair 1991-92), Bucknell U. Alumni Assn. (bd. dirs. 1971-80, pres. 1976-78, Outstanding Achievement 1991), Indian Trail Club, Phi Kappa Psi, Phi Kappa Phi. Office: Ramapo Coll 505 Ramapo Valley Rd Mahwah NJ 07430-1623

SCOTT, ROBERT CORTEZ, congressman, lawyer; b. Washington, Apr. 30, 1947; s. Charles Waldo and Mae (Hamlin) S. BA, Harvard U., 1969; JD, Boston U., 1973; LLD (hon.), Commonwealth Coll., Hampton, Va., 1988. Pvt. practice Newport News, 1973—; del. Va. Ho. Dels., Richmond, 1978-83, senator, 1983-92; mem. 103rd-104th Congresses from 3rd Va. dist., Washington, D.C., 1993—; mem. econ. & ednl. opportunity com., judiciary com. Br. pres. NAACP, Newport News, 1974-80; pres. bd. Peninsula Legal Aid Ctr., Hampton, 1977-81; mem. state exec. bd. March of Dimes, Va., 1987—; chmn. 1st dist. Dem. Party Va., 1980-85; bd. dirs. Hampton Roads March of Dimes; adv. com. Peninsula Boy Scouts Am. Recipient Brotherhood Citation award Nat. Conf. Christians & Jews, 1985, Child Adv. award Va. Acad. Pediatrics, 1987, Disting. Svc. award Va. State Fraternal Order Police, 1987, Outstanding Legislator award So. Health Assn., 1989. Mem. Peninsula C. of C., Alpha Phi Alpha, Sigma Pi Phi. Democrat. Office: US House of Reps 501 Cannon Bldg Washington DC 20515-0003*

SCOTT, ROBERT HAL, minister; b. Floydada, Tex., Apr. 2, 1930; s. Samuel Price and Fannie (Miller) S.; m. Carolyn Weaver, July 31, 1950; children: Vicki Lynette Reese, Steven Robert Scott. BA, Pasadena Coll., 1950; DD, Point Loma Coll., 1983. Ordained to ministry Ch. of the Nazarene, 1953. Pastor various Chs. of the Nazarene, Calif., 1950-75; dist. supt. Ch. of the Nazarene/So. Calif. Dist., Orange, Calif., 1975-86; dir. internat. missions Ch. of the Nazarene, Kansas City, Mo., 1986-94, dir. 21st Century Rsch. Inst., 1994—; trustee Pasadena (Calif.) Coll., 1964-75, Point Loma Coll., San Diego, Calif., 1975-86, Nazarene Bible Coll., Colorado Springs, 1976-80. Author: All Over the World, Our Family, 1994; contbr. articles to World Mission mag., 1986—.

SCOTT, ROBERT LANE, chemist, educator; b. Santa Rosa, Calif., Mar. 20, 1922; s. Horace Albert and Maurine (Lane) S.; m. Elizabeth Sewall Hunter, May 27, 1944; children: Joanna Ingersoll, Jonathan Armat, David St. Clair, Janet Hamilton. S.B., Harvard U., 1942; M.A., Princeton U., 1944, Ph.D., 1945. Sci. staff Los Alamos Lab., 1945-46; Frank B. Jewett fellow U. Calif., Berkeley, 1946-48; faculty UCLA, 1948—, prof. chemistry, 1960-92, prof. emeritus, 1993—, chmn. dept., 1970-75. Author: (with J.H. Hildebrand) Solubility of Nonelectrolytes, 3d edit, 1950, rev., 1964, Regular Solutions, 1962, Regular and Related Solutions, 1970; Contbr. articles to profl. jours. Guggenheim fellow, 1955; NSF sr. fellow, 1961-62; Fulbright lectr., 1968-69. Fellow AAAS, Am. Phys. Soc.; mem. Am. Chem. Soc. (Joel Henry Hildebrand award 1984), Royal Soc. Chemistry (London), Sigma Xi. Home: 11128 Montana Ave Los Angeles CA 90049-3509

SCOTT, ROBERT LEE, speech educator; b. Fairbury, Nebr., Apr. 19, 1928; s. Walter Everett and Ann Maria (Jensen) S.; m. Betty Rose Foust, Sept. 13, 1947; children—Mark Allen, Janet Lee, Paul Matthew. B.A., U. No. Colo., 1950; M.A., U. Nebr., 1951; Ph.D., U. Ill., 1955. Asst. prof. speech U. Houston, 1953-57; asst. prof. U. Minn., 1957-59, assoc. prof., 1959-63, prof., 1963—, chair dept. speech communication, 1971-89, chair dept. Spanish and Portuguese, 1992-94. Author: Rhetoric of Black Power, 1969, Moments in the Rhetoric of the Cold War, 1970; contbr. articles to profl. jours. Recipient Teaching award Coll. of Liberal Arts, U. Minn., 1981. Mem. Speech Comm. Assn. (editor Quar. Jour. Speech 1971-74, Winans-Wichelns Rsch. award 1970, Charles H. Woolbert Rsch. award, 1981, Douglas-Ehninger Disting. Scholar award 1989, Disting. Scholar of Assn. 1992), Ctrl. States Speech Assn., Internat. Soc. for Study of Rhetoric. Office: U Minn Dept Speech Communication Minneapolis MN 55455-0194

SCOTT, ROBERT MICHAEL, data processing executive; b. Swainsboro, Ga., May 6, 1950; s. William Hilton and Daphne (Fensom) S.; m. Marcia Lynne Norton, Dec. 20, 1972; children: Allison Marie, Bethany Diane, Katherine Anne. BA in Edn., Fla. Atlantic U., 1972. Consumer lending officer 1st Bank and Trust Co., Boca Raton, Fla., 1972-77; various mgmt. positions First Data Resources, Omaha, 1977-83, v.p., 1983-84, exec. v.p., 1984—; treas. First Data Resources, 1986—, also bd. dirs.; bd. dirs. Deposit Guarantee Bank, Omaha, Profl. On-Line Inc., Saginaw, Mich., Indeserv Inc., Omaha. Bd. dirs. Fontenelle Forest Assn., Omaha, 1986; mem. Salvation Army. Democrat. Office: 1st Data Resources Inc 11810 Nicholas St Omaha NE 68154-4477*

SCOTT, ROBERT MONTGOMERY, museum executive, lawyer; b. Bryn Mawr, Pa., May 22, 1929; s. Edgar and Helen Hope (Montgomery) S.; m. H. Gay Elliot, June 30, 1951 (separated); children: Hope Tyler Scott Rogers, Janny Scott Ritter, Elliot Montgomery. AB, Harvard U., 1951; LLB, U. Pa., 1954. Ptnr. Montgomery McCracken Walker & Rhoads, Phila., 1961-82, of counsel, 1982-88; spl. asst. to U.S. Amb. to Ct. of St. James, London, 1969-73; hon. Brit. consul Phila., 1979-83; pres., chief exec. officer Phila. Mus. Art, 1982—; mem. adv. bd. First Union Bancorp. No. Trustee Phila. Mus. Art, 1965—, Royal Oak Found., 1978-86, Inst. Cancer Rsch., Fox Chase Cancer Ctr., 1960-86, Lankenau Hosp., 1959-86, William Penn Found., 1986-91; pres. Mary Louise Curtis Book Fedn., 1989—, Curtis Inst. of Music, 1994—; bd. dirs. Glyndebourne Assn. Am., Inc. Recipient Superior Honor award Dept. State, 1973. Fellow Am. Bar Found.; mem. Am. Assn. Mus., Phila. Club, Knickerbocker Club, Locust Club, White's Club. Republican. Home: Ardrossan 807 Newtown Rd Villanova PA 19085-1031 Office: Phila Mus Art Benjamin Franklin Pky PO Box 7646 Philadelphia PA 19101-7646

SCOTT, RONALD WILLIAM, educator, physical therapist, lawyer, writer; b. Pitts., Dec. 19, 1951; s. Richard Jack and Leone Florence (Gore) S.; m. Maria Josefa Barba-Garces, Aug. 5, 1973; children: Ronald William Jr., Paul Steven. BS in Phys. Therapy summa cum laude, U. Pitts., 1977; JD magna cum laude, U. San Diego, 1983; MBA, Boston U., 1986; LLM, Judge Adv. Gen. Sch., Charlottesville, Va., 1988; postgrad., Samuel Merritt Coll., Oakland, Calif. Bar: Calif. 1983, Tex. 1994; cert. orthopaedic phys. therapist. Commd. 1st lt. U.S. Army, 1978, advanced through grades to maj.; atty.-advisor U.S. Army, Frankfurt, Germany, 1983-87; malpractice claims atty. U.S. Army, Ft. Meade, Md., 1988-89; chief phys. therapist U.S. Army, Ft. Polk, La., 1989-92; phys. therapist, clin. instr. Brooke Army Med. Ctr., San Antonio, 1992-94; assoc. prof. dept. phys. therapy Sch. of Allied Health Scis., U. Tex. Health Sci. Ctr., San Antonio, 1994—; presenter numerous profl. seminars on health law, ethics, and quality and risk mgmt.; guest lectr. phys. therapy program Hahnemann U., Phila., 1991—, Southwest Tex. State U., Tex. Woman's U., U.S. Army-Baylor U. Author: Healthcare Malpractice, 1990, Legal Aspects of Documenting Patient Care, 1994, Promoting Legal Awareness, 1996; editor: Law Rev., U. San Diego, 1982-83; also articles; mem. editl. adv. bd. PT: The Mag. of Phys. Therapy, 1991—. Merit badge counselor Boy Scouts Am. Mem. ABA, Am. Phys. Therapy Assn. (risk mgmt. advisor 1989—, jud. com. 1992—, McMillan scholar 1976), Am. Soc. Law, Medicine and Ethics, Nat. Health Lawyers Assn., Tex. Phys. Therapy Assn., Soc. for Human Resource Mgmt. (presenter Geriatric Rehab. Conf. Cambridge U. 1995, Trinity Coll., Dublin 1996). Democrat. Methodist. Avocations: guitar, collecting rare records and books, golf, skiing, hiking. Home: 5815 Spring Crown San Antonio TX 78247-5409 Office: U Tex Health Sci Ctr 7703 Floyd Curl Dr San Antonio TX 78284-6200

SCOTT, RUTH LOIS, dental hygiene educator; b. Chanute, Kans., Aug. 28, 1934; d. Walter Roy and Ruth Lois (Cunningham) Harder; m. Charles Calvin Scott, July 3, 1956 (div. July 1963); children: Valerie Elizabeth, Matthew Stuart, David Bruce. BA in Psychology and Theatre with honors, U. Kans., 1958; Cert., U. Mo., Kansas City, 1954, MS in Dental Hygiene Edn., 1972. Asst. prof. U. Iowa Coll. Dentistry, 1972-73; from instr. to clin. instr. dept. dental hygiene U. Mo.-Kansas City Sch. Dentistry, 1969-71; asst. prof. dept. preventive dentistry U. Mo. Kansas City Sch. Dentistry, asst. prof. comprehensive dentistry for adults, 1975-77, asst. prof. div. dental hygiene, 1977-81, assoc. prof., 1981—; pvt. practice dentistry Kansas City, 1954-90. Contbr. articles to profl. jours. Charter mem. Kansas City chpt. Parents Without Ptnrs., 1973—; mem. Ch. Without Walls. Recipient Dental Hygiene Alumni Svc. award U. Mo.-Kansas City, 1992. Mem. Am. Dental Hygienists Assn., Mo. Dental Hygienists Assn., Greater Kansas City Dental Hygiene Component Soc., Am. Assn. Dental Schs., Am. Assn. Dental Rsch., U. Mo.-Kansas City Dental Hygiene Alumni Assn., Phi Beta Kappa, Sigma Phi Alpha (exec. sec. 1990-96), Phi Psi, Phi Kappa Phi. Unitarian-Universalist. Office: U Mo-Kansas City 650 E 25th St Kansas City MO 64108

SCOTT, SANDRA LYNN (SANDY SCOTT), artist, sculptor, printmaker; b. Dubuque, Iowa, July 24, 1943; d. Jim and Dolly (Dillon) S. Student, Kansas City (Kans.) Art Inst., 1962-63. Animation background artist Calvin Motion Pictures, 1963-65; freelance portrait artist, illustrator Kona Coast, Hawaii, 1969, San Francisco, 1969; instr. Scottsdale Artists Sch., Ariz., 1987, Loveland Acad. Fine Art, 1992, The Fechin Inst., Taos, N.Mex., 1995. One woman shows include: Nat. Cowboy Hall Fame, 1978, Pen & Brush, N.Y., 1988; group shows include: Cheyenne Frontier Days Governor's Invitational Western Art Show, 1992, 93, 94, 95, Loveland Rotary's Colo. Invitational Art Show, 1992, 93, 94, 95, Nat. Wildlife Mus. Art Show, 1992, 93, 94, 95, Nat. Acad. Western Art, 1993, 94, Am. Women Artist Art Show, 1993, The West Show Tucson Mus. Art, 1993, Artist of Am. Denver Rotary Show, 1993, 94, 95, Nat. Cowboy Hall Fame, 1995, Western Art Exhibit, China; private collections include: Nat. Cowboy Hall Fame, Trammell Crow Corp., Mus. Arts and Crafts, Opryland Hotel, Miramichi Salmon Mus., Sebastiani Vineyards Collection, El Pasco Zoo, Vickers Oil Corp., Mustang Oil Corp., Ritz Carlton Hotel, Hillsdale Coll., Nat. Wildlife Mus., City Fort Collins, Brookgreen Gardens. Recipient Ann Huntington Sculpture award Catherine Lorillard Wolfe Art Club, 1982, Merit Sculpture award Northwest Rendezvous Group, 1987, 88, Hubbard Art Excellence award, 1991, Sculpture award Am. Profl. Artists League, 1991; recipient Sculpture prize Allied Artists, 1983, Catherine Lorillard Wolfe Art Club, 1983, Salmagundi Club, 1983, Am. Artists Profl. League, 1982, 83, Pen and Brush, 1984, Knickerbocker Artists, 1984, Ellen P. Speyer prize Nat. Acad. Design, 1988; recipient Gold medal for Sculpture Nat. Acad. Western Art, 1992.. Mem. Soc. Animal Artists, Am. Artist Profl. League, Pen & Brush, Northwest Rendezvous Group, Catherine Lorillard Wolfe Art Club. Home: 200 Gregory Rd Fort Collins CO 80524

SCOTT, STEPHEN CARLOS, academic administrator; b. Greenville, S.C., Sept. 20, 1949; s. Carlos O'Dell and Christina (Nikitas) S.; m. Patsy Jordan, Apr. 13, 1968; children: Stephanie Christina, Lance Stephen. BA, Clemson (S.C.) U., 1971, MEd, 1975, EdD, 1987. Owner, mgr. Scotty's Inc., restaurant, Clemson, 1967-71; tchr. math. Pickens (S.C.) Sr. High Sch., 1972-74; instr. bus. Tri-County Tech. Coll., Pendleton, S.C., 1974-76, head dept., 1976-78; dir. br. campus Tri-County Tech. Coll., Easley, S.C., 1978-80; dean bus. Greenville Tech. Coll., 1980-85, assoc. v.p., 1985-88; pres. Southeastern C.C., Whiteville, N.C., 1988—; cons. P.C.E. Fed. Credit Union, Liberty, S.C., 1975-88, Jacobs Mfg. Co., Clemson, 1979-80, Flat Rock Shelter Ctr., Easley, 1980-85. Contbr. articles to profl. jours. and mags. Pres. So. Shelter Ctr., Greenville, 1986—, Good Shepherd Found., Whiteville, 1990-92; bd. dirs. Good Shepherd, 1988-91; chmn. Columbus County Sch. Bond Dr., 1989, Am. Heart Fund Drive Columbus County, 1992; co-chmn. Columbus County Long Range Planning Com., 1989-91; vice chmn. Pvt. Industry Coun. Region O, 1992—; founding dir. Habitat for Humanity Columbus County, 1992; co-chmn. bd. dirs. Columbus County Rural Health Ctr., 1994. Recipient award for patriotism U.S. Savs. Bonds Program, 1987. Mem. Am. Assn. Community and Jrs. Colls. (Pres.'s Acad.), Rotary (bd. dirs. Whiteville 1990-92, pres. 1992-93). Presbyterian. Avocations: running, chess, numismatics, reading. Office: Southeastern CC RR 1, Hwy 74-76 Box 151 Whiteville NC 28472

SCOTT, STEVEN DONALD, geology educator, researcher; b. Fort Frances, Ont., Can., June 4, 1941; s. Donald West and Shirley Margaret (Casselman) S.; m. Barbara Joan Armstrong, Dec. 28, 1962; children: Susan Joan, Donald Montgomery. BSc, U. Western Ont., 1963, MSc, 1964; PhD, Pa. State U., State College, 1968. Rsch. assoc. Pa. State U., State Coll., 1968-69; asst. prof. geology U. Toronto, Ont., 1969-72, assoc. prof., 1972-79, prof., 1979—, chmn. geol. engring., 1988—; cross-apptd. prof. U. Bretagne Occidentale, France, 1994—; pres. 507999 Ont. Ltd., Toronto, 198—, Can. Sci. Submersible Facility, Toronto, 1995—; lectr. in field. Contbr. numerous articles to profl. jours. Recipient Hosler medal Pa. State U., 1996. Fellow Royal Soc. Can. (convenor for earth scis. 1989-90, Bancroft award 1990); mem. Soc. Economic Geologists (mem. coun. 1986-88, Lindgren award 1978, Silver medal 1995), Mineral Soc. Am., Geol. Assn. Can. (tech. program chmn. ann. meeting 1991), Mineral Assn. Can. (Past Pres.'s award 1988), Internat. Marine Mineral Assn. (pres. 1994—). Avocations: travel, fishing, swimming; researcher in marine geology and ore deposits. Office: U of Toronto, Dept Geology, Toronto, ON Canada M5S 3B1

SCOTT, STEVEN EVANS, journalist; b. Stockton, Calif., Sept. 7, 1961; s. Robert James and Betty Nadine (Evans) S.; m. Jeanne Marie Singer, Aug. 20, 1994. BA in Radio-TV Broadcasting, San Jose State U., 1983. Disc jockey, news anchor Sta. KRVE-FM, San Jose, Calif., 1980-82; asst. news dir., anchor Stas. KLIV and KARA-FM, San Jose, 1982-84; news dir., anchor Sta. KWSS-FM, San Jose, 1984-86, Sta. WRXR-FM, Chgo., 1986-87; news dir., morning anchor Sta. WCKG-FM, Chgo., 1987-93; news & traffic anchor Sta. WLS-AM-FM, Chgo., 1993—; dir. news ops. Shadow Broadcast Svcs., Chgo., 1993—; co-host Northwestern Reviewing Stand, 1988-92; freelance vo8ice talent, Chgo., 1988—; fill-in pub. address announcer Chgo. Bulls and Chgo. White Sox, 1990—; contbr. ABC Radio News, 1993—; instr. Columbia Coll., Chgo., 1991—. Mem. adv. bd. Make-A-Wish Found. No. Ill., Chgo., 1988—; host Nat. Runaway Switchboard, Chgo., 1992. Recipient best newscast awards UPI, 1988, 89, Gold Bell award Mental Health Assn. Ill., 1992, Best Feature award AP, 1993. Mem. AFTRA, Radio and TV New Dirs. Assn., Soc. Profl. Journalists, Ill. News Broadcasters Assn., Mus. Broadcast Comm., Nat. Eagle Scout Assn., Sigma Alpha Mu. Avocations: flying, travel, sports. Home: 320 W Illinois St Apt 1516 Chicago IL 60610-4132 Office: Sta WLS-AM-FM 190 N State St Chicago IL 60601

SCOTT, SUSAN, lawyer; b. Orange, N.J., July 25, 1943; d. Bailey Bartlett and Regina Margaret (Butler) S.; m. Robert John Gillispie, Aug. 20. 1966 (div. 1979); children: Robert John Jr., Megan Anne. BA in Math, Catholic U. Am., 1965; JD, Rutgers U., 1975. Bar: N.J. 1975, U.S. Dist. Ct. N.J. 1975, U.S. Ct. Appeals (3d cir.) 1988, U.S. Supreme Ct. 1993. Applied math. CIA, Washington, 1965-68; assoc. Pitney, Hardin, Kipp & Szuch, Morristown, N.J., 1975-76; assoc. Riker, Danzig, Scherer, Hyland & Perretti, Morristown, 1979-85, ptnr., 1986—; corp. counsel Allied-Signal, Inc., Morristown, 1977-78; mem. Child Placement Rev. Bd., Morristown,1992—; commr. Morris County Bd. Condemnation, Morristown, 1989—. Mem. ABA, N.J. State Bar Assn., Morris County Bar Assn. Democrat. Roman Catholic. Avocations: tennis, photography. Home: 20 Vinton Rd Madison NJ 07940-2506 Office: Riker Danzig Scherer Hyland & Perretti Headquarters Plz 1 Speedwell Ave Morristown NJ 07960-6845

SCOTT, SUZANNE, writer, artist; b. Athens, Ga., Mar. 1, 1940; d. Jane Scott (Terrell) Overby; divorced; children: Elizabeth Atwell, William F. Atwell Jr., Stephanie Atwell Zehr, David Allan Atwell; life ptnr. Lynne Mary Constantine. BA in English, Eastern Mennonite Coll., 1979; MA in English Lit., James Madison U., 1986. Continuity writer WSVA TV-AM-FM, Harrisonburg, Va., 1966-68, 71-72, WBTX-FM, Broadway, Va., 1972; instr. English as 2d lang. Eastern Mennonite Coll., Harrisonburg, 1977-78, instr. English, 1979; teaching asst. English James Madison U., Harrisonburg, 1979-81; writer Psychiatric Insts. Am., Washington, 1981-84; founding ptnr. Community Scribes, Arlington, Va., 1984—; founding ptnr., mng. editor Womans Monthly, 1992—; co-founder, ptnr. Women's Monthly, Arlington, 1992—; artist Arts & Space, Inc., Arlington, 1995—. Co-author: Migraine: The Complete Guide, 1994; contbr. articles to profl. jours. Mem. Nat. Gay & Lesbian Journalist Assn., Washington, 1995—; artist Arts and Space, Inc., 1995—. Meth. Ch. Coll. scholar, 1958; Teaching fellow James Madison U., 1979, 80. Mem. NAFE, Nat. Gay & Lesbian Journalists Assn., Arlington C. of C., Arlington Arts Ctr. Democrat. Methodist. Office: Community Scribes 1001 N Highland St Arlington VA 22201-2142

SCOTT, TERRY LEE, communications company executive; b. Rockford, Ill., Oct. 21, 1950; s. Wilson C. and Marie G. (Bunger) S.; divorced; 1 child, Andrea; m. Jenny Scarborough, Aug. 1, 1981; children: Brady, Tiffany. BS in Acctg. magna cum laude, Bradley U., 1972. CPA, Ill., Tex. Audit prin. Arthur Young and Co., Dallas, 1972-82; v.p. fin. and adminstrn., treas. Paging Network Inc., Dallas, 1982-90; sr. v.p. Paging Network, Inc., Dallas, 1990-92, pres., CEO, bd. dirs., 1993-95; pres., CEO, bd. dirs. Flash Comm., Inc., 1995—. Mem. AICPA, Tex. Soc. CPAs, Phi Kappa Phi, Zeta Pi. Methodist. Home: 1704 Riviera Dr Plano TX 75093-2910 Office: Flash Comm Inc 8214 Westchester Ste 905 Dallas TX 75225

SCOTT, THEODORE R., lawyer; b. Mount Vernon, Ill., Dec. 7, 1924; s. Theodore R. and Beulah (Flannigan) S.; m. Virginia Scott, June 1, 1947; children: Anne Laurence, Sarah Buckland, Daniel, Barbara Gomon. AB, U. Ill., 1947, JD, 1949. Bar: Ill. 1950. Law clk. to judge U.S. Ct. Appeals, 1949-51; pvt. practice Chgo., 1950—; assoc. Spaulding Glass, 1951-53, Loftus, Lucas & Hammand, 1953-58, Ooms, McDougall, Williams & Hersh, 1958-60; ptnr. McDougall, Hersh & Scott, Chgo., 1960-87; of counsel Jones, Day, Reavis & Pogue, 1987—. 2nd lt. USAAF, 1943-45. Decorated Air medal. Fellow Am. Coll. Trial Lawyers; mem. ABA, Ill. Bar Assn., Chgo. Bar Assn., 7th Cir. Bar Assn. (past pres.), Legal Club Chgo., Law Club Chgo., Patent Law Assn. Chgo. (past pres.), Union League Club, Exmoor Country Club (Highland Park, Ill.), Phi Beta Kappa. Home: 1569 Woodvale Ave Deerfield IL 60015-2350 Office: Jones Day Reavis & Pogue 77 W Wacker Dr Chicago IL 60601-1692

SCOTT, THOMAS CLEVENGER, lawyer; b. Columbus, Ohio, May 16, 1936; s. Willard Baldwin and Elizabeth (Clevenger) S.; m. Nancy Jo Tiberi, Nov. 11, 1961; children: Amy J., Molly M. BA, Ohio State U., 1958, JD, 1961. Bar: Ohio 1961. Ptnr. McLeskey & McLeskey, Columbus, 1961-79, Loveland, Callard, Clapham & Scott, Columbus, 1979-80, Scott, Kuehnle, Grace & Mills (and predecessor firm Scott, Walker & Kuehnle), Columbus, 1980-86; ptnr. Thompson, Hine & Flory, Columbus, 1986—, ptnr. in charge, 1992—; adj. prof. Ohio State U., Columbus; mem. bd. advisors North Ctrl. Bankruptcy Inst. Capital U. Law Ctr., 1987-90, Midwest Regional Bankruptcy Seminar, 1990—; mem. standing local rules adv. com. U.S. Bankruptcy Ct., 1987—. Contbr. articles to profl. jours., outlines for confs. and seminars. Mem. ABA, Columbus Bar Assn. (chmn. bankruptcy com. 1986-88), Ohio State Bar Assn., Lawyers Club (pres.). Office: Thompson Hine & Flory PLL One Columbus 10 W Broad St Columbus OH 43215-3418

SCOTT, THOMAS JEFFERSON, JR., lawyer, electrical engineer; b. Montgomery, Ala., Dec. 30, 1943; s. Thomas Jefferson Sr. and Irene (Feagin) S.; m. Betsy Sue Mackta, Apr. 25, 1981; children: Elspeth Watts, Marghuerita Taylor, Thomas Jefferson III. BEE, Yale U., 1966, BA in Econs., 1967; JD, Vanderbilt U., 1974. Bar: Va. 1974, D.C. 1975, N.Y. 1980, U.S. Dist. Ct. D.C. 1986, U.S. Dist. Ct. (ea. dist.) Va. 1993, U.S. Tax Ct. 1981, U.S. Ct. Fed. Claims, 1982, U.S. Ct. Appeals (fed. cir.) 1982, U.S. Ct. Appeals (4th cir.) 1993, U.S. Supreme Ct. 1984. Trial atty. civil div. U.S. Dept. of Justice, Washington, 1974-78; assoc. Cooper & Dunham, N.Y.C., 1978-80, sr. trial counsel civil div., 1980-85; ptnr. Pennie & Edmonds, Washington, 1985-90, Howrey & Simon, Washington, 1990—. Capt. USNR, 1966-71. Decorared D.F.C. Mem. ABA, Am. Intellectual Property Law Assn. Office: Howrey & Simon 1299 Pennsylvania Ave NW Washington DC 20004-2400

SCOTT, THOMAS WRIGHT, jazz musician, composer; b. Los Angeles, May 19, 1948; s. Nathan George and Margery (Wright) S. Student, U. So. Calif., 1966-67. Vis. prof. music U. Utah, 1971, Westminster Coll., 1975; clinician Capitol U., Columbus, Ohio, 1973-77. Instrumentalist on saxes, woodwinds, lyricon; rec. artist, arranger and performer on numerous albums, including with: Paul McCartney, George Harrison, Ringo Starr, Barbra Streisand, Carole King, Rod Stewart, Aretha Franklin, Joni Mitchell (as leader of L.A. Express), Steely Dan, Blues Bros., Quincy Jones, Ravi Shankar; producer albums by Doc Severensen, Chevy Chase; composer background music for TV shows: Dan August, Cannon, Barnaby Jones, Streets of San Francisco, Baretta, theme music for TV show Starsky and Hutch; composer TV movies Trouble Comes to Town, 1973, The Girls of Huntington House, 1973, Firehouse, 1973, Class of '63, 1973, Twin Detectives, 1976, Aspen, 1977, The Company Comedy, 1978, Our Family Business, 1981, Family Ties Vacation, 1985, Badge of the Assassin, 1985, The Leftovers, 1986, Not Quite Human, 1987, A Father's Homecoming, 1988, Run Till You Fall, 1988; composer for films The Culpepper Cattle Co., 1972, Conquest of The Planet of The Apes, 1972, Uptown Saturday Night, 1974, The Nine Lives of Fritz the Cat, 1974, Sidecar Racers, 1975, Americathon, 1979, Stir Crazy, 1980, Hanky Panky, 1982, Class, 1983, Going Berserk, 1983, Hard to Hold, 1984, Fast Forward, 1985, The Sure Thing, 1985, Just One of the Guys, 1985, Soul Man, 1986; sound man for films (with Mark Berger, Randy Thorn, David MacMillan) The Right Stuff, 1983 (Acad. Sound award 1983), (with Mark Berger, Todd Boelelheide, Chris Newman) Amadeus, 1984 (Acad. Sound award). Mem. Am. Fedn. Musicians, Nat. Acad. Rec. Arts and Scis. (dir. Los Angeles chpt. 1971-72, Grammy award 1974, chpt. Most Valuable Player 1973, 74, 75, 77), Composers and Lyricists Guild Am. (exec. bd. 1972-73, 80-81).

SCOTT, TOM, musician. Albums include New York Connection, Tom Cat, Bluestreak. Recipient Grammy award for Best Large Jazz Ensemble Performance ("All Blues"), 1996. Office: GRP Records Inc 555 W 57th St New York NY 10019*

SCOTT, TOM KECK, biologist, educator; b. St. Louis, Aug. 4, 1931; s. George Drake and Mary Ann (Keck) S.; children: David Seymour, Stephen Arthur, John Warner, Cynthia Keck; m. Margaret Ray, Apr. 7, 1990. AB, Pomona Coll., Calif., 1954; MA, Stanford U., 1959, Ph.D., 1961. Rsch. prof. Princeton U., 1961-63; asst. prof., then assoc. prof. biology Oberlin Coll., Ohio, 1963-69; mem. faculty U. N.C., Chapel Hill, 1969—; prof. botany U. N.C., 1972-82, prof. biology, 1982—, chmn. biology curriculum, 1970-75, chmn. dept. botany, 1972-82, dir. rsch., 1985-90; sr. scientist div. life/biomed. scis. and applications NASA, 1994—; vis. rsch. prof. U. Nottingham, Eng., 1967-68; Fulbright sr. lectr. Ege U., Izmir, Turkey, 1972-73; chmn. space biology panel NASA, 1984-89, chmn. plant growth working group, 1989-93, cons. space sta. freedon, 1984-88. Author: Plant Regulation and World Agriculture, 1979, The Functions of Hormones from the Level of the Cell to the Whole Plant, 1984, Plant Gravitational and Space Research, 1984. Served with AUS, 1954-56. Danforth assoc., 1974; NATO grantee, 1978; Japanese Soc. for Promotion of Sci. fellow, 1985. Fellow AAAS; mem. Am. Inst. Biol. Scis., Am. Soc. Plant Physiologists (trustee 1979-88, chmn. 84-86), Bot. Soc. Am., NAS (com. on space biology and medicine 1986-92), Am. Soc. Gravitational and Space Biology (bd. govs. 1985-88), Internat. Plant Growth Substance Assn. (bd. govs. 1985-88), Sigma Xi. Achievements include research on characteristics of growth development and hormone translocation in higher plants and gravitational plant biology. Home: 800 E Rosemary St Chapel Hill NC 27514-3722 Office: U NC Dept Biology Coker Hall Clb # 3280 Chapel Hill NC 27599

SCOTT, TONY, film director; b. Newcastle, England, June 21, 1944; m. Donna Wilson. Degree in Fine Arts, Sunderland Art School; postgrad., Leeds Coll. Art, 1969; MFA, Royal Coll. Arts, 1972. Film dir., 1972—. Dir. films including One of the Mission (half-hour film, Brit. Film Inst.), Loving Memory (1-hour feature, Albert Finney), The Hunger, 1983, Top Gun, 1986, Beverly Hills Cop II, 1987, Revenge, 1990, Days of Thunder, 1990, The Last Boy Scout, 1991, True Romance, 1993, Crimson Tide, 1995; formerly dir. TV commls. Recipient numerous Clios, Gold and Silver Lions and various other awards. Office: Totem Prodns 8009 Santa Monica Blvd Los Angeles CA 90046-5008 also: CAA 9830 Wilshire Blvd Beverly Hills CA 90212-1804

SCOTT, W. PETER, bishop. Bishop London (Ont.) Synod United Ch. Can. Office: United Church of Canada, 359 Windermere Rd, London, ON Canada N6G 2K3

SCOTT, WALDRON, mission executive; b. Kansas City, Kans., July 14, 1929; s. Waldron and Audrean (Spurgeon) S.; m. Georgia Dyke; children by previous marriage—Melody, Cheryl, Gregory, Douglas, Linda. B.A., Am. U., Beirut, 1953. Dir. The Navigators, Washington, 1954-59, Middle East and Africa, 1960-66, Asia/Australia, 1967-72; internat. field dir. The Navigators, Colorado Springs, Colo., 1973-74; gen. sec. World Evang. Fellowship, Colorado Springs, 1975-80; pres. Am. Leprosy Missions, Elmwood Park, N.J., 1981-84, Holistic Ministries Internat., Paterson, N.J., 1985—; chair Holistic Ministries Internat., 1994—, Greater Paterson YMCA, 1995—; adj. prof. world mission Eastern Bapt. Sem., Phila., 1995—; bd. dirs. Passaic County Cultural and Heritage Coun., Paterson Habitat for Humanity, Christian Leadership in Higher Edn.; adv. coun. Passaic County Human Svcs., Paterson YMCA, Scheffelin Rsch. and Tng. Ctr., Ch. World Svc., Div. Overseas Ministries' Nat. Coun. Chs., Vellore Christian Med. Coll., Paterson Community Health Ctr., Jubilee Svc. Author: Karl Barth's Theology of Mission, 1978, The Paterson Paradigm; Bring Forth Justice, 1980; editor: Serving our Generation, 1980. Chmn. Greater Paterson YMCA, Paterson Coun. Social Svcs., Citizens Alliance for a Drug Free Paterson. Mem. Leadership Paterson Alumni Assn., Am. Soc. Missiology, Nat. Assn. Evangelicals, Evangelicals for Social Action. Mem. Christian Reformed Ch.

SCOTT, WALTER, JR., construction company executive; b. 1931. BS, Colo. State U., 1953. With Peter Kiewit Sons, Inc., Omaha, 1953—, mgr. Cleve. dist., 1962-64, v.p., 1964, exec. v.p., 1965-79, chmn. bd. dirs., pres., 1979—; also pres. Joslyn Art Mus., Omaha. Served with USAF, 1954-56. Office: Peter Kiewit Sons Inc 1000 Kiewit Plz Omaha NE 68131-3302 also: Joslyn Art Mus 2200 Dodge St Omaha NE 68102-1208*

SCOTT, WALTER COKE, retired sugar company executive, lawyer; b. Norfolk, Va., July 20, 1919; s. Walter Coke and Rosemary (White) S.; m. Virginia Kemper Millard, May 14, 1949; children: Mary Lyman (Mrs. K. Logan Jackson), Roberta (Mrs. Frederick Warth), Alexander McRae, Buford Coke. B.S., Hampden-Sydney Coll., 1939; J.D., U. Va., 1948. Bar: Va. 1947, Ga. 1954. Atty. U.S. Dept. Justice, Jacksonville, Fla., 1948; commerce atty. S.A.L. Ry., Norfolk, 1948-54; commerce counsel, gen. solicitor Central of Ga. Ry., Savannah, 1954-60; v.p. Cen. of Ga. Ry., (Norfolk Southern), 1960-62, dir., 1960-88; ptnr. law firm Hitch, Miller & Beckmann, Savannah, 1956-60; sr. v.p., sec. Savannah Foods & Industries, Inc. (formerly Savannah Sugar Refining Corp.), 1962-72, exec. v.p., mem. exec. com., 1972-87, also dir.; exec. v.p., sec. mem. exec. com., dir. Everglades Sugar Refinery, Inc., Clewiston, Fla., 1964-87; sec., mem. exec. com., dir. The Jim Dandy Co., Birmingham, Ala., 1968-81; bd. dirs. 1st Union Nat. Bank Savannah, Atlanta, 1975-91. Pres., chmn. exec. com. Historic Savannah Found., 1963-64; bd. dirs. United Community Services, 1965-68, pres., 1967; gen. chmn. United Community Appeal, 1966; mem. Chatham-Savannah Met. Planning Commn., 1963-68; trustee, chmn. finance com. Telfair Acad. Arts and Scis., 1964-67; trustee, vice chmn. Savannah Country Day Sch., 1967-69, chmn., 1970-72; Bd. dirs., chmn. finance com. Savannah Speech and Hearing Center, 1967-70; bd. dirs. Savannah Symphony Soc., Inc. Mem. Va. State Bar, Ga. State Bar, St. Andrews Soc., Savannah Benevolent Assn. (pres. 1990-92), Kappa Sigma, Omicron Delta Kappa, Phi Alpha Delta, Chi Beta Phi, Pi Delta Epsilon. Episcopalian. Clubs: Chatham, Oglethorpe, Savannah Golf; Farmington Country (Charlottesville, Va.). Home: 56 E 54th St Savannah GA 31405-3314

SCOTT, WALTER DILL, management educator; b. Chgo., Oct. 27, 1931; s. John Marcy and Mary Louise (Gent) S.; student Williams Coll., 1949-51; BS, Northwestern U., 1953; MS, Columbia, 1958; m. Barbara Ann Stein, Sept. 9, 1961; children: Timothy Walter, David Frederick, Gordon Charles. Cons. Booz, Allen & Hamilton, N.Y.C., 1956-58; assoc. Glore, Forgan & Co., N.Y.C., 1958-63, ptnr., Chgo., 1963-65; ptnr. Lehman Bros., Chgo., 1965-72, sr. ptnr., 1972-73, also bd. dirs.; assoc. dir. econs. and govt. Office Mgmt. and Budget, Washington, 1973-75; sr. v.p. internat. and fin. Pillsbury Co., Mpls., 1975-78, exec. v.p., 1978-80, also bd. dirs.; pres., chief exec. officer Investors Diversified Services, Inc., Mpls., 1980-84, group mng. dir. Grand Met. PLC, 1984-86, also bd. dirs.; chmn. Grand Met U.S.A., 1984-86; prof., sr. Austin fellow Kellogg Grad. Sch. Mgmt., Northwestern U., 1988—; bd. dirs. Kairos, Inc., Chgo. Title and Trust, Intermatic, Inc., Ill. Power Co., Illinova Corp, Orval Kent Food Co. Bd. dirs. Chgo. Cities in Schs., Internat. Urban Assocs., Leadership for Quality Edn. Lt. (j.g.) USN, 1953-56. Home: 55 Meadowview Dr Northfield IL 60093-3547 Office: Northwestern U J L Kellogg Grad Sch of Mgmt Leverone Hall Evanston IL 60208

SCOTT, WILLARD HERMAN, radio and television performer; b. Alexandria, Va., Mar. 7, 1934; s. Willard Herman and Thelma Matti (Phillips) S.; m. Mary Ellen Dwyer, Aug. 7, 1959; children: Mary Phillips, Sally W. B.A. in Philosophy and Religion, Am. U., 1955. With NBC, 1950—; formerly staff announcer children's TV shows Voice of NASA radio show; weather reporter, performer Today Show and NBC Radio, N.Y.C., 1980—; host Willard Scott's Home and Garden Almanac (Cable TV); free-lance comml. actor, narrator. Active March of Dimes, Easter Seals, ARC, Am. Cancer Soc., Nat. Symphony of Washington, Nat. Park Service, Alzheimer's Found. Served with USN, 1956-58. Episcopalian. Club: De Molay. Office: NBC Today Program 30 Rockefeller Plz # 304 New York NY 10112

SCOTT, WILLIAM BEVERLEY, ichthyologist; b. Toronto, Ont., Canada, July 7, 1917; s. William James and Elsie Irene (Lowry) S.; m. Mildred Grace Fairfield, July 11, 1942; children: Paul James, Patricia Louise. B.Sc., U. Toronto, 1942, Ph.D., 1950; D.Sc., U. N.B., 1985, Queens U., 1994. Curator ichthyology dept. Royal Ont. Mus., Toronto, Ont., Can., 1948-77; assoc. dir. Royal Ont. Mus., 1973-75; dir. Huntsman Marine Lab., St. Andrews, N.B., Can., 1976-82; sr. scientist Huntsman Marine Sci. Centre, 1982—; assoc. prof. to prof. dept. zoology U. Toronto, 1962-83, prof. emeritus, 1983—; bd. dirs. Ont. Council Comml. Fisheries, Port Dover, Ont., Can., 1954-76, Can. Nat. Sportsmen's Shows, Toronto, 1974-78; research assoc. Royal Ont. Mus., Toronto, 1977—; hon. curator Royal Ont. Mus., 1994, curator emeritus, 1994. Author: Freshwater Fishes of Eastern Canada, 1954 (rev. 1974), Fishes Atlantic Coast of Canada, 1966, Freshwater Fishes of Canada, 1973, Atlantic Fishes of Canada, 1988; contbr. articles to profl. jours. Bd. dirs. Met. Toronto Zool. Soc., Can., 1970-75; bd. trustees Can. Nat. Sportsmen's Fund, 1977-85, Sunbury Shores Arts and Nature Ctr., St. Andrews (N.B., Can.), 1965-81, Ross Meml. Mus., 1979-94. Served to capt. Can. Army, 1942-45, PTO. Recipient Can. Centennial medal, 1967; recipient Can. Silver Jubilee medal, 1979. Fellow Royal Soc. Can.; mem. Toronto Sportsmens Assn. (life, bd. dirs. 1955-70); pres. Am. Soc. Ichthyologists and Herpetologists (1972), Can. Soc. Zoologists (hon. life mem., assoc. editor 1973-77), Am. Fisheries Soc. (Award of Excellence 1986), Internat. Game Fish Assn., Am. Inst. Fishery Rsch. Biologists, Nova Scotia Inst. Sci. Anglican. Home: PO Box 369, Brandy Cove Rd, Saint Andrews, NB Canada E0G 2X0

SCOTT, WILLIAM CLEMENT, III, entertainment industry executive; b. N.Y.C., Apr. 25, 1934; s. William Clement and Susan L. (Cameron) S.; m. Cindy L. Taylor, Dec. 5, 1981; children by previous marriage: Katherine Louise, David Campbell. A.B., Coll. William and Mary, Williamsburg, Va., 1956. Self-employed, 1956-64; v.p. Booz-Allen & Hamilton, N.Y.C., 1964-69; group v.p. Cordura Corp., Los Angeles, 1969-72; exec. v.p. Western Pacific Industries, N.Y.C., 1972-76; pres., chief operating officer Western Pacific Industries, 1976-87; pvt. investor N.Y.C., 1987-88; chmn., pres., chief exec. officer Panavision Internat. L.P., Lee Internat., Inc., N.Y.C., 1988—. Bd. dirs., pres. Opera Orch. of N.Y. Republican. Episcopalian. Clubs: Racquet and Tennis, Met. Opera (N.Y.C.); Hay Harbor; Fishers Island Country; Coral Beach (Bermuda). Office: Panavision Internat LP 140 E 45th St New York NY 10017-3144

SCOTT, WILLIAM CORYELL, medical executive; b. Sterling, Colo., Nov. 22, 1920; s. James Franklin and Edna Ann (Schillig) S.; m. Jean Marie English, Dec. 23, 1944 (div. 1975); children: Kathryn, James, Margaret; m. Carolyn Florence Hill, June 21, 1975; children: Scott, Amy Jo, Robert. AB, Dartmouth Coll., 1942; MD, U. Colo., 1944, MS in OB/GYN, 1951. Cert. Am. Bd. Ob-Gyn., 1956, 79, Am. Bd. Med. Mgmt., 1991. Intern USN Hosp., Great Lakes, Ill., 1945-46, Denver Gen. Hosp., 1946-47; resident Ob-Gyn St. Joseph's Hosp., Colo. Gen. Hosp., Denver, 1946-51; practice medicine specializing in Ob-Gyn Tucson, 1951-71; assoc. prof. emeritus U. Ariz. Med. Sch., Tucson, 1971-94, 1994; v.p. med. affairs U. Med. Ctr., Tucson, 1984-94. Contbr. articles to med. jours. and chpt. to book. Pres. United Way, Tucson, 1979-80, HSA of Southeastern Ariz., Tucson, 1985-87; chmn. Ariz. Health Facilities Authority, Phoenix, 1974-83. Served to capt. USNR, 1956-58. Recipient Man of Yr. award, Tucson, 1975. Fellow ACS, Am. Coll. Ob-Gyn, Pacific Coast Ob-Gyn Soc., Ctrl. Assn. of Ob-Gyn; mem. AMA (coun. on sci. affairs 1984-93, chmn. 1989-91), Am. Coll. Physician Execs., Am. Coll. Health Care Execs., Ariz. Med. Assn., La Paloma Country Club. Republican. Episcopalian. Avocations: golf, gardening, photography. Home: PO Box 805 Sonoita AZ 85637-0805

SCOTT, WILLIAM FRED, cultural organization administrator; b. Thomasville, Ga., 1953. B cum laude, Sch. Fgn. Svc., Georgetown U., 1974. Formerly assoc. condr., artistic adminstr. Opera Co. of Boston; artistic dir. The Atlanta Opera, 1985—; prin. condr. Opera New England; asst. condr. Atlanta Symphony Orch., 1981—, assoc. condr., 1987—; guest condr. various orgns. including Opera Co. of Boston, Wolf Trap Opera Co., N.Y.C. Opera at Lincoln Ctr., Boston Pro Arte Chamber Orch.; conducted opera workshop in Tel Aviv at request of Israeli Govt., 1983. Operatic debut as condr. Opera Company of Boston, 1975. Office: Atlanta Opera 1800 Peachtree St NW Ste 620 Atlanta GA 30309-2507*

SCOTT, WILLIAM HERBERT, state agency administrator; b. Estancia, N.Mex., Mar. 19, 1925; s. Chester Ray and Elizabeth Bryan (McNama) S.; m. Maryann Mavis Munro, Dec. 26, 1952 (div. 1980); children: Jean Ann, Megan Lynne; m. Dorothy Caroline Caster, Apr. 16, 1980. BS in Civil Engring., U. N.Mex., 1949, BBA in Acctg., 1949. CPA, Alaska. Field engr., office mgr. Kincaid & King Constrn., Anchorage, 1949-50; office mgr. M-B Contracting Co., Inc., Anchorage, 1951-52; staff acct. R.L. Rettig, CPA, Anchorage, 1952-54; ptnr. Rettig, Scott & Co., CPAs, Anchorage, 1955-60; mng. ptnr. Scott, McMahon & Co., CPAs, Anchorage, 1960-61, Peat, Marwick Mitchell & Co., Anchorage, 1961-83; cons., 1983-91; exec. dir. Alaska Indsl. Devel., Anchorage, 1991-92, Alaska Permanent Fund Corp., Juneau, 1992-94; sec. Alaska Bd. Pub. Accountancy, 1963-65. Mem. Com. on Operation U.S. Senate, Washington, 1976; honorary consul Denmark, Anchorage, 1963-88. Lt. j.g. USNR, 1942-46, PTO. Named Knight of Dannebrog Queen of Denmark, 1973, 83. Mem. Am. Arbitration Assn. (panel 1984—), Alaska Soc. CPAs (pres., founder 1961-62), AICPA (coun. 1961-62), Anchorage C. of C. (pres. 1966), Alaska State C. of C. (pres. 1968), Alaskan Air Command Civilian Affairs, Sigma Chi. Avocations: tennis, alpine skiing.

SCOTT, WILLIAM PAUL, lawyer; b. Staples, Minn., Nov. 8, 1928; A.L.A., U. Minn., 1949; B.S.L., St. Paul Coll. Law, 1952, J.D., 1954; m. Elsie Elaine Anderson, Feb. 7, 1968; 1 son, Jason Lee; children: William P., Mark D., Bryan D., Scott; stepchildren: Thomas J. (dec.), Terri L. Weeding-Berg. Bar: Minn. 1954. Atty. right of way div. Minn. Hwy. Dept., 1945-52, civil engr. traffic and safety div., 1953-55; practice law Arlington, Minn., 1955-61, Gaylord, Minn., 1963-67; sr. partner firm Scott Law Offices and predecessors, Pipestone, Minn., 1967—; probate, juvenile judge Sibley County, Minn., 1956-61; Minn. pub. examiner, 1961-63; county atty. Sibley County, 1963-68, city atty., Pipestone, 1978—. Formerly nat. committeeman Young Rep. League; Sibley County Rep. chmn., 1961. Served with USMCR, 1946-50; from 2d lt. to lt. col. USAF Res., 1950-77; ret. Recipient George Washington Honor medal Freedoms Found., 1970, 72. Mem. Minn. Bar Assn., TROA, Mensa, V.F.W., DAV, Am. Legion, Res. Officers Assn. Home: PO Box 704 Pipestone MN 56164-0704 Office: Park Plz Offices Pipestone MN 56164

SCOTT, WILLIAM PROCTOR, III, lawyer; b. Berkeley, Calif., Dec. 1, 1946; s. William Proctor Jr. and Marcia (Wood) S.; m. Helen Elizabeth Hiller, June 16, 1968; children: William Proctor IV, Jennifer Anne. BS, MIT, 1968; JD cum laude, U. Pa., 1975. Assoc. Ballard, Spahr, Andrews & Ingersoll, Phila., 1975-82, ptnr., 1982—; regional chmn. MIT Ednl. Coun., 1988—. Lt. (j.g.) USNR, 1969-72. Mem. ABA, Pa. Bar Assn., Phila. Bar Assn., MIT Club of Delaware Valley (mem. exec. com. 1991—). Office: Ballard Spahr Andrews & Ingersoll 1735 Market St Philadelphia PA 19103-7501

SCOTT, W(ILLIAM) RICHARD, sociology educator; b. Parsons, Kan., Dec. 18, 1932; s. Charles Hogue and Hildegarde (Hewit) S.; m. Joy Lee Whitney, Aug. 14, 1955; children: Jennifer Ann, Elliot Whitney, Sydney Brooke. AA, Parsons Jr. Coll., 1952; AB, U. Kans., 1954, MA, 1955; PhD, U. Chgo., 1961. Asst. prof. to assoc. prof. sociology Stanford (Calif.) U., 1960-69, prof., 1969—, chair dept. sociology, 1972-75; courtesy prof. Sch. Medicine, Stanford U., 1972—, Sch. Edn., Grad. Sch. Bus., 1977—; fellow Ctr. for Advanced Study in Behavioral Scis., 1989-90; dir. Orgns. Rsch. Tng. Program, Stanford U., 1972-89, Ctr. for Orgns. Rsch., 1988—; mem. adv. panel Sociology Program NSF, Washington, 1982-84; mem. epidemiol. and svc. rsch. rev. panel NIMH, Washington, 1984-88; mem. Commn. on Behavioral and Social Scis. and Edn., NAS, 1990—. Author: (with O.D. Duncan et al) Metropolis and Region, 1960, (with P.M. Blau) Formal Organizations, 1962, Social Processes and Social Structures, 1970, (with S.M. Dornbusch) Evaluation and the Exercise of Authority, 1975, Organizations: Rational, Natural and Open Systems, 1981, rev. edit., 1992, (with J.W. Meyer) Organizational Environments: Ritual and Rationality, 1983, edit., 1992, (with A.B. Flood) Hospital Structure and Performance, 1987, (with J.W. Meyer), Institutional Environments and Organizations: Structural Complexity and Individualism, 1994, Institutions and Organizations, 1995, (with S. Christinsen) The Institutional Construction of Organization, 1995; editor Ann. Rev. of Sociology, 1986-91. Fellow Woodrow Wilson, 1954-55; mem. Nat. Commn. Nursing, 1980-83; chair Consortium Orgns. Rsch. Ctrs., 1989-91; elder First Presby. Ch., Palo Alto, Calif., 1977-80, 83-86. Social Sci. Research Council fellow, U. Chgo., 1959; named Edmund P. Learned Disting. Prof., Sch. Bus. Adminstrn., U. Kans, 1970-71; recipient Cardinal Citation for Disting. Service, Labette Commmunity Coll, Parsons, 1981, Disting. Scholar award Mgmt. and Orgn. Theory div. Acad. Mgmt., 1988. Mem. Inst. Medicine, Am. Sociol. Assn. (chmn. sect. on orgns. 1970-71, mem. coun. 1989-92), Acad. Mgmt., Sociol. Rsch. Assn., Macro-Organizational Behavior Soc., Phi Beta Kappa. Democrat. Presbyterian. Home: 940

Lathrop Pl Stanford CA 94305-1060 Office: Stanford U Dept Sociology Bldg 120 Stanford CA 94305

SCOTTI, JAMES VERNON, astronomer; b. Bandon, Oreg., Aug. 22, 1960; s. Paul Carl and Elizabeth Louise (Garoutte) S.; m. Karriaunna K.-R. Harlan, May 15, 1983; children: Jennifer Anne, Christopher James. BS, U. Ariz., 1983. Planetarium asst. Flandrau Planetarium, Tucson, 1979-82; student rsch. asst. Lunar and Planetary Lab., Tucson, 1982-83, rsch. asst., 1983-93, sr. rsch. specialist, 1993—. Mem. Am. Astron. Soc. (assoc.), Div. for Planetary Scis., Assn. Lunar and Planetary Observers (asst. comets recorder). Achievements include being a leading observer of faint comets, being heavily involved in observing comet P/Shoemaker-Levy 9 before and during its impact on Jupiter in July 1994. Office: U Ariz Lunar and Planetary Lab Tucson AZ 85721

SCOTTI, MICHAEL JOHN, JR., medical association executive; b. N.Y.C., Oct. 30, 1938; s. Michael John and Florence (Ellis) S.; m. Susan Faye Suit, Aug. 25, 1961; children: Michael John III, Pamela Anne, Jennifer Beth. BS, Fordham Coll., 1960; MD, Georgetown U., 1965; postgrad., Indsl. Coll., Washington, 1982-83. Diplomate Am. Bd. Internal Medicine, Am. Bd. Family Practice; CAQ Geriat. Commd. 2d lt. U.S. Army, 1963, advanced through grades to maj. gen., 1990; dir. residency program Dept. Family Practice, Ft. Gordon, Ga., 1976-79; family practice cons. Surgeon Gen., Washington, 1979-80; dir. Grad. Med. Edn. U.S. Army, Washington, 1980-82; comdr. army hosp. Ft. Polk, La., 1983-86; dir. quality assurance Army Med. Dept., Washington, 1986-88; dir. profl. svcs. Army Med. Dept., 1988-90; comdg. gen. European 7th Med. Comd, Heidelberg, Fed. Republic Germany, 1990-95; ret. maj. gen., 1995; v.p. AMA, Chgo., 1996—; assoc. prof. Georgetown U. Sch. Medicine, 1986; chmn. Def. Med. Standardization, Ft. Detrick, Md., 1988-90; prof. Uniformed Svcs. U., Bethesda, Md., 1990. Health cons. Nat. PTA, Chgo., 1976-79. Named Person of Yr. Phi Delta Kappa, 1976. Fellow Am. Acad. Family Physicians (vice speaker 1988-90, speaker, bd. dirs. 1990-92), ACP; mem. AMA, Acad. Medicine. Office: AMA 515 N State St Chicago IL 60610

SCOTT MORTON, MICHAEL STEWART, business management educator; b. Mukden, Manchuria, Peoples Republic of China, Aug. 25, 1937; came to U.S., 1958; s. William and Alice (Gleysteen) S.M.; m. Mary Louise Mansell, June 20, 1964; children: Fiona Margaret, Lesley Elizabeth. Student, Glasgow U., Scotland, 1957-58; BS, Carnegie Mellon, 1961; DBA, Harvard U., 1967. Asst. prof. Sloan Sch. MIT, Cambridge, 1966-69, assoc. prof., 1969-75, Jay W. Forrester prof. mgmt., 1989—; bd. dirs. Sequent Computer Sys.; trustee Met. Life-State St. Author: Decision Support System, 1978, Strategic Control, 1986, Management in the 1990s, 1991, Information Technology and the Corporation, 1994; contbr. articles to profl. jours. Mem. Assn. for Computing Machinery, Inst. Mgmt. Sci., Handel and Haydn Soc. (gov.), Fidelco Guide Dog Found. (dir.), Somerset Club, Harvard Club (Boston). Avocations: sailing, walking. Home: 31 Somerset Rd Lexington MA 02173-3519 also: Ledgrianach, Appin, Argyll Scotland Office: MIT Sloan Sch Mgmt 50 Memorial Dr Cambridge MA 02142-1347

SCOTTO, RENATA, soprano; b. Savona, Italy, Feb. 24, 1935; m. Lorenzo Anselmi. Studied under, Ghirardini, Merlino and Mercedes Llopart, Accademia Musicale Savonese, Conservatory Giuseppe Verdi, Milan. Debut in La Traviata, Teatro Nuevo, Milan, 1954; then joined La Scala Opera Co.; appeared with Met. Opera, N.Y.C., 1965, Convent Garden, Hamburg (Fed. Republic of Germany) State Opera, Vienna (Austria) State Opera, Nat. Theatre Munich, San Francisco Opera, Chgo. Lyric Opera, 1988; roles include: Ballo in Maschera, La Sonnambula, I Puritani, L'Elisir d'amore, Lucia di Lammermoor, La Boheme, Turandot, Otello (Verdi), Trovatore, Le Prophete, Madama Butterfly, Adriana Lecouvreur, Norma, Tosca, Manon Lescaut, Rosenkavalier (Marschallin), La Voix Humaine, Pirata; dir. Madama Butterfly, N.Y. Met. Opera, 1986; recordings include Christmas at St. Patrick's Cathedral, French Arias with Charles Rosekrans, Live in Paris with Ivan Davis, Great Operatic Scenes with Jose Carreras. Office: care Robert Lombardo Assocs One Harkness Plaza 61 W 62d St Ste 6F New York NY 10023 also: care Il Teatro la Scala, via Filodrammatici 2, Milan Italy

SCOULAR, ROBERT FRANK, lawyer; b. Del Norte, Colo., July 9, 1942; s. Duane William and Marie Josephine (Moloney) S.; m. Donna V. Scoular, June 3, 1967; children—Bryan T., Sean D., Bradley R. B.S. in Aero. Engring., St. Louis U., 1964, J.D., 1968. Bar: Mo. 1968, Colo. 1968, N.D. 1968, U.S. Supreme Ct. 1972, Calif. 1979. Law clk. to chief judge U.S. Ct. Appeals (8th cir.), 1968-69; ptnr. Bryan, Cave, McPheeters & McRoberts, St. Louis, 1969-89; mng. ptnr. Bryan, Cave, McPheeters & McRoberts, Los Angeles, 1979-84, exec. com., 1984-85, sect. leader tech., computer and intellectual property law, 1985-89; ptnr. Sonnenschein, Nath, Rosenthal, Chgo., 1990—; mng. ptnr. Sonnenschein, Nath, Rosenthal, L.A., 1990—, mem. policy and planning com., 1995—; co-leader intellectual property practice, dir. Mo. Lawyers Credit Union, 1978-79. Contbr. articles to profl. jours. Bd. dirs. St. Louis Bar Found., 1975-76, 79; Eagle Scout, bd. dirs. L.A. Area Coun. Boy Scouts Am.; league commr. Am. Youth Soccer Orgn.; mem. alumni council St. Louis U., 1979-82. Mem. ABA (nat. dir. young lawyers div. 1977-78), Am. Judicature Soc., Bar Assn. Met. St. Louis (v.p. 1978-79, sec. 1979, chmn. young lawyers sect. 1975-76), Los Angeles County Bar Assn., Assn. Bus. Trial Lawyers, Calif. Bar. Assn., Mo. Bar (chmn. young lawyers sect. 1976-77, disting. svc. award), Computer Law Assn., Fed. Bar Assn. Home: 1505 Lower Paseo La Cresta Palos Verdes Estates CA 90274 Office: Sonnenschein Nath & Rosenthal 601 S Figueroa St Ste 1500 Los Angeles CA 90017-5720

SCOUTEN, WILLIAM HENRY, chemistry educator, academic administrator; b. Corning, N.Y., Feb. 12, 1942; s. Henry and M. Anna (Kimble) S.; m. Nancy Jane Coombs, July 16, 1965; children: Lisa, Linda, Michael, William Jr., Thomas, David. BA, Houghton Coll., 1964; PhD, U. Pitts., 1969. NIH postdoctoral fellow SUNY, Stony Brook, 1969-71; asst. prof. Bucknell U., Lewisburg, Pa., 1971-77; assoc. prof. Bucknell U., Lewisburg, 1977-83, prof., 1983-84; prof., chmn. dept. chemistry Baylor U., Waco, Tex., 1984-93; dir. biotech. ctr. Utah State U., Logan, 1993—; vis. scientist for minority inst. Fed. Am. Soc. Exptl. Biology, Washington. Author: Affinity Chromatography, 1981; editor: Solid Phase Biochem., 1983; assoc. editor Internat. Jour. Bio-Chromatography, 1994—; mem. editl. bd. Bioconjugate Chemistry, 1994—, Jour. Molecular Recognition, 1994—, Bioseparation, 1995. Fulbright fellow, 1976; Dreyfus Tchr. scholar, Dreyfus Found., 1976; NSF Sci. Devel. NSF, 1978; Lindbach Disting. Tchr. Bucknell U., 1975. Mem. Am. Soc. Biol. Chemists, Am. Chem. Soc., Internat. Soc. for Bioercognition Tech., Internat. Soc. for Molecular Recognition (pres. 1990-93), Assn. for Internat. Practical Tng. (bd. dirs. 1991—). Republican. Baptist. Office: Biotechnology Ctr Utah State U Logan UT 84322

SCOVIL, LARRY EMERY, minister; b. Conneaut, Ohio, Dec. 1, 1950; s. Lynn Edgar and Shirley Jean (Cook) S.; m. Kristine Adell Schulz, Dec. 19, 1970; children: Jennifer, Jarin, Lindsay. B. Music Edn., U. Wis., Oshkosh, 1972; MDiv, Bethel Theol. Sem., 1987. Ordained to ministry Conservative Congl. Christian Conv., 1976. Pastor Zoar Congl. Ch., Mott, N.D., 1975-81, Calvary Evang. Congl. Ch., St. Paul, 1981-86, Emmanuel Congl. Ch., Scottsbluff, Nebr., 1986—; bd. dirs. Conservative Congl. Christian Conf., St. Paul, 1988-91, rec. sec., 1991—, Rocky Mountain area rep., 1989—. Writer, arranger musical: Joy to the World, 1990, Christmas Carol, 1992, Little Town of Bethlehem, 1995. Mem. Panhandle Evang. Ministerial Assn. (pres. 1990-92). Republican. Office: Emmanuel Congl Ch 317 W 40th St Scottsbluff NE 69361-4634

SCOVIL, ROGER MORRIS, engineering company executive; b. Greenville, S.C., Apr. 23, 1929; s. Roger Peniston and Sophia Rose (Herbert) S.; m. Mary Earle Nock; children: Randolph, Frances, Elizabeth. Student, Davidson Coll., 1946-48; BS in Civil Engring., N.C. State U., 1951. Registered profl. engr., Ga., S.C., P.R. Project mgr. McKoy-Helgerson Co., Greenville, 1953-63; v.p., maintenance div. mgr. Daniel Constrn. Co., Greenville, 1963-66; v.p., Caribbean div. mgr. Daniel Internat. Corp., San Juan, P.R., 1966-74; v.p. Europe and Middle East Daniel Internat. Corp., Brussels and Jeddah, Saudi Arabia, 1974-79; v.p. internat. mkgt. Daniel Constrn. Co., Greenville, 1980; pres. Polysius Corp., Atlanta, 1981-88; sr. v.p., dir. Lockwood Greene Systems Corp., Atlanta, 1988—; sr. v.p., dir. Lockwood Greene Internat., Atlanta, 1991-95, pres., 1995—; mem. operating bd. Lockwood Greene Engrs., Inc., 1995—; bd. dirs. GLG Ingenieria Internacional, Mex.; chmn. bd. dirs. Alternica Lockwood Greene, Argentina. Capt. U.S. Army, 1951-53. Mem. Atlanta World trade Ctr. (bd. dirs.), Internat. Club Atlanta, Tau Beta Pi, Chi Epsilon. Episcopalian. Home: 6025 Riverwood Dr Atlanta GA 30328-3732 Office: Lockwood Greene Engrs 250 Williams St NW Ste 4000 Atlanta GA 30303-1032

SCOVIL, SAMUEL KINGSTON, mining company executive; b. Cleve., June 15, 1923; s. R. Malcolm and Dorothy Lee (Brown) S.; m. Barbara C. Baker, May 22, 1944; children—Emily, Malcolm (dec.), Samuel, Alexander. B.S., Yale U., 1945; grad., Advanced Mgmt. Program, Harvard, 1962. With Republic Steel Corp., 1947-50; with Cleveland Cliffs Inc., 1950—, mgr. sales, 1960-63, v.p. sales, 1963-69, sr. v.p. sales, 1970-72, sr. v.p., 1972-74, pres., 1974-83, chief exec. officer, 1976—, chmn. bd., 1983—, chmn. exec. com. of bd. dirs., 1988—; bd. dirs. Cleve.-Cliffs, Inc., Holnam Inc. Trustee Univ. Sch., Cleve., Cleve. Clinic Found. Office: Cleve-Cliffs Inc 1100 Superior Ave E Cleveland OH 44114-2518

SCOVILLE, JAMES GRIFFIN, economics educator; b. Amarillo, Tex., Mar. 19, 1940; s. Orlin James and Carol Howe (Griffin) S.; m. Judith Ann Nelson, June 11, 1962; 1 child, Nathan James. B.A., Oberlin Coll., 1961; M.A., Harvard U., 1963, Ph.D., 1965. Economist ILO, Geneva, 1965-66; instr. econs. Harvard U., Cambridge, Mass., 1964-65; asst. prof. Harvard U., 1966-69; assoc. prof. econs. and labor and indsl. relations U. Ill.-Urbana, 1969-75, prof., 1975-80; prof. indsl. rels. Indsl. Rels. Ctr., U. Minn., Mpls., 1979—, dir., 1979-82, dir. grad. studies, 1990—; cons. ILO, World Bank, U.S. Dept. Labor, Orgn. for Econ. Cooperation and Devel., AID; labor-mgmt. arbitrator. Author: The Job Content of the US Economy, 1940-70, 1969, Perspectives on Poverty and Income Distribution, 1971, Manpower and Occupational Analysis: Concepts and Measurements, 1972, (with A. Sturmthal) The International Labor Movement in Transition, 1973, Status Influences in 3rd World Labor Markets, 1991. Mem. Am. Econ. Assn., Indsl. Rels. Rsch. Assn., Internat. Indsl. Rels. Assn. Home: 4849 Girard Ave S Minneapolis MN 55409-2214 Office: U Minn Ind Rels Ctr 271 19th Ave S Minneapolis MN 55455-0430

SCOWCROFT, BRENT, retired air force officer, government official; b. Ogden, Utah, Mar. 19, 1925; s. James and Lucile (Ballantyne) S.; m. Marian Horner, Sept. 17, 1951 (dec. 1995); 1 dau., Karen. B.S., U.S. Mil. Acad., 1947; M.A., Columbia U., 1953, Ph.D., 1967; postgrad., Georgetown U., 1958. Commd. 2d lt. USAF, 1947, advanced through grades to lt. gen., 1974; asst. prof. dept. social sci. U.S. Mil. Acad., 1953-57; asst. air attache Am. Embassy, Belgrade, Yugoslavia, 1959-61; assoc. prof. dept. polit. sci. U.S. Air Force Acad., Colo., 1962-63; prof., head dept. U.S. Air Force Acad., 1963-64; mem. staff long range planning div. Office Dep. Chief Staff Plans and Ops., Washington, 1964-67; assigned Nat. War Coll., 1967-68; staff asst. Western Hemisphere region Office Asst. Sec. Def. Internat. Security Affairs, Washington, 1968-69; dep. asst. dir. plans for nat. security matters office Dep. Chief Staff Plans and Ops., 1969-70; spl. asst. to dir. Joint Staff, Joint Chiefs of Staff, 1970-71; mil. asst. to Pres., 1972-73, dep. asst. to Pres. for nat. security affairs, 1973-75, asst. to Pres. for nat. security affairs, 1975-77; mem. Pres.'s Gen. Adv. Com. on Arms Control, 1977-80; vice chmn. Kissinger Assocs., Inc., 1982-89; asst. to Pres. Nat. Security Coun., Washington, 1989-93; pres. Forum for Internat. Policy, Washington, 1993—; bd. dirs. Nat. Bank of Washington; chmn. Pres.' Commn. on Strategic Forces; mem. Pres.' Commn. on Def. Mgmt., Pres. Spl. Rev. Bd. on the Iran/Contra Affair; pres. The Scowcroft Group, 1994—. Bd. dirs. Atlantic Council U.S.; Bd. visitors U.S. Air Force Air U., 1977-79; mem. adv. bd. Georgetown Center for Strategic and Internat. Studies. Decorated D.S.M. with two oak leaf clusters, Legion of Merit with oak leaf cluster, Air Force Commendation medal, D.S.M. Dept. Def., Nat. Security medal; recipient Medal of Freedom, 1991; named Hon. Knight Brit. Empire, 1993. Mem. Council Fgn. Relations (bd. dirs.), UN Assn. U.S. (vice chmn.), Am. Polit. Sci. Assn., Acad. Polit. Sci. Mem. Ch. Jesus Christ of Latter-day Saints. Office: 1750 K St NW Ste 800 Washington DC 20006-2305

SCOZZIE, JAMES ANTHONY, chemist; b. Erie, Pa., Nov. 3, 1943. AB, Gannon Coll., 1965; MS, Case Western Res. U., 1968, PhD in Chemistry, 1970. Jr. rsch. chemist ctrl. rsch. dept. Lord Corp., 1965; rsch. chemist Diamond Shamrock Corp., 1970-72, sr. rsch. chemist, 1972-76, rsch. supr. pharmaceutics, 1976-78, group leader agrl. chemistry, 1978-81, assoc. dir. agrl. chemistry rsch., 1981-83; dir. agrl. chemistry rsch. SDS Biotech Corp., 1983-85, dir. corp. rsch., 1985—; pres. Ricerca, Inc., Painesville, Ohio, 1986—. Chmn. bd. trustees State of Ohio Edison Biotechnology Ctr.; bd. governance Edison Biotechnology Inst. Mem. Am. Chem. Soc. Achievements include research in structure and chemistry of peptide antibiotics, synthesis of biologically active compounds, pesticides, process studies of organic compounds, commercial evaluation, nutrition and animal health, herbicides, plant growth regulants, cardiovascular agents and anti-inflammatory agents. Office: Ricerca Inc PO Box 1000 7528 Auburn Rd Painesville OH 44077

SCRABECK, JON GILMEN, dental educator; b. Rochester, Minn., Dec. 6, 1938; s. Clarence and Nancy Alma (Brown) S.; m. DeAnn Louise Jacks, June 16, 1962; children: Joan Louise, Erik Jon. Student, Contra Costa Coll., San Pablo, Calif., 1964-66, U. Calif., Berkeley, 1966-67; DDS, UCLA, 1971; MA in Edn., U. Colo., 1985. Pvt. practice, Santa Rosa, Calif., 1971-78; sr. instr. U. Colo. Sch. Dentistry, Denver, 1978-79, asst. prof., 1980-86, dir. patient care, 1979-80, acting dir. clin. affairs, 1980-81; acting assoc. dean U. Colo. Sch. Dentistry, Denver, 1983-84; acting div. chmn. U. Colo. Sch. Dentistry, Denver, 1984-85; dept. chmn. Marquette U. Sch. Dentistry, Milw., 1986-90, assoc. prof., 1986—, assoc. prof. tenure, 1989, curricular head, 1990—; cons. Dental Student mag.,1983-86, Colo. Bd. Dentistry, Denver, 1985-86, Dentist mag., 1986-90, VA, Milw., 1987-90. Editor Jour. Colo. Dental Assn., 1980-86; contbr. articles and abstracts to dental jours. mem. vol. staff Morey Dental Clinic, Denver, 1982-85, Health Fair, Denver, 1983-85; ofcl. judge S.E. Wis. Sci. Fair, Milw., 1988—. Fellow Internat. Coll. Dentists, Acad. Dental Materials, Am. Coll. Dentists, Pierre Fauchard Acad.; mem. ADA (coun. on journalism 1984-86, coun. on dental rsch. 1986-88, manuscript reviewer 1988—), Acad. Operative Dentistry, Wis. Dental Assn. (assoc. editor Jour. 1987—), Omicron Kappa Upsilon, Alpha Gamma Sigma. Roman Catholic. Avocations: foreign and domestic travel, photography, boating, fishing, water skiing. Home: W349s10140 Bittersweet Ct Eagle WI 53119-1851 Office: Marquette U Sch Dentistry 604 N 16th St Milwaukee WI 53233-2117

SCRANTON, WILLIAM MAXWELL, manufacturing company executive, consultant; b. Scranton, Pa., Mar. 1, 1921; s. William Henry and Dorothy (Bessell) S.; m. Andrea Orne Abbott, Sept. 24, 1949 (dec. Oct. 1991); children: John Selden and Nancy Orne (Mrs. Don J. Sporborg) (twins), James Maxwell, Sarah Abbott. BS in Engring, Princeton U., 1942; MBA, Harvard U., 1948. With Pratt & Whitney Aircraft div. United Aircraft Crop., East Hartford, Conn., 1942-46, 48-50, MPB Corp., Keene, N.H., 1950-77; exec. v.p. MPB Corp., 1953-62, pres., 1962-77, dir., 1959-76; pres., dir. Beede Elec. Instrument Co. Inc., 1977-82; cons., 1983—; mem. adv. bd. Kearsarge Ventures, LP, Manchester, N.H.; dir. Summa Four, Inc.

SCRIBNER, BARBARA COLVIN, museum administrator; b. Bangor, Maine, Dec. 18, 1926; d. Howard Morton and May Josephine (Tierney) Colvin; m. Harold B. Scribner, Mar. 10, 1956 (dec. June, 1982); 1 child, Scott Colvin. Student Pratt Inst., 1945-46. Assoc. editor McCall's Mag., N.Y.C., 1950-59; assoc. editor Am. Home, N.Y.C., 1960-64, contbg. editor, 1964-67; free-lance writer-editor, N.Y.C., 1968-77; dir. pub. info. Stamford Mus. and Nature Ctr., Conn., 1978—, curator Going to Blazes exhbn., 1988-89, Music Mania exhbn., 1988-89, Antique Toy Banks exhbn., 1990-91, Antique Bottles exhbn., 1992-93, Toy Bldg. Sets Exhbn., 1994—, Bendel Estate Exhibit, 1994—, Puzzling Challenges Exhibit, 1996—; mem. attractions com. State of Conn., 1982—. Mem. product com. New Eng. U.S.A. Found., 1989-90; American Trail, 1990, Tourism Network Conn., 1992—; exec. bd. Council Darien Sch. Parents, Conn., 1974-82, Episcopal Ch. Women, Darien, 1970-78, Darien High Sch. Parents Assn., 1980-82. Republican. Lodge: Order Eastern Star. Home: 40 Maple St Darien CT 06820-5209 Office: Stamford Mus & Nature Ctr 39 Scofieldtown Rd Stamford CT 06903-4023

SCRIBNER, CHARLES, III, publisher, art historian, lecturer; b. Washington, May 24, 1951; s. Charles and Joan (Sunderland) S.; m. Ritchie Harrison Markoe, Aug. 4, 1979; children: Charles IV, Christopher Markoe. AB, Princeton U., 1973, MFA, 1975, PhD, 1977. Editor Charles Scribner's Sons, N.Y.C., 1975—, dir. subs. rights, 1978-82, pub. paperback div., 1982-83, exec. v.p., 1983-84; v.p. Macmillan Pub. Co., N.Y.C., 1984-94; instr. dept. art and archaeology Princeton U., 1976-77; mem. adv. council Princeton U. Library, 1981-90; mem. adv. council dept. art and archaeology Princeton U., 1983-91; trustee Princeton U. Press, 1984-90, Homeland Found., 1987—; bd. advisors Wethersfield Inst., 1985—; bd. dirs. Met. Opera Guild, 1990-92. Author: The Triumph of the Eucharist - Tapestries by Rubens, 1982, Rubens, 1989, Bernini, 1991. Trustee St. Paul's Sch., Concord, N.H., 1994—. Mem. Assn. Princeton U. Press. Roman Catholic. Clubs: Racquet and Tennis (N.Y.C.); Ivy (Princeton); Piping Rock (N.Y.). Avocations: music, art, opera. Office: Charles Scribners Sons 14th Fl 1230 Avenue of the Americas New York NY 10020

SCRIBNER, RODNEY LATHAM, state official; b. Rumford, Maine, May 6, 1935; s. Dwight Latham and Evaline May (House) S.; m. Evelyn Jean Sanborn, Feb. 28, 1963. B.S. in Marine Sci., Maine Maritime Acad., 1956. C.P.A., Maine. With Mobil Oil Co., N.Y.C., 1958-62; acct. Staples & Boyce, Portland, Maine, 1962-68; mem. Maine Ho. of Reps., 1967-68; dep. commr. Maine Dept. Fin. and Adminstrn., 1968-69, state controller, 1971-72, state budget officer, 1972-73; with Maine Leg. Fin. Office, 1973-74; treas. State of Maine, 1975-76, auditor, 1977; dep. dir. Office Revenue Sharing, U.S. Treas. Dept., Washington, 1977-79; commr. Dept. Fin. and Adminstrn., State of Maine, 1979-87; auditor State of Maine, 1987—; instr. U. Maine, 1971. Treas., United Way of Kennebec County; mem. Augusta Housing Authority, Maine, 1979-89; mem. planning com. Colby Coll. Mgmt. Inst., Waterville, Maine, 1973-89; past treas. Augusta Salvation Army; chmn. Maine Mcpl. Bond Bank, Augusta, 1976-77. Served to lt. (j.g.) USNR, 1956-58. Mem. AICPA, Maine Soc. CPAs (gov. 1983-84, 89—), Am. Soc. Pub. Adminstrn. (pres. Maine chpt. 1972-73), Rotary (treas. 1986-89). Democrat. Baptist. Home: 150 Green St Augusta ME 04330 Office: State of Maine Dept Audit Station #66 Augusta ME 04333

SCRICCA, DIANE BERNADETTE, principal; b. Flushing, N.Y., Mar. 18, 1951; d. Dominic John (Scricca) and Anne (Quinterno) Freohlich; m. Mark Scheinbart, Jan. 19, 1975 (div. Dec. 1988); 1 child, Mark Anthony. BA in Social Studies, St. John's U., 1973, MS in Curriculum and Teaching, 1977, D of Adminstrn. and Supervision, 1980. Tchr., social studies various high schs., N.Y.C., 1973-78; coord. spl. edn. Jamaica (N.Y.) High Sch., 1979-81, asst. prin., 1981-87; asst. prin. Ft. Hamilton High Sch., Bklyn., 1987-90; prin. Elmont (N.Y.) Meml. High Sch., 1990—; cons. in field; instr. new tchr., N.Y.C. Bd. Edn., 1982-90, instr., new suprs., 1988-90. Mem. ASCD, Nat. Assn. Secondary Sch. Prins. Roman Catholic. Avocations: tennis, travel, mus., reading. Home: 53 Corwin Ave New Hyde Park NY 11040-3953 Office: Elmont Meml High Sch 555 Ridge Rd Floral Park NY 11003-3524

SCRIGGINS, LARRY PALMER, lawyer; b. Englewood, N.J., Nov. 27, 1936; s. Thomas Dalby and M. Patricia (Fowler) S.; m. Victoria Jackola, Feb. 17, 1979; children: Elizabeth J., Thomas P. AB, Middlebury Coll., 1958; JD, U. Chgo., 1961. Bar: Md. 1962. Law clk. to chief judge Md. Ct. Appeals, 1962; assoc. Piper & Marbury L.L.P., Balt., 1962-69, ptnr., 1969—, vice chmn. 1988-93, mem. exec. com., CFO, 1993—; mem. legal adv. com. N.Y. Stock Exchange, 1992—; bd. dirs. USF & G Corp., 1979—, Center Stage Assocs., 1979-89, Balt. Choral Arts Soc., 1979—, Balt. Conv. Bur., 1982-95, YMCA of Greater Balt., 1987-94, Fund for Ednl. Excellence, 1990—, chmn. bd. trustees, 1993—; bd. dirs. Nat. Aquarium in Balt., bd. govs. 1987-93. Fellow Am. Bar Found.; mem. Md. Bar Assn. (coun. 1976-78, chmn. 1977-78, chmn. com. on corp. laws 1981-84), ABA (sect. on bus. law, council 1972-76, chair 1991-92, vice-chair and editor in chief The Bus. Lawyer 1989-90, chmn. law and acctg. com. 1985-88), Internat. Bar Assn., Am. Judicature Soc., Am. Law Inst., Task Force on Fin. Instruments, Fin. Acctg. Standards Bd., Am. Inst. CPAs Planning Com. (pub. mem. 1989-92). Contbr. articles to profl. jours. Home: 13 E Eager St Baltimore MD 21202-2513 Office: Piper & Marbury LLP 36 S Charles St Baltimore MD 21201-3020

SCRIMENTI, BELINDA JAYNE, lawyer; b. Dayton, Ohio, Jan. 30, 1956. BS in Journalism, Ohio U., 1978; JD, Ohio State U., 1981. Bar: Ohio 1981, U.S. Dist. Ct. (no. dist.) Ohio 1981, U.S. Dist. Ct. (ea. dist.) Mich. 1983, U.S. Ct. Appeals (3d and 6th cirs.) 1984, U.S. Dist. Ct. Md. 1988, D.C. 1989, U.S. Dist. Ct. D.C. 1989, U.S. Ct. Appeals (2d cir.), 1995. Assoc. Baker & Hostetler, Cleve., 1981-88; assoc. Baker & Hostetler, Washington, 1988-90, ptnr., 1991—. Contbr. articles to profl. jours. Sec. Chagrin Condominiums Homeowners' Assn., Chagrin Falls, Ohio, 1985-87. Mem. ABA (sect. on litigation, patent, trademarks and copyrights, entertainment and sports law), D.C. Bar Assn. (sects. on copyright, trademarks, patent and entertainment and sport law), Internat. Trademark Assn. (firm rep., coms. 1990—), Internat. Anti-Counterfeiting Coaliton (firm rep.), Womens Bar Assn. D.C. Office: Baker & Hostetler 1050 Connecticut Ave NW Washington DC 20036-5303

SCRIMSHAW, NEVIN STEWART, physician, nutrition and health educator; b. Milw., Jan. 20, 1918; m. Mary Ware Goodrich, 1941; 5 children. B.A. with honors, Ohio Wesleyan U., 1938; M.A. in Biology, Harvard U., 1939, Ph.D. in Physiology, 1941; M.D. with honors, U. Rochester, 1945; M.P.H. with honors, Harvard U., 1959. Diplomate Am. Bd. Med. Examiners. Intern Gorgas Hosp., C.Z., 1945-46; Rockefeller postdoctoral fellow U. Rochester, N.Y., 1946-47, Merck NRC fellow, 1947-49; asst. resident in ob-gyn Strong Meml. Hosp., Genesee Hosp., N.Y., 1948-49; cons. nutrition Pan-Am. San. Bur. WHO, 1948-49, regional advisor on nutrition, 1949-53; dir. Inst. Nutrition C.Am. and Panama, Guatemala, 1949-61, cons. dir., 1961-65, cons. 1965—; dir. Clin. Research Ctr., MIT, 1962-66, 79-85, dir. internat. food and nutrition program, 1976-88, prof. human nutrition, 1961-76, head dept. nutrition and food sci., 1961-79, inst. prof. emeritus, 1988—; vis. prof. Columbia U., N.Y., 1976-88; vis. lectr. 1961-66; vis. lectr. Harvard U., 1968-85; vis. prof. Tufts U; mem. govt. adv. com. NIH; chmn. internat. com. NRC; dir. devel. studies div. U.N. U., 1985-86, food nutrition program 1975—, mem. adv. com. WHO, Nutrition Found., others. Contbr. articles to profl. jours.; editor: (with others) Amino Acid Fortification of Protein Foods, 1971, Nutrition, National Development and Planning, 1973, The Economics, Marketing and Technology of Fish Protein Concentrate, 1974, Nutrition and Agricultural Development: Significance and Potential for the Tropics, 1976, Single-Cell Protein: Safety for Animal and Human Feeding, 1979, Nutrition Policy Implementation: Issues and Experience, 1983, Diarrhea and Malnutrition: Interactions, Mechanisms and Interventions, 1983, Chronic Energy Deficiency, 1987, Acceptability of Milk and Milk Products in Populations With Lactose Intolerance, 1988, Nutrition in the Elderly, 1989, Activity, Energy Expenditure and Energy Requirements of Infants and Children, 1990, RAP: Rapid Assessment Procedures: Qualitative Methodologies for Planning and Evaluation of Health Related Programs, 1992, Protein-energy Interactions, 1992, Community-based Longitudinal Nutrition and Health Studies: Classical Examples from Guatemala, Haiti, and Mexico, 1995, The Effects of Improved Nutrition in Early Childhood: The Institute of Nutrition of Central America and Panama Follow-up Study, 1995, The Nutrition and Health Transition of Democratic Costa Rica, 1995. Recipient Osborne and Mendal award, 1960, Internat. award Inst. Food Technologists, 1969, medal of honor Fundacion F. Cuenca Villoro, Spain, 1978, Bristol-Myers prize, 1988, Alan Shawn Feinstein award, 1991, World Food prize, 1991, also others. Trustee Rockefeller Found., 1971-83, Pan-Am. Health and Edn. Found., 1986-92; pres. Internat. Nutrition Found. for Developing Countries, 1982—. Fellow Am. Inst. Nutrition, Royal Soc. Health, AAAS, Am. Soc. Clin. Nutrition, Am. Pub. Health Assn. (v.p. 1978 award of excellence in promoting and protecting health of people 1974); mem. Am. Coll. Nutrition, NAS (ch. applied biol. section, 1973-76, 88-91), Inst. of Medicine, Am. Acad. Arts Scis., Am. Coll. Preventive Medicine, Am. Bd. Nutrition, Mass. Pub. Health Assn., New Eng. Pub. Health Assn., Mass. Med. Soc., Am. Physiol. Soc., Am. Epidemol. Soc., Internat. Union Nutritional Scis. (pres. 1978-81), Internat. Epidemol. Assn., also others. Home: Sandwich Mountain Farm PO Box 330 Campton NH 03223-0330 Office: Charles St Sta PO Box 500 Boston MA 02114-0500

SCRIMSHAW, SUSAN, dean. PhD in Anthropology, Columbia U., 1974. Dean U. Ill. Sch. Pub. Health, Chgo., 1995—. Recipient Margaret Mead award, 1985. Fellow AAAS; mem. Inst. Medicine-Nat. Acad. Sci., Am. Anthropology Assn., Soc. Applied Anthropology, Nat. Soc. Med. Anthropology (pres. 1985). Office: UCLA School of Public Health 405 Hilgard Ave Los Angeles CA 90024*

SCRIPPS, CHARLES EDWARD, newspaper publisher; b. San Diego, Jan. 27, 1920; s. Robert Paine and Margaret Lou (Culbertson) S.; m. Louann Copeland, June 28, 1941 (div. 1947); m. Lois Anne MacKay, Oct. 14, 1949 (dec. 1990); children: Charles Edward Jr., Marilyn Joy, Eaton Mackay, Julia Osborne; m. Mary Elizabeth Breslin, Sept. 7, 1993. Student, Coll. William and Mary, 1938-40, Pomona Coll., 1940-41. Reporter Cleve. Press, 1941; successor-trustee Edward W. Scripps Trust, 1945, chmn. bd. trustees, 1948—; v.p. E.W. Scripps Co., 1946—, chmn., 1953—, also bd. dirs., 1953-94; chmn. exec. com., 1994—; bd. dirs. various Scripps-Howard newspapers and affiliated enterprises. Mem. nat. adv. bd. Salvation Army; trustee Freedoms Found. Served to lt. (j.g.) USCGR, 1942-45. Mem. CAP, Theta Delta Chi. Office: Scripps Howard 312 Walnut St Ste 28 Cincinnati OH 45202-4024

SCRIPPS, EDWARD WYLLIS, newspaper publisher; b. San Diego, May 21, 1909; s. James G. and Josephine (Stedem) S.; m. Betty Jeanne Knight McDonnell, Jan. 31, 1950; children: Edward Wyllis III, Barry Howard. Student, Pomona Coll. Chmn. bd. Scripps League Newspapers, 1931—. Mem. St. Francis Yacht Club, Lyford Cay (Nassau, Bahamas), Boars Head Sports Club, Farmington Country Club, Everglades Club, Bath and Tennis Club, Colony Club, Mrs. Club (N.Y.C.). Home: Eagle Hill HCR 1 PO Box 38 Charlottesville VA 22901-0038 also: 947 N Ocean Blvd Palm Beach FL 33480-3325 Office: Dulles Corner Park 2411 Park S Ste 250 Herndon VA 22071

SCRIVEN, L. E.(DWARD), II, chemical engineering educator, scientist; b. Battle Creek, Mich., Nov. 4, 1931; s. L. Edward and Esther Mabel (Davis) S.; m. Dorene Bates Hayes, June 19, 1952; children: Ellen Dorene, Teresa Ann, Mark Hayes. BS, U. Calif., Berkeley, 1952; MChemE, U. Del., 1954, PhD, 1956. Rsch. engr. Shell Devel. Co., Emeryville, Calif., 1956-59; asst. prof. chem. engring. and fluid mechanics U. Minn., Mpls., 1959-62, assoc. prof., 1962-66, prof., 1966-89, Regents' prof., 1989—, assoc. dept. head, 1975-78, program dir. Ctr. Interfacial Engring., 1988—; cons. in fields; advisor to Humboldt Found., Fed. Republic of Germany; vis. com. to chem. engring. MIT, sci. assoc. Jet Propulsion Lab., 1977, 79; tech. expert UN Indsl. Devel. Orgn., Vienna, Austria, 1979-88; exec. com. on chem. engring. frontiers NRC, 1984-87; mem. NRC Bd. on Chem. Scis. and Tech., 1987-92, chmn., 1992; mem. NRC Commn. on Phys. Scis., Math. and Applications, 1994—; sci. adv. com. Packard Found., 1988—. Editor: Physio-chemical Hydrodynamics (V.G. Levich), 1992; assoc. editor Jour. Fluid Mechanics, 1970-75; adv. editor Jour. Coll. Interfluid Sci., Physics of Fluids, L.Am. Jour. Chem. Engring. and Applied Chemistry, Internat. Jour. Numerical Methods in Fluid Mechanics; contbr. numerous articles to sci. jours.; patentee in field. Recipient chem. engring. award Am. Soc. Engring. Edn., 1968, Minn. Achievement award, 1989, Murphree award Am. Chem. Soc., 1990; named Fairchild disting. scholar Calif. Inst. Tech., 1989; Guggenheim fellow, 1969-70, fellow Minn. Supercomputer Inst., 1984—. Mem. NAE, Am. Inst. Chem. Engrs. (mem. nat. program com. 1964-69, Colburn award 1960, Walker award 1977, Tallmadge award 1992), Am. Phys. Soc., Soc. Petroleum Engrs., Gordon Rsch. Confs., Chem. Soc. (Faraday div.), Soc. Indsl. and Applied Math., Soc. Rheology. Research in capillarity, fluid mechanics and coating processes, porous media, cold-stage electron microscopy, microstructured fluids and interfaces, origins of pattern and form, supercomputer-aided analysis. Office: Univ Minn 151 Amundson Hall 421 Washington Ave SE Minneapolis MN 55455-0373

SCRIVEN, MICHAEL, philosopher, evaluator; b. Beaulieu, United Kingdom, Mar. 28, 1928. BA in Math. with honors, U. Melbourne, Australia, 1948; MA in Math. and Philosophy, U. Melbourne, 1950; DPhil, Oxford (Eng.) U., 1956. Teaching asst. math. dept. U. Melbourne, 1949; instr. philosophy dept. U. Minn., 1952-56, rsch. assoc. Minn. Ctr. for Philosophy of Sci., 1953-56; asst. prof. philosophy Swarthmore Coll., 1956-60; prof. history and philosophy of sci. Ind. U., 1960-66; prof. philosophy U. Calif., Berkeley, 1966-78, spl. asst. to vice-chancellor, 1975-77, prof. edn., 1975-78; fellow Inst. Higher Studies, Santa Barbara, 1976-90; univ. prof., dir. Evaluation Inst. U. San Francisco, 1978-82; prof. dept. edn. U. Western Australia, 1982-90, dir. Ctr. Tertiary Edn. Studies, 1983-90; prof., dir. Evaluation Inst. Pacific Grad. Sch. Psychology, Palo Alto, Calif., 1989-92; fellow Ctr. Advanced Study in Behavioral Scis., Stanford, Calif., 1963; Alfred North Whitehead fellow for advanced study in edn. Harvard U., 1970-71; sr. nat. lectr. in evaluation Nova U., Ft. Lauderdale, Fla., 1973-90; disting. vis. scholar Ctr. for Advanced Study in Theoretical Psychology, U. Alta., Edmonton, Can., 1965, 80, Ednl. Testing Svc., Princeton, N.J., 1970; dir. model tng. program for evaluators Nat. Inst. Edn., 1972-73; cons. prof. Grad. Sch. Edn., Stanford U., 1990-92; adj. prof. philosophy Western Mich. U., 1990-94; sr. fellow in evaluation NSF, 1992-93. Co-author: The Gas Turbine in Automobile Design, 1956, Psychology, 1960, How to Buy a Word Processor: Electronic Typewriters, Personal Computer Systems and Dedicated Systems, 1982, Word Magic: Evaluating and Selecting Word Processing, 1983, Russian edit., 1987; author: Applied Logic: An Introduction to Scientific Method, 1965, Primary Philosophy, 1966, Philosophy of Science, 1970, Evaluation: A Study Guide for Educational Administrators, 1974, Reasoning, 1976, Evaluation Thesaurus, 1977, 4th edit., 1991, The Logic of Evaluation, 1981; editor: (with H. Feigl) The Foundations of Science and the Concepts of Psychology and Psychoanalysis, vol. 1, 1956, (with H. Feigl and G. Maxwell) Concepts, Theories and the Mind-Body Problem, vol. 2, 1958, Collected Papers of Eugene R. Wigner, 1966, Statistics as a Spectator Sport by R. Jaeger, 1982, (with George Madaus and Daniel Stufflebean) Evaluation Models, 1983; mem. editl. bd., editl. rev. panels and editorships to numerous jours. and mags. Grantee Nuffield Found., 1951-52, Carnegie Corp., 1960-61, NSF, 1965, 66-71, 74-75, 80, 92-93, U.S. Office Edn., 1971-72; recipient Pres.'s Prize Competition, Evaluation Network, 1980, Lazarsfeld medal Am. Evaluation Soc., 1986; hon. fellow Nat. Acad. Social Scis. in Australia, 1983. Home: 415 Drakes View Dr Inverness CA 94937-9708

SCRIVER, CHARLES ROBERT, medical scientist, human geneticist; b. Montreal, Que., Can., Nov. 7, 1930; s. Walter deM. and Jessie (Boyd) S.; m. E.K. Peirce, Sept. 8, 1956; children: Dorothy, Peter, Julie, Paul. B.A. cum laude, McGill U., Montreal, 1951, M.D.C.M. cum laude, 1955; DSc (hon.), U. Man., 1992, U. Glasgow, 1993, U. Montreal, 1993. Intern Royal Victoria Hosp., Montreal, 1955-56; resident Royal Victoria and Montreal Children's hosps., 1956-57, Children's Med. Center, Boston, 1957-58; McLaughlin travelling fellow Univ. Coll., London, 1958-60; chief resident pediatrics Montreal Children's Hosp., 1960-61; asst. prof. pediatrics McGill U., 1961, prof. biology Faculty of Sci., prof. pediatrics Faculty of Medicine, 1969—; Alva prof. human genetics, 1994—; mem. med. adv. bd. Howard Hughes Med. Inst., 1981-88; dir. Med. Rsch. Coun. Group in Genetics, 1972-94; assoc. dir. Can. Genetic Diseases Network, 1989—. Co-author: Amino Acid Metabolism and Its Disorders, 1973, Garrod's Inborn Factors in Disease, 1989; sr. editor Metabolic and Molecular Bases Inherited Disease, 1986—; contbr. more than 500 rsch. publs. in field. Decorated Order of Can.; recipient Wood Gold medal McGill U., 1955, Gairdner Internat. award Gairdner Found., 1979, Ross award Can. Pediatric Soc., 1990, Award of excellence Genet Soc. Can., 1992, Prix d'Excellence Inst. Rsch. Clin. de Montreal, 1993, Prix du Quebec, Wilder Penfield, 1995; Royal Coll. lectr., 1992, Markle scholar, 1962-67; Med. Rsch. Coun. assoc., 1968-95, Disting. Scientist, 1995—. Fellow AAAS, Royal Soc. Can. (McLaughlin medal 1981), Royal Soc. London (Can. Rutherford lectr. 1983); mem. Can. Soc. Clin. Investigation (pres. 1974-75, G. Malcolm Brown Meml. award 1979), Soc. Pediat. Rsch. (pres. 1975-76), Am. Soc. Human Genetics (dir. 1971-74, pres. 1986-87, William Allan award 1978), Am. Pediat. Soc. (pres. 1994-95), Am. Soc. Clin. Investigation, Assn. Am. Physicians, Brit. Pediat. Assn. (50th Anniversary lectr. 1978), Soc. Francaise de Pediat., Am. Acad. Pediat. (Mead Johnson award for rsch. in pediat. 1968). Office: McGill Univ-Montreal, Childrens Hosp Rsch Inst, 2300 Tupper St, Montreal, PQ Canada H3H 1P3

SCRIVNER, THOMAS WILLIAM, lawyer; b. Madison, Wis., Sept. 10, 1948; s. William H. and Jane (Gehrz) S.; m. Meredith Burke, Aug. 16, 1980; children: Allison, David. AB, Duke U., 1970, MAT, 1972; JD, U. Wis., 1977. Assoc. Michael, Best & Friedrich, Milw., 1978-85, ptnr., 1985—. Mem. ABA, Wis. Bar Assn., Milw. Bar Assn. (labor sect.), Corp. Practice Inst. (pres. 1989-92). Episcopalian. Home: 4626 N Cramer St Milwaukee WI 53211-1203 Office: Michael Best & Friedrich 100 E Wisconsin Ave Milwaukee WI 53202-4107

SCRUGGS, CHARLES G., editor; b. McGregor, Tex., Nov. 4, 1923; s. John Fleming and Adeline (Hering) S.; m. Miriam June Wigley, July 5, 1947; children—John Mark, Miriam Jan. B.S., Tex. A&M U., 1947. Assoc. editor Progressive Farmer, Dallas, 1947-61, editor, 1962—, v.p., 1964—, exec. editor, 1972, editorial dir., 1973—, editor-in-chief, 1982-87; editorial chmn. So. Progress Pubs., 1987-89; pres. Torado Land and Cattle Co., pres. Tex. Comml. Agr. Council 1953-54; chmn. bd. Sunlean Foods, Inc., 1989—. Author: The Peaceful Atom and the Deadly Fly, 1975, American Agricultural Capitalism. Founding gen. chmn. Chancellors' Century Coun., Tex. A&M U. System, 1987-90; Mem. Gov.'s Com. for Agr., 1950, Tex. Animal Health Council, 1955-61; chmn. So. Brucellosis Com., 1956; pres. Tex. Rural Safety Com., 1957-59; chmn. Nat. Brucellosis Com., 1958-59, 71-72; del. World Food Congress, 1963; pub. mem. U.S. del. 17th Biennial Conf. of FAO, UN, Rome, 1973; chmn. Joint Senate-House Interim Com. Natural Fibers, Tex. Legislature, 1971; mem. coordinating bd. Tex. Coll. and Univ. System, 1965-69; bd. regents Tex. Tech U., 1971-78; founding pres. S.W. Animal Health Research Found. 1961-63, trustee, 1961—. Served to lt. col. U.S. Army; Res., ret. Recipient Christian Svc. Mass Media award, 1955, Abilene Christian U., Southwestern Cattle Raisers award, 1962, Am. Seed Trade Assn. award, 1963, award of honor Am. Agrl. Editors Assn., 1964, Reuben Brigham award Am. Assn. Agrl. Coll. Editors, 1965, Disting. Svc. award Tex. Farm Bur., 1966, Journalistic Achievement award Nat. Plant Food Assn., 1967, Nat. award for agrl. excellence Nat. Agri-Mktg. Assn., 1983, Agrl. Vision award Nat. Forum for Agr., 1994; named Disting. Alumnus Tex. A&M U., 1982. Mem. Am. Agrl. Editors Assn. (pres. 1963), Am. Soc. Mag. Editors, Tex. Assn. Future Farmers Am. (pres. 1940-41), Dallas Agrl. Club (pres. 1951), Nat. Livestock Confedn. Mexico (hon.), The Austin Club, Headliners Club, Alpha Zeta, Sigma Delta Chi.

SCRUGGS, EARL EUGENE, entertainer; b. Cleveland County, N.C., Jan. 6, 1924; s. George Elam and Georgia Lula (Ruppe) S.; m. Anne Louise Certain, Apr. 18, 1948; children: Gary Eugene, Randy Lynn, Steven Earl. HHD in Folk Music (hon.), Gardner-Webb Coll., 1986. Banjo player, 1945—; formed Earl Scruggs Revue, 1969—; major performances include Carnegie Hall, N.Y.C., Wembley Festival, London, Washington Moratorium for Peace, 1969, also rock festivals, coll. concerts; TV appearances include NET-TV Spl. Earl Scruggs: His Family and Friends, 1971, Midnight Spl., NBC-Harper Valley U.S.A. Spl., NBC Country Music Awards Show, Phil Donahue Show, Mike Douglas Show, Austin City Limits, 1977, The Grand Ole Opry's 60th Anniversary Show, 1985, The Nashville Network spl. The American Music Shop, 1990, The Grand Ole Opry's 65th Anniversary Show, 1991, Country Music Assn. Awards Show, 1991, Country Music Assn. Hall of Fame 25th Anniversary TV show, 1992, The Legend of The Beverly Hillbillies, CBS-TV, 1993, Folk Sound USA-Revlon Revue, The Tonight Show, Les Crane Show, Mac Davis Special, The Johnny Cash Show, The Hootenanny Show, Frank McGee's Here and Now, Ernie Ford Show, Jimmy Dean Show, The Anatomy of Pop, Kraft's American Profile, The Roots of Country, CBS-TV, 1994, Red Hot and Country, TNN-TV, 1995, A Night at the Ryman, TNN-TV, 1995; rec. artist: Columbia Records, 1950—; albums include: Nashvilles Rock, Dueling Banjos, Kansas State, I Saw the Light, Earl Scruggs Revue, Rockin' Cross the Country, Family Portrait, Top of the World, Anniversary Special Vol. I and Vol. II, Live! At Austin City Limits, Earl Scruggs: His Family and Friends Soundtrack, Today and Forever, Bold and New, American-Made, World-Played, others; recorded theme song for TV series The Beverly Hillbillies, 1962, also made guest appearances; composer (with others) movie score Where The Lilies Bloom, 1973, also Earl Scruggs Revue rec. music soundtrack for movie; composer instrumental Foggy Mountain Breakdown (used in movie Bonnie and Clyde, Grammy award 1968, Broadcast Music, Inc. award 1969); star: (movie) Banjo Man, 1975; guest appearance (TV movie) Return of the Beverly Hillbillies, 1981; author: (book) Earl Scruggs and the 5-String Banjo, 1968. Apptd. hon. mem. Lt. Gov.'s Staff, State of Tenn., 1987. Named Artist of Yr. Hi-Fi Inst., 1975, Best Country and Bluegrass Banjoist, Frets mag., 1980; recipient Country Music award best instrumental group Billboard Mag., 1975, Cert. of Merit Internat. Bluegrass Music Assn., 1988, Order of the Long Leaf Pine award Gov. State of N.C., 1988, cert. appreciation Tenn. Gov. Ned McWherter, 1990, Spl. Citation of achievement recognition of nat. popularity over 1 million broadcasts of Foggy Mountain Breakdown, Broadcast Music, Inc., 1993, others; inducted into Gibson Hall of Fame, 1981, Country Music Assn. Hall of Fame, 1985, Internat. Bluegrass Music Assn. Hall of Honor, 1991; Nat. Heritage fellow NEA, 1989; Nat. Medal of Arts presented by Pres. George Bush at White House, 1992. Developer Scruggs style of banjo playing; inventor Scruggs Tuning Pegs.

SCRUGGS, JACK GILBERT, retired chemical executive; b. Cullman County, Ala., Sept. 9, 1930; s. Carlton Vann and Grace Blanche (Thoroman) S.; m. Anna Faye Thomas, Aug. 21, 1954; children: Pamela Ann, Linda Dianne. BS in Pharmacy, U. Mich., 1952, MS in Pharm. Chem., 1953, PhD in Organic Chem., 1956. Research and devel. mgr. Monsanto Fibers Div., Durham, N.C., 1956-66; tech. v.p. Phillips Fibers Corp., 1966-94. Patentee in polymers and fibers. Pres. Jr. Achievement, Greenville, 1985-86; active Boy Scouts Am.; coach, umpire Little League Baseball, Cary, N.C., 1963-65. Mem. Am. Chem. Soc., Phi Beta Kappa, Sigma Xi, Phi Eta Sigma, Rho Chi, Phi Lambda Upsilon. Republican. Mem. Ch. of Christ. Avocations: golf, racquetball, softball. Home: 614 Devenger Rd Greer SC 29650-3715

SCUDDER, DAVID BENJAMIN, economist, foundation administrator; b. Evanston, Ill., July 30, 1923; s. Guy and Ruth Marilla (Benjamin) S.; m. Marjorie Adell Buckland, Dec. 27, 1946; children: David Foster, Rexford Guy. BS, Bowling Green State U., 1948; AM, U. Chgo., 1950, postgrad., 1950-51. Economist CIA, Washington, 1951-81, econ. cons., 1981-84; editor, co-pub. World Amateur Dancer, McLean, Va., 1982-84; treas. The Scudder Assn., Inc., Arlington, Va., 1990-92, Boise, Idaho, 1992-96. Editor quarterly newsletter The Scudder Assn. Inc, 1989—; contbr. articles and reports to jours. Active Springfield Civic Assn., Fairfax County, Va., 1956-61. With USAF, 1943-45, ETO. Avocations: tennis, ballroom dancing, golf, amateur theater. Home: 1031 Strawberry Ln Boise ID 83712-7726

SCUDDER, EDWARD WALLACE, JR., newspaper and broadcasting executive; b. Newark, Dec. 8, 1911; s. Edward Wallace and Katherine (Hollifield) Scudder; m. Louise Bagby Fry, Jan. 19, 1945; children: Katherine Allison Tiballi, Mary Gale Doe, Edward, Robert. AB, Princeton, 1935. Treas. Newark Evening News, 1950-70; pres. Evening News Pub. Co., 1955-72, Newark Broadcasting, operating Sta. WVNJ, Newark, to 1978; chmn. of bd. Orange Mountain Comm., West Orange, N.J., 1971—. Trustee Paper Mill Playhouse, Millburn, N.J., Newark Mus.; treas. Lake Placid (N.Y.) Edn. Found. Lt. (j.g.) to lt. comdr. USNR Air Force, 1942-46. Mem. Short Hills Club, Gulfstream Golf Club, Gulfstream Bath and Tennis Club, Delray Beach Yacht Club. Home: 1171 N Ocean Blvd Delray Beach FL 33483-7273 Office: PO Box 79 Summit NJ 07902-0079 Summer home: Birchgate Lake Placid NY 12946

SCUDDER, RICHARD B., newspaper executive; b. Newark, May 13, 1913; s. Edward W. and Katherine (Hollifield) S.; m. Elizabeth A. Shibley, June 24, 944; children: Elizabeth H. (Mrs. Philip Difani), Charles A., Carolyn (Mrs. Peter M. Miller), Jean (Mrs. Joseph Fulmer). AB, Princeton U., 1935; LHD (hon.), Mon Coll. Reporter Newark News, 1935-37, v.p., 1941-51, pub., 1951-72; reporter Boston Herald, 1937-38; chmn. MediaNews Group, Gloucester County Times, Inc., Garden State Newspapers, Inc., Garden State Paper Co., Denver Newspapers, Inc. Trustee Riverview Hosp., N.J. Conservation Found., Monmouth County Conservation Found.; former trustee Rutgers U.; adv. com. Princeton (N.J.) Environ. Inst. Served from pvt. to maj. AUS, 1941-45. Decorated bronze star; recipient TAPPI award, 1971; Nat. Recycling award Nat. Assn. Secondary Materials Industries, 1972; Nat. Resource Recovery Man of Year award, 1978; Papermaker of Yr. award Paper Trade Jour., 1978; named to Paper Industry Hall of Fame, 1995. Mem. N.J. Audobon Soc. Clubs: Rumson Country, Seabright Beach, Seabright Lawn Tennis, Mill Reef, Adirondack League. Office: Denver Post 1560 Broadway Denver CO 80202

SCUDDER, THAYER, anthropologist, educator; b. New Haven, Aug. 4, 1930; s. Townsend III and Virginia (Boody) S.; m. Mary Eliza Drinker, Aug. 26, 1950; children: Mary Eliza, Alice Thayer. Grad., Phillips Exeter Acad., 1948; A.B., Harvard U., 1952, Ph.D., 1960; postgrad., Yale U., 1953-54, London Sch. Econs., 1960-61. Research officer Rhodes-Livingstone Inst., No. Rhodesia, 1956-57; sr. research officer Rhodes-Livingstone Inst., 1962-63; asst. prof. Am. U., Cairo, 1961-62; research fellow Center Middle East Studies, Harvard U., 1963-64; asst. prof. Calif. Inst. Tech., Pasadena, 1964-66; assoc. prof. Calif. Inst. Tech., 1966-69, prof. anthropology, 1969—; dir. Inst. for Devel. Anthropology, Binghamton, N.Y., 1976—; cons. UN Devel. Program, FAO, IBRD, WHO, Ford Found., Navajo Tribal Coun., AID, World Conservation Union, Lesotho Highlands Devel. Authority, South China Electric Power Joint Venture Corp., U.S. Nat. Rsch. Coun., Que.-Hydro. Author: The Ecology of the Gwembe Tonga, 1962; co-author: Long-Term Field Research in Social Anthropology, 1979, Secondary Education and the Formation of an Elite: The Impact of Education on Gwembe District, Zambia, 1980, No Place to Go: The Impacts of Forced Relocation on Navajos, 1982, For Prayer and Profit: The Ritual, Economic and Social Importance of Beer in Gwembe District, Zambia, 1950-1982, 1988, The IUCN Review of the So. Okavango Integrated Water Development Project, 1993. John Simon Guggenheim Meml. fellow, 1975. Mem. Am. Anthrop. Assn. (1st recipient Solon T. Kimball award for pub. and applied anthropology 1984, Edward J. Lehman award 1991), Soc. Applied Anthropology, Am. Alpine Club. Office: Calif Inst Tech # 228-77 Pasadena CA 91125

SCULFORT, MAURICE CHARLES, advertising agency executive; b. N.Y.C., Oct. 26, 1925; s. Edward and Marcelle (Bonnier) S.; children—Raymond J., Jack T. Student, N.Y. U., 1946-50. Sales Sears Roebuck & Co., 1946; advt. Donahue & Coe, 1947; with Compton Advt., Inc., N.Y.C., 1947-85; v.p. Compton Advt., Inc., 1959-69, sr. v.p., 1969-85. Contbr. articles to profl. publs. Active Boy Scouts Am., YMCA. Served with USNR, 1943-46, PTO; Served with USNR, ETO; Served with USNR, MTO. Republican. Home: 4476 NE Ocean Blvd 104C Jensen Beach FL 34957

SCULLEN, THOMAS G., superintendent. Supt. Indian Prairie Community Unit Sch. Dist. 204, Naperville, Ill. Recipient State Finalist for Nat. Supt. of Yr. award, 1993. Office: Indian Prairie CUSD204 PO Box 3990 Naperville IL 60567-3990

SCULLEY, DAVID W., food company executive; b. N.Y.C., July 17, 1946; s. John and Margaret Blackburn (Smith) S.; m. Paula Cook; children: Heather Kahrl, David. BA in Econs. cum laude, Harvard U., 1968. Group product mgr. Lever Bros. Co., N.Y.C., 1971-73; gen. mgr. mktg. H.J. Heinz-U.S.A., Pitts., 1974-77, v.p. mktg., 1978-81; dep. mng. dir. H.J. Heinz-U.K., Middlesex, Eng., 1982-85; pres., CEO Heinz U.S.A., Pitts., 1985-89, sr. v.p., 1989—, also bd. dirs. Trustee Sewickley Valley Hosp., Pa., 1981; trustee, chmn. Allegheny Gen. Hosp., Pitts., 1995—; chmn. D.T. Watson Home Charity Golf Tournament, Sewickley, 1986, Young Pres.'s Orgn. Mem. Allegheny Country Club, Duquesne Club, Laurel Valley Golf Club (Ligonier, Pa.). Republican. Episcopalian. Avocations: golf; tennis; jogging; gardening. Office: H J Heinz Co 600 Grant St Pittsburgh PA 15219-2857

SCULLIN, FREDERICK JAMES, JR., federal judge; b. Syracuse, N.Y., Nov. 5, 1939; s. Frederick James and Cleora M. (Fellows) S.; m. Veronica Terek Sauro, Aug. 31, 1984; children: Mary Margaret, Kathleen Susan, Kellie Anne, Rebecca Rose; 1 stepchild, Angel Jenette Sauro. B.S. in Econs., Niagara U., 1961; LL.B., Syracuse U., 1964. Bar: N.Y. 1964, Fla. 1976, U.S. Dist. Ct. (no. dist.) N.Y. 1967, U.S. Supreme Ct. 1971. Assoc. Germain & Germain, Syracuse, 1967-68; asst. dist. atty. Onondaga County, Syracuse, 1968-71; asst. atty. gen. N.Y. State Organized Crime Task Force, 1971-78; dir. regional office N.Y. State Organized Crime Task Force, Albany, 1974-78; chief prosecutor, dir. Gov.'s Council on Organized Crime State of Fla., Tallahassee, 1978—; sole practice Syracuse, 1979-82, U.S. atty. for No. Dist. N.Y., 1982-92; judge U.S. Dist. Ct. (no. dist.) N.Y., 1992—. With U.S. Army, 1964-67, Vietnam; col. USAR. Decorated Air medal, Bronze Star; Cross of Gallantry (Vietnam). Mem. Am. Judicature Soc., ABA, N.Y. State Bar Assn., Fla. Bar Assn., Fed. Bar Assn., Fed. Bar Coun. Office: US Dist Ct US Courthouse 100 S Clinton St Syracuse NY 13261-9211

SCULLION, ANNETTE MURPHY, lawyer, educator; b. Chgo., Apr. 6, 1926; d. Edmund Patrick and Anna (Nugent) Murphy; 1 son, Kevin. B.Ed., Chgo. Tchrs. Coll., 1960; J.D., DePaul U., 1964, M.Ed., 1966; M.Ed., Loyola U., Chgo., 1970; Ed.D., No. Ill. U., 1974. Bar: Ill. 1964, U.S. Dist. Ct. (no. dist.) Ill. 1965, U.S. Ct. Appeals (D.C. cir.) 1978. Lectr. Chgo. Community Coll., 1964-68; pvt. practice law, Chgo., 1964—; asst. prof. bus. edn. Chgo. State U., 1966-69, assoc. prof., 1970-73, prof., 1974—. Club founder, adviser Bus. Edn. Students Assn., Chgo. State U., 1976—; sch. law workshop coordinator Ill. Div. Vocat. and Tech. Edn., 1981. Mem. Nat. Bus. Edn. Assn., Women's Bar Assn. Ill., ABA, Am. Tchr. Edn., Beta Gamma Sigma Home: 386 Muskegon Ave Calumet City IL 60409-2347 Office: Chgo State U 95 And King Dr # 203 Chicago IL 60601

SCULLION, TSUGIKO YAMAGAMI, non-profit organization executive; b. China, June 30, 1946; d. Hajime and Akemi (Murazumi) Yamagami; m. William James Scullion, Nov. 26, 1971; 1 child, James. BA, Baldwin-Wallace Coll., 1970; MA, Sch. Internat. Tng., 1971. Area cons. Conn. AFS Internat./Intercultural Programs, N.Y.C., 1972-73, regional mgr. for Asia and Pacific, 1973-78, dir. internat. ops., 1978-81, v.p. Europe, Africa, Middle East, 1981-83, v.p. program svcs., 1083-85, exec. v.p., 1985-87; exec. v.p. U.S. Com. UNICEF, N.Y.C., 1988-95; mgmt. cons. strategic planning, mktg. and fundraising, 1995-96; chief oper. officer Synergos Inst., 1996—. Bd. dirs. Oberlin Shansi Meml. Assn. Avocations: golf, classical music, ballet. Home: 7 Chasmar Rd Old Greenwich CT 06870-1404

SCULLY, JOHN CARROLL, life insurance marketing research company executive; b. Springfield, Mass., Mar. 16, 1932; s. James and Frances (Carroll) S.; m. Barbara A. Fougere, Sept. 7, 1953; children: Kathleen, Margaret, John, James, Patricia, Mary Ellen, Susan. B.A., Holy Cross Coll., 1953; C.L.U., Boston U., 1963; postgrad., Dartmouth Inst., 1977. With John Hancock Mut. Life Ins. Co., 1953-92; gen. agent John Hancock Mut. Life Ins. Co., Indpls., 1966-75; sr. v.p. agency dept. John Hancock Mut. Life Ins. Co., Boston, 1975-80; pres. retail sector John Hancock Mut. Life Ins. Co., 1980-92; pres., chief. exec. officer Life. Ins. Mktg. Rsch. Assoc., Windsor, Conn., 1992—. Bd. dirs. Greater Boston YMCA, 1975-91; chmn. Mass. campaign Holocaust Meml. Mus., 1985—; div. chmn. United Way, 1985—; bd. dirs. Cath. Charities, 1986—; trustee Springfield Coll., 1986, Suffolk U., 1986. With U.S. Army, 1954-56. Mem. Am. Coll. Life Underwriters, Nat. Assn. Life Underwriters (v.p. Ind. 1973-75), Life Ins. Mktg. and Rsch. Assn. (past chmn.), Gen. Agts. and Mgrs. Assn. (past pres. Indpls. Nat. Mgmt. award 1973-75), Life Underwriter Tng. Coun. (past chmn.), Greater Boston C. of C. (bd. dirs. 1985—), Wellesley Club, Executives Club (past pres.), Algonquin Club (bd. dirs.), Farmington Country Club, Hartford Club, KC. Roman Catholic. Home: 2 Shibah Dr Bloomfield CT 06002-1527 Office: Limra Internat PO Box 208 Hartford CT 06141-0208

SCULLY, JOHN THOMAS, obstetrician, gynecologist, educator; b. N.Y.C., Mar. 11, 1931; s. John Thomas and Mildred Frances (Dunstrop) S.; children: John, Helen Mary, Thomas, Nora, James, Sara, Megan, Devin. B.S., Georgetown U., 1952; M.D., U. Mex., 1959. Diplomate Am. Bd. Ob-Gyn. Intern, Nassau Hosp., 1959-60, resident, 1960-63; practice medicine specializing in ob-gyn, 1963—; sr. attending dept. ob-gyn St. Peter's Med. Center, Robert Wood Johnson U. Hosp.; clin. prof. ob-gyn Rutgers U. Med. Sch., 1971—. Fellow ACS, Am. Coll. Ob-Gyn; mem. N.J. Med. Soc., Middlesex County Med. Soc., N.J. Ob-Gyn Soc., N.J. Right to Life (charter). Republican. Roman Catholic. Office: 23 Duke St New Brunswick NJ 08901-1738

SCULLY, JOSEPH C., bank executive; b. 1940. Grad., Loyola U., Chgo., 1962, MBA, 1972. With Dept. Urban Renewal City of Chgo., 1962-63; with St. Paul Bancorp., Inc., Chgo., 1963-80, pres., 1980—, now chmn. bd. Office: St Paul Bancorp Inc 6700 W North Ave Chicago IL 60635-3937*

SCULLY, MALCOLM GRIFFIN, editor, writer; b. Pitts., Nov. 25, 1941; s. Cornelius Decatur and Elinor Hilliard (Tucker) S.; m. Jane Carney, Sept. 11,

1965; children: Randolph Ferguson, Allen Tucker. BA in English, U. Va., 1963; MA in English, Cornell U., 1965. Reporter Norfolk Virginian-Pilot, 1963-64, The Charlotte (N.C.) Observer, 1965-67; asst. editor The Chronicle of Higher Edn., Washington, 1967-71, sr. editor, 1973-76, internat. editor, 1976-87, mng. editor, 1987—; freelance writer, Susan, Va., 1971-73; contbg. editor Saturday Review, San Francisco, 1972-73. With U.S. Coast Guard Reserve, 1964-70. Recipient 1st Prize Reporting award Edn. Writers Assn., 1969. Avocation: orinthology, tennis. Home: 321 Forest Dr Falls Church VA 22046 Office: The Chronicle of Higher Edn 1255 23d St NW Washington DC 20037

SCULLY, STEPHEN J., plastic surgeon; b. Lawrence, Mass., Jan. 29, 1937; s. Joseph A. and Frances M. (Hart) S.; m. Diane Loretta Lizotte, Apr. 22, 1967; children: Stephen, Christopher, Caroline, Jacqueline. AB summa cum laude, Merrimack Coll., 1958; MD cum laude, Georgetown U., 1962. Surg. resident Tufts New Eng. Med. Ctr., Boston, 1962-67; plastic surg. resident NYU, N.Y.C., 1969-72. Trustee Holy Family Hosp., Methuen, Mass., 1993, Merrimack Coll., North Andover, Mass., 1993. Lt. comdr. USNR, 1967-69. Fellow ACS; mem. Am. Soc. Reconstructive Surgeons, Am. Soc. Aesthetic Plastic Surgery. Roman Catholic. Avocations: photography, skiing. Office: Plastic Cosmetic Reconstr Surgery Inc 451 Andover St North Andover MA 01845-5044

SCULLY, THOMAS FRANCIS, lawyer; b. Orange, N.J., Jan. 10, 1952. BA in English, Fairfield U., 1974; JD, U. Bridgeport, 1980. Bar: N.J., U.S. Dist. Ct., Supreme Ct. of N.J.; cert. criminal trial atty. Staff atty. N.J. Office Adminstrv. Law, Trenton, 1981-83; asst. coun. N.J. Sch. Bds. Assn., Trenton, 1983-84; assoc. Law Firm of Kenney & McManus, Red Bank, N.J., 1984-85; dep. pub. defender N.J. Office of Pub. Defender, Trenton, 1985—; co-chmn. Monmouth County Bar Assn., 1991-92, mem. criminal practice com. 1992-93. Co-Author: (book) Basic School Law, 2d edit. 1983. Roman Catholic. Home: 57 Dogwood Ln Fair Haven NJ 07704 Office: Office of Pub Defender RH Justice Complex 25 Market St CN850 Trenton NJ 08625

SCULLY, VINCENT EDWARD, sports broadcaster; b. Bronx, N.Y., Nov. 29, 1927; s. Vincent Aloysius and Bridget (Freehill) S.; m. Sandra Hunt, Nov. 11, 1973; children: Michael, Kevin, Todd, Erin, Kelly, Catherine Anne. B.A., Fordham U., 1949. Sports announcer Bklyn. Dodgers Profl. Baseball Team, 1950-57, L.A. Dodgers Profl. Baseball Team, 1957—, CBS-TV, 1975-82, NBC-TV, 1982-89. Served with USNR, 1944-45. Recipient TV award Look mag., 1959; named Sportscaster of Year in Calif., 1959, 60, 63, 69, 71, 73-75; Nat. Sportscaster of Year, 1966, 78, 82; named to Fordham U. Hall of Fame, 1976. Mem. AFTRA, Screen Actors Guild, Catholic Actors, TV Acad. Arts and Scis. Roman Catholic. Clubs: Lambs (N.Y.C.); Bel Air Country, Beach. Office: LA Dodgers 1000 Elysian Park Ave Los Angeles CA 90012-1112

SCURLOCK, ARCH CHILTON, chemical engineer; b. Beaumont, Tex., Jan. 29, 1920; s. Marvin and Mary (Chilton) S.; m. Maurine Spurbeck, Nov. 27, 1945 (div.); children: Arch, Susan, Marvin Curtis; m. Nancy Morrison Yonick, Nov. 16, 1962; children: Mary, Nancy, Margaret Ann. B.S. in Chem. Engring, U. Tex., 1941, A.B. in Physics, 1941; M.S., Mass. Inst. Tech., 1943, Sc.D., 1948; spl. course meteorology, U. Chgo., 1944. Research asso. chem. engring. dept. Mass. Inst. Tech., 1946-48; asst. dir. chemistry Engring. Research Assocs., 1948-49; pres. Atlantic Research Corp., Alexandria, Va., 1949-62; chmn. bd. Atlantic Research Corp., 1962-65; pres., dir. Research Industries Inc., Alexandria, 1968—; chmn. TransTechnology Corp., 1969-92, Halifax Corp. Served to lt. (s.g.) USNR, 1943-46. Mem. AAAS, AIAA, Am. Inst. Chem. Engrs., Am. Chem. Soc., Am. Phys. Soc., Am. Meteorol. Soc., Am. Def. Preparedness Assn., Combustion Inst., Univ. Club (Washington), Belle Haven (Va.) Country Club, Army Navy Country Club (Va.), Mid-Ocean Club (Tuckers Town, Bermuda), Phi Beta Kappa, Sigma Xi, Tau Beta Pi. Home: 1753 Army Navy Dr Arlington VA 22202-1633 Office: 123 N Pitt St Alexandria VA 22314-3133

SCURRY, RICHARDSON GANO, JR., real estate company financial executive; b. Dallas, June 7, 1938; s. Richardson Gano and Josephine (DuVall) S.; m. Pamela Ruth Edith McGinley, Oct. 11, 1975; children: Richardson, Kristina. BA, U. Tex., 1961; MBA, Stanford U., 1963. Mktg. rep. DP div. IBM, Dallas, 1963-68; mgr. fin. planning, DP group IBM, Harrison, N.Y., 1968-72; exec. asst., group exec. IBM, Armonk, N.Y., 1973; mgr. fin. planning office products div. IBM, Franklin Lakes, N.Y., 1974; mgr. fin. analysis, antitrust litigation IBM, N.Y.C., 1975; controller system communication div. IBM, White Plains, 1976-80; dir. plans, controls internal info. systems & communications IBM Corp., Purchase, N.Y., 1981-84; sr. v.p. fin. Chem. Bank, N.Y.C., 1985-89; pres., chief exec. officer Pearce, Mayer & Greer Realty Corp., N.Y.C., 1989—; v.p. fin., ptnr. Wicker Garden's Children, 1984—; bd. dirs. Info. Mart, Dallas, Firecom, Woodside, N.Y.; treas., bd. dirs. 1158 Fifth Ave. Corp., N.Y.C., 1985-90; mem. real estate coms. Lincoln Ctr., N.Y.C., 1990—. Mem. bus. com. Met. Mus. Art, N.Y.C., 1986—; deacon Brick Presbyn. Ch. Mem. Fin. Exec. Inst. (com. info. mgmt. 1979—, dir. N.Y.C. chpt. 1988-90), Salesmanship Club of Dallas, Union League Club of N.Y.C., Phi Delta Theta. Republican. Home: 1158 Fifth Ave New York NY 10029-6917 Office: Pearce Mayer & Greer Realty Corp 1318 Madison Ave New York NY 10128-1303

SCUSERIA, GUSTAVO ENRIQUE, theoretical chemist; b. San Fernando, Buenos Aires, Argentina, July 30, 1956; came to U.S., 1985; s. Eraldo L. and Alicia (Capitanelli) S.; m. Ana Inés Ilvento, Apr. 17, 1982; children: Ignacio, Tomás. BS, MS, U. Buenos Aires, 1979, PhD in Physics, 1983. Grad. asst. U. Buenos Aires, 1979-83, asst. prof., 1983-85; rsch. assoc. U. Calif., Berkeley, 1985-87; sr. rsch. assoc. U. Ga., Athens, 1987-89; asst. prof. Rice U., Houston, 1989-93, assoc. prof., 1993-95, prof., 1995—. Camille and Henry Dreyfus Teacher scholar Camille and Henry Dreyfus Found., 1992. Mem. AAAS, Am. Chem. Soc., Am. Phys. Soc., Materials Rsch. Soc., Electrochemical Soc. Office: Rice U Dept Chemistry 6100 Main St MS60 Houston TX 77005-1892

SCZUDLO, RAYMOND STANLEY, lawyer; b. Olean, N.Y., July 5, 1948; s. Raymond Stanley and Ann Marie (Frisina) S.; children: Gregory Martin, Edward James. BChemE, U. Detroit, 1971; JD, Georgetown U., 1974. Bar: D.C., 1975., U.S. Dist. Ct. (fed. dist.) D.C. 1975, U.S. Ct. Appeals (D.C. cir.) 1975, U.S. Ct. Appeals (5th cir.) 1980, U.S. Supreme Ct. 1981. Assoc. Martin, Whitfield, Thaler & Bebchick, Washington, 1974-78, Verner, Liipfert, Bernhard & McPherson, Washington, 1978-80; ptnr. Verner, Liipfert, Bernhard, McPherson & Hand, Washington, 1981-87, Weil, Gotshal & Manges, Washington, 1987—; bd. dirs. Benlink, Inc., Washington, 1984—; adj. prof. banking law George Washington U. Nat. Law Ctr., 1991—. Contbr. articles on banking to profl. jours. Bd. dirs. Children's Nat. Med. Ctr., Washington, 1985—, chmn. fin. com., 1988-92, vice chmn. bd., 1989-92, chmn-elect, 1992, chmn. bd., 1993-95; chmn. bd. Children's Hosp. Found., 1996—; trustee Monsignor Smyth Endowment Fund, Washington, 1994—, Fedn. Am. Scientists Fund, 1994—. Mem. ABA, D.C. Bar Assn., Am. Coll. Investment Coun., Univ. Club. Office: Weil Gotshal & Manges 1615 L St NW Ste 700 Washington DC 20036-5610

SEAB, CHARLES GREGORY, astrophysicist; b. Ft. Benning, Ga., May 26, 1950; s. James A. and Ruby (Jones) S.; m. Peggy R. McConnell, May 9, 1979; 1 child, Jenna R. McConnell-Seab. BS in Physics, La. State U., 1971, MS in Physics, 1974; PhD in Astrophysics, U. Colo., 1982. Engring. analyst, programmer Mid. South Svcs., New Orleans, 1974-77; NRC rsch. assoc. NASA Ames Rsch. Ctr., Mountain View, Calif., 1983-85; rsch. scientist U. Calif., Berkeley, 1985, Va. Inst. Theoretical Astronomy, Charlottesville, 1985-87; vis. asst. prof. U. New Orleans, 1987-89, asst. prof., 1989-91, assoc. prof. astrophysics, 1991-96; prof., 1996—; bd. dirs. Freeport McMoran Obs., New Orleans, 1991—. Author: Astronomy, 1994; contbr. articles to profl. jours., chpts. to books. Capt. USAR, 1971-80. Nat. Merit scholar, 1967-71. Mem. Am. Astron. Soc., Pontchartrain Astronomy Soc., Phi Kappa Phi. Avocations: amateur astronomy, tennis. Office: U New Orleans Physics Dept Lakefront New Orleans LA 70148

SEABORG, DAVID MICHAEL, evolutionary biologist; b. Berkeley, Calif., Apr. 22, 1949; s. Glenn Theodore and Helen Lucille (Griggs) S.; m. Adele Fong Yee, June 17, 1990. BS, U. Calif., Davis, 1972; MA, U. Calif., Berkeley, 1974. Biology tchr. U. Calif., Berkeley, 1972-73; biol. rschr., photographer Trans Time Labs., Berkeley, 1978; self-employed, 1974—; hypnosis and self-hypnosis tchr. Open Edn. Exchange, Oakland, Calif., 1978-81; biol. tchr. Oakland Mus., Calif., 1983-87, rsch. biologist, dept. ecology and evolutionary biology U. Calif., Irvine, 1987; pres., dir. rsch. Found. for Biol. Conservation and Rsch., Lafayette, Calif., 1983—; radio talk show host Sta. KPFA, Berkeley; vol. asst. to curator Smithsonian Instn., 1966-67, Lab. Chem. Biodynamics, U. Calif., Berkeley, 1975; comedian, 1969—; lectr. sci., philos., environ. issues, 1974—. Contbr. articles to profl. jours. Inventor game, Sum-It, 1981. Chmn. Com. for Arts and Lectures, U. Calif., Berkeley, 1974-75; chmn., master of ceremonies, Bastille Day, Lafayette (Calif.)-Langeac Soc., 1982-86. Recipient Meritorious Service award Smithsonian Inst., 1967, Animal Photography award Soc. Photographic Scientists and Engrs., 1967. Democrat. Mem. Calif. Acad. Scis., World Wildlife Fund, Earth Island Inst., Greenpeace, Nat. Resources Def. Coun., Desert Tortise Preserve Com., Rainforest Action Network, Save the Bay Assn., Sierra Club, Nature Conservancy, Zero Population Growth, Calif. Alumni Assn., Calif. Aggie Alumni Assn., Lafayette Langeac Soc., Club of Rome-USA (bd. dirs.), Lafayette gen. plan adv. com. Address: 1888 Pomar Way Walnut Creek CA 94598

SEABORG, GLENN THEODORE, chemistry educator; b. Ishpeming, Mich., Apr. 19, 1912; s. H. Theodore and Selma (Erickson) S.; m. Helen Griggs, June 6, 1942; children: Peter, Lynne Seaborg Cobb, David, Stephen, John Eric, Dianne. AB, UCLA, 1934; PhD, U. Calif.-Berkeley, 1937; numerous hon. degrees; LLD, U. Mich., 1958, Rutgers U., 1970; DSc, Northwestern U., 1954, U. Notre Dame, 1961, John Carroll U., Duquesne U., 1968, Ind. State U., 1969, U. Utah, 1970, Rockford Coll., 1975, Kent State U., 1975; LHD, No. Mich. Coll., 1962; DPS, George Washington U., 1962; DPA, U. Puget Sound, 1963; LittD, Lafayette Coll., 1966; DEng, Mich. Technol. U., 1970; ScD, U. Bucharest, 1971, Manhattan Coll., 1976, U. Pa., 1983. Rsch. chemist U. Calif., Berkeley, 1937-39, instr. dept. chemistry, 1939-41, asst. prof., 1941-45, prof., 1945-71, univ. prof., 1971—, leave of absence, 1942-46, 61-71, dir. nuclear chem. research, 1946-58, 72-75, asso. dir. Lawrence Berkeley Lab., 1954-61, 71—; chancellor Univ. (U. Calif.-Berkeley), 1958-61; dir. Lawrence Hall of Sci. U. Calif., Berkeley, 1982-84, chmn. Lawrence Hall of Sci., 1984—; sect. chief metall. lab. U. Chgo., 1942-46; chmn. AEC, 1961-71, gen. adv. com., 1946-50; research nuclear chemistry and physics, transuranium elements.; chmn. bd. Kevex Corp., Burlingame, Calif., 1972-87, Advanced Physics Corp., Irvine, Calif., 1988—; mem. Pres.'s Sci. Adv. Com., 1959-61; mem. nat. sci. bd. NSF, 1960-61; mem. Pres.'s Com. on Equal Employment Opportunity, 1961-65, Fed. Radiation Council, 1961-69, Nat. Aeros. and Space Council, 1961-71, Fed. Council Sci. and Tech., 1961-71, Nat. Com. Am.'s Goals and Resources, 1962-64, Pres.'s Com. Manpower, 1964-69, Nat. Council Marine Resources and Engring. Devel., 1966-71; chmn. Chem. Edn. Material Study, 1959-74, Nat. Programming Council for Pub. TV, 1970-72; dir. Ednl. TV and Radio Center, Ann Arbor, Mich., 1958-64, 67-70; pres. 4th UN Internat. Conf. Peaceful Uses Atomic Energy, Geneva, 1971, also chmn. U.S. del., 1964, 71; U.S. rep. 5th-15th gen. confs. IAEA, chmn., 1961-71; chmn. U.S. del. to USSR for signing Memorandum Cooperation Field Utilization Atomic Energy Peaceful Purposes, 1963; mem. U.S. del. for signing Limited Test Ban Treaty, 1963; mem. commn. on humanities Am. Council Learned Socs., 1962-65; mem. sci. adv. bd. Robert A. Welch Found., 1957—; mem. Internat. Orgn. for Chem. Scis. in Devel., UNESCO, 1981-92, pres., 1981-92, pres. emeritus, 1992—; mem. Nat. Commn. on Excellence in Edn., Dept. Edn., 1981-83; co-discoverer elements 94-102 and 106: plutonium, 1940, americium, 1944-45, curium, 1944, berkelium, 1949, californium, 1950, einsteinium, 1952, fermium, 1953, mendelevium, 1955, nobelium, 1958, seaborgium, 1974; co-discoverer nuclear energy isotopes Pu-239, U-233, Np-237, other isotopes including I-131, Fe-59, Te-99m, Co-60; originator actinide concept for placing heaviest elements in periodic system. Author: (with Joseph J. Katz) The Actinide Elements, 1954, The Chemistry of the Actinide Elements, 1957, (with Joseph J. Katz and Lester R. Morse) 2d ed. Vols. I & II, 1986, The Transuranium Elements, 1958, (with E.G. Valens) Elements of the Universe, 1958 (winner Thomas Alva Edison Found. award), Man-Made Transuranium Elements, 1963, (with D.M. Wilkes) Education and the Atom, 1964, (with E.K. Hyde, I. Perlman) Nuclear Properties of the Heavy Elements, 1964, (with others) Oppenheimer, 1969, (with Ben Loeb) Stemming the Tide, 1987, (with W.R. Corliss) Man and Atom, 1971, Nuclear Milestones, 1972, (with Ben Loeb) Kennedy, Khruschev and the Test Ban, 1981, (with Walt Loveland) Elements beyond Uranium, 1990, (with Ben Loeb) The Atomic Energy Commission Under Nixon, 1992, (with Ray C. Colvig) Chancellor at Berkeley, 1994, (with Ronald L. Kathren, Jerry B. Gough, Gary T. Benefiel) The Plutonium Story: The Journals of Professor Glenn T. Seaborg 1939-1946, 1994; editor: Transuranium Elements: Products of Modern Alchemy, 1978, (with W. Loveland) Nuclear Chemistry, 1982, Modern Alchemy: The Seleced Papers of Glenn T. Seaborg, 1994; assoc. editor Jour. Chem. Physics, 1948-50; mem. editorial adv. bd. Jour. Inorganic and Nuclear Chemistry, 1954-82, Indsl. Rsch., Inc, 1967-75; mem. adv. bd. Chem. and Engring. News, 1957-59; mem. editorial bd. Jour. Am. Chem. Soc., 1950-59, Ency. Chem. Tech., 1975—, Revs. in Inorganic Chemistry, 1977—; mem. hon. editorial adv. bd. Internat. Ency. Phys. Chemistry and Chem. Physics, 1957—, Nuclear Sci. and Techniques, Chinese Nuclear Soc., 1989—; mem. panel Golden Picture Ency. for Children, 1957-61; mem. cons. and adv. bd. Funk and Wagnalls Universal Standard Ency, 1957-61; mem. Am. Heritage Dictionary Panel Usage Cons., 1964-80; contbr. articles to profl. jours. Trustee Pacific Sci. Ctr. Found., 1962-77, Sci. Svc., 1965, pres., 1966-68, chmn., 1988—; trustee Am.-Scandinavian Found., 1968—, Ednl. Broadcasting Corp., 1970-72; bd. dirs. Swedish Coun. Am., 1976—, chmn. bd. dirs., 1978-82; bd. dirs. World Future Soc., 1969—, Calif. Coun. for Environ. and Econ. Balance, 1974-83; bd. govs. Am. Swedish Hist. Found., 1972—; hon. chair spl. panel Protection and Mgmt. Plutonium, 1994—. Decorated officier Legion of Honor (France); recipient John Ericsson Gold medal Am. Soc. Swedish Engrs., 1948; Nobel prize for Chemistry (with E.M. McMillan), 1951, John Scott award and medal City of Phila., 1953, Perkin medal Am. sect. Soc. Chem. Industry, 1957, U.S. AEC Enrico Fermi award, 1959, Joseph Priestley Meml. award Dickinson Coll., 1960, Sci. and Engring. award Fedn. Engring. Socs., Drexel Inst. Tech., Phila., 1962; named Swedish Am. of Year, Vasa Order of Am., 1962; Franklin medal Franklin Inst., 1963; 1st Spirit of St. Louis award, 1964; Leif Erikson Found. award, 1964; Washington award Western Soc. Engrs., 1965; Arches of Sci. award Pacific Sci. Center, 1968; Internat. Platform Assn. award, 1969; Prometheus award Nat. Elec. Mfrs. Assn., 1969; Nuclear Pioneer award Soc. Nuclear Medicine, 1971; Oliver Townsend award Atomic Indsl. Forum, 1971; Disting. Honor award U.S. Dept. State, 1971; Golden Plate award Am. Acad. Achievement, 1972, Daniel Webster medal, 1976, John R. Kuebler award Alpha Chi Sigma, 1978; Founders medal Hebrew U. Jerusalem, 1981; Great Swedish Heritage award, 1984, Ellis Island Medal of Honor, 1986, Seaborg medal UCLA, 1987, Vannevar Bush award NSF, 1988, Nat. Medal of Sci. NSF, 1991, Royal Order of the Polar Star Sweden, 1992, Profl. Fraternity Assn. Career Achievement award, 1993; Minor Planet 4856-Asteroid Seaborg named in his honor, 1995. Fellow Am. Phys. Soc., Am. Inst. Chemists (Pioneer award 1968, Gold medal award 1973), Chem. Soc. London (hon.), Royal Soc. Edinburgh (hon.), Am. Nuclear Soc. (hon. chair Spl. Panel on Protection and Mgmt. of Plutonium 1994—, Henry DeWolf-Smyth award 1982, Seaborg award 1984, hon. chair Spl. Panel on Protection and Mgmt. of Plutonium 1994—), Calif. Acad. Scis., N.Y. Acad. Scis., Washington Acad. Scis., AAAS (pres. 1972, chmn. bd. 1973), Royal Soc. Arts (Eng.); mem. Am. Chem. Soc. (award in pure chemistry 1947, William H. Nichols medal N.Y. sect. 1948, Charles L. Parsons award 1964, Gibbs medal Chgo. sect. 1966, Madison Marshall award No. Ala. sect. 1972, Priestley medal 1979, pres. 1976, George C. Pimentel award in chem. edn., 1994), Am. Philos. Soc., Royal Swedish Acad. Engring. Scis. (adv. council 1980), Am. Nat., Argentine Nat., Bavarian, Polish, Royal Swedish, USSR acads. scis., Royal Acad. Exact, Phys. and Natural Scis. Spain (acad. fgn. corr.), Soc. Nuclear Medicine (hon.), World Assn. World Federalists (v.p. 1980), Fedn. Am. Scis. (bd. sponsors 1980—), Deutsche Akademie der Naturforscher Leopoldina (East Germany), Nat. Acad. Pub. Adminstrn., Internat. Platform Assn. (pres. 1981-86), Am. Hiking Soc. (bd. dirs. 1979-84, v.p. 1980, adv. com. 1984—), Phi Beta Kappa, Sigma Xi, Pi Mu Epsilon, Alpha Chi Sigma (John R. Kuebler award 1978), Phi Lambda Upsilon (hon.); fgn. mem. Royal Soc. London, Chem. Soc. Japan, Serbian Acad. Sci. and Arhemian (San Francisco); Chemists (N.Y.C.); Cosmos (Washington), University (Washington); Faculty (Berkeley). Office: U Calif Lawrence Berkeley Lab 1 Cyclotron Rd Berkeley CA 94720

SEABROOK, CHARLES, reporter. Sci. and tech. reporter Atlantic Jour. Constn., Atlanta. Office: Atlanta Journal & Constitution 72 Marietta St NW Atlanta GA 30303-2804

SEABROOK, JOHN MARTIN, retired food products executive, chemical engineer; b. Seabrook, N.J., Apr. 16, 1917; s. Charles Franklin and Norma Dale (Ivins) S.; m. Anne Schlaudecker, Apr. 5, 1939 (div. 1951); children: Carol Ormsby (Mrs. Jacques P. Boulanger), Elizabeth Anne; m. Elizabeth Toomey, 1956; children: John Martin, Bruce Cameron. B.S. in Chem. Engring, Princeton, 1939; LL.D. (hon.), Gettysburg Coll., 1974. Registered profl. engr., N.J., Del. Engr. Deerfield Packing Corp., 1939-41; v.p. Seabrook Farms Co., 1941-50, exec. v.p., 1950-54, dir., 1941-59, pres., 1954-59, chief exec. officer, 1955-59; cons. IU Internat. Corp., Wilmington, Del., 1959; v.p. IU Internat. Corp., 1960-65, dir., 1963-87, pres., 1965-73, 74-78, chief exec., 1967-80, chmn. bd., 1969-82, chmn. exec. com., 1982-87; pres., bd. dirs. Cumberland Automobile & Truck Co., 1954-59, Cumberland Warehouse Corp., 1954-59, Salem Farms Corp, N.J., 1948—; chmn. bd. dirs. Frick Co., Waynesboro, Pa., 1959-68; chmn., bd. dirs. S.W. Fabricating & Welding Co., Inc., Houston, 1964-68; chmn. Divcon, Inc., Houston, 1967-69; pres. bd. dirs. Internat. Utilities Overseas Capital Corp., Wilmington, 1966-82, chmn., 1970-80; v.p. Gen. Waterworks Corp., Phila., 1959-66, pres., 1966-68, chmn., 1968-71; chmn. bd. dirs. GWC Inc., Phila., 1971-73; pres. Brown Bros. Contractors, Inc., Phila., 1960, chmn. bd. dirs., 1965-67; pres. Am. Portable Irrigation Co., Eugene, Oreg., 1961, chmn. bd. dirs., 1966-68; chmn. bd. dirs. Gotaas-Larsen Shipping Corp., 1963, chmn., 1979, pres., CEO, 1982-88; chmn. bd. dirs. Amvit Corp., Cleve., 1964-68; bd. dirs. Echo Bay Mines Ltd., South Jersey Gas Co., Folsom, N.J., South Jersey Industries, Inc., Folsom, Bell Atlantic Corp.; dir. emeritus Bell Atlantic-N.J., Inc. Mem. N.J. Migrant Labor Bd., 1945-67, chmn., 1955-67; mem. N.J. Bd. Higher Edn., 1967-70, Pres.' Air Quality Adv. Bd., 1968-70; bd. dirs. Brandywine Conservancy, Inc., 1972-95, pres., 1992-93; trustee Eisenhower Exch. Fellowships, 1974-85; trustee Hitchcock Found., 1991-96, chmn., 1993-96. Mem. Phi Beta Kappa. Clubs: Racquet and Tennis (N.Y.C.), The Philadelphia, Wilmington (Del.), Toronto (Ont.). Home and Office: 55 Nimrod Rd Salem NJ 08079-4323

SEADEN, GEORGE, civil engineer; b. Cracow, May 26, 1936; s. Simon and Mary (Guttman) S.; m. Linda Helen Mutch, Mar. 18, 1978; children: Amy Elisabeth, Maia Claire. BE, McGill U., Montreal, Que., Can., 1958; MS, Harvard U., 1968; postgrad., Northwestern U., 1992. Engr. Gatineau Power, Hull, Que., 1958-59, Ent. Fougerolle, Paris, 1960-62; mgr. Warnock Hersey Ltd., Montreal, 1959-60; assoc. Cartier, Coté, Piette, Montreal, 1962-67; sr. advisor Ministry Urban Affairs, Ottawa, Ont., Can., 1969-71; pres. Archer, Seaden & Assoc., Inc., Montreal, 1971-84; dir. gen. Inst. Rsch. in Constrn. Nat. Rsch. Coun., Ottawa, 1985—; chief Constrn. Tech. Group NRC, 1995—; vis. prof. U. Ottawa, 1969-73; mem. Can. Constrn. Rsch. Bd., 1985-91, Constrn. Industry Devel., Can., 1988-93, Civil Engring. Rsch Found., 1993—, Rsch. Bd. Am. Pub. Works Assn., 1994—; pres. Conseil Internat. du Bâtiment, Rotterdam, The Netherlands, 1989-92; vice-chair Constrn. for Sustainable Devel. in the Twenty First Century (CIB), Washington, 1996; mem. jury to select best Can. constrn. projects and engring. design; lectr. numerous univs., rsch. ctrs. Co-editor: Trends in Building Construction Worldwide, 1989; mem. editl. bd. Bldg. Rsch. and Practice, 1990-94, Constrn. Bldg. Rev., 1991—; contbr. numerous articles to profl. publs. Chmn. bd. dirs. St. Andrew's Sch., Westmount, Que., 1975-82. Home: 80 Lyttleton Gardens, Rockcliffe Park, ON Canada K1L 5A6 Office: Inst for Rsch in Construction, Montreal Rd Bldg M-20, Ottawa, ON Canada K1A 0R6

SEADER, JUNIOR DEVERE, chemical engineering educator; b. San Francisco, Aug. 16, 1927; s. George Joseph and Eva (Burbank) S.; m. Sylvia Bowen, Aug. 11, 1961; children: Steven Frederick, Clayton Mitchell, Gregory Randolph, Donald Jeffrey, Suzanne Marie, Robert Clark, Kathleen Michelle, Jennifer Anne. BS, U. Calif., Berkeley, 1949, MS, 1950; PhD, U. Wis., 1952. Instr. chem. engring. U. Wis., Madison, 1951-52; group supr. chem. process design Chevron Rsch. Corp., Richmond, Calif., 1952-57; group supr. engring. rsch. Chevron Rsch. Corp., 1957-59; prin. scientist heat transfer and fluid dynamics rsch. Rocketdyne div. N.Am. Aviation, Canoga Park, Calif., 1959-65, sr. tech. specialist, summer 1967; prof. chem. engring. U. Idaho, 1965-66; prof. chem. engring. U. Utah, Salt Lake City, 1966—, chmn. dept. chem. engring., 1975-78; tech. cons.; trustee CACHE Corp., Austin, Tex.; inst. lectr. Am. Inst. Chem. Engrs., 1983, also dir., 1983-85. Author 5 books; assoc. editor IEC Rsch. jour.; contbr. articles to profl. jours. Served with USNR, 1945-46. Recipient Disting. Teaching award U. Utah, 1975, Donald L. Katz lectureship, 1990. Fellow Am. Inst. Chem. Engrs. (Computing in Chem. Engring. award 1988); mem. ACS, Sigma Xi, Phi Lambda Upsilon. Heat transfer rsch. connected with the devel. of rocket engines associated with the Apollo and Space Shuttle projects, 1960-65; rsch. on tar sands, process synthesis, catalyst effective factors, finding all roots to systems of nonlinear equations. Home: 3786 Viewcrest Dr Salt Lake City UT 84124-3930 Office: U Utah Dept Chem Engring Meb # 3290 Salt Lake City UT 84112-1180

SEADLER, STEPHEN EDWARD, business and computer consultant, social scientist; b. N.Y.C., 1926; s. Silas Frank and Deborah (Gelbin) S.; AB in Physics, Columbia U., 1947, postgrad. in atomic and nuclear physics, 1947; postgrad. with George Gamow in relativity, cosmology and quantum mechanics, George Washington U., 1948-50; m. Ingrid Linnea Adolfsson, Aug. 7, 1954; children: Einar Austin, Anna Carin. Legal rsch. asst., editor AEC, Washington, 1947-51; electronic engr. Cushing & Nevell, Warner, Inc., N.Y.C., 1951-54; seminar leader, leader trainer Am. Found. for Continuing Edn., N.Y.C. 1955-57; exec. dir. Medimetric Inst., 1957-59; mem. long range planning com., chmn. corporate forecasting com., mktg. rsch. mgr. W. A. Sheaffer Pen Co., Ft. Madison, Iowa, 1959-65; founder Internat. Dynamics Corp., Ft. Madison and N.Y.C., 1965, pres., 1965-70; orginator DELTA program for prevention and treatment of violence, 1970; founder ID Ctr., Ft. Madison, now N.Y.C., 1968, pres., 1968—; mgmt. cons. in human resources devel. and conflict reduction, N.Y.C., 1970-73; pres. UNICONSULT computer-based mgmt. and computer scis., N.Y.C., 1973—; speaker on decision support systems, internat. affairs and ideological arms control; author/speaker (presentation) Holocaust, History and Arms Control; originator social sci. of ideologies and computer based knowledge systems sci. of ideotopology; spl. works collection accessible via On-line Computer Libr. Ctr. Instr. polit. sci. Ia. State Penitentiary, 1959-62. Served with AUS, 1944-46. Recipient 20th Century Achievement award Internat. Biographical Ctr., 1995. Mem. Am. Phys. Soc., Am. Statis. Assn., Acad. Polit. Sci., Am. Sociol. Assn., IEEE, N.Y. Acad. Scis., Am. Mgmt. Assn. (lectr. 1963-68), Internat. Platform Assn. Unitarian. Lodges: Masons (32 deg.), Shriners. Author: Holocaust, History and Arms Control II, 1990; contbr. Ideologics and ideotopology sects. to Administrative Decision Making, 1977, Societal Systems, 1978; Management Handbook for Public Administrators, 1978; also articles profl. jours. Statement on ideological arms control in Part 4 of Senate Fgn. Relations Com. Hearings on Salt II Treaty, 1979, Ideologics extended to treat ethnic, racial, religious conflict, 1992, with first call for Western Ecumenical Reformation at Morristown, N.J., Unitarian Ch., 1993. Recipient 20th Century Achievement award Internat. Biog. Ctr., 1995. Office: 521 Fifth Ave Ste 1700 New York NY 10175-0001 *In retrospect, a single, predominant thread has woven through my entire life since childhood, sometimes as primary track, sometimes as parallel, but always as relentless destiny; to gain such learning and skills as to enable me to revolutionize Mankind's thinking, slay the dragons of racism, religionism, ethicism and other ideologies of malevolence, oppression and war, and bring true Peace for the first time. To accomplish that mission requires development of a single comprehensive framework, which has become the new field of ideologics, and a single comprehensive, revolutionary work employing that framework, to appear at the foothills of the new millennium. That work, it is now clear, shall be the book on which I have been laboring for several years: Principia Idealogica.*

SEAGAL, STEVEN, actor; b. Lansing, Mich., Apr. 10, 1951; m. Kelly LeBrock; children: Anna Aliza, Dominick, Arissa. Studied martial arts under masters, Japan. Founded Aikido Ten Shin Dojo, L.A. Martial arts choreographer The Challenge, 1982; actor, prodr., martial arts choreographer Above the Law, 1988, Marked for Death, 1990; actor, martial arts choreographer Hard to Kill, 1990; actor, prodr. Out for Justice, 1991, Under Siege, 1992, Under Siege 2, 1995; actor, dir., co-prodr. On Deadly Ground,

1994; fight scene choreographer various films. First non-Asian to open martial arts acad. in Japan; black belt numerous martial arts. *

SEAGER, DANIEL ALBERT, university librarian; b. Jacksonville, Fla., Jan. 1, 1920; s. Harry James and Albertina Adeline (Klarer) S.; m. Helen Ruthe Medearis, Mar. 6, 1943; children: Mary Adele, Susan Kathleen, Dana Ruthe. AA, St. John's Coll., Winfield, Kans., 1941; AB, Okla. Bapt. U., 1948; BA in L.S, U. Okla., 1950, MA, 1953; postgrad., Colo. State Coll. (now U. No. Colo.), 1956-59. Head librarian, prof. English Southwest U., Bolivar, Mo., 1949-53; head librarian, asst. prof. library sci., chmn. dept. Ouachita U., Arkadelphia, Ark., 1953-56; head librarian, head library sci. edn., assoc. prof. library sci. U. No. Colo., Greeley, 1956-66; dir. library services U. No. Colo., 1966-71, coordinator library research and devel., 1971—, prof. library sci., 1984—, chief bibliographer/editor library publns., cons., instr. ednl. media program, 1968-71; libr. cons., 1968—; cons. Ency. Brit. ultramicrofiche project, 1967-69; lectr. in field. Contbr. articles to profl. jours. Mem. book adv. coun. Edn. for Freedom Found.; mem. Com. library standards Colo. pub. schs., 1960-62; mem. exec. bd. Rocky Mountain Bibliog. Ctr. Research, 1959-60, 65-74, sec., 1961-63; sec. Colo. Council Librarians State-Operated Instns., 1966, chmn., 1968-70; mem. exec. bd. Weld County Assn. Mental Health, 1966, mem. library com., 1969; mem. Colo. Civil Service Examining Bd., 1961—; mem. U. N.C. Friends Libr., 1984—; Rep. com. chmn., Weld County, 1985-86; deacon, elder Christian Ch. With U.S. Army Signal Corps, WWII, 1942-44, ETO, 1944-45. Recipient several citations of merit profl. orgns. Fellow Intercontinental Biog. Assn.; mem. NEA, AAUP, Am. Library Assn. (library recruitment com. 1957—), Nat., Colo. assns. higher edn., United Profs. for Acad. Order Nat. Hist. Soc., Colo. Assn. Sch. Librarians (cons.), Spl. Libraries Assn., ALA (region recruitment rep. 1958—), Utah Library Assn., Kans. Library Assn., Wyo. Library Assn., Nebr. Library Assn., N.D. Library Assn., S.D. Library Assn., Nev. Library Assn., Mountain Plains Library Assn. (treas. 1959-63, exec. sec. 1963-76, spl. hons. plaque 1968, archivist 1974-84, constitution com. 1979, 83, chmn. nominating com. 1980, awards com. 1984, bylaws and amendments coms. 89-91, Pres.'s and Assn.'s Spl. award 17 Years Service award, Spl. Presdl. award 1994), Colo. Library Assn. (auditor), Tex. Library Assn., Southwestern Library Assn., Ill. Library Assn., Calif. Library Assn., Cath. Library Assn., Mich. Library Assn., Ohio Library Assn., N.Y. Library Assn., Pa. Library Assn., Midcontinent Med. Library Assn., Library Automation Research and Cons. Assn., U N.C. Friends of the Libr., 1984, Intercollegiate Studies Inst., Am. Security Council, Alumni Assn. U. No. Colo., Black Silent Majority Com. (hon.), Colo. Council Higher Edn., Colo. Edn. Assn. (mem. coms., del. to convs.), U. No. Colo. Edn. Assn. (treas. 1980-84, sec.-treas. 1984-85), U. Colo. Safety Com., Assn. Coll. and Reference Libraries, Colo. Hist. Soc., Assn. Research Libraries, Colo. Audiovisual Assn., Air Force Assn., Internat. Platform Assn., Acad. Polit. Sci. Columbia, Nat. Geog. Soc., Weld County Assn. Mental Health (mem. bd., chmn. library com.), Am. Judicature Soc., Emeritus Faculty Assn. U. No. Colo., Am. Numis. Assn., Am. Sci. Affiliation, Council on Consumer Info., Smithsonian Assocs., Chem. Abstracts Service Panel, Colo. Gerontol. Soc., Western Gerontol. Soc., Am. Assn. Retired Persons (vote com.), Audubon Nature Program, Forest History Soc., Journalism Edn. Assn., Greeley Numis. Club, Greeley C. of C., U. No. Colo. Emeritus Faculty Assn., Nat. Travel Club, Civitan (lt. gov. Mountain Plains dist. 1960-62), Knife and Fork Club, Rep. Club (Washington), Rep. Congl. Club (Washington), Eagles Club, Phi Delta Kappa. Mem. Reformed Christian Ch. Am. Home: 1230 24th Ave Greeley CO 80631-3516

SEAGER, FLOYD WILLIAMS, medical educator; b. Ogden, Utah, July 1, 1921; s. Roy Alfred and Florence (Williams) S.; m. Beth Anne Seager, Feb. 6, 1943 (div. June 1965); m. Dauna Gayle Olson, July 7, 1973; children: Stephen, Nancy, Candice, Pamela, Kevin, Karen; stepchildren: Jeff Stokes, John Stokes, Jeannettes Memmott. AS, Weber State U., 1941; BS in Chemistry, U. Utah, 1943; MD, Hahnemann U., 1947. Diplomate Nat. Bd. Med. Examiners. Pvt. practice Ogden, 1949-51; founder Ogden Clinic, 1951; chief of staff McKay Hosp., Ogden, 1979-81, trustee, 1989—; clin. prof. medicine U. Utah Med. Sch., Salt Lake City, 1990—. Editor: (med. jours.) Sub Q, 1980—, Ad Libitum, 1989. Capt. USMC, 1951-53, Korea. Decorated 6 Battle Stars, Bronze Star; Dr. Seager Day named in his honor Mayor of Ogden, 1991; named Dr. of Yr., Utah State Med. Soc., 1993, Quiet Pioneer, Gov. Utah, 1991; recipient Point of Light award Pres. Bush, 1992. Mem. Am. Legion, Dixieland Jazz Soc. (chmn. bd. dirs.), Rotary Club Ogden, Elks. Republican. Mormon. Avocations: playing piano, chess and bridge tournaments. Home and Office: 4046 S 895 E Ogden UT 84403-2416

SEAGRAM, NORMAN MEREDITH, corporate executive; b. Toronto, Ont., Can., July 10, 1934; s. Norman Oliver and Constance Beatrice (Mills) S.; m. Joyce Elizabeth McMackon, Aug. 21, 1958; children: Susan Elizabeth, Norman Philip, Joseph Frederick, Samantha. Student, Trinity Coll., Port Hope, Ont.; BASc, U. Toronto, 1958; MSc, U. Birmingham, Eng., 1964. Cons. Associated Indsl. Cons. Ltd. and Mgmt. Scis. Ltd., London, Nairobi, Kenya, Moshi, Tanzania, Harari, Zimbabwe, Halifax, N., S., Can., Toronto, Ont., Can., 1960-68; various mktg. and planning positions The Molson Cos., Molson Breweries of Can. Ltd., 1968-78; pres. Seaway/Midwest Ltd., Toronto, 1978-82, Molson Western Breweries Ltd., Calgary, Alta, Can., 1983-85, Molson Ont. Breweries Ltd., Toronto, 1985-86; exec. v.p. The Molson Cos., Toronto, 1986-92; chmn., CEO Can. Liquid Air, Toronto, 1993—; chmn. Molson Breweries Can. Ltd., Club de Hockey Can. Inc., Vancouver (Can.) Baseball Ltd., Santa Fe Beverage Co., 1986-88; bd. dirs. Harbourfront Ctr., VitalAire Co. Mem. Bus. Coun. on Nat. Issues, Coun. for Can. Unity, Coun. for Bus. and Arts in Can., Can. Found. for Internat. Mgmt., Inst. Corp. Dirs., Olympic Trust Can., Trinity Coll. Sch. Mem. Assn. Profl. Engrs. Ont., Alpha Delta Phi, Toronto Club, Toronto Badminton and Racquet Club, Montreal Badminton and Squash Club, Hillside Tennis Club, Empire Club, The Mount Royal Club. Conservative. Anglican. Avocations: tennis, squash, golf, skiing, hockey. Office: 20 York Mills Rd Ste 400, Toronto, ON Canada M2P 2C2

SEAGRAVE, JANET LEE, economic developer; b. Okinawa, Japan, Dec. 31, 1951; (parents Am. citizens); d. Rodman Gamble and Patricia Jane (McDonald) S. Student, Maple Woods Coll., 1974-78, Del Mar Coll., 1978-79. Cert. econ. developer. Exec. sec. Am. Indsl. Devel. Coun., Kansas City, Mo., 1973-78; dir. western sales Indsl. Properties Report, Corpus Christi, Tex., 1978-79; indsl. devel. location cons. Amarillo (Tex.) Bd. Devel., 1979-81; dir. econ. devel. divsn. Roswell (N.Mex.) C. of C., 1981-86; exec. dir. Sheridan (Wyo.) County Econ. Devel. Coun., 1986-90, High Plains Devel. Authority, Great Falls, Mont., 1990-94, Indsl. Devel. Corp. of Lea County, Hobbs, N.Mex., 1994—; mem. faculty Ariz. Basic Econ. Devel. course, U. Ariz., Tucson, 1983-94. Bd. regents Am. Indsl. Devel. Coun., 1981-83, bd. dirs., 1984-88; chmn., bd. dirs., mediator, treas. Great Falls Area Labor/Mgmt. Com., 1991-94; mem. Pres.'s coun. Coll. of Great Falls, 1991-94. 9th woman in N.Am. to obtain Cert. Econ. Developer designation, 1982. Mem. Mont. Profl. Econ. Devel. Assn. (bd. dirs. 1993-94), Am. Devel. Coun. (bd. dirs. 1982-86, bd. regents 1982-84), N.Mex. Indsl. Devel. Execs. (bd. dirs. 1994—), N.Mex. Commerce and Industry Assn., Hobbs Rotary, Order of Eastern Star. Republican. Baptist. Avocations: gardening, walking, working with children, church activity. Home: PO Box 294 Hobbs NM 88241-0294 Office: 2702 N Grimes St # B Hobbs NM 88240-1804

SEAGREN, ALICE, state legislator; b. 1947; m. Fred Seagren; 2 children. BS, SE Mo. State U. Mem. Minn. Ho. of Reps., 1993—. Active Bloomington (Minn.) Sch. Bd., 1989-92. Mem. Bloomington C. of C. (bd. dirs. 1990-92), Phi Gamma Nu, Alpha Chi Omega. Republican. Home: 9730 Palmer Cir Bloomington MN 55437-2017 Office: Minn Ho of Reps State Capital Building Saint Paul MN 55155-1606

SEAGREN, STEPHEN LINNER, oncologist; b. Mpls., Mar. 13, 1941; s. Morley Raymond and Carol Christine (Linner) S.; m. Jill Garrie; 1 child, Sean Garrie. AB, Harvard U., 1963; MD, Northwestern U., 1967. Diplomate Am. Bd. Internal Medicine, Am. Bd. Med. Oncology, Am. Bd. Radiology. From asst. prof. to assoc. prof. radiology and medicine U. Calif., San Diego, 1977-88, prof., 1988—. Contbr. over 80 articles to profl. jours. Bd. dirs. Wellness Cmty., San Diego, 1988—, chair profl. adv. com., 1988—; chair radiol. oncology com. Cancer and Acute Leukemia Group, Chgo., 1986—. Lt. comdr. USNR, 1971-73. Fellow ACP. Avocations: physical fitness, bridge, skiing, golf, tennis. Office: U Calif San Diego Med Ctr 200 W Arbor Dr San Diego CA 92103

SEAL, popular musician; b. London. Recipient Song of Yr. Grammy award, 1996, Record of Yr. Grammy award, 1996, Best Male Pop Vocal Performance Grammy award, 1996. Office: Warner Bros Records Inc 75 Rockefeller Plz New York NY 10019-4500*

SEALE, JAMES MILLARD, religious organization administrator, clergyman; b. Middlesboro, Ky., Oct. 4, 1930; s. Albert Tyler and Edith Josephine (Buchanan) S.; m. Mary Dudley Harrod; children: William Alan, Ann Lynn Seale Hazelrigg. BA, Transylvania U., 1952; BD, Lexington Theol. Sem., 1955, MDiv, 1963, D Ministry, 1981. Ordained to ministry Christian Ch. (Disciples of Christ), 1951. Student pastor various Christian Chs., Ky., 1949-54; pastor 1st Christian Ch., Pikeville, Ky., 1954-58, Erlanger (Ky.) Christian Ch., 1958-61; sr. minister 1st Christian Ch., Mt. Sterling, Ky., 1961-70, Paris, Ky., 1978-82; stewardship sec. Gen. Office Christian Ch., Indpls., 1970-74; adminstr. Christian Ch. Home of Louisville, 1974-77; dir. devel. Christian Ch. Homes Ky., Louisville, 1978; pres. Disciples of Christ Hist. Soc., Nashville, 1983-95. Author: A Century of Faith and Caring, 1983, Forward From The Past, 1991; editor jour. Discipliana, 1983-92. Pres. Kiwanis Club, Pikeville, 1957, Mt. Sterling, 1963, lt. gov., Ctrl. Ky., 1965. Avocations: writing, photography, golf, fishing.

SEALE, JOHN CLEMENT, director, cinematographer; b. Warwick, Queensland, Australia, Oct. 5, 1942; s. Eric Clement and Marjorie Lyndon (Pool) S.; m. Louise Lee Mutton, Sept. 23, 1967; children: Derin Anthony, Brianna Lee. Grad. high sch., Sydney, Australia. Camera asst. film dept. Australian Broadcasting Com., 1962-68; freelance technician, camera operator various films, series, commls., 1968-76, dir. photography various film cos., 1976; dir. feature film, Till There Was You, 1989-90. Dir. photography: Goodbye Paradise (Golden Tripod 1982), Careful, He Might Hear You (Best Cinematography 1983), Witness, 1984 (Golden Tripod 1984, Oscar nomination 1986, Brit. Acad. award nomination 1986), The Hitcher, 1985, Children of a Lesser God, 1985 (Golden Tripod 1987), The Mosquito Coast, 1986, Stakeout, 1987, Gorillas in the Mist (Brit. Acad. award nomination 1989, Premier Mag. Cinematographer of the Yr. 1989), Rainman, 1988 (Acad. award nomination 1988, Artistic Achievement award 1989), Dead Poets Society, 1989, The Doctor, 1991, Lorenzo's Oil, 1992, The Firm, 1993, The Paper, 1993, Beyond Rangoon, 1994, The American President, 1995, The English Patient, 1995. Recipient Film Critics Cir. Australia 1990 Tribute. Mem. Australian Cinematographers Soc. (named Cinematographer of Yr. 1982, 84). Avocations: building boats, sailing.

SEALE, MARY LOUISE, medical, surgical and geriatrics nurse; b. Wills Point, Tex., Nov. 30, 1930; d. Paul DeWitt and Beatrice Earl (Coplen) S.; div.; children: Raymond L. McDowell, Mary E. McDowell Graves, Audrey E. Smith Whisenhunt, Carol Jean Smith Baker, Jerry D. Smith. Lic. vocat. nurse, Fanning County Sch., Bonham, Tex., 1974; student, Navarro Jr. Coll., Corsicanna, Tex., 1951-52; ADN, Grayson County Coll., Denison, Tex., 1979-80; AS, Paris (Tex.) Jr. Coll., 1986. Lic. vocat. nurse, Tex. Lic. vocat. nurse II Scott and White Hosp., Temple, Tex.; lic. vocat. nurse Fannin County Hosp., Bonham, Tex.; attendant, student psychiat. nurse technician Tex. Terrell State Hosp., 1951-52; lic. vocat. nurse Sam Rayburn Meml. Vets. Hosp., Bonham, Tex. Vol. ARC, Denison, Tex. Mem. DAV Aux., Am. Assn. Ret. Persons. Baptist. Home: PO Box 285 Bonham TX 75418-0285

SEALE, ROBERT L., state treasurer; b. Inglewood, Calif., Oct. 4, 1941; m. Judy Seale (dec.). BSA, Calif. Poly. U. Former contr. and sr. fin. officer Rockwell Internat.; sr. accountant Ernst & Ernst, L.A.; mng. ptnr. Pangborn & Co., Ltd. CPA's, 1985-88; now state treas. State of Nev. Former treas. Nev. Rep. Com. Mem. Nat. Assn. State Treas. (pres.). Office: Office of State Treas Capital Complex Carson City NV 89710

SEALE, WILLIAM EDWARD, finance educator; b. Lynchburg, Va., Feb. 10, 1941; s. Frank Earl and Viola Elizabeth (Parks) S.; m. Patricia Jeanette Marquart, 1962 (div. 1990); children: William E. Jr., James Anthony, Patricia Jeanette; m. Marguerite E. Pelissier, 1992. A.B. in Chemistry, U. Ky., 1963, M.S. in Agrl. Econs., 1969, Ph.D. in Agrl. Econs., 1975. Farm mgmt. specialist U. Ky., Lexington, 1969-74; legis. asst. U.S. Senate, Washington, 1975-79; v.p. Commodity Exchange Inc., N.Y.C., 1979-83; commr. Commodity Futures Trade Commn., Washington, 1983-88; prof. fin., chmn. dept. Sch. Bus. and Pub. Mgmt. George Washington U., Washington, 1988—. Contbr. articles to profl. jours. and mags. Mem. So. Agrl. Econs. Assn., Am. Agrl. Econs. Assn., Am. Fin. Assn., Fin. Mgmt. Assn. Democrat. Roman Catholic. Avocations: yachting, amateur radio. Home: 1936 Franklin Ave Mc Lean VA 22101-5307 Office: George Washington U Dept Fin Washington DC 20052

SEALL, STEPHEN ALBERT, lawyer; b. South Bend, Ind., Oct. 24, 1940; s. Stephen Henry and Mildred Rita (MacDonald) S.; m. Barbara Ann Halloran, June 25, 1966; children: John Paul, Edward Andrew, Ann Marie. BA, Purdue U., 1963; postgrad., Cornell U. Grad. Sch. Bus. Adminstrn., 1963; LLB, U. Notre Dame, 1966. Bar: Ind. 1966, U.S. Claims Ct. 1973, U.S. Tax Ct. 1968, U.S. Ct. Appeals (6th cir.) 1980, U.S. Ct. Appeals (7th cir.) 1969, U.S. Supreme Ct. 1973. Assoc. Thornburg, McGill, Deahl, Harman, Carey & Murray, South Bend, 1966-71; ptnr. Barnes & Thornburg and predecessor firm Thornburg, McGill, Deahl, Harman, Carey & Murray, 1972—, vice chmn. exec. and mgmt. coms., 1985—; speaker in field. Mem. editorial bd. Notre Dame Law Rev., 1964-66. Mem. Mayor's Com. on Downtown Devel., South Bend, 1975-77, Mayor's Com. on Utilization of Downtown Bldgs., South Bend, 1988—; trustee Project Future, South Bend, 1986—; dir. Meml. Health Found., 1992—, United Way of St. Joseph County, Inc., 1992—. Fellow Am. Coll. Tax Counsel, Ind. Bar Found.; mem. ABA (taxation sect.), Ind. State Bar Assn. (chmn. taxation sect. 1977-78), Summit Club (chmn. 1976-77), Morris Park Country Club. Democrat. Roman Catholic. Avocations: weightlifting, softball, golf. Home: 17705 Waxwing Ln South Bend IN 46635-1328 Office: Barnes & Thornburg 600 1st Source Bank Ctr 100 N Michigan St South Bend IN 46601-1630

SEALS, DAN WAYLAND, country music singer; b. McCarney, Tex., Feb. 8, 1948. With England Dan & John Ford Coley, 1969-80; recording artist A&M, 1971-80, EMI Records, 1985-86, Liberty Records, 1988-92, Warner Bros., 1992—. Albums (with John Ford Coley) Nights are Forever Without You, 1976, Dowdy Ferry Road, 1977, Dr. Heckle & Mr. Jive, 1979; solo albums Won't Be Blue Anymore, 1985, The Best, 1988, Rage On, 1988, On Arrival, 1990, The Songwriter, 1992, Walking the Wire, 1992, Best of Dan Seals, 1994, Fired Up, 1994; gold #1 single (with John Ford Coley) I'd Really Love To See You Tonight, 1976. Recipient Duet of Yr. award (with Marie Osmond) for Meet Me in Montana from Country Music Assn., 1985, Single of Yr. award for Bop from Country Music Assn., 1988. Office: Warner Bros Records 3300 Warner Blvd Burbank CA 91505-4632

SEALS, MARGARET LOUISE, newspaper editor; b. Buckhannon, W.Va., Oct. 27, 1944; d. James Richard and Helen Margaret (Brown) Crumrine; m. Harry Eugene Seals, Jan. 10, 1975. BS in journalism, W. Va. U., 1966; MS in mass. comm., Va. Commonwealth U., 1983. Reporter, copy editor Democrat & Chronicle, Rochester, N.Y., 1966-67, Dayton (Ohio) Daily News, 1967-68; copy editor Richmond (Va.) Times-Dispatch, 1968-75, copy desk slot editor, 1975-81, exec. news editor, 1981, asst. mng. editor, 1982-92, deputy mng. editor, 1992-93, mng. editor, 1994—; adv. bd. Sch. Mass Comms., Va. Commonwealth U., 1988-93. Named Outstanding Woman in Comms. YWCA Met. Richmond, 1989. Mem. Am. Soc. Newspaper Editors, Soc. Profl. Journalists, Va. Press Women Inc. (pres. 1990-92, 2d v.p. 1988-90, treas. 1986-88, Press Woman of Yr. 1986); Assoc. Press Mng. Editors (dir. 1993-95, editor APME News 1993-94, treas. 1996). Avocations: history, historical fiction, jazz, walking. Office: Richmond-Times Dispatch 333 E Grace St Richmond VA 23219-1000

SEALY, ALBERT HENRY, lawyer; b. Columbus, Ohio, Oct. 23, 1917; s. Albert H. and Lillian E. (Stock) S.; m. Flora Kinkel, Aug. 23, 1947; children: Catherine Ann, Thomas P., Joan Deborah. BA summa cum laude, Ohio State U., 1938; LLB (JD), Harvard Coll., 1941; DL (hon.), Wright State U., 1982. Bar: N.Y. 1942, Ohio 1955. With Simpson, Thacher & Bartlett, N.Y.C., 1941-43, 46-55, Smith and Schnacke, Dayton and Columbus, Ohio, 1955-89; sec. Mead Corp., 1964-75. Author: Macro Blueprint, 1986; contbr. articles to profl. jours. Mem. Ohio Ho. Reps., 1966-68; chmn. Ohioans for Fair Taxation, 1972—, Ohio Inst. on Pub. Fin., 1973—; chmn. bd. trustees Wright State U., 1977—; exec. dir. Inst. Nat. Econ. and Social Dialogue, 1982-87. Lt. USNR, 1943-46. Mem. ABA, Assn. of Bar of City of N.Y., Phi Beta Kappa, Sigma Chi. Home: 3105 Burr St Fairfield CT 06430-1853

SEALY, JOSEPHINE SYLVIA DOREEN, primary care nurse; b. Ebenezer, Antigua, W.I., Apr. 15, 1935; d. John James Emanuel and Margaret Elizabeth (John) Nanton; m. Vernol S. Sealy, May 8, 1965; children: Vernetta, Vernol Jr. Diploma in Nursing, Howard U., 1970; BS in Sociology, BSW, Ea. Mich. U., 1982. RN, Washington, Mich.; cert. BCLS, med.-surg. nurse. Staff nurse Howard U. Med. Ctr., Washington, 1971, Hutzel Hosp., Detroit, 1973-76; charge nurse Kith Haven Convalescent, Ypsilanti, Mich., 1981; staff nurse U. Mich., Ann Arbor, 1983—. Mem. ANA, Mich. Nurses Assn., Am. Soc. Plastic and Reconstructive Surg. Nurses. Seventh-day Adventist. Avocations: writing poetry, walking, Biblical studies, travel. Home: 3667 Helen St Ypsilanti MI 48197-3760 Office: Univ Mich Med Ctr 1500 E Medical Center Dr Ann Arbor MI 48109-0999

SEAMAN, ALFRED BARRETT, journalist; b. Rockville Ctr., N.Y., July 4, 1945; s. Alfred Jarvis and Mary Margaret (Schill) S.; m. Laura Powers Maxwell, Apr. 25, 1970; children: Katherine Maxwell, Margaret Elise, Elizabeth Barrett. BA, Hamilton Coll., 1967; MBA, Columbia U., 1971. Reporter Life mag., N.Y.C., 1971-72, Fortune mag., N.Y.C., 1972; corr. Time mag., N.Y.C., 1973, Chgo., 1973-76, Bonn, Germany, 1976-78; bur. chief Time mag., Detroit, 1978-81; dep. bur. chief Time mag., Washington, 1981-83, White House corr., 1984-88; dep. chief corrs. Time mag., N.Y.C., 1988-91, sr. editor, 1991-94, spl. projects editor, 1994—. Co-author: Going for Broke: The Chrysler Story, 1981. Alumni trustee Hamilton Coll., Clinton, N.Y., 1990-93, 94—; trustee Village of Irvington, N.Y., 1992-94. With USNR, 1969-71. Mem. Ardsley County Club. Episcopalian. Avocations: squash, tennis, golf. Home: Ardsley Ave W Ardsley On Hudson NY 10503 Office: Time Mag Rockefeller Ctr New York NY 10020

SEAMAN, ALFRED JARVIS, retired advertising agency executive; b. Hempstead, L.I., N.Y., Sept. 17, 1912; s. Alfred J. and Ellen (Delaney) S.; m. Mary M. Schill, Sept. 26, 1937 (dec. June 1975); children: Marilyn Hollingsworth, Susan, Barry, Deborah; m. Honor S. Mellor, July 16, 1977. BS, Columbia U., 1935; LittD, L.I. U., 1987. Account exec. Fuller & Smith & Ross, Inc., N.Y.C., 1937-41; partner Knight & Gilbert. Inc., Boston, 1941-43; with Compton Advt., Inc., N.Y.C., 1946-59; exec. v.p., creative dir., dir. Compton Advt., Inc., 1954-59; vice chmn. bd., chmn. exec. com. SSC & B, Inc., 1959-60, pres., chief exec. officer, 1960-79, chmn., chief exec. officer, 1979-81; dir., mem. exec. com. Interpublic Group of Cos., Inc. Hon. bd. dirs., adv. council, founding chmn. Advt. Ednl. Found.; bd. dirs., hon. dir. com. Advt. Council.; chmn. planning bd., 1962—, mayor Village Upper Brookville, 1966—; chmn. emeritus Samuel Waxman Cancer Research Found. Lt. USNR, 1943-46. Named to Advt. Hall of Fame, 1983. Clubs: U.S. Sr. Golf Assn., Creek (Locust Valley, L.I.) (pres.), Piping Rock (Locust Valley, L.I.), Racquet and Tennis (N.Y.C.), Links (N.Y.C.), Brook (N.Y.C.), Jupiter Island (Fla.), Nat. Golf Links Am. (Southampton, N.Y.), Seminole (Fla.), Hobe Sound Yacht (Fla.). Home: Wolver Hollow Rd Upper Brookville Oyster Bay NY 11771 also: Jupiter Island 126 Gomez Rd Hobe Sound FL 33455-2424 Office: 220 E 42nd St New York NY 10017-4011

SEAMAN, BARBARA (ANN ROSNER), author; b. N.Y.C., Sept. 11, 1935; d. Henry Jerome and Sophie Blanche (Kimels) Rosner; m. Gideon Seaman, Jan. 13, 1957 (div.); children: Noah Samuel, Elana Felicia, Shira Jean. B.A. (Ford Found. scholar), Oberlin Coll., 1956, L.H.D. (hon.), 1978; cert. in advanced sci. writing (Sloan-Rockefeller fellow), Columbia U. Sch. Journalism, 1968. Columnist Brides Mag., N.Y.C., 1964-68; columnist, contbg. editor Ladies' Home Jour., N.Y.C., 1965-69; editor child care and edn. Family Circle, N.Y.C., 1970-73; contbg. editor Omni mag., 1978; cons. FYI, ABC-TV, 1979-80; v.p. for devel. David Brooks Prodns., 1990-94; contbg. editor MS Mag., 1993—; cons. U.S. Senate subcom. on monopoly: Nelson pill hearings, 1970; presented testimony to Senate and Congl. coms., 1970—; lectr. in field; participant TV discussion shows; tchr. Coll. New Rochelle, 1975, Sagaris Inst., 1975, CUNY, 1993; founding mem. N.Y. Women's Forum, 1973—; co-founder Nat. Women's Health Network, 1975—, Comm. Consultants for Choice, 1985-86, Nat. Task Force Sexual Malpractice, 1985-86, Families Against Sexually Abusive Therapists and Other Profls., 1992—; v.p. Women's Med. Ctr., N.Y.C., 1971-73; mem. ERA Emergency Task Force, 1979; mem. adv. coun. Feminist Press, Old Westbury, N.Y., 1975; mem. adv. bd. Feminist Ctr. for Human Growth and Devel., 1979, Women's History Libr., Berkeley, Calif., 1973-75; mem. steering com. Women's Forum, 1974; mem. adv. bd. NOW, N.Y., 1973, Women's Guide to Books, 1974, Jewish Women for Affirmative Action, Evanston, Ill., 1973—, Jour. Women and Health, 1975, Jewish Feminist Orgn., N.Y.C., 1975; chair com. domestic violence Nat. Coun. Women's Health, 1993—; judge for various journalism awards. Author: The Doctors' Case Against the Pill, 1969, rev. edit., 1980, 25th anniversary edit., 1995, Free and Female, 1972, (with G. Seaman) Women and the Crisis in Sex Hormones, 1977, Lovely Me: The Life of Jacqueline Susann, 1987, 10th anniversary edit., 1996; contbg. author: foreword to Lunaception, 1975; The Bisexuals, 1974, Career and Motherhood, 1979, The Hormone Industry, 1994; author (play) I Am a Woman, 1972; contbr. various anthologies including Rooms with No View, 1974, Women and Men, 1975, Seizing Our Bodies, 1978, Encyclopaedia of Childbirth, 1992; narrator (film) Taking Our Bodies Back, 1974; contbr. editorials and revs. to newspapers, popular mags.; books and articles translated into Spanish, German, Dutch, Turkish, Japanese, Hebrew, French, Italian. Alumni cons. women's studies program Oberlin Coll., 1975; mem. motivation com. Am. Cancer Soc., 1973; mem. adv. com. Older Women's Health Project, NYU Med. Ctr., 1980; bd. dirs. Safe Transp. of People, N.Y.C., 1975, Women's Health Newsletter, 1983; adv. bd. DES Action, 1977; cons. Nat. Task Force on DES, 1978; contraceptive research br. HEW, 1980; v.p., bd. dirs. ARM (Abortion Rights Moblzn.), 1981—; mem. hon. bd. Carcinogen Info. Program, St. Louis, 1981; trustee Nat. Coun. on Women in Medicine, 1990—; chmn. adv. bd. Coalition for Family Justice, 1991—; co-chair Domestic Violence com. N.Y. Women's Agenda, 1992-93. Recipient citation for books as first to raise issue of sexism in health care as world-wide issue Libr. of Congress, 1973, citation as author responsible for patient package inserts on prescriptions HEW, 1970, Matrix award, 1978, Pioneer Woman award Resources Divsn. of Am. Assn. Retired Persons, 1986, Athena award Nat. Coun. Women's Health, 1992, Health Advocacy award Health Policy Adv. Ctr., APHA, 1994, Project Censored award, 1996; inviting com. Am. Writers Congress. Mem. PEN, Internat. Women's Forum, Authors League, Nat. Assn. Sci. Writers. Address: 110 West End Ave Apt 5D New York NY 10023-6348

SEAMAN, DARYL KENNETH, oil company executive; b. Rouleau, Sask., Can., Apr. 28, 1922. BSME, U. Sask., 1948, LLD (hon.), 1982; LLD (hon.), U. Calgary, 1993. Cert. mech. engr. CEO Bow Valley Industries Ltd., Calgary, Alta., Can., 1962-70, 85-91, chmn., chief exec. officer, 1970-82; chmn. Box Valley Industries Ltd., Calgary, Alta., Can., 1982-85; pres. Bow Valley Industries Ltd., Calgary, Alta., Can., 1985-87; chmn. Bow Valley Industries Ltd., 1991-92; bd. dirs. Renaissance Energy Ltd., Calgary, Trimac Ltd., Potash Corp. Sask. Inc., Encal Energy Ltd., Can. Chem. Reclaiming Ltd., Abacan Resource Corp., Basic Industries Corp.; co-owner, bd. dirs. Calgary Flames Hockey Club; chmn., pres. Dox Investments, Inc. Mem. Royal Commn. Econ. Union and Devel. Prospects for Can., 1982-85; active numerous coms. for fundraising U. Sask.; hon. chmn. The Western Heritage Centre Soc.; chmn. nat. adv. com. Banff Sch. Mgmt. Served with RCAF, 1941-45, North Africa, Italy. There is no repetition since it is indicated as an award you received and as a membership. Mem. Assn. Profl. Engrs., Geologists and Geophysicists (hon. life, Frank Spragins award, 1985, McGill Mgmt. Achievement award, 1979), Order of Canada 1993, Western Heritage Centre Soc., Ranchmen's Club, RAF Club, Earl Grey Golf Club, Calgary Petroleum Club, Calgary Golf and Country Club, U. Calgary Chancellor's Club. Progressive Conservative. Mem. United Ch. Can. Avocations: ranching, golf, hunting, skiing. Home and Office: Dox Investments Inc, 500 333 5th Ave SW, Calgary, AB Canada T2P 3B6

SEAMAN, DONALD ROY, investment company executive; b. b., Rouleau, Sask., Can., July 26, 1925; s. Byron Luther and Letha Mae (Patton) S.; m. Eleanor Victoria Lee, Nov. 4, 1950; children: Victoria Anne, Donna Jane, Lauraine Suzanne (dec.), Marilou Kathleen. B.S.M.E., U. Sask., 1947. Indsl. engr. Canadian Industries Ltd., Kingston, Ont., Can., 1947-50; v.p.

Bow Valley Industries, Calgary, Alta., Can., 1950-75, dir., 1950-89, sr. v.p., 1986-87; pres. Bow Valley Resource Services, Calgary, 1976-87; bd. dirs. NuGas Ltd., Northstar Energy Corp., Dominion Explorers Inc., Artisan Drilling Ltd., Best Pacific Resources Ltd., Flowtech Energy Corp., Piper Petroleums Ltd., Ryan Energy Techs., Inc. Trustee Alta. Heritage Found. for Med. Research. Mem. Profl. Engrs. Alta. Clubs: Petroleu, Glencoe, Earl Grey Golf (dir. 1966-72). Office: D R S Resource Investments Inc, 333-5 Ave SW # 500, Calgary, AB Canada T2P 3B6

SEAMAN, EMMA LUCY, artist, poet; b. West Freedom, Pa., Dec. 5, 1932; d. Roger Leslie and Lillian Emeline (Phillips) Eddinger; m. Roger John Seaman, Sept. 14, 1958; 1 child, Roger Kent. Grad. H.S., Seneca, Pa. Sec. to supt. Cranberry H.S., Seneca, 1951-56; flight attendant, hostess Trans World Airlines, Newark, 1956-57; copy writer Radio St. WFRA, Franklin, Pa., 1957-58. Works have been exhibited at Art League of Marco Island, Fla., 1985-93, Sussex County Arts and Heritage Coun. Fine Arts Exhbns., Newton, 1990-94, N.J. Herald Art Show, Newton, 1990, Annual Sparta (N.J.) Day Event, 1990, St. Mary's Art Festival, Sparta, 1991-94, Hilltop Art Exhibit, Sparta, 1991-94, Edison Festival of Light, Ft. Myers, Fla., 1992; represented in permanent collection of Fame Mus. Teterboro (N.J.) Airport; one woman show: Sparta Libr., N.J., 1994; contbr. numerous poems to publs. Sunday sch. tchr., Sparta, 1965-74; organizer, operator Paper Drives, Sparta, 1965-74. Recipient First Pl. Beginners Oils award Creative Canvas Art Assn., Newton, 1982, Purchase award St. Mary's Art Festival, Sparta, N.J., 1991, honorable mention, 1993. Mem. ASPCA, AARP, People for the Ethical Treatment Animals, Art League Marco Island, Sussex County Arts and Heritage Coun., Sussex County Arts Assn., Studio A Art Assn., Edison Festival of Light, Nat. Humane Edn. Soc., Human Soc. U.S., Doris Day Animal League, Animal Legal Def. Fund, Women's Mus. Art, Smithsonial Assn., Antique Airplane Assn., Newton (N.J.) Meml. Hosp. Aux., Sparta (N.J.) Woman's Club, Lake Mohawk Country Club. Avocations: flying, reading, cooking, sewing, traveling. Home: 54 Alpine Trl Sparta NJ 07871-1509

SEAMAN, IRVING, JR., public relations consultant; b. Milw., July 14, 1923; s. Irving and Anne (Douglas) S.; m. June Carry, June 24, 1950; children: Peter Stewart, Marion Carry, Irving Osborne, Anne Douglas. B.A., Yale U., 1944. With Continental Ill. Nat. Bank & Trust Co., Chgo., 1947-61; v.p. Continental Ill. Nat. Bank & Trust Co., 1959-61; pres., chief exec. officer, dir. Nat. Boulevard Bank, Chgo., 1961-65; chmn. exec. com., chief exec. officer, dir. Nat. Boulevard Bank, 1966-76; vice chmn. bd., dir. Sears Bank and Trust Co., Chgo., 1976-77; pres., chief operating officer, dir. Sears Bank and Trust Co., 1977-82; sr. cons. Burson-Marsteller, Chgo., 1982-94; chmn. bd. Associated Bank Chgo., 1985—. Mem. Northwestern U. Assn.; life mem. bd. dirs. Lake Forest Hosp.; bd. dirs. United Way of Chgo., 1975-89, pres., 1979; bd. dirs. United Way/Crusade of Mercy, 1980-89, 94-95, vice chmn., 1980-81; trustee Chgo. Symphony Orch., 1987—. Lt. (j.g.) USNR, WWII. Mem. Commonwealth Club, Econ. Club, Chgo. Club, Comml. Club, Racquet Club, Onwentsia Club, Winter Club, Old Elm Club (Highland Park, Ill.), Shoreacres Club (Lake Bluff, Ill.), Augusta Nat. Golf Club (Ga.), Marsh Landing Club (Fla.). Home: 946 Elm Tree Rd Lake Forest IL 60045-1410 Office: 1 E Wacker Dr Chicago IL 60606

SEAMAN, JEFFREY RICHARD, academic administrator; b. Roslyn, N.Y., Feb. 22, 1949; s. Richard MacAvoy and Jane Louise (Decker) S.; m. I. Elaine Allen, Jan. 21, 1978; children: Christopher, Julia. BS, Cornell U., 1971, MA, MS, 1977, PhD, 1984. Lectr. Cornell U., Ithaca, N.Y., 1976-77; rsch. assoc. U. Pa., Phila., 1978-86, lectr. stats., 1979-84, dir. rsch. project, 1982-84, dir. microcomputer svcs., 1984-85, dir. computing resource, 1985-92, assoc. vice provost, 1990-92; prin. Pond View Assocs., Dover, Mass., 1992—; exec. dir. tech. Lesley Coll., Cambridge, Mass., 1994—; cons. Schuykill Twp., Valley Forge, Pa., 1990-92; mem. adv. bd. Apple Computer, 1985-90, Word Perfect, Orem, Utah, 1989-91, IBM, 1984-86. Office: Lesley Coll 29 Everett St Cambridge MA 02138-2790

SEAMAN, PEGGY JEAN, lawyer; b. New Orleans, Nov. 21, 1949; d. William David and Leah Catherine (Bourdet) Smith; m. Terry Noako Seaman, Dec. 22, 1970; children: Vanya Lianne, Ember Catherine. BA, Rutgers U.-Camden, 1974; JD, N.Y. Law Sch., 1978. Bar: N.Y. 1978, Va. 1980, U.S. Dist. Ct. Va., 1980, U.S. Dist. Ct. (so. and ea. dists.) N.Y. 1978. Pvt. practice, N.Y.C., 1978-79; gen. atty. Merit Systems Protection Bd., Office of Appeals, Washington, 1980-82, presiding ofcl., Washington regional office, Falls Church, Va., 1982-85, adminstrv. judge St. Louis regional office, 1985-87; atty. Office of Dep. Exec. Dir. for Regional Ops., Washington, 1987-89; gen. atty. Office of Appeals Counsel, Washington, 1989-95; adminstrv. judge Denver Field Office, 1995—. Recipient Sustained Superior Performance awards Merit Systems Protection Bd., Spl. Act award, 1988, Chmn.'s Honor award, 1991). Mem. ABA, Athenaeum Honor Soc., Mensa. Democrat. Home: 383 Van Gordon St Apt 11-357 Denver CO 80228 Office: Denver Field Office 12567 W Cedar Ave Denver CO 80228

SEAMAN, ROBERT LEROY, retired technology company executive, consultant; b. Auburn, N.Y., Mar. 26, 1924; s. LeRoy John and Alice Mary (Smith) S.; m. Jacqueline Bailey, June 27, 1949; children: Peter B. (dec.), David S., Richard J. B. Mgmt. Engring., Rensselaer Poly. Inst., 1950; M.S., MIT, 1968. With Ford Motor Co., Detroit, 1950-55; div. controller Curtiss-Wright Corp., Princeton, N.J., 1956-58; internal cons. CBS, Inc., N.Y.C., 1958-60; asst. controller Raytheon Co., Lexington, Mass., 1960-68, dir. planning, 1968, v.p. strategic planning, 1969-89; cons. in field, 1989—. Co-author: a computer-aided, on-line, planning and analysis system, STEPS, 1968. Served as lt. (j.g.) USNR, 1942-45. Decorated DFC, Air medal with 3 oak leaf clusters. Mem. Fin. Execs. Inst., Planning Forum, Rensselaer Soc. Engrs., Sigma Xi, Tau Beta Pi, Epsilon Delta Sigma. Club: N.Y., Univ., Econ. (N.Y.), El Conquistador Country. Home: 4455 Bay Club Dr Bradenton FL 34210

SEAMAN, TONY, university athletic coach. Head coach NCAA Divsn. 1A lacrosse Johns Hopkins Blue Jays, Balt., 1990—. Office: Johns Hopkins U Charles And # 34th Sts Baltimore MD 21218*

SEAMAN, WILLIAM BERNARD, physician, radiology educator; b. Chgo., Jan. 5, 1917; s. Benjamin and Dorothy E. S.; m. Veryl Swick, February 26, 1944; children—Cheryl Dorothy, William David. Student, U. Mich., 1934-37; M.D., Harvard U., 1941. Diplomate: Am. Bd. Radiology. Intern Billings Hosp., U. Chgo., 1941-42; asst. radiology Yale U. Sch. Medicine, 1947-48, instr., 1948-49; instr. radiology Washington U. Sch. Medicine, St. Louis, 1949-51, assoc. prof., 1951-55, prof., 1955-56; prof. radiology, chmn. dept. Coll. Phys. and Surg., Columbia U., 1956-82; James Picker prof. emeritus Columbia U., 1982—; dir. radiology service, trustee Presbyn. Hosp., N.Y.C. Served as maj. USAAF, 1942-46; flight surgeon. Recipient W.B. Cannon medal Soc. Gastro-intestinal Radiologists, 1979, Gold medal Am. Coll. Radiology, 1983. Mem. Radiol. Soc. N.A., Am. Roentgen Ray Soc. (pres. 1973-74, gold medal 1988), Am. Coll. Radiology (pres. 1980-81), Assn. U. Radiologists (pres. 1955-56, Gold medal 1979), N.Y. Roentgen Soc. (pres. 1961-62), N.Y. Gastroent. Soc. (pres. 1965-66), Soc. Chmn. Academic Radiology Depts. (pres. 1967-68), Eastern Radiol. Soc. (pres. 1985-86). Presbyterian. Home: Olympic K 9129 SE Riverfront Ter Tequesta FL 33469-1159

SEAMAN, WILLIAM CASPER, retired news photographer; b. Grand Island, Nebr., Jan. 19, 1925; s. William H. and Minnie (Cords) S.; m. Ruth Witwer, Feb. 14, 1945; 1 son, Lawrence William. Grad. high sch. Photographer Leschinsky Studio, Grand Island; news photographer Mpls. Star & Tribune, 1945-82; ret., 1982. Recipient Pulitzer prize, 1959; also awards Nat. Headliners Club; also awards Nat. Press Photographers Assn.; also awards Inland Daily Press Assn.; also awards Kent State U.; also awards Mo. U.; also awards Local Page One; State A.P. contest; Silver Anniversary award Honeywell Photog. Products, 1975. Mem. Nat. Press Photographers Assn., Sigma Delta Chi. Home: 8206 Virginia Cir S Minneapolis MN 55426-2458

SEAMANS, ANDREW CHARLES, editorial and public relations consultant, columnist, author; b. Hillside, N.J., Sept. 10, 1937; s. Thomas Randall and Marie Josephine (Mazur) S.; m. Marion Gloria Lufbery, Aug. 25, 1956 (div. June 1986); children: Andrew Charles, Darryl Wayne, Marion Gloria Seamans Raynor, Dawn Louise Seamans Wheeler. AS cum laude, No. Va. Community Coll., Annandale, 1989. Lic. real estate salesman, Va. Editorial writer U.S. Press Assn., McLean, Va., 1968-70; pub. rels. asst. Nat. Right to Work Com., Washington, 1970; assoc. editor Human Events, Washington, 1970-81; mng. editor Heritage Features Syndicate, Washington, 1981-91; syndicated columnist The Answer Man Creators Syndicate, L.A., 1985—; bd. dirs., pub. rels. cons. Marine Learning Inst., St. Louis, 1980—. Author: Who, What, When, Where, Why In the World of American History, 1991, Who, What, When, Where, Why In the World of World History, 1991, Who, What, When, Where, Why In the World of Nature, 1992; co-author: Whose FBI?, 1974. Bd. dirs. McLean Little League Baseball, Inc., 1975-83, pres., 1982-83; pres. Rahway (N.J.) Young Rep. Club, 1964-66; chmn. platform com. Union County Young Reps., N.J. Young Reps., various other Rep. orgns. Recipient cert. of appreciation McLean Little League Baseball, 1978, named to Hall of Fame, 1985. Mem. Pub. Rels. Soc. Am., Soc. Profl. Journalists (bd. dirs. D.C. chpt. 1986-87, membership dir. 1986-87, 89-90, dir. pub. info. 1988), No. Va. Assn. Historians, Va. Hist. Soc., Internat. Platform Assn., Nat. Press Club. Episcopalian. Home and Office: 1921 Westmoreland St Mc Lean VA 22101-5529

SEAMANS, ROBERT CHANNING, JR., astronautical engineering educator; b. Salem, Mass., Oct. 30, 1918; s. Robert Channing and Pauline (Bosson) S.; m. Eugenia Merrill, June 13, 1942; children: Katherine (Mrs. Louis Padulo), Robert Channing III, Joseph, May (Seamans Baldwin), Daniel M. BS, Harvard U., 1939; MS, MIT, 1942, ScD, 1951; grad. exec. program bus. adminstrn., Columbia U., 1959; DSc, Rollins Coll., 1962, NYU, 1967; DEng, Norwich Acad., 1971, Notre Dame U., 1974, Rensselaer Poly. Inst., 1974, U. Wyo., 1975, George Washington U., 1975, Lehigh U., 1976, Thomas Coll., 1980, Curry Coll., 1982. Successively instr. dept. aero. engring., staff engr. instrumentation lab., asst. prof., project leader instrumentation lab., asso. prof. Mass. Inst. Tech., 1941-55; chief engr. Project Meteor, 1950-53, dir. flight control lab., 1953-55; mgr. airborne systems lab., chief systems engr. airborne systems dept. RCA, 1955-58, chief engr. missile electronics and controls div., 1958-60; asso. adminstr. NASA, 1960-68, dep. adminstr., 1965-68, cons., 1968-69; vis. prof. MIT, 1968, Hunsaker prof., 1968-69; sec. air force, 1969-73; pres. Nat. Acad. Engring., 1973-74; adminstr. ERDA, Washington, 1974-77; Henry R. Luce prof. environment and pub. policy MIT, 1977-84, sr. lectr. dept. aeros. and astronautics, 1984—, dean Sch. Engring., 1978-81; mem. sci. adv. bd. USAF, 1957-62, assoc. adviser, 1963-67. Bd. overseers Harvard U., 1968-74; trustee Mus. Sci., Boston, Sea Edn. Assn.; trustee emeritus Nat. Geog. Soc., Carnegie Inst., Washington, Woods Hole Oceanographic Inst. Recipient naval ordnance devel. award 1945, Godfrey L. Cabot award Aero Club New Eng., 1965, disting. svc. medal NASA, 1965, 69, Robert H. Goddard meml. trophy, 1968, disting. pub. svc. medal Dept. Def., 1973, exceptional civilian svc. award Dept. Air Force, 1973, Gen. Thomas D. White U.S. Air Force Space Trophy, 1973, Ralph Coats Roe medal ASME, 1977; achievement award Nat. Soc. Profl. Engrs., Thomas D. White Nat. Def. award, 1980, exceptional svc. award Dept. Air Force, 1985, Arthur M. Bueche award Nat. Acad. Engring., 1994, Daniel Guggenheim award, 1995. Fellow Am. Acad. Arts and Scis., Am. Astron. Soc., IEEE, AIAA (hon., Lawrence Sperry award 1951); mem. Internat. Acad. Astronautics, Am. Soc. Pub. Adminstrn., Nat. Acad. Engring. (Arthur M. Bueche Award, 1994, Daniel Guggenheim award 1996), AAAS, Air Force Acad. Found., Fgn. Policy Assn., Coun. on Fgn. Rels., Sigma Xi. Clubs: Harvard (Boston); Manchester Yacht (Mass.); Essex County (Mass.); Chevy Chase, Metropolitan (Washington); Cruising of Am. (Boston Sta.). Office: MIT 33 406 Dept Aeros & Astronautics Cambridge MA 02139

SEAMANS, WARREN ARTHUR, museum director; b. Loveland, Colo., Aug. 8, 1935; s. James Lamott and Eleanor Caroline (Baechler) S. BS, Colo. State U., 1957. Pers. officer Stone & Webster Engring. Co., Boston, 1963-64; pers. officer MIT, Cambridge, 1964-66, adminstrn. officer dept. humanities, 1966-71, founding dir. mus., 1971—. Capt. USAF, 1958-63. Mem. Am. Mus. Assn. Democrat. Avocations: theatre, musical theatre recordings, history, gardening. Home: 1401 Quincy Rd Rumney NH 03266-9706 Office: MIT Mus 265 Massachusetts Ave Cambridge MA 02139-4109

SEAMANS, WILLIAM, writer, commentator, former television-radio journalist; b. Providence, July 8, 1925; s. William and Mary Seamans; m. Jane Kingsbury, Sept. 15, 1951; children: Laurie, Jonathan, Adam. AB, Brown U., 1949; MS, Columbia U., 1952. Freelance journalist, 1952-53; journalist CBS News, 1953-63; producer evening news ABC News, 1963-65; European producer ABC News, London, 1965-70; field producer ABC News, N.Y.C., 1970-72; corr., bur. chief ABC News, Tel Aviv, 1972-92; commentator Vt. Pub. Radio, lectr., freelance writer, 1992—. Producer Nightline in Israel Week (including Palestinian-Israeli town meeting) (Emmy award, Dupont award). Served with inf. AUS, 1942-45. Decorated Bronze Star medal; CBS Murrow News fellow Columbia U., 1961-62. Mem. Writers Guild Am., Nat. Acad. TV Arts and Scis. (Emmy award 1961, 89), Overseas Press Club Am. (award for best radio reporting invasion of Cyprus 1974, award for best fgn. affairs documentary Yitzhak Rabin biography 1975), Nat. Press Club (Washington), Fgn. Corrs. Assn. in Israel.

SEAMONS, QUINTON FRANK, lawyer; b. Idaho Falls, Idaho, Mar. 5, 1945; s. Eldon Monroe and Lois (Merrill) S.; m. Michele Geyer Seamons. BA cum laude with honors, Brigham Young U., 1968; JD, U. Utah, 1971. Bar: Utah 1971, D.C. 1976, Ill. 1977, U.S. Supreme Ct. 1975, U.S. Ct. Appeals (7th cir.) 1979, U.S. Dist. Ct. (no. dist.) Ill. 1978. Legis. asst. to Senator Wallace F. Bennett of Utah U.S. Senate, Washington, 1969-71; law clk. Utah Atty. Gen., Salt Lake City, 1970-71; staff atty. divsn. mkt. regulation, legal counsel SEC, Washington, 1971-76; ptnr. Wilson & McIlvaine, Chgo., 1976—; arbitrator NASD Proceedings; adj. prof. Chgo. Kent Coll. Law, 1996—. Asst. editor: The Summation: A Journal of Utah Law; Contbr. articles to profl. jours. Trustee Riverwoods Homeowners Assn., Ill., 1992, Ill. Cancer Coun., 1980-84; bd. dirs. Vol. Legal Svcs., Chgo., 1993; coach Northfield Park Dist., 1978-84. Hinckley scholar, U. Utah, 1969; recipient Outstanding Young Men of Am. award, 1970, Am. Jurisprudence award Bancroft-Whitney Co. and U. Utah, 1971. Mem. ATLA, ABA (bus. law sect., litigation sect.), Chgo. Bar Assn. (securities law com., corps. com., class actions com.), Blue Key, Phi Kappa Phi, Phi Alpha Delta, Phi Sigma Alpha. Avocations: sports memorabilia, reading and research of Civil War, Renaissance & Medieval history, book collecting, basketball, health club. Office: Wilson & McIlvaine 500 W Madison St Ste 3700 Chicago IL 60661-2511

SEAPKER, JANET KAY, museum director; b. Pitts., Nov. 2, 1947; d. Charles Henry and Kathryn Elizabeth (Dany) S.; m. Edward F. Turberg, May 24, 1975. BA, U. Pitts., 1969; MA, SUNY, Cooperstown, 1975. Park ranger Nat. Park Svc., summers 1967-69; archtl. historian N.C. Archives and History, Raleigh, 1971-76, hist. preservation adminstr., 1976-77, grant-in-aid adminstr., 1977-78; dir. Cape Fear Mus. (formerly New Hanover County Mus.), Wilmington, N.C., 1978—; bd. dirs. Bellamy Mansion Found., Wilmington, 1986-89, 91—, Lower Cape Fear Hist. Soc., Wilmington, 1985-88; N.C. rep. S.E. Mus. Conf., 1986-90; field reviewer Inst. Mus. Svcs., 1982—. Contbr. articles to profl. jours. Bd. dirs. Downtown Area Revitalization Effort, Wilmington, 1979-81, Thalian Hall Ctr. for Performing Arts, 1996—; bd. dirs. Hist. Wilmington Found., 1979-84, pres., 1980-81; mem. Cmty. Appearance Commn., Wilmington, 1984-88, 250th Anniversary Commn., Wilmington, 1986-90. Grad. program fellow SUNY, Cooperstown, 1969-70; recipient Profl. Svc. award N.C. Mus. Coun., 1982, Woman of Achievement award YWCA, 1994. Mem. Am. Assn. Mus. (accreditation vis. com. 1983—, reviewer mus. assessment program 1982—), Nat. Trust Hist. Preservation, Southeastern Mus. Conf. (N.C. state rep. 1986-90), N.C. Mus. Coun. (sec.-treas. 1978-84, pres. 1984-86), Hist. Preservation Found N.C. (sec. 1976-78). Democrat. Presbyterian. Home: 307 N 15th St Wilmington NC 28401-3813 Office: Cape Fear Mus 814 Market St Wilmington NC 28401-4731

SEAQUIST, ERNEST RAYMOND, astronomy educator; b. Vancouver, B.C., Can., Nov. 19, 1938; s. Egron Emanuel and Sigrid Alice (Back) S.; m. Gloria Stewart Jenkins, June 11, 1966; children: Jonathan William, Carolyn Suzanne. BASc, U. B.C., Vancouver, 1961; MA, U. Toronto, Ont., Can., 1962, PhD, 1966. Lectr. astronomy U. Toronto, 1965-66, asst. prof., 1966-72, assoc. prof., 1972-78, prof., 1978—, assoc. chmn. dept., 1974-88, chmn., 1988—; dir. David Dunlap Obs. U. Toronto, Richmond Hill, Ont., 1988—. Contbr. author: Classical Novae, 1989; also over 150 articles. Rsch. grantee Natural Scis. and Engring. Rsch. Coun. Can., 1967—. Mem. Internat. Astron. Union, Am. Astron. Soc., Can. Astron. Soc. (pres. 1986-88). Avocations: painting and sketching, collecting antiques. Office: U Toronto Dept Astronomy, 60 St George St, Toronto, ON Canada M5S 1A7

SEAR, MOREY LEONARD, federal judge, educator; b. New Orleans, Feb. 26, 1929; s. William and Yetty (Streiffer) S.; m. Lee Edrehi, May 26, 1951; children: William Sear II, Jane Lee. J.D., Tulane U., 1950. Bar: La. 1950. Asst. dist. atty. Parish Orleans, 1952-55; individual practice law Stahl & Sear, New Orleans, 1955-71; spl. counsel New Orleans Aviation Bd., 1956-60; magistrate U.S. Dist. Ct. (ea. dist.) La., 1971-76, judge, 1976—, chief judge, 1992—; judge Temp. Emergency Ct. of Appeals, 1982-87; adj. prof. Tulane U. Coll. Law; former chmn. com. on adminstrn. of bankruptcy sys., former chmn. adv. com. on bankruptcy rules, former mem. com. on adminstrn. of fed. magistrate sys. Jud. Conf. U.S.; former mem. Jud. Conf. of U.S. and Its Exec. Com.; mem. cir. coun. 5th Cir. of U.S.; founding dir. River Oaks Pvt. Psychiat. Hosp., 1968. Pres. Congregation Temple Sinai, 1977-79; bd. govs. Tulane Med. Ctr., 1977—; former chmn. Tulane Med. Ctr. Hosp. and Clinic, 1980-85. Mem. ABA, La. Bar Assn., New Orleans Bar Assn., Order of Barristers, Order of the Coif (hon.). Office: US Dist Ct C-256 US Courthouse 500 Camp St New Orleans LA 70130-3313

SEARCY, ALAN WINN, chemist, educator; b. Covina, Calif., Oct. 12, 1925; s. Claude Winn and Esther (Scofield) S.; m. Gail Vaught, Oct. 30, 1945; children: Gay, William, Anne. A.B., Pomona Coll., 1946; Ph.D., U. Calif. at Berkeley, 1950. Faculty Purdue U., 1949-54, asst. prof. chemistry, 1950-54; faculty U. Calif., Berkeley, 1954—, prof., 1958-91, prof. materials sci., 1960-91, prof. emeritus, 1991—, assoc. div. head inorganic materials div. Lawrence Radiation Lab., 1961-64, asst. to chancellor, 1963-64, vice-chancellor, 1964-67, chmn. faculty Coll. Engring., 1969-70, Miller rsch. prof., 1970-71, acting chmn. dept. materials sci. and engring., 1973; assoc. dir. Lawrence Berkeley Lab., head materials and molecular research div., 1980-84; Fulbright lectr. phys. chemistry Inst. Physics, Bariloche, Argentina, 1960; cons. Gen. Motors Tech. Center, 1956-64, Union Carbide, 1956-72, Gen. Atomic, 1957-72; Mem. com. high temperature chemistry NRC, 1961-70. Editor: (with D.V. Ragone, U. Colombo) Chemical and Mechanical Behavior of Inorganic Materials, 1970; assoc. editor Jour. Am. Ceramic Soc., 1996—; editl. adv. bd. High Temperature High Pressure, 1969-93, High Temperature Sci., 1969-94, Advanced in High Temperature Chemistry, 1971-75, Materials Chemistry and Physics, 1976-87, Reactivity of Solids, High Temperature and Materials Science, 1994—; contbr. numerous articles to profl. jours. Served with AUS, 1944-46. Recipient citation for distinction in rsch. U. Calif., Berkeley, 1991; Guggenheim fellow, 1967-68. Fellow Am. Ceramic Soc., AAAS; mem. Am. Chem. Soc., Acad. of Ceramics (charter), Materials Rsch. Soc., Phi Beta Kappa, Sigma Xi. Home: 24 Northampton Ave Berkeley CA 94707-1715

SEARCY, JANE BERRY, educational administrator; b. Birmingham, Ala., Dec. 21, 1951; d. Francis Clifford and Mary Jacqueline (Meeks) Berry; m. Joseph Alexander Searcy III, July 3, 1982; children: Margaret Alice, Joseph Alexander IV. BA in Elem. Edn., Birmingham So. Coll., 1973; MA in Spl. Edn., U. Ala., 1975, EdS in Spl. Edn., 1977, EdD in Spl. Edn., 1982. Cert. elem. and spl. edn. tchr., Ala. Tchr. spl. edn. Tuscaloosa (Ala.) County Schs., 1974-75, Montgomery (Ala.) County Schs., 1975-77; tchr. spl. edn. Tuscaloosa City Schs., 1977-79, curriculum assoc., 1979-86, dir. spl. edn., 1986—; instr. Livingston (Ala.) U. Coll. Edn., 1985-87, adj. prof., 1988—; cons. L.E.A.D. Acad., Montgomery, 1989-90; agy. rep. Child Protection Team, Tuscaloosa, 1986—, Tuscaloosa Autism Coun., 1988—; mem. Ala. Legis. Task Force, West Ala. Early Intervention Coun., Tuscaloosa, 1982—. Mem. adv. bd. Rural Infant Stimulation Environment, U. Ala., Tuscaloosa, 1988—; bd. dirs. Tuscaloosa Assn. for Retarded Citizens, 1987-94, Children's Ctr. of Tuscaloosa, 1989—, Miracle Riders of West Ala., 1994—; sec. bd. dirs. Ala. Choir Sch., 1993-94; bd. dirs. Tombigbee coun. Girl Scouts U.S., 1994—, disabilities coord., fin. com., 1993—. Recipient Profl. of the Yr. award Tuscaloosa Assn. for Retarded Citizens, 1994. Mem. ASCD, Coun. Exceptional Children, Ala. Coun. Exceptional Children (Outstanding SPE Coord. in Ala. 1995), Tuscaloosa Coun. Exceptional Children (bd. dirs. 1994—), Ala. Coun. Sch. Adminstrn. and Supervision, Ala. ASCD, Nat. Coun. Adminstrs. in Spl. Edn. (nat. bd. dirs.), Ala. Coun. Adminstrs. in Spl. Edn. (state pres. 1992-94, CASE del. to Sino-Am. conf. on exceptionality, Beijing, China 1995, Southeastern area CASE conf. chair 1996), Leadership Tuscaloosa (bd. dirs. 1996—), Alpha Delta Kappa (v.p. Epsilon chpt. 1984-86, pres. 1986-88, State Leadership Appreciation award 1988), Phi Delta Kappa, Alpha Omicron Pi, Kappa Delta Pi. Office: Tuscaloosa City Schs 1100 21st St E Tuscaloosa AL 35404

SEARCY, JARRELL D. (JAY), sportswriter; b. Stevenson, Ala., Mar. 26, 1934; s. Harley Johnson and Dovie Mae (Ryan) S.; m. Jackie Lou Hildebrand, Nov. 17, 1957; children—Michael Jarrell, Mark William. Student, U. Tenn., 1953-54, East Tenn. State U., 1956-57. Reporter Kingsport Times-News, Tenn., 1956-57; reporter Chattanooga Times, 1958-64, sports editor, 1964-71; editor/reporter N.Y. Times, N.Y.C., 1972-75; exec. sports editor Phila. Inquirer, 1975-86, sr. writer, 1986—. Author: (with Sam Goldaper) Golden State Warrior, 1975. Mem. Nat. Turf Writers' Assn., Nat. Boxing Writers Assn., Nat. Sportswriters and Broadcasters Assn., AP Sports Editors Assn. (pres. 1984-85), Quality Life Assn. (pres. 1990). Avocations: tennis; golf; gardening. Office: Phila Inquirer 400 N Broad St Philadelphia PA 19130-4015

SEARIGHT, PATRICIA ADELAIDE, retired radio and television executive; b. Rochester, N.Y.; d. William Hammond and Irma (Winters) S. BA, Ohio State U. Program dir. Radio Sta. WTOP, Washington, 1952-63, gen. mgr. info., 1964; radio and TV cons., 1964-84; ret., 1984; producer, dir. many radio and TV programs; spl. fgn. news corr. French Govt., 1956; v.p. Micro Beads, Inc., 1955-59; sec., dir. Dennis-Inches, Corp., 1955-59; exec. dir. Am. Women in Radio and TV, 1969-74; fgn. service officer U.S. Dept. State, ret., AEC, ret. Mem. pres.'s coun. Toledo Mus. Art. Recipient Kappa Kappa Gamma Alumna achievement award. Mem. Am. Women in Radio and TV (program chmn.; corrs. sec.; dir. Washington chpt.; pres. 1958-60, nat. membership chmn. 1962-63, nat. chmn. Industry Info. Digest 1963-64, Mid-Eastern v.p. 1964-66), Soc. Am. Travel Writers (treas. 1957-58, v.p. 1958-59), Nat. Acad. TV Arts and Scis., Women's Advt. Club (Washington, pres. 1959-60), Nat. Press Club, Soroptimist, Kappa Kappa Gamma. Episcopalian. Home: 9498 E Via Montoya Dr Scottsdale AZ 85255-5074 *Personal philosophy: "There is no such word as can't."*

SEARING, MARJORY ELLEN, government official, economist; b. N.Y.C., Mar. 29, 1945; d. William Edgar Searing and Jean Frances (Smith) Searing Fusaro; m. Warren Eugene Lane, Mar. 3, 1977; children—Gary Francis, Jennifer Rebecca, Stephanie Anne. B.A. in Econs., SUNY-Binghamton, 1966; M.A. in Econs., Georgetown U., 1969, Ph.D. in Econs., 1972. Economist Bur. Econs. Analysis U.S. Dept. Commerce, Washington, 1967-73, internat. economist Bur. East-West Trade, 1973-74, dir. Office Internat. Sector Policy, 1980-84, dir. Office Industry Assessment, 1984-86, acting dep. asst. sec. sci. and electronics, 1984-85, dir. Office Multilateral Affairs, 1986-90; dep. asst. sec. for Japan U.S. Dept. Commerce, 1991—; sr. internat. economist Office Trade Policy U.S. Dept. Treasury, Washington, 1974-76, dir. Office East-West Econ. Policy, 1976-79. Contbr. numerous articles to profl. publs. N.Y. State Regents scholar, 1962-65; Georgetown U. fellow, 1966-71. Office: US Dept Commerce 14th Pl SE Rm 2320 Washington DC 20230

SEARLE, ELEANOR MILLARD, history educator; b. Chgo., Oct. 29, 1926; married. BA, Harvard U., 1948; Licentiate Medieval Studies, Pontifical Inst. Medieval History, 1961, D Medieval Studies, 1972; D honoris causa, Pontifical Inst., 1994. Lectr. history Calif. Inst. Tech., Pasadena, 1962-63, prof. history, 1979-87, Edie and Lou Wasserman prof. history, 1987—; rsch. fellow Rsch. Sch. Social Sci., Australian Nat. U., 1963-65, fellow, 1965-68; assoc. prof. UCLA, 1969-72, prof., 1972-79; vis. fellow Cambridge U., 1976, 81; sr. rsch. fellow Hungtington Libr., 1986—; cons. Huntington Libr., 1980-82. Author: Lordship and Community: Battle Abbey and Its Banlieu, 1066-1538, 1974; editor: The Chronicle of Battle

Abbey, 1980; co-editor: Accounts of the Cellarers of Battle Abbey, 1967, Predatory Kinship and the Creation of Norman Power, 840-1066, 1988; contbr. articles to profl. jours. Fellow Royal Hist. Soc., Royal Soc. Antiquaries of London; mem. Am. Hist. Soc., Medieval Acad. Am. (pres. 1985-86), Econ. History Soc., Am. Soc. Legal History, Haskins Soc. (bd. dirs. 1982—, pres. 1990-96). Office: Calif Inst Tech Dept History Pasadena CA 91125

SEARLE, LEONARD, astronomer, researcher. Office: Carnegie Observatories 813 Santa Barbara St Pasadena CA 91101-1232

SEARLE, PHILIP FORD, bank executive; b. Kansas City, Mo., July 23, 1924; s. Albert Addison and Edith (Thompson) S.; m. Jean Adair Hanneman, Nov. 22, 1950 (dec. Nov. 1990); 1 child, Charles Randolph; m. Jean Walker, Oct. 4, 1992 (dec. Oct. 1993); m. Elizabeth Gordon, Nov. 4, 1994. AB, Cornell U., 1949; grad. in banking, Rutgers U., 1957, 64. With Geneva (Ohio) Savs. and Trust Co., 1949-60, pres., 1959-60; pres., sr. trust officer Northeastern Ohio Nat. Bank, Ashtabula, 1960-69; pres., chief exec. officer BancOhio Corp., Columbus, 1969-75; chmn., chief exec. officer Flagship Banks, Inc., Miami, Fla., 1975-84; chmn. bd. Sun Banks, Inc., Orlando, Fla., 1984-85, cons., 1986-94; mem. faculty Sch. Banking, Ohio U., 1959-70, Nat. Trust Sch., Northwestern U., Evanston, Ill., 1965-68; mem. corp. adv. com. Nat. Assn. Securities Dealers, 1981-83; v.p., mem. fed. adv. coun. to bd. govs. FRS, 1983-85; chmn. Nat. Adv. Bd. to Oversight Bd. for Resolution Trust Corp., 1991-92. Co-author: The Management of a Trust Department, 1967. Past chmn. bd. regents Stonier Grad. Sch. Banking, Rutgers U., 1974-76, past mem. faculty; trustee Fin. Acctg. Found., Norwalk, Conn., 1989-93. Capt. AUS, 1943-46, 51-52, ETO. Decorated Bronze Star; named Outstanding Citizen in Ashtabula County, 1967. Mem. Am. Bankers Assn. (bd. dirs. 1972-74, governing coun.), Bank Adminstrn. Inst. (nat. chmn. 1987-88, bd. dirs. Chgo., Ill. 1985-89), Fla. Bankers Assn. (bd. dirs. 1979-81, coun. 1981), Ohio Bankers Assn. (pres. 1970-71), Assn. Bank Holding Cos. (bd. dirs. 1979-81, exec. com. 1981), Fla. Assn. Registered Bank Holding Cos. (pres. 1979-81), Fla. C. of C. (bd. dirs. 1978-82), Royal Poinciana Golf Club (Naples, Fla.), Catawba Island Club (Port Clinton, Ohio), Phi Kappa Tau.

SEARLE, RODNEY NEWELL, state legislator, farmer, insurance agent; b. Camden, N.J., July 17, 1920; s. William Albert and Ruby Marie (Barrus) S.; m. Janette Elizabeth Christie, May 17, 1941; children: R. Newell Jr., Linda Jennison, Alan John. B.A., Mankato State U., 1960. Prodn. coordinator Johnson & Johnson, New Brunswick, N.J., 1940-47; farmer Waseca, Minn., 1947—; spl. agt. John Hancock Mut. Ins. Co., Waseca, Minn., 1961-84; mem. Minn. Ho. of Reps., St. Paul, 1957-80, speaker, 1979—. Author: Minnesota Standoff—The Politics of Deadlock, 1990. Lay reader St. John's Episcopal Ch., 1952—; chmn. Upper Mississippi River Basin Commn., 1981-82; pres. Minn. State U. Bd., 1981-92; chmn. Minn. Higher Edn. Bd., 1991-92; bd. dirs. Minn. Wellsprings, 1984-90; emeritus mem. adv. bd. Hubert H. Humphrey Inst.; emeritus mem. coun. Minn. Hist. Soc.; bd. dirs. Minn. Agrl. Interpretive Ctr., 1983—. Named Minn. State Tree Farmer of Yr., 1978. Mem. Am. Tree Farm System, Nat. Conf. State Legislators, Minn. Forestry Assn. (bd. dirs. 1991—), Masons, Rotary (pres. club 1968). Republican.

SEARLE, RONALD, artist; b. Cambridge, Eng., Mar. 3, 1920; s. William James and Nellie (Hunt) S.; m. Monica Koenig, 1967. Ed., Cambridge Sch. Art. Author: pub. in U.S. The Female Approach, 1954, Merry England, 1957; (with Kaye Webb) Paris Sketchbook, 1958, The St. Trinian's Story, 1959, Refugees, 1960, (with Alex Atkinson) The Big City, 1958, U.S.A. for Beginners, 1959, Russia for Beginners, 1960, Escape from the Amazon, 1964, Which Way Did He Go?, 1962, From Frozen North to Filthy Lucre, 1964, Those Magnificient Men in Their Flying Machines, 1965, (with Heinz Huber) Haven't We Met Before Somewhere?, 1966, Searle's Cats, 1968, The Square Egg, 1969, Hello: Where Did All the People Go?, 1970, (with Kildare Dobbs) The Great Fur Opera, 1970, The Addict, 1971, More Cats, 1975, Zoodiac, 1978, Ronald Searle Album, 1979, The Situation is Hopeless, 1981, The Big Fat Cat Book, 1982, Winespeak, 1983, Ronald Searle in Perspective, 1985, To the Kwai-- and Back, 1986, Something in the Cellar, 1988, Ah Yes, I Remember It Well: Paris 1961-75, 1988, Ronald Searle's Non-Sexist Dictionary, 1989, Slightly Foxed- But Still Desirable, 1989, The Curse of St. Trinian's, 1993, Marquis de Sade Meets Goody Two-Shoes, 1994; contbr. to New Yorker; 1st pub. work appeared in Cambridge Daily News, 1935-39; subject of Ronald Searle: a biography by Russell Davies, 1992; one-man shows include Leicester Galleries, London, 1948, 50, 54, 57, Kraushaar Gallery, N.Y.C., 1959, Blanchini Gallery, N.Y.C., 1963, city mus. Bremen, Hannover, Dusseldorf, Stuttgart, Berlin, 1965, 3d Biennale, Tolentino, Italy, 1965, Galerie Pro Arte, Delmenhorst, Germany, Mus. Art, Bremerhaven, Germany, Galerie Münsterberg, Basle, Switzerland, Galerie Pribaut, Amsterdam, Holland, Wolfgang-Gurlitt Mus., Linz, Austria, Galerie La Pochade, Paris, 1966-71, Art Alliance Gallery, Phila., 1967, Galerie Gurlitt, Munich, 1967-76, Grosvenor Gallery, London, 1968, Galerie Obere Zaune, Zurich, 1968, Galerie Hauswedell, Baden-Baden, 1968, Galerie Brumme, Frankfurt, 1969, Konsthallen, Södertälje, Sweden, 1969, Rizzoli Gallery, N.Y.C., 1969-81, Kunsthalle, Konstanz, 1970, Würzburg, 1970, Galerie Welz, Salzburg, 1971, Galerie Rivolta, Lausanne, 1972, Galerie Gaëton, Geneva, 1972, Bibliothèque Nationale, Paris, 1973, Galerie Würthle, Vienna, 1973, Kulterhaus Graz, Austria, 1973, 79, Galerie Rivolta, Lausanne, 1974, 78, Galerie l'Angle Aigu, Brussels, 1974, 77, Galerie Carmen Casse, Paris, 1975-77, Staatliche Museen Preussicher Kulturbesitz, Berlin, 1976, Galerie Bartsch and Chariau, Munich, 1981, Neue Galerie Wien, Vienna, 1985, 1988, Imperial War Mus., London, 1986, British Mus., London, 1986, Fitzwilliam Mus., Cambridge, 1987, Fine Arts Mus., San Francisco, 1987, Heineman Galleries, N.Y., 1994, Wilhelm Busch Mus., Hannover, 1996, Stadtmus., Munich, 1996, others; contbr. to nat. publs., 1946—; theatre artist: Punch, 1949-61; created series of cartoons on fictitious girls sch., 1941, which became a film series called Belles of St. Trinian's, 1954, Blue Murder at St. Trinian's, 1957, The Pure Hell of St. Trinian's, 1960, The Great St. Trinian's Train Robbery, 1965, Wildcats of St. Trinian's, 1980; films designs include John Gilpin (Brit. Film Inst.), 1951, On the Twelfth Day, 1954 (nominated Acad. award), Energetically Yours, 1957, The Kings Breakfast, 1963, Those Magnificient Men in Their Flying Machines, 1965, Monte Carlo or Bust, 1969, Scrooge, 1970, Dick Deadeye, or Duty Done, 1975. Recipient medal Art Dirs. Club Los Angeles, 1959, medal Art Dirs. Mem. Club Phila., Pa., 1959, gold medal 3d Biennale, Tolentino, Italy, 1965, Prix de la Critique Belge, 1968, medaille de la ville d'Avignon, 1971, Prix de l' Humour S.P.H. Festival d' Avignon, 1971, Prix de l' Humour Noir Grandville France, 1971, Prix Internationale Charles Huard France, 1972, Best Advt. Illustration award Nat. Cartoonists Soc., 1988. Club: The Garrick (London). Home: care Tessa Sayle, 11 Jubilee Pl, London SW 3-3TE England Office: care John Locke Studio 15 E 76th St New York NY 10021-1719

SEARLE, STEWART A., transportation equipment holding company executive; b. Winnipeg, Man., Can., 1923; s. Stewart Augustus and Sally Elizabeth (Appleyard) S.; m. Maudie Jessiman, Nov. 9, 1949; children: Stewart A., David J. Student, Trinity Coll., Port Hope, Ont., Queen's U., Kingston, Ont. Chmn. bd. dirs. Fed. Industries, Ltd., Winnipeg. Served to lt. RCAF. Office: Fed Industries Ltd, 1 Lombard Pl, Winnipeg, MB Canada R3B 0X3

SEARLE, WILLIAM LOUIS, investment company executive; b. Evanston, Ill., Mar. 4, 1928; s. John Gideon and Frances (Crow) S.; m. Sally Burnett, Dec. 4, 1953; children: Marion, Elizabeth Searle Reichert, Louise Searle Klarr. B.A., U. Mich., 1951; postgrad., Harvard, 1969. With G. D. Searle & Co., Chgo., 1953-83; v.p. marketing G. D. Searle & Co., 1965-68, v.p., gen. mgr., 1968-70, sr. v.p., gen. mgr., 1970-72, chmn. bd., 1972-77, vice chmn., 1977-78, chmn. pension com., 1978-83; dir. Kinship Corp., Northbrook, Ill., 1983—. Served with Chem. Corps AUS, 1951. Clubs: Chicago (Chgo.). Office: Kinship Corp 400 Skokie Blvd Ste 300 Northbrook IL 60062

SEARLES, ANNA MAE HOWARD, educator, civic worker; b. Osage Nation Indian Terr., Okla., Nov. 22, 1906; d. Frank David and Clara (Bowman) Howard; A.A., Odessa (Tex.) Coll., 1961; BA, U. Ark., 1964; M.Ed., 1970; postgrad. (Herman L. Donovan fellow), U. Ky., 1972—; m. Isaac Adams Searles, May 26, 1933; 1 dau., Mary Ann Rogers (Mrs. Herman Lloyd Hoppe). Compiler news, broadcaster sta. KJBC, 1950-60; corr. Tulsa Daily World, 1961-64; tchr. Rogers (Ark.) H.S., 1964-72; tchr. adult class rapid reading, 1965, 80; tchr. adult edn. Learning Center Benton County (Ark.), Bentonville, 1973-77, supr. adult edn., 1977-79; tchr. North Ark. C.C., Rogers, 1979-90, CETA, Bentonville, 1979-82; tchr. Joint Tng. Partnership Act, 1984-85; coordinator adult edn. Rogers C. of C. and Rogers Sch. System, 1984—. Sec. Tulsa Safety Council, 1935-37; leader, bd. dirs. Girl Scouts U.S.A., Kilgore, Tex., 1941-44, leader, Midland, Tex., 1944-52, counselor, 1950-61; exec. sec. Midland Community Chest, 1955-60; gray lady Midland A.R.C., 1958-59; organizer Midland YMCA, Salvation Army; dir. women's div. Savings Bond Program, Midland; mem. citizens com. Rogers Hough Meml. Library, women's aux. Rogers Meml. Hosp.; vol. tutor Laubach literacy orgn., 1973—; sec. Beaver Lake Literacy Council, Rogers, 1973-83, Little Flock Planning Commn., 1975-77, Benton County Hist. Soc., 1981—; pub. relations chmn. South Central region Nat. Affiliation for Literacy Advance, 1977-79; bd. dirs. Globe Theatre, Odessa, Tex., Midland Community Theatre, Tri-County Foster Home, Guadalupe, Midland youth centers, DeZavala Day Nursery, PTA, Adult Devel. Center, Rogers CETA, 1979-81; vol. recorder Ark. Hist. Preservation Program, 1984—; docent Rogers Hist. Mus., 1988—. Recipient Nice People award Rogers C. of C., 1987, Thanks badge Midland Girl Scout Assn., 1948, Appreciation Plaque award Ark. Natural Heritage Commn., 1988; Cert. of recognition, Rogers Pub. Schs., 1986, Cert. of Recognition, Beaver Lake Literacy Coun., 1993; Instr. of Yr. award North Ark. Community Coll. West Campus, Conservation award Woodmen of the World Life Ins. Soc., 1991, Vol. of Yr. award Rogers Hist. Mus., 1993. Mem. NEA (del. conv. 1965), Ark. Assn. Public Continuing and Adult Edn. (pres. 1979-80), South Central Assn. for Lifelong Learning (sec. 1980-84), PTA (life), Future Homemakers Am. (life; sec. 1980—), Delta Kappa Gamma (Disting. Acheivement award Beta Pi chpt. 1992). Episcopalian. Clubs: Altrusa (pres. 1979—), Apple Spur Community (Rogers), Garden Club Rogers (publicity chmn. 1994-95, garden therapy 1994-96). Home: 2808 N Dixieland PO Box 03319400 Rogers AR 72756

SEARLES, DEWITT RICHARD, retired investment firm executive, retired air force officer; b. Birmingham, Ala., Aug. 7, 1920; s. DeWitt Richard and Miriam (Hostetler) S.; m. Barbara Elizabeth Brown, Jan. 28, 1949; children: Ann Hampton, DeWitt Richard III, Elizabeth Alison. Student, Coll. William and Mary, 1939-41; B.A., U. Md., 1949; M.A., George Washington U., 1964; grad., Army Command and Gen. Staff Sch., Ft. Leavenworth, Kans., 1945, USAF Command and Gen. Staff Coll., Maxwell AFB, Ala., 1956, Nat. War Coll., Washington, 1964. Commd. 2d lt. USAAF, 1942; advanced through grades to maj. gen. USAF, 1971; fighter pilot and squadron comdr. New Guinea and Philippines, 1943-45; wing comdr. 81st Tactical Fighter Wing, Eng., 1965-67; insp. gen. Tactical Air Command, Langley AFB, Va., 1967-69; comdr. 327th Air Div., Taiwan, Republic of China, 1969-71; dep. comdr. 7/13 Air Force, Udorn AFB, Thailand, 1971-72; dep. insp. gen. Hdqrs. USAF, Washington, 1972-74, ret.; asst. v.p. Merrill Lynch, Pierce, Fenner & Smith, Washington, 1974-87, ret., 1987. Decorated D.S.M. with 2 oak leaf clusters, Legion of Merit with oak leaf cluster, D.F.C., Air medal with 7 oak leaf clusters. Home: 1605 Dunterry Pl Mc Lean VA 22101-4318

SEARLES, RICHARD BROWNLEE, botany educator, marine biology researcher; b. Riverside, Calif., June 19, 1936; s. Nathan Francis and Margaret Louise (Ashbrook) S.; m. Georgiana Elizabeth Miller, June 11, 1957; children: Timothy Edward, Andrew Nathan, Elizabeth Louise. AB, Pomona Coll., Claremont, Calif., 1958; PhD, U. Calif., Berkeley, 1965. Asst. prof. botany Duke U., Durham, N.C., 1965-69, assoc. prof., 1969-83, prof., 1983—, chmn. dept., 1991—. Co-author: Seaweeds of the Southeastern U.S., 1991. Served to 2d lt. U.S. Army, 1961-63, capt. Res. ret. Mem. Internat. Phycol. Soc., Phycol. Soc. Am. (Gerald W. Prescott award, 1993), Brit. Phycol. Soc., Oceanographic Soc. Am., Phi Beta Kappa, Sigma Xi. Unitarian. Home: 1800 Woodburn Rd Durham NC 27705-5725 Office: Duke Univ Dept Botany Durham NC 27706-0338

SEARLS, EILEEN HAUGHEY, lawyer, librarian, educator; b. Madison, Wis., Apr. 27, 1925; d. Edward M. and Anna Mary (Haughey) S.; BA, U. Wis., 1948, JD, 1950, MS in Libr. Sci., 1951. Bar: Wis. 1950. Cataloger Yale U., 1951-52; instr. law St. Louis U., 1952-53, asst. prof., 1953-56, asso. prof., 1956-64, prof., 1964—, law librarian, 1952—. Mem. Am. Lib. Assn., Wis. Bar Assn., Bar Assn. Met. St. Louis, Am. Assn. Law Librs., Mid-Am. Assn. Law Librs., Southwestern Assn. Law Librs., Altrusa Club. Office: 3700 Lindell Blvd Saint Louis MO 63108-3412

SEARS, BRADFORD GEORGE, landscape architect; b. Philmont, N.Y., June 21, 1915; s. Russell Lockwood and Alla (Scutt) S.; m. Ruth Ellen Fox, July 5, 1936; children—Bradford Alan, Brian Scutt, Patricia Ruth. B.S., N.Y. State Coll. Forestry, 1939, M.S., 1948. With State U. N.Y., Syracuse, 1941-76; prof. landscape architecture State U. N.Y., 1950-76, dean landscape architecture, 1968-76, dean emeritus, 1976—; pvt. practice landscape architecture, 1945—; vis. lectr. Sch. Design, N.C. State U., 1978-83; mem. bd. landscape architecture N.Y. State Dept. Edn., 1967-79. Contbr. articles to profl. jours. and manuals. Fellow Am. Soc. Landscape Architects; mem. (past pres. N.Y. Upstate chpt., past chmn. nat. accreditation bd. for profl. programs), Am. Camping Assn. Methodist. Address: 116 Wellwood Dr Fayetteville NY 13066-2353

SEARS, CURTIS THORNTON, JR., educational administrator; b. Wareham, Mass., Aug. 3, 1938; s. Curtis Thornton Sr. and Ruth (Blake) S.; m. Martha Wilda Colvin, July 5, 1960 (div. May 1977); children: Amy Elizabeth, Leslie Edward; m. Ronnie Spilton, Mar. 23, 1980. AB, W.Va. Wesleyan U., 1961; PhD, U. N.C., 1966. NATO postdoctoral fellow Bristol (Eng.) U., 1966-67; asst. prof. chemistry U. S.C., Columbia, 1967-71; from asst. to assoc. prof. Ga. State U., Atlanta, 1977, assoc. chmn. chemistry dept., 1986-91, assoc. v.p. rsch. and info. tech., 1993-94; reviewer NSF, Washington, 1975—, vis. scientist, 1991-92, 94. Author: Inquiries in Chemistry, 1977, Chemistry for the Health Sciences, 1976, 2d edit., 1982, Aspects of Chemistry, 1979. NATO fellow NSF, 1966; Recipient Teaching award Nat. Sci. Tchrs. Assn., 1973, Arts and Scis. Teaching award Ga. State U., 1977. Mem. Am. Chem. Soc., Royal Soc. Chemistry, Exams. Inst. of Am. Chem. Soc. (chair commn. 1986-91). Methodist. Avocations: cooking, gardening. Office: Ga State U Atlanta GA 30303

SEARS, DONNA MAE, technical writer and illustrator; b. St. Paul, Oct. 23, 1951; d. Raymond and Shirley Marie (Dupre) Waldoch; m. Mark D. Sears, Sept. 4, 1993. BA in Art and Edn., Cardinal Stritch Coll., Milw., 1969-73; postgrad., Rock Valley Coll., Rockford, Ill., 1985, 87, 89-90, So. Ill. U., 1983; cert. of tng., Computervision Tech. Ctr., Itasca, Ill., 1986, 88. Electronic assembler Warner Electric Co., Marengo, Ill., 1973-75, machine hand, 1976-78, quality assurance lead insp., 1978-80, draftswoman, 1980-86, CAD-sr. draftswoman, 1986-87; tchr. art Stephen Mack Sch. Dist., Rockford, 1975, Harrison Sch. Dist., Wonder Lake, Ill., 1975-76; CAD specialist Greenlee Textron Inc., Rockford, 1988-89, resigned, 1989; asst. buyer Ingersoll Milling, Rockford, 1989-90; asst. office mgr. and sign maker Shake-A-Leg Signs, Rockford, 1990-92; tech. writer and illustrator Mathews Co., Crystal Lake, Ill., 1992; tech. writer and CAD support Clinton Electronics, Loves Park, Ill., 1993—. Author: (with others) Treasured Poems of America, 1990, Poetic Voices of America, spring 1992, Anthonology of American Poetry, fall 1991 (awards of Poetic Excellence 1992), Distinguished Poets of America, spring 1993, The Sound of Poetry, spring 1993. Vol. Boone County Conservation Dist.; mem. choir St. James Ch., Belvidere, Ill., 1985-93; assoc. mem. Spl. Olympics, Macktown Restoradion Found. Recipient Leadership award YWCA, Rockford, 1988. Mem. Internat. Soc. Poets, Exptl. Aircraft Assn., Nat. Right to Life Assn., Macktown Restoration Found. Roman Catholic. Avocations: bicycling, art, gardening, fishing.

SEARS, EDWARD MILNER, JR., newspaper editor; b. Bluefield, W.Va., Dec. 28, 1944; s. Edward Milner and Helene (Stras) S.; m. Jo Ann Langworthy, May 15, 1971; 1 child, Helene Mateer. B.S. in Journalism, U. Fla., 1967. Makeup editor Atlanta Constn., 1970, news editor, 1971-73, feature editor, 1974, city editor, 1975-76, asst. mng. editor, 1977, mng. editor, 1978-80; mng. editor Atlanta Jour., 1980-82, Atlanta Jour. and Atlanta Constn., 1982-85; editor Palm Beach Post, 1985—. Served with U.S. Army, 1968-69. Mem. Fla. Soc. Newspaper Editors, Am. Soc. Newspaper Editors, Sigma Delta Chi. Home: 230 Dyer Rd West Palm Beach FL 33405-1218 Office: Palm Beach Post 2751 S Dixie Hwy West Palm Beach FL 33405-1233

SEARS, GEORGE AMES, lawyer; b. Chehalis, Wash., Oct. 17, 1926; s. Briton Wallis and Merle (Kelso) S.; m. Mary Ann Deggeller, May 5, 1951; children: Kathrin Elizabeth, Geoffrey John. BA, Yale U., 1949; JD, Stanford U., 1952. Bar: Calif. 1952. Assoc. Pillsbury, Madison and Sutro, San Francisco, 1952-58, ptnr., 1959—, chmn. firm, 1984-89. Bd. dirs. Bay Area Coun., San Francisco, 1984-89, Invest-in-Am. No. Calif. Coun., San Francisco, 1988-90, Marin Conservation League, 1992—; trustee Marin Country Day Sch., Corte Madera, Calif., 1961-65; mem. exec. com. bd. visitors Stanford (Calif.) U. Law Sch., 1982-86; mem. bd. visitors Brigham Young U. Law Sch., Provo, Utah, 1986-88; pres. Stanford U. Law Fund, 1985-86; pres. Legal Aid Soc., San Francisco, 1969-70; mem. Coun. Friends of Bancroft Libr., 1993—. With USN, 1945-46. Fellow Am. Coll. Trial Lawyers, Am. Bar Found.; mem. ABA, Calif. Bar Assn. (chmn. adminstrn. of justice com. 1973-74), San Francisco Bar Assn., Pacific-Union Club, Belvedere Tennis Club. Avocations: reading, music, hiking, tennis. Home: 161 Harrison Ave Sausalito CA 94965-2043 Office: Pillsbury Madison & Sutro 225 Bush St San Francisco CA 94104-4207

SEARS, JOHN PATRICK, lawyer; b. Syracuse, N.Y., July 3, 1940; s. James Louis and Helen Mary (Fitzgerald) S.; m. Carol Jean Osborne, Aug. 25, 1962; children: James Louis, Ellen Margaret, Amy Elizabeth. B.S., Notre Dame U., 1960; LL.B., J.D., Georgetown U., 1963. Bar: N.Y. bar 1963. Clk. N.Y. Ct. Appeals, 1963-65; asso. firm Nixon, Mudge, Rose, Guthrie, Alexander & Mitchell, 1965-66; mem. staff Richard M. Nixon, 1966-69; dep. counsel to Pres. Nixon, 1969-70; ptnr. Gadsby & Hannah, Washington, 1970-75, Baskin & Sears, Washington, 1977-84; pvt. practice Washington, 1984—; mgr. Ronald Regan's Presdl. Campaign, 1975-76, 79-80; polit. analyst NBC Today Show, 1984-89; mem. Wall Street Jour. bd. of polit. experts, 1984—; columnist LA Times, Newsday, 1992—. Fellow Kennedy Inst. Politics, Harvard, 1970. Home: 2801 New Mexico Ave NW Washington DC 20007-3921 Office: 2021 K St NW Washington DC 20006-1003

SEARS, JOHN WINTHROP, lawyer; b. Boston, Dec. 18, 1930; s. Richard Dudley and Frederica Fulton (Leser) S.; m. Catherine Coolidge, 1965 (div. 1970). AB magna cum laude, Harvard U., 1952, JD, 1959; MLitt, Oxford U., 1957. Bar: Mass. 1959, U.S. Dist. Ct. Mass. 1982. Rep. Brown Bros. Harriman, N.Y.C., 1959-63, Boston, 1963-66; mem. Mass. Ho. Reps. 1965-68; sheriff Suffolk County, Mass., 1968-69; chmn. Boston Fin. Commn., 1969-70, Met. Dist. Commn., 1970-75; councillor-at-large Boston City Coun., 1980-82; trustee Sears Office, Boston, 1975—; apptd. bd. dirs. Fulbright Scholarship, 1991-93. Contbr. articles to profl. jours. Trustee Christ's Ch., Longwood, Brookline Mass., 1965—, Sears Trusts, Boston, 1975—; hon. trustee J.F. Kennedy Libr., 1991—; bd. dirs. Middlesex Club, Ripon Soc., Mus. Am. Textile Heritage, 1987—, Shirley-Eustis Assoc., Environ. League Mass., 1994—. Rep. candidate Mayor of Boston, 1967, Sec. State, Mass., 1978, Gov. of Mass., 1982; vice chmn. Ward 5 Rep. Com., 1965-69, 75-85; chmn. Rep. State Com., 1975-76, mem., 80-85; del. Rep. Nat. Conv., 1968, 76, State Conv., 1966-92; mem. U.S. Electoral Coll., 1984; bd. dirs. United South End Settlements, 1966—, chmn., 1977-78. Lt. comdr. USNR, 1952-54, 61-62. Rhodes scholar, 1955; recipient Outstanding Pub. Servant award Mass. Legis. Assn., 1975. Mem. Mass. Bar Assn., New Eng. Hist. and Geneal. Soc. (bd. dirs., councillor 1977-82), Mass. Hist. Soc., Handel and Haydn Soc. (gov. 1982-87), Signet Soc., Boston Atheneum, Tennis and Racquet Club, Somerset Club, The Country Club (Brookline), St. Botolph Club, Wed. Evening Club of 1777, Spee Club (Cambridge chpt., pres., trustee), Phi Beta Kappa. Republican. Home: 7 Acorn St Boston MA 02108-3501 *As the working years come to an end, some of us look for ways to teach, to help neighbors, especially those in need, and to build up the beauty and excellence we may have encontered in our own lives.*

SEARS, MARVIN, ophthalmologist, educator; b. N.Y.C., Sept. 16, 1928; s. Louis and Blanche Sears; children: Anne, David, Jonathan, Edward, Benjamin. AB, Princeton U., 1949; MD, Columbia U., 1953. Intern Bellevue Hosp., N.Y.C., 1954; resident in ophthalmology Johns Hopkins Hosp., 1954-61; fellow NIH, 1959-60; chmn. sect. ophthalmology Yale-New Haven (Conn.) Hosp., 1961-71; asst. prof. dept. ophthalmology and visual sci. Yale U. Sch. Medicine, 1961-64, assoc. prof., 1964-69, prof., 1969—, chmn., 1971-93; cons. Vets. Meml. Med. Ctr., Meriden, Conn., 1986—, Princess Margaret Hosp., Nassau, 1982—, Waterbury (Conn.) Hosp., 1975—, William W. Backus Hosp., Norwich, Conn., 1974—, Hosp. Albert Schweitzer, Des Chapelles, Haiti, 1968-83, Jenkins (Ky.) Clinic Hosp., 1968, Hosp. St. Raphael, New Haven, New Britain (Conn.) Gen. Hosp.; chief cons. VA Med. Ctr., West Haven, Conn., 1961—; instr. Johns Hopkins Hosp., 1959-61; vis. prof. dept. ophthalmology U. Puerto Rico; mem. numerous adv. coms. Editorial bd.: Am. Jour. Ophthalmology, 1967-82, Investigative Ophthalmology, 1966-78, Jour. Ocular Pharmacology, 1985—; contbr. articles to profl. jours. Recipient McKosh prize/Epistemology, Princeton U., 1949, Schwentker medal Johns Hopkins Hosp., 1958, Alcon Rsch. Inst. award, 1985, Method to Extend Rsch. in Time award Nat. Eye Inst., 1990—; named Gifford lectr. Chgo. Ophthal. Soc., 1985; endowed professorship established in Sears' name Yale U., 1993. Fellow ACS, Pierson Coll. Yale U.; mem. Am. Acad. Ophthalmology, Am. Ophthal. Soc., Assn. for Rsch. in Vision and Ophthalmology (Jonas S. Friedenwald award 1977), Assn. Univ. Profs. Ophthalmology, Conn. State Med. Soc., Internat. Agy. for Prevention Blindness, Internat. Soc. for Eye Rsch., New England Ophthal. Soc. (award 1969), Pan Am. Assn. Ophthalmology, Soc. Eye Surgeons, Wilmer Residents Assn., Appalachian Mountain Club, Audubon Soc., Lions (Melvin Jones fellow). Jewish. Avocation: mountaineering. Office: Yale Eye Ctr PO Box 208061 330 Cedar St New Haven CT 06520-8061

SEARS, MARY HELEN, lawyer; b. Syracuse, N.Y.; d. James Louis and Helen Mary (Fitzgerald) Sears. AB, Cornell U., 1950; JD with honors, George Washington U., 1960. Bar: Va. 1960, D.C. 1961, U.S. Supreme Ct. 1963. Chemist Allied Chem. and Dye Corp., Syracuse, 1950-52, Hercules Powder Co., Wilmington, Del., 1952-55; patent examiner U.S. Patent Office, Washington, 1955-60; pvt. practice Washington, 1960-61; assoc. Irons, Birch, Swindler & McKie, Washington, 1961-69; mem. firm Irons and Sears, Washington, 1969-84; chmn. trade regulation practice dept. Memel, Jacobs, Pierno, Gersh & Ellsworth, Washington, 1984-87; ptnr., chmn. intellectual property and unfair competition practice dept. Ginsburg, Feldman & Bress, Washington, 1987-91; ptnr., chmn. intellectual property and telecomm. practice group Reid & Priest, Washington, 1991-94; founder, chmn. M. H. Sears Law Firm, 1994—; mem. adv. bd. Boardroom Reports, Inc., N.Y.C., 1980-85; mem. Cornell U. Coun., 1981-87, 89-93, life mem., 1995—, mem. adminstrv. bd., 1984-86. Contbr. articles to various publs. Recipient Outstanding Performance award U.S. Dept. Commerce, 1957. Mem. ABA (co-chmn. appellate practice com., litigation sect. 1989-92), Am. Intellectual Property Law Assn., Am. Chem. Soc., Am. Soc. Internat. Law, Licensing Execs. Soc., Internat. Trademark Assn., Va. State Bar Assn., D.C. Bar Assn., George Washington U. Law Alumnae Assn. (bd. dirs. 1995—), Order of Coif, Phi Alpha Delta. Republican. Office: M H Sears Laro Firm Chartered 2300 N St NW Washington DC 20037-1122

SEARS, RICHARD BRUCE, speech and language pathologist; b. London, Ont., Can., Mar. 20, 1950; came to U.S., 1953; s. Edward Mervin and Helen Barbara (MacNamara) S.; m. Mary Lynn Power, Jan. 21, 1972; children: Evan, Ethan, Erin. BS, Ea. Mich. U., 1978, MA, 1979. Clin. intern VA Med. Ctr., Allen Park, Mich., 1979; speech and lang. diagnostician Lake-McHenry Regional Program, Crystal Lake, Ill., 1980; tchr. speech and lang. impaired Dearborn (Mich.) Pub. Schs., 1980-83, 85—; speech and lang. pathologist St. Joseph's Hosp., Sarnia, Ont., Can., 1983-85, Sarnia Gen. Hosp., 1983-85; speech and lang. pathologist, cons. Sarnia-Lambton Home Care, 1983-85; adv. bd. Metrostaff home Care, Southfield, Mich., 1986-90. Lyricist, songwriter various music, 1986—. Chmn. Local Spiritual Assembly, Bahá'í, Dearborn, 1991—. Mem. Am. Speech, Lang. and Hearing Assn. Bahá'í. Avocations: songwriting, golf, skiing. Office: Dearborn Pub Schs 18700 Audette St Dearborn MI 48124-4222

SEARS, ROBERT STEPHEN, finance educator; b. Odessa, Tex., May 27, 1950; s. William Bethel and Leola Vernon (Little) S.; Reva Dana Flournoy, Aug. 17, 1973; children: Matthew Stephen, Elizabeth Rea. AAS, Odessa Jr. Coll., 1970; BA summa cum laude, Tex. Tech. U., 1973, MS, 1976; PhD, U. N.C., 1980. Supr. Bethel Enterprises, Odessa, Tex., 1973-74; teaching asst. Tex. Tech. U., Lubbock, 1974-76, Lubbock Bankers Assn. prof., dir. Inst.

Banking and Fin. Studies, 1988—; teaching asst. U. N.C., Chapel Hill, 1976-79; asst. prof. U. Ill., Champaign, 1979-85, assoc. prof., 1985-88; rsch. prof. Bur. Econ. and Bus., Champaign, 1984; cons. Cameron Brown Mortgage Co., Raleigh, N.C., 1978-80, Howard Savings Bank, Livingston, N.J., 1980; asset mgr., trustee, pvt. investors, 1984—. Author: Investment Management, 1993, (chpt), Modern Real Estate, 1980, 84; assoc. editor Rev. of Bus. Studies, 1989-95, Jour. of Fin. Rsch., 1990—, Internat. Jour. of Bus., 1995—; contbr. articles to profl. jours. Chmn. fin. com. Temple Bapt. Ch., Champaign, Ill., 1982, bd. deacons, 1982-88, chmn. deacons, lay leader, 1983; Sunday sch. tchr. Carrboro (N.C.) Bapt. Ch., 1977-79; bd. deacons Ind. Ave. Bapt. Ch., Lubbock, 1989—, Sunday sch. tchr., 1991-92, master design com., 1993—; trustee All Saints Episcopal Sch., 1995—. Rsch. grantee Cameron Brown Mortgage Co., Raleigh, N.C., 1978-80, U. Ill, Champaign, 1980-84, 86-87, Investors in Bus. Edn., Champaign, 1980-81, 84. Mem. Southwestern Fin. Assn. (pres. 1989-90, v.p. and program chmn. 1988-89, sec., treas. 1986-88, dir. 1984-86, program com. 1985-86, 89—), Fin. Mgmt. Assn. (ptogram com. 1986, 89-94), So. Fin. Assn. (program com. 1986, 95), Western Fin. Assn. (program com. 1986), Am. Fin. Assn., Ea. Fin. Assn., Alto Lakes Country Club, Lake Ridge Country Club. Republican. So. Baptist. Avocations: golf, walking, participating in sports with my children. Office: Tex Tech U COBA PO Box 4320 Lubbock TX 79409-4320

SEARS, ROLLIN GEORGE, wheat geneticist, small grains researcher; b. Salem, Oreg., Dec. 15, 1950; s. George Lestor and Margret (Mead) S.; m. Donna Jean DeNoma, Sept. 12, 1971; children: Stephanie L., Mark C., Scott N. BS, Montana State U., 1972, MS, 1974; PhD, Oreg. State U., Corvallis, 1979. Asst. prof. N.D. State U., Fargo, 1979-80; asst. prof. Kansas State U., Manhattan, 1980-84, assoc. prof., 1984-89, prof., 1989—; chmn. Nat. Wheat Improvement Com., 1991-92. Vestry Episc. Ch., Manhattan, Kans., 1982-85, sr. warden, 1985-87; pres. Manhattan Marlins, 1986-90. Mem. Am. Soc. Agronomy (bd. rep. 1992—), Crop Sci. Soc. Am., Tissue Culture Soc. Am., Internat. Soc. Plant Milec. Biology, Sigma Xi, Alpha Zeta. Avocations: reading, fishing, golf. Office: Kansas State U Agronomy Dept TH Hall Manhattan KS 66506-5501

SEARS, WILLIAM REES, engineering educator; b. Mpls., Mar. 1, 1913; s. William Everett and Gertrude (Rees) S.; m. Mabel Jeannette Rhodes, Mar. 20, 1936; children—David William, Susan Carol. BS in Aero. Engring, U. Minn., 1934; Ph.D., aeronautics, Calif. Inst. Tech., 1938; DSc (hon.), U. Ariz., 1987. Asst. prof. Calif. Inst. Tech., 1939-41; chief aerodynamics Northrop Aircraft, Inc., 1941-46; dir. Grad. Sch. Aero. Engring., Cornell U., Ithaca, N.Y., 1946-63; dir. Center Applied Math., 1963-67, J.L. Given prof. engring., 1962-74; prof. aerospace and mech. engring. U. Ariz., Tucson, 1974-88, prof. emeritus, 1988—; F. W. Lanchester lectr. Royal Aero. Soc., 1973, Gardner lectr. MIT, 1987, Guggenheim lectr. Internat. Congress Aero. Scis., 1988; cons. aerodynamics. Author: The Airplane and its Components, 1941, Stories from a 20th-Century Life, 1994; editor: Jet Propulsion and High-Speed Aerodynamics, vol. VI, 1954, Jour. Aerospace Scis., 1956-63, Ann. Revs. of Fluid Mechanics, Vol. I. Recipient Vincent Bendix award Am. Soc. Engring. Edn., 1965, Prandtl Ring Deutsche Gesellschaft für Luft- und Raumfahrt, 1974, Von Karman medal AGARD (NATO), 1977, ASME medal, 1989, NAS Award in Aeronautical Engrng Nat. Acad of Sciences, 1995; named to Ariz. Aviation Hall of Fame, 1996. Fellow AIAA (hon., G. Edward Pendray award 1975, S.A. Reed Aeros. award 1981, Von Karman lectr. 1968); mem. Nat. Acad. Engring. Mex. (fgn.), Am. Phys. Soc. (Fluid Dynamics prize 1992), Nat. Acad. Scis. (award in aero. engring. 1995), Sigma Xi. Home: Santa Catalina Villas 8202 7500 N Calle Sin Envidia Tucson AZ 85718

SEASE, GENE ELWOOD, public relations company executive; b. Portage, Pa., June 28, 1931; s. Grover Chauncey and Clara Mae (Over) S.; m. Joanne D. Cherry, July 20, 1952; children: David Gene, Daniel Elwood, Cheryl Joanne. A.B., Juniata Coll., 1952; B.D., Pitts. Theol. Sem., 1956, Th.M., 1959; Ph.D., U. Pitts., 1965, M.Ed., 1958; LL.D., U. Evansville, 1972, Butler U., 1972; Litt.D., Ind. State U., 1974; DD, U. Indpls., 1989. Ordained to ministry United Methodist Ch., 1956; pastor Grace United Meth. Ch., Wilkinsburg, Pitts., 1952-63; conf. dir., supt. Western Pa. Conf. United Meth. Ch., Pitts., 1963-68; lectr. grad. faculty U. Pitts., 1965-68; mem. staff U. Indpls., 1968—, asst. to pres., 1968-69, pres., 1970-88, chancellor, 1988-89, pres. emeritus, 1989—; chmn. Sease, Gerig & Assocs., Indpls., 1989—; bd. dirs. Indpls. Life Ins. Co., Nat. City Bank of Ind. Author: Christian Word Book, 1968; also numerous articles. Pres. Greater Indpls. Progress Com., 1972-75; pres. Marion County Sheriff's Merit Bd.; mem. Ind. Scholarship Commn.; cons. Am. Cablevision Indpls.; bd. dirs. Indpls. Conv. Bur., Ind. Law Enforcement Tng. Acad., 500 Festival, Crossroads coun. Boy Scouts Am., Community Hosp. Indpls., St. Francis Hosp. Mem. Internat. Platform Assn., English Speaking Union, Japan-Am. Soc. Ind., Ind. C. of C. (bd. dirs.), Indpls. C. of C. (bd. dirs.), Ind. Schoolmen's Club, Econ. Club of Indpls. (bd. dirs.), Phi Delta Kappa, Alpha Phi Omega, Alpha Psi Omega. Clubs: Mason (Indpls.) (33 deg., Shriner), Kiwanian. (Indpls.), Columbia (Indpls.).

SEASE, JOHN W(ILLIAM), chemistry educator; b. New Brunswick, N.J., Nov. 10, 1920; s. Virgil Bernard and Rosalyn (Summer) S.; m. Mary Lieurance, June 5, 1943; children—Margaret, Catherine, Ann, John Lieurance. A.B., Princeton U., 1941; Ph.D., Calif. Inst. Tech., 1946. Research asst. Nat. Def. Research Com., Calif. Inst. Tech., Pasadena, 1942-45; instr. chemistry Wesleyan U., Middletown, Conn., 1946-48, asst. prof. chemistry, 1948-52, assoc. prof. chemistry, 1952-58, prof. chemistry, 1958-82, E.B. Nye prof. chemistry, 1982-88, prof. emeritus, 1988—. Mem. Portland Sch. Bd., Conn., 1959-65. Mem. AAAS, Am. Chem. Soc. (councilor, sec. chmn. Conn. Valley sect.), Phi Beta Kappa, Sigma Xi. Office: Wesleyan U Dept Chemistry Middletown CT 06459

SEASHORE, MARGRETTA REED, physician; b. Red Bank, N.J., June 20, 1939; d. Robert Clark Reed and Lillie Ann (Heaviland) R.; m. John Seashore, Dec. 26, 1964; children: Robert H., Carl J., Carolyn L. BA, Swarthmore Coll., 1961; MD, Yale U., 1965. Diplomate Am. Bd. Pediatrics, Am. Bd. Med. Genetics, Nat. Bd. Med. Examiners. Intern in pediatrics Yale U. Sch. Medicine, Haven, Conn., 1965-66, asst. resident in pediatrics, 1966-68; postdoctoral fellow in genetics and metabolism, depts. of pediatrics and medicine Yale U. Sch. Medicine, 1968-70; clin. asst. prof. pediatrics U. Fla. Coll. Medicine, Gainesville, 1970-71; attending physician Hope Haven Children's Hosp., Jacksonville, Fla., 1970-73; asst. prof. pediatrics Duval Med. Ctr., Jacksonville, Fla., 1970-71; attending physician Duvall Med. Ctr. U. Hosp. Jacksonville, 1970-73; asst. prof. pediatrics U. Fla. Coll. Medicine, 1971-73; attending physician Shands Teaching Hosp., Gainesville, Fla., 1971-73; asst. clin. prof. human genetics and pediatrics Yale U. Sch. Medicine, 1974-78; attending physician Yale-New Haven Hosp., 1974—; cons. physician Bridgeport (Conn.) Hosp., 1974—; attending physician Danbury (Conn.) Hosp., 1977—; dir. Genetic Consultation Svc. Yale-New Haven Hosp., 1977-86; from asst. prof. to assoc. prof. human genetics and pediatrics Yale U. Sch. Medicine, 1978-90; cons. physician Lawrence and Meml. Hosp., New London, Conn., 1979—, Norwalk (Conn.) Hosp., 1981—; dir. Genetic Consultation Svc. Yale-New Haven Hosp., 1989—; prof. genetics and pediatrics Yale U. Sch. Medicine, 1990—. Contbr. chpts. to books. Fellow Am. Acad. Pediatrics (chair com. on genetics 1990-94, mem. screening com. Conn. chpt. 1977—, mem. genetics com. 1989—), Am. Coll. Med. Genetics (founder, mem. screeing subcom. 1993—); mem. AMA, AAAS, Am. Soc. Human Genetics (mem. genetic svcs. com. 1986-91), Soc. Inherited Metabolic Disorders (bd. dirs. 1989—, sec. 1991-96, pres.-elect 1996), Soc. for Study of Inborn Errors of Metabolism, New Eng. Genetics Group (co-dir. 1992-95, chmn. outreach com. 1979-89, chmn. screening com. 1989-93, mem. steering com. 1979—). Avocations: music, gardening, sewing, computers. Office: Yale U Sch Med Dept Genetics 333 Cedar St New Haven CT 06510-3206

SEASTRAND, ANDREA H., congresswoman; b. Chgo., Aug. 5, 1941; m. Eric Seastrand (dec.); children: Kurt, Heidi. BA in Edn., DePaul U., 1963. Prof. religion U. Santa Barbara; mem. Calif. Assembly, 1990-94, U.S. Ho. of Reps., 1995—; asst. Rep. leader; mem. Rep. caucus; mem. edn. com., agr. com., consumer protection com., new tech. com., govtl. efficiency com., and ways and means com.; mem. rural caucus and select com. on marine resources. Mem. Calif. Fedn. Rep. Women (past pres.). Office: US Ho of Reps 1216 Longworth HOB Washington DC 20515-0522*

SEATON, EDWARD LEE, newspaper editor and publisher; b. Manhattan, Kans., Feb. 5, 1943; s. Richard Melvin and Mary (Holton) S.; m. Karen Mathisen, Sept. 4, 1965; children: Edward Merrill, John David. AB cum laude, Harvard U., 1965; postgrad., U. Cen., Quito, Ecuador, 1965-66, U. Mo., 1966-67. Staff writer Courier-Jour., Louisville, 1968-69; editor-in-chief, pub. Manhattan Mercury, 1969—; bd. dirs., officer 12 other newspaper and broadcasting affiliates; mem. adv. com. Knight Internat. Press Fellowship Program; mem. Pulitzer Prize bd. Contbr. articles to profl. jours. Chmn. Alfred M. Landon lecture patrons Kans. State U.; chmn. Latin Am. Scholarship Program Am. Univs., Cambridge, Mass., 1986-87. Decorated comendador Order of Christopher Columbus (Dominican Republic); Fulbright scholar, 1965; recipient Cabot prize Columbia U., 1993. Mem. Am. Soc. Newspaper Editors (sec., pres. found.), Inter-Am. Press Assn. (pres. 1989-90), Internat. Ctr. Journalists (bd. dirs.), Internat. Press Inst., Kans. C. of C. and Industry (pres. 1987), Fly Club (Harvard U.). Avocations: tennis, cooking. Office: Manhattan Mercury Osage At N 5th # 5th St Manhattan KS 66502

SEATON, RICHARD MELVIN, newspaper and broadcasting executive; b. Washington, Jan. 25, 1913; s. Fay Noble and Dorothea Elizabeth (Schmidt) S.; m. Mary Holton, June 1, 1936 (dec. 1989); children: Richard H., Frederick D., Elizabeth, Edward L.; m. Eva Lee Sanborn, May 18, 1991. B.S. in Journalism, Kans. State U., 1934. Officer and dir. various cos. comprising Seaton News Media Group, 1937—. Trustee William Allen White Found., Kans. State U., Found.; mem. initial Kans. State Water Resources Bd., 1954-61, initial Kans. Cultural Arts Commn., 1965-67; founder Coffeyville Hist. Mus. Mem. Kans. Press Assn. (pres. 1949), Kans. AP (chmn. 1953), Am. Soc. Newspaper Editors, Internat. Press Inst., Coffeyville C. of C. (pres. 1950-51), Kans. State Hist. Soc. (dir. 1979—), Sigma Delta Chi, Phi Kappa Phi, Beta Theta Pi. Republican. Unitarian. Established R.M. Seaton profl. journalism chair Kans. State U., 1978, Dalton Defenders Meml. Mus., Coffeyville, Kans., 1953, Brown Mansion Mus., Coffeyville, 1973. Office: 218 W 8th St Coffeyville KS 67337-5808

SEATON, ROBERT FINLAYSON, retired planned giving consultant; b. Hancock, Mich., Nov. 28, 1930; s. Donald W. and Mary Lucille (Finlayson) S.; m. Helen Jean Robarts, Apr. 18, 1954; children: Scott, Sandy. BS, Mich. Technol. U., 1952; MBA, Stanford, 1956; postgrad., Ind. U., 1966, U. So. Calif., 1973. Asst. sec. Palo Alto (Calif.) Mut. Savs. and Loan Assn., 1956-60; asst. v.p. Am. Savs. and Loan Assn. No. Calif., 1960-63; v.p. 1st Western Savs. and Loan Assn., Las Vegas, 1963-67; v.p., sec. Fed. Home Loan Bank, Cin., 1967-72; pres., chief exec. officer 2d Fed. Savs. and Loan Assn., Cleve., 1973; pres., chief exec. officer Cardinal Fed. Savs. Bank, Cleve., 1973-87, chmn., 1987-88; sr. v.p. Planned Giving Systems, Inc., Cleve., 1989—, pres., 1990-94. Pres. The Orange Schs. Edn. Found.; trustee Univ. Circle, Inc.; v.p. Luth. Housing Corp., N.E. Ohio Coun. Higher Edn.; trustee, exec. com. Clean-Land-Ohio. Lt. USNR, 1952-54. Republican. Methodist. Home: 16 Pepper Creek Dr Cleveland OH 44124-5248

SEATON, SANDRA JEANNE, women's health nurse; b. St. Louis, Apr. 29, 1945; d. Lloyd Otto Hampe and Yvonne Jacqueline (Wagenbach) Reiner; m. Francis Bruce Seaton, Jan. 30, 1971; children: Theresa, Kyle. BA, Webster U., 1968; MA, St. Louis U., 1972; ADN, SUNY, Albany, 1980; BSN, Barry U., 1993. RN, Fla., cert. inpatient obstet. nurse, profl. healthcare quality, instr. neonatal resuscitation providers, cardiopulmonary resuscitation and emergency cardiac care instr. Staff nurse Baptist Hosp. of Miami, 1979-91, nurse clinician, 1991—, care coord., clinician Mother/Baby Unit, 1994—; expert witness Cohen, Berke, Bernstein, Brodie, Kondell & Laslo, P.A., Miami, 1993. Deacon Pinecrest Presbyn. Ch., Miami, 1990-93; mem. Bapt. Hosp. Environ. Task Force, Miami, 1990-94. Mem. AWHONN, Nat. Assn. Healthcare Quality, Dade Assn. for Healthcare Quality, South Fla. Perinatal Network, Macrobiotic Found. of Fla., Sigma Theta Tau Internat. Avocations: hiking, antiques, art appreciation, sailing, macrobiotics. Office: Bapt Hosp of Miami 8900 N Kendall Dr Miami FL 33176-2118

SEATON, VAUGHN ALLEN, veterinary pathology educator; b. Abilene, Kans., Oct. 11, 1928; m. Clara I. Bertelrud; children: Gregory S., Jeffrey T. BS, Kans. State U., 1954, DVM, 1954; MS, Iowa State U., 1957. Pvt. practice Janesville, Wis., 1954; instr. pathology Vet. Diagnostic Lab. Iowa State U., Ames, 1954-57, from asst. to assoc. prof. pathology Vet. Diagnostic Lab., 1957-64, prof., head Vet. Diagnostic Lab., 1964—; lab. coord. regional emergency animal disease eradication orgn. Animal and Plant Health Inspection Svc. USDA, 1974—; mem. rsch. com. Iowa Beef Industry Coun., 1972-85; mem. adv. bd. Iowa State Water Resources Rsch. Inst., 1973-80; cons. several orgns. Co-author: (monographs) Feasibility Study of College of Veterinary Medicine, 1972, Veterinary Diagnostic Laboratory Facilities-State of New York, 1970; bd. dirs. Iowa State U. Press, 1985-88, mem. manuscript com., 1982-85; contbr. articles to profl. jours. Trustee Ames Pub. Libr., 1979-85; mem. Iowa State Bd. Health, 1971-77, v.p., 1976-77. Mem. AVMA, Am. Assn. Vet. Lab. Diagnosticians (bd. govs. 1973-88, pres. 1968, E.P. Pope award 1980), Am. Coll. Vet. Toxicologists, U.S. Animal Health Assn., Iowa Vet. Med. Assn. (pres. 1971), North Cen. Assn. Vet. Lab. Diagnosticians, Western Vet. Conf. (exec. bd. 1986-90, v.p. 1994, pres.-elect 1995, pres. 1996), World Assn. Vet. Lab. Diagnosticians (pres. 1980-86), masons (bd. dirs. 1985-88), Ames C. of C. (bd. dirs. 1970-73), Phi Kappa Phi, Phi Zeta (pres. 1964), Alpha Zeta, Gamma Sigma Delta. Office: Iowa State U Coll Vet Medicine Vet Diagnostic Lab Ames IA 50011

SEAU, JUNIOR (TIANA SEAU, JR.), professional football player; b. Samoa, Jan. 19, 1969. Student, U. So. Calif. Linebacker San Diego Chargers, 1990—; player Super Bowl XXVIV, 1994. Named to Sporting News Coll. All-Am. Team, 1989, to Pro Bowl Team, 1991, 92, 93, to Sporting News NFL All Pro Team, 1992, 93. Office: San Diego Chargers PO Box 609609 San Diego CA 92160-9609

SEAVER, JAMES EVERETT, historian, educator; b. Los Angeles, Oct. 4, 1918; s. Everett Herbert and Gertrude Lillian (Sharp) S.; m. Virginia Stevens, Dec. 20, 1940; children—Richard Everett, William Merrill, Robert Edward. A.B., Stanford U., 1940; Ph.D., Cornell U., 1946. Asst. instr. history Cornell U., 1940-42, 44-46; instr. Mich. State U., 1946-47; mem. faculty U. Kans., Lawrence, 1947—; prof. history U. Kans., 1960—; prof. emeritus, 1989—; pres. faculty U. Kans., 1972-74, 82-83. Author: The Persecution of the Jews in the Roman Empire, 313-438 A.D, 1952, also articles. Fulbright-Hays grantee Italy, 1953-54; Fulbright-Hays grantee Israel, 1963-64; Carnegie grantee Costa Rica, 1966-67. Mem. Am. Hist. Assn., Am. Philol. Assn., Archaeol. Inst. Am., Am. Numismatic Soc., AAUP, Am. Acad. Rome, U.S. Archives of Recorded Sound. Democrat. Episcopalian. Clubs: Alvamar Tennis, Alvamar Country. Home: 600 Louisiana St Lawrence KS 66044-2336 Office: U Kans Dept History Lawrence KS 66045

SEAVER, RICHARD CARLTON, oil field equipment company executive, lawyer; b. Los Angeles, June 10, 1922; s. Byron D. and Mary Louise (Schmidt) Seaver; children: Richard Carlton, Christopher T., Patrick T., Victoria, Martha. B.A., Pomona Coll., 1946; J.D., U. Calif.-Berkeley, 1949. Bar: Calif. 1950. Assoc. Thelen, Marrin, Johnson & Bridges, Los Angeles, 1950-57; sec., counsel Hydril Co., Los Angeles, 1957-64, pres., 1964-86, chmn., 1986—; dir. DeAnza Land & Leisure Corp. Vice chmn., bd. dirs. Seaver Inst.; trustee Los Angeles County Mus. Natural History, Episcopal Diocesan Investment Trust, Doheny Eye Inst., Pomona Coll., Calif. Inst. Arts; bd. dirs. Hosp. of Good Samaritan; bd. dirs., pres. L.A. Music Ctr. Opera Assn.; bd. overseers Hoover Inst., Palo Alto. Served to capt. inf. AUS, 1942-46, PTO. Decorated Bronze Star with oak leaf cluster. Mem. ABA, Calif. Bar Assn., Los Angeles Bar Assn. Republican. Clubs: St. Francis Yacht, Los Angeles Country, Los Angeles Yacht, California (Los Angeles); Newport Harbor Yacht (Balboa). Office: Hydril Co 714 W Olympic Blvd Los Angeles CA 90015-1469*

SEAVER, ROBERT LESLIE, law educator; b. Brockton, Mass., June 13, 1937; s. Russell Bradford and Lois (Marchant) S.; m. Marjorie V. Rote, Aug. 21, 1960 (div. 1974); children: Kimberly, Eric, Kristen; m. Elizabeth A. Horwitz, May 22, 1984. AB cum laude, Tufts U., Medford, Mass., 1958; JD, U. Chgo., 1964. Bar: Ohio 1964, U.S. Ct. Appeals (6th cir.) 1964, U.S. Dist. Ct. (so. dist.) Ohio 1965. Assoc. Taft, Stettinius and Hollister, Cin., 1964-66; v.p., sec., gen. counsel IDI Mgmt. Inc., Cin., 1966-74; pvt. practice Cin., 1974-75; prof. law No. Ky. U. Salmon P. Chase Coll. Law, Highland Heights, 1975—; of counsel Cors & Bassett, Cin., 1993—; cons. in field, 1975—. Author/editor: Ohio Corporation Law, 1988; contbr. chpts. to books. Advisor subcom. on pvt. corps of Ky. Commn. on Constl. Rev., 1987. With USMC, 1958-61. Recipient Justice Robert O. Lukowsky award of Excellence Chase Law Sch. Student Bar Assn., 1986. Mem. ABA, Ohio Bar Assn., Cin. Bar Assn., No. Ky. Bar Assn., U. Chgo. Law Sch. Alumni Assn. (regional v.p. 1976—). Republican. Unitarian. Avocations: duplicate bridge, history. Home: 826 Woodscene Ct Cincinnati OH 45230-4334 Office: Northern Kentucky U Salmon Chase Coll Law Highland Heights KY 41099

SEAVER, TOM (GEORGE THOMAS SEAVER), former professional baseball player; b. Fresno, Calif., Nov. 17, 1944; s. Charles H. and Betty Lee (Cline) S.; m. Nancy Lynn McIntyre, June 9, 1966; children: Sarah, Anne Elizabeth. Student, Fresno City Coll., 1964, U. So. Calif., 1965-68. Pitcher Jacksonville (Fla.) Suns, 1966; pitcher N.Y. Mets, 1967-77, 83-84, 87, mem. World Series Championship team, 1969; pitcher Cin. Reds, 1977-82, Chgo. White Sox, 1984-86, Boston Red Sox, 1986; announcer N.Y. Yankees WPIX-TV, N.Y.C. Author: (with Lee Lowenfish) The Art of Pitching, 1984, (with Alice Seigel) Tom Seaver's Baseball Card Book, 1985, (with Herb Resnicow) novel Beanball, 1989. Served with USMCR, 1963. Recipient Cy Young award Nat. League, 1969, 73, 75; named Rookie of Yr. Baseball Writers Assn. Am., 1967, Nat. League Pitcher of Yr. Sporting News, 1969, 73, 75, Sportsman of Yr. Sports Illustrated, 1969; named to Nat. League All-Star team, 1969-73, 75-78, to Baseball Hall of Fame Baseball Writers Assn. Am., 1992. Credited with more than 300 career victories; pitched over 3,000 career strikeouts. Office: care Matt Mendola 185 E 85th St Apt 18G New York NY 10028-2146

SEAWELL, THOMAS ROBERT, artist, retired educator; b. Balt., Mar. 17, 1936; s. Robert James and Cynthia Edith (Bass) S.; m. Barbara Louise Frey, Nov. 30, 1985; children: James Bradford, Lee Thomas, Gustin Charles, Jay Turner Frey. B.F.A., Washington U., 1958; M.F.A., Tex. Christian U., 1960. Mem. faculty dept. art SUNY-Oswego, 1963-91, prof., 1973-91; vis. artist Ox Bow Print Symposium, 1985, Ann. Matrix Artist, U. Dallas, 1989, Midwestern State U., 1993; juror 50th Cooperstown Nat., 1985, Nat. Print Exhbn., Minot State U., N.D., 1985., Rochester Print Club Annual, Meml. Art Gallery U. Rochester, 1988. One-man exhbns. include retrospective U. Md., Baltimore County, 1983, Schoharie County Arts Ctr., 1991, Tyler Art Gallery, SUNY, Oswego, 1991, Univ. Gallery, ETSU, Commerce, Tex., 1995; group exhbns. include Contemporary Am. Prints in Leningrad, USSR, 1983-84, The Collagraph, U. Mont., 1987, SUNY, Oswego, 1988, U. Dallas, 1989, DeCordova Mus., 1991; traveling exhbn. So. Arts Fedn. Traveling Exhbn. "A Sense of Place," 1986—; represented in permanent collections Bklyn. Mus., DeCordova Mus. Art, Rochester Meml. Art Gallery, Pushkin Mus., USSR, Brit. Mus., Munson-Williams-Proctor Inst., Library of Congress, Portland Art Mus.; commd. print editions: Geldermann Securities Ltd., 1985-92. Mem. Boston Printmakers, Phila. Water Color Club, Soc. Am. Graphic Artists. Home (summer): PO Box 14 Sterling NY 13156-0014

SEAWELL, WILLIAM THOMAS, former airline executive; b. Pine Bluff, Ark., Jan. 27, 1918; s. George Marion and Harriet (Aldridge) S.; m. Judith Alexander, June 12, 1941; children: Alexander Brooke, Anne Seawell Robinson. B.S., U.S. Mil. Acad., 1941; J.D., Harvard U., 1949. Commd. 2d lt. U.S. Army, 1941; advanced through grades to brig. gen. USAF, 1959; comdr. 401st Bombardment Group, ETO, World War II, 11th Bomb Wing SAC, 1953-54; dep. comdr. 7th Air Div., 1954-55; mil. asst. to sec. USAF, 1958-59, to dep. sec. def., 1959-61; comdt. cadets U.S. Air Force Acad., 1961-63; ret., 1963; v.p. operations and engring. Air Transport Assn. Am., Washington, 1963-65; sr. v.p. ops. Am. Airlines, N.Y.C., 1965-68; pres. Rolls Royce Aero Engines Inc. U.S. subsidiary Rolls Royce, Ltd., 1968-71; pres., chief operating officer Pan Am. World Airways Inc., N.Y.C., 1971-72; chmn. bd. Pan Am. World Airways Inc., 1972-81. Decorated Silver Star, D.F.C. with three oak leaf clusters, Air medal with three oak leaf clusters; Croix de Guerre with palm France). Clubs: Wings (N.Y.C.), Pine Bluff Country. Home: 21 Westridge Dr Pine Bluff AR 71603-7149

SEAWRIGHT, JAMES L., JR., sculptor, educator; b. Jackson, Miss., May 22, 1936; s. James L. and Josephine (Power) S.; m. Mabelle M. Garrard, June 22, 1960; 1 child, James Andrew. Student, U. of South, 1953-54, Delta State Coll., 1954-55; B.A. in English, U. Miss., 1957; postgrad., Art Students League of N.Y., 1961-62. Tech. supr. Columbia-Princeton Electronic Music Center, N.Y.C., 1963-69; tchr. Sch. Visual Arts, 1967-69; dir. visual arts program Princeton U., 1972—, prof. coun. of humanities and visual arts, 1992—. Asst. to choreographer, Henry St. Playhouse, N.Y.C., 1962-63, spl. effects, tech. cons., Mimi Garrard Dance Co., N.Y.C., 1964—; sculptor represented in permanent collections, Mus. Modern Art, N.Y.C., Whitney Mus., N.Y.C., N.J. State Mus., Trenton, Guggenheim Mus., N.Y.C., Wadsworth Atheneum, Hartford, Conn., others; pub. commns. for SEA-TAC Internat. Airport, Seattle, Logan Internat. Airport, Boston; also pvt. collections. Served with USN, 1957-61. Recipient Theodoron award Guggenheim Mus., 1969; Graham Found. Advanced Study in Arts fellow, 1970. Mem. Am. Abstract Artists, Phi Delta Theta. Democrat. Episcopalian. Office: 185 Nassau St Princeton NJ 08544-2003

SEAY, FRANK HOWELL, federal judge; b. Shawnee, Okla., Sept. 5, 1938; s. Frank and Wilma Lynn Seay; m. Janet Gayle Seay, June 2, 1962; children: Trudy Alice, Laura Lynn. Student, So. Meth. U., 1956-57; B.A., U. Okla., 1960, LL.B., 1963. Bar: Okla. 1963. Atty. Seminole County, 1963-66; asst. dist. atty., 1967-68, assoc. dist. judge, 1968-74; judge Okla. Dist. Ct. 22, 1974-79; judge ea. dist. U.S. Dist. Ct., Okla., 1979—, now chief judge. Mem. ABA, Okla. Bar Assn., Seminole County Bar Assn. Democrat. Clubs: Masons, Elks, Lions. Office: US Dist Ct PO Box 828 Muskogee OK 74401*

SEBASCO, SALVADOR MONASTRA, safety engineer; b. Phila., Mar. 13, 1961; s. Sal Monastra and Elizabeth Sebasco Bauer; m. Berta J. Monastra, Oct. 13, 1983 (div. July 1994); children: Anthony, Samantha. BS in Occupl. Safety and Health, Mont. Tech., 1984. Registered profl. engr., Mass.; bd. cert. safety profl. Sr. safety engr. Lockheed Idaho Inc., Idaho Falls, 1991-95, Sci. Applications Internat. Corp., Pleasanton, Calif., 1995—; engring. adv. bd. N.Mex. Highlands U., Las Vegas, 1994—. Co-author: Bloodbourne Pathogens (booklet), 1993. Bd. dirs. Bonneville County Crime Stoppers, Idaho Falls, 1992-95. Mem. ASME (nat. nominating com.), Am. Soc. Safety Engrs. (pub. rels. chair 1992—), Soc. Hispanic Profl. Engrs. (bd. dirs. 1993-95), Internat. Conf. Bldg. Code Ofcls. Ch. of the Nazarene. Avocations: chess, hiking, swimming, theatre, cooking. Office: Sandia Nat Lab ORG 8643 7011 East Ave MS9223 Livermore CA 94550

SEBASTIAN, LUCIA VILLA, principal; b. Osaka, Japan, Sept. 27, 1951; d. Frank Benedict and Margaret (Jacob) Villa; m. Richard J. Sebastian; children: Matthew John, Shanna Maria. BS, East Carolina U., Greenville, N.C., 1973; MA Ed, Coll. William and Mary, Williamsburg, Va., 1986, EdS in Adminstrn., 1992, EdD candidate, 1995—. Cert. elem., mid., secondary prin., elem. supr., dir. instrn., gen. supr., asst. supt. instrn., tchr. K-7. Tchr. 1st grade Williamsburg-James City County Pub. Schs., 1973-74; kindergarten tchr. Walsingham Acad., 1974-75; tchr. 6th grade York County Pub. Schs., Yorktown, Va., 1982-88, instrnl. specialist, 1988-92, asst. prin. Bethel Manor Elem. and Dare Elem. Schs., 1992—, prin. elem. summer sch., 1992-95; prin. Clara Byrd Baker Elem., Williamsburg, Va., 1995—; fellow Hampton Rds. Ctr. for Advancement of Teaching, Norfolk, Va., 1987—. Campaign chair United Way, York County, 1992; prenatal instr. March of Dimes; Lamaze instr. Health Dept.; singer St. Bede's Folk Group. Mem. NEA, ASCD, Va. Edn. Assn., York Edn. Assn., York Mgmt. Assn., Va. Assn. Supervision and Curriculum Devel. (conf. chair 1991-94, treas. 1992, pres. elect 1993, pres. 1994), Delta Kappa Gamma (sec. 1990, Emily Nelson scholarship 1994), Phi Kappa Phi, Kappa Delta Pi. Roman Catholic. Avocations: singing, soccer. Home: 105 Little John Rd Williamsburg VA 23185-4907 Office: Clara Byrd Baker Elem Sch 3131 Ironbound Rd Williamsburg VA 23185

SEBASTIAN, MICHAEL JAMES, retired manufacturing company executive; b. Chgo., July 8, 1930; s. Michael and Larraine (DeAmicis) S.; m. Sally Ervin, Nov. 29, 1953; children: Michael, Mark, Lisa. B.S. in M.E., Santa Clara U., 1952; A.M.P., Harvard U., 1972. Div. mgr. FMC Corp, Indpls., 1953-77; pres. Rotek, Aurora, Ohio, 1977-78; v.p. Gardner-Denver, Dallas, 1978-79; group pres. Cooper Industries, Dallas, 1979-81; v.p. Cooper Industries, Houston, 1981-82, exec. v.p., 1982—; bd. dirs. Quanex Corp., Gardner Denver Machinery, Inc. Past dir. Weatherford Internat.; mem. adv. bd. U. Houston Ctr. Pub. Policy. Republican. Roman Catholic. Clubs: Petroleum,

Lakeside Country (Houston). Avocations: golf; gardening; tennis. Home: 11511 Shadow Way Houston TX 77024-5216 Office: Cooper Industries Inc PO Box 4446 1001 Fannin St Fl 40 Houston TX 77002-6706*

SEBASTIAN, PETER, international affairs consultant, former ambassador; b. June 19, 1926; m. Harvel Huddleston, Dec. 11, 1951; 1 child, Christopher. B.A., U. Chgo., 1950; postgrad., U. d'Aix-Marseille, Nice, France, 1949, New Sch. for Social Research, N.Y.C., 1950, Nat. War Coll., 1969-70. Dir., owner cons. co., N.Y.C., 1950-57; U.S. Fgn. Service officer Dept. State, Washington, 1957-76, dep. exec. sec., 1976-77, sr. seminar, 1977-78; U.S. consul gen. Casablanca, Morocco, 1978-80; minister, counselor Am. embassy, Rabat, Morocco, 1980-82; dir. for North Africa Dept. State, Washington, 1982-84; ambassador to Tunisia Tunis, 1984-87; ambassador-in-residence Ctr. for Strategic Internat. Studies, Georgetown U., Washington, 1987-88; cons in fgn. affairs to the public and pvt. sector, lectr., 1988—. Contbr. poems to Osmose, 1949; author studies for U.S. Dept. State and other U.S agys. Served to sgt. AUS, 1944-46. Decorated Ouissam Alaouite (Morocco), numerous U.S. mil. decorations; recipient Presdl. Meritorious Service award, 1985. Mem. Am. Fgn. Svc. Assn., Nat. Geog. Soc., Mid. East Inst. Episcopalian. Avocations: painting; drawing; photography.

SEBASTIAN, RICHARD LEE, physicist, executive; b. Hutchinson, Kans., June 22, 1942; s. Leroy Clarence and Marion Alta (Brown) S.; m. Judy Ann French, Dec. 29, 1964; children: Todd Winslow, Alison Louise. A.B. in Math, Princeton U., 1964; Ph.D. in Physics, U. Md., 1970. Staff scientist ENSCO, Inc., Springfield, Va., 1969-72; chief scientist ENSCO, Inc., 1972-73, v.p. research, 1973-83; pres. Wackenhut Research Corp., Springfield, 1980-81; pres., chmn. Digital Signal Corp., Springfield, 1983-91; corp. v.p., gen. mgr. Digital Signal div. Coleman Rsch. Corp., Springfield, 1991-95; pres. Digitat Forecasting Corp., 1996—. Mem. Am. Phys. Soc., IEEE, Soc. Exploration Geophysicists. Home: 6128 River Dr Mason Neck VA 22079-4124 Office: Coleman Rsch Corp Digital Signal Div 6551 Loisdale Ct Springfield VA 22150-1808

SEBELIUS, KATHLEEN GILLIGAN, insurance commissioner; b. Cin., May 15, 1948; d. John J. and Mary K. (Dixon) Gilligan; m. Keith Gary Sebelius, 1974; children: Edward Keith, John McCall. BA, Trinity Coll., 1970; MA, U. Kans., 1977. Dir. planning Ctr. for Cmty. Justice, Washington, 1971-74; spl. asst. Kans. Dept. Corrections, Topeka, 1975-78; mem. Kans. Ho. of Reps., 1987-95. Founder Women's Polit. Caucus; mem. Friends of Cedar Crest, Florence Crittendon Svcs.; precinct committeewoman, 1980-86; mayor-elect, Potwin, 1985-87; exec. com. NAIC, Kans. Health Care Commn. Mem. Common Cause (state bd., nat. gov. bd. 1975-81), Kans. Trial Lawyers Assn. (dir. 1978-86). Democrat. Roman Catholic. Home: 224 SW Greenwood Ave Topeka KS 66606-1228

SEBEOK, THOMAS ALBERT, linguistics educator; b. Budapest, Hungary, Nov. 9, 1920; came to U.S., 1937, naturalized, 1944; s. Dezso and Veronica (Perlman) S.; m. Eleanor Lawton, Sept. 1947; 1 child, Veronica C.; m. Jean Umiker, Oct. 1972; children: Jessica A., Erica L. B.A., U. Chgo., 1941; M.A., Princeton, 1943, Ph.D., 1945; PhD honoris causa, U. Budapest, Hungary, 1990; Dr. honoris causa, U. Nacional de Rosario, Argentina, 1991; DSc honoris causa, U. So. Ill., 1991. Mem. faculty Ind. U., Bloomington, 1943—, Disting. prof. linguistics, 1967-78, Disting. prof. linguistics and semiotics, 1978-91, Disting. prof. emeritus, 1991—, prof. anthropology, prof. Uralic and Altaic studies, fellow Folklore Inst., mem. Russian and East European Inst., chmn. Research Center for Lang. and Semiotic Studies, 1956-91, chmn. emeritus Grad. Program in Semiotic Studies, 1991—; mem.-at-large NAS-NRC, also mem. various coms.; lectr. various acads. and univs., U.S. and abroad; vis. prof. U. Mich., 1945, 58, U. P.R., 1949, U. N.Mex., 1953, U. Ariz., 1958-59, U. Vienna, 1963, U. Besançon, 1965, U. Hamburg, 1966, U. Bucharest, 1967, 69, U. Ill., 1968, U. Colo., 1969, Stanford U., 1971, U. South Fla., 1972, Linguistic Soc. Am. prof., 1975, Internat. Christian U., Tokyo, 1985, U. Quebec, 1985, El Colegio de Mexico, 1987, U. of Republic, Montevideo, Uraguey, 1987, others; Disting. vis. prof. Internat. Summer Inst. for Semiotic and Structural Studies, 1980-88; cons. Ford Found., Guggenheim Found., Wenner-Gren Found. for Anthrop. Research, U.S. Office Edn., NSF, fellowship div. Nat. Acad. Scis., Can. Council; panel mem. for linguistics Nat. Endowment for Humanities, 1966-67; mem. U.S. del. to permanent council Internat. Union Anthrop. and Ethnol. Scis., 1970-73; U.S. del. Comité International Permanent des Linguistes, 1972—; mem. internat. sci. council Royaumont Center for Sci. of Man, 1973—; exch. prof. NAS-USSR Acad. Scis., 1973; Regents fellow Smithsonian Instn., 1983-84; adj. fellow Woodrow Wilson Internat Ctr. for Scholars, 1983-84, mem. program on history, culture and soc., 1986-87. Author: Perspectives in Zoosemiotics, 1972, Structure & Texture: Selected Essays in Cheremis Verbal Art, 1974, The Play of Musement, 1981, others; editor-in-chief: Semiotica, 1968—, Current Trends in Linguistics, 1963—, Approaches to Semiotics, 1968-74; editor: Studies in Semiotics, 1974—, others; gen. editor: Advances in Semiotics, 1974—, others; contbr. numerous articles to profl. and scholarly jours. Mem. vis. com. Harvard U., 1973, Simon Fraser U., 1975, Georgetown U., 1977, Vanderbilt U., 1977-78. Recipient Pres.'s medal of excellence Ind. U., 1991, Profl. Achievement citation U. Chgo., 1992; John Simon Guggenheim Meml. Found. fellow, 1958-59, 81-82, Ctr. for Advanced Study in Behavioral Scis. fellow, 1960-61, 66-67, 71, NSF sr. postdoctoral fellow, 1966-67, NEH fellow, 1973-74, 80-81, Netherlands Inst. for Advanced Study fellow, 1973-74, Nat. Humanities Ctr. fellow, 1980-81, Smithsonian Instn. Regents fellow, 1983-84, Rsch. Assoc., 1984-87, Woodrow Wilson Internat. Ctr. for Scholars adj. fellow, 1983-84, Com. for Sci. Investigation of Claims of Paranormal fellow, 1983—; Fulbright grantee Germany, 1966, 71, Italy, 1969, 71, 87, Argentina, 1987, Uruguay, 1987, Am., Am. Coun. Learned Socs. grantee, Ford Found., Wenner-Gren Found. Anthrop. Rsch., USIA, other fed. agys. Fellow Am. Anthrop. Assn. (disting. service award 1984), Am. Folklore Soc., Soc. Cultural Anthropology, AAAS, Explorers Club, also fgn. linguistic socs.; mem. Internat. Assn. Semiotic Studies (editor-in-chief 1968—, exec. com. 1969—), Linguistic Soc. Am. (sec.-treas. 1969-73, v.p. 1974, pres. 1975, asso. dir. Linguistic Inst. 1958, 75, dir. 1964), Central States Anthrop. Soc. (pres. 1956), Am. Assn. Machine Translation and Computational Linguistics (exec. bd. 1964-66), Animal Behavior Soc. (exec. bd. 1968—), Semiotic Soc. Am. (sec.-treas. 1975, exec. dir. 1976-85, pres. 1984), Sigma Xi, others. Clubs: Cosmos (Washington); University (Chgo.); Princeton (N.Y.C.) ; Internat. House (Tokyo). Home: 1104 S Covenanter Dr Bloomington IN 47401-6043 Office: Indiana U PO Box 10 Bloomington IN 47402-0010

SEBOK, GYORGY, pianist, educator; b. Szeged, Hungary, Nov. 2, 1922; came to U.S., 1962; s. Vilmos and Klara (Krausz) S.; m. Eva Mandel, Jan. 29, 1957. Ed., Franz Liszt Acad. Music, Budapest, Hungary. Prof. piano Bela Bartok Conservatory, Budapest, 1949-56; prof. piano Ind. U., Bloomington, 1962—, disting. prof., 1985—; guest prof. Hochschule der Künste, Berlin; hon. life mem. Toho Gakuen Sch. Music, Tokyo; founder, dir. Festival der Zukunft, Ernen, Switzerland. First pub. appearance, 1936, concerts throughout Europe, N.Am., Japan, Africa, 1957—; rec. artist for, Erato, Mercury, Philips records. Recipient Internat. Prize Berlin, Germany, 1951, Liszt Prize, Budapest, 1952, Grand Prix du Disque, Paris, 1958, Gold medal City of Paris, 1995, Prix de Consécration of the Canton Wallis, Switzerland, 1996; named hon. citizen City of Ernen, 2d Order of Merit, Republic of Hungary. Home: Woodcrest Ct 2610 E 2nd St Bloomington IN 47401-5349

SEBOLD, DUANE DAVID, food manufacturing executive; b. Dorchester, Wis., Mar. 25, 1945; s. Louis J. and Geraldine M. (Herman) S.; m. Kathrin Saunders, June 6, 1970 (dec. Sept. 1973); m. Marcia K. Church, Mar. 19, 1989. BS, U. Wis., Stevens Point, 1967; degree advanced mgmt., Wharton Bus. Sch., 1989. Salesman Ciba-Geigy Corp., San Diego, 1970-73, sales mgr., 1973-76; dir. sales and mktg. Tombstone Pizza Corp., Medford, Wis., 1976-77, v.p. mktg., 1977-80, exec. v.p., gen. mgr., 1980-86, pres., chief exec. officer, 1986-89; chief exec. officer Sebold Enterprises, Medford, 1990—; pres. Nat. Frozen Pizza Inst., McLean, Va., 1985-87; chmn. Tombstone Pizze Found., Medford, 1983—; chmn. policy adv. coun. Marshfiel Med. Rsch. Found.; chmn. Tombstone Pizze Exec. Com., Medford, 1986-89; dir. Accrediting Commn. on Edn. for Health Svcs. Adminstrn., Marshfield Med. Rsch. Found., U. Wis.-Stevens Point Found. Contbr. articles to mags. mem. Rep. Senatorial Inner Circle, Washington, 1987-88; bd. dirs. Arthritis Found., Milw., 1985-86; guest spkr. U. Wis.-Madison Exec. Program, 1984-90. With USN, 1967-70. Recipient Disting. Alumni award U. Wis., 1994. Mem. Am. Mktg. Assn., Am. Mgmt. Assn., Nat. Mgmt. Assn. (Marketer of Yr. 1979, Gold Knight award of Mgmt. 1988), Safari Club Internat., Ducks Unltd., Found. for N.Am. Wild Sheep, Toastmasters. Roman Catholic. Avocations: hunting, fishing, golf. Home and Office: 5369W N Chelsea Ave Medford WI 54451

SEBOLD, RUSSELL PERRY, III, Romance languages educator, author; b. Dayton, Ohio, Aug. 20, 1928; s. Russell Perry and Mary (Kiger) S.; m. Jane Norvell Hale, Nov. 24, 1955; children: Mary Norvell, Alice Hale. Student, U. Chgo., 1945-47; B.A., Ind. U., 1949; M.A. (Woodrow Wilson fellow), Princeton U., 1951, Ph.D., 1953; D.Phil. and Letters (hon.), U. Alicante, Spain, 1984. Instr. Spanish, Duke U., 1955-56; instr. Spanish, U. Wis., 1956-58, asst. prof., 1958-62, assoc. prof., 1962-66; prof. Spanish, chmn. dept. fgn. langs. and lits. U. Md., 1966-68; prof. Spanish, U. Pa., 1968-88, chmn. dept. Romance langs., 1968-78, Edwin B. and Leonore R. Williams prof. Romance langs., 1988—; mem. adv. coun. Soc. Ibero-Am. Enlightenment, 1968—, treas., 1969—; steering com. Am. Soc. Eighteenth Century Studies, 1970—; corresponding academician Royal Spanish Acad., 1993—, Royal Acad. Humane Letters of Barcelona, 1993—. Author: Tomás de Iriarte: poeta de rapto racional, 1961, El rapto de la mente, 1970, 2nd edit., 1989, Colonel Don José Cadalso, 1970, Cadalso: el primer romántico europeo de España, 1974, Novela y autobiografía en la Vida de Torres Villarroel, 1975, Trayectoria del romanticismo español, 1983, Descubrimiento y fronteras del neoclasicismo español, 1985, Bécquer en sus narraciones fantásticas, 1989, De Ilustrados y románticos, 1992; author, editor: Fray Gerundio de Campazas (José Francisco de Isla), 4 vols, 1960-64, 2d edit., 1992, Visiones y visitas de Torres con don Francisco de Quevedo por la Corte (Diego de Torres Villarroel), 1966, 2d edit., 1991, Numancia destruida (Ignacio López de Ayala), 1971, Poética (Ignacio de Luzán), 1977, Comedias (Tomás de Iriarte), 1978; Gustavo Adolfo Bécquer (antología crítica), 1985, Vida (Diego de Torres Villarroel), 1985, Rimas (Gustavo Adolfo Bécquer), 1991, (with David T. Gies) Ilustración y neoclasicismo, 1992, Noches lúgubres (José de Cadalso), 1993, (with Jesus Perez Magallon) El hombrre practico (Conde de Fernan Nunez), 1996 ; gen. editor: Hispanic Rev.; adv. editor Eighteenth Century Studies, 1983, Cuadernos para Investigación de la Literatura Hispánica, 1987—, Discurso Literario, 1987—, El Gnomo, 1992—, Siglo XIX, 1995; columnist ABC newspaper, Madrid, 1985—; contbr. articles to profl. jours. Served with AUS, 1953-55. Guggenheim fellow, 1962-63; Am. Philos. Soc. grantee, 1971, 76, 82; Am. Council Learned Socs. fellow, 1979-80. Mem. Am. Assn. Tchrs. Spanish and Portuguese, Am. Assn. Tchrs. French, Ctr. 18th Century Studies (Oviedo, Spain), Sociedad de Literatura Española del Siglo XIX, Hispanic Soc. Am. (corr. mem.), Phi Beta Kappa, Phi Gamma Delta, Sigma Delta Pi. Episcopalian. Home: 16 Flintshire Rd Malvern PA 19355-1108 Office: U Pa Dept Romance Langs Philadelphia PA 19104-6305

SEBOROVSKI, CAROLE, artist; b. San Diego, June 16, 1960; d. Stanley and Eleanor Frances (Ononska) S. BFA, Calif. Coll. Arts and Crafts, 1982; MFA, Hunter Coll., 1987. Artist: solo exhibitions include: Damon Brandt Gallery, N.Y.C., 1986, Hunter Coll. Art Gallery, N.Y.C., 1986, Lorence-Monk Gallery, N.Y.C., 1988, 89, Galerie Karsten Greve, Paris, 1991, 94, Cologne, 1992, Milan, 1995, Angles Gallery, Santa Monica, Calif., 1991, 92, 93, 96, Betsy Senior Contemporary Prints, N.Y.C., 1993, John Weber Gallery, N.Y.C., 1993, 95, John Berggruen Gallery, San Francisco, 1994; group exhbns. at: Willard Gallery, N.Y.C., 1984, Nora Haime Gallery, N.Y.C., 1985, 86, 93, 95, Manhattan Arts Ctr., N.Y.C., 1985, Hillwood Art Gallery L.I. Univ., Brookville, N.Y., 1985, Damon Brandt Gallery, 1985, 86 (2), 87, Mus. de Arte, La Tertuila, Columbia, 1986, Weatherspoon Gallery, Greensboro, N.C., 1986, Barbara Krakow Gallery, Boston, 1986, 88, 90 (travels to John C. Stoller & Co., Mpls.), Anne Plumb Gallery, N.Y.C., 1987, Am. Acad. and Inst. Arts and Letters, 1987, Bklyn. Mus., 1987, Lorence-Monk Gallery, 1987, 89 (3), 90, 91 (2), Carnegie Mellon U. Art Gallery, Pitts., 1988, Reynolds/ Minor Gallery, Richmond, Va., 1988, John Good Gallery, N.Y.C., 1988, 92, Pamela Auchincloss Gallery, N.Y.C., 1988, Dart Gallery, Chgo., 1988, Angles Gallery, 1989, Persons & Lindell Gallery, Helsinki, Finland, 1989, Anderson Gallery Va. Commonwealth U., Richmond, 1989, Baxter Gallery, Richmond, 1989, Hillwood Art Gallery, Brookville (travels through 1991 to Blum Helman Gallery, N.Y.C., Richard F. Brush Gallery, Canton, N.Y., Contemporary Mus. Art, Caracas, Venezuela), Cheryl Haines Gallery, San Francisco, 1989, 94, Security Pacific Corp. Gallery, Santa Monica, 1990, Meml. Art Gallery U. Rochester, N.Y., 1990, Hood Mus. Art Dartmouth Coll., Hannover, N.H., 1990, San Francisco Mus. of Art, 1991, Pfizer, Inc. (Mus. Modern Art, N.Y. Collection), 1991, John Berggruen Gallery, 1991, travelling exhbn. to Anthony Ralph Gallery at Earl McGrath, L.A., Mars Gallery, Tokyo, Katonah Mus. Art, N.Y., Ind. U. Fine Arts Gallery, Kerr Gallery, Alberta Coll. of Art, Can., Huntsville Mus. Art, Ala., Worcester Art Mus., Mass., Lamont Gallery N.H., San Diego State U. Gallery, 1992, Barbara Mathes Gallery, N.Y.C., 1993, Transamerica Pyramid Lobby, San Francisco, 1993, travelling exhbn. to The Drawing Ctr., N.Y., Corcoran Gallery Art, Washington, Santa Monica Mus., L.A., The Forum, St. Louis, Am. Ctr., Paris, 1993, Addison Gallery, Andover, Mass., 1994, John Weber Gallery, 1994, Huntington Gallery Mass. Coll. Art, Boston, 1995, Rice U. Art Gallery, Houston, 1995, The Altered Stages, N.Y., 1995, Brooke Alexander Gallery, N.Y.C., 1995. Grantee Pollock-Krausner Found., 1986, NEA, 1991; named Artist in Residence, Villa Monalvo, Saratoga, Calif., 1989, Djerassi Found., Calif., 1990; Agnes Bourne fellow in visual arts, 1990. Achievements include works in permanent collections of: Weatherspoon Art Gallery, Greensboro, N.C., Whitney Mus. of Art, N.Y.C., Refco Collection, Chgo., Met. Mus. of Art, MIT Visual Ctr., Fogg Art Mus., Harvard U., Cleve. Ctr. for Contemporary Art, Carnegie Mus. of Art, Pitts., Bklyn. Mus., Balt. Mus., Addison Gallery, Phillips Acad., Andover, Mass. Home: Box 171 S Anson Rd Stanfordville NY 12581

SEBRING, PATRICIA LOUISE, technical writer and editor; b. N.Y., Oct. 3, 1956; d. Ray McCarty and Louise Arlene (Bender) S. BA, Wilkes Coll., 1978; MS, East Stroudsburg State U., 1981. Environ. compliance coord. Bechtel Power Corp., Berwick, Pa., 1981-84; safety engr. Dynamac Corp., Rockville, Md., 1984; exec. dir. Susquehanna-Wyoming Counties Solid Waste Authority, Tunkhannock, Pa., 1985-88; bus. devel. rep. Bechtel Civil, Inc., Vienna, Va., 1988-89; supr. pubs. Bechtel Power Corp., Gaithersburg, Md., 1989-94; bus. devel. rep. Bechtel Power Corp., 1994—; strategic planning coord. Grace United Meth. Ch., Gaithersburg, Md., 1995-96. Adult ministries coord., 1994-96, strategic planning chairperson, 1996—, Grace United Meth. Ch., Gaithersburg, Md., 1994-95. Mem. Nat. Mgmt. Assn. (chmn. bd. dirs. 1993-95). Methodist. Avocations: classical piano, hiking, swimming. Office: Bechtel Power Corp 9801 Washingtonian Blvd Gaithersburg MD 20878-5355

SECADA, JOHN, musician. Recipient Music award for Best Latin Pop Performance, 1996. Office: Capitol Records Inc EMI Latin 1750 N Vine St Hollywood CA 90028-5274*

SECCARECCIA, LUCILLE DINA, game manufacturing company executive; b. Hartford, Conn., June 27, 1958; d. Dino and Lucille (Gallicchio) S. BFA, U. Hartford. Lic. master type-setter Printing Industry Am. Paste-up artist, typesetter Gamer Publications, West Hartford, Conn., 1980; typesetter, supr. system Allied Printing Svc., Manchester, Conn., 1980-88; v.p. Lombard Mktg., Bloomfield, Conn., 1988-93; COO Gamewright, Inc., Chestnut Hill, Mass., 1993—. vol. career counselor U. Hartford, 1991—. Avocations: gourmet cooking, English perennial gardening, biking, drawing, painting. Office: Gamewright, Inc PO Box 370219 West Hartford CT 06137-0219

SECHRIST, CHALMERS FRANKLIN, JR., electrical engineering educator; b. Glen Rock, Pa., Aug. 23, 1930; s. Chalmers F. and Lottie V. (Smith) S.; m. Lillian Beatrice Myers, June 29, 1957; children: Jonathan A., Jennifer N. BEE, Johns Hopkins U., 1952; MS, Pa. State U., 1954, PhDEE, 1959. Sr. engr. Bendix Corp., summers 1952, 53, 54; instr. elec. enging. Pa. State U., 1954-55; staff engr. HRB-Singer, Inc., State College, Pa., 1959-65; asst. prof. elec. enging. U. Ill., Urbana, 1965-67, assoc. prof., 1967-71, prof., 1971-96, assoc. head instructional programs dept. elec. and computer engring., 1984-86, asst. dean engring., 1986-96; program dir. divsn. undergrad. edn. NSF, Washington, 1992-96; acting sci. sec. Sci. Com. on Solar-Terrestrial Physics, 1981; chmn. publs. com. Middle Atmosphere Program, 1980-86, editor handbook, 1981-86. Editor: Proc. Aeronomy Confs, 1965, 69, 72; contbr. articles to profl. jours. NSF grantee. Mem. Edn. Soc. of IEEE (v.p. 1989-90, pres. 1991-92, mem. IEEE edn. activities bd. 1990, 92, 93, mem. tech. activities bd. 1991-92), Am. Geophys. Union, Am. Meteorol. Soc., Am. Soc. for Engrng. Edn. Home: 12767 Yacht Club Cir Fort Myers FL 33919

SECK, MAMADOU MANSOUR, ambassador, career officer; b. Dakar, Senegal, July 3, 1935. Attended, St. Cyr Milit. Acad., France, Salon Air Force Acad., French Air War Coll., Institut des Hautes Etudes de la Def. Nat. Commanding officer 1st Senegalese Air Force Squad, 1966; comdr. 1st Senegalese Air Force, 1972; dep. chief gen. staff, 1980-84, spl. chief of staff to Pres. of Republic of Senegal, chief of staff of Sene-Gambia Confedn., 1984, gen. chief of staff, gen. chief Confedn., 1988, amb. to U.S., chmn., 1993—. Decorated Senegal, France, Gabon, Hollan, Luxembourg. Office: Embassy of Republic of Senegal 2112 Wyoming Ave NW Washington DC 20008-3906

SECKEL, BROOKE RUTLEDGE, plastic surgeon; b. Columbus, Ohio, Oct. 2, 1943; s. Raymond Clyde and Virginia Caine (Rutledge) S.; m. Deborah Anne Johnson, May 8, 1982; children: Laura, Thomas. BS summa cum laude, Ohio U., 1965; MD, Med. Coll. of Va., 1969. Diplomate Am. Bd. Psychiatry and Neurology, Am. Bd. Emergency Medicine, Am. Bd. Plastic Surgery, Nat. Bd. Med. Examiners; lic. physician, Va., Calif., Mass. Internship in surgery Univ. Hosp., San Diego, 1969-70; jr. asst. resident in neurology, jr. resident Boston City Hosp., Harvard Neurol. Unit, 1971-72, 72-73, chief resident in neurology, 1973-74; instr. in neurology Harvard Med. Sch., Cambridge, Mass., 1974-77; jr. resident in surgery, sr. resident New Eng. Med. Ctr., Boston, 1978-79, 79-80; sr. resident plastic/reconstructive surgery, chief resident Brigham and Women's Hosp. and The Children's Hosp., Boston, 1980-81, 81-82; instr. in surgery Harvard Med. Sch., Cambridge, 1982-85, clin. instr. in surgery, 1986-89, asst. prof. surgery, 1990-93; chmn. dept. plastic and reconstructive surgery Lahey Clinic Med. Ctr., Burlington, Mass., 1986—; courtesy staff The Children's Hosp., Boston, 1982—, New Eng. Deaconess Hosp., Boston, 1986—; assoc. surgeon Brigham and Women's Hosp., Boston, 1982—; dir. Microsurgical Ctr. Lahey Clinic Med. Ctr., 1986—, Plastic Surgery Rsch. Lab., Lahey Clinic Med. Ctr., 1986—, Plastic Surgery Residency Tng. Program, Lahey Clinic Med. Ctr., 1989—. Assoc. editor Jour. of Plastic and Reconstructive Surgery, 1988-94; expert reviewer Jour. of Muscle and Nerve, 1989—; assoc. editor Jour. of Reconstructive Microsurgery, 1990—; author: Plastic Surgery Research Directory, 1990, Facial Danger Zones: Avoiding Nerve Injury in Facial Plastic Surgery, 1993; author of numerous non-print materials including videotapes; contbr. numerous articles to profl. jours. and chpts. to books. Grantee Am. Assn. Plastic Surgeons, 1983, Plastic Surgery Ednl. Found., 1984, Eleanor Naylor Dana Charitable Trust, 1986-90, Donaldson Charitable Trust, 1990, Charles E. Culpeper Found., 1991, 92, The Robert Leet and Clara Guthrie Patterson Trust, 1993, 94. Fellow Am. Coll. Emergency Physicians, Am. Coll. Surgeons; mem. New Eng. Surg. Soc., Soc. Microsurgical Specialists, Assn. Acad. Chmn. Plastic Surgery, Am. Soc. for Aesthetic Plastic Surgery, Am. Assn. Plastic Surgeons, Northeastern Soc. Plastic Surgeons, The Sunderland Soc., Boston Surg. Soc., Plastic Surgery Rsch. Coun., Am. Soc. Plastic and Reconstructive Surgeons, New Eng. Soc. Plastic and Reconstructive Surgeons, Mass. Soc. Plastic Surgery, Mass. Med. Soc., Am. Coll. Emergency Physicians. Achievements include pioneer in the development of the Superpulser CO2 laser for use in aesthetic plastic surgery; research in plastic surgery and biophysiology of nerve regeneration. Home: 21 River St Concord MA 01742-2223 Office: Lahey Clin Med Ctr Plastic Surgery 41 Mall Rd Burlington MA 01805-0001

SECOR, DONALD TERRY, JR., geologist, educator; b. Oil City, Pa., Nov. 22, 1934; s. Donald Terry and Mary Elizabeth (LaRue) S.; m. Dorothy Eisenhart, June 15, 1959; children: Beth Ann, Jane Marie, Carol Lynn. B.S., Cornell U., 1957, M.S., 1959; Ph.D., Stanford U., 1963. Asst. prof. geology U. S.C., Columbia, 1962-66, assoc. prof., 1966-79, prof., 1979—, chmn. dept., 1966-68, 77-81. Am. Assn. Petroleum Geologists Disting. lectr., 1978-79; recipient U. S.C. Ednl. Found. award, 1991; NSF grantee, 1966-70, 76-94, U.S. Geol. Survey grantee, 1979-82. Fellow Geol. Soc. Am.; mem. Am. Geophys. Union, AAAS. Home: RR 1 Box 251 Newberry SC 29108-9738 Office: U SC Dept Geol Scis Columbia SC 29208

SECORD, LLOYD DOUGLAS, healthcare administrator; b. Lachine, Que., Can., Nov. 22, 1946; s. George William and Gladys Mable (Wilson) S.; m. Louise Margaret Morrison, Dec. 21, 1966; children: Steven Lloyd, Gordon Arthur, Mary Elizabeth. BS in Chemistry, U. New Brunswick, 1968; M of Adminstrn., U. Toronto, Ont., Can., 1970. Cert. accreditation surveyor Can. Coun. on Health Facilities, 1990-92. Adminstrv. resident Toronto East Gen. and Orthopaedic Hosp., 1969-70; adminstrv. asst. Moncton Hosp., summer 1968, asst. adminstr., 1970-75; exec. dir. Kiwanis Nursing Home Inc., 1975—; facility adminstr. Region 2 Hosp. Corp., Sussex, N.B., Can., 1975—; sec. Sussex Health Ctr. Svcs. Inc., Bryant Dr. Holdings Inc., 1975—, CEO, adminstr. hosp., 1975—; chmn. adv. com. Min. Health; mem. Fundy Linen Svcs. Inc., 1976-92; mem. regional hosp. planning com. Health Region II, 1974-76; commr. of oaths, 1975—. Bd. dirs. Atlantic Bapt. Sr. Citizen's Home Inc., 1973-79, original bldg. com., 1971-74, rec. sec., 1971-74, chmn. bldg. com.; founding chmn. Comty. Based Svcs. Coord. Com. for Sussex, 1981; founding pres. Sussex Sr. Housing Inc., 1981, 82; established Sussex Health Ctr. Svcs. Inc., 1991, Bryant Dr. Holdings Inc., 1992-93; bd. trustees, bd. deacons Sussex United Bapt. Ch.; dir. Sussex br. Order of St. John, 1976-78, 90-92; trombonist Sussex Comty. Adult Band, 1989—. Lord Beaverbrook scholar, Leonard Found. scholar. Fellow Am. Coll. Health Care Execs. (affiliate, regent for Atlantic provinces 1992—, membership oral examiner 1984, 85, 86, 88, 93, 95, 96, mem. ethics com. 1985-88), Can. Coll. Health Svc. Execs. (various provincial coms.), Soc. Mgmt. Accts. Can. (cert., mem. provincial coun. 1977-88, provincial sec.-treas. 1982, provincial chmn. 1987, nat. edn. svcs. com. 1985, 86, nat. bd. dirs. 1986, 87, nat. strategic planning com. 1986); mem. New Brunswick Hosp. Assn. (numerous provincial coms.), New Brunswick Assn. Nursing Homes (numerous provincial coms.), Northeastern Can./Am. Health Coun. (Can. co-chmn. 1991-94, co-chair internat. mini conf. on rural health care New London, N.H. 1988, chair bi-ann. conf. Montreal 1991), Provincial Ambulance Operators Assn. (exec. com. 1990—), Sussex and Dist. C. of C. (pres. 1985), Kiwanis Club Sussex Inc. (pres. 1985—). Avocations: band, golf, gardening, painting, education. Office: Sussex Health Ctr, PO Box 5006/Leonard Dr, Sussex, NB Canada E0E 1P0

SECREST, RONALD DEAN, lawyer; b. Kansas City, Mo., Nov. 13, 1951; s. William Francis and Corrine Elizabeth (Clarke) S. BS, Stanford U., 1974; JD, U. Va., 1977. Bar: Tex. 1979, U.S. Dist. Ct. (so. dist.) Tex. 1979, U.S. Ct. Appeals (5th cir.) 1980, U.S. Ct. Appeals (11th cir.) 1981, U.S. Dist. Ct. (no. dist.) Tex. 1986, U.S. Dist. Ct. (we. dist.) Tex. 1989, U.S. Ct. Appeals (10th cir.) 1989, U.S. Supreme Ct. 1990. Law clk. to presiding justice U.S. Ct. Appeals (5th cir.), Houston, 1977-78; ptnr. Fulbright & Jaworski, Houston, 1978-92, Beck, Redden & Secrest, Houston, 1992—. Fellow Tex. Bar Found., Houston Bar Found.; mem. ABA, Internat. Assn. Def. Counsel, Tex. Assn. Def. Counsel, Tex. Bar Assn., Houston Bar Assn. Home: 11682 Arrowwood Cir Houston TX 77063-1402 Office: Beck Redden & Secrest 1331 Lamar St Ste 1570 Houston TX 77010-3028

SECRIST, RICHARD A., industrial company executive; b. N.Y.C., Oct. 1, 1945; m. Patricia Aljoe; children: Richard Jr., Ryan, Robin, Rudd. BS, U. Fla., 1966, MA, 1967. Sr. mgr. Price Waterhouse, N.Y.C., 1967-77; pres. Gold Fields Am. Corp., N.Y.C., 1977-86; chmn., pres., chief exec. officer Blue Tee Corp., N.Y.C., 1986—, also dir. Mem. Baltusrol Golf Club (Springfield, N.J.), Univ. Club (N.Y.C.). Republican. Episcopalian. Office: Blue Tee Corp 250 Park Ave S New York NY 10003-1402*

SECULAR, SIDNEY, federal agency administrator, procurement analyst; b. N.Y.C., Dec. 20, 1940; s. Benjamin and Mollie (Stern) S.; m. Mildred Lucille Vance, Nov. 1, 1969. BA, SUNY, Stony Brook, 1962. Cert. high sch. tchr. Contract asst. U.S. Army, Bklyn., 1962-66; contract specialist USN, Washington, 1966-67, FDA, Washington, 1967-68; contracting officer Dept. Justice, Washington, 1968-81; procurement ctr. rep., counselor to small bus. SBA, Washington, 1986—; mem. consumer bd. Giant Food Corp., WSSC Water Utility; freelance resume writer Silver Spring, Md., 1985-86, 89—; weather forecaster Washington Weatherline, Bethesda, Md., 1982-91, Comprehensive Weather Svcs., 1982-85, Bell Atlantic Telephone Co., 1991—. Activist Citizens to Preserve Old Silver Spring, 1981—, East Silver Spring Citizens Assn., 1981—; vice chmn. Md. Libertarian Party, 1977-78. With

U.S. Army, 1963-69. Recipient performance and suggestion awards U.S. DEA and SBA. Mem. Am. Soc. Pub. Adminstrn., Nat. Contract Mgmt. Assn., Am. Meteorol. Soc., Am. Numis. Assn., Area Small and Disadvantaged Bus. Coun., Ctr. Hiking Club (trails dir. 1975), Masons. Avocations: natural health studies and counseling, meteorology, American history, environmental improvement. Home: 740 Silver Spring Ave Silver Spring MD 20910-4661 Office: US SBA Code SBA Arlington VA 22245-5200

SECUNDA, EUGENE, marketing communications executive, educator; b. Bklyn., June 15, 1934; s. Sholom and Betty (Almer) S.; m. Shirley Carol Frummer, Sept. 23, 1961; children—Ruthanne, Andrew. Comml. degree, N.Y. Inst. Photography, 1955; B.S., NYU Sch. Bus., 1956; M.S., Boston U., 1962; PhD, NYU, 1988. News editor Sta.-WBMS, Boston, 1956-57; reporter New London (Conn.) Daily Day, 1958-59; publicist various Broadway shows, 1959-62; sr. publicist 20th Century Fox Film Corp., N.Y.C., 1962-65; with J. Walter Thompson Co., N.Y.C., 1965-73; dir. corp. and public affairs J. Walter Thompson Co., 1974-78, sr. v.p., dir. entertainment group, 1974-80; dir. entertainment div. J. Walter Thompson Co., N.Y.C., 1978-80; sr. v.p., dir. communications services N.W. Ayer Internat., N.Y.C., 1980-82; pres. Barnum/Secunda Assocs., N.Y.C., 1982-85, Secunda Mktg. Communications, N.Y.C., 1985—; adj. prof. advt. NYU, N.Y.C., 1972-85; prof. mktg. and advt. NYU Grad. Sch. Bus., N.Y.C., 1985-88, Baruch Coll., CUNY, 1988-93; prof. mktg. Adelphi U., Garden City, N.Y., 1993—; guest lectr. FBI Acad., Columbia U., UCLA; pres. Secunda Mktg. Communication, N.Y.C., 1985—. Contbr. articles to profl. jours. Mem. Greenwich Village Trust. Served with USAR, 1957-63. Mem. NATAS, Internat. Comm. Assn., Internat. Advt. Assn., Am. Acad. Advt., Mcpl. Arts Soc., Am. Mktg. Assn. Address: 30 Fifth Ave New York NY 10011-8859

SEDAKA, NEIL, singer, songwriter; b. Mar. 13, 1939; s. Mac and Eleanor (Appel) S.; m. Leba Margaret Strassberg, Sept. 11, 1962; children: Dara Felice, Marc Charles. Grad., Juilliard Sch. Music. Composer numerous popular songs including Breaking Up Is Hard to Do, Stupid Cupid, Calendar Girl, Oh! Carol, Stairway to Heaven, Happy Birthday Sweet Sixteen, Laughter in the Rain, Bad Blood, Love Will Keep Us Together, Solitaire, The Hungry Years, Lonely Night (Angel Face); solo performer worldwide, 1959—; appeared in NBC-TV Special, 1976; recorded numerous albums including In the Pocket, Sedaka's Back, The Hungry Years, Steppin' Out, A Song, All You Need Is the Music, Come See About Me, Greatest Hits, 1988, Oh! Carol and Other Hits, 1990, Timeless, 1992 (Platinum LP). Recipient numerous gold records and industry awards; named to Songwriters' Hall of Fame, 1980; received star on Hollywood Walk of Fame. Mem. AGVA, Am. Fedn. Musicians, AFTRA. Office: c/o Neil Sedaka Music 888 7th Ave Ste 1600 New York NY 10106-1699

SEDARES, JAMES L., conductor; b. Chgo., Jan. 15, 1956. BMusEd, Webster U., 1977; MMusEd, Washington U., St. Louis, 1979. Assoc. condr. San Antonio Symphony, 1979-89; music dir. Phoenix Symphony Orch., 1989—, also prin. condr. Office: Phoenix Symphony Orch Symphony Hall 3707 N 7th St Ste 107 Phoenix AZ 85014-5062

SEDDON, JOHANNA MARGARET, ophthalmologist, epidemiologist; b. Pitts.; m. Ralph Hingson, 1974. BS, U. Pitts., 1970, MD, 1974; MS in Epidemiology, Harvard U., 1976. Intern Framingham (Mass.) Union Hosp., 1974-75; resident Tufts New Eng. Med. Ctr., Boston, 1976-80; fellow ophthalmic pathology Mass. Eye and Ear Infirmary, Boston, 1980-81, clin. fellow vitreoretinal Retina Svc., 1981-82; instr. clin. ophthalmology Harvard Med. Sch., Boston, 1982-84, asst. prof., asst. surgeon ophthalmolgy, 1984, assoc. prof., 1989—; assoc. surgeon, dir. ultrasound svc. Mass. Eye and Ear Infirmary, Boston, 1989—, orgn. epidemiology rsch. unit, 1984-85, dir. epidemiology unit, 1985—, surgeon in ophthalmology, 1992—; assoc. prof. faculty dept. epidemiology Harvard Sch. Pub. Health, Boston, 1992—; mem. com. vision Commn Behavioral and Social Scis. and Edn., NRC, NAS, Washington, 1984; mem. divsn. rsch. grants NIH, 1987-89, 94—; mem. sci. adv. bd. Found. for Fighting Blindness, 1985—, Mecular Internat., 1994—. Author books and articles in field; mem. editl. staff ophthalmic jours. Recipient NIH Nat. Svc. Rsch. awards, 1975, 80-81, Lewis R. Wasserman merit award from rsch. to prevent blindness for contbns. to ophthalmic rsch., 1996; grantee, prin. investigator Nat. Eye Inst., 1984-96, Nat. Cancer Inst., 1986; med. sch. scholar, 1970-74, Henry H. Clark Med. Edn. Found. scholar, 1973. Mem. AMA, APHA, Am. Acad. Ophthalmology (Honor award 1990), Am. Med. Women's Assn., Assn. Rsch. in Vision and Ophthalmology (elected, chair epidemiology sect. 1990, trustee clin. vision epidemiology sect. 1992—), Soc. Epidemiologic Rsch., New Eng. Ophthal. Soc., Am. Coll. Epidemiology, Retina Soc., Macula Soc. Home: 4 Louisburg Sq Boston MA 02108-1203

SEDELMAIER, JOHN JOSEF, film director, cinematographer; b. Orrville, Ohio, May 31, 1933; s. Josef Heinrich and Anne Isabel (Baughman) S.; m. Barbara Jean Frank, June 6, 1965; children: John Josef, Nancy Rachel, Adam Frederich. BFA, Art Inst. Chgo. at U. Chgo., 1955. Dir. art Young and Rubicam, Chgo., 1955-61; dir. art, assoc. creative dir. Clinton E. Frank, Chgo., 1961-64; dir. art, producer J. Walter Thompson, Chgo., 1964-67; pres. Sedelmaier Film Prodns., Chgo., 1967—. Retrospective exhibits Mus. Broadcast Communications, Chgo., 1988, Mus. Broadcasting, L.A., 1991, Mus. TV and Radio, N.Y.C., 1992. Recipient Golden Ducat award for short film MROFNOC Mannheim Film Festival, 1968, Golden Gate award for short film Because That's Why, San Francisco Film Festival, 1969, numerous Clio awards, 1968-92, numerous Gold, Silver and Bronze Lion awards Cannes Film Festival, 1972-90, Gold Hugo award Chgo. Film Festival, 1976, 91, 2d Ann. IDC Creative award, Chgo., 1980, Internat. Broadcasting award for world's best TV comml., 1980, 86, Clio award for dir. of yr., 1981, London Internat. Advt. awards, 1986-88, numerous awards Internat. Festival of N.Y., 1984-93, Ann. Achievement award Assn. Ind. Comml. Producers, 1988, British Design and Art Direction silver pencils, 1989; named Advt. Person of Yr., Chgo. Advt. Club, 1984, Jewish Communicator of Yr., 1985; named one of 50 Pioneers & Visionaries Who Made TV America's Medium, Advt. Age Mag., 1995; profiled in Communication Arts mag., Mar. 1976, Print mag., Jan. 1982, Fortune mag., June 1983, Newsweek mag., Nov. 1986, numerous others; featured on 60 Minutes, 48 Hours; subject of cover story Esquire mag., Aug. 1983. Office: Sedelmaier Film Prodns Inc 858 W Armitage Ave # 267 Chicago IL 60614-4329

SEDER, ARTHUR RAYMOND, JR., lawyer; b. Oak Park, Ill., Apr. 20, 1920; s. Arthur Raymond and Mary Aline (Grantham) S.; m. Marion Frances Heltzel, Feb. 28, 1942; children: James A., Susan J., Elizabeth A. Student, U. Minn., 1938-39; BSL, Northwestern U., 1946, LLB, 1947. Bar: Ill. 1948, Mich. 1961. Law clk. to Justice Vinson U.S. Supreme Ct., 1948-50; mem. Sidley & Austin., Chgo., 1950-72; pvt. practice Washington, 1985—; pres. Am. Natural Resources Co., Detroit, 1973-76; chmn., chief exec. officer, dir. Am. Natural Resources Co., 1976-85; bd. dirs. EnviroSource, Inc. Life trustee Northwestern U., Evanston, Ill. Mem. ABA, Ill. Bar Assn., Mich. Bar Assn. Home: 11221 Crest Hill Rd Marshall VA 22115-2713

SEDERBAUM, ARTHUR DAVID, lawyer; b. N.Y.C., Sept. 14, 1944; s. William and Harriet (Warschauer) S.; m. Francine Haba, Dec. 30, 1967 (div. Aug. 1982); children: Rebecca, David; m. Phyllis Padow, Jan. 18, 1986; 1 child, Elizabeth. AB cum laude, Columbia U., 1965, JD, 1968; LLM, NYU, 1972. Bar: N.Y. 1968, Fla. 1980, U.S. Dist. Ct. (so. and ea. dists.) N.Y. 1972. Assoc. Zissu, Halper & Martin, N.Y.C., 1968-70, Berlack, Israels & Liberman, N.Y.C., 1970-72, Rubin Baum Levin Constant & Friedman, N.Y.C., 1972-76; ptnr. Certilman, Haft, Balin, Buckley, Kremer & Hyman, N.Y.C., 1976-88, Olshan, Grundman, Frome, Rosenzweig & Orens, N.Y.C., 1988-92, Patterson, Belknap, Webb & Tyler, L.L.P., 1992—. Mem. adv. bd. NYU Inst. Fed. Taxation, CCH Fin. and Estate Planning. Author: Setting Up and Executing Trusts, 1988. Recipient J.K. Lasser Tax prize NYU Inst. Fed. Taxation, 1968. Fellow Am. Coll. Trusts and Estates Coun.; mem. ABA, N.Y. State Bar Assn. (vice-chmn. com. on estate planning trusts and estates law sect.), Assn. Bar City N.Y. (com. surrogates cts.), Practising Law Inst. (chmn. income taxation of estates and trusts program). Home: 5 Pheasant Dr Armonk NY 10504-1321 Office: Patterson Belknap Webb & Tyler LLP 1133 Ave of the Americas New York NY 10036

SEDERBAUM, WILLIAM, marketing executive; b. N.Y.C., Dec. 22, 1914; s. Harry and Sarah (Steingart) S.; m. Harriet Warschauer, Aug. 29, 1940; children: Arthur David, Caroline Joan. B.S., NYU, 1936, M.A., 1943, Ph.D. Assoc. Sigmund Pines Co., Pub. Accts., 1935-38; tchr. N.Y.C. pub. schs., 1935-39; restaurant propr., 1939-41; v.p. Schenley Distillers Co., N.Y.C., 1941-61; pres. Distbrs. New Eng., 1956-61, Melrose Distillers Co., 1959-60, Park & Tilford Distillers Co., 1959-61; exec. v.p. Meade & Co., 1961-62; v.p., mktg. dir. J. T. S. Brown Distillers Co., 1962-65; mktg. cons., 1965-67; exec. v.p., gen. mgr. Fulton Distbg. Co., 1967-77; asst. gen. mgr., dir. spl. projects Am. Distbrs. Fla., 1977—; instr. acctg. Fla. Jr. Coll., 1984-89. Mem. Eleanor Roosevelt Cancer Com.; mem. U.S. Olympic Games Com.; exec. com. Fedn. Jewish Charities, March of Dimes; bd. dirs. Jacksonville Urban League, 1975-87; mem. Com. of 100; bus. cons. Jr. Achievement Project, Jacksonville; chmn. bd. trustees, pres. men's club Reform Cong. of Merrick, L.I. Recipient Arch award NYU; named Chevalier, Confrerie de la Chaine des Rotisseurs, Bailliage de Jacksonville, Fla. Mem. Jacksonville Wholesale Liquor Assn. (pres. 1970-76), Jacksonville Symphony Assn., Jacksonville Civic Music Assn., Jacksonville C. of C. (econ. edn. com., airline svc. com., hon. adm. of flag ship Am. Airlines), Kappa Phi Kappa. Clubs: River, Carriage (N.Y.C.); NYU, Playboy, Key. Home: 4305 Plaza Gate Ln Apt 201 Jacksonville FL 32217-4439 Office: Am Distbrs Fla 6867 Stuart Ln S Jacksonville FL 32254-3438 *Live life the way it should be-not the way it is.*

SEDERHOLM, SARAH KATHLEEN (KATHY SEDERHOLM), primary education educator; b. Herrin, Ill., Apr. 17, 1945; d. Clifford Clark and Sarah Kathleen (Cockrum) Hatcher; m. Karl Alexander Sederholm, Aug. 12, 1966; 1 child, Scott Alexander. BS in Edn., No. Ariz. U., 1967; MEd, U. Ariz., 1972. Primary classroom tchr. Tucson Unified Sch. Dist., 1967-69, Marana (Ariz.) Unified Sch. Dist., 1978—. Mem. Ariz. Edn. Assn. (student rels. com. 1992-94), Marana Edn. Assn. (assn. rep. 1985-89, 91-93, treas. 1993-95), Delta Kappa Gamma (pres. chpt. 1992-94, treas. chpt. 1994—). Home: 4302 N Stanley Pl Tucson AZ 85705-1734 Office: Marana Unified Sch Dist 11279 W Grier Rd Marana AZ 85653-9776

SEDGWICK, ALEXANDER, historian, educator; b. Boston, June 8, 1930; s. William Ellery and Sarah (Cabot) S.; m. Charlene Mary Maute, June 24, 1961; children—Catherine Maria, Alexander Cameron. BA, Harvard U., 1952, PhD in History, 1963. Asst. prof. history Dartmouth Coll., 1962-63; assoc. prof. U. Va., Charlottesville, 1963-66, 1966-74, prof., 1974—; chmn. history dept. U. Va., 1979-85, dean Coll. Arts and Scis., 1985-90; dean grad. studies U. Va., Charlottesville, 1990-95, univ. prof., 1995—; mem. adv. com. in history Sr. Fulbright Awards Council for Internat. Exchange of Scholars. Author: The Ralliment in French Politics 1890-98, 1965, The Third French Republic, 1870-1914, 1968, Jansenism in Seventeenth Century France, Voices in the Wilderness, 1977; co-author: (with others): Church, State and Society Under the Bourbon Kings of France, 1982, For Want of a Horse, 1985, That Gentle Strength, 1980, Les Discour sur les Révolutions, 1991, History Today, 1991, Chroniques de Port-Royal, 1993, 95. Served with U.S. Army, 1952-54. Fulbright fellow, 1960-62; recipient Am. Coun. Learned Socs. grant-in-aid, 1967-78, Am. Philos. Soc. grant-in-aid, 1971. Mem. AAUP (nat. council 1976-79), Soc. French Hist. Studies (sec. 1979-83, pres. 1983-84), Am. Hist. Assn., Century Assn. Home: 1409 Rugby Rd Charlottesville VA 22903-1240 Office: U Va Dept History Randall Hall Charlottesville VA 22903

SEDGWICK-HIRSCH, CAROL ELIZABETH, financial executive; b. Cin., Apr. 16, 1922; d. Howard Malcolm Sedgwick and Lucile Alleen (Willard) Sedgwick-Schenk; m. Donald Sebastian Freeman, Nov. 25, 1944 (div. July 1968); children: Elizabeth P. Freeman Closson, Lucy S. Freeman; m. William Christian Hirsch, June 16, 1983. BS, U. Cin., 1944, postgrad., 1972; postgrad., Art Acad. of Cin., 1953-56; MEd, Xavier U., 1966; MS in Criminal Justice, Xavier U., Cin., 1990. Dir., head tchr. Sacred Heart Acad. PreSch., Cin., 1952-53; caseworker dependent children Hamilton County Welfare Dept., Cin., 1959-62; instr. ednl. psychology and child devel. Wright State U., Fairborn, Ohio, 1970-71, 71-72; pres., chief exec. officer Joseph England Hutton Enterprises, Cin., 1979—. Mem. Cin. Women's Club, Coll. Club of Cin., Kappa Alpha Theta. Avocations: golf, swimming, needlework, creative writing. Home: 9092 Lake St Alanson MI 49706-9733 also: 605 E Epworth Ave Cincinnati OH 45232-1705 Office: Joseph England Hutton Enterprises 605 E Epworth Ave Cincinnati OH 45232-1705

SEDKY, CHERIF, lawyer; b. Alexandria, Egypt, Dec. 10, 1943; came to U.S. 1958; s. Abdalla and Mona Frances (Smith) S.; m. Julie A. Greer, Dec. 18, 1964 (div.); children: Tarik, Mona, Sarah; m. Linda M. Jackson, Dec. 26, 1987. BA, Stanford U., 1966; JD, Georgetown U., 1969. Bar: D.C. 1969, U.S. Ct. Appeals (D.C. cir.) 1969, U.S. Supreme Ct. 1974, Va. 1993. Assoc. Surrey Karasik Greene & Hill, Washington 1969-71, Hill Christopher & Phillips, Washington 1971-72, 73-75; ptnr. Kirkpatrick & Lockhart and predecessor firms, Washington, 1976-92; pvt. practice, Washington, 1992-94; ptnr. Sedky, Wittie & Letsche, 1994—; gen. cousel Al-Murjan Group, Jeddah, Saudi Arabia, 1994—; asst. gen. counsel MCI Communications Corp., Washington, 1972-73. Bd. Dirs. Arab-Am. Cultural Found., Am. Near East Refugee Aid. Mem. ABA, D.C. Bar Assn., Nat. U.S. Arab C. of C. (chmn.), Met. Club, Phi Delta Phi. Moslem. Office: 1615 New Hampshire Ave NW Washington DC 20009

SEDLAK, VALERIE FRANCES, English language educator/university administrator; b. Balt., Mar. 11, 1934; d. Julian Joseph and Eleanor Eva (Pilot) Sedlak; 1 child, Barry. AB in English, Coll. Notre Dame, Balt., 1955; MA, U. Hawaii, 1962; PhD, U. Pa., 1992. Grad. teaching fellow East-West Cultural Ctr. U. Hawaii, 1959-60; adminstrv. asst. Korean Consul Gen., 1959-60; tchr. Boyertown (Pa.) Sr. High Sch., 1961-63; asst. prof. English U. Balt., 1963-69; assoc. prof. Morgan State U., Balt., 1970—, asst. dean Coll. Arts and Scis., 1995—, sec. to faculty, 1981-83, faculty research scholar, 1982-83, 92-93, communications officer, 1989-90, dir. writing for TV program, 1990—; cons. scholar Md. Humanities Coun., 1992—. Author poetry and lit. criticism; asst. editor Middle Atlantic Writer's Assn. Rev., 1989—; assoc. editor Md. English Jour., 1994—, Morgan Jour. Undergrad. Rsch., 1995—. Coord. Young Reps., Berks County, Pa., 1962-63; chmn. Md. Young Reps., 1964; election judge Baltimore County, Md., 1964-66; regional capt. Am. Cancer Soc., 1978-79; mem. adv. bd. Md. Our Md. Anniversary, 1984, The Living Constitution: Bicentennial of the Fed. Constitution, 1987. Fellow Morgan-Penn Faculty, 1977-79, Nat. Endowment Humanities, 1984; named Outstanding Teaching Prof., U. Balt. Coll. Liberal Arts, 1965, Outstanding Teaching Prof. English, Morgan State U., 1987. Mem. MLA, South Atlantic MLA, Coll. Lang. Assn., Coll. English Assn. (v.p. Mid-Atlantic Group 1987-90, pres. 1990-92, exec. bd. 1992—), Women's Caucus for Modern Langs., Md. Coun. Tchrs. English, Md. Poetry and Lit. Soc., Md. Assn. Depts. English (bd. dirs. 1992—), Mid. Atlantic Writers' Assn. (founding mem. 1981, asst. editor Mid. Atlantic Writers' Assn. Rev. 1989—), Delta Sigma Epsilon (v.p. 1992-94, pres. 1994-96). Roman Catholic. Home: 102 Gorsuch Rd Lutherville Timonium MD 21093-4318 Office: Morgan State U Coll Arts & Scis Dean Baltimore MD 21239

SEDLIN, ELIAS DAVID, physician, orthopedic researcher, educator; b. N.Y.C., Jan. 21, 1932; s. Arnold Boris and Sonia Lipschitz Sedlin; m. Barbara Sue Zidell, July 9, 1960; children: Faith Avril, Adrian. BS in Biology, U. Ala., 1951; MD, Tulane U., 1955; D.Med. Sci., U. Gothenburg, Sweden, 1966. Diplomate: Am. Bd. Orthopedic Surgery. Intern Mobile (Ala.) Gen. Hosp., 1955-56; resident Charity Hosp., New Orleans, 1956-57; chief resident Bronx (N.Y.). Mcpl. Hosp., 1959-60; sr. resident Henry Ford Hosp., Detroit, 1960-61, rsch. assoc., emergency room lectr., 1961-63, NIH fellow, 1963-64; jr. attending physician Detroit Receiving Hosp., 1962-63; spl. NIH fellow dept. orthopedic surgery Sahlgrenska Sjukhuset, Gothenburg, 1964-66; asst. prof. dept. orthopaedic surgery Albert Einstein Coll. Medicine, 1966-69, assoc. prof., 1969-75, prof., 1975—, dir. orthopaedic surgery, 1969-79; prof. orthopaedic surgery Mt. Sinai Sch. Medicine, 1980—, dir. orthopaedic edn. Contbr. to multiple symposia, profl. meetings, also articles to profl. jours. Served to capt. AUS, 1957-59. Fulbright scholar, 1962; NSF postdoctoral fellow, 1964; recipient P.D. McGehee award Mobile Gen. Hosp., 1956; Ludvic Hektoen gold medal AMA, 1963; Nicholas Andry award Assn. Bone and Joint Surgeons, 1964. Fellow ACS, AAAS, Am. Acad. Orthopaedic Surgeons; mem. Orthopaedic Rsch. Soc., Phi Beta Kappa. Office: 5 E 98th St New York NY 10029-6501

SEDRA, ADEL SHAFEEK, electrical engineering educator, university administrator; b. Assuout, Egypt, Nov. 2, 1943; arrived in Can., 1966; s. Chafik and Hélène (Monsour) S.; m. Doris M. Barker, May 5, 1973; children: Paul Douglas, Mark Andrew. BSEE, Cairo U., 1964; MASc in Elec. Engring., U. Toronto, Ont., Can., 1968, PhDEE, 1969. Registered profl. engr., Ont. Instr. Cairo U., 1964-66; asst. prof. elec. engring. U. Toronto, 1969-72, assoc. prof., 1972-78, prof., 1978—, chmn. dept., 1986-93, v.p., provost, 1993—; pres. Elec. Engring. Consociates Ltd., Toronto, 1979-81; bd. dirs. Info. Tech. Rsch. Ctr., Toronto, 1988-93. Co-author: Filter Theory and Design, 1978, Microelectronic Circuits, 1982, 3d edit., 1991 (also Spanish, Korean, Greek, Italian, Portuguese and Hebrew transls.); contbr. over 120 articles to sci. jours. Operating grantee Nat. Scis. and Engring. Rsch. Coun. Can., 1970—; Ryerson Poly. Inst. fellow, 1988. Fellow IEEE (Darlington best paper award 1984, Edn. medal 1996, Cir. and Sys. Soc. Edn. award 1994, Guillermina Cauer paper award 1987); mem. Am. Soc. Engring. Edn. (Terman award 1988), Info. Tech. Assn. Can. (Tech. Achievement award 1993), Assn. Profl. Engrs. Ont. Home: 18 High Park Blvd, Toronto, ON Canada M6R 1M4 Office: U Toronto Simcoe Hall, 27 Kings College Cir, Toronto, ON Canada M5S 1A1

SEDWICK, (BENJAMIN) FRANK, language educator; b. Balt., Apr. 7, 1924; s. Benjamin Frank and Louise (Lambert) S.; m. Alice Elvira Magdeburger, June 4, 1949; children: Eric, Lyn, Coralie, Daniel. A.B., Duke, 1945; M.A., Stanford, 1947; Ph.D., U. So. Cal., 1953. Instr. Spanish U. Md., College Park, 1947-49; asst. prof. Spanish and Italian U.S. Naval Acad., 1951-53; asst. prof. Spanish U. Wis.-Milw., 1953-58; prof. Spanish and Italian Ohio Wesleyan U., Delaware, 1958-63; prof. Spanish, head dept. fgn. langs. Rollins Coll., Winter Park, Fla., 1963-80; dir. overseas programs Rollins Coll., 1963-80; freelance writer, 1980—. Author: The Tragedy of Manuel Azaña and the Fate of the Spanish Republic, 1963, A History of the Useless-Precaution Plot in Spanish and French Literature, 1964, El otro and Raquel encadenada, 1960, La forja de los sueños, 1960, La gloria de don Ramiro, 1966, Selecciones de Madariaga, 1969, Conversation in Spanish (co-author French, Italian, English and German edits.), 5th edit., 1988, Conversaciones con madrileños, 1973, Spanish for Careers, 1980 (co-author French and German edits.), The Practical Book of Cobs, 1987, 3d edit., 1995, The Gold Coinage of Gran Colombia, 1991; contbr. articles to profl. jours. Served to lt. USNR, 1942-46, PTO. Recipient Heath Lit. award Am. Numismatic Assn., 1994. Home: 2033 Cove Trl Winter Park FL 32789-1158

SEDWICK, JOHN W., judge; b. Kittanning, Pa., Mar. 13, 1946; s. Jack D. and Marion (Hilton) S.; m. Deborah Brown, Aug. 22, 1966; children: Jack D. II, Whitney Marie. BA summa cum laude, Dartmouth Coll., 1968; JD cum laude, Harvard U., 1972. Bar: Alaska 1972, U.S. Dist. Ct. Alaska 1972, U.S. Ct. Appeals (9th cir.) 1973. Lawyer Burr, Pease and Kurtz, Anchorage, 1972-81, 1982-92; dir. div. lands State of Alaska, Anchorage, 1981-82; judge U.S. Dist. Ct. Alaska, Anchorage, 1992—. Mem. Commonwealth North, Anchorage, 1985; bd. dirs. South Addition Alaska R.R. Com., Anchorage, 1984. Sgt. USNG, 1969-72. Mem. ABA, Alaska Bar Assn. (chmn. environ. law sect. 1984, law examiners com. 1986-89, civil rules com. 1990-92, fee arbitration com. 1991-92). Episcopalian. Office: US Dist Ct Box 32 222 W 7th Ave Anchorage AK 94513

SEE, CAROLYN, English language educator, novelist, book critic; b. Pasadena, Calif., Jan. 13, 1934; d. George Newton Laws and Kate Louise (Sullivan) Daly; m. Richard Edward See, Feb. 18, 1955 (div. June 1959); 1 child, Lisa Lenine; m. Tom Sturak, June 11, 1959; 1 child, Clara Elizabeth Marya. BA, Calif. State U., L.A., 1958; PhD, UCLA, 1963. Prof. English, Loyola Marymount Coll., L.A., 1970-85, UCLA, L.A., 1985—; book critic L.A. Times, 1981-93, Washington Post, 1993—. Author: (novels) Rhine Maidens, 1980, Golden Days, 1986, Making History, 1991, Dreaming: Hard Luck and Good Times In America, 1995, also 3 others. Bd. dirs. Calif. Arts Coun., L.A., 1987-91, Day Break, for homeless, Santa Monica, Calif., 1989—, Friends of English, UCLA, 1990—; buddy for life AIDS Project Los Angeles, AIDS relief, L.A., 1990—. Recipient award Sidney Hillman Found., 1972, Robert Kirsch award L.A. Times, 1994; grantee Nat. Endowment for Arts, 1980, Guggenheim fellow, 1990-91. Mem. Writers Guild Am., Libr. Found. Calif., PEN Ctr. USA West (pres. 1990-91), Nat. Book Critics Cir. (bd. dirs. 1986-90). Democrat. Avocations: gardening, sailing, dancing, brush clearing. Home: PO Box 107 Topanga CA 90290-0107 Office: UCLA Dept English 405 Hilgard Ave Los Angeles CA 90024-1301

SEE, EDMUND M., lawyer; b. Marietta, Ohio, Oct. 9, 1943; s. Edgar Thorpe and Katherine M. (Merriam) S.; m. Ellen Engler, June 5, 1976; children: Kevin, Gregory, Tyler. BA, Wesleyan U., Middletown, Conn., 1965; JD, Harvard U., 1971. Bar: Conn. 1971. Assoc. Day, Berry & Howard, Hartford, Conn., 1971-77; ptnr. Day, Berry & Howard, Hartford, 1978—. Vol. Peace Corps, Gabon, 1965-67, Vista, 1968-69; trustee St. Joseph Coll., 1991—. Mem. Nat. Assn. Bond Lawyers, Conn. Govtl. Fin. Officers Assn. Office: Day Berry & Howard Cityplace 25th FL Hartford CT 06103-3499

SEE, ROBERT FLEMING, JR., lawyer; b. Kansas City, Mo., Apr. 23, 1942; s. Robert Fleming and Betty (Conard) S.; m. Leslie, Apr. 26, 1985. BA with honors, U. Tex., 1964, JD with honors, 1966. Bar: Tex. 1966. Assoc. Locke, Purnell, Rain, Harrell and predecessor, Dallas, 1966, ptnr., 1972, pres., 1989—; speaker in field. Contbg. author: Loan Documentation Guide, 1990. Bd. commrs. Dallas Housing Authority; bd. dirs., chair affordable housing com. Dallas Citizens Coun. Mem. ABA, Tex. Bar Assn., Dallas Bar Assn., Greater Dallas C. of C., North Dallas C. of C., Salesmanship Club Dallas. Office: Locke Purnell Rain Harrell 2200 Ross Ave Ste 2200 Dallas TX 75201-6766*

SEE, SAW-TEEN, structural engineer; b. Georgetown, Penang, Malaysia, Mar. 23, 1954; came to U.S., 1974; d. Hock-Eng and Ewe-See (Lim) S.; m. Leslie Earl Robertson, Aug. 11, 1982; 1 child, Karla Mei. BSc in Civil Engring., Cornell U., 1977, M in Civil Engring., 1978. Registered profl. engr., N.Y., Calif., Conn., Fla., Md., N.J., Ohio, Pa., Wash. Design engr. Leslie E. Robertson Assocs., N.Y.C., 1978-81, assoc., 1981-85, ptnr., 1986—, mng. ptnr., 1990—; profl. cons. M of Engring. class Cornell U., 1994-95; project dir., project mgr. Shinji Shumeikai Mus., Kyoto, Japan, West Side H.S., N.Y.C., Jr. H.S. 234, Bklyn., Jewelry Trade Ctr., Bangkok, Bilbao (Spain) Emblematic bldgs., Internat. Trade Ctr., Barcelona, Spain, Seattle Art Mus., San Jose (Calif.) Convention Ctr., San Jose Arena; project dir. Balt. Conv. Ctr., Rock 'N Roll Hall of Fame and Mus., Cleve., Pontiac Marina Hotel and Retail, Singapore, acad. bldgs. and greenhouse, SUNY, Binghamton, N.Y.; project mgr. Coll. of Law bldg. U. Iowa, Iowa City, Neiman-Marcus store, San Francisco, AT&T Exhbn. bldg., N.Y.C., Bank of China Tower, Hong Kong, PPG Hdqs., Pitts., AT&T Corp. Hdqs., N.Y.C. Contbr. articles to profl. jours. Named to Those Who Made Marks in the Constrn. Industry in 1988, Engring. News Record, N.Y.C., 1989. Mem. ASCE, Archtl. League, Coun. on Tall Bldgs. and Urban Habitat (past chairperson com. on gravity loads and temperature effects 1982-85), Architects, Designers, Planners for Social Responsiblity, N.Y. Assn. Cons. Engrs. (dir. 1989-93, structural codes com. 1991—). Avocations: sailing, skiing, reading, photography. Home: 45 E 89th St Apt 25C New York NY 10128-1230 Office: Leslie E Robertson Assocs 211 E 46th St New York NY 10017-2935

SEEBA, HINRICH CLAASSEN, foreign language educator; b. Hannover, Germany, Feb. 5, 1940; came to U.S., 1967; s. Hinrich and Irmgard (Witte) S. Student, Göttingen, Zürich, Tübingen univs., 1960-67; staatsexamen, U. Tübingen, Fed. Republic of Germany, 1966, PhD, 1967. Asst. prof. German U. Calif., Berkeley, 1968-72, assoc. prof., 1972-76, prof., 1976—, chmn. dept. German, 1977-81, 89-91; vis. prof. Free U. Berlin, 1992, Stanford (Calif.) U., 1994. Author: Kritik des ästhetischen Menschen, 1970, Die Liebe zur Sache, 1973; author, editor: Kleist: Dramen I, 1987, II, 1991; co-editor Politzefs, 1975, Brinkmanfs, 1981; contbr. scholarly papers on German lit. to jours.; editorial bd. Lessing Yearbook, 1979—, Eighteenth Century Studies, 1982-85, The German Quar., 1988-92, 94—, South Cen. Rev., 1988—; adv. bd. German Studies Rev., 1990—, Zeitschrift für Germanistik, 1991—, U. Calif. Press Modern Philology Series, 1992—. Studienstiftung fellow, 1963-68, Guggenheim Found. fellow, 1970-71. Mem. MLA, Am. Assn. Tchrs. German, German Studies Assn., Philol. Assn. of Pacific, Lessing Soc. (pres. 1985-87), Heine Soc., Grillparzer Gesellschaft, Herder Gesellschaft. Lutheran. Office: U Calif Dept German Berkeley CA 94720

SEEBACH, LYDIA MARIE, physician; b. Red Wing, Minn., Nov. 9, 1920; d. John Henry and Marie (Gleusen) S.; m. Keith Edward Wentz, Oct. 16, 1959; children: Brooke Marie, Scott. BS, U. Minn., 1942, MB, 1943, MD, 1944, MS in Medicine, 1951. Diplomate Am. Bd. Internal Medicine. Intern Kings County Hosp., Bklyn., 1944; fellow Mayo Found., Rochester, Minn., 1945-51; pvt. practice Oakland, Calif., 1952-60, San Francisco, 1961—; asst. clin. prof. U. Calif., San Francisco, 1981—; mem., vice chmn. Arthritis Clinic, Presbyn. Hosp., San Francisco, 1961-88, pharmacy com., 1963-78; chief St. Mary's Hosp. Arthritis Clinic, San Francisco, 1968-72; exec. bd. Pacific Med. Ctr., San Francisco, 1974-76. Contbr. articles to med. jours. Fellow ACP; mem. AMA, Am. Med. Womens Assn. (pres. Calif. chpt. 1968-70), Am. Rheumatism Assn., Am. Soc. Internal Medicine, Pan Am. Med. Womens Assn. (treas.), Calif. Acad. Medicine, Calif. Soc. Internal Medicine, Calif. Med. Assn., San Francisco Med. Soc., San Francisco Med. Assn., San Francisco Soc. Internal Medicine, No. Calif. Rheumatism Assn., Internat. Med. Women's Assn., Mayo Alumni (bd. dirs. 1983-89), Iota Sigma Pi. Republican. Lutheran. Avocations: music, cooking, gardening, needlepoint. Office: 490 Post St Ste 939 San Francisco CA 94102-1410

SEEBASS, ALFRED RICHARD, III, aerospace engineer, educator, university dean; b. Denver, Mar. 27, 1936; s. Alfred Richard Jr. and Marie Estelle (Wright) S.; m. Nancy Jane Palm, June 20, 1958; children: Erik Peter, Scott Gregory. BS in Engring. magna cum laude, Princeton U., 1958, MS in Engring., 1961; PhD, Cornell U., 1962. Rsch. asst. Cornell U., Ithaca, N.Y., 1960-62, asst. prof. aerospace engring., 1962-64, assoc. prof., 1964-72, prof. aerospace engring., assoc. dean, 1972-75; hdqrs. staff rsch. divsn. NASA, 1966-67; prof. aerospace engring., mech. engring. and math. U. Ariz., Tucson, 1975-81; dean Coll. Engring. & Applied Sci. U. Colo., Boulder, 1981-94, prof. aerospace engring. scis., 1994—, also chair, 1995—; faculty assoc. Boeing Sci. Rsch. Labs., 1970; cons. in field; mem. coms. NAE, NAS, NRC, NASA, Dept. Transp., sci. adv. bd. Air Force, Aeros. and Space Engring. Bd., Los Alamos Nat. Lab; grant investigator NASA, Office Naval Rsch., Air Force Office Sci. Rsch., 1966—; mem. univ. com. on applied math. U. Ariz., 1976-81; mem. aeronautics and space engring. bd. NRC, 1977-84, vice-chmn., 1979-81, chmn., 1981-83, mem. Commn. on Engring. and Tech. Sys., 1982-83; mem. Numerical Aerodynamics Simulator Adv. Group, 1978—; chmn. Air Force Office Scientific Rsch. rev. panel Flight Dynamics Lab., Wright-Patterson AFB, 1979; mem. NASA adv. coun., 1981-83; mem. survey com. on plasma physics and fluids, subcom. on fluids NRC, 1983-84; mem. engring. rsch. bd. Panel on Transp. Sys. Rsch., 1984-85; mem. sci. adv. bd. USAF, 1984-88, chmn. Air Force Operational Test & Evaluation Ctr. Divsn. Adv. Group, 1986-88, mem. Arnold Engring. & Devel. Ctr. Divsn. Adv. Group, 1984-88, mem. aerospace vehicles panel, 1984-88; mem. adv. coun. univ. study planning group NASA, 1988-89; bd. dirs. Boulder Tech. Incubator; mem. mech. and electronic external adv. com. Los Alamos (N.Mex.) Nat. Lab., 1991-93, chair divsn. rev. com. Engring. Scis. & Applications, Los Alamos, 1995; mem. NASA Adv. Coun. U. Rels. Task Force, 1991-93, mem. NASA Ames-Stanford Ctr. for Turbulence Rsch. Adv. Com., 1993; mem. Commn. on Phys. Scis., Math. & Applications NRC, 1992-95. Editor: Sonic Boom Research, 1967, Nonlinear Waves 1974, Russian, 1977; assoc. editor: Physics of Fluids, 1978-80; mem. editl. bd. Ann. Rev. Fluid Mechanics, Phys. Fluids, AIAA Jour.; editor-in-chief (book series) Progress Astronautics and Aeronautics, 1990—; contbg. author: Handbook of Applied Mathematics, 1974; contbr. articles to profl. jours., chpts. to books; reviewer Jour. Fluid Mechanics, Physics of Fluids, Jour. Acoustical Soc. Am., AIAA Jour., Jour. Aircraft, Jour. Applied Mechanics, NSF, others. Recipient Daniel and Florence Guggenheim fellow Princeton U., 1958-59, Woodrow Wilson fellow Cornell U., 1959-60, Disting. Engring. Alumni award U. Colo., 1983, Meritorious Civilian Svc. award Dept. Air Force, 1988, (with H. Sobieczky) Max Planck Rsch. prize, Germany, 1991, Internat. Astro. Fed. Frank J. Malina Astronautics medal 1994, U. Colo. medal 1994, U. Colo. Coll. of Engring. Centennial medal 1994, Frank J. Malina medal Internat. Astronautics Fedn., 1994; NASA grantee, 1966-82, 88-91, 92-93. Fellow AAAS (mem. engring. sect. nominating com. 1987-90, chair 1990, coun. del. engring. sect. 1991-94), AIAA (mem. fluid mechanics tech. com. 1977-80, tech. dir. bd. dirs. 1978-81, exec com. 1980-81, assoc. editor jour. 1981-83, Biannual Durand lecturer and medalist 1994); mem. Nat. Acad. Engring. (aerospace peer com. 1987-90, chair 1990, mem. com. on membership 1991-93, vice chmn. 1991, chair 1992), Am. Soc. Engring. Edn. (mem. sr. rsch. award com. 1990-93, chair 1993), Sigma Xi, Tau Beta Pi. Office: U Colo Campus Box 429 Coll Aerospace Engring Sci Boulder CO 80309

SEED, ALLEN H., elementary and secondary education educator, science educator; b. Lakewood, Ohio, June 9, 1953; s. Hugh A. and Patricia (Peattie) S.; m. Laura Seed, Aug. 11, 1979; children: David, Vicki. BS, Miami U., Oxford, Ohio, 1975; MEd, Miami U., 1980, PhD, 1994. Tchr. Hamilton (Ohio) city schs., Summit County Day Sch., Cin.; sci. curriculum coord. Maderia City Schs., Cin.; tchr. Maderia City Schs.; mem. adj. faculty Bowling Green State U., Miami U.; asst. prof. mid. grades edn. No. Ky. U. Greater Cin. Found. grantee; recipient Ohio Gov.'s award for sci., 1987, 88. Mem. ASCD, Nat. Staff Devel. Coun., Nat. Sci. Tchrs. Assn., Staff Devel. Coun. Ohio, Nat. Mid. Sch. Assn., Am. Ednl. Rsch. Assn., Ky. Mid. Sch. Assn., Hamilton Classroom Tchrs. Assn. Home: 151 Hidden Hills Dr Fairfield OH 45014-8607

SEEDLOCK, ROBERT FRANCIS, engineering and construction company executive; b. Newark, Feb. 6, 1913; s. Frank Andrew and Mary Elizabeth (Prosner) S.; m. Hortense Orcutt Norton, Sept. 1, 1937; children: Robert Francis, Elizabeth Munsell Seedlock Morrissette, Walter Norton, Mary Marion. Student Case Inst. Tech., 1931-33; BS, U.S. Mil. Acad., 1937; MS in Civil Engring., MIT, 1940; grad. Armed Forces Staff Coll., 1948, Nat. War Coll., 1958. Registered profl. engr., D.C., Pa. Commd. 2d lt. U.S. Army, 1937, advanced through grades to maj. gen., 1963; asst. to dist. engr., Pitts., 1937-39, Tulsa Aircraft Assembly Plant, 1941; regtl. exec. bn. comdr. Engr. Unit Tng. Ctr., Camp Claiborne, La., 1942; asst. theatre engr., CBI, also comdr. Burma Road Engrs., also chief engr. Shanghai Base Command, 1943-45; mem. Gen. Marshall's Mediation Mission, Peking, 1946-47; mem. gen. staff U.S. Army, Mem. Am. del. Far Eastern Commn., 1948-49; aide to chief staff U.S. Army, 1949-54; mem. U.S. del. NATO Ministerial Conf., 1952-53; dep. div. engr. Mediterranean div., 1954-57; mil. asst. to asst. sec. def. for pub. affairs, 1958-62; div. engr. Missouri River, Omaha, 1962-63; sr. mem. UN Mil. Armistice Commn., Korea, 1963-64; dir. mil. personnel Office dep. chief of staff for personnel Dept. Army, 1964-66; dir. mil. constrn. Office Chief of Engrs., 1966; comdg. gen. U.S. Army Engr. Center and Ft. Belvoir, Va., and comdt. U.S. Army Engr. Sch., Ft. Belvoir, 1966-68, ret., 1968; pres. Yuba Industries, 1968-69, v.p. Standard Prudential Corp. (merged with Yuba Industries), 1969-70; v.p., dir. Petro-Chem. Devel. Co., Inc., N.Y.C., 1968-70, Petchem Constrn. Co., N.Y.C., 1968-70, Petrochem. Isoflow Furnaces, Ltd. (Can.), 1968-70; dir. constrn. and devel. Port Authority of Allegheny County, Pitts., 1970-73; assoc. Parsons, Brinckerhoff, Quade & Douglas, N.Y.C., 1973-75, mgr. So. region, 1975-77; dep. project dir. Parsons, Brinckerhoff-Tudor-Bechtel, Atlanta, 1973-77; program dir. Ralph M. Parsons Co., Pasadena, Calif., Phila. and Washington, 1977-83; cons. engr. 1983—; dir. T.Y. Lin Intl., 1985-89; chief liaison, cons. Chinese Acad. Sci. for Beijing Inst. Mgmt., 1985-89; U.S. rep. to Permanent Tech. Com. Number 1 of Permanent Intl. Assn. of Navigation Congresses, 1984-93; pres. First Am. chapt. Burma Star Assn., 1984—; chmn. Sino-Am. Ventures, Inc., 1987—; cons. The Knowledge Co., 1989—, Dove & Assocs., 1990; mem. radio engring. adv. com. Voice of Am., 1990-93. Contbr. to mil. and engring. jours. Bd. dirs. Army and Air Force Exchange and Motion Picture Svc., 1964; mem. Miss. River Commn., 1962-63, Bd. Engrs. Rivers and Harbor, 1962-63, Def. Adv. Commn. Edn., 1964; chmn. Mo. Basin Inter-Agy. Com., 1962-63; fed. rep., chmn. Big Blue River Compact Commn., 1962-63; mem. U.S. Com. on Large Dams, 1962-82; exec. bd. Nat. Capital Area council Boy Scouts Am., 1967-68, Atlanta Area council, 1975-77. Decorated DSM, Legion of Merit with oak leaf cluster; chevalier Legion of Honor (France); 1st class, grade A medal Army, navy, air force, also spl. breast order Yun Hui (China); named Engr. of Yr., Met. Atlanta Engring. Soc., 1976; Ga. Engr. of Yr. in Govt., Ga. Soc. Profl. Engrs., 1976; recipient Silver Beaver award Boy Scouts Am., 1977, Case Alumni Assn. Gold medal, 1985. Fellow Soc. Am. Mil. Engrs. (nat. dir., Cathedral Latin Alumni Assn. Man of the Yr. award 1992); mem. ASCE (hon., aerospace div. program com. 1980-82, sec. exec. com. 1982-83, chmn. 1984-85, editor Jour. Aerospace Engring., 1986-93), Assn. U.S. Army, West Point Soc. N.Y. (life), West Point Soc. Atlanta (pres. 1976), Burma Star Assn. (pres. 1st Am. chpt., 1982—), Sigma Xi, Tau Beta Pi. Roman Catholic. Clubs: Army-Navy Country (sec., chmn. bd. govs. 1952-54, 61-62) (Arlington, Va.); MIT (pres. Shanghai 1946); Met. (N.Y.C.); Oglethorpe (Savannah, Ga.), Ansley Golf (Atlanta). Home and Office: 3 Plantation Ct Savannah GA 31419-2731 *Live by Duty, Honor and Country and you will live forever.*

SEEFELDT, CAROL, education educator; b. St. Louis, May 3, 1935; d. George and Mary (Reznicek) Wohanka; m. Eugene Seefeldt; children: Paul, Andrea. BA, U. Wis., Milw., 1956; MA, U. South Fla., 1968; PhD, Fla. State U., 1971. Reg. tng. officer Fla. Project Head Start, Tallahassee, 1968-71; prof. U. Md., College Park, 1971—. Author: Social Studies for the Preschool and Primary Child, 1992, Continuing Issues in Early Childhood Education, 1990, Early Childhood Education, 1994. Bd. dirs. Md. Com. for Children, Balt., 1988-90. Named Disting. Scholar/Tchr., U. Md., 1983—. Mem. Nat. Assn. for Edn. of Young Children (tchr. edn. commn. 1986—), Assn. for Childhood Edn. Internat., Am. Ednl. Research Assn., Phi Delta Kappa. Home: 881 Mt Airy Rd Davidsonville MD 21035-2225 Office: U Md Inst for Child Study College Park MD 20742

SEEGAL, HERBERT LEONARD, department store executive; b. Brookline, Mass., Aug. 13, 1915; s. Morris and Rose (Beerman) S.; m. Dorothy Goldstein, June 27, 1941 (div. June 1954); children: Jane Laura, Norma Ann; m. Juanita C. Steele, Feb. 4, 1987. AB, U. Mich., 1937. With R.H. White's, Boston, 1937-41; with Thalhimer's, Richmond, Va., 1941-53, v.p. charge gen. merchandising, 1949-53; sr. v.p. merchandising, dir. Macy's N.Y., N.Y.C., 1953-62; pres. Bamberger's N.J., Newark, 1962-71; dir. R.H. Macy & Co., Inc., 1965—, vice chmn. bd. dirs., 1971-72, pres., 1972-80. Mem. Princeton Club (N.Y.C.), Century Country Club (Purchase, N.Y.). Home: 128 Central Park S New York NY 10019-1565 also: 2451 Windsor Way Ct West Palm Beach FL 33414-7035

SEEGAL, JOHN FRANKLIN, lawyer; b. Newton, Mass., May 21, 1946; s. Samuel Melbourne and Martha (Lewenberg) S.; m. Barbara Ellen Wayne, Apr. 2, 1982; children: Sarah Rachel, Laura Rose.B.A., Harvard U., M.B.A., 1973, J.D., 1973. Assoc. Orrick, Herrington & Sutcliffe, San Francisco, 1973-78, ptnr., 1979—. Mem. ABA, Calif. Bar Assn. Republican. Jewish. Office: Orrick Herrington & Sutcliffe 400 Sansome St San Francisco CA 94111-3308

SEEGER, GUENTER OTTO, chef; b. Loffenau, Baden, Germany, Mar. 23, 1949; s. Otto Emil and Margarete (Temme) S.; m. Marion Boehmlander (div. Aug. 1991); children: Diana, Denise. Student, Cook and Hotel Sch., Lucerne, Switzerland. Apprentice Hotel Funk, Dobel, Germany, 1963-66; cook various locations, Switzerland, 1966-77; owner, operator restaurant Pforz Heim, Germany, 1977-84; exec. chef maifar Regent Hotel, Washington, 1984-85; exec. chef dining rm. Ritz-Carlton Hotel, Atlanta, 1985—; pres., cons., produce developer Smi, Inc., Atlanta, 1993. Editor calendars, 1982, 83 (award 1982). Named Best Chef of Atlanta, Atlanta Mag., 1993. Mem. Chefs Collaborative 2000 (bd. overseers 1994). Avocations: Kung fu. Office: The Ritz-Carlton Buckhead 3434 Peachtree Rd NE Atlanta GA 30326-1172

SEEGER, LEINAALA ROBINSON, law librarian, educator; b. Wailuku, Hawaii, July 2, 1944; d. John Adam and Anna Hiilani (Leong) Robinson; 1 child, Maile Lea. BA, U. Wash., 1966; JD, U. Puget Sound, 1977; M in Law Librarianship, U. Wash., 1979. Bar: Wash. 1977. Reference librarian U. Puget Sound Sch. Law., Tacoma, 1977-79, assoc. law librarian, 1981-86; asst. librarian McGeorge Sch. Law, U. of Pacific, Sacramento, 1979-81; assoc. librarian pub. svc. Harvard Law Sch., Cambridge, Mass., 1986-89; dir. law library, assoc. prof. law U. Idaho Coll. Law, Moscow, 1989—; bd. dirs. Inlan, Spokane, Wash., 1989—. Mem. Palouse Asian-Ams. Assn., Moscow, 1989—. Mem. Wash. STate Bar Assn., Am. Assn. Law Librs. (chmn. minority com. 1990-91, v.p., pres.-elect Western Pacific chpt. 1985-86, 90-91, pres. 1991-92, vice chmn. edn. com. 1991-92, chmn. 1992-93), Idaho Coun. Acad. Librs. Avocations: scuba, snorkeling, wine education, flying, aerobics. Office: U Idaho Coll Laws Moscow ID 83844-2324

SEEGER, MICHAEL, musician, singer, folklorist; b. N.Y.C., Aug. 15, 1933; s. Charles Louis and Ruth Porter (Crawford) S.; m. Marjorie L. Ostrow, Dec. 20, 1960 (div. 1968); children: Kim, Arley, Jeremy; m. Alice L. Gerrard, Aug. 16, 1970 (div.). guest lectr. English dept. U. Calif., Fresno, 1974; mem. jazz/folk/ethnic music sect. Nat. Endowment for Arts, 1973-77; dir. Am. Old Time Music Festival, 1975-78, Rockbridge Mountain Music Conv., Buena Vista, Va., 1986—. Performs Appalachian vocal and instrumental music in a variety of styles at concerts, folk festivals, on radio and TV in U.S. and abroad; also numerous record albums and documentary recordings from traditional folk musicians and dancers; founding mem. New Lost City Ramblers, 1958—, Strange Creek Singers, 1968-76, Bent Mountain Band, 1981. Trustee John Edwards Meml. Found., UCLA, 1962—; bd. dirs. Newport (R.I.) Folk Festival, 1963-71, Nat. Folk Festival, Washington, 1972-78, Smithsonian Am. Folklife Co., 1970-76. Recipient 1st prize banjo category Galax Va. Old Time Fiddlers conf., 1975, Ralph J. Gleason Meml. award Rex Found., 1994; award of merit Internat. Bluegrass Music Assn., 1995; Grammy nominee for best traditional folk album, 1986, 91, 94; Nat. Endowment Arts grantee, 1975, 82, 84, 87; vis. scholar Smithsonian Instn., 1983; Guggenheim fellow, 1984. Home: PO Box 1592 Lexington VA 24450-1592

SEEGER, PETE, folk singer, songwriter; b. N.Y.C., May 3, 1919; s. Charles Louis and Constance de Clyver (Edson) S.; m. Toshi-Aline Ohta, July 20, 1943; children: Daniel Adams, Mika Salter, Tinya. Student, Harvard U., 1936-38. Teamed with Woody Guthrie, toured south and southwest; an organizer, Almanac Singers, 1940, toured U.S. with group, 1941-42; collaborated on writing labor and anti-Fascist songs; sang on overseas broadcasts, OWI; became nat. dir., People's Songs, Inc., 1946; performed: motion picture film To Hear My Banjo Play, 1946; toured with Progressive Party candidate Henry Wallace; helped organize the Weavers, 1948; appeared nat. radio and TV shows until blacklisted from networks, night clubs and theaters; rec. for, Decca, 1949-52, Folkways, 1953-80, Columbia, 1961-73 toured schs., summer camps, colls., univs. U.S.A. and 35 other countries; assisted orgn., Newport (R.I.) Folk Festivals; songwriter: Where Have All the Flowers Gone, 1961, If I Had a Hammer, (in collaboration with Lee Hays) Kisses Sweeter than Wine, (in collaboration with Weavers) Turn, Turn, Turn, 1959; recent albums include Sing Along, 1980, (with John Hammond) Waist Deep in the Big Muddy and other Love Songs, 1994; TV series Rainbow Quest, 1965; producer ednl. short subjects, Folklore Research Films; performed global singing tour including 24 countries, 1963-64; appeared: Smothers Bros. Show, as network blacklist was lifted, 1967; appeared in: film Tell Me That You Love Me, Junie Moon, 1970; author: American Favorite Ballads, 1961, The Bells of Rhymney, 1964, How To Play The Five-String Banjo, Henscratches and Flyspecks, 1973, The Incompleat Folksinger, 1973, (with Charles Seeger) The Foolish Frog, 1973, Abiyoyo, 1983, (with Robert Reiser) Carry It On, 1986, (with Robert Reiser) Everybody Says Freedom., 1990, Where Have All the Flowers Gone, 1993. Served with U.S. Army, 1942-45. Recipient: Nat. Medal of the Arts, 1994, Kennedy Center Honor, 1994. Pioneered the appreciation of Southern folk music through over 45 years of concerts, recordings and writings, interested many others in the idea of making their own music, revived old music of many types and used music as a means of speaking out against war, racism, poverty, pollution, etc. Office: care Harold Leventhal 250 W 57th St New York NY 10107

SEEGER, SONDRA JOAN, artist; b. L.A., May 27, 1942; d. Reinhold Josheph and Bertha Catherine (Monese) S.; m. Richard John Pahl, Aug. 18, 1961 (div. 1974); children: Catherine Marie, Douglas Richard, Angela Gay, Susan Joan; m. David Ernest Matteson, Apr. 25, 1990. Student, Marylhurst Coll., 1960. Pvt. practice musician various locations, 1973-81; security guard MGM Hotel, Las Vegas, 1981-82; real estate salesperson Century 21, Kent, Wash., 1983-85; mgr. Viera Land & Cattle, Inc., La Grande, Oreg., 1984-92; freelance artist, Casper, Wyo., 1991—; ptnr. Old West Saddle Shop, Casper, 1989-93, Casper, Wyo., 1993—; com. mem. Oreg. State Forest Practices Com., N.E. Region, 1990-91. Named Union Co. Tree Farmer of Yr., Am. Tree Farm System, 1987. Mem. NRA, Nat. Soc. Artists, Women Artists of the West, Allied Artists, Cider Painters of Am., Australian Soc. of Miniature Art, Small Woodlands Assn., Knickerbocker Artists (assoc.), United Pastelists of Am. (signature), Nat. Soc. Artists (signature), Women Artists of the West, Pacific Art League, The Art League of Alexandria, Va., Miniature Art Soc. Fla., Oil Painters Am., Wyo. Artists Assn., Cody Country Art Guild, Am. Soc. Classical Realism, Gen. Artist Mem., Internat. Platform Assn., Oreg. Forest Resources Inst., Am. Artists' Profl. League. Republican. Avocations: dog obedience tng., hunting, wildlife habitat enhancement. Home and Office: Old West Saddle Shop PO Box 4300 Casper WY 82604-0300

SEEGMILLER, JARVIS EDWIN, biochemist, educator; b. St. George, Utah, June 22, 1920; m. Roberta Eads, 1950; children: Dale S. Maudlin, Robert E., Lisa S. Taylor, Richard L. AB, U. Utah, 1942; MD, U. Chgo., 1948. Asst. U.S. Bur. Mines, Utah, 1941; asst. nat. def. rsch. com. Northwestern Tech. Inst., 1942-44; asst. medicine U. Chgo., 1947-48; intern John Hopkins Hosp., 1948-49; biochemist Nat. Inst. Arthritis and Metabolic Diseases, 1949-51; rsch. assoc. Thorndike Meml. Lab. Harvard Med. Sch., 1952-53; vis. investigator Pub. Health Rsch. Inst., N.Y.C., 1953-54; chief sect. human biochemistry, genetics, asst. sci. dir. Nat. Inst. Arthritis and Metabolic Diseases, 1954-69; prof. dept. medicine, dir. divsn. rheumatology U. Calif., San Diego, 1969-90, prof. emeritus dept. medicine, assoc. dir. Stein Inst. Rsch., 1990—; vis. scientist U. Coll. Hosp. Sch. Medicine, London, 1964-65; Harvey Soc. lectr., 1970. Contbr. numerous articles to profl. jours. Macy scholar Basel Inst. Immunology; Guggenheim fellow Swiss Inst. Exptl. Cancer Rsch., Lausanne, 1982-83, John Simon Guggenheim Meml. Found. fellow, 1982, Fogarty Internat. fellow Oxford U., 1989. Mem. Nat. Acad. Sci., Harvey Soc. (hon.), Am. Soc. Biol. Chemists, Am. Rheumatism Assn., Am. Fedn. Clin. Rsch., Am. Soc. Human Genetics, Am. Soc. Clin. Investigation, AAAS, Assn. Am. Physicians, Am. Acad. Arts and Sci. Office: U Calif at San Diego Stein Inst Rsch on Aging 0664 5094 BSB La Jolla CA 92093*

SEEHRA, MOHINDAR SINGH, physics educator, researcher; b. Panjab, Pakistan, Feb. 14, 1940; came to U.S., 1963; s. Bakhshish Singh and Rattan (Kaur) S.; m. Harbhajan Kaur, May 12, 1963; children: Jasmeet, Parveen. BS, Panjab U., 1959; MS, Aligarh (India) U., 1962; PhD, U. Rochester, 1969. Instr. chemistry Arya Coll., Nawanshahr, India, 1959-60; lectr. physics Jain Coll., Ambala City, India, 1962-63; asst. prof. physics W.Va. U., Morgantown, 1969-73, assoc. prof., 1973-77, prof., 1977-91, Eberly disting. prof. physics, 1992—. Contbr. numerous articles to profl. jours. Rsch. fellow A.P. Sloan Found., 1973-75, ORAU Summer fellow, 1976, 77, 84, 85; recipient Outstanding Rsch. award Coll. Arts and Scis., U. W.Va., 1985. Fellow Am. Phys. Soc., Materials Rsch. Soc., Carbon Soc., ASM Internat. Office: WVa State U Dept Physics PO Box 6315 Morgantown WV 26506-6315

SEELENFREUND, ALAN, distribution company executive; b. N.Y.C., Oct. 22, 1936; s. Max and Gertrude (Roth) S.; m. Ellyn Bolt; 1 child, Eric. BME, Cornell U., 1959, M. in Indsl. Engring., 1960; PhD in Mgmt. Sci., Stanford U., 1967. Asst. prof. bus. adminstrn. Grad. Sch. Bus. Stanford U., Palo Alto, Calif., 1966-71; mgmt. cons. Strong, Wishart and Assocs., San Francisco, 1971-75; various mgmt. positions McKesson Corp., San Francisco, 1975-84, v.p., chief fin. officer, 1984-86, exec. v.p., chief fin. officer, 1986-89, chmn., chief exec. officer, 1989—, also bd. dirs.; bd. dirs. Armor All Products Corp., Pacific Gas and Electric Co. Bd. dir. Golden Gate Nat. Park Assn. Mem. World Affairs Coun. No. Calif., Bus. Roundtable, Bay Area Coun., Calif. Bus. Roundtable, Bankers Club, St. Francis Yacht Club, Villa Taverna Club, Pacific Union Club. Avocations: sailing, skiing. Office: McKesson Corp 1 Post St San Francisco CA 94104-5203

SEELEY, DONALD L., human resources specialist; b. 1944. With United Airlines, N.Y.C., 1974-84; pres., CEO Alexander Cons. Group, Inc., 1984—.

SEELEY, HARRY WILBUR, JR., microbiology educator; b. Bridgeport, Conn., Mar. 5, 1917; s. Harry W. and Genevieve (Quinlan) S.; m. Margaret Johnson, Dec. 21, 1940; children: Gail Seeley Fox, Beth (dec.), Carol Seeley-Teboe. B.S., U. Conn., 1941, M.S., 1942; Ph.D., Cornell U., 1947. Mem. faculty Cornell U., 1947—, prof. bacteriology, 1955—, chmn. sect. microbiology, 1964-68, prof.-in-charge microbiology, 1974-77, acting chmn. dept. microbiology, 1977-78, ret., 1979. Author: Microbes in Action, 1962, 4th edit., 1991, Microbes and Man, 1974. Guggenheim fellow, 1958. Mem. Soc. Gen. Microbiology, Am. Soc. Microbiology, Am. Acad. Microbiology, Soc. Applied Bacteriology, Internat. Oceanographic Found., AAAS, Am. Inst. Biol. Scientists, AAUP, Sigma Xi, Phi Kappa Phi. Home: Park Ln Jacksonville NY 14854-0001 Office: Cornell U Dept Microbiology Wing Hall Ithaca NY 14853

SEELEY, ROD RALPH, physiology educator; b. Rupert, Idaho, Dec. 29, 1945; s. Earl W. Seeley and Alice E. (Hall) Walker; m. Jeanette Brady, Aug. 27, 1965; children: Teri, Alicia, Christopher, Kara. BS, Idaho State U., 1968; MS, Utah State U., 1971, PhD, 1973. Asst. prof. dept. biol. scis. Idaho State U., Pocatello, 1973-78, assoc. prof., 1978-83, prof., 1983—, chmn. dept., 1986—. Author: Human Anatomy and Physiology, 1989, 3d edit., 1995, Essentials of Anatomy and Physiology, 1991, 2d edit., 1995, Understanding Anatomy and Physiology, 1994; contbr. articles on reproductive physiology to profl. jours. Mem. bd. Sch. Dist. 25, Pocatello, 1982-88, chmn. bd., 1985-87. Recipient Disting. Tchr. award Idaho State U., 1986. Mem. AAAS, Idaho Acad. Sci., Human Anatomy and Physiology Soc., Soc. Study Reproduction, Sigma Xi. Avocations: running, fishing, backpacking, hunting. Office: Idaho State U Dept Biol Scis PO Box 8007 Pocatello ID 83209-8007

SEELIG, GERARD LEO, management consultant; b. Schluchtern, Germany, June 15, 1926; came to U.S., 1934, naturalized, 1943; s. Herman and Bella (Bach) S.; m. Lorraine Peters, June 28, 1953; children: Tina Lynn, Robert Mark and Carol Ann (twins). BEE, Ohio State U., 1948; MS in Indsl. Mgmt, N.Y. U., 1954. Registered profl. engr., Ohio. Electronics engr. Martin Corp., Balt., 1948-50; sr. engr. Fairchild Aircraft Co., Farmingdale, N.Y., 1950-54; program mgr. RCA, Moorestown, N.J., 1954-59, Van Nuys, Calif., 1959-61; div. mgr. Missile & Space Co. div. Lockheed Aircraft Corp., Van Nuys, 1961-63; v.p., gen. mgr. Lockheed Aircraft Corp. (Lockheed Electronics div.), Los Angeles, 1963-68; exec. v.p. Lockheed Electronics Co., Inc., Plainfield, N.J., 1968-69; pres. Lockheed Electronics Co., Inc., 1969-71; group exec., exec. asst. to office of pres. ITT, N.Y.C., 1971-72; corp. v.p. ITT, 1972-79, sr. v.p., 1979-81, exec. v.p., 1981-83; pres. indsl. and tech. sector Allied Corp.; exec. v.p. Allied Corp., Morristown, N.J., 1983-87; disting. exec. lectr. Rutgers Grad. Sch. Mgmt.; exec.-in-residence, vis. prof. Columbia U. Grad. Sch. Bus.; bd. dirs. 5 corps.; cons. various investment firms. Served with AUS, 1944-46. Recipient Disting. Alumnus award Ohio State U., 1987. Fellow AIAA (assoc.); mem. IEEE (sr.).

SEELIG, STEVEN ALFRED, government financial executive; b. N.Y.C., Dec. 24, 1944; s. Henry Walter and Hilde (Oster) S.; m. Gloria Phylis Shidler, June 8, 1969; children: Katherine, Karen, Joanne. BA with hons., Clark U., 1966, PhD, 1971; MA, Washington U., 1968. Instr. Merrimack Coll., North Andover, Mass., 1970-71; economist Fed. Res. Bank of N.Y., N.Y.C., 1971-75; from asst. to assoc. prof. Fordham U., Bronx, N.Y., 1975-78; with Fed. Deposit Ins. Corp., Washington, 1978—, CFO, 1992—, dir. divsn. of liquidation, 1989-92, dir. divsn. of fin., 1992—; mem. adj. faculty Fairleigh Dickinson U., Teaneck, N.J., 1972-77, George Washington U., Washington, 1979-89; cons., lectr. in field. Author: Bank Holding Companies & The Public Interest, 1977; contbr. articles to profl. jours. Pres. Jr. High Sch. PTA, Potomac, Md., 1987-89; mem. adv. com. Appraisal Standards Bd., 1989-91. Mem. Am. Econ. Assn., Am. Fin. Assn., Nat. Soc. Real Estate Fin. (cert.), Omicron Delta Epsilon. Avocation: fishing. Office: Fed Deposti Ins Corp 550 17th St NW Washington DC 20429-0001

SEELIN, JUDITH LEE, rehabilitation specialist; b. Bklyn., Feb. 22, 1941; d. Sidney and Helene Agnes (Minkowitz) S.; m. Mel Schwartz, Sept. 30, 1965 (div. 1983); children: Jeffrey, Robin; m. Arnold Seelin, Oct. 16, 1983. AAS, SUNY, Farmingdale, 1972; BSN, SUNY, Stony Brook, 1973. CRRN, CIRS, CCM. Staff nurse surg. unit L.I. Jewish Med. Ctr., New Hyde Park, N.Y., 1962-67; DON Home Health Aids, Inc., Hempstead, N.Y., 1973-78, Able Home Health Care, Wantagh, N.Y., 1978-84; nursing adminstr. Aides at Home, Inc., Hicksville, N.Y., 1984-86; asst. ADON Savana Cay Manor, Port Saint Lucie, Fla., 1986; Fla. state supr. CCM, Hollywood, Fla., 1987-93; med. team leader Resource Opportunities, Fort Lauderdale, Fla., 1993-95; ind. med. case mgr., 1993-95; W.C. resource nurse Humana Health Care Plan, Mirama, Fla., 1995—; spkr. Am. Inst. Med. Law; adv. bd. mem. Whithal, Boca Raton. Mem. AARN, CMSA. Avocations: painting, sculpting, reading, antiquing. Home: 14090 Fair Isle Dr Delray Beach FL 33446-3395

SEELY, JAMES MICHAEL, consultant, retired naval officer, small business owner; b. Los Angeles, Oct. 15, 1932; s. Louis K. and Mary Edith (Gleason) S.; m. Gail Margaret Deverman, July 13, 1957; children: Ted Andrew, Nina Marie. BS, UCLA, 1955; MS, George Washington U., 1976. Commd. ensign USN, 1955, advanced through grades to rear adm.; student pilot, 1955-56, attack pilot, 1957-75; comdg. officer Attack Squadron 165, Naval Air Sta. Whidbey Island, Wash., 1972-73; comdr. Carrier Air Wing 9, Naval Air Sta. Lemoore, Calif., 1974-75; comdg. officer U.S. Naval Air Sta., Whidbey Island, 1977-79; dep. dir. DCNO (Air Warfare, OP-50), Pentagon, Washington, 1979-82; dir. Joint Analysis Directorate, Office Joint Chiefs Staff, Washington, 1982-84; comdr. Medium Attack Tactical Electronic Warfare Wing, Pacific Fleet, Naval Air Sta. Whidbey Island, 1984-86; dir. DCNO (Air Warfare, OP-50), Pentagon, 1986-88; dep. comptr. of Navy, Pentagon, 1988-89; ret. Pentagon, 1989; with RRP Def. Cons. Assocs., Arlington, Va., 1989—; Vietnam combat duty with Attack Squadrons 93, 152, 165 flying from aircraft carriers USS Enterprise, Hancock, Bon Homme Richard, Shangri-La and Constellation; 447 combat missions. Decorated Defense Superior Service, Legion of Merit (2), D.F.C. (4), Bronze Star, Air Medal (43). Mem. Naval Inst., Tailhook Assn., Assn. Naval Aviation, Marine Corps Aviation Assn., Red River Valley Fighter Pilots Assn., Navy League, Am. Legion, Am. Def. Preparedness Assn., Assn. Old Crows. Republican. Roman Catholic. Avocations: sports, automobiles. Home: 5730 Shropshire Ct Alexandria VA 22315-4027 Office: RRP Def Cons Assocs 2171 Crystal Dr Arlington VA 22202-3705

SEELY, JOHN F., dean. Dean faculty medicine U. Ottawa, Ont., Can. Office: U Ottawa, Faculty Medicine, 451 Smyth Rd, Ottawa, ON Canada K1H 8M5*

SEELY, ROBERT DANIEL, physician, medical educator; b. Woodmere, N.Y., Nov. 4, 1923; s. Harry and Ethel (Weil) S.; m. Marcia Ann Wells, June 19, 1953; children: Ellen Wells, Anne Wells. B.S., NYU, 1943; M.D., Columbia U., 1946. Intern Mt. Sinai Hosp., N.Y.C., 1946-47, asst. resident in medicine, 1950-51, resident in pathology, 1951-52, chief resident in medicine, 1952-53; Sara Welt fellow in cardiovascular research Presbyn. Hosp., N.Y.C., 1953-54; instr. dept. physiology, cardiovascular research Western Res. U., Cleve., 1947-48; chief rheumatic heart disease clinic Mt. Sinai Hosp., N.Y.C., 1961-70, attending physician medicine and cardiology, 1978—, chief of service dept. medicine, 1979—, clin. prof. medicine, cardiology Sch. Medicine, 1970—; practice medicine specializing in cardiovascular disease N.Y.C., 1953—. Contbr. articles to profl. jours. Served to capt. M.C. AUS, 1948-50. Recipient Solomon Berson Meml. award Mt. Sinai Hosp., 1977. Fellow Am. Coll. Cardiology, ACP; mem. N.Y. Heart Assn., AMA, N.Y. County Med. Soc., Soc. Cert. Internists N.Y., Phi Beta Kappa, Alpha Omega Alpha, Beta Lambda Sigma. Office: 994 5th Ave New York NY 10028-0100

SEELY, ROBERT FLEMING, lawyer; b. Englewood, N.J., June 21, 1944; s. Harry Gedney and Katharine Elizabeth (Fleming) S.; m. Rebeccah S., June 19, 1976; 1 child, Edward Smith. BA, Princeton U., 1966; JD, Cornell U., 1975. Bar: N.Y. 1976, D.C. 1988, Ill. 1990. Atty. U.S. Customs Svc. Hdqtrs., Washington, 1975-79, U.S. Dept. Commerce, Washington, 1980-87; assoc. Miller & Blume, Washington, 1987-88; ptnr. Katten, Muchin & Zavis, Chgo., 1989—. 1st lt. U.S. Army, 1968-71, Korea. Mem. ABA, Chgo. Bar Assn., Fed. Bar Assn., Internat. Trade Assn. of Greater Chgo. (bd. dirs. 1990—). Office: Katten Muchin & Zavis 525 W Monroe St Ste 1600 Chicago IL 60661-3629*

SEEMAN, MELVIN, sociologist, educator; b. Balt., Feb. 5, 1918; s. Morris and Sophie (Kostman) S.; m. Alice Ruth Zerbola, June 30, 1944; children—Teresa E., Paul D. B.A., Johns Hopkins U., 1944; Ph.D., Ohio State U., 1947. Asst. prof. sociology Ohio State U., 1947-52, assoc. prof., 1953-59; prof. UCLA, 1959-88, prof. emeritus, 1988—. Mem. Am. Sociol. Assn. Home: 21532 Paseo Serra St Malibu CA 90265-5112 Office: Dept Sociology UCLA 405 Hilgard Ave Los Angeles CA 90024-1301

SEESSEL, ADAM H., writer, journalist; b. Hopewell, N.J., May 18, 1964; s. Thomas Vining and Diane (Weiner) S.; m. Sadie Bridger, May 4, 1991. BA in Religion summa cum laude, Dartmouth Coll., 1985. Staff writer The News and Observer, Raleigh, N.C., 1985-89, The Independent, Raleigh, Durham, N.C., 1989-91; writer Rochester, N.Y., 1991-94, Hoboken, N.J., 1995—. Recipient George Polk award L.I. U., 1991. Mem. The Authors Guild, Phi Beta Kappa. Democrat. Avocations: baseball, soccer, rugby, poetry. Home: 422 Hudson St Apt #1 Hoboken NJ 07030

SEESSEL, THOMAS VINING, nonprofit organization executive; b. Chattanooga, Nov. 16, 1937; s. Ben Adolph and Dorothy Anne (Parham) S.; m. Diane Farnham Wiener, Jan. 26, 1963; children: Adam Humphreys, Jessica Parham, Ben Vining. BA, Dartmouth Coll., 1959; MPA, Princeton U., 1964. Asst. to dir. Community Progress, Inc., New Haven, 1964-67; exec. dir. N.J. Housing Fin. Agy., Trenton, 1967-70; sr. program officer The Ford Found., N.Y.C., 1970-74; dep. commr. N.J. Dept. Environ. Protection, Trenton, 1974-75; exec. v.p. Manpower Demonstration Res. Corp., N.Y.C., 1975-78; owner, mgmt. cons. T.V. Seessel Assocs., Hopewell, N.J., 1979-85; exec. dir. Nat. Coun. on Alcoholism, N.Y.C., 1985-88, pres., 1988; pres. Seedco, N.Y.C., 1988—, treas., 1986-88; vis. lectr. Cornell U., Ithaca, N.Y., 1966-68, Princeton (N.J.) U., 1968-69; adj. prof. New Sch. Social Rsch., N.Y.C., 1978-79; mem. tech. adv. com. Adolescent Sch.-based Health Care Svcs. program Robert Wood Johnson Found., Princeton, 1986-91, and nat. adv. com. "Fighting Back" program to combat substance abuse, 1989—. Author numerous articles, speeches and reports on alcoholism, and other health topics and community devel. Mem. bd. edn. Hopewell Valley Regional Sch. Dist., Pennington, N.J., 1971-74; trustee Thomas Edison Coll. N.J., 1979-92, chmn. bd. dirs., 1987-89; bd. trustees Thomas Edison Coll. N.J. Found., 1992—; bd. dirs. Bus. Employment Found., Paterson, N.J., 1979-87, Freedom Inst., N.Y.C., 1988-91, Nat. Neighborhood Coalition, 1995—; bd. dirs. Ctr. for Sci. in Pub. Interest, 1990-93, treas., 1991-93. Assoc. fellow Branford Coll., Yale U., 1965-70. Mem. Princeton Grad. Alumni (chmn. nominating and awards com. 1978-80), Phi Beta Kappa. Democrat. Club: N.Y. Princeton. Office: Seedco 915 Broadway New York NY 10010-7106

SEEVERS, CHARLES JUNIOR, foundation executive, psychologist; b. Seward, Nebr., May 13, 1925; s. Ferdinand Carl and Hilda Anna (Schultz) S.; m. Florine Marie Viets, June 5, 1949 (dec. 1991); children: Steven, Roger, Sandra, Jane; m. Ruth Ann Krohn Rehschuh, Aug. 28, 1993. AA, St. John's Coll., 1945; BA, Concordia Sem., St. Louis, 1949; MS magna cum laude, St. Francis Coll., Ft. Wayne, Ind., 1965, postgrad., 1966; PhD, U. Notre Dame, 1970. Ordained to ministry Lutheran Ch., 1949; asst. pastor Immanuel Luth. Ch., Balt., 1949-50; pastor St. Paul's Luth. Ch., Kingsville, Md., 1950-57, Bethlehem Luth. Ch., Richmond, Va., 1957-63; sr. pastor Zion Luth. Ch., Ft. Wayne, 1963-66; exec. dir. Assn. for Disabled of Elkhart County, Ind., 1966-82; exec. dir. Aux Chandelles Found., 1982-93, exec. dir. emeritus, 1993; adj. prof. psychology and spl. edn. Ind. U., South Bend, 1972-76; speaker Pres.'s Com. on Mental Retardation 3d Internat. Congress on Prevention of Mental Retardation, Buenos Aries, Argentina, 1986; apptd. del. health psychologist Ind. People to People Internat. Study Mission to Russia, People's Republic China, 1987; l cons. Kans. Developmental Disabilities Div., 1972-79, Accreditation Council for Facilities for the Mentally Retarded, Chgo., 1972-80; cons. on assessment of developmentally disabled in various states, 1974—, cons. Leicester, Eng., 1974-75; mem. Ind. Gov.'s Planning and Adv. Bd. for Mental Retardation and Other Developmental Disabilities, 1973-78, chmn., 1976-78; mem. Gov.'s Preventive Health and Handicap Services Coordination Study Commn., 1987-90, Devel. Disabilities Planning Council on Child Health, 1987-90, No. Ind. Health Systems Agy. Central Sub-Area Adv. Council, 1976-78, vice chmn., 1977-78; cons. psychonutrition, 1981-93, emeritus 1993—; regional psychologist Youth for Understanding, 1985-87. Contbr. articles to profl. publs. Chmn. United Way Execs., Elkhart, 1971-73; bd. dirs. Mill Neck Manor Sch. for the Deaf, L.I., N.Y., 1950-57, Assn. for Retarded Citizens Ind., 1983-89, No. Ind. Health Found., 1981-87; charter mem. Area Vocat. Edn. Adv. Bd., 1973-76; mem. state adv. bd. Prevention: To Be Born Well Curriculum Project, 1977-80; mem. residential services and facilities com. Nat. Assn. Retarded Citizens, 1973-78; mem. No. Ind. Developmental Disabilities Adv. Council, 1977-81, chmn., 1980-81; mem. Dept. Mental Health Multi-Disciplinary Screening Team, 1983-84; mem. bd. teenage parents adv. bd. Elkhart Community Schs., 1984-87; chmn. state policy Ind. Healthy Mothers/Healthy Babies Coalition, 1986-87; hon. chmn. Michiana Fetal Alcohol Syndrome Week, 1986. Recipient United Way Exec. of Yr. award, 1979; Eli Lilly fellow in religion and mental health Ind. U. Med. Center, Indpls., 1964-65; Recipient Liberty Bell award Elkhart Bar Assn., 1974, Outstanding Kindness award Elkhart County Assn. for Retarded, 1974, Concerned for Mankind in Our Nation award Jaycees, 1975, State of Ind. Citizen Participation award Gov.'s Voluntary Action Program, Sagamore of Wabash award Gov. of State of Ind., 1990; elected to Wall of Fame Assn. for Disbaled Elkhart County, Ind., 1985. Mem. Nat. Conf. Execs. of Assns. for Retarded Children (chmn. 1974-75), Am. Psychol. Assn., Soc. Behavioral Medicine, Am. Pub. Health Assn., Nat. Fedn. Parents for Drug Free Youth, Luth. Acad. for Scholarship, Internat. Psychol. Assn., United Cerebral Palsy Am., Luth. Human Relations Assn. Am., Ctr. for Sci. in Pub. Interest, Am. Orthopsychiat. Assn., Elkhart C. of C. (bd. dirs. 1974-76), Am. Council on Drug Edn., Assn. Birth Defect Children, Healthy Mothers/Healthy Babies Coalition, Internat. Council Psychologists. Lodge: Rotary (v.p. 1986, chmn. world affairs conf. dist. 654, 1985-87, pres.-elect 1987-88, gen. chmn. dist. assembly conf. 1986-87, Gov's. award 1987, Chmn. of Yr. 1987). Home: 2103 Norwood Dr Mountain Home AR 72653 *I believe I am a uniquely individual child of God, born to fulfill a purpose for which God continues to give me life each new day. We are joined together in a common effort to fulfill the purpose for which each of us is given life.*

SEFCIK, JOHN DELBERT, financial services executive; b. Temple, Tex., Jan. 21, 1921; s. John J. and Annie (Chaloupka) S.; m. Norma Marie Kuzel, May 22, 1942 (div. Sept. 1985); children: John D. Jr., Camille Freitas; m. Christine Gajdica Goodlett, Dec. 13, 1987. Student, Temple Jr. Coll., 1938-39; acctg. grad., Four C. Bus. Coll., 1948-50; A in Mgmt., Brewster Coll., 1956-59; student, So. Meth. U., 1958-70; grad., Civil Def. Staff Coll., Assn. Logistics Ex Sch., Command & Gen. Staff Coll., Indsl. Coll. Armed Forces, Arty. and Civil Affairs Mil. Govt. Sch. Cert. Army logistician. Placement mgr., tax auditor Tex. Employment Commn., 1945-51; with Phoenix Life Ins. Co., 1951-53; mktg. and dist. mgr. Armour Pharm. Co., Inc., 1953-86; regional mgr. ins. and investments, real estate broker Primerica Fin. Svcs., 1987-96. Bd. dirs., gen. chmn. 1st Dallas Mil. Ball, 1965, past pres., 1992-93, mem. to date. Master sgt. U.S. Army, 1940-45; col. USAR, 1948-78. Decorated Legion of Merit, Bronze Star. Mem. 102d Inf. Divsn. Assn. (life, pres., v.p., bd. dirs. , reunion gen. chmn. 1983-89), Res. Officers Assn. (life, nat. chmn. civil preparedness com. 1989-94, numerous other coms., Brigade of Vols., Wall of Gold, Waco chpt. pres. 1951-53, Dallas chpt. pres. 1963-65, Army Tex. dept. v.p. 1863-67, 90th divsn. arty. chpt. pres. 1965-66, pres. 1967-68, Tex. dept. nat. councilman 1968-69, Tex. ROA Conv. Gen. chmn. 1981), Mil. Order World Wars (life), Am. Legion (life), Ret. Officers Assn. (life), 2d INF Indian Head Divsn. Assn., KC (4th degree, Sir Knight Abram J. Ryan Assembly Coun. No 799).

SEFF, LESLIE S., securities trader; b. N.Y.C., Oct. 3, 1950; s. Fredric and Dorothy (Jacobson) S.; children: Dylan, Cortney, Blake, Matthew. BBA in Fin. cum laude with high honors, Hofstra U., Hempstead, N.Y., 1971; MBA, Baruch Coll., N.Y.C., 1980. Co-mgr. Muller & Co., N.Y.C., 1974-88; dir. over-the-counter trading Gruntal & Co., N.Y.C., 1988-92; dir. over-the-counter trading dept. Wagner Stott Mercator Ptnrs., N.Y.C., 1992—. Trustee Saddle River (N.J.) Recreation Commn., 1988; active Rep. Eagles, Washington, 1986-87. allied mem. N.Y. Stock Exch. Avocations: tennis, bicycling, playing the harmonica. Office: Wagner Stott Mercator Ptnrs 14 Wall St New York NY 10005-2101

SEFFRIN, JOHN REESE, medical society executive; b. Hagerstown, Ind., May 19, 1944; s. Theodore H. and Mary Ellen (Reese) S.; m. Carole Sue Washburn, Apr. 16, 1966; 1 child, Mary. BS in Edn., Ball State U., 1966; MS, U. Ill., 1967; PhD in Health Edn., Purdue U., 1970; DSc (hon.), Ball State U., 1994. Asst. prof. health edn. Purdue U., West Lafayette, Ind., 1970-76; asso. prof. Purdue U., 1976-79; prof., chmn. dept. applied health sci. Ind. U., Bloomington, 1979-92; chief exec. officer Am. Cancer Soc., Atlanta, 1992—; cons. Ind. Dept. Public Instrn., 1979-81, ADA, 1972—; guest lectr. various public health orgns. and schs., 1970—. Contbr. numerous articles on health edn. to profl. publs.; chmn. editorial bd.: Jour. Sch. Health, 1982-85, Smoking and Health Reporter, 1983-88; mem. editorial bd.: Health Edn., 1981-85; cons. editor: Jour. ADA, 1980—. Pres. State Welfare Bd., Dept. Public Welfare, Ind., 1979-80, 83-85; treas. Midwest Nuclear Bd., 1973-76; bd. dirs. Wabash Center for the Mentally Retarded, 1970-73; chmn. community edn. com. Am. Lung Assn., 1981-83, v.p., 1986-88, nat. bd. dirs., 1980—; bd. dirs. Partnership for Prevention...of Premature Death, Disease and Disability, 1991—, Acordia Small Bus. Benefits, Inc., 1992—. Recipient Cert. of Recognition, ADA, 1975, Cert. Appreciation Surgeon Gen. of Pub. Health Svc., 1992; named Sagamore of Wabash, State of Ind., 1980, 88; Outstanding Alumnus award Ball State U., 1982. Fellow Am. Sch. Health Assn. (mem. governing coun. 1978-81, pres. 1987-88, Howe award 1991); mem. AMA, Nat. Assn. State Bds. of Edn. (commn. on the sch. community role in improving adolescent health 1989—), Assn. for Advancement Health Edn. (bd. dirs. 1989-92), Ind. Assn. Health Educators (pres. 1975-76), Ind. Family Health Coun. (dir. 1979-81, v.p. 1980-81, pres. 1981), Ind. Thoracic Soc. (mem. governing coun. 1977—), Am. Cancer Soc. (dir. Ind. Div. 1977—, chmn. nat. bd. dirs. 1989-91, dir.-at-large to nat. bd. dirs., chmn. nat. pub. edn. com., nat. v.p. 1986-87), Ind. Assn. for Health, Phys. Edn. and Recreation (pres. 1976, Cert. of Appreciation 1977, Honor award 1982), Nat. Interagy. Coun. on Smoking and Health (bd. dirs. 1979—), Phi Delta Kappa, Eta Sigma Gamma. Roman Catholic. Office: Am Cancer Soc 1599 Clifton Rd NE Atlanta GA 30329-4250

SEGAL, BERNARD GERARD, lawyer; b. N.Y.C., June 11, 1907; s. Samuel I. and Rose (Cantor) S.; m. Geraldine Rosenbaum, Oct. 22, 1933; children: Loretta Joan Segal Cohen, Richard Murry. A.B., U. Pa., 1928, LL.B., 1931, LL.D., 1969; LL.D., Franklin and Marshall Coll., 1953, Temple U., 1954, Dropsie U., 1966, Jewish Theol. Sem. Am., 1977, Vt. Law Sch., 1978, Villanova U., 1980, Georgetown U., 1983; J.S.D., Suffolk U., 1969; D.H.L., Hebrew Union Coll., 1970. Bar: Pa. 1932, D.C. 1976. Mem. faculty U. Pa., 1928-35, 45-47; Am. reporter on contracts Internat. Congress of Law, The Hague, The Netherlands, 1932; asst. dep. atty. gen. Commonwealth of Pa., 1932-33, dep. atty. gen., 1933-34; co-founder Schnader Harrison Segal & Lewis, Phila., 1935—; instr. grad. bus., govt. Am. Inst. Banking, 1936-39; chmn. Schnader Harrison Segal & Lewis, Phila., 1968-86, sr. ptnr., 1986-88, of counsel, 1988-94; mem. Bd. Law Examiners, Phila., 1940-46; chmn. Commn. Jud. and Congl. Salaries, U.S. Govt., 1953-55; mem. Atty. Gen.'s Nat. Com. to Study Antitrust Laws, 1953-55; mem. exec. com. Atty. Gen.'s Nat. Conf. on Ct. Congestion, 1958-61; mem. standing com. on rules of practice and procedure Jud. Conf. U.S., 1959-76; co-chmn. Lawyers Com. on Civil Rights Under Law, 1963-65 (Founder award, 25th Anniversary, 1988); chmn. Pa. Jud. Nominating Commn., 1964-66; mem. Nat. Citizens Com. on Community Rels., 1964-74; mem. adv. com. U.S. mission to UN, 1967-68; mem. adv. panel internat. law U.S. Dept. State, 1967-79; mem. Adminstrv. Conf. U.S., 1968-74; chmn. nat. adv. com. on legal svcs. U.S. OEO, 1968-76, chmn. exec. com., 1971-74; chmn. bd. Coun. Legal Edn. Opportunities, 1968-71; mem. Jud. Coun. Pa., 1968-71; coun. World Peace Through Law Ctr., chmn. 1st demonstration trial, Belgrade, Yugoslavia, 1971, coun., 1973-94, participant world confs., Athens, Greece, Washington, Geneva, Bangkok, Abidjan, Ivory Coast, Manila and Cairo, chmn. com. on internat. communications, world chmn. World Law Day, Madrid, 1979, Berlin, 1985; mem. U.S. Commn. on Exec., Legis. and Jud. Salaries, 1972-73, 76-77; mem. Appellate Ct. Nominating Commn., 1973-79; mem. U.S. Commn. Revision Fed. Ct. Appellate System, 1974-75; chmn. World Conf. on Peace and Violence, Jerusalem, 1979. Editor-in-chief: Pennsylvania Banking and Building and Loan Law, 3 vols., 1941; editor: The Belgrade Spaceship Trial, 1972; mem. internat. hon. bd. Ency. Judaica; contbr. articles to law revs., other publs. Life trustee, mem. exec. bd. U. Pa., 1959-77, life trustee emeritus, 1977—; emeritus mem. bd. overseers U. Pa. Law Sch., 1959—; mem. Commn. on Anti-Poverty Program for Phila., 1967-71, Bus. Leadership Organized for Cath. Schs., 1979—, Commonwealth Commn. on Bicentennial of U.S. Constn., 1986-87; chmn. bd. Coun. Advancement Legal Edn., 1972-77; coun. trustees Hebrew U. Jerusalem; bd. dirs. So. Africa Legal Svcs. and Legal Edn. Project, 1979—, NAACP Legal Def. and Ednl. Fund, Found. Fed. Bar Assn.; bd. govs. emeritus, past. v.p., past treas. Dropsie Coll.; trustee emeritus, former exec. com. Albert Einstein Med. Ctr.; trustee Phila. Martin Luther King, Jr. Ctr. Nonviolent Social Change (Drum Major award for legal justice, 1984), 1984—, Found. for the Commenoration of the U.S. Constn., 1986-88, Found. for U.S. Constn., 1988—, bd. dirs. Chapel of Four Chaplains; mem. planning commn. Miracle at Phila., 1986-87. Recipient Arthur von Briesen medal Nat. Legal Aid and Defender Assn., 1970, Nat. Human Rels. award NCCJ, 1972, Herbert Lewis Harley award, Am. Judicature Soc., 1974, World Lawyer award World Peace through Law Ctr., 1975, Judge William H. Hastie award NAACP Legal Def. Fund, 1986, Legion Honor Gold Medallion award Chapel of Four Chaplains, 1988, Nat. Civil Rights award U.S. Atty. Gen. and Lawyers Com. for Civil Rights Under Law, 1969, Ford Found. award to our Counselor on Pub. Interest, 1979, Nat. Award of Merit Fed. Adminstrv. Law Judges Conf., 1984, Pa. Bar Assn. award for Dedicated and Disting. Service, Field of Jurisprude Admin. of Justice, 1962, 10th Anniversary award Pub. Interest Law Ctr. Phila., 1984; co-recipient Nat. Neighbors Disting. Leadership in Civil Rights award, 1988, ACLU Civil Liberties award, 1991, U. Pa. Law Alumni award of Merit, 1991. Fellow Am. Coll. Trial Lawyers (pres. 1964-65), ABA (pres. 1976-78, Gold medal 1976), Inst. Jud. Adminstrn. (bd. dirs. 1968-86), Am. Bar Found. (pres. 1976-78); mem. Jewish Fed. Greater Phila. (mem. emeritus exec. com.), Pa. Bar Assn., Phila. Bar Assn. (chancellor 1952, 53), Pa. Urban Affairs Partnership, Fed. Bar Assn. (nat. coun.), Assn. of Bar of City of N.Y., D.C. Bar Assn., Am. Arbitration Assn. (former dir.), Am. Law Inst. (1st v.p. 1976-86, 2nd v.p. 1970-75, treas. 1955-69, counselor emeritus 1987—), Am. Judicature Soc. (chmn. 1958-61, bd. dirs. 1956—), Coun. Legal Edn. for Profl. Responsibility (dir.), Fed. Juc. Conf. 3d Cir. (life), World Assn. Lawyers (pres. for Ams. 1976-86), Nat. Conf. Bar Pres., Taxpayers Forum Pa. (past pres.), Allied Jewish Appeal (past pres., hon. pres.), Legal Aid Soc. Phila.)bd. dirs.), Jewish League Israel (nat. bd.), Jewish Pub. Soc. Am. (life trustee, mem. exec. com.), Jewish Family Svc. (hon. dir.), Order of Coif, Tau Epsilon Rho, Delta Sigma Rho. Republican. Clubs: Locust, Union League, Faculty, Metropolitan (Washington). Home: Philadelphian Apt 19-C-44 2401 Pennsylvania Ave Philadelphia PA 19130-3001 Office: Schnader Harrison Segal & Lewis 1600 Market St Ste 3600 Philadelphia PA 19103-4252

SEGAL, BERNARD LOUIS, physician, educator; b. Montreal, Que., Can., Feb. 13, 1929; came to U.S., 1961, naturalized, 1966; s. Irving and Fay (Schecter) S.; m. Idajane Fischman, Feb. 17, 1963; 1 dau., Jody Segal. B.Sc. cum laude, McGill U., 1950, postgrad., 1950-51, M.D., C.M. high standing, 1955. Diplomate: Am. Bd. Internal Medicine. Intern Jewish Gen Hosp., Montreal, 1955-56; resident Balt. City Hosp., 1956-57, Beth Israel Hosp., Boston, 1957-58, Georgetown Med. Center, Washington, 1958-59, St. George's Hosp., London, Eng., 1959-61; practice medicine specializing in internal medicine and cardiology Phila., 1961—; prof. medicine Med. Coll. Pa., Hahnemann U., 1996—; prof., sr. attending physician med. Hahnemann Med. Coll., Phila., 1964—; dir. Phila. Heart Inst., 1987; prof. med. Med. Coll. Pa., Hahnemann U., 1996—. Author: Auscultation of the Heart, 1965; Editor: Theory and Practice of Auscultation, 1964, Engineering in the Practice of Medicine, 1966, Your Heart, 1972, Arteriosclerosis and Coronary Heart Disease, 1972; Editorial bd.: Am. Jour. Cardiology, 1970—, Clin. Echocardiography, 1978; Contbr. numerous articles on cardiology to med. jours. Fellow ACP, Am. Coll. Cardiology (chmn. scholar-trainee com., trustee 1969-71), Am. Coll. Chest Physicians; mem. N.Y. Acad. Scis., Alpha Omega Alpha. Home: 1156 Red Rose Ln Villanova PA 19085-2121 Office: 1320 Race St Philadelphia PA 19102 also: 401 City Line Ave Ste 610 Bala Cynwyd PA 19004

SEGAL, CHARLES PAUL, classics educator, author; b. Boston, Mar. 19, 1936; s. Robert and Gladys (Barsky) S.; m. Esther Rogers, Dec. 20, 1961 (div. June, 1979); children: Joshua H., Thaddeus G.; m. Nancy Ann Jones, Jan. 9, 1988; 1 child, Cora M. A.B., Harvard U., 1957, Ph.D., 1961; A.M. (hon.), Brown U., 1969. teaching fellow, classics tutor Harvard U., Cambridge, Mass., 1959-61, instr., 1963-64; asst. to assoc. prof. classics U. Pa., Phila., 1964-67; assoc. prof. to prof. Brown U., Providence, 1968-78; prof. classics and comparative lit., 1978-86; chmn. classics dept., 1978-81; Benedict prof. classics, prof. comparative lit., 1980-86; prof. classics, comparative lit. Princeton U., 1987-90; prof. Greek and Latin, Harvard U., Cambridge, Mass., 1990-96, Walter C. Klein Prof. of the Classics, 1996—. chmn. classics grad. studies U. Pa., 1967; jr. fellow Ctr. for Hellenic Studies, 1967-68; vis. prof. Intercollegiate Ctr. for Classical Studies, Rome, 1970-72; vis. prof. Brandeis U., 1974; vis. dir. Ecole des Hautes Etudes, Paris, 1975-76; Fulbright exchange lectr. U. Melbourne, Australia, 1978; vis. prof. Greek Columbia U., N.Y.C., 1979; participant 1st and 2d Soviet/Am. Semiotics Colloquia, Am. Council Learned Socs./USSR Acad. Sci., 1980, 83; cons. in field; mem. jury Classical Sch. Am. Acad. Rome, 1972-74, resident in classics, spring 1986; mem. exec. council Ctr. Semiotics, Brown U., 1979-85; chmn. curriculum revision com. Brown U., 1982-84. Author: Landscape in Ovid's Metamorphoses, 1969, The Theme of Mutilation in the Iliad, 1971, Tragedy and Civilization: An Interpretation of Sophocles, 1981, Poetry and Myth in Ancient Pastoral: Essays on Theocritus and Virgil, 1981, Dionysiac Poetics and Euripides' Bacchae, 1982, Pindar's Mythmaking, 1986; Language and Desire in Seneca's Phaedra, 1986; Interpreting Greek Tragedy, 1986, La Musique du Sphinx, 1987, Orpheus: The Myth of the Poet, 1989, Italian translation 1995, Lucretius on Death and Anxiety, 1990, Ovidio e la poesia del mito, 1991, Oedipus Tyrannus: Tragic Heroism and the Limits of Knowledge, 1993, Euripides and the Poetics of Sorrow, 1993, Singers, Heroes and God in the Odyssey, 1994, Sophocles' Tragic World, 1995; editor: The Heroic Paradox, 1982, The Rhetoric of Imitation, 1986, Roads to Paradise: Reading the Lives of the Early Saints, 1987; editorial bd. Am. Jour. Semiotics, 1985, Scholars Press, 1982-90, Helios, 1984—, MD, 1985—, Lexis, 1987—, Harvard Studies in Classical Philology, 1994—; contbr. articles to profl. jours. Am. Council Learned Socs. fellow, 1975; NEH grantee, 1977, fellow 1985-86; Guggenheim fellow, 1981-82; sr. fellow Ctr. Hellenic Studies, 1987-92; fellow Ctr. for Advanced Study in Behavioral Scis., 1989-90, fellow Nat. Humanities Center, 1993-94; recipient Prix de Rome Am. Acad. in Rome, 1961-63. Fellow Am. Acad. Arts and Scis.; mem. Am. Philol. Assn. (bd. dirs. 1982-86, pres. 1994), Societa Italiana per lo Studio dell' Antichita Classica (hon.), Virgilian Soc., Classical Assn. New Eng., Internat. Ovid Soc. Office: Harvard U Dept Classics 319 Boylston Hall Cambridge MA 02138

SEGAL, DONALD E., lawyer; b. Houston, Nov. 13, 1947. BA with honors, Brandeis U., 1969; JD, Boston Coll., 1972. Bar: Mass. 1972, D.C. 1973, U.S. Supreme Ct. 1976, U.S. Dist. Ct. (D.C. dist.) 1976. Assoc. chief counsel FDA, Washington, 1979-91; ptnr. Baker & Hostetler, Washington, 1991-93, Akin, Gump, Strauss, Hauer & Feld, Washington, 1993—. Editor law review; mem. Law Rev. Boston Coll. Mem. ABA, FBA, Food and Drug Inst. Office: Akin Gump Ste 1100 1333 New Hampshire Ave NW Washington DC 20036-1500

SEGAL, GEORGE, actor; b. N.Y.C., Feb. 13, 1934; m. Linda Segal. BA, Columbia U., 1955. Actor: (films) The Last Married Couple in America, The Knack, 1961, The Young Doctors, 1961, The Longest Day, 1962, Act One, 1963, The New Interns, 1964, Invitation to a Gunfighter, 1964, Who's Afraid of Virginia Woolf?, 1965, King Rat, 1965, Ship of Fools, 1965, The Lost Command, 1966, The Quiller Memorandum, 1966, The St. Valentines Day Massacre, 1967, Bye Bye Braverman, 1968, No Way To Treat A Lady, 1968, The Southern Star, 1969, The Bridge at Remagen, 1969, The Girl Who Couldn't Say No, 1969, Loving, 1970, The Owl and the Pussycat, 1970, Where's Poppa?, 1970, Born To Win, 1971, The Hot Rock, 1972, A Touch of Class, 1973, Blume in Love, 1973, The Terminal Man, 1974, California Split, 1974, Russian Roulette, 1975, Blackbird, 1975, Duchess and Dirt Water Fox, 1976, Fun With Dick and Jane, 1977, Rollercoaster, 1977, Who Is Killing The Great Chefs of Europe?, 1978, Lost and Found, 1979, Carbon Copy, 1981, Stick, 1985, All's Fair, Look Who's Talking, 1989, For the Boys, 1991, Me, Myself, and I, 1992, Look Who's Talking Now, 1993, (TV movies) including Death of a Salesman, The Desperate Hours, Of Mice and Men, 1981, The Cold Room, 1984, The Zany Adventures of Robin Hood, 1984, Not My Kid, 1985, Many Happy Returns, 1986, Killing 'em Softly, 1986, Of Mice and Men, Trackdown: Finding the Goodbar Killer, 1983, Four Minute Mile, (play) Henceforward, 1987, others; TV series: Murphy's Law, 1988. Recipient Jewish Cultural Achievement award, 1990. Office: Care Ken Starr Star & Co 350 Park Ave New York NY 10022-6022*

SEGAL, GEORGE, sculptor; b. N.Y.C., Nov. 26, 1924; s. Jacob and Sophie (Gerstenfeld) S.; m. Helen Steinberg, Apr. 7, 1946; children—Jeffrey, Rena. BS in Art Edn., N.Y. U., 1950; MFA, Rutgers U., 1963, PhD in Fine Art (hon.), 1970; PhD in Fine Art (hon.), SUNY, Purchase, 1992. One man shows include Hansa Gallery, N.Y.C., 1956-59, Rutgers U., 1958, 63, Green Gallery, N.Y.C., 1960-62, 64, Sonnabend Gallery, Paris, 1963, Schmela Gallery Dusseldorf, 1963, Janis Gallery, N.Y.C., 1965, 67, 68, 70, 71, 73-74, 77, 78, 80, 82, 84, 88, 89, 91, 93, Mus. Contemporary Art, Chgo., 1968, Galerie Speyer, Paris, 1969, 71, Princeton U., 1969, Western Gallery Western Wash. State Coll., 1970, Onnasch Galerie, Cologne, 1971, also European mus. tour, 1971-73, U. Wis., Milw., 1973, Onnasch Galerie, Switzerland, 1974, Andre Emmerich, Zurich, 1975, Dartmouth Coll., 1975, Inst. Contemporary Art, 1976, Nina Freudenheim Gallery, Buffalo, 1976, Art Assn. Newport, R.I., 1976, Suzette Schochet Gallery, 1976, Santa Barbara Mus. Art, 1976, Whitney Mus. Am. Art, N.Y.C., 1979, Jacksonville Art Mus., 1982, U. Miami, 1983, Jewish Mus., N.Y.C., Makler Gallery, Phila., 1983, 84, Galleria Il Ponte, Rome, 1984, Evelyn Aimis Fine Art, Toronto, 1984, Galerie Esperanza, Toronto, 1985, 87, Galerie Brusberg, Berlin, 1986, Richard Gray Gallery, Chgo., 1987, Riva Yares Gallery, Scottsdale, Ariz., 1988, Casino Knokke, Belgium, 1989, Galerie Tokoro, Tokyo, 1990, Marguiles/Taplin Gallery, Bay Harbor, Fla., 1990, Art Gallery U. Rochester, N.Y., 1991; retrospective group shows include Sao Paulo Bienal, Janis Gallery, Jewish Mus., N.Y.C., Carnegie Internat., Whitney Mus., others; represented in permanent collections including Mus. Modern Art, Whitney Mus., Mint Mus., Charlotte, N.C., Albright-Knox Mus., Mus. Modern Art, Stockholm, Sweden, Met. Mus. Art, N.Y.C., Guggenheim Mus., N.Y.C., Bklyn. Mus., Art Inst. Chgo., Cleve. Mus. Art, Detroit Mus. Art, Modern Art Mus., Ft. Worth, Newark Mus., Weisman Mus. Contemporary Art, L.A., Pa. Acad. Fine Arts, Phila., Carnegie Mus. Art, Pitts., Portland (Oreg.) Mus. Art, San Francisco Mus. Modern Art, Hirschorn Mus. & Sculpture Garden, Washington, Libr. Congress, Washington, Nat. Gallery Art, Washington, Nat. Mus. Am. Art, Washington, Nat. Portrait Gallery, Washington, Musee d'Art Contemporain, Montreal, Nat. Gallery Art, Ottawa, Can., Art Gallery Ontario, Can., Vancouver Art Gallery, Can., Tamayo Mus., Mexico, Museo de Arte Contemporaneo, Caracas, Venezuela, Musees Royaux des Beaux-Arts, Brussels, Art Mus. of Atenaeum, Helsinki, Finland, Centre Nat. d'Art Contemporain, Paris, Neue Galerie der Stadt Aachen, Germany, Kolnisches Stadtsmuseum, Cologne, Germany, Stadtische Kunsthalle Mannheim, Germany, Staatsgalerie Moderner Kunst, Munich, Germany, Museum Boymans-van Beuningen, The Netherlands, Mus. Modern Art, Teheran, Iran, Israel Mus., Jerusalem, Kunsthaus Zurich, Switzerland, Fukuoka Mcpl. Mus. Art, Japan, Hiroshima (Japan) City Mus. Contemporary Art, Mus. Modern Art, Seibu Takanawa, Karuizawa, Japan, Nat. Mus. Art, Osaka, Japan, Tokyo Ctrl. Mus., Shiga Mus. Art, Japan, and numerous others. Recipient 1st prize Art Inst. Chgo., 1966, award Walter H. Gutman Found., 1962. Office: care Sidney Janis Gallery 110 W 57th St New York NY 10019-3319

SEGAL, GERALDINE ROSENBAUM, sociologist; b. Phila., Aug. 26, 1908; d. Harry and Mena (Hamburg) Rosenbaum; m. Bernard Gerard Segal, Oct. 22, 1933; children: Loretta Joan Cohen, Richard Murry. BS in Edn., U. Pa., 1930, MA in Human Rels., 1963, PhD in Sociology, 1978; MS in Libr. Sci., Drexel U., 1968; Dr. Letters (Hon.), Franklin & Marshall Coll., 1990. Social worker County Relief Bd., Phila., 1931-35; sociologist, Phila., 1935—; cons. and lectr. in field. Author: In Any Fight Some Fall, 1975; Blacks in the Law, 1983. Bd. dirs. NCCJ, 1937-47, 82—, sec., 1983-91; bd. overseers U. Pa. Sch. Social Work, 1983—; bd. dirs., Juvenile Law Ctr., 1984—; chair Phila. Tutorial Project, 1966-68; 1st v.p. U. Pa. Alumnae Assn., 1967-70. Co-recipient Nat. Neighbors Disting. Leadership in Civil Rights award, 1988; recipient Drum Major award for Human Rights, Phila. Martin Luther King, Jr. Assn. for Nonviolence, 1990, Brotherhood Sisterhood award NCCJ, 1994. Democrat. Jewish. Home: 2401 Pennsylvania Ave Apt 19-C-44 Philadelphia PA 19130-3001

SEGAL, GORDON I., retail executive; b. Chgo., Dec. 27, 1938; s. Zalman and Ida (Glick) S.; m. Carole Browe, June 18, 1961; children: Christopher, Katherine, Robert. BS in Bus., Northwestern U., 1960. Founder, pres. Crate & Barrel, Chgo., 1962—; bd. dirs. Continental Bank, Chgo., L. Karp & Sons, Elk Grove Village, Ill., Bio-Logic Systems, Wheeling, Ill. Trustee Northwestern U., Evanston, Ill., 1990, Golden Apple Found., Chgo., 1988, Sta. WTTW-TV, Chgo., 1990, Chgo. Hist. Soc., 1991, Children's Meml. Hosp., Chgo., 1990. Named Man of Yr. City of Hope, 1984; recipient Alumni Merit award Northwestern U., 1988, Brotherhood award Nat. Coun. Christians & Jews, 1990, Steuart Henderson Britt award Am. Mktg. Assn., 1991. Mem. Chgo. Pres. Orgn., Chief Execs. Orgn., World Bus. Coun., The Comml. Club, Econ. Club of Chgo. Office: Crate & Barrel 725 Landwehr Rd Northbrook IL 60062-2349*

SEGAL, HELENE R., editor; b. L.A., Jan. 31, 1955; d. Alan and Lila E. Segal; m. David Scott Wright, May 6, 1979. Student, Calif. State U., Fullerton, 1973-75; BA in English, U. Calif., Santa Barbara, 1978. Library asst. ABC-CLIO, Santa Barbara, 1979-80, editorial asst., 1980-81, asst. editor, 1981-83; mng. editor ABC POL SCI, ABC-CLIO, Santa Barbara, 1983—. Mem. Am. Polit. Sci. Assn., Current World Leaders (adv. bd. 1989—). Avocations: reading, collecting, swimming. Home: 142 La Vista Grande Santa Barbara CA 93103-2817 Office: ABC-CLIO 130 Cremona Dr Santa Barbara CA 93117-3075

SEGAL, IRVING EZRA, mathematics educator; b. N.Y.C., Sept. 13, 1918; s. Aaron and Fannie Segal; m. Osa Skotting, 1955 (div. 1977); children: William, Andrew, Karen; m. Martha Fox., 1985; 1 child, Miriam Elizabeth. A.B., Princeton U., 1937; Ph.D., Yale U., 1940. Instr. Harvard U., 1941; research asst. Princeton U., 1941-42, assoc., 1942-43; asst. to O. Veblen, Inst. for Advanced Study, 1945-46; asst. prof. to prof. U. Chgo., 1948-60; prof. MIT, Cambridge, 1960—; vis. assoc. prof. Columbia U., 1953-54; vis. fellow Insts. Math. and Theoretical Physics, Copenhagen, 1958-59; vis. prof. Sorbonne, Paris, France, 1965, U. Lund, Sweden, 1971, Coll. de France, 1977. Author: Mathematical Problems of Relativistic Physics, 1963, (with R.A. Kunze) Integrals and Operators, 1968, Mathematical Cosmology and Extragalactic Astronomy, 1976, (with J.C. Baez and Z. Zhou) Introduction to Algebraic and Constructive Quantum Field Theory, 1992; editor: (with W.T. Martin) Analysis in Function Space, 1964, (with Roe Goodman) Mathematical Theory of Elementary Particles, 1988; contbr. articles to profl. jours. Served with AUS, 1943-45. Recipient Humboldt award, Germany, 1982-83; Guggenheim fellow, 1947, 51-52, 67-68. Mem. Am. Math. Soc., Am. Phys. Soc., Am. Acad. Arts and Sci., Royal Danish Acad. Scis., Am. Astron. Soc., Nat. Acad. Sci. Home: 25 Moon Hill Rd Lexington MA 02173-6139 Office: MIT Rm 2-244 Cambridge MA 02139

SEGAL, IRVING RANDALL, lawyer; b. Allentown, Pa., Oct. 15, 1914; s. Samuel I. and Rose (Kantor) S.; m. Eleanor F. Smolens, Dec. 26, 1943; children: Betsy A. Segal Carter, Kathy J., Robert J. BA, U. Pa., 1935; LLB, 1938. Bar: Pa. 1938. Instr. polit. sci. U. Pa., 1938-42; law clk. Ct. Common Pleas No. 4, Phila. County, Pa., 1938-39; assoc. Schnader, Harrison, Segal & Lewis, Phila., 1939-49, ptnr., 1949-92, sr. counsel, 1993—; Permanent mem. Jud. Conf. 3d Circuit U.S. Ct. Appeals; regional rationing atty. OPA, 1942. V.p. Nat. Kidney Disease Found., 1954-59, hon. life del., 1959-64; pres. Nephrosis Found., Phila., 1953-56; bd. mgrs. Woman's Hosp. Phila., 1957-64, v.p., 1962-63; bd. Jewish Edn., Phila., 1948-72; trustee YMHA, YWHA, 1954-58. Served to capt. Judge Adv. Gen. Dept. AUS, 1942-46. Decorated Mil. Commendation medal. Fellow Am. Coll. Trial Lawyers (regent 1976-79, sec. 1979-80); mem. ABA (corrections com. 1980-87, jud. selection tenure and compensation com. 1988-93), Pa. Bar Assn., Phila. Bar Assn. (chmn. sr. lawyers), Am. Law Inst., Am. Bar Found., Phila. Bar Found., Am. Judicature Soc., World Peace Through Law, Am. Acad. Polit. and Social Sci., Order of Coif, Phi Beta Kappa, Phi Gamma Mu (pres., 1934-35), Delta Sigma Rho. Jewish (dir., v.p. temple). Clubs: Phila. Lawyers, Art Alliance, Locust, Army and Navy of Washington. Home: 210 W Rittenhouse Sq Apt 2306 Philadelphia PA 19103-5726

SEGAL, JACK, mathematics educator; b. Phila., May 9, 1934; s. Morris and Rose (Novin) S.; m. Arlene Stern, Dec. 18, 1955; children: Gregory, Sharon. B.S., U. Miami, 1955, M.S., 1957; Ph.D., U. Ga., 1960. Instr. math. U. Wash., Seattle, 1960-61; asst. prof. U. Wash., 1961-65, assoc. prof., 1965-70, prof., 1970—, chmn. dept., 1975-78. Author: Lecture Notes in Mathematics, 1978, Shape Theory, 1982. NSF postdoctoral fellow Inst. Advanced Study, Princeton, N.J., 1963-64; Fulbright fellow U. Zagreb, Croatia, 1969-70, U. Coll. London hon. rsch. fellow, 1988; Nat. Acad. Sci. exch. prof. U. Zagreb, Croatia, 1979-80. Mem. Am. Math. Soc. Home: 8711 25th Pl NE Seattle WA 98115-3416 Office: U Washington Dept Mathematics Seattle WA 98195

SEGAL, JOAN SMYTH, library association executive, consultant, organization adminstrator; b. Bklyn., Sept. 14, 1930; d. John Patrick and Anna Catherine (Green) Smyth; m. William Segal, June 25, 1955; children: Harold M., Nora A. BA, Douglass Coll., Rutgers U., 1951; MS in LS, Columbia U., 1955; PhD, U. Colo., 1978. Cert. assn. exec., 1988. Librarian, Math Inst., NYU, 1955-58, Western Interstate Commn. for Higher Edn., Boulder, Colo., 1970-76; libr. cons., Boulder, 1976-78; resource sharing program mgr. Bibliog. Ctr. for Rsch., Denver, 1978-80, exec. dir., 1980-84; exec. dir. Assn. of Coll. and Rsch. Librs., ALA, Chgo., 1984-90; assoc. exec. dir. programs ALA, 1990-93; owner Vintage Ventures, 1993—; trainer library automation, group devel., resource sharing; cons. in field. Contbr. articles to profl. publs. Named Colo. Librarian of Yr., Colo. Library Assn., 1984; named to Douglass Soc. Mem. ALA, Spl. Libraries Assn. (chmn. edn. div. 1981-82, pres. Rocky Mountain chpt. 1981-82, 1994—, bd. dirs. 1983-86), OCLC Network Dirs. (chmn. 1983), Mountain Plains Library Assn., Am. Soc. Assn. Execs. Colo. Soc. Assn. Execs.

SEGAL, JOEL MICHAEL, advertising executive; b. N.Y.C., Sept. 2, 1933; s. Michel M. and Ethel (Meshaloff) S.; m. Alix Hegeler, Aug. 9, 1968; children: Mark J., Gregg F.; 1 grandchild, Nina. B.A., Cornell U., 1954; M.B.A., Columbia U., 1960. Media supr. Benton & Bowles, 1960-63; dir. network TV presentations NBC, 1963-65; successively network negotiator, network supr. and v.p., sr. v.p. then exec. v.p. network cable and syndicated broadcasting and dir. Ted Bates & Co., Inc., N.Y.C., 1965-87; exec. v.p. nat. broadcasting McCann-Erickson, N.Y.C., 1988—; bd. dirs. Rigel Inc. Served with AUS, 1956-58. Office: McCann-Erickson USA 750 3rd Ave New York NY 10017-2703

SEGAL, JONATHAN BRUCE, editor; b. N.Y.C., May 12, 1946; s. Clement and Florence Lillian (Miller) S.; m. Haidi Kuhn, June 30, 1974. B.A., Washington Coll., 1966. Writer, editor N.Y. Times, N.Y.C., 1966-73; editor Quadrangle/N.Y. Times Book Co., N.Y.C., 1974-76; sr. editor Simon & Schuster, N.Y.C., 1976-81; exec. editor, editor-in-chief, editorial dir., v.p. Times Books, N.Y.C., 1981-89; editor-at-large Random House, N.Y.C., 1985-89; v.p., sr. editor Alfred A. Knopf, N.Y.C., 1989—. Contbr. articles to popular jours. Democrat. Jewish. Home: 115 E 9th St Apt 12E New York NY 10003-5428 Office: Alfred A Knopf 201 E 50th St New York NY 10022-7703

SEGAL, LORE, writer; b. Vienna, Austria, Mar. 8, 1928; came to U.S., 1951, naturalized, 1956; d. Ignatz and Franzi (Stern) Groszmann; m. David I. Segal, Nov. 3, 1960 (dec.); children: Beatrice Ann, Jacob Paul. B.A. in English, Bedford Coll., U. London, Eng., 1948. Prof. writing div. Sch. Arts, Columbia U., also Princeton U., Sarah Lawrence Coll., Bennington Coll.; prof. English U. Ill., Chgo., 1978-92, Ohio State U., 1992—. Author: Other People's Houses, 1964; Lucinella, 1976, Her First American, 1985; (children's book) Tell Me A Mitzi, 1970, All the Way Home, 1973, Tell Me a Trudy, 1977; The Story of Mrs. Brubeck and How She Looked for Trouble and Where She Found Him, 1981, The Story of Mrs. Lovewright and Purrless Her Cat, 1985; translator: (with W.D. Snodgrass) Gallows Songs, 1968, The Juniper Tree and Other Tales from Grimm, 1973, The Book of Adam to Moses, 1987, The Story of King Saul and King David, 1991; contbr. short stories, articles to N.Y. Times Book Rev., Partisan Rev., New Republic, The New Yorker, others. Guggenheim fellow, 1965-66; Council Arts and Humanities grantee, 1968-69; Artists Public Service grantee, 1970-71; CAPS grantee, 1975; Nat. Endowment Arts grantee, spring 1982, 1987; NEH grantee, 1983; Acad. Arts and Letters award, 1986. Address: 280 Riverside Dr New York NY 10025-9010

SEGAL, MARTIN ELI, retired actuarial and consulting company executive; b. Vitebsk, Russia, Aug. 15, 1916; came to U.S., 1921, naturalized, 1928; s. Isidor and Anna (Title) S.; hon. degrees: L.H.D., Pratt Inst., 1976, Mus.D., Mannes Coll. Music, 1976, L.H.D., Grad. Center CUNY, 1979; LHD (hon.) L.I. U., 1986, NYU, 1988; m. Edith Levy, June 17, 1937; children: Susan Segal Rai, Paul. Various positions ins. industry, 1935-39; founder The Segal Co., consultants and actuaries, N.Y.C., 1939, pres., chief exec. officer, 1939-67, chmn. bd., 1967-91, chmn. emeritus, 1991—; pres. Wertheim Asset Mgmt. Svcs., Inc., N.Y.C., 1972-75, chmn., bd., 1975-82; ptnr. Wertheim & Co., investment bankers, N.Y.C., 1967-82. Bd. dirs. Helena Rubinstein Found., 1972-95; founding chmn. The N.Y. Internat. Festival of the Arts, Inc., 1985—; chmn. bd. Lincoln Ctr. Performing Arts, Inc., 1981-86, chmn. emeritus, 1986—; bd. dirs. Pub. Radio Internat., 1981-94, dir. emeritus, 1994—, co-chmn. Conf. on Intellectual Property The Arts and Tech., 1994, chmn. arts and culture com., N.Y. 92, N.Y. 93, N.Y. 94, N.Y. 95; mem., bd. dirs. Nat. Bldg. Mus., 1983-91; bd. advisers Libr. of Am., 1984—; trustee Am.-Scandinavian Found., 1986-91, adv. trustee, 1991—; bd. visitors Grad. Sch. and Univ. Ctr., CUNY, 1983—; bd. trustees, chmn. exhibitions com. Mus. Modern Art, 1978-81; trustee Inst. for Advanced Study, Princeton, N.J., 1972-91, trustee emeritus, 1991—; pres. Cultural Assistance Ctr., Inc., 1977-82, chmn., 1982-84; founding pres. Film Soc. of Lincoln Ctr., 1968-78, pres. emeritus, 1978—; mem. adv. bd. The Alliance for New Am. Musicals, 1991—; mem. adv. coun. Theatre Devel. Fund, 1992—; bd. dirs. N.Y. Conv. and Visitors Bur., Inc., 1981—; mem. Nat. Bd. of Young Audiences, Inc., 1979—; founding mem. publs. com. The Pub. Interest, 1965—; mem. vis. com., Harvard U. Sch. Pub. Health, 1979-92, dean's coun. Sch. Pub. Health, 1990—; chmn. mayor's Com. on Cultural Policy, 1974; founding chmn. Commn. for Cultural Affairs City of N.Y., 1975; chmn. pub. svc. awards com. Fund for City of N.Y., 1978, 79, bd. dirs, 1978-87; mem. leadership Coun. Nat. Cultural Alliance, 1993—. Decorated Royal Swedish Order of Polar Star, 1984; officer of Arts and Letters, Ministry of Culture of French Govt., 1985; recipient cert. of merit Mcpl. Art Soc., 1974, spl. award Internat. Film Importers and Distbrs. Am., 1973, N.Y.C. Mayor's award of honor for arts and culture, 1982, Ann. award of distinction Mus. City of N.Y., 1982, Concert Artists Guild award, 1983, Disting. Am. of Fgn. Birth award Internat. Ctr. N.Y.C., 1985, John H. Finley medal Alumni Assn. CCNY, 1985, Town Hall Friend of the Arts award, 1987, Drs. Emeriti award Lincoln Ctr. for Performing Arts, Inc., 1987, N.Y. State Gov.'s Arts award, 1989, Pres.'s award Grad. Sch. and Univ. Ctr. of City of N.Y., 1990, City of N.Y. Edn. Fund award LWV, 1984, Songwriter's Hall of Fame Patron of the Arts award, 1988, Nat. Fedn. Music Clubs Presdl. Citation award, 1989, Creative Arts Rehab. Ctr. Pub. Spirit award, 1989, Honor medal The Nat. Arts Club, 1992, Ellis Island medal of honor, 1996. Mem. Century Assn., City Athletic Club, Players Club. Democrat. Jewish. Office: 1 Park Ave New York NY 10016-5802

SEGAL, MORTON, public relations executive; b. N.Y.C., Mar. 3, 1931. BA, Kenyon Coll., England, 1953; MFA in Dramatic Lit., Columbia U., 1956. Mgr. publicity Paramount Pictures, 1961-63; dir. worldwide publicity and pub. rels. 20th Century Fox, 1963-65; v.p. advt. and publicity MGM, 1965-72; with Allen, Ingersoll, Segal and Henry, 1973-75; prin. ICPR, 1975-79, pres., 1978-85; vice chmn., prin. Dennis Davidson Assocs., 1986—; with L.A. Internat. Film Exposition, 1982-84. Mem. Acad. Motion Picture Arts and Scis. Office: Dennis Davidson Assocs Inc 5670 Wilshire Blvd Ste 700 Los Angeles CA 90036-5607

SEGAL, PHYLLIS NICHAMOFF, lawyer, federal agency administrator; b. Bklyn., Apr. 18, 1945; d. Sidney and Theresa Helen (Uroff) Nichamoff; m. Eli J. Segal, June 13, 1965; children—Jonathan, Mora. Student, Brandeis U., 1962-65; B.A., U. Mich., 1966; J.D., Georgetown U., 1973. Bar: N.Y. 1974, U.S. Dist. Ct. (so. and ea dists.) N.Y. 1975, Mass 1983, U.S. Supreme Ct. 1979. Assoc. Weil, Gotshal and Manges, N.Y.C., 1973-77; legal dir. NOW Legal Def. and Edn. Fund, N.Y.C., 1977-82; gen. counsel, 1986—; now chmn. Fed. Labor Rels. Auth., Washington; gen. counsel Exec. office Transp. and Constrn., Commonwealth of Mass., 1984-86; past dep. Atty. Gen. State of Mass., Boston; adj. asst. prof. law NYU, 1980-82; fellow Bunting Inst. Radcliffe Coll., 1982-83; cons. U.S. Commn. Civil Rights. Mem. Commn. on Party Reform Nat. Democratic Party, 1972-73, mem. Compliance Rev. Commn., 1974-76; mem. adv. bd. Mass. Commn. Against Discrimination, 1983—. Mem. ABA, Fedn. Women Lawyers Jud. Screening Panel, Mass. Bar Assn. Contbr. articles to profl. jours. Home: 314 Dartmouth St Ph Boston MA 02116-1809 Office: Fed Labor Rels Auth 607 14th St NW Washington DC 20424-0001

SEGAL, ROBERT MANDAL, lawyer; b. Worcester, Mass., Mar. 21, 1915; s. Abe Charles and Bella (Perry) S.; m. Sharlee Mysel, June 17, 1941; children: Terry P., Ellen Huvelle. AB, Amherst Coll., 1936; postgrad., U. Chgo., 1936-38; JD, Harvard U., 1942. Bar: Mass. 1942, U.S. Dist. Ct. Mass. 1946, U.S. Supreme Ct. 1952. Economist U.S. Steel Corp., 1939; sr. ptnr. Segal & Flamm, Boston, 1955-72; New Eng. counsel AFTRA, 1946-86; sr. ptnr. Segal, Roitman & Coleman, Boston, 1972—; lectr. labor law Harvard U. Bus. Sch., 1962-82, Boston Coll. Law Sch., 1979-81, Northeastern U. Labor Inst., U.S. State Dept., 1971, 73; trustee Mass. Continuing Legal Edn., 1970-83; counsel Mass. State Labor Coun., AFL-CIO, 1948-85. Co-author: History of Labor and Employment Section of the ABA, 1946-86, 1986; contbr. articles to profl. jours. Chmn. Harvard U. Law Sch. Rec. Alumni Com., 1973-93; pres. Jewish Cmty. Coun. of Boston, 1975; mem. film Commn. Mass., 1990—; mem. adv. coun. Mass. Prepaid Legal Svcs., 1984—. With U.S. Army, 1943-45. Recipient Cushing-Gavin Labor award, 1986; Brookings Instn. fellow, 1938-39. Mem. ABA (ho. of dels. 1957-58, mem. consortium 1975-80, chmn. labor and employment sect. 1957, co-chmn. membership and fin. com. labor sect. 1978—, forum com. 1984-86), AFTRA (New Eng. counsel 1947-85), Am. Guild of Musical Artists (N.E. counsel 1970—), Screen Actors Guild (New Eng. counsel 1955-88), Mass. Bar Assn., Boston Bar Assn. (mem. coun. 1960-84, co-chmn. labor law sect. 1957-85), Mass. Adv. Bd. of Film Bur., Mass. Prepaid Legal Svcs. Inst. (adv. bd. 1980—), Indsl. Rels. Assn., Mass. Ams. for Dem. Action (chmn. 1960), Harvard U. Law Sch. Alumni Assn. (mem. coun. 1970-73), Phi Beta Kappa, Delta Sigma Rho. Jewish. Home: 50 Longwood Ave Apt 1112 Brookline MA 02146-5227 also: 6750 Gulf Mexico Dr Longbeach Key FL 34228 Office: Segal Roitman & Coleman 11 Beacon St Boston MA 02108-3002

SEGAL, ROBERT MARTIN, lawyer; b. Atlantic City, N.J., Apr. 7, 1935; s. Nathan Albert and Edna (Dutkin) S.; m. Rhoda Sue Luber, June 8, 1958; children—Deborah Ann, William Nathan, Elizabeth Ann. Student, Cornell U., 1953-54; B.S. in Econs., U. Pa., 1957; LL.B. cum laude, Harvard Law Sch., 1960. Bar: Pa. 1961. Assoc. Wolf, Block, Schorr & Solis-Cohen, Phila., 1960-69, ptnr., 1969—, chmn., exec. com., 1978-79, 82-83, 86-87, 89—; hon. pres. Jewish Employment and Vocat. Svc. Contbr. articles to profl. jours. and mags. Constable of elections Lower Merion Twp., Pa., 1970-72; mem. Rep. Jewish Coalition, 1984-85; bd. dirs. Jewish Family and Children's Agy., Am. Jewish Com., Rosenbach Mus. and Libr., Greater Phila. Urban Affairs Coalition, Phila. Rehab. Plan, Inc. Mem. ABA, Pa. Bar Assn., Phila. Bar Assn., Internat. Coun. Shopping Ctrs., Urban Land Inst. (assoc.), Am. Coll. Real Estate Lawyers, Phila. Bar Found. (trustee 1981-87), Am. Law Inst., Harvard Law Sch. Assn. Phila., Assn. Governing Bds. Univs. and Colls., The Federalist Soc. (bd. advisors Phila. chpt.), Atlantic City Country Club, Gov.'s Club, Chaine des Rotisseurs, Sunday Breakfast Club, La Coquille Club, Harvard Club, Beta Gamma Sigma. Avocations: golf, swimming. Home: 1130 Red Rose Ln Villanova PA 19085-2121 Office: Wolf Block Schorr & Solis-Cohen 12th Fl Packard Bldg SE Corner 15th and Chestnut Philadelphia PA 19102-2678

SEGAL, SHELDON JEROME, biologist, educator, foundation administrator; b. N.Y.C., Mar. 15, 1926; s. Morris M. and Florence (Bogan) S.; m. Harriet Ellen Feinberg, May 22, 1961; children: Amy Robin, Jennifer Ann, Laura Jane. BA, Dartmouth Coll., 1947; postgrad., U. Geneva, 1947-48; MS, U. Iowa, 1951, PhD, 1952; MD (hon.), U. Tampere, Finland, 1984, U. Uppsala, Sweden, 1985. Rsch. scientist William S. Merrill Co., Cin., 1952-53; rsch. assoc., asst. prof. U. Iowa, 1953-56; asst. med. dir. Population Coun., N.Y.C., 1956-63, med. dir., 1963-78, v.p., 1969-76, sr. v.p., 1976-78; affiliate Rockefeller U., N.Y.C., 1956-76, adj. prof., 1977-87; dir. population scis. Rockefeller Found., 1978-91; disting. scientist Population Coun., N.Y.C., 1991—; lectr. Columbia U., 1959-61; vis. prof. All-India Inst. Med. Scis., New Delhi, 1962-63, Amir Chand lectr., 1975; mem. Marine Biol. Lab, Woods Hole, Mass.; cons. World Bank, WHO, NIH, Ford Found., Indian Govt., UN Office Sci. and Tech., UN Fund Population Activities; mem. com. on contraceptive tech. NAS, 1977-80, com. on health effects of marijuana Inst. Medicine, 1981-82, NAS com. on demographic impact of contraceptive tech., 1988-89, nat. rsch. con., overview com. for Indo-U.S. sci. initiative, 1985—; adv. com. on human reproduction FDA; cons. to dir. Nat. Inst. Child Health and Human Devel., 1978-80; plenary lectr. 3d World Congress Endocrinology, 1968, Upjohn lectr. Am. Fertility Soc., 1971, plenary lectr. World Fertility Congress, 1975, Sigma Xi lectr. U. Idaho, 1976, plenary lectr. World Congress on Ob-Gyn., 1976, lectr. Chinese Acad. Scis., 1977, Carl Gemzell lectr. U. Uppsala, 1982, Pierre Soupart lectr. Axel Munthe Found., 1988, Alpha Omega Alpha lectr. U. Pa. Coll. Medicine, 1989, plenary lectr. World Congress on Human Reproduction, 1990; hon. prof. Peking Union Med. Coll., Beijing, 1987, Chinese Acad. Scis., 1988; trustee Marine Biol. Lab., 1985—, chmn. bd. trustees, 1991—. Co-editor 8 books; contbr. numerous articles to profl. jours. Trustee Rye Country Day Sch., 1979—, pres. bd. trustees, 1981-85; trustee Ctr. for Reproductive Law and Policy, 1992—. Lt. (j.g.) USNR, 1943-45. Decorated Order Comdr. of Lion (Finland); recipient Honor award Innsbruck U., Austria, hon. citation Pres. of India, 1978, Clarence J. Gamble award World Acad. Arts and Scis., 1980, Joseph C. Wilson award Rochester Assn. for UN, 1981, UN Population award, 1984, Axel Munthe award in medicine Axel Munthe Found., Italy, 1985, Sci. award Planned Parenthood Fedn. Am., 1990, Dmitirus N. Chorafas award in medicine Swiss Acad. Scis., 1995. Fellow AAAS; mem. Royal Coll. Obstetricians and Gynecologists (hon.), Am. Fertility Soc. (hon. v.p. 1975-76, trustee found. 1975-77), Endocrine Soc., Am. Assn Anatomists, Internat. Soc. for Study Reprodn. (pres. 1968-72), Internat. Inst. Embryology, Am. Soc. Zoologists, Coun. Fgn. Rels., Mexican Acad. Medicine (hon.), Inst. Medicine, Dartmouth Club N.Y., Woods Hole Yacht Club. Home: 9 Topland Rd Hartsdale NY 10530-3001 Office: Population Coun One Dag Hammarskjold Plz New York NY 10017

SEGAL, SYLVIA OZNER, songwriter, publisher, producer, inventor; b. Bronx, N.Y.; m. Melvin Casey Segal; children: Michael Ozner, Laurence Ozner. Grad. high sch., Bronx. Pres., founder Glamortop Fashions Miami dba Ostel Enterprises, Inc., Fla., 1952-79; pres. SOS Worldwide Prodns., Inc., 1985; CEO, pres. children's divsn. Ednl. Songs. Internat., Inc., 1994—; founder Indie Label. Music writer, pub., prodr. records including My Love Song (recorded by Vic Damone 1952, a.k.a. You Belong To Me), Olympic Fever (song of U.S. Olympic Team 1988), Winning Fever, We Must Unite World, USA's For Me, others; creator The Safe Song Program, audio, video, booklet package, all langs. Recipient various awards Billboard Mag. Patentee for 12 Fashion Glamortop scarf. Mem. ASCAP, Songwriters Guild, Assn. Fla. Poets, Inc. Office: 20416 NE 10th Court Rd Miami FL 33179-2524

SEGALAS, HERCULES ANTHONY, investment banker; b. N.Y.C., Mar. 21, 1935; s. Anthony Spiros and Katherine A. (Michas) S.; m. Margaret Wharton, Sept. 18, 1956; children: Donnell Anthony, Stephen Wharton, Katherine Lacy Devlin. BS, Yale U., 1956. Various engring. and mfg. positions Procter & Gamble Co., Cin., 1956-65; pres. for Latin Am., mgr. Internat. Flavors and Fragrances, N.Y.C., 1965-68; exec. v.p., mem. bd. dirs. William D. Witter Inc., N.Y.C., 1969-76; sr. v.p. Drexel Burnham Lambert Inc., N.Y.C., 1976-87, mng. dir., 1987-88, also bd. dirs., 1976-88; mng. dir. head consumer products investment banking group PaineWebber Inc. Investment Banking Group, N.Y.C., 1988—, also bd. dirs. Bd. dirs. Nantucket Land Coun., Mass., 1982-85; mem. corp. Nantucket Cottage Hosp., 1984-85. Mem. Morristown Field Club, Nantucket Yacht Club (bd. govs. 1987-93, mem. exec. com. 1988-93). Republican. Avocations: tennis, sailing, languages, woodworking. Home: 17 Hilltop Cir Morristown NJ 07960-6312 Office: Paine Webber Inc 1285 Avenue Of The Americas New York NY 10019-6028

SEGALEWITZ, SCOTT I., biomedical engineer; b. Tucson, Apr. 1, 1961; s. Ira and Zelda (Kapustein) S.; m. Caryl Ann Stein, Jan. 1, 1994. BSEE, Rutgers U., 1983; MS in biomed. engring., N.J. Inst. Tech., 1986. Cert. profl. engr., Pa. Computer system mgr. St. Barnabas Med. Ctr., Livingston, N.J., 1984-85; instr. elec. engring. N.J. Inst. Tech., Newark, 1985-86, asst. program dir. biomed. camp, 1986; program chair biomed. engring. tech. Pa. State U., New Kensington, 1986—; v.p. systems devel. Micro Power Systems, Apollo, Pa., 1988-89; adj. instr. cardiovasc. tech. Mt. Aloysius Coll., Cresson, Pa., 1991-93; expert witness med. instrumentation and edn.; program evaluator Tech. Accreditation Commn. Accreditation Bd. Engring. and Tech., 1991—. Author: Reference Guide for Biomedical Technicians, 1985; editor: (newsletter) Affinity, Newsletter of Marquette Electronics, 1992—, Med. Equipment Tech. Soc., 1989-93; contbr. articles to profl. jours.

Mem. IEEE, Am. Soc. Healthcare Engring., Assn. Advancement Med. Instrumentation, Soc. Biomed. Equipment Techs. (bd. dirs. 1986—), Clin. Engring. Soc. Pa. (v.p., bd. dirs., editor 1988—). Avocations: woodworking, cooking, multimedia and internet software development. Office: Pa State U 3550 7th St Rd New Kensington PA 15068

SEGALL, HAROLD ABRAHAM, lawyer; b. N.Y.C., May 22, 1918; s. Morris and Mildred (Borkan) S.; m. Edith S. Besser, Jan. 27, 1952; children—Mark E., Grant D., Bruce K. BA with distinction, Cornell U., 1938; LLB cum laude, Yale U., 1941. Bar: N.Y. 1941. Practiced in N.Y.C., 1946—; assoc. mem. firm Gilbert, Segall and Young, 1946-49, ptnr., 1949-93, sr. counsel, 1994—; vis. lectr. Yale U. Law Sch., 1974-75, Yale U. Sch. Orgn. and Mgmt., 1983-85. Author: (with R.B. Kelley) Estate Planning for the Corporate Executive, 1971, Representing the Seller of a Closely-Held Business, 1973, reprint, 1976; (with J.A. Arouh) How to Prepare Legal Opinions-Boldness and Caution, 1979, reprint, 1990; (with M.S. Sirkin) Providing for Withdrawal from a Joint Venture, 1982, Seventeen Suggestions for Improving Communications with Clients and Colleagues, 1994, reprint, 1995, How to Keep Improving a Highly Successful Law Firm, 1994; contbr. articles to profl. jours. Mem. council State U. N.Y. at Purchase, 1974-79; Counsel United Republican Finance Com., N.Y. State, 1955-61, Rep. City Com., N.Y.C., 1961, Nat. Rep. Citizens Com., 1962, Keating for Senator Com., 1964, Eisenhower 75th Birthday Com., 1965, Friends of the Gov. Wilson Team, 1974, Gov.'s Club, N.Y., 1965-75; trustee, v.p., treas. Philip D. Reed Found. Inc., 1989—; bd. dirs. Oneita Knitting Mills, 1973-83. Served to maj. AUS, World War II, ETO and PTO. Recipient Edgar M. Cullen prize, 1939. Mem. ABA, Bar City N.Y. (com. on trademark and unfair competition 1967-69, chmn. subcom. legislation 1968-69), Jewish Community Center, Order of Coif, Phi Beta Kappa, Phi Kappa Phi, Phi Sigma Delta. Clubs: University (N.Y.C.); Elmwood Country (gov. 1966-70, 73-75). Home: 60 Woodlands Rd Harrison NY 10528-1419 Office: 430 Park Ave New York NY 10022-3505

SEGAR, GEOFFREY, retired lawyer; b. Indpls., Jan. 13, 1926; s. Louis H. and Beatrice (Felsenthel) S.; m. Janet Blatt, Jan. 7, 1949; children: Judith Segar Shepherd, Robert, Ann Leh. BS in Bus., Ind. U., 1948, JD, 1952. Bar: Ind. 1952, U.S. Dist. Ct. (so. dist.) Ind. 1952, U.S. Ct. Appeals (7th cir.) 1978, U.S. Supreme Ct. 1983, U.S. Ct. Appeals (8th cir.) 1986. Ptnr. Ice Miller Donadio & Ryan, Indpls., 1952-77, 79-91, ret., 1991; gen. counsel Samaritan Health Svc., Phoenix, 1978; mem. deans adv. com. Ind. U. Med. Sch., 1986—, adv. bd. Ctr. for Law, 1987—; mem. Commn. on Health Policy, Indpls., 1989. Bd. dirs. Hooverwood Nursing Home, Indpls., 1969-88, 92—, Ctrl. Ind. Coun. Aging, 1977, St. Vincents Hosp. and Health Care Ctr., 1991—; pres. Regency Apts. for Elderly, Indpls., 1989-90. With USN, 1944-46. Fellow Am. Coll. Trial Lawyers; mem. Nat. Health Lawyers, Am. Acad. Hosp. Attys. Office: Ice Miller Donadio & Ryan PO Box 82001 Indianapolis IN 46282

SEGARS, TRUDY W., mathematics educator; b. Baton Rouge, July 17, 1953; d. Augustus Ray and Ethel Mae (Smith) Williams; m. Leandrew Segars Jr., Dec. 18, 1976 (div. May 13, 1992); children: Tamara, Tara, Teresa. BS, Southern U., Baton Rouge, 1973; MA, Atlanta U., 1977. Math. tchr., sci. tchr. E. Baton Rouge Sch. Bd., 1974-78; LSM clk. U.S. Postal Svc., Baton Rouge, 1978-79; math. tchr. E. Baton Rouge Sch. Bd., 1979-93; site coord. Southern U., Baton Rouge, 1993—; middle sch. math. task. force E. Baton Rouge Sch. Bd., 1984—; cons. D.C. Health Textbooks, Inc., Austin, 1990; La. Math. Assessment Panel, La. State Dept. Edn., Baton Rouge, 1993—. Co-author: E. Baton Rouge School Math Guide, 1987. Mem. Parkwood Terrace Improvement Assn. Baker, La., 1990—; sec. 1st PResbyn. Ch. Scotland, Baton Rouge, 1993—. Named Tchr. of Yr. Northwestern Middle Sch., Zachary, La., 1985-86, 90; Black Role Model of Baton Rouge, 1st Presbyn. Ch. Scotland, Baton Rouge, 1994. Mem. NEA, Nat. Coun. Tchr. Math., Baton Rouge Area Coun. Tchrs. Math., Math. for Edn. Reform, La. Edn. Assn., La. Assn. Tchrs. Math. Presbyterian. Avocations: cross-stitch, reading, playing piano. Home: 13445 Ector Dr Baker LA 70714-4655 Office: Southern University PO Box 9759 Baton Rouge LA 70813

SEGEL, JOSEPH M., broadcasting executive; b. Phila., Jan. 9, 1931; s. Albert M. and Fannie B. (Scribner) S.; m. Renee A., June 1, 1951 (div. 1960); 1 child, Marvin; m. Doris Usem, Dec. 20, 1963; 1 child, Alan; 1 stepchild, Sandy Stern. BS in Econs., U. Pa., 1951. Chmn. Nat. Bus. Services, Inc., Phila., 1950-63; chmn., cons. Franklin Mint Corp., Franklin Center, Pa., 1963-85; chmn. Presdl. Airways Corp., Phila., 1975-79, QVC Network Inc., West Chester, Pa., 1986—; chmn. Software Digest, Inc., Wynnewood, Pa., 1983-86, Nat. Software Testing Labs., Inc., Phila., 1984-86. Editor The Counselor mag., 1951-61. Chmn. UN Assn. U.S.A., N.Y.C., 1973-75; mem. U.S. delegation UN Gen. Assembly, , 1974. Republican. Jewish. Club: LeMirador Country (Switzerland) (chmn. 1974-89). Office: QVC Network Inc Goshen Pk 1365 Enterprise Dr West Chester PA 19380-5959

SEGER, THOMAS M., lawyer; b. Cleve., Oct. 11, 1946. BA, Miami U., 1968; JD, Harvard U., 1972. Bar: Ohio 1972. Law clk. to Hon. Ed McEntree U.S. Ct. Appeals (1st cir.) Ohio, 1972-73; ptnr. Baker & Hostetler, Cleve. Office: Baker & Hostetler 3200 Nat City Ctr 1900 E 9th St Cleveland OH 44114-3485*

SEGERSTEN, ROBERT HAGY, lawyer, investment banker; b. Boston, June 24, 1941; s. Wendell C. and Claire H. S.; m. Marie E. Makinen, Feb. 13, 1965; children: Amanda Beth, Vanessa Bryce. A.B., Bates Coll., 1963; J.D., Boston U., 1970. Bar: Mass. 1970. Assoc. Nessen & Csaplar, Boston, 1970-75; v.p. March Co., Boston, 1975-77; pres. March-Eton Corp., Concord, Mass., 1977-82; ptnr. Nessen, Goodwin & Segersten, Concord, 1977-82, Kane & Segersten, Dedham, Mass., 1983-85; pres. Woodbine Optical Corp., Sharon, Mass., 1990—; adj. prof. Sch. Am. Studies, Boston U.; adj. prof. real estate law Bentley Coll. Officer, bd. dirs. Friends of The Jimmy Fund, Boston. Served to lt. USN, 1963-67. Mem. ACLU, Mass. Bar Assn. Democrat. Episcopalian. Home: 64 Folsom Ave Hyannis MA 02601-4823 Office: 41 Brooks Dr Braintree MA 02184

SEGESVÁRY, VICTOR GYÖZÖ, retired diplomat; b. Miskolc, Hungary, Feb. 20, 1929; came to U.S., 1984; s. Viktor and Margit (Kovács) S.; m. Andrea Bárczay, Jan. 20, 1955 (div. Nov. 1957); 1 child, Gábor; m. Monika Schwarz, Dec. 28, 1968. PhD in Polit. Sci., Grad. Inst. Internat. Studies, Switzerland, 1968; DD, U. Geneva, 1973. Asst., libr. Reformed Theol. Acad., Budapest, Hungary, 1953-56; sec. gen. African Inst., Geneva, 1961-63; asst. editor, market rsch. officer Bus. Internat. S.A., Geneva, 1963-66; market rsch. officer SESAF S.A., Geneva, 1967-68; chief rsch. dept. Henry Dunant Inst. Internat. Red Cross, Geneva, 1968-71; cons. Internat. Trade Ctr., UNCTAD/GATT, Geneva, 1969-71; tech. advisor market rsch.-market study Internat. Trade Ctr., Algiers, Algeria, 1971-72; sr. trade promotion advisor, project mgr. UNCTAD/GATT/ITC, Algiers, 1973-74; chief advisor in internat. econ. rels., project mgr. UNCTAD/GATT/ITC, Kabul, Afghanistan, 1975-79, Bamako, Mali, 1979-83; sr. advisor, cons. UN Devel. Programme, African countries, 1984-93; sr. advisor, cons. dept. for tech. cooperation for devel. UN, N.Y.C., 1985-88. Author: Le réalisme khrouchtchévien-Politique soviétoque au Proche-Orient, 1968, La Rèforme et l'Islam, 1500-1550, 1973, A Raday Kömuvtár 18. századi törtènete, 1992, Inter-Civilizational Relations and the Destiny of the West: Dialogue or Confrontation?, 1996. Sec.-gen. Internat. Fedn. Students in Polit. Sci., Geneva, 1958-59. Home: 330 E 39th St Apt 21/E New York NY 10016-2123

SEGGER, MARTIN JOSEPH, museum director, art history educator; b. Felixtowe, Eng., Nov. 22, 1946; s. Gerald Joseph and Lillian Joan (Barker-Emery) S.; m. Angele Cordonier, Oct. 4, 1968; children: Cara Michelle, Marie-Claire, Margaret Ellen. B.A., U. Victoria, 1969, Diploma in Edn., 1970; M. in Philosophy, U. London, 1973. Prof. art history U. Victoria, B.C., 1970-74; museologist Royal B.C. Mus., Victoria, 1974-77; dir. Maltwood Art Mus., prof. art history U. Victoria, B.C., 1977—; cons. Nat. Mus. Corp., Ottawa, 1977, UNESCO, O.E.A., Cairo, 1983. Author: exhbn. catalogue House Beautiful, 1975, Arts of the Forgotten Pioneers, 1971, Victoria: An Architectural History, 1979, (commendation Am. Assn. State and Local History 1980), This Old House, 1975, This Old Town, 1979, British Columbia Parliament Buildings, 1979, The Heritage of Canada, 1981, Samuel Maclure: In Search of Appropriate Form, 1986 (Hallmark award 1987), (a guide) St. Andrew's Cathedral, 1990, The Development of Gordon Head Campus, 1988, An Introduction to Museum Studies, 1989, An Introduction to Heritage Conservation, 1990, Botswana Live, 1994; editl. bd. mem. Managing Leisure: an International Journal, U.K., 1994—. Bd. govs. Heritage Can. Found., 1979-83; chmn. City of Victoria Heritage Adv. Com., 1975-79; bd. dirs. Heritage Trust, 1977-86, B.C. Touring Coun., Sta. CFUV Radio, B.C. Govt. House Found., 1987-93; mem. B.C. Heritage Adv. Bd., 1973-83; councillor City of Victoria, 1987-93; vice-chair Provincial Capital Commn., 1991—; pres. Assn. Vancouver Island Municipalities, 1993-94. Decorated knight Equestrian Order of Holy Sepulchre of Jerusalem; recipient award Heritage Can. Communications, 1976, Heritage Conservation award Lt. Gov. B.C., 1989, Harley J. McKee award Assn. Preservation Technology, 1994. Fellow Royal Soc. Arts; mem. Can. Mus. Assn. (counsellor 1975-77), Internat. Coun. Mus. (chair internat. com. for tng. of pers. 1995—), Internat. Coun. Monuments and Sites (bd. dirs. 1980-92), Soc. Study Architecture Can. (bd. dirs. 1979-81), Authors Club (London), Can Mus. Dirs. Orgn., Carnavon Club. Roman Catholic. Avocations: travel, motor mechanics, walking. Home: 1035 Sutlej St, Victoria, BC Canada V8V 3P2 Office: U Victoria Art Hist Dept, PO Box 3025, Victoria, BC Canada V8W 2P2

SEGGERMAN, ANNE CRELLIN, foundation executive; b. Los Angeles, May 13, 1931; d. Curtin Vergil and Yvonne (LaGrave) Crellin; m. Harry G.A. Seggerman, Apr. 14, 1951; children: Patricia, Henry, Marianne, Yvonne, Suzanne, John. Studies with Albert Levesque, Paris, 1948-50; Student, Sch. Decorative Arts, Paris, 1950, Sch. of the Louvre, Paris, 1950, Albert Magnus Coll., 1951; D.H.L. (hon.), Sacred Heart U., 1980. French tchr. Beverly Hills, Calif., 1958-60; translator World Affairs Council, Los Angeles, 1958-60; staff mem. West Side Sch. Gifted Children, Beverly Hills, 1958-60; pres. Huxley Inst. for Bio-Social Research, Fairfield, Conn., 1972—, 4th World Found. Interfaith Media Action, Fairfield, 1977—, Steiner Prodns., Fairfield, 1981—; founder The Com. for Guadalupe Research, Fairfield, 1982—; bd. dirs. Anuk, Inc. co-founder Christian/Jewish Ctr. Understanding Sacred Heart U., Fairfield, Conn.; active Pres. Reagan's Health Task Force Resources Com. on Health Adv. Couns. of U.S. Dept. Health and Human Svcs.; mem. Pres.'s Com. Mental Retardation, 1981-86, Com. Housing Handicapped Families, 1989; mem. Nat. Coun. on Disability, 1992-95; bd. dirs. Easter Seal Rehab. Ctr., Fairfield, Internat. Coll. Applied Nutrition, World Health Med. Group, Cath. League for Religion and Civil Rights. Recipient Am. Assn. Sovereign Mil. Order of Malta, 1991, Lady of Equestrian Order of Holy Sepulchre of Jerusalem, 1991. Mem. Nat. Health Fedn., The Inst. for Study of Human Knowledge, Am. Holistic Med. Inst., Internat. Acad. Preventive Medicine, Calif. Orthomolecular Soc., Am. Phys. Rsch., Fairfield County Organic Gardeners.

SEGIL, LARRAINE DIANE, former materials company executive; b. Johannesburg, South Africa, July 15, 1948; came to U.S., 1974; d. Jack and Norma Estelle (Cohen) Wolfowitz; m. Clive Melwyn Segil, Mar. 9, 1969; 1 child, James Harris. BA, U. Witwatersrand, South Africa, 1967, BA with honours, 1969; JD, Southwestern U., L.A., 1979; MBA, Pepperdine U., 1985. Bar: Calif. 1979, U.S. Supreme Ct. 1982. Cons. in internat. transactions, L.A., 1976-79; atty. Long & Levit, L.A., 1979-81; chmn., pres. Marina Credit Corp., L.A., 1981-85; pres., chief exec. officer Electronic Space Products Internat., L.A., 1985-87; mng. ptnr. The Lared Group, L.A., 1987—. Bd. govs. Cedars Sinai Med. Ctr., L.A., 1984—; bd. dirs. So. Calif. Tech. Execs. Network, 1984-86. Mem. ABA (chmn. internat. law com. young lawyers div. 1980-84), Internat. Assn. Young Lawyers (exec. coun. 1979-81, coun. internat. law and practice 1983-84), World Tech. Execs. Network (chmn.), Regency Club (house com. 1986). Avocations: piano, horseriding. Office: The Lared Group 1901 Avenue Of The Stars Los Angeles CA 90067-6004

SEGNER, EDMUND PETER, III, natural gas company executive; b. Dallas, Oct. 23, 1953; s. Edmund Peter Jr. and Martha Fairfax (Smith) S.; m. Kathryn Louise Daily, July 10, 1976; children: Peter Michael, Christian James. BSCE, Rice U., 1976; MA in Econs., U. Houston, 1980. CPA, Tex. Acct. Touche Ross & Co., Houston, 1976-78; asst. v.p. planning United Gas Pipe Line Co., Houston, 1978-86; asst. v.p. rsch. Drexel Burnham Lambert, N.Y.C., 1986-88; v.p. pub. and investor rels. Enron Corp., Houston, 1988-90; sr. v.p. pub. and gov. rels., investor Enron Corp, Houston, 1990-92, exec. v.p., chief staff, 1992—; lectr. civil engring. Rice U., Houston, 1983-85. Bd. dirs. Zool. Soc. Houston, 1992-95, Greater Houston Partnership for Ednl. Excellence, 1991-93, Rice U. Fund Coun., 1992—, Sam Houston Area coun. Boy Scouts Am.; treas. Tex. Nature Conservancy, 1992—; chmn. Cmty. Ptnrs., 1993-95. Mem. AICPA, Houston Soc. Fin. Analysts, Petroleum Investor Rels. Assn., Houston City Club, Briar Club, Braeburn Country Club, Coronado Club, Old Baldy Club. Republican. Lutheran. Home: 4130 Tennyson St Houston TX 77005-2750 Office: Enron Corp 1400 Smith St Houston TX 77002

SEGRÈ, NINA, lawyer; b. New Haven, Apr. 4, 1940; d. Victor M. and Naomi (Berlin) Gordon; m. Gino Segrè, Dec. 31, 1962 (div. 1983); children: Katia, Julie, Michele; m. Frank F. Furstenberg, Jr., Feb. 2, 1985; stepchildren: Sarah Furstenberg, Ben Furstenberg. BA, Radcliffe Coll., 1961; MAT, Harvard U., 1963; JD, U. Pa., 1974. Bar: Pa. 1974, U.S. Dist. Ct. (ea. dist.) Pa. 1974. Law clk. U.S. Ct. Appeals (3d cir.), Phila., 1974-75; assoc. Dechert Price & Rhoads, Phila., 1976-83, ptnr., 1983-93; ptnr. Segrè & Senser, P.C., Phila., 1993—; bd. dirs., course preparer, panelist Phila. (Pa.) Bar Edn. Ctr., 1994—. Trustee Radcliffe Coll., Cambridge, Mass., 1991-95, chair fund com., chair program com.; mem. fin. com. Lynn Yeakel for U.S. Senate, Phila., 1992, Lynn Yeakel for Gov. Pa., 1994. Mem. Phila. Bar Assn. (mem. real property sec., mem. exec. bd.), The Harvard-Radcliffe Club (v.p., mem. exec. bd.), College Works (founder, bd. dirs.). Home: 2316 Delancey Pl Philadelphia PA 19103-6407 Office: Segrè & Senser PC 2 Penn Center Plz Ste 414 Philadelphia PA 19102-1704

SEGUIN, LILLIAN ANGELIN, secondary school educator, mathematics educator; b. Brownsville, Tex., May 28, 1954; d. Frank DeWaine and Victoria Angelin (Muschamp) Preston; m. James William Seguin, Dec. 18, 1988. BS in Math., Tex. A&M U., 1976, MS in Math., 1992. Cert. tchr., Tex., Tex. Supr. Cert. Math. tchr. Pace H.S., Brownsville, 1984-86; math. tchr., dept. chair Hanna H.S., Brownsville, 1986-92; math. specialist Brownsville Ind. Sch. Dist., 1992-94; math. tchr., dept. chair Porter H.S., Brownsville, 1994—; adj. instr. U. Tex., Brownsville, 1987—; textbook reviewer Houghton Mifflin, 1992. Deaconess Seventh Day Adventist Ch., Brownsville, 1990, 91. Mem. ASCD, Nat. Coun. Tchrs. Math., Tex. Assn. Suprs. Math., Rio Grande Valley Coun. Tchrs. Math., Assn. Tex. Profl. Edn., Alpha Delta Kappa.

SEHN, SUSAN CLEARY, psychiatrist; b. Denver, Feb. 2, 1943; d. Herbert J and Helen (Wetherill) Cleary; m. George James Sehn, Jan. 23, 1965 (div. 1985); children: Natalie, Michael. BA, U. Colo., 1965; MS, Pa. State U., 1974; MD, Med. Coll. Pa., 1978. Diplomate in gen. psychiatry and child and adolescent psychiatry Am. Bd. Psychiatry and Neurology. Intern in pediatrics Hahnemann U. Hosp., Phila., 1978-79; resident in gen. psychiatry Med. Coll. Pa., Phila., 1979-81, fellow in child psychiatry, 1981-83; attending physician Horsham Clinic, Ambler, Pa., 1984-89; dir. adolescent psychiatry Eugenia Hosp., Lafayette Hill, Pa., 1988-90; attending physician Northwestern Inst., Ft. Washington, Pa., 1983-93; dir. adolescent psychiatry Warminster (Pa.) Psychiat. Ctr., 1990-91; attending psychiatrist Phila. Child Guidance Ctr., 1992—; v.p., treas. Askelpios Ltd., Levittown, Pa., 1990-91; sec. bd. dirs. United Psychiat. Svc., Lafayette Hill, 1988-90; mem. bd. med. dirs. Guillain Barré Found., Wynnewood, Pa., 1983—. Mem. Psyciat. Physicians Pa. (co-chair com. on women 1988-94), Regional Coun. Child and Adolescent Psychiatry (treas. 1993-95), Phila. Adolescent Soc. (v.p. 1988-93). Avocations: personal computing, singing, music, birding. Home: 4005 Fairway Rd Lafayette Hill PA 19444-1303

SEIBEL, ERWIN, oceanographer, educator; BS, CCNY, 1965; MS, U. Mich., 1966, PhD, 1972. Asst. research oceanographer U. Mich., Ann Arbor, 1972-75, assoc. research oceanographer, 1975-78, asst. dir. sea grant, 1975-78; environ. lab dir. San Francisco State U., 1978-81, chmn. dept. geoscis., 1981-88, dean undergraduate studies, 1988—. commr. Calif. Commn. on Tchr. Credentialing; sr. scientist cruises U. Mich., 1971-78; mem. sea grant site rev. teams Nat. Sea Grant Program, Washington, 1978—; bd. govs. Moss Landing Marine Labs., Calif., 1981—; mem. adv. com. Ctr. Advancement Mercantile Spacefaring; coord. Biology Forum Calif. Acad. Scis., 1988-89; exec. sec. Oceans 83 Marine Tech. Soc., IEEE, San Francisco, 1982-83; coord. Symposium for Pacific AAAS El Nino Effect, 1983-84; dir. environ. monitoring nuclear power plant, 1972-78; mem. sci. adv. panel Calif. Commn. Tchr. Credentialing, 1988-93; mem. steering com. Pacific Basin Studies Ctr., 1990-93; commr. Calif. Commn. on Teaching Credentialing, 1993—, fiscal planning & policy com., 1994—, performance stds. com., 1995—. Contbr. articles to profl. jours.; developer photogrammetric technique for continuous shoreline monitoring. Advisor MESA program for Minority Students, San Francisco area, 1981-88; vol. San Francisco Bay Area council Girl Scouts U.S., 1982-86. Served to capt. U.S. Army, 1967-71, Vietnam. Grantee Am. Electric Power Co., 1972-78, Gt. Lakes Basin Commn., 1975-76, Calif. Div. Mines and Geology, 1986-88, Am. Coun. Edn. and Ford Found., 1990-94. Recipient Exceptional Merit Service award San Francisco State U., 1984. Fellow AAAS, Calif. Acad. Scis., Geol. Soc. Am.; mem. N.Y. Acad. Scis., Am. Geophys. Union, Marine Tech. Soc. (pres. San Francisco Bay chpt. 1982-83), Western Assn. Schs. and Colls. (mem. student learning and teaching effectiveness task force 1994-95), U. Mich. Alumni Assn., Gold Key (hon.), Sigma XI (pres. San Francisco State U. chpt. 1982-84, 90-92, Chautauqua coord. 1989—, faculty athletic rep. NCAA, NCAC, 1991-93). Office: San Francisco State U Dean of Undergrad Studies 1600 Holloway Ave San Francisco CA 94132-1722

SEIBERLICH, CARL JOSEPH, retired naval officer; b. Jenkintown, Pa., July 4, 1921; s. Charles A. and Helen (Dolan) S.; m. Trudy Germi, May 29, 1952; children: Eric P., Heidi M., Curt A. B.S., U.S. Mcht. Marine Acad., 1943; grad., Armed Forces Staff Coll., 1959. Commd. ensign U.S. Navy, 1943, advanced through grades to rear adm., 1971; designated naval aviator, 1947, carrier ops. Heavier-than-Air, Lighter-than-Air and helicopters; comdg. officer Airship ZPM-1, 1949, Air Anti-Submarine Squadron 26, 1961, U.S.S. Salamonie, 1967, U.S.S. Hornet, 1969; dir. recovery astronauts Apollo 11 and 12 lunar missions, 1969; comdr. anti-submarine warfare group 3 Flagship U.S.S. Ticonderoga, 1971; comdr. task force 74 Viet Nam Ops., 1972; asst. dep. chief naval ops. for air warfare Navy Dept., 1975-77; dep. chief naval personnel, 1977-78; comdr. Naval Mil. Personnel Command, 1978-80; with VSE Corp., 1980-82; pres. U.S. Maritime Resource Ctr.; dir. mil. program Am. Pres. Lines, 1983—. Vice pres. Naval Aviation Mus. Found.; active Boy Scouts Am. Decorated Legion of Merit (6), Air medal; recipient Harmon Internat. trophy for devel. 1st variable depth towed sonar, 1951. Mem. AIAA, Am. Soc. Naval Engrs., Am. Helicopter Soc., U.S. Naval Inst., U.S. Naval Sailing Assn. (commodore 1979), Am. Angus Assn., Tailhook Assn., Navy Helicopter Assn., Naval Airship Assn., Early and Pioneer Naval Aviators Assn., Nat. Def. Transp. Assn., Am. Def. Preparedness Assn., Navy League U.S. (chmn. maritime affairs com.), Propeller Club, Order of Daedalians, U.S. Mcht. Marine Acad. Alumni Assn., Assn. Naval Aviation, Am. Legion, N.Y. Yacht Club, Nat. Space Club, Delta Sigma Pi. Clubs: N.Y. Yacht, Capital Yacht, Nat. Space. Home: Seagate Farm 1510 Loudoun Dr Haymarket VA 22069-1120 Office: Am Pres Lines 1101 17th St NW Ste 400 Washington DC 20036-4704 *Maintain a clear set of moral values, prepare yourself professionally, maintain physical fitness, persevere as you move toward your goal. Value personal relationships. Never give less than your best; never accept less than the best. Don't trade on the accomplishments of yesterday. Have fun and at times pause and admire the flowers.*

SEIBERLING, DANIEL R., principal; b. Akron, Ohio, Aug. 22, 1946; s. Carol J. Flemm, June 28, 1969; children: Phillip, Kurt. BS in Edn., Wittenberg U., Springfield, Ohio, 1968; MEd, Kent (Ohio) State U., 1972, Edn. Specialist in Adminstrn., 1977. Tchr. Cuyahoga Falls (Ohio) City Schs., 1968-69; tchr. Hudson (Ohio) Local Schs., 1969-76, 80-88, tech. coord./math. cons., 1976-80, adminstrv. asst., tchr., 1988-91, asst. prin., 1991-92, prin., adminstrv. asst., 1992-94, prin., pupil svcs. adminstr., 1994—; tchr., author, team mem. indsl arts activities integrated in curriculum Tech. for Children, 1970-73. Author, coord. study packets/primary aged gifted children Packets for Advancing Thinking Skills, 1982. Coach Stow (Ohio) Soccer Assn., 1985-94; com. chmn. troop 273 Boy Scouts Am., 1988—; dir. leader MOE dist. Day camp, Akron, Ohio, 1992, 93, 94. Jennings Found. scholar, Cleve., 1984-85. Mem. ASCD, Ohio Assn. Elem. Sch. Adminstrs., Phi Delta Kappa. Avocations: reading, camping, travel. Office: Hudson Local Schs 34 N Oviatt St Hudson OH 44236-3042

SEIBERLING, JOHN FREDERICK, former congressman, law educator, lawyer; b. Akron, Ohio, Sept. 8, 1918; s. J. Frederick and Henrietta (Buckler) S.; m. Elizabeth Pope Behr, June 4, 1949; children—John B., David P., Stephen M. AB, Harvard U., 1941; LLB, Columbia U., 1949. Bar: N.Y. 1950, Ohio 1955. Assoc. mem. firm Donovan, Leisure, Newton, Lumbard & Irvine, N.Y.C., 1949-53; atty. Goodyear Tire & Rubber Co., Akron, 1954-71; mem. 92d-99th Congresses from 14th Ohio Dist.; mem. com. on judiciary, com. on interior and insular affairs, chmn. subcom. on public lands; vis. prof. law U. Akron, 1987, 90, dir. Ctr. for Peace Studies, 1991-96; ptnr. Goldman, Seiberling, Davis & Tsarnas, Akron, 1988-89. Served to maj. AUS, 1942-46. Mem. ABA. Mem. United Ch. of Christ. Home: 2370 Martin Rd Akron OH 44333-2014

SEIBERT, ALBERT FRANK, chemical engineer; b. Houston, Oct. 29, 1958; s. Albert Frank and Cecilia Ruth (Williams) S. BSChemE, U. Houston, 1982; MSChemE, U. Tex., Austin, 1984, PhD in Engring., 1986. Rsch. assoc. Separations Rsch. Program, Austin, 1986-92, rsch. engr., 1993, tech. mgr., 1993—; cons. J.L. Humphrey & Assocs., Austin, 1987—. Author: Fluid Mixture Separation Technologies for Cost Reduction and Process Improvement, 1986; contbr. articles to profl. jours. Getty Oil scholar, 1981-82; recipient Excellence award ARCO, 1982. Mem. AIChE, N.Am. Membrae Soc. Achievements include discovery of method of cleaning produced water with carbon dioxide in a countercurrent contractor; contributed to the development of the membrane extractor and high capacity co-current distillation tray. Office: U Tex CES Bldg 133 10100 Burnet Rd Austin TX 78730

SEIBERT, RUSSELL JACOB, botanist, research associate; b. Shiloh Valley, Ill., Aug. 14, 1914; s. Erwin W. and Helen A. (Renner) S.; m. Isabelle L. Pring, Dec. 26, 1942; children: Michael, Donna, Lisa. A.B., Washington U., St. Louis, 1937, M.S., 1938, Ph.D., 1947. With U.S. Dept. Agr., 1940-50; botanist-geneticist rubber plant investigations U.S. Dept. Agr., Haiti, 1941-42; botanist-geneticist U.S. Dept. Agr., Peru, 1943-46, Costa Rica, 1947-49; dir. Los Angeles State and County Arboretum, Arcadia, Calif., 1950-55, Longwood Gardens, Kennett Square, Pa., 1955-79; adj. curator tropical horticulture Marie Selby Bot. Garden, Sarasota, Fla., 1979—; adj. prof. bot. garden mgmt. U. Del., 1967-79; head dept. arboreta and bot. gardens, Los Angeles County, 1952-55; Am. del. Internat. Soc. Hort. Sci., 1960-70; chmn. Am. Hort. Council-U.S.A. (hort. exhbn.), 1960; (floriade), Rotterdam, Holland; v.p. XVII Internat. Hort. Congress, 1966; chmn. Am. Hort. Film Festival, 1964-69. Recipient Frank N. Meyer Meml. medal Am. Genetic Soc., 1966, Arthur Hoyt Scott Garden and Horticulture medal Swarthmore Coll., 1975, Disting. Svc. awrd Hort. Soc. N.Y., 1969, award of merit Am. Assn. Bot. Gardens and Arboreta, 1982. Mem. AAAS, Am. Hort. Soc. (pres. 1964-65, Liberty Hyde Bailey medal 1975), Am. Inst. Biol. Scis., Rotary, Sigma Xi, Phi Sigma, Gamma Sigma Delta. Home: 1613 Caribbean Dr Sarasota FL 34231-5305 Office: Marie Selby Bot Garden Sarasota FL 34230

SEIBOLD, JAMES RICHARD, physician, researcher; b. Washington, Apr. 5, 1950; s. Herman Rudolph and Clara Bond (Taylor) S.; m. Margaret Frances Bennett, Jan. 20, 1968; children: Jon Drew, Zachary Bennett. BS, La. State U., 1972; MD, SUNY, Stony Brook, 1975. Diplomate Am. Bd. Internal Medicine, Am. Bd. Rheumatology. Intern in medicine L.I. Jewish Hosp., New Hyde Park, N.Y., 1975-76, resident in medicine, 1976-78; fellow in rheumatology U. Pitts., 1978-80; asst. prof. medicine Robert Wood Johnson Med. Sch. U. Medicine and Dentistry of N.J., New Brunswick, 1980-86, assoc. prof. medicine Robert Wood Johnson Med. Sch., 1986-92, chief rheumatology Robert Wood Johnson Med. Sch., 1986-91, dir. clin. rsch. ctr. Robert Wood Johnson Med. Sch., 1989-95; mem. adv. bd. Ctr. for Advanced Biotech. and Medicine, Piscataway, N.J., 1989-95, dir. Scleroderma program 1995—; W.H. Conzen chair clin. pharmacology Schering-Plough Found., Inc., 1989. Author: (chpt.) Rheumatology, 1988, 91, 94, 95; contbr. over 200 articles to profl. jours. Fellow ACP, Am. Coll. Rheumatology (regional coun. 1985). Mem. Soc. of Friends. Home: 16 Durham Rd Skillman NJ 08558-1805 Office: U Medicine & Dentistry NJ Robert

Wood Johnson Med Sch 1 Robert Wood Johnson Pl # 19cn New Brunswick NJ 08901-1928

SEIBOLD, RONALD LEE, sociologist, writer; b. Kansas City, Mo., May 8, 1945; s. Dean Phillip and Helen H. (Haney) S.; m. Christine Herbst, June 23, 1971 (div. July 1975). BS, Emporia State U., 1967; MA, Colo. State U., 1969. Dir. chpt. services Alpha Kappa Lambda, Ft. Collins, Colo., 1969-71; v.p. Siever & Assocs., Ft. Collins, 1971-72; pvt. practice sociology research Colo., 1972-75; coodinator Pines Internat., Lawrence, Kans., 1975—, sec., treas., 1976-87, pres., 1987—; pres. Live Foods Co., Lawrence, 1978—. Author: AKL Manual, 1969, Pines...The Wheat Grass People, 1982, Condominium Farming, 1986; editor: Cereal Grass: What's in it for You, 1990, Ceral Grass: Nature's Greatest Health Gift, 1993; contbr. articles to profl. mags. Founder, pres. Midwestern Interfraternity Coun., Emporia, Kans., 1966; pres. Interfraternity Coun., Emporia, 1965; v.p. Collegiate Young Reps., Emporia, 1965; mem. Kans. Organic Producers, 1978—, Organic Crop Improvement Assn., 1990—; pres. Wilderness Cmty. Edn. Found., 1989—. George Meredith scholar Emporia State U., 1963. Mem. Nat. Nutritional Foods Assn., Nutritional Products Quality Assurance Assn. (co-chmn. green foods group 1992—), Organic Crop Improvement Assn., Lawrence C. of C., U.S. C. of C., Kappa Mu Epsilon, Xi Phi. Presbyterian. Home: 1992 E 1400 Rd Lawrence KS 66044-9803 Office: Pines Internat Inc PO Box 1107 Lawrence KS 66044-8107

SEIDE, PAUL, civil engineering educator; b. N.Y.C., July 22, 1926; s. Julius David and Sylvia (Eiler) S.; m. Joan Cecilia Matalka, Jan. 7, 1951; children: Richard Laurence, Wendy Jane Seide Kielsmeier. B.C.E., CCNY, 1946; M. Aero. Engring, U. Va., 1952; Ph.D., Stanford U., 1954. Aero. research scientist Nat. Adv. Commn. for Aeros., Langley AFB, Va., 1946-52; research asst. Stanford Calif. U., 1952-53; research engr. Northrop Aircraft Co., Hawthorne, Calif., 1953-55; head methods and theory sect. TRW Inc., Los Angeles, 1955-60; head methods and research sect. Aerospace Corp., El Segundo, Calif., 1960-65; prof. civil engring. U. So. Calif., L.A., 1965-91, prof. emeritus, 1991—, assoc. chmn. dept. civil engring., 1971-73, 81-83; Albert Alberman vis. prof. Technion-Israel Inst. Tech., Haifa, 1975; vis. prof. U. Sydney, Australia, 1986, U. Canterbury, N.Z., 1986; cons. Northrop Inc., 1972-77, Aerospace Corp., 1966-68, Rockwell Inc., El Segundo, 1982-85. Author: Small Elastic Deformations of Thin Shells, 1975; contbr. numerous articles to profl. jours. NSF fellow, 1964-65. Fellow ASME, Am. Acad. Mechanics; mem. ASCE (life), Tau Beta Pi, Sigma Xi. Democrat. Jewish. Home: 300 Via Alcance Palos Verdes Peninsula CA 90274-1105 Office: U So Calif University Park Civil Engring Dept Los Angeles CA 90089-2531

SEIDEL, FREDERICK LEWIS, poet; b. St. Louis, Feb. 19, 1936; s. Jerome Jay and Thelma (Cartun) S.; children: Felicity, Samuel. AB, Harvard U., 1957. occasional lectr., Rutgers U., New Brunswick, 1964—; Paris editor, Paris Review, 1961, advisory editor, 1962. Author: (poetry) Final Solutions, 1963, Sunrise, 1979 (Lamont Poetry prize Acad. Am. Poets 1980, Am. Poetry Rev. prize 1980, Nat. Book Critics Circle award for poetry 1981), Men and Woman: New and Selected Poems, 1984, Poems 1959-1979, 1989, These Days, 1989, My Tokyo, 1993. Guggenheim Fellow, 1993.

SEIDEL, GEORGE ELIAS, JR., animal scientist, educator; b. Reading, Pa., July 13, 1943; s. George E. Sr. and Grace Esther (Heinly) S.; m. Sarah Beth Moore, May 28, 1970; 1 child, Andrew. BS, Pa. State U., 1965; MS, Cornell U., 1968, PhD, 1970; postgrad., Harvard U. Med. Sch., Boston, 1970-71. Asst. prof. physiology Colo. State U., Ft. Collins, 1971-75, assoc. prof., 1975-83, prof., 1983—; vis. scientist Yale U., 1978-79, MIT, 1986-87; mem. bd. on agr. NRC. Co-editor: New Technologies in Animal Breeding, 1981; contbr. articles to profl. jours. Recipient Alexander Von Humboldt award, N.Y.C., 1983, Animal Breeding Research award Nat. Assn. Animal Breeders, Columbia, Mo., 1983, Clark award Colo. State U., 1982, Upjohn Physiology award, 1986; Gov's. award for Sci. and Tech., Colo., 1986. Mem. AAAS, NAS, Am. Dairy Sci. Assn., Am. Soc. Animal Sci. (Young Animal Scientist award 1983), Soc. for Study of Reprodn., Internat. Embryo Transfer Soc. (pres. 1979). Home: 3101 Arrowhead Rd Laporte CO 80535-9374 Office: Animal Reprodn Biotechnol Lab Colo State U Fort Collins CO 80523

SEIDEL, MILTON JOSEPH, government administrator; b. Milw., July 3, 1931; s. Lawrence John and Anna (Norville) S.; m. Katherine Vukelic, Aug. 18, 1956; 1 child, Joseph Lawrence. BS cum laude, St. Louis U., 1956; MS, Washington U., St. Louis, 1963, postgrad., 1963-64. Spl. project engr. Alton (Ill.) Box Bd. Co., 1960-68; dir. mfg. engring. Colt Industries, St. Louis, 1968-71, Kuhlman Corp., Lexington, Ky., 1971-72; mgr. engring. edn. program U.S. Postal Service, Washington, 1972-74; chief Bur. Engraving and Printing, Office of Engring., Washington, 1974-79, asst. dir. research and engring., 1979-88, asst. dir. tech., 1988—; assoc. prof. Grad. Sch. Engring., George Washington U., Washington, 1973—; author, chmn. proceedings Internat. Conf. Machine Inspection Printed Security Documents, 1986, Internat. Conf. on Security Documents in 21st Century, 1987. Author: Economic Analysis for Capital Investment, 1972, Volume Forecasting, 1973, Network Analysis, 1973, Manpower Scheduling, 1974, Electronics Scanning, 1981, Electronic Quality Examination, 1981, Progress of Manufacturing Operation, 1985, Technology Innovation and Development Program, 1987. Served with U.S. Army, 1948-52. Mem. ASME, Ops. Research Soc. Am., Tech. Assn. Graphic Arts, Am. Soc. Pub. Adminstrn., Sigma Xi, Alpha Eta Rho. Home: 14412 Ansted Rd Silver Spring MD 20905-4410 Office: Bur Engraving and Printing 14th C St SW Washington DC 20228

SEIDEL, SELVYN, lawyer, educator; b. Long Branch, N.J., Nov. 6, 1942; s. Abraham and Anita (Stoller) S.; m. Deborah Lew, June 21, 1970; 1 child, Emily. BA, U. Chgo., 1964; JD, U. Calif., Berkeley, 1967; Diploma in Law, Oxford U., 1968. Bar: N.Y. 1970, U.S. Dist. Ct. (so. and ea. dists.) N.Y. 1970, D.C. Cir. Appeals, 1982. Ptnr. Latham & Watkins, N.Y.C., 1984—; adj. prof. Sch. Law, NYU, 1974-85; instr. Practicing Law Inst., 1980-81, 84. Mem. ABA, New York County Bar Assn., N.Y.C. Bar Assn. (mem. fed. cts. com. 1982-85, internat. law com. 1989-92, 95—), Boalt Hall Alumni Assn. (bd. dirs. 1980-82), Contbr. articles to profl. jours. Office: Latham & Watkins 885 3rd Ave New York NY 10022-4834

SEIDELMAN, ARTHUR ALLAN, director; b. N.Y.C.; s. Theodore and Jeanne (Greenberg) S. BA, Whittier (Calif.) Coll., 1958; MA, UCLA, 1960. Adminstr. Forum Theater, Lincoln Ctr., N.Y.C., 1970-72; pres. LSV Prodns., N.Y.C., 1972-76; v.p. Golden Eagle Prodns., N.Y.C., 1977-79; pres. Entertainment Profls., Inc., L.A., 1980-92, Entpro, Inc., L.A., 1992—. Dir.: (feature films) Rescue Me, The Caller, Children of Rage, Echoes, Ivye, (TV episodes) Hill Street Blues (Emmy, Humanitas awards for "Doris in Wonderland"), Murder She Wrote, Magnum, P.I., Knots Landing, Trapper John, M.D., Fame, A Year in the Life, L.A. Law, Capital News, WIOU, F.B.I. The Untold Stories, Sweet Justice, Amazing Grace, others, (TV movies) Which Mother is Mine? (Emmy award, Christopher award, Golden Halo award), I Love Liberty (Writer's Guild award), Schoolboy Father, Having a Baby, Look Away (Emmy nomination), Macbeth, A Matter of Time (Emmy award, Chgo. Film Festival Silver plaque, N.Y. Internat. Film Festival Silver plaque), She Drinks a Little (Emmy award, Golden Halo award), Strange Voices, A Place at the Table, An Enemy Among Us (Nancy Susan Reynolds award), Poker Alice, Sin of Innocence, Kate's Secret, A Friendship in Vienna (Grand prize N.Y. Internat. Film Festival), The People Across the Lake, Addicted to His Love, The Glory Years, False Witness, The Kid Who Loved Christmas, Body Language, Dying to Remember, Trapped in Space, The Secrets of Lake Success, Amazing Grace (pilot), Harvest of Fire; dir. Broadway and Off-Broadway plays Hamp. Ceremony of Innocence, Awake and Sing, Billy, Inherit the Wind, Justice Box, Vieux Carrè, The Mose Happy Fella for the N.Y.C. Opera, Gypsy Princess for Opera Pacific, The Sisters at the Pasadena Playhouse, others; host TV series Actors on Acting (Emmy award). Bd. dirs. ACLU So. Calif., L.A., 1986-94. Democrat. Office: Entpro, Inc 1015 Gayley Ave # 1149 Los Angeles CA 90024-3424

SEIDELMAN, SUSAN, film director; b. Pa., Dec. 11, 1952. Student, Drexel U., NYU. Dir. films, including: Smithereens, 1982, Desperately Seeking Susan, 1985, Making Mr. Right, 1987, Cookie, 1989, She-Devil, 1990, The Dutch Master (nominee Acad. award in dramatic short category), 1994, The Barefoot Executive, 1995; directorial debut with short film: You Act Like One, Too (Student Film award AMPAS). Office: care Michael Shedler 225 W 34th St Ste 1012 New York NY 10122-0049 also: William Morris Agy 151 El Camino Los Angeles CA 90048

SEIDEMANN, ROBERT SIMON, manufacturing company executive; b. Cleve., Jan. 25, 1938; s. Hans and Ilse (Cohn) S.; m. Anita Claire Rudolph, Dec. 27, 1959; children: Lisa Eiduson, Teri Robbins. AB, U. Mich., 1959; MA, Ohio State U., 1962. CPA, Ohio. Staff acct. Soloway & von Rosen, Cleve., 1962-68; controller, v.p. fin. Hunting Oil Co., Lakewood, Ohio, 1968-72; dir. devel. Second Fed. Savs. & Loan, Cleve., 1972-74; v.p. Fin. Am., Inc., Cleve., 1974-76; v.p. fin., CFO Tokyo Shapiro Inc., Cleve., 1976-80; chmn. bd., CEO Seidemann & Assoc., Inc., Cleve., 1980-88; dir. Price Waterhouse, Cleve., 1988-92; nat. ptnr. Arthur Andersen, Cleve., 1992-94; chmn., CEO Vicon Fabricating Co., 1994—. Co-author: Workouts and Turnarounds, 1991. Bd. trustees Fairmont Temple, Beachwood, 1980—. Mem. Turnaround Mgmt. Assn. (bd. dirs. 1985-93), Assn. Insolvency Accts. (bd. dirs. 1984-88). Home: 3122 Bremerton Rd Pepper Pike OH 44124-5345 Office: Vicon Fabricating Co 150 Parker Ct Chardon OH 44024

SEIDEN, ANDY, lawyer; b. N.Y.C., Sept. 16, 1956; s. Stanley and Dorothy Rose. BS in Indsl. and Labor Rels., Cornell U., 1978; vis. student, Harvard Law Sch., 1980-81; JD, U. Calif., Berkeley, 1981. Bar: Calif. 1981, N.Y. 1993. Assoc. Donovan Leisure Newton & Irvine, L.A., 1981-85, Curtis Mallet-Prevost Colt & Mosle, N.Y.C., 1987-89, Pettit & Martin, San Francisco, 1989-91; pvt. practice San Francisco, 1991-93; ptnr. Whitehead & Porter, San Francisco, 1993-95; v.p. bus. devel. and bus. affairs, gen. counsel Big Top Prodns., San Francisco, 1995—. Bd. dirs. L.A. League of Conservation Voters, L.A., 1983-85. Mem. ABA (com. on negotiated acquisitions 1994—), Multimedia Devel. Group, Phi Kappa Phi. Democrat. Avocations: world travel, skiing, cultural anthropology, computers. Home: 2677 Larkin St San Francisco CA 94109 Office: Big Top Prodns 548 Fourth St San Francisco CA 94107

SEIDEN, HENRY (HANK SEIDEN), advertising executive; b. Bklyn., Sept. 6, 1928; s. Jack S. and Shirley (Berkowitz) S.; m. Helena Ruth Zaldin, Sept. 10, 1949; children: Laurie Ann, Matthew Ian. BA, Bklyn. Coll., 1949; MBA, CCNY, 1954. Trainee Ben Sackheim Advt. Agy., 1949-51; nat. promotion mgr. N.Y. Post Corp., 1951-53; promotion mgr. Crowell-Collier Pub. Co., Inc., 1953-54; copy group head Batten, Barton, Durstine & Osborn, Inc., 1954-60; v.p., creative dir. Keyes, Madden & Jones, 1960-61; sr. v.p., assoc. creative dir. McCann-Marschalk, Inc., 1961-65, chmn. plans bd., 1964-65; creative dir., dir., prin. Hicks & Greist, Inc., N.Y.C., 1965—, sr. v.p., 1965-74, exec. v.p., 1974-83, COO, 1983—, pres., 1986—; CEO Ketchum/Hicks & Greist Inc., 1987-89; chmn., CEO Ketchum Advt., 1989-91; exec. v.p. Ketchum Comm. Inc., also bd. dirs.; vice chmn. Jordan, McGrath, Case & Taylor, Inc., 1992—; chmn., CEO The Seiden Group, Inc.; bd. dirs. Ketchum Internat. Inc.; guest lectr. Bernard M. Baruch Sch. Bus. and Pub. Adminstrn., CCNY, 1962—, Baruch Coll., 1969—, New Sch. Social Scis., 1968, 72,73, Sch. Visual Arts, 1979, 80—, Lehman Coll., CCNY, 1980—, Ohio U., 1981, Newhouse Grad. Sch., Syracuse U., 1981, NYU, 1983; cons. pub. rels. and comm. to mayor City of New Rochelle, N.Y., 1959—; cons. mktg. dept. Ohio State U.; cons. to pres. N.Y.C. City Coun., 1972-73; cons. Postmaster Gen. U.S., 1972-74; comm. advisor to commr. N.Y.C. Police Dept., 1973—, hon. dept. commr., 1991—, spl. cons. to commr., 1992—. Author: Advertising Pure and Simple, 1976, Advertising Pure and Simple: The New Edition, 1990; contbg. editor: Madison Ave. mag, 1966—, Advt. Age, Mag. Age; guest columnist: N.Y. Times, 1972. Vice commr. Little League of New Rochelle; bd. dirs. Police Res. Assn. N.Y.C., 1973—, pres. exec. com.; bd. dirs. Cancer Rsch. and Treatment Fund, Inc., pres., 1992—, Transmedia Network, Inc.; bd. dirs., pres. New York's Finest Found., 1975—, pres., 1996; bd. dirs., sr. v.p. Drug Enforcement Agy. Found., 1995—. Recipient award Four Freedoms Found., 1959, award Printers Ink, 1960, promotion award Editor and Pub., 1955, Am. TV Commls. Festival award, 1963-69, Effie award Am. Mktg. Assn., 1969, 70, award Art Dirs. Club N.Y., 1963-70, award Am. Inst. Graphic Arts, 1963, Starch award, 1969, spl. award graphic art lodge B'nai B'rith Greater N.Y., 1971, 87, award of highest honor FBI Nat. Acad., 1994. Mem. NATAS, Am. Inst. Mgmt. (assoc.), Drug Enforcement Agts. Found. (sr. v.p. 1995), Advt. Club N.Y. (exec. judge Andy awards, award 1963-65), Advt. Writers Assn. N.Y. (Gold Key award for best newspaper and mag. advts. 1962-640, Copy Club (co-chmn. awards com., Gold Key award for best TV comml. 1969), Alpha Phi Omega. Home: 1056 5th Ave New York NY 10028-0112 Office: The Seiden Group 445 Park Ave New York NY 10022-2606 *Be yourself but don't take yourself too seriously.*

SEIDEN, STEVEN ARNOLD, executive search consultant; b. N.Y.C., Feb. 18, 1936; s. Leon and Eleanor (Troy) S.; m. Katherine Cohen, June 8, 1965; children: Lisa Brooke, Hilary Anne. AB, Yale U., 1958. Pres. Seiden Krieger Assocs., 1984—; mem. N.Y. Stock Exchange Regulatory Adv. Com., 1981-83, policy com. Am. Council for Capital Formation, 1982-87. Mem. adv. bd. Registered Rep. Mag., 1982-84. Served with U.S. Army, 1961-62. Mem. Wall St. Tax Assn. (bd. dirs. 1981-83), Assn. Corp. Growth (bd. dirs., asst. v.p. 1987-88), Securities Industry Assn. (bd. dirs. 1981-83), N.Y. Soc. Security Analysts, Turnaround Mgmt. Assn. (program co-chair N.Y. chpt. 1991-92), Internat. Assn. Corp. and Profl. Recruiters (editorial bd. 1993-95), U.S. C. of C. (small bus. coun. 1985-89), Century Country Club, Bond Club. Republican. Office: Seiden Krieger Assocs 375 Park Ave New York NY 10152

SEIDENBERG, IVAN G., telecommunications company executive; b. N.Y.C., Dec. 10, 1946; s. Howard and Kitty (Zaretsky) S.; m. Phyllis A. Maisel, Dec. 13, 1969; children: Douglas, Lisa. BS in Math., CUNY, 1972; MBA in Mktg. Mgmt., Pace U., 1980. Various engring. positions N.Y. Tel., 1966-74; dist. mgr. transmission design AT&T, Basking Ridge, N.J., 1974-76; dist. mgr. tech. planning AT&T, Basking Ridge, 1976-78; div. mgr. fed. regulatory AT&T, N.Y.C., 1978-81, asst. v.p. mktg., 1981-83; v.p. fed. relations Nynex Corp., Washington, 1983-86, former v.p. external affairs, former pres. and vice chmn., chmn., 1995—. Served as sgt. U.S. Army, 1966-68, Vietnam. Mem. U.S. Telephone Assn. (bd. dirs. 1985—), Rockland Bus. Council (trustee 1987). Office: Nynex Corp 1095 Avenue of the Americas New York NY 10036*

SEIDENSTICKER, EDWARD GEORGE, Japanese language and literature educator; b. Castle Rock, Colo., Feb. 11, 1921; s. Edward George and Mary Elizabeth (Dillon) S. B.A., U. Colo., 1942; M.A., Columbia U., 1947; postgrad., Harvard U., 1947-48; LittD (hon.), U. Md., 1991. With U.S. Fgn. Service, Dept. State, Japan, 1947-50; mem. faculty Stanford U., 1962-66, prof., 1964-66; prof. dept. Far Eastern langs. and lit. U. Mich., Ann Arbor, 1966-77; prof. Japanese Columbia U., 1977-85, prof. emeritus, 1986—. Author: Kafu the Scribbler, 1965, Japan, 1961, Low City, High City, 1983, Tokyo Rising, 1990, Very Few People Come This Way, 1994; transl.: (by Murasaki Shikibu) The Tale of Genji, 1976. Served with USMCR, 1942-46. Decorated Order of Rising Sun Japan; recipient Nat. Book award, 1970; citation Japanese Ministry Edn., 1971; Kikuchi Kan prize, 1977; Goto Miyoko prize, 1982; Japan Found. prize, 1984; Tokyo Cultural award, 1985; Yamagata Banto prize, 1992. *"Make yourself a routine and stick to it," said my childhood piano teacher when I went off to college. I have never had, as some people seem to have, great plans for my future; but if a person has a serious routine and sticks resolutely with it, something is bound to get accomplished.*

SEIDERMAN, ARTHUR STANLEY, optometrist, consultant; b. Phila., Nov. 28, 1936; s. Morris and Anne (Roseman) S.; m. Susan Levin, Aug. 19, 1965; children: David, Leeann, Scott. Student, U. Vienna (Austria) Med. Sch., 1965; OD, Pa. Coll. of Optometry, 1963; AB, W.Va. Wesleyan Coll., 1959; MA, Fairleigh Dickinson U., 1973. Pvt. practice Elkins Park, Pa., 1971-94, Plymouth Meeting, Pa., 1994—; vision cons. U.S. Olympic Teams, Phila. Flyers Hockey Team. Co-author: The Athletic Eye, 1983, 20/20 Is Not Enough, 1990; mem. editoral adv. bd. Jour. of Learning Disabilities, 1979—. Vice pres. Jewish Nat. Fund, Phila., 1988—. Capt. U.S. Army, 1963-68. Fellow Am. Acad. Optometry, Coll. of Optometrists in Vision Devel.; mem. Multidisciplinary Acad. of Clin. Edn. (pres.), Internat. Reading Assn. (pres. disabled group 1987-89). Home: 155 Sawgrass Dr Blue Bell PA 19422 Office: 919 E Germantown Pike Ste 4 Norristown PA 19401-2442

SEIDERS, JOSEPH ROBERT, service company corporate executive, lawyer; b. Reading, Pa., Oct. 21, 1948; s. Harry Robert and Evelyn Kathryn (Knauer) S.; m. Sharon Ann Hunter, Aug. 21, 1976. BA, LaSalle Coll., Phila., 1970, MBA, 1982; JD, Temple U., Phila., 1974. Bar: Pa. 1974, U.S. Dist. Ct. (ea. dist.) Pa. 1974. Sole practice, Horsham, Pa., 1974-78; of counsel CDI Corp., Phila., 1978—, v.p., sec., 1980-87, sr. v.p., sec., 1987—. Pres., bd. dirs. Lafayette Place Homeowners Assn., 1986—. Mem. ABA, Pa. Bar Assn., Phila. Bar Assn., Nat. Tech. Services Assn. (pres., chmn. legal and legis. com. 1984-87). Republican. Home: 11 Bunker Hill Dr Washington Crossing PA 18977-1415 Office: CDI Corp 1717 Arch St Fl 35 Philadelphia PA 19103-2713

SEIDL, FREDRICK WILLIAM, dean, social work educator; b. Buffalo, Sept. 29, 1940; s. Wolfgang and Anna Clara (Schneider) S.; m. Ann Jane Hazlewood, Apr. 19, 1963; children: Andrew, Barbara. AB, Ohio U., 1962; MSW, SUNY, Buffalo, 1964; PhD, U. Wis., 1970. Asst. prof. U. Minn., Morris, 1964-68; assoc. prof. Wilfred Laurier U., Waterloo, Ont., Can., 1970-72; assoc. prof. U. Wis., Madison, 1972-78, prof., 1978-84, dir. Sch. Social Work, 1980-82; dean, prof. Sch. Social Work SUNY, Buffalo, 1985—; resident Toynbee Hall, London, England, 1991. Author: The Wisconsin Experiment, 1984; contbr. articles on social issues, edn., to jours., 1964—; author, performer: (musical) Hull House: A Folk Music Celebration, 1988, Songs of New Horizons, 1989, Letter From America, 1992, 3 albums of Folk Revival music, 1990-92. Bd. dirs. Child and Family Svcs., Buffalo, 1989—, Gateway Youth and Family Svcs., Williamsville, N.Y., 1989—, United Way, Buffalo, 1989—, Urban League, Buffalo, 1989—; bd. visitors Ohio U., Athens; chair edn. div. Buffalo Philharm. Ann. Appeal; mem. editorial com. Social Work Encyclopedia. Recipient Alumnus of Yr. award SUNY, Buffalo, 1985. Mem. Nat. Assn. Social Workers, Nat. Assn. Deans and Dirs. Social Work Schs., Coun. Social Work Edn. Democrat. Avocations: folk music, canoeing. Home: 69 Symphony Cir Buffalo NY 14201-1203 Office: SUNY Buffalo Sch Social Work 285 Almont Ave Buffalo NY 14224-2203

SEIDL, JANE PATRICIA, lawyer; b. Stamford, Conn., June 9, 1958; d. Francis Xavier and Frances (Nizolek) S. BA magna cum laude, Boston Coll., 1980; JD, U. Conn., 1985. Bar: Conn. 1985, U.S. Dist. Ct. Conn. 1985. Fin. editor Fin. Acctg. Standards Bd., Stamford, 1980-82; assoc. Schatz & Schatz, Ribicoff & Kotkin, Hartford, Conn., 1985-92; sr. counsel Northeast Utilities, Hartford, Conn., 1992—. Mem. ABA, Conn. Bar Assn., Hartford County Bar Assn., Hartford Assn. Women Attys. (pres. dir 1992—). Avocations: photography, water sports, literature. Office: Northeast Utilities PO Box 270 Hartford CT 06141-0270

SEIDLER, B(ERNARD) ALAN, lawyer; b. N.Y.C., Nov. 26, 1946; s. Aaron H. and Ethel T. (Berkowitz) S.; m. Lynne Aubrey, Jan. 21, 1978; children—Jacob A., Morgan H., Lily R. B.A., Colgate U., 1968; J.D., Seton Hall U., 1972. Bar: N.Y. 1973, U.S. Dist. Ct. (ea. and so. dists.) N.Y. 1975, U.S. Ct. Appeals (2d cir.) 1976, U.S. Supreme Ct. 1977, U.S. Ct. Appeals (3rd cir.) 1984. Staff atty. N.Y. Legal Aid Soc., N.Y.C., 1972-75; sole practice, N.Y.C. and Nyack, N.Y., 1975—. Mem. ABA, N.Y. County Lawyers Assn. Club: Snedens Landing Tennis Assn. (Palisades, N.Y.). Office: 127 S Broadway Nyack NY 10960-4411

SEIDLER, DORIS, artist; b. London, Nov. 26, 1912; m. Bernard Seidler, Sept. 5, 1935; 1 son, David. Group exhbns. include Bklyn. Mus. Bi-Ann., Vancouver Internat., Honolulu Acad. Arts, Pa. Acad. Fine Arts, Phila., Soc. Am. Graphic Artists, Assoc. Am. Artists Gallery, Jewish Mus., N.Y.C., Bklyn. Mus., Albright-Knox, 1994; represented in permanent collections Libr. of Congress, Smithsonian Instn., Washington, Phila. Mus. Art, Bklyn. Mus., Seattle Mus. Art, Whitney Mus., Nat. Gallery Art, Nassau County (N.Y.) Mus. Fine Arts, Brit. Mus., London, Victorial and Albert Mus. London, Pallant House Coll., Eng., Portland Mus. Art, Oreg. Mem. Soc. Am. Graphic Artists (rec. sec. 1964-71, past v.p.). Address: 14 Stoner Ave Great Neck NY 11021-2101

SEIDMAN, DAVID N(ATHANIEL), materials science and engineering educator; b. N.Y.C., July 5, 1938; s. Charles and Jeanette (Cohen) S.; m. Shoshanah Cohen-Sabban, Oct. 21, 1973; children: Elie, Ariel, Eytan. BS, NYU, 1960, MS, 1962; PhD, U. Ill., Urbana, 1965. Postdoc. assoc. Cornell U., Ithaca, N.Y., 1964-66, asst. prof. materials sci. and engring., 1966-70, assoc. prof. materials sci. and engring., 1970-76, prof. materials sci. and engring., 1976-85; prof. materials sci. and engring. Northwestern U., Evanston, Ill., 1985-96, Walter P. Murphy prof. materials sci. and engring., 1996—; vis. prof. Technion, Haifa, 1969, Tel-Aviv U., Ramat-Aviv, 1972; Lady Davis vis. prof. Hebrew U., Jerusalem, 1978, 80-81, prof. materials sci., 1983-85; vis. scientist C.E. de Grenoble, 1981, C.N.E.T.-Meylan, 1981, C.E. de Scalay, 1989, U. Goettingen, 1989, 92; sci. cons. Argonne (Ill.) Nat. labs., 1985-94. Spl. issues editor, editl. bd. Interface Sci., 1993—; contbr. numerous articles on internal interfaces, atomic-scale imperfections in metals and semicondrs., radiation effects, field-ion, atom-probe and electron microscopy, 1964—. Recipient Max Planck Rsch. prize Max-Planck-Gesellschaft and the A. von Humboldt-Stiftung, 1993; Guggenheim fellow, 1972-73, 80-81, Humboldt fellow, 1989, 92; named chair for phys. metallurgy Gordon Conf., 1982. Fellow Am. Phys. Soc.; mem. AAAS, Metall. Soc. (Hardy Gold medal 1967), Materials Rsch. Soc., Microscopy Soc. Am., A. von Humboldt Soc. Am. Democrat. Jewish. Avocations: reading history and novels, travel. Home: 9056 Tamaroa Ter Skokie IL 60076-1928 Office: Northwestern U Engring Dept MLSF Bldg Evanston IL 60208-3108

SEIDMAN, ELLEN SHAPIRO, lawyer, government official; b. N.Y.C., Mar. 12, 1948; d. Benjamin Harry Shapiro and Edna (Eysen) Stern; m. Walter Becker Slocombe, June 14, 1981; 1 child, Benjamin William. AB, Radcliffe Coll., 1969; JD, Georgetown U., 1974; MBA, George Washington U., 1988. Bar: D.C., 1975. Law clk. U.S. Ct. of Claims, Washington, 1974-75; assoc. Caplin & Drysdale, Washington, 1975-78; atty., advisor U.S. Dept. of Transportation, Washington, 1978-79, dep. asst. gen. counsel, 1979-81; assoc. gen. counsel Chrysler Corp Loan Guaranty Bd., Washington, 1981-84; atty., advisor U.S. Dept. of Treasury, Washington, 1981-86, spl. asst. to the Under Sec. Fin., 1986-87; dir. strategic planning Fed. Nat. Mortgage Assn., Washington, 1987-88, v.p., asst. to chmn., 1988-91, sr. v.p. regulation rsch. and econs., 1991-93; spl. asst. to the pres. for econ. policy The White House, Washington, 1993—. Office: Federal Nat'l Mortgage Assoc 3900 Wisconsin Ave Washington DC 20016

SEIDMAN, HERTA LANDE, international trade and information company executive; married. BA in Econs. and Lit., McGill U. and U. Miami, 1959; MA, Cornell U., 1960. Mgr. shipping and internat. trade bus. devel. firm, 1962-76; dep. commr. N.Y. State Dept. of Commerce, 1976-79; asst. sec. for trade U.S. Dept. of Commerce Carter Adminstrn., 1979-81; mng. dir. Philipp Bros. (thereafter Phibro & Phibro-Salomon and Solomon Brothers), 1981-85; co-founder, chmn. Tradenet Corp., N.Y.C., 1985—; dir Atlantic Coun. of U.S.; chmn. Soros Bus. and Mgmt. Found.; vice chair N.Y. Gov.'s Coun. Internat. Bus. Bd. dirs. Jr. Achievement Internat., Albania Am. Enterprise Fund. Woodrow Wilson fellow, 1960. Mem. Coun. Fgn. Rels. Office: Tradenet Corp 520 Madison Ave New York NY 10022-4213

SEIDMAN, L(EWIS) WILLIAM, television commentator; b. Grand Rapids, Mich., Apr. 29, 1921; s. Frank E. and Esther (Lubetsky) S.; m. Sarah Berry, Mar. 3, 1944; children: Thomas, Tracy, Sarah, Carrie, Meg, Robin. A.B., Dartmouth Coll., 1943; LL.B., Harvard U., 1948; M.B.A., U. Mich., 1949. Bar: Mich. 1949, D.C. 1977. Spl. asst. fin. affairs to gov. of Mich., 1963-66; nat. mng. partner Seidman & Seidman C.P.A.s, N.Y.C., 1969-74; asst. for econ. affairs to Pres. Gerald R. Ford, 1974-77; dir., CEO Phelps Dodge Corp., N.Y.C., 1977-82; vice chmn. Phelps Dodge Corp., 1980-82; dean Coll. Bus. Adminstrn. Ariz. State U., Tempe, 1982-85; chmn. FDIC, Washington, 1985-91; chief commentator Sta. CNBC-TV, 1991; pub. Bank Dir. Mag., 1992; chmn. Detroit Fed. Res. Bank Chgo., 1970, RTC, 1989-91; co-chair White House Conf. on Productivity, 1983-84. Lt. USNR, 1942-46. Decorated Bronze Star. Mem. D.C. Bar Assn., Chevy Chase Club (Md.), Univ. Club (N.Y.C.), Crystal Downs Club (Mich.), Nantucket Yacht Club. Home: 1694 31st St NW Washington DC 20007-2924 Office: CNBC 1825 K St NW Washington DC 20006

SEIDMAN, MARIAN TAYLOR, adult education educator; b. Montclair, N.J., Oct. 25, 1954; d. John Albert and Virginia Anne (Cooney) Taylor; m. Stephen Michael Seidman, Aug. 17, 1979; 1 child, Julie Anne. BS in Elem. Edn., U. Hartford, West Hartford, Conn., 1976; MEd, West Chester (Pa.) U., 1990. Cert. reading specialist, elem. edn. tchr. Tchr. Our Lady of Mt.

Carmel Sch., Boonton, N.J., 1977-79, Catawba County Schs., Hickory, N.C., 1980-82, St. Joseph Sch., Big Bend, Wis., 1982-87; tchr., evaluator, asst. coord. Del. County Lit. Coun., Chester, Pa., 1991—. Mem. Internat. Reading Assn., Del. Valley Reading Assn., Keystone State Reading Assn., Laubach Lit. Action, Kappa Delta Pi. Avocations: gardening, crafts, baking, reading. Office: Del County Lit Coun Chester PA 19013

SEIDMAN, SAMUEL NATHAN, investment banker, economist; b. N.Y.C., Mar. 31, 1934; s. Hyman and Pauline (Seidman) S.; m. Herta Lande, Sept. 4, 1964. B.A., Bklyn. Coll., 1955; Ph.D., NYU, 1964. Instr. Douglass Coll., Rutgers U., New Brunswick, N.J., 1960-62; v.p. Lehman Bros. Internat., N.Y.C., 1962-70; pres. Seidman & Co. Inc., N.Y.C., 1970—; pres., dir. Prodn. Systems Acquisition Corp.; dir. Amrep Corp., N.Y.C., Harken Oil Corp., Dallas; dir., chmn. Victoria Station Corp., San Francisco, 1985-87. Trustee Mental Health Assn. N.Y., N.Y.C. 1980—. Served to pfc. U.S. Army, 1954-56. Univ. fellow Inst. Labor Relations, NYU, N.Y.C., 1957-58; Fulbright scholar U. Philippines, 1959-60. Mem. Am. Econ. Assn., Univ. Club (N.Y.C.), Lake Waramug Country Club (Conn.). Avocations: music; history of Asia. Office: 520 Madison Ave New York NY 10022-4213

SEIDNER, STANLEY S., academic administrator, educator; b. N.Y.C., June 26, 1945; m. Maria Medina Seidner, Feb. 24, 1980; children: Jacqueline Elinor, Ariel Joseph. BA, Bklyn. Coll., 1968; MA, St. John's U., 1970, PhD, 1975; 6th yr. degree, CUNY, Richmond, 1976; MEd, U. Ulster, No. Ireland, 1992. Adminstr. N.Y.C. schs., 1971-75; assoc. prof. Tchrs. Coll., Columbia U., N.Y.C., 1975-79; dir. bilingual tchr. tng. U. Miami, Fla., 1979-80; acad. dean Nat. Coll. Edn., Chgo., 1980-85; supt. Caribbean Schs., P.R., 1985-86; v.p. M.S. Assocs., Chgo., 1986-88; dean/dir. acad. rsch. and 2nd lang. programs DeVry Inst. Tech., Chgo., 1988-92; prof., univ. supr. S.W. Tex. State U., San Marcos, 1993—; cons. IBM Corp., P.R., 1980-92, Ministry of Edn., Spain, 1989-91. Author: In the Wake of Conservative Reaction, 1982, Issues of Language Assessment, 3 vols., 1981-88; (with others) Teaching the Soviet Child, 1980, Handbook for Secondary Bilingual Education, 1981. Recipient award Polish Acad. Arts and Scis., 1978, Italian Acad. Arts and Scis., Rome, 1987; recipient Acad. Recognition award NEA, 1983, Outstanding Acad. Achievement award U.S. Sec. of Edn., Washington, 1986; named NAAS Educator of Yr., 1985. Avocations: judo (3rd degree black belt), jiu jitsiu (2nd degree black belt), classical piano.

SEIFER, JUDITH HUFFMAN, sex therapist, educator; b. Springfield, Ill., Jan. 18, 1945; d. Clark Lewis and Catherine Mary (Fisher) Huffman; married; children: Christopher, Patrick, Andrea. RN, St. John's Hosp./Quincy Coll., 1965; MHS, Inst. Advanced Study Human Sexuality, 1981, PhD, 1986. RN, Ohio; Diplomate Am. Bd. Sexology. Charge nurse Grandview Hosp., Dayton, Ohio, 1967-70; v.p. Sego, Inc., Dayton, 1970-84, pres., 1984—; marital and sex therapist Grandview Ob-Gyn., Inc., Dayton, 1975-87; asst. clin. prof. psychiatry and ob-gyn Wright State U. Sch. Medicine, Dayton, 1985-93; edn. cons., screenwriter The Learning Corp., Ft. Lauderdale, Fla., 1990—; COO Am. Sex Inst., Hillsborough Beach, Fla., 1995—; CEO In Good Co., Inc., Lewisburg, W.Va., 1995—; adj. prof. psychology U. dayton, 185-90; profl. spkr. The Upjohn Co., Kalamazoo, 1986—, CIBA-GEIGY Co., 1987-90; chmn. tech. adv. com. Mercari Comm., Inc., Englewood, Colo., 1988-89; cons. dept. psychology VA Hosp., Dayotn, 1990-93. Author, screenwriter film script: Mercari Communications, 1988; editor: Jour. Sexuality and Relationships, 1995—; author, screenwriter film script: In Good Co., Inc., 1994—; guest editor: The D.O., 1985; contbr. articles to profl. jours. Pres. Dayton Osteopathic Aux., 1974-75, Aux. Ohio Osteopathic Assn., Columbus, 1981-82, Sister City Assn., Oakwood, Ohio, 1985-86; bd. dirs. Grace House Sexual Abuse Resource Ctr., Dayton, 1987-89, Planned Parenthood Miami Valley, Ohio, 1985-86, Social Health Assn., Dayton, 1976-87. Grantee Dayton Found., 1980-82; fellow Masters and Johnson Inst., 1984. Fellow Internat. Coun. Sex Educators, Am. Acad. Clin. Sexologists; mem. Am. Assn. Sex Educators, Counselors and Therapists (cert., rec. sec. 1986-91, pres. 1994—), Am. Coll. Sexologists. Roman Catholic. Avocation: public speaking. Office: Sego Corp 2 Deerfield Rd PO Box 426 Lewisburg WV 24901-0426

SEIFERT, BLAIR WAYNE, clinical pharmacist; b. Regina, Sask., Can., June 5, 1955; s. John Martin and Lottie P. S. (Murray) S. BS in Pharmacy, U. Sask., Saskatoon, 1977; PharmD, U. Tex., 1981. Hosp. pharmacy resident Regina Gen. Hosp., 1977-78; clin. pharmacy resident Bexar County Hosp., San Antonio, 1978-81; asst. dir. pharmacy Thomason Gen. Hosp., El Paso, 1981-83; perinatal clin. pharmacist Victoria (B.C.) Gen. Hosp., 1983-84; pediat. clin. pharmacist Health Scis. Centre, Winnipeg, Man., Can., 1984—; asst. prof. pharmacy U. Man., Winnipeg, 1984—, asst. prof. pediat., 1994—; reviewer Am. Jour. Hosp. Pharmacy, 1988—, Clin. Pharmacy, 1988—, Can. Jour. Hosp. Pharmacy, 1989—; mem. panel examiners Pharmacy Examining Bd. Can., 1992-94; reviewer ind. learning material panel Can. Coun. on Continuing Edn. in Pharmacy, 1994—; lectr. family asthma program Man. Lung Assn., 1985—; spkr. KNOW Drug Program, Man. Pharm. Assn., 1989—; presenter in field. Vol. Man. Riding for the Disabled, Winnipeg, 1987-89, Teddy Bears' Picnic, Children's Hosp. Rsch. Found., 1987-90 92—, Children's Miracle Network Telethon, Children's Hosp. Rsch. Found., 1987—, Can. Nat. Inst. for the Blind, 1990—. Fellow Can. Soc. Hosp. Pharmacists (jr. chmn. Man. chpt. 1987-88, sr. chmn. com. 1988-89, v.p. 1989-90, pres. 1990-91, past pres. 1991-92, mem. corr. edn. com. 1988-89, host com. 1990 ann. gen. meeting 1989-90, stds. com. 1990-91, clin. pharmacy adv. com. 1991-93, chmn. intravenous admixture revision task force 1993-95), Man. Pharm. Assn. (edn. com. 1988-89, 91—, planning com. 1989-92). Avocations: reading, horseback riding, figure skating. Office: Health Scis Ctr Dept Pharm Svcs, 820 Sherbrook St, Winnipeg, MB Canada R3A 1R9

SEIFERT, GEORGE, professional football coach; b. San Francisco, Jan. 22, 1940; m. Linda Seifert; children: Eve, Jason. Grad., U. Utah, 1963. Asst. football coach U. Utah, 1964; head coach Westminster Coll., 1965; asst. coach U. Iowa, 1966, U. Oreg., 1966-71; secondary coach Stanford U., 1972-74; head coach Cornell U., 1975-76; from secondary coach to defensive coord. San Francisco 49ers, 1980-89, head coach, 1989—. With AUS, 1963. Named NFL Coach of Yr. The Sporting News, 1990, 94. Office: San Francisco 49ers 4949 Centennial Blvd Santa Clara CA 95054-1229*

SEIFERT, LAURENCE CURT, communications company executive; b. Jersey City, Feb. 17, 1938; s. Curt August and Mabelle Martha (Bissig) S.; m. Lucretia Lillian Morgan, June 21, 1969; children: Cynthia, Laura, Tanya, Thomas. BSEE, N.J. Inst. Tech., 1963. Communications systems engr. Western Electric (now AT&T), Newark, Sunnyvale, Calif., 1957-69; mfg. supr. Western Electric (now AT&T), North Andover, Mass., 1969-72; with engring. mgmt. Western Electric (now AT&T), N.Y.C., 1972-77; with mktg. mgmt. AT&T, Morristown, N.J., 1977-78; mfg. engring. dir. Western Electric (now AT&T), Morristown, N.J., 1979-81, North Andover, Mass., 1981-83, Oklahoma City, 1983-85; mfg. R & D v.p. AT&T, Princeton, N.J., 1985-87; v.p. engring. AT&T, Berkeley Heights, N.J., 1987-89, sr. v.p. sourcing and mfg., 1989—; bd. dirs. Am. Ridge Ins. Co., Burlington, Vt., AT&T Consumer Products, Ltd., Singapore, AT&T Telecommunications Products, Ltd., Thailand. Author 7 published papers in field. Recipient Weston medal, Disting. Alumni award N.J. Inst. Tech., 1990; M. Eugene Merchant Manufacturing Medal of ASME/SME, Am. Soc. of Mechanical Engineers, 1995. Mem. NAE, Mfg. Studies Bd. NRC, IEEE, Inst. Indsl. Engrs., Soc. Mfg. Engrs. Avocations: golf, reading.

SEIFERT, LUKE MICHAEL, lawyer; b. Smyrna, Tenn., Apr. 8, 1957; s. Donald R. and Joan (Clemas) S.; m. Kathleen Louise Schaffer, Aug. 1, 1980; children: Joseph, Nicholas, Peter, Rachel. BA, Creighton U., 1979; JD, William Mitchell Sch. of Law, St. Paul, 1983. Bar: U.S. Dist. Ct. Minn., Minn. Page Minn. Ho. of Reps., St. Paul, 1980, com. adminstr., 1981-82; assoc. Holmen Law Office, St. Cloud, Minn., 1983-87; pvt. practice St. Cloud, 1987—. Mem. ABA, Minn. Bar Assn., Minn. Trial Lawyers Assn., Stearns Benton Bar Assn. (sec., treas. 1986-87, v.p. 1987-88, pres. 1988-89), K.C. (guard 1986-87, advocate 1987-90), Delta Theta Phi. Home: 1305 W Oakes Dr Saint Cloud MN 56303-0741 Office: 125 11th Ave N Saint Cloud MN 56303-4643

SEIFERT, THOMAS LLOYD, lawyer; b. Boston, June 6, 1940; s. Ralph Frederick and Hazel Bell (Harrington) S.; m. Ann Cecelia Berg, June 19, 1965. BS cum laude, Ind. U., 1962, JD cum laude, 1965. Bar: Ill. 1965, Ind. 1965, N.Y. 1979. Assoc. law firm Keck, Mahin & Cate, Chgo., 1965-67; atty. Essex Group, Inc., Ft. Wayne, Ind., 1967-70, Amoco Corp., Chgo., 1970-73; assoc. gen. counsel, asst. sec. Canteen Corp., Chgo., 1973-75; sec., gen. counsel The Marmon Group, Inc. (and predecessor cos.), Chgo., 1975-78; v.p., gen. counsel, sec. Hanson Industries, Inc., N.Y.C., 1978-82; sr. v.p. law, chief fin. officer Petrie Stores Corp., N.Y.C., 1982-83; mem. Finley, Kumble, Wagner, Heine, Underberg, Manley, Myerson & Casey, N.Y.C., 1983-87, Paul, Weiss, Rifkind, Wharton & Garrison, N.Y.C., 1987-91; gen. counsel, chief legal officer Sterling Grace Capital Mgmt., L.P. and affiliated cos., N.Y.C., 1991—. Note editor Ind. Law Jour., 1964-65. Named to Ind. Track and Cross Country Hall of Fame, 1993. Mem. ABA, N.Y. State Bar Assn., Order of Coif, The Creek, Beta Sigma Gamma. Home: Museum Tower 15 W 53rd St Apt 31 E New York NY 10019-5410 Office: Sterling Grace Capital Mgmt 515 Madison Ave Rm 2000 New York NY 10022-5403

SEIFERTH, DORIS JANE, controller, consultant; b. Roslyn, N.Y., Nov. 10, 1959; d. Kenneth Russell and Doris (Schlegel) S. BBA, St. Johns U., Jamaica, N.Y., 1985. Supr. Viacom Internat., N.Y.C., 1977-80; controller fin. On-Line Media, Inc., N.Y.C., 1980-84; controller Norman Gershman Cons., Inc., N.Y.C., 1984—; pvt. practice fin. cons. N.Y.C., 1983—. Republican. Roman Catholic. Avocations: hiking, running, paddleball. Office: Norman Gershman Cons Inc 74 Trinity Pl New York NY 10006

SEIFF, ALVIN, planetary, atmospheric and aerodynamics scientist; b. Kansas City, Mo., Feb. 26, 1922; s. Harry Louis and Sara Dorothy (Silverstone) S.; m. Robbye Walker, Mar. 27, 1948 (div. Oct. 1959); children: David Wilson, Deborah Ellen Seiff Hedgecock; m. Julia Gwynne Hill, June 23, 1968; children: Michael Harry, Geoffrey Bernard. BS ChemE, U. Mo., 1942; postgrad., U. Tenn., 1946-48, Stanford U., 1959-60. Chem. engr. TVA, Florence, Ala., 1942-43; tech. supr. uranium isotope separ. Tenn. Eastman Corp., Oak Ridge, 1944-45; instr. physics U. Tenn., Knoxville, 1945-48; aero. rsch. scientist NACA Ames Aero. Lab., Moffett Field, Calif., 1948-57; chief supersonic free flight rsch. br. NACA, Moffett Field, 1952-63; chief vehicle environment div. NASA Ames Rsch. Ctr., Moffett Field, 1963-72, sr. staff scientist dir.'s office, 1972-77, sr. staff scientist space sci. div., 1977-86; sr. rsch. assoc. San Jose (Calif.) State U. Found., 1987—; mem. entry sci. team Viking Mars Mission Langley Rsch. Ctr., NASA, Hampton, Va., 1972-77, mem. sci. steering group Pioneer Venus Project Ames Rsch. Ctr., Moffett Field, 1972-82, Galileo Project, sci. group Jet Propulsion Lab., Pasadena, 1979—, mem. sci. team Soviet-French Vega Venus Balloom Mission, 1984-87, chmn. sci. adv. team atmosphere structure and meteorology Mars Pathfinder Mission, 1993—; mem. basic Rsch. Coun., NASA, Washington, 1973-76; Von Karman lectr., 1990; prin. investigator structure of Jupiter's atmosphere, Galileo entry probe, 1995. Author and editor: Ballistic Range Technology, 1972; (with others) Venus, 1983; contbr. articles to profl. jours. Recipient Exceptional Scientific Achievement medals NASA, 1978, 81, H. Julian Allen award Ames Rsch. Ctr., 1982. Fellow AIAA (assoc.); mem. Am. Astron. Soc. (div. planetary sci.), Am. Geophys. Union. Avocations: music, piano, gardening, home design and construction. Office: Ames Rsch Ctr Mail Stop 245-2 Moffett Field CA 94035

SEIFF, ERIC A., lawyer; b. Mt. Vernon, N.Y., Apr. 25, 1933; s. Arthur N. and Mathilde (Cohen) S.; m. Sari Ginsburg, June 26, 1960 (div. Oct. 1983); children: Judith C., E. Kenneth, Dean A.; m. Meredith Feinman, Jan. 15, 1984; children: Abigail, Sarah. BA, Yale U., 1955; LLB, Columbia U., 1958. Bar: N.Y. 1958, U.S. Dist. Ct. (so. dist.) N.Y. 1960, U.S. Dist. Ct. (ea. dist.) N.Y. 1981, U.S. Ct. Appeals (2d cir.) 1965, U.S. Supreme Ct. 1967. Assoc. Bower and O'Connor, N.Y.C., 1959-60, Yellin, Kramer & Levy, N.Y.C., 1961; asst. dist. atty. N.Y.C. Dist. Atty.'s Office, 1962-67; asst. counsel Agy. for Internat. Devel., Washington, 1967-70; counsel Agy. for Internat. Devel., Rio de Janeiro, 1970-72; gen. counsel N.Y. State Divsn. Criminal Justice Svcs., 1972-74; dep. chief atty. Legal Aid Soc. Criminal Def., N.Y.C., 1974-75; first dep. commr. N.Y. State Investigation Commn., 1975-77; chmn. N.Y. State Investigation Commn., N.Y.C., 1977-79; ptnr. Seiff & Kretz (formerly Scoppetta & Seiff), N.Y.C., 1981—; spl. dist. atty. Bronx County, 1986-89; spl. asst. atty. gen. State of N.Y., Gov.'s Task Force Investigating Conduct of Attica Prosecutions, 1975. Bd. dirs. Legal Aid Soc., N.Y.C., 1994—; Prisoners' Legal Svcs., N.Y.C., 1989—, Lawyers Fund for Client Protection, N.Y., 1980—. Recipient Frank S. Hogan Meml. award Frank S. Hogan Assn., 1994. Mem. N.Y. Criminal Bar Assn. (bd. dirs. 1980—, past pres.). Office: Seiff & Kretz 645 Madison Ave New York NY 10022

SEIGEL, JERROLD EDWARD, historian, writer; b. St. Louis, June 9, 1936; s. William and Katherine (Ginsberg) S.; m. Jayn Rosenfeld, Aug. 28, 1966; children: Micol, Jessica. A.B., Harvard U., 1958; Ph.D., Princeton U., 1963. Instr. Princeton (N.J.) U., 1962-65, asst. prof., 1965-68, assoc. prof., 1968-78, prof. history, 1978-88; prof. history NYU, N.Y.C., 1988—; Kenan prof., 1994—; vis. prof. history Maitre d'Etudes, Ecoles des hautes études, Paris, 1988-94; finalist Nat. Book Critics Cir., 1987. Author: Rhetoric and Philosophy, 1968, Marx's Fate, 1978, Bohemian Paris, 1986, Private Worlds of Marcel Duchamp, 1995. Fulbright fellow Inst. Internat. Edn., 1961-62; NEH fellow, 1979-80, 87-88. Mem. N.Y. Inst. for Humanities, Phi Beta Kappa. Home: 48 Horatio St New York NY 10014-1614 Office: NYU History Dept 19 University Pl New York NY 10003-4501

SEIGEL, STUART EVAN, lawyer; b. N.Y.C., Mar. 25, 1933; s. Philip Herman and Betty Sarah (Leventhal) S.; m. Joyce Roberta Meyers (div.); children: Charles Meyers, Lee Bennett, Suzanne Marcie; m. Sherry Diane Jackson,Sept. 24, 1989. BS, N.Y. U., 1953, LLB, 1957; LLM in Taxation, Georgetown U., 1960. Bar: N.Y. 1958, D.C. 1958. Atty. Office Chief Counsel, IRS, Washington, 1957-65, Office Tax Legis. Counsel, Dept. Treasury, Washington, 1965-69; assoc. tax legis. counsel Office Tax Legis. Counsel, Dept. Treasury, 1968-69; ptnr. firm Cohen and Uretz, Washington, 1969-77; chief counsel IRS, Washington, 1977-79; ptnr. firm Williams and Connolly, Washington, 1979-89, Arnold and Porter, N.Y.C., 1989—; lectr. George Washington U. Sch. Law, 1970-73; adj. prof. law Antioch Sch. Law, 1973-76, Georgetown U. Sch. Law, 1981. Mem. ABA, Am. Law Inst., Am. Judicature Soc., Am. Coll. Tax Counsel, N.Y. State Bar Assn., Assn. of Bar of City of N.Y. Club: Metropolitan (Washington). Office: Arnold and Porter 399 Park Ave New York NY 10022-4614

SEIGLER, DAVID STANLEY, botanist, chemist, educator; b. Wichita Falls, Tex., Sept. 11, 1940; s. Kenneth R. and Floy M. (Wilkinson) S.; m. Janice Kay Cline, Jan. 20, 1961; children: Dava, Rebecca. BS in Chemistry, Southwestern (Okla.) State Coll., 1961; PhD in Organic Chemistry, U. Okla., 1967. Postdoctoral assoc. USDA No. Regional Lab., Peoria, Ill., 1967-68; postdoctoral fellow dept. botany U. Tex., Austin, 1968-70; asst. prof. botany U. Ill., Urbana, 1970-76, assoc. prof., 1976-79, prof. botany, 1979—, head dept. plant biology, 1988-93; curator U. Ill. Herbarium, 1993—. Editor: Crop Resources, 1977, Phytochemistry and Angiosperm Phylogeny, 1981; contbr. numerous articles to profl. jours. Recipient Fulbright Hays Lecturer award Fulbright Commn., Argentina, 1976, (alternate) Germany, 1995-96, study award Deutsche Akademischer Austauschdienst, Germany, 1995. Mem. Phytochem. Soc. N.Am. (pres. 1988-89), Bot. Soc. Am., Am. Chem. Soc., Am. Soc. Plant Taxonomists, Internat. Soc. Chem. Ecology (pres. 1990-91). Mem. Assembly of God Ch. Avocation: genealogy. Home: 510 W Vermont Ave Urbana IL 61801-4931 Office: U Ill Dept Plant Biology 265 Morrill Hall 505 S Goodwin Ave Urbana IL 61801-3707

SEIKEL, OLIVER EDWARD, lawyer; b. Akron, Ohio, July 6, 1937; s. Herman William and Josephine Marie (Weaver) S.; m. Meredith Miller. B.S., Mass. Inst. Tech., 1959; J.D., U. Mich., 1962; postgrad. (fellow), U. Hamburg, 1962-63. Bar: Ohio 1963. Assoc. Falsgraf, Reidy, Shoup & Ault, Cleve., 1963-68, ptnr., 1969-71; legal mgr. internat. ops. Midland-Ross Corp., Cleve., 1971-73; sole practice Cleve., 1974-78; ptnr. Seikel & Stinson, Cleve., 1978-86; prin. Burke, Haber & Berick Co., Cleve., 1986-90, McDonald, Hopkins, Burke & Haber Co., L.P.A., Cleve., 1990-95; Bulgaria Liaison, Ctrl. and East European Law Initiative ABA, Sofia, Bulgaria, 1995-96; sec. Bearings, Inc. and subs., Cleve., 1974-90, gen. counsel, 1974-89. Trustee Our Lady of the Wayside Home, Avon, Ohio, 1969-88, Gilmour Acad., Gates Mills, Ohio, 1970—; trustee, mem. exec. com. Cath. Charities Corp., Cleve., 1975-88. Fellow Am. Bar Found.; mem. ABA, Ohio Bar Assn., Greater Cleve. Bar Assn., Rotary, Delta Theta Phi. Roman Catholic. Clubs: Cleve. Athletic (Cleve.), Cleve. Yachting (Cleve.), Cleve. City (Cleve.), Cleve. Playhouse (Cleve.). Home: 2 Bratenahl Pl Cleveland OH 44108-1183 Office: McDonald Hopkins Burke Haber Co LPA 2100 Bank One Center 600 Superior Ave E Cleveland OH 44114-2611

SEIL, FREDRICK JOHN, neuroscientist, neurologist; b. Nove Sove, Yugoslavia, Nov. 9, 1933; s. Joseph and Theresa (Krieger) S.; m. Daryle Faith Wolfers, July 2, 1955; children: Jonathan Fredrick, Joel Philip Timothy. BA, Oberlin Coll., 1956; MD, Stanford U., 1960. Intern Kaiser Found. Hosp., San Francisco, 1960-61; resident in neurology Stanford (Calif.) U., 1961-64, fellow in neurology, 1964-66; staff neurologist VA Med. Ctr., Palo Alto, Calif., 1969-76; clin. investigator VA Med. Ctr., Portland, Oreg., 1976-79, staff neurologist, 1979-81, dir. VA office regeneration research programs, 1981—; asst. prof. neurology Stanford U., 1969-75, assoc. prof. neurology Oreg. Health Sci. U., Portland, 1976-78, prof. neurology, 1978—, prof. cell biology and anatomy, 1990—. Editor: Nerve, Organ and Tissue Regeneration: Research Perspectives, 1983, Neural Regeneration, 1987, 94, Current Issues in Neural Regeneration and Transplantation, 1989, Advances in Neural Regeneration Research, 1990, Neural Injury and Regeneration: 1993, Multiple Sclerosis: Current Status of Research and Treatment, 1994; contbr. articles to profl. jours. Served to capt. U.S. Army, 1966-68. Grantee VA, 1970—, NIH, 1986—. Mem. Internat. Brain Rsch. Orgn., Internat. Soc. Develop. Neurosci., Am. Neurol. Assn., Am. Assn. Neuropathologists, Soc. Neurosci., Soc. Exptl. Neuropathology. Democrat. Home: 10306 SW Radcliffe Rd Portland OR 97219-7956 Office: VA Med Ctr Office Regeneration Rs Portland OR 97201

SEILER, JAMES ELMER, judge; b. LaCrosse, Wis., Sept. 2, 1946; s. Elmer Bernard and Margaret Theresa (Mader) S.; m. Sonia Gonzales, Feb. 9, 1968; children: Rebecca, Cristina. BA, U. Wis., LaCrosse, 1968; JD, U. Wis., 1973. Bar: Wis. 1973, Minn. 1981, U.S. Supreme Ct. 1985, Mo. 1986. Pvt. practice Balsam Lake, Wis., 1973-81; in-house counsel Farm Credit Banks, St. Paul, 1981-85; corp. counsel Hussmann Corp., St. Louis, 1985-94; adminstrv. law judge Social Security, Evansville, Ind., 1994-95, Office of Hearings and Appeals, Creve Coeur, Mo., 1995—. Candidate Dist. Atty., Polk County, Wis., 1980. With U.S. Army, 1969-71. Avocations: soccer coach, swimming, water skiing, running. Home: 18 Harbor Pt Ct Lake Saint Louis MO 63367 Office: 11475 Old Cabin Rd Saint Louis MO 63141

SEILER, STEVEN LAWRENCE, health facility administrator; b. Chgo., Dec. 30, 1941; married. B, U. Ariz., 1963; M, U. Iowa, 1965. Adminstrv. resident Rush-Presbyn.-St. Luke's Med. Ctr., Chgo., 1965, adminstrv. asst., 1965-68; asst. adminstr. Lake Forest (Ill.) Hosp., 1968-71, adminstr., 1971-73, pres., 1973-86; exec. v.p Voluntary Hosps. Am., Park Ridge, Ill., 1987-89, sr. v.p., 1986-92; CEO Good Samaritan Regional Med. Ctr., Phoenix, 1992—; adj. prof. Contbr. articles to profl. jours. Mem. AHA (svc. com.), Ill. Hosp. Assn. (chair 1980-81). Home: 3930 E Rancho Dr Paradise Vly AZ 85253-5025 Office: Good Samaritan Regional Med Ctr 1111 E Mcdowell Rd Phoenix AZ 85006-2612*

SEILHAMER, RAY A., bishop. Bishop United Brethren in Christ. Office: United Brethren in Christ 302 Lake St Huntington IN 46750-1264

SEILS, WILLIAM GEORGE, lawyer; b. Chgo., Aug. 9, 1935; s. Harry H. and Hazel C. (Sullivan) S.; m. Evelyn E. Oliver, Sept. 8, 1956; children: Elizabeth Ann, Ellen Carol, Eileen Alison. A.B., J.D., U. Mich., 1959. Bar: Ill. bar 1959. Since practiced in Chgo.; ptnr. Arvey, Hodes & Costello & Burman, 1968-87; gen. counsel, sec., sr. v.p. Richardson Electronics, Ltd., LaFox, Ill., 1986—. Contbr. articles to profl. jours.; asst. editor: Mich. Law Rev, 1958-59. Mem. Ill. Bar Assn., Order of Coif. Office: Richardson Electronics Ltd 40w267 Keslinger Rd Lafox IL 60147

SEINFELD, JOHN HERSH, chemical engineering educator; b. Elmira, N.Y., Aug. 3, 1942; s. Ben B. and Minna (Johnson) S. BS, U. Rochester, 1964; PhD, Princeton U., 1967. Asst. prof. chem. engring. Calif. Inst. Tech., Pasadena, 1967-70, assoc. prof., 1970-74, prof., 1974—, Louis E. Nohl prof., 1980—, exec. officer for chem. engring., 1973-90, chmn. engring. and applied sci. div., 1990—; Allan P. Colburn meml. lectr. U. Del., 1976; Camille and Henry Dreyfus Found. lectr. MIT, 1979; mem. coun. Gordon Rsch. Confs., 1980-83; Donald L. Katz lectr. U. Mich., 1981; Reilly lectr. U. Notre Dame, 1983; Dean's Disting. lectr. U. Rochester, 1985; Katz lectr. CUNY, 1985; McCabe lectr. N.C. State U., 1986; Lewis lectr. MIT, 1986; Union Carbide lectr. SUNY, Buffalo; Van Winkle lectr. U. Tex., 1988; Bicentennial lectr. La. State U., 1988; Ida Beam lectr. U. Iowa, 1989, David Mason lectr. Stanford U., 1989; Julian Smith lectr. Cornell U., 1990; Merck lectr. Rutgers U., 1991; Henske Disting. lectr. Yale U., 1991; mem. sci. adv. bd. EPA; lectr. AIChE, 1980; Centennial lectr. U. Pa., 1993; Miles Disting. lectr. U. Pitts., 1994; Kelly lectr. Purdue U., 1996. Author: Numerical Solution of Ordinary Differential Equations, 1971, Mathematical Methods in Chemical Engineering, Vol. III, Process Modeling, Estimation and Identification, 1974, Air Pollution: Physical and Chemical Fundamentals, 1975, Lectures in Atmospheric Chemistry, 1980, Atmospheric Chemistry and Physics of Air Pollution, 1986, Fundamentals of Air Pollution Engineering, 1988, Distributed Parameter Systems - Theory and Applications, 1989; assoc. editor Environ. Sci., Tech., 1981—; mem. editorial bd. Computers, Chem. Engring, 1974—, Jour. Colloid and Interface Sci, 1978—, Advances in Chem. Engring, 1980—, Revs. in Chem. Engring, 1980—, Aerosol Sci. and Tech., 1981—, Large Scale Systems, 1982—; assoc. editor: Atmospheric Environment, 1976—. Recipient Donald P. Eckman award Am. Automatic Control Coun., 1970, Pub. Svc. medal NASA, 1980, Disting. Alumnus award U. Rochester, 1989; Camille and Henry Dreyfus Found. Tchr. Scholar grantee, 1972. Fellow Japan Soc. Promotion Sci., AIChE (bd. dirs. 1988-91, mem. editl. bd. jours. 1985—, Allan P. Colburn award 1976, William H. Walker award 1986); mem. NAE, Am. Assn. Acad. Sci., Am. Soc. Engring. Edn. (Curtis W. McGraw Rsch. award 1976, George Westinghouse award 1987), Assn. Aerosol Rsch. (bd. dirs. 1983—, v.p. 1988-90, pres. 1990-92), Am. Acad. Arts and Scis., Air Waste Mgmt. Assn., Am. chem. Soc. (Svc. through Chemistry award 1988, Creative Advances in Environ. Sci. and Tech. award 1993), Sigma Xi, Tau Beta Pi. Home: 363 Patrician Way Pasadena CA 91105-1027 Office: Calif Inst Tech Div Engring and Applied Sci Pasadena CA 91125

SEIP, TOM DECKER, securities executive; b. St. Louis, Feb. 15, 1950; s. Norman Walter and Margaret Ann (Decker) S.; m. Linda Shinabarger, Sept. 1976 (div. 1987); children: Parker, Jared; m. Alexa Clay Giddings, Mar. 24, 1990. BA in Psychology, Pa. State U., 1972; postgrad., U. Mich., 1972-74. Regional human resources mgr. Merrill, Lynch, Pierce Fenner and Smith, Inc., N.Y.C., San Francisco, 1975-77; v.p., ptnr. Korn/Ferry Internat., Palo Alto, Calif., 1977-83; v.p. human resources Charles Schwab & Co., Inc., San Francisco, 1983-85; sr. v.p., nat. sales programs Charles Schwab & Co., Inc., San Francisco, 1985-86, sr. v.p. specialized bus., 1986-88, sr. v.p. ea. div., 1988-91; pres., COO Charles Schwab Investment Mgmt., Inc., San Francisco, 1991—; exec. v.p. The Charles Schwab Corp., San Francisco, 1992—; dir. Ridgefield Devel. Corp., Erie, Pa. Avocation: sailing. Office: Charles Schwab & Co Inc 101 Montgomery St San Francisco CA 94104-4122*

SEIPLE, ROBERT ALLEN, Christian relief organization executive; b. Harmony, N.J., Dec. 6, 1942; s. Chris and Gertrude (Crozier) S.; m. Margaret Ann Goebel, May 14, 1965; children: Chris, Amy, Jesse. AB, Brown U., 1965; LHD (hon.), Alderson-Broaddus, 1986, Sioux Falls Coll., 1986, Azusa Pacific U., 1993, Gordon Coll., 1995, Lawrence U., 1996. Sales rep. Boise Cascade, Mich., 1969-71; dir. athletics Brown U., Providence, 1972-79, v.p. devel., 1979-83; pres. Eastern Coll. and Eastern Bapt. Theol. Sem., St. Davids, Pa., 1983-87, World Vision, Inc., Monrovia, Calif., 1987—; bd. dirs. Stop Cancer, One to One Found.; bd. advisors World Impact, Young Life-Urban Phila., Opportunity Internat. Contbr. articles to mags. Capt. USMC, 1966-69, Vietnam. Decorated D.F.C., 28 Air medals, Vietnam Campaign medal with 5 Battle Stars, Navy Commendation award. Presbyterian. Avocations: deer hunting, trout fishing. Office: World Vision Inc 34834 Weyerhaeuser Way S Federal Way WA 98001-9716

SEIREG, ALI A(BDEL HAY), mechanical engineer; b. Arab Republic of Egypt, Oct. 26, 1927; came to U.S., 1951, naturalized, 1960; s. Abdel Hay and Aisha Seireg; m. Shirley Marachowsky, Dec. 24, 1954; children: Mirette Elizabeth LaFollette, Pamela Aisha. B.Sc. M.E., U. Cairo, 1948; Ph.D., U. Wis., 1954. Lectr. Cairo U., 1954-56; staff adv. engr. Falk Corp., Milw., 1956-59; assoc. prof. theoretical and applied mechanics Marquette U., 1959-64, prof., 1964-65; prof. (Kaiser chair) mech. engring. U. Wis., Madison,

1965—; Ebaugh Prof. U. Fla., Gainesville, 1986—; cons. industry, ednl. and govt. agys.; chmn. U.S. council Internat. Fedn. Theory of Machines, 1974—; co-chmn. 5th World Congress of Theory of Machines, 1979, 1st USSR-USA Conf. on Composite Materials, 1989. Author: Mechanical Systems Analysis, 1969, Biomedical Analysis of Musculoskeletal Structure for Medicine and Sports, 1989; editor Computers in Mechanical Engineering; editor in chief SOMA, Engineering for the Human Body, 1986-90: contbr. numerous articles to profl. jours. Recipient Kuwait prize for sci., 1987. Fellow ASME (Richards Meml. award 1973, Machine Design award 1978, Design Automation award 1990, chmn. div. design engrng. 1977-78, chmn. computer tech. 1978-81, mem. policy bd. communications 1978-80, mem. policy bd. gen. engrng. 1979-80, chmn. Century II Internat. Computer Tech. Conf. 1980, founding chmn. computer engrng. div. 1980-81, v.p. systems and design 1981-85, sr. v.p., chmn. council on engrng. 1985-90, pres. Gen. Research Inst. 1984—), Am. Soc. Engrng. Edn. (George Westinghouse award 1970), Soc. Exptl. Stress Analysis, Am. Inst. Med. and Biol. Engrng. (founding fellow), Am. Gear Mfg. Assn. (E. P. Connell award 1974), Automation Research Council; mem. Chinese Mech. Engrng. Soc. (hon.), USSR Acad. Sci. (fgn.), Russian Acad. Sci. (fgn.). Home: 2670 SW 14th Dr Gainesville FL 32608-2049 Office: 1513 University Ave Madison WI 53706-1539 *I have always tried my best to look beyond what I hear, to think beyond what I see, to give more than I receive, and to do good as its own reward.*

SEITEL, FRASER PAUL, public relations executive; b. Jersey City, June 6, 1946; s. Robert and Helen (Barmad) S.; m. Rosemary Kierstein, Dec. 20, 1969; children: Raina, David. BJ, U. Mo., 1964; MA, U. N.D., 1970; MBA, NYU, 1977. Pub. rels. officer Chase Manhattan Bank, N.Y.C., 1970-73, v.p., 1974-85, sr. v.p., dir. pub. affairs, 1985-92; mng. ptnr. Emerald Ptnrs., Ft. Lee, N.J., 1992—; sr. counselor Burson Marsteller, N.Y.C., 1992—; sr. counselor investor rels. and mktg. communications Greater N.Y. Savs. Bank, 1994—; pub. rels. cons. Hill and Knowlton, N.Y.C., 1973; instr. Profl. Devel. Inst., N.Y.C., Ragan Communications, Chgo., Estes Park Inst., Colo. Author: The Practice of Public Relations, 6th edit., 1995; pub. The Public Relations Strategist, 1995—; columnist U.S. Banker, 1989-94, Profit Mag., 1993-95; columns editor PRSA Tactics mag., 1994-95. Col. USAR, 1969-76. Mem. Pub. Rels. Soc. Am., Bank Mktg. Assn. Avocations: baseball, football, basketball, tai chi, rugby. Home: 12 King Pl Closter NJ 07624-2936 Office: 177 Main St Ste 215 Fort Lee NJ 07024-6936

SEITELMAN, MARK ELIAS, lawyer; b. N.Y.C., Apr. 14, 1955; s. Leo Henry and Pearl (Elias) S. BA, Bklyn. Coll., 1976; JD, Bklyn. Law Sch., 1979. Bar: N.Y. 1980, U.S. Dist. Ct. (ea., so., and we. dists.) N.Y. 1980, U.S. Supreme Ct. 1995, U.S. Ct. Mil. Appeals, 1995. Law asst. Criminal Ct., Bklyn., 1979; law clk. to Hon. Justice Aaron D. Bernstein N.Y. Supreme Ct., Bklyn., 1980; assoc. Lester, Schwab, Katz & Dwyer, N.Y.C., 1981-87, Weg and Myers, 1987-88, Kroll & Tract, 1988-90; pvt. practice N.Y.C., 1990—. Mem. ABA, ATLA, N.Y. State Bar Assn., N.Y. County Bar Assn. (ins. and supreme ct. coms.), N.Y. State Trial Lawyers Assn. (bd. dirs., mem. speakers bur.), Bklyn. Bar Assn. (mem. legis. com.). Office: Ste 901 233 Broadway New York NY 10279

SEITZ, CHARLES LEWIS, computer scientist and engineer; b. Phila., Jan. 1, 1943; s. Philip Franz Durham and Elaine Marie (Good) S.; m. Jean Marie Austin, July 5, 1963 (div. 1981); children: Elizabeth, Russell. BSEE, MIT, 1965, MS, 1967, PhD, 1971. Asst. prof. computer sci. U. Utah, Salt Lake City, 1970-72; cons. Burroughs Corp., LaJolla, Calif., 1971-78; prof. computer sci. Calif. Inst. Tech., Pasadena, Calif., 1977-94; pres. Myricom, Inc., Arcadia, Calif., 1994—; cons. Strategic Def. Initiative Orgn., Washington, 1985-87; panelist U.S. Congress Office Tech. Assessment, Washington, 1986-87; mem. Computer Sci. and Telecomms. Bd., NRC, 1992—. Contbr. articles to profl. jours; patentee in field. Recipient Goodwin medal MIT, 1968, Leonard G. Abraham award IEEE, 1971, Cert. Appreciation, City Oceanside, Calif., 1984. Mem. NAE, Assn. Computing Machinery, Sigma Xi. Avocation: hiking. Office: Myricom Inc 325 N Santa Anita Ave Arcadia CA 91006-2870

SEITZ, COLLINS JACQUES, federal judge; b. Wilmington, Del., June 20, 1914; s. George Hilary and Margaret Jane (Collins) S.; m. Virginia Anne Day; children: Virginia Anne, Collins Jacques, Mark, Stephen. A.B., U. Del., 1937, LL.D., 1962; LL.B., U. Va., 1940; LL.D., Widener Coll., 1975, Villanova U. Sch. Law, 1983, Cath. U., 1985, Dickinson Sch. of Law, 1988. Bar: Del. 1940. Vice chancellor Del., 1946; chancellor, 1951-66; judge U.S. Ct. Appeals, 3d Circuit, 1966-71, chief judge, 1971-84, judge, 1984-89, sr. judge, 1989—. Recipient James J. Hoey award, 1954, award NCCJ, 1957, Pro Ecclesia et Pontifice (papal award), 1965, award in law Thomas Jefferson Meml. Found., 1990. Mem. Am., Del. bar assns. Democrat. Roman Catholic. Club: Wilmington. Office: US Ct Appeals 844 N King St Ste 32 Wilmington DE 19801-3519*

SEITZ, FREDERICK, former university administrator; b. San Francisco, July 4, 1911; s. Frederick and Emily Charlotte (Hofman) S.; m. Elizabeth K. Marshall, May 18, 1935. AB, Leland Stanford Jr. U., 1932; PhD, Princeton U., 1934; Doctorate Hon. Causa, U. Ghent, 1957; DSc (hon.), U. Reading, 1960, Rensselaer Poly. Inst., 1961, Marquette U., 1963, Carnegie Inst. Tech., 1963, Case Inst. Tech., 1964, Princeton U., 1964, Northwestern U., 1965, U. Del., 1966, Poly. Inst. Bklyn., 1967, U. Mich., 1967, U. Utah, 1968, Brown U., 1968, Duquesne U., 1968, St. Louis U., 1969, Nebr. Wesleyan U., 1970, U. Ill., 1972, Rockefeller U., 1981; LLD (hon.), Lehigh U., 1966, U. Notre Dame, 1962, Mich. State U., 1965, Ill. Inst. Tech., 1968, N.Y. U., 1969; LHD (hon.), Davis and Elkins Coll., 1970, Rockefeller U., 1981, U. Pa., 1985, U. Miami, 1989. Instr. physics U. Rochester, 1935-36, asst. prof., 1936-37; physicist research labs. Gen. Electric Co., 1937-39; asst. prof. Randal Morgan Lab. Physics, U. Pa., 1939-41, assoc. prof., 1941-42; prof. physics, head dept. Carnegie Inst. Tech., Pitts., 1942-49; prof. physics U. Ill., 1949-57, head dept., 1957-64, dir. control systems lab., 1951-52, dean Grad. Coll., v.p. research, 1964-65; exec. pres. Nat. Acad. Scis., 1962-69; pres. Rockefeller U., N.Y.C., 1968-78; U. Miami (Fla.), 1989; trustee Ogden Corp., 1977—; dir. tng. program Clinton Labs., Oak Ridge, 1946-47; chmn. Naval Rsch. Adv. Com., 1960-62; vice chmn. Def. Sci. Bd., 1961-62, chmn., 1964-68; sci. adviser NATO, 1959-60; mem. nat. adv. com. Marine Biomed. Inst. U. Tex., Galveston, 1975-77; mem. adv. group White House Conf. Anticipated Advances in Sci. and Tech., 1975-76; mem. adv. bd. Desert Rsch. Inst., 1975-79, Ctr. Strategic and Internat. Studies, 1975-81; mem. Nat. Cancer Adv. Bd., 1976-82; dir. Akzona Inc. Author: Modern Theory of Solids, 1940, The Physics of Metals, 1943, Solid State Physics, 1955, The Science Matrix, 1992, On the Frontier: My Life in Science, 1994, Stalin's Captive: Nikolaus Riehl and the Soviet Race for the Bomb, 1995. Trustee Rockefeller Found., 1964-77, Princeton U., 1968-72, Lehigh U., 1970-81, Rsch. Corp., 1966-82, Inst. Internat. Edn., 1971-78, Woodrow Wilson Nat. Fellowship Found., 1972-82, Univ. Corp. Atmospheric Rsch., Am. Mus. Natural History, 1975—; trustee John Simon Guggenheim Meml. Found., 1973-83, chmn. bd., 1976-83; mem. Belgian Am. Edn. Found.; bd. dirs. Richard Lounsberry Found., 1980—. Decorated Order of the Brilliant Star (Republic of China); recipient Franklin medal Franklin Inst. Phila., 1965, Hoover medal Stanford U., 1968, Nat. Medal Sci., 1973, James Madison award Princeton U., 1978, Edward R. Loveland Meml. award ACP, 1983, Vannevar Bush award Nat. Sci. Bd., 1983, J. Herbert Holloman award Acta Metallurgica, 1993, Von Hippel award Materials Rsch. Soc., 1993. Fellow Am. Phys. Soc. (pres. 1961); mem. NAS, Am. Acad. Arts and Scis., AIME, Am. Philos. Soc., Am. Inst. Physics (chmn. governing bd. 1954-59), Inst. for Def. Analysis, Finnish Acad. Sci. and Letters (fgn. mem.), Phi Beta Kappa Assos. Address: Rockefeller U 1230 York Ave New York NY 10021-6307

SEITZ, HAROLD A., supermarket executive; b. 1938. Ba, Notre Dame U., 1960. With Jewel Cos., 1960-75; sr. v.p. Loblaw Cos. Ltd., Toronto, Can., 1975-85, Nat. Tea Co., New Orleans, 1985-88; pres. Nat. Tea Co., Hazelwood, Mo., 1989—. Office: Nat Tea Co PO Box 7123 Saint Louis MO 63177*

SEITZ, KARL RAYMOND, editor; b. Corpus Christi, Tex., Sept. 26, 1943; s. Kerlin McCullough and Martha Elizabeth (Tillman) S.; m. Patricia Jean Floyd, June 13, 1970; 1 child, Lee Kerlin. BA, Birmingham So. Coll., 1970. Copy editor Birmingham (Ala.) Post-Herald, 1967-70, asst. news editor, 1970-73, chief editorial writer, 1973-78, editor editorial page, 1978—; dir. Birmingham Post-Birmingham Typographical Union Pension Plan, 1983-90, chmn., 1986-90; dir. Goodfellow Fund, Inc., Birmingham, 1983—, v.p., 1986—. Active exec. in residence Birmingham So. Coll., 1987, Leadership Birmingham, 1986—. With USN, 1961-64. Mem. Am. Acad. Polit. and Social Sci., Nat. Conf. Editorial Writers, Acad. Polit. Sci. Home: 1308 Roseland Dr Birmingham AL 35209-3930 Office: Birmingham Post Herald PO Box 2553 Birmingham AL 35202-2553

SEITZ, MARY LEE, mathematics educator. BS in Edn. summa cum laude, SUNY, Buffalo, 1977, MS in Edn., 1982. Cert. secondary tchr., N.Y. Prof. math. Erie C.C.-City Campus, Buffalo, 1982—; Reviewer profl. jours. and coll. textbooks. Reviewer profl. jours. Mem. Nat. Coun. Tchrs. Maths., N.Y. Maths. Assn. Two Yr. Colls., Assn. Maths. Tchrs. N.Y., N.Y. Assn. Two Yr. Colls., Inc., Pi Mu Epsilon. Avocations: gardening, photography, bird watching. Office: Erie C C-City Campus 121 Ellicott St Buffalo NY 14203-2601

SEITZ, MELVIN CHRISTIAN, JR., distributing company executive; b. Indpls., Aug. 9, 1939; s. Melvin Christian and Francis Sue (Lee) S.; m. Bette Louise Pierson, May 5, 1941; children: David, Mark, Keith, Cindy. Student Butler U., 1957-60. Salesman, Service Supply Co., Inc., Indpls., 1963-71, sec.-treas., 1971-74, v.p., 1974-81, exec. vp., 1981-83, pres., 1983-94, COO, 1995, dir. corporate rels. Pres. Seitz-Owings Found.; active Met. Devel. Commn. Indpls., 1994—. Served with U.S. Army. Mem. Nat. Fastener Distributor Assn. (bd. dirs.), Cole Roster (bd. dirs.), Sigma Nu. Republican. Mem. Disciples of Christ. Lodges: Masons, Shriners, Scottish Rite. Home: 4716 Northeastern Ave Indianapolis IN 46239-1665 Office: Svc Supply Co Inc Ind 603 E Washington St Indianapolis IN 46204-2620

SEITZ, NICHOLAS JOSEPH, magazine editor; b. Topeka, Kans., Jan. 30, 1939; s. Frank Joseph and Lydia Natalie (Clerico) S.; m. Velma Jean Pfannenstiel, Sept. 12, 1959; children: Bradley Joseph, Gregory Joseph. BA, U. Okla., 1966. Sports editor Manhattan (Kans.) Mercury, 1960-62, Norman (Okla.) Transcript, 1962-64, Okla. Jour., Oklahoma City, 1964-67; mem. staff Golf Digest mag., Norwalk, Conn., 1967—; editor Golf Digest mag., 1973-82; editorial dir. Golf Digest and Tennis, 1982-90; editorial dir. Sports/Leisure div. N.Y. Times Co. Mag. Group, 1991-92, sr. v.p., editor in chief, 1992—; syndicated golf instrn. and commentary CBS Radio Network; commentary ESPN TV Network. Author: Superstars of Golf, 1978, (with Dave Hill) Teed Off, 1977, (with Tom Watson) Getting Up and Down, 1983, Getting Back to Basics, 1991, Tom Watson's Strategic Golf, 1993; contbr. articles to profl. jours.; anthologized in: Best Sports Stories. Named Okla. Sports Writer of Year Nat. Sportswriters and Sportscasters Assn., 1965; winner contests Nat. Basketball Writers Assn.; winner contests Golf Writers Assn.; recipient Lincoln A. Werden award for outstanding contbn. to golf journalism, 1993. Home: 36 Hunt St Norwalk CT 06853-1015 Office: 5520 Park Ave Trumbull CT 06611-3426

SEITZ, PATRICIA ANN, lawyer; b. Washington, Sept. 2, 1946; d. Richard J. and Bettie Jean (Merrill) S.; m. Alan Graham Greer, Aug. 14, 1981. BA in History cum laude, Kans. State U., 1968; JD, Georgetown U., 1973. Bar: Fla. 1973, D.C. 1975, U.S. Dist. Ct. (no., mid., so. dists., trial bar) Fla., U.S. Ct. Appeals (5th and eleventh cir.), U.S. Supreme Ct. Reporter Dallas Times Herald, Washington, 1970-73; law clk. U.S. Dist. Ct., Washington, 1973-74; assoc. Steel, Hector & Davis, Miami, Fla., 1974-79, ptnr., 1980—; adj. faculty U. Miami Law Sch., Coral Gables, Fla., 1984-88; faculty Nat. Inst. Trial Advocacy, Boulder, Colo., 1982, 83, 95, Chapel Hill, N.C., 1984, 87. Fla. region, 1989; lectr. in field. Contbr. numerous articles to law jours. Mem. Dade Munroe Mental Health Bd., Miami, 1982-84, United Way of Greater Miami comty. devel. com., 1984-87; chmn. family abuse task force United Way of Greater Miami, 1986; chmn. devel. com. Miami City Ballet, 1986-87, bd. dirs., 1986-90. Fellow Am. Bar Found., Am. Bd. Trial Advocacy, Internat. Soc. Barristers; mem. ABA (chmn. various coms. 1979-85, Ho. Dels. 1992—), Am. Arbitration Assn. (nat. bd. dirs. 1995—, complex case panel arbitrator), Fla. Bar Assn. (bd. govs. young lawyer divsn. 1981-82, bd. govs. 1986-92, pres. 1993-94, bd. cert. civil trial), Fla. Assn. Women Lawyers, Dade County Bar Assn. (pub. interest law bank). Democrat. Roman Catholic. Avocations: travel, art. Home: 224 Ridgewood Rd Miami FL 33133-6614 Office: Steel Hector & Davis 200 S Biscayne Blvd Ste 4000 Miami FL 33131-2310

SEITZ, TIM, church administrator. Pres. Luth. Youth Orgn. Evang. Luth. Ch. Am. Office: Evang Luthern Ch in Am 8765 W Higgins Rd Chicago IL 60631-4101

SEITZ, WALTER STANLEY, cardiovascular research consultant; b. L.A., May 10, 1937; s. Walter and Frances Janette (Schleef) S. BS in Physics and Math., U. Calif., Berkeley, 1959; PhD in Biophysics, U. Vienna, 1981, MD, 1982. Health physicist U. Calif. Radiation Lab., 1959-61; rsch. assoc. NIH at Pacific Union Coll., 1961-63; physicist Lockheed Rsch. Labs., Palo Alto, Calif., 1961-63; staff scientist Xerox Corp., Pasadena, Calif., 1963-66; sr. scientist Applied Physics Cons., Palo Alto, 1966-75; instr. clin. sci. U. Ill Coll. Medicine, Urbana, 1983-84; cons. cardiology Cardiovascular Rsch. Inst. U. Calif. Sch. Medicine, San Francisco, 1987—; sr. scientist Inst. Med. Analysis and Rsch., Berkeley, 1987—. Contbr. articles to profl. jours. Postdoctoral Rsch. fellow, U. Calif. San Francisco, 1984. Fellow Am. Coll. Angiography; mem. AAAS, Royal Soc. Medicine London, N.Y. Acad. Scis., Physicians for Social Responsibility. Avocations: reading, music, hiking. Office: IMAR Cons Inc 38 Panoramic Way Berkeley CA 94704-1828

SEITZ, WESLEY DONALD, agricultural economics educator; b. Wapakoneta, Ohio, Sept. 29, 1940; s. Donald Otto and Irene Katherine (Greubmeyer) S.; m. Janice Ann Parker, June 21, 1964; children: Kimberly, Matthew. BS, Ohio State U., 1962, MS, 1964; PhD, U. Calif., Berkeley, 1968. Asst. specialist, instr. U. Calif., Berkeley, 1967-68; asst. prof. bus. adminstrn. and agrl. econs. U. Ill., Urbana, 1968-72, assoc. prof. agrl. econs., 1972-74, assoc. dir. Inst. Environ. Studies, 1974-79, asst. head agrl. econs., 1979-81, head agrl. econs., 1981-87, prof. agrl. econs., 1987-92, assoc. head agrl. econs., 1992—; com. chmn. Nat. Acad. Sci., Washington, 1979-80, commn. mem., 1980, 85-86; cons. Dept. Interior, Ft. Collins, Colo., 1976; mem. Agrl. Task Force Ill. EPA, Springfield, 1978-80. Co-editor: Natural Resource Jour., vol. 15, no. 4, 1975; chmn.: Surface Mining: Soil, Coal and Society, 1981; contbr. chpts. to books. Bd. dirs. Univ. YMCA, Urbana, 1974-77; mem. adminstrv. com. Wesley Methodist Ch., 1981—. Served with USAFR, 1962-67. Recipient Disting. Service award Univ. YMCA, Urbana, 1980. Mem. Am. Agrl. Econs. Assn. (chmn. spl. publs. com.), Soil Conservation Soc. Am. (dir. Ill. chpt. 1980-82), North Central Research Strategy Com. (chmn. 1973-74), Am. Econs. Assn., Assn. Environ. and Resource Economists, Sigma Xi, Gamma Sigma Delta, Phi Kappa Phi (pres. Ill. chpt. 1989-90, chair Resource policy consortium). Home: 4014 Pinecrest Dr Champaign IL 61821-9216 Office: Dept Agrl Economics U Ill 1301 W Gregory Dr Urbana IL 61801-3608

SEITZ, WILLIAM HENRY, JR., orthopedic surgeon; b. N.Y.C., Jan. 12, 1950; s. William Henry and Catherine (Kehoe) S.; m. Susan Andrea Versenyi, June 4, 1972; children: David William, Eric Alexander, William Henry III, Elizabeth Andrea. BS, Fairfield U., 1971; grad. cert. phys. therapy, Columbia U., 1972, MD, 1979. Diplomate Am. Bd. Med. Examiners. Resident in gen. surgery St. Vincent's Med. Ctr., N.Y.C., 1979-81; resident in orthopaedic surgery Columbia Presbyn. Med. Ctr., N.Y.C., 1981-83, chief resident, 1983-84, Annie C. Kane fellow in hand surgery, 1984-85; clin. instr. Case Western Res. U., Cleve., 1985-87, asst. clin. prof., 1987-94, assoc. clin. prof., 1995—; head of hand and upper extremity surgery, orthop. rehab. Mr. Sinai Med. Ctr., Cleve., 1985—; cons. Nisonger Ctr. for Child Devel., Columbus, 1985—, Cuyahoga County Md. Mental Retardation, Cleve., 1986—. Editor Current Opinion in Orthops.-Hand and Wrist, 1994, 95; assoc. editor Jour. Hand Surgery, 1994—; reviewer JBJS, 1993—; contbr. articles to profl. jours. Pres. Shaker Heights (Ohio)ú Youth Soccer Assn., 1990-91, 91-92. Fellow Am. Acad. Orthopedic Surgeons; mem. Am. Soc. for Surgery of Hand (internat. traveling fellow 1992-93, Sterling Bunnell fellow 1992, Summer L. Koch award 1990), Am. Orthopedic Assn., Am. Shoulder and Elbow Surgeons Soc., Orthopedic Rsch. Soc., Orthopedic Trauma Assn. Roman Catholic. Home: 3398 Kenmore Rd Shaker Heights OH 44122 Office: Mount Sinai Med Ctr Dept Orthopaedic Surgery 1 Mount Sinai Dr Cleveland OH 44106-4191

SEITZER, KEVIN LEE, professional baseball player; b. Springfield, Ill., Mar. 26, 1962; m. Lisa Seitzer; 1 child, Brandon. BS in Indsl. Electronics, Ea. Ill. U., 1984. Baseball player Kansas City Royals (Am. League), 1986-91, Milwaukee Brewers, 1992, 93—, Oakland Athletics, 1993. Mem. Am. League All Star Team, 1987, 95. Office: Milwaukee Brewers County Stadium, PO Box 3099 Milwaukee WI 53201-3099*

SEIZINGER, BERND ROBERT, molecular geneticist, physician, researcher; b. Munich, Germany, Dec. 27, 1956; came to U.S., 1984; s. August and Mathilde (Haselbeck) S. MD, Ludwig-Maximilians U. Med. Sch, Munich, Germany, 1983; PhD summa cum laude, Max-Planck Inst., Munich, Germany, 1984. Postdoctoral rsch. assoc. Max Planck Inst. for Psychiatry, Munich, Germany, 1984; postdoctoral rsch. assoc. Harvard Med. Sch., Boston, 1984-86, instr. neurology, 1986-88, asst. prof., 1988-90, assoc. prof. neuroscience, 1990-95; dir. molecular neuro-oncology lab. Mass. Gen. Hosp., Boston, 1989-92, assoc. geneticist, 1990-95; v.p. oncology Bristol-Myers Squibb Pharm. Rsch. Inst., Princeton, N.J., 1992—, v.p. corp. and acad. alliances, 1995—; co-chmn. Internat. Consortium on Neurofibromatosis, N.Y.C., 1988—; chmn. Comm. on Gene Loss in Human Cancers Intern Human Gene Mapping Conf., Oxford, 1991, Rsch. Adv. Bd. Nat. Neurofibromatosis Found., N.Y.C., 1991—, co-chmn. 1993—; vis. rsch. scientist, assoc. mem. faculty Princeton (N.J.) U., 1993—. Recipient Otto Hahn Medal Max Planck Soc., Munich, 1983, Wilson S. Stone Meml. award Cancer Rsch., 1987, Rsch. Faculty Scholar award Am. Cancer Soc., 1989. Mem. Nat. Neurofibromatosis Found. (Von Recklinghausen award 1992, Jr. Investigators award 1985), Am. Soc. Human Genetics, Am. Assn. Cancer Rsch. Achievements include discovery of fundamental genetic mechanisms of tumor formation in the human nervous system, chromosomal location of the tumor suppressor genes causing neurofibromatosis type I and II, and von Hippel-Lindau disease; co-discovery of gene for neurofibromatosis type II. Office: Bristol-Myers Squibb Pharm Rsch Inst PO Box 4000 Princeton NJ 08543-4000

SEKANINA, ZDENEK, astronomer; b. Mlada Boleslav, Czechoslovakia, June 12, 1936; came to U.S., 1969; s. Frantisek Sekanina and Hedvika (Kolarikova) Sekaninova; m. Jana Soukupova, Apr. 1, 1966; 1 child, Jason. Diploma, Charles U., Prague, Czechoslovakia, 1959, PhD in Astronomy, 1963. Astronomer Stefanik Obs., Prague, 1959-66, Ctr. for Numerical Math., Charles U., Prague, 1967-68; vis. scientist Inst. d'Astrophysique, Univ. de Liege, Cointe-Ougree, Belgium, 1968-69; physicist Smithsonian Astrophys. Obs., Cambridge, Mass., 1969-80; mem. tech. staff Jet Propulsion Lab., Pasadena, Calif., 1980-81, rsch. scientist, 1981-84, sr. rsch. scientist, 1984—; assoc. Harvard Coll. Obs., Cambridge, 1969-80; mem. NASA Comet Sci. Working Group, 1977-80; cons. Jet Propulsion Lab., 1977-80; prin. U.S. co-investigator Particulate Impact Analyzer Experiment, Dust Impact Detector Sys. Experiment, European Space Agy.'s Giotto Mission to Comet Halley, 1980-89; mem. NASA-European Spacy Agy. Comet Halley Environ. Working Group, 1980-89; discipline specialist Near Nucleus Studies Network, Internat. Halley Watch, 1982-90; mem. imaging sci. subsys. team Comet Rendezvous Asteroid Flyby Mission, 1986-92; mem. sci. definition team ESA/NASA Comet Nucleus Sample Return Mission, 1988—; co-investigator STARDUST Discovery Mission, 1994—. Editor Comet Halley Archive, 1982-91; mem. editorial bd. Kosmicke Rozhledy, 1963-69. Recipient Exceptional Sci. Achievement medal NASA, 1985; minor planet named Sekanina, 1976. Mem. Internat. Astron. Union (mem. commns. 15, 10, 22, mem. organizing commn. 22 1976-82, organizing commn. 15 1979-85, mem. working group on comets 1988—, assoc. dir. Ctrl. Bur. for Astron. Telegrams 1970-80), COSPAR (working group 3, panel C, exec. mem. 1980-82). Roman Catholic. Office: Jet Propulsion Lab 4800 Oak Grove Dr Pasadena CA 91109-8001

SEKERKA, ROBERT FLOYD, physics educator, scientist; b. Wilkinsburg, Pa., Nov. 27, 1937; s. John Jacob and Vivian Mae (Smith) S.; m. Dianne Thompson, Apr. 30, 1960 (div. Apr. 1981); children: Lee Ann, Robert Thompson; m. 2d Carolyn Lee Confer, May 24, 1981. BS in Physics, U. Pitts., 1960; AM, Harvard U., 1961, PhD, 1965. Engr. Westinghouse Rsch. Labs., Pitts., 1965-68, mgr. materials growth and properties dept., 1968-69; lectr. Carnegie-Mellon U., Pitts., 1967-69, assoc. prof., 1969-72, prof. metallurgy and materials sci., 1972-82, dept. head, 1976-82, prof. physics and math., dean Mellon Coll. Sci., 1982-91, Univ. Prof., 1991—; mem. space studies bd. NRC, 1989-91. Assoc. editor Jour. Crystal Growth, 1971-94; Metallurgical Trans., 1970-76; editorial bd. Applied Microgravity Tech., 1987-90. Past bd. dirs. Forbes Health Sys., Pitts., Pitts. Regional Ctr. for Sci. Tchrs.; past vice chmn. bd. dirs. NMR Inst.; past mem. rsch. com. Allegheny Singer Rsch. Inst., Pitts. Recipient A.G. Worthing award U. Pitts., 1959, Philip M. McKenna Meml. award, 1980; Woodrow Wilson fellow, 1960, NSF fellow, 1962-65. Fellow Am. Soc. Metals; mem. Minerals Metals Materials Soc., Am. Phys. Soc., Am. Assn. Crystal Growth (mem. exec. com.), Internat. Assn. Crystal Growth (co-v.p., Frank prize 1992), Edgewood Country Club, Phi Beta Kappa, Sigma Xi, Omicron Delta Kappa. Home: 307 S Dithridge St Apt 407 Pittsburgh PA 15213-3514 Office: Carnegie Mellon U Dept Physics 6319 Wean Hall Pittsburgh PA 15213-3890

SEKI, HOKEN S., lawyer; b. Phoenix, Sept. 4, 1935; s. Hozen and Satomi (Shiomasu) S.; m. Frances C. Takamoto, Sept. 12, 1964; 1 child, Chandra. BA, Columbia U., 1957; LLB, Harvard U., 1964. Bar: N.Y., Ill., Calif., U.S. Supreme Ct., U.S. Ct. Appeals, U.S. Dist. Ct. Ptnr. Baker & McKenzie, Chgo., 1973-80, Seki, Jarvis & Lynch, Chgo., 1980-87, Bell, Boyd & Lloyd, Chgo., 1987-92, Foley & Lardner, Chgo., 1992—. V.p. bd. govs. Internat. House U. Chgo.; bd. overseers Ill. Inst. Tech. Chgo.-Kent Coll. Law, pres. bd. dirs. Libr. Internat. Rels.; chmn. bd. trustees Am. Buddhist Acad., N.Y.C.; bd. dirs. Japanese Am. Nat. Mus., L.A.; sec. Chgo.-Osaka Sister Cities Com., Chgo. Mem. Japan Am. Soc. Chgo. (bd. dirs.), Execs. Club Chgo., Chgo. Coun. Fgn. Rels. (mem. Chgo. com.), World Trade Ctr. Chgo. Assn. (bd. dirs.), Harvard Club (N.Y.C.), Univ. Club (Chgo.), Union League Club (Chgo.), Mid-Day Club (Chgo.), Mid-Am. Club (Chgo.). Republican. Office: Foley & Lardner 330 N Wabash Ave Chicago IL 60611

SEKITANI, TORU, otolaryngologist, educator; b. Kochi, Japan, May 5, 1932; s. Fusaharu and Miyoko (Tokushige) S.; m. Miyoko Uejo, Dec. 26, 1960; children: Miwako, Yoshiko, Tetsuko. MD, Yamaguchi Med. Sch., 1957. Intern Yamaguchi Med. Sch. Hosp., Ube, Japan, 1957-58, asst. prof., 1962, assoc. prof., 1971, prof., chmn. dept. otolaryngology, 1976-93; emeritus prof. Yamaguchi U., 1993—; dir. Nat Shimonoseki Hosp, Japan, 1993—; rsch. assoc. Univ. Iowa, Iowa City, 1969-71. Author: (with others) Vertigo: Basic and CLinic, 1976, Vastbular Mechanism in Health and Disease, 1978; editor: Vestibular Ganglia and Vestibular Neuronitis, 1988, Fundamentals of Galvanic Body Sway Test for Dizziness, 1995. Mem. Barany Soc. (Sweden), Prosper Meniere Soc. (U.S.A.), Otorhinolaryngological Soc. Japan, Japan Soc. equilibrium and Rsch. (exec. com. 1975—).

SEKLER, EDUARD FRANZ, architect, educator; b. Vienna, Austria, Sept. 30, 1920; came to U.S., 1954; s. Eduard Jakob and Elisabeth (Demmel) S.; m. Mary Patricia May, July 21, 1962. Dipl. Ing., Tech. U., Vienna, 1945; student, Sch. Planning and Regional Research, London, 1947; Ph.D., London U., 1948; A.M. (hon.), Harvard U., 1960; D Tech. Scis. (hon.), Fed. Inst. Tech., Zurich, Switzerland, 1988. Ptnr. archtl. firm Prehsler and Sekler, Vienna, 1945-95; teaching asst., lectr. faculty architecture Tech. U., Vienna, 1945-54; vis. prof. architecture Harvard U., Cambridge, Mass., 1955-56, assoc. prof., 1956-60, prof., 1960-91, prof. emeritus, 1991—, Osgood Hooker prof. visual art, 1970-91, prof. emeritus, 1991—; Beinecke-Reeves Disting. chair in archtl. preservation U. Fla., 1995-96; coord. studies Carpenter Ctr. Visual Arts, 1962-65, dir., 1966-76, chmn. dept. visual and environ. studies, 1968-70; expert mem. internat. com. hist. monuments UNESCO, 1951-54; UNESCO advisor to planning and archeology depts. Govt. of Nepal, 1972-94; cons. Hist. Monuments Office, Vienna, 1975, 89, 91-96; head UNESCO team for masterplan for Conservation Cultural Heritage of Kathmandu Valley, 1975; UNESCO cons. masterplan for Sukothai Hist. Park, Thailand, 1978, 84. Author: Point-houses in European Housing, 1952, Wren and His Place in European Architecture, 1956, Proportion, a Measure of Order, 1965, Historic Urban Spaces I-IV, 1962-71, Proposal for the Urbanistic Conservation of Patan Durbar Square, 1980, Jos. Hoffmann, The Architectural Work, 1982, Die Architektur und die Zeit, 1988; co-author: Kathmandu Valley, The Preservation of Physical Environment and Cultural Heritage, 2 vols., 1975, Le Corbusier at Work: The Genesis of the Carpenter Center for the Visual Arts, The Building and The Town: Essays for E. Sekler, 1994; archtl. works include restoration ch., Leopoldsberg, nr. Vienna, urban redevel., Alt Erdberg, 1956, Austrian Cultural Inst., N.Y.C., 1962, several housing schemes, Vienna, 1948-68, Telephone Exchange, Vienna, 1970. Mem. Cambridge Arts Council, 1975-84; bd. dirs. Archtl. Heritage, Inc., 1969-75; chmn. Kathmandu Valley Preservation Trust. Decorated Cross of Honor for Scis. and Art (Austria); recipient prize for humanities City of Vienna, 1983, Inst. honors AIA, 1989, Jean Tschumi prize Internat. Union Architects, 1990, Prechtl medal Vienna Tech. U., Gold medal City of Vienna, 1995, Medal of Honor, Austrian Soc. Archtl. Conservation, 1995; Guggenheim fellow, 1961-63. Fellow Am. Acad. Arts and Scis., U.S. Nat. Com. for Internat. Council of Monuments and Sites, Academia Scientiarum et Artium Europea; mem. Internat. Council Monuments and Sites, Soc. Archtl. Historians (dir. 1963-66, 70-73), Archtl. Assn. London, Austrian Chamber Architects, Royal Town Planning Inst. (hon. corr. mem. London), Signet Soc. Office: Grad Sch Design Gund Hall 48 Quincy St Cambridge MA 02138-3804

SEKULA, EDWARD JOSEPH, JR., financial executive; b. Brandonville, Pa., Sept. 2, 1937; s. Edward Joseph and Dorothy May (Fritz) S.; m. Carol Lee Helton, July 13, 1963; 1 child, David. BSBA, Pa. State U., 1961. Dep. fin. officer Aberdeen Proving Ground, Md., 1961-63; with Peat, Marwick, Mitchell & Co., N.Y.C., 1963-77; corp. cont. N.Y.C. Health & Hosp. Corp., 1977-78; dir. fin. Mt. Sinai Med. Ctr., N.Y.C., 1979-82; CFO Vis. Nurse Svc. N.Y., N.Y.C., 1982-86, Wallkill Valley Gen. Hosp., 1986-94; pres. EJ Sekula Ent. Inc.; sec.-treas. Planning Assistance Inc., N.Y.C., 1978—. Mem. parish coun. of deacons Abiding Peace Luth. Ch., 1972-89; cubmaster, com. chmn., Webelos leader Cub Scouts Am., 1974-78; scoutmaster Troop 186, Boy Scouts Am., 1978-85, asst. dist. commr.; vol. fireman Netcong Fire Co. 1, 1974—; co-treas. Lenape Valley Regional H.S. Band Parents Assn., 1981-83; chmn. environ. commn. Borough of Netcong, 1988—, Lake Musconetcong Regional Planning Bd., 1989—. With U.S. Army, 1961-63; capt. Res. (ret.). Recipient Dist. Award of Merit, Boy Scouts Am., Silver Beaver Mem. AICPA, Hosp. Fin. Mgmt. Assn., Home Care Assn., N.Y. Soc. CPAs, Musconetcong Club, Beta Alpha Psi, Phi Kappa Tau. Republican. Lutheran. Fishing, Trout Unltd., Rotary (Paul Harris fellow). Home: 39 Amendola Dr Netcong NJ 07857-1401

SEKULER, ROBERT WILLIAM, psychology educator, scientist; b. Elizabeth, N.J., May 7, 1939; s. Sidney and Mary (Siegel) S.; m. Susan Pamela Nemser, June 25, 1961; children: Stacia, Allison, Erica. A.B., Brandeis U., 1960; Sc.M., Brown U., 1963, Ph.D., 1964; postgrad. (NIH postdoctoral fellow), M.I.T., 1964-65. Prof. psychology Northwestern U., Evanston, Ill., 1973-89, chmn. dept., 1975-79, prof. ophthalmology Med. Sch., 1978-89, prof. neurobiology and physiology, 1982-89, assoc. dean Coll. Arts and Scis., 1985-89, John Evans prof. neurosci., 1986-89; v.p. Optronix, Inc., 1980-82; provost, dean of faculty Brandeis U., Waltham, Mass., 1989-91, Louis and Frances Salvage prof. psychology, 1989—; mem. Ctr. for Complex Systems, 1990—; rsch. prof. biomed. engrng. Boston U., 1992—; adj. prof. cognitive and neural systems Boston U., 1994—; cons. NSF, NIH, AAAS, USAF, U. Calif, Am. Psychol. Assn.; chmn. NRC-Nat. Acad. Sci. Vision Com.; chmn. NRC working Group on Visual Function and Aging; chmn. NRC Working Group on Aging Workers and Visual Impairment. Author: (with D. Kline and K. Dismukes) Aging and Human Visual Function, 1981, (with R. Blake) Perception, 1985, 2d edit., 1990, 3d edit., 1994; editor: Perception & Psychophysics, 1971-86, Jour. Exptl. Psychology, 1973-74, Vision Rsch. Jour., 1974-79, 80-92, Optics Letters, 1977-79, Am. Jour. Psychology, Ophthalmic and Physiol. Optics, 1986—, Intelligent Systems, 1986-92, Psychology and Aging, 1987-92; contbr. Handbook of Geriatric Medicine, 1992; contbr. articles to profl. jours. Grantee Nat. Inst. Neurol. Diseases and Stroke, USAF, NSF, Nat. Eye Inst., Nat. Inst. Aging, USN, James McDonnell Found. Fellow AAAS, Optical Soc. Am., Am. Psychol. Soc.; mem. Assn. Rsch. in Vision and Ophthalmology, Neurosci. Soc., Internat. Neural Network Soc., Psychonomic Soc., Knowles Inst. for Hearing Rsch. (bd. dirs. 1988-90), Sigma Xi. Home: 64 Strawberry Hill Rd Concord MA 01742-5502 Office: Brandeis U Ctr for Complex Systems Waltham MA 02254

SEKULOVICH, MALDEN See MALDEN, KARL

SEKULOW, JAY ALAN, lawyer; b. 1956. BA, JD, Mercer U. Bar: Ga. 1980. Chief counsel Am. Ctr. for Law and Justice, Virginia Beach; adj. prof. law Regent U. Author: From Intimidation to Victory, 1990, Knowing Your Rights, 1993, Students Rights and the Public School. Office: Am Ctr for Law & Justice PO Box 64429 Virginia Beach VA 23467-4429

SELANDER, LARRY, lawyer; b. Chgo., May 28, 1946. BS, U. Notre Dame, 1967; JD, U. Ill., 1972. Bar: Ill. 1972. Ptnr. Keck, Mahin & Cate, Chgo. Mem. ABA, Ill. State Bar Assn., Chgo. Bar Assn. Office: Keck Mahin & Cate 77 W Wacker Dr Ste 4900 Chicago IL 60601-1629*

SELBIN, JOEL, chemistry educator; b. Washington, Aug. 20, 1931; s. Abram Jacob and Rose (Aronson) S.; m. Marion F. Kilsheimer, Aug. 28, 1955; children: Eric Allyn, Jeffrey Lynn, Deborah Lyn, Jonathan David. BS, George Washington U., 1953; PhD, U. Ill., 1957. Asst. prof. chemistry La. State U., Baton Rouge, 1957-61, assoc. prof., 1961-67, prof., 1967-91, also dir. Summer Inst. for High Sch. Tchrs., 1984—; spl. vis. prof. U. Colo., Denver, 1991—; speaker Union of Concerned Scientists, 1980—. Author: Theoretical Inorganic Chemistry, 2d edit., 1969; patentee in field; contbr. articles to profl. jours. Grantee Am. Chem. Soc., NSF, Rsch. Corp. Fellow AAAS; mem. Am. Chem. Soc. (Charles E. Coates award 1973), Phi Beta Kappa, Sigma Xi. Office: U Colo Dept of Chemistry Denver CO 80304

SELBY, CECILY CANNAN, dean, educator, scientist; b. London, Feb. 4, 1927; d. Keith and Catherine Anne Cannan; m. Henry M. Selby, Aug. 11, 1951 (div. 1979); children: Norman, William, Russell; m. James Stacy Coles, Feb. 21, 1981. A.B. cum laude, Radcliffe Coll., 1946; Ph.D. in Phys. Biology, MIT, 1950. Teaching asst. in biology MIT, 1948-49; adminstrv. head virus study sect. Sloan-Kettering Inst., N.Y.C., 1949-50; asst. mem. inst. Sloan-Kettering Inst., 1950-55; research assoc. Sloan-Kettering div. Cornell U. Med. Coll., N.Y.C., 1953-55; instr. microscopic anatomy Cornell U. Med. Coll., 1955-57; tchr. sci. Lenox Sch., N.Y.C., 1957-58; headmistress Lenox Sch., 1959-72; nat. exec. dir. Girl Scouts U.S.A., N.Y.C., 1972-75; adv. com. Simmons Coll. Grad. Mgmt. Program, 1977-78; mem. Com. Corp. Support of Pvt. Univs., 1977-83; spl. asst. acad. planning N.C. Sch. Sci. and Math., 1979-80, dean acad. affairs, 1980-81, chmn. bd. advisors, 1981-84; cons. U.S. Dept. Commerce, 1976-77; dir. Avon Products Inc., RCA, NBC, Loehmanns Inc., Nat. Edn. Corp. pres. Am. Energy Ind., 1976; co-chmn. commn. precoll. math. and sci. Nat. Sci. Bd., 1982-83; adj. prof. NYU, 1984-86, prof. sci. edn., 1986—; mem. policy steering com. Gov. Cuomo's Conf. on Sci. and Engring., 1989-90. Contbr. articles to profl. jours., chpt. to book. Founder, chmn. N.Y. Ind. Schs. Opportunity Project, 1968-72; mem. invitational workshops Aspen Inst., 1973, 75, 77, 79; trustee MIT, Bklyn. Law Sch., Radcliffe Coll., Woods Hole Oceanographic Instn., Women's Forum N.Y., Skin Disease Found., N.Y. Hall of Sci., 1982—, vice chmn., 1989—, trustee Girls Inc., 1992—, Nat. Coun. Women in Medicine, 1990-94; mem. Yale U. Peabody Mus. Adv. Coun., 1981-89. Recipient Woman Scientist of Yr. award N.Y. chpt. Am. Women in Sci., 1992. Mem. Headmistresses of East (hon., pres. 1970-72), Sigma Xi, Phi Delta Kappa. Clubs: Cosmopolitan (N.Y.C.). Home and Office: 45 Sutton Pl S New York NY 10022-2444 also: 100 Ransom Rd Falmouth MA 02540-1652

SELBY, CLARK LINWOOD, JR., sales executive; b. Miami, Okla., Sept. 20, 1936; s. Clark Linwood and Edith Opal (Clark) S.; m. Patricia Ann Hayes, Dec. 22, 1952; children: Michael Lynn, Robert Clark. Sales engr. Carl Evans Co., Kansas City, Mo., 1962-70; asst. dir. traffic and parking U. Iowa, Iowa City, 1970-72; parking cons. De Leuw and Cather & Co., Chgo., 1972-77; pres. Enterprising Am. Corp., Hutchinson, Kans., 1978-82; dir. mfg. Duncan Industries, Harrison, Ark., 1982-85, dir. internat. sales, 1985-86, v.p. internat. sales, 1987-88, pres., 1988-90, v.p. sales and mktg., 1991-94; pres. Annell Corp., Wichita, Kans., 1991-95, bd. dirs., 1991-95; instr. free trade mktg. Kiev (USSR) Inst., 1991; chmn., sec. Florentine Corp., Flippin, Ark., 1994—; pres., CEO Worldwide Parking, Harrison, 1994—; dir. Eyewear Shoppe, Inc., Hutchinson; chmn. Florentine Corp., Flippin, Ark., 1994. Inventor in field. Served with USNG, 1955-60. Recipient Presdl. E award for excellences in exporting, 1988. Methodist. Home: 1801 Par Ln Harrison AR 72601-6708 Office: Worldwide Parking Security Plz Ste 203C Harrison AR 72601

SELBY, DIANE RAY MILLER, fraternal organization administrator; b. Lorain, Ohio, Oct. 11, 1940; d. Dale Edward and Mildred (Ray) Miller; m. David Baxter Selby, Apr. 14, 1962; children: Elizabeth, Susan, Sarah. BS in Edn., Ohio State U., 1962. Sec. Kappa Kappa Gamma Frat., Columbus, Ohio, 1962-63, editor, 1972-86; tchr. Hilliard (Ohio) High Sch., 1963-65; exec. dir. Mortar Bd., Inc. Nat. Office, Columbus, Ohio, 1986—. Editor The Key of Kappa Kappa Gamma Frat, 1972-86 (Student Life award, 1983, 84, 85). Founding officer Community Coordinating Bd., Worthington, Ohio, 1983; pres. PTA Coun., Worthington, 1984, Worthington Band Boosters, 1985; sec., treas. Sports and Recreation Facilities Bd., Worthington, 1986—; mem. sustaining com. Jr. League Columbus, 1991-93, docent Kelton House, 1979—. Mem. Mortar Bd., Inc., Twig 53 Children's Hosp. (assoc.), Assn. Coll. Honor Soc., Ladybugs and Buckeyes, Kappa Kappa Gamma. Republican. Lutheran. Home: 6750 Merwin Pl Columbus OH 43235-2838 Office: Mortar Bd Inc 1250 Chambers Rd Ste 170 Columbus OH 43212-1754

SELBY, HUBERT, JR., writer; b. N.Y.C., July 23, 1928; s. Hubert and Adalin (Layne) S.; m. Inez Taylor, Apr. 23, 1955 (div. 1960); children: Claudia, Kyle; Suzanne Schwartzman, Dec. 26, 1969; children: Rachel, William. Student public schs., Bklyn. Author: Last Exit to Brooklyn, 1964, The Room, 1971, The Demon, 1976, Requiem for a Dream, 1978, Song of the Silent Snow, 1986; screenwriter: Day and Night, 1986, Remember the Sabath Day, 1974, Love Your Buddy Week, 1978, Solder of Fortune, 1990. Served with U.S. Mcht. Marine, 1944-46. Mem. Writers Guild Am. (West chpt.), Authors Guild.

SELBY, JEROME M., mayor; b. Wheatland, Wyo., Sept. 4, 1948; s. John Franklin and Claudia Meredith (Hudson) S.; m. Gloria Jean Nelson, June 14, 1969; children: Tyan, Camerонn, Kalen. BS in Math., Coll. Idaho, 1969, MA in Ednl. Adminstrn., 1974; MPA, Boise State U., 1978. Assoc. engr. Boeing Co., Seattle, 1969-71; dir. evaluation WICHE Mountain States Regional Med. Program, Boise, 1971-74; dir. rsch., evaluation Mountain States Health Corp., Boise, 1974-76, with health policy analysis and accountability, 1976-78; dir. health Kodiak (Alaska) Area Native Assn., 1978-83; mgr. Kodiak Island Borough, 1984-85, mayor, 1985—; proprietor Kodiak Tax Svc., 1978—, Registered Guide, Kodiak, 1987—; cons. Nat. Cancer Inst., Washington, 1973-78, others. Contbr. articles to profl. jours. Treas. ARC, Kodiak, 1978-93, bd. dirs., 1978-95, chmn., 1989-90, mem. western ops. hdqrs. adv. bd., 1986-92, mem. group IV and V nat. adv. coj., 1986-89, nat. bd. govs., 1989-95, chmn. chpt. rels. com., 1994-95; pres. S.W. Alaska Mcpl. Conf., Anchorage, 1988-89, v.p., 1986-87, treas., 1996—, bd. dirs., 1986—; pres. Alaska Mcpl. League Investment Pool, Inc., 1992—; v.p. Alaska Mcpl. League, 1988-90, pres., 1990-91, bd. dirs., 1988—; bd. dirs. Alaska Mcpl. League Jt. Ins. Assn. Bd., 1995— mem. Alaska Resource Devel. Coun., 1987—, exec. com., 1989—; mem. policy com. of outer continental shelf adv. bd. U.S. Dept. Interior, 1990—; co-chair Alaska Task Force, 1995—; mem. Com. on Oil Pollution Act, 1995; mem. Nat. Assn. Counties, Cmty. and Econ. Devel. Steering Com., 1990—, Alaska govtl. roles task force, 1991-92; chmn. Kodiak Island Exxon Valdez Restoration Com., 1991-95; dir. Kodiak Health Care Found., 1992—; co-chmn. Arctic Power, 1993—; mem. bd. dirs. Western Interstate Region Nat. Assn. of Counties, 1993—. Paul Harris fellow, 1987, 88, 91, 92; recipient Outstanding Contbn. award Alaska Mcpl. League, 1994. Mem. Alaska Conf. Mayors, Nat. Soc. Tax Profls., Acad. Polit. Sci., Alaska Mcpl. Mgrs. Assn., Kodiak C. of C. (dir. 1983—), Rotary (bd. dirs., treas. 1989-93, v.p. 1993-94, pres.-elect 1994-95, pres. 1995-96). Office: Kodiak Island Borough 710 Mill Bay Rd Kodiak AK 99615-6340

SELBY, ROY CLIFTON, JR., neurosurgeon; b. Little Rock, Sept. 28, 1930; s. Roy Clifton Sr. and Annie Mae (Bular) S.; m. Marilyn Triffler, May 12, 1960; children: Brian M.T., Bretta L.T. BSc, MSc, La. State U., 1952; MD, U. Ark., Little Rock, 1956. diplomate Am. Bd. Neurol. Surgery. Intern Montreal Gen. Hosp., 1956-57; resident VA Hosp., Little Rock, Ark., 1957-58, U. Ill. Depart. Neurology and Neurosurgery, Chgo., 1958-61; sr. fellow Neurosurgery Lahey Clinic, Boston, 1961-62; dir. dept. neurosurgery Ministry Health Gen. Hosp., Kuala Lumpur, Malaysia, 1963-70; chmn. dept. neurosurgery Cook County Hosp., Chgo., 1970-74; practice medicine specializing in neurosurgery Texarkana, Tex., 1974-86; assoc. clin. prof. neurosurgery U. Ill., Chgo., 1970-74; prof. Cook County Postgrad. Sch. Med., 1970-74; vis. assoc. prof. Rush Presbyn. Med. Ctr., 1970-74; lectr. dept. psychology E. Tex. U., Texarkana, 1986—. Author short stories; contbr. chpts. to books. Fellow Royal Soc. Medicine; mem. Am. Assn. Neurol. Surgeons, N.Y. Acad. Scis., Soc. Neurol. Lange Francaise, N.Y. Acad. Medicine, French Soc. History of Medicine, Acad. Medicine (Paris), Internat. Soc. Surgery, Am. Osler Soc., Ark. Hist. Soc., Soc. Neurosci., Cen. Neuropsychiat. Soc., Inst. Charles DeGaulle, Ala. Hist. Soc., La. Hist. Soc., Sigma Xi, Alpha Omega Alpha. Avocations: reading, writing, gardening. Home: 7 Sweetbrush Ave Texarkana TX 75503-9999 Office: 1903 Mall Dr Texarkana TX 75503 *The more I learn, the less I feel separated from all creatures; believing in all forms of life highly specialized, though greatly diverse, require respect and reverence.*

SELCER, DAVID MARK, lawyer; b. Cleve., Feb. 12, 1943; s. Lester and Sylvia (Esral) S.; m. Belinda Weine, Aug. 8, 1968 (div. 1986); children: Daniel, Anne, Emily; m. Susan Merwin, Mar. 22, 1993. BA, Northwestern U., 1965; JD, Ohio State U., 1968. Bar: Ohio, 1968, Ill. 1969, U.S. Dist. Ct. (so. dist.) Ohio 1971, U.S. Dist. Ct. (no. dist.) Ohio 1973. Ptnr. Porter, Wright, Morris & Arthur, Columbus, Ohio, 1973-78, Krupman, Fromson & Selcer, Columbus, 1979-81, Baker & Hostetler, Columbus, 1981—; adj. prof. Capitol U. Law Sch., Columbus, 1973-74; bd. dirs. Consolidated Stores Corp., 1990-91. Trustee Temple Israel, Columbus, 1987-94; v.p. Jewish Family Svc., 1987-94. Recipient Disting. Service award Columbus Symphony Orch., 1986-87. Mem. ABA (equal employment opportunity subcom. of labor com 1978—), Nat. Labor Relations Bd (asst. bd. mem. 1967-68), Ohio Bar Assn., Columbus Bar Assn. Office: Baker & Hostetler 65 E State St Columbus OH 43215-4213*

SELDEN, RICHARD THOMAS, economist, educator; b. Pontiac, Mich., Mar. 31, 1922; s. Arthur Willis and Florence L. (Seeley) S.; m. Martha Mathiasen, Mar. 21, 1953 (div. June 1989); children: Phoebe Serena, Thomas Mathiasen; m. Louise H. Randolph, July 30, 1989; 1 stepdaughter, Laura Peyton Mosca. BA, U. Chgo., 1948, PhD, 1954; MA, Columbia U., 1949. Instr. U. Mass., Amherst, 1949-50; mem. faculty Vanderbilt U., Nashville, 1952-59; asso. prof. Vanderbilt U., 1955-59; research asso. Nat. Bur. Econ. Research, N.Y.C., 1958-59; asso. prof. banking Columbia, 1959-63; economist 1st Nat. City Bank, N.Y.C., 1962-63; prof. econs. Cornell U., 1963-69; Carter Glass prof. econs. U. Va., 1969-94, chmn. dept., 1972-79; Mem. adv. council banking and financial research com. Am. Bankers Assn., 1964-67; U. Va. rep. on univs. Nat. Bur. Com. for Econ. Research, 1969-79. Author: The Postwar Rise in the Velocity of Money, 1962, Trends and Cycles in the Commercial Paper Market, 1963, (with George R. Morrison) Time Deposit Growth and the Employment of Bank Funds, 1965; Contbr. articles to profl. jours. Guggenheim fellow, 1965; Fulbright Advanced Research scholar Brussels, Belgium, 1964-65; Ford Found. faculty fellow Cornell U., 1968-69; Indo-Am. fellow Bombay, India, 1981. Mem. Am. Econ. Assn. Home: PO Box 3 Ivy VA 22945-0003

SELDEN, ROBERT WENTWORTH, physicist, science advisor; b. Phoenix, Aug. 11, 1936; s. Edward English and Mary Priscilla (Calder) S.; m. Mary Tania Hudd, June 1958 (div. 1976); 1 child, Ian Scott; m. Marjorie Anne Harmon, Feb. 20, 1977; children: Brock, Thane, Shawna, Kirsten. BA in Physics cum laude, Pomona Coll., 1958; MS in Physics, U. Wis., 1960, PhD in Physics, 1964. Rsch. assoc. Lawrence Livermore (Calif.) Nat. Lab., 1965-67, staff mem., 1967-73, group leader, 1973-78, asst. assoc. dir., 1978-80; div. leader applied theoretical physics Los Alamos (N.Mex.) Nat. Lab., 1980-83, dep. assoc. dir. strategic def. rsch., 1983-84, assoc. dir. theoretical and computational physics, 1984-86, dir. Ctr. for Nat. Securities Studies, 1986-88, assoc. dir. for lab. devel., 1991-94; chief scientist USAF, Washington, 1991-94, panel chmn. sci. adv. bd., 1984-88, 91—; cons. Los Alamos, 1994—; chmn. study group on reactor materials and nuclear explosives U.S. Dept. Energy, 1976-78; mem. ballistic missile def. techs. adv. panel U.S. Congress Office Tech. Assessment, 1984-85, The Pres.'s Defensive Tech. Study Team, Washington, 1983. Editor Rsch. Jour. Lawrence Livermore Nat. Lab., 1976-77; contbr. sci. and tech. papers to profl. jours. Pres. Livermore Cultural Arts Coun., 1969-72; chmn. Livermore Sister City Orgn., 1973, Planning Commn. City of Livermore, 1971-76; bd. dirs. Orch. of Santa Fe, 1986-88. Capt. U.S. Army, 1964-67. Grad. fellow Edward John Noble Found., 1958-62; recipient Theodore von Karman award for outstanding contbn. to def. sci., 1989. Mem. AAAS, Am. Phys. Soc., N.Y. Acad. Sci., Air Force Assn. Avocations: tennis, hiking, music. Office: 624 La Bajada Los Alamos NM 87544-3805

SELDEN, WILLIAM KIRKPATRICK, retired educational administrator; b. Oil City, Pa., Nov. 11, 1911; s. Edwin van D. and Cornelia Fuller (Earp) S.; m. Virginia Barr, June 25, 1938; children: Edwin van Deusen, II, Joseph Barr. A.B., Princeton U., 1934; LL.D., Carthage Coll., 1954; Litt.D., Jacksonville U., 1964; L.H.D., Scholl Coll. Podiatric Medicine, 1984. Asst. to faculty dean, coll. dean Princeton U., 1934-37; clk. Eastman Kodak Co., Rochester, N.Y., 1937-38; asst. dir. admissions, admissions officer, asst. coll. dean Brown U., Providence, 1938-43; asst. to pres. Brown U., 1943-45; asst. dean students, dir. admissions Northwestern U., Evanston, Ill., 1945-52; univ. recorder Northwestern U., 1952-53; pres. Ill. Coll., 1953-55; exec. dir. Nat. Commn. on Accrediting, 1955-65; v.p. The Am. Assembly, 1965-66; former mem. various bds. and coms. concerned with issues in edn., mil., professions, and polit. affairs. Author: Accreditation--A Struggle Over Standards in Higher Education, 1960, Woodrow Wilson School, Princeton University, 1984, Princeton Summer Camp, 1987, Vignettes of Princeton University, 1987, Legacy of John Cleve Green, 1988, Its First 100 Years--Nassau Club of Princeton, 1989, From These Roots: The Creation of Princeton Day School, 1991, The Heritage of Isabella McCosh: A History of the Health Service at Princeton University, 1991, History of Princeton Theological Seminary, 1992, Drumthwalket, The Governors Mansion, 1993, Club Life at Princeton, An Historical Account of the Eating Clubs at Princeton University, 1995, Nassau Hall, Princeton University's National Historic Landmark, 1995. Home: Loe 105 Pennswood Village Newtown PA 18940-2401

SELDES, MARIAN, actress; b. N.Y.C.; d. Gilbert and Alice (Hall) S.; m. Julian Claman, Nov. 3, 1953 (div.); 1 child, Katharine; m. Garson Kanin, June 19, 1990. Grad., Neighborhood Playhouse, N.Y.C., 1947; D.H.L., Emerson Coll., 1979. Mem. faculty drama and dance div. Juilliard Sch. Lincoln Center, N.Y.C., 1969-91. Appeared with Cambridge (Mass.) Summer Theatre, 1945, Boston Summer Theatre, 1946, St. Michael's Playhouse, Winooski, Vt., 1947-48, Bermudiana Theatre, Hamilton, Bermuda, 1951, Elitch Gardens Theatre, Denver, 1953; Broadway appearances include Medea, 1947, Crime and Punishment, 1948, That Lady, 1949, Tower Beyond Tragedy, 1950, The High Ground, 1951, Come of Age, 1952, Ondine, 1954, The Chalk Garden, 1955, The Wall, 1960, A Gift of Time, 1962, The Milk Train Doesn't Stop Here Any More, 1964, Tiny Alice, 1965, A Delicate Balance, 1967 (Tony award for best supporting actress), Before You Go, 1968, Father's Day, 1971 (Drama Desk award), Mendicants of Evening (Martha Graham Co.), 1973, Equus, 1974-77, The Merchant, 1977, Deathtrap, 1978; off-Broadway appearances include Diff'rent, 1961, The Ginger Man, 1963 (Obie award), All Women Are One, 1964, Juana LaLoca, 1965, Three Sisters, 1969, Am. Shakespeare Festival, Stratford, Conn., Mercy Street at Am. Place Theater, N.Y.C., 1969, Isadora Duncan, 1976 (Obie award), Painting Churches, 1983, 84 (Outer Critics Circle award 1984), Other People, Berkshire Theatre Festival, 1969, The Celebration, Hedgerow Theater, Pa., 1971, Richard III, N.Y. Shakespeare Festival, 1983, Remember Me, Lakewood Theatre, Skowhegan, Maine, Gertrude Stein and a Companion, White Barn Theatre, Westport, Conn., 1985, Lucile Lortel Theatre, N.Y.C., 1986, Richard II, N.Y. Shakespeare Festival, 1987, The Milk Train Doesn't Stop Here Anymore, WPA Theatre, N.Y.C., 1987, Happy Ending, Bristol (Pa.) Riverside Theatre, 1988, Annie 2 John F. Kennedy Ctr., Washington, 1989-90, Goodspeed Opera House, Chester, Conn., 1990, A Bright Room Called Day, N.Y. Shakespeare Festival, 1991, Three Tall Women, River Arts, Woodstock, N.Y., 1992, Another Time, Am. Jewish Theatre, 1993, Breaking the Code, Berkshire Theatre Festival, 1993, Three Tall Women, Vineyard Theatre, N.Y.C., 1994, Promenade Theatre, 1994-95; engaged in nat. tour Medea, 1947; U.S. entry Berlin Festival, 1951, nat. tour Three Tall Women, 1995-96; motion picture appearances include The Greatest Story Ever Told, Gertrude Stein and a Companion, 1988, In a Pig's Eye, 1988, The Gun in Betty Lou's Handbag, 1992, Tom and Huck, 1995; (ABC series) Good and Evil, 1991, Murphy Brown, 1992, Truman, 1995; also appeared on CBS Radio Mystery Theater, 1976-81, as well as numerous dramatic shows; author: The Bright Lights, 1978, Time Together, 1981. Bd. dirs. Neighborhood Playhouse, The Acting Co., nat. repertory theatre. Inducted into Theater Hall of Fame, 1996. Mem. Players Club, Century Assn. Home: Apt 19 D 210 Central Park West New York NY 10019

SELDIN, DONALD WAYNE, physician, educator; b. N.Y.C., Oct. 24, 1920; s. Abraham L. and Laura (Ueberal) S.; m. Muriel Goldberg, Apr. 1, 1943; children: Leslie Lynn, Donald Craig, Donna Leigh. BA, NYU, 1940; MD, Yale U., 1943; DHL (hon.), So. Meth. U., 1977; DSc (hon.), Med. Coll. Wis., 1980, Yale U., 1988; D honoris causa, Univ. de Paris VI, Pierre et Marie Curie, 1983. Diplomate Am. Bd. Internal Medicine (test com. on nephrology 1970-73). Intern New Haven Hosp., Yale U., 1943-44, resident, 1944-46, instr. medicine, 1948-50, asst. prof. internal medicine, 1950-51; mem. faculty U. Tex. Southwestern Med. Sch., Dallas, 1951—, William Buchanan prof. internal medicine, 1969—, Univ. Tex. System prof., 1988—, chmn. dept. internal medicine, 1952-88; chief med. service Parkland Meml. Hosp., Dallas, 1952—; chmn. dept. medicine Lisbon VA Hosp., Dallas; pres. Southwestern Med. Found., 1988—; cons. Baylor Hosp., St. Paul's Hosp., Presbyn. Hosp., Dallas, Brooke Army Hosp., Ft. Sam Houston, Walter Reed Army Hosp., Washington, also to Surgeon Gen. U.S., Surgeon Gen. USAF, and Eli Lilly Co., 1972—; mem. Bur. Budget, Exec. Office of Pres., 1966-67, chmn. dialysis and transplantation com. of sci. adv. bd. Nat. Kidney Found.; mem. bd. sci. councillors Nat. Inst. Arthritis and Metabolic Diseases, NIH, 1968-71; trustee Rand Corp., 1975-93, adv. trustee, 1993—. Editorial bd.: Jour. Lab. and Clin. Medicine, 1958-60, Nephron, The Clinician, Medicine, Mineral and Electrolyte Metabolism, 1977-79; cons. editor: Am. Jour. Medicine; assoc. editor: Kidney Internat., 1973-79; contbr. articles to profl. jours. Served as capt. U.S. Army, 1946-48. Recipient Disting. Achievement award Modern Medicine, 1977, John P. Peters award Am. Soc. Nephrology, 1983, Disting. U.S. Scientist award Alexander von Humboldt Found., 1989, John K. Lattimer award Am. Urol. Assn., 1989; Friedrich Von Muller hon. lectr. U. Munich, 1968. Master ACP (Disting. Teaching award 1980); Fellow Royal Soc. Medicine, Am. Acad. Arts and Sci.; mem. AMA, Dallas County Med. Soc., Tex. Med. Assn., Dallas Diabetes Assn., So. Soc. Clin. Investigation (pres. 1964, Founders medal 1975), Central Soc. Clin. Research (pres. 1963), Am. Fedn. Clin. Research, Am. Soc. Clin. Investigation (pres. 1966), Assn. Profs. Medicine (pres. 1971, Robert H. Williams Disting. Chmn. Medicine award 1977), Assn. Am. Physicians (pres. 1980, Kober medal 1985), Am. Physiol. Soc., Am. Soc. Nephrology (pres. 1968), Nat. Kidney Found. (David Hume award 1981), Am. Heart Assn., Am. Clin. and Climatol. Assn., Soc. Med. Cons. to Armed Forces, Internat. Soc. Nephrology (councillor 1973-78, pres. 1984-87), Southwestern Med. Found. (pres. 1988-93, vice chmn. 1993—), Australian Soc. Nephrology (hon.), Gesellschaft für Nephrologie, (Volhard medal 1986), Alpha Omega Alpha. Office: 5323 Harry Hines Blvd Dallas TX 75235-7200

SELDMAN, NEIL NORMAN, cultural organization administrator; b. Bklyn., Aug. 2, 1945; s. Fred Herman and Sylvia (Flaster) S.; m. Laura Jane Klugherz, Feb. 22, 1968; children: Oliver, Chloe. BS in Indsl. and Labor Rels., Cornell U., 1966; MS in Internat. Communism, George Washington U., 1968, PhD in Internat. Rels., 1974. Asst. to pres. B.H. Krueger Co., Bklyn., 1969-72; assoc. prof., lectr. George Washington U., Washington, 1974-76, asst. dir. exptl. program, 1976-77; founder Inst. for Local Self-Reliance (ILSR), Washington, 1974—, pres., 1980—; cons. World Bank/UN Environ. Program, Washington, 1980-81, City Coun., Phila., 1984-90. Author: Common Sense Radicalism, 1976, Waste to Wealth: A Guide for Community Enterprise, 1985; co-author: Integrated Resource Recovery-Recycling from Municipal Refuse: A State-of-the-Art Review and Annotated Bibliography, 1985, Proven Profits from Pollution Prevention, 1986, Garbage in Europe: Economics, Technologies, Trends, 1987; contbr. article to Ency. of Energy Tech. and the Environment, 1995. Fabrangen Cheder Jewish Community Orgn.; elected chair Neighborhood Planning Coun., Washington, 1976-82; co-founder D.C. Interracial Coalition for Environ. Equity, Washington, 1989. With NG, 1968-74. Grantee Moriah Fund, 1990-95, Pew Charitable Trusts, 1991, NSF, 1979-80, H. Heinz Endowment, 1995-96,

U.S. EPA, 1993-96. Jewish. Avocations: fast pitch softball, nineteenth-century literature, French and Russian revolutions. Office: Inst Local Self-Reliance 2425 18th St NW Washington DC 20009-2003

SELDNER, BETTY JANE, environmental engineer, consultant, aerospace company executive; b. Balt., Dec. 11, 1923; d. David D. and Miriam M. (Mendes) Miller; m. Warren E. Gray, June 20, 1945 (div. 1965); children: Patricia, Deborah; m. Alvin Seldner, Nov. 15, 1965; children: Jack, Barbara. BA in Journalism, Calif. State U., Northridge, 1975, MA in Communications, 1977. Dir. pub. info. United Way, Van Nuys, Calif., 1958-63; dir. edn. United Way, Los Angeles, 1963-68; dir. pub. relations, fin. San Fernando Valley Girl Scout Council, Reseda, Calif., 1968-73; asst. dir. pub. info. Calif. State U., Northridge, 1973-75; dir. environ. mgmt. HR Textron Corp., Valencia, Calif., 1975-87; environ. engr. Northrop Aircraft, Hawthorne, Calif., 1987-88, EMCON Assocs., Burbank, Calif., 1988-92, Atkins Environ., 1992-93, Seldner Environ., Valencia, Calif., 1993—; prin. Seldner Environ. Svcs., 1993—. Author non-fiction. Mem. Santa Clarita Valley Environ. Mgrs. Soc. (chmn. bd. dirs. 1984), San Fernando Valley Round Table (pres. 1971-72), Hazardous Materials Mgrs.' Assn., Zonta Internat. Republican. Jewish. Avocation: sailing.

SELECMAN, CHARLES EDWARD, business executive; b. Dallas, Sept. 17, 1928; s. Frank A. and Eloise (Olive) S.; m. Nan Harton Nash, May 11, 1951 (div. 1975); children: Mary Lucinda, Nan Elizabeth, Amy Eloise; m. Judith Wallace Pollard, Feb. 6, 1976 (div. 1984); m. Barbara Ann Calvert, Apr. 18, 1985. B.A., So. Meth. U., 1951. Bus. mgmt. clk. Buick Motor div. Gen. Motor Corp., Dallas, 1951-52; pers. dept. Chance Vought Aircraft, Inc., Dallas, 1952-56; div. pers. mgr. U.S. Industries, Inc., Longview, Tex., 1956-64; div. v.p. mktg. U.S. Industries, Inc., 1964-66; div. exec. v.p. Axelson div. U.S. Industries, Inc., 1966-67, div. pres., 1967; corp. v.p. U.S. Industries, Inc., N.Y.C., 1967-68, corp. exec. v.p., dir., 1968-70, pres., 1970-73; vice chmn., CEO U.S. Industries, Inc., 1973-74, also dir.; pres., CEO E.T. Barwick Industries, Inc., 1975-78; ptnr. Marshalsea Texas Partners, Dallas, 1978-83; chmn., pres., CEO Input/Output Inc., Houston, 1984-93, chmn., 1993—; dir. Triton Oil & Gas Corp., 1975-93. Mem. Soc. Exploration Geophysicists, Sigma Alpha Epsilon. Office: Input/Output Inc 12300 Parc Crest Dr Stafford TX 77477-2419

SELES, MONICA, tennis player; b. Novi Sad, Yugoslavia, Dec. 2, 1973; came to U.S., 1986; d. Karol and Esther Seles. Winner Italian Open, 1990, German Open, 1990, French Open, 1990, 91, 92, Va. Slims, 1990, 91, 92, U.S. Open, 1991, 92, Australian Open, 1991, 92, 93, 96, Italian Open Doubles (with Kelesi) 1990, (with Capriati) 1991, (with Sukova), 1992; named Yugoslavia's sportswoman of yr., 1985, World #1 ranked player, 1991, 92, #3 players in terms of career titles as a teenager, 1993; recipient 1990 Rado Topspin award, Ted Tinling Diamond award Va. Slims, 1990, Grand Slam Title, 1996; named Tennis Mag./Rolex Watch Female Rookie of Yr., 1989, World Champion, 1991, 92, Tennis mag. Comeback Player of Yr., 1995, Profl. Female Athlete by Yr., 1995. 3rd player in the Open-era to capture the Australian and Roland Garros in same calendar year; named youngest #1 ranked player in tennis history for women and men at 17 years, 3 months, 9 days. Office: care Internat Mgmt Group 1 Erieview Plz Cleveland OH 44114-1715

SELF, CHARLES EDWIN, financial consultant, retail company executive; b. Roanoke, Va., June 6, 1934; s. Loy Evry and Louzelle (Childers) S.; m. Phyllis Ann Stevens, Sept. 2, 1961; children: Tim, Randy, Betsy. BA, Randolph Macon Coll., 1956. Budget specialist Gen. Electric Co., Schenectady, N.Y., 1960-64; merchandise contr. Montgomery Ward & Co., N.Y.C., 1964-67; contr. The Hecht Co., Washington, 1967-70; v.p., fin. contr. Zayre Corp., Framingham, Mass., 1970-79; v.p. fin. Wal-Mart Stores, Inc., Bentonville, Ark., 1979-87; pvt. practice fin. cons. Bellingham, Wash., 1987—; mem. fin. steering com. Nat. Mass Retail Inst., N.Y.C., 1980-86; chmn. Nat. Capital Group of Contrs., Washington, 1969; chmn., bd. dirs. Consumers' Choice Inc., Bellingham, Wash., 1990-94; bd. dirs. Bank of Bellingham, No. Automotive Corp., Phoenix. Commr. Conservation Commn., Mass., 1976-79; bd. dirs. Am. Field Svc., Ark., 1984, Whatcom Mus. History and Art, Bellingham, 1990-95, pres., 1994-95; trustee Western Found., Western Wash. U., 1991—, St. Luke's Found., 1994—. Lt. USNR, 1956-60. Mem. B'Ham (Wash.) Yacht Club. Republican. Episcopalian. Avocations: boating, fishing, stained glass, woodwork. Home and Office: 324 Bayside Rd Bellingham WA 98225-7802

SELF, JAMES REED, librarian; b. Greeneville, Tenn., May 14, 1944; s. Rex Clive and Ethel (Reed) S.; m. Charlotte Clifford, Mar. 18, 1967; children—Jennifer Reed, Abigail Clifford. B.S., U. Tenn., 1967, M.A. in History, 1970; M.A. in Librarianship, U. Denver, 1971. Reference librarian Ind. U., Bloomington, 1971-78, head undergrad. library, 1978-81; dir. Clemons Library U. Va., Charlottesville, 1982—. Contbr. articles to profl. jours. Mem. ALA, Va. Library Assn. Office: University of Virginia Clemons Library Charlottesville VA 22904

SELF, LARRY DOUGLAS, architectural firm executive; b. Cleburne, Tex., Aug. 14, 1943. BArch, Tex. Tech U., 1968. Registered arch., Mo., Tex.; cert. Nat. Coun. Archtl. Registration Bds. Project designer Hellmuth, Obata & Kassabaum, Inc., St. Louis, 1968—; overseas dir. Hellmuth, Obata & Kassabaum, Inc., Riyadh, Saudi Arabia; dir. design, mng. prin. Hellmuth, Obata & Kassabaum, Inc., Dallas, 1980-91; exec. dir. Europe, bd. dirs. Hellmuth, Obata & Kassabaum, Inc., London, 1992-95, dir. corp. ops., 1995-96; exec. v.p. Hellmuth, Obata & Kassabaum, Inc., St. Louis, 1996—. Prin. works include Am South/Harbert Plz., Birmingham, Ala., Zale Corp. World Hdqrs., Dallas, Arco Exploration & Prodn., Rsch. Ctr., Plano, Tex., Collin County C.C., Plano, Cmty. Fedn. Ctr., St. Louis, Plano Civic Ctr., Xerox Rsch. Ctr., Palo Alto, Calif., Tuscon Mall, Aetna Life & Casualty Group Benefits Divsn. Hdqrs., Middletown, Conn., Albuquerque Plz. Hyatt Hotel, Riverchase Galleria Wyndham Hote, Birmingham, King Saud Univ., Riyadh, Saudi Arabia, others. Fellow AIA. Office: Hellmuth Obata & Kassabaum 211 N Broadway Saint Louis MO 63102-2733 Home: 7057 Kingsbury Blvd Saint Louis MO 63130-4305

SELF, MADISON ALLEN, chemical company executive; b. Ozawkie, Kans., June 30, 1921; s. Benjamin B. and Margaret E. (Allen) S.; m. Lila M. Reetz, Sept. 1, 1943; 1 son, Murray A. B.S. in Chem. Engring, U. Kans., 1943. Engr. York Corp., 1943-44; salesman and researcher Sharples Chems., Inc., 1944-47; with Bee Chem. Co., Lansing, Ill., 1947-84; chmn. bd., chief exec. officer Bee Chem. Co., until 1984; pres. Allen Fin., Inc., 1984—; chmn. bd. dirs. Tioga Internat., Inc., 1989—. Life trustee Ill. Inst. Tech. Mem. Chief Exec. Orgn., World Pres.'s Orgn., Hinsdale Golf Club. Office: Allen Fin Inc 1440 Huntington Dr Calumet City IL 60409-5464

SELF, PHYLLIS C., library director; b. Moline, Ill., Dec. 5, 1946; d. Charles Arthur and Henrietta Mary (Youngvorst) K.; m. David Alfred Self, June 22, 1968; 1 child, Linnea Christine. A.S., Black Hawk Coll., 1966; B.S., U. Ill., 1969, M.L.S., 1974, PhD, 1990. Jr. librarian R.I. Pub. Library, Rock Island, Ill., 1969-70; unit librarian Rockridge Sch. Unit, Edgington, Ill., 1970-71; biology tchr. Northwestern High Sch., Sciota, Ill., 1971-73; asst. phys. sci. librarian U. Ill., Urbana, 1974-75, asst. health scis. librarian, 1975-77, health scis. librarian, 1977-87, asst. dir. pub. services, 1980-84; health scis. libr., vis. instr. U. N.C., Chapel Hill, 1987-89; dir. Health Scis. Libr., U. Cin., Cin., 1989-91; head Tompkins-McCaw Libr., Va. Commonwealth U., Richmond, 1991—; cons. in Sudan WHO, Alexandria, Egypt, 1982. Editor: Physical Disabilities, 1984 (Presdl. commn. award 1985); contbr. articles to profl. jours. Mem. Med. Library Assn. (com. chmn. 1979—, pres. 1980 Midwest chpt.), Internat. Fedn. Librarians. Methodist. Avocations: travel; cooking; golf. Home: 320 Farnham Dr Richmond VA 23236-4025 Office: Va Commonwealth U - Med Coll Va Campus Tompkins McCaw Libr 509 N 12th St Richmond VA 23298-5015

SELF, W. M., textile company executive. Pres. Greenwood (S.C.) Mills. Inc., also bd. dirs. Office: Greenwood Mills Inc PO Box 1017 Greenwood SC 29648-1017*

SELFE, EDWARD MILTON, lawyer; b. St. Paul, Sept. 26, 1921; s. Edward Milton and Eleanor (Moen) S.; m. Rena Hill McMurry, July 10, 1950 (div. Oct. 1979); children: Murry, Edward, James; m. Jane Comer Bowron, Dec. 31, 1979. BA, Presbyn. Coll., Clinton, S.C., 1943; LLB, U. Va., 1950. Bar: N.Y., Va., Ala. Asst. prof. law Law Sch., U. Va., Charlottesville, 1950-51; assoc. Shearman & Sterling, N.Y.C., 1951-52; assoc. Bradley Arant Rose White, Birmingham, Ala., 1952-57, ptnr., 1957—; vice chmn. Secor Bank, Birmingham, 1988-91, gen. counsel, 1991-93. Chmn. Birmingham-Jefferson County Transit Authority, 1972-82. Served to capt., inf. U.S. Army, 1943-47, ETO. Decorated Silver Star, Bronze Star (V), Purple Heart. Fellow Am. Coll. Tax Counsel; mem. ABA, Ala. Bar Assn., Birmingham Bar Assn. Democrat. Avocation: tennis (ranked 25th nationally in men's singles-age 70). Home: 2600 Arlington Ave Unit 84 Birmingham AL 35205 Office: Bradley Arant Rose & White PO Box 830709 Birmingham AL 35283-0709

SELFRIDGE, GEORGE DEVER, dentist, retired naval officer; b. Pitman, N.J., Sept. 24, 1924; s. William John and Edith (Gorman) S.; m. Ruth Motisher, 1948; children: Pamela Ruth, Kimberly Dawn, Cheryl Beth. Student, Gettysburg Coll., 1942-43, Muhlenburg Coll., 1943-45; DDS, U. Buffalo, 1947; MA, George Washington U., 1974. Commd. lt. (j.g.) USN, 1948, advanced through grades to rear adm., 1973; intern Naval Dental Sch., Bethesda, Md., 1948-49, Naval Hosp., St. Albans, N.Y., 1949-50; various dental positions USN, 1951-64; sr. dental officer U.S.S. Cadmus, 1964-65, U.S.S. Vulcan, 1965-66, Svc. Force, 1964-66, Submarine Force, Atlantic Fleet, 1967-69; asst. dir. grad. edn. Navy Grad. Dental Sch., Bethesda, 1969-72, comdg. officer, 1973-76; dep. exec. officer Norfolk (Va.) Navy Dental Clinic, 1972-73; ret. USN, 1976; dean Dental Sch., Washington U., St. Louis, 1976-86; dir. dental services Barnes Hosp., St. Louis, 1976-87, Children's Hosp., St. Louis, 1976-87; exec. dir. Am. Bd. Orthodontics, 1986—; mem. adv. bd. VA Hosp., St. Louis, 1977-79; mem. exec. coun. Cen. Region Testing Svc., 1976-86; mem. adv. com. St. Louis Jr. Coll. Dist., 1976-86. Contbr. articles to med. jours. Decorated Legion of Merit; recipient commendation medals, Greater St. Louis Gold Medallion award, 1995, Spl. Recognition award Am. Bd. Orthopedics, 1996. Mem. ADA, Am. Coll. Dentists, Internat. Coll. Coll. Dentists (dep. registrar, sec. U.S. sect.), Assn. Mil. Surgeons U.S., Omicron Kappa Upsilon (dir. St. Louis Gold Medallion award for dir. of yr.). Republican. Home: 14545 Foxham Ct Chesterfield MO 63017-5620 Office: Am Bd Orthodontics 401 N Lindbergh Blvd Ste 308 Saint Louis MO 63141-7839

SELIG, ALLAN H. (BUD SELIG), professional baseball team executive; b. Milw., July 30, 1934; s. Ben and Marie Selig; m. Suzanne Lappin Steinman, Jan. 18, 1977; children: Sari, Wendy. Grad., U. Wis., Madison, 1956; LHD (hon.), Lakeland Coll., 1989. With Selig Ford (became Selig Chevrolet 1982), West Allis, Wis., 1959-90, pres., owner, 1966-90; with Selig Exec. Leasing Co., West Allis, 1959—, pres., owner, 1977—; part owner Milw. Braves (became Atlanta Braves 1965), 1963-65; co-founder Teams, Inc., 1964; co-owner, pres., chief exec. officer Milw. Brewers Baseball Club, Inc., 1970—; interim commr. Maj. League Baseball, 1991—; bd. dirs. Green Bay Packers Profl. Football Team. Co-founder Child Abuse Prevention Fund, 1988. With U.S. Army, 1956-58. Recipient Major League Exec. of Yr. award UPI, 1978, Internat. B'nai B'rith Sportsman of Yr. award 1981, Sportsman of Yr. award U.S. Olympic Com., 1988, August A. Busch, Jr. award for long and meritorious svc. to baseball, 1989, Ellis Island Congl. medal of honor, 1993, Anti-Defamation League's "A World of Difference Award" 1994. Office: Milw Brewers Milw County Stadium PO Box 3099 Milwaukee WI 53201-3099

SELIG, KARL-LUDWIG, language and literature educator; b. Wiesbaden, Germany, Aug. 14, 1926; naturalized, 1948; s. Lucian and Erna (Reiss) S. B.A., Ohio State U., 1946, M.A., 1947; postgrad., U. Rome, Italy, 1949-50; Ph.D., U. Tex., 1955. Asst. prof. Romance langs. and lit. Johns Hopkins U., Balt., 1954-58; assoc. prof. U. N.C., Chapel Hill, 1958-61, U. Minn., Mpls., 1961-63; vis. prof. U. Tex., Austin, 1963-64, prof. Romance langs. and lit., 1964-65; Hinchliff prof. Spanish lit. Cornell U., Ithaca, N.Y., 1965-69; dir. grad. studies in Romance lit. Cornell U., Ithaca, 1966-69; prof. Spanish lit. Columbia U., N.Y.C., 1969—; Brown Found. fellow, vis. prof. Spanish and comparative lit. U. of the South, Sewanee, Tenn., 1990; vis. prof. U. Munich, 1963-64, U. Berlin, 1967, U. Greifswald, Germany, 1992—; cons. prof. Ohio State U., Columbus, 1967-69; vis. lectr. U. Zulia, Maracaibo, Venezuela, 1968; dir. summer seminar NEH, 1975, cons., 1975-77; vis. scholar Ga. U. Sys., 1977; vis. rsch. scholar Fondation Hardt, Vandoeuvres, Switzerland, 1959, Herzog August Bibliothek Wolfenbüttel, Fed. Repubic Germany, 1979—; mem. com. grants-in-aid Am. Coun. Learned Soc., 1969-73; chmn. Comparative Lit. Program and Colloquia, Columbia Coll., 1976-88. Author: The Library of Vincencio Juan de Lastanosa, Patron of Gracián, Geneva, 1960, Studies on Alciato in Spain, 1990, Studies on Cervantes, 1992; also numerous articles, revs.; editor: (Thomas Blundeville) of Councils and Counselors, 1963, (with A. G. Hatcher) Studia Philologica et Litteraria in Honorem L. Spitzer, 1958, (with J. E. Keller) Essays in Honor of N. B. Adams, 1966, (with R. Brinkmann) Theatrum Europaeum. Festschrift E. M. Szarota, 1982, (with S. Neumeister) Theatrum Mundi Hispanicum, 1986, (with R. Somerville) Florilegium Columbianum: Essays in Honor of Paul Oskar Kristeller, 1987, (with E. Sears) The Verbal and the Visual: Essays in Honor of William Sebastian Heckscher, 1990, Polyanthea Essays on Art and Literature in Honor of William Sebastian Heckscher, 1993; assoc. editor Modern Lang. Notes, 1955-58; mng. editor Romance Notes, 1959-61; editor: U. N.C. Studies in Comparative Lit, 1959-61, Bull. Comediantes, 1959-64, assoc. editor 1964-68, 79—; co-editor Yearbook of Comparative Lit., Vol. IX, 1960; editorial bd. Colección Támesis, London, 1962-79, Romanic Rev., 1969-89, Teaching Lang. Through Lit, 1978-88; assoc. editor Hispania, 1969-74, Ky. Romance Quar, 1973-85; gen. editor Revista Hispánica Moderna, 1971-86; mem. nat. adv. bd. MLA Internat. Bibliography, 1978-88; editorial bd. Yale Italian Studies, 1976-80. Recipient Mark Van Doren award Columbia, 1974, spl. citation Columbia Coll. Alumni Assn., 1991; fellow Fulbright Found., Rome, 1949-50, Newberry Library, 1958, Folger Shakespeare Library, 1959, 63, Belgian Am. Ednl. Found., 1961, 62; sr. fellow Mediaeval and Renaissance Inst. Duke U., 1978; Fulbright research scholar Utrecht, The Netherlands, 1958-59. Mem. MLA (sec., then chmn. Romance sect. 1965-66, chmn. comparative lit. 1973, James Russell Lowell prize com. 1989-90, chmn. 1990), Am. Friends of Herzog August Bibliothek (bd. dirs.), Internat. Assn. Hispanists, Am. Comparative Lit. Assn., Coll. Art Assn., Acad. Lit. Studies, Phi Beta Kappa (hon.). Home: 30 E 37th St New York NY 10016-3019

SELIGER, MARK ALAN, photographer; b. Amarillo, Tex., May 23, 1959; s. Maurice and Carol Lee (Singer) S. BS, East Tex. State U., 1981. Contbg. photographer Rolling Stone Mag., N.Y.C., 1989-93, chief photographer, 1993—. Recipient Excellence in Journalism award Page One, 1988, Excellence awards Comm. Arts, 1988, 89, 90, 91, 92, 93, Creativity certs. Distinction Art Direction Mag., 1989, 93, Merit award Art Dirs. Club, 1991, Distinctive Merit award 1991, 92, Excellence certs. Am. Photography, 1991, 92, Distinctive Merit awards Soc. Pub. Designers, 1992, Distinguished Alumni award East Tex. State U., 1993; Mark Seliger Photography Scholarship named in his honor East Tex. State U., 1994. Mem. Am. Soc. Mag. Photographers. Office: Rolling Stone Mag 1290 Avenue Of The Americas New York NY 10104*

SELIGMAN, DANIEL, editor; b. N.Y.C., Sept. 25, 1924; s. Irving and Clare (O'Brien) S.; m. Mary Gale Sherburn, May 23, 1953; children: Nora, William Paul. Student, Rutgers U., 1941-42; A.B., NYU, 1946. Editorial asst. New Leader, 1946; asst. editor Am. Mercury, 1946-50; asso. editor Fortune, 1950-59, editorial bd., 1959-66, asst. mng. editor, 1966-69, exec. editor, 1970-77, asso. mng. editor, 1977-87, contbg. editor, 1988—; sr. staff editor all Time, Inc. (publs.), 1969-70. Author: A Question of Intelligence: The IQ Debate in America, 1992. Home: 190 E 72nd St New York NY 10021-4370 Office: care Fortune Time And Life Bldg New York NY 10020

SELIGMAN, FREDERICK, lawyer; b. Bklyn.; s. Martin and Florence (Alperin) S.; m. Delice Felice. AB, Clark U., 1957; JD, N.Y. Law Sch., 1972. Bar: N.Y. 1973, U.S. Dist. Ct. (so. and ea. dists.) N.Y. 1974, U.S. Tax Ct. 1974, U.S. Ct. Appeals (2d cir.) 1975, U.S. Supreme Ct. 1979. Atty. N.Y.C. (N.Y.) Police Dept., 1972-73; asst. dist. atty. N.Y. County, N.Y.C., 1973-79; pvt. practice N.Y.C., 1980-85; ptnr. Seligman & Seligman, N.Y.C., 1986—. Mem. N.Y. Criminal Bar Assn., N.Y. State Defenders Assn. Home: Runge Rd Shokan NY 12481 Office: Seligman & Seligman 26 Broadway New York NY 10004

SELIGMAN, JOEL, law educator; b. N.Y.C., Jan. 11, 1950; s. Selig Jacob and Muriel (Bienstock) S.; m. Friederike Felber, July 30, 1981; children: Andrea, Peter. AB magna cum laude, UCLA, 1971; JD, Harvard U., 1974. Bar: Calif. 1975. Atty., writer Corp. Accountability Rsch. Group, Washington, 1974-77; prof. law Northeastern U. Law Sch., 1977-83, George Washington U., 1983-86, U. Mich., Ann Arbor, 1987-95; dean law U. Ariz., Tucson, 1995—; prof. law U. Mich., Ann Arbor, 1986-87; cons. Fed. Trade Commn., 1979-82, Dept. Transp., 1983, Office Tech. Assessment, 1988-89. Author (with others) Constitutionalizing the Corporation: The Case for the Federal Chartering of Giant Corporations, 1976, The High Citadel: The Influence of Harvard Law School, 1978, The Transformation of Wall Street: A History of the Securities and Exchange Commission and Modern Corporate Finance, 1982, The SEC and the Future of Finance, 1985, (multi-volume) Securities Regulation; contbr. articles to profl. jours. Mem. State Bar Calif., Am. Law Inst. (adv. com., advisor corp. governance project). Office: U Ariz Law Sch Speedway & Mountain Tucson AZ 85721

SELIGMAN, MARTIN E. P., psychologist; b. Albany, N.Y., Aug. 12, 1942; s. Adrian and Irene Seligman; A.B., Princeton U., 1964; Ph.D. in Psychology, U. Pa., 1967; PhD (hon.) Uppsala U., Sweden, 1989; m. Mandy M. Seligman; children—Amanda, David, Lara, Nicole, Darryl. Asst. prof. Cornell U., 1967-70; assoc. prof. psychology U. Pa., 1972-76, prof., 1976—, dir. clin. program, 1980-94; vis. fellow Maudsley Hosp. Inst. Psychiatry, U. London, 1975. Recipient MERIT award, 1991, JAmes McKeen Cattell Fellow award Am. Psychol. Soc., 1995; NIMH grantee, 1969—; NSF fellow, 1963-64, Woodrow Wilson fellow, 1964-65, Guggenheim fellow, 1974-75; Center Advanced Study in Behavioral Scis. fellow, 1978-79; lic. psychologist, Pa. Fellow AAAS, Am. Psychol. Assn. (pres. divsn. clin. psychology 1993-95, William James Fellow award 1992); mem. Eastern Psychol. Assn., Psychonomic Soc., Assn. Advancement Behavior Therapy, Am. Psychopathol. Assn., Am. Psychosomatic Soc., Phi Beta Kappa, Sigma Xi. Author: Helplessness, 1975, Learned Optimism, 1991, What You Can Change & What You Can't, 1993, The Optimistic Child, 1995; contbr. numerous articles to profl. jours. Office: 3815 Walnut St Philadelphia PA 19104-3604

SELIGMAN, RICHARD MICHAEL, lawyer; b. N.Y.C., Feb. 3, 1945; s. Alexander and Sophie (Goldblatt) S.; m. Dana Leslie Corman, Mar. 13, 1969 (div. June 1975); m. Jody Lynn Wittenberg, May 24, 1985. BS, U. Wis., 1966, MBA, 1968; JD, DePaul U., 1973. Bar: Ill. 1973, U.S. Dist. Ct. (no. dist.) Ill. 1973, U.S. Dist. Ct. (so. dist.) Ill. 1975. Asst. counsel Marsh & McLennan Cos., Chgo., 1973-75; sole practice Chgo., 1975; chief counsel Ill. Dept. Ins., Springfield, 1975-76; ptnr. Schiff, Hardin & Waite, Chgo., 1976-85, Katten Muchin & Zavis, Chgo., 1985—. Mem. ABA, Ill. Bar Assn., Chgo. Bar Assn. Democrat. Jewish. Avocations: scuba diving, flying, motorcycling. Home: 1908 Mccraren Rd Highland Park IL 60035-2229 Office: Katten Muchin & Zavis 525 W Monroe St Ste 1600 Chicago IL 60661-3629*

SELIGMAN, THOMAS KNOWLES, museum administrator; b. Santa Barbara, Calif., Jan. 1, 1944; s. Joseph L. and Peggy (Van Horne) S.; children: Christopher, Timothy, Dylan. BA, Stanford U., 1965; BFA with honors, San Francisco Acad. Art, 1967; MFA, Sch. Visual Art, N.Y.C., 1968. Tchr., mus. dir. Peace Corps, Liberia, 1968-70; curator dept. Africa, Oceania and Ams. Fine Arts Museums, San Francisco, 1971-88; dep. dir. edn. and exhbns. Fine Arts Museums, 1972-88, dep. dir. ops. and planning, 1988-91; dir. Stanford (Calif.) U. Mus. Art, 1991—; mem. cultural property adv. com. USIA, 1988-92, Nat. Endowment for Art Indemnity Panel, 1992-95. Author mus. catalogues, articles in field. Trustee Internat. Coun. Mus./Am. Assn. Mus., 1990-94, Am. Fedn. Arts; mem. adv. coun. Acad. Art Coll. Grad. Program. Fellow Nat. Endowment Arts, 1974-75, 87. Mem. Assn. Art Mus. Dirs., Am. Assn. Mus., Leaky Found. Address: Stanford U Mus Art Stanford CA 94305-5060

SELIGMANN, WILLIAM ROBERT, lawyer, author; b. Davenport, Iowa, Oct. 10, 1956; s. William Albert and Barbara Joyce (Carmichael) S.; m. Carole Lee Francis; children: D Anna, Matthew. BA, U. Calif., Santa Barbara, 1979; JD, Santa Clara U., 1982. Bar: Calif. 1983, U.S. Dist. Ct. (no. dist.) Calif. 1983. Assoc. Office of J.R. Dempster, Cupertino, Calif., 1983-85; city atty. City of Campbell, Calif., 1985—; ptnr. Dempster, Seligmann & Raineri, Los Gatos, Calif., 1985—; pro tem Mcpl. Ct. Calif., Los Gatos, 1992—. Mem. ABA, Santa Clara County Bar Assn., Am. Trial Lawyers Assn., Better Bus. Bur. Avocations: cross country skiing, scuba diving, swimming, writing. Office: Dempster Seligmann & Raineri 3 1/2 N Santa Cruz Ave # A Los Gatos CA 95030-5916

SELIGSON, CARL HAROLD, management consultant; b. N.Y.C., Feb. 25, 1935; s. Harold P. and Lilian (Yohalem) S.; m. Joan Escott, May 19, 1957 (div. Nov. 1969); children: Susan S. Pattenaude, Barbara C.; m. Bonnie Laskin, Mar. 6, 1983. AB, Brown U., 1956; postgrad., NYU Grd. Sch. Bus. Adminstrn., 1961-63. Textile salesman Cohn, Hall, Marx Co., Montreal, Can., 1958-61; security analyst Burnham & Co., N.Y.C., 1961-67, Kuhn, Loeb & Co, N.Y.C., 1967-71; mng. dir. Merrill Lynch Capital Markets, N.Y.C., 1971-87, Kidder, Peabody & Co., N.Y.C., 1987-90; sr. exec. cons. regulated industries Deloitte & Touche, N.Y.C., 1990-92; mng. dir. Prudential Securities, N.Y.C., 1992-95; sr. advisor Anderson Consulting, N.Y.C., 1996—. Contbr. articles to profl. jours. including Pub. Utilities Fortnightly, Telephony, Fin. Exec., The Southern Banker, Coal Monthly and Energy News. Bd. dirs. Nuclear Energy Inst., Washington, 1988—. With U.S. Army Counter Intelligence Corps. Fellow Fin. Analysts Fedn.; mem. Brown U. Club. Avocations: water sports, travel, theatre. Home: 40 E 94th St New York NY 10128-0709

SELIGSON, MITCHELL A., Latin American studies educator; b. Hempstead, N.Y., Nov. 12, 1945; s. Morris and Ethel (Finkel) S.; m. Susan Berk, June 18, 1967; 1 child, Amber Lara. BA, Bklyn. Coll., 1967; MA, U. Fla., 1968; PhD, U. Pitts., 1974. Vol. U.S. Peace Corps, Costa Rica, 1968-70; asst. prof./assoc. prof. U. Ariz., Tucson, 1974-85; prof. U. Pitts., 1986-93, Daniel H. Wallace prof. polit. sci., 1994—, dir. Latin Am. studies, 1986-92, rsch. prof., 1992—; cons. to U.S. AID, Guatemala, Honduras, Nicaragua, Costa Rica, Ecuador, Jamaica, Panama, El Salvador, 1980—. Author, editor: Peasants of Costa Rica and the Development of Agrarian Capitalism, 1980, The Gap Between Rich and Poor, 1984, Authoritarians and Democrats, 1987, Elections and Democracy in Central America, 1989, rev. edit. 1995, Development and Underdevelopment, 1993. Fulbright fellow, Costa Rica, 1986, Rockefeller Found. fellow, 1985-86; grantee Social Sci. Rsch. Coun., Ford Found., NSF, Mellon Found., Heinz Endowment. Mem. Am. Polit. Sci. Assn., Latin Am. Studies Assn. (chmn. fin. com. 1991). Office: U Pitts Dept Polit Sci Pittsburgh PA 15260

SELIGSON, THEODORE H., architect, interior designer, art consultant; b. Kansas City, Mo., Nov. 10, 1930; s. Harry and Rose (Haith) S.; m. Jacqueline Rose, Dec. 27, 1964 (div. 1976). BArch, Washington U., St. Louis, 1953. Registered architect, Mo., Kans. Intern Marshall & Brown, Kansas City, Mo., 1949-54; designer, head design Kivett & Myers, Kansas City, Mo., 1954-62; prin. Design Assocs., 1955—, Atelier Seligson, Kansas City, Mo., 1962-64; pres. Seligson, Eggen, Inc., Kansas City, 1964-73, Seligson Assocs., Inc., Architects Planners, Kansas City, 1973—; vis. lectr. adult edn. U. Mo.-Kansas City, 1958-61, vis. prof. arch., U. Mo. Kansas City, 1989-96; tchr., critic Kansas City Art Inst., Mo., 1961-64, 71-72, adj. prof. 1986, 89, 91, 92; adj. prof. Kansas State U., 1991-92, vis. prof. Washington U., 1975, 77, 78, 81, 86, 91, U. Kans., Lawrence, 1978, 79, 80, 91, 92; art cons. Design Assocs., Kansas City, Mo., 1955—. Projects pub. in archtl. jours. V.p. Friends of Art Nelson-Atkins Mus. Art, Kansas City, bd. dirs. 1963-67, chmn. selections com., 1981, vis. curator, 1972, 87; chmn. Capitol Fine Arts Commn. Mo., 1983-90, Kansas City Worlds Fair goals and themes subcom., 1985-90; bd. dirs. Westport Tomorrow, Kansas City, 1980-87, Hist. Kansas City Found., 1984-90; pres. Native Sons of Kansas City, 1989, bd. dirs. 1978-94, Westport Cmty. Coun., 1973-75. Recipient Urban Design award Kansas City Mcpl. Art Commn., 1968, 74, 78; Nat. Archtl. award Am. Inst. Steel Constrn., 1970; Nat. award ASID/DuPont Corian, 1989. Fellow AIA, Kansas City chpt. AIA (pres. 1983, bd. dirs. 1979-84, Design Excellence award 1966, 68, 70, 74, Cen. States Regional award 1974, 78, Honor award for outstanding service to chpt. and profession 1982-83); mem. Mo. Council Architects, Am. Soc. Interior Designers, Nat. Coun. Archtl. Registration Bds. (task analysis adv. com. 1988-90), Soc. Archtl. Historians (pres. 1973-

75). Jewish. Office: Seligson Assocs Inc 106 W 14th St Kansas City MO 64105-1906

SELIN, IVAN, entrepreneur; b. N.Y.C., Mar. 11, 1937; s. Saul and Freda (Kuhlman) Selin; m. Nina Kallet, June 8, 1957; children: Douglas, Jessica. B.E., Yale U., 1957, M.E., 1958, Ph.D., 1960; Dr. es Sciences, U. Paris, 1962. Rsch. engr. Rand Corp., Santa Monica, Calif., 1960-65; systems analyst Dept. Def., Washington, 1965-67, dep. asst. sec. def., 1967-69, acting asst. sec. for systems analysis, 1969-70; founder, chmn. bd. Am. Mgmt. Systems, Inc., Arlington, Va., 1970-89; undersec. state Dept. State, Washington, 1989-91; chmn. NRC, Washington, 1991-95; chmn., CEO Phoenix Internat., Washington, 1995—; lectr. UCLA, 1961-63; chmn. mil. econ. adv. panel to CIA, 1978-89. Author: Detection Theory, 1964; contbr. articles to profl. jours. Pres. Corp. Against Drug Abuse, 1988—; bd. dirs., gov. UN Assn. U.S., 1979-89; mem. exec. com. Greater Washington Research Ctr., Fed. City Council. Decorated Disting. Civilian Svc. medal, 1970; recipient Disting. Svc. medal Sec. of State, 1991; Fulbright scholar, 1959-61; Ford Found. grantee, 1952-54. Mem. Council Fgn. Relations, Fed. City Council Washington (trustee), IEEE (editor Trans. on Ifo. Theory 1960-65), Sigma Xi, Tau Beta Pi. Clubs: Yale, Cosmos. Home: 2905 32nd St NW Washington DC 20008-3526 Office: Phoenix Internat 1050 17th St NW Washington DC 20036

SELINE, REX, reporter. Bus. reporter The Miami Herald, Fla. Office: The Miami Herald Pub Co One Herald Plz Miami FL 33132-1693

SELK, ELEANOR HUTTON, artist; b. Duboise, Nebr., Oct. 21, 1918; d. Anderson Henry and Florence (Young) Hutton; R.N., St. Elizabeth Hosp., Lincoln, Nebr., 1938; m. Harold Frederick Selk, Aug. 3, 1940; children: Honey Lou, Katherine Florence. Nurse, Lincoln, 1938-40, Denver, 1940-50; with Colo. Bd. Realtors, 1956-66; owner, mgr. The Pen Point, graphic art studio, Colorado Springs, 1974-94; instr. history and oil painting, 1994—; one-woman shows: Colo. Coll., 1970, 72, Nazarene Bible Coll., 1973, 1st Meth. Ch., 1971 (all Colorado Springs); exhibited in group shows: U. So. Colo., 1969, 70, 71, 72, Colorado Springs Art Guild, 1969-72, Pike's Peak Artists Assn., 1969-73, Mozart Art Festival, Pueblo, Colo., 1969-74, numerous others; represented in permanent collection U.S. Postal Service, Pen-Arts Bldg., Washington, Medic Alert Found. Internat. Hdqrs., Turlock, Calif. Rec. sec. Colo. chpt. Medic Alert Found. Internat., 1980-90, chairperson El Paso County and Colorado Springs chpt., 1980-90, Colo. bd. dirs., 1980-89, rec. sec., 1980-89. Recipient 3d pl. award Nat. Tb and Respiratory Disease and Christmas Seal Art Competition, 1969, finalist award Benedictine Art competition Hanover Trust Bank, N.Y.C., 1970, numerous awards and certs. for pub. service and art, award Music of the Baroque, 1991, Editors Choice award Nat. Libr. Poetry, 1993. Mem. Nat. League Am. Pen Women (rec. sec. 1972-74, travelling art slide collection 1974—, designer jewelry, awards for book cover art, numerous Gold Bangle awards). Contbr. med. articles, short stories, poetry to newspapers. Home and Studio: 518 Warren Ave Colorado Springs CO 80906-2343

SELKIRK, JAMES KIRKWOOD, biochemist; b. N.Y.C., Dec. 3, 1938; s. James Kirkwood and Doris (Schuler) S.; m. Carole Ann Bozzone, Sept. 16, 1961; children: James Kirkwood, David Edward. BS, Coll. Environ. Sci. and Forestry, Syracuse (N.Y.) U., 1964; PhD, Syracue U. Upstate Med. Ctr., Syracuse, 1969. Postdoctoral fellow McArdle Lab. Cancer Rsch., U. Wis., Madison, 1969-72; staff fellow Nat. Cancer Inst., NIH, Bethesda, Md., 1972-74, sr. staff fellow, 1974-75; sr. staff scientist unit leader chem. carcinogenesis biology divsn. Oak Ridge (Tenn.) Nat. Lab., 1975-85; chief carcinogenesis and toxicology evaluation br. nat. toxicology program Nat. Inst. Environ. Health Scis., 1985—, assoc. dir. divsn. toxicology rsch. and testing, 1989-92, chmn. carcinogen mechanism group Lab. Molecular Carcinogenesis, 1992—; adj. prof. Oak Ridge Biomed. Grad. Sch., U. Tenn., 1975-85; mem. breast cancer task force NIH, 1979-82; mem. com. on pyrenes and analogs NAS, 1981-83; chmn. Interagy. Testing Commn., 1986-90. Author rsch. articles, chpts. in books; mem. editorial bd. Carcinogenesis Jour., 1984-87, 91—, Cancer Rsch., 1981-86, Environ. Perspectives, 1993—. With AUS, 1959-61. Recipient U.S. Interagy. Testing Com. Exemplary Svc. award, 1992. Mem. Am. Cancer Soc. (carcinogenesis study sect. 1992—). Home: 113 Basswood Ct Chapel Hill NC 27514-1610 Office: Nat Inst Environ Health Scis PO Box 12333 Research Triangle Park NC 27709

SELKOE, DENNIS JESSE, neurologist, researcher, educator; b. N.Y.C., Sept. 25, 1943; s. Herbert E. and Mary P. (Lille) S.; m. Polly Ann Strasser, June 24, 1967; children: Gregory, Kimberly. BA, Columbia U., 1965; MD, U. Va., 1969. Diplomate Am. Bd. Psychiatry and Neurology, Nat. Bd. Med. Examiners. Intern in medicine Hosp. U. Pa., Phila., 1969-70; rsch. assoc. NIH, Bethesda, Md., 1970-72; resident in neurology Peter Bent Brigham/Children's Hosp., Boston, 1972-74, chief resident in neurology, 1974-75; rsch. assoc. Harvard U. Med. Sch., Boston, 1975-78, asst. prof. neurology, 1978-82, assoc. prof., 1982-85, assoc. prof. neurology and neurosci., 1985-90, faculty mem. div. on aging, 1980—, prof. neurology and neurosci., 1990—; co-dir. Ctr. Neurologic Diseases Brigham and Women's Hosp., Boston, 1985—; mem. sci. adv. bd. Alzheimer's Disease Assn., Chgo., 1983-89; mem. Gov.'s Commn. on Alzheimer's Disease, Mass., 1985-87. Author over 200 articles, book chpts. on biochemistry and molecular biology of Alzheimer's Disease. Asst. surgeon USPHS, 1970-72. Recipient Wood-Kalb Found. prize Alzheimers Disease Assn., 1984, Med. Rsch. award Met. Life Found., 1986, LEAD award Nat. Inst. on Aging, 1988, NIH Merit award, 1991—; grantee Bristol-Myers Squibb Neurosci., 1990. Fellow Am. Acad. Neurology (Potamkin prize 1989); mem. Am. Neurol. Assn., Soc. for Neurosci., Am. Assn. Neuropathologists, World Fedn. Neurologists, AAAS. Office: Harvard Med Sch Brigham & Womens Hosp 221 Longwood Ave Boston MA 02115-5817

SELKOWITZ, ARTHUR, advertising agency executive; b. N.Y.C., May 26, 1943; s. Harry and Anne (Lichten) S.; m. Betsey Wattenberg, Apr. 15, 1967; children: Adam, Jed. AB, Syracuse (N.Y.) U., 1965. Account exec. Dancer Fitzgerald Sample, 1969-71; with Benton & Bowles, Inc., N.Y.C., 1971-82; v.p., account supr. Benton & Bowles, Inc., 1972-75, sr. v.p., mgmt. supr., 1975-81, sr. v.p., account dir., 1981-82; founder, pres. Penchina, Selkowitz Inc., N.Y.C., 1982-90; exec. v.p. internat. Benton & Bowles, N.Y.C., 1990-94, pres. Asia and Pacific, 1995-96, pres. N.Am., 1996—96; also bd. dirs. D'Arcy, Masius, Benton & Bowles, N.Y.C.; bd. dirs. Medicus Group Internat. Dancer Fitzgerald Sample, N.Y.C., 1966-71. Office: 1675 Broadway New York NY 10019-5820

SELL, EDWARD SCOTT, JR., lawyer; b. Athens, Ga., Mar. 13, 1917; s. Edward Scott and Nettie Ruth (Whatley) S.; m. Mary Deupree Eckford, Sept. 14, 1940; 1 son, Edward Scott. A.B., U. Ga., 1937, J.D. cum laude, 1939. Bar: Ga. bar 1938. Ptnr. firm Lewis & Sell, 1940-55, Lane & Sell, 1955-56, Sell & Comer, Macon, Ga., 1956-69, Sell, Comer & Popper, Macon, 1969-80, Sell & Melton, 1980—; city atty., Macon, 1947-53; atty. Macon-Bibb County Planning & Zoning Commn., 1953-65; county atty. Bibb County, Ga., 1965—; lectr. law Mercer U., 1958-60. Trustee Wesleyan Coll., Macon, 1973—. Served with U.S. Army, 1942-46. Decorated Bronze Star, Army Commendation medal. Fellow Am. Bar Found.; mem. State Bar Ga. (bd. govs. 1947-50), Macon Bar Assn. (past pres.), Macon Cir. Bar Assn. (past pres.), City Club of Macon, River North Club, Lions, Shriners, Masons, Phi Beta Kappa, Phi Kappa Phi, Phi Delta Phi. Clubs: City Club of Macon, Lions, Shriners, Masons, River North. Home: 1644 Hawthorne Rd Macon GA 31211-1213 Office: PO Box 229 Macon GA 31297-2899

SELL, ROBERT EMERSON, electrical engineer; b. Freeport, Ill., Apr. 23, 1929; s. Cecil Leroy and Ona Arletta (Stevens) S.; m. Ora Lucile Colton, Nov. 7, 1970. B.S., U. Nebr., 1962. Registered profl. engr., Nebr., Mo., Ill., Ind., Ohio, W.Va., Ky., Ark., Tex., Oreg., Wash., Calif. Chief draftsman Dempster Mill Mfg. Co., Beatrice, Nebr., 1949-53; designer-engr. U. Neb., Lincoln, 1955-65; elec. design engr. Kirkham, Michael & Assos., Omaha, 1965-67; elec. design engr. Leo A. Daly Co., Omaha, St. Louis, 1967-69; mech. design engr. Hellmuth, Obata, Kassabaum, St. Louis, 1969-70; chief elec. engr. Biagi-Hannan & Assos., Inc., Evansville, Ind., 1971-74; elec. project engr. H.L. Yoh Co., under contract to Monsanto Co., Creve Coeur, Mo., 1974-77; elec. project engr. Dhillon Engrs., Inc., Portland, Oreg., 1978-85; project coordinator Brown-Zammit-Enyeart Engring., Inc., San Diego, 1985-88; elec. engr. Morgen Design, Inc., San Diego, 1988; lead elec. engr. Popov Engrs., Inc., San Diego, 1988-89; mech. and elect. specialist Am. Engring. Labs., Inc. div. Prof. Svc. Industries, Inc., San Diego, 1990—; instr. Basic Inst. Tech., St. Louis, 1971. Mem. ASHRAE, IEEE. Home: PO Box 261578 San Diego CA 92196-1578 Office: AEL/PSI 7940 Arjons Dr Ste A San Diego CA 92126-6303

SELL, WILLIAM EDWARD, legal educator; b. Hanover, Pa., Jan. 1, 1923; s. Henry A. and Blanche M. (Newman) S.; m. Cordelia I. Fulton, Aug. 20, 1949; 1 son, Jeffrey Edward. AB, Washington and Jefferson Coll., 1944, LHD, 1973; JD, Yale U., 1947; LLD, Dickinson Sch. Law, 1968. Bar: D.C. 1951, Pa. 1952. Instr. law U. Pitts., 1947-49, asst. prof. law, 1949-51, assoc. prof. law, 1953-54, prof. law, 1954-77, assoc. dean, 1957-63, dean, 1966-77, disting. svc. prof. law, 1977-94; emeritus dean, disting. svc. prof. law, 1994—; sr. counsel firm Meyer, Unkovic & Scott, Pitts., 1977-94; vis. prof. U. Mich. Law Sch., 1957; past pres. Pa. Bar Inst.; chmn. bd. St. Clair Health Corp. Author: Fundamentals of Accounting Lawyers, 1960, Pennsylvania Business Corporations, 3 vols., 1969, revised, 1991, Sell on Agency, 1975, also articles; editor: Pennsylvania Keystone Lawyers Desk Library. Past pres., bd. dirs. St. Clair Meml. Hosp.; chmn. St. Clair's Health Corp. With USAAF, WWII. Fellow Am. Bar Found. (life); mem. ABA, Pa. Bar Assn., Allegheny County Bar Assn., Assn. Am. Law Schs., Am. Law Inst. (life), Univ. Club, Phi Beta Kappa, Order of Coif, Pi Delta Epsilon, Phi Gamma Delta, Phi Delta Phi, Omicron Delta Kappa. Presbyterian (elder, deacon). Home: 106 Seneca Dr Pittsburgh PA 15228-1029 Office: U Pitts Sch Law 531 Law Bldg Pittsburgh PA 15260 also: St Clair Health Corp 1000 Bower Hill Rd Pittsburgh PA 15243-1873

SELLAND, HOWARD M., manufacturing executive; b. 1943. BA, Spring Arbor Coll., 1979; MBA, U. Mich., 1983. Pres. Aeroquip Corp., Maumee, Ohio, 1963-81, 89—, also bd. dirs.; pres. Sterling Engineered Pdts. Inc., 1984-89; exec. v.p. Trinova Corp., 1981-84, 89—. Office: Aeroquip Corp 3000 Strayer Rd Maumee OH 43537-0631*

SELLECK, TOM, actor; b. Detroit, Jan. 29, 1945; s. Robert D. and Martha S.; m. Jacquelyn Ray, 1970 (div. 1982); 1 stepson, Kevin; m. Jillie Joan Mack, Aug. 7, 1987; 1 child, Hannah Margaret. Student, U. So. Calif. TV appearances include The Rockford Files, Gypsy Warriors; TV series Magnum P.I. 1980-88; films include Myra Breckinridge, 1970, Seven Minutes, 1971, Daughters of Satan, 1972, Midway, 1976, Coma, 1982, High Road to China, 1983, Lassiter, 1984, Runaway, 1985, Three Men and a Baby, 1987, Her Alibi, 1989, An Innocent Man, 1989, Quigley Down Under, 1990, Three Men and a Little Lady, 1990, Folks!, 1992, Christopher Columbus: The Discovery, 1992, Mr. Baseball, 1992; TV films include Returning Home, 1975, Most Wanted, 1976, The Sacketts, 1979, The Concrete Cowboys, 1979, Divorce Wars, 1982, Louis L'Amour's "The Shadow Riders", 1982; exec. prodr. (series) B.L. Stryker, 1989-90, (TV movie) Revealing Evidence, 1990. Office: ICM care Chris Andrews 8942 Wilshire Blvd Beverly Hills CA 90211*

SELLER, ROBERT HERMAN, cardiologist, family physician; b. Phila., Mar. 21, 1931; s. David and Elsie (Straussman) S.; m. Maxine Schwartz, June 3, 1956; children: Michael, Douglas, Stuart. A.B., U. Pa., 1952, M.D., 1956. Intern. Grad. Hosp. of U. Pa., Phila., 1956-57; research asst. dept. pharmacology U. Pa., 1953-55; resident in cardiology, research fellow Am. Heart Assn., Phila. Gen. Hosp., 1957-58; resident in internal medicine Albert Einstein Med. Ctr., Phila., 1958-59; chief resident Albert Einstein Med. Ctr., 1959-60; instr. medicine Hahnemann Med. Coll. and Hosp., Phila., 1960-64; asst. prof. Hahnemann Med. Coll. and Hosp., 1964-69, assoc. prof., 1969-72, dir. Service F, 1962-67, asst. coordinator mil. edn. for nat. def., 1961-64, dir. div. family medicine, 1967-72, acting chmn. dept. family medicine and community health, 1972-74, prof. medicine, family medicine and community health, 1973-74; practice medicine, specializing in cardiology Buffalo, 1974—; prof., chmn. dept. family medicine, prof. medicine SUNY-Buffalo, Deaconess Hosp., 1974-82, chmn. dept. family practice and dir. family practice residency program, 1974-82; prof. medicine and family medicine SUNY-Buffalo, 1974—. Author: Differential Diagnosis of Common Complaints, 1986, 3d edit., 1996; contbr. articles to profl. jours. NIH grantee, 1972-75; Deaconess Hosp. family practice resident tng. grantee, 1975—; health professions spl. projects grantee, 1975—. Fellow ACP, Am. Coll. Cardiology, Am. Acad. Family Physicians, Phila. Coll. Physicians; mem. AMA, N.Y. Med. Soc., Erie County Med. Soc., Am. Fedn. Clin. Research, Am. Heart Assn., Soc. of Tchrs. of Family Medicine, N.Y. Acad. Sci., N.Y. Acad. Family Physicians. Home: 125 Crestwood Ln Buffalo NY 14221-1462 Office: 1542 Maple Rd Buffalo NY 14221-3625

SELLERS, BARBARA JACKSON, federal judge; b. Richmond, Va., Oct. 3, 1940; m. Richard F. Sellers; children: Elizabeth M., Anne W., Catherine A. Attended, Baldwin-Wallace Coll., 1958-60; BA cum laude, Ohio State U., 1962; JD magna cum laude, Capital U. Law Sch., Columbus, Ohio, 1979. Bar: Ohio 1979, U.S. Dist. Ct. (so. dist.) Ohio 1981, U.S. Ct. Appeals (6th cir.), 1986. Jud. law clk. Hon. Robert J. Sidman, U.S. Bankruptcy Judge, Columbus, Ohio, 1979-81; assoc. Lasky & Semons, Columbus, 1981-82; jud. law clk. to Hon. Thomas M. Herbert, U.S. Bankrupcty Ct., Columbus, 1982-84; assoc. Baker & Hostetler, Columbus, 1984-86; U.S. bankruptcy judge So. Dist. Ohio, Columbus, 1986—; lectr. on bankruptcy univs., insts., assns. Recipient Am. Jurisprudence prize contracts and criminal law, 1975-76, evidence and property, 1976-77, Corpus Juris Secundum awards, 1975-76, 76-77. Mem. ABA (corp., litigation sect. 1986—, banking and bus. law sect. 1981-94, jud. adminstrv. sect. 1983-84), Columbus Bar Assn., Comml. Law League of Am., Am. Bankruptcy Inst., Nat. Conf. Bankruptcy Judges, Order of Curia, Phi Beta Kappa. Office: US Bankruptcy Ct 170 N High St Columbus OH 43215

SELLERS, BARNEY, professional society administrator; b. Bklyn., June 12, 1941; s. Milton Theodore and Alice Margaret (Wilensky) S.; m. Rosalie Bono; children: David, Lori; m. Karla Young, Nov. 1, 1958. BA, CCNY, 1963; MS, Syracuse U., 1972; MLA, Johns Hopkins U., 1991. Rsch. analyst U.S. Commn. on Civil Rights, 1964-66; asst. to dir. Office Civil Rights HEW, 1966-68; dir. project enforcement A. Philip Randolph Inst., 1968-69; Washington rep. Am. Friends Svc. Com., 1969-70; dir. spl. projects Nat. Urban Coalition, 1970-71; staff dir. med. assistance adv. coun. HEW, 1972-74; dir. govt. rels. Nat. Health Coun., 1974-78; dep. dir. Am. Health Planning Assn., 1978-79; dir. office beneficiary svcs. HEW, 1979-82; exec. dir. Am. Soc. Parenteral & Enteral Nutrition, 1982—; cons. McGraw-Hill Health and Medicine Newsletters, Resource Mgmt. Corp., Roy Littlejohn Assocs., Washington Rsch. Project. Vol. Dukakis for Pres., 1988. Mem. Am. Soc. Assn. Execs. (cert., tech. com. Greater Washington 1994—), Second Tuesday Breakfast Club (founder, pres.). Avocations: racquetball, hiking. Home: 9512 Nightsong Ln Columbia MD 21046 Office: Am Soc Parenteral Enteral Nut 8630 Fenton St Ste 412 Silver Spring MD 20910-3803

SELLERS, FRED WILSON, banker; b. Alexander City, Ala., Apr. 29, 1942; s. Fred Wilson and Helen (Hagan) Sellers); m. Nancy Wilbanks, July 11, 1964; children: Fredrick Hagan, Robert Wilbanks. BS, U. Ala., 1964; MBA, L.I. U., 1966; postgrad., U. Wis., Madison, 1974. CPA, N.C., Ala.; cert. fraud examiner. Staff acct. Ernst & Young, Winston-Salem, N.C., 1966-69; comptr. Citibanc Group, Inc., Andalusia, Ala., 1969-73; various positions, then sr. v.p., dir. internal audit AmSouth Bankcorporation, Birmingham, Ala., 1973—; bd. dirs. Better Bus. Bur., Mobile, Ala., 1984-86. Mem. budget com. United Way, Birmingham, 1982-83. Mem. AICPA, N.C. Assn. CPAs, Ala. Assn. CPAs, Ala. United States Air Force Acad. Parents Club (pres. 1993-94, 94-95), Vestavia Country Club, The Club, Univ. Club (Tuscaloosa). Avocation: travel. Home: 2112 Viking Cir Birmingham AL 35216-3125 Office: AmSouth Bankcorporation PO Box 11007 Birmingham AL 35288

SELLERS, JAMES EARL, retired theological educator; b. Lucedale, Miss., Nov. 1, 1926; s. Lucius Earl and Grace (McVicar) S. BEE, Ga. Inst. Tech., 1947; MS, Fla. State U., 1954; PhD (Kent fellow), Vanderbilt U., 1958. Asst. prof. Christian ethics and theology Div. Sch. Vanderbilt U., Nashville, 1958-61; assoc. prof. Vanderbilt U., 1961-64, prof., 1964-71, dean Div. Sch., 1964-67; David Rice prof. ethics Rice U., Houston, 1971-93, prof. emeritus, 1993—; retired, 1993. Author: The Outsider and the Word of God, 1961, The South and Christian Ethics, 1962, Theological Ethics, 1966, Public Ethics, 1970, Warming Fires, 1975, The Polis in America as Imago Dei, 1984, Tensions in the Ethics of Interdependence, 1986, Medical Ethics and the Civil Rights Movement, 1989, Love and Justice Reconsidered, 1990, Essays in American Ethics, 1991; co-author: The Health-Care Community as a Reservoir of Potential Subjects, 1984; editor-at-large The Christian Century, 1971-86; contbr. articles to Ethical Issues in Am. Life, Lifeboat Ethics. Lt. USNR, 1944-54. Recipient Danforth Rsch. award, France, 1966. Mem. Soc. for Values in Higher Edn., Group for Research in Med-Ethics, AAUP. Home: 2601 S Braeswood Blvd Apt 1501 Houston TX 77025-2816 Office: Rice U Dept Religious Studies 6100 S Main Houston TX 77251 *After more than thirty years of teaching ethics to university students and churchmen, I have concluded that neither "morality" nor "religion" is as basic as the American tradition of justice. If we would rescue the oppressed here or elsewhere, indeed, if we would redeem mankind, we should begin by affirming life with dignity, liberty, and the right of all to the pursuit of happiness, the disadvantaged as well as the advantaged.*

SELLERS, JILL SUZANNE, lawyer; b. Baton Rouge, Oct. 24, 1967; d. Tommy Davis Sellers and Rhonda Lynn (Zimmerman) Ross. BA, La. State U., 1988; vis. student cum laude, Suffolk U. Sch. Law, 1991-92; JD, Franklin Pierce Law Ctr., 1992. Bar: Mass. 1993, U.S. Dist. Ct. 1993, U.S. Ct. Appeals (1st cir.) 1993. Summer assoc. Law Office of Robert Hernandez, Malden, Mass., 1990; vol. intern Disability Rights Ctr., Concord, N.H., 1990, N.H. Pub. Defender, Manchester, N.H., 1991, N.H. Appellate Defender, Concord, 1991; summer assoc. Law Office of David Bownes, Laconia, N.H., 1991; vol. legal asst. Com. for Pub. Counsel Svcs., Dedham, Mass., 1992; atty. Jill S. Sellers, Atty. at Law, Concord, 1994-95; atty., bar adv./pub. defender Middlesex Def. Attys., Inc., Concord, 1993-95; atty. Law Office of Robert S. Potters P.C., Boston, 1992-95; notary pub., Mass., 1994; pub. defender divsn. Com. for Pub. Counsel Svcs., 1995—. Vol./chair vols. Habitat for Humanity, Roxbury, Mass., 1994. Mem. ATLA (state gov. young lawyers sect. 1993-94, 94-95-96, liaison 1993-95-96, sec./treas. criminal law sect. 1993-94, 1st vice-chair criminal law sect. 1995—, Pub. Svc. award 1994), Mass. Acad. Trial Attys. (exec. com. young lawyers sect. 1994-95), Boston Bar Assn., Cen. Middlesex Bar Assn. Democrat. Avocations: gymnastics-coaching and participating, reading, cooking. Home: 72 Marion Rd Ext Marblehead MA 01945 Office: Ste 408 One Salem Green Salem MA 01970

SELLERS, SUSAN TAYLOR, assistant principal; b. Melrose, Mass., Jan. 8, 1948; d. Walter Edmund and Lucille (Clark) Taylor; m. Burton Chance Sellers, Oct. 6, 1989; children: Heather, Heidi. BA in English, Syracuse U., 1970; MA in Ednl. Leadership, Immaculata (Pa.) Coll., 1993. Cert. early childhood, elem., elem. prin. Dir. Head Start The Neighborhood Ctr., Utica, N.Y., 1970; tchr. Mt. Markham Sch. Dist., Bridgewater, N.Y., 1970-72; dir. Little People Day Sch., Malvern, Pa., 1987-88; tchr. Friendship Elem. Sch., Coatesville, Pa., 1988-93; asst. prin. Rainbow Elem. Sch., Coatesville, 1993—; grad. adv. bd. Immaculata Coll., 1993—. Recipient Artist in Edn. award Pa. Coun. Arts, 1990, 91, 92, Presdl. award for excellence in elem. math. Pa. Dept. Edn., 1991. Mem. ASCD, Nat. Assn. Edn. Young Children, Nat. Coun. Tchrs. Math., Pa. Coalition Arts in Edn., Pa. Lit. Coun., Local Children's Team. Avocations: classical music, opera, visiting museums, photography, football. Home: 10 Oak Hill Cir Malvern PA 19355-2017 Office: Coatesville Area Sch Dist Rainbow Elem Sch 50 Country Club Rd Coatesville PA 19320

SELLERY, J'NAN MORSE, English and American literature educator; b. Oakland, Calif., Jan. 3, 1928; d. Raymond Stephen and Minna Esther (Bourus) Morse; m. Austin R. Sellery, Aug. 30, 1947; children: Stephen Brooke, Edward Austin, Margaret Joan, John Merritt. BA, U. Calif., Riverside, 1965; MA, U. Calif., 1967, PhD, 1970. Asst. prof. Harvey Mudd Coll., Claremont, Calif., 1970-74, assoc. prof. Claremont grad. sch., 1974-80, prof. English Claremont grad. sch., 1980—, Louisa & Robert Miller chair prof. humanities, 1989—; coord. women's studies Claremont Coll., 1988-91; cons. UMI Press, 1989, Conn. Rev., 1988. Co-editor: Faust Part I, 1969, The Scapegoat, 1972, Bibliography of Elizabeth Bowen, 1981; editor (jours.) Women's Voices, 1986, Gender, 1990; sr. editor Psychol. Perspectives, 1969-95; contbr. articles and poetry to mags. and profl. jours. NDEA fellow U. Calif., 1967-70; rsch. grantee Harvey Mudd Coll., 1971-90, NEH summer grantee Yale U., 1979, Mellon grantee in curriculum Claremont Colls., 1989; vis. humanities scholar U. Calgary, Can., 1992. Mem. AAUW (nat. bd. mem. 1982-83, mem. fellowship panel 1989-93), MLA, Nat. Women's Studies Assn. (coord. coun. 1989-92, cons. jour. and book awards 1991—). Office: Harvey Mudd Coll Humanities Dept Kingston Hall Claremont CA 91711

SELLIN, ERIC, linguist, poet, educator; b. Phila., Nov. 7, 1933; s. Thorsten and Amy (Anderson) S.; m. Birgitta Sjöberg, Jan. 25, 1958; children: Frederick, Christopher. BA, U. Pa., 1955, MA, 1958, PhD, 1965. Asst. instr. French U. Pa., Phila., 1955-56, 1957-58, 1959-60; lectr. Am. lit. U. Bordeaux, France, 1956-57; instr. French Clark U., Worcester, Mass., 1958-59; lectr. creative writing U. Pa., 1960-62; instr. French Temple U., Phila., 1962-65; asst. prof. Temple U., 1965-67, assoc. prof., 1967-70, prof., 1970-91, chmn. dept. French and Italian, 1970-73, founder, dir. Center for Study of Francophone Lit. of North Africa, 1981—; prof. French Tulane U., New Orleans, 1991—; chmn. dept. French and Italian, 1995—; USIS lectr., Africa and Near East, 1981-83, 85, 88-91, manuscript reader, cons. to various profl. jours., univ. presses, and founds.; sr. Fulbright-Hays lectr., Algiers, Algeria, 1968-69, Dakar, Senegal, 1978-79. Author: The Dramatic Concepts of Antonin Artaud, 1968, The Inner Game of Soccer, 1976, Soccer Basics, 1977, Reflections on the Aesthetics of Futurism, Dadaism and Surrealism-a Prosody Beyond Words, 1993, (poetry) Night Voyage, 1964, Trees at First Light, 1973, Tanker Poems, 1973, Borne Kilométrique, 1973, Marginalia, 1979, Crépuscule prolongé à El Biar, 1982, Nightfall over Lubumbashi, 1982, Night Foundering, 1985, Dead of Noon, 1992; editor: Africana Jour., 1983-87, CELFAN Edit. Monographs, 1987—, CELFAN Rev., 1981—; contbr. over 150 articles to profl. jours. and anthologies. Recipient faculty prize in Romance langs. U. Pa., 1955; Am. Philos. Soc. fellow, 1970, 82, NEH sr. fellow, 1973-74; Temple U. rsch. grantee, 1970, 82; sr. Fulbright-Hays Rsch. scholar Francophone Lit., Rabat, Morocco, 1989. Mem. Am. Assn. Tchrs. French, African Lit. Assn., Phi Beta Kappa. Office: Tulane U Dept French New Orleans LA 70118

SELLIN, IVAN ARMAND, physicist, educator, researcher; b. Everett, Wash., Aug. 16, 1939; s. Petrus and Amelia Fanny (Josephson) S.; m. Helen Kathleen Gill, June 16, 1962; children: Peter Bennington, Frank Erick. Student, Harvard U., 1956-59; MS, U. Chgo., 1960, PhD, 1964. Instr., rsch. assoc. U. Chgo., 1960-65; asst. prof. NYU, 1965-67; rsch. physicist Oak Ridge (Tenn.) Nat. Lab., 1967-70; assoc. prof. U. Tenn., Knoxville, 1970-74, prof., 1974-83, dist. prof., 1983—; adj. rsch. physicist Oak Ridge Nat. Lab., 1970—; program dir. NSF, Washington, 1988-89; mem. com. on atomic and molecular sci. NAS-NRC, 1973-76, chmn., 1980-83, mem. panel on accelerator related atomic and molecular sci., 1978-80; mem. panel on atomic, molecular adn optical physics NAS-NRC Physics Survey, 1983-86; Orgn. Am. States vis. prof. Centro Atomico, Bariloche, Argentina, 1972, 81-82, Inst. fur Kernphysik der Univ. Frankfurt, Germany, 1977, Rsch. Inst. for Physics, Stockholm, 1977-78, 83; invited visitor Harvard Smithsonian Instn. Astrophys. Obs., 1995; spkr., presenter in field. Editor, co-author: (with others) Advances in Atomic and Molecular Physics, 1976, McGraw-Hill Annual Yearbook of Science and Technology, 1978, McGraw-Hill Encyclopedia of Science and Technology, 5th edit., 1982, 7th edit., 1992, Beam Foil Spectroscopy: Vol 1, Atomic Structure and Lifetimes Vol. 2, Collisional and Radiative Processes, 1976, Structure and Collisions of Ions and Atoms, 1978, Forward Electron Ejection in Ion Collisions, 1984, Physics Through the 1990's; Atomic, Molecular and Optical Physics, 1986; contbr. more than 200 articles to profl. jours. Concert mgr. Oak Ridge Civic Music Assn., 1973. Grantee Office of Naval Rsch., 1972-82, NASA, 1972-73, 73-78, NSF, 1973—, Internat. Union Pure and Applied Physics, 1975, Dept. Energy, 1979-83, Oak Ridge Nat. Lab., 1980-82, NSF Divsn. Internat. Programs, 1986-92, 96—; recipient Sr. U.S. Scientist awrad Alexander von Humboldt Found., 1977, 86, 88; Fulbright scholar, 1977; rsch. scholar Japan Ministry of Edn., Sci. and Culture, 1994, Manne Siegbahn Nat. Lab., Stockholm, 1996-97. Fellow Am. Phys. Soc. (vice chmn. 1981, chmn. 1982-83, mem. com. on constn. and bylaws, mem. com. on meetings 1991-93, coun. advisor 1989-93, councillor 1979-83, chmn. publs. com. divsn. electron and atomic physics 1974-76, mem. program com. 1976-78, mem. nominating com. 1979-83, mem. fellowship com. 1979-83, mem. exec. com. 1979-83, mem. exec. com. S.E. sect. 1979-93, vice chmn. 1990-91, program chmn. 1990-91, chmn. 1991-92, Jesse Beams medal 1983), Acad. European, Cosmos Club. Achievements include research in highly ionized heavy ions, modes of formation and destruction in collisions with target atoms and molecules, and the excitations they induce in dilute gas and dense solid media; use of synchrotron radiation to form and study cold, multiply ionized ions using heavy ion accelerators, synchrotron storage rings, electron spectrometers, x-ray, soft x-ray, and extreme ltra-violet spectrometers, heavy particle spectrometers, and two-dimensional position-sensitive detectors.

SELLIN, THEODORE, foreign service officer, consultant; b. Phila., June 17, 1928; s. Thorsten and Amy (Anderson) S.; m. Taru Jarvi, July 10, 1965; 1 child, Derek. Student, U. Uppsala, Sweden, 1946-48; BA, U. Pa., 1951, MA, 1952. Joined Fgn. Svc., Dept. State, 1952; vice consul Copenhagen, 1952-56; rsch. analyst Dept. State, Washington, 1956-58; program officer Office Internat. Confs., 1965-67; acad. tng. staff U. Ind., 1958-59; 2d sec. Am. Embassy, Helsinki, Finland, 1959-64, 1st sec., polit. officer, 1971-73; 1st sec., labor-polit. officer Am. Embassy, Oslo, 1967-71; polar affairs officer Dept. State, 1975; consul gen. Goteborg, Sweden, 1978-80; fgn. rels. cons. Dept. State, Washington, 1980—. Office: Dept State IS/FPC/CDR Washington DC 20520

SELLMYER, DAVID JULIAN, physicist, educator; b. Joliet, Ill., Sept. 28, 1938; s. Marcus Leo and Della Louise (Plumhoff) S.; m. Catherine Joyce Zakas, July 16, 1962; children: Rebecca Ann, Julia Maryn, Mark Anthony. BS, U. Ill., 1960; PhD, Mich. State U., 1965. Asst. prof. MIT, Cambridge, 1965-72, assoc. prof., 1972; assoc. prof. U. Nebr., Lincoln, 1972-75, prof., 1975—, chmn. dept. physics, 1978-84, George Holmes disting. prof., 1987, dir. Ctr. Materials Rsch., 1988—; cons. Dale Electronics, Norfolk, Nebr., 1980—. Contbr. articles, book revs. to refereed jours. Recipient tech. award NASA, 1972; disting. vis. prof. S.D. Sch. Mines and Tech., Rapid City, 1981. Fellow Am. Phys. Soc. Office: U Nebr Ctr Materials Rsch 112 Brace Lab Lincoln NE 68588-0113

SELLO, ALLEN RALPH, oil company executive; b. Winnipeg, Man., Can., June 22, 1939; m. Mary Lou Sello, June 3, 1972; children: Clint, Monique, Daren. B of Commerce (hon)., U. Man., 1963; MBA, U. Toronto, Ont., Can., 1964. Mgr. mktg. analysis Ford Motor Co. of Can., Oakville, Ont., Can., 1972-75, mgr. product plans, 1975-78, asst. treas., 1978-79; dir. acctg. Gulf Can. Ltd., Toronto, 1979-81, dir. fin. planning, 1981-82, contr., 1982-85; v.p., contr. Gulf Can. Corp., Calgary, Alta., Can., 1985-86; v.p. fin. Gulf Can. Resources, Ltd., Calgary, 1986-88, v.p. fin., chief fin. officer, 1988-95; prin. Allen Sello & Assocs. Ltd., 1996—. Mem. Fin. Execs. Inst., Glencoe Golf and Country Club, Calgary Petroleum Club. Avocations: squash, skiing, tennis, golf.

SELLS, BOAKE ANTHONY, private investor; b. Ft. Dodge, Iowa, June 24, 1937; s. Lyle M. and Louise (Gadd) S.; m. Marian S. Stephenson, June 20, 1959; children: Damian, Brian, Jean Ann. BSC, U. Iowa, 1959; MBA, Harvard U., 1969. Bus. office mgr. Northwestern Bell Tel., Des Moines, 1959-63; salesman Hydraulic Cos., Ft. Dodge, 1964-67; pres. Cole Nat. Corp., Cleve., 1969-83; vice chmn. Dayton Hudson Corp., Mpls., 1983-84, pres., 1984-87; chmn., pres., chief exec. officer Revco D.S., Inc., Twinsburg, Ohio, 1987-92; bd. dirs. Promus Cos. Trustee Cleve. Ctr. for Contemporary Art, Cleve. Play House.

SELLS, BRUCE HOWARD, biomedical sciences educator; b. Ottawa, Ont., Can., Aug. 15, 1930; s. Charles Henry and Nell (Worth) S.; m. Bernice May Romain, Sept. 19, 1953; children: Jennifer, Monica, David, Lisa. B.S., Carleton U., 1952; M.A., Queen's U., 1954; Ph.D., McGill U., 1957. Demonstrator McGill U., Montreal, Ont., Can., 1954-57; research assoc. Columbia U., N.Y.C., 1961-62; asst. prof. St. Jude Children's Hosp.-U. Tenn., Memphis, 1962-64; assoc. prof. St. Jude Children's Hosp., Memphis, 1964-72, staff, 1968-72; prof., dir. molecular biology Meml. U. Nfld., St. John's, Can., 1972-83, assoc. dean, 1979-83; prof. molecular biology U. Guelph, Ont., Can., 1983—, dean biol. sci., 1983-95; mem. adv. com. Ont. Health Rsch. Coun., 1992. Contbr. numerous articles to various publs. Adv. Com. Ont. Health Rsch. Coun., 1992—. Research fellow Damon Runyon Meml. Fund, Brussels, 1957-59; research fellow Damon Runyon Meml. Fund, Copenhagen, 1959-60; Killam sr. research fellow U. Paris, 1978-79; grantee NIH, 1963-72, NSF, 1965-69, Med. Research Council Can., 1972, Damon Runyon Meml. Fund for Cancer Research, 1962-76, Nat. Found.-March of Dimes, 1974-78, Muscular Dystrophy Assn. Can., 1974, Nat. Cancer Inst. Can., 1979, Vis. Prof. award Institut Pasteur, Paris, 1989; Exchange fellow Natural Scis. and Engring. Rsch. Coun. of Can., 1994. Fellow Royal Soc. Can. (rapporteur microbiology and biochemistry divsn. 1985-87, convenor 1987-89); mem. Acad. Sci. of Royal Soc. Can. (life scis. divsn. fellowship rev. com. 1990-92), Am. Soc. Microbiologists, Can. Assn. Univ. Tchrs., Am. Soc. Biol. Chemists, Am. Soc. Cell Biology, Can. Biochemistry Soc. (Ayerst award selection com. 1990), Med. Rsch. Coun. (Centennial fellowships com., chmn. com. on biotech. devel. grants 1983-85, standing com. for Can. Genetic Disease Network 1991-92, chmn., 1992—), Nat. Rsch. Coun. Can. (biol. phenomena subcom. 1983-86, chmn. steering group, sci. criteria for environ. quality com. 1986, E.W.R. Steacie Prize com. 1986-88), Assn. Can. Deans of Sci. (co-founder 1989). Home: Rural Rte 6, Guelph, ON Canada N1H 6J3 Office: U Guelph, 577 Gordon St, Guelph, ON Canada N1G 2W1

SELMAN, ALAN LOUIS, computer science educator; b. N.Y.C., Apr. 2, 1941; s. Dan and Rose (Grass) S.; m. Sharon Jevotovsky, July 7, 1963; children: Jeffrey, Heather. BS in Math. cum laude, City Coll., CUNY, 1962; MA, U. Calif., Berkeley, 1964; PhD, Pa. State U., 1970. Asst. prof. computer sci. Fla. State U., Tallahassee, 1972-77; assoc. prof. Iowa State U., Ames, 1977-82; prof. Fern U., Hagen, Germany, 1982, Iowa State U., 1982-86; prof. Northea. U., Boston, 1986-90, acting dean, 1988-89; prof., chmn. dept. computer sci. SUNY, Buffalo, 1990—. Editor: Complexity Theory Retrospective, 1990; assoc. editor Jour. Computer and Sys. Scis.; mem. editl. bd. Math. Sys. Theory. NSA grantee, 1987-90; Fulbright award, 1981-82. Mem. Am. Math. Soc., Assn. Computing Machinery, IEEE. Office: SUNY Dept Computer Sci 226 Bell Hall Buffalo NY 14260-2000

SELMAN, JOE B., insurance company executive; b. Oklahoma City, Jan. 31, 1946; s. Paul J. and Letita G. (Whisler) S.; m. Eleanor J. Selman, Aug. 26, 1983; children: Karen L. Hartigan, Linda D. Coker, James J. Student, U. Okla., 1964-66, Elon Coll., 1968, Am. Coll., 1984, 88. Asst. athletic trainer U.S. Naval Acad., Annapolis, Md., 1966-68; assoc. distbr. Zimmer-Baxter, Roanoke, Va., 1968-73; distbr. Zimmer-Selman, Roanoke, 1973-75; pres. Joe B. Selman, Inc., Roanoke, 1975-76; agt. Equitable Life, 1977-95; dist. mgr. Equitable Life, Charlottesville, Va., 1978-81; pres. Benefits Mgmt., Charlottesville, 1981-94; CEO Duke Benefit Svcs., Inc., Charlottesville, 1995—; Am. Sports Underwriters cons. for catastrophic med. ins. plan for student athletes to Nat. Coll. Athletic Assn., Kansas City, Kans., 1983-84. Pres. Charlottesville dist. Va. Student Aid Found., 1991. With USN, 1966-68. Mem. Million Dollar Round Table (life). Episcopalian. Avocation: University of Virginia football. Office: Duke Benefit Svcs Inc 2975 Ivy Rd Charlottesville VA 22903

SELMAN, MINNIE CORENE PHELPS, elementary school educator; b. Freedom, Okla., Mar. 25, 1947; d. Maxwell Jack and Mary Elizabeth (Mountain) Phelps; m. Thomas O. Selman, Aug. 8, 1966; children: T. Justin, Jeffrey L. BS in Elem. Edn., Northwestern Okla. State U., 1969. Cert. elem. tchr., early childhood edn. tchr., elem. sci. tchr., Okla.; cert. early experiences insci., Okla. Tchr. Woodward (Okla.) Pub. Sch., 1969-72; pre-sch. tchr. Free Spirit Pre-sch., Woodward, 1974-75; tchr. Montessori Discovery World Pre-sch., Woodward, 1975-78; tchr. kindergarten Woodward Pub. Sch., Woodward, 1978—; host Leaderhip Okla. in the Classroom, 1991; tng. tchr. Okla. State U., Stillwater, 1987, 90. Benefit vol. Western Plains Shelter Orgn., Woodward, 1990, 91; life mem. Plains Indians and Pioneers Hist. Found., Woodward. Woodward Pub. Schs. Ednl. Found. grantee, 1990, 91, 92, NASA/NSTA grantee, 1995. Mem. NEA, Okla. Edn. Assn., Woodward Edn. Assn. (pub. rels. com. 1990—), Nat. Sci. Tchr. Assn. (cert. in elem. sci.), Okla. Sci. Tchrs. Assn. Democrat. Home: 318 Spruce Park Dr Woodward OK 73801-5945

SELMAN, ROLAND WOOTEN, III, lawyer; b. Kansas City, Mo., Aug. 16, 1941; s. Roland Wooten Jr. and Dixie R. (Chambliss) S.; 1 child, Kellee Harris. Student, U. Kans., 1959-61, Stetson U., 1961-62; BA, U. Mo., Kansas City, 1963; JD, U. Calif., Hastings, 1971. Bar: Calif. 1972, U.S. Ct. Appeals (9th cir.) 1975, U.S. Supreme Ct. 1975, D.C. 1979, U.S. Ct. Appeals (D.C. cir.) 1980, U.S. Ct. Appeals (Fed. cir.) 1983. Assoc. Pillsbury, Madison & Sutro, San Francisco, 1971-79, gen. ptnr., 1979-95; commn. counsel Calif. Commn. on Jud. Performance, San Francisco, 1995—; judge pro tem Mcpl. Ct., San Francisco, 1984-95. Bd. dirs. Marin Svcs. for Women; planning commr. City of Sausalito, Calif., 1991-93; chmn. Sausalito Planning Commn., 1992-93. Lt. USN, 1963-68. Decorated D.F.C., Air medal. Mem. San Francisco Bar Assn., Aircraft Owners and Pilots Assn., Harley Owners Group (life), Silver Wings Fraternity, Order of Coif. Mem. Christian Ch. Avocations: flying, scuba diving. Home: 28 Greenwood Bay Dr Belvedere Tiburon CA 94920-2252 Office: Commn on Jud Performance 100 Howard St Ste 300 San Francisco CA 94105 Office: Commn on Jud Performance Ste 300 101 Howard St San Francisco CA 94105

SELOVER, WILLIAM CHARLTON, corporate communications and governmental affairs executive; b. Long Beach, Calif., Dec. 12, 1938; s. John Jesse and Myrtis Charlton (Holmes) S.; m. Mary-Louise Hutchins, Jan. 5, 1963 (div. 1985); children: Victoria, Edward. BA, Principia Coll., 1960; MA, U. Va., 1962. Mem. editorial staff Christian Sci. Monitor, from Congl. corr. to diplomatic corr., 1964-71; spl. asst. to sec. of the navy USN, 1971; mem. White House Coun. on Internat. Econ. Policy, Washington, 1971-72; history and archives divsn. chief Cost of Living Coun., Exec. Office of the Pres., Washington, 1973-74; asst. to adminstr. U.S. EPA, Washington, 1974-75, 77-78; from staff mem. White House Domestic Coun. to asst. to V.P. Nelson Rockefeller White House, Washington, 1975-76; speechwriter Pres. Gerald R. Ford, Washington, 1976; pub. affairs exec. Ford Motor Co., Detroit, 1978-88; pub. affairs mgr. diversified products ops. Ford Motor Co.; regional pub. affairs mgr. Ford Motor Co., L.A., 1988-91; v.p. corp. comms. and govtl. affairs USL Capital Corp. (subs. Ford Fin. Svcs. Group), 1991—. Speechwriter for chmn. and CEO of Ford Motor Co., Henry Ford II; editor autobiography former Pres. Richard M. Nixon, 1977. Helen Dwight Reid Found. fellow, Carnegie Found./Maxwell Grad. Overseas fellow, 1962. Mem. Conference Bd. (coun. corp. comm. execs.), Nat. Press Club, Press Club Detroit, Press Club L.A., Motor Press Guild, Internat. Motor Press Assn., Leadership Detroit Alumni Assn., Am. Polit. Sci. Assn. Office: USL Capital Corp 733 Front St San Francisco CA 94111-1909

SELSKY, SAMUEL, film producer, consultant; b. Chgo., Nov. 11, 1909; arrived in France, 1947.; s. Abraham and Sonia S.; m. Marcella Siegel (div.); m. Lillian Hopkins (dec.); m. Liliane Stoumon (div.). BA, Johns Hopkins U., 1929, postgrad., 1930-32; MA, U. Md., 1942. Sci. tchr. Balt. Sch. Sys., 1935-41; Geologist State Geodetic Survey, Md., D.C., 1930-31; geologist Columbian Mining Enterprises, Colombia, 1933-34; dep. dir. dist. 4 Nat. Youth Adminstrn., Washington, 1942-43; placement officer War Manpower Commn., Washington, 1943-45; dir. War Relocation Authority, L.A., 1945-46; adminstr. UN, 1946-47; dir. pers. UNESCO, Paris, 1947-51; European prodr. "You Asked for It", Paris, 1951-58; film prodr. Les Films ABC, Paris, 1959—; dep. dir. Gen. Inst. Internat. de Biologie Humaine, Paris, Brussels, 1963-65. Editor: Sci. Trade Jour. Assn. U.S.; contbr. articles to profl. jours.; author radio scripts for nat. edn. U.S., 1942. Vol. USCGR, 1944-45. Recipient Medaille Argent Arts Scis. Lettres, Paris, 1966. Phi Delta Kappa. Jewish. Avocations: bridge, golf, travel, dramatics. Home & Office: Francam Interservice Co, 4 Rue Villehardouin, 75003 Paris France

SELTSER, RAYMOND, epidemiologist, educator; b. Boston, Dec. 17, 1923; s. Israel and Hannah (Littman) S.; m. Charlotte Frances Gale, Nov. 16, 1946; children: Barry Jay, Andrew David. MD, Boston U., 1947; MPH, Johns Hopkins U., 1957. Diplomate Am. Bd. Preventive Medicine (trustee, sec.-treas. 1974-77), Am. Bd. Med. Specialties (mem. exec. com. 1976-77). Asst. chief med. info. and intelligence br. U.S. Dept. Army, 1953-56; epidemiologist div. internal health USPHS, 1956-57; from asst. prof. to prof. epidemiology Johns Hopkins U. Sch. Hygiene and Pub. Health, 1957-81, assoc. dean, 1967-77, dep. dir. Oncology Ctr., 1977-81; dean U. Pitts. Grad. Sch. Pub. Health, 1981-87, prof. epidemiology, 1981-88, emeritus dean, prof. epidemiology, 1988—; assoc. dir. USPHS Ctrs. for Disease Control, Rockville, Md., 1988-90; assoc. dir. Ctr. for Gen. Health Svcs. Extramural Rsch. Agy. for Health Care Policy and Rsch., Rockville, 1990—; cons. NIMH, 1958-70, also various govtl. health agys., 1958-79; expert cons. Pres.'s Commn. on Three Mile Island, 1979-80; mem. Three Mile Island Adv. Panel Health, Nat. Cancer Inst. Cancer Control Grant Rev. Com., Pa. Dept. Health Preventive Health Service Block Grant Adv. Task Force, Gov.'s VietNam Herbicide Info. Commn. Pa.; chmn. Toxic/Health Effects Adv. Com., 1985-87. Trustee, mem. exec. com., chmn. profl. adv. com. Harmarville Rehab. Ctr., Pitts., 1982-87; bd. dirs. Health Edn. Ctr., Media Info. Service. Served to capt. AUS, 1951-53, Korea. Decorated Bronze Star; recipient Centennial Alumni citation Boston U. Sch. Medicine, 1973; elected to Johns Hopkins Soc. of Scholars, 1986. Fellow AAAS, APHA (mem. governing coun. 1975-77, chmn. EPI sect. coun. 1979-80), Pa. Pub. Health Assn. (bd. dirs. 1985-88, pres.-elect 1986-88), Am. Coll. Preventive Medicine, Am. Heart Assn.; mem. Am. Epidemiol. Assn., Internat. Epidemiol. Assn., Am. Soc. Preventive Oncology, Am. Cancer Soc. (bd. dirs. Pa. divsn. 1985-87, mem. exec. com. 1986-87), Assn. Schs. Pub. Health (sec. 1969-71, mem. exec. com., chmn. edn. com. 1983-87), Soc. Med. Cons. Armed Forces, Soc. Epidemiologic Rsch., Nat. Coun. Radiation Protection and Measurements (consociate), Johns Hopkins Alumni Coun. (mem. exec. com. 1994—), Am. Disability Prevention and Wellness Assn. (bd. dirs. 1996—), Sigma Xi, Delta Omega. Office: Agy Health Care Policy Rsch 2101 E Jefferson St Rockville MD 20852

SELTZER, LEO, filmmaker, educator, lecturer; b. Montreal, Que., Can., Mar. 13, 1910; came to U.S., 1916; s. Boris and Atalia (Gerowitz) S.; m. Elaine Basil, Apr. 15, 1941 (div. 1950); children: Janzie, John; m. Dicky Ransohoff, 1951 (div. 1963). BA, U. Mass., 1979. Faculty CCNY, 1949-54, New Sch. Social Research, 1949-51; pres. Leo Seltzer Assocs., Inc., N.Y.C., 1950-90; faculty Columbia U., 1954-60, Phila. Coll. Art, 1955-56, NYU, N.Y.C., 1966-67; dir. audio-visual therapy program pediatrics ward Univ. Hosp., N.Y.C., 1970-76; instr. film prodn. workshop Sch. Visual Arts, N.Y.C., 1969-84; asst. prof. performing and creative arts CUNY, 1977-78; prof. film Bklyn. Coll., 1978-83, prof. emeritus film, 1983—; adj. prof. film Coll. S.I., N.Y.C., 1976-78; lectr. in U.S. and abroad, including Mus. Modern Art, N.Y.C., Marymount Coll., Ghent U., others. Producer, dir. over 60 documentary, social, informational, theatrical and TV films in 35 countries, including First Steps, UN Divsn. Social Affairs, 1947 (Acad. award for best documentary 1948), Fate of a Child, 1949, For the Living, 1952, (with Walter Cronkite) Conquest of Aging, 1958, All the Years, 1959, Jacqueline Kennedy's Asian Journey, 1962, Progress through Freedom (pres. Kennedy's visit to Mex.), 1962, (with Edward R. Murrow) The American Commitment, 1963, Report on Acupuncture, 1977, (with John Huston) Let There Be Light; producer, dir.: Nat. Film Bd. Can., 1941; chief cons. visual aids City of N.Y., 1941-42; producer: N.Y.C. Mcpl. Film and TV Unit Sta. WNYC, 1949-50; film biographer to White House for Pres. Kennedy; exec. producer Quadrant Comms., Inc., 1973-75 (7 citations Cannes and Edinburgh Film Festivals 1948-63); films are in Nat. Archives, Libr. of Congress, in collection and distributed by Mus. Modern Art; photographs are in Houston Mus. Fine Arts collection, Nat. Gallery Can., Visual Studies Workshop, Rochester, N.Y.; reconstructed 6 Am. social documentary films of 1930's for Mus. Modern Art Film Collection, 1976-77; subject of TV program by Bill Moyers, A Walk Through the Twentieth Century; contbr. film footage to Nat. Geographic, Blackside Prodns.; producer TV series The Great Depression. Served as 1st lt. Signal Corps. U.S. Army, 1943-46, ETO. Recipient Acad. award for best documentary, 1948, Silver medals Venice Film Festival, 1949, 63, Freedom's Found. award, 1953, Golden Reel award Scholastic Mag., 1955, Robert Flaherty award CCNY, 1956, Silver medal Atlanta Internat. Film Festival, 1977; honored in Leo Seltzer tribute Mus. Modern Art, 1990. Mem. Dirs. Guild Am. (charter). Research on Early Am. social documentary films. Home and Office: 368 E 69th St New York NY 10021-5706

SELTZER, PHYLLIS ESTELLE, painter, printmaker; b. Detroit, May 17, 1928; d. Max and Lillian (Weiss) Finkelstein; m. Gerard Seltzer, May 31, 1953; children: Kim, Hiram. BFA, U. Iowa, 1949, MFA, 1952; postgrad., U. Mich., 1953-55, Case Western Res. U., 1966-70. Faculty U. Iowa, 1950-52, U. Mich., Ann Arbor, 1954-55, Case Western Res. U., Cleve., 1966-70; program coord. arts and humanities Cleve. State U., 1969-71, Lake Erie Coll., Painesville, Ohio, 1970-72; art interior designer Dalton, VanDijk, Johnson, Cleve., 1973-74; pvt. practice as designer Cleve., 1975-87; lectr. Scuola di Grafica, Venice, Italy, 1994. Designer poster Cleve. Bicentennial, 1975; executed elevator murals Stouffer Inn on Sq. Cleve, wall murals Bistrot des Artistes, Cleve., 1987, Highland Grill, Chgo., 1990, Indian's Administration Bldg. Gateway Commn., Cleve., 1994; 3 commd. paintings for Soc. Nat. Bank, Cleve.; 4 commns. on video for New Cleve. Campaign, 1994-95; one-person shows include Vixseboxse Gallery, 1983, Old Detroit Gallery, 1985, Women's City Club, 1987, Bonfoey's, Cleve., 1989, 91, Jane Haslem Gallery, Washington, 1990, Galerie Bubaco, Venice, Italy, 1993, Bonfoey Gallery, Cleve., 1994, SG Gallery, Venice, Italy, 1994, 1995; group shows include Mitchell Mus., Mt. Vernon, Ill., 1979, Associated Am. Artists, N.Y.C., 1986, Nat. Print Exhbn., Trenton, N.J., 1988, Butler Inst. Am. Art, Youngstown, Ohio, 1989, S.W. Tex. State U., San Marcos, 1989, Cleve. Mus. Art, 1990, 93, Art Expo, N.Y.C., 1990, Artlink Contemporary Art Space, Ft. Wayne, Ind., 1990, Jan Cicero Gallery, Chgo., 1991, Bolton Gallery, Cleve. Playhouse, 1992, Wasmer Gallery, Ursuline Coll., Cleve., 1992, N.D. Print and Drawing Annual, U. N.D., 1992, 93, Mansfield Art Center, Ohio, 1992, Americana '92, Hong Kong, 1992, N.Y. Print Fair, 1992, 94, The Hammond Galleries, Lancaster, Ohio, Urban-Suburban, Bonfoey Co., Cleve., Great No. Corp. Ctr., Cleve., Dutchess County Art Assn., Poughkeepsie, N.Y., 1992, Michael Ingbar Gallery of Architecture, N.Y.C., 1992, Jane Haslem, Washington, 1993, Hunterton Art Ctr., Clinton, N.J., 1993, Ctrl. Pa. Festival of Arts, 1993, Northeastern Ohio Art Dealers Assn. Fine Arts Expo., 1993, Fla. Printmakers Soc., 1993, Cleve. Ctr. Contemporary Arts, 1993, 94, 95, Alexandria Mus. Art, 1993, Cleve. Mus. Art, 1993, Ctrl. Pa. Festival of Arts, 1993, Jan Cicero Gallery, Chgo., 1993, Trenton (N.J.) State Coll., 1993, Bonfoey Co., Cleve., 1993, Hunterdon Art Ctr., Clinton, N.J., 1993, Nat. Printmaking Exhibition, 1993, Jan Cicero Gallery, Chgo., 1994, Hunterdon Art Ctr., Clinton, N.J., 1994, NOADA Expo., Tower City, Ohio, 1994, 95, Art Multiple Dusselforf, Germany, 1994, Jane Haslem Gallery, Washington, Palm Springs (Calif.) Desert Mus., 1995, Jayson Gallery, Chgo., 1995, Citysights, 1995, Cleve. Play House, 1996, Print Biennial, Silvermine Guild Arts Ctr., New Canaan, Conn., 1996, The Park Synagogue, Cleveland Heights, Oh., 1996, Hunterdon Art Ctr., Clinton, N.J., 1996. Sec. Edgewater Homeowners Assn., Cleve., 1976-78. Tiffany fellow, 1952; recipient Cleve. Health Dept. award, 1975, Print Exhbn. award Hudson River Mus., 1987, Printmaking award Nat. Congress Art and Design, 1988, Juror's Merit award Chattahoochee Valley Art Mus., 1991, Purchase award Cleve. Mus. Art, 1993. Mem. Am. Soc. Aesthetics, New Orgn. Visual Arts Cleve. (v.p. 1974), Cleve. Soc. Contemporary Art, Print Club of Cleve. Mus. Art. (pres. 1983-84). Studio: 7431 Detroit Ave Cleveland OH 44102-2862 *I am guided mainly by a need to make a visual contribution to society by adding innovative ways of seeing, as well as by utilizing the new techniques and technologies that are available to the visual artist. In my particular area this means the utilization of new printing processes-e.g. the mylar print, the 2080 Xerox print and the 6500 color Xerox and the laser Canon copier (with heat transfer printing). These new media also lend themselves to the continuance of painting in traditional methods, nevertheless expanding the horizon of surface and color on a single plane.*

SELTZER, RICHARD C., lawyer; b. N.Y.C., Sept. 3, 1943; s. Edward and Beatrice (Fishman) S.; m. Carol Reische, Aug. 31, 1969; children: Wendy, Mark. BA, Harvard U., 1965; JD, Columbia U., 1968. Bar: N.Y. 1969, U.S. Dist. Ct. (so. and ea. dists.) N.Y. 1969, U.S. Ct. Appeals (5th cir.) 1978, U.S. Ct. Appeals (2nd cir.) 1987, U.S. Supreme Ct. 1995. Ptnr. Kaye Scholer Fierman Hays and Handler, N.Y.C., 1969—. Mem. ABA, Assn. of Bar of City of N.Y. Office: Kaye Scholer Fierman Hays and Handler 425 Park Ave New York NY 10022-3506

SELTZER, RONALD, retail company executive; b. Boston, Nov. 16, 1931; s. Harold and Molly (Scheinberg) S.; m. Leila Podell, Feb. 24, 1957; children: Marjory, Michael, Barbara, Janet. B.B.A., Boston U., 1953. Asst. employment mgr. Gilchrist Co., Boston, 1956-59; personnel mgr. Bamberger's, Plainfield, N.J., 1959-61; employment and employee relations mgr. Bamberger's, Newark, 1961-66, v.p., store mgr., 1966-67, dir. sales promotion, 1967-70, sr. v.p., dir. stores, 1970-71; exec. v.p. Bamberger's, 1971-81, dir., 1969—; chmn. bd. R.H. Macy, N.Y.C., 1971-81; exec. v.p. ops. Macy N.Y., 1979-80; pres., chief exec. officer Lionel Leisure Inc., 1981-82; Louis Dryfus Retail Inc., 1981-90, bus. cons., 1990—; DWS. Retail Mgmt., Toronto; dir. Bradford Nat. Corp.; cons., pres. R & L Seltzer Assocs. Trustee Urban Coalition, N.J. Safety Council Inc., Garden State Ballet. Served with USNR, 1950-53; Served with AUS, 1953-55. Mem. Greater Newark C. of C. (dir. 1970—, mem. tax task force 1970—). Home: 278 Garfield Ave Oakhurst NJ 07755-1734

SELTZER, RONALD ANTHONY, radiologist, educator; b. Washington, Mar. 7, 1935; s. Lawrence H. and Sarah (Levin)S.; m. Adele Wishnow, June 25, 196l; children: Jeffrey David, Lauren Jill. AB with distinction, U. Mich., 1956; MD with high distinction, Wayne State U., 1960. Diplomate Am. Bd. Radiology. Resident in radiology Mass. Gen. Hosp., Boston, 1961-62, 64-66; asst. prof. radiology Stanford (Calif.) U. Med. Sch., 1966-67, asst. clin. prof., 1967-73, assoc. clin. prof., 1974-89; pvt. practice San Mateo, Redwood City,, Calif., 1967; mem. med. staff Mills Meml. Hosp., San Mateo, Calif., 1967-69; mem. med. staff Sequoia Hosp., Redwood City, 1969—, pres., 1986-88; cons. on radiation exposure divsn. radiol. health USPHS, 1964-67; cons. on nuclear medicine Palo Alto VA Hosp., 1967-75; cons. on computerized reporting in radiology GE, 1975-78; cons. advanced imaging divsn. Xerox Corp., 1978-82; cons. on electronic imaging Stanford Rsch. Internat., 1980-84; bd. dirs. Hosp. Consortium San Mateo County, 1986-88. Contbr. articles on biol. behavior and radiation dosimaty of radioactive materials, diagnostic radiology and uses of computers in medicine to med. jours. Sr. asst. surgeon USPHS, 1962-64. Fellow Inst. Cardiology Gt. Britain; mem. AMA, Calif. Med. Assn., Radiol. Soc. N.Am., Am. Roentgen Ray Soc., Western Angiography Soc. (pres. 1976-78), San Mateo County Ind. Practice Assn. (bd. dirs. Bay Pacific Health Plan 1979-84), Alpha Omega Alpha. Home: 140 Degas Rd Portola Vally CA 94028-7709 Office: Sequoia Hosp Redwood City CA 94062

SELTZER, VICKI LYNN, obstetrician-gynecologist; b. N.Y.C., June 2, 1949; d. Herbert Melvin and Marian Elaine (Willinger) S.; m. Richard Stephen Brach, Sept. 2, 1973; children: Jessica Lillian, Eric Robert. BS, Rensselaer Poly. Inst., 1969; MD, NYU, 1973. Diplomate Am. Bd. Ob-Gyn. Intern Bellevue Hosp., N.Y.C., 1973-74, resident in ob-gyn, 1974-77; fellow gynecol. cancer Am. Cancer Soc., N.Y.C., 1977-78, Meml. Sloan Kettering Cancer Ctr., N.Y.C., 1978-79; assoc. dir. gynecol. cancer Albert Einstein Coll. Medicine, N.Y.C., 1979-83; assoc. prof. ob-gyn., SUNY, Stony Brook, N.Y.C., 1983-89; prof. ob-gyn. Albert Einstein Coll. Medicine, 1989—; chmn. ob-gyn. L.I. Jewish Med. Ctr., 1993—; dir. ob-gyn., Queens Hosp. Ctr., Jamaica, N.Y., 1983-93, pres. med. bd., 1986-89. Author: Every Woman's Guide to Breast Cancer, 1987; editor-in-chief: Primary Care Update for the Ob-Gyn, 1993—; editor: Women's Primary Health Care, 1995; mem. editorial bd. Women's Life mag., 1980-82, Jour. of the Jacobs Inst. Women's Health, 1990—; contbr. over 75 articles to profl. jours.; host Weekly Ob-Gyn. TV Program, Lifetime Med. TV. Chmn. health com. Nat. Coun. Women, N.Y.C., 1979-84; mem. Mayor Beame's Task Force on Rape, N.Y.C., 1974-76; bd. govs. Regional Coun. Women in Medicine, 1985—; chmn. Coun. on Resident Edn. in Ob-Gyn., 1987-93. Galloway Fund fellow 1975; recipient citation Am. Med. Women's Assn., 1973, Nat. Safety Coun., 1978, Achiever award Nat. coun. Women, 1985, Achiever award L.I. Ctr. Bus. and Profl. Women, 1987. Fellow N.Y. Obstet. Soc., Am. Coll. Ob-Gyn (v.p. 1993-94, pres.-elect 1996-97, gynecol. practice com. 1981, examener Am. Bd. Obstetrics and Gynecology 1988—); mem. Women's Med. Assn. (v.p. N.Y. 1974-79, editorial bd. jour. 1985—, resident review com. for obstetrics and gynecology 1993—), Am. Med. Women's Assn. (com. chmn. 1975-77, 78-79, editorial bd. jour. 1986—), N.Y. Cancer Soc., NYU Sch. Med. Alumni Assn. (bd. govs. 1979—, v.p. 1987-91, pres. 1992-93), Alpha Omega Alpha. Office: LI Jewish Med Ctr New Hyde Park NY 11040

SELTZER, WILLIAM, statistician, social researcher, former international organization director; b. N.Y.C., Sept. 22, 1934; s. William B. Seltzer and Edith S. (Goldman) Alt.; m. Jane E. Berger, Nov. 20, 1970; children: Benjamin, Ezra. BA, U. Chgo., 1956. Rsch. asst. Health Info. Found., N.Y.C., 1957-60; statistician U.S. Bur. Census, Suitland, Md., 1960-64; advisor Pakistan Inst. Devel., Econs. and Cen. Statis. Office, Karachi, 1964-68; staff assoc. Population Coun., N.Y.C., 1968-74; br. chief UN Statis. Office, N.Y.C., 1974-86, dir., 1986-93; sr. advisor to under-sec.-gen. Dept. Econ. and Social Info. and Policy Analysis, N.Y.C., 1993-94; sr. rsch. schlar Fordham U., N.Y.C., 1995—; mem. com. on population and demography, chair panel on data collection NAS, Washington, 1977-82; cons. UN Population Fund, 1995—, Internat. Criminal Tribunal for Rwanda, 1996.

Author: Poems, 1960, Politics and Statistics, 1994; co-author: Population Growth Estimation, 1973; also various UN documents, jour. articles, reports. Fellow Am. Statis. Assn. (chair social stats. sect. 1983-84, chair com. on internat. rels. 1986-87), Royal Statis. Soc. (hon.); mem. Population Assn. Am., Internat. Statis. Inst., Internat. Assn. Official Statisticians. Mem. Soc. of Friends. Office: Fordham U Dept Sociology and Anthropology Dealy Hall Rm 522 441 E Fordham Rd Bronx NY 10458-5149

SELVADURAI, ANTONY PATRICK SINNAPPA, civil engineering educator, applied mathematician, consultant; b. Matara, Sri-Lanka, Sept. 23, 1942; arrived in Can., 1975; s. Kanapathiyar Sinnappa and W. Mary Adeline (Fernando) S.; m. Sally Joyce; children: Emily, Paul, Mark, Elizabeth. Diploma in Engring., Brighton Poly., U.K., 1964; Diploma, Imperial Coll./London U., 1965; MS, Stanford U., 1967; PhD in Theoretical Mechanics, U. Nottingham, 1971; DSc, U. Nottingham, Eng., 1986. Registered profl. engr., Can.; chartered mathematician, U.K. Staff rsch. engr. Woodward Clyde Assocs., Oakland, Calif., 1966-67; rsch. assoc. dept. theoretical mechanics U. Nottingham, 1969-70; lectr. dept. civil engring. U. Aston, Birmingham, Eng., 1971-75; asst. prof. civil engring. Carleton U., Ottawa, Ont., Can., 1975-76, assoc. prof., 1976-81, prof., 1982-93, chmn. dept., 1982-90, Davidson Dunton Rsch. lectr., 1987; prof., chmn. dept. civil engring./applied mechanics McGill U., Montreal, 1993—; vis. rsch. scientist Bechtel Group, Inc., San Francisco, 1981-82; vis. prof. U. Nottingham, 1986, Inst. de Mécanique de Grenoble, France, 1990; cons. Atomic Energy of Can. Ltd., Pinawa, Man., 1983—, Ministry of Transp. Ont., Toronto, 1984—, Fleet Tech., Ottawa, 1988—, Atomic Energy Control Bd., 1987—. Author: Elastic Analysis of Soil Foundation Interaction, 1979, (with R.O. Davis) Elasticity and Geomechanics, 1996; editor: Mechanics of Structured Media, 1981, (with G.Z. Voyiadjis) Mechanics of Material Interfaces, 1986, Developments of Mechanics, 1987, (with M.J. Boulon) Mechanics of Geomaterial Interfaces, 1995, Mechanics of Poroelastic Media, 1996. King George VI Meml. fellow English Speaking Union of Commonwealth, 1965, rsch. fellow SRC, U.K., 1969, Erskine fellow U. Canterbury, New Zealand, 1992. Fellow Am. Acad. Mechanics, Can. Soc. Civil Engring. (Leipholz medal 1991), Assoc. Prof. Engrs. of Ont. (Engring. medal for rsch. 1993), Engring. Inst. Can., Inst. Math. and Its Applications, Internat. Assn. for Computer Methods and Advances in Geomechanics (award for significant paper in the category theory computational analytical 1994). Roman Catholic. Office: McGill U, Dept Civil Engring, Montreal, PQ Canada H3A 2K6

SELVER, PAUL DARRYL, lawyer; b. N.Y.C., May 28, 1947; s. Rene T. Selver and Marilyn (Steiner) Pomerance; m. Ellen J. Roller, Jan. 22, 1984; children: Adam, Max, Katelyn. BA magna cum laude, Harvard U., 1969, JD, 1972. Bar: N.Y. 1973. Assoc. Hale Russell & Gray, N.Y.C., 1972-74; ptnr. Brown and Wood (formerly Tufo and Zuccotti), N.Y.C., 1974-94, Battle Fowler, N.Y.C., 1994—; lectr. of law Columbia U. Law Sch., 1994—; assoc. adj. prof. Sch. Architecture, Planning and Preservation Columbia U., N.Y.C., 1986-88. Author: (N.Y. practice guide book) Real Estate: Land Use Regulations, 1986; edit. bd. Metroplis Mag., 1983-86. Mem. Manhattan Cmty. Bd. #6, N.Y.C., 1974-76, Westside Transit Com., N.Y.C., 1987; bd. dirs. Manhattan Bower Corp., N.Y.C., 1992-95. Mem. ABA, Assn. of Bar of City of N.Y., Am. Planning Assn. Office: Battle Fowler 75 E 55th St New York NY 10022-3205

SELVY, BARBARA, dance instructor; b. Little Rock, Jan. 20, 1938; d. James Oliver and Irene Balmat Banks; m. Franklin Delano Selvy, Apr. 15, 1959; children: Lisa Selvy Yeargin, Valerie Selvy Miros, Lauren, Franklin Michael. Student, U. Ctrl. Ark., 1955-57. Founder, dir. Carolina Ballet Theater, Greenville, S.C., 1973—; Advisory bd. dirs. Met. Arts Council and S.C. Governors Sch. Appeared in numerous TV commls., on Goodson-Toddman game show Play Your Hunch, 1958-59; toured Far East with TV show Hit Parade, 1958; named Miss Ark., 1956, Mrs. S.C., 1981; dir. and staged Mrs. Va., Mrs. N.C., Mrs. S.C. pageants; choreographed Little Theater prodns., Furman U. Opera. Mem. So. Assn. Dance Masters (ballet adviser, regional dir.), Dance Educators Am., Dance Masters of Am., Profl. Dance Tchrs. Home: 206 Honey Horn Dr Simpsonville SC 29681-5814 Office: Carolina Ballet Theatre 872 Woodruff Rd Greenville SC 29607-3538

SELWOOD, PIERCE TAYLOR, lawyer; b. Evanston, Ill., July 31, 1939; s. Pierce Wilson and Alice (Taylor) S.; m. Alexis Fuerbringer, June 8, 1964; children: Allison, Jonathan. AB, Princeton U., 1961; JD, Harvard U., 1964. Bar: Calif. 1965, U.S. Dist. Ct. (cen. dist.) Calif. 1965, U.S. Dist. Ct. (no. dist.) Calif. 1966, US. Dist. Ct. (ea. dist.) Calif. 1989, U.S. Ct. Appeals (9th cir.) 1970. Assoc. Sheppard, Mullin, Richter & Hampton, L.A., 1964-70, ptnr., 1971—, chmn. litigation dept., 1986-91; lectr. Calif. Continuing Edn. Bar, Berkley, 1970-84, Practicing Law Inst., N.Y.C., 1980s, ABA Nat. Inst., Chgo., 1986. Mem. ABA (chmn. various subcoms. 1984-89), Calif. Bar Assn., L.A. County Bar Assn., Assn. Bus. Trial Lawyers (bd. gov.s 1977-79), Jonathan Club (L.A.), Princeton Club So. Calif. (pres. 1970-72). Republican. Episcopalian. Avocations: tennis, hiking, camping, travel. Office: Sheppard Mullin Richter & Hampton 333 S Hope St Fl 48 Los Angeles CA 90071-1406

SELWYN, DONALD, engineering administrator, researcher, inventor, educator; b. N.Y.C., Jan. 31, 1936; s. Gerald Selwyn and Ethel (Waxman) Selwyn) Moss; m. Delia Nemec, Mar. 11, 1956 (div. Mar. 1983); children—Laurie, Gerald, Marcia; m. Myra Rowman Markoff, Mar. 17, 1986. B.A., Thomas A. Edison Coll. N.J., 1977. Service engr. Bendix Aviation, Teterboro, N.J., 1956-59; service mgr. Bogue Electric Mfg. Co., Paterson, N.J., 1959; proposal engr. advanced design group Curtiss-Wright Corp., East Paterson, N.J., 1960-64; ind. bioengr., rehab. engring. cons. N.Y.C., 1964-67; pres. bd. trustees, exec. tech. and tng. dir. Nat. Inst. for Rehab. Engring., Hewitt, N.J., 1967—; cons. N.Y. State Office Vocat. Rehab., 1964—, Pres.'s Com. on Employment of Handicapped, 1966—, bus. and industry and for Am. with Disabilities Act compliance, also numerous state rehab. agys., health depts., vol. groups, agys. for handicapped in fgn. countries; cons., trainer computer applications. Contbr. articles on amateur radio, rehab. of severely and totally disabled to profl., gen. mags. Trustee Nat. Inst. for Rehab. Engring., Rehab. Research Center Trust. Decorated Knight of Malta; recipient Humanitarian award U.S. Ho. of Reps., 1972, Bicentennial Pub. Service award, 1975. Mem. Am. Acad. Consultants, I.E.E.E. (sr.), Soc. Tech. Writers and Pubs. (sr.), Nat. Rehab. Assn., N.Y. Acad. Scis., Mensa. Achievements include being the developer or co-developer field-expander glasses for hemianopsia, tunnel and monocular vision, electronic speech clarifiers, electronically guided wheelchairs, off-road vehicles and cars for quadriplegics, others; patentee indsl., mil. and handicapped rehab. inventions; expert, cons. on handicapped employment, handicapped product safety including design, manufacture, labelling and user instrnl. material, 1990—. Office: Nat Inst Rehab Engring PO Box T Hewitt NJ 07421-1020 *As I travel the road of life, it becomes more and more evident to me that people matter most, and technology is useful and good only so long as it serves man, and man is not made to serve technology. From technician I have evolved to humanist, using technology only as a tool. Always think positive. Don't waste your time or emotional energy on people who do not appreciate your good will. Think only about those who do, and you'll achieve more and enjoy life.*

SELYA, BRUCE MARSHALL, federal judge; b. Providence, May 27, 1934; s. Herman C. and Betty (Brier) S.; m. Ellen Hazel Barnes, Feb. 27, 1965; children: Dawn Meredith Selya Sherman, Lori Ann. BA magna cum laude, Harvard U., 1955, JD magna cum laude, 1958. Bar: D.C. 1958, R.I. 1960. Law clk. U.S. Dist. Ct. R.I., Providence, 1958-60; assoc. Gunning & LaFazia, Providence, 1960-62; ptnr. Gunning, LaFazia, Gnys & Selya, Providence, 1963-74, Selya & Iannuccillo, Providence, 1974-82; judge U.S. Dist. Ct. R.I., Providence, 1982-86, U.S. Ct. Appeals (1st cir.), Providence, 1986—; judge Lincoln Probate Ct., R.I., 1965-72; mem. R.I. Jud. Council, 1964-72, sec., 1965-70, chmn., 1971-72; mem. Gov.'s Commn. on Crime and Adminstrn. Justice, 1967-69; del. Nat. Conf. on Revisions to Fed. Appellate Practice, 1968-82; mem. various spl. govtl. commns. and adv. groups. Chmn. bd. trustees Bryant Coll., Smithfield, R.I., 1986-92; bd. dirs. Lifespan Health Sys., chmn. bd. dirs., 1994—, mem. bd. trustees R.I. Hosp. subs. Recipient Louis Dembitz Brandeis medal for disting. legal svc. Brandeis U., 1988, Neil Houston award Justice Assistance of Am., 1992. Mem. ABA, FBA, Fed. Judges Assn., R.I. Bar Assn. (chmn. various coms.), R.I. Bar Found., U.S. Jud. Conf. (mem. com. on jud. br.), Am. Arbitration Assn., Am. Judicature Soc. (bd. dirs.). Jewish. Home: 137 Grotto Ave Providence RI 02906-5720 Office: US Ct Appeals 311 Fed Bldg & US Courthouse Providence RI 02903 also: 1704 McCormack Boston MA 02109

SELZ, PETER HOWARD, art historian, educator; b. Munich, Germany, Mar. 27, 1919; came to U.S., 1936, naturalized, 1942; s. Eugene and Edith S.; m. Thalia Cheronis, June 10, 1948 (div. 1965); children: Tanya Nicole Eugenia, Diana Gabrielle Hamlin; m. Carole Schemmerling, Dec. 18, 1983. Student, Columbia U., U. Paris; MA, U. Chgo., 1949, PhD, 1954; DFA, Calif. Coll. Arts and Crafts, 1967. Instr. U. Chgo., 1951-56; asst. prof. art history, head art edn. dept. Inst. Design, Ill. Inst. Tech., Chgo., 1949-55; chmn. art dept., dir. art gallery Pomona Coll., 1955-58; curator dept. painting and sculpture exhbns. Mus. Modern Art, 1958-65; dir. univ. art mus. U. Calif., Berkeley, 1965-73, prof. history of art, 1965—; Zaks prof. Hebrew U., Jerusalem, 1976; vis. prof. CUNY, 1987; mem. pres.'s council on art and architecture Yale U., 1971-76. Author: German Expressionist Painting, 1957, New Images of Man, 1959, Art Nouveau, 1960, Mark Rothko, 1961, Fifteen Polish Painters, 1961, The Art of Jean Dubuffet, 1962, Emil Nolde, 1963, Max Beckmann, 1964, Alberto Giacometti, 1965, Directions in Kinetic Sculpture, 1966, Funk, 1967, Harold Paris, 1972, Ferdinand Holder, 1972, Sam Francis, 1975, The American Presidency in Political Cartoons, 1976, Art in Our Times, 1981, Art in a Turbulent Era, 1985, Chillida, 1986, Twelve Artists from the GDR, 1989, Max Beckmann: The Self Portraits, 1992, William Congdon, 1992, Beckmann, 1996; co-author: Theories and Documents of Contemporary Art, 1996; editor: Art in Am., 1967—, Art Quar., 1969-75, Arts, 1981-92; contbr. articles to art publs. Trustee Am. Crafts Coun., 1985-89, Creators Equity Found., 1980—, Marin Mus. Assn., 1993—, Marin County Art Assn. 1993—; pres. Berkeley Art Project, 1988-93; mem. adv. coun. archives Am. Art, 1971—; project dir. Christo's Running Fence, 1973-76; commr. Alameda county Art Commn., 1990-95; mem. acquisitions com. Fine Arts Mus. San Francisco, 1993—. With OSS AUS, 1941-46. Decorated Order of Merit Fed. Republic Germany; Fulbright grantee Paris, 1949-50; fellow Belgian-Am. Ednl. Found.; sr. fellow NEH, 1972; resident Rockefeller Found. Study Ctr., Bellagio, 1994. Mem. Coll. Art Assn. Am. (dir. 1959-64, 67-71), AAUP, Internat. Art Critics Assn. Office: U Calif Dept Art History Berkeley CA 94720

SEMAK, MICHAEL WILLIAM, photographer, educator; b. Welland, Ont., Can., Jan. 9, 1934; s. John and Lena (Roketsky) S.; m. Annette Antoniuk, Jan. 30, 1960; children: James, Arlene. Student archtl. tech., Ryerson Poly. Inst., 1956-58. Freelance photographer Toronto-Pickering, 1961—; mem. faculty York U., Toronto, 1971—, assoc. prof. photography, 1977—. Exhibitor one-man shows, Image Gallery, N.Y.C., 1972, Il Diaframma Canon Gallery, Milan, Italy, 1976, Enjay Gallery, Boston, 1977, Ukraina Soc., Kiev, U.S.S.R., 1980, 81, group shows, Ont. Art Gallery, 1967, Expo '67 Internat. Exhbn., Montreal, 1967, Neikrug Gallery, N.Y.C., 1971; represented in permanent collections, Nat. Film Bd. Can., Ottawa, Nat. Gallery Can., Ottawa, Mus. Modern Art, N.Y.C., UN, Geneva. Recipient Photo Excellence Gold medal Nat. Film Bd., 1969; recipient Excellence award Pravda newspaper, Moscow, 1970, 71, Excellence diploma Fedn. Intenationale de l'art Photographique, Switzerland, 1972. Home: 1796 Spruce Hill Rd, Pickering, ON Canada L1V 1S4 Office: Dept Photography York U, 4700 Keeles St, Toronto, ON Canada M3J 1P3 *I see many contradictions around us, social realities which I believe rob us of our self-esteem and individuality. Must we continually accept and succumb to the never-ending hot baths for the mind society offers us? I wish my photography and words to disturb the complacent and the sleeper. I offer you cold showers for the mind.*

SEMANS, MARY DUKE BIDDLE TRENT, foundation administrator; b. N.Y., Feb. 21, 1920; d. Anthony Joseph Drexel and Mary (Duke) B.; m. Josiah Trent; m. James H. Semans. Attended, Hewitt Sch., N.Y.; AB in History, Duke U.; LLD (hon.), N.C. Cen. U., 1963; HHD (hon.), Elon Coll., 1965; degree (hon.), Davidson Coll., N.C. Wesleyan Coll., 1982, U.N.C. at Chapel Hill, Duke U., 1983; LLD (hon.), Furman U., 1993. trustee emeritus Duke U., 1961-81; chmn. The Duke Endowment, 1960—; various positions N.C. Sch. Arts, 1981—; former trustee Davidson Coll., N.C. Mus. Art, 1961-83, Shaw U., Converse U., Lincoln Hosp.; vice chmn. The Mary Duke Biddle Found., 1960—; chmn. Angier B. Duke Meml., Exec. Mansion Fine Arts Com., 1965—, Friends of Duke U. Library; pres. Durham Homes, Inc., 1968; mem. bd. dirs. Goodwill Industries of the Rsch. Triangle Area, 1964—, First Union Corp., 1980-82, N.C. State Library, 1958-61, Durham Pub. Library; numerous other positions. mem. Durham City Coun., 1951-55; mayor pro-tem City of Durham, 1953-55; commencement speaker Duke U., 1983. Recipient Merit award Duke U. Health and Hosp. Adminstrn. Alumni Assn., 1989, Giannini medal for meritorious svc. to N.C. Sch. of the Arts, 1990, Alan Keith-Lucas Friend of Children award N.C. Childcare Assn., 1991, Elna Spaulding award Women-in-Action, 1993, Outstanding Philanthropist award Triangle Chpt. Nat. Soc. Fund Raising Execs., 1993, Sam Ragan award St. Andrews Coll., 1993. Mem. LWV, Bus. and Profl. Women's Club, Altrusa Club, Half Century Club, Rotary Club. Democrat. Methodist. Home: 1415 Bivins St Durham NC 27707-1519 Office: The Mary Duke Biddle Found 1044 W Forest Hills Blvd Durham NC 27707-1678*

SEMAS, PHILIP WAYNE, editor; b. Gilroy, Calif., Feb. 23, 1946; s. Louis Alexander and Marian (Crapper) S.; m. Robin Lucille Tuttle, Sept. 7, 1967; children: Katherine Lucille, Anna Marian, Ellis Jeremy. Student, U. Oreg., 1963-67. Editor Coll. Press Service, Washington, 1967-68; free-lance writer Berkeley, Calif., 1968-69; asst. editor Chronicle of Higher Edn., Balt. and Washington, 1969-76, sr. editor, 1976-78, mng. editor, 1978-88; editor Chronicle of Philanthropy, Washington, 1988—. Recipient Higher Edn. Writers award, AAUP, 1974. Mem. Am. Soc. Mag. Editors. Home: 3403 Notre Dame St Hyattsville MD 20783-1910 Office: Chronicle of Philanthropy 1255 23rd St NW Washington DC 20037-1125

SEMAYA, FRANCINE L., lawyer; b. N.Y.C., Mar. 26, 1951; d. Julie and Ann (Tannenbaum) Levitt; m. Richard Semaya, Aug. 3, 1975; children: Stefanie Rachel, David Steven, Scott Brian. BA magna cum laude, Bklyn. Coll., 1973, MS magna cum laude, 1975; JD, N.Y. Law Sch., 1982. Bar: N.Y. 1983, U.S. Dist. Ct. (ea. and so. dists.) N.Y. 1983. Sr. legal analyst, atty. Am. Internat. Group, Inc., N.Y.C., 1977-83; assoc. counsel, asst. v.p. Beneficial Ins. Group, Inc. (formerly Benico, Inc.), Peapack, N.J., 1983-87; v.p., counsel Am. Centennial Ins. Co., Peapack, 1985-87; legal/reins. cons. Peapack, 1987; counsel reins. Integrity Ins. Co. in Liquidation, Paramus, N.J., 1988-91; ptnr. Werner & Kennedy, N.Y.C., 1991—. Editor: Law and Practice of Insurance Insolvency Revisited, 1989; contbg. editor Reference Handbook Ins. Co. Insolvency, 3rd edit., 1993. Mem. ABA (TIPS coun. 1994—, chair TIPS task force on ins. insolvency 1995—, chmn. pub. regulation of ins. law com. 1990-91, chair ABA/TIPS pub. rels. com. 1993-94, co-editor State Regulation Ins. 1991), N.Y. State Bar (PLI ins. law adv. com. 1995—), Phi Beta Kappa. Avocations: reading, travel. Office: Werner & Kennedy 1633 Broadway New York NY 10019-6708

SEMBER, JUNE ELIZABETH, retired elementary education educator; b. Apr. 3, 1932; d. Charles Benjamin and Cora Emma (Miller) Shoemaker; m. Eugene Sember, Oct. 18, 1975. BS with honors, Ea. Mennonite, 1957; postgrad., Columbia U., 1958, U. W.Va., 1960. Tchr. grades 1-6 Cross Roads Pvt. Sch., Salisbury, Pa., 1953-55; tchr. grade 5 Connellsville (Pa.) Area Schs., 1957-58, tchr. grade 2, 1958-66, tchr. grade 1, 1967-92, classroom vol., 1992—; supervising tchr. California (Pa.) U., 1970-90. Mem. Delta Kappa Gamma (pres. 1978-80). Presbyterian. Avocations: writing, traveling, reading nonfiction. Home: 1125 Pittsburgh St Scottdale PA 15683-1630 Office: Connellsville Area Schs 7th Ave Connellsville PA 15425

SEMBLER, MEL, company executive, former ambassador; b. 1930; m. Betty Schlesinger; children: Steve, Brent, Greg. BS, Northwestern U., 1952. Developer shopping ctrs.; amb. to Australia, Canberra, 1989-93; chmn. bd. The Sembler Co., St. Petersburg, Fla., 1962—; committeeman Rep. Nat. Com., Fla., S.E. regional chmn., nat. adv. coun. Team 100; bd. trustees George Bush Presdl. Libr. Found., Eckerd Coll., Internat. Coun. Shopping Ctrs.; bd. dirs. Pratt Industries, First Union Nat. Bank Fla., Pro Hispanic Polit. Action Com., Bush/Quayle Alumni Assn., Nat. Jewish Coalition, Holocaust Meml. Mus. Madiera Beach; resident mem. Fla. Coun. of 100. Mem. Internat. Coun. Shopping Ctrs. (pres. 1986-87). Office: 5858 Central Ave Saint Petersburg FL 33707-1728

SEMEGEN, PATRICK WILLIAM, lawyer; b. Akron, Ohio, Dec. 23, 1946; s. Stephen T. and Jane F. (Schmiedel) S.; m. Joann Kucharski, Jan. 10, 1975; children: Michael, Peter. B.S. in Econs., U. Pa., 1968; J.D., U. Mich., 1971. Bar: Ohio 1971, Calif. 1974. Chief crim. div. Summit County Prosecutor, Akron, Ohio, 1972-74; sole practice, Akron, and San Diego, 1974-77; litigation counsel Beneficial Corp., Peapack, N.J., 1977-81; v.p. gen. counsel, sec. Western Auto Supply Co., Kansas City, Mo., 1981—, also dir. Contbr. articles to profl. jours. Served to capt. USAR, 1968-71. Mem. ABA, Internat. Franchise Assn., Am. Fin. Services Assn., Am. Corp. Counsel Assn. Office: Western Auto Supply Co 2107 Grand Blvd Kansas City MO 64108-1806

SEMEL, TERRY, entertainment company executive; b. N.Y.C., Feb. 24, 1943; s. Ben and Mildred S.; m. Jane Bovingdon, Aug. 24, 1977; children: Eric Scott, Courtenay Jane, Lily Bovingdon Semel, Kate Bovingdon Semel. BS in Acctg., L.I.U., 1964; postgrad. in market research, CCNY, 1966-67. Domestic sales mgr. CBS Cinema Center Films, Studio City, Calif., 1970-72; v.p., gen. mgr. Walt Disney's Buena Vista, Burbank, Calif., 1972-75; pres. W.B. Distbn. Corp., Burbank, 1975-78; exec. v.p., chief operating officer Warner Bros., Inc., Burbank, 1979-80, pres., chief operating officer, from 1980;, 1980-94, chmn., co-CEO, 1994—; chmn., co-CEO Warner Music Group, 1995—; bd. dirs. Revlon. Vice chmn. Pres.'s Com. for the Arts and Humanities; vice chair San Diego Host Com. for 1996 Rep. Nat. Conv.; bd. dirs. Solomon R. Guggenheim Mus., Edn. First, Cedars Sinai Med. Ctr., Environ. Media Assn. Pioneer of the Year, 1990, Found. of Motion PicturesPioneers. Office: Warner Bros Inc 4000 Warner Blvd Burbank CA 91522-0001

SEMERAD, ROGER DALE, management consultant; b. Troy, N.Y., Sept. 9, 1940; s. Ralph Donald and Marjorie (Burdekin) S.; m. Cathryn Lucille Crangle, Nov. 27, 1965; 1 child, Samantha. B.A., Union Coll., 1962. Staff asst. to the Pres. White House, Washington, 1974-76; chmn., chief exec. officer Semerad Assocs. Inc., Washington, 1977-81; chmn. bd. 70001 Ltd., Washington, 1976-85; exec. v.p., trustee Brookings Instn., Washington, 1981-85; asst. sec. labor Dept. Labor, Washington, 1985-87; sr. v.p. policy devel. Am. Express Co., 1988-89; sr. v.p. RJR Nabisco, Inc., 1989-94; pres. RJR Nabisco Found., 1989-94. Co-author: Reinventing Education, 1994. Exec. sec. adv. policy councils Republican Nat. Com., Washington, 1977-80, exec. dir. platform com., 1980; bd. dirs. Bryce Harlow Found., Washington, 1982—, Hudson Inst., Indpls., 1993—; treas. New Am. Schs. Devel. Corp., Va., 1991—; mem. Sec.'s Commn. on Achieving Necessary Skills, Washington, 1990-92; mem. Nat. Coun. on Standards and Testing, Washington, 1991-92. Club: Metropolitan (Washington). Avocation: farming.

SEMERJIAN, HRATCH GREGORY, research and development executive; b. Istanbul, Turkey, Oct. 22, 1943; came to U.S., 1966; s. Krikor and Diruhi (Semerciyan) S.; m. Sona Kohar Kurkciyan, July 12, 1969 Idec. 1983); children: Tamar, Ara; m. Ayda Karabal, Feb. 8, 1986 (div. 1994). BSME, Robert Coll., Istanbul, 1966; MSc in Engring., Brown U., 1968, PhD in Engring., 1972. Rsch. asst. div. engring. Brown U., Providence, 1966-70; lectr. chemistry U. Toronto, Ont., Can., 1971-73; rsch. engr. Pratt & Whitney Aircraft United Technologies Corp., East Hartford, Conn., 1973-77; group leader Ctr. for Chem. Tech. Nat. Bur. Standards (now Nat. Inst. Standards and Tech.), Gaithersburg, Md., 1977-87, divsn. chief Chem. Sci. and Tech. Lab., 1987-92, dir. Chem. Sci. and Tech. Lab., 1992—; organizer tech. sessions, confs. and symposiums for various profl. orgns., 1978—. Contbr. rsch. articles to profl. publs.; editor numerous conf. procs. Mem. parish coun. St. George Armenian Apostolic Ch., Hartford, Conn., 1975-77; chmn. parish coun., dir. choir St. Mary Armenian Apostolic Ch., Washington, 1977—; coach youth soccer Montgomery Soccer Inc., Rockville, Md., 1978-81; mem. Ani Armenian Choral Group, Washington, 1988—. Hagopian scholar Robert Coll., 1961-64, A.M.&F. corp. fellow, 1965, C.B. Keen fellow Brown U., 1969; recipient Silver medal Dept. Commerce, Washington, 1984, Gold medal Dept. Commerce, Washington, 1995; named Fed. Engr. of Yr., NSPE, Washington, 1991. Mem. AAAS, AIAA, ASME, AIChE, Am. Chem. Soc., Combustion Inst. Avocations: soccer, singing, boating. Office: Nat Inst Standards and Tech Bldg 222 Rm A317 Gaithersburg MD 20899

SEMION, A. KAY, editor; b. New Castle, Ind., July 27, 1944; d. Lowell Ernest and T. Byrneta (Byrne) Hooker; m. William Alexander Semion, June 21, 1969; children: Justin Alexander, Sonja Katherine. BA, Purdue U., 1966; AA, Delta Coll., 1974; MA, Wayne State U., 1981. Reporter The Flint (Mich.) Jour., 1966-70, The Daily Eagle, Wayne, Mich., 1970-71, The Bay City (Mich.) Times, 1971-72; copy editor The Ann Arbor (Mich.) News, 1979-83, editl. page editor, 1983—. Newsletter chmn. Lamaze Wayne County, Canton, Mich., 1977-80; leader La Leche League, Canton, 1978-81. Recipient Orthy awards Ch. 19 PBS, Bay City, 1973, 74. Mem. Soc. Profl. Journalists, Nat. Conf. Editl. Writers (chair mgmt. com., 1993-95, co-chair, mem. svcs. com. 1995—). Home: 41629 Larimore Ln Canton MI 48187-3921 Office: The Ann Arbor News PO Box 1147 Ann Arbor MI 48106-1147

SEMLER, DEAN, cinematographer. Productions include: (fims) Let the Balloon Go, 1976, Hoodwink, 1980, The Road Warrior, 1980, Kitty and the Bagman, 1981, Razorback, 1984, The Coca-Cola Kid, 1986, Mad Max Beyond Thunderdome, 1985, TV Film: Passion Flower, 1985, Going Sane 1985, Bulls Eye, 1986, The Lighthorsemen, 1986, Cocktail, 1988, Young Guns, 1988, Farewell to the King, 1987, Dead Calm, 1987, K-9, 1988, Impulse, 1990, Young Guns II, 1990, Dances with Wolves, 1990 (Academy award 1991), City Slickers, 1991, Power of One, 1991, Super Mario Bros, 1992, Last Action Hero, 1992, The Three Musketeers, 1993, The Cowboy Way, 1993, Waterworld, 1994. Mem. Australian Cinematographers Soc.. Office: 4324 Promenade Way Apt 317 Marina Del Rey CA 90292 Office: Smith/Gosnell/Nicholson & Assoc PO Box 1166 1515 Palisades Dr Pacific Palisades CA 90272

SEMLER, DEAN RUSSELL, food company executive; b. East St. Louis, Ill., Mar. 25, 1929; s. Ray Russell and Margaret Mildred (Swindler) S.; m. Mary Ann Millhoff, Feb. 10, 1961; 1 son, James R. Student, Dyke Spencerian Bus. Coll., 1947-48, Akron U., 1950-56. Plant contr. Ohio Match Co., Wadsworth, O., 1948-58; corp. contr. Ohio Match Co., 1958-61; regional contr. Hunt-Wesson Foods, Inc., Gretna, La., 1961-63; ops. contr. Hunt-Wesson Foods, Inc., Fullerton, Calif., 1963-68; corp. controller Hunt-Wesson Foods, Inc., 1968-78, v.p., contr., 1978-84, sr. v.p. fin., 1984-90; ret., 1990. Mem. Nat. Assn. Accountants. Home: 106 Demmer Dr Placentia CA 92670-2514

SEMLER, JERRY D., insurance company executive; b. Indpls., Mar. 5, 1937; m. Rosemary Semler; children: Mary, Jack, Kristin, Kimberly, Michael, Jeffrey, Sally. BS, Purdue U., 1958; postgrad. bus. exec. program, Stanford U., 1984. CLU; registered health underwriter. With Am. United Life Ins. Co., Indpls., 1959—, pres., 1980-84, pres., chief oper. officer, 1984-89, pres., chief exec. officer, 1989—, chmn. bd., pres., chief exec. officer, 1991—, also bd. dirs.; bd. dirs. MDRT Found. Bd. dirs. United Way Cen. Ind., Indpls. Conv. and Visitors Bur., Ind. Sports Corp., Ind. C. of C.; bd. dirs., mem. exec. com. Indpls. Downtown Inc.; chmn. bd. Ctr. for Leadership Devel. Inc., Noble Found.; chmn. bd. Ind. Repertory Theatre, Am. Coll. of Sports Medicine Found., Jenn Found.; mem. dean's adv. council Purdue U. Krannert Sch. Mgmt.; hon. dir. "500" Festival Assocs., Purdue Univ. Pres.'s Coun.; bd. advisors Ind. U. Sch. Medicine; trustee Eiteljorg Mus.; bd. trustees Indpls. Parks Found.; bd. assocs. Rose Hulman Inst. Tech., bd. dirs. IWC Resources Corp. With U.S. Army. Mem. Health Ins. Assn. Am., Am. Coll. Life Underwriters, Nat. Assn. Life Underwriters, Million Dollar Round Table (life), Ind. C. of C. (bd. dirs.), Life Office Mgmt. Assn. (bd. dirs.), Assn. Ind. Life Ins. Cos. (pres., mem. exec. com.), Life Ins. Mktg. and Rsch. Assn. (bd. dirs., chmn. bd.), Alpha Tau Omega. Roman Catholic. Office: Am United Life Ins Co 1 American Sq PO Box 368 Indianapolis IN 46206

SEMLYEN, ADAM, electrical engineering educator; b. Gherla, Romania, Jan. 10, 1923; came to Can., 1969; naturalized, 1974; s. Aurel and Anna (Gyorgy) S.; m. Mary Semlyen; 1 dau., Georgeta. Dipl. Ing., Poly. Inst. Timisoara, Romania, 1949; Ph.D., Poly. Inst. Iasi, Romania. Engr. Regional Power Authority, Timisoara, Romania, 1949-51; mem. faculty Poly. Inst. Timisoara, 1949-69, prof., 1968-69; prof. dept. elec. engring. U. Toronto, Ont., Can., 1969-88, prof. emeritus, 1988—. Fellow IEEE. Home:

65 High Park Ave # 2203, Toronto, ON Canada M6P 2R7 Office: U Toronto Dept Elec & Computer Engring, 10 King's College Rd, Toronto, ON Canada M5S 3G4

SEMM, KURT KARL, obstetrics & gynecology researcher/department head; b. 1927. MD, U. Munich. Prof. ob-gyn. univ. clinic U. Munich, 1953-70; dir. dept. ob-gyn. Michaelis Midwifery Sch., Christian Albrechts U., Kiel, Germany, 1970—. Mem. German-French Soc. for Ob-Gyn. (pres. 1976-88), Internat. Fed. of Fertility Socs. (sec.-gen. 1976-84, v.p. 1984—), European Sterility Congress Orgn. (sec.-gen. 1965—), Internat. Fedn. of Gynaecologic Endoscopists (v.p. 1984—). Office: Frauen Klinik, 24143 Kiel Germany*

SEMMEL, BERNARD, historian, educator; b. N.Y.C., July 23, 1928; s. Samuel and Tillie (Beer) S.; m. Maxine Loraine Guse, Mar. 19, 1955; 1 child, Stuart Mill. B.A., CCNY, 1947; M.A., Columbia U., 1951, Ph.D., 1955; postgrad., London Sch. Econs., 1959-60. With Nat. Citizens Commn. for Pub. Schs. and Coun. for Fin. Aid to Edn., N.Y.C., 1951-55; asst. prof. history Park Coll., Parkville, Mo., 1956-60; mem. faculty SUNY, Stony Brook, 1960-91; prof. history SUNY, 1964-91, chmn. dept., 1966-69; Disting. prof. Grad. Sch. CUNY, 1991-96; vis. prof. Columbia U., 1966-67. Author: Imperialism and Social Reform, 1960, Jamaican Blood and Victorian Conscience, 1963, The Rise of Free Trade Imperialism, 1970, The Methodist Revolution, 1973, John Stuart Mill and the Pursuit of Virtue, 1984, Liberalism and Naval Strategy, 1986, The Liberal Ideal and The Demons of Empire, 1993, George Eliot and the Politics of National Inheritance, 1994; editor: Occasional Papers of T.R. Malthus, 1963; editor, translator: Halévy's The Birth of Methodism in England, 1971; editor Jour. Brit. Studies, 1969-74, Marxism and the Science of War, 1981. Rockefeller Found. grantee, 1959-60; Am. Council Learned Socs. fellow, 1964-65; Guggenheim fellow, 1967-68, 74-75; Nat. Humanities Ctr. fellow, 1986-87. Fellow Royal Hist. Soc.; mem. Am. Hist. Assn. (profl. divsn. 1984-86), Conf. Brit. Studies, Phi Beta Kappa. Club: Cosmos. Home: PO Box 1162 Stony Brook NY 11790-0749

SEMMEL, JOAN, artist, educator; b. N.Y.C., Oct. 19, 1932; d. Lawrence and Sarah (Zucker) Alperstein; children: Patricia, Andrew. Diploma, Cooper Union Art Sch., N.Y.C., 1952; student, Art Students League, N.Y.C., 1958-59; BFA, Pratt Inst., 1963, MFA, 1972. Teaching positions Md. Inst. Art, Balt., 1973, Rutgers U., Livingston, N.J., 1974-75, Bklyn. Mus. Art Sch., 1976-78, Mason Gross Sch. Arts, Rutgers U., New Brunswick, N.J., 1978—; mem. jury Nat. Endowment for Arts, Washington, 1983, N.J. State Coun. on the Arts, 1990, 93. Solo exhbns. include Ateneo de Madrid, 1966, Mus. Plastic Arts, Montevideo, Uruguay, 1968, Juana Mordo Gallery, Madrid, 1969, Pratt Inst., N.Y.C., 1972, Lerner-Heller Gallery, N.Y.C., 1975, 78, 79, Manhattanville Coll., Purchase, N.Y., 1985, BentonGallery, Southampton, N.Y., 1987, Skidmore Coll., Saratoga Springs, N.Y., 1992, SUNY Albany, 1992, SUNY Oswego, 1992, Pratt Manhattan Ctr., N.Y.C., 1993; exhibited in group shows at Mus. Modern Art, Barcelona, Salon Nacional, Madrid, Concurso Nacional, Madrid, Moravian Coll., Bethlehem, Pa., Bronx Mus., Whitney Mus., N.Y.C., Bklyn. Mus., Mus. of U. Tex., Chrysler Mus., Norfolk, Va., Henry St. Settlement, N.Y.C., Ball State U. Art Gallery, Ft. Wayne (Ind.) Art Mus., Indpls. Art League, Hudson Ctr. Gallery, N.Y.C., Mint Mus., Charlotte, N.C., L.I. U., Brookville, N.Y., Tampa (Fla.) Mus. Art, Richard Anderson Gallery, N.Y.C., David Zwirmer Gallery, N.Y.C., N.J. State Mus., Trenton, numerous others; represented in collections at Mus. Contemporary Art, Houston, Tex., Mus. of Univ. Tex., Austin, Chrysler Mus., Norfolk, Va., N.J. State Mus. Art, Mus. of Women in the Arts, Greenville County Mus., Greenville, S.C., numerous others; numerous commns, especially for portraits; subject of articles and book chpts. Grantee Nat. Endowment for the arts, 1980, 85, Yaddo Colony, 1980, MacDowell Colony, 1977, others. Address: 109 Spring St New York NY 10012

SEMON, WARREN LLOYD, retired computer sciences educator; b. Boise, Ida., Jan. 17, 1921; s. August and Viola Lorreta (Eastman) S.; m. Ruth Valerie Swift, Dec. 1, 1945; children—Warren Lloyd, Nolan David, Jonathan Richard, Sue Anne. Student, Hobart Coll., 1940-43; S.B., U. Chgo., 1944; M.A., Harvard, 1949, Ph.D., 1954. Lectr. applied math. Harvard U., Cambridge, Mass., 1956-61, asst. dir. computation lab., 1954-61; head applied math. dept. Sperry Rand Research Ctr., Sudbury, Mass., 1961-64; mgr. computation and analysis lab. Burroughs Research Ctr., Paoli, Pa., 1964-67; prof. computer sci. Syracuse (N.Y.) U., 1967-84, prof. emeritus, 1984—, dir. system and information sci., 1968-76, dean Sch. Computer and Info. Sci., 1976-84; cons. USAF, 1957, NSA, 1957, Lockheed Electronics Corp., 1967, Monsanto Co., 1972. Contbr. profl. jours. Served to 1st lt. USAAF, 1943-46, MTO. Fellow IEEE; mem. Assn. Computing Machinery, Math. Assn. Am., IEEE Computer Soc. (chmn. publs. com. 1972-74, bd. govs. 1973-74, editor-in-chief 1975-76), Sigma Xi. Address: F54807 PO Box 44209 Cincinnati OH 45244-0209

SEMONIN, RICHARD GERARD, retired state official; b. Akron, Ohio, June 25, 1930; s. Charles Julius and Catherine Cecelia (Schooley) S.; m. Lennie Stuker, Feb. 3, 1951; children: Cecelia C., Richard G. Jr., James R., Patricia R. BS, U. Wash., 1955. With Ill. State Water Survey, Champaign, 1955-91, chief, 1986-91, chief emeritus, 1991—; adj. prof. U. Ill., 1975-91; chmn. Ill. Low-Level Radioactive Waste Task Group, 1994-96. Contbr. chpts. to books and articles to profl. jours.; co-editor: Atmospheric Deposition, 1983. Staff sgt. USAF, 1948-52. Grantee NSF, 1957-76, U.S. Dept. Energy, 1965-90. Fellow AAAS, Am. Meteorol. Soc. (councilor 1983-86); mem. Nat. Weather Assn. (councilor 1978-81), Weather Modification Assn., Ill. Acad. Scis., Sigma Xi. Roman Catholic. Avocations: Civil war, golf, fishing, genealogy. Home: 1902 Crescent Dr Champaign IL 61821-5826 Office: Ill State Water Survey 2204 Griffith Dr Champaign IL 61820-7463

SEMORE, MARY MARGIE, abstractor; b. Cowlington, Okla., Feb. 11, 1920; d. William Leonard and Bessie Mae (Bellah) Barnett; m. Jack Sanford Semore, Mar. 3, 1940 (dec. Jan. 1985). Grad. high sch., Wagoner, Okla., 1938. Legal sec. W.O. Rittenhouse, Wagoner, Okla., 1938-40; abstractor Wagoner County Abstract Co., 1941—. Mem. Title Industry Polit. Action Com., Washington, 1986, Am. Legion Women's Aux., Wagoner Hist. Soc. Mem. Okla. Land Title Assn., Am. Land Title Assn., Wagoner C. of C., DAR, Daus. Am. Colonists. Democrat. Methodist. Avocations: photography, hunting, fishing, golf, swimming. Home: 902 S White Ave Wagoner OK 74467-7239 Office: Wagoner County Abstract Co 219 E Cherokee PO Box 188 Wagoner OK 74477

SEMPLE, CECIL SNOWDON, retired manufacturing company executive; b. Assam, India, Aug. 12, 1917; came to U.S., 1927, naturalized, 1948; s. Fordyce B. and Anne (Munro) S. B.A., Colgate U., 1939. Buyer R.H. Macy & Co., 1939-42, 46-48; buyer, div. supt. Montgomery Ward, 1948-50; v.p. Nachman Corp., Chgo., 1950-55; sales mgr. radio receiver dept. Gen. Elec. Co., Bridgeport, Conn., 1955-60; mktg. cons. merchandising Gen. Elec. Co., N.Y.C., 1966-67, gen. mgr. audio products dept., 1967-68, dep. div. gen. mgr. housewares div., 1968-69, gen. mgr. housewares div., 1969, v.p., 1969-71, v.p. corp. customer relations, 1971-85; v.p. Rich's Inc., Atlanta, 1960-62, sr. v.p., dir., 1962-66; trustee Peoples Bank., Bridgeport, 1975-89, trustee emeritus. Bd. dirs. Nat. Jr. Achievement Inc., 1974-86, Bridgeport Area Found., 1970-91, dir. emeritus, 1991—; bd. dirs. Bridgeport Hosp., 1970-93, chmn., 1983-89, dir. emeritus, 1993—; bd. trustees Colgate U., 1970-84, vice chmn. 1978-84; trustee emeritus, past pres., bd. dirs. Alumni Corp., chmn. So. Conn. Health Svc. Inc., 1990-93. Served to maj. USAAF, 1942-46. Mem. St. Andrews Soc. State N.Y. (chmn. bd. mgrs. 1968-70), Delta Kappa Epsilon. Clubs: Brooklawn Country (Fairfield, Conn.), Fairfield Country. Home: 25 Cartright St Bridgeport CT 06604

SEMPLE, JAMES WILLIAM, lawyer; b. Phila., Nov. 18, 1943; s. Calvin James and Marie (Robinson) S.; m. Ellen Burns, Nov. 26, 1966; children: Megan Ward, Luke Robinson. AB, St. Josephs U., Phila., 1965; JD, Villanova U., 1974. Bar: Del. 1974, U.S. Dist. Ct. Del. 1974, D.C. 1975, U.S. Ct. Appeals (3d cir.) 1982. Ptnr. Morris, James, Hitchens & Williams, Wilmington, 1983—; lectr. numerous seminars; mediator Superior Ct. Voluntary Mediation Program. Mem. ABA (bus. law sect., litigation sect., torts and ins. practice sect.), Del. Bar Assn. (mem. exec. com. 1978, 80, 81, asst. sec. 1980, sec. 1981, chmn. torts and ins. practice sect. 1982-84), Am. Bd. Trial Advs., Fedn. Ins. and Corp. Counsel, Am. Judicatrue Soc., Def. Counsel Del. (charter pres. 1988), Am. Soc. Law and Medicine, Assn. Internat. de Droit d'Assurance, Am. Inns of Ct. (Richard Rodney chpt.). Democrat. Roman Catholic. Clubs: Wilmington Country (Greenville, Del.). Home: 103 Brookvalley Rd Wilmington DE 19807-2003 Office: Morris James Hitchens & Williams PO Box 2306 Wilmington DE 19899-2306

SEMPLE, LLOYD ASHBY, lawyer; b. St. Louis, June 7, 1939; s. Robert B. and Isabelle A. S.; m. Cynthia T. Semple, Aug. 26, 1961; children: Whitney, Sarah, Lloyd Jr., Terrell. BA, Yale U., 1961; JD, U. Mich, 1964. Bar: Mich. 1964. Assoc. Dykema Gossett, Detroit, 1964-70, ptnr., 1971-94; chmn., 1994—; gen. counsel Daedalus Enterprises, Inc., Ralph Wilson Enterprises, Copper & Bass Sales; bd. dirs. Interface Sys., Inc. Councilman, mayor pro tem City of Grosse Pointe Farms, Mich, 1975-83; chmn. bd., trustee Harper Hosp.; bd. trustees Detroit Med. Ctr. Corp.; bd. dirs. Detroit Zool. Soc.; dir., trustee Karmanos Cancer Inst. Mem. ABA, Mich. Bar Assn., Detroit Bar Assn., Country Club, Yondotega Club, Detroit Athletic Club, Yale Club (N.Y.C.), Bohemian Club (San Francisco). Episcopalian. Home: 57 Cambridge Rd Grosse Pointe MI 48236-3004 Office: Dykema Gossett 400 Renaissance Ctr Detroit MI 48243-1507

SEMPLE, ROBERT BAYLOR, JR., newspaper editor, journalist; b. St. Louis, Aug. 12, 1936; s. Robert B. and Isabelle Ashby (Neer) S.; m. Susan Riker Kirk, Aug. 19, 1961 (div. Feb. 1980); children: Robert Baylor III, Elizabeth, William, Mary; m. Lisa Pulling, Jan. 10, 1981. Grad., Phillips Acad., 1954; B.A., Yale U., 1959; M.A., U. Calif., Berkeley, 1961. Reporter Nat. Observer, 1961-63; corr. N.Y. Times, 1963-68, White House corr., 1968-72, dep. nat. editor, 1973-75, London bur. chief, 1975-77; fgn. editor N.Y. Times, N.Y.C., 1977-82, op-ed page editor, 1982-88, assoc. editor editorial page, 1988—. Recipient Pulitzer prize for editorial writing, 1996; Carnegie fellow, 1959-60; Woodrow Wilson fellow, 1960-61. Mem. Coun. Fgn. Rels., Century Assn. (N.Y.C.), Yale Club (N.Y.C.). Episcopalian. Office: 229 W 43rd St New York NY 10036-3913

SEMPLE, THOMAS CARL, physical-organic chemist; b. Attleboro, Mass., July 16, 1959; s. Alan R. and Janice L. (Jordan) S.; m. Antoinette Marie Gambini, Nov. 17, 1990; children: Alana G., Alexandra C. ScB, MIT, 1981; PhD, Brown U., 1986. Rsch. fellow Yale U., New Haven, 1986-88; process rsch. chemist Shell Chem. Co., Houston, 1988—. Contbr. articles to profl. jours. Mem. AAAS, Am. Chem. Soc., NYAS, Sigma Xi. Achievements include patents on new methods for hydroformylation, alkoxylation, and PET recycle processes. Home: 401 Falling Leaf Dr Friendswood TX 77546-4521 Office: Shell Chem Co WTC 3333 Highway 6 S Houston TX 77082-3101

SEMROD, T. JOSEPH, banker; b. Oklahoma City, Dec. 13, 1936; s. L.J. and Theda Jo (Hummel) S.; m. Janice Lee Wood, June 1, 1968 (div. 1988); children: Ronald, Catherine, Christopher, Elizabeth; m. Jaye Patricia Hewitt, May 27, 1989; 1 child, Kelsey. B.A. in Polit. Sci., U. Okla., 1958, LL.B., 1963. Bar: Okla. 1963. With Liberty Nat. Bank, Oklahoma City, 1963-81; v.p. Liberty Nat. Bank, 1967-69, sr. v.p., 1969-71, exec. v.p., 1971-73, pres., 1973-81; pres. Liberty Nat. Corp., Oklahoma City, 1976-81; chmn. bd., pres., chief exec. officer United Jersey Banks (name now UJB Fin. Corp.), Princeton, N.J., 1981-96; chmn., CEO, Summit Bancorp. (merged with UJB Fin. Corp.), Princeton, 1996—; chmn. bd. dirs. United Jersey Bank, Hackensack, N.J., 1981—; chmn. Internat. Fin. Conf., 1994. Bd. dirs. Fed. Res. Bank of N.Y., 1983-86; trustee, mem. exec. com. Nat. Urban League; mem. bd. advisors Outward Bound, Inc., 1984—, Ind. Coll. Fund N.J., 1986-90; commr. Citizens Commn. on Aids, 1988-90; chmn. bd. regents Stonier Grad. Sch. Banking, Rutgers U., 1983; mem. N.J. Transp. Trust Fund Authority, 1985-87; chmn. The Partnership for N.J., 1989-90, trustee; mem. N.J. Com.-U.S. Savings Bonds com.; chmn. banking industry U.S. Savs. Bonds campaign, 1992-93. 1st lt. U.S. Army, 1958-60. Mem. Am. Bankers Assn., N.J. Bankers Assn., N.J. Bar Assn., Okla. Bar Assn., Baankers Roundtable (bd. dirs. 1995—), Regional Plan Assn. (bd. dirs. 1989-91), Young Pres. Orgn., Am. Running and Fitness Assn. (bd. dirs. 1983-86), N.J. C. of C. (bd. dirs., vice chmn.), Drumthwacket Found. (chmn. 1990-94), Bedens Brook Club (Skillman, N.J.), River Club (N.Y.C.), Metedoconk Club (Jackson, N.J.), Coral Beach Club (Bermuda), Nassau Club, Tournament Players Club. Democrat. Roman Catholic. Office: Summit Bancorp PO Box 2066 301 Carnegie Ctr Princeton NJ 08543-2066

SEN, AMARTYA KUMAR, economist, educator; b. Santiniketan, India, Nov. 3, 1933; s. Ashutosh and Amita S. BA, Calcutta U., 1953; BA, Cambridge U., 1955, PhD, 1958; D.Litt. (hon.), U. Sask., 1979, Visva-Bharati U., 1983, U. Essex, 1984, Georgetown U., 1989, Jødavpur U., 1990, Kalyani U., 1990, Athens U. of Econs. and Bus., 1991, Williams Coll., 1991, London Guildhall U., 1991, New Sch. Social Rsch., 1992, Calcutta U., 1992, Oberlin Coll., 1993, Syracuse U., 1994, Wesleyan U., 1995, U. Oxford, 1996; D.Sc. (hon.), U. Bath, 1984, U. Edinburgh, 1995, Docteur Honoris Causa U. Caen, 1987, Louvain, 1989, U. Valencia, 1994, U. Zurich, 1994, U. Antwerp, 1995, U. Stockholm, 1996; Dottore ad honorem, U. Bologna, 1988; LL.D. (hon.) U. Tulane, 1990, Queen's U., 1993. Prof. econs. Jadavpur U., Calcutta, 1956-58; fellow Trinity Coll., Cambridge U., 1957-63; prof. econs. Delhi U., 1963-71, London Sch. Econs., 1971-77; prof. econs. Oxford U., 1977-80, Drummond prof. polit. economy, 1980-88; prof. econs. and philosophy Harvard U., 1987—; Lamont U. prof. Harvard U., 1988—, vis. prof., 1968-69; vis. prof. U. Calif., Berkeley, 1964-65; Andrew D. White prof.-at-large Cornell U., Ithaca, N.Y., 1978-84; chmn. expert group role advanced skill and tech. UN, 1967; hon. fellow Trinity Coll., Cambridge, Inst. Social Studies, The Hague, Inst. Devel. Studies, U. Sussex, London Sch. Econs., U. London. Fellow Brit. Acad., Econometric Soc. (past pres.); mem. AAAS (fgn. hon. mem), Am. Econ. Assn. (past pres.), Indian Econ. Assn. (past pres.), Royal Econ. Soc. (v.p.), Indian Econometric Conf., Devel. Studies Assn. (past pres.), Internat. Econ. Assn. (pres. 1986-89, hon. pres.), Agnelli Internat. prize 1990, Alan Shawn Feinstein World Hunger award 1990. Author: Choice of Techniques, 1960; Collective Choice and Social Welfare, 1970, Growth Economics, 1970, On Economic Inequality, 1973, Employment, Technology and Development, 1975, Poverty and Famines: An Essay on Entitlement and Deprivation, 1981, Utilitarianism and Beyond, 1982, Choice, Welfare and Measurement, 1982, Resources, Values and Development, 1984, Commodities and Capabilities, 1985, On Ethics and Economics, 1987, The Standard of Living, 1987, Hunger and Public Action, 1989, Inequality Reexamined, 1992, Quality of Life, 1993, India: Economic Development and Social Opportunity, 1995; contbr. articles to profl. jours. Office: Harvard U Dept Econs Cambridge MA 02138

SEN, ASHISH KUMAR, urban planner, educator; b. Delhi, India, June 8, 1942; came to U.S., 1967, naturalized, 1985; s. Ashoka Kumar and Arati Sen; m. Colleen Taylor. BS with honors, Calcutta U., 1962; MA, U. Toronto, Ont., Can., 1964, PhD, 1971. Research assoc., lectr. dept. geography Transp. Center, Northwestern U., 1967-69; mem. faculty Center Urban Studies, U. Ill., Chgo., 1969—; prof. Center Urban Studies, U. Ill., 1978—, dir. Sch. Urban Planning, 1991; dean Center Urban Studies, U. Ill. (Sch. Urban Scis.), 1977-78, acting dir., 1992; pres. Ashish Sen. and Assocs., Chgo., 1977—. Author: Regression Analysis: Theory, Methods and Applications, 1990, Gravity MOdels of Spatial Interaction Behavior, 1995; also articles. Mem. Chgo. Bd. Edn., 1990-95; chmn. budget com. 1992-94; bd. trustees Asian Inst., 1993—. Fellow Royal Statis. Soc.; mem. Am. Statis. Assn., Inst. Math. Stats., Am. Soc. Planning Ofcls., Regional Sci. Assn., Transp. Rsch. Forum, Transp. Rsch. Bd., Cliffdwellers. Hindu. Home: 2557 W Farwell Ave Chicago IL 60645-4617

SEN, PARESH CHANDRA, electrical engineering educator; b. Patiya, Chittagong, Bangladesh, June 30, 1938; arrived in Can., 1963; s. Judhistir and Jaya Sen; m. Maya Dey, July 21, 1968; children: Sujit, Priya, Debashis. BSc with honors, Calcutta (India) U., 1958, MSc Tech., 1961; MASc., U. Toronto, Ont., Can., 1965; PhD, U. Toronto, 1967. Registered profl. engr., Ont. Elec. engr. TISCO, Dhanbad, India, 1961-62, DVC, Maithon, India, 1962-63; teaching asst. U. Toronto, 1963-65, 65-67; rsch. asst. Northern Electric Co., Ottawa, Ont., 1965; profl. assoc. Queen's U., Kingston, Ont., 1967-68; asst. prof. elec. engring. Queen's U., Kingston, 1968-73, assoc. prof., 1973-79, prof., 1979—; cons. Urban Transp. Devel. Corp., Alcan Ltd., Kingston, 1975-80; sr. indsl. fellow Inverpower Control Ltd., Toronto, 1985-86. Author: Thyristor DC Drives, 1981, Principles of Electric Machines and Power Electronics, 1989. Fellow IEEE (prize paper award indsl. drive com. 1986). Hindu. Avocations: oil painting, reading novels. Office: Queens Univ, Dept Elec Engring, Kingston, ON Canada K7L 3N6

SENAHA, EIKI, English literature educator, university dean; b. Nago, Okinawa, Japan, Nov. 20, 1928; s. Eiko and Kami (Toguchi) S.; m. Shizu Kishimoto, Feb. 15, 1954; children: Yoko Shayesteh, Eijun, Tatsuko. BS, Ctrl. Mo. State U., 1959, MA, 1959; MPhil, U. Kans., 1971, PhD, 1977. Asst. prof. Okinawa (Japan) U., 1959-65; prof. U. Ryukyus, Japan, 1965-94, dir. librs., 1983-85, dean edn., 1985-89, chair internat. programs, 1991-94; prof., dean Meio (Japan) U., 1994—; interviewer Soc. for Testing English Proficiency, Japan, 1978—; examiner Okinawa Human Resources Devel. Found., Japan, 1982—; screener Fulbright Found., Japan, 1986—; sec. gen. VII Pacific Sci. Inter-Congress, Japan, 1990-94. Author: (book) Essays for Professor Genshu Asato, 1972, Japanese Responses to Wordsworth's Concept of Nature, 1976; contbr. articles to profl. jours. Scholar Govt. of U.S., 1957-59, 67-71; rsch. grantee Govt. of Japan, 1976-77. Mem. English Lit. Soc. Japan, English Romantic Soc. Japan, English Romantic Soc. Okinawa (pres. 1994—), Pacific Sci. Assn. (Japan nat. com. 1990—, coun. 1990—). Avocations: sports, travel. Office: Meio U, 1220-1 Biimata, Nago 905, Japan

SENCHAK, MARLISA, financial organization. V.p., asst. to chmn. Fed. Nat. Mortgage Assn., Washington, 1994—. Home: Fed Nat Mortgage Assn Office of Chmn 3900 Wisconsin Ave NW Washington DC 20016-2899

SENDAK, MAURICE BERNARD, writer, illustrator; b. Bklyn., June 10, 1928; s. Philip and Sadie (Schindler) S. Student, Art Students League, N.Y.C., 1949-51; LHD, Boston U., 1977; hon. degree, U. So. Miss., 1981, Keene State Coll., 1986. Window display artist Timely Svc., N.Y.C., 1946; display artist FAO Schwartz, N.Y.C., 1948-51; co-founder, artistic dir. The Night Kitchen, 1990—. One-man shows include Gallery Sch. Visual Arts, N.Y.C., 1964, Rosenbach Found., Phila., 1970, 75, Trinity Coll., 1972, Galerie Daniel Keel, Zurich, 1974, Ashmolean Mus., Oxford, 1975, Am. Cultural Center, Paris, 1978, Pierpont Morgan Library, N.Y.C., 1981; author, illustrator: Kenny's Window, 1956 (Spring Book Fesitval honor book 1956), Very Far Away, 1957, The Acrobat, 1959, The Sign on Rosie's Door, 1960, The Nutshell Library (contains Chicken Soup with Rice, One Was Johnny, Alligators All Around, Pierre: A Cautionary Tale), 1962, Where The Wild Things Are, 1963 (N.Y. Times Best Illustrated Book award 1963, Caldecott medal 1964, Lewis Carroll Shelf award 1964, Internat. Bd. on Books for Young People award 1966, Art Books for Children award 1973, 74, 75, Best Young Picture Books Paperback award Redbook Mag. 1984, Children's Choice award 1985), Hector Protector and As I Went Over the Water: Two Nursery Rhymes, 1965, Higglety, Pigglety, Pop!; or, There Must Be More to Life, 1967 (Am. Book award nomination 1980), In the Night Kitchen, 1970 (N.Y. Times Best Illustrated Book award 1970, Caldecott medal nomination 1971, Art Books for Children award 1973, 74, 75, Redbook Mag. award 1985), Ten Little Rabbits: A Counting Book with Mino the Magician, 1970, Pictures by Maurice Sendak, 1971, Maurice Sendak's Really Rosie, 1975, Some Swell Pup; or, Are You Sure You Want A Dog, 1976, Seven Little Monsters, 1977, Outside Over There, 1981 (N.Y. Times Best Illustrated Book award 1981, Boston Globe/Horn Book award 1981, Caldecott medal nomination 1982, Am. Book award 1982), We Are All in the Dumps with Jack and Guy, 1993, Tsippi, 1994, Moishe, 1994, Max, 1994; illustrator: Atomics for the Millions, 1947, Good Shabbos, Everybody!, 1951, The Wonderful Farm, 1951, A Hole is to Dig, 1952 (N.Y. Times Best Illustrated Book award 1952), Maggie Rose: Her Birthday Christmas, 1952, The Giant Story, 1953, Hurry Home Candy, 1953, Shadrach, 1953, A Very Special House, 1953 (Caldecott medal nomination 1954), I'll Be You and You Be Me, 1954 (N.Y. Times Best Illustrated Book award 1954), Happy Hanukkah, Everybody, 1954, The Tin Fiddle, 1954, Magic Pictures, 1954, Mrs. Piggle-Wiggle's Farm, 1954, The Wheel on the School, 1954, Charlotte and the White Horse, 1955, The Little Cow and the Turtle, 1955, Singing Family of the Cumberlands, 1955, What Can You Do With a Shoe?, 1955, Happy Rain, 1956, The House of Sixty Fathers, 1956, I Want to Paint My Bathroom Blue, 1956 (N.Y. Times Best Illustrated Book award 1956), Birthday Party, 1957 (N.Y. Times Best Illustrated Book award 1957), Circus Girl, 1957, You Can't Get There From Here, 1957, Little Bear, 1957, Along Came a Dog, 1958, No Fighting, No Biting!, 1958, Somebody Else's Nut Tree, 1958, What Do You Say, Dear?, 1958 (N.Y. Times Best Illustrated Book award 1958, Caldecott medal nomination 1959), The Moon Jumpers, 1959 (Caldecott medal nomination 1960), Father Bear Comes Home, 1959 (N.Y. Times Best Illustrated Book award 1959), Seven Tales, 1959, Dwarf Long-Nose, 1960, Little Bear's Friend, 1960, Open House for Butterflies, 1960 (N.Y. Times Best Illustrated Book award 1960), Let's Be Enemies, 1961, The Tale of Gockel, Hinkel and Gackeliah, 1961, What Do You Do, Dear?, 1961, Little Bear's Visit, 1961 (Caldecott medal nomination 1962), Schoolmaster Whackwell's Wonderful Sons, 1962, Mr. Rabbit and the Lovely Present, 1962 (Caldecott medal nomination 1963), The Singing Hill, 1962 (N.Y. Times Best Illustrated Book award 1962), Nikolenka's Childhood, 1963, She Loves Me, She Loves Me Not, 1963, The Bat-Poet, 1964 (N.Y. Times Best Illustrated Book award 1964), How Litte Lori Visited Times Square, 1964, Pleasant Fieldmouse, 1964, Lullabies and Night Songs, 1965, The Animal Family, 1965 (N.Y. Times Best Illustrated Book award 1965), Zlateh the Goat, 1966 (N.Y. Times Best Illustrated Book award 1966), The Golden Key, 1967, Poems from William Blake's Songs of Innocence, 1967, The Big Green Book, 1968, Griffin and the Minor Canon, 1968, A Kiss for Little Bear, 1968 (N.Y. Times Best Illustrated Book award 1968), The Light Princess, 1969 (N.Y. Times Best Illustrated Book award 1969), The Bee-Man of Orn, 1971, Sarah's Room, 1971, The Juniper Tree and Other Tales from Grimm, 1973 (N.Y. Times Best Illustrated Book award 1973), Fortunia: A Tale by Mme. D'Aulnoy, 1974, Fly by Night, 1976 (N.Y. Times Best Illustrated Book award 1976), King Grisly-Beard: A Tale from the Brothers Grimm, 1978, The Nutcracker, 1984 (N.Y. Times Best Illustrated Book award 1984), In Grandpa's House, 1985, The Children's Books of Randall Jarrell, 1988, Dear Mili, 1988, I Saw Esau, 1992, The Ubiquitous Pig, 1992; author: Fantasy Sketches, 1970, Collection of Books, Posters, and Original Drawings, 1984, The Love for Three Oranges: The Glyndebourne Version, 1984, Posters, 1986, Caldecott & Co.: Notes on Books and Pictures, 1988, Maurice Sendak Book and Poster Package: Wild Things, 1991; editor: Maxfield Parrish Poster Book, 1974, The Disney Poster Book, 1977; contbr.: The Publishing Archive of Lothar Meggendorfer, 1975, Babar's Anniversary Album, 1981, Masterworks of Children's Literature, Vol. 7, 1984, Victorian Color Picture Books, 1985, Winsor McCay: His Life and Art, 1987, Mickey Mouse Movie Stories, 1988; dir., lyricist: Really Rosie, 1975; lyricist, set designer: Really Rosie, 1978; lyricist, set designer, costume designer: Where the Wild Things Are, 1980, Higglety, Pigglety, Pop!, 1984; set designer, costume designer: The Magic Flute, 1980, The Cunning Little Vixen, 1981, Love for Three Oranges, 1982, The Goose of Cairo, 1984, Idomeneo, 1988, L'Enfant et les Sortileges, 1989, L'Heure Espagnol, 1989, It's Alive!, 1994, So, Sue Me, 1994; photographer: The Cunning Little Vixen, 1985; designer: (film) The Nutcracker, 1986. Recipient Chandler Book Talk Reward of Merit, 1967, Hans Christian Andersen Internat. medal, 1970, Laura Ingalls Wilder award Assn. Libr. Svc. to Children, 1983. Office: Harper & Row 10 E 53rd St New York NY 10022-5244*

SENDAX, VICTOR IRVEN, dentist, educator, dental implant researcher; b. N.Y.C., Sept. 14, 1930; s. Maurice and Molly R. S.; m. Deborah deLand Cobb, Dec. 17, 1969 (div. June 1976); 1 child, Jennifer Reiland; m. Marcia Ayer Pearson, Dec. 13, 1986; children: Anneliese Chase, Cordelia Ayer. Grad., Tanglewood Music Ctr., 1953; BA, NYU, 1951, DDS, 1955; postgrad., Harvard U. Sch. Dental Medicine, 1969-72. Diplomate Am. Bd. Oral Implantology/Implant Dentistry (pres. 1996). Commr. N.Y. State Dental Svc. Corp., 1969-73; pres., dir. BioDental Rsch. Found., Inc., N.Y.C., 1975—; pres. Victor I. Sendax, D.D.S., P.C., N.Y.C., 1972—, Mini Dental Implant Ctrs. Mgmt., Inc., 1985—; assoc. attending implantologist St. Lukes-Roosevelt Hosp. Dental Implant Ctr., N.Y.C., 1979—; vol. attending implantologist Beth Israel Hosp., N.Y.C., 1991—, Beth Israel North Hosp., N.Y.C., 1991—; adj. assoc. prof. implant prosthodontics Columbia U. Sch. Dental and Oral Surgery, N.Y.C., 1974-92; vis. lectr. dept. implant dentistry NYU Coll. Dentistry; faculty 1st Dist. Dental Soc. Sch. for Continuing Dental Edn.; mem. dental implant rsch. programs adv. com. Nat. Inst. Dental Rsch., HHS; cons. Julliard Sch. Voice and Drama, N.Y.C., 1972—, Vocal Dynamics Lab. Dept. Otolaryngology, Lenox Hill Hosp., N.Y.C., 1970-90; founder Sendax Seminars; 1st dir. implant prosthodontics resident program Columbia U. Sch. Dental and Oral Surgery and Columbia Presbyn. Hosp. Editor: Dental Clinics of North America: HA-Coated Dental Implants, 1992; mem. editl. bd. Oral Implantology, 1979—; patentee in oral implant magnetics, mini-implants, implant abutments and sinus graft implant stabilizers. Bd. dirs. City Ctr. Music and Drama, Inc. divsn. Lincoln Ctr. Performing Arts, N.Y.C., 1966-75; mem. adv. bd. Amagansett (N.Y.) Hist. Assn., 1969-89; trustee Leukemia Soc. Am., N.Y.C., 1967; bd. dirs. Schola Cantorum, 1980-90, Soc. Asian Music, 1965-76. Capt. Dental Corps USAF, 1955-57. Recipient Spl. Recognition, Am. Fund Dental Health, 1981, Cert. of Honor, Brit. Dental Implant Assn., 1988. Fellow Am. Coll. Dentists, Internat. Coll. Dentists, Am. Acad. Implant Dentistry (nat. pres. 1981), Royal Soc. Medicine Gt. Britain; mem. ADA (ho. of dels. 1969), Am. Assn. Dental Schs. (chmn. interdisciplinary group on dental implant edn.), Acad. of Osseointegration, Am. Prosthodontic Soc., Am. Equilibration Soc., Am. Analgesia Soc., Fedn. Dentaire Internat., Am. Assn. Dental Rsch. (implant group), Internat. Assn. Dental Rsch., N.Y. Acad. Scis., Japan Soc., Century Assn., Players Club (N.Y.C.), Sigma Epsilon Delta. Home: 70 E 77th St Apt 6A New York NY 10021-1811 Office: Parkview Dental Implant Condominium Ste 14B 30 Central Park S New York NY 10019-1628 *I stand in awe of mankinds' eternal need to innovate and push back the frontiers of knowledge, while tempering the harsher realities of existence with a perspective born of our cultural heritage.*

SENDERLING, JON TOWNSEND, journalist, public affairs specialist; b. Phila.; s. John Chester and Elizabeth (Nogle) S.; m. Elizabeth Marie Broadbent, Mar. 27, 1965; children: Jon, Tracy. Student, Ursinus Coll., 1960, Temple U., 1961-64; student (fellow), Stanford U., 1970. Reporter Bucks County Courier Times, Levittown, Pa., 1966-68, Wilmington (Del.) News-Jour., 1968-70; reporter, mag. writer, columnist, spl. projects editor Trenton (N.J.) Times, 1970-76; gen. assignments editor, state editor, nat.-fgn. editor Dallas Times Herald, 1976-80, editorial page dir., 1981-86; dep. fgn. editor Newsday, Melville, L.I., N.Y., 1987-89; pub. affairs mgr. EDS Corp., Dallas, 1989—. Author: play The Trashman, 1970. Recipient disting. service award for editorial writing Sigma Delta Chi, 1982, also 16 awards state press assns. Office: 5400 Legacy Dr Plano TX 75024-3105

SENDLEIN, LYLE V. A., geology educator; b. St. Louis, May 11, 1933; s. Lyle Vernon and Bernice Kathrine (Le Fevre) S.; m. Louise Pauline Darr; children: Lyle Scott, Todd Lockard, Erik Le Fevre. BS in Geol. Engring., Washington U., St. Louis, 1958, AM in Geology, 1960; PhD Geology-Soil Engring., Iowa State U., 1964. From instr. to prof. geology Iowa State U., Ames, 1960-77; prof. civil engr. Middle East Tech. U., Ankara, Turkey, 1973-74; asst. div. chief Ames Lab. Iowa State U., Ames, 1974-77; prof., dir. Coal Rsch. Ctr., So. Ill. U., Carbondale, 1977-82; prof. geology U. Ky., Lexington, 1982—, acting chmn. dept. geol. scis., 1989-91, dir. Inst. Mining and Minerals Rsch., 1982-94; dir. Ky. Water Resources Rsch. Inst., 1991—; pres. Forest Ridge Maintenance Assocs. Inc., Lexington, 1989-90. Author: Introduction to Geology, 1970; editor: Surface Mining Handbook, 1983; mem. editorial bd. Groundwater, 1977-80. With U.S. Army, 1953-55. Recipient best paper award Nat. Water Well Assn., 1971, 75. Fellow Geol. Soc. Am.; mem. Am. Geophys. Union, Assn. Groundwater Scientists and Engrs.. Rotary. Avocations: scuba diving, sailing. Home: 108 South Dr Key Largo FL 33037 Office: Water Resources Rsch Inst 233 Mining & Mineral Bldg Lexington KY 40506

SENDLER, DAVID ALAN, magazine editor; b. White Plains, N.Y., Dec. 12, 1938; s. Morris and Rose Sendler; m. Emily Shimm, Oct. 17, 1965; 2 children. BA, Dartmouth Coll., 1960; MS, Columbia U., 1961. Assoc. editor Sport mag., 1964-65; editor Pageant mag., 1965-71, exec. editor, 1969-71; editor Today's Health, 1971-74; sr. editor Parade, N.Y.C., 1974-75; articles editor Ladies Home Jour., 1975-76; mng. editor TV Guide mag., Radnor, Pa., 1976-79, exec. editor, 1979-80, co-editor, 1981-89; exec. editor Rediscover America Project Time Inc., 1990-91; editor-in-chief New Choices Mag., N.Y.C., 1992—. With U.S. Army, 1961-63. Mem. Am. Soc. Mag. Editors. Avocations: movies, public affairs, tennis, fitness.

SENDO, TAKESHI, mechanical engineering educator, researcher, author; b. Ena City, Japan, Aug. 5, 1917; s. Shigeyoshi and Michie (Yamamoto) S.; m. Hide Okamoto, Apr. 16, 1945; children: Mitsuyoshi, Sachiko, Kazuyasu. B of Engring., Tokyo U., 1941. Prof. mech. engring. Meijo U., Nagoya City, Japan, 1959-90, hon. prof., 1990—; curator libr. Meijo U., Nagoya City, 1975-80. Author: Treatise of High Speed Deformation of Metal, 1993, 2nd edit., 1994, Experiment: Behavior of Al Column by Drop Hammer Test, 1959-90; contbr. over 60 articles to profl. jours. Mem. cmty. activity com. Local Self-Governing Orgn., Moriyama City, Japan, 1990, 91. Served to lt. comdr. Japanese Navy, 1941-45. Fellow Japan Soc. Mech. Engring., Japan Soc. Precision Engring. Avocations: composing Haiku and Tanka, trying essay, jogging. Home: 21-8 Choei Moriyama-ku, Nagoya 463, Japan

SENDROVIC, ISRAEL, bank executive; b. Liberece, Czechoslovakia, June 19, 1947; s. Jacob Solomon and Frieda (Hirsch) S.; m. Esther Leah Karsh, June 15, 1969; children—Barry Dov, Karen Sue, Rochelle Beth, Deena. B.S. in Math., Bklyn. Coll., 1968; Rabbinical degree, Torah Vodaath Sem., Bklyn., 1969; M.S. in Ops. Research, NYU, 1970. Mem. research staff Riverside Research Inst., N.Y.C., 1968-70; exec. v.p. Fed. Res. Bank N.Y., N.Y.C., 1970—. Avocations: Talmudic studies, Judaica. Office: Fed Res Bank NY 33 Liberty St New York NY 10005-1011

SENECHAL, ALICE R., judge, lawyer; b. Rugby, N.D., June 25, 1955; d. Marvin William and Dora Emma (Erdman) S. BS, N.D. State U., 1977; JD, U. Minn., 1984. Bar: Minn. 1984, U.S. Dist. Ct. Minn. 1984, N.D. 1986, U.S. Ct. Appeals (8th cir.) 1987. Law clk. U.S. Dist. Judge Bruce M. Van Sickle, Bismarck, N.D., 1984-86; assoc. Robert Vogel Law Office, Grand Forks, N.D., 1986—; U.S. magistrate judge, 1990—. Office: Robert Vogel Law Office 106 N 3rd St Ste M102 Grand Forks ND 58203-3798

SENELICK, LAURENCE PHILIP, theatre educator, director, writer; b. Chgo., Oct. 12, 1942; s. Theodore Senelick and Evelyn Marder. BA, Northwestern U., Evanston, Ill., 1964; AM, Harvard U., 1965, PhD, 1972. Asst. prof. English Emerson Coll., Boston, 1968-72; from asst. to prof. drama, Fletcher prof. drama and oratory Tufts U., Medford, Mass., 1972—; hon. curator Russian drama & theatre Harvard Theatre Collection, Cambridge, Mass., 1991—. Author: A Cavalcade of Clowns, 1978, Tchaikovsky's Sleeping Beauty, 1978, Gordon Craig's Moscow Hamlet: A Reconstruction, 1982, Serf Actor: The Life and Art of Mikhail Shchepkin, 1984, Anton Chekhov, 1985, The Prestige of Evil: The Murderer as Romantic Hero, 1987, (with P. Haskell) The Cheese Book, 1985, The Chekhov Theatre, 1996; editor: National Theatre in Northern and Eastern Europe 1743-1900, Cabaret Performance: Europe 1890-1940, 2 vols., Gender in Performance, Wandering Stars, (plays) The Merchant of Venice, Dead Souls, You Never Can Tell, Tartuff, The Magic Flute, Le Nozze de Figaro, Il Barbiere di Siviglia, numerous others; contbr. articles to profl. jours. Recipient rsch. award NEH, 1994-96, George Freedley award Theatre Libr. Assn., 1988; fellow Guggenheim Found., 1979-80, 87-88, Wissenschaftskolleg zu Berlin, 1984-85. Mem. Am. Soc. Theatre Rsch. (exec. bd. dirs. 1992—), Internat. Fedn. Theatre Rsch. (univ. commn. 1992—). Avocations: collecting theatricalia, cooking. Office: Tufts U Dept of Drama Leir Hall Medford MA 02155

SENER, JOSEPH WARD, JR., securities company executive; b. Balt., June 30, 1926; s. Joseph Ward and Clara (Hodshon) S.; m. Ann Clark TenEyck, May 3, 1952 (dec. Oct. 1967); children: J. TenEyck, Beverley T., Joseph Ward III; m. Jean Eisenbrandt-Johnston, Feb. 6, 1971. A.B., Haverford (Pa.) Coll., 1950; diploma, Inst. Investment Banking, U. Pa., 1954. With John C. Legg & Co., Balt., 1950-70; gen. partner John C. Legg & Co., 1961-70; exec. v.p., dir. Legg, Mason & Co., Inc., Balt., 1970-72; vice chmn. bd. dirs., chief adminstrv. officer Legg Mason Wood Walker, Inc., Balt., 1976-80; bd. dirs. Legg Mason, Inc.; chmn. bd. dirs. Chesapeake Bank and Trust, Chestertown, Md., Chesapeake Bancorp. Trustee Boys' Latin Sch., Balt., pres. bd. trustees, 1980-82; chmn. bd. govs. Chesapeake Bay Maritime Mus. Served with USAAF, 1944-46. Mem. Nat. Assn. Securities Dealers (past dist. chmn.), Balt. Security Analysts Soc. (past pres.), Md. Club (Balt.). Republican. Episcopalian. Office: PO Box 511 Chestertown MD 21620-0511

SENESE, DONALD JOSEPH, former government official; b. Chgo., Apr. 6, 1942; s. Leo Carl and Joan (Schaffer) S.; m. Linda Faye Wall, Dec. 29, 1973; 1 dau., Denise Nicole. B.S. in History, Loyola U., 1964, M.A., 1966; PhD, U. S.C., 1970; postgrad., Sophia U., Tokyo, 1970, Nat. Chengchi U., Taipei, Taiwan, 1971; cert. in adminstrv. procedures, U.S. Dept. Agr. Grad. Sch., 1976. Assoc. prof. history Radford (Va.) U., 1969-72; legis. asst. to senator from Va. Senator from Va., 1973; legis. dir. to Rep. from Tex., 1973-76; sr. research assoc. House Republican Study Com., U.S. Ho. of Reps., Washington, 1976-81; asst. sec. for ednl. research and improvement U.S. Dept. Edn., Washington, 1981-85; pres. Senese Edn. Enterprises, Inc., 1985—; dep. asst. sec. to asst. sec. Office Territorial and Internat. Affairs, Dept. Interior, Washington, 1989-93; writer, cons. SEE, Inc., Alexandria, Va.; instr. U.S.Dept. of Agrl. Grad. Sch., 1995-96; mem. child care liability task force study, Dept. Labor, 1989; instr. U.S. Dept. Agrl. Grad. Sch., 1995—. Author: Indexing the Inflationary Impact of Taxes, 1978, Modernizing the Chinese Dragon, 1980, Asianomics: Challenge and Change in Northeast Asia, 1981; editor: Ideas Confront Reality, 1981, Sweet and Sour Capitalism, 1985, Democracy in Mainland China, 1986; co-author: Can The Two Chinas Become One?, 1989; editor: George Mason and The Legacy of Constitutional Liberty, 1989. Vice chmn. Alexandria (Va.) Rep. Com., 1976-78, staff Rep. Nat. Com., 1987-89; mem. Alexandria Hist. Records Commn., 1979-84; mem. Fairfax County History Commn., 1985—, chmn., 1990-91; Fairfax County Bicentennial of U.S. Constn. Com., 1986-91; dir. Nat. Ctr. for Presdl. Rsch., 1987—; dir. opposition rsch. Rep. Nat. Com., 1995-96; dir. of rsch Co-Chairman Rep. Nat. Com., 1996—. Recipient William P. Lyons Master Essay award, 1967; Freedoms Found. award, 1981, 85, 90; named Outstanding Man of Yr. Jaycees, 1976, 78, Sec. Labor Exceptional Achievement award, 1990. Mem. Univ. Profs. for Acad. Order, Order Sons of Italy, Pi Gamma Mu, Phi Alpha Theta, Delta Sigma Rho-Tau Kappa Alpha. Roman Catholic. Office: PO Box 6886 Alexandria VA 22306-0886 *It has been important to have a philosophy of government which emphasizes honesty, integrity, a Ciceronian concept of duty, cost-effective public service, and a committment to the American heritage and traditions. These views have been reinforced by the support of family, friends, and a spiritual faith.*

SENFF, MARK D., lawyer; b. Wooster, Ohio, Aug. 13, 1945. BS, Ohio State U., 1968, JD summa cum laude, 1971. Bar: Ohio 1971. Ptnr. Baker & Hostetler, Columbus, Ohio. Editor-in-chief Ohio State Law Jour., 1970-71. Office: Baker & Hostetler Capital Sq 65 E State St Ste 2100 Columbus OH 43215-4213

SENG, ANN FRANCES, civic organization executive; b. Chgo., Jan. 5, 1936; d. William John and Helen Christine (Steger) S. BA, Alverno Coll., Milw., 1957; MA, Loyola U., Chgo., 1970. Tchr. Alvernia High Sch., Chgo., 1958-65; exec. dir. Community House Cath. Charities, Chgo., 1965-67; adminstr. Sch. Sisters St. Francis, Chgo., 1967-69; dir. uptown advocacy program Chgo. Cath. Interracial Coun., 1970-71; community devel. dir. Uptown Ctr. Hull House, Chgo., 1971-81; dir. rsch. and pub. policy Hull House Assn., Chgo., 1981-88; pres., chief exec. officer Chgo. Coun. Urban Affairs, 1988—; bd. dirs. Jane Addams Conf., Chgo., 1987—, Chgo. Capital Fund, 1988-95, Women Employed Inst., Chgo., 1988-91. Mem. Pvt. Industry Coun., Chgo., 1988-95; vice-chair Chgo. Com. Urban Opportunity, 1988-92. Mem. LWV, NOW, Ill. Women's Agenda (chair 1983-84). Office: Chgo Coun Urban Affairs 6 N Michigan Ave Ste 1308 Chicago IL 60602-4808

SENGSTACKE, JOHN HERMAN HENRY, publishing company executive; b. Savannah, Ga., Nov. 25, 1912; s. Herman Alexander and Rosa Mae (Davis) S.; 1 son, Robert Abbott. B.S., Hampton (Va.) Inst., 1933; postgrad., Ohio State U., 1933. With Robert S. Abbott Pub. Co. (publishers Chgo. Defender), 1934—, v.p., gen. mgr., 1934-40, pres., gen. mgr., 1940—; chmn. bd. Mich. Chronicle, Detroit; pres. Tri-State Defender, Defender Publs., Amalgamated Pubs., Inc.; pub. Daily Defender; pres. Sengstacke Enterprises, Inc., Sengstacke Publs., Pitts. Courier Newspaper Chain; dir. Ill. Fed. Savs. & Loan Assn., Golden State Mut. Life Ins. Co. Mem. exec. bd. Nat. Alliance Businessmen; bd. govs. USO; mem. Ill. Sesquicentennial Commn., Pres.'s Com. on Equal Opportunity in Armed Services; mem. pub. affairs adv. com. Air Force Acad.; trustee Bethune-Cookman Coll., Daytona Beach, Fla., Hampton Inst.; bd. dirs. Washington Park YMCA, Joint Negro Appeal; chmn. bd. Provident Hosp. Recipient Two Friends award Nat. Urban League, 1950; Hampton Alumni award, 1954; 1st Mass. Media award Am. Jewish Com. Mem. Negro Newspaper Pubs. Assn. (founder), Nat. Newspaper Pubs. Assn. (founder, pres.), Am. Newspaper Pubs. Assn., Am. Soc. Newspaper Editors (dir.). Congregationalist. Clubs: Royal Order of Snakes, Masons, Elks, Econs, Chgo. Press. Office: Sengstacke Enterprises Inc 2400 S Michigan Ave Chicago IL 60616-2329

SENGUPTA, DIPAK LAL, electrical engineering and physics educator, researcher; b. Bengal, India, Mar. 1, 1931; came to U.S., 1959; s. Jayanta Kumar and Pankajini Sengupta; m. Sujata Basu, Aug. 31, 1962; children: Sumit, Mita. BSc in Physics with honors, Calcutta U., India, 1950, MSc in Radio Physics, 1952; PhD, U. Toronto, Ont., Can., 1958. Assoc. rsch. physicist dept. elec. engring. U. Mich., Ann Arbor, 1959-63, rsch. physicist, 1965-75, rsch. scientist, prof. dept. elec. engring., 1975-86; asst. prof. dept. elec. engring. U. Toronto, 1963-64; asst. dir. Cen. Electronics Engring. Rsch. Inst., Pilani, India, 1964-65; prof., chmn. dept. elec. engring. and physics U. Detroit Mercy, 1986-95; prof. elec. engring. U. Detroit, Mercy, 1996—; Fulbright vis. lectr. in India, 1992-93; cons. Ford Motor Co., Dearborn, Mich., 1976-77, Battelle Pacific N.W. Labs., Richland, Wash., 1978. Author: Radar Cross Section Analysis and Control, 1991; contbr. articles to profl. jours. Fellow IEEE (Contbn. award 1969, recognition awards 1978-79); mem. Internat. Radio Scientists Union (sec. commn. B 1976-78), Sigma Xi, Eta Kappa Nu. Office: U Detroit Mercy Dept Elec Engring 4001 W Mcnichols Rd Detroit MI 48219-0900

SENGUPTA, MRITUNJOY, mining engineer, educator; b. Cuttack, Orissa, India, Oct. 24, 1941; came to U.S., 1968; s. Chandi P. and Bani S.; m. Nupur Bagchi, Jan. 15, 1981; children: Shyam S. ME, Columbia U., 1971, MS, 1972; PhD, Colo. Sch. of Mines, 1983. Mining engr. Continental Oil Co., Denver, 1977-78, United Nuclear Corp., Albuquerque, 1978-80, Morrison-Knudson Co., Boise, Idaho, 1975-77, 80-82; assoc. prof. U. Alaska, Fairbanks, 1983-88, prof., 1989—; cons. UN Devel. Program, 1987. Author: Mine Environmental Engineering, vols. I and II, 1989, Environmental Impacts of Mining, 1992; contbr. articles to profl. publs. Recipient Gold medal Mining Metall. Inst. of India, 1976, Nat. Merit scholarship Govt. of India, 1959-63. Mem. NSPE, So. Mining Engrs. Achievements include development of new concepts for mine design in oilshale in Colo. Home: 421 Cindy Dr Fairbanks AK 99701-3220 Office: Univ Alaska Dept Engring Fairbanks AK 99775

SENHAUSER, DONALD A(LBERT), pathologist, educator; b. Dover, Ohio, Jan. 30, 1927; s. Albert Carl and Maude Anne (Snyder) S.; m. Helen Brown, July 22, 1961; children: William, Norman. Student, U. Chgo., 1944-45; BS, Columbia U., 1948, MD, 1951; grad. with honors, U.S. Naval Sch. Aviation Medicine, 1953. Diplomate Am. Bd. Pathology. Intern Roosevelt Hosp., N.Y.C., 1951-52; resident Columbia-Presbyn. Hosp., N.Y.C., 1955-56, Cleve. Clinic, 1956-60; instr. in pathology Columbia U., 1955-56; fellow in immuno-pathology Middlesex Hosp. Med. Sch., London, 1960-61; mem. dept. pathology Cleve. Clinic Found., 1961-63; assoc. prof. pathology U. Mo., 1963-65; prof., asst. dean Sch. Medicine U. Mo., 1969-70, dir. teaching labs., 1968-70, prof., vice-chmn. dept. pathology, 1965-75; prof., chmn. dept. pathology Coll. Medicine Ohio State U., 1975-92, chair emeritus, 1992, prof. Sch. Allied Med. Professions, 1975—; prof. emeritus, 1995—; dir. labs. Ohio State U. Hosps., 1975-92; pres. Univ. Reference Lab., Inc., 1984-86, CEO, 1986-92; bd. dirs. Columbus area chpt. ARC, 1978-82; cons. in field; WHO-AMA Vietnam med. edn. project mem. U. Saigon Med. Sch., 1967-72; vis. scientist HEW, 1972-73; acting dir. Ctrl. Ohio Regional Blood Ctr., 1976-79. Mem. editorial bd. Am. Jour. Clin. Pathology, 1965-76. With USN, 1945-46; lt. M.C. USNR, Korea, China; now capt. USNR ret. Served with USN, 1945-46; served as lt. M.C. USNR, Korea, China; now capt. USNR, Ret. Recipient Lower award Bunts Ednl. Found., 1960-61. Mem. AAAS, Coll. Am. Pathologists (bd. govs. 1980-86, v.p. 1989-90, pres.-elect 1990-91, pres. 1991-93, immediate past pres. 1993—, Pathologist of Yr. 1994), Am. Soc. Clin. Pathologists, Assn. Pathology Chmn., Am. Assn. Pathology, Internat. Acad. Pathology, Assn. Am. Med. Colls., Am. Assn. Blood Banks, Ohio Soc. Pathologists (gov. 1979, pres. 1987-89), Ohio Hist. Soc., Columbus Art League, Masons, Sigma Xi. Lutheran. Home: 1256 Clubview Blvd N Columbus OH 43235-1226 Office: 333 W 10th Ave Columbus OH 43210-1239

SENHAUSER, JOHN CRATER, architect; b. New Philadelphia, Ohio, Apr. 7, 1947; s. Edwin Crater and Margaret Jean (Huffman) S.; m. Teri A. Schleyer, June 25, 1988. BS in Architecture, U. Cin., 1971. Registered architect, Ohio, Ky. Designer Jones, Peacock, Garn & Ptnrs., Cin., 1971-72; project architect Smith Stevens Architects, Cin., 1972-76; project mgr. Herrlinger Enterprises, Cin., 1976-79; prin., owner John C. Senhauser, Architect, Cin., 1979—; adj. assoc. prof. Sch. Architecture and Interior Design, U. Cin., 1992—. Exhibited in group shows at Toni Birckhead Gallery, 1990, Contemporary Arts Ctr., Cin., 1993, Canton (Ohio) Art Inst., 1993; prin. works include residences. Mem. historic conservation bd. City of Cin., 1986—; mem. dean's adv. coun. Coll. Design Architecture Art and Planning U. Cin., 1990. Recipient Merit award Builder mag., 1985, 88, 94, Grand award, 1990, Grand Best in Region award Profl. Builder, 1990. Fellow AIA (pres. 1991, Honor award Cin. chpt. 1983, 85, 90, 91, 92, 93, 94, 95, Merit award 1990, 93, 94); mem. Architects Soc. Ohio (bd. dirs., Honor award 1985, 90, 91, 93, 94). Office: 1118 Saint Gregory St Cincinnati OH 45202-1724

SENHOLZI, GREGORY BRUCE, secondary school educator; b. Amityville, N.Y., Apr. 16, 1952; s. Joseph Bruce and Beverly Ann (Sullivan) S.; m. Rochelle Ann Birnbaum, Nov. 20, 1976; children: David, Vicki. BA, Iona Coll., 1974; MLS, SUNY, Stony Brook, 1976. Salesman, printer R.H. Macy's, Huntington, N.Y., 1967-74; math. and computer tchr. Sachem Sch. Dist., Lake Ronkonkoma, N.Y., 1974—; computer specialist Tex. Instruments, N.Y., 1982-84; audio video specialit Dart Audio Video, Centereach, N.Y., 1984-88; consulate, curriculum specialist Sachem Sch. Dist., 1978—. Deacon local Roman Cath. ch., Wading River, N.Y., 1989—. Mem. Adoptive Parents Com. (bd. dirs., workshop leader 1984—), K.C. (treas. 1988—). Avocations: swimming, acting, skiing, singing, travel. Home: 129 Gregory Way Calverton NY 11933 Office: Sachem Sch Dist Main St Holbrook NY 11742

SENIOR, ENRIQUE FRANCISCO, investment banker; b. Havana, Cuba, Aug. 3, 1943; came to U.S., 1960; s. Frank and Dolores (Hernandez) Senior; m. Robin Suffern Gimbel, Sept. 7, 1977; children: Tailer, Heather, Fern, Seanna. BA in Architecture, Yale U., 1964, BS in Elec. Engring., 1967; MBA, Harvard U., 1969. Corp. fin. exec. White, Weld & Co., N.Y.C., 1969-73; v.p. Allen & Co., Inc., N.Y.C., 1973-80, exec. v.p., mng. dir., 1980—; bd. dirs. Allen & Co., Inc., Air & Water Techs. Corp., Somerville, N.J., Dick Clark Prodns., Inc., Burbank, Calif. Mem. The Brook Club, Piping Rock Club, Farmington Country Club, Phi Beta Kappa, Tau Beta Pi. Avocations: flying, fishing, hunting, skiing, woodworking. Office: Allen & Co Inc 711 Fifth Ave New York NY 10022*

SENIOR, SHEILA MATHILDA, nurse; b. Phila., May 28, 1947; d. Robert F. and Georgiana Marie (Stewart) Riskie; children by previous marriage: Harry Brooks, Georgianna Brooks; m. Matthew J. Senior (div. 1979); 1 child, Melissa. AAS, Delaware County Community Coll., Media, Pa., 1979. Staff med.-surg. nurse Hahnemann U. Hosp., Phila., 1979, cardiology staff nurse, 1979-82, nurse educator, cardiology, 1982-83, rsch. nurse clinician, clin. cardiac electrophysiology, 1983—, head rsch. nurse sudden death prevention program and clin. cardiac electrophysiology, 1985-86; clin. rsch. assoc. DuPont Pharm., 1986-88; cardiovascular rsch. coord. Beecham Labs., 1988-93; clin. rsch. mgr. microbiology-virology Abbott Labs., 1989-93, medical liason infectious diseases Abbott Labs, 1993—; staff nurse Lake Forest Hosp., Chgo., 1992-93; staff nurse cardiology Princeton Med. Ctr., 1993—, grad. asst. Dale Carnegie, 1995—; numerous presentations in field; coord. First Nursing Presentation of the Yugoslav-U.S. Med. Assn., 1982; acting chmn. Third European Symposium on Cardiac Pacing, Torremolinos, Malaga, Spain, 1985. Author: (with P. Wilson) Understanding your Heart: Facts, Testing, Treatment, 1985; also articles; reviewer jours. Vol. instr. for prison inmate reform Thresholds, 1977; mem. St. Francis Players. Recipient Mayor's Svc. award, Phila., 1980, Humanitarian award Optimists Internat., 1980, Citizen of Yr. award Am. Legion, 1980. Mem. ACA. Avocations: skiing; target shooting; dancing. Home: 515 Brickhouse Rd Princeton NJ 08540-7349 Office: Abbott Labs 1 Abbott Park Rd North Chicago IL 60064-3500

SENIOR, THOMAS BRYAN A., electrical engineering educator, researcher, consultant; b. Menston, Yorkshire, Eng., June 26, 1928; came to U.S., 1957; s. Thomas Harold and Emily Dorothy (Matthews) S.; m. Heather Margaret Golby, May 4, 1957; children—Margaret, David, Hazel, Peter. B.Sc., Manchester U., 1949, M.Sc., 1950; Ph.D., Cambridge U., 1954. Sr. sci. officer Royal Radar Establishment, Malvern, Eng., 1952-57; rsch. scientist U. Mich., Ann Arbor, 1957-69, prof. elec. engring., 1969-84, prof. elec. and computer sci., 1984—, Arthur F. Thurnau prof., 1990—, dir. radiation lab., 1975-87, assoc. chmn. elect. engring. & computer sci. dept., 1984-90, acting chmn., 1987-88, assoc. chmn. acad. affairs, 1991—; cons. in field. Author: (with Bowman and Uslenghi) Electromagnetic and Acoustical Scattering by Simple Shapes, 1969; Mathematical Methods in Electrical Engineering, 1986; (with Volakis) Approximate Boundary Conditions in Electromagnetics, 1995; contbr. articles to profl. jours. Fellow IEEE; mem. Internat. Sci. Radio Union (chmn. U.S. nat. com. 1982-84, vice chmn. Com. B. 1985-87, chmn. 1988-90, v.p. 1993—, Van der Pol Gold medal 1993). Home: 1919 Ivywood Dr Ann Arbor MI 48103-4527 Office: U Mich Dept Elec Engring Comp S Ann Arbor MI 48109

SENKIER, ROBERT JOSEPH, foundation administrator, educator; b. Poughkeepsie, N.Y., May 31, 1916; s. Michael J. and Mary Gilberta (Perrin) S.; m. Mary Theresa Kelly, Mar. 21, 1941; children—Pamela Jeanne Senkier Scott, Deborah Ann. A.B., Columbia U., 1939, M.A., 1940, Ed.D., 1961. Mem. bus. faculty Columbia U., 1948-61; asst. dean Columbia U. (Sch. Bus.), 1958-61; prof. mgmt., dean Sch. Bus. Adminstrn. Seton Hall U., South Orange, N.J., 1962-74; prof. mgmt., dean Grad. Sch. Bus., Fordham U., N.Y.C., 1975-79; exec. dir. Mathers Found., 1982-84; found. cons., 1985—. Author: Revising a Business Curriculum—The Columbia Experience, 1961; contbr. articles to profl. jours. Mem. alumni bd. dirs. Columbia Coll.; mem. John Jay Assocs.; Holy See del. to U.N., 1980-83; trustee Marymount Coll. Va., 1983-85, Molloy Coll., 1986-89. Served to lt. comdr. USN, 1940-45. Mem. Acad. Internat. Bus., Columbia Alumni Assn., Phi Delta Kappa, Alpha Kappa Psi, Alpha Sigma Phi, Beta Gamma Sigma. Republican. Roman Catholic. Club: Princeton (N.Y.C.). Home: 6 Amherst Ct Glen Rock NJ 07452-1302 Office: Mathers Found 105 S Bedford Rd Mount Kisco NY 10549-3441

SENNEMA, DAVID CARL, museum consultant; b. Grand Rapids, Mich., July 6, 1934; s. Carl Edward and Alice Bertha (Bieri) S.; m. Martha Amanda Dixon, Feb. 22, 1958; children—Daniel Ross, Julia Kathryn, Alice Dixon. B.A., Albion Coll., 1956. Mgr., Columbia Music Festival Assn., 1964-67; exec. dir. S.C. Arts Commn., Columbia, 1967-70; assoc. dir. Federal-State Partnership and Spl. Projects programs Nat. Endowment for the Arts, Washington, 1971-73; prof. arts adminstrn., dir. community arts mgmt. program Sangamon State U., Springfield, Ill., 1973-76; dir. S.C. Mus. Commn. Columbia, 1976-85; bus. mgr. Palmetto Mastersingers, 1986—; cons. in field. Mem. adv. panel Nat. Endowment for the Arts Music, 1968-70. Chmn. Springfield Arts Commn., 1975-76. Served with U.S. Army, 1957-58. Lodge: Rotary (chmn. cultural affairs com. 1978-80).

SENNETT, HENRY HERBERT, JR., theatre arts educator and consultant; b. Atlanta, Feb. 28, 1945; s. Henry Herbert and Betty Ruth (Wilson) S.; m. Beverly Ann Rodgers, Dec. 9, 1967; children: Cristie Aline, Herbert Alan. BS in Edn., Ark. State U., Jonesboro, 1968; MA, Memphis State U., 1971; MDiv, So. Bapt. Sem., Louisville, 1978; DMin, Midwestern Bapt. Sem., Kansas City, Mo., 1988; MFA, Fla. Atlantic U., 1989. Cert. tchr. Tchr. speech and English Covington (Tenn.) High Sch., 1971-72; freelance designer Lighting by Herb, Memphis, 1972-73; tchr. speech and English Augusta (Ark.) High Sch., 1973-76; instr. drama Jefferson Community Coll., Louisville, 1977-78; pastor Dublin (Ohio) Bapt. Ch., 1979-83, Trinity Bapt. Ch., Searcy, Ark., 1983-85; asst. prof. theatre arts, dept. chair Palm Beach Atlantic Coll., West Palm Beach, Fla., 1985-96; pres. S&R Prodns., Inc., 1995—; stress mgmt. cons. Palm Beach County Bd. Edn., West Palm Beach, 1988—; freelance cons. theatrical lighting and design, West Palm Beach, 1986—; cons. drama edn. Fla. Dept. Edn., 1991-94; vis. prof. Midwestern Bapt. Sem., Kansas City, Mo., 1988; pres. S & R Prodns., Inc., 1995—. Author: Theatre in the Church, 1992, Religion and Dramatics: Essays on the Relationship Between Christianity and Theatrical Arts, 1994, How to Direct a Play Without Going Insane, 1996; author: (play) Stars, 1989. 1st lt. U.S.

Army, 1968-70, Vietnam; chaplain USAR, 1984—. Mem. Nat. Assn. Schs. Theatre, Fla. Theatre Edn., Fla. Theatre Conf., South Western Theatre Conf., Assn. Theatre Higher Edn., Blue Key Nat. Honor Soc., Theatre Comm. Group, Pi Kappa Phi (pres. 1965-66). Republican. Baptist. Avocations: pastor, author. Office: 3504 Tamarack Trl West Palm Beach FL 33406-4984

SENNETT, RICHARD, sociologist, writer; b. Chgo., Jan. 1, 1943; s. Maurice and Dorothy S. B.A. in History summa cum laude, U. Chgo., 1964; Ph.D., Harvard U., 1969. Asst. prof. Yale U., 1967-68; dir. Urban Family Study, Cambridge, Mass., 1969-71; mem. faculty NYU, 1971—, Univ. prof. of the humanities, 1984—; founder, dir. N.Y. Inst. Humanities, 1976-79, 81-84; chmn. adv. com. on urban studies UNESCO, 1988-93; Sigmund Freud Meml. lectr. U. London, 1977; disting. vis. prof. Coll. de France, Paris, 1980; Henry Luce lectr. Yale U., 1986; vis. prof. humanities Harvard U., 1984; Goethe lectr. U. Frankfurt, Germany, 1991-92; scholar-in-residence Am. Acad., Rome, 1992; rep. Internat. Social Sci. Coun. to UN, 1992—. Author: Families Against the City, 1970, The Uses of Disorder, 1970, The Hidden Injuries of Class, 1972, The Fall of Public Man, 1977, Authority, 1980, The Frog Who Dared to Croak, 1982, An Evening of Brahms, 1984, Palais Royal, 1986, The Conscience of the Eye, 1990, Flesh and Stone, 1994, The Darwin Lectures, 1996. Fellow Guggenheim Found., 1973, Inst. Advanced Study, 1973-74, 79-80, Nat. Endowment for the Humanities, 1976, Woodrow Wilson Ctr.-Smithsonian Instn., Washington, 1993. Fellow Royal Soc. Lit. (Gt. Britain), Am. Sociol. Assn., Nat. Acad. Arts and Scis.; mem. Internat. Sociol. Assn., Nat. Coun. Family Rels., PEN (dir. 1977—, v.p. 1979-82). Clubs: Century Assn. (N.Y.C.); Signet Soc. (Harvard). Office: 26 Washington Pl Rm 777 New York NY 10003-6642

SENOS, JEANNE ANN, geriatrics services professional; b. Chester, Pa., Apr. 11, 1942; m. Carl Andre Senos, Aug. 26, 1961; children: René Senos, Lori Dare. Student, Goldey-Beacom Coll., 1960; GPN, Del. Tech. and C.C., 1973, ADN, 1979. Co-owner, mgr. Heritage Farm Nursery, Landscape Svc., and Florist, Harrington, Del., 1973-89; nurse Milford (Del.) Meml. Hosp., 1973-79; staff nurse Kent Gen. Hosp., Dover, Del., 1979-83, per-diem staff and transport nurse, 1989-90; staff nurse Profl. Home Health Care, Salisbury, Md., 1984-90; charge nurse, supr. Wesleyan Health Care Ctr., Denton, Md., 1985-89, supr., assessment coord., 1991-92; staff devel. coord. Meridian-Corsica Hills, Centreville, Md., 1992-94; asst. dir. nursing Mallard Bay Nursing Ctr., Cambridge, Md., 1994; staff devel. coord. Integrated Health Svcs. of Del. at Kent, Smyrna. Active Caroline Hist. Soc. Mem. ANA (cert. in gerontology), Alzheimers Assn., Md. Nurses Assn. Avocations: reading, sailing, camping, crafts. Home: 675 Vernon Rd Harrington DE 19952 Office: IHS of Del at Kent 3034 S DuPont Blvd Smyrna DE 19974

SENSE, KARL AUGUST, physicist, educator; b. Kiel, Schleswig-Holstein, Germany, Mar. 6, 1917; came to U.S., 1929; s. Carl Richard and Charlotte Irma (Neuenfeldt) S.; m. Rita Evelyn Sharp, June 5, 1948 (div. Jan. 1971); children: Karl D., Nancy C., Kurt A., Janet E., Eric M. BA, SUNY, Albany, 1939; MS, U. Minn., 1951. Asst. div. cons. Battelle Meml. Inst., Columbus, Ohio, 1951-58; sr. physicist Atomics Internat. (Rockwell), Canoga Park, Calif., 1958-61; rsch. scientist Astropower subs. Douglas Aircraft, Newport Beach, Calif., 1961-64; project mgr., staff engr. TRW Systems Group, Redondo Beach, Calif., 1964-69; pvt. practice cons. Garden Grove, Calif., 1969-80; engring. specialist satellite systems div. Rockwell Internat., Seal Beach, Calif., 1981-84, ret., 1984; lectr. in physics Calif. State U., Long Beach, 1986. Author: Theory on Determination of Molecular Complexes of Vapors of Binary Systems, 1957, Power Failure Analysis of Satellites in GPS Orbit, 1981; mgr., author: Nuclear-Magnetohydrodynamic Power Systems, 1967; patentee thermionic emitter. Comdr. Am. Legion Post # 286, Garden Grove, 1977; pres. Worthington (Ohio) Luth. Ch., 1957; co-chmn., bd. dirs. Luth. High Sch. Assn. of Orange County, Calif., 1968. 2d lt. USAAF, 1943-45. Fellow AIAA (assoc., Membership award 1991); mem. Am. Phys. Soc. (sr.). Avocations: eschatology, music. Home: 37 Marion Hts Galax VA 24333-4500

SENSEMAN, RONALD SYLVESTER, architect; b. Collingswood, N.J., Oct. 19, 1912; s. Raphael and Louise (Tanner) S.; m. Lois Hatt, Aug. 18, 1935 (dec. Aug. 1979); children: Marilyn Louise (Mrs. John Whitson Rogers), Peggy June (Mrs. James Orvil Hutchinson); m. Claire M. Stoehr, Sept. 8, 1980; children: Deborah Stoehr (Mrs. Tim Darrin), Darice (Mrs. Kevin Lang), Darla (Mrs. Jeffrey Schultz), D'Lynn Stoehr (Mrs. Shean Phelps). Student, Columbia Union Coll., 1931-34, Cath. U. Am., 1934-36. Pvt. practice architecture Met. Washington area, 1935-89; ret.; cons. architect Silver Spring, 1989—; dir. Park Motels Inc., Manor Care, Inc.; pres. Reef Properties Inc., St. Croix, V.I.; lectr. Columbia Union Coll., Seventh Day Adventist Theol. Sem. Archtl. works include: Nat. Indsl. Coll., Army War Coll., Ft. McNair, Washington, Naval War Coll., Newport, R.I., Atlantic Union Coll., South Lancaster, Mass., Columbia Union Coll., Takoma Park, Md., Shady Grove Adventist Hosp., Gaithersburg, Md., others. Republican candidate Md. State Legislature, 1958; Mem. univ. councillors Loma Linda U.; trustee Atlantic Union Coll. Fellow AIA (pres. Md. div. met. Washington chpt. 1947-49, pres. Potomac Valley chpt.); mem. Guild Religious Architecture, Washington Bd. Trade, Washington Building Congress, Prince George's County C. of C., Cath. U. Alumni Assn. (Archtl. Achievement award 1967). Lodge: Rotary. Home: 10718 Gatewood Ave Silver Spring MD 20903-1013

SENSENBRENNER, FRANK JAMES, JR., congressman, lawyer; b. Chgo., June 14, 1943; s. Frank James and Margaret Anita (Luedke) S.; m. Cheryl Lynn Warren, Mar. 26, 1977; children: Frank James III, Robert Alan. AB in Polit. Sci., Stanford U., 1965; JD, U. Wis., 1968. Bar: Wis. 1968, U.S. Supreme Ct. 1972. Mem. firm McKay and Martin, Cedarburg., Wis., 1970-75; mem. Wis. Assembly, 1969-75; mem. Wis. State Senate, 1975-79, asst. minority leader, 1977-79; mem. 96th-104th Congresses from 9th Wis. dist., Washington, 1979—; mem. House Jud. Com., House Sci. Com., chmn. subcom. on space and aeronautics. Mem. Am. Philatelic Soc. Republican. Episcopalian. Club: Capitol Hill. Office: US Ho of Reps 2332 Rayburn House Bldg Washington DC 20515-4909

SENSENICH, ILA JEANNE, magistrate judge; b. Pitts., Mar. 6, 1939; d. Louis E. and Evelyn Margaret (Harbourt) S. BA, Westminster Coll., 1961; JD, Dickinson Sch. Law, 1964, JD (hon.), 1994. Bar: Pa. 1964. Assoc. Stewart, Belden, Sensenich and Herrington, Greensburg, Pa., 1964-70; asst. pub. defender Westmoreland (Pa.) County, 1970-71; U.S. magistrate judge for We. Dist. Pa., Pitts., 1971—; adj. prof. law Duquesne U., 1982-87. Trustee emeritus Dickinson Sch. Law. Mem. ABA, Fed. Magistrate Judges Assn. (sec. 1979-81, sec. 1988-89, treas. 1989-90, 2d v.p. 1990-91, pres.-elect 1992-93, pres. 1993-94), Pa. Bar Assn., Allegheny County Bar Assn. (fed. ct. sect.), Nat. Assn. Women Judges, Westmoreland County Bar Assn., Allegheny Bar Assn. (civil litigation sect., com. women in law), Womens Bar Assn. of We. Pa., Am. Judicature Soc. Democrat. Presbyterian. Avocations: skiing, sailing, bicycling, classical music, cooking. Author: Compendium of the Law of Prisoner's Rights, 1979; contbr. articles to profl. jours. Office: 518B US PO And Courthouse Pittsburgh PA 15219

SENSIPER, SAMUEL, consulting electrical engineer; b. Elmira, N.Y., Apr. 26, 1919; s. Louis and Molly (Pedolsky) S.; m. Elaine Marie Zwick, Sept. 10, 1950; children—Martin, Sylvia, David. B.S.E.E., M.I.T., 1939, Sc.D., 1951; E.E., Stanford U., 1941. Asst. project engr. to sr. project engr., cons. Sperry Gyroscope, Garden City, Great Neck, N.Y., 1941-51; sect. head and sr. staff cons. Hughes Aircraft, Culver City, Malibu, Calif., 1951-60; lab. div. mgr. Space Gen. Corp., Glendale, Azusa, Los Angeles, 1960-67; lab. mgr. TRW, Redondo Beach, Calif., 1967-70; cons. elec. engr., Los Angeles, 1970-73; dir. engring. Transco Products, Venice, Calif., 1973-75; cons. elec. engr. in pvt. practice, Los Angeles, 1975—; faculty U. So. Calif., Los Angeles, 1955-56, 79-80. Contbr. articles to profl. jours. Recipient Cert. of Commendation U.S. Navy, 1946; indsl. electronics fellow M.I.T., 1947-48. Fellow IEEE, AAAS; mem. Calif. Soc. Profl. Engrs., Fedn. Am. Scientists, M.I.T. Alumni Assn., Stanford Alumni Assn., Electromagnetics Acad., Sigma Xi, Eta Kappa Nu. Patentee in field. Home: 6011 S Holt Ave Los Angeles CA 90056-1415 Office: PO Box 3102 Culver City CA 90231-3102

SENSOR, MARY DELORES, hospital official, consultant; b. Erie, Pa., July 20, 1930; d. Sergie Pavl Malinowski and Leocadia Mary Francis (Machalinski) Harner; m. Robert Louis Charles Sensor, Apr. 21, 1945; children—Robert Louis Paul, Stephen Maxmillian Augustus, Therese Blaze, Katryn Anne. Student in Pre-Medicine, Gannon U., 1968-72, M.S. in Health Care Adminstrn., 1986; B.S. in Hosp. Adminstrn., Daemon Coll., 1972. Intern in hosp. adminstrn. Harvard U., Boston, 1972; dir. med. records St. Mary Hosp., Langhorne, Pa., 1972-74, Moses Taylor Hosp., Scranton, Pa., 1975-77, Erie County Geriatric Ctr., Fairview, Pa., 1988-92; dir. utilization rev. Millcreek Community Hosp., Erie, Pa., 1983—; bd. dirs. Christian Health Care Ctr., Erie, 1983-84; cons. prof. in-hosp. adminstrn. and med. records U. Pitts. and Temple U., 1972-74; contbr. paper 6th World Congress Automated Med. Data, Washington; presenter paper, Computer Adaption of SNOMed to DRG Assignment, to 12th Annual Symposium on Computer Application in Med. Care, Washington., Bd. dirs St. John Kanty Prep. Sch., Erie, 1970-71, pres. Ladies Aux., 1970-71. Mem. Am. Med. Rec. Assn., Pa. Med. Record Assn., NW Pa. Med. Record Assn. (sec. treas. 1982-84), Nat. Assn. Quality Assurance Profls., Pa. Assn. Quality Assurance Profls. Roman Catholic. Club: Siebenburger Singing Soc. Avocations: Profl. classical dancing; researcher early man's migration patterns; gourmet cooking; collecting jazz. Home: 3203 Regis Dr Erie PA 16510-2612

SENTELLE, DAVID BRYAN, federal judge; b. Canton, N.C., Feb. 12, 1943; s. Horace Richard, Jr., and Maude (Ray) S.; m. Jane LaRue Oldham, June 19, 1965; children: Sharon Rene, Reagan Elaine, Rebecca Grace. AB, U. N.C., 1965, JD with honors, 1968. Bar: N.C. 1968, U.S. Dist. Ct. (we. dist.) N.C. 1969, U.S. Ct. Appeals (4th cir.) 1970. Assoc. Uzzell & Dumont, Asheville, N.C., 1968-70; asst. U.S. atty. City of Charlotte, N.C., 1970-74, dist. judge, 1974-77; ptnr. Tucker, Hicks, Sentelle, Moon & Hodge, P.A., Charlotte, 1977-85; judge U.S. Dist. Ct. (we. dist.) N.C., Charlotte, 1985-87, U.S. Ct. Appeals D.C., 1987—; adj. prof. Fla. State U. Coll. Law; presiding judge Spl. Divsn. for Appointment of Ind. Counsels, 1992—. Contbr. articles to profl. jours. Chmn. Mecklenburg County Rep. Com., 1978-80; chmn. N.C. State Rep. Conv., 1979-80. Dameron fellow, 1967. Mem. ABA, Fed. Bar Assn. (chpt. pres. 1975), Mecklenburg County Bar Assn. Baptist. Lodges: Masons, Scottish Rite, Shriners. Office: US Court of Appeals 333 Constitution Ave NW Washington DC 20001-2802*

SENTENNE, JUSTINE, corporate ombudsman; b. Montreal, Que., Can.; d. Paul Emile and Irene Genevieve (Laliberte) S. MBA, U. Que., Montreal, 1993, postgrad. McGill U., Ecole Nat. d'Adminstrn. Publique, 1989-91. Fin. analyst, assoc. mgr. portfolio Bush Assocs., Montreal, 1970-82; city councillor, mem. exec. com. City of Montreal and Montreal Urban Com., 1978-82; adminstrv. asst. Montreal Conv. Ctr., 1983; dir. sponsorship Cen. Com. for Montreal Papal Visit, 1984; dir. pub. rels. Coopers & Lybrand, Montreal, 1985-87; exec. dir. Que. Heart Found., 1987-89; corp. ombudsman Hydro-Que., Montreal, 1991—; tchr. DSA program Concordia U.; v.p., bd. dirs. Armand Frappier Found., Can., Chateau Dufresne Mus. Decorative Arts, Montreal, 1985-90; chmn. bd. Wilfrid Pelletier Found., Montreal, 1986-91; bd. dirs. St. Joseph's Oratory, 1979-92, Caisse Populaire Desjardins Notre Dame de Grace, Montreal, 1980—; mem. jury John Labatt Ltd., London, Ont., 1982-86. Notre Dame de Grace v.p. riding assoc. Liberal Party of Can., chairperson Women's Commn.; mem. bd. govs. Youth and Music Can., Montreal, 1981-86; chmn. bd. The Women's Ctr., Montreal, 1986-88, Vol. Bur. Montreal, 1986-87; bd. dirs. Palais des Congres de Montreal, 1981-89, Port of Montreal, 1983-84, Can. Ctr. for Ecumenism, Montreal, 1968-85, Villa Notre-Dame de Grace, Montreal, 1979-87, v.p. Montreal Diet Dispensary, 1989—, Pathways to Faith, 1990—; bd. mgmt. Saidye Bronfman Ctr. for Arts, 1994—. Named Career Woman of Yr., Sullivan Bus. Coll., 1979; recipient Silver medal Ville de Paris, 1981, Women's Kansas City Assn. for Internat. Rels. and Trade medal, 1982. Fellow Fin. Analysts Fedn. N.Y., Inst. Fin. Analysts, Montreal Soc. Investment Analysts; mem. Cercle Fin. et Placement, Corporation Professionelle des adminstrs. agrées, Assn. Profl. Adminstrs., The Ombudsman Assn. Roman Catholic.

SENTER, ALAN ZACHARY, communications company executive; b. N.Y.C., Nov. 8, 1941; s. Hyman B. and Reva (Cooperwasser) S.; m. Karen G. Yellin, Dec. 26, 1965; children: Marc G., Elise J. BS, U. R.I., 1963; MBA, U. Chgo., 1965. Dir. internat. fin. Xerox Corp., Stamford, Conn., 1975-77; v.p. fin. Latin Am. Xerox Corp., Greenwich, Conn., 1977-79; v.p. fin. bus. products Xerox Corp., Rochester, N.Y., 1979-80; asst. contr. Xerox Corp., Stamford, 1981-85, v.p., treas., 1985-90, v.p. fin., 1990-92; exec. v.p., CFO Internat. Specialty Products/GAF Corp., Wayne, N.J., 1993—, Nynex Corp., N.Y.C., 1994—; bd. dirs. XL Ins., Bermuda, Nynex CableCom., Eng. Capt. USAR, 1966-68, Vietnam. Jewish. Avocations: skiing, tennis. Office: Nynex Corp 1113 Westchester Ave White Plains NY

SENTER, JACK, art director, production designer. Art dir.: (TV movies) Kung Fu, 1972, The Execution, 1985, Desperate, 1987, Nutcracker: Money, Madness, and Murder, 1987, (films) No Deposit, No Return, 1976, Obsession, 1976, Freaky Friday, 1976, Oh, God!, 1977, Greased Lightning, 1977, Return from Witch Mountain, 1978, Go Tell the Spartans, 1978, Love and Bullets, 1979, The Man Who Loved Women, 1983, Micki & Maude, 1984, Far and Away, 1992; prodn. designer: (films) Modern Problems, 1981, The New Adventures of Pippi Longstocking, 1988. Office: care Tom Miller The Miller Agency 23236 Lyons Ave Ste 219 Santa Clarita CA 91321-2635

SENTER, LYONEL THOMAS, JR., federal judge; b. Fulton, Miss., July 30, 1933; s. L. T. and Eva Lee (Jetton) S.; married. B.S., U. So. Miss., 1956; LL.B., U. Miss., 1959. Bar: Miss. 1959. County pros. atty., 1960-64, U.S. commr., 1966-68; judge Miss. Circuit Ct., Circuit 1, 1968-80, U.S. Dist. Ct. (no. dist.) Miss., 1980—. Mem. Miss. State Bar. Democrat. Office: US Dist Ct PO Box 925 Aberdeen MS 39730-0925

SENTER, MERILYN P(ATRICIA), former state legislator and freelance reporter; b. Haverhill, Mass., Mar. 17, 1935; d. Paul Barton and Mary Etta (Herrin) Staples; m. Donald Neil Senter, Apr. 23, 1960; children: Karen Anne Hussey, Brian Neil. Grad., McIntosh Bus. Coll., 1955. Sec. F.S. Hamlin Ins. Agy., Haverhill, Mass., 1955-60; free lance reporter Plaistow-Hampstead News, Rockingham county newspapers, Exeter and Stratham, N.H., 1970-89; mem. N.H. Gen. Ct., Rockingham Dist. 9, 1988-96. Sec. Hwy. Safety Com., Plaistow, N.H., 1976—; sec., bd. dirs. Region 10 Commn. Support Svcs. Inc., Atkinson, N.H., 1982-88; chmn. Plaistow Area Transit Adv. Com., 1990-93; active Devel. Disabilities Coun., 1993—; mem. Plaistow Bd. Selectmen, 1996-99. Named Woman of Yr., N.H. Bus. and Profl. Women, 1983, Nat. Grange Citizen of Yr., 1992. Republican. Avocations: nature, grandchildren, handicapped issues. Home and Office: 11 Maple Ave Plaistow NH 03865-2221

SENTER, WILLIAM JOSEPH, publishing company executive; b. N.Y.C., Dec. 4, 1921; s. Joseph and Sarah (Greenglass) S.; m. Irene Phoebe Marcus, Aug. 3, 1952; children: Adam Douglas, Caren Amy. B.B.A., CCNY, 1947. Chmn. bd., mng. editor Deadline Data, Inc., N.Y.C., 1962-66; pres. Unipub, Inc. (merged with Xerox Corp. 1971), N.Y.C., 1966-72; v.p. planning and devel. Xerox Info. Resources Group (includes AutEx Systems, R.R. Bowker Co., Ginn & Co., Univ. Microfilms Internat., Unipub Inc., Xerox Edn. Publs., Xerox Learning Systems, Xerox Computer Services), Greenwich, Conn., 1973-74; v.p. info. pub. Xerox Info. Resources Group, Greenwich, 1974-75; pres. Xerox Info. Resources Group, 1976-80, chmn., 1980-86; v.p. Xerox Corp., Stamford, Conn., 1978-86; pres. R.R. Bowker Co., N.Y.C., 1974-75. Served with U.S. Army, 1942-46. Mem. Assn. Am. Pubs. (dir. 1978-81), Info. Industry Assn. (dir. 1980-83). Office: PO Box 364 Cos Cob CT 06807-0364 *Always remember that life, in all its many stages, is truly a continuous series of adventures into the unknown and unexpected. Accordingly, the key to the fullness of life is each person's ability to daily generate a sense of excitement and discovery that one is able to overcome fears and the rebuffs of occasional failure.*

SENTER, WILLIAM OSCAR, retired air force officer; b. Stamford, Tex., June 15, 1910; s. William Oscar and Mary Ellen (Futrell) S.; m. Ruth Jane Tinsley, Apr. 10, 1937 (dec. Apr. 1967); children: Suellen, Ruth Jane; m. Carolyn C. Fallon, Jan. 2, 1973. Student, Hardin-Simmons U., 1929; BS, U.S. Mil. Acad., 1933; postgrad., Mass. Inst. Tech., 1938, Air War Coll., 1948-49; Aero. Engr., U. Okla., 1957. Commd. 2d lt. Coast Arty. Corps U.S. Army, 1933, attached to air corps and apptd. student officer, 1933; advanced through grades to lt. gen. USAF, 1963; comdr. Oklahoma City Air Material Area, 1954-57; dir. Procurement and Prodn. Hdqrs., Air Materiel Command Wright-Patterson AFB, 1957-59; asst. dep. chief staff materiel Hdqrs. USAF, 1959-63; dir. petroleum logistics policy Dept. Def., 1963-66, ret., 1966; exec. v.p. Natural Gas Supply Assn., 1966-74. Decorated D.S.M., Legion of Merit with oak leaf cluster. Mem. Air Force Assn., Assn. Grads. U.S. Mil. Acad., Air Force Hist. Found., Order Daedalians, Monarch Country Club. Roman Catholic. Home: 1100 SW Shoreline Dr Apt 200 Palm City FL 34990-4543

SENTURIA, YVONNE DREYFUS, pediatrician, epidemiologist; b. Houston, Jan. 16, 1951. BA in Biology and Sociology, Rice U., 1973; MD, U. Tex., San Antonio, 1977; MSc in Epidemiology, London Sch. Hygiene and Tropical Medicine, 1985. Diplomate Am. Bd. Pedias. Pediat. resident Shands Tchg. Hosp., Gainesville, Fla., 1977-79, Tex. Children's Hosp., Houston, 1979-80; instr., asst. prof. Coll. Medicine, Baylor U., Houston, 1980-82; sr. clin. med. officer Hammersmith and Fulham Health Authority, London, 1982-83; cons. pediatrician Kingston (Eng.) Hosp., 1983, Northwick Park Hosp., London, 1983; rsch. pediatrician Charing Cross Hosp. Med. Sch., London, 1984-85; clin. lectr. Inst. Child Health, London, 1985-88; attending pediatrician and epidemiologist Children's Meml. Hosp., Chgo., 1989—. Fellow Am. Acad. Pediats.; mem. Ambulatory Pediat. Assn., Midwest Soc. Pediat. Rsch. Office: Children's Meml Hosp 2300 Childrens Plz Box 208 Chicago IL 60614

SENZEL, MARTIN LEE, lawyer; b. Rochester, N.Y., June 21, 1944; s. Albert Benjamin and Besse (Lipson) S.; m. Dagni Maren Belgum, Feb. 17, 1979; 1 child, Whitney. BA, Yale U., 1966, LLB, 1969. Bar: N.Y. 1971, U.S. Dist. Ct. (so. dist.) N.Y., U.S. Ct. Appeals (2nd cir.) 1973. Assoc. Cravath, Swaine & Moore, N.Y.C., 1969-77; ptnr. Cravath, Swaine & Moore, 1977—. Mem. ABA, N.Y. State Bar Assn., Assn. Bar City N.Y. Home: 101 Central Park W New York NY 10023-4204 Office: Cravath Swaine & Moore Worldwide Plaza 825 8th Ave New York NY 10019-7416

SEPAHPUR, HAYEDEH C(HRISTINE), investment executive; b. Lincoln, Nebr., Dec. 8, 1958; d. Bahman and Marylin Lou (Duffy) S.; m. Bahman Robert Kosrovani, May 2, 1992; 1 child, Cyrus Thomas Simonson Kosrovani. BS, Lehigh U., 1983. V.p. Drexel Burnham Lambert Inc., N.Y.C., 1982-90, Donaldson, Lufkin & Jenrette, New York City, 1990-92, Lehman Bros., Inc., N.Y.C., 1992—. Sponsor Jr. Statesmen of Am. Found., Washington, 1976—; charter mem. Nat. Mus. Women in the Arts, Washington, 1985—; bd. dirs. Coll. Express Project, Bronx, N.Y., 1987—; mem. Inst. Asian Studies, St. Thomas Episc. Ch. Mem. Nat. Trust Hist. Preservation, The Asia Soc., Women's Campaign Fund, N.Y. Soc. Libr., French Inst., WISH List, Parents League, N.Y. Women's Found., Fin. Women's Assn. (N.Y. chpt.), Persian Heritage Found., Mensa, Gamma Phi Beta. Club: Downtown Athletic (N.Y.C.). Home: 220 E 67th St Apt 12-d New York NY 10021-6255 Office: Lehman Bros Inc 3 World Fin Ctr 200 Vesey St Fl 6 New York NY 10285-0600

SEPESI, JOHN DAVID, artist; b. Monessen, Pa., Aug. 12, 1931; s. John Lloyd and Gizella Elizabeth (Gnip) S. AA, San Bernardino Valley Coll., 1957; BA, Mexico City Coll., 1958. head cashier Club Cal-Neva Casino, Reno, 1983-90. One-man shows include Washoe County Libr., 1987, Reno City Hall Gallery, 1990, Town Ctr. Gallery, 1992; exhibited in group shows at Wilbur D. May Mus., Reno, 1986, Reno City Hall Gallery, 1987, 88, Shoppers Sq., Reno, 1990-91, Brewery Art Ctr., Carson City, 1991-93, Las Vegas Hist. Soc. Mus., 1990, El Wiegand Mus., Reno, 1990, Town Ctr. Gallery, 1992-93, Nev. State Fair, Reno, 1993-95, River Gallery, Reno, 1994-95, Glenn Duncan Sch., Reno, 1995; contbr. articles to profl. jours. Staff sgt. USAF, 1952-56. Mem. Nev. Artists Assn. (v.p. 1990—, exec. bd. 1991—), Sierra Watercolor Soc., Sierra Arts Found., Nev. Mus. Art, Nev. State Coun. on the Arts, Nev. Alliance for the Arts. Republican. Home and Office: 280 Island Ave Apt 1007 Reno NV 89501-1804

SEPKO, KAREN LUCIA, chemical engineer, consultant; b. Moses Lake, Wash., Apr. 9, 1962. BS in Chem. Engring., U. Ariz., 1987. Project engr. Manville Sales Corp., Corona, Calif., 1987-90; plant engr. NCR Corp., Brea, Calif., 1990-91; process engr. Martin Marietta Magnesia Specialties, Woodville, Ohio, 1994—; environ. cons., Fontana, Calif., 1991. Author: (book) Paint Tng. Manual, 1985. Avocations: stained glass, golf, real estate investor. Home: 8945 Rolling Hill Dr Holland OH 43528 Office: 8945 Rollins Hill Holland OH 43528

SEPPALA, KATHERINE SEAMAN (MRS. LESLIE W. SEPPALA), retail company executive, clubwoman; b. Detroit, Aug. 22, 1919; d. Willard D. and Elizabeth (Miller) Seaman; B.A., Wayne State U., 1941; m. Leslie W. Seppala, Aug. 15, 1941; children: Sandra Kay, William Leslie. Mgr. women's bldg. and student activities adviser Wayne State U., 1941-43; pres. Harper Sports Shops, Inc., 1947-85, chmn. bd., treas., sec., v.p. 1985—; ptnr. Seppala Bldg. Co., 1971—. Mich. service chmn. women grads. Wayne State U., 1962—, 1st v.p., fund bd., Girl and Cub Scouts; mem. Citizen's adv. com. on sch. needs Detroit Bd. Edn., 1957—, mem. high sch. study com., 1966—; chmn., mem. loan fund bd. Denby High Sch. Parents Scholarship; bd. dirs., v.p. Wayne State U. Fund; precinct del. Rep. Party, 14th dist., 1956—, del. convs.; mem. com. Myasthenia Gravis Support Assn. Recipient Ann. Women's Service award Wayne State U., 1963. Recipient Disting. Alumni award Wayne State U., 1971. Mem. Intercollegiate Assn. Women Students (regional rep. 1941-45), Women Wayne State U. Alumni (past pres.), Wayne State U. Alumni Assn. (dir., past v.p.), AAUW (dir. past officer), Council Women as Public Policy Makers (editor High lights) Denby Community Ednl. Orgn. (sec.), Met. Detroit Program Planning Inst. (pres.), Internat. Platform Assn., Detroit Met. Book and Author Soc. (treas.), Mortar Bd. (past pres.), Karyatides (past pres.), Anthony Wayne Soc., Alpha Chi Alpha, Alpha Kappa Delta, Delta Gamma Chi, Kappa Delta (chmn. chpt. alumnae adv. bd.). Baptist. Clubs: Zonta (v.p., dir.); Les Cheneaux. Home: 22771 Worthington Ct Saint Clair Shores MI 48081-2603 Office: Harper Sport Shop Inc 23208 Greater Mack Ave Saint Clair Shores MI 48080-3422 *Being successful has made it possible for me to help so many others along the way.*

SEQUEIRA, LUIS, plant pathology educator; b. San Jose, Costa Rica, Sept. 1, 1927; s. Raul and Dora (Jenkins) S.; m. Elizabeth Steinvorth, May 27, 1954; children: Anabel, Marta, Robert, Patricia. AB, Harvard U., 1949, AM, 1950, PhD, 1952. Plant pathologist United Fruit Co., Coto, Costa Rica, 1953-60; research assoc. N.C. State U., Raleigh, 1960-61; prof. plant pathology U. Wis., Madison, 1961-82, J.C. Walker prof. of plant pathology and bacteriology, 1982—; cons. Agracetus, Madison, 1982-93; mgr. competitive grants program USDA, Washington, 1984-85, chief scientist, 1987-88. Contbr. numerous articles to profl. jours. Recipient E. C. Stakman award U. Minn., 1992. Fellow Am. Phytopathological Soc. (editor-in-chief jour. 1979-81, St. Paul sect. v.p. 1984, pres. elect 1985, pres. 1986, Award of Distinction 1994), Am. Acad. Microbiology; mem. Nat. Acad. Scis., Linnean Soc. London. Democrat. Roman Catholic. Home: 10 Appomattox Ct Madison WI 53705-4202 Office: U Wis Dept Plant Pathology 1630 Linden Dr Madison WI 53706-1520

SEQUIN, CARLO H., computer science educator; b. Winterthur, Switzerland, Oct. 30, 1941; came to U.S., 1970; s. Carl R. and Margarit (Schaeppi) S.; m. Margareta Frey, Oct. 5, 1968; children: Eveline, Andre. B.S., U. Basel, Switzerland, 1965, Ph.D., 1969. Mem. tech. staff Bell Labs., Murray Hill, N.J., 1970-76; vis. Mackay lectr. U. Calif.-Berkeley, 1976-77, prof. elec. engring. computer scis., 1977—, assoc. chmn. computer sci., 1980-83. Contbr. 150 articles to profl. jours.; author first book on charge-coupled devices; patentee integrated circuits. Fellow IEEE; mem. Assn. Computing Machinery, Swiss Acad. Engring. Scis. Office: U Calif Dept EECS Computer Scis Divsn Berkeley CA 94720-1776

SERAFIN, BARRY D., television news correspondent; b. Coquille, Oreg., June 22, 1941; s. Peter B. and Ina V. Serafin; m. Lynn Van Camp, Aug. 24, 1963; children—Lisa Marie, Sandra Lynn. B.A., Wash. State U., 1964. Producer, dir. Sta. KOAP-TV, Portland, Oreg., 1964-65; reporter Sta. KOIN-TV, Portland, 1965-68, Sta. KMOX-TV, St. Louis, 1968-69; corr. CBS News, Washington, 1969-79; nat. corr. ABC News, Washington, 1979—. (Recipient Emmy award 1974). Office: ABC News Washington Bureau 1717 Desales St NW Washington DC 20036-4407

SERAFIN, DONALD, plastic surgeon; b. N.Y.C., Jan. 18, 1938; s. Stephen Michael and Julia (Sopko) S.; A.B., Duke U., 1960, M.D., 1964; m. Patricia Serafin; children: Allison Elizabeth, Christina Julia, Donald Stephen, Lara

Leigh. Surg. intern Grady Meml. Hosp., Atlanta, 1964-65; resident in surgery Emory U. Hosp., Atlanta, 1965-69; asst. resident in plastic and reconstructive surgery Duke U. Med. Center, Durham, N.C., 1971-73, chief resident, 1973-74; Christine Kleinert fellow in hand surgery U. Louisville Hosp., 1972-73; practice medicine specializing in plastic surgery, Durham; mem. staff Durham County Gen. Hosp.; asst. prof. plastic, reconstructive and maxillofacial surgery Duke U., 1974-77, assoc. prof., 1977-81, prof., 1981—, chief div. plastic, reconstructive and maxillofacial surgery; chmn. Plastic Surgery Rsch. Council, 1983. Assoc. editor Jour. Reconstructive Microsurgery. Contbr. articles to profl. jours. Served to maj. M.C., USAF, 1969-71, col. M.C., USAR. Diplomate Am. Bd. Surgery, Am. Bd. Plastic Surgery. Recipient Air Force commedation medal, 1971, U.S. Army commendation medal, 1990. Fellow ACS; mem. Internat. Soc. Reconstructive Microsurgery, Am. Soc. Plastic and Reconstructive Surgeons, Am. Assn. Plastic Surgeons, Am. Burn Assn., AMA, Plastic Surgery Research Council, N.C. Soc. Plastic, Maxillofacial and Reconstructive Surgeons, Southeastern Soc. Plastic and Reconstructive Surgeons, Southeastern Med. Dental Soc., Sigma Xi. Office: Duke U Med Ctr PO Box 3708 Durham NC 27710

SERAFIN, JOHN ALFRED, art educator; b. Washington, Nov. 3, 1942; s. John Bernard and Elizabeth (Pichette) S.; m. Josephine Azzarello, Apr. 12, 1969 (div. 1990); children: John Calvin, Michael Joseph, Mary Elizabeth. Student, Syracuse U., 1967-69, MS, 1974; BFA, U. Utah, 1971. Cert. tchr., N.Y. Graphic artist Sears, Roebuck and Co., Syracuse, 1967-68; dir. advt. Around the Town mag., Syracuse, 1969; tchr. art Blodgett Jr. High Sch., Syracuse, 1971-76, Roberts Elem. Sch., Syracuse, 1986-87, Fowler High Sch., Syracuse, 1976—; yearbook adviser Blodgett Jr. High Sch., 1971-75, coach track, 1971-74, coach cross-country, 1972-74; jr. class adviser Fowler High Sch., 1977-78. Artist mag. cover design U. Utah Pharmacy Mag., 1970, Fine Art Index Internat., 1995 edit., Chgo.; group exhbns. include Syracuse State, 1989-92, N.Y. State Fair, 1977, 89, 90, Everson Mus., Syracuse, 1985, Cooperstown (N.Y.) Nat. Show, 1991, Westmoreland Nat. Art Show, Latrobe, Pa., 1995, Nat. Design Congress of Art & Design Exhbn. Art Reach '95, Salt Lake City, Tex. Nat. Show, Stephen Austin State U., 1996, Stad Diksmuide World Show, Brussels, 1996; represented by Montserrat Art Gallery, N.Y.C., Limner Gallery, N.Y.C., Agora Gallery, N.Y.C. Recipient award of Excellence, Manhattan Arts Mag., N.Y.C. Mem. N.Y. State United Tchrs., Syracuse Tchrs. Assn. (rep. 1972-75), Associated Artists Galleries, Allied Artists of Am., Nat. Art Educators Assn., Syracuse U. Orange Pack and Alumni Assn., Crimson Club U. Utah Alumni Assn., N.Y. State Art Tchrs. Assn., Cooperstown Art Assn., Elks, Moose. Democrat. Avocations: Syracuse University sports, brewing, blues music, working out, travel. Home: 1205 Teall Ave Syracuse NY 13206-3467 Office: Fowler H S 227 Magnolia St Syracuse NY 13204-2707 *The artist can turn the not yet into reality.*

SERAFIN, ROBERT JOSEPH, science center administrator, electrical engineer; b. Chgo., Apr. 22, 1936; s. Joseph Albert and Antoinette (Gazda) S.; m. Betsy Furgerson, Mar. 4, 1961; children: Katherine, Jenifer, Robert Joseph Jr., Elizabeth. BSEE, U. Notre Dame, 1958; MSEE, Northwestern U., 1961; PhDEE, Ill. Inst. Tech., 1972. Engr. Hazeltine Rsch. Corp. Ill. Inst. Tech. Rsch. Inst., 1960-62; assoc. engr., rsch. engr., sr. rsch. engr. Nat. Ctr. for Atmospheric Rsch., Boulder, Colo., 1962-73, mgr. field observing facility, 1973-80; dir. atmospheric tech. div. Nat. Ctr. for Atmospheric Rsch., Bouulder, Colo., 1981-89, dir. ctr., 1989—; chair Nat. Weather Svc. Modernization Com. Author: Revised Radar Handbook, 1989; contbr. numerous articles to profl. jours.; editl. bd./com. Acta Meteorologica Sinica; editl. founder Jour. Atmospheric and Oceanic Tech.; patentee in field. Speaker various civic groups in U.S. and internationally. Fellow Am. Meteorol. Soc. (mem. exec. com.); Mem. IEEE (sr.), NAE, NAS (human rights com.), Boulder C. of C., Sigma Xi. Avocations: golf, fishing, skiing. Office: Nat Ctr Atmospheric Rsch PO Box 3000 1850 Table Mesa Dr Boulder CO 80303-5602

SERAMUR, JOHN C., bank executive; b. 1943. With First Fin. Corp., Stevens Point, Wis., 1966—, now pres., CEO. Office: First Fin Corp 1305 Main St Stevens Point WI 54481-2830*

SERAPHINE, DANNY PETER, drummer; b. Chgo., Aug. 28, 1948; s. John and Valentine and Mary (Colangelo) S.; m. Rosemarie Stevenson, June 3, 1967; children: Christine, Danielle. Grad. high sch. Owner night club B. Ginnings, Schaumburg, Ill., from 1974; owner clothing store Peabody's, Chgo., from 1974. Mem. musical group, Chicago, 1967—; co-composer: Lowdown, 1972, Devil's Sweet, 1974, Aire, 1974; albums include Chicago I through Chicago XVIII; (with group Chicago) Chicago 19, 1988, Chicago Transit Authority, 1989, Liberation, 1990. Address: care Warner Bros 75 Rockefeller Plz New York NY 10019-6908

SERBAROLI, FRANCIS J., lawyer, educator, writer; b. N.Y.C., Feb. 8, 1952. AB, Fordham U., 1973, JD, 1977. Bar: N.Y. 1978, U.S. Dist. Ct. (ea. and so. dists.) N.Y. 1978, U.S. Ct. Appeals (2d and D.C. cirs.) 1979, U.S. Supreme Ct. 1983. Asst. atty. gen. N.Y. State Dept. Law, 1978-80; ptnr. Cadwalader Wickersham & Taft, N.Y.C.; vice chmn. N.Y. State Pub. Health Coun., 1995—; health law columnist The N.Y. Law Jour. Bd. trustees Loyola Sch., N.Y.C. Fellow N.Y. Acad. Medicine; mem. Nat. Health Lawyers' Assn., N.Y. State Bar Assn., Assn. of Bar of City of N.Y. Office: Cadwalader Wickersham Taft 100 Maiden Ln New York NY 10038

SERBEIN, OSCAR NICHOLAS, business educator, consultant; b. Collins, Iowa, Mar. 31, 1919; s. Oscar Nicholas and Clara Matilda (Shearer) S.; m. Alice Marie Bigger, Sept. 16, 1952; children: Mary Llewellyn Serbein Parker, John Gregory. BA with highest distinction, U. Iowa, 1940, MS, 1941; PhD, Columbia U., 1951. Grad. asst. math. U. Iowa, Iowa City, 1940-41; clk. Met. Life Ins. Co., N.Y.C., 1941-42; lectr. U. Calif., Berkeley, summer 1948, 50; lectr., asst. prof., assoc. prof. Columbia U., N.Y.C., 1947-59; prof. ins. Stanford (Calif.) U., 1959-89, dir. doctoral program Grad. Sch. Bus., 1960-64, prof. emeritus ins., 1989—; cons. Ins. Info. Inst., N.Y.C., 1971-78, N.Am. Re-Assurance Life Service Co., Palo Alto, 1973, SRI Internat., Menlo Park, Calif., 1980-81, other bus.; cons., expert witness various law firms. Author: Paying for Medical Care in the U.S., 1953, Educational Activities of Business, 1961; co-author: Property and Liability Insurance, 4 ed., 1967, Risk Management: Text and Cases, 2 ed., 1983; also articles. Bd. dirs. Sr. Citizens Coord. Coun., Palo Alto, 1986-89, dir. emeritus, 1990—. Maj. USAF, WWII. Decorated Bronze Star, 1944. Mem. Am. Risk and Ins. Assn., Western Risk and Ins. Assn., Phi Beta Kappa, Sigma Xi, Beta Gamma Sigma. Democrat. Methodist. Club: Stanford Faculty. Avocation: gardening. Home: 731 San Rafael Pl Stanford CA 94305-1007 Office: Stanford U Grad Sch Business Stanford CA 94305

SERBUS, PEARL SARAH DIECK, former free-lance writer, former editor; b. Riverdale, Ill.; d. Emil Edwin and Pearl (Kaiser) Dieck; m. Gerald Serbus, Jan. 26, 1946 (dec. Aug. 1969); children—Allan Lester, Bruce Alan, Curt Lyle. Mem. home econs. staff, writer Chgo. Herald Examiner, 1934-39; operator test kitchen Household Sci. Inst., Mdse. Mart, Chgo., 1940-45; free-lance writer grocery chains, Chgo., 1945-49; Riv.-Dolton corr. Calumet Index, Chgo., 1953-58, editorial asst., 1958-60, asst. editor, 1960-68, editor, 1968-72; with Suburban Index, Chgo., 1959-72, editor, 1960-72; mng. editor Index Publs., 1972-74; free lance writer, 1974-94, ret., 1994. Public relations vol. New Hope Sch., 1959-67; bd. dirs. United Fund of Riverdale, Roseland Mental Health Assn., Thornton chpt. Am. Field Service; cmty. rels. vol. Ctrl. Ark. Therapy Inst. Recipient Disting. Service Meml. scroll PTA, 1959, Sch. Bell award Ill. Edn. Assn., 1965, Outstanding Citizen award Chgo. South C. of C., 1972. Named Outstanding Civic Leader Am.; recipient Vol. citation Ctrl. Ark. Radiation Therapy Inst., 1994. Mem. Ill. Woman's Press Assn. (past pres. Woman of Distinction 1968, recipient 46 state awards, 3 nat. awards), Ark. Press Women (Communicator of Achievement award 1991, honored 50 Yr. member 1994), Nat. Fedn. Press Women (past pres. parley past presidents 1981, past dir. protocol, Honors 50 Yrs. Membership 1994), Riverdale (v.p. 1966-68), Chgo. South (v.p., dir.) chambers commerce. Home: 1421 N University Ave Apt 215N Little Rock AR 72207-5241

SEREBRIER, JOSÉ, musician, conductor, composer; b. Montevideo, Uruguay, Dec. 3, 1938; came to U.S., 1956; s. David and Frida (Wasser) S.; m. Carole Farley, Mar. 29, 1969; 1 child, Lara Adriana Francesca. Diploma, Nat. Conservatory, Montevideo, 1956, Curtis Inst. Music, 1958; BA, U. Minn., 1960; studied with Aaron Copland, Anatal Dorati, Pierre Monteux. Ind. composer, condr., 1955—; apprentice condr. Minn. Orch., 1958-60; assoc. condr. Am. Symphony Orch., N.Y.C., 1962-66; music dir. Am. Shakespeare Festival, 1966; composer-in-residence Cleve. Orch., 1968-71; artistic dir. Internat. Festival of Ams., Miami, 1984—, Festival Miami, 1985—; guest condr. numerous orchs. including London Symphony, London Philharm., Paris Radio, Cleve. Symphony Orch., Phila. Symphony Orch., Pitts. Symphony Orch.; founder, artistic dir. Festival Miami (internat. arts festival), 1984. Composer: (for orch.) Variations on a Theme from Childhood, (for chamber) Symphony for Percussion, Concerto for Violin and Orch. (recorded by Royal Phila. Orch. on ASV), also works for chorus, voice, keyboard; recs. for RCA, CRI, ASV, KEM, Disc, Trax Classique, EMI, Tioch, Chandos, Varese-Sarabande Decca, IMG, Pickwick, with various orchs.; condr. for many recs. including Sibelius Symphony No. 1, Holst's The Planets, Carmen, Poulenc's opera La Voix Humaine, Shostakovich Film Suites vol. 1 (Deutsche Schallplatten award 1988), Carole Farley Sings French Songs (Deutsche Schallplaten award 1988), (home video) Kultur, Prokoviev's Alexander Nevsky, Beethoven's Eroica and Tchaikovsky Symphony No. 1 with Sydney and Melbourne Symphony Orch., Mendelssohn Symphonies, Beethoven Symphonies, Bloch's Violin Concerto and Serebrier's Poema Elegiaco CD, 1992, Laserdisc of Operas The Telephone by Menotti and La Voix Humaine by Poulenc with Scottish Chamber Orch., 1992, Royal Philharm. Orch., 1992, Dvŏrak Symphonies with Czech State Philharm. for Conifer/BMG, Music of Janacek and Chadwick (4 CDs) for R.R., Hindemith CD with Philharmonia Orch. for ASV. Recipient Ford Found. Condr.'s award, Alice M. Ditson award, 1976, commn. award Nat. Endowment Arts, 1978, Deutsche Schall Platten Critics award, Music Retailers Assn. award for Best Symphony Rec., 1991; Guggenheim fellow, 1958-60; Rockefeller Found. grantee, 1968-70. Mem. Am. Symphony Orch. League, Am. Music Ctr., Am. Fedn. Musicians. Home and Office: 20 Queensgate Gardens, London SW7 5LZ, England *A composer has the duty to communicate with his audience. The academic-intellectual composer of the 50's has become obsolete. Writing just for one's colleagues has fortunately been proven a dead-end.*

SERENBETZ, WARREN LEWIS, financial management company executive; b. N.Y.C., Mar. 27, 1924; s. Lewis E. and Estelle (Weygand) S.; m. Thelma Randby, Apr. 10, 1948; children: Warren Lewis, Paul Halvor, Stuart Weygand, Clay Raymond. B.S., Columbia U., 1944, M.S., 1949. Cons. Emerson Engrs., N.Y.C., 1949-51; with Oliver Corp., 1951-53; with REA Express, 1953-68, sr. v.p., 1966-68; v.p., dir. REA Leasing Corp., 1961-68; chmn. exec. com., chief exec. officer Interpool, Ltd., 1968-86; pres., chief exec. officer Radcliff Group, Inc., 1986—; pres. Containerization and Intermodal Inst., 1986-87; bd. dirs. Containerization and Intermodal Inst., Interpool Ltd., Interpool Inc., Microtech Corp., Trac Lease Inc. Trustee St. Cabrini Nursing Home. Served to lt. (j.g.) USNR, World War II. Named CEO of Yr., Fin. World, 1976; recipient key to city Savannah, Ga. Mem. Am. Mgmt. Pres. Assn., Larchmont Yacht Club, Univ. Club Larchmont, Union League Club. Presbyterian. Home: Hunter Hill West St Harrison NY 10528 Office: Radcliff Group Inc 695 West St Harrison NY 10528-2508

SERENO, PAUL C., paleontologist, educator; b. 1958. Ph.D. in paleontology, Columbia U, NY. Asst. prof. U Chicago, 1987—. Recipient Player of the Yr., Tempo All-Professor Team, Chicago Tribune, 1993. Achievements include discovering Eoraptor, the earliest known dinosaur, in the Argentine foothills of the Andes mountains, and two new species of dinosaur, Afrovenator abakensis and a new type of sauropod, in the Saharan desert about 600 miles northeast of Niamey, Niger. Recent discoveries include another new predatory species and the largest skull of a carnivorous dinosaur, Carcharodontosaurus saharicus, at 5 feet 4 inches long, both found in the Sahara in Morocco. Office: U Chgo Dept Organismal Biology/ Anatomy 1027 E 57th St Chicago IL 60637-1508

SERFAS, RICHARD THOMAS, architecture educator, urban planner, county official; b. Reading, Pa., Nov. 24, 1952; s. Clifford Donald and Helen Catherine (McGovern) S. Student, Jacksonville U., 1970-72; BA, Colo. State U., 1974; MPA, Pa. State U., 1977; MS in Real Estate Devel., Columbia U., 1995. Project coord. ACTION Peace Corps, VISTA, Gary, Ind., 1974-75; city adminstr. City of Beverly Hills, Mo., 1975; grad. rsch. asst. dept. pub. adminstrn. Pa. State U., Middletown, 1976-77; community planner St. Louis County Dept. Planning, 1977-78; mgmt. analyst Clark County Sanitation Dist., Las Vegas, Nev., 1978-79; environ. planner Clark County Dept. Comprehensive Planning, Las Vegas, 1979-80, prin. planner, 1980-84, asst. coord. planning, 1984-85, coord. advance planning, 1985-89, asst. dir., 1989-94; instr. U. Nev. Sch. Architecture, Las Vegas, 1989—; student advisor Las Vegas chpt. AIA, 1989—. Staff advisor Clark County Comprehensive Plan Steering Com., 1980—, Environ. Task Force, Las Vegas, 1984—, Archtl. Design Task Force, Las Vegas, 1984—, Devel. Sector Task Force, Las Vegas, 1984—; mem. Transit Tech. Com., Las Vegas, 1989—. Recipient achievement award Nat. Assn. Counties, 1983-90. Mem. Am. Inst. Cert. Planners, Urban Land Inst., Nat. Assn. Corp. Real Estate Execs., Nat. Coun. for Urban Econ. Devel., Am. Planning Assn. (treas. Nev. chpt. 1979-91, pres. 1992—, Appreciation award 1981, 83, 85, 87, 89, 91, Outstanding Pub. Sector Planning Accomplishment award 1987, 88, 90, 91), Cmty. Assns. Inst. So. Nev. (bd. dirs. 1990-92, sec. 1993—). Democrat. Roman Catholic. Avocations: tennis, skiing, hiking, photography.

SERFLING, SCOTT ROGERS, commodities executive; b. Lake Forest, Ill., Jan. 30, 1951; s. Arthur Carl and Ruth (Rogers) S. BS, Colo. State U., 1973, MS, 1974. Account exec. Merrill Lynch, N.Y.C., 1972-73; account exec. Merrill Lynch, Colorado Springs, Colo., 1973-74, sr. account exec., 1977-78; mgr. A.G. Edwards, Colorado Springs, 1974-75; account exec. E.F. Hutton, Colorado Springs, 1975-77; mgr. Smith, Barney, Colorado Springs, 1978-79; pres. Serfling Securities Inc., Denver, 1979-82, Serfling and Assocs. Inc., Chgo., 1980—, Serfling Internat. Commodities, Chgo., 1982—; mem. gold com., mem. option com., mem. fin. com. Chgo. Mercantile Exch., 1982-88; mng. dir. Moscow Stock Exchange, 1991-92; pres. Moscow Internat. Community exchange, East-West, 1992. Contbr. numerous articles to profl. jours. Mem. Lincoln Park Zoo, Chgo. Opera Soc., Goodman Theatre, Shedd Aquarium, Northlight Theatre. Named Top 100 Stock Brokers, 1983, U.S. Trading Championship Top Commodity Trader, 1984, 85, 86, Future Trader of the Month Futures Mag., 1986. Avocations: golf, sailing, racing, zoo, opera. Office: Serfling and Assocs 20 S Wacker Dr Chicago IL 60606-7409

SERGEY, JOHN MICHAEL, JR., manufacturing company executive; b. Chgo., Nov. 17, 1942; s. John Michael and Helen Ann (Bruchan) S.; m. Sharon Lee Ourada (div. 1982); children: John Michael III, Elisabeth Ann, Mark William, Tanya Ruth; m. Pamela Lynne Murphy, Aug. 8, 1987; children: Brian M., Sarah L. BA in Bus., Northwestern U., 1968; MBA, U. Chgo., 1976. Mgr. rolled products A. M. Castle, Chgo., 1959-74; v.p. Dietzgen Corp., Chgo., 1974-78; dir. sales and mktg. Avery Label, Azusa, Calif., 1978-80; v.p., gen. mgr. Fasson Roll div. Avery, Painesville, Ohio, 1980-84; group v.p. Soabar Products Group div. Avery, Phila., 1984-87, Materials Group div. Avery, Painesville, 1987-89; pres., CEO GAF Materials Corp., Wayne, N.J., 1989—. Office: GAF Materials Corp 1361 Alps Rd Bldg 2-2 Wayne NJ 07470-3700

SERI, ISTVAN, physician, researcher; b. Szombathely, Hungary, Apr. 15, 1951; came to U.S., 1986; s. Istvan and Katalin (Orszagh) S.; m. Eva Novoszel, Oct. 11, 1975; children: David, I. Adam. MD, Semmelweis Med. Sch., Budapest, 1976; PhD, Hungarian Acad. Scis., Budapest, 1985. Resident in pediatrics Semmelweis Med. Sch., Budapest, 1976-79, instr. in pediatrics, 1979-84, asst. prof. in pediatrics, 1984-91; rsch. fellow Karolinska Inst., Stockholm, Sweden, 1984-86; rsch. fellow in nephrology Harvard Med. Sch., Boston, 1986-88, fellow in neonatology, 1988-91, instr. in pediatrics, 1991-94; asst. prof. in pediatrics U. Pa., Phila., 1994—; clin. dir. neonatal svcs. Children's Hosp. Phila., U. Pa., 1994—. Contbr. over 30 articles to profl. jours. Recipient Janeway award Children's Hosp. Boston, 1991-92, CHRC award NIH, Washington, 1991-92, Clin. Investigator award NIH, 1992-94. Fellow Am. Acad. Pediatrics; mem. AMA, Am. Heart Assn., European Soc. Pediatric Rsch., Hungarian Med. Assn., Soc. Pediat. Rsch. Avocations: soccer, tennis, sailing. Office: Children's Hospital Phila 34th St & Civic Ctr Blvd Philadelphia PA 19104

SERKIN, PETER, pianist; b. N.Y.C., July 24, 1947; s. Rudolf and Irene (Busch) S. Student, Curtis Inst. Music, 1958-64. Instr. piano Mannes Coll. of Music, N.Y.C. Debut in, N.Y.C., 1959, appearances including with, Phila., Cleve., N.Y.C., London (Eng.), Zurich (Switzerland), Paris (France), Casals Festival orchs., recitals in, N.Y.C., London, Japan, maj. European and Am. cities; premiered works composed for him by Takemitsu, Berio, Lieberson; appearances including with benefit performances for pacifism, aid to victims of war; rec. artist for, RCA, ProArte, New World Records, CBS records, Boston Records. Recipient prize Premio Accademia Musicale Chigian Siena, 1983. also: Mannes Coll Music 150 W 85th St New York NY 10024

SERNA, JOE, JR., mayor; b. Stockton, Calif.; m. Isabel Serna; children: Phillip, Lisa. BA in Social Sci., Govt., Sacramento State Coll., 1966; postgrad., U. Calif., Davis. Vol. Peace Corps., Guatemala, 1966; edn. advisor Lt.-Gov. Mervyn Dymally, 1975-77; prof. govt. Calif State U., Sacramento, 1969—; mayor City of Sacramento, 1992—. Mem. Sacramento City Coun. 5th Dist., 1981-92, law and legis. com., 1989-92, Housing & Devel. Commn., Sacramento, chmn. budget and fin. com., 1981-89, transp. and cmty. devel. com., 1989-92; dir. United Farmworkers Am.'s Support Com. in Sacramento County, 1970-75; co-trustee Crocker Art Mus. Assn.; founder Thursday Night Market, Mayor's Summer Reading Camp; mem. Sacramento Housing & Devel. Commn.; bd. dirs. Regional Transit. Office: Office of the Mayor 915 I St Sacramento CA 95814-2608*

SERNAQUE, JOSE DAVID, cardiothoracic and vascular surgeon; b. Chiclayo, Peru, Sept. 10, 1944; came to U.S., 1973; s. David and Juana Maria (Tesen) S.; m. Clara Isabel Alcantara; children: David Antonio, Jose Manuel. MD, U. San Marcos, Lima, Peru, 1991. Lic. physician, Md., Ill., Calif. Intern U. San Marcos Affiliated Hosps., 1969-70, resident in cardiology, 1970-72; resident in gen. surgery Luth. Hosp. Md., Balt., 1973-77; resident in cardiovascular and thoracic surgery U. Ill. Med. Ctr., Chgo., 1977-79; pvt. practice cardiovascular and thoracic surbery, 1981—; mem. staff L.A. Cmty. Hosp., East L.A. Drs. Hosp., Santa Martha Hosp., Charter Suburban Hosp., Beverly Hosp, Montebello. Contbr. articles to med. jours. Fellow Am. Coll. Angiology, Internat. Coll. Surgeons; mem. Am. Heart Assn. (sci. coun. in cardiovascular surgery), Los Angeles County Med. Assn., InterAm. Coll. Physicians and Surgeons, Peruvian Am. Med. Soc. Avocations: billiards, pool, poetry. Office: 16660 Paramount Blvd Ste 203 Paramount CA 90723-5458

SERNETT, RICHARD PATRICK, lawyer; b. Mason City, Iowa, Sept. 8, 1938; s. Edward Frank and Loretta M. (Cavanaugh) S.; m. Janet Ellen Ward, Apr. 20, 1963; children: Susan Ellen, Thomas Ward, Stephen Edward, Katherine Anne. BBA, U. Iowa, 1960, JD, 1963. Bar: Iowa 1963, Ill. 1965, U.S. Dist. Ct. (no. dist.) Ill. 1965, U.S. Supreme Ct. 1971. House counsel, asst. sec. Scott, Foresman & Co., Glenview, Ill., 1963-70; sec., legal officer Scott, Foresman & Co., Glenview, 1970-80; v.p., law sec. SFN Cos., Inc., Glenview, 1980-83, sr. v.p., sec., gen. counsel, 1983-85, exec. v.p., gen. counsel, 1985-87; pvt. practice Northbrook, Ill., 1988-90; v.p., sec., gen. counsel Macmillan/McGraw-Hill Sch. Pub. Co., 1990-92; v.p. Bert Early Assoc., Chgo., 1992-93; ptnr. Sernett & Blake, Northfield, Ill., 1993-95; ret., 1995; mem. U.S. Dept. State Adv. Panel on Internat. Copyright, 1972-75. Chmn. bd. dirs. Iowa State U., Broadcasting Co., 1987-94. Mem. ABA (chmn. copyright div. 1972-73, com. on copyright legis. 1967-68, 69-70, com. on copyright office affairs 1966-67, 79-81, com. on program for revision copyright law 1971-72), Am. Intellectual Property Law Assn., Am. Soc. Corp. Secs., Ill. Bar Assn. (chmn. copyright com. 1971-72), Chgo. Bar Assn., Patent Law Assn. Chgo. (bbd. mgrs. 1979-82, chmn. copyright law com. 1972-73, 77-78), Copyright Soc. U.S.A. (trustee 1972-75, 77-80), North Shore Country Club (Glenview, Ill.), Eagle Ridge Country Club (Galena, Ill.), Wyndemere Country Club (Naples, Fla.), Met. Club Chgo. Home: 2579 Fairford Ln Northbrook IL 60062-8101

SERNOFF, LOUIS R., lawyer; b. Sellersville, Pa., Dec. 23, 1940. BA, U. Pa., 1962, LLB, 1965. Bar: D.C. 1966. With Bur. Competition FTC, Washington, 1966-74, atty. advisor to Commr., 1974; ptnr. Baker & Hostetler, Washington. Mem. ABA, Fed. Bar Assn., D.C. Bar. Office: Baker & Hostetler Washington Sq 1050 Connecticut Ave NW Ste 1100 Washington DC 20036-5303*

SEROKA, JAMES HENRY, social sciences educator, university administrator; b. Detroit, Mar. 5, 1950; s. Henry S. and Mary (Wyoral) S.; m. Carolyn Marie White, June 27, 1970; children: Mihail, Maritsa. BA, U. Mich., 1970; MA, Mich. State U., 1972, PhD, 1976. Labor mkt. analyst U.S. Dept. of Labor, Washington, 1970-71; asst. prof. U. N.C., Greensboro, 1976-77, Appalachian State U., Boone, N.C., 1977-79, So. Ill. U., Carbondale, 1979-81; assoc. prof. So. Ill. U., 1981-87, prof., dir., 1987-88; prof., head div. humanities and social scis. Pa. State U., Erie, 1988-90; prof. U. North Fla., Jacksonville, 1990—; also dir. Ctr. for Pub. Leadership, Jacksonville; dir. Master of Pub. Affairs Program Soc. Ill. U., 1987-88, Rural and Small Town Adminstrn. Project, 1980-85; asst. dir. Appalachian Regional Bur. Govts., Boone, N.C., 1977-79; manpower planning analyst U.S. Dept. Labor, Washington, 1970-71; exchange prof. Fakultet Politickih Nauka, Univerzitet u Beogradu, Yugoslavia, 1986; sr. researcher Coun. for the Internat. Exchange Scholars Yugoslavia, 1980; mem. state adv. com. Gov.'s Rural Affairs Coun. for State of Ill., 1988. Co-author: Political Organizations in Social Yugoslavia, 1986 (Choice award 1987); editor Rural Public Adminstration, 1986; co-editor: Developed Socialism, 1982, Comparative Political Systems, 1990, Yugoslavia: The Failure of Democratic Transformation, 1992; contbr. numerous articles to profl. jours. Recipient Akademischer Austausch Dienst Lang. scholar Fed. Republic of Germany, 1988 and numerous other grants, traveling fellows. Mem. Am. Soc. Pub. Adminstrn. (so Ill. chpt. 1982-83), Nat. Civic League, Am. Polit. Sci. Assn., Internat. Polit. Sci. Assn., Midwest Polit. Sci. Assn., So. Polit. Sci. Assn., Southwestern Polit. Sci. Assn., Western Polit. Sci. Assn., Policy Studies Orgn., Acad. Polit. Sci., Rural Sociol. Assn., Internat. Studies Assn., Am. Assn. Advancement of Slavic Studies, Western Social Sci. Assn., Cmty. Devel. Soc. Office: U North Fla Ctr Local Govt Adminstn 4567 Saint Johns Bluff Rd S Jacksonville FL 32224-2646

SERONDE, ADELE HERTER, artist; b. Manchester, Mass., June 17, 1925; d. Christian A. and Mary Caroline (Pratt) Herter; m. Joseph Seronde, Aug. 26, 1945; children: Antoine, Jacques, Pierre, Dorée, Jeanne. Student, Bennington Coll., 1943-45. One-woman show DeCordova Mus., Lincoln, Mass., 1956, Nova Gallery, Boston, 1958, Galleria Vigna Nuova and Gallerie Santa Croce, Florence, Italy, 1964, 66, Herbert Benevy Gallery, N.Y.C., 1976; 2-person show Art Directions Gallery, N.Y.C., 1966, S.W. Symphony Gallery, Sedona, 1985; exhibited in group shows Sedona (Ariz.) Arts Ctr., 1988, 92; one-woman show and group shows Wingspread Gallery, Gallery 68, Belfast, Maine, 1969, 73, 76, 80, 83, 88, 90, 93; also others; represented in permanent collections Phillips Mus., Washington, also numerous pub. and pvt. instns. Co-coord. visual arts Summerthing, neighborhood arts program, Boston, 1968-71; pres. Christian Herter Ctr.; mem. Sedona Cultural Arts Commn., 1989-90; sec., v.p., bd. dirs. Internat. Friends of Transformative Art, Phoenix, 1989-95; organizer show Sedona Art Mus., 1993. Avocations: poetry, gardening, teaching. Home and Studio: 345 Longwood Dr Sedona AZ 86351-7208

SEROTA, JAMES IAN, lawyer; b. Chgo., Oct. 20, 1946; s. Louis Henry and Phyllis Estelle (Horner) S.; m. Susan Perlstadt, May 7, 1972; children: Daniel Louis, Jonathan Mark. AB, Washington U., St. Louis, 1968; JD cum laude, Northwestern U., 1971. Bar: Ill. 1971, U.S. Dist. Ct. (no. dist.) Ill. 1972, D.C. 1978, U.S. Supreme Ct. 1978, U.S. Ct. Appeals (D.C. cir.) 1978, U.S. Dist. Ct. (D.C. dist.), U.S. Ct. Claims 1980, N.Y. 1981, U.S. Dist. Ct. (so. dist.) N.Y. 1981, (ea. dist.) N.Y. 1981, U.S. Ct. Appeals (2d cir.) 1983. Trial atty. Antitrust div. U.S. Dept. Justice, Washington, 1971-77; assoc. Bell, Boyd & Lloyd, Washington, 1977-81; ptnr. Werner, Kennedy & French, N.Y.C., 1982-85, Levitsky & Serota, 1985-86, Huber, Lawrence & Abell, N.Y.C., 1987—. Recipient Spl. Achievement award U.S. Dept. Justice, 1976. Mem. ABA (chmn. ins. industry com. 1987-90, vice chair program com. 1990-91, chair annual mtg. program 1991-94, chair fuel & energy com. 1994—), N.Y. State Bar Assn., Assn. of Bar of City of N.Y. (antitrust and trade regulations com. 1988-91), Fed. Bar Council. Contbr. articles to profl. jours. Editor Law Rev. Northwestern U.

SEROTA, SUSAN PERLSTADT, lawyer; b. Chgo., Sept. 10, 1945; d. Sidney Morris and Mildred (Penn) Perlstadt; m. James Ian Serota, May 7, 1972; children: Daniel Louis, Jonathan Mark. AB, U. Mich., 1967; JD,

NYU, 1971. Bar: Ill. 1971, D.C. 1972, N.Y. 1981, U.S. Dist. Ct. (no. dist.) Ill. 1971, U.S. Dist. Ct. (so. dist.) N.Y. 1981, U.S. Dist. Ct. (ea. dist.) N.Y. 1985, U.S. Ct. Claims 1972, U.S. Tax Ct. 1972, U.S. Ct. Appeals (D.C. cir.) 1972. Assoc. Gottlieb & Schwartz, Chgo., 1971-72, Silverstein & Mullens, Washington, 1972-75, Cahill Gordon & Reindel, N.Y.C., 1975-82; assoc. Winthrop, Stimson, Putnam & Roberts, N.Y.C., 1982, ptnr., 1983--; adj. prof. Sch. Law, Georgetown U., Washington, 1974-75; mem. faculty Practicins Law Inst., N.Y.C., 1983—. Editor: ERISA Fiduciary Law, 1995; assoc. editor Exec. Compensation Jour., 1973-75; dep. editor Tax Mgmt., Estate and Gift Taxation and Exec. Compensation, 1973-75; mem. editl. adv. bd. Benefits Law Jour., 1988—, Tax Mgmt. Compensation Jour., 1993—; mem. bd. editor ERISA and Benefits Law Jour., 1992—; contbr. articles to profl. jours. Fellow Am. Coll. Tax Counsel; mem. ABA (chmn. joint com. employee benefits taxation sect. 1991-92, coun. mem. taxation sect. 1994—), Internat. Pension and Employee Benefits Lawyers Assn. (co-chair 1993-95), N.Y. State Bar Assn. (exec. com. tax sect. 1988-92), Am. Bar Retirement Funds (dir. 1994—). Democrat. Office: Winthrop Stimson Putnam & Roberts One Battery Park Pla New York NY 10004-1490

SEROW, WILLIAM JOHN, economics educator; b. N.Y.C., Apr. 8, 1946; s. William John and Dorothea (Goyette) S.; m. Elizabeth Goetz, Aug. 24, 1968; 1 child, Erika. BA, Boston Coll., 1967; MA, Duke U., 1970, PhD, 1972. Rsch. dir. Univ. Va., Charlottesville, 1970-81; prof., dir. Fla. State U., Tallahassee, 1981—. Editor: Handbook of International Migration, 1990; author: Population Aging in the United States, 1990. Capt. U.S. Army, 1967-73. Recipient grants Fla. Health Care Cost Containment Bd., 1988-90, Nat. Instn. Aging, 1983-89, Nat. Inst. Mental Health, 1984-86, Govt. Indonesia, 1992-97. Mem. Internat. Union for Scientific Study of Population, Population Assn. Am., Am. and So. Econ. Assns., So. Demographic Assn. (pres. 1986-87), So. Regional Sci. Assn. (pres. 1982-83), Gerontol. Soc. Am. Avocations: railroads, Sherlock Holmes, baseball rsch. Office: Fla State U Ctr for Study of Population Tallahassee FL 32306-4063

SERRA, ANTHONY MICHAEL, nursing home administrator; b. Willoughby, Ohio, June 22, 1940; s. Enrico and Paulina (Schiaffino) S.; m. Carol Frances Heintz, July 22, 1962; children: Lisa Marie, Steven Anthony. BBA, Fenn Coll., 1965. CPA, Ohio. Staff acct. Walthall and Drake CPA's, Cleve., 1962-67; adminstr., exec. dir. Health Hill Hosp., Cleve., 1967-80; adminstr. Madison (Ohio) Village Manor, 1978—; gen. practice acctg., Madison, 1980—. Adminstr. Child Abuse and Neglect Project, Cleve., 1972-74. Mem. Am. Inst. CPA's, Ohio Soc. CPA's, Ohio Health Care Assn., Cleve. Area League for Nursing (bd. dirs. 1976-79). Republican. Roman Catholic. Home: 1845 Ridgewick Dr Wickliffe OH 44092-1632 Office: PO Box 17080 Cleveland OH 44117-0080

SERRA-BADUE, DANIEL FRANCISCO, artist, educator; b. Santiago de Cuba, Sept. 8, 1914; came to U.S., 1962; s. Daniel Serra and Eloisa Badue; m. Aida Betancourt, Mar. 8, 1944; 1 dau., Aida Victoria. Licenciate in Law, U. Barcelona, 1936; LL.D., U. Havana, 1938, Dr. in Social, Polit. and Econ. Scis., 1949; M.F.A., Nat. Sch. Fine Arts, Havana, 1943. Prof. Sch. Fine Arts, Santiago de Cuba, 1945-60, Nat. Sch. Fine Arts, Havana, 1960-62; lectr. Columbia U., N.Y.C., 1962-63; instr. Bklyn. Mus. Art Sch., N.Y.C., 1962-85; prof. St. Peter's Coll., Jersey City, 1967—; asst. dir. culture Ministry Edn., Havana, 1959-60. Exhibited over 40 one-man shows and over 250 group shows. Bd. dirs. Cintas Found., N.Y.C. Recipient Pa. Acad. prize, 1941; recipient Bienal Hispano Americana prize, 1954; Guggenheim Found. fellow, 1938, 39; Cintas Found. fellow, 1963, 64. Mem. AAUP, Coll. Art Assn. Am. Home: 15 W 72nd St Apt 10T New York NY 10023-3444 Office: St Peter's Coll 2641 John F Kennedy Blvd Jersey City NJ 07306-5943

SERRAGLIO, MARIO, architect; b. Bassano, Veneto, Italy, Apr. 13, 1965; came to U.S., 1972; s. Luciano G. and Maria P. (Bellon) S. BS in Architecture, Ohio State U., 1988. Real estate agent Four Star Realty, Columbus, Ohio, 1984—; treas. Columbus Masonry, Inc., 1985-86; v.p. Serraglio Masonry, Inc., Columbus, 1986—; pres. Serraglio Builders, Inc., Columbus, 1987—; residential designer Gary A. Bruck, SGR, Inc., Columbus, 1988-89, Sullivan Gray Ptnrs., Columbus, 1989-92; project mgr. John Regan Architects, Columbus, 1992-93. Mem. AIA, Columbus Bd. Realtors. Office: Mario Serraglio Inc 155 Green Meadow Dr S Westerville OH 43081

SERRANI, THOM, contracting company executive; b. Glens Falls, N.Y., Nov. 5, 1947; s. Italo N. and Florence Rosemary (LaPointe) S.; m. Beth Burgeson, June 24, 1978. B.A. in Liberal Arts, Sacred Heart U., Bridgeport, Conn., 1970; postgrad., Fairfield U., 1970-72. Mem. Stamford Bd. Reps., Conn., 1973-75; mem. Conn. Ho. of Reps., 1975-81, Conn. Senate, 1981-84; mayor City of Stamford, Conn., 1983-91; bus. cons. Ludlow Assocs., Stamford, 1991-95; exec. v.p. Associated Gen. Contractors of Vt., Montpelier, 1995—; mem. Nat. Conf. State Legislators, 1975-83, vice chmn. transp. com., 1981-83. Mem. Springdale Vol. Fire Co., Stamford, 1973—; apptd. mem. Gov's. Task Force on Safety in Pub. Spaces, Hartford, 1986, Gov's. Fire Marshall Tng. Council, Hartford, 1986; chmn. Met. Planning Orgn., Conn., 1986; vice chmn. Stamford Econ. Assistance Corp., Conn., 1986; del. Dem. Nat. Conv., N.Y., 1976, San Francisco, 1984; chmn. bd. (ex officio) Stamford Ctr. Arts. Recipient legis. award State Firemen's Assn., Conn., 1976, Community Svc. award Sacred Heart U., 1984, Outstanding Svc. award Easter Seal Rehab. Ctr., 1987, Equal Opportunity award NAACP, 1989, Aid for Retarded Recognition award, Disting. Community Svc. award B'nai Brith, 1988, Pitney Bowes Foreman's Club Merit award, 1987; named Legislator of Yr., Conn. Caucus of Dems., 1980, Downtown Man of Yr., 1985. Mem. Piedmont Assocs., Glenbrook Athletic Assn. Avocations: cross country skiing, construction, gardening. Home: 112 Ellison Rd Ludlow VT 05149 Office: Assoc Gen Contractors Vt 47 Court St Montpelier VT 05601

SERRANO, ANDRES, artist; b. N.Y.C., Aug. 15, 1950; s. Andres and Eulalia (Negual) S. Artist. Solo shows include Leonard Perlson Gallery, N.Y.C., 1985, Stux Gallery, N.Y.C., 1988, 89, 90, Gallery Hibbel, Tokyo, 1990, Seibu Mus. Art, Tokyo, 1990, Saatchi Mus., London, 1991, Thomas Segal Gallery, Boston, 1991, Galleri Susanne Ottesen, Copenhagen, 1991, Yvon Lambert Gallery, Paris, 1992, Inst. Contemporary Art, Amsterdam, 1992, Paula Cooper Gallery, N.Y.C., 1994, Mus. Contemporary Art, Montreal, 1994, Mus. Contemporary Art, Chgo., 1994, 95, New Mus. Contemporary Art, N.Y.C., 1995, Reykjavik, Iceland, 1996, Sala Mendoza, Venezuela, 1996, Barcelona, 1996, Ark., 1996, Malmö, 1996; exhibited in group shows at Temple U., Phila., Lehman Coll., Bronx, N.Y., Jan Kesner Gallery, L.A., Henry St. Settlement, N.Y.C., Greg Kucera Gallery, Seattle, Interat. Ctr. for Photography Midtown, N.Y.C., Galerie Antoine Candau, Paris, Wadsworth Atheneum, Hartford, Conn., Mus. Moderner Kunst, Vienna, Nat. Mus. Art, Osaka, Japan, Mus. Fine Arts, Boston, Musee de la Poste, Paris, Whitney Mus. Am. Art, N.Y.C., U. Que., Montreal, Cleve. Ctr. for Contemporary Art, U. Pa., Joslyn Art Mus., Omaha, numerous others. Grantee Nat. Endowment for the Arts, 1986, N.Y. Found. for the Arts, 1987, Louis Comfort Tiffany Found., 1989, Cintas Found., 1989, N.Y. State Coun. on the Arts, 1990, others. Office: care Paula Cooper Gallery 155 Wooster St New York NY 10012

SERRANO, JOSE E., congressman; b. Mayaguez, P.R., Oct. 24, 1943; s. Jose E. and Hipolita (Soto) S.; m. Mary Serrano; children: Lisa Marie, Jose Marco, Justine, Jonathan, Benjamin. With Mfrs. Hanover Trust Co., 1961-69; mem. Bd. Edn. N.Y., 1969-74; former N.Y. State Assemblyman Albany, from 1975; mem. 102nd-104th Congresses from 18th (now 16th) N. Y. dist.N.Y., Washington, D.C., 1991—; mem. appropriations com., subcom. fgn. ops., export financing and related programs, subcom. labor, health, human svcs. and edn., 1993-94, mem. subcom. constitution, judiciary com., 1995-96; chmn. Congl. Hispanic Caucus, 1993-94; mem. appropriations com., 1996—. Roman Catholic. Office: 2342 Rayburn Hob Washington DC 20515 also: 890 Grand Concourse Bronx NY 10451-2828

SERRIE, HENDRICK, anthropology and international business educator; b. Jersey City, July 2, 1937; s. Hendrick and Elois (Edge) S.; m. Gretchen Tipler Ihde, Sept. 3, 1959; children: Karim Jonathan, Keir Ethan. BA with honors, U. Wis., 1960; MA, Cornell U., 1964; PhD with distinction, Northwestern U., 1976. Dir. Solar Energy Field Project, Oaxaca, Mex., 1961-62; instr. U. Aleppo, Syria, 1963-64; asst. prof. Beloit (Wis.) Coll., 1964-69, Calif. State U., Northridge, 1969-70, Purdue U., West Lafayette, Ind., 1970-72, New Coll./U. South Fla., Sarasota, 1972-77; tchr. Pine View Sch., Sarasota, 1978; prof. anthropology, internat. bus. Eckerd Coll., St. Petersburg, Fla., 1978—; dir. internat. bus. overseas programs Eckerd Coll., 1981—; sr. rsch. assoc., Human Resources Inst., St. Petersburg, 1988—. Author, editor: Family, Kinship, and Ethnic Identity Among the Overseas Chinese, 1985, Anthropology and International Business, 1986, What Can Multinationals Do for Peasants, 1994; writer, dir. films: Technological Innovation, 1962, Something New Under the Sun, 1963; contbr. articles to Wall Street Jour. and Wall Street Jour. Europe. Tchr. Sunday sch., North United Methodist Ch., Sarasota, 1977—. Exxon scholar, So. Ctr. for Internat. Issues, Atlanta, 1980-81; Presdl. fellow Am. Grad. Sch. Internat. Mgmt., 1991; recipient Leavy award, Freedoms Found., Valley Forge, Pa., 1989. Fellow Am. Anthropol. Assn., Soc. Applied Anthropology; mem. So. Ctr. Internat. Issues, Acad. Internat. Bus., Tampa Bay Internat. Trade Coun., Internat. Soc. Intercultural Edn., Tng. and Rsch. Democrat. Avocations: singing, drawing, beach walking, cycling, sailing. Home: 636 Mecca Dr Sarasota FL 34234-2713 Office: Eckerd Coll Dept Internat Bus Saint Petersburg FL 33733

SERRIN, JAMES BURTON, mathematics educator; b. Chgo., Nov. 1, 1926; s. James B. and Helen Elizabeth (Wingate) S.; m. Barbara West, Sept. 6, 1952; children: Martha Helen Stack, Elizabeth Ruth, Janet Louise Sucha. Student, Northwestern U., 1944-46; BA, Western Mich. U., 1947; MA, Ind. U., PhD, 1951; DSc, U. Sussex, 1972; DSc in Engring., U. Ferrara, Italy, 1992; DSc in Math., U. Padova, Italy, 1992. With MIT, Cambridge, 1952-54; mem. faculty U. Minn., Mpls., 1955—, prof. math., 1959—, Regents prof., 1968—, head Sch. Math., 1964-65; vis. prof. U. Chgo., 1964, 75, Johns Hopkins U., 1966, U. Sussex, 1967-68, 72, 76, U. Naples, 1979, U. Modena, 1988, Ga. Inst. Tech., 1990. Author: Mathematical Principles of Classical Fluid Mechanics, 1957. Mem. Met. Airport Sound Abatement Council, Mpls., 1969—. Recipient Disting. Alumni award Ind. U., 1979. Fellow AAAS; mem. NAS, Am. Math. Soc. (G.D. Birkhoff prize 1973), Math. Assn. Am., Soc. for Natural Philosophy (pres. 1969-70), Finnish Acad. Sci. and Letters. Home: 4422 Dupont Ave S Minneapolis MN 55409-1739

SERRITELLA, JAMES ANTHONY, lawyer; b. Chgo., July 8, 1942; s. Anthony and Angela (Deleonardis) S.; m. Ruby Ann Amoroso, Oct. 3, 1981. B.A., SUNY-S.I., 1965, Pontifical Gregorian U., Rome, 1966; postgrad., DePaul U., 1966-67; M.A., U. Chgo., 1968, J.D., 1971. Bar: Ill. 1971, U.S. Supreme Ct. 1976, U.S. Tax Ct. 1985. Ptnr. Kirkland & Ellis, Chgo., 1978; ptnr. Reuben & Proctor, Chgo., 1978-86, Mayer, Brown & Platt, Chgo., 1986—; lectr. in field. Contbr. articles to profl. jours. Mem. exec. bd. govt. rels. com. United Way of Chgo., 1979-84; bd. dirs. Child Care Assn. Ill., 1975-79, Lyric Opera Guild, 1979-84; v.p. Comprehensive Community Svcs. of Met. Chgo., 1976-81; chmn. adv. bd. DePaul U. Coll. Law Ctr. Ch./State Studies, 1982—, mem. dean's vis. com., 1982—; trustee Mundelein Coll., 1982-86, St. Xavier Coll., St. Mary of the Lake Sem., 1982-83, Sta. WTTW Chgo. Pub. TV, 1978-81, Loretto Hosp., 1989-91; mem. geriatrics/gerontology steering com. McGaw Med. Ctr. Northwestern U., 1981-82; mem. adv. bd. N.Am. Coll., 1990—; mem. Bus. Execs. for Econ. Justice, 1988—, State wide citizens com. on Child Abuse and Neglect, 1988—; mem. bd. advisors Alzheimer's Ctr. Rush-Presbyn.-St. Luke's Med. Ctr., 1990—; founder, chmn. bd. Chgo. Ctr. for Peace Studies, 1990—; mem. adv. coun. Charitable Trust div. Ill. Atty. Gen., 1991—; cons. Union of Bulgarian Founds., 1992, Internat. Acad. for Freedom of Religion and Belief, Budapest, Hungary, 1992; active Ill. State Hist. Soc. Coun. for Ill. History, 1994—. Fellow Am. Bar Found.; mem. ABA, FBA, NCCJ (adv. com. on ch., state and taxation), Am. Assn. homes for Aging, Nat. Health Lawyers Assn., Ill. State Bar Assn. (bd. govs., spl. com. on jud. redistricting), Ill. Bar Found. (charter), Chgo. Bar Assn. (com. on evaluation of jud. candidates), Cath. Lawyers Guild (bd. govs.), Canon Law Soc. Am. (active mem.), Diocesan Attys. Assn. (exec. com.), Nat. Cath. Cemetery Conf., Cath. Health Assn., The Park Ridge Ctr., The Chgo. Club, Econ. Club, Tavern Club. Office: Mayer Brown & Platt 190 S La Salle St Chicago IL 60603-3410

SERRITELLA, WILLIAM DAVID, lawyer; b. Chgo., May 16, 1946; s. William V. and Josephine Dolores (Scalise) S. J.D., U. Ill., Champaign, 1971. Bar: Ill. 1971, U.S. Dist. Ct. (no. and cen. dists.) Ill. 1972, U.S. Dist. Ct. (ea. and we. dists.) Wis. 1995, U.S. Ct. Appeals (7th cir.) 1974, U.S. Supreme Ct. 1979. Law clk. U.S. Dist. Ct., Danville, Ill., 1971-72; ptnr. Ross & Hardies, Chgo., 1972—; arbitrator Am. Arbitration Assn. Mem. ABA, Ill. Bar Assn., Chgo. Bar Assn., Nat. Assn. R.R. Trial Counsel (Ill.), Soc. Trial Lawyers, Defense Rsch. Inst., Legal Club, Trial Lawyers Club (Chicago). Office: Ross & Hardies 150 N Michigan Ave Ste 2500 Chicago IL 60601-7525

SERT, STEVE YAVUZ, geotechnical engineering consultant; b. Istanbul, Turkey, Apr. 8, 1947; arrived in the U.S., 1980; m. Linda Diane Frost. BS in Civil Engring., Am. Robert Coll., Istanbul, 1971; MS, King's Coll., London, 1972, PhD, 1977. Registered civil engr., Calif., Nev. Geotechnical engr. James Willamson & Ptnrs., Glasgow, Scotland, 1978-80, Raytheon Engrs., N.Y.C., 1980-82; materials testing supr. Raytheon Engrs., Kodiak, Alaska, 1982-84; prin. engr. Raytheon Engrs., Sacramento, 1984-90; br. mgr. Herzog Assoc., Sacramento, 1990-91; owner, prin. Sert Consulting, Folsom, Calif., 1991—. Mem. ASCE (shallow founds. com. 1995), ASTM, Am. Concrete Inst. Achievements include research that showed increasing the lift thickness of roller compacted concrete placements as opposed to decreasing it to obtain better quality concrete. Office: Sert Consulting 212 Briggs Ranch Dr Ste 100 Folsom CA 95630-5259

SERVAAS, BEURT RICHARD, corporate executive; b. Indpls., May 7, 1919; s. Beurt Hans and Lela Etta (Neff) S.; m. Cory Jane Synhorst, Jan. 7, 1950; children: Eric, Kristin, Joan, Paul, Amy. Student, U. Mex., Mexico City, 1938-39; AB, Ind. U., 1940, MD, 1970; postgrad., Purdue U., 1941; D Bus. Mgmt., Ind. Inst. Tech.; LHD (hon.), Butler U. Agt. CIA, China, 1946; v.p. constrn. Vestar Corp., N.Y.C., 1948; founder, chief exec. officer No. Vernon Forge, Inc. Rev. Pub. Co., SerVaas Labs., Indpls., 1949—; chmn. bd. SerVaas, Inc., Indpls. and affiliated cos. Curtis Pub. Co., Forge Mexicana, Edgerton Tool, Dependable Engring., SerVaas Mgmt., SerVaas Rubber, Premier, Indpls. Rubber Co., Bridgeport Brass Co.; bd. dirs. Bank One Ind. Pres. City-County Coun., Indpls.; chmn. Ind. State Commn. Higher Edn.; chmn. Kirksville Coll. Osteopathic Medicine; bd. dirs. Coll. Univ. Corp., Ind. Pub. Health Found., Robert Schuller Ministries; past bd. dirs. Indt. State Bd. Health, Nat. Fgn. Rels. Commn. With USNR, 1941-45. Decorated Bronze Star; recipient Horatio Alger award, 1980. Mem. NAM, Am. Acad. Achievement (Golden Plate award 1973), Assn. Am. Med. Colls., Ind. C. of C., Indpls. C. of C., Marion County Hist. Soc., Ind. Hist. Soc., Newcomen Soc. N.Am., U.S. Naval Res. Assn., World Future Soc., Am. Legion, Columbia Club, Econ. Club, Indpls. Athletic Club, Indpls. Press Club, Meridian Hills Country Club, Phi Delta Kappa. Presbyterian. Home: 2525 W 44th St Indianapolis IN 46208-3249 Office: Office of the City County Coun 241 City-County Bldg 200 E Washington St Indianapolis IN 46204-3307

SERVAN-SCHREIBER, JEAN-JACQUES, engineer, author; b. Paris, Feb. 13, 1924; s. Emile and Denise (Bresard) Servan-S.; grad. Ecole Polytechnique, Paris, 1947; children: David, Emile, Franklin, Edouard. Sr. writer, fgn. affairs editor Le Monde, Paris, 1948-53; Groupe Expres, mags. L'Express, 1953-73; mem. nat. Parliament from Nancy; pres. Radical Party; pres. Lorraine region 1970-79; founder, 1979, chmn. Groupe de Paris (Europe, Japan, Arabia); chmn. World Center for Informatics and Human Resources, Paris, 1982-85; chmn. internat. com. Carnegie-Mellon U., Pitts., 1985—. Served as fighter pilot Free French Forces, World War II. Decorated Cross of Mil. Valor. Author: Lieutenant in Algeria, 1957, The American Challenge, 1967, The Radical Manifesto, 1971, The World Challenge, 1981, Passions I, 1991, Les Fossoyeurs, 1993.

SERVICE, ROBERT E., ambassador; b. Beijing, 1937; m. Karol Kleiner; children: Jennifer, John. BA, Oberlin Coll., 1958; MA, Princeton U., 1960; postgrad., Stanford U., Nat. War Coll. Head office so. cone affairs Dept State, Washington, 1980-82; polit. counselor Am. Embassy, Madrid, Spain, 1982-87; dep. chief of missions Am. Embassy, Buenos Aires, 1987-89, Brasilia, Brazil, 1989-92; coun. to asst. sec. fin. and mgmt. policy, under sec. mgmt. Am. Embassy, Brasilia, 1992; head reinventing govt. task force Dept. State, 1993; amb. to Parguay Am. Embassy, Asuncion, 1994—. Office: Am Embassy Paraguay Unit 4711 APO AA 34036-0001 also: US Dept State Paraguay Washington DC 20521-3020

SERVISON, ROGER THEODORE, investment executive; b. Columbus, Ohio, June 6, 1945; s. Theodore Calvin and Hilda Augusta (Longmack) S.; m. Kristin Landsteiner, Jan. 8, 1972. BA, U. Iowa, 1967; MBA, Harvard U., 1972. Chmn. Tax Man, Inc., Cambridge, Mass., 1970-72; v.p. Continental Investment Corp., Boston, 1972-75, Phoenix Investment Counsel, Boston, 1975-76; mng. dir. Fidelity Investments, Boston, 1976—; bd. dirs. Tax Man, Cambridge, Boston Fin. Group, Longwood Covered Coats, Brookline. Dir. First Night, Inc., Boston, 1985. Mem. Longwood Cricket Club, Sippican Club, Federal Club, City Club, Piney Point Beach Club. Avocations: art, antiques, tennis, aerobics. *

SERVODIDIO, PAT ANTHONY, broadcast executive; b. Yonkers, N.Y., Nov. 9, 1937; s. Pasquale and Catherine (Verdisco) S.; m. Ulla I. Schalien, May 4, 1968; children: Christian, Alexa. BS, Fordham U., 1959; postgrad., St. John's U., N.Y.C., 1960-63. Asst. to bus. mgr. Sta. WCBS-TV, N.Y.C., 1960-64; account exec. Sta. WTNH-TV, New Haven, 1964-66; account exec., N.Y. sales mgr. RKO TV Reps., N.Y.C., 1967-74; v.p., N.Y. sales mgr. Sta. WOR-TV, N.Y.C., 1974-79, v.p., gen. sales mgr., 1979-81; v.p., gen. mgr. Sta. WNAC-TV, Boston, 1981-82; pres. RKO TV, N.Y.C., 1982-87; pres. RKO Gen., Inc., N.Y.C., 1987-91, also bd. dirs.; v.p., gen. mgr. Sta. WKYC-TV, Cleve., 1991-92; pres. Multimedia Broadcasting Co., Cin., 1992-94; broadcast cons., 1995—. Bd. regents St. Peter's Coll., 1983—; mem. com. future financing Rutgers U., New Brunswick, N.J., 1983-85; dir. TV bur. Advt. Bd., 1993—; bd. dirs. Internat. Radio and TV Found., 1983-93, Assn. for Maximum Svc. TV, Inc., 1993—. With U.S. Army, 1959-62. Office: Multimedia Broadcasting Co 140 W 9th St Cincinnati OH 45202-1905

SERWATKA, WALTER DENNIS, publishing executive; b. Irvington, N.J., July 19, 1937; s. Walter F. and Grace R. (Sheehan) S.; m. Beverly M. Farrell, Aug. 10, 1963 (div. Feb. 1988); children—David, Nora, Nancy. BBA in Acctg., Upsala U., 1959; MBA in Fin., Fairleigh Dickinson U., 1966; postgrad. in bus., Harvard U., 1978, Columbia U., 1979, Stanford U., 1985. With treas.'s dept. WESTVACO, N.Y.C., 1964-68; dir. fin. analysis Random House Co., N.Y.C., 1968-72; with McGraw-Hill Info. Systems Co., 1972-83; contr. Sweet's div. McGraw-Hill, Inc., N.Y.C., 1972-73, dir. profit planning, 1973-75, asst. contr., 1975-76, sr. v.p.-contr., 1976-79, group v.p. real estate info. svcs., 1979-83, sr. v.p. group mfg. and circulation svcs., 1985, exec. v.p., chief fin. officer, 1985-88, exec. v.p. ops., 1989—; exec. v.p. fin. and svcs. McGraw-Hill Publs. Co., N.Y.C., 1983-84; pres. McGraw-Hill Info. Svcs., N.Y.C., 1988-89. Trustee Upsala Coll., East Orange, N.J. Served with U.S. Army, 1959-62. Mem. Fin. Exec. Inst., Mag. Pubs. Assn., Am. Inst. Accts., Planning Execs. Inst., Pvt. Sector Council. *

SERWER, ALAN MICHAEL, lawyer; b. Detroit, Aug. 31, 1944; s. Bernard Jacob and Marian (Borin) S.; m. Laurel Kathryn Robbert, June 6, 1968; children: David Matthew, Karen Anne. BA in Econs., U. Mich., 1966; JD, Northwestern U., 1969. Bar: Ill. 1969, D.C. 1980, U.S. Dist. Ct. (no. dist.) Ill. 1970, U.S. Ct. Appeals (7th cir.) 1979, U.S. Supreme Ct. 1979, U.S. Ct. Appeals (6th cir.) 1982, U.S. Ct. Appeals (5th cir.) 1983, U.S. Ct. Appeals (11th cir.) 1984, U.S. Ct. Appeals (9th cir.) 1986. Trial atty. U.S. Dept. Labor, Chgo., 1969-78, counsel safety and health, 1978-79; assoc. Haley, Bader & Potts, Chgo., 1979-82, ptnr., 1983-87; ptnr. Bell, Boyd & Lloyd, Chgo., 1987—. Mem. Ill. Bar Assn., Chgo. Bar Assn., Assn. Trial Lawyers Am., Fed. Bar Assn. (recipient Milton Gordon award 1977). Home: 233 Woodland Rd Highland Park IL 60035-5052 Office: Bell Boyd & Lloyd 70 W Madison St Ste 3200 Chicago IL 60602-4207

SESNO, FRANK, executive editor; married; 3 children. BA in Am. History, Middlebury Coll. Dir., reporter Sta. WCFR, Springfield, Vt.; with Voice of Am.; nat. corr. AP Radio; corr. White House CNN, Washington, 1984-90, anchor chair, 1991—, co-anchor The Internat. Hour, host Late Edition. Recipient First Place Reporting of Econs. Unity awards in Media, Spl. Jury award Best of Festival Worldfest-Houston Film Festival, Joan Shorenstein Barone award, Cable ACE award Nat. Acad. Cable Programming, Houston Internat. Film Festival award, Ben Grauer award for Best Spot News Reporting Overseas Press Club, Best Spot News Reporting award AP Broadcast, Nat. Press Club award. Office: CNN Am Inc Washington Bur 820 1st St NE Washington DC 20002-4243

SESONSKE, ALEXANDER, nuclear and chemical engineer; b. Gloversville, N.Y., June 20, 1921; s. Abraham and Esther (Kreitzer) S.; m. Marjorie Ann Mach, Apr. 17, 1952 (dec. Jan. 1995); children: Michael Jan, Jana Louise. B.Chem. Engring., Rensselaer Poly. Inst., 1942; M.S., U. Rochester, 1947; Ph.D., U. Del., 1950. Engr. Chem. Constrn. Corp., N.Y.C., 1942; chem. engr. Manhattan Project, 1943-45, Columbia-So. Chem. Corp., 1945-46; staff Los Alamos Sci. Lab., 1950-54, 60-61, cons., 1961-63; faculty Purdue U., Lafayette, Ind., 1954; prof. nuclear and chem. engring. Purdue U., 1959-86, prof. emeritus, 1986—, asst. chmn. dept. nuclear engring., 1966-73; Cons. Oak Ridge Nat. Lab., 1963-67, Electric Power Research Inst., 1974; mem. rev. com. Argonne (Ill.) Nat. Lab., 1965-67, 75-81; ind. cons. 1986—. Author: (with Samuel Glasstone) Nuclear Reactor Engineering, 1963, 4th edit., 1994, Nuclear Power Plant Design Analysis, 1973; mem. editorial bd. Advances in Nuclear Sci. and Tech., 1972—; contbr. numerous articles to profl. jours. Recipient Wall of Fame award U. Del., 1988. Fellow Am. Nuclear Soc. (Arthur H. Compton award 1987); mem. Am. Inst. Chem. Engrs., Am. Soc. Engring. Edn., Sigma Xi, Omega Chi Epsilon. Research on nuclear fuel mgmt., liquid metal heat transfer and nuclear reactor engring. Home and Office: 16408 Felice Dr San Diego CA 92128-2804

SESSAMEN, DONALD WILLIAM, communications company executive; b. Whitpain Twp., Pa., Sept. 3, 1932; s. Guy Raymond and Sylvia Marion (Harlan) S.; m. Sandra Roberta MacFarland, Apr. 2, 1954 (div. Aug. 1972); children: Victoria Leigh, Deborah Reneé, Pamela Suzanne, Guy Raymond II; m. Alice Catherine Cusumano, Nov. 10, 1974. Student, Glassboro State U., 1964-65. Various positions-plant, engring., mktg. N.J. Bell Telephone Co., 1954-69; v.p., gen. mgr. Princeton (N.J.) Timesharing Services Inc., 1970-72; western region v.p. Telecommunications Systems of Am., Oklahoma City, 1973-75; cen. region ops. mgr. So. Pacific Communications Co., McLean, Va., 1975-79; nat. ops. mgr. So. Pacific Communications Co., Burlingame, Calif., 1979-80; v.p. ops. Sprint Communications, Burlingame, 1980-82, sr. v.p. planning and bus. devel., 1982-83; sr. v.p. ops. Allnet Communication Services Inc., Birmingham, Mich., 1983-88, exec. v.p., 1988-89; pres., chief operating officer FiberTel, Inc., Columbus, Ohio, 1989—; mem. telecommunications adv. bd. U. Colo., Boulder, 1981—. Chmn. Cape May (N.J.) County Young Republicans, 1965; pres. Stone Harbor (N.J.) Lions Club, 1966; bd. dirs. Am. Speech-Lang.-Hearing Assn., Palo Alto, Calif., 1982-84, Am. Social Health Assn. Served to sgt. major USNG. Republican. Methodist. Home: 5605 Upper Ridge Way Auburn CA 95602-9248 Office: ALC Communications Corp 30300 Telegraph Rd Franklin MI 48025-4507

SESSIONS, JEFFERSON BEAUREGARD, III, state attorney general; b. Selma, Ala., Dec. 24, 1946; s. Jefferson Beauregard and Abbie (Powe) S.; m. Mary Montgomery Blackshear, Aug. 9, 1969; children: Mary Abigail, Ruth Blackshear, Samuel Turner. B.A., Huntingdon Coll., Montgomery, Ala., 1969; J.D., U. Ala., 1973. Bar: Ala. 1973. Assoc. Guin, Bouldin & Porch, Russellville, Ala., 1973-75; asst. U.S. atty. U.S. Dept. Justice, Mobile, Ala., 1975-77, U.S. atty., 1981-93; assoc., ptnr. Stockman & Bedsole Attys., Mobile, Ala., 1977-81; ptnr. Stockman, Bedsole & Sessions, Mobile, 1993-94; atty. gen. State of Ala., 1995—; mem. U.S. atty's. com. on legis. and rules, 1983-85; mem. U.S. atty. gen's. adv. com., 1987-89, vice chmn. 1989; chmn. controlled substances subcom. U.S. atty. gen's. adv. com., 1992-93. Presdl. elector State of Ala., 1972; mem. bd. trustees, exec. com. Mobile Bay Area Partnership for Youth, 1981—; chmn. adminstrv. bd. Ashland Pl. United Meth. Ch., Mobile, 1982; mem. bd. dirs. Mobile Child Advocacy Ctr., 1988—; chmn. com. on govt., judiciary and law enforcement Coalition for a Drug Free Mobile, 1990-93; 1st v.p. Mobile Lions Club, 1993-94. Capt. USAR, 1975-85. Recipient U.S. Atty. Gen's. award for significant achievements in the war against drug trafficking U.S. Atty. Gen. William P. Barr, 1992. Mem. ABA, Ala. Bar Assn., Mobile Bar Assn., Omicron Delta Kappa. Home: 16 S Lafayette St Mobile AL 36604-1714 Office: Office of Atty General 11 S Union St Montgomery AL 36130*

SESSIONS, JUDITH ANN, librarian, university library dean; b. Lubbock, Tex., Dec. 16, 1947; d. Earl Alva and Anna (Mayer) S. BA cum laude, Cen. Fla. U., 1970; MLS, Fla. State U., 1971; postgrad., Am. U., 1980, George

Washington U., 1983. Head libr. U. S.C., Salkehatchie, 1974-77; dir. Libr. and Learing Resources Ctr. Mt. Vernon Coll., Washington, 1977-82; planning and systems libr. George Washington U., Washington, 1981-82, asst. univ. libr. for adminstrn. svcs., acting head tech. svcs., 1982-84; univ. libr. Calif. State U., Chico, 1984-88; univ. libr., dean of libr. Miami U., Oxford, Ohio, 1988—; cons. Space Planning, S.C., 1976, DataPhase Implementation, Bowling Green U., 1982, TV News Study Ctr., George Washington U., 1981; asst. prof. Dept. Child Devel., Mt. Vernon Coll., 1978-81; mem., lectr. U.S.-China Libr. Exch. Del., 1986, 91; lectr., presenter in field. Contbr. articles, book revs. to profl. jours. Trustee Christ Hosp., Cin., 1990-94, Deaconness Gamble Rsch. Ctr., Cin., 1990-94; bd. dirs. Hamilton YMCA, 1994—, pres., 1995-96. Recipient award for outstanding contbn. D.C. Libr. Assn., 1979; rsch. grantee Mt. Vernon Coll., 1980; recipient Fulbright-Hayes Summer Travel fellowship to Czechoslovakia, 1991. Mem. ALA (Olofson award 1978, councillor-at-large policy making group 1981-94, coun. com. on coms. 1983-84, intellectual freedom com. 1984-88, directions and program rev. com. 1989-91, fin. and audit subcom. 1989-90, mem. exec. bd. 1989-94), Assn. Coll. and Rsch. Librs. (editorial bd. Coll. and Rsch. Librs. jour. 1979-84, nominatins and appointments com. 1983-85, faculty status com. 1984-86), Libr. and Info. Tech. Assn. (chair legis. and regulation com. 1980-81), Libr. Adminstrn. and Mgmt. Assn. (bd. dirs. libr. orgn. and mgmt. sect. 1985-87), Calif. Inst. Librs. (v.p., pres. elect 1987-88), Mid-Atlantic Regional Libr. Fedn. (mem. exec. bd. 1982-84), Jr. Mems. Round Table (pres. 1981-82), Intellectual Freedom Round Table (sec. 1984-85), Freedom to Read Found. (trustee 1984-88, v.p. 1985-86, treas. 1986-87, pres. 1987-88), Rotary, Beta Phi Mu. Home: 45 Waters Way Hamilton OH 45013-6324 Office: Miami U Edgar W King Oxford OH 45056

SESSIONS, ROBERT PAUL, former college president and administrator, retired educator, writer; b. Hardy, Ark., Oct. 5, 1926; s. Adolphus Wann and Mattie Orel (Gibson) Jernigan; adopted son Loys Rutherford S.; m. Martha Rae Rutledge, 1950 (div. 1957); children: Laura Elizabeth Sessions Stepp, Teresa Rae Sessions Kramer; m. Julia Margaret Anderson, Dec. 26, 1960; children: Kathryn Grace, Sarah Ruth Sessions Lundal. A.B., So. Meth. U., 1948, Th.M., 1950; Ph.D., Boston U., 1968. Ordained to ministry Meth. Ch., 1950. Pastor St. John's Meth. Ch., Van Buren, Ark., 1950-56, 1st Meth. Ch., Booneville, Ark., 1956-62, East Braintree Meth. Ch., Mass., 1962-67; asst. prof. sociology and religion W.Va. Wesleyan Coll., Buckhannan, 1967-70; prof., dept. chmn. East Tenn. State U., Johnson City, 1970-81; pres. Southwestern Coll., Winfield, Kans., 1981-84; dean Grad. Sch., dir. institutional planning Kearney State Coll., Nebr., 1984-88; prof. U. Richmond, 1988-92; cons. W.Va. Dept. Edn., Charleston, 1967-70, Tenn. Com. for the Humanities, Nashville, 1974, McCormick Theol. Sem., Chgo., 1976-77. Author: The Heart of the Bible, 1976; editor: Great Lakes Bulletin, 1945-46; co-editor: Updating Intergroup Education in Public Schools, 1970; contbr. articles to mags., religious jours. Bd. dirs. Broadside TV, Johnson City, Tenn., 1974-76; trustee Richard Young Psychiat. Hosp., Kearney, Nebr., 1985-88, chmn. 1987-88. Served with USN, 1944-46. Human Relations Inst. grantee, 1968; Updating Interethnic Edn. grantee, 1969. Mem. Am. Sociol. Assn., So. Sociol. Soc., Soc. for the Study of Social Problems, Soc. of Christian Ethics, Religious Research Assn., Phi Kappa Phi, Alpha Kappa Delta, Pi Gamma Mu, Phi Delta Kappa. Democrat. Lodges: Rotary Masons.

SESSIONS, ROY BRUMBY, otolaryngologist, educator; b. Houston, July 28, 1937; s. Roy Brumby and Elizabeth (Compton) S.; m. Mary Cousart, Aug. 28, 1976; children: Kate, Elizabeth, Abigail, Matthew. BS, La. State U., Baton Rouge, 1958; MD, La. State U., New Orleans, 1962. Resident gen. surgery and otolaryngology Washington U. Sch. Medicine, St. Louis, 1965-69; asst. prof. Baylor Coll. Medicine, Houston, 1969-73, assoc. prof., 1973-83; prof. head and neck surgery Meml. Sloan Kettering Cancer Ctr., N.Y.C., 1983-89; prof., chmn. dept. otolaryngology, head and neck surgery Gerogetown U. Med. Sch., Washington, 1989—. Contbr. articles to profl. jours., chpts. to books. Lt. comdr. USN, 1962-65. Roman Catholic.

SESSIONS, WILLIAM LAD, philosophy educator, administrator; b. Somerville, N.J., Dec. 3, 1943; s. William George and Alice Edna (Billhardt) S.; m. Vicki Darlene Thompson, Aug. 28, 1965; children: Allistair Lee, Laura Anne. BA magna cum laude, U. Colo., 1965; MA in Comparative Study of Religion, Union Theol. Sem., N.Y.C., 1967; postgrad., Oxford (Eng.) U., 1967-68; PhD, Yale U., 1971; postdoctoral studies, Stanford U., 1976, Harvard U., 1977-78. Teaching fellow Yale U., 1969; instr. U. Conn., Waterbury, 1970-71; asst. prof. philosophy Washington and Lee U., 1971-77, assoc. prof., 1977-83, prof., 1983—; instr. So. Sem., 1972, vis. prof. St. Olaf Coll., 1985-86, assoc. dean Coll. Washington and Lee U., 1992-95, acting dean, 1995-96. Author: The Concept of Faith, 1994; contbr. articles to religious and philos. jours. Ruling elder Lexington (Va.) Presbyn. Ch., 1983-89, tchr. Sunday sch., 1984-95. Glenn grantee Washington and Lee U., 1975—, Babcock Found. grantee, 1976, NEH grantee, 1977, 83, 86, Mellon Found. grantee, 1978-79, Mellon East Asian Studies grantee, 1990. Mem. Am. Philos. Assn., Va. Philos. Assn., Soc. for Philosophy of Religion (exec. coun. 1988-94, v.p. 1991, pres. 1992), Soc. Christian Philosophers (steering com. ea. region 1986-90, 92-95, exec. com. 1987-90), Phi Beta Kappa (exec. com. Va. chpt. 1986-95, v.p. 1989-91, pres. 1991-93). Office: Washington & Lee U Office of Dean Lexington VA 24450

SESSIONS, WILLIAM STEELE, former government official; b. Fort Smith, Ark., May 27, 1930; s. Will Anderson and Edith A. (Steele) S.; m. Alice Lewis, Oct. 5, 1952; children: William Lewis, Mark Gregory, Peter Anderson, Sara Anne. BA, Baylor U., 1956, JD, 1958; hon. degree, John C. Marshall Law Sch., St. Mary's U. Sch. of Law, Dickinson Sch. of Law, Flager Coll., Davis & Elkins Coll. Bar: Tex. 1959. Ptnr. McGregor & Sessions, Waco, Tex., 1959-61; assoc. Tirey, McLaughlin, Gorin & Tirey, Waco, 1961-63; ptnr. Haley, Fulbright, Winniford, Sessions & Bice, Waco, 1963-69; chief govt. ops sect. criminal divsn. U.S. Dept. Justice, Washington, 1969-71; atty. U.S. Dist. Ct., San Antonio, 1971-74; dist. judge U.S. Dist. Ct. (we. dist.) Tex., San Antonio, 1974-87, chief judge, 1980-87; dir. FBI, Washington, 1987-93; ptnr. Sessions & Sessions, San Antonio, 1995—; bd. dirs. Fed. Jud. Ctr., Washington, chmn. bench book com., 1981—; hon. bd. dirs. MLK, Jr. Fed. Holiday Corp., 1993—; mem. Tex. Comm. on Judicial Efficiency, 1995. Contbr. articles to profl. jours. Commr. Dr. Martin Luther King Jr. Fed. Holicy Commn., 1991-93, 94—. Lt. USAF, 1951-55; capt. USAFR,. Recipient Rosewood Gavel award St. Mary's U. Sch. Law, San Antonio, 1982, Disting. Alumni award Baylor U., Golden Plate award Am. Acad. Achievement, 1988, Law Enforcement Leadership award Assn. Fed. Investigators, 1989, medal of honor DAR, 1989, Disting. Eagle Scout award Boy Scouts Am., 1990, Person of Yr. award Am. Soc. for Indsl. Security, 1990, Magna Charta award Baronial Order of Magna Charta, 1990; named Lawyer of Yr., Baylor Law Sch., 1988, Father of Yr., Nat. Fathers Day Com., 1988, Ellis Island Congl. Medal of Honor, 1992. Mem. ABA, Jud. Conf. U.S. (com. on ct. adminstrn., chmn. jud. improvements subcom. 1983-85, ad hoc com. on automation to subcom. 1984-87, mem. ad hoc ct. reporter com. 1984-87), San Antonio Bar Assn. (bd. dirs. 1973-74), Fed. Bar Assn. (pres. San Antonio sect. 1974), Am. Judicature Soc. (exec. com. 1982-84), Dist. Judges Assn. of 5th Cir. (pres. 1982-83), State Bar of Tex. (chmn. com. to develop procedures for cert. state law questions to Supreme Ct. by Fed. Cts. 1983-85), Waco McLennan County Bar Assn. (pres. 1968), San Antonio Inns of Ct. (pres. 1986), William S. Sessions Inns of Ct. Republican. Methodist. Avocations: hiking, climbing, canoeing. Office: Sessions & Sessions 112 E Pecan St 30th Fl San Antonio TX 78205

SESSLE, BARRY JOHN, university administrator, researcher; b. Sydney, NSW, Australia, May 28, 1941; immigrated to Can., 1971; s. Frederick George and Sadie Isobel (Lawson) S.; m. Mary Baldwin; children from previous marriage: Erica Jane, Claire Marie. BDS, Sydney U., New South Wales, 1963, MDS, 1965, MSc, 1965; PhD, U. New South Wales, 1969. Scholar Dental Found. Sydney U., 1963-64; teaching fellow U. New South Wales, 1965-68; vis. assoc. U.S. Nat. Inst. Dental Research, Bethesda, Md., 1968-70; assoc. prof. U. Toronto Dental Sch., Ont., Can., 1971-76, prof., 1976-85, chmn. div. biol. scis., 1978-84, assoc. dean research, 1985-90, dean, 1990—; mem. com. on dental scis. Can. Med. Research Council, Ottawa, 1979-82. Author: The Neural Basis of Oral and Facial Function, 1978; editor: Mastication and Swallowing, 1976, Oro-facial Pain and Neuromuscular Dysfunction, 1985, Effects of Injury of Trigeminal and Spinal Somatosensory Systems, 1987, Trigeminal Neuralgia: Current Concepts Regarding Pathogenesis and Treatment, 1991, Temporomandibular Joint and Masticatory Muscle Disorders and Related Pain Conditions, 1995; mem. editl. bd. Arch. Oral Biol. Jour., 1988—, Pain Jour., 1986-90, assoc. editor, 1990-93, Dysphagia Jour., 1990—, Pain Rsch. and Mgmt. Jour., 1995—. Recipient Tchr. award Can. Fund for Dental Edn.; grantee Canadian Med. Research Council, 1971—, NIH, 1974—. Mem. Internat. Assn. Study Pain (sec. Can. chpt. 1982-87, mem. coun. 1993—), Soc. Neurosci. (pres. South Ont. chpt. 1982-83), Internat. Assn. Dental Rsch. (pres. Can. divsn. 1977-78, sec.-treas. 1976-79, pres. neurosci. group 1985-86, pres. 1994-95, Oral Sci. award 1976, Pindborg Oral Biol. prize 1994), Internat. Union Physiol. Sci. (sec. oral physiology commn. 1983—). Office: Faculty Dentistry U Toronto, 124 Edward St, Toronto, ON Canada M5G 1G6

SESSLER, ANDREW MARIENHOFF, physicist; b. Bklyn., Dec. 11, 1928; s. David and Mary (Baron) S.; m. Gladys Lerner, Sept. 23, 1951 (div. Dec. 1994); children: Daniel Ira, Jonathan Lawrence, Ruth. BA in Math. cum laude, Harvard U., 1949; MA in Theoretical Physics, Columbia U., 1951, PhD in Theoretical Physics, 1953. NSF fellow Cornell U., N.Y., 1953-54; asst. prof. Ohio State U., Columbus, 1954, assoc. prof., 1960; on leave Midwestern Univs. Research, 1955-56; vis. physicist Lawrence Rediation Lab., 1959-60, Niels Bohr Inst., Copenhagen, summer 1961; researcher theoretical physics U. Calif. Lawrence Berkeley Lab., Berkeley, 1961-73, researcher energy and environment, 1971-73, dir., 1973-80, sr. scientist plasma physics, 1980—; U.S. advisor Panjab U. Physics Inst., Chandigarh, India; mem. U.S.-India Coop. Program for Improvement Sci. Edn. in India, 1966, high energy physics adv. panel to U.S. AEC, 1969-72, adv. com. Lawrence Hall Sci., 1974-78; chmn. Stanford Synchrotron Radiation Project Sci. Policy Bd., 1974-77, EPRI Advanced Fuels Adv. Com., 1978-81, BNL External Adv. Com. on Isabelle, 1980-82; mem. sci. pol. bd. Stanford Synchrotron Radiation Lab., 1991-92; L.J. Haworth dist. scientist Brookhaven Nat. Lab., 1991—. Mem. editorial bd. Nuclear Instruments and Methods, 1969—; correspondent Comments on Modern Physics, 1969-71; contbr. articles in field to profl. jours. Mem. hon. adv. bd. Inst. Advanced Phys. Studies, LaJolla Internat. Sch. Physics, 1991—; mem. Superconducting Super Collider Sci. Policy Com., 1991-94. Recipient E.O. Lawrence award U.S. Atomic Energy Commn., 1970, U.S. Particle Accelerator Sch. prize, 1988, Nicholson medal for Humanitarian, APS, 1994; fellow Japan Soc. for Promotion Sci. at KEK, 1985. Fellow AAAS (nominating com. 1984-87), Am. Phys. Soc. (chmn. com. internat. freedom scientist 1982, study of directed energy weapons panel 1985-87, chmn. panel pub. affairs 1988, chmn. divsn. physics of beams 1990, chmn. com. applications of physics 1993, v.p. 1996); mem. NAS, IEEE, Fedn. Am. Scientists Coun. (vice chmn. 1987-88, chmn. 1988-92), N.Y. Acad. Sci., Assoc. Univ. Inc. (bd. dirs. 1991-94). Home: 225 Clifton St Apt 313 Oakland CA 94618-1468 Office: U Calif Lawrence Berkeley Labb 1 Cyclotron Rd M/S 71-259 Berkeley CA 94720

SESSOMS, ALLEN LEE, academic administrator, former diplomat, physicist; b. N.Y.C., Nov. 17, 1946; s. Albert Earl and Lottie Beatrice (Leff) S.; m. Csilla Manette von Csiky, Apr. 18, 1990; children: Manon Elizabeth, Stephanie Csilla. BS, Union Coll., Schenectady, N.Y., 1968; PhD, Yale U., 1972. Sci. assoc. CERN, Geneva, Switzerland, 1973-78; asst. prof. physics Harvard U., Cambridge, Mass., 1974-81; sr. tech. advisor OES, State Dept., Washington, 1980-82; dir. Office Nuclear Tech. & Safeguards, State Dept., Washington, 1982-87; counselor for sci. and tech. U.S. Embassy, Paris, 1987-89; polit. minister, counselor U.S. Embassy, Mexico City, 1989-91, dep. chief of mission, 1991-93; exec. v.p., v.p. for acad. affairs U. Mass. Sys., Boston, 1993-95; pres. CUNY Queens Coll., Flushing, N.Y., 1995—; mem. adv. com. U.S. Sec. Energy; mem. fusion energy adv. bd. Dept. of Energy. Contbr. articles to profl. jours. Adv. com. mem. U.S. Sec. of Energy. Ford Found. travel/study grantee, 1973-74; Alfred P. Sloan Found. fellow, 1977-81. Mem. AAAS, Am. Phys. Soc., N.Y. Acad. Sci., Cosmos Club.

SESSOMS, STUART MCGUIRE, physician, educator, retired insurance company executive; b. Autryville, N.C., July 16, 1921; s. Edwin Tate and Lillian Olive (Howard) S.; m. Thelma Ernestine Call, June 21, 1944; children: Stuart McGuire, Cristi Kay. B.S., U. N.C., 1943; M.D., Med. Coll. Va., 1946; postgrad., Johns Hopkins U. Diplomate: Am. Bd. Internal Medicine. Intern U.S. Marine Hosp., Balt., 1946-47; resident internal medicine U.S. Marine Hosp., 1947-50, asst. chief med. service, charge med. outpatient dept., 1950-52; asst. resident medicine Meml. Center Cancer and Allied Diseases, N.Y.C., 1952-53; with NIH, Bethesda, Md., 1953-68; mem. clin. medicine, surgery Nat. Cancer Inst., 1953-54, acting chief gen. medicine, 1954, asst. dir., 1958, asso. dir. collaberative research, 1961-62; chief cancer chemotherapy Nat. Service Center, 1958-62; asst. dir. clin. center NIH, 1955-57, dep. dir., 1962-68; clin. instr. medicine George Washington U., 1953-54; asso. dean, prof. medicine Duke Sch. Medicine, Durham, 1968-75; dir. Duke U. Hosp., 1968-75, prof. health adminstrn., 1973-75; sr. v.p. Blue Cross and Blue Shield of N.C., 1976-87. Contbr. articles to profl. jours. Active PTA. Recipient Distinguished Service award U.S. Jr. C. of C., 1957. Mem. AMA, Assn. Mil. Surgeons U.S., Am. Hosp. Assn., Am., N.C. hosp. assns., Am. Pub. Health Assn., N.Y. Acad. Sci., Phi Delta Chi, Rho Chi, Alpha Kappa Kappa. Presbyterian. Home: 3432 Dover Rd Durham NC 27707-4520

SESSOMS, WALTER WOODROW, telecommunications executive; b. Darlington, S.C., Jan. 14, 1934; s. Frank Darlington and Maggie (Garrison) S.; m. HArriet Floyd, June 14, 1957; children: Lee, Kay. BA, Wofford Coll., 1956. Asst. engr. So. Bell, Columbia, S.C., 1956-64; forecast supr. So. Bell, Greenville, S.C., 1964-65; mgr. pub. rels. So. Bell, Spartanburg, S.C., 1965-66; dist. engr. So. Bell, Florence, S.C., 1967-69; gen. mktg. mgr. So. Bell, Charlotte, N.C., 1974-77; v.p. So. Bell, Miami, Fla., 1978-79; v.p. So. Bell, Atlanta, 1979-89, sr. v.p., 1989-91; fin. supr. AT&T, N.Y.C., 1969-73; pres. svcs. group BellSouth Telecomm. Inc., Atlanta, 1991—; practitioner, lectr. U. Ga., Athens, 1984—. Trustee Ga. Bd. Edn., Atlanta, 1989—; chmn. bd. trustees Wofford Coll., Spartanburg, 1990-91; chmn. bd. dirs. Metro Atlanta chpt. Salvation Army, 1990—; chmn. Atlanta Partnership Bus. and Edn., 1990-91; mem. Ga. Edn. 2000, 1991—. 1st lt. U.S. Army, 1957-59. Recipient U.S. Fed. Govt. Pres. Outstanding Svc. award, 1974. Mem. Telephone Pioneers of Am. (sr. vice pres., 1995), Ga. C. of C. (chmn. bd. dirs. 1991-92), Presdl. Exec. Interexch. Assn., Commerce Club, Ashford Club, Rotary. Methodist. Home: 5995 River Chase Cir NW Atlanta GA 30328-3562 Office: BellSouth Telecomm 675 W Peachtree St NW Rm 4502 Atlanta GA 30308-1952

SESTINI, VIRGIL ANDREW, biology educator; b. Las Vegas, Nov. 24, 1936; s. Santi and Merceda Francesca (Borla) S. BS in Edn., U. Nev., 1959; postgrad., Oreg. State U., 1963-64; MNS, U. Idaho, 1965; postgrad., Ariz. State U., 1967, No. Ariz. U., 1969; cert. tchr., Nev. Tchr. biology Rancho High Sch., 1960-76; sci. chmn., tchr. biology Bonanza High Sch., Las Vegas, 1976-90; ret., 1990; co-founder, curator exhibits Meadows Mus. Nat. History, 1993-94; part-time tchr. Meadows Sch., 1987-94; ret., 1994; edn. specialist, cell biologist SAGE Rsch., Las Vegas, 1993; founder Da Vinci Enterprises, Las Vegas, 1995. Served with USAR, 1959-65. Recipient Rotary Internat. Honor Tchr. award, 1965, Region VIII Outstanding Biology Tchr. award, 1970, Nev. Outstanding Biology Tchr. award Nat. Assn. Biology Tchrs., 1970, Nat. Assn. Sci. Tchrs., Am. Gas Assn. Sci. Teaching Achievement Recognition award, 1976, 1980, Gustov Ohaus award, 1980, Presdl. Honor Sci. Tchr. award, 1983; Excellence in Edn. award Nev. Dept. Edn., 1983; Presdl. award excellence in math. and sci. teaching, 1984, Celebration of Excellence award Nev. Com. on Excellence in Edn., 1986, Hall of Fame award Clark County Sch. Dist., 1988, Excellence in Edn. award, Clark County Sch. Dist., 1987, 88, Spl. Edn. award Clark County Sch. Dist., 1988, NSEA Mini-grants, 1988, 89, 92, World Decoration of Excellence medallion World Inst. Achievement, 1989, Cert. Spl. Congl. Recognition, 1989, Senatorial Recognition , 1989, mini-grant Jr. League Las Vegas., 1989, Excellence in Edn. award, Clark Country Sch. Dist., 1989; named Nev. Educator of Yr., Milken Family Found./Nev. State Dept. Edn., 1989; grantee Nev. State Bd. Edn., 1988, 89, Nev. State Edn. Assn., 1988-89. Author: Lab Investigations For High School Honors Biology, 1989, Microbiology: A Manual for High School Biology, 1992, Laboratory Investigations in Microbiology, 1992, Genetics Problems for High School Biology, 1995, Science Laboratory Report Data Book, 1995, Field and Museum Techniques for the Classroom Teacher, 1995, Selected Lab Investigations and Projects for Honors and AP Biology, Vol. I Microbiology, 1995, Telecommunications: A Simulation for Biology Using the Internet, 1995; co-author: A Biology Lab Manual For Cooperative Learning, 1989, Metrics and Science Methods: A Manual of Lab Experiments for Home Schoolers, 1990, Experimental Designs in Biology I: Botany and Zoology, 1993, Designs in Biology: A Lab Manual, 1993, Integrated Science Lab Manual, 1994; contbr. articles to profl. jours. Mem. AAAS, NEA, Nat. Assn. Taxidermists, Nat. Sci. Tchrs. Assn. (life, Nev. State chpt. 1968-70), Nat. Assn. Biology Tchrs. (life, OBTA dir. Nev. State 1991—), Am. Soc. Microbiology, Coun. for Exceptional Children, Am. Biographic Inst. (rsch. bd. advisors 1988), Nat. Audubon Assn., Nat. Sci. Suprs. Assn., Am. Inst. Biol. Scis., Internat. Bank Modelers Soc., So. Nev. Scale Modelers (region VIII coord. Modeloberfest, 1995). Avocations: scale models, military figures, scale model circus, photography, chess. Office: Sage Rsch 2250 E Tropicana Ave Ste 19 452 Las Vegas NV 89119

SESTRIC, ANTHONY JAMES, lawyer; b. St. Louis, June 27, 1940; s. Anton and Marie (Gasparovic) S.; student, Georgetown U., 1958-62; JD, Mo. U., 1965; m. Carol F. Bowman, Nov. 24, 1966; children: Laura Antonette, Holly Nicole, Michael Anthony. Bar: Mo. 1965, U.S. Ct. Appeals (8th cir.) 1965, U.S. Dist. Ct. Mo., 1966, U.S. Tax Ct. 1969, U.S. Supreme Ct. 1970, U.S. Ct. Appeals (7th cir.) 1984, U.S. Dist. Ct. (no. dist.) Tex. 1985, U.S. Claims Ct. 1986. U.S. Dist. Ct. Ill., 1994, Minn. 1996. Law clk. U.S. Dist. Ct., St. Louis, 1965-66; ptnr. firm Sestric, McGhee & Miller, St. Louis, 1966-77; spl. asst. to Mo. atty. gen., St. Louis, 1968; ptnr. Fordyce and Mayne, 1977-78, Sestric & Garvey, St. Louis, 1978-96, Sestric Law Firm, 1996—; hearing officer St. Louis Met. Police Dept.; active Fed. Jud. Selection Commn., 1993; bd. dirs. Marquett Learning Ctr.; gen. chmn. 22nd jud. cir. bar com., 1995. Contbr. articles to profl. jours. Mem. exec. com. Nat. Caucus of Met. Bar Leaders, 1987-90; mem. Fed. Judicial Commn., 1993, mem. St. Louis Air Pollution Bd. Appeals and Varience Rev., 1966-73, chmn., 1968-73; mem. St. Louis Airport Commn., 1975-76; dist. vice chmn. Boy Scouts Am., 1970-76; bd. dirs. Full Achievement, Inc., 1970-77; bd. dirs. Legal Aid Soc. of St. Louis, 1976-77, Law Library Assn. St. Louis, 1976-78; v.p. bd. St. Elizabeth Acad., 1985-86; bd. dirs. Thomas Dunn Memls., 1995—, Marquette Learning Ctr., 1995—; mem. U.S. Judicial Selections Commn., 1993—. Mem. ABA (state chmn. judiciary com. 1973-75, cir. chmn. com. condemnation, zoning and property use 1975-77, standing com. bar activities 1982-88), Nat. Conf. Bar Pres.'s (exec. coun. 1987-90), Mo. Bar (vice chmn. young lawyers sect. 1973-76, bd. govs. 1974-77), Bar Assn. Met. St. Louis (chmn. young lawyers sect. 1974-75, exec. com. 1974-83, 94-95, pres. 1981-82, bd. govs. 1995—). Home: 3967 Holly Hills Blvd Saint Louis MO 63116-3135 Office: Sestric & Garvey 22 Morgan St Saint Louis MO 63102-2558

SESVOLD, RONALD LOUIS, business service company executive; b. Clarkston, Mich., Jan. 14, 1941; s. William and Thelma Yvonne (Mou Feis) S.; children: Mark Joel, Terry Scott, Chad Louis. BBA, Ea. Mich. U., 1967; BSBA, Cleary Coll., DSc in Bus. Adminstrn. Dir. faculty and student affairs Ea. Mich. U., Ypsilanti, 1966-68; mgr. retail advt. Oakland (Mich.) Press, 1968-71; gen. mgr. Tel-Twelve Mall, Southfield, Mich., 1971-78; dir. shopping ctrs. and pub. affairs Ramco-Gershenson, Inc., 1979-84, v.p. spl. projects and pub. affairs, 1984—; pres., owner Mainstreet Video; mem. faculty, chair Mich. conv., mem. admissions com., mem. governing bd. Council Shopping Ctrs., 1972. Contbr. articles to trade publs. Vice chmn. United Fund North Oakland County, 1969-70; bd. dirs. Southfield Arts Council, pres., 1974; trustee Cleary Coll., 1975-77, treas., 1976; chmn. Oakland County Week, 1975—, Southeastern Mich. Week, 1977—, State of Mich. Mich. Week, 1982; bd. govs. Greater Mich. Found., 1977—; founder Greater West Bloomfield Council for Arts, 1977, Lakes Area Council for Arts, 1977-79; chmn. adv. council LWV, 1979-81; mem. career, vocat. and placement adv. council Southfield Pub. Schs., 1980-81; bd. dirs. Lake Orion Stadium Elem. Sch., 1980-81, pres., 1981-82; bd. dirs. Oakland County Traffic Improvement Assn., 1973—, Oakway Symphony, 1974-84, West Bloomfield Symphony, 1976-78; treas. Walled Lake Schs. Bd. Edn. 1984-85; pres. Union Lake Shores Assn. 1973—, Union Lake Subdivision Property Owners Assn., 1973, 76, 79, 86—, Native Am. Vocat. and Cultural Orgn.; treas. Walled Lake Cen. High Sch. PTSA 1987-88. Mem. Southfield C. of C. (bd. dirs. 1973-76, v.p. 1974), Spirit of Detroit Assn. (commodore 1978), Ea. Mich. U. Alumni Assn. (pres. 1976), Civitan. Lodge: Civitan. Home: 7860 Barnsbury St West Bloomfield MI 48324-3618

SETH, OLIVER, federal judge; b. Albuquerque, May 30, 1915; s. Julien Orem and Bernice (Grefe) S.; m. Jean MacGillivray, Sept. 25, 1946; children: Sandra Bernice, Laurel Jean. A.B., Stanford U., 1937; LL.B., Yale U., 1940. Bar: N.Mex. 1940. Practice law Santa Fe, 1940, 46-62; judge U.S. Ct. Appeals 10th Circuit, 1962—, chief judge, from 1976, now senior judge; dir. Santa Fe Nat. Bank, 1949-62; chmn. legal com. N.Mex. Oil and Gas Assn., 1956-59, mem. regulatory practices com., 1960-62; counsel N.Mex. Cattlegrowers Assn., 1950-62, N.Mex. Bankers Assn., 1952-62; govt. appeal agent SSS, 1948-52. Mem. bd. regents Mus. of N.Mex., 1956-60; Bd. dirs. Boys Club, Santa Fe, 1948-49, New Mex. Land Resources Assn., 1956-60, Ghost Ranch Mus., 1962—; mng. bd. Sch. Am. Research, 1950—. Served from pvt. to maj. AUS, 1940-45, ETO. Decorated Croix de Guerre (France). Mem. Santa Fe C. of C. (dir.), N.Mex., Santa Fe County bar assns., Phi Beta Kappa. Presbyterian. Office: US Ct Appeals 10th Circuit PO Drawer I Santa Fe NM 87501

SETHI, SHYAM SUNDER, management consultant; b. Rawalpindi, Pakistan, July 11, 1942; s. Balraj and Shakuntala (Sawhney) S.; m. Kiran Nair, Oct. 17, 1972; children: Seema, Shana. B.E. in Mech. Engring., Birla Inst. Tech., Ranchi, India, 1964; M.S.I.E., U. Wis., 1970. Cert. mgmt. cons. V.p. Drake Sheahan/Stewart Dougall, N.Y.C., 1970-80; pres., ptnr. Distbn. Mgmt. Assocs., Inc., Princeton, N.J., 1980—; cons. in logistics, inventory mgmt., ops. for maj. indsl. cos. and retailers, Europe, S.Am. and U.S.; spkr. internat. logistics conf. Contbr. articles to profl. jours. Pres. N.J. chpt. Coun. Logistics Mgmt., 1987-88, N.J. chpt. Inst. Mgmt. Consultants, 1987-88. Mem. Yacht Assn. India. Hindu. Avocations: tennis, sailing. Home: 4 Haelig Ct Bridgewater NJ 08807-2377 Office: Distbn Mgmt Assocs Inc 22 Wall St Princeton NJ 08540-1513

SETHNA, BEHERUZ NARIMAN, university president, marketing, management educator; b. Bombay, July 31, 1948; came to U.S., 1973; s. Nariman Dhanjishaw and Mithu Nariman (Mistry) S.; m. Madhavi Kaji, May 25, 1974; children: Anita B., Shaun B. B in Tech. with honors, Indian Inst. Tech., Bombay, 1971; MBA, Indian Inst. Mgmt., Ahmedabad, 1973; MPhil, Columbia U., 1975, PhD in Bus., 1976; cert., Ind. U., 1986, Harvard U. Inst. Educ. Mgmt., 1991. Engring. and mgmt. trainee various corps., Bombay, 1968-69, 70-72; case writer, trainee Clarion Advt., Bombay, 1973; project mgr., cons. Lever Bros. Co., N.Y.C., 1974-76; prof., chair mktg. and mgmt. info. systems Clarkson U., Potsdam, N.Y., 1976-89, dir. grad. programs, 1978-80; mktg., rsch. and strategic planning mgr. Procter & Gamble (India)/Richardson Hindustan (Vicks), Bombay and Westport, Conn., 1980-81; interim exec. v.p. acad. and student affairs; interim exec. v.p. ASA; dean Coll. of Bus. and chief academic officer Lamar (Tex.) U., 1989-94, Gulf States Utilities prof. bus., 1991-94; pres. State U. W. Ga., Carrollton, 1994—; mem. adv. coun. SUNY-Canton (N.Y.) Coll., 1975-89; cons. in field. Author: Research Methods in Marketing, 1984; contbr. articles to profl. jours. Scoutmaster Boy Scouts Am., Potsdam, 1987-89, pack com. chair, den leader, 1987-89, mem. dist. bd., 1991-94, Pres.'s Scout Gold Cord, 1966; leader Girl Scouts U.S., Beaumont, 1989-94. Recipient Instrl. Innovation award Decision Scis. Inst., 1984, 85, 86, 87, 88, 89, Minority Achiever's award Role Model award, 1991, Dean's Leadership award Acad. Bus. Adminstrn., 1993, Nat. Svc. award, 1996; Fulbright scholar U.S. Info. Agy., 1986-87; U.S. Dept. Energy grantee, 1980, IBM Corp. grantee, 1984, AT&T grantee, 1985. Mem. Decision Scis. Inst., Rotary (pres. elect, edn. chair). Avocations: family, scouting. Home: 107 Wind Song Ct Carrollton GA 30117-4122 Office: Office of Pres State U W Ga Carrollton GA 30118-4500

SETHNESS, CHARLES OLIN, international financial official; b. Evanston, Ill., Feb. 24, 1941; s. Charles Olin and Alison Louise (Burge) S.; 1 son, Peter Worcester; m. Geraldine Greene, June 25, 1977; stepchildren: John, Carla, Sarah Houseman. A.B., Princeton U., 1963; M.B.A. with high distinction (Baker scholar), Harvard U., 1966. Sr. credit analyst Am. Nat. Bank & Trust Co., Chgo., 1963-64; research asst. Harvard Bus. Sch., 1966-67; assoc. Morgan Stanley & Co., N.Y.C., 1967-71; v.p. Morgan Stanley & Co., 1972, mng. dir., 1975-81; mgr. Morgan & Cie Internat., S.A., Paris, 1971-73; U.S. exec. dir. World Bank; and spl. asst. to sec. treasury Washington, 1973-75; assoc. dean for external relations Harvard U. Bus. Sch., Boston, 1981-85; asst. sec. treasury for domestic fin. Dept. Treasury, Washington, 1985-88; dir. capital markets dept. Internat. Fin. Corp., 1988-89; chief fin. officer Inter-Am. Devel. Bank, 1990—. Home: 6219 Garnett Dr Chevy Chase MD

20815-6617 Office: Inter-Am Devel Bank 1300 New York Ave NW Washington DC 20577-0001

SETLIN, ALAN JOHN, entrepreneur; b. N.Y.C., Oct. 27, 1933; s. Samuel and Alyce (Inginito) S.; children: Susan Marie, Peggy Ann, Gina Marie, Alycia Ruth, Alana Jean; m. Deborah Ann Kozlowski, Oct. 14, 1986. Student, U. Miami. CLU. V.p. Figurette, Ltd., Miami, Fla., 1956-60; ptnr. Robins & Clarke, N.Y.C., 1960-63; leading agt. Equitable Life Ins. Co., N.Y.C., 1963; gen. agt. Madison Life Ins. Co., N.Y.C., 1963-66, Beneficial Nat. Life Ins. Co., N.Y.C., 1967-72; pres., chief exec. officer Alliance Assoc., Inc., Beverly Hills, Calif., 1972—; ptnr. McMutry & Bell, Inc., Beverly Hills, 1982—; chief exec. officer Emergency Help, Inc., Beverly Hills, 1989-91; COO, dir. Clinica Medica Familiar, L.A., 1993—; bd. dirs. Six Million Dollar Forum, 1979-80. Mem. Rep. Senatorial Inner Circle, 1988-90. Sgt. AUS, 1952-54. Mem. Nat. Assn. Life Underwriters (fed. legis. chmn. Western States div. 1980-81, pres. L.A. chpt. 1979-80), CLU Assn. (pres. county chpt. 1979-80), Million Dollar Round Table (life), Golden Key (nat. com.). Roman Catholic. Avocations: weightlifting, boxing, skiing, white water rafting, motorcycling. Office: Clinica Medica Familiar 600 Wilshire Blvd Ste 700 Los Angeles CA 90017-3219

SETLOW, JANE KELLOCK, biophysicist; b. N.Y.C., Dec. 17, 1919; d. Harold A. and Alberta (Thompson) Kellock; m. Richard Setlow, June 6, 1941; children—Peter, Michael, Katherine, Charles. B.A., Swarthmore Coll., 1940; Ph.D. in Biophysics, Yale U., 1959. With dept. radiology Yale U., 1959-60; with biology div. Oak Ridge Nat. Lab., 1960-74; biophysicist Brookhaven Nat. Lab., Upton, N.Y., 1974—; mem. recombinant DNA molecule program adv. com. NIH, chmn., 1978-80. Author articles; mem. editorial bd. jours. Predoctoral fellow USPHS, 1957-59; postdoctoral fellow, 1960-62. Mem. Biophys. Soc. (pres. 1977-78), Am. Soc. Microbiology. Democrat. Home: 57 Valentine Rd Shoreham NY 11786-1243 Office: Biology Dept Brookhaven Nat Lab Upton NY 11973

SETLOW, RICHARD BURTON, biophysicist; b. N.Y.C., Jan. 19, 1921; s. Charles Meyer and Elsie (Hurwitz) S.; children: Peter, Michael, Katherine, Charles; m. Neva Delihas, Mar. 3, 1989. AB, Swarthmore Coll., 1941; PhD, Yale U., 1947; DSc, U. Toronto, 1985; MD, U. Essen, 1993. Assoc. prof. Yale U., 1956-61; biophysicist Oak Ridge (Tenn.) Nat. Lab., 1961-74, sci. dir. biophysics and cell physiology, 1969-74; dir. U. Tenn.-Oak Ridge Grad. Sch. Biomed. Scis., 1972-74; sr. biophysicist Brookhaven Nat. Lab., Upton, N.Y., 1974—, chmn. biology dept., 1979-87, assoc. dir. life scis., 1985—; prof. biomed. scis. U. Tenn., 1967-74; adj. prof. biochemistry SUNY, Stony Brook, 1975—. Author: (with E.C. Pollard) Molecular Biophysics, 1962; editor: (with P.C. Hanawalt) Molecular Mechanisms for Repair of DNA, 1975. Recipient Finsen medal Internat. Assn. Photobiology, 1980, Enrico Fermi award U.S. Dept. Energy, 1988. Mem. NAS, Am. Acad. Arts and Scis., Biophys. Soc. (pres. 1969-70), Internat. Com. Photobiology (pres. 1972-76), Radiation Rsch. Soc., Am. Soc. Photobiology, Am. Soc. Biochemistry and Molecular Biology, Am. Soc. Cancer Rsch., Environ. Mutagen Soc., 11th Internat. Congress on Photobiology (hon. pres. 1992), Phi Beta Kappa. Home: 4 Beachland Ave East Quogue NY 11942-4941 Office: Brookhaven Nat Lab Dept Biology Upton NY 11973

SETO, WILLIAM RODERICK, public accounting company executive; b. N.Y.C., July 2, 1954; s. James and Dorothy (Tsang) S. BS, U. Pa., 1976; JD, Cornell Law Sch., 1979. Bar: N.Y. 1980; CPA. Ptnr. Ernst & Young, Atlanta; S.E. area dir. internat. tax, 1986—; lectr. in field. Mem. editl. bd. Atlanta Internat. Mag., 1992-94. Mem. Leadership Atlanta. Named one of Top Tax Advisors in U.S., Internat. Tax Rev. mag., 1995. Mem. ABA, AICPA, N.Y. Bar Assn., Soc. Internat. Bus. Fellows, Internat. Fiscal Assn., Fgn. Sales Corp./Domestic Internat. Sales Corp. Tax Assn. (bd. advisors). Office: Ernst & Young 2800 Nations Bank Plz 600 Peachtree St Atlanta GA 30308

SETON, CHARLES B., lawyer; b. Bridgeport, Conn., Oct. 1, 1910; s. Charles Hillison and Stella (Rosen) Shapiro; m. Suzanne Alexia Maimin, Mar. 7, 1948; children: Pam Elinor Seton Lorenzo, Charles B. B.A., Yale U., 1931, LL.B., 1934. Bar: N.Y. 1934. Pvt. practice N.Y. 1934-55, Larchmont, N.Y., 1955—; assoc. firm Rosenman, Goldmark, Colin & Kaye (and predecessors), 1935-51; partner Rosen & Seton, 1955-58, 74-79, Rosen, Seton & Sarbin, 1958-74; sec. Ziff-Davis Pub. Co., 1974-77, gen. counsel, 1958-79; sec. Ziff Corp., 1976-77; ann. guest lectr. Advanced Copyright Seminar, N.Y. U. Law Sch., 1953-76, Practising Law Inst., 1955-74; past chmn. bd. trustees Fed. Bar Coun.; mem. Consular Law Soc., 1959-91. Participating author: The Business and Law of Music, 1965, Internat. Music Industry Conference, 1969; contbr. articles to profl. jours. V.p., founding dir. Music for Westchester, Inc., 1962-75, Arthur Judson Found., Inc., 1959-96; founding trustee Copyright Soc. U.s., v.p., chmn. Copyright Luncheon Circle (co-chmn. 1952-82). Lt. comdr. USNR, 1942-45. Mem. ABA, Westchester County Bar Assn. (atty./client econ. dispute com.), Assn. of Bar of City of N.Y., Guadalcanal Campaign Vets. (N.Y. state rep. 1987-92), Mory's Club, Yale Club. Home: 33 W Putnam Ave Greenwich CT 06830-5333 Office: 1890 Palmer Ave Ste 403 Larchmont NY 10538-3031

SETON, FENMORE ROGER, manufacturing company executive, civic worker; b. Bridgeport, Conn., Nov. 27, 1917; m. Phyllis Winifred Zimmerman, Apr. 5, 1942; 1 child, Diana Seton Adams Wakerley. BA in English, Yale U., 1938; EdM, So. Conn. State Coll./Yale U., 1956; LLD (hon.), U. New Haven, 1990; DHL (hon.), Albertus Magnus Coll., 1994. Asst. prof. air sci. and tactics Yale U., New Haven, 1952-56; pres., chief exec. officer Seton Name Plate Corp., New Haven, 1956-81; pres. Nat. Assn. Metal Etchers, Washington, 1968-69, Internat. Mktg. Device Assn., Chgo., 1973-74, mfrs. div. New Haven C. of C., 1974-79; chmn. Am. Nat. Standards Com. A13, N.Y.C., 1972-82. Apptd. Pres.'s Com. on Employment of People With Disabilities, Washington, 1973—; world pres. Rehab. Internat., World Secretariat in N.Y.C., 1988-92; bd. govs. U. New Haven, 1979—; treas. Save the Children Fedn., Westport, Conn., 1984-88; assoc. fellow Calhoun Coll. Yale U., 1976—. Recipient Citation of Honor Sec. HEW, Washington, 1976, Preminger medallion People-To-People program Com. for Handicapped, Washington, 1988, Elm and Ivy award Yale U., 1985, Pub. Svc.award Social Security Adminstrn., 1992, Yale medal Pres. Yale U. on behalf of Bd. Govs. Assn. Yale Alumni, 1992, Disting. Svc. award Pres. of U.S., 1992. Fellow Inst. Dirs. (U.K.); mem. Cercle de l'Union Interallié (Paris), Explorers Club (N.Y.C.), Circumnavigators Club (N.Y.C.), Elizabethan Club (New Haven), Mory's Assn. (New Haven), New Haven Country Club. Republican. Home: 2 Old Orchard Rd North Haven CT 06473-3022

SETRAKIAN, BERGE, lawyer; b. Beirut, Lebanon, Apr. 14, 1949; came to U.S. 1976; s. Hemayak and Arminee S.; m. Vera L. Nazarian, Nov. 22, 1975; children: Ani, Lara. Diplome d'Etudes de Doctorat, U. Lyons, France, 1973; Diplome d'Etudes de Doctorat Droit Compare, F.I.E.D.C., Strasbourg, France, 1974; Licence en Droit Francais, U. St. Joseph, Beirut, 1972, Licence en Droit Libanais, 1972. Bar: Beirut 1972, N.Y. 1983. Assoc. Tyan & Setrakian, Beirut, 1972-76; ptnr. Whitman & Ransom, N.Y.C., 1976-93, Whitman, Breed, Abbott & Morgan, N.Y.C., 1993—; bd. dirs. Cedars Bank, Calif., 1987—, Bank Audi, U.S.A., 1991; fgn. law cons., N.Y., 1978. Bd. dirs., v.p., sec. Armenian Gen. Benevolent Union, N.Y.C., 1977—; pres. Worldwide Youth orgns., 1978—; bd. dirs. Armenian Assy. of Am., Washington, 1978-87; bd. dirs. Am. Task Force for Lebanon, 1988—; bd. dirs. Am. U. Armenia, 1992—. Mem. ABA, N.Y. Bar Assn., Beirut Bar Assn., U.K. Law Soc., Am. Fgn. Law Assn., Englewood Field Club. Office: Whitman Breed Abbott Morgan 200 Park Ave New York NY 10166-0005

SETSER, CAROLE SUE, food science educator; b. Warrenton, Mo., Aug. 26, 1940; d. Wesley August and Mary Elizabeth (Meine) Schulze; m. Donald Wayne Setser, June 2, 1969; children: Bradley Wayne, Kirk Wesley, Brett Donald. BS, U. Mo., 1962; MS, Cornell U., 1964; PhD, Kans. State U., 1971. Grad. asst. Cornell U., Ithaca, N.Y., 1962-64; instr. Kans. State U., Manhattan, 1964-72, asst. prof., 1974-81, assoc. prof., 1981-86, prof., 1986—. Recipient Rsch. Excellence award Coll. of Human Ecology, Manhattan, 1990. Mem. Am. Assn.Cereal Chemists (assoc. editor 1989-93), Inst. Food Techs. (chmn. sensory evaluation divsn. edn. com. 1989-92, continuing edn. com. 1992—, other offices), Kappa Omicron Nu (Excellence for Rsch. award 1987), Sigma Xi, Phi Upsilon Omicron, Gamma Sigma Delta, Phi Tau Sigma. Office: Kansas State U Justin Hall Dept Foods Nutrition Manhattan KS 66506

SETSER, DONALD WAYNE, chemistry educator; b. Great Bend, Kans., Jan. 2, 1935; s. Leo Wayne and Velma Irene (Hewitt) S.; m. Carole Sue Schulze, June 2, 1969; children: Bradley Wayne, Kirk Wesley, Brett Donald. BS, Kans. State U., 1956, MS, 1958; PhD, U. Wash., 1961. Asst. prof. Kans. State U., Manhattan, 1963-66, assoc. prof., 1966-68, prof. chemistry, 1968—, Alumni Disting. prof. chemistry, 1984—; vis. prof. U. Grenoble, France, 1981, 84, 87, 91. Editor Reactive Intermediates, 1976; contbr. 240 articles to profl. jours. Recipient Rank prize electro-optics divsn., 1992. Fellow Am. Phys. Soc.; mem. Am. Chem. Soc. (Midwest award St. Louis sect. 1984), British Chem. Soc. Home: 414 Wickham Rd Manhattan KS 66502-3751 Office: Kans State U Dept Of Chemistry Manhattan KS 66506

SETTERHOLM, JEFFREY MILES, systems engineer; b. Rochester, N.Y., May 8, 1946; s. Vernon Miles and Grace Lorraine (Bogema) S.; m. Donna Jean Stollenwerk, July 6, 1974; children: Gregory Todd, Vincent Michael. BS in Engring. & Applied Sci. cum laude, Yale U., 1968; MS in Sys. Sci. and Math., Washington U., 1976. Electronic engr. McDonnell Douglas Aircraft Divsn, St. Louis, 1974, sr. engr. flight simulation, 1976-78; prin. devel. engr. mil. avionics divsn. Honeywell Inc., Mpls., 1978-84; prin. engr. aerospace divsn. Rosemount, Inc., Burnsville, Minn., 1984-92; ind. software tech. cons. Lakeville, Minn., 1992-94; geodetic scientist Geospan Corp., Mpls., 1994—. Author: The Philosophy Works Manual, 1993. Capt. USAF, 1969-73. Decorated Disting. Flying Cross, USAF, Thailand, 1973. Mem. AIAA, Soc. Automotive Engrs. Lutheran. Achievements include patents in field; origination of the computer configurable six-axis hand controller concept; research in virtual cockpit concepts. Home: 8095 230th St E Lakeville MN 55044-8287 Office: Geospan Corp 2905 Northwest Blvd Ste 60 Plymouth MN 55441-2644

SETTIPANI, FRANK G., news correspondent; b. Bklyn., July 18, 1948; s. Gaspare and Marion (Caronna) S.; m. Laura A. Czachor, Aug. 21, 1982; children: Cara, Paul. BA in Polit. Sci., Bklyn. Coll., 1968. Reporter UPI, N.Y.C., 1969-70; anchor, reporter Sta. WHLI Radio, L.I., N.Y., 1970-74, Sta. WNEW Radio, N.Y.C., 1975-80; anchor Sta. WGBB-Radio, L.I., 1974-75, Sta. WINS Radio, N.Y.C., 1980-81; reporter Dow Jones, N.Y.C., 1981; corr. CBS News, N.Y.C., 1982—. Trustee N.J. Ctr. for Outreach and Svcs. for Autism Cmty., Ewing, 1991-94. Recipient Champion-Tuck Econ. award for radio reporting Dartmouth Coll., 1984. Mem. AFTRA, TV and Radio Working Press Assn. Roman Catholic. Avocation: advocacy for handicapped and developmentally disabled. Office: CBS News 524 W 57th St New York NY 10019-2902

SETTLES, F. STAN, JR., manufacturing executive, educator; b. Denver, Oct. 3, 1938; s. Frank S. and Dorothy Marie (Johnson) S.; m. Evelyn Brown, June 10, 1961; children: Frank S. III, Richard, Charles, Michael. BS in Prodn. Tech., Indsl. Engring., LeTourneau Coll., Longview, Tex., 1962; MS in Indsl. Engring., Ariz. State U., 1967, PhD in Indsl. Engring., 1969. Sr. systems analyst AiResearch Mfg. Co., Phoenix, 1968-70, project mgr., 1970-74, mgr. operational planning, 1974-80; mgr. indsl. engrs. Garrett Pneumatic Systems, Phoenix, 1980-83; mgr. indsl. mfg. engring. Garrett Turbine Engring. Co., Phoenix, 1983-85; v.p. mfg. ops. AiResearch Mfg. Co., Torrance, Calif., 1985-87; dir. indusl. mfg. engring. The Garrett Corp., Phoenix, 1987-88; dir. planning Garrett Engine Div., Phoenix, 1988-92; asst. dir. White House Office of Sci. and Tech. Policy, 1992-93; program dir. NSF, 1992-94; prof., chmn. indsl. and systems engring. dept. U. So. Calif., L.A., 1994—; faculty assoc. Ariz. State U., Tempe, 1974-85, 90-92, rsch. prof., 1992-94. Mem. sch. bd. Tempe Elem. Sch. Dist., 1976-80; mem. YMCA Indian Guides, nat. chief, 1978-79. Fellow Inst. Indsl. Engrs. (pres. 1987-88, Ops. Rsch. award 1980); mem. Nat. Acad. Engrs., Soc. Mfg. Engrs. (sr.), Inst. Mgmt. Sci. (sr.), Am. Soc. Quality Control, Am. Soc. Engring. Edn., Quality and Productivity Mgmt. Assn. Republican. Presbyterian. Home: 1750 E Ocean Blvd #713 Long Beach CA 90802-6019 Office: Univ So Calif Dept Indsl and System Engring Los Angeles CA 90089-0193

SETTONNI, MICHAEL FRANCIS, broadcast journalist; b. Cleve., Aug. 13, 1959; s. Frank John and Marie Angela (Rodi) S.; m. Margaret Mary Greco, Aug. 9, 1986; children: Mario Francis, Rocco Michael. Degree in journalism, Ohio State U. Fellow Coll. Journalism U. Md., 1992; election supr. NBC News, N.Y.C., 1984-86; TV anchor WECT-TV, Wilmington, N.C., 1986-88; TV anchor WGME-TV, Elmira, N.Y., 1988-89, Portland, Maine, 1989-91; TV anchor WEWS-TV, Cleve., 1995—; TV anchor, environ. reporter KNSD-TV, San Diego, 1991-94; investigative reporter The Crusaders, Hollywood, Calif., 1994, WHDH-TV, Boston, 1995; cons. Nat. Environ. Mgmt. Assn., Washington, 1994, 95, 96. Bd. dirs. Midpark H.S., Middleburg Heights, Ohio, 1996. Recipient 4 Golden Microphone awards Calif. News Assn., 1991, 92, 93, 6 awards San Diego Press Club, 1991, 92, 93. Mem. NATAS (7 Emmy awards, 1991, 92, 93, 94, 95). Roman Catholic. Avocations: photography, sports. Home: 6973 Big Creek Pkwy Middleburg Heights OH 44130 Office: WEWS TV 3001 Euclid Ave Cleveland OH 44115

SETZEKORN, WILLIAM DAVID, retired architect, consultant, author; b. Mt. Vernon, Ill., Mar. 12, 1935; s. Merrett Everet and Audrey (Ferguson) S.; m. Georgia Sue Brown, Feb. 4, 1958 (div. 1968); children: Jeffrey Merle, Timothy Michael. BArch, Kans. State U., 1957; cert. in computer graphics, Harvard U., 1968; BA with MA equivalency in Humanities, Western Ill. U., 1982. Registered arch., Calif. Coord. design and constrn. Cal-Expo, Sacramento, 1968; pvt. practice Los Altos and Seattle, Calif., 1968-85; cons. Contra Costa County, Martinez, Calif., 1985-89, El Dorado County, Placerville, Calif., 1985-89, Somerset, Calif., 1989—; cons. Fed. Emergency Mgmt. Agy., The Presidio, San Francisco, 1989-95, Gov. Keating's task force dor disaster recovery, Oklahoma City, 1995. Author: Formerly British Honduras: A Profile of the New Nation of Belize, 1975, 4 other titles; contbr. articles to mags. Mem. Pi Kappa Alpha Alumni chpts., Manhattan, Kans. and Davis, Calif., 1957—. Recipient Ofcl. Commendation, State of Calif., 1968, U.S. Presdl. Medal of Merit, Ronald Reagan, 1988. Fellow Augustan Soc. (bd. dirs. 1994-96; mem. Noble Co. of the Rose (knight 1979, lt. magister Rosae 1995—), numerous other internat. orders of chivalry, Family Setzekorn Assn. (prin. officer 1979—), Kiwanis. Republican. Unitarian. Avocations. Genealogy, medieval history, heraldry, travel. Home and Office: PO Box 706 Somerset CA 95684-0706

SETZER, HERBERT JOHN, chemical engineer; b. N.Y.C., Oct. 23, 1928; s. Leo and Barbara (Hafner) S. m. Elizabeth Bernadette Curran, May 30, 1957; children: Stephen Lawrence, Robert Drew, John Herbert, Brian Edmund. BChemE, CUNY, 1951; MChemE, NYU, 1958. Engr. U.S. Army Ordnance Corps Redstone Arsenal, Huntsville, Ala., 1955-57; rsch. asst. NYU, 1958-61; rsch. engr. Internat. Fuel Cells (joint venture United Techs. Corp., Hartford, Conn. and Toshiba Corp., Tokyo), 1962-92; vis. lectr. Am. Internat. Coll., Conn., 1993—. Holder 21 U.S. patents chem. processing and hydrogen generation, other patents in Can., Europe, Africa, Asia, Australia; contbr. tech. papers in field to publs. Chmn. troop com. Long Rivers coun. Boy Scouts Am., 1971-81, com. mem., 1973-81. With U.S. Army, 1951-56. Recipient Mason award, NYU, 1962, Spl. award United Techs. Corp., 1980. Mem. Catalyst Soc. New Eng., Sigma Xi, Elks. Roman Catholic. Office: 17 Virginia Dr Ellington CT 06029-3432

SETZER, KIRK, religious leader. Pres. Amana (Iowa) Ch. Soc. Office: Amana Church Society Amana IA 52203

SETZLER, EDWARD ALLAN, lawyer; b. Kansas City, Mo., Nov. 3, 1933; s. Edward A. and Margaret (Parshall) S.; m. Helga E. Friedemann, May 20, 1972; children: Christina, Ingrid, Kirstin. BA, U. Kans., 1955; JD, U. Wis., 1962. Bar: Mo. 1962, U.S. Tax Ct. 1962. Assoc. Spencer, Fane, Britt & Browne, Kansas City, 1962-67, ptnr., 1968—, mng. ptnr., 1974-77, 78-82, chmn. trust and estate sect., 1974—; lectr. U. Mo. and Kansas City Sch. Law Continuing Edn. programs, 1983-95; mem. Jackson County Probate Manual com., 1988—; Mo. State rep. Joint Editl. Bd./Uniform Probate Code, 1989—. Co-author: Missouri Estate Administration, 1984, supplements, 1985-93; co-author, co-editor, reviewer Missouri Estate Planning, 1986, supplements, 1987-93; contbg. editor: A Will Is Not The Way -- The Living Trust Alternative, 1988; contbg. editor: Understanding Living Trusts, 1990, expanded edit., 1994; bd. editors Wis. Law Rev., 1961-62. Amb., bd. govs., bd. dirs., chmn. found. com. Am. Royal, 1982—; mem. planning giving com., bus. coun. Nelson Atkins Mus. Art, 1984—; mem. deferred giving com. Children's Mercy Hosp., 1991—; mem. Kansas City Estate Planning Symposium Com., 1984-92, chmn., 1991. Fellow Am. Coll. Trust and Estate Counsel (state chmn. 1992—); mem. ABA, Mo. Bar Assn. (lectr., vice chmn. probate and estate planning com. 1994—), Lawyers Assn. Kansas City, Kansas City Met. Bar Assn. (lectr., chmn. probate and trust 1979, 92, vice chmn. 1983-85, 91, legis. rev. com. 1991—), Estate Planning Soc. Kansas City (co-founder 1965, pres. 1983-84, dir. 1984-85, mem. social com. 1968—), Order of Coif, Sigma Chi, Phi Delta Phi. Office: Spencer Fane Britt & Browne 1000 Walnut St Ste 1400 Kansas City MO 64106-2140

SETZLER, WILLIAM EDWARD, chemical company executive; b. Bklyn., Dec. 20, 1926; s. William Edward and Gertrude A. (Seyer) S.; m. Dorothy C. Kress, Dec. 2, 1950 (dec. Mar. 1987); children: William John, Heather A.; m. Lenore Kelly, July 13, 1991. B of Chem. Engring., Cooper Union, 1950; MS in Liberal Studies, Columbia U., 1993. V.p. ops. Argus Chem. Corp., N.Y.C., 1950-66; v.p. engring., then group v.p. Witco Chem. Corp. (now Witco Corp.), N.Y.C., 1966-75, exec. v.p., 1975-90, ret., 1990, also bd. dirs.; chmn. and CEO Faimount Chem. Inc., 1993—. Author and patentee in field. Served with USAAF, 1945-46. Mem. Am. Inst. Chem. Engrs., Soap and Detergent Assn. (bd. dirs.). Home: 3921 Lincoln St Seaford NY 11783-2115

SEUFERT, EDWARD CECIL, librarian, military officer, retired; b. Newark, Apr. 16, 1933; s. Edward William and Dorothy Marie (Mussehl) S.; m. Shirley Ann Pratt, Oct. 20, 1963; children: Edward Roy, Janet Arlene. BS in Forestry, U. Maine, 1955; Cert. in Teaching, Lambuth Coll., 1977; MLS, Vanderbilt U., 1979; MA in Edn., Western Ky. U., 1982. Commd. 2d lt. U.S. Army, 1955, advanced through grades to lt. col., 1970; infantry and field artillery unit leader U.S. Army, U.S. and Korea, 1955-62; mobile tng. team leader U.S. Army, Vietnam, 1962-63; instr. Artillery Sch. U.S. Army, Ft. Sill, Okla., 1964-66; officer-in-charge Range Control Element U.S. Army, Baumholder Tng. Area, Fed. Republic of Germany, 1967-69; faculty chmn. combat arms br. Ordnance Sch. U.S. Army, Aberdeen Proving Ground, Md., 1970-73; dean adminstrn. Judge Adv. Gen.'s Sch. U.S. Army, Charlottesville, Va., 1973-75; ret. U.S. Army, 1975; head libr. Lindsey Wilson Coll., Columbia, Ky., 1979—. Tchr. adult Sunday sch. United Meth. Ch.; vol. county vets. assistance officer Ky. Divsn. Vets. Affairs; vol. dist. commr. Boy Scouts Am. Decorated Army Commendation medals (2), Legion of Merit, Combat Infantryman badge, Meritorious Svc. medal. Mem. ALA, Ret. Officers Assn., Columbia Men's Club (pres.), Nat. Eagle Scout Assn. (Eagle Scout 1949), Xi Sigma Pi, Alpha Gamma Rho. Home: 452 Jack Smith Rd Fairplay KY 42735-8728 Office: Lindsey Wilson Coll Libr Columbia KY 42728

SEUNG, THOMAS KAEHAO, philosophy educator; b. Jungju, Korea, Sept. 20, 1930; m. Kwihwan Hahn, May 29, 1965; children: Hyunjune Sebastian, Kwonjune Justin, Haesue Florence. BA, Yale U., 1958, MA, 1961, PhD, 1965. Instr. Yale U., 1963-65; asst. prof. Fordham U., 1965-66; mem. faculty dept. philosophy U. Tex., Austin, 1966—; prof. in philosophy U. Tex., 1972—, prof. in govt., 1985—, prof. in law, 1993—, Jesse H. Jones prof. liberal arts, 1987—. Author: The Fragile Leaves of the Sybil, 1962, Kant's Transcendental Logic, 1969, Cultural Thematics, 1976, Structuralism and Hermeneutics, 1982, Semiotics and Thematics, 1982, Intuition and Construction, 1993, Kant's Platonic Revolution, 1994, Plato Rediscovered, 1996. Served as officer Korean Army, 1950-53. Recipient Wilbur Lucius Cross medal Yale Grad. Sch. Alumni Assn., 1988; Soc. Religion in Higher Edn. fellow, 1969-70; Am. Council Learned Soc. fellow, 1970-71; NEH fellow, 1977-78. Office: U Tex Dept Philosophy Austin TX 78712

SEVALSTAD, SUZANNE ADA, accounting educator; b. Butte, Mont., Mar. 26, 1948; d. John Cornelius and Ivy Jeanette (Cloke) Pilling; m. Nels Sevalstad, Jr., Mar. 11, 1975. BS in Bus. with high distinction, Mont. State U., 1970, MS in Bus., 1972. CPA, Mont. Internal auditor Anaconda Co., Butte, 1970-71; mgr. Wise River (Mont.) Club, 1976-79; instr. acctg. Bozeman (Mont.) Vocat./Tech. Ctr., 1970-72, Ea. Mont. Coll., Billings, 1972-73, Mont. State U., Bozeman, 1973-76, U. Nev., Las Vegas, 1979—. Recipient Women of Month award Freshman Class Women, 1976, Disting. Tchr. Coll. Bus. U. Nev., 1983, 86, 89, 93, Prof. of Yr. award Student Acctg. Assn. U. Nev., 1984, 87, 88, 90, 91, Outstanding Acctg. Prof. award Acctg. Students of U. Nev., 1987, 88, 89, Spanos Disting. Teaching award, 1989, 94. Mem. AICPA, Am. Acctg. Assn., Nat. Inst. Mgmt. Acctg. (campus coord. 1988—), Inst. Mgmt. Accts., Assn. for Female Execs., Golden Key Soc. (hon.). Avocations: horseback riding, hiking, tennis, golf. Office: U Nev Dept Acctg 4505 S Maryland Pky Las Vegas NV 89154-9900

SEVCENKO, IHOR, history and literature educator; b. Radosc, Poland, Feb. 10, 1922; came to U.S., 1949, naturalized, 1957; s. Ivan and Maria (Cherniatynska) S.; m. Oksana Draj-Xmara, Apr., 1945 (div. 1953); m. Margaret M. Bentley, July 16, 1953 (div. 1966); m. Nancy Patterson, June 18, 1966 (div. 1995); children: Catherine, Elisabeth. Dr.Phil., Charles U., Prague, Czechoslovakia, 1945; Doct. en Phil. et Lettres, U. Louvain, Belgium, 1949; PhD (hon.), U. Cologne, Germany, 1994. Fellow in Byzantinology Dumbarton Oaks, 1949-50, dir. studies, 1966, prof. Byzantine history and lit., 1965-75, sr. research assoc., 1975—; lectr. Byzantine and ancient history U. Calif., Berkeley, 1950-51; fellow Byzantinology and Slavic lit., research program USSR, 1951-52; instr., then asst. prof. Slavic langs. and lit. U. Mich., 1953-57; mem. faculty Columbia U., 1957-72, prof., 1962-65, adj. prof., 1965-72; vis. prof. Harvard U., 1973-74, prof., 1974-92, emeritus, 1992; vis. fellow All Souls Coll., Oxford U., 1979-80, Wolfson Coll., Oxford U., 1987, 93; vis. mem. Princeton Inst. for Advanced Study, 1956; vis. prof. Munich U., 1959, Coll. de France, spring 1985, Cologne U., fall 1992, Ctrl. European U., Budapest, spring and fall 1995; treas., acting treas., bd. dirs. Am. Rsch. Inst. in Turkey, 1964-66, 67, 75—; assoc. dir. Harvard Ukrainian Rsch. Inst., 1973-89, acting dir., 1977, 85-86; chmn. Nat. Com. Byzantine Studies, 1966-77; mem. Internat. Com. for Greek Paleography, 1983—. Author: Etudes sur la polémique entre Théodore Métochite et Nicéphore Choumnos, 1962, Society and Intellectual Life in Late Byzantium, 1981, Ideology, Letters and Culture in the Byzantine World, 1982, Byzantium and the Slavs in Letters and Culture, 1991; co-author: Der Serbische Psalter, 1978, Life of St. Nicholas of Sion, 1984; contbr. articles to profl. jours. Guggenheim fellow, 1963, Humboldt-Forschungspreistraeger, 1985. Fellow Mediaeval Acad. Am., Brit. Acad. (corr.); mem. Am. Philos. Soc., Am. Acad. Arts and Scis., Ukrainian Acad. Arts and Scis., Sci. Sevcenko Soc., Société des Bollandistes Belgium (adj.), Accademia di Palermo (fgn.), Internat. Assn. Byzantine Studies (v.p. 1976-86, pres. 1986—), Christian Archeological Soc. of Athens (hon.), Austrian Acad. Sci. (corr.), Accademia Pontaniana of Naples (fgn.), Acad. Sci. Ukrainian SSR (fgn.), Cosmos Club (Washington), Harvard Club (N.Y.C.), Phi Beta Kappa (hon.). Office: Harvard Univ 319 Boylston Hall Cambridge MA 02138

SEVER, TOM, labor union administrator; b. West Newton, Pa., Aug. 13, 1935; widowed; children: Margaret, Josephine, Thomas, Paul. Student, St. Vincent Coll., Latrobe, Pa. Trustee local 30 Internat. Brotherhood Teamsters, Jeanette, Pa., 1973-75, bus. agt. local 30, 1979-91, pres. local 30, 1985—; gen. sec.-treas. Internat. Brotherhood Teamsters, Washington, 1992—. Mem. VFW, NRA, Eagles, Moose. Avocations: hunting, fishing. Office: Int Brotherhood Teamsters 25 Louisiana Ave NW Washington DC 20001-2130

SEVERDIA, ANTHONY GEORGE, chemistry research investigator; b. Sharon, Pa., Sept. 20, 1946; s. George Anthony and Angela Mary (Tomich) S. BS, Pa. State U., 1968; MS, Case Western Reserve U., 1971, PhD, 1974. Rsch., teaching assoc. Rensselaer Poly. Inst., Troy, N.Y., 1975-77; chemist N.Y. U., 1977-79, 82-83, Columbia U., N.Y.C., 1979-82; analytical chemist Mallinckrodt Vet., Terre Haute, Ind., 1983-92; rsch. investigation analytical sci. Sanofi Rsch., Gt. Valley, Pa., 1992—. Contbr. articles to profl. jours.; presenter in field. Recipient Summer fellowship NSF, Cleve., 1971. Mem. Am. Chem. Soc. (exec. com., treas. Terre Haute sect. 1991-92), Soc. Applied Spectroscopy, The Internat. Soc. for Optical Engring. Home: 209 Glendale Rd Upper Darby PA 19082

SEVERINO, ROBERTO, foreign language educator, academic administration executive; b. Catania, Italy, July 19, 1940; s. Giuseppe and Alba (Scroppo) S. Student, State U. Catania, Italy, 1960-62; BA, Columbia Union Coll., 1967; MA, U. Ill., 1969, PhD, 1973. Head acct., pers. dir. Industria Nazionale Apparecchiature Scientifiche, Milan, 1961-63; teaching asst., lang.

lab. supv. Columbia Union Coll., Takoma Park, Md., 1965-67; grad. teaching asst. U. Ill., Urbana, 1967-70, coord. Corr. Sch., 1970-71; instr. dept. French and Italian U. Mass., Amherst, 1971-73; prof. dept. Italian Georgetown U., Washington, 1973—, acting chmn., 1987, chmn. dept., 1988—; pres., co-founder Nat. Inst. Contemporary Italian Studies, 1986—; co-founder Associazione Internazionale del Diritto e dell'Arte, 1994—; pres. Am. U. of Rome, 1990-93; lit. dir. Georgetown U. Elec. Text Repository, Italian Archive, 1988—, Ultramarina, 1992—; mem. adv. bd. Nat. Italian Am. Found. Nat. Christopher Columbus 1992 Celebration; mem. U.S. delegation to 1st Conf. on Italian lang. and culture in U.S., 1987; lectr., speaker in field. Author: Le soluzioni immaginarie, 1985, The Signs and Sounds of Italian, 1985, A carte scoperte, 1990, Presente imperfetto ed altri tempi, 1992, The Battle for Humanism, 1994, A Dumas: Mariano Stabile Sindaco di Palermo, 1994; co-author: Periscopio, 1986, International Nuclear Agreements Multilingual Glossary, 1988, United Nations Organization Multilingual Glossary, 1988, Regularizing the Irregular Italian Verb, 1990; translator; The Next 6000 Days by Saverio Avveduto, 1987; editor: (serials) Segni, 1985-88, Hispano-Italic Studies, 1976, 79; guest editor: Forum Italicum, 1989; mem. editorial bd. Educazione Comparata, 1993—; contbr. articles to profl. jours. Trustee Joel Nafuma Refugee Ctr., Rome, 1993—. Rsch. grantee Interuniversity Ctr. European Studies, 1977; recipient Accademia Internazionale di Lettere, Scienze, Arti medal, 1983, Internat. Poetry prize, 1986, Gold Cross Cavaliere dell'Ordine al Merito della Repubblica Italiana, 1983, Gold medal Italian Ministries of Univs. and Sci. Rsch., 1988, Marranzano d'Argento prize, 1989, Gold Commander class Cross al Merito della Repubblica Italiana, 1990, Georgetown U. Vicennial Disting. Svc. medal, 1994. Mem. MLA, So. Atlantic Modern Lang. Assn., Nat. Assn. Secondary Sch. Prins. (mem. sch. partnerships internat. Italian adv. coun. 1988—), Italian Am. Cultural Found., Italian Cultural Soc. (pres. 1979-81, 83-85, Outstanding Svc. award 1983, chmn. acad. policy com. 1981—), Assn. Internationale Critiques Literaires and Associazione Italiana Critici Letterari, Greater Washington Assn. Tchrs. Fgn. Langs. (mem. award selection com. 1983-85), Manuscript Soc., Renaissance Soc. Am., Circolo Culturale Italiano (hon.), Am. Club (Rome), Touring Club Italiano (hon.), Gamma Kappa Alpha (v.p. 1990—, sec.-treas. and chpt. advisor 1985-90), World Jurist Assn. Ctr. Assocs. (U.S. pres. 1993—), Associazione Internazionale del Diritto e dell'Arte (v.p. 1994—). Home: 4949 Quebec St NW Washington DC 20016-3230 Office: Georgetown U Dept Italian 37th and O Sts NW Washington DC 20057

SEVERINSEN, DOC (CARL H. SEVERINSEN), conductor, musician; b. Arlington, Oreg., July 7, 1927; m. Emily Marshall, 1980; children—Nancy, Judy, Cindy, Robin, Allen. Ptnr. Severinsen-Akwright Co.; pops condr. The Phoenix (Ariz.) Symphony Orchestra. Mem., Ted Fio Rito Band, 1945, Charlie Barnet Band, 1947-49, then with, Tommy Dorsey, Benny Goodman, Norro Morales, Vaughn Monroe; soloist network band: Steven Allen Show, NBC-TV, 1954-55; mem., NBC Orch. Tonight Show, 1962-67 , music dir., 1967-92 ; past host of: NBC-TV show The Midnight Special; recs., RCA Records, including; albums: Brass Roots, 1971, Facets, 1988, The Tonight Show Band, Night Journey. Address: care Thomas Cassidy Inc 366 Horseshoe Dr Basalt CO 81621-9104 also: c/o William Morris Agency 151 S El Camino Dr Beverly Hills CA 90212-2704 also: The Phoenix Symphony Orch Symphony Hall 2498 3707 N 7th St Phoenix AZ 85014-5059

SEVERNS, PENNY L., state legislator; b. Decatur, Ill., Jan. 21, 1952. BS in Polit. Sci. and Internat. Relations, So. Ill. U., 1974. Spl. asst. to adminstr. AID, Washington, 1977-79; city councilwoman Decatur, from 1983; mem. 51st dist. Ill. State Senate, 1987—, chief budget negotiator for Senate Dems., 1993—, minority spokesperson appropriations com., 1994—. Office: Ill State Senate State Capitol Springfield IL 62706

SEVERO, RICHARD, writer; b. Newburgh, N.Y., Nov. 22, 1932; s. Thomas and Mary Theresa (Farina) S.; m. Emöke Edith de Papp, Apr. 7, 1961. B.A., Colgate U., 1954; postgrad., NYU Inst. Fine Arts, 1955-56, Columbia U. Sch. Architecture and Urban Planning, 1964-65. News asst. CBS, N.Y.C., 1954-55; reporter Poughkeepsie (N.Y.) New Yorker, 1956-57, A.P., Newark, 1957-61, N.Y. Herald Tribune, 1961-63; writer TV news CBS, N.Y.C., 1963-66; reporter Washington Post, 1966-68; investigative reporter N.Y. Times, N.Y.C., 1968-71; fgn. corr. N.Y. Times, Mex., C. Am. and Caribbean, 1971-73; investigative and environ. reporter N.Y. Times, 1973-77, sci. and environ. reporter, 1979—; assoc. Seminar on the City, Columbia U., 1966-69; vis. lectr. Am. culture Vassar Coll., 1985—; bd. dirs. Colgate U. Alumni Corp., 1988-92. Author: Lisa H., 1985; (with Lewis Milford) The Wages of War, 1989 (Am. Legion Nat. Comdr.'s award 1990); contbr. articles to mags. Poynter fellow-in-residence Vassar Coll., 1974 75; CBS News fellow, 1964-65; Recipient Front Page award Washington-Balt. Newspaper Guild, 1967; Journalistic award H.A.V.E.N., 1969; Schaeffer Gold Typewriter award N.Y. Newspaper Reporters Assn., 1969; Page One award Newspaper Guild of N.Y., 1970; hon. mention Mike Berger award Columbia U., 1970; Leone di San Marco award Italian Heritage and Culture Com., 1982; George Polk Meml. award L.I. U. Sch. Journalism, 1975; Hudson River Fisherman's Assn. award, 1976; Mike Berger award Columbia U., 1976; James Wright Brown award Deadline Club, Sigma Delta Chi, N.Y.C., 1976; Feature award N.Y. Press Club, 1977; Page One award Newspaper Guild N.Y., 1977, 82; Media award Am. Cancer Soc., 1977; hon. mention Heywood Broun Meml. award Am. Newspaper Guild, 1977; Penney-Mo. Newspaper award U. Mo. Sch. Journalism, 1978; Media award Agt. Orange Victims Internat., 1982; Page One award N.Y. Newspaper Guild, 1982; Gift of Life award N.Y. Blood Ctr., 1991, Spl. Writing award Soc. of the Silurians, 1992. Home: 81 Balmville Rd Newburgh NY 12550-1917

SEVERS, CHARLES A., III, lawyer; b. N.Y.C., Sept. 16, 1942; s. Charles A. and Gertrude (O'Neill) S.; m. Regina Ferrone, Sept. 4, 1965; children: Charles A. IV, Cornelius Forsythe, Rudyard Pierrepont, Olivia Consuelo. BA, Georgetown U., 1964, JD, 1967. Bar: N.Y. 1968, D.C. 1985. Ptnr. Dewey Ballantine, N.Y.C., 1967—; lectr. various continuing legal edn. programs. Contbr. articles to profl. jours. Dir., trustee various orgns. Fellow Am. Coll. Trust and Estate Counsel; mem. ABA, N.Y. State Bar Assn., Assn. of Bar of City of N.Y., D.C. Bar Assn., Union Club, Downtown Assn. Home: 1095 Park Ave New York NY 10128-1154 also: High Meadow Old Chatham NY 12136 Office: Dewey Ballantine 1301 Avenue Of The Americas New York NY 10019*

SEVERS, WALTER BRUCE, pharmacology educator, researcher; b. Pitts., June 10, 1938; s. Walter Bruce and Pauline Marie (Sever) S.; m. Anne Elizabeth Daniels, Apr. 25, 1970; children—Mary, Jane, Steven, William, Katherine. B.S., U. Pitts., 1960, M.S., 1963, Ph.D., 1965. Postdoctoral fellow NIH, Bethesda, Md., 1966-68; asst. prof. pharmacology Coll. Medicine, Pa. State U., Hershey, 1968-71, assoc. prof., 1971-77, prof., 1977—; ad hoc grant cons. NIH, U.S. Army, NSF. Mem. editorial bd. Am. Jour. Physiology, 1978—, Pharmacology, 1978—. Contbr. numerous articles, chpts., revs. to profl. pubs. Recipient Disting. Alumnus award U. Pitts., 1978, I.M. Setchenov medal Acad. Med. Sci. USSR, 1983, Blue medal for sci. Acad. Med. Sci., Bulgaria, Medal for Sci. U. Belgrade; NASA grantee, 1976—. Mem. Am. Physiol. Soc., Am. Soc. Pharmacology and Exptl. Therapeutics, Soc. for Neurosci., Pavlovian Soc. Am., Sigma Xi (pres. Pa. State U. chpt. 1981-82). Republican. Roman Catholic. Lodge: Kiwanis (pres. Hershey area 1980, bd. dirs.). Avocations: reading; camping; hiking; fishing. Home: 1011 Grubb Rd Palmyra PA 17078-3510 Office: Pa State U Coll Medicine Dept Pharmacology 850 University Dr Hershey PA 17033

SEVERS, WILLIAM FLOYD, actor; b. Britton, Okla., Jan. 8, 1932; s. Harry Lysander Fletcher and Katherine Lucinda (McAuliffe) S.; m. Mary Anne Proctor, Jan. 18, 1964 (div. 1971); 1 child, Pilar; m. Barbara Alice Schonger, Sept. 9, 1978; children: Katherine Meghan, Erin Christine. AA, Pasadena Playhouse Coll., 1956. Appeared on Broadway in Cut of the Axe, 1959-60, On Borrowed Time, 1991-92, nat. tour Look Homeward, Angel, 1960; co-star nat. tour Spoon River, 1964; actor Secret Storm, All My Children, One Life to Live, Guiding Light, Texas, Search for Tomorrow, Another World, Loving, 1963-93; other TV appearances include Armstrong Circle Theatre, 1963, The Defenders, 1964, World War II, A GI Diary, 1978, Nurse, 1980, Muggable Mary, 1986, Law and Order, recurring role as Hon. Henry Fillmore, 1990-96; appeared in film Funny Farm, 1988, Regarding Henry, 1991; actor European tour West Side Story, 1990-91, 94; actor, voice artist numerous commls., 1964—. Staff sgt. USAF, 1946-53. Mem. Actors Equity Assn., Screen Actors Guild, Am. Fedn. Television and Radio Artists, Pasadena Playhouse Alumni Assn. Democrat. Avocations: reading, golf. Home: 4007 Park Ave Fairfield CT 06432-1264 Office: Michael Hartig Agency Ltd 156 Fifth Ave New York NY 10010

SEVERSON, ROGER ALLAN, bank executive; b. Thief River Falls, Minn., Sept. 2, 1932; s. Alfred Gerhard and Esther Olga (Landro) S.; m. Beverly Diane Hays, Aug. 30, 1953; children: Eric Hays, Holle Diane. BS, U. Minn., 1954. Group v.p. First Nat. Bank, Mpls., 1952-73; pres. FBS Fin., Inc., Mpls., 1974-77; exec. v.p. F&M Savs. Bank, Mpls., 1977-82; sr. v.p. First Nat. Bank, St. Paul, 1983-85; exec. v.p. Shelard Nat. Bank, Mpls., 1985-86, TCF Bank Savs., Mpls., 1986-92; ret., 1992; mem. Robert Morris Assocs., 1980-92; trustee Heitman Mortgage Investors, Chgo., 1970-71, Mass. Mut. Mortgage Realty Investors, Springfield, 1972-85. Vice chmn. bd. of trustees The Am. Luth. Ch., Mpls., 1976-81; trustee Children's Health Ctr., Mpls., 1971-72; bd. dirs. Goodwill Industries, Mpls., 1967-70. Fellow Versterheim Mus.; mem. Ethics in Pub. Policy Ctr., Ctr. for Am. Experiment, Sons of Norway. Home: 8321 Essex Rd Chanhassen MN 55317-8705

SEVERY, LAWRENCE JAMES, psychologist, educator; b. Detroit, Mar. 30, 1943; m. Linda Andrea Anstensen, Aug. 20, 1966; children: Beth Andrea, Lisa Ellen. BS in Psychology, Wayne State U., 1965; MA in Psychology, U. Colo., 1970, PhD in Psychology, 1970. Rsch. asst. Inst. Behavioral Sci., U. Colo., Denver, 1968-69; predoctoral trainee Inst. Genetics and Behavior for Psychologists, U. Colo., Denver, 1969; asst. prof. psychology, sr. rsch. scientist Ark. Rehab. Rsch. and Tng. Ctr., U. Ark., 1970-71; various positions to prof., dept. psychology U. Fla., Gainesville, 1971—, R. David Thomas Endowed Legis. prof. psychology, 1988, assoc. dean for student affairs Coll. Liberal Arts and Scis., 1990—; rsch. fellow Inst. Population Studies, U. Exeter, Devon, Eng., 1982, sr. rsch. assoc. Behavioral Rsch. Inst., 1976-77, postdoctoral trainee, U. N.C. Population Ctr.'s summer inst., 1973 and others; cons. in field. Author: A Contemporary Introduction to Social Psychology, 1976, Advances in Population: Psychosocial Perspectives, Vol. 1 1993, Vol. 2, 1994; contbr. articles, book chpts. and monographs to profl. pubs. Recipient numerous grants in population and health fields. Fellow APA (numerous coms.); mem. Southeastern Psychol. Assn., Population Assn. Am. (psycho-social workshop program chmn. 1982, 92), Assn. Consumer Rsch., Internat. Assn. Applied Psychology. Home: 4242 SW 94th Dr Gainesville FL 32608-4164 Office: Coll Liberal Arts & Scis U Fla Gainesville FL 32611

SEVETSON, DONALD JAMES, minister, church administrator; b. Oak Park, Ill., Oct. 4, 1933; s. Earl Winfred and Lillian Ione (Anderson) S.; m. Mary Louise Frank, Nov. 30, 1957; children: Philip Curtis, Andrea Lyle, Erika Linnea. BA, Macalester Coll., 1954; BDiv, Chgo. Theol. Sem. and U. Chgo., 1957. Ordained to ministry Congl. Ch., 1958. Minister Raymond Congl. Ch., Franksville, Wis., 1959-62; assoc. minister 1st Congl. Ch., Mpls., 1957-59, Dekalb, Ill., 1962-65, Appleton, Wis., 1965-69; minister Parkview United Ch. of Christ, White Bear Lake, Minn., 1969-73; assoc. conf. minister Minn. Conf. United Ch. of Christ, Mpls., 1973-80; conf. minister Ctrl. Pacific Conf. United Ch. of Christ, Portland, Oreg., 1980-96; chairperson coun. conf. ministers United Ch. of Christ, Cleve., 1994-96, chairperson, bd. dirs. office of comm., 1989-93. Author: The First Century, 1994. Chair Oreg. Holocaust Resource Ctr., Portland, 1989-91, bd. dirs., 1984-91, 94-95; trustee Pacific U. Forest Grove, Oreg., 1989-96, Pacific U., Forest Grove, Oreg., 1989-96. Mem. Chgo. Theol. Sem. Alumni Assn. (pres. 1962-64). Democrat. Avocations: long distance running, golf, historical research. Office: United Ch of Christ Ctrl Pacific Conf 0245 SW Bancroft St Ste E Portland OR 97201

SEVEY, ROBERT WARREN, retired broadcasting executive, journalist; b. Mpls., Dec. 6, 1927; s. Benjamin Warren and Helen Margaret (Benham) S.; m. Rosalie Fergueson Thomas, Jan. 28, 1950; children: Michael Warren, David Ellis. BA, U. Calif., Santa Barbara, 1951. Announcer, newscaster WOI and KASI, Ames, Iowa, 1947-49; sports dir. KIST, Santa Barbara, 1949-51; prodn. asst. CBS-TV, Hollywood, Calif., 1951-52; producer, announcer KPHO-TV, Phoenix, 1952-54; prodn. mgr. KULA-TV, Honolulu, 1954-57; prodn. mgr. radio-TV Holst & Male Inc., Honolulu, 1957-59; sta. mgr. KGMB-TV, Honolulu, 1959-61; news dir. Sta. KHVH-TV, Honolulu, 1961-65, Sta. KGMB-TV, Honolulu, 1966-86; v.p. news/corporate affairs Heftel Broadcasting Co., Honolulu, 1987-90; with Heftel Broadcasting Co., L.A., 1990-91; ret., 1991. S/sgt. U.S. Army, 1945-47. Mem. Radio-TV News Dirs. Assn., Honolulu Press Club (pres. 1969-70, mem. Hall of Fame 1987—). Avocation: golf.

SEVIER, ERNEST YOULE, lawyer; b. Sacramento, June 20, 1932; s. Ernest and Helen Faye (McDonald) S.; m. Constance McKenna, Apr. 12, 1969; children: Carolyn Stewart, Katherine Danielle. A.B., Stanford U., 1954, J.D., 1956. Bar: Calif. 1956, U.S. Supreme Ct. 1965. Asso. mem. firm Sedgwick, Detert, Moran & Arnold, San Francisco, 1958-62; mem. firm Severson & Werson, San Francisco, 1962—. Served with USAF, 1956-57. Fellow Am. Bar Found.; mem. ABA (chmn. tort and ins. practice sect. 1982-83, exec. coun. 1976-84, chmn. standing com. on assoc. comms. 1988-90, chmn. coord. com. on Outreach to Pub. 1989-90, chmn. standing com. on lawyers responsibility for client protection 1991-94, commn. on non-lawyer practice 1992-95), Calif. Bar Assn., Internat. Assn. Def. Counsel, Fedn. Ins. and Corp. Counsel. Office: Severson & Werson 1 Embarcadero Ctr Ste 2500 San Francisco CA 94111-3714

SEVIK, MAURICE, acoustical engineer, researcher; b. Istanbul, Turkey, Mar. 19, 1923; s. Benjamin and Esther (Barzilai) S.; m. Jacqueline Delannoy, June 2, 1953; children: Michele, Martine. DIC, Imperial Coll. Sci. Tech., London, 1946; PhD, Pa. State U., 1963. Registered profl. engr., Ont. With Bristol Aircraft Corp., U.K., 1946-51; sr. structures engr. Avro Aircraft Ltd., Can., 1952-59; prof. aerospace engring., dir. Garfield Thomas Water Tunnel, Pa. State U., University Park, 1959-72; mem. assoc. tech. dir. ship signatures directorate David Taylor Rsch. Ctr., Bethesda, Md., 1972—; vis. prof. Cambridge (Eng.) U., 1970; cons. USAF Office Sci. Rsch. 1965. Contbr. articles to profl. jours. Fellow Churchill Coll., Cambridge U., 1970; recipient Gold Medal award The Am. Soc. of Naval Engrs., 1990, Disting. Alumni award Central Pa. chpt. Acoustical Soc. of Am., Charles B. Martell Tech. Excellence award Nat. Security Indsl. Assn., 1992. Fellow ASME (Raleigh lectr. 1995), Acoustical Soc. Am., Sigma Xi; mem. Nat. Acad. Engring. Home: 7817 Horseshoe Ln Rockville MD 20854-3828 Office: David Taylor Rsch Ctr Bethesda MD 20084

SEVILLA, STANLEY, lawyer; b. Cin., Apr. 3, 1920; s. Isadore and Dienna (Levy) S.; m. Lois A. Howell, July 25, 1948; children: Stanley, Susan, Donald, Carol, Elizabeth. B.A. in Econs. with high honors, U. Cin., 1942; J.D., Harvard U., 1948. Bar: Calif. 1949. Since practiced in Los Angeles; assoc. Williamson, Hoge & Curry, 1948-50; mem. firm Axelrod, Sevilla and Ross, 1950-75, Stanley Sevilla (P.C.), 1975—; gen. counsel La.-Pacific Resources, Inc., 1970-90. Bd. dirs. Caesars World, Inc., 1989-95. With USAAF, 1942-46. Mem. Los Angeles County Bar Assn., Beverly Hills Bar Assn., Phi Beta Kappa, Tau Kappa Alpha. Home: 16606 Merivale Ln Pacific Palisades CA 90272-2236 Office: PO Box 308 Pacific Palisades CA 90272-0308

SEVIN, EUGENE, engineer, consultant, educator; b. Chgo., Jan. 5, 1928; s. Sol and Rella (Yastrow) S.; m. Ruth H. Hirschson, June 12, 1951 (dec. Dec. 1989); children: Lori J. Sevin Gunter, Lynne M. Sevin Bossart, Lisa C.; m. Phyllis Robbins, Feb. 20, 1994. B.S. in M.E., Ill. Inst. Tech., 1949, Ph.D., 1958; M.S. in M.E., Calif. Inst. Tech., 1951. Research engr. Armour Research Found., Chgo., 1951-65; research dir. Research Inst. Ill. Inst. Tech., Chgo., 1965-69, adj. prof., 1967-70; cons. E. Sevin Assocs., Olympia Fields, Ill., 1969-70; prof., head dept. mech. engring. Ben Gurion U., Beer-Sheva, Israel, 1970-74; asst. to dep. dir. Def. Nuclear Agy., Washington, 1974-86; asst. dep. undersec. research and engring. Dept. Def., Washington, 1986-91; dep. dir. Missiles and Space Systems, Office Undersec. Def., Washington, 1992-94; cons. Lundhurst, Ohio, 1994—. Author: (with W.D. Pilkey) Optimum Shock and Vibration Isolation, 1971; contbr. papers to confs., articles to profl. jours.; monograph series. Mem. NAE, ASME, AIAA, Sigma Xi (Disting. lecture 1985), Tau Beta Pi, Pi Tau Sigma. Avocations: computer software development; handball. Home: 1782 Kenton Circle Lyndhurst OH 44124

SEVOLD, GORDON JAMES, savings and loan executive; b. Randall, Iowa, Sept. 26, 1926; s. Oscar Theodore and Elvira (Guest) S.; m. Nell Ruth Reeves, Jan. 7, 1978; children: Deborah, Louise, Robert. B.S., Drexel U., 1958. Controller, treas. Frank H. Fleer Corp., Phila., 1952-66; v.p. fin. plumbing products div. Borg Warner Co., Mansfield, Ohio, 1966-71; treas., chief fin. officer Centran Corp., Cleve., 1971-82; chmn. bd., pres. Investors Income Ins. Co., Dallas, 1975-82; exec. v.p. Am. Savs. and Loan Assn., Salt Lake City, 1982-85; chief fin. officer Northwestern region FSLIC Receivership, 1985-88; dep. dir. Ea. Region FSLIC Receivership, 1988-89; chief fin. officer FDIC, Atlanta, 1989-92; sr. acct. FDIC, Orlando, Fla., 1992-94; ret., 1994. Treas. Centran Polit. Action Com., 1975-79. Served with USAAF, 1944-45. Mem. Fin. Execs. Inst., Budget Execs. Inst. Republican. Club: Willow Creek Country. Home: 1808 Danbury Dr Sun City Center FL 33573-5251

SEVY, ROGER WARREN, retired pharmacology educator; b. Richfield, Utah, Nov. 6, 1923; s. Carl Spencer and Maude (Malmquist) S.; m. Barbara Florence Snetsinger, Aug. 16, 1948; children—Pamela Jane, Jonathan Carl. Student, Utah State U., 1941-43, Harvard, 1943-45; M.S., U. Vt., 1948; Ph.D., U. Ill., 1951, M.D., 1954. Asst. physiology U. Ill., 1948-51, instr., 1951-54; asst. prof. pharmacology Temple U., Phila., 1954-56, prof., 1956-89, chmn. dept., 1957-73, dean Sch. Medicine, 1973-79, prof. emeritus, 1989—. Served with AUS, 1943-45. Mem. Am. Soc. Pharmacology and Exptl. Therapeutics, Am. Physiol. Soc., Endocrine Soc., AAAS, Sigma Xi, Alpha Omega Alpha. Research on hypertension and cardiovascular pharmacology. Home: 242 Mather Rd Jenkintown PA 19046-3129 Office: Temple U 3420 N Broad St Philadelphia PA 19140-5104

SEWALL, TINGEY HAIG, banker; b. N.Y.C., Aug. 3, 1940; s. George Tingey and Mary (Bossidy) S.; m. Lucy M. Roosevelt, Oct. 10, 1964 (div. Sept. 1989); 1 child, Margaret Haig; m. Joan S. Law, Feb. 7, 1993. BA, Bowdoin Coll., 1962; grad. in banking, Rutgers U., 1974. Various positions State Street Bank & Trust Co., Boston, 1964-76, v.p., 1976-82; v.p. BankBank Norfolk, Dedham, Mass., 1982-84, sr. v.p., sr. lending officer, 1984-86, exec. v.p., sr. lending officer, 1986-90; exec. v.p. BayBank South, Dedham, 1990-91, BayBank, Burlington, Dedham, Mass., 1991-95, BayBank N.A., Boston, 1995—. Bd. overseers Dana Farber Cancer Inst., Boston, 1984—; trustee FCD Ednl. Svcs., Inc., Needham, Mass., 1991—. Served to capt. USAR, 1962-64. Mem. Robert Morris Assocs. (sr. assoc., bd. dirs. 1987-89 New Eng. chpt.), Newcomen Soc. U.S., Union Boat Club (Boston), Mahkeenac Boating Club (Stockbridge, Mass.). Home: 11 Spindrift Ln Cohasset MA 02025-1022

SEWALL, WILLIAM DANA, data processing manager; b. Boston, Jan. 17, 1948; s. Charles Hull Sewall and Mary (Butler) Spring; m. Lucinda Thames, Oct. 24, 1981; children: Rebecca, Alyssa, Holly, Madeline. BA, Dartmouth Coll., 1970; JD, Boston Coll., 1977. Bar: Mass. 1978, Calif. 1979. Tchr. Concord (N.H.) Sch. Dist., 1970-74; assoc. Csapler & Bok, Boston, 1977-81; gen. counsel LEF & C Corp., San Francisco, 1981-83; sr. v.p. technology Citicorp Bankers Leasing, Foster City, Calif., 1983—; also bd. dirs. Bankers Leasing, San Mateo. Editor Boston Coll. Law Rev., 1975-77. Mem. Am. Assn. Equipment Lessors (bd. dirs.). Avocations: gardening, sailing, jogging. Home: 25 Trace Ln Half Moon Bay CA 94019 Office: Citicorp Bankers Leasing 989 E Hillsdale Blvd Ste 300 Foster City CA 94404

SEWARD, GEORGE CHESTER, lawyer; b. Omaha, Aug. 4, 1910; s. George Francis and Ada Leona (Rugh) S.; m. Carroll Frances McKay, Dec. 12, 1936 (dec. 1991); children: Gordon Day, Patricia McKay (Mrs. Dryden G. Liddle), James Pickett, Deborah Carroll (Mrs. R. Thomas Coleman). Grad., Louisville Male High Sch., 1929; BA, U. Va., 1933, LLB, 1936. Bar: Va. 1935, N.Y., Ky., D.C., U.S. Supreme Ct. With Shearman & Sterling, N.Y.C., 1936-53, Seward & Kissel, N.Y.C., 1953—; founder, hon. chmn. Internat. Capital Markets Group of Internat. Fedn. Accts., Fedn. Internat. des. Bourses de Valeurs, Internat. Bar Assn.; legal adv. com. N.Y. Stock Exch., 1984-87; trustee The N.Y. Geneal. and Biog. Soc. Author: Basic Corporate Practice, Seward and Related Families; co-author: Model Business Corporation Act Annotated, We Remember Carroll. Trustee Arts and Scis. Coun. U.Va., 1983-93, pres., 1991-93. Elected to Louisville Male High Sch. Alumni Assn. Hall of Fame, 1991; named Ky. Col., 1993. Fellow Am. Bar Found. (chmn. model corp. acts com. 1956-65), N.Y. State Bar Found.; mem. Internat. Bar Assn. (hon. life pres., founder sect. on bus. law, lectr. series named in his honor, New Delhi 1988, Lisbon 1992, Budapest 1993, Geneva 1994), ABA (chmn. bus. law sect. 1958-59, chmn. sect. com. corp. laws 1952-58, chmn. sect. banking com. 1960-61, mem. ho. of dels. 1959-60, 63-74, mem. joint com. with Am. Law Inst. on continuing legal edn. 1965-74), Athenaeum Lit. Assn. (Louisville), Downtown Assn. (N.Y.C.), Knickerbocker Club, N.Y. Yacht Club, University Club (Chgo.), Met. Club (Washington), Bohemian Club (San Francisco), Shelter Island Yacht Club, Gardiner's Bay Country Club, Greencroft Club (Charlottesville, Va.), Cum Laude Soc., Raven Soc., Order of Coif, Phi Beta Kappa Assocs. (pres. 1969-75), Phi Beta Kappa, Theta Chi, Delta Sigma Rho. Home: 48 Greenacres Ave Scarsdale NY 10583-1436 Office: Seward & Kissel One Battery Park Plz New York NY 10004 also: Internat Bar Assn, 271 Regent St, London W1R 7PA, England

SEWARD, WILLIAM W(ARD), JR., author, educator; b. Surry, Va., Feb. 2, 1913; s. William Ward and Elizabeth (Gwaltney) S.; m. Virginia Leigh Widgeon, Dec. 27, 1941; children: Virginia R. Godwin, Leigh W. Huston. AB, U. Richmond, 1934, MA, 1935; grad. fellow, Duke U., 1938-39, 40-41. English tchr. pub. schs., 1935-38; instr. U. Richmond, 1939-40, summer 1944; head English dept. Greenbrier Mil. Sch., 1941-42; prof., head English dept. Tift Coll., 1942-45; faculty Old Dominion U., Norfolk, Va., 1945, 47—; prof. Old Dominion U., 1957-77, prof. emeritus, 1977—, head dept. English, 1947-61; lectr. U. Va. extension div., 1952-54. Author: The Quarrels of Alexander Pope, 1935; editor: The Longer Thou Livest the More Fool Thou Art (W. Wager), 1939, Literature and War, 1943, Skirts of The Dead Night, 1950, Foreword to Descent of the White Bird (Barbara Whitney), 1955, Contrasts in Modern Writers, 1963, My Friend Ernest Hemingway, 1969; contbr. to book: The True Gen: An Intimate Portrait of Hemingway by those Who Knew Him (Denis Brian), 1988; mem. editorial bd.: Lyric Virginia Today, 1956; contbr. articles to profl. jours. Recipient Charles T. Norman medal for best grad. in English U. Richmond, 1934. Mem. Poetry Soc. Va. (pres. 1952-55), Poetry Soc. Am., Hemingway Soc., Internat. Mark Twain Soc. (hon.), Va. Writers Club (emeritus), Princess Anne County Club, Virginia Beach Sports Club, Phi Beta Kappa, Kappa Alpha, Pi Delta Epsilon. Methodist. Home: 701 Cavalier Dr Virginia Beach VA 23451-3837

SEWELL, BETTY DAVENPORT, special education educator; b. Birmingham, Ala., Feb. 15, 1953; d. William Harry and Edna Earl (Staggs) Davenport; children: David, Daniel. Dental technician, Carrer Acad., Atlanta, 1973; BS in Spl. Edn. with honors, Auburn U., Montgomery, 1992, M in Mild Learning Handicapped, 1994. Cert. spl. edn. tchr., Ala. Dental technician Clanton (Ala.) Dental Lab., 1973-86; tchr. asst. Clanton Elem. Sch., 1988—, tchr. spl. edn., 1992—; tchr. emotionally conflicted Children's Harbor (Ala.) Sch.; edn. coord. Cmty. Intensive Treatment for Youth, Clanton, Ala., 1995—. Sec. Thorsby (Ala.) Band Boosters, 1989-91; parade organizer Thorsby Swedish Heritage Com., 1992-93. Mem. NEA, Ala. Edn. Assn., Coun. for Exceptional Children, Kappa Delta Phi, Phi Kappa Phi. Baptist. Avocations: crafts, playing piano, singing, special olympics. Home: 804 Ware Ave Clanton AL 35045-2444

SEWELL, BEVERLY JEAN, financial executive; b. Oklahoma City, July 10, 1942; d. Benjamin B. Bainbridge and Faith Marie (Mosier) Allison; m. Ralph Byron Sewell, Jan. 23, 1962; children: M. Timothy, Pamela J. Student, U. Okla., 1960-61, Jackson C.C., 1973-77; BA in Bus., Mesa Coll., 1982; cert., Coll. Fin. Planning, 1984, MS in Fin. Planning, 1994. Sole practice fin. planning Grand Junction, Colo., 1985-87; fin. planner, broker Interpacific Investors Services, Grand Junction, 1987-88; investment broker A.G. Edwards & Sons, Inc., Grand Junction, 1988-92, v.p., 1992—. Mem. ctrl. com. Grand Junction Rep. Orgn., 1988; mem. Grand Junction Planning Commn., 1987-89; bd. dirs. Grand Junction Symphony, 1991-94, Downtown Devel. Authority, St. Mary's Hosp. Mem. Inst. Cert. Fin. Planners, Internat. Assn. Fin. Planning. Avocations: tennis, jogging. Home: 717 Wedge Dr Grand Junction CO 81506-1866 Office: A G Edwards & Sons Inc 501 Main St Grand Junction CO 81501-2607

SEWELL, CHARLES HASLETT, banker; b. Buford, Ga., Jan. 16, 1928; s. Grover C. and Jennie G. (Haslett) S.; m. Margaret Gillespie, Sept. 9, 1985; children: Anna E., William H., John L. B.A., Emory U., 1951. Econs., mgmt. cons. Rsch. and Cons. Corp., Atlanta, 1952-72; sr. v.p. Deposit Guaranty Nat. Bank, Jackson, Miss., 1972—, exec. v.p., 1974—; chmn., chief exec. officer Deposit Guaranty Mortgage Co., Jackson, Miss., 1976-91; cons. in field; chmn. Miss. Econ. Council, 1983—; chmn. Sml. Bus. Devel. Ctr. U. Miss, Oxford, 1979—. Contbr. articles to profl. jours. Trustee Miss. State Libr. Commn., 1983—; chmn. Miss. Com. for Humanities, 1983—; pres. Miss. Symphony Orch., 1988-89; chmn. Miss. internat. adv. bd. Emory U. Coll. Arts and Scis., 1992—; exec.-in-residence Else Sch. Mgmt., Millsaps Coll. Mem. University Club (Jackson). Republican. Presbyterian. Home: 25 Village Green Cir Jackson MS 39211-2927 Office: Millsaps Coll Grad Sch Mgmt Jackson MS 39210

SEWELL, DARREL LESLIE, art museum curator; b. Cushing, Okla., Dec. 21, 1939; s. William Leslie and Irma Lena (Upp) S.; B.A., U. Chgo., 1962, M.A., 1965. Instr. art history Ohio State U., 1966-67, U. Ill. Chgo. Circle, 1968-70; curator edn. Nat. Collection Fine Arts, 1970-73; curator Am. Art, Phila. Mus. Art, 1973-76; The Robert L. McNeil Jr. curator of Am. Art, 1976—; exhibitions: Pa.: Three Centuries of Am. Art, 1976, Reinstallation of Am. Galleries, 1977, The U. Pa.: Collector and Patron of Art, 1779-1979, 1979, Copley from Boston, 1980; Thomas Eakins: Artist of Phila., 1981-82, One Hundred Yrs. of Acquisitions, 1983, Benjamin West in Pa. Collections, 1986, Modern Jewelry, 1964-86; The Helen Drutt Collection, 1986-87, The Fairmount Waterworks, 1988, Henry O. Tanner, 1991. Author: Philadelphia: Three Centuries of American Art, 1976; Thomas Eakins, Artist of Philadelphia, 1982; Henry O. Tanner, 1991. Office: Phila Mus Art PO Box 7646 Philadelphia PA 19101-7646

SEWELL, ELIZABETH, author, English educator; b. Coonoor, India, Mar. 9, 1919; came to U.S., 1949; d. Robert Beresford Seymour and Dorothy (Dean) S. BA, Cambridge U., Eng., 1942, MA, 1945, PhD, 1949; LittD (hon.), Fordham U., N.Y.C., 1968, U. Notre Dame, 1984. Lectr. English Vassar Coll., Poughkeepsie, N.Y., 1951-52; vis. prof. Fordham U., 1954-55, 58-59, chair Bensalem Experimental Coll., 1967-69; lectr. Christian Gauss sem. Princeton U., N.J., 1957; vis. prof. English Bennett Coll., Greensboro, N.C., 1960-61, Tougaloo Coll., Miss., 1963-64; prof. English, Hunter Coll. CUNY, 1971-74; Rosenthal prof. humanities U. N.C., Greensboro, 1974-77. Author 4 novels, 1952, 55, 62, 95, 3 poetry collections, 1962, 68, 84 (nat. award AAAL 1981). Recipient Zoe Brockman Kincaid award N.C. Poetry Soc., 1985; fellow Howald Rsch., 1949-50, Sr. Simon, 1955-57, Ashley, 1979. Mem. Assn. Literary Scholars and Critics, The Polanyi Soc., Lewis Carroll Soc. N.Am., PEN Am. Ctr. Home: 854 W Bessemer Ave Greensboro NC 27408-8404

SEWELL, JOHN WILLIAMSON, research association executive; b. Cleve., Dec. 19, 1935; s. William and Hilda F. (Gaunt) S.; m. Maryann Strauss, July 19, 1958; children: Gregory J., Michael P. B.A., U. Rochester, 1957; M.A., NYU, 1967. Fgn. service officer Dept. State, 1961-68; asst. to dir. Bur. Intelligence Research, Dept. State, Washington, 1968-70; asst. to pres. Brookings Inst., Washington, 1970-71; v.p. Overseas Devel. Council, Washington, 1971-77; exec. v.p. Overseas Devel. Council, 1977-79, pres., 1980—; mem. Bretton Woods Com.; mem. Interaction, North-South Roundtable, Internat. Ctr. for Rsch. on Women, Internat. Adv. Group for 1995 World Summit for Social Devel.; spl. advisor to the adminstrn. UNDP. Author: U.S. Foreign Policy and the Third World Agenda, 1985-86; Growth, Exports, & Jobs in a Changing World Economy: Agenda 1988; co-editor: United States Budget for a New World Order, FY, 1992, Challenges and Priorities in the 1990s: An Alternative U.S. International Affairs Budget, FY, 1993; contbr. articles to jours. Mem. World Resources Inst., The Carter Ctr., The Kellogg Inst.; pres. Nat. Choral Found., 1969-75. With U.S. Army, 1958-60. Mem. Coun. on Fgn. Rels., Cosmos Club. Home: 7614 Morningside Dr NW Washington DC 20012-1557 Office: Overseas Devel Council Ste 1012 1875 Connecticut Ave NW Washington DC 20009

SEWELL, PHYLLIS SHAPIRO, retail chain executive; b. Cin., Dec. 26, 1930; d. Louis and Mollye (Mark) Shapiro; m. Martin Sewell, Apr. 5, 1959; 1 child, Charles Steven. B.S. in Econs. with honors, Wellesley Coll., 1952. With Federated Dept. Stores, Inc., Cin., 1952-88, research dir. store ops., 1961-65, sr. research dir., 1965-70, operating v.p., research, 1970-75, corp. v.p., 1975-79, sr. v.p., research and planning, 1979-88; bd. dirs. Lee Enterprises, Inc., Davenport, Iowa, Pitney Bowes, Inc., SYSCO Corp. Bd. dirs. Nat. Cystic Fibrosis Found., Cin., 1963—; chmn. divsn. United Appeals, Cin., 1982; mem. bus. adv. coun. Sch. Bus. Adminstrn., Miami U., Oxford, Ohio, 1982-84; trustee Cin. Cmty. Chest, 1984-94, Jewish Fedn., 1990-92, Jewish Hosp., 1990—; mem. bus. leadership coun. Wellesley Coll., 1990—, Fordham U. Grad. Sch. Bus., 1988-89. Recipient Alumnae Achievement award Wellesley Coll., 1979, Disting. Cin. Bus. and Profl. Woman award, 1981, Directors' Choice award Nat. Women's Econ. Alliance, 1995; named one of 100 Top Corp. Women Bus. Week mag., 1976, Career Woman of Achievement YWCA, 1983, to Ohio Women's Hall of Fame, 1982.

SEWELL, RICHARD HERBERT, historian, educator; b. Ann Arbor, Mich., Apr. 11, 1931; s. Herbert Mathieu and Anna Louise (Broene) S.; m. Natalie Paperno, Jan. 13, 1971; 1 child, Rebecca Elizabeth. A.B., U. Mich., 1953; M.A., Harvard U., 1954, Ph.D., 1962. Asst. prof. No. Ill. U., DeKalb, 1962-64; asst. prof. history U. Wis., Madison, 1965-67, assoc. prof., 1967-74, prof, 1974-95, prof. emeritus, 1995—; vis. lectr. U. Mich., Ann Arbor, 1964-65; adv. bd. Lincoln and Soldiers Inst., Gettysburg Coll., Pa., 1990—. Author: John P. Hale and the Politics of Abolition, 1965, Ballots for Freedom, 1976, A House Divided, 1988; mem. editorial bd. Revs. in Am. History, 1981—; contbr. articles to profl. jours. Served to lt. (j.g.) USNR, 1954-57. Mem. Soc. Civil War Historians, So. Hist. Assn., Hist. Soc. Wis., Phi Beta Kappa, Phi Kappa Phi. Avocation: whitewater rafting. Home: 2206 Van Hise Ave Madison WI 53705-3822

SEWELL, ROBERT DALTON, pediatrician; b. Newman, Calif., Apr. 28, 1950; s. James Dalton and Mary Louise (Hartwell) S.; m. Esther Madiedo, Oct. 26, 1975; children: Kevin, David. BA magna cum laude, Pacific Union Coll., 1972; MD, Loma Linda U., 1975. Diplomate Am. Bd. Pediatrics. Pediatric intern and resident White Meml. Med. Ctr., L.A., 1975-77; pediatric resident, chief resident Milton S. Hershey Med. Ctr., Pa. State U., Hershey, 1977-80; pediatrician Children's Med. Ctr. Asheville, N.C., 1980-81, Lincoln City Med. Ctr. P.C., Lincoln City, Oreg., 1982-95; examining physician C.A.R.E.S. Ctr. Emanuel Hosp. & Health Ctr., Portland, Oreg., 1988-90; asst. prof. Loma Linda (Calif.) U. Sch. Medicine, 1995—; chmn. child protection team North Lincoln Hosp., Lincoln City, 1983-89, sec. med. staff, 1990-92, pres. med. staff, 1992-94; mem. Citizens' Rev. Bd. Lincoln County, Newport, Oreg., 1982-92, Early Intervention adv. com., Newport, 1986-90. Mem. North Lincoln Local Sch. Com., Lincoln City, 1983-94, chmn., 1986-90; bd. dirs. Lincoln Shelter & Svcs., Inc., Lincoln City, 1983-89, chmn., 1987-89; mem. North Lincoln divsn. Am. Heart Assn., Lincoln City, 1986-89, v.p., 1987-89; mem. Drug and Alcohol Task Force, Lincoln City, 1988; mem., 2d vice-chmn. Yr. 2000 Plan housing com. Lincoln City Planning Commn., 1987-88; mem. AIDS task force Lincoln County Sch. Dist., 1987-89; mem. Lincoln County Children's Agdnea Taskforce, 1988; mem. med. rev. com. Oreg. Med. Assn., 1990-95, mem.-at-large med. staff sect. gov. bd., 1993-95. Named Citizen of Yr. child protection com. Lincoln County, 1984, Man of Yr. Lincoln City C. of C., 1988. Mem. Am. Acad. Pediatrics (sect. on child abuse), Oreg. Pediatric Soc., Am. Profl. Soc. of Abuse of Children (charter mem.), Nat. Assn. Counsel for Children, Internat. Soc. for Prevention Child Abuse and Neglect, N.Am. Oreg. Profl. Soc. on Abuse of Children (founding pres. 1992-94), Calif. Profl. Soc. on Abuse of Children. Democrat. Seventh-day Adventist. Avocations: music, sports, boating, auto racing. Office: Loma Linda U Med Ctr Dept of Pediatrics 11262 Campus St West Hall Lima Linda CA 92354

SEWELL, WILLIAM HAMILTON, sociologist; b. Perrington, Mich., Nov. 27, 1909; s. Will H. and Lulu (Collar) S.; m. Elizabeth Shogren, June 13, 1936; children: Mary, William, Robert. A.B., Mich. State U., 1933, A.M., 1934, D.Sc. (hon.), 1973; Ph.D., U. Minn., 1939. Instr. U. Minn., 1934-37; asst. prof. sociology Okla. State U., 1937-38, assoc. prof., 1938-40, prof., 1940-44; prof. sociology, rural sociology U. Wis., 1946-64, Vilas research prof. sociology, 1964—, chmn. dept., 1951-53, chmn. social sci. research com., 1952-55, social sci. div., 1950-53, chmn. dept. sociology, 1958-63, univ. chancellor, 1967-68; vis. scholar Russell Sage Found., 1968-69; Walker-Ames vis. prof. U. Washington, 1954; vis. prof. U. Tex., 1941, U. P.R., 1949, Garrett Inst., 1950, Columbia U., 1952; Ford Found. vis. prof. Delhi, Bombay, Poona univs., 1956-57; cons. human resources Sec. War, Research and Devel. Bd., Dept. Def., 1946-54; cons. Nat. Inst. Mental Health, USPHS, 1957-80; chmn. behavioral scis. study sect., 1959-63 ; chmn. behavioral scis. tng. com. NIH, 1962-67, mem. metal health research adv. com., 1968-70; exec. com. behavorial sci. div. NRC, 1966-70; chmn. Nat. Commn. on Research, 1978-80; Trustee Chatham Coll., Am. Coll. Testing Program Reseach Inst., Nat. Opinion Research Center; bd. dirs. Social Sci. Research Council. Author: Construction and Standardization of a Scale for the Measurement of Farm Family Socioeconomic Status, 1941, (with others) Scandinavian Students on An American Campus, 1961, Attitudes and Facilitation in Status Attainment, 1972, Education, Occupation and Earnings: Achievement in the Early Career, 1975; co-editor: Uses of Sociology, 1967, Schooling and Achievement in American Society, 1976; assoc. editor: Am. Sociol. Rev, 1954-57, Sociometry, 1955-58, Human Resources, 1967-83, Sociology of Edn., 1983-87; contbr. articles, monographs on sociology to profl. jours. Served as lt. USNR, 1944-46. Recipient Outstanding Achievement award U. Minn., 1972, Disting. Rsch. award Am. Ednl. Rsch. Assn., 1975, Commonwealth award for disting. contbns. to sociology , 1983; fellow Center for Advanced Study in Behavioral Scis., 1959-60; rsch. fellow East-West Population Inst. Fellow AAAS (chmn. sect. 1975-76), Am. Sociol. Assn. (chmn. social psychology sect. 1960-61, v.p. 1961-62, pres. 1970-71, Cooley-Mead award in social psychology 1988, Willard Waller award in sociology edn. 1990), Am. Acad. Arts and Scis., Am. Philos. Soc.; mem. NAS (chmn. social and polit. scis. sect. 1981-84), Am. Statis. Assn., Rural Sociol. Soc. (pres. 1955), Southwestern Sociol. Soc. (pres. 1941), Midwestern Sociol. Soc. (pres. 1954), Sociol. Rsch. Assn. (pres. 1954), Soc. Rsch. in Child Devel. Clubs: Blackhawk Country, University. Home: 1005 Merrill Springs Rd Madison WI 53705-1314

SEWELL, WINIFRED, pharmaceutical librarian; b. Newport, Wash., Aug. 12, 1917; d. Harold Arthur and Grace (Vickerman) S. BA, State Coll. Wash., Pullman, 1938; BS in LS, Columbia U., 1940; DSc (hon.), Phila. Coll. Pharmacy and Sci., 1979. Asst. Columbia U. Library, N.Y.C., 1938-42; asst. librarian Wellcome Research Labs., Tuckahoe, N.Y., 1942-43; librarian Wellcome Research Labs., 1943-46, Squibb Inst. Med. Research, 1946-61; subject heading specialist Nat. Library of Medicine, 1961-62, dep. chief bibliog. services div., 1962-65, head drug literature program, 1965-70; adj. asst. prof. U. Md. Sch. Pharmacy, 1970-85; adj. lectr. U. Md. Coll. Libr. and Info. Svcs., 1969-92; cons. Nat. Health Planning Info. Ctr., 1975-81; instr. pharm. lit. and librarianship Columbia U., summer 1959; mem. com on modern methods for handling chem. info. Nat. Acad. Scis.-NRC; mem. Martindale Databank Adv. Panel, 1981-82. Editor: Unlisted Drugs, 1949-59, 62-64; author: Guide to Drug Information, 1976 (Ida and George Eliot award Med. Library Assn. 1977), (with Merle Harrison) Using MeSH for Effective Searching: a Programmed Guide, 1976, (with Sandra D. Teitelbaum) Micromanual for Casual Users of National Library of Medicine Databases, 1986, Reader in Medical Librarianship, 1973; editor: Health Affairs Series, Gale Info. Guides, 1971-80; mem. editorial bd.: Drug Info. Jour. Active Excerpta Medica adv. com., 1985-88. Fellow AAAS; mem. ALA, Am. Soc. for Info. Sci. (chmn. spl. interest group/classification rsch. 1974-75), Med. Libr. Assn. (chmn. Rittenhouse award com. 1975-76, chmn. recert. com. 1979-80, chmn. pub. health and health adminstrn. sect. 1979-80, chmn. med. librs. edn. sect. 1981-82), Spl. Librs. Assn. (chmn. pharm. sect., sci.-tech. divsn. 1952-53, pres. 1960-61, publs. award sci. and tech. divsn. 1966), Drug Info. Assn. (v.p. 1966-67, pres. 1970-71), Am. Assn. Colls. Pharmacy (chmn. librs./ednl. resources sect. 1979-80, del. coun. on sects. adv. bd. 1980-83). Home and Office: 6513 76th Pl Cabin John MD 20818-1413

SEWER, DORIS E., critical care nurse, educator; b. Charlotte, St. Thomas, V.I., Oct. 23, 1934; d. Richard and Rachel (Callwood) Donovan; m. Edmundo Valerius Sewer, Mar. 19, 1959; children: Milagros Holden, Melinda Muganzo Mignel Sewer, Maria Vantine. Diploma, Bella Vista Sch. Nursing, Mayaguez, P.R., 1969; BSN, Andrews U., 1975; MA in Edn., Counseling, Calif. State U., San Bernardino, 1979; cert. in clin. pastoral edn., Loma Linda U., 1989; postgrad., Walden U., 1995—. Staff nurse ICU Lincoln (Nebr.) Gen. Hosp., 1969-72; charge nurse ICU Loma Linda (Calif.) Community Hosp., 1974-75; staff nurse ICU Loma Linda U. Med. Ctr., 1975-77; dir. nursing Mountain View Child Care Ctr., Loma Linda, 1977-79; asst. prof. nursing Chaffey Coll., Ont., Calif., 1979-82; nursing instr., missionary nurse Antillian Coll., Mayaguez, P.R., 1982—; counselor, lectr. Suicide and Crisis Intervention, San Bernardino, Calif., 1977-80; part-time clin. instr. psychiat. nursing Riverside (Calif.) City Coll., 1976-78; instr. ICU course Bella Vista Hosp., Mayaguez, 1984, 86, 88, 89; participating instr. Intensive Care Course Antillian Coll., Mayaguez, 1989; mem. San Bernardino Adv. Com. Drug Abuse, 1979-82; vis. prof. nursing U. V.I., St. Thomas, 1991; pres. Tutorial Nursing and Edn. Unlimited. Mem. Nat. League Nursing.

SEXSON, STEPHEN BRUCE, educational writer, educator; b. Silver City, N.Mex., May 29, 1948; s. Ralph Dale and Wanda Claudean (McMahan) S.; m. Barbara Jane Davis, May 24, 1968; children: David Paul, Linda Carol. BA in Rhetoric and Pub. Address, Pepperdine U., 1969, MA in Pub. Comm., 1975; EdD in Higher Edn., Okla. State U., 1990. Asst. to supt. Morongo Unified Sch. Dist., 29 Palms, Calif., 1973-77; corp. trainer Merrill Lynch Realty, Dallas, 1979-81; sch. psychologist Texhoma (Tex.) Sch. Dist., 1982-83; assoc. prof., dir. Christian Student Ctr. Okla. Panhandle State U., Goodwell, 1982-84; rsch. resident Okla. State U., Stillwater, 1984-87; mem. spl. programs staff L.A. Unified Sch. Dist., 1987-93; dir. Edwest Edn. Rsch., Burbank, Calif., 1991—; guest lectr. edn. Okla. State U., Stillwater, 1993-94, U. Tulsa, 1993-94; conv. spkr. Merrill Lynch Realty-Relo, Atlanta, 1979. Author: The Magic Classroom, 1995, The Values Rich Teacher, 1996; contbr. articles to profl. jours. Mem. ASCD, Am. Assn. Sch. Adminstrs., Nat. Assn. of Sch. Psychologists, Lions Club, Phi Delta Kappa. Avocations: computing, travel, theatre. Home: 400 Clermont Dr Edmond OK 73003-3124

SEXTER, DEBORAH RAE, lawyer; b. Bklyn., May 28, 1939; d. Benjamin and Minnie (Popkewitz) Rochkin; m. Jay Sexter, Apr. 14, 1957; children: David, Michael. BBA, CCNY, 1961; AAS, Bergen C.C., 1975; MS, Fordham U., 1978, JD, 1987; profl. diploma, United Hosps. Sch. Nurse Anesthesia, 1980. Bar: N.J. 1987, U.S. Dist. Ct. N.J. 1987, N.Y. 1988; RN, N.J., N.Y.; cert. RN anesthetist, Am. Assn. Nurse Anesthetists; cert. fraud examiner, Assn. Cert. Fraud Examiners. Community organizer N.Y.C., 1965-70; staff nurse community hosps., Bergen County, N.J., 1975-78; staff anesthetist Columbia-Presbyn. Med. Ctr., N.Y.C., 1980-83, Manhattan Eye, Ear, Throat Hosp., N.Y.C., 1983-84; chief nurse anesthetist Anesthesia Assocs., Nyack, N.Y., 1984-87; pvt. practice law Grand View-on-Hudson, N.Y., 1987-90; sr. asst. gen. counsel, inspector gen. Met. Transp. Authority, N.Y.C., 1990-94; pvt. practice Irvington, N.Y., 1994—. Village justice Village of Grand View-on-Hudson, 1986-92; vice chmn. ethics com. Village of Irvington, N.Y., 1992—; mem. ethics com. Cmty. Hosp., Dobbs Ferry, N.Y., 1995—. Mem. Nat. Assn. Scholars, Fedn. Am. Immigration Reform, N.Y. State Magistrates Assn. Home: 2 Hudson Rd E Irvington NY 10533-2612 Office: 2 Hudson Rd E Irvington NY 10533-2612

SEXTON, CAROL BURKE, financial institution executive; b. Chgo., Apr. 20, 1939; d. William Patrick and Katharine Marie (Nolan) Burke; m. Thomas W. Sexton Jr., June 30, 1962 (div. June 1976); children: Thomas W., J. Patrick, M. Elizabeth. BA, Barat Coll., 1961; cert. legal, Mallinckrodt Coll., 1974. Tchr. Roosevelt High Sch., Chgo., 1961-63, St. Joseph's Sch., Wilmette, Ill., 1975-80; dir. Jane Byrne Polit. Com., Chgo., 1980-81; mgr. Chgo. Merc. Exch., 1981-84, sr. dir. govt. and civic affairs, 1984-87, v.p. pub. affairs, 1987-94, exec. v.p. corp. rels., 1994—; mem. internat. trade an investment subcom. Chgo. Econ. Devel. Commn., 1989, 90. Bd. dirs. Chgo. Sister Cities, 1992—; chmn. Chgo.-Toronto Sister Cities Com., 1992—; bd. dirs. Ill. Ambs., 1991—, pres., 1994; bd. dirs., sec. Internat. Press Ctr., 1992—, chmn. bd., 1994. Mem. Exec.'s Club of Chgo. (bd. dirs.), Chgo. Conv. and Tourism Bur. (sec. 1989—, exec. com. 1987—, chmn.-elect 1990, chmn. 1991-92), Econ. Club of Chgo. Roman Catholic. Avocations: books, gardening, travel, mountain hiking. Office: Chgo Merc Exch 30 S Wacker Dr Chicago IL 60606-7402

SEXTON, CHARLES EDMUND, consulting company executive; b. Binghamton, N.Y., Apr. 2, 1932; s. Charles Glenn and Marjorie Christine (Bentley) S.; m. Ruth Ann Wendolowski, Feb. 27, 1954 (dec. Feb. 1977); children: Glenn Alexander, Charles David, Mary Kathleen, Patrick Edmund; m. Mary Jane Czyzewski, Dec. 3, 1977. Student, Broome Tech. Coll., Binghamton, 1961-64, Syracuse U., 1970-71. Tech. planning mgr. field engring. div. IBM, Franklin Lakes, N.J., 1954-83; mgr. telecom. for nat. distbn. div. IBM, Princeton, N.J., 1983-88; owner, mgr. Sexton Assocs., Hawley, Pa., 1991—. Capt. USN, 1951-53, Korea. Recipient Meritorious Svc. award Dept. Navy, 1991. Mem. Naval Res. Assn., Ret. Officers Assn., Am. Legion, KC. Avocations: formula Ford automobile racing, competition handgunning, racquetball. Home: Box 421 99 Dewberry Dr Hawley PA 18428 Office: PO Box 421 Hawley PA 18428-0421

SEXTON, DONALD LEE, business administration educator; b. New Boston, Ohio, June 14, 1932; s. Benjamin Franklin and Virgie Marie (Jordan) S.; m. Levonne Bradley, June, 1954 (div. June 1964); 1 child, Rhonda Jane; m. Carol Ann Schwaller, Dec. 18, 1965; children: David Lee, Douglas Edward. BS in Math. and Physics, Wilmington Coll., 1959; MBA, Ohio State U., 1966, PhD in Mgmt., 1972. Indsl. engr. Detroit Steel Corp., Portsmouth, Ohio, 1959-61; sr. rsch. engr. Rockwell Internat., Columbus, Ohio, 1961-68; v.p. merchandising R.G. Barry Corp., Columbus, 1968-74; v.p., gen. mgr. Henri Fayette, Inc., Chgo., 1976; gen. mgr. M.H. Mfg. Co., Jackson, Miss., 1976-77; assoc. prof. Sangamon State U., Springfield, Ill., 1977-79; Caruth prof. entrepreneurship Baylor U., Waco, Tex., 1979-86; Davis prof. free enterprise Ohio State U., Columbus, 1986-94; dir. applied rsch. Ctr. for Entrepreneurial Leadership Inc. Kauffman Found., Kansas City, Mo., 1994—; mem. adv. bd. SBA, Columbus, 1986-94; rsch. adv. bd. U. So. Calif., L.A., 1986-90. Co-author: Entrepreneurship Education, 1981, Experiences in Small Business, 1982, Starting A Business in Texas, 1983; co-editor: Encyclopedia of Entrepreneurship, 1981, Art and Science of Entrepreneurship, 1986, Women Owned Businesses, 1989, Entrepreneurship: Cretivity and Growth, 1990, The State of the Art of Entrepreneurship, 1991, Leadership and Entrepreneurship, 1996. Served to staff sgt. USAF, 1951-55. Recipient Leavy Free Enterprise award Freedoms Found. Valley Forge, 1985, Cert. Appreciation SBA, Washington, 1984, 85, Outstanding Contbn. to Entrepreneurship Edn. award Assn. Coll. Entrepreneurs, 1991, Disting. Alumni award Wilmington Coll., 1993; named Adv. of Yr.-Innovation SBA, Dallas, 1982, 83, 84. Mem. Internat. Coun. for Small Bus. (sr. v.p. 1986), U.S. Assn. for Small Bus. (v.p. pub. rels. 1987), Acad. Mgmt. (chmn. entrepreneurship com. 1981, mem. adv. bd. 1984-85), Masons, Shriners, Eagles, Am. Legion, Alpha Tau Omega. Republican. Baptist. Avocation: golf. Home: 11006 W 127th Ter Overland Park KS 66213-3418 Office: Kauffman Found 4900 Oak St Kansas City MO 64112-2702

SEXTON, OWEN JAMES, vertebrate ecology educator, conservationist; b. Phila., July 11, 1926; s. Gordon and Elizabeth May (Evans) S.; m. Mildred Lewis Bloomsburg, Apr. 5, 1952; children: Kenneth, Jean, Ann, Carolyn. Student, Sampson Coll., 1947-48; BA, Oberlin Coll., 1951; MA, U. Mich., 1953, PhD, 1956. Sr. teaching fellow Washington U., St. Louis, 1955-56, instr., 1956-57, asst. prof., 1957-62, assoc. prof., 1962-68, prof. vertebrate ecology, 1968—, dir. Tyson Rsch. Ctr., 1996—; vis. prof. U. Mich. Biol. Sta., Pellston, 1975-83; cons. UNESCO, 1974-75; adj. curator St. Louis Sci. Ctr., 1986-88. Pres., bd. dirs. Mo. Prairie Found., Columbia, 1968—; pres. Wild Canid Survival and Research Ctr., St. Louis, 1971-73; sec. Contemporary Art Soc., 1972-73; bd. dirs. Creve Coeur Figure Skating Club, 1982-89; mem. membership com. U.S. Figure Skating Assn., 1987-90. NSF fellow, 1966-67; vis. research fellow U. New Eng., 1984. Fellow Herpetologists League; mem. Am. Soc. Icthyologists and Herpetologists, Ecol. Soc. Am., Soc. Study of Amphibians and Reptiles, Orgn. Tropical Studies (bd. dir. 1976-85). Democrat. Home: 13154 Greenbough Dr Saint Louis MO 63146-3622 Office: Washington Lindell & Skinker Dept Biology Saint Louis MO 63130

SEXTON, RICHARD, lawyer; b. Madison, Wis., 1929; s. Joseph Cantwell and Eleanor Carr (Kenny) S.; m. Joan Fleming, 1957; children: Molly, Joseph, Lucy, Michael, Ann, Katherine. Student, Amherst Coll., 1947-49; B.S., U. Wis., 1951; LL.B., Yale U., 1958. Bar: N.Y. 1959, U.S. Supreme Ct. 1968. Assoc. firm Sullivan & Cromwell, N.Y.C., 1958-64; with SCM Corp., N.Y.C., 1964-86; asst. counsel SCM Corp., 1964-67, div. gen. counsel Smith-Corona Marchant div., 1967-72, v.p., gen. counsel parent co., 1972-86, sec., 1977-86; pvt. practice, bus. cons., 1986—. Bd. dirs. Commonweal Mag. Bd. dirs. Advocates for Children of N.Y.C. Served to lt. (j.g.) USNR, 1951-55. Mem. Assn. Bar N.Y.C., ABA. Home: 532 3rd St Brooklyn NY 11215-3003 Office: 220 Fifth Ave Ste 1500 New York NY 10001

SEXTON, ROBERT FENIMORE, educational organization executive; b. Cin., Jan. 13, 1942; s. Claude Fenimore and Jane (Wisenall) S.; m. Pam Peyton Papka, Sept. 15, 1985; children: Rebecca, Robert B., Ouita Papka, Paige Papka, Perry Papka. BA, Yale U., 1964; MA in History, U. Wash., Seattle, 1968, PhD in History, 1970; DHL (hon.), Berea Coll., 1990, Georgetown Coll., Ky., 1993. Asst. prof. history Murray (Ky.) State U., 1968-70; dir. Office Acad. Programs, Commonwealth of Ky., Frankfort, 1970-73; assoc. dean, exec. dir. Office Exptl. Edn. U. Ky., Lexington, 1973-80; dep. exec. dir. Ky. Coun. Higher Edn., Frankfort, 1980-83; exec. dir. Prichard Com. for Acad. Excellence, Lexington, 1983—; founder, pres. Ky. Ctr. Pub. Issues, Lexington, 1988—; vis. scholar Harvard U., Cambridge, Mass., 1992, 94; chair Nat. Ctr. for Internships, Washington, 1973-80, Coalition for Alternatives in Post-Secondary Edn., Washington, 1977-80; bd. dirs. Editl. Projects in Edn., Ky. Long Term Policy Rsch. Ctr., Coun. for Advancement Exptl. Learning, 1976-80, Edn. Commn. of the States; adv. bd. Consortium for Prodn. in Schs., 1992—. Pub. The Ky. Jour., 1988—; editor book series: Public Papers of Governors of Kentucky, 1973-86; author reports in field. Co-chair Carnegie Ctr. for Literacy, Lexington, 1990-93; mem. Gov.'s Task Force on Health Care, Frankfort, 1992—; bd. dirs. Ky. Inst. Edn. Rsch. Fund for Improvement in Postsecondary Edn., 1993—; chair Bluegrass Edn. Work Coun., Lexington, 1978-80; founder, mem. steering com. Gov.'s Scholars Program, Frankfort, 1983-85. Recipient Charles A. Dana award for pioneering achievement, 1994. Mem. Am. Assn. Higher Edn. (bd. dirs. 1979-83). Democrat. Avocations: fishing, travel. Office: Prichard Com Acad Excell 167 W Main St Ste 310 Lexington KY 40507-1702

SEXTON, THOMAS JOHN, science administrator, research physiologist; b. Mt. Holly, N.J., Aug. 11, 1942; married, 1964; 3 children. BS, Delaware Valley Coll., 1964; MS, U. N.H., 1966; PhD in Dairy Sci., Pa. State U., 1972. Rsch. asst. U. N.H., 1964-66, U. Conn., 1966-67; rsch. assoc. Pa. State U., 1967-71; rsch. physiologist USDA, 1971-83, rsch. leader, 1983-88, dir. Livestock & Poultry Sci. Inst., Agr. Rsch. Svc., 1988—; adj. prof. Auburn U., Ala., 1984—. Mem. Poultry Sci. Assn. (Rsch. award 1982), World's Poultry Sci. Assn., Soc. Cryobiology, Sigma Xi. Achievements include research on critical problems that limit the reproductive efficiency of the avian male, cryogenic preservation of semen, artificial insemination and isolation of female gamete. Office: USDA Agr Rsch Ctr Livestock & Poultry Sci Inst B-200 Beltsville Beltsville MD 20705

SEXTON, VIRGINIA STAUDT, retired psychology educator; b. N.Y.C., Aug. 30, 1916; d. Philip Henry and Kathryn Philippa (Burkard) Staudt; m. Richard J. Sexton, Jan. 21, 1961. B.A., Hunter Coll., 1936; MA, Fordham U., 1941, PhD, 1946; LHD, Cedar Crest Coll., 1980. Elem. tchr. St. Peter and St. Paul's Sch., Bronx, N.Y., 1936-39; clk. N.Y.C. Dept. Welfare, 1939-44; lectr., asst. prof., assoc. prof. psychology Notre Dame Coll. of S.I., 1944-52; instr. Hunter Coll. of CUNY, 1953-56, asst. prof., 1957-60, assoc. prof., 1961-66, prof., 1967-68; prof. psychology Herbert H. Lehman Coll., 1968-79, prof. emeritus, 1979—; disting. prof. St. John's U., Jamaica, N.Y., 1979-92; mem. profl. conduct rev. bd. N.Y. State Bd. for Psychology, 1971-78; mem. adv. bd. Archives of History Am. Psychology, 1966—. Author: (with H. Misiak) Catholics in Psychology; A Historical Survey, 1954, History of Psychology: An Overview, 1966, Historical Perspectives in Psychology: Readings, 1971, Phenomenological, Existential and Humanistic Psychologies: A Historical Survey, 1973, Psychology Around the World, 1976. Editor: (with J. Dauben) History and Philosophy of Science: Selected Papers, 1983, (with R. Evans, T. Cadwallader) 100 Years: The American Psychology Assn., 1992, (with J. Hogan) International Psychology: Views From Around The World, 1992; mem. editorial bd. Jour. Phenomenological Psychology, 1977—, Jour. Mind and Behavior, 1979—, Interamerican Jour. Psychology, 1982—, The Humanistic Psychologist, 1984—, Professional Psychology: Research and Practice, 1984-89, Clinician's Research Digest, 1984-92.

Contbr. articles to profl. jours. Fellow Am. Psychol. Assn., AAAS, N.Y. Acad. Scis., Charles Darwin Assocs.; mem. Am. Hist. Assn., AAUP, AAUW, Am. Assn. for Advancement Humanities, Internat. Assn. Applied Psychology, Internat. Council Psychologists (pres. 1981-82), Interam. Soc. Psychology, Internat. Soc. History of Behavioral and Soc. Scis., Eastern Psychol. Assn., N.Y. Soc. Clin. Psychologists, N.Y. Psychol. Assn., N.Y. Assn. Applied Psychologists, Assn. for Women in Psychology, N.Y. Acad. Scis., Psychologists Social Responsibility, Phi Beta Kappa, Psi Chi (v.p. eastern region 1982-86; pres. 1986-87). Roman Catholic. Avocation: stamp collecting. Home: 188 Ascan Ave Flushing NY 11375-5947

SEXTON, WILLIAM COTTRELL, journalist; b. Balt., Sept. 22, 1928; s. Hardigg and Grace Dean (Cottrell) S.; m. Bonnie Stone, Dec. 18, 1976; 1 child, Paul Norman. Student, U. N.C., 1946-47. With UPI, 1948-62, mgr. N.Y. bur., 1959-62; assoc. dir. Am. Press Inst., Columbia U., 1963-66; mng. editor Louisville Courier Jour., 1966-67; mng. editor, then editor World Book Sci. Service, 1967-69; editor Publishers-Hall Syndicate, N.Y.C., 1969-70; with Newsday, Inc., Melville, N.Y., 1970-91, asst. to editor, 1972-73, assoc. editor, 1973-86, Asia bur., Peking, 1979-83, Asia bur., Tokyo, 1986-89, diplomatic corr., N.Y.C., 1989-91, editorial columnist, 1983-86; dir. Ford Found. seminar for African newspaper execs., 1965; vice chmn. N.Y. State Fair Trial Free Press Conf., 1977-79, mem., 1984-87. Pres. Richmond Hist. Soc., 1991—, Berkshire Bach Soc., 1993-94; co-chair Boston Symphony Assn. Vols. Tanglewood, 1995-96. With AUS, 1951-53. Mem. Coun. Fgn. Rels., Am. Radio Relay League. Home: 105 West Rd Richmond MA 01254-0428

SEYAM, NABIL AHMAD, engineering inspector; b. Kuwait, Jan. 25, 1961; came to U.S., 1980; s. Ahmad Hassan and Ameinha Mustaffa (Saad) S.; m. Carrie Lenee Allen, Nov. 5, 1982; children: Melissa, Ahmad, Yusef, Anisa. AA, Ft. Scott (Kans.) C.C., 1982; BSc in Inds. Engring., Wichita State U., 1985; Local Pub. Authority lic., Kans. State U., 1993; postgrad. in safety engring., Kennedy-Western U., 1994—. Safety supr. Kuwait Entertianment City, Doha, 1986-88, Kuwait Metal Pipe Industries, Sulybia, 1988-90; engring. inspector Sedgwick County Govt., Wichita, Kans., 1991—. Mem. Am. Soc. Safety Engrs. (pub. resl. com.), Kuwait Soc. Engrs., Isnt. Indsl. Engrs., Internat. Soc. Martial Arts. Home: 3143 N Rushwood St Wichita KS 67226-1228 Office: Sedgwick County Govt 1250 S Seneca St Wichita KS 67213-4445

SEYBERT, JOANNA, federal judge; b. Bklyn., Sept. 18, 1946; married; 1 child. BA, U. Cin., 1967; JD, St. John's U., 1971. Bar: N.Y. 1972, U.S. Dist. Ct. (ea. and so. dists.) N.Y. 1973, U.S. Ct. Appeals (2d cir.) 1973. Trial staff atty. Legal Aid Soc., N.Y.C., 1971-73; sr. staff atty. Legal Aid Soc., Mineola, N.Y., 1976-80; sr. trial atty. Fed. Defender Svc., Bklyn., 1973-75; bur. chief Nassau County Atty's Office, Mineola, 1980-87; judge Nassau County Dist. Ct., Hempstead, N.Y., 1987-92, Nassau County Ct., Mineola, 1992-94, U.S. Dist. Ct. (ea. dist.) N.Y., Bklyn., 1994—. Past mem. environ. bd. Town of Oyster Bay; mem. Rep. com. Nassau County, 1979-87. Recipient Norman F. Lent award Criminal Cts. Bar Assn., 1991. Mem. ABA, N.Y. State Bar Assn., Bar Assn. Nassau County, Nassau County Women's Bar Assn., Theodore Roosevelt Am. Inns of Ct., Fed. Judges Assn., Nassau Lawyer's Assn. (past pres.), Nat. Assn. Women Judges. Office: 2 Uniondale Ave Uniondale NY 11553-1259

SEYFERTH, DIETMAR, chemist, educator; b. Chemnitz, Germany, Jan. 11, 1929; came to U.S., 1933; s. Herbert C. and Elisabeth (Schuchardt) S.; m. Helena A. McCoy, Aug. 25, 1956; children—Eric Steven, Karl Dietmar, Elisabeth Mary. B.A. summa cum laude, U. Buffalo, 1951, M.A., 1953; Ph.D., Harvard, 1955; Dr. honoris causa, U. Aix-Marseille, 1979, Paul Sabatier Univ., Toulouse, France, 1992. Fulbright scholar Tech. Hochschule, Munich, Germany, 1954-55; postdoctoral fellow Harvard U., 1956-57; faculty MIT, 1957—, prof. chemistry, 1965—, Robert T. Haslam and Bradley Dewey prof., 1983—; cons. to industry, 1957—. Author: Annual Surveys of Organometallic Chemistry, 3 vols, 1965, 66, 67; regional editor: Jour. Organometallic Chemistry, 1963-81; coordinating editor revs. and survey sects., 1964-81; editor: Organometallics, 1981—; contbr. research papers to profl. lit. Recipient Disting. Alumnus award U. Buffalo, 1964, Alexander von Humboldt Found. sr. award, 1984, Clifford C. Furnas Meml. award SUNY-Buffalo, 1987; Guggenheim fellow, 1968. Fellow AAAS, Am. Inst. Chemists, Inst. Materials, Am. Acad. Arts and Scis.; mem. Am. Chem. Soc. (Frederic Stanley Kipping award in organosilicon chemistry 1972, disting. svc. award advancement inorganic chemistry 1981, award in organometallic chemistry, 1996), Materials Rsch. Soc., Am. Ceramic Soc., Royal Soc. Chemistry, Gesellschaft Deutscher Chemiker, German Acad. Scientists-Leopoldina, Phi Beta Kappa, Sigma Xi. Office: MIT 77 Massachusetts Ave Rm 4-382 Cambridge MA 02139-4301

SEYKORA, MARGARET S., psychotherapist; b. N.Y.C., June 18, 1947; d. Stanley Sneider and Janet Pick (Sneider) Smith; m. Sern A. Seykora, Jan. 19, 1968 (div. 1984); m. H. Lester Mower, Jr., Nov. 19, 1993. BS in Journalism, U. Fla., 1970; MA in Edn. and Human Devel. Counseling, Rollins Coll., 1991. Lic. mental health counselor, Fla.; lic. mortgage broker, Fla.; lic. real estate broker, Fla. Advt. profl. Gainesville (Fla.) Sun, 1968-75, TV mag. editor, 1968-75, Sunday/lesiure/book editor, 1970; stoneware potter, owner Old Town (Fla.) Pottery, 1975-82; real estate salesperson Jack McCormick Realty, Chiefland, Fla., 1982-85, Coldwell Banker, Orlando, Fla., 1985-90; real estate broker The Hood Group, Inc., Orlando, 1990-92; psychotherapist, facilitator, pres. Personal Dynamics Inst., Altamonte Springs, Fla., 1989—; career instr. The Knowledge Shop, Winter Park, Fla., 1992—; outpatient clin. svcs. supr. Lakeside Alternatives, Winter Park, Fla., 1992—; adj. instr. Seminole C.C., Sanford, Fla., 1992—, Valencia C.C., Winter Park, 1992—. Author/facilitator workshops in field. Mem. Nat. Bd. Counselors, Am. Counseling Assn., Assn. for Specialists in Group Work, Nat. Bd. Realtors. Mem. Ch. of Religious Sci. Avocations: travel, pub. speaking, cooking. Office: Personal Dynamics Inst 421 Montgomery Rd Ste 105 Altamonte Springs FL 32714-3140

SEYMORE, JAMES W., JR., magazine editor. Mng. editor Entertainment Weekly, N.Y.C. Office: Entertainment Weekly 1675 Broadway New York NY 10019-5820

SEYMOUR, ARTHUR HALLOCK, retired newspaper editor; b. Des Moines, Oct. 22, 1928; s. Forrest Wilson and Pearl Bernice (Yeager) S.; m. Ann Adele Ulness, Aug. 19, 1977; children—Forrest Wilson, Macy Yeager, Andrew Hallock. B.A., Harvard U., 1952. Reporter AP, Cheyenne, Wyo., 1952-53, Denver, 1953-55; mem. staff Mpls. Star and Tribune, 1955-90, bus. news editor, 1965-70, asst. news editor, 1970-72, news editor, 1972-78, dep. mng. editor, 1978-90, ret. Served with USMCR, 1946-49. Home: 29562 Orchard Rd Red Wing MN 55066-6164

SEYMOUR, BRIAN RICHARD, mathematics educator, researcher; b. Chesterfield, Derby, Eng., Sept. 25, 1944; came to U.S., 1968, Can., 1973; s. Douglas and Hilda (Ball) S.; m. Rosemary Jane Pembleton, Sept. 23, 1943; children—Mark, Jane, Richard. B.Sc. with honors, U. Manchester, 1965; Ph.D., U. Nottingham, 1968. Asst. prof. Lehigh U., 1969-70, N.Y. U., 1970-73, U. B.C., 1973-76; assoc. prof. U. B.C., 1976-81, Vancouver, Can., prof. math., 1981—, dir. inst. applied math, 1986-93; vis. prof. Ctr. Water Rsch. U. Western Australia, 1993-94. Contbr. research papers to profl. jours. Sci. Research Council sr. research fellow Oxford U., 1978; Killam sr. fellow Killam Trust, Monash U., 1984. Mem. Can. Applied Math. Soc., Soc. Indsl. & Applied Math. Avocation: field hockey. Office: U BC, 222-1984 Mathematics Rd, Vancouver, BC Canada V6T 1Z2

SEYMOUR, DALE GILBERT, publisher, author, speaker, consultant; b. Hugo, Colo., Sept. 30, 1931; s. Earl Daniel and Alice Edna (Andersen) S.; m. Linda Lou Horn, June 9, 1953 (div. Sept. 1969); children: Luanne, Douglas, Jill; m. Margo Lee Draper, Dec. 27, 1974. BS, U. Colo., 1953, MA, 1961; postgrad., Calif. State U., Hayward, San Jose State U. Tchr., coach Bayard (Nebr.) Pub. Schs., 1953-54, Longmont (Colo.) High Sch., 1956-62; tchr. Palo Alto (Calif.) Unified Sch. Dist., 1962-69; founder, pub., CEO, Creative Publs., Palo Alto, 1968-79; pub. Dale Seymour Publs., Palo Alto, 1979—, CEO., 1979-92; cons., author, speaker, 1994—; speaker over 600 state, nat. and internat. tchr. confs., 1968—; instr. East Tenn. State U., U. Hawaii; chmn. math. dept. Jordan Jr. High Sch., Palo Alto, 1963-69, assoc. math. curriculum, 1965-69; mem. addendum com. Calif. Math. Framework, 1979-80; mem. Calif. Model Curriculum Standards Com., 1984. Author, co-author numerous supplemental math. books and publs., 1965—; designer over 100 ednl. products, 1968—. 1st lt. C.E., U.S. Army, 1954-56. Mem. Nat. Coun. Tchrs. Math. (curriculum and evaluation standards commn. 1987-88), Nat. Coun. Suprs. Math. (Glen Gilbert award 1993).

SEYMOUR, HARLAN FRANCIS, healthcare industry executive; b. East Saint Louis, Mo., Jan. 25, 1950; s. Harlan Edward and Agnes Wilhelmina (Noakes) S.; m. Ellen Katheleen Schmitt, Aug. 17, 1973; children: Melissa Ann, Harlan Francis Jr. BA in Math., U. Mo., 1973; MBA, Keller Grad. Sch. Mgmt., 1980. Corp. v.p. Statis. Tabulating Corp., Chgo., 1973-80; dist. mgr. Datacorp, Chgo., 1980-83; exec. v.p. 1st Fin. Mgmt. Corp., Atlanta, 1983-94; pres., CEO 1st Health Svcs. Corp., Richmond, Va., 1989-94; exec. v.p., COO Trigon Blue Cross/Blue Shield, Richmond, 1994—; mem. mgmt. info. systems adv. bd. U. Ga., Athens, 1986-89, Va. Commonwealth U., 1991-93; bd. dirs. J. Sargeant Reynolds C.C., 1991—. V.p. St. Joseph's Home and Sch., Marietta, Ga., 1987-88. Mem. Nat. Assn. Bank Servicers, Bank Mktg. Assn., Richmond Metro C. of C., (past bd. dirs.), Assn. for Corp. Growth (bd. dirs. 1996—), Soc. Internat. Bus. Fellows. Roman Catholic. Avocations: sailing, tennis, jogging. Home: 12106 Country Hills Ct Glen Allen VA 23060-5347 Office: Trigon Blue Cross/Blue Shield 7130 Glen Forest Dr Richmond VA 23226-3757

SEYMOUR, JANE, actress; b. Hillingdon, Middlesex, Eng., Feb. 15, 1951; came to U.S., 1976; d. John Benjamin and Mieke Frankenberg; m. David Flynn, July 18, 1981 (div. 1991); 2 children; m. James Keach, May 15, 1993. Student, Arts Ednl. Sch., London. Appeared in films Oh What A Lovely War, 1968, The Only Way, 1968, Young Winston, 1969, Live and Let Die, 1971, Sinbad and the Eye of the Tiger, 1973, Somewhere in Time, 1979, Oh Heavenly Dog, 1979, Lassiter, 1984, Head Office, Scarlet Pimpernel, Haunting Passion, Dark Mirror, Obsessed with a Married Woman, Killer on Board, The Tunnel, 1988, The French Revolution; TV films include Frankenstein, The True Story, 1972, Captains and The Kings, 1976 (Emmy nomination), 7th Avenue, 1976, The Awakening Land, 1977, The Four Feathers, 1977, Battlestar Galactica, Dallas Cowboy Cheerleaders, 1979, Our Mutual Friend, PBS, Eng., 1975, Jamaica Inn, 1982, Sun Also Rises, 1984, Crossings, 1986, Keys to Freedom, Angel of Death, 1990, Praying Mantis, 1993; A Passion for Justice: The Hazel Brannon Smith Story, 1994; Broadway appearances include Amadeus, 1980-81, I Remember You, 1992, Matters of the Heart, 1991, Sunstroke, 1992, Praying Mantis, 1993, Heidi, 1993; TV mini-series include East of Eden, 1980, The Richest Man in the World, 1988 (Emmy award), The Woman He Loved, 1988, Jack the Ripper, 1988, War and Remembrance, 1988, 89; host PBS documentary, Japan, 1988; TV series: Dr. Quinn: Medicine Woman, 1993— (Emmy nomination, Lead Actress - Drama, 1994); author: Jane Seymour's Guide to Romantic Living, 1986. Named Hon. Citizen of Ill., Gov. Thompson, 1977. Mem. Screen Actors Guild, AFTRA, Actors Equity, Brit. Equity. Office: Metropolitan Talent Agency 4526 Wilshire Blvd Los Angeles CA 90010-3801*

SEYMOUR, JOYCE ANN, elementary school educator; b. Lafayette, Ind., Nov. 24, 1947; d. Richard Max and Helen Lois (North) Taylor; m. Timothy Joe Seymour, Dec. 27, 1969; children: Christy Nicole, Chad Richard. BS, Purdue U., 1970; MS, Wright State U., 1974. Cert. tchr. elem. edn.; cert. counselor. Tchr. grade 5 Fairborn (Ohio) City Schs., 1970-84, elem. guidance counselor, 1984-94, tchr. grade 6, 1994-95, elem. guidance counselor, 1995—; adv. com. Sch. Counseling, Wright State U., Dayton, 1986—. Mem. Phi Delta Kappa. Lutheran. Avocations: flying (pvt. pilot), water skiing. Home: 1100 Medway-Carlisle Rd Medway OH 45341

SEYMOUR, MARY FRANCES, lawyer; b. Durand, Wis., Oct. 20, 1948; d. Marshall Willard and Alice Roberta (Smith) Thompson; m. Marshall Warren Seymour, June 6, 1970; 1 foster child, Nghia Pham. BS, U. Wis., LaCrosse, 1970; JD, William Mitchell Coll., 1979. Bar: Minn. 1979, U.S. Dist. Ct. Minn. 1979, U.S. Ct. Appeals (8th cir.) 1979, U.S. Supreme Ct. 1986. With Cochrane and Bresnahan, P.A., St. Paul, 1979-94, Loper & Seymour, P.A., 1994—. Mem. ATLA, Minn. Bar Assn., Ramsey County Bar Assn., Minn. Trial Lawyers Assn., Assn. of Cert. Fraud Examiners. Office: Loper & Seymour PA 24 4th St E Saint Paul MN 55101-1002

SEYMOUR, MCNEIL VERNAM, lawyer; b. St. Paul, Dec. 21, 1934; s. McNeil Vernam and Katherine Grace (Klein) S.; children—Margaret, McNeil Vernam, James, Benjamin; m. Mary Katherine Velner, May 15, 1993. A.B., Princeton U. 1957; J.D., U. Chgo., 1960. Bar: Minn. 1960, U.S. Dist. Ct. Minn. 1960. Mem. Seymour & Seymour, St. Paul, 1960-71; mem. firm Briggs & Morgan, St. Paul, 1971—, ptnr., 1976—. Trustee Oakland Cemetery Assn.; pres., treas. White Bear Unitarian Ch., 1964-65; sec., bd. dirs. Ramsey County Law Library, 1972-76. Served with U.S. Army, 1960-62. Mem. Ramsey County Bar Assn., Minn. Bar Assn. Republican. Unitarian. Clubs: Somerset Country Club. Home: 886 S Highview Cir Mendota Hts MN 55118-3686 Offices: Briggs & Morgan 2200 1st Nat Bank Bldg Saint Paul MN 55101

SEYMOUR, MICHAEL, production designer. Prodn. designer: (films) Gumshoe, 1971, Theatre of Blood, 1973, Rosebud, 1975, Alien, 1979 (Academy award nomination best art direction 1979), Eureka, 1984, The Bride, 1985, Mr. Destiny, 1990, (with Benjamin Fernandez) Revenge, 1990, (with Hector Romero, Jr.) Gunmen, 1992, (with Thomas Wilkins) The Thing Called Love, 1993, Beverly Hills Cop III, 1994. Office: Judy Marks Agency 650 N Bronson Ave Ste 148 Los Angeles CA 90004-1404

SEYMOUR, RICHARD KELLOGG, linguist, educator; b. Hinsdale, Ill., June 21, 1930; s. William and Katharine (Fifield) S.; m. Nancy Ann Nutt, June 23, 1951; children: Michael Bradley, William David. B.A., U. Mich., 1951, M.A., 1952; cert., U. Tübingen, Tübingen, Germany, 1953; Ph.D., U. Pa., 1956, postgrad. linguistics, 1957. Asst. instr. U. Pa., 1952-55; instr. Princeton U., 1954-58; linguist NDEA Summer Inst., 1963; asst. prof. Duke U., 1958-63, asso. prof., 1963-67, endowment fellow, 1966; prof., chmn. dept. European langs. and lit. U. Hawaii, Honolulu, 1967-75, prof., 1977-95; ret., 1995; dean Coll. Langs., Linguistics and Lit. U. Hawaii, Honolulu, 1981-95; prof. German dept. Pa. State U., University Park, 1975-77; vis. prof. Cologne (Germany) U., 1974. Author: A Bibliography of Word Formation in the Germanic Languages, 1968; asst. editor Unterrichtspraxis, 1969-80; editor Am. Jour. Germanic Linguistics and Lit., 1989-95; co-editor: Interdisciplinary Jour. for Germanic Linguistics and Semiotic Analysis, 1995—; contbr. articles to profl. jours. Princeton Research Council grantee, 1958; Am. Council Learned Socs. grantee, 1957; Fulbright travel award, 1981. Mem. Linguistic Soc. Am., Internat. Linguistic Assn., Am. Dialect Soc., Am. Assn. Tchrs. German, MLA, S. Atlantic MLA (exec. sec. 19662-67), Delta Phi Alpha (nat. sec.-treas. 1968-95). Congregationalist (bd. deacons, sec. 1970-71).

SEYMOUR, STEPHANIE KULP, federal judge; b. Battle Creek, Mich., Oct. 16, 1940; d. Francis Bruce and Frances Cecelia (Bria) Kulp; m. R. Thomas Seymour, June 10, 1972; children: Bart, Bria, Sara, Anna. BA magna cum laude, Smith Coll., 1962; JD, Harvard U., 1965. Bar: Okla. 1965. Practice Boston, 1965-66, Tulsa, 1966-67, Houston, 1968-69; assoc. Doerner, Stuart, Saunders, Daniel & Anderson, Tulsa, 1971-75, ptnr., 1975-79; judge U.S. Ct. Appeals (10th cir.) Okla., Tulsa, 1979—, now chief justice; assoc. bar examiner Okla. Bar Assn., 1973-79; trustee Tulsa County Law Library, 1977-78; mem. U.S. Jud. Conf. Com. Defender Svcs., 1985-91, chmn., 1987-91. Mem. various task forces Tulsa Human Rights Commn., 1972-76, legal adv. panel Tulsa Task Force Battered Women, 1971-77. Mem. Am. Bar Assn., Okla. Bar Assn., Tulsa County Bar Assn., Phi Beta Kappa. Office: US Courthouse 333 W 4th St Rm 4-562 Tulsa OK 74103-3819*

SEYMOUR, THADDEUS, English educator; b. N.Y.C., June 29, 1928; s. Whitney North and Lola Virginia (Vickers) S.; m. Polly Gnagy, Nov. 20, 1948; children—Elizabeth Halsey, Thaddeus, Samuel Whitney, Mary Duffie, Abigail Comfort. A.B., U. Calif., 1950; M.A., U. N.C., 1951, Ph.D., 1955; D.H.L. (hon.), Wilkes Coll., 1968; LL.D. (hon.), Butler U., 1971, Ind. State U., 1976; LLD (hon.), Wabash Coll., 1984, U. Cen. Fla., 1990, Stetson U., 1990; DHL (hon.), Rollins Coll., 1990. Mem. faculty Dartmouth Coll., 1954-69, prof. English, dean coll., 1959-69; pres. Wabash Coll., Crawfordsville, Ind., 1969-78; pres. Rollins Coll., Winter Park, Fla., 1978-90, prof. English, 1978—; pres. Ind. Conf. Higher Edn., 1977; v.p. Assoc. Colls. Ind., 1978; vice-chmn. Fla. Ind. Colls. Fund. Past mem. Ind. Bicentennial Commn.; del. N.H. Republican Conv., 1958, 64; vice-chmn. N.H. Rep. Com., 1967-68; trustee Park-Tudor Sch., 1970-78, Bach Festival Soc.,; chmn. Fla. selection com. Rhodes Scholarship Trust, 1983-88. Mem. Nat. Rowing Found. (dir.), Ring 219 (charter), Internat. Brotherhood Magicians, Ind. Colls. and Univs. Fla. (sec.), Fla. Assn. Colls. and Univs., Century Assn., Omicron Delta Kappa. Home: 1350 College Pt Winter Park FL 32789-5700

SFAT, MICHAEL RUDOLPH, biochemical engineer; b. Timisoara, Romania, Oct. 28, 1921; came to U.S., 1924; s. Peter and Emilia (Iovin) S.; m. Jane Buckridge, Nov. 24, 1948; children: Gail Buckridge Sergent, Mary Anne Bauer. B Chem. Engring., Cornell U., 1943, M Chem. Engring., 1947; postgrad., Princeton U., 1949-50. Registered profl. engr., Wis. Rsch. assoc. Cornell U., Ithaca, N.Y., 1943-44; asst. microbiologist Merck & Co., Inc., Rahway, N.J., 1947-51, sr. microbiologist, 1951-52; dir. devel. pilot plant Pabst Brewing Co., Milw., 1952-54; rsch. dir. Rahr Malting Co., Manitowoc, Wis., 1954-58, coord. R&D, 1958-60, v.p. R&D, 1960-69; pres. Bio-Tech. Resources, Manitowoc, 1962-89, pres. emeritus, 1989—; mem. Gov.'s Counl on Biotech., Wis., 1990. Contbr. articles to profl. jours.; patentee in field. 2nd lt. U.S. Army, 1944-46. Recipient Schwarz prize for brewing tech., 1966, Disting. Svc. award Coll. Engring., U. Wis., 1993. Fellow Nat. Acad. Engring., Am. Acad. Microbiology, Am. Inst. Med. and Biol. Engrs.; mem. Am. Chem. Soc., Am. Inst. Chem. Engrs., Am. Soc. Brewing Chemists (pres. 1974-75), Am. Soc. Microbiology, Inst. Food Technologists, Master Brewers Assn. Am., Soc. Indsl. Microbiology, Manitowoc-Two Rivers C. of C. (dir. 1970-78), Branch River Country Club (dir. 1972-78), Elks. Republican. Presbyterian. Avocations: golf, tennis, skiing, windsurfing, barn restoration. Home: 1030 W Crescent Dr Manitowoc WI 54220-2420 Office: Bio-Technical Resources 1035 S 7th St Manitowoc WI 54220-5301

SFEKAS, STEPHEN JAMES, lawyer, educator; b. Balt., Feb. 12, 1947; s. James Stephen and Lee (Mesologites) S.; m. Joanne Lorraine Murphy, May 27, 1973; children: James Stephen, Andrew Edward Stephen, Christina Marie. BS in Fgn. Svc., Georgetown U., 1968; MA (Danforth fellow, Woodrow Wilson fellow) Yale U., 1972; JD, Georgetown U., 1973. Bar: Md. 1973, U.S. Dist. Ct. Md. 1974, U.S. Ct. Appeals (4th cir.) 1974. Law clk. U.S. Dist. Ct., Balt., 1973-74; assoc. firm Frank, Bernstein, Conaway & Goldman, Balt., 1974-75; asst. atty. gen. State of Md., Balt., 1975-81; assoc. firm Tydings & Rosenberg, Balt., 1981-82, ptnr., 1983-86, with firm Miles & Stockbridge, 1986-90; ptnr. Weinberg & Green, 1991—; instr. legal writing Community Coll. Balt., 1976-79; instr. legal ethics Goucher Coll., Balt., 1979; adj. prof. adminstrv. law U. Md., Balt., 1981-93, health, 1993—, law sch., 1993—. Editor Georgetown Law Jour., 1972-73; contbr. articles to legal publs. Bd. dirs. Md. region NCCJ, 1981-89, co-chmn. Md. region, 1986-89; mem. Piraeus Sister City Com., City of Balt., 1983-89; mem. parish council Greek Orthodox Cathedral of Annunciation, Balt., 1981-84; mem. internat. com. Balt. region ARC, 1984-85; mem. adv. com. on bread for the world, Dept. Ch. and Soc., Greek Orthodox Archdiocese N. and S.Am., 1984—; pres. Greek Orthodox Counseling and Social Services of Balt., 1984-88; bd. dirs. Orthodox Christian Laity, 1990—, Cen. Md. Ecumenical Coun., 1991—; mem. bylaw com. Girl Scouts of Cen. Md., 1989-91. WHO fellow, London, 1979. Fellow Soc. for Values in Higher Edn.; mem. ABA (Grant Morris fellow 1979, forum com. on health law), Md. Bar Assn., Bar Assn. Balt. City, Nat. Health Lawyers Assn., Am. Soc. Hosp. Attys. Democrat. Office: Weinberg & Green 100 S Charles St Baltimore MD 21201-2725

SFIKAS, PETER MICHAEL, lawyer, educator; b. Gary, Ind., Aug. 9, 1937; s. Michael E. and Helen (Thureanos) S.; m. Freida Platon, Apr. 24, 1966; children—Ellen M., Pamela C., Sandra N. BS, Ind. U., 1959; JD, Northwestern U., 1962. Bar: Ill. 1962, U.S. Dist. Ct. (no. dist.) Ill. 1963, U.S. Ct. Appeals (7th cir.) 1963, U.S. Supreme Ct. 1970, U.S. Ct. Appeals (9th cir.) 1976, U.S. Ct. Appeals (3d cir.) 1981, U.S. Ct. Appeals (D.C. cir.) 1984, U.S. Dist. Ct. (cen. dist.) Ill. 1988. Atty. Legal Aid Bur., United Charities Chgo., 1962-63; sr. ptnr. Peterson & Ross, Chgo., 1970-95; gen. counsel, assoc. exec. dir. div. legal affairs ADA, Chgo., 1995—; sr. ptnr. Bell, Boyd & Lloyd, Chgo., 1996—; prosecutor Village of LaGrange Park, Ill., 1969-74; mem. rules com. Ill. Supreme Ct., 1975-95, mem. spl. joint com. on discovery rules, 1995; arbitrator Nat. Panel Arbitrators, 1972—; adj. prof. Loyola U. Sch. Law, 1978—; guest lectr. U. Ill. Coll. Dentistry, 1988—; lectr. 23d ann. corp. counsel inst. Northwestern U. Sch. Law, 1984, lectr. 16th ann. Ray Garret Jr. Corp. and Securities Law Inst., 1996. Contbr. articles to profl. jours. Mem. Ill. steering com. Ct. Watching Project, LWV, 1975-77; pres. Holy Apostles Greek Orthodox Ch. Parish Coun., 1987-89; co-pres. Oak Sch. PTO, 1989-90; mem. com. to select sch. supr., dist. 86, DuPage County, Ill., 1993-94. Recipient Chgo. Bar Found. Maurice Weigle award 1973. Fellow Am. Bar Found., Am. Coll. Trial Lawyers, Chgo. Bar Found. (life); mem. ABA (editor in chief Forum Law Jour. sect. ins., negligence and compensation law 1972-76), Ill. Bar Found. (bd. dirs.), Northwestern U. Law Alumni Assn. (1st v.p. 1985-86, pres. 1986-87, Svc. award 1990), Ill. State Bar Assn. (bd. govs. 1970-76, chmn. antitrust law sect. coun. 1986-87), Chgo. Bar Assn. (editl. bd. Chgo. Bar Record 1973-84), Bar Assn. 7th Fed. Cir., Ill. Inst. Continuing Legal Edn. (chmn. profl. antitrust problems program 1976, author program on counseling corps., antitrust and trade regulation), Legal Club Chgo. (sec.-treas, 1984-86, v.p. 1989-90, pres. 1990-91), Law Club. Office: Bell Boyd & Lloyd Ste 3300 70 W Madison Chicago IL 60602-4207

SGANGA, JOHN B., furniture holding company executive; b. Bronx, N.Y., Nov. 21, 1931; s. Charles and Marie (Crusco) S.; B.S. in Acctg. cum laude, Bklyn. Coll., 1961; postgrad. Bernard Baruch Coll.; m. Evelyn Joan Battilana, Jan. 19, 1957; children: Mark, John B. Jr., Matthew. Systems analyst DIVCO, Wayne, N.Y., 1965-67; mgr. mgmt. cons. services Coopers & Lybrand, C.P.A.s, N.Y.C., 1967-74; sr. v.p. fin. and adminstrn. Aurora Products Co. subs. RJR Nabisco, West Hempstead, N.Y., 1974-79; controller Gt. Lakes Carbon Corp., N.Y.C., 1979-80, v.p., 1980-81, sr. v.p. fin., CFO, 1981-86; v.p. Cunard Line, Ltd., N.Y.C., 1988; exec. v.p., CFO Consolidated Furniture Corp. (formerly Mohasco Corp.), Wilmington, Del., 1989—, also bd. dirs. Served with USNR, 1950-54. Mem. Inst. Cert. Mgmt. Cons. (a founder), Inst. Mgmt. Accts., Fin. Execs. Inst. (past chmn. com. M.I.S.). Clubs: Treas.'s, Brookside Racquet and Swim. Contbr. articles to jours. in field; editl. adv. to Financial Management mag. Home: 255 Davidson Ave Ramsey NJ 07446-1003 Office: Consolidated Furniture Corp One Commerce Ctr 1201 N Orange St Ste 790 Wilmington DE 19801-1119

SGARLAT, MARY ANNE E. A., marketing professional; b. Boston, Apr. 5, 1958; d. Francis Abbott and Elizabeth Maria (Paragallo) S. Diploma, Milton Acad., 1974; student, Roedean Sch., Brighton, Eng., 1975; BA, Bennington Coll., 1979. Adminstr. Harvard U., Cambridge, Mass., 1979-86; pub. rels. dir. Graham Gund Architects, Cambridge, 1986-89; mktg. and comms. mgr. Elkus/Manfredi Architects, Boston, 1989-90; comms. mgr. Turan Corp., Boston, 1990-92; mktg. mgr. The Design Partnership of Cambridge, 1992—. Mem. LWV, Bennington Coll. Alumni Assn. (regional dir. 1993—, exec. com. 1986-93). Avocations: politics, figure skating, dancing, skiing, collecting rare books. Home: 1214 Brook Rd Milton MA 02186-4136

SGRO, JOSEPH ANTHONY, psychologist, educator; b. New Haven, Conn., Nov. 22, 1937; s. Fred and Tullia (Francesconi) S.; m. Beverly Ann Huston, Feb. 1, 1964; children: Anthony, Jennifer. BA, Trinity Coll., 1959; MS, Lehigh U., 1961; PhD, Tex. Christian U., 1966. Asst. prof. Old Dominion U., Norfolk, Va., 1965-67; asst. prof. Va. Poly. Inst. & State U., Blacksburg, 1967-71, assoc. prof., 1971-79, prof., 1979—, dept. head psychology, 1982-96, mem. exec. bd., sec.-treas. coun. grad. dept. psychology, 1990-92, chmn., 1992-93; vice-chmn. Va. Bd. Psychologists Examiners, Richmond, 1970-75. Editor: Virginia Tech Symposium on Applied Behavioral Science, 1980. Mem. Am. Psychol. Assn., Am. Psychol. Soc., Psychonomic Soc., Southeastern Psychol. Assn. (chmn. assn. heads depts. psychology 1987-89), Ea. Psychol. Assn., So. Soc. for Philosophy & Psychology, Va. Psychol. Assn. (pres. 1974-76), Omicron Delta Kappa, Psi Chi, Sigma Xi. Avocations: golf, cooking. Home: 4185 Pearman Rd Blacksburg VA 24060-8549 Office: Va Poly Inst & State U Dept Psychology Blacksburg VA 24061

SGROI, MARIO, publishing executive. With Calgary Sun and Toronto Sun, 1970-90; pres., dir. Fla. Sun Publs., Inc., Bradenton, 1991—. Office: Fla Sun Publs Inc 717 1st St Bradenton FL 34208-1947

SHAAR, H. ERIK, academic administrator. V.p. acad. affairs Shippensburg U. of Pa., until 1986; pres. Lake Superior State U., Sault Sainte Marie, Mich., 1986-92, Minot (N.D.) State U., 1992—. Office: Minot State U Office of Pres Minot ND 58707

SHABAZ, JOHN C., federal judge; b. West Allis, Wis., June 25, 1931; s. Cyrus D. and Harriet T. Shabaz; children: Scott J., Jeffrey J., Emily D., John D. Student, U. Wis., 1949-53; LLB, Marquette U., 1957. Pvt. practice law West Allis, Wis., 1957-81; mem. Wis. Assembly, 1965-81; judge U.S. Dist. Ct. (we. dist.) Wis., 1981—. With U.S. Army, 1954-64. Office: US Dist Ct PO Box 591 Madison WI 53701-0591

SHABAZZ, AIYSHA MUSLIMAH, social work administrator; b. Columbia, S.C., Aug. 9, 1942; d. Jerry James Gadson and Edna Louise (Bellinger) Gadson Smalls; m. Abdullah Muslim Shabazz, July 28; children: Ain, Wali. BA, Fed. City Coll., Washington, 1973; MSW with honors, U. S.C., 1994, postgrad., 1994-95. Cert. child protective svcs. investigator, S.C., adoption investigator, S.C.; lic. social worker and ACBSW; cert. AIDS instr. ARC; lic. notary pub., S.C. Social work asst. Family Service Ctr., Washington, 1966-68; admission counselor Washington Tech. Inst., Washington, 1968-70; program dir. Park Motor Community Ctr., Washington, 1970-75; adminstrv. asst. Neighborhood Planning Council, Washington, 1974-75; substitue tchr. D.C. Pub. Sch. System, Washington, 1974-75; substitute tchr. Dist. I Pub. Schs., Columbia, 1977; home sch. program dir. Community Care, Inc., Columbia, 1977-81; monitor summer program U. S.C., Columbia, 1982; program dir. Dept. Social Services, Columbia, 1984—, case auditor, 1987-88, social worker supr., 1988—; writer Acad. of Bacholu-Social Workers Exam, 1991; cons. substance abuse resch. program evaln., 1994—. substance abspeaker in field. Bd. dirs. Frederick Douglas Inst., Washington, 1968-69; pres. Park Motor Resident Coun., Washington, 1972-75; expert witness Family Ct.; bd. dirs. Coun. on Child Abuse and Neglect; adv. com., v.p. Benedict Coll. Sch. Social Work, S.C. Protection and Advocacy Handicapped Children; vol. AIDS instr. ARC, 1994; chairperson coordinating com. Voice of the Customer, 1995—. Mem. NASW (bd. dirs. 1993-95), S.C. Child Abuse and Neglect Task Force, AIDS Task Force (chmn. 1987-89). Democrat. Office: Dept Social Services 3220 Two Notch Rd Columbia SC 29204-2826

SHABICA, CHARLES WRIGHT, earth science educator; b. Elizabeth, N.J., Jan. 3, 1943; s. Anthony Charles and Eleanor (Wright) S.; m. Susan Ewing, Dec. 30, 1967; children: Jonathan, Andrew, Dana. BA in Geology, Brown U., 1965; PhD, U. Chgo., 1971. Prof. earth sci. Northeastern Ill. U., Chgo., 1971—; disting. prof., 1991; pres. Shabica & Assocs., Inc., Northfield, Ill., 1985—; chmn. bd. dirs. Aesti Corp.; rsch. collaborator Nat. Park Svc., 1978-82, 89—; adj. prof. Coll. V.I., St. Thomas, 1980; Kellogg fellow Northeastern Ill. U., 1979—; chmn. Task Force on Lake Michigan, Chgo., 1986-89; mem. Chgo. Shoreline Protection Commn., 1987-88; cons. Shedd Aquarium, Chgo., 1991; mem. Ft. Sheridan Commn., 1989-90. Commr., packmaster Boy Scouts Am., Winnetka, Ill., 1984-88. Coop. Inst. for Limnology and Ecosystems Rsch. Lab. fellow. Mem. Internat. Assn. for Great Lakes Rsch., Am. Shore and Beach Preservation Assn. (bd. dirs.), Sigma Xi. Home: 326 Ridge Ave Winnetka IL 60093 Office: 345 Walnut St Northfield IL 60093-4127

SHACHAR, AVISHAI, lawyer; b. Bklyn., Oct. 29, 1953; s. Zeev and Natasha (Kisler) S. m. Orly Eylan, Sept. 6, 1977; children: Carmel, Tal, Abigail. LLB, Tel-Aviv U., 1980; SJD, Harvard U., 1984. Bar: Israel 1983, N.Y. 1984. With Prof. Yuval Levi Law Offices, Tel-Aviv, 1979-80, Herzog, Fox, Neeman & Co., Tel-Aviv, 1980-81; assoc. Davis, Polk & Wardwell, N.Y.C., 1984-86, ptnr., 1987—. Recipient acad. award Yad Avi Ha-Yeshuv, Israel, 1982. Mem. ABA, Internat. Fiscal Assn., Israeli Bar Assn.

SHACK, WILLIAM ALFRED, anthropology educator, researcher, consultant; b. Chgo., Apr. 19, 1923; s. William and Emma (McAvoy) S.; m. Dorothy Nash, Sept. 1, 1960; 1 child, Hailu A. B.A.E., Sch. of the Art Inst., Chgo., 1955; M.A., U. Chgo., 1957; Ph.D., London Sch. Econs., 1961. Asst. prof. sociology and anthropology Northeastern Ill. State Coll., Chgo., 1961-62; asst. prof. sociology Haile Sellassie I Univ., Addis Ababa, Ethiopia, 1962-65; assoc. prof. anthropology U. Ill., Chgo., 1966-70; prof. anthropology U. Calif.-Berkeley, 1970-91, dean, grad. div., 1979-85. Author: The Gurage, 1966, The Central Ethiopians, 1974; co-author: Gods and Heroes, 1974; co-editor: Strangers in African Societies, 1979. Trustee, bd. dirs. World Affairs Council of No. Calif., San Francisco. Served with USCG, 1943-46; PTO. Fellow AAAS, Calif. Acad. Scis. (trustee, v.p. 1993), Am. Anthrop. Assn., Royal Anthrop. Inst. (pres. N.Am. com. 1983-86), Internat. African Inst. (econ. coun. 1984—, vice chmn. 1985-87, chmn. 1987—, Chevalier l'Ordre Nationale du Merite 1987), Athenaeum (London); mem. Faculty Club U. Calif.-Berkeley (pres. 1991-94). Avocation: vintage motor racing. Home: 2597 Hilgard Ave Berkeley CA 94709-1104 Office: U Calif-Berkeley Dept Anthropology 232 Kroeber Hall Berkeley CA 94720

SHACKELFORD, BARTON WARREN, retired utility executive; b. San Francisco, Oct. 12, 1920; s. Frank Harris and Amelia Louise (Schilling) S.; m. Charlaine Mae Livingston, July 24, 1949; children: Frank, Joan, Linda, Ann. B.S. in Civil Engring, U. Calif., Berkeley, 1941. Jr. engr. Todd-Calif. Shipbldg. Corp., 1941-44; with Pacific Gas & Electric Co., 1946-85; sr. v.p., then exec. v.p. Pacific Gas & Electric Co., San Francisco, 1976-79; pres. Pacific Gas & Electric Co., 1979-85; bd. dirs. Harding Assocs., Inc., CalEnergy Co., Inc. (emeritus). Office: Pacific Gas & Electric Co 123 Mission St PO Box 770000 Mail Code H17 San Francisco CA 94177

SHACKELFORD, GEORGE GREEN, historian; b. Orange, Va., Dec. 17, 1920; s. Virginius Randolph and Peachy Gascoigne (Lyne) S.; m. Grace Howard McConnell, June 9, 1962. B.A., U. Va., 1943, M.A., 1948, Ph.D., 1955; postgrad., Columbia U., 1949-51; cert., Attingham, Eng., 1957. Asst. prof. history Birmingham (Ala.) So. Coll., 1948-49; rsch. fellow Va. Hist. Soc., Richmond, 1951-53; instr. Va. Poly. Inst. and State U., Blacksburg, 1954-55; asst. prof. history Va. Poly. Inst. and State U., 1955-58, assoc. prof., 1958-68, prof., 1968-90, prof. emeritus, 1990—; cons. hist. mgmt. Westmoreland Davis Meml. Found., Leesburg, Va., 1967-73, 77-81; vis. scholar Am. Acad., Rome, 1996. Author: George Wythe Randolph and the Confederate Elite, 1988, Jefferson's Adoptive Son: William Short, 1993, Jefferson's Travels in Europe, 1995; editor: Monticello Assn. Collected Papers Vol I., 1965, Vol II, 1984; co-editor Va. Social Sci. Jour., 1967-68; contbr. articles to profl. jours. Mem. Va. Commn. on Bicentennial of The U.S. Constitution, 1987-92. Lt. USNR, 1943-49. Recipient award Va. soc. Am. Inst. Architects for Hist. Preservation, 1985. Mem. Am. Hist. Assn., English Speaking Union (pres. S.W. Va. br. 1979), Nat. Trust for Hist. Preservation (bd. advisors 1976-79), Assn. Inst. Early Am. History and Culture, Attingham Assocs., Assn. Preservation Va. Antiquities (bd. dirs. 1960-64, 67-77), Monticello Assn. (pres. 1969-71), So. Hist. Assn., Va. Hist. Assn., Soc. Archl. History, Farmington Country Club. Democrat. Episcopalian. Home and Office: Westminster Canterbury 250 Pantops Mount Rd 55 Charlottesville VA 22911

SHACKLEFORD, WILLIAM ALTON, JR., minister; b. Red Springs, N.C., Aug. 5, 1947; s. Purcell and Pearl (Walton) S.; m. Rebecca Belsches, Dec. 2, 1972; children: Kristal Lynn, William Alton Jr. Student, Hampton U., 1965-67, U. Richmond, 1969, 70; DD (hon.), Va. Sem. and Coll., 1990. Ordained to ministry Unity Bapt. Mins.' Conf., 1977. Pastor Cedar Grove Bapt. Ch., Charles City, Va., 1979-82, St. Paul High Street Bapt. Ch., Martinsville, Va., 1986—; past pres. Bapt. Sunday sch. and Bapt. Tng. Union Congress of Va., Sunday sch. Union of Hampton and Adjoining Cities, Unity Bapt. Min.'s Conf., Newport News, Va.; corr. sec. Va. Bapt. State Conv., 1986-96; sr. technician tech. svc. Badishe Corp., Williamsburg, Va., 1967-81, asst. supr. corp. office svcs., 1981-86. Contbr. articles to Martinsville Bull. Apptd. supt. Schs. Adv. Coun.; mem. Child Abuse and Neglect Multidiscipline Team; mem. exec. bd. Martinsville Voter's League, 1987—; mem. overall econ. devel. com., ad hoc drug and alcohol abuse com., past mem. adminstrv. bd. Martinsville Dept. Social Svcs.; mem. adv. coun. Good News Jail and Prison Ministries; past chmn. bd. dirs., mem. adv. com., mem. editl. bd. Patrick Henry Drug and Alcohol Coun.; vice chmn. Martinsville City Sch. Bd., 1991—; past chmn. bd. trustees Va. Sem. and Coll., Lynchburg, Va., 1992-96; v.p. Va. One Ch. One Child, 1992—; mem. edn. com. Va. Mcpl. League, 1993-95. Named Outstanding Min. Nat. Hairston Clan, 1988; recipient Dedicated Svc. award Va.'s One Ch. One Child Program, 1989, numerous others. Mem. NAACP, Smith River Bapt. Assn. (vice moderator), Martinsville and Henry County Ministerial Alliance (various positions). Home: 405 3rd St Martinsville VA 24112-3416 Office: St Paul High Street Bapt Ch PO Box 1003 401 Fayette St Martinsville VA 24114 *I live with the assurance that the invisible hand of God works to bless and exalt those who commit the totality of their existence to serve God and benefit humanity.*

SHACKMAN, DANIEL ROBERT, psychiatrist; b. N.Y.C., Nov. 15, 1941; s. Nathan H. and Dorothy K. Shackman. BA, Columbia U., 1962, MD, 1966. Diplomate Am. Bd. Psychiatry and Neurology. Intern Mount Sinai Hosp., N.Y.C., 1966-67, resident, chief resident, fellow, 1967-70; psychiatrist USAF, Spokane, Wash., 1970-72; clin. and adminstrv. staff Brentwood VA Hosp., L.A., 1972-79; pvt. practice psychiatry L.A., 1975-87, Santa Barbara, Calif., 1984—; asst. clin. prof. UCLA Sch. Medicine, L.A., 1975=87; psychiat. cons. Calif. Dept. Rehab., L.A., 1975-87; cons. psychiatrist Sanctuary Psychiat. Ctrs., Santa Barbara, 1984—; chmn. dept. psychiatry Santa Barbara (Calif.) Cottage Hosp., 1990-92. Bd. dirs. Family Counseling Svc., Spokane, 1971-72. Maj. USAF, 1970-72. Mem. Am. Psychiat. Assn., Am. Acad. Child/Adolescent Psychiatry, So. Calif. Psychiat. Soc. (dist. councillor 1989-92). Avocations: music appreciation and performance, computer science. Office: 924 Anacapa St Santa Barbara CA 93101

SHACTER, DAVID MERVYN, lawyer; b. Toronto, Ont., Can., Jan. 17, 1941; s. Nathan and Tillie Anne (Schwartz) S. BA, U. Toronto, 1963; JD, Southwestern U., 1967. Bar: Calif. 1968, U.S. Ct. Appeals (9th cir.) 1969, U.S. Supreme Ct. 1982. Law clk., staff atty. Legal Aid Found., Long Beach, Calif., 1967-70; asst. city atty. City of Beverly Hills, Calif., 1970; ptnr. Shacter & Berg, Beverly Hills, 1971-83, Selwyn, Capalbo, Lowenthal & Shacter Profl. Law Corp., 1984—; del. State Bar Conf. Dels., 1976—; lectr. Calif. Continuing Edn. of Bar, 1977, 82, 83, 86; judge pro tem L.A. and Beverly Hills mcpl. cts.; arbitrator L.A. Superior Ct., 1983—, also judge pro tem; disciplinary examiner Calif. State Bar, 1986. Bd. dirs. and pres. Los Angeles Soc. Prevention Cruelty to Animals, 1979-89. Mem. Beverly Hills Bar Assn. (bd. govs. 1985—, editor-in-chief jour., sec. 1987-88, treas. 1988-89, v.p. 1989-90, pres.-elect 1990-91, pres. 1991-92), Am. Arbitration Assn. (nat. panel arbitrators, NASD arbitration panel), City of Hope Med. Ctr. Aux., Wilshire C. of C. (bd. dirs., gen. counsel 1985-87). Office: Selwyn Capalbo Lowenthal & Shacter Profl Law Corp 8383 Wilshire Blvd Ste 510 Beverly Hills CA 90211

SHADBOLT, DOUGLAS, architecture educator, administrator; b. Victoria, B.C., Can., Apr. 18, 1925; s. Edmund and Alice Mary Maude (Healy) S.; m. Sidney Osborne Craig, June 29, 1960; stepchildren: James Osborne Craig, Catherine Shand Craig. B. Arch., U. Oreg., 1957; D. Eng. (hon.), N.S. Tech. Coll., 1969, Carleton U., 1982. Archtl. asst. Montreal, Que., Can., Ottawa, Ont., Vancouver, B.C., Victoria, B.C., Seattle, Boston, 1942-58; lectr. U. Oreg., 1955-57; asst. prof. McGill U., Montreal, 1958-60, assoc. prof., 1960-61; prof., dir. Sch. Architecture N.S. Tech. Coll., Halifax, Can., 1961-68; prof., dir. Sch. Architecture Carleton U., Ottawa, 1968-77, dir. Archtl. Research Group, 1977-79; prof., dir. Sch. Architecture, U. B.C., Vancouver, 1979-90, prof. emeritus, 1990—; pvt. practice cons. architect, 1961—. Author: Ron Thom, The Shaping of an Architect, 1995. Recipient Disting. Prof. award Assn. Collegiate Sch. Architecture, 1987. Fellow Royal Archtl. Inst. Can. (Gold medal 1992); mem. Archtl. Inst. B.C.

SHADDIX, JAMES W., lawyer; b. 1946. BBA, U. Tex., 1968, JD, 1971. Bar: Tex. 1971. Spl. agent U.S. Treasury-IRS, 1972-77; asst. gen. counsel Pennzoil Co., 1979-90, gen. counsel, 1990—. Office: Pennzoil Co PO Box 2967 Houston TX 77252-2967

SHADDOCK, CARROLL SIDNEY, lawyer; b. Beaumont, Tex., July 7, 1940; s. Carroll Bitting Jr. and Hulda Martha (Gaertner) S.; m. Dorothea Schulze, Nov. 30, 1963; children: Carroll Christian, Peter Eric, Matthew Nolan. BA, Rice U., 1962; JD, Yale U., 1965. Ptnr. Liddell, Sapp, Zivley, Hill & LaBoon L.L.P., Houston, 1967—. Chmn. Scenic Am., Washington, 1985-92, Scenic Tex., 1992—, Trees for Houston, 1982—, Billboards Limited, Houston, 1982-92. Republican. Lutheran. Avocations: church music, golf, travel. Home: 1715 South Blvd Houston TX 77098-5419 Office: Liddell Sapp Zivley Hill & LaBoon LLP Tex Commerce Tower 600 Travis Ste 3200 Houston TX 77002-3095

SHADEGG, JOHN B., congressman; b. Phoenix, Oct. 22, 1950; s. Stephen and Eugenia Shadegg; m. Shirley Shadegg; children: Courtney, Stephen. BA, U. Ariz., 1972, JD, 1975. Advisor U.S. Sentencing Commn.; spl. asst. atty. gen. State of Ariz., 1983-90; spl. counsel Ariz. Ho. Rep. Caucus, 1991-92; pvt. practice; mem. 104th Congress from 4th Ariz. dist., 1995—, mem. various coms., asst. whip; mem. Victims Bill of Rights Task Force, 1989-90; mem. Fiscal Accountability and Reform Efforts Com., 1991-92; counsel Arizonian's for Wildlife Conservation, 1992; chmn. Proposition 108-Two-Thirds Tax Limitation Initiative, 1992. Rep. Party Ballot Security chmn., 1982; active Corbin for Atty. Gen., 1982-86; Rep. Precinct committeeman; chmn. Ariz. Rep. Caucus, 1985-87; chmn. Ariz. Lawyers for Bush-Quayle, 1988; mem. steering com., surrogate spkr. Jon Kyl for Congress, 1988-92; former pres. Crime Victim Found.; founding dir. Goldwater Inst. Pub. Policy; chmn. Ariz. Juvenile Justice Adv. Coun.; mem. adv. bd. Salvation Army; mem. vestry Christ Ch. of Ascension, 1989-91; mem. class II Valley Leadership; bd. dirs. Ariz. State U. Law Soc. Office: US House Reps 503 Cannon House Office Bldg Washington DC 20515-0304*

SHADER, RICHARD IRWIN, psychiatrist, educator; b. Mt. Vernon, N.Y., May 27, 1935; s. Myer and Beatrice (Epstein) S.; m. Aline Brown, Sept. 21, 1958; children: Laurel Beth, Jennifer Robin, Robert Andrew. Student, Harvard U., 1952-56; M.D., NYU, 1960; grad., Boston Psychoanalytic Inst., 1970. Diplomate Am. Bd. Psychiatry and Neurology (dir. 1977-84, treas. 1982-83, pres. 1984). Intern Greenwich Hosp., Conn., 1960-61; resident in psychiatry Mass. Mental Health Ctr., Boston, 1961-62, 64-65, NIMH, Bethesda, Md., 1962-64; assoc. prof. psychiatry Harvard Med. Sch., 1970-79; prof. dept. psychiatry Tufts U. Med. Sch., Boston, 1979—, chmn. dept., 1979-91; psychiatrist in chief New Eng. Med. Ctr. Hosp., Boston, 1979-91; prof. pharmacology Tufts U. Med. Sch., Boston, 1989—, chmn. dept. pharmacology and exptl. therapeutics, 1991-93. Author: (with A. DiMascio) Psychotropic Drug Side Effects, 1970, (with D.J. Greenblatt) Benzodiazepines in Clinical Practice, 1974, Manual of Psychiatric Therapeutics, 1975, 2d edit., 1994; editor: Psychiatric Complications of Medical Drugs, 1972, (with A. DiMascio) Clinical Handbook of Psychopharmacology, 1970, (with D.J. Greenblatt) Pharmacokinetics in Clinical Practice, 1985, (with A. DiMascio) Butryophenones in Psychiatry, 1972, MAOI Therapy, 1988, (with J.P. Tupin and D.S. Harnett) Handbook of Clinical Psychopharmacology, 1988, (with others) Drug Interactions in Psychiatry, 1989, 2d edit., 1995, Clinical Manual of Chemical Dependence, 1991; editor in chief Jour. Clin. Psychopharmacology, 1980—. Bd. dirs. Med. Found., Inc., 1980-87. Served with USPHS, 1962-64. Joseph J. Michaels merit scholar, 1968-69; fellow Ctr. for Advanced Study in Behavioral Scis., Stanford, Calif., 1990-91; recipient Seymour Vestermark award Am. Psychiat. Assn., 1988, 90. Mem. AMA, Mass. Med. Soc., Am. coll. Neuropsychopharmacology (v.p. 1984, pres. 1990), Am. Soc. Clin. Pharmacology & Therapeutics, Am. Soc. Pharmacology and Exptl. Therapeutics. Democrat. Jewish. Office: Tufts U Sch Medicine 136 Harrison Ave Boston MA 02111-1800

SHADID, RANDEL COY, lawyer; b. Dallas, Sept. 28, 1947; s. Coy Constant and Jimmie Lee (Burrow) S.; m. Dana Hieronymus, Mar. 9, 1996; children from previous marriage: Jerame Scott, Jerod Ryan. BBA, U. Okla., 1969, JD, 1972. Bar: Okla. 1973, U.S. Dist. Ct. (we. dist.) Okla. 1973. Researcher Okla. Employment Security Commn., Oklahoma City, 1969-72; pvt. practice Edmond, Okla., 1973—; adj. prof. Ctrl. State U., Edmond, 1975-78, 94-96. Mayor pro tem Edmond City Coun., 1979—, mayor, 1991-95; deacon First Christian Ch.; mem. Edmond Econ. Devel. Authority. Named to Edmond Hall of Fame, 1995. Mem. Okla. County Bar Assn., Edmond C. of C. (pres. 1984, Citizen of Yr. 1986)), Ambucs, Rotary (treas. 1978), Delta Theta Phi, Delta Sigma Pi, Omicron Delta Kappa, Beta Gamma Sigma. Avocations: tennis, skiing, fishing, gardening, art & antique collecting. Home: 507 Timberdale Ter Edmond OK 73034-4215 Office: 19 N Broadway St # 100 Edmond OK 73034-3732

SHADLE, DONNA A. FRANCIS, principal; b. Canton, Ohio, Oct. 29, 1944; d. Gerald W. and Virginia M. (Kerker) Francis; m. Joseph E. Shadle, Apr. 24, 1965; children: Joseph, Paul, Ann, Mary. Student, Walsh Coll., 1964; BS in Edn., Kent State U., 1980, MS in Edn., 1989. Cert. early childhood, kindergarten, elementary edn., Ohio. Tchr. grade 4 St. Joseph's Elem., Canton, Ohio, 1964-65; dir., administr. Community Pre-sch., Canton, 1969-79; substitute tchr., K-8 Diocese of Youngstown, Canton, 1965-80; tchr. kindergarten St. Paul's Elem., North Canton, Ohio, 1980-95; prin. Sacred Heart of Mary Elem. Sch., Harrisburg, Ohio, 1995—; reading pubs. cons.; tchr. rep. Home & Sch. Assn., North Canton, 1985; tech. com., 1992—; dir. drama Ctrl. Cath. H.S., Canton, 1987—; workshop presenter various ednl. conventions, 1989—; adv. bd. ADD Partnership of Ohio, North Canton, 1992—; invited to participate in various dept. projects Ohio State Dept. Edn.; cons. Sadlier Pub. editor, pub. (newsletter) KinderKindlings, 1989—, pub. cons., 1994. Troop Leader Girl Scouts Am., North Canton, 1977-93; dir. Mime Easter drama, North Canton, 1983-89; vol. United Way, March of Dimes, Heart Fund Canton, Canton, 1965—. Recipient spl. recognition award for Ohio Tchr. of Yr. Ashland Oil, 1989. Mem. ASCD, Assn. Childhood Edn. Internat., Nat. Assn. Edn. Young Children, Nat. Cath. Ednl. Assn., Ohio Assn. Edn. Young Children, Canton Area Assn. Edn. Young Children. Home: 5544 Frazer Ave NW North Canton OH 44720-4040 Office: Sacred Heart of Mary 8276 Nickel Plate Ave NE Louisville OH 44641

SHADOAN, GEORGE WOODSON, lawyer; b. Galesburg, Ill., July 4, 1933; s. William Parker and Hortense (Lewis) S.; m. June Faith Spiegelman, May 16, 1969; 1 child, Jesse; 1 stepchild, Jenny Ducaud. B.S., U. Ky., 1958, LL.B., 1960; LL.M., Georgetown U., 1961. Bar: Ky., 1960, D.C. 1960, Md. 1963. Ptnr. Shadoan and Michael, LLP, Rockville, Md.; prof. law Georgetown U. Law Ctr., 1962-66. Author, editor: Law and Tactics in Federal Criminal Cases, 1964; Maryland Tort Damages, 1983, 85, 90, 94. Named Lawyer of Yr., Assn. Plaintiffs Trial Attys. of D.C., 1974. Fellow Am. Bar Found., Am. Bd. Trial Advocates, Am. Bd. Profl. Liability Attys.; mem. ATLA (gov. 1982-85), Md. Bar Assn., D.C. Bar Assn. (Young Lawyer of Yr. award 1963), Inner Circle of Advocates (pres. 1983-85), Trial Lawyers Pub. Justice (pres. 1984, Pub. Justice award 1994), Md. Trial Lawyers Assn. (pres. 1978-79), Internat. Soc. Barristers (chmn. Md. State Bar Assn. civil pattern jury instructions subcom.), Internat. Acad. Trial Lawyers, Am. Law Inst. Home: 4445 29th St NW Washington DC 20008-2307 Office: 108 Park Ave Rockville MD 20850-2619

SHADUR, MILTON I., judge; b. St. Paul, June 25, 1924; s. Harris and Mary (Kaplan) S.; m. Eleanor Pilka, Mar. 30, 1946; children: Robert, Karen, Beth. B.S., U. Chgo., 1943, J.D. cum laude, 1949. Bar: Ill. 1949, U.S. Supreme Ct. 1957. Pvt. practice practice Chgo., 1949-80; assoc. Goldberg, Devoe & Brussell, 1949-51; ptnr. Shadur, Krupp & Miller and predecessor firms, 1951-80; judge U.S. Dist. Ct. (no. dist.) Ill., Chgo., 1980—; commr. Ill. Supreme Ct. Character and Fitness, 1961-72, chmn., 1971; gen. counsel Ill. Jud. Inquiry Bd., 1975-80. Editor-in-chief: U. Chgo. Law Rev., 1948-49. Chmn. visiting com. U. Chgo. Law Sch., 1971-76, mem. vis. com., 1989-92; bd. dirs. Legal Assistance Found. Chgo., 1972-78; trustee Village of Glencoe, 1969-74, Ravinia Festival Assn., 1976-93, exec. com. 1983-93, vice chmn. 1989-93, life trustee, 1994—. Lt. (j.g.) USNR, 1943-46. Fellow Am. Bar Found.; mem. ABA (spl. com. on youth edn. for citizenship 1975-79), Ill. State Bar Assn. (joint com. on rules of jud. conduct 1974), Chgo. Bar Assn. (chmn. legis. com. 1963-65, jud. com. 1970-71, profl. ethics com. 1975-76, sec. 1967-69), Chgo. Council Lawyers, Order of Coif. Office: US Dist Ct 219 S Dearborn St Chicago IL 60604*

SHADUR, ROBERT H., lawyer; b. Chgo., June 17, 1947. Upper 2d degree, U. Birmingham, Eng., 1968; BA magna cum laude, UCLA, 1969; JD, U. Chgo., 1972. Bar: Ill. 1973. Former ptnr. Winston & Strawn, Chgo. Mem. ABA, Ill. State Bar Assn., Chgo. Bar Assn., Phi Beta Kappa. Office: Shadur and Assocs Ste 1650 333 W Wacker Dr Chicago IL 60606-1614

SHADWELL, WENDY JOAN, curator, writer; b. N.Y.C., Feb. 5, 1942; d. Howard and Phyllis Lilian (Jenner) S. BA with honors, Mary Washington Coll., 1963; postgrad. dept. art and archeology Columbia U., 1963-66. Curator Middendorf Collection, N.Y.C., 1966-73; cons. N.Y. Hist. Soc., N.Y.C., 1971-73, asst. editor, 1973-74, curator of prints, 1974—. Author: American Printmaking: The First 150 Years, 1969; Prized Prints, 1986. Contbr. articles to profl. jours. Sec. collections com. S.I. Hist. Soc., 1983—; v.p. Friends of Alice Austen House, S.I., 1983-85. Mem. Print Council Am., Am. Hist. Print Collectors Soc. (1st v.p.), Archivists Round Table, N.Am. Print Conf., Grolier Club, Phi Beta Kappa. Republican. Episcopalian. Office: NY Hist Soc 170 Central Park W New York NY 10024-5102

SHAEFFER, CHARLES WAYNE, investment counselor; b. Bridgeton, Pa., Dec. 12, 1910; s. Bartram Augustus and Carolyn I. (Morton) S.; m. Ruth S. Smyser, Oct. 2, 1937; children—Charles Wayne, Ann B. (Mrs. Clark F. MacKenzie), Julia P. B.A., Pa. State U., 1933; M.B.A., Harvard, 1935; LL.D., Loyola Coll., 1974. Investment counselor Mackubin Legg & Co., Balt., 1935-37; with T. Rowe Price Assos., Inc. (formerly T. Rowe Price & Assos., Inc.), Balt., 1938—; chmn. bd. T. Rowe Price Assos., Inc. (formerly T. Rowe Price & Assos., Inc.), 1966-76, pres., 1963-74, cons., 1976—; pres. T. Rowe Price Growth Stock Fund, Inc., 1968-74, chmn. bd., 1974-76; chmn. bd. Rowe Price New Income Fund, 1973—; dir. Rowe Price New Horizons Fund, Inc., 1966—, Rowe Price New Era Fund, Inc., Rowe Price Prime Res. Fund; trustee Monumental Properties Trust; lectr. investment mgmt. Balt. Coll. Commerce, 1938-70, Johns Hopkins, 1960-72. Trustee Pa. State U., Franklin Sq. Hosp.; bd. mgrs. Bryn Mawr Sch., U. Balt.; bd. dirs. Md. chpt. Nature Conservancy; chmn. bd. dirs. Md. Shock-Trauma Found. Recipient Distinguished Alumni award Pa. State U. Coll. Bus. Adminstrn., 1971-72. Mem. Investment Counsel Assn. Am. (pres. 1970-73, gov. 1965—), No-Load Mut. Fund Assn. (pres. 1972-75), Investment Co. Inst. (gov. 1968—, chmn. 1975-76), Alpha Sigma Phi, Pi Gamma Mu, Delta Sigma Pi. Episcopalian. Clubs: Maryland (Balt.), L'Hirodelle (Balt.), Merchants (Balt.), Center (Balt.), Elkridge (Balt.); Green Spring Valley Hunt (Garrison, Md.); Laurel Fish and Game Assn. (York, Pa.), Lafayette (York, Pa.); Seaview Country (Absecon, N.J.); Farmington Country (Charlottesville, Va.). Home: 603 Brightwood Club Dr Lutherville Timonium MD 21093-3632 Office: 100 E Pratt St Baltimore MD 21202-1009

SHAEFFER, THELMA JEAN, primary school educator; b. Ft. Collins, Colo., Feb. 1, 1949; d. Harold H. and Gladys June (Ruff) Pfeif; m. Charles F. Shaeffer, June 12, 1971; 1 child, Shannon Emily. BA, U. No. Colo., 1970, MA, 1972. Cert. profl. tchr., type B, Colo. Primary tchr. Adams County Dist #12 Five Star Schs., Northglenn, Colo., 1970-84; chpt. I (lang. arts) tchr. Adams County Dist #12 Five Star Schs., Northglenn, 1984-92, chpt. I, read succed tchr., 1992—; mem. policy coun. Adams County Dist. # 12 Five Star Schs., Northglenn, 1975-79, dist. sch. improvement team, 1987-89; presenter Nat. Coun. Tchrs. of English, 1990. Vol. 1992 election, Denver, alumni advisor for Career Connections U. No. Colo., 1993—. Mem. Colo. Tchrs. Assn. (del. 1992), Dist. Tchrs. Edn. Assn. (exec. bd. mem. 1991-93), Internat. Reading Assn. (pres. Colo. coun. 1988), Internat. Order of Job's Daughters (coun. mem.), Order of Eastern Star, Delta Omicron. Episcopalian. Home: 6502 Perry St Arvada CO 80003-6400 Office: Hulstrom Elem Sch 10604 Grant Dr Northglenn CO 80233-4117

SHAEVSKY, MARK, lawyer; b. Harbin, Manchuria, China, Dec. 2, 1935; came to U.S., 1938, naturalized, 1944; s. Tolio and Rae (Weinstein) S.; m. Lois Ann Levi, Aug. 2, 1964; children: Thomas Lyle, Lawrence Keith. Student, Wayne State U., 1952-53; BA with highest distinction, U. Mich., 1956, JD with highest distinction, 1959. Bar: Mich. 1959. Law clerk to presiding judge U.S. Dist. Ct., Detroit, 1960-61; assoc. Honigman Miller Schwartz & Cohn, Detroit, 1961-64; ptnr. Honigman, Miller, Schwartz & Cohn, Detroit, 1965-69, sr. ptnr., 1969—; instr. law Wayne State U. Law Sch., Detroit, 1961-64; comml. arbitrator Am. Arbitration Assn., Detroit; bd. dirs. Charter One Fin. Inc., Charter One Bank. Contbr. Wayne State U. Law Rev., U. Mich. Law Rev., 1957-59, asst. editor, 1958-59. Dir. Detroit Mens Orgn. of Rehab. through Tng., 1969-79; mem. exec. bd. Am. Jewish Com., Detroit, 1965-74; trustee Jewish Vocat. Svcs., Detroit, 1973-76; sec., dir. Am. Friends Hebrew Univ., Detroit, 1976-84; mem. capital needs com. Jewish Welfare Fedn., Detroit, 1986—. With U.S. Army, 1959-60. Burton Abstract fellow, 1959. Mem. ABA, Mich. Bar Assn., Franklin Hills Country Club, Order of the Coif, Phi Beta Kappa. Home: The Hills of Lone Pine

4750 N Chipping Gln Bloomfield Hills MI 48302-2390 Office: Honigman Miller Schwartz & Cohn 2290 First National Bldg Detroit MI 48226

SHAFER, DALLAS EUGENE, psychology gerontology educator, minister; b. Holyoke, Colo., Jan. 26, 1936; s. Howard C. and Mary M. (Legg) S.; m. Opal Iline Bruner, Aug. 22, 1954; children: Kim, Jana, Amy. BA, Nebr. Christian, 1958; postgrad., U. Colo., Colorado Springs, 1968-72, U. So. Calif., L.A., 1973; PhD, Walden U., 1978. Cert. clin. pastoral counseling; ordained to ministry Christian Ch., 1958. Minister Christian Ch., Colorado Springs, 1960-62, Julesburg, Colo., 1962-67; instr. of honors program U. Colo., Colorado Springs, 1974, 75; instr. psychology-gerontology Coll. of St. Francis, Colorado Springs, 1982, 84, 93; adj. grad. prof. U. Colo., Colorado Springs, 1992—; sr. minister counseling Christian Ch., Security, Colo., 1967-93; pastor of counseling Woodman Valley Chapel, Colorado Springs, 1995; prof. psychology/gerontology Pikes Peak C.C., Colorado Springs, 1969-96, dept. chair psychology/gerontology, 1969-92, pres. faculty assn., 1992-94, 95-96; vice chair devel. team Westley White Rehab. Ctr., Julesburg, 1966-67; trainer-cons. Pikes Peak Hospice, Colorado Springs, 1980-81; cons. St. Thomas Moore Hospice, Canon City, Colo., 1982, Sante Cristo Hospice, Pueblo, Colo., 1983-84; trainer for grief teams in U.S. mil. pers., Hawaii, Japan, 1994. Author: Approaches to Palliative Care, 1978, 92, Delphi-80-Study of Ministry, 1981; contbr. articles to Christian Standard. Bd. dirs. Colo. State Bd. Examiner for Nursing Home, Denver, 1977-83, chmn., 1981-83; moderator Conf. on Prevention of Violence-Sch. Dist. # 3, Security, 1992. Mem. Colo. Edn. Assn. (mem. higher edn. com. 1992-94). Avocations: cross country skiing, hi country 4 wheeling, antiques. Office: Pikes Peak CC 5675 S Academy Blvd Colorado Springs CO 80906-5422

SHAFER, ERIC CHRISTOPHER, minister; b. Hanover, Pa., Apr. 10, 1950; s. B. Henry and Doris M. (Von Bergen) S.; m. Kristi L. Owens, Nov. 24, 1973. BA, Muhlenberg Coll., 1972; MDiv, Hamma Sch. Theology, 1976. Ordained to ministry Luth. Ch. Am., 1976. Pastor Holy Trinity Meml. Luth. Ch., Catasauqua, Pa., 1976-83; asst. to Bishop Northeastern Pa. Synod, Wescosville, Pa., 1983-92; staff commn. for fin. support Evang. Luth. Ch. in Am., Chgo., 1988-92, asst. dir. dept. for comm., 1992-93, dir. dept. for comm., 1993—. Contbg. editor The Lutheran mag., 1989-92. Trustee Muhlenberg Coll., Allentown, Pa., 1972-83; chmn. Luth. Film Assn., 1995—; bd. govs. Religious Pub. Rels. Coun., Inc., 1993—; chmn. Comm. Commn., Nat. Coun. Chs. in USA, 1996—, mem. exec. bd., 1996—. Democrat. Avocations: running, computers, photography, travel. Office: Evang Luth Ch in Am 8765 W Higgins Rd Chicago IL 60631-4178

SHAFER, EVERETT EARL, business administration educator; b. Oelwein, Iowa, Apr. 19, 1925; s. Paul Emerson and Maude Blanche (Lovell) S.; m. Kathryn Elaine Rose, Sept. 4, 1949. B.S., Iowa State U., 1948; J.D., U. Iowa, 1951; M.B.A., U. Chgo., 1960. Bar: Iowa bar 1951, Ill. bar 1952. Mem. legal staff Motorola, Inc., Chgo., 1951-54; fin. adminstr. Motorola Fin. Corp., Chgo., 1954-60; asst. treas., credit mgr. Motorola Consumer Products, Inc., Chgo., 1960-68; assoc. prof. bus. adminstrn. Buena Vista Coll., Storm Lake, Iowa, 1968-72; chmn. faculty senate Buena Vista Coll., 1970-71; treas. Admiral Corp., Chgo., 1972-74; asst. treas. Addressograph Multigraph Corp., Cleve., 1975-76; pres., treas. Addressograph Multigraph Finance Corp., 1976-80; prof. bus. adminstrn. Buena Vista Coll., Storm Lake, Iowa, 1980-92, ret., 1992. Trustee Upper Iowa U. Served with USAAF, 1943-45. Decorated D.F.C., Air medal; recipient Outstanding Tchr. award Buena Vista Coll., 1972. Methodist. Home: 314 Forest Dr Bellevue NE 68005-2044 Office: Buena Vista Coll Off Bus Adminstrn Storm Lake IA 50588

SHAFER, JEFFREY RICHARD, federal official; b. Lake Forest, Ill., Sept. 10, 1944; s. William McKinley and Betty (Schuchert) S.; m. Mary Louise Terenzio, Sept. 7, 1968; 2 children. AB cum laude, Princeton U., 1966; MPhil, Yale U., 1972, PhD, 1976. Economist internat. fin. divsn. bd. govs. Fed. Res. System, 1972-77, dep. assoc. dir., 1978-81; sr. internat. staff economist Pres.'s Coun. Econ. Advisers, 1977-78; v.p. rsch. function Fed. Res. Bank N.Y., 1981-84; dep. dir. econs. dept. Orgn. Econ. Cooperation and Devel., 1984-93; asst. sec. internat. affairs Dept. of Treasury, Washington, 1993-95; undersec. Internat. Affairs, 1996—. 1st lt. U.S. Army, 1966-68, Vietnam, capt. USAR. Decorated Bronze Star with oak leaf cluster. Office: Undersec for Internat Affairs 15th & Pennsylvania Ave Washington DC 20220

SHAFER, NORMA R., financial consultant; b. Mt. Carmel, Pa., May 31, 1938; d. Daniel and Pearl E. Smigel; m. Charles Shafer, Feb. 10, 1962 (div. 1980); children: Lawrence Joseph, Adele Deborah, Dina Marlene. BS in Acctg., Temple U., 1962; postgrad., Ariz. State U., Phoenix Coll. CFP. Inventory control clk. U.S. Dept. Def., Phila., 1962; individual income tax return reviewer H & R Block, Phoenix, 1975; staff acct. Seely, Mullins & Assocs., P.C., CPAs, Glendale, Ariz., 1976-81; head tax dept. Price & Weidner, CPAs, Phoenix, 1981-82; acctg. and fin. planning staff Pioneer Securities, Phoenix, 1982-83; corp. income tax auditor Ariz. Dept. Revenue, Phoenix, 1983-84, spl. agt./acting chief, 1984-87, programs and projects specialist, 1988-91; fin. cons. Ariz. Dept. Environ. Quality, Phoenix, 1991—; registered rep. H.D. Vest, Inc., Irvine, Tex. Editor Ariz. Tax News newsletter, 1988-91; contbr. articles to profl. jours. Bd. dirs. Epilepsy Soc. Ariz., Phoenix, 1985-86. Mem. Internat. Assn. Fin. Planners, Inst. Cert. Fin. Planners, Nat. Soc. Pub. Accts., Assn. MBA Execs., Am. Soc. Profl. and Exec. Women, Am. Soc. Women Accts. Avocation: classical concert mgmt.

SHAFER, R. DONALD, church official; b. May 22, 1936; married; children: Bernice Elaine Worley, Bruce Eric. BA, Messiah Coll., 1958; BDiv, Ea. Bapt. Sem., 1962; D of Ministry, Fuller Sch. Theology, 1979. Assoc. pastor Brethren in Christ Ch., Elizabethtown, Pa., 1957-59, pastor, 1959-65; dir. Christian edn. Brethren in Christ Ch., 1964-72, bishop Midwest and Pacific regional confs., 1972-84, moderator, 1976-78, 82-84, adminstrv. dir. bd. Brotherhood concerns, 1992-94, gen. sec., 1984—; tchr. Mennonite Sch. Discipleship, Lancaster, Pa., summer 1980, Azusa (Calif.) Pacific Sch. Theology, Evang. Sch. Theology, Myerstown, Pa., Mennonite Bib., Fresno, Calif., winters 1980-92, Brethren in Christ Ch., 1983—; facilitator women in leadership seminar Grantham Brethren in Christ Ch., 1993; leader numerous seminars on Christian edn., ch. growth, worship and conflict mgmt., 1972—. Bd. trustees Messiah Coll., Grantham, 1972—; mem. U.S. and internat. Mennonite Cen. Com., 1984—; gen. conf. gen. sec., mem. gen. conf. bd. of adminstrn. Brethren in Christ Ch., 1984—; sec. Coun. Moderators & Secs., 1989-94; mem. Messiah Coll. Presdl. Search Com., 1993. Avocations: hiking, golf, camping, sports, reading. Office: Brethren in Christ Ch PO Box 290 431 Grantham Rd Grantham PA 17027-0290

SHAFER, RAYMOND PHILIP, lawyer, business executive; b. New Castle, Pa., Mar. 5, 1917; s. David Philip and Mina Belle (Miller) S.; m. Jane Harris Davies, July 5, 1941; children: Diane Elizabeth, Raymond Philip, Jane Ellen. AB cum laude, Allegheny Coll., 1938, LLD, 1963; LLB, Yale, 1941; numerous hon. LLD degrees. Bar: N.Y., Pa. Asso. firm Winthrop, Stimson, Putnam & Roberts, N.Y.C.; practice law Meadville, Pa., 1945-63; counsel Shafer, Swick, Bailey, Irwin and Stack; dist. atty. Crawford County, 1948-56; mem. Pa. Senate from 50th Dist., 1959-63; lt. gov. Pa., 1963-67; gov. Commonwealth Pa., 1967-71; vis. prof. U. Pa., 1973—; counselor to v.p. of U.S., 1975-77; ptnr., sr. counselor Coopers & Lybrand, 1977-88; former pres. and chmn. bd. trustees Allegheny Coll., Meadville, Pa. Chmn. Nat. Commn. on Marijuana and Drug Abuse; chmn. Nat. Com. U.S.-China Rels.; chmn. Nat. Coun. on Pub. Svc.; world bd. govs. USO; mem. adv. bd. Am. Enterprise Inst.; active charitable, cmty. drives; bd. dirs., vice chmn. Atlantic Coun. U.S., Am.-China Soc.; trustee Cleve. Clinic Found., Freedoms Found. With USNR, 1942-45, PTO. Recipient Gold Medal award Soc. Family of Man, 1972, numerous humanitarian and civic awards. Mem. ABA, Pa. Bar Assn., Crawford County Bar Assn. (pres. 1961-63), Council Fgn. Relations, Phi Beta Kappa, Phi Kappa Psi. Republican. Club: Mason (33 deg.). Office: Dunaway & Cross 1146 19th St NW Washington DC 20036-3703 *One makes a living by what one gets. One makes a life by what one gives.*

SHAFER, ROBERT TINSLEY, JR., judge; b. Cin., Sept. 11, 1929; s. Robert Tinsley and Grace Elizabeth (Welsh) S.; m. Barbara Jean Hough, Dec. 27, 1950; children: Richard Hough, Janet Lee Shafer Davis, Charles Welsh. BA, Coll. of Wooster, 1951; JD, U. Cin., 1956. Bar: Fla. 1956, U.S. Ct. Appeals (5th cir.) 1963, U.S. Dist. Ct. (so. dist.) Fla. 1961, U.S. Supreme Ct. 1965. Asst. trust officer 1st Nat. Bank, Ft. Myers, Fla., 1956-57; ptnr. Henderson, Franklin, Starnes & Holt, P.A., Ft. Myers, 1957-77; cir. judge 20th Jud. Cir. State of Fla., Ft. Myers, 1977-92, chief cir. judge, 1985-89, sr. judge, 1992—. Contbr. article to Corp. Law, 1955-56 (Goldsmith Corp. Law prize, 1956). Elder Covenant Presbyn. Ch., 1982-85; mem. jud. commn. Fla. Presbyn. Synod, 1960-63; chmn. Lee County chpt. Red Cross, Ft. Myers, 1963. 2nd lt. USMCR, 1951-53, PTO, Korea. Mem. ABA, Fla. Conf. Cir. Judges (exec. com. 1986-88), Fla. Bar Assn. (bd. govs. Jr. Bar sect. 1961-64), Lee County Bar Assn. (pres. 1968), Am. Judges Assn., Am. Judicature Soc., Nat. Conf. Met. Cts. Calusa Inn of Ct. Republican. Avocations: running races, bicycle racing, bicycle touring, travel, reading. Home: 2704 Shriver Dr Fort Myers FL 33901-5931

SHAFER, SUSAN WRIGHT, retired elementary school educator; b. Ft. Wayne, Dec. 6, 1941; d. George Wesley and Bernece (Spray) Wright; 1 child, Michael R. BS, St. Francis Coll., Ft. Wayne, 1967, MS in Edn., 1969. Tchr. Ft. Wayne Community Schs., 1967-69, Amphitheatre Pub. Schs., Tucson, 1970-96; ret., 1996; Odyssey of the Mind coord. Prince Elem. Sch., Tucson, 1989-91, Future Problem Solving, 1991-95. Tchr. Green Valley (Ariz.) Cmty. Ch., Vacation Bible Sch., 1987-89, dir. vacation bible sch., 1989-93. Mem. AAUW, NEA (life), Delta Kappa Gamma (pres. Alpha Rho chpt.), Alpha Delta Kappa (historian Epsilon chpt. 1990—), Phi Delta Kappa (life, Tucson chpt.). Republican. Methodist. Avocations: reading, traveling, walking. Home: 603 W Placita Nueva Green Valley AZ 85614-2827

SHAFFER, ALFRED GARFIELD TERRY, service organization executive; b. Sunbury, Pa., Jan. 5, 1939; d. Alfred G. and Betty Marjorie (Vogel) S.; m. Nancy Jane Dawson, Aug. 29, 1976. BS, Susquehanna U., 1961. Cert. tchr., Pa. Tchr., Danville Sch. Dist. (Pa.), 1962-69; mgr. club service Kiwanis Internat., Chgo., 1969-74, dir. program devel., 1974-81, dir. program services, Indpls., 1982-85, dir. spl. services, 1985-87, asst. sec. for spl. svcs., 1987-88, asst. to internat. sec., 1988-94, internat. sec. 1994—; corp. affairs cons. Nat. Easter Seal Soc., Chgo., 1981-82; adminstr. Circle K Internat., Chgo., 1982; mem. Pres.'s Com. on Employment of Handicapped, 1983-86. Chmn. adv. council 70001 Ltd., Indpls., 1984-86; active adv. coun. Salvation Army, Indpls. Recipient Gold Key of Svc., Pa. Dist. Key Clubs, 1964. Lutheran. Mem. Ind. Assn. Event Profls., Indpls. Athletic Club, 500 Festival Assocs., Kiwanis (pres. Selinsgrove, Pa. 1964, lt. gov. Pa. 1966-67, pres. Chgo. 1970-72, pres. Northwest Indpls. 1991-92, Outstanding Svc. award 1981, Kiwanian of Yr. 1966, 85). Home: 5688 Broadway St Indianapolis IN 46220-3073 Office: Kiwanis International 3636 Woodview Terrace Indianapolis IN 46268-1168

SHAFFER, BERNARD WILLIAM, mechanical and aerospace engineering educator; b. N.Y.C., Aug. 7, 1924; s. Abraham and Eva (Ellinsky) S.; m. Florence Solow, Feb. 23, 1947 (dec. Oct. 29, 1986); children: Janet Ilene, Roberta Franceen. B in Mech. Engring., CCNY, 1944; MS in Mech. Engring., Case Inst. Tech., 1947; PhD, Brown U., 1951. Registered profl. engr., N.Y., R.I. Aero. rsch. scientist Flight Propulsion Rsch. NACA (now NASA), Cleve., 1944-47; spl. lectr. applied mechanics Case Inst. Tech., Cleve., 1946-47; rsch. assoc., grad. div. applied math. and engring., instr. Brown U., Providence, 1947-50; asst. prof. mech. engring. NYU, N.Y.C., 1950-53, assoc. prof., 1953-58, prof., project dir. rsch. div., 1958-73; prof. dept. mech. and aerospace engring. Poly. U., Bklyn. and Farmingdale, N.Y., 1973-93; prof. emeritus Poly. U., Bklyn. and Farmingdale, 1993—; cons. in field; mem. adv. coun. Coll. Aeros., N.Y.C., 1982—; vis. rsch. prof. mech. engring. Fla. Atlantic U., Boca Raton, 1992, Disting. vis. rsch. prof., 1993-95. Contbr. articles to profl. jours. Bd. dirs. Harbor Hills Civic Assn., Great Neck, N.Y., 1968-71. With USAAF, 1944-47. Recipient various govt. grants. Fellow ASME (Richards Meml. award 1968), AIAA (assoc.); mem. Sigma Xi, Tau Beta Pi, Pi Tau Sigma. Avocations: golf, swimming. Home and Office: 18 Old Field Ln Great Neck NY 11020-1265

SHAFFER, DAVID JAMES, lawyer; b. Springfield, Ohio, July 30, 1958; s. Frank James Shaffer and Martha Isabelle (Hardman) Matthews; m. Julie Renee Shaffer, Oct. 8, 1995. BA, Wittenberg U., 1980; JD, Stanford U., 1983. Bar: Calif. 1984, U.S. Dist. Ct. (no. and ea. dists.) Calif. 1984, U.S. Ct. Appeals (9th cir.) 1984), U.S. Dist. Ct. (so. dist.) Calif. 1985, U.S. Dist. Ct. (we. dist.) Wash. 1986, D.C. 1988, U.S. Dist. Ct. D.C. 1988, U.S. Ct. Appeals (D.C. cir.) 1988, U.S. Dist. Ct. (no. dist.) Tex. 1991, U.S. Supreme Ct. 1993, Md. 1994. Supr. field ops. U.S. Census Bur., Columbus, Ohio, 1980; legal intern Natural Resources Def. Coun., Inc., San Francisco, 1982-83; assoc. Gibson, Dunn & Crutcher, San Jose, Calif., 1983; law clk. to Judge Betty B. Fletcher, U.S. Ct. Appeals for 9th Cir., Seattle, 1983-84; assoc. Gibson, Dunn & Crutcher, San Jose, 1984-87, Arnold & Porter, Washington, 1987-92; ptnr. Semmes, Bowen & Semmes, Washington, 1992-94, Arter & Hadden, Washington, 1995—. Campaign mgr. Clark County Dem. Party, Springfield, 1978-80; organizer Citizens for Sensible County Planning, Fairfax, Va., 1989-94. Alumni scholar Wittenberg U., 1976. Mem. ABA, Fed. Bar Assn. (chair EEO com. 1992-94, chair individual rights and responsibilities 1994-95, co-chair alt. dispute resolution 1995—, mem. governing bd. labor law and labor rels. sect., Outstanding Svc. award 1992, editor newsletter Labouring Oar), D.C. Bar Assn., Calif. Bar Assn., Order of Coif. Avocations: music, hiking, nature study. Office: Arter & Hadden 1801 K St NW Ste 400K Washington DC 20006

SHAFFER, DEBORAH, nurse; b. Tampa, Fla., Jan. 20, 1954; d. Frank Solomon and Mary Louise (Swann) Shaffer; children: Danny, Dionne. LPN, Suwanee-Hamilton Nursing Sch., Live Oak, Fla., 1984; student, Hillsborough CC, 1992—. LPN, Fla. Nursing experience various hosps. and nursing homes, 10 yrs. Author poems, songs and short stories. Active Neighborhood Crime Watch, Parents Without Ptnrs., The Spring, Literacy Vols. Am.; ESL tutor First Bapt. Ch.; activities instr. A.D.C. Osborne Ctr. Avocations: writing, painting, photography, gardening, guitar.

SHAFFER, DONALD S., retail executive; b. Philippi, W.Va., Mar. 22, 1943; m. Leslie Stalker; 1 child. AA, Potomac State Coll.; BS in Acctg., W.Va. U. Mgmt. trainee Sears, Roebuck and Co., USA, 1968-70; pers. mgr. Sears, Roebuck and Co., USA, Washington, 1970-72, Landover, Md., 1972-73; asst. store mgr. Sears, Roebuck and Co., USA, Washington, 1973-75, soft lines mdse. mgr., 1975-78; store mgr. Sears, Roebuck and Co., USA, Watertown, N.Y., 1978-81; zone oper. mgr. Sears, Roebuck and Co., USA, Albany, N.Y., 1981-82; store mgr. Sears, Roebuck and Co., USA, New Brunswick, N.J., 1982-83; with planning dept. nat. hdqs. Sears, Roebuck and Co., USA, Chgo., 1983-86; regional mgr. Sears, Roebuck and Co., USA, Hawaii, 1986-87; v.p. field sales ops. Sears Can. Inc., Toronto, 1987; v.p. field sales ops. and real estate Sears Can. Inc., 1988; regional gen. mgr. Sears, Roebuck and Co., USA, Detroit, 1989; nat. bus. mgr. womens apparel, accessories nat. hdqs. Sears, Roebuck and Co., USA, Chgo., 1989-90; nat. mdse. mgr. furniture Sears, Roebuck and Co., USA, 1990-93; exec. v.p., COO Sears Can. Inc., Toronto, Ont., 1993—; pres., CEO Sears Can. Inc.; bd. dirs. Sears Acceptance Co.; bd. mem. Retail Coun. Can. Bd. govs. Jr. Achievement Can. 1st lt. U.S. Army, 1965-67. Office: Sears Can Inc, 222 Jarvis St, Toronto, ON Canada M5B 2B8*

SHAFFER, DOROTHY BROWNE, retired mathematician, educator; b. Vienna, Austria, Feb. 12, 1923; d. Hermann and Steffy (Hermann) Browne; arrived U.S., 1940; m. Lloyd Hamilton Shaffer, July 25, 1943 (dec. 1978); children: Deborah Lee, Diana Louise, Dorothy Leslie. AB, Bryn Mawr Coll., 1943; MA, Harvard U., 1945, PhD, 1962. Mathematician, MIT, Cambridge, 1945-47; tchg. fellow, research asso., Harvard U., Cambridge, 1947-48; asso. mathematician Cornell Aeronautical Lab, Buffalo, N.Y., 1952-56; mathematician Dunlap & Assoc., Stamford, Conn., 1958-60; lectr. grad. engring. U. of Conn. at Stamford, 1962; prof. math Fairfield (Conn.) U., 1963-92, prof. emeritus, 1992—; vis. prof. Imperial Coll. Sci. and Tech., London, fall 1978, U. Md., College Park, spring 1981; vis. prof. U. Calif.-San Diego, summer 1981; vis. scholar, 1986; NSF faculty fellow IBM-T.J. Watson Research Center, Yorktown Heights, N.Y., 1979. Contbr. numerous papers in math. analysis. Mem. Am. Math. Soc., Math. Assn. of Am., Assn. for Women in Math., London Math. Soc. Achievement include patent in Viscosity Stabilized Solar Pond. Home: 156 Intervale Rd Stamford CT 06905-1311 Office: Fairfield U Dept Math & Computer Sci Fairfield CT 06430

SHAFFER, GAIL DOROTHY, secondary education educator; b. Summit, N.J., May 7, 1936; d. Franklin Clifford Jr. and Mildred Edna (Burgmiller) S. AB, Hood Coll., 1958. Tchr. Sherman Sch., Cranford, N.J., 1959-60, Gov. Livingston High Sch., Berkeley Heights, N.J., 1960—. Vol. intake worker Covenant House, N.Y.C., 1982-92, spkrs. bur., 1986—, bd. dirs., Newark, 1993—; mem. juvenile conf. Family Ct. Union County, Elizabeth, N.J., 1968—; project dir. Berkeley Heights (N.J.) Alliance Against Drugs and Alcohol, 1990-95; active Berkeley Heights Youth Com., 1960-65. Named Berkeley Heights Citizen of Yr. by Jr. C. of C., Speaker of Yr. by Covenant House Corp., Vol. of Yr. by Covenent House, Union County Tchr. of Yr., 1992-93, N.J. State Tchr. of Yr., 1992-93. Mem. NEA, N.J. Edn. Assn., N.J. State Tchrs. of the Yr. (pres.), Union County Edn. Assn. Republican. Methodist. Avocations: reading, travel, U.S. history, needlework, Victoriana. Home: 522 Plainfield Ave Berkeley Heights NJ 07922-1919 also: 7 Embury Ave Ocean Grove NJ 07756-1354 Office: Gov Livingston High Sch 175 Watchung Blvd Berkeley Heights NJ 07922-2726

SHAFFER, JAMES BURGESS, communications executive; b. Boston, May 6, 1945; s. Robert Howard and Marjorie Jane (Fitch) S.; m. Lynn Elliott Eitzen, June 3, 1967; children: Derek Bruce, Ryan Brooke. B.S. in Mech. Engrng, Purdue U., 1967; M.B.A., Ind. U., 1969. Staff engr. Aerospace Research Applications Center, Bloomington, Ind., 1967-69; ops. analyst Mpls. Star & Tribune Co., 1970-71, research planning analyst, 1972-73, research planning mgr., 1974, dir. acctg., 1975-77; pres., pub. Stromberg Publs., Inc. subs., Ellicott City, Md., 1977-79; sr. v.p., assoc. pub. Buffalo Courier-Express Co., Inc. subs., 1979-82; v.p., chief fin. officer L.A. Times, 1983-84, v.p. fin. and planning, 1985-89; exec. v.p. The Sun-Times Co., 1989-91; pres., chief exec. officer Guy Gannett COmmunications, Portland, Maine, 1991—; vice-chmn. bd. dirs. Better Bus. Bur. Western N.Y., 1980. Trustee Wildwood Sch., Santa Monica, Calif., 1987; mem. bd. trustees Portland (Maine) Symphony , 1993-95; bd. dirs. Maine Coalition Excellence in Edn., 1993—, Conf. & Visitors Bur., 1993—. Home: 12 Russell Rd Cumb Foreside ME 04110-1404 Office: Guy Gannett Comm Box 15277 1 City Ctr Portland ME 04112-5277

SHAFFER, JAY CHRISTOPHER, lawyer; b. Brookville, Pa., Sept. 18, 1947; s. John Rienard and Laverne (Berding) S.; m. Janice Rita McKenney, May 24, 1972; 1 child, Justin. BA, Ohio State U., 1969; JD, Harvard U., 1974. Bar: Ohio 1974, U.S. Supreme Ct. 1978. Atty. office gen. counsel FTC, Washington, 1974-77; counsel subcom. on oversight, interstate and fgn. com. U.S. Ho. of Reps., Washington, 1977-79; atty. antitrust div. U.S. Dept. of Justice, Washington, 1979-82, dep. dir. policy planning antitrust div., 1982-84, chief legal adv. unit antitrust div., 1984-86; dep. dir. bur. competition FTC, Washington, 1986-88; dep. gen. counsel Office of Gen. Counsel FTC, Washington, 1988—. Served to sgt. U.S. Army, 1970-72, Korea. Mem. ABA, Fed. Bar Assn. Home: 7016 Leewood Forest Dr Springfield VA 22151-3930 Office: FTC Rm 564 Washington DC 20580

SHAFFER, JEROME ARTHUR, philosophy educator; b. N.Y.C., Apr. 2, 1929; s. Joseph and Beatrice (Leibowitz) S.; m. Olivia Anne Connery, Sept. 3, 1960 (div. 1985); children: Diana, David; m. Eliana Bar-shalom, Aug. 7, 1994. BA, Cornell U., 1950; PhD, Princeton U., 1952; MA in Marital and Family Therapy, U. Conn., 1996. Prof. philosophy Swarthmore (Pa.) Coll., 1955-67; prof. U. Conn., Storrs, 1967-94, prof. emeritus, 1994—, head dept. philosophy, 1976-94; individual, marital, and family therapist, 1995—; exec. sec. Council Philos. Studies, 1965-72. Author: The Philosophy of Mind, 1968, Violence, 1970, Reality, Knowledge, and Value, 1971; contbr. articles to profl. jours. Served with U.S. Army, 1953-55. Fulbright fellow, 1952-53, fellow Ctr. for Advanced Study Behavioral Scis., 1963-64, NEH sr. fellow, 1973-74, Cambridge Clare Hall vis. fellow, 1987. Mem. Am. Philos. Assn., Phi Beta Kappa, Phi Kappa Phi. Home: 36 Clearview Dr Mansfield Center CT 06250 Office: U Conn Dept Philosophy # U-54 Storrs CT 06268

SHAFFER, PAUL, musician, bandleader; b. Thunder Bay, Ont., Can., Nov. 28, 1949; m. Cathy Vasapoli; 1 child, Victoria Lily. Mem. band Fabulous Fugitives, Thunder Bay, 1964-68; keyboardist NBC's Saturday Night Live, 1975-80; musical dir. Blues Bros. Band, 1978-79; leader, keyboardist The World's Most Dangerous Band NBC's Late Night with David Letterman, 1982-1993; music director The Late Show with David Letterman (CBS), 1993—. Mus. dir. (Toronto, Ont. prodn.) Godspell, 1972; musician: (N.Y.C. prodn.) The Magic Show, 1974, (Gilda Radner's mus. revue, also co-composer) Live in New York, 1979, (off-Broadway prodn.) Leader of the Pack, 1984; rec. artist, keyboardist: (with Barry Manilow) This One's For You, 1976, (with National Lampoon) Good-Bye Pop, 1976, (with the Jeff Healey Band) Feel This, 1977, (Blues Bros.) Briefcase Full of Blues, 1978, Made in America, 1980, (with Jaon Armatrading) Me Myself, 1980, (with Nina Hagen) Nunsexmonkrock, 1980, (with Diana Ross) Silk Electric, 1981, (with Yoko Ono) It's Alright, 1982, (Honey Drippers) The Honey Drippers, 1985, (film soundtrack) The Karate Kid II, 1986, (with Dion, Ben. E. King, Bobby Womack and Wilson Pickett) Coast to Coast, 1991, (with Blues Traveler) Save His Soul, 1993, (with the Party Boys of Rock 'n' Roll) The World's Most Dangerous Party, 1993; regular mem. cast (TV series) A Year at the Top, 1977; film appearances include This Is Spinal Tap, 1984; solo album Coast to Coast, 1989 (2 Grammy nominations). Office: Late Show w/ David Letterman CBS 530 W 57th St New York NY 10019-2902

SHAFFER, PAUL E., retired banker; b. Rockford, Ohio, Aug. 3, 1926; s. Randall J. and Zelah V. (Alspaugh) S.; m. Dorothy L. Schumm, June 26, 1951; children: Paula Kay, Patti Lee. Grad., U. Wis. Sch. Banking, 1954; cert., Am. Inst. Banking; DHL (hon.), Purdue U., 1985. With Rockford Nat. Bank, 1945-48; asst. nat. bank examiner Treasury Dept., 1948-52; with Ft. Wayne (Ind.) Nat. Bank, 1952-65, from exec. v.p. to vice-chmn., 1965-93, chmn. emeritus, 1993-95, ret., 1995; ret., 1996; bd. dirs. Old First Nat. Bank, Bluffton, Ind. Pres. Downtown Fort Wayne Assn., 1965, Credit Bur., Fort Wayne, 1962, Jr. Achievement, 1967-69; treas. Fort Wayne Better Bus. Bur., 1968, Ind.-Purdue Devel. Fund; mem. regional adv. com. Comptroller Currency, 1968-70; commr. Ft. Wayne Conv. and Tourism Authority.; past bd. dirs. Fort Wayne Conv. Bur., Fort Wayne Philharmonic Orch., Parkview Meml. Hosp.; bd. dirs. Caylor-Nickel Hosp., Ft. Wayne campus Ind. U., Ind.-Purdue Found., Taxpayers Research Assn.; past bd. dirs. United Community Services, chmn. drive, 1970-71; past bd. dirs. Fort Wayne YMCA, v.p., 1964-67; bd. adviser Ind. U.-Purdue U., Ft. Wayne; mem. fin. adv. bd. Luth. Social Services; bd. govs. Assn. Colls. Ind.; chmn. vol. com. U.S. Savs. Bonds, Allen County, Ind., numerous other civic activities. Served with USAAF, 1945. Mem. Am. Inst. Banking (past pres. Ft. Wayne chpt.), Am. Bankers Assn. (governing coun. 1978-79), Ind. Bankers Assn. (past pres., bd. dirs.), Ft. Wayne C. of C. (past v.p., bd. dirs.), Ind. C. of C. (state dir.), Execs. Club (past pres.), Ft. Wayne Country Club, Summit Club, Quest Club, Ft. Wayne Press Club, Mad Anthonys Club, Sycamore Hills Country Club, Masons, Shriners. Home: 11132 Carnoustie Ln Fort Wayne IN 46804-9014

SHAFFER, PETER LEVIN, playwright; b. Liverpool, Eng., May 15, 1926; s. Jack and Reka (Fredman) S. BA, Cambridge U., Eng., 1950. Conscript coal mines, Eng., 1944-47; with N.Y. Pub. Libr., N.Y.C., 1951-54, Bosey & Hawkes, London, 1954-55; lit. critic Truth, 1956-57; music critic Time and Tide, 1961-62; vis. prof. contemporary drama Oxford (Eng.) U., 1994-95. Author: (plays) Five Finger Exercise, 1958 (Evening Standard Drama award 1958, N.Y. Drama Critics Cir. award 1960), The Private Ear, 1962, The Public Eye, 1962, It's About Cinderella, 1963, The Royal Hunt of the Sun, 1964, Black Comedy, 1965, The White Liars, 1967, The Battle of Shrivings, 1970, Equus, 1973 (Best Play Tony award 1975, Outer Critics Cir. Best Play award 1975), Amadeus, 1979 (Evening Standard Drama award 1979, London Drama Critics award 1979, Best Play Tony award 1980, Plays and Players Best Play award 1980), Yonadab, 1985, Lettice and Lovage, 1987 (Evening Standard Drama award 1988), The Gift of the Gorgon, 1992, (screenplays) Follow Me!, 1971, Equus, 1977 (Acad. award nomination for best screenplay adaptation 1977), Amadeus, 1984 (Acad. award for best screenplay adaptation 1984), (TV plays) The Salt Land, 1955, Balance of Terror, 1957, (radio plays) The Prodigal Father, 1955, Whom Do I Have the Honor of Addressing?, 1989, (novels, with Anthony Shaffer) The Woman in the Wardrobe, 1951, How Doth the Little Crocodile?, 1952, Withered Murder, 1955. Decorated comdr. Order Brit. Empire, 1987; recipient Hamburg Shakespeare prize, 1987, William Inge award for disting. achievement in Am. theatre, 1992. Fellow Royal Soc. Lt. (London chpt.). Address: 173 Riverside Dr New York NY 10024-1615

SHAFFER, PETER THOMAS BARNUM, consultant; b. McKeesport, Pa., Oct. 24, 1929; s. Charles Holmes and Anne Barbara (Brubaker) S.; m.

Suzanne Chesney, Aug. 25, 1962; children: Tanya Anne Shaffer Onori, Scott Peter. BS, MIT, 1951; PhD, Pa. State U., 1955; postdoctoral, Baylor U., 1974. Sr. engr. E I duPont de Nemours & Co., Niagara Falls, N.Y., 1955-58; sr. rsch. assoc. Carborundum, Niagara Falls, 1958-81; v.p., co-founder Advanced Refractory Techs., Buffalo, 1981-90; v.p. tech. Tech. Ceramics Labs., Alpharetta, Ga., 1985-94; cons. Cumming, Ga., 1994—; pres. Hartstoffe, Buffalo; pres., cons. Heany Hartstoffe, Scottsdale, N.Y.; mem. Internat. Com. on Silicon Carbide, 1966; mem. materials tech. adv. com. U.S. Dept. Commerce, 1987-94. Contbr. articles to profl. jours. Recipient 6 Indsl. Rsch. IR-100 awards, N.Y., 1963, 64, 65, 74, 80, 87, Advanced Tech. award Inventors Clubs Am., 1990. Mem. ASTM, NRA (life), Am. Ceramic Soc., Am. Chem. Soc., Am. Soc. Materials, Izaac Walton League, Nat. Wildlife Fedn., Ducks Unltd., Trout Unltd. (chpt. pres., state coun., state chmn., nat. dir.), Am. Soc. Metals, Nat. Inst. Ceramic Engrs., Sigma Xi. Achievements include numerous U.S. patents and foreign equivalents; development of first process for the mass production of silicon carbide whiskers, single crystals exhibiting strengths in execss of one million psi; instrumental in first recovery and identification of a chlorine resistant strain of poliovirus from a drinking water supply system; responsible for development of a chlorine resistant strain of polio vaccine virus; instrumental in showing the direct correlation between algae and the presence of chloroform in finished drinking water. Avocations: fishing, hiking, photography, shooting (pistol, rifle, shotgun, archery). Home and Office: 3225 Chimney Cove Dr Cumming GA 30131-7711

SHAFFER, RICHARD JAMES, lawyer, former manufacturing company executive; b. Pe Ell, Wash., Jan. 26, 1931; s. Richard Humphrys and Laura Rose (Faas) S.; m. Donna M. Smith, May 13, 1956; children: Leslie Lauren Shaffer and Stephanie Jane Athenton. B.A., U. Wash.; LL.B., Southwestern U. Bar: Calif. Vice pres., gen. counsel, sec. NI, Inc., Long Beach, Calif., 1974-89; gen. counsel Masco Bldg. Products Corp., Long Beach, 1985-89; pvt. practice Huntington Beach, Calif., 1989—; mem. ltd. liability co. drafting com. and task force Calif. State Bar, 1992-94; lectr. on ltd. liability cos. Trustee Ocean View Sch. Dist., 1965-73, pres., 1966, 73; mem. fin. adv. com. Orange Coast Coll., 1966; mem. Long Beach Local Devel. Corp., 1978-89, Calif. Senate Commn. on Corp. Governance, Shareholders' Rights and Securities Transactions, 1986—, chmn. drafting com. ltd. liability co. act for senate com., 1991-93. Mem. ABA, Nat. Assn. Securities Dealers (bd. arbitrators), Calif. Bar Assn. (exec. com. corp. law dept. com. bus. sect. 1981-88, mem. drafting com. ltd. liability co. act), Orange County Bar Assn., Huntington Harbour Yacht Club, Wanderlust Skiers of Huntington Harbour, Huntington Harbour Ski Club. Office: 17111 Beach Blvd Ste 103 Huntington Beach CA 92647-5941

SHAFFER, RUSSELL K., advertising agency executive; b. N.Y.C., Apr. 12, 1933; s. Russell Parl and Alice (Cole) S.; m. Leslie Van Nostrand, July 28, 1956; children—Cole Van Nostrand, Wendel L., Daniel W., Russell W. A.B., Brown U., 1954; M.B.A., Harvard U., 1958. Account exec. McCann-Erickson, N.Y.C., 1958-62; account supr. Grey Advt., N.Y.C., 1962-66; exec. v.p. Richard K. Manoff, Inc., N.Y.C., 1966-71; pres. Richard K. Manoff, Inc., 1971-77, also dir.; pres. David H. Mann, Inc., 1977-80; exec. v.p. F.W. Free Inc. (now Laurance, Charles & Free, Inc.), N.Y.C., 1980-86; sr. v.p. SSC&B, N.Y.C., 1986—. Served to lt. USNR, 1954-56. Home: 2 Richards Ave Norwalk CT 06854-2318 Office: One Dag Hammarskjold Pla New York NY 10017

SHAFFER, SHEILA WEEKES, mathematics educator; b. Syracuse, N.Y., Oct. 20, 1957; d. Carroll Watson and Reina Lou (Yonkers) Judd; m. Jason Craig Shaffer, June 4, 1983 (div. Sept. 1994). BA, SUNY, Albany, 1979, MS, 1983. Cert. tchr. English/Math., N.Y.; cert. advanced profl. cert. in English and Math, Md. English tchr. Cortland (N.Y.) HS, 1979-81; English tchr. Prince George's County, Upper Marlboro, Md., 1984-86, math. tchr., 1986-87; math. tchr./coord. Prince George's County, 1990-95; math./English tchr. Camden HS, St. Mary's, Ga., 1988-90; math tchr. Frederick County, Va., 1995-96, Prince George's County, Upper Marlboro, Md., 1996—; mem. SAT Com., The Coll. Bd., N.Y.C., 1993-96. Mem. Nat. Coun. Tchrs. Math. Avocations: reading, hiking, gardening. Office: Potomac High Sch 5211 Boydell Ave Oxon Hill MD 20745

SHAFFER, SHERRILL LYNN, economist; b. Tyler, Tex., Aug. 1, 1952; s. Douglas Marsene and Ethel Elizabeth (Green) S.; m. Margaret Jane Ahrens, Jun 20, 1987; 1 child, David Carsten. BA, Rice U., 1974; MA, Stanford U., 1978, PhD, 1981. Rsch. asst. Stanford (Calif.) U., 1976-79, instr., 1979-80; from economist to chief Fed. Res. Bank N.Y., N.Y.C., 1980-88; from rsch. officer/economist to asst. v.p./discount officer Fed. Res. Bank Phila., 1988—; violinist solo and with orchs., Calif., N.Y., 1976-88; cons. asst. Rosse & Olszewski, Palo Alto, Calif., 1978-80. Assoc. editor to editor Jour. Econs. and Bus., 1993—; contbr. numerous articles to profl. jours. Sec. bd. dirs. N.Y. Arts Group, N.Y.C., 1982-83; mem. program com. So. Fin. Assn., 1996. Recipient Messier cert. Astronomical League, 1993. Mem. AAAS, Am. Econ. Assn., Am. Math. Soc., Math. Assn. Am., N.Am. Econs. and Fin. Assn., Indsl. Orgn. Soc., N.Y. Acad. Scis., Fin. Mgmt. Assn. (program com. 1991), So. Fin. Assn. (program com. 1996), Delaware Valley Amateur Astronomers (observing chmn. 1993, publicity chmn. 1994, 95, 96). Episcopalian. Avocations: hiking, theology, number theory, astronomy, computer programming. Home: 1529 N Fiedler Rd Ambler PA 19002-2718 Office: Fed Res Bank Phila 10 Independence Mall Philadelphia PA 19106

SHAFFER, THOMAS LINDSAY, lawyer, educator; b. Billings, Mont., Apr. 4, 1934; s. Cecil Burdette and Margaret Jeanne (Parker) S.; m. Nancy Jane Lehr, Mar. 19, 1954; children: Thomas, Francis, Joseph, Daniel, Brian, Mary, Andrew, Edward. B.A., U. Albuquerque, 1958; J.D., U. Notre Dame, 1961; LL.D., St. Mary's U., 1983. Bar: Ind. 1961. Assoc. Barnes, Hickam, Pantzer, & Boyd, Indpls., 1961-63; prof. law U. Notre Dame, Ind., 1963-80, assoc. dean, 1969-71, dean, 1971-75, Robert and Marion Short prof., 1988—; supervising atty. Notre Dame Legal Aid Clinic, 1991—; prof. law Washington and Lee U., 1980-87, Robert E.R. Huntley prof. law, 1987-88; vis. prof. UCLA, 1970-71, U. Va., 1975-76, U. Maine, 1982, 87, Boston Coll., 1992; bd. dirs. Cornerstone Found.; mem. Ind. Constl. Revision Commn., 1969-70, Ind. Trust Code Study Commn., 1968-71; reporter Ind. Jud. Conf., 1963, 67. Author: Death, Property, and Lawyers, 1970, The Planning and Drafting of Wills and Trusts, 1972, 3d edit., 1991, Legal Interviewing and Counseling, 1976, 2d edit., 1987, On Being a Christian and a Lawyer, 1981, American Legal Ethics, 1985, Faith and the Professions, 1987, American Lawyers and Their Communities, 1991; co-author: Lawyers, Law Students, and People, 1977, Cases in Legal Interviewing and Counseling, 1980, Property Cases, Materials and Problems, 1992, Lawyers, Clients, and Moral Responsibility, 1994; co-editor: The Mentally Retarded Citizen and the Law, 1976; contbr. articles to legal jours. Served with USAF, 1953-57. Frances Lewis scholar Washington and Lee U., 1979; recipient Emil Brown Found. Preventive Law prize, 1966, Presdl. citation U. Notre Dame, 1975, St. Thomas More award St. Mary's U., 1983, Law medal Gonzaga U., 1991, Jour. Law and Religion award, 1993. Mem. Ind. State Bar Assn., Soc. Christian Ethics, Jewish Law Assn. Roman Catholic. Home: 1865 Champlain Dr Niles MI 49120-8935 Office: U Notre Dame Law Sch Notre Dame IN 46556

SHAFFNER, PATRICK NOEL, architectural engineering executive; b. Burlington, N.C., Nov. 1, 1939; s. Samuel Hubert and Martha Jane (Noel) Shaffner; m. Patricia Anne Anders, June 12, 1961; children: Scott Anders, Kimberly Page, Melissa Hope. BS, Va. Poly. and State U., 1961. Registered profl. engr., Va. and others. Structural engr. Hayes, Seay, Mattern & Mattern, Roanoke, Va., 1963-68; sr. structural engr. Sherertz & Franklin, Roanoke, 1968-72; ptnr. Sherertz, Franklin, Crawford, Shaffner, Roanoke, 1972-87; chmn., CEO Sherertz, Franklin, Crawford, Shaffner, Inc., Roanoke, 1988—. Bd. dirs. Delta Dental, Mill Mt. Theatre, Va. Tech. Coll. Engring. Com. 100, Am. Heart Assn.; chmn. ARC. Capt. Corps. Engrs., U.S. Army, 1961-63. Paul Harris fellow. Fellow ASCE; mem. AIA (assoc.), Soc. Am. Mil. Engrs., Roanoke Regional C. of C. (Small Bus. Person of Yr. 1991), Rotary (pres. Roanoke club 1986). Republican. Baptist. Lodge: Rotary (Roanoke) (pres. 1986). Home: 2635 Turnberry Rd Salem VA 24153-7483 Office: Sherertz Franklin Crawford Shaffner Inc 305 S Jefferson St Roanoke VA 24011-2000

SHAFRAN, HANK, public relations executive; b. Boston, Nov. 13, 1945; s. Milton and Pauline (Hoffman) S.; m. Jane D. Shafran, Aug. 11, 1969 (div. Apr. 1982); children: Michael, Debra; m. Antoinette M. Delisi, July 26, 1987. BS, Boston U., 1968. Account exec. Burson-Marsteller, N.Y.C., 1968-71; exec. asst. to dir. Gov.'s Com. on Criminal Justice, Boston, 1971-77; dir. communications Computer Libr. Systems Inc., Newton, Mass., 1977-78; dir. pub. rels. Arnold & Co., Boston, 1979-83; dep. commr. Mass. Dept. Commerce, Boston, 1983-84; exec. v.p., ptnr. Cone Comms., Boston, 1984-91; comms. and pub. rels. cons., 1991—. V.p. Ronald McDonald House, Brookline, Mass., 1979—. Mem. Counselors Acad. Pub. Rels. Soc. Am., Pub. Rels. Soc. Am. (v.p. Boston chpt.), New Eng. Broadcasting Assn., Advt. Club of Greater Boston, Publicity Club of New Eng. Democrat. Jewish. Avocation: music.

SHAFRITZ, DAVID ANDREW, physician, research scientist; b. Phila., Oct. 5, 1940; s. Saul and Ethel (Kohn) S.; m. Sharon C. Klemow, Aug. 16, 1964; children: Gregory S., Adam B., Keith M. AB in Chemistry with honors, U. Pa., 1962, MD, 1966. Diplomate Nat. Bd. Med. Examiners, Am. Bd. Internal Medicine. Intern, then asst. resident U. Md. Hosp., Balt., 1966-68; rsch. assoc. NIH, Bethesda, Md., 1968-71; clin. and rsch. fellow Mass. Gen. Hosp., Boston, 1971-73; instr. Harvard Med. Sch., Boston, 1971-73, asst. prof. medicine, 1973; asst. prof. medicine and cell biology Albert Einstein Coll. Medicine, Yeshiva U., Bronx, N.Y., 1973-76, assoc. prof., 1976-81, prof. medicine and cell biology, 1981—, dir. Marion Bessin Liver Rsch. Ctr., 1985—, Herman Lapota prof. liver disease rsch., 1992—; cons. integrated Genetics, Inc., Framingham, Mass., 1981-86, Immuno, Vienna, Austria, 1986-91, Innovir, Inc., N.Y.C., 1991—, Eugenetech Internat., Inc., Ramsey, N.J., 1991-93; temp. advisor WHO, Geneva, 1983; mem. Nat. Com. for Clin. Lab. Stds., Villanova Pa., 1983—, sci. adv. bd. com. liver cancer program Inst. for Cancer Rsch., Fox Chase and Phila., 1987—, mem. rev. panel C. study sect. Nat. Inst. Diabetes and Digestive Kidney Diseases, 1988-92; mem. cen. coord. com. Liver Tissue Procurement and Distbn. Sys., 1986, Nat. Inst. Health Metabolic Pathology Study sect., 1995—; mem. Nat. Bd. Med. Examiners and U.S. Med. Exam. Com., 1996—. Co-author: The Liver: Biology and Pathobiology, 1982, 3rd edit., 1993, Hepatobiliary Diseases, 1991; assoc. editor Hepatology, 1981-86; mem. editl. bd. Jour. Med. Virology, 1982-93, Hepatology, 1990—, Jour. Virology, 1992—; contbr. numerous rsch. articles and revs. to profl. publs.; contbr. chpts. to books; patentee in field. Trustee Westchester Jewish Ctr., Mamaroneck, N.Y., 1980-86. Lt. comdr. USPHS, 1968-71. Recipient Merck award U. Pa., 1962, Morton McCutcheon Meml. Rsch. prize Sch. Medicine, 1966, Career Scientist award Irma T. Hirschl Trust, N.Y.C., 1974-79, NIH Merit award, 1994; European Molecular Biology Orgn. fellow, 1978; recipient Rsch. Career Devel. award NIH, 1975-80, spl. rsch. fellow, 1971-73, rsch. grantee, 1974—. Mem. Am. Assn. for Study of Liver Diseases, Internat. Assn. for Study of Liver, Am. Gastroenterol. Assn., Am. soc. Biochemistry and Molecular Biology, Am. Soc. Investigative Pathology, Am. Soc. Clin. Investigation, Assn. Am. Physicians, N.Y. Acad. Scis., Harvey Soc., Interurban Clin. Club. Democrat. Jewish. Avocations: jogging, tennis. Home: 4 Pheasant Run Larchmont NY 10538-3423 Office: Yeshiva U Albert Einstein Coll Med Marion Bessin Liver Rsch Ctr 1300 Morris Park Ave Bronx NY 10461-1926

SHAFTMAN, FREDRICK KRISCH, telephone communication executive, lawyer; b. Roanoke, Va., Apr. 9, 1948; s. Sydney and Rosalie (Krisch) S.; m. Diane Hasson, Dec. 27, 1970; children: Stephanie, Emily. BSBA, U. Ala., 1970, JD, 1973. Bar: Va. 1973. Gen. counsel Bell South Communication Systems (formerly Universal Communication Systems, Inc.), Roanoke, 1973-74, v.p., gen. counsel, 1974-79, pres., 1979-84, chief exec. officer, 1984—, also bd. dirs.; v.p. Am. Motor Inns, Inc. Bd. dirs. United Way of Roanoke Valley, Roanoke Mill Mountain Zoo; trustee North Cross Country Day Sch., Roanoke, Roanoke Valley Sci. Mus., Roanoke Valley Red Cross. Recipient Pres.'s Disting. Service award N.Am. Telecommunication Assn., 1985, Achievement award United Jewish Assn., 1989. Mem. N.Am. Telephone Assn. (bd. dirs.), Western Va. Better Bus. Bur. (bd. dirs.), ABA, Va. State Bar Assn. Lodge: Rotary. Office: Bellsouth Comm Systems 1936 Blue Hills Dr NE Roanoke VA 24012-8608

SHAFTO, ROBERT AUSTIN, insurance company executive; b. Council Bluffs, Iowa, Sept. 15, 1935; s. Glen Granville and Blanche (Radigan) S.; m. Jeanette DeFino, Dec. 17, 1954; children: Robert, Dennis, Teri, Shari, Michael. BS in Actuarial Sci., Drake U., Des Moines, 1959. Mgr. computer svcs. Guarantee Mut. Life Ins. Co., Omaha, 1959-65; v.p. Beta div. Electronic Data Systems, Dallas, 1965-71; from 2d v.p. to v.p. for computer systems devel. and info. svcs. New England Mutual Life Ins. Co., Boston, 1972-75, sr. v.p. policy holder and computer svcs., 1975-81, adminstrv. v.p., 1981-82, exec. v.p. individual ins. ops., 1982-86, exec. v.p. ins. and employee benefits ops., 1986-88, pres. ins. and personal fin. svcs., 1988-90, pres., chief oper. officer, 1990-92, pres., CEO, 1992-93, pres., CEO, chmn., 1993—, also bd. dirs.; bd. dirs., pres. New Eng. Variable Life, Fleet Bank of Mass., Am. Coun. Life Ins. Bd. overseers Children's Hosp., Boston, 1989—; mem. corp. Dana Farber Cancer Inst., Northwestern U.; bd. dirs. United Way of Mass; trustee Am. Coll. Mem. Greater Boston C. of C. (bd. dirs.). Roman Catholic. Avocations: tennis, golf, scuba diving, jogging. Office: New Eng Mut Life Ins Co 501 Boylston St Boston MA 02116-3706*

SHAGAM, MARVIN HÜCKEL-BERRI, private school educator; b. Monongalia, W.Va.; s. Lewis and Clara (Shagam) S. AB magna cum laude, Washington and Jefferson Coll., 1947; postgrad., Harvard Law Sch., 1947-48, Oxford (Eng.) U., 1948-51. Tchr. Mount House Sch., Tavistock, Eng., 1951-53, Williston Jr. Sch., Easthampton, Mass., 1953-55, Westtown (Pa.) Sch., 1955-58, The Thacher Sch., Ojai, Calif., 1958—; dept. head Kurasini Internat. Edn. Centre, Dar-es-Salaam, Tanzania, 1966-67, Nkumbi Internat. Coll., Kabwe, Zambia, 1967-68; vol. visitor Prisons in Calif., 1980—, Calif. Youth Authority, 1983—; sr. youth crisis counsellor InterFace, 1984—. 1st lt. M.I. res. U.S. Army, 1943-56. Danforth Found. fellow, 1942; Coun. for the Humanities fellow, Tufts U., 1983. Mem. Western Assn. Schs. and Colls. (accreditation com.), Great Teaching (Cooke chair 1977—), Phi Beta Kappa, Delta Sigma Rho, Cum Laude Soc. Republican. Avocations: hiking, camping, travel.

SHAGAN, STEVE, screenwriter, novelist, film producer; b. N.Y.C., Oct. 25, 1927; s. Barnet Harry and Rachel (Rosenzweig) S.; m. Elizabeth Leslie Florance, Nov. 18, 1956; 1 son, Robert William. Grad. high sch. Film technician Consol. Film, Inc., N.Y.C., 1952-56, RCA, Cape Canaveral, Fla., 1956-59; asst. to publicity dir. Paramount Pictures, Hollywood, Calif., 1962-63. Prodr.: (TV series) Tarzan, 1966; prodr., writer movies for TV, Universal and CBS, Hollywood, Calif., 1968-70; writer original screenplay: Save the Tiger, 1972 (Writers Guild award, Acad. award nominee 1973); prodr. film, author screenplay: City of Angels (produced as movie Hustle), 1975, novel, screenplay The Formula, 1979, screenplay Voyage of the Damned, 1976 (Acad. award nominee); writer, prodr. film The Formula, 1980; author: (novels) Save the Tiger, 1972, City of Angels, 1975, The Formula, 1979, The Circle, 1982, The Discovery, 1985, Vendetta, 1986, Pillars of Fire, 1989, A Cast of Thousands, 1993, (screenplays) Primal Fear, 1996, The John Gotti Story, 1996. Served with USCG, 1944-46. Mem. Writers Guild Am. (bd. dirs. West chpt. 1978-82). Office: care Michael Mesnick CPA 11300 W Olympic Blvd Los Angeles CA 90064-1637

SHAH, BIPIN CHANDRA, banker; b. Bombay, July 23, 1938; s. Manilal and Keshar Shah; m. Fay Shah, 1962 (div. 1985); m. Ellen T. Dever, Sept. 20, 1985 (div. 1992); children: Nelie, Sarah Lynn, Genevieve. BA, Baldwin-Wallace Coll., 1962; MA, U. Pa., 1965. Pres. Vertex Systems, Inc., King of Prussia, Pa., 1970-74; sr. v.p. Fed. Res. Bank, Phila., Pa., 1974-78, Am. Express, N.Y.C., 1979-80; exec. v.p. Phila. Nat. Bank, 1980-84; exec. v.p. CoreStates Fin. Corp., Phila., 1984-86, vice chmn., 1986-89, COO, 1990-91; pres., CEO Gensar Holdings, Inc., Ft. Washington, Pa., 1991—; bd. dirs. VISA, USA, San Matteo, Calif., Franklin Inst., Phila., Phila. Internat. Bank, N.Y.C., U.S. Pro Indoor Tennis, Phila.; chmn. bd. dirs. CoreStates Bank Del., Wilmington. Fund raiser Phila. Indoor Tennis, 1985-88. Mem. Union League. Republican. Avocations: reading, golf, tennis, fishing. Office: Gensar Holdings Inc Highland Office Ctr 550 Pinetown Rd Fort Washington PA 19034-9999

SHAH, HARESH C., civil engineering educator; b. Godhra, Gujarat, India, Aug. 7, 1937; s. Chandulal M. and Rama Shah; m. Mary-Joan Dersjant, Dec. 27, 1965; children: Hemant, Mihir. BEngring., U. Poona, 1959; MSCE, Stanford U., 1960, PhD, 1963. From instr. to assoc. prof. U. Pa., Phila., 1962-68; assoc. prof. civil engring. Stanford (Calif.) U., 1968-73, prof., 1973—, chmn. dept. civil engring., 1985-94, John A. Blume prof. engring., 1988-91, Obayashi prof. engring., 1991—, dir. Stanford Ctr. for Risk Analysis, 1987-94; bd. dirs. 1st Indo Am. Bank, San Francisco, Stanford Mgmt. Group, Inc., Risk Mgmt. Solutions, Inc.; cons. in field; pres. World Seismic Safety Initiative, 1994——. Author 1 book; contbr. over 250 articles to profl. jours. Mem. ASCE, Am. Concrete Inst., Earthquake Engring. Rsch. Inst., Seismol. Soc. Am., Sigma Xi, Tau Beta Pi. Avocations: hiking, climbing, travel. Office: Stanford U Dept Civil Engring Stanford CA 94305

SHAH, JAMES M., actuarial consultant; b. Amadhara, India, Feb. 4, 1943; came to U.S., 1980; s. Manekchand Keshrichand and Kamuben Manekchand Shah S.; m. Urmila Jashwantlal Shah, May 16, 1966; children: Meeta, Keena, Jatin. BS, Gujarat U., India, 1965; MS, Gujarat U., 1969; MA, Georgetown U., 1983; MS, U. Nebr., 1986. Sr. rsch. asst. Nat. Inst. Rural Devel., Hyderabad, India, 1972-74; rsch. officer Population Ctr. World Bank Population Project, Bangalore, India, 1974-77; actuarial analyst Shelby (Ohio) Ins. Co., 1987-90; actuary ins. dept. State of N.D., Bismarck, 1990-91; pres. A S D Consulting Svcs., Mansfield, Ohio, 1991—. Contbr. articles to profl. jours. UN fellow Ministry of Fgn. Affairs, 1978; recipient Outstanding Young Person award Garden City Jaycees, 1977, 7th Summer Seminar award U. Hawaii, 1976. Mem. Internat. Union for Sci. Study of Population, Soc. Actuaries (cert. 1994), Am. Acad. Actuaries (cert. 1994). Avocations: travel, reading, table tennis. Home: 3381 Clearview Ave Columbus OH 43221-1623 Office: A S D Consulting Svcs 91 S Ireland Blvd Mansfield OH 44906-2220

SHAH, MANU HIRACHAND, civil and structural engineer; b. Bardoli, Gujrat, India, May 14, 1936; came to U.S., 1959; s. Hirachand N. and Gulabben H. Shah; m. Ila M. Shah, Dec. 14, 1962; children: Paras, Pamona, Punam. BE Civil, Victoria Jubilee Tech. Inst., Bombay, 1958; MS Structural, U. Ill., 1960. Registered structural engr., Ill; registered profl. engr., 16 states. Design engr. Patel Engring., Bombay, 1958-59; project engr. Skidmore Owings & Merril, Chgo., 1960-73, Alfred Benesch & Co., Chgo., 1974-75; owner, pres. Shah Engring., Inc., Chgo., 1976—; pres. Chgo. Archtl. Assistance Ctr., 1985, bd. dirs., 1976-85. Mem. Zoning Bd. of Appeal, Village of Oak Brook, 1992—; pres. India Assn. Met. Chgo., 1965. Mem. ASCE, NSPE, Am. Concrete Inst. (bd. dirs. Chgo. chpt. 1984-85), Structural Engrs. Assn. Ill. (bd. dirs. 1982-85), Jain Soc. (coord. Chgo. 1986-887), Jain Social Group (pres. Chgo. 1986-87), Midwest Club (Oak Brook) (trustee, chmn. archtl. com. 1986-90, 1993—), Toastmasters (pres. Speakers Forum 1976-77). Achievements include constrn. inspection of Kennedy Expressway and Lake Shore Dr., design and constrn. mgmt. of Metra's Kensington Yard facility, design of improvements on CTA Lake St. and North Main Line, rehab. of high rise bldg. at Cabrini Green. Home: 1510 Midwest Club Pky Oak Brook IL 60521-2521 Office: Shah Engring Inc 1 E IBM Plz Ste 3200 Chicago IL 60611-3586

SHAH, RAMESH KESHAVLAL, engineering educator, researcher; b. Bombay, India, Sept. 23, 1941; came to U.S., 1963; s. Keshavlal M. and Hiraben K. (Kothari) S.; m. Rekha R. Maniar, Jan. 22, 1968; children: Nilay R., Nirav R. BME, Gujarat U., Ahmedabad, Gujarat, 1963; MS, Stanford U., 1964, ME, 1970, PhD in Mech. Engring., 1972. Project engr. Air Preheater Co., Wellsville, N.Y., 1964-66, Avco-Lycoming, Charleston, S.C., 1968-69; rsch. engr. Delphi Harrison Thermal Systems GM, Lockport, N.Y., 1971-75; tech. dir. rsch. Delphi Harrison Thermal Systems GM, Lockport, N.Y., 1983-88; sr. staff rsch. scientist Harrison Radiator Div., GM, Lockport, N.Y., 1989-95; chmn. dept. mech. engring. U. Ky., Lexington, 1995—; tchr. short courses, presenter keynote lectrs., seminars on heat exchanger design at various univs. and rsch. insts. in U.S., India, Can., U.K., Turkey, Yugoslavia, Fed. Republic of Germany, People's Republic of China, Japan, Australia, Argentina, Brazil, Portugal, Czechoslovakia, Hungary, Taiwan, South Korea, Israel, Belgium, Sweden, Lithuania, Russia, Greece, Italy, Malta, Singapore, Ukraine. Author: (with A.L. London) Laminar Flow Forced Convection in Ducts, Suppl. 1 to Advances in Heat Transfer, 1978; editor: (with S. Kakac and A.E. Bergles) Low Reynolds Number Flow Heat Exchangers, 1983, (with S. Kakac and W. Aung) Handbook of Single-Phase Convective Heat Transfer, 1987, (with E.C. Subbarao and R.A. Mashelkar) Heat Transfer Equipment Design, 1988, (with E.N. Ganic and K.T. Yang) Experimental Heat Transfer, Fluid Mechanics and Thermodynamics, 1988, (with A.D. Kraus and D.E. Metzger) Compact Heat Exchangers: A Festschrift for Professor A.L. London, 1990, (with H. Md. Roshan, V.M.K. Sastri and K.A. Padmanabhan) Thermomechanical Aspects of Manufacturing and Materials Processing, 1991, (with J.F. Keffer and E.N. Ganic) Experimental Heat Transfer, Fluid Mechanics and Thermodynamics, 1991, (with A. Hashemi) Aerospace Heat Exchanger Technology, 1993, (with M.D. Kelleher, K.R. Sreenivasan and Y. Joshi) Experimental Heat Transfer, Fluid Mechanics and Thermodynamics, 1993, (with S.P. Sukhatme, V. Venkat Raj and V.M.K. Sastri) Heat and Mass Transfer, 1994, (with G.P. Celata) Two-Phase Flow Modelling and Experimentation, 1995; editor 12 symposium vols.; founding co-editor, editor-in-chief Exptl. Thermal and Fluid Sci., 1987-95; tech. papers reviewer ASME Jour. Heat Transfer, Internat. Jour. Heat and Mass Transfer, Jour. Numerical Heat Transfer, AIChE Jour., ASME Jour. Fluids Engring., Heat Transfer Engring. Jour., numerous fgn. jours. NSF grantee (9) 1981-95; NATO grantee (4) 1980-87; UN grantee 85-86, 88-89. Fellow ASME (Region III Tech. Achievement award 1979, Valued Svc. award 1986, 87, 92, 50th Anniversary award of Heat Transfer Divsn. 1988, Charles Russ Richards Meml. award 1989); mem. Soc. Automotive Engrs., Indian Soc. Heat and Mass Transfer (life), Associacao Brasileira de Ciencias Mechanicas, Niagara Frontier Assn. R and D Dirs. Jain. Avocations: travel, reading, bridge. Office: University of Kentucky Dept Mechanical Engineering Lexington KY 40506-0108

SHAH, SHIRISH ANANTLAL, pharmacist; b. Bombay, India, Apr. 26, 1938; s. Anantlal T. and Lilavati A. (Choksi) S.; m. Portia Rose Dahling, Apr. 30, 1966; children: Sanjay, Kishan, Kinnari. BS in Pharmacy, U. Bombay, 1961; MS, U. Conn., 1964; PhD, U. Iowa, 1975. Scientist product devel. Armour Pharm. Co., Kankakee, Ill., 1963-69; head pharm. product devel. sect. Pennwalt Corp., Rochester, N.Y., 1969-72; sr. pharm. scientist USV Pharm. Corp., Tuckahoe, N.Y., 1975-76; asst. mgr. pharm. research Johnson & Johnson Baby Products Co., Piscataway, N.J., 1976-79; dir. research and tech. services Zenith Labs., Inc., Northvale, N.J., 1979-85; v.p. devel. and tech. affairs Lemmon Co., Sellersville, Pa., 1985-87; dir. product devel. Ciba Consumer Pharm., Edison, N.J., 1988-89; mgr. R&D DuPont Pharm., Garden City, N.Y., 1990-91; mgr. new product devel. Perrigo Co., Allegan, Mich., 1992—. Mem. Am. Assn. Pharm. Scientists, Am. Pharm. Assn., Drug Info. Assn., Am. Chem. Soc., Rho Chi, Phi Lamda Upsilon. Hindu. Lodge: Masons. Home: 607 Springwood Dr Kalamazoo MI 49009-9390

SHAH, SHIRISH KALYANBHAI, computer science educator, chemistry and environmental science educator; b. Ahmedabad, India, May 24, 1942; came to U.S., 1962, naturalized, 1974; s. Kalyanbhai T. and Sushilaben K. S.; B.S. in Chemistry and Physics, St. Xavier's Coll., Gujarat U., 1962; PhD in Phys. Chemistry, U. Del., 1968; cert. in bus. mgmt. U. Va., 1986; PhD in Cultural Edn. (hon.) World U. West, 1986; m. Kathleen Long, June 28, 1973; 1 son, Lawrence. Asst. prof. Washington Coll., Chestertown, Md., 1967-68; dir. quality control Vita Foods, Chestertown, 1968-72; asst. prof., assoc. prof. sci., adminstr. food, marine sci. and vocat. programs Chesapeake Coll., Wye Mills, Md., 1968-76; assoc. prof., prof. sci., chmn. dept. tech. studies Community Coll. of Balt., 1976-91; assoc. prof. chemistry Coll. Notre Dame of Md., 1991—; advisor to Young Republicans, 1992—; chmn. computer systems and engring. techs., 1982-89, coord. tech. studies, 1989-91; mem. Balt. City Adult Edn. Adv. Com., 1982-89; chmn. Coll. wide computer user com., 1985-91; permanent mem. Rep. Senatorial Com.; charter mem. Rep. Presdl. Task Force. Mem. com. Am. Lung Assn., 1971-80; mem. Congl. Adv. Com., 1983—. Fellow Am. Inst. Chemists; mem. IEEE, APHA, Am. Chem. Soc., (chmn.-elect Md. sect. 1995-96, chmn. 1996), Assn. Indsl. Hygiene, Data Processing Mgmt. Assn., Nat. Environ. Tng. Assn., Nat. Sci. Tchrs. Assn., Nat. Assn. Indsl. Tech. (dir. local region, bd. accreditors), Am. Vocat. Assn., Am. Tech. Edn. Assn., Am. Fedn. Tchrs., Md. State Tchrs. Assn., Md. Assn. Community and Jr. Colls. (v.p. 1977-78, pres. 1978—), Sigma Xi, Epsilon Pi Tau, Iota Lambda Sigma Nu. Jain, Roman Catholic. Contbr. articles on sci. and tech. to profl. jours. Home: 5605 Purlington Way Baltimore MD 21212-2950 Office: Coll Notre Dame Dept Chem 4701 N Charles St Baltimore MD 21210-2404

SHAH, SURENDRA POONAMCHAND, engineering educator, researcher; b. Bombay, Aug. 30, 1936; s. Poonamchand C. and Maniben (Modi) S.; m. Dorothie Crispell, June 9, 1962; children: Daniel S., Byron C. BE, B.V.M. Coll. Engring., India, 1959; MS, Lehigh U., 1960; PhD, Cornell U., 1965. Asst. prof. U. Ill., Chgo., 1966-69, assoc. prof., 1969-73, prof., 1973-81; prof. civil engring Northwestern U., Evanston, Ill., 1981—, dir. Ctr. for Concrete and Geomaterials, 1987—; dir. NSF Sci. and Tech. Ctr. for Advanced Cement-Based Materials Northwestern U., 1989—, Walter P. Murphy prof. of engring., 1992—; cons. govt. agys. and industry, U.S.A., UN, France, Switzerland, People's Republic China, Denmark, The Netherlands; vis. prof. MIT, 1969, Delft U., The Netherlands, 1976, Denmark Tech. U., 1984, LCPC, Paris, 1986, U. Sidney, Australia, 1987; NATO vis. sci. Turkey, 1992. Co-author: Fiber Reinforced Cement Composites, 1992, High Performance Concrete and Applications, 1994, Fracture Mechanics of Concrete, 1995; contbr. more than 400 articles to profl. jours.; editor 12 books; mem. editorial bds. 4 internat. jours.; editor-in-chief Jour. Advanced Based Materials. Recipient Thompson award ASTM, Phila., 1983, Disting. U.S. Vis. Scientist awrd Alexander von Humboldt Found., 1989, Swedish Concrete award, Stockholm, 1993, Engring. News Record award of Newsmaker, 1995. Fellow Am. Concrete Inst. (chmn. tech. com., Anderson award 1989), Internat. Union Testing and Rsch. Labs. Materials and Structures (chmn. tech. com. 1989—, Gold medal 1980); mem. ASCE (past chmn. tech. com., mem. exec. com.). Home: 921 Isabella St Evanston IL 60201-1773 Office: Northwestern U Tech Inst Rm A130 2145 Sheridan Rd Evanston IL 60208-0834

SHAH, VINOD PURUSHOTTAM, research scientist; b. Baroda, Gujarat, India, Sept. 2, 1939; came to U.S., 1960; s. Purushottam and Taraben Shah.; m. Manjula Shah, Feb. 18, 1965; children: Manish, Sujata. B in Pharmacy, U. Madras, 1959; PhD in Pharm. Chemistry, U. Calif., San Francisco, 1964. Pharm. R & D chemist Sarabhai Chems., Baroda, India, 1964-69; postdoctoral rsch. fellow U. Calif., San Francisco, 1969-75; sr. rsch. chemist, tech. coord. FDA, Washington, 1975-81; pharmacokinetic reviewer FDA, Rockville, Md., 1981-84, br. chief, 1984-88, asst.. dir., 1988-90, assoc. dir., 1990-94, sr. rsch. scientist, 1994—. Editor: Integration of Pharmocokinetics, Pharmacodynamics and Toxicokinetics in Reational Drug Development, 1993, Topical Drug Bioavailability, Bioequivalence and Penetration, 1993; contbr. articles to profl. jours.; adv. bd. Skin Pharmacology Jour., 1987-92. Recipient Gold medal U. Madras, 1959. Fellow Am. Assn. Pharm. Scientists (co-chair sci. workshops 1986—), Am. Pharm. Assn. Achievements include development of vitro release/dissolution methodology for topical, transdermal and water insoluble drug dosage forms for use as a quality control test. Home: 11309 Dunleith Pl North Potomac MD 20878 Office: FDA 7500 Standish Pl Rockville MD 20855

SHAHEEN, GEORGE T., management consultant; b. 1944. Mng. ptnr.-cons. for N.Am., Andersen Worldwide Orgn., until 1989; mng. ptnr. Andersen Cons. LLP, Chgo., 1989—. Office: Arthur Andersen & Co 69 W Washington St Chicago IL 60602-3004*

SHAHEEN, MICHAEL EDMUND, JR., lawyer, government official; b. Boston, Aug. 5, 1940; s. Michael Edmund and Dorothy Wallace (Cameron) S.; m. Polly Adair Dammann, Sept. 11, 1976; children: Michael Edmund, Timothy Andrew. B.A., Yale U., 1962; LL.B., Vanderbilt U., 1965. Bar: Tenn. 1968. Dir. ann. capital support fund, instr. physics Memphis Univ. Sch., 1965-66; law clk. Judge Robert M. McRae, Jr., Memphis, 1966-68; individual practice law Tenn., Miss., 1968-73; dep. chief voting and public accomodations sect. Dept. Justice, Washington, 1973-74, dep. chief fed. programs sect., civil rights div., 1974-75; counsel to Atty. Gen. for Intelligence, 1975; spl. adv. to atty. gen., counsel, dir. Office Profl. Responsibility, 1975—; mayor, Como, Miss., 1970-73; pres. Como Resources, Inc., 1971-72; mcpl. judge, Como, 1970-73; chmn. Como Indsl. Devel. Commn., 1970-73. Mem. Phi Delta Phi, Zeta Psi. Office: Dept Justice 10th Constitution Ave NE Washington DC 20530-0001

SHAIMAN, MARC, composer, arranger, orchestrator; b. Newark, Oct. 22, 1959; s. William Robert and Claire (Goldfein) S. Composer (films) Misery, 1990, City Slickers, 1991, The Addams Family, 1991, Father of the Bride, 1991, Sister Act, 1992, A Few Good Men, 1992, Mr. Saturday Night, Sleepless in Seattle, 1992 (Acad. award nominee for best song), A Wink and a Smile, City Slickers II, 1994, Heart and Souls, 1993, Addams Family Values, 1993, North, Speechless, The American President, 1995 (Acad. award nominee for best achievement in music 1996); (Broadway and off Broadway shows) Bette Midler's Divine Madness, Harry Connick Jr. in Concert, Peter Allen in Concert, Leader of the Pack, Legends with Mary Martin and Carol Channing; record producer, arranger Bette Midler's Thighs and Whispers, Divine Madness, Beaches, When Harry Met Sally, We Are in Love, Some Peoples Lives; producer various concerts by artists including Barbara Streisand, Billy Crystal, Barry Manilow, Luther Vandross, Raquel Welch; film music adaptations, supervision include When Harry Met Sally, Beaches, Scenes from a Mall, For the Boys; composer, arranger (TV shows) Saturday Night Live, various Acad., Grammy, and Emmy awards shows, (HBO spls.) Martin Short, Robin Williams, Bette Midler, Billy Crystal; actor (films) Broadcast News, Hot Shots. Address: Kelly Bush Pub Rels 2047 Glencoe Way Los Angeles CA 90068-3129 also: The Kraft-Benjamin Agency 8491 W Sunset Blvd Ste 492 West Hollywood CA 90069-1911

SHAIN, HAROLD, magazine publisher. Publisher Newsweek, N.Y.C. Office: Newsweek Inc The Washington Post Co 251 W 57th St New York NY 10019*

SHAIN, IRVING, retired chemical company executive and university chancellor; b. Seattle, Jan. 2, 1926; s. Samuel and Selma (Blockoff) S.; m. Mildred Ruth Udell, Aug. 31, 1947; children—Kathryn A., Steven T., John R., Paul S. B.S. in Chemistry, U. Wash., 1949, Ph.D. in Chemistry, 1952. From instr. to prof. U. Wis., Madison, 1952-75, vice chancellor, 1970-75, chancellor, 1977-86; provost, v.p. acad. affairs U. Wash., Seattle, 1975-77; v.p. Olin Corp., Stamford, Conn., 1987-92, ret., 1992; mem. tech. adv. bd. Johnson Controls, Inc., Milw., 1980—; bd. dirs. Olin Corp., Stamford, Conn., 1982—; trustee Univ. Rsch. Park, Inc., Madison, pres., 1984-86, v.p., 1987—; mem. Nat. Commn. on Superconductivity, 1989-90. Contbr. articles on electroanalytical chemistry to profl. jours. Bd. dirs. Madison Gen. Hosp., 1972-75; v.p. Madison Cmty. Found., 1984-86. Served with U.S. Army, 1943-46, PTO. Fellow AAAS, Wis. Acad. Scis., Arts and Letters; mem. Am. Chem. Soc., Electrochem. Soc., Internat. Soc. Electrochemistry, Conn. Acad. Sci. and Engring., Phi Beta Kappa, Sigma Xi, Phi Kappa Phi. Home: 2820 Marshall Ct # 8 Madison WI 53705-2270 Office: Univ Wis Univ Rsch Park 610 Walnut St Madison WI 53705-2336

SHAINE, THEODORE HARRIS, advertising agency executive; b. N.Y.C., Apr. 8, 1947; s. Bernard Leonard and Edna (Zeman) S. B.F.A., Pratt Inst., Bklyn., 1968. Art dir. Doyle Dane Bernbach, N.Y.C., 1968-73; art supr. Carl Ally, N.Y.C., 1973-75; creative supr. Young & Rubicam, N.Y.C., 1975-77; sr. v.p. Marschalk Co., N.Y.C., 1977-79; assoc. creative dir. Della Femina, Travisano, N.Y.C., 1979-81; sr. v.p. Doyle Dane Bernbach, N.Y.C., 1981-86, Ammirati & Puris, N.Y.C., 1986-90; exec. v.p., creative dir. Hill Holiday, Boston, 1990-92; exec. v.p. BBDO, N.Y.C., 1992—; advt. cons. to V.P. George Bush 1988 Presdl. campaign; instr. Pratt Inst., Bklyn., 1979-80; lectr., instr. Sch. Visual Arts, N.Y.C., 1973-77; lectr. One Club for Art and Copy N.Y.C. 1983. Poster design represented in collection Mus. Modern Art N.Y. Named to Clio Hall of Fame, 1977, 78; recipeint One Show Gold award, One Club, 1974, 83, Art Dirs. Show Gold award, 1973, Gold Lion award Cannes Film Festival, 1989. Home: PO Box 632 Montauk NY 11954-0502 Office: BBDO NY 1285 Avenue Of The Americas New York NY 10019*

SHAINESS, NATALIE, psychiatrist, educator; b. N.Y.C., Dec. 2, 1915; d. Jack and Clara (Levy-Hart) S.; div.; children: David Spiegel, Ann Spiegel. BA in Chemistry, NYU, 1936; MD, Va. Commonwealth U., 1939. Diplomate in psychiatry; cert. in psychoanalysis. Pvt. practice N.Y.C., 1955—; faculty William Alanson White Inst. Psychiatry, Psychoanalysis, N.Y.C., 1961-81; asst. clin. prof. psychiatry N.Y. Sch. Psychiatry, N.Y.C., 1964-67; faculty med. edn. div. N.Y. Acad. Medicine, 1966-67; lectr. psychiatry Columbia U. Coll. Physicians and Surgeons, N.Y.C., 1966-80; faculty, supervising analyst L.I. Inst. Psychoanalysis, N.Y., 1980—; invited participant 1st and 2nd Internat. Conf. on Abortion, 1967, 68; research project on menstruation. Editorial bd. Jour. of the Am. Women's Med. Assn., 1985—; author: Sweet Suffering: Woman as Victim, 1984; contbr. over 100 articles to profl. jours. and over 90 profl. book revs. Mem. Physicians for Social Responsibility, Nuclear Freeze, several other anti-nuclear orgns. Fellow Am. Acad. Psychoanalysis (past trustee, organizer several panels), Am. Psychiat. Assn. (life mem., organizer several panels), N.Y. Acad. Medicine (hon.), Soc. Med. Psychoanalyst (councillor, honored for keen erudition, lively imagination and professionalism 1993); mem. Assn. for Advancement Psychotherapy, Women's Med. Assn. N.Y.C. (fin. assistance com., 1st President's award 1990). Avocations: music, the arts. Home and Office: 140 E 83rd St New York NY 10028-1931

SHAINMAN, IRWIN, music educator, musician; b. N.Y.C., June 27, 1921; s. Samuel and Gussie (Pollack) S.; m. Bernice Cohen, Aug. 29, 1948; children—Joan, Jack. B.A., Pomona Coll., 1943; M.A., Columbia, 1948; Premier Prix, Conservatoire Nat. de Musique de Paris, France, 1950. Prof. music, curator Paul Whiteman collection Williams Coll., Williamstown, Mass., 1948-91, prof. emeritus, 1991—; chmn. music dept., 1971-77, dean faculty, 1972-73, coordinator performing arts, 1973-76, Class of 1955 prof. music, 1980-91; tchr. ext. U. Mass., 1952-55, Mass. State Coll., North Adams, 1957, also Bennington Coll. Composer's Conf. and Chamber Music Ctr.; cons. advanced placement program Coll. Entrance Exam. Bd., 1969-75; mem. edn. com. Saratoga Performing Arts Ctr., 1967-68; pres. Williamstown Theatre Found., 1972-77, South Mountain Concert Assn., 1980-96. Condr., Berkshire Symphony, 1950-65, also Williams Coll. band, brass ensemble and woodwind ensemble, 1st trumpet, Albany (N.Y.) Symphony Orch., 1960-65, Vt. Symphony Orch., 1954-58; contbr. articles to profl. jours.; columnist: Berkshire Eagle; author: Avoiding Cultural Default and Other Essays, 1991. Mem. merit aid panel Mass. Arts Council, 1984. Served with AUS, 1942-45. Decorated Purple Heart, Combat Inf. badge.; N.Y. Philharmonic scholar, 1934-35; Recipient Danforth Found. Tchrs. award, 1957-58. Mem. Am. Musicological Soc., Coll. Music Assn., Music Critics Assn. Home: 88 Baxter Rd Williamstown MA 01267-2111

SHAKELY, JOHN BOWER (JACK SHAKELY), foundation executive; b. Hays, Kans., Jan. 9, 1940; s. John B. and Martha Jean (Gaston) S.; 1 child, Benton. BA, U. Okla., 1962. Vol. Peace Corps., Costa Rica, 1963-64; editor publs. Dept. Def., 1967-68; dir. devel. U. Okla., 1968-70, Resthaven Mental Health Ctr., L.A., 1970-74; pres. Jack Shakely Assocs., L.A., 1974-75; sr. adv. Grantsmanship Ctr., L.A., 1975-79, Coun. on Founds., Washington, 1979; pres. Calif. Community Found., L.A., 1980—; lectr. in field. Bd. dirs. Emergency Loan and Assistance Fund, 1985—, chair bd. dirs., 1988-93; mem., vice chair L.A. Am. Indian Commn.; bd. dirs. So. Calif. Assn. Philanthropy, 1980—, Comic Relief, 1987—; chmn. bd. dirs. Nonprofit Channel. Served to 1st lt. U.S. Army, 1965-68. Decorated Army Commendation medal; named Nat. Philanthropy Day Outstanding Exec., L.A. Com. Nat. Philanthropy Day, 1989.

SHAKESPEARE, FRANK, ambassador; b. N.Y.C., Apr. 9, 1925; s. Francis Joseph and Frances (Hughes) S.; m. Deborah Anne Spaeth, Oct. 9, 1954; children: Mark, Andrea, Fredricka. BS, Holy Cross Coll., 1945; D.Eng. (hon.), Colo. Sch. Mines, 1975; DCS (hon.), Pace U., 1979; LLD (hon.), Del. Law Sch., 1980, Sacred Heart U., 1985, U. Dallas, 1987, Pepperdine U., 1990, Nichols Coll., 1991, Marquette U., 1993, Hillsdale Coll., 1996. Formerly pres. CBS-TV Services; exec. v.p. CBS-TV Stas.; dir. USIA, 1969-73; exec. v.p. Westinghouse Electric Corp., 1973-75; pres. RKO Gen. Inc., N.Y.C., 1975-85, vice chmn., 1983-85; U.S. ambassador to Portugal Lisbon, 1985-87; U.S. ambassador to The Holy See Vatican City, 1987-89. Chmn. Heritage Found., 1975-85, dir., 1989—; chmn. Radio Free Europe/Radio Liberty, Inc., 1976-85; dir. Bradley Founhd., 1989—. Served to lt. (j.g.) USNR, 1945-46. Club: Union League. Home: 303 Coast Blvd La Jolla CA 92037-4630

SHAKLAN, ALLEN YALE, broadcast executive; b. Newark, July 10, 1945; s. David George and Esther (Sweet) S.; m. Marlene Sokoloff, July 11, 1968; children: Steven, Daniel. AB, Rutgers U., Newark, 1967, JD, 1969; LLM, NYU, 1974. Bar: N.Y., D.C. Atty. FTC, N.Y.C., 1969-71, CBS, N.Y.C., 1971-84; v.p., asst. to pres. CBS TV, N.Y.C., 1984-86, v.p. programming, news adminstrn. and sta. services, 1986-88; v.p., gen. mgr. Sta. WFOR-TV, Miami, Fla., 1989—. Mem. Nat Assn. TV Programming Execs., Fla. Assn. Broadcasters. Office: Sta WFOR-TV 8900 NW 18th Ter Miami FL 33172-2696

SHAKNO, ROBERT JULIAN, hospital administrator; b. Amsterdam, Holland, Aug. 15, 1937; came to U.S., 1939, naturalized, 1944; s. Rudy C. and Gertrude (Loeb) S.; m. Elka Linda Baum, June 10, 1962; children: Steven Lee, Deborah Sue. B.B.A. (scholar 1955), So. Methodist U., 1959; M.H.A., Washington U., St. Louis, 1961. Adminstrv. asst. Mt. Sinai Hosp., Chgo., 1961-63; assoc. adminstr. Tex. Inst. Rehab. and Research, Houston, 1963-65; asst. adminstr. Michael Reese Hosp., Chgo., 1965-70; v.p., hosp. dir. Michael Reese Hosp., 1970-73; asso. exec. dir. Cook County Hosp., Chgo., 1973-75; pres. Hackensack Med. Center, N.J., 1975-85, Mt. Sinai Med. Ctr., Cleve., 1985—; oper. trustee, sec. LAurelwood Hosp., Willoughby, Ohio; clin. instr. Washington U., St. Louis, U. Chgo., Northwestern U., Columbia U.; bd. dirs. Ohio Hosp. Ins. Co. Mem. editorial bd. Mgmt. Series, Am. Coll. Healthcare Execs. Mem. Leadership Cleve.; bd. dirs. Premier Hosp. alliance, chmn., 1994—; bd. dirs. The New Cleve. Inc., Univ. Circle Inc., Cleve., Cleve. Sight Ctr.; bd. trustees Hope Lodge, Cleve. chpt. Am. Cancer Soc.; chmn. social svcs. divsn. United Jewish Appeal, Cleve., 1987-88, chmn. health cabinet, 1990, gen. co-chmn., 1990—; chmn. Hosp. Pacesetter campaign United Way, chmn. health svcs. portfolio, 1988-89, oversight commn., 1992-93. Served to 1st lt. USAR, 1960-66. Named Young Adminstr. of Yr., Washington U., 1968. Fellow Am. Coll. Hosp. Adminstrs.; mem. Am. Hosp. Assn. (coun. urban hosps., del. coun. on met. hosps., rep. regional policy bd.), Washington U. Alumni Assn. (past pres.), Greater Cleve. Hosp. Assn. (bd. dirs.), Ohio Hosp. Assn. (bd. dirs.), Cleve. Sight Ctr. (trustee, bd. dirs.), Sigma Alpha Mu (past pres.). Home: 32050 Meadow Lark Way Pepper Pike OH 44124-5508 Office: Mt Sinai Med Ctr 1 Mount Sinai Dr Cleveland OH 44106-4191

SHAKOW, DAVID JOSEPH, law educator; b. 1945. BA, Harvard U., 1967, JD, 1970; LLM, NYU, 1976. Bar: N.Y. 1971. Law clk. to Hon. William H. Hastie Phila., 1970-71; assoc. Davis, Polk & Wardwell, N.Y.C., 1971-77; atty., adviser Office Tax Legis. Counsel U.S. Treasury, D.C., 1977-79, assoc. tax legis counsel, 1979-80, dep. tax legis. counsel, 1980-81; assoc. prof. U. Pa., Phila., 1981-87, prof. law, 1987—. Author: The Taxation of Corporation and Their Shareholders, 1991. Office: U Pa Law Sch 3400 Chestnut St Philadelphia PA 19104-6204

SHALALA, DONNA EDNA, federal official, political scientist, educator, university chancellor; b. Cleve., Feb. 14, 1941; d. James Abraham and Edna (Smith) S. AB, Western Coll., 1962; MSSC, Syracuse U., 1968, PhD, 1970; 16 hon degrees, 1981-91. Vol. Peace Corps, Iran, 1962-64; asst. to dir. met. studies program Syracuse U., 1965-69; instr. asst. to dean Syracuse U. (Maxwell Grad. Sch.), 1969-70; asst. prof. polit. sci. CUNY, 1970-72; assoc. prof. politics and edn. Tchrs. Coll. Columbia U., 1972-79; asst. sec. for policy devel. and research HUD, Washington, 1977-80; prof. polit. sci., pres. Hunter Coll., CUNY, 1980-88; prof. polit. sci., chancellor U. Wis., Madison, 1988-93; sec. Dept. HHS, Washington, 1993—. Author: Neighborhood Governance, 1971, The City and the Constitution, 1972, The Property Tax and the Voters, 1973, The Decentralization Approach, 1974. Bd. govs. Am. Stock Exch., 1981-87; trustee TIAA, 1985-89, Com. Econ. Devel., 1981-93; bd. dirs. Inst. Internat. Econs., 1981-93, Children's Def. Fund, 1980-93, Am. Ditchley Found., 1981-93, Spencer Found., 1988-93, M&I Bank of Madison, 1991-93, NCAA Found., 1991; mem. Trilateral Commn., 1988-93, Knight Commn. on Intercollegiate Sports, 1990-93; trustee Brookings Inst., 1989-93. Ohio Newspaper Women's scholar, 1958, Western Coll. Trustee scholar, 1958-62; Carnegie fellow, 1966-68; Nat. Acad. Edn. Spencer fellow, 1972-73; Guggenheim fellow, 1975-76; recipient Disting. Svc. medal Columbia U. Tchrs. Coll., 1989. Mem. ASPA, Am. Polit. Sci. Assn., Nat. Acad. Arts & Scis., Nat. Acad. Pub. Adminstrn., Coun. Fgn. Rels., Nat. Acad. Edn., Nat. Acad. Arts and Scis. Office: Dept Health and Human Svcs Office of Sec 200 Independence Ave SW Rm 615F Washington DC 20201-0004

SHALES, THOMAS WILLIAM, writer, journalist, television and film critic; b. Elgin, Ill., Nov. 3, 1953; s. Clyde LeRoy and Hulda Louise (Reko) S. BA, Am. U., 1973. Entertainment editor Washington Examiner, 1968-71; arts reporter Washington Post, 1971-77, TV editor and chief TV critic, 1977—; film critic, modular arts service Nat. Public Radio, 1970-79, film critic, Morning Edit., 1979—; adj. prof. Am. U., 1978; syndicated columnist On the Air, Washington Post Writers Group, 1979—. Author: The American Film Heritage, 1972, On the Air!, 1982, Legends, 1989. Recipient Disting. Alumnus award Am. U., 1978. Recipient Pulitzer Prize, 1988. Office: Washington Post Co 1150 15th St NW Washington DC 20071-0001

SHALHOUB, MICHAEL See SHARIF, OMAR

SHALIKASHVILI, JOHN MALCHASE, military career officer; b. Warsaw, Poland, June 27, 1936; s. Dimitri and Maria (Ruediger) S.; m. Gunhild Bartsch, Apr. 18, 1963 (dec. Aug. 1965); m. Joan E. Zimpelman, Dec. 27, 1966; 1 child, Brant. BSME, Bradley U., 1958; attended, Naval War Coll., 1969-70, U.S. Army War Coll., 1977-78; MA in Internat. Affairs, George Washington U., 1970; LLD (hon.), U. Md., 1993, Bradley U., 1994. Joined U.S. Army, 1958, advanced through grades to gen., 1992—, various troop and staff assignments Alaska, U.S., Fed. Republic of Germany, Vietnam, Korea, 1959-75; battalion comdr. 9th infantry div. U.S. Army, Ft. Lewis, Wash., 1975-77; asst. chief of staff ops. So. European Task Froce U.S. Army, Vicenza, Italy, 1978-79; comdr. div. arty., 1st Armored Div. U.S. Army, Nuernberg, Fed. Republic of Germany, 1979-81; chief., politico-mil div. U.S. Army, Washington, 1981-84; asst. div. comdr. 1st. Armored div. U.S. Army, Nuernberg, Fed. Republic of Germany, 1984-86; dir. strategy, plans, policy U.S. Army, Washington, 1986-87; comdg. gen. 9th inf. div. Ft. Lewis, Wash., 1987-89; dep. comdr.-in-chief Hdqrs. USAREUR and 7th Army, Heidelberg, Fed. Republic of Germany, 1989-91; asst. to chmn. Joint Chiefs of Staff, Washington, 1991-92; Supreme Allied Comdr. Europe, Comdr.-in-Chief U.S. Forces Europe, 1992-93; chmn. Joint Chiefs of Staff, 1993—. Bd. govs. ARC; bd. trustees Bradley U. Decorated Def. D.S.M. with two oak leaf clusters, D.S.M., Legion of Merit with two oak leaf clusters, Bronze Star with V device, Meritorious Svc. medal with three oak leaf clusters, Air medal, Joint Svc. Commendation medal, Army Commendation medal, Nat. D.S.M. with bronze svc. star, Armed Forces Expeditionary medal, Humanitarian Svc. medal, Army Svc. ribbon, Order of Combat Infantry badge, Parachutist badge, Army Staff Identification badge, Overseas Svc. ribbon with bronze Arabic numeral 5, Inter-Am. Def. Bd. medal, Vietnam Svc. medal with silver svc. star, S.W. Asia Svc. medal with bronze svc. star, Republic of Vietnam Gallantry Cross with two silver and one bronze stars, Republic of Vietnam Armed Forces Honor medal 1st class, Republic of Vietnam Campaign medal; grand cordon Order of Leopold (Belgium), (2) Order of the Mil. Merit (Brazil), grand cross with star and sash Order of Merit (Germany), grand officer Nat. Order of Merit (France), grand cordon Order of Rising Sun (Japan), May Decoration of Mil. Merit (Argentina), Nat. Security Merit Tongil (Korea); recipient Disting. Alumni Achievement award George Washington U., 1994. Mem. Assn. U.S. Army, Field Arty. Assn., Ret. Officers Assn., Coun. Fgn. Rels., Am. Acad. Achievement. Home: 110 Grant Ave Arlington VA 22211-1204

SHALITA, ALAN REMI, dermatologist; b. Bklyn., Mar. 22, 1936; s. Harry and Celia; m. Simone Lea Baum, Sept. 4, 1960; children: Judith and Deborah (twins). AB, Brown U., 1957; BS, U. Brussels, 1960; MD, Bowman Gray Sch. Medicine, 1964; DSc (hon.), L.I. U., 1990. Intern Beth Israel Hosp., N.Y.C., 1964-65; resident dept. dermatology NYU Med. Ctr., 1967-68, NIH tng. grant fellow dept. dermatology, 1968-70, instr. dermatology, 1970-71; asst. prof. NYU, 1971-73, Columbia U., N.Y.C., 1973-75; assoc. prof. medicine, head divsn. dermatology SUNY Downstate Med. Ctr., Bklyn., 1975-79, prof., 1979—, head divsn. dermatology, 1979-80, chmn. dept. dermatology, 1980—, asst. dean, 1977-83; acting dean Queens campus SUNY Downstate Med. Ctr., 1983-84; assoc. dean clin. affairs SUNY Health Sci. Ctr., Bklyn., 1989-92, assoc. provost for clin. affairs, 1992-93, assoc. v.p. clin. affairs, 1993—, disting. tchg. prof., 1996—; disting. prof. SUNY Health Sci. Ctr., Bklyn., 1996; asst. attending in dermatology Univ. Hosp., N.Y.C., 1970-73, Bellevue Hosp. Ctr., 1970-73, Manhattan VA Hosp., 1971-73, Presbyn. Hosp., 1973-75; mem. med. bd. Kings County Hosp. Ctr.; cons. dermatology Bklyn. VA Hosp., 1975—; chief dermatology Brookdale Med. Ctr., 1977-90; chief dermatology Univ. Hosp. of Bklyn., 1975—; chief dermatology Kings County Hosp. Ctr., Bklyn., 1975—, acting med. dir., 1989-92; med. dir. Univ. Hosp. Bklyn., 1992-96. Pres. Temple Shaaray Tefila, N.Y.C., 1982-86, chmn. bd. trustees, 1987-95. Lt. M.C. USNR, 1965-67. Recipient Torch of Liberty award Anti-Defamation League, 1987, Surg. and Pediatric awards Beth Israel Hosp., N.Y.C., 1965; spl. fellow NIH, 1970-73. Dem. AMA, ACP, AAAS, Am. Acad. Dermatology (bd. dirs. 1983-87, v.p. 1995-96), Soc. Investigative Dermatology, Dermatology Found. (past trustee), Am. Dermatol. Assn. (asst. sec.-treas. 1995-96, sec.-treas. 1996—), Am. Soc. Dermatol. Surgery (past bd. dirs.), Soc. Cosmetic Chemists, Assn. Profs. of Dermatology (sec.-treas. 1988-94, pres.-elect 1994-96), Internat. Soc. Tropical Dermatology, N.Y. Acad. Scis., N.Y. State Med. Soc., N.Y. Acad. Medicine, N.Y. State Dermatol. Soc., Dermatol. Soc. Greater N.Y. (pres. 1980-81), N.Y. Dermatol. Soc. (pres. 1989-90). Republican. Home: 70 E 77th St New York NY 10021-1811 Office: 450 Clarkson Ave Brooklyn NY 11203-2012 *Treat others with compassion, dignity and respect, add a little humor to everyone's life. Speak up for what you truly believe, be charitable.*

SHALKOP, ROBERT LEROY, retired museum consultant; b. Milford, Conn., July 30, 1922; s. Bertram Leroy and Dorothy Jane (Boardman) S.; m. Antoinette Joan Benkowsky, Dec. 7, 1963; 1 son, Andrew Goforth. Student, Maryville (Tenn.) Coll., 1940-42; M.A., U. Chgo., 1949; postgrad., Sorbonne, 1951-52. Dir. Rahr Civic Center, Manitowoc, Wis., 1953-56, Everhart Mus., Scranton, Pa., 1956-62, Brooks Meml. Art Gallery, Memphis, 1962-64; assoc. dir. Colorado Springs (Colo.) Fine Arts Center, also curator Taylor Mus., 1964-71; dir. Anchorage Mus. History and Art, 1972-87; pvt. practice mus. cons. Salisbury, N.C., 1987-94; archaeologist Smithsonian Instn., 1948, 50, Am. Found. Study Man, 1951, U. Wash., 1953, State U. Idaho, 1960. Author: Wooden Saints, the Santos of New Mexico, 1967, A Comparative View of Spanish Colonial Sculpture, 1968, Arroyo Hondo, the Folk Art of a New Mexican Village, 1969, A Comparative View of Spanish Colonial Painting, 1970, A Show of Color: 100 Years of Painting in the Pike's Peak Region, 1971, Russian Orthodox Art in Alaska, 1973, Sydney Laurence, an Alaskan Impressionist, 1975, Eustace Ziegler, 1977, Contemporary Native Art of Alaska, 1979, Henry Wood Elliott, 1982; Editor: An Introduction to the Native Art of Alaska, 1972; assoc. editor: Exploration in Alaska, 1980. Served with USAAF, 1942-45. Mem. Am. Assn. Museums, Internat. Council Museums. Home and Office: 309 W Marsh St Salisbury NC 28144-5345

SHALLENBERGER, GARVIN F., lawyer; b. Beloit, Wis., Jan. 7, 1921; s. Garvin D. and Grace (Hubbell) S.; m. Mary L., May 15, 1945; children: Diane, Dennis Clark. BA in Pre-law, U. Mont., 1942; JD, U. Calif., Berkeley, 1949; LLD (hon.), Western State U., Fullerton, Calif., 1988. Bar: Calif. 1949, U.S. Dist. Ct. (cent. dist.) Calif. 1949, U.S. Ct. Appeals (9th cir.) 1949, U.S. Supreme Ct. 1961, U.S. Dist. Ct. (no. and so. dists.) Calif. 1963. Rutan & Tucker, Costa Mesa, Calif.; chmn. spl. adv. com. state bar legal svcs. program, 1979-89, pub. law ctr Orange County, 1979-90. Recipient distinguished svc. award Boalt Hall (U. Calif. Berkeley); Judge Learned Hand Human Rel. award Nat. Jewish Com., 1990. Fellow Am. Coll. Trial Lawyers; mem. Am. Bd. Trial Advs. (founder and 1st sec.),Calif. Bar Assn. (bd. govs. 1975-76, pres. 1977-78; mem. com. on jud. nominees 1978-79, pres. 1980), mem. Orange County Bar Assn. (bd. dirs. 1970-71, pres. 1972, Franklin West award 1979). Democrat. Avocations: tennis, writing. Office: Rutan & Tucker 611 Anton Blvd PO Box 1950 Costa Mesa CA 92626

SHALOWITZ, ERWIN EMMANUEL, civil engineer; b. Washington, Feb. 13, 1924; s. Aaron Louis and Pearl (Myer) S.; m. Elaine Mildred Langerman, June 29, 1952; children—Ann Janet, Aliza Beth, Jonathan Avram. Student, U. Pa., U. Notre Dame, 1944-45; B.C.E., George Washington U., 1947, postgrad., 1948-49; grad. soil mechanics, Cath. U., 1951; M.A. in Pub. Adminstrn. (fellow U.S. Civil Service Commn.), Am. U., 1954. Registered profl. engr., Washington. Engr. Klemitt Engring. Co., N.Y.C., 1947; with cons. firm Whitman, Requardt & Assos., Balt., 1947-48; chief structural research engr., head def. research sect., project officer and tech. adviser for atomic tests Bur. Yards and Docks, Dept. Navy, Washington, 1948-59; supervisory gen. engr. spl. asst. for protective constrn. programs, project mgr. for bldg. systems, chief research br., chief mgmt. information, chief contracting procedures and support, chief contract evaluation and analysis, Pub. Bldgs. Service, Gen. Services Adminstrn., Washington, 1959—; also team leader/project mgr. Electronic Acquisition Sy. Pub. Bldgs. Service, Gen. Services Adminstrn., Washington; chmn. fed. exec. tng. program U.S. Civil Service Commn., 1950; fallout shelter analyst Dept. Def.; chmn. GSA Fire Safety Com., GSA Fallout Protection Com., GSA Bldg. Evaluation Com.; mem. Interagy Com. on Housing Rsch. and Bldg. Tech.; mem. Nat. Evaluation Bd. Architect-Engr. Selections; mem. standing com. on procurement policy Nat. Acad. Sci. Bldg. Research Adv. Bd. and Interagency Com. on Procurement Curriculum Rev.; coordinator pub. bldgs. design and constrn. Small Bus. Program and Minority Enterprise and Minority Subcontracting Programs. Contbr. articles profl. jours. Served to engring. officer USNR, 1944-46. Recipient Commendable Svc. award GSA, 1968, Outstanding Performance recognition, 1976, 77, 79, 83, 87, 93, 94, 95, Superior Accomplishment award, 1995, others; Engr. Alumni Achievement award George Washington U., 1985. Fellow ASCE, Am. Biog. Inst.; mem. Soc. Advancement Mgmt., Am. Biog. Inst. (nat. bd. advisors), Soc. Am. Mil. Engrs., Sigma Tau, Pi Sigma Alpha. Jewish. Home: 5603 Huntington Pky Bethesda MD 20814-1132 Office: 19th and F Sts NW Washington DC 20405 *PRINCIPLES: Look beyond the material for lasting values and meaning, optimize managerial effectiveness by creating an objective and challenging climate in an organization, delve into the underlying causes of problem areas for meaningful solutions, and persevere in spite of obstacles. IDEAS: Cultural pluralism; the intrinsic potential of each individual; and love, appreciation, and support of one's family as indispensable for real accomplishment. GOALS: To attain the highest level of professional accomplishment within my capabilities and to continue to have a rich, happy, and fulfilling family life. STANDARDS OF CONDUCT: To be fair, consistent, and straightforward; and to avoid over-reacting.*

SHAM, LU JEU, physics educator; b. Hong Kong, Apr. 28, 1938; s. T.S. and Cecilia Maria (Siu) Shen; m. Georgina Bien, Apr. 25, 1965; children: Kevin Shen, Alisa Shen. GCE, Portsmouth Coll., Eng., 1957; BS, Imperial Coll., London U., Eng., 1960; PhD in Physics, Cambridge U., Eng., 1963. Asst. rsch. physicist U. Calif. at San Diego, La Jolla, 1963-66, assoc. prof., 1968-75, prof., 1975—, chair dept. physics, 1995—, dean div. natural scis., 1985-89; asst. prof. physics U. Calif. at Irvine, 1966-67; rsch. physicist IBM Corp., Yorktown Heights, N.Y., 1974-75; reader Queen Mary Coll., U. London, 1967-68. Assoc. editor Physics Letters A., 1992—; contbr. sci. papers to profl. jours. Recipient Churchill Coll. studentship, Eng., 1960-63, Sr. U.S. Scientist award Humboldt Found., Stuttgart, Germany, 1978; fellow Guggenheim Found., 1984, Chancellor Assocs. award for Excellence in Rsch., 1995. Fellow Am. Phys. Soc.; mem. AAAS. Democrat. Avocation: tennis, folk dancing. Office: U Calif San Diego Dept Physics 0319 La Jolla CA 92093-0319

SHAMANSKY, ROBERT NORTON, lawyer; b. Columbus, Ohio, Apr. 18, 1927; s. Harry Solomon and Sarah (Greenberg) S. BA Polit. Sci. cum laude, Ohio State U., 1947; JD, Harvard U., 1950. Bar: Ohio 1950, U.S. Supreme Ct. 1963. Ptnr. Feibel, Feibel, Shamansky & Rogovin, Columbus, 1954-81; mem. U.S. House Reps., Washington, 1981-83; ptnr. Guren, Merritt, Sogg & Cohen, Columbus, Ohio, 1981-84, Benesch, Friedlander, Coplan & Aronoff, Columbus, Ohio, 1984-93; of counsel Penesch, Friedlander, Coplan & Aronoff, Columbus, Ohio, 1993; mem. Nat. Security Edn. Bd., 1994—; pres., founder Legal Aid and Defender Soc., Columbus, 1955-58; spkr. in field. Contbr. articles to newspapers. Mem. Rickenbacker Port Authority, Franklin County, Ohio, 1983-86; chmn. Indsl. Tech. and Enterprise adv. bd. State Ohio, Columbus, 1983-89. With U.S. Army, 1950-52. Mem. ABA, Ohio State Bar Assn. (chmn. legal ethics and profl. conduct com. 1970-73), Columbus Bar Assn., Columbus Housing Partnership, Inc. (sec. 1987-91, bd. dirs. 1987-95), Coun. Ethics in Econs. (bd. dirs. 1983-93), Phi Beta Kappa. Democrat. Jewish. Avocations: fgn., domestic travel, pub. policy. Home: 678 Mohawk St Columbus OH 43206 Office: Benesch Friedlander Coplan & Aronoff 88 E Broad St Columbus OH 43215-3506

SHAMASH, YACOV, dean, electrical engineering educator; b. Iraq, Jan. 12, 1950; m. Linda Shamash, June 21, 1976; children: Aharon, Hela. BSEE, Imperial Coll., London, 1970; PhD in Control Systems, Imperial Coll., 1973. Postdoctoral fellowin elec. engring. Tel-Aviv U., 1973-75, from lectr. elec. engring. to sr. lectr. elec. engring., 1975-78; prof. elec. engring. Fla. Atlantic U., Boca Raton, 1977-85; prof., chair dept. elec. engring. dept. Wash. State U., Pullman, 1985-92; dean engring. SUNY, Stony Brook, 1992—; bd. dirs. KeyTronics, Spokane, Wash., 1990—; vis. asst. prof. U. Pa., Phila., 1976-77. Contbr. over 100 articles to profl. jours., book chpts. Fellow IEEE (sr.). Office: SUNY Coll Engring & Applied Sci Stony Brook NY 11790-2200

SHAMBAUGH, GEORGE ELMER, III, internist; b. Boston, Dec. 21, 1931; s. George Elmer and Marietta Susan (Moss) S.; m. Katharine Margaret Matthews, Dec. 29, 1956 (dec.); children: George, Benjamin, Daniel, James, Elizabeth; m. Martha Repp Davis, Jan. 3, 1987. B.A., Oberlin Coll., 1954; M.D., Cornell U., 1958. Diplomate Am. Bd. Internal Medicine. Gen. med. intern Denver Gen. Hosp., 1958-59; research fellow physiologic chemistry U. Wis.-Madison, 1968-69; asst. prof. medicine Northwestern U. Med. Sch., Chgo., 1969-74, assoc. prof., 1974-81, prof., 1981—; mem. Ctr. for Endocrinology, Metabolism and Molecular Medicine, 1969—; chief endocrinology and metabolism VA Lakeside Med. Ctr., Chgo., 1974—; attending physician Northwestern Meml. Hosp., Chgo., 1969—. Contbr. articles to text books and profl. jours. Served with M.C., U.S. Army, 1959-67. NIH spl. postdoctoral fellow, 1967-69; Schweppe Found. fellow, 1972-75. Fellow ACP; mem. Am. Fedn. Clin. Rsch., Sci. Rsch. Soc., am. Endocrine Soc., Am. Thyroid Assn., Am. Inst. Nutrition, Am. Soc. Clin. Nutrition, Am. Physiol. Soc., Ctrl. Soc. Clin. Rsch., Inst. Medicine Chgo., Taipei Internat. Med. Soc. (pres. 1960), N.Y. Acad. Sci., Euro Diabetes Assn., Am. Men and Women of Sci., Sigma Xi, Nu Sigma Nu. Home: 530 S Stone Ave La Grange IL 60525-2720 Office: Northwestern Med Faculty Found Inc 303 E Ohio St Fl 460 Chicago IL 60611-3317 also: VA Lakeside Med Ctr 333 E Huron St Chicago IL 60611-3004

SHAMBUREK, ROLAND HOWARD, physician; b. Adell, Wis., June 7, 1928; s. William and Catherine (Illig) S.; m. Gladys Irene Gibbons, June 21, 1952; children: Steven J., Robert D., Daniel J. BS, U. Wis., 1950, MD, 1953; MPH, Harvard U., 1960. Diplomate: Am. Bd. Preventive Medicine. Commd. 1st lt. M.C., U.S. Army, 1953, advanced through grades to col., 1968; intern St. Joseph's Hosp., Marshfield, Wis., 1953-54; grad. U.S. Naval Sch. of Aviation Medicine, Pensacola, Fla., 1957; resident in preventive medicine USAF Sch. Aerospace Medicine, Brooks AFB, 1960-63; service in Europe, 1955-56, 63-66; comdr. 67th EVAC Hosp., Vietnam, 1970-71, U.S. Army Med. Pers. Support Agy., 1975-77; ret., 1977; exec. v.p. Aerospace Med. Assn., 1977-79; clin. practice Pentagon Health Clinic, Washington, 1981-85; med. researcher Office of Army Surgeon Gen., 1985-87. Contbr. papers in field. Decorated Legion of Merit with oak leaf cluster, Commendation medal, Meritorious Service medal. Mem. AMA (del. 1978), Assn. Mil. Surgeons (John Shaw Billings award 1968), Am. Coll. Preventive Medicine (v.p. 1968-69), Aerospace Med. Assn. (v.p. 1968-69), Soc. Med. Cons. Armed Forces, Soc. U.S. Army Flight Surgeons, Soc. NASA Flight Surgeons, Internat. Acad. Aviation and Space Medicine, Internat. Health Soc. Address: 3700 Moss Dr Annandale VA 22003-1915

SHAMES, HENRY JOSEPH, lawyer; b. Milw., Jan. 20, 1921; s. Aron and Jennie (Greenberg) S.; m. Beverly Cleveland Van Wert, June 9, 1972; children: Stephen H., Suzanne Shames Sattelmeyer, Sarah Shames Phillips, Diana Shames Strandberg. A.B., U. Chgo., 1942; J.D., Harvard U., 1948. Bar: Ill. 1949, Calif. 1962. Mem. firm Arvey, Hodes & Mantynband, Chgo., 1949-61; partner Pacht, Ross, Warne, Bernhard & Sears, Los Angeles, 1962-75, Grossman & Shames, Los Angeles, 1975-83, Rosenfeld, Parnell & Shames Inc., Los Angeles, 1984-86; counsel Patterson, Belknap, Webb and Tyler, Los Angeles, 1986-87; chmn. bd. Switzer Center, Los Angeles, 1966-73. Served with USNR, 1943-46. Mem. Assn. Bus. Trial Lawyers (bd. govs. 1973-76, v.p. 1973-76), Calif. State Bar Assn., So. Def. Counsel, Los Angeles County Bar Assn., Phi Beta Kappa. Home: 4906 La Ramada Dr Santa Barbara CA 93111-1518 Office: 1875 Century Park E Los Angeles CA 90067-2501

SHAMES, IRVING HERMAN, engineering educator; b. Oct. 31, 1923; married; 2 children. BSME, Northeastern U., 1948; MS in Applied Mechanics, Harvard U., 1949; PhD in Applied Mechanics, U. Md., 1953. Instr. U. Md., College Park, 1949-53, asst. prof. mech. engring., 1953-55; asst. prof. Stevens Inst. Tech., Hoboken, N.J., 1955-57; prof., chmn. dept. engring. sci. Pratt Inst., Bklyn., 1957-62, acting chmn. dept. physics, 1960-61; prof., chmn. div. interdisciplinary studies and research Sch. Engring. SUNY, Buffalo, 1962-70, faculty prof. engring., applied sci., 1970-73, 79—, prof., chmn. dept. engring. scis., aerospace engring. and nuclear engring., 1973-83, disting. teaching prof., 1980—; prof. George Washington U., Washington, 1995—; lectr. Naval Ordnance Lab, 1952-55; vis. prof. materials dept. Technion, Israel, 1969, mech. engring. dept., 1976; Disting. vis. prof. George Washington U., 1993. Author: Engineering Mechanics: Statics, 1959, 3d rev. edit., 1980, Engineering Mechanics: Dynamics, 1959, 3d rev. edit., 1980, Mechanics of Fluids, 1962, rev. edit., 1982, 3d edit., 1992, Mechanics of Deformable Solids, 1964, (with C. Dym) Solid Mechanics- A Variational Approach, 1973, Introduction to Statics, 1971 Introduction to Solid Mechanics, 1975, (with C. Dym) Energy and Finite Elements in Structural Mechanics, 1985, (with F. Cozzarelli) Elastic and Inelastic Stress Analysis, 1992; editor McGraw-Hill Series in Advanced Engineering; contbr. numerous articles to profl. jours.; several books translated in Portuguese, Spanish, Japanese, Korean, Chinese, Arabic. Mem. Sigma Xi, Tau Beta Pi, Phi Eta Sigma, Pi Tau Sigma, Golden Key. Home: 1113 Fairview Ct Silver Spring MD 20910-4148

SHAMMAS, NAZIH KHEIRALLAH, environmental engineering educator, consultant; b. Homs, Syria, Feb. 18, 1939; came to U.S., 1991; s. Kheirallah Hanna and Nazha Murad (Hamwi) S.; m. Norma Massouh, July 28, 1968; children: Sarmed Erick, Samer Sam. Engring. degree with distinction, Am. U., Beirut, Lebanon, 1962; MS in Sanitary Engring., U. N.C., 1965; PhD in Civil Engring., U. Mich., 1971. Instr. Civil Engring. Am. U., Beirut, Lebanon, 1965-68; asst. prof. Civil Engring. Am. U., Beirut, 1972-76; tchg. fellow U. Mich., Ann Arbor, 1968-71; asst. prof. Civil Engring. King Saud U., Riyadh, Saudi Arabia, 1976-78; assoc. prof. King Saud U., Riyadh, 1978-91; prof. Environ. Engring. Lenox (Mass.) Inst. Water Tech., 1991—, dean edn., 1992-93; sr. prof. Sr. U., 1994—; cons., ptnr. Cons. and Rsch. Engrs., Beirut, 1973-76; advisor, cons. Riyadh Water and Sanitary Drainage Authority, 1979-83, Ar-Riyadh Devel. Authority, 1977-93, Associated Consulting Engring. Team, 1994—; assoc. cons. Vakakis Internat., 1995—. cons., ptnr. Cons. and Rsch. Engrs., Beirut, 1973-76; advisor, cons. Riyadh Water and San. Drainage Authority, 1978-83, Ar-Riyadh Devel. Authority, 1977-93, Associated Cons. Engring. Team, 1994—; assoc. cons. Vakakis Internat., 1995—. Recipient block grant U. Mich., 1968-70, Excellence in Teaching award King Saud U., 1981, 84. Mem. ASCE, Water Environ. Fedn., Am. Water Works Assn., European Water Pollution Control Assn., Internat. Assn. Water Quality, Assn. Environ. Engring. Profs. Achievements include research on biological and physicochemical remediation processes, math. modeling of nitrification process, water and wastewater mgmt. in developing countries, water conservation, wastewater treatment and reuse, appropriate tech. for developing countries, multidisciplinary studies in environmental management and planning. Home: 14 Joan Dr Pittsfield MA 01201-8417 Office: Lenox Inst Water Tech 101 Yokun Ave Lenox MA 01240

SHAMMAS, NICOLAS WAHIB, internist, cardiologist; b. Amyoun, El-Koura, Lebanon, Jan. 31, 1963; came to U.S., 1988; s. Wahib Nicolas and Vera Yousuf (El-Helou) S.; m. Gail Ann Hanson, Feb. 22, 1991; children: Waheeb John, Andrew Nicolas. BSc with distinction, Am. U. Beirut, Lebanon, 1983, MD, 1987, MSc in Physiology, 1987, Diploma in Computer Programming, 1985. Postdoctoral rsch. fellow Am. U. Beirut, 1987-88; resident in internal medicine U. Iowa Hosps., Iowa City, 1988-91; instr. medicine, clin. fellow cardiology U. Rochester (N.Y.) Med. Ctr., 1991-94; fellow assoc. in cardiology U. Iowa Hosps., Iowa City, 1994-95; mem. staff Genesis Med. Ctr., Davenport, Iowa, 1995—; founder Mastermind Pub. Author: (with others) Flavors of Lebanon, 1995; contbr. articles to profl. jours. Am. U. Beirut Univ. Rsch. Bd. awardee, 1986-87, John C. Sable Meml. Heart award J.C. Sable Fund, 1993, Trainee Investigator award for clin. rsch. meeting, Balt., 1994. Mem. AMA, ACP, Am. Fedn. Clin. Rsch., Am. Soc. Internal Medicine, Am. Coll. Cardiology (affiliate), Iowa Med. Soc. Achievements include research in basic cardiology: prostacyclin inhibits aminoacid transport in myocardial cells and modulates transmembrane calcium movements; dopamine binding sites are increased in hypertrophied rat hearts induced by renovascular hypertension; myocardial viability in hybernating myocardium cannot be predicted by clinical and exercise hemodynamic criteria; coronary flow reserve is underestimated if blood flow changes are assessed using flow velocity measurements alone; pretreatment with intracoronary nitroglycerin corrects this problem. Office: Cardiovasc Medicine PC Ste 305 1230 E Rusholme Davenport IA 52803-2484

SHAMOO, ADIL ELIAS, biochemist, biophysicist, educator; b. Baghdad, Iraq, Aug. 1, 1941; came to U.S., 1964, naturalized, 1973; s. Elias M. and Mariam T. (Mansour) S.; m. Joan Hutchison, Dec. 16, 1967; children: Abraheem, Zachary, Jessica. B.Sc. in Physics, U. Baghdad, 1962; M.S. in Physics (grad. fellow), U. Louisville, 1966; Ph.D. in Biophysics, CUNY, 1970. Instr. engring. physics Speed Sch., U. Louisville, 1965-68; asst. prof. physiology City U. N.Y., 1971-73; guest worker Lab. Biophysics and Neurochemistry, NIH, Bethesda, Md., 1972-73; asst. prof. radiation biology and biophysics U. Rochester, 1973-75; guest prof. Max-Planck Inst. Biophysics, Frankfurt, West Germany, 1977-78; assoc. prof. radiation biology and biophysics U. Rochester, 1975-79; prof., chmn. dept. biol. chemistry U. Md., Balt., 1979-82, head membrane biochemistry research lab., 1982—; cons. div. biol. scis. Kodak Co., Rochester, 1976-77; NIH tng. fellow U. Louisville, 1967; investigator Am. Heart Assn., 1976-79; Neurosci. Rsch. Program fellow, Boulder, Colo., summer 1977; pres. Sci. Profls. Inc.; chmn. symposia, various coms. in field; mem. organizing coms. workshops in field. Editor (with M.W. Miller) Membrane Toxicity, 1977, Carriers and Channels in Biological Systems, 1975, Carriers and Channels in Biological Systems-Transport Proteins, 1980, Regulation of Calcium Transport Across Muscle Membranes, 1985, Principles of Research Data Audit, (with R. Verna) Biotechnology Today, 1995; editor in chief Membrane Biochemistry, 1977-83, Accountability in Research: Policies and Quality Assurance, 1988—; mem. editl. bd. Molecular and Cellular Biochemistry, 1987-94, Quality Assurance: Good Practice Regulation and Law, 1991—; contbr. articles and abstracts to profl. jours. Bd. dirs. Alliance for Mentally Ill of Md., 1990-93, Friends Med. Rsch. Ctr., Inc., 1994-97; mem. rsch. monitoring com. Nat. Alliance for Mentally Ill, bd. dirs. 1994-97; pres. faculty senate U. Md., Balt., 1993-94; mem. coun. univ. systems U. Md., 1994—; mem. adv. com. Vantage Pl., 1995—. Recipient Advocacy award Mental Health Assn. Md., 1994, Disting. Svc. award Alliance for Mentally Ill of Md., 1994. Mem. AAAS, AAUP (chpt. sec. 1971-72), Basic Sci. Council of Am. Heart Assn., Am. Soc. Biol. Chemists and Mol. Biol., Am. Coll. Sports Medicine, Am. Assn. Physics Tchrs., Am. Physiol. Soc., Biophys. Soc. (Cole Membrane Award Com. 1983-84, chmn. biophysics subgroup 1982-83, council 1986-89), Membrane Biophys. Group (chmn. 1982-83, sec.-treas. 1983-85, co-chmn. U.S. bioenergetics group 1979-80), Md. Acad. Scis. (chmn. com. programs and exhbns. 1986-87, sci. council 1985-89), N.Y. Acad. Scis., Coun. of Biology (editor 1989—), Soc. Quality Assurance. Achievements include patents for liquid scintillators. Office: 108 N Greene St Baltimore MD 21201-1503

SHAMOS, MORRIS HERBERT, physicist educator; b. Cleve., Sept. 1, 1917; s. Max and Lillian (Wasser) S.; m. Marion Jean Cahn, Nov. 26, 1942; 1 son, Michael Ian. AB, NYU, 1941, MS, 1943, PhD, 1948; postgrad., MIT, 1941-42. Faculty NYU, 1942—, prof. physics, 1959-83, prof. emeritus, 1983—; chmn. dept. Washington Sq. Coll., 1957-70; sr. v.p. research and devel. Technicon Corp., 1970-75, chief sci. officer, 1975-83, also dir., prin. sci. cons., 1983-92; pres. M.H. Shamos & Assocs., 1983—; chmn. Protein Databases, Inc., 1985-90, Sci. Imaging Corp., 1985-88; Med. Mktg. Internat., 1992-94; dir. Anagen Ltd., 1989-92, Nat. Assn for Sci., Tech. & Soc., 1990-91, Anagen Holdings, Ltd., 1992—, Xsirius, Inc., 1993—; chmn. Med. Mktg. Internat., 1992-94; Cons. pvt. industry; cons. Armament Center, USAF, 1955-57, Tung-Sol Electric, Inc., 1949-65, Office Pub. Information, UN, 1958, NBC, 1957-67, AEC, 1957-70, N.Y. Eye and Ear Infirmary, 1961-64, 79—, L.I. Jewish Hosp., 1962—, N.Y.C. Health Dept., 1961-70, Technicon Instruments Corp., 1964-70, U.S. Office Edn., 1964-72. Author: Great Experiments in Physics, 1959, The Myth of Scientific Literacy, 1995 (Ness award 1995); co-editor: Recent Advances in Science, 1956, Industrial and Safety Problems of Nuclear Technology, 1950; cons. editor Addison-Wesley Pub. Co., 1965-69; adv. bd. Jour. Coll. Sci. Teaching, 1971-80, Clin Lab. Guide Am. Chem. Soc., 1972-76. Dir. tng., N.Y.C. Office Civil Def., 1950-54; subscribing mem. N.Y. Philharmonic Soc.; mem. adv. council Pace U., 1971—, N.Y. Poly. Inst., 1980—; trustee Hackley Sch., 1971-80, Westchester Arts Council. Poly. U. fellow. Fellow N.Y. Acad. Scis. (past chmn. phys. sci., bd. govs. 1977-83, rec. sec. 1978-80, v.p. 1980-81, pres. 1982), AAAS; mem. IEEE, AAUP, AFTRA, NSTA (pres. 1967), Am. Chem. Soc., Nat. Assn. Ednl. Broadcasters, Am. Phys. Soc., Assn. Physics Tchrs. Britain, Chemist's Club, Am. Assn. Clin. Chemists, Cosmos Club, Phi Beta Kappa, Sigma Xi, Pi Mu Epsilon, Sigma Pi Sigma. Clubs: Cosmos, Chemists. Spl. research atomic and nuclear physics, biophysics. Home: 3515 Henry Hudson Pky Bronx NY 10463-1326

SHANAFELT, NANCY SUE, organizational development specialist, career counselor; b. Northampton, Mass., Nov. 21, 1947; m. John D. Shanafelt; children: Amy, Nicholas. BS, U. Mass., 1969; MA in Human Resources/Orgnl. Devel., U. San Francisco, 1991. Tchr. Southwick (Mass.) Pub. Schs., 1969-70; acctg. asst. Maricopa County Schs., Phoenix, Ariz., 1973-74; tax auditor to br. chief IRS, San Jose, 1974-89; enrolled agt., 1984-85; OD specialist IRS, San Jose, 1991-93; creator IRS Women's Network, San Francisco, 1981—. Leader Girl Scouts U.S., Santa Clara, 1980-96, Golden Valley, 1996—, cons., 1981-82, svc. mgr., 1982-84, trainer, 1982-84; leader Boy Scouts Am., 1992-96; facilitator Unwed Parents Anonymous, 1992—; master catechist Diocese of San Jose, 1992-96. Recipient Disting. Performance award IRS, 1993. Mem. AAUW, NAFE, ASTD, Calif. Assn. for Counseling and Devel., Federally Employed Women, Commonwealth Club Am., Italian Cath. Fedn. (sec. 1991—), Bay Area Orgnl. Devel. Network, Medugorje PGL. Avocations: antique cars, travel. Office: Mail Stop FR4300 821 M St Fresno CA 93721

SHANAFIELD, HAROLD ARTHUR, educator; b. South Bend, Ind., Nov. 26, 1912; s. Harry Bacon and Anna (Paulsen) S.; m. Margaret Ann Goodman, Nov. 23, 1939; 1 child, Harold A. BA, U. Notre Dame; MSJ, MA, Northwestern U.; MEd, Chgo. State U. Copy editor Chgo. Herald Am., 1945-46; night picture editor Chgo. Sun-Times, 1946-47; mng. editor Elec. Dealer, Chgo., 1947-52; editor, mgr. Florists' Transworld Delivery News, Detroit, 1952-61; asst. mng. editor AMA Jour., Chgo., 1961-62; asst. dean Northwestern U., Chgo.-Evanston campus, evening divs., 1962-73; with Chgo. Bd. Edn., 1973—. Editor-in-chief news bull. Retired Tchrs. Assn. Chgo., 1984—; Vice chmn., bd. visitors Freedoms Found. at Valley Forge. Served to capt. USCG, 1945—. Bd. dirs. Ret. Tchrs. Assn. Chgo., Northwestern U. and Alumni Coun., Am. Bus. Writing Assn., Assn. Evening Univs., Quill and Scroll (lifetime faculty mem.), Nat. Sojourners (pres. Chgo. chpt. 1971), Ind. Soc. Chgo. (resident v.p. 1975—), U.S. Coast Guard League (nat. comdr. 1954-55, 59-60, Res. Officers Assn., Am. Legion, Mol. Order of World Wars, Masons (33 degree, editor Scottish Rite mag. 1973—, meritorious svc. award 1986, St. John's conclave, red cross of Constantine, 1989, knight of the York rite cross of honor, 1991, Sovereign Grand Insp. Gen. 33rd degree, 1992— hon. mem. Scottish Rite Supreme Coun. 1992—), Shriners (pres. 1970, editor Medinah Temple mag. 1987-91), KT (comdr. 1981), Societas Rosicruciana Civitatibus Foederatis, Chgo. Press Club, Chgo. Headline Club, Star Craft Club of Ill. (sec. 1972-77, pres. 1977-78), SAR (Ft. Dearborn chpt.), Delta Mu Delta, Phi Chi Theta, Delta Sigma Pi, Sigma Delta Chi, Iota Sigma Epsilon. Home: 2515 Marcy Ave Evanston IL 60201-1111

SHANAHAN, EDMOND MICHAEL, savings and loan executive; b. Omaha, Oct. 20, 1926; s. Jeremiah H. and Agnes (Corcoran) S.; m. Regina E. Johansing; children: Michael, Mary Elizabeth, Thomas, Terrence (dec.). B. Econs., St. Mary's Coll., Winona, Minn.; M.B.A., U. Chgo., 1965. Customer rels. and employee tng. ofcl. Peoples Gas Light & Coke Co., Chgo., 1949-59; instr. DePaul U. Evening Sch., 1957-59; v.p. savs. and advt. Bell Fed. Savs. & Loan Assn., Chgo., 1959-79, pres., COO, dir., 1979-84, pres., CEO, dir., 1984-93, chmn. bd., 1993—. Served with USNR. Mem. Rolling Green Country Club. Office: Bell Bancorp 79 W Monroe St Chicago IL 60603-4901

SHANAHAN, EILEEN FRANCES, secondary education educator; b. Bethlehem, Pa., Sept. 10, 1949; d. Edward Vincent and Geraldine Mary (Gilligan) S. BA, Moravian Coll., 1971. Cert. secondary tchr. in Spanish, English, N.J. Tchr. Kingsway Regional High Sch. Dist., Swedesboro, N.J., 1971—. Mem. NEA, N.J. Edn. Assn., Gloucester County Edn. Assn., Fgn. Lang. Educators N.J., Kingsway Edn. Assn. (sec. membership), Hellertown Hist. Soc. Democrat. Roman Catholic. Avocations: archaeology, historical research, genealogy.

SHANAHAN, ELIZABETH ANNE, art educator; b. High Point, N.C., Apr. 5, 1950; d. Joe Thomas and Nancy Elizabeth (Moran) Gibson; m. Robert James Shanahan, Aug. 31, 1969 (div. Mar. 1987); children: Kimberly Marie Shanahan Conlon, Brigette Susanne. Student, Forsyth Tech. Coll., 1974-83, Tri-County Tech. Coll., 1989, Inst. of Children's Lit., 1989. Owner cleaning bus. Winston-Salem, N.C., 1985-86, 87; instr. Anderson (S.C.) Arts Coun., 1987—, Tri-County Tech. Coll., Pendleton, S.C., 1987—. Artist Wild Geese, 1985 (Best in Show). Active Libr. of Congress, 1994. Mem. Anderson Art Assn. (con. 1987—), Met. Arts Coun. (Upstate Visual Arts divsn.), Triad Art Assn. (pres. Kernersville, N.C. chpt. 1984-85), Nat. Mus. Women in Arts (charter), Libr. of Congress (charter). Avocations: writing, sewing, traveling, decorating. Home: 7 Woodbridge Ct Anderson SC 29621-2260 Office: Tri County Tech Coll PO Box 587 Pendleton SC 29670-0587

SHANAHAN, EUGENE MILES, flow measurement instrumentation company executive; b. Great Falls, Mont., Sept. 18, 1946; s. Raymond Eugene and Helen Marjorie (Graham) S.; m. Beverly Ann Braaten, Sept. 8, 1967; children—Bret Allen, Shaun Eugene, Shae Erin. B.S. in Mech. Engring., Mont. State U., 1968; M.S., Mont. State U., 1969; M.B.A., Portland State U., 1976. Registered profl. engr., Oreg. Mech. engr. Tektronix, Beaverton, Oreg., 1968-71; mech. engr. Shell Oil Co., Martinez, Calif., 1967; chief mech. project engr. Mears Controls, Beaverton, 1971-76; mktg. mgr. Mears Controls, 1976-79; v.p., gen. mgr. Eaton Corp., Beaverton, 1979-87; pres. Dieterich Standard (a Dover Co.), Boulder, Colo., 1987—. Served with N.G., 1969-75. NSF trainee, 1969. Mem. ASME, Instrumentation Soc. Am., Tau Beta Pi, Phi Kappa Phi, Pi Tau Sigma. Home: 8417 Sawtooth Ln Niwot CO 80503-7281 Office: Dieterich Standard PO Box 9000 Boulder CO 80301-9000

SHANAHAN, MICHAEL FRANCIS, manufacturing executive, former hockey team executive; b. St. Louis, Oct. 29, 1939; m. Mary Ann Barrett; children: Megan Elizabeth, Michael Francis Jr., Maureen Patricia. BS in Commerce, St. Louis U.; postgrad., Wash. U., St. Louis; LHD (hon.), St. Louis Rabbinical Coll., 1987. With McDonnell Douglas Automation Co., St. Louis, 1962-73, sales mgr., 1969-71, br. mgr., 1971-72, mktg. dir. cen. region, 1972-73; mktg. v.p. Numerical Control Inc., St. Louis, 1973-74, pres., 1974-79; v.p. Cleve. Pneumatic Co. (formerly Numerical Control Inc.), St. Louis, 1979-82; chmn., chief exec. officer Engineered Air Systems Inc., St. Louis, 1982—; former chmn., ceo St. Louis Blues Hockey Team; bd. dirs. Engineered Air Systems Inc. (chmn.), St. Louis Blues Hockey Inc. (chmn.); adv. com. Nat. Hockey League; mem. U.S. Senatorial Bus. Adv. Bd.; bd. dirs. Capital Bank and Trust of Clayton, The Graphic Arts Ctr. Inc., Kilo Rsch. Found. (vice chmn.). Bd. dirs. Am. Heart Assn., St. Louis Ambassadors, Catholic Charities of St. Louis, Galway Sister City Com., The Backstoppers, Christmas in St. Louis Found.; nat. bd. dirs. Boys Hope; bd. trustees, pres. coun. St. Louis U.; adv. bd. Safe Kids; hon. bd. Paraquad; hon. chmn. Small Bus. Week in St. Louis, 1989; hon. co-chmn. Veteran's Day Observance and Parade, 1989; co-chairperson AMC Cancer Rsch. Ctr. Community Svc. award. Named St. Louis Ambassador of Yr., 1986, Olivette Businessman of Yr., 1987, St. Louis Bus. Leader of Yr. Coll. Bus. Adminstrn., So. Ill. U. at Carbondale, 1987,Outstanding Philanthropist St. Louis chpt., Nat. Soc. Fund Raising Execs., 1987; recipient Spirit of Life award City of Hope Labor Mgmt., 1987, St. Louis U. Alumni Merit award, 1987, Meritorious Svc. to Sports award MS Soc., 1987, Presdl. Sports award Maryville Coll., 1987, Sales Exec. of Yr. award Sales and Mktg. Execs. of Met. St. Louis, 1988, St. Louis Port Coun.'s Mgmt. Man of the Yr. award Greater St. Louis Area and Vicinity Port Council, Maritime Trades Dept., AFL-CIO, , 1989. Mem. Alzeimer's Disease and Related Disorders Assn. (hon.), St. Louis Counts, Hawthorn Found., St. Louis Club, Mo. Athletic Club, Old Warson Country Club, Norwood Hills Country Club. Office: Engineered Air Systems Inc 1270 N Price Rd Saint Louis MO 63132-2316*

SHANAHAN, MICHAEL GEORGE, police officer; b. Seattle, Oct. 14, 1940; s. Raymond Roderick and Carletta (Anderson) S.; m. Jo-Anne

Genevieve David, Sept. 16, 1961; children: Patrick, Matthew, Raymond. BA in Psychology, Stanford U., 1962. Asst. police chief U. Wash., Seattle, 1971-75, vol. police cons. and mgmt. pvt. sector issues, 1995—; mem. law enforcement task force interim mcpl. com. Wash. State Legis., 1970-71, campus law enforcement task force-higher edn. com., 1970-71; co-chmn. Wash. Law Enforcement Standards Task Force; founding chmn. Washington Law Enforcement Exec. Forum, 1981, Operation Bootstrap, 1985, others. Author: Private Enterprise and the Public Police: The Professionalizing Effects of a New Partnership, 1985; contbr. articles to profl. jours. Mem. nat. exploring com. Boy Scouts Am., 1977, exec. bd., chief Seattle council, 1984-88; mem. Blanchet High Sch. Bd., Seattle, 1978-79, Gov.'s Coun. on Criminal Justice, 1980-81, Gov.'s Coun. Food Assistance, 1983-86. Major U.S. Army, 1963-70, Vietnam. Decorated Bronze Star; recipient award for pub. svc. U.S. Dept. Transp., 1984, Humanitarian award Seattle chpt. NCCJ, 1985, Silver Beaver award Boy Scouts Am., 1986, St. Matthew award Northwest Harvest, 1987, Paul J. Breslin award Internat. Security Mgrs. Assn., 1990, Criminal Justice award of excellence Wash. State U., 1989. Mem. FBI Nat. Acad. Assocs., Nat. Inst. Justice (peer rev. program), Internat. Assn. Chiefs of Police (life, bd. officers 1983-84, gen. chmn. divsn. state assns. 1983-84, co-chmn. pvt. sector liaison com.), Police Exec. Rsch. Forum, Wash. Assn. Sheriffs and Police Chiefs, Rotary Internat. (pres. Univ. Rotary Club Seattle 1985-86, founding chmn. Rotary Op. First Harvest, Svc. Above Self award 1988). Roman Catholic. Avocations: fishing, gardening.

SHANAHAN, MIKE, professional football coach; b. Oak Park, Ill., Aug. 24, 1952; m. Peggy, children: Kyle, Krystal. BS Phys. Edn., Eastern Illinois U., Charleston, Ill., 1974; MS Phys. Edn., 1975. Student coach Eastern Illinois U.; asst. coach U. Oklahoma, 1975-76; offensive coord., No. Ariz. U., 1976-77, Ea. Ill. U., 1977-78, U. Minn., 1979-80, offensive coord., U. Fla., 1980-84, asst. head coach, 1983-84; receivers coach Denver Broncos, 1984-87; head coach Los Angeles Raiders, 1988-89; asst. coach Denver Broncos, NFL, 1989-91; offensive coordinator San Francisco 49ers, 1992-94; head coach Denver Broncos, 1995—. Golf, travel. Office: care Denver Broncos 13655 Broncos Pky Englewood CO 80112*

SHANAHAN, ROBERT B., banker; b. Buffalo, Jan. 8, 1928; s. Bart J. and Florence (Dietrich) S.; m. Janet I. Mulholland, Feb. 6, 1954; children: Maureen Shanahan DeRose, Timothy, Karin Halpern, Molly Healy, Colleen Collins, Mark, Ellen Becker. BS in Econs., U. Pa., 1951. New bus. rep. Assocs. Discount Corp., Buffalo, 1951-55; pres. Universal Time Plan, Inc., Buffalo, 1956-67; v.p. Norstar Bank, Buffalo, 1967-69, sr. v.p., 1969-72, exec. v.p., dir., 1972-91; dir. Eastern States Bankcard Assn., Lake Success, N.Y., Chase Fed. Bank, Miami, Fla. Contbg. author: The Bankers Handbook, 1978; mem. adv. coun. Banking Mag., 1978-84; contbr. articles to profl. jours. Pres. Multiple Sclerosis Assn. Western N.Y., Buffalo, 1982-86; trustee Theodore Roosevelt Inaugural Site, Inc., Buffalo, 1983—; pres. Buffalo Council on World Affairs, 1984-86; chmn. Catholic Charities Buffalo, 1986-87, 89-90. Served with U.S. Army, 1944-46. Decorated Knight of Holy Sepulchre Order, 1991; recipient Past Pres.'s award Multiple Sclerosis Assn., 1985. Mem. Am. Bankers Assn. (bd. dirs. 1977-84, chmn. installment lending divsn. 1978-79, edn., policy and devel. coun. 1983-84, Eagle award 1978), N.Y. State Bankers Assn. (mem. exec. com. consumer divsn. 1988-90), Buffalo Area C. of C., U. Pa. Club Western N.Y. (bd. dirs.), Buffalo Club, Cherry Hill Club (Ridgeway, Ont., Can.) (pres. 1992-93). Republican. Roman Catholic. Home: A-3 109 Half Moon Cir Lantana FL 33462

SHANAHAN, THOMAS M., judge; b. Omaha, May 5, 1934; m. Jane Estelle Lodge, Aug. 4, 1956; children: Catherine Shanahan Trofholz, Thomas M. II, Mary Elizabeth, Timothy F. A.B. magna cum laude, U. Notre Dame, 1956; J.D., Georgetown U., 1959. Bar: Nebr., Wyo. Mem. McGinley, Lane, Mueller, Shanahan, O'Donnell & Merritt, Ogallala, Nebr.; assoc. justice Nebr. Supreme Ct., Lincoln, 1983-93; judge U.S. Dist. Ct. Nebr., Omaha, 1993—. Office: US Dist Ct PO Box 457 Omaha NE 68101-0457

SHANAHAN, WILLIAM STEPHEN, consumer products company executive; b. Cin., Apr. 15, 1940; s. William Stephen and Dorothea (Murken) S.; children: Kimberly, Michael Erika, Alejandra. B.A., Dartmouth Coll., 1962; postgrad., U. Calif.-Berkeley, 1962-63, Internat. Christian U., Tokyo, 1963-64, U. Philippines-Manila, 1964-65. Pres., gen. mgr. Colgate-Palmolive Co., Sao Paulo, Brazil, 1972-76; v.p. mktg. services div. Colgate U.S.A. Colgate-Palmolive Co., N.Y.C., 1976-78, v.p. western hemisphere, group v.p., sr. exec. v.p. ops., until 1989, now chief oper. officer, 1989—; pres., chief exec. officer Helena Rubinstein, N.Y.C., 1978-80; pres. Mennen Co. Office: Mennen Co 300 Park Ave 11th Fl New York NY 10022*

SHANAMAN, FRED CHARLES, JR., business consultant; b. Tacoma, June 21, 1933; s. Fred Charles and Marjorie Blanch (Jeffries) S.; m. Jane Francis Aram, July 7, 1962; children: Fred C. III, Mara Shanaman Burke. BA, Dartmouth Coll., 1957; postgrad., U. B.C., Vancouver, 1958. Sales rep. Air Reduction Co., San Francisco, 1958-62; pres. Bulk Distbrs., Tacoma, 1962-75, Pyrodyne Corp., Tacoma, 1964-75, Toys Galore, Tacoma, 1964-75, Youth Entrepreneurship Corp., Tacoma, 1978-86; pres., owner Rainier Mgmt. Corp., Tacoma, 1970—; bd. dirs. Puget Sound Bancorp., Tacoma, Bellingham (Wash.) Nat. Key Bank of Wash., Tacoma Rockets Hockey Club, Puget Sound Hockey Ctrs.; presdl. appt. to commerce sec. Elliot Richardson's Regional Rep. in N.W., 1975-77; sec. of commerce spokesman and prin. liaison, 1975-77; mem. Commerce Dept. rep. Fed. Regional Coun. and Pacific N.W. River Basins Comm., 1975-77. Author: 101 Money Making Ideas for Young Adults 10 to 18 Year of Age, 1980, The First Official Moneymaking Book for Kids of All Ages, 1983, The Best is Yet to Come: Retirement A Second Career, 1984. Chmn. NCAA Womens Final Four, Tacoma, 1988-89; commr. Ice Hockey Goodwill Games, Seattle, 1990; past bd. dirs. Annie Wright Sch., Faith Home, United Way, Tacoma Symphony, Bellarmine Preparatory Sch., Greater Lakes Mental Health Clinic, Tacoma Actors Guild, Assn. of Washington Bus., Mary Bridge Hosp., Tacoma Leukemia Soc., Vt. Acad., and others. Mem. Tacoma Country Club, Canterwood Country Club, Elks, Lakes Club, Gyro Club, Le Mirador (Switzerland). Republican. Episcopalian. Avocations: fishing, skiing, antique collecting, Christmas decoration collection. Office: Tacoma Rockets 222 E 26th St Ste 104 Tacoma WA 98421-1102

SHANAPHY, EDWARD JOHN, publishing executive; b. Jersey City, Mar. 8, 1938; s. Edward Joseph and Angela (Giordano) S.; m. Kathleen Mavourneen Gately, Oct. 22, 1966; children: Edward Joseph, Meghan Gately, Kate Colleen. MusB, Cath. U., 1959, MusM, 1961. Pianist Glenn Miller Orch., N.Y.C., 1964-65; dir. mktg. Columbia House div. CBS, N.Y.C., 1965-73, Charles Hansen Music and Books, N.Y.C., 1974-76; pres. Shacor, Inc., Katonah, N.Y., 1976—; pres., pub. Sheet Music mag., Katonah, 1976—; pres. Good Music Record Co., Katonah, 1981—; pres., pub. Keyboard Classics mag., Katonah, 1981—. Author: Piano Stylings, 1985, Speed Reading at the Keyboard, 1987; editor (periodical) Jazz and Keyboard Workshop; composer various songs. With U.S. Army, 1961-64. Mem. ASCAP, Nat. Assn. Music Merchandisers, Dutch Treat Club, Waccabuc Country Club (N.Y., sec., gov. 1985-93), Players Club, Friars Club, Phi Beta Kappa. Republican. Roman Catholic. Office: Shacor Inc 223 Katonah Ave Katonah NY 10536-2139

SHANAS, ETHEL, sociology educator; b. Chgo., Sept. 6, 1914; d. Alex and Rebecca (Rich) S.; m. Lester J. Perlman, May 17, 1940; 1 child, Michael Stephen. AB, U. Chgo., 1935, AM, 1937, PhD, 1949; LHD (hon.), Hunter Coll., N.Y.C., 1985. Instr. human devel. U. Chgo., 1947-52, rsch. assoc. prof., 1961-65; sr. rsch. analyst City of Chgo., 1952-53; sr. study dir. Nat. Opinion Rsch. Ctr., Chgo., 1956-61; prof. sociology U. Ill., Chgo., 1965-82, prof. emerita, 1982—; vice chmn. expert com. on aging UN, 1974; mem. com. on aging NRC, Washington, 1978-82, panel on statistics for an aging population, 1984-86; mem. U.S. Com. on Vital and Health Stats., Washington, 1976-79. Author: The Health of Older People, 1962; (with others) Old People in Three Industrial Societies, 1968; editor: (with others) Handbook of Aging and the Social Sciences, 1976, 2d edit., 1985. Bd. govs. Chgo. Heart Assn., 1972-80; mem. adv. council on aging City of Chgo., 1972-78. Keston lectr. U. So. Calif., 1975; recipient Burgess award Nat. Council on Family Relations, 1978; Disting. Chgo. Gerontologist award Assn. for Gerontology in Higher Edn., 1988. Fellow Gerontol. Soc. Am. (pres. 1974-75, Kleemeier award 1977, Brookdale award 1981), Am. Sociol. Assn. (chmn. sect. on aging 1985-86 Disting. Scholar award, 1987); mem. Midwest Sociol. Soc. (pres. 1980-81), Inst. Medicine of Nat. Acad. Scis. (sr. mem.). Home: 222 Main St Evanston IL 60202-2467 Office: U Ill Chgo Dept Sociology M/C 312 4112 Behavioral Sci Bldg Chicago IL 60607-7140

SHANDLING, GARRY, comedian, scriptwriter, actor; b. Chgo., Nov. 29, 1949; s. Irving and Muriel S. Grad., U. Ariz. TV screenwriter: Sanford and Son, Welcome Back Kotter, Three's Company; guest host The Tonight Show, 1986-88; host Emmy Awards 1987, 88, Grammy Awards 1990, 91, 92; writer, prodr. Garry Shandling: Alone in Las Vegas, 1984; exec. prodr., writer It's Garry Shandling's Show 25th Anniversary Special, 1986, It's Garry Shandling's Show, 1986-90 (Ace award best comedy series 1989, 90, Ace award best actor in a comedy series 1990), Garry Shandling: Stand-Up, 1991, The Larry Sanders Show, 1992— (CableAce award, Writing in a Comedy Series, 1994); actor: (film) Love Affair, 1994, Mixed Nuts, 1994. Office: Brillstein/Grey 9150 Wilshire Blvd Ste 350 Beverly Hills CA 90212-3430

SHANDS, COURTNEY, JR., lawyer; b. St. Louis, Mar. 17, 1929; s. Courtney and Elizabeth W. (Jones) S.; m. Frances Jean Schellfeffer, Aug. 9, 1952 (div. 1976); children: Courtney III, E.F. Berkley, Elizabeth V.; m. Nancy Bliss Lewis, Oct. 25, 1980. AB, Washington U., St. Louis, 1951; LLB, Harvard U., 1954. Assoc. Thompson and Mitchell, St. Louis, 1954-62, ptnr., 1962-63; ptnr. Thompson, Walther and Shewmaker, St. Louis, 1963-69, Kohn, Shands, Elbert, Gianoulakis & Giljum, St. Louis, 1970—. Trustee Frank G. and Florence V. Bohle Scholarship Found., Edward Chase Garvey Meml. Found., L.F. Jones Charitable Trust, 1958-60; bd. dirs. St. Louis Fund, 1972—, Law Libr. St. Louis, 1988—, Hope Ednl. & Rsch. Found., 1989—, pres. 1995—, Citizenship Edn. Clearing House, St. Louis, 1985-87, pres. 1986-87, Mark Twain Summer Inst., St. Louis, 1968-89, pres., 1974-79; Andrews Acad., 1989—, v.p., 1989—; pres. com. Goldwater for Pres., Met. St. Louis, 1964, Ea. Mo. chpt. ACLU, 1966-69, nat. bd. dirs. 1969-72. Mem. ABA, Mo. Bar Integrated, Bar Assn. of Met. St. Louis, Selden Soc., Law Libr. Assn. (Mo. sect.), Noonday Club, Racquet Club, St. Louis Club. Republican. Episcopalian. Home: 507 N Taylor Ave Saint Louis MO 63122-4458 Office: Kohn Shands Elbert 1 Mercantile Ctr Fl 24 Saint Louis MO 63101-1643

SHANDS, HENRY LEE, plant geneticist, administrator; b. Madison, Wis., Aug. 30, 1935; s. Ruebush George and Elizabeth (Henry) S.; m. Catherine Miller, Nov. 20, 1962; children: Deborah A., Jeanne A., James L. BS, U. Wis., 1957; MS, Purdue U., 1961, PhD, 1963. NSF fellow Swedish Seed Assn., Svalov, 1962-63; asst. prof. Purdue U., West Lafayette, Ind., 1963-66, asst. prof. botany and plant pathology, 1965-66; rsch. agronomist, leader ea. wheat project Dekalb Hybrid Wheat, Inc., Lafayette, 1966-79; rsch. agronomist, dir. sunflower rsch. Dekalb-Pfizer Genetics and predecessor firms, Glyndon, Minn., 1979-86; nat. program leader for plant germplasm USDA Agrl. Rsch. Svc., Beltsville, Md., 1986-92, assoc. dep. adminstr. for genetic resources, 1992—; mem. AID Project, Minas Gerais, Brazil, 1963-65. 1st lt. U.S. Army, 1957-59. Recipient 1st Victor M. Bendelow Meml. Lectr. award U. Man., 1992. Fellow AAAS, Am. Soc. Agronomy, Crop Sci. Soc. Am. (Frank N. Meyer medal for plant genetic resources 1992); Am. Genetic Assn., Genetics Soc. Can., Am. Phytopath. Soc. Office: USDA-ARS Bldg 005 BARC-W Beltsville MD 20705-2350

SHANDS, WILLIAM RIDLEY, JR., lawyer; b. Richmond, Va., Nov. 23, 1929; s. William Ridley and Josephine (Winston) S.; m. Lynneth Williams, May 31, 1958; children: William Tyler, Laura Sawyer. B.A., Hampden-Sydney Coll., 1952; LL.B., U. Va., 1958. Bar: Va. 1958. Atty., asso. firm Christian, Barton, Epps, Brent & Chappell, Richmond, 1958-61; counsel The Life Ins. Co. of Va., Richmond, 1961-66; asst. gen. counsel The Life Ins. Co. of Va., 1966-68, asso. gen. counsel, 1968-71, gen. counsel, 1971-73, v.p., gen. counsel, 1973-78, sr. v.p., gen. counsel, 1978-79; sr. v.p. law and public affairs Continental Fin. Services Co., Richmond, 1980-85; sr. v.p., sec. Life Ins. Co. Va., Richmond, 1985-88; counsel Sands, Anderson, Marks & Miller, Richmond, 1988—. Chmn. Eastern Appeal Bd. Selective Svc. System, 1969; pres., chmn. bd. dirs. Trinity Episcopal High Sch., 1971-72; bd. dirs. Richmond Area Heart Assn., 1965-71, Southampton Cotillion, 1970-72; vestryman St. Michael's Episc. Ch., 1965-68, sr. warden, 1968. Served with AUS, 1952-55, Philippines. Mem. Va. Bar Assn., Richmond Bar Assn., Assn. Life Ins. Counsel (pres. 1987-88), Am. Coun. Life Ins. (chmn. legal sect. 1982-83), Commonwealth Club, Country Club Va. Home: 3811 Darby Dr Midlothian VA 23113-1318 Office: Sands Anderson Marks & Miller 801 E Main St # 1998 Richmond VA 23219-2901

SHANE, JOHN MARDER, endocrinologist; b. Kansas City, Mo., Oct. 5, 1942; s. Henry Kamsler and Ruth (Marder) S.; m. Eileen Goodart, June 18, 1967; children: Robert M., Edward G. BS, U. Okla., 1964, MD, 1967. Diplomate Am. Bd. Ob-Gyn., Am. Bd. Reproductive Endocrinology. Resident Harvard Med. Sch., Boston, 1970-73, fellowship, 1973-75, instr., 1970-75, asst. prof., 1975-78; pvt. practice Tulsa, 1978—; lectr., cons. Tutorial Svcs. Internat., England, 1984—; bd. dirs. St. Francies G.I.F.T. Lab., Tulsa; cons. to preimplantation genetics project Chapman Genetics Inst., Children's Med. Ctr., Tulsa. Author: CIBA Symposium Infertility: Diagnosis and Treatment; contbr. articles to profl. jours. and publs. Mem. Tulsa Garden Ctr., 1988—; bd. dirs. Temple Israel, Tulsa, 1985-86. Captain USAF, 1967-69. Recipient Annual award Boston Obstet. Soc., 1977. Mem. ACS, Tulsa Gynecol. Soc. (past pres. 1986-87), Soc. Reproductive Endocrinologists, Tulsa bonsai Soc. (bd. dirs. 1988—), Am. Coll. Ob-Gyn. (v.p. 1971-92, pres. New England Jr. divsn. 1972-73), Am. Bonsai Soc. (nat. bd. dirs.), Chanie des Rotisseurs (l'Ordre Mondial, Tulsa v.p.), Southside Rotary of Tulsa (bd. dirs.), Nat. Arboretum (nat. bd. dirs.). Republican. Jewish. Avocations: bonsai, collector oriental arts. Office: 1705 E 19th St Ste 703 Tulsa OK 74104-5418

SHANE, PETER MILO, law educator; b. Oceanside, N.Y., July 12, 1952; s. Albert and Ann (Semanoff) S.; m. Martha Elisabeth Chamallas, June 27, 1981; 1 child, Elisabeth Ann. AB, Harvard U., 1974; JD, Yale U., 1977. Bar: N.Y. 1978, U.S. Ct. Appeals (5th cir.) 1978, D.C. 1979, U.S. Ct. Appeals (8th cir.) 1983, U.S. Supreme Ct. 1984, Pa. 1995. Law clk. to judge U.S. Ct. Appeals (5th cir.), New Orleans, 1977-78; atty., advisor office of legal counsel, U.S. Dept. Justice, Washington, 1978-81; asst. gen. counsel Office of Mgmt. and Budget, Washington, D.C., 1981; assoc. prof. law U. Iowa, Iowa City, 1981-85, prof., 1985-94; dean, prof. law U. Pitts., 1994—; adj. lectr. Am. U., Washington, D.C., 1979-80; vis. prof. law Duke U., Durham, N.C., 1986; cons. U.S. Dept. Edn., Washington, D.C., 1980, MacArthur Justice Found., Chgo., 1987; active Adminstrv. Conf. U.S., 1991, pub. mem. 1995; cons. Nat. Commn. Jud. Discipline and Removal, 1992-93; cooperating atty. Iowa Civil Liberties Union, Des Moines, 1982-94, bd. dirs., 1987-89; active Coun. on Legal Edn. Opportunity, 1996—. Author: (with H.H. Bruff) The Law of Presidential Power: Cases and Materials, 1988, (with J. Mashaw and R. Merrill) Administrative Law: The American Public Law System, 1992, (with H.H. Bruff) Separation of Powers Law, 1996. Mem. Dem. cen. com. Johnson County, Iowa, 1982-88. Old Gold Summer fellow U. Iowa, 1981-84, Mellon Found fellow, 1982. Mem. ABA (coun. sect. adminstrv. law and regulatory practice 1993-96, chmn. com. on govt. orgn. and separation of powers 1987-91), Assn. Am. Law Schs. (chair adminstrv. law 1990, chair remedies 1992). Jewish. Office: U Pitts Sch Law 3900 Forbes Ave Pittsburgh PA 15260

SHANE, RITA, opera singer; b. N.Y.C.; d. Julius J. and Rebekah (Milner) S.; m. Daniel F. Tritter, June 22, 1958; 1 child, Michael Shane. BA, Barnard Coll., 1958; postgrad., Santa Fe Opera Apprentice Program, 1962-63, Hunter Opera Assn., 1962-64; pvt. study with, Beverly Peck Johnson, Elizabeth Schwartzkopf, Bliss Hebert. Adj. prof. voice Manhattan Sch. of Music, 1993-95; prof. voice Eastman Sch. Music Rochester U., 1989—; pvt. teachng, N.Y.C., 1978—. Performer with numerous opera cos., including profl. debut, Chattanooga Opera, 1964, Met. Opera, San Francisco Opera, N.Y.C. Opera, Chgo. Lyric Opera, San Diego Opera, Santa Fe Opera, Teatro alla Scala, Milan, Italy, Bavarian State Opera, Netherlands Nat. Opera, Geneva Opera, Vienna State Opera, Phila., New Orleans, Balt. Opera, Opera du Rhin, Strasbourg, Scottish Opera, Teatro Reggio, Turin, Opera Metropolitana, Caracas, Portland Opera, Minn. Opera, also others; world premiere Miss Havisham's Fire, Argento; Am. premieres include Reimann-Lear, Schat-Houdini, Henze-Elegy for Young Lovers; participant festivals, including Mozart Festival, Lincoln Center, N.Y.C., Munich Festival, Aspen Festival, Handel Soc., Vienna Festival, Salzburg Festival, Munich Festival, Perugia Festival, Festival Canada, Glyndebourne Festival, performed with orchs. including Santa Cecilia, Rome, Austrian Radio, London Philharmn., Louisville, Cin., Cleve., Phila., RAI, Naples, Denver, Milw., Israel Philharm., rec. artist, RCA, Columbia, Louisville, Turnabout labels, also radio and TV. Recipient Martha Baird Rockefeller award, William Matheus Sullivan award. Mem. Am. Guild Mus. Artists, Screen Actors Guild. Office: care Daniel F Tritter 330 West 42nd St New York NY 10036

SHANE, ROBERT SAMUEL, chemical engineer, consultant; b. Chgo., Dec. 8, 1910; s. Jacob and Selma (Shayne) S.; m. Jeanne Felice Lazarus, Aug. 21, 1936; children: Stephen H., Susan R., Jacqueline G. SB, U. Chgo., 1930, PhD, 1933. Plant supt. Amecco Chems., Rochester, N.Y., 1941-42; plant chemist Bausch & Lomb Optical Co., Rochester, 1942-46; project supr. Wyandotte (Mich.) Chems. Corp., 1952-54; assoc. dir. rsch. Davis & Geck div. Am. Cyanamid, Danbury, Conn., 1954-55; mgr. chem., ceramics, powder metals Westinghouse Atomic Power, Forest Hills, Pa., 1955-57; nucleonics specialist Bell Aircraft Co., Niagara Falls, N.Y., 1958-59; mgr. parts, materials, process engring. GE, Valley Forge, Pa., 1959-69; staff cons. Nat. Materials Adv. Bd., Washington, 1969-80; prin. Shane Assocs., Stuart, Fla., 1980-95; dist. dir. S. Fla. Mfg. Tech. Ctr., Stuart, 1995—; cons. in field; editor material engring. Marcel Dekker, Inc., N.Y.C., 1983—. Author, editor: Space Radiation Effects on Materials, 1962, Predictive Testing, 1972, Materials and Processes, 1985; author: Technology Transfer & Innovation, 1982; mem. editorial bd. Jour. Testing and Evaluation, 1985—; editor: Testing for Prediction of Material Performance, 1972; contbr. articles to profl. jours. Adult leader Boy Scouts Am.; organizer Literacy Coun., Ardmore, Pa., 1988. Recipient Joseph Stewart award Am. Chem. Soc., 1987, medal Swedish Royal Acad. Engring., 1972; named to space tech. hall of fame NASA, 1995. Fellow ASTM (award of merit 1973, F-15 com. on consumer product stds.), AIChE; mem. Am. Soc. for Metals Internat. (life), Sigma Xi. Home and Office: 1904 NW 22nd St Stuart FL 34994-9270

SHANE, RONALD, financial company executive; b. Chgo., May 9, 1953. A.A., Miami Dade Jr. Coll., 1972; B.A., Fla. Internat. U., 1974. Pres. Trans Leasing of Fla., Ft. Lauderdale, 1976-77; co-founder, pres. Assoc. Leasing Internat. Corp., Ft. Lauderdale, 1977—; v.p., dir. Assoc. Fin. Internat. Corp., Ft. Lauderdale, 1977—, Assoc. Mortgage Internat. Corp., Ft. Lauderdale, 1980—. Contbr. articles to fin. trade jours. Sec., mem. bd. dirs. Manors of Inverrary CondoAssn., Lauderhill, Fla., 1971, 72; mem. archtl. com. San Simeon Homeowners Assn., Boca Raton, Fla., 1984—. Recipient Personalities of Am. award, 1986. Mem. Internat. Machine Tool Assn. (assoc.), Graphic Arts and Printing Soc. (assoc.), Radiol. Soc. N.Am. (assoc.), Roll Royce Owners Cub Club, Antique Automobile Club, Classic Car Club, Riviera Owners Club, Fraternal Order of Police (assoc. Nat. Grand Lodge, chartered), Woodlands Country Club (Tamarac, Fla., jr. mem.). Avocations: collecting and restoring classic cars, power boating, golf, travel. Office: Assoc Leasing Internat Corp 1489 W Palmetto Park Rd Ste 475 Boca Raton FL 33486-3326

SHANE, SANDRA KULI, postal service administrator; b. Akron, Ohio, Dec. 12, 1939; d. Amiel M. and Margaret E. (Brady) Kuli; m. Fred Shane, May 30, 1962 (div. 1972); 1 child, Mark Richard; m. Byrl William Campbell, Apr. 26, 1981 (dec. 1984). BA, U. Akron, 1987, postgrad., 1988-90. Scheduler motor vehicle bur. Akron Police Dept., 1959-62; flight and ops. control staff Escort Air, Inc., Akron and Cleve., 1972-78; asst. traffic mgr. Keen Transport, Inc., Hudson, Ohio, 1978-83; mem. ops. and mktg. staff Shawnee Airways and Essco, Akron, 1983-86; in distbn. U.S. Postal Svc., Akron, 1986—; rec. sec. Affirmative Action Coun., Akron, 1988-90. Asst. art tchr. Akron Art Mus., 1979; counselor Support, Inc., Akron, 1983-84; com. chmn. Explorer post Boy Scouts Am., Akron, 1984-85. Mem. Bus. and Profl. Women's Assn. (pres.), Delta Nu Alpha. Democrat. Roman Catholic. Avocations: painting, sculpting, fabric design. Home: 455 E Bath Rd Cuyahoga Falls OH 44223-2511

SHANEFIELD, DANIEL JAY, ceramics engineering educator; b. Orange, N.J., Apr. 29, 1930; s. Benjamin and Nan (Leichter) S.; m. Elizabeth Davis, June 28, 1964; children: Alison, Douglas. BS in Chemistry, Yale U., 1952; PhD in Chemistry, Rutgers U., 1962. Sr. project engr. ITT Group, Nutley, N.J., 1962-67; sr. mem. tech. staff AT&T Bell Labs., Princeton, N.J., 1967-86; disting. prof. Rutgers U., New Brunswick, N.J., 1986—; adv. panel NSF, 1990—; course dir. Ctr. for Profl. Advancement, U.S. and The Netherlands, 1993—; cons. in field; presenter at profl. confs. Author: Organic Additives and Ceramic Processing, 1995; co-author: Defects in Gold Plating, 1981; contbr. 4 chpts. to tech. books, articles to profl. jours.; co-inventor 17 patents; assoc. editor Jour. Am. Ceramic Soc., 1987—. With U.S. Army, 1952-54, Korea. Fellow Am. Inst. Chemists, Am. Ceramic Soc. (Best Paper award); mem. IEEE (chmn. standards com. 1984—), Am. Chem. Soc. Republican. Avocations: modifying sports cars, writing audio, stereo articles. Home: 119 Jefferson Rd Princeton NJ 08540-3373 Office: Rutgers U Ceramics Engring Dept PO Box 909 Piscataway NJ 08855-0909

SHANER, LESLIE ANN, lawyer; b. Lynchburg, Va., Oct. 1, 1948; d. George Leslie and Ruby Ann (Ward) S.; 1 child, Jennifer Ann; m. Harris Sol Levy, Mar. 15, 1992. BA, Randolph-Macon Women's Coll., 1989; JD, Washington & Lee U., 1992. Bar: U.S. Dist. Ct. (we. dist.) Va. 1993, U.S. Ct. Appeals (4th cir.) 1993. Assoc. Singleton & Deeds, Warm Springs, Va., 1992-94, O'Keefe & Spies, Lynchburg, Va., 1994—. Chmn. Ctrl. Shenandoah Disabilities Svcs. Bd., 1993-94; bd. dirs. Highland Med. Ctr., Inc., 1992-93, Valley Cmty. Svcs. Bd., 1993—. Recipient Nat. Collegiate Humanities award, Am. Jurisprudence award, Future Interests. Mem. ABA, Va. State Bar Assn., Va. Bar Assn., Va. Trial Lawyers Assn., Allegheny-Bath-Highland Bar Assn. (sec.-treas. 1993-94, chmn. social com. 1993-94), Lynchburg Bar Assn., The Federalists Soc. (sec.), Phi Delta Phi, Phi Beta Kappa, Omicron Delta Kappa (pres.), Eta Sigma Phi, Phi Alpha Phi. Avocations: reading, needlework, gardening, travel. Office: O'Keefe & Spies 828 Main St Ste 1803 Lynchburg VA 24504

SHANG, CHARLES YULIN, medical physicist; b. Shanghai, May 6, 1956; came to U.S., 1987; s. Jian and Ming (gong) S.; m. Monica Jinhong Meng, Aug. 1, 1985; children: Stephen, Michael. MD, 2nd Med. Coll., Shanghai, China, 1983; postdoctoral cert., Chgo. Med. Sch., North Chgo., Ill., 1988; MS in Radiation, Health/Med. Physics, U. Pitts., 1990. Diplomate in Radiological Physics, Am. Bd. Radiology. Resident 301 Gen. Hosp., Beijing, China, 1983-85; radiologist 301 Gen. Hosp., Beijing, 1985-87; vis. radiologist Evanston (Ill.) Univ. Hosp., 1988; vis. radiologist Allegheny Gen. Hosp., Pitts., 1988-89, med. physicist, 1991; grad. student rschr. Presbyn. Univ. Hosp., Pitts., 1989-90; med. physicist St. Mary's Hosp., Waterbury, Conn., 1991-93; sr. med. physicist Boca Raton (Fla.) Comty. Hosp., 1993—. Contbr. articles to profl. jours. including Radiology, Neurosurgery, Annals N.Y. Acad. Scis., IEEE Transactions on Biomed. Engring. Recipient grad. scholarship U. Pitts., 1989-90. Mem. Am. Assn. Physicists in Medicine, Am. Coll. Radiology. Achievements include patents on a handheld body stereotactic guider for interventional radiology, China and U.S. Home: 9340 Lake Serena Dr Boca Raton FL 33496-6510 Office: Boca Raton Cmty Hosp Lynn Regional Cancer Ctr 16313 Military Trl Delray Beach FL 33484-6628

SHANG, ER-CHANG, acoustician; b. Sheng Yain, Liaonin, China, Feb. 5, 1932; came to U.S., 1986.; BS in Theoretical Physics, Peking U., Beijing, China, 1958; PhD equivalent, Inst. Acoustics, Acad. Sinica, Beijing, 1982. Asst. prof. Inst. of Acoustics, Beijing, 1958-62, assoc. prof., 1962-75, prof., 1975-82, dep. dir., 1982-86; sr. rsch. assoc. AOML/NOAA, Miami, Fla., 1983-84, Wave Propagation Lab./NOAA, Boulder, Colo., 1987-88; NRC postdoctoral advisor Wave Propagation Lab./NOAA, 1991—; rsch. assoc. CIRES/U. Colo./NOAA, Boulder, 1988-91, rsch. prof., supervisor, 1991—; vis. scientist Scripps Inst. Oceanography, U. Calif. San Diego, La Jolla, 1982-83; vis. prof. U. Wis., Madison, 1983, Yale U., New Haven, 1986-87. Author: Underwater Acoustics, 1981. Recipient Nat. award for sci. Nat. Com. of Sci, Beijing, 1982, 89. Fellow Acoustical Soc. Am. Achievements include new method of source localization in ocean waveguides--matched mode processing; modal ocean acoustic tomography and applied for El Nino monitoring; impact of mode-coupling on modal travel time in ocean waveguide; modal theory in shallow water acoustics. Office: ETL/NOAA 325 Broadway St Boulder CO 80303-3337

SHANGE, NTOZAKE (PAULETTE WILLIAMS), playwright, poet; b. Trenton, N.J., Oct. 18, 1948; d. Paul T. and Eloise Williams; m. David Murray, July 4, 1977 (div.); 1 child: Savannah. BA in Am. Studies cum laude, Barnard Coll., 1970; MA in Am. Studies, U. So. Calif., 1973. mem. faculty Sonoma State U., 1973-75, Mills Coll., 1975, CCNY, 1975, Douglass Coll., 1978; lectr. in field. Author: (plays) for colored girls who have considered suicide/when the rainbow is enuf, 1975 (Obie award for best play 1977, Outer Critics Circle award for best play 1977, Audelco award 1977, Tony award nomination for best play 1977, Grammy award nomination for best spoken word rec. 1977), Melissa and Smith, 1976, A Photograph: A Study of Cruelty, 1977, (with Thulani Nkabinde and Jessica Hagedorn) Where the Mississippi Meets the Amazon, 1977, Boogie Woogie Landscapes, 1978, From Okra to Greens, 1978, Spell #7: A Geechee Quick Magic Trance Manual, 1979, Black and White Two Dimensional Planes, 1979, Mouths, 1981, A Photograph: Lovers in Motion, 1981, Three For a Full Moon, 1982, Bocas, 1982, Three Views of Mt. Fuji, 1987; (adaptations) Mother Courage and Her Children (Brecht), 1980 (Obie award for best play 1981), Educating Rita, 1982; (operetta) Carrie, 1981; (novels) Sassafrass, 1976, Sassafrass, Cypress and Indigo, 1982, Betsey Brown, 1985, Liliana: Resurrection of the Daughter, 1994; (poems) Natural Disasters and Other Festive Occasions, 1977, Nappy Edges, 1978, Three Pieces, 1981 (L.A. Book prize for poetry 1981), A Daughter's Geography, 1983, From Okra to Greens, 1984, The Love Space Demands, 1991, I Live in Music, 1994; (non-fiction) See No Evil: Prefaces, Essays and Accounts 1976-1983, 1984, Ridin' the Moon in Texas: Word Paintings, 1987; contbr. poetry, essays and short stories to numerous mags. and anthologies, including Third World Women, Chgo. Rev., Am. Rag, Sojourner, Womansports; actress: For Colored Girls Who Have Considered Suicide/When the Rainbow is Enuf, 1976, Where the Mississippi Meets the Amazon, 1977; dir.: The Mighty Gents, 1979, A Photograph: A Study in Cruelty, 1979, The Issue, 1979, The Spirit of Sojourner Truth, 1979; writer: An Evening with Diana Ross: The Big Event, 1977 (Emmy award nomination 1977); performing mem.: Sounds in Motion Dance Co.; performed in various jazz/poetry collaborations; dancer with Third World Collective, Raymond Sawyer's Afro-American Dance Co., Sound in Motion, West Coast Dance Works; founder, dancer For Colored Girls Who Have Considered Suicide. Recipient Frank Silvera Writer's Workshop award, 1978, Excellence medal Columbia U., 1981, Taos World Poetry Heavyweight Champion, 1992, 93, 94; NDEA fellow, 1973, Guggenheim fellow, 1981. Mem. Actors Equity, Nat. Acad. TV Arts and Scis., Acad. Am. Poets, Dramatist's Guild, PEN Am Center, Poets and Writer's, Inc., N.Y. Feminist Art Guild. Office: care St Martins Press 175 5th Ave New York NY 10010-7703

SHANGRAW, CLARENCE FRANK, museum official; b. Burlington, Vt., Aug. 9, 1935; s. Eugene and Hazel Bernice (Fuller) S.; m. Sylvia Chen, Dec. 23, 1961 (dec.); children—Lea Lihsia, Lin Ethan. Grad., Yale U. Inst. Far Eastern Langs., 1955; A.B. with high honors, U. Calif.-, Berkeley, 1963, M.A., 1965. Tchr. U. Calif.-, Berkeley, 1964-65; art research asst. M.H. de Young Mus., 1965; asst. curator Avery Brundage Collection, 1966-68; sr. curator Asian art Asian Art Mus. San Francisco, 1968-85, acting dir., chief curator, 1985, chief curator, 1986-89, dep. dir., chief curator, 1989-92, chief curator emeritus, 1992; dir. Tsui Mus. Art, Hong Kong, 1992-93; Asian art cons., 1993—; adj. prof. Sch. Mus. Studies John F. Kennedy U., 1980—. Author: Origins of Chinese Ceramics, 1978, Masterworks of Ming: 15th Century Chinese Blue and White Porcelains, 1985, Marvels of Medieval China: Those Lustrous Song and Yuan Lacquers, 1986; co-author: Chinese Blue and White Porcelains from the Voyages of Drake and Cermeno Found. at Drakes Bay, California, 1982; editor: Legacy of Chenghua, Hong Kong, 1993; contbr. sect.: Chinese, Japanese and Korean Sculptures in the Avery Brundage Collection, 1974, 5,000 Years of Korean Art, 1979, The Art of Japan: Masterworks in the Asian Art Mus. of San Francisco, 1991, Vol. I, Tsui Museum of Art: Early Chinese Ceramics, Reflections on Early Chinese Ceramics, 1992, A Chorus of Colors: Chinese Glass from Three American Collections, 1995; contbr.: catalog Treasures from the Shanghai Museum: 6, 000 Years of Chinese Art, 1983, Looking at Asian Art Patronage, 1989, Beauty, Wealth, and Power: Jewels and Ornaments of Asia, 1992, Some Reflections on the Beginnings of China's Ceramic Traditions, 1993; contbr. numerous articles to profl. jours. Served with USAF, 1954-58. Mem. Am. Assn. Mus., Internat. Council Mus., Oriental Ceramics Soc. London, Am. Inst. Archaeology, Assn. Asian Studies. Republican. Conglist. Home: 5517 Diamond Heights Blvd San Francisco CA 94131-2642 Office: Asian Art Mus Golden Gate Park San Francisco CA 94118

SHANIES, HARVEY MICHAEL, pulmonologist, medical educator; b. N.Y.C., Nov. 17, 1944; s. William and Helen (Friedman) S.; children: Tabitha Amity, David Bradley. BS, George Washington U., 1966; MS, NYU, 1968, PhD, 1970, MD, 1973. Diplomate Am. Bd. Med. Examiners, Am. Bd. Internal Medicine, Am. Bd. Critical Care Medicine, Subspecialty Bd. in Pulmonary Diseases. Intern Bronx (N.Y.) Mcpl. Hosp. Ctr., 1973-74, med. resident, 1974-75, resident chest medicine, 1975-76, chief resident chest medicine, 1976-77; med. dir. respiratory care svcs. San Dimas (Calif.) Community Hosp., 1977-88, Foothill Prebyn. Hosp., Glendora, Calif., 1983-88; dir. respiratory ICU Mt. Sinai Svcs., Elmhurst (N.Y.) Hosp. Ctr., 1988-93, chief pulmonary medicine, 1993—; asst. prof. medicine Mt. Sinai Sch. Medicine, N.Y.C., 1988—. Author: Pulmonary Emergencies, 1993; editor: Medicine Stat! Cards, 1992. Fellow NSF, 1961, NIH, 1968-70. Fellow Am. Coll. Chest Physicians, Am. Coll. Angiology; mem. Am. Thoracic Soc. (bd. dirs. joint rev. com. for respiratory therapy edn. 1996—). Office: Elmhurst Hosp Ctr 79-01 Broadway Elmhurst NY 11373-1329

SHANK, CLARE BROWN WILLIAMS, political leader; b. Syracuse, N.Y., Sept. 19, 1909; d. Curtiss Crofoot and Clara Irene (Shoudy) Brown; m. Frank E. Williams, Feb. 18, 1940 (dec. Feb. 1957); m. Seth Carl Shank, Dec. 28, 1963 (dec. Jan. 1977). B in Oral English, Syracuse U., 1931. Tchr., 1931-33, merchandising exec., 1933-42; Pinellas County mem. Rep. State Com., 1954-58; life mem. Pinellas County Rep. Exec. Com.; exec. com. Fla. Rep. Com., 1954-64; Fla. committeewoman Rep. Nat. Com., 1956-64, mem. exec. com., 1956-64, asst. chmn. and dir. women's activities, 1958-64; alt., mem. exec. arrangements com., major speaker Rep. Nat. Conv., Chgo., 1960; alt., program and arrangement coms. Rep. Nat. Conv., 1964. Pres. St. Petersburg Women's Rep. Club, 1955-57; Mem. Def. Adv. Com. on Women in Services, 1959-65; trustee St. Petersburg Housing Authority, 1976-81. Recipient George Arents medal Syracuse U., 1959; citation for patriotic civilian service 5th U.S. Army and Dept. Def.; 1st woman to preside over any part of nat. polit. conv., Rep. Nat. Conv., Chgo., 1960. Mem. AAUW, DAR, Gen. Fedn. Women's Clubs, Colonial Dames 17th Century, Fla. Fedn. Women's Clubs (dist. pres. 1976-78), Women's Club (St. Petersburg, pres. 1974-76, Yacht Club, Lakewood Country Club (St. Petersburg). Methodist. Home: 939 Beach Dr NE Apt 409 Saint Petersburg FL 33701-2009

SHANK, FRED ROSS, federal agency administrator; b. Harrisonburg, Va., Oct. 11, 1940; m. Peggy Anne Westbrook, June 1967; children: Virginia Anne, Fred Ross III. BS in Agriculture, U. Ky., 1962, MS in Nutrition, 1964; PhD, U. Md., 1969. Dep. dir. Office Nutrition and Food Sci. FDA, Washington, 1979-86, dir. Office Phys. Sci., 1986-87, dep. dir. Ctr. for Food SAfety and Applied Nutrition, 1987-89, dir., 1989—. Fellow Inst. Food Technologists; mem. Am. Assn. Cereal Chemists, Am. Inst. Nutrition, Am. Soc. for Clin. Nutrition, Assn. Food and Drug Ofcls. Home: 2621 Steeplechase Dr Reston VA 22091-2130 Office: FDA Ctr Food Safety and Applied Nutrition 200 C St SW Washington DC 20204-0001

SHANK, JAMES WILLIAM, II, electrical engineer; b. Lexington, Ky., Dec. 27, 1965; s. James William Shank and June Estella (Howe) Folk; m. Kimberly Denise Hanhurst, Nov. 14, 1992; children: Dylan James, Amanda Brooke. BSEE, Pa. State U., 1988; MSEE, Rensselaer Polytech. Inst., 1991. Engr. Gen. Dynamics/Electric Boat, Groton, Conn., 1989-91, Carolina Power & Light Co., Raleigh, N.C., 1991-93; lead engr. Pub. Svc. Electric & Gas Co., Hancocks Bridge, N.J., 1994—; cons. CHAR Svcs., Inc., Lebanon, Pa., 1993—. Mem. IEEE, Internat Council Syss. Am. (SP67.16 WGI chair). Republican. Avocations: automobile racing and repair, football. Home: 3 Nottingham Way Turnersville NJ 08012 Office: Pub Svc Electric & Gas Co PO Box 236 Hancocks Bridge NJ 08038

SHANK, MAURICE EDWIN, aerospace engineering executive, consultant; b. N.Y.C., Apr. 22, 1921; s. Edwin A. and Viola (Lewis) S.; m. Virginia Lee King, Sept. 25, 1948; children: Christopher K., Hilary L. Shank-Kuhl, Diana L. Boehm. B.S. in Mech. Engring., Carnegie-Mellon U., 1942; D.Sc., MIT, 1949. Registered profl. engr., Mass. Assoc. prof. mech. engring. MIT, Cambridge, 1949-60; with Pratt & Whitney, East Hartford, Conn., 1960-87, dir. engine design and structures engring., 1980-81, dir. engring. tech., 1981-85, dir. engring. tech. assessment, 1985-86; v.p. Pratt Whitney of China, Inc., East Hartford, 1986-87; pvt. exec. cons. to industry and govt., 1987—; cons. editor McGraw-Hill Book Co., N.Y.C., 1960-80; adv. com. to mechanics div. Nat. Bur. Standards, Washington, 1964-69; vis. com. dept. mech. engring. Carnegie-Mellon U., Pitts., 1968-78; corp. vis. coms. depts. materials sci. and engring., dept. aeros. and astronautics MIT, 1968-74, 79-92; mem. rsch. and tech. adv. coun. com. on aero. propulsion NASA, Washington, 1973-77, mem. aero. adv. com., 1978-86; mem. aero. and space engring. bd. NRC, 1989-92; lectr. in field. Contbr. articles to profl. jours. Served to maj. U.S. Army, 1942-46. Fellow AIAA, ASME, AIME, Am. Soc. Metals; mem. Nat. Acad. Engring., Conn. Acad. Sci. and Engring. Episcopalian. Club: Cosmos. Avocations: boating; fishing.

SHANK, ROBERT ELY, physician, preventive medicine educator emeritus; b. Louisville, Sept. 2, 1914; s. Oliver Orlando and Isabel Thompson (Ely) S.; m. Eleanor Caswell, July 29, 1942; children: Jane, Robert Oliver, Bruce. A.B., Westminster Coll., 1935; M.D., Washington U., 1939. Diplomate: Am. Bd. Nutrition. Intern, house physician Barnes Hosp., 1939-41; asst. resident physician, asst. in research Hosp. Rockefeller Inst. Med. Research, 1941-46; research asso. div. nutrition and physiology Pub. Health Research Inst. City N.Y., 1946-48; prof. preventive medicine Washington U. Sch. Medicine, 1948-55, Danforth prof. preventive medicine, 1955-83, prof. emeritus preventive medicine, 1983—; Cutter lectr. preventive medicine Harvard, 1964; Mem. food and nutrition bd. NRC, 1949-69; spl. cons. nutrition USPHS, 1949-53; chmn. adv. bd. health and hosps., St. Louis County, 1949-54; med. adv. bd. St. Louis Vis. Nurses Assn., 1950-86; mem. com. food and nutrition nat. adv. bd. health services A.R.C., 1950-53; mem. adv. com. metabolism Office Surgeon Gen., 1956-60, mem. adv. com. on nutrition, 1964-72; mem. Am. Bd. Nutrition, 1955-64, sec., treas., 1958-64; mem. Nat. Bd. Med. Examiners, 1957-58; co-dir. nutrition survey NIH, Peru, 1959, N.E. Brazil, 1963; mem. sci. adv. bd. Nat. Vitamin Found., 1958-61; mem. nutrition study sect. NIH, 1964-68, chmn. sect., 1966-68; mem. gastroenterology and nutrition tng. com., 1968-69, mem. nat. adv. child health and human devel. council, 1969-73; mem. clin. application and prevention adv. com. Nat. Heart, Lung and Blood Inst., 1976-80. Author sects. in med. textbooks, sci. papers relating to nutritional, metabolic disorders.; Asso. editor: Nutrition Revs, 1948-58; editorial adv. bd.: Nutrition Today, 1966-76, Hepatology, 1980-85. Served as lt. comdr. M.C. USNR, 1942-46. Recipient Alumni Achievement award Westminster Coll., 1970, Alumni Faculty award Washington U., 1989. Fellow Am. Pub. Health Assn. (governing council 1955-56), Am. Inst. Nutrition; mem. N.Y. Acad. Scis., Harvey Soc., Am. Soc. Biol. Chemists, Soc. Exptl. Biology and Medicine (council 1952-54), Central Soc. Clin. Research, Am. Soc. Clin. Investigation, Assn. Tchrs. Preventive Medicine (v.p. 1955-57, pres. 1957-58), A.M.A. (council on foods and nutrition 1960-69, chmn. 1963-66), Gerontological Soc., Assn. Am. Physicians, Am. Soc. Clin. Nutrition (council 1963-65, pres. 1967-68), Am. Dietetic Assn. (hon.), Am. Soc. for Study Liver Diseases (council 1963-66, pres. 1966), Am. Heart Assn. (chmn. nutrition com. 1973-76, award of merit 1981), Sigma Xi, Alpha Omega Alpha. Presbyterian. Home: 1325 Wilton Ln Saint Louis MO 63122-6940 Office: Wash U Sch Medicine 4566 Scott Ave Saint Louis MO 63110-1031

SHANK, RUSSELL, librarian, educator; b. Spokane, Wash., Sept. 2, 1925; s. Harry and Sadie S.; m. Doris Louise Hempfer, Nov. 9, 1951 (div.); children: Susan Marie, Peter Michael, Judith Louise. B.S., U. Wash., 1946, B.A., 1949; M.B.A., U. Wis., 1952; Dr.L.S., Columbia U., 1966. Reference libr. U. Wash., Seattle, 1949; asst. engring. libr. U. Wis.-Madison, 1949-52; chief pers. Milw. Pub. Libr., 1952; engring.-phys. scis. libr. Columbia U., N.Y.C., 1953-59; sr. lectr. Columbia U., 1964-66, assoc. prof., 1966-67; asst. univ. libr. U. Calif.-Berkeley, 1959-64; dir. sci. libr. N.Y. Met. Reference and Rsch., 1966-68; dir. librs. Smithsonian Instn., Washington, 1967-77; univ. libr. prof. UCLA, 1977-89, asst. vice chancellor for libr. and info. svcs. planning, 1989-91, univ. libr., prof. emeritus, 1991—; cons. Indonesian Inst. Sci., 1970; bd. cons. Pahlavi Nat. Library, Iran, 1975-76; pres. U.S. Book Exchange, 1975; bd. trustees Freedom to Read Found., 1989—. Trustee OCLC, Inc., 1978-84, 87, chmn., 1984; mem. library del. People's Republic of China, 1979; bd. dirs. Am. Council on Edn., 1980-81. Served with USNR, 1943-46. Recipient Disting. Alumnus award U. Wash. Sch. Librarianship, 1968, Role of Honor award Freedom to Read Found., 1990, Disting. Alumnus award Columbia U. Sch. Libr. Sci., 1992; fellow Coun. on Libr. Resources, 1973-74. Fellow AAAS; mem. ALA (pres. 1978-79, coun. 1961-65, 74-82, exec. bd. 1975-80, chmn. internat. rels. com. 1980-83, pres. info. sci. and automation div. 1968-69), Assn. Coll. and Rsch. Librs. (pres. 1972-73, Hugh Atkinson award 1990), Assn. Rsch. Librs. (bd. dirs. 1974-77). Home: 12919 Montana Ave Apt 101 Los Angeles CA 90049-4843 *Intellectual freedom is the paramount human right. It is the American's premier heritage. Without it the claim to democracy is a sham. Should the principles of our society fade or perish, the survival of this freedom alone would justify the nation's experience. The freedom to think, to read, and to speak will be our enduring monument. Their diffusion throughout the world must be our unending crusade.*

SHANK, THOM LEWIS, real estate executive, entertainment consultant, author; b. Butler, Pa., Apr. 23, 1953; s. Berdyne Delmont and Florence Elizabeth (Glasser) S. BA in Sociology, U. Pa., 1974; MBA, Pepperdine U., 1981. Negotiator Worldmark Travel, N.Y.C. and Phila., 1971-76; retail ops. mgr. Just Plants, Inc., Roxborough, Pa., 1973-79; founder, mgr. The Best-direct mail sales, Edgemoor, Del., 1974-79; property mgr. Moss and Co., Westwood, Calif., 1977-82; talent mgr. Thom Shank Assocs., Brentwood, Calif., 1979-84; pres., founder The Great Am. Amusement Co., Palm Desert, Calif., 1979-84; sales exec. Fred Sands Realtors, Brentwood, 1981-85; sales and mktg. dir. Coldwell Banker, Newport Beach, Calif., 1985-86, Great Western Ranches, Burbank, Calif., 1988-95; dist. and regional mgr. E.R.A. Real Estate, Pasadena, Calif., 1986; owner Century 21 Realtors, Tarzana, Calif., 1987-89; resorts dir. Prudential Jon Douglas Co., Beverly Hills, Calif., 1996—. Lutheran. Avocations: tennis, flying, reading, film, photography. Office: 301 N Canon Dr Beverly Hills CA 90210

SHANK, WILLIAM O., lawyer; b. Hamilton, Ohio, Jan. 11, 1924; s. Horace Cooper and Bonnie (Winn) S.; m. Shirleen Allison, June 25, 1949; children—Allison Kay, Kristin Elizabeth. BA, Miami U., Oxford, O., 1947; JD, Yale, 1950. Bar: Ohio, Ill. bars, also U.S. Supreme Ct. bar. Pvt. practice Hamilton, Ohio, 1951-55, Chgo., 1955—; mem. firm Shank, Briede & Spoerl, 1951-55; assoc. Lord, Bissell & Brook, 1955-58; atty. Chemetron Corp., 1958-60, sr. atty., 1960-61, gen. atty., asst. sec., 1961-71, sec., gen. counsel, 1971-78; v.p., gen. counsel, sec. Walgreen Co., Deerfield, Ill., 1978-89; ptnr. Burditt & Radzius, Chartered, Chgo., 1989—; exec. v.p. Internat. Bus. Resources, Inc., Chgo., 1993—; mem. bus. adv. coun. Miami U., Oxford, Ohio, 1975—. Bd. dirs. Coun. for Cmty. Svcs. Met. Chgo., 1973-77; trustee Libr. Internat. Rels., 1971-78; bd. dirs. Chgo. Civic Fedn., 1984-89, Walgreen Drug Stores Hist. Found., 1990—; mem. Chgo. Crime Commn., 1985-89. 1st lt., pilot 8th Air Force, USAAF, World War II, ETO. Fellow Am. Bar Found. (life); mem. ABA (corp. gen. counsel), Ill. Bar Assn., Chgo. Bar Assn. (chmn. com. on corp. law depts. 1971-72, 89-90), Am. Soc. Corp. Secs. (pres. Chgo. regional group 1983-84, nat. bd. dirs. 1984-87), Yale U. Law Sch. Assn. (pres. Ill. Alumni, formerly exec. com. New Haven), Walgreen Alumni Assn. (pres. 1992-94), Legal Club (pres. 1979-80), Law Club, Univ. Club, Econ. Club, Yale Club of Chgo., Omicron Delta Kappa, Phi Delta Phi, Sigma Chi. Home: 755 S Shore Dr Crystal Lake IL 60014-5530 Office: Burditt & Radzius Chartered 333 W Wacker Dr Ste 2600 Chicago IL 60606-1227

SHANKEL, GERALD MARVIN, professional society administrator; b. Alma, Mich., Jan. 1, 1943; s. Marvin A. Shankel and Ruth E. (Walworth) Heppner; m. Lois M. Herzberg, June 22, 1963; children: Cheryl A., Jill M., Steven G. BA, Alma Coll., 1965; MBA, U. Mich., 1966. Auditor Ernst & Ernst, Detroit, 1966-68; mng. dir. fin. and adminstrn. Soc. Mfg. Engrs., Dearborn, Mich., 1968-87; assoc. exec. dir. fin. and adminstrn. ASME, N.Y.C., 1988-92; exec. dir. Nat. Assn. Corrosion Engrs. Internat., Houston, 1992—; bd. dirs. Greater Houston (Tex.) Visitors & Conv. Bur., 1994—. Mem. Am. Soc. Assn. Execs. (cert. assn. exec.), Coun. Engring. and Sci. Soc. Execs. (treas. 1978-86). Avocations: swimming, reading, traveling. Home: 3414 Cinco Lakes Dr Katy TX 77450-5775 Office: NACE Internat 1440 S Creek Dr Houston TX 77084-4906*

SHANKER, ALBERT, labor union official; b. N.Y.C., Sept. 14, 1928; s. Morris and Mamie S.; m. Edith Gerber, 1960; children: Carl, Adam, Jennie, Michael. B.A., U. Ill., 1949; postgrad., Columbia U.; Dr. Pedagogy (hon.), R.I. Coll., 1980; D.H.L. (hon.), CUNY Grad. Sch., 1983, Adelphi U., 1985; LL.D., U. Rochester, 1985. Tchr. elementary schs., jr. high sch. math. pub. schs. N.Y.C., 1952-59; pres. United Fedn. Tchrs., N.Y.C., 1964-86, Am. Fedn. Tchrs., Washington, 1974—; founding pres. Edn. Internat.; v.p. AFL-CIO, Washington, 1973—; chair dept. profl. employees, chmn. bd. AFL-CIO; chmn. bd. AFL-CIO; v.p. N.Y. State AFL-CIO, 1973—, mem. N.Y.C. Ctrl. Labor Coun., sec. Jewish Labor Com., 1965—; assoc. Univ. Seminar on Labor Columbia U.; hon. vice chmn. Am. Trade Union Coun. for Histradrut; mem. exec. com. Workers Def. League; mem. group Nat. Bd. Profl. Teaching Stds., 20th Century Fund; mem. labor adv. com. U.S. Holocaust Mus.; tchr. Hunter Coll., Harvard Grad. Sch. Edn.; scholar-in-residence U. Chgo., Claremont Coll., UCLA; apptd. White House Competitiveness Policy Coun., 1990; elected Ind. Sectr. Bd., 1990. Columnist (weekly) Where We Stand; contbr. articles to profl. and popular publs. Mem. labor com. Boy Scouts Am., 1969; bd. dirs. A. Philip Randolph Inst., 1965—, Internat. Rescue Com., 1973—, Com. for the Free World, 1980—; mem. internat. adv. coun. Population Inst., 1976—. Recipient Disting. Svc. medal Columbia U. Tchrs. Coll., Annual Labor Mgmt. award The Work Am. Inst., 1990. Mem. Nat. Acad. Edn., Nat. Bd. Profl. Teaching Standards. Democrat. Jewish. Avocations: reading, music, gardening, gourmet cooking. Office: Am Fedn Tchrs 555 New Jersey Ave NW Washington DC 20001-2029

SHANKER, MORRIS GERALD, lawyer, educator; b. Cleve., Aug. 23, 1926; s. Hyman and Anna (Kaplan) S.; m. Bernice Jacobs, Dec. 16, 1956; children: Chari, Jaymie Ann. BSEE, Purdue U., 1948; MBA, JD, U. Mich., 1952. Bar: Ohio 1952. Assoc. Grossman, Schlesinger & Carter, Cleve., 1952-61; prof. law Case Western Res. U., Cleve., 1961—, acting dean Law Sch., 1972—, John Home Kapp prof. law, 1975—; vis. prof. law U. Mich., 1964, U. Calif., Berkeley, 1966, Wayne State U., 1969, U. London, 1971, 87; cons., asst. reporter adv. com. on bankruptcy rules U.S. Supreme Ct., 1965-68, mem. com., 1969-77; mem. Nat. Bankruptcy Conf., 1966—; comml. and labor arbitrator; spl. master R.R. reorgn. procedures; lectr. comml. and bankruptcy law throughout U.S., Can. and U.K., 1961—. Contbr. articles to profl. jours. With USNR, 1944-46. Fellow Am. Coll. Bankruptcy; mem. ABA, Ohio Bar Assn., Cleve. Bar Assn., Am. Law Inst., Nat. Bankruptcy Conf., Order of Coif, Tau Beta Pi, Eta Kappa Nu. Home: 15712 Chadbourne Rd Cleveland OH 44120-3334 Office: Sch Law Case Western Res U Cleveland OH 44106

SHANKLIN, RICHARD VAIR, III, mechanical engineer; b. Bklyn., Feb. 12, 1937; s. Richard Vair and Sue Hall (Morfit) S.; m. Margaret Krogstad Courtney, July 3, 1981; children by previous marriage: Carolyn Dennett Shanklin Payne, Anne Landon Scott Weaver. B.S.M.E., Duke U., 1959; M.S., U. Tenn., 1965, Ph.D., 1971. Engring. asst. Phillips Petroleum Co., Tex., 1959-60; assoc. engr. Boeing Co., Seattle, 1960-62; design engr. Aro Inc., Arnold Air Force Sta., Tenn., 1962-64; chief engr. J.B. Dicks & Assos., Inc., Tullahoma, Tenn., 1967-70; assoc. prof. mech. engring. technology Nashville State Tech. Inst., 1971-72; asst. prof. U. Tenn., Tullahoma, 1972-73; sr. scientist Systems Research Labs., Dayton, Ohio, 1973-75; asst. dir. MHD div. ERDA, Washington, 1975-77; sr. staff engr. Energy Systems Group, TRW Inc., Morgantown, W.Va., 1977-78; dir. MHD div. Dept. Energy, Washington, 1978-79; mgr. combustion programs Energy Systems Group, TRW, Inc., Redondo Beach, Calif., 1979-80; asst. ops. mgr. for process devel. Energy Systems Group, TRW, Inc., McLean, Va., 1980-82; project officer U.S. Synthetic Fuels Corp., Washington, 1982-86; cons. to industry, 1986-89; dir. planning and facility transition BDM Fed., Inc., McLean, Va., 1989-95; cons. to industry, 1995—. Author papers and reports in field. Recipient Spl. Achievement awards ERDA, 1976, 77. Mem. ASME (George Westinghouse silver medal 1976), Cosmos Club Washington, Sigma Xi. Episcopalian. Home: 6206 Hardy Dr Mc Lean VA 22101-3113

SHANKS, CARROLL D., insurance company executive. With IBM Corp., 1954-65; with Nat. Life & Accident Ins. Co., 1965-82; sr. v.p. NLT Corp., 1982; pres., chief operating officer Am. Gen. Cos., Nashville, 1982-84, pres., chief exec. officer, 1984-85; now chmn. Equitable Life Ins. Co., Nashville, 1986—; chmn., chief exec. officer Am. Gen. Life and Accident, Life and Casualty Ins. Co. of Tenn., AGC Life Ins. Co., Am. Gen. of Okla. Office: Am Gen Life & Accident Ins Co Am Gen Ctr-Nashville Nashville TN 37250 also: Equitable Life Ins Co PO Box 900 Mc Lean VA 22101-0900

SHANKS, DAVID, publishing executive. Pres. Berkley Pub. Co., N.Y.C. Office: Berkley Pub Group 200 Madison Ave New York NY 10016-3903*

SHANKS, HERSHEL, editor, writer; b. Sharon, Pa., Mar. 8, 1930; s. Martin and Mildred (Freedman) S.; m. Judith Alexander Weil, Feb. 20, 1966; children: Elizabeth Jean, Julia Emily. BA, Haverford (Pa.) Coll., 1952; MA, Columbia, 1953; LLB, Harvard, 1956. Bar: D.C. 1956. Trial atty. Dept. Justice, 1956-59; pvt. practice Washington, 1959-88; ptnr. Glassie, Pewett, Beebe & Shanks, 1964-88; editor Bibl. Archaeology Rev., Washington, 1975—; pres. Bibl. Archaeology Soc., 1974—, Jewish Ednl. Ventures Inc., 1987—. Author: The Art and Craft of Judging, 1968, The City of David, 1973, Judaism in Stone, 1979, Jerusalem--An Archaeological Biography, 1995, also articles; co-editor: Recent Archaeology in the Land of Israel, 1984; editor: Ancient Israel, A Short History, 1988, Christianity and Rabbinic Judaism, 1992, Understanding the Dead Sea Scrolls, 1992; editor Bible Rev., 1985—, Moment mag., 1987—. Mem. ABA, D.C. Bar Assn., Am. Schs. Oriental Rsch., Nat. Press Club, Phi Beta Kappa. Home: 5208 38th St NW Washington DC 20015-1812 Office: Bibl Archaeology Soc 4710 41st St NW Washington DC 20016-1700 *I try to take time to identify what is important in my life, to focus on that and ignore the rest when it conflicts. It takes conscious effort not to dissipate energy on activities and attitudes that don't matter in the big picture of my priorities. Free to concentrate on what I value most, I try to accomplish something each day in a regular, habitual way.*

SHANKS, JUDITH WEIL, editor; b. Montgomery, Ala., Nov. 2, 1941; d. Roman Lee and Charlotte (Alexander) Weil; m. Hershel Shanks, Feb. 20, 1966; children: Elizabeth Jeannette, Julia Emily. BA in Econs., Wellesley Coll., 1963; MBA, Trinity Coll., 1980. Econs. asst. Export-Import Bank, Washington, 1963-68; cons. econs. and social sci., 1968-76; researcher Time-Life Books, Alexandria, Va., 1976-80, prin. researcher, 1980-83, illustrations editor, 1983, adminstrv. editor, 1984-95, dir. editl. adminstrn., 1996. Vol. dinner program for homeless women, Mentors, Inc., vol. mentor with Mentors, Inc.; bd. dirs. Anne Frank House, for formerly homeless women. Mem. Garden Writers Am., Internat. Alliance, Washington Alliance Bus. Women, Leadership Greater Washington, Washington Wellesley Club (career caucus). Democrat. Jewish. Avocations: hiking, scuba diving, dancing, gardening, research on women in finance and business area. Home: 5208 38th St NW Washington DC 20015-1812

SHANKS, KATHRYN MARY, health care administrator; b. Glens Falls, N.Y., Aug. 4, 1950; d. John Anthony and Lenita (Combs) S. BS summa cum laude, Spring Hill Coll., 1972; MPA, Auburn U., 1976. Program evaluator Mobile Mental Health, Ala., 1972-73; dir. spl. projects Ala. Dept. Mental Health, Montgomery, 1973-76; dir. adminstrn. S.W. Ala. Mental Health/Mental Retardation, Andulusia, Ala., 1976-78; adminstr. Mobile County Health Dept., 1978-82; exec. dir. Coastal Family Health Ctr., Biloxi, Miss., 1982-95; cons. med. group practice, 1995—; ptnr. Shanks & Allen, Mobile, 1979—; healthcare consulting pvt. practice, 1995—; cons. S.W. Health Agy., Tylertown, Miss., 1984-86; preceptor Sch. Nursing, U. So. Miss., Hattiesburg, 1983, 84; advisor Headstart Program, Gulfport, Miss., 1984—, LPN Program, Gulf Coast C.C., 1984—; lectr. Auburn U., Montgomery, 1977-78. Bd. dirs. Mobile Cmty. Action Agy., 1979-81, Moore Cmty. House; mem. S.W. Ala. Regional Goals Forum, Mobile, 1971-72, Cardiac Rehab. Study Com., Biloxi, Miss., 1983-84, Mothers and Babies Coalition, Jackson, Miss., 1983—, Gulf Coast Coalition Human Svcs., Biloxi, Miss., 1983—; exec. dir. Year for Miss., 1993-94. Spring Hill Coll. Pres.'s scholar, 1972. Mem. Miss. Primary Health Care Assn. (pres.), Med. Group Mgmt. Assn., Biloxi C. of C., ACLU, Soc. for Advancement of Ambulatory Care, Spring Hills Alumni Assn. Avocations: tennis, home restoration, golf. Office: Coastal Family Health Ctr PO Box 475 1046 Division St Biloxi MS 39533

SHANKS, ROBERT BRUCE, lawyer; b. Gallipolis, Ohio, Jan. 2, 1950; s. William and Kathryn (Morrow) S.; m. Margaret Elizabeth McCloskey, Sept. 15, 1984; children: Bruce, Brennan, Grace. AB, Brown U., 1972; JD, U. Va., 1975. Bar: D.C. 1977, U.S. Dist. Ct. D.C. 1977, U.S. Ct. Appeals (D.C. cir.) 1977, U.S. Supreme Ct. 1981. Law clk. to hon. judge Edward A. Tamm U.S. Ct. Appeals (D.C. cir.), 1975-76; law clk. to assoc. justice William J. Brennan Jr. U.S. Supreme Ct., 1976-77; assoc. Steptoe and Johnson, Washington, 1977-78, Latham and Watkins, Washington, 1978-81; dep. asst. atty. gen. Dept. Justice, Washington, 1981-84; v.p., gen. counsel Overseas Pvt. Investment Corp., 1984-87; ptnr. Sidley & Austin, Washington, 1987-91, Latham & Watkins, Washington, 1991-95, Morrison & Foerster, Washington, 1995—; adj. prof. Sch. Law Georgetown U., Washington, 1982-85. Contbr. articles to profl. jours. Mem. ABA (chmn. com.), D.C. Bar Assn. (steering com. 1986-87), Washington Fgn. Law Soc. (bd. govs.), Internat. Law Inst. (bd. dirs.), Order of Coif, Phi Beta Kappa. Avocations: skiing, running, sailing. Office: Morrison & Foerster 20th & Penn Ave NW Washington DC 20008

SHANKS, STEPHEN RAY, architectural and structural engineering consultant; b. San Antonio, Nov. 1, 1956; s. Leroy and Jane Adams (Coats) S.; m. Vickie Lynn Morrow, Aug. 6, 1977; 1 child, Erin Monette. Student pub. schs., Corpus Christi, Tex. Engring. technician Gulf Coast Testing Lab., Inc., Corpus Christi, part-time, 1971-75, full-time, 1975-78; projects mgr., quality control adminstr. Shilstone Engring. Testing Lab. div. Profl. Service Industries, Tex. and La., 1978-86; assoc., sr. cons., quality assurance mgr., corp. radiation safety officer Bhate Engring. Corp., 1987—. Author: Procedures and Techniques for Construction Materials Testing, 1978, Inspection and Testing of Asphaltic Concrete, 1979, Concrete Barges: Construction and Repair Techniques, 1984, Management and Marketing Strategies for Branch Offices with Rural Influences, 1985, How to Improve Profitability and Increase the Quality of Services, 1986, Quality and Process Control Systems for Federal Highway Administration Projects, 1990, Causes and Prevention of Efflorescence in Masonry Construction, 1992, It's Coming Unglued: Case Studies in the Failure of White Marble Veneers, 1992, Ultrasonic Examination and Evaluation of Tubular T-, Y-, and K-Connections, 1993, Qualification and Certification of Nondestructive Testing Personnel, 1994; editor: (lit. mag.) Viva!, 1975; contbr. articles to profl. jours. Lay Eurcharistic min. St. Francis of Assisi Episc. Ch., Pelham, Ala.; bd. dirs. Episc. diocese Ala. Dept. Architecture, AIDS Task Force. Mem. ASTM, Am. Soc. of Nondestructive Testing (cert. ASNT NDT level III, bd. dirs. Birmingham sect.), Am. Concrete Inst., Am. Mgmt. Assn., Am. Welding Soc. (cert. welding inspector), Nat. Inst. for Cert. in Engring. Technologies (cert. sr. engring. technician), Constrn. Specifications Inst., Constrn. Mgmt. Assn. Am., Roof Cons. Inst. (reg. roof observer). Democrat. Episcopalian. Lodge: Rotary. Home: 19 King Valley Rd Pelham AL 35124-1915 Office: 5217 5th Ave S Birmingham AL 35212-3515

SHANLEY, JOHN PATRICK, screenwriter; b. N.Y., Oct. 13, 1950; m. Jayne Haynes (div.). Playwright: Ketchup, 1980, Rockaway, 1982, Welcome to the Moon, 1982, Danny and the Deep Blue Sea, 1984, Savage in Limbo, 1985, the dreamer examines his pillow: A Heterosexual Homily, 1985, Women of Manhattan, 1986, All for Charity, 1987, Italian-American Reconciliation, 1988, The Big Funk, 1990, Beggars in the House of Plenty, 1991, four dogs and a bone, 1993; screenwriter: Moonstruck, 1987 (Academy award best original screenplay 1987, Writers Guild of Am. award 1987), Five Corners, 1988 (Special Jury prize Barcelona Film Festival 1989), The January Man, 1989, Alive, 1993, We're Back!: A Dinosaur's Story, 1993; screenwriter, dir.: Joe Versus the Volcano, 1990; appeared in film Crossing Delancey, 1988. Office: care William Morris Agy 151 S El Camino Dr Beverly Hills CA 90212-2704

SHANMAN, JAMES ALAN, lawyer; b. Cin., Aug. 1, 1942; s. Jerome D. and Mildred Louise (Bloch) S.; m. Marilyn Louise Glassman, June 11, 1972; 1 child, Ellen Joan. BS, U. Pa., 1963; JD, Yale U., 1966. Bar: N.Y. 1967, U.S. Ct. Mil. Appeals 1971, U.S. Supreme Ct. 1971, U.S. Ct. Appeals (2d cir.) 1972, U.S. Dist. Ct. (so. and ea. dists.) N.Y. 1972, U.S. Ct. Internat. Trade 1976, U.S. Ct. Appeals (fed. cir.) 1987, U.S. Dist. Ct. (ea. dist.) Mich. 1989. Assoc. Cahill Gordon & Reindel, N.Y.C., 1971-74, Freeman, Meade, Wasserman, Sharfman & Schneider, N.Y.C., 1974-76; mem. firm Sharfman, Shanman, Poret & Siviglia, P.C., N.Y.C., 1976-95; ptnr. Camhy Karlinsky & Stein LLP, N.Y.C., 1995—; speaker on reins. law topics. Capt. USAF, 1966-71. Mem. ABA, N.Y. State Bar Assn., Assn. of Bar of City of N.Y. (com. ins. law 1985-88, 90-92, com. profl. liaibility ins. 1988-92, com. on assn. ins. plans 1989—), Am. Arbitration Assn. (comml. panel arbitrators 1980—). Office: Camhy Karlinsky & Stein LLP 16th Fl 1740 Broadway New York NY 10019-4315

SHANNAHAN, JOHN HENRY KELLY, energy consultant; b. Sparrows Point, Md., Nov. 1, 1913; s. John Henry Kelly and Beulah Williams (Day) S.; m. Mary Reynolds Kline, Apr. 222, 1939 (dec. Feb. 1995); children: John H.K., James R., Jennifer K. (Mrs. Bernard R. Koerner, Jr.). AB, Princeton U., 1934; postgrad., U. Mich., 1954. Sr. exec. program Mass. Inst. Tech., 1959; Comml. mgr. Ind.-Mich. Electric Co., 1955-59; asst. v.p. Am. Electric Power Service Corp., 1959-61; asst. to pres. Kans. Power & Light Co., 1961-63; v.p., exec. dir. Electric Heating Assn., 1964-72; pres. Electric Energy Assn., 1972-75; sr. v.p. Edison Electric Inst., N.Y.C., 1975—; cons. energy matters, 1975-80. Trustee Suttons Bay Congl. Ch. Maj. F.A., AUS, 1942-45, ETO. Decorated Bronze Star with oak leaf cluster; recipient Trend Maker award Elec. Info. Publs. Inc., 1967. Presbyterian (elder). Club: Marines Memorial (San Francisco), Suttons Bay Rotary. Home: 2393 N Lake Leelanau Dr Lake Leelanau MI 49653-9707

SHANNON, ALBERT JOSEPH, educator; b. Pitts., Apr. 12, 1949; s. William Park and Dorothea B. (Brown) S.; m. Mary Jean Boblick, May 22, 1971; children: Erica Lynne, Sean Paul. BA summa cum laude, Marquette U., 1971; MEd, Boston U., 1972; PhD, Marquette U., 1978; grad. mgmt. devel. program Harvard U., 1989. Tchr. reading North Div. High Sch., Milw., 1972-76; reading cons. sch. dists. Wis., 1976-78; mem. faculty St. Mary's Coll., Notre Dame, Ind., 1978-83, asst. prof. dept. edn., 1978-83; assoc. prof. Sch. Edn., Rider U., Lawrenceville, N.J., 1983-86; chmn. dept. edn., dir. grad. edn. St. Joseph's U., Phila., 1986-88, chmn., grad. dir. edn. and health svcs., 1988-92; v.p. acad. affairs St. Joseph's Coll., Rensellaer, 1992-93, pres. 1993—; cons. on reading edn., 1978—; cons. computer edn., N.J. Contbr. articles to profl. jours. Recipient Outstanding Secondary Teaching award, 1975; Nat. Endowment for Humanities fellow Middlebury Coll., 1987-88, Am. Coun. on Edn. fellow U. Pa., 1990-91; named Sagamore of the Wabash, Gov. Office in Ind., 1995. Mem. ACE, Nat. Collegiate Athletics Assn. (presdl. commn.), Ind. Coll. Found. (dir.), Phi Beta Kappa, Phi Delta Kappa. Roman Catholic. Home: 215 E Thompson St Rensselaer IN 47978-3133 Office: St Joseph's Coll Box 869 Rensselaer IN 47978

SHANNON, CLAUDE ELWOOD, mathematician, educator; b. Gaylord, Mich., Apr. 30, 1916; s. Claude Elwood and Mabel Catherine (Wolf) S.; m. Mary Elizabeth Moore, Mar. 27, 1949; children: Robert James, Andrew Moore, Margarita Catherine. BS, U. Mich., 1936, DSc, 1961; MS, PhD in Math., MIT, 1940; MS (hon.), Yale U., 1954; DSc, Princeton U., 1962, U. Edinburgh, Scotland, 1964, U. Pitts., 1964, Northwestern U., Evanston, Ill., 1970, Oxford (Eng.) U., 1978, East Anglia U., 1982, Carnegie Mellon U., 1984, Tufts U., 1987; DSc (hon.), U. Pa., 1991. Staff Carnegie Instn., Washington, 1939, Bolles fellow, 1939-40; Nat. Research fellow Princeton U., N.J., 1940; cons. Nat. Def. Research Com., 1941; research mathematician Bell Telephone Labs., 1941-72; vis. prof. elec. communications MIT, 1956, prof. communications scis. and math., 1957—, Donner prof. sci., 1958-78, prof. emeritus, 1978—; vis. fellow All Souls Coll., Oxford, 1978; Vanuxem lectr. Princeton U., 1958; Steinmetz lectr., Schenectady, 1962; Gibbs lectr. Am. Math. Soc., 1965; Shannon lectr. IEEE, 1973; Chichele Lectr. Oxford U., 1978. Author: Mathematical Theory on Communication, 1949; editor: (with J. Mccarthy) Automata Studies, 1956, Collected Papers, 1993; contbr. papers on math. subjects to profl. jours. Recipient AIEE award, 1940, Morris Liebmann Meml. award, 1949, Stuart Ballantine medal Franklin Inst. Phila., 1955, Research Corp. award, 1956, Mervin J. Kelly award AIEE, 1962, medal of honor IEEE, 1966, Harvey prize Am. Soc. for Technion, 1972, Eduard Rhein prize, 1991; medal of honor Rice U., 1962, Nat. Medal Sci., 1966, Golden Plate award, 1967, Jacquard award, 1978, Harold Pender award, 1978, John Fritz award, 1983, Audio Engring. Soc. Gold medal, 1985, Kyoto prize Basic Sci., 1985, Marquis Achievement award, 1985, Lord Found. award, 1989; fellow Ctr. Advanced Study Behavioral Scis., Stanford, Calif., 1957-58. Fellow IEEE; mem. Am. Acad. Arts. and Scis., Nat. Acad. Scis., Leopoldina Acad., Royal Netherlands Acad. Arts & Scis., Nat. Acad. Engring., Am. Philos. Soc., Royal Irish Acad., Royal Soc. of London, Tau Beta Pi, Sigma Xi, Phi Kappa Phi. Home: 5 Cambridge St Winchester MA 01890-3703

SHANNON, DAVID THOMAS, academic administrator; b. Richmond, Va., Sept. 26, 1933; s. Charlie Lee and Phyllis (Gary) S.; m. Shannon P. Averett, June 15, 1957; children—Vernitia Averett, Davine Belinda S. Sparks, David Thomas Jr. B.A., VA. Union U., 1954, B.D., 1957; S.T.M., Oberlin Grad. Sch. Theology, 1959; D. Min., Vanderbilt U., 1974; D.D. (hon.), U. Richmond, 1983; Ph.D., U. Pitts., 1975; LHD (hon.), Interdenominational Theol. Ctr., 1992; LLD (hon.), Tuskegee U., 1993. Pastor Fair Oaks (Va.) Bapt. Ch., 1954-57; student asst. Antioch Bapt. Ch., Cleve., 1957-59; grad. asst. Oberlin (Ohio) Grad. Sch. Theology, 1958-59; univ. pastor Va. Union U., Richmond, 1960-61, lectr. humanities and history, 1959-69; pastor Ebenezer Bapt. Ch., Richmond, 1960-69; eastern dir. Christian Higher Edn. Services Am. Bapt. Bd. Edn. and Publ., Valley Forge, Pa., 1969-71; vis. prof. St. Mary's Sem. Urban Tng. Program, Cleve., 1969-72; assoc. prof. religion and dir. minority studies Bucknell U., Lewisburg, Pa., 1971-72; dean faculty Pitts. Theol. Sem., 1972-79; Bibl. scholar Hartford (Conn.) Sem. Found., 1979; pres. Va. Union U., Richmond, 1979-85; vice pres. for acad. services, dean faculty Interdenominational Theol. Ctr., Atlanta, 1985-91; pres. Andover Newton Theol. Sch., Newton Centre, Mass., 1991-94, Allen U, Columbia, S.C., 1994—; co-chmn. internat. dialogue Secretariat of Roman Catholic Ch. Bapt., Rome and Washington, 1985-90; co-chmn. task force on witnessing apostolic faith World Council of Chs., Geneva, 1984—; mem. faith and order commn. Nat. Council of Chs., N.Y.C., 1984; mem. commn. on doctrine and inter-ch. cooperation Bapt. World Alliance, Washington, 1980—; active Faith and Order Commn. World Coun. Chs. Author: Studies in the Life and Works of Paul, 1961, Old Testament Experience of Faith, 1977; co-editor: (with G. Wilmore) Black Witness to the Apostolic Faith, 1985; contbr. articles to profl. jours., chpts. to books. Life mem. NAACP, N.Y., 1950. Recipient Nat. Clergy award Opportunities Industrialization Ctrs. Am., 1993; named Man of Yr., NCCJ, 1981. Mem. Am. Assn. Higher Edn., Am. Acad. Religion, Soc. for Study of Black Religion, Soc. Bibl. Lit., Newton Rotary Club, Alpha Kappa Mu, Phi Beta Sigma, Theta Phi. Home: 3072 Pavillion Tower Cir Columbia SC 29201-2367 Office: Allen U 1530 Harden St Columbia SC 29204

SHANNON, DONALD HAWKINS, retired newspaperman; b. Auburn, Wash., Feb. 1, 1923; s. Ernest Victor and Fern (McConville) S.; m. Sally van Deurs, June 13, 1952; children—John McConville, Susanna Shepard. B.A., Stanford, 1944; postgrad., Law Sch., 1946-47. Reporter Brazil Herald, Rio de Janeiro, 1947-48, U.P.I., London, Eng., 1949-51, Western Reporters, Washington, 1951-53; mem. staff Los Angeles Times, 1954-92; bur. chief Los Angeles Times, Paris, France, 1962-65, Africa, 1965-66, Tokyo, Japan, 1966-71; bur. chief UN, N.Y.C., 1971-75, UN (Washington bur.), 1975-92. Served with AUS, 1944-46, PTO. Mem. Phi Gamma Delta. Clubs: Federal City (Washington), City Tavern (Washington); Overseas Press (N.Y.C.); Foreign Correspondents (Tokyo). Address: 1068 30th St NW Washington DC 20007-3822

SHANNON, EDGAR FINLEY, JR., English language educator; b. Lexington, Va., June 4, 1918; s. Edgar Finley and Eleanor (Duncan) S.; m. Eleanor H. Bosworth, Feb. 11, 1956; children—Eleanor, Elizabeth, Lois, Susan, Virginia. A.B., Washington and Lee U., 1939, Litt.D., 1959; A.M., Duke U., 1941, Harvard U., 1947; Rhodes scholar, Merton Coll., Oxford, 1947-50; D.Phil., Oxford U., 1949, DLitt, 1996; LL.D., Rhodes Coll., 1960, Duke U., 1964, Hampden-Sydney Coll., 1971; H.H.D., Wake Forest U., 1964; D.H.L., Thomas Jefferson U., Phila., 1967, U. Hartford, 1981, Ohio State U., 1981; Litt.D., Centre Coll., 1968, Coll. William and Mary, 1973; L.H.D., Bridgewater Coll., 1970. Assoc. prof. naval. sci. and tactics Harvard U., 1946, instr. English, 1950-52, asst. prof. English, 1952-56; assoc. prof. English U. Va., Charlottesville, 1956-59; prof. English U. Va., 1959-74, pres., 1959-74, pres. emeritus, 1988—, Commonwealth prof. English, 1974-86, Linden Kent Meml. prof. English, 1986-88, prof. emeritus, 1988—, chmn. dept. English, 1980-81; mem. state and dist. selection coms. Rhodes scholars; pres. Council So. Univs., 1962-64, 71-72; pres. State Univs. Assn., 1963-64; exec. com. Nat. Assn. State Univs. and Land-Grant Colls., 1964-67, chmn. exec. com., 1966-67, pres., 1965-66; mem. So. Regional Edn. Bd., 1963-71; bd. govs. Nat. Commn. on Accrediting, 1961-67; mem. U.S. Nat. Commn. for UNESCO, 1966-67, Pres.'s Commn. on CIA Activities within U.S., 1975. Author: Tennyson and the Reviewers, 1952; editor: (with Cecil Y. Lang) The Letters of Alfred, Lord Tennyson, vol.I, 1981, vol. II, 1987, vol. III, 1990; contbr. articles to various jours. Bd. visitors U.S. Naval Acad., 1962-64, USAF Acad., 1965-67; bd. cons. Nat. War Coll., 1968-71; bd. dirs. Am. Council on Edn., 1967-70, vice chmn., 1971-72; trustee Thomas Jefferson Meml. Found., 1973-88, hon. trustee, 1988—, pres., 1980-83, chmn. 1987-88; trustee Washington and Lee U., 1973-85, Darlington Sch., 1966-76, Mariners Mus., 1966-75, Colonial Williamsburg Found., 1975-88; chmn. Va. Found. Humanities and Pub. Policy, 1973-79; v.p. Oceanic Edn. Found., 1968-83; bd. adminstrs. Va. Inst. Marine Sci., 1963-71; hon. v.p. Tennyson Soc., 1960—; mem. council White Burkett Miller Center for Pub. Affairs, 1975—; mem. Gov. Va.'s Task Force on Sci. and Tech., 1982-83. Served from midshipman to lt. comdr. USNR, 1941-46; capt. Res. ret. Decorated Bronze Star, Meritorious Service medal; Distinguished Eagle Scout, 1973; named Va. Cultural Laureate, 1987; recipient Distinguished Service award Va. State C. of C., 1969; Medallion of Honor Virginians of Md., 1964; Thomas Jefferson award U. Va., 1965; Algernon Sydney Sullivan award Washington and Lee U., 1939; Algernon Sydney Sullivan award U. Va., 1975; Jackson Davis award Va. chpt. AAUP, 1977, Disting. Alumnus award Darlington Sch., 1986; Guggenheim fellow, 1953-54; Fulbright research fellow Eng., 1953-54. Mem. MLA, Assn. Va. Colls. (pres. 1969-70), Raven Soc., Signet Soc., Jefferson Soc., Soc. Cin., Am. Soc. Order of St. John of Jerusalem, Phi Beta Kappa (senator 1967-85, vis. scholar 1976-77, v.p. 1976-79, pres. 1979-82, chmn. Coun. Nominating Com. 1988-94), Omicron Delta Kappa (Laurel Crowned Cir. award 1980), Phi Eta Sigma, Beta Theta Pi, Century Assn. Club, University Club (N.Y.C.). Presbyterian. Home: 250 Pantops Mountain Rd # 3 Charlottesville VA 22911-8600

SHANNON, JAMES PATRICK, foundation consultant, retired food company executive; b. South St. Paul, Minn., Feb. 16, 1921; s. Patrick Joseph and Mary Alice (McAuliffe) S.; m. Ruth Church Wilkinson, Aug. 2, 1969. B.A. in Classics, Coll. St. Thomas, St. Paul, 1941; M.A. in English, U. Minn., 1951; Ph.D., Yale U., 1955; J.D., U. N.Mex., 1973; LL.D., U. Notre Dame, 1964, Macalester Coll., 1964, Lora Coll., 1964, DePaul U., 1965, St. Mary's Coll., 1965, Carleton Coll., 1965, Creighton U., 1966, Northland Coll., Ashland, Wis., 1979, William Mitchell Coll. Law, 1980; Litt.D., Seton Hall, 1965, Coe Coll., Cedar Rapids, Iowa, 1966, U. Minn., 1966; J.U.D., Lawrence U., 1969. Ordained priest Roman Catholic Ch., 1946; asst. prof. history Coll. St. Thomas, 1954-56, pres., 1956-66; aux. bishop Archdiocese of St. Paul, 1965-68; pastor St. Helna Parish, Mpls., 1966-68; tutor Greek St. John's Coll., Santa Fe, 1969-70; v.p. St. John's Coll., 1969-70; mem. firm Sutin, Thayer & Browne, Albuquerque, Santa Fe, 1973-74; exec. dir. Mpls. Found., 1974-78; v.p. Gen. Mills, Inc., 1980-88; columnist, writer, found. cons., 1970-79, 88—; dir. Midwest Importers, Inc., 1988-96. Author: Catholic Colonization on the Western Frontier, 1957. Bd. dirs. James H. Hill Libr., St. Paul, 1985-94, Inst. Ecumenical and Cultural Rsch., Collegeville, Minn., 1985—, chmn., 1990-94; bd. dirs. Ind. Sector, Washington, 1988-94, N.Mex. Cmty. Found., 1991-95, Gen. Svc. Found., 1991-94; coun. Conf. Bd., 1982-88; chmn. Rhodes Scholarship Selection Com. for Upper Midwest Selection Com., 1976-86; chmn. coun. founds., Washington, 1984-85; vice chmn. Found. Ctr., N.Y.C.; sr. cons. Coun. on Founds. Mem. D.C. Bar Assn., N.Mex. Bar Assn., Minn. Bar Assn., Mpls. Club (bd. govs. 1989-96, pres. 1994-95). Democrat. Address: PO Box 112 Wayzata MN 55391-0112

SHANNON, LAWANDA BOOGHREY, elementary school educator; b. Shreveport, La., Aug. 2; d. Albert Banks and Elizabeth (Ford) Booghrey; m. Wilkin Ronald Shannon, July 1, 1989. BA, Grambling State U. Cert. tchr., Tex. Tchr. Carroll Peak Elem. Sch., Ft. Worth, 1990—; mem. dist. textbook adv. com. Ft. Worth Ind. Sch. Dist., 1993-94, mem. math. cadre, 1992—, tech. coord., 1994. Mem. Rainbow Coalition, Dallas, 1994, Allied Cmtys. of Tarrant, 1991—. Named Carroll Peak Tchr. of Yr., 1992-93, 95-96. Mem. United Educators Assn. (bldg. rep. 1993—), Nat. Coun. Tchrs. Math., Gamma Theta Upsilon (sec. Grambling chpt. 1977-79), Delta Sigma Theta (scholarship Shreveport chpt. 1975). Democrat. Baptist. Avocations: reading, playing tennis, listening to music. Home: 109 Nonesuch Pl Irving TX 75061 Office: Carroll Peak Elem Sch 1201 E Jefferson Ave Fort Worth TX 76104-5775

SHANNON, LYLE WILLIAM, sociology educator; b. Storm Lake, Iowa, Sept. 19, 1920; s. Bert Book and Amy Irene (Sivits) S.; m. Magdaline W. Shannon, Feb. 27, 1943; children: Mary Shannon Will, Robert William, John Thomas, Susan Michelle. BA, Cornell Coll., Mount Vernon, Iowa, 1942; MA, U. Wash., 1947, PhD, 1951. Acting instr. U. Wash., 1950-52; mem. faculty dept. sociology U. Wis., Madison, 1952-62, assoc. prof., 1958-62; prof. sociology U. Iowa, Iowa City, 1962—, chmn. dept. sociology and anthropology, 1962-70, dir. Iowa Urban Community Research Ctr., 1970—, prof. emeritus, 1991—; vis. prof. Portland State U., Wayne State U., U. Wyo., U. Colo. Author: Underdeveloped Areas, 1957, Minority Migrants in the Urban Community, 1973, Criminal Career Continuity: Its Social Context, 1988, Changing Patterns of Delinquency and Crime: A Longitudinal Study in Racine, 1991, Developing Areas, 1995, Socks and Cretin: Two Democats Helping Bill with the Presidency, 1995; editor: Social Ecology of the Community series, 1974-76. With USNR, 1942-46. Mem. AAAS, Am. Sociol. Assn., Midwest Sociol. Soc., Urban Affairs Assn., Population Assn. Am., Soc. Applied Anthropology, Am. Soc. Criminology, Phi Beta Kappa. Democrat. Lodge: Kiwanis. Home: River Heights Iowa City IA 52240 Office: Univ Iowa Iowa Urban Cmty Rsch Ctr 170W Seashore Hall Iowa City IA 52242-1402

SHANNON, MARGARET ANNE, lawyer; b. Detroit, July 6, 1945; d. Johannes Jacob and Vera Marie (Spade) Van De Graaf; m. Robert Selby Shannon, Feb. 4, 1967. Student Brown U., 1963-65; B.A. in History, Wayne State U., 1966, J.D., 1973. Bar: Mich. 1973. Housing aide City of Detroit, 1967-68; employment supr. Sinai Hosp., Detroit, 1968-69; assoc. gen. counsel regulatory affairs Blue Cross Blue Shield of Mich., Detroit, 1969-80; ptnr. Honigman Miller Schwartz and Cohn, Detroit, 1980-95, of counsel, 1996—. Nat. Merit scholar, 1963-66. Mem. Detroit Bar Assn., Mich. State Bar (chmn. health care com. 1991, 92, co-chmn. payor subcom. health law sect.), Nat. Health Lawyers Assn., ABA (vice chmn. pub. regulation of ins. law com. 1981-82), U. Liggett Sch. Alumni (bd. govs.). Home: 825 Park Ln Grosse Pointe MI 48230-1852 Office: Honigman Miller Schwartz and Cohn 2290 First National Bldg Detroit MI 48226

SHANNON, MARGARET T., nursing administrator, educator; b. New Haven, June 23, 1939; d. Michael Joseph and Ellen (McNamara) S. MS in Chemistry, St. Louis U., 1967; BSN, Northwestern State U. of La., Nachitoches, 1978; MN, La. State U., New Orleans, 1981; PhD., U. New Orleans, 1987. Staff nurse Touro Infirmary, New Orleans, 1978-80; instr. nursing Touro Infirmary Sch. Nursing, New Orleans, 1980-85; asst. prof. nursing La. State U. Med. Ctr., New Orleans, 1985-87; dean divsn. nursing Our Lady of Holy Cross Coll., New Orleans, 1988—. Author: (with B.A. Wilson) Giovani & Hayes Drugs and Nursing Implications, 8th edit., 1995, (with B.A. Wilson and C. Stang) Nurses' Drug Guide, 1993, 94, 95, 96. Mem. ANA, NLN, La. League for Nursing, La. State Nurses Assn., Sigma Theta Tau, Phi Kappa Phi, Phi Delta Kappa.

SHANNON, MARY LOU, adult health nursing educator; b. Memphis, Apr. 4, 1938; d. Sidney Richmond Shannon and Lucille (Gwaltney) Cloud. BSN, U. Tenn., 1959; MA, Columbia U., 1963, MEd, 1964, EdD, 1972. Staff nurse City of Memphis Hosps., 1959-60, instr. Sch. Nursing, 1960-62; asst. prof. U. Tenn., Memphis, 1964-70, assoc. prof., 1970-73, prof., 1973-89; prof., chair adult health dept. Sch. Nursing U. Tex., Galveston, 1989—; bd. dirs. Nat. Pressure Ulcer Adv. Panel, Buffalo, 1987-96; vis. prof. U. Alta., Edmonton, Can., 1982; mem. project adv. bd. RAND, Santa Monica, Calif., 1994. Contbr. chpts. to books in field and to periodicals; mem. editl. bd. Advances in Wound Care, 1987—. Trustee Nurses Edn. Funds, N.Y.C., 1972-86. Mem. ANA, Nat. League Nursing (bd. of rev. 1983-86), Orthopedic Nurses Assn., So. Nursing Rsch. Soc., Am. Assn. for History of Nursing. Avocations: travel, reading. Office: U Tex Sch Nursing 301 University Blvd Galveston TX 77550-2708

SHANNON, MICHAEL EDWARD, specialty chemical company executive; b. Evanston, Ill., Nov. 21, 1936; s. Edward Francis and Mildred Veronica (Oliver) S.; m. A. Laura McGrath, July 4, 1964; children: Claire Oliver Mary, Kathryn Ann Elizabeth. BA, U. Notre Dame, 1958; MBA, Stanford U., 1960. With Continental Oil Co., Houston, 1960-62; with Gulf Oil Corp., 1962-75, asst. treas., 1970-75; treas. Gulf Oil Co. U.S., Houston, 1970-72, Gulf Oil Co.-Ea. Hemisphere, London, 1972-75; treas. Republic Steel Corp., Cleve., 1975-84, v.p., 1978-82, exec. v.p., 1982-84; exec. v.p., chief fin. officer Ecolab Inc., St. Paul, 1984, chief fin. and adminstrv. officer, 1984-90; pres. ChemLawn Svcs. Corp., Columbus, Ohio, 1988-90; CFO Ecolab Inc., 1990-92, pres. Residential Svcs. Group, 1990-92, vice chmn., chief fin. and adminstrv. officer, 1992-95, chmn. bd., chief fin. and adminstrv. officer, 1996—; Bd. dirs. Minn. Pub. Radio, St. Paul, Minn. Orchestral Assn., Mpls., chair. Bd. dirs. Minn. Pub. Radio, St. Paul, Minn. Orchestral Assn., Mpls., chair-elect. Mem. Fin. Execs. Inst., Nat. Assn. Mfrs. (bd. dirs.), Univ. Club, Rolling Rock Club, Mpls. Club, Minikahada Club, Minn. Club. Roman Catholic. Office: Ecolab Inc 370 N Wabasha St Saint Paul MN 55102

SHANNON, PETER MICHAEL, JR., lawyer; b. Chgo., Oct. 13, 1928; s. Peter Michael Sr. and Marian (Burke) S.; m. Anne M. Mueller, April 3, 1969; children: Peter III, Stephen, Heather, Eamon. BA, St. Mary of the Lake, Mundelein, Ill., 1949, MA, 1952, STL, 1953; JCL, Gregorian U., Rome, 1958; JD, U. Calif., Berkeley, 1971. Bar: Calif. 1972, D.C. 1972, Ill. 1988, U.S. Dist. Ct. Md. 1972, U.S. Dist. Ct. D.C. 1972, U.S. Dist. Ct. (no. dist.) Ill. 1988, U.S. Ct. Appeals (1st, 2d, 3d, 4th, 5th, 6th, 7th, 8th, 9th and 10th cirs.) 1972-75, U.S. Supreme Ct. 1975. Supervisory atty. litigation U.S. Dept. of Justice, Washington, 1971-75; ptnr. Shannon, et al, Washington, 1980-82, Keck, Mahin & Cate, Chgo., 1982-96; with Arnstein & Lehr, Chgo., 1996—; sr. appellate atty. ICC, Washington, 1975-77, dir. enforcement, 1977-80. Author: Energy and Transportation Implications of Ratemaking Policy Concerning Sources of Energy, 1980, Disposition of Real Estate by Religious Institutions, 1987, The Dual Approach of Civil Law Courts to Ecclestical Related Disputes, 1988. Mem. ABA (chmn. transp. com., adminstrv. law and regulatory practice sect. 1984-87, coun. mem. 1988-91), Am. Acad. Hosp. Attys., Assn. Transp. Law, Logistics and Policy, Canon Law Soc. (pres. 1965-66). Office: Arnstein & Lehr 120 S Riverside Plz Ste 1200 Chicago IL 60606-3913

SHANNON, ROBERT RENNIE, optical sciences center administrator, educator; b. Mt. Vernon, N.Y., Oct. 3, 1932; s. Howard A. and Harriebell S.; m. Helen Lang, Feb. 13, 1954; children: Elizabeth, Barbara, Jennifer, Amy, John, Robert. B.S., U. Rochester, 1954, M.A., 1957. Dir. Optics Lab., ITEK Corp., Lexington, Mass., 1959-69; prof. Optical Scis. Ctr., U. Ariz., 1969—, dir., 1983-92, prof. emeritus, 1992—; cons. Lawrence Livermore Lab., 1980-90; trustee Aerospace Corp., 1985-94, 96—; mem. Air Force Sci. Adv. Bd., 1986-90; mem. NRC Commn. on Next Generation Currency, 1992-94; mem. com. on def. space tech. Air Force Studies Bd., 1989-93, Hubble Telescope recovery panel, 1990; bd. dirs. Precision Optics Corp. Editor: Applied Optics and Optical Engineering, Vol. 7, 1980, Vol. 8, 1981, Vol. 9, 1983, Vol. 10, 1987, Vol. 11, 1992. Fellow Optical Soc. Am. (pres. 1985, mem. engring. coun. 1989-91), Soc. Photo-Optical Instrumentation Engrs. (pres. 1979-80, recipient Goddard award 1982, Gold medal, 1996); mem. NAE, Tucson Soaring Club (past pres.), Sigma Xi. Home: 7040 E Taos Pl Tucson AZ 85715-3344 Office: U Ariz Optical Scis Ctr Tucson AZ 85721

SHANNON, STEPHEN QUINBY, broadcasting and human resources executive; b. Feb. 20, 1934; s. Stephen Quinby and Elsie Elaine (Vetter) S.; m. Laurine Shannon, July 29, 1968; children: Debbie Lynn, Stephen Quinby, Kathleen Elaine, Logan Michelle. BS, U. Ariz., 1956. Promotion mgr. Sta. KPHO-TV-Radio, Phoenix, 1956-61; adminstrv. mgr. Meredith Broadcasting, Omaha, 1961-62; dir. pub. rels. Sta. WHEN-TV-Radio, Syracuse, N.Y., 1962-63; v.p., gen. mgr. Meredith-Avco, Inc., 1964-69; adminstrv. mgr. Meredith Broadcasting, N.Y.C. and Omaha, 1969-72; gen. mgr. Sta. KCMO-KCEZ, v.p. broadcasting group Meredith Broadcasting, Kansas City, Mo., 1975-83; v.p. staff ops. Broadcasting Group Meredith Broadcasting, Kansas City, 1984-85; v.p., gen. mgr. Sta. WOW/KEZO, Omaha, 1972-75; exec. v.p. Sunbelt Communications, Colorado Springs, Colo., 1985-86; v.p.-radio

Palmer Communications, Inc., Ft.Myers, Fla., 1986-90; gen. mgr. Sta. WHO/KLYF, Des Moines, 1986-88; mng. dir. Exec. Group Inc., Boca Raton, Fla., 1991-93; sr. cons. EnterChange, Inc., Boca Raton, Fla., 1993-94; broadcast and human resource cons. Quinby Skylur, Inc., 1994—. Bd. dirs. Urban League of Greater Kansas City, 1979-83; bd. dirs., treas. Pers. Assn. Palm Beach County; mem. exec. com. Rep. Party of Palm Beach County; mem. Boca Raton Men's Rep. Club. Recipient Bernard Powell Community Service award C. of C. Greater Kansas City, 1981. Mem. Fla. Assn. Broadcasters, Employment Mgrs. Assn. U.S.A., Soc. Human Resource Mgmt., Rotary (bd. dirs. 1993-95 Boca Raton Noon Club). Home: 3825 Sabal Lakes Rd Delray Beach FL 33445-1214

SHANNON, THOMAS ALFRED, educational association administrator; b. Milw., Jan. 2, 1932; s. John Elwood and Eleanor Ann (Mitchell) S.; m. Barbara Ann Weidner, June 26, 1954; children: Thomas Alfred, Paul J., Suzanne L., Terrence D. BS, U. Wis, 1954; JD, U. Minn., 1961. Bar: Minn. 1961, Calif. 1963, U.S. Supreme Ct. 1965, D.C. 1977, Va. 1984; Life cert. as sch. adminstr., Calif.; cert. assoc. exec. Am. Soc. Assn. Execs. Practiced law Mpls., 1961-62; schs. atty. San Diego City Schs., 1962-73; dept. supt., gen. counsel, 1973-77; exec. dir. Nat. Sch. Bds. Assn., Washington, 1977—; adj. prof. law and edn. U. San Diego; vis. prof. edn. U. Va.; adv. mem. Edn. Commn. of States; prof. Nat. Acad. Sch. Execs., 1971—; legal counsel Am. Assn. Sch. Adminstrs., 1973-77. Exec. pub. The American School Board Jour, 1977—, Exec. Educator, 1978—, Sch. Bd. News, 1981—. Chmn. San Diego County Juvenile Justice Commn., 1973-74; mem. nat. coun. Boy Scouts Am., 1979—; bd. dirs. Found. for Teaching Econ., San Francisco, 1993—. With USN, 1954-59. Mem. VFW (life), Am. Bar Assn. (chmn. com. public edn. 1978-82), Nat. Orgn. on Legal Problems of Edn. (pres. 1973), Nat. Sch. Bds. Assn. (chmn. council sch. attys. 1967-69). Home: 3811 26th St N Arlington VA 22207-5241 Office: NSBA 1680 Duke St Alexandria VA 22314-3455

SHANNON, THOMAS FREDERIC, German language educator; b. Cambridge, Mass., Mar. 16, 1948; m. Christine D. Höner. BA in German summa cum laude, Boston Coll., 1969; MA in German Lit., SUNY, Albany, 1973; MA in Theoretical Linguistics, Ind. U., 1975, PhD in Germanic Linguistics, 1982. Instr. in German Boston Coll., 1969-70; teaching fellow in German SUNY, Albany, 1971-73; univ. fellow Ind. U., Bloomington, 1973-74, assoc. instr., 1974-76, 1979-80; acting asst. prof. in Germanic linguistics U. Calif., Berkeley, 1980-82, asst. prof., 1982-87, assoc. prof., 1987-94, prof., 1994—, dir. lang. lab., 1989-92, assoc. dir. Berkeley Lang. Ctr., 1994-95; co-organizer Berkeley Confs. on Dutch Lang. & Lit., 1987, 89, 91, 93, 95; econs., presenter, speaker in field. Contbr. articles to profl. jours. With USAR, 1970-76. Grantee U. Calif. Berkeley, 1983-84, 94-95, ACLS, 1987, Internat. Assn. Netherlandic Studies, 1988, 91, 94, Fulbright Found., 1976-78; NDEA fellow, 1969; Fulbright rsch./lectr. grante Rijksuniversiteit Groningen, Netherlands, 1992-93. Mem. MLA (exec. com. discussion group in Germanic philology 1989-94, discussion group for Netherlandic Studies 1995—, divsn. on lang. change 1995), Am. Assn. Netherlandic Studies (exec. com. 1988—, editor newsletter 1989-95, series editor publs. 1994—), Am. Assn. Tchrs. German, Assn. Computers and Humanities, Internat. Assn. Netherlandic Studies, Internat. Assn. Germanstik, Internat. Soc. Hist. Lingusitics, Linguistic Soc. Am., Netherlands Am. U. League, Pacific Ancient & Modern Lang. Assn., European Linguistic Soc., Soc. Germanic Philology (v.p. 1991-92, 95—), Alpha Sigma Nu. Home: 770 Rose Dr Benicia CA 94510-3709 Office: U Calif Dept German 5317 Dwinelle Hall Berkeley CA 94720-3243

SHANNON, WILLIAM NORMAN, III, marketing and international business educator, food service executive; b. Chgo., Nov. 20, 1937; s. William Norman Jr. and Lee (Lewis) S.; m. Bernice Urbanowicz, July 14, 1962; children: Kathleen Kelly, Colleen Patricia, Kerrie Ann. BS in Indsl. Mgmt., Carnegie Inst. Tech., 1959; MBA in Mktg. Mgmt., U. Toledo, 1963. Sales engr. Westinghouse Electric Co., Detroit, 1959-64; regional mgr. Toledo Scale, Chgo., 1964-70; v.p. J. Lloyd Johnson Assoc., Northbrook, Ill., 1970-72; mgr. spl. projects Hobart Mfg., Troy, Ohio, 1972-74; corp. v.p. mktg. Berkel, Inc., La Porte, Ind., 1974-79; gen. mgr. Berkel Products, Ltd., Toronto, Can., 1975-78; chmn. Avant Industries, Inc., Wheeling, Ill., 1979-81; chmn., pres. Hacienda Mexican Restaurants, South Bend, Ind., 1978—; chmn. Ziker Shannon Corp., South Bend, 1982-88, Hacienda Franchising Group, Inc., South Bend, Ind., 1987—; assoc. prof. mktg. and internat. bus. St. Mary's Coll., Notre Dame, Ind., 1982—; chmn. Hacienda Franchise Group, Inc., 1987—, Hacienda Mex. Restaurants Mgmt., Inc., 1994—; mem. London program faculty, 1986, 89, 92, 94, coord. internat. bus. curriculum, 1989—, mktg. curriculum, 1983, 88, 95—; advisor Coun. Internat. Bus. Devel., Notre Dame, 1991—; mng. dir. Alden & Torch Lake Railway, 1995—. Co-author: Laboratory Computers, 1971; columnist small bus. Bus. Digest mag., 1988—; bd. editors Jour. Bus. and Indsl. Mktg., 1986—; mem. bd. editorial advisors South Bend Tribune Business Weekly, 1990—; contbr. articles to profl. jours. V.p. mktg. Jr. Achievement, South Bend, Ind., 1987-90; pres. Small Bus. Devel. Coun., South Bend., 1987-90; bd. dirs. Ind. Small Bus. Coun., Indpls., 1986—, Mental Health Assn., South Bend, 1987-90, Michiana World Trade Orgn., Internat. Bus. Edn., 1989-91; Entrepreneurs Alliance Ind., 1988-92, Nat. Small Bus. United, Washington, 1989-92, Women's Bus. Initiative, 1986-90, dir. ednl. confs., 1986-90; chmn. bd. trustees, Holy Cross Coll., Notre Dame, Ind., 1987—, chmn. edn. com., 1993—; chmn. St. Joseph County Higher Edn. Coun., 1988-91, Nat. Coun. Small Bus., Washington, 1988—; Midwest region adv. coun. U.S. SBA, 1988-91; at-large mem. U.S. Govt. Adv. Coun. on Small Bus., Washington, 1988-90, 1994—, chmn. Bus. and Econ. Devel. Com., 1988-90, 1994—; vice chmn. Internat. Trade Com., 1994—; mem. nat. adv. coun. Women's Network for Entrepreneur Tng., 1991—; mem., vice chmn. State of Ind. Enterprise Zone Bd., 1991—; elected del. White House Conf. Small Bus., Washington, 1986; bd. dirs. Ind. Small Bus. Devel. Ctrs. Adv. Bd. Named Small Bus. Person of the Yr., City of South Bend, 1987, Small Bus. Advocate of the Yr., State of Ind., 1987, Ind. Entrepreneur Advocate of the Yr., 1988. Mem. Am. Mktg. Assn. (chmn. Mich./Ind. chpt., pres. 1985-86), U.S. Assn. Small Bus. and Entrepreneurship (nat. v.p. for entrepreneurship edn. 1991-92, nat. v.p. entrepreneurship devel. 1992—), Ind. Inst. New Bus. Ventures (mktg. faculty 1987-91), Michiana Investment Network (vice chmn. 1988-91), SBA (adminstrn. adv. coun. 1988—, contbg. editor Our Town Michiana mag. 1988-91), U.S. C. of C., Nat. Coun. Small Bus. (Washington), South Bend C. of C. (bd. dirs. 1987—, vice chmn. membership 1993—), Assn. for Bus. Communications (co-chmn. Internat. Conf. 1986), Univ. Club Notre Dame (vice chmn.), Shamrock Club Notre Dame (exec. dir., trustee 1993—), Rotary. Roman Catholic. Home: 2920 S Twyckenham Dr South Bend IN 46614-2116 Office: Saint Mary's Coll Dept Bus Adminstrn Eco Notre Dame IN 46556 *Enjoy good fortune resulting from LUCK, an acronym for (L) Learning how to (U)Use your talents with genuine (C) Concern on how your (K) Knowlege can benefit others.*

SHANOR, CLARENCE RICHARD, clergyman; b. Butler, Pa., Dec. 26, 1924; s. Paul L. and Marion (McCandless) S.; B.A., Allegheny Coll., 1948; S.T.B., Boston U., 1951, Ph.D., 1958; m. Anna Lou Watts, June 23, 1948; 1 son, Richard Watts. Ordained to ministry Methodist Ch., 1950; pastor Meth. Ch., South Hamilton, Mass., 1951-54; research asso. Union Coll., Schenectady, 1954-55; prof. Christian edn. Nat. Coll., Kansas City, Mo., 1956-58; asso. minister First United Meth. Ch., St. Petersburg, Fla., 1958-61, First United Meth. Ch., Fullerton, Calif., 1961-66; coord. Metro dept. San Diego dist. United Meth. Union, San Diego, 1966-87, ret., 1987; pres. Human Svcs. Corp., 1972-77. Treas. San Diego County Ecumenical Conf., 1970-71, pres., 1975-77; chmn. Coalition Urban Ministries, 1970-71, Cultural and Religious Task Force Rancho San Diego, 1970-74; chmn. western jurisdiction Urban Network United Meth. Ch., 1978. Chmn. San Diego Citizens Com. Against Hunger, 1969-72; bd. dirs. Interfaith Housing Found., chmn., 1979, pres. 1988—; v.p. North County Interfaith Coun., 1987—; mem. Gaslamp Quarter Project Area Com., San Diego, 1978, mem. coun., 1980-84; chmn. bd. Horton House Corp., 1978; mem. Mayor's Task Force on the Homeless, 1983-84; chmn. Downtown Coordinating Coun., 1983-84; mem. regional Task Force on Homeless, 1986-87; vice-chmn. Community Congress, 1987, ret., 1987; bd. dirs. North County Interfaith Coun., 1987-92, Redwood Ter. Town Ct., 1995—; pres., bd. dirs. North County Housing Found., 1987-96. Recipient San Diego Inst. for Creativity award, 1969, Boss of Yr. award Am. Bus. Women's Assn., 1972, Christian Unity award Diocesan Ecumenical Commn., 1984, Congl. Disting. Svc. award, 1984, Helen Beardsley Human Rights award, 1986, Mayor O'Connor's Seahorse award 1989, Ecumenical Conf. award San Diego County, 1991, Vol. Extraordinaire award No. County Interfaith Coun., 1993. Author: (with Anna Lou Shanor) Kindergartner Meet Your World, 1966. Home: 1636 Desert Gln Escondido CA 92026-1849

SHANSBY, JOHN GARY, investment banker; b. Seattle, Aug. 25, 1937; s. John Jay and Jule E. (Boyer) S.; m. Joyce Ann Dunsmore, June 21, 1959 (div.); children: Sheri Lee, Kimberly Ann, Jay Thomas; m. Barbara Anderson De Meo, Jan. 1, 1983 (div.); m. Jane Robinson Dettner, May 1, 1990. B.A., U. Wash., 1959. Sales exec. Colgate-Palmolive Co., N.Y.C., 1959-67; subs. pres. Am. Home Products Corp., N.Y.C., 1968-71; v.p. Clorox Co., Oakland, Calif., 1972-73; ptnr. Booz, Allen & Hamilton, San Francisco, 1974-75; chmn. bd., chief exec. officer, dir. Shaklee Corp., San Francisco, 1975-86; mng. gen. ptnr. The Shansby Group, San Francisco, 1986—; bd. dirs. The Sharper Image. Chmn. Calif. State Commn. for Rev. of Master Plan Higher Edn.; founder J. Gary Shansby chair mktg. strtegy U. Calif., Berkeley; trustee Calif. State U. Mem. San Francisco C. of C. (past pres.), Villa Traverna Club, Pennask Lake Fishing Club (B.C.), Sky Club of N.Y.C., Sigma Nu. Republican. Office: The Shansby Group 250 Montgomery St San Francisco CA 94104-3401

SHANSTROM, JACK D., federal judge; b. Hewitt, Minn., Nov. 30, 1932; s. Harold A. and Willian (Wendorf) S.; m. June 22, 1957; children: Scott S., Susan K. BA in Law, U. Mont., 1956, BS in Bus., 1957, LLB, 1957. Atty. Park County, Livingston, Mont., 1960-65; judge 6th Jud. Dist. Livingston, 1965-82; U.S. magistrate Billings, Mont., 1983-90, U.S. Dist. judge, 1990—. Capt. USAF, 1957-60. Office: US Dist Ct PO Box 985 Billings MT 59103-0985*

SHANTZ, CAROLYN UHLINGER, psychology educator; b. Kalamazoo, Mich., May 19, 1935; d. James Roland and Gladys Irene (Jerrett) Uhlinger; m. David Ward Shantz, Aug. 17, 1963; children: Catherine Ann, Cynthia Anne. BA, DePauw U., 1957; MA, Purdue U., 1959, PhD, 1966. Rsch. assoc. Merrill-Palmer Inst., Detroit, 1965-71; prof. Wayne State U., Detroit, 1971—; com. mem. grant rev. panel NIMH, NIH, Washington, 1979-81, 84-86; reviewer grant proposals NSF, Washington, 1978—; cons. Random House, Knopf, Guilford, others. Editor Merrill-Palmer Quar., 1981—; contbr. articles to profl. jours. Rsch. grantee NSF, NICHHD, OEO, Edn., Spencer Found., 1966-89. Fellow Am. Psychol. Assn. (pres. div. on devel. psychology 1983-84), Am. Psychol. Soc.; mem. Soc. for Rsch. in Child Devel., Sigma Xi, Phi Beta Kappa. Office: Wayne State U Dept Psychology Detroit MI 48202

SHAO, OTIS HUNG-I, corporate executive, educator; b. Shanghai, China, July 18, 1923; came to U.S., 1949, naturalized, 1956; s. Ming Sun and Hannah (Chen) S.; m. Marie Sheng, Apr. 2, 1955. B.A., St. John's U., 1946; M.A., U. Colo., 1950; Ph.D., Brown U., 1957. From instr. to prof. polit. sci. Moravian Coll., Bethlehem, Pa., 1954-62; assoc. prof., then prof. polit. sci. Fla. Presbyn. Coll., St. Petersburg, 1962-68; prof. internat. politics, dean (Grad. Sch., U. Pacific), 1968-74; dir. Pub. Affairs Inst., 1969-74; provost Callison Coll., 1974-76; dean faculty, v.p. Occidental Coll., 1976-78; asso. exec. dir. sr. commn. Western Assn. Schs. and Colls., 1978-80; v.p., dean Hawaii Loa Coll., 1980-85; pres. Sheng Shao Enterprises Calif., 1985-92; CEO, chmn. D.S. Capital Internat., Calif., 1993-94; Mem. grad. students relations com. Council Grad. Schs. U.S., 1970-73; mem. exec. council undergrad. assessment program Ednl. Testing Service, 1978-80. Contbr. articles to profl. jours. Chmn. bd. dirs. Fgn. Policy Assn. Lehigh Valley, 1961-62; bd. dirs. World Affairs Council, San Joaquin County, 1969-77; trustee Inst. Med. Scis., Pacific Med. Center, San Francisco, 1968-72, optical scis. group of Profl. and Pub. Service Found., 1969-72; Resident fellow Harkness House, Brown U., 1953-54, Danforth Asso., 1958-85. Recipient Distinguished Service award Fgn. Policy Assn. Lehigh Valley, 1962. Mem. AAUP (pres. Fla. Presbyn. Coll. chpt. 1965-66), Am. Assn. Higher Edn., Rho Psi, Tau Kappa Epsilon. Democrat. Presbyn. Home: 6218 Embarcadero Dr Stockton CA 95219-3824

SHAO, SHIU, financial executive; b. Taipei, Taiwan, Rep. of China, Nov. 13, 1951; came to U.S., 1975; s. Chi-Ching and Tintz (Yu) S.; m. Misara Chan; 1 child, G.R. BS in Physics, Chan Yuan U., 1973; MBA in Fin., U. Pitts., 1977. Programmer analyst Standard Brands, Inc., Burlingame, Calif., 1977-78; acctg. analyst Watkins Johnson Co., Palo Alto, Calif., 1978-81; controller Oromeccanica Inc., Burbank, Calif., 1981-82; v.p. fin., CFO Oroamerica, Inc., Burbank, 1982—; dir. Am. Internat. Chain Co., Emex Corp. Author: Financial Credit Line Tie to Commodity Index for Precious Metals Industries, 1982. Jr. Achievement advisor, Santa Clara County, Calif., 1979. Served to 2d lt. Chinese Marine Corps, 1973-75. Mem. Nat. Assn. Accts. Home: 1568 Scenic Dr Pasadena CA 91103 Office: Oroamerica Inc 443 N Varney St Burbank CA 91502-1733

SHAPAZIAN, ROBERT MICHAEL, publishing executive; b. Fresno, Calif., Nov. 3, 1942; s. Ara Michael and Margaret (Azhderian) S. BA, U. Calif., 1964; AM, Harvard U., 1965, PhD in Renaissance English and Fine Arts, 1970. Design assoc. Arthur Elrod Assocs., L.A., 1971-73; v.p. El Mar Corp, Fresno, Calif., 1973-87; dir., art dir. The Lapis Press, Venice, Calif., 1987—; mem. photographic forum San Francisco Mus. Art, 1982-85, Mus. Modern Art, N.Y.C., 1985; mem. photographic com. Met. Mus. Art, N.Y.C., 1994; assoc. Gagosian Gallery, N.Y.C. Author: Metaphorics of Artificiality, 1970, Maurice Tabard, 1985; editor: Surrealists Look at Art, 1991 (AIGA award 1991, N.Y. Art Dirs. award 1991), A Witch, 1992 (AIGA award 1992, N.Y. Art Dirs. award 1992, L.A. Art Dirs. award 1992), Pacific Wall (AIGA award 1993), Albucius (We. Art Dirs. award 1993, N.Y. Art Dirs. award 1994). Bd. dirs. Big Brothers/Big Sisters, Fresno, Calif., 1980-82, Film Forum, L.A., 1984-86. Recipient Individual Achievement award Lit. Market Pl., N.Y.C., 1992, 23 awards for art direction and design; named Chevalier in Order of Arts and Letters, Govt. of France. Mem. Harvard Club (N.Y.C.). Avocations: twentieth century art, illustrated books, experimental photography. Office: PO Box 36821 Los Angeles CA 90036-0821

SHAPELL, NATHAN, financial and real estate executive; b. Poland, Mar. 6, 1922; s. Benjamin and Hela S.; m. Lilly Szenes, July 17, 1948; children: Vera Shapell Guerin, Benjamin (dec.). Co-founder Shapell Industries, Inc., Beverly Hills, Calif., 1955; now chmn. bd. Shapell Industries, Inc.; mem. adv. bd. Union Bank, Beverly Hills; mem. residential bldgs. adv. com. Calif. Energy Resources Conservation and Devel. Commn.; speaker in field. Mem. Calif. Commn. Govt. Reform, 1978; Atty. Gen. Calif. Adv. Council, Dist. Atty. Los Angeles County Adv. Council; chmn. Calif. Govt. Commn. Orgn. and Economy, 1975—, Gov.'s Task Force on Affordable Housing, 1980—; mem. adv. council Pres.'s Commn. on the Holocaust, 1979; pres. Am. Acad. Achievement, 1975—; mem. deans council UCLA Sch. Architecture and Urban Planning, 1976—. Author: Witness to the Truth, 1974. Trustee U. Santa Clara, Calif., 1976—; bd. councillors U. So. Calif. Med. Sch., 1973—. Recipient Golden Plate award Am. Acad. Achievement, 1974, Fin. World award, 1977. Jewish. Club: Hillcrest Country (Los Angeles). Prisoner in Auschwitz, 1943-45. Address: Shapell Industries Inc 8383 Wilshire Blvd Ste 700 Beverly Hills CA 90211-2406*

SHAPER, STEPHEN JAY, finance company executive; b. Houston, Oct. 7, 1936; s. Charles Harry and Ruth (L.) S.; m. Sue Z. Shaper, June 6, 1959; children: Peter, Park, Page, Penn. BS, Rice U., 1958; MBA, U. Harvard, 1960. Mfg. engr. Tex. Instruments, Houston, 1960-61; pres. El Patio Products Corp., Houston, 1961-87; chmn. Seville Industries, Ft. Worth, 1982-87; COO TeleCheck Internat., Inc., Houston, 1987—, also bd. dirs.; bd. dirs. Trussway Inc., Houston, CDP Corp., Dallas, Assoc. Bldg. Svcs., Houston, SSCI. Bd. dirs. Rice U.; chmn. Rice Fund Coun., Houston, 1989-90. Capt. U.S. Army, 1961. Mem. Breakfast Club Houston, Houston Racquet Club, April Sound Country Club. Avocations: handball, jogging, skiing, bridge. Home: 325 Ripple Creek Dr Houston TX 77024-6931 Office: TeleCheck Internat 5251 Westheimer Rd Ste 1000 Houston TX 77056-5405

SHAPERE, DUDLEY, philosophy educator; b. Harlingen, Tex., May 27, 1928; s. Dudley and Corinne (Pupkin) S.; m. Hannah Hardgrave; children—Hannah Elizabeth, Christine Ann; children by previous marriage: Alfred Dudley, Catherine Lucretia. B.A., Harvard U., 1949, M.A., 1955, Ph.D., 1957. Instr. philosophy Ohio State U., 1957-60; asst. prof. U. Chgo., 1960-65, asso. prof., 1965-67, prof., 1967-72, mem. com. on evolutionary biology, 1969-72, chmn. undergrad. program in history and philosophy of sci., 1966-72, chmn. com. on conceptual founds. sci., 1970-72; prof. U. Ill., Urbana, 1972-75, chmn. program in history and philosophy of sci. U. Ill., 1972-75; prof. U. Md., College Park, 1975-84; Z. Smith Reynolds prof. philosophy and history of sci. Wake Forest U., 1984—; mem. com. on history and philosophy of sci. U. Md., 1975-84; chmn. program in history and philosophy of sci. U. Md., 1983-84.; vis. prof. Rockefeller U., 1965-66, Harvard U., 1968; mem. Inst. Advanced Study, Princeton, N.J., 1978-79, 81, 89; spl. cons. (program dir.) program in history and philosophy of sci. NSF, 1966-75; Sigma Xi nat. biocentennial lectr., 1974-77. Author: Philosophical Problems of Natural Science, 1965, Galileo: A Philosophical Study, 1974, Reason and the Search for Knowledge, 1984; editorial bd.: Philosophy of Sci., Studies in History and Philosophy of Sci.; rev. bd.: Philosophy Research Archives; contbr. articles to profl. jours. Served with AUS, 1950-52. Recipient Quantrell award for excellence in undergrad. teaching U. Chgo., 1968; Disting. Scholar-Tchr. award U. Md., 1979-80. Fellow AAAS (sec. sec. 1972); mem. APA, Philosophy of Sci. Assn., History of Sci. Soc., Am. Philos. Assn., Acad. Internat. de Philosophie des Scis. Home: 3125 Turkey Hill Ct Winston Salem NC 27106-4951 Office: Wake Forest U PO Box 7229 Winston Salem NC 27109-7229

SHAPERO, HAROLD (SAMUEL), composer, pianist, educator; b. Lynn, Mass., Apr. 29, 1920; m. Esther Geller, 1945. Attended, Malkin Conservatory, Boston, 1936-37; studied composition with Ernst Krenek, 1937, studied piano with Eleanor Kerr; studied composition with Walter Piston, Harvard U., 1938-41; studied composition with Paul Hindemith, Berkshire Music Ctr., Tanglewood, Mass., 1970; studied composition with Nadia Boulanger, Longy Sch., 1942-43. Founding prof. music dept. Brandeis U., Waltham, Mass., 1952-85. Compositions include: (symphonies/orchestral) Nine-Minute Overture, 1940 (Am. Prix de Rome 1941), Serenade in D for string orch., 1945, Symphony for Classical Orch., 1947, The Travellers Overture, Sinfonia in C, 1948, Concerto for Orch., 1950, Credo, 1955, Lyric Dances, 1955, Partita in C. for piano and small orch., 1960, On Green Mountain, 1981; (chamber/instrumental) String Trio, 1938, Three Pieces for Three Pieces, 1939, Sonata for trumpet and piano, 1940, Sonata for piano, 1941, String Quartet, 1941, Sonata for violin and piano, 1942, Three Amateur Sonatas for piano, 1944, Variations in C for piano, 1947, Sonata in F for piano, 1948, American Variations for piano, 1950, On Green Mountain for jazz group, 1957, Three Improvisations in B for piano and synthesizer, 1968, Three Studies in C# for piano and synthesizer, 1969, Four Pieces in B flat for piano and synthesizer, 1970; (vocal/choral) Four Baritone Songs for voice, piano and cummings, 1942, Two Psalms, 1952, Hebrew Cantata, 1954, Two Hebrew Songs, 1973. Naumberg fellow, 1942, Guggenheim fellow, 1947, 48, Fulbright fellow, 1948; recipient Arthur George Knight prize, 1938, 40, Gershwin prize, 1946, Bearns prize, 1946. Office: Brandeis U Dept Music 415 South St Waltham MA 02254

SHAPEY, RALPH, composer, conductor, educator; b. Phila., Mar. 12, 1921; s. Max and Lillian (Paul) S.; m. Vera Shapiro, Oct. 28, 1957; 1 child, Max Klement; m. Elsa Charlston, Oct. 12, 1985. Student violin with Emanuel Zetlin; composition with, Stefan Wolpe. Prof. music U. Chgo., 1964-85, Disting. prof., 1985-91; ret., 1991; vis. prof. Queens Coll., 1973; chmn. admissions com. MacDowell Colony. Dir. Contemporary Chamber Players, Chgo., ret. 1994; asst. condr., Phila. Nat. Youth Adminstrn. Symphony Orch., 1938-42; guest condr., Phila. Symphony Orch. at Robin Hood Dell, 1942 (winner Phila. Finds Contest); condr. 1st performance saxophone quartet by Wolpe, McMillan Theatre, N.Y.C., 1950, repeat performance, Times Hall, N.Y.C., 1950; condr. clarinet concerto, N.Y. Philharmonic Chamber Soc., 1955, Internat. Soc. Contemporary Music, N.Y.C., 1961, 62, Phila., 1961-63, Fromm Found. Concert, N.Y.C., 1962; guest condr., London Symphony Orch. for BBC, mus. dir. orch. and chorus, U. Pa., 1963-64, mus. dir., Contemporary Chamber Players, U. Chgo., 1964—; Composer: Challenge-The Family of Man, for symphony orchestra, 1955, Mutations, for piano, 1956, Duo for Viola and Piano, 1957, Ontogeny for symphony orchestra, 1958, Form for piano, 1959, Rituals for symphony orchestra, 1959, Dimensions for soprano and 23 instruments, 1960, Incantations for soprano and 10 instruments, 1961, Convocation for chamber group, 1962, Birthday Piece for piano, 1962, Brass Quintet, 1963, String Quartet VI, 1963, VII, Sonance for carillon, 1964, Configurations for Flute and Piano, Praise, oratorio, Variations for piano, O Jerusalem, for soprano and flute, Songs of Eros, for soprano, orch. and tape, Covenant for Soprano, 16 players and tape, 1977, 21 Variations for Piano, 1978, Song of Songs 1, 1979, II, 1980, III, 1980, Evocation for cello, piano and percussion, 1979, Evocation III for viola and piano, 1981, Fanfare for 2 trumpets, horn, trombone and tuba, Concerto Grosso for woodwind quintet, 1981, Songs for Soprano and Piano, 1982, Passacaglia for Piano, 1982, Double Concerto for Violin, Cello and Orchestra, 1983, Discourse II for Violin, Clarinet, Cello, and Piano, 1983, Fantasy for Violin and Piano, 1983, Mann duo for Violin and Viola, 1983, Songs for Soprano and Four Instruments, 1984, Gottlieb Duo for Piano and Percussion, 1984, Variations for Organ, 1985, Duo Variations for Violin and Cello, 1985, Psalm I for Soprano and Piano, 1986, Psalm II for Baritone and Piano, 1986, Duo Variations for violin and cello, 1985, Soli for percussion, 1985, Kroslish Sonata for cello and piano, 1985, Symphonie Concertante for symphony orch. (commd. Phila. Orch.), 1986, Songs of Love (I am My Beloved's) for baritone and piano, 1986, Songs of Love (And My Beloved is Mine) for baritone and piano, 1986, Concerto for cello, piano and string orch., 1986, In Memorium for soprano,baritone and 9 players, 1987, Theme and Variations for harpsicord, 1987, Concertante #II for alto saxophone and 14 players, 1987, Songs of Joy for soprano and piano, 1987, Variations on a Cantus for piano, 1987, Kroslish Sonate for cello and piano, 1987, Concertante #I for trumpet and 10 players, 1987, Variations for Viola and 9 Players, 1987, 2 For 1 Solo for Snare Drum, 1988, Concerto Fantastique for Symphony Orch., 1989, Chgo. Symphony Orch., Intermezzo for Dulceme & piano/Celesta, 1990, Duo for 6 Winds, Two Players, 1991, Centennial Celebration for soprano, mezzo soprano, tenor, baritone and 12 players, 1991, Movement of VariedMoments for Two-flute and vibraphone, 1991, Trio 1992 for violin, cello, piano,1992, Trio Concertant for Violin, Piano and Percussion, 1992, Inventions for Clarinet and Percussion, 1992, Dinosaur Annex for Violin, Vibraphone & Marimba/Glock, 1993, String Quartet VIII, Naumberg, 1993, Constellations for Bang on the Can All-Stars, 1993, Rhapsody for Cello and Piano, 1993, Evocations # IV for Violin, Cello, Piano & Percussion, others: Recs. include: Music for a 20th Century Violinist, Fromm Variation: 31 Variations for Piano, 1973, Three for Six, 1980, 21 Variations for Piano. "Sonata Appassionata", "Sonata Profondo", 1995; "Stony Brook Concerto", Woodwinds brass, percussion, violin, 1996—. Served with AUS, 1942-45. Mac Arthur fellow, 1982, Inst. of Arts and Letters fellow, 1989; grantee Italian govt., 1959-60; recipient Creative Arts award Brandeis U., 1962, Nat. Found. Arts and Letters award, 1966, Norlin Found. award, 1978, 1st prize Friedheim award, 1990, Fromm award Outstanding contbn. 20th century Music, 1993. Mem. ASCAP, AAAL, Am. Acad. Arts and Scis., Internat. Soc. Contemporary Music (dir.). Office: U Chgo Dept Music 5845 S Ellis Ave Chicago IL 60637-1404 *My credo: Great art is a miracle! The music must speak for itself.*

SHAPIRA, DAVID S., food chain executive; b. 1942; married. B.A., Oberlin Coll., 1964; M.A., Stanford U., 1966. V.p. Giant Eagle, Inc. (formerly Giant Eagle Markets, Inc.), Pitts., 1974-81, pres., 1981-1994, chief exec. officer, also bd. dirs.; chmn. & CEO Giant Eagle, Youngstown; chmn. bd. Phar-Mor Inc., Youngstown. Office: Giant Eagle Inc 101 Kappa Dr Pittsburgh PA 15238-2809 Office: Tamarkin Company PO Box 1588 Youngstown OH 44501-1588*

SHAPIRO, ALVIN PHILIP, physician, educator; b. Nashville, Dec. 28, 1920; s. Samuel and Mollie (Levine) S.; m. Ruth Thomson, 1951; children: Debra, David. A.B., Cornell U., 1941; M.D., L.I. Coll. Medicine, Bklyn., 1944. Diplomate Nat. Bd. Med. Examiners.; cert. Am. Bd. Internal Medicine. Intern L.I. Coll. Hosp., Bklyn., 1944-45; asst. resident internal medicine Goldwater Meml. Hosp., N.Y.C., 1945-46; asst. resident psychiatry L.I. Coll. Hosp. and Kings County Hosp., 1947-48; practice acad. medicine specializing in internal medicine Cin., 1948-51, Dallas, 1951-56, Pitts., 1956—; research fellow Cin. Gen. Hosp., 1948-49; med. teaching fellow Commonwealth Fund Psychosomatic Program, 1949-51, attending physician, 1949-51; attending physician Parkland, VA hosps., Dallas, 1951-56, Presbyn.-Univ. Hosp., Pitts., 1957-61; sr. staff Presbyn.-Univ. Hosp., 1962—; attending physician VA Hosp., Pitts., 1960-66; cons. VA Hosp., 1967—; attending physician Shadyside Hosp., 1986—; co-dir. hypertension-renal clinic Falk Clinic U. Pitts., 1956-65, dir. hypertension clinic, 1965-86; instr. dept. internal medicine U. Cin. Coll. Medicine, 1949-51; asst. prof.

Southwestern Med. Sch., U. Tex., 1951-56; asst. prof. depts. clin. sci. and medicine U. Pitts. Sch. Medicine, 1956-60, assoc. prof. dept. medicine, 1960-67, prof., 1967-93, prof. emeritus, 1993—, dir. psychosomatic program dept. medicine, 1960-71, interim chief renal sect., 1962-65, chief clin. pharmacology-hypertension sect., 1960-71, assoc. dean acad. affairs, 1971-75, vice-chmn. dept. medicine, 1975-79, interim chmn. dept. medicine, 1977-79; dir. Internal Medicine Residency program, Shadyside Hosp., 1986-93; cons. AMA Council on Drugs, 1959, Med. Letter of Drugs and Therapy, 1960; Fulbright vis. prof. U. Utrecht, The Netherlands, 1968; chmn. spl. projects study com. Nat. Heart Inst., 1970, chmn. policy adv. bd. nat. hypertension study, 1972-82. Author: (with S.O. Waife) Clinical Evalution of New Drugs, 1959, Hypertension-Current Management, 1963, 77, Hypertension in Renal Disease, 1969, Pharmacologic Mechanisms in Control of Hypertension, 1971; assoc. editor: Psychosomatic Medicine, 1963-92; assoc. editor Integrative Physiol. and Behavioral Sci., 1990; contbr. articles to profl. jours. Served as capt. M.C. AUS, 1946-47. Co-recipient Albert Lasker spl. pub. health award, 1980. Fellow ACP (Laureate award for teaching excellence Pa. chpt. 1988), AAAS (elected 1989); mem. Am. Fedn. Clin. Rsch., Am. Psychosomatic Soc. (sec.-treas. 1969-73, pres. 1975), AMA, Am. Heart Assn. (med. adv. bd. coun. high blood pressure, coun. on circulation, coun. on epidemiology), Pa. County Med. Soc., Allegheny County Med. Soc., N.Y. Acad. Sci., Am. Diabetes Assn., Am. Soc. Clin. Investigation, Soc. for Exptl. Biology and Medicine, Am. Soc. for Pharmacology and Exptl. Therapeutics, Cen. Soc. Clin. Rsch., Internat. Soc. Hypertension, Acad. Behavioral Medicine (coun. 1986, pres. 1987), Alpha Omega Alpha. Achievements include research in hypertension and related diseases and in behavioral sciences. Office: Shadyside Hosp Pittsburgh PA 15232

SHAPIRO, ANNA, microbiologist, researcher; b. N.Y.C., Jan. 11, 1910; d. Samuel and Esther (Cohen) Lewis; m. Joseph Shapiro, Feb. 7, 1933 (dec. 1985); children: Joan Elisabeth Brandston (dec.), Joel Elias. BS in Biology and Chemistry, NYU, 1931, MS in Bacteriology, 1934, PhD in Microbiology, 1971. Lab. asst. Bellevue Med. Sch., NYU, 1931-33, instr., 1933-36; lectr. Hofstra U., L.I., 1963, Queensborough U., CUNY, Queens, 1964; rsch. asst. Haskins Lab. of Pace Univ., N.Y.C., 1971-80, rsch. assoc., 1980-83. Author: Methods of Enzymology, 1980, The In Vitro Cultivation of Pathogens of Tropical Diseases, 1980; contbr. articles to profl. jours. Mem. AAAS, N.Y. Acad. Sci. (Disting. Svc. award 1992), Sigma Xi. Achievements include rsch. in the conversion of Nitrobacter agilis from a strict autotroph to a heterotroph by using replica plating techniques which can be considered an adaptive mutation; blockade of respiratory systems of parasites by using iron chelators--this work led to further research in pathogenic African trypanosomes. Home: 2 Fifth Ave Apt 9J New York NY 10011

SHAPIRO, ASCHER HERMAN, mechanical engineer, educator, consultant; b. Bklyn., May 20, 1916; s. Bernard and Jennie (Kaplan) S.; m. Sylvia Charm, Dec. 24, 1939 (div. 1959); children: Peter Mark, Martha Ann, Bernett Mary; m. Regina Julia Lee, June 4, 1961 (div. 1972); m. Kathleen Larke Crawford, Sept. 6, 1985. Student, CCNY, 1932-35; SB, MIT, 1938, ScD, 1946; DSc (hon.), Salford U., Eng., 1978, Technion-Israel Inst. Tech., 1985. Asst. mech. engring. MIT, 1938-40, faculty, 1940—, prof. mech. engring., 1952—, prof. charge fluid mechanics divsn., mech. engring. dept., 1954-65, Ford prof. engring., 1962-75, chmn. faculty, 1964-65, head dept. mech. engring., 1965-74, inst. prof., 1975-86, inst. prof. emeritus, sr. lectr., 1986—; vis. prof. applied thermodynamics U. Cambridge, Eng., 1955-56; Akroyd Stuart Meml. lectr. Nottingham (Eng.) U., 1956; editor Acad. Press, Inc., 1962-65; cons. United Aircraft Corp., M.W. Kellogg Co., Arthur D. Little, Inc., Hardie-Tynes Mfg. Co., Carbon & Carbide Chems. Corp., Oak Ridge, Rohm & Haas Co., Ultrasonic Corp., Jackson & Moreland (Engrs.), Stone & Webster, Bendix Aviation, Oak Ridge Nat. Lab., Acushnet Processing Co., Kennecott Copper Co., Welch Sci., Sargent-Welch, Bird Machine Co., Organogenesis, Inc., CARR Separations, Inc., others; served on subcoms. on turbines, internal flow, compressors and turbines NACA; mem. Lexington Project to study and report on nuclear powered flight to AEC, summer 1948; dir. Project Dynamo to study and report to AEC on technol. and econs. nuclear power for civilian use, 1953, Lamp Wick study Office Naval Research, 1955; mem. tech. adv. panel aeronautics Dept. Def.; cons. ops. evaluation group Navy Dept.; sci. adv. bd. USAF, 1964-66; founder, mem. Nat. Com. for Fluid Mechanics Films, 1962—, chmn., 1962-65, 71—; chmn. com. on ednl. films Commn. on Engring. Edn., 1962-65; dir. lab. for devel. power plants for use in torpedoes Navy Dept., 1943-45; mem. ad hoc med. devices com. FDA, HEW, 1970-72; mem. com. Nat. Council for Research and Devel., Israel, 1971—; mem. com. sci. and pub. policy Nat. Acad. Scis., 1970-74. Author: The Dynamics and Thermodynamics of Compressible Fluid Flow, vol. 1, 1953, vol. 2, 1954 (with Chinese translation), Shape and Flow, 1961 (Japanese, Italian, German and Spanish translations); also 3 ednl. films, 39 videotape lecture series: Fluid Dynamics, 1984; contbr. over 130 articles to sci. jours.; mem. editl. bd. Applied Mechanics, 1955-56; mem. editl. com. Ann. Rev. Fluid Mechanics, 1967-71; mem. editl. bd. MIT Press, 1977-87, chmn., 1982-87. Mem. Town Meeting Arlington, Mass.; chmn. 1st Mass. chpt. Atlantic Union Com., 1951-52, mem. council, 1954—; bd. govs. Technion, Israel Inst. Tech., 1968-89. Recipient Naval Ordnance Devel. award, 1945; joint certificate outstanding contbn. War and Navy depts., 1947; Richards Meml. award ASME, 1960; Worcester Reed Warner medal, 1965; Fluids Engring. award, 1981; Townsend Harris medal Coll. City N.Y., 1978. Fellow AIAA, Am. Acad. Arts and Scis. (councillor 1967-71), ASME; mem. Am. Sci. Films Assn., Nat. Acad. Scis. (com. on sci. and pub. policy 1973-77), Nat. Acad. Engring. (adv. com. on edn. 1985-89), Am. Inst. Med. and Biol. Engring. (founding fellow), Biomed. Engring. Soc. (charter mem. 1968), AAAS, Am. Soc. Engring. Edn. (Lamme medal 1977), MIT Faculty Club, Cavendish Club (Brookline, Mass.), Sigma Xi, Tau Beta Pi, Pi Tau Sigma. Patentee fluid metering equipment, combustion chamber, propulsion apparatus, gas turbine aux., magnetic disc, magnetic disc storage device, vacuum pump, low-density wind tunnel, recipe calculator, decanter centrifuges (6). Home: 111 Perkins St Apt 86 Jamaica Plain MA 02130-4321

SHAPIRO, BABE, artist; b. Newark, N.J., May 4, 1937; s. George and Sarah (Kay) S. BA, N.J. State Tchrs. Coll., 1952; MA, CUNY-Hunter Coll., 1958. dir. Mount Royal Grad. Sch. Art, Md. Inst. Coll. Art, Balt., 1974—. One-man shows include Stable Gallery, N.Y.C., 1962-69, Gertrude Kasle Gallery, Detroit, 1971, 73, 75, A.M. Sachs Gallery, N.Y.C., 1971, 73, 75, 77, 80, Paula Allen Gallery, N.Y.C., 1986, Md. Art Place, Balt., 1990, Irving Gallery, Palm Beach, Fla., 1993; group shows include Newark Mus., 1958, 65, Pa. Acad. Fine Arts, 1962, Phila. Mus. Art, 1965, N.J. State Mus., Trenton, 1965, Cin. Mus. Art, 1966, Flint (Mich.) Inst. Art, 1969, Balt. Mus. Art, 1970, U. Md. Art Gallery, 1971, Colorado Springs Fine Arts Mus., 1972, Tex. Tech. U., 1974, Philbrook Art Ctr., Tulsa, 1975, Carnegie Inst., 1975, Anita Shapolsky Gallery, N.Y.C., 1994, Meyerhoff Gallery, Balt., 1995; represented in permanent collections Albright Knox Gallery, Buffalo, N.Y., Cooper Hewitt Mus., N.Y.C., Corcoran Gallery Art, Washington, Newark Edinburgh, Balt. Mus. Art, Storm King Art Ctr., Mountainville, N.Y., numerous others. Ford Found. grantee, 1966. Address: 31 Walker St New York NY 10013-3595

SHAPIRO, BARRY ROBERT, lawyer; b. Bklyn., Apr. 10, 1947; s. Sam and Jean (Moak) S.; m. Marjorie Spiegelman, Dec. 24, 1968; children: Andrew, Daniel. BA, Hofstra U., 1968; JD, Columbia U., 1973. Bar: N.Y., U.S. Dist. Ct. (so. dist.) N.Y., U.S. Ct. Appeals (2d cir.). Assoc. Shereff, Friedman et al, N.Y.C., 1973-74; v.p., gen. counsel Avis, Inc., Garden City, N.Y., 1974-83; ptnr. Farrell, Fritz, Caemmerer, Cleary, Barnosky & Armentano P.C., Uniondale, N.Y., 1983-88; sr. ptnr. Rivkin, Radler & Kremer, 1988—. Contbr. article to profl. jours. Chmn. bd. dirs. L.I. Philharmonic, Melville, N.Y., 1986—; bd. dirs. L.I. Coalition Fair Broadcasting, 1989—, Inst. Cmty. Devel., 1992-94, New Ctr. Wholistic Health Edn. Rsch., 1992—. Mem. ABA, N.Y. State Bar Assn., Nassau County Bar Assn. (lectr. 1985-86, 93), Hofstra Club (Hempstead, N.Y.). Avocations: sports, music. Office: Rivkin Radler & Kremer EAB Plz Uniondale NY 11556

SHAPIRO, BENNETT MICHAELS, biochemist, educator; b. Phila., July 14, 1939; s. Simon and Sara (Michaels) S.; m. Fredericka Foster, Mar. 13, 1982; children: Lisa, Lise, Jonathan. BS, Dickinson Coll., 1960; MD, Jefferson Med. Coll., 1964. Research assoc. NHLI, NIH, 1965-68, med. officer, 1970-71; vis. scientist Inst. Pasteur, Paris, 1968-70; from assoc. prof. to full prof. biochemistry U. Wash., 1971-90, chmn. biochemistry dept., 1985-90; exec. v.p. for worldwide basic rsch. Merck Rsch. Labs., Rahway, N.J., 1990—. Contbr. articles to profl. jour. Served as surgeon USPHS, 1968-70. John S. Guggenheim fellow, 1982; Japan Soc. for Promotion Sci., 1984. Mem. Am. Soc. Biol. Chemists, Am. Soc. Cell Biology, Am. Soc. Devel. Biology, Phi Beta Kappa, Alpha Omega Alpha. Office: Merck Rsch Labs PO Box 2000 Rahway NJ 07065-0900

SHAPIRO, BURTON LEONARD, oral pathologist, geneticist, educator; b. N.Y.C., Mar. 29, 1934; s. Nat Lazarus and Fay Rebecca (Gartenhouse) S.; m. Eileen Roman, Aug. 11, 1958; children—Norah Leah, Anne Rachael, Carla Faye. Student, Tufts U., 1951-54; D.D.S., NYU, 1958; M.S., U. Minn., 1962, Ph.D., 1966. Faculty U. Minn. Sch. Dentistry, Mpls., 1962—; assoc. prof. div. oral pathology U. Minn. Sch. Dentistry, 1966-70, prof., chmn. div. oral biology, 1970-79, prof., chmn. dept. oral biology, 1979-88, prof. dept. oral pathology and genetics, 1979-88, dir. grad. studies, mem. grad. faculty genetics, 1966—, prof. dept. oral sci., 1988—, mem. grad. faculty pathobiology, 1979; prof. dept. lab. medicine and pathology U. Minn. Sch. Medicine, 1985—, mem. Human Genetics Inst., 1988—, univ. senator, 1968-72, 88-93; also mem. med. staff U. Minn. Health Scis. Center; exec. com. Grad. Sch. U. Minn., chmn. health scis. policy rev. council, chmn. univ. faculty consultative com., 1988-92; chmn. univ. fin. and planning com. Grad. Sch. U. Minn., 1988; hon. research fellow Galton Lab. dept. human genetics Univ. Coll., London, 1974; spl. vis. prof. Japanese Ministry Edn., Sci. and Culture, 1983. Mem. adv. editorial bd.: Jour. Dental Research, 1971—; Contbr. articles to profl. jours. Served to lt. USNR, 1958-60. Am. Cancer Soc. postdoctoral fellow, 1960-62; advanced fellow, 1965-68; named Century Club Prof. of Yr., 1988. Fellow Am. Acad. Oral Pathology, AAAS; mem. Internat. Assn. Dental Research (councilor 1969), Am. Soc. Human Genetics, Craniofacial Biology Soc. (pres. 1972), Sigma Xi, Omicron Kappa Upsilon. Home: 148 Nina St # 2 Saint Paul MN 55102-2160 Office: U Minn Sch Dentistry Dept Oral Sci Minneapolis MN 55455

SHAPIRO, CHERYL BETH, lawyer; b. Neptune, N.J., July 11, 1962; d. Bernard D. and Marcia K. (Goldstein) S.; m. David B. Lebowitz, Nov. 22, 1992. BA, George Washington U., 1983; JD, Widener U., 1986. Bar: Pa. 1986, N.J. 1986. Law clk. Sanuel Shevlin, Phila., 1986; coord. planning & devel. Goldco Devel. C., Lakewood, N.J., 1986-87; law clk. Ct. Common Pleas, Phila., 1988-89; corp. atty. CSS Inds., Inc., Phila., 1989—. Pa. Bar Assn., Phila. Bar Assn., Phi Delta Phi. Avocations: theatre, travel. Office: CSS Inds Inc 1845 Walnut St Ste 800 Philadelphia PA 19103-4755

SHAPIRO, DAVID, artist, art historian; b. N.Y.C., Aug. 28, 1916; s. Jacob and Ida (Katz) S.; m. Cecile Peyser, June 18, 1944; children: Deborah Jane, Anna Roberta. Student, Ednl. Alliance Art Sch., 1933-35, Am. Artists Sch., 1936-39. Instr. Smith Coll., 1946-47, Bklyn. Coll., summer, 1947; asst. prof. art U. B.C., 1947-49; mem. faculty dept. art Hofstra U., 1961-81, prof. emeritus, 1981—; prof. fine art New Coll., 1972-81; prof. fine art, artist-in-residence U. Belgrade, Yugoslavia, 1981; vis. critic Vt. Studio Ctr., Johnson, Vt., 1990. Author: Social Realism: Art as a Weapon, 1973, Abstract Expressionism: A Critical Record, 1989; one-man shows include Ganso Gallery, N.Y.C., 1955, Milch Gallery, N.Y.C., 1958, 61, 63, Galleria Dell'Orso, Milan, 1971, Tweed Art Mus., Duluth, Minn, 1978, U. Belgrade Gallery, 1981; 50 yr. retrospective T.W. Wood Art Gallery, Vt. Coll. Arts Ctr., 1987; represented in permanent collections Bklyn. Mus., Met. Mus., Libr. Congress, Nat. Mus., Smithsonian Instn., Phila. Mus. Art. Fulbright grantee, 1951-52, 52-53; MacDowell fellow, 1976; Tamarind fellow, 1976; Nat. Endowment Arts, grantee, 1978; Fulbright grantee, 1980-81. Mem. Soc. Am. Graphic Artists (pres. 1968-70), Coll. Art Assn. Home: RR 1 Box 77 Cavendish VT 05142-9730 *My work and my family are the main interests in my life. Both make it very worthwhile.*

SHAPIRO, DAVID L., lawyer; b. Corsicana, Tex., May 19, 1936; s. Harry and Alice (Laibovitz) S. BA, U. Tex., 1967; JD, St. Mary's U., 1970. Bar: Tex. 1970, U.S. Dist. Ct. (we. dist.) Tex. 1972, U.S. Supreme Ct. 1975, U.S. Ct. Appeals (5th cir.) 1981. Assoc. Law Office Jim S. Phelps, Houston, 1971; pvt. practice Austin, 1972—; spl. counsel com. human resources Tex. Ho. Reps., Austin, 1973-74; counsel subcom. health svcs. Tex. Senate, Austin, 1983-87. With U.S. Army, 1959-61. Mem. State Bar Tex. (chmn. lawyer referral svc. com. 1980-82, adminstrn. of justice com. 1990-93, contbr. Media Law Handbook supplement 1986), Travis County Bar Assn. (sec.-treas. 1977-78, dir. 1979, pres. family law sect. 1980-81), Coll. of State Bar of Tex., Austin Criminal Def. Lawyers Assn. Democrat. Avocations: automobiles, reading. Home: 920 E 40th St #106 Austin TX 78751-4821

SHAPIRO, DAVID LOUIS, lawyer, educator; b. N.Y.C., Oct. 12, 1932; s. Louis and Sara (Grabelsky) S.; m. Jane Wilkins Bennett, June 19, 1954; 1 child, Lynn Mayson. Grad., Horace Mann Sch., 1950; A.B. magna cum laude, Harvard U., 1954, LL.B. summa cum laude, 1957. Bar: D.C. 1957, Mass. 1964. Assoc. atty. firm Covington & Burling, Washington, 1957-62; law clk. Supreme Ct. Justice John M. Harlan, 1962-63; faculty Harvard Law Sch., 1963—, prof. law, 1966—, William Nelson Cromwell prof. law, 1984—, assoc. dean, 1971-76; dep. solicitor gen. U.S. Dept. Justice, 1988-91; mem. labor arbitration and comml. arbitration panels Am. Arbitration Assn., 1966-89; reporter, adv. com. on fair trial and free press ABA, 1965-68. Author: (with others) The Federal Courts and the Federal System, 1973, 88, 96, Federalism: A Dialogue, 1995; editor: The Evolution of a Judicial Philosophy: Selected Opinions of Justice John M. Harlan, 1969; directing editor Found. Press, Univ. Casebook Series, 1980—; contbr. articles to profl. jours. Mem. Am. Law Inst. (asst. reporter study of div. of jurisdiction 1963-65, reporter Restatement of Judgments 2d 1970-74). Home: 17 Wendell St Cambridge MA 02138-1816 Office: Law Sch Harvard U Cambridge MA 02138

SHAPIRO, DEBBIE LYNN (LYNN SHAPIRO), singer, actress, dancer; b. Santa Monica, Calif., Sept. 29; d. Morton Harold and Anne (Lipsman) S.; m. Beau Gravitte, Sept. 21, 1986. Appeared in Broadway shows including Jerome Robbins' (Tony award 1989, N.Y. Women Stopper award 1989), Zorba, Blues in the Night, Perfectly Frank (Drama Desk nomination); (Broadway debut) They're Playing our Song; Annie Get Your Gun, Spotlight, Swing, King's Tapestry, Berlin to Broadway, Gentleman Prefer Blondes, Mack and Mabel; TV shows include Broadway Plays Washington, CBS Cable Songwriters Series, Trial and Error; TV appearances Pat Sajak, Merv Griffin Show; recs. include Mack and Mabel in Concert; Zorba (with Anthony Quinn), The Songs of Stephen Sondheim, The Songs of N.Y., Jerome Robbins Broadway, They're Playing Song, The First Nudie Musical; nightclubs acts include Sands Hotel, Atlantic City, Harrah's, Atlantic City, Freddy's Supper Club, N.Y.C., Rainbow and Stars, Rockefellar Ctr., N.Y.C., Les Mouches, N.Y.C., The St. Regis Hotel, N.Y.C., others.

SHAPIRO, EDWARD MURAY, dermatologist; b. Denver, Oct. 6, 1924; s. Isador Benjamin and Sara (Berezin) S.; student U. Colo., 1941-43; m. Ruth Young, Oct. 14, 1944; children: Adrian Michael, Stefanie Ann; m. Dorothy Rosmarin, July 22, 1990. AB with honors, U. Tex., 1948, MD, 1952. Intern, Jefferson Coll. Medicine Hosp., Phila., 1952-53; resident in dermatology U. Tex. Med. Br., Galveston, 1953-55; resident in dermatology Henry Ford Hosp., Detroit, 1955-56, asso. in dermatology div. dermatology, 1956-57; clin. instr. dermatology Baylor U. Coll. Medicine, Houston, 1957-68, assoc. clin. prof., 1968—; staff Jefferson Davis Hosp., Houston, 1958—; active staff Pasadena Bayshore Hosp., 1962—, Southmore Hosp., Pasadena, 1958—. Served with USAAF, 1943-46. Henry J. N. Taub research grantee, 1958-60; diplomate Am. Bd. Dermatology. Fellow Am. Acad. Dermatology; mem. AMA, Tex. Med. Assn., Tex. Dermatol. Soc. (pres.-elect 1988, pres. 1989-90), South Cen. Dermatol. Assn. (bd. dirs. 1987-88), Harris County Med. Assn. (pres. S.E. br. 1968-69), Houston Dermatology Assn., Houston Art League, Gulf Coast Art Soc., Am. Physicians Art Assn. (v.p. 1993). Jewish. Clubs: B'nai B'rith, Rotary Internat. (Paul Harris fellow 1995). Contbr. articles in field to med. jours. Home: 2506 Potomac Dr Houston TX 77057-4548 Office: 1020 Pasadena Blvd Pasadena TX 77506-4700

SHAPIRO, EDWARD ROBERT, psychiatrist, educator, psychoanalyst; b. Boston, Sept. 13, 1941; s. Jacob and Ruth (Yankelovich) S.; m. Donna Elmendorf; 1 child, Joshua Jackson; 1 child from previous marriage, Jacob Matthew; 1 stepchild, Zachary Andrew Robbins. BA magna cum laude, Yale U., 1962; MA in Anthropology, Stanford U., 1966; MD, Harvard U., 1968. Diplomate Am. Bd. Psychiatry and Neurology. Intern in medicine Beth Israel Hosp., Boston, 1968-69; resident in psychiatry Mass. Mental Health Ctr., Boston, 1969-72, chief resident in psychiatry, 1971-72; clin. assoc. NIMH, Bethesda, Md., 1972-74; dir. Adolescent and Family Treatment and Study Ctr. McLean Hosp., Belmont, Mass., 1974-89, dir. Psychosocial Tng. and Consultation, 1989-91; bd. dirs. Ctr. for Study of Groups and Social Systems, Boston, 1983-90; bd. dirs. A.K. Rice Inst., Washington, 1983-90, dir. Nat. Group Rels. Conf., 1989-91; faculty mem. Boston Psychoanalytic Inst., 1978—; assoc. clin. prof. psychiatry Harvard Med. Sch., Boston, 1982—; med. dir. The Austen Riggs Ctr., Stockbridge, Mass., 1991—. Co-author: (with A.W. Carr) Lost in Familiar Places: Creating New Connections Between the Individual and Society, 1991; mem. editorial bd. Jour. Adolescence, 1977-82, Psychiatry, 1988—; assoc. editor Jour. Adolescence, 1982-84; contbr. articles to profl. jours. Mem. Yale Russian Chorus. With USPHS, 1972-74. Recipient Isenberg Teaching award McLean Hosp., 1980, Rsch. prize Soc. for Family Therapy and Rsch., 1984, Felix and Helen Deutsch Sci. prize Boston Psychoanalytic Inst., 1980. Fellow Am. Psychiat. Assn., Am. Psychoanalytic Assn., Am. Family Therapy Assn., Am. Coll. Psychoanalysis, A.K. Rice Inst.; mem. Group for Advanced Study of Psychiatry. Avocation: music. Office: The Austen Riggs Ctr PO Box 962 25 Main St Stockbridge MA 01262-0962

SHAPIRO, ELI, business consultant, educator, economist; b. Bklyn., June 13, 1916; s. Samuel and Pauline (Kushel) S.; m. Beatrice Ferbend, Jan. 18, 1946; 1 child, Laura J. A.B., Bklyn. Coll., 1936; A.M., Columbia U., 1937, Ph.D., 1939. Instr. Bklyn. Coll., 1936-41; rsch. assoc. Nat. Bur. Econ. Rsch., 1938-39; cons. Nat. Bur. Econ. Research, 1939-42; mem. rsch. staff Nat. Bur. Econ. Rsch., 1955-62; asst. prof. fin. U. Chgo., 1946-47, asso. prof., 1948-52, prof., 1952; prof. fin. Mass. Inst. Tech., 1952-61; assoc. dean Mass. Inst. Tech. (Sch. Indsl. Mgmt.), 1954-58, Alfred P. Sloan prof. mgmt., 1976-84, Alfred P. Sloan prof. emeritus, 1984—; prof. fin. Harvard Bus. Sch., 1962-72, Sylvan C. Coleman prof. fin. mgmt., 1968-72; chmn. fin. com., dir. Travelers Ins. Cos., Hartford, Conn., 1971-78; vice chmn. bd., dir. Travelers Ins. Cos., 1976-78; chmn. bd. Mass. Co., 1971-72; pres. Nat. Bur. Econ. Research, 1982-84; chmn. bd. Fed. Home Loan Bank Boston, 1970-89; econ. analyst div. monetary rsch. U.S. Dept. Treasury, 1941-42; economist rsch. div. OPA, 1941-42; staff cons. Com. Econ. Devel., 1950-51, mem. rsch. adv. com., 1961-64, 69—, project dir., 1966-69; cons. to sec. treasury; mem. enforcement commn. WSB, 1952-53; cons. Inst. Def. Analyses; dep. dir. Rsch. Com. on Money and Credit, 1959-61. Author: (with others) Personal Finance Industry and Its Credit Standards, 1939, (with Steiner) Money and Banking, 1941, Development of Wisconsin Credit Union Movement, 1947, Money and Banking, 1953, (with others), 1958, (with D. Meiselman) Measurement of Corporate Sources and Uses of Funds, 1964, (with others) Money and Banking, 1969, (with Wolf) The Role of Private Placement in Corporate Finance, 1972; Editor: (with W.L. White) Capital for Productivity and Growth, 1977. Served from ensign to lt. USNR, 1942-46. Recipient Econ. Dept. award Bklyn. Coll., 1936, Honors Day award for distinguished alumni, 1949. Fellow Am. Acad. Arts and Scis.; mem. Nat. Bur. Econ. Research (pres.), Am. Econ. Assn., Council Fgn. Relations, Am. Fin. Assn. Home and Office: 180 Beacon St Boston MA 02116-1401

SHAPIRO, ELLEN MARIE, graphic design company executive, writer; b. L.A., June 26, 1948; d. Leon E. and Elizabeth (Nussbaum) S.; m. Jerry Miller, Oct. 10, 1980 (div. 1986); 1 child, Alex Miller; m. Julius Rabinowitz, Sept. 6, 1992. BA, UCLA, 1970. Art dir. UCLA Alumni and Devel. Ctr., 1970-72; sr. designer Lubalin Smith Carnase, Inc., N.Y.C., 1972-74; art dir. Barton-Gillet Co., N.Y.C., 1974-76; ptnr. Design Concern, N.Y.C., 1976-78; pres. Shapiro Design Assocs. Inc., N.Y.C., 1978—, Shapiro Communications, Inc., 1992—; mem. faculty dept. communication design, Parsons Sch. Design, N.Y.C., 1986—; judge design and advt. shows, U.S. and Can. Art dir., Upper & Lower Case, 1988; author: Clients and Designers, 1989; contbr. numerous articles to mags. Recipient over 60 awards from profl. orgns. Mem. Am. Inst. Graphic Arts (v.p. N.Y. chpt. 1987-89), N.Y. Art Dirs. Club (Gold and Silver awards), N.Y. Type Dirs. Club. Avocations: cooking, gardening, tennis, swimming. Office: Shapiro Design Assocs Inc 10 E 40th St New York NY 10016-0200

SHAPIRO, FRED DAVID, lawyer; b. Cleve., Nov. 10, 1926; s. Isadore R. and Lottie (Turetsky) S.; m. Helen Solomon, Sept. 5, 1948; children—Gary N., Ira R., Diane S. B.A. cum laude, Ohio State U., 1949; LL.B., Harvard U., 1954. Bar: Ohio 1954. Since practiced in Cleve.; sr. partner firm Shapiro, Turoff & Belkin, 1976-94; prin. Fred D. Shapiro Co., L.P.A., 1994—. Served with USNR, 1945-46. Mem. Ohio Bar Assn., Greater Cleve. Bar Assn., Cuyahoga County Bar Assn., The Rowfant Club, Phi Beta Kappa. Jewish. Home: 29226 S Woodland Rd Cleveland OH 44124-5737

SHAPIRO, FRED LOUIS, physician, educator; b. Mpls., Aug. 18, 1934; s. Ralph Samuel and Dora (Cullen) S.; m. Merle Sandra Rosenzweig, June 23, 1957; children: Wendy Judith, Richard Scott. BA magna cum laude, U. Minn., 1958, BS, 1961, MD, 1961. Intern Hennepin County Med. Ctr., Mpls., 1961-62, resident in internal medicine, 1962-65, instr., 1965-68, chief nephrology, 1965-84; med. dir. Regional Kidney Disease Program, 1966-84; asst. prof. U. Minn., Mpls., 1968-71, assoc. prof., 1971-75, prof., 1975—; pres. Hennepin Faculty Assocs., 1983-95. Contbr. articles to profl. jours. With USNR, 1953-55. Mem. Am. Soc. Nephrology, Am. Soc. Artificial Internal Organs, Nat. Kidney Found., Mpls. Soc. Internal Medicine, Phi Beta Kappa, Sigma Xi, Alpha Omega Alpha. Home: 3490 Fairway Ln Minnetonka MN 55305-4451 Office: Hennepin Facility Assocs 600 HFA Bldg 914 S 8th St Minneapolis MN 55404-1204

SHAPIRO, GARY MICHAEL, philosophy educator; b. St. Paul, June 17, 1941; s. Irving H. and Florence Beverly (Gleckman) S.; m. Anne Goll, 1961 (div. 1966); 1 child, Marya Suzanne; m. Lynne Margolies, 1968 (div. 1991); children: David Benjamin, Rachel Shulamith. B.A. magna cum laude, Columbia U., 1963, Ph.D., 1970; postgrad., Yale U., 1963-64. Instr. Columbia U., N.Y.C., 1967-70; asst. prof. U. Kans., Lawrence, 1970-75, assoc. prof., 1975-81, prof., 1981-91; prof. philosophy, Tucker Boatwright prof. in humanities U. Richmond, Va., 1991—. Author: Nietzschean Narratives, 1989, Alcyone, 1991, Earthwards: Robert Smithson and Art after Babel, 1995; editor: After the Future, 1990; mem. editl. adv. bd. Philosophy and Literature, 1982—, Contemporary Studies in Philosophy and Literature, Jour. History of Philosophy; co-editor: Hermeneutics: Questions & Prospects, 1984; contbr. articles to profl. jours. Woodrow Wilson fellow. Am. Coun. Learned Socs. fellow, 1978, U. Calif., Irvine Sch. of Criticism and Theory fellow, 1976; sr. rsch. fellow Wesleyan U. Ctr. for the Humanities, 1985, Nat. Humanities Ctr. fellow, 1993-94. Mem. Internat. Assn. for Philosophy and Lit. (exec. com. 1984-89), N. Am. Nietzsche Soc. (exec. com. 1983-89), Am. Philo. Assn. (com. on lectrs. pub. and research 1985-88), Phi Beta Kappa. Office: U Richmond Dept Philosophy Richmond VA 23173

SHAPIRO, GEORGE HOWARD, lawyer; b. St. Louis, Nov. 10, 1936; s. Isadore T. and Alice (Schucart) S.; m. Mary Kenney Leonard, 1977 (div. 1994); 1 child, Ellen Leonard. B.A., Harvard U., 1958, LL.B., 1961; postgrad., London Sch. Econs., 1961-62. Bar: Ga. 1960, D.C. 1963. Atty. U.S. Dept. Labor, Washington, 1962-63; assoc. Arent Fox Kintner Plotkin & Kahn, Washington, 1963-69, ptnr., 1970—. Co-author: 'Cable Speech' The Case for First Amendment Protection, 1983; editor: New Program Opportunities in the Electronic Media, 1983, Current Developments in CATV, 1981. Served with USAR, 1962-68. Frank Knox Meml. fellow Harvard U., 1961-62. Mem. D.C. Bar Assn., Fed. Communications Bar Assn., Fed. Bar Assn. (dep. chmn. communications law com. 1970-71), ABA (vice chmn. cable TV com. 1982-83). Democrat. Jewish. Avocation: skiing. Home: 3249 Sutton Pl NW # D Washington DC 20016-3507 Office: Arent Fox Kintner Plotkin & Kahn 1050 Connecticut Ave NW Washington DC 20036-5303

SHAPIRO, GEORGE M., lawyer; b. N.Y.C., Dec. 7, 1919; s. Samuel N. and Sarah (Milstein) S.; m. Rita V. Lubin, Mar. 29, 1942; children: Karen Shapiro Spector, Sanford. BS, LIU, 1939; LL.B. (Kent scholar), Columbia U., 1942; LL.D. (hon.), L.I. U., 1986. Bar: N.Y. 1942. Mem. staff gov. N.Y., 1945-51, counsel to gov., 1951-54; ptnr. Proskauer, Rose, Goetz & Mendelsohn, N.Y.C., 1955—, mem. exec. com., mng. ptnr., 1974-84, co-chmn. corp. dept., 1980-90; pres. Edmond de Rothschild Found., 1964-92; dir. Bank of Calif., 1973-84; counsel, majority leader N.Y. Senate, 1955-59; counsel N.Y. Constl. Revision Commn., 1960-61. Chmn. council State U. Coll. Medicine, N.Y., 1955-71; mem. Gov.'s Com. Reapportionment, 1964, Mayor's Com. Jud. Selection, 1966-69; chmn. Park Ave. Synagogue, 1973-81; mem. Coun. on Fgn. Rels., 1974-92. Served with USAAF, 1943-45. Club: Harmonie. Home: 1160 Park Ave New York NY 10128-1212 Office: Proskauer Rose Goetz & Mendelsohn 1585 Broadway New York NY 10036-8200

SHAPIRO, GILBERT LAWRENCE, orthopedist; b. Lewiston, Maine, June 14, 1931; s. Samuel and Freda (Meyer) S.; m. Frima Lee Goldman, Aug. 28, 1955; children: Beth S. Lewyckyi, Karen S. Goldaber, Ruth A. BA, Dartmouth Coll., 1953; MD, Tufts U., 1957. Diplomate Am. Bd. Orthopaedic Surgery. Pvt. practice orthopaedic surgery New Bedford, Mass., 1963—. Bd. dirs. NBIS Savings Bank, New Bedford, 1982—; trustee St. Luke's Hosp., New Bedford, 1989—; pres. bd. trustees. Pilgrim Healthcare (HMO), Norwell, Md., 1991—, Old Dartmouth Hist. Soc. (whaling mus.), New Bedford, 1991—. Mem. ACS, Am. Acad. Orthopaedic Surgeons, New England Orthopaedic Soc. (pres. 1988-90), Ea. Orthopaedic Soc. Office: 84 Grape St New Bedford MA 02740-2143 also: New Bedford Whaling Mus 18 Johnny Cake Hl New Bedford MA 02740-6317

SHAPIRO, GLENN ALAN, marketing executive, consultant; b. Bklyn., Apr. 4, 1953; s. Abraham L. and Roslyn Shapiro; m. Judy Lynn Levine, Nov. 7, 1976; children: Valerie, Jamie. BA in Econs., NYU, 1974, JD, MBA in Mktg. and Fin., 1977. Bar: N.Y. 1977. Mgr., adminstr. dir. mktg. card divsn. Am. Express, N.Y.C., 1976-78; dir. advt. Am. Express Travel Related Svcs., N.Y.C., 1978-80, v.p. bus. devel. comm. divsn., 1980-83; v.p. mkt. planning, direct mktg. Am. Mgmt. Assn., N.Y.C., 1983-85; dir. direct mktg. Prodigy divsn., IBM/Sears Co., N.Y., 1985-87; sr. v.p. mktg. Family Shopping Network, White Plains, 1987-88; sr. v.p. subscription mktg. Bur. Bus. Practive divsn. Prentice Hall-Simon and Schuster, Waterford, Conn., 1988-93; v.p. mktg. market data retrieval Dun & Bradstreet, Shelton, Conn., 1994-96; CEO Exec. Enterprises, N.Y.C., 1996—; prof. direct mktg. New Sch., N.Y.C., 1982-83; bd. dirs., cons. Ad Net Corp., Lebanon, Ohio, 1984-94. Mem. N.Y. State Bar Assn., Direct Mktg. Assn. Avocations: tennis, skiing, boating. Home: 21 Mackinnon Pl East Lyme CT 06333-1534 Office: Exec Enterprises 22 W 21st St New York NY 10010

SHAPIRO, HAROLD DAVID, lawyer, educator; b. Chgo., Apr. 15, 1927; s. Charles B. and Celia (Nierenberg) S.; m. Beatrice Cahn, June 6, 1950; children: Matthew D., Michael Ann, Nicholas J. BS, Northwestern U., 1949; JD, Northwestern U., Chgo., 1952. Adminstrv. asst. State of Ill. Dept. Fin., Springfield, 1952; assoc. Sonnenschein Nath & Rosenthal, Chgo., 1953-59; ptnr. Sonnenschein Nath & Rosenthal, 1959—; Edward A. Harriman adj. prof. law Northwestern U., Chgo., 1970—; sec., bd. dirs. West Side Affordable Housing, Inc., West Side Village, Inc. Trustee, mem. exec. com., sec. Jr. Achievement of Chgo.; bd. dirs. Schwab Rehab. Ctr., Chgo.; pres. Homan & Arthington Found.; pres. Northwestern U. Law Sch. Alumni Assn., Chgo., 1984-85. Served with Seabees, USNR, 1945-50, PTO. Recipient Merit award Northwestern U., 1988. Mem. Ill. Bar Assn., ABA, Chgo. Bar Assn., Chgo. Council Lawyers, Legal Club of Chgo. (pres.), Law Club of Chgo., Order of Coif, Wigmore Key, Standard Club, Met. Club, Cliff Dwellers, Chicago Club, Lake Shore Country Club. Democrat. Jewish. Home: 34 Linden Ave Wilmette IL 60091-2837 Office: Sonnenschein Nath & Rosenthal 8000 Sears Tower 233 S Wacker Dr Chicago IL 60606-6306 *Clients need to believe that you care and that you can relate to their problems. You must be able to explain the most complex analysis in understandable language which is both concise and complete. Colleagues respect truthfulness and an adherence to the highest standards of professionalism. Above all, it is important to be actively involved in government and organizations which address the cultural.*

SHAPIRO, HAROLD TAFLER, academic administrator, economist; b. Montreal, Que., Can., June 8, 1935; s. Maxwell and Mary (Tafler) S.; m. Vivian Bernice Rapoport, May 19, 1957; children: Anne, Marilyn, Janet, Karen. BComm, McGill U., Montreal, 1956; PhD in Econs. (Harold Helm fellow, Harold Dodds sr. fellow), Princeton U., 1964. Asst. prof. econs. U. Mich., 1964-67, assoc. prof., 1967-70, prof., 1970-76, chmn. dept. econs., 1974-77, prof. econs. and pub. affairs, from 1977, v.p. acad. affairs, 1977-79, pres., 1980-87; research adv. Bank Can., 1965-72; prof. econ. and pub. affairs, pres. Princeton U., 1988—; bd. dirs. Dow Chem.; trustee Univs. Rsch. Assn., 1988—; mem. exec. com. Assn. Am. Univs., 1985-89, N.J. Commn. on Sci. and Tech., 1988-91; mem. Pres.'s Coun. Advisors on Sci. and Tech., 1990-92; chmn. com. on employer-based health benefits Inst. Medicine, 1991. Trustee Alfred P. Sloan Found., 1980—, Interlochen Ctr. for Arts, 1988-95, U. Pa. Med. Ctr., 1992—, Ednl. Testing Svc., 1994—; dir. Am. Coun. Edn., 1989-92; chmn. Spl. Presdl. Com., The Research Libraries Group, 1980-91; mem. Gov.'s High Tech. Task Force, Mich., 1980-87; mem. Gov.'s Commn. on Jobs and Econ. Devel. (Mich.), 1983-87; mem. Carnegie Commn. on Coll. Retirement, 1984-86. Recipient Lt. Gov.'s medal in commerce McGill U., 1956. Fellow Am. Acad. Arts and Scis., Mich. Soc. Fellows (sr.); mem. Inst. Medicine of NAS, Am. Philos. Soc., Nat. Bur. Econ. Rsch. (bd. dirs.). Office: Princeton U 1 Nassau Hall Princeton NJ 08544-0015

SHAPIRO, HARRY DEAN, lawyer; b. Louisville, June 21, 1940; s. Herman Shapiro and Toby (Spector) Levy; m. Linda Siegel, Dec. 19, 1970; 1 child, Deborah Anne. BS, U. Louisville, 1962, JD, 1964. Bar: Ky. 1964, D.C. 1968, Md. 1970. Trial and appellate atty. U.S. Dept. Justice, Washington, 1964-70; assoc. Venable, Baetjer & Howard, Balt., 1970-74, ptnr., 1975-87; sr. ptnr., head of tax practice Weinberg & Green, Balt., 1987—, chmn. corp. dept., 1993-95; transaction group coord., 1995—. Author: Federal Tax Liens, 1981; contbr. articles to profl. jours. Mem. Md. State Bd. Edn., 1990—; v.p. Assoc. Jewish Charities of Balt., Inc. 1991-94; vice chmn. The Assoc. Jewish Cmty. Fedn. Balt. 1987-89, asst. treas., 1989-91, mem. exec. com., 1993—; trustee Sinai Hosp., Balt., 1987-90; trustee, counsel Balt. Mus. Art, 1984—, sec., 1985-92, v.p., sec., 1992-94, v.p., 1994—; dir., 1989—; chmn. Joint Budgeting Coun., 1993—, Coun. Jewish Fedns. Capt. USAR, 1967-70. Mem. ABA (tax sect.), Md. State Bar Assn., Ky. Bar Assn., D.C. Bar Assn., Md. Club, Center Club. Home: 7903 7 Mile Ln Baltimore MD 21208-4306 Office: Weinberg & Green 100 S Charles St Baltimore MD 21201-2725 *Our country is at a crossroads in its history, and it is becoming clear that a sea change is necessary. Basic reforms must occur in our governmental and educational structures. The question is whether we have the intelligence to reject the cries for bigger government and more taxes to solve these problems when fundamental action is required.*

SHAPIRO, HARVEY, poet; b. Chgo., Jan. 27, 1924; s. Jacob J. and Dorothy (Cohen) S.; m. Edna Lewis Kaufman, July 23, 1953; children—Saul, Dan. B.A., Yale U., 1947; M.A., Columbia U., 1948. Instr. English Cornell U., 1949-50, 51-52; creative writing fellow Bard Coll., 1950-51; mem. editorial staff Commentary, New Yorker, 1955-57; editorial staff N.Y. Times Mag., N.Y.C., 1957; asst. editor N.Y. Times Mag., 1964-75; editor N.Y. Times Book Rev., 1975-83; dep. editor N.Y. Times Mag., 1983-96, sr. editor, 1996—. Author: The Eye, 1953, The Book and Other Poems, 1955, Mountain, Fire, Thornbush, 1961, Battle Report, 1966, This World, 1971, Lauds, 1975, Nightsounds, 1978, The Light Holds, 1984, National Cold Storage Company, 1988, A Day's Portion, 1994. Served with USAAF, World War II. Decorated D.F.C., Air medal with 3 oak leaf clusters.; Rockefeller Found. grantee in poetry, 1967. Club: Elizabethan (New Haven), Century (N.Y.). Office: NY Times 229 W 43rd St New York NY 10036-3913

SHAPIRO, HOWARD ALAN, lawyer; b. Albany, N.Y., May 12, 1932; s. Ralph and Estelle (Warshak) S.; m. Eleanor Siegel, June 20, 1954; children: David Todd, Andrew Neil, Diane Graser. A.B. magna cum laude, Harvard U., 1953, LL.B. magna cum laude, 1956. Bar: N.Y. 1956. Assoc. Proskauer Rose Goetz & Mendelsohn, N.Y.C., 1956-65, ptnr., 1965—; lectr. Practicing Law Inst., 1971-79. Editor Harvard Law Rev., 1954-56, note editor, 1955-56. Mem. Assn. of Bar of City of N.Y. (com. on corp. law 1971-74, com. on banking law 1978-81, 86-89), N.Y. State Bar Assn., ABA, N.Y. County Lawyers' Assn. Home: 140 E 72nd St New York NY 10021-4243 Office: Proskauer Rose et al 1585 Broadway New York NY 10036-8200

SHAPIRO, HOWIE, newspaper editor. Cultural arts editor The Phila. Inquirer. Office: The Philadelphia Inquirer 400 N Broad St Philadelphia PA 19130-4015

SHAPIRO, IRVING S., medical think-tank executive. Chmn. of the trustees The Howard Hughes Medical Inst., Bethesda, Md. Office: Skadden Arps Slate Meagher & Flom PO Box 636 Wilmington DE 19899

SHAPIRO, IRVING SAUL, lawyer; b. Mpls., July 15, 1916; s. Sam I. and Freda (Lane) S.; m. Charlotte Farsht, Mar. 1, 1942; children: Stuart Lane, Elizabeth Irene. B.S., U. Minn., 1939, LL.B., 1941. Bar: Minn. 1941, Del. 1958. Atty. criminal div. Dept. Justice, 1943-51; with E.I. duPont de Nemours & Co., Inc., 1951-81; v.p. E.I. du Pont de Nemours & Co., Inc., 1970-73, vice chmn. bd., 1973, chmn., chief exec. officer, 1974-81, also dir., chmn. exec. com., chmn. pub. affairs com., until 1981; ptnr. firm Skadden, Arps, Slate, Meagher & Flom, N.Y.C., 1981-89, of counsel, 1990; bd. dirs. AEA Investors Inc., J.P. Morgan Fla. Fed. Savs. Bank. Chmn. bd. trustees Howard Hughes Med. Inst., Ohmicron Corp., Pediat. Scvs. of Am. Inc., Sola Internat. Inc. Office: Skadden Arps Slate Meagher & Flom 1 Rodney Sq Wilmington DE 19801 Office: Skadden Arps Slate Meagher Flom PO Box 636 Wilmington DE 19899

SHAPIRO, IRWIN IRA, physicist, educator; b. N.Y.C., N.Y., Oct. 10, 1929; s. Samuel and Esther (Feinberg) S.; m. Marian Helen Kaplun, Dec. 20, 1959; children: Steven, Nancy. A.B., Cornell U., 1950; A.M., Harvard U., 1951, Ph.D., 1955. Mem. staff Lincoln Lab. MIT, Lexington, 1954-70; Sherman Fairchild Distinguished scholar Calif. Inst. Tech., 1974; Morris Loeb lectr. physics Harvard, 1975; prof. geophysics and physics MIT, 1967-80, Schlumberger prof., 1980-84; Paine prof. practical astronomy, prof. physics Harvard U., 1982—; sr. scientist Smithsonian Astrophys. Obs., 1982—; dir. Harvard-Smithsonian Ctr. for Astrophysics, 1983—; cons. NSF, NASA. Contbr. articles to profl. jours. Recipient Albert A. Michelson medal Franklin Inst., 1975, award in phys. and math. scis. N.Y. Acad. Scis., 1982, Einstein medal Einstein Soc. Bern, 1994; Guggenheim fellow, 1982. Fellow AAAS, Am. Geophys. Union (Charles A. Whitten medal 1991, William Bowie medal 1993), Am. Phys. Soc.; mem. AAAS, NAS (Benjamin Apthorp Gould prize 1979), Am. Astron. Soc. (Dannie Heineman award 1983, Dirk Brouwer award 1987), Internat. Astron. Union, Phi Beta Kappa, Sigma Xi, Phi Kappa Phi. Home: 17 Lantern Ln Lexington MA 02173-6029 Office: Harvard-Smithsonian Ctr Astrophysics 60 Garden St Cambridge MA 02138-1516

SHAPIRO, ISAAC, lawyer; b. Tokyo, Jan. 5, 1931; s. Constantine and Lydia (Chernetzky) S.; m. Jacqueline M. Weiss, Sept. 16, 1956; children: Tobias, Alexandra, Natasha. A.B., Columbia U., 1954, LL.B., 1956; post-grad., Inst. de Droit Compare, U. Paris, 1956-57. Bar: N.Y. 1957, U.S. Supreme Ct. 1971, Paris 1991. Assoc. Milbank, Tweed, Hadley & McCloy, N.Y.C., 1956-65, ptnr., 1966-86; resident ptnr. Milbank, Tweed, Hadley & McCloy, Tokyo, 1977-79; ptnr. Skadden Arps Slate Meagher and Flom, N.Y.C., 1986—; resident ptnr. Skadden Arps Slate Meagher and Flom, Paris, 1990—; teaching fellow comparative law NYU, 1959-61; lectr. Soviet law, 1961-67; adj. asst. prof. NYU, 1967-69, adj. assoc. prof., 1969-71, 74-75; bd. dirs. Bank of Tokyo Mitsubishi Trust Co., N.Y.C., Carl Zeiss, Inc., Thornwood, N.Y., PRT Corp., N.Y.C. Author: (with Hazard and Maggs) The Soviet Legal System, 1969; author: Japan: The Risen Sun (in Japanese), 1982; editor: The Middle East Crisis-Prospects for Peace, 1969; contbr. articles to periodicals. Mem. Joint Com. U.S.-Japan Cultural and Ednl. Cooperation, Washington, 1972-78; mem. Japan-U.S. Friendship Commn., 1975-78; trustee Nat. Humanities Ctr., Triangle Park, N.C., 1976-89; trustee, v.p. Chamber Music Soc. Lincoln Ctr., 1980-86; trustee, pres. Isamu Noguchi Fedn., 1985—; trustee, chmn. Ise Cultural Fedn., 1984—; bd. dirs. Bus. Coun. for Internat. Understanding, 1989-95, Nat. Com. for U.S.-China Rels., 1989-95. Fulbright scholar, 1956-57. Mem. ABA, N.Y. State Bar Assn., Assn. Bar City N.Y., Japan Soc. (pres. N.Y. 1970-77), Coun. Fgn. Rels. Home: 6 rue Goethe, 75116 Paris France Office: Skadden Arps Slate et al, 105 rue faubourg St Honore, 75008 Paris France

SHAPIRO, ISADORE, materials scientist, consultant; b. Mpls., Apr. 25, 1916; s. Jacob and Bessie (Goldman) S.; m. Mae Hirsch, Sept. 4, 1938; children: Stanley Harris, Jerald Steven. BChemE. summa cum laude, U. Minn., 1938, PhD, 1944. Asst. instr. chemistry U. Minn., 1938-41, rsch. fellow, 1944-45; rsch. chemist E. I. duPont de Nemours and Co., Phila., 1946; head chem. lab. U.S. Naval Ordnance Test Sta., Pasadena, Calif., 1947-52; dir. rsch. lab. Olin-Mathieson Chem. Corp., 1952-59; head chemistry Hughes Tool Co., Aircraft div., Culver City, Calif., 1959-62; pres. Universal Chem. Systems Inc. 1962—, Aerospace Chem. Systems, Inc., 1964-66; dir. contract rsch. HITCO, Gardena, Calif., 1966-67; prin. scientist Douglas Aircraft Co. of McDonnell Douglas Corp., Santa Monica, Calif., 1967; prin. scientist McDonnell Douglas Astronautics Co., 1967-70; head materials and processes AiResearch Mfg. Co., Torrance, Calif., 1971-82, cons., 1982—; inaugurated dep. gov. Am. Biog. Inst. Rsch. Assn., 1988; dep. dir. gen. Internat. Biog. Ctr., 1989, Eng. Rater U.S. Civil Svc. Bd. Exam., 1948-52. Served 1st lt. AUS, 1941-44. Registered profl. engr., Calif. Fellow Am. Inst. Chemists, Am. Inst. Aeros and Astronautics (assoc.); mem. AAAS, Am. Ordnance Assn., Am. Chem. Soc., Soc. Rheology, Soc. Advancement Materials and Process Engring., Am. Inst. Physics, AIM, Am. Phys. Soc., N.Y. Acad. Sci., Am. Assn. Contamination Control, Am. Ceramic Soc., Nat. Inst. Ceramic Engrs., Am. Powder Metallurgy Inst., Internat. Plansee Soc. for Powder Metallurgy, Sigma Xi, Tau Beta Pi, Phi Lambda Upsilon. Author articles in tech. publs. Patentee, discoverer series of carborane compounds; created term carborane; formulator of universal compaction equation for powders (metals, ceramics, polymers, chemicals). Home: 5624 W 62nd St Los Angeles CA 90056-2009

SHAPIRO, IVAN, lawyer; b. N.Y.C., Nov. 11, 1928; s. Archie M. and Auguste (Reiff) S.; m. Florence Goodstein, June 24, 1951 (div. Oct. 1958); 1 child, Lisa J. Kubiske; m. Maria Schaffner, Sept. 16, 1960; 1 child, Alexandra. B.S.S., CCNY, 1948; J.D., Harvard U., 1951. Bar: N.Y. 1952. Assoc. Wien, Lane, Klein & Purcell, N.Y.C., 1954-59; ptnr. Wien, Lane & Klein, 1959-74, Greenbaum, Wolff & Ernst, N.Y.C., 1974-81, Willkie Farr & Gallagher, N.Y.C., 1981-91; lectr. Real Estate Inst., NYU Sch. Continuing Edn., N.Y.C., 1978-81. Author: Case Studies in Real Estate Finance, 1980; author pamphlets on ethical issues, 1973-80, articles on civil liberties issues, 1966-80. Trustee Ethical Culture Soc., N.Y.C., 1970—, pres., 1972-78; pres. Ethical Culture Schs., N.Y., 1976-82; bd. visitors Grad. Sch., Univ. Ctr. CUNY, 1986—, vice chmn., 1992—; mem. Asia Watch Com. Human Rights Watch, 1990-95; bd. dirs., pres. Urban Pathways, Inc. (formerly West Side Cluster Inc.), 1991-95; bd. dirs. Bklyn. Navy Yard Devel. Corp., 1991-95, chmn. bylaws com., 1992-94; bd. dirs. Abortiion Rights Assn. N.Y., 1970-71, Nat. Assn. for Repeal of Abortion laws, 1971-74. Mem. ACLU (bd. dirs. N.Y. chpt. 1966-80, 87—, treas. 1989-95), Assn. Bar of City of N.Y., Phi Beta Kappa. Democrat. Office: 1 CitiCorp Ctr 153 E 53rd St New York NY 10022-4602

SHAPIRO, JAMES EDWARD, judge; b. Chgo., May 28, 1930; s. Ben Edward and Rose (Slate) S.; m. Rhea Kahn, Dec. 28, 1958; children—Jeffrey Scott, Steven Mark. B.S., U. Wis., 1951; J.D., Harvard U., 1954. Bar: Wis. 1956, U.S. Dist. Ct. (ea. dist.) Wis. 1956, U.S. Ct. Appeals (7th cir.) 1962, U.S. Supreme Ct. 1971. Sole practice, Milw., 1956-57; resident house counsel Nat. Presto Industries, Eau Claire, Wis., 1957-60; ptnr. Bratt & Shapiro, Milw., 1960-64; sole practice, Milw., 1964-74; ptnr. Frank, Hiller & Shapiro, Milw., 1974-82; judge U.S. Bankruptcy Ct., Milw., 1982—; mem. Bayside Bd. Appeals, Wis., 1969-77; Milw. county ct. commr., 1969-78; dir. Milw. Legal Aid Soc., 1969-77. Served to 1st lt. U.S. Army, 1954-56. Mem. State Bar Assn. Wis. (chmn. bankruptcy, insolvency, creditors rights sect.), Milw. Bar Assn. (past chmn., past vice chmn. bankruptcy sect.). Jewish. Office: US Courthouse 140 Fed Bldg 517 E Wisconsin Ave Milwaukee WI 53202

SHAPIRO, JEROME GERSON, lawyer; b. N.Y.C., May 12, 1924; s. Joseph Louis and Beatrice Rebecca S.; m. Marjorie Kemble Mackay, Dec. 31, 1959; children—Jeffrey Kemble, Jill Dara, Eric Paul. A.B. summa cum laude, N.Y. U., 1946; LL.B. magna cum laude, Harvard U., 1948. Bar: N.Y. State bar 1949, U.S. Supreme Ct. bar 1955. Assoc. mem. firm Hughes Hubbard & Reed, N.Y.C., 1949-51, 52-57; spl. asst. atty. gen., sr. asst. counsel N.Y. State Crime Commn., 1951-52; ptnr. firm Hughes Hubbard & Reed, N.Y.C., 1957-95; chmn. Hughes Hubbard & Reed, 1975-90; counsel, 1995—; prof. law N.Y. Law Sch., 1951-53. Vice chmn. trustees James W. Johnson Community Centers, Inc., N.Y.C., 1975-78; trustee Lawyers Com. for Civil Rights Under Law, 1976—. Served with AUS, 1943-45. Decorated Purple Heart, Bronze Star. Fellow Am. Coll. Trial Lawyers; mem. Assn. of Bar of City of N.Y. (exec. com. 1967-73), Am. Bar Found. (rsch. com.), Harvard Club, Phi Beta Kappa. Jewish. Office: Hughes Hubbard & Reed 1 Battery Park Plz New York NY 10004-1405

SHAPIRO, JEROME HERBERT, radiologist, educator; b. Cleve., Aug. 5, 1924; s. Louis and Rose (Hamburgher) S.; m. Amy Elizabeth Alderman, June 16, 1948 (dec. Jan. 1991); children: Nancy Lee, Mathew Paul, Wendy Jane, Deborah Gail; m. Meredith Pearlstein, Dec. 16, 1993. Student, Western Res. U., 1942-44; M.D., Yale U., 1948. Intern Mt. Sinai Hosp., Cleve., 1948-49; resident radiology Montefiore Hosp., N.Y.C., 1949-52; fellow X-ray diagnosis Meml. Center, N.Y.C., 1952; attending radiologist Montefiore Hosp., 1952-63; assoc. clin. prof. radiology N.Y. U., 1960-63; prof. radiology Boston U. Sch. Medicine, 1963—, chmn. dept. radiology, 1963-92; dir. radiology Boston City, Univ. hosps., 1963-92; Lectr. radiology Harvard, Tufts med. schs., 1963—. Sr. author: Cardiac Calcifications, 1963; Contbr. numerous articles to profl. jours. Vice pres. Wellesley (Mass.) Symphony Orch., 1980-82, pres., 1982-86. Fellow Am. coll. Radiology (chancellor 1973-79, 89-90, v.p. 1980-81, pres. 1989-90, gold medal 1992), Coun. Med. Splty. Socs. (pres. 1992-93); mem. AMA, Radiol. Soc. N.Am., Am. Roentgen Ray Soc. (pres. 1974-75), Assn. Univ. Radiologists, Am. Soc. Neuroradiology, Mass. Radiol. Soc. (pres. 1970-71). Jewish (pres. temple 1968-72). Home: 416 Commonwealth Ave #505 Boston MA 02215-2811 Office: Univ Hosp Dept Radiology 88 E Newton St Boston MA 02118-2308

SHAPIRO, JOAN ISABELLE, laboratory administrator, nurse; b. Fulton, Ill., Aug. 26, 1943; d. Macy James and Frieda Lockhart; m. Ivan Lee Shapiro, Dec. 28, 1968; children: Audrey, Michael. RN, Peoria Methodist Sch. Nursing, Ill., 1964. Nurse, Grant Hosp., Columbus, Ohio, 1975-76; nurse Cardiac Thoracic and Vascular Surgeons Ltd., Geneva, Ill., 1977—, mgr. non-invasive lab., 1979—; owner, operator Shapiro's Mastiff's 1976-82; sec.-treas. Sounds Svcs., 1976—, Mainstream Sounds Inc., 1980-84; co-founder Cardio-Phone Inc., 1982—, Edgewater Vascular Inst., 1987-89, Associated Profls., 1989-92; v.p., bd. dir. Computer Specialists Inc., 1986-89; founder, pres. Vein Ctr., Edema Ctr. Ltd. Mem. Soc. Non-invasive Technologists, Soc. Peripheral Vascular Nursing (community awareness com. 1984—), Oncology Nursing Soc., Internat. Soc. Lymphology, Kane County Med. Soc. Aux. (pres. 1983-84, adviser, 1984-85). Lutheran. Office: Cardiac Thoracic and Vascular Surgeons Ltd PO Box 564 Geneva IL 60134-0564

SHAPIRO, JOEL ELIAS, artist; b. N.Y.C., Sept. 27, 1941; s. Joseph and Anna (Lewis) S.; m. Ellen Phelan; 1 dau., Ivy Bess. B.A., NYU, 1964, M.A., 1969. One-person shows include Paula Cooper Gallery, N.Y.C., 14 shows 1970-89, 90-92, Inst. Art and Urban Resources, N.Y.C., 1973, Mus. Contemporary Art, Chgo., 1976, Albright-Knox Art Gallery, Buffalo, 1977, Gallery M. Bochum, W. Ger., 1977, Galerie Mukai, Tokyo, 1980, 81, 88, Asher/Faure, L.A., 1980, 89, Whitechapel Gallery, London, 1980, Hans Lange, Krefeld, W. Ger., 1980, Moderna Museet, Stockholm, 1980, Brown U., 1980, Ackland Art Mus., Chapel Hill, N.C., 1981, Contemporary Arts Ctr., Cin., 1981, Israel Mus., Jerusalem, 1981, Portland Ctr. Visual Arts, Oreg., 1982, Whitney Mus. Am. Art, N.Y.C., 1982, Galerie Aronowitsch, Stockholm, 1983, Delahunty Gallery, Dallas, 1983, Donald Young Gallery, Chgo., 1984, Stedelijk Mus., Amsterdam, 1985, Kunstmuseum, Dusseldorf, 1985, Staatliche Kunsthalle, Baden-Baden, 1985, Seattle Art Mus., 1986, Galerie Daniel Templon, Paris, 1986, 88, The John and Mable Ringling Mus., Sarasota, 1986, John Berggruen Gallery, San Francisco, Hirshhorn Mus. and Sculpture Garden, Washington, 1987, Hans Strelow, Dusseldorf, Germany, 1988, Toledo Mus. Art, 1989, Waddington Gallery, London, 1989, Museet I Varberg, Sweden, 1990, Balt. Art Mus., 1990, Des Moines Art Ctr., 1991, Ctr. for Fine Arts, Miami, 1991, IVAM Centre Julio Gonazlez, Valencia, Spain, 1990, Ctr. for the Fine Arts, Miami, 1991, Asher-Faure, L.A., 1991, Gallery Mukai, Tokyo, 1991, John Berggruen Gallery, San Francisco, 1991, Pace Gallery, 1993, Galerie Karsten Greve, Cologne, Germany, 1993, Gallery Seomi, Seoul, 1994, Glerie Aronowitsch, Stockholm, 1995, Karsten Greve, Paris, 1995, Pace Gallery, N.Y., 1995, Walker Art Ctr./Mpls. Sculpture Garden, 1995, Nelson-Atkins Mus. Art/Kansas City Sculpture Park, 1996, Pace Wildenstein Gallery, L.A., 1996; numerous group exhibits; permanent collections and commns. include Mus. Modern Art, N.Y.C., Whitney Mus. Art, N.Y.C., Walker Art Center, Mpls., Met. Mus. Art, N.Y.C., Albright Knox Art Gallery, Buffalo, Detroit Inst. Art, Stedelijk Mus., Amsterdam, Moderna Museet, Stockholm, Dallas Mus. Art, Centre Pompidou, Paris, Nat. Gallery Art, Washington, Brit. Mus., London, Bklyn. Mus., Cocoran Gallery, Washington, Fogg Art Mus. at Harvard U., Cambridge, Mass., High Mus. Art, Atlanta, Hirshhorn Mus. and Sculpture Garden at Smithsonian Instn., Washington, Israel Mus., Jerusalem, Kunsthaus Zürich, Switzerland, Mus. Contemporary Art, L.A., Mus. Fine Arts, Boston, Mus. Modern Art, Friuli, Italy, Parrish Art Mus., Southampton, N.Y., Phila. Mus. Art, Tate Gallery, London, commissions include Cigna Corp., Phila., 1983-84, Fukuoka (Japan) Sogo Bank, 1988, Creative Artists Agy., L.A., 1988-89, Kawamura Meml. Mus. Art, Chiba, Japan, 1988-89, Govt. Svc. Adminstrn., L.A., 1988-90, Hood Mus. Art at Dartmouth Coll., Hanover, N.H., 1989-90, U.S. Holocaust Meml. Mus., Washington, 1993, Sony Music Entertainment, N.Y.C., 1994-95, Friedrichstadt Passagen, Berlin, 1994-95, Kansas City (Mo.) Internat. Airport, 1995-96; represented by Pace Gallery, N.Y.C., Cleve. Mus. Art, N.C. Mus. Art, Raleigh, Des Moines Art Ctr., Pace Gallery, N.Y.C. Recipient Nat. Endowment for Arts award, 1975, Brandeis award, 1984, Skowhegan medal, 1986, Award of Merit, Am. Acad. and Inst. of Arts and Letters, 1990. Mem. Swedish Royal Acad. Art. Office: care Pace Gallery 32 E 57th St New York NY 10022-2513

SHAPIRO, JONATHAN SALEM, electrical engineer; b. N.Y.C., July 9, 1943; s. Harold Roland and Pauline (Wolinsky) S.; m. Rosalind Elaine Miller, Jan. 24, 1974; children: Pauline, Rebecca. BEEE, CCNY, 1965; MA, MSEE, PhD, Princeton U., 1968. Sr. engr. Microstate Electronics, Murray Hill, N.J., 1968-70; chief engr. Pollution Control Inc., Stamford, Conn., 1970-73; engring. mgr. Machlett Labs. (Divsn. of Raytheon), Stamford, Conn., 1973-84; v.p. tech. AFP Imaging, Elmsford, N.Y., 1984-85; sr. project engr. Philips Med. Systems, Shelton, Conn., 1985-86; dir. engring. Mikron Instrument Co., Wyckoff, N.J., 1986-88; engring. mgr. EDO Corp./Barnes Engring. Div., Shelton, Conn., 1988-90; pres. Greenwich (Conn.) Instrument Co. Inc., 1988—. Author chpt.: Handbook of Intelligent Senors, 1992; patentee for x-ray system tester, x-ray tube control system, radiographic system, sterilizing device, others. Mem. Am. Assn. Physicists in Medicine, IEEE, Am. Phys. Soc. Jewish. Avocations: photography, music. Office: Greenwich Instrument Co 128 Old Church Rd Greenwich CT 06830-4821

SHAPIRO, JUDITH R., anthropology educator, university official; b. N.Y.C., Jan. 24, 1942. Student Ecole des Haute Etudes Institut d'Etudes Politiques, Paris, 1961-62; BA, Brandeis U., 1963; PhD, Columbia U., 1972. Asst. prof. U. Chgo., 1970-75; postdoctoral fellow U. Calif.-Berkeley, 1974-75; Rosalyn R. Schwartz lectr., asst. prof. anthropology Bryn Mawr Coll., Pa., 1975-78, assoc. prof., 1978-85, prof., 1985—, chmn. dept., 1982-85, acting dean undergrad coll., 1985-86, provost, 1986-94; pres. Barnard Coll., N.Y., 1994—; contbr. articles to profl. jours., chpts. to books. Fellow Woodrow Wilson Found., 1963-64, Columbia U., 1964-65, NEH Younger Humanist, 1974-75, Am. Coun. Learned Socs., 1981-82, Ctr. for Advanced Study in the Behavioral Scis., 1989; grantee NSF summer field tng., 1965, Ford Found. 1966, NIMH, 1974-75, Social Sci. Rsch. Coun., 1974-75. Mem. Phila. Anthrop. Soc. (pres. 1983), Am. Ethnol. Soc. (nominations com. 1983-84, pres. elect 1984-85, pres. 1985-86), Am. Anthrop. Assn. (ethics com. 1976-79, bd. dirs. 1984-86, exec. com. 1985-86), Social Sci. Rsch. Coun. (com. social sci personnel 1977-80), mem. bd. dirs. consortium on financing higher edn.; dir. Fund for the City of N.Y.; mem. exec. com. Women's Coll. Coalition; mem. nat. adv. com. Woodrow Wilson Nat. Fellowship Found., Women's Forum, Phi Beta Kappa, Sigma Xi. Office: Barnard Coll Office of the Pres 3009 Broadway New York NY 10027-6598

SHAPIRO, KARL JAY, poet, former educator; b. Balt., Nov. 10, 1913; s. Joseph and Sarah (Omanski) S.; m. Evalyn Katz, Mar. 25, 1945 (div. Jan. 1967); children: Katharine, John J., Elizabeth (dec. Jan. 1993); m. Teri Kovach, July 31, 1967 (dec. July 1982); m. Sophie Wilkins, Apr. 25, 1985. Student, Johns Hopkins U., 1937-39. Cons. poetry Library of Congress, 1946-47; assoc. prof. writing Johns Hopkins U., 1947-50; editor Poetry: A Magazine of Verse, 1950-56; prof. English U. Nebr., Lincoln, 1956-66, U. Ill. Circle Campus, Chgo., 1966-68, U. Calif. at Davis, 1968-85; now ret. Author: Poems, 1935, New and Selected Poems, 1940-46, Person, Place and Thing, 1942, The Place of Love, 1942, V-Letter and Other Poems, 1944, Essay on Rime, 1945, Trial of a Poet, 1947, Bibliography of Modern Prosody, 1948, Poems, 1942-53, 1953, Beyond Criticism, 1953, Poems of a Jew, 1958, In Defense of Ignorance, 1960, (with James E. Miller, Jr. and Bernice Slote) Start with the Sun, 1960, Prose Keys to Modern Poetry, 1962, The Bourgeois Poet, 1964, A Prosody Handbook, 1964, (with Robert Beum) Selected Poems, 1968, To Abolish Children, 1968, White-Haired Lover,

1968, The Poetry Wreck, Selected Essays 1950-70, 1975, Adult Bookstore, 1976, Love & War, Art & God, 1984, Collected Poems 1940-1978, 1978, New and Selected Poems, 1940-86, 1987, The Younger Son, 1988, Reports of My Death, 1990, The Old Horsefly, 1993; (novel) Edsel, 1971: (film) Karl Shapiro's America, 1976. Served with AUS, 1941-45. Recipient Jeanette S. Davis prize, 1942, Levinson prize, 1943, Contemporary Poetry prize, 1943, Pulitzer prize for poetry, 1945, Shelley Meml. prize, 1945, Bollingen prize for poetry, 1969, Robert Kirsch award L.A. Times, 1989, Charity Randall citation, 1990; grantee Am. Acad. Arts and Letters, 1944; fellow Kenyon Sch. Letters, 1956, 57, Guggenheim fellow, 1953-54, fellow Libr. of Congress. Mem. PEN, Nat. Acad. Arts and Letters, Am. Acad. Arts and Scis.

SHAPIRO, KENNETH, insurance executive; b. 1946. With USPHS, Bethesda, Md., 1968-71, Penn Mut. Life Ins., Phila., 1971-74; CEO Hay/Huggins Co., Inc., 1974—. Office: 229 S 18th St Ste 6 Philadelphia PA 19103

SHAPIRO, KENNETH PAUL, actuary, company executive; b. N.Y.C., Mar. 20, 1946; s. Harry and Esther (Forman) S.; m. Hazel Paula Neuwirth, Sept. 20, 1970; children: Seth, Matthew, Elissa. BS in Math., Bklyn. Coll., 1967; MS in Math., U. Mich., 1968. Actuary Penn Mutual Life Ins. Co., Phila., 1971-74; v.p. Hay/Huggins Co., Inc., Phila., 1974-82, pres., chief exec. officer, 1982—; bd. dirs. The Hay Group, 1987—. Columnist Bus. Insur., 1980-85. Lt. USPH, 1968-71. Fellow Soc. Actuaries, Conf. Actuaries; mem. Am. Acad. Actuaries, Acutaries Club of Phila. (pres. 1982-83). Avocations: sports, coin and stamp collecting. Home: 48 Cameo Dr Cherry Hill NJ 08003-5126 Office: Hay/Huggins Co Inc 229 S 18th St Philadelphia PA 19103-6144

SHAPIRO, LARRY JAY, pediatrician, scientist, educator; b. Chgo., July 6, 1946; s. Philip and Phyllis (Krause) S.; m. Carol-Ann Uetake; children: Jennifer, Jessica, Brian. A.B., Washington U., St. Louis, 1968, M.D., 1971. Diplomate Am. Bd. Pediatrics, Am. Bd. Med. Examiners, Am. Bd. Med. Genetics. Intern St. Louis Children's Hosp., 1971-72, resident, 1971-73; research assoc. NIH, Bethesda, Md., 1973-75; asst. prof. Sch. Medicine, UCLA, 1975-79, assoc. prof., 1979-83, prof. pediatrics and biol. chemistry, 1983-91; investigator Howard Hughes Med. Inst., 1987-91; prof., chmn. dept. pediat. U. Calif.-San Francisco Sch. Medicine, 1991—, chief pediat. svcs. U. Calif. San Francisco Med. Ctr., 1991—. Contbr. numerous articles to profl. publs. Served to lt. comdr. USPHS, 1973-75. Fellow AAAS, Am. Acad. Pediatrics (E. Mead Johnson award in rsch. 1982); mem. Inst. Medicine-NAS, Soc. Pediatric Rsch. (coun. 1984-87, pres. 1991-92), Western Soc. for Pediatric Rsch. (coun. 1983-87, Ross award in rsch. 1981, pres. 1989-90), Soc. for Inherited Metabolic Disease (coun. 1983-88, pres. 1986-87), Assn. Am. Physicians, Am. Soc. Human Genetics (council 1985-88, pres. elect 1995), Am. Soc. Clin. Investigation, Am. Pediatric Soc., Am. Acad. Arts & Scis. Office: U Calif Third Ave & Parnassus San Francisco CA 94143

SHAPIRO, LEE TOBEY, planetarium administrator, astronomer; b. Chgo., Dec. 12, 1943; s. Sydney Harold and Ruth Iva (Levin) S.; m. Linda Susan Goldman, Aug. 16, 1970; children: Steven Robert, Aaron Edward. BS in Physics, Carnegie Inst. Tech., 1966; MS in Astronomy, Northwestern U., 1968, PhD, 1974. Lectr. Adler Planetarium, Chgo., 1967-74; asst. prof. astronomy Mich. State U., East Lansing, 1974-79, assoc. prof., 1979-82; bd. dirs. Abrams Planetarium, 1974-82, Morehead Planetarium U. N.C.-Chapel Hill, 1982—, adj. assoc. prof., 1983—; vis. prof. Duke U., Durham, N.C., summers 1987-89, 93-94. Fellow Royal Astron. Soc.; mem. Am. Astron. Soc., Am. Assn. Mus., Astronomical Soc. of the Pacific, Internat. Planetarium Soc., Great Lakes Planetarium Assn. (pres. 1980). Jewish. Office: Morehead Planetarium # 3480 U of NC Chapel Hill NC 27599-3480

SHAPIRO, LEO J., social researcher; b. N.Y.C., July 8, 1921; m. Virginia L. Johnson, Feb. 9, 1952; children: David, Erik, Owen, Amy. BA, U. Chgo., 1942, PhD, 1952. Survey specialist Fed. Govt. Agy., Washington, 1941-45, Sci. Rsch. Assn., Chgo., 1948-52; prin., founder Leo J. Shapiro and Assocs., Chgo., 1952-91; pres. Greenhouse, Inc., 1991—; bd. dirs. Coop. Mktg. Mem. vis. com. bd. trustees U. Chgo. Fellow U. Chgo., 1949. Fellow Social Sci. Research Council; mem. Am. Mktg. Assn., Am. Assn. Pub. Opinion Research, Am. Sociol. Assn., AAAA, Phi Beta Kappa.

SHAPIRO, LUCILLE, molecular biology educator; b. N.Y.C., July 16, 1940; d. Philip and Yetta (Stein) Cohen; m. Roy Shapiro, Jan. 23, 1960 (div. 1977); 1 child, Peter; m. Harley H. McAdams, July 28, 1978; stepchildren: Paul, Heather. BA, Bklyn. Coll., 1961; PhD, Albert Einstein Coll. Medicine, 1966. Asst. prof. Albert Einstein Coll. Medicine, N.Y.C., 1967-72, assoc. prof., 1972-77, Kramer prof., chmn. dept. molecular biology, 1977-86, dir. biol. scis. div., 1981-86; Eugene Higgins prof., chmn. dept. microbiology, Coll. Physicians and Surgeons Columbia U., N.Y.C., 1986-89; Joseph D. Grant prof., chmn. dept. devel. biology Sch. Medicine, Stanford U., 1989—; bd. dirs. Silicon Graphics; bd. sci. counselors NIH, Washington, 1980-84, DeWitt Stetten disting. lectr., 1989; bd. sci. advisors G.D. Searle Co., Skokie, Ill., 1984-86; sci. adv. bd. Mass. Gen. Hosp., 1990-93, SmithKline Beecham, 1993—, PathoGenesis, 1995—; bd. trustees Scientists Inst. for Pub. Info., 1990-94; lectr. Harvey Soc., 1993; commencement address U. Calif., Berkeley, 1994. Editor: Microbiol. Devel., 1984; mem. editorial bd. Jour. Bacteriology, 1978-86, Trends in Genetics, 1987—, Genes and Development, 1987-91, Cell Regulation, 1990-92, Molecular Biology of the Cell, 1992—, Molecular Microbiology, 1991—, Current Opinion on Genetics and Devel., 1991—; contbr. articles to profl. jours. Mem. sci. bd. Helen Hay Witney Found., N.Y.C., 1986-94; co-chmn. adv. bd. NSF Biology Directorate, 1988-89; vis. com., bd. overseers Harvard U., Cambridge, Mass., 1987-90; mem. sci. bd. Whitehead Inst., MIT, Boston, 1988-93; mem. sci. rev. bd. Howard Hughes Med. Inst., 1990-94, Cancer Ctr. of Mass. Gen. Hosp., Boston, 1994; mem. Presidio Coun. City of San Francisco, 1991-94; mem. Pres. Coun. U. Calif., 1991—. Recipient Hirschl Career Scientist award, 1976, Spirit of Achievement award, 1978, Alumna award of honor Bklyn. Coll., 1983, Excellence in Sci. award Fedn. Am. Soc. Exptl. Biology, 1994; Jane Coffin Child fellow, 1966. Fellow AAAS, Am. Acad. Arts and Scis., Am. Acad. Microbiology; mem. NAS, Inst. Medicine of NAS, Am. Soc. Biochemistry and Molecular Biology (nominating com. 1982, 87, coun. 1990-93), Am. Heart Assn. (sci. adv. bd. 1984-87). Avocation: watercolor painting. Office: Stanford U Sch Medicine Beckman Ctr Dept Devel Biology Stanford CA 94305

SHAPIRO, MARCIA HASKEL, speech and language pathologist; b. N.Y.C., Nov. 6, 1949; d. Ben and Edna Haskel; m. Louis Shapiro, Aug. 1, 1981. BA, Hunter Coll., 1982; MA, NYU, 1983; MA in Speech Pathology, U. Cen. Fla., 1991. Cert. deaf educator, Fla. Tchr. deaf Pub. Sch. 47, N.Y.C., 1983-84; speech pathologist St. Francis Sch. for the Deaf, Bklyn., 1984-86, Seminole County Schs., 1986-87, Lake County Schs., 1987-89, Orange County Schs., Orlando, Fla., 1989-91, West Volusia Meml. Hosp., Deland, Fla., 1991-93, Orlando Regional Med. Ctr., 1993, Sand Lake Hosp., 1993—; staff head swallowing dept. Leesburg Regional Med. Ctr., 1994; dir. speech pathology Fla. Hosp., Waterman, 1994—. Mem. ASHA, AFTRA, EQITY, Annals of Deaf, CAID, Alexander Graham Bell Assn. for Deaf.

SHAPIRO, MARJORIE MACKAY, musicologist, educator; b. Jamaica, N.Y., Nov. 3, 1929; d. Hugh Alexander and Violet (Kemble) Mackay; m. Jerome Gerson Shapiro, Dec. 31, 1959; children: Jeffrey Kemble, Jill Dara, Eric Paul. BS, SUNY, Oswego, 1950; MA, Columbia U., 1954; MusM, Manhattan Sch. Music, 1982; postgrad., CUNY, 1989—. Lic. tchr., N.Y. Tchr. various pub. schs., New Canaan, Conn., 1950-54; tchr. high sch. music and English various pub. schs., Great Neck, N.Y., 1954-56; tchr. Le Coll. de Jeunes Filles, St. Gauthier, France, 1956-57; singer various light opera houses and chs., Paris, 1957-59; singer, prin. Village Light Opera Group, N.Y.C., 1959-64; singer Ch. of the Resurrection, N.Y.C., 1959-74; founder, prin. singer The Hopewell Consort, N.Y.C., 1970-76; founder ednl. co. Ventures in Music, N.Y.C., 1984-90; mem. Am. Recorder Soc., N.Y.C., 1979-85; staff lectr. on music Manhattan Sch. of Music, N.Y.C., 1984-86, Berkshire Choral Inst., Sheffield, Mass., 1984-86, Aristocrat Tours, Inc., 1984-87, AAUW, 1986-89, The New Sch., N.Y.C., 1986-91, The N.Y. Philharmonic, N.Y.C., 1987-91. Performer (record album) The Art of Heinrich Schutz Vol. I and II, 1965; contbr. articles to profl. publs. Organizer Head Start program James Weldon Johnson Settlement House, N.Y.C., 1970-74; rschr., active mem. Citizens' Com. for Children, N.Y.C., 1972—. Frick Mus. fellow, 1990-95. Mem. AAUW, Am. Composers Orch. (adv. coun. 1982—), Am. Music Ctr., Music Libr. Assn., Sonneck Soc. for Am. Music (area rep. 1983—, bd. trustees, chair Nat. Am. Music Week Com.), English Speaking Union, Cosmopolitan Club (music com. 1986-89, 92), Bohemian Club. Episcopalian. Avocations: tennis, chess. Home: 200 E 66th St # A-701 New York NY 10021-6728

SHAPIRO, MARK HOWARD, physicist, educator, academic dean, consultant; b. Boston, Apr. 18, 1940; s. Louis and Sara Ann (Diamond) S.; m. Anita Rae Lavine, June 8, 1961; children: David Gregory, Diane Elaine, Lisa Michelle. A.B. with honors, U. Calif., Berkeley, 1962; M.S. (NSF coop. fellow), U. Pa., 1963, Ph.D., 1966. Research fellow Kellogg Radiation Lab., Calif. Inst. Tech., Pasadena, 1966-68; vis. assoc. Kellogg Radiation Lab., Calif. Inst. Tech., 1976—; research assoc. Nuclear Structure Research Lab. U. Rochester (N.Y.), 1968-70; mem. faculty Calif. State U., Fullerton, 1970—, prof. physics, 1978—, acting assoc. dean Sch. Math., Sci. and Engring., 1985-86, acting dir. Office Faculty Research and Devel., 1986-87, chmn. physics dept., 1989-96; dir. tchr. enhancement program NSF, Washington, 1987-88; tour speaker Am. Chem. Soc., 1983-85. Contbr. over 125 articles to profl. jours. Pres. Pasadena Young Democrats, 1967-68; mem. pub. info. and edn. com. Calif. Task Force on Earthquake Preparedness, 1981-85; bd. dirs. Calif. State U. Fullerton Found., 1982-85. Grantee Research Corp., 1971-74, Calif. Inst. Tech., 1977-78, U.S. Geol. Survey, 1978-85, Digital Equipment Corp., 1982, NSF, 1985-87, 90—. Mem. AAAS, Am. Phys. Soc., Am. Assn. Physics Tchrs. (profl. concerns com. 1990-93, chmn. 1991-93), Am. Geophys. Union, N.Y. Acad. Scis., Materials Rsch. Soc., Coun. on Undergrad. Rsch. (physics/astronomy councillor 1993—). Achievements include research in experimental nuclear physics, experimental nuclear astrophysics, geophysics and atomic collisions in solids. Office: Calif State Univ Physics Dept Fullerton CA 92634

SHAPIRO, MARTIN, retired university administrator, musician; b. 1933. B.A., UCLA, 1955; Ph.D., Harvard U., 1961. Instr. polit. sci. Harvard U., Cambridge, Mass., 1960-62; prof. Harvard U., 1971-74; asst. prof. Stanford U., Calif., 1962-65; assoc. prof. U. Calif.-Irvine, 1965-70, prof., 1970; prof. stringed instruments Grove City (Pa.) Coll., 1971; prof. law U. Calif.-Berkeley, 1977—; prof. U. Calif.-San Diego, 1974-77; bd. dirs. Nat. Bank N.E., Pa., dir. N.E. Bancorp; musician throughout U.S., 1956—; permanent guest condr. to Shandong Provincial Symphony Orch., Jinan, China; mem. Erie Philharm. Author: Law and Politics in the Supreme Court, 1964, Freedom of Speech, The Supreme Court and Judicial Review, 1966, Supreme Court and Administrative Agencies, 1968, Courts, 1981, Who Guards the Guardians, 1987. Mem. Law and Soc. Assn. (trustee 1992-95), Western Polit. Sci. Assn. (pres. 1978), Am. Acad. Arts and Scis., Am. Polit. Sci. Assn. (v.p. 1988). Office: U Calif Law Sch 225 Boalt Hall Berkeley CA 94720

SHAPIRO, MARVIN SEYMOUR, lawyer; b. N.Y.C., Oct. 26, 1936; s. Benjamin and Sally (Book) S.; m. Natalie Kover, July 12, 1959; children: Donna, Meryl. AB, Columbia U., 1957, LLB, 1959. Bar: D.C. 1959, Calif. 1962. Atty. appellate sect. Civil Div. U.S. Dept. Justice, Washington, 1959-61; ptnr. Irell & Manella, L.A., 1962—, mng. ptnr., 1992—; lectr. U. So. Calif. Tax Inst., Calif. Continuing Edn. of the Bar, Practising Law Inst. Articles editor Columbia Law Rev., 1958-59. V.p., bd. dirs. Jewish Fedn. Coun., L.A., 1985-95; treas. Alan Cranston Campaign, 1974, 80, 86; chmn. credentials com. Dem. Nat. Com., 1972-76. Mem. L.A. County Bar Assn., Beverly Hills Barristers (pres. 1970). Avocations: travel, golf. Home: 432 N Cliffwood Ave Los Angeles CA 90049-2620 Office: Irell & Manella 1800 Avenue Of The Stars Los Angeles CA 90067

SHAPIRO, MAURICE MANDEL, astrophysicist; b. Jerusalem, Israel, Nov. 13, 1915; came to U.S., 1921; s. Asher and Miriam R. (Grunbaum) S.; m. Inez Weinfield, Feb. 8, 1942 (dec. Oct. 1964); children: Joel Nevin, Elana Shapiro Ashley Naktin, Raquel Tamar Shapiro Kislinger. B.S., U. Chgo., 1936, M.S., 1940, Ph.D., 1942. Instr. physics and math. Chgo. City Colls., 1937-41; chmn. dept. phys. and biol. scis. Austin Coll., 1938-41; instr. math. Gary Coll., 1942; physicist Dept. Navy, 1942-44; lectr. physics and math. George Washington U., 1943-44; group leader, mem. coordinating council of lab. Los Alamos Sci. Lab., U. Calif., 1944-46; sr. physicist, lectr. Oak Ridge Nat. Lab., Union Carbon and Carbide Corp., 1946-49; cons. div. nuc. energy for propulsion aircraft Fairchild Engine & Aircraft Corp., 1948-49; head cosmic ray br. nucleonics div. U.S. Naval Research Lab., Washington, 1949-65, supt. nucleonics div., 1953-65, chief scientist Lab. for Cosmic Ray Physics, 1965-82, apptd. to chair of cosmic ray physics, 1966-82, chief scientist emeritus, 1982—; lectr. U. Md., 1949-50, 52—, assoc. prof., 1950-51, vis. prof. physics and astronomy, 1986—; vis. prof. physics and astronomy U. Iowa, 1981-84; vis. prof. astrophysics U. Bonn, 1982-84; vis. scientist Max Planck Inst. für Astrophysik, W. Ger., 1984-85; cons. Argonne Nat. Lab., 1949; cons. panel on cosmic rays U.S. nat. com. IGY; lectr. physics and engring. Nuclear Products-Erco div. ACF Industries, Inc., 1956-58; lectr. E. Fermi Internat. Sch. Physics, Varenna, Italy, 1962; vis. prof. Weizmann Inst. Sci., Rehovoth, Israel, 1962-63, Inst. Math. Scis., Madras, India, 1971; Inst. Astronomy and Geophysics Nat. U. Mex., 1976; vis. prof. physics and astronomy Northwestern U., Evanston, Ill., 1978; cons. space rsch. in astronomy Space Sci. Bd., Nat. Acad. Scis., 1965; cons. Office Space Scis., NASA, 1965-66, 89; prin. investigator Gemini S-9 Cosmic Ray Expts., NASA, 1964-69, Skylab, 1967-76, Long Duration Exposure Facility, 1977—; mem. Groupe de Travail de Biologie Spatiale, Council of Europe, 1970—; mem. steering com. DUMAND Consortium, 1976—, mem. exec. com., 1979-82, mem. sci. adv. com., 1982—; lectr. Summer Space Inst., Deutsche Physikalische Gesellschaft, 1972; dir. Internat. Sch. Cosmic-Ray Astrophysics, Ettore Majorana Centre Sci. Culture, Erice, Italy, 1977—, also sr. corr., 1977—; chmn. U.S. IGY com. on interdisciplinary research, mem. nuclear emulsion panel space sci. bd.; Nat. Acad. Scis., 1959—; chief U.S. rep., steering com. Internat. Coop. Emulsion Flights for Cosmic Ray Research; cons. CREI Atomics, 1959—; vis. com. Bartol Research Found., Franklin Inst., 1967-74; mem. U.S. organizing com. 13th and 19th Internat. Confs. on Cosmic Rays; mem. sci. adv. com. Internat. Confs. on Nuclear Photography and Solid State Detectors, 1966—; mem. Com. of Honor for Einstein Centennial, Acad. Naz. Lincei, 1977; mem. Internat. Organizing com. Tex. Symposia on Relativistic Astrophysics, 1976—; Regents lectr. U. Calif. Riverside, 1985; Edison lectr. Naval Rsch. Lab award, 1990; Victor Hess Meml. lectr., Rome, 1995. Mem. editorial bd. Astrophysics and Space Sci., 1968-75; assoc. editor: Phys. Rev. Letters, 1977-84; editor (NATO) ASI Series on Cosmic-Ray Astrophysics; contbr. to Am. Inst. Handbook of Physics, various encys. Mem. exec. bd. Cong. Beth Chai, Washington, 1987—; trustee Nat. Capital Astronomers, Washington, 1989—; mem. internat. panel Chernobyl World Lab., 1988. Recipient Disting. Civilian Svc. award Dept. Navy, 1967, medal of honor Soc. for Encouragement au Progrès, 1978, publs. award Naval Rsch. Lab., 1970, 74, 76, Dir.'s Spl. award, 1974, Sr. U.S. Scientist award Alexander von Humboldt Found., 1982, Profl. Achievement citation U. Chgo., 1992. Fellow Am. Phys. Soc. (chmn. organizing com. div. cosmic physics, chmn. 1971-72, com. on publs. 1977-79), AAAS, Washington Acad. Scis. (past com. chmn., Disting. Career in Scis. award, 1993); mem. Am. Astron. Soc. (exec. com. div. high-energy astrophysics 1978—, chmn. 1982), Philos. Soc. Washington (past pres.), Am. Technion Soc. (Washington bd.), Assn. Los Alamos Scientists (past chmn.), Assn. Oak Ridge Engrs. and Scientists (past chmn.), Fedn. Am. Scientists (past mem. exec. com., nat. council), Internat. Astron. Union (organizing comm. on high-energy astrophysics), Internat. Conf. on Cosmic Rays (Victor Hess Meml. lectr., 1995), Phi Beta Kappa, Sigma Xi (Edison lectr. 1990). Club: Cosmos (Washington). Achievements include patents in field; discovery of first definitive evidence for production of cosmic ray secondaries in the interstellar medium; research in cosmic radiation, composition, origin, propagation, and nuclear transformations; in high-energy astrophysics; in particles and fields; in nuclear physics, neutron physics and fission reactors; in hydrodynamics and gamma-ray and neutrino astronomy. Office: 205 S Yoakum Pky Ste 1514 Alexandria VA 22304-3838 *In scientific achievement, good judgement (e.g., in choice of research problems)is sometimes more important than brilliance.*

SHAPIRO, MEL, playwright, director, drama educator; b. Bklyn., Dec. 16, 1935; s. Benjamin Shapiro and Lillian (Lazarus) Bestul; m. Jeanne Elizabeth Shapiro, Feb. 23, 1963; children: Joshua, Benjamin. BFA, Carnegie-Mellon U., 1961, MFA, 1961. Resident dir. Arena Stage, Washington, 1963-65; producing dir. Tyrone Guthrie Theater, Mpls., 1968-70; master tchr. drama NYU, N.Y.C., 1970-80; guest dir. Lincoln Ctr. Repertory, N.Y.C., 1970; dir. N.Y. Shakespeare Festival, N.Y.C., 1971-77; prof. Carnegie Mellon U., Pitts., 1980-90, head. dept., 1980-87; bd. dirs. Pitts. Pub. Theater, 1982—; head acting UCLA Sch. Theater, Film and TV, 1990—; founder Onstage Co., L.A., 1993. Dir. N.Y.C. prodns. The House of Blue Leaves, 1970, Bosoms and Neglect, 1978; co-adaptor mus. Two Gentlemen of Verona, 1971 (Tony award); author: (plays) The Price of Admissions, 1984 (Drama-Logue mag. award), The Lay of the Land (Joseph Kesselring award 1990), A Life of Crime, 1993. With U.S. Army, 1955-57. Recipient N.Y. Drama Critics award, 1971, 72, Obie award Village Voice, 1972, Drama Desk award, 1973, Drama-logue award, 1993. Mem. Soc. Stage Dirs. and Choreographers (founder, editor The Jour. 1978). Office: UCLA Sch Theatre Film & TV 405 Hilgard Ave Los Angeles CA 90024-1301

SHAPIRO, MICHAEL, supermarket corporate officer; b. N.Y.C., Mar. 3, 1942; s. Jack and Celia (Schwartzbaum) S.; m. Sara Louise Ress, Mar. 22, 1964; children: Jeffrey, Lisa, Kenneth. BS, CCNY, 1962. CPA, N.Y., N.J. Acct. Sidney Kaminsky & Co., N.Y.C., 1964-68; supr. Hurdman Cranston, Penney & Co. (C.P.A.s), N.Y.C., 1968-71; with Mayfair Super Markets Inc., Elizabeth, N.J., 1971-87; v.p. fin. and adminstrn. Mayfair Super Markets Inc., 1978-80, sr. v.p. fin. and adminstrn., 1980-86, exec. v.p. fin. and corp. devel., 1986-87, also dir.; self employed ins. cons., 1988-89; v.p. Fin. Fidelity Land Devel. Corp., Chatham, N.J., 1989-92; v.p. fin. and ops. Apex One Inc., Piscataway, N.J., 1992-94; sr. v.p., CFO, treas. Foodarama Supermarkets, Inc., Freehold, N.J., 1994—. Mem. AICPA, N.Y. State Soc. CPAs. Office: Foodarama Supermarkets Inc 922 Hwy 33 Bldg 6 Ste 1 Freehold NJ 07728

SHAPIRO, MICHAEL EDWARD, museum administrator, curator, art historian; b. N.Y.C., Nov. 15, 1949; s. Edward Aaron and Sylvia (Fishman) S.; m. Elizabeth Harvey, 1977; 2 children. BA, Hamilton Coll., 1972; MA, Williams Coll., 1976, Harvard U., 1978; PhD, Harvard U., 1980. Asst. prof. dept. art history Duke U., Durham, N.C., 1980-84; curator 19th-20th century art St. Louis Art Mus., 1984-92, chief curator, 1987-92; dir. Los Angeles County Mus. Art, 1992-93; dir. mus. programs Chief Curator High Mus. of Art, Atlanta, 1994-95. Author: Bronze Casting and American Sculpture, 1985; contbg. author: Frederic Remington: The Masterworks, 1988, George Caleb Bingham, 1990; mng. curator, editor Rings: Five Passions in World Art, 1996.

SHAPIRO, MICHAEL HENRY, government executive; b. Bayonne, N.J., Sept. 23, 1948; s. William and Sophie (Slotkin) S. BS, Lehigh U., 1970; MS, Harvard U., 1972, PhD, 1976. Assoc. prof. Harvard U., Cambridge, Mass., 1976-82, analyst, 1980-81, br. chief, 1981-83, dir. econs. and tech. divsn., 1983-89; dep. asst. adminstr., air and radiation EPA, Washington, 1989-93; dir. Office of Solid Waste, Washington, 1993—. Office: EPA 401 M St SW # 5301 Washington DC 20460-0001

SHAPIRO, MURRAY, structural engineer; b. N.Y.C., July 5, 1925; s. Samuel and Fanny (Korman) S.; m. Florence Morrison, June 16, 1951; children: Fred Richard, Alan Neil. BCE, CCNY, 1947. Registered profl. engr., N.Y., N.J., Pa., Md., Ga., N.C., Mass., Conn. Steel detailer Knopf & Amron, N.Y.C., 1947-48; asst. engr. N.Y.C. Bd. Transp., 1948-50; designer James Ruderman cons. engrs., N.Y.C., 1950-53, sr. engr., 1953-58, assoc., 1958-65; jr. ptnr. Office of James Ruderman, N.Y.C., 1965-66, sr. ptnr., 1966—. Structural designer many highrise office buildings, including GM Bldg., N.Y.C., Pan Am Bldg., N.Y.C., also schs., apartment houses, theaters. With U.S. Army, 1943-45, ETO. Decorated Purple Heart, Bronze Star. Mem. N.Y. Cons. Engrs. Assn. (trustee 1972-77, sec. 1974-76), Am. Concrete Inst., N.Y. Acad. Scis., Fresh Meadow Country Club. Republican. Jewish. Home: 170 West End Ave Apt 15D New York NY 10023-5448 Office: Office of James Ruderman 15 W 36th St New York NY 10018-7910

SHAPIRO, NORMA SONDRA LEVY, federal judge; b. Phila., July 27, 1928; d. Bert and Jane (Kotkin) Levy; m. Bernard Shapiro, Aug. 21, 1949; children: Finley, Neil, Aaron. BA in Polit. Theory with honors, U. Mich., 1948; JD magna cum laude, U. Pa., 1951. Bar: Pa. 1952, U.S. Supreme Ct. 1978. Law clk. to presiding justice Pa. Supreme Ct., 1951-52; instr. U. Pa. Law Sch., 1951-52, 55-56; assoc. Dechert Price & Rhoads, Phila., 1956-58, 67-73; ptnr. Dechert Price & Rhoads, 1973-78; judge U.S. Dist. Ct. (ea. dist.) Pa., 1978—; assoc. trustee U. Pa. Law Sch., 1978-93; former trustee Women's Law Project, Albert Einstein Med. Ctr.; v.p. Jewish Pub. Soc.; trustee Fedn. Jewish Agys., 1980-83; mem. lawyers adv. panel Pa. Gov.'s Commn. on Status of Women, 1974; legal adv. regional Coun. Child Psychiatry, bd. dirs. Women Judges' Fund for Justice. Guest editor: Shingle, 1972. Mem. Lower Merion County (Pa.) Bd. Sch. Dirs., 1968-77, pres., 1977, v.p., 1976; v.p. Jewish Community Relations Council of Greater Phila., 1975-77; chmn. legal affairs com., 1978; pres. Belmont Hills Home and Sch. Assn., Lower Merion Twp.; legis. chmn. Lower Merion Sch. Dist. Intersch. Council; mem. Task Force on Mental Health of Children and Youth of Pa.; treas., chmn. edn. com. Human Relations Council, Lower Merion; v.p., parliamentarian Nes Ami Penn Valley Congregation, Lower Merion Twp. Named Woman of Yr., Oxford Circle Jewish Community Center, 1979, Woman of Distinction, Golden Slipper Club, 1979; Gowen fellow, 1954-55; recipient Hannah G. Solomon award Nat. Coun. Jewish Women, 1992. Mem. Am. Law Inst., Am. Bar Found., ABA (ho. dels. 1990—, coun./chmn. conf. fed. judges 1986-87, vice-chmn. com. law and mental health sect. family law), Pa. Bar Assn. (ho. of dels. 1979-81), Phila. Bar Assn. (chmn. com. women's rights 1972, 74-75, chmn. bd. govs. 1977-78, chmn. pub. rels. com. 1978), Fed. Bar Assn. (Bill of Rights award 1991), Nat. Assn. Women Lawyers, Phila. Trial Lawyers Assn., Am. Judicature Soc., Phila., Nat. Assn. Women Judges, Fellowship Commn., Order of Coif (chpt. pres. 1973-75), Tau Epsilon Rho, Jurisprudence. Office: US Dist Courthouse Independence Mall West 601 Market St Rm 10614 Philadelphia PA 19106*

SHAPIRO, NORMAN RICHARD, Romance languages and literatures educator; b. Boston, Nov. 1, 1930; s. Harry Alexander and Eva (Goldberg) S. B.A., Harvard U., 1951, M.A., 1952, Ph.D., 1958; de Langue et Lettres Françaises, Université d'Aix-Marseille, 1956, M.A. (hon.), 1972. Instr. French Amherst Coll., 1958-60; asst. prof. romance langs. and lits. Wesleyan U., 1960-65, assoc. prof., 1965-71, prof., 1971—. Editor: Echos, 1965, Palabres, 1973; translator, editor: Négritude, 1971; translator: Four Farces by Georges Feydeau, 1970, Comedy of Eros, 1971, Kamouraska by Anne Hébert, 1973, Virginie, or the Dawning of the World by Joseph Majault, 1974, The Camp of The Saints by Jean Raspail, 1975, Feydeau, First to Last, 1982, Fables from Old French: Aesop's Beasts and Bumpkins, 1983, A Fitting Confusion by Georges Feydeau, 1985, The Pregnant Pause, or Love's Labor Lost, by Georges Feydeau, 1987, The Brazilian by Henry Meilhac and Ludovic Halévy, 1987, A Slap in the Farce by Eugène Labiche, 1988, A Matter of Wife and Death by Eugène Labiche, 1988, Fifty Fables of La Fontaine, 1988, The Fabulists French: Verse Fables of Nine Centuries, 1992, La Fontaine's Bawdy: Of Libertines, Louts and Lechers, 1992, A Flea in Her Rear, or Ants in Her Pants, and Other Vintage French Farces, 1994; composer: Three Songs, 1961; contbr. articles, transls. and revs. to profl. jours. Mem. African Studies Assn., Am. Assn. Tchrs. French, Universala Esperanto-Asocio, Esperanto League N.Am., Judezmo Soc., Am. Lit. Transl. Assn. (Disting. Translation award 1992), Am. Translators Assn., Dramatists Guild, Beast Fable Soc. (editorial bd. Bestia), Signet Soc. of Harvard, Delta Kappa Epsilon. Jewish. Home: 214 High St Middletown CT 06457-3242

SHAPIRO, PAUL SAUVEUR, chemical engineer, researcher; b. Pitts., Dec. 4, 1942; s. Carl Lynwood and Lillian Ruth (Simon) S.; m. Melissa Friedland, Jan. 19, 1986; 1 child, Felix Benjamin. SB in Chem. Engring., MIT, 1963, SM in Chem. Engring., 1965, postgrad., 1967-71; EdM in Ednl. Planning, Harvard U., 1966. Expert cons. HEW and Action, Washington, 1972-76; sr. staff officer NRC, Washington, 1976-77; cons. Office Sci. and Tech. Adviser World Bank, Washington, 1977-80; cons. on nat. and internat. sci. and tech. AID, NSF and other agys., Washington, 1980-81; cons. Office Toxic Substances EPA, Washington, 1981-82, environ. engr. Office of Solid Waste, 1983-84, program mgr. Office R&D, 1985-94, CSI coord. office R&D, 1994—; vis. sr. rschr. Tel Aviv (Israel) U., 1979. Contbr. over 20 articles to profl. publs. Vol., advisor Vols. in Tech. Assistance, Arlington, Va., 1978-81; chmn. career edn. adv. coun. Washington Pub. Schs.; vice chmn. Early Environs., inc. Fellow NDEA, NDFL, 1967, 70. Mem. AIChE (program coord.), Fed. Water Quality Assn. (sec.), Air and Waste Mgmt. Assn. (work group leader), MIT Club of Washington (pres.), MIT Luncheon Club (pres.), Sigma Xi, Phi Delta Kappa. Democrat. Jewish. Achievements include development of mitigation research programs for radon, indoor air pollution, stratospheric ozone protection, global climate change, and mixed hazardous and radioactive wastes; development of pollution prevention research programs with metal finishing and electronics industries; co-development and implement of EPA's highest priority program, The Common Sense Initiative. Avocations: mysteries, swimming, singing, computers. Home: 1312 4th St SW Washington DC 20024 Office: EPA Office R&D 401 M St SW Washington DC 20460

SHAPIRO, PERRY, economics educator; b. Los Angeles, Jan. 15, 1941; s. Abraham and Ann (Warshaw) S.; m. Jody Silverstein, June 25, 1994; children: Elizabeth Naomi, Samuel Robert, Sarah Gertrud. BA in Econs., U. Calif.-Berkeley, 1962, PhD in Econs., 1968. Postdoctoral fellow in urban econs. Washington U., St. Louis, 1967-68; lectr. London Sch. Econs., 1968-69; asst. prof. econs. U. Calif.-Santa Barbara, 1969-74, assoc. prof., 1974-78, prof., 1978—, chair dept. econs., 1987-93; vis. prof. U. Mich., Ann Arbor, 1979-80; vis. scholar Federalism Rsch. Ctr. Australian Nat. U., 1992, adj. prof. Rsch. Sch. Social Scis., 1994—. Author: An Analytical Framework for Regional Policy, 1970. Vis. scholar U.S. Bur. Labor Stats., Washington, 1975-76; grantee NSF, 1979—, Nat. Inst. Justice, 1980-85; Fulbright sr. rsch. scholar Australia Nat. U., 1990-91. Mem. Am. Econs. Assn., Econometric Soc., Nat. Tax Assn. Office: U of Calif Dept Econs Santa Barbara CA 93016

SHAPIRO, RAYMOND L., lawyer; b. N.Y.C., Aug. 1, 1934; s. Alexander and Sadye (Morrison) S.; m. Judith Manis, Dec. 23, 1956; children: Joel, Todd, Lisa. BS, Temple U., 1956, LLB, 1959. Ptnr. Wexler, Weisman, Forman & Shapiro, Phila., 1959-84, Blank, Rome, Comisky & McCauley, Phila., 1984—. Author: Dunlap-Hanna Pa. Forms, 1963-83, Pa. Civil Practice Handbook, 1973-83; contbg.-author: Business Workouts Manual. Trustee Phila. Fedn. Jewish Agys., 1979—, treas., 1984-87, v.p., 1987-90; pres. Jewish Pub. Group, 1992-95. Fellow Am. Coll. Bankruptcy (bd. dirs.); mem. Nat. Bankruptcy Conf., ABA, Pa. Bar Assn., Phila. Bar Assn., Locust Club (bd. dirs. 1990). Office: Blank Rome Comisky & McCauley 4 Penn Center Plz 10-13 Fl 4 Philadelphia PA 19103-2599

SHAPIRO, RICHARD CHARLES, sales and marketing executive; b. Bklyn., May 28, 1936; s. Isidore and Sylvia (Rappaport) S.; m. Marilyn Joyce Bialy, Feb. 17, 1957 (div. 1974); children: Joseph, Scott; m. Francine L. Shaw, Sept. 19, 1975. BS in Edn., Golden State U., 1978, MBA, 1981; PhD in Bus. Adminstrn., Honolulu U., 1987. Lic. real estate broker, Ill. Affiliate Effective Motivation Assocs./Success Motivation inst., Bethpage, N.Y., 1965-68; v.p. sales Field Enterprises, Chgo., 1962-78; pres., CEO Snack-In, Inc., Detroit, 1978-82; sr. ptnr. Directions Growth and Strategy Cons., Chgo., 1982-95; CEO America's Home Detailing Corp., 1995—; v.p. domestic & internat. mktg. & sales Ency., oper. officer Ency. Brit.-Compton's Learning Co., 1991-93, specialist network mktg. & relationship mktg., pres., bd. dirs.; CEO Am.'s Home Detailing Corp., 1995, 1995—; pres., COO Am.'s Master Deep Clean Divsn., Deerfield, Ill., 1995—; instr. planning Life Underwriter Tng. Coun., L.I., 1965-66; assoc. editor Media Technics Pub. Assn., Lake Forest, 1988; bd. dirs. Master Deep Clean Co., Nat. Video Libr.; spkr. on mktg., sales and leadership. Author various self-improvement cassettes; contbr. articles to profl. jours. Active Explorers, high schs., youth clubs, 1965-74; founder, pres. Abundance and Goodwill Soc., 1968—. Served with USAF, 1957-60. Recipient Leadership award Am. Sales Masters, 1968; named Sales/Mktg. Execs. Leadership Recruiter/Trainer of Decade award. Mem. Salesmen With a Purpose, Chgo. Computer Soc., Effective Motivation Assocs. Avocations: wild-water rafting, white-water canoeing, camping, tennis, writing.

SHAPIRO, RICHARD GERALD, retired department store executive, consultant; b. N.Y.C., Apr. 24, 1924; s. David and Sophie (Hayflich) S.; m. Lila Eig, July 27, 1951; children—Judith, Amy, Donald. B.A., U. Mich., 1946; M.B.A., Harvard, 1948. With Lord & Taylor, N.Y.C., 1948-64; v.p. Lord & Taylor, 1959-63, sr. v.p., 1963-64; also mem. adv. bd.; pres. Wm. Filene's Sons Co., Boston, 1965-68; chief exec. officer, chmn. bd. Wm. Filene's Sons Co., 1968-73; pres. Gimbel Bros. Corp., N.Y.C., 1973-76; v.p. W.R. Grace & Co., pres. sporting goods div., 1977-79, pres. splty. store div., 1979-84; pres. Richard Shapiro Assocs., 1979—; sr. v.p. Montgomery Ward, Inc., 1986-88; bd. dirs. Assoc. Merchandising Corp., Nitrotec Corp., Capital Market Fund; retail chmn. Greater N.Y. Fund, 1963; chmn. merc. div. Mass. Bay United Fund, 1967. Mem. corp. Simmons Coll., Boston Mus. Fine Arts (permanent); bd. dirs. Mass. Mchts.; bd. dirs Family Counseling and Guidance Centers, 1969-72, v.p., 1970; trustee Brandeis U. Served with AUS, 1942-46. Mem. Harvard Bus. Sch. Assn. (gov.). Home: 10019 Gable Manor Ct Potomac MD 20854-5000

SHAPIRO, RICHARD STANLEY, physician; b. Moline, Ill., June 11, 1925; s. Herbert and Esther Dian (Grant) S.; BS, St. Ambrose Coll., 1947; BS in Pharmacy, U. Iowa, 1951, MS in Preventive Medicine and Environ. Health, 1951, M.D., 1957; m. Arlene Blum, June 12, 1949; children: Michele Pamela, Bruce Grant, Gary Lawrence; m. Merry Lou Cook, Oct. 11, 1971. Pharmacist, Rock Island, Ill., 1951-53; research asst. U. Iowa Coll. Medicine, Iowa City, 1950-51, 53-57; practice medicine specializing in allergy, Beverly Hills, Calif., 1958-62, Lynwood, Calif., 1962—; attending physician Good Hope Found. Allergy Clinic, Los Angeles, 1958-62, Cedars of Lebanon Hosp., Hollywood, Calif., 1959-68, U. So. Calif.-Los Angeles County Med. Center, 1962—; physician St. Francis Hosp., Lynwood, 1962—; assoc. clin. prof. medicine U. So. Calif., 1978-84, emeritus, 1984—. Bd. dirs. Westside Jewish Community Center, 1961-65, Camp JCA, 1964-65. Served with USNR, 1943-45; PTO. Diplomate Am. Bd. Allergy and Immunology. Fellow Am. Geriatric Soc., Am. Coll. Allergy, Am. Assn. Clin. Immunology and Allergy; mem. Am. Soc. Tropical Medicine and Hygiene, Am. Acad. Allergy, Los Angeles Allergy Soc., AMA, Calif., Los Angeles County med. assns., West Coast Allergy Soc., AAAS, Am., Calif. socs. internal medicine, Calif. Soc. Allergy, Am. Heart Assn., Sierra Club, Sigma Xi. Jewish. Mason; mem. B'nai B'rith. Contbr. articles to profl. jours. Office: 8301 Florence Ave Ste 104 Downey CA 90240-3946

SHAPIRO, ROBERT ALAN, retail executive; b. Denver, Dec. 24, 1946; s. George and Ruth Bearnice (Horn) S.; m. Jan Laurelle Tilker, Nov. 8, 1980; children: Aaron Phillip, Michael Samuel. BA, U. Denver, 1968; student, Northwestern U. Law Sch, 1968-70. V.p. Draper and Kramer, Inc., Chgo., 1970-73; asst. v.p. Urban Investment & Devel. Co., Chgo., 1973-75; dir. real estate The Limited, Columbus, Ohio, 1975-78; pres. Robert A. Shapiro & Assocs., Chgo., 1978-85; sr. v.p., corp. ops. asst. sec. County Seat Stores, Inc., Dallas, 1985—; lectr. Northwestern U., Evanston, Ill., Ohio State U., Columbus, 1976-78; mem. retail adv. bd. Shopping Ctr. Bus. mag. Mem. Internat. Coun. Shopping Ctrs. (tenant com. 1975-78), Nat. Retail Fedn. (splty. store task force com.). Jewish. Avocations: swimming, reading, skiing. Office: County Seat Stores 17950 Preston Rd Dallas TX 75252-5793

SHAPIRO, ROBERT B., manufacturing executive; b. N.Y.C., Aug. 4, 1938; s. Moses and Lilly (Langsam) S.; m. Berta Gordon, Mar. 27, 1964; children: James Gordon, Nina Rachel. A.B., Harvard U., 1959; LL.B., Columbia U., 1962. Bar: N.Y. 1963. Assoc. in law Columbia U., 1962-63; atty. firm Poletti Freidin Prashker Feldman & Gartner, N.Y.C., 1963-67; spl. asst. to gen. counsel and undersec. U.S. Dept. Transp., Washington, 1967-69; assoc. prof. law Northeastern U., Boston, 1969-71; asst. prof. law U. Wis., Madison, 1971-72; v.p., gen. counsel Gen. Instrument Corp., N.Y.C., 1972-79, G.D. Searle & Co., Skokie, Ill., 1979-82; pres. NutraSweet Group div. G.D. Searle & Co., Skokie, Ill., 1982-85; chmn., pres., chief exec. officer Nutra Sweet Co. subs. Monsanto, Skokie, Ill., 1985-95, also bd. dirs; now chmn., pres. Monsanto Co., St. Louis, 1995—. Mem. Mass. Gov.'s Transp. Task Force, 1970-71; mem. com. on procedure CAB, 1975-76; mem. bus. adv. com. White House Domestic Policy Rev. on Indsl. Innovation, 1978-79; Nat. Bd. Trustees Boys Clubs of Am. Recipient John R. Miller award as outstanding corporate mktg. exec., 1984; Outstanding Achievement award Sales and Mktg. Mgmt. Mag., 1984. Mem. Am. Bar Assn. (vice chmn. com. on corp. counsel 1981-82), U.S. C. of C. (council on antitrust policy 1981-82), N.Y. State Bar Assn. Office: Monsanto Co 800 N Lindbergh Blvd Saint Louis MO 63167*

SHAPIRO, ROBERT FRANK, investment banking company executive; b. St. Louis, Dec. 19, 1934; s. Eugene J. and Clara (Katz) S.; m. Anna Marie Susman, Dec. 21, 1960; children: Albert Andrew, Robert Jr., Jeanne Savitt. Grad., St. Louis Country Day Sch., 1952; BA, Yale U., 1956. Assoc. Lehman Bros., N.Y.C., 1956-67, ptnr., 1967-73, dir., sr. mng. dir., 1970-73; ptnr. Wertheim & Co., 1974; exec. v.p. Wertheim & Co., Inc., N.Y.C., 1974-75, pres., 1975-86; co-chmn. Wertheim Schroder & Co., Inc., 1986-87; chmn. RFS and Assocs., Inc., N.Y.C., 1988—, New Street Capital Corp., 1992-94; bd. dirs. TJX Cos., Inc., The Burnham Fund, Am. Bldgs. Co.; ind. gen. ptnr. Equitable Capital Ptnrs.; chmn. nominating com. N.Y. Stock Exch., 1980, mem. regulatory adv. com., 1988—, surveillance com., 1989—; bd. govs. Am. Stock Exch., 1970-76. Trustee Lenox Hill Hosp., Skowhegan; mem. gov. bd. Yale U. Art Gallery, New Haven, 1993—. Mem. Securities Industry Assn. (chmn. 1985, Bond Club N.Y. (pres. 1987-88, Yale Culb, Rockefeller Ctr. Club, Century Country Club. Office: RFS & Assocs 375 Park Ave Ste 2602 New York NY 10152-2699

SHAPIRO, ROBERT LESLIE, lawyer; b. Plainfield, N.J., Sept. 2, 1942. BS in Fin., UCLA, 1965; JD, Loyola U., L.A., 1968. Bar: Calif. 1969, U.S. Ct. Appeals (9th cir.) 1972, U.S. Dist. Ct. (cen., no. & so. dists.) Calif. 1982. Dep. dist. atty. Office of Dist. Atty., L.A., 1969-72; sole practice L.A., 1972-87, 88—; of counsel Bushkin, Gaims, Gaines, Jonas, L.A., 1987-88; Christensen, White, Miller, Fink & Jacobs, L.A., 1988-95; ptnr. Christensen, White, Miller, Fink, Jacobs, Glaser & Shapiro, L.A., 1995—. Author: Search for Justice, 1996. Recipient Am. Jurisprudence award Bancroft Whitney, 1969. Mem. Nat. Assn. Criminal Def. Lawyers, Calif. Attys. for Criminal Justice, Trial Lawyers for Pub. Justice (founder 1982), Century City Bar Assn. (Best Criminal Def. Atty. 1993). Office: 2121 Avenue Of The Stars Fl 19 Los Angeles CA 90067-5010

SHAPIRO, ROBYN SUE, lawyer, educator; b. Mpls., July 19, 1952; d. Walter David and Judith Rae (Sweet) S.; m. Charles Howard Barr, June 27, 1976; children: Tania Shapiro-Barr, Jeremy Shapiro-Barr, Michael Shapiro-Barr. BA summa cum laude, U. Mich., 1974; JD, Harvard U., 1977. Bar: D.C., 1977, Wis., 1979, U.S. Supreme Ct., 1990. Assoc. Foley & Lardner, Washington, 1977-79; ptnr. Barr & Shapiro, Menomonee Falls, Wis., 1980-87; assoc. Quarles & Brady, Milw., 1987-92; ptnr. Michael Best & Friedrich, Milw., 1992—; adj. asst. prof. law Marquette U., Milw., 1979-83; assoc. dir. bioethics ctr. Med. Coll. Wis., Milw., 1982-85, dir., 1985—; asst. prof. bioethics Med. Coll. Wis., 1984-89, assoc. prof. bioethics, 1989—; dir. Wis. Ethics Com. Network, 1987—; bd. mem. Wis. Health Decisions, 1990-93. Editorial bd. mem: Cambridge Quarterly, 1991—, HEC Forum, 1988-91; contbr. articles to profl. jours. Mem. ethics com. St. Luke's Hosp., Milw., 1983—, Elmbrook Meml. Hosp., Milw., 1983-86, Cmty. Meml. Hosp., Menomonee Falls, 1984—, Sinai Samaritan Hosp., Milw., 1986—, Milw. County Med. Complex, 1984—, Froedtert Meml. Luth. Hosp., 1985—; mem. subcom. organ transplantation Wis. Health Policy Coun., Madison, 1984, bioethics com., 1986-89; mem. com. study on bioethics Wis. Legis. Coun., Madison, 1984-85; bd. dirs. Jewish Home and Care Ctr., 1994—, chair ethics com., 1994—; chair Bayside Ethics Bd., 1994—; bd. dirs. Milw. area chpt. Girl Scouts U.S., Am. Bioethics Assn., 1995—. James B. Angell scholar, 1971-72. Mem. ABA (forum com. health law, individual rights and responsibilities sec., health rights com. chair 1994—, mem. coordinating com. on bioethics and law, chair 1995—), Nat. Health Lawyers Assn., Am. Soc. Law & Medicine, Am. Hosp. Assn. (bioethics tech. panel 1991-94, spl. com. HIV & practitioners 1991-93), Wis. Bar Assn. (coun. Wis. health law sect. 1988-89, individual rights sect. coun. 1987-90), Assn. Women Lawyers, ACLU, Wis. Found. (Atty. of Yr. 1988), Milw. Acad. Medicine (coun. 1992—, chair bioethics com. 1992—), Milw. AIDS Coalition (steering com. 1988-91), Internat. Bioethics Assn. (chair task force on ethics coms.), Profl. Dimensions (Golden Compass award 1994), Phi Beta Kappa, others. Home: 9474 N Broadmoor Rd Milwaukee WI 53217-1309 Office: Med Coll Wis Bioethics Ctr 8701 W Watertown Plank Rd Milwaukee WI 53226-3548

SHAPIRO, SAM, health care analyst, biostatistician; b. N.Y.C., Feb. 12, 1914; married, 1938; 2 children. BS, Bklyn. Coll., 1933. Chief natality analysis br. Nat. Office Vital Stats., USPHS, 1947-54; sr. study dir. Nat. Opinion Rsch. Ctr., 1954-55; assoc. dir. div. rsch. and stats. Health Ins. Plan Greater N.Y., 1955-59, v.p., dir., 1959-73; dir. Health Svc. R & D Ctr., Balt., 1973-83; prof. health policy and mgmt. Johns Hopkins Sch. Hygiene and Pub. Health, Balt., 1973-85; emeritus prof. Johns Hopkins Sch. Hygiene and Pub. Health, 1985—; lectr. in pub. health Columbia U. Sch. Pub. Health and Adminstrv. Medicine, 1961-80; adj. prof. medicine Mt. Sinai Sch. Medicine, N.Y.C., 1972-78. Recipient prize GM Cancer Rsch. Found., 1988, Disting. Achievement award Am. Soc. Preventive Oncology, 1985. Fellow AAAS, APHA (award for excellence 1977), Am. Statis. Assn., Am. Coll. Radiology (hon.); mem. Inst. Medicine, Assn. for Health Svcs. Rsch. (Disting. Career in Health Svcs. Rsch. award 1985). Office: Johns Hopkins U Sch Hygiene and Pub Health 624 N Broadway Baltimore MD 21205-1901

SHAPIRO, SAMUEL BERNARD, management consultant; b. Chgo., Nov. 15, 1909; s. Bernard and Ida (Schwartz) S.; m. Mary Heller, Dec. 24, 1933; children: Judith Shapiro DeGraff, Richard B. B.S., U. Chgo., 1935. Asst. to mgr. Greater Chgo. Safety Council, 1928-33; exec. sec. Authorized Ford Dealers Assn., 1933-38; mgr. Chgo. Automobile Trade Assn. and Chgo. Auto Shows, 1938-43; chief research and planning, automobile rationing br. (OPA), 1943; exec. dir. Linen Supply Assn. Am., 1946-75; pres. Samuel B. Shapiro Cons. Inc., 1975—; v.p. Seminars, Speakers, Travel, Inc., Washington, 1976-82; Sr. v.p., treas., dir. Am. Soc. Assn. Execs., 1958-62, pres., 1962-63; chmn. bd. trustees CAE-ASAE, 1972; pres. Assn. Execs. Forum Chgo., 1956-57; chmn. exec. operating council Insts. Orgn. Mgmt., Mich. State U., 1957; mem. exec. adv. council Fla. Atlantic U., 1974-84. Co-author: textbook Association Management, 1958, Forward Planning, 1969, Future Perspectives, 1985, Handbook for Corporate Directors, 1985; author: The Whys of Association Executive Success (and Failure), 1977, Before and After Retirement, 1978, Financial Incentives for Association Executives, 1983, From the Past Comes the Future, 1986, Coming of Age of the Association Profession, 1987; mem. adv. bd.: Adult Edn. mag, 1956-58; contbr. articles and monographs to profl. lit.; lectr. in field. Served with AUS, 1943-45. Recipient Key award Cert. Assn. Exec.-Am. Soc. Assn. Execs., 1960. Mem. ACLU, Am. Soc. Assn. Execs. (1st hon. mem. 1988), Internat. Soc. Gen. Semantics (charter mem., v.p. 1969-82), Am. Vets. Com., Phi Beta Kappa. Home: 5945 N Bay Rd Miami FL 33140

SHAPIRO, SANDER WOLF, lawyer; b. St. Louis, Sept. 24, 1929; s. Robert and Bess (Fisher) S.; m. Lottie F. Frankel, Aug. 14, 1955; children: Julie A. Shapiro Schechter, Susan B. Shapiro Schmitz. BA, Rice U., 1951; postgrad., Columbia U., 1951-52; JD, U. Tex., 1954. Atty. tax div. Dept. Justice, Washington, 1955-57; atty. advisor U.S. Tax Ct., Washington, 1957-58; ptnr. Clark, Thomas, Winters & Shapiro, Austin, Tex., 1958-84; sr. ptnr. Shapiro, Edens & Cook, Austin, 1984-91; of counsel Jenkens & Gilchrist, P.C., Austin, 1991—; adj. prof. law U. Tex., 1975—; lectr. in tax field. Author, editor Tex. Franchise Earned Surplus and Tax, 1985—, Family Solutions to Family Concerns, 1991—, A Walk Through Form 706, 1991—; co-editor Tex. Tax Svc., 1986-94. Bd. dirs. Austin Symphony Orch. Soc., 1974—, fin. v.p., 1980-95; bd. dirs. U. Tex. Coll. Fine Arts Adv. Coun., 1987-95, pres., 1991-94; bd. dirs. Capital of Tex. Pub. Telecomm. Coun., 1988—, pres., 1994-95; bd. dirs. Ronald McDonald House of Ctrl. Tex., Austin, 1990—, pres., 1994-95; bd. dirs. Capital Met. Transit Authority, 1988-91, chair, 1990; bd. dirs. Austin Cmty. Found., 1985-92, pres., 1991. Sander W. Shapiro Presdl. Scholarship in Law at U. Tex. endowed in his honor by Jenkens & Gilchrist, 1992. Fellow Am. Bar Found. (life), Am. Coll. Trust and Estate Counsel, Am. Coll. Tax Counsel, Tex. Bar Found. (sustaining life); mem. ABA, State Bar Assn. Tex., Am. Law Inst., Internat. Acad. Estate and Trust Law (academician), Nat. Assn. State Bar Tax Sects. (bd. dirs., vice-chair, 1996), Tex. Law Rev. Assn. (pres. 1992-93). Avocations: reading, music, golf. Office: Jenkens & Gilchrist 600 Congress Ave Ste 2200 Austin TX 78701-3248

SHAPIRO, SANDOR SOLOMON, hematologist; b. Bklyn., July 26, 1933. BA, Harvard U., 1954, MD, 1957. Intern Harvard med. svc. Boston City Hosp., 1957-58, asst. resident, 1960-61; asst. surgeon divsn. biol. std. NIH, USPHS, 1958-60; NIH spl. fellow MIT, 1961-64; from instr. to assoc. prof. Cardeza found. Jefferson Med. Coll., Phila., 1964-72, prof. medicine, 1972—, assoc. dir., 1978-85, dir., 1985—; mem. hematology study sect. NIH, 1972-76, 78-79; mem. med. adv. coun. Nat. Hemophilia Found., 1973-75; chmn. Pa. State Hemophilia Adv. Com., 1974-76. Mem. Am. Soc. Clin. Investigation, Am. Soc. Hematology, Am. Assn. Immunologists, Assn. Am. Physicians, Internat. Soc. Thrombosis and Hemostasis. Achievements include research in hemostasis and thrombosis, prothrombin metabolism, hemophilia, lupus anticoagulants, endothelial cells. Office: Thomas Jefferson U Cardeza Found Hematologic Rsch 1015 Walnut St Philadelphia PA 19107

SHAPIRO, SANDRA, lawyer; b. Providence, Oct. 17, 1944; d. Emil and Sarah (Cohen) S. AB magna cum laude, Bryn Mawr Coll., Pa., 1966; LLB magna cum laude, U. Pa., 1969. Bar: Mass. 1970, U.S. Dist. Ct. Mass. 1971, U.S. Ct. Appeals (1st cir.) 1972, U.S. Supreme Ct. 1980. Law clk. U.S. Ct. Appeals (1st cir.), Boston, 1969-70; assoc. Foley, Hoag & Eliot, Boston, 1970-75, ptnr., 1976—; bd. dirs. Mass. Govt. Land Bank; mem. Bd. Bar Overseers Mass. Supreme Judicial Ct., 1988-92, Gender Bias Study Com., 1986-89. Contbr. articles to profl. jours. Bd. dirs. Patriots' Trail coun. Girl Scouts U.S., 1994—; mem. bd. overseers Boston Lyric Opera, 1993—, New England Conservatory of Music, 1995—. Woodrow Wilson fellow, 1966. Mem. ABA (ethics, professionalism and pub. edn. com. 1994—), Women's Bar Assn. of Mass. (prs. 1985-86), New Eng. Women in Real Estate, Nat. Women's Law Ctr. Network, Mass. Bar Assn. (chmn. real property sect. coun., com. on profl. ethics), Boston Bar Assn. (mem. coun.), U. Pa. Law Sch. Alumni Assn. (bd. mgrs. 1990—), Order of Coif, Boston Club. Office: Foley Hoag & Eliot 1 Post Office Sq Boston MA 02109-2170

SHAPIRO, STANLEY, materials scientist; b. Bklyn., Jan. 3, 1937; s. George Israel and Dora (Richman) S.; m. Janet Esther Skolnick, Aug. 24, 1958; children: Shari Lynne, David Elliot, Jill Diane. BSChemE, CCNY, 1960; MS in Engring. Sci., Rensselaer Poly. Inst., Troy, N.Y., 1964; PhD in Metallurgy and Materials Sci., Lehigh U., 1966. Rsch. engr. Pratt & Whitney Aircraft Co., 1960-61; rsch. scientist United Aircraft Corp., 1961-64; instr., rsch. asst. Lehigh U., 1964-66; rsch. scientist, supr. metals rsch. lab. Olin Metals Rsch., New Haven, 1966-79; pres. Revere Rsch. Inc. subs. Revere Copper & Brass, Inc., Edison, N.J., 1979-84; v.p. R & D Nat. Can Corp., Des Plaines, Ill., 1984-87; v.p. R & D ops. Am. Nat. Can Co., Barrington, Ill., 1987-89; cons. Mergers & Acquisitions, Skokie, Ill., 1989-93; corp. contr. Metamor Techs. Ltd., Chgo., 1993-94; chief fin. officer Metamor Techs., Ltd., Chgo., 1994—. Patentee in field. Mem. AAAS, ASTM, Metall. Soc., Am. Soc. Metals, Am. Mgmt. Assn., Electron Microscopy Soc., Inst. Metals, Sci. Research Soc., N.Y. Acad. Scis., Packaging Inst., Inst. Food Technologists, Research Dirs. Chgo., Indsl. Research Inst., Sigma Xi. Achievements include 30 patents in field. Office: One N Franklin Chicago IL 60606

SHAPIRO, STEPHEN MICHAEL, lawyer; b. Chgo., May 3, 1946; s. Samuel H. and Dorothy A. (D'Andrea) S.; m. Joan H. Gately, Oct. 30, 1982; children: Dorothy Henderson, Michael Clifford. BA magna cum laude, Yale U., 1968, JD, 1971. Bar: Ill. 1971, Calif. 1972, D.C. 1991, U.S. Dist. Ct. (no. dist. trial bar) Ill. 1992, U.S. Ct. Appeals (all cirs.), U.S. Supreme Ct. 1975. Law clk. U.S. Ct. Appeals (9th cir.), San Francisco, 1971-72; ptnr., sr. mem. appellate practice Mayer, Brown & Platt, Chgo., 1972-78, 83—; asst. to solicitor gen. U.S. Dept. Justice, Washington, 1978-80, dep. solicitor gen., 1981-82; trustee Product Liability Adv. Found. Co-author: Supreme Court Practice, 1993; contbr. articles to profl. jours. Mem. ABA, Am. Law Inst., Am. Acad. Appellate Lawyers, Supreme Ct. Hist. Soc., Phi Beta Kappa. Republican. Jewish. Office: Mayer Brown & Platt 190 S La Salle St Chicago IL 60603-3410

SHAPIRO, STEPHEN RICHARD, retired air force officer, physician; b. Bklyn., Dec. 30, 1934; s. George Daniel and Bertha Brinna (Bazerman) S.; m. Myrna Farber, May 28, 1960; children: David C., Robert S., Marc E. BA, Bklyn. Coll., 1956; MD, SUNY Downstate Med. Ctr., 1960. Diplomate Am. Bd. Internal Medicine, Am. Bd. Allergy and Immunology, Am. Bd. Med. Mgmt. Commd. 2nd lt. USAF, 1960, advanced through grades to brig. gen., 1987; intern, then resident and fellow Walter Reed Gen. Hosp., Washington, 1960-65; asst. chief allergy Wilford Hall USAF Med. Ctr., San Antonio, 1965-73; chief clin. svc. Ramstein (Germany) Clinic, 1973-74; chief divsn. clin. medicine Hdqrs. USAFE/SG, Ramstein, 1974-76; comdr. USAF Hosp. RAF, Upper Heyford, Eng., 1976-80; dep. surgeon Hdqrs. AFSC/SG, Andrews AFB, Md., 1980-82; surgeon Hdqrs. AFRES/SG, Robins AFB, Ga., 1982-84; command surgeon Hdqrs. AFSC/SG, Andrews AFB, Md., 1984-87; comdr. Malcolm Grow USAF Med. Ctr., Andrews AFB, 1987-89; command surgeon Hdqrs. AFLC/SG, Wright-Patterson AFB, Ohio, 1989-92, Hdqrs. AFMC, 1991-92; chief of staff VA Health Care Ctr., El Paso, Tex., 1992—. Fellow Aerospace Med. Assn. (assoc.); mem. Am. Coll. Physician Execs., Am. Acad. Allergy and Immunology, Air Force Soc. Flight Surgeons, Air Force Soc. Physicians, Alpha Omega Alpha. Jewish. Avocations: gardening, reading, travel. Office: 5001 N Piedras St El Paso TX 79930-4211

SHAPIRO, STUART CHARLES, computer scientist, educator; b. N.Y.C., Dec. 30, 1944; s. Louis M. and Bertha (Rubinstein) S.; m. Caren Dee Knight, July 16, 1972. BS, MIT, 1966; MS, U. Wis., 1968, PhD, 1971. Lectr. computer scis. dept. U. Wis., Madison, 1971; vis. asst. prof. Ind. U., Bloomington, 1971-72, asst. prof., 1972-77, assoc. prof., 1977-78; asst. prof. SUNY, Buffalo, 1977-78, assoc. prof., 1978-83, prof., 1983—, chmn., 1984-90; cons. Calspan UB Rsch. Ctr., Buffalo; rsch. scientist Nat. Ctr. for Geographic Info. and Analysis, 1989—. Author: Techniques of Artificial Intelligence, 1979, LISP: An Interactive Approach, 1986, Common Lisp: An Interactive Approach, 1992; editor: Encyclopedia of Artificial Intelligence, 1987, paperback edit., 1990, 2d edit., 1992; contbr. articles to profl. jours. Grantee NSF, 1971—; recipient numerous grants for computer sci. research, 1971—. Fellow Am. Assn. Artificial Intelligence; mem. IEEE (sr.), Assn. Computing Machinery (chmn. spl. interest group on artificial intelligence 1991-95), Assn. Computational Linguistics, Cognitive Sci. Soc., Sigma Xi. Home: 142 Viscount Dr Buffalo NY 14221-1770 Office: SUNY at Buffalo Dept of Computer Sci 226 Bell Hall Buffalo NY 14260-2000

SHAPIRO, SUMNER, retired naval officer, business executive; b. Nashua, N.H., Jan. 13, 1926; s. Maurice David and Hannah (Goodman) S.; m. Eleanor S. Hymen, June 14, 1949; children: Martha, Steven, Susan. B.S., U.S. Naval Acad., 1949; M.S., George Washington U., 1966; postgrad., Naval War Coll., 1966, U.S. Army Inst. Advanced Soviet and Eastern European Studies, 1961. Commd. ensign U.S. Navy, 1949; advanced through grades to rear adm.; asst. naval attache U.S. Navy (Am. embassy), Moscow, 1963-65; dep. asst. chief of staff for intelligence U.S. Naval Forces Europe, London, 1967-69; comdg. officer Naval Intelligence Processing System Support Activity, Washington, 1969-72; asst. chief staff for intelligence U.S. Atlantic Command and U.S. Atlantic Fleet, Norfolk, Va., 1972-76; dep. dir. naval intelligence, 1976-77; comdr. Naval Intelligence Command, Washington, 1977-78; dir. naval intelligence Washington, 1978-82; ret., 1982; v.p. for advanced planning BDM Internat., 1983-89; pres. The Sumner Group Inc., 1989—. Pres. Naval Intelligence Found. Decorated D.S.M., Legion of Merit and others., Nat. Intelligence D.S.M., Netherlands Order Orange-Nassau, Brazil Order Naval Merit, French Nat. Order Merit, others. Mem. Naval Intelligence Found. (pres.), Naval Intelligence Profls. (bd. dirs.), U.S. Naval Inst., Assn. Former Intelligence Officers, Nat. Mil. Intelligence Assn., Nat. Security Industries Assn., U.S. Naval Acad. Alumni Assn., Naval Submarine League.

SHAPIRO, THEODORE, psychiatrist, educator; b. N.Y.C., Feb. 26, 1932; s. Herman Alexander and Nettie (Rosenblatt) S.; m. Joan May Itkin, June 26, 1955; children: Susan, Alexander Herman. BA, Wesleyan U., 1953; MD, Cornell U., 1957. Diplomate Am. Bd. Psychiatry and Neurology, Am. Bd. Child Psychiatry, Am. Psychoanalytic Assn. Intern Montefiore Hosp., N.Y.C., 1957-58; resident in psychiatry NYU-Bellevue Hosp., 1958-61, rsch. assoc. child psychiatry, 1961-65; instr. to prof. NYU Sch. Medicine, 1960-76; prof. psychiatry and pediatrics Cornell U. Med. Coll., N.Y.C, 1976—; vice chair for child and adolescent psychiatry, 1995—; asst. lectr. N.Y. Psychoanalytic Inst., N.Y.C., 1970-86, tng. and supervising analyst, 1986—; cons. Alcohol, Drug Abuse and Mental Health Adminstrn., WHO, Washington, Geneva, Copenhagen, 1980-82, Am. Acad. Child and Adolescent Psychiatry, Washington; chair com. on stewardship Task Force Future, 1980-82, acad. sec., 1981-83, chair work group on sci. issues, 1988-89, chair com. editorship and stewardship of jour., 1984-86, 90-92; participant in APA bilateral exch. in Ea. Europe, 1992; reviewer child psychopathology and treatment rev. com. NIMH, 1994—. Author: Clinical Psycholinguistics, 1979; co-editor: Infant Psychiatry, 1976; editor: Psychoanalysis and Contemporary Science, 1976, Structure in Psychoanalysis, 1991, Affect: Psychoanalytic Perspectives, 1992; editor Jour. Am. Psychoanalytic Assn., 1984-93; book rev. editor Internat. Jour. Psychoanalysis, 1993—; co-editor

Research in Psychoanalysis, 1995; contbr. articles to profl. jours. Recipient Sandor Rado lectureship Columbia Psychoanalytic Clinic, 1991, Prager lectureship George Washington U. Sch. Medicine; NIMH residency tng. grantee, 1976-86; recipient Wilfred C. Hulse N.Y. Coun. Child Psychiatry, 1982, Harry Bakwin Meml. NYU, 1982, Maurice Laufer lectureship E.P. Bradley Hosp., 1982. Fellow Am. Acad. Child Psychiatry (sec. 1981-83), Am. Psychiat. Assn.; mem. Soc. Profs. Child Psychiatry (chmn. com. on edn. 1982—), Group for Advancement of Psychiatry (chmn. com. on child psychiatry 1985-90), Am. Bd. Psychiatry & Neurology (com. on child and adolescent psychiatry 1987-93, chmn. 1992-93), N.Y. Psychoanalytic Soc. Jewish. Office: Cornell U Med Coll Payne Whitney Clinic Box 147 525 E 68th St New York NY 10021-4873

SHAPIRO, VICTOR LENARD, mathematics educator; b. Chgo., Oct. 16, 1924; s. Joseph E. and Anna (Grossman) S.; m. Florence Gilman, Mar. 21, 1948; children—Pamela Sue Shapiro Baer, Laura Fern Shapiro Young, Charles R., Arthur G. B.S., U. Chgo., 1947, M.S., 1949, Ph.D., 1952. Mem. faculty Rutgers U., 1952-60, prof. math., 1959-60; mem. Inst. Advanced Studies, Princeton, N.J., 1953-55, 58-59; mem. faculty U. Oreg., Eugene, 1960-64; prof. math. U. Calif., Riverside, 1964—; faculty research lectr. U. Calif., 1978. Author: Topics in Fourier and Geometric Analysis, 1961, also articles. Served with AUS, 1943-46. NSF postdoctoral fellow, 1954-55. Mem. Am. Math. Soc., Math. Assn. Am., Am. Soc. Indsl. and Applied Math. Office: U Calif Math Dept Riverside CA 92521

SHAPIRO, WALTER ELLIOT, political reporter; b. N.Y.C., Feb. 16, 1947; s. Salem Seeley and Edith Geraldine (Herwitz) S.; m. Meryl Gordon, Aug. 24, 1980. BA, U. Mich., 1970, postgrad., 1970-71. Reporter Congl. Quarterly, Washington, 1969-70; editor Washington Monthly, 1972-76; spl. asst. U.S. Sec. Labor, Washington, 1977-78; Presdl. speechwriter The White House, Washington, 1979; reporter Washington Post, 1979-83; gen. editor Newsweek, N.Y.C., 1983-87; sr. writer Time Mag., N.Y.C., 1987—; Contbg. editor Washington Monthly, 1976—. Contbr. numerous articles to mags. Leadership fellow Japan Soc., U.S.-Japan, 1991. Mem. Judson Welliver Soc. Jewish. Avocations: social critic, art collector. Home: 201 W 86th St Apt 1105 New York NY 10024-3351 Office: Time Mag Time & Life Bldg Rockefeller Ctr New York NY 10020

SHAPLEY, LLOYD STOWELL, mathematics and economics educator; b. Cambridge, Mass., June 2, 1923; s. Harlow and Martha (Betz) S.; m. Marian Ludolph, Aug. 19, 1955; children—Peter, Christopher. A.B., Harvard U., 1948; Ph.D., Princeton U., 1953; PhD (hon.), Hebrew U., Jerusalem, 1986. Mathematician Rand Corp., Santa Monica, Calif., 1948-50; 54-81; prof. depts. math. and econs. UCLA, 1981—; instr. Princeton U., 1952-54; sr. research fellow Calif. Inst. Tech., 1955-56; fellow Inst. Advanced Studies, Hebrew U., Jerusalem, 1979-80; mem. faculty Rand Grad. Inst. for Policy Studies, 1970-86. Author: (with S. Karlin) Geometry of Moment Spaces, 1953, (with R. Aumann) Values of Non-Atomic Games, 1974; editor: (with others) Advances in Game Theory, 1964; mem. editorial bd. Internat. Jour. Game Theory, 1970—, Math. Programming, 1971-80, Jour. Math. Econs, 1973—, Math. Ops. Research, 1975—, Games and Econ. Behavior, 1988—. Served with AC U.S. Army, 1943-45. Decorated Bronze Star. Fellow Econometric Soc., Am. Acad. Arts and Scis.; mem. Nat. Acad. Scis., Ops. Research Soc. Am., Am. Math. Soc., Math. Programming Soc. Research in game theory, math., econs., polit. sci. Office: UCLA Dept Math Los Angeles CA 90024

SHAPLEY, ROBERT MARTIN, neurophysiology and perception educator; b. N.Y.C., Oct. 7, 1944; s. Benjamin and Florence Edith (Rosenthal) S.; m. Laurie Rose Sigal, July 31, 1966; children: Nina Claire, Alice Eve. AB, Harvard U., 1965; PhD, Rockefeller U., 1970. Postdoctoral fellow Northwestern U., Evanston, 1970-71, Cambridge U., Eng., 1971-72; asst. prof. Rockefeller U., N.Y.C., 1972-76, assoc. prof., 1976-87; prof. neural sci. NYU, N.Y.C., 1987—, Spencer prof. for sci., 1992—, dir. Ctr. for Neural Sci., 1991-94, dir. Ctr. for Theoretical Neurobiology, 1994—; chmn. Visual Scis. B. Study Sect., Bethesda, Md., 1990-92. Assoc. editor Jour. Gen. Physiology, 1983-95, Visual Neurosci., 1988-91; sensory editor Exptl. Brain Rsch. (Hamburg, Fed. Republic Germany), 1990—; editor Contrast Sensitivity, 1993; contbr. articles to profl. jours. Recipient Career Devel. award NIH, 1977-82; Helen Hay Whitney Found. fellow, 1970-72; John and Catherine MacArthur Found. fellow, 1986. Mem. Assn. for Rsch. in Vision and Ophthalmology, Soc. for Neurosci. Jewish. Avocations: tennis, history of art. Home: 1 Washington Square Vlg New York NY 10012-1632 Office: NYU Ctr for Neural Sci 4 Washington Pl New York NY 10003-6621

SHAPO, HELENE S., law educator; b. N.Y.C., June 5, 1938; d. Benjamin Martin and Gertrude (Kahaner) Seidner; m. Marshall S. Shapo, June 21, 1959; children: Benjamin Mitchell, Nathaniel Saul. BA, Smith Coll., 1959; MA in Teaching, Harvard U., 1960; JD, U. Va., 1976. Bar: Va. 1976, U.S. Dist. Ct. (we. dist.) Va. 1977, Ill. 1993. Tchr. Dade County, Miami, Fla., 1960-64; assoc. Robert Musselman & Assocs., Charlottesville, Va., 1976-77; law clk. to presiding justice U.S. Dist. Ct. Va., Charlottesville, 1977-78; asst. prof. law Northwestern U., Chgo., 1978-81, assoc. prof. law, 1981-83, prof. law, 1983—; instr. Sweet Briar Coll., Va., 1976-77, U. Va., Charlottesville, 1976-78; mem. com. law sch. admissions council/testing and devel., 1983—; cons. in field. Mem. ABA, Va. Bar Assn., Assn. of Am. Law Schs. (sect. chairperson 1985—), Women's Bar Assn. Chgo. Office: Northwestern U Sch Law 357 E Chicago Ave Chicago IL 60611-3008*

SHAPO, MARSHALL SCHAMBELAN, lawyer, educator; b. Phila., Oct. 1, 1936; s. Mitchell and Norma (Schambelan) S.; m. Helene Shirley Seidner, June 21, 1959; children: Benjamin, Nathaniel. AB summa cum laude, U. Miami, 1958, JD magna cum laude, 1964; AM, Harvard U., 1961, SJD, 1974. Bar: Fla. 1964, Va. 1977. Copy editor, writer Miami (Fla.) News, 1958-59; instr. history U. Miami, 1960-61; asst. prof. law U. Tex., 1965-67, asso. prof., 1967-69, prof., 1969-70; prof. law U. Va., 1970-78, Joseph M. Hartfield prof., 1976-78; Frederic P. Vose prof. Northwestern U. Sch. Law, Chgo., 1978—; of counsel Sonnenschein, Nath & Rosenthal, Chgo., 1991—; vis. prof. Juristisches Seminar U. Gottingen (Fed. Republic Germany), 1976; cons. on med. malpractice and tort law reform U.S. Dept. Justice, 1978-79; mem. panel on food safety Inst. Medicine, NAS, 1978-79; vis. fellow Centre for Socio-legal Studies, Wolfson Coll., Oxford, vis. fellow of Coll., 1975, Wolfson Coll., Cambridge, 1992; mem. Ctr. for Advanced Studies, U. Va., 1976-77; cons. Pres.'s Commn. for Study of Ethical Problems in Medicine and Biomed. and Behavioral Rsch., 1980-81; reporter Spl. Com. on Tort Liability System Am. Bar Assn., 1980-84; del. leader People to People Citizen Amb. program delegation to East Asia Tort and Ins. Law, 1986; lectr. appellate judges' seminars ABA, 1977, 83, 90; reporter symposium on legal and sci. perspectives on causation, 1990; advisor Restatement of the Law, Third, Torts: Products Liability, 1992—. Author: Towards a Jurisprudence of Injury, 1984, Tort and Compensation Law, 1976, The Duty to Act: Tort Law, Power and Public Policy, 1978, A Nation of Guinea Pigs, 1979, Products Liability, 1980, Public Regulation of Dangerous Products, 1980, The Law of Products Liability, 1987, Tort and Injury Law, 1990, The Law of Products Liability, 2 vols., 2d edit., 1990, 3d edit., 1994, supplements, 1991, 92, 93, Products Liability and the Search for Justice, 1993; (with Page Keeton) Products and the Consumer: Deceptive Practices, 1972, Products and the Consumer: Defective and Dangerous Products, 1970; mem. editl. bd. Jour. Consumer Policy, 1980-88, Products Liability Law Jour.; author: A Representational Theory of Consumer Protection: Doctrine, Function and Legal Liability for Product Disappointment, 1975; mem. adv. bd. Loyola Consumer Law Reporter; contbr. articles to legal and med. jours. NEH sr. fellow, 1974-75. Mem. Am. Law Inst., Am. Assn. Law Schs. (chmn. torts compensation systems sect. 1983-84, torts round table coun. 1970). Home: 1910 Orrington Ave Evanston IL 60201-2910 Office: Northwestern U Sch Law 357 E Chicago Ave Chicago IL 60611-3008

SHAPOFF, STEPHEN H., financial executive; b. N.Y.C., Nov. 1, 1944; s. Barney and Freda Shapoff; m. Andrea Dorin, May 30, 1967; 1 child, Matthew F. BBA, Pace U., 1967. CPA, N.Y. With audit dept. Ernst & Young, N.Y.C., 1967-72; asst. controller Seeburg Industries, Inc., 1972-74, 1967-72; with Estee Lauder, Inc., N.Y.C., 1974-78; controller Coleco Industries, Inc., Hartford, Conn., 1978-79; sr. v.p. fin. Ivy Hill Corp. subs. of Time Warner Inc., N.Y.C., Conn., 1979-85; exec. v.p. Ivy Hill Corp., N.Y.C., 1985—; adj. asst. prof. Pace U., N.Y.C., 1971—. Mem. AICPA, Fin. Exec. Inst. (pres. L.I. chpt. 1988, 92-94, chair nat. membership com.), N.Y. Soc. CPAs, Nat. Assn. Accts. Office: Ivy Hill Corp 375 Hudson St New York NY 10014-3658

SHAPPELL, VAUGHN SCOTT, education director, educator; b. Allentown, Pa., Feb. 18, 1953; s. Scott Henry and Elizabeth Susan (Gruver) S.; m. Janile Martinez, Aug. 27, 1983. BA, Susquehanna U., 1975; MEd, Lehigh U., 1977. Cert. spl. edn. tchr., supr. of spl. edn., elem. and secondary prin., Pa. Tchr. Carbon-Lehigh Intermediate Unit 21, Schnecksville, Pa., 1976-79; tchr. Wiley House, Bethlehem, Pa., 1979-83, supr. of edn., 1983-85, dir. edn., 1985—. Mem. Coun. for Exceptional Children (pres. 1981), Pa. Assn. Fed. Program Coords., Coun. Adminstrs. of Spl. Edn., Mid. States Assn. Colls. and Schs. (vis. team chairperson 1987-94). Avocations: running, cross country skiing, hiking, camping. Office: Kids Peace Nat Ctrs Kids in Crisis 5300 Kidspeace Dr Orefield PA 18069-2044

SHAPPIRIO, DAVID GORDON, biologist, educator; b. Washington, June 18, 1930; s. Sol and Rebecca (Porton) S.; m. Elvera M. Bamber, July 8, 1953; children: Susan, Mark. B.S. with distinction in Chemistry, U. Mich., 1951; A.M., Harvard U., 1953, Ph.D. in Biology, 1955. NSF postdoctoral fellow in biochemistry Cambridge U., Eng., 1955-56; research fellow in physiology Am. Cancer Soc.-NRC, U. Louvain, Belgium, 1956-57; mem. faculty U. Mich., Ann Arbor, 1957—, prof. zool. and biology, 1967—, Arthur F. Thurnau prof., 1989—; assoc. chmn. div. biol. scis. U. Mich., 1976-83, acting chmn., 1978, 79, 80, 82, 83, coordinator NSF undergrad. sci. edn. program, 1962-67, dir. honors program Coll. Lit. Sci. and Arts, 1983-91; vis. lectr. Am. Inst. Biol. Scis., 1966-68; reviewer, cons. to pubs. on textbook devel.; reviewer grant proposals NSF, NIH, mem. program site visit teams. Author rsch. on biochemistry and physiology growth, devel., dormancy; invited spkr., rsch. symposia of nat. and internat. orgns. in field. Recipient Disting. Teaching award U. Mich., 1967, Excellence in Edn. award, 1991, Bausch & Lomb Sci. award, 1974; Lalor Found fellow, 1953-55; Danforth Found. assoc. Fellow AAAS; mem. Am. Inst. Biol. Scis. (vis. lectr. 1966-68), Am. Soc. Cell Biology, Biochem. Soc., Am. Soc. Zoologists, Soc. Exptl. Biology, Soc. Gen. Physiologists, Assn. Biol. Lab. Edn., Xerces Soc., Assn. Biol. Computing, Phi Beta Kappa (v.p. U. Mich. chpt. 1995—). Office: U Mich Dept Biology 1123 Natural Sci Bldg Ann Arbor MI 48109-1048

SHARBAUGH, THOMAS J., lawyer; b. Mar. 7, 1952. BS, Pa. State U., 1973; JD, U. Mich., 1976. Bar: Pa. 1976. Ptnr. Morgan, Lewis & Bockius LLP, Phila. Office: Morgan Lewis & Bockius One Logan Sq Ste 2000 Philadelphia PA 19103

SHARBEL, JEAN M., editor; b. Lansford, Pa.; d. Joseph and Star (Nemr) Sharbel. BA in Journalism, Hunter Coll., N.Y.C. Editorial dir., v.p. Dauntless Books, N.Y.C., 1962-75; editor romance mags., True Confessions Mag., Macfadden Holdings, Inc., N.Y.C., 1976-92; freelance editor fiction and nonfiction books, 1989—. Home: 165 E 66th St New York NY 10021-6132

SHARBONEAU, LORNA ROSINA, artist, educator, author, poet, illustrator; b. Spokane, Wash., Apr. 5, 1935; d. Stephen Charles Martin and Midgie Montana (Hartzel) Barton; m. Thomas Edward Sharboneau, Jan. 22, 1970; children: Curtis, Carmen, Chet, Cra, Joseph. AA in Arts, Delta Coll., 1986; studies with Steve Lesnick, Las Vegas, Nev.; studies with Bette Myers/Zimmerman, Phoenix and Bonners Ferry, Idaho. Prin. Sharboneau's Art Gallery, Spokane, 1977-80; tchr. art Michell's Art Gallery, Spokane, 1978-79; art therapist Vellencino Sch. Dist., Calif., 1981-83; ind. artist Lind, Wash., 1948—; dir., producer, stage designer Ch. of Jesus Christ of LDS, San Jose, Sonora, Modesto, Calif., 1978 (1st. place road show San Jose); dir. Sharboneau's Art Show, Spokane, 1979, Hands On-Yr. of the Child; platform spkr., poet, fundraiser, libr., 1984-87; asst., apprentice to Prof. Rowland Cheney, Delta Coll., Stockton, Calif., 1985, 86, 87; demonstrated drip oil technique, Bonners Ferry, Idaho, Spokane, Wash., Stockton, Calif., Delta Coll. Author, illustrator: Through the Eyes of the Turtle Tree, The One-Armed Christmas Tree, The Price of Freedom, William Will, Bill Can, Song of the Turtle Tree, Chet's Ottle-Bottle: The Unbreakable Bottle, One Drop of Water and a Grain of Sand; poet; prolific artist completed over 4000 paintings and drawings, displayed works in galleries through western states; featured in Magnolia News, Seattle, Delta Coll. Impact, Stockton, Calif., Stockton Record, Union Democrat, Sonora, Calif., Lincoln Center Chronicle, Stockton, Calif., Spokesman Rev., Spokane, Wash., Modesto (Calif) Bee, Angels Camp, Calif., Union Democrat, Sonora, Calif., New-Letter, Ch. of Jesus Christ of L.D.S 1st ward, Sonora; artist mixed media, oil, drip oil works, sculptures, pastel, watercolor; illustrations pen and ink, acrylic; sculptor bronze, lost wax method, ceramic art, soap stone, egg-tempra, original techniques, collage, variation on a theme. Dir., programmer, fundraiser Shelter Their Sorrows, Sonora, Calif., 1989-92, vol. Community Action Agency and Homeless Shelter. Recipient Golden Rule award J.C. penny, 1991, Recognition award Pres. George Bush, cert. Spl. Congl. Recognition Congressman Richard H. Lehman, 3rd Pl. Best Show East Valley ARtists/Pala Show, 1973, 74, 75, 3d Pl. Artist of Yr., 1974, Valley Fair, Santa Clara, Calif., 1974, 1st and 2d Pl. Spokane County Fair, 1978, 3 honorable mentions, 4 premiums, 1979, 3 1st Pl., 3 2d Pl., 2 3rd Pl., honorable mention Calaveras County Fair/Angels Camp, Calif., 1983, 1st and 3rd Pl. Unitarian Art Festival, Stockton, Calif., 1984, 2d Pl., 1985, 3d Pl., 1986, 1st Pl. Lodi Art Ann., 1985, 3rd Pl., 1986, 1st Pl. 1987, 1st Pl., 1988, honorable mention SJCAC Junque Art Show, Stockton, 1985, 1st Pl Ctrl. Calif. Art League, Modesto, 1986, 88, 2d Pl. 1995; 3d Pl. Camilla Art Show, San Jose, Calif., 1974, and numerous others; 1st, 2d, and 3d Pl., Spokane County Fair, 1978; 4 honorable mentions, Sonora, Calif., 1993, 2nd Pl. Ctrl. Calif. Art Show, 1996. Mem. Ctrl. Sierra Arts Coun., Mother Lode Artists Assn., Sacramento Fine Arts Ctr., Inc., Internat. Platform Assn. (Judges Choice conv. arts competition 1993), The Planetary Soc., The Nat. Mus. of Women of Arts. Mem. Ch. of Jesus Christ of LDS. Achievements include: homeless shelter kitchen named in her honor, Sonora. Avocations: mathematics, astronomy, baseball, archeology. Home and Studio: 400 Mono Way Sonora CA 95370-5235 Office: Internat Platform Assn PO Box 250 Winnetka IL 60093-0250

SHARE, RICHARD HUDSON, lawyer; b. Mpls., Sept. 6, 1938; s. Jerome and Millicent S.; m. Carolee Martin, 1970; children: Mark Lowell, Gregory Martin, Jennifer Hillary, Ashley. B.S., UCLA, 1960; J.D., U. So. Calif., 1963. Bar: Calif. Sup. Ct. 1964, U.S. Dist. Ct. (cen. and so. dists.) Calif., U.S. Supreme Ct. 1974. Field agt. IRS, 1960-63; mem. law div., asst. sec. Avco Fin. Services, 1963-72; founder Frandzel and Share, Los Angeles, 1972—; lectr. in field. Mem. Calif. Bankers Assn., Cmty. Bankers of So. Calif. Clubs: Rivera Tennis, Pacific Palisades. Office: 17th Fl 6500 Wilshire Blvd Los Angeles CA 90048 also: 26th Fl 100 Pine St San Francisco CA 94111-5212

SHARER, JOHN DANIEL, lawyer; b. Bklyn., Sept. 19, 1950; s. Albert Robert and Alda Loretta (Tapiro) S.; m. Kathleen Gail Donaldson, Feb. 14, 1981; 1 child, Stephanie Erin. AB, Dartmouth Coll., Hanover, N.H., 1972; JD, U. Pa., 1975. Bar: Pa. 1975, N.J. 1975, D.C. 1976, N.Y. 1989, Va. 1994. Law clk. Superior Ct. Pa., Hon. Edmund B. Spaeth, Jr., Phila., 1975-76; assoc. Sutherland, Asbill & Brennan, Washington, 1976-82, ptnr., 1982-94; counsel Christian, Barton, Epps, Brent & Chappell, Richmond, Va., 1994-95, ptnr., 1996—. Bd. dirs. Wakefield Sch., Marshall, Va., 1990-94; dist. enrollment dir. Dartmouth Club of Ctrl. Va. Mem. Phi Beta Kappa. Republican. Avocations: classical piano, computers, dogs. Home: 12317 Northlake Ct Richmond VA 23233-6635 Office: Christian & Barton LLP 909 E Main St Ste 1200 Richmond VA 23219-3095

SHARETT, ALAN RICHARD, lawyer, environmental mediator and arbitrator, law educator; b. Hammond, Ind., Apr. 15, 1943; s. Henry S. and Frances (Givel) Smulevitz; children: Lauren Ruth, Charles Daniel; m. Cherie Ann Vick, Oct. 15, 1993. Student Ind. U., 1962-65; J.D., DePaul U., 1968; advanced postgrad. legal edn. U. Mich. and U. Chgo., 1970-71. Bar: N.Y. 1975, Ind. 1969, U.S. Ct. Appeals (2d cir.) 1975, U.S. Ct. Appeals (7th cir.) 1974, U.S. Supreme Ct. 1973. Assoc. Call, Call, Borns & Theodoros, Gary, Ind., 1969-71; judge protem Gary City Ct., 1970-71; environ. dist. atty. 31st Jud. Cir., Lake County, Ind., 1971-75; counsel Dunes Nat. Lakeshore Group, 1971-75; mem. Cohan, Cohan & Smulevitz, 1971-75; town atty., Independence Hill, Ind., 1974-75; judge pro tem Superior Ct., Lake County, Ind., 1971-75; professorial dir. NYU Pub. Liability Inst., N.Y.C., 1975-76; speaker, guest lectr., adj. faculty ATLA, Purdue U., N.Y. U., Ind. U., De Paul U., Valparaiso U., St. Joseph Coll., U. Miami; Coll. paralegal instr., 1970-89; adj. faculty prof. constl. law Union Inst., Miami, Cin., 1990-92; adj. prof. environ. litigation and alternative dispute resolution Ward Stone Coll., Miami, 1994; guest prof. internat. environ. law Dept. Internat. and Comparative Law, U. Miami, 1992—; mem. adv. panel, seminar speaker on internat. issues Interamerican Dialogue on Water Mgmt., 1993; spkr. on environ. transactions and litigation North Dade County Fla. Bar Assn., 1995—; seminar spkr. on environ. politics U. Miami Dept. Environ. Sci., 1995—; gen. counsel Marjory Stoneman Douglas Friends of Everglades, 1992-93; asst. atty. gen., chair fed. and constnl. practice, N.Y. State, N.Y.C., 1976-78; pvt. practice, Flushing, N.Y., 1980-82, Miami Beach, Fla., 1988—, lead trial counsel, chmn. lawyers panel for No. Ind., ACLU, 1969-71; liaison trial counsel Lake County and Ind. State Health Depts. and Atty. Gen., 1971-75; mem. Nat. Dist. Attys. Assn., 1972-75, mem. environ. protection com; pres. ESI Group, Nat. Environ. Responsibility Cons, Inc.; spkr. in field. Editor in chief DePaul U. The Summons, 1967-68; mem. staff DePaul Law Rev., 1968; contbr. articles to profl. jours. Mem. coalition Fla. Save Our Everglades Program. Recipient Honors award in forensic litigation Law-Sci. Acad. Am., 1967. Mem. ABA (nat. article editor law student div. 1967-68, nat. com. environ. litigation, com. fed. procedure, com. toxic torts, hazardous substances and environ. law, com. energy resources law, com. internat. environ. law, com. internat. litigation, environ. interest group, sect. natural resources, energy and environ. law, judge negotiation competition championship round, law student divsn., midyear meeting 1995, sect. sci. and tech., nat. toxic and hazardous substances and environ. law com., sect. tort and ins. practice, 1996, corp. gen. counsel com., 1996, media law and defamation torts com., 1996, tort and hazardous substances and environ. law com., 1996), Am. Arbitration Assn., Soc. Profls. in Dispute Resolution, Assn. Bar of City of N.Y., N.Y. County Lawyers Assn. (com. on fed. cts. 1977-82), Am. Judicature Soc., ATLA (nat. coms. toxic, environ. and pharm. torts, environ. litigation), Environ. Law Inst., Am. Immigration Lawyers Assn., Ill. State Bar Assn. (staff editor 1967-68), N.Y. State Bar Assn. (environ. law sect., family law sect.), Ind. State Bar Assn. (environ. law sect., internat. law sect., trial practice sect.), Nat. Fla. Assn. Environ. Profls., Greater Miami C. of C. (coms. on environ. awareness, environ. econs., biomedical exch., planning and zoning growth mgmt., internat. econ. devel., bus. and industry econ. devel., govtl. affairs, ins., internat. banking, Europe/Pacific rim), AAAS (physics, math., astronomy), Am. Acad. Poets. Office: ESI Group Nat Environ Responsibility Cons Inc 6421 Cow Pen Rd Ste M 107 Miami Lakes FL 33014

SHARF, STEPHAN, automotive company executive; b. Berlin, Dec. 30, 1920; came to U.S., 1947; s. Wilhelm and Martha (Schwartz) S.; m. Rita Schantzer, June 17, 1951. Degree in Mech. Engring., Tech. U., Berlin, Fed. Republic Germany, 1947. Tool and die maker Buerk Tool & Die Co., Buffalo, 1947-50; foreman Ford Motor Co., 1950-53; gen. foreman Ford Motor Co., Chgo., 1953-58; with Chrysler Corp., Detroit, 1958-86, master mechanic Twinsburg stamping plant, 1958-63, mfg. engring. mgr., 1963-66, mfg. prodn. Twinsburg stamping plant, 1966-68, plant mgr. Warren stamping plant, 1968-70, plant mgr. Sterling stamping plant, 1970-72, gen. plants mgr. stamping, 1972-78, v.p. Engine and Casting div., 1978-80, v.p. Power Train div., 1980-81, exec. v.p., mfg., dir., 1981-85, exec. v.p. internat., 1985-86, also bd. dirs.; pres. SICA Corp., Troy, Mich., 1986—; bd. dirs. Medar, Inc., Gecamex Tech., Can., Channel 56 Pub. TV. Bd. dirs. Jr. Achievement, Detroit council Boy Scouts Am.; trustee, v.p. Oakland U. Mem. Soc. Auto Engrs., Detroit Engring. Soc. Club: Wabeek Country. Home: 966 Adams Castle Dr Bloomfield Hills MI 48304-3713 Office: SICA Corp PO Box 623 Troy MI 48099-0623

SHARFSTEIN, STEVEN SAMUEL, health care executive, medical director; b. N.Y.C., July 2, 1932; s. Sidney J. and Beverly (Zevie) S.; m. Margaret Shiling, June 13, 1965; children: Joshua, Daniel, Sarah. BA magna cum laude, Dartmouth Coll., 1964; MD, Albert Einstein Coll. Medicine, 1968; MPA, Harvard U., 1973. Diplomate Nat. Bd. Med. Examiners. Intern in pediatrics Bronx (N.Y.) Mcpl. Hosp. Ctr., 1968-69; jr. resident Mass. Mental Health Ctr., Boston, 1969-70, sr. resident, 1970-71, chief resident, 1971-72; dir. mental health svcs. Brookside Park Family Life Ctr., Jamaica Plain, Mass., 1972-73; spl. asst. to dir. Office Planning & Evaluation Nat. Inst. Mental Health, 1973-74, dir. program analysis and evaluation Office Program Devel. and Analysis, 1974-76, dir. divsn. mental health svc. programs, 1976-80, attending psychiatrist clin. ctr., 1980-82, assoc. dir. behavioral medicine, 1980-82; dep. med. dir. Am. Psychiat. Assn., 1983-86; exec. v.p., COO, med. dir. The Sheppard & Enoch Pratt Hosp., Balt., 1986-91, pres., CEO, med. dir., 1992—; lectr. in psychiatry Johns Hopkins U., Balt., 1987—; professorial lectr. in psychiatry dept. psychiatry Georgetown U., Washington, 1984—; clin. prof. U. Md., College Park, 1986—; cons. Neighborhood Employment Ctr. and Barbara Street Welfare Office, 1970-71, Allegheny County Mental Health/Retardation Bd., Pitts., 1973-74; examiner Am. Bd. Psychiatry and Neurology, 1979—; active Gov. Adv. Coun. on Mental Hygiene, 1987—, Inst. Medicine Bd. on Biobehavioral Scis. & Mental Disorders, 1993—. Co-author: Madness and Government: Who Cares for the Mentally Ill, 1983, Maintaining and Improving Psychiatric Insurance Coverage: An Annotated Bibliography, 1983, Coverage for Mental and Nervous Disorders, 1983, Health Insurance and Psychiatric Care, 1984; author chpts. to books; co-editor: Neighborhood Psychiatry, 1977, The New Economics and Psychiatric Care, 1985, Prospective Payment & Psychiatric Care, 1988; assoc. editor Am. Jour Psychiatry, 1993; mem. ednl. adv. bd. Cmty. Mental Health Jour., 1980—; mem. editl. bd. Jour. Mental Health Adminstrn., 1989—, Relapse, 1993; contbr. articles to profl. jours. Served with USPHS, 1970-73. Recipient Andrew Edison prize in govt. Dartmouth Coll., 1964; Harry C. Solomon prize Harvard U. Med. Sch., 1974; Adminstr.'s award for meritorious achievemnet Alcohol, Drug Abuse and Mental Health Adminstrn., 1980; Sr. Exec. Service Bonus award, 1981. Fellow Am. Psychiat. Assn. (mem. commn. on stds. and third party payments 1976-82, chmn. budget com. 1987-90, chmn. com. on managed care 1990—, sec. 1991—), Am. Coll. Psychiatrists (mem. pubs. com. 1984-87, mem. budget com. 1987-89, chair Dean award com. 1990—), Am. Orthopsychiat. Assn., Am. Coll. Mental Health Adminstrn.; mem. AMA, AAAS, Am. Assn. Gen. Hosp. Psychiatrists, Am. Assn. Psychiat. Adminstrs. (Significant Contbns. in Adminstrn. award 1987), Am. Psychosomatic Soc., Washington Psychiat. Soc. (mem. coun. 1982—, Outstanding Svc. award 1984), Md. Assn. Private Practicing Psychiatrists, Md. Psychiat. Soc., Balt.-Washington Soc. for Psychoanalysis (affiliate), Washington Psychoanalytic Soc. (hon.), Med. Soc. D.C. Office: Sheppard and Enoch Pratt Hosp 6501 N Charles St Baltimore MD 21204-6819

SHARICK, MERLE DAYTON, JR., mortgage insurance company executive; b. Bloomington, Ill, May 5, 1946; s. Merle Dayton and Joyce Madeline (Reed) S.; m. Cheryl Jean Easterday, Dec. 28, 1966; children: Amber Dawn, Cami Nicole. BA, Southwestern Coll., Winfield, Kans., 1968; MS in Edn., U. Kans., 1970. Tchr., coach Kans. High Schs., Lawrence, Hutchinson, 1968-73; asst. prin., prin. Kans. High Schs., Buhler, Inman, Leoti, 1973-77; auctioneer, real estate salesman R.E.I.B., Inc., Hutchinson, Kans., 1977-78; account exec. Mortgage Guaranty Ins. Co., Hutchinson, 1978-81; regional sales mgr. Mortgage Guaranty Ins. Co., Shawnee Mission, Kans., 1981-83, Houston, 1983-86; div. risk mgr. Mortgage Guaranty Ins. Co., Atlanta, 1986-90; regional dir. Mortgage Guaranty Ins. Co., Charlotte, N.C., 1990-93; v.p., mgr. risk mgmt. Republic Mortgage Ins. Co., Winston-Salem, N.C., 1993—; sports editor Winfield (Kans.) Daily Couier, 1966-68; grad. asst. U. Kans., Lawrence, 1968-70; owner, operator Riverside Home Style Laundry, South Hutchinson, Kans., 1975-79, founder, owner, The Sport Shack, Hutchinson, Kans., 1977-79; guest speaker various orgns. Active in Rep. support groups, Houston, Atlanta, 1983—. Fellow Inst. for Devel. Ednl. Adminstrs.; mem. Nat. Assn. Rev. Appraisers and Mortgage Underwriters (bd. dirs. 1989-95, Ark. Traveler award 1995), Mortgage Bankers Am., Ga. Mortgage Bankers, Mortgage Bankers Carolinas, N.C. Alliance Cmty. Fin. Instns., S.C. League Savs. Instns., Fla. Mortgage Bankers, Tex. Mortgage Bankers, Charlotte Mortgage Bankers, The Housing Roundtable, The Piedmont Club. Baptist.

SHARIF, OMAR (MICHAEL SHALHOUB), actor; b. Alexandria, Egypt, Apr. 10, 1932; s. Joseph and Claire (Saada) Shalhoub; m. Faten Hamama, Feb. 5, 1955; 1 child, Tarek. Attended, Victoria Coll., Cairo. Appeared in numerous Egyptian, French and Am. films including (debut) Ciel d' enfer, 1953, The Mamluks, The Blazing Sun, Goha, Lawrence of Arabia, 1962 (Golden Globe award for best supporting actor), Behold a Pale Horse, 1964, The Fall of the Roman Empire, 1964, Genghis Khan, 1965, The Yellow Rolls Royce, 1965, Doctor Zhivago, 1966 (Golden Globe award best actor), Night of the Generals, 1967, More Than a Miracle, 1967, Funny Girl, 1968,

Mayerling, 1969, Che!, 1969, MacKenna's Gold, 1969, The Appointment, 1969, The Horsemen, 1970, The Last Valley, 1971, The Burglars, 1972, The Tamarind Seed, 1974, The Mysterious Island of Captain Nemo, 1974, Juggernaut, 1974, Funny Lady, 1975, Crime and Passion, 1975, Ace Up The Sleeve, The Pink Panther Stikes Again, The Right To Love, Ashanti, 1979, Bloodline, 1979, Oh Heavenly Dog, 1980, The Baltimore Bullet, 1980, Green Ice, Chanel Solitaire, Top Secret, 1984, The Rainbow, 1989, Mountains of the Moon, 1990, Journey of Love, 1990; TV appearances include S*H*E*, Pleasure Palace, The Far Pavillion, Mrs. 'arris Goes to Paris, 1992, (miniseries) Peter the Great, 1986, Anastasia: The Mystery of Anna, 1986, Grand Larceny, Omar Sharif Returns to Egypt, The Mysteries of the Pyramids (host). Author: The Eternal Male, 1977; author syndicated columns on bridge. Office: William Morris Agy care Ames Cushing 151 S El Camino Dr Beverly Hills CA 90212-2704*

SHARIF-EMAMI, JAFAR, former prime minister of Iran; b. Tehran, Iran, Sept. 8, 1910; s. Haji Mohammad Hossein and Banu (Kobra) Sharif-E.; m. Eshrat Moazzami, Nov. 16, 1946; children: Shirin, Simin, Ali. Ed., Reichsbahn Zentralschule, Brandenburg, Germany, Statens Tekniskaskolan, Boras, Sweden; Dr.H.C., Seoul U., 1978; diploma in computer programming, Internat. Corr. Sch., 1990. Joined Iranian State Rys., 1931, tech. dep. gen. dir., 1942-46; chmn., mng. dir. Ind. Irrigation Corp., 1946-50, gen. dir., 1950-51; undersec. to Minister Roads and Communications, 1950-51, minister roads and communications, 1951; mem. Senate of Iran from Tehran, 1955-57, 63—, pres. senate house, 1963-78; pres. 3d Constituent Assembly, 1967; minister industries and mines, 1957-60, prime minister of Iran, 1960-61, 78—; dep. custodian Pahlavi Found., 1962-78; pres. chamber of industries and mines, 1962-67; chmn. bd. Indsl. and Mining Devel. Bank, 1963-78. Mem. high council Plan Orgn., 1951-52, mng. dir., chmn. high council, 1953-54; pres. 22d Internat. Conf. Red Cross, 1973; bd. dirs. Royal Orgn. Social Services, 1962-78; trustee Pahlavi U., Shiraz, 1962-78, Nat. U., Tehran, 1962-78, Aria Mehr Tech. U., 1965-78, Queen Pahlavi's Found., 1966-78; bd. founders Soc. Preservation Nat. Monuments, 1966-78. Decorated 1st grade Order Taj, Iran; decorated 3d and 1st grade Order Homayoon, Iran, 1st grade Order Social Services, Iran, 1st grade Order Land Reform, Iran, 1st grade Order Labour, Iran, 1st grade Order Cooperative, Iran, 1st grade Order Coronation, Iran, 1st grade Order 25th Shahrivar, Iran, 1st grade Order of Celebration 2500th Anniversary Founding of Persian Empire by Cyrus the Great, Iran, chevalier de Grand Croix Italy, das Gross-Kreuz Verdienstorden Germany, grand officer Legion of Honor, France, grand cross Legion of Honor, France, Stora Korset av Kingl. Nordstjarneoden Sweden, grand cross Order de la Courone, Belgium, grand cordon Order Leopold, Belgium, Das Grosse Golden Ehrenzelchen am Bande Austria, Order St. Michael and St. George U.K., Order Sacred Treasure 1st grade Japan, Order of Rising Sun 1st grade Japan, Tudor Vladimirescu 1st grade Romania, knight grand cross Most Exalted Order of White Elephant 1st grade, Thailand, Alesteghlal 1st grade Tunisia, Den Kgl. Norske St. Olavs Orden 1st grade Norway, Order of Danbrok 1st grade Denmark, Order Al-Arsh 1st grade Morocco, Order Jugoslovenske Zvenzde Za Lentom Yugoslavia, Krzyz Wielki Order Odrodzenia Polski Poland, Di-Peliharakan Allah Panckuan Necara Malaysia, grand condon Order Menelik Second, Ethiopia, Order of Banner of Hungarian Peoples Republic 1st grade, Ghaede Azam Pakistan, 1st grade Veshahol Malek Abdol-Aziz Saudi Arabia, Order Nile 1st grade Egypt, Grand Croix Ordre du Merite Senegal, Esteghlal Qatar. Fellow ASCE; mem. Red Lion and Sun (dir 1963, dep. chmn. 1966-78), Internat. Bankers Assn. (pres. 1975), Iranian Engrs. Assn. (pres. 1966-78).

SHARIR, YACOV, artistic director, choreographer; b. Casablanca, Morocco, Aug. 22, 1940; came to U.S., 1978; s. Simon and Rene Sharir. Student, Jerusalem Acad. Music, 1962-65, Bat-Sheva Dance Co. Sch., 1965-67; grad., Jerusalem Besalel Acad. F.A., 1966. Instr. Bat-Sheva Dance Co., 1966-74; ballet instr. Israeli Ballet Co. & Kibbutz Dance Co., 1970-73; founder, artistic dir. Am. Deaf Dance Co., Austin, Tex., 1977-82, Sharir Dance Co., Austin, 1982—; sr. lectr. U. Tex., Austin, 1977—; faculty dance Jerusalem Rubin Acad. Music & Dance, 1988—; arts fellow for dance & virtual reality project Banff Ctr. For the Arts, 1992-94; choreographer over 70 pieces for various dance companies. Choreographer Homage to Jerome Robbins, Mechanical Doll, Quadroped, Right to Left, others. Choreography fellow NEA, 1989, 89-90.. Avocations: ceramics, sculpting, gardening. Home: 5406 Mount Bonnell Rd Austin TX 78731-4610 Office: U Tex Dept Theatre & Drama Austin TX 78712

SHARITS, DEAN PAUL, motion picture company executive; b. Mankato, Minn., Feb. 6, 1944; s. Loran Ross and June Banita (Timmerman) S.; m. Patricia Ann Taylor, June 14, 1966 (div. 1973); 1 child, James Dean; m. Adela Zamora, July 23, 1988. AS in Engring., L.A. Trade Tech., 1974; BS in Bus., Calif. State U., Northridge, 1979; MBA, Mankato State U., 1980. Prodn. mgr. Walt Disney Imagineering, Glendale, Calif., 1980-84; gen. mgr. Recreation Entertainment Comml., Burbank, Calif., 1984-85; pres., CEO Apogee Prodns., Inc., Van Nuys, Calif., 1985-90; sr. v.p. Landmark Entertainment Group, L.A., 1990-92; pres., CEO Gold Springs Enterprises, Inc., San Diego, 1992-93; exec. v.p. Scenic Techs., Las Vegas, 1994-95; pres. Sharits & Assocs., Las Vegas, 1995—; dir. Internat. Kinetics Corp., Altadena, Calif., 1990—, Concerned Calif. for Motion Pictures and TV, Hollywood, Calif., 1986-88; cons. Technifex, Inc., Sun Valley, Calif., 1989-91, Water Entertainment Tech., Universal City, Calif., 1989-91. Contbr. articles to profl. jours. With USN, 1961-65. Republican. Avocations: golf, tennis, skiing, running. Home and Office: 7808 Riviera Beach Dr Las Vegas NV 89128

SHARKEY, KATHLEEN, accountant; b. Phila., Jan. 25, 1951; d. Joseph Philip and Florence Veronica (Noykoff) Sharkey; m. Joel David Delpha, Sept. 24, 1977; children: Daniel Joseph, Madeleine Day. BA, John Carroll U., 1973. Tchr. St. Michael's Sch., St. Louis, 1976-79; acct. Citicorp Acceptance, St. Louis, 1986-89; fin. dir., adminstr. Women's Self Help Ctr., St. Louis, 1989—. Bd. dirs. Mo. Religious Coalition for Reproductive Choice, St. Louis, 1992—; co-chair St. Louis Caths. for a Free Choice, 1992—; treas. Shaw Neighborhood Improvement Assn., 1994—, Mo. Coalition Against Domestic Violence, 1995—. Democrat. Roman Catholic. Home: 4047 Magnolia Pl Saint Louis MO 63110-3914 Office: Women's Self Help Ctr Inc 2838 Olive St Saint Louis MO 63103-1428

SHARKEY, THOMAS DAVID, educator, botanist; b. Detroit, Jan. 28, 1953; s. Robert Hugh and Patricia June (Elliot) S.; m. Paulette Marie Bochnig June 21, 1974; 1 child, Jessa Sung. BS in Biology, Mich. State U., 1974, PhD in Botany and Plant Pathology, 1980. Postdoctoral fellow Australian Nat. U., Canberra, 1980-82; assoc. rsch. prof. Desert Rsch. Inst., Reno, Nev., 1982-87; asst. prof. U. Wis., Madison, 1987-88, assoc. prof., 1988-91, prof., 1991—; assoc. dir. Biolog. Scis. Ctr., Reno, Nev., 1983-87; chmn. dept. botany U. Wis., Madison, 1992-94; dir. Biotron, U. Wis., Madison, 1993—. Editor: (book) Trace Gas Emissions from Plants, 1991; contbr. more than 80 articles to profl. peer-reviewed jours. Mem. AAAS, Am. Soc. Plant Physiologists, Internat. Photosynthesis Soc. Home: 5901 S Highlands Ave Madison WI 53705 Office: Univ Wis Dept Botany 430 Lincoln Dr Madison WI 53706

SHARKEY, VINCENT JOSEPH, lawyer; b. Newport, R.I., May 25, 1944; s. Vincent Joseph and Dorothy (Auvil) S.; m. Joyce Toomey, Dec. 27, 1969; children: Alison, Christina, John, Julia. BA in Econs., Yale U., 1966; JD, U. Va., 1971. Bar: N.J. 1971, U.S. Ct. Appeals (3d cir.) 1985. Asst. prosecutor Bergen County Prosecutor's Office, Hackensack, N.J., 1971-72; pvt. practice, Bergen County, 1972-75; ptnr. Riker, Danzig, Scherer, Hyland & Perretti, Morristown, N.J., 1975—. Lt. U.S. Army, 1966-68. Mem. ABA, N.J. Bar Assn., Bergen County Bar Assn., Yale U. Alumni Assn. (pres. Bergen County chpt. 1986-88). Office: Riker Danzig Scherer 1 Speedwell Ave Morristown NJ 07962-1981

SHARMA, ARJUN DUTTA, cardiologist; b. Bombay, June 2, 1953; came to U.S., 1981; s. Hari D. and Gudrun (Axelsson) S.; m. Carolyn D. Burleigh, May 9, 1981; children: Allira, Eric, Harison. BSc, U. Waterloo, Ont., Can., 1972; MD, U. Toronto, Ont., 1976. Intern Toronto Gen. Hosp., 1976-77, resident in medicine, 1978-80; resident in medicine St. Michael's Hosp., Toronto, 1980-81; residency medicine Toronto Gen. Hosp., 1977-78; Rsch. assoc. Washington U., St. Louis, 1981-83; asst. prof. pharmacy and toxicology U. Western Ont., London, 1985-89, asst. prof. medicine, 1983-89, assoc. prof. medicine, 1989-90; dir. interventional electrophysiology Sutter Meml. Hosp., Sacramento, 1990-95; abstract reviewer, faculty of ann. sci. sessions N.Am. Soc. for Pacing and Electrophysiology, 1993; assoc. clin. prof. U. Calif., Davis, 1988-95; cons. Medtronic Inc., Mpls., 1985—, Telectronics Pacing Sys., Inc., 1990-94; mem. rsch. com. Sutter Inst. Med. Rsch., 1991—; mem. exec. com. Sutter Heart Inst., 1992. Reviewer profl. jours., including Circulation, Am. Jour. Cardiology; contbr. articles to profl. publs. Mem. coun. for basic sci. Am. Heart Assn., chmn. ann. sci. session, 1989. Recipient John Melady award, 1972, Dr. C.S. Wainwright award, 1973-75, Rsch. prize Toronto Gen. Hosp., 1979, 80, Ont. Career Scientist award Ont. Ministry of Health, 1983-89; Med. Rsch. Coun. Can. fellow, 1981-83. Mem. Am. Fedn. Clin. Rsch., Sacramento Med. Soc., Eldorado Med. Soc. Avocations: skiing, tennis, philately. Office: 3941 J St Ste 260 Sacramento CA 95819-3633

SHARMA, BHU DEV, mathematics educator, researcher; b. Bijnor, North, India, June 21, 1938; came to U.S., 1987; s. Janki Prasad and Shanti Devi Sharma; m. Kusum Lata, July 9, 1959; children: Ritu, Swati, Harsh. Student, Govt. Inter Coll., Bijnor, 1951, Govt. Inter Coll., Moradabad, India, 1953; BS, Agra U., India, 1955, MS, 1957; PhD, Delhi U., 1971. Lectr. in math. NAS Coll., Agra U., Meerut, 1957-63; head maths. dept. Mcpl. Coll., Agra U., Mussoorie, India, 1963-64; head math. dept. Vaish Coll., Agra U., Shamli, India, 1964-66; lectr. in math. U. Delhi, 1966-72, reader in math., 1972-79; prof. math. U. W.I., St. Augustine, Trinidad, 1979-88; prof. math. Xavier U., New Orleans, 1988—, chair dept. math., 1994—; vis. postdoctoral fellow Colo. State U., Ft. Collins, 1976; vis. prof. U. Santa Caterina, Florianapolis, Brazil, 1985, U. P.R., Rio Piedras, 1982, 85, 89, U. Bielefeld, Germany, 1991, Chinese Acad. Scis., Inst. Systems Scis., Beijing;. Chief editor: Jour. Combinatories Info. and System Sci., 1976—; editor-in-chief: Vishva-Vivek mag.; adv. editor: Jour. Info. and Optimization Sci., 1979-94; editor: Caribbean Jour. of Math., 1981—, Jour. Ramanu. Trustee Hindu Temple Soc. of Greater New Orleans, 1992-94. Mem. Am. Math. Soc., Math. Assn. Am., Indian Math. Soc. (life), Soc. Indian Academics in Am. (nat. rep. 1993-94), Hindu Ednl. and Religious Soc. Am., Inc. (pres.), Calcutta Math. Soc. (life), Operational Rsch. Soc. (life), Forum for Interdisciplinary Math. (life, pres. 1987-91, pres. 1996—), Hindi Nidhi (Trinidad chmn. acad. com. 1986-88, v.p. 1988-89), Lokenath Divine Fellowship La. (pres. 1995—). Hindu. Office: Xavier U La 7325 Palmetto St New Orleans LA 70125-1056

SHARMA, BRAHAMA D., chemistry educator; b. Sampla, Punjab, India, June 5, 1931; naturalized Am. citizen; s. Des Raj and Kesara Devi (Pathak) S.; m. Millicent M. Hewitt, Dec. 22, 1956 (div. 1996); children: Nalanda V. Sharma Bowman, Renuka D. BS with honors, U. Delhi, India, 1949, MS, 1951; PhD, U. So. Calif., 1961. Chemist Govt. Opium Factory, Ghazipur, India, 1951-52; lab. assoc., sci. asst. Nat. Chem. Lab., Poona, India, 1952-55; lab. assoc. U. So. Calif., L.A., 1955-61; research fellow Calif. Inst. Tech., Pasadena, 1961-65; asst. prof. chemistry U. Nev., Reno, 1963-64, Oreg. State U., Corvallis, 1965-70; asst. prof. chemistry Calif. State U., Northridge, 1973-75, assoc. prof., 1975-76; prof. L.A. Pierce Coll., Woodland Hills, Calif., 1976—; part-time assoc. prof. chemistry Calif. State U., L.A., 1973-85, prof., 1985—; vis. assoc. Calif. Inst. Tech., 1979, 82; pres. L.A. Pierce Coll. Senate, 1981-82, chmn. profl. and acad. stds., 1989-92. Contbr. articles to profl. jours. Grantee E.I. duPont de Nemours, L.A., 1961, Am. Chem. Soc. Petroleum Rsch. Fund, Washington, 1965-69, NSF, Washington, 1967-69. Mem. Am. Chem. Soc. (chmn. edn. com. So. Calif. chpt. 1981-82), Royal Soc. Chemistry (chartered chemist), Am. Inst. Parliamentarians (sec., adminstr., lt. gov. region VII, exec. lt. gov.), Nat. Assn. Parliamentarians, Calif. State Assn. Parliamentarians (pub. rels. chmn., statewide edn. chmn. So. area, pres. Calif. Sigma unit). Avocations: playing bridge, reading, history, classical music, crystal models. Office: LA Pierce Coll Chem Dept Woodland Hills CA 91371

SHARMA, DHARMENDRA K., federal agency administrator , electrical engineer. BTech with honors, Indian Inst. Tech., Kharagpur; MEE, U. Windsor, Ont., Can.; M and PhD in Electric Power Engring., Rensselaer Poly. Inst. Registered profl. engr., Mass. With Heavy Elecs. Ltd., Bhopal, India, Gen. Electric Co., Calif., N.Y., Mass., EPRI, Palo Alto, Calif.; IEEE Congl. fellow U.S. Senate, 1992; tech. liaison with Congress and industry Electric power Rsch. Inst., Washington, 1993-94; adminstr. rsch. and spl. programs adminstrn. U.S. Dept. Transp., 1994—. Pres. bd. edn. Morgan Hill Unified Sch. Dist., 1984-85. Fellow IEEE; mem. various profl. engring. socs. Office: US Dept Transp Rsch & Spl Prog Adminstrn 400 7th St SW Washington DC 20590*

SHARMA, RASHMI, toxicologist, researcher; b. Mathura, India, Aug. 10, 1960; came to U.S., 1989; d. Ghanshiam Nath and Gomati (Ramnathji) S. BSc, U. Allahabad, India, 1979, MSc, 1981, PhD, 1989. Rsch. assoc. U. Miss., Jackson, 1989-91; postdoctoral fellow U. Tex. Med. Br., Galveston, 1991—; attendee workshops and meetings Congress Zoology, Gwalior (India) U., 1983, Meerut (India) U., 1985, Indian Sci. Congress Assn., Lucknow (India), 1984, Delhi U., 1985, Bangalore (Karnataka) India, 1986, USA Internat. Conf., Stanford (Calif.) U., 1987, Young Scientist Workshop on Environ. Nematology, U. Allahabad, India, 1987, South Ctrl. Soc. Toxicology, Oxford (Miss.) U., 1989, Nat. Ctr. for Toxicol. Rsch., Jefferson, Ark., 1990, Miss. Acad. Sci., Biloxi, 1990, Jackson, Miss., 1991, Soc. Toxicology, Dallas, 1991, New Orleans, 1993, Am. Assn. Cancer Rsch., San Diego, 1992, Orlando, Fla., 1993, San Francisco, 1994, Toronto, Can., 1995. Contbr. articles to profl. jours. Fellow Coun. Sci. and Indsl. Rsch., Govt. of India, 1984-87; grantee NIH, 1989-91. Mem. AAAS, Am. Assn. for Cancer Rsch. Home: 515 1st St Apt 335 Galveston TX 77550-5743 Office: U Tex Med Br 7 138 MRB Rt J-67 Galveston TX 77555-1067

SHARMA, SHIV KUMAR, geophysicist; b. India, July 2, 1946; came to U.S., 1977; m. Madhu Malaviya, Aug. 10, 1974; 2 children. BSc, Jiwaji U., 1968; MSc, Jiwaji (India) U., 1973; PhD, Indian Inst. Tech., Delhi, 1980. Rsch. fellow IIT, Delhi, India, 1969-74; rsch. assoc. U. Leicester, 1974-77; with Geophysics Lab., Washington, 1977-80; with Hawaii Inst. Geophysics & Planet U. Hawaii, 1980—. Contbr. over 140 rsch. papers to profl. jours; patentee in field. Carnegie Postdoctoral fellow; rsch. grantee. Fellow Nat. Acad. Sci.; mem. Am. Geophys. Union, Am. Ceramic Soc., Am. Electrochem. Soc., Mineral Soc. Am., Optical Soc. Am., Pacific Congress, Soc. for Applied Spectroscopy. Avocations: reading, writing, travel. Office: U Hawaii Sch Ocean & Earth Sci & Tech Hawaii Inst Geophys & Planet 2525 Correa Rd Honolulu HI 96822

SHARMAN, RICHARD LEE, telecommunications executive, consultant; b. Warren, Pa., Oct. 23, 1932; s. Scott Albert Sr. and Viola Lena Marie (Kittner) S.; m. Diane Lee Van Patten, Nov. 3, 1973; children: Daria Lee, Deedra Lee; children by previous marriage, Suzanne Annette, Cynthia Lee. BS in Engring. Physics, U. Toledo, 1959; MS in Elec. Engring., Cornell U., 1961. Project engr. advanced electronics ctr. GE, Syracuse, N.Y., 1965-68, mgr. infrared and optics, electronics lab., 1965-68; mgr. info. networks, info. systems div. GE, Bethesda, Md., 1968-73; mgr. comml. analysis Xerox Corp., Rochester, N.Y., 1973-78; mgr. mktg. systems Xerox Corp., Rochester, 1978-80; v.p. bus. sector GTE Corp., Stamford, Conn., 1980-84; v.p. mktg. GTE Mobilnet Inc., Houston, 1984-87, gen. mgr. Tex. region, 1987-90; v.p. ops. GTE Mobilnet Inc. Hdqrs., Houston, 1990-92; pres., COO Guidry Group, Houston, 1992-93; pres., owner Mgmt. Consulting Svcs. Co., The Woodlands, Texas, 1993—; pres., founder Mgmt. Cons. Svcs., The Woodlands, Tex., 1993—; bd. dirs. Cellular Communications Corp., Irvine, Calif., 1985-87. Contbr. articles profl. jours. Bd. dirs. Houston unit ARC. With USCG, 1951-54. Mem. Am. Mktg. Assn. (exec. mem.), Houston C. of C. (mem. region mobility com.), Houston Grand Opera (patron 1990—), Tau Beta Pi, Forum Club (Houston), Cornell Alumni Assn. Republican. Episcopalian. Avocation: photography. Home and Office: 26 Fernglen Dr The Woodlands TX 77380-3968

SHARMAN, WILLIAM, professional basketball team executive; b. Abilene, Tex., May 25, 1926; m. Joyce Sharman; children by previous marriage: Jerry, Nancy, Janice, Tom. Student, U. So. Calif. Basketball player Washington Capitols, 1950-51, Boston Celtics, 1951-61; coach Los Angeles/Utah Stars, 1968-71; coach Los Angeles Lakers, 1971-76, gen. mgr., 1976-82, pres., 1982-88, spl. cons., 1991—. Author: Sharman on Basketball Shooting, 1965. Named to Nat. Basketball Assn. All Star First Team, 1956-59, 2d Team, 1953, 55, 60, All League Team, 7 times; named Coach of Year Nat. Basketball Assn., 1972, Naismith Basketball Hall of Fame, 1976. Home: 27996 Palos Verdes Dr East Rancho Palos Verdes CA 90275 Office: LA Lakers PO Box 10 3900 W Manchester Blvd Inglewood CA 90306

SHARON, NATHAN, biochemist; b. Brisk, Poland, Nov. 4, 1925; arrived in Israel, 1934; m. Rachel Itzikson, 1948; children: Esther, Osnat. MS, Hebrew U., Jerusalem, 1950, PhD, 1953; Dr. (hon.), U. Rene Descartes, Paris, 1990. Rsch. asst. Agrl. Rsch. Sta., Rehovot, Israel, 1949-53; rsch. asst. dept. biophysics Weizmann Inst. Sci., Rehovot, Israel, 1954-57, rsch. assoc. dept. biophysics, 1957-60, sr. scientist dept. biophysics, 1960-65, assoc. prof. dept. biophysics, 1965-68, prof. dept. biophysics, 1968—; vis. scientist numerous univs. and colls. Author: Complex Carbohydrates: Their Chemistry, Biosynthesis and Functions, 1975; co-editor: Biotechnological Applications of Proteins and Enzymes, 1977, The Lectins: Properties, Functions and Applications in Biology and Medicine, 1986; co-author: Lectins, 1989; contbr. over 400 articles to profl. jours. Recipient Laundau prize Mifal Hapyis, Israel, 1973, Weizmann prize in exact scis. City of Tel Aviv, 1977, Olitzki prize Israel Soc. Microbiology, 1989, Datta lectureship award Fedn. European Biochem. Socs., 1987, Bijvoet medal Utrecht U., 1989, Israel Prize in Biomedical and Medical Research, 1994. Mem. Am. Chem. Soc., Biochem. Soc. Eng., Am. Soc. Biol. Chemists (hon.), European Molecular Biology Orgn., Israel Acad. Scis. and Humanities, Internat. Sci. Writers Assn., Israel Biochem. Soc. (pres. 1969-70), Soc. for Complex Carbohydrates, Fedn. European Biochem. Socs. (chmn. 1980-81), Internat. Glycoconjugate Orgn. (pres. 1989-91). Avocation: swimming. Home: 77 Mishmeret, Afeka Tel Aviv 69012, Israel Office: Weizmann Inst Sci Dept, Membrane Rsch/Biophysics, Dept Membrane Rsch & Biophysics, Rehovot 76100, Israel

SHARP, AARON JOHN, botanist, educator; b. Plain City, Ohio, July 29, 1904; s. Prentice Daniel and Maude Katharine (Herriott) S.; m. Cora Evelyn Bunch, July 25, 1929; children: Rosa Elizabeth, Maude Katharine, Mary Martha (dec.), Fred Prentice, Jennie Lou. AB, Ohio Wesleyan U., 1927, DSc, 1952; MS, U. Okla., 1929; PhD, Ohio State U., 1938. Instr. botany U. Tenn., Knoxville, 1929-37, asst. prof., 1937-40, assoc. prof., 1940-46, prof., 1946-65, Disting. Service prof., 1965-74, prof. emeritus, 1974—, curator herbarium, 1949-68, assoc. curator herbarium, 1968—, head dept. botany, 1951-61; assoc. editor The Bryologist, 1938-42, 45-53, acting editor, 1943-44; assoc. editor Castanea, 1947-66; trustee Highlands (N.C.) Biol. Lab., 1934-38, 48-64, bd. mgrs., 1946-52; Cecil Billington lectr. Cranbook Inst. Sci., 1947; sec. sect. Inter-Am. Conf. on Conservation of Renewable Natural Resources, Denver, 1948; vis. prof. Stanford U., 1951, U. Mich. Biol. Sta., 1954-57, 59-64, U. Minn. Biol. Sta., 1971, U. Mont. Biol. Sta., 1972, Nat. U. Taiwan, 1965, Instituto Universitario Pedagógico Experimental, Maracay, Venezuela, 1976, U. Va. Biol. Sta., 1980; mem. staff Hattori (Japan) Bot. Lab., 1956—; vis. lectr. Am. Inst. Biol. Scis., 1967-70; mem. nat. adv. bd. Ministry of Ecology, 1975-81; cons. Time-Life Books, 1975, Brit. Broadcasting Corp., 1984, Nat. Geog. Books, 1985; hon. curatorship in the Inst. of Systematic Botany of the N.Y. Bot. Garden, 1994; hon. life mem. Save-the-Redwoods League, 1995. Assoc. editor: Hattori Bot. Jour., Nichinan, Japan, 1961—; contbr. articles to sci. jours. and Ency. Britanica. Bd. dirs. Nature Conservancy, 1955-61, Gt. Smoky Mountains Nat. Hist. Assn., 1979-81. Decorated officer Order of Rising Sun (Japan); Guggenheim Found. fellow, 1944-46; recipient Merit award Tenn. Environ. Edn. Assn., 1991, Disting. Achievement award Ohio Wesleyan U., 1992, Eloise Payne Luquer medal Garden Club Am., 1983, Appreciation cert. Great Smoky Mountains Nat. Park, 1994. Fellow AAAS (v.p. 1963), Linnean Soc. London; mem. AAUP, New Eng. Bot. Club, Internat. Soc. Phytomorphologists, Internat. Assn. Plant Taxonomy, So. Appalachian Bot. Club (pres. 1946-47), Sullivant Moss Soc. (pres. 1935), Am. Bryol. and Lichen. Soc., Am. Fern Soc., Bot. Soc. Am. (editorial com. 1948-53, treas. 1957-62, v.p. 1963, pres. 1965, Merit award 1972), Soc. for Study Evolution, Soc. Botánica de México (hon.), Soc. Mexicana de Historia Natural, Tenn. Acad. Sci. (exec. com. 1943-44, v.p. 1952, pres. 1953), Am. Soc. Plant Taxonomists (pres. 1961), Assn. Southeastern Biologists (v.p. 1956, Meritorious Tchr. award 1972, Bartholomew award 1989), Ecol. Soc. Am. (v.p. 1958-59), Torrey Bot. Club, Nature Conservancy (gov. 1955-61), Am. Soc. Naturalists, Bot. Brit. Bryol. Soc., Internat. Soc. Tropical Ecology, Internat. Phycolog. Soc., Nat. Assn. Biology Tchrs., Palynolog. Soc. India, Phycolog. Soc. Am., Systematics Assn., Am. Assn. Stratigraphic Palynol., Soc. Latino-Americano de Briologia (hon.), Tenn. Nat. Plant Soc. (hon.), Gt. Smoky Mountains Conservation Assn., (bd. dirs. 1960—), U. Tenn. Arboretum Soc. (bd. dirs. 1979—), Explorers Club, Phi Beta Kappa, Phi Kappa Phi, Sigma Xi, Phi Sigma, Phi Epsilon Phi, Sigma Delta Pi. Home: 1105 Tobler Rd Knoxville TN 37919-8164 Office: U Tenn Dept Botany Knoxville TN 37996 *The Universe is so constructed that for every error committed someone must pay a penalty now or in the future.*

SHARP, ALLEN, chief federal judge; b. Washington, D.C., Feb. 11, 1932; s. Robert Lee and Frances Louise (Williams) S.; children: Crystal Catholyn, Scarlet Frances. Student, Ind. State U., 1950-53; AB, George Washington U., 1954; JD, Ind. U., 1957; MA, Butler U., 1986. Bar: Ind. 1957. Practiced in Williamsport, 1957-68; judge Ct. of Appeals Ind., 1969-73; judge U.S. Dist. Ct. (no. dist.) Ind., South Bend, 1973—, now chief judge. Bd. advisers Milligan (Tenn.) Coll. Served to JAG USAFR. Mem. Ind. Judges Assn., Blue Key, Phi Delta Kappa, Pi Gamma Mu, Tau Kappa Alpha. Republican. Mem. Christian Ch. Club: Mason. Office: US Dist Ct 124 Fed Bldg 204 S Main St South Bend IN 46601*

SHARP, ANNE CATHERINE, artist, educator; b. Red Bank, N.J., Nov. 1, 1943; d. Elmer Eugene and Ethel Violet (Hunter) S. BFA, Pratt Inst., 1965; MFA (teaching fellow 1972), Bklyn. Coll., 1973. tchr. art Sch. Visual Arts, 1978-89, NYU, 1978, SUNY, Purchase, 1983, Pratt Manhattan Ctr., N.Y.C., 1982-84, Parsons Sch. Design, N.Y.C., 1984-90, Visual Arts Ctr. of Alaska, Anchorage, 1991, Anchorage Mus. Hist. and Art, 1991, 93, 94, 95, U. Alaska, Anchorage, 1994—; lectr. AAAS, The 46th Arctic Divsn. Sci. Conf., U. Alaska, Fairbanks, 1995. One-person shows Pace Editions, N.Y.C., Ten/Downtown, N.Y.C., Katonah (N.Y.) Gallery, 1974, Contemporary Gallery, Dallas, 1975, Art in a Public Space, N.Y.C., 1979, Eatontown Hist. Mus., N.J., 1980, N.Y. Pub. Library Epiphany Br., 1988, Books and Co., N.Y., 1989, The Kendall Gallery, N.Y.C., 1990, Alaska Pacific U., Carr-Gottstein Gallery, Anchorage, 1993, Internat. Gallery Contemporary Art, Anchorage, 1993, Art Think Tank Gallery, N.Y.C., 1994, U.S. Geol. Survey, Reston, Va., 1994, Stonington Gallery, Anchorage, 1994; group shows include Arnot Art Mus., Elmira, N.Y., 1975, Bronx Mus., 1975, Mus. Modern Art, N.Y.C., 1975-76, Nat. Arts Club, N.Y.C., 1979, Calif. Mus. Photography, Riverside, 1983-92, Jack Tilton Gallery, N.Y.C., 1983, Lincoln Ctr., N.Y.C., 1983, Cabo Frio Print Biennale, Brazil, 1983, Pratt Graphic Ctr., N.Y.C., 1984, State Mus. N.Y., Albany, 1984, Kenkeleba Gallery, N.Y.C., 1985, Hempstead Harbor Art Assn., Glen Cove, N.Y., 1985, Mus. Mod. Art, Weddel, Fed. Republic of Germany, 1985, Kenkeleba Gallery, N.Y.C., 1985, Paper Art Exhbn. Internat. Mus. Contemporary Art, Bahia, Brazil, 1986, Mus. Salon-de-Provence, France, 1987, Mus. Contemporary Art, Sao Paulo, Brazil, 1985-86, Salon de Provence, France, 1987, Adirondack Lakes Ctr. for Arts, Blue Mountain Lake, N.Y., 1987, Kendall Gallery, N.Y.C., 1988, Exhibition Ctr. Parsons Sch. Design, N.Y.C., 1989, F.M.K. Gallery, Budapest, Hungary, 1989, Galerie des Kulturbundes Schwarzenberg, German Dem. Republic, Q Sen Do Gallery, Kobe, Japan, 1989, Anchorage Mus. History and Art, 1990-91, 94, U. Alaska, Anchorage, 1990, 91, Coos Art Mus., Coos Bay, Oreg., 1990, Spaceship Earth, Mus. Internat. de Neu Art, Vancouver, Can., 1990, Councourse Gallery, Emily Carr Coll. Art and Design, 1990, Nat. Mus. Women in the Arts, Washington, 1991, Visual Arts Ctr. Alaska, 1991, 92, Nomad Mus., Lisbon, Portugal, 1991, Mus. Ostdeutsche Gallery, Regensberg, Germany, 1991, Mcpl. Mus. Cesley Krumlov (So. Bohemia) CSFK, Czechoslovakia, 1991, Böltmiche Dörter Exhbn. Hochstrass 8, Munich, 1992, BBC-TV, Great Britain, U.K., Sta. WXXI-TV, Rochester, N.Y., 1992-93, Site 250 Gallery Contemporary Art., Fairbanks, 1993, Santa Barbara (Calif.) Mus. Art, 1993, The Rochester (N.Y.) Mus. and Sci. Ctr., 1990-94, Space Arc: The Archives of Mankind, Time Capsule in Earth Orbit, Hughes Comm., Divec TV Satellite Launch, 1994, Stonington Gallery, Anchorage, 1994, 95, UAA Art Galley U. Alaska, 1995, Arctic Trading Post, Nome, Alaska, 1995, Lawrenceville (N.J.) Sch., 1996; represented in permanent collections Smithsonian Instn., Nat. Air and Space Mus., Washington, Albright Knox Gallery, Buffalo, St. Vincent's Hosp, N.Y.C., N.Y. Pub. Libr., N.Y.C., U.S. Geol. Survey, Reston, Va., White House (Reagan, Bush adminstrns.), Site 250 Gallery Contemporary Art, Anchorage Mus. History and Art, others; Moon Shot series to commemorate moon landing, 1970-76, Cloud Structures of the Universe Painting series, 1980-86, Am. Landscape series, 1987-89, Thoughtlines, fall 1986,

Swimming in the Mainstream with Her, U. Va., Charlottesville; author: Artist's Book - Travel Dreams U.S.A., 1989, Artworld-Welt Der Kunst, Synchronicity, 1989—, Art Think Tank: Projects in Art and Ecology, 1990—, The Alaska Series, 1990—, Potraits in the Wilderness, 1990—; columnist: Anchorage Press, 1995—. Sponsor IDITOROD Trail Com., Libby Riddles. Artist-in-residence grantee Va. Center for Creative Arts, 1974, Artpark, Lewiston, N.Y., 1980, Vt. Studio Colony, 1989; recipient Pippin award Our Town, N.Y.C., 1984, certificate of Appreciation Art in Embassy program U.S. Dept. State, 1996. Mem. Nat. Space Soc., Nat. Mus. Women in Arts, Alaska Photography Ctr., Pratt Inst. Alumni Assn., The Planetary Soc., Internat. Assn. Near-Death Studies, Art and Sci. Collaborations, The Internat. Gallery of Contemporary Art. Address: PO Box 100480 Anchorage AK 99510-0480 Gallery: 621 W 6th Ave Anchorage AK 99501 also: 250 Custaman St Ste 2A Fairbanks AK 99701 *As an active painter I explore the mysteries of the 20th century space adventure in my American landscapes, painted directly from nature and in planetary landscapes, fantastic pictures of the cosmos. I believe it is in the reconciliation between inner and outer experience, through a personal sense of humor and use of universal symbols that a mystical or cosmic harmony can be expressed in art.*

SHARP, BERT LAVON, retired education educator, retired university dean; b. Philadelphia, Miss., Nov. 4, 1926; s. Bert L. and Louie (McBeath) S.; m. Mary Warren, Dec. 24, 1948; children—Kenneth, Richard. B.S., Miss. Coll., Clinton, 1949; M.Ed., U. Fla., Gainesville, 1953, D.Ed., 1960. Tchr., dir. guidance Miss. and Fla., 1945-55; dir. ednl. research Pinellas County, Fla., 1955-56; dir. secondary curriculum and ednl. services, 1958-61; assoc. prof., chmn. counselor edn. Auburn (Ala.) U., 1961-63; mem. faculty U. Fla., Gainesville, 1956-58, prof. edn., 1963-85, prof. emeritus, 1985—, dean Coll. Edn., 1968-78, dean emeritus, 1978—; cons. in field. Contbr. articles to profl. jours. Mem. Am. Assn. Colls. Tchr. Edn. (dir. 1973-76, exec. com. 1974-76, 78-81, pres. 1979), Assn. Colls. Schs. Edn. in State Univs. and Land-Grant Colls (pres. 1976), Am. Personnel and Guidance Assn., Am. Assn. Counselor Edn. and Supervision, Fla. Council Deans, Am. Sch. Counselor Assn., Assn. Deans Edn. Land Grant Coll. and State Univs., Fla. Council Tchrs. Edn., Am. Assn. Sch. Adminstrs., Gov. Fla. Council Tchr. Edn. Centers, Internat. Council for Edn. of Tchrs. (bd. dirs. 1980—), Phi Kappa Phi, Phi Delta Kappa, Alpha Kappa Delta. Home: Richland Pl Apt 115 500 Elmington Ave Nashville TN 37205-2518

SHARP, DANIEL ASHER, foundation executive; b. San Francisco, Mar. 29, 1932; s. Joseph C. and Miriam (Asher) S.; m. Jacqueline Borda, 1967 (div. 1975); 1 son, Benjamin Daniel; m. Revelle Pergament Allen, 1989. B.A., U. Calif.-Berkeley, 1954; J.D., Harvard U., 1959. Bar: Calif. 1959. Dep. atty. gen. State of Calif., San Francisco, 1959-61; with U.S. Peace Corps, 1961-68; asst. dir. internat. programs U.S. Peace Corps, Washington, 1961-62; assoc. dir. U.S. Peace Corps, Cuzco, Peru, 1962-64; acting dir. Peace Corps, La Paz, Bolivia, 1964; creator, dir. Staff Tng. Ctr. Peace Corps, Washington, 1965-68; dir. div. edn. resources U.S. Peace Corps, 1966;, 1988—; dir. edn. and Latin Am. programs, asst. dir. Adlai Stevenson Inst. Internat. Affairs, U. Chgo., 1968-70; dir. tng. ITT, Latin Am., 1970-72; mgr. mgmt. devel. ITT World Hdqrs., N.Y.C., 1973; with Xerox Corp., 1973-88; dir. human resources devel. Xerox Corp. (Xerox LatinAm. group), 1973-75, chmn. overhead value analysis task force, 1975-76; dir. ops. support Xerox Corp. (Xerox Latinam. group), 1976, dir. Inter-Am. affairs, 1977-79; dir. internat. affairs Xerox Corp. Hdqrs., 1979-85, dir. internat. and pub. affairs, 1985-87, internat. cons., 1988-93, sr. internat. advisor InterMatrix Group, 1990—; pres. Am. Assembly Columbia U., 1987—; adj. prof. internat. and pub. affairs Columbia U., 1991—; faculty Aspen Inst., 1995—; cons. U.S. Dept. State, fgn. govts., corps., founds.; mem. U.S. del. to UN Econ. and Social Coun., Geneva, 1961; mem. U.S. del. to OAS, San Juan, 1986; negotiated 6 treaties U.S. Govt.; U.S. rep. Internat. Conf. on Vol. Programs, The Hague, Netherlands, 1961; mem. outside bd. adv. coun. Macmillan Ltd. (U.K.), 1982; rep. U.S. bus. cmty. nat. task force on Europe Bus. and Industry Adv. Com., regional trade blocs, Paris, 1989. Editor: United States Foreign Policy and Peru, 1972, Los Estados Unidos y La Revolucion Peruaña, 1972, U.S. editor European Business Journal, 1988-95; contbr. articles to N.Y. Times, Wall St. Jour., Internat. Herald Tribune, and chapters in several books. Chmn. adv. bd. Coun. of Ams., 1978-85; bd. dirs. Overseas Devel. Coun., 1980—, Internat. Ctr. of N.Y., 1980-88, Fund for Multinat. Mgmt. Edn., 1979-85, Accion, 1980-88, World Press Inst., 1986-89, Forum for World Affairs, 1987-95, Stamford Symphony, 1987-91; bd. advs. Landegger Program in Internat. Bus. Diplomacy, Sch. Fgn. Svc., Georgetown U., 1981-92, Econ. Growth Ctr., Yale U., 1987, Consortium on Competitiveness and Coop., U. Calif., 1987-90, Fletcher Sch. Law and Diplomacy, 1984-89; bd. visitors Duke U. Inst. of Policy Scis. and Pub. Affairs, 1988-91; mem. U.S./Mex. Bus. Coun., 1981-87. Served with U.S. Army, 1954-55; capt. Res. Recipient Medalla de Oro y Diploma de Honor del Consejo Provincial del Cuzco, 1963, Manchester Leadership award, 1992; Woodrow Wilson fellow Princeton, N.J., 1981-85. Mem. State Bar Calif., Coun. on Fgn. Rels., Mid-Atlantic Club (bd. dirs.). Home: 94 Campbell Dr Stamford CT 06903-4032 Office: Am Assembly Columbia U 475 Riverside Dr Ste 456 New York NY 10115-0456 *Changing careers frequently keeps life exciting, as one must constantly learn new roles and ideas and organizations. Public service and the not-for-profit sector are ultimately more satisfying, but the management skills learned in the private sector are practically indispensable.*

SHARP, ELAINE CECILE, obstetrician, gynecologist; b. Hoven, S.D., Feb. 19, 1952; d. Lewis Ralph and Bernadette Teresa (Bastien) Arbach; m. Walton H. Sharp, Oct. 26, 1979 (div.); m. Shane Daigle, Nov. 1991; 1 child, Sean Patrick Daigle. BA, No. State U., 1974, BS, 1976; MD, U. Tex., Houston, 1985. Diplomate Am. Bd. Ob-Gyn. Pvt. practice Pensacola, Fla., 1989—; speaker, chmn. Body Talk, Milton, Fla., 1989—. Mem. Am. Med. Womens' Assn., Am. Diabetes Assn., Am. Bus. Womens' Assn., Am. Coll. Ob-Gyn, Soc. Laparoendoscopic Surgeons, Fla. Ob-Gyn Soc., Exec. Club (asst. chmn. cancer com.). Republic. Roman Catholic. Avocations: biking, running, swimming, boating, racquetball. Office: PO Box 17062 Pensacola FL 32522-7062 also: Elaine Sharp MD PA 1717 N E St # 436 Pensacola FL 32501-6339

SHARP, GEORGE KENDALL, federal judge; b. Chgo., Dec. 30, 1934; s. Edward S. and Florence S.; m. Mary Bray; children: Florence Kendall, Julia Manger. BA, Yale U., 1957; JD, U. Va., 1963. Bar: Fla. 1963. Atty. Sharp, Johnston & Brown, Vero Beach, Fla., 1963-78; pub. defender 19th Cir. Ct., Vero Beach, 1964-68; sch. bd. atty. Indian River County, Fla., 1968-78; Fla. circuit judge 19th Cir., 1978-83; judge U.S. Dist. Ct. (mid. dist.) Fla., Orlando, 1983—. Office: US Dist Ct 635 US Courthouse 80 N Hughey Ave Orlando FL 32801*

SHARP, J(AMES) FRANKLIN, finance educator, academic administrator; b. Johnson County, Ill., Sept. 29, 1938; s. James Albert and Edna Mae (Slack) S. B.S. in Indsl. Engring., U. Ill., 1960; M.S., Purdue U., 1962, Ph.D., 1966, cert. mgmt. acctg., 1979. Chartered fin. analyst, 1980. Asst. prof. engring., econs. Rutgers U., New Brunswick, N.J., 1966-70; assoc. prof. NYU Grad. Sch. Bus., N.Y.C., 1970-74; supr. bus. research AT&T, N.Y.C., 1974-77, dist. mgr. corp. planning, 1977-81, dist. mgr. fin. mgmt. and planning, 1981-85; prof. fin. Grad. Sch. Bus. Pace U., N.Y.C., 1975-91; chmn. Sharp CFA Rev. & Inst. for Investment Edn., 1987-96, Sharp Seminars, 1996—; speaker, moderator meetings, 1965—; cons. Sharp Investment Mgmt., 1967—. Contbr. numerous articles to profl. publs.; corr.: Interface, 1975-78; fin. editor: Planning Rev., 1975-78. Mem. N.Am. Soc. Corp. Planning (treas. 1976-77, bd. dirs. at large 1977-78), Inst. Mgmt. Sci. (chpt. v.p. acad. 1972-74, chpt. v.p. program 1974-75, chpt. v.p. membership 1975-76, chpt. pres. 1976-77), Internat. Affiliation Planning Socs. (coun. 1978-84), N.Y. Soc. Security Analysts (CFA Rev. 1985-87), Ops. Rsch. Soc. Am. (pres. corp. planning group 1976-82), AAUP (v.p. Pace U. chpt. 1988-90), Theta Xi. Republican. Office: 315 E 86th St # 7H New York NY 10028-4714

SHARP, JOEL H., JR., lawyer; b. Salem, Ohio, Aug. 25, 1935. BS, Yale U., 1957; LLB, Stanford U., 1960. Bar: Calif. 1961, Fla. 1964. Ptnr. Baker & Hostetler, Orlando, Fla. Fellow Am. Coll. Trust and Estate Coun., Am. Coll. Tax Coun.; mem. ABA (vice chmn. corp. com., tax sect. 1984-86, chmn. 1986-88), State Bar Calif., Fla. Bar (mem. exec. coun. tax sect. 1965—; chmn. 1976-77, mem. bd. govs. 1975-79), Orange County Bar Assn. (mem. exec. coun. 1967-74, pres. 1972-73). Office: Baker & Hostetler Sun-Bank Ctr 200 S Orange Ave Ste 2300 Orlando FL 32801 Office: Baker & Hostetler PO Box 636 Orlando FL 32802*

SHARP, JOHN LEWIS, oil industry executive, geologist; b. Warren, Ark., Nov. 1, 1959; s. Billy Ray and Jerry Lynn (Lewis) S.; m. Kyoung Sun Kim, June 20, 1981; 1 child, Alex Lewis. BS in Geology with high hons., U. Ark., Fayetteville, 1981, MS in Geology, 1983. Exploration geologist Marathon Oil Co., Houston, 1983-88; ops. geologist Marathon Petroleum Korea, Ltd., Houston, 1988-90; sr. geologist ArkLa Exploration Co., Houston, 1990-93; geol. cons. Houston, 1993; exploration mgr. Transfuel Resources, Inc., Houston, 1993-94, v.p. exploration, 1994-95; co-owner Praxis Resources LLC, Houston, 1996—. Mem. Am. Assn. Petroleum Geologists (cert. petroleum geologist), Houston Geolog. Soc. Republican. Avocation: golf. Office: Praxis Resources LLC 10700 Richmond Ste 100 Houston TX 77042

SHARP, MITCHELL WILLIAM, advisor to prime minister; b. Winnipeg, Man., Can., May 11, 1911; s. Thomas and Elizabeth (Little) S.; m. Daisy Boyd, Apr. 23, 1938 (dec.); 1 son, Noel; m. Jeannette Dugal, Apr. 14, 1976. B.A., U. Man., 1934, LL.D. (hon.), 1965; postgrad., London Sch. Econs., 1937-38; hon. Dr. Social Sci., U. Ottawa, 1970; LLD (hon.), U. Western Ont., 1977, Carleton U., 1994, McMaster U., 1995. Statistician Sanford Evans Statis. Service, 1926-36; economist James Richardson & Sons, Ltd., 1936-42; officer Canadian Dept. Fin., Ottawa, 1942-51; dir. econ. policy div. Canadian Dept. Fin., 1947-51; assoc. dep. minister Canadian Dept. Trade and Commerce, 1951-57, dep. minister, 1957-58; v.p. Brazilian Traction, Toronto, Can., 1958-62; mem. Can. Ho. of Commons, from 1963; minister trade and commerce, 1963-65, minister fin., 1965-68, sec. state external affairs, 1968-74, pres. Privy Council, house leader, 1974-76, resigned, 1978; commr. No. Pipeline Agy., 1978-88. Decorated officer Order of Can. Address: 33 Monkland Ave, Ottawa, ON Canada K1S 1Y8

SHARP, PAUL DAVID, institute administrator; b. Youngstown, Ohio, Nov. 3, 1940; s. Robert Henderson and Kathryn (Tadsen)S.; m. Carole G. Graff, Sept. 16, 1967; children: David Allen, Kathryn Elizabeth. BA cum laude, Kenyon Coll., Gambier, Ohio, 1962; MPA, Auburn U., 1974. Commd. 2d lt. USAF, 1962, advanced through grades to col., 1983, intelligence officer, 1962-80; comdr. Detachment 1, 7450th Intelligence Squadron USAF, Neubruecke, Germany, 1980-83; comdr. 480th Reconnaissance Tech. Group USAF, Langley AFB, Va., 1983-85, dir. intelligence systems HQ Tactical Air Command, 1985-86, dep. chief intelligence Tactical Air Command, 1986-88; mgr. operational intelligence group Battelle Meml. Inst., Columbus, Ohio, 1988-89, mgr. fgn. tech. assessment group, 1989-91, mgr. intelligence projects/programs, 1991-92, v.p. bus. devel. fgn. sci. and tech., 1992-95; dir. fgn. sci. and tech. programs Batelle Meml. Inst., Columbus, Ohio, 1995—; mem. student career coun. Kenyon Coll., Columbus, 1992-95. Trustee Brandywine Assn., Yorktown, Va., 1987, Chase Assn., Powell, Ohio, 1991. Decorated Legion of Merit, Meritorious Svc. medals. Mem. Nat. Mil. Intelligence Assn., Armed Forces Communications and Electronics Assn., Air Force Assn., Sigma Pi (pres. Lambda chpt. 1961-62). Republican. Episcopalian. Avocations: golf, woodworking, photography, music. Office: Battelle Meml Inst 505 King Ave Columbus OH 43201-2696

SHARP, PAUL FREDERICK, former university president, educational consultant; b. Kirksville, Mo., Jan. 19, 1918; s. Frederick J. and L. Blanche (Phares) S.; m. Rosella Ann Anderson, June 19, 1939; children: William, Kathryn, Paul Trevor. AB, Phillips U., 1939; PhD, U. Minn., 1947; LLD (hon.), Tex. Christian U., 1961, Austin Coll., 1978, Drake U., 1980; LHD (hon.), Buena Vista Coll., 1967, U. Nev., Towson State U., 1980, Oklahoma City U., 1996; LittD (hon.), Limestone Coll., 1971; HHD, Okla. Christian U. Sci. & Arts, 1992. Instr. U. Minn., 1942, 46-47, vis. lectr., 1948; asso. prof. Am. history Iowa State U., 1947-54; prof. Am. history, chmn. Am. Instns. program U. Wis., 1954-57, vis. lectr., 1953; vis. lectr. San Francisco State Coll., 1950, U. Oreg., 1955; Fulbright lectr. Am. Instns., univs. Melbourne, Sydney, 1952; pres. Hiram Coll., 1957-64; chancellor U. N.C., Chapel Hill, 1964-66; pres. Drake U., Des Moines, 1966-71; pres. U. Okla., Norman, 1971-78, pres. emeritus, Regents' prof., 1978-88, pres. emeritus, Regents' prof. emeritus, 1988—; disting. prof. history U. Sci. and Arts, Okla., 1990—; dir. Am. Coun. on Edn. Insts. for Coll. and Univ. Presidents, 1977-79; vis. lectr. Harvard U. Bus. Sch. summer session, 1970-72. Author: Agrarian Revolt in Western Canada, 1948, Old Orchard Farm, Story of an Iowa Boyhood, 1952, Whoop-Up Country, Canadian American West, 1955; cons. author: Heritage of Midwest, 1958; Editor: Documents of Freedom, 1957; Contbr. articles to profl. jours. Pres. Norman Cmty. Found., 1995-96. USN liaison officer His Majesty's Australian Ship, Hobart, 1943-46. Recipient Iowa State U. Alumni Fund award, 1952, award of merit Am. Assn. State and Local History, 1955, Silver Spur award Western Writers Am., 1955, Fulbright award to Australia, 1952; named to Okla. Higher Edn. Hall of Fame, 1995; Minn. Hist. Soc. grantee, 1947, 48, Social Sci. Rsch. Coun. grantee, 1949, 51; Ford Faculty fellow, 1954, Guggenheim fellow, 1957. Mem. Phi Beta Kappa, Phi Kappa Phi, Phi Delta Kappa, Pi Gamma Mu, Phi Alpha Theta. Mem. Disciples of Christ Ch. Home: 701 Mockingbird Ln Norman OK 73071-4829 Office: U Okla 630 Parrington Oval Rm 105 Norman OK 73019-0375

SHARP, PHILLIP ALLEN, academic administrator, biologist, educator; b. Ky., June 6, 1944; s. Joseph Walter and Katherin (Colvin) S.; m. Ann Christine Holcombe, Aug. 29, 1964; children: Christine Alynn, Sarah Katherin, Helena Holcombe. BA, Union Coll., Barbourville, Ky., 1966, LHD (hon.), 1991; PhD, U. Ill., 1969. NIH postdoctoral fellow Calif. Inst. Tech., 1969-71; sr. research investigator Cold Spring Harbor (N.Y.) Lab., 1972-74; assoc. prof. MIT, Cambridge, 1974-79, prof. biology, 1979—, head dept. biology, 1991—, dir. Ctr. Cancer Rsch., 1985-91; co-founder, mem. sci. bd., dir. BIOGEN, 1978—; chmn. sci. bd., 1987—; mem. Pres.' Adv. Coun. on Sci. and Tech., 1991—; mem. bd. trustees Alfred P. Sloan Found., 1995—. Mem. editl. bd. Cell, 1974-95, Jour. Virology, 1974-86, Molecular and Cellular Biology, 1974-85. Co-recipient Nobel Prize in Physiology or Medicine, 1993; recipient awards Am. Cancer Soc., 1974-79, awards Eli Lilly, 1980, awards Nat Acad. Sci./U.S. Steel Found., 1980, Howard Ricketts award U. Chgo., 1985, Alfred P. Sloan Jr. prize Gen. Motors Research Found., 1986, award Gairdner Found. Internat., 1986, award N.Y. Acad. Scis., 1986, Louisa Horwitz prize, 1988, Albert Lasker Basic Med. Rsch. award, 1988, Dickson prize U. Pitts., 1990; awarded Class of '41 chair, 1986-87, John D. MacArthur chair, 1987-92, Salvador E. Luria chair, 1992—. Fellow AAAS; mem. Am. Chem. Soc., Am. Soc. Microbiology, NAS (councilor 1986), Am. Acad. Arts and Scis, European Molecular Biology Orgn. (assoc.), Am. Soc. Biochemistry and Molecular Biology (elected mem. coun.), Am. Philos. Soc. (elected mem.), Inst. of Medicine of NAS (elected mem.). Home: 36 Fairmont Ave Newton MA 02158-2506 Office: MIT Ctr for Cancer Rsch 40 Ames St Rm E17 529B Cambridge MA 02139-4307

SHARP, RICHARD L., retail company executive; b. Washington, Apr. 12, 1947. Student, U. Va., 1965-66, Coll. of William and Mary, 1968-70. Programmer Group Health Inc., Washington, 1970-75; founder, pres. Applied Systems Corp., Washington, 1975-81; with Circuit City Stores, Inc., Richmond, Va., 1982—, exec. v.p., 1982-84, pres., 1984-86, pres., CEO, 1986-94, chmn. pres., CEO, 1994—; bd. dirs. Flextronics Internat., James River Corp. With USAF, 1967-70. Office: Circuit City Stores Inc 9950 Mayland Dr Richmond VA 23233-1464

SHARP, ROBERT PHILLIP, geology educator, researcher; b. Oxnard, Calif., June 24, 1911; s. Julian Hebner Sharp and Alice Sharp Darling; m. Jean Prescott Todd, Sept. 7, 1938; adopted children—Kristin Todd, Bruce Todd. B.S., Calif. Inst. Tech., Pasadena, 1934, M.S., 1935; M.A., Harvard U., Cambridge, Mass., 1936, Ph.D., 1938. Asst. prof. U. Ill., Urbana, 1938-43; prof. U. Minn., Mpls., 1946-47; prof. Calif. Inst. Tech., Pasadena, 1947-79, chmn., 1952-67, prof. emeritus, 1979—. Author: Glaciers, 1960, Field Guide-Southern California, 1972, Field Guide-Coastal Southern California, 1978, Living Ice-Understanding Glaciers and Glaciation, 1988, (with A.F. Glazner) Geology Under Foot in Southern California, 1993. Served to capt. USAF, 1943-46. Recipient Exceptional Sci. Achievement medal NASA, 1971, Nat. Medal Sci., 1989, Charles P. Daly medal Am. Geog. Soc., 1991; Robert P. Sharp professorship Calif. Inst. Tech., 1978. Fellow Geol. Soc. Am. (councilor, Kirk Bryan award 1964, Penrose medal 1977), Am. Geophys. Union; hon. fellow Internat. Glaciological Soc.; mem. NAS. Republican. Avocations: flyfishing, snorkeling, camping. Home: 1901 Gibraltar Rd Santa Barbara CA 93105-2326 Office: Calif Inst Tech 1200 E California Blvd Pasadena CA 91125

SHARP, ROBERT WEIMER, lawyer; b. Cleve., Feb. 12, 1917; s. Isaac Walter and Ruth (Weimer) S.; m. Norine Wines, Nov. 13, 1948; children: Kathleen L. Sharp Samuel, Pamela J. Sharp Adamson, Janet E. Sharp Schoon, Andrea S. Sharp Bobak, Gail N. Sharp Henderson. A.B. magna cum laude, Oberlin Coll., 1939; LL.B., Harvard U., 1942. Bar: Ohio 1944. Practiced in Cleve; ptnr. Gallagher, Sharp, Fulton & Norman and predecessors, 1958-92; pres. Bulkley Bldg. Co., 1966-70. Trustee emeritus St. Luke;s Hosp. Assn.; trustee emeritus, hon life mem. Ohio divsn. Am. Cancer Soc.; trustee emeritus Ohio East Area United Meth. Found., 1974—, sec., 1967-74, 83-86, pres., 1974-80. Mem. ABA, Ohio Bar Assn., Cleve. Bar Assn., Phi Beta Kappa. Republican. Methodist. Home: 3090 Fairmount Blvd Cleveland OH 44118-4129 Office: Gallagher Sharp Fulton & Norman 600 Bulkley Bldg Cleveland OH 44115

SHARP, RONALD ALAN, English literature educator, author; b. Cleve., Oct. 19, 1945; s. Jack Trier and Florence (Tenenbaum) S.; m. Inese Brutans, June 22, 1968; children: Andrew Janis, James Michael. BA, Kalamazoo Coll., 1967; MA, U. Mich., 1968; PhD, U. Va., 1974. Instr. in English Western Mich. U., Kalamazoo, 1968-70; instr. Kenyon Coll., Gambier, Ohio, 1970-72, asst. prof. English, 1974-78, assoc. prof., 1978-85; prof. Kenyon Coll., 1985-90, John Crowe Ransom prof. English, 1990—, chmn. dept. English, 1984-86, co-editor Kenyon Rev., 1978-82; dir. Keats Bicentennial Conf., Harvard U., 1995. Author: Keats, Skepticism and the Religion of Beauty, 1979, Friendship and Literature: Spirit and Form. 1986; translator: Teatro Breve (Garcia Lorca), 1979, editor (with Eudora Welty) The Norton Book of Friendship, 1991, (with Nathan Scott) Reading George Steiner, 1994; contbr. articles to profl. jours. Recipient award for editl. excellence Ohioana Assn., 1980; fellow Nat. Humanities Ctr., 1981, 86, NEH, 1981, 84-87, 93, 94, 95, Ford Found., 1971, Mellon Found., 1980, Danforth Found., 1971, English Speaking Union, 1973, Am. Coun. Learned Socs., 1986. Mem. MLA, NEH (chmn's. adv. group humanities edn. 1987), Wordsworth-Coleridge Assn., Keats-Shelley Assn. Jewish. Home: 11671 Kenyon Rd Mount Vernon OH 43050-9207 Office: Kenyon Coll Dept English Gambier OH 43022

SHARP, RONALD ARVELL, sociology educator; b. Vivian, La., Sept. 29, 1941; s. Walter Arvell and Virginia (Refield-King) S.; m. Imelda Idalia Pena, Sept. 16, 1967; children: Ronald Arvell II, Donald Allen. BS in Edn., Cameron U., 1976; BA in Sociology, SUNY, Albany, 1977; MEd in Counseling Psychology, U. Okla., 1978; PhD in Sociology, Clayton U., 1985. Ret. U.S. Army, 1960-82; radiologic technologist VA Hosp., Temple, Tex., 1983-84; vets. counselor Vets. Outreach Program, San Antonio, Tex., 1982-83; dir. personnel & mktg. Heran Pharms., San Antonio, Tex., 1988-91; prof. sociology Ctrl. Tech. Coll., Killeen, 1991-95; instr. sociology Tex. State Tech. Coll., Waco, 1995-96, Academia Assocs., 1996—; part-time instr. Ctrl. Tex. Coll., 1980-82, City Coll. Chgo., 1981, Big Bend C.C., Mannheim, Germany, 1981-82; instr. Acad. Health Scis., 1977-79. Contbr. articles to profl. jours. Coach Youth Soccer Orgns., San Antonio and Mannheim, 1976-82. Nat. Coll. Radiology Technologists fellow, 1968. Mem. AAUP, Am. Sociol. Assn., Soc. Applied Sociology, Am. Polit. Sci. Assn., La. Archeological Soc., Choctaw Nation of Okla., Order of Alhambra, KC, Masons, Soc. for the Study of Social Problems, Psi Beta (chpt. sponsor), Alpha Kappa Delta, Psi Chi, Sigma Eta Sigma (nat. dir.). Roman Catholic. Avocations: soccer, golf, paleo-historic anthropology. Home: 9310 Oak Hills Dr Temple TX 76502-5272 Office: Academia Assocs Waco TX 76705

SHARP, SHARON LEE, gerontology nurse; b. Beatrice, Nebr., Jan. 14, 1939; d. Clarence Alfred and Edna Clara (Grosshuesch) Wolters; m. Philip Butler, June 27, 1959 (div. 1964); m. Ted C. Sharp, Sept. 21, 1966 (div. 1988); children: Sheryl Butler, Philip Butler. Diploma, Lincoln Gen. Hosp., 1959. RN Nebr. Charge nurse Mary Lanning Meml. Hosp., Hastings, Nebr., 1960-61; asst. head nurse Ingleside State Hosp., Hastings, Nebr., 1961-62; charge nurse Rio Hondo Meml. Hosp., Downey, Calif., 1969-71, Santa Barbara (Calif.) Cottage Hosp., 1974-78; supr. Marlora Manor Convalescent Hosp., Long Beach, Calif., 1979-80; supr. Marlinda Nursing Home, Lynwood, Calif., 1982-84, dir. nursing, 1984-89; dir. nursing Ramona Care Ctr., El Monte, Calif., 1989-90, Oakview Convalescent Hosp., Tujunga, Calif., 1990-91, North Valley Nursing Ctr., Tujunga, Calif., 1992—; asst. dir. nursing Skyline Health Care Ctr. (Gran Care), L.A., 1993-94; resident assessment coord. Country Villa Rehab. Ctr., L.A., 1994-95; case mgr. Vitas Innovative Hospice Care, West Covina, Calif., 1995—; mem. adv. bd. Regional Occupational Program, Downey, 1985-86. Avocations: metaphysics, paranormal experiences, reading, alternative ways of healing, healing touch practitioner. Home: 2875 E Del Mar Blvd Pasadena CA 91107-4314

SHARP, WALTER LEN, secondary educator; b. Norfolk, Va., Nov. 26, 1943; s. Thomas Leonard and Mary Josephine (Messick) S.; m. Melodie Lynn Lambert, July 1, 1967; children: Lara, Ryan. BS in Secondary Edn., Old Dominion U., 1967; MS in Sci. Edn., Syracuse U., 1971; cert. advanced study in adminstrn., SUNY, Brockport, 1980. Cert. permanent earth sci. and biology tchr., supervision, adminstrn., N.Y. Dir. swimming and gymnasium Boys Clubs Norfolk, 1962-67; tchr. sci. Norfolk City Schs., 1967-69; tchr. earth sci. West Genesee Cen. Schs., Camillus, N.Y., 1969-72; tchr. sci., chmn. dept. Virginia Beach (Va.) City Schs., 1972-76; tchr. earth sci. Liverpool (N.Y.) Cen. Schs., 1976—; regent's writer N.Y. State Edn. Dept., Albany, 1988, 89, 90; mem. sci. com. N.Y. new Compact for Learning, Albany, 1991—; mem. earth sci. statement com. Am. Geol. Union, Washington, 1992; mem. NSTA for high schs. and tours; sci. tchr., manuscript renew and task force on exemplary programs; earthquake cons., writer NCEER SUNY, Buffalo; writer/contbr. for NSTA/NASA Meteor "Impacts" Act. Man. Author slide and script program Natural History of Central New York, 1987; contbg. writer AGU/FEMA National Earthquake Curriculum Guide, 1993. Contbr., advisor World Resources Inst., Washington, 1992. Recipient Tchr. Field award Earthwatch, Alaska, 1987, Excellence in Sci. Teaching award Prentice Hall/Stanys, 1988; Close-Up Found. fellow, 1993, Sci-Mat fellow, 1993, Presdl. awardee for N.Y., 1995. Mem. NSTA (STANYS liaison, 1994-96, Newmast award 1987, award for Innovations in H.S. Tchg. of Sci. 1993), Nat. Earth Sci. Tchrs. Assn. (pres. 1992-94, Disting. Svc. award 1993), Nat. Assn. Geol. Tchrs. (ea. sect. Outstanding Earth Sci. Tchr. award 1988), Sci. Tchrs. Assn. N.Y. (pres. 1991-92, Disting. svc. award 1988), Am. Fedn. Tchrs., Greenpeace, Optimists, Phi Delta Kappa (Tchr. of Yr. award 1990). Baptist. Avocations: travel, photography, collecting fossils, writing, sports. Home: 2731 Rolling Hills Rd Camillus NY 13031-8634 Office: Liverpool High Sch HSE 5 Wetzel Rd Liverpool NY 13090

SHARPE, AUBREY DEAN, college administrator; b. Miami, Fla., Oct. 4, 1944; s. William Gibson and Ila-Mae (Albritton) S.; m. Linda Lee Rush, Dec. 22, 1973. BA, E. Tex. Bapt. U., 1967; MDiv, Southwestern Bapt. Theol. Sem., Ft. Worth, 1970; MA, southwestern Bapt. Theol. Sem., Ft. Worth, 1972; EdD, U. No. Tex., 1993. Assoc. pastor edn. Trinity Bapt. Ch., Ft. Worth, Tex., 1970-72; minister edn. Polytechnic Bapt. Ch., Ft. Worth, Tex., 1972-73; dean community svcs. Tarrant County Jr. Coll., Ft. Worth, Tex., 1973-84; religion inst. Tarrant County Jr. Coll., Ft. Worth, 1976-78; nat. dir. tng. Presbyn. Ministers Fund, Phila., 1984-89; v.p. The Pat Petersen Collection, Ft. Worth, 1984-91; owner ADS Investments, Ft. Worth, 1984—; exec. dir. Regional Tng. and Devel. Complex Tyler (Tex.) Jr. Coll., 1989—. Pres. Ft. Wroth Boys Club, 1979; allocaitons chmn. United Way Tarrant County, Ft. Worth, 1981-87, Sr. Citizens, Inc., Ft. Worth, 1985-86, Tyler Metro YMCA, 1992-93; bd. dirs. United Way Tyler and Smith County, 1991-96, v.p. allocations/funding, bd. dirs., trainer for loaned exec. program, 1991-95; adv. bd. North Tex. Small Bus. Devel. Ctr., 1995-96. Recipient Nat. Sales Achievement award Nat. Assn. Life Underwriters, 1987, Nat. Sales Leader award 1987; recipient Achievers award Presbyn. Ministers Fund, 1987, Vol. Svc. Award, United Way of Tarrant County, 1987. Mem. ASTD (pres.-elect 1991, pres. 1992-93), Tex. Assn. Community Svcs. and Continuing Edn., Tex. Jr. Coll. Tchrs. Assn., Nat. Coun. for Community Svcs./Continuing Edn., Tex. Adminstrs. Continuing Edn., Tyler Area C. of C., Phi Delta Kappa. Republican. Baptist. Avocations: reading, collecting old books, landscaping. Home: 503 Towne Oaks Dr Tyler TX 75701-9536 Office: Tyler Jr Coll Regional Training Complex 1530 Ssw Loop # 323 Tyler TX 75701

SHARPE, CHARLES RICHARD, retail company executive; b. St. Catharines, Ont., Can., Feb. 11, 1925; s. James Walter and Anna B. (Clark) S.; m. Marjorie Agnes Pepler, Apr. 22, 1954; children: Lisette, David, Catherine, Sarah. BA in Bus. Adminstrn. with honors, U. Western Ont., 1950. Trainee Simpsons-Sears, Ltd. (now Sears Can., Inc.), Toronto, Ont., 1950-52, buyer, 1952-55, buying supr., 1955-62, gen. mdse. mgr., 1962-70, v.p. merchandising, 1970-79, chmn., chief exec. officer, dir., 1979-89, chmn., dir., 1989—; bd. dirs. Sears Can. Inc., Sears Acceptance Co. Inc., BCE Inc., Bell Can., Can. Imperial Bank Commerce, Mediacom Inc., Noranda Forest Inc., Omers Realty Corp. Bd. dirs. Sir Edmund Hillary Found., Wellesley Hosp.; mem. adv. coun. Sch. Bus. Adminstrn., U. Western Ont. With RCAF, 1943-46,92, (hon. col. 436T squadron). Mem. Toronto Club, York Club, Univ. Club, Toronto Golf Club. Anglican. Home: 759 Cardinal Pl, Mississauga, ON Canada L5J 2R8 Office: Sears Can Inc, 222 Jarvis St, Toronto, ON Canada M5B 2B8*

SHARPE, DANIEL ROGER, lawyer; b. Detroit, Mar. 13, 1948; s. Roger Holdsworth and Dorothy Jane Donner S.; m. Jane Paula Marinsky, Aug. 25, 1972; children: Leah, Rebecca, Anna. BA, U. Rochester, 1970; JD, Ohio State U., 1975. Bar: N.Y. 1976, U.S. Dist. Ct. 1976, U.S. Tax Ct. 1978. Assoc. Hodgson, Russ, Andrews, Woods & Goodyear, Buffalo, 1975-79, ptnr., 1980—; instr. Canisius Coll., Buffalo, 1987, 91; pres. N.Y. Employee Benefits Conf., Syracuse, N.Y., 1988-90. Author: (with others) Individual Retirement Plans, 1988, (with others) Taxation of Distributions from Qualified Plans, 1991. Bd. dirs., tax cons. Allentown Assn., Inc., Buffalo, 1977-78; tax cons. Parkside Cmty. Assn., Inc., Buffalo, 1980; bd. dirs. Concerned Ecumenical Ministry Upper West Side, Inc., Buffalo, 199397, v.p., 1996-97. Mem. ABA (employee benefits com. tax sect. 1989-96). Office: Hodgson Russ Andrews Woods & Goodyear 1800 One M & T Plz Buffalo NY 14203-2391

SHARPE, DONALD EDWARD, lawyer; b. Edmonton, Alta., Can., Oct. 24, 1937; came to U.S., 1945; s. Eldon Durwood Sharpe and Bertha Evelyn (Johnston) Skinner; m. JoAnn Firth; children: Jennifer, William, Gregory. BA, U. Md., 1960, LLB, 1963. Bar: Md. 1963, U.S. Dist. Ct. Md. 1964, U.S. Ct. Appeals (4th cir.) 1964, U.S. Dist. Ct. D.C. 1981. Law clk. to presiding judges U.S. Dist. Ct. Md., Balt., 1963-64; assoc. Piper & Marbury, Balt., 1964-67, 69-71, ptnr., 1971—; asst. U.S. atty. U.S. Atty.'s Office, Balt., 1967-69. Recent Decisions editor Md. Law Rev., 1963. Mem. ABA (chmn. products-torts and ins. practice sect. 1985-86, membership com. 1988-89, task force on selection and performance standards of counsel 1988-89), Order of Coif. Democrat. Presbyterian. Avocations: golf, volleyball, woodworking, gardening, fishing. Office: Piper & Marbury LLP 36 S Charles St Baltimore MD 21201-3020

SHARPE, HENRY DEXTER, JR., manufacturing company executive; b. Providence, May 5, 1923; s. Henry Dexter and Mary Elizabeth (Evans) S.; m. Peggy Plumer Boyd, Aug. 1, 1953; children: Henry Dexter, Douglas, Sarah. Grad., Brown U., Providence, 1945. With Brown & Sharpe Mfg. Co., Providence, 1946—, v.p., 1950-51, pres., 1951-76, chmn., chief exec. officer, 1976-80, chmn., 1980—; bd. dirs., mem. exec. com. Providence Jour. Co.; vice chancellor Brown U., 1986-87. Bd. dirs. R.I. Pub. Expenditure Coun.; trustee, fellow Brown U.; trustee Coll. of the Atlantic, 1992—. Lt. (j.g.) USNR, 1943-46. Mem. Am. Soc. Tool Engrs., Nat. Machine Tool Builders Assn. (pres. 1969-70), ASME, Machinery and Allied Products Inst. (ret. mem. exec. com.). Office: Pojac Point Rd North Kingstown RI 02852-1031

SHARPE, JAMES SHELBY, lawyer; b. Ft. Worth, Sept. 11, 1940; s. James Henry and Wanzel (Vanderbilt) S.; m. Martha Moudy Holland, June 9, 1962; children: Marthanne Freeman, Caren Roark, Stephen. BA, U. Tex., 1962, JD, 1965. Bar: Tex. 1965, U.S. Dist. Ct. (no. dist.) Tex. 1966, U.S. Dist. Ct. (ea. dist.) Tex. 1993, U.S. Ct. Appeals (5th and 6th cirs.) 1982, U.S. Ct. Appeals (fed. cir.) 1983, U.S. Ct. Appeals (10th cir.) 1992, U.S. Supreme Ct. 1972. Briefing atty. for chief justice Supreme Ct. of Tex., Austin, 1965-66; ptnr. Brown, Herman, Scott, Dean & Miles, Ft. Worth, 1966-84, Gandy Michener Swindle Whitaker & Pratt, Ft. Worth, 1984-87; shareholder Sharpe & Tillman, Ft. Worth, 1988—; adj. prof. polit. sci. Tex. Christian U., Ft. Worth, 1969-79, Dallas Bapt. U., 1987, 1992-94; gen. counsel U.S.A. Radio Network, Internat. Christian Media, Denton Pub. Co. Pres. Ft. Worth-Tarrant County Jr. Bar, 1969-70, bd. dirs., 1968, sec., 1968, v.p., 1968-69; head marshal USA-USSR Track and Field Championships, Ft. Worth, USA-USSR Jr. Track and Field Championships, Austin, Tex., Relays, Austin, 1963—, NCAA Nat. Track and Field Championships, 1976, 80, 85, 92, 95, S.W. Conf. Indoor Track and Field Championships, 1987-96, Olympic Festival, San Antonio, 1993, Colorado Springs, 1995; 12 time head marshal S.W. Conf. Track and Field Championships. USA/Mobil Track Championship, 1994, 95; USA Nat. Jr. Track Championship, 1994, 95. Mem. ABA, State Bar of Tex. (dist. 7-A grievance com. 1983-85, com. adminstrn. of justice 1985-92, com. on ct. rules 1992—, chmn. 1992-93, 93-94). Baptist. Home: 8304 Crosswind Dr Fort Worth TX 76179-3003 Office: Sharpe & Tillman 500 Throckmorton St Ste 2400 Fort Worth TX 76102-3811

SHARPE, KEITH YOUNT, retired lawyer; b. Hiddenite, N.C., July 11, 1930; s. Ruel Yount and Eileen Lois (Lackey) S.; m. Margaret Joyce Land, Aug. 27, 1955 (div.); children: Jonathan, Matthew, Leonora, Felicia. A.B., Duke U., 1952; J.D., Wake Forest U., 1957, M.B.A., 1982. Bar: N.C. 1957. Practiced law Winston-Salem, N.C., 1957-62, 82-94; asst. solicitor Mcpl. Ct. of Winston-Salem, 1958-60; with Pilot Freight Carriers Inc., Winston-Salem, 1962-82; sr. v.p. Pilot Freight Carriers Inc., 1967-76, v.p., 1976-82; also dir.; v.p., dir. Comml. Automotive Co., 1967-76, Terminal Warehouse Corp., 1967-82; bd. govs. So. Motor Carriers Rate Conf., 1977-81. Served with inf. U.S. Army, 1952-54. Mem. Assn. Transp. Practitioners, Phi Alpha Delta, Theta Chi. Democrat. Episcopalian. Home: Box 19633 Asheville NC 28815

SHARPE, MYRON EMANUEL, publisher, editor, writer; b. Chester, Pa., Sept. 10, 1928; s. Abraham Maxwell and Emma (Friedman) S.; m. Jacqueline Steiner, 1959 (div.); children: Susanna, Matthew; m. Carole S. Brafman, 1983; children: Elizabeth, Hannah. B.A., Swarthmore Coll., 1950; M.A., U. Mich., 1951, postgrad., 1951-54. Pres. Modern Factors Corp., Phila., 1957; founder, chmn. bd., pres. M.E. Sharpe, Inc. (Pub.), Armonk, N.Y., 1958—, writer, editor, 1955—; founder, exec. dir. Com. to Save the Life of Henry Spetter, 1974; co-founder, coord. Initiative Com. for Nat. Econ. Planning, 1974-76; participant in drafting Full Employment and Balanced Growth Act of 1978; co-founder, pres. M.E. Sharpe, Ltd. (Arts and Antiques), New Canaan, Conn., 1981-83. Author: John Kenneth Galbraith and the Lower Economics, 1973. Chmn. Pro Arte Chamber Singers of Conn., 1982-83; pres. Waveny Chamber Music Soc., 1987—; econ. advisor to Senator Birch Bayh for presdl. campaign, 1975. Office: M E Sharpe Inc 80 Business Park Dr Armonk NY 10504-1710

SHARPE, RICHARD SAMUEL, architectural company executive; b. New Haven, Conn., Aug. 7, 1930; s. Herman and Betty (Silberman) S.; m. Anne Johnson; children: Peter, Andrew, Rebecca. BArch, U. Pa., 1953; postgrad., U. Liverpool, Eng., 1953-54. Registered architect, Conn., N.Y., R.I., Mass. Prin. Richard Sharpe Assocs. P.C., Norwich, Conn., 1957—; v.p. Pan-Am. Fedn. Architects, 1972-78. Bd. dirs. Conn. Humanities council, 1974-78; pres. Conn. Habitat, 1978-79; pres. Thames River Devel. Corp., 1982-83. Recipient Ann. award Producers Council, 1974-78, Ann. Craft award Slater Mus., Norwich, 1986, spl. citation AIA, 1978. Fellow Am. Inst. Archs.; mem. Conn. Soc. Archs. (v.p. 1963, pres. 1966), Hist. Dist. Com. (com. chmn.), S.E. Conn. Grievence Comm., Rotary. Avocations: wood pottery, photography, pre-Columbian art collecting, sailing. Office: Richard Sharpe Assocs PC 30 Connecticut Ave Norwich CT 06360-1502

SHARPE, ROBERT F., SR., writer, lecturer, educator, consultant, publisher; b. Florence, Ala., Sept. 8, 1926; s. Thomas Leslie and Lida (Gammill) S.; m. Jane A. Sharpe, Dec. 28, 1948; children: Susan, Robert Jr., Paul, Timothy. BS, Memphis State U., 1957. Life ins. agt. Pilot Life Ins. Co., Greensboro, N.C., 1950-54; agt., supr. Vol. Life Ins. Co., Chattanooga, 1954; agt. Crown Life Ins. Co., Toronto, Can., 1954-59; sec. stewardship Good News Broadcasting Assn., Lincoln, Nebr., 1959-63; exec. dir. Reformed Presbyn. Fedn., St. Louis, 1963-65; founder Robert F. Sharpe & Co. Inc., Memphis, 1963-93, sr. cons., 1993—; founder, exec. dir. The Nat. Planned Giving Inst., 1967-93, The Nat. Planned Giving Assn., 1985. Author: The Planned Giving Idea Book, Before You Give Another Dime, 27 Plus Ways to Increase Giving to Your Church; pub. monthly newsletter Give and Take; contbr. articles to publs. Bd. trustees Ch. Health Ctr., Memphis, Endowment Assn. Coll. William and Mary, Williamsburg, Va.; pres. Memphis Mus. Inc., 1994-95. With USN, 1944-47, PTO. Recipient Disting. Svc. award Memphis State U., 1970. Mem. Soc. Entrepreneurs. Methodist. Avocations: sailing, music. Office: 5050 Poplar Ave Fl 7 Memphis TN 38157-0101 Office: College of William & Mary 519 Richmond Rd Williamsburg VA 23185

SHARPE, ROBERT FRANCIS, equipment manufacturing company executive; b. Buffalo, Mar. 29, 1921; s. Bertram Francis and Agnes (Coppinger) S.; m. Audrey Rembe, July 10, 1943; 1 son, Robert Francis. B.S. in Chem. Engring, Rensselaer Poly. Inst., 1942. With Duriron Co., 1946—; mgr. pump sales Duriron Co., Dayton, 1955-58; dir. research, devel. Duriron Co., 1958-63, v.p. plastics ops., 1963-65, exec. v.p., 1967-68, pres., chief operating officer, 1968-69, pres., 1969-76, chief exec. officer, 1969-79, chmn. bd., 1978-83. Served with USAAF, 1943-46. Mem. Am. Inst. Chem. Engrs., Hydraulic Inst. Home: 15520 Whitney Ln Naples FL 33963-7611 also: PO Box 8820 Dayton OH 45401-8820

SHARPE, ROCHELLE PHYLLIS, journalist; b. Gary, Ind., Apr. 27, 1956; d. Norman Nathaniel and Shirley (Kaplan) S. BA, Yale U., 1978. Reporter Concord (N.H.) Monitor, 1979-81; statehouse rep. Wilmington News Jour., Dover, Del., 1981-85; statehouse corr. Gannett News Svc., Albany, N.Y., 1985; nat. reporter Gannett News Svc., Washington, 1986-93; staff reporter social issues The Wall St. Jour., Washington, 1993—. Contbr. articles to profl. jours. Recipient Pulitzer prize for series in child abuse, Columbia U., 1991. Home: 2500 Q St NW Apt 315 Washington DC 20007-4360 Office: Wall St Jour Washington Bur 1025 Connecticut Ave NW Ste 800 Washington DC 20036-5405

SHARPE, ROLAND LEONARD, retired engineering company executive, earthquake and structural engineering consultant; b. Shakopee, Minn., Dec. 18, 1923; s. Alfred Leonard and Ruth Helen (Carter) S.; m. Jane Esther Steele, Dec. 28, 1946; children: Douglas Rolfe, Deborah Lynn, Sheryl Anne. BS in Civil Engring., U. Mich., 1947, MSE, 1949. Registered civil engr. and structural engr., Calif. Designer, Cummins & Barnard, Inc., Ann Arbor, Mich., 1947-48; instr. engring. U. Mich., 1948-50; exec. v.p. John A. Blume & Assocs., engrs., San Francisco, 1950-73; chmn., founder Engring. Decision Analysis Co., Inc., Cupertino, 1974-87; cons. earthquake engr., 1987—; mng. dir. EDAC, GmBH, Frankfurt, Germany, 1974-82; dir. EDAC; pres. Calif. Devel. & Engring. Co., Inc., Las Vegas, Nev., 1973-81; mem. nat. earthquake hazard reduction program adv. com. overviewing Fed. Emergency Mgmt. Agy., U.S. Geol. Survey, NSF and Nat. Inst. Stds. and Tech., 1990-93. Author: (with J. Blume, E.G. Kost) Earthquake Engineering for Nuclear Facilities, 1971. Mem. Planning Commn., Palo Alto, 1955-60; mng. dir. Applied Tech. Coun., Palo Alto, 1973-83; dir. Earthquake Engring. Rsch. Inst., 1972-75, now mem.; project dir., editor Tentative Provisions for Devel. of Seismic Regulations for Buildings, 1978; tech. mgr., contbr., editor Data Processing Facilities: Guidelines for Earthquake Hazard Mitigation, 1987. Served with USMC, 1942-46. Author, co-author over 200 engring. papers and reports; author of chpts.: (with others) Seismic Safety Guide, 1995. Fellow ASCE (hon. mem. 1994, chmn. dynamic effects com., 1978-80, exec. com. structural div. 1980-84, 89-93, chmn. 1983, mgmt. group B 1989-93, Earnest E. Howard award 1994); mem. Japan Structural Cons. Assn. (hon. mem. 1992), Structural Engrs. Assn. Calif. (dir. 1971-73, chmn. seismology com. 1972-74), Structural Engrs. No. Calif. (dir. 1969-71, life mem.), Am. Concrete Inst. (life), Structural Engrs. World Congress (pres. 1995—). Recipient citation for contbn. to constrn. industry Engring. News Record, 1978-79, 86-87; chmn. U.S. Joint Com. on Earthquake Engring., 1982-88. Home: 10320 Rolly Rd Los Altos CA 94024-6520 Office: Sharpe Struct Engrs 10051 Pasadena Ave Cupertino CA 95014 *Personal philosophy: One's conduct should be beyond reproach both morally and ethically and I should serve each of my clients to the best of my ability.*

SHARPE, SHANNON, professional football player; b. Chgo., June 26, 1968. Student, Savannah State U. Tight end Denver Broncos, 1990—; player AFC Championship Game, 1991. Named to Pro Bowl Team, 1992, 93, Sporting News NFL All-Pro Team, 1993. Office: Denver Broncos 13655 E Broncos Pkwy Englewood CO 80112

SHARPE, STERLING, professional football player; b. Chgo., Apr. 6, 1965. BA, U. S.C., 1987. With Green Bay Packers, 1988-95. Named to Sporting News Coll. All-Am., 1987; named receiving leader NFL, 1989, 92, wide receiver All-Pro Team NFL, 1989. Played in Pro Bowl, 1989, 90, 92; named to Pro Bowl, 1993.

SHARPE, WILLIAM FORSYTH, economics educator; b. Cambridge, Mass., June 16, 1934; s. Russell Thornley Sharpe and Evelyn Forsyth (Jillson) Maloy; m. Roberta Ruth Branton, July 2, 1954 (div. Feb. 1986); children: Deborah Ann, Jonathan Forsyth; m. Kathryn Dorothy Peck, Apr. 5, 1986. AB, UCLA, 1955, MA, 1956, PhD, 1961. Economist Rand Corp., 1957-61; asst. prof. econs. U. Wash., 1961-63, assoc. prof., 1963-67, prof., 1967-68; prof. U. Calif., Irvine, 1968-70; Timken prof. fin. Stanford U., 1970-89, Timken prof. emeritus, 1989-92; prin. William F. Sharpe Assocs., 1986-92; prof.fin. Stanford U., 1993-95, STANCO 25 prof. of fin., 1995—. Author: The Economics of Computers, 1969, Portfolio Theory and Capital Markets, 1970; co-author: Fundamentals of Investments, 1989, 2d edit., 1993, Investments, 5th edit., 1995. With U.S. Army, 1956-57. Recipient Graham and Dodd award Fin Analysts' Fedn., 1972, '73, '86-88. Nicholas Molodovsky award, 1989. Nobel prize in econ. scis., 1990. Mem. Am. Fin. Assn. (v.p. 1979, pres. 1980), Western Fin. Assn. (Enduring Contbn. award 1989), Ea. Fin. Assn. (Disting. Scholar award 1991), Am. Econ. Assn., Phi Beta Kappa.

SHARPE, WILLIAM NORMAN, JR., mechanical engineer, educator; b. Chatham County, N.C., Apr. 15, 1938; s. William Norman and Margaret Horne (Womble) S.; m. Margaret Ellen Strowd, Aug. 21, 1959; children: William N., J. Ashley. BS, N.C. State U., 1960, MS, 1961; PhD, Johns Hopkins U., 1966. Registered profl. engr., Mich., La., Md. Assoc. prof. Mich. State U., East Lansing, 1970-75, prof., 1975-78; prof., chmn. dept. mech. engring. La. State U., Baton Rouge, 1978-83; prof., dept. mech. engring. Johns Hopkins U., Balt., 1983—, Decker prof. mech. engring., 1985—. Recipient Alexander von Humboldt award, Fed. Republic Germany, 1989. Fellow ASME (Nadai award 1993), Soc. Exptl. Mechanics (Tatnall award, exec. bd. 1979-81, pres. 1984-85); mem. ASTM, Am. Soc. Engring. Edn. Home: 220 Ridgewood Rd Baltimore MD 21210-2539 Office: Johns Hopkins U Dept Mech Engring Latrobe Hall Rm 126 Baltimore MD 21218

SHARPLES, WINSTON SINGLETON, automobile importer and distributor; b. Springfield, Mass., Oct. 24, 1932; s. Winston Singleton and Carmela (Parrino) S.; m. Jeanette Williams, July 1961 (div. Apr. 1981); children: John, Hadley, Gillian; m. Ruth Emily Lissak, June 26, 1981. BA, Harvard Coll., 1953; postgrad. drama, Yale U., 1956-57; MFA, Carnegie Mellon U., 1959; postgrad., Univ. Md., 1978-80. Freelance writer, 1959—; producer, dir. Mon. Valley Playhouse, Charleroi, Pa., 1959, Robin Hood Theater, Arden, Del., 1960-61; pres., film and music editor Synchro-Sound Inc., N.Y.C., 1961-71; prof. CUNY, N.Y.C., 1969-74, Temple Univ., Phila., 1974-76, U. Md., College Park, 1978-79; adminstr. film preservation and documentation Am. Film Inst., Washington, 1976-78; prof. Howard Univ., Washington, 1978-80; pres. Cantab Motors, Ltd., Round Hill, Va., 1984—. Author: (with others) A Primer for Film-Making, 1971—; supr. Am. Film Inst. Catalog of Feature Films, 1960-69, 77; editor, music editor films and cartoons; contbr. articles to profl. jours. and mags. With U.S. Army, 1953-56. Nat. Endowment for the Humanities grantee, 1977. Mem. ASCAP, Archeol. Soc. Va., Am. Studies Assn., Univ. Film Assn. (v.p. 1975-76), Soc. for Cinema Studies, Soc. Automotive Engrs., Washington Automotive Press Assn., Morgan Car Club, Land Rover Owners Assn. Va., British Automobile Mfrs. Assn., Harvard Club (N.Y.C.). Democrat. Avocations: forestry, archeology. Home: 16657 Tree Crops Ln Round Hill VA 20141-9310 Office: Cantab Motors Ltd Valley Indsl Park 12 E Richardson Ln Purcellville VA 20132-3500

SHARPLESS, JOSEPH BENJAMIN, former county official; b. Takoma Park, Md., Feb. 4, 1933; s. William Raiford and Julia Maude (Rouse) S.; m. Nancy Kathleen Steffen, July 28, 1962 (dec. Feb. 1988); 1 child, Carole Marie. BA, Earlham Coll., 1955; MS, Pa. State U., 1960. Instr. recreation Montgomery County Recreation Dept., Rockville, Md., 1957-58; from program supr. to dir. Recreation and Parks Dept., Livingston, N.J., 1959-70; chief recreation svc. Md.-Nat. Capital Park and Planning Commn. Prince George's County, Riverdale, Md., 1970-77, parks and recreation div. chief, 1977-95; ret., 1995—. Contbr. articles to profl. jours. V.p. Montpelier Cmty. Assn., South Laurel, Md., 1983-84, pres., 1985; mem. Md. Sports Adv. Com., 1988-92; Md. State Games Commr., 1986-91; bd. regents, instr. Sch. Sports Mgmt., N.C. State u., 1989-92; nat. volleyball chmn. AAU, 1966-69, 72, volleyball chmn. N.J. chpt. 1961-70, volleyball chmn. Potomac Valley chpt., 1971-73; mem. volleyball games staff 1996 Olympic Games, Atlanta; staff for FNB World Congress, 1996; dir. volleyball Spl. Olympics Internat., 1994—. Mem. U.S. Volleyball Assn. (bd. dirs. 1973—, mem. exec. com. 1976-80, 85-89, 92-96, v.p. 1973-90, regional commr. 1965-78, nat. ofcl. 1967-96, exec. cons. 1989-91, corp. sec. 1992-96, mng. editor pubs. 1994—, numerous awards), Nat. Intercollegiate Soccer Ofcls. Assn. 9sec. 1966-68, treas. 1968-70), Nat. Recreation and Pks. Assn. (Disting. Svc. award Mid-Atlantic fellow), Am. Pk. & Recreation Soc. (bd. dirs. 1977-80, nat. coun., coun. affiliate pres.), N.J. Recreation and Pks. Assn. (sec. 1965, v.p. 1965, pres. 1967), Md. Recreation and Pk. Assn. (v.p. 1975-77, pres. 1977-78, Mem. of Yr. 1975, Citation 1985), Ret. Life Profl. (Disting. Fellow award 1996), N.J. Soccer Ofcls. Assn. (sec. 1966-70), Nat. Capitol Area Bd. Volleyball Ofcls. (sec. 1985-89). Republican. Mem. Soc. of Friends. Home: 8754 Oxwell Ln Laurel MD 20708-2469

SHARPLESS, RICHARD KENNEDY, lawyer; b. Springdale, Pa., Mar. 30, 1911; s. Charles Thomas and Luella Lincoln (Kennedy) S.; m. Eleanor Ridgway Crowther, Mar. 4, 1946; m. Nancy Jean Sleight, July 23, 1948; children: Kendall Deborah, Richard Kennedy, Lincoln Kennedy. AB, Boston U., 1932; LLB, Harvard U., 1935, JD, 1969. Bar: Pa. 1936, Calif. 1947, Hawaii 1949, U.S. Ct. Appeals (9th dist.) 1964, U.S. Supreme Ct. 1960. With firm Dalzell, McFall & Pringle, Pitts., 1936-42; mem. legal sect. trust dept. Bank of Am., Los Angeles, 1946-48; atty. Office Dist. Engr., Honolulu, 1948-49; with Office Atty. Gen., T.H., 1949-55, atty. gen., 1956-57; mem. Lewis, Saunders & Sharpless (and predecessor firm), 1957-68; mng. dir. City and County of Honolulu, 1968-72, 75-78, corp. counsel, 1973-75, 78-80; of counsel firm Case, Kay & Lynch, Honolulu, 1980-81. Mem. Planning Commn. City and County of Honolulu, 1966-68, chmn., 1968; asst. to Town Atty. of Chapel Hill, 1984-93; bd. dirs. United Way, 1982-85, Pub. Sch. Found., 1984-89, Village Cos. Found., 1987-89; mem. exec. com. PTA Thrift Show, 1986-90. Capt. C.E., AUS, 1942-46. Mem. Bar Assn. Hawaii (pres. 1960-61), Chapel Hill-Carrboro C. of C. (v.p. 1982-85), SAR (pres. Hawaii 1961), Kiwanis. Episcopalian. Home: 134 Berry Patch Ln Chapel Hill NC 27514

SHARPTON, ALFRED CHARLES, minister, political activist. Founder, pres. Nat. Action Network, Inc., Bklyn., 1991—. Office: Nat Action Network Inc 1133 Bedford Ave Brooklyn NY 11216

SHARROW, LEONARD, musician, educator; b. N.Y.C., Aug. 4, 1915; s. Saul and Sonia (Berson) S.; m. Emily M. Kass, Oct. 22, 1942; 1 son, Neil Jason. Grad., Juilliard Sch. Music, 1935. Prin. bassoonist Nat. Symphony Orch., Washington, 1935-37; bassoonist NBC Symphony, N.Y.C., 1937-41; prin. bassoonist NBC Symphony, 1947-51, Detroit Symphony, 1946-47, Chgo. Symphony Orch., 1951-64, Pitts. Symphony Orch., 1977-87; mem. faculty Juilliard Sch. Music, 1949-51; mem. faculty, performer Gunnison Music Camp, Western State Coll., Colo., 1962-63; pvt. teaching, 1946—; tchr. bassoon Ind. U. Sch. Music, Bloomington, Ind., part-time 1963-64; prof. music (bassoon) Ind. U. Sch. Music, 1964-77; assoc. prof. Indiana U. of Pa., 1979-80; part-time faculty Pa. State U., 1979-80, 80-81; adj. prof. Sch. of Music, Carnegie Mellon U., 1981-86; mem. bassoon faculty New Eng. Conservatory Music, Boston, 1986-89; faculty, performer New Coll. Summer Music Festival, 1976, 77, 79-86, Aspen Music Festival, 1967—, Waterloo Music Festival, 1979, 80, 83, 86, Banff Ctr. for Arts, Can., 1982, Johannesen Internat. Sch. Arts Summer Festival, Victoria, B.C., Can., 1984; solo bassoonist World Philharm. Orch., Stockholm, 1985; Alan R. Rose fellow, guest artist, lectr., performer Victorian Coll. Arts, Melbourne, Canberra, Sydney, Australia, 1989; mem. faculty, performer Nagano Aspen Music Festival, Japan, 1990-94; mem. faculty Marrowstone Music Festival, Port Townsend, Wash., 1995—. Mem. Am. Woodwind Quintet, 1964-77; Editor: major works for bassoon; performances chamber music groups, Washington, N.Y.C., Chgo. others; participant, Pablo Casals Festival, Prades, France, 1953, soloist, NBC Symphony, Chgo. Symphony Orch., Pitts. Symphony, Aspen Festival Orch.; TV concerts, Chgo. and Pitts. symphonies; solo recs.: Mozart Bassoon Concerto in B flat Major, with Arturo Toscanini and NBC Symphony, Vivaldi Concerti for Bassoon with Max Goberman and N.Y. Symphonietta, Leonard Sharrow Plays Bassoon Solos, with piano, Concerto da Camera for Bassoon and Orch. (Dan Welcher), Concerto for bassoon and orch. (Ray Luke); assisting artist: A Baroque Trumpet recital with Gerard Schwarz. Served with AUS, 1941-45. Recipient award Toscanini Collection Assn., 1985. Mem. AAUP, Pi Kappa Lambda. Office: 3153 Coppertree Dr Bloomington IN 47401-9699

SHARROW, MARILYN JANE, library administrator; bd. Oakland, Calif.; d. Charles L. and H. Evelyn S.; m. Lawrence J. Davis. BS in Design, U. Mich., 1967, MALS, 1969. Librarian Detroit Pub. Libr., 1968-70; head fine arts dept. Syracuse (N.Y.) U. Librs., 1970-73; dir. libr. Roseville (Mich.) Pub. Libr., 1973-75; asst. dir. librs. U. Wash., 1975-77, assoc. dir. librs., 1978-79; dir. libraries U. Man., Winnipeg, Can., 1979-82; chief libr. U. Toronto, Can., 1982-85; univ. libr. U. Calif., Davis, 1985—. Recipient Woman of Yr. in Mgmt. award Winnipeg YWCA, 1982; named Woman of Distinction, U. Calif. Faculty Women's Rsch. Group, 1985. Mem. ALA, Assn. Rsch. Librs. (bd. dirs., v.p., pres-elect 1989-90, pres. 1990-91, chair sci. tech. work group 1994—, rsch. collections com. 1993-95), Online Computer Libr. Ctr.-Rsch. Librs. Adv. Com. (vice chmn. 1992-93, chair 1993-94), Calif. State Network Resources Lib. Com. Office: U Calif Shields Lib Davis CA 95616

SHARTLE, KEITH ROBERT, producer. BA, UCLA, 1974. Purchasing agt. Profl. Photosystems Corp., 1970, v.p., gen. mgr. retail and photo supply div.; with client rels. and contracts, photography and film editing depts. Dream Quest Images, Simi Valley, Calif., 1982, bus. mgr., 1987, exec. producer Film divsn., 1987-94, pres. Film Group, 1994-96; sr. v.p. Dream Quest Images subs. Walt Disney Co., Simi Valley, 1996—. Exec. producer of visual effects for films including The Abyss, Total Recall, Scrooged, Short Circuit 2, Big Business, The Lost Boys, Crimson Tide; overseer prodn. of effects for feature films, TV episodes and movies, numerous film attractions worldwide theme parks. Office: Dream Quest Images 2635 Park Center Dr Simi Valley CA 93065-6212

SHARWELL, WILLIAM GAY, retired university president and company executive; b. Newark, July 26, 1920; s. William G. Sharwell and Lillian Kenny; m. Jacqueline Larocque, Oct. 22, 1960; children: William L., Paul L. BS, Seton Hall U., 1941, DBA (hon.), 1980; MBA, NYU, 1950, Harvard U., 1952; DCS, Harvard U., 1960; LLD (hon.), Pace U., 1979. V.p., comptr. N.Y. Tel., N.Y.C., 1967-68, exec. v.p. ops., 1968-76; sr. v.p. AT&T, N.Y.C., 1976-84; pres. Pace U., N.Y.C., 1984-90; ret., 1990; bd. dirs. U.S. Life Corp., N.Y.C., U.S. Life Ins. Co., N.Y.C., Am. Biogenetic Scis., Inc., Copiague, N.Y., Associated Solo Artists, TII Industries, Inc., Toa Alta, P.R.; gen. ptnr. Equitable Capital Ptnrs., L.P. Mem. editorial bd. Ency. of Profl. Mgmt., 1978. Bd. dirs. Internat. House; trustee Coll. New Rochelle, N.Y. Mem. Harvard Club (N.Y.C.). Avocations: tennis, kite flying, video editing.

SHASHOUA, VICTOR E., pharmaceutical company executive; b. Kermanshah, Persia, Nov. 15, 1929; s. Ezra S. and Violet S. (Mouallem) S.; m. Angela M. Saleh, June 9, 1955; children: Karen, Edward, Michael. BSc, London U., 1952; PhD, U. Del., 1956. Rsch. assoc. DuPont Exptl. Sta., Wilmington, Del., 1952-64, MIT, Cambridge, 1964-70; assoc. prof. neurosci. Harvard Med. Sch., Boston, 1970-92, lectr., 1993—; assoc. biochemist McLean Hosp., Belmont, Mass., 1970-92; chief scientific officer, chmn. Neuromedica Inc., Cambridge, 1992—; adj. prof. pharmacology and exptl. therapeutics Tufts U. Sch. Medicine, Boston, 1993-95. Contbr. articles to profl. jours.; patentee in field; mem. editorial bd. Jour. Neurochem. Rsch., 1992—. Recipient award KcKnight Found., Grant Found., 1971-73. Mem. Soc. for Neurosci., Am. Soc. for Neurochemistry, Internat. Soc. for

Neurochemistry, Am. Assn. for Sci. Avocations: skiing, fishing, music, tennis. Office: Neuromedica Inc 99 Erie St Cambridge MA 02139-4534

SHASTEEN, DONALD EUGENE, government official; b. Englewood, Colo., Dec. 3, 1928; s. George Donald and Frances True (Meyers) S.; m. Shirley Mae Johnson, Aug. 8, 1954; children: Jon Randolph, Ron Winston, Sherilyn Sue. B.A. in Journalism, U. Colo., 1950. Reporter Omaha World-Herald, Des Moines, 1954-58, Lincoln, Nebr., 1958-66; exec. asst. to Senator Carl T. Curtis of Nebr., Washington, 1966-73, adminstrv. asst., 1973-78; adminstrv. asst. to Sen. Gordon J. Humphrey, 1979-80; with transition group Senate Republican Conf., 1980; dep. under sec. for legislation and intergovtl. affairs Dept. Labor, 1981-83, dep. asst. sec. for vets. employment, 1983-85, asst. sec. for vets. employment and tng., 1985-89; chmn. exec. com. Am. World Svcs., Inc.; v.p. Cocke & Phillips, Inc. Rep. nominee for U.S. Senate Nebr., 1978. Served with U.S. Army, 1951-52. Mem. Am. Legion, VFW, Am. Vets., Disabled Am. Vets., Phi Delta Theta. Republican. Lutheran.

SHASTID, JON BARTON, wine company executive; b. Hannibal, Mo., Nov. 21, 1914; s. Jon Shepherd and Mary (Barton) S.; m. Natalie Kiliani, Dec. 16, 1944; children—Lucinda, Jon G.H., Victoria A., Thomas Bartwyn. Bar: Calif. bar 1959; C.P.A., Calif., Kans. Pub. accountant Dodge City, Kans., 1938-42; v.p. finance Johnson Bronze Co., New Castle, Pa., 1946-54; exec. v.p., treas. E. & J. Gallo Winery, Modesto, Calif., 1954-88; pres. Gallo Wine Co. of La. at New Orleans, 1960-89. City councilman, Modesto, 1961-69. Served to capt. USAAF, 1942-46. Mem. State Bar of Calif., Am. Bar Assn., Calif. Soc. C.P.A.'s. Home and Office: PO Box 3808 Modesto CA 95352-3808

SHATIN, JUDITH, music composing educator; b. Boston, Nov. 11, 1949; d. Leo and Harriet Evelyn (Sommer) S.; m. Michael Kubovy, June 28, 1992. AB, Douglass, Coll., 1971; MM, Julliard Sch., 1974; PhD, Princeton U., 1979. Asst. prof. U. Va., Charlottesville, 1979-85, assoc. prof., 1985-92, prof., 1992—; dir. Va. Ctr. Computer Music, 1988—. Composer (piano concerto) Passion of St. Cecilia, 1985, (flute concerto) Ruan, 1985, (soprano and tape) Three Summers Heat, 1989 (Barlow Found. Commn.), Piping the Earth (commd. by Women's Philharm.), 1990, Stringing the Bow (commd. Va. Chamber Orch.), 1992, COAL (commd. as part of 2-yr. retrospective of work, sponsored by Lila Wallace-Readers Digest Arts Ptnrs. Program), 1994, (string quartet) Janus Quartet, 1994, (string quartet and electronic playback) Elijah's Chariot (commd. Kronos Quartet). Nat. Endowment for Arts Composer fellow, 1980, 85, 89, 92; recipient award Va. Commn. for the Arts, 1989. Mem. Am. Music Ctr., Am. Women Composers (pres. 1989-93), Am. Composers Alliance (bd. dirs. 1993—). Avocations: swimming, yoga, hiking.

SHATKIN, AARON JEFFREY, biochemistry educator; b. Providence, July 18, 1934; s. Morris and Doris S.; m. Joan A. Lynch, Nov. 30, 1957; 1 son, Gregory Martin. A.B., Bowdoin Coll., 1956, D.Sc. (hon.), 1979; Ph.D., Rockefeller Inst., 1961. Sr. asst. scientist NIH, Bethesda, Md., 1961-63; research chemist NIH, 1963-68; vis. scientist Salk Inst., La Jolla, Calif., 1968-69; assoc. mem. dept. cell biology Roche Inst. Molecular Biology, Nutley, N.J., 1968-73; full mem. Roche Inst. Molecular Biology, 1973-77, head molecular virology lab., 1977-86, head dept. cell biology, 1983-86; dir. N.J. Ctr. Advanced Biotech. Medicine, 1986—; prof. molecular genetics UMDNJ, 1986—; univ. prof. molecular biology Rutgers U., New Brunswick, N.J., 1986—; adj. prof. cell biology Rockefeller U.; vis. prof. molecular biology Princeton U. Mem. editl. bd. Jour. Virology, 1969-82, Archives of Biochemistry and Biophysics, 1972-82, Virology, 1973-76, Comprehensive Virology, 1974-82, Jour. Biol. Chemistry, 1977-83, 94—, RNA Jour., 1995—; editor Advances in Virus Research, 1983—, Jour. Virology, 1973-77; editor-in-chief Molecular and Cellular Biology, 1980-90. Served with USPHS, 1961-63. Recipient U.S. Steel Found. prize in molecular biology, 1977, N.J. Sci. and Tech. Pride award, 1989, Thomas Edison Sci. award State of N.J., 1991; Rockefeller fellow, 1956-61. Fellow Am. Acad. Microbiology, N.Y. Acad. Scis.; mem. NAS, AAAS, Am. Soc. Microbiology, Am. Soc. Biol. Chemists, Am. Soc. Virology, Am. Chem. Soc., Am. Soc. Cell Biology, Harvey Soc. Home: 1381 Rahway Rd Scotch Plains NJ 07076-3452 Office: Ctr Advanced Biotech and Medicine 679 Hoes Ln Piscataway NJ 08854-5638

SHATNER, WILLIAM, actor; b. Montreal, Que., Can., Mar. 22, 1931; s. Joseph and Anne S.; m. Gloria Rand, Aug. 12, 1956 (div. Mar. 1969); m. Marcy Lafferty, Oct. 20, 1973; 3 daus. B.A., McGill U., 1952. Stage debut, 1952; appeared Montreal Playhouse, summers 1952, 53; played juvenile roles Canadian Repertory Theatre, Ottawa, 1952-53, 53-54; appeared Stratford Shakespeare Festival, Ont., 1954-56; Broadway appearances include Tamburlaine the Great, 1956, The World of Suzie Wong, 1958, A Shot in the Dark, 1961; films include The Brothers Karamazov, 1958, The Explosive Generation, 1961, Judgement at Nuremburg, 1961, The Intruder, 1962, The Outrage, 1964, Dead of Night, 1974, The Devil's Rain, 1975, Star Trek, 1979, The Kidnapping of the President, 1979, Star Trek: The Wrath of Khan, 1982, Star Trek III: The Search for Spock, 1984, Star Trek IV: The Voyage Home, 1986, (director) Star Trek V: The Final Frontier, 1989, Star Trek VI: The Undiscovered Country, 1991, National Lampoon's Loaded Weapon, 1992, Star Trek: Generations, 1994; also TV movies and appearances on The Andersonville Trial, The Bastard, 1978, Disaster on the Coastliner, 1979, Secrets of a Married Man, 1984, North Beach and Rawhide, 1985, Columbo, 1993; star of TV show Star Trek, 1966-69, animated series, 1973-75; TV series Barbary Coast, 1975-76, The Babysitter, 1979, T.J. Hooker; host (TV series) Rescue 911, CBS, 1989—; dir. TV movie TekWar; author: (novels) TekWar, 1989, TekLords, 1991, TekLab, 1991, Tek Vengeance, 1992, Tek Secret, 1993, (memoirs) Star Trek Memories, 1993, Star Trek Movie Memories, 1994, Tek Power, 1994. Recipient Tyrone Guthrie award, 1956, Theatre World award, 1958. Mem. Actors Equity Assn., AFTRA, Screen Actors Guild, Dirs. Guild. Address: care of Lemli Prodns 760 N La Cienega Blvd Los Angeles CA 90069-5231

SHATTO, GLORIA MCDERMITH, academic administrator; b. Houston, Oct. 11, 1931; d. Ken E. and Gertrude (Osborne) McDermith; m. Robert J. Shatto, Mar. 19, 1953; children: David Paul, Donald Patrick. BA with honors in Econs., Rice U., 1954, PhD (fellow), 1966. Mkt. rsch. Humble Oil & Refining Co., Houston, 1954-55; tchr. pub. sch. C.Z., 1955-56; tchr. Houston Ind. Sch. Dist., 1956-60; asst. prof. econs. U. Houston, 1965-69, assoc. prof., 1969-72; prof. econs., assoc. dean Coll. Indsl. Mgmt., Ga. Inst. Tech., Atlanta, 1973-77; George R. Brown prof. bus. Trinity U., San Antonio, 1977-79; pres. Berry Coll., Mt. Berry, Ga., 1980—; sml. bus. adv. com. U.S. Treasury, 1977-81; trustee Joint Coun. Econ. Edn., 1985-88; dir. Ga. Power Co., So. Co., Becton Dickinson and Co., Tex. Instruments, Inc. Contbr. articles to profl. jours.; Editor: Employment of the Middle-Aged, 1972; mem. editorial bd.: Ednl. Record, 1980-82. Mem. Tex. Gov.'s Commn. on Status of Women, 1970-72, Gov.'s Commn. on Economy and Efficiency in State Govt., 1991; trustee Ga. Tech. Rsch. Inst., 1975-77, Berry Coll., Ga., 1975-79, Ga. Forestry Commn., 1987-95; mem. Ga. Gov.'s Commn. on Status of Women, 1975; mem. commn. on women in higher edn. Am. Coun. on Edn., 1980-82, chmn., 1982; mem. Ga. Study Com. on Pub. Higher Edn. Fin., 1981-82; v.p. Ga. Found. Ind. Colls., 1981, pres. 1982, 94; mem. adv. bd. to Sch. Bus. Adminstrn., Temple U., Phila., 1981-83; mem. Study Com. on Ednl. Processes, Soc. Assn. Colls. and Schs., 1981-82, Ga. United Meth. Commn. on Higher Edn. and Campus Ministry, 1981-82; trustee Redmond Park Hosp., Rome, Ga., 1981-87, 1st United Meth. Ch., 1986-89. Recipient Disting. Alumni award Rice U., 1987; OAS fellow, summer 1968. Mem. Royal Econ. Assn., Am. Econ. Assn., So. Econ. Assn., Southwestern Econ. Assn. (pres. 1976-77), Am. Fin. Assn. (nominating com. 1976), Southwestern Social Scis. Assn., Fin. Execs. Inst. (chmn. Atlanta edn. com. 1976-77, mem. com. on profl. devel. 1981), AAUW (area rep. 1967-68, Tex. chmn. legis. program 1970-71, mem. internat. fellowships-awards com. 1970-76, chmn. 1974-76), Ga. Newcomen Soc. (chmn. 1991—), Newcomen Soc. U.S. (trustee), Phi Beta Kappa, Phi Kappa Phi, Omicron Delta Epsilon. Office: Berry Coll Office of the President 39 Mount Berry Sta Mount Berry GA 30149-0159

SHATTUCK, CATHIE ANN, lawyer, former government official; b. Salt Lake City, July 18, 1945; d. Robert Ashley S. and Lillian Culp (Shattuck). B.A., U. Nebr., 1967, J.D., 1970. Bar: Nebr. 1970, U.S. Dist. Ct. Nebr. 1970, Colo. 1971, U.S. Dist. Ct. Colo. 1971, U.S. Supreme Ct. 1974, U.S. Ct. Appeals (10th cir.) 1977, U.S. Dist. Ct. D.C. 1984, U.S. Ct. Appeals (D.C. cir.) 1984. V.p., gen. mgr. Shattuck Farms, Hastings, Nebr., 1967-70; asst. project dir. atty. Colo. Civil Rights Commn., Denver, 1970-72; trial atty. Equal Employment Opportunity Commn., Denver, 1973-77; vice chmn. Equal Employment Opportunity Commn., Washington, 1982-84; pvt. practice law Denver, 1977-81; mem. Fgn. Svc. Bd., Washington, 1982-84, Presdl. Personnel Task Force, Washington, 1982-84; ptnr. Epstein, Becker & Green, L.A. and Washington, 1984—; lectr. Colo. Continuing Legal Edn. Author: Employer's Guide to Controlling Sexual Harrassment, 1992; mem. editorial bd. The Practical Litigator, 1988—. Bd. dirs. KGNU Pub. Radio, Boulder, Colo., 1979, Denver Exchange, 1980-81, YWCA Met. Denver, 1979-81. Recipient Nebr. Young Career Woman Bus. and Profl. Women, 1967; recipient Outstanding Nebraskan Daily Nebraskan, Lincoln, 1967. Mem. ABA (mgmt. chair labor and employment law sect. com. on immigration law 1988-90, mgmt. chair com. on legis. devels. 1990-93), Nebr. Bar Assn., Colo. Bar Assn., Colo. Women's Bar Assn., D.C. Bar Assn., Nat. Women's Coalition, Delta Sigma Rho, Tau Kappa Alpha, Pi Sigma Alpha, Alpha Xi Delta, Denver Club.

SHATTUCK, GEORGE CLEMENT, lawyer; b. Syracuse, N.Y., Sept. 2, 1927; s. Frank M. and Geneveive Mary (Hannon) S.; m. Sheila Eagan, Sept. 21, 1957 (div. 1985); children: Edward, George, Frank, Mark, Patrick; m. Carla A. Amussen, June 16, 1987; 1 child, Morgan. BS in Mgmt., Syracuse U., 1950, JD, 1953. Bar: N.Y. 1954, U.S. Supreme Ct. 1973. Ptnr., estate planning splty. practice group Bond, Schoeneck & King Law Firm, Syracuse, 1954—. Author: Oneida Land Claims, 1991, Estate Planning for the Small Business Owner, 1993. Mem. Syracuse Bd. Edn., 1968-75. Roman Catholic. Avocations: writing, reading history and philosophy, fishing, biking. Home: 5158 W Lake Rd Cazenovia NY 13035-9633 Office: Bond Schoeneck & King One Lincoln Ctr Syracuse NY 13202

SHATTUCK, JOHN, federal official; m. Ellen Hume; 4 children. BA magna cum laude, Yale U., JD; MA with 1st-class honors, Cambridge U., Eng. Law clk. to Hon. Edward Weinfeld U.S. Dist. Ct. (so. dist.) N.Y., 1970-71; nat. counsel ACLU, 1971-77, dir. Washington office, 1977-84; v.p. govt., community and pub. affairs Harvard U., 1984-93, sr. assoc. sci. tech. and pub. policy program John F. Kennedy sch. govt., 1984-93; asst. sec. of state bur. human rights and humanitarian affairs Dept. of State, Washington, 1993—; lectr. Harvard U.; vis. lectr. Princeton U. Editor Yale U. Law Jour.; contbr. articles to profl. jours. Recipient H.L. Mencken award Free Press Assn., Pub. Svc. award Yale U., Roger Baldwin medal. Mem. Leadership Conf. Civil Rights (mem. exec. com.). Office: Dept of State Office of the Secretary 2201 C St NW Rm 7802 Washington DC 20520-0001*

SHATTUCK, LAWRENCE WILLIAM, recruitment director; b. Nashua, N.H., Aug. 24, 1951; s. Fred and Shirley (Lundeen) S. AS, Middlesex C.C., Mass., 1975; MEd, Cambridge (Mass.) Coll., 1990. Admissions officer Tufts U. Sch. Dental Medicine, Boston, 1976-90; dir. recruitment New Eng. Coll. Optometry, Boston, 1990—. Mem. Nat. Assn. Grad. Admissions Profls. (mem. membership com.), Nat. Assn. Advisors for the Health Professions, N.E. Assn. Advisors to the Health Professions. Home: 278 Manning St #904 Hudson MA 01749 Office: New Eng Coll Optometry 424 Beacon St Boston MA 02115-1129

SHATTUCK, MAYO ADAMS, III, investment banking executive; b. Boston, Oct. 7, 1954; s. Mayo Adams Jr. and Jane (Bergwall) S.; children: Mayo Adams IV, Kathleen Elizabeth. BA, Williams Coll., 1976; MBA, Stanford U., 1980. Analyst Morgan Guaranty Trust Co., N.Y.C., 1976-78; mgr. Bain & Co., Menlo Park, Calif., 1980-83; v.p. to mng. dir. and head of corp. fin. Alex Brown & Sons, San Francisco, 1985-91; pres. and COO Alex Brown & Sons, Balt., 1991—; bd. dirs. Alex Brown, Inc., Balt., Constellation Holdings Inc. subs. Balt. Gas and Electric. Trustee Gilman Sch., Wellness Cmty., Balt., 1991—; chmn. bd. dirs. Columbus Ctr., Balt., 1992—; adv. dir. U. Md., Balt., 1992—. Mem. Am. Bus. Conf. Avocations: tennis, golf. Office: Alex Brown & Sons 135 E Baltimore St Baltimore MD 21202-1607

SHATTUCK, ROGER WHITNEY, author, educator; b. N.Y.C., Aug. 20, 1923; s. Howard Francis and Elizabeth (Colt) S.; m. Nora Ewing White, Aug. 20, 1949; children—Tari Elizabeth, Marc Ewing, Patricia Colt, Eileen Shepard. Grad., St. Paul's Sch., Concord, N.H., 1941; B.A., Yale, 1947; Doctorat honoris causa, U. Orléans, France, 1990. Information officer UNESCO, Paris, France, 1947-48; asst. editor Harcourt, Brace & Co., 1949-50; mem. Soc. Fellows, Harvard, 1950-53, instr. French, 1953-56; faculty U. Tex., Austin, 1956-71; prof. English, French U. Tex., 1968-71, chmn. dept. French and Italian, 1968-71; Commonwealth prof. French U. Va., Charlottesville, 1974-88; univ. prof., prof. modern fgn. langs. Boston U., 1988—; mem. adv. bd. Nat. Translation Center, 1964-69, chmn., 1966-69; provediteur gen. Coll. de Pataphysique, Paris, 1961—; Fulbright prof. U. Dakar, Senegal, 1984-85. Author: The Banquet Years, 1958; poems Half Tame, 1964, Proust's Binoculars, 1963, Marcel Proust, 1974 (Nat. Book award 1975), The Forbidden Experiment, 1980, The Innocent Eye, 1984, Forbidden Knowledge, 1996; editor or co-editor: Selected Writings of Guillaume Appollinaire, 1950, Mount Analogue, (René Daumal), 1959, The Craft and Context of Translation (with William Arrowsmith), 1961, Selected works of Alfred Jarry, 1965, Occasions by Paul Valèry, 1970; mem. editl. bd. PMLA, 1977-78. Served to capt. USAAF, 1942-45. Decorated Ordre Palmes Academiques (France).; Guggenheim fellow, 1958-59; Fulbright research fellow, 1958-59; Am. Council Learned Socs. research fellow, 1969-70. Fellow AAAS; mem. Assn. Literary Scholars and Critics (pres. 1995-96). Office: Boston U Univ Profs Program 745 Commonwealth Ave Boston MA 02215-1401

SHATZ, STEPHEN SIDNEY, mathematician, educator; b. Bklyn., Apr. 27, 1937; s. Nathan and Agusta S.; children: Geoffrey, Adria. A.B., Harvard U., 1957, A.M., 1958, Ph.D., 1962; A.M. (hon.), U. Pa., 1971. Instr. Stanford U., 1962-63, acting asst. prof., 1963-64; asst. prof. U. Pa., Phila., 1964-67; assoc. prof. U. Pa., 1967-69, prof. math., 1969—, chmn. dept. math., 1983-86; vis. prof. U. Pisa, 1966-67. Author: Profinite Groups, Arithmetic and Geometry, 1972; contbr. articles to profl. jours. Mem. Am. Math. Soc. (editor Trans. 1975-78, coun. 1975-80, exec. com. coun. 1979-80). Office: U Pa Dept Math Philadelphia PA 19104-6395

SHATZKIN, LEONARD, publishing consultant; b. Warsaw, Poland, July 16, 1919; came to U.S., 1920, naturalized, 1922; s. Isaac and Helen (Feiman) S.; m. Eleanor Oshry, Aug. 4, 1940; children: Michael, Karen, Nancy. Student, CCNY, 1935-38; B.S., Carnegie Inst. Tech., 1941. Prodn. mgr. House Beautiful Mag., N.Y.C., 1941-43; research scientist Manhattan Project, N.Y.C., 1943-45; prodn. mgr. Viking Press, N.Y.C., 1945-50; asst. to dir. mfg. Doubleday & Co., N.Y.C., 1950-55; dir. research Doubleday & Co., 1955-60; v.p. Crowell-Collier Macmillan Co., N.Y.C., 1960-63; dir. mfg. McGraw-Hill Book Co., N.Y.C., 1963-68; v.p. McGraw-Hill Book Co., 1968-70; pres. Planned Prodn., N.Y.C., 1970-78, Two Continents Pub. Group, Ltd., N.Y.C., 1972-78; prin. Shatzkin & Co. (Cons.), Croton-on-Hudson, N.Y., 1979—; instr. div. gen. studies NYU, 1948-53; bd. dirs. Yates Industries, 1965-72; instr. Pratt Inst., 1971-72; cons. George Banta Co., Avon Industries, Macmillan Co., Orbis Books, Doubleday & Co., Grove Press, St. Martin's Press, Thomas Nelson, Grolier, Inc., CBS Internat., Dodd Mead, N.Y. Bot. Garden, Pahlavi Nat. Libr., Teheran, Iran., Ford Found., Gen. Mills, USIA, Raben & Sjogren, Stockholm, Sweden, Nat. Endowment for Arts, John Wiley & Sons, Ediouro Pub. Co., Rio de Janeiro, Curio Bookstore, Rio de Janeiro, Internat. Trademark Assn., N.Y.; cons. to Christian Lit. Assn. of Malawi, Internat. Exec. Svc. Corps re-book distbn. in Russia. Editor and translator: The Stars Bear Witness, 1947; author: In Cold Type, 1982; contbr.: articles to Publishers Weekly, others. Mem. Am. Inst. Graphic Arts (treas. 1952-59), Trade Book Clinic, Christian Literature Assn., Publishers Round Table, Tamiment Inst., Amnesty Internat. Mem. Democratic Socialists of Am. Patentee field of book binding. Home: 132 Old Post Rd N Croton On Hudson NY 10520-1934

SHAUB, HAROLD ARTHUR, food products executive; b. Lancaster County, Pa., Nov. 28, 1915; s. Arthur and Clara (Cramer) S.; m. Eileen Bair, Aug. 5, 1939; children: John A., Carole Sue Shaub Hoffman, Lynn Eileen Shaub Benton. BS in Commerce, Drexel U., 1939. Indsl. engr. Talon, Inc., 1941-42; gen. supt. Camden (N.J.) plant, then other supervisory positions Campbell Soup Co., Camden and Chgo., 1942-57; v.p., gen. mgr. Campbell Soup Co. Ltd. (subs. Campbell Soup Co.), Toronto, Ont., Can., 1957-58, pres., 1961-66; pres. Pepperidge Farm subs. Campbell Soup Co., Norwalk Conn., 1966-68; sr. v.p., frozen food ops. and Can. and Pepperdige Farm subs. Campbell Soup Co., Camden, 1968-69, exec. v.p., 1969, pres., chief exec. officer, 1972-80; former mem. internat. adv. coun. Can. Imperial Bank Commerce, Toronto, industries adv. com. Advt. Coun. and The Conf. Bd.; food mfg. industry chmn. U.S. Indsl. Payroll Savs. Com., 1976-77. Trustee Drexel U., Coriell Inst. Med. Rsch.; former trustee Valley Forge Mil. Acad. and Jr. Coll.; bd. dirs. Citizens Crime Commn. Phila., 1987-89; former mem. bd. mgrs. Franklin Inst. Phila. Named Bus. Leader of the Yr. Drexel U., 1973. Office: 25 Chestnut St Ste 108 Haddonfield NJ 08033-1874

SHAUD, JOHN ALBERT, association executive, former air force officer; b. Cleve., Dec. 15, 1933; s. Albert Grant and Helen Katherine (Meek) S.; m. Janelle Marie Ohlenbusch, July 19, 1958; children: Patricia, James, Katherine. BS, U.S. Mil. Acad., 1956; MS, George Washington U., 1967; PhD, Ohio State U., 1971. Commd. 2d lt. USAF, 1956, advanced through grades to gen., 1988; pilot B-47, B-52, RF-4C USAF, Ariz., Ohio, Thailand, Vietnam, 1957-71; mem. faculty Air Command and Staff Coll., Montgomery, Ala., 1971-73; student, rsch. assoc. Nat. War Coll., Washington, 1973-74; dep. comdr. for ops., vice wing comdr. 449 Bomb Wing, Kinross, Mich., 1974-75; staff officer plans and ops. USAF Hdqrs., Pentagon, Washington, 1975-78; wing comdr. 92 Bomb Wing, Spokane, Wash., 1978-80; air div. comdr. 47th/57th Air Div., Wash. and N.D., 1980-81; dep. dir., dir. plans, plans and ops. USAF Hdqrs., Pentagon, 1981-85; dep. chief of staff, pers. Hdqrs., Pentagon, 1985-86; comdr. Air Tng. Command, San Antonio, 1986-88; chief of staff Supreme Hdqrs. Allied Powers Europe (SHAPE), Mons, Belgium, 1988-91; ret., 1991; dir. Air Force Aid Soc., Arlington, 1991-95; exec. dir. Air Force Assn., Arlington, Va., 1995—. Decorated Def. D.S.M., Air Force D.S.M. with one oak leaf cluster, DFC, Legion of Merit with one oak leaf cluster, Air medal with 5 oak leaf clusters. Mem. Air Force Assn., Order of Daedalians, Mil. Order of Carabao, Beta Gamma Sigma, Alpha Tau Omega. Lutheran. Office: Air Force Assn 1501 Lee Highway Arlington VA 22209-1198

SHAUGHNESSY, EDWARD LOUIS, Chinese language educator; b. Sewickley, Pa., July 29, 1952; s. James Francis and Marie Rosalie (Kraus) S.; m. Gina Lynn Look, May 15, 1976 (div. Sept. 1992). BA, U. Notre Dame, 1974; MA, Stanford U., 1980, PhD, 1985. Asst. prof. U. Chgo., 1985-90, assoc. prof., 1990-96, prof., 1996—. Assoc. editor: Early China, 1985-88, editor, 1988—; editor: Paleographic Sources of Early Chinese History, 1995; author: Sources of Western Zhou History: Inscribed Bronze Vessels, 1991, (with Robert Poor and Harrie A. Vanderstappen) Ritual and Reverence: Chinese Art at the University of Chicago, 1989, (with Cai Fangpei and James F. Shaughnessy) A Concordance of the Xiaotun Nandi Oracle-Bone Inscriptions, 1988; contbr. essays to books. Andrew W. Mellon fellow for Chinese studies, 1984-85, divsn. of humanities jr. faculty fellow U. Chgo., 1986. Home: # 506 711 S Dearborn Chicago IL 60605 Office: U Chgo East Asian Langs/Civilizat 1050 E 59th St Chicago IL 60637

SHAUGHNESSY, THOMAS WILLIAM, librarian, consultant; b. Pitts., May 3, 1938; s. Martin T. and LaVerne (O'Brien) S.; m. Marlene D. Reuben, Aug. 11, 1968; 1 child, Mark Andrew. AB, St. Vincent Coll., 1961; MLS, U. Pitts., 1964; PhD, Rutgers U., 1970. Asst. dean Rutgers U., New Brunswick, N.J., 1969-71; libr. dir. Rutgers-Newark, 1971-74; assoc. dean U. So. Calif., L.A., 1974-78; asst. libr. dir. U. Houston, 1978-82; libr. dir. U. Mo.-Columbia, 1982-89; univ. libr. and dir. U. Minn., Mpls.-St. Paul, 1989—; rsch. dir. Chgo. Pub. Libr. Survey, 1968-69; cons. U. Tulsa Libr., 1982-83; adv. com. OCLC Rsch. Librs., 1988-92. Author: (with Lowell A. Martin) Library Response to Urban Change, 1969, Developing Leadership Skills: A Source Book for Librarians, 1990. U.S. Office Edn. grantee Rutgers U., 1971; fellow Coun. Libr. Resources, 1973, sr. fellow, 1985; recipient Hugh C. Atkinson Meml. award, 1996. Mem. ALA, Assn. Coll. and Rsch. Librs., Assn. Rsch. Librs. (cons. tng. fellow 1981, bd. dirs. 1989-92), Minn. Libr. Assn., Beta Phi Mu. Home: 5705 Wycliffe Rd Minneapolis MN 55436-2264 Office: U Minn Wilson Libr Minneapolis MN 55455-0414

SHAULL, RICHARD, theologian, educator; b. Felton, Pa., Nov. 24, 1919; s. Millard and Anna (Brenneman) S.; m. Mildred Miller, May 17, 1941 (div. May 1975); children: Madelyn, Wendy; m. Nancy Johns, Apr. 14, 1981. B.A., Elizabethtown Coll., 1938, D.D., 1958; B.Th., Princeton Theol. Sem., 1941, Th.M., 1946, Th.D., 1959. Ordained to ministry Presbyn. Ch., 1941; pastor in Wink, Tex., 1941-42; missionary in Colombia, 1942-50, U. Brazil, 1952-62; prof. ch. history Campinas (Brazil) Presbyn. Sem., 1952-60; v.p. Mackenzie Inst., São Paulo, Brazil, 1960-62; prof. ecumenics Princeton Theol. Sem., 1962-80, prof. emeritus, 1980—; cons. internat. programs, 1960—; chmn. N.Am. Congress Latin Am., 1966-89, World Student Christian Fedn., 1968-73; acad. dir. Instituto Pastoral Hispano, N.Y.C., 1983-89. Author: Encounter with Revolution, 1955, (with Carl Oglesby) Containment and Change, 1967, (with Gustavo Gutierrez) Liberation and Change, 1977, Heralds of a New Reformation, 1984, Naming the Idols, 1988, The Reformation and Liberation Theology, 1991, also 3 books in Portuguese. Home and Office: 46 Morgan Cir Swarthmore PA 19081-2214

SHAVELSON, MELVILLE, writer, theatrical producer and director; b. N.Y.C., Apr. 1, 1917; s. Joseph and Hilda (Shalson) S.; m. Lucille T. Myers, Nov. 2, 1938; children: Richard, Carol-Lynne. AB, Cornell U., 1937. Author: How to Make a Jewish Movie, 1970, Lualda, 1975, The Great Houdinis, 1976, The Eleventh Commandment, 1977, Ike, 1979, Don't Shoot, It's Only Me, 1990; writer Bob Hope Pepsodent Show, NBC radio, 1938-43; screenwriter The Princess and the Pirate, 1944, Wonder Man, 1944, Room for One More, 1951, I'll See You in My Dreams, 1952; screenwriter, dir. The Seven Little Foys, 1954, Beau James, 1956, Houseboat, 1957, The Five Pennies, 1958, It Started in Naples, 1959, On the Double, 1960, Yours, Mine and Ours, 1968, The War Between Men and Women, 1972, The Legend of Valentino, 1975, Deceptions, 1985; screenwriter, dir., producer The Pigeon That Took Rome, 1962, A New Kind of Love, 1963, Cast a Giant Shadow, 1966, Mixed Company, 1974, The Great Houdinis, 1976, Ike, 1979; dir. The Other Woman, 1983; creator TV shows including Danny Thomas Show, ABC-TV, 1953, My World—and Welcome To It, NBC-TV, 1969; author Broadway mus. Jimmy, 1969. Recipient Screen Writers Guild award, 1959, Christopher award, 1959, Sylvania TV award, 1953, Acad. Award nominations (screenplay), 1955, 58, Screen Writers Ann. award nominations (screenplay), 1952 (2), 58, 59, 62, 68, 72, 75, Screen Writers award (best written Am. mus.), 1959, Award of Merit United Jewish Appeal, 1966. Mem. Dirs. Guild Am., Writers Guild Am. (exec. bd. dirs 1960-75, 78, pres. screen writers br. 1967, pres. found. 1975—), Acad. Motion Picture Arts and Scis. (mem. bd. govs.), Writer Guild Am. West (pres. 1969-70, 79-81, 85-87, Valentine Davies award 1979, Laurel award 1984), Sigma Delta Chi. Home and Office: 11947 Sunshine Ter Studio City CA 91604-3708

SHAVER, JAMES PORTER, education educator, university dean; b. Wadena, Minn., Oct. 19, 1933. BA magna cum laude, U. Wash., Seattle, 1955; MA in Teaching, Harvard U., 1957, EdD, 1961. Instr. Grad. Sch. Edn., Harvard U., 1961-62; assoc. prof., dir. Social Studies Curriculum Ctr., Ohio State U., Columbus, 1964-65; mem. faculty Utah State U. Coll. Edn., Logan, 1962-64, prof., 1965—, chmn. Bur. Rsch. Svcs., 1965-93, assoc. dean rsch., 1978-93, acting dean Sch. Grad. Studies, 1990-91, 92-93, dean, 1993—; mem. Comm. Youth Edn. for Citizenship, ABA, 1975-81; mem. edn. task force Am. Hist. Assn.-Am. Polit. Sci. Assn. Project '87, 1981-84; tech. advisor Nat. Ctr. on Effective Secondary Schs., 1988-91; mem. adv. bd. program in civic and moral edn. Inst. for Philosophy and Pub. Policy, U. Md., 1992—; mem. steering com. Nat. Assessment Ednl. Progress Civics Consensus Project, 1995-96. Co-author: Teaching Public Issues in the High School, 1966, 2d edit., 1974, Facing Value Decisions: Rationale-building For Teachers, 1976, 2d edit., 1982; editor: Building Rationales for Citizenship Education, 1977, Handbook of Research on Social Studies Teaching and Learning, 1991; co-editor: Democracy, Pluralism, and the Social Studies, 1968; also others. Mem. AAAS, AAUP, Nat. Coun. Social Studies (pres. 1976), Am. Ednl. Rsch. Assn. Home: PO Box 176 Hyrum UT 84319-0176 Office: Utah State U Main 132 Logan UT 84322-0900

SHAVER, KELLY G., psychology educator; b. Highland Park, Ill., Oct. 30, 1941. BS, U. Wash., 1963, MS, 1965; PhD, Duke U., 1969. Teaching asst. U. Wash., 1963-64, rsch. asst., 1964-65; rsch. asst. Duke U., 1965-68; asst. prof. Coll. William and Mary, Williamsburg, Va., 1968-73, assoc. prof., 1973-82, prof., 1982—, rsch. dir. Tech. Entrepreneurship Ctr., 1989-90; dir. social and devel. psychology program divsn. behavioral and neural scis. NSF,

1977-79; chair Hampton-Roads Innovation and Tech. Edn. Consortium, 1990-94; issues facilitator Va. sect. White House Conf. Small Bus., 1994; mem. adv. com. Va. Assembly on Adult Corrections, 1983-84; mem. oversight review com. programs in cognitive sci. divsn. behavioral and neural scis. NSF, 1984, mem. adv. panel social psychology divsn. social scis., 1973-75, mem. presdl. young investigator awards review panel divsn. behavioral and neural scis., 1989, mem. review panel undergrad. faculty enhancement program divsn. undergrad. sci., engring. and math. edn., 1990, mem. rsch. tng. groups adv. panel for biol., behavioral and social scis., 1991, mem. rsch. experiences undergrads. adv. panel for biol., behavioral and social scis., 1991, mem. adv. panel undergrad. course and curriculum devel. program divsn. undergrad. sci., engring., and math. edn. directorate for edn. and human resources, 1992, mem. small bus. innovation rsch. adv. panel, decision risk and mgmt. scis. program divsn. social and econ. sci., 1992, rep. to interagy. panel for rsch. adolescence, 1977-79, leader behavioral and neural scis. review panel, 1980, mem. adv. panel social and devel. psychology divsn. behavioral and neural scis., 1982; cons. Commonwealth Fund, 1986; lectr. Kendon Smith meml. lectrs. U. N.C., Greensboro, 1988; ad-hoc reviewer behavioral scis. rsch. review com. Nat. Inst. Mental, 1990; ad-hoc reviewer rsch. review com. on human devel., Nat. Insts. Health, 1990, human devel. and aging spl. study sect., 1990, 91, 92; chair social scis. review panel La. Ednl. Quality Support Fund, Bd. Regents, 1991-92, 94; lectr. psychology seminar series Coll. Charleston, 1982; mem. program review com. dept. psychology Bucknell U., 1982; mem. editorial bd. Entrepreneurship and Regional Devel., 1992—, Entrepreneurship: Theory and Practice, 1989-92, editor 1994—, Jour. Personality, 1983-87, Jour. Applied Social Psychology, 1983—, Jour. Personality and Social Psychology, 1977-88; proposal reviewer various orgns.; editor Entrepreneurship: Theory and Practice, 1994—; outside evaluator various colls. and univs.; presenter in field. Author: An Introduction to Attribution Processes, 1975, Principles of Social Psychology, 1977, Attribution of Blame: Causality, Responsibility, and Blameworthiness, 1985, (with E. Stotland and S. Sherman) Empathy and Birth Order: Some Experimental Explorations, 1971, (with R.M. Tarpy) Psychology, 1993; author: (with others) New Directions in Attribution Research, 1981, Life Crises and Experiences of Loss in Adulthood, 1992; contbr. 30 articles to profl. jours. Mem. Am. Psychol. Soc., Am. Psychology-Law Soc., Ea. Psychol. Assn. (program com. 1991-94), Capital Area Social Psychology Assn., Acad. Mtmg. Soc. Exptl. Social Psychology, Soc. Psychol. Study Social Issues, Soc. Advancement Social Psychology (steering com. 1984-85), Richmond Venture Capital Club (bd. dirs.), Small Bus. Devel. Ctr. Greater Hampton Rds. (bd. dirs.). Office: Coll William and Mary Williamsburg VA 23187-8795

SHAW, ALAN, lawyer, corporate executive; b. Long Branch, N.J., July 23, 1930; m. Margaret Knight, Oct. 15, 1959; children: Andrew Macbeth, Adriane Macbeth. AB, U. Mich., 1952; LLB, Harvard U., 1955. Bar: Mass. 1955, N.Y. 1958. Assoc. Skadden, Arps, Slate, Meagher & Flom, N.Y.C., 1958-65; v.p., gen. counsel, sec. Athlone Industries Inc., Parsippany, N.J., 1966-93, also bd. dirs.; Adjunct assoc. prof. of Law, Fordham U., 1996—. Served as cpl. U.S. Army, 1955-57. Mem. ABA (sect. on corps.), N.J. Gen. Counsel Group, Assn. Bar City N.Y., Morristown (N.J.) Club, Washington Assn. (Morristown), Morris County Golf Club (Convent Station, N.J.). Home: 490 S Maple Ave Basking Ridge NJ 07920 Office: Woodmont Park Ste 104 601 Jefferson Rd Parsippany NJ 07054-2823

SHAW, ALAN ROGER, financial executive, educator; b. Bklyn., July 7, 1938; s. Sewall S. and Vera (Dimmick) S.; children: Stephen S., Todd J., Bradley C.; married 2d, Mary Elizabeth Hogg, May 30, 1987. Student, Susquehanna U., 1957, Adelphi U., 1963-66. Analyst Harris Upham & Co., N.Y.C., 1958-71, asst. v.p., 1971-73, v.p., 1973-75; 1st v.p. Smith, Barney, Harris, Upham & Co., N.Y.C., 1975-80; sr. v.p., mng. dir. Smith Barney, N.Y.C., 1980—; tchr. N.Y. Inst. Fin., 1966—. Mem. Market Technicians Assn. (pres. 1974), N.Y. Soc. Security Analysts, Securities Industry Assn. Inst. (trustee 1986-92), Southward Ho Country Club, Unqua Corinthian Yacht Club (commodore 1988-90). Home: 87 Wagstaff Ln West Islip NY 11795-5206 also: 322 W 57th St New York NY 10019-3701 also: 2123 Fisher Island Dr Fisher Island FL 33109-0052 Office: Smith Barney Inc 388 Greenwich St New York NY 10013-2375

SHAW, ANGUS ROBERTSON, III, minister; b. Charlotte, N.C., Oct. 7, 1932; s. Angus Robertson Jr. and Claudia (Morrison) S.; m. Carolyn Farmer, Aug. 14, 1965; children: Karen, Rob. BA, Bob Jones U., 1955; MDiv, Columbia Theol. Sem., 1958, DMin, 1989; DD (hon.), King Coll., 1965. Asst. pastor 1st Presbyn. Ch., Pulaski, Va., 1956-62; pastor Seagle Meml. Ch., Pulaski, 1956-62, Royal Oak Ch., Marion, Va., 1962-69; sr. pastor 1st Presbyn. Ch., Dothan, Ala., 1969-78, Johnson City, Tenn., 1978—; chmn. bd. Salvation Army, Johnson City, Tenn., 1986, Contact Teleministries, Johnson City, 1987-88. Trustee Lees-McRae Coll., Banner Elk, N.C., 1979-84; chmn. ch., coll. coun. Montreat (N.C.)-Anderson Coll., 1980; chmn. ann. fund King Coll., Briston, Tenn., 1985-86; bd. trustees Tusculum Coll., 1993—, chair coun. on ch. rels., 1992, chair Ptnrs. in Ministry Drive, 1996; bd. dirs. United Way, 1991—. Mem. Watauga Mental Health Assn. (bd. dirs. 1990-96, chair 1992-93), Kiwanis (pres. 1990-91), Soc. Theta Pi. Home: 1013 Somerset Dr Johnson City TN 37604-2919 Office: 1st Presbyn Ch 105 S Boone St Johnson City TN 37604-6262

SHAW, ARTIE, musician, writer, lecturer; b. N.Y.C., May 23, 1910; s. Harry and Sarah Shaw; m. Margaret Allen; m. Lana Turner; m. Elizabeth Kern; 1 son, Steven Kern; m. Ava Gardner (div. Oct. 1946); m. Kathleen Winsor, (ct. 28, 1946; 1 son, Jonathan; m. Evelyn Keyes, 1957 (div. June 1985). Extension work in lit., Columbia U.; MusD (hon.), U. Nebr., 1938, LittD (hon.); LHD (hon.), Calif. Luth. U., 1987; DFA (hon.), U. Ariz., 1995. former owner firm Shooters Svc. and Dewey (gun mfrs.); pres. Arixo Prodns., Ltd. (film distbn. co.); lectr. colls. and univs.; ann. lectr. U. Calif., Santa Barbara, Oxnard Coll., Camarillo, Calif., Yale U., U. Pa., Memphis U. Orch. leader, 1936-54; appeared in motion pictures Dancing Coed, Second Chorus; also engaged in film, theatrical prodn.; producer Broadway mus. The Great Gatsby; recipient Downbeat award best Am. swing band, Esquire Mag. Poll award as favorite band of armed services, Hall of Fame award for rec. Begin the Beguine; Stardust, Nat. Acad. Rec. Arts and Scis. 1977); condr., composer numerous songs and orchestral works including Concerto for Clarinet; author: A Clarinet Method; The Trouble with Cinderella; I Love You, I Hate You, Drop Dead! Three Variations on a Theme; The Best of Intentions, and Other Stories, 1989. Former mem. exec. council, bd. Hollywood Ind. Citizens Com. Arts, Scis. and Professions. Served with USNR, 1942-44. Recipient Presdl. award Am. Soc. Mus. Arrangers, 1990. Subject of film: Artie Shaw: Time is All You've Got (Acad. award Best Feature-length Documentary 1986). *I'm still trying to figure life out and will let you know when, as, or if I ever do. But don't hold your breath; I imagine it'll take some 80 years more for me to find an answer.*

SHAW, BERNARD, television journalist; b. Chgo., 1940; m. Linda Shaw; children: Anil, Amar. Corr. Washington bur. CBS News, 1971-77; fgn. corr., bur. chief ABC News, 1977-80; anchor Cable News Network, Washington, 1980—. Served with USMC. recipient, Cable Ace award: Best Newscaster, 1994. Office: CNN 820 1st St NE Washington DC 20002-4243

SHAW, BREWSTER HOPKINSON, JR., astronaut; b. Cass City, Mich., May 16, 1945; m. Kathleen Mueller; children: Brewster H. III, Jessica Hollis, Brandon Robert. BS in Engring. Mechanics, U. Wis., 1968, MS in Enginrg. Mechanics, 1969. Commd. USAF, 1969, advanced through grades to col.; student pilot Craig AFB, Ala., 1970; assigned to F-100 replacement tng. unit Luke AFB, Ariz., 1970-71; served as F-100 combat fighter pilot, 352d Tactical Fighter Squadron Phan Rang Air Base, Republic of Vietnam, 1971; assigned to F-4 Replacement Tng. Unit George AFB, Calif., 1971; served with 25th Tactical Fighter Squadron Ubon Republic Thailand AFB; F-4 flight instr. 20th Tactical Fighter Tng. Squadron George AFB, Calif., 1973; student USAF Test Pilot Sch., Edwards AFB, Calif., 1975-76, instr., operational test pilot 6512th Test Squadron, 1977-78; astronaut NASA, 1978—, mem. support crew and Entry CAPCOM for STS-3 and STS-4, head Orbiter fleet, astronaut office liaison with Dept. Def., staff mem. Roger's Presdl. Commn. investigating STS 51-1, Challenger accident, pilot STS-9/Spacelab-1, 1983; spacecraft comdr. STS-61B, 1985, STS-28, 1989, completing total of 534 hours in space; dep. dir. Space Shuttle Ops. Kennedy Space Ctr., Fla., 1989-93, dir. Space Shuttle Ops., 1993—, chmn. Mission Mgmt. Team, 1989—. Decorated DFC with 7 oak leaf clusters, Def. Superior Svc. medal, Def. Meritorious Svc. medal, Air medal with 20 oak leaf clusters, Cross of Gallantry Republic Vietnam, NASA Space Flight medals, 1983, 85, 89, numerous other mil. and NASA awards; recipient Flight Achievement award Am. Astronautical Soc., 1983, Nat. Space award VFW, 1984. Avocations: running, skiing, flying, hunting. Office: care JF Kennedy Space Ctr NASA Orlando FL 32899*

SHAW, BRYAN P. H., retired investment company executive; b. Kwongtung, China, Aug. 16, 1921; came to U.S., 1947, naturalized, 1962; s. Ying-Chow (Chung-ching) and Sui-ming (Soo) S.; m. Linda L.T. Tan, Apr. 4, 1953 (dec. 1976). B.A., St. John's U., Shanghai, China, 1946; M.A., Fordham U., 1955. Vice pres., treas. Counselled Funds Distbr. Inc., N.Y.C., 1959-61, also dir.; sec., treas. Axe Sci. Mgmt. Co., Inc., Tarrytown, N.Y., 1960-74; treas. Axe Sci. Corp., Tarrytown, 1960-74, Axe-Houghton Found., Tarrytown, 1968-70, Axe-Houghton Income Fund, Inc., Tarrytown, 1968-86, Axe-Houghton Fund B, Inc., Tarrytown, 1969-86, Axe-Houghton Stock Fund, Inc., Tarrytown, 1970-86, Axe-Houghton Money Market Fund, Inc., Tarrytown, 1982-86; v.p. Axe-Houghton Mgmt., Inc., Tarrytown, 1977-86. Clubs: Fordham U. (Bronx); Fordham U. Wall Street (N.Y.C.). Home: Coral Ridge Towers S 3333 NE 34th St Apt 819 Fort Lauderdale FL 33308-6909

SHAW, BRYCE ROBERT, author; b. Mansfield, Pa., Feb. 22, 1930; s. Wilford Walter and Genevieve (Cox) S.; m. Sally Ruth Prutsman, June 29, 1952; children: David Bryce, Jody Lynn McMillin, Erin Suzanne Hunsinger. AB, Muhlenberg Coll., Allentown, Pa., 1952; MA, U. Mich., 1953, postgrad., 1959-64. Cert. secondary edn. tchr. Teaching fellow U. Mich., Ann Arbor, 1953-55; math. analyst Willow Run Rsch. Ctr., Ypsilanti, Mich., 1954-59; tchr. math. Mt. Morris (Mich.) Bd. Edn., 1959-60, Flint (Mich.) Bd. Edn., 1960-64; lectr. math. U. Mich, Flint, 1961-68; coord. math. Flint Bd. Edn., 1964-75, dir. math. and computer systems, 1975-77; author in residence Houghton Mifflin Co., Boston, 1977-81, sr. author, 1970—; rsch. mathematician sch. dists., univs., Houghton Mifflin, others, Flint, Boston, L.A., 1961—; math. cons. sch. bds., state edn. depts., univs., U.S., Can., Mex., 1965—, Am. Sch. Found., Mexico City, 1965-68; lectr. edn. Ea. Mich. U., Ypsilanti, 1964-67; lectr. math. Nat. and Regional Math. Couns., Mich. State U., East Lansing, 1965-67; chmn. math. dept. Flint Bd. Edn., 1960-64; lectr. math. curriculum Flint Bd. Edn., 1960-80; lectr. math. curriculum devel. bds. edn., sch. math. staffs. Author: (textbooks) General Math I, 2d edit., 1979, Mathematics Plus, 1980, Fundamentals of Mathematics, 2d edit., 1986, Personalized Computational Skills Program, Vol. I, 1980, vol. II, 1981, Personalized Computational Skills Program--Skills and Applications, 1982, Personalized Computational Skills Program: Module A, B, C, D, E, and F, 3d edit., 1982, Mathematics Plus!, 1982, Computer Math Program, Computational Skills Program, 1988, Brush-Up: Mathematics Program, 1995; contbr. articles to profl. jours. Recipient Citation of Meritorious Acheivement in laser rsch., Internat. Man of Yr. award, 1991-92, Key of Success; Profl. Performance Achievement Rsch. and Notable Author award Biog. Honor award in Math., Internat. Cultural Diploma of Honor, others; named Disting. Lectr. Coll. Mathematicians. Mem. Math. Assn. Am., Nat. Coun. Tchrs. Math., Textbook Authors Assn., Phi Delta Kappa, Omicron Delta Kappa, Alpha Kappa Alpha. Avocations: music, chess. Home and Office: PO Box 531 Venice FL 34284-0531

SHAW, CAROLE, editor, publisher; b. Bklyn., Jan. 22, 1936; d. Sam and Betty (Neckin) Bergenthal; m. Ray Shaw, Dec. 27, 1957; children: Lori Eve Cohen, Victoria Shaw Locknar. BA, Hunter Coll., 1962. Singer Capitol Records, Hilton Records, Rama Records, Verve Records, 1952-65; TV appearances Ed Sullivan, Steve Allen, Jack Paar, George Gobel Show, 1957; owner The People's Choice, L.A., 1975-79; founder, editor-in-chief Big Beautiful Woman mag., Beverly Hills, Calif., 1979—; creator Carole Shaw and BBW label clothing line for large-size women. Author: Come Out, Come Out Wherever You Are, 1982. Avocations: piano, painting, swimming, travel. Office: BBW Mag PO Box K-298 Tarzana CA 91356

SHAW, CHARLES ALDEN, engineering executive; b. Detroit, June 8, 1925; s. Fred Alden and Amy (Ellis) S.; m. Barbara Loveland, Mar. 9, 1963 (div. 1979); children: Amy Elizabeth, Polly Nicole; m. Jeanne Steves Partridge, Apr. 22, 1989. BS, Harvard U., 1945; MSEE, Syracuse U., 1958. Test and design engr. G.E., Syracuse-Schenectady, N.Y., 1947-51; chief engr. Onondaga Pottery Co., Syracuse, 1951-60; mgr. semiconductor div. G.E., Syracuse-Schenectady, 1960-66; cons. to gen. dir. Bull-G.E., Paris, 1966-69; mgr. CAD sect. integrated cir. product dept. G.E., Syracuse, 1969-71, mgr. CAD ctr. solid state applied ops., 1971-78, mgr. computer support solid state applied ops., 1978-81; dir. CAD G.E. Intersil, Cupertino, Calif., 1981-88; cons. in field Cupertino, 1988-89; mgr. tech. program Cadence Design Systems, Santa Clara, Calif., 1989—. Trustee Hidden Villa, Los Altos Hills, Calif., 1986-92; vol. tech. KTEH Channel 54 pub. TV, 1984—. With USN, 1942-45, PTO. Mem. IEEE, Assn. Computing Machinery (chmn. spl. interest group SIGDA 1986-91), Design Automation Conf. (exec. bd. 1985-95), Harvard Club of Peninsula. Democrat. Unitarian. Avocations: skiing, scuba diving, music. Home: 4925 Monaco Dr Pleasanton CA 94566-7671 Office: 555 River Oaks Pky San Jose CA 95134-1917

SHAW, CHARLES ALEXANDER, judge; b. Jackson, Tenn., Dec. 31, 1944; s. Alvis and Sarah (Weddle) S.; m. Kathleen Ingram, Aug. 17, 1969; 1 child, Bryan Ingram. BA, Harris Stowe State Coll., 1966; MBA, U. Mo., 1971; JD, Cath. U. Am., 1974. Bar: D.C. 1975, Mo. 1975, U.S. Ct. Appeals (8th and D.C. cirs.) 1975, U.S. Dist. Ct. (ea. dist.) Mo. 1976, U.S. Ct. Appeals (6th and 7th cirs.) 1976. Tchr. St. Louis Pub. Schs., 1966-69, D.C. Pub. Schs., Washington, 1969-71; law clk. U.S. Dept. Justice, Washington, 1972-73; law clk. NLRB, Washington, 1973-74, atty., 1974-76; assoc. Lashly, Caruthers, Theis, Rava & Hamel, St. Louis, 1976-80, asst. U.S. atty., 1980-87; judge Mo. Cir. Ct., St. Louis, 1987-94, asst. presiding judge, 1993-94; judge U.S. Dist. Ct., St. Louis, 1994—; hearing officer Office of the Mayor, Washington, 1973-74; instr. U. Mo., St. Louis, 1980-81. State bd. dirs. United Negro Coll. Fund, St. Louis, 1979-83; trustee St. Louis Art Mus., 1979-82, 89-96; bd. dirs. Arts and Edn. Coun., 1992-95, Metro Golf Assn., Landmarks Assn., St. Louis, 1980-82. Danforth Found. fellow, 1978-79; Cath. U. Am. scholar, 1971-74. Mem. D.C. Bar Assn., Mo. Bar Assn., Mound City Bar Assn., Bar Assn. Metro. St. Louis, Harris-Stowe State Coll. Alumni Assn. (bd. dirs., Disting. Alumni 1988), Phi Alpha Delta (Svc. award 1973-74). Avocations: golf, tennis. Office: 1114 Market St Saint Louis MO 63101-2043

SHAW, CHARLES RAYMOND, journalist; b. Phila., Feb. 2, 1951; s. Charles Raymond Sr. and Dorothy Blanche (Buckman) S.; m. Francine Ruth Pennock, Jan. 14, 1983. BS in Journalism, Temple U., 1972; MS in Journalism, Columbia U., 1973. Staff writer Intelligencer Jour., Lancaster, Pa., 1973-83, asst. news editor, 1983-88, news editor, 1989—. Mem. Pa. Soc. of Newspaper Editors. Office: Lancaster Newspapers Inc Intelligencer Jour 8 W King St Lancaster PA 17603-3824

SHAW, CHARLES RUSANDA, government investigator; b. Detroit, Aug. 17, 1914; s. Leonard George and Harriet (Kratzer) S.; m. Sally Madeline Jock, May 3, 1947; children: Patrick R., Sandra L. Keding (dec.), Janice L., Lisa Keding; stepchildren: Lillian Genna, Ruth Czenkus. Cert., Wicker Sch. of Fine Arts, 1936, Mich. Acad. Advt. Art, 1937; student, Intelligence Corps Sch., 1947. Freelance artist Detroit, 1936-39; spl. agt. U.S. Army Counter Intelligence Corps, Washington, 1947-48, Office Spl. Investigations, USAF, Washington, 1948-66; pvt. investigator Charles Shaw Assocs., Mt. Clemens, Mich., 1966-84; contract investigator USAF & U.S. Customs Svc., Washington, 1984-94; entrepreneur-inventor neoteric products, patents pending, 1994—. Master sgt. U.S. Army, 1939-45, PTO, ETO. Mem. Assn. Former OSI Spl. Agts. (chartered). Democrat. Roman Catholic. Avocations: fine arts, photography, gardening, home improvements. Home and Office: 59295 Bates Rd New Haven MI 48048-1728

SHAW, DAVID ELLIOT, financial executive; b. Chgo., Mar. 29, 1951; s. Charles B. Jr. and Marilyn (Baron) S. BA, U. Calif., San Diego, 1972; MS, Stanford U., 1975, PhD, 1980. Pres. Stanford Systems Corp., Palo Alto, Calif., 1976-79; assoc. prof. Columbia U., N.Y.C., 1980-86; v.p. Morgan Stanley & Co., N.Y.C., 1986-88; chmn. D.E. Shaw & Co., Inc., N.Y.C., 1988—. Contbr. articles to profl. jours. Chmn. N.Y.C. Mayor's Panel on Tech. and Fin., 1987; mem. N.Y.C. Partnership Subcom. on Tech. and Fin., 1987; apptd. to Pres. Clinton's Com. of Advisors on Sci. and Tech., 1994; chmn. Pres. Clinton's Panel on Ednl. Tech., 1995. Mem. Am. Fin. Assn., N.Y. Acad. Scis. (bd. govs. 1993-95). Democrat. Jewish.

SHAW, DAVID LYLE, journalist, author; b. Dayton, Ohio, Jan. 4, 1943; s. Harry and Lillian (Walton) S.; m. Alice Louise Eck, Apr. 11, 1965 (div. Sept. 1974); m. Ellen Torgerson, July 17, 1979 (dec.); stepchildren: Christopher, Jordan; m. Lucy Stille, Apr. 14, 1988; 1 child, Lucas. BA in English, UCLA, 1965. Reporter Huntington Park Signal (Calif.), 1963-66, Long Beach Independent (Calif.), 1966-68; reporter L.A. Times, 1968-74, media critic, 1974—. Aauthor: WILT: Just Like Any Other 7-Foot, Black Millionare Who Lives Next Door, 1973, The Levy Caper, 1974, Journalism Today, 1977, Press Watch, 1984, The Pleasure Police, 1996; contbr. numerous articles to mags. including Gentlemen's Quar., Esquire, TV Guide, New York. Recipient Mellet Fund Nat. award, 1983, PEN West award, 1990, Calif. Bar Assn. Gold Medallion, 1990, Pulitzer Prize for disting. criticism, 1991. Office: LA Times Times Mirror Sq Los Angeles CA 90012

SHAW, DAVID TAI-KO, electrical and computer engineering educator, university administrator; b. China, Mar. 13, 1938; came to U.S., 1960, naturalized, 1972; m. Katharine Lin-Yee Yang; children: Albert, Stanley. B.S.M.E., Nat. Taiwan U., Taipei, 1959; M.S. in Nuclear Engring., Purdue U., 1961, Ph.D., 1964. Asst. prof. div. interdisciplinary studies and research Sch. Engring., SUNY-Buffalo, 1964-67, assoc. prof. faculty engring. and applied scis., 1967-74, prof. elec. engring. and nuclear engring., aerospace and engring. sci., 1974-77, prof. elec. and computer engring., 1974—, dir. lab. for power and environ. studies, 1978—; exec. dir. N.Y. State Inst. on Superconductivity, 1987—; vis. prof. U. Paris, 1976-77; vis. scientist Centre d'Études Nucleairs de Fontenay-aux-Roses (France) Commissariat a L'Energie Atomique, 1976-77; vis. assoc. dept. environ. health engring. Calif. Inst. Tech., 1970-71; mem. U.S. del. French Commissariat a L'energie ATomique, 1974, U.S. del. Joint Nuclear Energy Agy. IAEA Internat. Liaison Group on Thermionic Elec. Power Generation, Paris, 1974; mem. U.S. vis. team USSR Acad. Scis.;. Editor: Fundamentals of Aerosol Science, 1978, Recent Developments in Aerosol Science, 1978, Assessment of Airborne Radioactivity, 1978; editor-in-chief: Jour. Aerosol Sci. and Tech., 1982-93; contbr. numerous articles to profl. publs. Mem. IEEE, ASME, AAAS, Am. Assn. Aerosol Rsch. (pres. 1982-85, Assn. award 1984, Internat. Aerosol Fellow award 1994), Am. Nuclear Soc., Air Pollution Control Assn., Assn. Aerosol Rsch. (Germany), Sigma Xi, Sigma Pi Sigma. Office: SUNY-Buffalo NYS Inst Superconductivity 330 Boner Hall Buffalo NY 14260

SHAW, DENIS MARTIN, university dean, former geology educator; b. St. Annes, Eng., Aug. 20, 1923; emigrated to Can., 1948; s. Norman Wade and Alice Jane Sylvia (Shackleton) S.; m. Pauline Mitchell, Apr. 6, 1946 (div. 1975); children—Geoffrey, Gillian, Peter; m. Susan L. Evans, Apr. 9, 1976. BA, Emmanuel Coll., Cambridge, Eng., 1943, MA, 1948; Ph.D., U. Chgo., 1951. Lectr. McMaster U., Hamilton, Ont., Can., 1949-51; asst. prof. McMaster U., 1951-55, asso. prof., 1955-60, prof. geology, 1960-89, prof. emeritus, 1989—, chmn. dept., 1953-59, 62-66, dean grad. studies, 1978-84; assoc. prof. Ecole nationale supérieure de géologie appliquée, U. Nancy, France, 1959-60; invited prof. Inst. de Minéralogie, U. Genève, 1966-67. Exec. editor: Geochimica et Cosmochimica Acta, 1970-88; asso. editor: Handbook of Geochemistry, 1966—; Author: Masson Et Cie, 1964. Served with RAF, 1943-46. Fellow Royal Soc. Can. (W.G. Miller medal 1981); mem. Geol. Assn. Can., Geochem. Soc., Mineral. Assn. Can. (pres. 1964, Past Pres.' medal 1985), Am. Geophys. Union, AAAS. Address: McMaster U, Dept Geology, Hamilton, ON Canada L8S 4M1

SHAW, DONALD HARDY, lawyer; b. Oelwein, Iowa, June 1, 1922; s. John Hardy and Minnie (Brown) S.; m. Elizabeth Jean Orr, Aug. 16, 1946; children: Elizabeth Ann, Andrew Hardy, Anthony Orr. B.S., Harvard U., 1942; J.D., U. Iowa, 1948. Bar: Ill. 1949, Iowa 1948, cert. fin. planner 1983. With firm Sidley & Austin, Chgo., 1948-55; with Iowa-Ill. Gas & Electric Co., Davenport, Iowa, 1956-87; treas. Iowa-Ill. Gas & Electric Co., 1960-72, v.p. finance, 1973-87, also dir.; of counsel Walton, Creen, Curry and Robertson, Davenport, Iowa, 1987-88, Newport, Bell & Oxley, Davenport, 1989—. Mem. Iowa State Bd. Regents, 1969-81, Iowa State TV-Radio Com., 1976-81; trustee St. Luke's Hosp., Davenport, 1966-91. Served to capt. USAAF, 1942-45. Recipient Philo Sherman Bennett award, 1942. Mem. Scott County Iowa Bar Assn., Rock Island Arsenal Club, Outing Club, Harvard Club N.Y.C., Order of Coif, Delta Thata Phi. Democrat. Congregationalist. Home: 29 Hillcrest Ave Davenport IA 52803-3726 Office: Newport Bell & Oxley 246 W 3rd St Davenport IA 52801-1902

SHAW, DONALD LESLIE, Spanish language educator; b. Manchester, Eng., Feb. 11, 1930; s. Stephen Leslie and Lily (Hughes) S.; m. Maria Concetta Cristini, June 30, 1958; children: Andrew Leslie, Sylvia Maria Pierina. BA, U. Manchester, Eng., 1952, MA, 1953; PhD, U. Dublin, Ireland, 1960. Asst. lectr. U. Dublin, 1955-57; lectr. U. Glasgow, Scotland, 1957-64, U. Edinburgh, Scotland, 1964-69, sr. lectr., 1969-72, reader, prof. Spanish, 1972-86; prof. Spanish, U. Va., Charlottesville, 1986—; vis. prof. Brown U., Providence, 1967, U. Va., Charlottesville, 1983. Author: Historia de la Literatura Española, 1973, La Generación del 98, 1977, Nueva Narrativa Hispanoamericana, 1981, Alejo Carpentier, 1985, Borges' Narrative Strategies, 1992, Antonio Skármeta and the Post-Boom, 1994. Served with RAF, 1953-55. Avocation: cycling. Home: 1800 Jefferson Park Ave Charlottesville VA 22903 Office: U Va 402 Cabell Hall Charlottesville VA 22903

SHAW, DORIS BEAUMAR, film and video producer, executive recruiter; b. Pitts., July 13, 1934; d. Emerson C. and Doris Llorene (Rees) Beaumar; m. Robert Newton Shaw, July 6, 1957. BA summa cum laude, Lindenwood Coll., St. Charles, Mo., 1955. Writer, asst. to pres. Baker Prodns., Benton Harbor, Mich., 1955; asst. prodn. mgr. Condor Films, Inc., St. Louis, 1955-57; chief editor, asst. to v.p. Frederick F. Watson Inc., N.Y.C., 1957-58; v.p. Gen. Pictures Corp., Cleve., 1958-71; dir., editor, unit mgr. Cinecraft Inc., Cleve., 1971-72; mgr. audio-visual dept. Am. Greetings Corp., Cleve., 1972-73; proprietor Script to Screen Svcs., Chagrin Falls, Ohio, 1973-76; pres. D & B Shaw, Inc., Chardon, Ohio, 1976-87, Hudson, Ohio, 1987—; pres. Execusearch, Inc., Hudson, 1987—, Infosearch, Inc., Hudson, 1994—, Cybersearch, Inc., Hudson, 1995—; film festival judge, tchr. Martha Holden Jennings Found./Hawken Sch., Gates Mills, Ohio, 1970-85; advisor teenage film contests, seminars Cleve. Bd. Edn., 1970-88; contest judge/film and video WVIZ-TV, Channel 25, Parma, Ohio, 1971—; guest lectr. Lindenwood Coll., 1973-80; adj. prof. U. Akron, 1990—. Writer, dir., editor, prodr. film, video, multi-image, multi-media, audio/visual prodn., radio, TV, commls. and programs; contbr. articles to profl. jours. Bd. trustees Ohio Boys Town, Cleve., 1957-68; mem. alumnae coun. Lindenwood Coll., 1973-77; publicity chmn. Geauga County Preservation Soc., 1984-91; active various charitable orgns. Named Outstanding Young Woman of Am., Fedn. of Women's Clubs, 1965, Alumna of Yr. Merit award Lindenwood Coll., 1971; recipient numerous awards and grants for film, video projects including Gold Camera Best Documentary award, 1979. Mem. Soc. Motion Picture and TV Engrs., Info. Film Prodrs. Am., Assn. for Multi Image (charter), Detroit Prodrs. Assn., Internat. TV and Video Assn. (charter), Internat. Comm. Industries Assn., Alpha Epsilon Rho. Republican. Avocations: computers, reading, travel, physical fitness, environmental issues. Office: D & B Shaw Inc 118 E Streetsboro Rd Hudson OH 44236-2029

SHAW, E. CLAY, JR. (CLAY SHAW), congressman; b. Miami, FL, Apr. 19, 1939; s. E. Clay and Rita (Walker) S.; m. Emilie Costar, Aug. 22, 1960; children: Emilie, Jennifer, E. Clay, John C. B.S., Stetson U., 1961, J.D., 1966; M.B.A., U. Ala., 1963. Bar: Fla. 1967; CPA, Fla. Asst. city atty. City of Ft. Lauderdale, 1968, chief city pros., 1968-69, assoc. mcpl. judge, 1969-71, city commr., 1971-73, vice mayor, 1973-74, mayor, 1975-80; mem. 97th-102nd Congresses from 15th Fla. dist., 1981—; mem. Ways and Means com. 97th-104th Congresses from 15th (now 22nd) Fla. dist.; chmn. Ways and Means subcom. on human resources; U.S. spl. ambassador to Papua New Guinea Independence; pres. U.S. Conf. Republican Mayors; mem. adv. and exec. bd. U.S. Conf. Mayors.; former chmn. mcpl. div. Ft. Lauderdale United Fund Campaign, 1971; former Young Rep. Club Broward County, Ft. Lauderdale Rep. Exec. Com.; past mem. exec. com. Rep. Nat. Com.; former mem. House Selects Com. Narcotics Abuse and Control; past bd. dirs. Broward County Traffic Assn.; mem judiciary com. Pub. Works and Transp. Bd. overseers Stetson Coll. Law. Home: 700 Coral Way Fort Lauderdale

FL 33301-2532 Office: US Ho of Reps 2267 Rayburn Bldg Washington DC 20515-0005*

SHAW, ELEANOR JANE, newspaper editor; b. Columbus, Ohio, Mar. 23, 1949; d. Joseph Cannon and Wanda Jane (Campbell) S. BA, U. Del., 1971. With News-Jour. newspapers, Wilmington, Del., 1970-82, editor HEW desk, asst. met. editor, 1977-80, bus. editor, 1980-82; topics editor USA Today, 1982-83; asst. city editor The Miami Herald, 1983-85; projects editor The Sacramento Bee, 1985-87, news editor, 1987-91, exec. bus. editor, 1991-93, editor capitol bureau news, 1993-95, state editor, 1995—. Bd. dirs. Del. 4-H Found., 1978-83. Mem. Calif. Soc. Newspaper Editors (bd. dirs. 1990-96), No. Calif. Wine Soc. (v.p. 1987-93, pres. 1993—). Office: The Sacramento Bee PO Box 15779 Sacramento CA 95852-0779

SHAW, GAYLORD, newspaper executive; b. El Reno, Okla., July 22, 1942; m. Judith Howard, 1960; children: Randall, Kristine, Kelly. Attended, Cameron Coll., 1960-62, U. Okla., 1962-64. Night police reporter Lawton (Okla.) Constitution Press, 1960-62; Okla. City bur. night editor, statehouse correspondent AP, 1962-66, Washington bur. night editor, investigative reporter, spl. assignment team editor, White House correspondent, 1966-75; asst. mng. editor to mng. editor/news Dallas Times Herald, 1981-83; editor-in-chief Shaw Comms. Inc., Charlotte, N.C., 1983-85; correspondent Washington, Denver L.A. Times, 1975-81, correspondent, projects coord. Washington bur., 1985-88; Washington bur. chief Newsday, 1988-95; sr. corr. for projects Newsday, Washington, 1995—. Recipient Pulitzer Prize Nat. Reporting, 1978, Disting. Svc. award for Washington correspondence Sigma Delta Chi/Soc. Profl. Journalists, 1978, Loeb award Disting. Bus. Reporting, 1978, Disting. Reporting award Merriman Smith/White House Correspondents Assn., 1974, Worth Bingham Disting. Reporting award, 1968, Washington Correspondence award Nat. Press Club, 1991. Home: 2815 Otsego Dr Herndon VA 22071-2444 Office: Washington Bur Newsday Ste 850 1730 Pennsylvania Ave NW Washington DC 20006

SHAW, GEORGE BERNARD, consulting engineer, educator; b. Dayton, Ohio, Feb. 25, 1940; s. William E. and Edna E. (Hartley) S.; m. Carol M. Crawford, Aug. 6, 1966. A in Mech. Engring., U. Dayton, 1963, BCE, 1967, MSCE, 1971. Diplomate Am. Acad. Environ. Engrs.; registered profl. engr., Ohio, Va., Ind., Ky., Tenn., W.Va., Fla., Kans., Mich., Mo., Okla., Ill., Tex.; lic. profl. surveyor, Ohio. Asst. to chief engr. Northmont Engrs., Vandalia, Ohio, 1960-66; estimator Oberer Constrn., Dayton, 1966-67; sanitary engr. Alden E. Stilson & Assocs., Columbus, 1967-68; staff cons. Miami Conservancy Dist., Dayton, 1969-71; assoc. prof. civil and environ. engring. U. Dayton, 1967—; pres., CEO Shaw, Weiss & De Naples, Dayton, 1968—; pres., CEO GBS Environ., 1989—; chmn. Panterra Corp., 1990—. Contbr. articles to profl. jours. Treas. Engrs. Club Dayton Found. Mem. NSPE, ASCE, Am. Consulting Engrs. Coun., Soc. Am. Mil. Engrs., Water Environment Fedn., Inter-Am. Assn. Sanitary Engring., Am. Water Works Assn. Avocation: travel. Office: Shaw Weiss & De Naples PC 14 W 1st St Dayton OH 45402-1213

SHAW, GRACE GOODFRIEND (MRS. HERBERT FRANKLIN SHAW), publisher, editor; b. N.Y.C.; d. Henry Bernheim and Jane Elizabeth (Stone) Goodfriend; m. Herbert Franklin Shaw (dec. 1992); 1 son, Brandon Hibbs. Student, Bennington Coll.; BA magna cum laude, Fordham U., 1976, MS, 1991. Reporter Port Chester (N.Y.) Daily Item; editorial coordinator World Scope Ency., N.Y.C.; assoc. editor Clarence L. Barnhart, Inc., Bronxville, N.Y.; freelance-writer for reference books; editing supr. World Pub. Co., mng. editor, sr. editor; mng. editor Peter H. Wyden Co., N.Y.C., 1969-70; assoc. editor Dial Press, N.Y.C., 1971-72; sr. editor Dial Press, 1972, David McKay Co., N.Y.C., 1972-75, Grosset & Dunlap, 1975-79; chief editor Today Press (Grosset), 1977-79; sr. editor, coll. dept. Bobbs-Merrill, N.Y.C., mng. editor, exec. editor trade div., 1979-80; pub. Bobbs-Merrill, 1980-84; mng. editor Rawson Assocs. div. Macmillan Pub., 1985-91; pres. Grace Shaw Assocs., Scarsdale, N.Y., 1991—. Home and Office: 85 Lee Rd Scarsdale NY 10583-5212

SHAW, (FRANCIS) HAROLD, performing arts administrator; b. Hebron, N.Y., June 11, 1923. Student, Ithaca Coll., 1942, Columbia, 1944, N.Y. U. Extension, 1948. Former assoc. Hurok Concerts, Inc., N.Y.C.; chmn., owner Shaw Concerts, Inc., N.Y.C., 1969—; performing arts dir. Seattle World's Fair, 1961-62; former mgr. Nathan Milstein, Vladimir Horowitz, Dame Janet Baker, others; now mgr. Jessye Norman, Helen Donath, Jacqueline duPre, Wolfgang Holzmair, Jard van Nes, Mitsuko Uchida, Garrick Ohlsson, Shura Cherkassky, Horacio Gutiérrez, Julian Bream, John Williams, Elmar Oliveira, Kyoko Takezawa, Robert Shaw, Andrew Davis, and over 100 artists and attractions; exec. dir. President's Shakespeare Ann. Com., 1964. Dir. exec. staff, mem. performing arts com. Cultural Commn., N.Y.C., 1966; nat. chmn. Performing Arts Energy Commn., 1974; chmn. bd. trustees Am. Shakespdare Theatre, Straftord, Conn., 1974. With USAAF, 1942-43. Mem. Internat. Performing Arts Adminstrs., Am. Symphony Orch. League, Assn. Coll., Univ. and Community Arts Adminstrs., Actors Equity Assn., Am. Summer Stock Mgrs. Assn. (co-founder), Players Club, Bohemians, N.Y. Athletic Club, Phi Mu Allpha Sinfonia. Office: Shaw Concerts Inc 1900 Broadway 2nd FL New York NY 10023-7004

SHAW, HELEN LESTER ANDERSON, university dean; b. Lexington, Ky., Oct. 18, 1936; d. Walter Southall and Elizabeth (Guyn) Anderson; m. Charles Van Shaw, Mar. 14, 1988. BS, U. Ky., 1958; MS, U. Wis., 1965, PhD, 1969. Registered dietitian. Dietitian Roanoke (Va.) Meml. Hosp., 1959-60, Santa Barbara (Calif.) Cottage Hosp., 1960-61; dietitian, unit mgr. U. Calif., Santa Barbara, 1961-63; rsch. asst., NIH fellow U. Wis., Madison, 1963-68; from asst. prof. to prof. U. Mo., Columbia, 1969-88, assoc. dean, prof., 1977-84; prof., chair dept. food and nutrition U. N.C., Greensboro, 1989-94, dean Sch. Human Environ. Scis., 1994—; cluster leader Food for 21st Century rsch. program U. Mo., 1985-88. Contbr. articles to rsch. publs. Elder 1st Presbyn. Ch., Columbia, 1974-89, Greensboro, 1992—. Recipient Teaching award Home Econ. Alumni Assn., 1981, Gamma Sigma Delta, 1984; rsch. grantee Nutrition Found., 1971-73, NIH, 1972-75, NSF, 1980-83. Mem. Am. Inst. Nutrition, Am. Bd. Nutrition, Am. Soc. for Clin. Nutrition, Am. Dietetic Assn., Am. Family and Consumer Sci. Assn., Soc. for Nutrition Edn., Sigma Xi, Phi Upsilon Omicron, Kappa Omicron Nu. Democrat. Avocations: tennis, choral singing.

SHAW, HERBERT JOHN, physics educator emeritus; b. Seattle, June 2, 1918; s. Herbert John and Nell Grace (Cayley) S.; m. Francel Harper, Apr. 25, 1943; children: John Joseph, Kathleen, Karen. BA, U. Wash., 1941; MS, Stanford U., 1943, PhD, 1948. Test engr. GE, Schenectady, 1940-41; rsch. assoc. elec. engring. dept. Stanford (Calif.) U., 1948-50, rsch. assoc. Microwave Lab., 1950-57, sr. rsch. assoc., 1957-74, assoc. dir., 1968-77, adj. prof., 1974-83, rsch. prof. applied physics dept., 1983-88, prof. emeritus, 1989—; liaison scientist U.S. Office Naval Rsch., London, 1968-69; cons. to numerous electronics and optics cos. and govt. agys., 1950—. Fellow IEEE (Morris N. Liebmann Meml. award 1976, achievement award group on sonics and ultrasonics 1981); mem. NAE, Tau Beta Pi. Home: 719 Alvarado Row Stanford CA 94305-1037 Office: Stanford U Edward L. Ginzton Lab Stanford CA 94305

SHAW, IAN ALEXANDER, accountant, mining company executive; b. Toronto, Feb. 28, 1940; m. JoAnne Millyard, Dec. 22, 1967; children: Julia, Martin, Laura. B.Comm., U. Toronto, 1964. Chartered acct. Deloitte Touche & Sells, Toronto, 1964-68; v.p. fin. A.G.F. Mgmt. Ltd., Toronto, 1968-75; treas. Sherritt Gordon Mines Ltd., Toronto, 1975-86; v.p., treas. Curragh Inc., Toronto, 1986-93; CFO Caribgold Resources, Inc., Metallica Resources, Inc., Pelangio-Larder Mines, Ltd., AMT Internat. Mining corp. Office: Ste 905 Box 22, 26 Wellington St E, Toronto, ON Canada M5E 1S2

SHAW, JACK ALLEN, communications company executive; b. Auburn, Ind., Jan. 1, 1939; s. Marvin Dale and Vera Lucille (Harter) S.; m. Martha Sue Collins, Aug. 24, 1963; 1 child, Mark Allen. BSEE, Purdue U., 1962, hon. doctorate Capitol Coll., 1994, DS (hon.), 1995. Project engr. Hughes Aircraft Co., El Segundo, Calif., 1962-69; dir. program mgmt. ITT Space Communications, Ramsey, N.J., 1969-74; v.p., corp. devel. Digital Communications Corp., Gaithersburg, Md., 1974-78, exec. v.p., COO, Germantown, Md., 1978-81, pres., CEO, 1981-84, pres., CEO M/A-com Telecom. divsn., 1984-87; chmn., CEO Hughes Network Systems Inc., 1988—; chmn. also bd. dirs. 1978—, Hughes Network Systems Inc., Germantown, 1987—; bd. dirs. DCC Ltd., Milton Keyes, Eng., Hughes Software Systems, Pvt. Ltd., New Delhi; sr. v.p., mem. office of chmn. Hughes Electronics; co-chmn. U.S.-India Comml. Alliance. Vice chmn. United Fund Campaign Montgomery County, 1982. Named Disting. Engring. Alumni Purdue U., 1994, Outstanding Electrical Engr. Purdue U., 1994. Mem. IEEE (sr.), Radio Club of Am.(honored 1993). Republican. Clubs: Lakewood Country, Aspen Hill Racquet. Home: 11504 Lake Potomac Dr Potomac MD 20854-1223 Office: Hughes Network Systems Inc 11717 Exploration Ln Germantown MD 20876-2700

SHAW, JAMES, church administrator. Exec. dir. Ministry to the Armed Forces Standing Committee of the Lutheran ChurchMO Synod International Ctr., St. Louis. Office: Lutheran Church 1333 S Kirkwood Rd Saint Louis MO 63122-7226

SHAW, JAMES, computer systems analyst; b. Salt Lake City, June 26, 1944; s. James Irvin and Cleo Lea (Bell) S. Student, San Antonio Coll., 1962-64; BA in History, St. Mary's U., San Antonio, 1966. With VA Automation Ctr., Austin, Tex., 1967—, sr. computer programmer analyst, 1984-87, supervisory computer programmer analyst, 1987-88, computer systems analyst, 1988-94, sr. computer systems analyst, 1994—; conversion team manual to computerized acctg. VA, 1974-76; participant conversion computerized acctg. sys. to database, 1984-88; participant complete replacement of VA computerized acctg. sys., 1989-95. Active Smithsonian Institution, Planned Parenthood, Met. Mus. Art, Austin Mus. Art. Mem. Am. Assn. Individual Investors. Democrat. Home: 11500 Jollyville Rd Apt 1312 Austin TX 78759-4070 Office: VA Automation Ctr 1615 Woodward St Austin TX 78772-0001

SHAW, JAMES HEADON, nutritionist, educator; b. Sharon, Ont., Can., Jan. 1, 1918; came to U.S., 1939, naturalized, 1948; s. Merton and Myrtle (Foord) S.; m. Vera Gwendolyn Chapman, Dec. 18, 1943; children—Sandra Yvonne, James Stephen. BA, McMaster U., Hamilton, Ont., 1939; MS, U. Wis., 1941, PhD, 1943; AM (hon.), Harvard U., 1955. Postdoctoral research fellow U. Wis., 1943-45; mem. faculty Sch. Dental Medicine, Harvard U., 1945-84, prof. nutrition, 1965-84; prof. emeritus Harvard U., 1984—; chmn. com. postdoctoral edn. Sch. Dental Medicine, Harvard U. (Sch. Dental Medicine), 1974-85; mem. com. dentistry, med. sci. div. NRC, 1953-62; mem. com. on dietary phosphates and dental caries Food and Nutrition Bd., 1958-63; mem. com. nutrition edn. schs. dentistry Internat. Union Nutritional Scis., 1967-69; panel 1V-2 advanced teaching nutrition White House Conf. Food, Nutrition and Health, 1969; panel to evaluate nat. caries program Nat. Inst. Dental Research, chmn. sub-panel on modifying diet, 1979. Author textbooks; contbr. articles to profl. publs.; asst. editor Nutrition Revs., 1946-49, contbg. editor, 1971-89. Recipient Rsch. Career award Nat. Inst. Dental Rsch., 1964-84; Shenstone scholar McMaster U., 1939, Wis. Rsch. Alumni Found. scholar, 1939-43. Fellow AAAS; mem. ADA (biochemistry test constrn. com. nat. bd. examiners 1964-70), Soc. Exptl. Biology and Medicine (editorial bd. procs. 1969-85), Internat. Assn. Dental Research, Am. Inst. Nutrition, Soc. Nutrition Edn. (charter), Sigma Xi, Omicron Kappa Upsilon (hon.). Office: Countway Libr Medicine Harvard Med Area Countway Libr Medicine Fl 4 Boston MA 02115

SHAW, JAMES SCOTT, astronomy research administrator; b. Grand Junction, Colo., Oct. 13, 1942; 1 child. AB, Yale U., 1964; PhD in Astronomy, U. Pa., 1970. Asst. prof. U. Ga., Athens, 1970-77, assoc. prof. astronomy, 1977—. Mem. Internat. Astron. Union, Am. Astron. Soc., Sigma Xi. Office: Univ of Georgia Dept Physics & Astronomy Athens GA 30602*

SHAW, JEANNE OSBORNE, editor, poet; b. Stone Mountain, Ga., June 1, 1920; d. Virgil Waite and Daisy Hampton (Scruggs) Osborne; m. Harry B. Shaw, Dec. 10, 1982; children: Robert Allan Gibbs, Marilyn Osborne Gibbs Barry. BA, Agnes Scott Coll., 1942. Mem. editl. staff Atlanta Constitution, 1942; feature writer New London (Conn.) Day, 1943; book reviewer Atlanta Constitution, 1940-42, Atlanta Jour., 1945-48; poetry editor Banner Press, Emory U., 1957-59; book editor Georgia Mag., Decatur, 1957-73. Pres., Newton class Druid Hills Bapt. Ch., 1973-74, dir. ch. tng., 1978-79, ch. clk., 1995-96. Recipient Internat. Narrative Poem award Poets and Patrons, Inc., Chgo., 1992, Robert Martin, Burke, Otto, In Praise of Poetry awards N.Y. Poetry Forum, 1973, 79, 81; Westbrook award Ky. Poetry Soc., 1976; Ariz. award, 1981, Ind. State Fedn. of Poetry Clubs award, Ala. State Poetry Soc. award, 1990, Nat. Fedn. State Poetry Socs. Mem. Ga. Writers Assn. (lit. achievement award 1971), Poetry Soc. Ga. (John Clare prize 1955, Katharine H. Strong prize 1975, Eunice Thomson prize 1976, Jimmy Williamson prize 1977, Capt. Frank Spencer prize 1985, 88, Conrad Aiken prize, 1987, 88, Sarah Cunningham prize 1989, 94, Soc. prize 1989, Lucy McEntire prize 1990, 94, Grace Schley Knight prize 1991, 93, Gerald Chan Sieg prize 1991, 95, Eunice Thompson prize 1992, Harriet Ross Colquitt prize 1994, 95, Eva Tennyson Forbes Meml. prize 1996), Atlanta Writers Club (pres. 1949-50, named Aurelia Austin Writer of Year in poetry 1971, Wyatt award 1986, 95, Light Verse award 1989, Edward Davin Vickers award, Light Verse award 1990, Daniel Whitehead Hicky award, 1991, 95, F. Levering Neely award 1991, Poet Laureate's award 1993, Ben Willingham award, Gerry Crocker award 1995), Ga. State Poetry Soc. (Traditional award 1984, Cole and Ledford award 1986, Goreau award, 1987, 93, Melissa Henry award 1989, Charles and Virginia Dickson award 1990, Jo Ann Yeager Adkins award 1991, Poem About Atlanta award 1992, 14th Aniv. Free Verse award 1993, My Very Best Poem award 1995), Phi Beta Kappa. Author: The Other Side of the Water (Author of Year in Poetry award Dixie Coun. of Authors and Journalists), 1970; Unravelling Yarn, 1979; co-author: Noel! Poems of Christmas, 1979; They Continued Steadfastly, History of Druid Hills Baptist Church, 1987; author: Faithbuilders, 1982-84; contbr. poems, pen and ink sketches to mags. Home: 809 Pinetree Dr Decatur GA 30030-2332

SHAW, JIAJIU, chemist; b. Taichung, Taiwan, China, Jan. 21, 1950; came to U.S., 1979; s. Pei-Fan and Yu-Jane (Lin) S.; m. Shu-Chin, Mar. 5, 1982; children: Allen J., Cindy Y. BS in Chemistry, Tsing Hua U., China, 1972; PhD in Chemistry, U. Kans., 1984. Postdoctoral rsch. assoc. U. N.C., Chapel Hill, 1984-86; sr. chemist Nat. Analytical Labs., Rockville, Md., 1986-87; sr. rsch. scientist Ciba-Geigy Corp., Summit, N.J., 1987-89, staff scientist, 1990-93; dir. Lannett Co., Phila., 1993-94, Caraco Pharms., Detroit, 1994—. Contbr. articles to profl. jours. Recipient Ray I. Brewster award U. Kans., 1984. Mem. Am. Chem. Soc., Am. Assn. Pharm. Scientists. Republican. Achievements include design of new pharmaceutical controlled release system. Avocation: painting. Office: 3166 Shamrock Ct Ann Arbor MI 48105

SHAW, JOHN ARTHUR, lawyer; b. San Antonio, June 6, 1922; s. Samuel Arthur and Ellen Agnes (Lawless) S.; m. Margaret Louise Strudell, June 9, 1951; children: John Richard, Barbara Ann, David William. Student, Loyola U., Chgo., 1940-41, U. N.C., 1943-44; LL.B., St. Louis U., 1948, J.D., 1969. Bar: Mo. 1948. Assoc. firm Pollock, Tenney & Dahman, St. Louis, 1948-51; atty. St. Louis Probate Ct., 1951-53; ptnr. firm Pollock, Ward, Klobasa & Shaw, St. Louis, 1953-63; gen. counsel Reliable Life Ins. Co., Webster Groves, Mo., 1967-83, sr. v.p., 1969-80, sec., 1980-83, dir., 1968-83, also dir., officer, gen. counsel subs. cos., 1967-85. Contbg. author: Basic Estate Planning, 1957; editor: Missouri Probate Law and Practice, 1960. Bd. dirs., sec. Tatman Found., 1967-84; committeeman Boy Scouts Am., 1969-77; bd. dirs. Mo. Ins. Guaranty Assn., 1973-87, sec. 1983-87. Served as lt. AUS, 1943-46, ETO; maj. U.S. Army Res., (ret.). Mem. Mo. Bar, Met. St. Louis Bar Assn., Assn. Life Ins. Counsel, Ret. Officers Assn., Mil. Order of the World Wars, Alpha Sigma Nu, Delta Theta Phi. Home and Office: 306 Luther Ln Saint Louis MO 63122-4647

SHAW, JOHN FIRTH, orchestra administrator; b. Chesterfield, U.K., June 28, 1948; s. Jack Firth and Mary Stuart (MacPherson) S.; m. Julia Valette Phillips, Dec. 29, 1973; children: Mary Valette, Mark Firth, Andrew Nicholas. Licentiate Royal Acad. Music, 1968; grad. Royal Schs. of Music, 1970. Freelance musician, 1966-70; prin. musician Calgary Philharm. Orch., 1970-77, asst. mgr., 1977-78, asst. gen. mgr., 1978-79, gen. mgr., 1979-93; mng. dir. Hamilton Philharm. Orch., 1993-95. Bd. dirs. Calgary Philharm. Soc., 1974-77, Calgary Centre for Performing Arts, 1980-85, Choral Music Assn. Calgary, 1991-92; mem. adv. com. Mount Royal Coll. Conservatory of Music, 1990-93. Recipient Alta. Achievement award, 1991, Disting. Citizen Calgary award, 1993. Mem. Assn. Can. Orchs. (dir. 1982-84, 86—, pres. 1988-92, dir. 1992—). Home: 52 Markland St, Hamilton, ON Canada L8P 2J7

SHAW, JOHN FREDERICK, retired naval officer; b. Dallas, Oct. 14, 1938; s. John Frederick and Sarah E. (Crouch) S.; m. Janice Muren, July 14, 1962; children: Elizabeth Lee, Suzanne Michele. BS, U.S. Naval Acad., 1960; MS in Mgmt. with distinction, Naval Postgrad. Sch., Monterey, Calif., 1970; grad., Armed Forces Staff Coll., 1971. Commd. ensign USN, 1960, advanced through grades to rear adm., 1983; exec. officer USS Long Beach (CGN 9), 1978-79; comdg. officer USS Bainbridge (CGN 25), 1980-83; dir. guided missile destroyer 51, Arleigh Burke program Comdr. Naval Sea Systems Command, Washington, 1983-85, mgr. AEGIS shipbldg. program, 1985-87; comdr. Cruiser-Destroyer Group One, San Diego, 1987-88; dep. chief staff plans and policy Supreme Allied Comdr., Atlantic, Norfolk, Va., 1988-89, chief staff, 1989-91; ret., 1991; prof. joint mil. ops. Coll. Continuing Edn., Naval War Coll., San Diego, 1992-94; bd. advisors United Svc. Benefit Assn., Kansas City, Kans., 1987-93. Decorated Def. D.S.M., Legion of Merit with two gold stars, Meritorious Svc. medal with gold star, Navy Commendation medal with gold star. Mem. U.S. Naval Inst.(life), U.S. Naval Acad. Alumni Assn. (life, pres. Washington chpt. 1986). Avocations: golf, reading, economics.

SHAW, JOHN MALACH, federal judge; b. Beaumont, Tex., Nov. 14, 1931; s. John Virgil Shaw and Ethel (Malach) Newstadt; m. Glenda Ledoux, Nov. 10, 1970; children: John Lewis, Stacy Shaw Walpole. Student, Tulane U., 1949-50; B.S. with spl. attainments in Commerce, Washington and Lee U., 1953; LL.B., J.D., La. State U., 1956. Bar: La. 1956; U.S. Dist. Ct. (we. dist.) La. 1958, U.S. Ct. Appeals (5th cir.) 1966. Ptnr. firm Lewis and Lewis, Opelousas, La., 1958-79; U.S. dist. judge Western Dist. La., Opelousas, 1979—; now chief judge Western Dist. La., Lafayette, 1991—; Govt. appeal agt. Local Bd. 60, La., 1965-72. Mem.: La. Law Rev, 1954-56; asso. editor, 1955-56; author articles, 1954-56. Served with U.S. Army, 1956-58. Recipient Presdl. cert. of appreciation for services as appeal agt. Mem. Fed. Judges Assn., Fifth Cir. Dist. Judges Assn. Democrat. Methodist. Club: Kiwanis. *

SHAW, JOHN W., lawyer; b. Mo., 1951. BA, U. Mo., 1973, MA, 1973, JD, 1977. Bar: Mo. 1977. Ptnr. Bryan Cave, Kansas City. Mem. ABA, Securities Industry Assn. (legal and compliance group), Mo. Bar, Def. Rsch. Inst. (chmn. firearms litigation subcom.), Order of Coif. Office: Bryan Cave LLP 3500 One Kansas City Pl 1200 Main St Kansas City MO 64105-2100

SHAW, JOSEPH THOMAS, Slavic languages educator; b. Ashland City, Tenn., May 13, 1919; s. George Washington and Ruby Mae (Pace) S.; m. Betty Lee Ray, Oct. 30, 1942; children: David Matthew, Joseph Thomas, James William. AB, U. Tenn., 1940, AM, 1941; AM, Harvard, 1947, PhD, 1950. Asst. prof. Slavic langs. Ind. U., 1949-55, assoc. prof., 1955-61; prof. Slavic langs. U. Wis., 1961-89, prof. emeritus, 1989—, chmn. dept. Slavic langs., 1962-68, 77-86, chmn. div. humanities, 1964-65, 72-73, assoc. dean Grad. Sch., 1965-68. Author: The Letters of Alexander Pushkin, 1963, Pushkin's Rhymes: A Dictionary, 1974, Baratynskii: A Dictionary of the Rhymes and a Concordance to the Poetry, 1975, Batiushkov: A Dictionary of the Rhymes and a Concordance to the Poetry, 1975, Pushkin: A Concordance to the Poetry, 1985, American Association Teachers Slavic and East European Languages: The First Fifty Years 1941-91, 1991, Pushkin's Poetry of the Unexpected: The Nonrhymed Lines in the Rhymed Poetry and the Rhymed Lines in the Nonrhymed Poetry, 1994, Pushkin, Poet and Man of Letters, and His Prose (Collected works, vol. 1), 1995; editor: The Slavic and East European Jour., 1957-70; contbr. articles to profl. jours. Served to capt. USNR, 1942-46, 51-53. Mem. Am. Assn. Tchrs. Slavic and East European Langs. (mem. exec. council 1953-70, 73-80, pres. 1973-74). Home: 4505 Mineral Point Rd Madison WI 53705-5071

SHAW, JULIUS C., SR., carpet manufacturing company executive; b. 1929. Student, Ga. Inst. Tech. Supt. Crown Cotton Mills Inc., 1950-57; with Rocky Creek Mills, 1957-63; v.p., gen. mgr. Dan River Carpets, Danville, Va., 1965-67; pres. Sabre Carpets Inc. (merged into Shaw Industries), Dalton, Ga., 1967—; now chmn. Emeritus, dir. Shaw Industries, Dalton, Ga. Office: Shaw Industries Inc PO Box 429 Cartersville GA 30120*

SHAW, (GEORGE) KENDALL, artist, educator; b. New Orleans, Mar. 30, 1924; s. George Kendall and Florence Gladys (Worner) S.; m. Frances Glenn Fort, Oct. 31, 1955. Student, Ga. Inst. Tech., 1944-46; B.S. in Chemistry, Tulane U., 1949, M.F.A. in Painting, 1959; postgrad., La. State U., 1950. instr. Columbia U., 1961-66, Hunter Coll., 1966-68, Parsons Sch. Design, N.Y.C., 1966-86, Lehman Coll., 1968-70, Bklyn. Mus. Art Sch., 1970-76. One-man shows include Columbia U., 1965, Bienville Gallery, New Orleans, 1968, Tibor de Nagy Gallery, N.Y.C., 1964, 65, 67, 68, Southampton Coll., 1969, John Bernard Myers Gallery, 1972, Alessandra Gallery, 1976, Lerner/Heller Gallery, N.Y.C., 1979, 81, 82, Bernice Steinbaum Gallery, N.Y.C., 1991, Artists Space, N.Y.C., 1992; group shows include P.S.I., N.Y.C., 1977, Gladstone-Villani Gallery, N.Y.C., 1978, Galerie Habermann, Cologne, 1979, Modern Art Gallery, Vienna, 1980, Jacksonville Art Mus. (Fla.), 1983, others; represented in permanent collections Peter Ludwig, Aachen, Bklyn. Mus., Albright-Knox Gallery, Buffalo, Mus. Contemporary Art, Nagaoka, Japan, Everson Mus., Syracuse, Chase Manhattan Bank, N.Y.C., Chem. Bank, N.Y.C., N.Y. U., N.Y.C. Served with USN, 1943-46. Mem. Coll. Art Assn., Artists Equity Assn. Democrat. Address: 458 Broome St New York NY 10013-2611

SHAW, KENNETH ALAN, university president; b. Granite City, Ill., Jan. 31, 1939; s. Kenneth W. and Clara H. (Lange) S.; m. Mary Ann Byrne, Aug. 18, 1962; children: Kenneth William, Susan Lynn, Sara Ann. BS, Ill. State U., 1961, DHL, 1987; EdM, U. Ill., 1963; PhD, Purdue U., 1966, EdD (hon.), 1990; DHL, Towson State, 1979, Ill. Coll., 1986. Tchr. history, counselor Rich Twp. High Sch., Park Forest, Ill., 1961-63; residence hall dir., instr. edn. Ill. State U., 1963-64; counselor Office Dean of Men, Purdue U., 1964-65, Office Dean of Men, Purdue U. (Office Student Loans), 1965-66; asst. to pres., lectr. sociology Ill. State U., 1966-69; v.p. acad. affair, dean Towson State U., Balt., 1969-76; pres. So. Ill. U., Edwardsville, 1977-79; chancellor So. Ill. U. System, Edwardsville, 1979-86; pres. U. Wis. System, Madison, 1986-91; chancellor Syracuse U., 1991—. Trustee CICU, Albany, N.Y., 1993—, Am. Coll. Testing, 1990—; bd. dirs. Unity Mutual Life Ins. Co., 1992—, Syracuse (N.Y.) C. of C., 1991—, NCAA Pres. Commn., 1993—, Met. Devel. Assn., 1991—, Key Bank of Ctrl. N.Y., 1995—. Recipient Young Leader in Edn. award, 1980, Citizen of Yr. award So. Ill. Inc., 1985, Silver Anniversary award NCAA, 1986, Coaches Silver Anniversary award Nat. Assn. of Basketball, 1986; named to Ill. Basketball Hall of Fame, 1983. Mem. Am. Assn. State Colls. and Univs. (external rels. com. 1986-88), Am. Coun. Edn. (com. on minorities in higher edn. 1987-91), Am. Social. Assn., Am. Higher Edn. Assn., State Higher Edn. Exec. Officers Assn., Phi Delta Kappa, Pi Gamma Mu. Office: Syracuse Univ Off of Chancellor Syracuse NY 13244-1100

SHAW, L. EDWARD, JR., lawyer; b. Elmira, N.Y., July 30, 1944; s. L. Edward and Virginia Anne (O'Leary) S.; m. Irene Ryan; children—Christopher, Hope, Hillary, Julia, Rory. B.A. in Econs., Georgetown U., Washington, 1966; J.D., Yale U., New Haven, 1969. Bar: N.Y. 1969. Assoc. Milbank, Tweed, Hadley & McCloy, N.Y.C., 1969-77, ptnr., 1977-83; sr. v.p., gen. counsel Chase Manhattan Corp., N.Y.C., 1983-85, exec. v.p., gen. counsel, 1985-96; gen. counsel Natwest Market, N.Y.C., 1996—. Mem. Assn. Bar City N.Y., Winged Foot Golf Club, Phi Beta Kappa. Roman Catholic. Avocations: youth athletics; golf. Office: Natwest Market 175 Water St New York NY 10038*

SHAW, LAURIE JO, grant project director; b. Morris, Minn., Feb. 23, 1956; d. Edgar Allen and Dorothy Ruth (Harms) S.; m. Grant William Carlson, July 23, 1983 (div. Feb. 1986). Tchr. aide degree, Hutchinson Area Vocat. Tech., Minn., 1975; audio visual prodn., Hutchinson (Minn.) AVTI, 1976; BA in Psychology, S.W. State U., 1982; MA in Counseling, N.Mex. State U., 1987. Libr. tech. S.W. State U., Marshall, Minn., 1976-84; student svcs. coord. Mohave C.C., Bullhead City, Ariz., 1987-91; counselor, instr. Prestonsburg C.C., Pikeville, Ky., 1992-93; project dir. So. W.Va. C.C., Williamson, 1993—. Mem. AAUW (v.p. 1990-92), Nat. Assn. Student Pers. Adminstrs., Ky. Assn. Student Fin. Aid Adminstrs., Bus. and Profl. Women (pres. 1990-91, Young Career Woman award 1989), W.Va. Assn. Edn. Opportunity Program Pers., Mid.-East Assn. Edn. Opportunity Program Pers. Democrat. Methodist. Avocations: cross country skiing, oriental cooking, collecting Hummels. Office: So WV Community Coll Armory Dr Williamson WV 25661

SHAW, LEANDER JERRY, JR., state supreme court justice; b. Salem, Va., Sept. 6, 1930; s. Leander J. and Margaret S.; m. Vidya B. Lye. BA, W.Va. State Coll., 1952, LLD (hon.), 1986; JD, Howard U., 1957; PhD (hon.) in Pub. Affairs, Fla. Internat. U., 1990; LLD (hon.), Nova Law Sch., 1991, Washington & Lee Law Sch., 1991. Asst. prof. law Fla. A&M U., 1957-60; sole practice Jacksonville, Fla., 1960-69, 72-74; asst. pub. defender Fla., 1965-69; asst. state's atty. Fla., 1969-72; judge Fla. Indsl. Relations Commn., 1974-79, Fla. Ct. Appeals (1st dist.), 1979-83; justice Fla. Supreme Ct., Tallahassee, 1983—, chief justice, 1990-92. Office: Fla Supreme Ct Supreme Ct Bldg Tallahassee FL 32399

SHAW, LEE CHARLES, lawyer; b. Red Wing, Minn., Feb. 17, 1913; s. Marvil Thomas and Bernice (Quinland) S.; m. Lorraine Schroeder, July 1, 1939; children—Lynda Lee, Robert, Candace Jean, Lee Charles. B.A., U. Chgo., 1936, J.D., 1938. Bar: Ill. 1938. Assoc. Pope & Ballard, Chgo., 1938-44, ptnr., 1944-45; founding ptnr. Seyfarth, Shaw, Fairweather & Geraldson, Chgo., 1945—; mem. arbitration svcs. adv. com. Fed. Mediation and Conciliation Svc. Contbr. articles on labor law to profl. jours. Mem. ABA, Chgo. Bar Assn. (bd. mgrs. 1956-57), U. Chgo. Alumni Assn., Tavern Club, Union League Club (Chgo.). Republican. Episcopalian. Home: Pacific Regent La Jolla 3890 Nobel Dr Apt 1702 San Diego CA 92122-5784 Office: Seyfarth Shaw Fairweather 55 E Monroe St Ste 4200 Chicago IL 60603-5702

SHAW, LEONARD GLAZER, electrical engineering educator, consultant; b. Toledo, Aug. 15, 1934; s. A. Daniel and Mary (Glazer) S.; m. Susan Gail Weil, Dec. 24, 1961; children: Howard Benjamin, Mitchell Bruce, Jenny Louise. BSEE, U. Pa., 1956; MSEE, Stanford U., 1957, PhD, 1961. From asst. prof. to assoc. prof. Polytech. U., N.Y., Bklyn., 1960-1975, prof., 1975—, head dept. elec. engring. and computer sci., 1982-90, dean sch. elec. engring. and computer sci., 1990-94; vice provost for undergraduate studies, 1995—. vis. prof. Tech. U., Eindhoven, Netherlands, 1970, Ecole Nationale Superieure de Mecanique, Nantes, France, 1977; cons. Sperry Systems Mgmt. Div., Great Neck, N.Y.; mem. grant rev. panels NSF, 1986—. Author: (with others) Signal Processing, 1975. Contbr. articles to profl. jours. Research grantee NSF, 1973, 81. Fellow IEEE (various coms., editorial bd. 1961-92, editor-in-chief, IEEE Press 1988-91, gen. chmn. Conf. on Decision and Control, Dec. 1989, v.p. Fin. Control System Soc., 1992-93, chair Tech. Field Award Coun., 1995-96; mem. AAAS, Am. Soc. for Engring. Edn. Office: Polytech U Jacobs Coll Engring & Sci 6 Metrotech Ctr Brooklyn NY 11201-2990

SHAW, LILLIE MARIE KING, vocalist; b. Indpls., Nov. 27, 1915; d. Earl William and Bertha Louise (Groth) King; m. Philip Harlow Shaw, June 26, 1940. Student, Jordan Conservatory Music, Indpls., 1940-43; BA, Ariz. State U., 1959; MA, Denver U., 1962; pvt. vocal study, 1944-70. Educator, libr. Glendale (Ariz.) Schs., 1959-67; lectr. libr. sci. Ariz. State U., Tempe, 1962-68. Concertizing, oratorio, symphonic soloist, light opera, 1965-82; soloist First Ch. of Christ Scientist, Sun City West, Ariz., 1980—. Monthly lectr. Christian Women's Fellowship, Phoenix, 1989—; World Conf. del. Soc. of Friends, 1967. Mem. Nat. Soc. Arts and Letters (sec. 1990-94, nat. del. 1992), Am. Philatelic Assn. (life), Am. Topical Assn., Phoenix Philatelic Soc., Auditions Guild Ariz. (sec. 1989-92), Phoenix Opera League, Phoenix Symphony Guild (bd. mem. youth activities 1986—), Sigma Alpha Iota Alumnae (Phoenix chpt., life, treas. 1988-94, Sword of Honor 1972, Rose of Honor 1982, Rose of Dedication 1995). Republican. Avocations: philately, gardening. Home: 6802 N 37th Ave Phoenix AZ 85019-1103

SHAW, M. THOMAS, bishop; s. M.T. and T. Jaynes Shaw. Ed., Alma (Mich.) Coll., Notre Dame U., Gen. Theol. Sem. Ordained priest Episcopal Ch., 1970. Parish priest Milw., from 1970; with Co. of Mission Priests, Eng.; with Soc. St. John the Evangelist, Cambridge, Mass., now novice master, superior; bishop of Mass. Episcopal Diocese. Address: 980 Memorial Dr Cambridge MA 02138

SHAW, MARGERY WAYNE SCHLAMP, geneticist, physician, lawyer; b. Evansville, Ind., Feb. 15, 1923; d. Arthur George and Louise (Meyer) Schlamp; m. Charles Raymond Shaw, May 31, 1942 (div. Nov. 1972); 1 dau., Barbara Rae. Student, Hanover Coll., 1940-41; A.B. magna cum laude, U. Ala., 1945; M.A., Columbia U., 1946; postgrad., Cornell U., 1947-48; M.D. cum laude, U. Mich., 1957; J.D., U. Houston, 1973; D.Sc. (hon.), U. Evansville, 1977, U. So. Ind., 1986. Intern St. Joseph Mercy Hosp., Ann Arbor, Mich., 1957-58; practice medicine specializing in human genetics Ann Arbor, 1958-67; instr. dept. human genetics Med. Sch. U. Mich., 1958-61, asst. prof., 1961-66, assoc. prof., 1966-67; assoc. prof. dept. biology Grad. Sch. Biomed. Scis., U. Tex., Houston, 1967-69; prof. Grad. Sch. Biomed. Scis., U. Tex., 1969-88, dir. Med. Genetics Ctr., 1971-83, acting dean, 1976-78, prof. emeritus, 1988—; mem. genetics study sect. NIH, Bethesda, Md., 1966-70, mem. genetics tng. com., 1970-74, adv. com. to dir., 1979-82; chromosome studies astronauts NASA, 1970-71; mem. med. adv. bd. Nat. Genetics Found., 1972-88; rsch. adv. bd. Planned Parenthood, Houston, 1972-79; vis. scholar Yale Law Sch., 1974; Andrew D. White prof.-at-large Cornell U., 1982-88; vis. prof. U. Utah, 1983; adj. prof. U. Houston Law Ctr., 1986-88. Asso. editor: Am. Jour. Human Genetics, 1962-68; editorial bd.: Am. Jour. Med. Genetics, 1977-87, Am. Jour. Law and Medicine, 1977-88; contbr. articles to profl. jours. First aid instr. ARC, 1962-67; unit chmn. United Fund, 1966. Recipient Billings Silver medal AMA, 1966; Achievement award AAUW, 1970-71; Am. Jurisprudence award, 1973. Mem. Am. Soc. Human Genetics (past sec., dir., pres. 1982), Genetics Soc. Am. (sec. 1971-73, pres. 1977-78, Wilhelmene Key award 1977), Tissue Culture Assn. (trustee 1970-72), Environ. Mutagen Soc. (coun.), Am. Soc. Cell Biology, Am. Soc. Law Medicine (trustee 1980-88), Phi Beta Kappa, Alpha Omega Alpha. Home: 2617 Pine Tree Dr Evansville IN 47711-2117

SHAW, MARI GURSKY, lawyer; b. Chgo., 1947. BA, U. Ill., 1969; JD, U. Wis., 1973. Bar: Wis. 1973, Pa. 1973. Ptnr. Dechert Price & Rhoads, Phila.; chmn. Wilma Theater, 1991-93; chmn. adv. bd. Paly-Levy Gallery, Moore Coll. of Art, 1993—. Office: Dechert Price & Rhoads 4000 Bell Atlantic Tower 1717 Arch St Philadelphia PA 19103-2713

SHAW, MARILYN MARGARET, artist, photographer; b. San Diego, Dec. 19, 1933; d. George Louis and Helen Frances (Wright) Mitchell; m. Robert Dale Shaw, Feb. 19, 1952; children: Austin Allen, Kenneth Duane, Frank Lloyd. BA in Fine Arts and Photography, Juniata Coll., 1989. Photographer The Daily News, Huntingdon, Pa., 1988-92; owner, tchr. Marilyn Shaw Studios, Tyrone, Pa., 1989-95; photographer The Jamesyouth, St. James. Luth. Ch., Huntingdon, 1987-92; photojournalist Easter Seals Telethon, 1991-92; art dir. Allegheny Riding Camp-The GrierSch., Tyrone, Pa., 1992. One-woman shows include Shoemaker Gallery, Huntingdon, 1989; group shows include Standing Stone Art League, Huntingdon, 1978-92, Washington St. Art Gallery, Huntingdon, 1991, 94; author, illustrator The Prize, 1989. Vol. The Huntingdon House, 1992—, Presbyn. Ch., Huntingdon, 1992-95, Tyrone Presbyn. Ch., 1995—. Recipient numerous ribbons Huntingdon County Fair, 1978, 90, 91, Sinking Valley Farm Show, 1992, 94, 95, Huntingdon County Arts Coun., 1989, 90, 91, Merit cert. Photographers Forum, 1989, Vila Gardner Metzger art award, 1989, others. Mem. Standing Stone Art League, Huntingdon County Arts Coun., Women's League Juniata Coll., , Nat. Mus. of Women in the Arts (charter mem.). Avocations: hunting, fishing, needlecrafts, camping, travel. Home and Office: 104 W 12th St Tyrone PA 16686-1634

SHAW, MARY M., computer science educator; b. Washington, Sept. 30, 1943; d. Eldon Earl and Mary Lewis (Holman) Shaw; m. Roy R. Weil, Feb. 15, 1973. BA cum laude, Rice U., 1965; PhD, Carnegie Mellon U., Pitts., 1972. Asst. prof. to prof. computer sci. Carnegie Mellon U., Pitts., 1972—, assoc. dean computer sci. for profl. programs, 1992—, Alan J. Perlis chair computer sci.; chief scientist Software Engring. Inst., Carnegie Mellon U., Pitts., 1984-88; mem. Computer Sci. and Telecommunications Bd., NRC, Washington, 1986-93. Author: Fundamental Structures of Computer Science, 1981, The Carnegie Mellon Curriculum for Undergraduate Computer Science, 1985, (with David Garlan) Software Architecture: Perspectives on an Emerging Discipline, 1996; contbr. articles to profl. jours. Recipient Warnier prize, 1993; named Woman of Achievement, YWCA of Greater Pitts., 1973. Fellow AAAS, IEEE (disting. lectr.), Assn. for Computing Machinery (SIGPLAN exec. com. 1979-83, Recognition of Svc. award 1985, 90); mem. Sigma Xi. Office: Carnegie Mellon U Dept Computer Sci Pittsburgh PA 15213

SHAW, MELVIN PHILLIP, physicist, engineering educator, psychologist; b. Bklyn., Aug. 16, 1936; s. Harry and Yetta (Stutsky) S.; m. Carol Joan Phillips, Sept. 5, 1959 (div. Feb. 1987); children: Adam, Evan; m. Bernetta Berger, May 16, 1987. BS, Bklyn. Coll., 1959; MS, Case Western Res. U., 1963, PhD, 1965; MA, Ctr. for Humanistic Studies, 1988. Research scientist United Techs. Research Labs., E. Hartford, Conn., 1964-68, scientist-in-charge, 1966-70; prof. Wayne State U., Detroit, 1970—; adminstrv. dir. Assocs. of Birmingham/Kingswood Hosp., 1991-93; cons. Energy Conversion Devices, Troy, Mich., 1970-92. Co-author: The Gunn-Hilsum Effect, 1979, The Physics and Applications of Amorphous Semiconductors, 1988, The Physics of Instabilities in Solid State Electron Devices, 1992, Creativity and Affect, 1994. Fellow Am. Phys. Soc.; mem. IEEE (sr.), Am. Psychol. Assn. (assoc.). Avocations: cooking, walking, travel.

SHAW, MICHAEL, biologist, educator; b. Barbados, W.I., Feb. 11, 1924; s. Anthony and Myra (Perkins) S.; m. Jean Norah Berkinshaw, Oct. 16, 1948; children—Christopher A., Rosemary E., Nicholas R., Andrew L. B. Sc., McGill U., 1946, M. Sc., 1947, Ph.D., 1949, D.Sc., 1975. Nat. Research Council Can. postdoctoral fellow Botany Sch., Cambridge U., 1949-50; Assoc. prof. biology U. Sask., 1950-54, prof., 1954-67, prof., head dept. biology, 1961-67; dean faculty agrl. scis. U. B.C., 1967-75, v.p. acad. devel., 1975-81, acad. v.p., provost, 1981-83, univ. prof., 1983-89, univ. prof. emeritus, 1989—; mem. Sci. Council Can., 1976-82, Natural Scis. and Engring. Research Council Can., 1978-80. Contbr. articles to profl. jours. Recipient Queen's Silver Jubilee medal, 1977, gold medal Biol. Coun. Can., 1983. Fellow Royal Soc. Can. (Flavelle medal 1976), Can. Phytopath. Soc., Am. Phytopath. Soc., N.Y. Acad. Scis.; mem. Can. Bot. Assn., Can. Soc. Plant Physiologists (gold medal 1971), Am. Soc. Plant Physiologists. Home: 1792 Western Pky, Vancouver, BC Canada V6T 1V3 Office: U BC, Dept Plant Sci, Vancouver, BC Canada V6T 1Z4

SHAW, MICHAEL ALLAN, lawyer, mail order company executive; b. Evanston, Ill., July 14, 1940; s. Frank C. and Mabel I. (Peacock) S.; m. Genevieve Schrodt, Aug. 16, 1964; children: M. Ian, Trevor A. BA, Colo. State U., 1962; JD, U. Denver, 1965; MBA, DePaul U., 1969; postgrad., Columbia U., 1970. Bar: Ill. bar 1965. Practiced in Chgo., 1965-83; asst. counsel, staff asst. to v.p. traffic Jewel Cos., Inc., Melrose Park, Ill., 1965-71; corp. sec., asst. treas., house counsel Wieboldt Stores, Inc., Chgo., 1972-83; pvt. practice law Naperville, Ill., 1983-89; pres. Kingston Korner, Inc., Naperville, Ill., 1983—, Aztec Corp., Naperville, Ill., 1989—. Pres. Folk Era Prodns., producers folk music concert series, records, 1985—; editor Folk Music Editor, 1984; contbr. articles to legal jours. Mem. Village Planning Commn., Itasca, Ill., 1973-77; bd. dirs. Crimestoppers, Naperville, 1984—, chmn., 1988-94; session mem. Naperville Lumen Christi United Presbyn. Ch., 1984-85; chmn. bldg. fin. com. Naperville Presbyn. Ch., 1989-93. Mem. Fox Valley Folklore Soc. (bd. dirs. 1991—). Home: 6 S 230 Cohasset Rd Naperville IL 60540 Office: Aztec Corp 705 S Washington St Naperville IL 60540-6654

SHAW, MICHAEL LEE, social studies educator; b. Joliet, Ill., July 27, 1954; s. Richard James and Geneva B. (Briggs) S. AAS, Joliet Jr. Coll., 1979; BS, Ea. Ill. U., 1982. Cert. tchr. K-9. Tchr. 6th grade social studies St. Clement, Chgo., 1982—. With U.S. Army, 1975-77. Recipient Heart of Sch. award Archdiocese of Chgo., 1989-90. Mem. Nat. Coun. for Social Studies. Home: 715 W Barry Ave Apt 2D Chicago IL 60657-4579 Office: St Clement Sch 2524 N Orchard St Chicago IL 60614-2512

SHAW, MILTON CLAYTON, mechanical engineering educator; b. Phila., May 27, 1915; s. Milton Fredic and Nellie Edith (Clayton) S.; m. Mary Jane Greeninger, Sept. 6, 1939; children—Barbara Jane, Milton Stanley. B.S. in Mech. Engring, Drexel Inst. Tech., 1938; M.Eng. Sci., U. Cin., 1940, Sc.D., 1942; Dr. h.c., U. Louvain, Belgium, 1970. Research engr. Cin. Milling Machine Co., 1938-42; chief materials br. NACA, 1942-46; with Mass. Inst. Tech., 1946-61, prof. mech. engring., 1953-61, head materials processing div., 1952-61; prof., head dept. mech. engring. Carnegie Inst. Tech., Pitts., 1961-75; univ. prof. Carnegie Inst. Tech., 1974-77; prof. engring. Ariz. State U., Tempe, 1977—; Cons. indsl. cos.; lectr. in, Europe, 1952; pres. Shaw Smith & Assos., Inc., Mass., 1951-61; Lucas prof. Birmingham (Eng.) U., 1961; Springer prof. U. Calif. at Berkeley, 1972; Distinguished guest prof. Ariz. State U., 1977; mem. Nat. Materials Adv. Bd., 1971-74; bd. dirs. Engring. Found., 1976, v.p. conf. com., 1976-78. Recipient Outstanding Research award Ariz. State U., 1981; Am. Machinist award, 1972; P. McKenna award, 1975; Guggenheim fellow, 1956; Fulbright lectr. Aachen T.H., Germany, 1957; OECD fellow to Europe, 1964—. Fellow Am. Acad. Arts and Scis., ASME (Hersey award 1967, Thurston lectr. 1971, Outstanding Engring. award 1975, ann. meeting theme organizer 1977, Gold medal 1985, hon. 1980), Am. Soc. Lubrication Engrs. (hon., nat. award 1964), Am. Soc. Metals (Wilson award 1971, fellow 1981); mem. Internat. Soc. Prodn. Engring. Research (pres. 1960-61, hon. mem. 1975), Am. Soc. for Engring. Edn. (G. Westinghouse award 1956), Soc. Mfg. Engrs. (hon. mem. 1970, Gold medal 1958, internat. edn. award 1980), Nat. Acad. Engring., Polish Acad. Sci., Am. Soc. Precision Engrs. (hon.). Home: C119 2625 E Southern Ave Tempe AZ 85282-7633 Address: Arizona State Univ Engring Dept Tempe AZ 85287-6106

SHAW, MILTON HERBERT, conglomerate executive; b. Phila., June 16, 1918; s. Milton Herbert and Ethel (Shane) S.; m. Rita P. Revins, Nov. 24, 1971. BS, U. Pa., 1949. cons. indsl. safety and workmen's compensation. Accountant Franklin Sugar Refinery, Phila., 1945-52; with Kaiser Metal Products, Inc., Bristol, Pa., 1952-61; mgr. ins. and taxes Kaiser Metal Products, Inc., 1955-61; with Kidde Consumer Durables Corp., Bala Cynwyd, Pa., 1961-88; asst. v.p. Kidde Consumer Durables Corp., 1968-88, dir. corp. svcs. and risk mgmt., 1977-88; cons. Indsl. Safety-Workmans Compensation, 1988; owner Golden Grain Goldens; co-owner Potpourri Promotions, Rita P. Shaw Porcelain Studio. Served with USNR, 1936-45. Mem. NRA, VFW (treas. home assn. post 9788), Nat. Wildlife Fedn., Sigma Kappa Phi. Home and Office: 2209 Blackhorse Dr Warrington PA 18976-2118

SHAW, MONTGOMERY THROOP, chemical engineering educator; b. Ithaca, N.Y., Sept. 11, 1943; s. Robert William and Charlotte (Throop) S.; m. Stephanie Habel, Sept. 5, 1966 (dec. 1989); 1 child, Steven Robert; m. Maripaz Nespral, June 25, 1994. BChemE, Cornell U., 1966, MS, 1966; MS, Princeton (N.J.) U., 1968, PhD, 1970. Engr., project scientist Union Carbide Corp., Bound Brook, N.J., 1970-76; assoc. prof. Dept. Chem. Engring., U. Conn., Storrs, 1977-83, prof., 1983—; sabbatical prof. Sandia Nat. Labs., Albuquerque, 1983-84; vis. scientist E.I. Dupont de Nemours and Co., Experimental Station, Wilmington, Del., 1991-92; adv. bd. Jour. of Applied Polymer Sci., 1984-89. Co-author: Polymer-Polymer Miscibility, 1977, Computer Programs for Rheologists, 1994. Grantee Alcoa Found., 1985, Exxon Edn. Found., 1986. Mem. IEEE (sr. mem., assoc. editor transactions on dielectrics and elec. insulation), Soc. Rheology (sec. 1977-81), Am. Chem. Soc., Am. Phys. Soc. Achievements include patents on rheological measurement method and apparatus and low density microcellular foams. Office: U Conn IMS 97 S Eagleville Rd Storrs Mansfield CT 06268-2502

SHAW, NANCY RIVARD, museum curator, art historian, educator; b. Saginaw, Mich.; d. Joseph H. and Jean M. (O'Boyle) Marcotte; m. Danny W. Shaw, Feb. 29, 1980; 1 stepchild, Christina Marie. BA magna cum laude, Oakland U., 1969; MA, Wayne State U., 1973. Asst. curator Am. art Detroit Inst. Arts, 1972-75, curator, 1975—; adj. prof. art and art history Wayne State U., Detroit, 1991—. Contbg. author: American Art in the Detroit Institute of Arts, 1991; contbr. articles to exhbn. catalogues and profl. jours. Mem. Wayne State U. Alumni Assn. Roman Catholic. Avocations: knitting, painting, golf. Office: Detroit Inst Arts 5200 Woodward Ave Detroit MI 48202-4008

SHAW, SIR NEIL MCGOWAN, sugar, cereal and starch refining company executive; b. Montreal, Que., Can., May 31, 1929; s. Harold LeRoy and Fabiola Marie (McGowan) S; m. Frances Audrey Robinson, July 6, 1952; children: David, Michael, Cynthia, Andrea, Sonia; m. 2nd Elizabeth Mudge Massey, Sept. 15, 1985. Student, Lower Coll. With Tate & Lyle plc, London, 1986—, chmn., 1992-93; vice chmn. Redpath Industries Ltd., Toronto, 1981; bd. dirs. United Biscuits Holdings, plc, U.K., Alcantara, Portugal, Can. Imperial Bank of Commerce, Toronto, Tate & Lyle Mgmt. and Fin. Ltd., Bermuda, Tunnel Refineris, Inst. of Dirs., mem. adv. com., 1991; chmn. Tate & Lyle Holdings, London, 1981-91; mem. adv. coun. Prince's Youth Bus. Trust, 1990—; chmn., dir. World Sugar Rsch. Orgn., U.K., 1982, 94; dir. A.E. Staley, Decatur, 1988-91. Gov. Reddy Meml. Hosp., Montreal Gen. Hosp., World Econ. Forum, World Food Argo Forum; mem. adv. coun. Youth Enterprise Scheme, 1986; chmn. Anglo Can. Support Group Care, 1989; mem. Can. Meml. Found., 1989; mem. adv. coun. London Enterprise Agy., 1986; chmn. Bus. in Cmty., 1991-96; trustee Royal Botanic Gardens Kew Found., 1990—, chmn. Trustees and Friends Royal Botanic Gardens Kew, 1994; dir. Theatre Royal Windsor, 1991—. Named Knight Bachelor; honored at Queen of Eng. Birthday, 1994. Fellow Inst. Grocery Distbn.; mem. Food Assn. Can. Univs. Soc. Gt. Britain (adv. coun. 1989), Brit. N.Am. Com., Ptnrs. of the World, Brit. Inst. Mgmt. (companion 1981—), Home-Start Consultancy (v.p.), Toronto Golf Club, Brooks Club, Toronto Club, Wentworth Golf Club, Taymouth Estate Golf Club (Scotland), Per Cent Club (joint chmn.). Avocations: skiing, golf, sailing. Office: Tate & Lyle PLC, Sugar Quay Lower Thames St, London EC3R 6DQ, England

SHAW, RANDALL FRANCIS, state legislator; b. Concord, N.H., Sept. 5, 1931; s. Joseph F. and Irma A. (Randall) S.; m. Margaret J. Geary, Dec. 23, 1942; children: Randall J., Joel T. BS, Franklin Pierce Coll., Rindge, N.H., 1983. Supervising field auditor U.S. PFO, Concord, 1965-75, supervising computer specialist, 1975-85; asst. U.S. Property and Fiscal Office, Concord, 1985-90; mem. N.H. Ho. of Reps., Concord, 1990—. Mem. N.H. Republican Com., Concord, 1994, Merrimack County Exec. Com., Concord, 1994. Served to lt. col. U.S. Army Res., 1954-86. Mem. Res. Officers Assn., Am. Legion, Masons. Home: 425 Deerpath Ln Pembroke NH 03275-3214 Office: State Legislature State House Concord NH 03301

SHAW, RICHARD ALLAN, lawyer; b. Portland, Oreg., Oct. 14, 1937; s. Leland B. and Vena (Gaskill) S.; m. Jo-Ann O. Shaw, Mar. 23, 1959; 1 child, Kevin A. BS, U. Oreg., 1959, JD, 1962; LLM in Taxation, NYU, 1963. Bar: Oreg. 1962, Ariz. 1967, Calif. 1969. Assoc. Kramer, Roche, Burch, Streich & Cracchiolo, Phoenix, 1966-68, Hewitt & Greaves, San Diego, 1968-71; ptnr. Hewitt & Shaw, San Diego, 1972-77; pres., sr. mem. Shenas, Shaw & Spievak A.P.C., San Diego, 1978-96; ptnr. Shaw & O'Brien, LLP, San Diego, 1996—; teaching fellow NYU Sch. Law, N.Y.C., 1962-63; disting. adj. prof. advanced bus. planning and advanced corporate tax problems U. San Diego Sch. Law, 1978—; founding incorporator, dir. San Diego County Bar Found., 1979; lectr. insts. and programs nationally. Editor Oreg. Law Rev., 1961-62, The Fed. Bar Jour., 1964-68, The Tax Lawyer, 1973-74, Jour. of S Corp. Taxation, 1988—; contbr. articles in field to profl. jours. Pres. San Diego County Boy Scouts, 1982-84; chmn. Washington-Lincoln Laurels for Leaders, San Diego, 1986-87; chmn. Corp. Fin. Coun., 1993-94; chmn. Eagle Scout Alumni Assn., 1978. Capt. JAGC, U.S. Army, 1963-66. Recipient Silver Beaver award Boy Scouts Am., San Diego, 1979, Silver Antelope award, 1982, Disting. Eagle Scout award, 1988. Fellow Am. Coll. Tax Counsel, ABA (chmn. tax. com. on S corps. 1974-76, coun. dir. taxation sect. 1988-94, vice-chmn. taxation sect. 1991-94); chair Taxation Taskforce White House Conf. on Small Bus.; mem. Oreg. State Bar, Ariz. State Bar, Calif. State Bar (chmn. taxation sect. 1981-82, V. Judson Klien award 1985), Western Region Tax Bar Assn. (chmn. 1988), San Diego County Bar Assn. (chmn. bus. law sect. 1974), Kiwanis (disting. past pres. 1985-86). Republican. Avocations: skiing, painting, stained glass. Office: Shaw & O'Brien 701 B St Ste 2200 San Diego CA 92101-8111

SHAW, RICHARD DAVID, marketing and management educator; b. Pitts., Kans., Aug. 25, 1938; s. Richard Malburn and Jessie Ruth (Murray) S.; m. Adolphine Catherine Brungardt, Aug. 21, 1965; children: Richard David Jr., John Michael, Shannon Kathleen. BSBA, Rockhurst Coll., 1960; MS in Commerce, St. Louis U., 1964. Claims adjuster Kemper Ins. Group, Kansas City, Mo., 1961; tchr. acctg. Corpus Christi High Sch., Jennings, Mo., 1961-63; assoc. prof. econs. Fontbonne Coll., St. Louis, 1963-70; chmn. social behavioral sci. dept. Fontbonne Coll., 1968-70; mem. faculty, chmn. bus. div. Longview Community Coll., Lee's Summit, Mo., 1970-81, coord. mktg., 1979-81; assoc. prof. mktg. Rockhurst Coll., Kansas City, 1981—, chmn. mgmt. and mktg., 1983-85; workshop leader Rockhurst Coll., 1975—, faculty moderator Jr. Execs. Assn., The Rock yearbook, Students in Free Enterprise, Rockettes; pvt. cons., 1981—, chmn. freshman seminar com., 1994; instr. principles of mktg. on The Learning Channel on Cable TV for the PACE Program, 1994; chmn. sch. mgmt. curriculum com., 1993—. Author: Personal Finance, 1983, Principles of Marketing Study Guide, 1993, Contemporary Marketing Study Guide, 1994, Consumer Behavior Study Guide, Instructor's Manual for Michael Solomon's Consumer Behavior; cooperating author: Philip Kotler's Marketing Management. Mem. alumni bd. assessment task force Rockhurst Coll., 1971-73, 78-80, chmn. 30 yr. reunion com., 1990, 35 yr. reunion com., 1995, chmn. curriculum com., curriculum task force; chmn. Eastwood Hills Coun., Kansas City, 1974-76, bd. dirs., 1988-91, co-chmn. of Solid Rocks Faculty-Staff Fund Raising Campaign, 1994; lead couple Marriage Preparation Classes, Kansas City St. Joseph Dioceses; co-chmn. Kansas City Vols. Against Hunger, 1975-80; campaign mgr. Larry Ferns for City Coun., Kansas City, 1975; bd. govs. Citizens Assn., 1976—. With USAR, 1960-64. Recipient Gov.'s Excellence in Teaching award, Mo., 1993; Hallmark fellow Rockhurst Coll.; faculty devel. grantee Sch. Mgmt., Rockhurst Coll., 1984, 93, 95. Mem. Am. Mktg. Assn., Soc. for Advancement of Mgmt., Mid-Am. Mktg. Assn., Alpha Sigma Nu. Roman Catholic. Avocations: racquetball, gardening, photography, sand volleyball. Home: 11014 Washington St Kansas City MO 64114-5177 Office: Rockhurst Coll 1100 Rockhurst Rd Kansas City MO 64110-2508

SHAW, RICHARD EUGENE, cardiovascular researcher; b. Springfield, Ohio, Jan. 20, 1950; s. Eugene Russell and Marjorie Catherine (Lewe) S.; m. Christine Elizabeth Costa, Nov. 26, 1976; children: Matthew, Brian. BA, Duquesne U., 1972; MA, U.S. Internat. U., San Diego, 1977; PhD, U. Calif., San Francisco, 1984. Cert. nuclear med. technologist. Staff nuclear med. technician Scripps Meml. Hosp., La Jolla, Calif., 1975-79; rsch. asst. U. Calif. San Francisco Sch. Medicine, 1980-85; mgr. rsch. programs San Francisco Heart Inst., Daly City, Calif., 1985-87, dir. rsch., 1988-90, dir. rsch. and ops., 1991—; sr. advisor steering com. for databases Daus. of Charity Nat. Health Systems, St. Louis, 1993—; cons. HealthLink SmartPhone comms. informatics project, San Francisco, 1992—. Editor-in-chief Jour. Invasive Cardiology, King of Prussia, Pa., 1989—; contbr. more than 200 articles and book chpts. to med. lit. Coach Am. Youth Soccer Orgn., Burlingame, Calif., 1990—. Fellow Am. Coll. Cardiology; mem. Am. Heart Assn., Soc. for Clin. Trials, N.Y. Acad. Scis., Am. Statis. Assn., Soc. Behavioral Medicine. Avocation: music. Office: San Francisco Heart Inst-Seton Med Ctr 1900 Sullivan Ave Daly City CA 94015-2200

SHAW, ROBERT E., carpeting company executive; b. Cartersville, GA, 1931. Pres., chief exec. officer Star Finishing Co. Inc. (merged into Shaw Industries Inc.), Dalton, Ga., until 1969; now pres., chief exec. officer Shaw Industries Inc., Dalton, Ga., 1969—, also bd. dirs., 1969—. Office: Shaw Industries Inc 616 E Walnut Ave Dalton GA 30721-4409*

SHAW, ROBERT EUGENE, minister, administrator; b. Havre, Mt., Apr. 8, 1933; s. Harold Alvin and Lillian Martha (Kruse) S.; m. Marilyn Grace Smit, June 14, 1957; children—Rebecca Jean, Ann Elizabeth, Mark David, Peter Robert. B.A., Sioux Falls Coll., 1955; M.Div., Am. Baptist. Sem. of West, 1958; D.D. (hon.), Ottawa U., 1976, Judson Coll., 1984. Ordained to ministry Am. Bapt. Chs. U.S.A., 1958; pastor First Bapt. Ch., Webster City, Ia., 1958-63, Community Bapt. Ch., Topeka, Kans., 1963-68; sr. pastor Prairie Bapt. Ch., Prairie Village, Kans., 1968-78; pres. Ottawa U., Kans., 1978-83; exec. minister Am. Bapt. Chs. Mich., East Lansing, 1983—; mem. gen. bd. Am. Bapt. Chs. U.S.A., Valley Forge, Pa., 1972-80, nat. v.p., 1978-80; nat. v.p. Am. Bapt. Minister Council, Valley Forge, 1969-72, nat. pres., 1972-75; nat. chair Am. Bapt. Evang. Team, 1988—; mem. Internat. Commn. on Edn. and Evangelism, Bapt. World Alliance, 1990—; mem. nat. exec. com. Am. Bapt. Adminstrs. Colls. and Univs., 1980-82; bd. dirs. Kans. Ind. Colls. Assn., 1980-82. Trustee No. Bapt. Theol. Sem., Lombard, Ill.,

1983—, Kalamazoo Coll., Mich., 1983—, Judson Coll, Elgin, Ill., 1983—; dir. Webster City C. of C., 1961-62, Ottawa C. of C., 1980-82. Office: Am Baptist Chs of Mich 4578 S Hagadorn Rd East Lansing MI 48823-5355

SHAW, ROBERT FLETCHER, retired civil engineer; b. Montreal, Que., Can., Feb. 16, 1910; s. John Fletcher and Edna Mary Baker (Anglin) S.; m. Johann Alexandra MacInnes, Dec. 24, 1935; 1 son, Robert Fletcher (dec.). B.C.E., McGill U., Montreal, 1933; D.Sc. (hon.), McGill U., 1985; Sc.D. (hon.), McMaster U., 1967, U. N.B., 1986; D.Eng. (hon.), Tech. U. of N.S., 1967. Registered profl. engr., Que. With Found. Co. Can. Ltd., Montreal, 1933-63; pres. Found. Co. Can. Ltd., 1962-63, dir., 1968-71; shipyard mgr. Found. Maritime Ltd., Pictou, N.S., 1943-45; on loan to Govt. Can. as v.p., chief engr. Def. Constrn. (1951) Ltd., 1951-52; on loan as mem. working party mil. airfields NATO, 1952; dep. commr. gen., also dir. Expo '67, Montreal, 1963-68; v.p. adminstrn. McGill U., 1968-71; chmn. bd., dir. Found. Can. Engring. Corp., 1968-71; dep. minister environment Govt. Can., 1971-75; pres., dir. Monenco Pipeline Cons. Ltd., 1975-78; adv. Nfld. Dept. Indsl. Devel., 1978-80; sr. cons. Montreal Engring. Co. Ltd., 1975-92; chmn. rsch. policy com. Ctr. Cold Ocean Resources Engring. Meml. U. Nfld., 1981-82. Bd. govs. McGill U., 1964-68; bd. govs. U. N.B., 1973-85, chmn., 1978-80; bd. govs. Montreal Gen. Hosp., 1963-94; pres. Can. Assn. Mentally Retarded, 1963-65; bd. dirs. Montreal Internat. Music Competition, 1967-87. Decorated companion Order Can., 1967; recipient Can. Centennial medal, 1967, citation Engring. News Record, 1967, Queen's Jubilee medal, 1977; named Hon. Chmn. Can. Engring. Centennial Bd., 1984-87. Fellow Engring. Inst. Can. (pres. 1975-76, Julian C. Smith award 1967, Keefer medal 1979), Can. Soc. Civil Engrs., fellow Can. Acad. of Engring, 1987—, mem. Order Engrs. Que. (pres. 1953), Can. Council Profl. Engrs. (v.p. 1954, gold medal 1979), Grads. Soc. McGill U. (pres. 1964-65, Gold medal 1968), Royal Montreal Golf. Home: Apt C29, 3980 Cote des Neiges Rd, Montreal, PQ Canada H3H 1W2 *Exploding population is creating a heavy demand on the world's resources. If species man is to survive and improve, he must innovate, mass produce, provide the additional energy required, enhance the environment, and learn the value of interdependence. So far we are losing ground. The human reaction to these problems seems to be confrontation, conflict, fragmentation and increased social and economic nationalism. I hope that I have made a contribution to increasing productivity, better management and more interdependent action.*

SHAW, ROBERT GILBERT, restaurant executive, senator; b. Erwin, N.C., Nov. 22, 1924; s. Robert Gilbert B. and Annie Elizabeth (Byrd) S.; m. Grace Lee Wilson, Jan. 29, 1951 (div. 1976); children: Ann Karlen, Barbara Jean; m. Linda Owens, May 27, 1982. AA, Campbell U., 1948; postgrad., U. N.C., 1948-50. Restauranteur, 1951—. County commr. County of Guilford, Greensboro, N.C., 1968-76; chair N.C. Rep. Ctrl. Com., Raleigh, 1975-77; minority leader N.C. Senate, Raleigh, 1984—; chair Guilford County Rep. Ctrl. Com., 1973-75; active Rep. Nat. Ctrl. Com., Washington, 1975-77. With U.S. Army, 1943-46. Named Legislator of Yr. Nat. Fedn. Wildlife, 1990. Mem. Elks (life, bd. govs. 1953—). Presbyterian. Avocations: fishing, hunting, politics. Home: 4901 Tower Rd Greensboro NC 27410-5724 Office: NC Senate 1129 Legislative Bldg Raleigh NC 27611

SHAW, ROBERT LAWSON, symphony orchestra conductor; b. Red Bluff, Calif., Apr. 30, 1916; s. Shirley Richard and Nelle Mae (Lawson) S.; m. Maxine Farley, Oct. 15, 1939 (div. 1973); children: Johanna, Peter Thein, John Thaddeus; m. Caroline Sauls Hitz, Dec. 19, 1973; 1 child, Thomas Lawson. AB, Pomona Coll., 1938; hon. degree, Coll. of Wooster, 1951, Pomona Coll., 1953, St. Lawrence U., 1955, Mich. State U., 1960, Kenyon Coll., 1962, U. Alaska, 1963, Cleve. Inst. Music, 1966, Case Western Res. U., 1966, Emory U., 1967, Fla. State U., 1968, Westminster Choir Coll., 1975, U. Akron, 1976, Morehouse Coll., 1977, Oglethorpe U., 1977, Baldwin-Wallace Coll., 1980, Stetson U., 1983, New Eng. Conservatory, 1983, St. Olaf Coll., 1985, Duke U., 1988, Atlanta Coll. Art., 1988, Fla. So. Coll., 1989, Baylor U., 1990, Rhodes Coll., 1990, Johns Hopkins U., 1990, Eastman Sch. Music, 1991, State U. of N.Y., 1993, Ind. Univ., 1993, Boston U., 1994. Dir. choral music Juilliard Sch. Music, N.Y.C., 1945-48; founder, condr. Robert Shaw Chorale, 1948-65; condr. San Diego Symphony, 1953-57; music dir. Alaska Festival, Anchorage, 1956-75; assoc. condr., dir. choruses Cleve. Orch., 1956-67; condr., music dir. Atlanta Symphony Orch., 1967-88, music dir. emeritus and conductor laureate, 1988—; vis. prof. U. Tex, Austin, 1988. Dir. Fred Waring Glee Clubs, 1938-45; founder, condr. Collegiate Chorale, N.Y.C., 1941-60, choral dir.: Aquacades, 1942-43, Carmen Jones, 1943, Seven Lively Arts, 1944, Berkshire Music Ctr., Tanglewood, Mass., 1945-48; guest condr. numerous orchs. including, Chgo. Symphony, Cin. Symphony, Minn. Orch., N.Y. Philharm., Phila. Orch., Boston Symphony, NBC Symphony, Dallas Symphony, others; recs. on RCA Victor, Telarc, Vox (Turnabout), Pro Arte and New World labels including (with Robert Shaw Chorale) Mass in B Minor by Bach (Grammy award 1961), Ceremony of Carols by Britten (Grammy award 1964), Handel's Messiah (Grammy award 1966), Gloria by Poulenc (Grammy award 1965), Symphony of Psalms by Stravinsky (Grammy award 1965), (with Atlanta Symphony) Pellaes et Melisande by Faure (Grammy award 1986), Requiem by Berlioz (2 Grammy awards 1986), Verdi Requiem, 1989 (2 Grammy awards, Gramaphone award), Rorem String Symphony, 1989 (Grammy award). Recipient ASCAP award 1976, 81, 86, Alice M. Ditson award Columbia U., 1955, Govs. award in the arts, Ga., 1973, 75, Disting. Svc. award Atlanta Boys Club, 1975, Nat. Fedn. Music Clubs award, 1975, Samuel Simons Sanford medal Yale U., 1980, Am. Choral Dirs. Assn. award, 1981, Martin Luther King Jr. award for artistic achievement, 1982, Fulton County (Ga.) Arts Coun. award, 1985, Gold Baton award Am. Symphony Orch. League, 1988, George Peabody medal for outstanding contbn. to music in Am. Peabody Conservatory, 1990, Kennedy Ctr. Honors, 1991, Nat. Medal of Arts award White House, 1992, Theodore Thomas award Conductor's Guild, 1993; Guggenheim fellow, 1944, Ind. U. fellow, 1983; Housewright Eminent scholar Fla. State U., 1986; named Outstanding Am. Born Condr. of Yr., 1943, Musician of Yr. in Musical Am., 1992. Office: Atlanta Symphony Orch 1293 Peachtree St NE Atlanta GA 30309-3525

SHAW, ROBERT WILLIAM, JR., management consultant, venture capitalist; b. Ithaca, N.Y., Aug. 10, 1941; s. Robert William and Charlotte G. (Throop) S.; m. Anne P. Meads, Aug. 29, 1964; children: Mark Andrew, Christopher Matthew. B of Engring. Physics, Cornell U., 1964, MSEE, 1964; PhD, Stanford U., 1968; MPA, Am. U., 1981. Postdoctoral fellow Cavendish Lab., Cambridge, Eng., 1968-69; mem. tech. staff Bell Tel. Labs., Murray Hill, N.J., 1969-72; with Booz Allen Hamilton, Bethesda, Md., 1972-83, sr. v.p. energy and environ. divsn., 1979-83, mem. oper. coun., 1981-83, also bd. dirs.; pres. Arete Ventures, Inc., 1983—, Utech Venture Capital Corp., 1985—; gen. ptnr. Utech Venture Capital Corp. Fund I, 1985—, Utech Venture Capital Corp. Fund II, 1988—, Utech Venture Capital Corp. I Parallel Fund L.P., 1988—, Utech Venture Capital Corp. II Parallel Fund, L.P., Rockville, Md., 1991—, Utech Climate Challenge Fund, L.L.C., 1995—; v.p. Can. Energy and Environment Ventures, Inc., 1993-95; mem. energy com. Aspen Inst. Humanistic Studies, Investor's Cir.; chmn. bd. dirs. Superconductivity, Inc., Evergreen Solar, Inc.; bd. dirs. Nanophase Tech. Corp. Contbr. articles to profl. jours. NASA trainee; Office Sci. rsch. fellow USAF, 1968-69. Mem. AAAS, Am. Phys. Soc. (mem. investment com.), Nat. Venture Capital Assn., Orgnl. Devel. Network, Assn. Humanistic Psychology, Inst. Noetic Scis., Internat. Transactional Analysis Assn., Sigma Xi, Tau Beta Pi, Phi Kappa Phi, Pi Alpha Alpha, Kappa Delta Rho. Home: 9405 Falls Bridge Ln Rockville MD 20854-3953 Office: 6110 Executive Blvd Ste 1040 Rockville MD 20852-3903

SHAW, RONALD AHREND, physician, educator; b. Toledo, July 20, 1946; s. Harold Michael and Eve Helen (Ganch) S.; m. Carol Ann Rapp, June 13, 1970; children: Robert, Benjamin, Daniel. BS, U. Toledo, 1968; MD, Washington U., 1972. Diplomate Am. Bd. Emergency Medicine. Intern, then resident in surgery St. Luke's Hosp., St. Louis, 1972-73, resident in surgery, 1973; mem. staff Bapt. Med. Ctr.-Montclair, Birmingham, Ala., 1976-81, chief emergency svc., 1979-81; assoc. dir. lifesaver flight ops. Caraway Meth. Med. Ctr., Birmingham, 1981-85; dir. emergency svc. sch. medicine U. Ala., 1985-89; asst. dir. emergency svc. R.I. Hosp., Providence, 1989-95; cons. U. Tex., Houston, 1986, Bell Helicopter, Ft. Worth, 1986, Mut. Assurance, Birmingham, 1986-89, NYU, 1988-89, R.I. State Med. Examiners Office, 1991—, Fla. Dept. Health, EMS Office, 1991—, Joint Underwriters Assocs. of R.I., 1991—; chmn. adv. bd. emergency svc. Ala. Dept. Pub. Health, 1986-89; med. dir. Emergency Med. Svcs. div. R.I. Dept. Health, 1990-95; med. dir. Health Care Rev., Inc., 1995—. Bd. dirs. MADD, Ala., 1986, Univ. Emergency Medicine Found., 1995—; mem. planning com. Youth Baseball, Vestavia Hills, ala., 1986, 87; mem. disaster com. City of Birmingham, 1984-89; mem. 911 Commn., State of R.I., 1991—. Recipient Disting. Achievement award Birmingham Emergency Med. Svc., 1988. Fellow Am. Coll. Emergency Physicians (bd. dirs. Ala. chpt. 1984-89, steering com. EMS sect. 1991-94, sec.-treas. R.I. chpt. 1995—); mem. AAAS, ACS (state com. on trauma R.I. chpt. 1990—), N.Y. Acad. Sci., Med. Assn. Ala. (mem. coun. med. svc. 1985-86). Republican. Avocations: hunting, stamp and record collecting. Office: RI Hosp Dept Emergency Medicine 593 Eddy St Providence RI 02903-4923

SHAW, ROSLYN LEE, elementary education educator; b. Bklyn., Oct. 1, 1942; d. Benjamin Biltmore and Bessie (Banilower) Deretchin; m. Stephen Allan Shaw, Feb. 1, 1964; children: Laurence, Victoria, Michael. BA, Bklyn. Coll., 1964; MS, SUNY, New Paltz, 1977, cert. advanced study, 1987; cert. gifted edn., Coll. New Rochelle, 1986. Cert. sch. adminstr., supr., sch. dist. adminstr., reading tchr., tchr. N-6. Tchr. Hillel Hebrew Acad., Beverly Hills, Calif., 1965-66, P.S. 177, 77, Bklyn., 1964-65, 66-67; tchr. Middletown (N.Y.) Sch. Dist., 1974-77, reading specialist, 1977—, compensatory edn. reading tchr., 1977-95, tchr. gifted children, 1984-87, asst. project coord. pre-K, 1988-89, instrnl. leader, 1989-93. Pres. Middletown H.S. Parents' Club, 1983-86; bd. dirs. Mental Health Assn., Goshen, N.Y., 1980-81; mem. Middletown Interfaith Coun., 1983-85. Mem. ASCD, Amy Bull Crist Reading Coun. (pres. 1989-91, 93-95), N.Y. State Reading Assn. (Coun. Svc. award 1990, regional dir. 1991-94, bd. dirs. 1991—, chair reading tchrs. spl. interest group 1993-94, newsletter editor The Empire State Reading Scene), Internat. Reading Assn., Univ. Women's Club, Delta Kappa Gamma. Avocations: swimming, photography, walking, reading. Home: 133 Highland Ave Middletown NY 10940-4712 Office: Liberty St Sch 6 Liberty St Middletown NY 10940-5508

SHAW, RUSSELL BURNHAM, association executive, author; b. Washington, May 19, 1935; s. Charles Burnham and Mary (Russell) S.; m. Carmen Hilda Carbon, July 19, 1958; children: Mary Hilda, Emily Anne, Janet, Charles, Elizabeth. BA, Georgetown U., 1956, MA, 1960. Staff writer Cath. Standard, Washington, 1956-57; reporter Nat. Cath. News Svc., 1957-66; dir. publs., pub. info. Nat. Cath. Ednl. Assn., 1966-69; dir. Nat. Cath. Office for Info., 1969-73; assoc. sec. for communication U.S. Cath. Conf., 1973-74, sec. for pub. affairs Nat. Conf. Cath. Bishops, 1975-87; dir. pub. info. KC, 1987—; consultor Pontifical Commn. for Social Communications, 1984-89. Author: The Dark Disciple, 1961, Abortion on Trial, 1968, Church and State, 1979, Choosing Well, 1982, Why We Need Confession, 1986, Renewal, 1986, Signs of the Times, 1986, Does Suffering Make Sense?, 1987, To Hunt, To Shoot, To Entertain, 1993, Understanding Your Rights, 1994; co-author: S.O.S. for Catholic Schools, 1970, Beyond the New Morality, 3d edit., 1988, Fulfillment in Christ, 1991, others; columnist (monthly mag.) Washington Report, 1966—; Washington corr. Our Sunday Visitor, 1988—. Mem. Pub. Rels. Soc. Am., Nat. Press Club, Equestrian Order of Holy Sepulchre of Jerusalem, Phi Beta Kappa. Roman Catholic. Home: 2928 44th Pl NW Washington DC 20016-3555 Office: Knights of Columbus 401 Michigan Ave NE Washington DC 20017

SHAW, RUSSELL CLYDE, lawyer; b. Cleve., Mar. 19, 1940; s. Clyde Leland and Ruth Arminta (Williams) S.; BS, Ohio State U., 1962; JD, Ohio State U., 1965; m. Jane Ann Mohler, Feb. 15, 1969 (div. 1988); children: Christopher Scott, Robin Nicole, Curtis Russell; m. Lynn Baird Breuer, Oct. 21, 1989; stepchildren: Heather Breuer, Matthew Breuer, Russell Breuer. Bar: Ohio 1965, U.S. Supreme Ct. 1968. Assoc., Thompson, Hine & Flory, Cleve., 1965, 69-74, ptnr., 1979-93, chmn. area specialty group, 1988-90; ptnr. Walter & Haverfield (formerly Walter, Haverfield, Buescher & Chockley), Cleve., 1993—, chmn. area specialty group, 1993—. Mem. Geauga United Way Svcs. Council, 1980-87, officer, 1982-87, chmn. (chief vol. officer), 1984-87; trustee United Way Svcs. of Cleve., 1983-88, assoc. v.p., 1986-88; trustee Cleve. Community Fund, 1986-88, Ohio Citizen's Council; trustee Ohio United Way, 1986—, v.p., 1987-90, chmn., 1990-92, mem. exec. com., 1990—; chmn. Ohio Citizen's Council Welfare Reform Task Force, 1987-90, mem. United Way of Am. Welfare Reform Task Force; mem. Ohio Adv. Coun. for the Aging, 1990—, vice chmn., 1992-93, chmn., 1993—; mem. Gov. Ohio's Ops. Improvement Task Force, 1991-93; Nat. Inst. for Responsible Fatherhood and Family Devel., 1990—, trustee, exec. com. mem. Fairmount Presbyn. Ch.; del. White House Conf. on Aging, Washington, 1995. Served to capt. AUS, 1965-69. Recipient Harvey H. Hebert Meml. award Delta Sigma Phi, 1989; named to Honorable Order of Ky. Cols. Commonwealth of Ky. Mem. ABA (employee benefits com. taxation sect.), Def. Rsch. Inst. (employee benefits com.), Fed. Bar Assn., Ohio Bar Assn., Nat. Lawyers Club, Internat. Found. Employee Benefit Plans, Employee Benefits Attys. Forum Cleve., Old English Sheepdog Club Am. (nat. officer 1972-74), Fedn. Ohio Dog Clubs (pres. 1978-82), Sugarbush Kennel Club (pres. 1975-78, 81—), Midwest Pension Conf., Delta Sigma Phi (nat. officer 1975—, nat. officer Found. 1978—, trustee Found. 1983—, Herbet Meml. award), Pres.'s (Ohio State U.). Presbyterian. Office: Walter & Haverfield 50 Public Sq 1300 Terminal Tower Cleveland OH 44113

SHAW, SAMUEL ERVINE, II, retired insurance company executive, consultant; b. Independence, Kans., Apr. 10, 1933; s. Samuel Ervine and Jessie Elizabeth (Guernsey) S.; m. Dale Foster Dorman, June 19, 1954; children: Samuel Ervine III, Christopher Atwood, Elizabeth Foster. BA, Harvard U., 1954; JD, Boston Coll., 1965. Bar: Mass. 1965, U.S. Supreme Ct. 1971; enrolled actuary 1976-93; cons. actuary, 1987. With John Hancock Mut. Life Ins. Co., Boston, 1957-87, group pension and ins. actuary, 2d v.p., 1979-85, v.p., group ins. actuary, 1985-87; dir. Health Reins. Assn. Conn., Hartford, 1980-87; cons. Internat. Exec. Service Corps, Guayaquil, Ecuador, 1973, Jakarta, Indonesia, 1988, Perm, Russia, 1994, Pension Benefit Guaranty Corp., Washington, 1974-75, Nat. Hosp. Ins. Fund, Nairobi, Kenya, 1990. Mem. Brookline Hist. Commn. (Mass.), 1981-88, Brookline Retirement Bd., 1985-90; chmn. Brookline Com. on Town Orgn. and Structure, 1975-79. Served to maj. USAF, 1954-57. Fellow Soc. Actuaries; mem. Am. Acad. Actuaries, Internat. Actuarial Assn., ABA, Mass. Bar Assn., Boston Bar Assn. Episcopalian. Home and Office: 131 Sewall Ave Brookline MA 02146-5314

SHAW, SCOTT ALAN, photojournalist; b. Danville, Ill., 1963. BS in Journalism, So. Ill. U., 1985. Formerly with The Comml. News, Danville; with The Paragould (Ark.) Daily Press, 1985-86; staff photographer The Odessa (Tex.) Am., 1986-89; with St. Louis Sun, 1989-90; now staff photographer The Plain Dealer, Cleve., 1990—. Recipient Pulitzer Prize for spot news photgraphy, 1988. Office: The Plain Dealer 1801 Superior Ave E Cleveland OH 44114-2107

SHAW, SONDRA ANN, English language and business educator; b. Louisville, Aug. 31, 1944; d. Sam Vernon Williams and Katie Cozine (Robards) Clay; m. Roosevelt Shaw, Nov. 24, 1962 (div. 1982); children: Kevin, Roosevelt Jr., Mark, Patrick, Sonya, Rafiq, Sharifah, Sabriya. BS, Medaille Coll., 1987; postgrad., Buffalo State Coll., 1989. Peer tutor Medaille Coll., Buffalo, 1984-87; peer mentor Buffalo State Coll., 1988, media specialist, 1988-89; supr., asst. dir. Buffalo Pub. Access Ctr., 1989-91; instr. Erie C.C., Buffalo, 1992-93; adminstrv. svcs. clk. Buffalo Correctional Facility, 1992-93; instr. U. Buffalo, 1992—; supr. U.S. Census Bur., Buffalo, 1990; instr. Bryant & Stratton Bus. Inst., 1994—. Editor: (newsletters) Mt. Calvary Holy Church, 1979-86, Buffalo Public Access, 1990-91; contbr. articles and poetry to jours. Pub. rels. rep. Help A Neighbor Orgn., Buffalo, 1983-85; community adv. Victim Witness Asst., Buffalo, 1987; founder black history club Medaille Coll., Buffalo, 1987. Recipient Media scholarship Urban League, Buffalo, 1986. Mem. Urban Christian Ministries (women's aux., vice chair), Just Buffalo Lit. Soc., Soc. Profl. Journalists. Democrat. Avocations: soloist, catering, interior decorating. Home: 325 Winslow Ave Buffalo NY 14211-1254

SHAW, STANLEY MINER, nuclear pharmacy scientist; b. Parkston, S.D., July 4, 1935; s. George Henry and Jensina (Thompson) S.; m. Excellda J. Watke, Aug. 13, 1961; children: Kimberly Kay, Renee Denise, Elena Aimee. BS, S.D. State U., 1957, MS, 1959; PhD, Purdue U., 1962. Instr. S.D. State U., 1960-62; asst. prof. bionucleonics Purdue U., West Lafayette, Ind., 1962-66; assoc. prof. Purdue U., 1966-71, prof. nuclear pharmacy, 1971—, head. Div. Nuclear Pharmacy, 1990—, acting head Sch. Health Scis., 1990-93; mem. Bd. Pharm. Spltys., Splty. Council Nuclear Pharmacy, 1978-82. Contbr. sci. articles to profl. jours. Recipient Lederle Pharmacy faculty awards, 1962, 65, Parenteral Drug Assn. rsch. award, 1970, Henry Heine Outstanding Tchr. award Sch. Pharmacy Purdue U., 1989, 93, Disting. Alumnus award S.D. State U., 1991, Disting. Pharmacy Educator award AACP, 1994. Fellow Acad. Pharmacy Practice (chmn. sect. nuclear pharmacy 1979-80, historian 1981-85, mem.-at-large 1993-95, chair-elect 1995-96, chair 1996—), Am. Soc. Hosp. Pharmacy; mem. Health Physics Soc., Am. Pharm. Assn. (ho. of dels. 1977, 79, 86, 92, Founder's award nuclear pharmacy sect.), Sigma Xi, Phi Lambda Upsilon, Phi Lambda Sigma, Rho Chi. Assembly of God. Home: 7208 W Greenview Dr Battleground IN 47920 Office: Purdue U Sch Pharmacy West Lafayette IN 47907-1333

SHAW, STEPHEN LYNN, geoscientist; b. San Angelo, Tex., May 28, 1949; s. Joe William and Verda D. (Tankersley) S.; m. Nancy Berry Keeling; children: Katherine Lynn, William Keeling. BS in Geology, U. Tex., Austin, 1971, MA in Geology, 1974. Cert. profl. geol. scientist Am. Inst. Profl. Geologists. Ground water hydrologist William F. Guyton & Assocs., Austin, 1973-79; exploration geologist Superior Oil, Midland, Tex., 1979-81, exploration supr., 1981; exploration geologist Buckeye Energy, Midland, Tex., 1981-82, Conquest Exploration, Midland, Tex., 1982-86; adj. geology instr. U. Tex. Permian Basin, Odessa, 1983-84; petroleum geologist Meridian Oil, Midland, 1986-93, regional geoscientist, 1993—. Contbr. articles to Tex. Jour. Sci., West Tex. Geol. Soc. Bull. Bd. dirs. Permian Basin Grad. Ctr., Midland, 1986-87, Midland Energy Libr., 1990—, West Tex. Geology Found., Midland, 1992-95, Midland Habitat for Humanity, 1994—; vestry mem. St. Nicholas Episcopal Ch., Midland, 1990-92. Mem. Am. Assn. Petroleum Geologists (cert., vice-chmn. elect ho. of dels. 1995—, del.), Geol. Soc. Am., West Tex. Geol. Soc. (pres.), Nat. Ground Water Assn., Midland Lee Football Booster Club (pres., v.p., adviser). Episcopalian. Home: 3513 Stanolind Midland TX 79707 Office: Meridian Oil 3300 N A St Bldg 6 Midland TX 79705

SHAW, STEVEN JOHN, retired marketing educator, academic administrator; b. Hamilton, N.Y., Nov. 16, 1918; s. Constantine J. and Agnes (Tilicki) S.; m. Aracelis Goberna, June 8, 1952. B.S., N.Y. State U., 1941; M.S. in Retailing, N.Y. U., 1946, Ph.D., 1955. Instr. mktg. U. Miami, Coral Gables, Fla., 1948-52; asst. prof. Tulane U., New Orleans, 1954-55, U. Fla., Gainesville, 1955-57; assoc. prof., then prof. U. S.C., Columbia, 1957-89, Disting. prof. emeritus, 1989—, dir. dept. mktg., 1968-72; cons. Hoffman LaRoche, Nutley, N.J.; exec. dir. S.C.-Southwestern Colombia chpt. Ptnrs. of Ams., 1977-79, asst. exec. dir., 1987-91, also bd. dirs. Author: Salesmanship: Modern Viewpoints on Personal Communication, 1960, Marketing in Business Management, 1963, Cases in Marketing Management Strategy, 1971. Recipient N.Y. U. Founders Day award, 1956, Steven J. Shaw award for most scholarly article in Jour. Bus. Research. Mem. So. Marketing Assn. (pres. 1964), Beta Gamma Sigma (pres. 1965). Home and Office: 7600 Tryall Dr Hialeah FL 33015-2931

SHAW, TALBERT O., university president. BD, Andrews U., 1963; MA, U. Chgo., 1968, PhD, 1973. Dean of students Oakwood Coll., Huntsville, Ala., 1965-71; dean Howard U., Washington, 1971-76; dean Coll. Arts and Scis. Morgan State U., Balt., 1976-87; pres. Shaw U., Raleigh, N.C., 1987—. Office: Shaw U 118 E South St Raleigh NC 27601-2341

SHAW, TIMOTHY MILTON, political science educator; b. Frimley, Surrey, Eng., Jan. 27, 1945; came to Can., 1971; s. Arnold J. and Margaret E. (Milton) S.; m. Jane L. Parpart, Sept. 2, 1983; children—Laura, Lee Parpart; m. Susan M. Sturt, July 8, 1967 (div. 1980); children—Benjamin, Amanda. B.A., Sussex U., Brighton, Eng., 1967; M.A., East Africa U., Kampala, Uganda, 1969; M.A., Princeton U., 1971, Ph.D., 1975. Vis. faculty mem. Makerere U., Kampala, 1966-70, U. Zambia, Lusaka, 1973-74, Carleton U., Ottawa, Ont., Can., 1978-79, U. Ife, Nigeria, 1979-80, U. Zimbabwe, 1989, Rhodes U., South Africa, 1993; prof. polit. sci. Dalhousie U., Halifax, N.S., Can., 1971-73, 74-78, 80—; dir. Centre African Studies, Halifax, 1983-89, dir. Centre for Fgn. Policy Studies, Halifax, 1993—; dir. Internat. Devel. Studies Program, 1986-89; dir. Pearson Inst., Halifax, 1985-87, Canadian Internat. Devel. Agy., 1994-95; cons. UN Econ. Commn. for Africa, Addis Ababa, Ethiopia, 1983-88; editor Macmillan Press Internat. Polit. Economy Series, London, 1984—. Author: Reformism and Revisionism in Africa's Political Economy in the 1990s, 1993; co-editor (with Julius Nyang'oro) Beyond Structural Adjustment in Africa, 1992, Corporatism in Africa, 1988, Political Economy of NICs, 1988, (with Larry A. Swatuk) The South at the End of the Twentieth Century, 1994, (with Julius E. Okolo) The Politcal Economy of Foreign Policy in ECOWAS, numerous others. Mem. New Democratic party, Halifax, 1984—. Research grantee Social Scis. & Humanities Research Council of Can., Africa, 1981—. Mem. Internat. Polit. Sci. Assn. (chair study group # 3 on New World Orders?), Can. Assn. Devel. Studies (pres. 1993-94), Can. Assn. African Studies (pres. 1984-85), Internat. Studies Assn. (pres. global devel. sect. 1995-96), Waegwoltic Club (Halifax). Avocations: jogging; cooking; building; traveling. Home: 1143 Studley Ave, Halifax, NS Canada B3H 3R8 Office: Dalhousie University, Halifax, NS Canada B3H 4H6

SHAW, VALEEN JONES, special education educator, elementary school educator; b. Coalville, Utah, June 19, 1930; d. G. Allen and Mabel Leon (Clark) Jones; m. Melvin Francis Shaw, June 21, 1948; children: C. Allene Shaw Fuhriman, Denise Ellen Shaw Call, Sharon Marie Shaw Williams. BS, Weber State U., Ogden, Utah, 1966; postgrad., U. Utah, Utah State U., Brigham Young U. Cert. tchr. elem. edn., early childhood edn., spl. edn. Tchr. 3rd grade Morgan (Utah) Sch. Dist., 1965-66; tchr. 6th grades N. Summit Sch. Dist., Coalville, Utah, 1966-67, tchr. 2d grades, 1967-82, tchr. resource, spl. edn., 1982-92, teaching specialist elem. summer sch. prog., 1967-92; elementary resource and spl. edn. tchr. North Summit Sch. Dist., Coalville, 1982-92; mentor N. Summit Elementary Sch., 1988-89. Tchr./trainer Coalville Ch. of Jesus Christ of Latter-day Saints. &D. Mem. NEA, ASCD Inst., Utah Edn. Assn., Morgan Edn. Assn., North Summit Edn. Asssn, Utah Fedn. Coun. for Exceptional Children.

SHAW, WARD ERIC, information company executive; b. Boston, Dec. 8, 1945; s. Erwin and Barbara (Ward) S.; m. Janet Seeley; children: Eric, Tucker; m. 2d Heather Cameron; 1 child, Geoffrey. AB, Hamilton Coll., 1967; SM, Simmons Coll., 1968; LLD (hon.), U. No. Colo., 1990. Asst. dir. Colby Coll. Libr., Waterville, Maine, 1968-72; assoc. dir. U. Denver Libr., 1972-78; exec. dir. Colo. Alliance of Rsch. Libr., Denver, 1978-88; chmn., CEO Carl Corp., Denver, 1988—; cons. in field; mem. various bds. Author, editor various publs. Recipient Lita Gaylord award for excellence in libr. and info. tech. ALA, 1989. Home: 2202 S Milwaukee St Denver CO 80210-4830 Office: Carl Corp 3801 E Florida Ave Denver CO 80210-2571

SHAW, WILLIAM FREDERICK, statistician; b. Bklyn., Feb. 24, 1920; s. Charles Peter and Josephine Veronica (Seusing) S.; m. Josephine Cannington Kerbey, Jan. 18, 1947; children—William Frederick, Teresa Anne. B.B.A., U. Miami, 1949; M.A., George Washington U., 1953; postgrad. studies in econometrics, math. and computer scis., U.S. Dept. Agr. Grad. Sch., 1964-74; Ph.D. (fellow), Walden U., 1977. Research asst. U. Miami, 1948-49; with Research and Stats. div. FHA, Washington, 1950-73; chief statistician Research and Stats. div. FHA, 1969—; chief statistician, dir. Advanced Statis. Analysis and Computer Applications Staff HUD, 1974-82, chief statistician, dir. housing stats. div., 1982-89, chief statistician, dir. info. systems div., 1990-91, chief statistician, dir. Office of Evaluation, 1991—; pres. Kerbey-Shaw Assos. Served with F.A. AUS, 1943-45. Decorated D.S.C., Silver Star and Bronze Star medals for heroism; recipient Superior Performance award HUD, 1977; named by Info. Resources Adminstrn. Council as Fed. Office Systems Profl. of Yr., 1983. Mem. AAAS, Am. Statis. Assn., Am. Risk and Ins. Assn., Western Fin. Assn., Am. Real Estate and Urban Econ. Assn., So. Econ. Assn., Va. Assn. Economists, Am. Econ. Assn., Am. Fin. Assn., Assn. Computing Machinery, Am. Ednl. Rsch. Assn., N.Y. Acad. Scis., Nat. Assn. Rev. Appraisers and Mortgage Underwriters, So. Fin. Assn., Soc. Cost Estimating and Analysis, Res. Offcers Assn. U.S., 101st Airborne Divsn. Assn., Air Force Assn., Alpha Kappa Psi. Roman Catholic. Home: 6527 Byrnes Dr Mc Lean VA 22101-5227 Office: HUD 7th and D Sts SW Washington DC 20411

SHAW, WILLIAM VAUGHAN, architect; b. Los Angeles, Apr. 12, 1924; s. Norman Tooker and Elizabeth Allison (Kennedy) S.; m. Mary Morse, Sept. 14, 1967; stepchildren: Susan Osborne, Charles D. Osborne, Polly

Osborne, Ellen Osborne. BA in Architecture, U. Calif. at Berkeley, 1950. Practice architecture Carmel, Calif., 1951-55; partner Walter Burde, Burde Shaw & Assos., Carmel, 1955-69; founder, prin. Will Shaw & Assos., Monterey, Calif., 1969—; trustee Monterey Bay Aquarium. (Recipient Calif. Gov.'s award in environmental design for Shell Ser. Sta., Carmel 1964, Urban Renewal Design Award Progressive Architecture mag. 1973). Pres. Calif. 7th Agr. Dist., 1964-65; founder, pres. Monterey County Citizens Planning Assn., 1960-65; chmn. design adv. com. Monterey County, 1960-65; exec. dir. Found. Environmental Design, 1963-69; chmn. exec. com. Monterey Found., 1965-67, pres., 1972-73; bd. dirs. Pebble Beach Corp., 1976—; pres., founding mem. Big Sur Found., 1977—. Served to lt. USNR, 1944-47, PTO. Fellow Am. Acad. in Rome, 1968. Fellow AIA (pres. Monterey chpt. 1964, AIA Honor award for Merchant Built houses 1968). Clubs: Old Capital (Monterey), Pacific Biol. Lab. (Monterey). Office: 225A Cannery Row Monterey CA 93940-1436

SHAW-COHEN, LORI EVE, magazine editor; b. Manhattan, N.Y., Apr. 22, 1959; d. Ray and Carole (Bergenthal) Shaw; m. Robert Mark Cohen, Sept. 20, 1981; children: Joshua Samuel, Drew Taylor, Logan Shaw. BA in Journalism, U. So. Calif., 1981. Editorial asst., writer BBW: Big Beautiful Woman Mag., Los Angeles, 1979-80; editorial asst., writer Intro Mag., Los Angeles, 1980-81; mng. editor 'Teen Mag., Los Angeles, 1981-86; writer, interviewer Stan Rosenfeld & Assocs. Pub. Relations, Los Angeles, 1980-81; cons. BBW: Big Beautiful Woman Mag., Los Angeles, 1981—, Media Research Group, Los Angeles, 1984; condr. seminars Women in Communication, Los Angeles, 1983, Pacific N.W. Writers Conf., Seattle, 1984. Patentee children's toy, 1971; lyricist for songs, 1977—; contbr. articles and poems to profl. jours. and mags. Avocations: travel; reading; photography; horseback riding. Office: BBW: Big Beautiful Woman Mag 19528 Ventura Blvd # 298 Tarzana CA 91356-2917

SHAWL, S. NICOLE, hypnobehavioral scientist; b. South Amboy, N.J., July 26, 1940; d. Michael Joseph and Kathleen Shawl; life ptnr. Donna J. Talcott. BA, Georgian Court Coll., 1971; MA, Kean Coll. of N.J., Union, 1975; PhD, Calif. Coast U., Santa Ana, 1992; postgrad., Saybrook Inst., San Francisco; postgrad. studies in hypno-behavioral psychology, The Union Inst., Cin. Joined Sisters of Mercy, 1958, left, 1966; cert. student pers. svcs. adminstr., prin., supr., dir. student pers. svcs., substance awareness coord. Georgian Ct. Coll., substance awareness coord. State of N.J.; cert. hypnobehavioral therapist. Tchr. pub. and parochial schs., Monmouth & Ocean Counties, N.J., 1960-79; interviewer, pub. rels. mgr. ARC, Toms River, N.J., 1980; editor, writer Prentice-Hall, Englewood Cliffs, N.J., 1980; counselor, asst. dir. coll. program Georgian Court Coll., Lakewood, N.J., 1980—; adj. instr. UCLA, 1975-76; owner, pres. Auntie Nuke Enterprises. Active NOW. Mem. AAUW, ACLU, ACA, NOW, So. Poverty Law Ctr., Mercy Higher Edn. Colloquium Assn., Nat. Guild Hypnotists, Am. Soc. Clin. Hypnosis, Nat. Psychology Adv. Assn., Nat. Bd. for Cert. Clin. Hypnotherapists, Inc., Nat. Coun. of Ednl. Oppty. Assn., Union Inst. Ctr. for Women. Democrat. Avocations: singing opera,. sailing, fishing and crabbing, gardening, carpentry. Office: Georgian Court Coll 900 Lakewood Ave Lakewood NJ 08701-2600

SHAWN, WALLACE, playwright, actor; b. N.Y.C., Nov. 12, 1943; s. William and Cecille (Lyon) S. BA., Harvard U., 1965; BA, Oxford U., Eng., 1968, MA, 1975. Instr. English Indore Christian Coll., Madhya Pradesh, India, 1965-66; tchr. English, Latin, drama Ch. of Heavenly Rest Day Sch., N.Y.C., 1968-70; shipping clk. Laurie Love Ltd., N.Y.C., 1974-75; machine operator Hamilton Copy Ctr., N.Y.C., 1975-76. Author: (plays) Our Late Night, 1975 (Obie award for disting. playwriting 1975), Summer Evening, 1976, The Youth Hostel, 1976, Mr. Frivolous, 1976, (libretto) In the Dark, 1976, (trans.) The Mandrake, 1977, Marie and Bruce, 1980, The Hotel Play, 1981, Aunt Dan and Lemon, 1985; (monologue) The Fever, 1990 (Obie award for best play 1991); (screenplay) My Dinner with Andre, 1981; actor: (theatre) The Mandrake, 1977, The Master and Margarita, 1978, Chinchilla, 1979, The First Time, 1983, Ode to Napoleon Bonaparte, 1984, Aunt Dan and Lemon, 1985, The Fever, 1991; (films) Manhattan, 1979, Starting Over, 1979, All That Jazz, 1979, Simon, 1980, Atlantic City, 1981, My Dinner with Andre, 1981, A Little Sex, 1982, The First Time, 1983, Deal of the Century, 1983, Lovesick, 1983, Strange Invaders, 1983, Saigon-Year of the Cat, 1983, Crackers, 1984, The Hotel New Hampshire, 1984, The Bostonians, 1984, Micki and Maude, 1984, Heaven Help Us, 1985, Head Office, 1986, Radio Days, 1987, The Bedroom Window, 1987, Nice Girls Don't Explode, 1987, Prick Up Your Ears, 1987, The Princess Bride, 1987, The Moderns, 1988, She's Out of Control, 1989, Scenes From the Class Struggle in Beverly Hills, 1989, We're No Angels, 1989, Shadows and Fog, 1992, Mom and Dad Save the World, 1992, Nickel and Dime, 1992, The Cemetary Club, 1993, Un-Becoming Age, 1993, The Meteor Man, 1993, Vanya on 42nd Street, 1994, Mrs. Parker and the Vicious Circle, 1994, Canadian Bacon, 1995, Clueless, 1995; (TV) The Cosby Show, Taxi, How To Be Perfect In Three Days. Fulbright scholar, India, 1956-66. Office: care Rosenstone/Wender 3 E 48th St New York NY 10017-1027 Office: William Morris Agy 151 S El Camino Dr Beverly Hills CA 90212-2704

SHAY, JOHN E., JR., academic administrator; b. Rochester, N.Y., July 29, 1933; m. Patricia Kopacz; children: Maria, John, David. B.A., U. Fla., 1955; M.A., Tchrs. Coll., Columbia U., 1960; Ph.D. in Higher Edn., U. Mich., 1966. Asst. dir. student activities Harpur Coll., SUNY, 1960-62; dean men Marshall U., 1964-65, dean student affairs, 1965-67; dean student Coll. Holy Cross, 1967-71, v.p. student affairs, 1969-71; v.p. student affairs U. R.I., 1971-80; pres. Marygrove Coll., Detroit, 1980—; v.p. student pers. adminstr. W.Va. Coll. and Univs., 1966-67. Contbr. articles to profl. jours. Trustee Detroit Symphony Orch. Hall; bd. dirs. Sta. WTVS-Pub. TV, Detroit, Greater Detroit Interfaith Roundtable NCCJ. Mem. NAACP, Nat. Assn. Student Pers. Adminstrs. (edn. bd. 1967-70, region I v.p. 1970-71), Mich. Colls. Found. (exec. com.), Nat. Assn. Ind. Colls. and Univs. (bd. dirs.), Assn. Ind. Coll. and Univs. Mich. (treas., exec. com.). Office: Marygrove Coll Office of the Pres 8425 W Mcnichols Rd Detroit MI 48221-2546

SHAY, ROSHANI CARI, political science educator; b. Milw., Oct. 5, 1942; d. Walter John and Dorothee May (Dahnke) O'Donnell; 1 child, Mark Sather. Student, Willamette U., 1960-63; BA, U. Oreg., 1968, MA, 1971, PhD, 1974. Adminstrv. asst. Dept. of Youth Svcs., Lubbock, Tex., 1963; teaching asst., instr. U. Oreg., Eugene, 1969-72; vis. asst. prof. Oreg. State U., Corvallis, 1973-74, Willamette U., Salem, Oreg., 1973-79, Lewis and Clark Coll., Portland, Oreg., 1976, 78; from asst. prof. to prof. Western Oreg. State Coll., Monmouth, 1979—, chair history, polit. sci., pub. adminstrn. dept., 1991-94; chair social sci. divsn., 1994—. Author: (with others) The People of Rajneeshpuram, 1990, Annual Yearbook on the Sociology of Religion, 1995, (simulation) European Unity Project, 1982. Co-founder, v.p., sec.-treas Ind. Opportunities Unltd., Salem, 1986—; co-founder, sec. Inst. for Justice and Human Rights, San Francisco, 1988-94; bd. dirs. Oreg. UN Assn., Portland, 1982—, Salem UN Assn., 1982-91; v.p., pres., bd. dirs. Garten Found. for Disabled, Salem, 1989—; pres. Assn. Oreg. Faculties, 1989-91; mem. adv. bd. Connections Program for Disabled Deaf, Salem, 1989—; pres., bd. dirs. Model UN of the Far West, San Diego, 1981-84, 86-88, 95—; mem. Oreg. Women's Polit. Caucus. Danforth Found. fellow, 1968-74; named Woman of Achievement YMCA Tribute, Salem, 1990, Mem. of Yr., Oreg. Rehab. Assn., 1995. Mem. Am. Fedn. Tchrs. (v.p., legis. officer local 2278 1982-88), Western Polit. Sci. Assn., Communal Studies Assn., Mental Health Assn. Oreg., Oreg. Acad. Sci., Oreg. Internat. Coun., Phi Kappa Phi (hon.). Democrat. Avocations: volunteer work with multiply disabled deaf, reading, meditation. Home: 348 S Main St Falls City OR 97344-9763 Office: Western Oreg State Coll 345 Monmouth Ave N Monmouth OR 97361-1314

SHAYE, ROBERT KENNETH, cinema company executive; b. Detroit, Mar. 4, 1939; s. Max Mendle and Dorothy (Katz) S.; m. Eva G. Lindsten, 1970; children: Katja, Juno. B.B.A., U. Mich., 1960; postgrad., Sorbonne, 1961; J.D., Columbia U., 1964. Bar: N.Y. 1967. Chmn. of the bd. New Line Cinema Corp., N.Y.C., 1967—; trustee Neurosci. Inst., Coneucon Film Inst.; dir. Mind, Body Found., Turner Broadcasting Sys. Mem. Gov. Adv. Bd. on Motion Pictures and TV. Recipient 1st prize Rosenthal competition Soc. Cinematologists, 1964; recipient cert. of merit Inst. Copyrights and Patents, U. Stockholm, 1966; Recipient award ASCAP/Nathan Burkan Meml. competition, 1964; Fulbright scholar, 1964-66. Mem. Motion Picture Pioneers (bd. dirs.). Club: Friar's (N.Y.C.). Office: New Line Cinema 116 N Robertson Blvd West Hollywood CA 90048-3103 also: New Line Cinema Corp 888 7th Ave New York NY 10106 *Life is a lot tougher than television watching in the '50's led me to believe.*

SHAYKIN, LEONARD P., investor; b. Chgo., Nov. 17, 1943; s. Lawrence L. and Rose (Yaker) S.; m. Norah Josephine Kan, June 26, 1966; children: Benjamin, Gabriel, Rebecca. BA, U. Chgo., 1965, MA, 1966, MBA, 1973; postgrad., U. Sussex, Brighton, Eng., 1970. Investment officer First Capital Corp., Chgo., 1970-74; asst. to chmn. Apeco Corp., Chgo., 1975-76; div. pres. Brown Mfg. Co., Woodstock, Ill., 1976-78; v.p. Citicorp Venture Capital, N.Y.C., 1978-79; v.p., dir. Citicorp Capital Investors, N.Y.C., 1979-82; mng. ptnr. Adler & Shaykin, N.Y.C., 1983—; bd. dirs. Addiction Recovery Corp. Waltham, Mass., GP Tech. Inc., Somerville, N.J., Joy Techs., Inc., Pitts., Best Products, Inc., Richmond, Folger-Adam Inc., Ill., Athena Ptnrs., Israel; chmn., bd. dirs. Peterson Outdoor Advt., Inc., Orlando, 1986-88, Chicago Sun-Times, 1986—; chmn., pres. N.Y. Venture Capital Forum, N.Y.C., 1983; chmn. USIL Investments, Israel. Chmn. Hebrew Arts Sch. and Merkin Concert Hall, N.Y.C., 1983-86. Avocations: sailing, skiing. Home: 101 Central Park W Apt 2F New York NY 10023-4204 Office: Shaykin and Co 375 Park Ave New York NY 10152 Also: Chgo Sun-Times Inc 401 N Wabash Ave Rm 110 Chicago IL 60611-3532*

SHAYMAN, JAMES ALAN, nephrologist, educator; b. Chgo., June 14, 1954; s. Benjamin and Chernie (Abrams) S.; m. Deborah Berko, May 30, 1976; children: Rebecca Lynn, David Aaron. AB, Cornell U., 1976; MD, Washington U., St. Louis, 1980. Intern and resident Barnes Hosp., St. Louis, 1980-83; instr. Washington U., St. Louis, 1985-86; asst. prof. U. Mich., Ann Arbor, 1986-92, assoc. prof., 1992—. Mem. Am. Soc. Nephrology, Internat. Soc. Nephrology, Am. Diabetes Assn., Am. Soc. Clin. Investigation, Am. Physiol. Soc., Phi Beta Kappa, Phi Kappa Phi, Alpha Omega Alpha. Achievements include research in renal inositol phosphate metabolism and renal glycolipid metabolism. Office: U Mich Med Ctr 1500 E Med Ctr Dr Ann Arbor MI 48109

SHAYNE, ARNIE See SCHWARTZ, ARNOLD

SHAYNE, STANLEY H., lawyer. Ptnr. Baker & Hostetler, Columbus, Ohio; mng. ptnr. Shayne & Greenwald, 1995—. Office: Shayne & Greenwald 221 High St Columbus OH 43215*

SHAYS, CHRISTOPHER, congressman; b. Stamford, Conn., Oct. 18, 1945; m. Betsi deRaismes, 1968; 1 child. BA, Principia Coll.; MBA, MPA, NYU. Vol. U.S. Peace Corps, 1968-70; state rep. State of Conn. (Dist. 147), Stamford, 1974-87; mem. 100th-103rd Congresses from 4th Conn. Dist., Washington, 1987—. Republican. Office: House of Reps 1502 Longworth Bldg Washington DC 20515-0004*

SHAYS, RONA JOYCE, lawyer; b. N.Y.C., July 16, 1928; d. Samuel and Beatrice (Fleischer) Eskin; children: Douglas, Sharon; m. Henry C. Shays, Sept. 15, 1974. Student, U. Mich., 1944-47; LLB, Bklyn. Law Sch., 1950; MA, Columbia U., 1968. Bar: N.Y. 1950, U.S. Dist. Ct. (so. and ea. dists) N.Y. 1952. Law clk., assoc. Arthur Bardack, Esquire, Bklyn., 1947-51; assoc. Legal Aid Soc., Mineola, N.Y., 1951-52; legal asst. Mut. Life Ins. Co., N.Y.C., 1959-63; assoc. Hays, Sklar & Herzberg, N.Y.C., 1963-68; from assoc. to ptnr. Mitchell Salem Fisher & Shays, N.Y.C., 1968-76; ptnr. Shersky, Kalman & Shays, N.Y.C., 1976-77, Rosenthal & Shays, N.Y.C., 1977-95, Shays Kemper, N.Y.C., 1995—. Named Matrimonial Law Arbitrator, Am. Acad. Matrimonial Lawyers, 1992. Fellow Am. Acad. Matrimonial Lawyers (sec. N.Y. state chpt. 1975-82, 90-91, v.p. N.Y. state chpt. 1984-85, 89-90, chair admissions com. N.Y. state chpt. 1986-91, counsel N.Y. state chpt. 1992-93, nat. co-chair interdisciplinary rels. com. 1990-94), Internat. Acad. Matrimonial Lawyers; mem. Assn. Bar City of N.Y. (matrimonial law com. 1982-85, 86-89, 92-95), Nat. Forum on Mental Health and Family Law (co-chair 1990-93), N.Y. State Interdisciplinary Forum on Mental Health and Family Law (co-chair 1986—). Office: Shays Kemper 276 5th Ave New York NY 10001-4509

SHEA, BERNARD CHARLES, retired pharmaceutical company executive; b. Bradford, Pa., Aug. 7, 1929; s. Bernard and Edna Catherine (Green) S.; m. Marilyn Rishell, Apr. 12, 1952; children—David Charles, Melissa Leone. BS in Biology, Holy Cross Coll., Worcester, Mass. Dir. mktg. Upjohn Co., Kalamazoo, Mich., 1954-80; pres. pharm. div. Pennwalt Corp., Rochester, N.Y., 1980-86; v.p. health div. Pennwalt Corp., Phila., 1986, sr. v.p. health div., 1987-88, sr. v.p. chemicals, 1988-89; group pres. Atochem N.Am., Inc., Phila., 1989-90, pharm. cons., 1990-93. Served to lt. (j.g.) USN, 1951-54, Korea.

SHEA, DANIEL BARTHOLOMEW, JR., English language educator, actor; b. Mpls., Oct. 29, 1936; s. Daniel Bartholomew and Dorothea (Lonergan) S.; m. Kathleen Anne Williams, June 3, 1978; children: Timothy, Matthew, Catherine, Daniel, Emily. B.A. summa cum laude, Coll. St. Thomas, 1958; M.A., Stanford U., 1962, Ph.D., 1966. Teaching asst. Stanford U., 1959-61; instr. to prof. English Washington U., St. Louis, 1962—; chmn. dept. Washington U., 1978-84, 95—; acting chair performing arts, prof. drama, 1995; Fulbright-Hays lectr. Univs. of Caen and Nice, France, 1968-69; vis. fellow Clare Hall, U. Cambridge, Eng., 1984-85. Author: Spiritual Autobiography in Early America, 1968, 2d edit., 1988; editorial bd.: Early Am. Lit, 1972-74; sect. editor: Columbia Literary History of the United States; contbr. chpts. to books. Woodrow Wilson fellow, 1958; NEH summer grantee, 1971. Mem. MLA (del. gen. assembly 1977-78), AFTRA, Equity. Home: 6138 Kingsbury Blvd Saint Louis MO 63112-1102 Office: Washington Univ Dept of English Saint Louis MO 63130

SHEA, DAVID MICHAEL, state supreme court justice; b. Hartford, July 1, 1922; s. Michael Peter and Margaret (Agnes) S.; m. Rosemary Anne Sasseen, Apr. 28, 1956; children—Susan, Kathleen, Margaret, Rosemary, Christina, Michael, Maura, Julie. B.A., Wesleyan U., 1944; LL.B., Yale U., 1948. Bar: Conn. 1948. Assoc. Tunick & Ferris, Greenwich, Conn., 1948-49; assoc. Bailey & Wechsler, Hartford, 1949-57; ptnr. Bailey, Wechsler & Shea, Hartford, 1957-65; judge Conn. Superior Ct., Hartford, 1966-81; justice Conn. Supreme Ct., Hartford, 1981-92, trial referee, 1992—. Served with U.S. Army, 1943-46. Democrat. Roman Catholic. Office: Conn Superior Ct 95 Washington St Hartford CT 06106-4406

SHEA, DION WARREN JOSEPH, fraternal organization administrator; b. New London, Conn., June 10, 1937; s. Frank Steven and Violette Marie (Dion) S.; m. Elizabeth M. Siaba, Dec. 31, 1986; children from previous marriage: Dion Warren Joseph, Nancy Wallace. A.B., Sc.B. in Physics, Brown U., 1959; M.A. in Physics, Boston U., 1962; Ph.D., U. Colo., 1968. Mem. tech. staff RCA, 1959-62; asst. prof. physics Creighton U., 1967-68; NRC/Environ. Sci. Svcs. Adminstrn. fellow, rsch. assoc. Environ. Sci. Svcs. Adminstrn., Boulder, Colo., 1968-70; exec. dir. Soc. Physics Students, Am. Inst. Physics, 1970-87, mgr. edn. div., 1972-87; cons. ednl. and computer sytems, 1988—; dir. alumni affairs U.S. Merchant Marine Acad., Kings Point, N.Y., 1989-93; asst. dir. devel. CUNY Grad. Sch., 1993—. Author sci. articles. Fellow AAAS; mem. Am. Phys. Soc., Am. Assn. Physics Tchrs., Assn. Coll. Honor Socs. (exec. com. 1984-86), Am. Soc. Assn. Execs., N.Y. Soc. Assn. Execs., Nat. Soc. Fund Raising Execs. (greater N.Y. chpt.), Planned Giving Group Greater N.Y., Coun. Advancement and Support Edn., Sigma Xi, Sigma Pi Sigma, Sigma Chi, Huntington Bicycle Club, Appalachian Mountain Club, Port Dive Club (treas. 1980-83). Home: 1 Doone Dr Syosset NY 11791-6308 Office: Office of Devel Grad Sch and Univ Ctr CUNY 33 W 42nd St New York NY 10036-8003

SHEA, DONALD FRANCIS, state supreme court justice; b. Pawtucket, R.I., Sept. 14, 1925; s. Edward Leo and Lucy Rose (Read) S.; m. Ursula V. Rafferty, June 17, 1950; children: Donald Edward, Michaela Theresa, Christopher John, Sara Elizabeth, Ellen Marie. A.B., Providence Coll., 1950; J.D., Georgetown U., 1954. Bar: R.I. Trial atty. firm Boss, Conlan, Keenan, Bulman and Rice, Providence, 1955-72; assoc. justice Superior Ct. R.I., 1972-81, Supreme Ct. R.I., 1981—; part-time law instr. Roger Williams Coll., Bristol; mem. R.I. Ho. of Reps., 1960-68; exec. asst. to gov. R.I., 1968-72. Served with USNR, 1943-46. Mem. ABA, R.I. Bar Assn.

SHEA, DONALD RICHARD, political science educator; b. Mpls., July 15, 1926; s. John James and Marjorie (Jennings) S.; m. Mary Patricia Donovan, June 4, 1948; children: Barbara, John, Marjorie, Kathleen. B.A., U. Minn., 1947, M.A., 1949, Ph.D., 1953. Prof. polit. sci. U. Wis., Milw., 1949-89, prof. emeritus, 1989—, chmn. dept. polit. sci., 1957-61, dir. Inst. for World Affairs, 1960-63, spl. asst. to chancellor, 1962-64, adminstr. Peace Corps Tng. Center, 1962-69, dean Internat. Studies and Programs, 1963-70, dir. Ctr. for Latin America, 1976-89, dir. Inst. World Affairs, Summer Fgn. Student Seminar, 1962, 63, 71, 72; cons. Ford Found., 1966-68. Author: The Calvo Clause: A Problem of Inter-American and International Law and Diplomacy, 1955; editor: Business and Legal Aspects of Latin America Trade and Investment, 1976; sr. editor: Reference Manual on Doing Business in Latin America, 1979; co-editor: Mass Communication in the Americas: Focus on the New World Information and Communication Order, 1985; contbr. to Ency. Americana, The Univ. of Wis.-Milw.: A Hist. Profile, 1992. Bd. dirs. World Affairs Council Milw., Inst. World Affairs, Milw. Internat. Student's Center. Served with USNR, 1944-46. Doherty fellow for rsch. in Latin Am., 1955-56; recipient Kiekhofer Meml. Tchg. award, 1975, Donald R. Shea scholarship in Latin Am. studies established in 1995. Mem. Am. Soc. for Internat. Law, Am. Polit. Sci. Assn., Latin Am. Studies Assn. Home: 3346 N Summit Ave Milwaukee WI 53211-2929

SHEA, DONALD WILLIAM, career officer; b. Butte, Mont., Apr. 15, 1936; s. Edward Joseph and Agnes C. (Stanton) S. BA, Carroll Coll., 1958; BTh, St. Paul (Minn.) Sem., 1962; MA in Human Rels., U. Okla., 1984; MEd, L.I. U., 1975; MA in Pers. Mgmt., Cen. Mich. U., 1981. Ordained priest Roman Cath. Ch., 1962. Commd. 1st lt. U.S. Army, 1966, advanced through grades to maj. gen.; student Basic Chaplain Officer Sch., Ft. Hamilton, N.Y., 1966, Airborne Sch., Ft. Bragg, N.C., 1966; with 3d Brigade, 5th Inf. Div. Dept. of the Army, Ft. Carson, Colo., 1966; student spl. forces officer course Ft. Bragg, N.C., 1967; chaplain 10th Spl. Forces Group Dept. of the Army, Bad Toelz, Germany, 1967; chaplain 5th Spl. Forces Group Dept. of the Army, Vietnam, 1968; chaplain 1st Brigade, 7th Inf. Div. Dept. of the Army, Republic of Korea, 1969; chaplain 15th Field Arty. Group Dept. of the Army, Vietnam, 1970; chaplain 4th Bn., 10th Inf. Dept. of the Army, Panama, 1972; chaplain 2d Bn., 9th Inf. Div. Dept. of the Army, Ft. Lewis, Wash., 1975; chaplain 1st Brigade, 1st Armored Div. Dept. of the Army, Germany, 1977; student Command and Gen. Staff Coll., Ft. Leavenworth, Kans., 1978; div. chaplain 1st Armored Div. Dept. of the Army, Germany, 1978; with office Chief of Chaplains Dept. of the Army, Washington, 1979; student U.S. Army War Coll., Carlisle Barracks, Pa., 1984; chaplain VII Corps U.S. Army, Germany, 1984; staff chaplain U.S. Army Europe, 7th Army U.S. Army War Coll., Germany, 1986; exec. officer, chief of chaplains U.S. Army, Washington, 1989; dep. chief of chaplains U.S. Army War Coll., Washington, 1990-94; chief of chaplains U.S. Army, 1994—. Apptd. Domestic Prelate Pope John Paul II, 1992. Office: Office Chief of Chaplains US Army The Pentagon Washington DC 20310-2700

SHEA, EDWARD EMMETT, lawyer, educator, author; b. Detroit, May 29, 1932; s. Edward Francis and Margaret Kathleen (Downey) S.; m. Ann Marie Conley, Aug. 28, 1957; children: Michael, Maura, Ellen. AB, U. Detroit, 1954; JD, U. Mich., 1957. Bar: Mich. 1957, Fla. 1959, N.Y. 1961. Assoc. Simpson Thacher & Bartlett, N.Y.C., 1960-63, Dykema, Wheat, Spencer, Detroit, 1963-69, Cadwalader Wickersham & Taft, N.Y.C., 1969-71; v.p., gen. counsel, chmn. Reichhold Chems., White Plains, N.Y., 1971-81; adj. prof. Grad. Sch. Bus. Pace U., N.Y.C., 1982—; counsel, ptnr. Windels, Marx, Davies & Ives, 1982-84, ptnr., 1986—; sr. v.p., gen. counsel GAF Corp., 1984-86; sec. Peridot Chems., 1988—; lectr. N.Y. Inst. Fin., 1995—. Co-author: Acquisitions, Mergers, Sales, Buyouts and Takeovers, 1991; author: An Introduction to the U.S. Environmental Laws, 1995; editor: The Acquisitions Yearbook, 1991, 92, 93; contbr. articles to profl. jours. Mem. adv. bd. N.Y. State Small Bus. Ctr. Program, 1988-93. 1st lt. JAGC, USAF, 1957-60. Mem. N.Y. Athletic Club, Chemist's Club. Office: Windels Marx Davies & Ives 156 W 56th St New York NY 10019-3800

SHEA, GERALD PATRICK, engineering executive; b. N.Y.C., May 10, 1935; s. William James and Mary M. (Fitzmaurice) S.; m. Joan Elaine Bergener, Mar. 3, 1938; children: Jerry, Kevin, Kathleen, William, Brian. BSCE, U. Notre Dame, 1956; MCE, NYU, 1963. Registered profl. engr., N.Y., N.J., Conn., Pa., Fla., Ark., S.C., Va. Bridge design engr. Parsons Brinckerhoff, N.Y.C., 1956-58; bridge engr. Bur. Pub. Roads, Richmond, Va., 1958-62; assoc. TAMS Consultants, N.Y.C., 1963-78; v.p. Louis Berger Internat. Inc., East Orange, N.J., 1978—; bd. dirs. Internat. Road Fedn.; pres. Internat. Road Ednl. Found. Contbr. numerous articles to profl. jours. Fellow Inst. Transp. Engrs.; mem. ASCE, Soc. Am. Mil. Engrs., MOLES. Roman Catholic. Avocations: golf, walking, travel, sailing. Home: 5 Placid Lake Ln Wesport CT 06880 Office: Louis Berger Internat Inc 100 Halsted St East Orange NJ 07019

SHEA, JAMES F., manufacturing executive. CEO Fairmont Homes, Nappanee, Ind. Office: Fairmont Homes 502 S Oakland Ave Nappanee IN 46550

SHEA, JAMES WILLIAM, lawyer; b. N.Y.C., July 10, 1936; s. William P. and Mildred E. (McCaffrey) S.; m. Ann Marie Byrne, June 6, 1964; children: James T., Kathleen A., Tracy A. BS, St. Peters Coll., 1957; JD, Fordham U., 1962; LLM in Taxation, NYU, 1965. Bar: N.Y. 1962, U.S. Dist. Ct. (so. and ea. dists.) N.Y. 1966, U.S. Supreme Ct. 1967. Revenue agent U.S. Treasury Dept., N.Y.C., 1961-63; tax atty. Kennecott Copper Corp., N.Y.C., 1963-67; tax counsel CBS Inc., N.Y.C., 1968-71; ptnr. Hunton & Williams and predecessor firm Conboy, Hewitt, O'Brien & Boardman, N.Y.C., 1971—; bd. dirs. Victory Van Lines Inc., N.Y.C. Rep. committeeman, Staten Island, N.Y., 1980; mem. adv. com. tax and fin. N.Y. State Charter Commn. City of S.I. Served to 1st lt. U.S. Army, 1957-61, to capt. USAR, 1962-72. Mem. ABA, N.Y. State Bar Assn. Republican. Roman Catholic. Club: Richmond County Country (Staten Island), 101 (sec. 1993—). Home: 399 Tysens Ln Staten Island NY 10306-2844 Office: Hunton & Williams 200 Park Ave New York NY 10166-0005

SHEA, JOHN J., catalog and retail company executive; b. Newark, NJ, 1938. BS, La Salle Coll., 1959; MBA, U. Pitts., 1960. With John Wanamaker, Phila., 1953-80; pres., chief exec. officer Spiegel, Inc., Hinsdale, Ill., 1981—, now also vice chmn. Office: Spiegel Inc 3500 Lacey Rd Downers Grove IL 60515*

SHEA, JOHN MARTIN, JR., business executive; b. Santa Barbara, Calif., Nov. 14, 1922; s. John Martin and Karmel Kathryn (Knox) S.; m. Marion Abie; children: Michael Knox, Patrick Campbell, Katherine Martin. B.A., U. Wash., 1944. Vice pres., gen. mgr. Yaras & Co., Far East, Manila, P.I., Hong Kong, Tokyo, Japan, 1946-52; pres. Shea Oil Co., Pasadena, Calif., 1953-57; v.p., dir. Am. Petrofina, Inc.; sr. v.p. mktg., refining, transp., crude oil, dir. Am. Petrofina Co. of Tex., 1957-64; pres. Colonial Oil Products Co., Des Moines, Osmond Oil Co., Waco, Tex., 1958-64; chmn. bd. Freeman, Gossage & Shea (advt. and cons.), San Francisco, 1964-65; chmn. bd., chief exec. officer Beacon Bay Enterprises Inc., Newport Beach, Calif., 1964—, Shea (S.A.), Buenos Aires, Argentina, 1968—; dir. Commercebank, Newport Beach. Trustee Newport Harbor Art Mus., Newport Beach, Calif., 1975—, chmn. bd.trustees 1986-88; pres. bd. trustees Valle Padrinos, Palm Springs, Calif., 1988—. Lt. (j.g.) USNR, World War II. Office: Beacon Bay Bldg 260 Newport Center Dr Newport Beach CA 92660-7520

SHEA, JOHN PETER, lawyer; b. Belleville, N.J., May 1, 1967; s. Edmund Joseph and Josephine (Sciortino) S. BS in Acctg., Providence Coll., 1989; JD, Villanova U., 1992. Bar: Pa. 1992, N.J. 1992, Conn. 1994, U.S. Dist. Ct. (ea. dist.) Pa. 1992, U.S. Dist. Ct. N.J. 1992. Assoc. firm Kent & McBride, P.C., Phila., 1992—; legal advisor Chester County Plumbers, Malvern, Pa., 1992—. Mem. ABA, Pa. Bar Assn., Phila. Bar Assn. Republican. Roman Catholic. Office: Kent & McBride PC Two Logan Sq Ste 600 Philadelphia PA 19103

SHEA, KEVIN MICHAEL, lawyer; b. Indpls., Dec. 23, 1951; s. James Louis and Elizabeth (Walker) S.; m. Marilyn Alkire, Nov. 27, 1985; children: Brendan Alkire, Maura Kathryn. BS, U. Colo., 1973; JD, U. Detroit, 1976. Bar: Colo. 1976, U.S. Dist. Ct. D.C. 1976, U.S. Ct. Appeals (10th cir. 1980), U.S. Supreme Ct. 1982. Dep. dist. atty. Boulder, Colo., 1976-79; shareholder, dir., assoc. Roath & Brega P.C., Denver, 1980-85; spl. counsel

Holme Roberts & Owen, Denver, 1985-87, ptnr., 1987-94; ptnr. Ballard, Sphar, Andrews & Ingersoll, Denver, 1995—. Mem. ABA (vice chair environ. crime sect. 1991—), Colo. Bar Assn. (chair criminal law sect. 1990-91), Denver Country Club. Democrat. Avocation: ranching. Office: Ballard Sphar Andrews Inger 1225 17th St Ste 2300 Denver CO 80202

SHEA, MEGAN CARROLL, arts lawyer; b. Lake Forest, Ill., Sept. 7, 1967; d. Barry Joseph and Barbara (Pehrson) C.; m. Timothy J. Shea II. Student, Middlebury Coll., Paris, 1987-88; BA in Philosophy, French Lit., Boston Coll., 1989, JD, 1992. Bar: Mass., 1993, Ill. 1994, D.C. 1995. Law clk. Middlesex County Probate & Family Ct., Cambridge, Mass., 1990-91; assoc. Powers & Hall, Boston, 1991; asst. dist. atty. Norfolk County, Mass., 1992; prin., owner Carroll Assocs., Counsel for the Arts, Boston, 1994—; bd. dirs. Carroll Internat. Corp., Des Plaines, Ill. Arts review writer various publs. Mem. Am. Ireland Fund, Boston, Chgo., 1985—, DAR, Chgo., 1985—, Phillips Acad. Alumni Coun., Andover, Mass., 1991-95; trustee Regency Pk. Condominiums, Brookline, Mass., 1989-91; sec. Phillips Acad. Alumni Class of 1985, Andover, 1989-95. Recipient Golden Key Nat. Honor Soc., Boston Coll., 1989, Order of the Cross and Crown, Scholar of the Coll., 1989. Mem. ABA, Arts and Media Law Assn. of Boston Coll. (pres., founder), Social Register, Woman's Athletic Club Chgo., Order of Malta Aux., Jr. Internat. Club Lauterbach (Germany), East Chop Beach Club, East Chgo. Yacht Club, East Chop Tennis Club, Phi Delta Phi. Republican. Roman Catholic. Avocations: classical ballet, choreography, scuba diving, flying (lic. pilot). Home: 24 Columbia St Wellesley MA 02181-1603 also: 55 Mayflower Rd Lake Forest IL 60045 Office: Carroll Assocs Two Park Plaza Ste 409 Boston MA 02116

SHEA, ROBERT MCCONNELL, lawyer; b. North Adams, Mass., May 28, 1924; s. Edward Michael and Margaret Frances (McConnell) S. AB cum laude, Harvard U., 1948, LLB, 1951; grad. sr. exec. program, MIT, 1962. Bar: Mass. 1951. With John Hancock Mut. Life Ins. Co., Boston, 1951-91, counsel, 1966-70, v.p., counsel, 1970-85; pvt. practice cons., 1986-91. Bd. trustees Labouré Coll., Boston, 1976-88, sec., 1981-88. Served with U.S. Army, 1943-46. Decorated Bronze Star; recipient Labouré medal Labouré Coll., 1989. Mem. Am., Boston bar assns., Assn. Life Ins. Co., Am. Life Ins. Assn., Health Ins. Assn. Am. Republican. Catholic. Club: Harvard. Home: 85 Grove St Apt 209 Wellesley MA 02181-7823

SHEA, STEPHEN MICHAEL, physician, educator; b. Galway, Ireland, Apr. 25, 1926; came to U.S., 1956, naturalized, 1966; s. Stephen and Margaret Mary (Cooke) S. B.Sc. in Anatomy and Pathology, Univ. Coll., Galway Nat. U. Ireland, 1948; M.B., B.Ch. in Medicine, 1950, M.Sc. in Pathology, 1951, M.D., 1959. Diplomate: Am. Bd. Pathology. Intern St. Vincent's Hosp., Dublin, Ireland, 1950-51; Dr. Keenan traveling scholar, dept. physiology Univ. Coll., London, 1951-53; asst. lectr. pharmacology Univ. Coll., Dublin, 1953-56; resident in pathology Mallory Inst. Pathology, Boston City Hosp., 1956-59, chief resident, 1958-59; asst. prof. pathology U. Toronto, Ont., Can., 1959-61; instr. Harvard U. Med. Sch., 1961-63, instr. math. biology, 1963-65, asso. in pathology, 1965-67, asst. prof. pathology, 1967-70, assoc. prof., 1970-73; assoc. pathologist Mass. Gen. Hosp. and Shriners Burns Inst., both Boston, 1972-73; prof. pathology Robert Wood Johnson Med. Sch., U.M.D.N.J., 1973—. Contbr. articles to profl. publs. Fellow Royal Coll. Pathologists (U.K.), Royal Coll. Physicians (Can.); mem. Am. Soc. Invest Pathologists, Internat. Acad. Pathology, Am. Soc. Cell Biology, Biophys. Soc., Soc. Math. Biology, Microcirculatory Soc., Harvard Club, Travellers Club, Harvard of Boston Club. Roman Catholic. Home: 1050 George St Apt 12L New Brunswick NJ 08901-1020 Office: UMDNJ-Robert Wood Johnson Med Sch Piscataway NJ 08854

SHEA, WALTER JAMES, labor union executive; b. Bklyn., Nov. 30, 1929; s. Walter Edmund and Madlyn (Baker) S.; m. Mary Ann Carr, Aug. 2, 1952; children: Michael, Kathleen, Sheila, Margaret, Patrick, Mary. A.B. in Edn., U. S.C., 1953. Claims adjuster, examiner Govt. Employees Ins. Co., Washington, 1956-57; research dept. asst. to dir. Eastern Conf. Teamsters, Washington, 1957-67; exec. asst. to gen. pres., v.p. Internat. Brotherhood of Teamsters, Chauffeurs, Warehousemen and Helpers of Am., 1967-92, chmn. Ea. Conf. Teamsters, 1991—; mem. Teamsters Nat. Freight Industry Negotiating Com., 1964-92; co-chmn. Nat. Automobile Negotiation Com., 1967-89; mem. exec .coun. AFL-CIO, 1990-94, sec./treas. Dept. Transp. Trades, 1990-94; retired, 1994. Mem. Presdl. Commn. for Drunk Driving, 1982—; mem. Nat. Coal Council, Dept. Energy; mem. Quadular Forum, Georgetown U. Ctr. Strategic Studies; mem. Panama Canal Commn. Served to capt. USAF, 1954-56. Mem. Kappa Sigma. Democrat. Roman Catholic. Home: 661A Windsurf Ln # 102 Naples FL 33963-8718

SHEA, WILLIAM RENE, historian, science philosopher, educator; b. Gracefield, Que., Can., May 16, 1937; s. Herbert Clement and Jeanne (Lafreniere) S.; m. Evelyn Fischer, May 2, 1970; children: Herbert, Joan-Emma, Louisa, Cecilia, Michael. B.A., U. Ottawa, 1958; L.Ph., Gregorian U., Rome, 1959; L.Th., Gregorian U., 1963; Ph.D., Cambridge U., Eng., 1968. Assoc. prof. U. Ottawa, Ont., Can., 1968-73; fellow Harvard U., Cambridge, Mass., 1973-74; prof. history and philosophy of sci. McGill U., Montreal, 1974—; dir. d'etudes Ecole des Hautes Etudes, Paris, 1981-82; sec.-gen. Internat. Union of History and Philosophy of Sci., 1983-89, pres., 1990-93; mem. gen. com. Internat. Coun. of Sci. Union, Paris, 1983-89; cons. Killam Found., Ottawa, Ont., 1983-85; mem. McGill Centre for Medicine, Ethics and Law, 1990-95; Hydro Que. prof. environ. ethics, 1992—; vis. prof. U. Rome, 1992; dir. Inst. History of Sci., U. Louis Pasteur, Strasbourg, 1995—. Author: Galileo Intellectual Revolution, 1972, The Magic of Numbers and Motion, 1991; co-author: Galileo Florentine Residences, 1979; editor: Nature Mathematized, 1983, Otto Hahn and the Rise of Nuclear Physics, 1983, Revolutions in Science, 1988, Creativity in the Arts and Science, 1990, Persuading Science: The Art of Scientific Rhetoric, 1991, Interpreting the World, Science and Society, 1991, Energy Needs in the Year 2000: Ethical and Environmental Perspectives, 1994. Can. Coun. fellow, 1965-68, Can. Cultural Inst. fellow, Rome, 1973, Social Scis. and Humanities Rsch. Coun. Can., 1980-81, Inst. of Advanced Studies in Berlin fellow, 1988-89; recipient The Alexandre Koyre medal Internat. Acad. of History of Sci., 1993, Knight of the Order of Malta, 1993. Fellow Royal Soc. Can.; mem. History of Sci. Soc. (coun. 1973-76), European Sci. Found. (standing com. for humanities 1989-95), Can. Nat. Com. of History and Philosophy of Sci. (coun. 1982-93), Can. Philos. Assn., Internat. Acad. History of Sci. (ordinary), McGill Faculty Club. Home: 6 Rue Gottfired, 6700 Strasbourg France Office: Inst d'Histoire des Scis, 7 Rue de L'Universite, 6700 Strasbourg France

SHEAFFER, CINDY ELAINE, lawyer; b. Mechanicsburg, Pa., July 5, 1958; d. Maynard Leroy and Ruth Geraldine (Walters) Sheaffer; 1 child, Matthew Thomas Priest; m. Dennis Anthony DeStadio, Aug. 5, 1995. Paralegal Cert., Harrisburg (Pa.) Area C.C., 1988; BS, Pa. State U., Harrisburg, 1990; JD, Dickinson Sch. Law, Carlisle, Pa., 1993. Bar: Pa. 1994. Legal sec. McNees, Wallace & Nurick, Harrisburg, 1988-90; law clk. Schmidt & Ronca, P.C., Harrisburg, 1991; cert. legal intern Family Law Clinic, Carlisle, 1992; law clk. The Underwriters' Group, Harrisburg, 1993; pvt. practice Enola, Pa., 1995—; atty./instr. Ctrl. Pa. Bus. Sch., Summerdale, 1993—; pro bono atty. Ctrl. Pa. Legal Svc., Harrisburg, 1994—. Atty. vol. Dauphin County Custody Clinic, Harrisburg, 1995—; bd. dirs. Ronny Powley Ctr. for Social Ministries, Enola, 1995. Mem. ABA, Pa. Bar Assn., Dauphin County Bar Assn. Avocation: watching son's sports. Office: PO Box 267 806 Wertzville Rd Enola PA 17025

SHEAFFER, WILLIAM JAY, lawyer; b. Carlisle, Pa., Jan. 18, 1948; s. Raymond Jay and Barbara Jean (Bell) S.; m. Carol Ann Madison, Jan. 5, 1974. BA cum laude, U. Cen. Fla., 1975; JD, Nova U., 1978. Bar: Fla. 1978, U.S. Dist. Ct. (mid. dist.) Fla. 1979, U.S. Dist. Ct. (so. and no. dists.) Fla. 1981, U.S. Ct. Appeals (5th and 11th cirs.) 1981, U.S. Supreme Ct. 1983. Atty. State of Fla., Orlando, 1978-79; pvt. practice, Orlando, 1979—; apptd. to merit selection panel to consider U.S. Magistrate Judge Applicants, 1995—. Served to ensign class 4 USN, 1967-71. Mem. ABA, FBA, Nat. Assn. Criminal Def. Lawyers, Fla. Bar Assn. (cert. criminal trial specialist, 9th jud. cir. grievance com.), Orange County Bar Assn. (Guardian Ad Litem of Yr. award 1994, award of excellence 1995), Fla. Assn. Criminal Def. Lawyers, Fed. Trial Lawyers Assn., Tiger Bay Club, Citrus Club. Republican. Avocations: boating, running, skiing, scuba diving, golf. Office: 609 E Central Blvd Orlando FL 32801-2948

SHEAHAN, JOAN A., long term care nursing administrator; b. Darby, Pa., Apr. 25, 1940; d. William P. and Beatrice Alta (Bell) Salter; m. John W. Sheahan, Dec. 4, 1976. Diploma in nursing, Thomas Jefferson U., 1961; AS, Camden County Coll., 1988. DON Abbey Convalescent Home, Warren, Mich., 1969-72, Clintonview Care, Mt. Clemens, Mich., 1972, Pine Crest Nursing Home, Sewell, N.J., 1973-86, Cinnaminson (N.J.) Manor Nursing Ctr., 1989-91, Beneva Nursing Pavillon, Sarasota, Fla., 1992-94, Hillhaven Rehab. Ctr. Ft. Myers, Fla., 1994—. Capt. USAFR, 1964-72. Thomas Jefferson U. scholar. Mem. Assn. Rehab. Nurses, Fla. Assn. Dirs. Nursing Adminstrs./Long Term Care, Thomas Jefferson U. Nurses Alumni Assn., Camden County Coll. Alumni Assn. Home: 19538 Ravines Ct Fort Myers FL 33903-9052 Office: Hillhaven Rehab Ctr of Ft Myers 3250 Winkler Ave Ext Fort Myers FL 33916

SHEAHAN, JOHN BERNARD, economist, educator; b. Toledo, Sept. 11, 1923; s. Bernard William and Florence (Sheahan) S.; m. Denise Eugénie Morlino, Nov. 29, 1946; children: Yvette Marie, Bernard Eugene. BA, Stanford U., 1948; PhD, Harvard U., 1954. Econ. analyst Office Spl. Rep. in Europe, ECA, Paris, France, 1951-54; mem. faculty Williams Coll., 1954-94; prof. econs. Williams Coll., Williamstown, Mass., 1966-94, prof. emeritus; mem. devel. adv. service Colombia adv. group Harvard, 1963-65; nat. research prof. Brookings Instn., 1959-60; vis. prof. El Colegio de México, Mexico City, 1970-71; Fulbright research scholar Institut de recherche économique et de planification, Université de Grenoble, France, 1974-75; vis. scholar Inst. Devel. Studies, U. Sussex, 1981-82; vis. fellow Ctr. for U.S.-Mexican Studies, U. Calif. at San Diego, 1991. Author: Promotion and Control of Industry in Postwar France, 1963, The Wage-Price Guideposts, 1967, An Introduction to the French Economy, 1969, Patterns of Development in Latin America, 1987, Conflict and Change in Mexican Economic Strategy, 1992. Mem. Presdl. Price Adv. Com., 1979-80. Mem. Am. Econ. Assn., Latin Am. Studies Assn., New England Coun. Latin Am. Studies (pres. 1989-90), Phi Beta Kappa. Home: Syndicate Rd Williamstown MA 01267 Office: Williams Coll Dept Econs Williamstown MA 01267

SHEAHAN, ROBERT EMMETT, lawyer, consultant; b. Chgo., May 20, 1942; s. Robert Emmett and Lola Jean (Moore) S.; m. Pati Smith, Mar. 20, 1991. BA, Ill. Wesleyan U., 1964; JD, Duke U., 1967; MBA, U. Chgo., 1970. Bar: Ill. 1967, La. 1975, N.C. 1978. Vol. VISTA, N.Y.C., 1967-68; trial atty. NLRB, Milw. and New Orleans, 1970-75; ptnr. Jones, Walker, Waechter, Poitevent, Carrere & Denegre, New Orleans, 1975-78; pvt. practice, High Point, N.C., 1978—; bd. dirs. Inst. for Effective Mgmt., Bus. Publs. Inst. Author: Employees and Drug Abuse: An Employer's Handbook, 1994, The Encyclopedia of Drugs in the Workplace, Labor and Employment Law in North Carolina, 1991, Personnel and Employment Law in North Carolina, 1992, Desk Book of Labor and Employment Law for Healthcare Employers, 1995, North Carolina's Healthcare Employers' Desk Manual, 1995; contbg. author: The Developing Labor Law, 1975—; editor: The World of Personnel; contbg. editor: Employee Testing and the Law. Bd. dirs. High Point United Way, 1979-83; mem. congressional action com. High Point C. of C., chmn., 1991—, bd. dirs., 1996—. Mem. ABA, N.C. Bar Assn., High Point Bar Assn., Ill. Bar Assn., La. Bar Assn. Republican. Roman Catholic. Clubs: Sedgefield (N.C.) Country, String and Splinter (High Point), Bald Head (N.C.) Island Club. Home: 101 Bellwood Ct Jamestown NC 27282-9446 Office: Eastchester Office Ctr 603B Eastchester Dr High Point NC 27262-7634

SHEALY, CLYDE NORMAN, neurosurgeon; b. Columbia, S.C., Dec. 4, 1932; s. Clyde Lemuel and Palma Leona (Padget) S.; m. Mary-Charlotte Bayles, June 13, 1959; children: Brock Allison, Craig Norman, Laurel Elizabeth. B.S. in Medicine, Duke U., 1956, MD, 1956; PhD, Humanistic Psychology Inst., San Francisco, 1977; DSc (hon.), Ryodomaku Rsch. Inst., Kansas City, 1979. Intern Duke U. Hosp., Durham, N.C., 1956-57; resident in neurosurgery Mass. Gen. Hosp., Boston, 1958-63; sr. instr., then asst. prof. neurosurgery Western Res. U. Med. Sch., 1963-66; chief neurosurgery Gundersen Clinic, LaCrosse, Wis., 1966-71; assoc. clin. prof. neurosurgery U. Minn. Med. Sch., 1970-75; asst. clin. prof. U. Wis. Med. Sch., 1967-74; dir. Pain and Health Rehab. Center, S.C., LaCrosse, 1971-81; pres. Holos Insts. Health, 1981—; founder, dir. Shealy Pain and Health Rehab. Inst., Springfield, Mo.; clin. prof., prof. clin. research Forest Inst. Profl. Psychology; adj. prof. Columbia Pacific U. Author: Occult Medicine Can Save Your Life, 1975, The Pain Game, 1976, 90 Days to Self Health, 1977 (with Mary-Charlotte Shealy), To Parent or Not, 1981, SpeedyGourmet, 1985, AIDS: Pathway to Transformation, 1987, The Creation of Health, 1988, Third Party Rape: The Conspiracy to Rob You of Health Care, 1993, The Self-Healing Workbook, 1993, The Self-Healing Workbook, 1993, Miracles Do Happen, 1995; also articles. Served with USNR, 1956-63. Fellow ACS, Am. Coll. Preventive Medicine; mem. AMA, Am. Acad. Pain Medicine, Am. Acad. Pain Mgmt., Mo. State Med. Assn., Greene County Med. Soc., Harvey Cushing Soc., Am. Holistic Med. Assn. (founder, past pres., chmn. edn. com.), Am. Assn. Study Headache, Internat. Assn. Study Pain, Internat. Acad. Preventive Medicine, Phi Beta Kappa, Alpha Omega Alpha. Address: 1328 E Evergreen St Springfield MO 65803-4400 *Preventing illness is infinitely more important than treating it. My belief and practice has evolved from the treatment of illness to a major educational role. Most illnesses are the result of unhealthy habits. We need to teach people how to deal with those at all levels: physical, chemical, emotional, mental and spiritual.*

SHEALY, DAVID LEE, physicist, educator; b. Newberry, S.C., Sept. 16, 1944; s. William Elmer and Elizabeth (Plaxico) S.; m. Elaine Wohlford, June 17, 1969; children: Bridget McGill, David McElwee. BS, U. Ga., 1966, PhD, 1973. Prof., chmn. dept. physics, U. Ala., Birmingham, 1984—; cons. Motorola, Phoenix, 1978-84, Jet Propulsion Lab., Pasadena, Calif., 1980-82, Los Alamos Nat. Lab., 1989-91, NASA Marshall Space Flight Ctr., 1989—. Contbr. articles to profl. jours. Faculty fellow NASA, ASEE, 1980, 81; recipient Silver Quill and Publ. award Motorola, 1982, 83. Mem. IEEE (adminstrv. com., 1988-90, research paper award Ala. Sect. 1984), Am. Assn. Physics Tchrs., Am. Physical Soc., Optical Soc. Am. (fellow 1988), Material Rsch. Soc., N.Y. Acad. Sci. Republican. Methodist. Avocations: running. Home: 2337 Morningstar Dr Birmingham AL 35216-2005 Office: U Ala-Birmingham Dept Physics CH-310 Birmingham AL 35294-1170

SHEAR, IONE MYLONAS, archaeologist; b. St. Louis, Feb. 19, 1936; d. George Emmanuel and Lella (Papazouglou) Mylonas; BA, Wellesley Coll., 1958; MA, Bryn Mawr Coll., 1960, PhD, 1968; m. Theodore Leslie Shear, June 24, 1959; children: Julia Louise, Alexandra. Research asst. Inst. for Advanced Study, Princeton, N.J., 1963-65; mem. Agora Excavation, Athens, 1967, 72-94; lectr. art and archaeology Princeton U., 1983-84; lectr. Am. Sch. Classical Studies, Athens, summers 1989—; also excavator various other sites in Greece and Italy. Mem. Archaeol. Inst. Am., Greek Archaeol. Soc. (hon.). Author: The Panagia Houses at Mycenae, 1987; contbr. articles to profl. jours. Address: 87 Library Pl Princeton NJ 08540-3015

SHEAR, THEODORE LESLIE, JR., archaeologist, educator; b. Athens, Greece, May 1, 1938; s. Theodore Leslie and Josephine (Platner) S.; m. Ione Doris Mylonas, June 24, 1959; children: Julia Louise, Alexandra. AB summa cum laude, Princeton U., 1959, MA, 1963, PhD, 1966. Instr. Greek and Latin Bryn Mawr Coll., 1964-66, asst. prof., 1966-67; asst. prof. art and archaeology Princeton (N.J.) U., 1967-70, assoc. prof., 1970-79, chmn. program in classical archaeology, 1970-85, assoc. chmn. dept. art and archaeology, 1976-78, 82-83, prof. classical archaeology, 1979—; prof. archaeology Am. Sch. Classical Studies, Athens, 1988-94; mem. mng. com. Am. Sch. Classical Studies, Athens, 1972—; mem. archaeol. expdns. to Greece and Italy, including Mycenae, 1953-54, 58, 62-63, 65-66, Eleusis, 1956, Perati, 1956, Corinth, 1960, Morgantina, Sicily, 1962; mem. Ancient Agora of Athens, 1955, 67, field dir., 1968-94; trustee William Alexander Procter Found., 1982-89, Princeton Jr. Sch., 1983—, pres., 1994—. Author: Kallias of Sphettos and the Revolt of Athens in 286 B.C., 1978; contbr. articles to profl. jours. White fellow Am. Sch. Classical Studies, 1959-60. Mem. Archaeol. Inst. Am., Am. Philol. Assn., Coll. Art Assn., Archaeol. Soc. Athens (hon.), Phi Beta Kappa. Republican. Episcopalian. Clubs: Century Assn. (N.Y.C.); Nassau (Princeton); Princeton (N.Y.C.); Hellenic Yacht (Piraeus, Greece). Home: 87 Library Pl Princeton NJ 08540-3015

SHEARER, CHARLES LIVINGSTON, academic administrator; b. Louisville, Ky., Nov. 23, 1942; s. Guy Cooper and Kathryn (Aufenkamp) S.; m. Susan Pulling Shearer, Nov. 30, 1968; children: Todd A., Mark G., Scott B. BS, U. Ky., 1964, MA, 1967; MA, Mich. State U., 1973, PhD, 1981. Instr. Henderson (Ky.) Community Coll., 1967-69; asst. prof. Ferris State Coll., Big Rapids, Mich., 1969-71; grad. asst. Mich. State U., East Lansing, 1971-73; dir. mgmt. program Albion (Mich.) Coll., 1973-75, dir. ops., 1975-79; v.p. fin. Transylvania U., Lexington, Ky., 1979-83, pres., 1983—; bd. dirs. Ky. Utilities, Lexington. Bd. dirs. Lexington Philharmonic Soc., 1983-89; mem. adv. bd. Salvation Army, Lexington, 1983-87; mem. Henry Clay Meml. Found., Lexington, 1983-89. Capt. U.S. Army Nat. Guard, 1966-76. Named One of Outstanding Young Men in Am., 1978. Mem. Am. Econs. Assn., Lexington C. of C. (bd. dirs. 1985—). Mem. Christian Ch. (Disciples of Christ). Lodge: Rotary.

SHEARER, DEREK N., international studies educator, diplomat, administrator; b. L.A., Dec. 5, 1946; s. Lloyd and Marva (Peterson) S.; m. Ruth Y. Goldway, July 8, 1976; 1 child, Casey; stepchildren: Anthony, Julia. BA, Yale U., 1968; PhD, Union Grad. Sch., Yellow Springs, Ohio, 1977. Lectr. U. Calif., L.A., 1979-81; dir. internat. and pub. affairs ctr., prof. of pub. policy Occidental Coll., L.A., 1981-94; dep. under sec. U.S. Dept. Commerce, Washington, 1993; U.S. ambassadorto Finland U.S. Dept. State, Washington, 1994—; fellow Econ. Strategy Inst., Washington, 1993; policy adv. to Presidential Candidate Bill Clinton, 1990-92. Contbr. articles to profl. publs. Planning commr. City of Santa Monica (Calif.), 1984; bd. mem. Nat. Consumer Bank, Washington, 1991. Recipient Guggenheim Fellowship Guggenheim Found., 1984, U.S.-Japan Leadership fellow Japan Soc., 1991. Democrat. Avocations: basketball, tennis, travel, mysteries. Home: 12725 Sunset Blvd Los Angeles CA 90049

SHEARER, JOHN CLYDE, economics consultant, labor arbitrator, international manpower consultant; b. Phila., June 24, 1928; s. John Dwight and Edna Mildred (Moser) S.; m. Mary Ann Shafer, Apr. 30, 1955; children—John Peter, Rachel Alicia. Student, Cornell, 1945-46, 48-52; B.S., N.Y. State Sch. Indsl. and Labor Relations, 1952; postgrad., U. Manchester, Eng., 1952-53; A.M., Princeton, 1958, Ph.D., 1960. Adminstrv. asst. indsl. relations Union Carbide Metals Co., Marietta, Ohio, 1952-56; research asst. indsl. relations Princeton, 1957-60; asst. prof. econs. Grad. Sch. Indsl. Adminstrn. Carnegie Inst. Tech., Pitts., 1960-65; assoc. prof. econs. Pa. State U., State College, 1965-67; prof. econs., dir. Manpower Research and Tng. Center Okla. State U., Stillwater, 1967-87, emeritus prof. econs., 1987—; prof., economist Latin Am. Inst. Econ. and and Social Planning, UN Econ. Commn. for Latin Am., Santiago, Chile, 1962-63; cons. OAS, UN, Ford Found., Inter-Am. Devel. Bank, Coun. Internat. Progress in Mgmt., ILO, AMA, others; mem. arbitration panels Fed. Mediation and Conciliation Svc., Am. Arbitration Assn., Employment Disputes Settlement Panel. Author: High-Level Manpower in Overseas Subsidiaries: Experience in Brazil and Mexico, 1960, La Importación y La Exportación de Los Recursos Humanos, 1964, (with Jacob Kaufman, Grant Farr) The Development and Utilization of Human Resources, 1967, Industrial Relations of American Corporations Abroad, 1967, (with Rafael Isaza) Employment and Unemployment in Colombia, 1969, Manpower Environments Confronting American Firms in Western Europe, 1970, Intra and International Movements of High-Level Human Resources, 1971, High-Level Human Resources in Economic Development, 1973, Arbitration and Changing Life Styles, 1974, Fact and Fiction Concerning Multinational Labor Relations, 1977, Dispute Settlement in the South, 1981, (with I.B. Helburn) Human Resources and Industrial Relations in China: A Time of Ferment, 1984, Reducing Cost of Arbitration Through Increasing the Parties' Options, 1985, Reinstatement without Back Pay: An Appropriate Remedy?, 1987; contbr. articles to profl. jours. Mem. for edn. Southwestern Regional Manpower Adv. Com. to Secs. Labor and HEW. Served with USMC, 1946-48. Fulbright fellow Eng., 1952-53; Owen D. Young fellow, 1956-57, 57-58; Ford Found. fellow, 1958-59. Mem. Am. Econ. Assn., So. Econ. Assn., Okla. Civil Liberties Union, Indsl. Relations Research Assn., Internat. Indsl. Rel. Assn., Soc. Internat. Devel., Nat. Acad. Arbitrators (bd. govs.), Am. Arbitration Assn., Soc. Profl. in Dispute Resolution. Home: 2020 N Crescent Dr Stillwater OK 74075-2801 also:: RR 1 Box 2210 Mount Vernon ME 04352-9720

SHEARER, P. SCOTT, government relations professional; b. Clinton, Ill., Feb. 27, 1948; s. Lloyd Jr. and Pauline Lucille (Glosser) S.; m. Barbara Boston, July 3, 1981; children: Jason J., Carrie K. Brunk. BS, U. Ill., 1970, MS, 1975. Asst. dir. cash mgmt. State Treas. Ill., Springfield, 1973-74, asst. chief fin. officer, 1974-77, chief fiscal officer, 1977-78; dir. vehicle svc. State of Ill., Springfield, 1978-81; legis. asst. Senator Dixon U.S. Senate, Washington, 1981-84; exec. dir. Nat. Corn Growers Assn., St. Louis, 1984-90; dir. govt. rels. Halfpenny, Hahn, Roche & Marchese, 1990-93; dir. legis. affairs Zeneca Inc., Washington, 1993; dep. asst. sec. congl. rels. USDA, 1993—; adv. com. Ill. Atty.'s Gen. Agr. Law, State of Ill., 1985-91, Dean Coll. Agr., U. Ill., 1989-90, U. Ill. Dept. Agrl. Econs., 1986-89. Del. Dem. Nat. Conv., 1978, Mo. Dem. State conv., 1988, Va. Dem. State Conv., 1992, 93, 94; mem. Police Bd. Commrs., Chesterfield, Mo., 1988-90; pres. Mo. river Dem. Club, 1987-89. Named to Hon. Order of Ky. Cols., 1990, Alpha Gamma Sigma nat. merit award, 1991. Mem. St. Louis Agr.-Bus. Club (sec.-treas. 1987-88, 2d v.p. 1988-89, v.p. 1989-90, pres. 1990), U. Ill. Alumni Assn., U. Ill. Coll. Agr. Alumni Assn. (dir. at large 1990), Ill. Group (chmn. 1993), Alpha Zeta. Methodist. Home: 2744 Clarkes Landing Dr Oakton VA 22124-1120 Office: Dept Agr 213-A Whitten Bldg 14th & Independence Ave Washington DC 20250

SHEARER, RICHARD EUGENE, industrial consultant; b. Connellsville, Pa., Dec. 30, 1919; s. H.D. and Florence (Prinkey) S.; m. Ruth Mansberger, June 16, 1944 (dec. Mar. 1993); children: Patricia (Mrs. Richard Wilson), Suzanne (Mrs. Terry Jones), Richard J.; m. Marilyn Likeness Erdman, May 7, 1994. A.B., Eastern Bapt. Coll. and Sem., Phila., 1943, D.D., 1953; B.D., New Brunswick Theol. Sem., 1945; M.A., Columbia, 1948, Ed.D., 1959; LL.D., Denison U., 1958; H.H.D., Bishop Coll., 1977. Ordained to ministry Bapt. Ch., 1943; minister Atlantic Highlands, N.J., 1943-45, New Brunswick, N.J., 1945-5O; pres. Alderson-Broaddus Coll., Philippi, W.Va., 1951-83; ind. cons., 1983—; cons., interim dir. W.Va. Found. Ind. Colls.; prin. resdl. devel. Bridgeport, W.Va., 1983—; v.p., exec. dir. United Health Found., Clarksburg, W.Va., 1987—; pres. R. Shearer & Assocs., Philippi, W.Va., 1984; lectr. Mex. Pastor's Conf., summer 1955; past pres. W.Va. Found. Ind. Colls.; mem. Commn. on Instnl. Funding, Am. Bapt. Chs., U.S.A.; coordinator (Central Europe Coll. Program); pres. Am. Bapt. Assn. Sch. and Coll. Adminstrs., 1977; mem. W.Va. Ednl. Found., W.Va. State Scholarship Commn. Bd. regents W.Va. Assn. Pvt. Colls.; bd. dirs. W.Va. Found. Independent Colls.; sr. min. Bridgeport (W.Va.) Bapt. Ch., 1988-93; bd. dirs. Eastern Bapt. Theol. Sem., Phila. Named Phi Delta Kappa Profl. Educator of Year, 1964. Mem. Am. Assn. Sch. Adminstrs., W.Va. Assn. Coll. and Univ. Presidents (sec. mem. exec. com. 1963—), Assn. Am. Colls. (commn. coll. and soc.), Kiwanis. Office: Alderson-Broaddus Coll RR 3 Box 27216 Philippi WV 26416-9803 *The joint impact of good religion and good education has been the dominant theme of my life and work. I feel that education is a powerful force which can be directed in either constructive or destructive directions. Good religion can assure that the power in education is constructive, and good education can assure that religion has depth.*

SHEARER, RICK LELAND, academic administrator; b. Wichita, Kans., Jan. 8, 1955; s. Jack Leland and Marjorie Louise (Pearson) S. BSc, U. Calgary, Alberta, Can., 1979; MBA in Fin., Nat. U., 1984; MA in Edn., San Diego State U., 1992. V.p., gen. mgr. Direction Holdings Ltd., Calgary, 1979-81; cons. Ethic Mgmt. Ltd., Calgary, 1981-82; from dir. computer based edn. to dir. rsch. and evaluation Nat. U., San Diego, 1985-92, dir. instl. rsch., founding assoc. distance edn. system, 1992—; presenter conf. procs. Distance Teaching and Learning, 1993-94, 95-96, Ed Media 93, 1993. Author: Am. Jour. Distance Edn., 1994. Mem. Assn. Edn. Comm. & Tech., Am. Coun. Distance Edn. Avocations: fitness, skiing, sailing, skating. Office: Nat Univ 4025 Camino Del Rio S San Diego CA 92108-4107

SHEARER, RONALD ALEXANDER, economics educator; b. Trail, C., Can., June 15, 1932; s. James Boyd and Mary Ann (Smith) S.; m. Renate Elizabeth Selig, Dec. 20, 1956 (dec.); children: Carl, Bruce. B.A., U. B.C., 1954; M.A., Ohio State U., 1955, Ph.D., 1959. Asst. prof. econs. U. Mich., 1958-62; economist Royal Commn. Banking and Finance, Toronto, 1962-63; mem. faculty U. B.C., Vancouver, 1963—; prof. econs. U. B.C., 1970—, head dept., 1972-76. Co-author: Money and Banking, 1975, The Economics of the Canadian Financial System, 1994; editor: Trade Liberalization and a Regional Economy, 1971. Mem. Am., Canadian econs. assns. Office: Univ BC, Dept Economics, Vancouver, BC Canada

SHEARER, WILLIAM KENNEDY, lawyer, publisher; b. Marysville, Calif., Jan. 21, 1931; s. William and Eva (Kennedy) S.; m. Eileen Mary Knowland; Nov. 25, 1956; 1 child, Nancy Lorena. BA, San Diego State U., 1955; JD, Western State U., 1975. Bar: Calif. 1975, U.S. Dist. Ct. (so. dist.) Calif. 1975, U.S. Ct. Claims 1976, U.S. Supreme Ct. 1982, U.S. Ct. Appeals (fed. cir.) 1982, U.S. Ct. Appeals (9th cir.) 1983. Legis. asst. to Congressman James Utt, 1953, 55-56; exec. dir. San Diego County Rep. Cen. Com., 1956-58; pub. Oceanside-Carlsbad Banner, Oceanside, Calif., 1958-63; adminstrv. asst. Assemblyman E.R. Barnes, Sacramento, Calif., 1963-65; polit. campaign cons. Banner Advt., San Diego, Los Angeles, 1964-75; atty. Duke, Gerstel, Shearer & Bregante, San Diego, 1975—. Pub. newsletters Calif. Statesman, 1962—, Legis. Survey, 1963—, Fgn. Policy Rev., 1972—, Am. Ind., 1974—. Rep. nominee for State Assembly, San Diego County, 1956, 58; state chmn. Am. Ind. Party, Calif., 1967-70, nat. chmn. 1968-71, 73-77; nat. vice chmn. U.S. Taxpayers Party, 1992—; Am. Ind. nominee for Gov., 1970; adv. com. Elections Com., Calif. Legislature, Sacramento, 1971-76; bd. dirs. San Diego Gilbert & Sullivan Co., 1984-90, pres. 1986-88, v.p., 1985-86, 88-90. With U.S. Army, 1953-55. Mem. ABA, Calif. Bar Assn., San Diego County Bar Assn. Avocations: ancient Near Eastern history, gardening, music. Home: 8160 Palm St Lemon Grove CA 91945-3028 Office: Duke Gerstel Shearer & Bregante 101 W Broadway Ste 600 San Diego CA 92101-8207

SHEARER, WILLIAM THOMAS, pediatrician, educator; b. Detroit, Aug. 23, 1937. BS, U. Detroit, 1960; PhD, Wayne State U., 1966; MD, Washington U., St. Louis, 1970. Diplomate Am. Bd. Pediatrics, Am. Bd. Allergy and Immunology (chmn. 1994-95, dir. 1990-95), Nat. Bd. Med. Examiners; cert. in diagnostic lab. immunology. Post-doctoral fellow in biochemistry dept. chem. Indiana U., Bloomington, 1966-67; intern in pediatrics St. Louis Children's Hosp., 1970-71, resident in immunology in pediatrics, 1971-72, dir. divsn. allergy and immunology, 1974-78; fellow in immunology in pediatrics Barnes Hosp., Washington U., St. Louis, 1972-74; spl. USPHA sci. rsch. fellow in medicine dept. medicine Washington U., 1972-74, assoc. prof., 1978, prof., 1978; prof. pediat., microbiology, immunology Baylor Coll. Medicine, Houston, 1978—, dir. AIDS rsch. ctr., 1991—; head sect. allergy & immunology Tex. Children's Hosp., Houston, 1978—; mem. ACTU Cmty. Adv. Bd., Tex. Children's Hosp., Houston, 1991—; chmn. pediat. core com. pediat. AIDS clin. trial group Nat. Inst. Allergy and Infectious Diseases NIH, Bethesda, Md., 1989—, ad hoc reviewer, 1991, mem. therapeutics subcom. AIDS rsch. adv. com., 1993—, chmn. pediat. AIDS clin. trial group immunology com., 1994—, mem. pediat. AIDS clin. trials group exec. com., 1991-95, mem. spl. rev. com. persons affected by chronic granulomatous disease, 1993; site visitor Gen. Clin. rsch. Ctr., NIH, Bethesda, 1993, vice chmn. pediat. AIDS clin. trials group exec. com., 1996—; chmn. study population/patient mgmt. com. Clin. Ctrs. for the Study of Pediat. Lung and Heart Complications of HIV Infection Nat. Heart, Lung and Blood Inst. NIH, Bethesda, 1989—, mem. AIDS ad hoc work group, 1991; dir. pediat. HIV/AIDS Clin. Rsch. Ctr., Houston, 1988—; chmn. exec. com. clin. trial intravenous gammaglobulin in HIV infected children Nat. Inst. Child and Health and Human Devel., Bethesda, 1989—. Editor: Pediatric Asthma, Allergy, and Immunology, 1989; editl. bd. Jour. of Allergy and Clin. Immunology, 1993—, Clin. and Diagnostic Lab. Immunology, 1994—; editor Pediatric Allergy and Immunology, 1995—, Allergy and Immunology Tng. Program Dir.; guest editor Seminar Pediatric Infectious Disease, 1990; contbr. intro.: Allergy: Principles and Practice, 1992; contbr. articles to profl. jours. including New Eng. Jour. Medicine. AIDS cons. Houston Ind. Sch. Dist., 1986—; med. adv. Spring Branch Ind. Sch. Dist., Houston, 1987—; chmn. community HIV/AIDS adv. group Tex. Med. Ctr., 1991—. Recipient faculty rsch. award Am. Cancer Soc., 1977-79, Myrtle Wreath award Hadassah, 1985, spl. recognition award Am. Acad. Allergy and Immunology, 1994; rsch. scholar Cystic Fibrosis Found., 1974-77; grantee NIH, 1988—. Mem. Am. Soc. Clin. Investigation, Am. Acad. Pediats. (mem. exec. com. sect. allergy and immunology 1991—), Tex. Allergy Soc. (exec. com. 1990—, Tex. Allergy and Immunology Soc. (chmn. nat. issues com. 1992-96, pres. 1994-96), Am. Acad. allergy and Immunology (chmn. clin. and lab. immunology com. 1994-96, chmn. tng. program dirs. nat. issues subcom. 1994-96), Am. Acad. Allergy, Asthma and Immunology (assoc. chmn. for planning of 1997-98 internat. meetings, profl. ednl. coun.). Achievements include research in half-matched T-cell-depleted bone marrow transplants, in membrane signal pathway of human B lymphcytes. Office: Tex Childrens Hosp A/I Svc 6621 Fannin St MC 1-3291 Houston TX 77030-2303

SHEARING, CLIFFORD DENNING, criminology and sociology educator; b. Durban, Natal, South Africa, Feb. 2, 1942; s. Cecil and Amy (Clifford) S.; children: Anthony Denning, Renée Anne. B Social Sci. in Psychology-nd Sociology, U. Natal, Durban, 1965, B Social Sci. in Sociology cum laude, 1967; MA in Sociology 1st class, U. Toronto, Ont., Can., 1968, PhD in Sociology, 1977. Assoc. Can. Inst. for Advanced Rsch., 1985-89; rsch. assoc. Ctr. Criminology U. Toronto, 1972-75, sr. rsch. assoc., 1976-83, coord. grad. studies, 1978-83, 89—, sr. fellow Woodsworth Coll., 1985—, assoc. prof. Ctr. Criminology, 1984-89, prof., 1989—, dir. Ctr. Criminology, 1993—, instr. Woodsworth Coll., 1976-81, assoc. prof., 1981-89, prof., 1989—, assoc. prof. dept. sociology, 1981-89, prof., 1989—; mem. bd. control Ctr. for Socio-Legal Studies, U. Natal, 1988-90, assoc. mem., 1990—; vis. rsch. prof. Cmty. Law Ctr., U. Western Cape, Cape Town, South Africa, 1991-93, dir., 1993—; vis. prof. faculty law U. Cape Town, 1992-93, vis. lectr., rsch. assoc. Inst. Criminology, 1992-93; vis. fellow dept. law Rsch. Sch. Social Sci., Australia Nat. U., 1992; faculty advisor Can. Criminology Forum, 1979-83, reviewer, 1983-85; reviewer Can. Jour. Sociology, 1982—, Social Problems, 1982—, Law and Society Rev., 1983-85, Am. Bar Found. Rsch. Jour./Law and Social Inquiry, 1988—, Can. Jour. Criminology, 1988—, Criminology, 1989—, Jour. Contemporary Ethnography, 1990—, Law and Policy, 1991—, Economy and Society, 1995—; assoc. cons. Jour. Criminal Law and Criminology, 1991—; cons. Can. Police Coll., 1979-80, Met. Toronto Housing Authority, 1987-89, Toronto Transit Commn., 1987, Office Pub. Compaints Commr., Ont., 1986-87, Hoppo Valley Estates, Zimbabe, 1986, Ont. Waste Mgmt. Corp., 1986, Law Reform Commn. Can., 1979-80, 84-85, Nat. Mus. Can., 1983; advisor police powers project Can. Human Rights Found., 1983; advisor Commn. of Inquiry Concerning Activities of the Royal Can. Mounted Police, 1977-81; numerous others. Author: (with Hilstan L. Watts) Blood Donation: Attitudes and Motivation, 1966, (with Margaret B. Farnell) Private Security: An Examination of Canadian Statistics, 1961-71, (with Philip C. Stenning) Police Training in Ontario: An Evaluation of Recruit and Supervisory Course, 1980, (with Farnell and Stenning) Contract Security in Ontario, 1980, (with Michael Brogden) Policing for a New South Africa, 1993; editor: Organizational Police Deviance: Its Structure and Control, 1981, -a-Cop: A Study of Police Mobilization, 1984; co-editor: Private Security and Private Justice: The Challenge of the 80's, 1983, Private Policing, 1987, Criminology: A Readers Guide, 1991; assoc. editor Can. Jour. Sociology, 1975-78, Critical Arts, 1986—; mem. editl. bd. Natal U. Law and Society Rev., 1985—, Policing and Society, 1988—, Jour. Regulatory Law and Practice, 1992—; contbr. articles and revs. to profl. jours., chpts. to books. Office: U Toronto, Ctr Criminology, 130 St George St Rm 8001, Toronto, ON Canada M5S 1A1

SHEARING, GEORGE ALBERT, pianist, composer; b. London, Aug. 13, 1919; came to U.S., 1947, naturalized, 1956; s. James Philip and Ellen Amelia (Brightman) S.; m. Beatrice Bayes, May 1, 1941 (div.); 1 child, Wendy Ann; m. Eleanor Geffert, July 28, 1984. Student, Linden Lodge Sch. for Blind, London; Hon. degree, Westminster Coll., Salt Lake City, 1975, Hamilton Coll., 1994. V.p. Shearing Music Corp. Composer: Lullaby of Birdland, numerous other popular songs; recs. English Decca and Parlophone, Am. Savoy, London, MGM Capitol, Sheba Records, Concord Jazz, Telarc; albums include: An Evening with George Shearing and Mel Torme, 1982, Top Drawer, 1983, An Evening at Charlie's, 1984, Grand Piano, 1985, An Elegant Evening, 1986, George Shearing and Barry Tuckwell Play the Music of Cole Porter, 1986, More Grand Piano, 1987, (with Marian McPartland) Alone Together, 1981, George Shearing and Dakota Staton: In the Night, A Vintage Year, 1987, George Shearing and Hank Jones: The Spirit of 176, 1989, George Shearing In Dixieland, 1989, I Hear a Rhapsody: Live at the Blue Note, 1994, On a Clear Day, 1980, How Beautiful is Night, 1993, Best of George Shearing, 1993, That Shearing Sound, 1994, Walkin' - Live at the Blue Note, 1995, The George Shearing Quintet: By Request, 1995, Jazz Moments, 1995, Paper Moon: Music of Nat King Cole, 1996, George Shearing and Friends, 1996; appearances at: London Symphony Pops Concerts, 1986, 87, London Paladium, 1987, Concord Jazz Festival, Japan, 1987, Hong Kong Cultural Ctr., 1992, European Jazz Festivals, 1995, Birmingham (Eng.) Symphony with Sir Simon Rattle, 1995, Japan Tour, 1996, New Eng. Jazz Festival, 1996, Tanglewood, Mass., 1996, Can. Tour, 1995, US Tour, 1996, others. Bd. dirs. Guide Dogs for Blind, San Rafael, Hadley Sch. for Blind, Winnetka, Ill. Voted top English pianist, 1941-47; winner all Am. jazz polls, also many pvt. awards; recipient Golden Plate award Am. Acad. of Achievement, 1968, Helen Keller Achievement award, 1995. Mem. Broadcast Music Inc. Club: Bohemian (San Francisco). Office: care Joan Shulman, 103 Avenue Rd Ste 301, Toronto, ON Canada M5R 2G9*

SHEARON, FORREST BEDFORD, humanities educator; b. Bolivar, Tenn., Sept. 7, 1934; s. George W. and Carrie Mae (Shinault) S.; m. Jeannette Brooks, June 5, 1955 (div. 1972); children: Angelia J. Shearon Schulte, Michael F.; m. Lynn Britton, June 11, 1981. AB in History, Union U., 1956; postgrad., Northwestern U., 1962-63; MA in English, U. Louisville 1965, PhD in English, 1973. English tchr. Halls (Tenn.) High Sch., 1956-58, Pleasure Ridge Park High Sch., Louisville, 1958-62, 63-65; asst. prof. English Ky. So. Coll., Louisville, 1965-68; instr. English U. Louisville, 1969-73; asst. prof., assoc. prof., prof. humanities Ea. Ky. U., Richmond, 1973—. Contbr. articles to profl. jours. Recipient Outstanding Grad. Student award U. Louisville, 1973; Ford Found. fellow, 1962-63, NEH fellow, 1979; Fulbright-Hays grantee, 1987. Mem. MLA, So. Humanities Coun. (co-chair 1995-96, sec. 1989—), Ky. Philological Assn. (exec. sec. 1983-84), South Atlantic MLA, South Asian Lit. Assn., Phi Kappa Phi. Democrat. Presbyterian. Avocations: travel, reading, writing. Home: 305 Summit St Richmond KY 40475-2133 Office: Ea Ky U Dept Humanities Case Annex 368 Richmond KY 40475-3140

SHEA-STONUM, MARILYN, judge; b. Anaconda, Mont., June 6, 1947. AB, U. Calif., Santa Cruz, 1969; JD, Case Western Res. U., 1975. Bar: Ohio 1975, Calif. 1976. Law clk. to Hon. Battisti U.S. Dist. Ct. (no. dist.), Ohio, 1975-76; ptnr. Jones, Day, Reavis & Pogue, Cleve., 1984-94; bankruptcy judge ea. divsn. U.S. Bankruptcy Ct. Ohio (no. dist.), Akron, 1984-94; bankruptcy judge U.S. Bankruptcy Ct. (no. dist.) Ohio, Akron, 1994—. Office: US Bankruptcy Ct No Dist Ohio Ea Divsn 2 S Main St Rm 240 Akron OH 44308*

SHEAVLY, ROBERT BRUCE, social worker; b. Detroit, Sept. 13, 1952; s. George Brown and Mary Jane (Hoover) S. BA, Georgetown U., 1974; MSW, U. Md., 1981. Lic. ind. clin. social worker; bd. cert. diplomate; ACSW. Bookkeeper, accounts payable mgr. Capitol Area Ins. Assocs., Silver Spring, Md., 1974-77; asst. cons. The Wyatt Co., Washington, 1977-79; counselor Whitman-Walker Clinic, Washington, 1977-79; social worker Dept. Social Svcs. City Balt., 1980; social worker Alcohol and Drug Abuse Program, U. Md. Sch. Medicine, Balt., 1980-81, instr. Sch. Medicine, asst. dir. Family Violence Unit, 1981-82; pvt. practice Balt., 1982-83; social worker alcohol/drug abuse prevention/control program U.S. Army, Giessen (Germany) Cmty. Counseling Ctr., 1983-84; clin. supr. alcohol/drug abuse prevention/control program U.S. Army, Giessen Milcom, Community Counseling Ctr., 1984-85; instr. drug and alcohol abuse divsn. 7th Army Tng. Ctr., Munich, Germany, 1985-91; dir. family program specialized treatment addiction recovery Walter Reed Army Med. Ctr., Washington, 1991-93, cons. dept. clin. pastoral edn., 1993—; assoc. dir. Bill Austin Day Treatment Ctr. for Persons with AIDS Whitman-Walker Clinic, Washington, 1993-94; pvt. practice, 1994—; presenter, guest lectr. in field. Ch. organist, dir. music Ch. of the Nativity, Washington, St. James Episcopal Ch., Washington, 1970-79; mem. diocesan commn. on liturgy and music Episcopal Diocese of Washington. Mem. NASW, AACD (European br.), Acad. Cert. Social Workers, Soc. Neuro-Linguistic Programming, Washington Soc. Jungian Psychology, Phi Kappa Phi. Episcopalian. Avocations: biking, scuba, sq. dancing, liturgics, ch. organist. Home: 2039 New Hampshire Ave NW Washington DC 20009-3479 Office: 1633 Q St Ste 200 Washington DC 20009

SHEBESTA, LYNN MARIE, school administrator; b. Manitowoc, Wis., Dec. 16, 1955; d. Joseph J. Shebesta and Shirley Ann (Pietras) Kent. BS, U. Wis., La Crosse, 1978; MS, Mankato State U., 1986; postgrad. study Admissions, Harvard Grad. Sch. Edn., 1992. Admissions counselor Silver Lake Coll., Manitowoc, Wis., 1980-83; asst. dir. admissions Mankato (Minn.) State U., 1983-88; dir. admissions Lakeland Coll., Sheboygan, Wis., 1988-90; dean of admissions and fin. aid Wayland Acad., Beaver Dam, Wis., 1990-95; econ. devel. profl. Northeast Wis. Tech. Coll., Green Bay, Wis., 1995—; cons. to admissions Northwestern Military/Naval Acad., Lake Geneva, Wis., 1992; presenter Nat. Assn. Luth. Coll. Admission Officers, Concordia U. Wis., Mequon, Wis., 1993. Editor, designer, publisher (ednl. insts. brochures, viewbooks), 1986-93. Bd. dirs., founder Civitan, Mankato, 1986-88; bd. dirs. Big Brothers/Big Sisters, Manitowoc, Wis., 1989, Girl Scouts, Green Bay, Wis., 1996. Mem. Wis. Assn. Secondary Sch. and Coll. Admissions Counselors, Secondary Sch. Admission Test Bd., Midwest Boarding Schs. (bd. dirs.), Nat. Assn. Student Affairs Profls. Avocations: skiing, camping, coaching softball, motorcycling, gardening. Home: 448 North Good Hope Rd De Pere WI 54115 Office: Northeast Wis Tech Coll PO Box 19042 2740 W Mason St Green Bay WI 54307-9042

SHECHTER, BEN-ZION, artist, illustrator; b. Tel Aviv, Aug. 7, 1940; s. Isaac and Elka (Demb) S.; m. Laura Judith Goldstein, Feb. 26, 1969; 1 child, Adam. B.F.A., Bezalel Acad. Fine Art, Jerusalem, 1966. Airplane mechanic Israeli aviation industry (Lod), 1961-62; free-lance comml. artist N.Y.C., 1966—, artist, illustrator, 1974—. Illustrator: Common Ground, 1980; one-man shows Martin Sumers Graphic, N.Y.C., 1983, Wustum Mus., Racine, Wis., 1982, Cayuga Community Coll., Auburn, N.Y., 1982, Suffolk County Community Coll., Selden, N.Y., 1984, Capricorn Gallery, Bethesda, Md., 1989, FDR Gallery, N.Y.C., 1993; exhibited in group shows U. Iowa Mus., 1983, Bklyn. Mus., 1980, 84, Minn. Mus. Art, St Paul, 1980, Elvchjem Mus., U. Wis.-Madison, 1983, Ark. Art Ctr., Little Rock, 1986, 92, Hunt Inst. (Carnegie Instn.), Pitts., 1988, Butlur Inst., Youngstown, Ohio, 1988, Kutztown (Pa.) U., 1989, Suffolk County C.C., Selden, N.Y., 1994; represented in permanent collections, Bklyn Mus., U. Iowa Mus., Boston Mus. Fine Art, Israel Mus., Jerusalem. Served with Israeli Air Force, 1958-61. City of Jerusalem scholar, 1963, 64; Israeli Ministry Edn. scholar, 1965, 66. Jewish. Home: 429 4th St Brooklyn NY 11215-2901

SHECHTER, LAURA JUDITH, artist; b. Bklyn., Aug. 26, 1944; d. Philip and Jeannette (Newmark) Goldstein; m. Ben-Zion Shechter, Feb. 26, 1969; 1 son, Adam. B.A. with honors in Art, Bklyn. Coll., 1965. Case worker Dept. Social Service, N.Y.C., 1965-73; artist N.Y.C., 1965—; lectr., 1978—; curator Forum Gallery, N.Y.C., 1978; tchr. Parson Sch. Design, N.Y.C., 1984, Nat. Acad. Design, N.Y.C., 1985-88, 94—. Exhibited one-woman shows Forum Gallery, N.Y.C., 1976, 80, 83, Greenville County Mus. Art, 1982, Wustum Mus., Racine, Wis., 1982, Schoelkopf Gallery, N.Y.C., 1985, Staempfli Gallery, N.Y.C., 1987, 88, Rahr West Mus., Manitowoc, Wis., U. Richmond, 1991, Perlow Gallery, N.Y.C., 1992, 94, Pucker Gallery, Boston, 1996; group shows include Akron Art Inst., 1974, Minn. Mus. Art, St. Paul, 1981, Pa. Acad. Art, Phila., 1982, Boston Mus., 1982, Bklyn. Mus., 1980, 84, Nat. Mus. Am. Art, Washington, 1985, San Francisco Mus. Modern Art, 1985, Huntsville Mus., Ala., 1987, Butler Inst., Youngstown, Ohio, 1987, 88, Ind. U. Art Mus., Joplin, Mo., 1991, Ark. Art Ctr., 1992; represented in pub. collections including Boston Mus. Fine Art, Bklyn. Mus., Carnegie Inst., Indpls. Mus., Israel Mus., others. Recipient Creative Artist Pub. Service award N.Y. State, 1982. Mem. Artists Equity, Nat. Acad. Art. Home: 429 4th St Brooklyn NY 11215-2901 *I believe that my work is always slowly changing through hard and consistent effort. There was a strong idea that initiated this work. Although that idea has been completely altered, it still exists.*

SHECTER, HOWARD L., lawyer; b. Boston, May 13, 1943. AB, Harvard U., 1965; JD, U. Pa., 1968. Bar: Pa. 1968. Assoc. Morgan, Lewis & Bockius, LLP, Phila., 1968-73; ptnr. Morgan, Lewis & Bockius, Phila., 1973—. Office: Morgan Lewis & Bockius LLP 2000 One Logan Sq Philadelphia PA 19103

SHEDD, BEN ALVIN, film producer, director, production company executive; b. Stockton, Calif., Jan. 27, 1947; s. Robert Alvin and Beverly Joyce (Ganeles) S.; 1 child, Nara Evelyn. B.A. in Radio-TV-Film, San Francisco State U., 1968; M.A. in Cinema, U. So. Calif., 1973. adj. prof. cinema U. So. Calif., 1979-89; faculty Calif. Inst. Arts, 1984-89, Dow Creativity Ctr., Northwood Inst., Mich., 1989; PNM endowed chair prof. media arts U. N.Mex., 1989-90. Filmmaker Churchill Films, Los Angeles, 1971-73; producer, dir., writer: pub. TV sci. documentary series NOVA, Sta.WGBH-TV, Boston, 1973-76; film and videotape dir./producer, pres. public TV sci. documentary series, Shedd Prodns., Inc., Los Angeles, 1976—, Shedd Prodns., Inc.; dir., writer, editor: documentaries The Flight of the Gossamer Condor, 1976-78, Poetry for People Who Hate Poetry; film series, Steffens/Shedd Poetry Films, 1979; producer commls. Newby's Movies, Los Angeles, 1980; producer Calif. Dream Series, Sta. KOCE, Huntington Beach, 1981, The Homefront, U. So. Calif./PBS TV Spl., Los Angeles, 1982; songwriter Making the Music, TriStar Pictures, N.Y., 1984; producer, dir., co-writer, co-editor Seasons, Imax/Omnimax Film Sci. Mus. Minn./Graphic Films, 1985-87; dir. Dealing with Feelings About Nuclear Age Issues, 1988; dir., co-producer Tropical Rainforest, 1987-91. Served with USAR, 1969-75. Co-recipient Peabody award U. Ga. Sch. Journalism and Bd. Regents, 1974; Acad. award for best documentary short subject Acad. Motion Picture Arts and Scis., 1978; also numerous U.S. and internat. film festival awards. Mem. Acad. Motion Picture Arts and Scis., Acad. Magical Arts. Office: PO Box 4220 Albuquerque NM 87196-4220

SHEDD, DENNIS W., federal judge; b. 1953. BA, Wofford Coll., 1975; JD, U. S.C., 1978; M of Laws, Georgetown U., 1980. Bar: S.C. Mem. staff U.S. Senator Strom Thurmond, 1978-88; chief counsel U.S. Senate Jud. Com., Washington, 1985-86; of counsel Bethea, Jordan & Griffin, Columbia, S.C., 1988-90; pvt. practice, 1989-90; judge U.S. Dist. Ct. S.C., Greenville, 1990-91; adj. prof. U. S.C., 1989-90. Mem. S.C. Bar Assn., Richland County Bar Assn., Phi Beta Kappa. Office: US District Court 1845 Assembly St Columbia SC 29201-2455*

SHEDD, DONALD POMROY, surgeon; b. New Haven, Aug. 4, 1922; s. Gale and Marion (Young) S.; m. Charlotte Newsom, Mar. 17, 1946; children: Carolyn, David, Ann, Laura. B.S., Yale U., 1944, M.D., 1946. Diplomate Am. Bd. Surgery. Intern Yale New Haven Hosp., 1946-47, asst. resident, resident, 1949-53; instr. surgery Yale U. Med Sch., New Haven, 1953-54, asst. prof., 1954-56, assoc. prof., 1956-67; chief dept. head and neck surgery Roswell Park Cancer Inst., Buffalo, 1967-96, prof. emeritus, 1996—. Co-editor: Surgical and Prosthetic Speech Rehabilitation, 1980, Head and Neck Cancer, 1985; contbr. numerous articles to profl. jours. Founding bd. dirs. Hospice Buffalo, Inc., 1973-83. Served to capt. U.S. Army, 1947-49. Mem. Soc. Univ. Surgeons, Soc. Surg. Oncology, New Eng. Surg. Soc., Soc. Head and Neck Surgeons (pres. 1976-77). Avocations: sailing; windsurfing; tennis. Home: 671 Lafayette Ave Buffalo NY 14222-1435 Office: Roswell Park Cancer Inst Elm & Carlton Sts Buffalo NY 14263-0001

SHEDLOCK, JAMES, library director, consultant; b. Detroit, Nov. 25, 1950. BA in English, U. Notre Dame, 1974; AM in LS, U. Mich., 1977. Reference and serials libr. St. Joseph Mercy Hosp., Pontiac, Mich., 1977-79; document delivery libr. Wayne State U. Med. Libr., Detroit, 1979-81; coord. online search svc. U. N.C. Health Scis. Libr., Chapel Hill, 1982-85; head pub. svcs. Med. Libr., Northwestern U., Chgo., 1985-88, assoc. dir., 1988-91, dir. Galter Health Scis. Libr., 1991—; cons. U.N. High Commr. for Refugees, Cyprus, 1993-94. Mem. ALA, Med. Libr. Assn., Am. Med. Informatics Assn., Assn. Acad. Health Scis. Libr. Dirs. (rep.), Acad. Health Info. Profls. (disting.). Offices: Northwestern U Galter Health Scis Libr 303 E Chicago Ave Chicago IL 60611-3008

SHEED, WILFRID JOHN JOSEPH, author; b. London, Eng., Dec. 27, 1930; came to U.S., 1947; s. Francis Joseph and Maisie (Ward) S.; m. Miriam Ungerer; children: Elizabeth, Francis, Marion. BA, Lincoln Coll., Oxford U., 1954, MA, 1957. Movie reviewer Jubilee mag., N.Y.C., 1959-61, assoc. editor, 1959-66; drama critic, book editor Commonweal mag., N.Y.C., 1964-71; movie critic Esquire mag., N.Y.C., 1967-69; columnist N.Y. Times, 1971—; vis. prof. Princeton, 1970-71; judge, mem. editorial bd. Book of Month Club, 1972-88. Author: Joseph, 1958, A Middle Class Education, 1960, The Hack, 1963, Square's Progress, 1965, Office Politics, 1966 (Nat. Book award nomination 1966), The Blacking Factory and Pennsylvania Gothic: A Short Novel and a Long Story, 1968, Max Jamison, 1970 (Nat. Book award nomination 1971), The Morning After, 1971, People Will Always Be Kind, 1973, Three Mobs: Labor, Church and Mafia, 1974, Vanishing Species of America, 1974, Muhammad Ali: A Portrait in Words and Photographs, 1975, Transatlantic Blues, 1978, The Good Word and Other Words, 1978, Clare Boothe Luce, 1982, Frank and Maisie, 1985, The Boys of Winter, 1987, The Kennedy Legacy: A Generation Later, 1988, Essays in Disguise, 1989, Face of Baseball, 1990, My Life as a Fan, 1993, In Love with Daylight, 1995; editor: G.K. Chesterton's Essays and Poems, 1957, Sixteen Short Novels, 1986, Baseball and Lesser Sports, 1991; contbr. to periodicals including N.Y. Times Book Rev., Esquire, Sports Illustrated, Commonweal. Recipient Nat. Inst. and Am. Acad. award in literature, 1971; Guggenheim fellow, 1971-72. Mem. PEN, Authors Guild. Roman Catholic. Address: Sag Harbor NY 11963

SHEEDY, ALLY (ALEXANDRA ELIZABETH SHEEDY), actress; b. N.Y.C., June 13, 1962; d. John and Charlotte (Baum) S.; m. David Lansbury. Student, U. So. Calif. Past ballet dancer. Film debut in Bad Boys, 1983; other films include Wargames, 1983, Oxford Blues, 1984, The Breakfast Club, 1985, St. Elmo's Fire, 1985, Twice in a Lifetime, 1985, Short Circuit, 1986, Blue City, 1986, Maid to Order, 1987, Heart of Dixie, 1989, Betsy's Wedding, 1990, Only the Lonely, 1991, Home Alone II: Lost in New York, 1992, The Pickle, 1992, Man's Best Friend, 1993, Tattle Tale, 1993; TV films include The Best Little Girl in the World, 1981, The Day the Loving Stopped, 1981, The Violation of Sarah McDavid, 1981, Splendor in the Grass, 1981, Dead Lessons, 1983, We Are the Children, 1987, Fear, 1990, The Lost Capone, 1990, Lethal Exposure, 1993, Chantilly Lace, 1993, The Hauting of Sea Cliff Inn, 1994, Ultimate Betrayal, 1994, Parallel Lives, 1994; author (children's book) She Was Nice to Mice, 1975, (poetry) Yesterday I Saw the Sun, 1991. Address: care William Morris Agency 151 El Camino Beverly Hills CA 90212*

SHEEDY, PATRICK THOMAS, judge; b. Green Bay, Wis., Oct. 31, 1921; s. Earl P. and Elsie L. (Brauel) S.; m. Margaret P. Mulvaney, Sept. 6, 1952; children: Michael, Mary, Kathleen, Patrick Thomas. BS in Bus. Adminstrn., Marquette U., 1943, JD, 1948; LLM in Taxation, John Marshall Law Sch., 1972. Bar: Wis. 1948. Pvt. practice Milw., 1948-80; judge Wis. Cir. Ct., Milw., 1980-90; chief judge 1st Jud. Dist., Milw., 1990—. Past vice chmn. Archdiocesean Sch. Bd., Milw., chairperson, 1986—. Served to col. USAR, 1942-73. Decorated Legion of Merit. Mem. ABA (state del. 1983-85, 89-92, bd. govs. 1985-88), Wis. Bar Assn. (pres. 1974-75, bd. govs., exec. com.). Roman Catholic. Club: Exchange (pres.).

SHEEHAN, CHARLES VINCENT, investment banker; b. London, Dec. 19, 1930; came to U.S., 1931; s. Charles Vincent and Mary Margaret (Stokes) S.; m. Susan Ellen Rosar, May 5, 1962. BS, Georgetown U., 1952. Chief fin. officer Gen. Electric Co., Tokyo, Sydney, Australia and Sao Paulo, Brazil, 1962-64, 64-66, 67-71; staff exec. Gen. Electric Co., Fairfield, Conn., 1972-83, v.p. corp. exec. office, 1983-87; sr. v.p., chief fin. and adminstrn. officer Kidder, Peabody Group, Inc., N.Y.C., 1987-90; bd. dirs. Fleet Trust Co. Chmn. Non-partisan Polit. Action Com. for Gen. Electric Co. employees, Fairfield, 1982-83. Served to lt. USN, 1952-54. Mem. Johns Island Club (Vero Beach, Fla.), Wildcat Cliffs Country Club (Highlands, N.C.). Republican. Roman Catholic. Avocations: golfing, surf fishing. Home: 884 Indian Ln Vero Beach FL 32963-1131

SHEEHAN, DEBORAH ANN, radio station and theater executive; b. Paterson, N.J., Mar. 29, 1953; d. John J. and Ruth (Badertscher) S.; m. Emidio S. Quattrocchi, Mar. 15, 1985; 1 child, Deirdre Emily Sheehan. B.A., William Paterson Coll., 1975. With radio Sta. WWDJ, Hackensack, N.J., 1980-83, Shadow Traffic, N.Y.C., 1981-83; dir. news, community affairs WPAT-AM/FM, N.Y.C., 1979—. Actress-tchr. Paterson Arts Ctr., 1975-79; host radio show Bus. Jour. N.J., 1984; host, producer radio show Debbie Sheehan mag., 1983; host FDU Focus, Cable Network N.J.; writer plays. Exec. dir., actress Learning Theater Co., Paterson, 1975—; sec. bd. dirs. YMCA Passaic Valley, Paterson, 1983-89; mem. N.J. Legal Bd., Montclair, N.J., 1984-86; mem. Paterson Edn. Found., 1984-89; bd. dirs. United Way

Passaic Valley, Conn., 1985, chair allocations com., 1985-92. Recipient Edward R. Murrow Gold medal B'nai B'rith, 1983, finalist 1984-85; Gold medal Internat. Radio Festival, 1983; Best Reporter award Sigma Delta Chi, 1985-87, Personality Profile award local chpt., 1987, Best Pub. Service award, 1987; Best Feature award AP, 1985, 87; Angel Excellence award, Los Angeles, 1985, 87; Internat. Press Assn. fellow, Japan, 1985, New Zealand, 1988. Club: Zonta. Avocations: weaving; travel; acting. Office: WPAT-AM-FM 1396 Broad St Clifton NJ 07013-4222

SHEEHAN, DENNIS WILLIAM, SR., lawyer; b. Springfield, Mass., Jan. 2, 1934; s. Timothy A. and H. Marjorie (Kelsey) S.; m. Elizabeth M. Hellyer, July 27, 1957; children: Dennis William Jr., Catherine Elizabeth, John Edward. BS, U. Md., 1957; JD, Georgetown U., 1960, LLM, 1962. Bar: D.C., Md. 1960, Mo. 1976, Ohio 1977. Legal asst. to chmn. NLRB, Washington, 1960-61; trial atty. U.S. SEC, Washington, 1962-63; corp. atty. Martin Marietta, Balt., N.Y.C., 1963-64; v.p., gen. counsel, sec. Bunker Ramo Corp., Oak Brook, Ill., 1964-73; exec. v.p., gen. counsel, dir. Diversified Industries, Inc., St. Louis, 1973-75; v.p., gen. counsel, dir. N-ReN Corp., Cin., 1975-77; v.p., gen. counsel, sec., dir. AXIA Inc., Oak Brook, Ill., 1977-84, chmn., pres., chief exec. officer, 1984—; bd. dirs. Andamios Atlas, Mexico City, Compagnie Fischbein (S.A.), Brussels, Greenfield Industries, Augusta, Ga., CST, Inc., Wheeling, Ill., Bradington-Young, Inc., Hickory, N.C.; chmn. Allied Healthcare Sys., St. Louis. Bd. dirs. St. Margaret's Sch. Found., MAPI, Washington; chmn. U.S. C. of C., Nat. Coun. on Crime and Delinquency. Mem. ABA, Chgo. Club, St. Louis Club, Econ. Club Chgo., Met. Club Washington, Downtown Club Richmond, Met. Club Chgo., Univ. Club Balt., Phi Delta Pi, Sigma Alpha Phi, Delta Sigma Phi. Republican. Home: 450 Lexington Dr Lake Forest IL 60045-1563 Office: Axia Corp 2001 Spring Rd Ste 300 Hinsdale IL 60521-1879

SHEEHAN, DONALD THOMAS, academic administrator; b. Winsted, Conn., Jan. 2, 1911; s. James J. and Louise (Coffey) S.; m. Betty Young, June 25, 1941; 1 son, Michael Terrence. Grad., Gilbert Sch., Winsted, 1931; B.S. in Edn, Syracuse U., 1935; student, Sch. Pub. Affairs, Am. U., 1936. Dir. health edn. D.C. Tb. Assn., 1937-39; dir. Washington office NCCJ, 1939-41; dir. Bur. Info. Nat. Cath. Welfare Conf., Washington, 194-42; spl. cons. to U.S. Commr. Edn., 1946; staff mem. John Price Jones Co., Inc. (pub. relations cons.), 1946-51; cons. civil def. edn. program, asst. adminstr. charge vol. manpower FCDA, 1951-54, cons. vol. manpower, 1954—; dir. pub. relations U. Pa., 1954-76, sec. corp., 1975-76, sec., v.p. emeritus, 1976—; spl. lectr. pub. relations Drexel U., 1957-72; cons. Nat. Bd. Med. Examiners, 1964—, Coll. Physicians Phila., 1973—, Citizens' Action Com. to Fight Inflation, 1974-75, Wistar Inst. Anatomy and Biology, 1979, Univ. Mus., U. Pa., 1982—, Inst. Environ. Medicine, 1983—; Mem. adv. com. Nat. Trust for Hist. Preservation; cons. Am. Philos. Soc., 1988—. Served from 1st lt. to lt. col. USAAF, 1942-46. Decorated Bronze Star medal. Fellow Coll. Physicians Phila. (hon. assoc.), ; mem. Public Relations Soc. Am., Pi Gamma Mu. Roman Catholic. Club: Nat. Press. Home: 201 W Evergreen Ave Apt 310 Philadelphia PA 19118-3830

SHEEHAN, EDWARD JAMES, technical consultant, former government official; b. Johnstown, Pa., Dec. 31, 1935; s. Louis A. and Ethel F. (Schaefer) S.; m. Florence Ann Hartnett, June 17, 1958; children—Edward, James, John, William, Mary. B.S. in Physics, St. Francis Coll., 1959; M.S. (Sloan fellow), Mass. Inst. Tech., 1972. Project engr. Electronics Command, Dept. Army, 1959-61, project team leader electro-optic equipment for tanks, 1961-63, project team leader electro-optic equipment for infantry, 1963-65, tech. area dir. electro-optic night vision equipment, 1965-73, asso. lab. dir. for devel. engring., 1973-76; lab. dir. Night Vision Lab., Fort Belvoir, Va., 1976-79; founder, pres. Sheehan Assos. Inc., Alexandria, Va., 1979-92; founder, CEO, chmn. Stardyne, Inc., Johnstown, 1992—; chmn. Nat. and Internat. Symposia for Electro-Optical Tech. and Applications; bd. dirs. Johnstown (Pa.) Corp. Recipient numerous awards including Meritorious Civilian Svc. award Dept. Army, Disting. Alumnus award in sci. St. Francis Coll., 1989; named Man of Yr., Combined Svc. Clubs, Johnstown, Pa., 1993. Home: 8502 Crestview Dr Fairfax VA 22031-2803

SHEEHAN, JAMES JOHN, historian, educator; b. San Francisco, May 31, 1937; s. James B. and Sally W. (Walsh) S.; m. 1960; 1 child, Michael L.; m. Margaret L. Anderson, Sept. 2, 1989. BA, Stanford U., 1958; MA, U. Calif., Berkeley, 1959, PhD, 1964. From asst. to assoc. prof. Northwestern U., Evanston, Ill., 1964-79; prof. Stanford (Calif.) U., 1979-86, chmn. dept., 1982-89, Dickason prof. in humanities, 1986—. Author: Lujo Brentano, 1966, German Liberalism, 1978, German History 1770-1866, 1989, Der Ausklang des alten Reiches, 1994; editor: The Boundaries of Humanity, 1991; contbr. articles to profl. jours. Fellow Am. Council Learned Socs., 1981-82, NEH, 1985-86, Wissenschaftskolleg Berlin. Fellow AAAS (Humboldt Rsch. prize 1995); mem. Am. Hist. Assn. (nominating com. 1979-81, chmn. conf. group on Ctrl. European history 1985-86). Office: Stanford U Dept of History Stanford CA 94305

SHEEHAN, JAMES PATRICK, media company executive; b. Jersey City, June 6, 1942; s. John Patrick and Helen Teresa (Woods) S.; m. Mary Ellen Finnell, July 1, 1967; children: James, Christopher. B.S., Seton Hall U., 1965; M.B.A., Wayne State U., 1973. Controller Otis Elevator Co. N.Am., Farmington, Conn., 1976-78; dir. mfg. Otis Elevator Co. N.Am., Yonkers, N.Y., 1978-80; v.p., controller Pratt & Whitney Aircraft, East Hartford, Conn., 1980-82; sr. v.p. A. H. Belo Corp., Dallas, 1982-84, chief fin. officer, 1984-86, pres., chief operating officer, 1987-93; ret., 1993; also dir. A. H. Belo Corp., ret., 1993. Mem. devel. bd. U. Tex.-Dallas, 1985—; bd. dirs. United Way, The Dallas Partnership, The Dallas Morning News Charities; trustee St. Paul Med. Ctr. Found. Served to Lt. (j.g.) USN, 1967-69, Vietnam. Mem. Am. Newspaper Pubs. Assn., So. Newspaper Pubs. Assn. Roman Catholic. Avocations: tennis; racquetball; golf; jogging.

SHEEHAN, JOHN FRANCIS, cytopathologist, educator; b. Portsmouth, N.H., July 28, 1906; s. John Thomas and Ellen Agnes (Lynes) S.; m. Grace Anne O'Neil, Aug. 3, 1935; 1 child, John Thomas. B.S., U. N.H., 1928, M.S., 1930; Ph.D., State U. Iowa, 1945; postgrad., McGill U., 1949. Grad. asst. U. N.H., 1928-30; instr. biology Creighton U., 1930-38, asst. prof., 1938-44, assoc. prof., 1944-49, chmn. biology dept., 1949-58, prof. biology, 1949-67, prof. pathology Sch. Medicine, 1967-88, prof. ob-gyn, 1975-88, prof. emeritus pathology and gynecology, 1988—; attending staff AMI St. Joseph Hosp.; dir. cytopathology St. Joseph Hosp., Omaha, 1978-82; dir. cytopathology emeritus St. Joseph Hosp., 1982—; prof. emeritus biology and pathology Creighton U., 1989. Recipient Golden Jubilee Svc. award Creighton U., 1981, Certificate award AAUP, 1988; Dept. Biology Creighton U. lecture hall named in his honor, 1984. Fellow Am. Soc. Colposcopy and Cervical Pathology; mem. AAUP, Am. Soc. Cytopathology, Internat. Coll. Surgeons (vice regent for Nebr. 1984), Am. Inst. Biol. Scis., Am. Micros Soc., Am. Men and Women of Sci., Am. Soc. Clin. Pathologists, Nebr. Heart Assn., Nebr. Acad. Scis., Smithsonian Nat. Assocs., Sigma Xi, Alpha Omega Alpha, Alpha Sigma Nu, Phi Rho Sigma. Home: 7300 Graceland Dr Apt 307A Omaha NE 68134-4341 Office: St Joseph Hosp 601 N 30th St Omaha NE 68131

SHEEHAN, LAWRENCE JAMES, lawyer; b. San Francisco, July 23, 1932. AB, Stanford U., 1957, LLB, 1959. Bar: Calif. 1960. Law clk. to chief judge U.S. Ct. Appeals 2d Cir., N.Y.C., 1959-60; assoc. O'Melveny & Myers, L.A., 1960-68, ptnr., 1969-94, of counsel, 1995—; bd. dirs. Van Kampen, Am. Capital Mut. Funds, FPA Mut. Funds, TCW Convertible Securities Fund Inc., Source Capital, Inc. Mem. ABA, Los Angeles County Bar Assn., Calif. Bar Assn., Order of Coif. Office: O'Melveny & Myers 1999 Avenue Of The Stars Los Angeles CA 90067-6022 Also: O'Melveny & Myers 400 S Hope St Los Angeles CA 90071-2801

SHEEHAN, LINDA SUZANNE, educational administrator; b. Dayton, Ohio, Aug. 1, 1950; d. Paul J. and Betty L. (Fowler) King; m. J. Scott Sheehan, Dec. 18, 1971. 1 child Amy Elizabeth. BS in Edn. with honors, Ohio State U., 1971; MEd, U. Tex., 1974; adminstrn. cert. Houston Bapt. U., 1983. Cert. tchr., Tex. Tchr. Upper Arlington Schs., Columbus, Ohio, 1971-72, Brown Sch., San Marcos, Tex., 1972-73, Comal Ind. Sch. Dist., New Braunfels, Tex., 1973-75, Alief Ind. Sch. Dist., Houston, 1975-79; asst. prin. Killough Mid. Sch., Houston, 1979-84; prin. Olle Mid. Sch., Houston, 1984-92, Holub Middle Sch., 1992—. Named Tchr. of Yr., Olle Mid. Sch., Houston, 1978. Mem. NEA, Nat. Mid. Sch. Assn., Nat. Assn. Secondary Sch. Prins., Tex. Assn. Secondary Sch. Prins., Tex. Mid. Sch. Assn. (dir. 1979-91, pres. 1991-92, state convention chair 1993-94), Houston Council Social Studies, Kappa Delta Pi (pres. 1984-85), Phi Delta Kappa. Roman Catholic. Home: 526 Nottingham Oaks Trl Houston TX 77079-6332 Office: Holub Mid Sch 9515 S Dairy Ashford St Houston TX 77099-4909

SHEEHAN, MICHAEL JARBOE, archbishop; b. Wichita, Kans., July 9, 1939; s. John Edward and Mildred (Jarboe) S. MST, Gregorian U., Rome, 1965; D of Canon Law, Lateran U., Rome, 1971. Ordained priest Roman Cath. Ch., 1964. Asst. gen. sec. Nat. Coun. Cath. Bishops, Washington, 1971-76; rector Holy Trinity Sem., Dallas, 1976-82; pastor Immaculate Conception Ch., Grand Prairie, Tex., 1982-83; bishop Diocese of Lubbock, Tex., 1983-93; archbishop Archdiocese of Santa Fe, Albuquerqe, N.Mex., 1993—; past chmn. Am. Bd. Cath. Missions, 1989-91; trustee Cath. Relief Svcs., 1992—. Contbr. articles to New Cath. Ency. Trustee St. Mary Hosp., Lubbock, 1983-89; bd. dirs. Tex. Conf. of Chs. Mem. Serra Club (chaplain 1983-93). Avocations: snow skiing, racquetball. Office: Archdiocese of Santa Fe 4000 Saint Josephs Pl NW Albuquerque NM 87120-1714

SHEEHAN, MICHAEL TERRENCE, arts administrator, historian, consultant; b. Washington, Dec. 15, 1942; s. Donald Thomas and Betty (Young) S. BA, U. Pa., 1965, MA, 1968, PhD, 1974. House mgr. Annenberg Ctr., Phila., 1968-72; mgr. Performing Arts Ctr. SUNY, Albany, 1972-76; mng. dir. Taconic Theatre Co., Spencertown, N.Y., 1973-77; exec. dir. Snug Harbor Cultural Ctr., N.Y.C., 1978-82; cons. Washington, 1984-87; pres. Oatlands Plantation, Leesburg, Va., 1987-89; dir. Woodrow Wilson House Nat. Trust for Historic Preserve, Washington, 1989—. Bd. dirs. Albany League of Arts, 1972-77, Loudon County League of Arts, Leesburg, 1988-89; mem. Loudon County Tourism Bd., 1987-89; consortium officer Historic House Museums of Met. Washington, 1992—. Mem. Am. Assn. Mus., League Historic Am. Theatres, Nat. Press Club Washington, Nat. Trust Historic Preservation, Internat. Coun. Mus. Office: Woodrow Wilson House 2340 S St NW Washington DC 20008-4015

SHEEHAN, NEIL, reporter, scholarly writer; b. Holyoke, Mass., Oct. 27, 1936; s. Cornelius Joseph and Mary (O'Shea) S.; m. Susan Margulies, Mar. 30, 1965; children—Maria Gregory, Catherine Fair. AB cum laude, Harvard, 1958; LittD (hon.), Columbia Coll., Chgo., 1972; LHD (hon.), Am. Internat. Coll., 1990, U. Lowell, 1991. Vietnam Bur. chief U.P.I., Saigon, 1962-64; reporter N.Y. Times, N.Y.C., Djakarta, Saigon, Washington, 1964-72. Author: The Arnheiter Affair, 1972, A Bright Shining Lie: John Paul Vann and America in Vietnam, 1988 (Nat. Book award 1988, Pulitzer Prize for gen. non-fiction 1989, Robert F. Kennedy book award 1989, Vetty award Vietnam Vets. Ensemble Theatre Co. 1989, Spl. Achievement award Vietnam Vets. Am. 1989, Outstanding Investigative Reporting award Investigative Reporters and Editors, Inc. of U. Mo. Sch. Journalism 1989, Amb. award English-Speaking Union 1989, John F. Kennedy award, Holyoke, Mass 1989), After the War Was Over: Hanoi and Saigon, 1992, also articles and book revs. for popular mags.; contbr. to The Pentagon Papers, 1971. Served with AUS, 1959-62. Recipient Louis M. Lyons award for conscience and integrity in journalism, 1964, Silver medal Poor Richard Club, Phila., 1964, certificate of appreciation for best article on Asia Overseas Press Club Am., 1967, 1st Ann. Drew Pearson prize for excellence in investigative reporting, 1971, Columbia Journalism awards, 1972, 89, Sidney Hillman Found. awards, 1972, 88, Page One award Newspaper Guild N.Y., 1972, Distinguished Service award and Bronze medallion Sigma Delta Chi, 1972, citation of excellence Overseas Press Club, 1972, Literary Lion award N.Y. Pub. Libr., 1992; Guggenheim fellow, 1973-74; Adlai Stevenson fellow, 1973-75; Lehrman Inst. fellow, 1975-76; Rockefeller Found. fellow in humanities, 1976-77; Woodrow Wilson Internat. Center for Scholars fellow, 1979-80. Mem. Soc. Am. Historians, Am. Acad. Achievement. Obtained Pentagon Papers, 1971. Home: 4505 Klingle St NW Washington DC 20016-3580

SHEEHAN, PATTY, professional golfer. 4th ranked woman LPGA Tour, 1992; winner U.S. Women's Open, 1992, 94, LPGA Championship, 1983-84, 93. Inductee LPGA Hall of Fame, 1993, Sports Illustrated Sportsman of the Yr., 1987. Winner 31 LPGA Tournaments including Mazda Japan Classic, 1981, 88, Inamori Classic, 1982-83, 86, Orlando Lady Classic, 1982, Safeco Classic, 1982, 90, 95, LPGA Corning Classic, 1983, LPGA Championship, 1983-84, 93, Henredon Classic, 1983-84, Elizabeth Arden Classic, 1984, McDonald's Kids Classic, 1984, 90, Sarasota Classic, 1985-86, 88, J&B Scotch Pro AM, 1985, Konica San Jose Classic, 1986, Rochester Internat., 1989-90, 92, 95, Jamaica Classic, 1990, Ping-Cellular One Championship, 1990, Orix Hawaiian Ladies Open, 1991, Jamie Farr Toledo Classic, 1992, Weetabix Women's Brit. Open, 1992, U.S. Women's Open, 1992, 94, Mazda LPGA Championship, 1993. Office: LPGA Ste B 2570 W Internat Speedway Blvd Daytona Beach FL 32114-1118*

SHEEHAN, ROBERT C., lawyer; b. N.Y.C., Oct. 12, 1944; s. John Edward and Mary Elizabeth (Trede) S.; m. Elizabeth Mary Mammen, Aug. 17, 1968; children: Elizabeth, Robert, William. BA, Boston Coll., 1966; LLB, Univ. Pa., Phila., 1969. Bar: N.Y. 1970. Ptnr. Skadden, Arps, Slate, Meagher & Flom, N.Y.C., 1978—, exec. ptnr., 1994—. Office: Skadden Arps Slate Meagher Flom 919 3rd Ave New York NY 10022

SHEEHAN, ROBERT W., lawyer; b. New London, Conn., Aug. 16, 1945; s. Eugene Francis Sheehan and Lucille Irene (Izbicki) Heard; m. Pauline Orr Vietor, July 27, 1968; children: Margaret O., William B., Thomas V., Arthur W., Eliza F. BA, Yale U., 1967; JD cum laude, NYU, 1974. Bar: N.Y. 1975, U.S. Dist. Ct. (so. dist.) N.Y. 1975, U.S. Tax Ct. 1994. Assoc. Milbank, Tweed, Hadley & McCloy, N.Y.C., 1974-81; assoc., ptnr. Breed, Abbott & Morgan, N.Y.C., 1981-91; ptnr. Chadbourne & Parke, N.Y.C., 1991—; Bar: N.Y. 1975, U.S. Dist. Ct. (so. dist.) N.Y. 1975, U.S. Tax Ct. 1994. Pres. N.Y.C. Mission Soc., 1993. 1st. lt. U.S. Army, 1969-72. Fellow Am. Coll. Trust and Estate Counsel; mem. N.Y. State Bar Assn. (chmn. trusts and estate sect., membership com. 1996—), Assn. of Bar of City of N.Y. (com. trusts, estates and surrogates cts. 1992-95). Office: Chadbourne & Parke 30 Rockefeller Plz New York NY 10112

SHEEHAN, STEPHEN D., airport commissioner; b. Oct. 29, 1942. BS, USAF Acad., 1965; M in Aviation Mgmt. with honors, Embry Riddle Aero. U.; postgrad., Air War Coll., 1982-83. Commd. officer USAF, 1965, advanced through grades to col., ret., 1992, chief test pilot, instr., flight examiner, 1965-75; chief Air Base Plans Divsn., Incirilik, Turkey, 1975-76; pilot, action officer, exec. officer, dept. chief staff Hdqrs. USAF Tactile Air Command, 1977-80; pilot, chief air ops. tng., comdr. air support ops. squadron, 1980-82; asst. inspector gen. Unified Command Hdqrs., 1983-86; group comdr. USAF, 1986-89, base comdr., 1989-91; faculty mem., dir. Tactical Air Ops., U.S. Army War Coll., 1991-92; dep. commr. ops. Safety and Security Cleve. Hopkins Internat. Airport, 1992-94; commr. Cleve. Hopkins Internat. Airport, 1994—. Decorated Legion of Merit, 3 Disting. Flying Crosses, 13 Air medals. Office: 5300 Riverside Dr Cleveland OH 44135

SHEEHAN, SUSAN, writer; b. Vienna, Austria, Aug. 24, 1937; came to U.S., 1941, naturalized, 1946; d. Charles and Kitty C. (Herrmann) Sachsel; m. Neil Sheehan, Mar. 30, 1965; children—Maria Gregory, Catherine Fair. BA (Durant scholar), Wellesley Coll., 1958; DHL (hon.), U. Lowell, 1991. Editorial researcher Esquire-Coronet, N.Y.C., 1959-60; free-lance writer N.Y.C., 1960-61; staff writer New Yorker mag., N.Y.C., 1961—. Author: Ten Vietnamese, 1967, A Welfare Mother, 1976, A Prison and a Prisoner, 1978, Is There No Place on Earth for Me?, 1982, Kate Quinton's Days, 1984, A Missing Plane, 1986, Life For Me Ain't Been No Crystal Stair, 1993; contbr. articles to various mags., including N.Y. Times Sunday Mag., Washington Post Sunday Mag., Harper's, Atlantic, New Republic, McCall's, Holiday, Boston Globe Sunday Mag., Life. Judge Robert F. Kennedy Journalism awards, 1980, 84; mem. lit. panel D.C. Commn. on Arts and Humanities, 1979-84; mem. pub. info. and edn. com. Nat. Mental Health Assn., 1982-83; mem. adv. com. on employment and crime Vera Inst. Justice, 1978-86; chair Pulitzer Prize nominating jury in gen. non-fiction for 1988, 1994, mem., 1991. Recipient Sidney Hillman Found. award, 1976, Gavel award ABA, 1978, Individual Reporting award Nat. Mental Health Assn., 1981, Pulitzer prize for gen. non-fiction, 1983, Feature Writing award N.Y. Press Club, 1984, Alumnae Assn. Achievement award Wellesley Coll., 1984, Carroll Kowal Journalism award NASW, 1993, Disting. Grad. award Hunter Coll. H.S., 1995, Pub. Awareness award Nat. Alliance for Mentally Ill, 1995; fellow Guggenheim Found., 1975-76, Woodrow wilson Internat. Ctr. for Scholars, 1981. Mem. Soc. Am. Historians, Phi Beta Kappa, Authors Guild. Home: 4505 Klingle St NW Washington DC 20016-3580 Office: New Yorker Mag 20 W 43rd St New York NY 10036-7400

SHEEHY, HOWARD SHERMAN, JR., minister; b. Denver, Mar. 19, 1934; s. Howard Sherman and Mildred Louise (Fishburn) S.; m. Thelma Florine Cline, Sept. 4, 1954; children: John Robert, Lisa Florine, Michael Howard. A.A., Graceland Coll., 1953; B.S., Central Mo. State Coll., 1955; M.S., U. Kans., 1960, postgrad. Ordained to ministry Reorganized Ch. of Jesus Christ of Latter-Day Sts., 1954. Youth dir. Reorganized Ch. Jesus Christ Latter-day Saints, Independence, Mo., 1960-64; pastor Des Moines, 1964-68; church supr. Haiti, 1968-70, Canada, 1970-74, Australia, 1970-75, N.Z., 1970-75, India, 1970-78, Japan, Korea, Republic of China, Philippines, 1976-78; mem. Council of Twelve Apostles, 1968-78, mem. 1st presidency, 1978—; mem. corp. body Outreach Internat., Restoration Trail Found. Editor-in-chief: Saints Herald. Mem. nat. Protestant com. on scouting Boy Scouts Am., 1964-66; trustee Independence Regional Health Ctr., 1979-88, 90-95. Lt. USNR, 1955-59. Mem. Pi Omega Pi, Phi Delta Kappa, Phi Kappa Phi. Republican. Home: 3403 S Crane St Independence MO 64055-2532 Office: The Temple PO Box 1059 Independence MO 64051-0559

SHEEHY, JEROME JOSEPH, electrical engineer; b. Hartford, Conn., Dec. 3, 1935; s. Jeremiah and Anna (Foley) S.; m. Jean Ann Baldassari, Oct. 13, 1962; children: Caroline, Jerome, Daniel, Carlene. BSEE, U. Conn., 1962, MSEE, 1967. Electronic engr. USN Underwater Sound Lab., New London, Conn., 1962-69; mem. tech. staff Rockwell Internat., Anaheim, Calif., 1969-74; staff engr. Hughes Aircraft Co., Fullerton, Calif., 1974-83; systems engr. Norden Systems, Santa Ana, Calif., 1983-89; advanced engring. specialist Lockheed Aircraft Svc., Ontario, Calif., 1990—. Contbr. articles to Jour. Acoustical Soc. Am. With USAF, 1954-57. Mem. Acoustical Soc. Am. Achievements include research in detection and estimation theory for non-gaussian noise, non-normal statistics. Home: 22951 Belquest Dr Lake Forest CA 92630-4007

SHEEHY, JOAN MARY, nurse; b. Newton, Mass., Sept. 14, 1931; d. Daniel Joseph and Mary Frances (Herlihy) Welch; m. James E. Sheehy, Sept. 14, 1969; children: James M., Robert E., Patricia A., Julie M. Diplomate in nursing, St. Mgts. Sch. Nursing, Dorchester, Mass., 1952; student, Boston Coll., 1952-56; cert. x-ray technician, Northeastern U., 1962. RN, Mass.; cert. sch. nurse. Staff nurse St. Margaret's Hosp., Dorchester, 1952-53, Newton (Mass.) Vis. Nursing Assn., 1953-54, Cambridge (Mass.) Health Dept., 1954-56, John Hancock Mut. Life Ins., Boston, 1956-68, Boston Sch. Dept., 1969-93; mem. staff Deutsches Altenheim, Boston, 1993—; aides educator, Boston, 1985-93. Mem. alumni assn. Our Lady's H.S., Newton, 1989, 93; assoc. Human Rights, Newton, 1985—. Mem. Nat. Sch. Nursing Assn. Roman Catholic. Avocations: caring for grandchild, knitting, sewing, crocheting, plays. Home: 16 Lucille Pl Newton MA 02164-1211

SHEEHY, PAT MURPHY, artistic director. BA, George Washington U., 1960; postgrad., Catholic U., 1980. Founding mem., dir. Trinity Players, 1977-82; mgr. Source Theatre Co., Washington, 1984-86, mng. dir., 1986, producing artistic dir., 1986—; apptd., mem. exec. com., major instns. panel, pers. com., commr.-convener visual arts panel D.C. Arts and Humanities Commn., 1984-87; chair D.C. Commn. on Arts, 1987-91; state rep. Nat. Assn. State Arts Agys., 1987-91, planning com., 1990; mem. steering com. 14th St. Arts Festival, 1992; mem. Mayor's Arts Task Force, 1978, Mayor's Adv. Task Force on Howard Theatre, 1989, Mayor's Cultural Transition Task Force, 1990, Mayor's Adv. Task Force on Lincoln Theatre, 1992-93, Mayor's Adv. Com. on Entertainment, 1993—; bd. dirs. Lincoln Theatre; presenter and panlist in field. Dir. stage prodns. Three Viewings, Distant Fires, Lloyd's Prayer, Mud, Beirut, Time Remembered, Dust Conspiracy, Busboy (Best Dir. award 1985), The Father, Ivory Pawns, Many Moons, Madonna of the Powder Room, Da, The Last Meeting of the Knights of the White Magnolia, The Bad Seed, Sherlock Holmes; asst. dir. stage prodsn. K-2, The Ephemeral is External; actress White Money, Dumb Stuff, True West, The Aunts, Beyond the Horizon, The Dining Room, Mirrors, And Miss Reardon Drinks a Little, The Mousetrap, Hands Across The Sea, Family Album. Chair spl. fundraising Rufus Phillips Congl. Campaign, Va., 1974; chair precinct fundraising ward 3 Marion Barry Mayoral Campaign, 1978; mem. exec. com. Cardozo-Shaw Neighborhood Com. Recipient Spl. Recognition award Mayor's Arts Awards, 1991, Washington Post award, 1993. Mem. League Washington Theatres (exec. com. 1989-91, chair advocacy com. 1989-91, pres. 1991-93), Cleve. Park Hist. Soc. (founding, bd. dirs. 1984-90). Home: 2941 Newark St NW Washington DC 20008-3339 Office: Source Theatre Co 1835 14th St NW Washington DC 20009-4425

SHEEHY, SIR PATRICK, tobacco and financial services executive; b. Sept. 2, 1930; s. Sir John Francis Sheehy and Jean Newton Simpson; m. Jill Patricia Tindall, 1964; 2 children. Grad., Ampleforth Coll., Yorkshire, Eng.; LHD (hon.), Va. Union U., 1985. Joined Brit.-Am. Tobacco Co., (BATCo) 1950, from mgmt. trainee to gen. mgr., Nigeria, Ghana, Ethiopia and W.I. 1950-62, mktg. advisor, London, 1962-67, gen. mgr., Holland, 1967-70, mem. group bd., 1970—, chmn. tobacco div. bd., N. Am. and Australia, 1975-76, dir. dep. chmn. B.A.T. Industries, 1976, vice chmn., 1981-82, chmn., 1982—, chmn. BATco, 1976-79, also bd. dirs. BAT Industries; dir. Brit. Petroleum Co. plc, 1984, Cluff Resources, 1992; mem. coun. internat. advisers Swiss Bank Corp., 1985; bd. dirs. The Spectator, 1988—. Chmn. South London Bus. Initiative, 1986—. Appointed chmn. Home Office Inquiry into Police Responsibilities and Rewards, 1992. 2d lt. Irish Guards, 1948-50. Mem. Confedn. Brit. Industry, Action Com. for Europe, European Round Table, Royal Inst. Internat. Affairs (coun. mem.). Avocations: golf, skiing, reading. Office: BAT Industries plc, Windsor House 50 Victoria St, London SW1H 0NL, England

SHEEHY, THOMAS DANIEL, apparel and textile manufacturing company executive; b. Lawrence, Mass., Dec. 9, 1946; s. Bernard Agustine and Frances Patricia (Noone) S.; m. Brenda J. Hutchey; children: Christine Judith, Matthew Thomas. BSBA, Suffolk U., 1969, MBA, 1974. R & D engr. Malden Mills, Inc., 1970-71, prodn. control mgr., 1972-77; corp. mgr. Champion Products, Inc., Rochester, N.Y., 1977-80, mgr. prodn. and inventory mgmt., 1980-81, dir. mfg. resource planning, 1981-83, dir. mfg., 1984-85, v.p. mfg., 1985-86, v.p. ops., 1986-89, v.p., gen. mgr. retail, 1989-90, exec. v.p., 1990; pres., chief oper. officer Signal Apparel Co., Chattanooga, Tenn., 1991-93; pres. T.D. Sheehy Consulting, 1993-95; pres., CEO. Eshco, LLC, 1995—. Area chmn. Suffolk U. Alumni Fund, 1975-77. With U.S. Army, 1970-71. Mem. Am. Prodn. and Inventory Control Soc. (cert. practitioner inventory mgmt.). Home: 2020 Clematis Dr Hixson TN 37343-3510

SHEEHY, VINCENT, automotive executive; b. 1928. V.p. Sheehy-Manassas, Inc., Manassas, Va., 1991—; pres. Sheehy Ford, Inc., Suitland, Md., 1966—; CEO Sheehy Automotive, Fairfax, Va., 1988—. Office: Ste 380 12450 Fair Lakes Cir Fairfax VA 22033

SHEEKS, BILL F., minister; b. Kannapolis, N.C., Mar. 10, 1934; s. Harley Grady and Sadie Pauline (Pethel) S.; m. Eleanor Stout, May 31, 1958; children: Cheryl Stansky, Randy. AA, Lee Coll., 1954; BA, Catawba Coll., 1956; MA, Calif. Grad. Sch. Theology, 1978, DMin, 1979. Pastor Camp Greene Ch. of God, Charlotte, N.C., 1959-64, state youth dir., 1964-68; pastor Ch. of God, Burlington, N.C., 1968-70; state evangelism dir. Ch. of God, Charlotte, 1970-74; state overseer Ch. of God, Aiea, Hawaii, 1974-78, Decatur, Ill., 1978-82, Birmingham, Ala., 1982-86; asst. dir. evangelism and home missions Ch. of God, Cleveland, Tenn., 1986-90, dir. of evangelism and home ministries, 1990—; dir. N.C. State Bible Sch. Ch. of God, Charlotte, 1967-73, mem. N.C. Children's Home Bd., Kannapolis, 1968-72, N.C. State Coun., Charlotte, 1968-72. Author: The Growth of the Church of God: America's Oldest Pentecostal Church, 1979, How to Plant a Church of God, 1987, Winning Everyone, 1993; editor: Winning Kids, 1988. Named one of Outstanding Young Men Am., 1964. Avocation: walking. Home: 5430 Chiltern Hill Trl Charlotte NC 28215 Office: Ch of God Internat Offices 2490 Keith St NW Cleveland TN 37311-1309

SHEELINE, PAUL CUSHING, hotel executive; b. Boston, June 6, 1921; s. Paul Daniel and Mary (Child) S.; m. Harriet White Moffat, May 23, 1948 (dec. 1962); children: Christopher White, William Emerson, Mary Child, Leonora Moffat; m. Sandra Dudley Wahl, July 24, 1965; 1 child, Abby

Tucker. B.S., Harvard U., 1943, J.D., 1948. Bar: N.Y. 1949, D.C. 1986. Assoc. Sullivan & Cromwell, N.Y.C., 1948-54; with Lambert & Co., N.Y.C., 1954-65, gen. ptnr., 1958-65; chief fin. officer Intercontinental Hotels Corp., N.Y.C., 1966-71, pres., 1971-74, chief exec. officer, 1971-85, chmn. bd., 1972-87, cons., 1987-90; of counsel Verner, Liipfert, Bernhard, McPherson & Hand, Washington, 1986-93; bd. dirs. Resorts Internat., Inc., 1991-94; mem. Presdl. Bd. Advisors on Pvt. Sector Initiatives, Washington, 1987-89. Vice chmn. Community Service Soc. of N.Y., 1962-63; dir. Am. Assn. for UN, 1951-58; former mem. Harvard Overseers Com. to visit Center for Internat. Affairs and Dept. Romance Langs.; trustee East Woods Sch., Oyster Bay Cove, N.Y., 1959-68, Camargo Found., St. Luke's/Roosevelt Hosp. Ctr.; bd. dirs. Bus. Council for Internat. Understanding., 1975-88, Fgn. Policy Assn., 1981-90, Scientists' Inst. Pub. Info., 1984-91, Battle of Normandy Found., 1986-91. Served to capt. USAAF, 1942-46. Decorated Silver Star medal, French Legion of Honor, Croix de Guerre with palm, Moroccan Ouissam Alaouite. Mem. Am.-Arab Assn. Commerce and Industry (chmn. bd. 1984-86), Phi Beta Kappa. Clubs: Cold Spring Harbor Beach; Harvard (N.Y.C.); Balsam Lake Anglers (N.Y.).

SHEEN, CHARLIE (CARLOS IRWIN ESTEVEZ), actor; b. N.Y.C., Sept. 3, 1965; s. Ramon (Martin Sheen) and Janet Estevez; m. Donna Peele, Sept. 3, 1995. Appearances include (film) Grizzly II: The Predator, 1984, Red Dawn, 1984, The Boys Next Door, 1985, Ferris Bueller's Day Off, 1986, Lucas, 1986, Platoon, 1986, Wisdom, 1986, The Wraith, 1986, Wall Street, 1987, No Man's Land, 1987, Three for the Road, 1987, Eight Men Out, 1988, Young Guns, 1988, Major League, 1989, Never on Tuesday, 1989, Courage Mountain, 1990, Navy Seals, 1990, Men At Work, 1990, The Rookie, 1990, Cadence, 1990, Backtrack, 1990, Hot Shots!, 1990, Hot Shots, Part Deux, 1993, The Three Musketeers, 1993, The Chase, 1994, Major League 2, 1994, Terminal Velocity, 1994, The Shadow Conspiracy, 1995, Shockwave, 1995; (TV movies) Silence of the Heart, 1984. Office: care Jeffrey Ballard Pub Relations 4814 Lemona Ave Sherman Oaks CA 91403

SHEEN, MARTIN (RAMON ESTEVEZ), actor; b. Dayton, Ohio, Aug. 3, 1940; s. Francisco and Mary Ann (Phelan) Estevez; m. Janet Sheen, Dec. 23, 1961; children: Emilio, Ramon, Carlos, Renee. Grad. high sch. Made N.Y. stage debut as mem. Living Theatre in The Connection, 1959; Broadway debut in Never Live Over a Pretzel Factory, 1964; other stage appearances include The Subject Was Roses, 1964-66, The Wicked Crooks, 1967, Hamlet, 1967, Romeo and Juliet, 1968, Hello and Goodbye, 1969, The Happiness Cage, 1970, Death of a Salesman, 1975, Julius Caesar, 1988; film appearances include The Incident, 1967, The Subject Was Roses, 1968, Catch-22, 1970, No Drums, No Bugles, 1971, Rage, 1972, Badlands, 1973, The Legend of Earl Durand, 1974, The Cassandra Crossing, 1976, The Little Girl Who Lives Down the Lane, 1977, Apocalypse Now, 1979, The Final Countdown, 1980, Gandhi, 1982, That Championship Season, 1982, The King of Prussia, 1982, No Place to Hide, 1983, The Dead Zone, 1983, Man, Woman, and Child, 1983, Enigma, 1983, Eagle's Wing, 1983, Firestarter, 1984, The Believers, 1987, Wall Street, 1987, Siesta, 1987, Judgement in Berlin, 1988, Walking After Midnight, 1988, Da, 1988, Beverly Hills Brats, 1989, Cadence, 1991 (also dir.), JFK, 1991 (narrator), Hot Shots, Part Deux!, 1993 (cameo), Hear No Evil, 1993, Gettysburg, 1993; regular: TV series As the World Turns; TV movies and miniseries include Then Came Bronson, 1969, The Subject Was Roses, 1969, Mongo's Back in Town, 1971, Welcome Home, Johnny Bristol, 1972, That Certain Summer, 1972, Catholics, 1973, The Execution of Private Slovik, 1974, The California Kid, 1974, The Story of Pretty Boy Floyd, 1974, The Missiles of October, 1974, Sweet Hostage, 1975, The Last Survivors, 1975, Blind Ambition, 1979, Taxi!!, 1978, The Long Road Home, 1980, Fly Away Home, 1981, Kennedy, 1982, Choices of the Heart, 1983, The Atlanta Child Murders, 1985, Consenting Adult, 1985, Out of Darkness, 1985, Shattered Spirits, 1986, Samaritan, 1986, News at Eleven, 1986, Conspiracy: The Trial of the Chicago 8, 1987, No Means No (exec. producer), Night Breaker, 1989; other TV appearances include Mannix, Murphy Brown (Emmy award, Guest Actor - Comedy Series, 1994). Roman Catholic. Office: Innovative Artists 1999 Ave of the Stars Los Angeles CA 90067*

SHEEN, ROBERT TILTON, manufacturing company executive; b. Phila., Dec. 10, 1909; s. Milton Roy and Emma Elizabeth (Tilton) S.; m. Dorothy Martha Dillenbeck, June 25, 1932; children—James D., Roberta Alace (Mrs. R. Donald Peterson); m. Mary Regina Orban, Aug 17, 1951; 1 dau., Regina Elizabeth (Mrs. Brian C. Ridgway); m. Frieda Marie Van Riter, July 19, 1972. B.S. in Chem. Engring, Lehigh U., 1931, Chem Engr., 1936. Registered profl. engr., Pa., N.J., Ohio, Ill. Chem. engr. Swann Chem. Co., Anniston, Ala., 1931-32; tech. dir., then dir. cons. div. W.H. & L.D. Betz Co., 1932-43; co-founder Milton Roy Co., Phila and St. Petersburg, Fla., 1946; pres., chmn. bd. Milton Roy Co., 1947-68, chmn. bd., chief exec. officer, 1968-72, chmn. bd., 1972-74, dir., chmn. exec. com., 1975-89. Author: Robert T. Sheen-His-Story, 1991; contbr. articles to profl. jours. Pres. Jr. Achievement of St. Petersburg, 1965-66; chmn. Bayfront Med. Center, Inc., St. Petersburg, 1968-72, hon. chmn. campaign for New Times, 1984-86; mem. Fla. Gov.'s Council on Productivity and Council on Profl. Regulation, 1980-83; bd. dirs. United Fund S. Pinellas, Fla., 1962; trustee Eckerd Coll., St. Petersburg, 1959—, chmn. bd., 1974-77, mem. Acad. Sr. Profls. Eckerd Coll., 1983—; hon. trustee Sci. Center Pinellas County; mem. Fla. Com. on Aging, 1984-86; hon. bd. dirs. Fla. Council on Econ. Edn., 1984—; mem. council advisers Fla. State U., Tallahassee, 1975-82; former dir., chmn. health care com. Fla. Council of 100, 1969-77, chmn. human affairs com., 1978-82. Recipient Diamond Jubilee award U.S. CSC, 1958, Outstanding Citizen award, 1967, West Coast Fla. Engr. of Yr. award, 1968, Silver Medallion Brotherhood award NCCJ, 1977, Top Mgmt. award Soc. Mfg. Engrs., St. Petersburg, 1981, Monroe J. Rathbone Alumni Achievement award Lehigh U., 1989, Robert T. Sheen award for Vol. Leadership, Bayfront Med. Ctr., 1993; Robert T. and Fran V.R. Sheen Conference Ctr., Bayfront Med. Ctr., named in his honor, 1995; inducted into Sr. Hall of Fame, City of St. Petersburg, Fla., 1996. Fellow Instrument Soc. Am. (pres. 1955-56); hon. mem. Am. Mgmt. Assn. (dir. 1962-67, 70-73, mem. exec. com. 1965-67, 70-73, life mem.); mem. Am. Chem. Soc., Nat. Soc. Profl. Engrs., Am. Inst. Chem. Engrs., Suncoasters Inc. (named Mr. Sun 1969, pres. 1974-75), Newcomen Soc. N.Am. Patentee chem. pumps, chem. feed systems. Home: 672 Boca Ciega Point Blvd N Saint Petersburg FL 33708-2730

SHEER, BARBARA LEE, nursing educator; b. Riverside, N.J., Dec. 16, 1946; d. David J. and Edna (Maher) Phelan; m. George W. Sheer, Nov. 15, 1969; 1 child, Jeffrey B. Grad., Phila. Gen. Hosp. Sch. Nursing, 1967; BSN, U. Pa., 1971; PNP, Rutgers U., 1976; MSN, SUNY, Binghamton, 1981; DNSc, Widener U., 1989. Cert. family nurse practitioner ANA, CRNP, Pa. Instr. Coll. Misericordia, Dallas, Pa.; asst. prof. U. Scranton (Pa.); nurse practitioner Maternal Health Svcs., Wilkes Barre, Pa.; assoc. prof. Wilkes U., Wilkes Barre; asst. prof. U. Del., coord. family nurse practitioner program. Author: Nurse Practitioners: A Review of the Literature. Recipient Del. C. of C. Superstar Educator of Yr., 1994; Pub. Health Svcs. Policy fellow, 1992. Mem. ANA, Nat. Alliance of Nurse Practitioners (mem. governing body 1990-94, chair 1994-95), Am. Acad. Nurse Practitioners (membership sec. 1987-90, pres. 1990-92, Outstanding Leadership and Svc. award 1994, State award for excellence 1995), Pa. Nurses Assn., Primary Health Care Nurse Practitioners N.E. Pa., Sigma Theta Tau. Home: Box 374 Grouse Hill Dalton PA 18414 Office: U Del McDowell Hall Newark DE 19716

SHEER, SHARON, publishing company executive. V.p. human resources Cahners Pub. Co., Newton, Mass. Office: Cahners Pub Co 275 Washington St Newton MA 02158*

SHEERAN, MICHAEL JOHN LEO, priest, college administrator; b. N.Y.C., Jan. 24, 1940; s. Leo John and Glenna Marie (Wright) S. AB, St. Louis U., 1963, PhL, 1964, AM in Polit. Sci., 1967, AM in Theology, 1971, STL, 1971; PhD, Princeton U., 1977. Joined Soc. Jesus, 1957; ordained priest Roman Catholic Ch., 1970. Exec. editor Catholic Mind, N.Y.C., 1971-72; assoc. editor Am. mag., N.Y.C., 1971-72; assoc. chaplain Aquinas Inst., Princeton, N.J., 1972-75; asst. dean Regis Coll., Denver, 1975-77, dean of Coll., 1977-82, v.p. acad. affairs, 1982-92, acting pres., 1987-88, pres., 1993—; retreat dir., cons. on governance for religious communities, 1970—. Author: Beyond Majority Rule, 1984. Contbr. articles and editorials to publs. Trustee Rockhurst Coll., Kansas City, Mo., 1982-91, Creighton U., Omaha, 1985-95, U. San Francisco, 1985-94, Loyola U., New Orleans, 1994—, Rocky Mountain Coll. of Art and Design, 1994—; active Mile High United Way, 1995—. Ford Found. scholar, 1963. Democrat. Home: 3333 Regis Blvd Denver CO 80221-1099 Office: Regis U 3333 Regis Blvd Denver CO 80221-1099

SHEERAN, THOMAS JOSEPH, education educator, writer, consultant, judge; b. N.Y.C., Feb. 24, 1947; s. John Joseph and Dorothy (McAdams) S.; m. Maureen Elizabeth Flynn, June 27, 1970; children: Meaghan, Brendan. BS, Ithaca (N.Y.) Coll., 1968, MS, 1969; MEd, Niagara U., 1976; EdD, SUNY, Buffalo, 1976. Cert. tchr., N.Y. Teaching asst. Ithaca Coll., 1968-69; instr. Niagara U., Lewiston, N.Y., 1969-81, men's swimming coach, 1969-80, asst. prof., 1969—, women's swimming coach, 1969-74; prof., 1980—; chmn. dept. phys. edn. Niagara U., Lewiston, N.Y., 1980-82, chmn. dept. edn., 1988-91; tchr. Niagara U. Campus Sch., Lewiston, 1969-81; cons. various colls. and high schs., 1984-90. Mem. water safety com. ARC, Niagara Falls, N.Y., 1970-81; mem. planning bd. Town of Lewiston, 1982-84, zoning bd., 1986-92; mem. zoning Bd. Town Justice, 1992—. Fellow Am. Coll. Sports Medicine; mem. ASCD, Am. Alliance Health and Phys. Edn. (rsch. fellow), Assn. Tchr. of Edn., N.Y. Assn. coll. Tchr. Edn. (pres. 1992-93), N.Y. Magistrates Assn., Niagara County Magistrates Assn. (sec.), Niagara Falls Tchrs. Ctr. (policy bd. 1993—), N.Y. Assn. Coll. Tchr. Edn. (pres. 1992-93), Am. Assn. Coll. Tchrs. Edn. (state rep. 1992-93), Niagara Falls Country Club (bd. govs., sec.), Phi Delta Kappa, Pi Lambda Theta. Democrat. Roman Catholic. Avocations: golf, tennis. Home: 5230 Hewitt Pky Lewiston NY 14092-1923 Office: Niagara U Dept Edn Niagara Falls NY 14109

SHEERAN-EMORY, KATHLEEN MARY, executive consultant; b. Wilmington, Del., Feb. 27, 1948; d. Stanley Robert and Eileen Ann (Walsh) Sheeran; m. MacInfy Ian Eakins Emory, Lord Renfrew, 1982 (dec. Mar. 1993). BA, St. Mary's Coll., Notre Dame, Ind., 1970. Asst. editor Conde Nast Publs., N.Y.C., 1970-76; account exec. Working Woman mag., N.Y.C., 1976-77; account exec. Foote Cone & Belding Communications, Inc., N.Y.C., 1977-78; v.p. John P. Holmes & Co., Inc., N.Y.C., 1978-83, Korn Ferry Internat., N.Y.C., 1983-84, Sheeran-Emory Assocs., N.Y.C., 1984—; mem. faculty YWCA, 53d St. chpt., N.Y.C., 1980—. Mem. nominating com. Girl Scouts Greater N.Y.; active Princess Grace Found. Fellow Internat. Biog. Assn.; mem. MIT Enterprise Forum, Nat. Assn. for Female Execs., Women's Nat. Rep. Club, Am. Soc. Profl. and Exec. Women. Roman Catholic. Home and Office: Sheeran-Emory Assocs 33 Douglas Rd #JOHN Kingston NJ 08528

SHEERR, DEIRDRE MCCRYSTAL, architectural firm executive; m. Clinton Jay Sheerr. BA, Monmouth Coll., 1969; MArch, U. Colo., 1978; MA in Counseling Psychology, Antioch U., 1995. Registered architect, N.H., Colo. Computer systems and program analyst, 1970-75; pres. McCrystal Design & Devel., Inc., Denver, 1976-83; ptnr., head housing divsn. Sheerr & McCrystal, Inc., New London, N.H., 1983—; instr. passive solar design Denver Free U.; cons. solar and low income housing design Capitol Hill Architects and Planners; solar cons. Bros. Redevelopment, Inc. Prin. works include Lawrence Berkeley (Calif.) Lab., Solar Homestead, Boulder, Colo. (Nat. Passive Solar Design award HUD), 1515 South Pearl St., Curtis Pk. Face Block Renovation Project, Denver (Nat. Honor award AIA), St. Paul's Episcopal Ch. (Archtl. award Gov.'s Commn. Handicapped 1987). Mem. pres.'s adv. coun. Colby Sawyer Coll., 1987-91; mem. fundraising com. Ausbon Sargent Land Preservation Trust, 1989—; co-chair ski-a-thon, 1990—, trustee, 1991—; bd. dirs. 1992—, vice-chmn. 1996—; mem. affordable housing task force charrette for City of Laconia, N.H. Housing Authority, 1989; mem. bus. adv. coun. Town of New London, 1990—; life mem. Upper Valley Humane Soc.; active Nature Conservancy, Wilderness Soc., Greenpeace, Connecticut River Watershed Coun., Sierra Club, Nat. Audubon Soc. Recipient Main St. Comml. Beautification award New London Garden Club, Best Restoration of Yr. award Denver Mag., 1983, Heritage Concord Grand award 1994; Nat. Hist. Preservation grantee Sec. of Interior, 1980. Mem. AIA (bd. dirs. N.H. chpt. 1984-89, sec. 1985, pres.-elect 1986, pres. 1987, immediate past pres. 1988, mem. exec. bd. New Eng. regional coun., 1986-87, spkr. N.W. regional conf., Denver Housing Authority Law Income Housing Design co-winner 1976, Western Regional Merit award 1981, 11 awards for Excellence in Architecture N.H. chpt. 1983, 85, 86, 88, 90, 91, 92, 93, 94, 95, Nat. Honor award 1983), Nat. Trust Hist. Preservation, Nat. Pks. and Conservation Assn., Homebuilder's Assn. N.H. (SAM Silver award), N.H. Hist. Soc., Boston Computer Soc., New London Hist. Soc., Urban Design Forum, Appalachian Mountain Club. Office: Sheerr & McCrystal Inc 177 Main St New London NH 03257-4551

SHEETS, HERMAN ERNEST, marine engineer; b. Dresden, Germany, Dec. 24, 1908; s. Arthur Chitz and Gertrude (Stern) S.; m. Norma Sams, Oct. 17, 1942 (dec. Dec. 1970); m. Paulann Hosler, May 29, 1982; children: Lawrence S., Michael R., Arne H., Diana E., Elizabeth J., Karn N. M.E., U. Dresden, 1934; Dr. Tech. Scis. in Applied Mechanics, U. Prague, Czechoslovakia, 1936. Engr. Prvni Brněnska Strojima, Brno, 1936-39; Chief engr. Chamberlin Research Corp., East Moline, Ill., 1939-42; mgr. research St. Paul Engring. & Mfg. Co., 1942- 44; project engr. Elliott Co., Jeannette, Pa., 1944-46; engring. mgr. Goodyear Aircraft Corp., Akron, Ohio, 1946-53; v.p. Electric Boat div. Gen. Dynamics Corp., Groton, Conn., 1953-69; v.p. engring, and research; prof. dept. ocean engring. U. R.I., Kingston, 1969-80, dept. chmn., 1971-79; dir. engring. Analysis and Tech., North Stonington, Conn., 1979-84; cons. engr. Groton, 1980—. Author numerous articles in field. Recipient citation sec. war. Fellow AIAA (asso.), ASME, AAAS; mem. N.Y. Acad. Scis., Nat. Acad. Engring., Soc. Naval Architects and Marine Engrs., Am. Soc. Naval Engrs., Marine Tech. Soc., Pi Tau Sigma. Home and Office: Mumford Cove 87 Neptune Dr Groton CT 06340

SHEETS, JOHN WESLEY, JR., research scientist; b. Jacksonville, Fla., Sept. 17, 1953; s. John Wesley and Alice Marie (Hagen) S.; m. Robin Adair Ritchie, June 27, 1987; 1 child, Camille Barbara. BS in Zoology, U. Fla., 1975, MS in Materials Sci., 1978, PhD in Materials Sci., 1983. Grad. rsch. asst. U. Fla., Gainesville, 1976-78, grad. rsch. assoc., 1978-82; biomaterials engr. Intermedics Intraocular, Pasadena, Calif., 1982-84, mgr. biomaterials rsch., 1984-87; dir. rsch. Pharmacia Ophthalmics, Pasadena, 1987-88; dir. new product and process devel. IOLAB Corp. Johnson & Johnson, Claremont, Calif., 1988-94; sr. dir. devel. Alcon Labs., Ft. Worth, 1994—; lectr. Calif. State Poly. U., Pomona, 1984; evaluator, chmn. subcom. Am. Nat. Standards Inst. Z80.7, Accreditation Bd. for Engring. and Tech. Contbr. articles to profl. jours. Mem. AAAS, Accreditation Bd. for Engring. and Technology, Am. Chem. Soc., Soc. Plastics Engrs., Soc. Biomaterials, Mensa, Sigma Xi, Tau Beta Pi, Alpha Sigma Mu. Avocations: weight training, swimming, cooking. Home: 4001 Sarita Dr Fort Worth TX 76109-4740 Office: Alcon Labs 6201 S Freeway R5-12 Fort Worth TX 76134 *Personal philosophy: Build from basics: strength and personal integrity. Challenge the obvious and trivial solutions. Continuously seek improvements.*

SHEETS, PAULANN HOSLER, lawyer, environmental law consultant; b. Ft. Wayne, Ind., Apr. 16, 1941; d. Paul Robert and Margaret Antoinette (Phillips) Hosler; m. David Caplovitz, June 8, 1968 (div. 1981); children: Abigail Phillips, Gideon Paul; m. Herman Ernst Sheets, May 29, 1982. AB, Ind. U., 1965, postgrad., 1965-67; JD, Columbia U., 1971. Bar: N.Y. 1973, Conn. 1983. Assoc. Weil, Gotshal and Manges, N.Y.C., 1973-80; asst. atty. gen. N.Y. Dept. Law, N.Y.C., 1980-82; cons. Tech. Audit Assocs., New Canaan, Conn., 1982-88; pro bono atty. Conn. Fund for Environment, New Haven, 1986—; pub. mem. Conn. Siting Coun., New Britain, 1988-94; ind. cons., Groton, Conn., 1988—. Author manual: Rising Electric Rates, 1974. Nat. sec. Com. to Aid Bloomington (Ind.) 3, 1963-65; mem. Groton Bd. Edn., 1985-93; appointee legal adv. com. Conn. Fund for Environ., New Haven, 1986—; town coord. Clinton for Pres. campaign, Groton, 1992. Harlan Fiske Stone scholar Columbia U., 1971; recipient Environ. Leadership award Conn. Gen. Assembly, 1987, Environ. Svc. award Conn. Fund for Environment, 1992. Mem. NAACP (exec. com., legal adviser New London unit 1990-92), Conn. Bar Assn., Mumford Cove Assn. (bd. dirs. 1984-88), The Sound Conservancy, Phi Beta Kappa. Democrat. Universalist. Avocations: writing poetry, reading biographies, public affairs. Home and Office: Sheets and Sheets Cons 87 Neptune Dr Groton CT 06340-5421

SHEETZ, MICHAEL PATRICK, cell biology educator; b. Hershey, Pa., Dec. 11, 1946; s. David Patrick and Mary Patricia (Blumer) S.; m. Katherine Elliott, Jan. 25, 1968; children: Jonathon Patrick, Jennifer Mikaere, Courtney Elizabeth. BA, Albion Coll., 1968; PhD in Chemistry, Calif. Inst. Tech., 1972. Postdoctoral rsch. fellow U. Calif., San Diego, 1972-74; asst. prof. cell biology dept. physiology U. Conn. Health Ctr., Farmington, 1974-79, assoc. prof., 1980-85; prof. dept. cell biology and physiology Sch. Medicine, Washington U., St. Louis, 1985-90; prof., chmn. dept. cell biology Med. Sch., Duke U., Durham, N.C., 1990—; presenter profl. confs. Contbr. chpt. to Erythrocyte Mechanics and Blood Flow, 1980; co-contbr. chpt. to The Red Cell, 1978, Motility in Cell Function, 1979, White Blood Cell Mechanics, 1984, The Cytoskeleton, 1985, Protein-Membrane Interactions, Current Topics in Membranes and Transport, Vol. 36, 1989; co-contbr. chpts. to Cell Movement, Vol. 2, 1988; contbr. articles to sci. jours. Established investigator Am. Heart Assn., 1981-86. NIH trainee, 1969-72; Dernham jr. fellow Calif. div. Am. Cancer Soc., 1973-74. Office: Duke U Med Ctr Dept Cell Bi PO Box 3011 Durham NC 27715-3011

SHEETZ, RICHARD LATRELLE, retired association executive; b. Macon, Mo., Aug. 10, 1906; s. Robert Karl and Lena M. (Fetter) S.; m. Aagot Velline, Aug. 12, 1939; children: Robert K., Susan S. Laitsch, Timothy R.; stepchildren: Ferne D. Holmes, Harold S. Austin, Geraldine M. Beck. A.B., Westminster Coll., 1928. Asst. sales mgr. Lowe and Campbell Athletic Goods Co., Kansas City, Mo., 1928-33; officer mgr., campaign asst. Kansas City Charities Fund, 1933-36; exec. dir. N.D. Community Chest, Fargo, 1936-39, Tex. Community Chest and Planning Council, Austin, 1939-43, Va. United Communities Fund, Norfolk, 1943-71, The Norfolk Found.-Community Trust, 1971-86; ret., 1986; pres. S.E. region Community Chests and Councils of Am., 1948-49, Va. Fedn., 1949-59; nat. bd. dirs. Community Chests and Councils of Am., 1953-59. Author: Savannah, Georgia, A Study of Community Organization, 1950. Named Mr. Citizen of his generation Norfolk Union Labor Council, 1971; recipient citation for outstanding service City of Norfolk, 1970, Golden Legion award Westminster Coll., 1978. Mem. Nat. Conf. Social Welfare, Beta Theta Pi. Club: Virginia. Home: 2545 Murray Ave Norfolk VA 23518-4521

SHEETZ, STANTON R., retail executive. Student, Bentley Coll. With Colt Industries, 1977-81; CEO Sheetz Inc., 1981—. Office: 5700 Sixth Ave Altoona PA 16602

SHEFFEL, DONALD DAVID, neurosurgeon; b. N.Y.C., Nov. 9, 1928; s. Joseph and Ethel (Homansky) S.; m. Sheila Alice Moffat; children: Jeffrey, Scott, Elissa. BA, Duke U., 1948; MD, U. Leiden, Netherlands, 1954. Diplomate Am. Bd. Neurol. Surgery. Resident in pathology U. Miami, 1956; resident in neurosurgery U. Tex., Galveston, 1958-63; NIH fellow in neurosurgery Harvard Med. Sch. and Mass. Gen. Hosp., Boston, 1962; neurosurgeon in pvt. practice Hollywood, Fla., 1963-86; asst. prof. U. Miami, 1964-66, clin. assoc. prof., 1966—; chief div. neurosurgery Meml. Hosp., Hollywood, 1986—; asst. prof. U. N.Mex., Albuquerque, 1974-75; past chmn. Joint Coun. of STae Neurosurg. Socs., 1992-94. Contbr. chpts.: The Development and Neurotrauma Systems and Centers, 1993; speaker in field. Site visitor Pa. Trauma Found. Lt. USN, 1956-58. Mem. AMA, Am. Assn. Neurol. Surgeons (bd. dirs. 1994—), Congress Neurol. Surgeons (exec. com. 1992-94), So. Neursurg. Soc., Fla. Neurosurg. Soc., Singleton Surg. Soc. Avocations: skiing, tennis, golf. Office: Meml Hosp Div Neurosurgery 1150 N 35th Ave Ste 300 Hollywood FL 33021

SHEFFEL, IRVING EUGENE, psychiatric institution executive; b. Chgo., July 5, 1916; s. Joseph and Jennie (Leibson) S.; m. Beth Silver, Aug. 2, 1942 (dec.); 1 child, Anita (dec.). A.B., U. Chgo., 1939; M.P.A., Harvard U., 1946; LHD (hon.), Washburn U., 1987. Insp., wage and hour div. Dept. Labor, Chgo., 1940-41; mgmt. and budget analyst VA, Washington, 1946-48; budget analyst U.S. Bur. of Budget, Washington, 1948-49; controller, treas. Menninger Found., Topeka, 1949-73; v.p. Menninger Found., 1973-93, v.p. emeritus, 1993—; instr. Menninger Sch. Psychiatry. Bd. dirs. Washburn U. Art Center, 1969—, pres., 1971-73; treas. Karl Menninger lect. series, 1983—. Served to maj. U.S. Army, 1942-45. Fellow Assn. Mental Health Adminstrs. (charter); mem. Am. Soc. Public Adminstrn. (charter), Topeka Opera Soc. (treas. 1985—). Jewish. Home: 1215 SW 29th Ter Topeka KS 66611-2192 Office: PO Box 829 Topeka KS 66601-0829

SHEFFIELD, GARY ANTONIAN, professional baseball player; b. Tampa, Fla., Nov. 18, 1968. Baseball player Milw. Brewers, 1986-92, San Diego Padres, 1992-93, Florida Marlins, 1993—. mem. Nat. League All-Star Team, 1992-93; Sporting News Player of the Year, 1992; Sporting News All-Star Team, 1992; recipient Silver Slugger award, 1992; named Minor League Co-Player of the Yr. Sporting News, 1988, Comeback Player of Yr., Sporting News, 1992. Nat. Batting League Champion, 1992. Office: Florida Marlins 2269 NE 199th St Miami FL 33180*

SHEFFIELD, LESLIE FLOYD, retired agricultural educator; b. Orafino, Nebr., Apr. 13, 1925; s. Floyd L. and Edith A. (Presler) S.; BS with high distinction in Agronomy, U. Nebr., 1950, MS, 1964; postgrad. U. Minn., summer 1965; PhD, U. Nebr., 1971; m. Doris Fay Fenimore, Aug. 20, 1947; children: Larry Wayne, Linda Faye (Mrs. Bernard Eric Hempelman), Susan Elaine (Mrs. Randy Thorman). County extension agt. Lexington and Schuyler, Nebr., 1951-52; exec. sec. Nebr. Grain Improvement Assn., 1952-56; chief Nebr. Wheat Commn., Lincoln, 1956-59; exec. sec. Great Plains Wheat, Inc., market devel., Garden City, Kans., 1959-61; asst. to dean Coll. Agr., U. Nebr. at Lincoln, 1961-66, supt. North Platte Expt. Sta., 1966-71, asst. dir. Nebr. Coop. Extension Service, Nebr. Agrl. Expt. Sta., Lincoln, 1971-75, asst. to vice chancellor Inst. Agr. and Natural Resources, 1975-84, also extension farm mgmt. specialist and assoc. prof. agrl. econs., 1975-94; ret. U. Nebr., Lincoln, 1994. v.p. U. Nebr. Found., 1982-86; sec.-treas. Circle 4S-L Acres, Wallace, Nebr., 1973-87; cons. econs. of irrigation in N.D., Minn., S.D. and Brazil, 1975, 88, Sudan, Kuwait and Iran, 1976, People's Republic of China, 1977, 81, Can., 1977, 78, 79, 80, Mex., 1978, 79, Argentina, 1978, Hong Kong, 1981, Japan, 1981, Republic of South Africa, 1985, Argentina, Brazil and Paraguay, 1992, Australia, 1994, New Zealand, 1994. Author: Economic Impact of Irrigated Agriculture, 1985; co-author: Flat Water-A History of Nebraska and Its Water, 1993; author chpt. to book; editor: Procs. of Nebr. Water Resources and Irrigation Devel. for 1970's, 1972; contbg. editor Irrigation Age Mag., St. Paul, 1974-86; contbr. articles to various publs. With U.S. Army, 1944-46; ETO. Recipient Hon. State Farmer award Future Farmers Am., 1955, Hon. Chpt. Farmer award, North Platte chpt., 1973; fellowship grad. award Chgo. Bd. Trade, 1964, Agrl. Achievement award Ak-Sar-Ben, 1969, Citizen award U.S. Dept. Interior Bur. Reclamation, 1984; Pub. Svc. award for contbns. to Nebr. agr. Nebr. Agribus. Club, 1984, Ditch Rider award Four States Irrigation Coun., 1988, Disting. Svc. award Am. Soc. Farm Mgrs. & Rural Appraisers Nebr. chpt., 1993, Alumnus of Yr. award U. Nebr.-Lincoln Coll. Agr. & Natural Resources Alumni Assn., 1993, Headgate award Four States Irrigation Coun., 1995, Pioneer Irrigation award Nebr. Water Conf. Coun. and U. Nebr. Lincoln, 1995 ; NASA Rsch. grantee, 1972-77; inducted Nebr. Hall of Agrl. Achievement, 1988; named Irrigation Man of Yr. Irrigation Assn., 1988; honoree Disting. Svc. Nebr. Hall Agrl. Achievement, 1996. Mem. Am. Agrl. Econs. Assn., Am., Nat., Nebr. Water Resources Assns. (Pres.'s award 1979, award for Commitment to Irrigated Agriculture 1993), Nebr. Irrigation Assn., Nebr. Assn. Resource Dists., Am. Soc. Farm Mgrs. Rural Appraisers, Orgn. Profl. Employees of U.S. Dept. Agr., Lincoln C. of C. (chmn. agrl. com. 1974-77), Rotary (dir. 1965-66), Gamma Sigma Delta, Alpha Zeta (v.p. Nebr. agrl. rels. coun., 1993-94). Home: 3800 Loveland Dr Lincoln NE 68506-3842

SHEFFIELD, RICHARD LEE, physicist; b. Dayton, Ohio, Sept. 22, 1950; s. Albert H. and Pauline E. (Schutte) S.; m. Antoinette M. Mals, Oct. 28, 1978; children: Nicole, Angela, Michael. BS, Wright State U., 1972; PhD, MIT, 1978. Staff mem. high energy high density physics Los Alamos (N.Mex.) Nat. Lab., 1978-82, staff mem. free electron laser tech., 1982-85, dep. group leader, 1985-89, group leader accelerator theory & free electron laser tech., 1989-93, prin. investigator advanced FEL initiative, 1990—; advisor UV/FEL adv. panel Brookhaven (N.Y.) Nat. Lab., 1991—, Project Leader Advanced Accelevator Tech., 1994—; lectr. U.S. Accelerator Summer Sch., 1989. Editorial bd. Particle Accelerators, 1991—; patentee photoinjector, high brightness electron accelerators. Pres. Los Alamos United Way, 1981-84; vice chmn. Los Alamos County Planning and Zoning Commn., 1983-86, exec. coun. for divsn. of Beams and Particles. Recipient R&D 100 award R&D 100 Mag., 1988, Strategic Def. Tech. Achievements award Strategic Def. Preparedness Assn., 1989. Fellow Am. Phys. Soc. (prize for Achievement in Accelerator Physics and Tech., 1993); mem. Sigma Pi Sigma.

SHEFFLER, DUDLEY, telecommunications industry executive. CEO Reltec Corp., Cleve. Office: Reliance Comm/Tec Corp 6065 Parkland Blvd Cleveland OH 44124-4186 Office: Reltec 5875 Landerbrook St Ste250 Cleveland OH 44124

SHEFLIN, MICHAEL JOHN EDWARD, environment and transportation official; b. Toronto, Ont., Can., Dec. 27, 1938; s. John Edward and Marguerite Christine (MacKinnon) S.; m. Elizabeth Anne Taylor, Apr. 19, 1965; children: Sydney Michelle Taylor, Siobahn Morgan Taylor. Diploma in engring., St. Francis Xavier U., Antigonish, N.S., 1959; B of Civil Engring., Tech. U. N.S., 1962; diploma, Banff Sch. Advanced Mgmt., Alta., 1972. Engr. USAF, Harmon AFB, 1962-65; town mgr. Town of Stephenville, Nfld., 1965-66; sr. engr. ops. City of St. Catharines, Ont., 1966-70; dir. engring. and works City of Halifax, N.S., 1970-75; transp. commr. Regional Municipality of Ottawa-Carleton, Ont., 1975-95; environ. and transp. commr. Regional Municipality of Ottawa-Carleton, Ont., 1995—; gov. Internat. Pub. Works Fedn., Washington, 1989-92; eminent overseas speaker Instn. of Engrs., Canberra, Australia, 1989. Co-author: Management of Local Public Works, 1986; contbr. articles to jours. V.p. Liberal Party of Nfld., Stephenville, 1966; chmn. Econ. Affairs, Jaycees, Can., 1966, 67, Niagara Regional Sci. Fair, St. Catharines, 1969, United Way City of Halifax, 1973. Fellow Inst. Transp. Engrs. (Outstanding Svc. award 1991); mem. Internat. Fedn. Mcpl. Engrs. (life mem. Oslo, 1st v.p. 1991-94, 2d v.p. 1985-88, pres. 1988-91), Transp. Assn. Can. (v.p. 1989, treas. 1990-93, award of merit 1991, hon. life mem. Calgary), Inst. Mcpl. Engrs. (pres. 1976-77, hon. mem.), Am. Pub. Works Assn (Leader of Yr. 1981). Avocations: history, traveling, walking. Home: 35 3d Ave, Ottawa, ON Canada K15 2J5 Office: Regional Municipality, 111 Lisgar St Cartier Sq, Ottawa, ON Canada K2P 2L7

SHEFTEL, ROGER TERRY, merchant banking executive; b. Denver, Sept. 10, 1941; s. Edward and Dorothy (Barnett) S.; m. Phoebe A. Sherman, Sept. 7, 1968; children: Tisha B., Ryan B. BS in Econs., U. Pa., 1963. Comml. lending officer Provident Nat. Bank, Phila., 1963-65; asst. to pres. Continental Finance Corp., Denver, 1965-68; v.p. Eastern Indsl. Leasing Corp., Phila., 1968-71, exec. v.p., dir., 1971-73; exec. v.p., dir. HBE Leasing Corp., Phila., 1971-73; dir. Kooly Kupp, Inc., Boyertown, Pa., 1974-77, pres., dir., 1977; prin. Trivest, Phila., 1973-77; pres. Trivest, Inc., Phila., 1977-78, 1670 Corp., mgmt. cons.'s, 1978-82; pres. Am. Cons. Group, Inc., 1982-83; exec. v.p., dir. Argus Rsch. Labs., Inc., 1982-83; pres. Leasing Concepts, Inc., 1983-87, Brice Capital Corp., 1987-92; pres. Rhodes Fin., Inc., 1992—. Mem. Nantucket Yacht Club, Friars Club, Rotary. Home: 414 Barclay Rd Bryn Mawr PA 19010-1218 Office: Rhodes Fin Inc PO Box 7338 Saint Davids PA 19087-7338

SHEFTMAN, HOWARD STEPHEN, lawyer; b. Columbia, S.C., May 20, 1949; s. Nathan and Rena Mae (Kantor) S.; m. Sylvia Elaine Williams, Nov. 30, 1974; children: Amanda Elaine, Emily Catherine. BS in Bus. Adminstrn., U. S.C., 1971, JD, 1974. Bar: S.C. 1974, U.S. Dist. Ct. 1975, U.S. Ct. Appeals (4th cir.) 1982. Assoc. Kirkland, Taylor & Wilson, West Columbia, S.C., 1974-75; ptnr. Sheftman, Oswald & Holland, West Columbia, 1975-77, Finkel, Goldberg, Sheftman & Altman, P.A., Columbia, 1977—. Mem. S.C. Bar Assn. (practice and procedure com. 1978—), S.C. Trial Lawyers Assn. (chmn. domestic rels. sect. 1982-83, bd. govs. 1987-93, 94—), Richland Bar Assn., Met. Sertoma Club (pres. 1986-87). Jewish. Office: Finkel Goldberg Sheftman & Altman PA PO Box 1799 Columbia SC 29202-1799

SHEH, ROBERT BARDHYL, environmental management company executive; b. N.Y.C., July 29, 1939; s. Talat and Nedime (Karali) S.; m. Mary Cheney Fleming, Dec. 29, 1961; children—Andrea K., Jonathan C., Robert R., Elisabeth F., Theresa N. BS in Civil Engring, Rennselaer Poly. Inst., 1960; grad. program for Mgmt. Devel., Harvard U., 1974. With The Ralph M. Parsons Co., 1971—; sr. v.p., mgr. petroleum, chem., mining and metall. div. The Ralph M. Parsons Co., Pasadena, Calif., 1981-88, pres., 1989-92, also bd. dirs.; pres., CEO Internat. Tech. Corp., Torrance, Calif., 1992—; mem. adv. bd. Sch. Chem. Engring., U. Calif., Berkeley, 1986—; bd. dirs. Davidson Assocs., 1993—; mem. adv. bd. Rensselaer Poly. Inst., 1995. Bd. regents Marymount Internat. Sch., London, 1979; bd. trustees Harvey Mudd Coll., 1992—. With USNR, 1960-64. Mem. Calif. Club (L.A.), Annandale Golf Club (Pasadena), L.A. Country Club. Office: Internat Tech Corp 23456 Hawthorne Blvd Torrance CA 90505-4716

SHEHADI, SAMEER IBRAHIM, plastic surgeon; b. Zahle, Lebanon, Mar. 3, 1931; came to U.S., 1984; s. Ibrahim A. and Mounira D. (Dumit) S.; m. Leila A. Nassif, June 18, 1960; children: Ramzi Richard, Kamal Sameer, Imad Edward. BA, Am. U. Beirut, 1952, MD, 1956. Diplomate Am. Bd. Surgery, Am. Bd. Plastic Surgery. Intern. Am. U. Hosp., Beirut, resident gen. surgery, 1956-59, chief resident gen. surgery, 1959-60; resident plastic surgery St. Louis U. Hosps., 1960-62; fellow hand surgery Pitts. U. Hosps., 1962; resident head and neck surgery Roswell Park Meml. Inst., Buffalo, N.Y., 1963; clin. asst. prof. Am. U. Beirut, 1963-79, clin. prof. surgery, 1979-84, chmn. dept. surgery, 1976-79, 81-84; prof., dir. div. plastic surgery St. Louis U., 1984—. Contbr. articles to profl. jours. Recipient Chevaliers award Order of the Cedars, Govt. Lebanon, 1968. Fellow ACS (gov. at large Lebanon chpt. 1981-84); mem. AMA, St. Louis Met. Med. Soc., St. Louis Surg. Soc., Mo. Med. Assn., Lebanese Order of Physicians, Am. U. Beirut Med. Alumni Assn., Am. Soc. Plastic and Reconstructive Surgeons, Am. Soc. Maxillofacial Surgeons, Am. Assn. Chmn. Plastic Surgery, Am. Assn. Plastic Surgeons, Am. Assn. Hand Surgeons, Lebanese Soc. Plastic and Reconstructive Surgeons (pres. 1974-84), Internat. Soc. Burn Injuries (Lebanon rep. 1968-84). Home: 12256 Ladue Woods Dr Saint Louis MO 63141-8159 Office: St Louis U Med Ctr PO Box 15250 Saint Louis MO 63110-0250

SHEHEEN, FRED ROUKOS, education agency administrator; b. Camden, S.C., July 7, 1936; s. Austin M. and Lucile (Roukos) S.; m. Rose Maria Serio, Nov. 26, 1966; children: Maria, Vincent, Margaret Rose. AB Polit. Sci., Duke U., 1958; postgrad., Harvard U., 1990; LLD (hon.), Claflin Coll., 1990; HHD, Lander Coll., 1992; AA honoris causa, Tech. Coll. Lowcountry, Beaufort, S.C., 1992. Bureau chief Charlotte (N.C.) Observer, Rock Hill, Columbia, S.C., 1958-63; press sec. to Gov. Donald Russell, Columbia, 1963-65; exec. asst. to Sen. Donald Russell, Washington, 1965-66; asst. to dir. S.C. State Devel. Bd., Columbia, 1967-68; v.p. & sec., pres. & publisher Banner Publishers Inc., Chronicle Publishers Inc., N.C., S.C., 1968-76; founder, pres., prin. owner Camden (S.C.) Co., 1976-87; commr. of higher edn. S.C. Commn. on Higher Edn., Columbia, 1987—; bd. dirs. S.C. Rsch. Authority, Columbia, 1983-86; mem. S.C. Commn. Human Affairs, 1971-72, S.C. Commn. Higher Edn., 1971-75, 79-86, (chmn. 1983-86), Edn. Improvement Act Selection com., 1983-86, Commn. Future S.C., Columbia, 1987-89. Contbr. chpt. to book, article to profl. jour. Pres. Kershaw County Mental Health Assn., Camden, S.C., 1971, 76; mem. S.C. Tuition Grants Commn., 1988—, Nat. Edn. Goals Panel task force Collegiate Attainment and Assessment, 1988—, S.C. Edn. Goals Panel, 1992—, So. Regional Coun. Coll. Bd., 1993—; adv. bd. Master Pub. Adminstrn. program U. S.C. Coll. Charleston, 1992—; trustee Springdale Sch., Camden, 1976-84, Boyland-Haven-Mather Acad., Camden, 1976-83, S.C. Gov's. Sch. Sci. and Mathematics, 1987—; bd. dirs. Kershaw County Cancer Soc. Recipient Sertoma Svc. to Mankind award Sertoma club, 1973; named Educator of Yr. S.C. Tech. Edn. Assn., 1990. Mem. State Higher Edn. Exec. Officers (exec. com. 1990—, Nat. Ctr. Edn. Statistics Network adv. com. 1990—), S.C. Agy. Dir's. Orgn. (pres. 1992). Roman Catholic. Avocations: racquetball, water sports, reading. Home: 2107 Washington Ln Camden SC 29020-1723 Office: SC Commn Higher Edn 1333 Main St Ste 200 Columbia SC 29201-3201

SHEIL, WILMA ROHLOFF, psychiatry, mental health nurse; b. N.Y.C., Oct. 10, 1937; d. William G.H. and Marjorie (Marshall) Rohloff; m. John James Sheil, July 6, 1958; children: Shawn William (dec.), Marjorie Katherine. LPN diploma, Wilson Tech., 1975; ASN, SUNY, Albany, 1985. Staff nurse Hoch Psychiatric Ctr., Brentwood, N.Y., 1976-77; staff nurse Huntington (N.Y.) Hosp., 1977-85, 85-87, asst. nurse mgr., 1988—. Mem. MADD, 1994—, Planned Parenthood, 1994—, U.S.O., 1994—. Mem. AARP, NRA, Nat. Wildlife Fedn., Humane Soc. U.S., Ctr. Marine Conservation, Internat. Soc. of Poets. Roman Catholic. Avocations: collecting carnival glass, dolls, carousel horses, crystal, reading, travel, writing poetry. Office: Huntington Hosp 270 Park Ave Huntington NY 11743

SHEIN, JAY LESING, financial planner; b. Chgo., Jan. 27, 1951; s. Garrett Melchior and Evelyn (Blitt) Hamm; m. Val Margaret Rich, Dec. 14, 1984; children: Melissa Loree, Blair Charles, Christina Anne, Allison Marie, Lindsay Gayle. Student, Broward C.C., Davie, Fla., 1969-71; CFP, Coll. for Fin. Planning, Denver, 1990; MS in Taxation and Fin., LaSalle U., 1994, PhD, 1994. Tech. technician Broward County Sch. Bd., Ft. Lauderdale, Fla., 1973-76; owner, mgr. Bus. and Tax Consulting Firm, Ft. Lauderdale, 1976-83; dist. mgr. United Group and Group One, Ft. Lauderdale, 1983-84; from account exec. to v.p. Compass Fin. Group, Inc., Lighthouse Point, Fla., 1984-90; pres. Compass Fin. Group, Inc., Lighthouse Point, 1990—; adv. bd. devel. coun., mem. Highlands Christian Acad., Pompano Beach, Fla., 1992—; adj. prof. Nova Southeastern U. Grad. Sch. Bus. Contbr. articles to newspapers and pubs. in field. Mem. Estate Planning Coun. of Broward County. Mem. Inst. CFP, Nat. Assn. Life Underwriters, Practising Law Inst. (assoc.), South Fla. Soc. of Inst. of CFPs (pres.-elect 1996, edn. chmn. 1994, dir. ethics 1993-94), Broward County Assn. Life Underwriters (v.p. 1992-94), Greater Ft. Lauderdale Tax Coun., Marine Industries of South Fla. Republican. Baptist. Avocations: volleyball, racquetball, travel. Office: Compass Fin Group Inc 3050 N Federal Hwy Ste 208 Lighthouse Point FL 33064-6866

SHEINBAUM, GILBERT HAROLD, international management consultant; b. N.Y.C., Apr. 20, 1929; s. Herman and Selma (Klimberg) S.; m. Inger Fredebo Thomsen, Aug. 28, 1971; children: Neil, Britt. AB in History, NYU, 1950; postgrad., CUNY, 1954-55, New Sch. for Social Rsch., 1955-56. Various fgn. svc. posts Washington, Laos, France, Vietnam, 1957-68; polit. officer Am. Embassy, Copenhagen, 1968-72, U.S. Dept. of State, Washington, 1972-75; chargé d'affaires Am. Embassy, Antananarivo, Madagascar, 1975-77; dep. chief of mission Am. Embassy, Lilongwe, Malawi, 1977-79; Am. consul Am. Consulate, Cebu, Philippines, 1979-83; polit. counselor U.S. Mission to the UN, Geneva, 1983-86; dir. Colombo Plan (internat. orgn.), Colombo, Sri Lanka, 1986-91; assoc. Global Bus. Access, Ltd., Washington, 1991; cons. Nat. Security Edn. Program, Washington, 1992-95, Internat. Found. for Election Sys., Washington, 1995—; internat. observor Sri Lankan elections, 1993, 94. Author and editor articles on econ. devel. in Asia. Trustee George Keyt Cultural Found., Colombo, 1987-91; bd. chmn. Overseas Children's Sch., Colombo, 1987-90; commr. Boy Scouts Am., Geneva, 1984-86; stage mgr. Am. Light Opera Co., Washington, 1962-64. 1st lt. U.S. Army, 1951-53. Recipient Award of Recognition, Mindanao State U., Marawi, Philippines, 1983. Mem. Am. Fgn. Svc. Assn., World Affairs Coun. of Washingotn DC, World Affairs Coun. of No. Calif., Asia Soc., Vietnamese-Am. C. of C. (bd. dirs. 1992—), Diplomatic and Consular Officers Ret. (treas.). Avocations: tennis, jogging, touring, reading. Home: 210 Patterson St Falls Church VA 22046-4631 Office: Internat Found Election Sys Electoral Systems 1101 15th St NW Washington DC 20006

SHEINBERG, ISRAEL, computer company executive; b. Fort Worth, Apr. 15, 1932; s. Samuel I. and Pauline C. (Fram) S.; m. Betty S. Topletz, Aug. 19, 1962; children—Amy, Karen, David, Paula. B.S. in Physics, U. Tex., 1953; student, UCLA, 1957-58, Arlington (Tex.) State Coll., 1960, Southwestern Med. Sch., 1961. Electronic engr. Hughes Aircraft Co., 1956-60, Nat. Data Processing Corp., 1961; also exec. v.p. and gen. mgr. European ops. Recognition Equipment Inc., 1961-90; pvt. cons. to industry Dallas, 1990—; bd. dirs. Tex. Commerce Bank, Balchem Corp.; mem. adv. coun. of engring. found., adv. coun. for natural scis. U. Tex., Austin; speaker on image technology, optical character recognition and related subjects. Contbr. articles to profl. jours. With AUS, 1954-56. Inducted into Assn. for Work Process Improvement Hall of Fame. Mem. Optical Soc. Am., Am. Mgmt. Assn. Jewish (bd. dirs. synagogue). Home: 5706 Watson Cir Dallas TX 75225-1653 Office: Sheinberg Assocs 5706 Watson Cir Dallas TX 75225-1653

SHEINBERG, SIDNEY JAY, recreation and entertainment company executive; b. Corpus Christi, Tex., Jan. 14, 1935; s. Harry and Tillie (Grossman) S.; m. Lorraine Gottfried, Aug. 19, 1956; children: Jonathan J., William David. A.B., Columbia Coll., 1955; LL.B., Columbia U., 1958. Bar: Calif. 1958. Assoc. in law UCLA Sch. Law, 1958-59; with MCA, Inc., Universal City, Calif., 1959—, pres. TV div., 1971-74, corp. exec. v.p., 1969-73, corp. pres., chief operating officer, 1973-95; ptnr. The Bubble Factory, Beverly Hills, CA, 1995—. Mem. Assn. Motion Picture and Television Producers (chmn. bd.). Office: The Bubble Factory 8840 Wilshire Blvd Beverly Hills CA 90210

SHEINFELD, DAVID, composer; b. St. Louis, Sept. 20, 1906; s. Joseph and Feige (Sandler) S.; m. Dorothy Jaffe, Apr. 12, 1942; children: Daniel, Paul. MusB, Am. Conservatory Music, Chgo., 1929; studies with Ottorino Respighi, Santa Cecilia Acad., Rome, 1929-31. Violinist, arranger various radio programs, Chgo., 1934-40; violist Pitts. Symphony, 1944-45; violinist San Francisco Symphony, 1945-71; ind. composer, tchr. San Francisco, 1971—. Composer orchestral and chamber music works including Adagio and Allegro, 1947, Patterns, 1962, Dualities, 1981, Dreams and Fantasies, 1982; commd. to compose work for San Francisco Symphony Assn. Orch.'s 60th anniversary, 1971 (Recipient Norman Fromm award for chamber music composition 1979), 2d string quartet Kronos Quartet, 1990; compositions performed by symphony orchs. in San Francisco, Chgo., Pitts., Phila., Phila. Chamber Symphony, chamber music performed, numerous cities in U.S., Can., Eng. Recipient Composer's award AAAL, 1993, award Koussevitzky Music Found., 1993; NEA grantee for orch. work, 1987-88. Mem. Broadcast Music, Inc. Avocations: astronomy, physics. Home and Office: 1458 24th Ave San Francisco CA 94122-3312 *Respect for the rights of others; respect for our cultural achievements and ideals; respect for the art of music; these principles have guided my life.*

SHEINGOLD, DANIEL H., electrical engineer; b. Boston, Sept. 26, 1928; s. Louis S. and Elsie (Frank) S.; m. Ann Silverman, Aug. 2, 1953 (dec. Feb. 1995); children: Mark J., Laura R. BSEE with distinction, Worcester Poly. Inst., 1948; MSEE, Columbia U., 1949. Engr. George A. Philbrick Rschs. Inc., Boston, 1949-55, application engring. mgr., 1957-63; v.p. George A. Philbrick Researches, Inc., Dedham, Mass., 1964-67; staff cons. Teledyne Philbrick, Dedham, 1967-68; tech. mktg. mgr. Analog Devices, Inc., Norwood, Mass., 1969—. Editor: Analog-Digital Conversion Handbook, 1972, 3d edit., 1986, Nonlinear Circuits Handbook, 1974, Transducer Interfacing Handbook, 1980; editor Analog Dialogue jour., 1969—, others. With AUS, 1955-57. Fellow IEEE; mem. IEEE Instrumentation and Measurement Soc. (sec.-treas. 1976, v.p. 1977, pres. 1978), AAAS. Jewish. Avocations: music, walking, crosscountry skiing, reading. Office: Analog Devices Inc PO Box 9106 3 Technology Way Norwood MA 02062-9106

SHEININ, ROSE, biochemist, educator; b. Toronto, Ont., Can., May 18, 1930; d. Harry and Anne (Szyber) Shuber; BA, U. Toronto, 1951, MA (scholar), 1953, PhD in Biochemistry, 1956, L.H.D., 1985; DHL (hon.), Mt. St. Vincent U., 1985; DSc (hon.) Acadia U., 1987, DSc (hon.) U. Guelph, 1991; m. Joseph Sheinin, July 15, 1951; children—David Matthew Khazanov, Lisa Basya Judith, Rachel Sarah Rebecca. Demonstrator in biochemistry U. Toronto (Ont., Can.), 1951-53, asst. prof. microbiology, 1964-75, asst. prof. med. biophysics, 1967-75, prof. microbiology, 1975-90, prof. med. biophysics, 1978-90, assoc. prof. med. biophysics, 1975-78, chmn. microbiology and parasitology, 1975-82, vice dean Sch. Grad. Studies, 1984-89; vice-rector acad., Concordia U., Montreal, Que., Can., 1989-94, prof. dept. biology, 1989—; mem. Health Scis. Com.; vis. rsch. assoc. chem. microbiology, Cambridge U., 1956-57, Nat. Inst. Med. Rsch., London, 1957-58; rsch. assoc. fellow div. biol. research Ont. Cancer Inst., 1958-67; sci. officer cancer grants panel Med. Research Council Can.; mem. Can. Sci. Del. to People's Republic of China, 1973; mem. adv. com. Provincial Lottery Health Research Awards; mem. adv. com. on biotech. NRC Can., 1984-87; mem. Sci. Council Can., 1984-87; adv. com. on sci. and tech. CBC, 1980-85; mem. bd. dirs. Can. Bacterial Disease Network, 1989-94; vis. prof. biochemistry U. Alta., 1971. Nat. Cancer Inst. Can. fellow, 1953-56, 58-61; Brit. Empire Cancer Campaign fellow, 1956-58; Recipient Queen's Silver Jubilee medal, 1978, Woman of Distinction award Health and Edn., YWCA, 1988; Josiah Macy Jr. Faculty scholar, 1981-82; fellow Ligue Contre le Cancer, France, 1981-82, Massey Coll. U. Toronto, 1981—, resident sr. fellow, 1994—; hon. fellow Ryerson Polytech. U., 1993. Fellow Am. Acad. Microbiology, Royal Soc. Can. (chair women in scholarship com. 1990-93); mem. Can. Biochem. Soc. (pres. 1974-75), Can. Soc. Cell Biology (pres. 1975-76), Am. Soc. Virology, Am. Soc. Microbiologists, Canadian Assn. Women in Sci., Internat. Assn. Women Bioscientists, Sigma Xi Rsch. Soc., Scitech, Soc. Complex Carbohydrates, Toronto Biochem. and Biophys. Soc. (pres. 1960-70, council 1970-74). Assoc. editor Can. Jour. Biochemistry, 1968-71, Virology, 1969-72, Intervirology, 1974-85; editorial bd. Microbiol. Revs., 1977-80; author, co-author various publs. Office: U Toronto Massey Coll, 4 Devonshire Pl, Toronto, ON Canada M5S 2E1

SHEINKMAN, JACK, union official, lawyer; b. N.Y.C., Dec. 6, 1926; s. Shaia and Bertha (Rosenkrantz) S.; m. Betty Francis Johnson, May 31, 1954; children: Michael, Joshua, Mark. B.S., Cornell U., 1948, LL.B., 1952; cert. in econs., Oxford U., 1949. Bar: N.Y. 1952. Atty. NLRB, Washington, 1952-53; atty. Amalgamated Clothing Workers Am., N.Y.C., 1953-58, gen. counsel, 1958-72, v.p., 1968-72, sec.-treas., 1972-76; sec.-treas. Amalgamated Clothing and Textile Workers Union, N.Y.C., 1976-87, pres., 1987-95, pres. emeritus, 1995—; chmn. bd. Amalgamated Bank of N.Y.; mem. exec. coun., v.p. AFL-CIO, 1987-95; mem. indsl. union dept. Internat. Textile, Garment and Leather Workers Fedn., Brussels, 1972—. Dir. internat. rescue com. N.Y. Hist. Soc.; bd. dirs. Martin Luther King Jr. Inst.; vice chmn. Coun. Competitiveness United Housing Found.; trustee Aspen Inst.; mem. Pres.'s Adv. Com. on Trade Policy Negotiations, 1987-95. Lt. (j.g.) USNR, 1944-46, PTO. Mem. Workers Def. League (dir.), Am. Arbitration Assn. (dir.) Coun. Fgn. Rels., UN Assn. U.S.A. (bd. dirs.), Brit.-N.Am. Com. (exec. com.), Nat. Planning Com. (exec. com.). Democrat. Jewish. Home: 52 W 76th St New York NY 10023-1517 Office: Amalgamated Bank NY 15 Union Sq W New York NY 10003

SHEINMAN, MORTON MAXWELL, editor, consultant, writer, photographer; b. N.Y.C., Oct. 7, 1933; s. Irving and Mollie (Feigenblatt) S.; m. Claire Rosenfeld, Aug. 27, 1967 (div.). BA in English, CCNY, 1954. Reporter Women's Wear Daily, N.Y.C., 1960-69, news editor, 1970-71, mng. editor, 1971—; mng. editor W Mag., N.Y.C., 1972-82, assoc. editor, 1982—; cons., writer ATT Sumer Olympics Exhibit, L.A., 1984, Cafe Concepts, N.Y.C., 1989—, Pru Ctr. Observatory, Boston, 1995; cons. MMD, N.Y.C., 1990—. Photographer Diverson Mag., 1979—. With U.S. Army, 1954-56. Mem. CCNY Comm. Alumni. Home: 60 Gramercy Park N New York NY 10010 Office: Women's Wear Daily 7 W 34th St New York NY 10001

SHELANSKI, MICHAEL L., cell biologist, educator; b. Phila., Oct. 5, 1941; s. Herman Alder and Bessie B.; m. Vivien Brodkin, June 9, 1963; children: Howard, Samuel, Noah. Student, Oberlin Coll., 1959-61; M.D. (Life Ins. Med. Research Fund fellow), U. Chgo., 1966, Ph.D., 1967. Intern in pathology Albert Einstein Coll. Medicine, N.Y.C., 1967-68; fellow in neuropathology Albert Einstein Coll. Medicine, 1968-70, asst. prof. pathology, 1969-74; staff scientist NIH, Bethesda, Md., 1971-73; vis. scientist Inst. Pasteur, Paris, 1973-74; assoc. prof. neuropathology Harvard U., Cambridge, Mass., 1974-78; sr. research assoc., asst. neuropathologist Children's Hosp. Med. Center, Boston, 1974-78; prof., chmn. dept. pharmacology N.Y. U. Med. Center, N.Y.C., 1978-86; Delafield Prof., chmn. dept. pathology Coll. Physicians and Surgeons, Columbia U., N.Y.C., 1987—; dir. pathology services Presbyn. Hosp., N.Y.C., 1987—; mem. Neurology A study sect. NIH, 1974-78; Pharmacological Scis. study sect., 1986-90; mem. sci. and med. adv. bd. Alzheimer's Disease and Related Disorders Assn., 1985-92, sec., 1987-92, mem. Zenith award panel, 1993-95; chmn. overhead powerline adv. panel State of N.Y., 1981-87; dir. Alzheimer's disease rsch. ctr. Columbia U., 1989—; mem. Am. Cancer Soc. IRG Panel, 1989-93, sci. adv. bd. Dystonia Assn., Amyotrophic Lateral Sclerosis Assn. Mem. editl. bd. Jour. Neurochemistry, 1982-90, Jour. Neuropathology and Exptl. Neurology, 1983-85, Neuroscis., 1985—, Neurobiology of Aging, 1988-95, Lab. Investigation, 1989—, Brain Pathology, 1990-93. Served as sr. asst. surgeon USPHS, 1971-73. Guggenheim fellow, 1973-74. Mem. Am. Soc. Cell Biology, Am. Assn. Neuropathologists, Assn. Med. Coll. Pharmacologists, Am. Soc. Neurochemistry, Am. Assn. Physicians. Achievements include research on fibrous proteins of brain, aging of human brain, devel. neurobiology. Office: Columbia U Coll Physicians and Surgeons Dept Pathology 630 W 168th St New York NY 10032-3702

SHELBY, JAMES STANFORD, cardiovascular surgeon; b. Ringgold, La., June 15, 1934; s. Jesse Audrey and Mable (Martin) S.; BS in Liberal Arts La. Tech. U., 1956; MD, La. State U., 1958; m. Susan Rainey, July 15, 1967; children: Bryan Christian, Christopher Linden. Intern, Charity Hosp. La., New Orleans, 1958-59, resident surgery and thoracic surgery, 1959-65; fellow cardiovascular surgery Baylor U. Coll. Medicine, Houston, 1965-66; practice medicine specializing in cardiovascular surgery, Shreveport, La., 1967—; mem. staff Schumpert Med. Ctr., Highland Hosp., Willis-Knighton Med. Ctr.; assoc. prof. surgery La. State U. Sch. Medicine, Shreveport, 1967—. With M.C., AUS, 1961-62. Diplomate Am. Bd. Surgery, Am. Bd. Thoracic Surgery. Recipient Tower of Medallion award La. Tech. U., 1982. Mem. Am. Coll. Cardiology, AMA, Soc. Thoracic Surgeons, Am. Heart Assn., Southeastern Surg. Congress, So. Thoracic Surg. Assn. Home: 6003 E Ridge Dr Shreveport LA 71106-2425 Office: 3300 Virginia Ave Ste 7B Shreveport LA 71103-3941

SHELBY, JEROME, lawyer; b. N.Y.C., Mar. 17, 1930; s. Morris and Rose Shelby; m. Adrian Austin, Nov. 24, 1957; children: Karen A. Anderson, P. Austin. AB, NYU, 1950; LLB, Harvard U., 1953. Bar: D.C. 1953, N.Y. 1954. Assoc. Cadwalader, Wickersham & Taft, N.Y.C., 1953-63, ptnr., 1963-92, of counsel, 1993—; sr. v.p. Marine Transport Lines Inc., N.Y.C., 1958-74, also dir., 1989-92, adv. dir., 1993—; exec. v.p., dir. Energy Transp. Corp., N.Y.C., 1973—; dir. Astro Tankers Ltd.; trustee Seamen's Ch. Inst. Mem. Assn. Bar City N.Y., Montclair Golf Club, Palm Beach Polo Club (Fla.). Home: 74 Highland Ave Montclair NJ 07042-1910 Office: Cadwalader Wickersham & Taft 100 Maiden Ln New York NY 10038-4818

SHELBY, RICHARD CRAIG, senator, former congressman; b. Birmingham, Ala., May 6, 1934; s. O.H. and Alice L. (Skinner) S.; m. Annette Nevin, June 11, 1960; children: Richard Craig, Claude Nevin. AB, U. Ala., 1957, LLB, 1963. Bar: Ala. 1961, D.C. 1979. Law clk. Supreme Ct. of Ala., 1961-62; practice law Tuscaloosa, Ala., 1963-79; prosecutor City of Tuscaloosa, 1964-70; spl. asst. atty. gen. State of Ala., 1969-70; U.S. magistrate No. Dist. of Ala., 1966-70; mem. Ala. State Senate, 1970-78, 96th-99th Congresses from 7th Ala. dist., 1979-87; mem. energy and commerce com., mem. vets. affairs com., U.S. senator from Ala., 1987—, mem. com. on appropriations, com. on banking, housing, and urban affairs, select com. on intelligence, spl. com. on aging. Active Boy Scouts Am.; pres. Tuscaloosa County Mental Health Assn., 1969-70; bd. govs. Nat. Legis. Conf., 1975-78. Mem. ABA, Ala. Bar Assn., Tuscaloosa County Bar Assn., D.C. Bar Assn., Exch. Club. Republican. Presbyterian. Home: 1414 High Forest Dr N Tuscaloosa AL 35406-2152 Office: US Senate 110 Hart Senate Bldg Washington DC 20510*

SHELBY, TIM OTTO, English educator; b. Longview, Wash., Mar. 23, 1965; s. William Richard and Ruth (Masser) S. BA in edn., Eastern Wash. U., 1989. Cert. grades 4-12 English tchr., Wash. Eng. tchr. Kahlotus (Wash.) H. S., 1989-90; tchr. various districts, 1990-92; Eng. tchr. Kalama (Wash.) H.S., 1992-95; tchr. English, head basketball coach Frazier Mountain High Sch., Lebec, Calif., 1995—; asst. basketball coach Kalama H.S., 1992-95, head basketball and football coach, 1989-90. Mem. Nat. Coun. Tchrs. Eng., Internat. Reading Assn., Nat. Assn. Basketballs Coachs, Wash. State Coaches Assn., Wash. Edn. Assn. (bldg. rep.), Assn. Supervision & Curriculem Devel. Roman Catholic. Avocations: traveling, reading, coaching sports, theatre, movies. Home: Box 113 Frazier Park CA 93225 Office: El Tajon Unified Sch Dist Box 876 Lebec CA 93243

SHELDON, BROOKE EARLE, librarian, educator; b. Lawrence, Mass., Aug. 29, 1931; d. Leonard Hadley and Elsie Ann (Southerl) Earle; m. George Duffield Sheldon, Mar. 28, 1955 (dec.); children: L. Scott, G. Stephen. B.A., Acadia U., 1952, D.C.L. (hon.), 1985; M.L.S., Simmons Coll., 1954; Ph.D., U. Pitts., 1977. Base librarian Ent AFB, Colorado Springs, Colo., 1955-57, U.S. Army, Germany, 1956-57; br. librarian Albuquerque Public Library, 1959-61; coordinator adult services Santa Fe Public Library, 1965-67; head library devel. N.Mex. State Library, Santa Fe, 1967-72; asst. dir. leadership tng. inst. U.S. Office Edn., Washington, 1971-73; head tech. svcs. and tng. Alaska State Library, Juneau, 1973-75; dean Sch. Library Info. Studies Tex. Woman's U., Denton, 1977-90; acting provost Library Info. Studies, Tex. Woman's U., Denton, 1979-80; dean Grad. Sch. Libr. Info. Sci. U. Tex., Austin, 1991—. Author: Leaders in Libraries: Styles and Strategies for Success, 1991; editor: Library and Information Science Education in the United States, 1996; contbr. articles to profl. jours. Bd. dirs. Am. Libr. in Paris, 1992—. Recipient Alumni Achievement award Simmons Coll., 1983; Disting. Alumni award Sch. Library Info. Sci., U. Pitts., 1986. Mem. ALA (pres. 1983-84, chmn. com. on accreditation 1995-96), Tex. Libr. Assn., Rotary Internat., Beta Phi Mu. Democrat. Episcopalian.

SHELDON, CHARLES HARVEY, political science educator; b. Jerome, Idaho, Aug. 2, 1929; s. Milo Francis and Martha Susan (McCorkle) S.; m. Patricia Ann Murphy, Dec. 31, 1970; children—Lee Ann, Christopher, Ross, Thomas. B.A., U. Wash., Seattle, 1952, M.A., 1957; Ph.D., U. Oreg., 1965. Instr. polit. sci. Boise (Idaho) Jr. Coll., 1958-61; asst. prof., chmn. dept., dir. Sch. Social Sci., U. Nev., Las Vegas, 1962-68; asso. prof., chmn. dept. Southampton (N.Y.) Coll., L.I. U., 1968-70; mem. faculty Wash. State U., Pullman, 1970—; prof. polit. sci. Wash. State U., 1974—, dir. div. govtl. studies and services, 1976, dept. chmn., 1993-94, Claudius O. and Mary W. Johnson disting. prof. polit. scis., 1994—. Author: The American Judicial Process: Models and Approaches, 1974, A Century of Judging: A Political History of the Washington Supreme Court, 1988, The Washington High Bench: A Biographical History of the State Supreme Court, 1992; co-author: Democracy at the Crossroads, 1978, Politicians, Judges and the People, 1980, Political Life in Washington, 1985, Government and Politics in the Evergreen State, 1992; editor: The Supreme Court: Politicians in Robes, 1969; co-editor: Postwar America: The Search for Identity, 1968, Government and Politics of Washington State, 1978; contbr. articles to profl. jours. and law revs. Served with AUS, 1952-55. Grantee Am. Philos. Soc., 1976; grantee Nat. Endowment Humanities, 1978; grantee NSF, 1982-83, 95. Mem. ACLU, Am. Polit. Sci. Assn., Am. Judicature Soc., Wash. State Com. Minority and Justice, Wash. State Hist. Soc., Western Polit. Sci. Assn., Law and Soc. Assn., U.S. Masters Swimming, Alpha Delta Phi. Nationally ranked masters swimmer, 1975-80, 85, 87. Address: SE 905th Spring St Pullman WA 99163

SHELDON, DAVID FREDERICK, museum director, headmaster; b. N.Y.C., Feb. 2, 1929; s. Seward Ross and Zue Mac (Bronaugh) S.; m. Judith West, June 18, 1954; children: Frederick William, Charles Seward, James Nias. A.B., Amherst Coll., 1951; M.B.A., Harvard U., 1953, M.A.T., 1958. Trainee, then account exec. McCann-Erickson Inc. (advt.), 1953-57; tchr. history and English Middlesex Sch., Concord, Mass., 1957-59; dir. admissions Middlesex Sch., 1961-64, headmaster, 1964-90; exec. dir. Shelburne (Vt.) Mus., 1990-96; Pres. Sch. Scholarship Service, 1963-65. Trustee Charles River Sch., Dover, Mass., 1965-68, Carroll Sch., Lincoln, Mass., 1972—, Interalp, Princeton, N.J., 1973—, Ind. Schs. Coun. for Religion; mem. corp. Emerson Hosp., Concord, Mass., 1970—; mem. overseers vis. com. Harvard U., 1966—; exec. com. Ind. Schs. Found. Mass., 1981—; mem. commn. for ind. schs. New Eng. Assn. Schs. and Colls., 1985-88; exec. dir. Shelburne (Vt.) Mus. Mem. Headmasters Assn., New Eng. Assn. Schs. and Colls. (commn. ind. schs. 1985-88, overseas schs. 1985-88, pres. 1990-91). Episcopalian (vestryman). Address: Shelburne Museum PO Box 10 Shelburne VT 05482-0010

SHELDON, ELEANOR HARRIET BERNERT, sociologist; b. Hartford, Conn., Mar. 19, 1920; d. M.G. and Fannie (Myers) Bernert; m. James Sheldon, Mar. 19, 1950 (div. 1960); children: James, John Anthony. AA, Colby Jr. Coll., 1940; AB, U. N.C., 1942; PhD, U. Chgo., 1949. Asst. demographer Office Population Rsch., Washington, 1942-43; social scientist USDA, Washington, 1943-45; assoc. dir. Chgo. Community Inventory, U. Chgo., 1947-50; social scientist Social Sci. Rsch. Coun., N.Y.C., 1950-51, rsch. grantee, 1953-55, pres., 1972-79; rsch. assoc. Bur. Applied Social Rsch. Columbia U., 1950-51, lectr. sociology, 1951-52, vis. prof., 1969-71; social scientist UN, N.Y.C., 1951-52; rsch. assoc., lectr. sociology UCLA, 1955-61; assoc. rsch. sociologist, lectr. Sch. Nursing U. Calif., 1957-61; sociologist, exec. assoc. Russell Sage Found., N.Y.C., 1961-72; vis. prof. U. Calif., Santa Barbara, 1971; dir. Equitable Life Assurance Soc., Mobil Corp., H.J. Heinz Co. Author: (with L. Wirth) Chicago Community Fact Book, 1949, America's Children, 1958, (with R.A. Glazier) Pupils and Schools in N.Y.C, 1965; editor: (with W.E. Moore) Indicators of Social Change, Concepts and Measurements, 1968, Family Economic Behavior, 1973; contbr. (with W.E. Moore) articles to profl. jours. Bd. dirs. Colby-Sawyer Coll., 1979-85, UN Rsch. Inst. for Social Devel., 1973-79; trustee Rockefeller Found., 1978-85, Nat. Opinion Rsch. Ctr., 1980-87, Inst. East-West Security Studies, 1984-88, Am. assembly, 1976-95. William Rainey Harper fellow U. Chgo., 1945-47. Fellow Am. Acad. Arts and Scis., Am. Sociol. Assn., Am. Statis. Assn.; mem. AAAS, U. Chgo. Alumni Assn. (Profl. Achievement award), Sociol. Rsch. Assn. (pres. 1971-72), Coun. on Fgn. Rels., Am. Assn. Pub. Opinion Rsch., Ea. Sociol. Soc., Internat. Sociol. Assn., Internat. Union Sci. Study of Population, Population Assn. Am. (2d v.p. 1970-71), Inst. of Medicine (chmn. program com. 1976-77), Cosmopolitan Club. Home and Office: 630 Park Ave New York NY 10021-6544

SHELDON, ERIC, physics educator; b. Pilsen, Bohemia, Oct. 24, 1930; s. Robert Bernard and Martha (Martin) S.; m. Sheila Harper, July 8, 1959; 1 child, Adrian. B.Sc., London (Eng.) U., 1951, B.Sc. in Physics, with honors, 1952, Ph.D., 1955, D.Sc., 1971. Chartered chemist; chartered physicist. Lectr., rsch. assoc. Acton Tech. Coll., London, 1952-55; assoc. physicist IBM Rsch. Lab., Switzerland, 1957-59; rsch. assoc. E.T.H., Zurich, Switzerland, 1959-62, lectr., 1962-64, prof., 1964-69; prof. physics and applied physics Lowell (Mass.) Technol. Inst. and U. Lowell, 1970-91, U. Mass. at Lowell, 1991-96; hon. dir., 1994-96, emeritus prof., 1996—; Univ. prof. U. Lowell, 1985-88; vis. prof., NSF sr. fgn. sci. fellow U. Va., 1968-69; vis. prof. U. Tex., 1969-70, U. Oxford (Eng.), 1989. Author: (with R. Szostak and P. Marmier) Kernphysik I, 1960, Kernphysik II, 1961, (with P. Marmier) Physics of Nuclei and Particles, Vol. I, 1969, Vol. II, 1970; editor Procs. Internat. Conf. on Interactions of Neutrons with Nuclei, 1976; contbr. articles to books, encys. and profl. jours. Mem. Convocation London U., 1951—. Decorated Order of Merit (Poland). Fellow AAAS, Am. Phys. Soc. (chmn. New Eng. sect. 1985-86, mem. exec. com. 1983-87), Inst. Physics, Royal Soc. Chemistry, Royal Astron. Soc.; mem. Zurich Physical Soc. (life), Royal Instn. Gt. Britain, Am. Assn. Physics Tchrs., Mensa. Anglican/Episcopalian (lay reader). Home: 38 Cathy Rd Chelmsford MA 01824-2043 *The benefits of happiness in my work and throughout my life, of health, contentment, fulfillment and zest for living, impose an obligation to repay this good fortune in some measure through direct service to the world around me. And still the wonder remains: Life has given me so much more than I ever could contribute—inspiration and love from family and friends, the grace of beauty in the world around me, vivacity and the radiant miracle of laughter. For all that is gentle, peaceful, wise, goodwilled, compassionate, spiritually inspiring and nobly idealistic in this wondrous universe, I feel deep reverence, appreciation and profound gratitude.*

SHELDON, GARY, conductor, music director; b. Bay Shore, N.Y., Jan. 21, 1953. Student, Wash. U., St. Louis, 1972; BMus, Juilliard Sch. Music, 1974; diploma, Inst. Hautes Etudes Musicales, Montreux, Switzerland, 1975. Prin. condr. Opera Theater, Syracuse, 1976-77; asst. condr. Syracuse Symphony Orch., 1976-77, New Orleans Symphony Orch., 1977-80; assoc. condr. Columbus (Ohio) Symphony Orch., 1982-89; music dir. Lancaster (Ohio) Festival, 1988—, Marin Symphony Orch., San Rafael, Calif., 1990—. Composer: Variations on a Theme of Handel, 1984, Mississippi River (for documentary film Miss. River Mus.), Memphis; rec. performances include Beauty and the Beast (with Frank DiGiacomo), 1977, Ballet Class with Karen Hebert, 1982. Recipient New Orleans Music and Drama Found. award, 1982, 3d prize Rupert BBC Symphony Found., London, 1982, 4th prize Leopold Stokowski Conducting Competition, 1986. Mem. Am. Symphony Orch. League (youth orch. div. bd. dirs. 1980—). Office: Marin Symphony Orchestra Marin Center Aud 4340 Redwood Hwy San Rafael CA 94903-2104

SHELDON, GEORGE F., medical educator; b. Dec. 20, 1934; s. Richard Robert and Helen Irene (Zerzan) S.; m. Ruth Guy, Aug. 28, 1959; children: Anne Anderson, Elizabeth, Julia. BA, U. Kans., 1957, MD, 1961; post-grad., Mayo Clinic Grad. Sch., 1965. Intern Kans. U. Med. Ctr.; resident in surgery U. Calif., San Francisco, 1965-69; fellow in surg. biology Harvard Med. Sch. of Peter Bent Brigham Hosp., 1969-71; from asst. to full prof. U. Calif., 1971-82; Dr. Zack D. Owens Disting. prof. surgery, dept. chmn. U. N.C., Chapel Hill, 1984—; chmn. residency rev. com. accreditation Coun. for Grad. Med. Edn.; mem. Coun. Grad. Med. Edn. of Health and Human Svcs., 1986; mem. adminstrv. bd. Coun. Acad. Socs. Author: (with J.B. Runnell) Pictorial History of Kansas Medicine, 1961, (with Jill Ridky) Managing in Academnics, 1993; editor: (with J.B. Davis) Clinical Surgery, 1995. With USPHS, 1962-64. Recipient Surgeon's awrd for Svc. to Safety, Nat. Safety Coun., 1993, Douglass Stubbs award Nat. Med. Assn., 1991. Hon. fellow Royal Coll. Surgeons of Edinburgh, European Surg. Assn., Assn. of Surgeons of Gt. Britain and Ireland; mem. ACS (regent 1983-92), Am. Bd. Surgery (chmn. 1989-90), Nat. Bd. Med. Examiners (test com. 1981-84), Am. Assn. Surgery of Trauma (pres. 1984), Am. Surg. Assn. (sec. 1989-94, pres. 1994-95), Inst. Medicine (sec. com. on employer based health ins. and tech. assessment edn. bds.), Merit Rev. Bd. for Surgery Va. (chmn.). Office: U NC at Chapel Hill 136 Burnett-Womack Bldg 229 Chapel Hill NC 27599

SHELDON, GILBERT IGNATIUS, clergyman; b. Cleve., Sept. 20, 1926; s. Ignatius Peter and Stephanie Josephine (Olszewski) S. Student, John Carroll U.; M.Div., St. Theol. Sem., 1970; D.Min., St. Mary Sem. and Ohio Consortium of Sems., 1974. Ordained priest Roman Cath. Ch., 1953, bishop, 1976. Assoc. pastor Cleve. Diocese, 1953-64, diocesan dir. propagation of faith, 1964-74; pastor, Episcopal vicar Lorain County, Ohio, 1974-76; aux. bishop Cleve., 1976—; vicar for Summit County, 1979-80, So. Region, 1980-92; bishop Steubenville, 1992—; bd. dirs. Soc. Propagation of Faith, 1968-74, Diocesan Presbyteral Coun.; instr. theology St. John Coll.; clergy adv. bd. econ. edn. Akron U.; mem. Bishop's Com. Latin Am.; bd. trustees St. Mary Seminary, Diocesan Health Ins. Adv. Bd., Cath. Charities Corp.; former mem. bd. trustees Borromeo Coll.; mem. acad. bd. St, Mary Seminary; bd. dirs. Bishops' Com. Latin Am., adminstrv. com. Nat. Conf. Cath. Bishops/USCC, Nat. Adv. Coun., Bishops' Com. for Missions, Nat. Bd. Soc. for Propagation of Faith; bd. trustees Pontifical Coll. Josephinum. Mem. adv. bd. Internat. Chem. Workers; mem. econ. adv. bd. Akron U. Clergy; mem. Summit Mental Health Adv. Bd.; mem. Summit chpt. Nat. Cancer Soc.; mem. Goals for Greater Akron. Served with USAAF, 1944-45. Mem. Nat. Conf. Cath. Bishops (adminstrv. bd. 1985—), Am. Legion, Cath. War Vets., Knights of Columbus, Order of Alhambra., Rotary Club Akron and Steubenville. Club: K.C. Lodge: Rotary (Akron). Avocations: golf, astronomy, photography, history, travel. Office: 40 University Ave Akron OH 44308-1613*

SHELDON, HARVEY M., lawyer; b. Chgo., Dec. 7, 1942; s. Richard A. and Beatrice (Gutensky) S.; m. Gail Harrington; children: Paul (dec.), Timothy, Victoria. AB, Amherst Coll., 1965; JD, Harvard U., 1968. Bar: Ill. 1968, U.S. Ct. Appeals (7th and D.C. cirs.) 1978, U.S. Supreme Ct. 1980. Assoc. Schiff, Hardin & Waite, Chgo., 1968-70; asst. atty. gen. spl. prosecutions State of Ill., 1970-71, chief environ. control div., 1972-73; regional counsel U.S. EPA, 1973-74; ptnr. Nisen, Elliott & Meier, Chgo., 1974-85; ptnr. Coffield, Ungaretti, Harris & Slavin, Chgo., 1985-88; capital ptnr., head environ. law group McDermott, Will & Emery, Chgo., 1988—; pres. Harvey M. Sheldon P.C., 1993—; instr. environ. law and equity law John Marshall Law Sch., 1974-76; adj. prof. environ. law Loyola U., Chgo., 1983-90. Mem. editl. bd. Environ. Compliance and Litigation Strategy, 1995—. Active Mayor's Task Force on Air Quality, 1978-82; spl. counsel Ill. Dept. Mines & Minerals, 1977-86; bd. dirs. Nature of Ill. Found.; bd. advisors The Environ. Counselor, 1988—. Mem. ABA, Ill. Bar Assn., Fed. Bar Assn., Chgo. Bar Assn., Air Pollution Control Assn., Environ. Law Inst. (assoc.), Chicagoland C. of C., (dir., chmn. environ. control com.), Chem. Indsl. Coun. of Ill. (assoc.), Ill. State C. of C. (environ. com.), Univ. Club (Chgo.). Republican. Contbr. to environ. law handbooks. Office: McDermott Will & Emery 227 W Monroe St Chicago IL 60606-5016

SHELDON, INGRID KRISTINA, mayor; b. Ann Arbor, Mich., Jan. 30, 1945; d. Henry Ragnvald and Virginia Schmidt (Clark) Blom; m. Clifford George Sheldon, June 18, 1966; children: Amy Elizabeth, William David. BS, Eastern Mich. U., 1966; MA, U. Mich., 1970. Cert. tchr., Mich. Tchr. Livonia (Mich.) Pub. Schs., 1966-67, Ann Arbor Pub. Schs., 1967-68; bookkeeper Huron Valley Tennis Club, Ann Arbor, 1978—; acct. F.A. Black Co., Ann Arbor, 1984-88; coun. mem. Ward II City of Ann Arbor, 1988-92, mayor, 1993—; chair Housing Bd. Appeals, Ann Arbor, 1988-91; chair fin. and budget com. S.E. Mich. Coun. Govts. Mem. Huron Valley Child Guidance Clinic, Ann Arbor, 1984—, Ann Arbor Hist. Found., 1985—, Parks Adv. Commn., 1987-92, Ann Arbor Planning Commn., 1988-89; excellence com. Ann Arbor Pub. Schs. reorgn., 1985; treas. SOS Cmty. Crisis Ctr., Ypsilanti, Mich., 1987-93; precinct ward city vice-chair Ann Arbor Rep. City Com., 1978—. Recipient Community Svc. award Ann Arbor Jaycees, 1980; AAUW fellowship, 1982. Mem. Mich. Mcpl. League (del. 1989—), Ann Arbor Women's City Club (chair endowment com. 1989-90, fin. com. 1987-90, treas.), Rotary (dir. Ann Arbor chpt.), Kappa Delta Pi, Alpha Omnicron Pi. Republican. Methodist. Avocation: musical theatre. Home: 1416 Folkstone Ct Ann Arbor MI 48105-2848

SHELDON, MICHAEL RICHARD, judge, law educator; b. Schenectady, Apr. 6, 1949; s. Richard Charles and Evelyn Marie (Delisle) S.; m. Diane Mary Micklos, May 29, 1971; children: Graham Andrew, Conor Michael, Rowan Richard, Cameron Ashleigh. AB, Princeton U., 1971; JD, Yale U., 1974; postgrad. Georgetown U., 1974-76. Bar: D.C. 1975, U.S. Dist. Ct. D.C. 1975, U.S. Ct. Appeals (D.C. cir.) 1975, U.S. Dist. Ct. (no. dist.) N.Y. 1976, Conn. 1976, U.S. Dist. Ct. Conn. 1976, U.S. Supreme Ct. 1978. Legal intern Georgetown U. Law Ctr., Washington, 1974-76; prof. law, dir. legal clinic U. Conn. Sch. Law, Hartford, 1976-91, adj. prof. law, 1991—; judge Conn. Superior Ct., 1991—; vis. scholar Yale U., New Haven, Conn., 1985-86; vis. prof. U. Aix-Marseille, 1986; bd. dirs. Conn. Civil Liberties Union, Hartford, 1979-83; ednl. cons. Office of Chief Pub. Defender, Hartford, 1978-91. Contbg. author: Handbook on the Connecticut Law of Evidence, 1982. Bd. dirs. Legal Aid Soc. of Hartford County, 1978-91; mem. Am. Leadership Forum, Hartford, 1988; mem. Dem. Town Com., Canton, Conn., 1988-91; mem. bd. fin., Canton, 1989-91; pres. Canton-Kuntsevo Exchange Com., Inc., 1990-92. Recipient Outstanding Faculty Mem. award Student Bar Assn. U. Conn. Sch. Law, 1979, 82, Alva P. Loiselle award Conn. Moot Ct. Bd., 1989; sr. fellow Am. Leadership Forum, 1989—. Mem. Conn. Bar Assn. (exec. com. sect. on human rights and responsibilities, exec. com. sect. on criminal justice 1978—), Conn. Prison Assn. (bd. dirs. 1993—, v.p. 1994—).

SHELDON, NANCY WAY, environmental management consultant; b. Bryn Mawr, Pa., Nov. 10, 1944; d. John Harold and Elizabeth Semple (Hoff) W.; m. Robert Charles Sheldon, June 15, 1968. BA, Wellesley Coll., 1966; MA, Columbia U., 1968, M in Philosophy, 1972. Cert. hazardous materials mgr., environ. auditor, Calif.; registered environ. profl., environ. assessor, Calif. Mgmt. cons. ABT Assocs., Cambridge, Mass., 1969-70; mgmt. cons. Harbridge House, Inc., 1970-79, L.A., 1977-79, v.p., 1977-79; mgmt. cons., pres. Resource Assessment, Inc., 1979—. Author: Social and Economic Benefits of Public Transit, 1973. Contbr. articles to profl. jours. Columbia U. fellow, 1966-68; recipient Nat. Achievement award Nat. Assn. Women Geographers, 1966. Mem. DAR, Nat. Environ. Health Assn., Air and Waste Mgmt. Assn., Nat. Ground Water Assn., Water Pollution Control Fedn., Water Environment Fedn., Fla. Pollution Control Assn., Grad. Faculties Alumni Assn. Columbia U. Office: Resource Assessment Inc 1192 Kittiwake Cir Sanibel FL 33957-3606

SHELDON, RICHARD ROBERT, Russian language and literature educator; b. July 12, 1932; s. Richard Robert and Helen Irene (Zerzan) S.; m. Karen Ryden Sears, Feb. 8, 1964; children: Katherine Palmer, John Ryden, Robert Charles, Rebecca Ann. BA, U. Kans., 1954; JD, U. Mich., 1960, MA, 1962; PhD, Mich. U., 1966. Chmn. Russian dept. Grinnell (Iowa) Coll., 1965-66; asst. prof. Dartmouth Coll., Hanover, N.H., 1966-70, assoc. prof., 1970-75, prof. Russian lang. and lit., 1975—, chmn. dept., 1970-81, 90—, formerly dir. fgn. studies programs, chmn. com. on orgn. and policy, com. on admissions, com. on diversity, com. on off-campus study, dean of humanities, 1984-89, acad. dir. alumni coll., 1990; vis. prof. U. Calif. Berkeley, 1968, Stanford (Calif.) U., 1974; cons. Coun. Internat. Ednl. Exchange, N.Y.C., 1967-83, Dept. Edn., Washington, 1979—, Cornell U. Press, Ithaca, N.Y., 1970—; sr. assoc. mem. St. Antony's Coll., Oxford, Eng., 1983-84. Translator, editor: (books by V. Shklovsky) A Sentimental Journey, 1970, Zoo or Letters Not About Love, 1971, Third Factory, 1977; compiler: Viktor Shklovsky: An International Bibliography of Works by and about Him, 1977; co-editor: Soviet Society and Culture, 1988; author articles, book revs., other transls. Chmn. bd. Norwich (Vt.) Day Care Ctr., 1980-81. Pfc. U.S. Army, 1955-57. Summerfield scholar, 1952-54; Nat. Def. Act fellow Dept. Edn., Washington, 1961-64, Alfred P. Lloyd fellow U. Mich., Ann Arbor, 1964-65, Ctr. Advanced Study fellow U. Ill., Urbana, 1969-70, Am. Coun. Learned Socs. fellow, 1970; Internat. Rsch. and Exchanges Bd. study grantee, USSR, 1964-65. Mem. Am. Assn. Advancement of Slavic Studies, Am. Assn. Tchrs. Slavic and East European Langs., Coun. of Mem. Instns. (exec. com., adv. com. to pres.), Phi Beta Kappa, Phi Alpha Theta, Phi Delta Theta (pres. 1953), Delta Sigma Rho. Democrat. Episcopalian. Home: 86 S Main St Hanover NH 03755-2029 Office: Dartmouth Coll Russian Dept 44 N College Hanover NH 03755-1801

SHELDON, SIDNEY, author; b. Chgo., Feb. 11, 1917; s. Otto and Natalie (Marcus) S.; m. Jorja Curtright, Mar. 28, 1951 (dec. 1985); 1 dau., Mary; m. Alexandra Kostoff, 1989. Ed., Northwestern U. Author Morning, Noon & Night, 1995. Started as reader, Universal and 20th Century Fox Studios; author: novels The Naked Face, 1970, The Other Side of Midnight, 1975, A Stranger in the Mirror, 1976, Bloodline, 1977, Rage of Angels, 1980, Master of the Game, 1982, If Tomorrow Comes, 1985, Windmills of the Gods, 1987, The Sands of Time, 1988, Memories of Midnight, 1990, The Dooms Day Conspiracy, 1991, The Stars Shine Down, 1992, Nothing Lasts Forever, 1994; creator, writer, producer: Nancy, The Patty Duke Show, I Dream of Jeannie; created TV show Hart to Hart; author: plays including Roman Candle, Jackpot, Dream With Music, Alice in Arms, Redhead; writer: screenplays including Billy Rose's Jumbo, The Bachelor and the Bobby-Soxer, Easter Parade, Annie Get Your Gun; writer, dir.: screenplays including Dream Wife, Buster Keaton Story; writer: screenplays including Anything Goes, Never Too Young; recipient Acad. award for screenplay The Bachelor and the Bobby-Soxer 1947, Tony award for Redhead 1959, Writers Guild Am. Screen awards for Easter Parade, 1948, Annie Get Your Gun 1950, Edgar Allan Poe award Mystery Writers Am. for Naked Face, 1970. Served with USAAF, World War II. Address: care William Morrow & Co Press Rels 1350 Avenue Of The Americas New York NY 10019-4702

SHELDON, TED PRESTON, library director; b. Oak Park, Ill., July 5, 1942; s. Preston and Marjorie Sheldon; m. Beverly Stebel; children: Kathy, Mark. BA, Elmhurst (Ill.) Coll., 1964; MA, Ind. U., 1965, PhD, 1976; MLS, U. Ill., 1977. Asst. archivist U. Ill., Urbana, 1976-77; reference librarian U. Kans., Lawrence, 1977-79, head collection devel., 1979-81; assoc. dir. libraries SUNY, Binghamton, 1981-83; assoc. dir. libraries U. Mo., Kansas City, 1983-85, dir. libraries, 1985—; pres. Mo. Libr. Network Corp., 1991-95, bd. dirs. Author: Population Trends, 1976, Kans. Coll. Devel. Policy, 1978, History, Sources Social Science, 1985. Mem. ALA, Mus. Libr. Assn., Internat. Assn. Sound Archives, Assn. Recorded Sound Collection (mng. editor jour 1988-95, pres. 1996—). Office: U Mo Libraries 5100 Rockhill Rd Kansas City MO 64110-2446

SHELDON, TERRY EDWIN, lawyer, business consultant, advisor; b. Sacramento, June 22, 1945; s. Earl M. and Christine M. S.; m. Jan L. Winters, Aug. 26, 1966; children: Jeffrey, Tiffini, Melissa. BS magna cum laude, Abilene Christian U., 1967; JD, So. Meth. U., 1970. Bar: Calif. 1970. Assoc. Bronson, Bronson & McKinnon, San Francisco, 1970-74; gen. counsel, also dir. Consol. Capital Cos., Emeryville, Calif., 1974-83, exec. v.p., chief oper. officer, 1984-85, cons., advisor, 1986-87; pres., trustee Consol. Capital Spl. Trust, 1980-85; exec. v.p., trustee Consol. Capital Realty Investors, 1975-85, Consol. Capital Income Trust, 1978-85, Consol. Capital Income Opportunity Trust, 1983-85, Consol. Capital Income Opportunity Trust 2, 1985; chmn. Nat. Syndication Forum (a div. of RESSI), 1981-82; real estate securities specialist RESSI; v.p., prin. Alpha Venture Corp., Walnut Creek, Calif., 1987; bus. cons., 1988—. Chmn. bd. visitors adv. com. Coll. of Bus. Adminstrn. Abilene Christian U., 1990. Mem. ABA, Calif. Bar Assn., Nat. Assn. Securities Dealers (direct participation programs com., real estate com., standing adv. com. to bd. govs. 1980-83), Nat. Syndication Forum. Republican. Mem. Ch. of Christ.

SHELDON, THOMAS DONALD, academic administrator; b. Canastota, N.Y., July 15, 1920; s. Harry Ellsworth and Sadie Joyce (McNulty) S.; m. Helen Elizabeth Kyser, Aug. 29, 1941; children: Thomas, Paul, Edward, Patricia, Curtis, Roberta, Kevin. B.S., Syracuse U., 1942, M.S., 1949, Ed.D., 1958; grad., USAF Air Command & Staff AirWar Coll., 1972. Tchr. sci., coach Split Rock (N.Y.) High Sch., 1942-43; tchr. sci., coach, vice prin., prin. Minoa (N.Y.) High Sch., 1946-59; prin., asso. supt. Hempstead (N.Y.) High Sch., 1959-63; supt. schs. Hempstead Public Schs., 1963-68; supt. Balt. City Schs., 1968-71; dep. commr. N.Y. State Edn. Dept., Albany, 1971-77; pres. Utica Coll. of Syracuse U., 1977-82; interim pres. Mohawk Valley Community Coll., 1983; then interim pres. Onondaga Community Coll., 1984, now hon. pres. emeritus; prof. ednl. adminstrn. Syracuse U., N.Y., 1984-85; supt. Sewanhaka Central High Sch. Dist., 1985-86; interim pres. Munson-Williams-Proctor Inst., 1990-91; exec. dir. Syracuse U. Relations, N.Y.C., 1987-93; chmn. Edn. Profls. Internat., 1977—. Co-author and editor various N.Y. State Regents publs., 1971-76. Served with U.S. Army, 1943-46; served to col. USAF, 1961-62, Berlin; to brig. gen. Air N.G. 1955-76. First recipient Outstanding Grad. award Syracuse U. Sch. Edn., 1977; recipient Outstanding Md. Educator award Md. State Council PTA's, 1969; Disting. Am. Educator award Freedoms Found., 1966; Conspicuous Service medal N.Y. State Gov., 1976; N.Y.C. PSAL medal, 1978; named to Balt. Afro-Am. Honor Roll, 1970. Mem. N.Y. State PTA (hon. life), N.Y. State Coaches Assn. (pres. 1957), Am. Legion, Lions (hon. life), Phi Delta Kappa. Clubs: Lions (hon. life).

SHELDRICK, GEORGE MICHAEL, chemistry educator, crystallographer; b. Huddersfield, Great Britain, Nov. 17, 1942; s. George and Elizabeth S.; m. Katherine E. Herford, 1968; 4 children. Student, Huddersfield New Coll., Jesus Coll., Cambridge. Lectr. Cambridge U., Eng., 1966-78; prof. inorganic chemistry U. Göttingen, Germany, 1978—; with Inst. Anorg Chemie, Göttingen, Germany. Contbr. numerous articles to profl. jours. Recipient Meldola and Corday-Morgan medals Royal Soc. Chemistry, Leibniz prize Deutsche Forschungsgemeinschaft, A.L. Patterson award Am. Crystallographic Assn., 1993. Achievements include authorship of widely used computer programs for crystal structure determination. Office: Institut für Anorganische Chemie, Tammannstrasse 4, D-37077 Göttingen Germany

SHELESKI, STANLEY JOHN, accountant, comptroller, consultant; b. Harleigh, Pa., Feb. 20, 1931; s. Stanley Joseph and Agnes Rose (Yeshmond) S.; m. Sandra Lee Atkins. BS in Fin. Acctg., Rider Coll., 1958. Treas., mgr. United Savs. and Loan, Trenton, N.J., 1958-62; mgr. acctg. dept. Allstates Engring. Co., Trenton, 1962-85, asst. treas., asst. sec., comptroller, 1985—; v.p. fin. Allstates Design and Devel. Co., Trenton, 1988—; bd. dirs. Allstates Credit Union, Trenton, 1966—, treas. and gen. mgr. Allstates Credit Union, 1968—. Planner Jr. C. of C., Trenton, 1959. Served to sgt. USMC, 1952-54, Korea. Mem. Nat. Assn. Accts., Ewing Bus. Assn. (treas. 1959-62). Republican. Roman Catholic. Lodge: North Star Club (v.p. 1953-58). Avocation: raising airedale terriers.

SHELL, ART, professional football team coach; b. Charleston, S.C.; m. Janice Shell; 2 children. Student, Md. State Coll. Player L.A. Raiders, 1968-83, coach, 1983-89, head coach, 1989-94; offensive line coach Kansas City Chiefs, 1995—. Inducted into Pro Football Hall of Fame, 1989; recipient, Jackie Robinson Award for Athletics (Ebony mag.), 1990; named N.F.L. Coach of Yr., 1991. Office: Kansas City Chiefs One ArrowheadDr Kansas City MO 64129*

SHELL, BILLY JOE, retired university president; b. Ecorse, Mich., Sept. 2, 1925; s. Millard Wootson and Flossie Mae (Evans) S.; m. Edythe Lorraine Roach, Dec. 25, 1948; children: Deborah Shell Wilkinson, Brian Jeffrey. B.S., Mich. State U., 1947, M.S., 1949, Ph.D., 1955. Registered profl. engr., Ariz., Miss., Tex. Faculty U. Ariz., 1949-53, Mich. State U., 1955; v.p., chief engr. San Xavier Rock & Sand Co., Tucson, 1956-66; asso. dean engring. Miss. State U., 1966-70, acting v.p. for research, 1969-70; dean engring. Calif. State Poly. U., Pomona, 1970-73, acting v.p. acad. affairs,

1971-72; pres. Northrop U., Inglewood, Calif., 1973-89, ret., 1989, also trustee; pres. Calif. Engring. Found., 1982-85; vice chmn. Ariz. Bd. Tech. Registration, 1965-66; chmn. Calif. Council for Pvt. Postsecondary Ednl. Instns. Mem. Environ. Quality Control Com., Los Angeles County, 1971; chmn. bd. dirs. Tucson Boys Chorus, 1965-66. Served with USMCR, 1943-45. Recipient Engr. of Year award So. chpt. Ariz. Soc. Profl. Engrs., 1965, Outstanding Service award, 1966, Educator of Year award Region VII, Soc. Mfg. Engrs., 1973; Skill, Integrity and Responsibility award Asso. Gen. Contractors Calif., 1975. Fellow ASCE, Inst. for Advancement Engring.; mem. NSPE, AAAS, AAUP, Calif. Soc. Profl. Engrs. (Outstanding Svc. award 1973, Edn. Achievement award 1975), Nat. Coun. Engring. Examiners, Am. Water Works Assn., Water Pollution Control Fedn., Am. Soc. Engring. Edn., Inglewood C. of C. (pres. 1986-87, bd. dirs.), Sigma Xi, Chi Epsilon, Sigma Pi Alpha, Delta Theta Phi, Tau Beta Pi. Clubs: Mason, Rotarian. Home: 1182 Steele Dr Brea CA 92621-2233

SHELL, KARL, economics educator; b. Paterson, N.J., May 10, 1938; s. Joseph J. and Grace (De Young) S.; m. Susan Witherow Schulze, Jan. 27, 1962; children: Stephanie Shell Read, Jason Anthony. AB in Math. with honors, Princeton U., 1960; PhD in Econs., Stanford U., 1965; MA (hon.), U. Pa., 1971. Asst. and assoc. prof. econ. MIT, Cambridge, 1964-68; assoc. prof. U. Pa., Phila., 1968-70, prof., 1970-87; Robert Julius Thorne Prof. Econs. Cornell U., Ithaca, N.Y., 1986—; vis. prof. Stanford U., Calif., 1972-73, Autonomous U. Barcelona, 1989, Bocconi Inst. Mgmt., Milan, Italy, 1990, U. Calif., San Diego, 1992; adj. prof. U. Paris, 1979-81, 91; rschr. CEPREMAP, Paris, 1977-78; dir. Ctr. for Analytic Rsch. in Econs. and the Social Scis., Phila., 1975-86; Ctr. for Analytic Econs., Ithaca, 1986-92; pvt. practice econ., Ithaca, 1964—. Co-author: Economic Theory of Price Indices, 1972; editor: Optimal Economic Growth, 1967, Jour. Econ. Theory, 1968—; co-editor: Investment and Finance, 1972, Hamiltonians, 1976, Economic Complexity, 1989. Woodrow Wilson Found. fellow, 1960-61, 63-64; Ford Found. faculty rsch. fellow, 1967-68; Guggenheim fellow, 1977, Ctr. for Advanced Study in Behavioral Sci. fellow, 1984; Fulbright scholar, Barcelona, Spain, 1989. Fellow Econometric Soc.; mem. Am. Econ. Assn., European Econ. Assn., Econ. Study Soc., Soc. for Promotion of Econ. Theory, Elm Club (Princeton), Princeton Club (N.Y.C.), Statler Club (Ithaca), Sigma Xi. Republican. Episcopalian. Home: 917 Wyckoff Rd Ithaca NY 14850-2130 Office: Cornell U Dept Econs 402 Uris Hall Ithaca NY 14853-7601

SHELL, OWEN G., JR., banker; b. Greenville, S.C., June 19, 1936; s. Owen and Katherine S.; m. Mary Ruth Trammell, Aug. 9, 1980; children: Katherine Sloan, Mary Carroll, Robert Owen, James Walker. B.S., U. S.C., 1960; post grad., Stonier Grad. Sch. Banking, 1971; grad., Advanced Mgmt. Program, Harvard U., 1979. Tech. supt. Deering-Milliken, Inc., 1962-63; v.p. Citizens & So. Nat. Bank S.C., Columbia, 1968-71; sr. v.p. Citizens & So. Nat. Bank S.C., 1971-74, exec. v.p., 1974-79; pres., dir., chief exec. officer First Am. Nat. Bank, Nashville, 1979-86; vice chmn. bd., dir. First Am. Corp., 1979-86; chmn., pres., chief exec. officer Sovran Bank/Tenn., Nashville, 1986-91; pres. Nations Bank of Tenn. (formerly Sovran Bank), Nashville, 1992—; chmn. NationsBank of Ky.; dir. Nashville br. Fed. Res. Bank of Atlanta. Adv. bd. INROADS/Nashville; active Leadership Nashville, Tenn. Performing Arts Found., Mid. Tenn. coun. Boy Scouts Am., Vanderbilt U. Owen Grad. Sch. Mgmt.; trustee Met. Nashville Pub. Edn.; bd. dirs. Tenn. Bus. Roundtable, Tenn. Tomorrow. Mem. Assn. Res. City Bankers, Nashville Area C. of C., Kappa Alpha, Omicron Delta Kappa. Presbyterian. Clubs: Rotary, Cumberland, Belle Meade Country. Home: 4412 Chickering Ln Nashville TN 37215-4915

SHELL, ROBERT EDWARD LEE, photographer, writer; b. Roanoke, Va., Dec. 3, 1946; s. James Ralph and Mary (Terry) S.; m. Darlene Bridget. Student, Va. Poly. Inst. and State U., 1965-68, Elkins Inst., 1972, Nat. Camera Inst., 1973. Staff SMithsonian Inst., Washington, 1968-72; photographer Sta. WBRA-Pub. TV, Roanoke, 1972-74; owner Camera, Inc., Salem, Va., 1974-76; photographer, technician Gentry Studios, Blacksburg, Va., 1976-81; tech. editor Shutterbug Mag., Patch Communications, Radford, Va., 1984-91; editor Shutterbug Mag., Patch Communications, Titusville, Fla., 1991—, tech. editor, 1984-91, editor, 1991—; U.S. corr. Asahi Camera, Tokyo, 1986—, Color Foto, Munich, 1989—, Photo Answers, U.K., 1989—; pub. PIC Mag., U.K., 1994—. Author: Photography with Canon EOS System, 1990, Hasselblad Camera System Guide, 1991, Mamiya Camera System Guide, 1992, Photo Business Careers, 1992, Canon Compendium, 1994, Metz Flash System Handbook, 1994, Olympus IS System Handbook, 1994, Canon Rebel Handbook, 1994; tech. editor numerous publs; contbr. articles to profl. jours. Smithsonian Inst. grantee, Washington, 1968. Mem. Photo Mktg. Assn. Internat., German Photographers Soc., Megapress. Avocations: painting, drawing, classic automobiles. Home and Office: Bob Shell Photography 1601 Grove Ave Radford VA 24141-1624

SHELLEDY, JAMES EDWIN, III, editor; b. Spencer, Iowa, Nov. 11, 1942; s. James E. Jr. and Patricia L. (Cornwall) S.; m. Susan Emily Thomas, Mar. 7, 1986; 1 child, Ian Whittaker. BA, Gonzaga U., 1966. Reporter Spkesman-Rev., Spokane, Wash., 1963-66; tchr., coach Kootenai High Sch., Harrison, Idaho, 1967-71; reporter AP, Boise, Idaho, 1971-72; reporter, editor Lewiston (Idaho) Morning Tribune, 1973-80; editor, pub. Idahonian, Moscow, Idaho, 1981-91, Daily News, Pullman, Wash., 1981-91; editor The Salt Lake Tribune, Salt Lake City, 1991—; juror Pulitzer Prize Com., Columbia U., 1987-88; dir. Investigative Reporters and Editors, 1978-82; bd. dirs. New Directions for News, 1989—, Newspaper Agy. Corp., 1994—; mem. AP audit com., N.Y.C., 1982-91. Dir. Idaho Parks Found., Boise, 1976-78, Idaho-Washington Symphony, Pullman, Wash., 1986-89; commr. Idaho Lottery Commn., Boise, 1990-91; adv. bd. Utah YWCA, 1992—. Roman Catholic. Avocations: golf, sailing. Office: The Salt Lake Tribune 143 S Main St Salt Lake City UT 84111-1917

SHELLER, JOHN WILLARD, lawyer; b. L.A., Oct. 29, 1950; s. Willard Newton and Barbara (Tremaine) S.; m. Mary Elizabeth Hodor, Aug. 9, 1975; children: Matthew John, James Henry. BA, Stanford U., 1972; JD, Loyola U., L.A., 1975. Bar: Calif. 1975. Ptnr. Haight, Brown & Bonesteel, Santa Monica, Calif., 1975—; mem. Am. Bd. Trial Advs. Contbr. articles to profl. jours. Mem. Calif. State Bar Assn., Los Angeles County Bar Assn., So. Calif. Assn. Def. Counsel, Fedn. Ins. and Corp. Counsel, L.A. Country Club. Avocation: golf. Home: 15461 De Pauw St Pacific Palisades CA 90272-4370 Office: Haight Brown & Bonesteel PO Box 680 1620 26th St Santa Monica CA 90406-0680

SHELLEY, CAROLE AUGUSTA, actress; b. London, Aug. 16, 1939; came to U.S., 1964; d. Curtis and Deborah (Bloomstein) S.; m. Albert G. Woods, July 26, 1967 (dec.). Student, Arts Ednl. Sch., 1943-56, Prepatory Acad. Royal Acad. Dramatic Art, 1956-57; studies with Iris Warren. Studied with Iris Warren and Eileen Thorndike; Trustee Am. Shakespeare Theatre., 1974-82. Appeared in revues, films, West End comedies, including Mary Mary at the Globe Theatre; first appeared as Gwendolyn Pigeon in stage, film and TV versions of The Odd Couple, Absurd Person Singular; The Norman Conquests (L.A. Drama Critics Circle award 1975); appeared as Rosalind in As You Like It, as Regan in King Lear, as Neville in She Stoops to Conquer, Stratford, Ont., Can., 1972, as Mrs. Margery Pinchwife in The Country Wife, Am. Shakespeare Festival, Stratford, Conn., 1973, as Nora in A Doll's House, Goodman Theatre, Chgo., as Ann in Man and Superman, as Lena in Misalliance, Zita in Grand Hunt; appeared at Shaw Festival, 1977, 80, Stepping Out, 1986 (Tony nomination 1986), Broadway Bound, 1987-88; appeared in: The Play's the Thing, Bklyn. Acad. Music, 1978; played Eleanore in stage prodn. Lion in Winter, 1987; other stage appearances include Nat. Co. of The Royal Family (L.A. Drama Citics Circle award 1977), The Elephant Man (Outer Critics Circle award 1978-79 season, Tony award for best actress 1978-79 season), What the Butler Saw, 1989; appeared inaugural season, Robin Phillips Grand Theatre Co., London, Ont., Can., 1983-84, Broadway and Nat. Co. of Noises Off, 1985, Waltz of the Toreadors, 1986, Oh Coward, 1986-87 ; appeared as Kate in Broadway Bound by Neil Simon The Nat. Co. and L.A. Premiere, 1987-88; played Lettice in Lettice and Lovage Globe Theatre, London, 1989-90, Frosine in The Miser, 1990, Cabaret Verboten, 1991, The Destiny of Me, 1992-93, Later Life, 1993 (Outer Critics nominee), Richard II, 1994, London Suite (Neil Simon) 1995, N.Y. Shakespeare Festival, Show Boat, 1995; films include: The Boston Strangler, The Odd Couple, The Super, 1990, Devlin, 1991, Quiz Show, 1993, The Road to Wellville, 1993; created: voice characters in Walt Disney films Robin Hood, The Aristocats. Recipient Obie Award for Twelve Dreams N.Y. Shakespeare Festival, 1982. Jewish. Office: care Duva-Flack Assocs Inc 200 W 57th St New York NY 10019-3211

SHELLEY, EDWARD HERMAN, JR., retired insurance company executive; b. Harrisburg, Pa., Oct. 14, 1919; s. E. Herman and Elizabeth (Workman) S.; m. Dorothy M. Treier, Feb. 14, 1942; children: David, Martha. A.B., Franklin and Marshall Coll., Lancaster, Pa., 1941. Office mgr. Nationwide Ins. Co., Harrisburg, Pa., 1941-50; head systems dept. Nationwide Ins. Co., Columbus, 1950-57, Agway, Ithaca, N.Y., 1958-60; v.p. data processing State Farm Ins. Co., Bloomington, Ill., 1960-83; bd. dirs. Bank One, Bloomington/Normal. Bd. dirs. Project Oz, Bloomington, 1980; with Vol. Income Tax Assistance, 1987-95. Served with AUS, 1944-46. Mem. Nat. Office Mgmt. Assn., Assn. for Computing Machinery, Life Office Mgmt. Assn. (mem. property and casualty systems com. 1981-83), Phi Sigma Kappa, Pi Gamma Mu. Republican. Lutheran. Home: RR 2 Box 168 Lexington IL 61753-9548 Office: State Farm Ins Cos 1 State Farm Plz Bloomington IL 61701-4300

SHELLEY, ELBERT VERNELL, professional football player; b. Tyronza, Ark., Dec. 24, 1964. Student, Ark. State U. Cornerback Atlanta Falcons, 1987—. Named to Pro Bowl Team, 1992, 93. Office: Atlanta Falcons 2745 Burnette Rd Suwanee GA 30174-2127

SHELLEY, HERBERT CARL, lawyer; b. Stamford, Tex., Jan. 28, 1947; s. Carl B. and Lourena A. (Whitley) S.; m. Jerilyn S. Ray, Aug. 9, 1969; children: Megan, Caitlyn, Daniel. BA, Columbia Coll., 1969; JD, Vanderbilt U., 1972; LLM Internat. and Comparative Law magna cum laude, Vrije Universiteit Brussel, Brussels, Belgium, 1973. Bar: D.C. 1973, Md. 1985, U.S. Ct. Appeals (fed. cir.) 1981, U.S. Ct. Internat. Trade 1982, U.S. Supreme Ct. 1987. Atty./adv. U.S. Tariff Commn., Washington, 1973-74; Internat. trade specialist, asst. Office dir. Office Tariff Affairs U.S. Dept. Treasury, Washington, 1974-76; internat. trade negotiator Office Spl. Trade Reps., Geneva, Switzerland, 1976-79; ptnr. Plaia & Schaumberg, Washington, 1979-86, Howrey & Simon, Washington, 1986—. Mem. ABA, D.C. Bar Assn., Md. Bar Assn., City Club Washington. Avocations: skiing, golf, cooking, travel. Office: Howrey & Simon 1299 Pennsylvania Ave NW Washington DC 20004-2400

SHELLEY, JAMES LAMAR, lawyer; b. Joseph City, Ariz., Dec. 8, 1915; s. Thomas Heber and Eva (Tanner) S.; m. Virginia Rand, Nov. 21, 1942; children: Carol (Mrs. Danny Parker Boyle), Marlene (Mrs. J. Robert Tolman), Jana (Mrs. Gunn B. McKay), Mary (Mrs. Mark Hutchings), Gerald LaMar, James Rand. B.A., Ariz. State Coll., 1936; J.D., U. Ariz., 1949. Bar: Ariz. 1948. Asst. city atty. City of Mesa, Ariz., 1948-49, city atty., 1950-87; ptnr. Johnson & Shelley, Mesa, 1951-88; gen. counsel League Ariz. Cities and Towns, Phoenix, 1959—; ptnr. Shelley & Bethea, Mesa, 1988—. Adv. bd. Theodore Roosevelt coun. Boy Scouts Am., 1962-92, adv. coun. Grand Canyon coun., 1993—, Mesa Dist. chmn., 1967-68; v.p. Mesa United Fund, 1967-69, pres., 1970; pres. bd. mgmt. Mesa br. YMCA; pres. Mesa Christmas Basket Assn., Mesa Fine Arts Assn., 1978-80; mem. religious adv. com. Ariz. Dept. Corrections, 1981. Lt. USNR, 1942-45. Named Mesa Man of Year, 1965. Mem. Ariz. Acad., Nat. Inst. Mcpl. Law Officers (past pres.). Republican. Mem. Ch. of Jesus Christ of Latter-day Saints (former regional rep.). Clubs: Exchange (past pres.), Southside Dinner (past pres. Mesa). Home: 550 N Emerson St Mesa AZ 85201-5516 Office: Shelley & Bethea 1201 S Alma School Rd Ste 3400 Mesa AZ 85210-2010

SHELLEY, JOHN FLETCHER, lawyer; b. Des Moines, Oct. 7, 1943; s. John DeWane and Catherine Hilma (Fletcher) S.; m. Karan Antoinette Early, Aug. 27, 1966 (div. 1994); children: Jack, Joseph; m. Patricia Burgess, Dec. 28, 1994. AB, Harvard U., 1965; LLB., Harvard U., 1968. Bar: Ohio 1968. Assoc., Squire, Sanders & Dempsey, Cleve., 1968, 72-78, ptnr., 1978—; practice area coord. Estates, Trusts, and Employee Benefits Practice Area, 1984-94. V.p., trustee Child Guidance Ctr. of Cleve., 1980-86; trustee Univ. Circle, Inc., 1988—. Trustee Cleve. Inst. Music, 1987—. With USNR, 1968-71. Mem. ABA, Bar Assn. Greater Cleve. (mem. coun. estate planning and probate sect.), Ohio State Bar Assn., Bar Assn., Union Club, Club at Soc. Ctr. Democrat. Home: 3283 Norwood Rd Cleveland OH 44122-3439 Office: Squire Sanders & Dempsey 4900 Society Ctr 127 Public Sq Cleveland OH 44114-1216

SHELLEY, WALTER BROWN, physician, educator; b. St. Paul, Feb. 6, 1917; s. Patrick K. and Alfaretta (Brown) S.; m. Marguerite H. Weber, 1942 (dec.); children: Peter B., Anne E. Kiselewich, Barbara A. (dec.); m. E. Dorinda Loeffel, 1980; children: Thomas R., Katharine D., William L. B.S., U. Minn., 1940, Ph.D., 1941, M.D., 1943; M.A. honoris causa, U. Pa., 1971; M.D. honoris causa, U. Uppsala, Sweden, 1977. Diplomate: Am. Bd. Dermatology (pres. 1968-69, dir. 1960-69). Instr. physiology U. Pa., Phila., 1946-47; asst. instr. dermatology and syphilology U. Pa., 1947-49, asst. prof. dermatology, 1950-53, assoc. prof., 1953-57, prof., 1957-80, chmn. dept., 1965-80; prof. dermatology U. Ill. Peoria Sch. Medicine, 1980-83; prof. medicine (dermatology) Med. Coll. Ohio, 1983—; instr. dermatology Dartmouth Coll., 1949-50; Regional cons. dermatology VA, 1955-59; mem. com. on cutaneous system NRC, 1955-59, Commn. Cutaneous Diseases, Armed Forces Epidemiological Bd., 1958-61, dep. dir., 1959-61; cons. dermatology Surgeon Gen. USAF, 1958-61, U.S. Army, 1958-61; mem. NRC, 1961-64. Author: (with Crissey) Classics in Clinical Dermatology, 1953, (with Pillsbury, Kligman) Dermatology, 1956, Cutaneous Medicine, 1961, (with Hurley) The Human Apocrine Sweat Gland in Health and Disease, 1960, (with Botelho and Brooks) The Endocrine Glands, 1969, Consultations in Dermatology with Walter B. Shelley, 1972, Consultations II, 1974 (with Shelley) Advanced Dermatologic Therapy, 1987, Advanced Dermatologic Diagnosis, 1992, A Century of International Dermatological Congresses, 1992; mem. editorial bd.: Jour. Investigative Dermatology, 1961-64, Archives of Dermatology, 1961-62, Skin and Allergy News, 1970-93, Excerpta Medica Dermatologica, 1960—, Cutis, 1972—, Jour. Geriatric Dermatol, 1993; assoc. editor: Jour. Cutaneous Pathology, 1972-81; editorial cons.: Medcom, 1972—. Served as capt. M.C. AUS, 1944-46. Recipient Spl. award Soc. Cosmetic Chemists, 1955, Hellerstrom medal, 1971, Am. Med. Writers Assn. Best Med. Book award, 1973, Dohi medal, 1981, Rothman medal Soc. for Investigative Dermatology, 1987, Rose Hirschler award, 1990. Master A.C.P.; fellow Assn. Am. Physicians, St. John's Dermatol. Soc. London (hon.); mem. AMA (chmn. residency rev. com. for dermatology 1963-67, chmn. sect. dermatology 1969-71), Assn. Profs. Dermatology (pres. 1972-73), Pacific Dermatol. Assn. (hon.), Am. Dermatol. Assn. (hon., dir., pres. 1975-76), Soc. Investigative Dermatology (hon. pres. 1961-62), Am., Phila. physiol. socs., Brit. Dermatol. Soc. (hon.), Phila. Dermatol. Soc. (pres. 1960-61), Mich. Dermatol. Soc., Ohio Dermatol. Soc. (hon.), Am. Acad. Dermatology (Gold medal 1992, hon. pres. 1971-72), Pa. Acad. Dermatology (pres. 1972-73), Am. Soc. for Dermatologic Surgery, North Am. Clin. Dermatol. Soc. (hon.), Noah Worcester Dermatological Soc., Royal Soc. Medicine; corr. mem. Nederlandse Vereniging Van Dermatologen, Israeli Dermatol. Assn., Finnish Soc. Dermatology, Swedish Dermatol. Soc., French Dermatologic Soc.; fgn. hon. mem. Danish Dermatol. Assn., Japanese Dermatol. Assn., Dermatol. Soc. S.Africa. Home: 21171 W River Rd Grand Rapids OH 43522-9703 Office: Med Coll Ohio PO Box 10008 3000 Arlington Ave Toledo OH 43614-2595

SHELLHASE, LESLIE JOHN, social work educator; b. Hardy, Nebr., Jan. 12, 1924; s. John Clayton and Sanna Belle (Muth) S.; m. Fern Eleanor Kleckner, June 8, 1948; children: Jeremy Clayton, Joel Kleckner. Student, U. Calif.-Berkeley, 1943-44; A.B., Midland Coll., 1947; M.S.W., U. Nebr., 1950; D.Social Work, Catholic U. Am., 1961. Lic. social worker, Ala. Parole supr. Child Welfare, Omaha, 1948-49; psychiat. social work intern Letterman Gen. Hosp. San Francisco, 1950-51; commd. 2d lt. U.S. Army, 1949, advanced through grades to lt. col., 1966; chief social worker (6th Inf. Div.), Ft. Ord, Calif., 1952-55; chief med. social worker Walter Reed Gen. Hosp. Washington, 1955-57, research investigator Walter Reed Inst. Research, 1957-63; head social work faculty Med. Field Service Sch., Ft. Sam Houston, Tex., 1963-66; chief sociologist U.S. Army, Washington, 1966-68; prof. Sch. Social Work, U. Ala., Tuscaloosa, 1968-89; prof. emeritus Sch. Social Work, U. Ala., 1989—; pvt. practice social work, 1968—; dir. tour, interpreter to surgeon gen. Belgium Armed Forces, 1961; lectr. Cath. U. Am., 1961-63, 66-68; rsch. dir. Jewish Social Svc. Fedn., San Antonio, 1963-66; rep. to internat. social and behavioral scis. cmty. Dept. Army, 1966-68; cons. Family Svc. Assn. Am., 1969—, Ala. Mental Health Dept., 1989—; mem. expert group on social welfare UN, 1975—; mem. Internat. Rels. Forum, 1981—; rsch. fellow U. Exeter, 1981-82; mem. social work tng. com. NIMH, 1983—; mem. Interfaith Com. on AIDS, 1993; newscaster Radio Reading Svc., Ala. Pub. Broadcast, 1989—; condr. workshops; cons. on group psychotherapy Ala. Dept. Mental Health, 1989—. Author: The Group Life of the Schizophrenic Patient, 1961, Bibliography of Army Social Work, 1962; book rev. editor Social Perspectives, 1979-83; editorial reviewer Social Work Papers, mem. editorial bd., 1986—; editorial reviewer Mac Millan Press, 1990—, Families in Society, 1992—, Oxford U. Press, 1994; internat. editorial bd. Internat. Abstracts Social Sci.; contbr. articles on social and behavioral sci. to nat. and internat. profl. jours., chpts. to books. Bd. dirs. Crisis Intervention Ctr.; bd. dirs., chmn. Soc. for Crippled Children and Adults. Served with inf. U.S. Army, 1942-46. Decorated Legion of Merit, Bronze Star, Purple Heart; recipient letter of commendation from Pres. of U.S., 1968, letter of commendation from Surgeon Gen., 1961. Fellow Am. Sociol. Assn.; mem. NASW (mem. nat. task force on ethics 1976-79, chmn. 1976-77, dir. 1963-66), Coun. social Work Edn., Acad. Cert. Social Workers, Brit. Sociol. Assn., Brit. Assn. Social Workers, Ret. Officers Assn., So. Sociol. Soc. Democrat. Home: 3823 Somerset Pl Tuscaloosa AL 35405-5436 Office: PO Box 870314 Tuscaloosa AL 35487-0314

SHELLHORN, RUTH PATRICIA, landscape architect; b. L.A., Sept. 21, 1909; d. Arthur Lemon and Lodema (Gould) S.; m. Harry Alexander Kueser, Nov. 21, 1940. Student dept. landscape architecture, Oreg. State Coll., 1927-30; grad. landscape architecture program, Cornell U. Coll. Architecture, 1933. Pvt. practice landscape architecture, various cities Calif., 1933—; exec. cons. landscape architect Bullocks Stores, Calif., 1945-78, Fashion Sqs. Shopping Ctrs., Calif., 1958-78, Marlborough Sch., L.A., 1968—, El Camino Coll., Torrance, Calif., 1970-78, Harvard Sch., North Hollywood, Calif., 1974-90; cons. landscape architect, site planner Disneyland, Anaheim, Calif., 1955, U. Calif., Riverside Campus, 1956-64, numerous others, also numerous gardens and estates; landscape architect Torrance (Calif.) City Goals Com., 1969-70; cons. landscape architect City of Rolling Hills (Calif.) Community Assn., 1973-93. Contbr. articles to garden and profl. publs.; subject of Oct. 1967 issue Landscape Design & Constrn. mag. Named Woman of Year, Los Angeles Times, 1955, Woman of Year, South Pasadena-San Marino (Calif.) Bus. Profl. Women, 1955; recipient Charles Goodwin Sands medal, 1930-33, Landscape Architecture award of merit Calif. State Garden Clubs, 1984, 86, Horticulturist of the Yr. award So. Calif. Hort. Inst., numerous nat., state, local awards for excellence. Fellow Am. Soc. Landscape Architects (past pres. So. Calif. chpt.), Phi Kappa Phi, Kappa Kappa Gamma (Alumni Achievement award 1960). Projects subject of Oct. 1967 issue of Landscape Design and Constrn. Mag. Home and Office: 362 Camino De Las Colinas Redondo Beach CA 90277-6435 *Integrity, honesty, dependability, sincerity, dedication, and a willingness to give more than is expected in service, are the basic principles which have guided my career. Never losing sight of the importance of the individual, I have tried to create total environments of harmony and beauty to which each individual can relate in a very personal and pleasureable way, and for a little while, can find a calm oasis in a busy and demanding world.*

SHELLMAN, EDDIE J., ballet dancer, teacher, choreographer; b. Tampa, Fla., May 10, 1956; s. Eddie J. and Elizabeth (Coleman-Smith) Lucas. Ed., High Sch. Performing Arts, N.Y.C. Dancer Pepsie Bethel Jazz Co., N.Y.C., 1972-73; dancer U.S. Terpsichore, N.Y. Sch. Ballet, N.Y.C., 1974-75; prin. dancer Dance Theatre Harlem, N.Y.C., 1975—, also choreographer, bd. dirs.; guest artist The Royal Ballet, London, Iowa U. Gala, Ballet New Eng. Performed in Internat. Ballet Festival of Havana, 1986, 66th Acad. Awards. Recipient Key to City, Birmingham, Ala., 1981, Resolution, City of Balt., 1981. Club: 4 Sevens (N.Y.C.). Avocations: Photography; cars; swimming; refinishing wood furniture. Office: Dance Theatre Harlem 466 W 152nd St New York NY 10031-1814

SHELLMAN-LUCAS, ELIZABETH C., special education educator, researcher; b. Thomas County, Ga., Feb. 5, 1937; d. Herbert and Juanita (Coleman) Smith; m. John Lee Lucas, Jr. (div.); 1 child, Sandie Juanita Lucas Boyce; m. Eddie Joseph Shellman; 1 child, Eddie Joseph Shellman, Jr. MS in Edn., CUNY, 1990. Pvt. practice cosmetologist N.Y.C., 1959—; tchr. N.Y.C. Bd. of Edn. High Sch. Dist., 1984—. Vol. various community orgns.; citizen amb. del. People to People Internat., 1994. Mem. Coun. for Exceptional Children. Avocations: reading, music, dancing, jogging, languages.

SHELLOW, ROBERT, management service company executive, consultant; b. Milw., Sept. 22, 1929; s. Henry G. and Sadie (Myers) S.; m. Dorothea Laadt, Aug. 30, 1963; children: Sarah Katherine, Leslie Suzzane. BA, Reed Coll., 1951; MA, U. Mich., 1952, PhD, 1956. Commd. USPHS, Bethesda, Md., 1955, advanced through grades to commdr., Psychol. U.S. Bureau Prisons, 1955-58; asst. dep. dir. Nat. Adv. Commn. on Civil Disorders, 1967-68; dir. pilot programs D.C. Dept. Pub. Safety, 1968-70; prof. Carnegie-Mellon U., Pitts., 1970-76; pres. IMAR Corp., Washington, 1978—; cons. in field; expert witness psychol. deterence, security negligence cases, state and fed. cts., 1978—; mng. dir. Cross-Continent Assocs., Ltd., 1993—. Author: Issues in Law Enforcement, 1976; contbr. numerous articles to profl. jours. USPHS fellow U. Mich., 1953. Fellow Am. Psychol. Assn. ; mem. Nat. Bus. Aircraft Assn., Internat. Assn. Profl. Security Cons. (v.p. 1987-89, pres. 1989-91), Sigma Xi. Avocations: sailing; automobile and boat restoration. Office: IMAR Corp PO Box 34528 Bethesda MD 20827-0528

SHELLY, CHRISTINE DEBORAH, foreign service officer; b. Pontiac, Mich., May 1, 1951; d. Chester Price and Margaret Alice (Neafie) S.; m. Jose Manuel San-Bento Menezes, July 19, 1987; 1 stepchild, Ana Ferreira San-Bento Menezes. BA cum laude, Vanderbilt U., 1973; MA, Tufts U., 1974, MA in Diplomacy, 1975. Fgn. affairs analyst Intelligence and Rsch. Bur. Dept. State, Washington, 1975-77, desk officer Near Eastern Affairs, 1977-79; fin. attache Am. Embassy Dept. State, Cairo, 1979-81; asst. v.p. BankAmerica Internat., N.Y.C., 1981-82; spl. asst. Near Eastern Affairs Dept. State, Washington, 1982-83; econ., polit. officer Am. Embassy Dept. State, Lisbon, Portugal, 1983-87; dep. econ. advisor U.S. Mission to NATO, Brussels, 1987-90, dep. cabinet dir. Sec. Gen., 1990-93; dep. spokesman, dep. asst. sec. pub. affairs Dept. State, Washington, 1993-95; mem. Sr. Exec. Seminar U.S. State Dept., 1995-96. Avocation: equestrian. Office: Dept of State 2201 C St NW Washington DC 20520-0001

SHELNUTT, JOHN MARK, lawyer; b. Gainesville, Ga., Jan. 19, 1963; s. Dumas Broughton and Georgia Texana (Ruff) S.; m. Leila Christine Ricketson, June 24, 1989; children: John Mark Jr., Sarah. AA, Emory U., 1983, BA, 1985, JD, 1988. Bar: Ga. 1988, U.S. Dist. Ct. (mid. dist.) Ga. 1994. Asst. dist. atty. Dist. Atty.-Dougherty Jud. Cir., Albany, Ga., 1988, Dist. Atty.-Chattahoochee Jud. Cir., Columbus, Ga., 1989-94; ptnr. Berry and Shelnutt, Columbus, 1994—; faculty basic litigation course Prosecuting Atty.'s Coun., Forsyth, Ga., 1992—. Mem. ABA, State Bar Ga., Columbus Bar Assn., Ga. Trial Lawyers Assn., Ga. Assn. Criminal Def. Lawyers. Methodist. Home: 6451 S Branch Ct Columbus GA 31909 Office: Berry & Shelnutt 1024 2nd Ave Columbus GA 31901

SHELOKOV, ALEXIS PAUL, orthopedic spine surgeon; b. Washington, June 19, 1954; s. Alexis Ioann and Paula (Helbig) S.; m. Georgiana Gibson, Mar. 15, 1986. BA, U. Tex., 1978; MD, U. Tex. Southwestern Med. Sch., 1982. Intern internal medicine Parkland Hosp., Dallas, 1982-83; resident in surgery Harvard Deaconess Hosp., Boston, 1983-84; resident in orthopedics Tufts New Eng. Med. Ctr., Boston, 1984-87; chief resident orthopedics Jamaica Plains VA Hosp., Boston, 1987; fellow in pediat. spinal surgery Tex. Scottish Rite Hosp., Dallas, 1988; fellow Tex. Back Inst., Dallas, 1988-89, ptnr., co-dir. scoliosis ctr., 1989—, adv. bd., 1989—; fellow Orthop. Rsch. and Edn. Found., Paris, 1989; dir. TBI Inc., Dallas; bd. dirs. Intellipage Inc., Dallas. Bd. dirs. Dallas Easter Seals, 1992-93. Mem. N.Am. Spine Soc., Tex. Spine Soc., Beta Beta Beta. Home: 10010 Gaywood Rd Dallas TX 75229-6601

SHELTON, BESSIE ELIZABETH, school system administrator; b. Lynchburg, Va.; d. Robert and Bessie Ann (Plenty) Shelton; B.A. (scholar), W.Va. State Coll., 1958; student Northwestern U., 1953-55, Ind. U., 1956; M.S., SUNY, 1960; diploma Profl. Career Devel. Inst., 1993. Young adult libr. Bklyn. Pub. Libr., 1960-62; asst. head cen. ref. div. Queens Borough

Pub. Libr., Jamaica, N.Y., 1962-65; instructional media specialist Lynchburg (Va.) Bd. Edn., 1966-74; ednl. research specialist, 1974-77; ednl. media assoc. Allegany County Bd. Edn., Cumberland, Md., 1977—. Guest singer Sta. WLVA, 1966—, WLVA-TV Christmas concerts, 1966—;cons. music and market rsch. Mem. YWCA, Lynchburg, 1966—, Fine Arts Ctr., Lynchburg, 1966—; ednl. adv. bd., nat. research bd. Am. Biog. Inst.; mem. U.S. Congl. Adv. Bd., USN Nat. Adv. Coun.; amb. goodwill Lynchburg, Va., 1986. Named to Nat. Women's Hall of Fame. Mem. AAUW, NEA, NAFE, Md. Tchrs. Assn., Allegany County Tchrs. Assn., Va. Edn. Assn., State Dept. Sch. Librarians, Internat. Entertainers Guild, Music City Songwriters Assn., Vocal Artists Am., Internat. Clover Poetry Assn., Internat. Platform Assn., Nat. Assn. Women Deans, Adminstrs. and Counselors, Intercontinental Biog. Assn., World Mail Dealers Assn., N.Am. Mailers Exch., Am. Assn. Creative Artists, Am. Biog. Inst. Research Assn., Tri-State Community Concert Assn. Pi Delta Phi, Sigma Delta Pi. Contbr. poems to various publs. Democrat. Baptist. Clubs: National Travel, Gulf Travel. Home: PO Box 187 Cumberland MD 21501-0187

SHELTON, DAVID HOWARD, economics educator; b. Winona, Miss., Nov. 30, 1928; s. Tuttle M. and Kate (Moss) S.; m. Margaret Murff, Feb. 4, 1951; children: David Keith, Sarah Katherine, Susan Esther. B.A., Millsaps Coll., 1951; M.A., Ohio State U., 1952, Ph.D., 1958. Instr. Ohio State U., 1958; asst. prof. U. Del., 1958-63, assoc. prof., 1963-65; prof. U. N.C., Greensboro, 1965—, head dept. econs., bus. adminstrn., 1967-70, dean Sch. Bus. and Econs., 1970-83, head dept. econs., 1988-93; Cons. Joint Council on Econ. Edn., 1969-72, N.C. Dept. Pub. Instrn., 1970-73. Trustee N.C. Council on Econ. Edn., 1971—, chmn., 1971-75, pres., 1975-85. Served with USNR, 1946-48. M.D. Lincoln fellow, 1956-57; H.L. and Grace Doherty fellow, 1957. Mem. Beta Gamma Sigma, Omicron Delta Kappa, Kappa Sigma. Episcopalian. Home: 3609 Dogwood Dr Greensboro NC 27403-1010 Office: U NC Greensboro 462 Greensboro Greensboro NC 27412

SHELTON, KARL MASON, management consultant; b. Lincolnton, N.C., June 8, 1933; s. Karl and Annie (Grace) S.; m. Deloris Hundley, May 8, 1954; children: Melanie Dwain, Leslie Elaine, Kevin Karl. Grad., Am. Inst. Banking, 1960, Carolinas Sch. Banking, 1963, Stonier Grad. Sch. Banking, 1967. Vice pres. N.C. Nat. Bank, Charlotte, 1954-71; sr. v.p., treas. Seattle-First Nat. Bank, 1971-79; pres. Citizens Fidelity Corp., Louisville, 1979-82; exec. v.p. Southeast Bank, N.A., Miami, Fla., 1982-86; pres., chmn. bd. Shelton Mgmt. Services, Panama City, Fla., 1987-88, 89—; pres., chief operating officer Sec. Fed. Savs. Bank, Columbia, S.C., 1988-89. Contbg. editor: Bankers Handbook, 1978. Served with AUS, 1952-54. Methodist.

SHELTON, MURIEL MOORE, religious education administrator; b. Freeport, N.Y., May 29, 1921; d. Samuel Talbott and Agnes Jerolean (Trigg) Payne; m. Ernest William Moore, May 29, 1944 (dec. Apr. 2, 1978); children: Diana Moore Williams, David E. Moore, Cathi Moore Mount, Douglas L. Moore; m. Malcolm Wendell Shelton, Aug. 9, 1987. AB, Eastern Nazarene Coll., 1942; MusM, U. Tex., 1966. Cert. educator gen. and choral music, English, Tex., Tenn., Ark., Kans. Music dir. Coll. Ave. United Meth. Ch., Manhattan, Kans., 1969-71, Cen. United Meth. Ch., Lawrence, Kans., 1971-75, First United Meth. Ch., Horton, Kans., 1975-78; dir. Christian edn. St. Mark's United Meth. Ch., Bethany, Okla., 1980—; chmn. bd. dirs. Northwest Food Pantry, Oklahoma City, 1987-88; rep. St. mark's United Meth. Ch. Labor Link Ctr., 1989—; lectr. in field. Contbr. articles to quar. mags.; author: Song of Joy, 1985, Promises of Good, 1989, Healing in His Wings, 1992. Mem. Christian Educators' Fellowship. Home: 6404 NW 35th St Bethany OK 73008-4136 Office: St Mark's United Meth Ch 8140 NW 36th St Bethany OK 73008-3526 *A life for God is eternally significant.*

SHELTON, PHILIP ANDERSON, criminal investigator, writer; b. Coeur d'Alene, Idaho, July 3, 1938; s. Philip Anderson and Mildred Evelyn (Wendt) S.; m. Sharon Lee Hopkins, Feb. 15, 1973 (div. Sept. 1985); 1 child, Thane Kevit. Student, Chico (Calif.) State Coll., 1957, U. Calif., Davis, 1960-62, Sacramento State U., 1973-75; BS in Criminology, U. Ala., 1996; postgrad. in Writing, Norwich U., 1996—. Cert. criminal investigator, Calif.; lic. pvt. investigator, Calif. Fraud investigator Philip A. Shelton Profl. Investigations, Sacramento, 1960-64, owner, operator, 1964-77; chief investigator Yolo County Conflict Def., Woodland, Calif., 1966-69; investigator Fed. Pub. Defender, Sacramento, 1975; chief investigator Fed. Pub. Defender, Fresno, 1977-78, Santa Barbara (Calif.) County Pub. Defender, 1978—. Author short stories and novella. Bd. dirs. Santa Barbara Mus. of Art, 1980-84; founding mem. G.A.T.E. Sch. Program, Santa Barbara, 1980-85; mem., group leader City/County Disaster Svcs., Santa Barbara, 1980-89. Recipient Honor for Bravery World Secret Svc. Orgn., 1960; grantee Calif. Cattlemen's Assn., 1956, Fed. Defender Program, Washington, 1978. Mem. World Assn. Detectives, Assn. Brit. Detectives, Coun. Internat. Investigators, Calif. Assn. Lic. Investigators (co-founder 1966, Svc. award 1969), Inst. Personal Injury Investigators (dir., co-founder 1966—), Def. Investigators Assn. Avocations: printing, designing, amateur radio, lecturing, acting. Office: Santa Barbara County Pub Defender 1100 Anacapa 3d Fl Santa Barbara CA 93101

SHELTON, RICHARD FOTTRELL, investment executive; b. Cebu, Philippines, May 23, 1929; s. Edward Mason and Emily (Fottrell) S.; m. Nan Dodson, 1955 (div. 1962); children: Leslie, Anita; m. Patricia Brooks, 1964 (dec. 1968); 1 child, Celia; m. Sydney Walton, 1973 (dec. 1994); stepchildren: Suzanne, Peter, Jenny. A.B., Stanford U., 1950. Account exec. Merrill Lynch, Pierce Fenner & Smith, 1954-63; br. mgr., then regional partner Paine, Webber, Jackson & Curtis, Inc., San Francisco, 1963-71; sr. v.p., div. dir. Paine, Webber, Jackson & Curtis, Inc., 1972-82, also dir.; gen. ptnr., then sr. v.p., mng. dir. Hambrecht & Quist, 1982-85; pres. Calif. Investment Trust Fund Group, San Francisco, 1985—. Pres. bd. trustees Children's Cancer Research Inst., San Francisco, 1980-82, Katherine Burke Sch., 1976-78; pres. The Guardsmen, 1964-65; treas. bd. trustees Santa Catalina Sch., 1982-85; commr. Asian Art Mus., San Francisco, 1987—, Asian Art Mus. Found., 1987—. Served to 1st lt. USAF, 1950-54. Decorated Air medal with 2 oak leaf clusters. Mem. Burlingame Country Club (Hillsborough, Calif.), Pacific-Union Club, Bohemian Club, Kappa Sigma. Republican. Episcopalian. Office: 44 Montgomery St Ste 2100 San Francisco CA 94104-4708

SHELTON, RICKY VAN, country music singer, songwriter; b. Danville, Va., Jan. 12, 1952; s. Jenks Dewitt and Julia Eloise (Simpson) S.; m. Bettye Witt, Aug. 4, 1986. Grad. high sch., Gretna, Va., 1970. Various pipefitting and constrn. jobs various cos., 1970-86; car salesman Alta Vista (Va.) Ford Co., 1972-74; plumber J.H. Cothran Plumbing Co., Alta Vista, Va., 1980-84; country music singer Columbia Records, Nashville, 1985—. Albums: Wild-Eyed Dream, 1987, Loving Proof, 1988, Ricky Van Shelton Sings Christmas, 1989, RVS III, 1990, Backroads, 1991, Don't Overlook Salvation, 1992, Greatest Hits Plus, 1992, A Bridge I Didn't Burn, 1993, Love and Honor, 1994. Recipient TNN/Music City News Awards Entertainer of the Yr., 1990, 91. Mem. Country Music Assn. (Horizon award 1988, Male Vocalist of Yr. 1989), Acad. County Music. Recipient Male Vocalist of Yr. award, Album of Yr. award Nashville Network Viewer's Choice, 1989. Avocations: farming, fishing, raising beefalo. Office: care Michael Campbell & Assocs 40 Music Sq E Nashville TN 37203-4323

SHELTON, ROBERT NEAL, physics educator, researcher; b. Phoenix, Oct. 5, 1948; s. Clark B. and Grace M. (McLaughlin) S.; m. Adrian Ann Millar, Aug. 30, 1969; children: Christian, Cameron, Stephanie. BS, Stanford U., 1970; MS, U. Calif., San Diego, 1973, PhD, 1975. Postdoctoral researcher U. Calif.-San Diego, La Jolla, 1975-76, asst. rsch. physicist, 1976-78; asst. prof. Iowa State U., Ames, 1978-81, assoc. prof., 1981-84, prof. physics, 1984-87; prof. physics, chmn. dept. U. Calif.-Davis, 1987-90, vice chancellor for rsch., 1990—. Contbr. over 200 articles to profl. jours. Fellow Am. Phys. Soc.; mem. Sigma Xi. Office: U Calif Dept Physics Davis CA 95616

SHELTON, ROBERT WARREN, marketing executive; b. Albuquerque, Apr. 26, 1943; s. Eugene and Rusty M. (Jentsch) S.; children: Elise Straus, Samantha; m. Ginger Lee Rapp, Feb. 14, 1984. BBA in Mktg., St. Mary's U., San Antonio, 1969; postgrad., Ga. State U., 1972-73, postgrad. in fin. and internat. bus., 1973. Field mgr. Ford Motor Co., Atlanta, 1969-78; dir. fleet ops. Rollins, Inc., Atlanta, 1978-81; v.p. sales and ops. Lease Plan U.S.A., Atlanta, 1981-85; v.p. mktg. Spencer Services, Inc., Roswell, Ga., 1985-87; v.p. FX-10 Corp., 1987-88; pres. Shiloh Capital Corp., 1989—; pres. Victory Svcs., Inc., 1998—, Shiloh Capital Corp., 1989, Interactive Telenet USA, Inc., 1994, The Phone Co., Inc., 1993. Mem. Lost Forest Civic Assn. (pres. 1980-81). Mem. Nat. Assn. Fleet Adminstrs., Am. Fleet and Leasing Assn., NRA. Republican. Christian. Avocations: golf, racquetball, tennis, shooting. Office: 1201 Peachtree St NE Atlanta GA 30361-3500

SHELTON, SLOANE, actress; b. Hahira, Ga., Mar. 14, 1934; d. Clarence Duffie and Ruth Evangeline (Davis) S. Student, Berea Coll., 1955; honors diploma, Royal Acad. Dramatic Art, London, 1959. Mem. O'Neill Found., Waterford, Conn., 1981-83, 85, 89, 91, 94; mem. theater panel N.Y. State Coun. on the Arts, 1979-81. Producer: (with Kevin Brownlow and Norma Millay Ellis) (documentary film) Millay at Steepletop, 1976; appearances in Broadway plays include: I Never Sang for My Father, Sticks & Bones, The Runner Stumbles, The Shadow Box, Orpheus Descending, Passione, Open Admissions; films include: All That Jazz, All the President's Men, Tiger Warsaw, Running on Empty, Jacknife, Lean on Me. Pres. Berilla Kerr Found., N.Y.C., 1993—. Mem. SAG, AFTRA, Actors Equity Assn., Actors Fund Am. Democrat.

SHELTON, STEPHANI, broadcast journalist, consultant; b. Boston; d. Phil and Babette (Belloff) Saltman; m. Frank Herold. BS, Boston U. Reporter, news broadcaster Sta. WPAT, Paterson, N.J., 1972-73; corr. CBS News, N.Y.C., 1973-84; news corr. WWOR-TV, N.Y.C., 1984-88; corr., anchor Fin. News Network, N.Y.C., 1989-91; ind. broadcast journalist, producer, cons., 1991—; freelance reporter Sta. WPIX-TV, 1991-95, Sta. WNBC-TV, 1993—; freelance radio documentary writer Westinghouse Group W Broadcasting, N.Y.C., 1970-73. Recipient Peabody award, 1972, N.J. Best Spot News award AP, 1987, 88, N.J. Working Press award, 1992, 93, 94; Emmy nominee, 1994-95. Mem. Radio and TV Working Press Assn. (v.p. 1985—), Soc. Profl. Journalists, Radio and TV News Dirs. Assn., N.Y.C. Press Club. *Guiding principles: a questioning mind, a refusal to take no for an answer and the memory of 28 marathons. Whatever happens the important thing is to survive.*

SHELTON, WAYNE VERNON, professional services and systems integration company executive; b. Mpls., Nov. 27, 1932; s. Olen George and Evelyn Ruth (Karpen) S.; m. Mary Kay Schwappach, Dec. 29, 1956; children: William David, Susan Evelyn. BS, U. Minn., 1954. Instr. U. Minn., Mpls., 1954-56; tchr. Mpls. Pub. Schs., 1956-57; mathematician Rand Corp., Santa Monica, Calif., 1957-62; sr. assoc. Planning Research Corp., Los Angeles, 1963-72; v.p. Planning Research Corp., McLean, Va., 1972-83, sr. v.p., 1983-85, pres., chief operating officer, 1985-87, chmn., pres. and chief exec. officer, 1987-90; v.p. Emhart Corp., Farmington, Conn., 1987-88; exec. v.p., pres. Emhart Info. and Electronics Systems, Towson, Md., 1988-90; v.p., sr. v.p. Hughes Aircraft Co., 1990—; pres. Hughes Info. Systems, Reston, Va., 1994—; instr. data processing Santa Monica (Calif.) Coll., 1960-62; pres. Assn. Ind. Software Cos., McLean, 1970-71; bd. dirs. Profl. Svcs. Coun., Washington, 1972—, vice chmn., 1993-95; bd. dirs. Security Affairs Support Assn., Annapolis, Md., 1983-85, chmn., 1983-84. Bd. dirs. No. Va. Tech. Coun., 1992—. Mem. Armed Forces Comm. and Electronics Assn. (bd. dirs. 1987—, internat. v.p. 1994—), Navy League (life), Assn. U.S. Army, Air Force Assn., Nat. Security Indsl. Assn., Am. Electronics Assn. (bd. dirs. 1988-89, 93—). Republican. Avocations: gardening, personal investments, personal computers, running. Home: 8578 Brickyard Rd Rockville MD 20854-4833

SHELTON, WILLIAM CHASTAIN, retired government statistician, investor; b. Athens, Ga., May 5, 1916; s. William Arthur and Effie Clyde (Landrum) S.; m. Helen Higgins, Dec. 17, 1938; children: Stuart H., Terry Ann Shelton Coble, Jean R. Shelton Jaffray, Alvin C. AB, Princeton U., 1936; postgrad. U. Chgo., 1937-38. Economist, statistician Fed. Govt., Washington, 1936-48; chief stats. sect. USRO-Marshall Plan, Paris, France, 1948-55; mgr. bus. research Fla. Devel. Com., Tallahassee, 1956-60; asst. com. foreign labor Bur. Labor Stats., Washington, 1960-75; spl. asst. statis. policy div. Office Mgmt. and Budget, 1975-77. Author: (with Joseph W. Duncan) Revolution in U.S. Government Statistics, 1926-76, 1978; contbr. articles to profl. jours. Mem. Am. Statis. Assn., Washington Soc. Investment Analysts, Nat. Economists Club, Sigma Xi, Phi Beta Kappa. Republican. Presbyterian. Home: 8401 Piney Branch Rd Silver Spring MD 20901-4353

SHELTON, WILLIAM EVERETT, university president; b. Batesville, Miss., Sept. 6, 1944; s. Loyd Taylor and Merle Golden (Barlow) S.; m. Sharon Nordengreen, Apr. 23, 1965; 1 child, William Bradley. BS, Memphis State U., 1967, MA, 1970; EdD, U. Miss., 1975. Tchr. Olive Branch (Miss.) High Sch., 1967-68; prin. Oakland (Tenn.) Elem. Sch., 1968-70; adminstr., instr. N.W. Miss. Jr. Coll., Senatobia, 1970-76; dean for student devel. Henderson State U., Arkadelphia, Ark., 1976-78, v.p., 1978-83; v.p. Kent (Ohio) State U., 1983-89; pres. Ea. Mich. U., Ypsilanti, 1989—. Vice chmn. Ohio Pub. TV, 1986-89. Mem. Am. Assn. for Higher Edn., Am. Assn. State Colls. and Univs., Kent Area C. of C. (pres. 1986). Avocations: flying, golf. Office: Ea Mich U 202 Welch Hall Ypsilanti MI 48197-2214*

SHEMIN, BARRY L., insurance company executive; b. Bklyn., Dec. 17, 1942. AB magna cum laude, Brown U., 1963; MA, U. Mich., 1964. With John Hancock Mut. Life Ins. Co., Boston, 1968—, sr. v.p., corporate actuary; bd. dirs. John Hancock Property and Casualty Holding Co., Hancock Natural Resource Group. Bd. dirs. ARC of Mass. Bay. Fellow Soc. Actuaries; mem. Am. Acad. Actuaries, Internat. Actuarial Assn., Phi Beta Kappa, Sigma Xi. Club: Brown Univ. (Boston). Office: John Hancock Mut Life Ins Co PO Box 111 Boston MA 02117-0111

SHEN, BENJAMIN SHIH-PING, scientist, engineer, educator; b. Hangzhou, China, Sept. 14, 1931; s. Nai-cheng and Chen-chiu (Sun) S.; m. Lucia Elisabeth Simpson, 1971; children: William, Juliet. AB, Assumption Coll., Mass., 1954, ScD (hon.), 1972; AM in Physics, Clark U., 1956; DSc d'Etat in Physics, U. Paris, 1964; MA (hon.), U. Pa., 1971. Asst. prof. physics SUNY, Albany, 1956-59; assoc. prof. space sci., dept. aeros. and astronautics Engring. Sch., NYU, 1964-66; assoc. prof. U. Pa., Phila., 1966-68, prof., 1968-72, Reese W. Flower prof. astronomy and astrophysics, 1972—, assoc. provost, 1979-80, chmn. coun. grad. deans, 1979-81, provost, 1980-81, chmn. dept. astronomy and astrophysics, 1973-79, dir. Flower and Cook Obs., 1973-79, mem. Ctr. for Energy and Environment, 1976-93, chmn. roundtable on sci., industry and policy, 1976—, prof. Sch. Engring. and Applied Sci., 1980-85; mem. U.S. Nat. Sci. Bd., 1990-94, chmn. U.S. sci. and engring. indicators, 1990-92, chmn. task force on sci. literacy, 1992-94; mem. Nat. Coun. on Sci. and Tech. Edn., 1996—; cons. GE, 1961-68, Office Tech. Assessment, U.S. Congress, 1977-78; sci. and tech. adviser Budget Com., U.S. Senate, 1976-77; guest staff Brookhaven Nat. Lab., 1963-64, 65-70; chmn. commn. on pub. understanding on sci. N.Y. Acad. Scis., 1972-75; mem. adv. com. Mt. John Obs., New Zealand, 1978-84. Author: Nuclear Problems in Radiation Shielding in Space, 1963, Passage des Protons dans des Milieux Condenses, 1964; editor, co-author: High-Energy Nuclear Reactions in Astrophysics, 1967; co-editor, co-author: Spallation Nuclear Reactions and Their Applications, 1976; mem. editorial bd. Earth and Extraterrestrial Scis., 1974-78, assoc. editor, 1978-79; assoc. editor: Comments on Astrophysics, 1979-85; contbr. articles to profl. jours. Mem. Hayden Planetarium com. of bd. trustees Am. Mus. Natural History, 1978—; mem. sci. adv. bd. Children's TV Workshop, N.Y.C., 1977, 79—; mem. ABA-AAAS Nat. Conf. Bd. Lawyers and Scientists, 1986-92; former trustee or bd. dirs. N.Y. Acad. Scis., University City Sci. Ctr. Rsch. Park, Phila., U. Pa. Rsch. Found., Morris Arboretum, Phila., Univ. Mus., Phila., Pa. Ballet Co. Decorated Ordre des Palmes Académiques (France); recipient Vermeil medal for sci. Soc. d'Encouragement au Progres, France, 1978. Fellow Am. Phys. Soc., AAAS (com. on sci. engring. and pub. policy 1978-84, chmn. subcom on fed. research and devel. budget 1978-81), Royal Astron. Soc. (U.K.); mem. Internat. Astron. Union. Office: U Pa David Rittenhouse Lab Philadelphia PA 19104-6396

SHEN, CHIA THENG, former steamship company executive, religious institute official; b. Chekiang, China, Dec. 15, 1913; came to U.S., 1952, naturalized, 1964; s. Foo Sheng and Wen Ching (Hsai) S.; m. Woo Ju Chu, Apr. 21, 1940; children: Maria May Shen Jackson, Wilma Way Shen George, David Chuen-Tsing, Freda Foh. BEE, Chiao Tung U., 1937; LittD (hon.), St. John's U., 1973. With Central Elec. Mfg. Works, China, 1937-44; factory mgr. Central Elec. Mfg. Works, 1942-44; dep. coordinating dept. Nat. Resources Commn., Govt. of China, 1945-47; pres. China Trading and Indsl. Devel. Corp., Shanghai, 1947-49; mng. dir. China Trading & Indsl. Devel. Co. Ltd., Hong Kong, 1949-53; with TransAtlantic Financing Corp., 1954-62, pres., 1958-62; pres. Pan-Atlantic Devel. Corp., N.Y.C., 1955-70; with Marine Transport Lines Inc., N.Y.C., 1958-70; sr. v.p. Marine Transport Lines Inc., 1964-70; with Am. Steamship Co., Buffalo, 1967-80; chmn. bd., chief exec. officer Am. Steamship Co., 1971-80. Trustee Inst. Advanced Studies World Religions, N.Y., 1970—, chmn. bd., chief exec. officer, 1970-92, pres., 1970-84, 90—; trustee China Inst. in Am., N.Y.C., 1963-90, vice chmn., 1970-79, chmn., 1979-80, mem. exec. com., 1963-84; trustee, v.p. Buddhist Assn. U.S., N.Y.C., 1964—. Mem. Chinese Inst. Engring. Home and Office: RD 2 Rte 301 Carmel NY 10512-9802 *To benefit all human beings and to work toward freeing them from fear is my goal. The collective wisdom of all world religions furnishes us the direction and means to achieve that goal. To introduce such wisdom into the daily life of mankind in general and America in particular, is therefore what I devote my energy to.*

SHEN, HUNG TAO, hydraulic engineering educator; b. Shanghai, China, May 4, 1944; s. Chin Mei and Ai-Yuan (Chen) S.; m. Hayley Hsi, May 26, 1973; children: Scott P., June P. BSCE, Chung Yuan U., Chungli, Taiwan, 1965; ME, Asian Inst. Tech., Bangkok, 1969; PhD in Mechanics and Hydraulics, U. Iowa, 1974. Engring. analyst Sargent & Lundy, Chgo., 1974-76; asst. prof. Clarkson U., Potsdam, N.Y., 1976-81, assoc. prof., 1981-83, prof. civil and environ. engring., 1983—, chair fluid mechanics and thermal sci. program, 1980-88; expert, cons. U.S. Army Cold Regions Rsch. and Engring., Hanover, N.H., 1984—; vis. prof. Lulea (Sweden) U., 1990-91; advisor China Inst. Water Resources and Hydropower Rsch., Beijing, 1994—. Editor: Frontiers in Hydraulic Engineering, 1983; assoc. editor Jour. Cold Regions ASCE, 1994—; mem. editorial bd. Jour. Hydraulic Rsch., 1993—; contbr. articles to Jour. Hydraulic Engring., Geophys. Rsch., Hydraulic Rsch., Fluid Mechanics. Bd. dirs. Asian Inst. Tech. Found., N.Y., 1984-90. U.S. Nat. Acad. Sci. vis. scholar, 1991; grantee NSF, U.S. Army Rsch. Office, NOAA, Dept. Transp., World Bank. Mem. ASCE (tech. coms. 1980—), Am. Geophys. Union, Internat. Assn. Hydraulic Rsch. (ice rsch. and engring. com. 1986-94), Internat. Assn. Great Lakes Rsch. Achievements include development of first comprehensive computer model on river ice, and theories on frazil jam evolution, and dynamic transport and jamming of surface ice in rivers; computer models on oil/chemical spills in rivers. Office: Clarkson U Dept Civil & Environ Engr Box 5710 Potsdam NY 13699-5710

SHEN, JEROME TSENG YUNG, pediatrician; b. Shanghai, China, Aug. 5, 1918; came to U.S., 1947; s. John G.K. and Agnes (Yao) S.; m. Theresa D.S. Yao, Oct. 10, 1938; children: Jerome L., Elizabeth Burke, Frances Schuman, Li Poppen, Thomas. BS, St. John's U., Shanghai, 1942, MD, 1945; MS in Pediatrics, St. Louis U., 1949. Lic. physician, Mo.; diplomate Am. Bd. Pediatrics 1951. Instr. dept. pediatrics St. Louis U. Sch. Medicine, 1949-52, sr. instr., 1952-60, asst. clin. prof., 1960-70, assoc. clin. prof., 1970-76, clin. prof., 1976-93, clin. prof. emeritus, 1994—; grad. fellow adolescent medicine Harvard Grad. Sch., Boston, 1958-59; vis. prof. Nat. Coll. Juvenile Ct. Judges, Reno, Nev., 1973, adj. prof. jud. adminstrn., 1981-82; cons. adolescent medicine St. Louis State Hosp. and Mo. Inst. Psychiatry, St. Louis, 1973-80; head dept. pediatrics St. Louis City Hosp., 1959-63; chief dept. pediatrics and outpatient dept. Scott Field Air Force Hosp., Belleville, Ill., 1956-58; chief dept. pediatrics St. Lous Labor Health Inst., 1967-90; sr. cons. adolescent clinic Cardinal Glennon Children's Hosp., St. Louis, 1977-90; hon. staff Cardinal Glennon Children's Hosp., St. Mary's Health Ctr., St. John's Mercy Health Ctr.; emeritus staff Jewish Hosp. St. Louis, 1993—; chmn., Expert Advisors Medicine and Pub. Health Rep. China (Taiwan), 1978; bd. dirs., mem. exec. com. Children's Lobby, Washington, 1972; mem. planning com. Mo. State Conf. on Crime, Delinquency and System of Justice; mem. adv. com. Mo. Divsn. Family Svcs., 1973-80; pres. Bi-State Interagy. Coun. on Smoking and Health, 1971-74; Mo. del. to White House Conf. on Children and Youth, 1970; mem. Gov. Com. for Children and Youth, chmn. subcom. on health, 1972-81; chmn. Midwest Regional Conf. Smoking and Health, 1972. Author, editor: Clinical Practice of Adolescent Medicine, 1980, Spanish edit., 1983; editorial bd. Postgrad. Medicine, 1977-88; contbr. articles to profl. jours. Coord. Mother Teresa's Gift of Mary Ctr., St. Louis; founder, bd. dirs. past pres. Pro Life Citizens Polit. Action Com., St. Louis, 1986—; chmn. Mo. Task Force on Unwed Adolescent Sexual Activity and Pregnancy, Jefferson City, 1987; hon. mem. Nat. Coun. Juvenile and Family Ct. Judges, Reno, 1982—; bd. dirs. Birthright Counseling, 1965—; Westminster Day Ctr. for the Poor, St. Louis, 1969-72, St. Louis Archdiocesan Pro Life Com., 1974—, co-chmn. 1981-82; Lady's Inn, St. Louis, 1981—, co-chmn, 1974-75; bd. dirs.; Mo. and Nat. Drs. for Life, 1980—; mem. Bd. of Health, City of University, 1974-80; bd. dirs. Our Lady's Inn, St. Louis, 1981—; chmn. Midwest Regional Conf. on Smoking and Health, 1972. Maj. USAF, 1956-58. Recipient Cardinal Carberry Pro Life award Archdiocese of St. Louis, 1978, Citation for Outstanding Achievement Senate State of Mo., Jefferson City, 1988, Svc. award St. Louis U. Fellow Am. Acad. Pediat. (now emeritus; liaison rep. to various coms., mem. Nat. Com. on Youth 1970-76, com. on adolescence 1977-80, chmn. Mo. com. on youth 1969-70, co-chmn. youth and sch. com. 1971); charter mem. Soc. Adolescent Medicine (treas. 1973-75, chmn. pvt. practice com. 1969-75, historian 1982-90). Republican. Roman Catholic. Avocations: photography, insects, collection of miniatures, stamps, coins. Home: 7132 Kingsbury Blvd University City MO 63130-4306

SHEN, LIANG CHI, electrical engineer, educator, researcher; b. China, Mar. 17, 1939; came to U.S., 1962; s. Kuang Huai and ting Chin (Yu) S.; m. Grace Liu, June 26, 1965; children: Michael, Eugene. BSEE, Nat. Taiwan U., Taipei, 1961; PhD, Harvard U., 1967. Registered profl. engr., Tex. Prof., chmn. electrical engring. dept. U. Houston, 1977-81, prof., dir. well logging lab., 1978—. Author: Applied Electromagnetism, 1987, 3d edit., 1995. Fellow IEEE (assoc. editor geosci. and remote sensing 1986—). Office: U Houston Dept Elec Engring Houston TX 77204

SHEN, MASON MING-SUN, medical center administrator; b. Shanghai, Jiang Su, China, Mar. 30, 1945; came to U.S., 1969; s. John Kaung-Hao and Mai-Chu (Sun) S.; m. Nancy Hsia-Hsian Shieh, Aug. 7, 1976; children: Teresa Tao-Yee, Darren Tao-Ru. BS in Chemistry, Taiwan Normal U., 1963-67; MS in Chemistry, S.D. State U., 1971; PhD in Biochemistry, Cornell U., 1977; MS in Chinese Medicine, China Acad., Taipei, Taiwan, 1982; OMD, San Francisco Coll Acupuncture, 1984; AMD (hon.), Asian Am. Acupuncture Coll., San Diego, 1985; MD (Medicina Alternativa), Internat. U., Colombo, Sri Lanka, 1988. Diplomate Nat. Commn. for Cert. of Accupuncturists; lic. acupuncturist. Rsch. assoc. Lawrence Livermore (Calif.) Lab., 1979-80; assoc. prof. Nat. Def. Med. Coll., Taipei, 1980-82; prof. Inst. of Chinese Medicine China Acad., Taipei, 1981-82, San Francisco Coll. Acupuncture, 1983-85; chief acupuncturist Acupuncture Ctr. of Livermore, 1982-93; prof. Acad. Chinese Culture & Health Scis., Oakland, Calif., 1985-86; dir. Pain & Stress Mgmt. Ctr., Danville, Calif., 1989-90; adminstr. Ea. Med. Ctr., Pleasanton, Calif.; chief acupuncturist Acupuncture Ctr. Pleasanton, 1993—, Acupuncture Ctr. Tracy, Calif., 1995—; pres. Florescent Inst. Traditional Chinese Medicine, Oakland, 1995—; adminstr. Am. Ea. Med. Inst., Pleasanton, 1993—; chmn. adminstrn. subcom., 1991-92, acupuncture com. State of Calif., 1988-92; dir. United Calif. Practitioners of Chinese Medicine, San Francisco, 1995—; bd. dirs. Five Branches Inst., Coll. of Traditional Chinese Medicine, Santa Cruz, Calif., 1996—. Contbr. articles to profl. jours. Rep. Republican Party, Danville, 1988-93; bd. dirs. Asian Rep. Assembly, 1989—; mem. presdnl. adv. com. Republican Presdl. Task Force, 1992; mem. chmn's. adv. bd. Republican Nat. Com., 1993. Recipient Nat. Rsch. Svc. award NIH, 1977, Presdl. Order of Merit, Pres. of the U.S., 1991. Mem. AAAOM, N.Y. Acad. Sci., Calif. Cert. Acupuncturists Assn. (bd. dirs. 1984-88, pres. 1984-85, mem. polit. action com. 1995—), Acupuncture Assn. Am. (bd. dirs. 1986-90, v.p. 1987-89), Am. Assn. Acupuncture and Oriental Medicine (bd. dirs. 1987-92, pres. 1989-90), Nat. Acupuncture Detoxification Assn. (cons. 1987—), Presdl. Round Table (presdl. adv. com.), Hong Kong and Kowloon Chinese Med. Assn. (hon. life pres. 1985). Republican. Avocations: travel, horse back riding, rifles. Home: 3240 Touriga Dr Pleasanton CA 94566-6966 Office: Eastern Med Ctr 3510 Old Santa Rita Rd Ste D Pleasanton CA 94588-3466

SHEN, MICHAEL, lawyer; b. Nanking, Jiangsu, Peoples Republic of China, Aug. 15, 1948; came to U.S. 1951; s. James Cheng Yee and Grace

(Pai) S.; m. Marina Manese (div.); m. Pamela Nan Bradford, Aug. 12, 1983; 1 child, Jessica Li. BA, U. Chgo., 1969; MA, U. Pa., 1970; JD, Rutgers U., 1979. Bar: U.S. Dist. Ct. N.J. 1979, N.Y. 1980, U.S. Dist. Ct. (so. and ea. dists.) N.Y. 1980, N.J. 1981, U.S. Ct. Appeals (2d cir.) 1987, U.S. Supreme Ct. 1988, U.S. Ct. Appeals (3rd cir.). Staff atty. Bedford Stuyvesant Legal Svcs., Bklyn., 1979-80, Com. for Interns and Residents, N.Y.C., 1980-81; ptnr. Shneyer & Shen, P.C., N.Y.C. 1981—; pres. bd. dirs. Asian Am. Legal Def. and Edn. Fund, N.Y.C.; of counsel 318 Restaurant Workers Union, N.Y.C., 1984—. Bd. dirs. Nat. Asian Pacific Am. Legal Consortium, N.Y.C., Nat. Employment Law Project; bd. dirs. N.Y. Civil Liberties Union, N.Y.C., 1987—. Mem. Nat. Employees Lawyers Assn., N.Y. State Bar Assn., N.Y. County Bar Assn., Nat. Lawyers Guild. Avocations: squash, reading. Office: Shneyer & Shen PC 2109 Broadway Ste 206 New York NY 10023 Also: 1085 Cambridge Rd Teaneck NJ 07666-4926

SHEN, NELSON MU-CHING, fiber optics communications scientist; b. Taiwan, Sept. 2, 1946; came to U.S., 1971; s. Mao-Chang and Ching (Chang) S.; m. Jane Chu; children: Helen Diana, Basil Francis. BS in Physics, Chung Yuan Christian U., Taiwan, 1969; MS in Physics, North Western State U., La., 1972; PhD in Physics, U. Tex., Dallas, 1977. Rsch. assoc. U. So. Calif., L.A., 1977-79; chief scientist, dir. techs. Kaptron corp., Palo Alto, Calif., 1979-81; sr. engr. GTE Corp., Mountain View, Calif., 1981-82; sr. scientist Raychem Corp., Menlo Park, Calif., 1982—. Patentee in fiber optics; contbr. papers to profl. publs. Chmn. bd. trustee, Canaan Ch., Mountain View, 1986—. Mem. Optical Soc. Am., Internat. Soc. for Optical Engring. Home: 4131 Old Trace Rd Palo Alto CA 94306-3728 Office: Raychem Corp 300 Constitution Dr Menlo Park CA 94025-1140

SHEN, RONG-NIAN, physician; b. Hunan, China, July 29, 1934; came to U.S., 1980; s. Zhan-Wei Shen and Show-Yin Tan; m. Li Lu, Feb. 15, 1963; 1 child, Yuan Shen. MD, Zhong Shan Med. Coll., Guang Zhou, China, 1961; Fellow Therapeutic Radiation, Montefiore Med. Coll., 1983. House staff, dept. medicine Peking Union Med. Coll., China, 1961-62; resident in radiation oncology Chinese Acad. of Med. Sci., Beijing, 1967-76, attending physician in oncology, 1977-80; fellow Columbia U., N.Y.C., 1980-81; rsch. assoc. Ind. U., Indpls., 1984-85, asst. scientist, 1985-89, assoc. scientist, 1989-92, sr. scientist, 1992—; vis. prof. Meml. Sloan Kettering Cancer Ctr., N.Y.C., 1982-84; cons. Greenland, Inc., Seattle, 1990. Contbr. articles to profl. jours. Recipient awards for nat. scientific advances, Nat. Sci. Com. of China, 1985, award Cancer Rsch. Inst., Inc., N.Y.C., 1981. Fellow Cancer Soc./Little Red Door; mem. Internat. Clin. Hyperthermia Soc. (v.p. Indpls. chpt. 1989, chmn. 6th conf. Yugoslavia 1986), Am. Assn. Cancer Rsch., Am. Soc. Hematology, Overseas Conf. Office of Internat. Programs Fund. Achievements include finding that mice infected with retrovirus can be cured by low-dose total body irradiation (TBI). TBI may be effective in those diseases in which the viral agt. causes immune suppression. Predicated on the report Shen, et al., del regato initiated low-dose TBI clin. trail with AIDS patients; whole body hyperthermia: a potent radioprotector in vivo. These findings have important implications for radiation, hyperthermia and potentially chemotherapy. Office: Ind Univ Walther Oncology Ctr 975 W Walnut St IB501 Indianapolis IN 46202

SHEN, THEODORE PING, investment banker; b. N.Y.C., Feb. 18, 1945; s. Shih-Chang and Clara Grace (Low) S.; m. Carol Lee Wing, June 13, 1968; 1 child, Carla Patricia. B.A. in Econs., Yale U., 1966; M.B.A. in Fin., Harvard U., 1968. V.p., securities analyst Donaldson, Lufkin & Jenrette, N.Y.C., 1968-78, mng. dir. research, 1978-81, mng. dir. equities div., 1981-84, pres. DLJ Capital Markets Group, 1984-86, chmn. DLJ Capital Markets Group, 1986—; bd. dirs. Donaldson, Lufkin & Jenrette, Inc., N.Y.C., 1984—; bd. dirs. N.Y. Urban Coalition; chmn. bd. trustees The Packer Collegiate Inst., Bklyn.; trustee Phillips Exeter Acad. Mem. N.Y. Soc. Securities Analysts, The Bond Club of N.Y., Heights Casino Club (Brooklyn Heights, N.Y.). Office: Donaldson Lufkin & Jenrette Securities Corp 140 Broadway New York NY 10005-1101

SHEN, YUEN-RON, physics educator; b. Shanghai, China, Mar. 25, 1935; came to U.S.,; BS, Nat. Taiwan U., 1956; MS, Stanford U., 1959; PhD, Harvard U., 1963. Rsch. asst. Hewlett-Packard Co., Palo Alto, Calif., 1959; rsch. fellow Harvard U., Cambridge, Mass., 1963-64; asst. prof. U. Calif., Berkeley, 1964-67, assoc. prof., 1967-70, full prof., 1970—; prin. investigator Lawrence Berkeley Lab., 1967—. Author: The Principles of Nonlinear Optics, 1984. Sloan fellow, 1966-68; recipient Guggenheim Found. fellowship, 1972-73, Charles Hard Townes award, 1986, Arthur L. Schawlow prize Am. Phys. Soc., 1992, Alexander von Humboldt award, 1984, Outstanding Rsch. award DOE-MRS Rsch., 1983, Sustained Outstanding Rsch. award, 1987. Fellow Am. Phys. Soc. (disting. traveling lectr. Laser Sci. Topical Group 1994—), Optical Soc. Am., Photonics Soc. Chinese-Ams.; mem. AAAS, NAS, Academia Sinica. Achievements include research in nonlinear optics and condensed matter physics. Office: U Calif Berkeley Dept Physics Berkeley CA 94720

SHENEFIELD, JOHN HALE, lawyer; b. Toledo, Jan. 23, 1939; s. Hale Thurel and Norma (Bird) S.; m. Judy Simmons, June 16, 1984; children: Stephen Hale, Christopher Newcomb. AB, Harvard U., 1960, LLB, 1965. Bar: Va. 1966, D.C. 1966. Assoc. Hunton & Williams, Richmond, Va., 1965-77; dep. asst. atty. gen. antitrust div. Dept. Justice, Washington, 1977; asst. atty. gen. Dept. Justice, 1977-79, assoc. atty. gen., 1979-81; assoc. Milbank, Tweed, Hadley & McCloy, 1981-86, Morgan, Lewis & Bockius, Washington, 1986—; assoc. prof. law U. Richmond, 1975; prof. law Georgetown Law Ctr., 1981-83; chmn. Nat. Commn. for Rev. Antitrust Law and Procedures, 1978-79. Co-author The Antitrust-Laws - A Primer, 2d edit., 1996; contbr. articles on law to profl. jours. Sec. Va. Dem. Com., 1970-72, treas., 1976-77; chmn. Richmond Dem. Party, 1975-77; bd. govs. St. Albans Sch., 1983-90, chmn. 1988-90; mem. chpt. Washington Cathedral, 1988—; pres. Nat. Cathedral Assn., 1993—; chmn. Va. Racing Commn., 1989—. 2d lt. U.S. Army, 1961-62; to capt. Res., 1965. Mem. ABA, Va. Bar Assn. Home: 220 Carrwood Rd Great Falls VA 22066-3721 Office: Morgan Lewis & Bockius 1800 M St NW Ste 6 Washington DC 20036-5802

SHENG, BRIGHT, composer, pianist, conductor; b. Shanghai, China, Dec. 6, 1954; came to U.S., 1982; s. David K-Y and Alice D-J (Cheng) S. BMus, Shanghai Conservatory Music, 1982; M. Mus. Arts, CUNY, 1984; Dr. Mus. Arts, Columbia U., 1993. Pianist/timpanist Folk Dance & Music Theater, Chinhai Province, China, 1971-78; instr. Columbia U., N.Y.C., 1985-89; Baldwin pianist/artist, 1988—; composer-in-residence Lycric Opera of Chgo., 1989-92, Seattle Symphony, 1992-95, LaJolla Chamber Music Summerfest, 1993, Santa Fe Chamber Music Festival, 1993; artistic dir. Wet Ink '93 Festival/San Francisco Symphony, 1993; artist-in-residence U. Wash., Seattle, 1994—; lectr. The Juilliard Sch., Peabody Conservatory, Princeton U., U. Chgo., U. Md., Northwestern U., Harvard U., others. Commns. and performances by N.Y. Philharmonic, Chgo. Symphony, Cleve. Orch., San Francisco Symphony, Seattle Symphony, Balt. Symphony, N.Y. Chamber Symphony, Honolulu Symphony Orch., Sinfonica dell'Accademia Nazionale di Santa Cecilia, Houston Symphony, Boston Symphony, Lyric Opera of Chgo., Houston Grand Opera, Chamber Music Soc. of Lincoln Ctr., Tanglewood Music Festival, Aspen Music Festival, Santa Fe Chamber Music Festival, LaJolla Chamber Music Summerfest, Seattle Chamber Music Festival, Seattle Internat. Music Festival, others; recordings include New World Records, Delos, Koch Internat. Recipient 1st prize Art Song Competition, Shanghai, 1979, 1st and 2d prizes chamber music composition competition, Shanghai, 1980, Am. Acad. and Inst. Arts and Letters, 1984, Alfred Knapp award Tanglewood Music Ctr., 1985; grantee The Mary Flagler Charitable Trust, 1987, Nat. Endowment of Arts, 1987, 90, 94, 95, Guggenheim Found., 1990, Naumberg Found., 1990, Rockefeller Found., 1991, Seattle Arts Commn., 1992. Home: 158-13 78 Rd Flushing NY 11366 Office: U Mich Sch Medicine Composition Dept Ann Arbor MI 48109-2085

SHENG, JACK TSE-LIANG, law librarian; b. Hsiang Ying, Hunan, China, Nov. 15, 1929; m. Helen S. Sheng, Sept. 20, 1939; children: Paul, Henry. LLB, Soochow U., Taiwan, 1963; LLM, Yale U., 1966; MS, La. State U., 1967; JD, Wayne State U., 1969. Teaching asst. Soochow U. Law Sch., Taipei, Taiwan, 1963-64; librarian I and II, cataloger Detroit Pub. Library, 1967-70; head librarian, assoc. prof. Soochow U., 1970-72; asst. law librarian Ohio No. U., Ada, 1972-75; law librarian Duval County Law Library, Jacksonville, Fla., 1975—; editorial asst. Gale Research Co., Detroit, 1969; law library cons. Del. Law Sch., Wilmington, 1973, CSX Corp., Jacksonville, Fla., 1983-85; instr. Fla. Jr. Coll., Jacksonville, 1976-83. Author: Index to Chinese Legal Periodicals, 1963-70, 1972. Mem. Am. Assn. Law Libraries. Democrat. Home: 4080 Old Mill Cove Trl W Jacksonville FL 32277-1569 Office: Duval County Law Libr 330 E Bay St Jacksonville FL 32202-2921

SHENG, TSE CHENG (TED C. SHENG), natural resources educator; b. Chia-Hsing, China, Oct. 16, 1924; came to U.S. 1984; s. Tsu Ming and Chen Hwa (Sze) S.; m. Chuan Shen, June 1, 1947; children: Tom Sze-Tsan, Richard Van. BSc, Nat. Chekiang U., 1947; MSc, Colo. State U., 1966. Soil conservation specialist Chinese-Am. Joint Commn. on Rural Reconstruction, Taipei, Republic of China, 1953-68; expert advisor Food and Agrl. Orgn. of UN, Rome, 1968-84; prof. watershed mgmt. Colo. State U., Ft. Collins, 1985—; internat. cons. UN Devel. Programme, N.Y.C., 1987—; cons. Computer Assisted Devel. Inc., Ft. Collins, 1988—. Author: Watershed Conservation I & II, 1986-90, Soil Conservation for Small Farmers in the Humid Tropics, 1989, Watershed Survey and Planning, 1990; editor: Conservation Policies for Sustainable Hillslope Farming, 1992. Recipient award Crown Zellerbach Found., 1965, Hugh Hammond Bennett award, 1991. Mem. Soil and Water Conservation Soc. (life, vice chair internat. affairs com. 1994-96), World Assn. Soil and Water Conservation, Chinese Soil and Water Conservation Soc. (bd. dirs. 1966-68). Avocations: writing poems, prose, articles for newspapers and journals. Home: 636 S Shields St Fort Collins CO 80521 Office: Dept of Earth Resources Colo State Univ Fort Collins CO 80523

SHENK, GEORGE H., lawyer; b. N.Y.C., Sept. 10, 1943; BA, Princeton U., 1965; M in Internat. Affairs, Columbia U., 1967; JD, Yale U., 1970. Bar: N.Y. 1971, Calif. 1985. Assoc. Coudert Bros., Paris, 1970, N.Y.C., 1970-73, Hong Kong, 1973-75, Tokyo, 1975-78, ptnr., N.Y.C., 1978-91, San Francisco, 1991-94, ptnr. Heller Ehrman, White & McAuliffe, 1994—. Contbr. articles to publs. Bd. dirs. alumni council Columbia Sch. Internat. Affairs, N.Y.C., 1982-85, French-Am. C. of C. of San Francisco, 1991-93, Internat. Ctr., N.Y.C., 1983-86. Mem. Bar Assn. City of N.Y., Calif. State Bar Assn., Council Fgn. Relations, San Francisco Tennis Club. Office: Heller Ehrman White & McAuliffe 333 Bush St San Francisco CA 94104-2806

SHENK, RICHARD LAWRENCE, real estate developer, photographer, artist; b. Columbus, Ohio, Jan. 26, 1940. BBA, Tulane U., 1961, U. of Va., 1961-62, Ohio State U., 1962-65. Plant mgr. S.A. Shenk Co., Columbia and U.S., 1962-65; v.p. Konter Corp., Cin., 1965-70; owner Richard L. Shenk Devel., Cin., 1970—; bd. dirs. Consol. Stores Corp., Columbus; co-founder Images Photographic Gallery, Cin., 1980; pres. Cmty. Improvement Corp., Springdale, Ohio, 1989-93; past. pres., bd. dirs., chmn. fin. com. Talbert House, Inc., Cin. Author: Different Way of Seeing, 1989. Mem. program com. Judaic studies program U. Cin.; mem. bd. overseers Cin. Campus Hebrew Union Coll.; bd. dirs., chmn. fin. com. Jewish Home of Cin., past campaign chmn., pres. Jewish Fedn. of Cin.; bd. dirs. Adath Israel Synagogue, Israil Ednl. Fund, Simon Wiesenthal Ctr., L.A. Mem. United Jewish Appeal (nat. vice chmn.), Rotary (past pres. Springdale chpt.). Home: 2349 Grandin Rd Cincinnati OH 45208

SHENK, WILLIS WEIDMAN, newspaper executive; b. Manheim, Pa., Nov. 2, 1915; s. John Horst and Amanda (Weidman) S.; m. Elsie Sherer, Aug. 31, 1940; 1 son, J. David. Acct. Raymond D. Shearer, Lancaster, Pa., 1937-39; sr. acct. Lancaster Newspapers, Inc., 1940-50, sec.-controller, 1950-61, v.p., sec., 1961-76, pres., 1977-83, chmn. bd., 1984—. Pres. United Way of Lancaster County, 1961; pres., bd. trustees Lancaster Country Day Sch., 1971-72; trustee Franklin and Marshall Coll., Lancaster, 1977-85; sec. Pequea Twp. Planning Commn., 1965-77. Mem. Nat. Assn. Accts., Pa. Inst. CPAs, Lancaster Country Club. Lutheran. Clubs: Hamilton, Masons. Office: Lancaster Newspapers Inc PO Box 1328 8 W King St Lancaster PA 17603-3824

SHENKAROW, BARRY L., professional hockey team executive. Pres., gov. Winnipeg (Man.) Jets (NHL), Can., 1983—. Office: Winnipeg Jets, 1661 Portage Ave 10th Fl, Winnipeg, MB Canada R3J 3T7

SHENKER, IRA RONALD, physician; b. N.Y.C., July 8, 1934; s. Morris and Rose (Wilner) S.; m. Caroline Cabin, June 22, 1958; children: Diane Amy, Mitchell Steven. B.S., U. Wis., 1955, M.D., 1958. Diplomate Am. Bd. Pediatrics. Intern, L.I. Jewish Med. Ctr., New Hyde Park, N.Y., 1958-59; resident pediat., 1959-61; resident pub. health Nassau County Health Dept., N.Y., 1961-62; coll. health physician Mt. Holyoke Coll., 1962-64; chief adolescent medicine L.I. Jewish Med. Ctr., 1965—; assoc. prof. pediat. SUNY-Stony Brook, 1979—; prof. pediat. Albert Einstein Coll. Medicine, 1989—. Author: Human Figure Drawings in Adolescence, 1972. Editor: Adolescent Medicine, 1981, Clinical Monographs in Pediatrics: Adolescent Medicine, 1994. Contbr. articles to profl. jours. Bd. dirs. Roslyn Sr. Citizens, N.Y., 1975-78. USPHS grantee, 1965-82. Fellow Am. Acad. Pediat.; mem. Queens Pediat. Soc. (pres. 1981-82), N.Y. Pediat. Soc., Nassau Pediat. Soc., Soc. for Adolescent Medicine (pres. 1986). Home: 5 Fairway Rd Roslyn NY 11576-1099 Address: 270-05 76th Ave New Hyde Park NY 11040-1433 Office: Schneider Children's Hosp of LI Jewish Med Ctr New Hyde Park NY 11042

SHENKER, JOSEPH, academic administrator; b. N.Y.C., Oct. 7, 1939; s. George and Isabelle (Schwartz) S.; m. Adrienne Green (div. 1979); children: Deborah, Karen; m. Susan Armiger, Jan. 2, 1988; children: Sarah Gabrielle, Jordan. BA in Psychology, Hunter Coll., 1962, MA in Econ., 1963; EdD in High Edn., Tchrs. Coll., 1969. Dean, community coll. affairs CUNY, 1967-69; acting pres. Kingsborough Community Coll., N.Y.C., 1969-70; chief negotiator for mgmt. CUNY, 1977; acting pres. Hunter Coll., N.Y.C., 1979-80; founding pres. LaGuardia Community Coll., N.Y.C., 1970-88; pres. Bank St. Coll. Edn., N.Y.C., 1988-95; provost C.W. Post Campus, L.I. U., 1995—; bd. dirs. Sch. & Bus. Alliance, N.Y.C.; ptnr. N.Y.C. Partnership, 1990—. chmn. Liberty Scholarship Adv. Com., Albany, N.Y., 1989—; co-chmn. Task Force on Early Childhood Edn., N.Y.C., 1989—, Agenda for Children Tomorrow, 1989—; chmn. Chancellor's Com. on U./Sch. Collaboratives, N.Y.C., 1988. Recipient Distinguished Alumni award Tchrs. Coll. Columbia, N.Y.C., 1990. Mem. Princeton Club. Office: C W Post Campus Long Island U 720 Northern Blvd Brookville NY 11548

SHENKIR, WILLIAM GARY, business educator; b. Three Rivers, Tex., June 27, 1938; s. William and Lydia (Jancik) S.; m. Missy Smith, Jan 1, 1973. B.B.A., Tex. A & M U., 1960; postgrad. (Rockefeller Bros. Theol. fellow), Drew U. Sem., 1960-61; M.B.A., U. Tex., 1962, Ph.D., 1964. Asst. prof. McIntire Sch. Commerce, U. Va., Charlottesville, 1967-69; assoc. prof. McIntire Sch. Commerce, U. Va., 1969-72, prof., 1972-73, dean, 1977-92; William Stamps Farish prof. McIntire Sch. Commerce U. Va., 1982—; project dir. Fin. Acctg. Standards Bd., Stamford, Conn., 1973-76; vis. prof. NYU Grad. Sch. Bus., N.Y.C., 1976-77; bd. dirs. 1st Union Nat. Bank Va., Roanoke. Editor: Carman Blough: His Professional Career and Accounting Thought, 1978; contbr. articles to profl. jours. Served to lt. USAF, 1964-67. Mem. AICPA, Am. Acctg. Assn. (former v.p., acctg. edn. change commn.), Am. Assembly Collegiate Schs. of Bus. (former bd. dirs., pres. 1990-91), Fin. Execs. Inst., Va. Soc. CPAs, Boar's Head Sports Club, Raven Soc., Landfall Club, Phi Delta Kappa, Beta Gamma Sigma, Phi Kappa Phi. Presbyterian. Home: 420 Rookwood Dr Charlottesville VA 22903-4732

SHENNUM, ROBERT HERMAN, retired telephone company executive; b. Scobey, Mont., Apr. 12, 1922; s. Joseph M. and Nellie M. Shennum; m. Doris Postlewait; children: Sharon, Keith, Marsha Shennum Burns. B.S.E.E., Mont. State U., 1944, M.S.E.E., 1948, D. Eng. (hon.), 1963; Ph.D. in Physics and Elec. Engring., Calif. Inst. Tech., 1954. Instr. engring. Mont. State U., Bozeman, 1946-50; rsch. assoc. engring. Calif. Inst. Tech., Pasadena, 1950-54; cons. Kelman Electric Co., Los Angeles, 1954; mem. tech. staff AT&T Bell Labs., Murray Hill, N.J., 1954-85; also dir. AT&T Bell Labs., Parsippany, N.J.; mem. adv. com. Internat. Telecommunications Energy Conf., 1974-87. Contbr. articles to profl. jours.; patentee pulse code modulation. Served to 1st lt. Signal Corps, U.S. Army, 1944-46, ETO. Recipient cert. of appreciation for patriotic services U.S. Army, 1975. Fellow IEEE (chmn. N.C. sect. 1973), Greensboro C. of C. (chmn. continuing edn. 1970-74). Republican. Home: 2888 Swan Hwy Bigfork MT 59911-6414

SHENOY, SUDHAKAR VENKATRAYA, computer software company executive; b. Kanhangad, India, Apr. 23, 1947; came to U.S., 1970; s. Konchady Venkatraya and Radha Bai Shenoy; m. Bina Sudhakar Prabhu; children: Sushma, Divya. BTech. with honors, Indian Inst. Tech., Bombay, India, 1970; MS, U. Conn., 1971, MBA, 1973. Tchr. U. Conn., Storrs, 1972-73; fin. mgr. Windsor (Conn.) Mfg. Co., 1973-78; sr. analyst, project mgr. Am. Mgmt. Systems, Arlington, Va., 1978-80; pres. Info. Mgmt. Cons., Inc., Falls Church, Va., 1981—. Office: Info Mgmt Cons Inc 7915 Westpark Dr Mc Lean VA 22102-4201

SHEON, AARON, art historian, educator; b. Toledo, Oct. 7, 1937; s. Benjamin William and Katherine (Rappoport) S.; m. Martine Bruel, Jan. 26, 1963 (div. 1986); children: Sandrine, Nicolas. B.A., U. Mich., 1959, M.A., 1960; M.F.A. (Wilson fellow), Princeton U., 1962, Ph.D., 1966; postgrad., U. Paris, 1962-63. Staff officer, dir. gen.'s cabinet UNESCO, Paris, 1963-66; asst. prof. U. Pitts., 1966-69, asso. prof., 1969-78, prof. art history, 1979—, acting chmn. dept. fine arts, 1969, 79-80; dir. univ. program U. Pitts., Rouen, France, 1974-75; vis. prof. Carnegie-Mellon U., 1981; Vis. exhbn. curator Mus. Art, Carnegie Inst., Pitts., 1977-81; program cons. Nat. Endowment Arts and Humanities, 1978-85; visual arts cons. Pa. Arts Council, 1981; vis. mem. Inst. for Advanced Study, Princeton, 1984-85. Author: The Gosman Collection, 1969, Monticelli, His Contemporaries, His Influence, 1978, Organic Vision, The Architecture of Peter Berndtson, 1980, Monticelli, 1986, Paul Guigou, 1987. Recipient Charles E. Merrill faculty award, 1968; Chancellor Bowman award, 1976; Honor award Pa. Soc. Architects, 1982; grantee Ford Found., 1967, NEH, 1979; Gould Arts Found. fellow, 1986. Mem. Coll. Art Assn., Société de l'histoire de l'art français, Am. Assn. of Mus. Office: U Pitts Dept Fine Arts Pittsburgh PA 15260

SHEPARD, ALAN BARTLETT, JR., former astronaut, real estate developer; b. East Derry, N.H., Nov. 18, 1923; s. Alan Bartlett and Renza (Emerson) S.; m. Louise Brewer, Mar. 3, 1945; children: Laura, Juliana. Student, Admiral Farragut Acad., 1940; B.S., U.S. Naval Acad., 1944; grad., Naval War Coll., 1958; M.S. (hon.), Dartmouth Coll.; D.Sc. (hon.), Miami U. Commd. ensign USN, 1944, advanced through grades to rear adm., 1971, designated naval aviator, 1947; assigned destroyer U.S.S. Cogswell, Navy Test Pilot Sch., Pacific, World War II, Fighter Squadron 42, aircraft carriers in Mediterranean, 1947-49; with USN Test Pilot Sch., 1950-53, 55-57, took part in high altitude tests, expts. in test and devel. in-flight refueling system, carrier suitability trials of F2H3 Banshee; also trials angled carrier deck ops. officer Fighter Squadron 193, Moffett Field (Calif.), carrier U.S.S. Oriskany, Western Pacific, 1953-55; test pilot for F4D Skyray, 1955, F3H Demon, F8U Crusader, F11F Tigercat, 1956; project test pilot F5D Skylancer, 1956; instr. Naval Test Pilot Sch., 1957; aircraft readiness officer staff Comdr.-in-Chief, Atlantic Fleet, 1958-59; joined Project Mercury man in space program NASA, 1959; first Am. in space, May 5, 1961, chief of astronaut office, 1965-74, selected to command Apollo 14 Lunar Landing Mission, 1971, became 5th man to walk on moon, hit 1st lunar golf shot; pres. Seven Fourteen Enterprises, 1986, Windward Coors Co., Deer Park, Tex., 1974; presdl. appointee, del. 26th Gen. Assembly UN, 1971. Author: (with Deke Slayton) Moon Shot: The Inside Story of America's Race to the Moon, 1994. Decorated D.S.M., D.F.C., Presdl. unit citation, NASA Disting. Service medal, Congressional Medal of Honor, 1978; recipient Langley medal Smithsonian Instn., 1964. Fellow Soc. Exptl. Test Pilots; mem. Order Daedlians, Soc. Colonial Wars, Lions, Kiwanis, Rotary.

SHEPARD, EARL ALDEN, retired government official; b. Aurora, Ill., Sept. 30, 1932; s. Ralph George and Marcia Louise (Phelps) S.; m. Carolyn Mae Borman, Sept. 1, 1959; 1 son, Ralph Lyle. AS in Bus. Adminstrn. magna cum laude, Southea. U., 1967, BSBA magna cum laude, 1969; MBA, U. Chgo., 1974. Chief program budget divsn. U.S. Army Munitions Command., Joliet, Ill., 1971-73; comptr., dir. adminstrn. U.S. Navy Pub. Works Ctr., Gt. Lakes, Ill., 1973-77; dep. comptr. U.S. Army Electronics Command/U.S. Army Communications Electronics Materiel Readiness Command, Ft. Monmouth, N.J., 1977-79; dir. resource mgmt., comptr., dir. programs U.S. Army, White Sands Missile Range, N.Mex., 1979-92; bd. dirs. 1st Nat. Bank of Dona Ana County, 1987—; mem. adv. com. Rio Grande Bancshares/First Nat. Bank of Dona Ana County, 1983-84; founding mem. White Sands Missile Range Hist. Found., 1992—. Mem. bd. govs. Southea. U. Ednl. Found., 1969-71; chmn. fin. com. No. Va. Assn. for Children with Learning Disabilities, 1966-67, treas., 1968-70; pres. West Long Branch (N.J.) Sports Assn., 1979. Fed. and local govt. employee scholar, 1967, Ammunition Procurement Supply Agy. fellow, 1974. Republican. Home: 2712 Topley Ave Las Cruces NM 88005-1334

SHEPARD, ELAINE ELIZABETH, writer, lecturer; b. Olney, Ill.; d. Thomas J. and Bernice E. (Shadle) S.; m. Terry D. Hunt, Apr. 16, 1938; m. George F. Hartman, Oct. 1, 1943 (div. June 1958). Covered nat. polit. convs. for Stas. WTTG-TV and WINS, Chgo., 1952, 1956; polit. reporter for NANA and WINS, Chgo. and Los Angeles, 1960; reporter Congo rebellion for N.Am. Newspaper Alliance and N.Y. Mirror, 1960-61; corr. covering Pres. Eisenhower's Middle East, Far East and S. Am. tour, 1959-60; Vietnam corr. MBS, 1965-66; granted interviews with Khrushchev, Castro, Tito, Chou En-lai, Nasser, Shah of Iran, King Hussein, King Faisel, Duvalier, Lumumba, Chiang-Kai-Shek, Nehru, Menzies, John F. Kennedy, Richard M. Nixon, others; mem. White House Press Corps accompanying Pres. Nixon to, Austria, Iran, Poland, Moscow, 1972. Film and theater actress, Hollywood, N.Y.C., Europe, 1939-50, cover girl, John Robert Powers, 1939-43, under contract to, RKO and Metro-Goldwyn-Mayer, 1940-45, guest commentator for, Voice of Am.; contbr.: feature articles to various mags., including N.Y. News Sunday Mag, 1953—; columnist, contbg. editor: feature articles to various mags., including Nat. Cath. Press, 1969-74; author: Forgive Us Our Press Passes, 1962, The Doom Pussy, 1967, The Doom Pussy II, 1991. Recipient 2 citations for participating in armed helicopter assaults with 145th Aviation Bn. Vietnam. Mem. Screen Actors Guild, AFTRA, Actors Equity. Club: Overseas Press (N.Y.C.). Home: 12 E 62nd St New York NY 10021-7218 *Happiness is the full use of your powers along lines of excellence in a life affording hope.*

SHEPARD, GEOFFREY CARROLL, insurance executive; b. Santa Barbara, Calif., Nov. 7, 1944; s. James J. and Barbara (Hoose) S.; m. Saundra Gayle Carlton, Jan. 10, 1973; children: Jonathan Pettus, William Dabney. B.A., Whittier Coll., 1966; J.D., Harvard U., 1969. Bar: Wash. 1970, D.C. 1972, Pa. 1977, U.S. Supreme Ct. 1973. White House fellow, 1969-70; staff asst. to Pres. White House, 1970-72, assoc. dir. domestic coun., 1972-75; sr. assoc. Steptoe & Johnson, Washington, 1975-77; sr. v.p., assoc. gen. counsel CIGNA Corp., Phila., 1977-91; sr. v.p., gen. counsel, corp. sec. Reliance Ins. Group, Phila., 1991-94; pres. comml. divsn. Karr Barth Assocs., Phila., 1994—; mem. pvt. security adv. coun. Dept. Justice, 1975-77. Adv. coun. on gen. govt. Rep. Nat. Com., 1977-78; Phila. Cmty. Leadership Seminar, 1978-79, exec. com. Boy Scouts Am., Phila, 1981-83, exec. bd. Valley Forge Coun., 1994—; bd. dirs. Sacred Heart Med. Ctr., 1983-85, Swarthmore Presbyn. Ch., 1984-86, Wallingford Hills Civic Assn., 1983-85, Com. of 70, 1985-87, Acad. Natural Scis., Phila., 1987-93, Pub. Affairs Coun., Washington, 1986-89, Episc. Acad., 1987-90; exec. com. White House fellows reg. selection panel, 1987-93; prin. counsel Excellence in Govt., 1994—. Mem. ABA, Assn. for Ad. Life Underwriting, Pa. Bar Assn., Phila. Assn. of Life Underwriters, D.C. Bar Assn., White House Fellows Alumni Assn., Met. Club (Washington), Union League Club (Phila.), Harvard Club (N.Y.C.). Office: Karr Barth Assocs Inc Comml Divsn 40 Monument Rd Bala Cynwyd PA 19004-1735

SHEPARD, HENRY BRADBURY, JR., lawyer; b. Exeter, N.H., Oct. 29, 1927; s. Henry Bradbury and Frances Gardner (Dudley) S.; m. Klaudia Ockert Steidle, July 26, 1958; children: Katherine Shepard Alexander, Emily Perry, Julia Bradbury. BA with honors, Yale U., 1949; postgrad., U. Goettingen, Germany, 1951-52; LLB with honors, Harvard U., 1957. Instr. Am. U. in Cairo (Egypt), 1949-51; asst. dir. Fridtjof Nansen Internat. Student House, Goettingen, Germany, 1951-52; instr. Interpreters Inst., Goettingen, Germany, 1951-52; assoc. Goodwin, Procter & Hoar, Boston, 1957-64, ptnr., 1964-93, counsel, 1994—; dir. Mass. Venture Capital Corp., Boston, 1973-88, The C.T. Main Corp., Boston, 1975-85, Neworld Bancorp, Inc., Boston, 1986-92, Neworld Bank, Boston, 1968-92. Author: Handbook of Recent Developments in Massachusetts Banking Law, 1983, Obligations and Liabilities of Bank Directors and Trustees, 1990. Trustee George R. Wallace Found., Boston, 1978—, N.H. Hist. Soc., Concord, 1991—; hon. trustee

Deree-Pierce Coll., Athens, Greece, 1970—. With U.S. Army, 1952-54. Mem. ABA (chmn. subcom. on regulatory liaison mut. savs. banks 1980-85), Mass. Bar Assn., Boston Bar Assn., Greater Boston C. of C. (bd. dirs. 1974-80, pres. 1979-80, hon. v.p. 1980-93), The Hamilton Trust (v.p. 1989, pres. 1990-91), New Bedford Yacht Club, The Country Club, Harvard Travellers Club, Phi Beta Kappa. Independent. Office: Goodwin Procter & Hoar Exch Pl Boston MA 02109

SHEPARD, JAMES EDWARD, physician; b. Laconia, N.H., Dec. 8, 1933; s. Robinson and Myra Ellen (Foster) S.; m. Sally-Jean Shupert, Oct. 4, 1958; children: Sandra Jean, Elizabeth Anne. BA, Wesleyan U., Middletown, Conn., 1955; MD, Cornell U., 1959. Diplomate Am. Bd. Nephrology, Am. Bd. Luteinal Medicine. Practice medicine specializing in internal medicine and nephrology Greenbrae, Calif., 1974—; chief medicine Marin (Calif.) Gen. Hosp., 1974-76; asst. clin. prof. medicine U. Calif., San Francisco, 1970—. Contbr. articles to profl. jours. Pres. Marin Heart Assn., 1969-71; active, founder Marin Kidney Assn., 1970-80; mem. San Francisco Graphic Arts Council, 1980-86. Fellow ACP; mem. Nat. Soc. Nephrology, Internat. Soc. Nephrology, Calif. Acad. Medicine, Sigma Xi. Club: Mill Valley (Calif.) Tennis. Office: Drs Shepard Lambert Hancock & Ley 5 Bar Ave Rd Ste 101 Larkspur CA 94939

SHEPARD, JEAN HECK, author, publishing company consultant; b. N.Y.C., Feb. 2, 1930; d. Chester Reed and Anna S. (Charig) Heck; m. Lawrence Vaeth Hastings, Mar. 29, 1950 (div. 1953); 1 child, Lance Clifford Hastings; m. Daniel A. Shepard, July 26, 1954 (div. 1981); 1 child, Bradley Reed. BA, Barnard Coll., 1950; postgrad., Columbia U., 1952. Mem. sch. and libr. svc. Viking Press, N.Y.C., 1956-57; asst. dir. sch. and libr. promotion E.P. Dutton, N.Y.C., 1957-58; dir. advt. publicity and promotion Thomas Y. Crowell Co., N.Y.C., 1958-62; dir. advt. and promotion Charles Scribner's Sons, N.Y.C., 1962-67; cons. Stephen Greene Press, Brattleboro, Vt., 1970-73; mktg. mgr. A&W Publishers, N.Y.C., 1979-80, Franklin Watts Publ., N.Y.C., 1980-82; pub. mags., divsn. advt. & promotion mgr. McGraw Hill Book Co., N.Y.C., 1983-85; cons. Monitor Publ. Co., N.Y.C., 1988—. Author: Simple Family Favorites, 1971, Herb and Spice Sampler, 1972, Cook With Wine!, 1973, Earth Watch: Notes on a Restless Planet, 1973, Harvest Home Steak Cookbook, 1974, Fresh Fruits and Vegetables, 1974, Yankee Magazine, 1972. Mem. Authors Guild, Pub. Ad Club, Am. Libr. Assn., Women's Nat. Book Assn. Methodist. Avocations: the dance, reading, writing, travel, music. Home: 73 Kingswood Dr Bethel CT 06801 Office: The Shepard Agy Ste 3 Pawling Savs Bank Bld Southeast Plz Brewster NY 10509

SHEPARD, JON MAX, sociologist; b. Ashland, Ky., July 15, 1939; s. Maxwell Irwin and Mabel Louise S.; m. Virginia Kay Vogel, July 16, 1961; 1 son, Jon Mark. B.A., Georgetown (Ky.) Coll., 1961; M.A., U. Ky., 1963; Ph.D., Mich. State U., 1968. Rsch. assoc. MIT, 1968-69; from asst. prof. to prof. sociology U. Ky., 1969-78, prof. mgmt. and sociology, 1978-88; prof. mgmt. and sociology Va. Poly. Inst. and State U., Blacksburg, 1989—, Pamplin prof. mgmt. Author: Automation and Alienation, A Study of Office and Factory Workers, 1971, Organizational Issues in Industrial Society, 1972, (with H. Voss) Social Problems, 1978, Sociology, 1996; contbr. articles to profl. jours. Recipient Gt. Tchr. award U. Ky., 1978. Mem. Am. Acad. Mgmt., Am. Sociol. Assn. Home: 2821 Chelsea Ct Blacksburg VA 24060-4120 Office: Va Poly Inst & State U Pamplin Hall Blacksburg VA 24061

SHEPARD, KATHRYN IRENE, public relations executive; b. Tooele, Utah, Jan. 6, 1956; d. James Lewis and Glenda Verleen (Slaughter) Clark; m. Mark L. Shepard, June 5, 1976. BA in History, Boise State U., 1980. On-air writer Sta. KTTV, Channel 11, L.A., 1982-85; publicity dir. Hollywood (Calif.) C. of C., 1985-87; pres. Kathy Shepard Pub. Rels., Burbank and Portland, 1987-93; dir. public relations Las Vegas Hilton, 1993-94; dir. comms. Hilton Gaming, 1994-96; dir. corp. comms. Hilton Hotels Corp., 1996—; instr. pub. rels. ext. program UCLA, 1991-92. Contbr. articles to profl. publs. Mem. Publicity Club L.A. (pres. 1991-92, bd. dirs. 1987-91), Pub. Rels. Assn. Am., Women in Comms. Avocations: genealogy, film, travel. Office: Hilton Hotels Corp PR Dept 9336 Civic Center Dr Beverly Hills CA 90210

SHEPARD, KENNETH SIHLER, physician, surgeon; b. Des Moines, Iowa, Oct. 21, 1922; s. Kenneth Eglin and Dorothy Marie (Sihler) S.; m. Helen Reis (dec. Oct. 1982); children: Ann, Helen, Kenneth, Mary, David; m. Colleen Gay Braker, Dec. 24, 1982; children: Christopher, Kevin. AB, BS, Duke U., 1943, MD, 1947. Diplomate Am. Bd. Pediatrics; ordained to ministry Roman Catholic Ch. as deacon, 1982. Intern St. Francis Hosp., Evanston, Ill.; resident in contagious disease Willard Parket Hosp., N.Y.C.; resident in pediatrics Duke U. Sch. Medicine, Durham, N.C.; resident in pathology Boston Children's Hosp.; fellow in psychosomatic pediatrics Duke U. Sch. Medicine, Durham; fellow in perinatology U. Vt., Burlington; sgt. U.S. Army Air Corps, 1943, commd. capt., 1950; advanced through grades to col., 1977, flight surgeon, cons. in pediat. to USAF surgeon gen., 1965-77; chief dep. warden Calif. Med. Facility, Vacaville, Calif., 1987-92; health care mgr. Folsom and Sacramento State Corrections, Vacaville, Calif., 1992-94; clin. dir. Calif. Youth Authority, 1991-94; deacon Epiphany Episcopal Ch., Vacaville, Calif., 1982—. Contbr. numerous articles to profl. jours.; presenter in field. Fellow Royal Acad. Health, Royal Acad. Pediatrics; mem. AMA, Assn. Am. Med. Authors, World Congress Pediatrics, Internat. Pediatric Soc., Aerospace Med. Soc., Am. Acad. Pediatrics, Soc. Air Force Physicians, Soc. Air Force Physicians, Aerospace Med. Assn., Soc. for Adolescent Medicine, Ill. Med. Soc., Chgo. Med. Soc., Cook County Med. Soc., Howland Pediatric Soc., Chgo. Pediatric Soc., Colston Soc. Med. Rsch. (Eng.), Univ. Club Evanston, Tex. Pediatric Soc., Lions, numerous others. Home: 124 Viewmont Ln Vacaville CA 95688 Office: CSP Sacramento PO Box 29 Represa CA 95671-7129

SHEPARD, PAUL HOWE, ecology educator, author, lecturer; b. Kansas City, Mo., July 12, 1925; s. Paul Howe and Clara (Grigsby) S.; m. Melba Wheatcroft, 1950 (div.); children: Kenton, Margaret, Jane; m. Florence Krall, 1988. A.B., U. Mo., 1949; M.S., Yale U., 1952, Ph.D., 1954. From instr. to asso. prof. biology and dir. Green Oaks, Knox Coll., 1954-64; lectr. biology Smith Coll., 1965-70; vis. prof. environ. perception Dartmouth Coll., 1971-73; Avery prof. natural philosophy and human ecology Pitzer Coll. and Claremont Grad. Sch., 1973-94, emeritus, 1994—; nat. lectr. Sigma Xi, 1984-86; NSF in-svc. inst. program dir., 1959. Author: The Pictorial History of the 493d Armored Field Artillery Battalion, 1945, Man in the Landscape: A Historic View of the Esthetics of Nature, 1967, 2d edit., 1990, The Subversive Science: Essays Toward an Ecology of Man, 1969, Environmental: Essays on the Planet as a Home, 1971, The Tender Carnivore and the Sacred Game, 1973, Thinking Animals, 1977, Nature and Madness, 1982, The Sacred Paw, The Bear in Nature, Myth and Literature, 1985, 2d edit., 1992, the Others, How Animals Made Us Human, 1995, Subject: The Company of Others: Essays in Celebration of Paul Shepard, 1995, The Only World We've Got: A Paul Shepard Reader, 1996, Traces of an Omnivore, 1996; mem. editorial adv. bd. Landscape and Urban Planning. Served with AUS, 1943-46. Fulbright rsch. scholar Wellington, N.Z., 1961; Guggenheim fellow, 1969; USPHS grantee, 1962; fellow Rockefeller Found., 1977, Coun. for Internat. Exch. Scholars, India, 1989; Disting. Vis. Lectr., India, 1985. Fellow Inst. Human Ecology. Home: PO Box 99 Bondurant WY 82922-0099

SHEPARD, RANDALL TERRY, judge; b. Lafayette, Ind., Dec. 24, 1946; s. Richard Schilling and Dorothy Ione (Donlen) S.; m. Amy Wynne MacDonell, May 7, 1988; one child, Martha MacDonell. AB cum laude, Princeton U., 1969; JD, Yale U., 1972; LLM, U. Va., 1995; LLD (hon.), U. So. Ind., 1995. Bar: Ind. 1972, U.S. Dist. Ct. (so. dist.) Ind. 1972. Spl. asst. to under sec. U.S. Dept. Transp., Washington, 1972-74; exec. asst. to mayor City of Evansville, Ind., 1974-79; judge Vanderburgh Superior Ct., Evansville, 1980-85; assoc. justice Ind. Supreme Ct., Indpls., 1985-87, chief justice, 1987—; instr. U. Evansville, 1975-78, Indiana U., 1995. Author: Preservation Rules and Regulations, 1980; contbr. articles to profl. publs. Bd. advisors Nat. Trust for Hist. Preservation, 1980-87, chmn. bd. advisors, 1983-85, trustee, 1987—; dir. Hist. Landmarks Found. Ind., 1983—, chmn., 1989-92, hon. chmn., 1992—; chmn. State Student Assistance Commn. on Ind., 1981-85; chmn. Ind. Commn. on Bicentennial of U.S. Constn., 1986-91; vice chmn. Vanderburgh County Rep. Ctrl. Com., 1977-80. Recipient Friend of Media award Cardinal States chpt. Sigma Delta Chi, 1979, Disting. Svc. award Evansville Jaycees, 1982, Herbert Harley award Am. Judicature Soc., 1992. Mem. ABA (coun. mem. sect. on legal edn. 1991—, vice chair appellate judges conf. 1992—), Ind. Bar Assn., Ind. Judges Assn., Princeton Club (N.Y.), Capitol Hill Club (Washington), Columbia Club (Indpls.). Republican. Methodist. Home: 4057 N Meridian St Indianapolis IN 46208-4012 Office: Ind Supreme Ct 304 State House Indianapolis IN 46204-2213

SHEPARD, ROBERT CARLTON, English language educator; b. Akron, Ohio, Dec. 20, 1933; s. Robert and Mildred Lucille (Stewart) S.; m. Marjorie Alma Mackey, June 9, 1956; children: Robert Lincoln, Donald Ward. BA, U. Oreg., 1970, MA, 1971; postgrad., England, 1979, 1991. Prof. English Southwestern Oreg. C.C., Coos Bay, 1971-94, chair divsn. English, 1976-78, prof. emeritus, 1994—; liaison Oreg. Com. for Humanities, 1985-86; judge statewide writing contests Nat. Coun. Tchrs. English, Urbana, Ill., 1987-88; founder Willamette Valley Vineyards, Turner, Oreg., 1991; co-founder Nor 'Wester Brewing Co., Portland, 1993, Breweries Across Am., Portland, 1994. Author, photographer, producer: (multi-image show) Christmas Fiestas of Oaxaca (Mexico), 1985; developer ednl. software, 1993—. With USMCR, 1954-58. Grad. Teaching fellow U. Oreg., 1970-71. Democrat. Avocations: bicycling, photography, music appreciation, world travel. Home: 3280 Sheridan Ave North Bend OR 97459-3043

SHEPARD, ROBERT M., lawyer, investment banker, engineer; b. Amityville, N.Y., Feb. 15, 1932; s. Sidney M. and Undine L. (Lehmann) Shapiro; m. Barbara S. Stannard, June 25, 1955 (div. 1980); children: Karen Michele Shepard Sweer, Daniel Robert; m. Joanne E. Devlin, May 16, 1981 (div. 1993). B.C.E., Cornell U., 1954; M.B.A., Hofstra Coll., 1960; LL.B., Yale U., 1963; LLM, NYU, 1988. Bar: N.Y. 1964; registered profl. engr., N.Y., Conn. Project engr. Lockwood Kessler & Bartlett, Syosset, N.Y., 1956-60; assoc. atty. Cravath, Swaine & Moore, N.Y.C. and Paris, 1963-70; gen. ptnr. Kuhn, Loeb & Co., N.Y.C., 1970-77; sr. v.p. Donaldson, Lufkin & Jenrette, N.Y.C., 1977-83; gen. ptnr. Donovan Leisure Newton & Irvine, N.Y.C., 1983-89, Adler & Shepard, N.Y.C., 1989-91, Shepard & van Essche, N.Y.C., 1991, Ballon Stoll Bader & Nadler, P.C., N.Y.C., 1992—. Note and comment editor: Yale Law Jour., 1962-63. Bd. dirs. N.Y. Grand Opera, 1987—. Recipient Fuertes Medal Cornell U., 1953. Mem. ABA, Am. N.Y. State Bar Assn., Pub. Power Assn., Nat. Assn. Bond Lawyers, Order of Coif, Tau Beta Pi, Chi Epsilon. Club: Union League. Home: 750 Park Ave Apt 12B New York NY 10021-4252 Office: Ballon Stoll Bader & Nadler 1450 Broadway New York NY 10018-2201

SHEPARD, ROGER NEWLAND, psychologist, educator; b. Palo Alto, Calif., Jan. 30, 1929; s. Orson Cutler and Grace (Newland) S.; m. Barbaranne Bradley, Aug. 18, 1952; children: Newland Chenoweth, Todd David, Shenna Esther. B.A., Stanford U., 1951; Ph.D., Yale U., 1955; A.M. (hon.), Harvard U., 1966; ScD (hon.), Rutgers U., 1992. Rsch. assoc. Naval Research Lab., 1955-56; rsch. fellow Harvard, 1956-58; mem. tech. staff Bell Telephone Labs., 1958-66, dept. head, 1963-66; prof. psychology Harvard U., 1966-68, dir. psychol. labs., 1967-68; prof. psychology Stanford U., 1968—, Ray Lyman Wilbur prof. social sci., 1989. Guggenheim fellow Center for Advanced Study in Behavioral Scis., 1971-72; recipient, N.Y. Acad. Scis. award, 1987, Nat. Medal of Sci., 1995. Fellow AAAS, Am. Psychol. Assn. (pres. exptl. div. 1980-81, Disting. Sci. Contbn. award 1976); mem. Am. Acad. Arts and Scis., Nat. Acad. Scis., Psychometric Soc. (pres. 1973-74), Psychonomic Soc., Soc. Exptl. Psychologists (Howard Crosby Warren medal 1981). Office: Stanford U Dept Psychology Bldg 420 Stanford CA 94305-2130

SHEPARD, SAM (SAMUEL SHEPARD ROGERS), playwright, actor; b. Ft. Sheridan, Ill., Nov. 5, 1943; s. Samuel Shepard and Jane Elaine (Schook) Rogers; m. O-Lan Johnson Dark, Nov. 9, 1969 (div.); 1 son, Jesse Mojo; children with Jessica Lange: Hannah Jane, Samuel Walker. Student, Mt. San Antonio Jr. Coll., Walnut, Calif., 1961-62. Playwright-in-residence Magic Theatre, San Francisco. Author: (plays) Cowboys, 1964, The Rock Garden, 1964, 4-H Club, 1965, Up to Thursday, 1965, Dog, 1965, Rocking Chair, 1965, Chicago, 1965 (Obie award 1966), Icarus's Mother, 1965 (Obie award 1966), Fourteen Hundred Thousand, 1966, Red Cross, 1966 (Obie award 1966), Melodrama Play, 1966 (Obie award 1968), La Turista, 1967 (Obie award 1967), Cowboys #2, 1967, Forensic and the Navigators, 1967 (Obie award 1968), The Holy Ghostly, 1969, The Unseen Hand, 1969, Operation Sidewinder, 1970, Shaved Splits, 1970, Mad Dog Blues, 1971, Terminal, 1971, (with Patti Smith) Cowboy Mouth, 1971, Black Bog Beast Bait, 1971, The Tooth of Crime, 1972 (Obie award 1973), Blue Bitch, 1973, (with Megan Terry and Jean-Claude van Itallie) Nightwalk, 1973, Geography of a Horse Dreamer, 1974, Little Ocean, 1974, Action, 1974 (Obie award 1975), Killer's Head, 1974, Suicide in B-Flat, 1976, Angel City, 1976, Curse of the Starving Class, 1977 (Obie award 1977), Buried Child, 1978 (Pulitzer Prize in drama 1979, Obie award 1979), Tongues, 1979, Savage/Love, 1979, Seduced, 1979, True West, 1981, Fool for Love, 1983 (Obie award 1984), Superstitions, 1983, The Sad Lament of Pecos Bill on the Eve of Killing his Wife, 1983, A Lie of the Mind, 1985 (New York Drama Critics' Circle award 1986), States of Shock, 1991, Simpatico, 1993; (collections of plays) Five Plays by Sam Shepard, 1967, The Unseen Hand and Other Plays, 1971, 2nd edit., 1986, Mad Dog Blues and Other Plays, 1972, The Tooth of Crime and Geography of a Horse Dreamer, 1974, Angel City, Curse of the Starving Class and Other Plays, 1976, Buried Child, Seduced, Suicide in B-Flat, 1979, Four Two-Act Plays by Sam Shepard, 1980, Chicago and Other Plays, 1981, Seven Plays, 1981, Fool for Love and The Sad Lament of Pecos Bill on the Eve of Killing His Wife, 1983, Fool For Love and Other Plays, 1984, 1986; contbr. to Oh! Calcutta, 1976; (screenplays) Me and My Brother, 1967, (with Michelangelo Antonioni, Tonino Guerra, Fred Graham, and Clare Peploe) Zabriskie Point, 1970, (with Murray Mednick) Ringaleevio, 1971, (with others) Oh! Calcutta!, 1972, (with Bob Dylan) Renaldo and Clara, 1978, Paris, Texas, 1984 (Golden Palm award Cannes Film Festival 1984), Fool for Love, 1985; (other writings) Rolling Thunder Logbook, 1977, Hawk Moon: A Book of Short Stories, Poems and Monologues, 1981, Motel Chronicles, 1982; writer, dir.: (plays) Fool for Love, 1983, A Lie of the Mind, 1985, (screenplays) Far North, 1988, Silent Tongue, 1993; actor: (films) Renaldo and Clara, 1978, Days of Heaven, 1978, Resurrection, 1980, Raggedy Man, 1981, Frances, 1982, The Right Stuff, 1983 (Academy award nomination best supporting actor 1984), Country, 1984, Fool for Love, 1985, Crimes of the Heart, 1986, Baby Boom, 1987, Steel Magnolias, 1989, Hot Spot, 1990, Bright Angel, 1991, Defenseless, 1991, Thunderheart, 1992, The Pelican Brief, 1993, Safe Passage, 1994, The Good Old Boys, 1995. Fellow U. Minn., 1966, Yale U., 1967; grantee Rockefeller Found., 1967, Guggenheim Found., 1968, 71; recipient Nat. Inst. and Am. Acad. Arts and Letters award for lit., 1974, Creative Arts award Brandeis U., 1975, Theater Hall of Fame, 1994. mem. Am. Acad. and Inst. of Arts and Letters, 92. Office: Internat Creative Mgmt 8942 Wilshire Blvd Beverly Hills CA 90211-1934*

SHEPARD, STEPHEN BENJAMIN, journalist, magazine editor; b. N.Y.C., July 20, 1939; s. William and Ruth (Tanner) S.; m. Lynn Povich, Sept. 16, 1979; children—Sarah, Ned. B.S., CCNY, 1961; M.S., Columbia U., 1963. Reporter, editor, writer Business Week, N.Y.C., 1966-75; asst. prof., dir. Walter Bagehot fellowship program econs. and bus. journalism Columbia U., N.Y.C., 1975-76; sr. editor Newsweek, N.Y.C., 1976-81; editor Saturday Rev., N.Y.C., 1981-82; exec. editor Business Week mag., N.Y.C., 1982-84, editor in chief, 1984—. Mem. Am. Soc. Mag. Editors (v.p. 1990-92, pres. 1992-94), Coun. Fgn. Rels., Century Assn. Home: 322 Central Park W New York NY 10025-7629 Office: Business Week McGraw Hill Inc 1221 Ave Of The Americas New York NY 10020-1001

SHEPARD, THOMAS HILL, physician, educator; b. Milw., May 22, 1923; s. Francis Parker and Elizabeth Rhodes (Buchner) S.; m. Alice B. Kelly, June 24, 1946; children: Donna, Elizabeth, Ann. A.B., Amherst Coll., 1945; M.D., U. Rochester, 1948. Intern Strong Meml. Hosp., Rochester, N.Y., 1948-49; resident Strong Meml. Hosp., 1950-52, Albany (N.Y.) Med. Center, 1949-50; pediatric endocrine fellow Johns Hopkins Hosp., 1954-55; pediatrician U. Wash., Seattle, 1955-61; embryologist dept. anatomy U. Fla., 1961-62; teratologist U. Wash., 1961—, prof. pediatrics, head central lab. for human embryology, 1961-93, prof. emeritus, 1993—; research assoc. dept. embryology Carnegie Inst., 1962, U. Copenhagen, 1963; cons. NIH, FDA, EPA, 1971—; vis. prof. pediatrics U. Geneva, 1972, 73-74. Author: A Catalog of Teratogenic Agents, 1973, 8th edit., 1995; contbr. articles to profl. jours. Served with U.S. Army, 1946-48; Served with USAF, 1952-54. Mem. Teratology Soc. (hon. mem. 1993, pres. 1968), Western Soc. Pediatric Rsch. (pres. 1970), Am. Pediatric Soc., Acad. Pediatrics. Home: 3015 98th Ave NE Bellevue WA 98004-1818 Office: U Wash Sch Medicine Dept Pediatrics Seattle WA 98195

SHEPARD, THOMAS ROCKWELL, JR., publishing consultant; b. N.Y.C., Aug. 22, 1918; s. Thomas Rockwell and Marie (Dickinson) S.; m. Nancy Kruidenier, Sept. 20, 1941; children: Sue Shepard Jaques, Molly Shepard Richard, Amy S. Knight, Thomas Rockwell III. B.A., Amherst Coll., 1940. Asst. sales promotion mgr. Vick Chemical Co., 1940-41; with Look mag., N.Y.C., 1946-72; advt. sales mgr. Look mag., 1961-64, advt. dir., 1964-67, pub., 1967-72; cons. Cowles Communications, Inc.; pres. Inst. Outdoor Advt., 1974-76. Co-author: The Disaster Lobby, 1973; contbr. articles to various publs. Pres. Greenwich Community Chest, 1964-65; chmn. Robert A. Taft Inst. Govt., 1978-81, Rep. Roundtable of Greenwich, 1981-85; bd. dirs. Advt. Coun., Lit. Vols. Am., 1989-91, Community Answers, 1988-91; chmn. Amherst Coll. Alumni Fund, 1986; mem. exec. com. alumni coun. Amherst Coll.; hon. pres. Soc. Amherst Coll. Alumni. Lt. comdr. USNR, 1941-45. Recipient George Washington honor medal for pub. address Freedoms Found., 1970, 73, Amherst Coll. medal for eminent svc., 1990. Republican. Clubs: Princeton (N.Y.C.); Bird Key Yacht (Fla.); Bell Haven; Round Hill. Home: 44 Lismore Ln Greenwich CT 06831-3760

SHEPARD, THOMAS ROCKWELL, III, advertising sales executive; b. Greenwich, Conn., Apr. 21, 1951; s. Thomas Rockwell, Jr. and Nancy (Kruidenier) S.; m. Margaret O'Neal, Sept. 1, 1972; children—Amanda Marie, Thomas Rockwell IV, Brian Dickinson. B.A., Amherst Coll., Mass., 1973. Hockey player Calif. Golden Seals, Oakland, 1973-74; salesman Union Carbide Battery Products, N.Y.C., 1974-78; became mem. advt. sales staff Hearst Mags., N.Y.C., 1978, became advt. dir. Good Housekeeping mag., 1984; now pub. Redbook mag. Republican. Clubs: Manursing (Rye, N.Y.); N.Y. Athletic (N.Y.C.). Office: Redbook Hearst Magazines 224 West 57th Street New York NY 10019*

SHEPARD, WILLIAM SETH, government official, diplomat; b. Boston, June 7, 1935; s. Robinson and Myra Ellen (Foster) S.; m. Lois Rosalie Burke, June 25, 1960; children—Stephanie Lee, Cynthia Robin, Warren Burke (dec.). A.B. cum laude, Wesleyan U., Middletown, Conn., 1957; J.D., Harvard U., Cambridge, Mass., 1961. Bar: N.H. 1961, U.S. Ct. Mil. Appeals 1962 U.S. Supreme Ct., 1970,. Aide to ambassadors Henry Cabot Lodge and Ellsworth Bunker U.S. embassy, Saigon, Vietnam, 1966-67; staff officer Exec. Secretariat Dept. of State, Washington, 1967-69; consul, polit. officer U.S. Embassy, Budapest, Hungary, 1970-73; desk officer Hungarian affairs Dept. State, Washington, 1973-75; desk officer Singapore and Malaysian affairs Dept. of State, Washington, 1975-77; dep. polit. counselor U.S. embassy, Athens, Greece, 1978-80; consul gen. consulate gen. U.S., Bordeaux, France, 1983-85; dir. office congressional affairs U.S. Arms Control and Disarmament Agy., 1987-89; cons. to the gen. counsel U.S. Dept. Agriculture, 1991-92; lectr. internat. law U. Singapore, 1965-66; CEO The Shepard Internat. Group, Inc., 1994—. Author: Au Revoir Bordeaux: Tales from the Consular Service, 1996; also articles. Candidate for Rep. nomination 8th Md. Congl. Dist., 1985-86, Rep. nominee for Gov. of Md., 1990, candidate, 1994; del. Rep. Nat. Conv., 1992; Md. co-chmn. Dole Presdl. Campaign, 1996. Recipient Pro Libertate Hungariae Commemorative medallion, 1981; French Govt. teaching asst. and Fulbright travel grantee, 1957-58; Congl. fellow Am. Polit. Sci. Assn. and fgn. policy legis. asst. to Senator Robert Dole, 1982-83. Mem. Am. Fgn. Service Assn., SAR, Soc. Mayflower Desc., Gov. Bradford Compact, Soc. Desc. Colonial Govs. (chancellor gen. 1993-95), Soc. Desc. Colonial Wars; corr. mem. Montesquieu Acad. France. Republican. Unitarian. Clubs: City Tavern (Washington), Flagon and Trencher, Les Chevaliers de Bretvin, Ordre des Compagnons de Bordeaux, Connetablie de Guyenne, La Jurade de St. Emilion, Bontemps Medoc et des Graves, Commanderie de Bordeaux (Washington), also others. Avocations: Plantagenet history, vintage Bordeaux wines, rose cultivation. Home: 8602 Hidden Hill Ln Potomac MD 20854-4225 *I remember Asian sunsets, Greek islands and Bordeaux vinyards. Hard work in a principled cause may ease the pain of family loss for a while, but it is Disneyland fantasy to believe in success. In the end, family life, a foyer, a book worth reading, pets and a glass of wine matter. So, perhaps, does God.*

SHEPHARD, MARK SCOTT, civil and mechanical engineering educator; b. Buffalo, Oct. 27, 1951; s. William N. and Beatrice (Hass) S.; m. Sharon L. Nirschel, Nov. 25, 1972; children: Steven W., Kari L. BS, Clarkson U., 1974; PhD, Cornell U., 1979. Asst. prof. civil engring. and mech. engring. Rensselaer Poly. Inst., Troy, N.Y., 1979-84, assoc. prof., 1984-87, prof., 1988—, dir. Sci. Computation Rsch. Ctr., 1990—, Samuel A. and Elisabeth C. Johnson Jr. prof. engring., 1993—; assoc. dir. Rensselaer Design Rsch. Ctr., Troy, N.Y., 1980-90; vis. rsch. fellow GE Corp., R & D Schenectady, 1985, cons., 1984-87; cons. GM Rsch. Lab., Detroit, 1980—, also other orgns.; mem. tech. adv. bd. Aries Tech., Lowell, Mass., 1987-89. Co-editor: Engring. with Computers; mem. editl. bd. Internat. Jour. Numerical Methods Engring., Engring. Applications of Artificial Intelligence, Internat. Jour. Engring. Analysis and Design, Computational Mechanics; contbr. articles to profl. jours., chpts. to books. Fellow AIAA (assoc.), U.S. Assn. for Computational Mechanics (treas.); mem. ASCE, ASME, Am. Soc. Engring. Edn., Am. Acad. Mechanics, Internat. Assn. for Computational Mechanics (exec. bd.), Sigma Xi, Tau Beta Pi, Phi Kappa Phi. Home: 305 Algonquin Beach Rd Averill Park NY 12018 Office: Rensselaer Poly Inst 110 8th St Troy NY 12180-3590

SHEPHERD, ALAN J., construction executive, management consultant; b. Bklyn., Jan. 15, 1942; s. Morris Elijah and Jean (Birnbaum) Shapiro; children: Robin Elyse, Kevin Peter. B.S. in Mech. Engring., Mich. State U.; M.S. in Indsl. Engring., Wayne State U., 1966. Mgmt. trainee Chrysler Corp., Detroit, 1964-65, product engr., 1965-66; exec. v.p. Bruce Erts & Assocs., Southfield, Mich., 1966-70; pres. Creative Mgmt. Group, Inc., Southfield, Mich., 1970-76, chmn. bd., 1976, pvt. cons., 1976-79; dir. planning and coordination Mgmt. Support Assocs., Tel Aviv, Israel, 1979-81, gen. mgr., 1981-82; mgmt. cons. MSA Consortium, Washington, 1982-83; regional mktg. dir. Hill Internat., Washington, 1983-84; mng. v.p. spl. projects CRS Sirrine, Inc., Washington, 1984-85; dir. advanced mgmt. program BDM Corp., McLean, Va., 1986-89; v.p. Hill Internat., Inc., Willingboro, N.J., 1989-90, AWD Techs., Inc., Rockville, Md., 1990-94; bd. dirs. Brown & Root, Inc., Washington; instr. Lawrence Inst. Tech., 1971, 73. Mem. Am. Inst. Indsl. Engrs., Project Mgmt. Inst., Soc. Am. Mil. Engrs. Office: Brown & Root Inc 1150 18th St NW Ste 200 Washington DC 20036-9999

SHEPHERD, CYBILL, actress, singer; b. Memphis, Feb. 18, 1950; d. William Jennings and Patty Shobe (Micci) S.; m. David Ford, Nov. 19, 1978 (div.); 1 child, Clementine; m. Bruce Oppenheim, March 1, 1987; children: Molly Ariel and Cyrus Zachariah (twins). Student, Hunter Coll., 1969, Coll. of New Rochelle, 1970, Washington Sq. Coll., NYU, 1971, U. So. Calif., 1972, NYU, 1973. Appeared in motion pictures Last Picture Show, 1971, The Heartbreak Kid, 1973, Daisy Miller, 1974, At Long Last Love, 1975, Taxi Driver, 1976, Special Delivery, 1976, Silver Bears, 1977, The Lady Vanishes, 1978, Earthright, 1980, The Return, 1986, Chances Are, 1988, Texasville, 1990, Alice, 1990, Once Upon a Crime, 1992, Married to It, 1993; star TV series The Yellow Rose, 1983-84, Moonlighting, 1985-89, Cybill, 1994—; TV films include A Guide for the Married Woman, 1978, Secrets of a Married Man, 1984, Seduced, 1985, The Long Hot Summer, 1985, Which Way Home, 1991, Memphis, 1992 (also co-writer, co-exec. prodr.), Stormy Weathers, 1992, Telling Secrets, 1993, There Was a Little Boy, 1993; record albums include Cybill Does It To Cole Porter, 1974, Cybill and Stan Getz, 1977, Vanilla with Phineas Newborn, Jr, 1978; appeared in stage plays A Shot in the Dark, 1977, Picnic, 1980, Vanities, 1981.

SHEPHERD, DANIEL MARSTON, executive recruiter; b. Madison, Ind., Apr. 8, 1939; s. Marston Vincent and Edith America (Brunson) S.; m. Bonnie Lynn Brawley, June 27, 1970 (div. Nov. 1987); children: Vincent, David, Christopher, Megan; m. Gail Lenore Sanborn, Oct. 3, 1989; children: Heather, Shannon. BS in Civil Engring., U. Ky., 1962; MBA, Harvard Bus. Sch., 1964. Mfg. and distbn. mgr. Procter & Gamble Co., Staten Island, N.Y., 1966-70; distbn. and ops. mgr. Mattel, Inc., Gardenia, Calif., 1970-73; gen. mgr., dir. ops. Fuqua Industries, Inc., Atlanta, 1973-76; v.p. product/market mgmt. Masonite Corp., Chgo., 1976-78; v.p. Heidrick & Struggles, Chgo., 1978-82, Lamalie Assocs., Chgo., 1982-86; prin. Sweeney Shepherd

Bueschel Provus Harbert & Mummert, Chgo., 1986-91, Shepherd Bueschel & Provus, Inc., Chgo., 1991—. Capt. U.S. Army, 1964-66. Decorated Army Commendation medal, 1966; recipient Am.'s Top 150 Recruiters award Harper Bus., N.Y.C., 1992. Mem. Assn. Exec. Search Cons., Inc., Union League Club, Harvard Bus. Sch. Club. Republican. Episcopalian. Avocations: coin and art collecting, skiing, baseball, food, wine. Home: 990 N Lake Shore Dr # 27E Chicago IL 60611-1345 Office: 401 N Michigan Ave Ste 3020 Chicago IL 60611-1345

SHEPHERD, FRANK ANDREW, lawyer; b. West Palm Beach, Fla, Dec. 11, 1946; s. Vernon Francis and Helen Veronica (Shaab) S.; children: Scott, Kristi, Sandra. BA, U. Fla., 1968; JD, U. Mich., 1972. Bar: Fla. 1972, D.C. 1975, U.S. Dists. Ct. (so., mid. and no. dists.) Fla., U.S. Ct. Appeals (5th and 11th cirs.), U.S. Supreme Ct. With Kimbrell & Hamann, P.A., Miami, Fla., 1972-90, Popham, Haik, Schnobrich & Kaufman Ltd, Miami, 1990—. Vice chmn. State Affairs Com., Miami, 1990-91. With U.S. Army Res., 1972-79. Mem. ABA, Dade County Bar Assn., Dade County Def. Bar Assn., Am. Jurisprudence Soc., Def. Rsch. Inst., U.S. Supreme Ct. Hist. Soc., Miami C. of C. Republican. Office: Popham Haik Schnobrich & Kaufman 4000 International Pl 100 SE 2nd St Miami FL 33131-2100

SHEPHERD, JAMES HAROLD, JR., hospital administrator, contruction executive; b. Atlanta, Jan. 26, 1951; s. James Harold and Alana (Smith) S. BBA in Fin., Mgmt., Bus. Law, U. Ga., 1973. V.p. Shepherd Constrn. Co., Inc., Atlanta, 1974—; chmn., pres. bd. Shepherd Ctr., Inc., Atlanta, 1980—; advisor Emory U. Rehab., Decatur, Ga., 1978-83; del. White House Conf. on Handicapped Indivuals, Washington; mem. Ga. Conf. of Handicapped Individuals, Atlanta. Bd. dirs. Ctr. for Rehab., Ga. Tech. U., Atlanta, 1981—, Goodwill Industries, Atlanta, 1980-82, Atlanta Paralympic Organizing Com., 1993—; mem. Ga. Gov. Coun. on Devel. Disabilities, Ga. State Health Planning and Devel. Task Force on Rehab. Svcs. Named One of Ten Outstanding Young Men in Am., U.S. Jaycees, 1985, One of Outstanding Young Persons of the World, Jaycee Internat., 1985. Mem. Young Pres. Orgn., Chi Phi. Home: 1800 Briarcliff Rd Atlanta GA 30309 Office: Shepherd Spinal Ctr Inc 2020 Peachtree St NW Atlanta GA 30309-1402

SHEPHERD, JOHN FREDERIC, lawyer; b. Oak Park, Ill., May 22, 1954; s. James Frederic Shepherd and Margaret Joanne (Crotchett) Woollen; children: Eliza Marion, Justine Catherine. AB magna cum laude, Dartmouth Coll., Hanover, N.H., 1976; JD, U. Denver, 1979. Bar: Colo. 1979, U.S. Dist. Ct. Colo. 1979, D.C. 1981, U.S. Dist. Ct. D.C. 1981, U.S. Ct. Appeals (10th cir.) 1981, U.S. Ct. Appeals (D.C. cir.) 1982, U.S. Ct. Appeals (9th cir.) 1990, U.S. Supreme Ct. 1984. Assoc. Holland & Hart, Denver, 1979-81; assoc. Holland & Hart, Washington, 1981-85, ptnr., 1985-87; ptnr. Holland & Hart, Denver, 1987—. Reporter Mineral Law Newsletter, 1985-92. Mem. 50 for Colo., Denver, 1989. Mem. ABA (chmn. pub. lands and land use com. 1991-93, mem. coun. for sect. of natural resources energy and environ. law 1993—), Rocky Mountain Oil and Gas Assn. (mem. pub. lands com. 1987—), Rocky Mountain Mineral Law Found. (mem. long-range planning com. 1988—, bd. trustees 1993-95), Dartmouth Alumni Club (pres. Washington chpt. 1985-86), Denver Athletic Club. Avocations: flyfishing, basketball, running. Home: 848 Monroe St Denver CO 80206 Office: Holland & Hart 555 17th St Ste 3200 Denver CO 80202-3929

SHEPHERD, JOHN THOMPSON, physiologist; b. No. Ireland, May 21, 1919; s. William Frederick and Matilda (Thompson) S.; m. Helen Mary Johnston, July 28, 1945; children: Gillian Mary, Roger Frederick John; m. Marion G. Etzwiler, Apr. 22, 1989. Student, Campbell Coll., Belfast, No. Ireland, 1932-37; M.B., B.Ch., Queen's U., Belfast, 1945, M.Chir., 1948, M.D., 1951, D.Sc., 1956, D.Sc. (hon.), 1979; M.D. (hon.), U. Bologna, 1984, U. Gent, 1985. Lectr. physiology Queen's U., 1948-53, reader physiology, 1954-57; assoc. prof. physiology Mayo Found., 1957-62, prof. physiology, 1962—, chmn. dept. physiology and biophysics, 1966-74; bd. govs. Mayo Clinic, 1966-80; trustee Mayo Found., 1969-81, dir. research, 1969-77, dir. for edn., 1977-83, chmn. bd. devel., 1983-88; dean Mayo Med. Sch., 1977-83; assoc. dir. Gen. Rsch. Ctr. Mayo Clinic, Rochester, 1992-94. Author, editor: Physiology of the Circulation in Human Limbs in Health and Disease, 1963, Cardiac Function in Health and Disease, 1968, Veins and Their Control, 1975, Human Cardiovascular System, 1979, Handbook of Physiology, The Cardiovascular System Peripheral Circulation and Organ Blood Flow, 1983, Vascular Diseases in the Limbs, 1993, Nervous Control of the Heart, 1995; mem. editl. bd. Hypertension, 1973—, Am. Jour. Physiology, Am. Heart Jour., Microvascular Rsch.; cons. editor Circulation Rsch., 1982; editor-in-chief News in Physiol. Sci., 1988-94; contbr. more than 590 sci. articles and 350 papers to profl. jours. Recipient NASA Skylab Achievement award, 1974, A. Ross McIntyre medal for achievement, 1991; Brit. Med. Assn. scholar, 1949-50, Fulbright scholar, 1953-54; Anglo-French Med. exchange bursar, 1957; Internat. Francqui chair, 1978; Einthoven lectr. 1981, Volhard lectr., 1990. Fellow Am. Coll. Cardiology (hon.), Royal Coll. Physicians (London), Royal Acad. Medicine (Belgium); mem. Am. Physiol. Soc. (Disting. Svc. award 1990), Louis Rapkine Assn., Am. Heart Assn. (dir. 1968—, pres. 1975-76, chmn. vascular medicine and biology task force 1990, hon. fellow council clin. cardiology), Physiol. Soc. Gt. Brit., Med. Research Soc. London, Nat. Acad. Scis. (space sci. bd. 1973-74, chmn. com. space biology and medicine 1973), Assn. Am. Physicians, Internat. Union of Angiology (hon.), Rappaport Inst. Israel (sci. adv. bd.), Sigma Xi. Home: 600 4th St SW Rochester MN 55902-3291 Office: Mayo Clinic 1043 Plummer Bldg Rochester MN 55905

SHEPHERD, KAREN, former congresswoman; b. Silver City, N.Mex., July 5, 1940; m. Vincent P. Shepherd. BA, U. Utah, 1962; MA, Brigham Young U., 1963. Former instr. Brigham Young U., Am. U., Cairo; former pres. Webster Pub. Co.; former adminstr. David Eccles Sch. Bus., U. Utah; former dir. Salt Lake County Social Svcs., Utah; former dir. continuing edn. Westminster Coll.; former mem. Utah Senate; mem. 103d Congress from 2d Utah dist., Washington, 1993-95, Nat. Common Cause Governing Bd., Washington, 1995—; founding mem. Utah Women's Polit. Caucus, Project 2000; mem. Internat. Delegation to Monitor Elections in West Bank and Gaza, Israel. Former mem. United Way, Pvt. Industry Coun.; former mem. adv. bd. U.s. West Grad. Sch. Social Work; trustee Westminster Coll. Recipient Women in Bus. award U.S. Small Bus. Assn., Woman of Achievement award, Pathfinder award, 1st place award Nat. Assn. Journalists, Disting. Alumni award U. Utah Coll. Humanities. Fellow Inst. Politics Kennedy Sch Govt.; Salt Lake Area C. of C. (pub. rels. com.). Home: PO Box 1049 Salt Lake City UT 84110 Office: 21 G St Salt Lake City UT 84103

SHEPHERD, KATHLEEN SHEAREN MAYNARD, television executive; b. N.Y.C., June 14, 1950; d. Theodore E. and Phyllis (Wildman) Shearer; m. Charles Dix Shepherd; m. Joseph Ashton Maynard (div. June 1977); 1 child, Natasha Candice. Student, Tufts U., Medford, Mass., 1968-69, Duke U., Durham, N.C., 1972-73, Westchester Community Coll., White Plains, N.Y, 1974-75, NYU, 1975-77. From administrv. asst. to assoc. producer WCBS-TV, N.Y.C., 1973-74, producer, 1975-76; from program devel. supr., exec. producer to dir. pub. affai WPIX TV, N.Y.C., 1977-84, v.p. pub. affairs, prodn., exec. producer; tchr. Montclair State Coll., 1985-88. Bd. dirs. Nat. Coalitin of 100 Black Women, lower Fairfield chpt., Conn., 1987, Childrens Village, Dobbs Ferry, N.Y., 1988. Mem. Nat. Acad. TV Arts, Sciences, Pvt. Industry Council, Archdiocese Communications Com. Democrat. Episcopalian. Avocations: jogging, exercise. Office: WPIX Inc 220 E 42nd St New York NY 10017-5806

SHEPHERD, MARK, JR., retired electronics company executive; b. Dallas, Jan. 18, 1923; s. Mark and Louisa Florence (Daniell) S.; m. Mary Alice Murchland, Dec. 21, 1945; children: Debra Aline Shepherd Robinson, MaryKay Theresa, Marc Blaine. BSEE, So. Meth. U., 1942; MSEE, U. Ill., at Urbana, 1947. Registered profl. engr., Tex. With GE, 1942-43, Farnsworth TV and Radio Corp., 1947-48; with Tex. Instruments, Dallas, 1948-88, v.p., gen. mgr. semicondr.-components div., 1955-61, exec. v.p., chief operating officer, 1961-66, pres., chief operating officer, 1967-69, pres., chief exec. officer, 1969-76, chmn. bd. dirs., chief exec. officer, 1976-84, chmn. bd. dirs., chief corp. officer, 1984-85, chmn., 1985-88; ret. Hon. trustee Com. for Econ. Devel.; councillor conf. Bd.; mem. Bus. Coun. Lt. (j.g.) USNR, 1943-46. Fellow IEEE; mem. NAE, Sigma Xi, Eta Kappa Nu.

SHEPHERD, PAUL H., elementary school educator; b. Salt Lake City, Sept. 6, 1955; s. Richard Lawrence and Janis (Hoskings) S.; m. Marlene Wade, Aug. 31, 1978; children: Janice, Faith, Matthew, Andrew, Luke, Christian. BS in Elem. Edn., U. Utah, 1981, MEd, 1985. Cert. elem. tchr., Utah. Printer Transamerica Film Svc., Salt Lake City, 1978-81; tchr. Granite Sch. Dist., Salt Lake City, 1981—; pres. Granite Fedn. Tchrs., 1985-87, treas., 1990-92. Active mem. State House of Reps., 1992-94; Bishop LDS Ch., West Jordan, Utah, 1988; mem. Oquivrh Shadows Community Coun., West Jordan, 1987; chmn. rels. com. Boy Scouts Am., 1972—. Recipient Outstanding Tchr. award Excel Found., 1985, Elem. Tchr. of Yr. award Utah Fedn. Tchrs., 1991. Mem. ASCD, Utah Assn Gifted Children. Democrat. Avocations: fishing, guitar. Home and Office: 6644 S 5095 W West Jordan UT 84084-6889

SHEPHERD, R. F., retired bishop; b. July 15, 1926; s. Herbert George and Muriel (Grant) S.; m. Ann Alayne Dundas, 1952; 6 children. BA with honors, U. B.C., 1948; postgrad., King's Coll., London; DD (hon.), St. John's Coll., Winnipeg, 1988. Curate St. Stephen's, London, 1952-57; rector St. Paul's, Glanford, Ont., 1957-59, All Sts., Winnipeg, 1959-65; dean, rector All Sts. Cathedral, Edmonton, Alta., 1965-69, Christ Ch. Cathedral, Montreal, 1970-83; rector St. Matthias, Victoria, B.C., 1983-84; Anglican Bishop of B.C., 1985-92. Fellow Coll. of Preachers. Home: 110 Ensilwood Rd, Salt Spring Island, BC Canada V8K 1N1

SHEPHERD, ROBERT JAMES, plant pathology researcher, retired educator; b. Clinton, Okla., June 5, 1930; s. Lee Fines and Ruby (Gilleland) S.; m. Shirley Ann Stuby, Sept. 6, 1955 (div. Sept. 1976); children: Steven L., Eudora Deidre, David A.; m. Mary Ann Sall, Mar. 18, 1978. Student, U. Okla., 1948-50; BS, Okla. State U., 1954, MS, 1955; PhD, U. Wis., 1959. Asst. prof. U. Wis., Madison, 1959-61; asst. prof. U. Calif., Davis, 1961-66, assoc. prof., 1966-72, prof. plant pathology, 1972-84; prof. plant pathology U. Ky., Lexington, 1984-96; ret., 1996; chmn. plant virus subcom. Internat. Com. Taxonomy of Viruses, 1971-76; mem. sci. bd. Calgene Inc., Davis, 1980-85; cons. Ohio Bd. Regents, 1985-86. Editor Virology jour., 1971-73; contbr. articles and revs. to profl. jours. With U.S. Army, 1950-52, Korea. Fulbright scholar, Cambridge, Eng., 1955-56. Fellow Am. Phytopathol. Soc. (Ruth Allen award 1981); mem. NAS. Democrat. Avocations: bird watching, gardening.

SHEPHERD, STEVEN STEWART, auditor, consultant; b. Pauls Valley, Okla., Aug. 7, 1956; s. Lloyd Thomas and Barbara Lou (Garton) S.; m. Dawn Rachelle Godwin, Aug. 22, 1981; children: Shane, Lauren. BBA, U. Tex., 1981, MBA, 1990. Internal auditor Ark-La. Gas Co., Shreveport, La., 1982-84; sr. constrn. auditor Cen. & S.W. Svcs., Inc., Dallas, 1984-87; constrn. audit supr. City of Ft. Worth, 1987—; cons. Constrn. Mgmt. Svcs., Arlington, Tex., 1990—, Eagle Tax Svcs., Arlington, 1990—; mem. adv. com. for acctg. program Tarrant County Jr. Coll., 1995-97; mem. internat. audit adv. bd. U. North Tex., 1993-96. Contbr. articles to profl. jours. Mem. allocation com. Tarrant County United Way, Ft. Worth, 1991; bd. dirs. Charlotte Anderson Elem. Sch. PTA, Mansfield, Tex., 1990-91. Mem. Inst. Internal Auditors (bd. govs. Ft. Worth chpt. 1990—, sec. 1990-91, treas. 1991-92, v.p. 1992-93, pres. 1993-94), Mansfield Youth Baseball Assn. (bd. dirs. 1993—), Delta Upsilon (bd. dirs. 1991—, sec. 1994). Republican. Mem. Ch. of Christ. Avocations: little league coach, horseback riding, water skiing, snow skiing, scuba diving.

SHEPHERD, STEWART ROBERT, lawyer; b. Chgo., Sept. 9, 1948; s. Stewart and LaVina Beatrice (Nereim) S.; m. Margaret Brownell Shoop, Aug. 14, 1970; children: Elisabeth Ashby, Megan Brownell, Blair Stewart. BA, Rockford Coll., 1970; JD, U. Chgo., 1973. Bar: Calif. 1973, U.S. Dist. Ct. (no. dist.) Calif. 1973, Ill. 1976, U.S. Dist. Ct. (no. dist.) Ill. 1976. Assoc. Heller, Ehrman, White & McAuliffe, San Francisco, 1973-75; assoc. Hopkins & Sutter, Chgo., 1975-79, ptnr., 1979-96; ptnr. Sidley & Austin, 1996—. Mem. ABA, Order of Coif, Phi Beta Kappa. Office: Sidley & Austin One First National Plz Chicago IL 60603

SHEPLEY, HUGH, architect; b. Boston, Mar. 17, 1928; s. Henry Richardson and Anna Lowell (Gardiner) S.; m. Mary Waters Niles, Dec. 27, 1950; children: Hamilton Niles, Philip Foster. B.A., Harvard U., 1951; BArch., Boston Archtl. Ctr., 1958; postgrad., Mass. Inst. Tech., 1958-59. Mem. archtl. firm Shepley, Bulfinch, Richardson & Abbott, Boston, 1955-63; ptnr. Shepley, Bulfinch, Richardson & Abbott, 1963-91. Bd. dirs. Greater Boston Red Cross, 1967-73, mem. exec. com., 1968-69; bd. dirs. Cmty. Music Ctr., Boston, 1966-72, Boston Ctr. for Blind Children, 1979-87; trustee New Eng. Conservatory Music, 1978-83, overseer, 1983—; trustee Univ. Hosp., 1980—, mem. exec. com., 1981-92, vice chmn. bd. dirs., 1985-89, chmn. bd. dirs., 1989-92; trustee Am. Coll. of Greece, 1983-92, treas., 1986-88; trustee, sec. Rotch Travelling Scholarship, 1987-93, v.p., 1993—; mem. adv. coun. Boston U. Med. Ctr., 1990—, Corp. Old South Assn., 1993—; v.p. Manchester (Mass.) Hist. Soc., 1994—. Fellow AIA; mem. Mass. Assn. Architects (pres. 1972), Boston Soc. Architects (pres. 1974), Boston Archtl. Ctr. (pres. 1969-71). Republican. Episcopalian. Clubs: Tavern (Boston); Manchester Yacht (commodore 1985-87). Home: 18 Forster Rd Manchester MA 01944-1420 Office: S B R & A 40 Broad St Fl 6 Boston MA 02109-4307

SHEPP, BRYAN EUGENE, psychologist, educator; b. Cumberland, Md., Sept. 13, 1932; s. Bryan Evert and Dorothy Lorene (Stell) S.; m. June Lee Langeluttig, Jan. 31, 1953; children—Karen Suzanne, David Bryan. B.S., U. Md., 1954, M.S., 1956, Ph.D., 1960; M.S. (hon.), Brown U., 1966. Research prof. U. Conn., 1961-63; asst. prof. psychology George Peabody Coll., 1963-64; asst. prof. Brown U., 1964-66, assoc. prof., 1966-69, prof., 1969—, chmn. dept. psychology, 1983-88, assoc. dean of faculty, 1988-91, dean of faculty, 1991—; cons. in field; vis. scientist Oxford (Eng.) U., 1970. Contbr. numerous articles to profl. publs.; ad hoc editor for several psychol. jours. Served with USN, 1955-59. Decorated letter of commendation Sec. of Navy; USPHS postdoctoral fellow, 1959-61; Nat. Inst. Child Health and Human Devel. grantee, 1965—. Fellow Am. Psychol. Assn.; mem. Psychonomic Soc., AAAS, AAUP. Club: Univ. Office: 89 Waterman St Providence RI 02912-9079

SHEPPARD, ALBERT PARKER, JR., mathematics educator; b. Griffin, Ga., June 6, 1936; s. Albert Parker and Cornelia (Cooper) S.; m. Judith Prosser, Sept. 9, 1957 (div. 1976); children: Albert Parker III, Frank Phillip; m. Eleanor C. Davis, Feb. 8, 1978 (dec. Oct. 1994); 1 stepchild, Phillip Hancock; m. Marjory W. Dewell, Nov. 18, 1995. B.S., Oglethorpe U., 1958; M.S., Emory U., 1959; Ph.D., Duke U., 1965. Sr. engr. Orlando (Fla.) rsch. div. Martin Marietta Co., 1960-63; physicist U.S. Army Rsch. Office, Durham, N.C., 1963-65; prin. rsch. engr., head spl. techniques br., electronics div. Ga. Inst. Tech., 1965-71, chief of chem. sci. lab., 1971-72, assoc. dean coll. engring., 1972-74, prof. elec. engring., 1972-89, assoc. v.p. for rsch., 1974-88, acting v.p. rsch., 1979-80, asst. to pres. info. tech., 1986, v.p. for interdisciplinary programs, 1988-89, acting v.p. info. tech., 1988-89; Charles and Mildred Jenkins prof. math. Fla. So. Coll., Lakeland, 1989—; mem. evening faculty DeKalb Coll., Clarkston, Ga., 1967-71; pres. APS Enterprises Corp., Lakeland, 1980—; cons. scholar IBM So. Area 8, 1990-93. Contbr. articles to profl. jours. Inventor linear down-draft biomass gasifier. Trustee Southeastern Univs. Research Assocs., 1983-86. Recipient Disting. Alumni award Oglethorpe U., 1974; Woodrow Wilson fellow, 1959. Mem. IEEE (sr.), Univ. Space Rsch. Assn. (vice chmn. coun. instns. 1980-81, chmn. 1981-82, trustee 1985-89, vice chmn. bd. dirs. 1986-87, chmn. 1987-88, chmn. engring. sci. coun. 1989-94), Ga. Tech. Rsch. Corp. (trustee), Math. Assn. Am., Lone Palm Golf Club, Sigma Xi, Sigma Pi Sigma, Kappa Mu Epsilon. Presbyterian. Home: 1240 Jefferson Dr Lakeland FL 33803-2300 Office: Fla So Coll Dept Math Lakeland FL 33801

SHEPPARD, CLAUDE-ARMAND, lawyer; b. Ghent, Belgium, May 26, 1935; m. Claudine Proutat; children—Jean-Pierre, Michel, Marie-Claude, Stephane, Annabelle. B.A., McGill U., 1955; B.C.L., 1958. Bar: Que. 1959. Partner firm Robinson, Sheppard & Shapiro, Montreal, 1965—; legal commentator for French and English radio and television networks in, Can.; lectr. various instns.; counsel various royal commns.; counsel to com. Canadian Ho. of Commons; legal supr. Que. Commn. of Inquiry Lang. Rights; dir. various orgns. and founds. Author: The Law of Languages in Canada, 1965, The Organization and Regulation of the Health and Social Welfare Professions in Quebec, 1970, Language Rights in Quebec, 1973, also numerous papers. Past pres. Canadian Civil Liberties Union; former mem. Canadian Adv. Council on Status of Women. Fellow C.B.A. Found. for Legal Rsch. Mem. ABA (assoc.), Can. Bar Assn., Internat. Inst. Comparative Linguistic Law (pres. 1987—), Que. Bar Found. (gov.), Found. André-Guerin (pres. 1991—), Found. Montreal 2000 (v.p. 1994—). Office: Robinson Sheppard & Shapiro, 800 Place Victoria Ste 4700, Montreal, PQ Canada H4Z 1H6

SHEPPARD, HAROLD LLOYD, gerontologist, educator; b. Balt., Apr. 1, 1922; s. Joseph and Anna Leslie (Levy) S.; m. Gloria Stefanowicz, July 27, 1986; children by previous marriages: Mark, Jenny. MA, U. Chgo., 1945; PhD, U. Wis., Madison, 1949. Assoc. prof. sociology Wayne State U., Detroit, 1947-59; rsch. and staff dir. spl. com. on aging U.S. Senate, Washington, 1959-61; asst. adminstr. area redevel. adminstrn. U.S. Dept. Commerce, Washington, 1961-63; staff social scientist W.E. Upjohn Inst. Employment Rsch., Washington, 1963-75; sr. rsch. fellow Am. Inst. Rsch., Washington, 1975-80; counselor on aging to Pres. Carter Washington, 1980-81; assoc. dir. Nat. Coun. on Aging, Washington, 1981-82; dir. Internat. Exchange Ctr. Gerontology U. South Fla., Tampa, 1983-91; prof. Dept. Gerontology U. South Fla., Tampa, 1983—; cons. U.S. Dept. Labor, Washington, Senate Com. on Unemployment and Poverty, Washington, ILO, Geneva, OECD, Paris. Author, editor: Towards an Industrial Gerontology, 1970; co-author: Where Have all the Robots Gone?, 1972, The Graying of Working America, 1979; editor: Poverty and Wealth in America, 1972, Future of Older Workers, 1990. Fulbright scholar, France, 1957-58. Fellow Gerontol. Soc. Am. Avocation: sailing.

SHEPPARD, JACK W., retired air force officer; b. Parkersburg, W.Va., Aug. 8, 1931; s. James Lee and Audrey Irene (Heiney) S.; m. Norma Ann Stutler, Sept. 4, 1953; children—Bradley, Gregory. B.A.C., U. Akron, Ohio, 1955; M.A. in Pub. Adminstrn., George Washington U., 1965. Commd. lt. U.S. Air Force, 1955, advanced through grades to maj. gen.; vice comdr. 60 Mil. Airlift Wing, USAF, Travis AFB, Calif., 1977-79; comdr. 1606 Air Base Wing, USAF, Kirtland AFB, N.Mex., 1979-81; dir. internat. staff Inter Am. Def. Bd., USAF, Washington, 1981-82; dep. chief staff for personnel USAF Mil. Airlift Command, Scott AFB, Ill., 1982-83, chief of staff, 1983-85; comdr. Twenty First Air Force, McGuire AFB, N.J., 1985-87; asst. dep. chief staff programs and resources Hdqrs. USAF, Washington, 1987-88, ret., 1988. Mem. Order of Daedalians, Air Force Assn., Airlift Assn., Theta Chi. Presbyterian. Home: PO Box 908 21 Beaver Ln Cedar Crest NM 87008-0908

SHEPPARD, JOHN WILBUR, computer research scientist; b. Pitts., Aug. 21, 1961; s. Harry Reid and Mary Jane (Amon) S.; m. Justine Anne Pape, Oct. 29, 1988. BS, So. Meth. U., 1983; MS, Johns Hopkins U., 1989, postgrad., 1990—. Systems analyst Sheppard Internat., Inc., Hermitage, Pa., 1979-86; prin. rsch. analyst ARINC Inc., Annapolis, Md., 1986—. Coauthor: System Test and Diagnosis, 1994; contbr. articles to profl. jours. Mem. YMCA, Hermitage, 1979-85, Md. Hall for the Creative Arts, Annapolis, 1988-90; pres. Univ. Chapel Campus Ministry, Dallas, 1982-83. Mem. IEEE, Am. Assn. for Artificial Intelligence, Internat. Neural Network Soc., Mensa, Kappa Mu Epsilon. Republican. Lutheran. Achievements include U.S. patent awarded and foreign patent pending for methods and apparatus for diagnostic testing; development of explanation-based learning approach for fault diagnosis. Home: 1203 Will-O-Brook Dr Pasadena MD 21122 Office: ARINC Inc 2551 Riva Rd Annapolis MD 21401-7435

SHEPPARD, LOUIS CLARKE, biomedical engineering educator; b. Pine Bluff, Ark., May 28, 1933; s. Ellis Allen and Louise (Clarke) S.; m. Nancy Louise Mayer, Feb. 8, 1958; children: David, Susan, Lisa. BS in Chem. Engring., U. Ark., 1957; PhD in Elec. Engring., U. London, 1976. Registered profl. engr., Ala., Tex. Devel. staff supr. Diamond Alkali Co., Deer Park, Tex., 1957-63; staff engr. IBM, Rochester, Minn., 1963-66; assoc. prof. surgery dept. U. Ala.-Birmingham, 1966-88, sr. scientist Cystic Fibrosis Research Ctr., 1981-87, prof., chmn. biomed. engring. dept., 1979-88; prof. phsiology and biophysics, asst. v.p. rsch. U. Tex., Galveston, 1988-90, assoc. v.p. rsch., 1990-92, assoc. v.p. bioengring. and biotech., 1992—, prof. biomed. engring., Austin; adj. prof. elec. engring. U. Houston; mem. med. adv. bd. Hewlett Packard, 1980-84; cons. IMED Corp., 1982-83, Oximetrix, 1982, 86-88, MiniMed, 1986-88; mem. sci. adv. bd. JJMI, 1992-94; dir. FBK Internat.; pres. S.E.A. Corp., 1984-94; mem. editorial bd. Med. Progress Through Tech., 1984-94, Springer-Verlag, Berlin; cons. Nat. Heart, Lung and Blood Inst. Bd. dirs. Birmingham Met. Devel. Bd. Served with AUS, 1958-66. Recipient Ayerton Premium award IEE (U.K.), 1984. Recipient Disting. Alumnus citation, U. Ark., 1987, Lifetime Achievement award M.D. Buyline, 1987. Fellow IEEE, Am. Inst. for Med. and Biol. Engring., Am. Coll. Med. Informatics; mem. Brit. Computer Soc., Biomed. Engring. Soc. (dir.), IEEE, Am. Inst. Chem. Engrs., Am. Med. Informatics Assn., Univ. Space Rsch. Assn. (bd. dirs. 1995—), Acad. Med. Arts and Scis., Blue Key, Sigma Xi, Tau Beta Pi, Alpha Pi Mu, Eta Kappa Nu, Theta Tau. Clubs: St. Andrews Soc. of Middle South, The Houstonian, The Yacht. Contbr. abstracts, chpts. to books, editorials; patentee method and system for estimation of arterial pressure. Home: 5 E Broad Oaks Ln Houston TX 77056-1218 Office: U Tex Med Br 626 Jennie Sealy Hosp Galveston TX 77555-0455

SHEPPARD, POSY (MRS. JEREMIAH MILBANK), social worker; b. New Haven, Aug. 23, 1916; d. John Day and Rose Marie (Herrick) Jackson; m. John W. Sheppard, May 16, 1936 (dec. Apr. 1990); children: Sandra S. (Mrs. Allan Gray Rodgers), Gail G. (Mrs. Gail Bidwell), Lynn S. (Mrs. William Muir Manger), John W.; m. Jeremiah Milbank, May 4, 1991. Student, Vassar Coll., 1938. Vol. field cons. Conn. A.R.C., 1955-60; vice chmn. bd. govs. Am. Nat. Red Cross, 1962-66; rep. League Red Cross Socs. to UN, 1957-80, Am. Nat. Red Cross to com. internat. social welfare Nat. Social Welfare Assembly, 1957-61; chmn. Non-Govtl. Orgn. Com. for UNICEF, 1963-64, 71-73; chmn. Non-Govtl. Orgn. Com. exec. com. for Office Pub. Information, UN, 1964-66; pres. conf. non-govtl. orgns. in consultative status with UN Econ. and Social Council, 1966-69. Mem. Am. Soc. Polit. and Social Sci., Soc. Internat. Devel., Nat. Soc. Colonial Dames, Descs. Signers of Declaration Independence, Round Hill Club, River Club (N.Y.). Home: 535 Lake Ave Greenwich CT 06830-3831

SHEPPARD, RICHARD MORGAN, chemical engineer; b. Birmingham, Ala., Mar. 5, 1949; s. Leon Morgan and Wands Penelope (Pacyna) S.; m. Joan Carrol Leach, Mar. 6, 1982; 1 child, Judy Ann. BS in Chem. Engring., U. Calif., Berkeley, 1975. Engr. Valecitos Nuclear Rsch. Ctr., Livermore, Calif., 1975-78; mgr. ops. SGS Control Svcs., Valdez, Alaska, 1978-80, Sapec Engring., Geneva, Switzerland, 1980-82; mgr. measurement assoc. Sohio, Cleve., 1982-85; mgr. measurement and quality assurance Buckeye Pipe Line Co., Allentown, Pa., 1986—. Contbr. articles to profl. jours. Mem. ASTM (chmn. 1988-90), Am. Petroleum Inst. (chmn. 1982-95, citation for svc. 1993), Mensa, Intertel. Avocations: golfing, skiing, basketball.

SHEPPARD, SCOTT, magazine publisher. Publisher Southern Living, Birmingham. Office: Southern Living 2100 Lakeshore Dr Birmingham AL 35209*

SHEPPARD, WALTER LEE, JR., chemical engineer, consultant; b. Phila., June 23, 1911; s. Walter Lee and Martha Houston (Evans) S.; m. Dorothy Virginia Cosby Vanderslice, Oct. 17, 1942 (div. Mar. 1947); m. Boudinot Atterbury Oberge Kendall, Mar. 24, 1953 (dec. Feb. 1996); stepchildren: Charles H. Kendall Jr., John Atterbury Kendall. BChem, Cornell U., 1932; MS, U. Pa., 1933. Registered profl. engr., Del., Calif.; diplomate Am. Acad. Environ. Engrs.; ordained deacon Liberal Cath. Ch., 1954, priest, 1955. Control chemist various cos., 1933-35; advt. writer N.W. Ayer & Son, 1936-37; asst. to editor The Houghton Line (E.F. Houghton Co.), 1937-38; salesman Atlas Mineral Products, 1938-48; plant mgr., cons. engr. Tanks & Linings, Ltd., Droitwich, Eng., 1948-49; sales engr., dist. mgr. ElectroChem. Engring. & Mfg., and successor cos., 1949-68; nat. accounts mgr., field sales mgr. Corrosion Engring. div. Pennwalt Corp., Phila., 1968-76; pres. C.C.R.M., Inc.; cons. on chemically resistant masonry, 1976—; profl. genealogist, 1936—. Author: Ancestry and Descendants of Thomas Stickney Evans and Sarah Ann Fifield, His Wife, 1940, Chemically Resistant Masonry, 1977, 2d edit., 1982, Ancestry of Edward Carleton and Ellen Newton, His Wife, 1978; author, editor: Corrosion and Chemical Resistant Masonry Materials Handbook, 1986; editor: Passengers and Ships Prior to 1684, 1965; successor editor: Ancestral Roots of 60 New England Colonists, 3rd to 7th edits., 1992, Magna Charta Sureties 1215, 2nd to 4th edits., 1991; contbg. editor Am. Genealogist, 1941-70, Nat. Geneal. Quar., 1961—; mem.

publs. com. Pa. Geneal. Mag., 1960-76; contbr. articles on corrosion resistant masonry constrn. to profl. jours. Dir. displaced persons camps UNRRA, also d.p. specialist, staff Chief of Mission, Vienna, Austria, 1945-46; founding trustee, v.p. Bd. Cert. Genealogists, 1965-82, pres., 1969-78, chmn., 1978-79. Served to maj. U.S. Army, 1941-45, UNRRA, 1945-46; lt. col., Res., ret. 1960. Named Hon. Mem. Class of 1928 U.S. Naval Acad., 1976. Fellow Am. Soc. Genealogists (sec. 1958-61, 66-67, v.p. 1967-70, pres. 1970-73), Nat. Geneal. Soc., Pa. Geneal. Soc.; mem. ASTM (membership sec. 1975-83, C-3 com.), NSPE, Am. Acad. Environ. Engrs., Welcome Soc. (pres. 1969-76), Illegitimate Sons and Daus. of Kings and Queens of Britain (founder, sec. 1950-68, pres. 1968-88), Flagon and Trencher Soc. (co-founder, pres. 1967-73), Nat. Assn. Corrosion Engrs. (cert. competence in corrosion engring., chmn. Phila. sect. 1962), New Eng. Historic Geneal. Soc. (com. on Heraldry, 1991—), Nat. Geneal. Soc. Quar. (contbg. editor), Geneal. Soc. Pa., Soc. Genealogists (London), Yorkshire Archeol. Soc., Savoy Co., Gilbert and Sullivan Soc. (founder, pres. Phila. br. 1957-63), Sovereign Order St. John of Jerusalem, Mil. Order Fgn. Wars, Mayflower Descs., Order of Three Crusades, Order of the Crown of Charlemagne in Am. (3rd v.p. 1989—), Ret. Officers Assn., Phi Kappa Psi (nat. v.p. 1964-68, pres. 1968-70), Alpha Chi Sigma. Home and Office: 923 Old Manoa Rd Havertown PA 19083-2610

SHEPPARD, WILLIAM STEVENS, investment banker; b. Grand Rapids, Mich., Apr. 29, 1930; s. James Herbert and Emily Gilmore (Stevens) S.; m. Jane Steketee, 1956 (dec. 1975); children: Stevens C., Elizabeth W., Emily R.; m. Patricia Gillis Bloom, Dec. 2, 1978. B.A. in Econs, U. Va., 1953. Trainee J.P. Morgan & Co., Inc., N.Y.C., 1955-58; investment adv. Delafield & Delafield, N.Y.C., 1958-71; from salesman to sr. v.p. and dir. F.S. Smithers & Co., N.Y.C., 1971-76; sr. v.p., dir. successor Paine, Webber, Jackson & Curtis, Inc., 1976-81; pres., chief exec. officer, dir. Paine Webber Real Estate Securities Inc., 1980-85; mng. dir. Paine Webber Capital Markets, N.Y.C., 1985-88; adv. dir. Berkshire Capital Corp., N.Y.C., 1988—; adminstr. Pequot Investment Advisors, Ic., Southport, Conn., 1995—; chmn. bd. dirs. Ea. Bancorp. An editor: Ginny Mae Manual, 1979; contbr. to handbooks. Trustee, treas. Riot Relief Fund City N.Y., 1970—. Served to lt. USNR, 1953-55. Republican. Clubs: N.Y. Yacht; Country of Fairfield (Conn.); Pequot Yacht; Mashomack Fish and Game, North Haven Casino. Home: 405 Sasco Rd Southport CT 06490 Office: Pequot Investment Advisors Box 139 Southport CT 06490

SHEPPARD, WILLIAM VERNON, transportation engineer; b. Harlan, Ky., Apr. 18, 1941; s. Vernon L. and Margaret M. (Montgomery) S.; m. Charlotte A. McGehee, Nov. 6, 1981; children: W. Kevin, Candice Gaye. BCE, The Citadel, 1964. Registered profl. engr., Pa., Calif. and 10 other states. Hwy. engr. Howard Needles, Tammen & Bergendoff, Kansas City, Mo., 1964-65; with Wilbur Smith & Assos., Columbia, S.C., 1967-80, various positions to western regional v.p., so. regional v.p.; v.p., dir. transp. Post Buckley, Schuh & Jernigan, Inc., Columbia, 1980-85; sr. v.p., Sverdrup Civil, 1985-94; sr. v.p., chmn. Surface Transp., HNTB, 1994—; guest lectr. U. So. Calif. Sch. Architecture and Urban Planning. Mem. engring. adv. bd. Clemson U., 1977-80. Served to capt. U.S. Army, 1965-67. Decorated AEM medal. Fellow ASCE, Inst. Transp. Engrs. (pres. S.C. div. 1979); mem. Nat. Soc. Profl. Engrs., S.C. Coun. Engring. Socs. (pres. 1978), Tau Beta Pi. Republican. Roman Catholic.

SHEPPERD, SUSAN ABBOTT, special education educator; b. Pekin, Ill., May 12, 1942; d. Robert Fred and Martha Mae (Abbott) Belville; m. Thomas Eugene Shepperd, Oct. 7, 1960; children: Scott Thomas, Allison Marie Shepperd-Henry, Michele Lea. BA, Maryville Coll., 1990; MEd, U. Mo., 1994. Cert. elem. edn. tchr. grades 1-8, spl. reading tchr. grades K-12. Resource tchr. reading grades K-8 St. Joseph Sch., Ardiocese of St. Louis, Cottleville, Mo., 1990—. Mem. Pi Lambda Theta (pres. 1992-94), Assn. in Edn. (Gamma Zeta chpt.), Phi Kappa Phi, Delta Epsilon Sigma. Episcopalian. Avocations: golfing, music, swimming. Home: 15977 Chamfers Farm Rd Chesterfield MO 63005-4717 Office: St Joseph Sch Motherhead Rd Cottleville MO 63304

SHEPRO, RICHARD W., lawyer; b. Berwyn, Ill., May 9, 1953; s. Justice Warren and Inez Marjorie (McKillip); m. Lindsay Ellen Roberts, Sept. 5, 1981; children: Claire Willoughby, Warren Boyd. AB, Harvard U., 1975, JD., 1979; MSc, London Sch. Econs., Eng., 1976. Bar: Ill. 1979, Calif. 1981, U.S. Ct. Appeals (9th cir.) 1981, U.S. Dist. Ct. (no. dist.) Ill. 1982, U.S. Supreme Ct. 1993. Teaching fellow Harvard U., Cambridge, Mass., 1979; law clk. to chief judge U.S. Ct. Appeals (9th cir.), San Francisco, 1979-81; assoc. Mayer, Brown & Platt, Chgo., 1981-85, ptnr., 1986—; lectr. law U. Chgo., 1992—; staff mem. U.S. Senate Judiciary Com., 1979; spl. asst. atty. gen., Ill., 1981-82; corr. on bus. law The Fin. Times, London, 1986—. Co-author: Bidders & Targets: Mergers and Acquisitions in the U.S., 1990; contbr. numerous articles to profl. jours. Del. nat. conv. NOW, Ind., 1982; bd. govs. Kohl Children's Mus.; vestryman St. Chrysostom's Ch., Chgo. Recipient U.S. Presdl. scholar Pres. of U.S., Washington, 1971, Greenman Prize Harvard U., 1975; named Harvard Law Rev. Supreme Ct. Editor, Harvard Law Rev. Assn., 1977-79; named to Am. Law Inst., 1993. Fellow Chgo. Bar Found.; mem. ABA, Chgo. Coun. Lawyers (bd. govs. 1986-89, chmn. election law com. 1987—), Chgo. Coun. Fgn. Rels., The Chgo. Ensemble (dir. and v.p.), Chgo. Club, LaSalle Club (dir. and mem. exec. com.), Les Nomades Club. Home: 837 W Oakdale Ave Chicago IL 60657-5121 Office: Mayer Brown & Platt 190 S La Salle St Chicago IL 60603-3410

SHER, GEORGE ALLEN, philosophy educator; b. N.Y.C., Nov. 10, 1942; s. Daniel and Clara (Landesberg) S.; m. Emily Fox Gordon, July 10, 1972; 1 child, Sarah Landesberg. BA, Brandeis U., 1964; PhD, Columbia U., 1972. Instr. philosophy Fairleigh Dickinson U., Teaneck, N.J., 1966-72, asst. prof. philosopy, 1972-74; assoc. prof. philosophy U. Vt., Burlington, 1974-80, prof., 1980-91; Herbert S. Autrey prof. philosophy Rice U., Houston, 1991—, chmn. dept. philosophy, 1993—; univ. scholar Univ. Vt., 1988-89; mem. Inst. for Advanced Study, Princeton, N.J., 1987-88. Author: (book) Desert, 1987, Beyon Neutrality: Perfectionism and Politics, 1996; editor: (book) Moral Philosophy: Selected Readings, 1989; contbr. articles to profl. jours. Named fellow Nat. Humanities Ctr., Rsch. Triangle Park, N.C., 1980-81. Mem. Am. Philos. Assn. Home: 2425 Dryden Rd Houston TX 77030 Office: Rice U Dept Philosophy 6100 S Main St Houston TX 77005-1892

SHER, LINDA ROSENBERG, lawyer; b. Chgo., May 16, 1938; d. Sidney and Rebecca Rosenberg; B.A., U. Chgo., 1959; LL.B., Yale U., 1962; m. Stanley O. Sher, Aug. 11, 1963; children—Jeremy Jay, Hellyn Sue. Admitted to D.C. bar, 1962; counsel constl. rights subcom. Senate Judiciary Com., 1962-64; atty. NLRB, 1964-77, asst. gen. counsel supreme ct. br., 1977-93, acting assoc. gen. counsel, 1994-95, assoc. gen. counsel, 1995—. Office: NLRB 1099 14th St NW Washington DC 20005-3419

SHER, PAUL PHILLIP, physician, pathologist; b. Bklyn., Oct. 25, 1939; s. Louis and Lottie (Kloner) S.; m. Joan E. Zeffren, June 9, 1964; children: Matthew, Andrew, Lawrence. BS cum laude, Hobart Coll., 1961; MD, Washington U., 1965. Diplomate Am. Bd. Pathology. Intern in pathology Columbia-Presbyn. Hosp., N.Y.C., 1965-66, resident in pathology, 1966-69; instr. pathology Columbia Presbyn. Hosp., N.Y.C., 1968-70; resident in pathology Englewood (N.J.) Hosp., 1969-70; dir. clin. chemistry Frances Delafeld Hosp., N.Y.C., 1970-71; dir. blood bank Bethesda Naval Hosp., Rockville, Md., 1971-72, dir. hematology, 1973; dir. clin. chemistry NYU Med. Ctr., Tisch Hosp., 1973, dir. clin. labs., 1980-93; clin. prof. pathology, prof. med. informatics Biomed. Info. Comm. Ctr. Oreg. Health Scis. U., Portland, 1993—. Editor Lab. Med.; contbr. articles, editorial, revs. to profl. jours.;. Lt. comdr. USN, 1971-73. Fellow Coll. Am. Pathologists, Am. Soc. Clin. Pathologists, Explorer's Club.

SHERAK, THOMAS MITCHELL, motion picture company executive; b. Bklyn., June 22, 1945; s. Myer and Freida (Rosenthal) S.; m. Madeleine Frankfurter, Nov. 22, 1967; children: Barbra, Melissa, William. A.A. in Mktg., N.Y. Community Coll., Bklyn., 1965. Salesman Paramount Pictures, N.Y.C., Washington, St. Louis, 1970-74; booker film R/C Theatres, Balt., 1974-77; dist. film buyer Gen. Cinema, Cherry Hill, N.J., 1977-78; v.p. film Gen. Cinema, N.Y.C., 1978-82; v.p. head film buyer Gen. Cinema, Cherry Hill, N.J., 1982-83; pres. domestic distbn. and mktg. 20th Century-Fox Pictures, Beverly Hills, Calif., 1983-85, pres. domestic distbn., 1985—. Served with U.S. Army, 1967-69. Mem. Motion Picture Bookers Club (hon.), Motion Picture Pioneer, Will Rogers. Democrat. Home: 4041 Declaration Ave Calabasas CA 91302-5742 Office: 20th Century-Fox Film Corp 1211 Avenue Of The Americas New York NY 10036-8701 Office: PO Box 900 Beverly Hills CA 90213-0900

SHEAR, JOSEPH WILLIAM, retired insurance broker, investor, research director; b. Fresno, Calif., Sept. 27, 1930; s. Joseph William Garland and Verna Irene (Kneeland) S.; BS, U.S. Naval Acad., 1952; JD, Loyola U., New Orleans, 1965; m. Nancy Barr Gooch, Nov. 6, 1954 (div. 1988); children: Deirdra Clarisse, William Gooch, David Kneeland (dec.), Lynne Fox; m. Judith H. Senac, 1989. Commd. ensign USN, 1952, advanced through grades to lt., 1958; destoyer officer, 1952-53; naval aviator, 1954; landing signal officer, 1956-57; aide to Vice Adm. James Thatch, Com Huk Lant, 1958; flight instr. Saufley Naval Air Sta., Pensacola, Fla., 1958; trainee Marine Office Am., 1958-59; marine broker Hardin and Ferguson, 1959-61; radar instr. U.S. Maritime Adminstrn., New Orleans, 1961-62; resigned, 1965; chmn. Ingram-Armistead & Co. SPA, Milan, Italy, 1976-78, Corroon & Black, Inc., New Orleans, 1979; pres. Shear, Cook & Gardner, Inc. (merger Hilb, Rogal & Hamilton Co. 1990), Metairie, La., 1979-90, sr. v.p., 1991-96, Sailing Sales Inc., New Orleans, 1972-84, Cathay Trading Corp., 1981-87, Altair Ins. Co. Ltd., 1981-84; mng. ptnr. Severn Assocs., 1981-93; now exec. v.p. and dir. Transp. Rsch. Inst.; lectr. and seminar chmn. in field; underwriting mem. Lloyd's of London. Edn. chmn. YPO, Rio de Janeiro, Brazil; former trustee U.S. Naval Acad. Sailing Found. Inc., 1984-90; chmn. Fales adv. com. U.S. Naval Acad., 1981; chmn. aviation com. C. of C. New Orleans, 1975-79. Bolero crew mem. 1956 Newport Bermuda Race Record. Mem. Maritime Law Assn., Young Pres.'s Orgn. (chmn. La. chpt. 1978-79), U.S. Naval Acad. Alumni Assn. (pres. New Orleans chpt. 1963), S.R., SAR (pres. George Washington chpt. 1994), Colonial Wars Soc. La. (treas. 1978-79), Delta Theta Phi (life mem.). Clubs: Cruising Am., Mil. Order of Fgn. Wars (L.A. chpt. sec. 1996), Royal Ocean Racing London (life), Naval Acad. Sailing Squadron (life), Storm Trysail, N.Y. Yacht (mem. race crew Royal Thames Yacht Club Team 1989, Royal Yacht Squadron Round the Island Race 1991), So. Yacht (Gulf Ocean Racing Champion, Boat of Yr.), The Corinthians, Essex (pres. 1971-72), Bienville. Contbr. articles to profl. jours.

SHERBELL, RHODA, artist, sculptor; b. Bklyn.; d. Alexander and Syd (Steinberg) S.; m. Mervin Honig, Apr. 28, 1956; 1 child, Susan. Student, Art Students League, 1950-53, Bklyn. Mus. Art Sch., 1959-61; also; pvt. study art, Italy, France, Eng., 1956. cons., coun. mem. Emily Lowe Gallery, Hofstra U., Hempstead, N.Y., 1978, pres., 1989-81, instr., 1991—, life mem. bd. friends, pres. bd. trustees; tchr. instr. Mus. Modern Art, N.Y.C., 1959, NAD Art Sch., N.Y.C., 1985—, Art Students League, N.Y.C., 1980—. Exhibited one-woman shows Country Art Gallery, Locust Valley, N.Y., Bklyn. Mus. Art Sch., 1961, Adelphi Coll., A.C.A. Galleries, N.Y.C., 1967, Capricorn Galleries, Rehn Gallery, Washington, 1968, Huntington Hartford Mus., N.Y.C., 1969, Morris (N.J.) Mus. Arts and Scis., 1980, Bergen Mus. Arts and Scis., N.J., 1984, William Benton Mus., Conn., 1985, Palace Theatre of the Arts, Stamford, Conn., Bronx Mus. Arts, 1986, Hofstra Mus. Art, L.I., N.Y., 1989, 90, County Art Gallery, N.Y.C., 1990; one-woman retrospective at N.Y. Cultural Ctr., 1970, Nat. Arts Collection, Washington, 1970, Montclair Mus. of Art, 1976, Nat. Art Mus. of Sport, 1977, Jewish Mus. of N.Y.C., 1980, Black History Mus., 1981, Queens Mus., 1981, 82, Nat. Portrait Gallery, Washington, 1981, 82, Bronx Mus., N.Y., Bklyn. Mus., Mus. Modern Art, N.Y.C., Country Art Gallery, 1990, Port Washington Library, Nat. Mus. Am. Art, The Smithsonian Instn., 1982, Nat. Acad. Design, N.Y.C., 1984, 89, Castle Gallery Mus., N.Y.C., 1987, Emily Lowe Mus., N.Y.C., 1987, Heckshire Mus., N.Y.C., 1989, Islip Art Mus., N.Y.C., 1989, Gallery Emanuel, N.Y.C., 1993, Sundance Gallery, Bridgehampton, N.Y., CASTIRON Gallery SoHo Show, 1995, Nat. Acad. Design Exhibition, 1995, Sundance Gallery, Bridgehampton, N.Y., 1995; exhibited group shows Heckscher Mus., 1989, Islip Mus., 1989, Nassau Dept. Recreation and Parks, 1989, Downtown Gallery, N.Y.C., Maynard Walker Gallery, N.Y.C., F.A.R. Gallery, N.Y.C., Provincetown Art Assn., Detroit Inst. Art, Pa. Acad. Fine Arts, Bklyn. and L.I. Artists Show, Old Westbury Gardens Small Sculpture Show, Audubon Artists, NAD, Allied Artists, Heckscher Mus., Nat. Art Mus. Sports, Mus. Arts and Scis., L.A., Am. Mus. Natural History, Post of History Mus., 1987, 88, Caslte Gallery Mus., N.Y.C., 1987, Emiloy Lowe Gallery Mus., N.Y., 1987, Bronx Mus. Arts, 1987, Chgo. Hist. Soc., Mus. of Modern Art, N.Y.C., 1988, Sands Point Mus., L.I., NAD, Hofstra Mus., 1990, Nat. Mus. Sports Art, 1991, Indpls. Art Mus., Phoenix Mus. Art, Corcoran Mus. Art, Washington, IBM, N.Y.C., Fire House Gallery Mus. Nassau Cmty. Coll., L.I., 1992, Nat. Arts Club Ann. Exhbn., 1992, Sports in Art From Am. Mus. at IBM, N.Y.C., 1992, Nat. Sculpture Soc. and The Regina A Quick Ctr. for The Arts Fairfield U.Centennial Anniversary Exbn., 1993, Mus. Modern Art, N.Y.C., Nat. Sculpture Soc. 100 Anniversary Exhbn., 1993, Italy, 1994, Provincetown Assn. and Art Mus., 1993, Kyoto (Japan) Mus. Sculpture Guild, 1993, Nat. Sculpture Soc. Exhbn. in Italy, Lucca, 1994, Sculptures Guild, N.Y.C., 1994-95, Cline Gallery, Santa Fe, 1995; represented permanent collections, Stony Brook Hall of Fame, William Benton Mus. Art, Colby Coll. Mus., Oklahoma City Mus., Montclair (N.J.) Mus., Schonberg Library Black Studies, N.Y.C., Albany State Mus., Hofstra U., Bklyn. Mus., Colby Coll. Mus., Nat. Arts Collection, Nat. Portrait Gallery, Smithsonian Instn., Baseball Hall of Fame Cooperstown, N.Y., Nassau Community Coll., Hofstra U. Emily Lowe Gallery, Art Students League, Jewish Mus., Queens Mus., Black History Mus., Nassau County Mus., Stamford Mus. Art and Nature Ctr., Jericho Pub. Library, N.Y., African-Am. Mus., Hempstead, N.Y., 1988, Stamford (Conn.) Mus. Art and Scis., Silvermine Artists North East exhibition, 1989, Nassau Community Coll. Fire House Gallery Exbn., 1992, Nat. Portrait Gallery Smithsonian Instn.; also pvt. collections, TV shows, ABC, 1968, 81; ednl. TV spl. Rhoda Sherbell-Woman in Bronze, 1977; important works include Sed Ballerina, portraits of Aaron Copland (Bruce Stevenson Meml. Best Portrait award Nat. Arts Club 1989), Eleanor Roosevelt, Variations on a Theme (36 works of collaged sculpture), 1982-86; appeared several TV shows; guest various radio programs; contbr. articles to newspapers, popular mags. and art jours. Council mem. Nassau County Mus., 1978, trustee, 1st v.p. council; asso. trustee Nat. Art Mus. of Sports, Inc., 1975—; cons., community liaison WNET Channel 13, cultural coordinator, 1975-83; host radio show Not for Artists Only, 1978-79; trustee Women's Boxing Fedn., 1978; mem. The Art Comm of The City of New York, 1993. Recipient Gold medal Allied Artists of Am., 1989, Alfred G. B. Steel Meml. award Pa. Acad. Fine Arts, 1963-64; Helen F. Barnett prize NAD, 1965, Jersey City Mus. prize for sculpture, 1961, 1st prize sculpture Locust Valley Art Show, 1966, 67, Ann. Sculpture prize Jersey City Mus., Bank for Savs. 1st prize in sculpture, 1950, Ford Found. purchase award, 1964, 2 top sculpture awards Mainstreams 77, Cert. of Merit Salmagundi Club, 1978, prize for sculpture, 1980, 81, award for sculpture Knickerbocker Artists, 1980, 81, top prize for sculpture Hudson Valley Art Assn., 1981, Sawyer award NAD, 1985, Gold medal of honor Audubon Artists, 1985, 39th Ann. Silvermine Exhbn. award, Gold medal Allied Artists Am., 1990, Pres' award Nat arts Club N.Y.C.; MacDowell Colony fellow, 1976 Am. Acad. Arts and Letters and Nat. Arts and Letters grantee, 1960, Louis Comfort Tiffany Found. grantee, 1962, Ford Found. grantee, 1964, 67, also award; named one of top 5 finalist World Wide Competition to do Monument of Queen Catherine of England, 1991. Fellow Nat. Sculpture Soc.; mem. Sculpture Guild (dir.), Nat. Assn. Women Artists (Jeffery Childs Willis Meml. prize 1978), Allied Artists Soc. (dir., Gold medal 1990), Audubon Artists (Greta Kempton Walker prize 1965, Chaim Gross award, award for disting. contbr. to orgn. 1979, 80, Louis Weskeem award, dir.), Woman's Caucus for Art, Coll. Art Assn., Am. Inst. Conservation Historic and Artistic Works, N.Y. Soc. Women Artists, Artists Equity Assn. N.Y., Nat. Sculpture Soc. (E.N. Richard Meml. prize 1989), Internat. Platform Assn., Profl. Artists Guild L.I., Painters and Sculptors Soc. N.J. (Bertrum R. Hulmes Meml. award), Am. Watercolor Soc. (award for disting. contbn. to orgn.), Catharine Lorillard Wolfe Club (hon. mention 1968), Nat. Arts Club (N.Y.C., Stevenson Meml. award 1989, Pres. award 1992), NAD Design (Leila Gordon Sawyer prize 1989; The Dessle Green Prize 1993). Home: 64 Jane Ct Westbury NY 11590-1410

SHERBINSKI, LINDA ANNE, nurse anesthetist, nursing educator; b. Rochester, N.Y., Jan. 17, 1956; d. Edward Marion and Helen Marie (Kindzera) S. Student, Genesee Hosp. Sch. Nursing, Rochester, N.Y., 1977; BSN, Alfred U., 1978; grad. in anesthesia, Univ. Health Ctr. Pitts., 1987; MSN, Duqusne U., 1991. RN, Pa. Leader day team CCU The Genesee Hosp., 1978-84, staff nurse operating rm., 1984-85; staff nurse ICU Forbes Met. Hosp., Pitts., 1985-87; staff anesthetist Presbyn. Univ. Hosp., Pitts., 1987-92, preceptor anesthetist, 1991-92; instr. Univ. Health Ctr. Pitts. Sch. Anesthesia, 1987-90, U. Pitts. Grad. Anesthesia Program, 1990-92; staff anesthetist Meml. Med. Ctr., Springfield, Ill., 1992-94; anesthetist Rochester (N.Y.) Gen. Hosp., Highland Hosp., Genesee Hosp., N.Y., 1994—; item writer Acad. Item Writers AANA, Chgo., 1991—. Contbr. articles to profl. jours., chpt. to book. Med. vol. Pitts. Marathon, 1990, 91. Mem. Am. Assn. Nurse Anesthetists (cert. nurse anesthetist, program dir. internship grant 1990), Nat. League Nursing, Sigma Theta Tau (sec. Delta Sigma chpt. 1978-80, Rsch. scholar Epsilon Phi chpt. 1991). Roman Catholic. Home: 27 Bella Dr Penfield NY 14526 Office: Rochester Gen Hosp Portland Ave Rochester NY 14621

SHERBOURNE, ARCHIBALD NORBERT, civil engineering educator; b. Bombay, India, July 8, 1929; s. Manekji and Sarah Agnes (Sherbourne) Bulsara; m. Jean Ducan Nicol, Aug. 15, 1959; children: Mary, Sarah, Jeffrey, Nicolas, Jonathan, Simon. B.Sc., U. London, 1953, D.Sc., 1970; B.S., Lehigh U., 1955, M.S., 1957; M.A., Cambridge U., 1959, Ph.D., 1960. Registered profl. engr., Ont.; chartered engr. U.K., European Engr. Mem. faculty U. Waterloo, Ont., Can., 1961—; prof. civil engring. U. Waterloo, 1963—; dean U. Waterloo (Faculty Engring.), 1966-74; dir. Sherbourne Consultants Ltd.; vis. prof. U. W.I., Trinidad, 1969-70, Nat. C.E. Lab., Lisbon, Portugal, 1970, Ecole Polytechnique Federale, Lausanne, Switzerland, 1975-77; DAAD vis. fellow, W. Ger., 1975, NATO sr. scientist fellow, vis. lectr., 1975-76; advisor-cons. Commonwealth Africa study group on tech. edn. in industry Commonwealth Secretariat London, 1978; Gledden vis. sr. fellow U. Western Australia, Perth, 1978; acad. adviser Centre for Sci. and Tech., Fed. U. Paraiba, Campina Grande, Brazil, 1979; prin. cons. acad. planning Faculty Engring., U. Victoria, B.C., Can., 1979-80; advisor Tata Sons Ltd., Bombay, 1980; vis. prof. civil engring. Mich. Technol. U., Houghton, 1980-81, 82-83, U. Melbourne, 1983; spl. cons. technol. edn. for developing countries Can. Internat. Devel. Agy.; vis. prof. ocean engring. Fla. Atlantic U., Boca Raton, 1985, archtl. engring. N.C. A & T State U., Greensboro, 1987; vis. prof. aerospace engring. I.I. Sci., Bangalore, India, 1990. Contbr. articles to profl. jours.; visting prof. civil engineering, U. Cape Town, S. Africa, 1995—. OECD fellow Switzerland, 1964; recipient Engring. medal Assn. Profl. Engrs., Province Ont., 1975. Fellow Instn. Structural Engrs. (London), Royal Soc. Arts, Can. Soc. Civil Engring., Can. Acad. Engring.; mem. Internat. Assn. Bridge & Structural Engring. Home: 131 Keats Way Pl, Waterloo, ON Canada N2L 5H4 Office: U Waterloo Dept Civil Engring, Faculty Engring, Waterloo, ON Canada N2L 3G1

SHERBURNE, DONALD WYNNE, philosopher, educator; b. Proctor, Vt., Apr. 21, 1929; s. Hermon Kirk and Alma May (Bixby) S.; m. Elizabeth Statesir Darling, July 30, 1955; children—Kevin Darling, Nancy Elizabeth, Lynne Darling. A.B., Middlebury Coll., 1951; B.A., Balliol Coll., Oxford U., 1953; M.A., Yale U., 1958, Ph.D., 1960. Instr. philosophy Yale, 1959-60; asst. prof. Vanderbilt U., Nashville, 1960-64, asso. prof., 1964-68, prof. philosophy, 1968-95, chmn. dept., 1973-80, 90-94, prof. emeritus, 1995; Cowling vis. prof. philosophy Carleton Coll., 1990; chmn. editorial adv. com. Vanderbilt U. Press, 1991-95. Author: A Whiteheadian Aesthetic, 1961, A Key to Whitehead's Process and Reality, 1966; editor: Soundings—An Interdisciplinary Jour, 1980-85; co-editor: Corrected Edition of Whitehead's Process and Reality, 1978. Troop leader Cub Scouts, 1965-67. Served with U.S. Army, 1954-56. Recipient Jeffrey Nordhaus award for excellence in teaching., 1984; Dutton fellow Oxford U., 1951-53; sr. fellow NEH, 1977-78. Mem. AAUP (pres. Vanderbilt chpt. 1966-67), Metaphys. Soc. Am. (governing coun. 1969-73, 86-90, pres.-elect 1992-93, pres. 1993-94), So. Soc. Philosophy and Psychology (governing coun. 1971-74, treas. 1974-77, pres.-elect 1977, pres. 1978, Jr. award for Excellence 1961), Am. Philos. Assn. (program com. 1982, com. on status and future of profession 1989-92, nominating com. 1994-95), Am. Soc. Aestheti cs, Phi Beta Kappa (pres. Vanderbilt chpt. 1975-77). Home: 3 Jefferson Ct S Saint Petersburg FL 33711

SHERBY, KATHLEEN REILLY, lawyer; b. St. Louis, Apr. 5, 1947; d. John Victor and Florian Sylvia (Frederick) Reilly; m. James Wilson Sherby, May 17, 1975; children: Michael R.R., William J.R., David J.R. AB magna cum laude, St. Louis U., 1969, JD magna cum laude, 1976. Bar: Mo. 1976. Assoc. Bryan Cave, St. Louis, 1976-85; ptnr. Bryan Cave LLP, St. Louis, 1985—. Contbr. articles to profl. jours. Bd. dirs Jr. League, St. Louis, 1989-90, St. Louis Forum, 1992—, pres., 1995—); vice chmn. Bequest and Gift Coun. of St. Louis U., 1995—. Fellow Am. Coll. Trust and Estate Coun., Estate Planning Coun. of St. Louis (pres. 1986-87), Bar Assn. Met. St. Louis (chmn. probate sect. 1986-87), Mo. Bar Assn. (probate coun. 1985-87, 89—, chmn. probate law revision subcom. 1988—). Episcopalian. Home: 47 Crestwood Dr Saint Louis MO 63105-3032 Office: Bryan Cave LLP 1 Metropolitan Sq Ste 3600 Saint Louis MO 63102-2733

SHERCK, TIMOTHY C., lawyer; b. Hamilton, Ohoi, Feb. 27, 1949. BA with honors, Northwestern U., 1971; JD magna cum laude, Harvard U., 1974. Bar: Ill. 1975, U.S. Dist. Ct. (no. dist.) Ill., 1975, U.S. Tax Ct. 1977, U.S. Dist. Ct. (ea. dist.) Wis. 1977, U.S. Ct. Appeals (7th cir.) 1979. Ptnr. Mayer, Brown & Platt, Chgo. Contbr. articles to profl. jours. Mem. ABA, Chgo. Bar Assn., Phi Beta Kappa. Office: Mayer Brown & Platt 190 S La Salle St Chicago IL 60603-3410*

SHERE, DENNIS, publishing executive; b. Cleve., Nov. 29, 1940; s. William and Susan (Luskay) S.; m. Maureen Jones, Sept. 4, 1965; children: Rebecca Lynn, David Matthew, Stephen Andrew. B.S. in Journalism, Ohio U., 1963, M.S. in Journalism, 1964. Staff writer Dayton (Ohio) Daily News, 1966-69; asst. prof. Sch. Journalism Bowling Green (Ohio) State U., 1969-70; fin. editor Detroit News, 1970-72, city editor, 1973-75; editor Dayton Jour. Herald, 1975-80; pub. Springfield (Ohio) Newspapers Inc., 1980-83, Dayton Newspapers, Inc., 1983-88; gen. mgr. Media Group Moody Bible Inst., 1989—. Served with AUS, 1964-66. Mem. Sigma Alpha Epsilon, Omicron Delta Kappa. Office: Moody Bible Inst 820 N La Salle Dr Chicago IL 60610-3214

SHERER, SAMUEL AYERS, lawyer, urban planning consultant; b. Warwick, N.Y., June 17, 1944; s. Ernest Thompson and Helen (Ayers) S.; m. Dewi Sudewinahidah, June 28, 1980. AB magna cum laude, Oberlin Coll., 1966; JD, Harvard U., 1970; M in City Planning, MIT, 1970. Bar: D.C. 1972, U.S. Supreme Ct. 1979. Atty., advisor HUD, Boston, 1970; sr. cons. McClaughry Assoc., Washington, 1970-71, 74-76; cons. Urban Inst., Washington, 1971-72; atty., urban planner IBRD Jakarta (Indonesia) Urban Devel. Study, 1972-74; atty., advisor Office Minority Bus. U.S. Dept. Commerce, Washington, 1976-77; ptnr. Topping & Sherer, Washington, 1977-90; pres. Sherer-Axelrod-Monacelli, Inc., Cambridge, Mass., 1978—; prin. The Washington Team, Inc., 1992—; bd. dirs. Optical Comm. Corp., PADCO, Inc., The Urban Agriculture Network; rep. Internat. Devel. Law Inst., Washington, 1983-90; sr. fellow Climate Inst., 1988—; cons. in field. Co-author: Urban Land Use in Egypt, 1977; editor: Important Laws and Regulations Regarding Land, Housing and Urban Development in the Arab Republic of Egypt, 1977, Important Laws and Regulations Regarding Land, Housing and Urban Development in the Hashemite Kingdom of Jordan, 1981. Bd. dirs. MIT Enterprise Forum of Washington-Balt., 1980-82; mem. D.C. Rep. Cent. Com., 1984-88; mem. nat. governing bd. Ripon Soc., Washington, 1977-83. Urban Studies fellow HUD, 1969-70. Mem. ABA, D.C. Bar Assn., Am. Planning Assn., Asia Soc., Phi Beta Kappa. Avocations: tennis, reading. Home: 4600 Connecticut Ave NW Apt 205 Washington DC 20008-5702 Office: 316 Pennsylvania Ave SE # 202 Washington DC 20003-1146

SHERESKY, NORMAN M., lawyer; b. Detroit, June 22, 1928; s. Harry and Rose (Lieberman) S.; m. Elaine B. Lewis, Oct. 30, 1977; 1 child, from previous marriage, Brooke Hillary. A.B., Syracuse U., 1950; LL.B., Harvard U., 1953. Bar: N.Y. 1953. Assoc. Gold & Pollack, N.Y.C., 1954-60; sole practice, N.Y.C., 1960-72; ptnr. Sheresky & Kalman, N.Y.C., 1972-77; ptnr. Colton, Hartnick, Yamin & Sheresky, N.Y.C., 1977-93; ptnr. Baer, Marks & Upham, N.Y.C., 1993-95; ptnr. Sheresky, Aronson, Mayefsky & Roday LLP, 1995—. adj. prof. matrimonial litigation N.Y. Law Sch., 1979-86; mem. judiciary com. N.Y.C. Bar Assn.; pres.-elect Am. Coll. Family Trial Lawyers. Mem. Internat. Acad. Matrimonial Lawyers (past treas., gov. N.Y. chpt.), Am. Acad. Matrimonial Lawyers (gov., past pres. N.Y. chpt., pres. elect.), N.Y. State Bar Assn., Assn. Trial Lawyers Am., Met. Trial Lawyers Assn., Internat. Acad. Matrimonial Lawyers (bd. govs. 1986—, com. to examine lawyer conduct in matrimonial actions 1992-95). Author:

(with Marya Mannes) Uncoupling, 1972; On Trial, 1977; contbr. editor: Fairshare mag. Office: Sheresky Aronson Mayefsky & Roday LLP 400 Park Ave New York NY 10022-4406

SHERIDAN, CHRISTOPHER FREDERICK, human resources executive; b. Syracuse, N.Y., June 7, 1953; s. Frederick John and Patricia Ann (McCormick) S.; m. Diane Marie Harman, Dec. 31, 1977; children: Ryan, Kelly. BS in Indsl. Relations, LeMoyne Coll., 1975. Employee rels. trainee Anaconda Co., Buffalo, 1975-76; employee rels. rep. Anaconda Co., Los Angeles, 1976-78; pers. mgr. HITCO, Gardena, Calif., 1978-80; labor rels. rep. Miller Brewing Co., Fulton, N.Y., 1980-82; labor rels. mgr. Miller Brewing Co., Los Angeles, 1982-90; employee rels. mgr. Ryder Distbn. Resources, Anaheim, Calif., 1990-91; dir. human resources Alta-Dena Cert. Dairy Inc., City of Industry, Calif., 1991—. Mem. Soc. Human Resources Mgmt., Am. Mgmt. Assn. Roman Catholic. Avocations: golf, basketball, reading, music. Office: Alta-Dena Cert Dairy Inc 17637 Valley Blvd La Puente CA 91744-5731

SHERIDAN, DIANE FRANCES, public policy facilitator; b. Wilmington, Del., Mar. 12, 1945; d. Robert Kooch and Eileen Elizabeth (Forrest) Bupp; m. Mark MacDonald Sheridan III, Dec. 7, 1968; 1 child, Elizabeth Anne. BA in English, U. Del., 1967. Tchr. English Newark (Del.) Sch. Dist., 1967-68, Lumberton (Tex.) Ind. Sch. Dist., 1969-71, Crown Point (Ind.) Sch. Dist., 1972-75; sr. assoc. The Keystone (Colo.) Ctr., 1986—; environ. policy facilitator Taylor Lake Village, Tex., 1986—; chair Keystone Siting Process Local Rev. Com. 1st v.p. LWV, Washington, 1992-94, sec. treas. voters edn. fund, sec. treas. Nat. LWV, 1994; pres. LWV of Tex., 1987-91, chair edn. fund, 1987-91, bd. dirs., 1983-87; pres. LWV of the Bay Area, 1981-83; mem. adv. com. Ctr. for Global Studies of Houston Advanced Rsch. Ctr., The Woodlands, Tex., 1991—, Ctr. for Conflict Analysis and Mgmt., bd. advisors Environ. Inst.; mem. U. Houston-Clear Lake Devel. Adv. Coun., 1989-95; mem. Bay Area Cmty. Awareness and Emergency Response Local Emergency Planning Com., 1988-92; active Tex. House-Senate Select Com. on Urban Affairs Regional Flooding Task Force, 1979-80, Congressman Mike Andrews Environ. Task Force, 1983-85, Gov.'s Task Force on Hazardous Waste Mgmt., 1984-85; dir. local PTAs, 1981-91; coord. Tex. Roundtable on Hazardous Waste, 1982-87; sec., v.p. Tex. Environ. Coalition, 1983-85; co-chair Tex. Risk Commn. Project, 1986-89; mem. Leadership Tex., Class of 1988. Mem. Soc. for Profls. in Dispute Resolution, Internat. Assn. for Pub. Participation Practitioners, Mortarboard, Pi Sigma Alpha, Kappa Delta Pi.

SHERIDAN, EILEEN, librarian; b. N.Y.C., Jan. 11, 1949; d. Edward John and Florence Veronica (Glennon) S. BA in English, U. Bridgeport, Conn., 1972; MLS, So. Conn. State U., 1974. Children's libr. I, Bridgeport Pub. Libr., 1974-80, children's libr. II, 1980-82, coord. youth svcs., 1982—. Pres. Sch. Vol. Assn., Bridgeport, 1987-89; bd. dirs. Action for Bridgeport Cmty. Devel., 1989-90; pres. Conn. Zool. Soc., 1989-91, v.p., 1991—. Recipient vol. award for contbn. to children Mt. Aery Bapt. Ch., 1988, Champion of Children award South End Cmty. Ctr., 1992. Mem. LWV. Avocations: writing, travel, reading. Home: Unit 11 3300 Park Ave Bridgeport CT 06604-1100 Office: Bridgeport Pub Libr 925 Broad St Bridgeport CT 06604-4812

SHERIDAN, JAMES EDWARD, history educator; b. Wilmington, Del., July 15, 1922; s. Phillip Lambert and Ida Alverna (Green) S.; m. Sonia Landy, Sept. 27, 1947; 1 son, Jamy. B.S., U. Ill., 1949, M.A., 1950; Ph.D., U. Calif. at Berkeley, 1961. Lectr. Chinese history Stanford U., 1960; mem. faculty Northwestern U., 1961—, prof. history, 1968—, chmn. dept., 1969-74, assoc. dean Coll. Arts and Scis., 1985-89, prof. emeritus, 1992—. Author: Chinese Warlord: The Career of Feng Yu-hsiang, 1966, China: A Culture Area in Perspective, 1970, China in Disintegration: The Republican Era in Chinese History, 1912-1949, 1975; editor: The Transformation of Modern China series, 1975—. Served to ensign USN, 1941-46. Fulbright fellow France, 1950-51; Ford Found. fellow, 1958-60; grantee Am. Council Learned Socs.-Social Sci. Research Council, 1966-67, 71-72. Home: 80 Lyme Rd Apt 429 Hanover NH 03755-1236 Office: Northwestern Univ Dept History Evanston IL 60201

SHERIDAN, JIM, director, screenwriter; b. Dublin, Ireland, 1949. Student, Univ. Coll., Dublin, NYU. Dir., writer Lyric Theatre, Belfast, No. Ireland; artistic dir. Project Arts Theatre, 1976-80, N.Y. Irish Arts Ctr., 1982-87; founder Children's Theatre Co., Dublin, Ireland. Scripts include (plays) Mobile Homes, Spike in the First World War (Edinburgh Festival Fringe Best Play award 1983); (film) Into the West, 1993; screenwriter, dir.: My Left Foot, 1989 (Acad. award nomination best dir. 1989, Acad. award nomination best adapted screenplay 1989), The Field, 1990, In the Name of the Father, 1993 (Acad. award nomination best dir. 1993, Acad. award nomination best adapted screenplay 1993). Office: Hells Kitchen Inc All Hallows Coll, Grace Park Rd, Dublin Ireland

SHERIDAN, PATRICK MICHAEL, finance company executive; b. Grosse Pointe, Mich., Apr. 13, 1940; s. Paul Phillip and Frances Mary (Rohan) S.; m. Diane Lorraine Tressler, Nov. 14, 1986; children: Mary, Patrick, Kelly, Kevin, James. BBA, U. Notre Dame, 1962; MBA, U. Detroit, 1975. Acct. Peat, Marwick, Mitchell & Co., Detroit, 1962-72, audit mgr., 1969-72; exec. v.p. fin. Alexander Hamilton Life Ins. Co., Farmington, Mich., 1973-76; sr. v.p. ops. Sun Life Ins. Co. Am., Balt., 1976-78, exec. v.p., 1978-79; pres. Sun Ins. Services, Inc., 1979-81; pres., chief exec. officer Am. Health & Life Ins. Co., Balt., 1981-85; chief exec. officer Gulf Ins. Co., 1985-86; sr. v.p., chief fin. officer Comml. Credit Co., 1985-86, sr. v.p. audit, 1987; exec. v.p., chief fin. officer Anthem, Inc., Indpls., 1987—. Rep. candidate for U.S. Congress, 1972; past pres. Charlesbrooke Cmty. Assn.; past. v.p. Jr. Achievement of Met. Balt., 1984-85; bd. dirs. Goodwill Industries of Balt., 1986, bd. govs. 1994; bd. dirs. Family Svcs. Assn., 1994, Goodwill Industries of Indpls., 1994; mem. adv. coun. Clowes Meml. Hall. Capt. AUS, 1963-65. Recipient various Jaycee awards. Fellow Life Mgmt. Inst.; mem. Am. Mgmt. Assn. (pres.'s assn.), AICPAs, Mich. Assn. CPAs, Md. Assn. CPAs, Am. Soc. CLUs, U.S. Jaycees (treas. 1973-74), Mich. Jaycees (pres. 1971-72), Detroit Jaycees (pres. 1968-69), Balt. C. of C. (bd. dirs.), Mensa, Notre Dame Club, Skyline Club.

SHERIDAN, PHILP HENRY, pediatrician, neurologist; b. Washington, June 29, 1950; s. Andrew James and Mildred Adele (Stohlman) S.; m. Margaret Mary Williams, Oct. 3, 1987; children: Gerard Andrew, Philip Henry, Kathleen Mary, Patrick Gerard, Mary Margaret Gerard, Mary Anne Gerard. BS magna cum laude, Yale U., 1972; MD cum laude, Georgetown U., 1976. Diplomate Am. Bd. Pediatrics, Am. Bd. Psychiatry and Neurology, Am. Bd. Qualification in Electroencephalography. Resident in pediatrics Children's Hosp. Phila., 1976-79; fellow in pediatric neurology Hosp. of U. Pa., Phila., 1979-82; med. staff fellow NIH, Bethesda, Md., 1982-84, neurologist, epilepsy br. Nat. Inst. Neurol. Disorders and Stroke, 1984—, health scientist adminstr., guest worker researcher, 1984-89, chief Devel. Neurology Br., 1989—, acting chief Epilepsy Br. NIH, 1995—; cons., lectr. Nat. Naval Med. Ctr., Bethesda, 1984—; med. dir. U.S. Pub. Health Svc. Contbr. articles on clin. and rsch. neurology to med. jours. Neurologist Div. Children's Splty. Svcs., Fairfax, Va., 1984—. Mem. Am. Acad. Neurology, Child Neurology Soc. (invited reviewer), Soc. for Neurosci., Alpha Omega Alpha. Roman Catholic. Current work: Planning and administering a comprehensive research program concerning epilepsy, pediatric neurology, developmental neurobiology, and neuromuscular disorders. Subspecialties: Neurology, Pediatrics. Office: NIH Fed Bldg Rm 516 Bethesda MD 20892

SHERIDAN, RICHARD BERT, economics educator; b. Emporia, Kans., Feb. 10, 1918; s. Bert and Olive Nancy (Davis) S.; m. Audrey Marion Porter, Oct. 18, 1952; children—Richard David, Margaret Anne. B.S., Emporia Kans. State U., 1940; M.S., U. Kans., 1947; Ph.D., London Sch. Econs. and Polit. Sci., 1951. Instr. to assoc. prof. U. Kans., Lawrence, 1947-62, prof. econs., 1963-88; emeritus prof. econs., 1988—; external examiner U. W.I., Kingston, Jamaica, 1964-74; vis. prof. Coll. V.I., St. Thomas, 1971, U. West Indies, St. Augustine, Trinidad, 1987. Author: Economic History of South Central Kansas, 1956, Chapters in Caribbean History, 1970, Sugar and Slavery, 1974, Doctors and Slaves, 1985; cons. editor: Jour. Caribbean History, 1971—; contbr. articles to profl. jours. Served to lt. USNR, 1942-46. Recipient Article award N.C. Bicentennial Contest, 1976, article award Kans. State Hist. Soc., 1989; honored with a festschrift, 1996; Fulbright scholar U. W.I., 1962-63; grantee NIH, Nat. Libr. Medicine, 1973. Fellow Royal Hist. Soc.; mem. Soc. for Human Econs., Assn. Caribbean History. Democrat. Congregationalist. Home: 1745 Louisiana St Lawrence KS 66044-4055 Office: U Kans Dept of Econ Lawrence KS 66045

SHERIDAN, SONIA LANDY, artist, retired art educator; b. Newark, Ohio, Apr. 10, 1925; d. Avrom Mendel and Goldie Cornelia (Hanon) Landy; m. James Edward Sheridan, Sept. 27, 1947; 1 son, Jamy. A.B., Hunter Coll., 1945; postgrad., Columbia U., 1946-48; M.F.A. with high honors, Calif. Coll. Arts and Crafts, 1961. Tchr. art public high schs. Calif., 1951-57; chmn. dept. art Taipei Am. Sch., Taiwan, 1957-59; instr. Calif. Coll. Arts and Crafts, 1960-61; asst. prof. art Sch. Art Inst. Chgo., 1961-67, assoc. prof., 1968-75, prof., 1976-80, prof. emeritus, 1980—, founder, head generative systems program, 1970-80; artist-in-residence 3M Corp., 1970, 76; cons. French Ministry of Culture, 1986; artist-in-residence Xerox Corp., 1981; lectr., univs., museums, art schs., workshops; lectr. Hungarian Acad. Scis. Symposium Collected Essays & Exhbn., Budapest, 1989. One-woman shows include Rosenberg Gallery, Chgo., 1966, Visual Studies Workshop, Rochester, N.Y., 1973, Iowa Mus. Art, Iowa City, 1976, Mus. Sci. Industry, Chgo., 1978; two-person show Mus. Modern Art, N.Y.C., 1974; exhibited in group shows at Print Ann, Boston Mus., 1963, Software, Jewish Mus., N.Y.C., 1969-70, Photography into Art, London, 1972-73, Photokino, Cologne, Germany, 1974, San Francisco Mus. Art, 1975, U. Mich. Mus. Art, 1978, Toledo Mus. Art, 1982-83, Mus. Modern Art, Paris, 1983, Siggraph, U.S., Japan, France, 1982, 83, Reina Sofia Mus., Madrid, Spain, 1986, Smithsonian Instn., 1990, Tokyo Met. Mus. Photography, 1991, Madrid City Cultural Ctr., 1992, Karl Ernst Osthaus Mus., Hagen, Germany, 1992, Circulo des Belles Artes, Madrid, 1992, Yale U. Art Gallery, 1995, Tokyo Intercom. Ctr., 1995, U. Montreal, 1995; represented in permanent collections Art Inst. Chgo., San Francisco Mus. Art, Mus. Sci. and Industry, Chgo., U. Iowa Mus. Art, Nat. Gallery Art, Ottawa, Can., Visual Studies Workshop, Rochester, Tokyo Met. Mus. Photography, Fundacion Arte y Technologia, Madrid; author: Energized Artscience: Sonia Landy Sheridan, 1978; co-editor Leonardo jour.; contbr. articles, essay to profl. jours. Guggenheim fellow, 1973; Nat. Endowment for Arts workshop grantee 1974, pub. media grantee, 1976, artist grantee 1981; Union Ind. Colls. Art grantee 1975. Mem. Coll. Art Assn., Internat. Soc. for Interdisciplinary Study of Symmetry.

SHERIDAN, THOMAS BROWN, mechanical engineering and applied psychology educator, researcher, consultant; b. Cin., Dec. 23, 1929; s. Mahlon Brinsley and Esther Anna (Brown) S.; m Rachel Briggs Rice, Aug. 1, 1953; children: Paul Rice, Richard Rice, David Rice, Margaret Lenore. BS, Purdue U., 1951; MS, UCLA, 1954; ScD, MIT, 1959; Dr. (hon.), Delft U. Tech., The Netherlands, 1991. Registered profl. engr., Mass. Asst. prof. mech. engring. MIT, Cambridge, 1959-65, assoc. prof., 1965-70, prof., 1970-78, prof. engring. and applied psychology, 1978-94, prof. aeronautics and astronautics, 1994—, Ford prof., 1995—; lectr. U. Calif., Berkeley, Stanford U., 1968; vis. prof. U. Delft, The Netherlands, 1972, Stanford U., 1989, Ben Gurion U., Israel, 1995; chmn. com. human factors, mem. com. aircrew-vehicle interaction, com. on commercially developed space facility, com. on human factors in air traffic control, NRC; mem. adv. com. on applied phys., math. and biol. scis. NSF; mem. life scis. adv. com., study group on robotics, oversight com. flight telerobotic servicer NASA; mem. task force on appropriate tech. U.S. Congress Office Tech. Assessment; mem. study sect. accident prevention and injury control NIH; mem. Def. Sci. Bd. Task Force on Computers, Tng. and Gaming, Nuclear Regulatory Commn. on Nuclear Safety Rsch. Rev. Com. Author: Telerobotics, Automation and Human Supervisory Control, 1992; co-author: Man Machine Systems, 1974; editor: (with others) Monitoring Behavior and Supervisory Control, 1976; assoc. editor Automatica, 1982-94; mem. edtl. adv. bd. Tech. Forecasting and Social Change, Computer Aided Design, Advanced Robotics, Robotics and Computer Integrated Mfg.; sr. editor Presence: Telerobots and Virtual Environments, 1991—. Served to 1st lt. USAF, 1951-53. Fellow IEEE (pres. Systems, Man and Cybernetics Soc. 1974-76, Centennial medal 1984, Norbert Wiener award 1993, Joseph G. Wohl award 1995), Human Factors Soc. (Paul M. Fitts award 1977, pres. 1990-91), Nat. Acad. Engring. Democrat. Mem. United Ch. of Christ. Office: MIT 77 Massachusetts Ave Cambridge MA 02139-4301

SHERIF, S. A., mechanical engineering educator; b. Alexandria, Egypt, June 25, 1952; came to U.S., 1978; s. Ahmed and Ietedal H. (Monib) S.; m. Azza A. Shamseldin, Feb. 6, 1977; children: Ahmed S., Mohammad S. BSME (hon.), Alexandria U., 1975, MSME, 1978; PhD in Mech. Engring., Iowa State U., 1985. Tchg. asst. mech. engring. Alexandria U., 1975-78; tchg. assoc. mech. and environtl. engring. U. Calif., Santa Barbara, 1978-79; rsch. asst. mech. engring. Iowa State U., Ames, 1979-84; asst. prof. No. Ill. U., Dekalb, 1984-87, mem. grad. faculty, 1985-87; mem. grad. faculty U. Miami, Coral Gables, Fla., 1987-91, asst. prof. civil, archtl. and mech. engring., 1987-91; assoc. prof. mech. engring. U. Fla., Gainesville, 1991—, mem. doctoral rsch. faculty, 1992-94; cons. Solar Reactor Techs., Inc., Miami, Fla., 1988-91, Dade Power Corp., Miami, 1988-91, Ind. Energy Sys., Miami, 1988-91, Carey Dwyer Eckhart Mason Spring & Beckham, P.A. Law Offices, Miami, 1988-89, Michael G. Widoff, P.A., Attys. at Law, Ft. Lauderdale, Fla., 1989-93, Law Offices Pomeroy and Betts, Ft. Lauderdale, 1991-92, Ctr. for Indoor Air Rsch., 1994—; adj. faculty cons. Kennedy Western U., Thousand Oaks, Calif., 1994—; resident assoc. Argonne (Ill.) Nat. Lab., Tech. Transfer Ctr., summer 1992; faculty fellow NASA Kennedy Space Ctr., Cape Canaveral, Fla., summer 1993; rsch. assoc. summer faculty rsch. program Air Force Office Sci. Rsch., Arnold Engring. Devel. Ctr., Arnold AFB, Tenn., 1994; reviewer 20 internal jours., 80 conf. procs. and several pub. cos. and rsch. svc. orgns. Co-editor: Industrial and Agricultural Applications of Fluid Mechanics, 1989, The Heuristics of Thermal Anemometry, 1990, Heat and Mass Transfer in Frost and Ice, Packed Beds, and Environmental Discharges, 1990, Industrial Applications of Fluid Mechanics, 1990, rev. edit., 1991, Mixed Convection and Environmental Flows, 1990, Measurement and Modeling of Environmental Flows, 1992, Industrial and Environment Applications of Fluid Mechanics, 1992, Thermal Anemometry-1993, 1993, Heat Transfer in Turbulent Flows-1993, 1993, Developments in Electroheological Flows and Measurement Uncertainty-1994, 1994, Heat, Mass and Momentum Transfer in Environmental Flows, 1995; contbr. numerous articles to profl. jours. Mem. environ. awareness adv. com., Dade County Pub. Schs., 1989-91, lab. dir. cmty. lab. rsch. program, 1989-91, also faculty liaison design svcs. dept.; active Com. for Nat. Inst. for Environ., 1992—; mem. senate U. Fla., 1994-95. Mem. ASME (mem. coord. group fluid measurements, fluids engring. divsn. 1987—, vice chmn. 1990-92, chmn. 1992-94, fluids engring. divsn. adv. bd. 1994—, honors and awards com. 1994—, mem. fluid mechs. tech. com. 1990—, fluid mech. com. 1987-90, environ. heat transfer com. heat transfer divsn. 1987—, mem. fluid applications and systems tech. com. 1990—, systems analysis tech. com. advanced energy sys. divsn., 1989—, newsletter editor advanced energy sys. divsn. 1995—, fundamentals and theory tech. com. solar energy divsn. 1990—, chmn. CGFM nominating com. 1992-94, mem. 1994—, chmn. profl. devel. com. Rock River Valley sect. 1987, tech. activities operating com. Gator sect. 1994—, MFFCC subcom. 1 on uncertainties in flow measurements 1995—), ASHRAE (mem. heat transfer fluid flow com. 1988-92, 93—, corr. mem. 1992-93, mem. thermodynamics and psychrometrics com. 1988-92, corr. mem. 1992—, vice chmn. 1990-92, mem. liquid to refrigerant heat exchangers com. 1989-93, sec. 1990-92, chmn. standards project com. on measurement of moist air properties 1989-95), AIAA (sr.), AIChE, Internat. Assn. Hydrogen Energy, Internat. Solar Energy Soc., Am. Solar Energy Soc., Internat. Energy Soc. (mem. sci. coun.), Assn. Energy Engrs. (sr.), European Assn. Laser Anemometry (ASME/FED rep., mem. steering com.), Internat. Inst. Refrigeration (U.S. nat. com.), ABI (hon. mem. rsch. bd. adv. 1994—), Sigma Xi. Moslem. Avocations: reading, soccer, basketball, history, astronomy. Home: 540-3 Gainesville FL 32606 Office: U Fla Dept Mech Engring 228 MEB Gainesville FL 32611-6300

SHERIFF, JIMMY DON, accounting educator, academic dean; b. Greenville, S.C., Dec. 8, 1940; s. James Donald and Gladys Ellie (Chapman) S.; BA, So. Wesleyan U., 1964; MBA, U. Ga., 1970, PhD, 1976; m. Gwen Anne Campbell, Aug. 31, 1969. Acct., Maremont Corp., Greenville, 1965-68; instr. U. Ga., Athens, 1970-73; asst. prof. Presbyn. Coll., Clinton, S.C., 1973-74; prof. Clemson (S.C.) U., 1974-87, assoc. dean, dir. rsch., 1987-92, acting dean, 1992-93, sr. assoc. dean, 1993—; U.S. rep. Network Internat. Bus. Schs. Chmn. Pickens County Aeros. Commn., 1980-91; founding pres. Pickens County Property Owners Assn. 1st lt. U.S. Army, 1964; brig. gen. USNG ret. Decorated U.S. Legion of Merit, Order of the Palmetto; named to Officer Candidate Sch. Hall of Fame. Mem. Inst. Mgmt. Accts. (Most Valuable Mem. 1978, dir. 1975—, pres. Anderson area 1979-80, nat. dir. 1984-86), Am. Acctg. Assn. (doctoral consortium fellow 1972), Soc. Rsch. Adminstrs., Nat. Coun. Rsch. Adminstrs., Acad. Sci., Acad. Acctg. Historians, Nat. Coun. Govtl. Acctg., S.C. Assn. Acctg. Instrs. (pres. 1974-75), So. Wesleyan U. Alumni Assn. (pres. 1970-72, Alumnus of Yr. 1994), 228th Brigade Assn. (pres.), Pickens County Hist. Soc., Pickens County Property Owners Assn. (founding pres.), Am. Legion, Beta Gamma Sigma, Beta Alpha Psi, Sigma Iota Epsilon, Delta Sigma Pi. Baptist. Clubs: University (pres. 1985-86), Commerce (Greenville). Lodges: Lions (pres.), Masons, Rotary, Shriners, Am. Legion. Author: Attitudes Toward Current Values, 1976. Republican. Home: 988 Old Shirley Rd Central SC 29630-9337 Office: Clemson U Coll Bus & Public Affairs Dean's Office 165 Sirrine Hall Clemson SC 29634-1301

SHERIN, EDWIN, theatrical and film director, actor; b. Danville, Pa., Jan. 15, 1930; s. Joseph and Ruth (Berger) S.; m. Jane Alexander, Mar. 29, 1975; children: Anthony J., Geoffrey B., Jonathan E.; 1 stepchild, Jason E. AB in History and Polit. Sci., Brown U., 1952. Acting tchr. Am. Theatre Wing, N.Y.C., 1962-64; acting tchr. Am. Theatre Tng. Inst. Southeastern Mass. U., South Dartmouth, 1974; Lucille Lortel Disting. guest artist U. Bridgeport (Conn.), 1980; dir. Sch. Theatre Arts Boston U., 1981; acting tchr. Okla. Summer Arts Inst., 1985-86, One on One, L.A., 1989, 90; exec. v.p. Altion Prodns., L.A., 1985-93; mem. nat. adv. for Mus. Am. Theatre; instr. Okla. Summer Arts Inst., guest dir. Calif. Inst. Arts. Actor with Houseman's troupe Phoenix Theatre, N.Y.C., 1957-58, actor N.Y. Shakespeare Festival, 1956-60; appeared as: Octavius Caesar in, Anthony and Cleopatra, 1958; appeared in Broadway plays Come Blow Your Horn, 1960, Desert Incident, 1961, Romulus, 1962, Face of a Hero, 1963; TV films Playhouse 90, 1956-58, Studio One, 1956-58, Omnibus, 1957-60, East Side/West Side, 1960; dir. Broadway plays including The Great White Hope, 1968, Glory Hallelujah, 1969, 6 RMS RIV VU, 1973, Find Your Way Home, Of Mice and Men, 1974, Red Devil Battery Sign, 1975, Sweet Bird of Youth, 1976, Eccentricities of a Nightingale, 1976, The First Monday in October, 1978, Goodbye Fidel, 1980, The Visit, 1992; assoc. producing dir. Washington's Arena Stage, 1964-68; dir. Cosi Fan Tutte, N.Y. City Opera Co., 1972, A Streetcar Named Desire, Piccadilly Theatre, London, 1973, Semmelweiss, Studio Arena Theatre, Buffalo, N.Y., 1978, Outrage, Kennedy Ctr., Washington, 1982; films including Valdez is Coming, 1970, My Old Man's Place, 1971; producing artistic dir. Showdown at Adobe Hotel, Semmelweiss, Hedda Gabler, Night Must Fall, A Streetcar Named Desire, Hartman Theatre, Stamford, Conn., 1980-85; dir. Chelsea Walls, Naked Angels, N.Y.C., 1990, TV programs Hill Street Blues, Moonlighting, WIOU, L.A. Law, Tour of Duty, MEN; co-exec. prodr. Law and Order, 1993-94, exec. prodr., 1994—, (TV films) The Father Clements Story, Lena, My 100 Children, Daughter of the Streets, Getting Even, A Marriage: Georgia O'Keeffe and Alfred Stieglitz, 1991. With USN, 1952-56, Korea. Recipient Outer Circle award, 1969; New Eng. Theatre award, 1969; Recipient N.Y. Drama Critics award, 1969, Drama Desk award, 1969, L.A. Drama Circle award, 1971, Recipient Tony nomination, 1974, London Evening Standard citation, 1973, Joseph Jefferson award, 1976, Buffalo drama award, 1978; New Eng. Theatre Conf. award; Ford Found. grantee, 1965-66. Mem. AFTRA, SAG, Actors Equity Assn., Dirs. Guild Am., Dramatists Guild, Soc. Stage Dirs. and Choreographers (v.p. 1970-80), Lincoln Soc., Phi Gamma Delta.

SHERK, KENNETH JOHN, lawyer; b. Ida Grove, Iowa, Feb. 27, 1933; s. John and Dorothy (Myers) Sherk; m. Virginia Kay Taylor, June 28, 1958; children: Karin Fulton, Katrina, Keith, Kyle. BSC, U. Iowa, 1955; JD, George Washington U., 1961. Bar: Ariz. 1962, U.S. Dist. Ct. Ariz. 1962, U.S. Ct. Appeals (9th cir.) 1966, U.S. Supreme Ct. 1974. Assoc. Moore & Romley, Phoenix, 1962-67, ptnr., 1967-79; ptnr. Romley & Sherk, Phoenix, 1979-85; dir. Fennemore Craig, Phoenix, 1985—. Served as 1st lt. U.S. Army, 1955-58, Korea. Recipient Profl. Achievement Svcs. award George Washington Law Assn., 1986, Ariz. Judges Assn., 1989, Disting. Svc. award Phoenix Assn. Def. Counsel, 1990. Fellow Am. Coll. Trial Lawyers, Am. Acad. Appellate Lawyers, Am. Bar Found., Ariz. Bar Found.; mem. ABA (ho. of dels. 1990-93), Ariz. Bar Assn. (pres. 1985-86), State Bar of Ariz. (Mem. of Yr. award 1994), Maricopa Bar Assn. (pres. 1978-79). Republican. Congregational. Avocations: fishing, hiking, bicycling. Home: 1554 W Las Palmaritas Dr Phoenix AZ 85021-5429 Office: Fennemore Craig 2 N Central Ave Ste 2200 Phoenix AZ 85004-4406

SHERLOCK, JOHN MICHAEL, bishop; b. Regina, Sask., Can., Jan. 20, 1926; s. Joseph and Catherine S. Student, St. Augustine's Sem., Toronto, Ont., Can., 1950; student canon law, Catholic U. Am., 1950-52; LLD (hon.), U. Windsor, 1986; DD (hon.), Huron Coll., London, Ont., 1986. Ordained priest Roman Catholic Ch., 1950, bishop, 1974; asst. pastor St. Eugene's, Hamilton, Ont., 1952-59, St. Augustine's, Dundas, Ont., 1959-63, Cathedral Christ the King, Hamilton, also, Guelph and Maryhill, Ont., 1950-52; pastor St. Charles Ch., Hamilton, 1963-74; aux. bishop London, Ont., 1974-78; bishop, 1978—; chaplain Univ. Newman Club, McMaster U., Hamilton, 1963-66; pres. Canadian Conf. Cath. Bishops, 1983-85, liaison with U. Chaplains Can. and Pres. Cath. Coll. and Univs.; chmn. social affairs com. commn. Ont. Conf. Cath. Bishops, edn. commn., family life com.; adv. judge for the Regional Marriage Truban, 1954-72. Mem. Wentworth County Roman Cath. Separate Sch. Bd., 1964-74, chmn., 1972-73; chmn. Nat. Cath. Broadcasting Found., 1995—. Fellow honoris cause U.St. Michael's Coll., Toronto, 1994. Address: Chancery Office, 1070 Waterloo St, London, ON Canada N6A 3Y2

SHERMAN, ALAN ROBERT, psychologist, educator; b. N.Y.C., Nov. 18, 1942; s. David R. and Goldie (Wax) S.; m. Llana Helene Tobias, Aug. 14, 1966 (div. 1989); children: Jonathan Colbert, Melissa Anne. BA, Columbia U., 1964; MS, Yale U., 1966, PhD, 1969. Lic. psychologist, Calif. Faculty psychology U. Calif., Santa Barbara, 1969—; clin. psychologist in pvt. practice Santa Barbara, 1981—; cons. in field. Author: Behavior Modification, 1973; contbr. articles to profl. jours. and chpts. in books. Pres. Santa Barbara Mental Health Assn., 1978, 84-85, 91, Mountain View Sch. Site Coun., Santa Barbara, 1978-84. Recipient Vol. of Yr. award Santa Barbara Mental Health Assn., 1979, Tchg. Excellence awards Delta Delta Delta, Alpha Chi Omega, Gamma Phi Beta, Santa Barbara; NIMH predoctoral rsch. fellow, 1964-69; grantee in field. Fellow Behavior Therapy and Rsch. Soc.; mem. APA, AAUP (chpt. pres. 1978-79), Calif. Psychol. Assn., Assn. for Advancement of Behavior Therapy, Santa Barbara County Psychol. Assn. (pres. 1985), Phi Beta Kappa (chpt. pres. 1977-78), Sigma Xi, Psi Chi (chpt. faculty advisor, 1979—). Office: Univ of Calif Dept Psychology Santa Barbara CA 93106-9660 *Pursuing a creative profession which allows one to help improve the condition of others, provides intrinsic rewards that make the work process satisfying in itself. I am fortunate to be involved in two such professions, college teaching and psychotherapy. When you genuinely enjoy what your are doing, you are likely to be successful at it.*

SHERMAN, ARTHUR, theater educator, writer, actor, composer; b. Dec. 5, 1920; s. Herman and Fay (Epstein) S.; m. Margery Frost Sherman, Apr. 15, 1974 (div. Sept. 1989); children: Claudia, Andrew Jay. MusB, Juilliard Sch. Music, 1955; M in Music Edn., Manhattan Sch. Music, 1957; Doctoral Equivalency, CUNY, 1962. Dir. performing arts N.Y.C. (N.Y.) Tech. Coll., 1964-72; prof. speech and theatre John Jay Coll., N.Y.C., 1990—, Borough Man C.C., N.Y.C., 1990—; judge Film Award Com., Australia, 1972-89, Acad. Awards, 1990; cons. Min. for Edn., Tasmania, Australia, 1977. Author (screenplays) Thistle and Thorn, 1982, Same Difference, 1983; composer of music; composer book, music lyrics Prisms in the Looking Glass, Once Upon a Crime; actor., dir. films, TV, theatre in U.S. and Australia; sculptures displayed YWCA, Hamilton, Ont., Can., 1967, Lincoln Ctr., N.Y.C., 1969, State Bank, Sydney, Australia, 1974. Pres. United Fedn. Coll. Tchrs., N.Y.C., 1971. With USN, 1943-46. Grantee Australian Film Commn., 1981. Mem. ASCAP, Australasian Performing Rights Assn., Actors' Equity U.S. and Australia. Home: 315 W 57th St New York NY 10019 Office: John Jay Coll 58th St 10th Ave New York NY 10019

SHERMAN, CHARLES DANIEL, JR., surgeon; b. Avon Park, Fla., Oct. 5, 1920; s. Charles Daniel and Mary Alice (Oliver) S.; m. Jean Riebling, Aug. 13, 1943; children: Rachel, Charles Daniel, Edward. B.S., U. Fla., 1942; M.D., Johns Hopkins U., 1945. Diplomate: Am. Bd. Surgery. Intern Duke U. Hosp., Durham, N.C., 1945-46; resident U. Rochester Med. Center, 1948-

52, instr., 1952-56, asst. prof., 1956-64, clin. assoc. prof. surgery, 1964-70, clin. prof., 1970—; fellow Meml. Center for Cancer, 1951; practice medicine specializing in cancer surgery Rochester, 1953—; mem. staff Highland Hosp., Rochester, N.Y.; v.p. Redd Labs., Clearwater, Fla., 1961-70; advisor N.Y. State Bur. Cancer Control, 1964-75; sec.-treas. Monroe County Health Planning Coun., 1967-69; mem. Monroe County Bd. Health, 1966-79; advisor to WHO, 1971, dir. Internat. Network of WHO Collaborating Ctrs. for Cancer Edn., 1996—; mem. advisory com. Nat. Cancer Insts.; dir. Internat. Union Against Cancer Project to Survey Cancer Edn. in L.Am., 1976, Asia, 1977; mem. hosp. adv. com. to Joint Com. on Accreditation of Hosps., 1980-88; organizer WHO/Internat. Union Against Cancer European Congress on Cancer Edn., 1981; mem. Accreditation Coun. for Continuing Med. Edn., 1983-89, vice-chmn., 1988, chmn., 1989; organizer Coordinating Coun. on Cancer Edn. in L.Am., 1986, in Asian-Pacific region, 1987; chmn. Coordinating Coun. for Cancer Edn. in Europe, 1987-88; bd. dirs. Nat. Resident Matching Plan, 1988-92, treas., 1989-90; mem. organizing com. Internat. Med. Scholar Program, 1987-89; keynote spkr. Internat. Cancer Congress, 1992; co-dir. WHO Internat. Network of Cancer Edn. Ctrs., 1996—; lectr. in field. Author: Clinical Concepts in Cancer Management, 1976; co-author: Clinical Oncology, 1974; editor, pub.: Directory of U.S. Oncologists, 1983—; editor: (with others) Programmed Instruction in Medical Education; Newsletter in Cancer, 1968-80; chmn. editorial bd. for 2d , 3d and 4th edits. Clinical Oncology (monograph): (with others) Internat. Union against Cancer, 1978-86; mem. editorial bd. Jour. Cancer Edn., 1984—, Greek Jour. Continuing Med. Edn., 1986—; participant movie on esophogeal reconstrn., 1957; producer exhibits on cancer treatment and cancer edn.; co-contbr. articles to profl. jours. Mem. adv. com. on Continuing Edn. in Oncology of the European Community, 1993; advisor European Sch. Oncology, European Med. Student Assn.; mem. internat. adv. com. Asian Pacific Cancer Congress, Beijing, 1991, Bangkok, 1993, Singapore, 1995, Malaysia, 1996. Fulbright fellow Mendoza, Argentina, 1963; recipient Health Edn. award N.Y. State Pub. Health Assn., 1973; cert. of merit. Rochester Acad. Medicine, 1982. Mem. ACS, AMA (N.Y. state del. to Ho. of Dels., coun. on med. edn. 1983-92, com. on med. liability 1984-85, com. on fgn. grads. 1984, com. on cancer 1970-74, exec. com. 1989-90), Am. Radium Soc., Soc. Head and Neck Surgeons, Royal Soc. Medicine, Am. Assn. Cancer Edn. (pres. 1975-76), Am. Fedn. Clin. Oncologic Socs. (bd. govs. 1974-77), N.Y. State Med. Soc. (councillor 1973-79, asst. treas. 1980-83, treas. 1983-85, v.p. 1986, pres.-elect 1987, pres. 1988-89, trustee 1990—, chair trustees 1994-95, liaison com. on med. edn. 1992-94), N.Y. Acad. Sci., N.Y. State Cancer Programs Assn. (pres. 1970-71, chmn. UICC prof. edn. program 1986-94, exec. coun. 1986-94), Monroe County Med. Soc. (pres. 1965, Edward Mott Moore award 1978), Monroe County Cancer and Leukemia Assn. (pres. 1962-66), European Assn. Cancer Edn. (bd. dirs. 1987-92), Soc. Surg. Oncology (chmn. residents award com. 1963-66), Am. Soc. Preventive Oncology, U.S. Squash Rackets Assn. (dir. 1963-65), Argentine Anti-Smoking Union (hon.), Blue Key Soc., Phi Beta Kappa, Alpha Phi Omega. Home: 127 Southern Pky Rochester NY 14618-1052

SHERMAN, CHARLES EDWIN, broadcasting executive, educator; b. Phila., Mar. 20, 1934; s. Abe and Rae (Ginsberg) S.; m. Elaine Landsburg, Sept. 11, 1960; children: Jean, Eric, David. BS, Temple U., Phila., 1960, MA, 1962; PhD, Wayne State U., Detroit, 1967. Announcer, program producer Sta. WHAT, Phila., 1957-62; mem. prodn. staff Sta. WFIL-TV, Phila., 1961; grad. asst. Temple U., 1960-62; TV producer-dir., prodn. supr. Wayne State U., 1962-64, instr. dept. speech, 1964-66, asst. to dir. div. mass communication, 1966-67; asst. prof. dept. speech U. Wis., 1967-70, assoc. prof. dept. communication arts, assoc. chmn., 1970-73, assoc. prof., acting chmn., 1974, prof., assoc. chmn. dept. communication arts, 1974-75; prof., chmn. dept. telecommunications Ind. U., Bloomington, 1975-79, adj. prof. telecommunications, 1980—; pres., gen. mgr. WTRF-TV, Wheeling, W.Va., 1979-84, WHOI-TV, Peoria, Ill., 1984-88; sr. v.p. TV Nat. Assn. of Broadcasters, Washington, 1988—; cons. Forward Communications, Inc., Wausaw, Wis., 1974-79; mem. CBS Network TV Affiliates Bd., 1982-84, ABC Network TV Affiliates Bd., 1986-88; bd. dirs. Bank of Wheeling, Nat. Assn. TV Program Execs. Ednl. Found., 1986—, Accreditating Council on Edn. in Journalism and Mass Communication, 1986—; chmn. Task Force on Citizens Rights and Access, Wis. Commn. on Cable TV, 1973; vice chmn. W.Va. Ednl. Broadcasting Authority, 1980-85. Contbr. articles on broadcasting to profl. jours. Bd. dirs. Upper Ohio Valley United Way, 1979-85, Heart of Ill. United Way, 1986-88, Peoria Human Services Ctr., 1986-88; bd. dirs., mem. exec. com. Wheeling Devel. Conf., 1980-85; trustee Ohio Valley Med. Ctr., 1980-85. With U.S. Army, 1955-57. Recipient Communications award Temple U., 1960, Sigma Delta Chi award Temple U., 1960, Disting. Service award in broadcasting Wayne State U., 1966. Mem. Speech Communication Assn., Broadcast Edn. Assn. (chmn. Internat. Seminar 1974, chmn. Internat. Interest Group 1974, dir., sec., treas. 1983-85, chmn. 1985-86), Nat. Assn. Ednl. Broadcasters, Nat. Assn. Broadcasters (chmn. rsch. com.), Wheeling C. of C. (bd. dirs. 1979-85), Alpha Epsilon Rho, Sigma Delta Chi. Jewish. Office: Nat Assn Broadcasters 1771 N St NW Washington DC 20036-2805

SHERMAN, CINDY, artist; b. Glen Ridge, N.J., 1954. Student, State Univ. Coll. Buffalo, 1972-76. One-woman exhbns. include Hallwalls Gallery, Buffalo, 1976, 77, Contemporary Arts Mus., Houston, 1980, The Kitchen, N.Y., 1980, Metro Pictures, N.Y., 1980, 83, Saman Gallery, Genoa, 1981, Young/Hoffman Gallery, Chgo., 1981, Chantal Crousel Gallery, Paris, 1982, Stedelijk Mus., Amsterdam, 1982, St. Louis Art Mus., 1983, Fine Arts Ctr. Gallery, SUNY-Stony Brook, 1983, Rhona Hoffman Gallery, Chgo., 1983, Douglas Drake Gallery, Kansas City, 1983, 84, Seibu Gallery Contemporary Art, Tokyo, 1984, Akron Art Mus., 1984, Linda Cathcart Gallery, Santa Monica, Calif., 1992, Museo de Monterrey, Mex., 1992; group exhbns. include Albright-Knox Art Gallery, Buffalo, 1975, Artists Space, N.Y., 1978, Max Protetch Gallery, N.Y., 1979, Castelli Graphics, N.Y., 1980, Lisson Gallery, London, 1980, Centre Pompidou, Paris, 1981; NIT, 1981, Renaissance Soc. U. Chgo., 1982, Metro Pictures, N.Y., 1982, La Ciennale de Venezia, Venice, Italy, 1982, Documenta 7, Kassel, West Germany, 1982, Chantall Crousel Gallery, Paris, 1982, San Francisco Mus. Modern Art, 1982, Inst. Contemporary Art, London, 1982, Grey Art Gallery, N.Y., 1982, Inst. Contemporary Art, Phila., 1982, Young Hoffman Gallery, Chgo., 1983, Hirshhorn Gallery, Washington, 1983, 1983, Whitney Mus. Am. Art, N.Y., 1983, 85, 91; represented in permanent collections Mus. Fine Arts, Houston, Albright/Knox Art Gallery, Buffalo, Dallas Mus. Fine Arts, Mus. Boymans-van Beuningen, Rotterdam, Akron Art Mus., Ohio, Mus. Modern Art, N.Y.C., Walker Art Ctr., Mpls., Tate Gallery, London, Rose Art Mus., Brandeis U., Centre Pompidou, Paris, Stedelijk Mus., Amsterdam, Met. Mus. Art, N.Y., St. Louis Art Mus., San Francisco Mus. Modern Art. Office: care Metro Pictures 150 Greene St New York NY 10012-3202*

SHERMAN, DEMING ELIOT, lawyer; b. Providence, July 22, 1943; s. Edwin Fisk and Martha Amy (Parkhurst) S.; m. Jane Catherine Bauer, Dec. 20, 1966; children: Melissa Jane, Nicholas Deming. BA, Amherst (Mass.) Coll., 1965; JD, U. Chgo., 1968. Bar: R.I. 1968, U.S. Dist. Ct. R.I. 1970, U.S. Supreme Ct. 1974, Mass. 1985, U.S. Dist. Ct. Mass. 1985. Ptnr. Edwards & Angell, Providence, 1969—, mng. ptnr., 1986-94. Trustee First Night Providence, 1988-93, pres., 1991-93; bd. dirs. R.I. Philharm. Orch., 1985—, pres., 1993-95; trustee Providence Preservation Soc., 1990—, v.p., 1994—; mem. R.I. Com. on Jud. Tenure and Discipline, 1992—; bd. dirs. Providence YMCA, 1975-85, Blackstone Pk. Improvement Assn., 1979—; corporator R.I. Hosp., 1989—. Fellow R.I. Bar Found.; mem. ABA, R.I. Bar Assn., Amherst Alumni Assn. R.I. (pres. 1980-91), Greater Providence C. of C. (bd. dirs. 1991-94). Home: 254 Irving Ave Providence RI 02906-5544 Office: Edwards & Angell 2700 Hospital Trust Towers Providence RI 02903

SHERMAN, DONALD H., civil engineer; b. Jackson, Wyo., May 14, 1932; s. Howard M. and Dorothy (Turner) S.; children: D. John, Cynthia Lynn Pierceall, Richard L., Sheila L. Bufmack; m. Patricia A. Hoffman, June 26, 1993. AA in Engring., Fullerton Jr. Coll., 1953; diploma in surveying and mapping, I.C.S., 1955; BS in Geology, U. Wyo., 1960, BS in Civil Engring., 1968. Registered profl. engr., Wyo., Colo. Geophysicist Texaco Geophysical, Casper, Wyo. and Billings, Mont., 1960-63; surveyor Wyo. Hwy. Dept., Jackson, 1963-64; engring. geologist Wyo. Hwy. Dept., Cheyenne, 1964-66, hydraulics engr., 1968-72; civil engr., rotation trainee U.S. Bur. Reclamation, Denver, 1972-73; civil engr. D.M.J.M.-Phillips-Reister-Haley, Denver, 1973-79, Stearns Roger, Inc., Glendale, Colo., 1980-82, Centennial Engring., Arvada, Colo., 1983-85; civil engr. land devel. York Assocs., Denver, 1986-87; civil engr. City of Colo. Springs, 1987—; owner Valley View Trailer Park, Jackson, 1965-96; advisor to U.S. Senator Clifford Hansen on Black 14 incident, 1969. Recipient Presdl. Legion of Merit Rep. Nat. Com., 1992-96, Presdl. Commn., Rep. Nat. Com., 1992-96, Cert. of Award Presdl. Adv. Commn., 1991-92, 94, 96. Mem. Citizens Against Govt. Waste (charter), Concerned Women of Am., Nat. Right to Life, Nat. Republican Congressional Com., Nat. Republican Senatorial Com., Reublican Presdl. Task Force, Rebublican Presdl. Trust, Nat. Taxpayers Union, Am. Conservation Union. Republican. Avocations: photography, hiking, writing government leaders, genealogy. Home: 131 N Roosevelt St Colorado Springs CO 80909-6547 Office: City Engring 30 S Nevada Ave Rm 403 Colorado Springs CO 80903-1825

SHERMAN, EDWARD FRANCIS, lawyer, educator; b. El Paso, Tex., July 5, 1937; s. Raphael Eugene and Mary (Stedmond) S.; m. Alice Theresa Hammer, Feb. 23, 1963; children—Edward F. Jr., Paul. AB, Georgetown U., 1959; MA, U. Tex.-El Paso, 1962, 67; LLB, Harvard U., 1962. SJD, 1981. Bar: Tex. 1962, Ind. 1976. Aide to gov. Nev., state govt. fellow, Carson City, 1962; law clk. to U.S. dist. judge Western dist. Tex., El Paso, 1963; ptnr. firm Mayfield, Broaddus & Perrenot, El Paso, 1963-65; teaching fellow Harvard Law Sch., Cambridge, Mass., 1967-69; prof. Ind. U. Sch. Law, Bloomington, 1969-77; Fulbright prof. Trinity Coll., Dublin, 1973-74; vis. prof. U. London, 1989, U. London, 1989, Chuo U., Tokyo, 1995; Edward Clark Centennial prof. law, U. Tex., Austin, 1977—; counsel Tex. County Jail Litigation, 1978-85; bd. dirs., officer Travis County Dispute Resolution Ctr., Austin, 1985-88; chmn. bd. dirs. Tex. Resource Ctr., 1989-95, Tex. Ctr. Pub. Policy Dispute Resolution, 1993—; mem. arbitrator panel, course dir. Internat. Ctrs. for Arbitration. Capt. U.S. Army, 1965-67, lt. col. Res., 1970-90. Fulbright lectr. in law Trinity Coll., Dublin, Ireland, 1973-74. Fellow Tex. Bar Found.; mem. ABA (reporter ABA civil justice improvements project 1993, offer of judgement task force, 1995), Am. Arbitration Assn. (arbitrator panel), AAUP (gen. counsel 1986-88), Am. Law Inst., Tex. State Bar Assn. (alternative dispute resolution com. 1985—, chair Pattern Jury Charge Com. 1983-94), Tex. Civil Liberties Union (gen. counsel 1985-91). Co-author: The Military in American Society, 1979, Complex Litigation, 1985, 2d edit., 1992, Processes of Dispute Resolution, 1989, 2d edit., 1996, Civil Procedure: A Modern Approach, 1989, 2nd edit., 1995, Rau & Sherman's Texas ADR and Arbitration Statutes, 1994. Home: 2622 Wooldridge Dr Austin TX 78703-2538 Office: U Tex Sch Law 727 E 26th St Austin TX 78705-3224

SHERMAN, ELAINE C., gourmet foods company executive, educator; b. Chgo., Aug. 1, 1938; d. Arthur E. and Sylvia (Miller) Friedman; m. Arthur J. Spiegel, Jan. 1989; children: Steven J., David P., Jaime A. Student, Northwestern U., 1956-58; diploma in cake decorating, Wilton Sch. Profl. Cake Decorating, 1973; diploma, Dumas Pere, L'école de la Cuisine Française. Tchr. cooking and adult edn. Maine, Oakton, Niles Adult and Continuing Edn. Program, Park Ridge, Ill., 1972-82; corp. officer The Complete Cook, Glenview, Ill., 1976-82, Madame Chocolate, Glenview, 1983-87; food columnist Chgo. Sun Times, 1985-87; dir. mktg. Sue Ling Gin, Chgo., 1987-88; co-owner Critical Eye, Chgo., 1988—; v.p., dir. merchandising, gen. mgr. Foodstuffs, Inc., Evanston, Ill., 1990-91, food cons. mgmt. and mktg., 1991—. Author: Madame Chocolate's Book of Divine Indulgences, 1984 (nominated Tastemaker award 1984). Bd. dirs. Chgo. Fund on Aging and Disability, 1989—; co-chmn. Meals on Wheels, 1989-90, 91. Mem. Les Dames D'Escoffier (founding pres.), Women's Foodservice Network (pres.), Confrerie de la Chaine Des Rotisseurs (vice conselliere gastronomique), Am. Inst. Wine and Food (bd. dirs.). Home and Office: 1728 Wildberry Dr # D Glenview IL 60025-1748

SHERMAN, EUGENE JAY, marketing executive, retired economist; b. N.Y.C., Jan. 10, 1935; s. Samuel and Sarah (Lavinsky) S.; m. Mary Eileen Van, Apr. 22, 1966; 1 child, Rebecca. BA, CCNY, 1956; MBA, NYU, 1959, postgrad., 1959-63. Economist Fed. Res. Bank N.Y., 1959-62, Chase Manhattan Bank, N.Y.C., 1962-65; v.p. Bank of N.Y., N.Y.C., 1965-72; sr. v.p., exec. dir., dir. rsch. Merrill Lynch and Co., N.Y.C., 1972-78; v.p., chief economist, mgr.internat. investment Internat. Gold Corp., N.Y.C., 1980-86; sr. v.p., chief economist Fed. Home Loan Bank N.Y., 1986-93; sr. v.p., dir. rsch. M.A. Schapiro & Co., Inc., N.Y.C., 1993-96; gold cons., N.Y.C., 1986—. Author: Gold Investment: Theory and Application, 1986; contbr. articles to profl. jours. Mem. Money Marketeers (pres. 1971-72. honored fellow 1987), Downtown Economist Club (chmn. 1988-89), Forecasters (winner 1986, 95), Treasury Securities Luncheon (pres. 1995-96), Nat. Assn. Bus. Econs., N.Y. Assn. Bus. Econs. Avocations: mountaineering, performing arts. Home: 115 E 9th St New York NY 10003-5414

SHERMAN, GEORGE M., manufacturing company executive; b. N.Y.C., Aug. 6, 1941; s. Joseph B. and Fredericka (Hand) S.; m. Betsy Rae Bicknell, Nov. 26, 1966; children: Jonathan, David, Michael, Matthew. B.S., L.I. U., 1963; M.B.A., U. Louisville, 1971. Product gen. mgr. Gen. Electric Co., Bridgeport, Conn., 1966-79; pres. Weed Eater div. Emersen Electric Co., Houston, 1979-80; pres. Skil Corp. div. Emerson Electric Co., Chgo., 1980-82; group v.p. U.S. power tools group Black & Decker Corp., Balt., 1985, sr. v.p., pres. power tools group, from 1986, then exec. v.p., pres. power tools group, until 1990; now chief exec. officer Danaher Corp, Washington, D.C., 1990—; mem. adv. bd. Nat. Home Ctr. Show, Chgo., 1987; bd. dirs. D.I.Y. Research Inst., Lincolnshire, Ill., 1988. Bd. dirs. Ctr. Stage, Balt., 1988. Served with U.S. Army, 1964-66. Mem. Am. Mgmt. Assn. (mem. gen. mgmt. council 1988). Clubs: Center (Balt.); Hillendale Country (Phoenix, Md.). Avocations: flying, skiing, scuba diving, racquetball, golf. Office: Danaher Corporation 1250 24th St NW Ste 800 Washington DC 20037-1124*

SHERMAN, GORDON RAE, computer science educator; b. Menomenee, Mich., Feb. 24, 1928; s. Gordon E. and Myrtle H. (Evenson) S.; m. Lois E. Miller, July 3, 1951; children—Karen Rae, Gordon Thorstein. B.S., Iowa State U., 1953; M.S., Stanford U., 1954; Ph.D., Purdue U., 1960. Instr. math. and research assoc. Statis and Computational Lab., Purdue U., Lafayette, Ind., 1956-60; dir. Computing Ctr., U. Tenn., Knoxville, 1960—, prof. computer sci., 1960—, prof. emeritus; program dir. techniques and systems Office of Computing Activities, NSF, 1971-72; chmn. membership com. EDUCOM Council, 1983-85. Served with USAF, 1946-49, 50-51. Recipient Chancellor's citation U. Tenn., 1983; NSF grantee, 1974. Fellow Brit. Computer Soc.; mem. Am. Statis. Assn., Assn. for Computing Machinery, Dta Processing Mgmt. Assn. (internat. computer sci. Man of Yr. award S.E. Region VIII, 1973; Profl. of Yr. Region VIII 1979), Ops. Research Soc. Am., Soc. for Indsl. and Applied Math., Sigma Xi, Phi Kappa Phi. Republican. Lutheran. Contbr. articles on computer sci. to profl. jours. Home: 301 Cheshire Dr Apt 105 Knoxville TN 37919-5849 Office: U Tenn 209 Stokely Mgmt Ctr Knoxville TN 37996

SHERMAN, IRWIN WILLIAM, biological sciences educator, university official; b. N.Y.C., Feb. 12, 1933; s. Morris and Anna (Ezaak) S.; m. Vilia Gay Turner, Aug. 25, 1966; children: Jonathan Turner, Alexa Joy. BS, CCNY, 1954; MS, Northwestern U., 1959, PhD, 1960. Asst. prof. U. Calif., Riverside, 1962-67, assoc. prof., 1967-70, prof. biology, 1970—, chmn. biology dept., 1974-79, dean Coll. Natural and Agrl. Scis., dir. agrl. expt. sta., 1981-88, exec. vice chancellor, 1993-94; instr. marine biol. lab., Woods Hole, Mass., 1963-68; mem. study sect. tropical medicine NIH, 1970-73; cons. Agy. Internat. Devel., 1978—; mem. ad hoc study group U.S. Army, 1975-78. Author: (book) The Invertebrates: Function and Form, 1976, Biology: A Human Approach, 1989. Mem. steering com. World Health Orgn., 1978-87. Served with U.S. Army, 1954-56. USPHS fellow Rockefeller Inst., 1960-62, Guggenheim fellow, 1967, NIH/Nat. Inst. Med. Rsch. fellow 1973-74, Walter and Eliza Hall Inst. for Med. Rsch. fellow, 1986; Wellcome Trust lectr. Brit. Soc. Parasitology, 1987, Scripps Rsch. Inst. fellow 1991. Mem. AAAS, Am. Soc. Tropical Medicine and Hygiene, Soc. Protozoology, Soc. Parasitology, Sigma Xi. Democrat. Jewish. Avocations: painting, reading. Office: Univ of Calif-Riverside Dept Biology Riverside CA 92521

SHERMAN, JEFFREY ALAN, dentist; b. Bklyn., June 16, 1947; s. Joseph G. and Gertrude P. S.; m. Roslyn B. Tillis, Aug. 15, 1970; children: Jodi Heather, Brett Andrew. BA, Adelphi U., 1969; DDS, Howard U., 1973. Diplomate Am. Bd. Oral Electrosurgery. Resident in gen. dentistry Del. State Hosp., 1974; pvt. practice, Oakdale, N.Y., 1975—; mem. faculty Albert Einstein Coll. Medicine; vis. lectr. Tufts U.; dir. Greater L.I. Dental Meeting, 1990—. Author: Oral Electrosurgery: An Illustrated Clinical Guide, 1992; contbr. to profl. publs. Fellow Internat. Coll. Dentists; mem. ADA (lectr. ann. meetings 1978—), Suffolk County Dental Soc. (bd. dels. 1989—, dental lab and trades com. 1989—, edn. com. 1989-91, photographer dental meeting 1990—), Acad. Gen. Dentistry (membership com. 1992—, area v.p. 1991-92), Am. Acad. Dental Electrosurgery (co-editor, pres. 1987), N.Y. State Acad. Gen. Dentistry (pub. info. officer 1992). Office: 1237 Montauk Hwy Oakdale NY 11769-1434

SHERMAN, JEFFREY BARRY, retail executive; b. Passaic, N.J., June 25, 1948; s. Maxwell and Elinor (Richman) S.; m. Karin Lynn Swann, May 1, 1971; children—Erik, Brett, Peter, Kristin. B.S. in Econs., CCNY, 1971; M.B.A., NYU, 1975. With Bloomingdale's, N.Y.C., 1971—; v.p. merchandising Bloomingdale's, 1982-83, sr. v.p., 1983-85, exec. v.p., 1985—, now pres. Avocations: skiing; sailing. Office: Bloomingdale's 59th St & Lexington New York NY 10022*

SHERMAN, JOHN CLINTON, geography educator; b. Toronto, Ont., Can., May 3, 1916; s. Harold C. and Grace (Ubbes) S.; m. Helen Jean Loyd, Mar. 15, 1941; children: Constance Sherman Newell, John Harold (dec.), Mary Helen (Mrs. Stephen Wood), Barbara Lillian (Mrs. David Graves). B.A., U. Mich., 1937; M.A., Clark U., 1942; Ph.D., U. Wash., 1947. Mem faculty U. Wash., Seattle, 1942—; prof. geography U. Wash., 1963-86, prof. emeritus, 1986—, chmn. dept., 1963-73; Mem. sub-com. on geography adv. to U.S. Geol. Survey space programs for earth observation Nat. Acad. Sci.-NRC, 1965—. Author: Atlas of a Single ERTS Image, 1975, (with others) Atlas of Marine Use for the North Pacific; Adv. co-editor: (with others) Oxford Regional Economic Atlas of U.S. and Can, 1967; visual and tactile map of met. Washington, tactile atlas of The Mall, Washington. Mem. Wash. State Bd. on Geog. Names. Mem. Assn. Am. Geographers, Assn. Pacific Coast Geographers, Internat. Cartographic Assn. (mem. U.S. com.). Research and publs. on maps for the blind, maps and graphics for partially seeing children. Home: 7424 55th Ave NE Seattle WA 98115-6220

SHERMAN, JOHN FOORD, biomedical consultant; b. Oneonta, N.Y., Sept. 4, 1919; s. Henry C. and Ruth (Foord) S.; m. Betsy Deane Murray, Feb. 8, 1944; children: Betsy Deane, Mary Ann. B.S., Albany Coll. Pharmacy of Union U., 1949, D.Sc., 1970; Ph.D., Yale U., 1953. With NIH, 1953-74; assoc. dir. extramural programs Nat. Inst. Neurol. Diseases and Blindness, 1961-62, Nat. Inst. Arthritis and Metabolic Disease, 1962-63; assoc. dir. for extramural programs Office Dir. NIH, 1964-68, dep. dir., 1968-74; v.p. Assn. Am. Med. Colls., Washington, 1974-91, exec. v.p., 1987-91, spl. cons., 1991-94; mem. bd. advisors Am. Bd. Internal Medicine, 1991—; sr. advisor Rsch!Am., 1994—. Asst. surgeon gen. USPHS, 1964-68; spl. rsch. chemotherapy and neuropharmacology; mem. panel on data and studies NRC, 1976-87; mem. biomed. libr. rev. com. NIH; bd. dirs. Spinal Cord Injury Edn. and Tng. Found., 1986-92, Musculoskeletal Transplant Found., 1987—. With U.S. Army, 1941-46. Decorated Bronze Star; recipient Meritorious Svc. award USPHS, 1965, Disting. Svc. award HEW, 1971, Sec.'s Spl. Citation award, 1973, award Nat. Civil Svc. League, 1973, Disting. Alumnus award Union U.-Pharmacy Coll. Coun., 1974, Lifetime Achievement award Nat. Assn. for Biomed. Rsch., 1990. Fellow AAAS; mem. Inst. Medicine NAS, Cosmos Club, Sigma Xi. Congregationalist.

SHERMAN, JONATHAN HENRY, lawyer; b. Washington, Jan. 4, 1963; s. Gerald Howard and Lola (Kay) S. BA in History magna cum laude, U. Rochester, 1984; MA in History, Yale U., 1989; JD, Stanford U., 1991. Bar: N.Y. 1992, U.S. Dist. Ct. (so. dist.) N.Y. 1992, U.S. Supreme Ct. 1995, U.S. Dist. Ct. (ea. dist.) N.Y. 1996, U.S. Ct. Appeals (11th cir.) 1996. Assoc. Cahill Gordon & Reindel, N.Y.C., 1991—; lectr. Stanford U., Palo Alto, Calif., 1991, Yale Coll., New Haven, 1993. Sponsor, mentor Student-Sponsor Partnership, N.Y.C., 1992—; contbr. The Cornerstone Sch., Jersey City, 1994. Mem. ABA, N.Y. State Bar Assn., Phi Beta Kappa. Democrat. Jewish. Avocations: writing, reading, cycling. Home: 600 W End Ave Apt 12E New York NY 10024-1645 Office: Cahill Gordon & Reindel 80 Pine St New York NY 10005-1702

SHERMAN, JOSEPH HOWARD, clergyman; b. Marion, S.C., June 14, 1923; s. Samuel and Alma (Cannon) S.; m. Daisy Lee Littles; children: Joseph Howard Jr., Beatrice Sherman Boone. D.D. (hon.), Trinity Hall Coll.; LL.D. (hon.), New Haven Theol. Appointed Jurisdictional Bishop of N.C., 2d Jurisdiction, 1963. Founder, pastor Pentecostal Temple Ch. of God in Christ, Charlotte, N.C.; pres. N.C. Youth Dept.; dist. supt. N.C. Jurisdiction, Wadesboro; chmn. Council of Bishops, Memphis, 1976—; pres. C. H. Mason System of Bible Colls., Charlotte, N.C., 1975; mem. Nat. Hymnal Com. Author: (book) Weapons of the Righteous; (phamplet) Witchcraft, The Work of the Devil; (album) Peace That Only Christ Can Give; editor The Mighty Voice That Crieth mag. pres., founder J. Howard Sherman Scholarship Fund, Charlotte, 1974—; bd. dirs. C. H. Mason Scholarship Found., Memphis, Saints Ctr.; mem. NAACP, Charlotte, Hiring of the Handicapped, Charlotte, 1984, Ch. of God in Christ Hosp. Fund; mem. grievance com. Housing Authority, Charlotte, 1983, 84; mem. steering com. Democratic Governorship, N.C., 1984. Named Knight of Queen City, Charlotte, 1976, hon. citizen City of Balt., 1981, hon. atty. gen. N.C., 1983; J.H. Sherman Day named in his honor, Charlotte, 1980-84. Mem. Ministerial Alliance (exec. Charlotte chpt. 1983—).

SHERMAN, JOSEPH OWEN, pediatric surgeon; b. Chgo., Aug. 15, 1936; s. Joseph Owen and Mary Elizabeth (Kelly) S.; m. June Marie Martin, Mar. 16, 1963; children: Brian William, Lee Ann. Student, U. Ill., 1955-58; BS, Northwestern U., 1959, MD, 1962. Diplomate Am. Bd. Surgery, Am. Bd. Pediatric Surgery; lic. physician, Ill. Rotating intern Passavant Meml. Hosp., Chgo., 1963-64; resident in gen. surgery VA Rsch. Hosp., Chgo., 1964-65, 67-68; Am. Cancer Soc. clin. fellow Northwestern U. Med. Sch., Chgo., 1965-66; resident in pediatric surgery Children's Meml. Hosp., Chgo., 1966, 68-69; resident in thoracic surgery Mcpl. Tb San., Chgo., 1967; from instr. to assoc. prof. surgery Northwestern U. Med. Sch., 1967-86, prof. clin. surgery, 1986—; emeritus staff dept. surgery Children's Meml. Hosp., 1995—, Evanston (Ill.) Hosp., 1995—. Contbr. articles to profl. jours. Served with Ill. Army N.G., 1953-69, Ill. Air N.G., 1966-67. Fellow ACS, Inst. Medicine Chgo.; mem. AMA, Am. Pediat. Surg. Assn., Assn. for Acad. Surgery, Chgo. Med. Soc., Chgo. Surg. Soc., Ill. Pediat. Surg. Assn., Ill. State Med. Soc. Avocations: photography, computer programing, indoor and outdoor gardening.

SHERMAN, JUDITH DOROTHY, producer, recording company owner, recording engineer; b. Cleve., Nov. 12, 1942; d. William Paul and Laverne (Spoerke) Luekens; m. Kenneth Sherman, Aug. 1, 1964 (div. Aug. 1972); m. Max Wilcox, Jan. 1, 1981 (div. Jan. 1988); m. Curtis Macomber, Apr. 29, 1988. BA, Valparaiso U., 1964; MFA, SUNY-Buffalo, 1971. Rec. engr. Edward at the Moog, N.Y.C., 1971-72; producer-music dir. WBAI-FM, N.Y.C., 1972-76; owner-producer Judith Sherman Prodns., N.Y.C., 1976—; rec. engr. Marlboro (Vt.) Music Festival, 1976-94; adminstrv. dir. La Musica di Asolo, Sarasota, Fla., 1986-88; vocalist Steve Reich and Musicians, 1971-72. Recipient Corp. Pub. Broadcasting award, 1976, two Grammy award nominations, 1991, Grammy award, Classical Prodr. of Yr., 1993, Grammy award nominations, 1994. Mem. NAFE, Chamber Music Am., NARAS. Democrat. Home and Office: 645 W 239th St Apt 6F and 2A Bronx NY 10463-1277

SHERMAN, JUDITH ZEHMAN, child advocate; b. Cleve., Sept. 9, 1931; d. Sidney and Irene (Ratner) Zehman; m. Harlan Edwin Sherman, Aug. 31, 1952; children: Charles Evan, Charna Eve, Scott Allen. BA in Econs., Case Western Res. U., 1953, MS in Edn., 1968. Spl. edn. tchr. Beachwood (Ohio) Bd. Edn., 1967-68; founder, dir. Suburban East Sch. for the Retarded, Cleve., 1969-75; planning assoc. Fedn. of Cmty. Planning, Cleve., 1977-84. Commr. Ohio Commn. for Children, Columbus, 1978-81; chmn. Ohio White House Conf. on Children, Columbus, 1980-81; bd. dirs. Cuyahoga County Bd. of Mental Retardation, Cleve., 1975-78; pres., founder Parent Vol. Assn.-Women's Aux., Cleve., 1970-73; mem. vis. com. Sch. Applied Social Scis., Case Western Res. U., Cleve., 1978-80; pres. Bellefaire/Jewish Children's Bur., Cleve., 1981-85; chmn. capital campaign, 1986-91; bd. dirs. Jewish Cmty. Fedn., 1980—, Fairmount Temple, v.p., 1978—. Mem. Child Welfare League of Am. (trustee 1986—, v.p. 1992—, Child Advocate of Yr. 1985).

Avocations: grandchildren, volunteering, art, travel. Home: 26720 Hendon Rd Beachwood OH 44122-2434

SHERMAN, JUDY, medical researcher; b. Darby, Pa., Apr. 7, 1942; d. Reynolds H. and Helen E. (Young) Wyatt; children from previous marriage: Alan, Pegi, Jason; m. Charles R. Sherman, Apr. 17, 1993. BSN, U. Tex., Houston, 1986, MS in Nursing, 1990. RN, Ga. Cardiology nurse specialist Cardiology Assn. Houston; network mgr. critical care Meml. City Med. Ctr., Houston; clin. instr. Sch. Nursing U. Tex. H.S.C., Houston; critical care clin. coord. Floyd Med. Ctr., Rome, Ga.; rsch. coord. Southeastern Cardiovascular Inst., Rome. Contbr. articles to profl. publs. Capt. U.S. Army, 1962-66. Mem. ANA, Ga. State Nurses Assn. (mem. pub. rels. com. 1990-92, mem. com. 1990-92, program rev. com. 1990-96, dist. bd. dirs. 1990-92), AACN (chpt. past pres., sec., treas., mem. and chair various coms., Nurse of Yr. Houston-Gulf Coast chpt. 1989). Home: 15 Rosalynn Dr SW Rome GA 30165-8589

SHERMAN, KENNETH, oceanographer; b. Boston, Oct. 6, 1932. BS, Suffolk U., 1954, DSc (hon.), 1979; MS, U. R.I., 1960; DSc, Morski Inst. Ryback, 1978. Instr. conservation edn. Mass. Audubon Soc., 1954-55; fishery aide U.S. Bur. Commn. Fisheries, Mass., 1955-56; fishery rsch. biologist zooplankton ecology U.S. Bur. Commn. Fisheries, Hawaii, 1960-63, Maine, 1963-71; tchr. high sch. Mass., 1959-60; coord. marine resources monitoring assessing and prediction program U.S. Dept. Commerce, NOAA, Nat. Marine Fisheries Svc., 1971-73; chief resource assessment divsn. U.S. Dept. Commerce, NOAA, Nat. Marine Fisheries Svc., Washington, 1973-75; lab. dir., chief marine ecosystems br. U.S. Dept. Commerce, NOAA, Nat. Marine Fisheries Svc., Narragansett, R.I., 1975—; mem. biol. oceanographic com. Internat. Coun. Exploration Sea, 1972-87; U.S. project officer Plankton Sorting Ctr., Szczecin, Poland, 1973—; adj. prof. grad. sch. oceanography U. R.I., 1980—. Co-editor: Variability & Management of Large Marine Ecosystems, 1986, Biomass Yields & Geography of Large Marine Ecosystems, 1989, Large Marine Ecosystems: Patterns, Processes & Yields, 1990, Food Chains Yields, Models, & Management of Large Marine Ecosystems, 1991, Large Marine Ecosystems, Stress, Mitigation and Sustainability, 1993. Recipient marine ecology award U. Szczecin, 1989, Silver medal U.S. Dept. Commerce, 1978, Bronze medal, 1995; decorated Order of Merit, Republic of Poland, 1993. Fellow AAAS; mem. Am. Soc. Limnology and Oceanography, Ecol. Soc. Am., Am. Soc. Zoology, Am. Soc. Ichthyology and Herpetology. Office: Nat Marine Fisheries Svc NE Fisheries Sci Ctr 28 Tarzwell Dr Narragansett RI 02882

SHERMAN, LOUIS ALLEN, biology educator; b. Chgo., Dec. 16, 1943; s. Stanley E. and Sarah R. Sherman; m. Debra Meddoff, June 15, 1969; children: Daniel, Jeff. BS in Physics, U. Chgo., 1965, PhD in Biophysics, 1970. Postdoctoral fellow Cornell U., Ithaca, N.Y., 1970-72; asst. prof. U. Mo., Columbia, 1972-78, assoc. prof., 1978-83, prof., 1983-88, dir. biol. scis., 1985-88; prof., head dept. biol. scis. Purdue U., West Lafayette, Ind., 1989—. Contbr. articles to profl. jours. NIH fellow, 1965-72; Fulbright Hayes scholar, The Netherlands, 1979-80; NSF travel grantee, Fed. Republic Germany, Japan; grantee NIH, USDA, Dept. Energy. Fellow AAAS, Am. Acad. Microbiology; mem. AAUP, Am. Soc. Microbiology, Am. Soc. Plant Physiology, Biophys. Soc., Plant Molecular Biology Soc. Office: Purdue U Dept Biol Scis Lilly Hall West Lafayette IN 47907

SHERMAN, MARTIN, entomologist; b. Newark, Nov. 21, 1920; s. Louis and Anna (Norkin) S.; m. Ruth Goldsmith, Sept. 25, 1943 (div. Nov. 1975); children: Laurel Deborah Sherman Englehart, Susan Leslie Sherman Kitakis. B.S., Rutgers U., 1941, M.S., 1943; Ph.D., Cornell U., 1948. Research fellow in entomology Rutgers U., 1941-43; research asst. Cornell U., 1945-48; entomologist Beech-Nut Packing Co., Rochester, N.Y., 1948-49; mem. faculty U. Hawaii, Honolulu, 1949—; prof. entomology U. Hawaii, 1958-86, prof. emeritus entomology, 1986—; Fulbright scholar U. Tokyo, 1956-57, Royal Vet. and Agrl. Coll. of Denmark, 1966; vis. prof. Rutgers U., 1973. Editorial bd.: Pacific Sci, 1962-66, Jour. Med. Entomology, 1968-72. Served to 1st lt. USAAF, 1943-45. Fellow Am. Inst. Chemists; mem. Entomol. Soc. Am. (gov. bd. 1974-77, pres. Pacific br. 1970), Am. Chem. Soc., Soc. Toxicology, Soc. Environ. Toxicology and Chemistry, Am. Registry Profl. Entomologists, Japanese Soc. Applied Entomology and Zoology, Hawaiian Entomology Soc. (pres. 1969-70), Internat. Soc. for Study Xenobiotics, Sigma Xi, Delta Phi Alpha, Phi Kappa Phi, Gamma Sigma Delta. Club: Torch. Address: 1121 Koloa St Honolulu HI 96816-5103

SHERMAN, MARY ANGUS, public library administrator; b. Lawton, Okla., Jan. 3, 1937; d. Donald Adelbert and Mabel (Felkner) Angus; m. Donald Neil Sherman, Feb. 8, 1958; children: Elizabeth Sherman Cunningham, Donald Neil II. BS in Home Econs., U. Okla., 1958, MLS, 1969. Br. head Pioneer Libr. System, Purcell, Okla., 1966-76; regional libr. Pioneer Libr. System, Norman, Okla., 1976-78, asst. dir., 1978-80, dir., 1987—. Named one of Distinguished Alumni Sch. Home Econs., U. Okla., 1980. Mem. ALA (councilor 1988-96, planning and budget assembly 1990-91, internat. rels. com. 1992-96), Pub. Libr. Assn. (divsn. of ALA, pres. pub. policy for pub. librs. sect. 1995-96), AAUW (pres. Okla. chpt. 1975-77, nat. bd. dirs. 1983-87, S.W. ctrl. region dir. 1983-85, v.p. nat. membership 1985-87, Woman of the Yr. Purcell chpt. 1982), Okla. Libr. Assn. (pres. 1982-83, interlibrary cooperation com. 1993-95, chair 1994-95, Disting. Svc. award 1986), Norman C. of C. (bd. dirs. 1988-96, pres. 1994-95), Rotary (program chair 1991-92, bd. dirs. 1993—, pres. 1995-96. Paul Harris fellow), Norman Assistance League Club (cmty. assoc.), Norman, Okla. Sister City Com. 1994—, Delta Gamma Mothers (pres. 1978-79), Kappa Alpha Theta (pres. Alpha Omicron House Corp. 1984-87, nat. dir. house corps. 1987-88), Beta Phi Mu, Phi Beta Kappa. Democrat. Methodist. Office: Pioneer Libr System 225 N Webster Ave Norman OK 73069-7133

SHERMAN, MONA DIANE, school system administrator; b. N.Y.C., Aug. 28, 1941; d. Hyman and Lillian (Baker) Ginsberg; m. Richard H. Sherman, May 9, 1964; children: Holly Baker, Andrew Hunter. BS, Hunter Coll., CUNY, 1962; MS, CUNY, 1965. Cert. elem. tchr., K-12 reading endorsement specialist, ESL tchr., elem. adminstrn. and supervision, instrnl. supervision, spl. edn. learning disabilities and neurologically impaired edn., Ind. Elem. tchr. N.Y.C. Pub. Schs., 1962-77; team leader Tchr. Corps Potsdam (N.Y.) State Coll., SUNY, 1977-79; dir. Tchr. Ctr., Sch. City of Hammond, Ind., 1979-87; lab. coord. PALS, Gary (Ind.) Sch. Corp., 1987-93, mentor, 1988—, facilitator of staff devel., 1993—; instr. Tex. Instrument Computer Co., Lubbock, 1983-84, Performance Learning Sys., Emerson, N.J., 1984—; cons. in classroom discipline and computer instrn. Gary Staff Devel. Ctr., 1987—; mentor Urban Tchr. Edn. program Ind. U. N.W., Gary, 1991—; chair sch. improvement team, tchr. of yr. com., 1993-94; mem., grantswriter Gary Tech. Com., Gary Distance Learning Com. Mem. Lake Area United Way Lit. Coalition NW Ind., 1990, Gary Reading Textbook Adoption Com.; sec. Martin Luther King Jr. Acad. PTSA, mem. sch. improvement team. Recipient Recognition NW Ind. Forum, 1988, Tchr. of Yr. award Merrillville (Ind.) Lions Club, 1988, Outstanding Tchr. of Yr. award Inland Ryerson, East Chicago, Ind., 1989. Mem. Ind. Reading Assn., Gary Reading Assn., Phi Delta Kappa, Delta Kappa Gamma. Avocations: theatre, crafts, tennis. Home: 1112 Fran Lin Pky Munster IN 46321-3607

SHERMAN, NORMAN MARK, advertising agency executive; b. N.Y.C., June 19, 1948; s. Sol and Rhoda (Kaplan) S.; m. Michelle Petnov, Jan. 8, 1978; 1 child, Michael Isaac. BA, U. Buffalo, 1970; MBA, Columbia U., 1972. Cert. tchr., N.Y. Product mgr. RCA Records, N.Y.C., 1972-73; dir. mktg. Shelter Records, N.Y.C., 1973-74; account exec. Rosenfeld Sirowitz & Lawson, N.Y.C., 1974-76; account exec. Benton & Bowles, N.Y.C., 1976-78, v.p. account supr., 1978-81, sr. v.p., mgmt. supr., 1981-84; exec. v.p., dir. account mgmt. Avrett, Free & Ginsberg, N.Y.C., 1984-85; sr. v.p., group account dir. D'Arcy, Masius, Benton & Bowles, 1985-93, mgn. dir., 1993—, also bd. dirs. Home: 330 W 72nd St New York NY 10023-2641 Office: D'Arcy Masius Benton & Bowles 1675 Broadway New York NY 10019-5820

SHERMAN, RANDOLPH S., lawyer; b. New Rochelle, N.Y., Nov. 19, 1944; s. Julius and Selma (Goldstein) S.; m. Joan E. Lauterbach, May 28, 1967; children: Elissa, Stephanie. BS in Indsl. Labor, Cornell U., 1966; JD, NYU, 1969. Bar: N.Y. 1970, U.S. Ct. Appeals (2d cir.) 1980, U.S. Ct. Appeals (3d cir.) 1983, U.S. Ct. Appeals (4th cir.) 1994, U.S. Ct. Appeals (8th cir.) 1986, U.S. Supreme Ct. 1984. Ptnr. Kaye Scholer, Fierman, Hays & Handler, N.Y.C., 1969—. Mem. ABA (antitrust sect., litigation sect.), U.S. Trademark Assn., N.Y.C. Bar Assn. Office: Kaye Scholer Fierman Hays & Handler LLP 425 Park Ave New York NY 10022-3598

SHERMAN, RICHARD ALLEN, lawyer; b. Atlanta, Mar. 16, 1946; s. Robert Hiram and Olivia Mae (Latham) S.; m. Mary Margaret Sawyer, June 23, 1973 (div. June 1994); children: Richard A. Jr., Jill Mary, James Warren; m. Catherine Agnes Oakley, May 4, 1996. BA, Tulane U., 1968, JD, 1972. Bar: Fla. 1974, La. 1973, U.S. Ct. Appeals (5th cir.) 1978, U.S. Ct. Appeals (11th cir.) 1981, U.S. Supreme Ct. 1981. Ptnr., head appellate divsn. Wicker, Smith, Blomqvist, Davant, Tutan, O'Hara, McCoy et al, Miami, 1973-83; pvt. practice Ft. Lauderdale, Fla., 1983—, practice limited to handling appeals in Fla. Active Rep. Nat. Com. Mem. ABA (vice-chmn. U.S. Ct. Appeals 5th cir. com. 1981), Fla. Bar Assn. (appellate rules com. 1979-81), Dade County Bar Assn. (chmn. appellate cts. com. 1982-83), Mensa, Pres. Club, Lauderdale Yacht Club, Upper Keys Sailing Club (bd. dirs.). Avocations: yacht racing, boating, scuba diving, travel, theatre. Office: 1777 S Andrews Ave Ste 302 Fort Lauderdale FL 33316-2517

SHERMAN, RICHARD BEATTY, history educator; b. Somerville, Mass., Nov. 16, 1929; s. James Beatty and Hilda Louise (Ford) S.; m. Hanni Fey, June 13, 1952; children: Linda Caroline, Alan Theodore. AB, Harvard U., 1951, PhD, 1959; MA, U. Pa., 1952. Instr. history Pa. State U., State College, 1957-60; asst. prof. Coll. of William and Mary, Williamsburg, Va., 1960-65, assoc. prof., 1965-70, prof. 1970-87, chancellor prof., 1987-92, Pullen prof., 1992-94, prof. emeritus, 1994—; Fulbright prof. Am. history U. Stockholm, 1966-67. Served with U.S. Army, 1952-54. Am. Philos. Soc. grantee, 1964, 66; faculty rsch. grantee, Coll. of William and Mary, 1962, 63, 65, 80, 87. Mem. AAUP, Phi Beta Kappa. Democrat. Author: The Negro and the City, 1970; The Republican Party and Black America, 1973, The Case of Odell Waller, 1992; co-author: The College of William and Mary: A History, 1993; contbr. articles to profl. jours. Home: 205 Matoaka Ct Williamsburg VA 23185-2810 Office: Coll William and Mary Dept History Williamsburg VA 23185

SHERMAN, RICHARD H., education educator; b. Yonkers, N.Y., Jan. 5, 1941; m. Mona D. Sherman, May 9, 1964; children: Holly Baker, Andrew Hunter. BA, Hunter Coll., 1962; MA, Iowa U., 1965; MS, Queens Coll., 1970; EdD, Yeshiva U., 1977. Cert. tchr., Ind., Ill., N.Y. Asst. prof. edn. SUNY, Potsdam; instr. Herbert H. Lehman Coll., CUNY; asst. prof. edn. Purdue U., Hammond, Ind.; assoc. dean Ind. Vocat. Tech. Coll., Gary; chmn., assoc. prof. Calumet Coll. St. Joseph, Whiting, Ind.; edn. dir. Mus. Broadcast Communications, Chgo.; dir. Zarem/Golde ORT TECH Inst., Chgo.; workshop leader; presenter and speaker in field; exec. dir. Allied Ednl. Svcs. Author, playwright, poet, critic. Bd. dirs. Jewish Fedn. N.W. Ind.; chmn. events "Walk for Israel", Lake Area United Way, v.p. mobilization and resources devel, needs and assessment priorities com., chmn. section campaign; active Lake County chpt. ARC, N.W. Ind. Film Commn. Recipient N.W. Ind. Forum Svc. Recognition award, Jewish Fedn. N.W. Ind. Young Leadership award, Harlem Arts Svc. award. Mem. Internat. Reading Assn., Am. Assn. Theatre Critics, Dramatists Guild, Ind. Reading Coun., Ind. Reading Profs. (treas.), Hammond Reading Coun. (pres.), Ind. State Coun., N.W. Ind. Arts Assn. (subcom.), Rotary Club, Sigma Tau Delta, Phi Delta Kappa.

SHERMAN, ROBERT B(ERNARD), composer, lyricist, screenwriter; b. N.Y.C., Dec. 19, 1925; s. Al and Rosa (Dancis) S.; student UCLA, 1943; BA, Bard Coll., 1949; MusD (hon.) Lincoln U., 1990; m. Joyce Ruth Sasner, Sept. 27, 1953; children: Laurie Shane, Jeffrey Craig, Andrea Tracy, Robert Jason. Popular songwriter, 1950-60, including Tall Paul, Pineapple Princess, You're Sixteen (Gold Record); songwriter Walt Disney Prodns., Beverly Hills, Calif., 1960-68, for 29 films including The Parent Trap, 1961, Summer Magic, 1963, Mary Poppins, 1964, That Darn Cat, 1965, Winnie The Pooh, 1965, Jungle Book, 1967, Bedknobs and Broomsticks, 1971; co-composer song It's A Small World, theme of Disneyland and Walt Disney World, Fla.; composer, lyricist United Artists, Beverly Hills, 1969—, songs for film Chitty, Chitty, Bang, Bang, 1969, Snoopy, Come Home!, 1972; song scores Charlotte's Web, 1972, Cabbage Patch Kids, 1974, Little Nemo, 1992, The Mighty Kong, 1996; composer for Walt Disney's Wonderful World of Color, TV, 1961—; co-producer NBC-TV spl. Goldilocks, 1970; v.p. Musi-Classics, Inc.; co-producer, composer, lyricist stage musical Victory Canteen, 1971; composer-lyricist Broadway show Over Here, 1975, Busker Alley, 1995; screenplay and song score Tom Sawyer, United Artists, 1972, Huckleberry Finn, 1974, The Slipper and the Rose, 1977, The Magic of Lassie, 1978. Served with inf. AUS, 1943-45; ETO. Decorated Purple Heart; recipient 2 Acad. awards best score for Mary Poppins, 1964, best song for Chim Chim Cheree, 1964; Grammy award, 1965; Christopher medal, 1965, 74; nine Acad. award nominations; Acad. award nomination for song score Bedknobs and Broomsticks, 1971, for best song The Age of Not Believing, 1971, others; 16 golden, 4 platinum and one diamond record album, 1965-83; first prize best composer song score Tom Sawyer, Moscow Film Festival, 1973, B.M.I. Pioneer award, 1977; Golden Cassette awards for Mary Poppins, Jungle Book, Bed Knobs and Broomsticks, 1983, Mouscar award Disney Studios, Disney Legend award, 1990, BMI Richard Kirk Achievment award, 1991. Mem. Acad. Motion Picture Arts and Scis. (exec. bd. music br. 12 yrs.), AFTRA, Nat. Acad. Rec. Arts and Scis., Composers and Lyricists Guild (exec. bd.), Dramatists Guild, Authors League. Office: 9030 Harratt St West Hollywood CA 90069-3858

SHERMAN, ROGER, economics educator; b. Jamestown, N.Y., Sept. 10, 1930; s. Claire Blanchard and Margaret Gertrude (Burke) S.; m. Charlotte Ann Murphy, Apr. 4, 1953 (div. Feb. 1995); children: Claire Randall, Thomas Allen. B.S. in Math., Grove City Coll., 1952; M.B.A. in Fin., Harvard U., 1959; M.S. in Econs., Carnegie-Mellon U., 1965, Ph.D., 1966. Mgr. mfg. control IBM Corp., N.Y.C., 1956-62; asst. prof., assoc. prof., prof. U. Va., Charlottesville, 1965-72, Brown Forman prof. econs., 1982—, chmn. dept. econs., 1982-90; vis. scholar Oxford U., 1987, Sydney U., 1988. Author: Oligopoly: An Empirical Approach, 1972, The Economics of Industry, 1974, Antitrust Policies and Issues, 1978, The Regulation of Monopoly, 1989; editor: Perspectives on Postal Service Issues, 1980; contbr. articles to profl. jours. Bd. dirs. McGuffey Art Ctr., Charlottesville, 1984-92. Lt. USNR, 1953-62. U. Bristol fellow, 1968-69; Fulbright lectr., Madrid, 1972; Sci. Ctr. Berlinfellow, 1975, 79, 80; Rockefeller Found. Vis. scholar, 1985. Mem. Am. Econ. Assn., Royal Econ. Soc., Econometric Soc. Home: 500 Court Sq Apt 807 Charlottesville VA 22902-5147 Office: U Va Rouss Hall Charlottesville VA 22903-3288

SHERMAN, ROGER TALBOT, surgeon, educator; b. Chgo., Sept. 30, 1923; s. Joseph Bright and Alice Elizabeth (Baur) S.; m. Ruth Kathryn Thieman, Aug. 23, 1952; children: Nann, Alice, Nina, John, Julie. A.B., Kenyon Coll., 1946; M.D., U. Cin., 1948. Diplomate Am. Bd. Surgery (mem.). Intern, fellow in pathology St. Luke's Hosp., Chgo., 1948-50; resident in surgery Cin. Gen. Hosp., 1950-56; chief dept. exptl. surgery Walter Reed Army Med. Center, 1956-59; asst. prof. to prof. surgery U. Tenn., Memphis, 1959-72; prof., chmn. dept. surgery U. South Fla., Tampa, 1972-82; prof. surgery Emory U. Sch. Medicine, Atlanta, 1983-93; chief surgery Grady Meml. Hosp., Atlanta, 1983-92; Whitaker prof. surgery Emory U. Sch. Medicine, Atlanta, 1993—; dir. surg. edn. Piedmont Hosp., Atlanta, 1993—; cons. Walter Reed Army Med. Center. Mem. editorial bd. Am. Surgeon, 1970-91, Jour. Trauma, 1970-93; contbr. articles to profl. jours., chpts. to books. Served to maj. M.C. AUS, 1956-59. Recipient Golden Apple Tchr. of the Yr. award, 1972, Williams Disting. Teaching award Emory U., 1984, Curtis P. Artz award, 1988. Fellow ACS (gov.); mem. Am. Assn. Surgery of Trauma (pres. 1979), Am. Surg. Assn., So. Surg. Assn., Southeastern Surg. Congress (pres. 1985), Internat. Surg. Soc., Soc. Surgery of Alimentary Tract, Am. Burn Assn., Shock Soc., Am. Trauma Soc., Sigma Xi, Psi Upsilon, Alpha Omega Alpha. Home: 1170 Woods Cir NE Atlanta GA 30324-2736 Office: Piedmont Hospital Department of Surgery 1984 Peachtree Rd NW Atlanta GA 30309-1231 *Surgery. The opening, exploration and repair of the living human body is an awesome responsibility afforded to only a few. To be privileged to be counted among those is a high honor, surpassed only by being trusted to teach others this demanding, and marvelous craft.*

SHERMAN, RON, photographer; b. Cleve., May 10, 1942; s. Hyman B. and Sheryl D. Sherman; m. Myra LeBell, Aug. 16, 1969; children: Scott Neal, Jonathan Harris, Hannah Beth. BFA in illustrative photography, Rochester Inst. Tech., 1964; MA in photographic commn., Syracuse U., 1971. Staff photographer Gannett Newspapers (Democrat, Chronicle and Times Union), Rochester, N.Y., 1961-64, U. Fla., Gainesville, 1964-66; photo-officer, military intelligence unit U.S. Army-Signal Corps, Vietnam, 1967-68; staff photographer Milw. Journal, Wis., 1969; photographer Syracuse U., Syracuse, N.Y., 1969-71; prin. Ron Sherman Photographer, Atlanta, 1971—, Computer Aided Photography, Inc., Atlanta, 1991—; adv. comml. photography Gwinett Tech. Inst., Lawrenceville, Ga., 1983—; cons. ABC TV, Alcoa, AT&T, CBS Sports, The Coca-Cola Co., Eastman Kodak, Ford Motor Co., IBM, TRW, Atlanta Com. for the Olympic Games, Bell-South, Southern Bell, Atlanta Gas Light Co., Nat. Hockey League, Sonat, Gen. Mills, Ga. Power, Southern Co., Phoenix Comms. Photographer; pub. in Life, Time, Newsweek, Inside Sports, Bus. Week, Forbes, Reader's Digest, Ford Times, America Illustrated, Med. World News, N.Y. Times, U. S. News and World Report, Venture; pub. works in Atlanta calendar, 1994, 95, 96, 97; Atlanta photos used to illustrate Peter Max's Super Bowl XXVIII poster; (hard cover books) Greater North Fulton and Atlanta, A Vision for the New Millenium. 1st Lt. U.S. Army 1968-69, Vietnam. Mem. Nat. Press Photographers Assn., Am. Soc. Media Photographers (pres. Atlanta chpt. 1980-81). Avocations: gardening, reading, classical and jazz music. Office: PO Box 28656 Atlanta GA 30358-0656

SHERMAN, RUTH TENZER, artist, fixtures company executive; b. Chgo., Sept. 11, 1920; d. Philip and Jennie (Greitzer) Tenzer; m. Samuel Sherman, May 18, 1946 (dec. Nov. 1974); children: Patricia (dec.), Randy Mitchell. Art student, Pratt Inst., 1938-42, Art Students League, N.Y.C., 1942-45; studies with Raphael Soyer, N.Y.C., 1943, studies with Harold Baumbach, 1947-49; studies with Ruth Connery, Mamaroneck, N.Y., 1955; studies with Rudolph Baranik, White Plains, N.Y., 1961-63, studies with George Koras, 1966. Cert. artist Dept. Cultural Affairs. Pres. Pioneer Fixture Corp., Paterson, N.J., 1975-86. Exhbns. include Mamaroneck Artists Guild, 1963, Jr. League Artists of North Westchester, 1964, Westchester C.C., Valhalla, N.Y., 1964, The New Rochelle (N.Y.) Art Assn., 1964, Silvermine Guild Artists, New Canaan, Conn., 1964-88, Westchester Art Soc., White Plains, 1964-72, Hudson River Mus., Yonkers, N.Y., 1965, First Westchester Nat. Bank, New Rochelle, 1967, Conn. Acad. Fine Arts, Hartford, 1967, Stern Bros., N.Y.C., 1967, Nat. Jewish Hosp. Denver, Woodmere, N.Y., 1968, Quaker Ridge Sch., Scarsdale, N.Y., 1970, Gallery Shop, Westport, Conn., 1978, Mari Gallery, Woodstock, N.Y., 1978, The Village Gallery, Ardsley, N.Y., 1979, Todd Gallery, Kiamesha Lake, N.Y., 1980, Norwalk Mchts. Bank, New Canaan, 1980, Mchts. Bank, Norwalk, 1980, Emery Air Freight Hdqrs., Conn., 1981, Mari Hube Gallery, N.Y., 1990, Helio Gallery, N.Y.C., 1991, Maska Gallery, Seattle, 1991, Rockefeller Town House, N.Y.C., 1992, Denise Bibro Fine Art Gallery, Shoho, N.Y., 1993, Museè D'Art Moderne, Tonniens, France, 1993, Salon du Vieux Colombier, Paris, 1993, Md. Fedn. Art, Cardinal Gallery Md. Hall, Annapolis, 1993, Mus. Modern Art, Coral Gables, Fla., 1994, Wirtz Gallery, South Miami, Fla., 1994, U.S. Dept. State-Art in Embassies, 1995. Recipient Merit award Westchester Art Soc., 1964, Cert. of Honor Museè d'Art Moderne, 1994, Disting. Visitor award Mayor of Miami, 1994, U.S. Dept. of State, Art in Embassies Program, 1995. Avocations: golf, opera, classical and contemporary music, travel. Home: 58 Village Dr Stroudsburg PA 18360-1566

SHERMAN, SIGNE LIDFELDT, portfolio manager, former research chemist; b. Rochester, N.Y., Nov. 11, 1913; d. Carl Leonard Broström and Herta Elvira Maria (Thern) Lidfeldt; m. Joseph V. Sherman, Nov. 18, 1944 (dec. Oct. 1984). BA, U. Rochester, 1935, MS, 1937. Chief chemist Lab. Indsl. Medicine and Toxicology Eastman Kodak Co., Rochester, 1937-43; chief rsch. chemist Chesebrough-Pond's Inc., Clinton, Conn., 1943-44; ptnr. Joseph V. Sherman Cons., N.Y.C., 1944-84; portfolio strategist Sherman Holdings, Troy, Mont., 1984—. Author: The New Fibers, 1946. Fellow Am. Inst. Chemists; mem. AAAS, AAUW (life), Am. Chem. Soc., Am. Econ. Assn., Am. Assn. Ind. Investors (life), Fedn. Am. Scientists (life), Union Concerned Scientists (life), Western Econ. Assn. Internat., Earthquake Engrng. Rsch. Inst., Nat. Ctr. for Earthquake Engrng. Rsch., N.Y. Acad. Scis. (life), Internat. Platform Assn., Cabinet View Country Club. Office: Sherman Holdings Angel Island 648 Halo Dr Troy MT 59935-9415

SHERMAN, STUART, physician; b. New York, N.Y., Feb. 21, 1955; s. Sol and Rhoda (Kaplan) S.; m. Leslie Jane Derus, Oct. 5, 1991; children: Matthew, Benjamin. BA, SUNY, Binghampton, 1977; MD, Washington U., St. Louis, 1982. Diplomate Am. Bd. Internal Medicine. Resident in internal medicine U. Pitts., 1982-85, rsch. fellow, 1985-86; gastroenterology fellow Sch. of Medicine UCLA, 1986-89; therapeutic endoscopy fellow Sch. Medicine Ind. U., 1989-90; asst. prof. medicine and pancreaticobiliary endoscopy UCLA, 1990-92; assoc. prof. medicine Ind. U., 1992—; cons. Bard Interventional Products Adv. Panel, Tewksbury, Mass., 1994—. Contbr. articles to profl. jours. Recipient Glaxo Award for excellence in gastroenterology Midwest Am. Fedn. Clin. Rsch., 1993, Young Scholars Rsch. award World Congress of Gastroenterology, L.A., 1994. Mem. ACP, Am. Coll. Gastroenterology, Am. Soc. for Gastrointestinal Endoscopy, Am. Gastroent. Assn. Avocations: traveling, skiing, tennis, golf. Office: Ind U Med Ctr 550 N Univ Blvd Ste 2300 Indianapolis IN 46202-5000

SHERMAN, WENDY RUTH, federal agency administrator; b. Balt., June 7, 1949; m. Bruce Edward Stokes; 1 child, Sarah Renee. BA, Boston U., 1971; MSW, U. Md., 1976. Former chief of staff Senator Barbara Mikulski; spl. sec. for children and youth State of Md., 1987, dir. Office Child Welfare; dir. Washington ops. Dukakis for Pres., 1987-88; dir. Campaign '88 Dem. Nat. Com., Washington, 1988; polit. and pub. policy cons. Ctr. Nat. Policy Foreman and Heidepriem, Washington, 1988-91; ptnr. Doak, Shrum, Harris, Sherman, Washington, 1991-93; asst. sec. state legis. affairs Dept. State, Washington, 1993—; now pres., ceo Fannie Mae Found. Office: Fannie Mae Foundation 4000 Wisconsin Ave Washington DC 20016*

SHERMAN, WILLIAM COURTNEY, foreign service officer; b. Edmonton, Ky., Sept. 27, 1923; s. George Frederick and Katherine Courtney (Kinnaird) S.; m. Mary Jane Hazelip, Apr. 28, 1945; children—Katherine Courtney, John Justin, Roger Woodson. AB, U. Louisville, 1946; student, U. Colo., 1945, Okla. A&M Coll., 1945-46, Nat. War Coll., 1967-68. With Mil. Govt., in Korea, 1946-48; ECA mission to Korea, 1948-50; joined Fgn. Service, Dept. State, 1951; vice consul Yokohama, Japan, 1952-54; 3d sec. embassy Tokyo, Japan, 1954-56; assigned State Dept., 1956-60; 1st sec. embassy Rome, Italy, 1960-65; spl. asst. to dep. under sec. state for adminstrn., 1966-67; consul gen. Kobe-Osaka, Japan, 1968-70; counselor for polit. affairs Am. embassy, Tokyo, 1970-73; minister-counselor, dep. chief mission Am. embassy, 1977-81; dir. for Japanese affairs State Dept., Washington, 1973-77; dep. U.S. rep. (with rank of amb.) UN Security Coun., 1981-84; dep. asst. sec. state for East Asian and Pacific Affairs, 1984-86; diplomat in residence Sch. Advanced Internat. Studies, Johns Hopkins U., 1986-94, sr. advisor Reischaver Ctr., 1994—. Served to lt. (j.g.) USNR, 1943-46, 50-51. Mem. Omicron Delta Kappa. Home and Office: 1702 Beaver Cir Reston VA 22090-4407

SHERMAN, WILLIAM DELANO, lawyer; b. White Plains, N.Y., Nov. 11, 1942; s. Edgar Jay S.; children from previous marriage: Jennifer W., Andrea B.; m. Vickie R. McGraw, July 31, 1982; children: Peter M., Sarah D. BA, Princeton U., 1964; MBA, JD, U. Calif., Berkeley, 1972. Bar: Calif., U.S. Dist. Ct., U.S. Ct. Appeals. Teaching, research asst. various orgns., 1961-72; assoc. Pillsbury, Madison & Sutro, San Francisco, 1972-79, ptnr., 1979-87; ptnr. Morrison & Foerster, San Francisco, 1987—; lectr. grad. sch. bus. U. Calif., Berkeley, 1976—; judge pro tem Mcpl. Ct., San Francisco, 1978-87; panelist, moderator various profl. orgns. Bd. dirs. Youth for Svc., 1975-76; bd. dirs. Town Sch. for Boys, pres. alumni assn., trustee, 1976-77; bd. dirs. Head-Royce Sch., Oakland, Calif., 1977-86, chmn., 1985-86, treas., 1979-82, chmn. devel. com. 1978-79, chmn. fin. com.; mem. alumni coun. Phillips Acad., Andover, Mass., 1984-87. Mem. ABA (fed. regulation of securities com., 1981—, state regulation securities com., 1981-85, banking and bus. law sect., charter mem. fed. securities law com. young lawyers div. 1977-80), Calif. Bar Assn. (corps. com. bus. law sect. 1986—), San Francisco Bar Assn. (bd. dirs. 1977-78, chmn. corps. com. Barristers club 1974-76, sec. bd. dirs. 1977-78). Episcopalian. Office: Morrison & Foerster 755 Page Mill Rd Palo Alto CA 94304-1018

SHERMAN, ZACHARY, civil and aerospace engineer, consultant; b. N.Y.C., Oct. 26, 1922; s. Harry and Minnie (Schulsinger) S.; m. Bertha

Leikin, Mar. 23, 1947; children: Gene Victor, Carol Beth. BCE, CCNY, 1943; MCE, Polytech. U. N.Y., Bklyn., 1953, PhD in Civil Engring. & Mechanics, 1969; MME, Stevens Inst. Tech., 1968. Registered profl. engr., N.Y., N.J. Stress analyst Gen. Dynamics, San Diego, 1943-45; sr. stress analyst Republic Aviation, Farmingdale, N.Y., 1945-47, 59-62; prof. civil engring. U. Miss., Oxford, 1954-59; lectr. civil engring. Stevens Inst. Tech., Hoboken, N.J., 1962-67, CUNY, 1967-69; assoc. prof. aerospace engring. Pa. State U., State College, 1969-73; prin. Dr. Zachary Sherman Cons. Engrs., Long Beach, N.Y., 1973—; aerospace engr. FAA, N.Y.C., 1980-86; designated engr. rep., FAA. Contbr. articles to profl. jours. NSF grantee, 1972. Fellow ASCE; mem. AIAA (v.p. Western Conn. chpt. 1977-78), N.Y. Acad. Scis., Sigma Xi. Achievements include development of beam/beam-column deck suspension bridge, prestressed aircraft wing. Home and Office: 25 Neptune Blvd Apt 7H Long Beach NY 11561-4657

SHERNOFF, ELISE RUBIN, special education educator; b. Savannah, Ga., Aug. 16, 1951; d. Irving and Madeline (Sadler) Rubin; m. Victor Harvey Shernoff, June 4, 1972; children: Jason Noah, Heather Toby. BA in History, Armstrong State Coll., 1973, MEd in Spl. Edn., 1977. Cert. spl. edn. tchr., Ga. Tchr. Myers Mid. Sch., Savannah, 1973, Bartlett Mid. Sch., Savannah, 1973-74, Jenkins High Sch., Savannah, 1976-81, Beach High Sch., Savannah, 1986—; bd. dirs. Rambam Day Sch., Savannah; presenter CEC conf., Denver, 1994, Indpls., 1995, NEA so. regional conf., Biloxi, Miss., 1995. Mem. Coun. for Exceptional Children, Jewish Edn. Alliance (bd. dirs. 1992—), Agudath Achim Synagogue-Sisterhood (life), Hadassah (life), B'nai B'rith Women. Democrat. Jewish. Avocations: cooking, baking, fitness walking.

SHERR, LYNN BETH, TV news correspondent; b. Phila., Mar. 4, 1942; d. Louis and Shirley (Rosenfeld) S.; m. Lawrence B. Hilford, Jan. 11, 1980. B.A., Wellesley Coll., 1963. Writer, editor Conde Nast Publications, N.Y.C., 1963-65; writer, reporter AP, N.Y.C., 1965-72; corre. Sta. WCBS-TV News, N.Y.C., 1972-74; anchor, corre. Pub. Broadcasting System, N.Y.C., 1975-77; nat. corre. ABC News, N.Y.C., 1977—. Co-author: (with Jurate Kazickas) The Liberated Woman's Appointment Calendar, 1971-82, The American Woman's Gazetteer, 1976, Susan B. Anthony Slept Here, 1994; author: Failure is Impossible: Susan B. Anthony in Her Own Words, 1995. Recipient Ohio State award Ohio State U., 1976; recipient spl. commendation Am. Women in Radio & TV, 1979, Emmy for Post Election Spl., 1980, Peabody, 1994; numerous others. Office: 20/20 147 Columbus Ave New York NY 10023-5900

SHERRATT, GERALD ROBERT, academic administrator; b. Los Angeles, Nov. 6, 1931; s. Lowell Heyborne and Elva Genevieve (Lamb) S. B.S. in Edn., Utah State U., 1953, M.S. in Edn. Adminstrn., 1954; Ph.D. in Adminstrn. Higher Edn., Mich. State U., 1975. Staff assoc. U. Utah, Salt Lake City, 1961-62; dir. high sch. relations Utah State U., Logan, 1962-64, asst. to pres., 1964-77, v.p. for univ. relations, 1977-81; pres. So. Utah U., Cedar City, 1982—; dir. Honeyville Grain Inc., Utah; mem. council pres. Utah System Higher Edn., 1982—; chmn. bd. Utah Summer Games, Cedar City, 1984—; chmn. pres.'s council Rocky Mountain Athletic Conf., Denver, 1984-85. Author hist. pageant: The West: America's Odyssey, 1973 (George Washington Honor medal 1973). Chmn. Festival of Am. West, Logan, Utah, 1972-82; chmn. bd. Utah Shakespearean Festival, Cedar City, 1982-86; chmn. bd. dirs. Salt Lake City Br. of the Fed. Res. Bank of San Francisco; trustee Salt Lake Organizing Com. Winter Olympics 2002. 1st lt. USAF, 1954-57. Recipient Editing award Indsl. Editors Assn., 1962, Robins award Utah State U., 1967, Disting. Alumnus award Utah State U., 1974, So. Utah U., 1991, Total Citizen award Cedar City C. of C., 1993; named to Utah Tourism Hall of Fame, 1989. Mem. Am. Assn. State Colls. and Univs., Cache C. of C. (bd. dirs. 1980-82), Phi Kappa Phi, Phi Delta Kappa, Sigma Nu (regent 1976-78). Mem. LDS Ch. Lodge: Rotary. Home: 331 W 200 S Cedar City UT 84720-3101 Office: So Utah U 351 W Center St Cedar City UT 84720-2470

SHERRELL, JOHN BRADFORD, lawyer; b. Indpls., Jan. 27, 1951; s. Carl and Mary Jean (Bell) S.; m. Sherry Naomi Calhoun, Apr. 28, 1974; children: David Alan, Corinne Elizabeth. BA, Yale U., 1973; JD, U. Mich., 1977. Bar: Calif. 1977. Ptnr. Latham & Watkins, Los Angeles, 1977—. Dep. gen. counsel to Ind. Commn. on L.A. Police Dept. Mem. ABA, Calif. Bar Assn. (co-chair real estate fin. subsect. of real property sec. 1990-92), L.A. County Bar Assn. (barrister's exec. com. 1978-80, bd. trustees 1991-93). *

SHERRER, CHARLES DAVID, college dean, clergyman; b. Marion, Ohio, Sept. 21, 1935; s. Harold D. and Catherine E. (Fye) S. A.B., U. Notre Dame, 1958, M.A., 1965; S.T.L., Gregorian U., 1962; Ph.D., U. N.C., 1969. Ordained priest Roman Cath. Ch., 1961. Instr. English U. Portland, Oreg., 1963-64, asst. prof., 1969-74, prof., 1990—, chmn. dept., 1970-74, dean Grad. Sch., 1982-87, mem. Bd. Regents, 1986-87, acad. v.p., 1987-96; pres. King's Coll., Wilkes Barre, Pa., 1974-81; bd. trustees Stonehill Coll., 1992—; dir. studies Holy Cross Fathers, Ind. Province, 1979-88. Office: U Portland Office of Acad Vice Pres Portland OR 97203

SHERRICK, DANIEL NOAH, real estate broker; b. Greenup, Ill., Mar. 28, 1929; s. Conrad Donovan and Helen Lorene (Neeley) S.; m. Dora Ann Moore, Aug. 11, 1957; children: Renata Ann Sherrick McBride, Sherrie Dee Sherrick Sierra. B.S. in Edn., Eastern Ill. U., Charleston, 1956. Owner Midwest Ins. Agy., Greenup, 1956-60; supt. agys. Midwest Life Ins. Co., Lincoln, Nebr., 1960-62; asst. v.p. Gulf Life Ins. Co., Jacksonville, Fla., 1962-71; pres. Bank of Carbondale, Ill., 1971-74, Prescription Learning Corp., Springfield, Ill., 1974-76; exec. v.p. Imperial Industries, Inc., Miami Lakes, Fla., 1976-88, pres., chief exec. officer, 1988-90; broker, salesman Coldwell Banker Residential Real Estate, 1990-91, 93—; pres., bd. dirs. Palmer State Bank, Taylorville, Ill., 1991-93; broker-salesman Coldwell Banker Hunter Realty, 1993—. Pres. Alderman Park Civic Assn., Jacksonville, 1968, Heritage Hills Home Owners Assn., Carbondale, 1973. With USAF, 1948-52. Mem. Am. Legion, Greater Sebring C. of C., VFW, Internat. Torch Club, Masons, Elks. Presbyterian. Home: 6228 Aquavista Dr Sebring FL 33870-7409 Office: Coldwell Banker Hunter Realty 2617 US 27 S Sebring FL 33870

SHERRIFFS, RONALD EVERETT, communication and film educator; b. Salem, Oreg., Apr. 10, 1934; s. Robert William and Margaret Kathleen (Tutt) S.; m. Mary Lona West, July 9, 1960; children: Ellen, Matthew. BA, San Jose State U., 1955, MA, 1957; PhD, U. So. Calif., 1964. Instr. theater Mich. State U., East Lansing, 1960-61; asst. prof. broadcasting Tex. Tech U., Lubbock, 1964-65; asst. prof. speech U. Oreg., Eugene, 1965-70, assoc. prof., 1970-79, prof. telecomm. and film, 1979-92, chmn. dept. speech, 1978-84, 88-90, prof. journalism and comm., 1993—. Author: (with others) Speech Communication via Radio and TV, 1971, TV Lighting Handbook, 1977, Small Format TV Production, 1985, 3d edit., Video Field Production and Editing, 1994, 4th edit., 1996; prodr., dir. TV programs, 1965—. Mem. Oreg. Pub. Broadcasting Policy Adv. Bd., 1980-88. Served to lt. comdr. USNR, 1957-68, PTO. Faculty enrichment program grantee Can., 1984, 91. Mem. Speech Communication Assn. Am., AAUP, Western States Communication Assn. Clubs: Oreg. Track; McKenzie Flyfishers (Eugene). Office: Univ Oreg Journalism Dept Eugene OR 97403

SHERRILL, H. VIRGIL, securities company executive; b. Long Beach, Calif., 1920. Grad., Yale U., 1942, JD, 1948. Sr. dir. Prudential Securities Inc., N.Y.C. Office: Prudential Securites 199 Water St Fl 34 New York NY 10292

SHERRILL, THOMAS BOYKIN, III, newspaper publishing executive; b. Tampa, Fla., Nov. 19, 1930; s. Thomas Boykin Jr. and Mary Emma (Addison) S.; m. Sandra Louise Evans, Dec. 27, 1969; children: Thomas Glenn, Stephen Addison. Circulation dir. Tampa (Fla.) Tribune, 1962-67, Sarasota (Fla.) Herald-Tribune, 1967-75; v.p. circulation The Dispatch Printing Co., Columbus, Ohio, 1975-78, v.p. mktg., 1978—, bd. dirs., 1977—; v.p., bd. dirs. Ohio Mag., Inc., Columbus, 1979—. Chmn. bd. dirs. Salvation Army; trustee, past chmn. bd. dirs. Better Bus. Bur. Ctrl. Ohio, Inc.; bd. dirs. Ctrl. Ohio Ctr. Econ. Edn.; v.p., trustee Columbus Dispatch Charities; exec. bd. mem. Simon Kenton coun. Boy Scouts Am.; past pres. Wesley Glen United Meth. Retirement Ctr.; pres.'s adv. bd. mem. Meth. Theol. Sch.. With USN, 1951-56. Recipient Disting. Svc. award Editor and Pub. Mag., 1978; named hon. pres. Troy State U., 1979, hon. Ky. Col., 1980, hon. lt. col. aide-to-camp to Gov. State of Ala., 1984. Mem. Internat. Circulation Mgrs. Assn. (pres. 1975, Pres's. award 1989), Internat. Newspaper Mktg. Assn., Ohio Newspaper Assn. (bd. dirs., pres. 1986-88, Pres.'s award 1990), So. Circulation Mgrs. Assn. (pres. 1967-68, C.W. Bevinger Meml. award 1972), Audit Bur. Circulations (bd. dirs. 1980-90), Am. Advt. Fedn., Navy League, Ohio Newspapers Found., Ohio Circulation Mgrs. Assn (Pres.' award 1989), Columbus Area C. of C., SAR, Internat. Platform Assn., Columbus Met. Club, Athletic Club of Columbus, Muirfield Village Country Club, Kiwanis (pres. 1982). Republican. Home: 5215 Hampton Ln Columbus OH 43220-2270 Office: Columbus Dispatch 34 S 3rd St Columbus OH 43215-4201

SHERROD, BLACKIE, newspaper sports columnist. Sports columnist Dallas Morning News. Office: Dallas Morning News Communications Ctr 508 Young St Dallas TX 75202-4808

SHERRY, GEORGE LEON, political science educator; b. Lodz, Poland, Jan. 5, 1924; came to U.S., 1939, naturalized 1945; s. Leon G. and Henrietta (Mess) S.; m. Doris H. Harf, Mar. 6, 1947; 1 child, Vivien Gail Sherry Greenberg. BA summa cum laude, CCNY, 1944; MA, Columbia U., 1951, MA, cert. Russian Inst., 1955, PhM, 1959. Reporter, radio news writer The N.Y. Times, N.Y.C., 1944-46; editor, interpreter, then sr. interpreter UN, N.Y.C., 1946-59, from polit. officer to dir. and dep. to under sec.-gen. for spl. polit. affairs, 1959-84; polit. advisor to missions Congo, Cyprus, India and Pakistan, 1962-66; asst. sec.-gen. for spl. polit. affairs UN (office in charge peacekeeping forces which won Nobel Peace Prize, 1988), N.Y.C., 1984-85; Stuart Chevalier prof. diplomacy and world affairs Occidental Coll., Los Angeles, 1985—; dir. Occidental at-the-UN program, N.Y.C., 1986—; U.S. del. staff Dartmouth Soviet-Am. confs., 1961-94; assoc. seminar on problem of peace Columbia U., N.Y.C.; cons. UN dept. peacekeeping ops., 1992, 93; leader UN tech. mission to Ga., 1993; UN envoy to follow Russian elections, 1993; advisor Internat. Peace Acad., 1993—. Author: The United Nations Reborn: Conflict Control in the Post-Cold War World, 1990; editorial adv. bd. Polit. Sci. Quar., N.Y.C., 1973-89; contbr. articles and revs. to profl. jours. Recipient Townsend Harris medal CCNY, 1993; UN Inst. for Tng. and Rsch. sr. fellow, 1985-93. Mem. Coun. on Fgn. Rels., Internat. Studies Assn., Acad. Coun. on UN Sys., UN Assn.-USA. Democrat. Avocations: piano playing; skiing; sailing. Home: 185 E 85th St Apt 3-c New York NY 10028-2140

SHERRY, HENRY IVAN, marketing consultant; b. Chgo., Aug. 10, 1930; s. Emmanuel H. and Dorothy Harriet S.; B.S. in Bus. Adminstrn., U. Ala., 1952; m. Maxine Rae Gould, Aug. 7, 1955; children—Dale Sara, Michael Jay. Account exec. Jones, Frankel Co., Chgo., 1954-60; account exec., account supr., v.p., group supr. Edward H. Weiss & Co., Chgo., 1960-66; v.p., account supr., sr. mgmt. officer Interpub. Group of Cos.-McCann Erickson, Inc., Atlanta, dir. Communications Counselors Network, 1966-69; sr. v.p., dir., exec. policy com. The Marchalk Co., Atlanta, N.Y.C., 1969-71; pres. Henry Sherry Assocs., Inc., Atlanta, 1971-88; chmn. Sherry & Bellows, Inc., Atlanta, 1988-91; pres. Sherry & Mitchell Inc., 1991—. Mem. assoc. bd. Mt. Sinai Hosp., 1965-66; chmn. pub. info. United Way, 1970; dir. The Temple, 1982—; mem. exec. com. Coverdell for Congress, 1976. Served with U.S. Army, 1952-54. Club: Standard (dir. 1967-68, 84-86). Office: Sherry & Mitchell Inc 1100 Circle 75 Pky NW Ste 800 Atlanta GA 30339-3097

SHERRY, PAUL HENRY, minister, religious organization administrator; b. Tamaqua, Pa., Dec. 25, 1933; s. Paul Edward and Mary Elizabeth (Stein) S.; m. Mary Louise Thornburg, June 4, 1957; children: Mary Elizabeth, Paul David. BA, Franklin and Marshall Coll., 1955; ThM, Union Theol. Sem., N.Y.C., 1958, PhD, 1969; hon. doctorate, Ursinus Coll., 1981, Elmhurst Coll., 1990, Defiance Coll., 1991, Lakeland Coll., Sheboygan, Wis., 1991, Reformed Theological Acad., Debrecen, Hungary, 1994, United Theol. Sem. Twin Cities, 1995. Ordained to ministry United Ch. of Christ, 1958. Pastor St. Matthew United Ch. of Christ, Kenhorst, Pa., 1958-61, Community United Ch. of Christ, Hasbrouck Heights, N.J., 1961-65; mem. staff United Ch. Bd. Homeland Ministry, N.Y.C., 1965-82; exec. dir. Community Renewal Soc., Chgo., 1983-89; pres. United Ch. of Christ, Cleve., 1989—; mem. gen. bd. Nat. Coun. Chs., N.Y.C., 1989—; mem. cen. com. World Coun. Chs., Geneva, 1991—, del. 7th Assembly, Canberra, Australia, 1991; bd. dirs. Ind. Sector, Washington, 1991—. Editor: The Riverside Preachers; editor Jour. Current Social Issues, 1968-80; contbr. numerous articles to religious jours.; host weekly radio programs local sta., 1974-78, 84-85, 93—. Mem. Soc. Christian Ethics. Democrat. Avocations: reading, hiking, cultural events. Home: 13400 Shaker Blvd Cleveland OH 44120-1599 Office: United Ch of Christ 700 Prospect Ave E Cleveland OH 44115-1131

SHERTZER, BRUCE ELDON, education educator; b. Bloomfield, Ind., Jan. 11, 1928; s. Edwin Franklin and Lois Belle S.; m. Carol Mae Rice, Nov. 24, 1948; children: Sarah Ann, Mark Eldon. B.S., Ind. U., 1952, M.S., 1953, Ed.D., 1958. Tchr., counselor Martinsville (Ind.) High Sch., 1952-56; dir. div. guidance Ind. Dept. Pub. Instrn., 1956-58; assoc. dir. project guidance of superior students North Central Assn. Coll. and Secondary Sch., 1958-60; asst. prof. Purdue U., 1960—, assoc. prof., 1962, prof., head dept. ednl. studies, 1989-95, prof. emeritus of counseling, 1995—; vis. prof. ednl. psychology U. Hawaii, 1967; Fulbright sr. lectr., Reading, Eng., 1967-68; vis. prof. U. So. Calif. Overseas Grad. Program, 1975, 82; chmn. Nat. Adv. Council for Career Edn., 1976. Author: Career Exploration and Planning 1973, 2d edit., 1976, Fundamentals of Counseling, 3d edit., 1980, Fundamentals of Guidance, 4th edit., 1981, Individual Appraisal, 1979, Career Planning, 3d edit., 1985, also articles. Chmn. bd. trustees Found. Am. Assn. of Counseling and Devel., 1986-87. With AUS, 1946-47. Mem. Am. Counseling Assn. (pres. 1973-74, Disting. Profl. Svc. award 1986). Home: 1620 Western Dr West Lafayette IN 47906-2236 Office: Purdue U Liberal Arts Edn Bldg West Lafayette IN 47907

SHERVA, DENNIS G., investment company executive; b. Mpls., Dec. 3, 1942; s. Garfield Theodore and Dorothy Genevive (Oberlander) S.; m. Cathleen Marybeth Tischer, Oct. 15, 1965. B.A., U. Minn., 1964; M.A., Wayne State U., 1965. Chartered fin. analyst. Fin. analyst 1st Nat. Bank, Mpls., 1965-67; fin. analyst Honeywell, Inc., Mpls., 1967; v.p. Smith, Barney & Co., N.Y.C., 1967-71, Baker, Weeks & Co., N.Y.C., 1971-77; mng. dir. Morgan Stanley & Co., Inc., N.Y.C., 1977—; bd. dirs. Morgan Stanley Ventures, San Francisco, Morgan Stanley Venture Capital, N.Y.C., Morgan Stanley Asset Mgmt. Inc., N.Y.C. Recipient All-Am. Research Team 1st place award Instl. Investor Mag., 1979, 81, 83, 84, 85, 87. Mem. Nat. Assn. Securities Dealers (instl. com. 1985—), N.Y. Athletic Club, Torrington Country Club. Home: 791 Park Ave New York NY 10021-3551 Office: Morgan Stanley & Co Inc 1221 Ave Of The Americas New York NY 10020-1001

SHERVHEIM, LLOYD OLIVER, insurance company executive, lawyer; b. Kensington, Minn., June 22, 1928; s. Lewis and Ruth Amanda (Thronson) S.; m. Ruth Elaine Rhodes, Oct. 29, 1950; children: Daniel, Anne, Heidi, Garold, Robette, Shanna, Bryce. Student, Gustavus Adolphus Coll., 1948-50, U. Minn., 1950-52; B.S., William Mitchell Coll. Law, 1958, LL.B., 1958. Bar: Minn. 1959. Supr., asst. to corp. sec. Investors Diversified Services, Inc., 1952-59; legal counsel Investors Syndicate Life Ins. Co., Mpls., 1959-66; gen. counsel Western Life Ins. Co., St. Paul, 1966-72; corporate sec. St. Paul Cos., Inc., 1969-82, chief legal officer, 1972-78, v.p. legal affairs, 1978-85, sr. v.p. law, corporate sec., 1985-89; corporate sec. St. Paul Fire and Marine Ins. Co., 1969-82; dir. St. Paul Ins. Co., Tex., St. Paul Surplus Lines Ins. Co., St. Paul Mercury Ins. Co., St. Paul Guardian Ins. Co., St. Paul Ins. Co., Ill. Charter patron Minn. Theatre Co., 1958; mem. Lake Elmo City Council, 1970-78; past chmn. protection open space task force Met. Open Space Adv. Bd., 1969-70; trustee William Mitchell Coll. Law, 1981-92, vice chmn., 1983-86, chmn., 1986-89; dir. Minn. Citizens Council on Crime and Justice, 1986-89. With U.S. Army, 1946-48. Mem. ABA, Minn. Bar Assn. (chmn. ins. com. 1964-65, gov. 1980-81), Fed. Bar Assn. (pres. Minn. chpt. 1978-79), Ramsey County Bar Assn. (ethics com. 1978-80), Assn. Life Ins. Counsel, Am. Soc. Corp. Secs., Am. Life Conv. (v.p. Minn. chpt. 1969-71), Am. Judicature Soc., Corp. Counsel Assn. Minn. (dir., pres. 1979-80), Pool and Yacht Club (St. Paul). Lutheran (chmn. bd. trustees). Home and Office: 2325 E Chelsea St Lake Havasu City AZ 86404-5911

SHERWIN, BYRON LEE, religion educator, college official; b. N.Y.C., Feb. 18, 1946; s. Sidney and Jean Sylvia (Rabinowitz) S.; m. Judith Rita Schwartz, Dec. 24, 1972; 1 child, Jason Samuel. BS, Columbia U., N.Y.C., 1966; B of Hebrew Lit., Jewish Theol. Sem. of Am., 1966, M of Hebrew Lit., 1968; MA, NYU, 1969; PhD, U. Chgo., 1978. Ordained rabbi, 1970. Prof. Jewish philosophy and mysticism Spertus Coll. Judaica, Chgo., 1970—, v.p. acad. affairs, 1984—. Author: Judaism, 1978, Encountering the Holocaust, 1979, Abraham Joshua Heschel, 1979, Garden of the Generations, 1981, Jerzy Kosinski: Literary Alarm Clock, 1981, Mystical Theology and Social Dissent, 1982, The Golem Legend, 1985, Contents and Contexts, 1987, Thank God, 1989, In Partnership with God: Contemporary Jewish Law and Ethics, 1990, No Religion Is an Island, 1991, Toward a Jewish Theology, 1991, How To Be a Jew: Ethical Teachings of Judaism, 1992, The Theological Heritage of Polish Jews, 1995, Sparks Amongst the Ashes: The Spiritual Legacy of Polish Jewry, 1996, also articles. Recipient Man of Reconciliation award Polish Coun. Christians and Jews, 1992, Presdl. medal, Officer of Order of Merit, Republic of Poland, 1995. Mem. Midwest Jewish Studies Assn. (founding pres.), Am. Philos. Assn., Assn. for Jewish Studies, Rabbinical Assembly, Am. Acad. Religion, Religious Ednl. Assn. Republican. Avocations: cooking, book collecting. Office: Spertus Coll Judaica 618 S Michigan Ave Chicago IL 60605-1901

SHERWIN, JAMES TERRY, lawyer, window covering company executive; b. N.Y.C., Oct. 25, 1933; s. Oscar and Stella (Zins) S.; m. Judith Johnson, June 21, 1955 (div. Apr. 1984); children—Miranda, Alison, Galen; m. Hiroko Inouye, June 15, 1985. BA, Columbia U., 1953, LLB (Stone scholar), 1956. Bar: N.Y. 1956, U.S. Supreme Ct. 1963. Assoc. Kaye, Scholer, Fierman, Hays & Handler, N.Y.C., 1957-60; with GAF Corp., N.Y.C., 1960-83, 84-90, asso. counsel, gen. mgr. European ops., 1969-71, group v.p. photography, 1971-74, exec. v.p. fin. and adminstrn., legal and investment svcs., 1974-83; vice chmn., chief adminstrv. officer GAF Corp., Wayne, N.J., 1984-90; exec. v.p., chief fin. officer Triangle Industries, Inc., 1983-84, Hunter-Douglas N.V., 1991—; exec. v.p., CFO. Bd. dirs. Internat. Rescue Com., chmn. exec. com., v.p. to 1990. Lt. comdr. USCGR, 1956-57. U.S. intercollegiate chess champion, 1951-53, N.Y. State champion, 1951, U.S. speed champion, 1956-57, 59-60, internat. master. Mem. Am. Chess Found. (pres., bd. dirs. to 1990), Marshall (N.Y.) Chess Club (pres. 1967-69, gov. to 1990), Phi Beta Kappa. Home: Stegenhöhe 24, CH 6048 Horw Switzerland Office: Hunter Douglas Mgmt AG, Adligenswilerstrasse 37, 6006 Lucerne Switzerland

SHERWIN, MICHAEL DENNIS, government official; b. Decorah, Iowa, Dec. 29, 1939; m. Diann May, Feb. 6, 1965; children: Catherine, Jennifer, Carolyn, Elizabeth. B.A., Coll. St. Thomas, 1962. Intelligence analyst CIA, Washington, 1963-66; copy editor St. Paul Pioneer Press, 1966-67; personnel mgr. Office Personnel Mgmt. U.S. Civil Service Commn., Washington, 1967-79; dir. human resources CAB, Washington, 1979-81, mng. dir., 1981-84; dir. mgmt. systems FAA, Washington, 1985-91, dep. asst. adminstr. for info. tech., 1991-92, dir. civil aviation security program mgmt., 1992-93; dep. asst. adminstr. USAID, Washington, 1993-96; dir. strategic devel. Oracle Corp., Herndon, Va., 1996—. Recipient Commrs. award U.S. CSC 1978, Adminstr.'s Spl. Achievement award for EEO, FAA, 1986, Meritorious Svc. award Sec. of Transp., 1990, Top 100 award Fed. Computer Week, 1990. Roman Catholic. Office: FAA AID 320 21st St NW Washington DC 20523-0002

SHERWOOD, AARON WILEY, aerodynamics educator; b. St. Louis, Jan. 13, 1915; s. Charles Vliet and Amelia Pauline (Kappler) S.; m. Helene M. Gysin, 1944; children—Susan Helene, Mark Wiley. M.E., Rensselaer Poly. Inst., 1935; M.S., U. Md., 1943. Exptl. engr. Wallace & Tiernan Co., Inc., 1936-38; devel. engr. Assoc. Engring., 1938-39; layout engr. Glenn L. Martin Co., 1939-40; instr. U. Md., 1940-44; aero. project engr. David Taylor Model Basin, 1944-46, prof. aerodynamics, 1946—, acting head dept. aero. engring., 1950-58, head dept. aerospace engring., 1958-67, prof. dept. aerospace engring., 1967-77; in charge wind tunnel lab. Glenn L. Martin Inst. Tech., 1946-55; owner, engring. cons. Aerolab. Author: Aerodynamics, 1946. Fellow ASME (chmn. Washington sect. 1954-55); mem. Am. Inst. Aeros and Astronautics (sect. chmn.), Am. Soc. Engring. Edn., Sigma Xi, Tau Beta Pi, Phi Kappa Phi, Phi Kappa Tau. Home: 3411 Chatham Rd Hyattsville MD 20783-1852 Office: Aerolab 9580 Washington Blvd N Laurel MD 20723-1372 *Instead of carefully planned progress toward long-term fixed goals, I advocate frequent modifications of both goals and access routes according to current circumstances. One should follow his interests, tempered only by the needs of his associates and by firm ethical standards —a sort of intelligent muddling along.*

SHERWOOD, ALLEN JOSEPH, lawyer; b. Salt Lake City, Sept. 26, 1909; s. Charles Samuel and Sarah (Abramson) Shapiro; m. Edith Ziff, Jan. 19, 1941; children—Mary (Mrs. John Marshall), Arthur Lawrence. Student, UCLA, 1927-30; AB, U. So. Calif., 1933, LLB, 1933. Bar: Calif. 1933, U.S. Supreme Ct. 1944. Pvt. practice law L.A., 1933-54, Beverly Hills, 1954-95; legal counsel Internat. Family Planning Rsch. Assn., Inc., 1970-76; bd. dirs. Family Planning Ctrs. Greater L.A., Inc., 1968-84, pres., 1973-76. Mem. editorial bd. So. Calif. Law Rev., 1932-33. Contbr. articles to profl. jours. Mem. Calif. Atty. Gen.'s Vol. Adv. Coun. and its legis. subcom., 1972-78. Mem. Med.-Legal Soc. So. Calif. (bd. dirs. 1966-74), ABA, L.A. County Bar Assn., Beverly Hills Bar Assn., State Bar of Calif., Am. Arbitration Assn. (nat. panel arbitrators 1965—), Order of Coif, Tau Delta Phi, Brentwood Country Club (L.A.), Masons. Home: 575 Moreno Ave Los Angeles CA 90049-4840

SHERWOOD, ARTHUR LAWRENCE, lawyer; b. L.A., Jan. 25, 1943; s. Allen Joseph and Edith (Ziff) S.; m. Frances Merele, May 1, 1970; children: David, Chester. BA magna cum laude, U. Calif.-Berkeley, 1964; MS, U. Chgo., 1965; JD cum laude, Harvard U., 1968. Bar: Calif. 1969, US. dist. cts. (cen. dist.) Calif. 1968 (no. dist.) Calif. 1971 (so. dist.) Calif. 1973 (ea. dist.) Calif. 1973, U.S. Ct. Appeals (9th cir.) 1973, U.S. Ct. Appeals (D.C. cir.) 1991, U.S. Supreme Ct., 1980. Instr. UCLA Law Sch., 1968-69; assoc. Gibson, Dunn & Crutcher, Los Angeles, 1968-75, ptnr., 1975—; judge pro tem Los Angeles Mcpl. and Superior Ct., 1980—; instr. law, UCLA, 1968-69, arbitrator N.Y. Stock Exchange., Nat. Futures Assn. Co-author: Civil Procedure During Trial, 1995, Civil Procedure Before Trial, 1990, contbr articles to profl. jours. NASA fellow U. Chgo., 1964-65; chmn. Far Ea. Art Coun., L.A. County Mus. Art, 1992—. Mem. ABA, L.A. County Bar Assn., Calif. Bar Assn., Phi Beta Kappa. Republican. Avocations include: art, 18th century Am. history. Office: Gibson Dunn & Crutcher 333 S Grand Ave Fl 45 Los Angeles CA 90071-1504

SHERWOOD, ARTHUR MORLEY, lawyer; b. Buffalo, Oct. 3, 1939; s. Frederick T. and Neva E. (Merrill) S.; m. Karen H. Hilstad, Apr. 2, 1964; children: Laurel Ann, Carolyn Margaret. BA, Harvard U., 1961; JD, U. Mich., 1964. Bar: Mich. 1965, N.Y. 1967, U.S. Supreme Ct. 1989. Law clk. to Hon. Ralph M. Freeman U.S. Dist. Ct. (ea. dist.) Mich., Detroit, 1964-66; pntr. Phillips, Lytle, Hitchcock, Blaine & Huber, Buffalo, 1971—. Contbr. articles to Trusts and Estates, N.Y. State Bar Jour. and N.Y. Tax Svc. Asst. chancellor Episcopal Diocese of Western N.Y., 1982—; mem. adv. com. N.Y. State Legislature on N.Y. Estates, Powers and Trusts Law, Surrogate's Ct. Procedure. Fellow Am. Coll. Trust and Estate Counsel, N.Y. Bar Found.; mem. N.Y. State Bar Assn. (chairperson trusts and estates law sect. 1987). Home: 3770 Windover Dr Hamburg NY 14075-6322 Office: Phillips Lytle Hitchcock Blaine & Huber 3400 Marine Midland Ctr Buffalo NY 14203-2887

SHERWOOD, JAMES ALAN, physician, scientist, educator; b. Oneida County, N.Y., Jan. 4, 1953; s. Robert Merriam and Sally (Trevett-Edgett) S. AB, Hamilton Coll., 1974; MD, Columbia U., 1978. Diplomate Nat. Bd. Med. Examiners, Am. Bd. Internal Medicine. Intern Duke U. Med. Ctr., Durham, N.C., 1978-79; resident physician Strong Meml. Hosp., Rochester, N.Y., 1979-81; fellow U. Rochester Sch. Medicine and Dentistry, 1981-83, NIH, Bethesda, Md., 1983-86; rsch. investigator Walter Reed Army Inst. Rsch., Washington, 1986-92; vis. scientist Clin. Rsch. Ctr. Kenya Med. Rsch. Inst., Nairobi, 1987-92; physician Saradidi Rural Health Programme, Nyilima, Kenya, 1987-92; rsch. cons. Rockville, Md., 1992-93; physician St. Mary's Hosp., Waterbury, Conn., 1993—; clin. instr. Sch. Medicine Yale U., 1994—. Contbr. chpt. to book, articles to profl. jours. Comty. svc. vol. The Door, N.Y.C., 1976-77; vol. physician Washington Free Clinic, 1985-87; charity Sisters of St. Joseph of Chambery. Lt. col. Med. Corps, USAR, 1986-92. Recipient Norton prize in chemistry, 1974, Underwood prize in chemistry, 1974. Fellow Am. Coll. Physicians; mem. Med. Soc. D.C., Am.

Fedn. Clin. Rsch., Am. Soc. Tropical Medicine and Hygiene, Muthaiga Club, Phi Beta Kappa, Sigma Xi. Avocations: drawing, book collecting. Office: PO Box 112 Waterbury CT 06720

SHERWOOD, KATHERINE D., artist, educator; b. New Orleans, Oct. 17, 1952; m. Jeff Adams; 1 child, Odette. BA, U. Calif., Davis, 1975; MFA, San Francisco Art Inst., 1979. Asst. prof. U. Calif., Berkeley, 1989—; adj. instr. NYU, 1983-89. One-woman shows include Anna Gardner Gallery, Stinson Beach, Calif., 1977, Nelson Gallery, Davis, Calif., 1981, ARC Gallery, Sacramento, 1982, Gallery Paule Anglim, San Francisco, 1982, M.O. David Gallery, N.Y.C., 1984, 8 B.C., N.Y.C., 1985, D.P. Fong Gallery, San Jose, 1994, others; group shows include Concord Gallery, N.Y.C., 1981, Eaton-Schoen Gallery, San Francisco, 1982, Protetch-McNeil Gallery, N.Y.C., 1983, Phila. Coll. Art, 1984, Avenue B. Gallery, N.Y.C., 1985, U. Santa Clara (Calif.), 1986, Washington Square Gallery, N.Y.C., 1987, Bruno Facchetto Gallery, N.Y.C., 1988, Worth Ryder Gallery, Berkeley, 1989, Otaru Mcpl. Mus., Hokkaido, Japan, 1991, San Francisco Art Commn. Gallery, 1992, Alexandria Mus. of Art, 1993 (Juror's Merit award 1993), Palm Springs (Calif.) Desert Mus., 1994 (Best of Show 1994), Microsoft Gallery, Beaverton, Oreg., 1995, others. U. Calif. Priorities in Edn. grantee, 1990, Faculty Mentor grantee, 1991, 93, Jr. Faculty Devel. Program grantee, 1991, Humanities Rsch. grantee, 1992; NEA Visual Artists fellow, 1989, MacDowell Colony fellow, 1984. Office: U Calif 238 Koreber Hall Berkeley CA

SHERWOOD, LILLIAN ANNA, librarian, retired; b. South Bend, Ind., Dec. 22, 1928; d. Julius Andrew and Mary (Kerekes) Takacs; m. Neil Walter Sherwood, May 31, 1953; children: Susan Kay Huff, Nancy Ellen Coney, James Walter. AB in Home Econs., Ind. U., 1951, postgrad., 1978-83. Cert. libr. IV, Ind., 1984. Lab. tech. Lobund Inst., Notre Dame (Ind.) U., 1951-53; substitute tchr. Plymouth (Ind.) Community Schs., 1969-73; bookkeeper, processing clk. Plymouth (Ind.) Pub. Libr., 1973-76, audio-visual coord., 1976-79, reference and genealogical libr., 1980-93; retired, 1994; project dir. Ind. Heritage rsch. grant, Ind. Humanities Coun. and Ind. Hist. Soc., 1992-93; orgn. and verification com. Geneal. Socs., Pioneer Soc., Marshall County, Ind., Plymouth, 1988—. Mem. bd. dirs. Child Day Care Ctr. of Plymouth, 1971-75, pres., 1974. Mem. AAUW (v.p. 1966-68, pres. 1971-73, 85-87, 91-93), Marshall County Geneal. Soc. (v.p. 1986-87), Omicron Nu. Methodist. Avocations: genealogy, music appreciation, gardening, travel. Home: 808 Thayer St Plymouth IN 46563-2859

SHERWOOD, (PETER) LOUIS, retail executive; b. London, Oct. 27, 1941; came to U.S., 1979; s. Peter and Mervyn (De Toll) S.; m. Nicole Dina, Aug. 22, 1970; children: Christopher, Anne, Isabelle. BA, Oxford U., 1963, MA, 1966; MBA, Stanford U., 1965. Fin. planning officer Morgan Grenfell & Co. Ltd., London, 1965-68; gen. mgr. Melias Ltd., Welwyn Garden City, Eng., 1969-72; dir. Anglo-Continental Investment & Fin. Co. Ltd., London, 1973-79; chmn., chief exec. officer Maidenhead Investments, London, 1977-79; sr. v.p. Grand Union Co., Elmwood Park, N.J., 1979-85; pres. Gt. Atlantic & Pacific Tea Co. Inc., Montvale, N.J., 1985-88; chmn., chief exec. officer Gateway Foodmarkets, Bristol, Eng., 1988-89; chmn. Airedale Holdings plc, Keighley, Yorkshire, Eng., 1990-92, HTV Group plc, Cardiff, Wales, 1991—, New Look plc, Weymouth, Dorset, 1994—. Harkness fellow Stanford U., 1965.

SHERWOOD, LOUIS MAIER, physician, scientist, pharmaceutical company executive; b. N.Y.C., Mar. 1, 1937; s. Arthur Joseph and Blanche (Burger) S.; m. Judith Brimberg, Mar. 27, 1966; children: Jennifer Beth, Arieh David. AB with honors, Johns Hopkins U., 1957; MD with honors, Columbia U., 1961. Diplomate Am. Bd. Internal Medicine, Subsplty. Bd. in Endocrinology and Metabolism. Intern Presbyn. Hosp., N.Y.C., 1961-62, asst. resident in medicine, 1962-63; clin. assoc. research fellow Nat. Heart Inst., NIH, Bethesda, Md., 1963-66; NIH trainee endocrinology and metabolism Coll. Physicians and Surgeons, Columbia U., N.Y.C., 1966-68; assoc. medicine Beth Israel Hosp. and Harvard Med. Sch., Boston, 1968-69; chief endocrinology Beth Israel Hosp., 1968-72; asst. prof. medicine Harvard U., 1969-71, assoc. prof., 1971-72; physician-in-chief, chmn. dept. medicine Michael Reese Hosp. and Med. Ctr., Chgo., 1972-80; prof. medicine, div. biol. scis. Pritzker Sch. Medicine, U. Chgo., 1972-80; Ted and Florence Baumritter prof. medicine and biochemistry Albert Einstein Coll. Medicine, 1980-88, vis. prof. medicine, 1989—, chmn. dept. medicine, 1980-87; physician-in-chief Montefiore Hosp. and Med. Ctr., N.Y.C., 1980-87; adj. prof. medicine U. Pa., 1993—; sr. v.p. med. and sci. affairs Merck, Sharp & Dohme Internat., 1987-89; exec. v.p. worldwide devel. Merck, Sharp & Dohme Rsch. Labs., 1989-92, sr. v.p. U.S. Med. and Sci. Affairs Merck Human Health, 1992—; bd. dirs. Physicians and Surgeons Corp., Michael Reese Med. Ctr., 1973-80, Barren Found., 1974-80; Josiah Macy Jr. Found. fellow and vis. scientist Weizmann Inst., Israel, 1978-79; assoc. mem. bd. on subcom. endocrinology and metabolism Am. Bd. Internal Medicine, 1977-83. Editor: Beth Israel seminars New Eng. Jour. Medicine, 1968-71; mem. editorial bd. Endocrinology, 1969-73; assoc. editor Metabolism, 1970-85, Gen. Medicine B Study Sect., NIH, 1975-79; mem. editorial bd. Yr. in Endocrinology, 1976-86, Calcified Tissue Internat., 1978-80, Internal Medicine Alert, 1979-89; contbr. numerous articles on endocrinology, protein hormones, calcium metabolism and ectopic proteins to jours. Trustee Michael Reese Med. Ctr., 1974-77; mem. vis. council CUNY Med. Sch., 1986—; mem. alumni council Columbia Coll. Physicians and Surgeons, 1986—. Served as surgeon USPHS, 1963-66. Recipient Joseph Mather Smith prize for outstanding alumni research Coll. Physicians and Surgeons, Columbia U., 1972, Sr. Class Teaching award U. Chgo., 1976, 77; grantee USPHS, 1968-88. Fellow ACP (Outstanding Contbn. to Internal Medicine award 1987); mem. AAAS, Am. Fedn. Clin. Rsch. (bd. dirs. Found. 1989-92, Spl. Recognition award 1992), Am. Inst. Chemists, Am. Soc. Biol. Chemists, Am. Soc. Clin. Investigation (pres. 1982-83), Assn. Am. Physicians, Endocrine Soc., Am. Physicians Fellowship for Medicine in Israel (pres. 1993—), N.Y. Acad. Medicine (bd. dirs. 1991-95), Am. Soc. Hypertension (bd. dirs. 1992—), Mass. Med. Soc., Ctrl. Soc. Clin. Rsch., Assn. Program Dirs. Internal Medicine (coun. 1979-85, pres. 1983-84), Assn. Profs. Medicine, Chgo. Soc. Internal Medicine, Assn. Prof. Med. Industry Roundtable, Interurban Clin. Club, Phi Beta Kappa, Alpha Omega Alpha. Achievements include research in protein and polypeptide hormones: structure, function and regulation of secretion; molecular studies of hormone biosynthesis; clinical pharmacology, new drug development, outcomes research and disease management. Office: Merck & Co US Human Health West Point PA 19486 *To be a successful leader, you must be willing to surround yourself with outstanding individuals, give them your full support and enjoy their growth.*

SHERWOOD, PATRICIA WARING, artist, educator; b. Columbia, S.C., Dec. 19, 1933; d. Clark du Val and Florence (Yarbrough) Waring; divorced; children: Cheryl Sherwood Kraft, Jana Sherwood Kern, Marikay Sherwood Taitt. BFA magna cum laude, Calif. State U., Hayward, 1970; MFA, Mills Coll., Oakland, Calif., 1974; postgrad., San Jose State U., 1980-86. Cert. tchr., Calif. Tchr. De Anza Jr. Coll., Cupertino, Calif., 1970-78, Foothill Jr. Coll., Los Altos, Calif., 1972-78, West Valley Jr. Coll., Saratoga, Calif., 1978—; artist-in-residence Centrum Frans Masereel, Kasterlee, Belgium, 1989. One-woman shows include Triton Mus., Santa Clara, Calif., 1968, RayChem Corp., Sunnyville, Calif., 1969, Palo Alto (Calif.) Cultural Ctr., 1977, Los Gatos (Calif.) Mus., 1992, Stanford U. faculty club, Palo Alto, 1993, d. P. Fong Gallery, San Jose, Calif., 1995, Heritage Bank, San Jose, Calif.; exhibited in group shows at Tressider Union Stanford U., 1969, Oakland (Calif.) Mus. Kaiser Ctr., 1969, Sonoma (Calif.) State Coll., 1969, Bank Am., San Francisco, 1969, San Francisco Art Festival, 1969, 70, U. Santa Clara, 1967, Charles and Emma Frye Mus., Seattle, 1968, Eufrat Gallery DeAnza Coll., Cupertino, 1975, San Jose (Calif.) Mus. Art, 1976, Lytton Ctr., Palo Alto, 1968 (1st award), Zellerbach Ctr., San Francisco, 1970, Works Gallery, San Jose, 1994; represented in permanent collections Mills Coll., Bank Am., San Francisco. Art judge studnet show Stanford U., Palo Alto, 1977; mem. d.p. Fong Gallery, San Jose, Calif., 1994. Nat. Endowment for Arts/We. States Art Fedn. fellow, 1994. Mem. Calif. Print Soc., Womens Caucus for Arts, Internat. Platform Assn. Home: 1500 Arriba Ct Los Altos CA 94024-5941 Office: West Valley Jr Coll Art Dept 14000 Fruitvale Ave Saratoga CA 95070-5640

SHERWOOD, ROBERT PETERSEN, retired sociology educator; b. Black Diamond, Wash., May 17, 1932; s. James Brazier and Zina (Petersen) S.; m. Merlene Burningham, Nov. 21, 1951; children: Robert Lawrence, Richard William, Rolene, RaNae. BS, U. Utah, 1956, MS, 1957; EdD, U. Calif., Berkeley, 1965. Tchr. Arden-Carmichael Sch. Dist., Carmichael, Calif., 1957-59; vice prin. jr. high Arden-Carmichael Sch. Dist., 1960-61, prin. jr. high, 1962-65; v.p., prin. San Juan Unified Sch. Dist., Sacramento, 1966-70; assoc. prof. Calif. State U., Sacramento, 1966-71; dir. outreach progs. Am. River Coll., Sacramento, 1971-73; acting assoc. dean of instrn. Am. River Coll., 1973-74, prof. sociology, 1970-92, chmn. sociology/anthropology dept., 1980-86, retired, 1992; pres. acad. senate Am. River Coll., 1990-91. With USN, 1953-55. Recipient Merit Recognition award, Boy Scouts Am., 1989. Mem. NEA, Calif. Tchrs. Assn., Faculty Assn. Calif. Community Colls., Western Assn. Schs. and Colls., Calif. Fedn. Coll. Profs., Phi Delta Kappa (life). Mem. LDS Ch. Avocations: reading, writing, woodworking, travel. Home: 4053 Esperanza Dr Sacramento CA 95864-3069

SHERZER, HARVEY GERALD, lawyer; b. Phila., May 19, 1944; s. Leon and Rose (Levin) S.; m. Susan Bell, Mar. 28, 1971; children: Sheri Ann, David Lloyd. BA, Temple U., 1965; JD with honors, George Washington U., 1968. Bar: D.C. 1970, U.S. Ct. Appeals (D.C. cir.) 1970, U.S. Ct. Fed. Claims 1970, U.S. Ct. Appeals (fed. cir.) 1970, U.S. Supreme Ct. 1974. Law clk. to trial judges U.S. Ct. Fed. Claims, Washington, 1968-69; law clk. to chief judge U.S. Ct. Appeals for Fed. Cir., Washington, 1969-70; assoc. Sellers, Conner & Cuneo, Washington, 1970-75, ptnr., 1975-80; ptnr. McKenna, Conner & Cuneo, Washington, 1980-82, Pettit & Martin, Washington, 1982-85, Howrey & Simon, Washington, 1985—; adv. bd. The Govt. Contractor, 1996—. Author: (with others) A Complete Guide to the Department of Defense Voluntary Disclosure Program, 1996; contbr. articles to profl. jours. Office: Howrey & Simon 1299 Pennsylvania Ave NW Washington DC 20004-2400

SHESTACK, ALAN, museum administrator; b. N.Y.C., June 23, 1938; s. David and Sylvia P. (Saffran) S.; m. Nancy Jane Davidson, Sept. 24, 1967. BA, Wesleyan U., 1961, DFA (hon.), 1978; MA, Harvard U., 1963. Mus. curator graphic art Nat. Gallery Art, Washington, 1965-67; assoc. curator prints and drawings Yale Art Gallery, New Haven, 1967-68; curator prints and drawings Yale Art Gallery, 1968-71, dir., 1971-85; adj. prof. history of art Yale U., 1971-85; dir. Mpls. Inst. Art, 1985-87, Boston Mus. Fine Arts, 1987-93; dep. dir. Nat. Gallery of Art, Washington, 1994—; mem. adv. com. Art Mus., Princeton, 1972-75; mem. vis. com. Harvard U. Art Mus., 1990-95; mem. mus. panel Nat. Endowment for the Arts, 1974-77; mem. com. prints and illustrated books Mus. Modern Art, N.Y.C., 1972—; mem. Fed. Arts and Artifacts Indemnification Panel, 1979-83. Author: Fifteenth Century Engravings of Northern Europe, 1967, The Engravings of Martin Schongauer, 1968, Master LCZ and Master WB, 1971, Exhibitions Organized and Catalogued: Master E.S, 1967, The Danube School, 1969, Hans Baldung Grien, Prints and Drawings, 1981; contbr. articles to profl. jours. Woodrow Wilson fellow Harvard U., 1963, David E. Finley fellow, 1963-65. Mem. Print Coun. Am. (bd. dirs., v.p. 1970-71), Coll. Art Assn. (bd. dirs. 1972-76), Am. Assn. Mus., Am. Fedn. Arts (trustee 1981-94), Alpha Delta Phi, Phi Beta Kappa. Office: Nat Gallery of Art Washington DC 20565

SHESTACK, JEROME JOSEPH, lawyer; b. Atlantic City, N.J., Feb. 11, 1925; s. Isidore and Olga (Shankman) S.; m. Marciarose Schleifer, Jan. 28, 1951; children: Jonathan Michael, Jennifer. A.B., U. Pa., 1944; LL.B., Harvard U., 1949. Bar: Ill. 1950, Pa. 1952. Teaching fellow Northwestern U. Law Sch., Chgo., 1949-50; asst. prof. law, faculty editor La. State Law Sch., Baton Rouge, 1950-52; dep. city solicitor City of Phila., 1952, 1st dep. solicitor, 1952-55; ptnr. Schnader, Harrison, Segal & Lewis, Phila. and Washington, 1956-91, Wolf, Block, Schorr & Solis-Cohen, Phila., 1991—; adj. prof. law U. Pa., 1956; U.S. amb. to UN Human Rights Commn., 1979-80; U.S. del. to ECOSOC, UN, 1980; sr. U.S. del. to Helsinki Accords Conf., 1979-80; mem. U.S. Commn. on Improving Effectiveness of UN, 1989—; chmn . Internat. League Human Rights, 1973—, U.S. del. to CSCE Conf., Moscow, 1991; bd. dirs., sec. Internat. Comm. Jurists Am.; founder, chmn. Lawyers Com. Internat. Human Rights, 1978-80, Jacob Blaustein Inst. Human Rights, 1988-92; mem. nat. adv. com. legal svcs. OEO, 1965-72; bd. dirs., exec. com. Laywers Com. Civil Rights. Editor: (with others) Rights of Americans, 1971, Human Rights, 1979, International Human Rights, 1985, Bill of Rights: A Bicentennial View, 1991, Understanding Human Rights, 1992, Thomas Jefferson; Lawyer, 1993, Abraham Lincoln, Circuit Lawyer, 1994. Mem. exec. com. Nat. Legal Aid and Defender Assn., 1970-80; trustee Eleanor and Franklin Roosevelt Inst., 1986—; bd. govs. Tel Aviv U., 1983—; v.p. Am. Jewish Com., 1984-89; chmn. bd. dirs. Am. Poetry Ctr., 1976-91; trustee Free Libr. Phila., vice chmn., 1989—. With USNR, 1943-46. Rubin fellow Columbia U. Law Sch., 1984; hon. fellow U. Pa. Law Sch., 1980. Mem. ABA (ho. of dels. 1971-73, 77—, mem. jud. com. 1985-90, bd. govs. 1992-95, exec. com. 1994-95, pres. elect 1996—), Pa. Bar Assn. (bd. govs.), Internat. Bar Assn. (chmn. com. on human rights), Am. Soc. Internat. Law (exec. com. 1993-95), Am. Law Inst., Am. Coll. Trial Lawyers, Am. Acad. Appellate Lawyers, Order of Coif. Home: Parkway House 2201 Pennsylvania Ave Philadelphia PA 19130-3513 Office: Wolf Block Schorr & Solis-Cohen Packard Bldg 12th Fl SE Corner 15th & Chestnut Sts Philadelphia PA 19102-2678

SHESTACK, MELVIN BERNARD, editor, author, filmmaker, television producer; b. Bklyn., Aug. 18, 1931; s. David and Sylvia Pearl (Saffran) S.; m. Jessica Gifford, Feb. 13, 1965; 1 dau., Victoria J.; 1 dau. by previous marriage, Lisa F. A.B., U. So. Calif., 1953; postgrad., U. Rochester, N.Y. U., New Sch. Social Research. Assoc. editor Sat. Eve. Post, 1965-67; staff producer CBS-TV News, 1967-69; asso. producer Sta. WOR-TV, 1970; exec. editor True mag., N.Y.C., 1971-75, editor-in-chief, 1975; editor In The Know mag., N.Y.C., 1975—; exec. dir. Ponca Inst. Am. Studies, 1976-80; exec. editor Antelope Classics, Empire Edits., 1977—; v.p., dir. spl. projects Montcalm Pub. Co., 1980-85; pres. Gifford-Shestack Assocs., 1985-89; exec. v.p., dir. creative devel. Gt. Western Entertainment Corp., N.Y.C., 1989—. Producer, writer: (documentary) The Forgotten American, 1967, Changing Health Care, 1986; dir., producer: (PBS series) America's Challenge, 1990; author: The Country Music Encyclopedia, 1974; co-author: (filmscript) The Soul, 1978, Secrets of Success, 1980, "How'm I Doing?": The Wit and Wisdom of Ed Koch, 1981, New Country Encyclopedia, 1993, (screenplay) 5 Rooms, 1992; pub. Fresh Ayer, 1994; contbr. articles to profl. pubs. Served with AUS, 1953-55. Recipient Brown-Nickerson award for best religious radio program, 1967. Mem. Pi Lambda Phi. Home: 4 Great Jones St New York NY 10012-1134 Office: Centuri Internat Prodns 825 8th Ave New York NY 10019-7416 *I have been blessed by a spectacular marriage. My wife is my best friend and continues to prove her devotion. I am an enthusiast. I meet a great many successful people and they share two qualities. They are serious about what they do and they're enthusiasts. They also work to the very top of their ability and rarely procrastinate. I am enthusiastic and serious, but I am given to procrastination. When I conquer that problem, there is no end to what I can accomplish.*

SHETH, JAGDISH NANCHAND, business administration educator; b. Rangoon, Burma, Sept. 3, 1938; came to U.S., 1961, naturalized, 1975; s. Nanchand Jivraj and Diwaliben Sheth; m. Madhuri Ratilal Shah, Dec. 22, 1962; children—Reshma J., Raju J. B.Com. with honors, U. Madras, 1960; M.B.A., U. Pitts., 1962; Ph.D., 1966. Research asso., asst. prof. Grad. Sch. Bus., Columbia U., 1963-65; asst. prof. M.I.T., 1965-66, Columbia U., 1966-69; asso. prof. bus. adminstrn. U. Ill., Urbana, 1969-71; acting head dept. U. Ill., 1970-72, prof. and research prof., 1971-73, I.B.A. Disting. prof. and research prof., 1973-79, Walter H. Stellner Disting. prof. and research prof., 1979-83; Robert E Brooker Disting. prof. mktg. and research U. So. Calif., Los Angeles, 1983-91; Charles H. Kellstadt prof. mktg. Emory U., Atlanta, 1991—; founder, dir. Ctr. for Telecommunications Mgmt. U. So. Calif, 1983—, Ctr. Relationship Mktg. Emory U.; vis. prof. Indian Inst. Mgmt., 1969; vis. lectr. Internat. Mktg. Inst., Harvard U., 1969; Albert Frey vis. prof. mktg. U. Pitts., 1974; condr. seminars for industry and govt.; cons. to industry. Author: (with John A. Howard) The Theory of Buyer Behavior, 1969, (with S.P. Sethi) Multinational Business Operations: Advanced Readings, 4 vols, 1973, (with A. Woodside and P. Bennett) Consumer and Industrial Buying Behavior, 1977; (with Bruce Newman): A Theory of Political Choice Behavior, 1986; (with Dennis Garrett) Marketing Theory, 1986; (with S. Ram) Bringing Innovation to Market; (with Gary Frazier) Theories of Marketing Practice; (with Milind Lele) The Customer is Key; editor: Models of Buyer Behavior, 1974, (with Peter L. Wright) Marketing Analysis for Societal Problems, 1974, Multivariable Methods for Market and Survey Research, 1977, Winning Back Your Market, 1984, (with David Gardener and Dennis Garrett) Marketing Theory: Evolution and Evaluation, 1988, also (with Abdol Reza and Goli Eslghi) 9 vols. on global bus., 1989-90, (with Bruce Newman and Barbara Gross) Consumption Values and Choice Behavior, 1990; series editor Research in Marketing, 1978—, Research in Consumer Behavior, 1984—; contbr. articles profl. jours. Recipient Viktor Mataja medal Austrian Rsch. Soc., 1976, Mktg. Educator award Sales and Mktg. Execs. Internat., 1991; Mgmt. Program for Execs. fellow, S & H Green Stamps fellow, 1963-64. Fellow APA, Acad. Mktg. Sci. (Disting. fellow 1996, Mktg. Educator award 1989); mem. Am. Mktg. Assn. (P.D. Converse award 1992). Home: 1626 Mason Mill Rd NE Atlanta GA 30329-4133

SHETLAR, JAMES FRANCIS, physician; b. Wichita, Dec. 26, 1944. MD, U. Kans., 1970. Resident in family practice Saginaw County Hosp., 1970-72; staff St. Luke's Gen. Hosp.; asst. clin. prof. Mich. State U. Mem. AMA, Am. Assn. Family Practioners, Mich. Assn. Family Practioners. Office: 163 Churchgrove Saginaw MI 48734-1025

SHETTLES, LANDRUM BREWER, obstetrician-gynecologist; b. Pontotoc, Miss., Nov. 21, 1909; s. Basil Manly and Sue (Mounce) S.; m. Priscilla Elinor Schmidt, Dec. 18, 1948; children—Susan Flora, Frances Louise, Lana Brewer, Landrum Brewer, David Ernest, Harold Manly and Alice Annmarie (twins). B.A., Miss. Coll., 1933, D.Sc. (hon.), 1966; M.S. (fellow 1933-34), U. N.M., 1934; Ph.D., Johns Hopkins, 1937, M.D., 1943. Diplomate: Am. Bd. Obstetrics and Gynecology, N. Am. sect. obstetrics and gynecology Pan Am. Med. Assn. Instr. biology Miss. Coll., 1932-33; biologist U.S. Bur. Fisheries, 1934; instr. biology Johns Hopkins, 1934-37, research fellow, 1937-38; research fellow Nat. Com. Maternal Health, N.Y.C., 1938-43; intern Johns Hopkins Hosp., 1943-44; resident Columbia-Presbyn. Med. Center, N.Y.C., 1947-51; attending obstetrician-gynecologist Columbia-Presbyn. Med. Center, 1951-73, Doctors, Polyclinic and Flower-Fifth Av hosps., N.Y.C., 1974-75; chief obstetrician-gynecologist Gifford Meml. Hosp., Randolph, Vt., 1975-81, Star Clinic, Las Vegas, Nev., 1981-82, Oasis Clinic, Las Vegas, Nev., 1982-85; attending gynecologist-obstetrician Women's Hosp., Las Vegas, Nev., 1981-94, Sunrise Hosp. and Med. Ctr., 1994—; Markle Found. scholar Columbia Coll. Phys. and Surg., 1951-56; assoc. prof. clin. obstetrics-gynecology Coll. Phys. and Surg., Columbia, 1951-73; individual practice, N.Y.C., 1951-75; dir. research N.Y. Fertility Research Found., 1974-75; Anglo-Am. lectr. Royal Coll. Obstetricians and Gynecologists, London, Eng., 1959; Research cons. Office Naval Research, Am. embassy, London, 1951-52. Author: Ovum Humanum, 1960, Your Baby's Sex, Now You Can Choose, 1970, From Conception to Birth, 1971, Choose Your Baby's Sex, 1976, The Rites of Life: The Scientific Evidence of Life Before Birth, 1983, How to Choose Your Baby's Sex, 1984, 89; also numerous articles. Served to maj., M.C. AUS, 1944-46. Editorial bd. Infertility. Recipient Ortho medal and award Am. Soc. Study Fertility, Sterility and Allied Subjects, 1960, Order of the Golden Arrow award Miss. Coll., 1993, Disting. Alumnus award Miss. Coll., 1993. Fellow ACS, AAAS, Am. Coll. Obstetricians and Gynecologists, World Med. Assn., Royal Soc. of Health (London), Royal Soc. Medicine (London); mem. AMA, Am. Soc. Zoologists, Am. Physiol. Soc., Soc. Exptl. Biology and Medicine, Vt. Med. Soc., Soc. U. Gynecologists, N.Y. Obstet. Soc., Harvey Soc., Wisdom Soc., N.Y. State Med. Assn., N.Y. County Nev. Med. Assn., Clarke County Med. Assn., 50 Yr. Club of Miss. Coll., 50 Yr. Club of Johns Hopkins U., 50 Year Club of Vt. State Med. Soc., 25 Yr. Club of Columbia-Presbyn. Med. Ctr., Phi Beta Kappa, Sigma Xi, Omicron Delta Kappa, Gamma Alpha. Spl. rsch. fisheries biology, physiology, human reprodn., fertility and sterility, hemorrhagic disease in newborn infants, sperm biology; discovered, identified male and female producing sperms; achieved gamete intrafallopian transfer, 1978; human in vitro fertilization, 1951; method for chorionic villi sampling, 1979. Home and Office: 2209 Pardee Pl Las Vegas NV 89104-3424

SHETTY, MULKI RADHAKRISHNA, oncologist, consultant; b. Hiriadka, Karnataka, India, July 10, 1940; came to U.S., 1974; s. Mulki Sunderram and Kusumavati Shetty. MBBS, Stanley Med. Coll., Madras, 1964; DTM, U. Liverpool, Eng., 1968; LMCC, Med. Coun., Can., 1975. House surgeon and physician Bombay Hosp., 1965-66; sr. house officer Manor Pk. Hosp., Bristol, Eng., 1966-67, Torbay Hosp., 1967-68, St. Lukes Hosp., Huddersfield, 1969-70; sr. resident Gen. Hosp. Meml. U., New Foundland, 1971-72; intern Ottawa Gen. Hosp., 1972-73; fellow in chemotherapy Ont. Cancer Found., Ottawa, Can., 1973-74; fellow in clin. oncology U. Fla., Gainesville, 1974-75; attending oncologist N.W. Community Hosp., Arlington Heights, Ill., 1975—; cons. N.W. Community Hosp., 1975—. Author: Lung Cancer, 1980, Recent Advances in Chemotherapy, 1985; contbr. numerous articles to profl. jours.; coined new ord calcifectomy; writer lyrics for Love Can Make a Grown Up Cry. Recipient Cert. for Outstanding Svc., Am Cancer Soc., 1982. Fellow Royal Soc. Medicine; mem. Internat. Assn. for Study of Lung Cancer, Chgo. Med. Soc. Hindu. Office: NW Community Hosp 800 W Central Rd Arlington Heights IL 60005-2349

SHEVEL, WILBERT LEE, information systems executive; b. Monessen, Pa., Oct. 26, 1932; s. Wilbert Lee and Lillian Marie (Palomaki) S.; m. Faye Elizabeth Johnston, Aug. 20, 1954; children: Lynn, Laurel, Kathleen, Amy. BSEE, Carnegie-Mellon U., 1954, MSEE, 1955, PhDEE, 1956. With IBM Corp., White Plains, N.Y., 1956-73; v.p. consumer electronics Motorola Corp., Franklin Park, Ill., 1973-74; v.p., gen. mgr. home electronics Rockwell Internat., Schaumburg, Ill., 1974-76; pres., chief exec. officer OMEX Inc., Santa Clara, Calif., 1976-80, Barrington Inc., San Jose, Calif., 1980-82; sr. v.p. corp. ops. Burroughs Corp., Detroit, 1982-84; v.p. systems and tech. Unisys (formerly Systems Devel. Corp.) div. Burroughs Corp., McLean, Va., 1984-88; pres Paramax Def. Systems Can., 1988-92; v.p. corp. info. systems Unisys Corp., 1992-94; mng. dir. EIM, San Diego, 1994—. Patentee in field. Mem. adv. bd. Carnegie Mellon U. Sch. Computer Sci., 1988-95. 1st lt. U.S. Army, 1957. Fellow IEEE. Office: EIM 16776 Bernardo Ctr Dr 110-B San Diego CA 92128

SHEVIN, ROBERT LEWIS, lawyer; b. Miami, Fla., Jan. 19, 1934; s. Aaron and Pauline (Bott) S.; m. Myrna Bressack, Jan. 27, 1957; children: Laura Dawn, Hilary Beth, Harry Alan. BA, U. Fla., 1955; JD magna cum laude, U. Miami, 1957. Bar: Fla. 1957, U.S. Dist. Ct. (so. and mid. dists.) Fla. 1963, U.S. Supreme Ct. 1971, U.S. Ct. Appeals (5th cir.) 1971, U.S. Dist. Ct. (no. dist.) Fla. Ptnr. Shevin, Goodman and Holtzman, 1957-67, Shevin and Shevin, 1967-70; mem. Fla. Ho. of Reps., 1963-65, chmn. interim com. on crime and law enforcement, 1965; mem. Fla. State Senate, 1966-70, chmn. select com. to investigate organized crime and law enforcemnt, 1967, mem. interim study com. on urban affairs, 1968; atty. gen. State of Fla., 1971-79; ptnr. Sparber, Shevin, Rosen, Shapo & Heilbronner, Miami, 1979-87, Stroock & Stroock & Lavan, Miami, 1988—; mem. Fla. Tax Reform Commn., 1968, Fla. Constl. Revision Commn., 1978; city atty. City of Miami Beach, Fla., 1979-80. Chmn. Housing Fin. Authority Dade County, Fla., 1980—, Fla. State Athletic Commn., 1984-87; mem. exec. com. Miami Citizens Against Crime; bd. dirs. Fla. Citizens Against Crime, 1985—; pres. Fla. Senate's Sunshine Adv. Com., 1988; chmn. Ptnrs. for Safe Neighborhoods, 1994; vis. com. U. Miami Law Sch. Recipient Allen Morris award, 1969, Intergovtl. award HUD, 1969, Conservationist of Yr. awards Fla. Wildlife Fedn., 1973, Audubon Soc., 1974, Furtherance of Justice award Fla. Prosecuting Attys. Assn., 1974, Disting. Svc. award Fla. Sheriff's Assn., 1976, Peace award State of Israel, 1977; named one of 10 Most Valuable Mems. Fla. Legislature Capital Press Corps, 1965. Mem. ABA, Internat. Bar Assn., Fla. Bar Assn., Dade County Bar Assn., Am. Trial Lawyers Assn., Am. Judicare Soc., Nat. Assn. Attys. Gen. (chmn. so. region 1981), Iron Arrow, Fla. Blue Key, Sertoma, Phi Delta Phi, Pi Lambda Phi, Phi Kappa Phi, Omicron Delta Kappa. Democrat. Jewish. Home: 7171 SW 56th St Miami FL 33155-5616 Office: Stroock & Stroock & Lavan 33rd Fl 200 S Biscayne Blvd Fl 33 Miami FL 33131-2310

SHEWARD, DAVID JOHN, newspaper editor and critic; b. Wilamatic, Conn., May 7, 1959; s. John Albert and Marjorie Patricia (Berry) S. Student, Carnegie-Mellon U., 1977-79; BA, Temple U., 1982. Actor, dir. stock and regional theatres, Phila., N.Y.C., 1982—; mng. editor, critic Back Stage newspaper, N.Y.C., 1984—. Author: It's A Hit: The Back Stage Book of Broadway's Longest Running Hits 1984 to the Present, 1994; contbr. articles to theatrical publs.; actor in Long Day's Journey into Night, The Crucible, A Midsummer Night's Dream; dir. As Is, Talking Wit, Plaza Suite. Mem. Drama Desk (treas. 1994, nominating com. 1995—), N.Y. Drama

Critics Circle, Outer Critics Circle. Avocations: acting, directing, travel. Office: Back Stage 1515 Broadway New York NY 10036

SHEWARD, RICHARD S., judge; b. Jackson, Ohio, May 21, 1944; s. D.J. and M.A. (Rapp) S.; m. Kathryn L. Wagner, Sept. 26, 1975; children: Carrin E., Alison M. BBA, Ohio U., 1967; JD, Capital U., 1974. Bar: Ohio 1974, U.S. Dist. Ct. (so. dist.) Ohio 1975, U.S. Supreme Ct. 1978. Asst. pros. atty. Franklin County (Ohio), 1974-76; ptnr. Sheward & Weiner, Columbus, Ohio, 1976-87; judge Franklin County Mcpl. Ct., 1987-91, Franklin County Ct. Common Pleas, 1991—, presiding judge, 1993—; instr. real estate law Columbus Tech. Inst., 1977-80. Mem. Upper Arlington (Ohio) Civic Assn.; mem. Franklin County Republican Central Com., 1978-87; bd. dirs. Easter Seal Soc. Columbus, 1990-93. Served with U.S. Army, 1968-71. Decorated Bronze Star, Air medal. Mem. ABA, Ohio Bar Assn., Columbus Bar Assn. (common pleas ct., chmn. criminal law com. 1985-86, 86-87), Franklin County Trial Lawyers Assn. (pres. 1984-85), Am. Arbitration Assn. (labor panel), Franklin County Pros. Atty. Alumni Assn. (chmn. 1979-87). Methodist. Clubs: Buckeye Rep. (pres. 1981), Touchdown, Agonis, Charity Newsies, Am. Inns Ct. (pres. Robert Duncan chpt. 1994-95). Lodge: Masons (32 deg.). Home: 2090 Cheltenham Rd Columbus OH 43220-4343 Office: Franklin County Common Pleas Ct 369 S High St Court Rm 9-C Columbus OH 43215

SHEWMAKER, JACK CLIFFORD, retired retail executive, rancher, consultant; b. Buffalo, Mar. 14, 1938; s. Clifford Verl and Pansy Louise (Brackley) S.; m. Melba June Prosser, Mar. 16, 1958; children: Daniel, Shari Shewmaker Steiger, Emily Shewmaker Loyd. Student, Ga. Tech. Inst.; hon. doctorate, S.W. Baptist U., 1985. Dist. mgr. Wal-Mart Stores, Inc., Bentonville, Ark., 1970-73, v.p. security, 1973-74, v.p. store ops., 1974-76, exec. v.p., 1976-78, pres., chief operating officer, 1978-84, vice-chmn., chief fin. officer, 1984-88, ret., 1988, also bd. dirs.; owner, operator Jac's Ranch, Bentonville, Ark., 1983—; cons. Edgars, South Africa, IMRA, Washington, Lowe's Cos., Inc., North Wilkesboro, N.C., Wal-Mart Stores, Inc., Bentonville, Ark., Big W Discount Stores, Sydney, Australia, ALH Australia & Pacific, Dunlop, Melbourne, Australia, Sonae, Portugal, Big C, Bangkok, Thailand. Contbr. articles to bus. jours. Vice chmn., bd. trustees Drury Coll., Springfield, Mo.; chmn. Students in Free Enterprise, Inc., Springfield, Mo., 1985-88, bd. dirs., 1985—. Named Discount Retailer of Yr., 1981; Retailer of Yr., Mass Market Retailer mag., 1985. Republican. Baptist. Avocations: hunting, fishing, skiing. Address: Jac's Ranch Rte 4 Box 313 10054 E Hwy 72 Bentonville AR 72712

SHEWMAKER, KENNETH EARL, history educator; b. L.A., June 26, 1936; s. James Virgil and Jeanette M. (Greenberg) S.; m. Elisabeth L. Spalteholz, June 12, 1960; children: Richard Glenn, Nancy Jeanette. BS, Concordia Tchrs. Coll., 1960; MA, U. Calif., Berkeley, 1961; PhD, Northwestern U., 1966. Instr. Northwestern U., Evanston, Ill., 1965-66; asst. prof. Coll. William and Mary, Williamsburg, Va., 1966-67; from asst. prof. to assoc. prof. Dartmouth Coll., Hanover, N.H., 1967-78, prof. history, 1978—, acting chair dept. history, 1985-86, chmn. dept. history, 1986-89. Author: Americans and Chinese Communists, 1927-45: A Persuading Encounter, 1971 (Stuart L. Bernath prize 1972); editor: Papers of Daniel Webster, Diplomatic Papers, Vol. 1, 1841-1843, 1983, Vol. 2, 1850-1852, 1987, Daniel Webster, The Completest Man, 1990; contbr. articles to profl. jours. Mem. Am. Hist. Assn., N.H. Hist. Soc., Orgn. Am. Historians, Soc. Historians Am. Fgn. Rels. Lutheran. Avocations: fly fishing, fly tying. Office: Dartmouth College Dept History Hanover NH 03755

SHIBASAKI, YOSHIO, chemistry educator, researcher; b. Gyoda, Japan, Mar. 21, 1934; s. Reiji and Shige (Kobayashi) S.; m. Teiko Ishizuka Shibasaki, Apr. 15, 1967; children: Hideaki, Miki. BS, Saitama U., Japan, 1959; DSc, U. Tokyo, 1980. Tech. official U. Tokyo, Japan, 1960-63, asst., 1963-67; lectr. Saitama U., Urawa, Japan, 1967-70, assoc. prof., 1970-92, prof., 1992—. Inventor: Kobunshi Kagaku, 1964, J. Polymer Science, 1967, 1980. Trustee Saitama U., Internat. Conf. Thermal Analysis & Calorimetry, Japan Soc. Calorimetry & Thermal Analysis. Avocations: appreciation of pictures. Home: 1642 Tsutsumine, Gyoda 361, Japan Office: Saitama U Faculty Sci, 255 Shimo-okubo, Urawa 338, Japan

SHIDELER, ROSS PATRICK, foreign language and comparative literature educator, author, translator, poet; b. Denver, Apr. 12, 1936. B.A., San Francisco State U., 1958; M.A., U. Stockholm, 1963; Ph.D., U. Calif., Berkeley, 1968. Instr. in comparative lit. U. Calif., Berkeley, 1967-68; asst. prof. English Hunter Coll., N.Y.C., 1968-69; asst. prof. Scandinavian lang. and comparative lit. UCLA, 1969-73, assoc. prof., 1973-79, prof., 1979—; chmn. program in comparative lit., 1979-86, 92—. Author: (monograph) Voices Under The Ground: Themes and Images in the Poetry of Gunnar Ekelof, 1973, Per Olov Enquist-A Critical Study, 1984; translator: (play) The Night of the Tribades (Per Olov Enquist), 1977, The Hour of the Lynx, 1990 (Per Olov Enquist), 1990; U.S. assoc. editor Swedish Book Rev., 1984—. Fellow NDFL, 1964; fellow NDEA, 1965; Fulbright-Hays fellow, 1966-67. Mem. MLA (exec. com. divsn. Scandinavian Langs. and Lits. 1993—), Soc. for Advancement Scandinavian Studies (exec. coun. 1985-89), Am. Comparative Lit. Assn., Assn. Depts. and Programs Comparative Lit. (exec. com. 1993-94, 94—). Office: UCLA Dept Comparative Lit Los Angeles CA 90024

SHIDELER, SHIRLEY ANN WILLIAMS, lawyer; b. Mishawaka, Ind., July 9, 1930; d. William Harmon and Lois Wilma (Koch) Williams; 1 dau., Gail Shideler Frye. LLB, Ind. U., 1964. Bar: Ind. 1964. Legal sec. Barnes, Hickam, Pantzer & Boyd, Indpls., 1953-63; assoc. Barnes & Thornburg, 1964-70, ptnr., 1971-92, of counsel, 1993—. Participant fund drives Indpls. Symphony, 1968-81, Indpls. Mus. Art, 1969-79, Marion County Libr. Restoration, 1985-88, Goodwill Industries, 1988-89; bd. dirs. bus. unit gals Indpls. Mus. Art, 1973-80; bd. dirs. Indpls. Legal Aid Soc., 1982-93, Community Hosp. Found., 1986-94, Cen. Newspapers Found. Fellow Am. Coll. Trust and Estate Counsel; mem. ABA, Ind. Bar Assn. (sec. 1975-76, chmn. probate, trust and real property sect. 1982), Nat. Conf. Bar Founds. (trustee 1988-94), Indpls. Bar Assn. (bd. mgrs. 1968-72, v.p. charge affairs 1972), Ind. Bar Found. (bd. mgrs. 1980-92, sec. 1981-82, treas. 1981-86, v.p. 1986-88, pres. 1988-90), Indpls. Bar Found. (bd. mgrs. 1970-82, sec. 1972-77), Estate Planning Coun., Women's Rotary (pres. Indpls. club 1969-71, dir. 1968-79). Home: 2224 Boston Ct Apt C Indianapolis IN 46208-3257 Office: Barnes & Thornburg 1313 Mchts Bank Bldg 11 S Meridian St Indianapolis IN 46204-3506

SHIEBER, STUART MERRILL, natural sciences educator; b. St. Louis, Apr. 27, 1959; s. William and Hortense (Rader) S.; m. Cassia Wyner, June 19, 1993. AB in Applied Math. summa cum laude, Harvard U., 1981; PhD in Computer Sci., Stanford U., 1989. Rsch. fellow Ctr. for Study of Lang. and Info., Stanford U., 1983-89; rsch. computer scientist Artificial Intelligence Ctr., SRI Internat., 1981-89; asst. prof. computer sci. Harvard U., Cambridge, Mass., 1989-93, John L. Loeb assoc. prof. natural scis., 1993—; founder Cartesian Products, Inc., 1991; vis. prof. U. Calif., Santa Cruz, summer 1991; founder, organizer The Computation and Lang. E-Print Archive. Author: An Introduction to Unification-Based Approaches to Grammar, 1986, Spanish transl., 1989, French transl., 1990; Constraint-Based Grammar Formalisms, 1992; (with Fernando C.N. Pereira) Prolog and Natural-Language Analysis, 1987, Italian transl., 1992; editor: (with Peter Sells and Thomas Wasow) Foundational Issues in Natural Language Processing, 1991; contbr. numerous articles to profl. jours.; mem. editl. bd. Computational Linguistics, 1990-93, Jour. Artificial Intelligence Rsch., 1993—. Named Presdl. Young Investigator, 1991-93; Presdl. Faculty fellow, 1993—. Mem. Assn. Computational Linguistics (mem. exec. com. 1993—), Phi Beta Kappa. Office: Harvard Univ Cambridge MA 02138

SHIEKMAN, LAURENCE ZEID, lawyer; b. Phila., Feb. 13, 1947; s. Morton and Roberta (Zeid) S.; m. Marjorie Kershbaum, Dec. 25, 1970; children: Wendy K., Thomas K. BS in Econs., U. Pa., 1968, JD, 1971. Bar: Pa. 1971. Law clk. to Hon. A. Leon Higginbotham, Jr. U.S. Dist. Ct. (ea. dist.) Pa., 1971-73; asst. prof. Fla. State U. Coll. Law, Tallahassee, 1973-75; assoc. Pepper, Hamilton & Scheetz, Phila., 1975-78, ptnr., 1978—. Chmn. 20th Yr. reunion com. U. Pa. Law Sch., Phila., 1995. Mem. ABA, Pa. Bar Assn., Phila. Bar Assn. Office: Pepper Hamilton & Scheetz 3000 Two Logan Sq 18th & Arch Sts Philadelphia PA 19103-2799

SHIELDS, ALLAN EDWIN, writer, photographer, retired educator; b. Columbus, Ohio, July 3, 1919; s. Richard Edwin and Eloessa (Smith) S.; m. Bernice Clark, Aug. 2, 1941; children—Allan Oakley, Richard Minter, Larry Michael, Catherine Marie. A.B., U. Calif.-Berkeley, 1941; M.A., U. So. Calif., 1947, Ph.D., 1951. Prof. philosophy San Diego State U., 1949-68, 70-78; emeritus prof. San Diego State Coll., 1978—; dean Coll. Humanities and Fine Arts U. No. Iowa, 1968-70; owner, pub. Jerseydale Ranch Press, 1992—; seasonal ranger naturalist Nat. Park Service, Yosemite Nat. Park, 1955-60; freelance writer, photographer, 1978—; violinist-violist, frequent recitalist; mem., sometime concertmaster Merced Symphony Orch., Calif., 1979-91; founder, with wife, Jerseydale Ranch Press, 1992. Author: Guide to Tuolumne Meadows Trails, 1960, rev. edit., 1973, (with Herbert Searles) A Bibliography of the Works of F.C.S. Schiller, 1969, (with Richard Shields) Tuolumne Profile: Yosemite, 1967, (novella) The Tragedy of Tenaya, 1974, new version 1992, A Bibliography of Bibliographies in Aesthetics, 1974, (poetry) A Horse in the House, 1985, Mariposa Now and Then, 1993, Tuffy, An Angel Hid in a Cloud, 1994, What Animals Taught Me, 1995, (with Bernice Shields) Into the Valley: A Brief History of Jerseydale Ranch, 1995, also numerous poems and articles; editor: A Yosemite Adventure in 1863, 1992, Wild Bill Neely and the Pagan Brothers' Golden Goat Winery, 1993, The Song of Sonora, 1993, O.S.S.: One Sad Sack--Pvt. Neely Disciplines the Military, 1994, A Yosemite Naturalist's Odyssey, 1994, Wilderness Treks by Foot, Chanoe, and Adobe Rocket, and Father's Far-Flung Fables, 1995; pub. various profl. jours. Bd. dirs. San Diego Symphony. Served with USAAF, 1942-45. Mudd fellow in philosophy U. So. Calif., 1948-49. Mem. Am. Soc. for Aesthetics (trustee), Phi Beta Kappa, Phi Kappa Phi, Phi Mu Alpha Sinfonia (hon.). Home: 6506 Jerseydale Rd Mariposa CA 95338-9638 *My greatest satisfactions have come with tasks completed to the best of my abilities. Whether raising children, building a building, nurturing a marriage, learning the violin, or writing, all have inherent standards demanding recognition. Though there is always joy in the process of doing, joy can be transformed into satisfaction only in completion evaluated against the standards of worth for that kind of undertaking.*

SHIELDS, BROOKE CHRISTA CAMILLE, actress, model; b. N.Y.C., May 31, 1965; d. Francis A. and Teri (Schmon) S. BA, Princeton U., 1987. Model for Ivory Soap commls. starting in 1966, later for Calvin Klein jeans and Colgate toothpaste commls.; actress: (films) Alice, Sweet Alice, 1975, Pretty Baby, 1977, King of the Gypsies, 1978, Wanda Nevada, 1978, Just You and Me Kid, 1978, Blue Lagoon, 1979, Endless Love, 1980, Sahara, 1983, Backstreet Strays, 1989, Brenda Starr, 1992, Seventh Floor, 1993, Running Wild, 1993, Freaked, 1993; (TV movies) The Prince of Central Park, 1977, After the Fall, Wet Gold, I Can Make You Love Me: The Stalking of Laura Black, 1993, Nothing Lasts Forever, 1995, (TV shows) The Tonight Show, Bob Hope spls., The Diamond Trap, 1988, Friends, 1996; appeared on Broadway in Grease, 1994-95. Office: Christa Inc Ste 630 2300 West Sahara Box 18 Las Vegas NV 89102

SHIELDS, CAROL ANN, writer, educator; b. Oak Park, Ill., June 2, 1935; came to Can., 1957, naturalized, 1974; d. Robert Elmer and Inez Adelle (Sellgren) Warner; m. Donald Hugh Shields, July 20, 1957; children: John, Anne, Catherine, Margaret, Sara. B.A., Hanover Coll., 1957; MA, U. Ottawa, Ont., Can., 1975. Editl. asst. Can. Slavonic Papers, Ottawa, 1972-74; lectr. U. Ottawa, 1976-77, U. B.C., Vancouver, Can., 1978-80; prof. U. Man., Winnipeg, Can., 1980—. Author: (poems) Others, 1972, Intersect, 1974, Coming to Canada, 1991; (novels) Small Ceremonies, 1976, The Box Garden, 1977, Happenstance, 1980, A Fairly Conventional Women, 1982; Various Miracles, 1985, Swann: A Mystery, 1987, The Orange Fish, 1989, The Republic of Love, 1992, The Stone Diaries, 1993 (Nat. Book Critics Circle award for fiction 1994, Pulitzer Prize for fiction 1995); (play) Women Waiting, 1983, Departures and Arrivals, 1984, Thirteen Hands, 1993, (with Catherine Shields) Fashion Power Guilt. Grantee Can. Council, 1973, 76, 78, 86, Man. Arts Council, 1984, 85; recipient prize CBC, 1983, 84, Nat. Mag. award, 1985, Arthur Ellis award, 1987, Can. Book Sellers'award 1994, Manitoba Book of the Yr., 1994, Marian Engel award Writers' Devel. Trust, 1990, Gov. Gen.'s award Can. Coun., 1993. Mem. PEN, Writers Union Can., Writers Guild Man., Jane Austen Soc., N.Am. Can. Coun. Bd. Quaker. Home: 701 237 Wellington Crescent, Winnipeg, MB Canada R3M 0A1 Office: care Bella Pomer Agency Inc, 22 Shallmar Blvd Penthouse 2, Toronto, ON Canada M5N 2Z8

SHIELDS, H. RICHARD, tax consultant,business executive; m. Frances Augenstein; 1 dau., Eileen. A.B., Bklyn. Coll.; LL.B., J.D., NYU; M.B.A., Harvard U. Bar: N.Y. bar 1940. Corp. practice law, 1940-60; sec., treas. Forbes Realty Corp., 1960-70; exec. v.p. Forbes Industries, Ltd., 1965-70; exec. v.p. Am. Diversified Industries Corp., 1964-66, pres., chmn. bd., 1966-76; exec. v.p. Daily Mirror, Sunday Mirror, N.Y.C.; chmn., chief exec. officer, dir. TTC Industries (also subs. Armstrong Glass Mfg. Corp.), Erwin, Tenn., 1970-76; pres., dir. Euro Industries, Ltd.; and dir.; pres., chief exec. officer, dir. Dairene Industries, Ltd., 1971-80; tax cons. Regal Cons., Ltd., Great Neck, N.Y., 1974-85; dir. Blue Ribbon Mktg. Corp.; govt. appeal agt. U.S. Selective Service; mem. N.Y. State Commn. on Human Rights; referee, arbitrator Civil Ct., N.Y.C. Served to maj. USAAF, 1942-46, CBI. Decorated Commendation medal, Legion of Merit, China War Meml. medal. Mem. Am. Inst. Mgmt., Nat. Assn. Accts., Nat. Tax Assn. (com. fed. taxation), Tax Inst. Am., Tax Execs. Inst., Nat. Assn. Corp. Dirs., Assn. Bar City N.Y. (legis. com.). Club: Harvard.

SHIELDS, JAMES JOSEPH, JR., educational administrator, educator, author; b. Phila., Feb. 11, 1935; s. James Joseph and Lena Josephine (Dyer) S. (dec.). BS in Polit. Sci., Saint Joseph's U., 1956; EdM, Temple U., 1959; EdD, Columbia U., 1963. Asst. to dir., internat. studies Tchrs. Coll., Columbia U., N.Y.C., 1961; rechr., Tchrs. for East Africa Program Tchrs. Coll., Columbia U., N.Y.C. and Kampala, 1961-62; asst. prof. history and philosophy of edn. SUNY, New Paltz, 1962-64; asst. prof. comparative and politics of edn. CUNY, 1964-69; assoc. prof. comparative and politics of edn. CUNY, N.Y.C., 1969-75, prof. comparative and politics of edn., 1975—, head, Sch. Adminstrn. Program, 1983-85, chair, dept. social and psychol. founds., 1988-90; dir. Japan Initiative, N.Y.C., 1986—; cons. Inst. for Ednl. Devel., N.Y.C., 1968-71, Equitable Life Ins. Co., N.Y.C., 1961, N.Y.C. Bd. Edn. Dist. 4, 1996; vis. rsch. prof. Tokyo Met. U., 1986—; vis. prof. Tchrs. Coll., Columbia U., 1965-67, 93-95; mem. evaluation bd. Nat. Coun. on Accreditation of Tchr. Edn., Washington, 1970-75; assoc. Columbia U., Univ. Seminar on Modern Japan, N.Y.C., 1987—, chair, 1990-91. Author: Education in Community Development: Its Function in Technical Assistance, 1967; editor: Problems and Prospects in International Education, 1968, Foundations of Education: Dissenting Views, 1974, Japanese Schooling: Patterns of Socialization Equality and Political Control, 1989 (nominated for Books on Japan award), rev. edit. 1993; author numerous book chpts., monographs and book reviews; contbr. numerous articles to profl. jours. Mem. Pub. Edn. Assn. Task Force on a Reconstructed Ednl. Sys., N.Y.C., 1977-78, Pub. Edn. Assn. Task Force on Tchr. Selection, N.Y.C., 1981; mem. N.Y. Urban Coalition, 1982-84, Alumni Coun., Tchrs. Coll. Columbia U., 1993—. With USAR, 1959-59. Grantee SUNY Rsch. Found., 1964, N.Y. State Edn. Dept., 1969-72, Rsch. Found. CUNY, 1980-81, Japan-U.S. Friendship Commn., 1986-89, The City Coll., Provost, 1988-89, 89-90; Fulbright travel grantee, 1964, 1964, Japan Found. Ctr. for Global Partnership, 1994, The U.S.-Japan Found., 1994-96; recipient Wyo. Gov.'s Youth Coun. award, 1974, Higher Edn. award Holy Family Coll., Phila., 1990, Ann. Gertrude Langsam Ednl. Reconstrn. award Adelphi U., 1992; postdoctoral fellow Yale U., New Haven, 1967-68. Hon. fellow Comparative and Internat. Edn. Soc. (N.E. region conf. coord. 1984, bd. dirs. 1992-95); mem. Am. Ednl. Studies Assn. (pres. 1973-74, exec. coun. 1970-75), Carnegie Coun. on Ethics and Internat. Affairs, Japan Soc. of N.Y., Internat. House of Japan, Soc. for Ednl. Reconstrn. (exec. com. 1973—), Am. Ednl. Rsch. Assn. Avocations: collecting Long Island painters (1850-1950), travel, gardening. Home: 562 W End Ave Apt 4D New York NY 10024-2718 Office: CUNY 138th St and Convent Ave New York NY 10031

SHIELDS, JERRY ALLEN, ophthalmologist, educator; b. Pride Station, Ky., June 9, 1937; s. Fendell Harris and Beulah Etta (Williams) S.; m. Carol Lally, Oct. 26, 1985; children: Jerry, Patrick, William, Margaret, John. BA, Murray State U., 1960; MD, U. Mich., 1964. Diplomate Am. Bd. Ophtalmology. Intern Denver Gen. Hosp., 1964-65; resident in ophthalmology Wills Eye Hosp., Phila., 1967-70, fellowship in retina, 1970, fellowship in pathology, 1971, dir. ocular oncology svc., 1973—; prof. ophthalmology Thomas Jefferson U. Hosp., Phila., 1980—. Author: Diagnosis and Management of Intraocular Tumors, 1983, Diagnosis and Management of Orbital Tumors, 1989, Intraocular Tumors: A Text and Atlas, 1991; contbr. articles to jours., chpts. to textbooks. Lt. MC, USN, 1965-67, Vietnam. Recipient Golden Apple award Sr. Residents Wills Eye Hosp., 1990; co-recipient award Brady Cancer Rsch. Inst., 1986. Mem. AMA, Am. Acad. Ophthalmology, Am. Assn. Rsch. Ophthalmology, Phila. Ophthalmic Club, Pa. Acad. Ophthalmology and Otolaryngology. Home: 617 Williamson Rd Bryn Mawr PA 19010-1932 Office: Wills Eye Hosp Dept Oncology 9th & Walnut Sts Philadelphia PA 19107*

SHIELDS, JOHN CHARLES, American studies and African American studies and literature educator; b. Phoenix, Oct. 29, 1944; s. Granville Blaine and Elizabeth Merle (Hartgraves) S. BA, U. Tenn., Knoxville, 1967, MA in Coll. Teaching, 1969, PhD, 1978; EdS, George Peabody Coll., 1975. Tchr. English Sevier County High Sch., Sevierville, Tenn., 1967-68; head dept. English Battle Ground Acad., Franklin, Tenn., 1969-71; dir. academics Brentwood Acad., Nashville, 1971-73, Columbia (Tenn.) Mil. Acad., 1973-74; instr. U. Tenn., Knoxville, 1978-79; asst. prof. Ill. State U., Normal, 1979-86, assoc. prof. English, 1986-93, prof. English, 1993—; cons. Ency. Britannica, Oxford Companion to African Am. Lit., Norton Anthology African American Literature, others; project dir. conf. on Phillis Wheatley NEH, 1983-85; faculty advisor Native Am. Student Soc. Ill. State U., 1990—. Assoc. editor Style, DeKalb, Ill., 1988-90, guest editor, 1990—; editor: The Collected Works of Phillis Wheatley, 1988, paperback, 1989; adv. editor, contbr. Oxford Companion to African Am. Lit., 1993—, Am. Nat. Biography, 20 vols., 1994—; contbr. New Dictionary of Nat. Biography, Great Britain, 1995—; contbr. articles to lit. jours. and chpts. to books; manuscript reviewer various presses and jours. Spokesperson for Native Am. citizens, 1990—. Ford Found. fellow, 1968-69, Soc. for Humanities fellow Cornell U., 1984-85, NEH fellow, 1983, 84, 89, 93, John. C. Hodges Teaching Excellence award, 1969. Mem. MLA, Internat. Soc. for 18th-Century Studies, Am. Studies Assn., Melville Soc., Coll. Lang. Assn., Phi Mu Alpha, Alpha Phi Omega, Sigma Nu. Unitarian. Avocations: piano, singing, Native American culture, archaeology, rare book collecting. Home: 1566D Hunt Dr Normal IL 61761-2109 Office: Ill State Univ Normal IL 61761

SHIELDS, JOHN JOSEPH, computer manufacturing executive; b. Worcester, Mass., Aug. 31, 1938; s. John Joseph Jr. and Pauline Shields; m. Judith A. Morse, Sept. 1980; 6 children. Student, Worcester Poly. Inst., hon. degree, 1989; grad. mgmt. devel. progam, Harvard U. Field svc. engr. to v.p. field svc. tng. Digital Equipment Corp., Maynard and Stow, Mass., 1961-79, v.p. customer svcs., 1979-81, group v.p. sales, svcs., mktg. and internat., 1981-86; sr. v.p. Digital Equipment Corp., Stow, Mass., 1986—; bd. dirs. Ionics, Inc., Watertown, Mass. Trustee, chmn. acad. affairs com. Clark U., Worcester, Mass. Roman Catholic. *

SHIELDS, LAWRENCE THORNTON, orthopedic surgeon, educator; b. Boston, Oct. 2, 1935; s. George Leo and Catherine Elizabeth (Thornton) S.; AB, Harvard U., 1957; MD, Johns Hopkins U., 1961; m. Karen S. Kraus, Sept. 21, 1968; children: Elizabeth Coulter, Laura Thornton, Sarah Daly, Michael Lawrence. Intern, Barnes Hosp., Washington U., St. Louis, 1961-62, resident, 1962-63; resident orthopedic surgeon Children's Hosp. Med. Ctr., Boston, 1966-67, Mass. Gen. Hosp., Boston, 1967-68, Peter Bent Brigham, Robert Breck Brigham hosps., Boston, 1968-69; resident orthopedic surgeon Harvard Med. Sch., Boston, 1965-69, instr., 1969—; orthopedic surgeon Peter Bent Brigham & Women's Hosp., Children's hosps., 1969—; orthopedic surgeon Waltham (Mass.) -Weston Hosp. and Med. Ctr., 1969—, also chief orthopedic surgery, pres. med. staff; mem. Waltham-Weston Orthopedic Assos.; proprietor Boston Athenaeum; mem. staffs Hahnemann Hosp., Boston, Newton-Wellesley (Mass.) hosps.; cons. orthopedic surgeon VA Hosp., Boston; mem. faculty Harvard Med. Sch.; vis. scholar Cambridge U., 1987; hon. prof. New Eng. Coll, Henniker, N.H. and Sussex, Eng., 1995; bd. dirs. Wal-West Health Systems, 1986—; pres. Massachusetts Bay Investment Trust; dir. Waltham Investment Group. Bd. dirs. Mass. Acad. Emergency Med. Technicians, Waltham Boys' Club; bd. of overseers Boston Lyric Opera, 1993—; trustee, exec. com. Waltham-Weston Hosp. and Med. Ctr. Lt. M.C., USNR, 1963-65. Diplomate Am. Bd. Orthopedic Surgery. Fellow ACS, Am. Acad. Orthopedic Surgeons, Mass. Hist. Soc. Libr., Mass. Hist. Soc.; mem. N.Y. Acad. Scis., Royal Soc. Medicine, Mass. Orthopaedic Assn. (bd. dirs., sec. 1986—), New Eng. Orthopaedic Club, Boston Orthopedic Club, Charles River Dist. (treas., exec. com., pres. 1982-83) Mass. (councillor; v.p. 1982-83) med. socs., R. Austen Freeman Soc. (v.p.), Thomas B. Quigley Sports Medicine Soc., Titanic Hist. Soc., Boston Opera Assns. (bd. dirs.), Harvard Mus. Assn., Thoreau Soc., Emerson Soc., Trollope Soc. (founding mem., bd. dirs., London), Handel and Hayden Soc. (bd. overseers), Waltham Hist. Soc., St. Botolph Club (Boston), Les Amis d'Escoffier Soc., Confrerie de La Chaine des Rotisseurs (elected 1996), Harvard Club, Algonquin Club of Boston (bd. dirs., pres. 1990—), St. Crispin's Soc. Boston (founding mem., pres. 1991—), English Speaking Union (bd. dirs.), Union Club of Boston, St. Botolph Club of Boston, Boston Lyric Opera (bd. overseers 1993), Rotary, Pi Eta (Harvard). Contbr. articles to med. jours. Home: 9 Beverly Rd Newton MA 02161-1112 Office: 721 Huntington Ave Boston MA 02115-6010 Also: 20 Hope Ave Ste 314 Waltham MA 02154-2717

SHIELDS, RANA COLLEEN, special education educator; b. Midland, Tex., Oct. 2, 1951; d. Robert Campbell and Edith Sue (Alexander) S.; m. Michael Leggett; children: Daniel Robert Tilly, Casey Michelle Leggett; 1 stepchild, Laurie Ayn Leggett. B of Journalism, U. Tex., 1974; JD magna cum laude, South Tex. U., 1984; MEd in Spl. Edn., S.W. Tex. State U., 1993. Bar: Tex., 1985; cert. generic spl. edn., reading, Tex. City editor Huntsville (Tex.) Item, 1976-78; asst. county atty. Travis County Atty.'s Office, Austin, Tex., 1986-87; tchr. spl. edn. Liberty Hill (Tex.) H.S., 1990-91, Tex. Sch. for the Blind, Austin, 1991-93; grad. rsch. asst. in spl. edn. U. Tex., Austin, spring 1994, tchg. asst. spl. edn., 1995-96. Asst. casenotes editor: South Tex. Law Jour., 1983. Recipient 1st Pl. Spot News Photography award AP Mng. Editors, 1978, Am. Jurisprudence awards, 1979, 82, 83; named Outstanding Sophomore Journalist, Women in Comm., 1971; Univ. fellow, 1996—. Mem. Assn. Tex. Profl. Educators, Kappa Delta Pi, Phi Kappa Phi.

SHIELDS, ROBERT EMMET, merchant banker, lawyer; b. Ridley Park, Pa., May 18, 1942; s. Joseph Leonard and Kathryn J. (Walsh) S.; m. Mary Katherine Reid, July 22, 1967; children: Christopher D., David R., Kevin M., Kathleen. AB, Coll. Holy Cross, 1964; LLB cum laude, NYU, 1967. Bar: Pa. bar 1968. Mem. faculty Boalt Hall Sch. Law U. Calif., Berkeley, 1967-68; assoc. Drinker Biddle & Reath, Phila., 1968-74; ptnr. Drinker Biddle & Reath, 1974-94, mng. ptnr., 1979-83, 85-94, head corp. and securities group, 1983-93, CFO, 1993-94; mng. dir., ptnr. Questor Gen. Ptnr., L.P., 1995—; mng. dir. Questor Ptnrs. Fund, L.P., 1995—; sec. Wallquest Inc. Author: (with Eliot B. Thomas) Federal Securities Act Handbook, 4th edit, 1977; (with Robert H. Strouse) Securities Practice Handbook, 1987. Mem. ABA, Am. Law Inst., Pa. Bar Assn., Phila. Bar Assn. Club: Union League (Phila.). Home: 206 Atlee Rd Wayne PA 19087-3836 Office: Questor Mgmt Co Ste 530 4000 Town Center Southfield MI 48075 Also: 1100 Phila Nat Bank Bldg 1345 Chestnut St Philadelphia PA 19107

SHIELDS, THOMAS CHARLES, lawyer; b. Evergreen Park, Ill., Apr. 26, 1941; s. Thomas James and Adelaide (McElligott) S.; m. Nicoline M. Murphy, Sept. 14, 1974; children: Thomas James II, Nicoline Margaret, Suzanne Adelaide, Kerry Anne. AB, Georgetown U., 1963; JD cum laude, Northwestern U., 1966. Bar: Ill. 1966, U.S. Dist. Ct. (no. dist.) Ill. 1966, U.S. Ct. Appeals (7th cir.) 1966, U.S. Tax Ct. 1968, U.S. Supreme Ct. 1977. Assoc. Hopkins & Sutter, Chgo., 1966-73; ptnr. Hopkins & Sutter, 1973-93; ptnr., head health care law group Bell, Boyd & Lloyd, Chgo., 1994—; gen. counsel Cath. Health Assn. U.S., St. Louis, 1994—; mem. adv. bd. Health Law Inst. Loyola U. Sch. Law, Chgo., 1984-89, Health Law Inst. DePaul U. Sch. Law, Chgo., 1985—; lectr. Ill. Inst. Continuing Legal Edn., 1973; adv. com. Cath. Hosp. Assn., 1974. Contbr. articles to profl. pubs., chpt. to book; mng. editor Northwestern Law Rev., 1965-66. Bd. dirs. Cancer Rsch. Found., Chgo., 1987—, Brother Louie and Fannie Roncoli Found., 1994—, Chgo. Zool. Soc., Cath. Charities Chgo. Mem. Am. Acad. Healthcare Attys. (bd. dirs. 1983-91, pres. 1989-90), Am. Soc. Law and Medicine, Am. Hosp. Assn. (tax adv. group 1987-90), Ill. Bar Assn., Ill. Assn. Healthcare Attys. (bd. dirs. 1983-89, pres. 1987-88), Chgo. Bar Assn., Univ. Club, Exec. Club

Chgo., Law Club Chgo., Mid-Am. Club Chgo., Order of Coif. Avocations: skiing, bicycling, golf, tennis. Office: Bell Boyd & Lloyd 3 First Nat Plz Ste 3200 Chicago IL 60602

SHIELDS, THOMAS WILLIAM, surgeon, educator; b. Ambridge, Pa., Aug. 17, 1922; s. John Jr. and Elizabeth (Flanagan) S.; m. Dorothea Ann Thomas, June 12, 1948; children: Thomas William, John Leland, Carol Ann. BA, Kenyon Coll., 1943, DSc (hon.), 1978; MD, Temple U., 1947. Resident surgery Northwestern U. Med. Sch., Chgo., 1949-55; prof. surgery Northwestern U. Med. Sch., 1968-92, prof. Emeritus of surgery, 1992—; practice medicine specializing in surgery Chgo., 1956—; chief of surgery VA Lakeside Hosp., Chgo., 1968-87; chief thoracic surgery VA Lakeside Med. Ctr., Chgo., 1987-90. Editor: General Thoracic Surgery, 1972, 4th edit., 1994, Bronchial Carcinoma, 1974, Mediastinal Surgery, 1991; assoc. editor Surgery, Gynecology and Obstetrics, Annals of Thoracic Surgery, 1993—; mem. editorial bd. Annals of Thoracic Surgery, Lung Cancer; contbr. articles to profl. jours. Served with U.S. Army, 1951-53. Mem. ACS, AMA, Am. Assn. for Thoracic Surgery, Soc. Thoracic Surgery, Central, Western Surg. Assns., Société Internationale de Chirurgie, Soc. for Surgery of Alimentary Tract, Internat. Assn. for Study Lung Cancer, Pan Pacific Surg. Assn., Phi Beta Kappa, Sigma Xi, Alpha Omega Alpha. Home: 1721 Jenks St Evanston IL 60201-1528 Office: 250 E Superior St Ste 201 Chicago IL 60611-2914

SHIELY, JOHN STEPHEN, company executive, lawyer; b. St. Paul, June 19, 1952; s. Vincent Robert and Mary Elizabeth (Hope) S.; m. Helen Jane Pauly, Aug. 29, 1981; children: Michael, Erin, Megan. BBA, U. Notre Dame, 1974; JD, Marquette U., 1977; M of Mgmt., Northwestern U., 1990. With Arthur Andersen & Co., Milw., 1977-79, Hughes Hubbard & Reed, Milw., 1979-83, Allen-Bradley Co., Milw., 1983-86, Rockwell Internat. Corp., Milw., 1985-86; with Briggs & Stratton Corp., Milw., 1986—, gen. counsel, 1986-90, v.p., gen. counsel, 1990-91, exec. v.p. adminstrn., 1991-94, pres., COO, 1994—. Dir., St. Charles, Inc., Milw., 1978—, Children's Hosp. of Wis., Inc., 1992—. Mem. Am. Corp. Counsel Assn. (past pres., bd. govs., Wis. chpt. 1984-94), Assn. for Corp. Growth (past pres., bd. dirs. Wis. chpt. 1988—). Office: Briggs & Stratton Corp PO Box 702 Milwaukee WI 53201-0702

SHIENTAG, FLORENCE PERLOW, lawyer; b. N.Y.C.; d. David and Ester (Germane) Perlow; m. Bernard L. Shientag, June 8, 1938. BS, NYU, 1940, LLB, 1933, JD, 1940. Bar: Fla. 1976, N.Y. Law aide Thomas E. Dewey, 1937; law sec. Mayor La Guardia, 1939-42; justice Domestic Relations Ct., 1941-42; mem. Tchrs. Retirement Bd., N.Y.C., 1942-46; asst. U.S. atty. So. dist. N.Y., 1943-53; cir. ct. mediator Fla. Supreme Ct., 1992; pvt. practice N.Y.C., 1994—, Palm Beach, Fla., 1994—; lectr. on internat. divorce; mem. Nat. Commn. on Wiretapping and Electronic Surveillance, 1973—, Task Force on Women in Cts., 1985-86; circuit ct. mediator Fla. Supreme Ct., 1992. Contbr. articles to profl. jours. Candidate N.Y. State Senate, 1954; bd. dirs. UN Devel. Corp., 1972-95, Franklin and Eleanor Roosevelt Inst., 1985—; bd. dirs., assoc. treas. YM and YWHA; hon. commr. commerce, N.Y.C. Mem. ABA, Fed. Bar Assn. (exec. com.), Internat. Bar Assn., N.Y. Women's Bar Assn. (pres., Life Time Achievement award 1994), N.Y. State Bar Assn., N.Y.C. Bar Assn. (chmn. law and art sect.), N.Y. County LAwyers Assn. (dir.), Nat. Assn. Women LAwyers (sec.). Home: 737 Park Ave New York NY 10021-4256 *Success is a product of self respect and hard work at what you do well.*

SHIER, GLORIA BULAN, mathematics educator; b. The Philippines, Apr. 20, 1935; came to U.S., 1966.; d. Melecio Cauilan and Florentina (Cumagun) Bulan; m. Wayne Thomas Shier, May 31, 1969; children: John Thomas, Marie Teresita, Anna Christina. BS, U. Santo Tomas, Manila, Philippines, 1956; MA, U. Ill., 1968; PhD, U. Minn., 1986. Tchr. Cagayan (Philippines) Valley Coll., 1956-58, St. Paul Coll., Manila, 1959-62, Manila Div. City Schs., 1958-64; asst. prof. U. of East, Manila, 1961-66; rsch. asst. U. Ill., Urbana, 1968-69; instr. Miramar Community Coll., San Diego, 1974-75, Mesa Community Coll., San Diego, 1975-80, Lakewood Community Coll., St. Paul, 1984, U. Minn., Mpls., 1986-87, North Hennepin Community Coll., Brooklyn Park, Minn., 1987—; cons. PWS Kent Pub. Co., Boston, 1989—. Chairperson Filipino Am. Edn. Assn., San Diego, 1978-79. Fulbright scholar U.S. State Dept., U. Ill., 1966-70; fellow Nat. Sci. Found., Oberlin Coll., 1967; recipient Excellence in Teaching award UN Ednl. Scientific Cultural Organ., U. Philippines, 1960-62, Cert. Commendation award The Gov. of Minn., 1990, Outstanding Filipino in the Midwest Edn. Cat. award 1992, Cavite Assn. Mem. Am. Math. Soc., Math. Assn. Am., Phi Kappa Phi, Sigma Xi Rsch. Honor Soc., Nat. Coun. Tchrs. Math., Am. Math. Assn. for Two Yr. Colleges, Internat. Group for Psychology of Math. Edn., Minn. Coun. of Tchrs. Math., Minn. Math. Assn. of Two Yr. Colleges, Fil-Minnesotan Assn (bd.dirs. 1991—), Am. Statistical Assn. Roman Catholic. Avocation: piano. Home: 1715 Heritage Ln New Brighton MN 55112-7109

SHIER, SHELLEY M., production company executive; b. Toronto, Mar. 15, 1957; d. Harry Shier and Rosaline (Cutler) Sonshine; m. Hank O'Neal, May 14, 1985. Student, H.B. Studio, N.Y.C., 1975-76, Stella Adler Conservatory, N.Y.C., 1976-80. Company mem., actor Soho Artists Theater, N.Y.C., 1976-81; casting dir. Lawrence Price Prodns., N.Y.C., 1981-82; pres. Hoss, Inc., N.Y.C., 1983—; v.p. Chiaroscuro Records, N.Y.C., 1987—; cons. Peter Martin Assocs., N.Y.C., 1983, Kloster Cruise Ltd., Miami, Fla., 1983—, Floating Jazz Festival, Big Bands At Sea, Rhythm & Blues Cruise, Dixieland At Sea, Oslo (Norway) Jazz Festival, 1986—, New Sch. for Social Rsch., N.Y.C., 1989—, Beacons In Jazz Awards Ceremony, A Tribute to the Music of Bob Wills and The Texas Playboys, Mardi Gras at Sea. Talent acquisition agt. Save the Children, N.Y.C., 1986, Tomorrow's Children, N.Y.C., 1990, Royal Caribbean Cruise Ltd., Miami, 1994—, Ultimate Caribbean Jazz Spectacular, Country Music Festival in the Caribbean, CUNARD N.Y.C., 1994—, Barcelona Olympics, NBC, 1992, others. Avocations: karate, photography, riding, fishing, weightlifting. Office: HOSS Inc 830 Broadway New York NY 10003-4827

SHIFF, ALAN HOWARD WILLIAM, judge; b. New Haven, June 2, 1934; s. Philip Robert and Harriet (Panikoff) S.; children: Daniel Stuart, Andrew Reuben; m. Carol Sweeterman Brumbaugh. BA, Yale U., 1957; LLB, U. Va., 1960. Bar: Conn. 1960, U.S. Dist. Ct. Conn. 1960, U.S. Ct. Appeals (2d cir.) 1969. Ptnr. Shiff, Shiff and Schancupp, New Haven, 1960-81; judge U.S. Bankruptcy Ct., Dist. Conn., Bridgeport, 1981—, chief judge, 1996—; mem. bankruptcy apppellate panel svc., 1996—; spl. counsel Conn. Gen. Assembly Energy and Pub. Utilities Com., 1979-80; lectr. to various bar assns.Mem. Conn. Bar Assn., Administrv. office of U.S. Cts. (adv. com. of bankruptcy judges 1991—, task force official on forms 1984-88, elected to serve 2nd cir. gov. Nat. Conf. Bankruptcy Judges, 1995—). Office: US Bankruptcy Court 915 Lafayette Blvd Bridgeport CT 06604-4706

SHIFFER, JAMES DAVID, utility executive; b. San Diego, Mar. 24, 1938; s. Kenneth Frederick and Thelma Lucille (Good) S.; m. Margaret Edith Rightmyer, Sept. 5, 1959 (div. July 1986); children: James II, Elizabeth Gonzales, Russell; m. Esther Zamora, Sept. 13, 1986; stepchildren: Bryan Boots, Jeremy Hellier, Marisol Boots. BS ChemE, Stanford U., 1960, MS ChemE, 1961. Registered profl. engr., Calif. Nuclear engr. Pacific Gas & Electric Co., Humboldt Bay Power Plant, Eureka, Calif., 1961-71; tech. mgr. Pacific Gas & Electric Co., Diablo Canyon Power Plant, Avila Beach, Calif., 1971-80; mgr. nuclear ops. Pacific Gas & Electric Co., San Francisco, 1980-84, v.p. nuclear power generation, 1984-90, sr. v.p., gen. mgr. nuclear power generation bus. unit, 1990-91; exec. v.p. Pacific Gas & Electric, San Francisco, 1991—; pres., CEO PG&E Enterprises, San Francisco, 1994-95, also bd. dirs.; bd. dirs. Nuclear Energy Inst., U.S. Oper. Svcs. Co., Math., Engring., Sci. Achievement. Mem. AIChE, Commonwealth Club of Calif. (bd. govs.). Republican. Episcopalian. Avocations: golf, music. Home: 2550 Royal Oaks Dr Alamo CA 94507-2227 Office: Pacific Gas & Electric Co PO Box 770000 77 Beale St B32 San Francisco CA 94177

SHIFFMAN, BERNARD, mathematician, educator; b. N.Y.C., June 23, 1942; s. Max and Bella (Manel) S.; m. Doris Judith Yaffe, July 11, 1965; children: Jonathan, Daniel. BS, MIT, 1964; PhD (NSF fellow), U. Calif., Berkeley, 1968. C.L.E. Moore instr. MIT, 1968-70; asst. prof. math. Yale U., 1970-73; assoc. prof. Johns Hopkins U., Balt., 1973-77, prof., 1977—, chair dept. math., 1990-93; mem. Inst. Advanced Study, Princeton, N.J., fall 1975, Math. Scis. Rsch. Inst., Berkeley, Calif., spring 1996; series lectr. U. Kaiserslautern, West Germany, 1977, Inst. Math., Academia Sinica, Beijing, China, 1978, U. Paris VI, 1979, Nordic Summer Sch., Joensuu, Finland, 1981; mem. Inst. des Hautes Etudes Scientifiques, Bures-sur-Yvette, France, June 1979; vis. prof. U. Paris VI, 1981, 85, U. Grenoble, June 1992, Nov. 1995. Editor Forum Mathematicum, 1989-95; assoc. editor Am. Jour. Math., 1990-92, editor, 1992-93, editor-in-chief, 1993—; rschr. publs. in complex analysis. Hon. Woodrow Wilson fellow, 1964; Alfred P. Sloan rsch. fellow, 1973-75; recipient Woodrow Wilson Faculty Devel. award, 1979. Mem. Am. Math. Soc. Office: Johns Hopkins U Dept Math Baltimore MD 21218

SHIFFRIN, STEVEN H., law educator; b. 1941. BA, Loyola U., Chgo., 1963, JD, 1975; MA, Calif. State U., Northridge, 1964. Assoc. Irell & Manella, Los Angeles, 1976-77; acting prof. UCLA, 1977-81, prof., 1981-87; prof. of law Cornell U., Ithaca, N.Y., 1987—; vis. prof. Boston U., 1982-83, Mich. U., 1984. Office: Cornell U Law Sch Myron Taylor Hall Rm 110 Ithaca NY 14853*

SHIH, BENEDICT CHESANG, investment company executive; b. Taipei, Taiwan, Jan. 3, 1935; s. Yun Ping and Chyu Ying (Shih) Chiu; m. Sophia Sufu Wu, Oct. 12, 1960; children: Vivian F. Shih Hauer, Peggy F., Phoebe F., Shih Sharp, Jonathan T. BA, Nat. Taiwan U., 1957. Pres. NOEC Corp., Taipei, 1973-78, chmn., CEO, 1995—; pres. KTT Corp., Irvine, Calif., 1983; pres. Nat. Investment Corp., Taipei, 1983—, also bd. dirs.; pres. Nat. Investment Co. (U.S.) Corp., Issaquah, Wash., 1990—; also bd. dirs. Shih Corp., Issaquah; cons. NCR Corp., Dayton, Ohio, 1979-83; ptnr. Blue Heron Assocs., Seabeck, Wash., 1989—. Mem. TRW Credentials Svc., 1989—. Mem. Taiwan C. of C. of Seattle, Taiwan Chiaw Chi Country Club, Taiwan First Country Club, Taiwan Golf and Country Club, Bankers Club Taipei, Sahalee Country Club. Avocations: golf, travel, horseback riding, reading. Office: NIC (US) Corp 611A 100th SW St Tacoma WA 98439-0159

SHIH, HSIENCHENG, medicinal chemist; b. Pingtung, Taiwan, Feb. 13, 1947; came to U.S., 1975; s. Ching-nan and Ching-Jui (Wang) S.; m. Weiyung Yoko Chan, Nov. 26, 1983; children: Renshy Alexis, Renshuay Justin. BS in Pharmacy, Kaohsiung Med. Coll., 1969; MS in Medicinal Chemistry, U. R.I., 1977; PhD in Medicinal Chemistry, SUNY, Buffalo, 1982. Postdoctoral fellow M.D. Anderson Hosp. & Tumor Inst., Houston, 1982, Med. U. S.C., Charleston, 1984; group leader Food & Drug Bur., Taipei, Taiwan, 1983; rsch. assoc. Marshall U., Huntington, W.Va., 1986-89; asst. mem. The Whittier Inst., La Jolla, Calif., 1989-90; rsch. staff U. Calif., San Diego, 1991—. Rsch. fellow Naylor Dana Inst., Am. Health Found., Valhalla, N.Y., 1984-86. Mem. Am. Chem. Soc., Am. Assn. Pharm. Scientists. Achievements include anti cancer agent patent development and patents in field. Home: 10735 Passerine Way San Diego CA 92121 Office: U Calif 9500 Gilman Dr La Jolla CA 92093

SHIH, J. CHUNG-WEN, Chinese language educator; b. Nanking, China; came to U.S., 1948, naturalized, 1960; d. Cho-kiang and Chia-pu (Fang) S. B.A., St. John's U., Shanghai, 1945; M.A., Duke U., 1949, Ph.D., 1955. Asst. prof. English Kings Coll. N.Y., 1955-56; asst. prof. U. Bridgeport, Conn., 1956-60; postdoctoral fellow East Asian Studies Harvard, 1960-61; asst. prof. Chinese Stanford, 1961-64; asso. prof. Chinese Pomona Coll., 1965-66; asso. prof. George Washington U., Washington, 1966-71, prof., chmn. dept. East Asian langs. and lit., 1971-93, prof. emeritus, 1993—, chmn. dept. East Asian langs. and lit., 1971-93, rsch. prof., 1994—. Author: Injustice to Tou O, 1972, the Golden Age of Chinese Drama: Yuan Tsa-chu, 1976, Return from Silence: China's Writers of the May Fourth Tradition, 1983. Bd. dirs. Sino-Am. Cultural Soc., Washington, 1971-80. AAUW fellow, 1964-65; Social Sci. Rsch. Coun. fellow, 1976-77; grantee NEH, 1979-80, 89-91, 96-97, Annenberg/CPB Project, 1989-92; sr. scholars exchange program NAS, China, Spring 1980. Mem. Assn. Asian Studies, Am. Council Fgn. Lang. Tchrs., Chinese Lang. Tchrs. Assn. (chmn. exec. bd. 1976-78). Home: 2500 Virginia Ave NW Washington DC 20037-1901 Office: George Washington U Dept East Asian Langs E Washington DC 20052

SHIH, JASON CHENG, architecture and engineering educator and consultant, university director; b. Taiwan, Republic of China, Sept. 19, 1942; s. Chuan C. Shih and Su G. Yeh; m. Janet Chin, May 22, 1971; children: Jennifer April, Jeffrey Alan. BS, Chung Kung U., Taiwan, 1963; MS, Va. Poly. Inst., 1966; PhD in Engring., Duke U., 1970. Registered profl. engr. and architect, Republic of China, Taiwan, N.C., Va., Caif., Tex., La., Mass. Sr. structural engr., project mgr. Hakan/Best & Assocs., Chapel Hill, N.C., 1968-71; v.p., sr. project mgr. John D. Latimer & Assocs., Durham, N.C. and Taunton, Mass., 1971-76; asst. prof. La. State U., Baton Rouge, 1976-78, assoc. prof., 1978-82, dir. Office of Bldg. Rsch., 1978—, prof., 1982—; grad. program coord., 1993—; engring. cons. Baton Rouge, 1976—; cons. NSF, Washington, 1979-82; bd. dirs. Archtl. Rsch. Ctrs. of Consortium, Washington, 1978-92; co-chmn. spl. project Nat. Inst. Bldg. Sci., Washington, 1982-83. Author: La. Solar Design Notes, 1983; co-author: Architectural Research, 1985; editor: Symposium on Architecture and ACSA tech. Conf. proceedings.; contbr. 72 tech. papers to profl. jours. Mem. Rep. Nat. Com., Washington, 1988. Co-recipient Design Honor award N.C. chpt. AIA, 1973, 74, 75, 76, 77; recipient Solar Project award La. Dept. Natural Resources, 1983, 84, 86, Nat. Energy Innovation award U.S. Dept. Energy, 1984. Mem. NSPE, La. Solar Design Assn. (pres. 1984—), Phi Kappa Phi. Avocations: golf, swimming, tennis, travel. Office: La State U Sch. Architecture Office of Bldg Rsch Baton Rouge LA 70803

SHIH, JASON CHIA-HSING, biotechnology educator; b. Chien-Chen, Hunan, China, Oct. 8, 1939; came to U.S., 1969; m. Jane Chu-Huei Chien, Aug. 31, 1966; children: Giles C., Tim C. BS, Nat. Taiwan U., Taipei, 1963; MS, Nat. Taiwan U., 1966; PhD, Cornell U., 1973. Lectr. Tunghai U., Taichung, Taiwan, 1966-69; rsch. asst. Cornell U., Ithaca, N.Y., 1969-73; sr. rsch. assoc. Cornell U., Ithica, N.Y., 1975-76; rshc. assoc. U. Ill., Urbana, 1973-75; asst. prof. N.C. State U., Raleigh, 1976-80; assoc. prof. N.C. State U., Raleigh, N.C., 1980-88, prof., 1988—; vis. fellow U. Coll. Cardiff, Wales, 1983; sci. advisor Shenyang Agrl. U., China, 1985—; vis. prof. Nat. Taiwan U., 1986, spl. advisor to the pres., 1994; vis. specialist UNDP, China, 1987-93; vis. prof. Bowman Gray Sch. Medicine, 1991. Patentee in field. Exec. com. mem. Triangle Area Chinese Am. Soc., Raleigh, 1979-82, pres., 1982-83, chmn. bd., 1992-93; coord. N.C. State U. exch. programs with China and Taiwan, 1985—; sci. exch. fellow to Spelderholt Poultry Rsch. Ctr., The Netherlands, USDA-Office of Internat. Coop. and Devel., 1994, 95. Recipient numerous rsch. grants, 1977—; Pew Nat. fellow faculty scholar, 1990-91. Fellow Am. Heart Assn., Arteriosclerosis Rsch. Coun.; mem. Am. Instn. Nutrition (Travel award 1981, 89), Am. Soc. for Microbiology, Poultry Sci. Assn., Soc. Chinese Bioscientists in Am. (sec. and treas. 1985-86), Phi Kappa Phi, Sigma Iota Rho (J. Rigney award for Internat. Svc. 1994). Office: N C State U Dept Poultry Sci Raleigh NC 27695-7608

SHIH, TSO MIN, mining engineering educator; b. Ying-Chen, Shantung, China, Apr. 4, 1935; s. Ren Ying and Sun Sum S.; m. Ching Chi Hsia, June 1, 1961; children: Rosa Hung-Chen, Kim Hung-Wei, Sophia Hung-Ren. BS, Nat. Cheng-Kung U., Tainan, Taiwan, 1958; MS, McGill U., Montreal, Can., 1965; postgrad., U. B.C., Vancouver, 1966-68. Rsch. asst. Nova Scotia Tech. Coll., Halifax, N.S., Can., 1965-66; lectr. Nat. Cheng-Kung U., Tainan, Taiwan, 1968-72, assoc. prof., 1972-74, dept. chmn., 1974-80, prof., 1980—; dir. Chinese Inst. Mining and Metal Engring., Taipei, 1976-78. 2d lt. ROTC, 1958-60. Recipient award Pi Epsilon Tao, 1989. Mem. Chinese Inst. Mining and Metal. Engring. (award 1972, 91), Mining Assn. Rep. of China (dir. 1988-94, 96—, award 1996), Chinese Inst. Engrs. Office: Nat Cheng-Kung U, Ta-Hsueh Rd, 700 Tainan Taiwan

SHIHATA, IBRAHIM FAHMY IBRAHIM, development banker, lawyer; b. Damietta, Egypt, Aug. 19, 1937; s. Ibrahim and Neamat (El Ashmawy) S.; m. Samia S. Farid, June 18, 1967; children: Sharif, Yasmine, Nadia. LL.B., U. Cairo, 1957, diploma in pub. law and fin., 1958, diploma in pvt. law, 1959; S.J.D., Harvard U., 1964, LLD (hon.), U. Dundee, Scotland, 1995. Mem. Conseil d'Etat, UAR, 1957-60; mem. Tech. Bur. of Pres., Egypt, 1959-60; from lectr. to assoc. prof. internat. law Ain-Shams U., Cairo, 1964-66, 70-72; legal adviser Kuwait Fund for Arab Econ. Devel., 1966-70, 72-76; dir. gen. OPEC Fund for Internat. Devel., Vienna, 1976-83; exec. dir. Internat. Fund for Agrl. Devel., Rome, 1977-83; v.p., gen. counsel World Bank, Washington, 1983—; sec. gen. Internat. Centre for Settlement of Investment Disputes, Washington, 1983—; chmn. bd. Internat. Devel. Law Inst., Rome, 1983—; bd. dirs. Internat. Fertilizer Devel. Ctr., Muscle Shoals, Ala., 1979-84, Vienna Devel. Inst.; mem. internat. law adv. council Am. U., Washington, 1984-86; adv. com. Rsch. Ctr. Internat. Law, Cambridge, Eng., 1985—; founding adv., bd. dir. Inst. Transnat. Arbitration, Houston, 1986—. Author: The Power of the International Court to Determine Its Own Jurisdiction, 1965, International Air and Space Law, 1966, International Economic Joint Ventures, 1969, International Guarantee for Foreign Investments, 1971, Treatment of Foreign Investments in Egypt, 1972, Secure and Recognized Boundaries, 1974, The Arab Oil Embargo, 1975, The Other Face of OPEC, 1982, The OPEC Fund for International Development-The Formative Years, 1983, A Program for Tomorrow-Challenges and Prospects of the Egyptian Economy in a Changing World, 1987, MIGA and Foreign Investment, 1988, The European Bank for Reconstruction and Development, 1990, The World Bank and the Arab World, 1990, The European Bank for Reconstruction and Development, 1990, The World Bank in a Changing World, vol. 1, 1991, Legal Treatment of Foreign Investment: The World Bank Guidelines, 1993, Towards a Comprehensive Reform, 1993, The World Bank Inspection Panel, 1994, The World Bank in a Changing World, vol. 2, 1995, My Will for My Country, vol. 1, 1995, vol. 2, 1995, vol. 3, 1996; editor ICSID Rev.-Fgn. Investment Law Jour. Decorated Grosses Silbernes Ehrenzeichen am Bande fuer Verdienste um die Republik Oesterreich (Austria), 1983; recipient Kuwait prize for sci. progress in social scis., 1983. Mem. Am. Soc. Internat. Law (exec. coun. 1984-87), Institut de Droit International (Geneva). Office: IBRD General Counsel 1818 H St NW Washington DC 20433-0001

SHIH-CARDUCCI, JOAN CHIA-MO, cooking educator, biochemist, medical technologist; b. Rukuan, Chunghua, Republic of China, Dec. 21, 1933; came to U.S., 1955; d. Luke Chiang-hsi and Lien-chin (Chang) Shih; m. Kenneth M. Carducci, Sept. 30, 1960 (dec. July 1988); children: Suzanne R., Elizabeth M. BS in Chemistry, St. Mary Coll., Xavier, Kans., 1959; intern in med. tech., St. Mary's Hosp., Rochester, N.Y., 1960. Med. researcher Strong Meml. Hosp. (U. Rochester), 1960-61; pharm. chemist quality control Strasenburgh Labs., Rochester, 1961-62; cooking tchr. adult edn. Montgomery County Pub. Schs., Rockville, Md., 1973-79; cooking tchr. The Chinese Cookery Inc., Rockville, 1975-86; cooking tchr. The Chinese Cookery Inc., Silver Spring, Md., 1986—, pres., bd. dirs., 1975—; chemist NIH, Bethesda, 1987—; analytical chemist NIH/WRAIR, Rockville, Md., 1994-96. Author: The Chinese Cookery, 1981, Hunan Cuisine, 1984. Mem. Am. Chem. Soc., Internat. Assn. Cooking Profls. (Woman of the Yr. 1994, 95). Republican. Roman Catholic. Avocations: piano, music, dance, flowers, vegetables. Home and Office: The Chinese Cookery Inc 14209 Sturtevant Rd Silver Spring MD 20905-4448

SHIKUMA, EUGENE YUJIN, travel agency executive; b. Tokyo, Nov. 18, 1948; came to U.S., 1957; s. Mitsuo and Yukiko (Kanaoka) S. BSEE, U. Hawaii at Manoa, Honolulu, 1971, MS in Computer Sci., 1975. Lab. test engr. and scientist McDonnell Douglas Astronautics, Inc., 1971-72; systems engr. Lear Siegler Astronics, 1972-73; jr. coord. Japan Travel Bur. Hawaii, Inc., Honolulu, 1978-83, sr. coord., 1983-84, supr., 1984-89, mgr., 1989—. Bd. dirs. Maui United Way, Kahului, Hawaii, 1988-89, Maui Hui Malama, Waiulku, 1989-90; bd. dirs., sec. Kamoa Views Apt. Owners Assn., 1991-96; mem. Maui County Visitor Task Force, 1995—. Mem. Maui C. of C., Maui Japanese C. of C. Avocations: swimming, coin collecting, fine art, antique prints.

SHILL, VICTOR LAMAR, architect; b. Phoenix, July 6, 1933; s. Victor David and Olive (Nielsen) S.: m. Patsy Ann Nelson, Nov. 7, 1952; children: Michael, Wayne, Mark, Curt, Tracy. BArch, Ariz. State U., 1955. Registered architect, Ariz. Architect Kistner, Wright & Wright, Los Angeles, 1955-56, Horlbeck, Hickman & Assocs., Mesa, Ariz., 1956-63; pres. Shill, Judd, Richards & Johnson Architects, Inc., Mesa, 1963—. Prin. works include Mesa Police Bldg., Mesa Cts. Bldg., Rhoder Jr. H.S., Mesa (AIA award 1978), Ariz. State U. Student Health Bldg., Tempe, Ea. Ariz. Coll. Fine Arts Ctr., Thatcher, Shepherd Jr. H.S., Brimhall Jr. H.S., Dobson H.S., Mohave H.S., River Valley H.S., over 100 ch. projects throughout Ariz. Mem. AIA. Republican. Mormon. Home: 2550 N Gilbert Rd Mesa AZ 85203-1304 Office: Shill Judd Richards & Johnson 1045 E Mckellips Rd Mesa AZ 85203-3001

SHILLESTAD, JOHN GARDNER, financial services company executive; b. Oak Park, Ill., Oct. 31, 1934; s. John Nelson and Isabel Blanche (Gardner) S.; m. Astri Cedervall; children—Christine C., Annette. B.B.A., Northwestern U., 1964, M.B.A., 1967. CLU; CPCU; ChFC. Mktg. dir. spl. plans CNA Ins., Chgo., 1958-66; asst. v.p. Montgomery Ward Life, Chgo., 1966-69; pres., chief exec. officer Fort Dearborn Life Ins. Co., Chgo., 1969-79; sr. v.p. Hartford Life Cos., Conn., 1979-85, also bd. dirs., 1985-87; pres. JGS Fin. Svcs., Inc., 1987—; pres., chmn. bd., CEO, Columbian Mut. Life Ins. Co., Binghamton, N.Y., 1987—; chmn., CEO Columbian Life Ins. Co.; chmn. bd. dirs., CEO Washington Nat. Life N.Y. Mem. Bd. Edn., Dist. 30, Northbrook, Ill., 1976-79; bd. dirs. Salvation Army, Binghamton; mem. adv. bd. SUNY Sch. Mgmt., Binghamton, Kellogg Sch. Bus., Northwestern U. With U.S. Army, 1954-56. Mem. Sunset Ridge Club (Northfield, Ill.), Binghamton Country Club, City Club of Binghamton, Sky Club (N.Y.C.). Republican. Congregationalist. Home: 25 Virginia Ave Binghamton NY 13905-4305 Office: Columbia Mut Life Ins Co Vestal Pkwy E Binghamton NY 13802

SHILLING, A. GARY, economic consultant, investment advisor; b. Fremont, Ohio, May 25, 1937; s. A. Vaughn and Lettie E. (O'Harrow) S.; m. Margaret E. Bloete, Dec. 22, 1962; children: Geoffrey B., Andrew J., Stephen E., Jennifer E. AB in Physics magna cum laude, Amherst (Mass.) Coll., 1960; MA in Econs., Stanford (Calif.) U., 1962, PhD in Econs., 1965. Economist Standard Oil Co. (N.J.), N.Y.C., 1963-67; chief economist Merrill Lynch, Pierce, Fenner & Smith, N.Y.C., 1967-71; rsch. dir. Estabrook & Co., N.Y.C., 1971-72; sr. v.p., chief economist White, Weld & Co., N.Y.C., 1972-78; chmn., pres., dir. A. Gary Shilling & Co., Inc., Springfield, N.J., 1978—; pres. Lakeview Econ. Svcs., Inc., Springfield, 1979—; owner Lakeview Svcs., Inc., Springfield, 1993—; bd. dirs. Nat. Life Vt., Montpelier, Am. Productivity and Quality Ctr., Houston, adv. dir. Austin (Tex.) Trust Co.; informal econ. advisor Former Pres. George Bush, 1978—; mem. Nat. Com. on Jobs and Small Bus., 1986-87; dir. The Heartland Group of Mutual Funds, 1995—, Palm. Harbor Homes, 1995—. Author: Is Inflation Ending? Are You Ready?, 1983, The World Has Definitely Changed: New Economic Forces and Their Implications for the Next Decade, 1986, After the Crash: Recession or Depression? Investment and Business Strategies for a Deflationary World, 1988; creator bd. game The Deflation Game, 1989; columnist Forbes, S&P Credit Week, Nihon Keizai Shimbun Jour. Bd. dirs. Aim Packaging Inc., 1986-89, Henry H. Kessler Found., Inc., West Orange, N.J., 1988-95, Episcopal Ch. Found., N.Y.C., 1989—; chmn. Episcopal Evangelism Found., N.Y.C., 1988—; trustee Bates Coll., Lewiston, Maine, 1988-91, Kent Pl. Sch., Summit, N.J., 1983-89; bd. dirs. The Gen. Theol. Episcopal Sem., N.Y.C., 1988—, treas., 1994—; bd. dirs. N.J. Shakespeare Festival, Madison, 1988-95, chmn. 1992-95; chmn. N.J. State Revenue Forecasting Adv. Commn., 1995—. Named Wall St. Top Economist, Instl. Investor Mag., 1975, 76, Top Commodity Trading Advisor, Futures Mag., 1993. Mem. Nat. Assn. Bus. Economists, N.Y. Soc. Security Analysts, Short Hills Club, Phi Beta Kappa, Sigma Xi. Republican. Episcopalian. Avocations: tennis, travel, gardening, hunting, fishing, beekeeping. Home: 33 Lakeview Ave Short Hills NJ 07078-2264 Office: A Gary Shilling & Co Inc 500 Morris Ave Springfield NJ 07081-1020

SHILLING, MARY EMILY, nursing administrator; b. Milford, Del., Aug. 25, 1931; d. Robert Edward and Mary Emma (Clifton) S. Diploma, Children's Hosp. Sch. Nursing, Boston, 1952; BSN, U. Va., 1966; MSN, U. Pa., 1968. Cert. nursing adminstr. Staff and head nurse Children's Hosp., Boston; assoc. adminstr., head nurse, supr. pediatrics Greenville (S.C.) Gen. Hosp.; assoc. adminstr. Greenville Meml. Hosp.; v.p. nursing and quality improvement Greenville Hosp. System, S.C.; past pres. S.C. State Bd. Nursing. Contbr. articles to profl. jours. Past bd. dirs., mem. nursing practice and standards com Nat. Coun. State Bds. Nursing; past mem. and chmn. S.C. Statewide Master Planning Com. for Nursing Edn. Mem. Am. Orgn. Nursing Execs., S.C. Orgn. Nursing Execs., Sigma Theta Tau. Home: 71 Briarview Cir Greenville SC 29615-2131

SHILLING, ROY BRYANT, JR., academic administrator; b. Enville, Okla., Apr. 7, 1931; s. Roy Bryant and Lila M. (Prestage) S.; m. Margaret

Riddle, Oct. 16, 1952; children: Roy Bryant III, Nancy Gale. BA, McMurry U., 1951, HHD, 1982; BD, So. Meth. U., 1957; MS, Ind. U., 1966, PhD, 1967. Presdl. asst. McMurry U., Abilene, Tex., 1959-61; asst. to pres. Tenn. Wesleyan Coll., 1961-64; asst. in devel. Ball State U., 1964-65; rsch. assoc. Ind. U., 1965-67; dir. planning and rsch. Baldwin Wallace Coll., 1967-68; exec. v.p. Southwestern U., 1968-69, pres., 1981—; pres. Hendrix Coll., 1969-81; mem. Nat. Commn. on United Meth. Higher Edn., 1975-77. Mem. Ark. Arts and Humanities Coun., 1970-76, chmn., 1974-75; bd. dirs. Ark. Children's Hosp., 1981; mem. bd. higher edn. and ministry United Meth. Ch., 1972-80, mem. univ. senate, 1980-88, v.p. 1983-84, pres., 1984-88; chmn. Gulf dist. Rhodes Scholarship Selection Com., 1992, Ark. chmn., 1973-74, Tex. chmn., 1985-91; mem. Young Pres. Orgn., 1975-81; mem. bd. visitors Air U., 1991-94. With U.S. Army, 1952-54. Recipient Disting. Alumnus award McMurry U., 1980, Perkins Disting. Alumnus award So. Meth. U., 1987, Owen B. Sherrill award for leadership in econ. devel. Georgetown, 1988; named one of Top 100 Most Effective Coll. Pres. in Nation, Bowling Green State U./Exxon Edn. Found., 1988. Mem. North Ctrl. Assn. Colls. and Schs. (vice chmn.-elect 1980-81), Nat. Assn Schs. and Colls. o United Meth. Ch. (v.p. 1975-76, pres. 1976-77), Nat. Coun. Ind. Colls. and Univs. (bd. dirs. 1984-88), So. U. Conf. (exec. com. 1974-78), 79-86, sec.-treas. 1979-86, v.p. 1991-92, pres. 1992-93), Am. Coun. Edn. (bd. dirs. 1989-91), Inst. for Humanities (bd. dirs. Salado, Tex. chpt. 1985-91, mem. internat. coun. advs. 1994), Philos Soc. Tex., Rotary, Masons, Alpha Chi, Phi Delta Kappa. Office: Southwestern U Georgetown TX 78626

SHILLINGLAW, GORDON, accounting educator, consultant, writer; b. Albany, N.Y., July 26, 1925; s. James McCombe and Margaret Blanche (Stephens) S.; m. Barbara Ann Cross, June 24, 1950; children—James McCombe, Laura Cross. A.B. magna cum laude, Brown U., 1945; M.S., U. Rochester, 1948; Ph.D., Harvard U., 1952. Asst. prof. Hamilton Coll., Clinton, N.Y., 1951-52; cons. assoc. Joel Dean Assocs., Yonkers, N.Y., 1952-55; asst. prof. MIT, Cambridge, 1955-61; assoc. prof. Columbia U., N.Y.C., 1961-66, prof. acctg., 1966-90, prof. emeritus, 1991—; vis. prof. Mgmt. Devel. Inst., Lausanne, Switzerland, 1964-65, 67-69; mem. U.S. Cost Acctg. Stds. Bd., 1978-80, U.S. R.R. Acctg. Prin. Bd., 1985-87; trustee Scudder Latin Am. Fund, Scudder Pacific Opportunities Fund, Scudder Value Fund, Scudder Capital Growth Fund, Scudder Devel. Fund, Am. Assn. Ret. Persons Growth Trust, Income Trust, Insured Tax Free Income Trust, Money Market Trust; dir. Scudder Internat. Fund, Scudder Small Co. Value Fund, Scudder Gold Fund; cons. in field. Author: Managerial Cost Accounting, 1961, 5th edit., 1982, Accounting: A Managment Approach, 1964, 9th edit., 1993, Financial Accounting: Concepts and Applications, 1989; contbr. articles to profl. jours. Mem. bd. advisors Fund Directions; bd. dirs., treas. Feris Found. Am., Stamford, Conn., 1970-94. Served with U.S. Navy. 1943-46. Recipient Disting. Teaching award Columbia U., 1970. Mem. Am. Acctg. Assn. (v.p. 1966-67), Inst. of Mgmt. Accts., Phi Beta Kappa, Beta Gamma Sigma. Avocations: tennis; travel; French and Italian language study. Home: 196 Villard Ave Hastings On Hudson NY 10706 Also: 109 Oakwood Dr Largo FL 34640-4056

SHILLINGSBURG, MIRIAM JONES, English educator, academic administrator; b. Balt., Oct. 5, 1943; d. W. Elvin and Miriam (Reeves) Jones; BA, Mars Hill Coll., 1964; MA, U. S.C., 1966, PhD, 1969; m. Peter L. Shillingsburg, Nov. 21, 1967; children: Robert, George, John, Alice, Anne Carol. Asst. prof. Limestone Coll., Gaffney, S.C., 1969; asst. prof. Mississippi State (Miss.) U., 1970-75, assoc. prof., 1975-80, prof. English, 1980-96, assoc. v.p. for acad. affairs, 1988-96, dir. summer sch., 1991-96; dean arts and scis. Lamar U., Tex., 1996—; vis. fellow Australian Def. Force Acad., 1989; Fulbright lectr. U. New South Wales, Duntroon, Australia, 1984-85. Nat. Endowment Humanities fellow in residence, Columbia U., 1976-77. Mem. Soc. Study So. Lit., Nat. Acad. Advising Assn., S. Ctrl. Modern Lang. Assn., Australia-New Zealand Am. Studies Assn., Phi Kappa Phi, Simms Soc. (pres.). Author: Mark Twain in Australasia, 1988; editor: Conquest of Granada, 1988; The Cub of the Panther, 1996; mem. editorial bd. Works of W.M. Thackeray; assoc. editor Miss. Quarterly; contbr. articles to profl. jours. and mags.

SHILLINGTON, EDWARD BLAIN, government official; b. Grayburn, Sask., Can., Aug. 28, 1944; s. Sterling Arthur and Dorothy Jennie (Henry) S.; m. Sonia Shirley Koroscil, Aug. 15, 1970; children: Ryan Sterling, Tara Dawn. BA, LLB, U. Sask., 1967. Mem. Sask. Legis. (Regina N.E.), 1975—, minister of coop. and coop. devel., 1975-77, minister of consumer affairs, 1975-76, minister of govt. svcs., 1976-78, minister of culture and youth, 1977-80, minister of edn., 1978-79, assoc. minister of fin., 1992, minister of labour, 1992-95, assoc. minister fin. and minister of crown investments, 1995, minister of justice and atty. gen., 1995, minister of intergovtl. rels. and provincial sec., 1995—, govt. house leader, 1995—; ptnr. Shillington-Doré Law Office, 1980-92. Avocations: reading, boating, fishing, flying. Office: Government of Saskatchewan, Rm 204 Legislative Bldg, Regina, SK Canada S4S 0B3

SHILS, EDWARD B., management educator, lawyer; b. Phila., May 29, 1915; s. Benjamin and Dinah (Berkowitz) S.; m. Shirley Seigle, July 31, 1942; children: Ronnie Lois, Nancy Ellen, Edward Barry. BS in Econs., U. Pa., 1936, MA in Polit. Sci., 1937, PhD, 1940, JD, 1986, LLM, 1990; LLD, Phila. Coll. Textiles and Sci., 1975; PhD (hon.), Tel-Aviv U., Israel, 1990. Bar: Pa. 1988, U.S. Dist. Ct. (ea. dist.) Phila. 1988. Research assoc. Pa. Economy League, 1938-42; cons. job classification and wage adminstrn. Phila. City Council, 1942-43; chief coordination and planning VA, Phila., 1947-48; cons. tchr. salary schedules Phila. Bd. Pub. Edn., 1948-50; dir. pub. edn. survey Greater Phila. Movement, 1950-51; sr. dept. head U.S. Wage Stabilization Bd., Phila., 1951; methods cons. Budget Office Gov. Pa., 1951-55; cons., dir. Dental Mfrs. of Am., Inc., 1952—; cons. Phila. County Med. Soc., 1955-56; chmn. social sci. dept. Community Coll., Temple U., Phila., grad. lectr. pub. adminstrn., 1948-56; mem. faculty Wharton Sch. U. Pa., Phila., 1956—, prof. mgmt., chmn. mgmt dept., 1968-76, George W. Taylor prof. emeritus entrepreneurial studies, 1979—, prof. emeritus polit. sci., 1985—, dir. Wharton Entrepreneurial Ctr., 1973-86, dir. emeritus, 1986—; judicial adminstr. U. Pa., 1986-90; pvt. practice law Phila., 1988—; of counsel Sarner and Assocs., Phila.; Disting. prof. entrepreneurial studies Tel Aviv U., 1991—; pers. cons. Phila. Bd. Pub. Edn., 1946-75, Phila. Psychiat. Ctr., 1971-76, Am. Bd. Internal Medicine, 1973-77, Girard Coll., 1974; cons. Royal Coll. Physicians and Surgeons Can., 1977-80; cons. on sports and econs., major league baseball, football, hockey and basketball, 1985-91; cons. labor rels. Phila. Pub. Sch. Dist., 1951-68; cons. econ. Phila. New Conv. Ctr., 1988-90; mgmt. advisor to Phila. Dist. Atty., 1992-93. Author: Finances and Financial Administration of Philadelphia's Public Schools 1923-1939, 1940, Automation and Industrial Relations, 1963, Teachers, Administrators and Collective Bargaining, 1968, Industrial Peacemaker: George W. Taylor's Contribution to Collective Bargaining, 1979; co-editor: Frontiers of Entrepreneurship Research, 1985. V.p. Fedn. Jewish Agys. for Phila., 1976-84, Life Trust fed. Jewish Agys., 1990—; pres. Jewish Publs. Soc. Am., 1978-81, Hon. pres., 1982; Life trustee, hon. chmn. trustee com. on edn. Phila. Coll. Textiles and Sci.; chmn. bd., hon. pres. Pathway Sch., Jeffersonville, Pa., 1970-84; pres. Philadelphians for Good Govt., 1991-93, hon. pres., 1992—. Served as officer Signal Corps U.S. Army, 1943-46. Honored with a chair in his name at U. Pa. Law Sch., The Edward B. Shils Professorship in Arbitration and Alternative Dispute Resolution, 1991. Mem. Union League Pa., Faculty Club U. Pa. (pres. 1966-69, 87-92), Green Valley Country Club (Plymouth, Pa.), Masons (32 degree). Home: 335 S Woodbine Ave Narberth PA 19072-1525 Office: U Pa Wharton Sch Philadelphia PA 19104 Also: 123 S Broad St Philadelphia PA 19109-1029

SHILS, MAURICE EDWARD, physician, educator; b. Atlantic City, Dec. 31, 1914; s. Samuel L. and Sarah (Harris) S.; m. Cylia Finkiel, Feb. 19, 1939 (dec. Sept. 1987); children: Loraine J., Jonathan R.; m. Betty Ann Bell, Sept. 24, 1988. BA, Johns Hopkins U., 1937, ScD, 1940; MD, NYU, 1958. Intern joint program Cornell divsn. Bellevue Hosp. and Meml. Hosp., N.Y.C., 1958-59; fellow in physiology Meml. Hosp., 1959-60; instr., asst. prof. nutrition Sch. Pub. Health Columbia U., N.Y.C., 1946-54; instr. biochemistry Sch. Hygiene Johns Hopkins U., Balt., 1940-42; head Ctrl. Metabolic Lab. Sloan Kettering Inst., N.Y.C., 1960-72; from asst. to assoc. attending physician Meml. Hosp., N.Y.C., 1962-72, attending physician, 1972-85; asst. prof. biochem. Sloan-Kettering divsn. Med. Coll. Cornell U., N.Y.C., 1959-62, from asst. prof. to prof. medicine Med. Coll., 1962-85, prof. emeritus, 1985—; adj. prof. nutrition dept. pub. health scis. Bowman Gray Sch. Medicine, Winston-Salem, N.C., 1989-94, cons., 1994—. Author, co-editor: Modern Nutrition in Health and Disease, 8th edit., 1994; contbr. more than 200 rsch. and review articles to profl. jours. Fellow Am. Inst. Nutrition, Am. Coll. Physicians, N.Y. Acad. Medicine (Acad. Plaque award 1987); mem. AMA (chmn. nutrition adv. group 1974-77, Goldberger award 1983), Am. Soc. Clin. Nutrition (pres. 1985-86, Excellence in Med. Sch. award 1994), Am. Bd. Nutrition, Phi Beta Kappa, Alpha Omega Alpha.

SHIM, SANG KOO, state mental health official; b. Tokyo, Japan, Oct. 1, 1942; came to U.S., 1968; s. Sang Taek and Kum Ryon (Bae) S.; m. Jae Hee Lee, July 12, 1972; children: Tammy, David. BS, Seoul Nat. U., Korea, 1967; MBA, No. Ill. U., 1970; MS, U. Wis., 1975. CPA, Ill., cert. govt. fin. mgr., Assn. Govt. Accts. Acct. Vaughn Mfg. Co., Chgo., 1970-72, Stewart-Warner Corp., Chgo., 1972-73; fin. cons. Cen. Acctg. Assn., New Baden, Ill., 1977-79; auditor Ill. Dept. Mental Health, Springfield, 1980-82, CFO, 1983—. Treas. Korean Assn. Greater St. Louis, 1982. Mem. Ill. CPA Soc., Assn. Govt. Accts. (cert. govt. fin. mgr.), Korean-Am. C. of C. (v.p. Greater St. Louis chpt. 1994-95). Home: 5 Settlers Ln Springfield IL 62707-7725 Office: Ill Dept Mental Health Bur Fin Svcs 401 S Spring St Springfield IL 62706-0002

SHIMA, HIROMU, management educator; b. Kyoto, Japan, June 20, 1929; s. Seitaro and Teru Shima; m. Atsuko Onogi, Mar. 26, 1961; children: Katsutoshi, Yukihiro. B in Commerce, Doshisha U., Kyoto, Japan, 1951, M in Commerce, 1953; D in Bus. Adminstrn., Kobe (Japan) U., 1982. Teaching asst. Doshisha U., Kyoto, 1953-55, lectr., 1955-58, assoc. prof., 1958-67, prof., 1967—. Author: The Research of Scientific Management, 1963, Personnel Management, 1981, Big Business and Management, 1991, Management in an International Economy, 1996. Libr. Doshisha U., 1989-91. Mem. Assn. for Study of Theory of Pers. Mgmt., Am. Acad. Mgmt., Assn. for Study of Bus. Adminstrn., Japan Soc. for Pers. and Labor Rsch. Home: 26 Hiraki-machi, Uji-shi Kyoto 611, Japan Office: Doshisha U, Karasuma-Imadegawa Kamikyo-ku, Kyoto 602, Japan

SHIMA, LARRY MITSURU, health facility administrator; b. Tokyo, Nov. 17, 1958; came to U.S., 1970; s. Masa and Amy A. (Narisawa) S.; m. Fran T. Shinsato, July 14, 1991; 1 child, Austin Y. BS in Med. Tech., U. Hawaii, 1981; MS in Health Svcs. Adminstrn., Cen. Mich. U., 1994. Med. technologist Kuakini Med. Ctr., Honolulu, 1980-86; chemistry specialist Straub Clinic and Hosp., Honolulu, 1986-89; chemistry supr. Health Care Internat., Aiea, Hawaii, 1989; from ops. supr. to ops. mgr. Pali Momi Med. Ctr., Aiea, Hawaii, 1990-94; ops. mgr. Clin. Labs. Hawaii, Honolulu, 1994—; quality assurance coun. mem. Kapiolani Health Systems, Honolulu, 1993-94, tissue, transfusion mem., 1992-94, cons. cholesterol testing, 1991-94; cons. lab. computer systems, 1990-91. Mem. Clin. Lab. Mgmt. Assn., Am. Assn. for Clin. Chemistry, Am. Soc. Clin. Pathologists, Acad. Med. Arts & Scis., John A. Burns Sch. Medicine Alumni Assn. Republican. Achievements include rsch. in HPLC applications in clin. toxicology, ethics and managed care, managed care and the lab. Home: 95-103 Mahuli Pl Mililani Town HI 96789 Office: Clin Labs Hawaii Kapiolani Med Ctr 1319 Punahou St Honolulu HI 96826

SHIMADA, HARUO, physical chemistry educator; b. Himeji, Hyōgo, Japan, Mar. 27, 1935; s. Shigeyoshi and Shige (Okamoto) S.; m. Ikuko Tanaka, Sept. 21, 1968; children: Yōko, Kenichiro. Grad., U. Tokyo, 1958, doctorate, 1968. Rschr. Yawata (Japan) Iron & Steel Co., 1958-72; sr. rschr. Nippon Steel Corp., Kawasaki, Japan, 1973-80; chief rschr. Nippon Steel Corp., Kawasaki, 1980-90; prof. Sci. U. Tokyo, Shinjuku, Japan, 1990—. Editorial mem.: (monthly jour.) Chem. Industry, 1972—; contbr. articles to profl. jours. Mem. Nat. Assn. Corrosion Engrs., Internat. Tech. Inst. (life mem.). Avocations: jogging, swimming. Home: Chuō 5-3-5, ōta 143, Japan Office: Sci Univ Tokyo, 1-3 Kagurazaka, Shinjuku 162, Japan

SHIMADA, TOSHIYUKI, orchestra conductor, music director; b. Tokyo, Dec. 23, 1951; came to U.S., 1966; s. Ron and Matsue Shimada; m. Eva Virsik, 1987; 1 child, Matias. MusB, Calif. State U., Northridge, 1977. Dir. music, condr. Youth Musicians Found. Debut Orch., L.A., 1978-81; assoc. condr. Houston Symphony Orch., 1981-86; dir. mus., condr. Rice U. Symphony Orch., Houston, 1982-85, Nassau (N.Y.) Symphony Orch., 1987-88, Portland (Maine) Symphony Orch., 1986—; artist cons. Tex. Inst. for Aesthetic Study, Houston, 1984-86; artist in residence U. So. Maine, Portland, 1986-88. Trustee Japan Am. Soc. Maine, Portland, 1990-91. Recipient Condrs. award Young Musicians Found., 1977; finalist Herbert von Karajan Competition, Berlin, 1979; Toshiyuki Shimada Day proclaimed by City of Houston, 1986. Office: Portland Symphony Orch 30 Myrtle St Portland ME 04101-4911

SHIMANSKI, CHARLES STUART, organization executive; b. Madison, Wis., Jan. 17, 1957; s. Stuart Thomas and Gloria Mae (Schindler) S.; m. Christiane Leitinger, May 30, 1992. BA in Econs., U. Wis., 1980. Float control mgr. United Bank of Denver, 1980-84; cash mgr. Oppenheimer, Denver, 1985-86, project mgr. office automation, 1987-93; sys. cons. Darlington Asset Mgmt., Geneva, 1986-87; exec. dir. Am. Alpine Club, Golden, Colo., 1993—; lectr. U. Colo., Boulder, U. Denver, Arapahoe C.C., Sierra Club, Denver Pub. Schs., Jefferson County Pub. Schs., Boy Scouts Am., Wilderness Med. Soc., Nat. Park Svcs., Nat. Ski Patrol, Nat. Forest Svc., Mountain Rescue Assn., Colo. Search and Rescue Bd., Colo. Mountain Club, Internat. Alpine Sch., also mountaineering outfitters and corps.; tech. cons., including Rescue 911, CBS, Unsolved Mysteries, NBC, Turning Point, Women of Valor, ABC, Tour de France, CBS, Emergency Call; published over 300 photographs in areas of alpine mountaineering, mountain rescue, med.-evacuation helicopter rescue, avalanche safety and rescue; EMT, State of Colo., 1985—; dir. Avalanche Awareness Week, Colo. Search and Rescue Bd., 1988-93, instr. Breckenridge Avalanche Sch., 1988—; mem. Alpine Rescue Team, Evergreen, Colo., 1983—, tng. and pub. rels. dir., 1991-92, pres., 1988-89, bd. dirs. 1987-91, dir. fund raising, 1987-89, sec., 1987-88. Author: Helicopters in Search and Rescue Operations—Basic, 1993, Intermediate, 1993, AVALANCHE!!!, 1993, General Back-Country Safety, 1993. Mem. Am. Assn. Avalanche Profls., Mountain Rescue Asssn. (vice chmn., tng. dir. Rocky Mountain region 1989-92, chmn. 1992-94, nat. exec. officer 1992-94, chmn. edn. com. 1994—), Wilderness Med. Soc., Emergency Med. Svcs. Assn. Colo., Am. Alpine Club, Colo. Mountain Club. Avocations: mountain climbing, including peaks in France, Italy, Switzerland, Canada and U.S., photography. Office: Am Alpine Club 710 10th St Ste 100 Golden CO 80401-1022

SHIMAZAKI, YOJI, civil engineering educator; b. Yokohama, Kanagawa, Japan, Dec. 5, 1948; s. Fumio and Fusae (Ishikawa) S.; m. Mitsuko Nagai, Feb. 17, 1980; children: Eriko, Yosuke. BS, Tokai U., Kanagawa, 1971, MS, 1973; PhD, Colo. State U., 1980; DEng, Tohoku U., Sendai, Japan, 1987. Lectr. civil engring. Tokai U., 1981-83, assoc. prof., 1983-93, prof., 1993—; cons. Idemitsu Petrochem. Co. Ltd., Chiba, Japan, The Yokohama Rubber Co. Ltd., Kanagawa. Contbr. articles to profl. jours. Mem. Japan Soc. Civil Engrs., Japan Soc. Mech. Engrs., Soc. Rheology. Avocations: skiing, tennis. Home: 2-2-25 Hiratsuka, Hinataoka 254, Japan Office: Tokai U, 1117 Kitakaname Hiratsuka, Kanagawa 259-12, Japan

SHIMER, DANIEL LEWIS, corporate executive; b. San Angelo, Tex., July 30, 1944; s. Lewis V. and Mary A. (Slick) S.; married. BS in Acctg. and Mktg., Ind. U., 1972; postgrad., Loyola U., New Orleans, 1977. CPA. Sr. acct. Peat, Marwick, Mitchell & Co., Indpls., 1973-75; asst. treas. LTV Corp., Dallas, 1975-79; v.p. fin. Stoller Chem. Co., Houston, 1979-81; v.p., CFO Petro-Silver, Inc., Denver, 1981-83; v.p., treas. FoxMeyer Corp., Denver, 1983-86; v.p., treas., sec. CoastAmerica Corp., Denver, 1986-88; exec. v.p. Bard & Co., Denver, 1989-90; pres. nat accounts divsn. I Can't Believe It's Yogurt/ Brice Foods, Inc., Dallas, 1991-93; exec. v.p., CFO COREStaff Inc., Houston, 1994—. Mem. AICPA, Nat. Assn. Corp. Treas. Roman Catholic. Avocations: sailing, carpentry, snow skiing, camping, fishing. Home: 11 Duncannon Ct Dallas TX 75225-1809

SHIMER, ZACHARY, lawyer; b. Bklyn., Sept. 13, 1933; s. Nathan and Ida (Antonowsky) S.; m. Susan Rosenthal, Feb. 26, 1961; children—Jennifer Shimer Piper, Robert Jay. A.B., UCLA, 1955, LL.B., 1960. Bar: Calif., N.Y. Atty. Antitrust div. U.S. Dept. Justice, Washington, 1960-62; assoc. firm Chadbourne, Parke, Whiteside & Wolff (now Chadbourne & Parke), N.Y.C., 1962-70, ptnr., 1970—. Contbr. articles to profl. jours. Served with U.S. Army, 1955-57. Mem. State Bar of Calif., Assn. Bar City of N.Y., ABA, Order of Coif. Democrat. Jewish. Office: Chadbourne & Parke LLP 30 Rockefeller Plz New York NY 10112-0127

SHIMIZU, REIJU, anesthesiology educator; b. Negi Misato-machi, Japan, Feb. 14, 1935; s. Kenju and Asayo (Yashiro) S.; m. Yukiko Sakae, May 25, 1964; children: Juichirou, Yumiko, Risaburou. Grad., Kyoto Univ., 1961; MD, Tokyo U., 1968. Asst. Tokyo U., 1968-73; assoc. prof. Kyoto U., 1973-80; prof., chmn. Jichi Med. Sch., Tochigi, Japan, 1980—. Grantee Ministry of Edn. Culture and Sci., 1990-92, 93-95, 94-95; recipient Astra Rsch. award, 1996. Mem. Japan Soc. of Anesthesiology (editor jour. 1987-92), Japan Soc. Clin. Anesthesiology, Japan Soc. Circulation Control in Medicine (pres. 1994). Avocations: gardening, classical music, cats. Home: 1-9-16 Nishibori 338, Urawa City 338, Japan Office: Jichi Med Sch, 3311-1 Yakushiji, Minamikawachi-machi, Kawachi 329-04, Japan

SHIMIZU, YOSHIAKI, art historian, educator; b. Tokyo, Feb. 27, 1936; came to U.S., 1953, U.S. resident, 1976; s. Mamoru and Michiko (Hayasaka) S.; children: Karen Akiko Marie, Kenneth Cuyler Norio, Katherine Kimie, Kei Robert. BA, Harvard U., 1963; MA, U. Kans., 1968; MFA, Princeton U., 1971, PhD, 1974. Asst. prof. dept. art and archaeology Princeton (N.J.) U., 1973-75, prof., 1984—, chmn. dept. art and archaeology, 1990-92, Marquand prof. art & archaeology, 1992—; asst. prof. U. Calif., Berkeley, 1975-78, assoc. prof., 1978-79; curator Japanese art Freer Gallery, Smithsonian Instn., Washington, 1979-84; guest curator Nat. Gallery Art, Washington, 1982-89; guest prof. U. of Heidelberg, 1993; mem. art adv. com. Japan Soc. Gallery, 1984—, adv. com. The Asia Soc. Galleries, N.Y.C., 1992—; vis. fellow dept. Comparative Culture Sophia U., Tokyo, 1993. Author: (with Suzan Nelson) Genji: The World of a Prince, 1982; (with John M. Rosenfield) Masters of Japanese Calligraphy, 1984; editor: (with Carolyn Wheelwright) Japanese Ink Paintings, 1976; author, editor: Japan: The Shaping of Daimyo Culture 1185-1858, 1988; mem. editorial bd. Archives of Asian Art, 1979—. Adv. bd. Asian Art, Smithsonian Inst., 1985-93; mem. vis. com. Arthur M. Sackler Gallery, Washington, 1984-94. Smithsonian Inst. fellow, 1967, Social Sci. Rsch. Coun./Am. Coun. Learned Socs. fellow, 1977-78, Asian Cultural Coun. fellow, 1995. Mem. Coll. Art Assn. (bd. dirs. 1987—), Japan Art History Assn., Japan Soc. N.Y., Ctr. for the Study of Japanese Woodblock Prints (mem. internat. adv. bd. 1983—). Home: 171 Nassau St Princeton NJ 08542-7007 Office: Dept Art & Archaeology Princeton U Princeton NJ 08540

SHIMM, MELVIN GERALD, law educator; b. 1926; s. Joseph George and Sadie Rosalie (Rosenblatt) S.; m. Cynia Brown, Aug. 15, 1948; children: David Stuart, Jonathan Evan. AB, Columbia U., 1947; LLB, Yale U., 1950. Bar: N.Y. 1950. Assoc., Cahill, Gordon, Zachry & Reindel, N.Y.C., 1950-51; atty. Wage Stblzn. Bd., Washington, 1951-52; Bigelow fellow U. Chgo., 1952-53; asst. prof. Duke U. Law Sch., Durham, N.C., 1953-56, assoc. prof., 1956-59, prof., 1959—, assoc. dean, 1978-83; vis. prof. NYU, 1957, U. So. Calif., 1965, U. Mich., Ann Arbor, 1973, U. Tex.-Austin, 1976; chmn. Durham (N.C.) Bd. Adjustment, 1966-70; dir. Assn. Am. Law Schs. Orientation Program in Am. Law, 1968-70, Duke Inst. in Transnat. Law, 1987-92; cons. The Brookings Instn., 1965-67; mem. N.C. Gen. Statutes Commn., 1984-88. Bd. dirs., vice-chmn. Lucy Daniels Found., 1989—; pres. Beth El Congregation, Durham, N.C., 1967-70, 1975-78. Lt. U.S. Army. 1943-46. Mem. Order of Coif, Phi Beta Kappa. Editor-in-chief Law & Contemporary Problems, Jour. Legal Edn., Am. Editor Jour. Bus. Law; editor Yale Law Jour. Office: Duke U Sch Law PO Box 90360 Durham NC 27708-0360

SHIMMIN, MARGARET ANN, women's health nurse; b. Forbes, N.D., Oct. 26, 1941; d. George Robert and Reba Aleda (Strain) S. Diploma in Nursing, St. Luke's Hosp. Sch. Nursing, Fargo, N.D., 1962; BSW, U. West Fla., 1978; cert. ob-gyn nurse practitioner, U. Ala., Birmingham, 1983, MPH, 1986. Lic. nurse, Fla., N.D., Ala. Head nurse, emergency room St. Luke's Hosps., Fargo, 1962-67; charge nurse, labor and delivery, perinatal nurse educator Sacred Heart Hosp., Pensacola, Fla., 1970-82; ARNP Escambia County Pub. Health Unit, Pensacola, 1983-89; cmty. health nursing cons. Dist. 1 Health and Rehab. Svcs., Pensacola, 1989—. Capt. nurse corps U.S. Army, 1967-70, Japan. Mem. NAACOG (cert. maternal-gynecol.-neonatal nursing 1978, ob-gyn nurse practitioner 1983), Fla. Nurses' Assn., ANA, N.W. Fla. ARNP (past sec./treas.), Fla. Perinatal Assn., Nat. Perinatal Assn., Healthy Mothers/Healthy Babies Coalition, Fla. Pub. Health Assn., U. West Fla. Alumni Assn., U. Ala. at Birmingham Sch. of Public Health Alumni Assn., Phi Alpha. Republican. Presbyterian. Avocations: cooking, music, travel, photography, reading. Home: 8570 Olympia Rd Pensacola FL 32514-8029 Office: Dist 1 HRS 160 Governmental Ctr Pensacola FL 32501

SHIMMYO, THEODORE TADAAKI, seminary president; b. Shiokawa-machi, Japan, Aug. 13, 1944; came to U.S. 1973; s. Shizuo and Tomiko (Saito) S.; m. Sumie Kurihara, Oct. 21, 1970; children: Keijo, Tatenaga, Keishin, Keika. BS in Nuclear Engring., U. Tokyo, 1971; diploma in religious edn., Unification Theol. Sem., Barrytown, N.Y., 1977; MPhil in Christian Theology, Drew U., Madison, N.J., 1981, PhD in Christian Theology, 1984. Asst. prof. theology Unification Theol. Sem., Barrytown, N.Y., 1984—, asst. dean faculty, 1987; asst. acad. dean Unification Theol. Sem., Barrytown, 1987-94, pres., 1994—. Author: Addressing Some of the Criticisms About the Divine Principle, 1985, Explorations in Unificationism, 1996; translator: The Divine Principle Study Guide Part II, 1975; contbr. articles to profl. jours. Mem. Ctr. for Process Studies, Soc. for Study of Process Philosophies, New Ecumenical Rsch. Assn., Unification Thought Inst. Am. (sec. gen.), Assn. Governing Bds. of Univs. and Colls., Karl Barth Soc. of N.Am. Mem. Unification Ch. Avocations: harmonica, classical guitar. Home: 20 Browning Ln Tarrytown NY 10591 Office: Unification Theol Sem 10 Dock Rd Barrytown NY 12507

SHIMODA, JERRY YASUTAKA, national historic park superintendent; b. Haleiwa, Hawaii, Mar. 21, 1930; s. Tamotsu and Sasai Shimoda; m. Clara H. Segawa, Aug. 7, 1954; children: Karen Marie K., Randall T., Shaun T., Teri Ellen H., Jacqueline Y., David Y. BA in Govt., U. Hawaii, 1952, MA in Far Ea. Area Studies, 1957; postgrad., St. Louis U., 1957-59. Historian Jefferson Nat. Expansion Meml. Nat. Hist. Site, St. Louis, 1957-60; chief historian, in charge hist. rsch. and visitor svcs. Saratoga Nat. Hist. Park, Stillwater, N.Y., 1960-66; chief historian Home of Franklin D. Roosevelt Nat. Hist. Site and, Frederick Vanderbilt Nat. Hist. Site, Hyde Park, N.Y., 1966-69; instr. Nat. Park Svc. Stephen T. Mather Tng. Ctr., Harpers Ferry, W.Va., 1969-72; supt. Pu'uhonua o Honaunau (Hawaii) Nat. Hist. Park, 1972—, Puukohola Heiau Nat. Hist. Site, Honaunau, 1972—; lectr. environ. edn. Pa. State U., U. W.Va., Shepherd Coll., 1969-72; acting supr. Kaloko-Honokohau Nat. Hist. Park, 1988-90; instr. environ. edn., interpretive and basic instructing techniques U. Hawaii, Hilo, Kapiolani C.C.; U.S. del. U.S.-Japan Panel on Nat. Parks and Equivalent Res., 1968—, World Conf. on Marine Parks, Tokyo, 1975; Japanese translator U.S. Nat. Park Svc.; mem. internat. bd. dirs. Heritage Interpretation Internat.; numerous presentations at confs. and tng. courses. Author booklets on nat. parks, mgmt. and history; contbr. numerous articles to profl. publs., mags. and newspapers. Bd. dirs. Volcano Art Ctr.; mem. adv. com. Wailoa State Ctr.; mem. Hawaii Gov.'s Task Force on Ocean and Recreation; chmn. restoration com. St. Benedict's Ch., Honounau, 1982-95. Recipient spl. achievement award Nat. Park Svc., 1964, 68, 70, resolution W.Va. Senate, 1971, Hawaii Ho. of Reps., 1982, sec.'s cert. Dept. Interior, 1971, Exec. of Yr. award West Hawaii chpt. Profl. Secs. Internat., 1981, cert. Govt. of Japan, 1981, staff plaque Pu'uhonua o Honaunau Nat. Hist. Park, Puukohola Heiau Nat. Hist. Site and Kaloko-Honokohau Nat. Hist. Park, 1988, cert. Japan Nat. Parks Assn., 1989, cert. of appreciation South Kona Aloha Lions Club, 1990, also others. Mem. Hawaii Mus. Assn. (bd. dirs. 1988-92), Kona Hist. Soc. (bd. dirs. 1988-92), Big Island Ocean Recreation and Tourism Assn. (exec. com.), Kona Judo Club (pres. 1977—), Rotary (pres. Kona Nauka 1978-79, Paul Harris fellow 1991, Disting. Svc. award 1992). Avocations: writing, reading, travel, teaching. Office: Pu'uhonua o Honaunau Nat Hist Pk PO Box 129 Honaunau HI 96726-0129

SHIMOYAMA, HIDEO, construction company executive; b. 1943. Grad., Osaka (Japan) U.; attended, Mich. State U. With Kajima Constrn. Svcs., Japan, 1967-81, Kajima Internat., 1981-91; pres., COO, exec. v.p. Kajima Constrn. Svcs., Englewood Cliffs, N.J., 1991—. Office: Kajima Constrn Svcs 900 Sylvan Ave Englewood Cliffs NJ 07632*

SHIMP, ROBERT EVERETT, JR., academic administrator, historian; b. Phila., Mar. 1, 1942; s. Robert Everett Sr. and Vivian (Myrtetus) S.; m. Marilyn Hopkins, Aug. 3, 1963; children: Gregory, Cecily, Jennifer. BA, Thiel Coll., 1964; MA, Ohio State U., 1965, PhD, 1970. Instr. history Ohio Wesleyan U., Delaware, Ohio, 1968-70, asst. prof., 1970-76, assoc. prof., 1976-82, prof. history, 1982-84, dir. off campus program, 1979-84; acad. dean Ky. Wesleyan Coll., Owensboro, 1984-88; provost, v.p. for acad. affairs Millikin U., Decatur, Ill., 1988-93; pres. McMurry U., Abilene, Tex., 1993—; vis. assoc. prof. Ohio State U., Columbus, summer 1978, Coll. of V.I., St. Croix, fall 1982; mem. Inst. for Ednl. Mgmt. Harvard U., 1985; reader and table leader European history AP, Princeton, N.J. 1976-83; dir. Newberry Libr. Program in the Humanities, Chgo., 1976-77. Contbr. articles to profl. jours. Mem. Leadership Owensboro, 1986-87; capt. drives United Way, Owensboro and Delaware, 1981-85, bd. dirs., Decatur and Abilene; trustee for Sears Retirement Systems and Abilene Higher Edn. Authority; bd. dirs. Abilene C. of C. Fellow Ohio State U., 1968, Newberry Libr., Chgo., 1976-77. Mem. Ohio Acad. History, Conf. on Brit. Studies. Democrat. Methodist. Avocations: fishing, reading. Office: McMurry U Office of Pres PO Box 98 Abilene TX 79604-0098

SHIMPFKY, RICHARD LESTER, bishop; b. Albuquerque, Oct. 18, 1940; m. Jamel Shimpfky, 1966; children: Trevor, Allison, Joshua. Grad., U. Colo., 1963, Va. Theol. Seminary, 1970. Ordained to diaconate Episc. Ch., 1970. With William L. Philips Found., Richmond, Va., 1963-67; curate St. Peter's Ch., Arlington, 1970-72; vicar All Saints' Sharon Chapel, Alexandria, Va., 1972-73, rector, 1973-77; rector Christ Ch., Ridgewood, N.J., 1977-90; bishop Diocese El Camino Real, Monterey, Calif., 1990—. Avocations: reading, traveling. Office: Diocese of El Camino Real PO Box 1093 Monterey CA 93942-1093*

SHIN, WILLIAM DONG MOON, brokerage house executive; b. Seoul, Korea, Apr. 12, 1944; came to the U.S., 1970; s. Kyung Soon and Il Soon (Kim) S.; m. Jeanie C. Youn, Jan. 30, 1971; children: Laura, Melissa. BSBA, Youngstown State U., 1977, MBA, 1986. Cert. money mgr. Payroll auditor Gen. Motors, Lordstown, Ohio, 1978-82; steel cost analyst Gen. Motors, Mansfield, Ohio, 1982-87; fin. cons. Merrill Lynch, Cleve., 1987-89, fin. mgr., 1989-90, asst. v.p., 1990-91, v.p., 1991-94; first v.p. Merrill Lynch, Pepper Pike, Ohio, 1994—. Pvt. Korean Army, 1966-69. Presbyterian. Avocations: golf, skiing, swimming. Home: 32081 Meadow Lark Way Pepper Pike OH 44124-5507 Office: Merrill Lynch 30100 Chagrin Blvd Pepper Pike OH 44124-5705

SHINAGEL, MICHAEL, English literature educator; b. Vienna, Austria, Apr. 21, 1934; came to U.S., 1941; s. Emanuel and Lilly (Hillel) S.; m. Ann Birdsey Mitchell, Sept. 1, 1956 (div. 1970); children: Mark Mitchell, Victoria Stuart; m. Rosa Joanne Bonanno, Dec. 6, 1973 (div. 1993); m. Marjorie Lee North, May 26, 1995. A.B., Oberlin Coll., 1957; A.M., Harvard U., 1959, Ph.D., 1964. Teaching fellow Harvard U., Cambridge, Mass., 1958-59, tutor in English, 1962-64, assoc. dir. career office, 1959-64, dean continuing edn., 1975—, lectr. extension, 1976—, sr. lectr. English, 1983—, master Quincy House, 1986—; asst. prof. English, Cornell U., Ithaca, N.Y., 1964-67; prof., chmn. dept. English, Union Coll., Schenectady, 1967-75; bd. dirs. Harvard Coop. Soc., publ. Harvard Rev.; pres. bd. dirs. Ednl. Exch. Boston, 1982-87. Author: Defoe and Middle-class Gentility, 1968; co-author: (handbook) Summer Institutes in English, 1965; editor: Concordance to Poems of Swift, 1972, Critical Edition of Robinson Crusoe, 1975 (revised 1993); co-editor: Harvard Scholars in English (1890-1990), 1991. Served with U.S. Army, 1952-54, Korea. Woodrow Wilson fellow, 1957; NEH grantee, 1965. Mem. Nat. Univ. Continuing Edn. Assn., Assn. Continuing Higher Edn., Mass. Hist. Soc., Old South Meeting House, The Johnsonians, The Saturday Club, Harvard Faculty Club (pres. 1985-87), Phi Beta Kappa. Avocations: reading; cooking; music; tennis. Home: Master's Residence Quincy House 58 Plympton St Cambridge MA 02138-6604 Office: Harvard U Div Continuing Edn 51 Brattle St Cambridge MA 02138-3701

SHINDELL, SIDNEY, medical educator, physician; b. New Haven, May 31, 1923; s. Benjamin Abraham and Freda (Mann) S.; m. Gloria Emhoff, June 17, 1945; children: Barbara, Roger, Lawrence, Judith. BS, Yale U., 1944; MD, L.I. Coll. Medicine, 1946; postgrad., Emory U., 1948-49; LLB, Geo. Washington U., 1951. Diplomate Am. Bd. Preventive Medicine, Am. Bd. Occupational Medicine. With USPHS, 1947-52; med. dir. Conn. Commn. on Chronically Ill and Aged, 1952-57, Am. Joint Distbn. Com., 1957-59; asst. prof. preventive medicine U. Pitts., 1960-65; dir. Hosp. Utilization project Western Pa., 1965-66; prof. dept. preventive medicine Med. Coll. Wis., Milw., 1966-93, chmn. dept., 1966-89, dir. office internat. affairs, 1989-93, prof. emeritus, 1993—; exec. dir. Health Svc. Data of Wis., 1967-73; bd. sci. advisers Am. Coun. on Sci. and Health, 1978-87, 92—; mem. Nat. Adv. Com. on Occupational Safety and Health, U.S. Dept. Labor, 1982-84; cons. Caribbean Epidemiology Ctr. Pan. Am. Health Orgn./WHO, 1988, field epidemiology tng. program, Thailand, 1989, Nat. Office Occupational and Environ. Medicine Royal Thai Ministry of Pub. Health, 1990—; mem. gov's white paper com. on health care reform, Wis., 1993; acad. cons. Faculties of Medicine, Padjadjaran U., Bandung, Airlangga U., Surabaya, Indonesia, 1993, 94; bd. dirs. Am. Coun. of Sci. and Health, 1987-89, chmn. 1989-92. Author: Statistics, Science and Sense, 1964, A Method of Hospital Utilization Review, 1966, The Law in Medical Practice, 1966, A Coursebook on Health Care Delivery, 1976; contbr. 120 articles to profl. jours. Mem. Sch. Bd. Fox Point-Bayside (Wis.), Sch. Dist., 1970-71; vice-chmn. Citizens' Adv. Com. Met. Problems, 1971-72; Bd. dirs. Med. Care Evaluation S.E. Wis., 1973-76. Served with AUS, 1943-46. Fellow Am. Coll. Preventive Medicine (bd. regents 1982-85), Am. Pub. Health Assn., Am. Coll. Occupational and Environ. Medicine, Am. Coll. Legal Medicine; mem. Am. Assn. Health Data Systems (sec. 1972-73), Assn. Tchrs. Preventive Medicine (dir. 1973-74, pres. 1976-77), Assn. Occupational Health Profls. (pres. 1980-90), Wis. State Med. Soc. (coun. on health care financing and delivery, coun. on govt. affairs, mem. ho. of dels.), Am. Coll. Physician Execs., Internat. Commn. on Occupational Health, Aircraft Owners and Pilots Assn., Masons, CAP. Home: 929 N Astor St # 2507 Milwaukee WI 53202-3490 Office: PO Box 26509 Milwaukee WI 53226-0509

SHINDLER, DONALD A., lawyer; b. New Orleans, Oct. 15, 1946; s. Alan and Isolene (Levy) S.; m. Laura Epstein, June 22, 1969; children: Jay, Susan. BSBA, Washington U., St. Louis, 1968; JD, Tulane U., 1971. Bar: La. 1971, U.S. Dist. Ct. (ea. dist.) La. 1971, U.S. Tax Ct. 1974, Ill. 1975, U.S. Dist. Ct. (no. dist.) Ill. 1975; CPA, La.; lic. real estate broker, Ill. Assoc. Pope, Ballard, Shepard & Fowle, Chgo., 1975-78; assoc. Rudnick & Wolfe, Chgo., 1978-81, ptnr., 1981—; seminar lectr. Chgo. Bar Assn., Ill. Inst. CLE, Profl. Edn. Sys., Inc., Internat. Assn. Corp. Real Estate Execs., Urban Land Inst., Am. Corp. Counsel Assn., Bldg. Owners and Mgrs. Assn., 1980—. Contbr. articles on real estate to legal jours. Trustee Glencoe (Ill.) Pub. Libr., 1981-87, pres., 1986-87; alumni bd. govs. Washington U., 1992-93; mem. Glencoe Zoning Commn./Bd. Appeals, 1994—. Lt. JAGC, USNR, 1971-75. Mem. ABA, La. State Bar Assn., Chgo. Bar assn. (com. chmn. 1979-80, 83-84, 90-94, editor land trust seminars 1984—), Urban Land Inst. (mem. exec. com. Chgo. dist. coun.), Internat. Assn. Corp. Real Estate Execs., Internat. Assn. Attys. and Execs. in Corp. Real Estate, Union League Club (chair real estate group 1993—), Order of Coif, Beta Gamma Sigma, Omicron Delta Kappa. Office: Rudnick & Wolfe 203 N La Salle St Ste 1800 Chicago IL 60601-1210

SHINDLER, MERRILL KARSH, writer, radio personality; b. N.Y.C., July 2, 1948; s. Joseph and Miriam (Karsh) S. BA, CCNY, 1970; MFA, NYU, 1971. Entertainment editor San Francisco Bay Guardian, 1972-75; music editor Rolling Stone mag., San Francisco, 1976-79; film critic Los Angeles mag., 1979-89; restaurant critic L.A. Examiner, 1979-88; editor Zagat Los Angeles Restaurant Survey, 1986—; restaurant critic L.A. Reader, 1990—, Daily Breeze, 1990—, Daily News, 1990—. Author: Best Restaurants of L.A., 1989, Zagat, L.A. Restaurant Survey, 1986—; writer (radio shows) Am. Top 40, 1979-89, Casey's Top 40, 1989—, Casey's Biggest Hits, 1990, USA Top 20, 1990—, (TV shows) Am. Top 10, 1980-93, Cinemattractions, 1990—, USA Music Today, 1990—; host radio show Dining Out with Merrill Shindler, 1988—; contr. to Gault-Millau Best of Los Angeles, 1988, Gault-Millau Best of Hong Kong, 1989; contbr. articles to jours. Avocations: restaurants, cooking, jogging, travel.

SHINE, HENRY JOSEPH, chemistry educator; b. London, Jan. 4, 1923; s. Nathan and Esther (Lewkovich) S.; m. Sellie Schneider, June 14, 1953; children: Stephanie, Trevor Paul. B.Sc., London U., 1944, Ph.D., 1947. Research chemist Shell Oil Co., Eng., 1944; research chemist U.S. Rubber Co., Passaic, N.J., 1951-54; asst. prof. chemistry Tex. Tech U., Lubbock, 1954-57; asso. prof. Tex. Tech U., 1957-60, prof., 1960—, Paul Whitfield Horn prof., 1968—, chmn. dept., 1969-75. Author: Aromatic Rearrangements, 1967; contbr. articles to profl. jours. Mem. Am. Chem. Soc. (exec. com. div. organic chemistry 1973-75, alt. councillor 1975-78, councillor 1978-80), Chem. Soc. London, AAAS (regional pres. 1979-80), Sigma Xi (pres. chpt. 1976-77), Phi Kappa Phi. Home: 4705 17th St Lubbock TX 79416-5707 Office: Dept Chemistry and Biochemistry Tex Tech U Lubbock TX 79409

SHINE, KENNETH IRWIN, cardiologist, educator; b. Worcester, Mass., 1935. Grad., Harvard Coll., 1957; MD, Harvard U., 1961. Diplomate Am. Bd. Internal Medicine. Intern Mass. Gen. Hosp., 1961-62, resident, 1962-63, 65-66, fellow in cardiology, 1966-68; surgeon USPHS, 1963-65; assoc. in medicine Beth Israel Hosp., Resont, Va., from 1969; instr. Harvard Med. Sch., from 1968; asst. prof. medicine UCLA Sch. Medicine, 1971-73, assoc. prof., 1973-77, prof., 1977-92, prof. emeritus, 1993—, dir. CCU, 1971-75, chief div. cardiology, 1975-79, vice chmn. dept. medicine, 1979-81, exec. chmn., 1981-86, dean, 1986-92; clin. prof. medicine Georgetown U. Med. Ctr., Washington, 1993—; provost for med. scis. UCLA Sch. Medicine, 1991-92; pres. Inst. Medicine, Washington, 1992—. Mem. Am. Heart Assn. (pres. 1986-87), Assn. Am. Med. Colls. (adminstrv. bd. coun. deans 1989-92, exec. bd. 1990-92, chmn. coun. deans 1991-92). Office: Institute of Medicine 2101 Constitution Ave NW Washington DC 20418-0007*

SHINE, NEAL JAMES, journalism educator, former newspaper editor, publisher; b. Grosse Pointe Farms, Mich., Sept. 14, 1930; s. Patrick Joseph and Mary Ellen (Conlon) S.; m. Phyllis Theresa Knowles, Jan. 24, 1953; children: Judith Ann, James Conlon, Susan Brigid, Thomas Patrick, Margaret Mary, Daniel Edward. BS in Journalism, U. Detroit, 1952; PhD (hon.), Cleary Coll., 1989, Siena Heights Coll., 1995, U. Mich., 1995, U. Detroit Mercy, 1996, Ctrl. Mich. U., 1996. Mem. staff Detroit Free Press, 1950-95, asst. city editor, 1963-65, city editor, 1965-71, mng. editor, 1971-82, sr. mng. editor, 1982-89, pub., 1990-95; prof. journalism Oakland U., Rochester, Mich., 1995—. Host, moderator Detroit Week in Rev., Sta. WTVS-TV, 1981-89, host Neal Shine's Detroit, 1989-91. Trustee, vice chmn. bd. trustees Youth for Understanding, 1973-75, chmn., 1975-78; mem. bd. for student publs. U. Mich.; bd. dirs. Children's Hosp., Econ. Club Detroit, Detroit Renaissance, New Detroit, Inc., Detroit Symphony Orch., Detroit Inst. Arts, Detroit Hist. Soc., United Way of Southeastern Mich., Met. Detroit Conv. and Visitors Bur., Operation ABLE, Detroit Press Club Found. With U.S. Army, 1953-55. Inducted Mich. Journalism Hall of Fame, 1990. Mem. Am. Soc. Newspaper Editors, Am. Newspapers Pubs. Assn., Mich. Press Assn. (bd. dirs. 1990-95), AP Mng. Editors, Sons of Whiskey Rebellion (comdr.-in-chief 1979—), Inc. Soc. Irish-Am. Lawyers, Detroit Press Club (charter, bd. govs. 1966-89, sec. 1957-68, v.p. 1969-71, pres. 1971-73). Home: 11009 Harbor Place Dr Saint Clair Shores MI 48080-1527 Also: Rathclaire, Gen Delivery, Pointe aux Roches, ON Canada N0R 1N0

SHINEFIELD, HENRY ROBERT, pediatrician; b. Paterson, N.J., Oct. 11, 1925; s. Louis and Sarah (Kaplan) S.; m. Jacqueline Marilyn Walker; children: Jill, Michael, Kimberley Strome, Melissa Strome. B.A., Columbia U., 1945, M.D., 1948. Diplomate: Am. Bd. Pediatrics (examiner, 1975—, bd. dirs., 1979-84, v.p., 1981-84). Rotating intern Mt. Sinai Hosp., N.Y.C., 1948-49; pediatric intern Duke Hosp., Durham, N.C., 1949-50; asst. resident pediatrician N.Y. Hosp. (Cornell), 1950-51, pediatrician to outpatients, 1953-59, instr. in pediatrics, 1959-60, asst. prof., 1960-64, asso. prof., 1964-65, asst. attending pediatrician, 1959-63, asso. attending pediatrician, 1963-65; pediatrician to outpatients Children's Hosp., Oakland, Calif., 1951-53; chief of pediatrics Kaiser-Permanente Med. Center, San Francisco, 1965-89, chief emeritus, 1989—; co-dir. Kaiser-Permanente Pediat4ric Vaccine Study Ctr., San Francisco, 1984—; asso. clin. prof. pediatrics Sch. Medicine U. Calif., 1966-68, clin. prof. pediatrics, 1968—, clin. prof. dermatology, 1970—; asso. attending pediatrician Paterson (N.J.) Gen. Hosp., 1955-59; chief of pediatrics Kaiser Found. Hosp., San Francisco, 1965—; attending Moffitt Hosp., San Francisco, 1967—; practice medicine specializing in pediatrics Paterson, 1953-59; cons. San Francisco Gen. Hosp., 1967—, Childrens Hosp., San Francisco, 1970—, Mt. Zion Hosp., San Francisco, 1970—; mem. research grants rev. br. NIH, HEW, 1970-74; med. dir. USPHSR, 1969—; bd. dirs. San Francisco Peer Rev. Orgn., 1975-81, sec., exec. com., 1976-81; chmn. Calif. State Child Health Disability Bd., 1973-82; mem. Inst. of Medicine, Nat. Acad. Scis., 1980—; cons. Bur. Drugs FDA, 1970, NIH, HEW, 1974—. Editorial bds. Western Jour. of Medicine, 1968-80, American Jour. of Diseases of Children, 1970-82; contbr. writings to profl. publs. Chmn. San Francisco Med. Adv. Com. Nat. Found. March of Dimes, 1969-80. Served with USPHS, 1951-53. Fellow Am. Acad. Pediatrics (com. of fetus and newborn 1969-76, mem. com. on drugs 1978-82); mem. AMA, Soc. Pediatric Research, Infectious Diseases Soc. Am., Western Pediatric Soc., Western Soc. Clin. Research, Am. Pediatric Soc., Phi Beta Kappa. Home: 2705 Larkin St San Francisco CA 94109-1117 Office: 2200 Ofarrell St San Francisco CA 94115-3357

SHINEMAN, EDWARD WILLIAM, JR., retired pharmaceutical executive; b. Canajoharie, N.Y., Apr. 9, 1915; s. Edward W. and Bertelle H. (Shubert) S.; m. H. Doris Thompson, Apr. 15, 1939; children: Edward T., Alan B. AB, Cornell U., 1937. With apparatus dept., acctg. dept. Gen. Electric Co., 1938-46, line auditor, 1942-46; with Beech-Nut, Inc. and predecessor cos., 1946-68, asst. treas., 1948-63, contr., 1959-63, treas., 1963-68; asst. sec.-treas. Squibb Corp., 1968-81; bd. dirs. Fenimore Asset Mgmt., Inc., Taconic Farms, Inc. Trustee, pres. Arkell Hall Found.; mem. emeritus coun. Cornell U. Mem. Fin. Execs. Inst., Inst. Mgmt. Accts. Republican. Home: 420 E 51st St Apt 14E New York NY 10022-8022

SHINN, ALLEN MAYHEW, retired naval officer, business executive; b. Niles, Calif., June 6, 1908; s. Joseph Clark and Florence Maria (Mayhew) S.; m. Sevilla Hayden Shuey, June 20, 1936; children: Allen Mayhew, James Washburn, Jonathan Hayden. BS, U.S. Naval Acad., 1932; grad., Nat. War Coll., 1953. Commd. officer USN, 1932, advanced through grades to vice adm.; served in battleships, 1932-36; naval aviator, 1937, served in various fleet aircraft squadrons, comdr. 3, also comdr. attack carrier air group, 1944-45; served on various staffs; comdr. 2 carriers USS Saipan, 1956, USS Forrestal, 1958; comdt. midshipmen U.S. Naval Acad., Annapolis, Md., 1956-58; comdr. Anti-Submarine Warfare Carrier Task Group, 1960-61, Attack Carrier Task Force, 1963-64; chief Bur. Naval Weapons, Washington, 1964-66; comdr. Naval Air Force Pacific Fleet, 1966-70; ret., 1970; chmn. bd. Harvard Industries, Inc., 1970-71, All-Am. Industries, 1973-78; pres., CEO Internat. Controls Corp., 1973-78, dir. 1973-79; dir. Loral Corp., 1973—, Pennzoil Co., 1970-94; bd. dirs. Navy Mut. Aid Assn., 1962-66; bd. mgrs. Navy Relief Soc., 1962-64; pres. Naval Acad. Athletic Assn., 1956-58, North Water St. Corp., Edgartown, Mass., 1948-50. Trustee Longfellow Sch. Boys, Bethesda, Md., 1950-53. Decorated D.S.M. Mem. Soc. Mayflower Descendants, Cosmos Club, N.Y. Yacht Club, Edgartown Yacht Club, Delta Tau Delta. Republican. Unitarian. Home: 3130 Roadrunner Dr Borrego Springs CA 92004

SHINN, CLINTON WESLEY, lawyer; b. Haworth, Okla., Mar. 7, 1947; s. Clinton Elmo and Mary Lucille (Dowdy) S.; m. Catherine Borne; children: Laura Kathryn, Clinton Wesley, Timothy Daniel. BS, McNeese State U., 1969; JD, Tulane U., 1972; LLM, Harvard U., 1973. Bar: La. 1972, U.S. Dist. Ct. (ea. dist.) La. 1975, U.S. Dist. Ct. (we. dist.) La. 1980, U.S. Ct. Appeals (5th cir.) 1981, U.S. Ct. Appeals (11th cir.) 1982, U.S. Tax Ct. (1982). Asst. prof. law Tulane U., New Orleans, 1973-75; assoc. Stone, Pigman et al, New Orleans, 1975-78, ptnr., 1979—; faculty advisor, 1974-75, editor in chief Tulane Law Rev., 1971-72. Editor in chief Tulane Law Rev., 1971-72. Co-founder, bd. dirs. Childhood Cancer Families Network, 1987-90; co-founder Camp Challenge, 1988; team leader Campaign for Caring, Children's Hosp., New Orleans, 1989-91; bd. dirs. Christ Episcopal Sch., Covington, 1988-91, chmn. long-range planning, 1990-91, exec. com. 1989-91, chmn. legal com., 1989-91, chmn. admissions/recruitment com., 1988-90, mem. headmaster search com., 1993; bd. dirs. Greater New Orleans YMCA, 1989—, exec. com. 1991—, asst. sec., 1994-95, sec. 1996—, mem. fin. com. 1994—, exec. dir. search com. 1996; active Indian Guides/Princesses; bd. dirs. West Side Tammany YMCA, 1987-95, exec. com. 1988-95, bd. chmn. 1989-90, 92-93; bd. dirs. Christwood, 1992—; bd. dirs. La. Air & Waste Mgmt. Assn., 1993—, chmn. corp. rels. com. 1992-93. Co-recipient Pals of the Yr. award Greater New Orleans YMCA Indian Guides/Princesses, 1987-88; named Vol. of Yr. West St. Tammany YMCA, 1990, 92. Mem. ABA, Nat. Assn. Securities Dealers (bd. arbitrators), Nat. Wildlife Fedn. (life), La. Bar Assn., La. Forestry Assn., New Orleans Bar Assn., New Orleans Estate Planning Coun., Assn. Employee Benefit Planners New Orleans, Assn. Henri Capitant, Air and Waste Mgmt. Assn., Order of Coif. Avocations: backpacking, gardening. Home: Dogwood Ridge Farm 20297 Brunning Rd Covington LA 70435-7579 Office: Stone Pigman Walther Wittman & Hutchinson 546 Carondelet St New Orleans LA 70130-3521 *In all things be firm but fair.*

SHINN, DAVID HAMILTON, diplomat; b. Yakima, Wash., June 9, 1940; s. Guy Wilson and Ada Louise (Gelvin) S.; m. Judy Karen Rolfe, Sept. 9, 1961; children: Steven Hamilton, Christopher Rolfe. AA, Yakima Valley Coll., 1960; BA, George Washington U., 1963, MA, 1964, PhD, 1980; cert. African studies, Northwestern U., Evanston, Ill., 1969. With U.S. State Dept., 1964—; rotational officer U.S. Embassy, Beirut, Lebanon, 1964-66; polit. officer Nairobi, Kenya, 1967-68; desk officer East African affairs Washington, 1969-72; polit. officer Dar es Salaam, Tanzania, 1972-74; dep. chief of mission Nouakchott, Mauritania, 1974-76, Office of Mayor, City of Seattle, 1977-78; dep. coord. state and local govt. U.S. Dept. State, Washington, 1978-81; dep. chief of mission Yaounde, Cameroon, 1981-83, Khartoum, Sudan, 1983-86; U.S. ambassador Ouagadougou, Burkina Faso, 1987-90; diplomat-in-residence Southern U., Baton Rouge, La., 1990-91; diplomat State Dept., Washington, 1991—. Recipient Superior Honor award State Dept., 1980, 85, 94, Alumnus of Yr. award Am. Assn. Cmty. Colls., 1994, Phi Theta Kappa, 1995. Mem. Internat. Studies Assn., Am. Fgn. Service Assn., Am. Philatelic Soc. Methodist. Avocations: philately, skiing, softball, tennis, volleyball. Office: US Dept State Washington DC 20520

SHINN, GEORGE, owner NBA franchise; b. Kannapolis, N.C.. Owner The Charlotte (N.C.) Hornets, Charlotte Knights Baseball. Recipient Horatio Alger award, 1975. Mem. Charlotte C. of C. (bd. dirs.). Office: Charlotte Hornets 100 Hive Dr Charlotte NC 28217

SHINN, GEORGE LATIMER, investment banker, consultant, educator; b. Newark, Ohio, Mar. 12, 1923; s. Leon Powell and Bertha Florence (Latimer) S.; m. Clara LeBaron Sampson, May 21, 1949; children: Deborah, Amy, Martha, Sarah, Andrew. AB, Amherst Coll., 1948; LLD (hon.), Denison U., 1975, Amherst Coll., 1982; MA, Drew U., 1990, PhD, 1992. Trainee Merrill Lynch, Pierce, Fenner & Beane, 1948-49; various exec. positions, 1949-75; pres. Merrill Lyncy & Co., Inc.; also pres. Merrill Lynch & Co., Inc., 1974-75; chmn. bd., chief exec. officer 1st Boston Corp., 1975-83, First Boston Inc., 1976-83; investment banking consultant, 1983—; adj. prof. philosophy Drew U., Madison, N.J., 1992—; mem. exec. com. President's Pvt. Sector Survey on Cost Control, 1982-84; exec.-in-residence Columbia U. Grad. Sch. Bus., 1983-85; bd. govs. Am. Stock Exch., 1970-74; bd. dirs., trustee Colonial Group Mut. Funds. Gen. chmn. United Hosp. Fund, N.Y.C., 1973-74; trustee Kent Pl. Sch., Summit, N.J., 1966-73, Carnegie Found. for Advancement Teaching, 1976-85, Pingry Sch., 1977-79, Lucille P. Markey Charitable Trust, 1985—, Rockefeller Family Office Trust, 1989—, N.J. Coun. for the Humanities, 1994—, Arts Coun. Morris Area, 1978-91, Philharmonic Symphony Soc. N.Y., 1983-91, Nat. Humanities Ctr., 1988-94; trustee emeritus Amherst Coll., 1968-82, chmn. bd. trustees, 1973-80; bd. dirs. Rsch. Corp., 1975-86. Capt. USMCR, 1943-52. Fellow Am. Acad. Arts and Scis., River Club, Century Assn., Morris County Golf Club. Office: CS First Boston 12 E 49th St New York NY 10017

SHINN, RICHARD RANDOLPH, former insurance executive, former stock exchange executive; b. Lakewood, N.J., Jan. 7, 1918; s. Clayton Randolph and Carrie (McGravey) S.; m. Mary Helen Shea, Nov. 8, 1941; children: Kathleen, Patricia, John; m. Marion Berenson Weitman, Nov. 30, 1985. B.S., Rider Coll., 1938. C.L.U., 1949. With Met. Life Ins. Co., 1939-83, 2d v.p., 1959-63, v.p., 1963-64, sr. v.p., 1964-66, exec. v.p., 1966-68, sr. exec. v.p., 1968- 69, pres., dir., 1969-83, chief exec. officer, 1973-83, chmn., 1980-83, ret., 1983; exec. vice chmn. NYSE, N.Y.C., 1986-91; chmn. Olympia & York USA, 1993; bd. dirs. Union Tex. Petroleum Co., Grey Advt. Bd. dirs. Lincoln Ctr. for the Performing Arts, Inc.; mem. Cardinal's Com. for the Laity. Mem. Met. Opera Assn., Knights of Malta. Clubs: The Blind Brook (Port Chester, N.Y.); Round Hill (Greenwich, Conn.); Riverside Yacht; Sky Club, Links (N.Y.C.); Gulfstream Golf (Fla.), Delray Yacht Club (Fla.). Home: 136 Parsonage Rd Greenwich CT 06830-3943 Office: MetLife Bldg 200 Park Ave Ste 5700 New York NY 10166-0005

SHINNAR, REUEL, chemical engineering educator, industrial consultant; b. Vienna, Austria, Sept. 15, 1923; came to U.S., 1962; s. Abraham Emil and Rosa (Storch) Bardfeld; m. Miryam Halpern, June 22, 1948; children—Shlomo, Meir. Diploma in Chem. Engring., Technion, Haifa, Israel, 1945, M.Sc. in Chem. Engring., 1954; Dr. Engring. Sci., Columbia U., 1957. Various position in chem. engring. Israel, 1945-58; adj. assoc. prof. Technion, Haifa, Israel, 1958-62; visiting research fellow Guggenheim Labs., Princeton (N.J.) U., 1962-64; prof. chem. engring. CCNY, 1964—, disting. prof., 1979—; Pinhas Naor lectr. Technion U., 1974; Wilhelm Meml. lectr. Princeton U., 1985, Kelly lectr. Purdue U., 1991; cons. to various oil and chem. cos. Contbr. numerous articles to profl. jours.; patentee in field. Fellow AICE (Founders award 1992, Alpha Chi Sigma award 1979), N.Y. Acad. Scis.; mem. AIAA, Am. Chem. Soc., Nat. Acad. Engring. Office: City Coll NY Dept Chem Engring 140th St and Convent Ave New York NY 10031

SHINNAR, SHLOMO, child neurologist, educator; b. Haifa, Israel, Nov. 11, 1950; s. Reuel and Miryam (Halpern) S.; m. Shoshana Ellen Cohen, Aug. 11, 1974; children: Ora Rivka, Aviva Batya, Avraham Ever. BA in Physics summa cum laude, Columbia Coll., 1971; PhD, Albert Einstein Coll. Medicine, 1977, MD, 1978. Diplomate Am. Bd. Pediatrics, Am. Bd. Psychiatry and Neurology. Intern, asst. resident in pediatrics, fellow Johns Hopkins Hosp., Balt., 1978-80, asst. resident, resident in neurology, fellow, 1980-83; from asst. prof. neurology and pediatrics to prof. neurology and pediatrics Albert Einstein Coll. Medicine, Bronx, 1983—; from asst. attending to attending neurology and pediatrics Montefiore Med. Ctr., Bronx Mcpl. & North Ctrl. Bronx Hosps., 1983—; dir. CERC Seizure Clinic R.K. Kennedy Ctr., Bronx, 1983—; co-dir. Epilepsy Mgmt. Ctr., Montefiore Med. Ctr., Albert Einstein Coll. Medicine, Bronx, 1983-86, dir., 1986—; mem. adv. bd. Epilepsy Inst., N.Y.C., 1984—, instnl. rev. bd. protection of human subjects Montefiore Med. Ctr., Bronx, 1985—, vice chmn., 1989—; adj. sch. scientist Gertrude Sergievsky Ctr., Columbia Coll. Physicians and Surgeons, N.Y.C., 1985—, Sergievsky Scholar, 1986—; cons. in field. Field editor Epilepsy Advances, 1987-93; editl. bd. The Neurologist, 1993—, Epilepsia, 1994—, Pediatric Neurology, 1995—; contbr. articles to profl. jours. N.Y. State Regents scholar, 1967-71; Martin and Emily L. Fisher fellow, 1991—. Fellow Am. Acad. Pediats.; mem. Am. Epilepsy Soc. (profl. adv. bd. chmn. childhood onset epilepsy com. 1993-95, councillor 1992-95, Rsch. Recognition award 1989), Am. Acad. Neurology, Child Neurology Soc., Eastern EEG Soc., Internat. Child Neurology soc., Nat. Assn. Epilepsy Ctrs., Soc. for Pediat. Rsch., Am. Neurol. Assn. Office: Montefiore Med Ctr 111 E 210th St Bronx NY 10467-2490

SHINNERS, STANLEY MARVIN, electrical engineer; b. N.Y.C., May 9, 1933; s. Earl and Molly (Planter) S.; m. Doris Pinsker, Aug. 4, 1956; children: Sharon Rose Cooper, Walter Jay, Daniel Lawrence. BEE, CCNY, 1954; MS in Elect. Engring., Columbia U., 1959. Equipment engr. Western Electric Co., N.Y.C., 1953-54; staff engr. electronics div. Otis Elevator Co., Bklyn., 1954-56; project engr. Consol. Avionics Corp., Westbury, N.Y., 1956-58; sr. rsch. sect. head tactical sys. sector Lockheed Martin Corp. (formerly Loral Corp., Unisys Corp.), Great Neck, N.Y., 1958—; adj. prof. engring. The Cooper Union, N.Y.C., 1966—, N.Y. Inst. Tech., Old Westbury, N.Y., 1972-92, Poly. Inst. Bklyn., 1959-72. Author: Control System Design, 1964, Techniques of Systems Engineering, 1967, A Guide to Systems Engineering and Management, 1976, Modern Control System Theory and Application, 1978, Modern Control System Theory and Design, 1992. Recipient Career Achievement medal CCNY Alumni Assn., 1980. Fellow IEEE; mem. Am. Soc. for Engring. Edn., Eta Kappa Nu, Tau Beta

Pi. Home: 28 Sagamore Way N Jericho NY 11753-2358 *I was very poor economically as a child, but I received an abundance of love and encouragement from parents and family. I have always tried to succeed and to help others succeed. Above all, I have always tried to do what is right whether the decision had to be made in the business world or in private and family matters.*

SHINOLT, EILEEN THELMA, artist; b. Washington, May 18, 1919; d. Edward Lee and Blanche Adele (Marsh) Bennett; m. John Francis Shinolt, June 14, 1956 (dec. Aug. 1969). Student, Hans Hoffman Sch Art, 1949, Pa. Acad. Arts, 1950, Corcoran Sch. Art, 1945-51, Am. U., 1973-77. Sect. chief Dept. Army, Washington, 1940-73, retired, 1973. One-woman shows include various locations, 1982, 83, 85, 90, 94, 96; group shows include Perlmutter & Co., 1981, Fitch Fox and Brown, 1986, Foundry Gallery, 1987, Ann. Add Arts, 1986, Westminster Gallery, London, 1995; represented in permanent collections Women's Nat. Mus., Washington, Cameo Gallery, Columbia, S.C., others. Mem. Woman's Nat. Dem. Club, Washington, 1980—. Mem. Am. Art League (editor newsletter 1985-86, 1st pl. 1987, 2d pl. 1986), Arts Club Washington (exhbn. com. 1985—, admissions com. 1987-88), Miniature Painters, Sculptors & Gravers Soc. (historian 1989—, editor newsletter 1986-89). Roman Catholic. Avocations: reading, studying art periodicals, art galleries. Home: 4119 Davis Pl NW Apt 203 Washington DC 20007-1254

SHIPLER, DAVID KARR, journalist, correspondent, author; b. Orange, N.J., Dec. 3, 1942; s. Guy Emery Jr. and Eleanor (Karr) S.; m. Deborah S. Isaacs, Sept. 17, 1966; children: Jonathan Robert, Laura Karr, Michael Edmund. AB, Dartmouth Coll., 1964; LittD (hon.), Middlebury Coll., 1988, Glassboro (N.J.) State Coll., 1988; AM (hon.), Dartmouth Coll., 1994. News clk. N.Y. Times, 1966-67, news summary writer, 1968, reporter met. staff, 1968-73, fgn. corr. Saigon bur., 1973-75, fgn. corr. Moscow Bur., 1975—, bur. chief Moscow Bur., 1977-79, chief Jerusalem bur., 1979-84, corr. Washington bur., 1985-87, chief diplomatic corr., 1987-88; sr. assoc. Carnegie Endowment for Internat. Peace, Washington, 1988-90; guest scholar Brookings Instn., 1984-85; adj. prof. Am. U. Sch. Internat. Svc., Washington, 1990; Ferris prof. journalism and pub. affairs, Princeton U., 1990-91; Woodrow Wilson vis. fellow, 1990—. Author: Russia: Broken Idols, Solemn Dreams, 1983 (Overseas Press Club award), Arab and Jew: Wounded Spirits in a Promised Land, 1986 (Pulitzer prize for Gen. Nonfiction 1987), exec. producer, prin. writer, narrator documentary film made from book, 1989 (Alfred DuPont-Columbia U. award for Broadcast Journalism 1990); contbr. articles to nat. mags. Trustee Dartmouth Coll. With USNR, 1964-66. Recipient award for disting. reporting Soc. Silurians, 1971; award for disting. pub. affairs reporting Am. Polit. Scis. Assn., 1971; award N.Y. chpt. Sigma Delta Chi, 1973; co-recipient George Polk award, 1982. Mem. Human Rights Watch Middle East (adv. com.). Office: 4005 Thornapple St Chevy Chase MD 20815-5037 *I have been governed professionally by the conviction that an open society needs open examination of itself to survive. Defining problems, inspecting blemishes, probing wounds, and exposing injustice are the required pastimes of a free people. Nothing intelligent can come from ignorance. If information does not guarantee wisdom, it is at least a prerequisite, for the only wise course is through knowledge. To write about current affairs, then, is to play a small role in a great endeavor. It is to measure one's own performance continually against the highest standards of honesty, fairness, thoroughness, intelligence, to search every day for a bit of truth, then share it. These are the ingredients of happiness, for such a job involves a life of constant learning, perpetual self-education. It keeps a man whole.*

SHIPLEY, DAVID ELLIOTT, university dean, lawyer; b. Urbana, Ill., Oct. 3, 1950; s. James Ross and Dorothy Jean (Elliott) S.; m. Virginia Florence Coleman, May 24, 1980; 1 child, Shannon C. BA, Oberlin Coll., 1972; JD, U. Chgo., 1975. Bar: R.I. 1975. Assoc. Tillinghast, Collins & Graham, Providence, 1975-77; asst. prof. U. S.C. Sch. Law, Columbia, 1977-81, assoc. prof., 1981-85, prof., 1985-90, assoc. dean, 1989-90; dean U. Miss. Sch. Law, University, 1990-93, U. Ky. Coll. Law, Lexington, 1993—; vis. prof. Coll. William and Mary, Williamsburg, Va., 1983-84, Ohio State U. Coll. Law, Columbus, 1986-87. Author: South Carolina Administrative Law, 1983, 2d edit., 1989; co-author Copyright Law, 1992. Pres. Shandon Neighborhood Assn., Columbia, 1988-90. Named Prof. of Yr., U. S.C. Sch. Law, 1990, faculty scholar, 1989-90. Mem. ABA, R.I. Bar Assn., S.C. Bar Assn. (assoc.). Methodist. Avocations: running, yardwork, gardening, reading. Home: 827 Lakeshore Dr Lexington KY 40502-3125 Office: U Ky Coll Law Lexington KY 40506-0048

SHIPLEY, L. PARKS, JR., banker; b. Orange, N.J., Aug. 2, 1931; s. L. Parks and Emily Catherine (Herzog) S.; m. Micheline Genevieve Oltramare, Apr. 2, 1966; children—Christiane, Daniel, Alix. B.A., Yale U., 1953. Vol. Moral ReArmament, Europe, Africa, S.Am., 1954-64; participant in founding Up With People Inc., 1964-69; from internat. banking officer to v.p. Marine Midland Bank, N.Y.C., 1969-76; v.p. Irving Trust Co., N.Y.C., 1976-84, exec. v.p., 1984-89; exec. v.p. Bank of N.Y., N.Y.C., 1989-90; pres. Ultramar Assoc., Inc., N.Y.C., 1990-91, Ultramar Group, Inc., 1991-92; U.S. rep., bd. advisor Banco Credito Argentino; pres. Shipley Assocs.; bd. dirs. The Keimei Fund for Internat. Edn. Inc. Trustee Young Life, 1991; mem. adv. bd. Ams. Soc. Corp. Program. Mem. Brazilian Am. C. of C., Yale Club, Baltusrol Golf Club, Nagelvoort and Co. Adv. Bd. Home: 77 Bellevue Ave Summit NJ 07901-2007 Office: 630 5th Ave Ste 3170 New York NY 10111-0001

SHIPLEY, LUCIA HELENE, retired chemical company executive; b. Boston, Oct. 26, 1920; d. Harry Jacob and Helen Merrill (Dillingham) Farrington; m. Charles Raymond Shipley, Oct. 11, 1941; children: Helen Merrill, Richard Charles. Student, Smith Coll., 1938-41. Chief exec. officer, treas. Shipley Co. Inc., Newton, Mass., 1957-92, also bd. dirs. Patentee for immersion tin, electroless copper. Recipient Winthrop Sears award Chem. Industry Assn., 1985, Semi award Semicon West, 1990. Mem. Garden Club (pres. 1954-56). Republican. Congregationalist. Avocations: gardening, shell collecting, dogs, cage birds.

SHIPLEY, SAMUEL LYNN, advertising and public relations executive; b. Marlborough, Mass., Nov. 14, 1929; s. Clifford Lynn and Esther (Jacobs) S.; m. Sue Finucan, Sept. 5, 1955; children—Jeffrey Lynn, Beth Ann, Amy. Student, Charles Morris Price Sch. Advt. and Journalism, U. N.H., 1948-50. Exec. dir. Democratic Party N.H., 1953-56; pres., chmn. Shipley Assos., Inc., Wilmington, Del., 1962—, Internat. Toy Shows, Inc., 1977—; pres. Cable TV Advt. Inc., 1982—; dir. Del. Devel. Dept., Dover, 1965-69. Del. U.S. Constl. Council of Thirteen Original States, 1976—; nominee for U.S. Congress, 1976; pub. relations dir. Del. Democratic Com., 1964-68; chmn. Del. Dem. Com., 1982-90; bd. dirs. Blood Bank of Del.; pres. Del. Heritage Found., 1980—; bd. trustees Grand Opera House; former chair Dem. State Com. Served with U.S. Army, 1951-53. Recipient Freedoms Found. Honor medal, 1966, Outstanding Grad. award Charles Morris Price Sch., 1974. Mem. Am. Advt. Fedn., Wilmington Advt. Club. Clubs: Mason. (Wilmington), Masonic of Del. (Wilmington). Home: 1196 Paper Mill Rd Newark DE 19711-2924 Office: 1300 Pennsylvania Ave Wilmington DE 19806-4311 *The ingredients for success are good health, average intelligence, a giving spirit, positive thinking, good imagination, self-discipline, hard work, and persistence.*

SHIPLEY, TONY L(EE), software company executive; b. Elizabethton, Tenn., July 19, 1946; s. James A. and Edith J. (Crowder) S.; m. Lynda Anne Jenkins, Nov. 19, 1971; children: Blake Alan, Sarah Robyn. BS in Indsl. Engring., U. Tenn., 1969; MBA, U. Cin., 1975. Indsl. engr. Monsanto Co., Pensacola, Fla., 1969-72; mktg. mgr. SDRC, Cin., 1972-76; v.p. sales and mktg. Anatrol Corp., Cin., 1977-81; pres. Entek Sci. Corp., Cin., 1981—. Named Small Bus. Person of Yr., Greater Cin. C. of C., 1994. Mem. ASME, The Exec. Com., Soc. Automotive Engrs., Vibration Inst., Greater Cin. Software Assn., Greater Cin. C. of C., Leadership Class XVIII, Terrace Park (Ohio) Country Club. Republican. Avocations: golf, family activities. Home: 7 Laurelwood Milford OH 45150-9748 Office: Entek Sci Corp 4480 Lake Forest Dr Ste 316 Cincinnati OH 45242-3753

SHIPLEY, VERGIL ALAN, political science educator; b. Amber, Okla., June 25, 1922; s. Guy and Ida Jean (Grant) S.; m. Zannie May Manning, May 3, 1947; children—Douglass Manning, John Grant. B.A., U. Okla., 1947, M.A., 1948; postgrad., U. Tex., 1947; Ph.D., London (Eng.) Sch. Econs., 1950. Assoc. prof. polit. sci. Wichita State U., 1950-56; asst. prof. govt. U. Miami, Coral Gables, Fla., 1957-61; assoc. prof. U. Miami, 1962-68, prof. politics and pub. affairs, 1968-89, prof. emeritus, 1989—, chmn. dept., 1970-77; acting dean Sch. Bus. Adminstrn., 1968-69; Polit. election analyst WTVJ-CBS, 1962-84; cons. to study commn. on local govt., 1971-72. Served to capt. AUS, 1942-46, ETO. Mem. Am. Polit. Sci. Assn., Am. Soc. Pub. Adminstrn., Phi Beta Kappa, Phi Eta Sigma, Pi Sigma Alpha, Beta Gamma Sigma (pres. U. Miami chpt. 1969), Delta Sigma Pi (faculty adviser 1968-76). Democrat. Home: 1127 Alberca St Miami FL 33134-2446 Office: U Miami Dept Politics Pub Affa Coral Gables FL 33124

SHIPLEY, WALTER VINCENT, banker; b. Newark, Nov. 2, 1935; s. L. Parks and Emily (Herzog) S.; m. Judith Ann Lyman, Sept. 14, 1957; children: Barbara, Allison, Pamela, Dorothy, John. Student, Williams Coll., 1954-56; BS, NYU, 1961. With Chem. Bank, N.Y.C., 1956-96, pres., 1982-83, chmn. bd., 1983-91, pres., 1992-93, chmn., CEO, 1994-96; chmn., CEO Chase Manhattan Corp., N.Y.C., 1996—; Bd. dirs. Champion Internat. Corp., NYNEX Corp., Reader's Digest Assn., Inc. Bd. dirs. Lincoln Ctr. for Performing Arts Inc., Goodwill Industries Greater N.Y. Inc., United Way Am., United Way Tri-State. Mem. The Bus. Coun., Bus Roundtable, Coun. Fgn. Rels., Trilateral Commn., Links, Augusta Nat. Golf Club, Baltusrol Golf Club (Springfield, N.J.). Office: Chase Manhattan Corp 270 Park Ave New York NY 10017-2070

SHIPMAN, CHARLES WILLIAM, chemical engineer; b. Phillipsburgh, N.J., Aug. 29, 1924; s. George Funk and Elizabeth (Johnston) S.; m. Louise Jean Hendrickson, Aug. 31, 1946; children—Nancy Ruth, Jane Louise, Robert Walter George. SB, MIT, 1948, SM, 1949, ScD, 1952. Instr. chem. engring. MIT, 1949-50, research assoc., 1955-58; asst. prof. U. Del., 1952-55; mem. faculty Worcester (Mass.) Poly. Inst., 1958-74, prof. chem. engring., 1964-74, dean grad. studies, 1971-74; engr. Cabot Corp., Billerica, Mass., 1974-87; mgr. Carbon Black R/D, 1980-86; cons., 1953-74, 1987—; bd. dirs. Knox Dist. Housing, Bar Harbor, Maine, 1988—, MDI Helpers, Bar Harbor, 1988-90, treas. 1989-90. Contbr. articles to profl. jours. Trustee Monteux Meml. Found., 1994—. With USMCR, 1944-46. Mem. Combustion Inst. (recipient Silver Combustion medal 1964, bd. dirs. 1978-90), Am. Chem. Soc., Am. Inst. Chem. Engrs., Sigma Xi, Alpha Chi Sigma, Chi Phi. Home and Office: PO Box 32 Prospect Harbor ME 04669-0032

SHIPPEY, SANDRA LEE, lawyer; b. Casper, Wyo., June 24, 1957; d. Virgil Carr and Doris Louise (Conklin) McC.; m. Ojars Herberts Ozols, Sept. 2, 1978 (div.); children: Michael Ojars, Sara Ann, Brian Christopher; m. James Robert Shippey, Jan. 13, 1991. BA with distinction, U. Colo., 1978; JD magna cum laude, Boston U., 1982. Bar: Colo. 1982, U.S. Dist. Ct. Colo. 1985. Assoc. Cohen, Brame & Smith, Denver, 1983-84, Parcel, Meyer, Schwartz, Ruttum & Mauro, Denver, 1984-85, Mayer, Brown & Platt, Denver, 1985-87; counsel western ops. GE Capital Corp., San Diego, 1987-94; assoc. Page, Polin, Busch & Boatwright, San Diego, 1994-95; v.p., gen. counsel First Comml. Corp., San Diego, 1995—. Active Pop Warner football and cheerleading. Mem. Phi Beta Kappa, Phi Delta Phi. Republican. Mem. Ch. of Christ. Avocations: tennis, photography. Home: 11878 Glenhope Rd San Diego CA 92128-5002 Office: First Comml Corp Ste 1000 550 West C St Ste 1000 San Diego CA 92101

SHIPTON, HAROLD WILLIAM, biomedical engineering educator, researcher; b. Birmingham, Eng., Sept. 29, 1920; came to U.S., 1957; Student, Shrewsbury (Eng.) Tech. Coll., 1938. Engr. Burden Neurol. Inst., Bristol, Eng., 1946-57; asst. prof. biomed. engring. U. Iowa, Iowa City, 1957-59, prof., 1959-79; prof. biomed. engring. Washington U., St. Louis, 1979-89, prof. emeritus, 1989—, chmn. dept., 1986-89, chmn. pro tem dept. elec. engring., 1986-87; mem. study sect. NIH, 1965-70. Assoc. editor Jour. EEG and Clin. Neurophysiology; contbr. articles to profl. jours. Served with RAAF, 1940-47. Grantee NIH, 1968-76. Fellow Am. EEG Soc. (hon.); mem. The EEG Soc. U.K. (hon.), Cen. Assn. EEG (pres. 1975). Unitarian. Avocation: literature; lic. pilot. Home: 4 N Kingshighway Blvd Saint Louis MO 63108-1358 Office: Washington U Dept Biomed Engring 1 Brookings Dr Saint Louis MO 63130-4862

SHIRA, ROBERT BRUCE, university administrator, oral surgery educator; b. Butler, Pa., Dec. 2, 1910; s. Thomas Plummer and Erla (Brown) S.; m. Anne Eileen Anderson, Mar. 27, 1933; children: Sharon Lu, Mary Ann, Linda Kay. Student, Bartlesville (Okla.) Jr. Coll., 1927-28; D.D.S., U. Mo., Kansas City, 1932; D.Sc., Georgetown U., 1976, Tufts U., 1979, U. Mo., Kansas City, 1982, U. Detroit, 1987. Diplomate: Am. Bd. Oral and Maxillofacial Surgery (pres. 1974-75). Pvt. practice dentistry Pawhuska, Okla., 1932-38; commd. 1st lt., Dental Corps U.S. Army, 1938, advanced through grades to maj. gen., 1967; chief oral surgery Walter Reed Gen. Hosp., 1954-64; dir. dental activities Walter Reed Army Med. Center, 1966-67; dental surgeon Europe, 1964-66; asst. surgeon gen., chief Army Dental Corps, 1967-71; ret., 1971; prof. oral surgery Tufts U., Boston, 1971-93; dean Sch. Dental Medicine, Tufts U., Boston, 1972-78; sr. v.p., provost Tufts U., Boston, 1979-82, asst. to pres., 1982-93; vis. prof. U. of Pacific, 1954-71, U. Pa., 1956-71; professorial lectr. Georgetown U., 1955-71. Contbr.: chpts. Textbook of Oral Surgery, 1973, Management of Office Emergencies, 1979, Improving Dental Practice through Preventive Measures, 1965; contbr. articles to profl. jours. Decorated D.S.M., Legion of Merit with 2 oak leaf clusters, Army Commendation medal, Army Disting. Svc. medal, Army Disting. Svc. medal; recipient Sword of Hope award Am. Cancer Soc., 1959; named Man of Yr. U. Mo., Kansas City, 1960. Mem. ADA (pres. 1975-76, cons. Council on Therapeutics, Disting. Service award), Am. Assn. Oral and Maxillofacial Surgery (pres. 1965-66), Am. Acad. Oral Pathology. Republican. Presbyterian. Home: Ste 814 3310 N Leisure World Blvd Silver Spring MD 20906

SHIRAI, SCOTT, communications executive; b. Honolulu, June 5, 1942; s. George Yoshio and Thelma Takeko (Tominaga) M.; children: Todd, Kimberly, Lance, Lyle. MusB, U. Hawaii, 1983; exec. dir. news, reporter Sta. KHON-TV, Honolulu, 1974-81; asst. gen. mgr. Vanguard Investments, Berkeley, Calif., 1976-79; newscaster Sta. KPOI, Honolulu, 1979-80; news dir. Sta. KGU, Honolulu, 1981-82; owner Visual Perspectives, 1981—; dir. pub. rels. Hawaiian Electric Co., Honolulu, 1982-90; dir. cmty. rels., Hawaiian Electric Industries, 1990—; instr. U. Hawaii, 1984—; dir. BBB of Hawaii, 1995, Hawaii Pub. Broadcasting, 1996. Bd. dirs., sec. Hawaii Com. For Freedom of Press, 1982—; bd. dirs. Mental Health Assn. in Hawaii, 1981—, Moanalua Gardens Found., 1981-84, Health and Cmty. Svcs. Coun., 1982-86, Friends of Father Damien, 1986; v.p. Mele Nani Singers, 1986—; mem. Mayors Adv. Com. on Mcpl. TV, 1987, Office of Hawaiian Affairs Pub. Rels. Adv. Com., 1987, (all Honolulu); sec., dir. Pro Geothermal Alliance, 1990-91. Recipient Jefferson award Honolulu Advertiser, 1985, Gold award Audio-Visual Producers Assn. Am., 1985, Audio-Visual Dept. of Yr. award Videography mag., 1986, Award of Excellence Nat. Hospice Orgn., 1987, Intre award Inst. Teleradial Atica Puerto Rico, Inc., 1988. Mem. ASTD, Internat. TV Assn. (pres. 1983—), Am. Film Inst., AFTRA (bd. dirs. 1980-83), Pub. Rels. Soc. Am. (immediate past pres. and del. 1995—), Hawaii Speakers Assn., Hawaii Film Bd., Honolulu Cmty. Media Council, Hawaii Cmty. TV Assn. (pres. 1990—). Clubs: Honolulu Press (bd. dirs. 1984—), Hui Luna (bd. dirs. 1986-90) (Honolulu). Avocations: martial arts, singing. Office: Hawaiian Electric Industries PO Box 730 1001 Bishop St Ste 811 Honolulu HI 96813

SHIRAI, SHUN, law educator, lawyer; b. Tokyo, June 18, 1942; s. Kyo and Tomi Shirai; m. Junko Matsushita, Apr. 10, 1969; children: Akiko, Yuko, Jin. LLB, Hitotsubashi U., Tokyo, 1966, LLM, 1969. Cert. atty. at law. Asst. prof. criminal law Kokugakuin U., Tokyo, 1974-81, prof., 1981—; atty. at law Tokyo (Japan) 2nd Bar Assn., 1992—. Author: Phenomenology of Crime, 1984, Thought on Criminal Law of Ancient India, 1985, Legal History on Criminal Law of Ancient India, 1990, Philosophy of Criminal Law in Ancient India, 1995. Mem. Indian History Congress. Buddhist. Home: 17-25 Matsudoshinden, Matsudo-shi Chiba Pref 271, Japan Office: Kokugakuin U, 4-10-28 Higashi Shibuya-Ku, Tokyo 150, Japan

SHIRBROUN, RICHARD ELMER, veterinarian, cattleman; b. Coon Rapids, Iowa, Oct. 22, 1929; s. Francis Clyde and Clara Mable (Bell) S.; m. Treva Margaret Teter (div.), Sept. 9, 1951; children: Randal Mark, Camille Lean, James Bradley; m. Wava Lynne Frank, Nov. 11, 1989. DVM, Iowa State U., 1952. Owner, vet. Shirbroun Vet. Med. Ctr., Coon Rapids, 1955—. Lt. USAF, 1952-55. Mem. AVMA (trustee 1982—), Am. Assn. Bovine Practitioners (bd. dirs. 1982—, Excellence Preventive Medicine award 1987), Am. Assn. Swine Practitioners, Iowa Vet. Med. Assn. (pres. 1981, Pres.' award 1985), Soc. for Theriogenology, N.Am. Limousin Found. (founding mem. 1968), Nat. Cattlemen Assn., Iowa Cattlemen Assn., Am. Legion, Rotary (pres. Coon Rapids 1965). Republican. Methodist. Home and Office: Shirbroun Vet Med Ctr 32284 Velvet Ave Coon Rapids IA 50058

SHIRE, DAVID LEE, composer; b. Buffalo, July 3, 1937; s. Irving Daniel and Esther Miriam (Sheinberg) S.; m. Talia Rose Coppola, Mar. 29, 1970 (div.); 1 child, Matthew Orlando; m. Didi Conn. Feb. 11, 1984; 1 child, Daniel Joshua. BA, Yale U., 1959. Film scores include The Conversation, 1974, The Taking of Pelham 1-2-3, 1974, Farewell, My Lovely, 1975, The Hindenburg, 1975, All the President's Men, 1977, Saturday Night Fever (adaptation and additional music), 1977, Norma Rae, 1979 (Acad. award for best original song It Goes Like It Goes), Only When I Laugh, 1981, The World According to Garp, 1982, Max Dugan Returns, 1983, 2010, 1984, Return to Oz, 1985, Short Circuit, 1986, 'Night, Mother, 1986, Vice Versa, 1988, Monkey Shines, 1988, Paris Trout, 1991, Bed and Breakfast, 1992, The Journey Inside (IMAX), 1993, One Night Stand, 1994; TV scores include Raid on Entebbe, 1977 (Emmy nomination), The Defection of Simas Kudirka, 1978 (Emmy nomination), Do You Remember Love?, 1985 (Emmy nomination), Promise, 1986, Echoes in the Darkness, 1987, The Women of Brewster Place, 1989, The Kennedys of Massachusetts, 1990 (Emmy nomination), Common Ground, 1990, Sarah Plain & Tall, 1991, Last Wish, 1992, Broadway Bound, 1992, Skylark, 1993, Remember, 1993, The Companion, 1994, My Brother's Keeper, 1995, Serving in Silence, 1995, The Heidi Chronicles, 1995, My Antonia, 1995, The Streets of Laredo, 1995; theatre scores include The Sap of Life, 1961, Graham Crackers, 1962, The Unknown Soldier and His Wife, 1967, How Do You Do, I Love You, 1968, Love Match, 1970, Starting Here, Starting Now, 1977, Baby, 1983 (Tony nominee best mus. and best original score), Urban Blight, 1988, Closer Than Ever, 1989 (Outer Critics Circle award best off-Broadway musical and best score), Big, 1996; composer Sonata for Cocktail Piano, 1965; recorded songs include Autumn, 1959, Starting Here, Starting Now, 1965, What About Today?, 1969, Manhattan Skyline, 1977, The Promise, 1978 (Acad. award nomination), It Goes Like It Goes, 1979 (Acad. award), With You I'm Born Again, 1979; albums include Saturday Night Fever, 1977 (Grammy award 1978), Starting Here, Starting Now, 1977 (Grammy nomination 1977), Baby, 1984, Return to Oz, 1985, Closer Than Ever, 1990, David Shire at The Movies, 1991. With Army N.G., 1960-66. Mem. Composers and Lyricists Guild Am., Am. Fedn. Musicians, Broadcast Music Inc., Acad. Motion Picture Arts and Scis., Nat. Acad. Rec. Arts and Scis., Nat. Acad. TV Arts and Scis. Jewish. Office: Savitsky Stain & Geibelson Ste 1450 1901 Avenue Of The Stars Los Angeles CA 90067-6015

SHIRE, DONALD THOMAS, retired air products and chemicals executive, lawyer; b. Boston, Jan. 13, 1930; s. Thomas J. and Nellie M. S.; m. Anne Court Bither, Nov 21, 1953; children: Jennifer Anne, Andrew Carter, Daniel Orchard. B.S. in Bus. Adminstrn, Boston U., 1951, LL.B., 1953; postgrad., Harvard Bus. Sch., 1985. Atty. Air Products and Chems., Inc., 1957-64, sec., atty., 1964-75, sec., asst. gen. counsel, 1975-78, v.p. energy and materials, 1978-85, v.p. human resources, 1986-90, sr. v.p. human resources and adminstrn., 1990-91, sr. v.p. adminstrn., 1991-93; ret., 1993; also bd. dirs. Air Products and Chems., Inc.; chmn. Air Products Found., 1991-93; bd. dirs., v.p. Exec. Svc. Corps of Lehigh Valley; bd. dirs. Lehigh Valley 2000: A Bus. Edn. Partnership. Trustee Muhlenberg Coll., 1976-95, Lehigh Valley Hosp. Lt. USNR, 1954-57. Mem. Am. Arbitration Assn. Episcopalian. Home: 1133 N Main St Allentown PA 18104-2913 Office: Air Products and Chems Inc 7201 Hamilton Blvd Allentown PA 18195-1526

SHIREMAN, JOAN FOSTER, social work educator; b. Cleve., Oct. 28, 1933; d. Louis Omar and Genevieve (Duguid) Foster; m. Charles Howard Shireman, Mar. 18, 1967; 1 child, David Louis. BA, Radcliffe Coll., 1956; MA, U. Chgo., 1959, PhD, 1968. Caseworker N.H. Children's Aid Soc., Manchester, 1959-61; dir. research Chgo. Child Care Soc., 1968-72; assoc. prof. U. Ill., Chgo., 1972-85; prof. Portland (Oreg.) State U., 1985—, dir. PhD program, 1992—; interim exec. dir. Partnership for Rsch., Tng. and Grad. Edn. in Child Welfare, 1994; research cons. child welfare orgns., Ill., 1968-85, Oreg. 1985—; lectr. U. Chgo., 1968-72. Co-author: Care and Commitment: Foster Parent Adoption Decisions, 1985; mem. editl. bd. Jour. Sch. Social Work, 1978-81, Social Work Rsch. and Abstracts, 1990-93, Children and Youth Svcs. Rev., 1990-95, Jour. Social Work Edn., 1990-95; contbr. articles to profl. jours., chpts. to books. Bd. dirs. Oreg. chpt. Nat. Assn. for Prevention Child Abuse, 1985-87; bd. dirs. Friendly House, Portland, 1991—, pres., 1995-96; mem. adv. com. children's svcs. divsn. State of Oreg., 1985-95. Grantee HEW, 1980-82, Chgo. Community Trust, 1982-86, Oreg. Children's Trust Fund, 1991-96. Mem. NASW, AAUP, Am. Profl. Soc. Abuse of Children, Children First Oreg., Acad. Cert. Social Workers, Coun. on Social Work Edn., Phi Beta Kappa. Home: 2535 SW Sherwood Dr Portland OR 97201-1679 Office: Portland State U Grad Sch Social Work PO Box 751 Portland OR 97207-0751

SHIRER, BRUCE EDWARD, pathologist; b. Chgo., Sept. 22, 1941; s. Benjamin Franklin and Thelma Katherine (Borgstrom) S.; m. Janett Margaret Jurasek, Sept. 16, 1967 (div. Nov. 1982); m. Linda Locke Sevcik, July 7, 1984; children: Brandt Stephen, Benjamin Stuart. Student, North Ctrl. Coll., Naperville, Ill., 1958-61; MD, U. Wis., 1965. Diplomate Am. Bd. Pathology. Resident internal medicine Northwestern U., Chgo., 1968-69, resident in pathology, 1969-73; pathologist, co-dir. San Diego Inst. Pathology, 1973-82; locum tenens pathologist various labs., San Diego, 1982-84; med. dir. Lab. Corp. Am., San Diego, 1984—; assoc. pathologist Yuma (Ariz.) Regional Med. Ctr., 1986—. Lt. comdr. USNR, 1966-68, Vietnam. Fellow Coll. AM. Pathologists, Am. Soc. Clin. Pathologists; mem. AMA, Calif. Med. Assn., San Diego County Med. Soc. Republican. Avocations: travel, skiing, classical music, opera, reading. Home: 5566 Rutgers Rd La Jolla CA 92037-7821 Office: Lab Corp Am 5601 Oberlin Dr San Diego CA 92121-3747

SHIRES, GEORGE THOMAS, surgeon, educator; b. Waco, Tex., Nov. 22, 1925; s. George Thomas and Donna Mae (Smith) S.; m. Robbie Jo Martin, Nov. 27, 1948; children: Donna Blain, George Thomas III, Jo Ellen. MD, U. Tex., Dallas, 1948. Diplomate Am. Bd. Surgery (dir. 1968-74, chmn. 1972-74). Intern Mass. Meml. Hosp., Boston, 1948-49; resident Parkland Meml. Hosp., Dallas, 1950-53; mem. faculty U. Tex. Southwestern Med. Sch. at Dallas, 1953-74, assoc. prof. surgery, acting chmn. dept., 1960-61, prof., chmn. dept., 1961-74; surgeon in chief surg. services Parkland Meml. Hosp., 1960-74; prof., chmn. dept. surgery U. Wash. Sch. Medicine, Seattle, 1974-75; chief of service Harborview Med. Center, Seattle, Univ. Hosp., Seattle, 1974-75; chmn. dept. surgery N.Y. Hosp.-Cornell Univ. Med. Coll., 1975-91; dean and provost for med. affairs Cornell U. Med. Coll., 1987-91; prof., chmn. surgery Tex. Tech. U., Lubbock, 1991-95; Canizaro Disting. prof. surgery Canizaro Disting. prof. surgery, Lubbock, 1995—; cons. Surgeon Gen. Army, 1965-75, Jamaica Hosp., 1978-91, Inst. Medicine Nat. Acad. Scis., 1975—; mem. com. metabolism and truama Nat. Acad. Scis.-NRC, 1964-71, com. trauma, 1964-71; mem. rsch. program evaluation com., reviewer clin. investigation applications career devel. program VA, 1972-76; mem. gen. med. rsch. program projects com. NIH, 1965-69; mem. Surgery A study sect., 1970-74, chmn., 1976-78; mem. Nat. Adv. Gen. Med. Scis. Coun., 1980-84; cons. editl. bd. Jour. Trauma, 1968—. Mem. editl. bd. Year Book Med. Publs., 1970-92, Annals of Surgery, 1972—, Surg. Techniques Illustrated: An International Comparative Text, 1974-75, Am. Jour. Surgery, 1968—, Contemporary Surgery, 1973-89; assoc. editor-in-chief Infections in Surgery, 1981; mem. editl. coun. Jour. Clin. Surgery, 1980-82; editor Surgery, Gynecology and Obstetrics, 1982-93. Lt. M.C. USNR, 1949-50, 53-55. Life Ins. Med. Rsch. fellow, 1947. Mem. ACS (bd. regents 1971-82, chmn. bd. regents 1978-80, pres. 1981-82), AMA, Dallas Soc. Gen. Surgeons (pres.-elect, pres. 1972-74), Am. Assn. Surgery Trauma, Am. Surg. Assn. (sec. 1969-74, pres. 1980), Digestive Disease Found. (founding mem.), Halsted Soc., Internat. Soc. Burn Injuries, Internat. Surg. Soc. (sec. 1978-81, v.p. 1982-83, pres. U.S. chpt. 1984-85), Pan-Am. Med. Assn. (surgery council 1971—), Pan Pacific Surg. Assn., Soc. Clin. Surgery, Soc. Surgery Alimentary Tract, Soc. Surg. Chairmen (pres. 1972-74), Soc. Univ. Surgeons (chmn. publs. com. 1969-71), So. Surg. Assn., Surg. Biology Club (sec. 1968-70), Western Surg. Assn., Allen O. Whipple Surg. Soc., James IV Assn. Surgeons (bd. dirs. 1980-81, sec. 1981-87, pres. 1987-91), Alpha Omega

Alpha, Alpha Pi Alpha, Phi Beta Pi. Office: Tex Tech U Med Coll Lubbock TX 79430

SHIRK, RICHARD D., insurance company executive; b. 1946; married. With Equitable Life Assurance, N.Y.C., Houston, 1967-86; pres. so. region Equicor Inc., Nashville, Houston, 1987-90; with Cigna Corp., Houston, 1990-92; pres., CEO Blue Cross & Blue Shield of Ga., Atlanta, 1992—. Office: Blue Cross & Blue Shield of GA 3350 Peachtree Rd NE Atlanta GA 30326-1040*

SHIRLEY, AARON, pediatrician; b. Gluckstadt, Miss., Jan. 3, 1933; married; 4 children. BS, Tougaloo Coll., 1955; MD, McHarry Med. Coll., 1959, U. Miss., 1968. Intern Herbert Hosp., Tenn., 1959-60; gen. practice Vicksburg, 1960-65; project dir. Jackson-Hinds Comprehensive Health Ctr., Jackson, Miss., 1980—; mem. faculty medicine Tufts U. Medicine, Mass., 1968-73, U. Miss. Med. Sch., 1970—; head start cons. Am. Acad. Pediats., 1969-74; adv. bd. rural practice project Robert Wood Johnson Found., 1974-78; mem. Select Panel Prom. Child Health, Washington, 1979-81. Mem. Inst. Medicine-NAS (mem. coun. 1988—). Office: Jackson-Hinds Comp Hlth Ctr 4433 Medgar Evers Blvd Jackson MS 39213*

SHIRLEY, COURTNEY DYMALLY, nurse; b. Trinidad, July 17, 1937; came to U.S., 1960; d. Andrew Hamid Dymally; m. Adolph Shirley, Apr. 8, 1960; children: Ingrid, Robyne, Andrea, Kirk, Sandra. Cert. mgmt./adminstrn. health facilities, UCLA, 1978; BBA, Calif. Coast U., 1980, MBA, 1983. Cert. critical care nurse, advanced critical care nurse, nursing home adminstr. Head nurse med. unit Prince of Wales Gen. Hosp., London, 1959-60; asst. head nurse, CCU staff nurse Cedars-Sinai Hosp., L.A., 1962-73; asst. dir. nursing, dir. in-svc. edn., staff nurse Beverly Glen Hosp., 1973-75; supr. ICU/CCU/house Imperial Hosp., 1975-76; house supr. Med. Ctr. of North Hollywood, 1976-77; dir. nursing Crenshaw Ctr. Hosp., 1977-78, Mid-Wilshire Convalescent, 1978-79; supr. ICU/CCU, coord. utilization rev. Temple U., 1979-80; house supr. East L.A. Doctors' Hosp., 1980-81; pvt. nurse various hosps. and homes, 1981-86; utilization rev. coord. Managed Care Resources, L.A., 1986-88; prof. rev. sys. utilization rev. coord., case mgr. Nat. Med. Enterprises, Santa Monica, Calif., 1988—, cert. case mgr., 1993—. Mem. AACN, Internat. Case Mgmt. Assn., Sci. of Mind, Toastmasters (sgt. at arms 1990). Avocations: reading, scrabble, dominoes, entertaining, blackjack. Office: Nat Med Enterprises 2700 Colorado Ave Santa Monica CA 90404-3521

SHIRLEY, DAVID ARTHUR, chemistry educator, science administrator; b. North Conway, N.H., Mar. 30, 1934; m. Virginia Schultz, June 23, 1956 (dec. Mar. 1995); children: David N., Diane, Michael, Eric, Gail; m. Barbara Cerny, Dec. 26, 1995. BS, U. Maine, 1955, ScD (hon.), 1978; PhD in Chemistry, U. Calif.-Berkeley, 1959; D honoris causa, Free U. Berlin, 1987. With Lawrence Radiation Lab. (now Lawrence Berkeley Lab.), U. Calif., Berkeley, 1958-92, assoc. dir., head materials and molecular research div., 1975-80, dir., 1980-89, lectr. chemistry, 1959-60, asst. prof., 1960-64, assoc. prof., 1964-67, prof., 1967-92, vice chmn. dept. chemistry, 1968-71, chmn. dept. chemistry, 1971-75; sr. v.p. rsch., dean grad. sch. Pa. State U., University Park, 1992—. Contbr. over 400 rsch. articles. NSF fellow, 1955-58, 66-67, 70; recipient Ernest O. Lawrence award AEC, 1972, Humboldt award (sr. U.S. scientist); listed by Sci. Citation Index as one of the world's 300 most cited scientists for work published during 1965-78. Fellow Am. Phys. Soc.; mem. Nat. Acad. Scis., Am. Chem. Soc., AAAS, Am. Acad. Arts and Scis., Sigma Xi, Tau Beta Pi, Sigma Pi Sigma, Phi Kappa Phi.

SHIRLEY, DENNIS LYNN, education educator; b. Columbia, S.C., Feb. 28, 1955; s. Edward Lynn and Margaret Jane (Farnham) S.; m. Laura Shelley Cochran, Jan. 5, 1960; children: Syke Atla, Gabriel Delayne. BA, U. Va., 1977; MA in Sociology, New Sch. for Social Rsch., 1980; EdD, Harvard U., 1988. Tchr. Ecole D'Humanité, Goldern, Switzerland, 1980-83; prof. Rice U., Houston, 1988—. Author: The Politics of Progressive Education: The Odenwaldschule in Nazi Germany, 1992. Fed. Chancellor's scholar Alexander von Humboldt Found., Bonn, Germany, 1990-91. Office: Rice Univ PO Box 1892 Houston TX 77251

SHIRLEY, GLENN DEAN, writer; b. Payne County, Okla., Dec. 9, 1916; s. Ellis Dean and Effie Teresa (Knorr) S.; m. Carrie Mabel Jacob, 1946; children: Glenda Lea, Kenneth Ellis. Diploma, N.Y. Inst. Photography, 1941, Internat. Criminologist Sch., 1948, Delehanty Inst., 1949, Okla. Inst. Tech., 1950; LL.B., LaSalle U., Chgo., 1940. Capt., asst. chief Stillwater Police Dept., (Okla.), 1936-57; criminal dep. Payne County Sheriff's Office, 1957-59; asst. chief security Okla. State U., Stillwater, 1959-69; publs. specialist, asst. dir. Okla. State U. Press, 1969-79, ret., 1980; freelance writer Stillwater, 1980—; now hist. cons. Western Publs., pub. True West, Old West mags., Stillwater; lectr. in field. Author: books of western history and personalities, including Toughest of Them All, 1953; Six-Gun and Silver Star, 1955, Law West of Ft. Smith: A History of Frontier Justice in the Indian Territory,, 1834-1896/1957, 9th edit., 1990, Pawnee Bill: A Biography of Gordon W. Lillie, 1958, 4th edit., 1981, rev. 1993, Buckskin and Spurs: A Gallery of Frontier Rogues and Heroes, 1958, Outlaw Queen, 1960, Heck Thomas, Frontier Marshal: The Story of a Real Gunfighter, 1962, rev. edit., 1981, Born to Kill, 1963, Henry Starr, Last of the Real Badmen, 1965, 2d edit., 1976, Buckskin Joe: The Unique and Vivid Memoirs of Edward Jonathan Hoyt, Hunter-Trapper, Scout, Soldier, Showman, Frontiersman and Friend of the Indians, 1840-1918, 1966, 2d édit., 1988, Shotgun for Hire: The Story of Deacon "Jim Miller", Killer of Pat Garrett, 1970, 2d edit., 1980, The Life of Texas Jack: Eight Years a Criminal—41 Years Trusting in God, 1973, Red Yesterdays, 1977, West of Hell's Fringe: Crime, Criminals and the Federal Peace officer in Oklahoma Territory 1889-1907, 1978, Temple Houston, Lawyer with a Gun, 1980, Belle Starr and Her Times: The Literature The Facts and The Legends, 1982, Guardian of the Law, The Life and Times of William Matthew Tilghman, 1988, Purple Sage, The Exploits, Adventures and Writings of Patrick Sylvester McGeeney, 1989, Hello, Sucker! The Story of Texas Guinan, 1989, Gunfight at Ingalls, Death of an Outlaw Town, 1990, They Outrobbed Them All, The Rise and Fall of the Vicious Martins, 1992, The Fighting Marlows, Men Who Wouldn't Be Lynched, 1994, Marauders of the Indian Nations: The Bill Cokk Gang and Cherokee Bill, 1994; contbr. numerous short stories, novelettes and factual articles to Western pulps, fact-detective and men's mags. and gen. markets, to anthologies; former contbg. editor: Westerner, Old Trails, Oklahoma Monthly; collector Western Americana. Recipient Okla. Literary Endeavor award, 1960, Am.'s Star award U.S. Marshal Svc., 1989, Profl. Writing award U. Okla., 1990; inducted into Okla. Journalism Hall of Fame, 1981, Okla. Profl. Writers Hall of Fame, 1992;. Mem. Okla. Writers Fedn. (past pres., life mem.), Indian Ter. Posse Westerners (past pres.), Western Writers Am., Western History Assn., Nat. Assn. Outlaw and Lawman History, Oklahoma Heritage Assn., Inst. Great Plains, Assocs. Western History Collections (trustee), Okla. State Hist. Soc., Kans. State Hist. Soc., Mont. State Hist. Soc. Address: PO Box 824 Stillwater OK 74076-0824

SHIRLEY, GRAHAM EDWARD, management executive; b. Starkville, Miss., Jan. 4, 1943; s. Herman Milford and Helen (Lang) S.; m. Deborah Kay Long, 1996; children: Jennifer, Caryn; 1 stepchild, Tyler. BS, USAF Acad., 1966; MA, U. So. Calif., 1973. Commd. 2d lt. USAF, 1966, advanced through grades to brig. gen., 1988; ops. officer 393d Bomb Squadron, Pease AFB, N.H., 1977-78; comdr. 84th Fighter Interceptor Squadron, Castle AFB, Calif., 1978-80, 86th Tactical Fighter Wing, Ramstein Air Base, Germany, 1984-85, 20th Tactical Fighter Wing, RAF Upper Heyford, Eng., 1985-88; with Hdqrs. USAF, Washington, 1980-83, dir. regional plans, 1988-90; assigned to Air War Coll., Maxwell AFB, Ala., 1983-84; vice comdr. Air Force Intelligence Command, San Antonio, 1990-92; ret. brig. gen. USAF, 1992; v.p. Kasten & Co., Washington, 1992-94; pres. Ettington Cons. Internat., McLean, Va., 1994—. Decorated DSM, Legion of Merit, DFC, Air medal. Mem. Air Force Assn., Internat. Inst. for Strategic Studies (London), Air Force Acad. Assn. Grads., Daedalians. Avocations: flying, reading, hunting, fishing, travel. Office: 1301 Dolley Madison Blvd Mc Lean VA 22101-3912 *An enlightened and progressive society cannot exist unless the leadership at all levels has compassion, integrity and courage. Compassion for the less fortunate—integrity to know what is right—courage to do what is right regardless of the personal consequences.*

SHIRLEY, ROBERT CLARK, university president, strategic planning consultant, educator; b. Jacksonville, Tex., July 1, 1943; s. James Cullen and Mary Jim (Clark) S.; m. Terrie Thomas, June 17, 1967; children: Robin, Deron. B.B.A., U. Houston, 1965, M.B.A., 1967; Ph.D., Northwestern U., 1972. Asst. dean faculties U. Houston, 1974-76; asst. to pres. SUNY-Albany, 1976-77, assoc. v.p. acad. affairs, 1977-79; assoc. prof. Central U. Iowa, Pella, 1979-81; prof. Trinity U., San Antonio, 1981-84; pres. U. So. Colo., Pueblo, 1984—; cons. on strategic planning and mgmt. to numerous colls. and univs. Author: Strategy and Policy Formation, 1981; contbr. articles to profl. publs. Mem. Pueblo Econ. Devel. Bd. Bill Laufman Meml. scholar U. Houston, 1965-66; Northwestern U. fellow, 1969-71; HEW research asst. grantee, 1971, 72; La. State U. Found. grantee, 1972, 73. Mem. Acad. Mgmt., Soc. Coll. and Univ. Planning, Pueblo C. of C. Presbyterian. Lodge: Rotary. Office: U So Colo 2200 Bonforte Blvd Pueblo CO 81001-4901

SHIRLEY, VIRGINIA LEE, advertising executive; b. Kankakee, Ill., Mar. 24, 1936; d. Glenn Lee and Virginia Helen (Ritter) S. Student, Northwestern U., 1960-61. With prodn. control dept. Armour Pharm., Kankakee, 1954-58; exec. sec. Adolph Richman, Chgo., 1958-61; mgr. media dept. Don Kemper Co., Chgo., 1961-63, 65-69; exec. sec. Playboy mag., Chgo., 1964-65; exec. v.p. SMY Media inc., Chgo., 1969-96, CEO, chmn. bd., 1996—. Mem. Pla. Club. Home: 1502-J S Prairie Ave Chicago IL 60605-2856 Office: SMY Media Inc 333 N Michigan Ave Chicago IL 60601-3901

SHIRLEY-QUIRK, JOHN, concert and opera singer; b. Liverpool, Eng., Aug. 28, 1931; came to U.S., 1990; s. Joseph Stanley and Amelia (Griffiths) S.-Q.; m. Patricia May Hastie, July 1955 (dec. Feb. 1981); children: Kate, Peter; m. Sara Van Horn Watkins, Dec. 29, 1981; children: Benjamin, Emily, Julia. BSc, Liverpool U., 1953, MusD (hon.), 1977; D Univ., Brunel U., 1981. Asst. lectr. Acton Tech. Coll., London, 1956-60; vicar choral St. Paul's Cathedral, London, 1960-61; profl. singer, 1960—; joint artistic dir. Aldeburgh Festival, 1981-84; mem. voice faculty Peabody Conservatory, Balt., 1991—; vis. artist Carnegie-Mellon U., Pitts., 1994—. Numerous recs. and 1st performances, especially works of Benjamin Britten. Mem. ct. Brunel U., 1977—. Flying officer RAF, 1952-55. Mem. Royal Acad. Music (hon.), Order of the British Empire (comdr. 1975).

SHIRTCLIFF, CHRISTINE FAY, healthcare facility executive; b. Greenfield, Mass.; d. Francis E. and Doris E. (Olsen) S.; 1 child, Danielle Elizabeth. BS in Pub. Health, U. Mass., 1973, MBA, 1987; MEd, Antioch U., 1978. Lic. nursing home adminstr., social worker. Health program rep. Fulton County Health Dept., Atlanta, 1973-74; home health aide supv. County Health Care, Greenfield, Mass., 1974-77; adminstrv. asst. Mary Lane Hosp. (now Mary Lane Hosp./Baystate Health Sys.), Ware, Mass., 1977-79; asst. exec. dir. Mary Lane Hosp., Ware, Mass., 1979-85, exec. v.p., 1985—; founder, mem. steering com. We. Mass. Healthcare Mgrs. Group, 1983-86; active Mass. Rural Devel. Social Svcs. Subcom., 1986, Mass. Coun. Homemaker/Home Health Aide Svcs., 1976-85, bd. dirs., 1976-77, We. Mass. Health Planning Coun., 1974-78. Trustee Congl. Ch. in Belchertown, Mass., 1993-95; mem. Belchertown Collaboration for Excellence in Edn., 1993; mem. blue ribbon com. on excellence in edn.; corporator Country Bank, 1996. Fellow Am. Coll. Healthcare Execs.; mem. New England Women Healthcare Execs. Office: Mary Lane Hosp 85 South St Ware MA 01082-1649

SHIRTUM, EARL EDWARD, civil engineer; b. Montague, Mich., Feb. 20, 1927; s. Earl Willard and Elizabeth Caroline (Boelke) S.; m. Martha Louise Wright, June 19, 1953. BS in Civil Engring., Ind. Tech. Coll., Ft. Wayne, 1950. Bridge design squad leader Mich. Dept. Transp., Lansing, 1952-63, transp. planning engr., 1963-96; mem. Bridge Replacement and Rehab. Com., Lansing, 1967-94. With U.S. Army, 1945-46, ETO. Mem. Mich. Profl. Engring. Soc. (rep. engr. in govt. 1974-77), Lansing Engr. Club (bd. mem. 1980-84). Republican. Methodist. Avocations: fishing, bridge. Home: 1617 Victor Ave Lansing MI 48910-6511 Office: Mich Dept Transp PO Box 30050 Lansing MI 48909-7550

SHIRVANI, HAMID, academic administrator, architecture educator; b. Tehran, Iran, Oct. 20, 1950; came to U.S., 1974, naturalized, 1986; s. Majid and Taji (Granpisheh) S. Diploma in architecture, Poly. of Cen. London, 1974; MArch, Pratt Inst., 1975; MS, Rensselaer Poly. Inst., 1977; MA, Harvard U., 1978, Princeton U., 1979; PhD, Princeton U., 1980. Project designer London Borough of Barnet, 1973-74; prin. Techonokam Inc., Tehran and N.Y.C., 1975-77; asst. prof. architecture Pa. State U., 1979-82; prof., dir. grad. studies SUNY, Syracuse, 1982-85; prof., dir. Sch. Urban Planning and Devel., U. Louisville, 1985-86; prof. architecture and urban design U. Colo., Denver, 1986-92, dean Sch. of Architecture and Planning, 1986-91; prof. philosophy, dean Coll. Arts and Scis. U. Mass., Lowell, 1992-95, prof. philosophy, dean Coll. Arts and Scis., 1992-95; v.p. grad. studies and rsch. CUNY Queens Coll., Flushing, 1995—; mem. vis. faculty So. Calif. Inst. Architecture, U. So. Calif.; lectr. numerous universities worldwide including U. Tex., San Antonio, Lehigh U., U. Waterloo (Can.), U. Sydney (Australia), Mo. State U., Columbia U., N.Y.C., Amsterdam Acad. Art, U. Venice (Italy), Chinese U. Hong Kong, So. China Inst. U., SUNY, Pratt Inst., Miss. State U., U. Calif., Irvine. Author: Urban Design: A Comprehensive Reference, 1981, Urban Design Review, 1981, Urban Design Process, 1985, Beyond Public Architecture, 1990; editor Urban Design Rev., 1982-85, Urban Design and Preservation Quar., 1985-88; mem. editorial bd. Jour. Archtl. Edn., 1988-94, Avant Garde, 1988-93, Jour. Planning Edn. and Rsch., 1987-93, Art and Architecture, 1974-78, Jour. Am. Planning Assn., 1982-88. Recipient Gold Medal in Architecture and Urbanism, Faculty Honor award, Acad. Leadership award, Faculty Rsch. award. Fellow Soc. for Values in Higher Edn., Royal Geog. Soc., Royal Soc. Arts; mem. Am. Studies Assn., Am. Soc. Landscape Architects (recognition award), Am. Inst. Cert. Planners, Am. Planning Assn. (chmn. urban design divsn. 1987-89, Disting. award 1984, Urban Design award 1985), Sigma Xi, Omicron Delta Epsilon, Tau Sigma Delta (Silver medal in archtl. edn. 1988), Tau Beta Pi, Sigma Lambda Alpha. Office: Queens Coll CUNY Flushing NY 11367-1597

SHISLER, ARDEN L., insurance and transportation company executive; b. 1941. Chmn. Nationwide Mut. Ins. Co., Columbus; also pres., CEO K&B Transport, Dalton, Ohio; also ptnr. Sweetwater Beef Farms, Dalton; v.p. Ohio Farm Bur., 1974-84; pres. Ohio Agriculture Mktg. Assn., 1982-84. Office: Nationwide Mut Ins Co 1 Nationwide Plz Columbus OH 43215*

SHISTER, JOSEPH, arbitrator, educator; b. Montreal, Can., Nov. 27, 1917; came to U.S., 1939, naturalized, 1943; s. Eli Harry and Pearl (Millman) S.; m. Edna Louise Tuck, Dec. 28, 1941; children—Neil Barry, Jayne Ellen, Gail Marjorie, Diane Marjorie. B.S., U. Montreal, 1939; M.A., Harvard, 1941, Ph.D., 1943. Instr. econs. Cornell U., 1942-43; research assoc. study trade-unionism Rockefeller Found., 1944-45; asst. prof. econs. Syracuse U., 1945-46; asst. prof., dir. research, labor and mgmt. center Yale U., 1946-49; mem. faculty SUNY, Buffalo, 1949-83; prof. SUNY, 1950-83, prof. emeritus indsl. relations, 1983—, chmn. dept. indsl. relations, 1950-78; vis. prof. Tufts U., Wesleyan U., Montreal U., 1949-55; moderator U. Buffalo Round Table of the Air, WBEN, WBEN-TV, WBEN-FM, 1952-72; labor arbitrator, 1944—; Cons. economist Nat. War Labor Bd., 1944; pub. mem. constrn. commn. Nat. Wage Stblzn. Bd., 1951-52; referee System Boards of Adjustment, 1959—; chmn. Presdl. Emergency Dispute Bd., 1961, 62, 64; spl. adviser labor legislation Gov. Conn., 1948-50; mem. social stratification com. Social Sci. Research Council, 1952-53; mem. N.Y. State Mediation Bd., 1966-69; spl. cons. N.Y. State Med. Bd., 1968-72; also spl. Mayor's Office Settlement Emergency Labor Disputes, 1959-70; spl. cons. Buffalo Full Employment Com., 1958-60; chmn. Erie County Grievance Bd., 1963-70; mem. N.Y. State Minimum Wage Bd. in Amusement and Recreation Industry, 1957-59, White House Conf. on Nat. Econ. Issues, 1962, White House Conf. on Indsl. World Ahead, 1972, Nat. Acad. Arbitrators, 1950—; arbitration panel Fed. Mediation and Conciliation Svc., 1952—, Am. Arbitration Assn., 1955—; mem. labor dispute panels various bds. and commns. Author: Economics of the Labor Market, rev. edit, 1956, Readings in Labor Economics and Industrial Relations, rev. edit, 1956; Co-author: Job Horizons, 1948, Conflict and Stability in Labor Relations, 1952; contbg. author: A Decade of Industrial Relations Research, 1958, Unions, Management and the Public, 1967, Problems de Planification, 1964, Economic Issues and Policies, 1965, Negotiation and Administration of Collective Bargaining Agreements, 1966, The Business World, 1967, Rights and Obligations of Parties Under Collective Agreements, 1967; Co-editor: Insight Into Labor Issues, 1948, Public Policy and Collective Bargaining, 1962; Contbr. articles to profl. jours. Served as pvt. AUS, 1943-44. Mem. Indsl. Rels. Rsch. Assn. (exec. bd. 1959-62), Phi Beta Kappa, Beta Gamma Sigma. Home: 2460 NW 15th St Delray Beach FL 33445-1359

SHIVAPUJA, BHAGYALAKSHMI GOVIND SETTY, auditory neurophysiologist; b. Mysore, Karnataka, India; came to U.S. 1974; d. Govind Setty V. and Jayamma (Maddagiri) S. BSc in Speech and Hearing, All India Inst. Speech Hearing, Mysore, 1974; MA in Audiology, Western Mich. U., Kalamazoo, 1976; PhD in Communication Diseases, U. Tex., Dallas, 1988. Audiologist I Pinecrest State Sch., Pineville, La., 1980-81, audiologist III, 1981-82; dir. otolaryngology rsch. divsn. Henry Ford Hosp., Detroit, 1990—; cons. Mandala Scis., Detroit, 1993—. Contbr. articles to profl. jours. Mem. Am. Speech, Lang. and Hearing Assn., Assn. for Rsch. in Otolaryngology. Avocations: reading, travel, observing natural animal behavior. Office: Henry Ford Hosp 2799 W Grand Blvd Detroit MI 48202-2608

SHIVE, PHILIP AUGUSTUS, architect; b. Luebo, Zaire, Apr. 14, 1938; came to U.S., 1955; s. Alexander M. and Jean B. (Setser) S.; m. Marilyn Ayce Miller, Aug. 3, 1968; children: Susannah, Heather. Student, Davidson Coll., 1956-58; BArch, N.C. State U., 1963; MArch, U. Pa., 1964. Registered architect, N.C., N.Y., Ga. Design architect I.M. Pei & Ptnrs., N.Y.C., 1964-68; ptnr. Gorman, Mixon & Shive, Atlanta, 1968-77; v.p. Wolf Assocs., Charlotte, 1977-83; v.p., dir. design J.N. Pease Assocs., Charlotte, 1983-88; pres. Shive/Bohm-NBBJ, Charlotte, 1988-91, Shive Assocs. Architects, Charlotte, 1991-95, Nix Mann Shive, 1995-96, Nix Mann Shive Perkins & Will, 1996—. Mem. citizen's adv. com. Charlotte-Mecklenburg Planning Commn., 1985-87. Fellow AIA (Kamphoefner prize 1992, 27 design awards); mem. Nat. Am. Inst. Architects (urban design com.), N.C. Arts Coun. Design (arts planning com.), Charlotte City Club. Democrat. Presbyterian. Office: Nix Mann Shive Inc 1130 E 3rd St Ste 200 Charlotte NC 28204-2624

SHIVE, RICHARD BYRON, architect; b. Cleve., Jan. 16, 1933; s. Roy Allen and Mary Elizabeth (Thompson) S.; m. Patricia Butler, Aug. 28, 1954; children: Lisa Ann, Laura Mary, John Thompson, Nancy Butler. BS, Rensselaer Poly. Inst., Troy, N.Y., 1954; postgrad., Newark (N.J.) Coll. Engring., 1957, Rutgers U., 1960-63. Registered architect, N.J., N.Y., Pa., Vt.; lic. profl. planner, N.J. Field engr. Wigton-Abbott Corp., Plainfield, N.J., 1954-55, The Glenwal Co., Rochelle Park, N.J., 1955; asst. supt. Wigton-Abbott Corp., Plainfield, 1955-57; archtl. draftsman Raymond B. Flatt, Architect, Bloomfield, N.J., 1957-58; chief draftsman Raymond B. Flatt, Architect, 1958-60; project architect Scrimenti/Swackhamer/Perantoni Architects, Somerville, N.J., 1960-66; assoc. Scrimenti/Swackhamer/Perantoni Architects, 1966-69; ptnr. Scrimenti, Shive, Spinelli, Perantoni Architects, Somerville, 1969-86, Shive/Spinelli/Perantoni & Assocs., Architects & Planners, Somerville, 1986—; adv. com. First Fidelity Bank, Bound Brook, N.J., 1989-91; chmn. bd. Somerset Health Care Corp., 1987-91. Contbr. articles to profl. jours. Bd. dirs., exec. com. N.J. Hosp. Assn., Princeton, 1986-92, 93—; chmn. bd. trustees Somerset Med. Ctr., Somerville, 1973—; mem. Nat. Trust for Hist. Preservation; bd. dirs. Ctr. for Health Affairs, Inc., 1992-93. Recipient award James F. Lincoln Arc Welding Found., 1973, President's award for outstanding svc. Rolling Hills coun. Girl Scouts U.S.A., 1988, Trustee of Yr. award N.J. Hosp. Assn., 1993, Outstanding Citizen of Yr. award Somerset County C. of C., 1993; Paul Harris fellow Bound Brook-Middlesex Rotary Club, 1993. Mem. AIA, ASTM, ASHRAE, ACI (chpt. bd. dirs. 1978-83), N.J. Soc. Architects, Illuminating Engring. Soc., Nat. Fire Protection Assn., Greater Somerset County C. of C. (v.p. 1985-86, 92—, Outstanding Citizen of Yr. award 1993), Rotary (pres. 1969-70, Paul Harris fellow 1993), Wash. Campground Assn. (pres. 1975-76, v.p. 1977-78, sec. 1978—), Chi Phi (sec. 1973). Republican. Congregationalist. Avocations: fishing, photography, skiing, canoeing, backpacking. Home: 1001 N Mountain Ave Bound Brook NJ 08805-1451 Office: Shive Spinelli Perantoni & Assocs PO Box 758 148 W End Ave Somerville NJ 08876-0758

SHIVELY, JOHN ADRIAN, pathologist; b. Rossville, Ind., Oct. 29, 1922; s. Henry Adam and Lucy (Gascho) S.; m. Lois Lorene Faris, Aug. 26, 1945; children—David A., Ann M., Theodore J., Janet S. B.A., Ind. U., 1944, M.D., 1946. Intern Phila. Gen. Hosp., 1946-47; resident internal medicine Clinic Hosp., Bluffton, Ind., 1949-50; resident pathology South Bend Med. Found., 1950-52; asst. prof. clin. pathology Ind. U. Sch. Medicine, 1954-57; assoc. prof. pathology U. Ky. Med. Sch., 1962-63; prof. pathology, chief clin. pathology U. Tex. M.D. Anderson Hosp., 1963-68; prof. pathology U. Mo. Med. Sch., 1968-71; prof. pathology, chmn. dept. U. Tenn. Coll. Medicine, 1971-76; vice chancellor for acad. affairs U. Tenn. Ctr. for Health Scis., 1976-82; med. dir. SmithKline Clin. Labs., Tampa, Fla., 1983-88; prof. pathology U.S. Fla. Coll. Medicine, 1988-93, assoc. dean, 1990-93, interim chmn. pathology, 1993-94; prof. emeritus, 1993—; pathologist-in-chief City of Memphis Hosps., 1971-76. Served with AUS, 1947-49. Mem. Am. Soc. Clin. Pathologists, Coll. Am. Pathologists, ACP, Am. Soc. Hematology, Am. Assn. Blood Banks (pres. 1967-68), Phi Beta Kappa, Sigma Xi, Alpha Omega Alpha. Research on platelet physiology. Office: 12901 N 30th St # 11 Tampa FL 33612-4742

SHIVELY, MERRICK LEE, pharmaceutical scientist, consultant; b. Alamagordo, N.Mex., Dec. 12, 1958; s. Milton Lee and Dorothy Jean (Garlock) S.; m. Maureen Lynch, Dec. 28, 1985; 1 child, Sierra Lange. BS in Pharmacy, U. Conn., 1982, PhD in Pharmaceutics, 1986. Registered pharmacist, Colo., Mass. Sr. rsch. assoc. Baxter Healthcare, Morton Grove, Ill., 1985-87; asst. prof. U. Colo., Boulder, 1987-93; sr. rsch. scientist Atrix Labs., Inc., Ft. Collins, Colo., 1993-94; sr. scientist Nexagen, Inc., Boulder, 1994-96; founder, mng. ptnr. Drug Delivery Solutions LLC, Louisville, Colo., 1996—; pharm. cons. Glaxo, Synergen, Chemex, Cell Tech., Lilly; del. U.S. Pharmacopeia, 1988-94. Contbr. articles to Pharm. Rsch., Jour. Colloid Interface Sci., Drug Devel. and Indsl. Pharmacy, Internat. Jour. Pharmaceutics, others. Mem. Denver Econ. Com., 1989. Richardson-Vicks fellow, 1982-85. Mem. Am. Assn. Pharm. Scientists, Soc. of Controlled Release, Am. Chem. Soc., Rocky Mountain Devel. Forum (treas. 1989—), Phi Kappa Phi, Rho Chi. Achievements include patents in field; discovery and method of manufacture of solid state emulsions; findings that the formation of multi-molecular inclusion compounds are responsible for unique properties. Home and Office: 10ll Turnberry Cir Louisville CO 80027-9594

SHIVELY, WILLIAM PHILLIPS, political scientist, educator; b. Altoona, Pa., Mar. 31, 1942; s. Arthur Willard and Ruth Phillips S.; m. Barbara Louise Shank, Aug. 29, 1964; children—Helen, David. B.A., Franklin and Marshall Coll., 1963; Ph.D., U. N.C., 1968. Mem. faculty U. Oreg., Eugene, 1967-68, Yale U., 1968-71; mem. faculty U. Minn., Mpls., 1971—; prof. polit. sci. U. Minn., 1979—, provost arts, scis. & engring., 1995—. Author: Craft of Political Research, 1974, rev. edit., 1989, Research Process in Political Science, 1985, Power and Choice, 1986, rev. edit., 1989, 4th edit., 1994, Comparative Governance, 1995, Cross-Level Inference, 1995; editor Am. Jour. Polit. Sci., 1977-79; contbr. articles on elections and voting to profl. jours. Home: 1572 Northrop St Saint Paul MN 55108-1322 Office: U Minn Dept Polit Sci Minneapolis MN 55455

SHIVERS, JANE, corporate communications executive, director; b. Georgetown, Tex., June 29, 1943; d. Marvin Bishop and Jewell (Petrey) Edwards; m. Harold E. Shivers; children: Clay Houston, Will Davis; m. Don Evans Hutcheson. BA, U. Md., 1965. Reseacher Amex Broadcasting Co., San Francisco, 1965-67; pub. info. officer Semester at Sea, Orange, Calif., 1967-69; dir. pub. rels. Atlanta Arts Alliance, 1974-78, RSVT, Atlanta, 1978-82; pres. Shivers Communications, Atlanta, 1982-84; exec. v.p., dir. Ketchum Pub. Rels., Atlanta, 1985—; pres. Midtown Bus. Assocs., Atlanta, 1987-91; bd. dirs. Crown Cryts, Inc. Trustee Alliance Theatre Co., Atlanta, 1980-93, Care, Internat., Atlanta, 1988-89; bd. dirs. Piedmont Park Conservancy, Emory Sch. Pub. Health. Recipient Mgmt. Woman Achievement award Women in Communication, Atlanta, 1984. Mem. Pub. Rels. Soc. Am. (bd. dirs.), Cen. Atlanta Progress Club, Commerce Club, Peachtree Club, Crown Crafts, Inc. (bd. dirs.). Episcopalian. Home: 238 15th St NE Atlanta GA 30309-3594 Office: Ketchum Pub Rels 999 Peachtree St NE Atlanta GA 30309-3964

SHIVLER, JAMES FLETCHER, JR., retired civil engineer; b. Clearwater, Fla., Feb. 17, 1918; s. James Fletcher and Estelle (Adams) S.; m. Katherine Lucille Howlett, Feb. 2, 1946; children: James Fletcher, Susan (Mrs. William J. Schilling). B.C.E., U. Fla., 1938, M.S., 1940. Registered profl. engr., Fla., Ga. Mem. engring. faculty U. Fla., 1940-41; with Reynolds, Smith & Hills Architects-Engrs.-Planners, Inc. (formerly Reynolds, Smith & Hills, architects and engrs.), Jacksonville, Fla., 1941-88, partner, 1950-69, pres., 1970-88, chmn. bd., 1983-88, ret.; ret., 1988; partner Lewis-Eaton Partnership (Architects-Engrs. & Planners), Jackson, Miss., 1969-88. Mem. Fla. Bd. Engr. Examiners, 1964-70, v.p., 1964-65, pres., 1965-70. Served to lt. j.g. USNR, 1943-46. Recipient Outstanding Service award Fla. Engring. Soc., 1971, Disting. Alumnus award U. Fla., 1972, citation for service to constrn. industry Engring. News Record, 1973. Fellow ASCE (pres. Fla. sect. 1952), Am. Cons. Engrs. Coun., Fla. Engring. Soc. (pres. 1960-61); mem. NSPE (pres. 1972-73, Meritorious Svc. award 1981), Am. Assn. Engring. Socs. (chmn. engring. affairs coun. 1982-83), Fla. C. of C. (dir.-at-large 1971-88), Jacksonville Exch. Club, Deerwood Club, Fla. Yacht Club, Tau Beta Pi. Presbyterian. Home: 8191 Hollyridge Rd Jacksonville FL 32256-7103

SHKLAR, GERALD, oral pathologist, periodontist, educator; b. Montreal, Que., Can., Dec. 2, 1924; came to U.S., 1950, naturalized, 1955; s. Louis and Ann (Schleifstein) S.; m. Judith Nisse, June 16, 1948 (dec. Sept. 18, 1992); children: David, Michael, Ruth. BS, McGill U., 1947, DDS, 1949; MS, Tufts U., 1952; MA (hon.), Harvard U., 1971. Diplomate Am. Bd. Oral Pathology, Am. Bd. Periodontology. Asst. prof. oral pathology Tufts U. Sch. Dental Medicine, Boston, Mass., 1953-59; assoc. prof. Tufts U. Sch. Dental Medicine, 1960-61, prof., 1961-71, research prof. periodontology, 1961-71, lectr. in oral pathology, 1971—; Charles A. Brackett prof. oral pathology Harvard U. Sch. Dental Medicine, Boston, 1971—, head dept. oral medicine and oral pathology, 1971-93; sr. clin. investigator Forsyth Dental Ctr., Boston, 1994—; cons. oral pathology Children's Hosp. Med. Ctr., Brigham and Women's Hosp., Mass. Gen. Hosp. Author books, articles on oral diseases, oral cancer, exptl. pathology, exptl. oral cancer. Fellow Am. Acad. Dental Sci., AAAS, Am. Acad. Oral Pathology, Am. Coll. Dentists, Internat. Coll. Dentists; mem. ADA, Internat. Assn. Dental Rsch., Am. Acad. Periodontology, Am. Cancer Soc., Am. Assn. Cancer Rsch., Am. Assn. Cancer Edn., Am. Acad. Oral Medicine, Am. Acad. History Dentistry, History of Sci. Soc., Sigma Xi, Omicron Kappa Upsilon. Avocations: playing flute and harpsichord. Home: 7 Chauncy Ln Cambridge MA 02138-2401 Office: 188 Longwood Ave Boston MA 02115-5819

SHLAUDEMAN, HARRY WALTER, retired ambassador; b. L.A., May 17, 1926; s. Karl Whitman and Florence (Pixley) S.; m. Carol Jean Dickey, Aug. 7, 1948; children: Karl Frederick, Katherine Estelle, Harry Richard. BA, Stanford U., 1952. Joined U.S. Fgn. Svc., 1955; vice consul Barranquilla, Colombia, 1955-56; polit. officer Bogotá, Colombia, 1956-58; assigned lang. tng. Washington, 1958-59; consul Sofia, Bulgaria, 1960-62; chief polit. sect. Santo Domingo, Dominican Republic, 1962-64; officer charge Dominican Affairs State Dept., 1964-66; asst. dir. Office Caribbean Affairs, 1965-66; sr. seminar fgn. policy State Dept., 1966-67, spl. asst. to sec. state, 1967-69; dep. chief of mission Santiago, Chile, 1969-73; dep. asst. sec. state for Inter-Am. affairs Washington, 1973-75; amb. to Venezuela, 1975-76, asst. sec. state for Inter-Am. affairs, 1976-77, amb. to Peru, 1977-80, amb. to Argentina, 1980-83; exec. dir. Nat. Bipartisan Commn. on Central Am., 1983-84; spl. amb. to Cen. Am., 1984-86; amb. to Brazil Brasilia, 1986-89; amb. to Nicaragua, 1990-92, ret., 1992. Served with USMCR, 1944-46. Recipient Disting. Honor award Dept. State, 1966, Pres. Disting. Svc. award, 1988, Pres. Medal Freedom, 1992. Mem. Am. Acad. Diplomacy, Bethesda Country Club, Phi Gamma Delta. Home: 3531 Winfield Ln NW Washington DC 20007-2378

SHMAVONIAN, GERALD S., association executive; b. L.A., June 26, 1945; s. Sarkis Neshan and Berje-Lucia (der Hareutunyan) S. Student, U. Calif., Berkeley, 1964-70. Leader archaeol. excavation team Guatemala, Turkey, 1970-75; pub. City Mags., 1975-80; special advisor Bicentennial Commission, Washington, D.C., 1987; chmn. Am. Nationalities Coun., Stanford U., 1983—. Mem. Calif. Scholarship Fedn. (life, pres. 1963), Nat. Forensic League (pres. 1963, degree of honor), Statesmen's Club. Home: 6219 N Prospect Ave Fresno CA 93711-1658

SHNAYERSON, ROBERT BEAHAN, editor; b. N.Y.C., Dec. 8, 1925; s. Charles and Madalene (Griffin) Beahan; m. Lydia Conde Todd, Dec. 23, 1950 (dec. Sept. 1973); children: Michael, Kate; m. Laurie Platt Winfrey, June 9, 1980; children: Maggie, Bonnie. AB, Dartmouth, 1950. Reporter N.Y. Daily News, 1946; reporter Life mag., N.Y.C., 1950-54; corr. Time-Life News Svc., 1954-56; contbg. editor Time mag., 1957-59, edn. editor, 1959-64, law editor, 1964-67, sr. editor, 1967-71; editor-in-chief Harper's Mag., N.Y.C., 1971-76; editor, pub. Quest mag., N.Y.C., 1976-81, Technology mag., N.Y.C., 1981-82; editorial dir. Sci. Digest mag., 1986-87; editl. cons. Lear's mag., 1987-90; cons. in mag. field; sr. advisor Travel Holiday mag., 1989-95. Author: Illustrated History of the Supreme Court, 1986; contbr. articles to various mags. With USNR, 1943-46. Home: 118 Riverside Dr New York NY 10024-3708

SHNEIDMAN, EDWIN S., psychologist, educator, thanatologist, suicidologist; b. York, Pa., May 13, 1918; s. Louis and Manya (Zukin) S.; m. Jeanne E. Keplinger, Oct. 1, 1944; children: David William, Jonathan Aaron, Paul Samuel, Robert James. A.B., UCLA, 1938, M.A., 1940; M.S., U. So. Calif., 1947, Ph.D., 1948. Diplomate: Am. Bd. Examiners Profl. Psychology (past v.p.). Clin. psychologist VA Center, Los Angeles, 1947-50; chief research VA Center, 1950-53; co-dir. Central Research Unit for Study Unpredicted Deaths, 1953-58; co-dir. Suicide Prevention Center, Los Angeles, 1958-66; chief Center Studies Suicide Prevention NIMH, Bethesda, Md., 1966-69; vis. prof. Harvard U., 1969; fellow Ctr. Advanced Study in Behavioral Scis., 1969-70; clin. assoc. Mass. Gen. Hosp., 1969, Karolinska Hosp., Stockholm, 1978; prof. med. psychology UCLA, 1970-75, prof. thanatology, 1975-88, emeritus, 1988—; vis. prof. Ben Gurion U. of Negev, Beersheva, 1983. Author: Deaths of Man, 1973, Voices of Death, 1980; Definition of Suicide, 1985, Suicide as Psychache, 1993, The Suicidal Mind, 1996; editor: Thematic Test Analysis, 1951; editor: (with N.L. Farberow) Clues to Suicide, 1957, The Cry for Help, 1961, Essays in Self-Destruction, 1967, (with M. Ortega) Aspects of Depression, 1969, On the Nature of Suicide, 1969, (with N.L. Farberow, L.E. Litman) Psychology of Suicide, 1970, Death and the College Student, 1972, Death: Current Perspectives, 1976, 80, 84, Suicidology: Contemporary Developments, 1976, Endeavors in Psychology: Selections From The Personology of Henry A. Murray, 1981, Suicide Thoughts and Reflections, 1981. Served to capt. USAAF, 1942-45. Recipient Harold M. Hildreth award Psychologists in Pub. Service, 1966; Louis I. Dublin award Am. Assn. Suicidology, 1969; Disting. Profl. Contbn. to Pub. Service award Am. Psychol. Assn., 1987. Mem. Am. Assn. Suicidology (founder, past pres.), Am. Psychol. Assn. (past div. pres.), Soc. Projective Techniques (past pres.), Melville Soc. Office: UCLA Neuropsychiat Inst 760 Westwood Plz Los Angeles CA 90024-8300

SHNEIDMAN, J. LEE, historian, educator; b. N.Y.C., June 20, 1929; s. Bernard Wolf and Fannia Abramova (Raskin) S.; m. Conalee Levine, Sept. 3, 1961; children—Philip, Jack. B.A., NYU, 1951, M.A., 1952; Ph.D., U. Wis., Madison, 1957. Lectr. CCNY, 1956-57, U. Md. Overseas, 1957-58; asst. prof. Fairleigh Dickinson U., 1958-62; prof. history Adelphi U., 1963—; chmn. seminar on hist., legal, and polit. thought Columbia U., 1985—. Author: Rise of the Aragonese-Catalan Empire, 2 vols, 1970, Spain and Franco, 1949-59, 1973, John F. Kennedy, 1974. Democratic N.Y. County committeeman, 1970—. Mem. Am. Hist. Assn., Medieval Acad. Am., Am. Philatel. Soc., Internat. Psychohist. Assn. (editor bull.), Rossica Soc., China Soc. Jewish. Home: 161 W 86th St New York NY 10024-3411 Office: History Dept Adelphi University Garden City NY 11530 *Only by understanding from where we came can we understand where we are and where we are going.*

SHNEOUR, ELIE ALEXIS, biochemist; b. Neuilly-sur-Seine, France, Dec. 11, 1925; came to U.S., 1941, naturalized, 1944; s. Zalman and Salomea (Landau) S.; m. Polly M. Henderson, 7 Sept. 1990; children from previous marriage: Mark Zalman, Alan Brewster. B.A., Columbia U., 1947; DSc (hon.), Bard Coll., 1969; M.A., U. Calif., Berkeley, 1955; Ph.D., UCLA, 1958. Teaching., research fellowship U. Calif., Berkeley, 1953-55, Am. Heart Assn. research fellow, 1958-62; teaching., research fellowship U. Calif., L.A., 1958; research fellow Nat. Cancer Inst., 1956-57; Am. Heart Assn. research fellow N.Y.U., 1958-59; research assoc. genetics Stanford U., 1962-65; assoc. prof. biology and neurosciences U. Utah, 1965-69; research neurochemist City of Hope Nat. Med. Ctr., Duarte, Calif., 1969-71; dir. rsch. Calbiochem., 1971-75; pres. Biosystems Insts., Inc., 1975—; dir. Biosystems Rsch. Inst., 1979—; mem. exec. com. Nat. Acad. Sci. Study Group on Biology and the Exploration of Mars, 1964; chmn. Western Regional coun. Rsch. in Basic Bioscis. for Manned Orbiting Missions, Am. Inst. Biol. Scis., NASA, 1966-69. Author: Extraterrestrial Life, 1965, (with Eric A. Ottesen) National Academy of Sciences, National Rsch. Coun., 1966, (with S. Moffat) Life Beyond the Earth, 1966, The Malnourished Mind, 1974; contbr. numerous articles to sci. and lay jours. Chmn. citizens adv. coun. San Diego Pub. Schs., 1971-72; mem. adv. coun. Cousteau Soc., 1977—; bd. dirs. Am.-Ukraine Trade Coun., 1991—, Lunar Power System Coalition, 1993—, Transinnova S.A. France, 1990—; chmn. sci. adv. bd. County of San Diego, 1995—. With U.S. Army, 1944-45. Recipient William Lockwood prize, 1947. Mem. IEEE, AAAS (chmn. So. Calif. Skeptics soc. Pacific divsn. 1988-90), Am. Chem. Soc., N.Y. Acad. Scis., Am. Inst. Biol. Scis., Am. Soc. for Biochemistry and Molecular Biology (chmn. sci. advisors program 1973-75, mem. com. on pub. policy 1974-76, congl. liaison 1992—), Am. Soc. Neurochemistry (mem. coun. 1971-73), Soc. Neurosci., Internat. Soc. Neurochemistry, U.S. C. of C. (bd. dirs. 1993—), La Jolla Chamber Music Soc. (bd. dirs. 1994—), Sigma Xi, Phi Sigma. Office: Biosystems Insts Inc CDM-608 700 Front St San Diego CA 92101-6009

SHNIDER, BRUCE JAY, lawyer; b. Lansing, Mich., Oct. 16, 1950; s. Harold A. and Raynor (Seidner) S.; m. Patricia Lynn Strandness, Dec. 28, 1973; 1 child, Ruth Strandness Shnider. AB magna cum laude, Dartmouth Coll., 1972; MPP, JD magna cum laude, Harvard U., 1977. Bar: Minn. 1977, U.S. Dist. Ct. Minn. 1977, U.S. Tax Ct., 1978, U.S. Ct. Appeals (8th cir.) 1980, U.S. Supreme Ct. 1981. Asst. to dir. Mich. Dept. Commerce, Lansing, 1972-73; law clk. United Mineworkers Am. Health/Retirement Funds, 1975; summer assoc. Robins, Davis & Lyon, Mpls., 1976; assoc. Dorsey & Whitney, Mpls., 1977-82, ptnr., 1983—; chmn. diversity com., 1990-93, chmn. tax practice group, 1994—; bd. dirs. Minn. Justice Found., Mpls., 1989-91. Mem. ABA, Minn. State Bar Assn., Hennepin County Bar Assn. Home: 1908 James Ave S Minneapolis MN 55403-2831 Office: Dorsey & Whitney 220 S 6th St Minneapolis MN 55402-4502

SHNIER, ALAN, real estate executive; b. Emerson, Man., Can., June 11, 1928; m. Rhona Ostrove, Oct. 15, 1949. Chmn. bd. Met. Equities Ltd., Winnipeg, Man., 1975—; chmn. S.W. United Holdings, Inc., United Fibre-Bond, Inc., United Woodframe, Inc. Office: Metropolitan Equities Ltd, 1175 Sherwin Rd, Winnipeg, MB Canada R3H 0V1

SHOAF, RICHARD ALLEN, medieval English professor; b. Lexington, N.C., Mar. 25, 1948; s. Henry Lee and Alma Lucille (Clodfelter) S.; m. Judith Patricia McNamara, May 17, 1975; children: Brian Diarmid, Alma Elaine. BA summa cum laude, Wake Forest U., 1970; BA with honors, U. East Anglia, Eng., 1972; MA, Cornell U., 1975, PhD, 1977. Editorial asst. Winston-Salem (N.C.) Jour. and Sentinel, 1970; teaching asst. Cornell U., Ithaca, N.Y., 1973-75; asst. prof. Yale U., New Haven, 1977-82, assoc. prof., 1982-85; prof. U. Fla., Gainesville, 1985—, coord. grad. studies, 1987-90, alumni prof. English, 1990—. Author: Dante, Chaucer, and the Currency of the Word: Money, Images, and Reference in Late Medieval Poetry, 1983, The Poem as Green Girdle: Commercium in Sir Gawain and the Green Knight, 1984, Milton, Poet of Duality: A Study of Semiosis in the Poetry and the Prose, 1985; founding editor Exemplaria; contbr. articles to profl. jours. Marshall scholar U.K., 1970-72; Morse fellow Yale U., 1980-81, NEH fellow, 1982-83. Mem. Dante Soc. Am. (prize com. 1981-83), Medieval Acad. Am., Modern Lang. Assn. Am., Phi Beta Kappa, Omicron Delta Kappa. Democrat. Avocations: singing, musical comedy, cycling, gardening. Office: U Fla English Dept Turlington Hall Gainesville FL 32611

SHOAFF, THOMAS MITCHELL, lawyer; b. Ft. Wayne, Ind., Aug. 21, 1941; s. John D. and Agnes H. (Hanna) S.; m. Eunice Swedberg, Feb. 7, 1970; children: Andrew, Nathaniel, Matthew-John. BA, Williams Coll., 1964; JD, Vanderbilt U., 1967. Bar: Ind. 1968. Assoc. Isham, Lincoln & Beale, Chgo., 1967-68; ptnr. Baker & Daniels, Ft. Wayne, Ind., 1968—; bd. dirs. Ft. Wayne Nat. Bank, Ft. Wayne Nat. Corp., Weaver Popcorn Co., Inc., Ft. Wayne, Dreibelbiss Title Co., Inc., Ft. Wayne, Am. Steel Investment Corp., Ft. Wayne. Bd. dirs. McMillen Found., Ft. Wayne, Wilson Found., Ft. Wayne. Mem. ABA, Allen County Bar Assn., Ind. State Bar Assn. Presbyterian. Avocations: golf, sailing. Office: Baker & Daniels Ste 800 111 E Wayne St Fort Wayne IN 46802

SHOBER, EDWARD WHARTON, bioscience company executive; b. Bryn Mawr, Pa., Nov. 16, 1926; s. Edward Wharton and Catherine Mather S.; m. Sandra Metcalf, May 27, 1978; children: Jorie, Edward, Paula. Student, Princeton U., 1950; DSc, Wilkes U., 1975. Pres., CEO Atec Corp., N.Y.C., 1957-71, Hahnemann Med. Coll., Phila., 1971-77; CEO, co-founder Gen. Arabian Medical, Riyadh, Saudi Arabia, 1978-88; chmn. Pioneer Bioscis. Ltd., Malmesbury, Wiltshire, Eng., 1990—; chmn. Drexel, Hahnemann, Jefferson Med. Coll. Pa. Cancer Ctr., 1973-77. Author: Blood Lost, 1990, Royal Treachery, 1993. Dir. Old Phila. Devel. Corp., 1972-78, Bryn Mawr Hosp., Phila., 1965-72; hon. consul Nicaragua, Phila., 1960-75; dir. English Speaking Union, Newport, R.I., 1960-85. 1st lt. C.E. German mil., 1950-52. Home: Charlton Park, Wiltshire SN16 9DG, England

SHOBERT, ERLE IRWIN, II, management consultant; b. DuBois, Pa., Nov. 19, 1913; s. Erle Irwin and Edna Mae (Gray) S.; m. Marjorie E. Sullivan, Apr. 6, 1939; children: Judith Ann (Mrs. Edward Marsden), Margaret (Mrs. William G. Hayes). AB summa cum laude, Susquehanna U., 1935, DSc, 1957; student, Georg August U., Goettingen, Germany, 1935-36; MA in Physics, Princeton, 1939. With Stackpole Carbon Co., St. Mary's, Pa., 1934-79, v.p. tech., 1971-79, cons., 1979—; bd dirs. Chemcut Corp., State College, Pa., 1968-83, chmn., 1978-80, Tech. Adv. Contact Tech., Inc., 1990—; mem. materials adv. panel Pa. Dept. Commerce, 1972; indsl. and adv. com. Pa. State U., 1968-71; adv. com. Am. Carbon Conf., 1967-73; bd. dirs. Engrs. Joint Council, 1969-72; exec. standards council Am. Nat. Standards Inst., 1973, bd. dirs., 1974-76; bd. dirs. Kaul Land Co. Author 3 books, tech. papers. Pres. Elk County Soc. Crippled Children and Adults; pres. St. Mary's Youth Council.; pres., bd. dirs. Susquehanna U., 1978—, chmn. 1978-86.; bd. dirs. Kaul Found., 1981—. Recipient Outstanding Alumni award Susquehanna U., 1969, named dormitory in honor of Mr. and Mrs. Shobert. Fellow ASTM (bd. dirs. 1966-74, pres. 1971-72), IEEE (Ragnar Holm Sci. Achievement award 1974, Armington Recognition award 1985, prize paper competition named in his honor, Outstanding Achievement award 1994), Soc. for Preservation of Old Tigers (sec.-treas. 1996—); mem. Masons, Sigma Xi, Omicron Delta Kappa. Patentee carbon products, electronic materials and applications. Home: PO Box 343 Saint Marys PA 15857-0343 *I am product of a Tom Sawyer youth and the scholarship and work opportunities of the American higher education system. My career was and continues to be with one organization, among people and work I liked and respected. My family, including my grandchildren and great grandchild, are my pride and joy. My wife and I try to repay some of the organizations and people who have helped us.*

SHOBE-WESTBROOK, KAREN LYNN, special education educator; b. Gainesville, Tex., Oct. 13, 1938; d. Paul Joseph and Linnie P. (Billingsley) Shobe; children: Tammy Rivera, Terrence Proffer, Sheree Shobe Hazlewood, Paula Brant, Dava Westbrook. BS, U. North Tex., 1959; cert., Tex. Women's U., 1976; postgrad., Tex. A&M, 1982. Cert. elem. edn. tchr., lang./learning disabilities tchr., mentally retarded and emotionally disturbed tchr. Tchr. Ft. Worth Christian Acad., 1958, Colleyville-Grapevine (Tex.) Schs., 1963, Malta (Europe) Internat. Sch., 1977-79; resource tchr. Tex. A&M Consolidated Sch., College Station, 1980-82, 85-89; cons. Jakarta (Indonesia) Internat. Sch., 1982-83; emotionally disturbed educator Midland (Tex.) Ind. Sch. Dist., 1989-91; resource tchr. Aransas County Ind. Sch. Dist., Rockport, Tex., 1991—. Mem. Tex. State Tchrs. Assn. (sec. 1993-94, membership com. 1991-92), Eastern Star (color station 1988-89, line officer, Svc. award 1989), Bus. and Profl. Women (Svc. award 1993), Am. Women's Club Malta (sec. 1977-78, Silver Tray Svc. award 1978). Avocations: crafts, painting, crocheting, travel, ceramics. Home: 11202 Hambleton Way Houston TX 77065-4143

SHOCHAT, STEPHEN JAY, pediatric surgeon; b. Balt., Dec. 17, 1938; s. Albert J. and Rose (Blechman) S.; m. Sheila Floam, July 1960 (div. July 1979); children: Francine Lynne, Alisa Joy; m. Carla Ann Centi, Jan. 26, 1980; children: David Robert, Sarah Elizabeth. BS, Randolph Mason Coll., 1959; MD, Med. Coll. Va., 1963. Surg. resident Washington U. Med. Ctr., St. Louis, 1963-68; pediatric surg. resident Boston Children's Hosp., 1968-70; thoracic surg. resident Queen Elizabeth Hosp., Birmingham, Eng., 1970, George Washington Hosp., Washington, 1972; chief pediatric surgery Hershey (Pa.) Med. Ctr., 1973-77, Stanford (Calif.) Med. Ctr., 1977-94; sr. surgeon Children's Hosp. Phila., 1994—. Lt. col. USAF, 1970-72. Office: Children's Hosp Phila 34th & Civic Ctr Blvd Philadelphia PA 19104

SHOCKEY, THOMAS EDWARD, real estate executive, engineer; b. San Antonio, Aug. 17, 1926; s. Verlie Draper and Margaret Ruth (Shuford) S.; BS (Davidson fellow Tau Beta Pi), Tex. A&M U., 1950; postgrad. St. Mary's U., 1964, San Antonio Coll., 1972, Pacific Western U., 1981; m. Jacqueline McPherson, June 4, 1949; children: Cheryl Ann, Jocelyn Marie, Valerie Jean. With Petty Geophys. Survey, 1947-49, J.E. Ingram Equipment Co., 1950-51; co-owner, archtl. engr., realtor Moffett Lumber Co., Inc., San Antonio, 1952-76; cons. gen. contracting, gen. real estate, 1964—, retailer wholesale bldg. material, 1951—, v.p., 1959—; real estate counselor, appraiser, 1972—; real estate appraiser Gill Appraisal Svc., San Antonio, 1977—; comml. loan appraiser, underwriter, analyst Gill Savs. Assn., Gill Cos., San Antonio, 1979; chief appraiser, underwriter, architect, engr., insp. Gill Cos., 1981, v.p., 1981-87, ret., 1987; v.p. La Hacienda Savs. Assn., 1988-91, ret., 1991. Fire chief Mico Vol. Fire Dept., 1993-95. With inf. Signal Corps, U.S. Army, 1944-46; ETO. Mem. San Antonio C. of C., Nat. Lumber Dealers, Nat. Home Builders, Nat. Real Estate Bd.. Nat. Inst. Real Estate Brokers, Internat. Soc. Real Estate Appraisers, Tex. Assn. Real Estate Insps., Real Estate Appraisers Tex., Nat. Assn. Rev. Appraisers and Mortgage Underwriters, Internat. Inst. Valuers, Internat. Platform Assn. Home: 126 County Road 2620 Mico TX 78056-5213

SHOCKLEY, CAROL FRANCES, psychologist, psychotherapist; b. Atlanta, Nov. 24, 1948; d. Robert Thomas and Frances Lavada (Scrivner) S. BA, Ga. State U., 1974, MEd, 1976; PhD, U. Ga., 1990. Cert. in gerontology; Diplomate Am. Bd. Forensic Examiners. Counselor Rape Crisis Ctr., Atlanta, 1979-80; emergency mental health clinician Gwinnett Med. Ctr., Lawrenceville, Ga., 1980-86; psychotherapist Fla. Mental Health Inst., Tampa, 1987-89, Tampa Bay Acad., Riverview, Fla., 1990-91; sr. psychologist State of Fla. Dept. of Corrections, Bushnell, 1991-92; ind. practice psychology Brunswick, Ga., 1992—; mem. Adv. Bd. for Mental Health/Mental Retardation, 1992-94. Author: (with others) Relapse Prevention with Sex Offenders, 1989. Vol. Ga. Mental Health Inst., Atlanta, 1972; leader Alzheimer's Support Group, Athens, Ga., 1984; vol. therapist Reminiscence Group for Elderly, Athens, 1984-85. Recipient Meritorious Svc. award Beta Gamma Sigma, 1975. Mem. Am. Psychol. Assn., Ga. Psychol. Assn., Sigma Phi Omega, Psi Chi. Avocations: astronomy, archeology, music, travel. Office: 14 Saint Andrews Ct Brunswick GA 31520-6764

SHOCKLEY, EDWARD JULIAN, aerospace company executive; b. Augusta, Ga., Oct. 31, 1924; s. Julian P. and Margaret (Epps) S.; m. Dorothy Elizabeth Holley, Nov. 24, 1945; children: Edward J., Steven Holley. B.Aero. Engring., Ga. Inst. Tech., 1950; postgrad. (Sloan fellow), Stanford U. Grad. Sch. Bus., 1962-63. Flight test engr. Douglas Aircraft Co., 1950-53; with Lockheed-Ga. Co., 1953-80, dir. quality and safety, 1965-74, dir. mktg., 1974-78, v.p., 1978-80; pres. Lockheed Aircraft Service Co. div. Lockheed Corp., Burbank, Calif., 1980-86, sr. advisor to pres., 1986-87, ret., 1987; pres. Millimeter Wave Tech., Inc., Marietta, Ga., 1988-90, vice chmn. bd. dirs., 1991-92; dir. Aerosurge Mgmt. Cons., 1991-92; pres. Lockheed-Ga. Fed. Credit Union, 1971-74. Mem. bus. adv. coun. Ga. So. U.; mem. adv. coun. Sch. Bus. and Econs., Coll. of Charleston. Served with USN, 1941-46. Mem. Cherokee Town and Country Club. Republican. Methodist.

SHOCKLEY, THOMAS DEWEY, electrical engineering educator; b. Haynesville, La., Nov. 2, 1923; s. Thomas Dewey and Inez (Hudson) S.; m. Willie Belle Austin, Feb. 13, 1947; children: Dianne, Cecilia. B.S. in Elec. Engring, La. State U., 1950, M.S. in Elec. Engring, 1952; Ph.D., Ga. Inst. Tech., 1963. Instr. La. State U., 1950-53; aerophysics engr. Gen. Dynamics, 1953-56; research engr., asst. prof. Ga. Inst. Tech., 1956-63; assoc. prof. U. Ala., 1963-64; prof. U. Okla., 1964-67; prof., chmn. dept. elec. engring. Memphis State U., 1967-83; pres. SSC, Inc., Germantown, Tenn., 1978—, chmn. bd., 1981—; system cons. ITT, Md. Co., State Farm Fire & Casualty Co., Aetna Ins. Cos., CNA Ins. Co. Mem. elec. code panel, Shelby County, Tenn., 1978-84; mem. Memphis-Shelby County Appeals Bd., 1984—. Served with AUS, 1942-46, 1950. Mem. IEEE (treas. Memphis sect. 1970-71, sec. 1971-72, vice chmn. 1972-73, chmn. 1973-74, Centennial medal 1984), Nat. Soc. Profl. Engrs., Tenn. Soc. Profl. Engrs., Nat. Fire Protection Assn. (com. 110), Sigma Xi (chpt. pres. 1969-71), Phi Kappa Phi (chpt. pres. 1973-74, 84-85). Home: 1526 Poplar Estate Pky Memphis TN 38138-1836 Office: SSC Inc Germantown TN 38138

SHOCKLEY, W. RAY, travel trade association executive; b. Apalachee, Ga., Aug. 19, 1924; s. Benjamin Arthur and Sophie Sarah (Harris) S.; m. Virginia Nell Davis, Sept. 21, 1946; children—Lisa Wray, David Wray, Jenifer Wray. B.A. in Journalism, U. Ga., 1956. News editor Athens (Ga.) Banner Herald and, Gainesville (Ga.) Daily Times, 1948; state news editor Augusta (Ga.) Chronicle, 1948-52; Sunday editor Atlanta Jour.-Constitution, 1952-54, 1954-56; field rep. pub. rels. Am. Textile Mfgs. Inst., Washington, 1956-58; asst. sec., treas. Am. Textile Mfgs. Inst., 1958-70, dep. exec. v.p., 1974-76, exec. v.p., 1976-84; exec. v.p. S.C. Textile Mfrs. Assn., Columbia, 1970-74; pres., chief oper. officer Am. Soc. Travel Agts., 1985-90; cons. pub. affairs, 1990-91; dir. industry and bus. affairs C. of C., Athens, 1991-95; ret., 1995. Served with USN, 1944-45, PTO. Mem. Am. Soc. Assn. Execs., Ga. Alumni Assn. (out-of-state v.p. 1967-69), Belle Haven Country Club (Alexandria, Va.), Athens C. of C. (dir. industry and small bus. affairs 1991—), Rotary (pres. Dilworth club 1964-65, Athens East 1991—). Methodist (treas. 1966-70). Home: 507 Cherokee Rd Winterville GA 30683-9566

SHOCKMAN, GERALD DAVID, microbiologist, educator; b. Mt. Clemens, Mich., Dec. 22, 1925; s. Solomon and Jennie (Madorsky) S.; m. Arlyne Taub, June 2, 1949; children—Joel, Deborah. B.S., Cornell U., 1947; Ph.D., Rutgers U., 1950; Docteur (hon.), U. Liege, 1991. Predoctoral fellow Rutgers U., 1947-50; research assoc. U. Pa., 1950-51; research fellow, research assoc. Inst. Cancer Research, Phila., 1951-60; asso. prof. Temple U. Sch. Medicine, Phila., 1960-66; prof. dept. microbiology and immunology Temple U. Sch. Medicine, 1966—, chmn. dept., 1974-90. Contbr. articles in field to profl. jours. Served with U.S. Army 1942-44. Recipient Research Career Devel. award NIH, 1965-70, Titular de la Chaire d'Actualité Scientifique U. Liège, Belgium, 1971-72; NRC fellow, 1954-55. Mem. Am. Soc. Biol. Chemists, Am. Acad. Microbiology, Am. Soc. Microbiology, AAAS, Sigma Xi. Home: 901 Rodman St Philadelphia PA 19147-1247 Office: Temple U Sch Medicine 3400 N Broad St Philadelphia PA 19140-5196

SHOCTOR, JOSEPH HARVEY, barrister, producer, civic worker; b. Edmonton, Alta., Can., Aug. 18, 1922. BA, LLB, U. Alta., 1946, LLD (hon.), 1981; diploma in theatre adminstrn. (hon.), Grant MacEwan Coll., 1986. Named to Queens Counsel, 1960. Barrister, solicitor, sr. counsel Duncan & Craig, Edmonton, 1993—; bd. dirs. Saxony Investments, Inc., Desa Stores Ltd.; pres., exec. officer Harvey Holdings Ltd. Prodr. Broadway plays including Peter Pan, 1965, Henry, Sweet Henry, 1967, Billy, 1969, Hamlet, 1969; founder, pres., exec. producer, bldg. chmn., campaign chmn. Citadel Theater; producer Circle 8 Theatre, Civic Opera, Red Cross Entertainment; panelist pub. affairs talk show and sports forum. Active United Cmty. Fund, 1968—; chmn. Downtown Devel. Corp., Edmonton, 1986; mem. Edmonton Jewish Welfare Bd.; past pres. Edmonton Jewish Cmty. Coun.; past nat. sec. Federated Zionist Orgn.; past nat. v.p. United Israel Appeal, Inc.; past bd. dirs. Can. Coun. Jewish Welfare Funds; chmn. divsn. Brit. Commonwealth Games Found., 1978; bd. govs. Nat. Theatre Sch. of Can., officer Order of Can., 1986. Inducted into Cultural Hall of Fame, 1987; named Man of Hr., Sta. CFRN-TV, 1966, Citizen of Yr., B'nai B'rith, 1966, one of Twelve Top Albertans of the 70's, The Alberta Report, U. Alberta Alumni Wall of Recognition, 1995, Disting. Citizen Grant MacEwan C.C., 1995; recipient Performing Arts award City of Edmonton, 1972, Theatre

Arts Achievement award Province of Alta., 1975, Prime Minister's medal State of Israel, 1978, Builder of Cmty. award City of Edmonton, 1979, Queen's Silver Jubilee medal, 1977, City of Edmonton Silver Ribbon award, 1985, Great Canadian award, 1992, Commemorative medal for 125th Anniversary Canadian Confederation, 1992; The Shoctor Theatre named in his honor, 1976; Alta. Order of Excellence. Mem. Edmonton C. of C. Clubs: The Edmonton, The Centre, Eskimo Football (founder, past sec.-mgr.). Office: Duncan & Craig, 10060 Jasper Ave 2800, Edmonton, AB Canada T5J 3V9

SHOE, MARGARET ELLEN, accountant; b. Phila., Feb. 10, 1944; d. Francis James and Margaret Edna (Hathaway) Wiedenmann; m. Richard Alan Shoe, Feb. 14, 1964 (div. Aug. 1975). Associates, Burlington County Coll., 1978; BS, Trenton State Coll., 1982. Lic. pub. acct.; lic. real estate salesperson. Acct., office mgr. Philmar Constrn. Co., Somerdale, N.J., 1967-72; acct. Microcircuit Engring., Medford, N.J., 1972-73, R.L. Fitzwater and Son, Inc., Merchantville, N.J., 1973-75; asst. contr. Bancroft Sch. and Instrn., Haddonfield, N.J., 1976-79; corp. contr. Paparone Constrn. Co. Inc., Mt. Laurel, N.J., 1979; asst. contr. Reutter Engring. Inc., Camden, N.J., 1979-80; corp. contr. CSI Electronics, Inc., Cinnaminson, N.J., 1980, Wagner Holm and Inglis, Inc., Mt. Holly, N.J., 1980-81; pub. acct. Shoe Acctg. and Consulting Svc., Mt. Laurel, N.J., 1981—; acctg. clk. Robert C. Perina, CPA, Camden, 1968-69; bookkeeper, acctg. clk. Lantern Lane Interiors, Cherry Hill, N.J., 1967; bookkeeper, cost acctg. clk. Drew Constrn. Co., Inc., Cherry Hill, 1964-66; bookkeeper, time study clk. Mailing Svcs., Inc., Pennsauken, N.J., 1963-64. Recipient Woman of Achievement award Burlington County Freeholders, 1990. Mem. N.J. Assn. Pub. Accts. (pres. 1992-93, bd. dirs. 1988—, Camden pres., v.p. 1988-91), N. J. Bd. Accountancy, N.J. Assn. Women Bus. Owners (bd. dirs. 1981—, del. White House conf. small bus. 1984), Burlington County Bd. Realtors, Inst. Managerial Accts. (assoc.), Cherry Hill C. of C., Rotary. Lutheran. Avocations: dancing, art, skiing, swimming, biking. Home and Office: Shoe Acctg and Consulting 623 Union Mill Rd Mount Laurel NJ 08054-9515

SHOEMAKER, BILL (WILLIAM LEE SHOEMAKER), retired jockey, horse trainer; b. Fabens, Tex., Aug. 19, 1931; s. B. B. and Ruby (Call) S.; 1 child, Amanda Elisabeth. Jockey, 1949-90, ret., 1990, trainer, 1990—. Author: Stalking Horse, 1994, Fire Horse, 1995, Dark Horse, 1996. Winner Ky. Derby, 1955, 59, 65, 86, Belmont Stakes, 1957, 59, 62, 67, 75, Preakness Stakes, 1963, 67; ret. with 8,833 wins, including over 1000 Stakes wins. Office: c/o Vincent Andrews Mgmt Ste 208 315 S Beverly Dr Beverly Hills CA 90212-4310

SHOEMAKER, CAROLYN SPELLMANN, planetary astronomer; b. Gallup, N.Mex., June 24, 1929; d. Leonard Robert and Hazel Adele (Arthur) Spellmann; m. Eugene Merle Shoemaker, Aug. 18, 1951; children: Christine Shoemaker Woodard, Patrick Gene, Linda Shoemaker Salazar. BA cum laude, Chico State Coll., 1949, MA, 1950; ScD (hon.), No. Ariz. U., 1990. Vis. scientist Br. astrogeology U.S. Geol. Survey, Flagstaff, Ariz., 1980—; rsch. asst. Calif. Inst. Tech., Pasadena, 1981-85; rsch. prof. astronomy No. Ariz. U., Flagstaff, 1989—; mem. staff Lowell Obs., Flagstaff, 1993—; guest observer Palomar Obs., Palomar Mountain, Calif., 1982-94; Emmons lectr. Colo. Sci. Soc., 1995; co-McGovern lectr. Cosmos Club Found., 1995. Co-recipient Rittenhouse medal Rittenhouse Astron. Soc., 1988, Scientist of Yr. awrd ARCS Found., 1995; recipient Woman of Distinction award Soroptimists, 1994, 20th Anniversary Internat. Women's Yr. award Zonta and 99s, 1995, NASA Exceptional Scientific Achievement medal, 1996; named Disting. Alumna of the Calif. State U., Chico, 1996. Fellow AAAS; mem. Astron. Soc. Achievements include discovery of 32 comets including Periodic Comet Shoemaker-Levy 9 which impacted Jupiter in July 1994, more than 500 asteroids including 41 Earth approachers and approximately 68 Mars crossers, meteorites at Veevers Crater, Australia and impactites at Wolfe Creek Crater, Australia. Home: RR 4 Box 998 Flagstaff AZ 86001-8346 Office: Lowell Obs 1400 W Mars Hill Rd Flagstaff AZ 86001-4470

SHOEMAKER, CYNTHIA CAVENAUGH JONES, academic director; b. Washington, Feb. 13, 1938; d. Robert LaTourrette and Herta (Wilson) Cavenaugh; m. Roger H. Jones, July 4, 1958 (div. Dec. 1984); children: Roger, Michael, Steve, Allison; m. Douglas B.G. Shoemaker, Oct. 21, 1989. BS in Human Ecology, Cornell U., 1959; MEd in Edn., U. Md., 1974, PhD in Edn., 1981, postgrad., 1987-91. Tchr. St. Raphael's Nursery Sch., Rockville, Md., 1971-72; sr. v.p. Home and Sch. Inst., 1972-75; exec. dir. Early Childhood Edn. Adminstrn. Inst., 1975-84; asst. to dean continuing edn. Cath. U., 1982; program dir. continuing edn. Montgomery Coll., 1983-84; assoc. dir. off-campus programs George Washington U., Washington, 1984—; parent-child presch. observation program tchr. Montgomery County (Md.) Pub. Schs., 1972-75; adj. prof. M.A. in Teaching Trinity Coll., Washington, 1974-78, asst. prof., 1978-84; adj. prof. Webster Coll., St. Louis, 1981; adj., assoc. prof. George Mason U., Fairfax, Va., 1989-95; speaker various meetings, confs. and workshops throughout U.S., 1970-94; exec. bd. Md. Coun. Staff Devel., 1987-89; chmn. Tri-County Staff Devel. Consortium, Charles County, St. Mary's County and Calvert Counties, Md.; program chmn. Assn. Fed. Info. Resource Mgmt., 1993-94; conf. chmn. AFFIRM/SIGCAT, 1994, exec. v.p., 1995—. Author: Leadership and the Use of Power in ECE Adminstration, 1980, Motivating Staff, Parents and Children, 1981, Home Learning Enablers and Other Helps, 1992, 94, Adminstration and Management of Programs for Young Children, 1994; co-author: (with Dorothy Rich) Success for Children Begins at Home, 1973, The Home New Educational Partnership, 1974, A Family Affair: Education, 1977; contbr. articles to profl. jours. Elder Rockville Presbyn. Ch. Grantee U.S. SBA, Montgomery C.C., 1983, 84, Md. State Dept Edn., Tri-County Staff Devel. Consortium, 1988; recipient nat. award Parent Coop. Preschs. Internat., 1970. Mem. ASCD, Nat. Assn. Edn. Young Children, Assn. Childhood Edn. Internat., assn. Fed. info. Resource Mgmt., Am. Soc.of Pub. Adminstr. Presbyterian. Office: George Washington U 2231 Crystal Dr Lbby 150 Arlington VA 22202-3711 *Helping children and adults develop to their full potential and helping east and west understand each other better are two very rewarding goals of my life.*

SHOEMAKER, DON (DONALD CLEAVENGER SHOEMAKER), columnist; b. Montreal, Que., Can., Dec. 6, 1912; (parents Am. citizens); s. Richard Samuel and Alberta (Stone) S.; m. Lyal Reynolds, Oct. 30, 1937 (dec. July 1968); 1 child, Elizabeth; m. Suzanne Statler, Aug. 2, 1969; 1 child, Charlotte. AB, U. N.C., 1934; LittD (hon.), Hollywood Coll., 1970. Assoc. editor Asheville Citizen, 1941-47, editor, 1947-55; exec. dir. So. Edn. Reporting Service, 1955-58; editor, editorial page The Miami Herald, 1958-62, editor, 1962-78; columnist Knight-Ridder Newspapers, 1978—. Editor: Henry George: Citizen of the World (by Anna George de Mille), 1950, Middle East Journey; The Case of the Lively Ghost, 1957, With All Deliberate Speed, 1957, Spanish Diary, 1974; contbr. to mags. and encys. Sec. Fla. World's Fair Authority; mem. Orange Bowl Com.; dir. Fla. Bicentennial Commn.; past vice chmn. Fla. Council of 100; chmn. N.C. Conf. Editorial Writers, 1951-52; pres. Buncombe County Community Chest, 1951; mem. Coun. on Fgn. Relations; chmn. Dade Coordinating Council, 1974-75; chmn. Fla. region NCCJ, also nat. trustee; trustee U. Miami, Mus. of Sci.; trustee United Way Dade County, pres., 1976, chmn. bd., 1977; dir., chief U.S. del. United Way Internat., Hong Kong, 1977; mem. Fla. Edn. Council, Fla. Task Force on Student Assessment; chmn. Fla. Profl. Tchr. Task Force, 1985-86. Recipient Silver medallion award NCCJ, 1970, medal of merit The Asheville Sch., Diamond Jubilee award Nat. Jewish Hosp., 1974, Disting. Eagle Scout award, 1978; named to N.C. Journalism Hall of Fame, 1982. Mem. Inter-Am. Press Assn., Asociacion de Amigos del Pais (Guatemala), Internat. Press Inst., Am. Soc. Newspaper Editors, Order of Golden Fleece (U. N.C.), Newcomen Soc., Bath Club, Pi Kappa Alpha, Sigma Delta Chi. Episcopalian. Home and Office: 617 Sabal Palm Rd Bay Point Miami FL 33137

SHOEMAKER, ELEANOR BOGGS, television production company executive; b. Gulfport, Miss., Jan. 20, 1935; d. William Robertson and Bessie Eleanor (Ware) Boggs; m. D. Shoemaker, April 9, 1955 (div. 1987); children: Daniel W., William Boggs. Student in protocol, Southeastern U., 1952-53; student, George Washington U., Washington, 1953-56; BA in Communications and Polit. Sci. with honrs, Goucher Coll., 1981; postgrad., Villanova U. Feature writer Washington Times Herald, 1951-54; dir. Patricia Stevens Modeling Agy., Washington, 1955-56; free-lance model Julius Garfinkel, Woodward & Lothrop, Washington, 1951-56; research analyst Balt. County Council, Towson, Md., 1980-81; feature news reporter Sta. WGCB-TV, Red Lion, Pa., 1980—; pub. speaker, protocol The Reliable Corp., Columbia, Md., 1982-86; media cons. The Enterprise Found., Columbia, Md., 1985-86; faculty, TV prodn. and communication St. Francis Prep Sch., Spring Grove, Pa., 1985-88; owner Windswept Prodns. Co., Felton, Pa., 1984—; mktg. svcs. coord. Yorktowne, Inc., Red Lion, Pa., 1993-95; mem. conservation bd. Pa. Parks and Recreation Soc., 1984—; prodr. The Pa. County TV Prodn., 1981; prodr., host Westar 4 Channel 9 half hour weekly news program Keystone Report. Prodr. The Pa. County TV Prodn., 1981, The Pa. County TV Prodn., 1981, documentary Human Rights: A Special Report, Sta. WGCB-TV, 1989; prodr., host Westar 4 Channel 9 half hour weekly news program Keystone Report, 1990. Bd. dirs. York (Pa.) County Parks and Recreation, 1972-87, YWCA, York, 1957-82, Hist. York, 1990—; mem. exec. com. York County Reps., 1972-82; accreditation adv. com. York Coll. of Pa.; instr. YWCA Women in Politics; founder, mem. Child Abuse Task Force, York, 1983—; mem. select com. Pa. Agrl. Zoning, 1988; mem. steering com. York Forum, 1989—; co-chmn. Cross Mill Restoration, 1987—; mem. Displaced Homemaker's Bd., 1989—, pres., 1993—; bd. dirs. Hist. York, 1990—; founder, host Old Rose Tree Pony Club, 1967—; chair Spring Valley County Pk. Task Force, 1972; master of fox hounds Mrs. Shoemaker's Hounds, 1969—; master of beagles Mrs. Shoemaker's Weybright Beagles, 1988—. Recipient pro bono child legal representation grant Pa. Bar Assn., 1983, Pa. Tree Farmer of Yr. award, 1987, Outstanding Achievement in Broadcasting award Am. Women in Radio and TV, 1992, Lay Person of Yr. award Pa. Recreation and Parks Assn. and Gov. Thornburg, 1982, Jefferson award, 1992, Matrix award Ctrl. Pa. Women in Comm., 1993, First pl. corp. video prodn. Ctrl. Pa. Women in Comm., 1993; selected journalist for Novosti Press USSR-U.S. Press Exch. program, 1989. Mem. Am. Polled Hereford Assn., York Area C. of C., York County C. of C. (publicity com. 1985—, agri. bus. com.), Masters of Foxhounds Assn. Episcopalian. Avocation: foxhunting, beagling. Home and Office: PO Box 167 Felton PA 17322-0167

SHOEMAKER, EUGENE MERLE, geologist; b. L.A., Apr. 28, 1928; s. George Estel and Muriel May (Scott) S.; m. Carolyn Jean Spellmann, Aug. 18, 1951; children: Christine Carol, Patrick Gene, Linda Susan. B.S., Calif. Inst. Tech., 1947, M.S., 1948; M.A., Princeton U., 1954, Ph.D., 1960; Sc.D., Ariz. State Coll., 1965, Temple U., 1967, U. Ariz., 1984. Geologist U.S. Geol. Survey, 1948-93, scientist emeritus, 1993—, exploration uranium deposits and investigation salt structures Colo. and Utah, 1948-50, regional investigations geochemistry, volcanology and structure Colorado Plateau, 1951-56, research on structure and mechanics of meteorite impact and nuclear explosion craters, 1957-60, with E.C.T. Chao, discovered coesite, Meteor Crater, Ariz., 1960, investigation structure and history of moon, 1960-73, established lunar geol. time scale, methods of geol. mapping of moon, 1960, application TV systems to investigation extraterrestrial geology, 1961—, geology and paleomagnetism, Colo. Plateau, 1969—, systematic search for planet-crossing asteroids and comets, 1973-94; with C.S. Shoemaker and D.H. Levy discovered Periodic Comet Shoemaker-Levy 9, 1993, discovered Trojan Asteroids, 1985-94; geology of satellites of Jupiter, Saturn, Uranus and Neptune, 1978—, investigating role of large body impacts in evolution of life, 1981—, impact craters of Australia,, 1983—; organized br. of astrogeology U.S. Geol. Survey, 1961; co-investigator TV expt. Project Ranger, 1961-65; chief scientist, center of astrogeology U.S. Geol. Survey, 1966-68; prin. investigator geol. field investigations in Apollo lunar landing, 1965-70, also television expt. Project Surveyor, 1963-68; prof. geology Calif. Inst. Tech., 1969-85, chmn. div. geol. and planetary scis., 1969-72; sci. team leader Clementine Mission to the Moon, 1993-94; staff mem. Lowell Observatory, Flagstaff, Ariz., 1993—. Recipient (with E.C.T. Chao) Wetherill medal Franklin Inst., 1965, Arthur S. Flemming award, 1966, NASA medal for exceptional sci. achievement, 1967, Honor award for meritorious svc. U.S. Dept. Interior, 1973, Disting. Svc. award, 1980, Disting. Alumni award Calif. Inst. Tech., 1986; co-recipient Rittenhouse medal, 1988, Nat. medal of Sci. Pres. Bus, 1992, McGovern award Cosmos Club Found., 1995. Mem. NAS, Internat. Astron. Union, Am. Acad. Arts and Scis., Geol. Soc. Am. (Day medal 1982, Gilbert award 1983), Mineral Soc. Am., Soc. Econ. Geologists, Geochem. Soc., Am. Assn. Petroleum Geologists, Am. Geophys. Union (Whipple award 1993), Am. Astron. Soc. (Kuiper prize 1984), Meteoritical Soc. (Barringer award 1984, Leonard medal 1985). Home: RR 4 Box 998 Flagstaff AZ 86001-8346 Office: US Geol Survey 2255 N Gemini Dr Flagstaff AZ 86001-1637

SHOEMAKER, FRANK CRAWFORD, physicist, educator; b. Ogden, Utah, Mar. 26, 1922; s. Roy Hopkins and Sarah Parker (Anderson) S.; m. Ruth Elizabeth Nelson, July 11, 1944; children—Barbara Elaine, Mary Frances. A.B., Whitman Coll., 1943, D.Sc. (hon.), 1978; Ph.D., U. Wis., 1949. Staff mem. Radiation Lab. MIT, 1943-45; instr. physics U. Wis., 1949-50; mem. faculty Princeton U., 1950-89, prof. physics, 1962-89, emeritus, 1989—; assoc. dir. Princeton U. Pa. Accelerator, 1962-66; vis. scientist Rutherford High Energy Lab., 1965-66; main accelerator sect. head Nat. Accelerator Lab., 1968-69; prin. investigator Dept. of Energy High Energy Physics Contract, 1972-85. Co-author proposal for 3 billion electron volt Princeton-Pa. Accelerator, 1955. Fellow Am. Phys. Soc.; mem. Phi Beta Kappa, Sigma Xi. Home: 361 Walnut Ln Princeton NJ 08540-3446

SHOEMAKER, GRADUS LAWRENCE, chemist, educator; b. Zeeland, Mich., Jan. 18, 1921; s. Corey and Hattie (Lubbers) S.; m. Florence Etta Wright, June 5, 1952; children—Robert Neil, Betty Lynn. A.B., Hope Coll., 1944; M.S., U. Ill., 1947, Ph.D., 1949. Mem. faculty U. Louisville, 1949—, prof. chemistry, 1965-88, prof. emeritus, 1988—, chmn. dept., 1963-64, 65-67, chmn. div. natural sci., 1967-79; mem. exec. bd. Covenant Housing, Inc., 1989—. Served as ensign USNR, 1944-45. Mem. Am. Chem. Soc. (councillor 1968-80), AAUP, Ky. Acad. Sci., Blue Key, Sigma Xi, Alpha Epsilon Delta, Phi Kappa Phi, Phi Lambda Upsilon. Presbyn. Home: 2815 Meadow Dr Louisville KY 40220-2406

SHOEMAKER, HAROLD LLOYD, infosystem specialist; b. Danville, Ky., Jan. 3, 1923; s. Eugene Clay and Amy (Wilson) S.; A.B., Berea Coll., 1944; postgrad. State U. Ia., 1943-44, George Washington U., 1949-50, N.Y. U., 1950-52; m. Dorothy M. Maddox, May 11, 1947 (dec. Feb. 1991). Research physicist State U., Ia., 1944-45, Frankford Arsenal, Pa., 1945-47; research engr. N.Am. Aviation, Los Angeles, 1947-49, Jacobs Instrument Co., Bethesda, 1949-50; asso. head systems devel. group The Teleregister Corp., N.Y.C., 1950-53; mgr. electronic equipment devel. sect., head planning for indsl. systems div. Hughes Aircraft Co., Los Angeles, 1953-58; dir. command and control systems lab. Bunker-Ramo Corp., Los Angeles, 1958-68, v.p. Data Systems, 1968-69, corp. dir. data processing, 1969-75; tech. staff R & D Assocs., Marina Del Rey, Calif., 1975-85; info. systems cons., 1985—. Served with AUS, 1945-46. Mem. IEEE. Patentee elec. digital computer. Home: PO Box 3385 Granada Hills CA 91394-0385

SHOEMAKER, INNIS HOWE, art museum curator; b. Reading, Pa.; d. William Erety and Jean (Miller) S. AB, Vassar Coll., 1964; MA, Columbia U., 1968, PhD, 1975. Curator Vassar Coll. Art. Gallery, Poughkeepsie, N.Y., 1965-68, 73-76; asst. dir. Ackland Art Mus., U. N.C., Chapel Hill, 1976-82, dir., 1983-86; sr. curator prints, drawings and photographs Phila. Mus. Art, 1986—; fellow in art history Am. Acad. in Rome, 1971-73; adj. prof. U. N.C., Chapel Hill, 1983-86; bd. dirs. Conservation Ctr., Phila., 1987—; vis. com. Frances Lehman Lueb Art Ctr., Vassar Coll., 1993—. Co-author: The Engravings of Marcantonio Raimondi, 1981, Paul Cézanne: Two Sketchbooks, 1989. Mem. vis. com. Muscarelle Mus., Coll. of William and Mary, 1995—; mem. vis. com. Lehman Loeb Art Ctr., Vassar Coll., 1993—; bd. dirs. Conservation Ctr. for Art and Hist. Artifacts, Phila., 1987—. Mem. Coll. Art Assn. Am., Am. Assn. Mus., Print Coun. Am. (bd. dirs. 1986-89). Office: Phila Mus Art PO Box 7646 Philadelphia PA 19101-7646

SHOEMAKER, SANDRA KAYE, aerospace executive; b. Dallas, July 13, 1954; d. Vondyl Claud and Billie Juanita (Pritchett) Willis; m. Carl Vernon Shoemaker, Aug. 16, 1975; children: Regan Amanda, Ryan Adam. BBA, Baylor U., 1975. Fin. coord. Tex. A&M U., College Station, 1975-77; from engring. planner to mgr. adminstrv. support Gen. Dynamics Corp., Ft. Worth, 1977-90; dir. engring. adminstrn. Lockheed Ft. Worth Co., 1990-94; dir. rsch. & engring. svcs. & process support, 1994—. Republican. Baptist. Avocations: music, snow skiing, water skiing, racquetball, snorkeling and scuba diving. Home: 5100 Dewdrop Ln Fort Worth TX 76123-1931 Office: Lockheed Ft Worth Co PO Box 748 Fort Worth TX 76101-0748

SHOEMAKER, SYDNEY S., philosophy educator; b. Boise, Idaho, Sept. 29, 1931; s. Roy Hopkins and Sarah Parker (Anderson) S.; m. Molly McDonald, Oct. 1, 1960; 1 son, Peter William. B.A., Reed Coll., 1953; postgrad., Edinburgh Univ., Scotland, 1953-54; Ph.D., Cornell Univ., 1958. Instr. Ohio State Univ., Columbus, 1957-60; asst. prof. Cornell Univ., Ithaca, N.Y., 1961-64, assoc. prof., 1964-67, prof., 1970—, Susan Linn Sage prof. philosophy, 1978—; assoc. prof. Rockefeller Univ., N.Y.C., 1967-70; John Locke lectr. Oxford U., England, 1972; Josiah Royce lectr. Brown U., 1993. Author: Self-Knowledge and Self-Identity, 1963, Identity, Cause, and Mind, 1984; co-author: Personal Identity, 1984; co-editor: Knowledge and Mind, 1983, Philso. Rev., 1964—(intermittently); gen. editor: Cambridge Studies in Philosophy, 1982-90. Fulbright scholar Edinburgh, Scotland, 1953-54; Santayana fellow Harvard Univ., Cambridge, Mass., 1960-61; fellow Ctr. Advanced Study in Behavioral Scis., Stanford, Calif., 1973-74, Nat. Endowment for Humanities, 1980-81, Guggenheim Found., 1987-88, Nat. Humanities Ctr., 1987-88. Mem. AAUP, Am. Acad. Arts and Scis., Am. Philos. Assn. (mem. exec. com. ea. div. 1977-80, v.p. 1992-93, pres. 1993-94). Home: 104 Northway Rd Ithaca NY 14850-2241 Office: Cornell Univ Dept Philosophy 218 Goldwin Smith Hall Ithaca NY 14853-3201

SHOEMAKER, WILLIAM EDWARD, financial executive; b. Charleston, W.Va., Sept. 17, 1945; s. Robert Edward and Janet Elizabeth (Hoglund) S. BBA, U. Notre Dame, 1967. Assoc. buyer Proctor & Gamble, Cin., 1971; gen. mgr. Eastwind Inc., Anchorage, 1972-73; pres., operator Golden Horn Lodge, Inc., Bristol Bay, Alaska, 1973-79; treas. Hawley Resource Group, Inc., Anchorage, 1979-88; treas., chief fin. officer Golden Zone Resources, Inc., Campbell, Calif., 1988-90; ptnr. Resort Mgmt. Corp., Anchorage, 1987-90; pres. Discovery Holdings, Inc., Ft. Lauderdale, Fla., 1991—; bd. dirs. Pacific Art & Design Cons., Inc. Bd. dirs. Anchorage Econ. Devel. Corp., 1988-90. Served to lt. (j.g.) USN, 1967-71. Mem. Quarter Deck Club (Anchorage). Republican. Avocations: boating, skiing, fishing. Home: 2301 Solar Plaza Dr Fort Lauderdale FL 33301

SHOEMATE, CHARLES RICHARD, food company executive; b. LaHarpe, Ill., Dec. 10, 1939; s. Richard Osborne and Mary Jane (Gillette) S.; m. Nancy Lee Gordon, Sept. 16, 1962; children: Steven, Jeffrey, Scott. BS, Western Ill. U., 1962; MBA, U. Chgo., 1973. Supr. Corn Products Co., Summit, Ill., 1962-72; comptroller Corn Products Unit of CPC Internat., Englewood Cliffs, N.J., 1972-74; plant mgr. Corn Products Unit of CPC Internat., Corpus Christi, Tex., 1974-76; v.p. ops. Corn Products Unit of CPC Internat., Englewood Cliffs, 1976-81; pres. Can. Starch Co., Montreal, Que., 1981-83; v.p. Corn Refining div. CPC Internat., Englewood Cliffs, 1983-86, pres., 1986-88; corp v.p. CPC Internat., Englewood Cliffs, 1983-88, pres., 1988—, chmn., chief exec. officer, 1990—. Office: CPC Internat Inc Box 8000 Internat Plz Englewood Cliffs NJ 07632*

SHOEN, EDWARD JOSEPH, transportation and insurance companies executive; s. Leonard and Anna (Carty) S. MBA, Harvard U. Pres., chmn. Amerco Nev. Corp., Phoenix; pres. U-Haul Internat., Inc., Phoenix. Office: Amerco Nev Corp PO Box 21502 Phoenix AZ 85036-1502 also: Amerco 1325 Airmotive Way Reno NV 89502-3201*

SHOENBERGER, ALLEN EDWARD, law educator; b. Waynesburg, Pa., Sept. 18, 1944; s. Allen Edward and Evelyn S.; m. Cynthia Grant (div. 1975); 1 child, Michael Grant; m. Caroline Orzac, Aug. 3, 1980; 1 child, Elisa Orzac. BA with honors, Swarthmore Coll., 1966; JD with honors, Columbia U., 1969; LLM, NYU, 1972. Bar: Ill. 1973, U.S. Dist. Ct. (no. dist.) Ill. 1973, U.S. Ct. Appeals (7th cir.) 1977, U.S. Supreme Ct. 1977. Vis. lectr. U. Nairobi, Kenya, 1969-71; fellow Internat. Legal Ctr., Nairobi, 1969-71; asst. prof. Loyola U., Chgo., 1972-77, assoc. prof., 1977-85, prof., 1985—, chmn. faculty coun., 1983—; cons. Adminstrv. Conf. U.S., Washington, 1988; mem. Ill. A.G. Task Force for Handicapped, 1982—; chmn. adv. bldg. com. Cir. Ct. of Cook County, Chgo., 1988-93. Editor Spina Bifida publ., 1985-93, East African Law Reports, 1969-71; contbr. articles to profl. publs. Mem. Ill. Spina Bifida Assn., Chgo., 1980-93; hearing officer Ill. Pollution Control Bd., 1974—, U.S. Dept. Energy, Ill., 1984-89. Recipient various grants, including NIE, 1973; fellow Ford Found., 1972, NEH, 1987. Mem. ABA, Fed. Bar Assn., Chgo. Bar Assn. (chmn. adminstrv. law com. 1985-86). Office: Loyola Sch of Law 1 E Pearson St Chicago IL 60611-2055

SHOFF, PATRICIA ANN, lawyer; b. Colby, Kans., Sept. 27, 1948; d. Clarence O. and Clara C. (Ortbal) Shoff; m. Thomas E. Salsbery, Oct. 6, 1979; children: Emily Anne, Edward Philip. BA with honors, U. Iowa, 1970, JD with distinction, 1973. Bar: Iowa 1973, U.S Dist. Ct. (no. and so. dists.) Iowa 1974. Law clk. Supreme Ct. of Iowa, Des Moines, 1973-74; assoc. Thoma Schoenthal Davis, Hockenberg & Wine, Des Moines, 1974-79; ptnr., shareholder Davis, Brown, Koehn, Shors & Roberts, P.C., Des Moines, 1979—; vice chair bd. law examiners Iowa Supreme Ct., 1991-95. Sec. bd. dirs. Iowa's Children and Families, 1980-91, v.p. 1981-82, pres. 1982-83, Very Spl. Arts Iowa, 1988—, sec. 1990, chair pers. com., 1990-92, pres. 1992, chair resource devel. com. 1992—; mem. Gov.'s Com. Child Abuse Prevention, 1982-92, chair 1987-92; pres. bd. govs. Greater Des Moines Leadership Inst., 1984-85; co-chair fundraising com. Hospice of Ctrl. Iowa, 1983-85; pub. rels. com. mem. St. Augustin's Ch., 1986-87; exec. bd. Mid-Iowa Coun. Boy Scouts Am., 1988—, nominating com., 1989-91, Homestead bd. dirs., 1993, pres.-elect, 1994, pres., 1995. Mem. ABA (family law sect., labor, employment law sect.), AAUW (juvenile justice com. 1974-76), Iowa Law Sch. Found. (bd. dirs. 1992—), Iowa State Bar Assn. (young lawyers sect., family law com. 1979-81, membership com. 1979-81, chair legal aid com. 1981-85, labor and employment law com. 1991-92, others), Iowa Supreme Ct. Bd. Law Examiners (vice-chair 1991-95), Polk County Bar Assn. (treas. 1989-92, v.p. 1992-93, pres. elect 1993, pres. 1994, Merit award 1990), Womens Fedn. Lawyers, Greater Des Moines C. of C. Fedn. (bd. dirs. 1984-85, bur. econ. devel. com. 1985—, exec. call com. 1985—), Polk County Women Attys., Iowa Orgn. Women Attys., Greater Des Moines C. of C. Leadership Inst. (pres. bd. govs. 1984-85, alumni orgn. 1984—), Jr. League (adv. planning 1983-84, placement advisor 1986-87, grants com. 1988), Phi Delta Phi. Democrat. Roman Catholic. Office: Davis Brown Koehn Shors & Roberts 2500 Fin Ctr 666 Walnut St Des Moines IA 50309-3904

SHOFF, WILLIAM HUDSON, emergency physician; b. Altoona, Pa., Oct. 5, 1946; s. James Wendel and Elizabeth Lenore (Robinson) S.; m. Jane Todd Cooper, Sept. 28, 1985; children: Eamon R. Raylor, Savannah Cooper-Ramsey. BS, Pa. State U., 1968, Md, 1973. Diplomate Am. Bd. Internal Medicine, Am. Bd. Emergency Medicine; cert. advanced trauma life support, advanced cardiac life support, pediatric advanced life support. Fellow cancer rsch. dept. pathology Pa. State U., 1970-71; intern in internal medicine Harrisburg (Pa.) Hosp., 1973-74, resident in internal medicine, 1974-76; clin. asst. prof. dept. medicine, emergency medicine Pa. State U., 1976-78, fellow in family medicine, 1979, asst. prof. dept. family and cmty. medicine Coll. Medicine, 1979-85; mini-resident occupational medicine UMDNJ-Robert Wood Johnson Med. Sch., Piscataway, N.J., 1991; lectr. dept. emergency medicine Hosp. of U. Pa., Phila., 1993; asst. prof. emergency medicine U. Pa., Phila., 1993—; attending physician dept. emergency med./internal med. Shamokin State Gen. Hosp., 1975-77, Maple Ave. Gen. Hosp., 1976, Harrisburg Hosp., 1976-78, Seidle Hosp., Mechanicsburg, Pa., 1976-85; attending physician dept. emergency and trauma medicine Polyclinic Med. Ctr., Harrisburg, 1985-88; attending physician dept. emergency medicine Good Samaritan Hosp., Lebanon, Pa., 1987-93; mem. med. adv. com. Emergency Health Svcs. Fedn., S. Ctrl. Pa., 1977-79; mem. med. adv. com. Pa. Emergency Health Svcs. Coun., 1978-81, mem. physician's edn. com., 1978-79; bd. dirs. Hospice of Ctrl. Pa., Camp Hill, 1982-85, med. dir., 1983-84. Guest reviewer Annals of Emergency Medicine, 1994—; contbr. articles to profl. jours. Bd. dirs. Women in Crisis, Hummelstown, Pa., 1979-85; mem. ctrl. program com. S. Ctrl. Pa. chpt. Am. Heart Assn., 1979-80. Mem. Am. Coll. Emergency Physicians, Am. Coll. Physicians, Soc. Acad. Emergency Medicine. Office: U Pennsylvania Med Ctr Dept Emergency Med 3400 Spruce St Philadelphia PA 19104

SHOFFER, JEFFREY DAVID, financial planner; b. Toledo, Ohio, Sept. 4, 1951; s. Norman and Marilyn (Fingerhut) S.; m. Kathleen R. Morrison, Sept. 20, 1975; children: Sarah E., Steven A., John E. BS, U. Toledo, 1975, MBA, 1976. Cert. fin. planner. Agt., registered rep. Mfrs. Life/Manequity, toledo, 1976-81; asst. br. mgr. Mfrs. Life/Manequity, New Orleans, 1981-83; dept. head, agt. Savage & Assocs. Inc., Toledo, 1983-86; fin. planner, v.p. Bolanis Fin. Planning Group, Toledo, 1989-94; fin. planner, pres. Strategic

Resources Planning, Toledo, 1986-89, 94—. Contbr. articles to profl. jours. Charter mem., mem. program com. Toledo Planned Giving Coun., 1994—; mem. fin. bd. Oblates of St. Francis, Toledo, 1991—; bd. dirs. St. Pius X Sch., Toledo, 1990—, Internat. Inst., Toledo, 1994—; fund raiser Republican Party, Toledo, 1989-90. Mem. Internat. Assn. for Fin. Planning (vice chair chpt. adv. coun. 1990—). Jewish. Avocations: golf, photography. Office: Strategic Resources Planning Inc 3341 W Bancroft St Toledo OH 43606

SHOFSTAHL, ROBERT MAXWELL, savings and loan executive; b. New Orleans, Feb. 8, 1942; s. Maxwell Frederick and Ellen Anna (Falkenstein) S.; m. Lois Alice Berrigan, June 6, 1964; children: Tyson Brahm, Elisia Ellette, Christian Aric. BA cum laude (scholar), Tulane U., 1964; postgrad., 1966. Mgr. So. Bell-South Central Bell, New Orleans, Baton Rouge, Shreveport, 1964-71; asst. to pres. Pelican Homestead Savs. & Loan, Metairie, La., 1971-73, exec. v.p., 1973-77, dir., 1973-92, pres., CEO, 1978-92; pres., COO, dir. AmWest Savs. Assn., Bryan, Tex., 1992-94, N.Y. Life, 1995—; dir. Eureka Homestead, 1996—; dir. Fed. Res. Bank of Atlanta, New Orleans br., 1986-88. Mem. future of industry task force U.S. League, 1987-88; mem. 9th dist. FHLB Com. on Mgmt. Consignment Program, 1985; mem. last carousel fin. com. Friends of City Park, 1986-87; bd. dirs. Neighborhood Housing Services of New Orleans, 1978-81, treas., 1979-81; trustee St. Martin Episcopal Sch., 1981-87, treas., 1984, v.p., 1985-86, capital funds tri-chmn., 1984, headmaster search com., 1985, bd. visitors, 1989—, chmn., 1996—; lectr. south grad. bus. sch. Loyola U., 1982—; mem. vis. com. Loyola U. Bus. Sch., 1991-92; speaker ann. conv. Deans So. Bus. Adminstn. Assn., 1989; apptd. to gov's. Thrift Industry Adv. Coun., 1981-84; mem. adv. bd. New Orleans Opera Ball, 1984; inaugural pres. New Orleans Aquatics, 1988; panelist New Orleans: The Decade Ahead, 1989; hon. econ. devel. ambassador State of La., 1985; La. Newsmaker of Yr., USA Today, 1983. Mem. U.S. League Savs. Instns. (vice chmn. ad hoc fl. ins. com., 1976-77, chmn. ins. and protective com., 1979-80), La. League Savs. Instns. (ins. com. 1974, exec. com. 1980-81, 87-89, legis. com. 1983-84), League Homestead/Savs. and Loan Assn. Greater New Orleans (pres. 1973), Nat. Assn. Bus. Economists (panelist nat. policy suvey 1989-92), New Orleans Coun. Bus. Economists, Bryan-College Station C. of C. (mem. inner circle 1993-94), Deutsches Haus, Bienville Club, Phi Beta Kappa, Phi Eta Sigma, Eta Sigma Phi. Episcopalian. Home: 324 Homestead Ave Metairie LA 70005-3707 Office: NY Life Ste 1900 739 Poydras St New Orleans LA 70113

SHOGAN, ROBERT, news correspondent; b. N.Y.C., Sept. 12, 1930; s. Albert and Millie (Jacobs) S.; m. Ellen Shrewsbury, May 26, 1959; children: Cynthia Diane, Amelia Ford. B.A., Syracuse U., 1951; postgrad., U. Mich. Inst. Pub. Adminstrn., 1951, Columbia U. Grad. Faculty Polit. Sci., 1952. Reporter Detroit Free Press, 1956-59; telegraph editor Miami (Fla.) News, 1959-61; asst. editor Wall St. Jour., N.Y.C., 1961-65; evaluation officer Peace Corps, Washington, 1965-66; corr. Newsweek, Washington, 1966-73; nation polit. corr. Los Angeles Times, Washington, 1973—; profl.-in-residence Annenberg Sch. Communication, U. Pa., 1993. Author: Question of Judgement, 1972, Promises to Keep, 1977, None of the Above, 1982, The Riddle of Power, 1991, Hard Bargain, 1995; co-author: (with Tom Craig) The Detroit Race Riot, 1964. Served with U.S. Army, 1952-54. McCormick fellow Hoover Presdl. Libr., 1993; recipient 1st prize Feature Writing, Mich. AP, 1959, Disting. Reporting Pub. Affairs award Am. Polit. Sci. Assn., 1969. Mem. Phi Beta Kappa. Home: 3513 Raymond St Chevy Chase MD 20815-3227 Office: 1875 I St NW Washington DC 20006-5409

SHOICHI, IDA, artist; b. Kyoto, Japan, Sept. 13, 1941; came to U.S., 1970; s. Ida Kikuji and Ida Yukie. BA, Kyoto Mcpl. U. Art, MFA, BA (hon.). Cert. mus. curator. lectr. dept. sculpture, printmaking Kyoto Mcpl. U. Art, 1965-68, 70-72, Ohio State U., Columbus, 1974, Columbus Inst. Printmaking, 1974, SUNY, New Paltz, 1974, Kala Art Inst., Berkeley, Calif. 1979, San Francisco Art Inst., 1979, Art Inst. Chgo., 1980, U. Alta., 1981, Calif. Coll. Art and Craft, 1986, Whitman Coll., Walla Walla, Wash., 1989, Art Mus. Cin., 1989, others; panelist in field. Solo exhbns. include Gallery Azuchi, Osaka, Japan, 1966, Dragon, Inc., Paris, 1970, Gallery Crews, N.Y.C., 1970, Himezi Gallery, Tokyo, 1974, 75, 76, Gallery Coco, Kyoto, Japan, 1976, Tokyo Gallery, 1977, 79, 82, 86, 92, Suzuki Gallery, N.Y.C., 1979, San Francisco Art Inst., 1979, Yoh Art Gallery, Osaka, 1979, 80, 82, 83, 84, 87, 88, 90, 92, Mary Baskett Gallery, Cin., 1981, 90, Gallery Ueda, Tokyo, 1983, 85, 87, 88, 89, 90, 92, Gallery 24, Osaka, 1983, 86, Chgo. Art Fair, 1993, Suzuki Gallery, N.Y., 1993, Life Gallery TEN, Fukuoka, Japan, 1994, Gallery Ueda, Tokyo, 1994, Perimeter Gallery, Chgo., 1994, Gallery Mori, Tokyo, 1994, many others; innumerable group exhbns. Japan, Europe, U.S, 1966—, include Kyoto Mcpl. Mus. Art, Mcpl. Mus. Mod. Art, Paris, Nat. Mus. Modern Art, Tokyo, Kyoto, San Jose (Calif.) Mus. Art, Mus. Modern Art, Chgo.; exhbns. Internat. Biennale Prints and Drawings; represented in collections Nat. Libr., Paris, Victoria and Albert Mus., London, MOMA, N.Y.C., Swedish Art Assn., Osaka (Japan) Contemporary Art Ctr., Museo de Arte Contemporaneo, Ibiza, Spain, Mus. Modern Art, Krakow, Poland, L.A. County Mus. Art, Art Acad. Cin., Smithsonian Internat.-Arthur M. Sackler Gallery, Deutsch Bank AG, Frankfurt, Ger., Hara Mus. Contemporary Art, Tokyo, numerous others. Recipient Peter Millard prize 7th Brit. Internat. Print Biennale, Bradford, Eng., 1982, (with Robert Rauschenberg) Award for Excellence Internat. Cultural Exchange NEA, Washington, 1986, Grand Priz Suntory Prize Suntory Found., 1989, Aequo Prize 12th Internat. Print Biennale, Krakow, Poland, 1988, The Suntry Grand prize, 1989, others; French Govt. grantee, 1968, Japan Soc. N.Y.C. grantee, 1974, Asian Cultural Coun. grantee, N.Y.C., 1986, Hitachi Found. grantee, Washington, 1986, Centrum Found. grantee, Commn. Centennial Wash. State, 1989. Office: care Perimeter Gallery Chicago IL 60610 also: 2924 Russell St Berkeley CA 94705-2334*

SHOLES, DAVID HENRY, laywer, former state senator; b. Providence, June 1, 1943; s. Leonard and Anna S. BA, Brown U., 1965; JD, Boston U., 1968. Bar: R.I. 1968, Mass. 1968. Pvt. practice law, Providence and Warwick, R.I., 1969-72; sr. ptnr. Sholes & Sholes, Warwick, 1970—; former lectr. U. R.I. Extension; mem. R.I. State Senate, 1976-92, chmn. senate com. on health, edn. & welfare; state adv. com. U.S. Civil Rights Commn.; former mem. Def. Civil Preparedness Adv. Coun., Cranston Gen. Hosp. Mem. R.I. Bar Assn., R.I. Trial Laywers Assn., Cranston Hist. Soc., Phi Alpha Delta. Democrat. Jewish. Clubs: Elks, Masons, Kiwanis, Touro Fraternal Assn. Home: 32 Mauran St Cranston RI 02910-1818 Office: 1375 Warwick Ave Warwick RI 02888-5066

SHON, FREDERICK JOHN, nuclear engineer; b. Pleasantville, N.Y., July 24, 1926; s. Frederick and Lucy (Stelz) S.; m. Dorothy Theresa Patterson, June 8, 1946; 1 son, Robert Frederick. BS, Columbia U., 1946; postgrad., Ohio State U., U. Calif., Berkeley. With Publicker Alcohol Co., Phila., 1946-47, Thermoid Co., Trenton, N.J., 1947-48, Mound Lab., Miamisburg, Ohio, 1948-51; radiation chemist Atomics Internat., Canoga Park, Calif., 1951-52; physicist, reactor ops. supr. Lawrence Radiation Lab., Livermore, Calif., 1952-61; chief exam br., div. licensing and regulations U.S. AEC, Washington, 1961-62, chief reactor safety br., div. operational safety, 1963-67, asst. dir. nuclear facilities, 1967-72; dep. chief adminstrv. judge-tech., vice-chmn. tech., atomic safety and licensing bd. panel U.S. Nuclear Regulatory Commn., Washington, 1972—; cons. various nuclear firms including Danish AEC, Risoe, Atomics Internat., Spanish AEC, IAEA; lect. nuclear engring. U. Calif., Berkeley, 1955-63. Mem. Am. Nuclear Soc., Tau Beta Pi. Home: 4212 Flower Valley Dr Rockville MD 20853-1808 Office: US Nuclear Regulatory Commn Washington DC 20555

SHONK, ALBERT DAVENPORT, JR., advertising executive; b. L.A., May 23, 1932; s. Albert Davenport and Jean Spence (Stannard) S.; BS in Bus. Adminstrn., U. So. Calif., 1954. Field rep. mktg. div. Los Angeles Examiner, 1954-55, asst. mgr. mktg. and field supr. mktg. div. 1955-56, mgr. mktg. div., 1956-57; account exec. Hearst Advt. Svc., Los Angeles, 1957-59; account exec., mgr. Keith H. Evans & Assos., San Francisco, 1959-65; owner, pres. Albert D. Shonk Co., L.A., 1965—; gen. ptnr. Shonk Land Co. LTD, Charleston, W.Va., 1989—; pres. Signet Circle Corp., Inc., 1977-81, dir., 1962-81, hon. life dir., 1981—, treas., 1989—. Bd. dirs. Florence Crittenton Ctr. for Young Women and Infants, sec., 1978, 1st v.p., 1978-79, exec. v.p., 1979-81, pres., 1981-83, chmn. bd., 1983-85, hon. life dir., 1986—; co-chair centennial com., founding chmn. Crittenton Assocs. Recipient Medallion of Merit Phi Sigma Kappa, 1976, Founders award, 1961,NIC Interfraternal award, 1989 . Mem. Advt. Club Los Angeles, Pubs. Rep. Assn. of So. Calif., Nat. Assn. Pubs. Reps. (past v.p. West Coast 1981-83), Jr. Advt. Club L.A. (hon. life, dir., treas., 1st v.p.), Trojan Club, Skull and Dagger, U. So. Calif., U. S.C. Commerce Assocs. (nat. bd. 1991-, treas. 1995—), U. S.C. Assocs., Inter-Greek Soc. (co-founder, hon. life mem. and dir., v.p. 1976-79, pres. 1984-86), Rotary, Phi Sigma Kappa (dir. grand council 1962-70, 77-79, grand pres. 1979-83, chancellor 1983-87, 90-91, recorder 1995, v.p. meml. found. 1979-84, pres. 1984, trustee pres. Phi Sigma Kappa found. 1984-95, honorary and trustee emeritus 1995—), Alpha Kappa Psi, Town Hall. Home: 3460 W 7th St Apt 806 Los Angeles CA 90005-2312 Office: Albert Shonk Co 3156 Wilshire Blvd Ste 7 Los Angeles CA 90010-1209

SHONS, ALAN RANCE, plastic surgeon, educator; b. Freeport, Ill., Jan. 10, 1938; s. Ferral Caldwell and Margaret (Zimmerman) S.; AB, Dartmouth Coll., 1960; MD, Case Western Res. U., 1965; PhD in Surgery, U. Minn., 1976; m. Mary Ella Misamore, Aug. 5, 1961; children: Lesley, Susan. Intern U. Hosp., Cleve., 1965-66, resident in surgery, 1966-67; research fellow transplantation immunology U. Minn., 1969-72; resident in surgery U. Minn. Hosp., 1972-74; resident in plastic surgery NYU, 1974-76; asst. prof. plastic surgery U. Minn., Mpls., 1976-79, assoc. prof., 1979-84, prof., 1984; dir. div. plastic and reconstructive surgery U. Minn. Hosp., St. Paul Ramsey Hosp., Mpls. VA Hosp., 1976-84; cons. plastic surgery St. Louis Park Med. Center, 1980-84; prof. surgery Case Western Res. U., Cleve., 1984-93; dir. div. plastic and reconstructive surgery Univ. Hosps. Cleve., 1984-92; prof. surgery U. South Fla., H. Lee. Moffitt Cancer Ctr. and Rsch. Inst., Tampa, 1993—. Served to capt. USAF, 1967-69. Diplomate Am. Bd. Surgery, Am. Bd. Plastic Surgery. Fellow ACS (chmn. Minn. com. on trauma); mem. Am. Soc. Plastic and Reconstructive Surgeons, Am. Assn. Plastic Surgeons, Minn. Acad. Plastic Surgeons (pres. 1981-82), AMA, Soc. Head and Neck Surgeons, Am. Assn. Surgery Trauma, Transplantation Soc., Plastic Surgery Research Council, Am. Soc. Aesthetic Plastic Surgery, Am. Soc. Maxillofacial Surgeons, Am. Assn. Immunologists, Soc. Exptl. Pathology, Am. Burn Assn., Am. Cleft Palate Assn., Am. Soc. Nephrology, Assn. Acad. Surgery, Central Surg. Assn., Fla. Soc. Plastic & Reconstructive Surgeons, Sigma Xi. Office: H Lee Moffitt Cancer Ctr & Rsch Inst 12902 Magnolia Dr Tampa FL 33612-9497

SHOOB, MARVIN H., federal judge; b. Walterboro, S.C., Feb. 23, 1923; s. Michael Louis and Lena (Steinberg) S.; m. Janice Paradies, Nov. 14, 1949; children: Michael, Wendy. J.D., U. Ga., 1948. Bar: Ga. 1948. Ptnr. Brown & Shoob, Atlanta, 1949-55; ptnr. Phillips, Johnson & Shoob, Atlanta, 1955-56, Shoob, McLain & Merritt, Atlanta, 1956-79; judge U.S. Dist. Ct., Atlanta, 1979—; chmn. Juvenile Ct. Com., 1964-70; mem. Ga. State Bar Grievance Tribunal, 1975-79; chmn. Ga. State Bar Fed. Legislation Com., 1977-79; guest lectr. Continuing Legal Edn., Athens, Ga., 1975-77. Chmn. 5th Dist. Democratic Exec. Com., 1974-76. Mem. Phi Eta Sigma, Phi Kappa Phi. Jewish. Office: US Dist Ct 1921 US Courthouse 75 Spring St SW Atlanta GA 30303-3309*

SHOOK, LANGLEY R., lawyer; b. Alexandria, Va., Dec. 22, 1947. AB, U. Mich., 1969, JD magna cum laude, 1974. Bar: Ill. 1974, U.S. Dist. Ct. (no. dist.) Ill. 1974, U.S. Ct. Appeals (7th cir.) 1974, D.C. 1977, U.S. Dist. Ct. (D.C. dist.) 1977, U.S. Ct. Appeals (D.C. cir.) 1977. Ptnr. Sidley & Austin, Washington. Office: Sidley & Austin 1722 I St NW Washington DC 20006-3705*

SHOOK, ROBERT LOUIS, business writer; b. Apr. 7, 1938; m. Elinor Marks; children: Carrie, RJ, Michael. BSBA, Ohio State U., 1959. Chmn. bd. Shook Assocs. Corp.; co-founder, chmn. bd. Am. Exec. Corp., Am. Exec. Life Ins. Co.; bd. dirs. Value City Dept. Stores; appearances on over 600 radio and TV talk shows, including CNN, The David Susskind Show, The Sally Jessy Raphael Show, The Today Show, others. Author: Winning Images, 1977, 2d edit., 1978, The Greatest Salespersons, 1978, 2d edit., 1980, The Entrepreneurs, 1980, The Real Estate People, 1980, The Chief Executive Officers, 1981, Why Didn't I Think of That!, 1982, The Shaklee Story, 1982, The Book of Why, 1983, Survivors: Living with Cancer, 1983, The Healing Family, 1984, The IBM Way...Insights into the World's Most Successful Marketing Organization, 1986, The Perfect Sales Presentation, 1986, Wheel of Fortune, 1987, Honda: An American Success Story, 1988, All You Need to Know About Patents, Copyrights and Trademarks, 1989, How to Close Every Sale, 1989, Turnaround: The New Ford Motor Company, 1990, The Wall Street Dictionary, 1990, Hardball: Subtle High-Pressure Selling Techniques That Work, 1990, The Book of Odds, 1991, America's Best Kept Secret, 1991, The Name of the Game is Life, 1992, The Winner's Circle, 1992, It's About Time, 1992, Franchising: The Business Strategy That Changed the World, 1993; co-author: How to be the Complete Professional Salesman, 1974, Total Commitment, 1975, Successful Telephone Selling in the 90's, 1990, Joe Gandolfo's How to Make Big Money Selling, 1984, The Greatest Sales Stories Ever Told, 1995, (with Britt Beemer) The Beemer Principle: Why Every Marketing Strategy Ultimately Fails, 1996. Past trustee Columbus Opera; chmn. bd., Franklin County Am. Cancer Soc., 1996. Home and Office: 261 S Columbia Ave Columbus OH 43209-1626

SHOOMAN, MARTIN LAWRENCE, electrical engineer, computer scientist, educator; b. Trenton, N.J., Feb. 24, 1934; s. Lou and Ada (Pearl) S.; m. Sylvia Rose Bashoff, Dec. 23, 1962; children: Andrew Michael, Alice Helen (Mrs. Mark Lebowitz). BS, MIT, 1956, MS, 1956; DEng, Poly. Inst. Bklyn., 1961. Test engr. GE Co., 1953-55; teaching fellow MIT, Cambridge, Mass., 1955-56, vis. assoc. prof. elec. engring., 1971; rsch. engr. Sperry Gyroscope Co., 1956-58; successively instr., asst. prof., assoc. prof. elec. engring. Poly. Inst. Bklyn., 1958-72; prof. elec. engring. and computer sci. Poly. U., 1973—, dir. computer sci. div., 1980-83; sr. lectr. IBM, Grumman Aerospace, Hazeltine Corp., U.S. Army, U. Calif., George Washington U., U. Md., Eng., France, Can., Israel, Belgium, Italy and others; cons. to govt. agys. and industry, including Bell Labs., NASA, GE, RCA; tech. chmn. IEEE Computer Soc. Symposium Software Reliability and Software Engring., 1973, 76, 79; gen. chmn., 1975, 85, chmn. com. software engring., 1975; prin. investigator Poly. U.; rsch. contracts with NASA, Office Naval Rsch., USAF, Dept. Transp., others. Author: Probabilistic Reliability, 1968, 2d edit. 1990, Software Engineering, 1983 (transl. Japanese and Chinese 1989), also chpts. in 6 textbooks, numerous rsch. papers and reports on reliability, safety, computers, software and control systems. Fellow IEEE (spl. lectr., mem. adminstrv. com. reliability soc., software reliability tech. com., Best Tech. Paper on Reliability award, 1967, 71, 77, 83, Ann. Reliability award 1977, Best Paper on Software award 1977, mem. adv. bd. ann. reliability and maintainability symposium 1985—), Sigma Xi, Tau Beta Pi, Eta Kappa Nu. Home: 12 Broadfield Pl Glen Cove NY 11542-2004 Office: 6 Metrotech Ctr Brooklyn NY 11201-3840

SHOOTER, ERIC MANVERS, neurobiology educator, consultant; b. Mansfield, Eng., Apr. 18, 1924; came to U.S., 1964; s. Fred and Pattie (Johnson) S.; m. Elaine Staley Arnold, May 28, 1949; 1 child, Annette Elizabeth. BA, Cambridge (Eng.) U., 1945, MA, 1949, PhD, 1950, ScD, 1986; DSc, U. London, 1964. Sr. scientist biochemistry Brewing Industry Rsch. Fedn., 1950-53; biochemistry lectr. Univ. Coll., London, 1953-63; assoc. prof. genetics Stanford U., 1963-68, prof. genetics and biochemistry, 1968-75, prof., chmn. neurobiology dept., 1975-87, prof. neurobiology, 1987—, chmn. Neurosci. PhD Program, 1972-82; assoc. Neurosci. Rsch. Program, N.Y.C., 1979-89; teaching staff Internat. Sch. Neurosci., Praglia, Italy, 1987-93; sr. cons. Markey Charitable Trust, Miami, Fla., 1985—; chair sci. adv. bd., and dir. Regeneron Pharm., Inc., Tarrytown, N.Y., 1988—. Assoc. editor: (book series) Ann. Rev. Neurosci., 1984—; contbr. numerous articles to profl. jours. Recipient Wakeman award Duke U., 1988; Faculty scholar Josiah Macy Jr. Found., N.Y.C., 1974-75. Fellow AAAS, Royal Soc. (London), Am. Acad. Arts and Scis.; mem. Inst. Medicine of NAS (fgn. assoc.), Biochem. Soc., Am. Assn. Biol. Chemists, Soc. for Neurosci. (Ralph W. Gerard prize 1995), Am. Soc. Neurochemistry, Internat. Soc. Neurochemistry, Internat. Brain Rsch. Orgn. Avocation: travel. Home: 370 Golden Oak Dr Portola Vally CA 94028-7757 Office: Stanford U Sch Medicine Dept Neurobiology Stanford CA 94305

SHOPE, ROBERT ELLIS, epidemiology educator; b. Princeton, N.J., Feb. 21, 1929; s. Richard Edwin Shope and Helen Madden (Ellis) Flemer; m. Virginia Elizabeth Barbour, Dec. 27, 1958; children—Peter, Steven, Deborah, Bonnie. BA, Cornell U., 1951, MD, 1954. Intern then resident Grace-New Haven Hosp., 1954-58; mem. staff Rockefeller Found., Belem, Brazil, 1959-65; dir. Belem Virus Lab., Brazil, 1963-65; from asst. to assoc. prof. epidemiology Yale Sch. Medicine, New Haven, 1965-75, prof., 1975-95; prof. pathology U. Tex. Med. Br., Galveston, 1995—; adv. bd. Gorgas Inst., Panema City, 1972-90; mem. WHO Expert Panel Arboviruses, Geneva, Switzerland, 1974—, U.S. del. U.S.-Japan Coop. Med. Scis. Program, Washington, 1977—, Pan Am. Health Orgn. Commn. for Dengue, Washington, 1980—. Served to capt. U.S. Army, 1955-57, Southeast Asia. Fellow Am. Acad. Microbiology; mem. Am. Soc. Tropical Medicine and Hygiene (pres. 1980, Bailey K. Ashford award 1974, Walter Reed award 1993), Am. Soc. Virology, Am. Soc. Epidemiology, Infectious Diseases Soc. Am. Democrat. Office: U Tex Med Br Dept Pathology 301 University Blvd Galveston TX 77555-0609

SHOR, GEORGE G., JR., geophysicist, oceanographic administrator, engineer; b. N.Y.C., June 8, 1923; s. George Gershon and Dorothy (Williston); m. Elizabeth Louise Noble, June 11, 1950; children: Alexander Noble, Carolyn Elizabeth, Donald Williston. B.S., Calif. Inst. Tech., 1944, M.S., 1948, Ph.D., 1954. Joined Seismic Explorations, Inc., Houston, 1948; party chief Seismic Explorations, Inc., 1949-50; asst. research geophysicist to research geophysicist Scripps Inst. Oceanography, La Jolla, Calif., 1953-69; prof. marine geophysics Scripps Inst. Oceanography, 1969-90, prof. emeritus, 1990—, assoc. dir., 1968-91; mgr. Calif. Sea Grant program, 1969-73; Mem. NAS-NRC panel on Mohole site selection, 1959; com. on underwater telecommunications, 1968, USN Marine Geophys. Survey Liaison Council, 1965-67; spl. adv. to Com. for Coordination of Joint Prospecting for Mineral Resources in Asian Offshore Areas, 1976-91; chmn. ship scheduling panel Univ. Nat. Oceanographic Lab. Systems, 1987-89; sci. leader oceanographic expdns. to various parts of Pacific and Indian oceans, 1955-82. Served to lt. (j.g.) USNR, 1943-46; now comdr. USNR Ret. Fellow Geol. Soc. Am., Am. Geophys. Union; mem. Soc. Exploration Geophysicists, Scholia Club, Am. Bamboo Soc. (pres. 1994—). Home: 2655 Ellentown Rd La Jolla CA 92037-1147

SHOR, SAMUEL WENDELL WILLISTON, naval engineer; b. N.Y.C., June 25, 1920; s. George Gershon and Dorothy (Williston) S.; m. Joan Bopp, June 21, 1958; children: Peter Williston, Molly Hathaway. Student, Harvard U., 1937-39; B.S., U.S. Naval Acad., 1942; Naval Engr., MIT, 1949; M.S. in Math., NYU, 1963. Commd. ensign U.S. Navy, 1942, advanced through grades to capt., 1962; served in cruisers Chicago, St. Louis, and Quincy, Pacific and Atlantic, 1942-46; assigned San Francisco Naval Shipyard, 1949-52, naval reactors br. AEC, 1952-53; AEC rep. for initial tests of submarines nuclear propulsion in U.S.S. Nautilus and U.S.S. Seawolf, 1953-57; AEC rep. for startup testing of Shippingport Atomic Power Sta., 1957-58; design supt., prodn. engring. officer N.Y. Naval Shipyard, 1958-63; dir. sonar systems office Naval Ship Systems Command, 1963-67, exec. dir. plans, 1967-69, dep. comdr. for engring., 1969-71; project mgr. electronic warfare Naval Electronic Systems Commd., 1971-73; with Bechtel Power Corp., San Francisco, 1973—. Author tech. papers. Mem. Soc. Naval Architects and Marine Engrs., Soc. Naval Engrs., Am. Math. Soc., Am. Phys. Soc., Sigma Xi. Home: 318 Montford Ave Mill Valley CA 94941-3313 Office: Bechtel Corp 50 Beale St San Francisco CA 94105-1895

SHORB, GARY SEYMOUR, hospital administrator; b. Memphis, Sept. 7, 1950; married. B, Clemson U., 1972; M, Memphis State U., 1985. Acting dir. Regional Med. Ctr., Memphis, 1986-87, pres., CEO, 1987-90; pres., CEO Meth. Hosps. of Memphis, 1990—. Contbr. articles to profl. jours. Home: 360 Bluff Ridge Cv Cordova TN 38018-7617 Office: Meth Hosps Memphis 1265 Union Ave Memphis TN 38104*

SHORE, HARVEY HARRIS, business educator; b. Cambridge, Mass., Apr. 14, 1940; s. Jacob and Freda Edna (Pearlman) S.; m. Roberta Ann Rogers, Jan. 29, 1967; children: Nina Ellen, Elissa Amy. BA cum laude, Harvard U., 1961; MS, MIT, 1963; DBA, Harvard U., 1966. Asst. prof. indsl. adminstrn. U. Conn., Storrs, 1966-72; assoc. prof. indsl. adminstrn. U. Conn., 1972-77; dir. Hartford MBA prog. U. Conn., Hartford, 1977-82; assoc. prof. mgmt. U. Conn., Storrs, 1982-95, assoc. prof. emeritus, 1995—. Contbr. articles to profl. jours.; editor Cubic Rev., 1975-78; author: Arts Administration and Management, 1987. Chmn. bus. adv. com. Tunxis Community Coll., Farmington, Conn., 1983-85; bd. dirs. Temple Beth Sholom, Manchester, Conn., 1987-90. Mem. Employee Assistance Soc. N.Am., Masons. Democrat. Jewish. Avocation: tennis.

SHORE, HERBERT, writer, poet, educator; b. Phila., June 6, 1924; s. Meyer and Frances (Smiler) S.; m. Yen Lu Wong, Dec. 23, 1977; children: Norman Jon, Pia Ilyen Wong. Maya Iming Wong. B.A., U. Pa., 1942; postgrad., Columbia U., 1946-48, Dramatic Workship New Sch., 1946-48; postgrad, Stanford U., 1948-53; M.A., Stanford U., 1958; Ph.D., Internat. Coll., 1983. Writer, poet, dramatist and dramaturg, 1956—; dir. Council Tech. and Cultural Transformation, 1974-88; prof., assoc. dean Sch. of Theatre U. So. Calif., 1979-93; founding dir. TNR: The New Repertory, 1972—; cons. UNESCO, 1974—; provost Internat. Coll., 1983-86; writer-in-residence Blue Mountain Centre, 1985, 86; dir. plays for theatre and TV, author plays, also cantatas; disting. vis. fellow La Trobe U., Australia, 1990; scholar in residence Eltham Coll., Australia, 1990; sr. rsch. scholar Ctr. for Multiethnic and Transnat. Studies, U. So. Calif., 1993—; fellow Mayibuye Ctr., South Africa, 1995; mentor global studies Immaculate Heart Coll. Ctr., 1993—; bd. dirs. Eduardo Mondlang Meml. Found., 1996. Author: Come Back Africa, 1970, Ashes Dark Antigone, 1972, Toward the World of Tomorrow, 1978, Cultural Policy, 1981, Cicada Images, Moulting, 1983, No Future Wrapped in Darkness, 1984; Seek to Be Human, 1985, Beginnings are Born in Memory, 1986, Shime, 1986, Trees Die Standing, 1987, And the Dogs Are Silent, 1988, Should the Grain Perish, 1989, Namashawala, Santa Claus and the Bagamoyo Cock, 1990, South African Township Theatre, 1990, Southern Africa: A Dream Deferred, 1990, Apartheid's Waning and Dangerous Years, 1990, Sounds in the Wind, 1991, Exile from El Salvador, Terra Infirma, 1992; also articles, short stories, poems. Adv. council Internat. Symposium on Arts, Banff Centre, 1984—; exec. com. Internat. Inst. Audio-Visual Media, Vienna, 1985—; assoc. Ctr. for African Studies, Eduardo Mondlane U., 1988—. Served with USMC, 1943-46. Recipient Writers Digest prize for fiction, 1963, medal of Bagamoyo, Nat. Assembly, Mozambique, 1989; Herbert Shore Collection established in his honor Immaculate Heart Coll. Ctr., 1991, Mayibuye Ctr., South Africa, 1995; grantee Ford. Found., 1978-79, 96, Africa Fund, 1995-96, Rockefeller Found., 1966-67, NEH, 1979-81, Helen Wurlitzer Found., 1958-60, Social Sci. Rsch. Coun., 1967-68, African and Am. Univs. Program, 1964-65, Kate Maremont Found., 1959-60, Centro Mexicano de Escritores, 1958. Mem. PEN Ctr. West, USA, LMDA, Assn. Theatre Higher Edn., Nat. Writers Union, Acad. Am. Poets, Soc. Writers and Poets, African Studies Assn. Office: U So Calif Ctr Multiethnic Transnat GFS 344 Los Angeles CA 90089-1694

SHORE, HOWARD LESLIE, composer; b. Toronto, Ontario, Canada, Oct. 18, 1946; s. Mac and Bernice (Ash) S.; m. Elizabeth Ann Cotnoir, Aug. 3, 1990; 1 child, Mac. Student, Berklee Sch. Music, 1965-67, Forest Hill Collegiate, Toronto, Ont., Can., 1961-64. Composer film scores including I Miss You, Hugs and Kisses, 1978, the Brood, 1979, Scaners, 1981, Videodrome, 1983, Nothing Lasts Forever, 1984, Places in the Heart, 1984, After Hours, 1985, Belizaire the Cajun, 1987, Fire with Fire, 1986, The Fly, 1986, Nadine, 1987, The Local Stigmatic, 1987, Heaven, 1987, Moving, 1988, Dead Ringers, 1988 (Genie award), Big, 1988, She-Devil, 1989, An Innocent Man, 1989, Signs of Life, 1989, Postcards from the Edge, 1990, The Silence of the Lambs, 1991, A Kiss Before Dying, 1989, Naked Lunch, 1990, Prelude to a Kiss, 1992, Single White Female, 1992, (TV score) Scales of Justice, 1990, Guilty as Sin, 1993, Sliver, 1993, M. Butterfly, 1993, Mrs. Doubtfire, 1993, Philadelphia, 1993, The Client, 1994, Ed Wood, 1994, Nobody's Fool, 1994, Moonlight and Valentino, 1995, White Man's Burden, 1995, Seven, 1995, Before and After, 1996, The Truth About Cats and Dogs, 1996, Looking for Richard, 1996, Crash, 1996; music dir. Saturday Night Live, 1975-80. Mem. ASCAP, Lighthouse (founding mem.). Home: Wee Wah Lodge Tuxedo Park NY 10987 Office: Prince in NY Music Corp Wee Wah Rd Tuxedo Park NY 10987-0836

SHORE, JAMES H(ENRY), psychiatrist; b. Winston-Salem, N.C., Apr. 6, 1940; s. James Henry and Ellen Elizabeth (Hayes) S.; m. Christine Lowenbach, Aug. 24, 1963; children—Ellen Ottilie, James Henry. M.D., Duke U., 1965. Diplomate Am. Bd. Psychiatry and Neurology. Intern U. Utah Med. Center, 1965-66; resident in psychiatry U. Wash., 1966-69; chief mental health office Portland (Oreg.) Area Indian Health Service, 1969-73;

assoc. prof. psychiatry, dir. community psychiatry tng. program U. Oreg. Health Scis. Center, 1973-75, prof., chmn. dept. psychiatry, 1975-85; chmn. dept. psychiatry U. Colo. Health Scis. Ctr., Denver, 1985—; interim chancellor, 1992-93; dir. Colo. Psychiatry Hosp., 1985—; interim dir. U. Colo. Hosp., Denver, 1987-88, interim exec. vice chancellor, 1994-95; mem. exptl. and spl. edn. com. NIMH-Internal Rev. Group, 1976-80; cons. in field. Contbr. numerous articles to profl. publs. Mem. Various community bds. Served with USPHS, 1969-73. Decorated USPHS Commendation medal; various grants. Fellow Am. Psychiat. Assn., Am. Coll. Psychiatry; mem. Am. Assn. Chmn. Depts. Psychiatry (pres. 1989), Am. Bd. Psychiatry and Neurology (dir. 1987—, pres. 1994), Residency Rev. Com. for Psychiatry (chmn. 1991-92). Office: U Colo Health Scis Ctr PO Box C-249 4200 E 9th Ave Denver CO 80262-0001

SHORE, MILES FREDERICK, psychiatrist, educator; b. Chgo., May 26, 1929; s. Miles Victor and Margaret Elizabeth S.; m. Eleanor M. Gossard, July 4, 1953; children: Miles Paul, Rebecca Margaret, Susanna Gladys. BA, U. Chgo., 1948; AB, Harvard U., 1950, MD, 1954. Intern U. Ill. Research and Edn. Hosp., Chgo., 1954-55; resident in psychiatry Mass. Mental Health Center, Beth Israel Hosp., Boston, 1956-61; asst. prof. psychiatry Tufts U. Sch. Medicine, Medford, Mass., 1964-68; assoc. prof. Tufts U. Sch. Medicine, 1968-71, prof., 1971-75, prof. community health, 1972-75; founder, dir. Tufts Community Mental Health Center, 1968-74, asso. dean community affairs, 1972-75; mem. faculty Boston Psychoanalytic Inst., 1973—; Bullard prof. psychiatry Harvard Med. Sch., Boston, 1975—, dir. div. mental health systems, 1993—; supt. Mass. Mental Health Ctr., 1975-93; vis. scholar John F. Kennedy Sch. Govt. Harvard U., 1993—; dir. program for chronic mental illness Robert Wood Johnson Found., 1985-92. Editl. bd. Psychat. Svcs. Jour., 1990; bd. editors Jour. Interdisciplinary History, 1975, Psycho History Rev., 1978; column editor Harvard Rev. Psychiatry, 1993; contbr. articles to profl. jours. Bd. dirs. Federated Dorchester Neighborhood Houses, Boston, 1975-78, Med. Found., Bosotn, 1987—, Ctr. House, Boston, 1995—; mem. Blue Ribbon Commn., Mass. Dept. Mental Health, 1979-80. Capt. U.S. Army, 1956-58. Community Mental Health Center grantee, 1964-75. Fellow Am. Psychiat. Assn. (life, joint commn. on pub. affairs, adminstrv. psychiatry award 1987), Am. Coll. Psychiatrists (chmn. fin. com. 1983-89, bd. regents 1988-90, 1st v.p. 1994, pres. 1996-97, Bowis award for svc. 1990, Arthur P. Noyes award 1994); mem. Boston Psychoanalytic Soc. and Inst. (chmn. bd. trustees 1970-73), Mass. Psychiat. Soc. (pres. 1970-71), Mass. Hosp. Assn. (trustee 1980-85), Am. Hosp. Assn. (governing coun. mental health and psychiat. svcs. 1985-87, chmn. governing coun. for psychiat. and substance abuse svcs. 1992-93), Roxbury Clinic Record Club, Aesculapian Club, Mass. Hist. Soc. Office: JFK Sch Govt 79 Jfk St Cambridge MA 02138-5801

SHORE, RICHARD ARNOLD, mathematics educator; b. Boston, Aug. 18, 1946; s. Philip M. and Miriam (Krensky) S.; m. Naomi J. Spiller, Aug. 3, 1969; children—Deena A., Aviva R. B. Jewish Edn., Hebrew Coll., 1966; A.B., Harvard U., 1968; Ph.D., MIT, 1972. Instr. U. Chgo., 1972-74; asst. prof. Cornell U., Ithaca, N.Y., 1974-78, assoc. prof., 1978-83; asst. prof. U. Ill.-Chgo., 1977; vis. assoc. prof. MIT, Cambridge, 1980; vis. prof. Hebrew U., Jerusalem, 1982-83; prof. math. Cornell U., Ithaca, 1983—; organizing com. Logic Yr. at MSRI, 1989-90, other internat. meetings. Author: (with A. Nerode) Logic for Applications; cons. editor Jour. Symbolic Logic, 1980-83, editor, 1984-93, coord. editor, 1989-91; editor: Recursion Theory: mng. editor: Bull. Symbolic Logic, 1993—; contbr. articles to profl. jours. V.p. for edn. Hillel Acad. Broome County, Binghamton, N.Y., 1985-89; treas. Beth David Synagogue, 1993—. NSF grantee, 1973—. Mem. Am. Math. Soc., Spl. Interest Group in Algorithms and Computation Theory, Assn. for Computing Machinery, Assn. for Symbolic Logic (coun. 1984—). Jewish. Home: 7 Avon Rd Binghamton NY 13905-4201 Office: Cornell U Dept Math White Hall Ithaca NY 14853

SHORE, STEPHEN, photographer; b. N.Y.C., Oct. 8, 1947; m. Ginger Cramer Seippel, 1980; 1 child, Nicholas; 1 stepchild, Alex Seippel. Student, Minor White, Workshop, 1970. Photographer, 1953—. One-man shows, Met. Mus. Art, N.Y.C., 1971, Light Gallery, N.Y.C., 1972, 73, 75, 77, 78, 80, Phoenix Gallery, San Francisco, 1975, Mus. Modern Art, N.Y.C., 1976, U. Akron, Ohio, 1978, Vision Gallery, Boston, 1978, La Photogaleria, Madrid, 1979, Ewing Gallery, Washington, 1979, Catskill Ctr. Photography, Woodstock, N.Y., 1980, Fraenkel Gallery, San Francisco, 1982, Mus. Arts and Scis., Daytona Beach, Fla., 1981, Polk Pub. Mus., 1982, ARCO Ctr. Visual Arts, L.A., 1982, N. Mex. State U. Art Gallery, Las Cruces, 1982, Art Inst. Chgo., 1984, Pace Wildenstein MacGill, N.Y.C., 1989, 95, Sprengel Mus., Hannover, 1995, Würt. Kunstverein, Stuttgart, 1995, Amerika Haus, Berlin, 1995, George Eastman House, Rochester, N.Y., 1996; group shows include, Met. Mus. Art, N.Y.C., 1973, 82, Internat. Mus. Photography, George Eastman House, 1975, Documenta 6, Kassel, W. Ger., 1977, Art Inst. Chgo., 1977, 79, 89, Mus. Modern Art, N.Y.C., 1978, 91, Corcoran Gallery, Washington, 1979, Kunsthaus, Zurich, Switzerland, 1980, U. Ariz. Mus. Art, Tucson, 1981, Nat. Gallery, Washington, 1989, Getty Mus., 1992; represented in permanent collections, Met. Mus. Art, N.Y.C., Mus. Modern Art, N.Y.C., Internat. Mus. Photography, George Eastman House, Rochester, N.Y., Mus. Fine Arts, Boston, Library of Congress, Washington, Art Inst. Chgo., in Permanent collections, Ctr. Creative Photography, U. Ariz., Tucson, in permanent collections, Stedelijk Mus., Amsterdam, Netherlands, Neue Sammlung, Munich, W.Ger., Australian Nat. Gallery, Canberra; author: Andy Warhol, 1968, Uncommon Places, 1982, The Gardens at Giverny, 1983, Stephen Shore: Luzzara, 1993, Stephen Shore: Photographs 1973-1993, 1995, The Velvet Years, 1995; portfolio 12 Photographs, 1976; contbr. articles to profl. jours. Nat. Endowment Arts grantee, 1974, 79; Guggenheim fellow, 1975; Am. Acad. (Rome) spl. fellow, 1980; MacDowell Colony fellow, 1993.

SHORE, STEVEN NEIL, physics educator, research astrophysicist; b. N.Y.C., July 16, 1953; m. Lys A. Taylor, 1974. MSc, SUNY, Stony Brook, 1974; PhD in Astronomy, U. Toronto, 1978. Rsch. assoc. astronomy Columbia U., 1978-79, lectr., 1979; assoc. prof., dir. Astrophys. Rsch. Ctr., 1985-89; asst. prof. astronomy Case Western Res. U., 1979-84; ops. astronomer Space Telescope Sci. Inst. Computer Sci. Corp., 1984-85, astrophysicist Goddard Space Ctr., 1989-93; assoc. prof. physics, chair dept. physics and astronomy Ind. U., South Bend, 1993—; Shapley lectr. astronomy Am. Astron. Soc., 1980—; vis. asst. prof. astronomy Ohio State U., 1981; vis. prof. Ecole Normale Superiure; vis. physicist Am. Inst. Physics, 1992—; adj. assoc. prof. physics Ariz. State U., 1992—; vis. prof. astrophysics U. Pisa, 1993—. Sci. editor: Astrophysics Jour. Mem. Am. Astron. Soc., Hist. Sci. Soc., Internat. Astron. Union, Brit. Soc. Hist. Sci., Sigma Xi. Office: Ind Univ Dept Physics & Astronomy South Bend IN 46634

SHORE, THOMAS SPENCER, JR., lawyer; b. Akron, Ohio, Jan. 1, 1939; s. T. Spencer and Harriet G. (Delicate) S.; m. Margaret F. Kudzma, Aug. 12, 1961; children—Thomas Spencer III, John Christopher, Daniel Andrew, Mary Margaret. B.A., Brown U., 1961; J.D., Northwestern U., 1964. Bar: Ohio 1964. Assoc. Taft, Stettinius and Hollister, Cin., 1964-69; asso. Rendigs, Fry, Kiely & Dennis, Cin., 1969-71; partner Rendigs, Fry, Kiely & Dennis, 1972—; adj. asst. prof. Chase Law Sch., U. No. Ky. Bd. dirs. United Cerebral Palsy of Cin., 1978—; bd. dirs., sec. Boys Club Am., Cin.; trustee emeritus Family Svc. of Cin. Area; past pres. Vis. Nurse Assn. of Cin., hon. trustee. Mem. Cin. Bar Assn., Ohio Bar Assn., Am. Bar Assn. Clubs: Cin. Country, Cin. Tennis, Queen City, Webhanet. Home: 3224 Columbia Pky Cincinnati OH 45226-1042 Office: 900 Central Trust Tower Cincinnati OH 45202

SHORENSTEIN, ROSALIND GREENBERG, physician; b. N.Y.C., Jan. 14, 1947; d. Albert Samuel and Natalie Miriam (Sherman) Greenberg; m. Michael Lewis Shorenstein, June 18, 1967; children: Anna Irene, Claire Beth. BA in Chemistry, Wellesley Coll., 1968; MA in Biochemistry and Molecular Biology, Harvard U., 1970, PhD in Biochemistry and Molecular Biology, 1973; MD, Stanford U., 1976. Diplomate Am. Bd. Internal Medicine. Resident in internal medicine UCLA Med. Ctr., 1976-79; pvt. practice internal medicine Santa Cruz, Calif., 1979—; mem. dept. internal medicine Dominican Hosp., Santa Cruz, 1979—; co-dir. med. svcs. Health Enhancement & Lifestyle Planning Systems, Santa Cruz, 1983—. Contbr. articles to profl. journals. Dir. Santa Cruz Chamber Players, 1993-94, pres., bd. dirs., 1994—. Recipient Charlie Parkhurst award Santa Cruz Women's Commn., 1989; NSF fellow, 1968-72, Sarah Perry Wood Med. fellow Wellesley Coll., 1972-76. Mem. Am. Soc. Internal Medicine (del. 1994, 95), Calif. Soc. Internal Medicine (trustee 1994—), Am. Med. Women's Assn. (Outstanding Svc. award 1987, br. #59 pres. 1986—), Calif. Med. Assn. (com. on women 1987-93), Santa Cruz County Med. Soc. (mem. bd. govs. 1993—), Phi Beta Kappa, Sigma Xi. Jewish. Office: 700 Frederick St Ste 103 Santa Cruz CA 95062-2239

SHORENSTEIN, WALTER HERBERT, commercial real estate development company executive; b. Glen Cove, N.Y., Feb. 23, 1915; m. Phyllis J. Finley, Aug. 8, 1945 (dec.); children: Joan (Dec.), Carole, Douglas. Student, Pa. State U., 1933-34, U. Pa., 1934-36; D Econs. (hon.), HanYang U., Seoul, 1988. With property sales mgmt. depts. Milton Meyer & Co., San Francisco, 1946-51, ptnr., 1951-60, owner, chmn. bd., 1960—; owner, chmn. bd. Shorenstein Group, San Francisco, Shorenstein Co., San Francisco, 1960—. Past chmn. bd. trustees Hastings Law Ctr., U. Calif., San Francisco; founding mem. exec. adv. com. Hubert H. Humphrey Inst. Pub. Affairs, U. Minn.; founder Joan Shorenstein Barone Ctr. on Press, Politics and Pub. Policy, Harvard U. Kennedy Sch. Govt.; past pres., hon. life bd. dirs. San Francisco Park and Recreation Commn.; chmn. Vietnam Orphans Airlift; bd. dirs. San Francisco Performing Arts Ctr.; trustee Asia Found.; fin. chmn. Dem. Nat. Conv., 1984; apptd. by Pres. Clinton to Nat. Svc. Commn., 1994; chmn. San Francisco UN50 nat. com., 1995, also numerous polit. activities. Maj. USAF, 1940-45. Named Leader of Tomorrow, Time mag., 1953, Calif. Dem. of Yr., 1985; recipient Nat. Brotherhood award NCCJ, 1982, Disting. Svc. award Dem. Nat. Com., 1983; Golden Plate award Am. Acad. Achievement. Mem. Calif. C. of C. (bd. dirs.), San Francisco C. of C. (past chmn. bd., life bd. dirs. Office: Shorenstein Co 555 California St Ste 4900 San Francisco CA 94104-1714

SHORNEY, GEORGE HERBERT, publishing executive; b. Oak Park, Ill., Dec. 16, 1931; s. George Herbert and Mary (Wallace) S.; m. Nancy Leith, Aug. 27, 1955; children: Cynthia, Herbert, John, Scott. BA, Denison U., 1954. Office mgr. Hope Pub. Co., Carol Stream, Ill., 1958-61, v.p., 1961-70, pres., 1970-91, chmn., 1992—; bd. dirs. Gary-Wheaton (Ill.) Bank. Contbr. New Grove Handbook of Music, 1989. Pres. West Suburban Choral Union, Wheaton, 1984-92; bd. govs. Ctrl. DuPage Hosp., Winfield, Ill., 1985-95; mem. gov. com. Chgo. Symphony Orch., 1986—; chmn. Wheaton Fire and Police Commrs., 1974-81, Wyndemere Retirement Cmty., Wheaton, 1989; chmn. bd. dirs. Healthcorp Affiliates, Naperville, Ill., 1982-95; chmn. bd. trustees Westminster Choir Coll., Princeton, N.J., 1988-91; trustee Denison U., Granville, Ohio, 1995—. With USN, 1954-56. Mem. Ch. Music Pubs. Assn. (pres. 1986-87), Denison Univ. Alumni Soc. (pres. 1976-78), Univ. Club (Chgo.), Nat. Liberal Club (London). Democrat. Presbyterian. Home: 160 W Elm St Wheaton IL 60187-6428 Office: Hope Pub Co 380 S Main Pl Carol Stream IL 60188-2448

SHORNEY, MARGO KAY, art gallery owner; b. Great Falls, Mont., July 5, 1930; d. Angus Vaughn McIver and Loneta Eileen Kuhn; m. James Thomas Shorney, Apr. 17, 1954; 1 child, Blair Angus. Student, Coll. Edn., Great Falls, Mont., 1948-50, U. Denver, 1950-53. Owner, dir. Shorney Gallery Fine Art, Oklahoma City, 1976—; pres. Mont. Inst. Arts, Great Falls, 1953-54, Okla. Art Gallery Owners Assn., Oklahoma City, 1981-83; lectr. Norman (Okla.) Art League, 1987-91; judge fine arts Ponca City (Okla.) 12th Ann. Fine Arts, 1986, Edmond (Okla.) Art Assn. Expo 1995, Fine Arts Festival 22nd Ann., 1996; appraiser Globe Life, Oklahoma City, Ponca City Juried Art Assn. 22nd Ann. Fine Arts. Works exhibited in group shows, various orgns., 1953-90. Mentor South Oklahoma City Coll., 1990; active Okla. Mus. Art, 1973-78. Mem. Nat. Assn. Women Bus. Owners, Okla. Sculpture Soc. (charter), Okla. Art Guild (bd. dirs. 1979-82, lectr. 1981, 82, 83, 92). Republican. Episcopalian. Avocations: swimming, figure skating, horseback riding, landscaping. Office: Shorney Gallery Fine Arts 6616 N Olie Ave Oklahoma City OK 73116-7318

SHORR, MIRIAM KRONFELDT, artist; b. N.Y.C.; m. Eli Yale Shorr, 1931. Student, Hunter Coll., 1921-25. Exhibited in ann. shows Audubon Artists, City Ctr. Gallery, N.Y.C., Nat. Soc. Painters in Casein; Knickerbocker, Whitney, Bklyn. and Norfolk Mus., Five Arts Soc., Sarasota, 1991-92; one man shows Brandeis U., Bklyn. Coll., U. Maine, Rutgers U., LaSalle Coll., Hillside U., Gettysburg Coll., U. Tampa, Miami, R.I., Albany, Ga. and Colby U. One-man shows throughout U.S.; one-man showing of tapestries Cen. Libr., St. Petersburg, Fla., 1982, Plymouth Harbor Gallery, Sarasota, 1990; one-man show paintings Ctr. Libr., Bradenton, Fla., 1988; numerous group shows. Recipient 1st prize for drawing Nat. Assn. Women Artists, 1962, Lena Newcastle award, 1961, 65, Aileen O. Webb prize, 1974, 1st prize Fibres and Fabrics, Longboat Key Art Assn., 1979, 1st prize enamels Venice (Fla.) Art Assn., 1982, 2d prize for painting Sarasota Art Assn., 1983, 1st prize Venice Art League, 1985, Ann. Parade of Prize Winners, 1982-88, Longboat Key Art Assn., 1982-88. Mem. Artists Equity Assn. (bd. dir. 1958-64), Nat. Assn. Women Artists (bd. dir. 1970-72), Sarasota Art Assn. (chmn. exhbns. 1976-78, editor The Bull. 1979-81), Art League Manatee County, Fla. Artists Group, Longboat Key Art Assn., Venice Art League. Home: 3435 Fox Run Rd Unit 102 Sarasota FL 34231-7384

SHORS, CLAYTON MARION, cardiologist; b. Beemer, Nebr., June 10, 1925; s. Jospeh Albert and Morva Edith (Clayton) S.; m. Arlene Towle, June 6, 1948; children—Susan Debra, Clayton Robert, Scott Towle. B.S., U. Nebr., 1950, M.D., 1952. Diplomate Am. Bd. Internal Medicine (subspecialty cardiovascular disease). Intern Detroit Receiving Hosp., 1952-53, resident, 1953-56; practice medicine specializing in cardiology Detroit; chief cardiology St. John Hosp., Detroit. Bd. dirs. Sedona Acad.; mem. Sedona 30. Served with U.S. Army, 1943-46. Fellow Am. Coll. Cardiology, Internat. Coll. Angiology, Am. Heart Assn. Council on Clin. Cardiology; mem. Alpha Omega Alpha. Home: 44 Rue De La Rose Sedona AZ 86336-5970 Office: 1785 W Us Highway 89A Sedona AZ 86336-5567

SHORT, ALEXANDER CAMPBELL, lawyer; b. Washington, July 26, 1940; s. Joseph Hudson and Beth (Campbell) S.; m. Patricia Graves Thompson, Aug. 24, 1968; children: Joseph Graves, Ashley Campbell, Justin Owen. BA, Amherst Coll., 1963; MA, U. Pa., 1968; JD, U. Va., 1972. Bar: Conn. 1972, Md. 1973. Field and site rep. U.S. Dept. of HUD, Phila., 1963-69; assoc. Reid & Riege P.C., Hartford, Conn., 1972-73, Piper & Marbury, Balt., 1973-79; assoc. Miles & Stockbridge, Balt., 1979-81, ptnr., 1981-94; pvt. practice Balt., 1994-95; ptnr. Hooper, Kiefer & Cornell, LLP, Balt., 1995—; bd. dirs., pres. Handel Soc. adv. bd. to Handel Choir, Balt., 1983-87; pres. Handel Choir, Balt., 1987-88. Bd. dirs. Homeland Assn., Balt., 1984-85, Kernewood Assn., Balt., 1995—; mem. bd. mgrs. Camp Dudley, YWCA, 1991-96. Mem. Md. Bar Assn. (real property planning and zoning sect., sec. 1982-84, chmn. elect 1984-86, chmn. 1986-88. Democrat. Presbyterian. Avocations: choral singing, scouting, gardening. Office: 343 N Charles St Baltimore MD 21201

SHORT, BETSY ANN, elementary education educator; b. Macon, Ga., Mar. 18, 1958; d. Garland Brooks Jr. and Mary Eleanor (Jordan) Turner; m. Lynn Robin Short, July 21, 1984. BS in Early Childhood Edn., Ga. Coll., Milledgeville, 1981, M in Early Childhood Edn., 1993, EdS, 1995. Cert. elem. tchr. and tchr. support specialist, Ga. Tchr. 3d grade Stockbridge (Ga.) Elem. Sch., 1983-84, tchr. kindergarten, 1984-93; tchr. augmented spl. instructional assistance Locust Grove (Ga.) Elem. Sch., 1993—. Author: Spinning Yarns, 1995; mem. editl. adv. bd. Ga. Jour. Reading; contbr. articles to profl. jours.; artist oil painting/pen and ink drawing. Mem. Profl. Assn. of Ga. Educators, Ga. Coun. Tchrs. Maths., Ga. Coun. Internat. Reading Assn., Ga. Coun. Social Studies, Ga. Sci. Tchrs. Assn., Henry Heritage Reading Coun. Baptist. Avocations: oil painting, cross-stiching, writing short stories, story telling. Office: Locust Grove Elem 1727 Griffin Rd Locust Grove GA 30248

SHORT, BOBBY See SHORT, ROBERT WALTRIP

SHORT, BYRON ELLIOTT, engineering educator; b. Putnam, Tex., Dec. 29, 1901; s. Samuel W. and Florence Gertrude (Sublett) S.; m. Mary Jo Fitzgerald, June 1, 1937; children: Mary Aileen Short Gauntt, Byron Elliott Jr. B.S., U. Tex., 1926, M.S., 1930; M.M.E., Cornell U., 1936, Ph.D., 1939. Cadet engr. Tex Co., summers 1926-27, mech. engr., summers 1928-30; instr. U. Tex., 1926-29, asst. prof., 1929-36, charge heat-power, fluid mechanics lab., 1930-65, mech. engr., summers 1932-36, 40, asso. prof., 1936-39, prof. mech. engring., 1939-73, prof. emeritus, 1973—, chmn. dept., 1945-47, 51-53; acting dean U. Tex. (Coll. Engring.), 1948-49; teaching fellow Cornell, 1935-36; cons. Oak Ridge Nat. Lab., research participant, 1956, 57. Author: Flow, Measurement and Pumping of Fluids, 1934, Engineering Thermodynamics, (with H.L. Kent, B.F. Treat), 1953, Pressure Enthalpy Charts (with H.L. kent and H.A. Walls), 1970; assoc. editor Design Volume, Am. Soc. Refrigerating Engrs. Databook, 1953-55, editor, 1957; contbr. articles to engring. Fellow ASME (life; chmn. South Tex. sect. 1938-39, mem. heat transfer and power test code com.), ASHRAE (life); mem. SAR, Am. Soc. Engring. Edn., Huguenot Soc. Am. (state pres. 1983-85), Masons (33d degree SR & KT), Shriners, Sigma Xi, Tau Beta Pi, Phi Kappa Phi, Pi Tau Sigma. Baptist. Home: 502 E 32nd St Austin TX 78705-3105 *As I look backward over the years relative to what I have done professionally and in home and civic life, I think of the men and women whom I admired and loved and thus influenced my life. An early admonition of my mother was "learn things while young before your mind becomes cluttered with non-essentials".*

SHORT, EARL DE GREY, JR., psychiatrist, consultant; b. Talladega, Ala., Jan. 11, 1933; s. Earl de Grey and Adeline Eugenia (McWilliams) S.; m. Martha Burt Rossiter, Oct. 12, 1963; children: Earl D III, Philip A., Catherine E., William R. BS, The Citadel, 1956; MD, Med. U. S.C., Charleston, 1959. Commd. 2d lt. USAR, 1956; entered active duty U.S. Army, 1961, advanced through grades to col., 1976; battalion surgeon 4th Armored BN, 8th Inf. div., Germany, 1961-62; resident psychiatry Walter Reed Army Med. Ctr., Washington, 1962-65; chief dept. psychiatry U.S. Army Hosp., Ft. Polk, La., 1965-68, U.S. Walson Army Hosp., Ft. Dix, N.J., 1968-70; student Command and Gen. Staff Coll., Ft. Leavenworth, Kans., 1970-71; divsn. surgeon, comdr. 2d Med. Bn., 2d Infantry divsn., Korea, 1971-72; chief psychiatry svc. Brooke Army Med. Ctr., Ft. Sam Houston, Tex., 1972-80; ret. U.S. Army, 1980; psychiatrist Mecklenburg County Mental Health Ctr., Charlotte, N.C., 1980-86; ret. Mecklenburg County, 1993; psychiatrist Carolinas Medical Ctr. Ctr. for Mental Health, Charlotte, N.C., 1986—; pvt. practice Carolinas Med. Group, Psychiat. and Psychol. Assocs., 1992—; psychiat. cons. Mecklenburg County, Charlotte, 1987—, Amethyst, Charlotte, 1993-95. Founder Philip Alexander Short Meml. Scholarship Fund, Wingate (N.C.) Coll., 1988, Short Endowment Fund, Wingate Coll., 1991, Philip Alexander Short Meml. Fund, Elon Homes for Children, Elon Coll., N.C., 1989. Decorated Meritorious Svc. medal with 1 oak leaf cluster, U.S. Army, 1972, 80, Army Commendation medal with 1 oak leaf cluster, U.S. Army, 1968, 70; recipient All Am. award The Citadel, 1956. Mem. AMA, Am. Psychiat. Assn., N.C. Med. Soc., N.C. Psychiat. Assn., Charlotte Psychiat. Soc., Assn. Mil. Surgeons, Mecklenburg County Med. Soc., Ret. Officers Assn., Am. Legion, VFW, Sons Am. Revolution, Nat. Assn. for Uniformed Svcs. Republican. Presbyterian. Avocations: genealogy, composing piano music, restoring ancestral homes, collecting stamps, books and coins. Office: PO Box 18773 Charlotte NC 28218-0773

SHORT, ELIZABETH M., physician, educator, federal agency administrator; b. Boston, June 2, 1942; d. James Edward and Arlene Elizabeth (Mitchell) Meehan; m. Herbert M. Short, Sept. 2, 1963 (div. 1969); 1 child, Timothy Owen; m. Michael Allen Friedman, June 21, 1976; children: Lia Gabrielle, Hannah Ariel, Eleanor Elana. BA Philosophy magna cum laude, Mt. Holyoke Coll., 1963; MD cum laude, Yale U., 1968. Diplomate Am. Bd. Internal Medicine, Am. Bd. Med. Genetics. Intern, jr. resident internal medicine Yale New Haven Hosp., 1968-70; postdoctoral fellow in human genetics Yale Med. Sch., 1970-72; postdoctoral fellow in renal metabolism U. Calif., San Francisco, 1972-73; sr. resident in internal medicine Stanford (Calif.) Med. Sch., 1973-74, chief resident in internal medicine, 1974-75; staff physician Palo Alto Veterans Med. Ctr., Stanford, Calif., 1975-80; asst. prof. of medicine Stanford Med. Sch., 1975-83, asst. dean Student Affairs, 1978-80, assoc. dean Students Affairs/Medical Education, 1980-83; dir. biomed. rsch. and faculty devel. Assn. Am. Med. Colls., Washington, 1983-87, dep. dir. dept. acad. affairs, 1983-87, dep. dir. biomedical rsch., 1987-88; dep. assoc. chief med. dir. for acad. affairs VA, Washington, 1988-92, assoc. chief medical dir. for acad. affairs, 1992—; vis. prof. Human Biology, Stanford U., 1983-86; resource allocation com. Veteran's Health Adminstrn., 1989-91; budget planning and policy review coun. 1991—: planning review com. Veterans Health Adminstrn., 1991—; chair resident work limit task force 1991—; managed care task force, 1993-94; co-chair com. status women Am. Fedn. Clin. Rsch., 1975-77; mem. numerous adminstrv. coms., Yale Med. Sch., Stanford U.; accreditation coun. grad. med. edn., 1988—; mem. public policy com. Am. Soc. Human Genetics, 1984—, chair, 1986-94; mem. White House Task Force on Health Care Reform, 1993-94. assoc. editor Clin. Rsch. Jour., 1976-79, editor elect, 1979-80, editor 1980-84; contbr. articles to profl. jours. Mem. nat. child health adv. coun. NIH, 1991—; mem. com. edn. and training Office Sci. and Tech. Policy, 1991—. Recipient Maclean Zoology award Mt. Holyoke Coll.; Munger scholar, Markle scholar, Sara Williston scholar Mt. Holyoke Coll., 1959-63, Yale Men in Medicine scholar, 1964-68; Bardwell Meml. Med. fellow, 1963. Mem. AAAS, Am. Soc. Human Genetics, Am. Fedn. Clin. Rsch. (bd. dirs. 1973-83, editor 1978-83, nat. coun., exec. com., pub. policy com. 1977-87), Am. Assn. Women in Scis., Western Soc. Clin. Investigation, Calif. Acad. Medicine, Phi Beta Kappa, Alpha Omega Alpha. Home: 6807 Bradley Blvd Bethesda MD 20817-3004 Office: Dept Veterans Affairs Health Adminstrn Acad Affairs 810 Vermont Ave VHA 14 Washington DC 20420

SHORT, EUGENE MAURICE, JR., lawyer, accountant; b. San Francisco, Sept. 4, 1932; s. Eugene Maurice and Emeline Inez (Cox) S.; m. Ann Page, Sept. 4, 1953 (div. 1962); children: Lawrence, David, Dale; m. Karol Fageros, Dec. 1, 1963 (dec. Apr. 1988); children: Kristin, Karri; m. Mary Marhoefer Lynch, Apr. 2, 1992. BBA, City Coll. San Francisco, 1952, U. Miami, Fla., 1954; JD, U. Miami, 1959. Bar: Fla. 1959, U.S. Ct. Mil. Appeals 1960, U.S. Supreme Ct. 1963, U.S. Ct. Appeals (5th and 11th cir.) 1967, U.S. Tax Ct. 1971. Assoc. Carey, Goodman, Terry, Dwyer & Austin, Miami, Fla., 1959-62; ptnr. Peters, Maxey, Short & Maxey, P.A., Coral Gables, Fla., 1963—. Capt., U.S. Army, 1954-63. Mem. ABA, Dade County Bar Assn., Coral Gables Bar Assn., SAR, Royal Palm Tennis Club (dir.), Surf Club, Phi Alpha Delta, Sigma Nu. Avocation: bridge. Home: 7041 SW 92nd St Miami FL 33156-1614 Office: Peter Maxey Short & Maxey PA 3001 Ponce De Leon Blvd Miami FL 33134-6824

SHORT, JANET MARIE, principal; b. Boston, Sept. 18, 1939; d. Robert Emmet and Getta Agnes (Mills) S. BS in Edn., Boston State Coll., 1962, MEd, 1967; LLD (hon.), Regis Coll., 1991. Tchr. Boston Pub. Schs., 1962-70, acting asst. dir. staff devel., 1970-71, tchr.-in-charge, 1971-75; prin. D.L. Barrett Sch., Boston, 1976-81; tchr. Boston Pub. Schs., 1981-82; prin. Maurice J. Tobin Sch., Boston, 1982—, lead cluster prin., 1995—; lectr. in field. Adv. bd. DiMaiti Stuart Found., Boston, 1990—; adv. bd. Mission Hill and Camp Mission Posible, 1984-87; community adv. bd. Harvard Sch. Pub. Health, Boston, 1990—; adv. bd. Boston Against Drugs, 1990-94. Recipient Women of Achievement award Big Sister Assn. of Greater Boston, 1994, Thankful Recognition award Channel 5, Boston, 1987, Recognition award Boston Women's Mag., 1988, Pub. Svc. award Henry L. Shattuck, Bus. Mcpl. Bur. Rsch. award, 1988, Freedom's Found. Honor medal, 1990, Annual Excellence in Edn. award Alpha Gamma chpt. Pi Lambda Theta, 1993 and others; movie based on J.M. Short, "A Matter of Principal", 1990. Mem. ASCD, Mass. Middle Level Adminstrs. Assn., Boston Assn. Sch. Adminstrs. (exec. bd. 1984-93), Boston Middle Sch. Assn., Boston Elem. Prins. Assn., MESPA, Delta Kappa Gamma (chpt. pres. 1978-80). Roman Catholic. Avocations: travel, bowling, reading. Home: 39 Ridgeway Dr Quincy MA 02169-2321 Office: Maurice Tobin Sch 40 Smith St Roxbury MA 02120-2702

SHORT, JOEL BRADLEY, lawyer, consultant, software publisher; b. Birmingham, Ala., Dec. 27, 1941; s. Forrest Edwin and Laura Elizabeth (Bradley) S.; m. Georgianna Pohl, June 5, 1965 (div. Apr. 1973); m. Nancy Ann Harty, Dec. 17, 1977; children: Christopher Bradley, Matthew Douglas. BA, U. Colo., 1963, LLB, 1966, JD, 1968. Bar: Kans. 1966, U.S. Dist. Ct. Kans. 1966, U.S. Ct. Appeals (10th cir.) 1975, U.S. Supreme Ct. 1976. Ptnr. Short & Short, Attys., Fort Scott, Kans., 1966-77, Nugent & Short, Overland Park, Kans., 1977-83; pvt. practice J. Bradley Short & Assoc., Overland Park, Kans., 1983-91; ptnr. Short & Borth, Overland Park, Kans., 1991—; owner Bradley Software; mem. tech. adv. com. Kans. Jud. Coun., Topeka, 1991-95. 1st lt. U.S. Army, 1967-73. Fellow Am. Acad. Matrimonial Lawyers; mem. Johnson County Bar Assn. (ethics and family law coms. 1983—). Avocation: sailing. Office: Short and Borth Attys 32/ 1111 Corporate Woods 9225 Indian Creek Pky Overland Park KS 66210-2009

SHORT, JOHN D., sports museum administrator. Grad., U. Notre Dame, 1974, U. Sch. of Law at Indpls. Bar: Ind. 1979. Pres., bd. govs. Nat. Art Mus. of Sport/Ind. U.-Purdue U., Indpls., 1994—; mem. com. 1997 NCAA Men's Basketball Finals; mem. White River State Park Commn.; mem. bd. Indpls. Convn. and Vis. Assn., Marian Coll. Internat. Student Leadership Inst./U. Notre Dame, Community Action of Greater Indpls., Cathedral H.S., Flanner House Ctr.; mem. com. for RCA Men's Hardcourts Tennis Championships. Office: Univ Place Conf Ctr 850 West Michigan St Indianapolis IN 46202-5198

SHORT, LINDA MATTHEWS, reading educator; b. Winston-Salem, N.C., Mar. 25, 1949; d. Edwin Kohl and Nannie Mae (Bowen) Matthews; m. James Coy Short, June 18, 1972. BS, Appalachian State U., 1971, MA, 1981. Cert. elem. edn. tchr. Tchr. Mount Airy City Schs., Mount Airy, N.C., 1971-72, 88—, Surry County Schs., Dobson, N.C., 1972-88; mem. Mt. Airy City Schs. Adv. Bd., 1994-95. Pres.-elect Foothills Reading Coun., 1992-93; active Mt. Airy Women's Club, 1970s, Mt. Airy Jaycettes, 1970s. Mem. Foothills Reading Coun. (pres. 1993-96), N.C. Reading Assn. (area dir. 1995-96), N.C. Assn. Educators (treas. 1992-94), Internat. Reading Assn., Mt. Airy N.C. Assn. Educators (treas. 1992-94). Democrat. Baptist. Avocations: music, painting, crafts, collecting dolls, ceramic cats. Home: 107 Brentwood Dr Mount Airy NC 27030 Office: BH Tharrington Elem Sch 315 Culbert St Mount Airy NC 27030

SHORT, MARTIN, actor, comedian; b. Mar. 26, 1951; s. Charles Patrick and Olive Short; m. Nancy Dolman; children: Katherine, Oliver, Henry. Degree in social work, McMaster U., 1972. Actor: (feature films) Three Amigos, 1986, Innerspace, 1987, Cross My Heart, 1987, Three Fugitives, 1989, The Big Picture, 1989, Pure Luck, 1991, Father of the Bride, 1991, Captain Ron, 1992, We're Back! A Dinosaur's Story, 1993 (voice), Clifford, 1994, The Pebble and the Penguin, 1995 (voice), Father of the Bride 2, 1995; (TV series) The Associates, 1979, I'm a Big Girl Now, 1980-81, SCTV Network 90, 1982-84, Saturday Night Live, 1985-86, The Completely Mental Misadventures of Ed Grimley, 1988-89 (voice), The Martin Short Show, 1994; (TV movies) The Family Man, 1979, Sunset Limousine, 1983, (TV spls.) Martin Short's Concert for the North Americas, 1985, Really Weird Tales, 1987, I, Martin Short Goes Hollywood, 1989; also numerous revues and cabaret appearances with Second City comedy troupe, 1977-78, appeared on Broadway in The Goodbye Girl, 1993.

SHORT, RAY EVERETT, minister, sociology educator emeritus, author, lecturer; b. Coffeyville, Kans., Jan. 5, 1919; s. Franklin Marion and Jennie (Messersmith) S.; m. Jeannette Louise Stephens, June 12, 1954; children: Glenn Alan, Linda Louise, Kenneth Ray, Timothy Wesley, Karen Amy; 1 stepdau., Mary Jennings. AB, Willamette U., 1944; postgrad., U. Chgo., 1946; BD, Duke, 1948, PhD, 1961; postgrad., U. Idaho, 1950-51. Ordained to ministry Meth. Ch., 1946. Dir. Westminster Found., Duke, 1944-46; co-pastor Interracial Meth. Ch., Durham, N.C., 1947; asst. prof. religion, dir. chapel programs Fla. So. Coll., Lakeland, 1947-48; exec. dir. Fla. br. United World Federalists, 1948-51; dir. Intermountain Region, 1953-54, Wesley Found., U. Idaho, 1950-51; exec. dir. Student YMCA-YWCA, U. Denver, 1951-53; pastor Fairmont Meth. Ch., Lockport, Ill., 1954-56; grad. asst. sociology Duke, 1956-57; assoc. prof. religion, head divsn. religion and philosophy, chaplain Tenn. Wesleyan Coll., 1957-60; assoc. prof. sociology and religion, head dept. sociology U. Dubuque, Iowa, 1960-65, acting chmn. div. social sci., 1962-65; assoc. prof. sociology, head dept. sociology and anthropology U. Wis., Platteville, 1965-70, prof. sociology, 1966-87, prof. emeritus, 1987—; prof. sociology and anthropology Copenhagen Study Ctr. U. Wis., spring 1974, nat. lectr., 1975—; chmn. Peace and World Order divsn. North Iowa Meth. Conf., 1963-69; rep. U.S. Jr. C. of C. in testimony before U.S. Senate Com. on Fgn. Rels., 1950; Midwest region rep. Nat. Coun. World Federalist Assn., 1964-73, pres. Midwest region, 1967-69, chmn. nat. coun., 1971-72, nat. v.p., 1991—; (with wife) WFA dels. to NGO Forum and 4th UN Conf. on Women, Beijing, 1995; mem. spl. Wis. Conf. called with Pres.'s Comn. for Observance of 25th Anniversary of UN, 1970-87; mem. Wis. U. Meth. Bd. on Ch. and Soc., 1973-80, chmn. World Peace divsn., mem. exec. com., 1975-80. Author: Sex, Love or Infatuation: How Can I Really Know?, 1978, on videocassette, 1987, 2nd edit., 1990 (Augsburg Bestseller), Sex, Dating and Love: Questions Most Often Asked, 1984, 2nd edit., 1994 (Augsburg Bestseller); contbr. articles to profl. jours. Dem. candidate for Wis. 3rd Dist. Congl. Seat, 1970, 72; del. Dist. and State Convs., 1969-87, mem. state platform com., 1975-87; bd. dirs. Dubuque Salvation Army, 1961-65; mem. nat. bd. Am. Freedom Assn.; nat. v.p. Campaign for UN Reform, 1983-87, 1st v.p., 1989—; dir., founder Wis. Ann. High Sch. World Peace Study Program, 1975-87. Recipient NSF grant Anthropology Inst., Fairmont State Coll., W.Va., 1962. Fellow Am. Sociol. Assn.; mem. AAUP, Nat. Coun. on Family Rels., Fedn. Am. Scientists, Nat. United Meth. Men (mem. peace adv. task force 1990—). Home: 505 S Miller Ave Lafayette CO 80026-1545 *Nuclear and chemical weapons, crises of environments. While my life has largely been spent helping others have a better future, I now know we have to help assure that they have a future at all.*

SHORT, ROBERT HENRY, retired utility executive; b. Klamath Falls, Oreg., Oct. 15, 1924; s. Judge Haywood and Henrietta Luella (Lyon) S.; m. Ruby Madalyn Rice, Aug. 1, 1946; children—Robert L., Victoria (Mrs. Gregory Baum), Casey. BS in Journalism, U. Oreg., 1950; PhD in Humane Letters (hon.), Linfield Coll., 1984. City editor Klamath Falls Herald and News, 1950-52; dir. pub. rels. Water and Elec. Bd., Eugene, Oreg., 1952-55; mgr. pub. info. Portland Gen. Electric Co., Oreg., 1955-57, asst. to chmn., 1957-62, v.p., 1962-71, sr. v.p., 1971-73, exec. v.p., 1973-77, pres., 1977-80, chmn. bd., chief exec. officer, 1980-88, ret., 1989; bd. dir. First Interstate Bank of Oreg. Bd. dirs. Oreg. Ind. Colls. Found., Oreg. Health Sci. U.; trustee Oreg. Grad. Inst. With USNR, 1942-45. Mem. Portland Golf Club, Arlington Club. Home: 1210 SW 61st Ct Portland OR 97221-1504 Office: One SW Columbia St Ste 555 Portland OR 97258

SHORT, ROBERT WALTRIP (BOBBY SHORT), entertainer, author; b. Danville, Ill., Sept. 15, 1924; s. Rodman Jacob and Myrtle (Render) S. Grad. high sch. Singing pianist as child and after high sch.; appeared in night clubs in U.S. and abroad, concerts in maj. cities; regular cabaret performer N.Y.C.; recordings include: Krazy for Gershwin, Live at Cate Carlyle, Loves Cole Porter, Short Celebrates Rodgers and Hart, Guess Who's in Town, 1987, 50 From Bobby Short, 1987, Late Night At The Cafe Carlyle, 1992, (with the Alden-Barret Quinlet) Swing That Music, 1993; appeared in TV movie Roots, The Next Generation, 1979; appeared in motion picture Splash, 1984; appeared in Broadway prodns., 1956—; appeared at White House for Duke and Duchess of Windsor at request of Pres. Nixon, 1970; Author: Black and White Baby, 1971; also articles. Grammy nomination, Best Jazz Vocal for "Swing That Music" (with the Alden-Barrett Quintet), 1994. Mem. NAACP (life). Address: care Cafe Carlyle Madison Ave at 76th St New York NY 10021

SHORT, STEVE EUGENE, engineer; b. Crockett, Calif., Oct. 17, 1938; s. Roger Milton and Ida Mae (Mills) S.; B.S. in Gen. Engring. with honors, U. Hawaii, 1972, M.B.A., 1973; M.S. in Meteorology, U. Md., 1980; m. Yumie Sedaka, Feb. 2, 1962; children: Anne Yumie, Justine Yumie, Katherine Yumie. With Nat. Weather Service, NOAA, 1964—, tech. cons. 1994—; govt. exec. Silver Spring, Md., 1974-81, program mgr. ASOS, 1981—, transition dir. 1991—; ind. tech. cons., 1994—; cons. enging. and mgmt.; cons. SBA. Contbr. articles to sci. jours. Served with USMC, 1956-60. Registered profl. engr., Hawaii. Recipient Gold Medal award U.S. Dept. Commerce, 1992, Presdl. Meritorious Exec. award, 1992. Mem. VFW, Am. Meteorol. Soc., Japan-Am. Soc., Am. Soc. Public Adminstrn. Home: 3307 Rolling Rd Chevy Chase MD 20815-4033 Office: Nat Weather Svc 1325 E West Hwy Silver Spring MD 20910-3280

SHORTELL, ANNABELLE PETERSEN, family nurse practitioner; b. Barnegrat, N.J., Nov. 14, 1924; d. Robert Charles and Mary Inman (Peterson) Petersen; m. Nicholas Emmett Shortell, Nov. 22, 1945 (dec. June 1992); children: Michael James, Susan Catherine, Nicholas Richard, Catherine Anne, Patricia Lynn. Diploma, Monmouth Meml. Hosp., 1946; cert. family nurse practitioner, Frontier Sch. Midwifery, Hyden, Ky., 1973. Cert. family nurse practitioner; lic. nurse practitioner with prescriptive privileges, Va. Nurse Va. Health Dept., Virginia Beach, 1968-71; family nurse practitioner Va. Health Dept., New Castle, 1973-87, 93—, Va. State Health Dept., Alleghany Dist., 1987-90, Va. Health Dept., Pennington Gap, Va., 1990-93, James Madison U., Harrisonburg, Va., 1994—. Bd. dirs. Am. Cancer Soc., Craig County, 1974-93; mem. planning com. Craig County Planning Commn., New Castle, 1978-93; pres. Craig County Cancer Unit, New Castle, 1983-84. Mem. Va. Health Dept. Nurses (continuing edn. com., judge ann. nurse practitioner award 1991—, dist. award as outstanding nurse practitioner for excellence 1990). Avocations: walking, reading, basket weaving. Home: 1915 Creekside Ct Mc Gaheysville VA 22840

SHORTELL, STEPHEN M., medical educator; b. New London, Wis., Nov. 9, 1944. BBA, U. Notre Dame, 1966; MPH, UCLA, 1968; MBA, U. Chgo., 1970, PhD in Behavioral Sci., 1972. Rsch. asst. Nat. Opinion Rsch. Ctr., 1969; instr., rsch. assoc. Ctr. Health Adminstrv. Studies, 1970-72; acting dir. grad. program hosp. adminstrn. U. Chgo., 1973-74, from asst. prof. to assoc. prof., 1974-79; prof. Sch. Pub. Health & Comty. Medicine, Dept. Health Svc. U. Wash., 1979-82; A. C. Buehler Disting. prof. health svc. mgmt. Northwestern U., Evanston, Ill., 1982—; cons. VA, Robert Wood Found., Henry Keiser found.; asst. prof. Health Svcs. Orgn., U. Chgo., 1972-74; adj. asst. prof. dept. sociology U. Wash., 1975-76, dir. doctoral program dept. health svcs. Sch. Pub. Health & Comty. Medicine, 1976-78; prof. sociology dept. sociology Northwestern U., 1982, prof. comty. medicine dept. comty. health & preventive medicine Sch. Medicine. Contbr. numerous publs. to profl. jours. Mem. APHA, Inst. Med.-NAS. Office: Northwestern U J L Kellogg Grad Sch Mgmt Leverone Hall Evanston IL 60208-2007*

SHORTER, BARBARA LUCILE, high school principal; b. St. Petersburg, Fla., May 29, 1936; d. Frank and Jannie (Willis) Cubby; m. Charles D. Shorter, Dec. 22, 1958 (div. July 1980); children: Gary T., Reginald C., Lynda C., Monica G. BS in Bus. Edn., Fla. A & M U., 1957, MS in Guidance, 1971; postgrad., U. South Fla., 1981. Cert. prin., Fla. Exec. sec. Fla. A & M U., Tallahassee, 1957-58, 59-61; tchr. Lincoln High Sch.-Manatee County, Palmetto, Fla., 1958-59; computer clk. Honeywell, Inc., St. Petersburg, 1961-65; vocat. counselor Fla. State Rehab./Health, St. Petersburg, 1965-67; tchr., counselor, dean, asst. prin. N.E. High Sch.-Pinellas County, St. Petersburg, 1968-85; asst. prin. Boca Ciega High Sch.-Pinellas County, St. Petersburg, 1985—. Mem. Dem. Women's Club of Pinellas County, St. Petersburg, 1980-88. Mem. Fla. Assn. Secondary Adminstrs., Pinellas Adminstr. Assn., Nat. Assn. of Secondary Prins., Pinellas County Asst. Prins. (sec., pres. 1982-91), Fla. A&M Alumni Assn. (sec. 1990—), Phi Delta Kappa, Delta Sigma Theta, Delta Kappa Gamma. Baptist. Avocations: gardening, reading, tutoring, cooking. Office: Gibbs Sr High Sch 850 34th St S Saint Petersburg FL 33711-2208

SHORTER, JAMES RUSSELL, JR., lawyer; b. N.Y.C., June 10, 1946; s. James Russell and Helen (Ibert) S. AB, Columbia Coll., 1968; JD, Harvard U., 1975; LLM in Taxation, NYU, 1979. Bar: N.Y. 1976, U.S. Dist. Ct. (so. and ea. dists.) N.Y. 1976, U.S. Tax Ct. 1987. Assoc. Thacher Proffitt & Wood, N.Y.C., 1975-84, ptnr., 1984—. Capt. USNR, 1968—. Mem. ABA (tax, bus. law sect.). Republican. Club: Harvard (N.Y.C.). Home: 345 E 80th St Apt 26C New York NY 10021-0671 Office: Thacher Proffitt & Wood 2 World Trade Ctr Fl 39 New York NY 10048-3998

SHORTER, WAYNE, musician; b. Newark, Aug. 25, 1933. B.A., NYU, 1956. Played saxophone with Art Blakey, 1959-63, Miles Davis, 1964-70, Weather Report, 1970-86, Miles Davis Tribute Band, 1992; solo albums include: Schizophrenia, 1968, Supernova, 1970, Native Dancer, 1974, Native Dancer, 1975, Etcetera, 1981, Atlantis, 1986, Phantom Navigator, 1987, Joy Rider, 1988, Native Dancer, 1990, The All Seeing Eye, 1994. Served with U.S. Army, 1956-58. Winner numerous Down Beat mag. awards., 1970-77, named Best Soprano Sax, 1984, 85; co-recipient Grammy award for best jazz instrumental composition, 1987. Office: care Blue Note Records 1750 Vine St Los Angeles CA 90028-5247

SHORTLIDGE, RICHARD LYNN, JR., human resources consultant, retired foreign service officer, economist; b. Charlotte, N.C., Dec. 4, 1941; s. Richard Lynn and Lalla (Spearman) S.; m. Gloria Ann McArn, Dec. 18, 1966; children: Seth Lynn, David Lynn. AA, U. Fla., 1962, BA, 1964; MSc, Cornell U., 1970, PhD, 1973. Sr. rsch. assoc. Ohio State U., Columbus, 1973-77; asst. prof., lectr. George Washington U., Washington, 1977-80; labor economist U.S. Agt. Internat. Devel., Washington, 1976-81, human resources officer, 1981-86; dep. dir. Mission to Malawi U.S. Agt. Internat. Devel., Lilongwe, Malawi, 1986-90; dep. dir. Mission to Botswana U.S. Agt. Internat. Devel., Gaborone, Botswana, 1990-91; AID rep. Mission to Namibia U.S. Agt. Internat. Devel., Windhoek, Namibia, 1991-93; dir. Ctrl. Asia Acad. Ednl. Devel., Almaty, Kazakhstan, 1993-95; sr. human resources adv. Acad. Ednl. Devel., Washington, 1996—. Author: Dual Careers: Study of Women, 1975-76; contbr. articles to profl. jours. Vol. U.S. Peace Corps., Agartala, Tripura, India, 1964-67. Democrat. Mem. Religious Soc. Friends. Avocations: mountain climbing, camping, bicycling, swimming. Home and Office: PO Box 674 Saint Augustine FL 32085-0674

SHORTLIFFE, EDWARD HANCE, internist, medical informatics educator; b. Edmonton, Alta., Can., Aug. 28, 1947; s. Ernest Carl and Elizabeth Joan (Rankin) S.; m. Linda Marie Dairiki, June 21, 1970; children: Lindsay Ann, Lauren Leigh. AB, Harvard U., 1970; PhD, Stanford U., 1975, MD, 1976. Diplomate Am. Bd. Internal Medicine. Trainee NIH, 1971-76; intern Mass. Gen. Hosp., Boston, 1976-77; resident Stanford Hosp., Palo Alto, Calif., 1977-79; asst. prof. medicine Stanford U. Sch. Medicine, Palo Alto, 1979-85, assoc. prof., 1985-90, prof., 1990—, chief div. gen. internal medicine, 1988-95; assoc. dean info. resources and tech. Stanford U. Sch. Medicine, 1995—; pres. SCAMC, Inc. (Symposium on Computer Applications in Med. Care), Washington, 1988-89; assoc. chair medicine Primary Care, 1993-95; bd. dirs. Smart Valley, Inc.; advisor Nat. Bd. Med. Examiners, Phila., 1987-93; mem. Nat. Fed. Networking Adv. Coun., NSF, 1991-93; mem. computer sci. and telecomm. bd. NRC, 1991-96; bd. regents ACP, 1996—. Editor: Rule-Based Expert Systems, 1984, Readings in Medical Artificial Intelligence, 1984, Medical Informatics: Computer Applications in Health Care, 1990; developer several medical computer programs including MYCIN, 1976 (Grace M. Hopper award Assn. Computing Machinery). Recipient Young Investigator award Western Soc. Clin. Investigation, 1987, rsch. career award Nat. Libr. of Medicine, 1979-84; scholar Kaiser Family Found., 1983-88. Fellow Am. Assn. Artificial Intelligence, Am. Coll. Med. Informatics (pres. 1992-94); mem. Soc. for Med. Decisionmaking (pres. 1989-90), Inst. Medicine, Am. Soc. for Clin. Investigation, Am. Med. Informatics Assn., Assn. Am. Physicians, Am. Clin. and Climatol. Assn. Avocation: skiing. Office: Stanford U Sch Medicine Sect on Med Informatics 300 Pasteur Dr Stanford CA 94305-5479

SHORTRIDGE, DEBORAH GREEN, lawyer; b. Balt., Sept. 5, 1952; d. Harry Joseph Green and Dorothy Marie (Eser) Diamond; children: Bretton, Dana. BA, U. Balt., 1980, JD, 1982. Bar: Md. 1982, U.S. Dist. Ct. Md. 1983, U.S. Ct. Appeals (4th cir.), D.C. 1987. Assoc. prof. U. Balt., 1982-83; assoc. Weinberg and Green, Balt., 1982-89, adminstrv. ptnr., 1989-93; in-house counsel Weinberg & Green LLC, Balt., 1993—; mem. U. Balt. law adv. coun., 1993—. Bd. dirs., v.p. AIDS Interfaith Residential Svcs., Balt., 1991-96, pres. 1996—; bd. govs. U. Balt. Alumni Assn., 1985-91 (H. Melbane Turner Svc. award 1991); mem. ACLU of Md., 1983-90. Recipient Law Faculty award U. Balt. Law Sch., 1982. Mem. ABA, Md. State Bar Assn. (pro bono sect.), Bar Assn. Balt. City. Office: Weinberg & Green LLC 100 S Charles St Baltimore MD 21201-2773

SHORTS, GARY K., newspaper publisher; b. Grove City, Pa., Feb. 26, 1951; s. Leonard and Sarah Maxine (Young) S.; m. Karen Healy; children: Steven A., Elizabeth H., Daniel C. BA in Journalism, Economics, Ohio Wesleyan U., 1973; MBA, U. Pa., 1975. Circulation dir. News Democrat, Belleville, Ill., 1977-80; mktg. dir. Oakland Press, Pontiac, Mich., 1981-83; v.p., gen. mgr. Times Pub. Co., Wichita Falls, Tex., 1983-85; v.p. mktg. Harte-Hanks Comms., San Antonio, 1985-86; pres. So. Calif. Newspapers, Inc., San Diego, 1986-87; pub., chief exec. officer The Morning Call, Allentown, Pa., 1987—; dir. Pa. Newspaper Pubs. Assn., treas. 1991-92, v.p. daily newspapers 1992-93, pres. 1993-94; dir. Lehigh County Indsl. Devel. Corp., Allentown Econ. Devel. Corp., sec. 1988—. Chmn. United Way, Allentown, 1991; trustee Cedarcrest Coll. Mem. Allentown-Lehigh County C. of C. Office: Morning Call PO Box 1260 101 N 6th St Allentown PA 18105

SHORTZ, RICHARD ALAN, lawyer; b. Chgo., Mar. 11, 1945; s. Lyle A. and Wilma Warner (Wildes) S.; m. Jennifer A. Harrell; children: Eric, Heidi. BS, Ind. U., 1967; JD, Harvard U., 1970. Bar: Calif. 1971, U.S. Supreme Ct. 1980. Assoc. Gibson, Dunn & Crutcher, L.A., 1970-73; sr. v.p., gen. counsel, sec. Tosco Corp., L.A., 1973-83; ptnr. Jones, Day, Reavis & Pogue, L.A., 1983-95, Rogers & Wells, L.A., 1995—. Mem. L.A. World Affairs Inst., 1983—, Town Hall L.A., 1983—. 2nd lt. U.S. Army, 1970-71. Mem. ABA, L.A. Bar Assn., Calif. Club, Beach Club (Santa Monica, Calif.), L.A. Country Club. Republican. Episcopalian. Home: 1343 Pavia Pl Pacific Palisades CA 90272-4047 Office: Roger & Wells 9th Fl 444 S Flower St Los Angeles CA 90071

SHORTZ, WILL, puzzle editor; b. Crawfordsville, Ind., Aug. 26, 1952; s. Lyle A. and Wilma Warner (Wildes) S. AB, Ind. U., 1974; JD, U. Va., 1977. Editor Penny Press, Stamford, Conn., 1977-78; assoc. editor Games Mag., N.Y.C., 1978-82, sr. editor, 1982-89, editor, 1989-93; crossword editor N.Y. Times, N.Y.C., 1993—; founder, dir. Am. Crossword Puzzle Tournament, Stamford, Conn., 1978—, World Puzzle Team Championship, N.Y.C., 1992; puzzlemaster Weekend Edit., Sunday NPR, Washington, 1987—; U.S. team capt. Internat. Crossword Marathon, Brno, Czechoslovakia, 1989, Bjelovar, Yugoslavia, 1990, World Puzzle Championship, Brno, 1993, Cologne, 1994, Brasov, Romania, 1995, Utrecht, The Netherlands, 1996; riddle writer Batman Forever, 1995. Author: Brain Games, 1979, The American Quiz Book, 1979, Brain Games 2, 1980, The Bantam Great Masters Winning Crossword Puzzles, vol. 1-3, 1980, World Class Championship Crosswords, 1982, Brain Games 3, 1963, Games Mag. Book of Crossword Puzzles, 1985, American Championship Crosswords, 1990, Games Mag. Giant Book of Games, 1991, Will Shortz's Best Brain Busters, 1991, Games Mag. Best Pencil Puzzles, 1992, The World's Most Ornery Crosswords, vol. 1, 1992, Brain Twisters from the First World Puzzle Championships, 1993, N.Y. Times Daily Crossword Puzzles, vol. 40-43, 1995—; (with Ron Osher) Brain Twisters From the World Puzzle Championship, vol. 2, 1995. Mem. Am. Antiquarian Soc., Am. Cryptogram Assn., Authors Guild, Nat. Puzzlers' League (pres. 1977, 81, historian 1992—). Avocations: table tennis, book collecting. Office: NY Times 229 W 43rd St New York NY 10036-3913

SHORY, NASEEB LEIN, dentist, retired state official; b. Birmingham, Ala., Sept. 27, 1925; s. Lein George and Fomeyi (Buhana) S.; m. Mary Jo Howard, Sept. 8, 1951; children: Lawrence G., Richard L., Carl B., Celeste Marie. B.S., U. Ala., 1948; D.D.S., Loyola U., Chgo., 1952; M.P.H., U. Mich., 1962. Diplomate: Am. Bd. Dental Pub. Health. Pvt. practice dentistry Montgomery, Ala., 1952-60; dir. Bur. Dental Health, Ala. Dept. Pub. Health, 1961-68, 73-88; assoc. clin. prof. Med. Coll. Ala., 1966-68; assoc. prof., head dept. community and preventive dentistry La. State U. Sch. Dentistry, 1968-70; prof., chmn. dept. community dentistry Loyola U. of New Orleans, 1968-70; lectr. Tulane U. Sch. Pub. Health and Tropical Medicine, 1968-70; prof., dir. div. health services Sch. Dental Medicine, So. Ill. U., Edwardsville, 1970-72; asst. to dean Sch. Dental Medicine, So. Ill. U., 1972-73, chmn. dept. health ecology, 1970-73; mem. Ala. Bd. Dental Scholarships, 1965-68, 73-87; dir. Ala. Smile Keeper Program, 1976-87; mem. Ala. State Health Advisory Commn., 1977-79; Pres. Profl. Men's Credit Assn., Montgomery, 1960-61; mem. Montgomery Community Council, 1960-61, Youth Adv. Council, Montgomery Police Dept., 1960-61. Contbr. articles to profl. jours. Bd. dirs. Cath. Charities, 1959, 65, 66, New Orleans Area Health Planning Coun., 1968-70; mem. Montgomery Cath. High Sch. Bd., 1975-76, State Com. Pub. Health, Ala., 1988-92; chmn. Parish Coun., St. Joseph Cath. Ch., 1990-92. Served with AUS, 1943-45, ETO. Decorated Purple Heart; recipient Most Excellent Fellow award Ala. Dental Assn., 1968; D.G. Gill award Outstanding Contbn. to Pub. Health in Ala., 1982. Fellow Internat. Coll. Dentists (dep. regent for Ala. 1986-88, dist. V vice regent 1987-88); mem. ADA (chmn. nat. task force on prohibition confection sales in schs. 1978-79, mem. council dental health and health planning 1984-86; Council on Community Health, Hosps., Instns. and Med. Affairs 1986-88), Ill. Dental Assn., La. Dental Assn. (chmn. council on dental health 1969-70), Ala. Dental Assn. (ho. of dels., trustee), Am. Assn. Pub. Health Dentists, Assn. State and Territorial Dental Dirs. (pres. 1980-82, Outstanding Achievement award 1991), Ala. Pub. Health Assn. (pres. 1984-85), Council on Dental Health (state com. on pub. health 1988-92), Optimist Club (v.p. Perdido Bay chpt. 1991-92), Svc. Corps Ret. Execs. Home: 34090 Kathryn Dr Lillian AL 36549-5100

SHOSID, JOSEPH LEWIS, government official; b. Ft. Worth, Aug. 27, 1927; s. Samuel and Lilly Minna (Schneider) S.; children: Sharon Suzann, Steven Stanford; m. Linda D. Johnson, Oct. 8, 1994. BA, Tex. Christian U., 1950, MA, 1952; grad., Indsl. Coll. Armed Forces, Washington. Former exec. prof. baseball with L.A. (Bklyn.) Dodgers farm orgn.; bus. mgr. Ft. Worth Baseball Club, 1950-54; with various newspapers, radio & TV stas. as sportscasting and advt. exec.; pres. Advt. Unlimited, Inc., Ft. Worth, 1954-76; spl. asst. to U.S. Ho. of Reps. Speaker of Ho. Jim Wright 12th Dist. Tex., 1955-89; pres., chief exec. officer Shosid & Assocs., Ft. Worth and Washington, 1981—; chmn. Ft. Worth Airpower Coun., 1972-74; mem. adv. coun. Pres.'s Nat. Com. for Employer Support of Guard and Res., 1971—; spl. asst. to Vice Pres. Hubert H. Humphrey, 1966-69. Basketball and football ofcl. NCAA, 1953—, including 13 football bowl games, 21 basketball playoffs, 21 Aloha Classics, 1989-90, Japan Classics, Osaka and Tokyo; liaison officer USAFE-Sports, Ramstein AB, Feb. Republic of Germany, 1964—. With AUS, WWII; maj. gen. USAF Ret. Decorated D.S.M., Air Force Legion of Merit, Exceptional Service award USAF, 1975. Mem. Air Force Assn. (past nat. pres. and chmn. bd., Nat. Man of Yr. 1963, Medal of Merit 1962, Exceptional Svc. Plaque 1971, life mem., nat. bd. dirs.), S.W. Basketball Ofcls. Assn. (past pres.), Congl. Staff Club, Aerospace Edn. Found. (Dolittle fellow), Ft. Worth C. of C., Res. Officers Assn., Am. Basketball Assn., Nat. Assn. Basketball Coaches, Fed. Internat. Basketball Assn., Naismith Basketball Hall of Fame, Am. Football Coaches Assn., Collegiate Sports Info. Dirs. Am., Atlantic Coast Football Ofcls. Assn. (life), Masons (32 degree), Shriners. Mem. Christian Ch. Home: 1612 Ems Rd W Fort Worth TX 76116-1828 *I had the good fortune of being schooled at an early age that a mind is a terrible thing to waste. And that every American has an obligation to serve his/her country in a constructive way, thus the inspiration for my interest in a military career. Parents who came to America from Lithuania, fleeing the Marxist Revolution didn't have to wait until post World War II to understand or be told about the "Soviet Threat." They saw it first hand. A major thesis of my life has been to be grateful that they had the great courage to immigrate to this great nation and thus allow me the freedom of thought and mind otherwise denied.*

SHOSS, CYNTHIA RENÉE, lawyer; b. Cape Girardeau, Mo., Nov. 29, 1950; d. Milton and Carroll Jane (Duncan) S.; m. David Goodwin Watson, Apr. 13, 1986; 1 child, Lucy J. Watson. BA cum laude, Newcomb Coll., 1971; JD, Tulane U., 1974; LLM in Taxation, NYU, 1980. Bar: La. 1974, Mo. 1977, Ill. 1978, N.Y. 1990. Law clk. to assoc. and chief justices La. Supreme Ct., New Orleans, 1974-76; assoc. Stone, Pigman et al, New Orleans, 1976-77, Lewis & Rice, St. Louis, 1977-79, Curtis, Mallet-Prevost, et al, N.Y.C., 1980-82; ptnr. LeBoeuf, Lamb, Greene & MacRae, L.L.P., N.Y.C., 1982—; mng. ptnr. London office LeBoeuf, Lamb, Leiby & MacRae, 1987-89; assoc. editor Tulane Law Rev., 1972-74; frequent speaker before profl. orgns. and assns. Contbr. articles to profl. jours. Mem. ABA, Internat. Tax Planning Assn., Am. Mgmt. Assn. (ins. and risk mgmt. coun.), Corp. Bar Westchester and Fairfield (pro bono steering com.), Tax Rev., Lawyers Alliance N.Y. (chair, bd. dirs.). Office: LeBoeuf Lamb Greene Et Al 125 W 55th St New York NY 10019-5369

SHOSTAKOVICH, MAXIM DMITRIYEVICH, symphonic conductor; b. Leningrad, USSR, May 10, 1938; came to U.S., 1981; s. Dmitri Dmitriyevich and Nina (Varzar) S.; 1 child, Dmitri; m. Marina Tisie; children: Maria, Maxim. Student, Leningrad Conservatory, 1961-62, Moscow Conservatory, 1963; DFA, U. Md., 1982. Asst. condr. Moscow Symphony Orch., 1963-66, Moscow State Symphony Orch., 1966-69; prin. condr., artistic dir. Orch. Radio and TV USSR, Moscow, 1971-81; mus. advisor Hartford Symphony Orch., Conn., 1985; prin. guest condr. Hong Kong Philharm., 1982—; music dir. New Orleans Symphony Orch., 1986-91; hon. music dir. La. Philharmonic Orch., 1993-94. Debut London Philharm. Orch., 1968; toured

Can., U.S., Mex. with USSR State Symphony Orch., 1969; guest condr., Europe, N.Am., Japan and Australia; pianist including Piano Concerto No. 2; rec. father's ballet compositions including Bolt, The Age of God, suites, music for films Zoya, Pirogov with Bolshoi Theater Orch., Shostakovich Symphonies; recs. EMI, Philips, Chandos including Shostakovich's Violin Concerto No. 1, Shostakovich's Symphony No. 5, Suite on Verses of Michelangelo, 1971, 77, Piano Concerti Nos. 1 and 2 rec. with Philips Shostakovich's Cello Concerti, 1984. Recipient Outstanding Performance for Arts award Combo Fund Campaign, 1982. Mem. Concert Artists Guild, Great Artists Series NYU (exec. bd. Gallatin div. N.Y.C.). Home: 173 Black Rock Tpke West Redding CT 06896-2519 Office: care Columbia Artists Inc 165 W 57th St New York NY 10019-2201

SHOTTS, WAYNE J., nuclear scientist, federal agency administrator; b. Des Plaines, Ill., Mar. 20, 1945; s. Norman Russell Shotts and Winnifred Mae (Averill) Shotts Goeppinger; m. Melinda Maureen Antilla, June 24, 1967 (dec. Feb. 1975); children: Kenneth Wayne Shotts, Jeffrey Alan Shotts; m. Jacquelyn Francyle Willis, Aug. 11, 1979. BA in Physics, U. Calif., Santa Barbara, 1967; PhD, Cornell U., 1973. Rsch. physicist E.I. duPont deNemours & Co., Wilmington, Del., 1973-74; physicist U. Calif., Livermore, Calif., 1974—, Lawrence Livermore (Calif.) Nat. Lab., 1974-79; group leader, thermonuclear design divsn. Lawrence Livermore Nat. Lab., Livermore, Calif., 1979-85, divsn leader, nuclear chemistry, 1985-86, divsn. leader, prompt diagnostics, 1986-88, prin. dep. assoc. dir., military applications, 1988-92, prin. dep. assoc. dir. def. and nuclear techs., 1992-95, assoc. dir. nonproliferation arms control/internat. security, 1995—. Recipient Ernest Orlando Lawrence Meml. award U.S. Dept. Energy, Washington, 1990. Mem. Am. Phys. Soc., Am. Assn. Advancement Sci. Office: Lawrence Livermore Nat Lab PO Box 808 Livermore CA 94551-0808

SHOTWELL, CHERRIE LEIGH, speech and language pathologist; b. Munich, Nov. 15, 1950; parents Am. citizens; d. William Bedford and Pauline Leona (Bainbridge) S. BA with distinction, U. Redlands, 1973, MS, 1975. Cert. lang., speech and hearing tchr., Calif. Speech and lang. therapist Hawaii Dept. Edn., Wahiawa, 1976-86; lang. and speech specialist L.A. County Dept. Edn., Downey, Calif., 1986-87; day treatment instr. Assn. Retarded Citizens, Honolulu, 1987-88; speech and lang. pathologist Honolulu Cmty. Action Program, 1988-89, Hawaii Speech Pathology, Honolulu, 1989-90, Med. Pers. Pool, Honolulu, 1990-94, Hawaii Dept. Edn., Waipahu, 1994—. Mem. Hawaii Speech Lang. Hearing Assn. (com. chairperson Licensure and Ethics 1978-79). Democrat. Avocations: swimming, sailing, fashion design. Home: 1015 Laakea Pl Honolulu HI 96818

SHOTWELL, MALCOLM GREEN, minister; b. Brookneal, Va., Aug. 14, 1932; s. John Henry and Ada Mildred (Puckett) S.; m. LaVerne Brown, June 19, 1954; children: Donna (dec.), Paula. BA in Sociology, U. Richmond, 1954; MDiv, Colgate Rochester Div. Sch., 1957; D Ministry, Ea. Bapt. Theol. Sem., 1990; DD (hon.), Judson Coll., 1990. Ordained to ministry Am. Bapt. Ch. in U.S.A., 1957. Student asst. Greece Bapt. Ch., Rochester, N.Y., 1954-57; pastor 1st Bapt. Ch., Cuba, N.Y., 1957-62; sr. pastor 1st Bapt. Ch., Galesburg, Ill., 1962-71, Olean, N.Y., 1971-81; area minister Am. Bapt. Chs. of Pa. and Del., 1981-90; regional exec. minister Am. Bapt. Chs. of Great Rivers Region, Ill. and Mo., 1990—; mem. Midwest Commn. on Ministry, Am. Bapt. Chs. U.S.A., 1990—, mem. task force for So. Bapt.Am. Bapt. Chs. Relationships, 1990—. Author: Creative Programs for the Church Year, 1986, Renewing the Baptist Principle of Associations, 1990. Trustee No. Bapt. Theol. Sem., Lombard, Ill., 1993—, Judson Coll., Elgin, Ill., 1990—, mem. gen. bd. ABC, 1990—, mem. gen. exec. coun., 1990—, regional exec. ministers coun., 1990—; bd. dirs. Cen. Bapt. Theol. Sem., Kansas City, Kans., 1990—; sec. bd. dirs. Shurtleff Fund, Springfield, Ill., 1990—. Walter Pope Binns fellow William Jewell Coll., Liberty, Mo., 1995. Mem. Ministers Coun. Ill. and Mo. Office: Am Bapt Chs of Great Rivers 225 E Cook St Springfield IL 62704-2509

SHOUB, EARLE PHELPS, chemical engineer, educator; b. Washington, July 19, 1915; m. Elda Robinson; children: Casey Louis, Heather Margaret Shoub Dills. BS in Chemistry, Poly. U., 1938, postgrad. 1938-39. Chemist, Hygrade Food Products Corp., N.Y.C., 1940-41, Nat. Bur. Standards, 1941-43; regional dir. U.S. Bur. Mines, 1943-62, chief divsn. Accident Prevention & Health, 1962-70; dep. dir. Appalachian Lab. Occupational Respiratory Diseases, Nat. Inst. Occupational Safety and Health, Morgantown, W.Va., 1970-77, dep. dir. div. safety research, 1977-79; mgr. occupational safety, indsl. environ. cons., safety products div. Am. Optical Corp., Southbridge, Mass., 1979; cons., 1979—; assoc. clin. prof. dept. anesthesiology W.Va. U. Med. Center, Morgantown, 1977-82, prof. Coll. Mineral and Energy Resources, 1970-79. Recipient Disting. Service award Dept. Interior and Gold medal, 1959. Registered profl. engr.; cert. safety profl. Fellow Am. Inst. Chemists; mem. AIME, ASTM, NSPE, ANSI, Am. Indsl. Hygiene Assn., Vets. of Safety, Am. Soc. Safety Engrs., Nat. Fire Protection Assn., Am. Conf. Govtl. Indsl. Hygienists, Internat. Soc. Respiratory Protection (past pres., William H. Revoir award 1993), Am. Nat. Standards Inst., Sigma Xi. Methodist. Contbr. articles to profl. jours. and texts. Home: 5850 Meridian Rd Apt 202C Gibsonia PA 15044-9690

SHOUP, ANDREW JAMES, JR., oil company executive; b. Monroe, La., Mar. 26, 1935; s. Andrew James Sr. and Ruth (Landis) S.; m. Sue Cowles, Sept. 12, 1959; children: Catherine Shoup Collins, Andrew James III. BS in Petroleum Engring., La. State U., 1957; M in Indsl. Adminstrn., Yale U., 1959. Registered engr., Tex. Prodn. engr. Continental Oil Co., Houston, 1959-65; v.p. DeGolyer and MacNaughton, Dallas, 1965-74; chmn., chief exec. officer Sabine Corp., Dallas, 1974-89; pres. Pacific Enterprises Oil Co. U.S.A, Dallas, 1989-90; pres., chief exec. officer The Wiser Oil Co., Dallas, 1991—. 2nd lt. U.S. Army, 1959-60. Mem. Am. Petroleum Inst., Ind. Prodrs. Assn. Am., Soc. Petroleum Engrs. of AIME, Dallas Petroleum Club, Dallas Country Club. Avocations: skiing, jogging, tennis. Office: The Wiser Oil Co 8115 Preston Rd Ste 400 Dallas TX 75225

SHOUP, CARL SUMNER, retired economist; b. San Jose, Calif., Oct. 26, 1902; s. Paul and Rose (Wilson) S.; m. Ruth Snedden, Sept. 27, 1924; children: Dale, Paul Snedden, Donald Sumner (dec.). AB, Stanford U., 1924; PhD, Columbia U., 1930; PhD (hon.), U. Strasbourg, 1967. Mem. faculty Columbia U., 1928-71; dir. Internat. Econ. Integration Program and Capital Tax Project, 1962-64; Editor Bull. Nat. Tax Assn., 1931-35; staff mem. N.Y. State Spl. Tax Commns., 1930-35; tax study U.S. Dept. Treasury, June-Sept. 1934, Aug.-Sept. 1937, asst. to sec. Treasury, Dec. 1937-Aug. 1938, research cons., 1938-46, 62-68; interregional adviser, tax reform planning UN, 1972-74; sr. Killam fellow Dalhousie U., 1974-75; staff Council of Econ. Advisers, 1946-49; dir. Twentieth Century Fund Survey of Taxation in U.S., 1935-37, Fiscal Survey of Venezuela, 1958, Shoup Tax Mission to Japan, 1949-50, Tax Mission to Liberia, 1969; co-dir. N.Y.C. finance study, 1950-52; pres. Internat. Inst. Pub. Finance, 1950-53; cons. Carnegie Ctr. for Transnat. Studies, 1976, Harvard Inst. for Internat. Devel., 1978-83, Venezuelan Fiscal Commn., 1980-83, Jamaica Tax Project, 1985, World Bank Value-Added Tax Study, 1986-87, Duke U. Tax Missions Study, 1987-88; vis. prof. Monash U., 1984. Author: The Sales Tax in France, 1930, (with E.R.A. Seligman) A Report on the Revenue System of Cuba, 1932, (with Robert M. Haig and others) The Sales Tax in the American States, 1934, (with Roy Blough and Mabel Newcomer) Facing the Tax Problem, 1937, (with Roswell Magill) The Fiscal System of Cuba, 1939, Federal Finances in the Coming Decade, 1941, Taxing to Prevent Inflation, 1943, Principles of National Income Analysis, 1947, (with others) Report on Japanese Taxation, 1949, (with others) The Fiscal System of Venezuela, 1959, Ricardo on Taxation, 1960,reprinted, 1992, The Tax System of Brazil, 1965, Federal Estate and Gift Taxes, 1966, Public Finance, 1969 (transl. into Japanese 1974, Spanish 1979), (with others) The Tax System of Liberia, 1970; Editor: Fiscal Harmonization in Common Markets, 1966. Decorated Order Sacred Treasure (Japan), Grand Cordon. Disting. fellow Am. Econ. Assn.; mem. Nat. Tax Assn. (pres. 1949-50, hon. mem.), Phi Beta Kappa. Address: 48 Heard Rd Center Sandwich NH 03227-9719

SHOUP, CHARLES SAMUEL, JR., chemicals and materials executive; b. Nashville, Dec. 10, 1935; s. Charles Samuel and Leola Ruth (Turner) S.; m. Frances Carolyn DiCarlo, June 7, 1958; children: Mark Steven, Elizabeth Ann Shoup Kehoe, Margaret Carol Shoup Meyer. AB, Princeton U., 1957; MS, U. Tenn., 1961, PhD, 1962. Rsch. chemist Oak Ridge (Tenn.) Natl. Lab., 1962-67; mgr. special projects Union Carbide Corp., N.Y.C., 1967-68; mgr. planning and controls Bell and Howell Co., Lincolnwood, Ill., 1968; v.p. Bell and Howell Sch. Inc., Chgo., 1968-69; mgr. tech. planning Cabot Corp., Boston and Cambridge, Mass., 1969-70, dir. corp. rsch., Mass., 1970-73, gen. mgr. E-A-R div., 1973-87, v.p., Indpls., 1984-87; pres. Alphaflex Ind. Inc., Indpls. 1987-88, bd. dirs., 1988, Cemkote Corp., Indpls., 1988-91; chmn. bd. dirs. Blasterz Corp., Carmel, Ind., 1992—; bd. dirs. Exec. Svc. Corps, Indpls., 1993—, mem. exec. com., 1994—; mem. bd. visitors Coll. Arts and Scis., U. Tenn., Knoxville, 1994—. Contbr. articles to profl. jours.; patentee in field. Treas. Oak Ridge Community Arts Ctr., 1965-67; pres. Sherborn Edn. Found., 1974-76; chmn. Met. Div. United Way, 1982; bd. trustees, Ind. Safety Equipment Assn. 1978-81. Fellow Am. Inst. Chemists; mem. AAAS, Am. Chem. Soc., Noise Control Products and Materials Assn. (trustee 1977-87, pres. 1982-84), Sigma Xi. Presbyterian. Home: 13019 Andover Dr Carmel IN 46033-2419

SHOUP, MICHAEL C., newspaper reporter, editor; b. Ringtown, Pa., July 17, 1940; s. Daniel George and Marie E (Fisher) S.; m. Mary Ellen Trimble, Jan. 2, 1965 (div. 1984); children: Rachael, Timothy; m. Mary Jo Crowley, July 22, 1988; stepchildren: David, Benjamin. BA, Moravian Coll., 1965; MS, Columbia U., 1966. Russian linguist intelligence svc. USAF, 1957-61; reporter, editor Phila. Bull., 1967-71; night city editor Phila. Inquirer, 1973, day city editor, 1974, mng. editor Phila. Inquirer Mag., 1975-79, travel editor, columnist, 1980—; travel columnist for Knight-Ridder newspapers, 1980—. Avocations: bicycling, running. Home: 2202 Wallace St Philadelphia PA 19130-3126 Office: Phila Inquirer 400 N Broad St Philadelphia PA 19130-4015

SHOVER, JOAN, secondary school educator; b. St. Joseph, Mo., Apr. 7, 1948; d. Jay S. and Clara Lillian (Burkett) Marquis; m. Rolland Craig Shover, May 31, 1975; children: Terra Jayne, Thomas Jay. BS in Edn., Ctrl. Mo. State U., 1971, MS in Edn., 1976, postgrad., 1989—. Cert. tchr., Mo. Phys. edn. tchr. Worth County H.S., Grant City, Mo., 1971-73, Blue Springs (Mo.) H.S., 1973—; mem. rev. com. Mo. Dept. Elem. and Secondary Edn., Jefferson City, 1993—. Named Am. Cancer Soc. Educator of Yr., 1989, Top 36 Am. Tchrs. award, Disney Corp., 1992. Mem. AAHPERD, NEA, Am. Coun. on Exercise, Internat. Dance Exercise Assn., Mo. Assn. Phys. Edn., Health, Recreation and Dance (Kansas City Dist. Phys. Educator award 1989, Prewsl. award, Kansas City rep. 1988—), Mo. State Tchrs. Assn., Pilot Club. Avocations: reading, dancing, skiing, running. Home: 1418 NW A St Blue Springs MO 64015-3605

SHOVLIN, JOSEPH PATRICK, optometrist. BA in Psychology, Gettysburg Coll., 1974; BS in Physiol. Optics, Pa. Coll. of Optometry, 1978, D of Optometry, 1980. Cert. optometrist Pa., N.Y., Va., Md. Assoc. Morrison Assocs., Harrisburg Pa., N.Y.C., 1980-85; clin. assoc. Northeastern Eye Inst., Scranton, Pa., 1985—; cons. Lancaster County Blind Assn., Lancaster, Pa., 1980-85, State Bd. of Optometry, Commonwealth of Pa., 1988-90, Ophthalmic Devices' Adv. Panel, Ctr. for Devices and Radiological Health, Food and Drug Adminstrn., 1987-88, 1992-93; adj. faculty Pa. Coll. of Optometry, 1981—; cons. and expert witness Bur. of Profl. and Occupational Affairs, Commonwealth of Pa., 1983-85; voting mem. Ophthalmic Devices Adv. Panel, Ctr. for Devices and Radiological Health, Food and Drugs Adminstrn., 1988-92; presenter over 175 formal lectures to major internat., nat., regional and state ophthalmic groups. Author: (with others) Problems in Optometry, 1990, Clinical Contact Lens Practice, 1991, Optometric Pharmacology, 1992, Anterior Segment Complications of Contact Lens Wear, 1994; contbr. numerous articles to profl. jours. including: Review of Optometry (contbg. editor 1984-88, assoc. clin. editor 1988—), Metabolic, Pediatric and Systemic Ophthalmology, Contact Lens Forum, Focus on Product News, International Contact Lens Clinic (contbg. editor 1988-93), Primary Care Optometry News, (cons. editor, 1995—), Contemporary Optometry, Contact Lens Spectrum (consulting editor 1988—), Optometric Management (contbg. editor 1992-95), Practical Optometry, Review of Ophthalmology, American Acad. of Optometry Newsletter; assoc. editor Making Contact, 1982-88, 94—; editl. bd. Contacto; mem. jour. rev. bd. Optometry Clinics, 1991—; cons. editor Primary Care Optometry News, 1995—; referee Jour. Am. Optometric Assn. and Optometry and Vision Sci. Mem. sci. adv. com. Pa. Lions' Sight Conservation and Eye Rsch. Found., nat. adv. eye coun. Nat. Eye Inst. Nat. Insts. Health, 1992-96. Fellow Am. Acad. Optometry (diplomate cornea and contact lens sect. 1985, mem. exec. bd., spkrs. bur., bd. dirs. Pa. chpt. past mem., numerous other coms.); mem. APHA, Internat. Soc. Refractive Surgery (assoc.), Am. Optometric Assn. (sec. contact lens sect. 1988-89, vice chair 1989-90, chair elect 1990-91, chair 1991-92, immediate past chair 1992-93, numerous other coms. and offices, Am. Optometric Recognition award 1980—), Pa. Optometric Assn. (chmn. continuing edn. com. 1993, Keystone contact lens conf. 1987—, com. on contact lenses 1986-94, others), The Assn. for Rsch. in Vision and Ophthalmology, Nat. Eye Rsch. Found., Am. Optometric Found. (bd. dirs. 1988-90), The Prentice Soc., Adv. Bd. Eye Vision Assocs., The Optometric Coun. of the State of N.Y. (Disting. Svc. award 1984). Home: 1308 Oakmont Rd Clark's Summit PA 18411 Office: Northeastern Eye Inst 200 Mifflin Ave Scranton PA 18503

SHOWALTER, BUCK (WILLIAM NATHANIEL SHOWALTER, III), major league baseball team manager; b. DeFuniak Springs, Fla., May 23, 1956. Student, Chipola Jr. Coll., Fla., Miss. State U. Player various minor league teams N.Y. Yankee orgn., 1977-83, minor league coach, 1984, minor league mgr., 1985-89; coach N.Y. Yankees, 1990-91, mgr., 1992-95. Named N.Y.-Pa. League Mgr. of Yr., 1985, Eastern League Mgr. of Yr., 1989, Am. League Mgr. of Yr., 1994. Office: Arizona Diamondbacks PO Box 2095 Phoenix AZ 85001*

SHOWALTER, ELAINE, humanities educator; b. Cambridge, Mass., Jan. 21, 1941; married; 2 children. BA, Bryn Mawr Coll., 1962; MA, Brandeis U., 1964; PhD in English, U. Calif., Davis, 1970. Teaching asst. English U. Calif., 1964-66, from instr. to assoc. prof., 1967-78; prof. English Rutgers U., from 1978; prof. English, Avalon Found. prof. humanities, Princeton (N.J.) U., 1984—; Avalon Found. prof. humanities Princeton (N.J.) U., 1987—; vis. prof. English and women's studies U. Del., 1976-77; vis. prof. Sch. Criticism and Theory, Dartmouth Coll., 1986; prof. Salzburg (Austria) Seminars, 1988; Clarendon lectr. Oxford (Eng.) U., 1989; vis. scholar Phi Beta Kappa, 1993-94; numerous radio and TV appearances. Author: A Literature of Their Own, 1977, The Female Malady, 1985, Sexual Anarchy, 1990, Sister's Choice, 1991; co-author: Hysteria Beyond Freud, 1993; editor: These Modern Women, 1978, The New Feminist Criticism, 1985, Alternative Alcott, 1987, Speaking of Gender, 1989, Modern American Women Writers, 1991, Daughters of Decadence, 1993; also articles and revs. Recipient Howard Behrman humanities award Princeton U., 1989; faculty rsch. coun. fellow Ruthers U., 1972-73, Guggenheim fellow, 1977-78, Rockefeller humanities fellow, 1981-82, fellow NEH, 1988-89. Mem. MLA. Office: Princeton U Dept of English Princeton NJ 08544

SHOWALTER, ENGLISH, JR., French language educator; b. Roanoke, Va., May 14, 1935; m. 1963; 2 children. B.A., Yale U., 1957, Ph.D. in French, 1964. Asst. prof. French Haverford Coll., 1961-64, U. Calif.-Davis, 1964-66, Princeton U., N.J., 1966-74; assoc. prof. Rutgers U., Camden, N.J., 1974-78; prof. Rutgers U., 1978-83, disting prof., 1985—; dir. MLA, N.Y.C., 1983-85. Author: The Evolution of the French Novel, 1641-1782, 1972, Voltaire et ses Amis, D'apres la Correspondance de Mme De Graffigny, 1975, Rousseau and Mme De Graffigny, 1978, Exiles and Strangers: A Reading of Camus's Exile and the Kingdom, 1984, Humanity and the Absurd: Camus' The Stranger, 1989, My Night at Maud's, 1993. Fellow NEH, 1977-78; Guggenheim fellow, 1982-83. Mem. MLA, Am. Assn. Tchrs. French, Am. Soc. 18th Century Studies, French Soc. 18th Century Studies. Office: Rutgers Univ French Dept Camden NJ 08102

SHOWALTER, ROBERT EARL, banker; b. Vienna, W.Va., Feb. 16, 1937; s. Clay and Edna Melinda (Mahaney) S.; m. Shirley Anita Tessmer, June 24, 1961; children: Brent Alan, Lynn Allison, Eric Michael, Dean Edward. BS, Marietta Coll., 1959; MBA, Case Western Res. U., 1964; postgrad. Advanced Mgmt. Program, Harvard U., 1983. Mgmt. trainee Republic Steel, Cleve., 1959-60; sr. v.p. Fed. Res. Bank, Cin., 1960-84; pres., CEO Commerce Nat. Bank, Lexington, Ky., 1984-90; pres., CEO Nat. City Bank, Toledo, 1990-95, Akron, Ohio, 1996—; trustee Ohio Council Econ. Edn., 1980-83. Trustee Good Samaritan Hosp., Cin., 1979-85, Rotary Found., 1982-84, ARC, 1981-85, Cardinal Hill Hops., 1985-90, sec., 1989-90, Med. Coll. Ohio, 1991-95; bd. dirs. United Way Bluegrass, 1985-90, campaign chmn., 1987, v.p., 1989. Named Disting. Alumnus, Marietta Coll., 1982. Mem. Thoroughbred of Am. Club, Toledo Club, Firestone C. of C., Glenmoor C. of C., Wilderness C. of C., Inverness Country Club. United Methodist. Home: 6301 Bertram Ave NW Canton OH 44718 Office: Nat City Bank 1 Cascade Plz Akron OH 44308

SHOWALTER-KEEFE, JEAN, data processing executive; b. Louisville, Mar. 11, 1938; d. William Joseph and Phyllis Rose (Reis) Showalter; m. James Washburn Keefe, Dec. 6, 1980. BA, Spalding U., 1963, MS in Edn. Adminstrn., 1969. Cert. tchr., Ky. Tchr., asst. prin. Louisville Cath. Schs., 1958-71; cons. and various editorial positions Harcourt Brace Jovanovich Co., Chgo. and N.Y.C., 1972-82; dir. editorial Ednl. Challenges, Alexandria, Va., 1982-83; mgr. project to cons. Xerox Corp., Leesburg, Va., 1983-88, mgr. systems edn., 1988-89; curriculum devel. mgr. corp. edn. and tng. Xerox Corp. Hdqrs., Stamford, Conn., 1989-94; mem. bd. Belcastle Cluster Assocs., Reston, Va., 1994—, pres. bd., 1995—, mgmt. and sys. cons., 1995—; mem. adv. bd. Have a Heart Homes for Abused Children, 1991-93; instr. Sales Exec. Club N.Y., 1974-79; cons., Houston, 1980-83. Moderator Jr. Achievement, Louisville, 1968-70; cons. Future Bus. Leaders Am., Dade County, Fla. 1983. Named Outstanding Young Educator Louisville Jaycees, 1968. Mem. Nat. Assn. Female Execs., Am. Soc. Tng. and Devel., Am. Mgmt. Assn. Avocations: gardening, classical music. Home: 1419 Belcastle Ct Reston VA 22094-1245 Office: 1419 Belcastle Ct Reston VA 22094-1245

SHOWER, ROBERT WESLEY, financial executive; b. Harvey, Ill., Sept. 5, 1937; s. Glenn Wesley and Chrissie Irene (Ford) S.; m. Sandra Marie Stough, June 27, 1959; children: David Wesley, Lynece Marie. B.S., U. Tulsa, 1960; P.M.D., Harvard Business Sch., 1972. Sr. auditor Arthur Andersen & Co., Tulsa, 1960-64; with The Williams Cos., Tulsa, 1964-86; asst. v.p. The Williams Cos., 1968-69, v.p. adminstrn., 1969-71, v.p., treas., 1971, v.p. fin., 1971-73, sr. v.p. fin., 1973-77, exec. v.p. fin. and adminstrn., dir., 1977-86; mng. dir. Shearson, Lehman, Hutton, Dallas, 1986-90; v.p. fin. Ameriserv Food Co., Dallas, 1990-91; sr. v.p. fin., CFO Seagull Energy Co., Houston, 1994-96, exec. v.p., CFO, 1994—. Mem. Okla. Soc. CPAs, Bent Tree Country Club (Dallas), Lambda Chi Alpha, Delta Sigma Pi. Home: 17224 Village Ln Dallas TX 75248-6047

SHOWERS, RALPH MORRIS, electrical engineer educator; b. Plainfield, N.J., Aug. 7, 1918; s. Ralph W. and Angelina (Jackson) S.; m. Beatrice Anne Cicko, July 11, 1944; children—Virginia Ann, Janet Lynne, Carolin Joan. B.S., U. Pa., 1939, M.S., 1941, Ph.D., 1950. Lab. asst. Farnsworth Radio & Television, 1939-40; test engr. Gen. Electric Co., Phila., Schenectady, 1940-41; lab. asst. U. Pa., Phila., 1941-43, instr. elec. engring., 1942-43, research engr., lab. supr., 1943-45, asst. prof. elec. engring., 1945-53, prof., 1959-89, prof. emeritus, 1989—; v.p. Internat. Spl. Com. on Radio Interference, 1973-79, chmn., 1979-85; v.p. U.S. nat. com. Internat. Electrotech. Commn., 1975-94, chmn. accredited stds. com. C63, 1968—, chmn. com. of action adv. com. on electromagnetic compatibility, 1986-91; cons. Dept. Navy; cons. interference reduction panel R & D bd. Dept. Def., 1945; mem. spl. mission OSRD, Washington, 1945. Contbr. articles to profl. jours. Recipient Astin-Polk Internat. Standards medal Am. Nat. Standards Inst., 1991, meritorious achievement award 1995. Fellow IEEE (Charles Proteus Steinmetz award 1982, Centennial medal 1984, Standards medallion 1991); mem. EMC Soc. (life), Ops. Research Soc. Am., Am. Soc. Engring. Edn., Am. Nat. Standards Inst., AAUP, Sigma Xi. Home: 223 Oxford Rd Upper Darby PA 19083-3906 Office: U Pa Moore Sch Elec Engring Philadelphia PA 19104-6390

SHOWS, CLARENCE OLIVER, dentist; b. nr. Brantley, Ala., Oct. 17, 1920; s. John Oliver and Cora (Nichols) S.; student Wis. State Coll., 1946-47; DDS, Northwestern U., 1951; m. Rita Silverman Orenstein, Nov. 25, 1987; children from previous marriage: Toni Cherie, Kristin Clare Shows Ball, Bradley Scott, Gregory Norman, Jeffery Ryan. Individual practice dentistry, Valparaiso, Fla., 1951-53, Pensacola, 1953—. Mem. Pensacola Art Assn.; past pres. Escambia County unit Am. Cancer Soc., now bd. dirs. Fla. unit, also hon. life mem.; mem. Eagle Scout Bd. Rev., Escambia County; sec. Gulf Breeze Vol. Fire Dept. Served with USCG, 1939-46. Fellow Royal Soc. Health, Internat. Coll. Dentists, Internat. Acad. Gen. Dentistry, Am. Coll. Dentists; mem. Am. AAAS, ADA, Acad. Gen. Dentistry (master, past pres. Fla. unit), Internat. Orthodontic Assn., Internat. Acad. Preventive Medicine, Am. Orthodontic Soc., Gulf Breeze C. of C. (past pres.), Fla. Soc. Dentistry for Children (past pres.), Acad. Gen. Dentistry, Am. Profl. Practice Assn., L.D. Pankey Dental Found., Fedn. Dental Internat., Am. Assn. Clin. Hypnosis, Northwestern U. Alumni Assn., Navy League (life), G.V. Black Soc. (life), Pensacola Jr. Coll. Found. (life), Psi Omega. Presbyterian (elder). Clubs: Masons, Shriners, Jesters, Elks; Pensacola (past pres.), Exchange. Home: 519 Navy Cove Blvd Gulf Breeze FL 32561-4025 Office: 3090 W Navy Blvd Pensacola FL 32505-8024

SHOWS, WINNIE M., public relations company executive, professional speaker; b. L.A., Apr. 2, 1947; d. William Marion Arvin and Joan Catherine (Sperry) Wilson; m. George Albert Shows, Mar. 18, 1967 (div. May 1980); 1 child, Sallie; m. Michael P. Florio, Jan. 1, 1990. BA in English, UCLA, 1969; MEd, Calif. State U., Long Beach, 1976. Tchr. St. Joseph High Sch., Lakewood, Calif., 1969-71; tchr. high sch. Irvine (Calif) Unified Sch. Dist., 1972-79; freelance writer, 1979-80; mgr. pub. rels. Forth, Inc., Hermosa Beach, Calif., 1980-81; account mgr., account supr., dir. mktg. Franson & Assoc., San Jose, Calif., 1981-84; v.p., pres. Smith & Shows, Menlo Park, Calif., 1984—. Author (newsletter) Smith & Shows Letter, 1989-94. Vol. Unity Palo Alto (Calif.) Cmty. Ch., 1989-94, Newcomers, Menlo Park, 1990-93, Kara, Palo Alto, 1991-94, Menlo Park Sch. Dist., 1993—. Named Woman of Vision, Career Action Ctr., 1994. Mem. Nat. Spkrs. Assn., Bus. Mktg. Assn. (program dir. 1985-87). Avocations: writing, reading, gardening. Office: Smith & Shows 28 Holbrook Ln Atherton CA 94027

SHPERLING, IRENA, internist; b. Tallin, USSR, Sept. 20, 1938; came to U.S., 1976; d. Ber Epstein and Maria Minkov; m. Betsalel R. Shperling, June 16, 1960; 1 child, Elena. MD, First Pavlov's Med. Inst., Leningrad, USSR, 1961. Diplomate Am. Bd. Internal Medicine. Med. dr. City Hosp., Leningrad, USSR, 1961-75; resident in internal medicine Winthrop U. Hosp. SUNY, 1977-80; gen. practice medicine Mineola, N.Y., 1980—. Mem. Am. Soc. Internal Medicine, N.Y. State Soc. Internal Medicine, Nassau County Soc. Internal Medicine, Am. Coll. Physicians, Am. Coll. Physicians, Nat. Assn. Female Execs. Avocations: art, travel, music. Office: Nassau Internists 134 Mineola Blvd Mineola NY 11501-3959

SHRADER, CHARLES REGINALD, historian; b. Nashville, July 3, 1943; s. Reginald Woodrow and Freda Olene (Presley) S.; m. Carole Anne Analore, Aug. 17, 1963; children: Peter Reginald, Sheila Lynne Shrader Bixby. BA cum laude, Vanderbilt U., 1964; MA History, Columbia U., 1970, M Phil, 1974, PhD History, 1976; Grad., U.S. Army Command/Gen. Staff, Coll., 1978, U.S. Army War Coll., 1982, NATO Def. Coll., 1984. Commd. 2d lt. U.S. Army, 1964, advanced through grades to lt. col., retired, 1987; asst. prof. history U.S. Mil. Acad., 1971-74; instr. European Div. U. Md., Pirmasens and Landstuhl, Germany, 1971-74; instr. U.S. Army Command and Gen. Staff Coll., 1977-80, U.S. Army War Coll., 1980-84; mem. staff NATO Def. Coll., Rome, 1984-85; independent historian, 1987—; exec. dir. Soc. for Mil. History, Carlisle, Pa., 1992—; adj. instr. Elizabethtown Coll., 1988-89, Penn State U.-Harrisburg, 1988-90; lectr. various Army svc. schs., CIA, U. Kans., U. Victoria/B.C., NATO Def. Coll. Mem. Carlisle Mcpl. Authority, 1993—. Mem. Army and Navy Club, Phi Kappa Psi, Phi Beta Kappa. Roman Catholic. Home and Office: 910 Forbes Rd Carlisle PA 17013

SHRADER, RALPH W., management consultant. Office: Booz Allen & Hamilton Inc 8283 Greensboro Dr Mc Lean VA 22102*

SHRADER, THOMAS HENRY, biologist; b. Marlinton, W.Va., July 12, 1943; s. George Henry and Lula Katherine (Wymer) S.; m. Michele H. Nguyen, Jan. 15, 1966; 1 child: Theodore Jack London. BS, U. Ariz., 1967, MS, 1972; postgrad., N.Mex. State U., 1972-77. Agronomist U.S. Bur. Reclamation, El Paso, Tex., 1972-73, conservation agronomist, 1974-77, ecologist, 1977-84, supervisory natural resource specialist, 1985-91; supervisory biologist U.S. Bur. Reclamation, Boulder City, Nev., 1991—; lectr. in field. Contbr.: Herbicide Manual, 1983; contbr. articles to profl.

jours. Dir. Celebrity Home Assn., Henderson, Nev., 1995; mem. Colo. River Work Group, 1993-95. Mem. Am. Soc. Agronomy, Weed Sci. Soc. Am., Ariz. Riparian Coun., Gamma Sigma Delta, Phi Kappa Phi. Avocations: civil war, rare books, photography. Home: 233 Jonquil Cir Henderson NV 89014-5244 Office: US Bureau of Reclamation PO Box 61470 Boulder City NV 89006-1470

SHRADER, WILLIAM WHITNEY, radar consulting scientist; b. Foochow, China, Oct. 17, 1930; came to U.S., 1932; s. Ralph Raymond and Elizabeth Talmadge (Hand) S.; m. Natalie Lucinda Hutchinson, July 21, 1984. BSEE, U. Mass., 1953; MSEE, Northeastern U., 1961. Rsch. engr. Boeing Airplane Co., Seattle, 1953-56; cons. scientist, tech. dir. numerous radar systems developed Raytheon Co., Wayland, Mass., 1956-1994; pvt. practice radar cons. Stow, Mass., 1994—. Author: (with others) Radar Handbook, 1970, 2d edit., 1990; contbr. articles to profl. jours.; holder 10 U.S. patents, numerous fgn. patents. Fellow IEEE. Avocation: sports car rallying. Home and Office: 144 Harvard Rd Stow MA 01775-1070

SHRAGE, LAURETTE, special education educator; b. Montreal, Jan. 15, 1951; d. Ivan and Adela (Zupnik) Benda; m. William Lee Shrage, Oct. 30, 1977; children: Robert, Jaclyn. BS in Elem. Edn., Adelphi U., 1972; MS in Reading, Coll. New Rochelle, 1994. Cert. elem. edn., spl. edn., reading, bilingual edn., N.Y. Mgr. Century Operating Corp., N.Y.C., 1973-82; substitute tchr. New Rochelle (N.Y.) Sch. Dist., 1992-93, bilingual spl. edn. tchr., 1993—; substitute tchr. Keller Sch., Yonkers, N.Y., 1992-93; parent rep. New Rochelle Com. Presch. Spl. Edn., 1990-91, New Rochelle Com. Spl. Edn., 1991-92; mem. adv. coun. Jefferson Sch., New Rochelle, 1993—, mem. Magnet Think Tank com., 1994—; mem. Ptnrs. in Policy Making N.Y. State, 1992. Pres. PTA Augustus St. Gardens Sch., N.Y.C., 1987-90; advt. mgr. Mitchell Lama Apt., N.Y.C., 1983-86; telethon vol. Channel 13, N.Y.C., 1977; sponsor Sagamore Children's Sch., Suffolk, N.Y., 1974. Recipient Parent Leadership award Coun. Suprs. and Adminstrs. City of N.Y., 1990. Avocations: Spanish, French, tennis, piano, opera. Home: 29 Reyna Ln New Rochelle NY 10804-1104 Office: Jefferson Sch 131 Weyman Ave New Rochelle NY 10805-1428

SHRAUNER, BARBARA WAYNE ABRAHAM, electrical engineering educator; b. Morristown, N.J., June 21, 1934; d. Leonard Gladstone and Ruth Elizabeth (Thrasher) Abraham; m. James Ely Shrauner, 1965; children: Elizabeth Ann, Jay Arthur. BA cum laude, U. Colo., 1956; AM, Harvard U., 1957, PhD, 1962. Postdoctoral researcher U. Libre de Bruxelles, Brussels, 1962-64; postdoctoral researcher NASA-Ames Rsch. Ctr., Moffett Field, Calif., 1964-65; asst. prof. Washington U., St. Louis, 1966-69, assoc. prof., 1969-77, prof., 1977—; sabbatical Los Alamos (N.Mex.) Sci. Lab., 1975-76, Lawrence Berkeley Lab., Berkeley, Calif., 1985-86; cons. Los Alamos Nat. Lab., 1979, 84, NASA, Washington, 1980, Naval Surface Weapons Lab., Silver Spring, Md., 1984. Contbr. articles on transport in semiconductors, hidden symmetries of differential equations, plasma physics to profl. jours. Mem. IEEE (exec. com. of standing tech. com. on plasma sci. applications), AAUP (local sec.-treas. 1980-82), Am. Phys. Soc. (divsn. plasma physics, exec. com. 1980-82, 96—), Am. Geophys. Union, Univ. Fusion Assn., Phi Beta Kappa, Sigma Xi, Eta Kappa Nu, Sigma Pi Sigma. Home: 7452 Stratford Ave Saint Louis MO 63130-4044 Office: Washington U Dept Elec Engring 1 Brookings Dr Saint Louis MO 63130-4862

SHREEVE, JEAN'NE MARIE, chemist, educator; b. Deer Lodge, Mont., July 2, 1933; d. Charles William and Maryfrances (Briggeman) S. BA, U. Mont., 1953, DSc (hon.), 1982; MS, U. Minn., 1956; PhD, U. Wash., 1961; NSF postdoctoral fellow, U. Cambridge, Eng., 1967-68. Asst. prof. chemistry U. Idaho, Moscow, 1961-65; assoc. prof. U. Idaho, 1965-67, prof., 1967-73, acting chmn. dept. chemistry, 1969-70, 1973, head dept., and prof., 1973-87, vice provost rsch. and grad. studies, prof. chemistry, 1987—; Lucy W. Pickett lectr. Mt. Holyoke Coll., 1976, George H. Cady lectr. U. Wash., 1993; mem. Nat. Com. Standards in Higher Edn., 1965-67, 69-73. Mem. editl. bd. Jour. Fluorine Chemistry, 1970—, Jour. Heteroatom Chemistry, 1988—, Accounts Chem. Rsch., 1973-75, Inorganic Synthesis, 1976—; contbr. articles to sci. jours. Mem. bd. govs. Argonne (Ill.) Nat. Lab., 1992—. Recipient Disting. Alumni award U. Mont., 1970; named Hon. Alumnus, U. Idaho, 1972; recipient Outstanding Achievement award U. Minn., 1975, Sr. U.S. Scientist award Alexander Von Humboldt Found., 1978, Excellence in Teaching award Chem. Mfrs. Assn., 1980; U.S. hon. Ramsay fellow, 1967-68, Alfred P. Sloan fellow, 1970-72. Mem. AAAS (bd. dirs. 1991-95), AAUW (officer Moscow chpt. 1962-69), Am. Chem. Soc. (bd. dirs. 1985-93, chmn. fluorine divsn. 1979-81, Petroleum Rsch. Fund adv. bd. 1975-77, women chemists com. 1972-77, Fluorine award 1978, Garvan medal 1972, Harry and Carol Mosher award Santa Clara Valley sect. 1992), Phi Beta Kappa. Office: U Idaho Rsch Office 111 Morrill Hall Moscow ID 83843

SHREEVE, SUSANNA SEELYE, educational planning facilitator. BA in Dance, Arts and Humanities, Mills Coll.; MA in Confluent Edn., U. Calif., Santa Barbara, 1989; postgrad., U. Calif., 1990, San Diego State U., 1992. Cert. elem. tchr., C.C. adminstr., tchr., Calif. Comm. instr. Brooks Inst., 1982; initiator Santa Barbara County Arts and Aging Forum, 1982; co-planner PARTners "How Kids Learn" Conf., 1985; dir. Los Ninos Bilingual Head Start Program, 1986-87; writing counselor Am. and internat. students S.B. City Coll., 1988, U. Calif., Santa Barbara, 1989-90; writing counselor Upward Bound, 1989-90; edn. coord. Santa Barbara County Urban Indian Project, Santa Barbara, 1990; instr. Santa Barbara Youth Cultural Arts, Santa Barbara, 1993; planner/staff Tri-County Regional Team Youth Summit, 1993-94; planner SIG confluent edn. AERA, 1994—; DQ-U. math/sci. resources for tchrs. Indian Edn., 1992—; multi-cultural cmty. Regional Alliance Info. Network Internet Youth Programs, Santa Barbara, 1991—; Pro-Youth Coalition planner, NAPF's Indigenous People's Issues Liaison to WWWebsite, City of Santa Barbara. Office: 527 Laguna St Santa Barbara CA 93101-1607

SHREM, CHARLES JOSEPH, metals corporation executive; b. Cairo, May 9, 1930; came to U.S., 1959; s. Joseph C. and Paula (Cadranel) S.; m. Vivian L. Chalom, Jan. 30, 1955; children: Jeff, Leslie Allen. Degree in bus. and economy, Coll. Français, Cairo, 1951. Export mgr. Stanton Ironworks U.K., Middle East, 1950-57; comml. mgr. Soc. Sovibor, Paris, 1957-59; purchasing dir. Montanore, Inc., N.Y.C., 1959-65; exec. v.p. Commonwealth Metal Corp., Englewood Cliffs, N.J., 1965-85, pres., chief exec. officer, 1985—. Bd. dirs. Adult Edn., Pequannock, N.J., 1970-80. Mem. U.S. C. of C. (econ. coun., exec. com. U.S. Polish Coun./U.S. C. of C.). Office: 560 Sylvan Ave Englewood Cliffs NJ 07632-3104

SHREVE, ALLISON ANNE, former air traffic control specialist; b. Sturgeon Bay, Wis., Aug. 29, 1961; d. Kendil McLaren and Barbara Gail (Kellner) S. Student, U. Wis., Oshkosh, 1979-82, 95—, Madison Area Tch. Coll., 1993. Cert. control tower operator. Air traffic asst. FAA, Green Bay, Wis., 1985-87, air traffic control specialist, 1987-96. Active Earth Share Fund, Humane Assn., ASPCA; animal care vol. Wildlife Sanctuary, Green Bay, Wis. Mem. Wis. Wildlife Rehabilitator's Assn. Avocations: animals, music and songwriting, reading, outdoor activities. Home: 411 S Francis St Brillion WI 54110-1338

SHREVE, PEG, state legislator, retired elementary educator; b. Spencer, Va., July 23, 1927; d. Hubert Smith and Pearl (Looney) Adams; m. Don Franklin Shreve, June 17, 1950 (dec. Sept. 1970); children: Donna, Jennifer, John, Don. BA, Glenville State U., 1948. Cert. elem. tchr., Va., Wyo. Reading tchr. Wood County Bd., Parkersburg, W.Va., 1948-50; elem. tchr. Mt. Solon, Va., 1950-52, Bridgewater, Va., 1952-53, Cody, Wyo., 1970-86; mem. Wyo. Ho. of Reps., 1983—, chmn.. com. travel, recreation and wildlife, 1983-91, majority whip, 1992-94, speaker pro tem, 1995—. Mem. coun. Girl Scouts U.S.A., White Sulpher Springs, W.Va., 1962-65; co-chmn. Legis. Exec. Conf., Wyo., 1987; mem. Nat. Com. State Legislatures, 1982—. Named Legislator of Yr., Wyo. Outfitters Assn., 1989, Ofcl. of Yr., Wyo. Wildlife Assn., 1990, Alumna of Yr., Glenville State Coll., 1994. Mem. AAUW (exec. bd.), Nat. Women Legislators, Soroptimists (Women Helping Women award 1985), Beta Sigma Phi (Lady of Yr. award 1986). Republican. Presbyterian. Avocations: golf, walking, needlepoint, knitting, bridge. Home: PO Box 2257 Cody WY 82414-2257

SHREVE, SUSAN RICHARDS, author, English literature educator; b. Toledo, May 2, 1939; d. Robert Kenneth and Helen (Greene) Richards; children—Porter, Elizabeth, Caleb, Kate. U. Pa., 1961; MA, U. Va., 1969. Prof. English lit. George Mason U., Fairfax, Va., 1976—; vis. prof. Columbia U., N.Y.C., 1982—, Princeton U., 1991, 92, 93. Author: (novels) A Fortunate Madness, 1974, A Woman Like That, 1977, Children of Power, 1979, Miracle Play, 1981, Dreaming of Heroes, 1984, Queen of Hearts, 1986, A Country of Strangers, 1989, Daughters of the New World, 1992, The Train Home, 1993, Skin Deep: Women & Race, 1995, The Visiting Physician, 1995; (children's books) The Nightmares of Geranium Street, 1977, Family Secrets, 1979, Loveletters, 1979, The Masquerade, 1980, The Bad Dreams of a Good Girl, 1981, The Revolution of Mary Leary, 1982, The Flunking of Joshua T. Bates, 1984, How I Saved the World on Purpose, 1985, Lucy Forever and Miss Rosetree, Shrinks, Inc., 1985, Joshua T. Bates In Charge, 1992, The Gift of the Girl Who Couldn't Hear, 1991, Wait for Me, 1992, Amy Dunn Quits School, 1993, Lucy Forever & the Stolen Baby, 1994, The Formerly Great Alexander Family, 1995, Zoe and Columbo, 1995, Warts, 1996; co-editor: Narratives on Justice, 1996, The Goalie, 1996. Recipient Jenny Moore award George Washington U., 1978; John Simon Guggenheim award in fiction, 1980; Nat. Endowment Arts fiction award, 1982. Mem. PEN/Faulkner Found. (pres.), Phi Beta Kappa.

SHRIBER, MAURICE NORDEN, research and manufacturing company executive; b. St. Louis, Oct. 24, 1943; s. Bernard and Yetta (Gitlin) S.; m. Nancy Jo Wood; children: Amy K., Rebecca D., Aaron L. BA, Washington U., St. Louis, 1965; MBA, St. Louis U., 1970. Sr. cons. Harbridge House, Boston, 1968-70; sr. staff analyst Office Sec. Def., Washington, 1970-78, dep. dir. material mgmt., 1978-79, chief aircraft systems div. Aviation Systems Command, St. Louis, 1979-80, staff dir. supply policy and programs, 1981-82, dir. supply mgmt. policy, 1982-84, dep. asst. sec. def. for spares program mgmt., 1984-85, dep. asst. sec. def. for logistics, 1985-87; corp. v.p. mfg. and logistics System Planning Corp., Rosslyn, Va., 1987-88, pres., corp. v.p., logistics div. mgr.; pres. System Planning Corp. Engring Svcs., Inc., Arlington, Va., 1988-91, COO, 1991-94, pres., 1994—. Assoc. author: Quantitative Analysis for Business and Economics, 1974. Served with U.S. Army, 1967-73. Recipient Presdl. Meritorious Rank award Office Personnel Mgmt., 1986, Disting. Civilian Service medal Dept. Def., 1987, Meritorius Civilian Svc. award U.S. Army.

SHRIBMAN, DAVID MARKS, editor; b. Salem, Mass., Mar. 2, 1954; m. Cynthia L. Skrzycki, Sept. 9, 1978; children: Elizabeth, Natalie. AB summa cum laude, Dartmouth Coll., 1976. Mem. city staff and Washington bur. Buffalo Evening News, 1977-80; mem. feature and nat. staff The Washington Star, 1980-81; with Washington bur. N.Y. Times, 1981-84; congl. reporter, nat. polit. corr. The Wall St. Jour., 1984-93; chief Washington bur., asst. mng. editor The Boston Globe, 1993—. Trustee Dartmouth Coll. James B. Reynolds scholar Jesus Coll.; recipient Pulitzer Prize for beat reporting, 1995. Mem. Phi Beta Kappa. Office: Globe Newspaper Co 1130 Connecticut Ave NW Washington DC 20036-3904*

SHRIER, ADAM LOUIS, investment firm executive; b. Warsaw, Poland, Mar. 26, 1938; came to U.S., 1943, naturalized, 1949; s. Henry Leon and Mathilda June (Czamanska) S.; m. Diane Kesler, June 10, 1961; children: Jonathan, Lydia, Catherine, David. BS, Columbia U., 1959; MS (Whitney fellow), MIT, 1960; D.Engr. and Applied Sci. (NSF fellow), Yale U., 1965; postdoctoral visitor, U. Cambridge, Eng., 1965-66; J.D., Fordham U., 1976. With Esso Research & Engring. Co., Florham Park and Linden, N.J., 1963-65, 66-72; head. environ. scis. research area Esso Research & Engring. Co., 1969-72; coordinator pollution abatement activities, tanker dept. Exxon Internat. Co., N.Y.C., 1972-74; project mgr., energy systems Exxon Enterprises Inc., N.Y.C., 1974-75; gen. mgr. solar energy projects Exxon Enterprises Inc., 1975-77, pres. solar thermal systems div., 1977-81; corp. planning cons., sec. new bus. investments Exxon Corp., N.Y.C., 1981-82; div. mgr. supply and transp. Exxon Internat. Co., N.Y.C., 1983-86, mgr. policy and planning, 1986-88; mng. dir. Splty. Tech. Assocs., Washington, 1988—; adj. lectr. chem. egnring. Columbia U., N.Y.C., 1967-69; industry adv. bd. Internat. Energy Agy., 1984-88, Energy and Environ. Policy Ctr., Harvard U., 1986-88, Internat. Energy Program, Johns Hopkins U., 1987-88; sr. assoc. Global Bus. Forum, 1988—, Cambridge Energy Rsch. Assocs., 1988—. Patentee in field; contbr. articles to profl. jours. Mem. AIChE, Am. Inst. Energy Economists, Cosmos Club, Sigma Xi, Tau Beta Pi, Phi Lambda Upsilon. Office: 4000 Cathedral Ave NW Washington DC 20016-5249

SHRIER, STEFAN, mathematician, educator; b. Mexico City, Nov. 7, 1942; s. Henry Leon Shrier and Mathilda June Czamanska; m. Helaine G. Elderkin, 1985. BS in Engring., Columbia U., 1964, MS in Ops. Rsch., 1966; PhD in Applied Math., Brown U., 1977. Chmn. computer sci. program Wellesley (Mass.) Coll., 1972-75; sr. engr. Booz, Allen and Hamilton, Bethesda, Md., 1977-79; dir. Latin Am. ops. SofTech, Inc., Springfield, Va., 1979-80; mem. rsch. staff Systems Planning Corp., Arlington, Va., 1980-83; tech. dir. Grumman-CTEC, Inc. subs. Grumman Data Systems, Inc. (absorbed by Grumman Data Systems, Inc. Jan. 1988), McLean, Va., 1983-85, dir. Lab. Machine Intelligence and Correlation, 1984-87, dir. R & D, 1985-87; asst. dir. tech. dept. Grumman Data Systems, Inc., McLean, Va., 1988-90, dep. dir. tech. dept. Washington ops., 1990-91; mem. tech. staff MRJ, Inc., Fairfax, Va., 1991—; professorial lectr. statistics George Washington U., 1981-84, adj. prof. stats., 1984-85; adj. prof. computer sci. George Mason U., 1985-87; sec. New Eng. Regional Computing Program, Cambridge, Mass., 1973-75. Contbr. articles to profl. jours. Fellow Washington Acad. Sci.; mem. Sigma Xi, Tau Beta Pi. Office: MRJ Inc 10560 Arrowhead Dr Fairfax VA 22030-7305

SHRINER, THOMAS L., JR., lawyer; b. Lafayette, Ind., Dec. 15, 1947; s. Thomas L. Sr. and Margaret (Kamstra) S.; m. Donna L. Galchick, June 5, 1971; children: Thomas L. III, John H. , Joseph P., James A. AB, Ind. U., 1969, JD, 1972. Bar: Wis. 1972, U.S. Ct. Appeals (7th cir.) 1972, U.S. Dist. Ct. (ea. dist.) Wis. 1973, U.S. Dist. Ct. (we. dist.) Wis. 1977, U.S. Supreme Ct. 1978, U.S. Ct. Appeals (8th cir.) 1989, U.S. Ct. Appeals (fed. cir.) 1990. Law clk to Hon. John S. Hastings U.S. Ct. Appeals (7th cir.), Chgo., 1972-73; assoc. Foley & Lardner, Milwaukee, Wis., 1973-79, ptnr., 1979—. Contbr. articles to profl. jours. Fellow Am. Coll. Trial Lawyers; mem. 7th Cir. Bar Assn. (pres. 1993-94), Phi Beta Kappa. Republican. Roman Catholic. Office: Foley & Lardner 777 E Wisconsin Ave Milwaukee WI 53202-5302

SHRINSKY, JASON LEE, lawyer; b. Pitts., June 15, 1937; s. Abe and Sylvia S.; children: Jeffrey, Steven, Stacy. BA, U. Pitts., 1959; JD, George Washington U., 1962. Sr. ptnr. Shrinsky, Weitzman & Eisen, Washington, 1971-87; ptnr., exec. com. mem. Kaye, Scholer, Fierman, Hays & Handler, Washington, 1987—; mem. exec. com., 1993-97; panelist Paul Kagan Seminars on Radio and TV Acquisitions, Inst. Soc. Internat. Rsch.; atty.-advisor Complaints and Compliance Div. Broadcast Bur. FCC, Washington, 1961-64; bd. dirs. U.S. Com. Sports for Israel, Phila., FCC Bar Assn. Contbr. articles to Radio and Records mag., Broadcast Cable Fin. Jour. Presdl. del. Mt. Sinai transfer ceremonies, 1978; U.S. basketball chmn. 12th, 13th and 14th Maccabiah games, Israel; bd. dirs. Washington Hebrew Congregation, 1978-85. Mem. Internat. Radio and TV Soc., Nat. Broadcaster's Club (past pres.), U. Pitts. Alumni Assn. (bd. dirs.). Jewish. Office: Kaye Scholer Fierman 901 15th St NW Washington DC 20005-2327

SHRIVER, DONALD WOODS, JR., theology educator; b. Norfolk, Va., Dec. 20, 1927; s. Donald Woods and Gladys (Roberts) S.; m. Peggy Ann Leu, Aug. 9, 1953; children: Gregory Bruce, Margaret Ann, Timothy Donald. B.A., Davidson Coll., 1951; B.D., Union Theol. Sem. Va., 1955; S.T.M., Yale U., 1957; Ph.D. (Rockefeller Doctoral fellow), Harvard U., 1963; L.H.D. (hon.), Central Coll., 1970, Davidson Coll., 1984, Union Medal, Union Theol. Sem. Am., 1991; D.D. (hon.), Wagner Coll., 1978, Southwestern Coll., Memphis, 1983, Colgate U., 1996; LHD (hon.), Jewish Theol. Sem., 1991; DD (hon.), Colgate U., 1996. Ordained to ministry Presbyterian Ch., 1955; pastor Linwood Presbyn. Ch., Gastonia, N.C., 1956-59; u. minister, prof. religion N.C. State U., Raleigh, 1963-72; dir. u. program on sci. and soc. N.C. State U., 1968-72; prof. ethics and soc. Emory U., Atlanta, 1972-75; William E. Dodge prof. applied Christianity Union Theol. Sem., N.Y.C., 1975—, pres. faculty, 1975-91; adj. prof. bus. ethics Sch. Bus. Adminstrn., Columbia U.; sr. fellow freedom forum Sch. Journalism, Columbia U., 1992-93; adj. prof. ethics, 1994—; lectr. Duke U., Va. State U., Ga. State U., numerous colls. and univs. in Can., Kenya, India, Japan and Korea. Author: How Do You Do and Why: An Introduction of Christian Ethics for Young People, 1966, Rich Man Poor Man: Christian Ethics for Modern Man Series, 1972, (with Dean D. Knudsen and John R. Earle) Spindles and Spires: A Restudy of Religion and Social Change in Gastonia, 1976, (with Karl A. Ostrom) Is There Hope for the City?, 1977, The Social Ethics of the Lord's Prayer, 1980, The Gospel, The Church, and Social Change, 1980, The Lord's Prayer: A Way of Life, 1983, An Ethic for Enemies: Forgiveness in Politics, 1995; co-author: Redeeming the City, 1982, Beyond Success: Corporations and Their Critics in the Nineties, 1991; editor: The Unsilent South, 1965, Medicine and Religion: Strategies of Care, 1979. Dir. Urban Policy Study N.C. State U., 1971-73; precinct chmn. Democratic Party, Raleigh, N.C., del. to nat. conv., 1968; mem. Mayor's Com. on Human Relations, Raleigh, 1967-71; chmn. Urban Policy Seminar, Center for Theology and Public Policy, 1978-82. Served with Signal Corps U.S. Army, 1946-47. Recipient The Union medal, Union Theol. Sem., 1991; Kent fellow in religion, 1959. Mem. Am. Soc. Christian Ethics (pres. 1979-80), Soc. for Values in Higher Edn., Soc. for Health and Human Values, Soc. for Sci. Study of Religion, AAAS, Am. Sociol. Assn., Am. Soc. Engring. Edn. (chmn. liberal arts div. 1972-73), United Christian Youth Movement of Nat. Council of Chs. (nat. chmn. 1951-53), Council on Fgn. Relations. Home: 440 Riverside Dr Apt 58 New York NY 10027-6830 Office: Union Theol Sem 3041 Broadway New York NY 10027-5710 *Modern people need to recover connections between memory and hope. The past we applaud pre-enacts the future we hope for, and the past we deplore forms our obligation, in the present, to make a different future. In a time when young people find it hard to envision a long human future, the connections of history and ethics are indispensable. The forging of such connections is my vocation as an educator.*

SHRIVER, DUWARD FELIX, chemistry educator, researcher, consultant; b. Glendale, Calif., Nov. 20, 1934; s. Duward Laurence and Josephine (Williamson) S.; m. Shirley Ann Clark; children: Justin Scott, Daniel Nathan. BS, U. Calif., Berkeley, 1958; PhD, U. Mich., 1961. From instr. to assoc. prof. chemistry Northwestern U., Evanston, Ill., 1961-70, prof., 1970-87, Morrison prof. of chemistry, 1987—, chmn. dept. chem., 1992-95; mem. Inorganic Syntheses Inc., 1974—, pres., 1982-85; vis. staff mem. Los Alamos (N.Mex.) Nat. Lab., 1976-85, cons., 1985-92; vis. prof. U. Tokyo, 1977, U. Wyo., 1978, U. Western Ont., Can., 1979. Author: The Manipulation of Air-Sensitive Compounds, 1969, edit., 1987; co-author: Inorganic Chemistry, 1990, 2d edit., 1994; editor-in-chief Inorganic Syntheses, vol. 19, 1979; co-editor: The Chemistry of Metal Cluster Complexes, 1990, Inorganic Synthesis, 1979—, Advances in Inorganic Chemistry, 1986—, Jour. Coordination Chemistry, Inorganic Chimca Acta, 1988—, Chemistry of Materials, 1988-90, 92—, Jour. Cluster Sci., 1990—, Organometallics, 1993-95; contbr. articles to profl. jours. Alfred P. Sloan fellow, 1967-69; Japan Soc. Promotion of Sci. fellow, 1977; Guggenheim Found. fellow, 1983-84. Fellow AAAS; mem. Am. Chem. Soc. (Disting. Svc. in Inorganic Chemistry award 1987), Royal Soc. Chemistry London (Ludwig Mond lectr. 1989), Electrochem. Soc., Materials Rsch. Soc. (medal 1990). Home: 1100 Colfax St Evanston IL 60201-2611 Office: Northwestern U Dept Chemistry Evanston IL 60208-3113

SHRIVER, EUNICE MARY KENNEDY (MRS. ROBERT SARGENT SHRIVER, JR.), civic worker; b. Brookline, Mass.; m. Robert Sargent Shriver, Jr., May 23, 1953; children: Robert Sargent III, Maria Owings, Timothy Perry, Mark Kennedy, Anthony Paul Kennedy. BS in Sociology, Stanford U., 1943; student, Manhattanville Coll. of Sacred Heart, LHD (hon.), 1963; LHD (hon.), D'Youville Coll., 1962, Regis Coll., 1963, Newton Coll., 1973, Brescia Coll., 1974, Holy Cross Coll., 1979, Princeton U., 1979, Boston Coll., 1990; LittD (hon.), U. Santa Clara, 1962; also hon. degrees, U. Vt., Albertus Magnus Coll., St. Mary's Coll. With spl. war problems div. State Dept. Washington, 1943-45; sec. Nat. Conf. on Prevention and Control juvenile Delinquency, Dept. of Justice, Washington, 1947-48; social worker Fed. Penitentiary for Women, Alderson, W.Va., 1950; exec. v.p. Joseph P. Kennedy, Jr. Found., 1956—; founder Spl. Olympics Internat.; social worker House of Good Shepherd, Chgo., also Juvenile Ct., Chgo., 1951-54; regional chmn. women's div. Community Fund-Red Cross Joint Appeal, Chgo., 1958; mem. Chgo. Commn. on Youth Welfare, 1959-62; cons. to Pres. John F. Kennedy's Panel on Mental Retardation, 1961; founder Community & Caring, Inc., 1986. Editor: A Community of Caring, 1982, 85, Growing Up Caring, 1990. Co-chmn. women's com. Dem. Nat. Conv., Chgo., 1956. Decorated Legion of Honor; recipient Lasker award, Humanitarian award A.A.M.D., 1973, Nat. Vol. Service award, 1973, Phila. Civic Ballet award, 1973, Prix de la Couronne Française, 1974, Presdl. Medal of Freedom, 1984, others.

SHRIVER, GARNER EDWARD, lawyer, former congressman; b. Towanda, Kans., July 6, 1912; s. Edward Arthur and Olive (Glass) S.; m. Martha Jane Currier, June 4, 1941; children: Kay Kwon, David Garner, Linda Ann Breeding. A.B., U. Wichita, 1934; J.D., Washburn U., 1940; D. Pub. Service, Friends U., Wichita, 1970. Bar: Kans. 1940. Instr. English and speech South Haven (Kans.) High Sch., 1936-37; mem. firm Bryant, Cundiff, Shriver & Shanahan, Wichita, 1940-61; Mem. Kans. Ho. of Reps. from Sedgwick County, 1947-51; atty. Wichita Bd. Edn., 1951-60; mem. 87th-94th Congresses, 4th Kans. Dist.; Mem. Kansas Interstate Coop. Commn., 1953-55, Kans. Senate, 27th Dist., 1953-61; mem. Kan. Legis. Council, 1955-60; minority counsel Senate Vet. Affairs Com., 1975-80, gen. counsel, 1981-82; of counsel Johnson, Shriver & Kinzel, McPherson, Kans, 1983-86, Law Offices of David G. Shriver, McPherson, Kans., 1986—. Trustee Murdock Art Collection of Wichita Art Mus.; bd. dirs. Kans. Dialysis Assn., DeMolay Legion of Honor. Lt. USNR, World War II. Recipient U. Wichita Alumni Achievement award, 1961; recipient Washburn Alumni Disting. Service award, 1967. Mem. ABA, Kans. Bar Assn., Wichita Bar Assn., VFW, Am. Legion, Nat. Sorjourners, Masons (33d degree), Shriners. Republican. Methodist. Home: 15205 Timber Lake Cir Wichita KS 67230-9214 Office: Law Offices of David G Shriver 100 S Main St Mc Pherson KS 67460-4852

SHRIVER, MARIA OWINGS, news correspondent; b. Chgo., Nov. 6, 1955; d. Robert Sargent and Eunice Mary (Kennedy) S.; m. Arnold Schwarzenegger, Apr. 26, 1986; children: Katherine Eunice, Christina Aurelia, Patrick. BA, Georgetown U. Coll. Am. Studies, Washington, 1977. News producer Sta. KYW-TV, 1977-78; producer Sta. WJZ-TV, 1978-80; nat. reporter PM Mag., 1981-83; news reporter CBS News, Los Angeles, 1983-85; news correspondent, co-anchor CBS Morning News, N.Y.C., 1985-86; co-host Sunday Today, NBC, 1987-90; anchor Main Street, NBC, 1987; co-anchor Yesterday, Today, and Tomorrow, NBC, 1989; anchor NBC Nightly News Weekend Edition, 1989-90, Cutting Edge with Maria Shriver, NBC, 1990, First Person with Maria Shriver, NBC, 1991—; co-anchor summer olympics, Seoul, Korea, 1988; substitute anchor NBC News at Sunrise, Today, NBC Nightly News with Tom Brokaw. Recipient Christopher award for "Fatal Addictions", 1990, Exceptional Merit Media award Nat. Women's Political Caucus. Democrat. Roman Catholic. Office: NBC News First Person with Maria Shriver 30 Rockefeller Plz New York NY 10112

SHRIVER, PAMELA HOWARD, professional tennis player; b. Balt., July 4, 1962. Profl. tennis player, 1979—; winner 21 career singles, 92 career doubles titles, 7 Australian Opens (with Martina Navratilova), 4 French Opens (with Navratilova), 5 Wimbledons (with Navratilova), 6 U.S. Opens, French Open mixed doubles (with Emilio Sanchez); mem. U.S. Fedn. Cup Team, 1986-87, 89, 92, U.S. Wightman Cup Team, 1978-81, 83, 85, 87. V.P. Internat. Tennis Hall of Fame; pres. of Women's Tennis Association, 1991, 92, 93. Recipient Gold medal 1988 Olympic Games in doubles (with Zina Garrison). Mem. Women's Tennis Assn. Tour Players Assn. Address: c/o PHS Ltd Ste 902 401 Washington Ave Baltimore MD 21204

SHRIVER, PHILLIP RAYMOND, academic administrator; b. Cleve., Aug. 16, 1922; s. Raymond Scott and Corinna Ruth (Smith) S.; m. Martha Damaris Nye, Apr. 15, 1944; children: Carolyn (Mrs. Richard Helwig), Susan (Mrs. Lester LaVine), Melinda (Mrs. David Williams), Darcy, Raymond Scott II. BA, Yale U., 1943; MA, Harvard U., 1946; PhD, Columbia U., 1954; LittD, U. Cin., 1966; LLD, Heidelberg Coll., 1966, Eastern Mich., 1972, Ohio State U., 1973; DH, McKendree Coll., 1973; DPS, Albion Coll., 1974; LHD, Central State U., 1976, No. Ky. State U., 1980, Miami U., 1984, U. Akron, 1988. Mem. faculty Kent (Ohio) State U.,

1947-65, prof. Am. history, 1960-65; dean Coll. Arts and Scis., 1963-65; pres. Miami U., Oxford, Ohio, 1965-81; pres. emeritus, prof. Am. history Miami U., 1981—; pres. Ohio Coll. Assn., 1974-75; chmn. coun. pres.'s Mid-Am. Conf., 1971-77; chmn. Ohio Bicentennial Commn. for NW Ordinance and U.S. Constn., 1985-89, Ohio Tuition Trust Authority, 1989-92; chmn. coun. pres.'s Nat. Assn. State Univs. and Land Grant Colls., 1975-76, mem. exec. coun., 1976-78. Author: The Years of Youth, 1960, George A. Bowman: The Biography of an Educator, 1963, (with D.J. Breen) Ohio's Military Prisons of the Civil War, 1964, A Tour to New Connecticut: The Narrative of Henry Leavitt Ellsworth, 1985. Bd. dirs. Cin. Ctr. Sci. and Industry, 1965-70; trustee Ohio Coll. Library Center, 1968-74; chmn. bd. Univ. Regional Broadcasting, 1975-76, 78-79. Served to lt. (j.g.) USNR, 1943-46, PTO. Decorated Order of Merit Grand Duchy of Luxembourg, 1976; recipient Disting. Acad. Svc. award AAUP, 1965, Gov.'s award 1969, A.K. Morris award, 1974, Ohioana Career medal, 1987, Converse award, 1990, Award of Merit, Am. Assn. for State and Local History, 1993. Mem. Orgn. Am. Historians, Ohio Acad. History (pres. 1983-84, Disting. Svc. award 1991), Archaeol. Inst. Am., Ohio Hist. Soc. (trustee 1982-91, v.p. 1983-84, pres. 1984-86), Ohio Humanities Council, Am. Studies Assn., Mortar Board, Phi Beta Kappa, Omicron Delta Kappa, Phi Alpha Theta, Alpha Kappa Psi, Kappa Delta Pi, Phi Eta Sigma, Phi Kappa Phi, Kappa Kappa Psi, Alpha Lambda Delta, Beta Gamma Sigma, Sigma Delta Pi, Alpha Phi Omega, Delta Upsilon (Disting. Alumni Achievement award 1985). Presbyterian. Club: Rotary. Home: 5115 Bonham Rd Oxford OH 45056-1428 Office: Miami U Oxford OH 45056

SHRIVER, ROBERT SARGENT, JR., lawyer; b. Westminster, Md., Nov. 9, 1915; s. Robert Sargent and Hilda (Shriver) S.; m. Eunice Mary Kennedy, May 23, 1953; children: Robert Sargent III, Maria, Timothy, Mark Kennedy, Anthony Paul Kennedy. Student, Canterbury Sch.; B.A. cum laude, Yale U., 1938, LL.B., 1941; LL.D., St. Procopius Coll., 1959, Notre Dame U., DePaul U., Seton Hall Coll., 1961, St. Louis U., Kansas State U., Brandeis U., 1962, St. Michael's Coll., Vt., Fordham U., Boston Coll., Yale U., Duquesne U., N.Y.U., Wesleyan U.; D.C.L., U. Liberia, 1963; H.H.D., Salem Coll., 1963, Bowling Green State U.; L.H.D., Springfield (Mass.) Coll., 1963, U. Scranton, Providence Coll.; Dr. Polit. Sci., Chulalongkorn U., Bangkok, Thailand. Bar: N.Y. State 1941, Ill. 1959, U.S. Supreme Ct. 1969, D.C. 1971. With Winthrop, Stimson, Putnam & Roberts, 1940-41; asst. editor Newsweek, 1945-46; assoc. Joseph P. Kennedy Enterprises, 1947-48; asst. gen. mgr. Merchandise Mart, Chgo., 1948-61; dir. Peace Corps., Washington, 1961-66, Office Econ. Opportunity, 1964-68; U.S. ambassador to France, 1968-70; spl. asst. to the Pres., 1965-68; sr. ptnr. law firm Fried, Frank, Harris, Shriver & Jacobson, N.Y.C., Washington, L.A., London, Eng., 1971-86; of counsel Fried, Frank, Harris, Shriver & Jacobson, 1986—; pres. Spl. Olympics, Washington, 1986-90, chmn., CEO, 1990—; mem. Am. Com. on East-West Accord, 1978—, Ams. for SALT, 1979—. Author: Point of the Lance, 1964. Pres. Chgo. Bd. Edn., 1955-60; mem.-at-large Nat. Coun. Boy Scouts Am.; pres. Cath. Interracial Coun. Chgo., 1955-60; chmn. Internat. Orgn. Patrons of Israel Mus., 1972-75, Democratic candidate for v.p., 1972, ran for Dem. presdl. election, 1976; bd. dirs. The Arms Control Assn., 1983—. Lt. comdr. USNR, 1940-45. Recipient Yale U. medal, 1957, Chgo. medal of merit, 1957, James J. Hoey award Cath. Interracial Coun. N.Y., 1958, Franklin D. Roosevelt Freedom from Want award, 1991, Presdl. Medal of Freedom, 1994; named Lay Churchman of Yr. Religious Heritage Am., 1963; recipient Golden Heart Presdl. award Philippines, 1964, Laetare medal U. Notre Dame, 1968. Mem. Yale U. Law Sch. Assn. (exec. com.), Navy League (life), Chgo. Council Fgn. Relations (dir.), Delta Kappa Epsilon. Roman Catholic. Clubs: Serra, Economic, Racquet, Executives (Chgo.); Onwentsia (Lake Forest, Ill.); Yale (N.Y.C.); University (Washington); Chevy Chase (Md.). Extensive world travel to visit Peace Corps projects, 1961-66. Office: Spl Olympics Internat 1325 G St NW Ste 500 Washington DC 20005

SHRODER, TOM, newspaper editor. Exec. editor sunday "tropic" sec. The Miami Herald, Fla. Office: The Miami Herald Pub Co One Herald Plz Miami FL 33132-1693

SHROFF, FIROZ SARDAR, merger and acquisition professional; b. Karachi, Pakistan, Feb. 27, 1950; s. Sardar Mohammad Shroff and Kulsum (Bano) Dhanji; m. Munira Firoz, Oct. 27, 1977; children: Khurram, Sara, Ally. Grad. high sch., Nairobi, Kenya. Apprentice, duty incharge Empire Investment Ltd., Nairobi, 1966-67; asst. mgr. to mgr. Trade Aids Inc., Karachi, 1967-69, asst. gen. mgr., 1969-72; gen. mgr. Canorient Overseas Distbrs. Ltd., London, 1972-74; dir., gen. mgr. Westland Securities Ltd., Nairobi, 1974-75; dep. mng. dir. Sasi Ltd., Karachi, 1975-78; dir. internat. expansion Sasi Group Cos., Karachi, 1978-80, mng. dir., 1984—; dir. operation Key Internat. S.A., London, 1980-84; participant Nat. Book Devel. Council, Singapore, 1980, Arthur D. Little Mgmt. Edn. Inst. and Pakistan Inst. Mgmt., 1986; trustee Sasi Found., Karachi, 1985; developer bus. info. and rsch. ctr.; advisor/cons. various corp. bodies on takeover acquisition of bus. in U.S., U.K. and the Pacific; involved in group discussions on internat. bus. opportunities, contacts in fin. circles. Recipient Cert. Recognition Asia-Pacific Real Estate Congress, 1987. Mem. Pakistan Pubs. and Booksellers Assn. (copyright com. 1975-80), Internat. Real Estate Fedn., Assn. Builders and Developers (convenor 1985), Internat. Real Estate Inst. (chpt. head 1986), Inst. Dirs., Pakistan C. of C. and Industry, United Coop. Credit Soc. (bd. dirs. 1977-79), Property Cons. Soc., Internat. Airline Passengers Assn. Clubs: Karachi Golf; Def. Lodge: Rotary. Avocations: reading, travel. Office: Sasi House G/2, Block 9, KDA Scheme No 5, Main Clifton Rd, Khayaban-e-Iqbal Kehkashan Karachi 75600, Pakistan also: 12 Wynwood Dr Princeton Junction NJ 08550

SHRONTZ, FRANK ANDERSON, airplane manufacturing executive; b. Boise, Idaho, Dec. 14, 1931; s. Thurlyn Howard and Florence Elizabeth (Anderson) S.; m. Harriet Ann Houghton, June 12, 1954; children: Craig Howard, Richard Whitaker, David Anderson. Student, George Washington U., 1953; LLB, U. Idaho, 1954; MBA, Harvard U., 1958; postgrad., Stanford U., 1969-70. Asst. contracts coordinator Boeing Co., Seattle, 1958-65, asst. dir. contract adminstrn., 1965-67, asst. to v.p. comml. airplane group, 1967-69, asst. dir. new airplane program, 1969-70, dir. comml. sales operations, 1970-73, v.p. planning and contracts, 1977-78; asst. sec. Dept. Air Force, Washington, 1973-76, Dept. Def., Washington, 1976-77; v.p., gen. mgr. 707/727/737 div. Boeing Comml. Airplane Co., Seattle, 1978-82, v.p. sales and mktg., 1982-84; pres. Comml. Airplane Co. Boeing Div., Seattle, 1986—; pres., chief exec. officer The Boeing Co., Seattle, 1986—, chmn., chief exec. officer, 1988—; bd. dirs. Citicorp, Boise Cascade Corp., 3M Co.; mem. The Bus. Coun., 1987; vice chmn. New Am. Schs. Devel. Corp. Mem., bus. policy com. Bus. Roundtable; trustee Smithsonian Instn. 1st lt. AUS, 1954-56. Mem. Phi Alpha Delta, Beta Theta Pi. Clubs: Overlake Golf and Country, Columbia Tower. Office: Boeing Co 7755 E Marginal Way S Seattle WA 98108-2207*

SHROPSHIRE, DONALD GRAY, hospital executive; b. Winston-Salem, N.C., Aug. 6, 1927; s. John Lee and Bess L. (Shouse) S.; m. Mary Ruth Bodenheimer, Aug. 19, 1950; children: Melanie Shropshire David, John Devin. B.S., U. N.C., 1950; Erickson fellow hosp. adminstrn., U. Chgo., 1958-59; LLD (hon.), U. Ariz., 1992; EdD (hon.), Tucson U., 1994. Personnel asst. Nat. Biscuit Co., Atlanta, 1950-52; asst. personnel mgr. Nat. Biscuit Co., Chgo., 1952-54; adminstr. Eastern State Hosp., Lexington, Ky., 1954-62; assoc. dir. U. Md. Hosp., Balt., 1962-67; adminstr. Tucson Med. Ctr., 1967-82, pres., 1982-92, pres. emeritus, 1992—, bd. dirs., 1995; pres. Tucson Hosps. Med. Edn. Program, 1970-71, sec., 1971-86; pres. So. Ariz. Hosp. Council, 1968-69; bd. dirs. Ariz. Blue Cross, 1967-76, chmn. provider standards com., 1972-76; chmn. Healthways Inc., 1985-92; bd. dirs. 1st Interstate Bank Ariz., Phoenix, Tucson Med. Found.; adv. bd. Steele Meml. Pediatric Rsch. Ctr., U. of Ariz. Coll. of Medicine, 1996—. Bd. dirs. Health Planning Coun. Tucson, 1992, mem. exec. com., 1969-74; chmn. profl. divsn. United Way, Tucson, 1969-70, vice chmn. campaign, 1988, Ariz. Health Faciltities Authority, bd. dirs., 1992—; chmn. dietary svcs. com., vice chmn., 1988, Md. Hosp. Coun., 1966-67; bd. dirs. Ky. Hosp. Assn., 1961-62, chmn. coun. profl. practice, 1960-61; past pres. Blue Grass Hosp. Coun.; trustee Assn. Western Hosps., 1974-81, pres., 1979-80; mem. accreditation Coun. for Continuing Med. Edn., 1982-87, chair, 1986; bd. govs. Piima C.C., 1970-76, sec., 1973-74, chmn., 1975-76, bd. dirs. Found., 1978-82, Ariz. Bd. Regents, 1982-90, sec., 1983-86, pres., 1987-88; mem. Tucson Airport Authority, 1987-95, bd. dirs., 1990-95, pres., 1995; v.p. Tucson Econ. Devel. Corp., 1977-82; bd. dirs. Vol. Hosps. Am., 1977-88, treas., 1979-82; mem. Ariz. Adv. Health Coun. Dirs., 1976-78; bd. dirs. Tucson Tomorrow, 1983-87, Tucons Downtown Devel. Corp., 1988-95, Rincon Inst., 1992—, Sonoran Inst., 1992—; dir. Mus. No. Ariz., 1988—; nat. bd. advisors Coll. Bus. U. Ariz., 1992—, chmn. Dean's Bd. Fine Arts, 1992-96, pres. Ariz. Coun. Econ. Edn., 1993-95; vis. panel Sch. Health Adminstrn. and Policy Ariz. State U., 1990-92; bd. dirs. Tuscon Cmty. Found., 1996—. Named to Hon. Order Ky. Cols.; named Tucson Man of Yr. 1987; recipient Disting. Svc. award Anti-Defamation League B'nai B'rith, 1989. Mem. Am. Hosp. Assn. (nominating com. 1983-86, trustee 1975-78, ho. dels. 1972-78, chmn. coun. profl. svc. 1973-74, regional adv. bd. 1969-78, chmn. joint com. with NASW 1963-64, Disting. Svc. award 1989), Ariz. Hosp. Assn. (Salisbury award 1982, bd. dirs. 1967-72, pres. 1970-71), Ariz. C. of C. (bd. dirs. 1988-93), Assn. Am. Med. Colls. (mem. assembly 1974-77), Tucson C. of C. (bd. dirs. 1968-69), United Comml. Travelers, Nat. League for Nursing, Ariz. Town Hall (bd. dirs. 1982-92, chmn. 1990-92, treas. 1985), Pima County Acad. Decathlon Assn. (dir. 1983-85), The Rotary Ctr. of Tucson (pres. 1993-94). Baptist (ch. moderator, chmn. finance com., deacon, ch. sch. supt., trustee, bd. dirs. ch. found.). Home: 6734 N Chapultepec Circle Tucson AZ 85750 Office: Tucson Med Ctr 2195 E River Rd Ste 202 Tucson AZ 85718-6586 *It seems important to put something back into life - for all we take from it.*

SHROPSHIRE, WALTER, JR., biophysicist emeritus, pastor; b. Washington, Sept. 4, 1932; s. Walter and Mary Virginia (Anderson) S.; m. Audrey Marie McConkey, June 28, 1958; children—Janet Marie, Susan Lynn, Edward Allen. BS in Physics, George Washington U., 1954, MS in Botany, 1956, PhD in Plant Physiology, 1958; MDiv summa cum laude, Wesley Theol. Sem., 1990; postdoctoral fellow biophysics, Calif. Inst. Tech., 1957-59. Ordained to ministry United Meth. Ch., 1977. Physicist Smithsonian Instn., Washington, 1959-63; asst. dir. Smithsonian Environ. Rsch. Ctr., Washington, 1963-86; Gast prof. U. Freiburg, Germany, 1968-69; biophysicist, dir. Omega Lab., Cabin John, Md., 1986—; professorial lectr. botany George Washington U., 1960-85; Gast prof. U. Zurich, Switzerland, 1985-86. Editor: Phytochrome, 1972, Joys of Research, 1981, Photomorphogenesis, Vol 16A, 16B, 1983, Photobiology, 1984-85; Contbr. articles to profl. jours. Pastor, Foundry United Meth. Ch., Washington, 1991—. Recipient Smithsonian Outstanding Performance award, 1967, Smithsonian Research award, 1968; NSF grantee, 1960-66. Fellow Explorers Club. Office: Omega Lab PO Box 189 Cabin John MD 20818-0189 *The world is an incredible place, rich with unexplored and unexplained interconnections between the biological and physical domains. I am fortunate to have been born when science has begun to unravel some of the mysteries of these interconnections and especially fortunate to have had teachers who shared their enthusiasm for learning. I also have benefited from mystical religious experiences of others and my own that enable me to work at the interface between science and religion. My belief is that the pursuit of both subjective and objective knowledge of ourselves and the universe we live in is necessary to enable humanity to develop to its fullest potential. This is an exciting pursuit I hope to continue to participate in a long time.*

SHTOFMAN, ROBERT SCOTT, lawyer; b. Phila., May 8, 1958; s. David S. and Lynne (Lamonosoff) S. BA, JD. Bar: Pa. 1985, N.J. 1987, Calif. 1988, U.S. Dist. Ct. (ctrl. dist.) Calif. 1988. Assoc. Law Office of Robert Wasserwald & Assocs., L.A., 1988-92; pvt. practice L.A., 1992—. Mem. ATLA, Calif. Trial Lawyers Assn., Consumer Attys. Assn. L.A., Million Dollar Advocates Forum. Jewish. Office: 445 S Figueroa # 2160 Los Angeles CA 90071

SHTOHRYN, DMYTRO MICHAEL, librarian, educator; b. Zvyniach, Ukraine, Nov. 9, 1923; came to U.S., 1950; s. Mykhailo and Kateryna (Figol) S.; m. Eustachia Barwinska, Sept. 3, 1955; children: Bohdar O., Liudoslava V. Student, Ukrainian Free U., Munich, 1947-48, U. Minn., 1954; M.A. in Slavic Studies, U. Ottawa, Can., 1958, B.L.S., 1959, Ph.D. in Slavic Studies, 1970. Slavic cataloger U. Ottawa, 1959; cataloger NRC Can., Ottawa, 1959-60; Slavic cataloger, instr. library adminstrn. U. Ill., Urbana, 1960-64, head Slavic cataloging, asst. prof. library adminstrn., 1964-68, head Slavic cataloging, assoc. prof., 1968-75, head Slavic cataloging, prof., 1975-85, assoc. Slavic librarian, prof., 1985-95, prof. Ukrainian lit., 1991—; lectr. Ukrainian lit. U. Ill., 1975-91; vis. prof. Ukrainian lit. U. Ottawa, 1974; assoc. prof. Ukrainian lit. Ukrainian Cath. U., Rome, 1978—; prof. Ukrainian lit. Ukrainian Free U., Munich, 1983—, Ukrainian lang. and lit., U. Ill., 1991—; chmn. Ukrainian Research Program U. Ill., 1984—. Editor: Catalog of Publications of Ukrainian Academy of Sciences, 1966, Ukrainians in North America: A Bibliographical Directory, 1975; author: Ukrainian Literature in the U.S.A.: Trends, Influences, Achievements, 1975, The Rise and Fall of Book Studies in Ukraine, 1986, Oleh Kandyba-Olzhych: Bibliography, 1992; editor: Bull. Ukrainian Libr. Assn. Am., 1982-88; mem. editl. bd. Ukrainian Historian, 1985—, Ethnic Forum, 1985-95, Crossroads, 1986—, Ukrainian Quar., 1993—. Counselor Boy Scouts Am., Champaign, Ill., 1967-85; bd. dirs. Ukrainian-Am. Found., Chgo., 1978-87. Recipient Grant Future Credit Union Toronto, 1956; recipient Grant U. Ill., 1977, 82, Silver medal Parliament of Can. Librarian, Ottawa, 1959, award Glorier Soc. Can., 1959. Fellow Shevchenko Sci. Soc. (exec. com.); mem. ALA (chmn. Slavic and East European sect. 1968-69), Ukrainian Libr. Assn. Am. (pres. 1970-74, 82-87), Ukrainian Acad. and Profl. Assn. (charter, sec. 1985-89, pres. 1989—), I. Franko Internat. Soc. (founding mem., pres. 1978-79, 81-82), Ukrainian-Am. Assn. Univ. Profs. (exec. com. 1981-96), Ukrainian Hist. Assn. (exec. com. 1983—), Ukrainian Acad. Arts and Scis. in U.S. (exec. com. 1993—), Ukrainian Congress Com. of Am. Scholarly Coun., Ukrainian Writers' Assn. Slovo. Ukrainian Catholic. Home: 403 Park Lane Dr Champaign IL 61820-7729 Office: Dept Slavic Langs & Lits 3092 Fgn Langs Bldg 707 S Mathews Ave Urbana IL 61801-3625

SHU, CHI-WANG, mathematics educator, researcher; b. Beijing, People's Republic of China, Jan. 2, 1957; came to U.S., 1982, naturalized, 1993.; s. Kuang-Yao and Ding-Zhen (Shi) S.; m. Din-Sui Loh, May 1, 1984; 1 child, Hai-Shuo. BS, U. Sci. and Tech. of China, 1982; PhD, UCLA, 1986. Rsch. assoc. U. Minn., Mpls., 1986-87; asst. prof. applied math. Brown U., Providence, 1987-91, assoc. prof., 1992-96; prof., 1996—; cons. ICASE, NASA Langley Rsch. Ctr., Hampton, Va., 1988—. Mem. editorial bd. Mathematics of Computation, SIAM Jour. Numerical Analysis, Jour. Computational Math., 1993—; contbr. articles to profl. jours. Grantee NSF, NASA, Army Rsch. Office; recipient NASA Pub. Svc. Group Achievement award for pioneer work in computational fluid dynamics, 1992, First Feng Kang prize of Sci. Computing Chinese Acad. Sci., 1995. Mem. Am. Math. Soc., Soc. for Indsl. and Applied Math. Achievements include research in numerical solutions for discontinuous problems. Home: 135 Woodbury St Providence RI 02906-3511 Office: Brown U Div Applied Maths 182 George St Providence RI 02912-9056

SHUART, JAMES MARTIN, academic administrator; b. College Point, N.Y., May 9, 1931; s. John and Barbara (Schmidt) S.; m. Marjorie Strunk, Apr. 5, 1953; children: James Raymond, William Arthur. BA, Hofstra U., 1953, MA, 1962; PhD, NYU, 1966. Group rep. Home Life Ins. Co., 1955-57; N.Y. Life Ins. Co., 1957-59; adminstr. Hofstra U., Hempstead, N.Y., 1959-70, asst. dir. admissions, asst. dean faculty, asst. pres., exec. dean student services, assoc. dean liberal arts scis., trustee, 1973-75; v.p. adminstrv. services Hofstra U., 1975-76, pres., 1976—; mem. higher edn. adv. com. N.Y. State Senate, 1979—; trustee Commn. on Ind. Colls. and Univs., N.Y. State, 1982-89, 92—, chmn., 1988-89; mem. Am. Coun. on Edn.'s Labor/Higher Edn. Coun., 1983-88, Am. Coun. on Edns. Commn. on Leadership Devel., 1987—, Peat Marwick Higher Edn. Pres.'s Adv. Com., 1988—; bd. dirs. Smith Barney World Funds, European Am. Bank; chair Nassau County Property Tax Relief Commn., 1990—; co-chair N.Y. State Temporary Commn. for L.I. Tax Relief. Trustee Molloy Coll., 1973-77; mem. adv. bd. Adelphi U. Sch. Social Work, 1973-84; dep. county exec. Nassau County, 1973-75, commr. social svcs., 1971-73, commr. L.I. Reg. Planning Bd., 1978-83, chmn., 1981-83; bd. dirs L.I. Assn., 1986-90; trustee Uniondale (N.Y.) Pub. Libr., 1967-78, L.I. Hosp. Planning Coun., 1971-75; pres., bd. dirs. Health Welfare Coun. Nassau County, 1971-80; chmn. Nassau Bd. Social Svcs., 1971-73; bd. dirs. Winthrop U. Hosp., 1979-86; mem. Nassau County Charter Revision Commn., 1993-94. Decorated officer Order of Orange Nassau (The Netherlands); recipient Founders Day award NYU, 1967, Alumnus of Yr. award Hofstra U., 1973, George M. estabrook Disting. svc. award Alumni Assn., 1974, Leadership in Govt. award C.W. Post coll., L.I. U., 1978, Man of Yr. award Hempstead C. of C., 1978, L.I. Pers. and Guidance Assn., award, 1977, Lincoln Day award Syosset-Woodbury Rep. Club, 1981, L.I. Bus. disting. Leadership award 1982, Joseph Giacalone award 1986, Medal of Honor L.I.A., 1988, L.I. Achievement award Pub. Rels. Profls. of L.I., 1995, Award L.I. Bus. Devel. Coun., 1994; others; named to L.I. Hall of Fame, 1985. Home: 25 Cathedral Ave Garden City NY 11530-4412 Office: Hofstra U Office of Pres Hempstead NY 11550

SHUBART, DOROTHY LOUISE TEPFER, artist, educator; b. Ft. Collins, Colo., Mar. 1, 1923; d. Adam Christian and Rose Virginia (Ayers) Tepfer; m. Robert Franz Shubart, Apr. 22, 1950; children: Richard, Lorenne. Grad., Cleve. Inst. Art, 1944-46; AA, Colo. Women's Coll., 1944; grad., Cleve. Inst. Art, 1946; student, Western Res. U., 1947-48; BA, St. Thomas Aquinas Coll., 1974; MA, Coll. New Rochelle, 1978. Art tchr. Denver Mus., 1942-44, Cleve. Recreation Dept., 1944-50; ind. artist, portrait painter, ceramist-potter Colo., Cleve., N.Y., and N.Mex., 1944—; adult edn. art tchr. Nanuet (N.Y.) Pub. Schs., 1950-65, Pearl River (N.Y.) Adult Edn., 1950-51; rec. sec. Van Houten Fields Assn., West Nyack, N.Y., 1969-74. Exhbns. include Hopper House, Rockland Ctr. for Arts, CWC, Cleve. Inst. Art, Coll. New Rochelle, Rockland County Ann. Art Fair, 1970-89. Leader 4-H Club, Nanuet, 1960-80, Girls Scouts U.S., Nanuet, 1961-68; mem. scholarship com., gen. com. PTA, Nanuet, 1964-68; rec. sec. Van Houten Fields assn., West Nyack, N.Y., 1969-74; com. mem. Eldorado (Santa Fe) Cmty. Improvement Assn.-Arterial Rd. Planning Com., 1992-94, Ams. for Dem. Action (coun. for a livable world), Environ. Def. Fund, Union of Concerned Scientists, Nat. Com. to Preserve Social Security and Medicare; capt. Neighborhood Watch; local organizer Eldorado chpt. Eldorado History Project Com.; worked for Jim Baca Gov.'s campaign, 1994; mem. Eldorado Hist. Com., 1995-96; mem. El Dorado Arterial Road Planning Com. Gund scholar Cleve. Inst. Art, 1946. Mem. AAUW, NOW, Audubon Soc., Ams. for Dem. Action, Environ. Def. Fund, Union Concerned Scientists, Nat. Com. To Preserve Social Security and Medicare, Action on Smoking and Health, Wilderness Club, Delta Tau Kappa, Phi Delta Kappa. Democrat. Avocations: books, gardening, photography, bicycling, camping. Home: 8 Hidalgo Ct Santa Fe NM 87505-8898 *Spring is eternal, life is very fragile.*

SHUBB, WILLIAM BARNET, lawyer; b. Oakland, Calif., May 28, 1938; s. Ben and Nellie Bernice (Fruechtenicht) S.; m. Sandra Ann Talarico, July 29, 1962; children: Alisa Marie, Carissa Ann, Victoria Ann. AB, U. Calif., Berkeley, 1960, JD, 1963. Bar: Calif., 1964, U.S. Ct. Internat. Trade 1981, U.S. Customs Ct. 1980, U.S. Ct. Appeals (9th cir.) 1964, U.S. Supreme Ct. 1972. Law clk. U.S. Dist. Ct., Sacramento, 1963-65; asst. U.S. atty., Sacramento, 1965-71; chief asst. U.S. atty. (ea. dist.) Calif., 1971-74; assoc. Diepenbrock, Wulff, Plant & Hannegan, Sacramento, 1974-77, ptnr., 1977-80, 81-90; U.S. atty. Eastern Dist. Calif., 1980-81; judge U.S. Dist. Ct. (ea. dist.) Calif., 1990—; chmn. com. drafting of local criminal rules U.S. Dist. Ct. (ea. dist.) Calif., 1974, mem. speedy trial planning com., 1974-80; lawyer rep. 9th Cir. U.S. Jud. Conf., 1975-78; mem. faculty Fed. Practice Inst., 1978-80; instr. McGeorge Sch. Law, U. Pacific, 1964-66. Mem. ABA, Fed. Bar Assn. (pres. Sacramento chpt. 1977), Calif. Bar Assn., Assn. Def. Counsel, Am. Bd. Trial Advs., Sacramento County Bar Council. Office: US Courthouse 650 Capitol Mall Sacramento CA 95814-4708*

SHUBERT, GABRIELLE S., museum executive director; b. Phila., Apr. 28, 1955; d. Albert H. and Florence (Reiff) S. B in Music, Oberlin Coll., 1977; M in Public Adminstrn., N.Y.U., 1989. Asst. to v.p./dir. of sales Columbia Artist Mgmt., N.Y.C., 1979-80; artist rep. Herbert Barrett Mgmt., N.Y.C., 1980-81; dir. sales Sheldon Soffer Mgmt., N.Y.C., 1981-87; dir. work study program The Parks Coun., N.Y.C., 1987-88; mgr. arts for transit Met. Transp. Authority, N.Y.C., 1988-91; exec. dir. N.Y. Transit Mus., N.Y.C., 1991—; guest lectr. N.Y.U., 1995, Yale U., New Haven, Conn., 1987; pub. art selection panel Dept. of Cultural Affairs, N.Y.C., 1992. Chmn. Concerned Citizens Upper Broadway, N.Y.C., 1983-85. Fellow Mus. Mgmt. Inst. Getty Mus., Berkeley, Calif., 1995, Mayor's Leadership Inst., N.Y.C., 1995. Fellow Mcpl. Art Soc. Office: NY Transit Museum 130 Livingston St Rm 9001 Brooklyn NY 11201-5106

SHUBERT, GUSTAVE HARRY, research executive, consultant, social scientist; b. Buffalo, Jan. 18, 1929; s. Gustave Henri and Ada Shubert (Smith) S.; m. Rhea Brickman, Mar. 29, 1952; children—Wendy J., David L. B.A., Yale U., 1948; M.A., NYU, 1951. Staff mem. Lincoln Lab., MIT, 1955-57; adminstr. systems engring. Hycon Eastern, Inc., Paris, 1957-59; with RAND Corp., Santa Monica, Calif., 1959—, corp. v.p. domestic programs, 1968-75, sr. corp. v.p. domestic programs, 1975-78, sr. corp. v.p., 1978-89, trustee, 1973-89, sr. fellow, corp. advisor and adv. trustee, 1989—; founding dir. Inst. Civil Justice, 1979-87; dir. equities trust Neuberger & Berman, N.Y.C., 1989—; cons. Keene Corp., N.Y.C., 1990-92; pres. N.Y.C. Rand Inst., 1972-73, trustee, 1972-79; trustee Housing Allowance Offices Brown County, Wis. and South Bend, Ind., 1973-80; mem. adv. coun. Sch. Engring., Stanford U., 1976-79; mem. policy adv. com. clin. scholars program UCLA, 1975, 88; mem. adv. group evaluation and methodology divsn. GAO, 1986—; mem. adv. commn. on professionalism ABA, 1985-87; mem. Calif. jud. system com. Los Angeles County Bar Assn., 1984-85; mem. com. on evaluation of poverty rsch. NAS. Mem. history dept. adv. bd. Carnegie Mellon U., 1995—. With USAF, 1951-55. Decorated Air medal with 3 oak leaf clusters, Commendation medal. Mem. AAAS, Am. Judicature Soc. (bd. dirs. 1987-90), Inst. Strategic Studies (London) World Affairs Coun. (L.A. chpt.), Coun. of Fgn. Rels., Commonwealth Club of San Francisco, Town Hall Club Calif., Jonathan Club, Yale Club. Home: 13838 W Sunset Blvd Pacific Palisades CA 90272-4022 Office: RAND Corp 1700 Main St Santa Monica CA 90401-3208

SHUBERT, JOSEPH FRANCIS, librarian; b. Buffalo, Sept. 17, 1928; s. Joseph Francis and Lena M. (Kohn) S.; m. Dorothy Jean Whearty, Feb. 5, 1955 (div. Feb. 1980); children: Julia Ellen, Alan Joseph. BS, State U. Tchrs. Coll., Geneseo, N.Y., 1951; MA, U. Denver, 1957. Reference and extension librarian Nev. State Library, Carson City, 1951-57; library cons. Nev. State Library, 1957-59, state librarian, 1959-61; asst. dir. internat. relations office ALA, 1962-66; state librarian Ohio, 1966-77; state librarian, asst. commr. libraries N.Y. State Edn. Dept., 1977—, sec., treas. chief officer state Library Agys., 1973-76, chmn., 1976-78; mem. adv. council to U.S. Pub. Printer, 1974-77; adv. com. White House Conf. Library and Info. Services, 1977-79; bd. dirs. Capital Dist. Regional Info. Svc. Network, State U. Albany; trustee Ohio Coll. Library Center, 1976-78; mem. adv. com. Center for the Book, Library of Congress, 1979-82, mem. network adv. coun., 1981—; Disting. Alumnus lectr. U. Denver, 1979; mem. adv. coun. Sch. Library and Info. Sci., Pratt Inst., 1980—; bd. dirs. N.E. Document Conservation Center, 1980-82, treas. 1986-89, mem. 1989—; chmn. chief officers State Libraries in the NE, 1987-89; mem. design task force White House Conf. on Library and Info. Svcs., 1985. Editor: The Bookmark, 1987—; contbr. to numerous periodicals. Mem. adv. com. U. Wis. Inst. on Edn., Federally Funded Literacy Program, 1992-94. Recipient Hall of Fame award Ohio Libr. Assn., 1991, Exceptional Achievement award ALA Assn. Specialized and Coop. Library Agy. Assn., 1985, Disting. Pub. Service award SUNY-Albany, Nelson A. Rockefeller Coll. of Pub. Affairs and Policy, 1987; named Disting. Alumnus, SUNY-Geneseo, 1985. Mem. ALA (grass roots advocate 1996), Nat. Ctr. for Ednl. Stats., Nat. Commn. on Librs. and Info. Svcs., Task Force on Pub. Libr. Stats. (adv. com. 1990—), Assn. of Specialized and Coop. Lit. Agys. (pres. 1988-89), Nev. Libr. Assn. (pres.), North Collins Libr. Assn. (N.Y.), Meml. Libr. Assn., N.Y. Libr. Assn., Chief Officers State Libr. Agys. (chmn. 1977-78), Nev. Congress Parents and Tchrs., Kappa Delta Pi. Roman Catholic. Home: 494 Madison Ave Albany NY 12208-3601 Office: NY State Libr State Edn Dept 33 Cultural Edn Ctr # 10A Albany NY 12230

SHUBIK, MARTIN, economics educator; b. N.Y.C., Mar. 24, 1926; s. Joseph Louis and Sara S.; m. Julia Kahn, Aug. 11, 1970; 1 child, Claire Louise. B.A., U. Toronto, 1947, M.A., 1949; Ph.D., Princeton U., 1953. Research asst. Princeton U., 1950-53, research asso., 1953-55; fellow Center for Advanced Study in Behavioral Scis., Palo Alto, Calif., 1955-56; cons. mgmt. consultation services Gen. Electric Co., 1956-60; adj. research prof. Pa. State U., 1957-59; vis. prof. econs. Yale U., New Haven, 1960-61; prof. econs. of orgn., dept. adminstrv. sci. Yale U., 1963-75, Seymour H. Knox prof. math. instl. econs., 1975—; bd. dirs. Equity Strategies, Third Ave. Fund; mem. staff T.J. Watson Rsch. Labs., IBM Corp., 1961-63; vis. prof. Escuela de Estudios Económicos U. Chile, Santiago, 1965, Inst. Advanced Studies, Vienna, Austria, 1968, 70, U. Melbourne, Australia, 1973; cons. Rand Corp., Santa Monica, Calif., 1963; dir. Cowles Found. for Rsch. In Econs., Yale U., 1973-76; mem. econs. bd. Santa Fe Inst., 1991—; cons. in field. Author or co-author: numerous books in field including The War Game, 1979, (with G. Brewer) The Aggressive Conservative Investor, 1979, (with M.J. Whitman) Market Structure and Behavior, 1980, (with R.E. Levitan) Game Theory in the Social Sciences, vol. 1, 1982, vol. 2, 1984; mem. editorial bd. Conflict Resolution; mem. editorial adv. bd. Internat. Studies Series; assoc. editor Mgmt. Sci, 1965-81; contbr. articles to profl. jours. Served to lt. Royal Can. Navy. Recipient Lanchester prize, 1983; named hon. prof. U. Vienna. Fellow Econometric Soc., World Acad. Arts and Scis.; mem. Social Systems Inc. (chmn. bd. dirs. 1978), Am. Acad. Arts and Scis., Conn. Acad. Arts and Scis. Home: 140 Edgehill Rd New Haven CT 06517-4011 Office: 30 Hillhouse Ave New Haven CT 06511-3704

SHUCART, WILLIAM ARTHUR, neurosurgeon; b. St. Louis, Oct. 23, 1935; s. Frank M. and Beatrice S.; m. Laura Huber, Dec. 16, 1971. AB, Washington U., 1957; MD, U. Mo., 1961. Diplomate Am. Bd. Neurol. Surgery. Intern U. Utah Hosp., Salt Lake City, 1961-62; resident in surgery Peter Bent Brigham Hosp., Boston, 1963-64; resident in neurosurgery Columbia-Presbyn. Hosp., N.Y.C., 1967-70, Hosp. for Sick Children, Toronto, Ont., Can., 1976-71; mem. faculty dept. neurosurgery Med. Sch. Tufts U., Boston, 1971-76, assoc. prof., 1976; prof., chmn. dept. neurosurgery SUNY, Downstate Med. Ctr., Bklyn., 1976-81; neurosurgeon Tufts-New England Med. Ctr., Boston, 1972-76, prof., chmn. dept. neurosurgery, 1981—. With U.S. Army, 1964-67. Mem. ACS, Am. Assn. Neurol. Surgeons, Soc. Neurol. Surgeons. Home: 100 Meadowbrook Rd Weston MA 02193-2406 Office: New England Med Ctr PO Box 178 750 Washington St Boston MA 02111

SHUCHAT, ALAN HOWARD, mathematician, educator; b. Bklyn., Oct. 6, 1942; s. Morris M. and Molly (Kuris) S.; S.B., M.I.T., 1963; M.S., U. Mich., 1965, Ph.D., 1969; m. Alix E. Ginsburg; children: Mark, Vera. Assoc. prof. math Wellesley (Mass.) Coll., 1974-83, prof., 1983—, chmn. dept., 1981-83; asst. prof. U. Toledo, 1968-71, Mt. Holyoke Coll., South Hadley, Mass., 1971-74, assoc. dean Wellesley Coll., 1989-92. Author: (with Fred Shultz Addison- Wesley) The Joy of Mathematica, 1994. U.S. Dept. Transp. faculty fellow, 1981; NSF grantee, 1979-80, 89. Mem. Am. Math. Soc., Math. Assn. Am., Ops. Research Soc. Am. Jewish. Research in functional analysis and operations research; curriculum devel. Office: Wellesley Coll Dept Math 106 Central St Wellesley MA 02181-8209

SHUCK, ANNETTE ULSH, education educator; b. Harrisburg, Pa., Apr. 4, 1946; d. David Addison and Florence (Scholl) Ulsh; children: Ryan David Summers, Kirsten Annette Shuck. BS, Bloomsburg U., 1967; MS, W.Va. U., 1968, EdD, 1976; sch. psychology cert., Coll. Grad. Studies, 1983. Cert. elem., secondary, spl. edn. tchr., Pa., W.Va., sch. psychologist, W.Va. Elem. tchr. Pa. and W.Va. schs., 1968-70; instr. W.Va. U., Morgantown, 1972, grad. asst., 1972-75, instr. spl. edn. dept., 1976-77, asst. prof., 1977-83, assoc. prof., 1983-87; vis. assoc. prof. div. edn. U. V.I., Charlotte Amalie, St. Thomas, 1987-88, assoc. prof., 1988, prof. div. edn., 1989—; part-time instr. Lebanon Valley Coll. and Temple U., Harrisburg, Pa., 1970-72; cons. sch. psychology program Coll. Grad. Studies, Institute, W.Va., 1986; mem. Gov. of V.I. Spl. Edn. Task Force, 1988—. Author: International Parent Interventionist Booklet, 1976, 1988; contbr. chpt. to book and articles to profl. jours. Mem. com. St. Thomas Hist. Soc., 1988—, Environ. Awareness and Action Com., St. Thomas, 1991—; hearing officer State Dept. Spl. Edn.; parent edn. interventionist, 1979—. NDEA fellow, 1967-68. Mem. Coun. for Exceptional Children, Am. Assn. Coll. Tchr. Edn., Phi Delta Kappa (v.p. 1975-76, pres. 1976-77). Avocations: research, writing, snorkeling, sailing, dancing. Office: U VI Tchr-Edn-208 Saint Thomas VI 00802

SHUCK, JERRY MARK, surgeon, educator; b. Bucyrus, Ohio, Apr. 23, 1934; s. James Edwin and Pearl (Mark) S.; m. Linda Wayne, May 28, 1974; children: Jay Steven, Gail Ellen, Kimberly Ann, Lynn Meredith, Steven James. BS in Pharmacy, U. Cin., 1955, MD, 1959, DSc, 1966. Intern Colo. Gen. Hosp., Denver, 1959-60; resident in surgery U. Cin. Integrated Program, 1960-66; mem. faculty dept. surgery U. N.Mex., Albuquerque, 1968-80; prof. U. N.Mex., 1974-80; founder burn and trauma unit; Oliver H. Payne prof. dept. surgery, chmn. dept. Case-Western Res. U., Cleve., 1980—; interim v.p. for med. affairs, 1993-95; dir. surgery Univ. Hosps. Cleve., 1980—; cons. FDA, 1972-77. Contbr. articles to profl. jours. Served to capt. U.S. Army, 1966-68. Mem. ACS, Am. Surg. Assn., Am. Bd. Surgery (bd. dirs., chmn. 1993-94), Soc. Univ. Surgeons, Am. Assn. Surgery Trauma, Am. Trauma Soc. (founding mem.), Univ. Assn. Emergency Medicine (founding mem.), Am. Burn Assn. (founding mem.), We. Surg. Assn., Cen. Surg. Assn. (pres. 1996—), Assn. Acad. Surgery, S.W. Surg. Assn., Cleve. Surg. Soc., Ohio Med. Assn., Acad. Medicine Cleve., Halsted Soc., Surg. Infection Soc. (founding mem.), B'nai Brith, Jewish Comty. Ctr. Club, The Temple Club. Democrat. Jewish. Office: Case Western Reserve U Dept Surgery 2074 Abington Rd Cleveland OH 44106-2602

SHUCK, LOLA MAE, retired secondary school educator; b. Eustis, Nebr., Mar. 22, 1929; d. Gust Adolf and Dora (Timm) Hueftle; m. Kenneth L. Shuck, Dec. 22, 1951 (div. Oct. 1969); children: David Lynn, Terri Kay, Lorie Jane Shuck Larson. BA, Nebr. Wesleyan U., 1951; MA, Ariz. State U., 1969. Elem. tchr. Springfield (Colo.) Pub. Sch., 1948-49; tchr. art David City (Nebr.) Pub. Schs., 1951-52, Alhambra Dist. 68 Pub. Schs., Phoenix, 1964-68, 69-92; ret., 1992. Vice pres. Women's Soc. Christian Svc., 1959-63; committeewoman Phoenix Rep. Com., 1976-77. Named Ms. Personality, Ms. Nebr. Contest, 1949. Mem. Alpha Delta Kappa (pres. Xi chpt. 1981-82, chmn. bylaws 1991-93). Democrat. Methodist. Avocations: china painting, acrylic, watercolor and oil painting. Home: 4766 W Palmaire Ave Glendale AZ 85301-2742

SHUCK, ROBERT F., financial executive; s. Robert F. II and Gertrude (Lehr) S.; m. Page Downe, May 30, 1969; children: Robert F. IV, Hollister A. BA in Acctg. with honors, S.E. Mo. Coll., 1959; MBA, Northwestern U., 1961. CPA, Ill.; cert. fin. planner. With Raymond James Fin., Inc., St. Petersburg, Fla., 1969—, vice chmn., 1991—; bd. dirs. RJ Comm., Inc. Trustee All Children's Hosp.; mem. long range devel. com. Fla. Coun. Econ. Edn.; mem. policy bd. Tampa Bay Partnership for Regional Econ. Devel.; mem. devel. found. St. Petersburg Jr. Coll.; stewardship chmn. Our Savior Luth. Ch., St. Petersburg. Mem. Securities Industry Assn. (sales and mktg. com.), Internat. Assn. for Fin. Planning (past bd. dirs.), Nat. Endowment for Fin. Edn. (trustee, mem. exec. com.). Office: Raymond James Fin 880 Carillon Pky Saint Petersburg FL 33716-1102

SHUE, ELISABETH, actress; b. Wilmington, Del., Oct. 6, 1963; m. Davis Guggenheim. Grad., Wellesley Coll., Harvard U.; studied with Sylvie Leigh. Appeared in Broadway plays including Some Americans Abroad, Birth and After Birth; appeared in films including The Karate Kid, 1984, Link, 1986, Adventures in Babysitting, 1987, Cocktail, 1988, Body Wars, 1989, Back to the Future Part II, 1989, Back to the Future Part III, 1990, Soapdish, 1991, The Marrying Man, 1991, Twenty Bucks, 1993, Heart and Souls, 1993, Radio Inside, 1994, Blind Justice, 1994, The Underneath, 1995, Leaving Las Vegas, 1995 (Oscar nominee for Best Actress), The Trigger Effect, 1996, The Saint, 1996; appeared in TV movies including Call to Glory, 1984, Double Switch, 1987; appeared in TV series Call to Glory, 1984. Office: Creative Arts Agy 9830 Wilkshire Blvd Beverly Hills CA 90212*

SHUER, LAWRENCE MENDEL, neurosurgery educator; b. Toledo, Apr. 12, 1954; s. Bernard Benjamin and Estelle Rose (Drukker) S.; m. Paula Ann Elliott, Sept. 4, 1976; children: Jenna, Tammy, Nichole. BA with high distinction, U. Mich., 1975, MD cum laude, 1978. Diplomate Am. Bd. Neurol. Surgery, Nat. Bd. Med. Examiners. Fellow in neurology Inst. Neurology, London, 1979; intern in surgery Stanford (Calif.) U. Sch. Medicine, 1978-79, resident in neuropathology, 1980, resident in neurosurgery, 1980-84, clin. asst. prof. surgery and neurosurgery, 1984-90, assoc. prof., 1990—, acting chmn. dept. neurosurgery, 1992-95; numerous presentations in field. Contbr. articles and abstracts to med. jours., chpts. to books. Recipient Kaiser tchr. award Stanford U., 1993; James B. Angell scholar. Mem. AMA, Am. Assn. Neurol. Surgeons, Congress Neurol. Surgeons, Western Neurosurg. Soc., Calif. Assn. Neurol. Surgeons (bd. dirs., treas. 1995—), Calif. Med. Assn., Am. Heart Assn. (fellow stroke coun.), Santa Clara County Med. Assn., San Francisco Neurol. Soc., Alpha Omega Alpha. Avocations: skiing, swimming, travel. Office: R155 Stanford U Med Ctr 300 Pasteur Dr Palo Alto CA 94304-2203

SHUEY, JOHN HENRY, diversified products company executive; b. Monroe, Mich., Mar. 14, 1946; s. John Henry and Bertha (Thomas) S.; children: Katherine, John Henry, John Joseph Satory. B.S. in Indsl. Engring., U. Mich., 1968, M.B.A., 1970. With Tex. Instruments Co., Dallas, 1970-74; asst. treas. The Trane Co., La Crosse, Wis., 1974-78, treas., 1978-81, v.p., treas., 1981-83, v.p. fin., chief fin. officer, 1983-86; also v.p., group exec. Am. Standard; sr. v.p. and chief fin. officer AM Internat. Inc., Chgo., 1986-91; exec. v.p. Amcast Indsl. Corp., Dayton, Ohio, 1991-93, pres., COO, 1993-95, pres., CEO, 1995—, also bd. dirs.; dir., chmn. audit com. State Bank of La Crosse, 1981-87. Bd. dirs. Pub. Expenditure Survey of Wis., La Crosse, 1980-83; bd. dirs., pres. Luth. Hosp. Found., 1983-87. Mem. Fin. Execs. Inst., Machinery and Allied Products Inst. Congregationalist. Office: Amcast Indsl Corp PO Box 98 Dayton OH 45401-0098 Also: Elkhart Products Corp 1255 Oak St Elkhart IN 46514-2277

SHUFORD, HARLEY FERGUSON, JR., furniture manufacturing executive; b. Norfolk, Va., Oct. 7, 1937; s. Harley Ferguson Sr. and Nancy (Pope) S.; m. Helgi Kuuskraa; children: Linda, David. BA, U. N.C., 1959. Engr. Century Furniture Co., Hickory, N.C., 1959-60, mgr. data processing, 1960-63, v.p. mfg., 1964-67, pres., 1967-95; chmn. Shuford Industries, Inc., Hickory, 1994—; bd. dirs. 1st Union Bank N.C., Charlotte. Trustee Catawba Meml. Hosp., Hickory, 1971-77, chmn., 1977-81; bd. dirs. U. N.C. Sys., Chapel Hill, 1975-83; bd. dirs. N.C. Citizens Bus. and Industry, Raleigh, 1982-95; chmn. N.C. Arts Coun., Raleigh, 1985-93. Mem. Am. Furniture Mfrs. Assn. (bd. dirs. 1968-92, pres., chmn. 1980-82), Catawba County C. of C. (pres. 1976), Phi Beta Kappa. Republican. Mem. United Ch. of Christ. Office: Shuford Industries PO Box 608 Hickory NC 28603-0608

SHUGART, ALAN F., electronic computing equipment company executive; b. L.A., Sept. 27, 1930. BS in Engring. and Physics, U. Redlands, 1951. Dir. engring. IBM, San Jose, Calif., 1952-69; v.p. Memorex Corp., Sunnyvale, Calif., 1969-73; pres. Shugart Assocs., 1973-78; chmn., pres., chief exec. officer Seagate Tech., Scotts Valley, Calif., 1978—, also bd. dirs., also pres., COO. Office: Seagate Tech 920 Disc Dr Scotts Valley CA 95066-4544*

SHUGART, CECIL GLENN, physics educator; b. Ennis, Tex., Oct. 13, 1930; s. Clifford Clarence and Ethel Hazel (Venable) S.; m. Theresa Lively, Aug. 26, 1955 (div. July 1981); children: David Neal, Peter Gregory; m. Anita Brumbelow, Dec. 14, 1985. Student, Navarro Coll., Corsicana, Tex., 1954-55; B.A., N. Tex. State U., 1957; M.A., U. Tex.-Austin, 1961, Ph.D., 1968. Research scientist Def. Research Lab., Austin, 1958-61; assoc. engr. IBM, San Jose, Calif., 1961-62; asst. prof., head dept. physics Hardin-Simmons U., Abilene, Tex., 1962-65; dir. Soc. Physics Students Am. Inst., N.Y.C., 1968-70; research assoc. U. Tex.-Austin, 1967-68; prof. physics, chmn. Northeast La. U., Monroe, 1970-77; prof. chmn. physics U. Memphis, 1977—; cons. Tech. Legal Assocs., Memphis, 1978—. Author: (with Bedell and Genusa) Experiments for General Physics, 1975; co-author: (with Johnston) The Phenomena of Physics, 1982, Phenomenal Physics and Astronomy, 1991; editor: (with P. Barker) After Einstein, 1981, (with J. Payne) Scientists and Public Policy, 1982. Served with USAF, 1948-52. NSF fellow, 1966-67; NSF grantee, 1974-75, 79-80. Fellow AAAS; mem. Am. Assn. Physics Tchrs., Am. Phys. Soc. (vice chmn. southeastern sect. 1982-83, sect. chmn. 1983-84, sect. sec., 1991-95, sec. ea. region 1991-95), Sigma Pi Sigma (pres. 1972-76). Republican. Methodist. Home: 3628 Beechollow Dr Memphis TN 38128-4272 Office: U Memphis Dept Physics Memphis TN 38152

SHUGART, HOWARD ALAN, physicist, educator; b. Orange, Calif., Sept. 21, 1931; s. Howard Ancil and Bertha Elizabeth (Henderson) S.; m. Elizabeth L. Hanson, Feb. 6, 1971. B.S., Calif. Inst. Tech., 1953; M.A., U. Calif.-Berkeley, 1955, Ph.D., 1957. Teaching asst. physics U. Calif.-Berkeley, 1953-56, assoc., 1957, lectr., 1957-58, acting asst. prof., 1958-59, asst. prof., 1959-63, assoc. prof., 1963-67, prof., 1967-93, prof. emeritus, 1993—, vice chmn., 1968-70, 79-87, 89—, acting chmn., summer 1979, 80, 81, 83, 84,87; atomic beam group leader Lawrence Berkeley Lab. Lawrence Berkeley Nat. Lab., 1965-79; cons. Convair divsn. Gen. Dynamics Corp., 1960-61; mem. com. nuclear constants NRC, 1960-63. Recipient Donald Sterling Noyce prize for excellence in undergrad. tchg. U. Calif., 1988, Berkeley citation, 1993. Fellow Am. Phys. Soc. (acting sec. Pacific Coast 1961-64, exec. com. div. electron and atomic physics 1972-74), Nat. Speleological Soc. (gov. 1954-56); mem. Sigma Xi. Office: U Calif Dept Physics Berkeley CA 94720-7300

SHUGART, JILL, school system administrator; b. Dallas, July 15, 1940; d. Claude Ernest and Allie Merle (Hamilton) S. BA, Baylor U., 1962; MA, Tex. Woman's U., 1972, PhD, 1980. Middle sch. English tchr. Garland (Tex.) Ind. Sch. Dist., 1962-63, high sch. social studies tchr., 1963-76, high sch. asst. prin., 1976-79, dir. communications, 1979-82, asst. supt., 1982-85, supt., 1985—; mem. legis. coun. U. Interscholastic League, Tex., 1989—; chmn. Dist. III music com., Tex., 1989-98; adj. prof. Tex. Women's U., Denton, 1983; chmn. Region X ESC Adv. Coun., rep. to commr.'s supt.'s com., 1993-95. Gen. chmn. Boy Scouts Am. Scouting Night, Dallas, 1988-89; chmn. City of Garland Comty. Rels. Coun., 1992; sec. Tex. Sch. Alliance, 1992-96; life mem. Tex. PTA; pres. Garland br. Am. Heart Assn., 1990-91; co-chmn. sustaining dr. Garland YMCA, 1995-96. Recipient Lamar award for excellence Masons, Award of Distinction, Tex. Ret. Tchrs. Assn.; named Top 100 Educators to Watch, Executive Educator mag., 1985, Finalist as Outstanding Tex. Sch. Supt., 1990, Woman of Distinction, Soroptomist Club; Paul Harris fellow. Mem. Am. Assn. Sch. Adminstrs. (suburban sch. com. 1990-93), Tex. Assn. Sch. Adminstrs., Tex. Assn. for Supr. Curriculum Devel., Garland Adminstr. Assn. (pres. 1978-79), Nat. Tex. PTA. Republican. Baptist. Avocations: snow skiing, tennis. Office: Garland Ind Sch Dist 720 Stadium Dr Garland TX 75040-4616

SHUGHART, DONALD LOUIS, lawyer; b. Kansas City, Mo., Aug. 12, 1926; s. Henry M. and Dora M. (O'Leary) S.; m. Mary I. Shughart, July 25, 1953; children: Susan C. Shughart Hogsett, Nancy J. Goede. AB, U. Mo., Columbia, 1949, JD, 1951. Bar: Mo. 1951, U.S. Dist. Ct. (we. dist.) Mo. 1951, U.S. Tax Ct. 1979. With Shughart, Thomson & Kilroy, P.C., Kansas City, Mo., 1951—; v.p. K.C. Mack Sales & Service Inc., R.D. Mann Carpet Co.; mem. Mo. Motor Carriers Assn. Pub. Service Com. Bd. dirs. Rockhurst Coll.; mem. adv. bd. St. Joseph Hosp. Served with AC, U.S. Army, 1944-47. Mem. Kansas City Bar Assn., Lawyers Assn. Kansas City, Mo. Bar Assn. (chmn. corp. com. 1980-81, 82-83), Kansas City Bar Assn. (chmn. bus. orgns. com. 1990-91), Internat. Assn. Ins. Counsel, Am. Judicature Soc., Mo. Orgn. Def. Lawyers (pres. 1971-72), U. Mo. Law Soc., Homestead Country Club, Brookfield Country Club, Phi Delta Phi. Republican. Roman Catholic.

SHUHLER, PHYLLIS MARIE, physician; b. Sellersville, Pa., Sept. 25, 1947; d. Raymond Harold and Catherine Cecilia (Virus) S.; m. John Howard Schwarz, Sept. 17, 1983; 1 child, Luke Alexander. BS in Chemistry, Chestnut Hill Coll., 1971; MD, Mich. State U., 1976; diploma of Tropical Medicine and Hygiene, U. London, 1980. Diplomate Am. Bd. Family Medicine. With Soc. Cath. Med. Missionaries, Phila., 1966-82; ward clk., nursing asst. Holy Family Hosp., Atlanta, 1971-72; resident in family practice Somerset Family Med. Residency Program, Somerville, N.J., 1976-79; physician East Coast Migrant Health Project, Newton Grove, N.C., 1980; physician, missionary SCMM, Diocese of Sunyani, Berekum, Ghana, West Africa, 1980-81; emergency rm. physician Northeast Emergency Med. Assn., Quakertown, Pa., 1981-82; founder, physician Family Health Care Ctr., Inc., Pennsburg, Pa., 1982-90; physician Lifequest Med. Group, Pennsburg, 1990-93; pvt. practice Pennsburg, 1993—. Fellow Royal Soc. Tropical Medicine and Hygiene; mem. Am. Acad. Family Practice, Am. Bd. Family Practice, Am. Med. Women Assn. Pa. Acad. Family Practice, Lehigh Valley Women Med. Assn. Roman Catholic. Avocations: guitar, reading, bicycling, hiking. Office: 101 W 7th St Ste 2C Pennsburg PA 18073

SHUKER, GREGORY BROWN, publishing and production company executive; b. Charleston, W.Va., Oct. 3, 1932; s. George and Florence (Brown) S.; m. Nancy Swift Frederick, June 9, 1956 (div. 1983); children: John Frederick, Allison Gregory, Frances Swift. B.S. in Journalism, Northwestern U., 1954. Corr. Life mag., 1959-60; producer Drew Assos., 1961-66, 73-78, Pub. Broadcast Lab., 1967-68; dir. programming CBS-EVR, 1969; program dir. Time-Life Video, RCA SelectaVision, 1970; exec. prod., v.p. Eden House Pub. Inc., N.Y.C., 1971—; exec. producer Playback Assos., Inc., 1972—, Communication for Edn. and Industry, 1981—; pres. GBS, Inc., media devel. group, 1991—; lectr. U. Mich. Sch. Comm., 1989-91; media devel., mgmt. cons. Am. Flywheel Sys., Inc., 1992; dir. corp. TV CEO Seminars, 1993, CD-ROM Devel. Series, 1994-95; exec. prodr. Brazil and Argentina Imax Documentary and Comms. Devel. Group, 1995—, Playback Holographic Data Storage, 1996; bd. dirs. The Loft Film and Theatre Ctr.; mng. dir. Tree-Free Print Out Devel. Group, 1995—. Producer: documentary films TV Crisis: Behind a Presidential Committment, 1963, The Chair, 1963 (Grand Prix Cannes), Faces of November, 1964 (1st prize Venice), Letters from Vietnam (ABC-TV), 1964, Free at Last, 1968 (1st prize Venice); exec. producer: documentary films TV What Do We Do Now? - The Need for Direction, 1976, Productivity Series, 1979-81, Corp. Media and HDTV Devel., 1984—; feature motion picture prodn., 1982—; producer, Aspira (AT&T), 1987, Lawrence of Arabia and Lowell Thomas, 1992, (TV series) Baltic Festival, 1994; line producer London-to-Peking, 1990; author: Learning by Television (Ford Found.), 1966. Served to lt. (j.g.) USNR, 1955-58. Mem. Deru, Sigma Delta Chi, Alpha Tau Omega, Kappa Tau Alpha. Clubs: Bronxville Field, Little Forum. Home and Office: 12 Sunset Ave Bronxville NY 10708-2215 also: care NS Bienstock Inc 1740 Broadway New York NY 10019-4315 *God grant me the serenity to accept the things I cannot change, courage to change the things I can, and wisdom to know the difference.*

SHULA, DAVID D., professional football team coach; b. Lexington, Ky., May 28, 1959; s. Donald F. and Dorothy (Bartish) S.; m. Leslie Ann Maglathlin, June 5, 1982; children: Dan, Chris, Matt. BA, Dartmouth Coll., 1981. Pro football player Balt. Colts, 1981; asst. coach Miami (Fla.) Dolphins, 1982-89, Dallas Cowboys, Irving, 1989-91; asst. coach Cin. Bengals, 1991, head coach, 1991—. Mem. NFL Alumni Assn. Republican. Roman Catholic. Office: Cincinnati Bengals 200 Riverfront Stadium Cincinnati OH 45204*

SHULA, DON FRANCIS, professional football coach; b. Grand River, OH, Jan. 4, 1930; s. Dan and Mary (Miller) S.; children: David, Donna, Sharon, Anne, Michael; m. Mary Anne Shula. B.S., John Carroll U., Cleve., 1951, H.H.D. (hon.), 1972; M.A., Case Western Res. U., 1953; Sc.D. (hon.), Biscayne Coll., 1974. Profl. football player Cleve. Browns, 1951-52, Balt. Colts, 1953-56, Washington Redskins, 1957; asst. coach U. Va., 1958, U. Ky., 1959, Detroit Lions, 1960-62; head coach Baltimore Colts, 1963-69, Miami (Fla.) Dolphins, 1970—. Author: The Winning Edge, 1972, (with Ken Blanchard) Everyone's A Coach, 1995. Fla. crusade chmn. Nat. Cancer Soc., 1975; co-chmn. Jerry Lewis March Against Dystrophy, 1975; nat. bd. dirs. Jesuit Program for Living and Learning, 1976; mem. nat. sports com. Multiple Schlerosis Soc., Muscular Dystrophy Assn.; bd. dirs. Heart Assn. Greater Miami; hon. chmn. Belen Jesuit Intercultural Fund Campaign To Build Schs.; established Don Shula Found., breast cancer rsch., 1991—; sponsor Don Shula Scholarship, 1978—. Coached 6 Superbowl teams, winning teams 1972, 73; recipient Coach of Yr. awards 1964, 66, 70, 71, 72, Coach of decade Profl. Football Hall of Fame, 1980, Pro Football's All-Time Winningest Coach, 1994, Brotherhood award Fla. region NCCJ, 1977, Light of Flames Leadership award Barry Coll., 1977, Concern award Cedars Med. Ctr., 1992, Solheim Lifetime Achievement award, 1992, Jim Thorpe award, 1993, Sportsman of Yr. Sports Illustrated, 1993, Horrigan award Pro Football Writers, 1994, Horatio Alger award, 1995; named Balt. Colts Silver Anniversary Coach, 1977. Roman Catholic. Office: Miami Dolphins 7500 SW 30th St Davie FL 33314-1020 *Success is never final; defeat is never fatal.*

SHULA, ROBERT JOSEPH, lawyer; b. South Bend, Ind., Dec. 10, 1936; s. Joseph Edward and Bertha Mona (Buckner) S.; m. Gaye Ann Martin, Oct. 8, 1978; children: Deirdre Regina, Robert Joseph II, Elizabeth Martin. BS in Mktg., Ind. U., 1958, JD, 1961. Bar: Ind. 1961; Diplomate Ind. Def. Trial Counsel. Ptnr. Bingham Summers Welsh & Spilman, Indpls., 1965-82, sr. ptnr., 1982-89; ptnr. Price & Shula, Indpls., 1989-91, Lowe Gray Steele & Hoffman, Indpls., 1991—; mem. faculty Nat. Inst. Trial Advocacy; guest lectr. Brit. Medicine and Law Soc., 1979, Ind. U. Sch. Law; medico-legal lectr. Ind. U. Schs. Medicine, Dentistry, and Nursing. Bd. dirs. Arts Ind., Indpls., pres. 1995—; pres. Oriental Arts Soc., Indpls., 1975-79, Meridian Women's Clinic, Inc., Indpls.; trustee Indpls. Mus. Art, 1975-78, life trustee, 1984—; bd. dirs. Ind. Repertory Theatre, Indpls., 1982-92, chmn. bd., pres., 1985-89; pres. Repertory Soc., 1993—; v.p., bd. dirs. Flanner House of Indpls., Inc., 1977-88, chmn., 1988—; pres. Internat. Ctr. of Indpls., Inc., 1993-96. Maj. JAGC, USAFR, 1961-65. Fellow Internat. Soc. Barristers; mem. ABA, Fed. Bar Assn., Ind. State Bar Assn., Indpls. Bar Assn., Am. Bd. Trial Advs., Am. Law Inst., Ind. Def. Lawyers Assn., Confrerie Chevaliers du Tastevin, Woodstock Country Club. Democrat. Episcopalian. Home: 4137 N Meridian St Indianapolis IN 46208-4014 Office: Lowe Gray Steele & Hoffman Bank One Ctr # 4600 111 Monument Cir Indianapolis IN 46204-5100

SHULAW, RICHARD A., lawyer; b. Bowling Green, Ohio, Oct. 14, 1934; s. Francis Marion and Mary Frances (Morehead) S. AA, Ferris State Coll., 1958; LLB, Detroit Coll. of Law, 1963, JD, 1968. Bar: Mich., U.S. Dist. Ct. (ea. and we. dists.) Mich., U.S. Ct. Appeals (6th cir.), U.S. Supreme Ct. Sole practice Owosso, Mich., 1963—; chief asst. pros. atty. Shiwassee County, Mich., 1971, cir. ct. commr., 1965-67. With U.S. Army, 1954-55. Mem. ABA, ATLA, Mich. Bar Assn. (ins. sect., negligence sect., law sect.), State Bar Mich. (grievance com., standing com. on character and fitness 1987-93, com. on arbitration of disputes between lawyers, elected twice to rep. assembly), Shiawassee County Bar Assn. (v.p.), Mich. Trial Lawyers Assn., Mich. Def. Trial Counsel Inc., Owosso Country Club, Elks, KC (4th degree), Moose, Delta Theta Phi (past pres.). Republican. Roman Catholic. Avocation: golf. Home: 815 W Oliver St Owosso MI 48867-2108

SHULER, ELLIE GIVAN, JR., museum administrator; b. Raleigh, N.C., Dec. 6, 1936; s. Ellie Givan and Berta (Williams) S.; m. Annette Fontaine Maury, Mar. 22, 1961; children—Ellie Givan III, Franklin Maury, Gray Hays. B.S.C.E., The Citadel, 1959; M.S. in Mgmt., Rensselaer Poly. Inst., 1967; grad., Squadron Officer Sch., Maxwell AFB, Ala., 1964; postgrad., Naval War Coll.; grad. command and staff course, Nat. War Coll., 1976; grad. cen. flight instr. course, Castle AFB, Calif. Engr. in tng., S.C. Commd. 2d lt. U.S. Air Force, 1959, advanced through grades to lt. gen., 1988, various positions and locations, 1959-68; F-4C pilot, asst. flight comdr. 558th Tactical Fighter Squadron U.S. Air Force, Cam Ranh Bay AFB, Republic of Vietnam, 1968-69; indsl. engr., then asst. dep. chief Engring. Mgmt. Div., Hdqrs. 2d Air Force U.S. Air Force, Barksdale AFB, La., 1969-71; asst. exec. officer to comdr. in chief U.S. Air Force in Europe, Lindsey Air Sta., West Germany, 1972-73; base civil engr., comdr. 86th Civil Engring. Squadron U.S. Air Force in Europe, Ramstein Air Base, Fed. Republic Germany, 1973-75; dir. ops. 3902d Air Base Wing, comdr. 3902d Ops. Squadron Offutt AFB, Nebr., 1976; dir. programs Office Dep. Chief of Staff for Engring. and Services SAC, Offutt AFB, Nebr., 1976-77, exec. to comdr. in chief, 1977-79; vice comdr., then comdr. 19th Bombardment Wing Robins AFB, Ga., 1979-80; comdr. 42d Bombardment Wing Loring AFB, Maine, 1980-81; comdr. 4th Air Div. F.E. Warren AFB, Wyo., 1981-84; comdr. 3rd Air Div. SAC, Andersen AFB, Guam, 1984-86; asst. dep. then dep. chief of staff, ops. SAC Hqrs., Offutt AFB, Nebr., 1986-88; comdr. 8th Air Force SAC, Barksdale AFB, 1988-91; retired, 1991; chmn. bd., CEO 8th Air Force Heritage Ctr., 1993—. Bd. dirs. Longs Peak coun. Boy Scouts Am., 1983-84; trustee Falcon Found., USAF Acad. Decorated D.S.M. with oak leaf cluster, Legion of Merit with oak leaf cluster, D.F.C., Air medal with five oak leaf clusters, Air Force Commendation medal with oak leaf cluster. Mem. Soc. Am. Mil. Engrs. (chpt. pres. 1971), Am. Def. Preparedness Assn. (regional bd. dirs. 1981-84), Order of Dadaelians (hon. flight capt. 1981-85), Council on Am.'s Mil. Past, Mil. Order of World Wars, Tau Beta Pi. Republican. Episcopalian. Lodge: Kiwanis. Avocations: numismatics, golf, hunting, fishing, military history. Office: 675 Willow Way West Alexander City AL 35010-9555

SHULER, HOWARD L., superintendent. Supt. Auburn-Washburn U.S.D. 437, Topka, Kans. Recipient State Finalist for Nat. Supt. of Yr. award, 1993. Office: Auburn-Washburn USD 437 5928 SW 53rd St Topeka KS 66610-9423

SHULER, KURT EGON, chemist, educator; b. Nuremberg, Germany, July 10, 1922; came to U.S., 1937, naturalized, 1944; s. Louis and Donie (Wald)

Schulherr; m. Beatrice Gwyn London, Nov. 11, 1944. B.S., Ga. Inst. Tech., 1942; Ph.D., Cath. U. Am., 1949; postdoctoral fellow, Johns Hopkins U., 1949-51. Sr. staff mem., asst. group supr., chem. physics group Applied Physics Lab., Johns Hopkins, 1951-55; supervisory phys. chemist Nat. Bur. Standards, 1955-58, cons. to dir., 1958-61, asst. dir., sr. research fellow, 1963-68; mem. research staff, sci. adviser to v.p. research Gen. Motors Corp., 1958; spl. asst. to dir. research Inst. Def. Analyses, 1961-63; vis. prof. chemistry U. Calif. at San Diego, La Jolla, 1966-67, prof. chemistry, 1968-91, prof. emeritus, 1991—, chmn. dept., 1968-70, 84-87; cons. to govt. and industry, 1956—; mem. Solvay Conf., 1962, 78; mem. adv. panel, chemistry div. NSF, 1973-75; assoc. Sotheby's, 1991—. Author, editor tech. books; assoc. editor: Jour. Math. Physics, 1963-66; bd. editors: Jour. Statis. Physics, 1968-80; mem. adv. bd.: Chem. Engring. News, 1967-70; contbr. articles to profl. jours. Served with U.S. Army, 1944-46. Recipient Distinguished Service award Nat. Bur. Standards, 1959, Gold medal award Dept. Commerce, 1968; Solvay Found. fellow, 1975. Fellow Am. Inst. Chemists, AAAS, Am. Phys. Soc., Washington Acad. Sci.; mem. Am. Chem. Soc., Washington Philos. Soc. Club: Rancho Santa Fe Golf. Home: PO Box 1504 Rancho Santa Fe CA 92067-1504 Office: Univ Calif at San Diego Dept Chemistry La Jolla CA 92093

SHULER, MICHAEL LOUIS, biochemical engineering educator, consultant; b. Joliet, Ill., Jan. 2, 1947; s. Louis Dean and Mary Clara (Boylan) S.; m. Karen Joyce Beck, June 24, 1972; children: Andrew, Kristin, Eric, Katherine. BSChemE, U. Notre Dame, 1969; PhDChemE, U. Minn., 1973. Asst. prof. biochem. engring. Cornell U., Ithaca, N.Y., 1974-79, assoc. prof., 1979-83, prof., 1984-91; Samuel B. Eckert prof. chem. engring. Cornell U., Ithaca, 1992—; dir. bioengring. program, 1994—; vis. scholar U. Wash., Seattle, 1980-81; vis. scientist U. Wis., Madison, 1988-89; guest prof. ETH, Zurich, Switzerland, 1995; bd. dirs. Phyton Catalytic Inc., Ithaca. Editor 6 books; contbr. numerous articles to profl. jours. and chpts. to books. Bd. dirs., treas., sec., v.p. Advs. for the Handicapped, Ithaca, 1978-88; sec., bd. dirs. Tompkins County Human Rights Commn., Ithaca, 1985-87; coach Spl. Olympics, 1994—; mem. adv. bd. Carnegie-Mellon Chem. Engring., Princeton U. Chem. Engring., Johns Hopkins U. Chem. Engring. Recipient Outstanding Paper award Am. Oil Chemist Soc., 1984, Coll. of Engring. Honor award U. Notre Dame, 1989. Fellow Am. Inst. Med. and Biol. Engrs. (founder, v.p. edn. com.); mem. NAE, AIChE (editor Biotech. Progress 1985-88, cons. editor jour. 1986—, mem. publ. com. 1988—, awards com. 1993—, chair Food Pharm. and Bioengring. divsn. 1994—, Food, Pharm., Engring. award 1989, Prof. Progress award 1991), Am. Acad. Arts and Scis., Am. Chem. Soc. (M.J. Johnson award 1986), Am. Soc. Microbiology, Am. Soc. Pharmacognosy, Biomed. Engring. Soc. Roman Catholic. Avocation: fishing. Office: Cornell U Dept Chem Engring 340 Olin Hall Ithaca NY 14853-5201

SHULER-DONNER, LAUREN, film producer; b. Cleveland, OH. B.S. in Film & Broadcasting, Boston U. TV films include: Amateur Night at the Dixie Bar and Grill, 1979; fmils include: Thank God It's Friday, 1978 (assoc. prodr.), Mr. Mon, 1983, Ladyhawke, 1985, St. Elmo's Fire, 1985, Pretty in Pink, 1986, Three Fugitives, 1989, Radio Flyer, 1992, Dave, 1993, Free Willy, 1993, The Favor, 1994, Free Willy 2: The Adventure Home, 1995, Assassins, 1995 (exec. prodr.). Office: Donner/Shuler-Donner Prodns Warner Bros 4000 Warner Blvd Burbank CA 91522-0001

SHULEVITZ, URI, author, illustrator; b. Warsaw, Poland, Feb. 27, 1935; came to U.S., 1959, naturalized, 1965; s. Abraham and Szandla (Hermanstat) S. Student, Tel-Aviv Art Inst., 1953-55; Tchrs. Cert., Tchrs. Coll. Israel, 1956; student, Bklyn. Museum Art Sch., 1959-61. Instr. illustrating and writing children's books The New Sch., 1970-86; dir. illustrating and writing children's books Hartwick Coll., 1974-92. Author, illustrator: The Moon In My Room, 1963, One Monday Morning, 1967, Rain Rain Rivers, 1969, Oh What a Noise, 1971, The Magician, 1973, Dawn, 1974, The Treasure, 1978, (Caldecott honor Book 1979), The Strange and Exciting Adventures of Jeremiah Hush, 1986, Toddlecreek Post Office, 1990, The Secret Room, 1993; author: Writing with Pictures: How to Write and Illustrate Children's Books, 1985; illustrator: The Fool of the World and the Flying Ship, 1968 (Caldecott medal 1969), The Twelve Dancing Princesses, 1966, SOldier and Tsar in the Forest, 1972, The Touchstone, 1976, Hanukah Money, 1978, The Lost Kingdom of Karnica, 1979, The Golem, 1982, Lilith's Cave: Jewish Tales of the Supernatural, 1988, The Diamond Tree, 1991, The Golden Goose, 1995. Served with Israeli Army, 1956-59. Mem Authors Guild. Office: Care Farrar Straus & Giroux Inc 19 Union Sq W New York NY 10003-3307

SHULGASSER, BARBARA, writer; b. Manhasset, N.Y., Apr. 10, 1954; d. Lew and Luba (Golante) S. Student, Sarah Lawrence Coll., 1973-74; BA magna cum laude, CUNY, 1977; MS, Columbia U., 1978. Feature writer Waterbury (Conn.) Rep., 1978-81; reporter, feature writer Chgo. Sun Times, 1981-84; film critic San Francisco Examiner, 1984—; freelance book critic N.Y. Times Book Rev., N.Y.C., 1983—. Co-author: (screenplay, with Robert Altman) Ready to Wear, 1994; freelance video columnist N.Y. Times Sunday Arts & Leisure, 1989, features for Vanity Fair, Glamour and Mirabella mags. Office: San Francisco Examiner 110 5th St San Francisco CA 94103-2918

SHULL, CLIFFORD G., physicist, educator; b. Pitts., Sept. 23, 1915; s. David H. and Daisy I. (Bistline) S.; m. Martha-Nuel Summer, June 19, 1941; children: John C., Robert D., William F. BS, Carnegie Inst. Tech., 1937; PhD, NYU, 1941. Research physicist Texas Co., 1941-46; chief physicist Oak Ridge Nat. Lab., 1946-55; prof. physics MIT, 1955-86, emeritus prof., 1986—; Chmn. vis. com. Brookhaven Nat. Lab., 1961-62; chmn. vis. com. Nat. Bur. Standard reactor, 1972-73; chmn. vis. com. solid state div. Oak Ridge Nat. Lab., 1974-75; chmn. policy com. Nat. Small-Angle-Scattering Center, 1978-81. Contbr. articles to sci. jours. Recipient award of merit Alumni Assn. of Carnegie Mellon U., 1968, Humboldt Sr. U.S. Scientist award, 1979, Disting. Scientist award Gov. of Tenn., 1986, Gregori Aminoff prize, 1993, Ilja Frank prize, 1993, Nobel Prize in Physics, 1994. Fellow Am. Phys. Soc. (Buckley prize 1956, chmn. solid state physics divsn. 1962-63), AAAS, Am. Acad. Arts and Scis., N.Y. Acad. Scis., Nat. Acad. Scis. (vice chmn. panel on neutron sci. 1977); mem. Am. Crystallographic Assn., Rsch. Soc. Am., Sigma Xi, Tau Beta Pi, Phi Kappa Phi, Phi Beta Kappa. Home: 4 Wingate Rd Lexington MA 02173-4516

SHULL, HARRISON, chemist, educator; b. Princeton, N.J., Aug. 17, 1923; s. George Harrison and Mary (Nicholl) S.; m. Jeanne Louise Johnson, 1948 (div. 1962); children: James Robert, Kathy, George Harrison, Holly; m. Wil Joyce Bentley Long, 1962; children: Warren Michael Long, Jeffery Mark Long, Stanley Martin, Sarah Ellen. A.B., Princeton U., 1943; Ph.D., U. Calif. at Berkeley, 1948. Assoc. chemist U.S. Naval Research Lab., 1943-45; asst. prof. Iowa State U., 1949-54; mem. faculty Ind. U., 1955-79, research prof., 1961-79, dean Grad. Sch., 1965-72, vice chancellor for research and devel., 1972-76, dir. Research Computing Center, 1959-63, acting chmn. chemistry dept., 1965-66, acting dean arts and scis., 1969-70, acting dean faculties, 1974; mem. faculty, provost, v.p. acad. affairs Rensselaer Poly. Inst., 1979-82; chancellor U. Colo., Boulder, 1982-85; prof. dept. chemistry U. Colo., 1982-88; provost Naval Postgrad. Sch., 1988-95; asst. dir. rsch., quantum chemistry group Uppsala (Sweden) U., 1958-59; vis. prof. Washington U., St. Louis, 1960, U. Colo., 1963; founder, supr. Quantum Chemistry Program Exchange, 1962-79; chmn. subcom. molecular structure and spectroscopy NRC, 1958-63; chmn. Fulbright selection com. chemistry, 1963-67; mem. adv. com. Office Sci. Personnel, 1957-60; chmn. First Gordon Research Conf. Theoretical Chemistry, 1962; mem. com. survey chemistry Nat. Acad. Sci., 1964-65; mem. adv. panel chemistry NSF, 1964-67; mem. adv. panel Office Computer Activities, 1967-70, cons. chem. information program, 1965-71, mem. adv. com. for research, 1974-76; mem. vis. com. chemistry Brookhaven Nat. Lab., 1967-70; mem. adv. com. Chem. Abstracts Service, 1971-74; dir. Storage Tech. Corp.; chief of Naval Ops. Exec. Panel, 1984-88. Assoc. editor: Jour. Chem. Physics, 1952-54; editorial adv. bd.: Spectrochimica Acta, 1957-63, Internat. Jour. Quantum Chemistry, 1967—, Proc. NAS, 1976-81; contbr. articles to profl. jours. Trustee Argonne U. Assn., 1970-75, Asso. Univs., Inc., 1973-76, U. Rsch. Assn., 1984-89, Inst. Defense Analysis, 1984—. Served as ensign USNR, 1945. NRC postdoctoral fellow phys. scis. U. Chgo., 1948-49; Guggenheim fellow U. Uppsala, 1954-55; NSF sr. postdoctoral fellow, 1968-69; Sloan research fellow, 1956-58. Fellow Am. Acad. Arts and Scis. (v.p. 1976-83, chmn. Midwest Ctr. 1976-79), Am. Phys. Soc.; mem. AAAS, Nat. Acad. Scis. (com. on sci. and pub. policy 1969-72, coun., exec. com. 1971-74, chmn. U.S.-USSR sci. policy subgroup for fundamental rsch. 1973-81, naval studies bd. 1974-79, 96—, chmn. Commn. on Human Resources, 1977-81, nominating com. 1978), Am. Chem. Soc., Assn. Computing Machinery, Royal Swedish Acad. Scis. (fgn. mem.), Royal Acad. Arts and Scis. Uppsala (corr. mem.), Cosmos Club (Washington), Old Capital Club (Monterey), Phi Beta Kappa, Sigma Xi, Phi Lambda Upsilon. Office: Naval Postgrad Sch Code 09/hs Monterey CA 93940

SHULL, RICHARD BRUCE, actor; b. Evanston, Ill., Feb. 24, 1929; s. Ulysses Homer and Zana Marie (Brown) S.; m. Margaret Ann Haddy, July 14, 1951 (div. 1956); m. Peggy Joan Barringer, June 9, 1957 (div. 1967); m. Marilyn Sandra Swartz, July 6, 1969 (div. 1985, remarried July 7, 1989). BA in Drama, State U. Iowa, 1950; AA in Humanities, Kemper Mil. Sch., 1986. exec. asst. producer Gordon W. Pollock Prodns., 1953-56; stage mgr. Hyde Park Playhouse, 1954-55; prodn. mgr. Kaufman Auditorium, N.Y.C., 1956; gen. mgr. Music Circle Theatre, Detroit, 1957; prodn. supr. Ford Motor Co. Am. Road Show, 1959; prodn. mgr. (film) Dana Prodns. Inc., 1959-60; dir. Lake Luzerne Playhouse, 1962, 64, Showboat Dinner Theatre, 1968-69; art dir. (film) Tears are for Tomorrow, 1960. Freelance theatrical stage mgr. and dir., N.Y.C., 1950-70; appeared in plays, N.Y.C., including Each in His Own Way, 1950, Wake Up Darling, 1956, Minnie's Boys, 1970, Goodtime Charley (Tony nominee, Drama Desk nomination), 1975, Fools, 1981, Oh, Brother!, 1981, Desire Under the Elms, 1983, Fade the Game, 1984, The Marriage of Bette and Boo (Obie award), 1985, The Front Page, 1986, Opera Comique, 1987, Rough Crossing, 1990, One of the All-Time Greats, 1992, Ain't Broadway Grand, 1993, The Gig, 1994, Victor/Victoria, 1995, plays in L.A., including Mr. Ferris and The Model, 1967, The Tempest, 1979; film appearances include The Anderson Tapes and B.S., I Love You, 1970, Hail to the Chief and Such Good Friends, 1971, Slither and Ssssss, 1972, Cockfighter, 1974, The Fortune, The Black Bird and The Big Bus, 1975, The Pack, 1977, Lovesick, 1983, Spring Break, 1983, Unfaithfully Yours, 1984, Splash, 1984, Garbo Talks, 1984, My Blue Heaven, 1990, Tune in Tomorrow, 1990, Housesitter, 1992, For Love or Money, 1993, Trapped in Paradise, 1994, Café Society, 1995; private parts, 1996—; appearances on TV include Your Hit Parade, 1950, Robert Montgomery Presents, 1950, Diana, 1973, Ironsides, 1975, Goodtimes, 1975, Holmes and YoYo, 1976, The Rockford Files, 1978, Ziegfeld, A Man and His Women, 1978, Studs Lonigan, 1979, Hart to Hart, 1979, Lou Grant, 1980, The Ropers, 1980, Alice, 1980, Nurse, 1981, Will There Really Be a Morning?, 1982, The Boy Who Loved Trolls, 1984, Keeping the Faith, 1984, Seize the Day, 1985, The Conan O'Brien Show, 1993; dir. Man Without a Shadow, 1958; author: motion picture story and screenplay Aroused, 1964, Pamela, Pamela You Are, 1967; program dir. Armed Forces Radio Sta. GYPSY; created AFKN Network program Concert in Jazz. Served with U.S. Army, 1951-53, Korea. Mem. AFTRA, Actors Equity Assn. (founding editl. bd., constl. rev. com. 1975), Screen Actors Guild, Acad. Motion Picture Arts and Scis., Episcopal Actors Guild (life), Actors Fund (life), SR, Soc. Colonial Wars, St. Nicholas Soc. (steward, bd. mgrs.), N.Y. Vet. Corps. Artillery (councillor), Gen. Soc. War of 1812 (pres. N.Y. State soc.), Colonial Order Acorn, Sons of Union Vets, Civil War (treas. Tilden Camp), First Families Ohio, Soc. Ind. Pioneers, Pioneer Assn. State Wash., Sons. Am. Colonists (gov. N.Y. chpt.), Hon. Order Ky. Cols., Lambs Club (life), Players Club, Friars Club, Dutch Treat Club, Univ. Club (N.Y.C.), Sloane Club (London), India House (N.Y.C.), Ends of the Earth, Pumpkin Papers Irregulars, Baker St. Irregulars. Democrat. Avocations: antique autos and railroading, animal protection. Office: Cheerieerie Ltd 1501 Broadway #1510 New York NY 10036

SHULMAN, ANITA, nurse midwife; b. Waterloo, Iowa, Mar. 14, 1957; d. Herbert and Deana Shulman. RN, Hasharon Sch. Nursing, Petah Tikva, Israel, 1979; Israel cert. midwife, Hebrew U. Jerusalem, 1981; cert. nurse midwife, Frontier Sch. Midwifery, Hyden, Ky., 1989. Staff nurse, midwife Hadassah Med. Orgn., Jerusalem, 1980-86; pvt. midwifery practice assoc. Cynthia K. Monshower & J. Emerling CNM, Balt., Balt., 1989-90; midwife Planned Parenthood, Balt., 1989-90; staff midwife Johns Hopkins Med. Svcs. Corp., Balt., 1990-93; midwife privileges Johns Hopkins Hosp., Balt., 1991—. Mem. Am. Coll. Nurse Midwives, HMO Hadassah Med. Orgn. (life). Democrat. Jewish. Home: 2213 Wicomico Rd Baltimore MD 21221-1545

SHULMAN, ARNOLD, judge, lawyer; b. Phila., Apr. 12, 1914; s. Edward Nathaniel and Anna (Leshner) S.; m. Mary Frances Johnson, Nov. 26, 1943; children: Diane Shulman Thompson, Warren Scott, Amy Lynn Shulman Haney. Student, Emory U., 1931; J.D., U. Ga., 1936. Bar: Ga. 1937. Mem. firm Shulman, Shulman, Bauer & Deitch (and predecessors), Atlanta, to 1977; judge Ga. Ct. Appeals, 1977-84, presiding judge, 1981-83, chief judge, 1983-84; of counsel Troutman, Sanders, Lockerman & Ashmore, Atlanta, 1984-87; appointed sr. appellate ct. judge, 1987—; chief judge settlement conf. div. Ct. Appeals Ga., 1989—; prof. Atlanta Law Sch., 1964-84; adj. prof. Ga. State U. Coll. Law, Atlanta. Author: (with Wiley H. Davis) Georgia Practice and Procedure, 1948, 3d edit., 1968, 4th edit, (with Warren S. Shulman), 1975; contbr. articles to legal jours. Chmn. DeKalb County (Ga.) Sch. Salary Commn., 1960-62, DeKalb County Sch. Study Commn., 1962-64; mem. Fulton County-Atlanta Ct. Study Commn., 1961-62. Served to capt. U.S. Army, 1941-46. Mem. ABA, Atlanta Bar Assn., Ga. State Bar, Lawyers Club (Atlanta). Home: 1527 September Chase Decatur GA 30033-1731 Office: 908 DeKalb County Courthouse Decatur GA 30030

SHULMAN, ARTHUR, communications executive; b. N.Y.C., Mar. 4, 1927; s. Jacob and Sarah (Hochman) S.; m. Jan. 30, 1958; children: James, Karen. BA, Syracuse U., 1950. Asst. to pub. TV Guide Mag., Radnor, Pa., 1958-72; pub. Seventeen Mag., N.Y.C., 1972-73; dir. regional ops. TV Guide, 1974-82; dir. comm. B'nai B'rith Internat., Washington, 1983—. Author: How Sweet It Was, 1966, The Television Years, 1972. Dir. Penn Wynne (Pa.) Civic Assn., 1965-66. S/Sgt. US Army, 1945-46, Japan. Mem. Radio & TV Execs. Soc., Nat. Press Club, Overseas Press Club, Nat. Acad. TV Arts & Scis. Jewish. Home: 4450 S Park Ave Chevy Chase MD 20815-3621 Office: B'Nai B'Rith Internat 1640 Rhode Island Ave NW Washington DC 20036-3278

SHULMAN, CAROLE KAREN, professional society administrator; b. Mpls., Nov. 25, 1940; d. Allen Eldon and Beulah Ovidia (Blomsness) Banbury; m. David Arthur Shulman, Mar. 26, 1962; children: Michael, Krista, Tracy, Robbyn. Student, Colo. Coll., 1958-61; California Coast U., 1983-84. Profl. instr. Rochester (Minn.) Figure Skating Club, 1962-84, dir. skating, 1964-79, cons., 1979—; exec. dir. Profl. Skaters Assn., Rochester, 1984—; master rating examiner Profl. Skaters Guild, Rochester, 1971—, world profl. judge, 1976, 79, 87-88. Editor Professional Skater mag., 1984—; prodr. U.S. Open Profl. Figure Skating Championships, 1987, 89—. Pres. Rochester Arts Council, 1983. Named triple gold medalist U.S. Figure Skating Assn., Colorado Springs, Colo., 1959, 63, Master Rated Coach Profl. Skaters Assn., 1970, Sr. Rated Coach in Dance Profl. Skaters Assn., 1970. Mem. Am. Harp Soc. Mem. Covenant ch. Avocations: harp, skiing. Office: Profl Skaters Assn Internat PO Box 5904 Rochester MN 55903-5904

SHULMAN, HYMAN, food service executive; b. 1920. With Max Starks Delicatessen and Liquors, Roselle, N.J., 1942-43, 46-49; mgr. Bardy Farms Supply Market, Union, N.J., 1949-53; with West Essex Supermarkets Inc., Caldwell, N.J., 1953—, now chmn. bd. dirs.; asst. treas., bd. dirs. Twin County Grocers, Inc., 1983-84, sec., bd. dirs., 1984-89, vice chmn., bd. dirs., 1989—. Served U.S. Armed Forces, 1943-46. Office: Twin County Grocers Inc 145 Talmadge Rd Edison NJ 08818*

SHULMAN, LAWRENCE EDWARD, biomedical research administrator, rheumatologist; b. Boston, July 25, 1919; s. David Herman and Belle (Tishler) S.; m. Pauline K. Flint, July 19, 1946; 1 son, Lawrence E.; m. Reni Trudinger, Mar. 20, 1959; children: Kathryn Verena, Barbara Corina. AB, Harvard U., 1941, postgrad., 1941-42; PhD, Yale U., 1945, MD, 1949. Nat. Bd. Med. Examiners. Intern Johns Hopkins Hosp., 1949-50, resident and fellow in internal medicine, 1950-53; dir. connective tissue div. Johns Hopkins U., 1955-75, assoc. prof. medicine, 1964—; assoc. dir. div. arthritis, musculoskeletal and skin diseases NIH, Bethesda, Md., 1976-82, dir., 1982—; dir. Nat. Inst. Arthritis & Musculoskeletal & Skin Diseases NIH, 1986-94, dir. emeritus, 1994—, emissary for clin. rsch., 1995—; chmn. med. adminstrn. com. Arthritis Found., Atlanta, 1974-75, exec. com., 1972-77; dir. Lupus Found. Am.; med. adv. bd. United. Scleroderma Found., Watsonville, Calif., 1977-88; chair sci. group rheumatic diseases WHO, 1989. Discoverer: Eosinophilic Fasciitis, 1974, new med. sign friction rubs in scleroderma, 1961. Recipient Sr. Investigator award Arthritis Found., 1957-62, Disting. Svc. award, 1979, Heberden medal for rsch., London, 1975, Superior Svc. award USPHS, 1985, Spl. Recognition award Nat. Osteoprosis Found., 1991, Spl. award Am. Acad. Orthop. Surgeons, 1992, Presdl. citation for leadership Am. Acad. Dermatology, 1993, Leadership award Lupus Found. Am., 1994, Career Achievement award Am. Coll. Rheumatology, 1994, Outstanding Support Rsch. award Am. Soc. Bone Mineral Rsch., 1994, Gold medal Am. Coll. Rheumatology; named W.R. Graham Meml. lectr., 1973, Cochrane Disting. lectr., 1993. Master Am. Rheumatism Assn. (pres. 1974-75); fellow ACP; mem. Soc. Clin. Trials, Pan-Am. League Against Rheumatism (pres. 1982-86)., Soc. Investigative Dermatology. Home: 6302 Swords Way Bethesda MD 20817-3350

SHULMAN, MAX L., corporate executive; b. N.Y.C., Oct. 18, 1908; s. Jacob and Dora (Silverman) S.; m. Sylvia C. Weinstein, June 25, 1939; children: Lloyd J., Gail P. Student CCNY, 1924; LLB, Nat. U., Washington, 1930. Bar: D.C. 1930, N.Y. 1942. Chief exec. officer, J.W. Mays, Inc., Bklyn., 1953-63, chmn., 1963—; pres. Weinstein Enterprises, Inc., Carmel, N.Y., 1963—; pres. Weinstein Found. Inc., Carmel, 1963—. With U.S. Army, 1930, WWII; maj. USAR, ret. 1946. Decorated Army Commendation medal with oak leaf clusters. Mem. Harmonie Club, Rotary. Office: JW Mays Inc 9 Bond St Brooklyn NY 11201-5805

SHULMAN, ROBERT GERSON, biophysics educator; b. N.Y.C., Mar. 3, 1924; s. Joshua S. and Freda (Lipshay) S.; m. Saralee Deutsch, Aug., 1952 (dec. Oct. 1983); children: Joel, Mark, James; m. Stephanie S. Spangler, May 11, 1986. AB, Columbia U., 1943, MA, 1947, PhD, 1949. Rsch. assoc. Columbia U. Radiation Lab., N.Y.C., 1949; AEC fellow in chemistry Calif. Inst. Tech., Pasadena, 1949-50; head semicondr. research sect. Hughes Aircraft Co., Culver City, Calif., 1950-53; mem. tech. staff Bell Labs., Murray Hill, N.J., 1953-66; head biophysics rsch. dept. Bell Labs., 1966-79; prof. molecular biophysics and biochemistry Yale U., 1979—, dir. divsn. biol. scis., 1981-87, Sterling prof. molecular biophysics and biochemistry, 1994—; Rask Oersted lectr. U. Copenhagen, 1959; vis. prof. Ecole Normale Superieur, Paris, 1962; Appleton lectr. Brown U., 1965; vis. prof. physics U. Tokyo, 1965; Reilly lectr. U. Notre Dame, Ind., 1969; vis. prof. biophysics Princeton U., 1971-72; Regents lectr. UCLA, 1978. Guggenheim fellow in lab. molecular biology MRC Cambridge (Eng.) U., 1961-62; recipient Havinga medal Leiden U., 1983, Gold medal Soc. Magnetic Resonance in Medicine, 1984,. Mem. Nat. Acad. Scis., Inst. Medicine. Achievements include research in spectroscopic techniques applied to physics, chemistry and biology. Office: Yale U MR Ctr Dept Molecular Bio PO Box 208043 New Haven CT 06520-8043

SHULMAN, ROBERT JAY, physician; b. Newark; s. Irving Jack and Shirley (Weinstock) S.; children: David Ian, Hannah Rachael. BA, Emory U., 1972; MD, Chgo. Med. Sch., 1976. Asst. prof. pediat. Baylor Coll. Medicine, Houston, 1982-89, assoc. prof., 1989—; dir. nutritional support team Tex. Children's Hosp., Houston, 1982—. Author: Yougn Chef's Nutrition Guide and Cookbook, 1990, Keys to Child Nutrition, 1991, (with others) Principles and Practice of Pediatrics, 1994, Physiology of the Gastrointestinal Tract, 1994; mem. editl. bd. Jour. Pediat. Gastroenterology and Nutrition, 1994—. Fellow Am. Acad. Pediat.; mem. Am. Gastroent. Soc., Am. Soc. Patenteral and Enteral Nutrition (pres. 1991-92), Am. Inst. Nutrition, N.Am. Soc. Pediat. Gastroenterology and Nutrition, Soc. Pediat. Rsch. Avocation: guitar. Office: Baylor Coll Medicine 1100 Bates Ave Houston TX 77030-2600

SHULMAN, STEPHEN NEAL, lawyer; b. New Haven, Apr. 6, 1933; s. Harry and Rea (Karrel) S.; m. Sandra Paula Still, Aug. 14, 1954; children—Harry, Dean, John. B.A., Harvard, 1954; LL.B. cum laude, Yale, 1958. Bar: Conn. 1958, D.C. 1960. Indsl. relations Bendix Aviation Corp., 1954-55; law clk. to Justice Harlan, U.S. Supreme Ct., 1958-59; vis. asst. pro. U. Mich. Law Sch., 1959; asso. firm Covington & Burling, Washington, 1959-60; asst. U.S. atty. Washington, 1960-61; exec. asst. to sec. labor, 1961-62, dept asst. sec. of def., 1962-65; gen. counsel U.S. Air Force, 1965-66; chmn. Equal Employment Opportunity Commn., 1966-67; mem. Kane, Shulman & Schlei, Washington, 1967-70; mem. firm Cadwalader, Wickersham & Taft, N.Y.C., also Washington, 1971-95, Freedman, Levy, Kroll & Simonds, Washington, 1995—; vis. prof. mgmt. U. Okla., 1965-66. Co-author: The Law of Equal Employment Opportunity, 1990; editor in chief Yale Law Jour., 1957-58. Mem. Book and Gavel, Order of Coif, Cum Laude Soc., Phi Alpha Delta. Home: 1332 Skipwith Rd Mc Lean VA 22101-1841 Office: Freedman Levy 1050 Connecticut Ave NW Washington DC 20036-5366

SHULMAN, YECHIEL, engineering educator; b. Tel Aviv, Jan. 28, 1930; came to the U.S., 1950; s. David and Rachel (Chonowski) S.; m. Ruth Danzig, June 29, 1950; children: Elinor D., Ron E., Orna L. BS in Aero. Engring., MIT, 1954, BS in Bus. and Engring. Adminstrn., 1954, MS in Aero. Engring., 1954, DSc Aero. and Astro., 1959; MBA, U. Chgo., 1973. Assoc. prof. mech. engring. Northwestern U., Evanston, Ill., 1959-67; v.p. adv. engring. Anocut, Inc., Elk Grove Vill., Ill., 1967-72; v.p. corp. devel. Alden Press, Elk Grove Vill., Ill., 1973-84; pres. MMT Environ., Inc., Shoreview, Minn., 1984-87; cons. Shulman Assocs., Mpls., 1987-89; prof. mech. engring. dept. U. Minn., Mpls., 1989—, H. W. Sweatt chair in technol. leadership and dir. ctr. for devel. technol. leadership, 1989—, dir. grad. studies mgmt. of tech. program, 1990—. Mem. Am. Soc. Mech. Engrs., Inst. Indsl. Engrs. Office: U Minn 107 Lind Hall Minneapolis MN 55455

SHULTIS, ROBERT LYNN, finance educator, cost systems consultant, retired professional association executive; b. Kingston, N.Y., June 30, 1924; s. Albert H. and Dorothy Elizabeth (Jenkins) S.; m. Bernice Elizabeth Johnson, Jan. 20, 1946; 1 son, Robert Lee. BS, Columbia Univ. Sch. Bus., 1949, postgrad., 1949-51. Staff acct. Price Waterhouse, N.Y.C., 1949-52; credit mgr., controller Organon, Inc., West Orange, N.J., 1952-68; v.p., treas., chief fin. officer Arwood Corp., Rockleigh, N.J., 1968-72; v.p., controller Technicon, Tarrytown, N.Y., 1972-80; exec. dir. Inst. of Mgmt. Accts., Montvale, N.J., 1980-86; faculty, exec. dir. Ctr. for Exec. Devel. Coll. William & Mary, Williamsburg, Va., 1987-91; instr. Rutgers U., 1964-74, Fairleigh Dickinson U., 1967-68; mem. Fin. Acctg. Standards Adv. coun., 1981-86; cons. Acctg. and Cost Sys. design, 1990—; lectr., seminar leader, cons. on controllership, activity-based costing, cost mgmt., cost sys. design U. Calif, Berkeley, U. Minn., Michigan State U., So. Meth. U., Baldwin Wallace Coll., George Mason U., James Madison U., others, 1990—. Editor: Management Accountants' Handbook, and supplements, 1991-94. Mem. bd. advs. U. Fla. Sch. Accountancy, James Madison U. Sch. Accountancy; mem. fin. and budget com. Kingsmill Community Svcs. Assn. Served with USAF, 1943-45. Decorated Presdl. Unit Citation. Mem. AAUP, Fin. Execs. Inst., Assn. Systems Mgmt., Inst. of Mgmt. Accts., Am. Acctg. Assn., Ross Inst. Acctg. Rsch., Kingsmill Club, Beta Alpha Psi (adv. forum).

SHULTS, ROBERT LEE, real estate executive, airline executive; b. Helena, Ark., Feb. 23, 1936; s. Albert and Mary S.; m. Belinda Housley, Aug. 21, 1965; children: Catherine Ann, Robert L. BS in Acctg. magna cum laude, U. Ark.-Fayetteville, 1961. CPA, Ark. Mgr., Arthur Andersen & Co., Memphis, 1961-70; exec. v.p. Allied Tel. Co., Little Rock, 1970-80; chmn. bd. Scheduled Skyways, Inc., Little Rock, 1980-88, chmn. bd., chief exec. officer, Fin. Ctr. Corp., Little Rock, 1980—, cons. Alltel Corp., Little Rock, 1980-90; chmn. bd., chief exec. Ranch Prop Inc., 1989—; chmn. bd. dir., chief exec. Fin. Ctr. Devel. Co., Air Midwest Inc.; past chmn. bd. Regional Airline Assn., Washington, 1984. Pres. bd. dirs. Ark. Children's Hosp., 1994—; bd. dirs., treas. Am. Cancer Soc., Ark., 1976-91, Inst. Pub. Utilities, Mich. State U., 1976-80; mem. Ark. Arts Ctr.; chmn. bd. trustees Trinity Cathedral, 1982-92, Fifty for Future Little Rock. With USMC, 1956-58. Recipient Pres.'s citation, U.S. Ind. Tel. Assn., 1978, 80. Mem. AICPA, Mo. Bd. Accts., Tenn. Bd. Accts., Met. Little Rock C. of C., Little Rock Club, The Capital Club, Summit Club, Little Rock Country Club, Rotary (bd. dirs. 1988-90). Episcopalian. Office: Fin Ctr Corp PO Box 56350 Little Rock AR 72215-6350

SHULTS, ROBERT LUTHER, JR., lawyer; b. Pine Bluff, Ark., Oct. 25, 1925; s. Robert Luther and Gay (Moseley) S.; m. Barbara Jo Taylor, Aug. 19, 1950; children—Steven Taylor, Elizabeth Gay. BSEE cum laude, La. State U., 1950; LLB cum laude, Harvard U., 1953; LLD (hon.), U. Ark., 1981. Bar: Ark. bar 1953. Assoc., ptnr. Wright, Lindsey, Jennings, Lester & Shults, Little Rock, 1953-65; ptnr. Lester and Shults, Little Rock, 1965-79, Shults, Ray & Kurrus, Little Rock, 1979—. Editor: Harvard Law Rev, 1952-53. Chmn. Little Rock Com. Fgn. Rels.; bd. dirs. Little Rock Ctrl. YMCA, Ark. chpt. Arthritis Found., Winrock Internat. Inst. for Agrl. Devel.; chmn. bd. Winthrop Rockefeller Found., Econ. Opportunity Agy. Pulaski County; trustee Winthrop Rockefeller Charitable Trust, Ark. Blue Cross-Blue Shield, Inc., Ark., Arts Ctr. 1st lt. AUS, 1943-46, ETO. Mem. ABA, Ark. Bar Assn. (chmn. legal edn. council 1963-66, chmn. exec. com. 1968-69), Am. Judicature Soc., Am. Inst. for Public Service (bd. of selectors), Nat. Audubon Soc. (dir. 1980-86), Sigma Chi, Tau Beta Pi, Omicron Delta Kappa. Democrat. Methodist. Clubs: Little Rock Country, Capital. Home: 11 Glenridge Rd Little Rock AR 72227-2208 Office: Shults Ray & Kurrus 200 W Capitol 1600 Boatmens Bank Bldg Little Rock AR 72201

SHULTS, THOMAS DANIEL, lawyer; b. Massena, N.Y., Apr. 18, 1955; s. Robert Daniel and Beverly Jean (Stowell) S.; m. Deborah Lynn Barmore, Nov. 17, 1979; children: Daniel, Timothy. BS, Fla. State U., 1977; JD, Washburn U., 1982. Bar: Fla. 1983, U.S. Dist. Ct. (mid. and so. dists.) Fla. 1984, U.S. Tax Ct. 1985, U.S. Ct. Appeals (11th cir.) 1985; cert. mediator Fla. Supreme Ct., mediator U.S. Dist. Ct. Asst. state atty. State of Fla. State's Atty. Office, Orlando, 1983-84; litigation assoc. Abel, Band, Brown, et al, Sarasota, Fla., 1984-87; ptnr. Shults & Pomeroy, P.A., Sarasota, 1988-94, Thomas D. Shults, P.A., Sarasota, 1995—; adj. prof. Manatee C.C., Bradenton, Fla., 1994-95; mem. individual rights com. Fla. Bar, 1987-88; chmn. pub. edn. com. Sarasota Bar, 1991-92; mem. counsel of attys. Am. Subcontractors Assn., Sarasota, 1990-96; v.p. Sarasota Cmty. Mental Health Resource Ctr., 1995. Contbr. articles to profl. publs. Capt. U.S. Army, 1977-86. Mem. Order of Barristers, Sarasota Inn of Ct. Avocations: photography, camera collecting, film making, film history. Office: Thomas D Shults PA 1800 2d St Ste 790 Sarasota FL 34236

SHULTS-DAVIS, LOIS BUNTON, lawyer; b. Elkton, Md., Sept. 29, 1957; d. Asa Grant Bunton and Carolyn Elizabeth Bunton Pate; m. David Reed Shults (Dec. 8, 1979 (div. Sept. 1990); children: Kenneth Grant, Joseph David, Lawrence Scott; m. Michael Howard Davis, June 14, 1992. BS, East Tenn. State U., 1977; JD, U. Tenn., 1980. Bar: Tenn. 1980, U.S. Dist. Ct. (ea. dist.) Tenn. 1985. Assoc. Jenkins & Jenkins, Knoxville, Tenn., 1980-82, R.O. Smith Law Offices, Erwin, Tenn., 1982-85; ptnr. Shults & Shults, Erwin, 1985—; gen. counsel Erwin Nat. Bank, 1985—. Bd. dirs. Unicoi County Heritage Mus., Erwin, 1986-87, Unicoi County Ambulance Authority, Erwin, 1990-91, YMCA, Erwin, 1991—; pres. Unicoi Elem. PTO, 1994; mock trial coach Mock Trial Competition Young Lawyers, 1993, 95-96. Recipient Contbn. to Edn. award Unicoi County Edn. Assn., 1994. Mem. Female Attys. of Mountain Empire, DAR (regent 1990-92). Republican. Methodist. Avocations: snow skiing, reading, travel, gardening, home improvement. Home: Rt 1 Box 258-B Unicoi TN 37692 Office: Shults & Shults Law Offices 111 Gay St Erwin TN 38650

SHULTZ, GEORGE PRATT, former government executive, economics educator; b. N.Y.C., Dec. 13, 1920; s. Birl E. and Margaret Lennox (Pratt) S.; m. Helena M. O'Brien, Feb. 16, 1946; children: Margaret Ann Shultz Tilsworth, Kathleen Pratt Shultz Jorgensen, Peter Milton, Barbara Lennox Shultz White, Alexander George. BA in Econs., Princeton U., 1942; PhD in Indsl. Econs., MIT, 1949; hon. degrees, U. Notre Dame, Loyola U., U. Pa., U. Rochester, Princeton U., Carnegie-Mellon U., Baruch Coll., N.Y.C., Northwestern U., Yeshiva U., U. Tel Aviv, Technion-Israel Inst. Tech. Mem. faculty M.I.T., 1949-57; assoc. prof. indsl. relations MIT, 1955-57; prof. indsl. relations Grad. Sch. Bus., U. Chgo., 1957-68, dean sch., 1962-68; fellow Ctr. for Advanced Study in Behavioral Scis., 1968-69; U.S. sec. labor, 1969-70; dir. Office Mgmt. and Budget, 1970-72; U.S. sec. treasury, also asst. to Pres., 1972-74; chmn. Council on Econ. Policy, East-West Trade Policy com.; exec. v.p. Bechtel Corp., San Francisco, 1974-75, pres., 1975-77; vice chmn. Bechtel Corp., 1977-81; also dir.; pres. Bechtel Group, Inc., 1981-82; prof. mgmt. and pub. policy Stanford U., 1974-82, prof. internat. econs., 1989-91, prof. emeritus, 1991—; chmn. Pres. Reagan's Econ. Policy Adv. Bd., 1981-82; U.S. sec. of state, 1982-89; disting. fellow Hoover Instn., Stanford, 1989—; bd. dirs. Bechtel Group, Inc., GM, Gulfstream Aerospace Corp., AirTouch Comm.; mem. Gilead Scis. Bd.; chmn. J.P. Morgan Internat. Coun.; chmn. adv. coun. Inst. Internat. Studies, Calif. Go.v's Econ. Policy Adv. Bd. Author: Pressures on Wage Decisions, 1951, (with Charles A. Myers) The Dynamics of a Labor Market, 1951, (with John R. Coleman) Labor Problems: Cases and Readings, 1953, (with T.L. Whisler) Management Organization and the Computer, 1960, (with Arnold R. Weber) Strategies for the Displaced Worker, 1966, (with Robert Z. Aliber) Guidelines, Informal Controls and the Market Place, 1966, (with Albert Rees) Workers and Wages in the Urban Labor Market, 1970, Leaders and Followers in an Age of Ambiguity, 1975, (with Kenneth W. Dam) Economic Policy Beyond the Headlines, 1977, Turmoil and Triumph: My Years as Secetary of State, 1993; also articles, chpts. in books, reports, and essays. Served to capt. USMCR, 1942-45. Mem. Am. Econ. Assn., Indsl. Relations Research Assn. (pres. 1968), Nat. Acad. Arbitrators. Office: Stanford U Hoover Instn Stanford CA 94305

SHULTZ, JOHN DAVID, lawyer; b. L.A., Oct. 9, 1939; s. Edward Patterson and Jane Elizabeth (Taylor) S.; m. Joanne Person, June 22, 1968; children: David Taylor, Steven Matthew. Student, Harvard Coll., 1960-61; BA, U. Ariz., 1964; JD, Boalt Hall, U. Calif., Berkeley, 1967. Bar: N.Y. 1968, Calif. 1978. Assoc. Cadwalader, Wickersham & Taft, N.Y.C., 1968-77; ptnr. Lawler, Felix & Hall, L.A., 1977-83, mem. exec. com., chmn. planning com., co-chmn. recruiting and hiring com.; ptnr. Morgan, Lewis & Bockius, L.A., 1983—, chmn. mgmt. com., mem. lateral entry com.; chmn. profl. evaluation com., chmn. bus. plan com., chmn. practice devel. com., chmn. recruiting com. Trustee St. Thomas Ch., N.Y.C., 1969-72, Shore Acres Point Corp., Mamaroneck, N.Y., 1975-77; mem. adv. bd. Internat. and Comparative Law Center, Southwestern Legal Found., 1981—; active Practicing Law Inst. Adv. Bd., Corp. and Securities Law, 1992—. Mem. ABA, Assn. Bar City N.Y., State Bar Calif., N.Y. State Bar Assn., Jonathan Club (L.A.), Phi Delta Phi, Sigma Chi. Episcopalian. Office: Morgan Lewis & Bockius 801 S Grand Ave Los Angeles CA 90017-4613

SHULTZ, LEILA MCREYNOLDS, botanist, educator; b. Bartlesville, Okla., Apr. 20, 1946; 1 child, Kirsten. BS, U. Tulsa, 1969; MA, U. Colo., 1975; PhD, Claremont Grad. Sch., 1983. Curator Intermountain Herbarium Utah State U., 1973-92; rschr. Harvard U., Cambridge, Mass., 1994—. Coauthor: Atlas of the Vascular Plants of Utah, 1988; taxon editor: Flora of North America (3 vols.), 1987. Mem. Am. Bot. Soc. (systematics rep. 1988-90), Am. Soc. Plant Taxonomists (coun. 1990-92). Office: Harvard U Herbaria 22 Divinity Ave Cambridge MA 02138-2020

SHUMACKER, HARRIS B., JR., surgeon, educator, author; b. Laurel, Miss., May 20, 1908; s. Harris B. and Corinne (Teller) S.; m. Myrtle E. Landau, Dec. 1, 1933; children—Peter D., James N. B.S., U. Tenn., Chattanooga, 1927; A.M., Vanderbilt U., 1928; M.D., Johns Hopkins U., 1932; D.Sc. (hon.), Ind. U., 1985. Diplomate Am. Bd. Surgery, Am. Bd. Thoracic Surgery. Asst. in surgery Johns Hopkins U., 1932-35, instr., 1938-41, asst. prof., 1941-46; asst. in surgery Yale U., 1936-37, instr., 1937-38, assoc. prof., 1946-48; prof. surgery Ind. U., 1948-70, chmn. dept., 1948-68, Disting. prof., 1970-78, Disting. prof. emeritus, 1978—; prof., sr. advisor Uniformed Svcs. U. of Health Scis., Bethesda, Md., 1981-87, Disting. prof. surgery, 1988—; pres. Uniformed Svcs U. Assocs., 1987-88; hon. mem. surg. faculties in Peoples Republic of China, 1979—; dir. sect. cardiovascular-thoracic surgery St. Vincent Hosp., 1973-78, sr. surg. cons., 1978-81. Served from capt. to lt. col. M.C., U.S. Army, 1942-46; cons. surgeon gen., 1949-60. Recipient Roswell Park award, 1968, Medal of Honor, Evansville U., 1970, Disting. Alumus award U. Chattanooga, Curtis medal, 1970, Spl. Alumnus award Johns Hopkins U., 1973, Disting. Svc. award Am. Soc. Abdominal Surgery, letter of commendation Surgeon-Gen. USN, 1987, Disting. Svc. medal Uniformed Svc. U. Health Scis., 1988, René Leriche prize Soc. Internat. de Chir., 1993. Fellow Royal Coll. Surgeons (hon.); mem. Am. Assn. Surgery of Trauma, Am. Surg. Assn. (1st v.p. 1961, sec. 1964-68), So. Surg. Assn., Central Surg. Assn., Pan-Pacific Surg. Assn. (trustee 1961-64, v.p., 1964-75, 78—, pres. 1975-78), AMA (chmn. sect. gen. surgery), Internat. Surg. Soc., Internat. Soc. Cardiovascular Surgeons (v.p. 1957-59, pres. N.Am. chpt. 1956-58), Soc. Clin. Surgery (pres. 1961-63), ACS (chmn. forum com. 1955-60, chmn. nat. TV com. 1964-68, Disting. Service award 1968), Soc. U. Surgeons (pres. 1951), Soc. for Vascular Surgery (pres. 1958-59), Am. Thoracic Surg. Assn., Soc. Thoracic Surgeons (hon.), Internat. Surg. Group (v.p. 1974-75, pres. 1975-76), Polish Surg. Assn. (hon.), Sociedad Cubana de Angiologia (hon.), Societa Italiana di Chirurgia (hon.), Internat. Surg. Group (hon.), Phi Beta Kappa, Sigma Xi, Alpha Omega Alpha.

SHUMAKER, JOHN WILLIAM, academic administrator; b. Pitts., Aug. 21, 1942; s. Thomas E. Shumaker and Sara Jane (Giffn) Cobun; children: Timothy, Brian. BA, U. Pitts., 1964; MA, U. Pa., 1966, PhD, 1969; LLD hon., Briarwood Coll., 1989; EdD (hon.), Kyung Hee U., 1992. Asst. assoc. prof. classics Ohio State U., Columbus, 1969-77, asst. dean Coll. Humanities, 1971-72, acting chmn. dept. classics, 1972-73, assoc. dean Coll. Humanities, 1973-77; dean Coll. Humanities and Fine Art SUNY, Albany, 1977-83, v.p. rsch. and ednl. devel., 1983-85, v.p. academic planning and devel., 1985-87; pres. Cen. Conn. State U., New Britain, 1987—; exec. dir. Capital Dist. Humanities Program, Albany, 1978-83; trustee, chmn. Conn. Inst. for the ARts in Edn., New Britain, 1988-91; trustee Nat. Commn. for Coop. Edn., Boston, 1987—, exec. com. 1993—. Bd. dirs. New Britain Gen. Hosp., 1988—, Hartford chpt. ARC, 1988-91, A.W. Stanley Found., New Britain, 1988-93, Fleet Bank Adv. Bd., 1993—, World Affairs Coun., Hartford, Conn., 1994—, New Britain Found. for Pub. Giving, 1994—. Mem. Internat. Assn. Univ. Pres. (exec. com. 1987—, vice chmn. N.Am. coun. 1990—), Internat. Assembly Coop. Edn., Am. Assn. State Colls. and Univs. (com. on internat. programs 1987-88, com. state reps. 1988-89, com. diversity 1993—), New Eng. Bd. Higher Edn. (bd. govs. 1990—), New Britain C. of C. (bd. dirs. 1988-89), Phi Beta Kappa. Avocation: swimming. Office: Cen Conn State U 1615 Stanley St New Britain CT 06053-2439

SHUMAN, JOSEPH DUFF, lawyer; b. Pitts., Dec. 27, 1942; s. Joseph and Anna Jane (Phillips) D.; m. Ann Stewart McMillan, Nov. 9, 1969; children: David Stewart, Lauren Forbes. BA, Yale U., 1964; LLB, Harvard U., 1967. Bar: Pa. 1968, U.S. Dist. Ct. (we. dist.) Pa. 1968. Assoc. Thorp, Reed & Armstrong, Pitts., 1967-73, ptnr., 1974—, co-chair, corp. and bus. law dept., 1990-94, chair, 1994—. Republican. Presbyterian. Office: Thorp Reed & Armstrong 1 Riverfront Ctr Pittsburgh PA 15222-4800

SHUMAN, LARRY MYERS, soil chemist; b. Harrisburg, Pa., Apr. 3, 1944; s. Mark P. and Opal I. (Myers) Shuman; m. Catherine A. Yost, Mar. 21, 1970; children: Karen, Rebecca. BS, Pa. State U., 1966, MS, 1968, PhD, 1970. Asst. prof. soil chemistry U. Ga., Experiment, 1972-79, assoc. prof., 1979-91, prof., 1991—; USDA-OICD Exch. scientist to People's Republic of China, 1992. Co-editor, contbg. author Micronutrients in Agriculture, 1991; contbg. author: Zinc in Soils, 1979, Plant Environment Interactions, 1994; contbr. articles to profl. jours. Capt. M.S., U.S. Army, 1970-72. U.S. Aid grantee, 1980-81, USDA-CSRS grantee, 1992-94, Dept. Energy, 1995-96. Fellow Soil Sci Soc. Am. (soil chemistry divsn. chair 1994, assoc. editor jour. 1986-91); mem. Am. Soc. Agronomy, Coun. Agrl. Sci. and Tech., Soc. Environ. Geochemistry and Health. Home: 447 Trice Rd Milner GA 30257-3427 Office: U Ga Ga Experiment Sta Griffin GA 30223-1797

SHUMAN, MARK SAMUEL, environmental and electroanalytical chemistry educator; b. Yakima, Wash., July 29, 1936; s. Samuel and Ardella (Martin) S.; children—Kim, Donna, Bryce. B.S., Wash. State U., 1959; Ph.D., U. Wis., 1966. Chemist Atlantic Research Corp., Alexandria, Va., 1960-62; asst. prof. chemistry Tex. Christian U., Ft. Worth, 1966-69; vis. prof. Whitman Coll., Walla Walla, Wash., 1969-70; asst. prof. environ. chemistry U. N.C., Chapel Hill, 1970-75; assoc. prof. U. N.C., 1975-80, prof, 1980-92, prof. emeritus, 1992—. Contbr. articles to profl. jours., chpts. to books. Served to capt. U.S. Army, 1960-61. EPA fellow, 1970. Mem. Am. Chem. Soc. Office: 6 Davie Ln Chapel Hill NC 27514-5909

SHUMAN, MICHAEL HARRISON, lawyer, policy analyst; b. N.Y.C., June 4, 1956; s. Jack Jacob and Bernadine Sydelle (Fine) S. AB, Stanford U., Palo Alto, Calif., 1979; JD, Stanford U., 1982. Bar: Calif. 1983, D.C. 1990. Intern NRDC, San Francisco, 1981-82; pres. Ctr. for Innovative Diplomacy, Irvine, Calif., 1982-91; fellow Inst. for Policy Studies, Washington, 1991-92, dir., 1992—. Author: Citizen Diplomats, 1987, Conditions of Peace, 1991, Technology for the Common Good, 1993, Security Without War, 1993, Towards A Global Village, 1994. Kellogg Found. fellow, 1987. Avocations: roller skating, moose paraphernalia, film making, juggling. Office: Inst Policy Studies 1601 Connecticut Ave NW Washington DC 20009-1035

SHUMAN, NICHOLAS ROMAN, journalist, educator; b. Chgo., June 30, 1921; s. Roman William and Pauline (Stasevich) S.; m. Marilyn Elaine Johnson, Feb. 23, 1952; children—Kristin Mary, Elizabeth Carol, Mark Nicholas. B.A., U. Ill., 1943. With Chgo. Jour. Commerce, 1938-46; mem. staff Herald-American, Chgo., 1946-51; asst. photo editor Herald-American, 1947-51; mem. staff Chgo. Daily News, 1951-78, fin. editor, 1961-65, asst. mng. editor, 1965-69, nat. and fgn. editor, 1969-77, chief editorial writer, 1977-78; editorial writer Chgo. Sun-Times, 1978-84; prof. journalism Columbia Coll., Chgo., 1984-92, cons., 1992—; columnist Chgo. Reporter, 1985-90; sr. editor World Book Ency., 1965-66; profl. instr. Medill Sch. Journalism, Northwestern U., 1954-61; freelance mag. writer, 1951—; TV commentator, 1958-61. Founding pres. Arlington Heights (Ill.) Human Relations Com., 1965. Served to 1st lt. AUS, 1943-46, ETO. Recipient awards Ill. AP, UPI, John Howard Assn., Inland Press Assn., Chgo. Newspaper Guild; nominated for Pulitzer prize 3 times. Mem. Alpha Kappa Lambda, Sigma Delta Chi. Home: 1001 W Clarendon Rd Arlington Heights IL 60004-4507 Office: Columbia Coll 600 S Michigan Ave Chicago IL 60605-1901

SHUMAN, R(OBERT) BAIRD, academic program director, writer, english language educator, educational consultant; b. Paterson, N.J., June 20, 1929; s. George William and Elizabeth (Evans) S. A.B. (Trustees scholar), Lehigh U., 1951; M.Ed., Temple U., 1953; Ph.D. (Univ. scholar), U. Pa., 1961; cert. in philology, U. Vienna, Austria, 1954. Tchr. Phila. Pub. Schs., 1953-55; asst. instr. English U. Pa., 1955-57; instr. humanities Drexel U., Phila., 1957-59; asst. prof. San José (Calif.) State U., 1959-62; asst. prof. English Duke U., 1962-63, asso. prof., 1963-66, prof. edn., 1966-77; prof. English, dir. English edn. U. Ill., Urbana-Champaign, 1977-85; dir. freshman rhetoric U. Ill., 1979-84, coord. Univ. Associates in Rhetoric Program, 1978-84, dir. devel., 1988-93, acting dir. Ctr. for Study of Writing, 1989-90, prof. emeritus, 1993—; vis. prof. Moore Inst. Art, 1958, Phila. Conservatory Music, 1958-59, Lynchburg Coll., 1965, King Faisal U., Saudi Arabia, 1978, 81, Bread Loaf Sch. English, Middlebury Coll., 1980, East Tenn. State U., Johnson City, 1980, Olivet Nazarene Coll., 1984, 86, 88, U. Tenn., Knoxville, 1987; cons. Ednl. Testing Svc., 1970—, Am. Coll. Testing Svc., 1975-82; cons. in lang. and lit. Coll. Engring., U. Ill., 1980—, Worldwide Youth in Sci. and Engring., 1995—; mem. William Inge Nat. Festival Com., 1989—. Author: Clifford Odets, 1962, Robert E. Sherwood, 1964, William Inge, 1965, rev. edit., 1989, Strategies in Teaching Reading: Secondary, 1978, (with Robert J. Krajewski) The Beginning Teacher: A Guide to Problem Solving, 1979, Elements of Early Reading Instruction, 1979, The First R: Strategies in Early Reading Instruction, 1987, rev. edit., 1989, Classroom Encounters: Problems, Case Studies, Solutions, 1989, (with Eric Hobson) Reading and Writing in High School, (with Denny T. Wolfe Jr.) Teaching English Through the Arts, 1990, Resources for Writers, 1992, American drama 1918-1960, 1992, Georgia O'Keeffe, 1993; editor: Nine Black Poets, 1968, An Eye for an Eye, 1969, A Galaxy of Black Writing, 1970, Creative Approaches to the Teaching of English: Secondary, 1974, Questions English Teachers Ask, 1977, Educational Drama for Today's Schools, 1978, Education in the 80's—English, 1980, The Clearing House: A Closer Look, 1984, 70th anniversary issue The Clearing House, 1995; exec. editor The Clearing House jour., 1976—; cons. editor Poet Lore, 1977-80, Cygnus, 1978—, Jour. Aesthetic Edn., 1978-82; contbg. editor Reading Horizons, 1975-85; editor quar. column Reading Horizons, 1975-85; editor Trends in English column Ednl. Leadership, 1989—. Active Nat. Trust Hist. Preservation. NEH researcher Trinity Coll., Dublin, Ireland, 1985. Mem. MLA, Nat. Coun. Tchrs. English (evaluator ERIC Clearing House, com. alt. careers for English profls.), Internat. Fedn. Tchrs. English, Internat. Coun. Edn. of tchrs., Nev. Coun. Tchrs. English, Conf. English Edn. (exec. com. 1976-79), Internat. Reading Assn. (coord. symposium on cultural literacy, Queensland, Australia 1988), Internat. Assn. Univ. Profs. English, Nat. Soc. Study Edn., Am. Fedn. Tchrs., Union Profl. Employees (editor newsletter 1988-92, exec. com. 1988-92). Democrat. Home: PO Box 27647 Las Vegas NV 89126-1647 Office: U Ill 208 English Bldg 608 S Wright St Urbana IL 61801-3613 *An education that does not produce people who are vibrantly alive, intoxicated with the wonder of existence, has fallen short. Joy of learning is the fulcrum upon which the human equation is balanced. I have always believed that emotion prevails over intellect and have led my life accordingly with the inevitable resultof being extraordinarily happy for most of my days.*

SHUMAN, SAMUEL IRVING, lawyer, law educator; b. Fall River, Mass., Aug. 7, 1925; s. Max and Fannie S.; m. Cynthia Webre, Mar. 25, 1990; children from previous marriage: Maxim Erric, Michael A. A.B., U. Pa., 1947, M.A., 1948, Ph.D., 1951; J.D., U. Mich., 1954; S.J.D., Harvard U., 1959. Bar: Mich. 1954, Tex. 1979. Research asst. Legis. Research Center, U. Mich., Ann Arbor, 1953-54; vis. prof. law Legis. Research Center, U. Mich., 1961; vis. prof. U. Rome, 1963-64; asst. prof. law Wayne State U., Detroit, 1954-55; assoc. prof. Wayne State U., 1955-56, prof., 1957-80; prof. dept. psychiatry Wayne State U. Med. Sch.; lectr. Internat. Faculty Comparative Law, Luxembourg, 1964; prof. forensic psychiatry, spl. counsel Lafayette Clinic, Mich. Dept. Mental Health; gen. counsel Mich. Psychiat. Assn., Epilepsy Center Mich. Author: Legal Positivism: Its Scope and Limitations, 1963, (with N.D. West) Introduction to American Law: Cases and Materials, 1971, Psychosurgery and the Medical Control of Violence: Autonomy and Deviance, 1977; editorial bd.: Am. Jour. Jurisprudence, 1969-79. Bd. dirs. Tex. Modern Art Found. Recipient Wayne State U. Bd. Govs. Faculty Recognition award, 1978; Probus Club award Disting. Acad. Achievement in Humanities, 1963; Fulbright fellow Italy, 1961; Rockefeller Found. grantee, 1959, 61; Fulbright travel grantee Germany, 1961; Wayne State U. research grantee, 1960-64; Internat. Research & Exchanges Bd. grantee, 1973. Mem. Am. Law Inst. (life). Office: Box D Camden ME 04843

SHUMAN, STANLEY S., investment banker; b. Cambridge, Mass., June 22, 1935; s. Saul A. and Sarah L. (Saxe) S.; m. Ruth H. Lande, 1967 (div. 1979); children—David Lande, Michael Adam. B.A., Harvard U., Boston, 1956, J.D., 1959, M.B.A., 1961. Bar: Mass. 1959, N.Y. 1991. Exec. v.p., mng. dir. Allen & Co., Inc., N.Y.C., 1961—; bd. dirs. Bayou Steel Corp., Global Asset Mgmt. (USA), Inc., Hudson Gen. Corp., News Corp. Ltd., News Am. Holdings Inc., Sesac Inc. Mem. Fin. Control Bd., N.Y.C., 1977—; trustee The Dalton Sch., 1977-84, hon. trustee, 1984—; class agt. Phillips Acad., Andover, Mass., 1972-90; pres. Wiliwyck Sch., 1971-78; v.p. exec. com. Jewish Guild for the Blind, 1973-80; trustee Jewish Publ. Soc., 1986-90, Channel 13 WNET, 1990—, Carnegie Hall, 1990—, N.Y. Law Sch., 1990—, The Markle Found., 1992—, Nat. Pub. Radio Found., 1992—; chmn. Nat. Econ. Devel. and Law Ctr., 1978-83; chmn. adv. bd. Inst. Policy Scis. and Pub. Affairs, Duke U., 1992—. Mem. ABA (comml. arbitration com., sect. corp. banking and bus. law 1974—). Clubs: Harvard (Boston); City Athletic, Quaker Ridge Golf, Harvard (N.Y.C.); East Hampton Tennis. Home: 17 E 73rd St New York NY 10021-3544 Office: Allen & Co Inc 711 5th Ave New York NY 10022-3109*

SHUMATE, CHARLES ALBERT, retired dermatologist; b. San Francisco, Aug. 11, 1904; s. Thomas E. and Freda (Ortmann) S.; B.S., U. San Francisco, 1927, H.H.D., 1976; M.D., Creighton U., 1931. Pvt. practice dermatology, San Francisco, 1933-73, ret., 1973; asst. clin. prof. dermatology Stanford U., 1956-62; pres. E Clampus Vitus, Inc., 1963-64; hon. mem. staff St. Mary's Hosp. Mem. San Francisco Art Commn., 1964-67, Calif. Heritage Preservation Commn., 1963-67; regent Notre Dame Coll. at Belmont, 1965-78, trustee, 1977-93; pres. Conf. Calif. Hist. Socs., 1967; mem. San Francisco Landmarks Preservation Bd., 1967-78, pres., 1967-69; trustee St. Patrick's Coll. and Sem., 1970-86; dir. U.S. Catholic Hist. Soc., 1988—. Served as maj. USPHS, 1942-46. Decorated knight comdr. Order of Isabella (Spain); knight Order of the Holy Sepulchre, knight of St. Gregory, knight of Malta. Fellow Am. Acad. Dermatology; mem. U. San Francisco Alumni Assn. (pres. 1955), Calif. Book Club (pres. 1969-71), Calif. Hist. Soc. (trustee 1958-67, 68-78, pres. 1962-64), Soc. Calif. Pioneers (dir. 1979—), Drum Found. (v.p. 1986—). Clubs: Bohemian, Olympic, Roxburghe (pres. 1958-59) (San Francisco); Zamorano (Los Angeles). Author: Life of George Henry Goddard; The California of George Gordon, 1976, Jas. F. Curtis, Vigilante, 1988, Francisco Pacheco of Pacheco Pass, 1977; Life of Mariano Malarin, 1980; Boyhood Days: Y. Villegas Reminiscences of California 1850s, 1983, The Notorious I.C. Woods of the Adams Express, 1986, Rincon Hill and South Park, 1988, Captain A.A. Ritchie, Pioneer, 1991, Stormy Life of Major William Gouverneur Morris, 1993, Lord Sholter Douglas, Clamgen, 1996. Mem. St. Andrew Soc. (hon. mem.). Home: 1901 Scott St San Francisco CA 94115-2613 Office: 490 Post St San Francisco CA 94102-1401

SHUMATE, PAUL WILLIAM, JR., communications executive; b. Phila., July 15, 1941; s. Paul William and Ruth (Bailey) S.; m. Randi Atkins, June 20, 1964; 1 child, Angela Lynn. BS in Physics, Coll. of William & Mary, 1963; PhD in Physics, U. Va., 1968. Scientist Nat. Bur. of Standards, Washington, 1963-64; asst. prof. physics U. Va., Charlottesville, 1968-69; mem. tech. staff Bell Telephone Labs., Murray Hill, N.J., 1969-75, supr., 1975-84; dist. mgr. Bellcore, Morristown, N.J., 1984-86; div. mgr. Bellcore, Morristown, 1986-91, exec. dir., 1991—; lectr. and pub. in field; mem. optoelectronics study team Japanese Tech. Evaluation Ctr. NSF, 1994—. Editor-in-chief Photonics Tech. Letters, 1988-94, Trans. Mag., 1972-79, Lightwave Tech. Steering Com., 1982—; contbr. chpts. to books. Fellow IEEE (E.H. Armstrong award 1993, Telephony Fiber-in-the-Loop award 1993); mem. Optical Soc. Am., Lasers and Electro-Optics Soc. (v.p. publs.), Sigma Xi, Phi Beta Kappa.

SHUMILA, MICHAEL JOHN, electrical engineer; b. Newark, Aug. 30, 1947; s. Michael John and Anne (Zavocki) S. AS, Essex County Coll., Newark, 1971; BSEE, N.J. Inst. Tech., 1974, MSEE, 1977. Systems engr. Lockheed Electronics, Plainfield, N.J., 1977-78; engr. group VI Reeves Teletape, N.Y.C., 1978-79; sr. mem. engring. staff G.E. Am. Communications, Princeton, N.J., 1979-81; mem. tech. staff David Sarnoff Rsch. Ctr., Princeton, N.J., 1981—. Author: NAB Engineering Handbook, 1985; contbr. articles to profl. jours. Recipient RCA Outstanding Tech. Achievement award David Sarnoff Rsch. Ctr., 1985, First Cut Silicon award VLSI Tech., Inc., 1991. Mem. Aircraft Owners and Pilots Assn., Exptl. Aircraft Assn., Soc. Motion Picture and TV Engrs. Lutheran. Achievements include contribution to the architecture and design of the RCA Digital Audio Transmission system; patents on real time median filter design, adaptive control of median filters. Home: 16 Pintinalli Dr Trenton NJ 08619-1538

SHUMWAY, JULIE FRISONI, news producer; b. Niagara Falls, N.Y., Apr. 6, 1964; d. David Nicholas and Helen Josephine (Basile) Frisoni; m. Jeffery Bue Shumway, Sept. 25, 1993; 1 child, Kelsey Paige. BA in Comm. summa cum laude, Ariz. State U., 1986. From prodr. to exec. prodr. KPNX-TV, Phoenix, 1985—. Team leader, committed ptnr., founding mem. Phoenix Youth at Risk, 1989-93. Recipient Emmy awards (7) Nat. Acad. TV Arts and Scis. (Rocky Mt. chpt.), 1987-92, AP awards (12), 1987—, N.Y. Film Festival awards (2), 1990, Nat. Gabriel award Nat. Cath. Assn. for Broadcasters, 1989. Mem. Am. Women in Radio and TV (Best Support Staff award). Lutheran. Avocations: snow skiing, boating, travel, water skiing. Office: KPNX TV 1101 N Central Ave Phoenix AZ 85004

SHUPACK, PAUL MARTIN, law educator; b. Bklyn., May 20, 1940; s. Ben and Florentina Marie (Leipniker) S.; m. Leslie Sloan, Dec. 23, 1989; stepchildren: Alexander Hoffert, Jason Hoffert. AB, Columbia U., 1961; postgrad., Harvard U., 1961-67; JD, U. Chgo., 1970. Bar: N.Y. 1971. Assoc. Cleary, Gottlieb, Steen & Hamilton, N.Y.C., 1970-77; asst. prof. Yeshiva U., N.Y.C., 1977-79, assoc. prof., 1980-84, prof., 1984—; vis. asst. prof. U. Chgo., 1979. Contbr. articles to profl. jours. Mem. Am. Law Inst., Assn. Bar City of N.Y. Home: 35 Sutton Pl Apt 7C New York NY 10022 Office: Yeshiva U 55 5th Ave New York NY 10003-4301

SHUPP, FRANKLIN RICHARD, economist; b. Palmerton, Pa., Apr. 9, 1934; s. Floyd Edwin and Mona Elizabeth (Williams) S.; m. Carol Ann Edwards, Sept. 27, 1959; children: Diedre Elaine, Ruth Louise, Robert Seth. BS, Lafayette Coll., 1954; PhD, Princeton U., 1960. Asst. lectr.

Edinburgh (Scotland) U., 1959-60; asst. prof. U. Ill., Urbana, 1960-64, assoc. prof., 1964-70, prof. econs., 1970—, chmn. dept. econs., 1986-89; Fulbright rsch. prof. U. Oslo, Norway, 1966-67; sr. economist bd. govs. FRS, Washington, 1970-71; vis. prof. U. York, Eng., 1973-74, U. Cambridge, Eng., 1981-82, U. Sydney, Australia, 1989-90, U. Beijing, Peoples U., China, 1992-93; cons. joint econ. com. U.S. Congress, Washington, 1978-80. Author monograph The Inflation Process, 1969-79, 1979; assoc. editor Jour. Econ. Dynamics and Control, 1979—; contbr. numerous articles to profl. jours., chpts. in books. Vis. fellow Wolfson Coll., Cambridge U., 1981, Gonville and Caius Coll., Cambridge U., 1982, U. Melbourne, Australia, 1990; recipient grants Ford Found., 1966, NSF, 1973, 79, Social Sci. Rsch. Coun., 1981, NAS, 1993. Mem. Soc. Econs. Dynamics and Control (sec.-treas. 1983-84, pres. 1984-86), Am. Econ. Assn., Royal Econ. Soc. Lutheran. Home: 507 W Vermont Ave Urbana IL 61801-4930 Office: U of Ill 193 Commerce W Champaign IL 61820

SHUR, GEORGE MICHAEL, lawyer; b. Portland, Maine, Nov. 10, 1942; m. Martha West, Nov. 14, 1970; children: Aaron, Rebecca. AB in Modern European History, Colby Coll.; JD, Boston U.; postgrad., Nat. Inst. for Trial Advocacy. Bar: Maine, 1968, U.S. Cist. Ct. Maine, 1968, U.S. Supreme Ct. 1980, U.S. Ct. Appeals (1st cir.) 1980, Ill. 1983, U.S. Dist. Ct. (no. dist.) Ill. 1983, U.S. Ct. Appeals (7th cir.) 1985. Assoc. Bernstein, Shur, Sawyer & Shur, 1968-72; ptnr. Bernstein, Shur, Sawyer & Nelson, Portland, Maine, 1972-83; gen. counsel, chief legal officer No. Ill. U., DeKalb, 1983—. Contbr. articles to profl. jours., chpts. to books. Mem. Cape Elizabeth (Maine) Town Dem. Com., del. State Dem. Conv., 1976-78, 80-82; mem. City of DeKalb Human Rels. Commn., 1985—, United Way Budget Com., 1972-77; faculty Nat. Small Craft Sch. ARC, summers 1963-70; bd. dirs. 1968-71; v.p. Children's Theatre of Maine, Inc., 1970-71, bd. dirs. 1968-72; pres. Portland Colby Alumni Club, 1979-82, Portland Players, Inc., 1972-74, bd. dirs. 1970-80, pres., Alumni Coun. Colby Coll., 1980-83; bd. dirs. Camp Fire Girls, 1969-72, ARC, Portland, 1968-72, DeKalb County Am. Cancer Soc., 1985—; bd. dirs., sec., mem. exec. com. Portland Boys' Club, 1977-83; asst. chmn. Bd. Zoning Appeals Town of Cape Elizabeth, Maine, 1978-83; mem. bd. trustees, exec. com. North Yarmouth Acad., 1980-83; mem. DeKalb Bd. of Edn., 1991—, v.p. 1992—. With USAR, 1968-76. Recipient Thomas S. Biggs award Stetson U. Coll. Law, 1994. Mem. ABA (local govt. law and legal edn. and admissions sects.), Maine State Bar Assn. (chmn. legal edn. and admissions com., bridging the gap program 1975-83, rep. commn. to examine bar admission process 1980-83), Ill. Bar Assn. (legal edn., admissions and competence com. 1984-94), DeKalb County Bar Assn. (chmn. rev. model rules of profl. conduct com. 1984-85), Nat. Coll. and Univ. Attys. (pres. 1988-89, pres. elect 1987-88, chmn. ann. conf. program and 1st v.p. 1986-87, 2d v.p. 1985-86, exec. bd. 1974-78, 83-85, mid-winter Continuing Legal Edn. workshop 1979, program com. 1980-81, program com. ann. confs. 1985, rep. conf. of solicitors instns. higher edn. Dalhousie U. 1975, chmn. spl. conf. New Eng. Bd. Higher Edn. 1977, chmn. spl. conf. legal presentations Wakefield (Mass.) chpt. 1978, chmn. site selection com. 1981-82, 1st ann. mid-winter Continuing Legal Edn. workshop com. 1980, New Eng. membership sect. 1971-73, 76-81, student affairs sect. 1980—), Nat. Orgn. Legal Problems, Assn. Trial Lawyers Am., Maine Trial lawyers Assn., Maine Econ. Soc. (charter mem., bd. dirs. 1980-83), Assn. Student Jud. Affairs (chair legis. affairs com. 1992-93, mem. faculty 1994—), Alpha Delta Phi. Home: 305 Forsythe Ln De Kalb IL 60115-2341 Office: No Ill U Lowden Hall Office Univ Legal Counsel De Kalb IL 60115-2880

SHUR, MICHAEL, electrical engineer, educator, consultant; b. Kamensk-Yralski, Sverdlovsk, USSR, Nov. 13, 1942; came to U.S., 1976.; s. Saul and Anna (Katz) S.; m. Paulina Gimmelfarb, Sept. 25, 1966; children: Luba, Natasha. MS, Leningrad Elec. Tech. Inst., 1965; PhD, Ioffe Inst., Leningrad, 1967; DSc, Ioffe Inst., St. Petersburg, 1992; Hon. Doctorate, St. Petersburg State Tech. U., 1994. Scientist Ioffe Inst., 1965-75; asst. prof. Wayne State U., Detroit, 1976-77, Oakland U., Rochester, Mich., 1978; prof. U. Minn., Mpls., 1979-92; John Marshall Money prof. U. Va., Charlottesville, Va., 1989-96; Patricia W. and C. Sheldon Roberts prof. Rensselaer Poly. Inst., 1996—; Author 9 books; co-editor-in-chief Internat. Jour. High Speed Electronics and Sys.; contbr. articles to profl. jours.; patentee in field. Author 7 books; contbr. articles to profl. jours.; patentee in field. Fellow IEEE (assoc. editor IEEE Trans. 1990-93), Am. Phys. Soc.; mem. Eta Kappa Nu, Tau Beta Pi. *When we were penniless refugees, the United States adopted me and my family with compassion and friendship, gave us work and citizenship. Our debt of gratitude to the American people who accepted us as their own we will be never able to repay.*

SHURBAJI, M. SALAH, pathologist; b. Cairo, Apr. 18, 1957; came to U.S., 1984; s. Muhammad B. and Salma Shurbaji; m. Hilda Touma, 1984; 2 children. BS with distinction, Am. U. Beirut, 1979, MS, 1981, MD with distinction, 1984. Diplomate Am. Bd. Pathology; lic. physician Md., Tenn., Mich. Intern Am. U. Beirut Med. Ctr., 1983-84; resident pathology Johns Hopkins Hosp., Balt., 1984-87, resident dept. lab. medicine, 1987-89; clin. fellow dept. pathology Johns Hopkins U. Sch. Medicine, Balt., 1984-89, rsch. fellow dept. pathology, 1989-90; asst. prof. pathology East Tenn. State U., Johnson City, 1990-94, assoc. prof. pathology, 1994—; staff pathologist Univ. Physicians Practice Group, Johnson City, 1990—; staff pathologist Vets. Affairs Med. Ctr., Johnson City, 1990—, acting chief pathology and lab. medicine svc., 1993-94, chief pathology and lab. medicine svc., 1994—. Contbr. articles to profl. jours. Recipient John Abi Hashem Pediatric award Am. U. Beirut, 1982. Fellow Am. Soc. Clin. Pathologists, Coll. Am. Pathologists; mem. AASA, A.P. Stout Soc. Surg. Pathologists, Am. Soc. Cytology, U.S. and Can. Acad. Pathology, Papanicolaou Soc. Cytopathology, Internat. Soc. Urologic Pathology, Sigma Xi, Alpha Omega Alpha. Achievements include contribution to understanding of certain factors that affect the prognosis of neoplasms especially prostate cancer. Office: 1905 Roundtree Dr Johnson City TN 37604

SHURE, MYRNA BETH, psychologist, educator; b. Chgo., Sept. 11, 1937; d. Sidney Natkin and Frances (Laufman) S.; student U. Colo., 1955; BS, U. Ill., 1959; MS, Cornell U., 1961, PhD, 1966. Asst. prof. U. R.I., head tchr. Nursery Sch., Kingston, 1961-62; asst. prof. Temple U., Phila., 1966-67, assoc. prof., 1967-68; instr. Hahneman Med. Coll., Phila., 1968-69, sr. instr. psychology, 1969-70, asst. prof., 1970-73, assoc. prof., 1973-80, prof., 1980—. NIMH research grantee, 1971-75, 77-79, 82-85, 87, 88-93. Recipient Lela Rowland Prevention award Nat. Mental Health Assn., 1982; . lic. psychologist, Pa. Fellow Am. Psychol. Assn. (Disting. Contbn. award div. community psychology 1984), Am. Psychol. Assn. (divsn. clin. psychology, child sect. 1994, Task Force on Prevention award 1987, Task Force on Model Programs award 1994); mem. Nat. Assn. Sch. Psychologists, Nat. Assn. Edn. Young Children, Soc. Research in Child Devel., Phila. Soc. Clin. Psychologists. Author: (with George Spivack) Social Adjustment of Young Children, 1974; (with George Spivack and Jerome Platt) The Problem Solving Approach to Adjustment, 1976; (with George Spivack) Problem Solving Techniques in Childrearing, 1978, (child curricula manual) I Can Problem Solve, 1992, (trade book) Raising a Thinking Child, 1994, (audiotape, workbook), 1996; mem. editl. bd. Jour. Applied Developmental Psychology; spl. cons. to The Puzzle Place PBS Children's TV Show.

SHURICK, EDWARD PALMES, television executive, rancher; b. Duluth, Minn., Dec. 15, 1912; s. Edward P. and Vera (Wheaton) S.; m. F(lossie) Dolores Pipes, Aug. 1, 1933; children—Patricia Annette (Mrs. Robert Dube), Sandra Sue Shurick Dryden, Linda Jean (Mrs. James Elsea), Edward P. III. Student, U. Minn., 1932-33; B.A. in Econs, U. Mo., 1946. Gen. sales mgr. Intermountain Network, Salt Lake City, 1937-41; advt. mgr. sta. KMBC, Kansas City, Mo., 1941-47; research mgr. Free & Peters, N.Y.C., 1947-49; v.p. CBS TV, N.Y.C., 1949-57; exec. v.p. Blair TV, N.Y.C., 1957-62; chmn., treas. H-R TV, N.Y.C., 1962-76; dir. Seltel, Inc., N.Y.C.; v.p., owner Sta. KXXX-AM-FM, Colby, Kans., 1963-84; v.p., treas. H-R Rep. Cos., 1970-73; pres. S&S Enterprises, Charlottesville, Va., 1959-89, S & S Ranch Corp., Aspen, Colo., 1965-82; mem. bd. Chgo. Internat. Live Stock Expn., 1972-76. Author: First Quarter-Century of American Broadcasting, 1946. Pres. Shurick Rsch. Found., Bridgewater, 1959-72; v.p., originator Internat. Radio and TV Found., N.Y.C., 1964-73. Recipient Alumnus award U. Mo. at Kansas City, 1968; ordre du merit for contbns. to agr. Govt. France, 1970; Ordre du Charolais Francais, 1971. Mem. Internat. Radio and TV Soc. N.Y. (pres. 1967-69), Am. Internat. Charolais Assn. (pres. 1968-69), Colonial Charolais Breeders (dir. 1967-71), World Fedn. Charolais (pres. 1973-74), Broadcast Pioneers Assn., Am. Nat. Cattlemen's Assn. (tax com. 1968-76), Internat. Wine and Food Soc. (bd. dirs. 1985-88), Masons (32 degree), Shriners. Episcopalian (lay reader). Address: 1006 Fearrington Post Fearrington Village NC 27312 *The opportunity to succeed as a self-made person still exists in the United States today. This may seem hackneyed and out-of-date, but it isn't. Honesty, dedication, long hours of hard work with an average amount of luck will build a fortune from a few cents to a million dollars.*

SHURLEY, JAY TALMADGE, psychiatrist, medical educator, administrator, behavioral sciences researcher, polar explorer, author, genealogist; b. Sonora, Tex., Dec. 20, 1917; s. Ira L. and Jewell L. (Choate) S.; m. Erwina Bode Cornelison, Dec. 20, 1986. BA in Zoology, U. Tex.-Austin, 1940; MD, U. Tex. Med. Br., Galveston, 1942. Diplomate Am. Bd. Psychiatry and Neurology. Intern. Ind. U.-Indpls. Med. Ctr., 1943; Rockefeller fellow in neuropsychiatry dept. mental and nervous disease Inst. for Mental Hygiene Pa. Hosp., Phila., 1944-47; dir. Markle Meml. Unit for Insulin Therapy dept. for mental and nervous disease Pa. Hosp., Phila., 1945-50; pvt. practice medicine specializing in psychiatry and psychoanalysis Phila., 1947-51, Austin, 1951-52; pvt. practice medicine specializing in psychiatry San Antonio, 1952-54, Chevy Chase, Md., 1955-57; pvt. practice medicine specializing in psychiatry, psychoanalysis and sleep disorders medicine Oklahoma City, 1978-90; acting chief lab. adult psychiat. investigation, clin. investigations NIMH, NIH, Bethesda, 1955-57; chief psychiatry service and mental hygiene clinic VA Hosp., Oklahoma City, 1957-62; sr. med. investigator in psychiatry, research service, dept. medicine and surgery VA, 1962-76; founder and dir. behavioral scis. labs VA Med. Ctr., Oklahoma City, 1962-78; med. dir. outpatient psychiatry clinics Okla. Meml. Hosp. and Clinics, Okla Health Scis. Ctr., Oklahoma City, 1978-81; sci. dir. Oklahoma Mental Health Research Inst., Oklahoma Dept. Mental Health, 1988-89; cons.-liaison in geropsychiatry O'Donoghue Rehab. Inst., Okla. Med. Ctr., 1990-91; med. dir. emeritus Willow View Mental Health Ctr., Oklahoma City, 1985-87; prof. psychiatry U. Okla., Oklahoma City, 1957-62, career research prof. psychiatry and behavioral scis., 1962-77, prof. psychiatry and behavioral scis. Coll. of Medicine and Grad. Coll., 1977-81; prof. emeritus psychiatry and behavioral scis. U. Okla. Coll. Medicine, Oklahoma City, 1981—; adj. prof. human ecology Coll. Health, U. Okla., 1967-81; mem. com. on polar rsch., chmn. panel on biology and medicine NAS/NRC, 1970-74; U.S. rep. Working Group on Biology XII Sci. Com. on Antarctic Rsch., Canberra and Melbourne, Australia, 1972; U.S. rep. Working Group on Human Biology and Medicine XIII Sci. Com. on Antarctic Rsch., Jackson Hole, Wyo., 1974; disting. vis. scientist Acad. Scis. USSR, Moscow and Leningrad, 1972; Centennial Yr. vis. prof. dept. psychol. medicine U. Otago, Dunedin, N.Z., 1975; mem. Health Rsch. Com., Okla. Ctr. for Sci. and Tech., 1986-91, Okla. Alzheimer Rsch. Adv. Coun., 1990-92. Editor: Relating Environment to Mental Health and Illness: The Eco-psychiatric Data Base, 1979, Symposium on Man on the South Polar Plateau, 1970; mem. editorial bd. Jour. Clin. Psychology, 1970-80; contbr. more than 100 articles to sci. publs. Served as capt. M.C. U.S. Army, 1952-54. Recipient Antarctic Svc. medal NSF/NAS, 1970, Disting. Profl. Svc. award Okla. Psychol. Assn., 1972, Sustained Superior Achievement cert. VA, 1974, Disting. Psychiatrist award Mid-Continent Psychiat. Assn., 1986, Okla. Psychiat. Assn., 1990, Sealy Inc. prize Assn. Profl. Sleep Socs., 1991; Shurley Ridge, Pensacola Mountains Antarctica named in his honor. Fellow Am. Psychiat. Assn. (life), Am. Coll. Psychiatrists (life); mem. AMA,Oklahoma County Med. Assn., Okla. State Med. Assn. (life), Okla. Psychiat. Assn. (pres. 1968, chair ethics com. 1989-91), Faculty House Club, Sigma Xi, Alpha Omega Alpha, Alpha Epsilon Delta. Democrat. Mailing Address: PO Box 1277 Bastrop TX 78602

SHURTLEFF, MALCOLM C., plant pathologist, consultant, educator, extension specialist; b. Fall River, Mass., June 24, 1922; s. Malcolm C. and Florence L. (Jewell) S.; m. Margaret E. Johnson, June 14, 1950; children: Robert Glen, Janet Lee, Mark Steven. BS in Biology, U. R.I., 1943; MS in Plant Pathology, U. Minn., 1950, PhD in Plant Pathology, 1953. Asst. plant pathologist Conn. Agrl. Expt. Sta., New Haven, 1942, R.I. Agrl. Expt. Sta., Kingston, 1943; asst. extension prof. U. R.I., Kingston, 1950-54; assoc. extension prof. Iowa State U., Ames, 1954-61; prof. plant pathology U. Ill., Champaign-Urbana, 1961-92, prof. emeritus, 1992—; cons., writer Urbana, 1992—. Author: How To Control Plant Diseases, 1962, 66 (award Am. Garden Guild 1961, 66), How To Control Lawn Diseases and Pests, 1973, How To Control Tree Diseases and Pests, 1975, Controlling Turfgrass Pests, 1987, 96, A Glossary of Plant Pathological and Other Terms Used by Plant Scientits, 1996; editor-in-chief Phytopathology News, 1966-69, Plant Disease, 1969-72; contbr. numerous articles to encys., profl. publs. and mags. Lt. (j.g.) USN, 1943-46, PTO. Recipient Disting. Svc. award U.S. Dept. Agriculture, Washington, 1986. Fellow Am. Phytopathological Soc. (councilor at large 1970-71, Excellence in Extension Plant Pathology award 1991); mem. Internat. Soc. Plant Pathology (chmn. extension com. 1975-80), Am. Phytopathological Soc. (mem. various coms.). Avocation: photography. Home: 2707 Holcomb Dr Urbana IL 61801-7724 Office: U Ill Dept Plant Pathology N-427 N Turner Hall Urbana IL 61801

SHURTLIFF, MARVIN KARL, lawyer; b. Idaho Falls, Idaho, Nov. 6, 1939; s. Noah Leon and Melba Dorothy (Hunting) S.; m. Peggy J. Griffin, Nov. 23, 1963; 1 dau., Jennifer Karyl. B.A., Idaho State Coll., 1962; J.D., U. Idaho, 1968. Bar: Idaho 1968. Tchr. pub. schs. Jefferson County, Idaho, 1964-65; atty. U.S. Dept. Justice, Washington, 1968-74; commr. Idaho Pub. Utilities Commn., 1974-75, pres., 1975-76; spl. asst., legal counsel Gov. of Idaho, Boise, 1977; U.S. atty. for Dist. of Idaho, Boise, 1977-81; practice law Boise, 1981—; mem. Idaho Ho. of Reps., 1962-64. Mem. Idaho State Bd. Edn., 1990-95. Mem. Idaho Bar Assn. Democrat. Home: 62 Horizon Dr Boise ID 83702-4419 Office: PO Box 1652 Boise ID 83701-1652

SHUSHKEWICH, KENNETH WAYNE, structural engineer; b. Winnipeg, Man., Sept. 22, 1952; m. Valdine Cuffe, Sept. 28, 1980. BSCE, U. Man., Winnipeg, 1974; MS in Structural Engring., U. Calif., Berkeley, 1975; PhD in Structural Engring., U. Alta., Edmonton, Can., 1985. Engr. Wardrop and Assocs., Winnipeg, 1974-78, Preconsult Can., Montreal, Que., 1978-80; prof. U. Alta., 1981-85, U. Man., 1985-87; engr. T.Y. Lin Internat., San Francisco, 1988-90, H.J. Degenkolb Assocs., San Francisco, 1990-92, Ben C. Gerwick, Inc., San Francisco, 1993-94, J. Muller Internat., Chgo., 1994-95, T.Y. Lin Internat., San Francisco, 1995—; mem. bridge design com., prestressed concrete com. ASCE-Am. Concrete Inst. Prin. works include design of prestressed concrete segmental bridges, seismic strengthening of San Francisco Ferry Building damaged in Loma Prieta earthquake, seismic retrofit of Presidio Viaduct in San Francisco; design mgr. for long-span west approach bridge of Northumberland Strait Crossing in Can.; contbr. articles to profl. jours. Recipient award for design of Vierendeel truss bridge, Man. Design Inst., 1977. Mem. ASCE, Am. Concrete Inst., Prestressed Concrete Inst., Internat. Assn. Bridge and Structural Engrs. Office: PO Box 2590 San Francisco CA 94126

SHUSTER, ALVIN, journalist, newspaper editor; b. Washington, Jan. 25, 1930; s. Fred and Dora (Levy) S.; m. Miriam Schwartz, June 22, 1952; children: Fred, Jessica, Beth. AB, George Washington U., 1951. Reporter Washington Bur. N.Y. Times, 1952-61, asst. news editor, 1961-66, reporter London Bur., 1967-70; bur. chief Saigon, Vietnam, 1970-71, London, 1971-75, Rome, 1975-77; dep. editor editorial pages L.A. Times, 1977-83, fgn. editor, 1983-95, sr. consulting editor, 1995—; pres. Fgn. Corrs. Assn., London, 1973-74; trustee Monterey (Calif.) Inst. Internat. Studies, 1983—. Editor: The Witnesses, 1964, Washington: The New York Times Guide to the Nations' Capital, 1967, International Press Institute Report, 1995—. Nieman fellow Harvard U., 1966-67. Mem. Reform Club (London). Office: Los Angeles Times Times Mirror Sq Los Angeles CA 90053

SHUSTER, BUD, congressman; b. Glassport, Pa., Jan. 23, 1932; s. Prather and Grace (Greinert) S.; m. Patricia Rommell, Aug. 27, 1955; children: Peg, Bill, Debbie, Bobby, Gia. B.S., U. Pitts., 1954; M.B.A., Duquesne U., 1960; Ph.D. in Econs. and Mgmt., Am. U., 1967. Nat. account mgr. Univac div. Sperry Rand, 1956, Univac div. Remington Rand Co. (name now Sperry Rand), 1956-60; dist. mgr. Western Pa. RCA, 1960-62; mgr. ops. RCA, Washington, 1962-65; v.p. EPD div. RCA, 1965-68; pres. computer terminal co., 1968-72; mem. 93rd-104th Congresses from 9th Pa. dist., Washington, D.C., 1973—; pres. 93d Congress Republican Freshman Class; chmn. Nat. Transp. Policy Study Commn., 1976; ranking mem. Pub. Works and Transp. com., 1995—, chmn. com. on transportation and infrastructure. Author: Believing in America, 1983. Del. Republican Nat. Conv., 1976, 80, 84, 88, 92; co-chair Energy, Environment & Transp. Platform Subcom.; sr. transp. advisor Bush-Quayle campaign; also mem. platform com.; chmn. Reagan-Bush Campaign in Western Pa.; sr. adviser to transition team for Dept. Transp., 1980-81; trustee J.F. Kennedy Ctr. for Performing Arts. Served with inf. and CIC AUS, 1954-56. Recipient Watchdog of Treasury award, Guardian of Small Bus. award, Golden Age Hall of Fame award. Mem. Pa. Soc., Chowder and Marching Soc., Phi Beta Kappa, Omicron Delta Kappa, Sigma Chi (Significant Sig award). Club: Capitol Hill. Office: US Ho of Reps 2188 Rayburn Bldg Ofc B Washington DC 20515-0005*

SHUSTER, JOHN A., civil engineer; b. Santa Fe, Jan. 18, 1939; s. William H. and Selma (Dingee) S.; m. Carol Habberley, July 1958 (div. Feb. 1960); m. Susan Handy, Aug. 20, 1962 (div. May 1992); children: David Brian, Karen. Student, U. N.Mex., 1961-63; BCE, U. Alaska, 1965; MCE, Stanford U., 1966. Registered profl. engr., Alaska, Calif., R.I., Mass., Va., Wash., Wis., Md., Del. Project engr. Woodward Clyde Assocs., Oakland, Calif., 1966-67, sr. project engr., 1969-72; resident project engr. Soil Cons. of S.E. Asia, Bangkok, Thailand, 1967-69; v.p. engring. Am. Drilling Co., Providence, 1972-74, also bd. dirs.; exec. v.p. Terrafreeze Corp., Lorton, Va., 1974-79, also bd. dirs.; pres. Geocentric Engring. Corp., Newington, Va., 1979-89; ind. profl. engr. Internat. Cons. Practice, Mason Neck, Va., 1989-91; pres. Geofreeze, Inc., Mason Neck, Va., 1991—; vis. lectr. on constrn. ground freezing and related techs., numerous univs. and profl. assns., 1975-88; bd. dirs. Geofreeze Corp., Lorton. Contbr. numerous tech. papers to internat. confs. Bd. dirs. Harbor View Civic Assn., Lorton, 1974-79; sect. dir. Operation Zap The Blackstone, Providence, 1972. Served with U.S. Army, 1957-61. Mem. ASCE, Internat. Soc. Soil Mechanics and Founds., Engring. Inst. Can., Am. Underground Space Assn. (charter), Deep Founds. Inst., Nat. Rsch. Coun. Transp. Rsch. Bd., Internat. Organizing Com. for Ground Freezing (internat. contractors rep.), Harbor View Recreation Club (bd. dirs. 1977-80). Democrat. Unitarian. Avocations: boating, fishing, skiing, motorcycling.

SHUSTER, ROBERT G., electronics company executive, consultant; b. N.Y.C., June 1, 1927; s. Robert Chandler and Therese G. (Giraud); m. Marianne B. Lynski, Apr. 20, 1970 (div. Jan. 1987); m. H. Elizabeth Young, May 20, 1989 (div. Dec. 1995). BSEE, CCNY, 1948; MSEE, Columbia U., 1955, postgrad., 1959-64. Test engr. Elec. Testing Labs., N.Y.C., 1948-50; project leader Sperry Gyroscope Co., Great Neck, N.Y., 1950-59; project mgr. RCA Advanced Communications Lab., N.Y.C., 1959-67; prin. scientist Tracor, Inc., Rockville, Md., 1967-75, v.p. electronics systems div., 1975-87; pres. Tracor Tech. Resources, Inc., Rockville, Md., 1984-90, RGS Assocs., McLean, Va., 1990—; v.p. C-Cubed Corp., Alexandria, Va., 1990-93; pres. C-Cubed Corp., 1993-95; sr. cons., 1996—. Mem. IEEE (sr.), AAAS, N.Y. Acad. Scis. Avocations: photography, hiking. Office: C-Cubed Corp 6800 Verser Ctr Springfield VA 22151-4177

SHUSTERMAN, MURRAY H., lawyer; b. Solochov, Ukraine, Sept. 8, 1913; came to U.S., 1922; s. Herman Shusterman and Esther Tsiboushnik; m. Judith Weiner, Nov. 10, 1940; children; Robert, Richard, Ronald. BS with honors, Temple U., 1933, JD with honors, 1936, MA, U. Pa., 1940, PhD, 1942. Bar: Pa., U.S. Supreme Ct. 1961. Atty. Bur. Mcpl. Rsch., Phila., 1936-42, Reconstructive Fin. Corp., Phila., 1942-49; spl. trial counsel Small Bus. Adminstrn., Phila., 1949-51; dep. city solicitor Phila., 1951-63, ptnr. various law firms, 1951-68; sr. ptnr. Fox, Rothschild, O'Brien & Frankel, Phila., 1968—; vice chmn. bd. Stenton Pl. Assocs., Atlantic City, N.J., 1978—; chmn. bd. Forum Mgmt. Corp., Phila., 1980—; adj. prof. law Temple U., 1962-94; former dep. solicitor Phila.; counsel Commn. Human Rels. Phila., City Coun. (citation Merit). Past pres. Law Alum. Temple U.; former chair Friends Ben Gurion U. (Phila. chpt.); former v.p. Phila. City Bd. Health; co-chmn. Nat. Conf. Christians and Jews (Phila.), sec. Fellowship Commn.; pres. Jewish Community Rels. Coun. Greater Phila., founder, 1st pres. Pa.; chair B'nai Brith Klutznick Mus., Internat. adv. coun., internat. bd. govs., pres. B'nai Brith World Ctr., Jerusalem., past pres. B'nai Brith Dist. 3; bd. overseers Gratz Coll.; bd. govs. Ben Gurion U., Beer Sheva, Israel; trustee Annenberg Rsch. Inst., 1980-93, Fedn. Jewish Agys.; hon. life trustee Temple U.; Anti-Defamation League B'nai Brith (life mem. commn., Met. award); sec. Ctr. Judaic Studies U. Pa., 1993—. Recipient Loyal Legion award Temple U., 1957, Disting. Alumnus award, 1995; Disting. Svc. award Phila. Commn. Human Rels., 1963, Tower award State of Israel, 1969, Met. award Anti-Defamation League, 1981, Justice Louis D. Brandeis award Zionist Orgn. Am., 1985. Mem. ABA, Pa. Bar Assn., Phila. Bar Assn. (chair civil rights com.), Lawyer's Club, Law Found. (pres.), B'nai Brith Internat. (v.p., sr. mem.). Jewish. Avocations: reading, golf, bridge, music. Home: 500 S Ocean Blvd Apt 2102 Boca Raton FL 33432-6212 Office: Fox Rothschild O'Brien & Frankel 2000 Market St Ste 10 Philadelphia PA 19103-3201

SHUSTERMAN, NEAL DOUGLAS, author, screenwriter; b. N.Y.C., Nov. 12, 1962; s. Milton and Charlotte Ruth (Altman) S.; m. Elaine Gale Jones, Jan. 31, 1987; children: Brendan, Jarrod. BA in Psychology and Drama, U. Calif., Irvine, 1985. Author, screenwriter, 1987—. Author: Guy Talk, 1987, The Shadow Club, 1988 (Children's CHoice award Internat. Reading Assn. 1989), Dissidents, 1989, Speeding Bullet, 1991 (Best Book for Teens award N.Y. Pub. Libr., nominated Calif. Young Reader Medal 1995-96), Kid Heroes, 1991, What Daddy Did, 1991 (Best Book for Young Adults award ALA, Outstanding Work of Fiction award So. Calif. Coun. Lit. for Children and Young People, Children's Choice award and Young Adult Choice award Internat. Reading Assn., Pick of the List award ABA, Best Book for Teens award N.Y. Pub. Libr., Okla. Sequoyah award 1994), The Eyes of Kid Midas, 1992 (ALA Best Book for Reluctant Readers), Darkness Creeping, 1993, Piggyback Ninja, 1994, Scorpion Shards, 1995, Darkness Creeping II, 1995, Mindquakes, 1996, Mindstorms, 1996; screenwriter: Time Scavengers, 1990, Double Dragon, 1992, Evolver, 1993, The Eyes of Kid Midas, 1993; dir. Heart on a Chain, 1991 (Golden Eagle award CINE), What About the Sisters, 1993 (Golden Eagle award CINE), Games: How to Host a Teen Mystery, 1994, (TV show) Goosebumps: The Werewolf of Fever Swamp, 1996. Mem. PEN, Writers Guild Am. West, Soc. Children's Book Writers and Illustrators. Avocations: swimming, tennis, storytelling. Office: PO Box 18516 Irvine CA 92713-8516

SHUTE, DAVID, retail executive, lawyer; b. Crystal, Mich., Feb. 6, 1931; s. Bert M. and Bessie M. (Gleason) S.; m. Lorna Mae Lesnick (div. Apr. 1976); children: David K., Douglas R.; m. Roxanne J. Decyk (div. June 1987); m. Gerri Hilt, May, 1989. BA, Princeton U., 1953; JD, U. Mich., 1959. Bar: Wis. 1959, D.C. 1971, Ill. 1981. Assoc., then ptnr. Foley & Lardner, Milw., 1959-81; sr. v.p., gen. counsel Seraco Enterprise Inc., Chgo., 1981, Coldwell Banker Real Estate Group, Chgo., 1982-84, Sears Consumer Fin. Corp., Lincolnshire, Ill., 1984-86; corp. gen. counsel Sears Roebuck and Co., Chgo., 1987—, v.p., 1987-88, sr. v.p., sec., gen. counsel, 1988—. Mem. adv. com. Corp. Counsel Ctr., Northwestern U. Sch. Law, Chgo., 1987—, mem. planning com. Corp. Counsel Inst., Chgo. Vol. Legal Svcs. Found., 1988; mem. lawyers com. Nat. Ctr. for State Cts., Washington, 1987; bd. trustees Library Internat. Rels., Chgo. Lt. (j.g.) USNR, 1953-56. Mem. ABA (com. on corp. law depts.), Ill. Bar Assn., Chgo. Bar Assn., Assn. Gen. Counsel, Am. Enterprise Inst. (mem. fin. svcs. adv. com.), The Law Club, Economic Club of Chgo., Saddle and Cycle Club, Metropolitan Club. Avocations: tennis, skiing, travel. Home: 1448 N Lake Shore Dr # 10C Chicago IL 60610-1625 Office: Sears Roebuck & Co 68th Floor Sears Tower Chicago IL 60684

SHUTE, RICHARD EMIL, government official, engineer; b. Bklyn., May 1, 1938; s. William Leonard and Doris (Schlichting) S.; m. Linda Janan McElhiney, Mar. 7, 1960. B.S. in Mech. Engring., U. Miami, 1960; M.B.A., Fla. State U., 1970. Registered profl. engr., Fla. Engr. Pratt and Whitney Aircraft, West Palm Beach, Fla., 1960-62, Gen. Dynamics Corp., San Diego, 1962-64; aerospace engr. NASA/Kennedy Space Ctr., Fla., 1964-71; dir. planning and evaluation Fla. Dept. Health and Human Services, Tallahassee, 1971-76; dir. office program devel. Office Human Devel., HHS, Washington, 1976-87; dir. office of mgmt. and info. systems U.S. Dept. Commerce, Washington, 1987-90; pres. Richard E. Shute and Assocs. Mgmt. Cons., 1990—. Recipient Superior Achievement award NASA, 1966; recipient Spl. Achievement award HHS, 1977, Sr. Exec. award HHS, 1982. Mem. SAE, Nat. Assn. Security Dealers (registered arbitrator).

SHUTER, BRUCE DONALD, lawyer; b. N.Y.C., Feb. 20, 1940; s. David C. and Lillian (Hermann) S.; m. Marsha Nan Ellen, Aug. 20, 1961 (div.

1989); children: David, Richard; m. Janis Lynn Klein, May 23, 1989. BA, Alfred U., 1961; JD, NYU, 1964. Bar: N.Y. 1964, Pa. 1971. Atty. Fed. Res. Bd., Washington, 1964-68, chief counsel divsn. supervision and regulation, 1968-70; assoc. Drinker Biddle & Reath, Phila., 1970-72, ptnr., chmn. banking dept., 1972-95, chmn. instnl. debt fin. dept., 1996—. Mem. Com. of Seventy, Phila., 1976-78. Mem. Pyramid Club of Phila., Wissahickon Skating Club (bd. dirs. 1992, treas. 1995, v.p. 1996). Office: Drinker Biddle & Reath 1345 Chestnut St Fl 2100 Philadelphia PA 19107-3426

SHUTIAK, JAMES, management consultant; b. Saskatoon, Sask., Can., July 1, 1932; s. Nicholas and Anna (Zabaczinski) S. MBA, Simon Fraser U., 1977. Chartered acct.; cert. mgmt. cons.; cert. fraud examiner. Ptnr. Winspear, Higgins, Stevenson & Co. (C.A.), 1951-61; comptroller, treas. Wainwright Producers & Refiners, Calgary, Alta., Can., 1961-63; sec., treas. Peace River Oil Pipeline Co., Ltd., Calgary, 1963-69; asst. to treas., asst. treas. Columbia Cellulose Co., Ltd., Vancouver, 1969-71; mgmt. cons. J. Shutiak (C.A.), Vancouver, 1971-73; asst. gen. mgr., dep. chmn. Man. Devel. Corp., Winnipeg, 1973-75; treas. Alta. Gas Trunk Line Co., Ltd., Calgary, 1975-79, also v.p. oil and gas subs., 1977-79; v.p. fin., CFO CDC Oil & Gas Ltd., Calgary, 1979-80; pres. IES Consulting, a divsn. of IES Resources Ltd., Calgary, 1980—; pvt. mgmt. cons., 1980—. Mem. Inst. Chartered Accts. Alta., Inst. Cert. Mgmt. Cons. Alta., Assn. Cert. Fraud Examiners, Fin. Execs. Inst., Simon Fraser U. Alumni Assn., Calgary Petroleum Club. Home: Box 1 Site 17 RR 1, De Winton, AB Canada T0L 0X0

SHUTLER, MARY ELIZABETH, academic administrator; b. Oakland, Calif., Nov. 14, 1929; d. Hal Wilfred and Elizabeth Frances (Gimbel) Hall; m. Richard Shutler Jr., Sept. 8, 1951 (div. 1975); children: Kathryn Allice, John Hall, Richard Burnett. BA, U. Calif., Berkeley, 1951; MA, U. Ariz., 1958, PhD, 1967. Asst., assoc., full prof. anthropology, chmn. dept. San Diego State U., 1967-75; prof. anthropology, dept. chmn. Wash. State U., Pullman, 1975-80; dean Coll. Arts and Scis., prof. anthropology U. Alaska, Fairbanks, 1980-84; vice chancellor, dean of faculty, prof. anthropology U. Wis. Parkside, Kenosha, 1984-88; provost, v.p. for acad. affairs, prof. anthropology Calif. State U., L.A., 1988-94; provost West Coast U., L.A., 1994—; mem. core staff Lahav Rsch. Project, Miss. State U., 1975—. Co-author: Ocean Prehistory, 1975, Deer Creek Cave, 1964, Archaeological Survey of Southern Nevada, 1963, Stuart Rockshelter, 1962; contbr. articles to jours. in field. Mem. coun. Gamble House. Fellow Am. Anthropol. Assn.; mem. Soc. for Am. Archaeology, Am. Schs. for Oriental Rsch., Am. Coun. Edn., Am. Assn. for Higher Edn., Am. Assn. State Colls. and Univs., Delta Zeta. Republican. Roman Catholic. Avocations: travel, gardening, cats. Office: West Coast U 440 Shatto Pl Los Angeles CA 90020-1704

SHUTT, FRANCES BARTON, special education educator; b. Pryor, Okla., Nov. 12, 1912; d. Edwin Harley and Bonnie (Heflin) Barton; m. John Paul Shutt, Dec. 24, 1932; children: Jon Edwin, Frances Paulette. BA, Northeastern Tchrs. U., 1941; MA, U. N.Mex., 1954, cert. in spl. edn., 1958. Classroom tchr. Pryor, Okla., 1932-40; classroom tchr. Albuquerque, 1941-55, homebound tchr. in spl. edn., 1955-72; substitute tchr. Las Cruces, N.Mex., 1973-75; ESL tchr. Las Cruces, 1974—. Author: First Grade Guide, 1952. Mem. AAUW, 1962-68, Daus. of Nile, 1953; mission work in Japan, 1964, Samoa, 1972. Mem. N.Mex. Assn. Ednl. Retirees, Coun. for Exceptional Children (state pres. 1963-65), Ret. Tchrs. N.Mex. (sec. 1996), Order Eastern Star (worthy matron 1938), Pi Lambda Theta (pres. 19658-60), Alpha Delta Kappa (pres. 1968-70), Delta Kappa Gamma (pres. 1986-88), Kappa Kappa Iota (pres. 1990-930. Democrat. Baptist. Home: PO Box 697 Mesilla Park NM 88047-0697

SHUTT, RALPH P., research physicist. Rsch. scientist Brookhaven Nat. Lab., Upton, N.Y. Recipient W.K.H. Panofsky prize Am. Phys. Soc., 1993. Office: Brookhaven National Laboratory Upton NY 11973

SHUTTLEWORTH, ANNE MARGARET, psychiatrist; b. Detroit, Jan. 17, 1931; d. Cornelius Joseph and Alice Catherine (Rice) S.; A.B., Cornell U., 1953, M.D., 1956; m. Joel R. Siegel, Apr. 19, 1959; children: Erika, Peter. Intern, Lenox Hill Hosp., N.Y.C., 1956-57; resident Payne Whitney Clinic-N.Y. Hosp., 1957-60; practice medicine, specializing in psychiatry, Maplewood, N.J., 1960—; cons. Maplewood Sch. System, 1960-62; instr. psychiatry Cornell U. Med. Sch., 1960; mem. Com. to Organize New Sch. Psychology, 1970. Mem. AMA (Physicians Recognition award 1975, 78, 81, 84, 87, 90, 93, 96), Am. Psychiat. Assn., Am. Med. Women's Assn., N.Y. Acad. Scis., Acad. Medicine N.J., Phi Beta Kappa, Phi Kappa Phi. Home: 46 Farbrook Dr Short Hills NJ 07078-3007 Office: 2066 Millburn Ave Maplewood NJ 07040-3715

SHUTZ, BYRON CHRISTOPHER, real estate executive; b. Kansas City, Mo., Feb. 16, 1928; s. Byron Theodore and Maxine (Christopher) S.; m. Marilyn Ann Tweedie, Mar. 30, 1957; children: Eleanor S. Gaines, Byron Christopher, Collin Reid, Allison S. Moskow, Lindley Anne Baile. A.B. in Econs, U. Kans., 1949. Ptnr. Herbert V. Jones & Co., Kansas City, Mo., 1953-72; pres. Herbert V. Jones Mortgage Corp., Kansas City, 1967-72, The Byron Shutz Co., Kansas City, 1973—; dir. 1st Am. Financial Corp., Rothschild's, Inc. Chmn. bd. trustees U. Kansas City, 1979-81; trustee Pembroke-Country Day Sch., 1974-77, Midwest Rsch. Inst., 1980-89; chmn., bd. govs. Kansas City Art Inst., 1960-62; chmn. bd. dirs. Ctr. for Bus. Innovation, Inc., 1985-87; bd. dirs. Kansas City Crime Commn. 1st lt. USAF, 1951-53. Mem. Mortgage Bankers Assn. Am. (bd. govs. 1966-74), Am. Inst. Real Estate Appraisers. Clubs: Kansas City Country, University, Mercury (pres. 1978-79); Fla. Yacht (Jacksonville), Ocean Reef (Key Largo, Fla.). Home: 1001 W 58th Ter Kansas City MO 64113-1159 Office: 800 W 47th St Kansas City MO 64112-1251

SHWARTZ, ROBERT N., lawyer; b. Bklyn., Apr. 20, 1950; s. Morton and Joyce (Rosenthal) S.; m. Susan J. Greenberg, Feb. 22, 1992. BA, Syracuse U., 1972; JD, Columbia U., 1975. Bar: N.Y. 1976, D.C., U.S. Dist. Ct. (so. and ea. dists.) N.Y., U.S. Dist. Ct. (ea. dist.) Mich., U.S. Ct. Appeals (2d and 3d cirs.). Clk. to Hon. Orrin G. Judd U.S. Dist. Ct. (ea. dist.) N.Y., Bklyn., 1975-76; assoc. Curtis, Mallet, Prevost, Colt & Mosle, N.Y.C., 1976-77; asst. U.S. atty. U.S. Dist. Ct. (so. dist.) N.Y., N.Y.C., 1977-83; assoc. Debevoise & Plimpton, N.Y.C., 1983-84, ptnr., 1985-87, 88—; assoc. ind. counsel, Iran-Contra Office Ind. Counsel, Washington, 1987-88. Contbr. articles to profl. jours. Office: Debevoise & Plimpton 875 3rd Ave New York NY 10022-6225

SHYER, CHARLES RICHARD, screenwriter, film director; b. Los Angeles, Oct. 11, 1941; s. Melville Shyer and Lois Jones. Co-writer: (films) Goin' South, 1977, Housecalls, 1978; co-writer, prodr.: (film) Private Benjamin, 1980 (Acad. award nominee for screenplay 1980, Best Original Comedy award Writers Guild 1980); co-writer, dir.: (films) Irreconcilable Differences, 1984, Baby Boom, 1987, Father of the Bride, 1991, I Love Trouble, 1994, Father of the Bride, Part II, 1995. Mem. ASCAP, Acad. Motion Picture Arts and Scis., Writers Guild Am., Writers Guild Am. West, Dirs. Guild Am.

SHYER, JOHN D., lawyer; b. Nashville, May 4, 1956; s. Michael and Hilda (Wertheim) S.; m. Marsha Anne Gisser, May 7, 1989; children: Allison Parcell, Michael Wertheim. AB, Princeton U., 1978; JD, Stanford U., 1981. Bar: N.Y. 1982, U.S. Ct. Appeals (2d cir.) 1983, U.S. Ct. Appeals (3d cir.) 1992. Assoc. Donovan, Leisure, Newton & Irvine, N.Y.C., 1981-85; assoc. Latham & Watkins, N.Y.C., 1985-89, ptnr., 1989—. Trustee Princeton (N.J.) Broadcasting Svc., 1985—. Mem. Assn. Bar City N.Y. Avocations: traveling, hiking, reading. Office: Latham & Watkins 885 3rd Ave Ste 1000 New York NY 10022-4834

SHYMANSKI, CATHERINE MARY, nursing education administrator; b. Omaha, Jan. 23, 1954; d. Leo Michael and Mildred Mary (Swank) Shymanski. AAS in Nursing, Iowa Western C.C., 1977; BSN, Pacific Western U., 1982; BFA, Drake U., 1980; MSN, Pacific Western U., 1992. Charge nurse Nebr. Psychiat. Inst., Omaha, 1977-78; staff nurse Menninger Found., Topeka, 1978-79; staff devel. instr., clin. coord. Stormont Vail Regional Med. Ctr., Topeka, 1979-80; charge nurse Allen County Hosp., Iola, Kans., 1980-81; asst. dir. nursing Arkhaven at Erie, Kans., 1980; dir. shift ops. Truman Med. Ctr., Kansas City, Mo., 1983; nursing supr. Osawatomie (Kans.) State Hosp., 1981-91; nursing orientation and insvc. coord. Topeka State Hosp., 1991-94, dir. nursing edn., 1993-94; coord. health occupation Kaw Area Tech. Sch., Topeka, Kans., 1994-95; supr. outpatient & partial hospitalization svcs. St. Catherine Hosp., Garden City, Kans., 1995—. Mem. River City Players, Osawatomie, 1984-88. Mem. Bus. & Profl. Women (pres. Osawatomie chpt. 1985-86, 88-89, dist. dir. 1987-88, Young Career Woman award 1982, 84, Woman of Yr., 1982-83), Am. Psychiat. Nurses Assn., Kans. State Nursing Assn. (pres. dist. 1985-86), Am. Cat Fanciers Assn., Topeka Cat Fanciers. Avocations: raise and show cats, gardening, reading. Office: Kaw Area Tech Sch 5724 Huntoon Topeka KS 66604

SHYY, WEI, aerospace, mechanical engineering researcher, educator; b. Tainan, Taiwan, China, July 19, 1955; came to U.S. 1979; s. Chiang-Chen and June-Hua (Chao) S.; m. Yuchen Shih; children: Albert, Alice, Andrew Chang, Kevin Chang. BS, Tsin-Hua U., Taiwan, 1977; MSE, U. Mich., 1981, PhD, 1982. Postdoctoral rsch. scholar U. Mich., Ann Arbor, 1982-83; rsch. scientist GE Corp. Rsch. and Devel. Ctr., Schenectady, N.Y., 1983-88; faculty mem. of aeronautics and astronautics Nat. Cheng-Kung U., Taiwan, 1987; assoc. prof. aerospace engring., mechanics and engring. sci. U. Fla., Gainesville, 1988-92, prof. aerospace engring., mechanics and engring. sci., 1992—, chmn. dept. aerospace engring, mechs. and engring. sci., 1996—; co-founder, pres. SCRAM Tech., Inc.; cons. numerous pvt., fed. agencies U.S., Taiwan; lectr. in field. Author: Computational Modeling for Fluid Flow and Interfacial Transport, 1994; co-author: Computational Fluid Dynamics with Moving Boundaries, 1996; editor: Recent Advances in Comoputational Fluid Dynamics, 1989; mem. editl. adv. bd. Numerical Heat Transfer Jour.; reviewer U.S. govt., other govts., indsl. labs., profl. jours.; contbr. numerous articles to profl. jours. Recipient GE Rsch. and Devel. Ctr. 1986 Pubs. award, Chinese Soc. of Mech. Engrs. 1987 Rsch. Paper award, NASA/ASEE 1991 Cert. of Recognition. Fellow AIAA (assoc.); mem. ASME (Combustion and Fuel Com. 1984 Hon. Paper award), Combustion Inst., APS, TMS, Consortium of Computational Fluid Dynamics for Propulsion. Achievements include research in computational fluid dynamics, combustion and propulsion, gravity-induced thermofluid transport processes, materials processing and solidification, microgravity sciences and engring. contributions to gas turbine, hydraulic turbine, high pressure lamp and electronic cooling. Office: U Fla Dept Aerospace Engring 231 Aero Bldg Gainesville FL 32611

SIA, DAVID S., advertising agency executive; b. Shanghai, China, 1943. BA, Brigham Young U., 1965. Exec. v.p., regional dir. Young & Rubicam; now chmn., CEO BBDO Asia Pacific, Bangkok, Thailand; also bd. dirs., exec. v.p. BBDO Worldwide. Office: BBDO Worldwide Inc 1285 Avenue Of The Americas New York NY 10019-6028

SIART, WILLIAM ERIC BAXTER, banker; b. Los Angeles, Dec. 25, 1946; s. William Ernest and Barbara Vesta (McPherson) Baxter; m. Noelle Ellen Reid, Sept. 17, 1966; children—Shayne Allison, Tiffany Ann. B.A. in Econs., U. Santa Clara, 1968; M.B.A., U. Calif., Berkeley, 1969. With Bank of Am., 1969-78; v.p. corp. banking Bank of Am., Brussels, 1977-78; sr. v.p. charge mktg. Western Bancorp, Los Angeles, 1978-81; pres., chief operating officer First Interstate Bank of Nev. N.A., Reno, 1981-82; pres., chief exec. officer First Interstate Bank of Nev. N.A., 1982-84, chmn. bd., pres., chief exec. officer, 1984; formerly chmn., pres., chief exec. officer First Interstate Bank Calif., L.A., also bd. dirs.; pres. First Interstate Bancorp, L.A., 1990—, CEO, 1994—. Trustee U. Nev.-Reno Found.; bd. dirs. Sierra Arts Found. Mem. Am. Bankers Assn. (mem. govt. relations council), Reno-Sparks C. of C. (dir.). Republican. Roman Catholic. Office: First Interstate Bancorp 633 W 5th St Los Angeles CA 90071-2005*

SIAS, JOHN B., multi-media company executive, newspaper publisher,publishing exec; b. 1927. A.B., Stanford U., 1949. Group v.p. Metromedia Inc., 1962-71; with Capital Cities Communications, 1971-93; pres. Fairchild Pubs. Inc., 1971-75, exec. v.p., pres. pub. div., 1975-85; pres. ABC-TV Network Group, N.Y.C., 1986-93; also former exec. v.p. Capital Cities/ABC Inc.(parent), N.Y.C.; pres., ceo Chronicle Pub. Co., San Francisco, 1993—. Served with AUS, 1945-46. Office: Chronicle Pub Co 901 Mission St San Francisco CA 94103-2988 also: Capital Cities/ABC Inc 24 E 51st St New York NY 10022-6801*

SIAU, JOHN FINN, wood scientist, educator; b. Detroit, Mar. 30, 1921; s. Robert H. and Marguerite L. (Finn) S.; children: John E., Mary M. B.S., Mich. State Coll., 1943; M.S., SUNY, Syracuse, 1964; Ph.D., SUNY-Syracuse, 1968. Engr. Utah Radio Products, Huntington, Ind., 1946-48; design engr. vacuum tubes Gen. Electric Co., Schenectady, 1948-58; prof. physics Paul Smith's (N.Y.) Coll., 1958-66; prof. wood products engring. SUNY Coll. Environ. Sci. and Forestry, Syracuse, 1966-85, emeritus prof., 1985-93; adj. prof. wood physics VPI, State U., Blacksburg, Va., 1993—; vis. prof. U. Aberdeen, U.K., 1978, Tech. U., Zvolen, Slovakia, 1994. Author: Flow in Wood, 1971, Transport Processes in Wood, 1984, Wood: Influence of Moisture and Physical Properties, 1995; editor Wood and Fiber Sci., 1994-95. Served with USNR, 1943-46. Recipient Wood award 2d pl. Forest Products Research Soc., 1968. Fellow Internat. Acad. Wood Sci.; mem. Forest Products Soc., Internat. Assn. Wood Anatomists, Soc. Wood Sci. and Tech., Tau Beta Pi. Roman Catholic. Club: Adirondack Mountain. Home: PO Box 41 Keene NY 12942

SIBBALD, JOHN RISTOW, management consultant; b. Lincoln, Nebr., June 20, 1936; s. Garth E.W. and Rachel (Wright) S.; BA, U. Nev., 1958; MA, U. Ill., 1964; m. Kathryn J. Costick ; children: Allison, John, Wright. Office mgr. Hewitt Assocs., Libertyville, Ill., 1964-66; coll. rels. mgr. Pfizer Inc., N.Y.C., 1966-69; pres., chief exec. officer Re-Con Systems, N.Y.C., 1969-70; v.p. Booz, Allen & Hamilton, N.Y.C., 1970-73, Chgo., 1973-75; pres., founder John Sibbald Assocs., Inc., Chgo., 1975; mem. Nat. Advisory Coun., Nat. Club Assn. Author: The Career Makers, 1990, 92, 94; contbr. articles to profl. jours. Served to capt. AUS, 1958-64. Mem. Mid-Day Club Chgo., St. Louis Club. Episcopalian. Office: 8725 W Higgins Rd Chicago IL 60631-2702

SIBITS, DAVID J., diversified financial services company executive; b. 1951. BS, Kent State U., 1972. CPA, Ohio. Various IRS, 1972-75; mng. ptnr. Hausser & Taylor, Cleve., 1976—. Office: Hausser & Taylor 1400 North Point Tower Cleveland OH 44114*

SIBLEY, ALDEN KINGSLAND, former organization executive, retired army officer; b. Tuscaloosa, Ala., Jan. 3, 1911; s. Frederick Hubbard and Annabelle (Pearson) S.; m. Elvira Trowbridge, Nov. 15, 1945; 1 child, Frederick Drake. Student, U. Nev., 1928-29; BS, U.S. Mil. Acad., 1933; BA, Oxford U., Eng., 1936, BSc, 1936, MA, 1943; postgrad., Engr. Sch., Ft. Belvoir, Va., 1937-38; grad., Nat. War Coll., 1957; doctoral study nuclear physics, George Washington U., 1955—; DSc, Coll. Advanced Sci., Canaan, N.H., 1962. Registered profl. engr. Mass. Commd. 2d lt. C.E. U.S. Army, 1933, advanced through grades to maj. gen., 1961; condr. sci. expdn. around world, 1935; bn. comdr. 1st Bn., 5th Engr. Regt. Ft. Belvoir, Va., 1936; mil. aide to pres., White House, 1937-38; exec. officer constrn. Conchas Dam N.Mex., 1938; chief, inspection constrn. John Martin Dam Colo., 1939; exec. officer St. Lawrence Seaway and Power Project, 1940-41; dist. engr. African Engr. Dist. Cairo, 1942, asst. chief staff G-4 (logistics), Middle-East Theater Ops., 1942; comdg. officer Eritrea and Tripoli Base commands N. Africa, 1943; chief Army component Joint Brit.-U.S. Operations Planning Group Middle East, 1943; dep. chief staff Middle East Theater Operations, 1943; exec. officer, asst. chief staff G-4 (logistics), SHAEF London, 1943-44; chief SHAEF Mission to France, 1944-45, dep. asst. chief staff G-4, War Dept. Gen. Staff, 1945, mem. joint logistics com. Joint Chiefs Staff, 1946, chief theaters br. Gen. Staff Army, 1946-48, chief ops. planning group Office Chief Staff Army, 1949, mil. sec. Army Policy Council, Office Sec. Army, also spl. asst. under sec. army for politico-mil. affairs, 1950-52; chief, logistic plans br. SHAPE Paris, 1952-55; dir. ednl. devel., faculty Nat. War Coll., 1955-57; chief staff U.S. del. for negotiations Fed. Republic of Germany Bonn, 1956; chief staff Philippine Base Negotiations Manila, 1956; div. engr. U.S. Army Engr. Div. New Eng., 1957-60; dep. chief Mil. Assistance Adv. Group Saigon, Vietnam, 1960-61; dep. chief engrs. Washington, 1961-62; comdg. gen. U.S. Army Mobility Command Center Line, Mich., 1962-64; dep. chief staff logistics, acting chief of staff U.S. Army Europe Heidelberg, Germany, 1964-66; comdg. gen. XI U.S. Army Corps St. Louis, 1966-67; dep. comdg. gen. 5th U.S. Army Chgo., 1967-68; exec. asst. to chmn. bd. Champion Internat. Corp., N.Y.C., 1968-74, Econ. Devel. Council, N.Y.C., 1974-78. Contbr. articles to profl. publs.; exhibited original oil paintings, Grand Palais, Société des Independents, 1954. Mem. Rhodes Scholarship selection com., Europe, 1954, Mass., 1958, Mich., 1963, Mo., 1966; dir. World Affairs Council, Boston ; bd. dirs. Isabel O'Neil Found. Decorated D.S.M., Legion of Merit, Bronze Star, Army Commendation ribbon with oak leaf cluster U.S.; Medal of Honor 1st class Vietnam; Order Brit. Empire; comdr. Legion of Honor; Croix de Guerre with palm France; recipient Diamond Jubilee Anniversary medal ASME, 1956, Author's award Automotive Industries, 1963-64; Rhodes scholar Oxford U., 1936. Mem. AAAS, ASME, Am. Def. Preparedness Assn., Armed Forces Mgmt. Assn., Assn. U.S. Army (pres. N.Y. chpt. 1972-73), Am. Soc. French Legion of Honor (exec. v.p., dir., chmn. exec. com., 1968-82), Pilgrims U.S., S.A.R., Nat. Aviation Hall of Fame, Soc. Am. Mil. Engrs. (founding pres. Saigon chpt., nat. dir., pres. Boston chpt. 1958-59), Soc. Am. Rhodes Scholars, Nat. Inst. Social Scis. (dir.), Chevalliers du Tastevin (grand officier), Sigma Xi, Phi Kappa Phi. Clubs: Army-Navy (Washington), Marco Polo (N.Y.C.). Home: 969 Park Ave New York NY 10028-0322

SIBLEY, CELESTINE (MRS. JOHN C. STRONG), columnist, reporter; b. Holly, Fla., May 23, 1917; d. W.R. and Evelyn (Barber) S.; m. James W. Little (dec. 1953); children: James W., Susan Little Bazemore, Mary Little Vance; m. John C. Strong (dec. 1988). Attended, U. Fla., Spring Hill Coll.; LHD (hon.), Spring Hill Coll. Columnist, reporter Atlanta Constitution, 1941—; twice juror Pulitzer Pirze newspaper awards. Author: The Malignant Heart, 1957, Peachtree Street, U.S.A.: An Affectionate Portrait of Atlanta, 1963, (stories) Christmas in Georgia, 1964, A Place Called Sweet Apple, 1967, Dear Store: An Affectionate Portrait of Rich's, 1967, Especially at Christmas, 1969, Mothers are Always Special, 1970, The Sweet Apple Gardening Book, 1972, Day by Day with Celestine Sibley, 1975, Small Blessings, 1977, Ah, Sweet Mystery: A Kate Mulcay Novel of Suspense, 1991, Straight As an Arrow: A Kate Mulcay Mystery, 1992, Dire Happenings at Scratch Ankle, 1993, A Plague of Kinfolks, 1995, others. Bd. vis. Grady Hosp.; mem. adv. bd. Neighborhood Justice Ctr.; mem. literary panel Ga. Coun. Arts; head fund appeal Atlanta Area Svcs. for Blind. Recipient Literary Achievement award Ga. Writers Assn., 1964, 2 Recognition awards Dixie Coun. Authors and Journalists, 2 AP awards, Radio and TV Big Story award Pall Mall, 2 awards Ga. Conf. Social Work, Nat. Christopher award, Wesley Woods award, Ralph McGill award Lifetime Achievement in Journalism by Soc. Profl. Journalists, numerous others; named Woman of Yr. in Arts, Atlanta, 1956. Democrat. Presbyterian. Office: Atlanta Constitution Metro Desk 72 Marietta St NW Atlanta GA 30303-2804

SIBLEY, CHARLES GALD, biologist, educator; b. Fresno, Calif., Aug. 7, 1917; s. Charles Corydon and Ida (Gald) S.; m. Frances Louise Kelly, Feb. 7, 1942; children: Barbara Susanne, Dorothy Ellen, Carol Nadine. A.B., U. Calif.—Berkeley, 1940, Ph.D., 1948; M.A. (hon.), Yale U., 1965. Biologist, USPHS, 1941-42; instr. zoology U. Kans., 1948-49; asst. prof. San Jose (Calif.) State Coll., 1949-53; assoc. prof. ornithology Cornell U., 1953-59, prof. zoology, 1959-65; prof. biology Yale U., 1965-86, prof. emeritus, 1986—, William Robertson Coe prof. ornithology, 1967-86, emeritus, 1986—; dir. div. vertebrate zoology, curator birds Peabody Mus., 1965-86, dir. mus., 1970-76; Dean's prof. sci., prof. biology San Francisco State U., 1986-92; cons. systematic biology, 1963-65; mem. adv. com. biol. medicine NSF, 1968—; exec. com. biol. agr. NRC, 1966-70. Co-author: (with Jon Ahlquist) Phylogeny and Classification of Birds, 1990, (with Burt Monroe) Distribution and Taxonomy of Birds of the World, 1990; mem. editorial bd. Jour. Molecular Evolution, 1983—, Molecular Biology and Evolution, 1986—. Served to lt. USNR, 1943-45. Guggenheim fellow, 1959-60. Fellow AAAS; mem. NAS (Daniel Giraud Elliot medal 1988), Soc. Study Evolution, Am. Soc. Naturalists, Soc. Systematic Biology, Am. Ornithologists' Union (pres. 1986-88, Brewster Meml. medal 1971), Royal Australian Ornithol. Union, Deutsche Ornithol. Gesellschaft, Internat. Ornithol. Congress (sec.-gen. 1962, pres. 20th congress 1986-90). Home: 433 Woodley Pl Santa Rosa CA 95409-6431

SIBLEY, HORACE HOLDEN, lawyer; b. Phila., Oct. 13, 1939; s. John Adams and Barbara (Thayer) S.; m. Beverly Bryan, Mar. 18, 1961; children: Clare, Holden, Eve. BA, Vanderbilt U., 1961; LLD, U. Ga., 1964; MBA, Ga. State U., 1971. Bar: Ga. 1964, U.S. Supreme Ct. 1975. Assoc. King and Spalding, Atlanta, 1968-72, ptnr., 1972—; chmn. Ga. Ctr. for Advance Telecom. Tech.; bd. dirs. So. Ctr. for Internat. Studies, Atlanta Com. for Olympic Games; bd. advisors Carter Ctr. Trustee, mem. exec. com. Agnes Scott Coll., Atlanta, 1977; adv. trustee Henrietta Egleston Hosp. for Children, Atlanta, 1974-77, trustee, mem. exec. com., 1977—, chmn. bd. dirs., 1983-90; mem. exec. com. Atlanta Organizing Com. Summer Olympics, 1989—; chmn. bd. dirs. Butler St. YMCA, Atlanta, 1981; past bd. dirs. United Way, Nat. Assn. of Childrens' Hosp. and various other charitable orgns.; participant Leadership Ga., 1978, Leadership Atlanta, 1973, Soc. Internat. Bus. Fellows, 1982—; elder Trinity Presbyn. Ch., 1969-73. Capt. inf. U.S. Army, 1965-68, Germany. Mem. ABA, Ga. Bar Assn., Atlanta Bar Assn., World Trade Club Atlanta (bd. dirs. 1988-92), Japan-Am. Soc. (bd. dirs. 1981-87), Rotary, Blue Key Svc. Soc., Phi Kappa Phi, Omicron Delta Kappa. Democrat. Presbyterian. Avocations: tennis, running, fishing. Office: King & Spalding 191 Peachtree St NE Atlanta GA 30303-1740

SIBLEY, JAMES MALCOLM, retired lawyer; b. Atlanta, Aug. 5, 1919; s. John Adams and Nettie Whitaker (Cone) S.; m. Karen Norris, Apr. 6, 1942; children: Karen Mariea, James Malcolm Jr., Jack Norris, Elsa Alexandria Victoria, Quintus Whitaker. A.B., Princeton U., 1941; student, Woodrow Wilson Sch. Law, 1942, Harvard Law Sch., 1945-46. Bar: Ga. 1942. Assoc. King & Spalding, Atlanta, 1942-47, ptnr., 1947-91; bd. dirs. Rock-Tenn. Co., Summit Industries, Inc.; dir. emeritus Life Ins. Co. of Ga.; exec. com., mem. pub. affairs com. Coca-Cola Co., 1979-91; chmn. exec. com. John H. Harland Co., 1963-91; chmn. exec. com., mem. compensation com. Trust Co. of Ga., 1975-92; mem. exec. com., mem. compensation com. SunTrust Banks, Inc., 1985-92. Trustee Joseph B. Whitehead Found., Lettie Pate Evans Found., Emory U., A.G. Rhodes Home, Inc., Robert W. Woodruff Found., Inc. (formerly Trebor Found.), John H. and Wilhelmina D. Harland Charitable Found., Inc.; bd. dirs. Callaway Gardens Found. With USAF, 1942-45. Mem. ABA, Ga. Bar Assn., Atlanta Bar Assn., Am. Coll. Probate Counsel, Am. Bar Found., Am. Law Inst. Episcopalian. Clubs: Piedmont Driving, Commerce. Home: 63 Peachtree Circle Atlanta GA 30309-3556 also: King & Spalding 191 Peachtree St NE Atlanta GA 30303-1763

SIBLEY, WILLIAM ARTHUR, academic administrator, physics educator, consultant; b. Ft. Worth, Nov. 22, 1932; s. William Franklin and Sada (Rasor) S.; m. Joyce Elaine Gregory, Dec. 21, 1957; children: William Timothy, Lauren Shawn, Stephen Marshall. B.S., U. Okla., 1956, M.S., 1958, Ph.D., 1960. Teaching and rsch. asst. U. Okla., 1956-60; postdoctoral rsch. in defect solid state Kernforschungsanlage Julich and Tech. U. Aachen, Germany, 1960-61; rsch. solid state div. Oak Ridge Nat. Lab., 1961-70; prof., head physics Okla. State U., Stillwater, 1970-76; dir. Sch. Phys. and Earth Scis. Okla. State U., 1976-78, asst. v.p. rsch., 1978-88; program dir. NSF, Washington, 1988-89; acting div. dir. Div. Materials Rsch., 1990; v.p. acad. affairs U. Ala.-Birmingham, 1990—; mem. solid state sci. com. NAS, 1977-83; bd. dirs. Oak Ridge Assoc. Univs., 1982-88, Coun. on Govt. Rels., 1987-93, Okla. Ctr. for Advancement Sci. and Tech., 1987-88; trustee, chmn. materials rsch. counsel Southeastern Univ. Rsch. Assn., 1992-95; cons. univ. edn. and rsch. Contbr. articles to profl. jours. Pres. Stillwater Indsl. Found., 1985-86. Served to lt. AUS, 1951-53; maj. Res. 1953-60. Fellow Am. Phys. Soc.; mem. Rotary Internat., Omicron Delta Kappa, Sigma Xi, Sigma Pi Sigma, Pi Mu Epsilon. Baptist. Home: 422 Delcris Dr Birmingham AL 35226-1979 Office: U Ala Birmingham Office Academic Affairs Birmingham AL 35294

SIBLEY, WILLIAM AUSTIN, neurologist, educator; b. Miami, Okla., Jan. 25, 1925; s. William Austin and Erna Johanna (Quickert) S.; m. Joanne Shaw, Sept. 4, 1954; children: John, Mary Jane, Peter, Andrew. B.S., Yale U., 1945, M.D., 1948. Intern Univ. Hosp., Cleve., 1948-50; asst. resident neurologist Neurol. Inst. Presbyn. Hosp., N.Y.C., 1953-55; chief resident neurologist Neurol. Inst. Presbyn. Hosp., 1955-56; asst. prof. neurology Western Res. U., Cleve., 1956-63; assoc. prof. Western Res. U., 1963-67; prof. U. Ariz. Coll. Medicine, Tucson, 1967—, head dept. neurology, 1967-82. Chmn. therapy com. Internat. Fedn. Multiple Sclerosis Socs., 1986-92, 96—. Served to capt. M.C. USAF, 1951-53. Recipient LaFayette B. Mendel prize in physiol. chemistry Yale U., 1945. Mem. Am. Neurol. Assn. (v.p.

1979-80), Am. Acad. Neurology (v.p. 1985-87), Central Soc. for Neurol. Research (pres. 1968). Helped establish effectiveness of beta-interferon therapy in multiple sclerosis. Home: 2150 E Hampton St Tucson AZ 85719-3810 Office: 1501 N Campbell Ave Tucson AZ 85724-0001

SIBLEY, WILLIS ELBRIDGE, anthropology educator, consultant; b. Nashville, Feb. 22, 1930; s. Elbridge and Elizabeth Reynolds (LaBarre) S.; m. Barbara Jean Grant, June 9, 1956; children: Sheila Katherine, Anthony Grant, Michael David. B.A., Reed Coll., 1951; M.A., U. Chgo., 1953, Ph.D., 1958. Instr. sociology and anthropology Miami (Ohio) U., 1956-58; asst. prof. anthropology U. Utah, 1958-60; from asst. prof. to prof. anthropology Wash. State U., 1960-71; prof. anthropology Cleve. State U., 1971—, chmn. dept., 1971-77, Cleve. (City) faculty fellow, 1987, interim chmn., 1989-90, prof. emeritus, 1990—; sr. program analyst EPA, Washington, 1977-78; Govtl. fellow Am. Coun. on Edn., 1978; Rockefeller Found. vis. prof. anthropology U. Philippines, Quezon City, 1968-69; postdoctoral fellow in society and tech. Carnegie-Mellon U., 1981-82. Fulbright grantee, 1954-55, 64; NIMH grantee, 1959-61; NSF grantee, 1964-71; Nat. Acad. Scis.-NRC travel grantee, 1966; Office Edn., HEW research grantee, 1967. Fellow AAAS, Am. Anthropol. Assn. (treas. 1989-91, alt. dir. Renewable Natural Resources Found.), Soc. Applied Anthropology (sec. 1977-80, pres. 1981-82); mem. AAUP (treas. Wash. State U. chpt. 1962-63, v.p. 1963-64, pres. 1965-66, pres. Cleve. State U. chpt. 1979-80, treas. 1980-81, interim pres. 1989-90), ACLU (pres. Pullman chpt. 1963, 66), Anthropol. Soc. Washington, Ctrl. States Anthropol. Soc. (past mem. exec. bd., treas. 1986-89), Wash. Assn. Profl. Anthropologists, Philos. Club Cleve. Home: 1190 Cedar Ave Shady Side MD 20764-9513 Office: Cleve State U Dept Anthropology Cleveland OH 44115

SIBOLSKI, ELIZABETH HAWLEY, academic administrator; b. Gt. Barrington, Mass., Aug. 18, 1950; d. William Snyder and Frances Harrington (Smith) Gallup; m. John Alfred Sibolski Jr., Aug. 15, 1970. BA, The Am. U., 1973, MPA, 1975, PhD, 1984. Acting dir. acad. adminstrn. The Am. U., Washington, 1974, planning analyst, 1974-79, asst. dir. budget and planning, 1980-83, dir. instl. rsch., 1984-85, dir. univ. planning and rsch., 1985—; trustee Mortar Bd. Nat. Found., 1989-95. Recipient Comencement award Am. U. Women's Club, 1973. Mem. ASPA, Assn. Instl. Rsch., Soc. Coll. and Univ. Planning (bd. dirs. 1995—), Am. Assn. for Higher Edn., Mortar Bd. (sect. coord. 1975-82), Pi Alpha Alpha, Phi Kappa Phi (chpt. officer 1986-92), Pi Sigma Alpha, Omicron Delta Kappa. Avocation: breed, raise and show Morgan horses. Home: 565 Wayward Dr Annapolis MD 21401-6747 Office: The Am Univ Office of Planning 4400 Massachusetts Ave NW Washington DC 20016-8001

SICHERMAN, MARVIN ALLEN, lawyer; b. Cleve., Dec. 27, 1934; s. Harry and Malvina (Friedman) S.; m. Sue Kovacs, Aug. 18, 1957; children: Heidi Joyce, Steven Eric. B.A., Case Western Res. U., 1957, LL.B., 1960, J.D., 1968. Bar: Ohio 1960. Mng. prin. Dettelbach, Sicherman & Baumgart, Cleve., 1971—. Editorial bd.: Case-Western Res. Law Rev, 1958-60; Contbr. articles to legal jours. Mem. Beachwood (Ohio) Civic League, 1972—; mem. Beachwood Bd. Edn., 1978-86, pres., 1981, 85, v.p., 1984; trustee Beachwood Arts Council, 1977-84. Mem. ABA, Ohio Bar Assn. (lectr. truth in lending 1969, lectr. bankruptcy 1972, 81, 84; Meritorious Service awards 1971, 77, 78, 79, 83, 84, 85, 86, 87), Cleve. Bar Assn. (lectr. practice and procedure clinic 1960-80, 82-87, chmn. bankruptcy ct. com. 1971-73), Jewish Chautauqua Soc., Tau Epsilon Rho, Zeta Beta Tau. Jewish (trustee Temple brotherhood 1968-76, sec. 1971-73). Home: 24500 Albert Ln Cleveland OH 44122-2302 Office: Dettelbach Sicherman & Baumgart 1100 Ohio Savings Plz Cleveland OH 44114

SICILIANO, ELIZABETH MARIE, secondary education educator; b. Mansfield, Ohio, Apr. 22, 1934; d. Samuel Sevario and Lucy (Sferro) S. BS in Edn., Ohio State U., 1957; MA in Edn., Ea. Mich. U., 1971; MFA, Bowling Green U., 1975. Cert. tchr., Mich. Instr. adult edn. The Toledo (Ohio) Mus. Art, 1972-81; tchr. art Monroe (Mich.) Pub. Schs., 1975-96; workshop facilitator, presenter in field, computer graphics art instr. Artist, working in oils, pastels and fabricating jewelry. Judge Monroe Bicentennial, Monroe Arts and Crafts League, other shows. Mem. NEA, Mich. Edn. Assn., Nat. Art Edn. Assn., Mich. Art Edn. Assn., Stratford Festival for the Arts, Toledo Craft Club, Toledo Fedn. Art Socs., Toledo Mus. Art. Avocations: swimming, skiing, classic cars, designing and creating jewelry, portraiture and landscape in oils. Home: 7179 Edinburgh Dr Lambertville MI 48144-9539 Office: Monroe High Sch 901 Herr Rd Monroe MI 48161-9702

SICILIANO, ROCCO CARMINE, institute executive; b. Salt Lake City, Mar. 4, 1922; s. Joseph Vincent and Mary (Arnone) S.; m. Marion Stiebel, Nov. 8, 1947; children: Loretta, A. Vincent, Fred R., John, Maria. B.A. with honors, U. Utah, 1944; LL.B., Georgetown U., 1948; LHD, Hebrew Union Coll. Bar: D.C. bar 1949. Legal asst. to bd. mem. NLRB, Washington, 1948-50; asst. sec.-treas. Procon Inc., Des Plaines, Ill., 1950-53; asst. sec. labor charge employment and manpower Dept. Labor, Washington, 1953-57; spl. asst. to Eisenhower for personnel mgmt., 1957-59; ptnr. Wilkinson, Cragun & Barker, 1959-69; pres. Pacific Maritime Assn., San Francisco, 1965-69; undersec. of commerce Washington, 1969-71; pres., chmn. bd., chief exec. officer Ticor, Los Angeles, 1971-84; chmn., exec. com. Ticor, 1984-85; of counsel Jones, Day, Reavis & Pogue, 1984-87; chmn. bd., chief exec. officer Am. Health Properties, Inc., 1987-88; chmn. Dwight D. Eisenhower World Affairs Inst., Washington, 1991—; chmn. Ctr. for Govtl. Studies, 1992—; commr. Calif. Citizens Budget Commn.; bd. dirs. United TV, Inc.; mem. Fed. Pay Bd., 1971-73; trustee emeritus J. Paul Getty Trust. Bd. dirs. Eisenhower Inst., L.A. Philharm. Assn.; past chmn. Calif. Bus. Roundtable; trustee Com. for Econ. Devel.; co-chmn. Calif. Commn. on Campaign Financing; bd. govs. Cedars-Sinai Med. Ctr. 1st lt. AUS, 1943-46, MTO, ETO. Decorated Bronze Star; Order of Merit (Italy). Mem. Nat. Acad. Pub. Adminstrn., Met. Club (Washington), Calif. Club (L.A.). Home: 612 N Rodeo Dr Beverly Hills CA 90210-3208 Office: 918 16th St NW Ste 501 Washington DC 20006-2902 also: PO Box 2249 Beverly Hills CA 90213-2249

SICK, WILLIAM NORMAN, JR., investment company executive; b. Houston, Apr. 20, 1935; s. William Norman and Gladys Phylena (Armstrong) S.; m. Stephanie Anne Williams, Sept. 14, 1963; children: Jill Melanie, David Louis. BA, Rice U., 1957, BSEE, 1958. With Tex. Instruments Inc., Dallas, Washington, Phila., 1958-70; pres. Tex. Instruments, Asia Ltd., Tokyo, 1971-74; asst. v.p. strategic devel., gen. mgr. Europe Tex. Instruments, Dallas, 1974-77; v.p., group mgr. materials and elec. products Tex. Instruments, Attleboro, Mass., 1977-80; v.p., group mgr. consumer products Tex. Instruments, 1980-82; pres. semicondr. products group Tex. Instruments Inc., Dallas, 1982-86; exec. v.p. Asia Pacific Region Tex. Instruments, Inc., Dallas, 1987; bd. dirs. Tex. Instruments, Inc., 1985-87; CEO Am. Nat. Can Co., Chgo., 1988-89; also bd. dirs. Am. Nat. Can. Co., Chgo., 1988-89; mem. exec. com. Pechiney, Paris, 1989; bd. dirs. Pechiney Internat., 1989; vice, chmn., bd. dirs. Triangle Industries, N.Y.C., 1988; chmn., CEO, Bus. Resources Internat., Winnetka, Ill., 1989—; chmn. bd. dirs. Power Trends, Batavia, Ill.; bd. dirs. Aware, Bedford, Mass., Metasolv, Dallas; guest lectr. Sophia U., Tokyo, 1973. Chmn. bd. trustees Shedd Aquarium, Chgo.; exec. com. adv. bd. Brown Sch. Enging., Rice U., 1983-94. Mem. IEEE, Japan-Am. Soc., Chgo. Com., Exec. Club Chgo., Glenview Club, Sigma Xi, Tau Beta Pi, Sigma Tau. Episcopalian. Office: Bus Resources Internat PO Box 500 Winnetka IL 60093-0500

SICKEL, JOAN SOTTILARE, foundation administrator; b. Jersey City, Dec. 29, 1941; d. Peter S. and Rose M. (Maresca) Sottilare; m. Walter F. Sickel Jr., Jan. 4, 1964 (div. July 1979); children: Walter F. III (dec.), Linda Hilaire. AB, Georgian Ct. Coll., 1963. Dir. ann. giving Tucson Med. Ctr. Found., 1980-87; dir. devel. and pub. rels. Ariz. Children's Home, Tucson, 1987-93; exec. dir. Ariz. Children's Home Found., Tucson, 1993-94; curator edn. program devel. Ariz. Aerospace Found., Tucson, 1995—. Mem. women's studies adv. coun. U. Ariz. Mem. Nat. Soc. Fund Raising Execs., Nat. Assn. for Hosp. Devel., Pub. Rels. Soc. Am., Planned Giving Round Table of So. Ariz., AAUW, Ariz. Assn. for Hosp. Devel. (treas. 1986-88), U. Ariz. Presidents Club, U. Ariz. Wildcat Club, Soroptimists Internat. (chair fin. com. 1985). Home: 4151 N Camino Ferreo Tucson AZ 85750-6358 Office: 6000 E Valencia Tucson AZ 85706

SICKELS, ROBERT JUDD, political science educator; b. Nyack, N.Y., June 26, 1931; s. Robert and Dorothy (Judd) S.; m. Alice Esterer; children: Stephen Judd, Wendy. B.A., U. Chgo., 1950, M.A., 1954; Ph.D., Johns Hopkins U., 1960. Asst. staff dir. Pres.'s Commn. on Registration and Voting Participation, Washington, 1963-64; asso. dir. exec. insts. U.S. CSC, Washington, 1964-65; asso. prof. polit. sci. Purdue U., West Lafayette, Ind., 1965-68; assoc. prof. polit. sci. U. N.Mex., Albuquerque, 1968-73; prof. U. N.Mex., 1973-95; prof. emeritus U. N.Mex., Albuquerque, 1995—; chmn. dept. U. N.Mex., 1976-81. Author: Race, Marriage, and the Law, 1972, Presidential Transactions, 1974, The Presidency, 1980, John Paul Stevens and The Constitution: The Search for Balance, 1988; contbr. articles to profl. jours. Home: 1514 Harvard Ct NE Albuquerque NM 87106-3712

SICKELS, WILLIAM LOYD, secondary educator; b. Porterville, Calif., Mar. 26, 1936; s. Roy Ernest and Lula Mae (Weaver) S.; m. Donna Louise Eilers; 1 child, Alan Michael. AA, Porterville (Calif.) Coll., 1956; BA, San Jose (Calif.) State U., 1960, MA, 1965. Tchr. Redwood High Sch., Visalia, Calif., 1962-68; instr. Victor Valley Coll., Victorville, Calif., 1968-70; athletic dir., tchr. Tulare (Calif.) Western High Sch., 1970—. Pres. Sequoia Lake Conf. of YMCA's (pres. 1990-91, bd. dirs. 1982—). With U.S. Army, 1960-62. Named to Hall of Fame Visalia YMCA, 1990, Man of Yr., 1984. Fellow Y's Men Internat. (pres. 1985—), Calif. State Athletic Dirs. Assn. (v.p. 1984-94, Athletic Dir. of Yr. 1981, pres. 1995-96). Republican. Methodist. Avocations: back-packing, hiking. Home: 2723 W Country Ave Visalia CA 93277-6114 Office: Tulare Western High Sch 824 W Maple Ave Tulare CA 93274-2609

SICOTTE, SHELDON, finance company executive, director; b. 1932. Acct. John Cummings & Co., San Francisco, 1956-65; pres., treas. Hemming Morse Inc., San Mateo, Calif., 1965—. Office: Hemming Morse Inc 160 Bovet Rd San Mateo CA 94402*

SICURO, NATALE ANTHONY, academic administrator; b. Warren, Ohio, July 19, 1934; s. Gaetano and Antonette (Montecalvo) S.; m. Linda Lou Rockman, Aug. 3, 1957; children: Michael, Christine, Paul. BS, Kent State U., 1957, PhD, 1964; MS in Pub. Health, U. N.C., Chapel Hill, 1958. Tchr., coach, recreation adminstr. schs. in N.E. Ohio, 1958-62; instr., grad. asst., teaching fellow Kent State U., 1962-64; asst. supt. Geauga (Ohio) County schs., 1964-65; dir. program planning, asst. dean regional campuses Kent State U., 1965-68, 70-72, dean continuing edn., assoc. provost med. affairs, 1972-78; sr. cons., mgr. Peat, Marwick, Mitchell, Washington and L.A., 1968-70; pres. So. Oreg. State Coll., Ashland, 1979-86, Portland State U., 1986-88, Roger Williams U., Bristol, R.I., 1989-93, Roger Williams U. Sch. Law, Bristol, 1992-93; Jones Disting. Univ. prof. Jones Inst. for Ednl. Excellence Tchrs. Coll., Emporia (Kans.) State U., 1993-94; pres. SICURO Ednl. Cons., 1994—; pres. Ohio Council Continuing Edn., 1975-76; bd. dirs. So. Oreg. Coll. Found., 1979-86; state rep., chmn. fed. relations com. Am. Assn. State Colls. and Univs., 1979-86, bd. dirs. 1987-88, chmn.-elect, 1988; chmn. Govtl. Relations Commn., Am. Council on Edn., 1983-86; mem. council of presidents Nat. Assn. Intercollegiate Athletics; chmn. council of presidents Evergreen Conf.; co-chmn. council of presidents Columbia Football League; dir. Rogue Valley Physicians Service. Pres. United Way of Jackson County, Oreg., 1982; bd. dirs. Ashland YMCA, 1980-81, Ashland Indsl. Devel. Corp., 1982-85; mem. Jackson County Econ. Devel. Com., 1981-86, Am. Council on Edn., 1986-87. Mem. Nat. Challenges Commn. Higher Edn., Ashland Rotary, Bristol Rotary, Phi Delta Kappa, Phi Kappa Phi. Roman Catholic. Office: 77628 Woodhaven Dr S Palm Desert CA 92211-8132

SIDAMON-ERISTOFF, ANNE PHIPPS, museum official; b. N.Y.C., Sept. 12, 1932; d. Howard and Harriet Dyer (Price) Phipps; m. Constantine Sidamon-Eristoff, June 29, 1957; children—Simon, Elizabeth, Andrew. B.A., Bryn Mawr Coll., 1954. Chmn., bd. dirs. Am. Mus. Natural History, N.Y.C.; dir.-at-large Black Rock Forest Consortium; trustee God Bless Am. Fund. Bd. dirs. Greenacre Found., Highland Falls (N.Y.) Pub. Libr., N.Y. Cmty. Trust, Storm King Art Ctr., Mountainville, N.Y., World Wildlife Fund.; former bd. dirs.Scenic Hudson, St. Bernard's Sch., N.Y.C., Mus. Modern Art, N.Y.C., Mus. Hudson Highlands. Home: 120 East End Ave New York NY 10028-7552

SIDAMON-ERISTOFF, CATHERINE B., securities broker; b. N.Y.C., Jan. 2, 1964; d. Comer Cash and Betty Nan (Carpenter) Baxter; m. Andrew Sidamon-Eristoff, Mar. 30, 1996. BA, Duke U., 1986, MBA, 1987. V.p. Morgan Stanley & Co., Inc., N.Y.C., 1987—; former alumni coun. mem. Fuqua Sch. Bus., Durham, N.C.; mem. alumnae bd. Hockaday Sch., Dallas. Chmn. bd.-elect Burden Ctr. for Aging, N.Y.C., 1991—; active Jr. League, N.Y.C., 1982—; mem. jr. coun. Am. Mus. Natural History. Mem. NAFE, Am. Women's Econ. Devel. Assn. Republican. Presbyterian. Avocations: skiing, travel, reading. Office: Morgan Stanley & Co Inc 1251 Avenue Of The Americas New York NY 10020-1104

SIDAMON-ERISTOFF, CONSTANTINE, lawyer; b. N.Y.C., June 28, 1930; s. Simon C. and Anne Huntington (Tracy) Sidamon-E.; m. Anne Phipps, June 29, 1957; children: Simon, Elizabeth, Andrew. B.S.E. in Geol. Engring, Princeton U., 1952; LL.B., Columbia U., 1957. Clk., then assoc. firm Kelley Drye Newhall Maginnes & Warren, N.Y.C., 1957-64; individual practice law N.Y.C., 1964-65, 74-77; exec. asst. to Congressman John V. Lindsay, 1964-65; city coordinator Lindsay Mayoral Campaign, N.Y.C., 1965; asst. to mayor City of N.Y., 1966, commr. hwys., 1967-68, transp. adminstr., 1968-73; ptnr. Sidamon-Eristoff, Morrison, Warren, & Ecker, N.Y.C., 1978-83; counsel Morrison & de Roos, 1984-88; pvt. practice N.Y.C., 1988-89; regional adminstr. Region II EPA, N.Y.C., 1989-93; of counsel Patterson, Belknap, Webb & Tyler, N.Y.C., 1993—; mem. N.Y. State Met. Transp. Authority Bd., 1974-89; commr. N.Y. State Jud. Commn. on Minorities, 1987-91; mem. Gov.'s Coun. on Hudson River Valley Greenway, 1989; trustee United Mut. Savs. Bank, N.Y.C., 1979-82; trustee Phipps Houses, N.Y.C., 1974—, chmn. 1986—. Trustee Allaverdy Found., N.Y.C., 1962—, Am. Farm Sch., Thessaloniki, Greece, 1973-79, Carnegie Hall, N.Y.C., 1967-92, Millbrook (N.Y.) Sch., 1971-89, hon. trustee, 1989—, Orange County (N.Y.) Citizens Found., 1974-81, Am. the Beautiful Fund (Washington), 1985—; bd. dirs. Caramoor Center for Music and Arts, Katonah, N.Y., 1961-80, Tolstoy Found., Inc., N.Y.C., 1975—, chmn., 1979-89, 94—, Boyce Thompson Inst. for Plant Rsch., Ithaca, N.Y., 1994—; bd. dirs., mem. exec. com. Mid-Hudson Pattern for Progress, Poughkeepsie, N.Y., 1975-89, chmn., 1981-85; bd. dirs. Coun. on Mcpl. Performance, N.Y.C., 1979-87, chmn., 1979-83, vice chmn., 1986, 87, N.Y. State Republican committeeman, 1980-89. Served to 1st lt. arty. AUS, 1952-54, Korea. Decorated Bronze Star; recipient Honor award Kings County chpt. N.Y. State Soc. Profl. Engrs., 1969, Honor award Greater N.Y. coun. Girl Scouts U.S., 1973, Board Leadership award Coun. Mcpl. Performance, 1984, Transp. Man of Yr. award Greater N.Y. March of Dimes, 1985, Award of Excellence Mid-Hudson Pattern for Progress, 1990, Honor award Nat. and N.Y. Parks and Conservation Assn., 1992, Bronze medal USEPA, 1993. Mem. ABA, N.Y. State Bar Assn., Assn. of Bar of City of N.Y., N.Y. County Lawyers Assn., Kent Moot Ct., AIME, Phi Delta Phi, Delta Psi. Eastern Orthodox. Clubs: Century Assn. (N.Y.C.), Knickerbocker (N.Y.C.), Racquet and Tennis (N.Y.C.). Office: Patterson Belknap Webb & Tyler LLP 1133 Ave of the Americas New York NY 10036-6710

SIDDAYAO, CORAZÓN MORALES, economist, educator, energy consultant; b. Manila, July 26, 1932; came to U.S., 1968; d. Crispulo S. and Catalina T. (Morales) S. Cert. in elem. teaching, Philippine Normal Coll., 1951; BBA, U. East, Manila, 1962; MA in Econs., George Washington U., 1971, MPhil and PhD, 1975. Cert. Inst. de Francais, 1989. Tchr. pub. schs. Manila, 1951-53; asst. pensions officer IMF, Washington, 1968-71; cons. economist Washington, 1971-75; rsch. assoc. Policy Studies in Sci. and Tech. George Washington U., Washington, 1971-72, teaching fellow dept. econs., 1972-75; natural gas specialist U.S. Fed. Energy Adminstrn., Washington, 1974-75; sr. rsch. economist, assoc. prof. Inst. S.E.A. Studies, Singapore, 1975-78; sr. rsch. fellow energy/economist East-West Ctr., 1978-81, project dir. energy and industrialization, 1981-86; vis. fellow London Sch. Econ., 1984-85; sr. energy economist in charge energy program Econ. Devel. Inst., World Bank, Washington, 1986-94, ret., 1994; affiliate prof. econs. U. Hawaii, 1979—; vis. prof. econs. U. Philippines, intermittently, 1989—; co-dir. UPecon Inst. of Resource Studies, 1995—; vis. prof. U. Montpelier, France, 1992-95; cons. internat. orgns. and govts., 1995—; spkr. at confs. and symposia. Author or co-author: Increasing the Supply of Medical Personnel, 1973, The Offshore Petroleum Resources of Southeast Asia: Some Potential Conflicts and Related Economic Factors, 1978, Round Table Discussion on Asian and Multinational Corporations, 1978, The Supply of Petroleum Resources in Southeast Asia: Economic Implications of Evolving Property Rights Arrangements, 1980, Critical Energy Issues in Asia and the Pacific: The Next Twenty Years, 1982, Criteria for Energy Pricing Policy, 1985, Energy Demand and Economic Growth, 1986; editor: Energy Policy and Planning series, 1990-92, Energy Investments and the Environment, 1993; co-editor: Investissements Energetiques et Environnement, 1993; co-editor: (series) Energy Projecy Analysis for the CIS Countries (Russian), 1993, Politique d'Efficacité de l'Énergie et Environnement, Expérience pratiques, 1994, Matérial Pedagogique sur la Politique d'Efficacité de l'Energie et Environnement, 1994; contbr. chpts. to books, articles to profl. jours. Grantee in field. Mem. Am. Econ. Assn., Internat. Assn. Energy Economists (charter), Alliance Francaise, Omicron Delta Epsilon. Roman Catholic. *Power and money never provided stimuli in my life. Rather, I have sought to do that which challenges, stimulates the spirit and the intellect, is useful - in the rather abstract global level or at the more concrete persoal level - and which I am happy doing. As much as I would like to write about the past, I feel that there is so much to do in the present and for our future not to keep going. Also the less advantaged the individuals I deal with, the more help I feel they should get.*

SIDDERS, PATRICK MICHAEL, financial executive; b. Duluth, Minn., Oct. 19, 1940; s. Blaine L. and Elizabeth M. (Murphy) S.; m. Barbara E. Powers, Aug. 31, 1963; children: Patrick Michael, Kevin, Jennifer. BABA, St. Benedict's Coll., Atchison, Kans., 1963; postgrad., U. Minn. Grad. Sch. Bus. Adminstrn. Investment analyst Prudential Ins. Co., 1964-68; v.p. corp. fin. Dain Bosworth, Inc., Mpls., 1968-73; v.p. fin., treas. Modern Merchandising Inc., Minnetonka, Minn., 1973-79, exec. v.p., acting chief operating officer, 1979-81; pres. Modern Merchandising, Minnetonka, Minn., 1982-83; also dir. Modern Merchandising Inc., Minnetonka, Minn.; pres., chmn. and chief exec. officer Drag Spltys., Inc., Minnetonka, 1983-89, also dir.; CFO Salkin & Linoff, Mpls., 1989-90; sr. v.p., mng. dir. corp. fin. John G. Kinnard & Co., Mpls., 1990-94; exec. v.p. adminstrn., CFO, dir. Casino Magic Corp., Bay St. Louis, Miss., 1994-95; sr. v.p., mng. dir. corp. fin. R.J. Steichen & Co., Mpls., 1995—. Mem. Fin. Execs. Inst. Republican. Roman Catholic. Home: 2940 Pelican Point Ct Mound MN 55364-9999 Office: 800 Marquette Ave Ste 1100 Minneapolis MN 55402-9999

SIDDIQUI, FAROOQ AHMAD, medical educator; b. Unnao, India, Jan. 1, 1951; came to U.S., 1976; s. Siddique Ahmad and Humra (Ahmad) S.; m. Yasmeen Siddiqui, June 24, 1979; children: Tazeen, Sanna. BS in Biology, M.U. Aligarh, India, 1969; MS in Biochemistry, M.U., Aligarh, India, 1971, MPhil in Biochemistry, 1972, PhD in Biochemistry, 1975. Sr. rsch. fellow in biochemistry Patel Chest Inst., Delhi, 1975-76; cancer rsch. affiliate Dept. Exptl. Therapeutics Roswell Park Meml. Inst., Buffalo, N.Y., 1976-79; vis. assoc. in biology McGill U., Montreal, Que., Can., 1979-80; rsch. assoc. biochemistry Georgetown U., Washington, 1980-81; rsch. assoc. medicine Divsn. Hematology U. Miami, 1981-83, rsch. instr. medicine Divsn. Hematology, 1983-85, rsch. asst. prof. medicine Divsn. Hematology/Oncology, 1985-94, rsch. assoc. prof. medicine divsn. hematology/oncology, 1994—; sci. presenter at nat. and internat. meetings. Contbr. articles to profl. jours. Mem. coun. on thrombosis Am. Heart Assn. Co-Prin. Investigator grantee NIH, 1988-93; fellow Coun. Sci. and Indsl. Rsch., New Delhi, 1971-72, Indian Coun. Med. Rsch., 1972-75. Mem. Soc. Biol. Chemists (India), Sigma Xi. Home: 13324 SW 115th Pl Miami FL 33176-4493 Office: U Miami/Va Med Ctr #R-151 Rm 2A122 1201 NW 16th St Miami FL 33125-1624

SIDDONS, SARAH MAE, chemist; b. Conway, S.C., July 20, 1939; d. Willie C. and Lelia (Parker) Crawford; m. John Lathan, June 26, 1958 (div.); m. Ronald Gladstone Siddons, June 26, 1965; 1 child, Ronald George. BA, Coll. New Rochelle, 1980; postgrad., Cornell U., 1975. Lab. technologist DC37-Local 144, Bronx, 1961-65, 65-82; jr. chemist DC37-Local 375, Bronx, 1982-85, assoc. chemist, 1985-90, assoc. chemist, supr., 1990—; del. DC37-Lcoal 144, 1962-84, DC37-Local 375, 1984—. Mem. Am. Assn. Clin. Chemistry, Dynamic Five Social Club (pres. 1988—, v.p. 1980-88). Home: 3924 Carpenter Ave Bronx NY 10466 Office: Lincoln Med Ctr 234 E 149th St Rm 432 Bronx NY 10451

SIDDOWAY, HENRY RALPH, company executive; b. Vernal, Utah, Oct. 9, 1905; s. William Henry and Emily Jane (Dunster) S.; m. Marsale Eunice Eaton, Apr. 21, 1924; children: William Ralph, Lynn Irvin, Charyl Anita. BS with honors, U. Utah, 1928, postgrad., 1963; postgrad., Brigham Young U., 1929-30. Cert. secondary tchr., music tchr., social svc. worker. Tchr. Uintah High Sch., Vernal, Utah, 1928-46, treas., 1928-44; acct., bus. mgr. Calder Motor Co.-S. Calder, Vernal, 1930-34; dir. and owners self interest 3000 sheep Utah, 1946-80; bus. mgr., dir. Vernal Milling Co., 1933-56; stockholder, dir., sec., treas. Ashley Coop. Merc. Inst., 1943-96; office mgr., acct. Calder Bros. Creamers, Vernal, 1947-50; office mgr. Uintah Oil Refinery, 1950-54; dir. S. Raven Oil & Refining co., Rangely, Colo., 1960-65; mem. U.S. Bur. Land Mgmt., Uintah, Duchesne Dagget County, Utah, 1943-60, sec., 3 County, 1943-60, mem. adv. bd., 1957-60. Mem. Utah State Adv. Bd.; mem. Uintah County Bd., Edn., 1942, pres., 1944-45; mayor City of Vernal, 1958-62; bd. dirs. Uintah County Coun. on Aging, 1970-78; dir. Area Agy. on Aging, 1978-89. Recipient Help Line Profl. Svc. award Dept. Social Svcs. Div. Alcohlism and Drugs, Salt Lake City, 1978. Mem. Lions Club (sec. 1945, pres. 1946, zone chmn. 1947). Republican. Mem. LDS Ch. Home: 673 N Vernal Ave Vernal UT 84078-3703 Office: Ashley Coop Merc Inst 22 W Main St Vernal UT 84078-2502

SIDER, HARVEY RAY, minister, church administrator; b. Cheapside, Ont., Can., June 20, 1930; s. Earl M. and Elsie (Sheffer) S.; m. Erma Jean Heise, July 20, 1957; children: Cheryl Sider Giles, Steven. BA, Western U., Ont., 1957; BD, Winona Lake Sch. Theology, Ind., 1962. Ordained to ministry Brethren in Christ Ch., 1953; cert. tchr., Ont. Pastor Brethren in Christ Ch., Toronto, Ont., 1957-61; missionary, adminstr. missions dept. Brethren in Christ Ch., Bihar, India, 1962-74; pastor Brethren in Christ Ch., Stayner, Ont., 1974-76; pres. Niagara Christian Coll., Ft. Erie, Ont., 1976-78; bishop Brethren in Christ Ch., Can., 1978-90; moderator Brethren in Christ Ch., N.Am., 1990—. Office: Brethren Christ Ch PO Box 290 Grantham PA 17027-0290

SIDER, RONALD J., theology educator, author; b. Stevensville, Ont., Can., Sept. 17, 1939; m. Arbutus Lichti Sider, Aug. 19, 1961; children: Theodore Ronald, Michael Jay, Sonya Maria. BA with honors, Waterloo Luth. U., 1962; MA in History, Yale U., 1963, BD, 1967, PhD in History, 1969. Lectr., asst. prof., then assoc. prof. Messiah Coll., 1968-78, acting dir., dean, 1971-75; assoc. prof. theology Ea. Bapt. Theol. Sem., Wynnewood, Pa., 1978-84, prof. theology, 1984—; coord., chair, convenor workshops in field; coord. Internat. Consultation on Simple Lifestyle, London, 1980; lectr. in field. Editor: Preaching on Peace, 1982, Lifestyle in the Eighties: An Evangelical Commitment to Simple Life-Style, 1982, Evangelicals and Development: Toward a Theology of Social Change, 1982, Living More Simply, 1980, Cry Justice: The Bible on Hunger and Poverty, 1988, 91; author: Christ and Violence, 1979, Karlstadt's Battle with Luther: Documents in a Liberal-Radical Debate, 1978, 82, Evangelism, 1985, Rich Christians in an Age of Hunger: A Biblical Study, 1977, rev. edit., 1984, 90, German edit., 1979, Dutch edit., 1980, Portuguese edit., 1984, Japanese edit., 1989, Korean edit., 1995, Andreas Bodenstein Von Karlstadt, 1974, (with Richard K. Taylor) Nuclear Holocaust and Christian Hope, 1982, English edit., 1984, (with Oliver O'Donovan) Peace and War: A Debate About Pacifism, 1985, (in chinese) Evangelical Faith and Social Ethics, 1986, Completely Pro-Life, 1987, (with Michael A. King) Preaching About Life in Threatening World, 1988, (with Kathleen Hayes), JustLife/88: A 1988 Election Study Guide for Justice, Life and Peace, 1988, Testing the Limits of Nonviolence, 1988, One-Sided Christianity? Uniting the Church to Heal a Lost and Broken World, 1993, Cup of Water, Bread of Life: Inspiring Stories About Overcoming Lopsided Christianity, 1994; editor, contbr.: The Chicago Declaration, 1974; contbr. numerous articles to profl. publs., chpts. to books. Head voter registration dr., New Haven, 1967; pres. Diamont St. Cmty. Ctr., 1986-91; exec. dir. Evangelicals for Social Action, 1987-92, pres., 1992—; exec. dir. Just Life, 1987-91, pres., 1991-94; bd. dirs. Bread for the World, 1978-84, Mennonite Ctrl. Com., 1978-80; co-chair Nat. Workshop on Race and Reconciliation, Atlanta, 1975. Malcolm Chase fellow, 1962-63, R.E. Darlin fellow, 1963-64, fellow Yale U., 1967-68, Inst. for Advanced Christian Studies, 1976. Mem. Nat. Assn. Evangelicals (mem. social action commn. 1975—). Mennonite. Home: 312 W Logan St Philadelphia PA 19144 Office: Ea Bapt Sem 6 Lancaster Ave Wynnewood PA 19096

SIDEROFF, BARRY, advertising executive; b. Mount Vernon, N.Y., Aug. 31, 1953; s. Milton and Beatrice (Plotkin) S.; m. Florence E. Flancbaum, July 25, 1979; children: Melissa Jane, Marc Adam. BA, SUNY, Binghamton, 1975; Mktg. and Advt. degree, NYU, 1982. Mgr. Comml. Investment Trust Fin. Corp., N.Y.C. and Livingston, N.J., 1980-83; asst. v.p. Mfrs. Hanover, N.Y.C., 1983-85; dir. mktg. Compu-U-Card Internat., Stamford, Conn., 1985-86; sr. v.p. D'Arcy, Masius, Benton & Bowles, Greenwich, Conn., 1986-93; sr. v.p./dir. mktg. Barry Blau & Ptnrs., Fairfield, Conn., 1993—; mem. Direct Mktg. Idea Exch., N.Y.C., 1983-86; guest lectr. in field. Mem. Direct Mktg. Assn. (moderator, spkr. nat. conv. 1992, Echo awards 1982, 84). Home: 18 Clover St Larchmont NY 10538 Office: Barry Blau & Ptnrs 1960 Bronson Rd Fairfield CT 06430

SIDES, JAMES RALPH, aerospace executive; b. Carbon Hill, Ala., Apr. 17, 1936; s. James Beatty and Ruby (Kilpatrick) S.; m. Martha Sue Ryland, Nov. 1, 1955; children: James R. Jr., Christopher Kent, Patrick Ryland. BS in Chemistry, U. Ala., 1958. Chemist Thiokol Chem. Corp., Huntsville, Ala., 1958-60; chemist, group leader Amcel Propulsion Co. (subs. Celanese), Asheville, N.C., 1960-65; head process engring., chief mfg. and engring., project office mgr. Atlantic Rsch. Corp., Gainesville, Va., 1965-69, dir. engring., 1969, asst. dir. propulsion div., mgr. engring dept., 1970-78, asst. gen. mgr. propulsion div., dir. engring. dept., 1978-80, v.p., gen. mgr. propulsion div., 1980-85, sr. v.p., gen. mgr. propulsion div., 1985-87, group pres., 1987—; bd. dirs. Atlantic Rsch. Corp., Prince William County Higher Edn. Bd.; mem. exec. com. Bendix-Atlantic Inflator Co. Contbr. articles to profl. jours.; patentee in field. Mem. Dulles Airport Task Force, Va., 1987. Recipient Cert. of Commendation USAF, 1964. Fellow AIAA (assoc., Wyld Propulsion award, 1989); mem. Am. Defense Preparedness Assn. (chmn. missiles and astronautics), Va. Mfrs. Assn. (bd. dirs.), Air Force Assn., Assn. U.S. Army, Field Artillery Assn., Navy League, Alpha Chi Sigma. Home: 11133 Tattersall Trl Oakton VA 22124-1927 Office: Atlantic Rsch Corp 1577 Spring Hill Rd Ste 600 Vienna VA 22182-2223*

SIDES, KERMIT FRANKLIN, furniture manufacturing company executive; b. Lee County, Miss., Feb. 13, 1932; s. Robert Franklin and Francis Jet (Cox) S.; grad. high sch., Wheeler, Miss.; m. Edna E. Heavener, Aug. 1, 1953; children: Connie Ann, Timothy Franklin. Mfg. supr. Futorian Mfg. Co., New Albany and Okolona, Miss., 1953-69; v.p., gen. mgr. Action Industries, Verona, Miss., 1969-79; exec. v.p., sec., treas. PeopLounger Inc., Nettleton, Miss., 1979—, also dir. Indsl. chmn. Lee United Neighbors div. United Way, Tupelo, Miss., 1969-73; v.p., bd. dirs. Northeast Miss. Community Relations Assn.; co-founder PeopLoungers, 1979. Recipient award for Outstanding Contbn. to Appearance of City, 1981. Baptist. Home: 2637 St Andrews Dr Belden MS 38826-9535 Office: PO Drawer 429 Nettleton MS 38858

SIDES, LARRY EUGENE, advertising executive; b. Albany, Ga., Nov. 14, 1946; s. Robert N. and Florine (Stewart) S.; m. Kathy Ashworth, Aug. 13, 1950. BA in Radio and TV, U. Southwestern La., 1970, MS in Communications, 1975. News reporter Sta. KATC-TV, Lafayette, La., 1970-71; account exec. Herbert S. Benjamin Assocs., Lafayette, La., 1971-76; pres. Sides & Assocs., Lafayette, La., 1976—. Vice-chmn. Crimestoppers, Lafayette, 1985; bd. dirs. Episcopal Sch. Acadiana, Lafayette, 1987; pres. Gateway Found., 1990; active Leadership La., 1989, 90; mem. Coun. for a Better La., 1991—; bd. dirs. La. Coun. on Child Abuse, 1992—; active Leadership Lafayette, 1995. Named one of Outstanding Young Men of Am., Lafayette Jaycees, 1976; recipient Disting. Alumni award dept. comms. U. Southwestern La., 1995. Mem. Am. Assn. Advt. Agys. (pres. La. coun., 1989-90), Am. Soc. Hosp. Pub. Rels., Pub. Rels. Soc. Am., La. Assn. Advt. Agys., Pub. Rels. Assn. La., Acadiana Advt. Fedn., Lafayette C. of C. (pres. 1989, Entrepreneur of Yr. 1983), Sigma Nu (alumni pres. Lafayette chpt. 1977). Club: Beaver (pres. 1986, Outstanding Club Mem. award 1976). Home: 1015 W St Mary Blvd Lafayette LA 70506-3420 Office: 404 Eraste Landry Rd Lafayette LA 70506-2324

SIDEY, HUGH SWANSON, correspondent; b. Greenfield, Iowa, Sept. 3, 1927; s. Kenneth H. and Alice Margaret (Swanson) S.; m. Alice Anne Trowbridge, Dec. 5, 1953; children—Cynthia Anne, Sandra, Bettina, Edwin. B.S., Iowa State U., 1950. Reporter Adair County (Iowa) Free Press, 1950, The Nonpareil, Council Bluffs, Iowa, 1950-51, Omaha World-Herald, 1951-55, Life mag., 1955-58; corr. Time mag., 1958—; columnist Time mag., Life mag. (The Presidency), 1966—; chief Time mag. (Washington Bur.), 1969-78, Washington contbg. editor, 1978—. Author: John F. Kennedy, President, 1963, A Very Personal Presidency, Lyndon Johnson in the White House, 1966, These United States, 1975, Portrait of a President, 1975, The Presidency, 1991; co-author: 1,000 Ideas for Better News Pictures, 1956, The Memories, 1961—JFK—1963, 1973; contbr.: The Kennedy Circle. Served with AUS, 1945-46. Office: 1050 Connecticut Ave NW Washington DC 20036-5303

SIDHU, JAY S., banking executive. CEO, pres. Sovereign Bancorp, Wyomissing, Pa. Office: Sovereign Bancorp Inc PO Box 12646 1130 Berkshire Blvd Reading PA 19612*

SIDHU, RAJINDER SINGH, molecular biologist, researcher; b. Bajoana, Punjab, India, May 1, 1949; came to U.S., 1982, naturalized, 1991.; s. Bhag Singh and Surjit Kaur (Chuhan) S.; m. Parmjit Kaur Dhaliwal, Mar. 5, 1978; children: Jaspreet Singh, Harsimran Singh. BS, Punjab Agrl. U., 1968; PhD, Haryana Agrl. U., Hissar, India, 1976. Postdoctoral fellow Osaka (Japan) U., 1979-80; postdoctoral fellow Wadley Inst. Molecular Medicine, Dallas, 1982-84, sr. scientist I, 1984-86, sr. scientist II, 1986-88; sr. scientist III Wadley Bioscis., Dallas, 1988-91; sr. scientist III, co-dir. gene expression Cytoclonal Pharms., Inc., Dallas, 1991—. Contbr. articles to profl. jours. Mem. AAAS, Am. Soc. Microbiology. Achievements include research on the regulation of protein synthesis and secretion of proteins by yeast production of Taxol and other secondary metabolites.

SIDLE, ROY CARL, research hydrologist; b. Quakertown, Pa., Oct. 31, 1948; s. Carl G. and Isabel (Ziegler) S.; children: Shelley, Bradley. BS, U. Ariz., 1970, MS, 1972; PhD, Pa. State U., 1976. Hydrologist Wright Water Engrs., Denver, 1972; rsch. asst. Pa. State U., University Park, 1972-76; rsch. soil scientist USDA-ARS, Morgantown, W.Va., 1976-78; watershed extension specialist Oreg. State U., Corvallis, 1978-80; rsch. hydrologist Forest Svc., PNW Rsch. Sta., USDA, Juneau, 1980-86; project leader (hydrologist) Forest Svc., INT Rsch. Sta., USDA, Logan, Utah, 1986-95; sr. rsch. hydrologist Geol. Survey of Denmark and Greenland, Copenhagen, 1995—; adj. prof. Utah State U., Logan, 1986—; symposium chmn. Am. Soc. Agronomy, Anaheim, Calif. and Las Vegas, Nev., 1982; vis. fellow Japanese Forestry and Forest Products Rsch. Inst., 1991. Sr. author: Hillslope Stability and Land Use, 1985; assoc. editor Jour. of Environ. Quality, 1990—; contbr. numerous articles to profl. jours. Grantee Water Resources Rsch. Inst. Oreg. State U., 1979, USDA-Forest Svc., 1979, Am. Geophys. Union, 1982, Am. Philos. Soc., 1982, Utah Fuel Co., 1992-96, Genwal Coal Co., 1993-95, Sci. and Tech. Agy. Japan, 1991, 92, 93, 94, Danish Natural Sci. Rsch. Coun., 1996; recipient Cert. of Merit Chief USDA-Forest Svc., 1989. Mem. Am. Soc. Agronomy, Soil Sci. Soc. Am., Am. Geophys. Union, Am. Water Resources Assn., Internat. Soc. Soil Sci., Sigma Xi, Gamma Sigma Delta. Avocations: skiing, weight lifting, baseball card collecting, antique collecting, biking. Office: GEUS, Thoravej 8, DK-2400 Copenhagen Denmark

SIDMAN, ROBERT JOHN, lawyer; b. Cleve., Aug. 4, 1943; s. Charles Frances and Louise (Eckert) S.; m. Mary Mato, July 29, 1967; children: Christa Mary, Alicia Mary. BA, Benedictine Coll., 1965; JD, U. Notre Dame, 1968. Bar: Ohio 1968, U.S. Dist. Ct. (so. dist.) Ohio 1970, U.S. Ct. Appeals (6th cir.) 1971, U.S. Supreme Ct. 1971. Law clk. U.S. Dist. Ct. (so. dist.) Ohio, Columbus, 1968-70; assoc. Mayer, Tingley & Hurd, Columbus, 1970-75; judge Bankruptcy Ct. U.S. Dist. Ct. (so. dits.) Ohio, Columbus, 1975-82; ptnr. Vorys, Sater, Seymour & Pease, Columbus, 1982—; prof. Ohio State U. Law Sch., Columbus, 1984, 85, 86. Mem. Nat. Conf. Bankruptcy Judges (bd. dirs. 1981-82), Assn. Former Bankruptcy Judges (bd. dirs. 1983-89, treas. 1986-87, pres. 1988-89). Office: Vorys Sater Seymour & Pease PO Box 1008 52 E Gay St Columbus OH 43215-3161

SIDNEY, SYLVIA (SOPHIA KOSSOW), actress; b. N.Y.C., Aug. 8, 1910; d. Victor and Rebecca (Saperstein) Kossow; m. Bennett Alfred Cerf, 1935 (div.); m. Luther Adler, 1938 (div.); 1 child, Jacob L.; m. Carlton Alsop, 1945 (div.). Attended, N.Y.C. pub. schs., Theater Guild Sch., 1925. Made stage debut starring as Prunella at the Garrick theater, 1926; subsequent stage appearances include The Challenge of Youth, Washington, 1926, The Squall, N.Y.C., 1927, Crime, 1927, Mirrors, 1928, The Breaks, 1928, The Gods of the Lightning, 1928, Nice Women, N.Y.C., 1929, Cross-Roads, 1929, Many a Slip, 1930, Bad Girl, 1930, To Quito and Back, N.Y.C., 1937, Pygmalion, 1938, The Gentle People, N.Y.C., 1939, Accent on Youth, 1941, Angel Street, 1942, 64, Pygmalion, 1943, Joan of Lorraine, 1947, Kind Lady, 1948, The Two Mrs. Carrolls, 1949, Pygmalion, 1949, O Mistress Mine, 1949, Goodbye My Fancy, 1950, Anne of the Thousand Days, 1950, Innocents, Black Chiffon, 1951, The Gypsies Wore High Hats, 1952, The Fourposter, 1952, A Very Special Baby, 1956, Auntie Mame, 1958, Enter Laughing, 1963, Silver Cord, 1964, Kind Lady, 1964, Come Blow Your Horn, 1968-69, Vieux Carré, Sabrina Fair, Morning's at 7, 1981, Shadow Box, 1981, Come Along with Me, 1981; appearances in Nat. Repertory Theatre plays includes The Rivals, 1965-66, The Little Foxes, 1966, The Importance of Being Earnest, 1966, She Stoops to Conquer, 1968; film career began in 1930; movie appearances include Beetlejuice, Summer Wishes Winter Dreams (Acad. award nominee for best supporting actress), I Never Promised You A Rose Garden, Accent on Youth, 30 Day Princess, Behold My Wife, Sabotage, 1/3 of a Nation, Damien: Omen 2, Hammett, City Streets, An American Tragedy, Street Scene, Merrily We Go to Hell, Mary Burns, Fugitive, Madame Butterfly, Trail of the Lonesome Pine, Fury, You Only Live Once, Dead End, The Searching Wind, Love from a Stranger, Les Miserables, Used People; TV appearances include My Three Sons, Whiz Kids, Magnum PI, Trapper John, M.D.; TV movies include The Shadow Box, 1980, Raid on Entebbe, 1977, Snowbeast, 1977, Siege, 1978, A Small Killing, 1981, An Early Frost, André's Mother, 1990 (Golden Globe nominee); author: Sylvia Sidney's Needlepoint Book, 1968, The Sylvia Sidney Question and Answer Book on Needlepoint, 1975. Bd. dirs. Nat. Amyotrophic Lateral Sclerosis Found. Avocations: needlepoint, reading, watching TV. Office: care John Springer 130 E 67th St New York NY 10021-6136

SIDNEY, WILLIAM WRIGHT, retired aerospace company executive; b. Anaconda, Mont., Dec. 31, 1929; s. Paul and Lily Maud (Wright) S.; divorced; children: Kay Elise, Paul Daniel. Student U. Calif., Berkeley, 1953-56. Supr. prodn. Kaiser Aerospace, San Leandro, Calif., 1953-57, project engr., 1957-67, chief engr., 1967-69, gen. mgr., 1969-77; pres. Kaiser Aerotech, San Leandro, Calif., 1977-95, Kaiser Space Products, Pueblo, Colo., 1988-95, ret., 1995. With USN, 1948-52. Recipient NASA Pub. Svc. medal 1981. Mem. U. Calif. Alumni Assn. Home: 6025 Ridgemont Dr Oakland CA 94619-3721

SIDO, KEVIN RICHARD, lawyer; b. Alton, Ill., Nov. 22, 1951; s. Robert Frederick and Mary (Colligan) S.; m. Mary O'Neil, July 28, 1984. BA, U. Ill., 1972, JD, 1975. Bar: Ill. 1975, U.S. Dist. Ct. (no. dist.) Ill. 1975, U.S. Tax Ct. 1976, U.S. Ct. Appeals (7th cir.) 1977, U.S. Supreme Ct. 1979. Assoc. Hinshaw, Culbertson, Moelmann, Hoban & Fuller, Chgo., 1975-82, ptnr., 1982—, mem. exec. com., 1988—; lectr. Ill. Inst. CLE, 1977—; arbitrator Cir. Ct. of Cook County. Contbr. articles to profl. jours. Bd. dirs. Lake Barrington Shores (Ill.) Homeowners Assn., 1979. Mem. ABA, Ill Bar Assn., Chgo. Bar Assn., Def. Rsch. Inst. (lectr. 1983—, state chmn. No. Ill. 1988-94), Ill. Def. Counsel Assn. (bd. dirs. 1982-83, 87-94, editor 1984-87), Internat. Assn. Def. Counsel, Am. Arbitration Assn. (arbitrator), Phi Beta Kappa. Avocations: photography, antiques. Office: Hinshaw and Culbertson 222 N La Salle St Ste 300 Chicago IL 60601-1005

SIDON, CLAUDIA MARIE, psychiatry, mental health nursing educator; b. Bellaire, Ohio, Feb. 6, 1946; d. Paul and Nell (Bernas) DePaulis; m. Michael Sidon; children: Michael II, Babe. Diploma, Wheeling (W.Va.) Hosp. Sch., 1966; BS in Nursing summa cum laude, Ohio U., Athens, 1979; MS in Nursing, W.Va. U., Morgantown, 1982. Cert. social worker. Various staff positions Bellaire City Hosp., 1966-67, 72-77; adj. nursing faculty W.Va. No. Community Coll., Wheeling, 1977-82; nurse clinician, psychotherapist Valley Psychol. and Psychiat. Svcs., Moundsville, W.Va., 1984; psychotherapist, nurse clinician, case mgr. No. Panhandle Behavioral Health Ctr., Wheeling, 1984-88; assoc. prof. ADN program Belmont Tech. Coll., St. Clairsville, Ohio, 1988—; presenter in field. Mem. Tri-State Psychiat. Nursing Assn. (pres., v.p., program chmn.), Nat. League for Nursing (presenter), Phi Kappa Phi, Sigma Theta Tau. Home: 52295 Sidon Rd Dillonvale OH 43917-9538 Office: Belmont Tech Coll 120 Fox Shannon Pl Saint Clairsville OH 43950-8751

SIDRAN, MIRIAM, retired physics educator, researcher; b. Washington, May 25, 1920; d. Morris Samson and Theresa Rena (Gottlieb) S. BA, Bklyn. Coll., 1942; MA, Columbia U., N.Y.C., 1949; PhD, NYU, 1956. Rsch. assoc. dept. physics NYU, N.Y.C., 1950-55, postdoctoral fellow, 1955-57; asst. prof. Staten Island Community Coll., Richmond, N.Y., 1957-59; rsch. scientist Grumman Aerospace Corp., Bethpage, N.Y., 1959-67; prof. N.Y. Inst. Tech., N.Y.C., 1967-72; NSF rsch. fellow Nat. Marine Fisheries Svc., Miami, Fla., 1971-72; assoc. prof. then prof. physics Baruch Coll., N.Y.C., 1972-89, chmn. dept. natural scis., 1983-89, prof. emerita, 1990—; v.p. Baruch chpt. Prof. Staff Congress, 1983-89. Contbr. numerous articles to profl. and govtl. publs., chpts. to books. N.Y. State Regents scholar, 1937-41; NSF summer fellow, Miami, 1970. Mem. N.Y. Acad. Scis., Am. Assn. Physics Tchrs. Avocations: French and Hebrew languages, music, bicycling. Home: 210 West 19 St Apt 5G New York NY 10011

SIDRANE, MICHELLE DIANA, publishing executive; b. Bklyn., Oct. 9, 1948; d. David Allen and Irene G. (Goldberger) Frenkel; m. Alan Paul Sidrane, June 12, 1970; children: Davida Jennifer, Andrew Elliot. B.A., SUNY-Stony Brook, 1970. Mgr. subs. rights Macmillan Pub. Co., N.Y.C., 1971-74; v.p., dir. subs. rights and spl. sales Crown Pubs., Inc., N.Y.C., 1974—, sr. v.p., pub., 1989—, exec. v.p., pub., 1990—. Mem. Civic Council Park Slope, Bklyn., 1981-82, 82-83; trustee Berkley-Carroll Sch., 1988—. Mem. Women's Media Group, Nat. Premium Sales Execs. Office: Crown Pubs Inc 201 E 50th St New York NY 10022-7703

SIDRANSKY, HERSCHEL, pathologist; b. Pensacola, Fla., Oct. 17, 1925; s. Ely and Touba (Bear) S.; m. Evelyn Lipsitz, Aug. 18, 1952; children: Ellen, David Ira. B.S., Tulane U., 1948, M.D., 1953, M.S., 1958. Diplomate: Am. Bd. Pathology. Intern Charity Hosp. La., New Orleans, 1953-54; vis. asst. pathologist Charity Hosp. La., 1954-58; practice medicine, specializing in pathology Washington, 1977—; pathologist Nat. Cancer Inst., NIH, Bethesda, Md., 1958-61; instr. pathology Tulane U., 1954-58; prof. pathology U. Pitts., 1961-72; prof., chmn. dept. pathology U. South Fla., Tampa, 1972-77, George Washington U., 1977—; cons. VA Hosp. and Children's Hosp., Washington. Mem. editl. bd. Jour. Nutrition, 1973-77, Cancer Rsch., 1974-77, Human Pathology, 1979-91, Am. Jour. Clin. Nutrition, 1979-82, Am. Jour. Pathology, 1980-85, Jour. Exptl. Pathology, 1982-92, Exptl. Molecular Pathology Jour., 1987—; contbr. articles to profl. jours. Served with AUS, 1944-46. Life Ins. Med. Research fellow, 1956-57; USPHS fellow, 1957-58, 67-68; NIH research grantee, 1961—. Mem. Am. Soc. for Investigative Pathology, Soc. Exptl. Biology and Medicine, Am. Assn. Cancer Rsch., Am. Inst. Nutrition, Am. Soc. Clin. Nutrition, U.S.-Can. Acad. Pathologists, Med. Mycology Soc. Ams., Reticuloendothelial Soc., N.Y. Acad. Scis., AAAS, Washington Acad. Medicine (pres. 1986-98), Washington Soc. Pathologists, Assn. Pathology Chmn., Intersoc. Com. on Pathology Info., Sigma Xi. Home: 5144 Macomb St NW Washington DC 20016-2612 Office: 2300 I St NW Washington DC 20037-2337

SIEBEL, MATHIAS PAUL, mechanical engineer; b. Witten, Germany, Mar. 6, 1924; came to U.S., 1957, naturalized, 1962; s. Franz and Marie-Luise S.; m. Katherine Elizabeth Jente, May 27, 1960. B.S. in Mech. Engring, U. Bristol, Eng., 1949, Ph.D., 1952. From research and devel. engr. to asst. plant mgr. Tube Investments Ltd., Birmingham, Eng., 1952-57; research asso. Columbia U., N.Y.C., 1958-59; mgr. pressure equipment Pall Corp., Glen Cove, N.Y., 1959-64; v.p. ops. RDI Co., Westbury, N.Y., 1964-65; dir. mfg. engring. lab., then mem. sci. staff Marshall Space Flight Center, NASA, Huntsville, Ala., 1965-79; mgr. NASA Michoud Assembly Facility, New Orleans, 1979-87, cons., 1987—; assoc. dean Coll. Engring. U. New Orleans, 1989-92. Author. Mem. Sigma Xi. Patentee in field. Home: 5204 Janice Ave Kenner LA 70065-3238

SIEBENBURGEN, DAVID A., airline company executive; b. Cin., Sept. 18, 1947; s. Joseph and Elsie (Diersing) S.; m. Marcia Altieri, Sept. 27, 1974, 1 child, Brian. BBA, Xavier U., 1972. CPA, Ohio. Acct. Arthur Andersen & Co., Ohio, Ohio, 1974—; pres., COO Comair, Inc., Cin., 1984—. Mem. St. James Ch., Cin., 1980—, Community Chest, Cin. Republican. Roman Catholic. Office: Comair Inc PO Box 75021 Cincinnati OH 45275

SIEBER, SUZANNE MAHONEY, sales executive; b. Pitts., Apr. 18, 1963; d. John Patrick and Naomi Ruth (O'Neil) Mahoney; m. Richard M. Sieber, Dec. 29, 1990; 1 child, Madison Margaret. BS in Elec. Engr., Pa. State U., 1985; MS in Indsl. Adminstrn., Carnegie Mellon U., Pitts., 1990. Project mgr. Otis Elevator Co., Pitts., 1986, svc. sales rep., 1986-89, new equipment sales rep., 1989—. Dir. Canevin High Sch. Musical, Pitts. 1987. Mem. Am. Mktg. Assn., Western Pa. Soc. Engrs., Pitts. Ski Club, Pa. State Alumni Assn., Delta Delta Delta Alumni Assn. Democrat. Roman Catholic. Avocations: skiing, reading, theater. Home: 1441 Pueblo Dr Pittsburgh PA 15228-1605 Office: Otis Elevator Co 50 13th St Pittsburgh PA 15222-4234

SIEBERT, CALVIN D., economist, educator; b. Hillsboro, Kans., Feb. 11, 1934; s. Ira and Margaret (Everett) S.; m. Valerie Dawn Nanninga, Feb. 18, 1960; children—Douglas Erik, Derek Christopher. BA, U. Kans., 1958, MA, 1960; PhD in Econs., U. Calif., Berkeley, 1966. Asst. prof. econs. U. Iowa, 1965-68, assoc. prof., 1968-75, prof., 1975—, chmn. dept., 1969-71, 75-79; Rockefeller Found. vis. asso. prof. U. Philippines, 1971-72. Contbr. articles to profl. jours. With U.S. Army, 1954-56. Ford Found. grantee, 1964-65. Mem. Am. Econ. Assn., AAUP, Phi Beta Kappa. Home: 341 N 7th Ave Iowa City IA 52245-6003 Office: U Iowa Dept Econs W276 Pbab Iowa City IA 52242

SIEBERT, DIANE DOLORES, author, poet; b. Chgo., Mar. 18, 1948; m. Robert William Siebert, Sept. 21, 1969. RN. Author: Truck Song, 1984 (Notable Childrens Book award ALA 1984, Sch. Libr. Jour. one of Best Books 1984, Outstanding Childrens Book award N.Y. Times Book Rev. 1984, Reading Rainbow Selection book 1991), Mojave, 1988 (Childrens Editors Choice 1988, Internat. Reading Assn. Tchrs. Choice award 1989, others), Heartland, 1989 (award Nat. Coun. for Social Studies/Childrens Book Coun. 1989, on John Burroughs List Nature Book for Young Readers 1989, Ohio Farm Bur. Women award 1991), Train Song, 1990 (Notable Childrens Book award ALA, 1990, Redbook Mag. one of Top Ten Picture Books 1990, one of Best Books award Sch. Libr. Jour. 1990, others), Sierra, 1991 (Outstanding Sci. Trade Book for Children award NSTA 1991, Notable Childrens Trade Book in Field Social Studies award Nat. Coun. Social Studies 1991, Beatty award Calif. Libr. Assn. 1992), Plane Song, 1993 (Outstanding Sci. Trade Book for Children 1994, Platinum award Oppenheim Toy Portfolio, Tchrs. Choice award Internat. Reading Assn. 1994). Avocations: environmental affairs, running, classical guitar, motorcycle, animals. Home: 9676 SW Jordan Rd Culver OR 97734

SIEBERT, KARL JOSEPH, food science educator; b. Harrisburg, Pa., Oct. 29, 1945; s. Christian Ludwig and Katharine (Springer) S.; m. Sui Ti Atienza, Mar. 14, 1970; children: Trina, Sabrina. BS in Biochemistry, Pa. State U., 1967, MS in Biochemistry, 1968, PhD in Biochemistry, 1970. Chemist Applied Sci. Labs., State College, Pa., 1968-70; rsch. assoc. Stroh Brewery Co., Detroit, 1971, head R & D sect., 1971-73, mgr. R & D lab., 1973-82, dir. rsch., 1982-90; v.p. Strohtech, Detroit, 1986-90; prof. Cornell U., Geneva, N.Y., 1990—, chmn. dept food sci. and tech., 1990-95; also assoc. dir. Cornell Inst. Food Sci. Cornell U., Ithaca, 1990-95. Contbr. articles to profl. jours. Bd. visitors Oakland U. Biology Dept., Rochester, Mich., 1985-89; bd. dirs. Cornell Rsch. Found., 1990—, Geneva Concerts Inc., 1991—. Capt. USAR, 1967-75. Recipient Presdl. award Master Brewers Assn., 1986, 90. Fellow NSF; mem. Am. Chem. Soc. (divsn. agrl. and food chemistry, computers in chemistry divsn.), Master Brewer Assn. Ams., Am. Soc. Brewing Chemists (chmn. tech. com. 1986-88, mem. editl. bd. 1983-91), Inst. Food Technologists (divsn. fruit and vegetable tech., food chemistry, sensory analysis), Internat. Chemometrics Soc. (N.Am. chpt.). Avocations: computers, electronics. Home: 9 Parkway St Geneva NY 14456-9765 Office: NY State Agrl Expt Sta Cornell U Dept Food Sci Geneva NY 14456

SIEBERT, MURIEL, business executive, former state banking official; b. Cleve.; d. Irwin J. and Margaret Eunice (Roseman) Siebert; student Western Res. U., 1949-52; DCS (hon.), St. John's U., St. Bonaventure U., Molloy Coll., Adelphi U., St. Francis Coll., Mercy Coll., Coll. New Rochelle, St. Lawrence U., Manhattan Coll. Security analyst Bache & Co., 1954-57; analyst Utilities & Industries Mgmt. Corp., 1958, Shields & Co., 1959-60; partner Stearns & Co., 1961, Finkle & Co., 1962-65, Brimberg & Co., N.Y.C., 1965-67; individual mem. (first woman mem.) N.Y. Stock Exchange, 1967; chmn., pres. Muriel Siebert & Co., Inc., 1969-77; trustee Manhattan Savs. Bank, 1975-77; supt. banks, dept. banking State of N.Y., 1977-82; dir. Urban Devel. Corp., N.Y.C., 1977-82, Job Devel. Authority, N.Y.C., 1977-82, State of N.Y. Mortgage Agy., 1977-82; chmn., pres. Muriel Siebert & Co., Inc., 1983—; assoc. in mgmt. Simmons Coll.; mem. adv. com. Fin. Acctg. Standards Bd., 1981-84; guest lectr. numerous colls. Former mem. women's adv. com. Econ. Devel. Adminstrn., N.Y.C.; former trustee Manhattan Coll.; v.p., former mem. exec. com. Greater N.Y. Area council Boy Scouts Am.; mem. N.Y. State Econ. Devel. Bd., N.Y. Coun. Economy; bd. overseers NYU Sch. Bus., 1984-88; former bd. dirs. United Way of N.Y.C.; trustee Citizens Budget Commn., L.I. U.; mem. bus. com. Met. Mus., bus. com. of N.Y. State Bus. Coun.; active Women's Campaign Fund; bd. dirs. N.Y. Women's Agenda. Recipient Spirit of Achievement award Albert Einstein Coll. Medicine, 1977; Women's Equity Action League award, 1978; Outstanding Contbns. to Equal Opportunity for Women award Bus. Council of UN Decade for Women, 1979; Silver Beaver award Boy Scouts Am., 1981; Elizabeth Cutter Morrow award YWCA, 1983; Emily Roebling award Nat. Women's Hall of Fame, 1984; Entrepreneurial Excellence award White House Conf. on Small Bus., 1986; NOW Legal Def. and Edn. Fund award, 1981, Brotherhood award Nat. Conf. of Christians and Jews, 1989, Women on the Move award Anti-Defamation League, 1990., award Borough of Manhattan, 1991, Benjamin Botwinick prize Columbia Bus. Sch.'s, 1992, Women in Bus. Making History award Women's Bus. Coun. N.Y. C. of C., 1993, Disting. Woman of the Yr. award Greater N.Y. Boy Scouts of Am., 1993, Woman of the Yr. award Fin. Women's Assn. N.Y., 1994, Medal of Honor award Ellis Island, 1994, Bus. Philanthropist of the Yr. award So. Calif. Conf. for Women Bus. Owner's,, 1990, Corning Excellence award N.Y.S. Bus. Coun., 1993, Star award N.Y. Women's Agenda, Established Siebert Entrepreneurial Philanthropic Plan, N.Y. Urban Coalition's Achievement award, 1994, Women of Distinction award Crohn's and Colitis Found., Entrepreneurial Leadership award Nat. Found. Teaching Entrepreneurship, 1994; inductee Nat. Woman's Hall of Fame, Seneca Falls, N.Y., 1994, Internat. Women's Forum Hall of Fame, 1994. Mem. Women's Forum (founding mem., pres.), Com. 200, Fin. Women's Assn. (Community Svc. award 1993), River Club, Doubles Club, Westchester County Club, West Palm Beach Polo and Country Club, Nat. Assn. Women Bus. Owners (Veuve Clicquot Bus. Women of Yr. award 1992, Lifetime Achievement award 1993), Econ. Club. Home: 435 E 52nd St New York NY 10022-6445 Office: Muriel Siebert & Co Inc 885 3rd Ave New York NY 10022-4834

SIEBERT, THOMAS L., ambassador; b. Cleve., May 2, 1946; m. Deborah Simpson; 4 children. BA, Georgetown U., JD. Intern Rep. Robert E. Sweeney, 1965-66; vol. Senator Robert F. Kennedy, 1966-68; aide Senator Carl Hayden, 1968-70; assoc. Pittman, Lovett, Ford & Hennessey, Washington, 1971-78; ptnr. Lovett, Ford, Hennessey, Stambler & Siebert, 1978-87; of counsel Besozzi & Gavin, 1987-93, Besozzi, Gavin & Craven, Washington, 1993; U.S. amb. to Sweden Dept. State, 1993—. Bd. Regents Cath. U.; bd. visitors St. John's Coll.; active U.S. Naval Acad. Midshipmen Program, Md. Hall for the Creative Arts. Mem. ABA, D.C. Bar, Fed. Comm. Bar Assn., Annapolis Assn. Office: Am Embassy, Strandvagen 101, S-115 89 Stockholm Sweden

SIEBERT, WILLIAM MCCONWAY, electrical engineering educator; b. Pitts., Nov. 19, 1925; s. Charles Theodore Jr. and Isabel (McConway) S.; m. Anne Decker, Sept. 10, 1949; children: Charles R. (dec.), Thomas McC., Peter W., Terry A., Theodore D. SB, MIT, 1943, ScD, 1952. Jr. engr.

Westinghouse Rsch. Labs., 1946-47; group leader Lincoln Lab. MIT, Cambridge, Mass., 1953-55, mem. faculty, 1952-95, prof. elec. engring., 1963-95, sr. lectr., 1995—; cons. to govt. and industry, 1952—. With USNR, 1943-46. Fellow IEEE; mem. Acoustical Soc. Am., Sigma Xi, Tau Beta Pi, Eta Kappa Nu. Research in applications of communication theory to radar and biol. systems. Home: 100 Keyes Rd Unit 304 Concord MA 01742-1633 Office: MIT 77 Massachusetts Ave Cambridge MA 02139-4301

SIEDLE, ROBERT DOUGLAS, management consultant; b. Canton, Ohio, Aug. 8; m. Beverly Rose Scholl, Mar. 18, 1972 (div. Oct. 1983). BA in Econs., Hiram Coll., 1956; profl. cert. edn., Kent State/Western Res. Univs., 1963. Tchr., prin. Ohio secondary schs., 1957-65; salesman, area rep. visual products divsn. 3M Co., 1966-68; mgr. market devel. and tng. AV divsn. Bell & Howell, 1968-69; Chgo. br. mgr. info. systems divsn. Am. Std., 1969-72; mgr. edn. systems divsn. Audiotronics Corp., 1972-76; gen. mgr. Niles Entertainment/Wardway Films, 1977-80; pres. The Ultimate Image, Lakeland, Fla., 1985—. Producer: (films) New Dimensions in Learning II, 1969, District 65: The Exceptional Child, 1969, Career Exploration: Health, 1976, The Wide World of Work, 1976; author: Multisensory Learning: A Training Guide, 1973, Alphabet Zoo, 1973, The Quick Job Hunt Guide, 1991; author, producer, dir.: (multimedia rd. show) "Rap" With Students, 1975; producer, editor: (film) Stampin' Ground, 1977; author poetry appearing in books and mags., 1983—; appeared on nat. radio and TV programs in U.S. and Can. Named Internat. Man of Yr., Internat. Biog. Ctr., Cambridge, Eng., 1992-93, recipient Internat. Order of Merit, 1993. Fellow Am. Biog. Inst. (Man of Yr. and Most Admired Man of Decade 1993); mem. Am. Biog. Inst. Rsch. Assn. (dep. gov. life), U.S. Naval Aviation Mus. (life), U.S. Naval Inst. (life), World Future Soc., Internat. Platform Assn., Sun 'n Fun Air Mus. (life), Am. Air Mus. in Britain (founding mem.), Aircraft Owners and Pilots Assn., Exptl. Aircraft Assn., Warbirds of Am., Soaring Soc. Am., Great Lakes Hist. Soc. (life). Baptist. Office: The Ultimate Image PO Box 91388 Lakeland FL 33804-1388

SIEDLECKI, NANCY THERESE, lawyer, funeral director; b. Chgo., May 30, 1954; d. LeRoy John and Dorothy Josephine (Wilczynski) Schielka; m. Jonathan Francis Siedlecki, June 18, 1977; children: Samantha Ann, Abigail Marie. Student Triton Jr. Coll., 1971-73; grad. funeral dir., Worsham Coll., 1974; student Loyola U., Chgo., 1974-76., U. Ill.-Chgo., 1976-77; JD with honors, Chgo.-Kent Coll. Law, 1980. Bar: Ill. 1980. Paralegal in real estate Rosenberg, Savner & Unikel, Chgo., 1974-77; pvt. practice law, Burr Ridge, Ill., 1980—; cons. probate and various small bus. corps., Chgo., 1980—. Mem. ABA, Ill. State Bar Assn., Chgo. Bar Assn. Roman Catholic. Office: 5300 Main St Downers Grove IL 60515

SIEDLER, ARTHUR JAMES, nutrition and food science educator; b. Milw., Mar. 17, 1927; s. Arthur William and Margaret (Stadler) S.; m. Doris Jean Northrop, Feb. 23, 1976; children: William, Nancy Siedler Wilhite, Sandra Siedler Lowman, Roxanne Rose Butler, Randy Rose. BS, U. Wis., 1951; MS, U. Chgo., 1956, PhD, 1959. Chief div. biochemistry and nutrition Am. Meat Inst. Found., Chgo., 1959-64; group leader Norwich (N.Y.) Pharmacal Co., 1964-65, chief physiology sect., 1965-69, chief biochemistry sect., 1969-72; acting dir. div. nutritional scis. U. Ill., Urbana, 1978-81, head dept. food sci., 1972-89, prof. food sci., internal medicine and nutritional scis., 1972-94, prof. emeritus, 1994—. With USCG, 1945-46, PTO. NIH research grantee, 1960-63; Nat. Livestock and Meat Bd. grantee, 1959-64. Mem. Inst. Food Technologists, Am. Chem. Soc., Am. Inst. Nutrition, Coun. for Agrl. Sci. and Tech., Eagles, Moose, Rotary, Sigma Xi. Patentee in field. Home: 8 Stanford Pl Champaign IL 61820-7620 Office: 382M Ag Eng Sci 1304 W Pennsylvania Ave Urbana IL 61801-4726

SIEFER, STUART B., architect; b. Detroit, Nov. 28, 1942; s. Louis and Esther (Ressler) S.; m. Nancy Ann Feldman, Apr. 23, 1967; children: Eric S., Jeremy M., Ted B. BA, Wayne State U., 1965; postgrad., U. Detroit, 1965-68; BArch, Ariz. State U., 1971. Registered architect, Ariz. Designer, draftsman various firms, Detroit, 1966-68; rschr. Detroit Bd. Edn., 1967; archtl. designer Peace Corps, Tegucigalpa, Honduras, 1968-70; designer, job capt. various firms, Phoenix, 1970-73; prin. Siefer Assocs., Tempe, Ariz., 1973—. Bd. dirs. Downtown Tempe Community, Inc., 1993—; vol. bd. mem. Tempe Ctr. for Habilitation, 1993—; mem. Ariz. Town Hall, Phoenix, 1993—. Recipient 11 design awards Tempe Beautification Com., 1975—, merit & Crescordia award Valley Forward Assn. AIA Ariz., 1988, 93, Beautification award City of Mesa, Ariz. Mem. AIA (pres. Rio Salado chpt.), Rio Salado Architecture Found. (exec. mem.), Tempe C. of C. (pres. 1992-93) Found. (founding bd. mem. 1995). Avocations: jogging, skiing, hiking, tennis.

SIEFERS, ROBERT GEORGE, banker; b. Pitts., Aug. 28, 1945; s. George Francis and Idella Alice (Eiler) S.; m. Janice Lynn Kirkpatrick, Mar. 25, 1970; children—Robert Scott, Jillian Stewart. B.A., Mt. Union Coll., 1967; M.B.A., Kent State U., 1971; J.D., Cleveland Marshall Law Sch., 1976. Security analyst Nat. City Bank, Cleve., 1971-76, v.p., investment rsch. dir., 1976-80, v.p. adminstrn. and rsch., 1980-82; sr. v.p. corp. planning Nat. City Corp., Cleve., 1982-85; sr. v.p. corp. banking Nat. City Bank, Cleve., 1985-86; pres., chief exec. officer Ohio Citizens Bank (affiliate Nat. City Corp.), Toledo, 1986-90; exec. v.p., chief fin. officer Nat. City Corp., Cleve., 1990—; bd. dirs. HCR Corp. Bd. trustees Mt. Union Coll. Republican. Presbyterian Club: Chagrin Valley Country. Home: 10 Pebblebrook Ln Chagrin Falls OH 44022-2380 Office: Nat City Corp Nat City Ctr Cleveland OH 44022

SIEFERT-KAZANJIAN, DONNA, corporate librarian; b. N.Y.C.; d. Merrill Emil and Esther (Levins) S.; m. George John Kazanjian, June 15, 1974; 1 child, Merrill George. BA, NYU, 1969; MSLS, Columbia U., 1973; MBA, Fordham U., 1977. Asst. librarian Dun & Bradstreet, N.Y.C., 1969-73; research assoc. William E. Hill & Co., N.Y.C., 1973-76; sr. info. analyst Info. for Bus., N.Y.C., 1976-77; librarian Handy Assocs., N.Y.C., 1979-90; mgr. Infoserve Fuchs Cuthrell & Co., Inc., N.Y.C., 1991-94; libr. Heidrick & Struggles, Inc., N.Y.C., 1994—. Mem. Spl. Librs. Assn., Rsch. Roundtable, Am. Mensa Ltd. Roman Catholic. Office: Heidrick & Struggles Inc 245 Park Ave New York NY 10167-0002

SIEG, ALBERT LOUIS, photographic company executive; b. Chgo., Mar. 25, 1930; s. Albert Fredrick and Louise Augusta (Strege) S.; m. Irma Alice Spencer, Sept. 3, 1955; children—Karen, Diane, Susan. B.S. in Chemistry, U. Ill., 1951; Ph.D. in Organic Chemistry, U. Rochester, 1954; P.M.D., Harvard Bus. Sch., 1971. Supr. emulsion Eastman Kodak Co., Rochester, N.Y., 1970-72, corp. mgr. instant., 1972-76, mgr. paper mgt., 1976-81, v.p., dir., 1981-84; pres. Kodak Japan K.K., Tokyo, 1984-89; pres., rep. dir. Eastman Kodak Japan, Tokyo, 1989-91, also bd. dirs.; pres., rep. dir. Eastman Chems. Japan Ltd., Tokyo, 1989-91; v.p., dir. strategic resources, sec. imaging bd. Eastman Kodak Co., Rochester, 1991-92, ret., 1992; prin., cons. Albert L. Sieg Assocs., Rochester, 1992—; bd. dirs. Kodak Japan Industries, Ltd.; sr. lectr. U. Rochester, 1960-69. Co-author: 8th Here's How, 1972; co-author (with S. Bennett, Oliver Wight) Tokyo Chronicles, 1994; inventor in field. Bd. dirs., chmn. corp. gifts Rochester Philharm. Orch., 1982-84; chmn. corp. gifts Internat. Mus. Photography at George Eastman House, 1993; pres. Reformation Luth. Ch., Rochester, 1978-83; bd. dirs. St. John's Home for the Aging, 1994—, St. John's Nursing Home, 1994—. Served with Med. Svc. Corps, U.S. Army, 1955-57. Recipient George Eastman Medal Kodak Camera Clubs, 1980; Kiwanis Club Chgo. fellow, U. Ill., 1947-51; Am. Cyanamide fellow, 1953-54. Fellow Am. Inst. Chemists, Photog. Soc. Am. (v.p. 1969-84, Harold Lloyd award 1978, exec. v.p. 1995, progress medal 1995); mem. Am. Chem. Soc., Soc. Photog. Scientists and Engrs., AAAS, Rochester C. of C., Am. C. of C. in Japan (bd. govs. 1988-91, v.p. 1989-91), Internat. Stereoscopic Union (pres. 1993). Republican. Club: American (Tokyo); Fgn. Correspondence. Avocations: skiing; photography; gardening. Home and Office: 159 Hillhurst Ln Rochester NY 14617-1938

SIEGAL, ALLAN MARSHALL, newspaper editor; b. N.Y.C., May 1, 1940; s. Irving and Sylvia Norma (Wrubel) S.; m. Gretchen M-P. Leefmans, May 31, 1977; children—Anna Marianita, Peter Bert. Grad., NYU, 1962. With New York Times, 1960—, editor Pentagon Papers, 1971, asst. fgn. editor, 1971-76, asst. to exec. editor, 1976-77, news editor, 1977-87, asst. mng. editor, 1987—, founding editor nat. edit., 1980; tchr. journalism NYU, 1966, Columbia U., 1967-69; juror Pulitzer Prize Nominating Com., 1987-89. Mem. Century Assn., Am. Soc. Newspaper Editors. Office: NY Times Co 229 W 43rd St New York NY 10036-3913

SIEGAL, BURTON LEE, product designer, consultant, inventor; b. Chgo., Sept. 27, 1931; s. Norman A. and Sylvia (Vitz) S.; m. Rita Goran, Apr. 11, 1954; children: Norman, Laurence Scott. BS in Mech. Engring., U. Ill., 1953. Torpedo designer U.S. Naval Ordnance, Forest Park, Ill., 1953-54; chief engr. Gen. Aluminum Corp., Chgo., 1954-55; product designer Chgo. Aerial Industries, Melrose Park, Ill., 1955-58; chief designer Emil J. Paidar Co., Chgo., 1958-59; founder, pres. Budd Engring. Corp., Chgo., 1959—; dir. Dur-A-Case Corp., Chgo.; design cons. to numerous corps. Holder more than 114 patents in more than 32 fields including multimemory for power seats and electrified office panel sys.; contbr. articles to tech. publs. Mem. math., sci. and English adv. bds. Niles Twp. High Schs., Skokie, Ill., 1975-79; electronic cons. Chgo. Police Dept., 1964. Winner, Internat. Extrusion Design Competition, 1975; nominated Presdl. Medal Technology Sen. Paul Simon and Rep. Dan Rostenkowski, 1986; named Inventor of Yr. Patent Law Assn. Chgo., 1986. Mem. ASME, Soc. Plastics Engrs., Soc. Mfg. Engrs., No. Ill. Indsl. Assn., Inventor's Coun., Soc. Automotive Engrs., Pres.'s Assn. Ill., Ill. Mfg. Assn. Office: 8707 Skokie Blvd Skokie IL 60077-2269 *A true professional can perform any time, any place, independent of his mood.*

SIEGAL, JACOB J., management and financial consultant; b. Phila., Apr. 4, 1929; s. Louis and Henrietta (Greenberg) S.; m. Dolores Berg, June 8, 1952; children: Marla, Karen, Leslie. B.S., Temple U., 1951, LL.B., 1954; postgrad., U. Chgo., 1973. Bar: Pa. 1955, Ill. 1973. With City of Phila., 1954-61, chief counselor, 1959-61, dep. city solicitor, 1958-61; pvt. practice law, partner firm Meltzer & Schiffrin, Phila., 1961-72; v.p., gen. counsel, dir. Bluebird Inc., Phila., 1972-74; exec. v.p. Bluebird Inc., 1974-78, pres., 1978-79, chmn., chief exec. officer, 1979; chmn. bd. Armen Cadillac-Osmobile, Inc. Mem. Am. Bar Assn., Am. Soc. Corp. Secs., Am. Meat Inst. (dir., conv. speaker 1978). Home: 101 Cheswold Ln Haverford PA 19041-1865 Office: PO Box 193 Plymouth Meeting PA 19462-0193

SIEGAL, KENNETH HARVEY, editor; b. Brookline, Mass., June 5, 1947; s. Samuel and Rose (Wolfson) S.; m. Jane Bolan, Mar. 29, 1970; children: Michele A., Joshua D. BS, Boston U., 1969. Reporter The Patriot Ledger, Quincy, Mass., 1969-75, copy editor, 1975-83; asst. mng. editor Boston Herald, 1983-88; mng. editor Digital News and Rev., 1988-93; dept. editor PC Week, 1993-95, mng. editor, 1995—. Officer Jaycees, Randolph, Mass., 1980-85. Home: 26 Katy Cir Randolph MA 02368 Office: PC Week 10 Presidents Landing Medford MA 02155

SIEGAL, RITA GORAN, engineering company executive; b. Chgo., July 16, 1934; d. Leonard and Anabelle (Soloway) Goran; m. Burton L. Siegal, Apr. 11, 1954; children: Norman, Laurence Scott. Student, U. Ill., 1951-53; BA, DePaul U., 1956. Cert. elem. tchr., Ill. Tchr. Chgo. Public Schs., 1956-58; founder, chief exec. officer Budd Engring. Corp., Skokie, Ill., 1959—; founder, pres. Easy Living Products Co., Skokie, 1960—; pvt. practice in interior design, Chgo., 1968-73; dist. sales mgr. Super Girls, Skokie, 1976; lectr. Northwestern U., 1983; guest speaker nat. radio and TV, 1979—. Contbr. to profl. jours. Mem. adv. bd. Skokie High Schs., 1975-79; advisor Cub Scouts Skokie coun. Boy Scouts Am., 1975; bus. mgr. Nutrition for Optimal Health Assn., Winnetka, Ill., 1980-82, pres., 1982-84, v.p. med./profl., 1985-93; leader Great Books Found., 1972; founder Profit Plus Investment, 1970; bd. dirs. Noha, Internat. Recipient Cub Scout awards Boy Scouts Am., 1971-72, Nat. Charlotte Danstrom award Nat. Women of Achievement, 1988, Corp. Achievement award, 1988. Mem. North Shore Women in Mgmt. (pres. 1987-88), Presidents Assn. Ill. (bd. dirs. 1990-94, membership chairperson 1991-93), No. Ill. Indsl. Assn., Ill. Mfrs. Assn., Inventors Coun. Office: Budd Engring Corp 8707 Skokie Blvd Skokie IL 60077-2269 *Believe in yourself, if others can do it so can you. Prioritize so you are not overwhelmed by your responsibilities.*

SIEGAN, BERNARD HERBERT, lawyer, educator; b. Chgo., July 28, 1924; s. David and Jeannette (Seitz) S.; m. Sharon Goldberg, June 15, 1952 (dec. Feb. 1985); m. Shelley Zifferblatt, Nov. 19, 1995. AA, Herzl. Jr. Coll., Chgo., 1943, 46; Student, Roosevelt Coll., Chgo., 1946-47; J.D., U. Chgo., 1949. Bar: Ill. 1950. Practiced in Chgo.; partner firm Siegan & Karlin, 1952-73; pres., sec. various small corps. and gen. partner in partnerships engaged in real estate ownership and devel., 1955-70; weekly columnist Freedom newspaper chain, other papers, 1974-79; cons. law and econs. program U. Chgo. Law Sch., 1970-73; adj. prof. law U. San Diego Law Sch., 1973-74, prof., 1974-75, Disting. prof., 1975—; adj. scholar Cato Inst., Washington, 1991—, Heritage Found., 1992—; cons. windfalls and wipeouts project HUD, 1973-74; cons. FTC, 1985-86, U.S. Justice Dept., dir. constl. bibliog. project, 1986-88; keynote speaker 5th Internat. Conf. on Urbanism, Porto Alegre, Brazil, 1989; nominated by Pres. Reagan to U.S. Ct. Appeals (9th cir.) Feb. 2, 1987, confirmation denied July 14, 1988 by party line vote Senate Judiciary Com. Author: Land Use Without Zoning, 1972, Spanish edit., 1995, Other People's Property, 1976, Economic Liberties and the Constitution, 1980, The Supreme Court's Constitution: An Inquiry Into Judicial Review and Its Impact on Society, 1987, Drafting a Constitution for a Nation or Republic Emerging into Freedom, 1992, 2d edit., 1994, Portuguese, Ukrainian, Polish and Spanish edits., 1993; editor: Planning without Prices, 1977, The Interaction of Economics and the Law, 1977, Regulation, Economics and the Law, 1979, Government, Regulation and the Economy, 1980. Mem. pres.-elect's Task Force on Housing, 1980-81; mem. Pres.'s Commn. on Housing, 1981-82; mem. Nat. Commn. on bicentannial of U.S. Constn., 1985-91; chmn. adv. com. Affordable Housing Conf., San Diego, 1985, Rights of Regulated Conf., Coronado, Calif., 1976; chmn. Conf. on the Taking Issue, 1976; mem. Houston Regional Urban Design Team, Study of Houston, 1990; mem. U.S. team Bulgarian Econ. Growth and Transition Project, 1990; mem. devel. bd. Mingei Internat. Mus. World Folk Art, 1981-84. Served with AUS, 1943-46. Research fellow law and econs. U. Chgo. Law Sch., 1968-69; Urban Land Inst. research fellow, 1976-86; recipient Leander J. Monks Meml. Fund award Inst. Humane Studies, 1972, George Washington medal Freedom Founds. at Valley Forge, 1981, Spl. award Liberal Inst. of Rio Grande do Sul, Porto Alegre, Brazil, 1989. Home: 6005 Camino De La Costa La Jolla CA 92037-6519

SIEGEL, ABRAHAM J., economics educator, academic administrator; b. N.Y.C., Nov. 6, 1922; s. Samuel J. and Dora (Drach) S.; m. Lillian Wakshull, Dec. 22, 1946; children: Emily Jean Siegel Stangle, Paul Howard, Barbara Ann Pugliese. B.A. summa cum laude, CCNY, 1943; M.A., Columbia U., 1949; Ph.D., U. Calif., Berkeley, 1961. Instr. dept. econs. CCNY, 1947-49; research economist Inst. Indsl. Relations, U. Calif., Berkeley, 1952-54; instr. dept. econs. M.I.T., Cambridge, 1954-56, asst. prof., 1956-59, assoc. prof., 1959-64, prof. dept. econs. Sloan Sch. Mgmt., 1964-93, assoc. dean Sloan Sch. Mgmt., 1967-80, dean, 1980-87, prof. emeritus, sr. lectr., 1993—; spl. lectr. Trade Union Program, Harvard U., 1961-64; vis. prof. Brandeis U., 1956-60; vis. prin. mem. div. Internat. Inst. Labour Studies, Internat. Labor Office, Geneva, 1964-65; asso. staff dir. Com. Econ. Devel., Study Group on Nat. Labor Policy, 1960-61; trustee, chmn. adminstrv. com. M.I.T. Retirement Plan for Staff Mems., 1970—. Co-author: Industrial Relations in the Pacific Coast Longshore Industry, 1956, The Public Interest in National Labor Policy, 1961, The Impact of Computers on Collective Bargaining, 1969, Unfinished Business: An Agenda for Labor, Management and the Public, 1978. Bd. dirs. Whitehead Inst. Biomed. Rsch., Analysis Group, Inc., Internat. Data Group; mem. adv. group Internat. Inst. for Applied Systems Analysis, Laxenburg, Austria; mem. Framingham Sch. Com., South Middlesex Regional Dist. Vocat. Sch. Com., 1968-71. With USAF, 1943-46. Mem. Am. Econ. Assn., Indsl. Relations Research Assn., Nat. Acad. Arbitrators, Am. Arbitration Assn. (mem. various panels), Inst. Mgmt. Scis. Bus. Roundtable (exec. com.), Phi Beta Kappa. Clubs: Comml, St. Botolph's. Home: 112 Gardner Rd Brookline MA 02146-4537 Office: MIT Sloan Sch Mgmt 50 Memorial Dr Cambridge MA 02142-1347

SIEGEL, ALLEN GEORGE, lawyer; b. Chgo., May 19, 1934; s. David Harry and Jeanette (Morris) S.; m. Rochelle Robin, Mar. 12, 1961; children: Dina Robin, Jonathan Joseph. B.B.A., CCNY, 1957; LL.B. with distinction, Duke U., 1960. Bar: Fla. 1960, D.C. 1965. Pvt. practice law Jacksonville, Fla., 1960-62; field atty. NLRB, 1962-64; assoc. Arent, Fox, Kintner, Plotkin & Kahn, Washington, 1964-70, ptnr., 1970-80, sr. ptnr., 1980—; sr. lectr. in law Duke U., Durham, N.C., 1979—. Author: Confidential Supervisors Guide to Labor Relations, 1980, Confidential Supervisors Guide to Equal Employment, 1981; contbr. articles. Past pres. United Cerebral Palsy D.C., founder David H. Siegel Meml. Scholarship Duke U. Sch. Law, bd. dirs. pvt. adjudicator ctr., 1986—; mem. bd. regents Cath. U. Am., 1990—; founder Rabbi Seymour Siegel Meml. Moot Ct. Competition Duke U. Law Sch.; founder Jeanette Siegel Meml. Scholarship, Phillip M. Siegel Meml. Scholarship; gen. counsel Jewish Social Svc. Agy. Washington, United Cerebral Palsy Assn. Washington and No. Va. Mordecai Soc. scholar. Mem. ABA, Fla. Bar Assn., D.C. Bar Assn., Am. Judicature Soc., Univ. Club Washington, Order of Coif. Republican. Jewish. Home: 7505 Connecticut Ave Chevy Chase MD 20815-4925 Office: Washington Square 1050 Connecticut Ave NW Washington DC 20036-5339

SIEGEL, ARTHUR HERBERT, accounting company executive; b. N.Y.C., Jan. 5, 1938; s. Joseph Kenneth and Gertrude Sylvia (Hecker) S.; m. Eleanor Novick, June 5, 1960; children: Joan Aileen, Linda Beth, Mark Eric. AB, Columbia, 1958, MBA, 1960. With Price Waterhouse, N.Y.C., 1960-61, mgr., L.I., 1961-72, ptnr., Boston, 1972—, nat. dir. acctg. svcs., N.Y.C., 1984-88, vice-chmn. bus. adv. and auditing svcs., 1988-95; mem. Fin. Acctg. Stds. Bd. Emerging Issues Task Force, 1985-88, Fin. Acctg. Stds. Adv. Coun., 1985-90; mem. adv. coun. Sch. Acctg. U. So. Calif., 1987-89; active World ABS Exec. Com., 1988-95, chmn., 1990, U.S. Mgmt. Com., 1988-95, World Mgmt. Coms., 1990-95. Past trustee, treas., 1st v.p. Temple Beth Avodah, Newton Centre, Mass.; bd. dirs. Nat. Multiple Sclerosis Soc., treas. exec. com., chmn. fin. com. Mem. AICPA (chmn. task force on risks and uncertainties, chmn. SEC practice exec. com.), N.Y. Soc. CPA's (Silver Medal award), Mass. Soc. CPA's (pres.-elect 1983), Beta Gamma Sigma. Home: 179 E 70th St New York NY 10021-5154 Office: Price Waterhouse 300 Atlantic St Stamford CT 06904-9316

SIEGEL, BARRY ALAN, nuclear radiologist; b. Nashville, Dec. 30, 1944; s. Walter Gross Siegel and Lillian B. (Tumbarello) Ivener; m. Pamela M. Mandel, Aug. 18, 1968 (div. Mar. 1981); children: Peter A., William A.; m. Marilyn J. Siegel, Jan. 29, 1983. AB, Washington U., St. Louis, 1966, MD, 1969. Diplomate Am. Bd. Nuclear Medicine, Am. Bd. Radiology. Intern Barnes Hosp., St. Louis, 1969-70; resident in radiology and nuclear medicine fellow Mallinckrodt Inst. Radiology, Washington U., 1970-73, dir. div. nuclear medicine, 1973—, asst. prof., 1973-76, assoc. prof., 1976-79, prof. radiology, 1979—, assoc. prof. medicine, 1980-83, prof. medicine, 1983—; dir. Am. Bd. Nuc. Medicine, L.A., 1985-90, sec., 1990; chmn. adv. com. on med. uses of isotopes NRC, Washington, 1990-96; chmn. radiopharm. drugs adv. com. U.S. FDA, Rockville, Md., 1982-85, radiol. devices panel, 1992-95; mem. U.S. Pharmacopeia Adv. Panel on Radiopharms., 1975—, Armed Forces Radiobiol. Rsch. Inst., Bethesda. Author, editor 26 books; contbr. articles to profl. jours., chpts. to books. Maj. USAF, 1974-76. Recipient Commr.'s Spl. citation U.S. FDA, 1988, Honor citation U.S. Pharmacopeial Conv., 1995. Fellow ACP, Am. Coll. Radiology (vice chmn. commn. on nuclear medicine 1981—, editor in chief self evaluation program 1988—), Am. Coll. Nuclear Physicians; mem. AMA, Am. Roentgen Ray Soc., Assn. Univ. Radiologists, Radiol. Soc. N.Am., Soc. Nuclear Medicine (trustee 1981-85, 87-91). Office: Washington U Mallinckrodt Inst Radiology 510 S Kingshighway Blvd Saint Louis MO 63110-1016

SIEGEL, BERNARD, foundation administrator. Pres. The Harry and Jeanette Weinberg Found., Inc., Balt. Office: Harry and Jeanette Weinberg Found 5518 Baltimore Nat Pike Baltimore MD 21228*

SIEGEL, BERNARD LOUIS, lawyer; b. Pitts., Sept. 15, 1938; s. Ralph Robert and Frieda Sara (Stein) S.; m. Marcia Margolis, Sept. 3, 1961 (div. Aug. 1982); children: Jonathan, Sharon. BA, Brandeis U., 1960; JD, Harvard U., 1963. Bar: Pa. 1964, U.S. Dist. Ct. (we. dist.) Pa. 1964, U.S. Dist. Ct. (ea. dist.) Pa. 1985, U.S. Ct. Appeals (3d cir.) 1985, U.S. Supreme Ct. 1985. Assoc. Silin, Eckert & Burke, Erie, Pa., 1963-66; ptnr. Silin, Eckert, Burke & Siegel, Erie, Pa., 1966-73; 1st asst. dist. atty. Erie County, 1972-76; dep. atty. gen. Pa. Dept. Justice, Phila., 1976-78; dep. dist. atty. Dist. Atty. of Phila., 1978-86; pvt. practice Phila., 1986—; adj. prof. La Salle U., Phila., 1986—; lectr. Fed. Law Enforcement Tng. Ctr., Glynco, Ga., 1986—, Mercyhurst Coll., Erie, 1974-76, Nat. Coll. Dist. Attys., Houston, 1978-85, Temple U. law sch., 1995—; mem. criminal rules com. Pa. Supreme Ct., Phila., 1976-85; commr. Pa. Crime Commn., Harrisburg, 1976-79. Author: (with others) Pennsylvania Grand Jury Practice, 1983, By No Extraordinary Means, 1986. Mem. ABA, Nat. Assn. Criminal Def. Lawyers, Pa. Assn. Criminal Def. Lawyers (bd. dirs. 1988—), Pa. Bar Assn. (chmn. criminal law sect. 1988-91), Phila. Bar Assn. (chmn. criminal justice sect. 1990-91). Democrat. Jewish. Avocations: bicycling, reading, hiking. Office: Packard Bldg 24th Fl 111 S 15th St Philadelphia PA 19102

SIEGEL, BETTY LENTZ, college president; b. Cumberland, Ky., Jan. 24, 1931; d. Carl N. and Vera (Hogg) Lentz; m. Joel H. Siegel, June 6; children: David Jonathan, Michael Jeremy. B.A., Wake Forest Coll., 1952; M.Ed., U. N.C., 1953; Ph.D., Fla. State U., 1961; postgrad., Ind. U., 1964-66; hon. doctorate, Miami U., 1985, Cumberland Coll., 1985, Ea. Ky. U., 1992. Asst. prof. Lenoir Rhyne Coll., Hickory, N.C., 1956-59; assoc. prof., 1961-64; asst. prof. U. Fla., Gainesville, 1967-70; assoc. prof. U. Fla., 1970-72, prof., 1973-76, dean acad. affairs for continuing edn., 1972-76; dean Sch. Edn. and Psychology Western Carolina U., Cullowhee, N.C., 1976-81; pres. Kennesaw State Coll., Marietta, Ga., 1981—; bd. dirs. Atlanta Gas Light Co., Equifax Inc., Nat. Services Industries, Acordia Benefits of the South Inc.; cons. numerous sch. systems. Author: Problem Situations in Teaching, 1971; contbr. articles to profl. jours. Bd. dirs. United Way Atlanta, Ga. Acad. Children and Youth Profls., Ga. Partnership for Excellence in Edn., Ga. Coun. Econ. Edn., Northside Hosp. Found., Atlanta Ballet. Recipient Outstanding Tchr. award U. Fla., 1969; Mortar Bd. Woman of Yr. award U. Fla., 1973, Mortar Bd. Educator of Yr., Ga. State U., 1983, CASE award, 1986, Alumna of Yr. award Wake Forest U., 1987, "Grad Made Good" award Fla. State U. Alumni Assn, Omicron Delta Kappa, 1991, Spirit of Life award City of Hope, 1992, Woman of Achievement award Cobb Chamber YWCA, 1992; named One of 100 Most Influential People in State of Ga., Ga. Trend Mag., Outstanding Alumni, Fla. State U. Coll. Edn. Alumni Assn., 1992. Mem. ASCD, Am. Psychol. Assn., Am. Assn. State Colls. and Univs. (bd. dirs., chmn. 1990), Am. Coun. Edn. (bd. dirs., bd. advisors), Am. Inst. Mng. Diversity (bd. dis.), Soc. Internat. Bus. Fellows, Internat. Alliance for Invitational Edn. (co-founder, co-dir.), Bus./Higher Edn. Forum 9mem. exec. com.), Assn. Tchrs. Educators' Commn. on Leadership in Interprofl. Edn. (task force on techr. edn.), Cobb C. of C. (chair 1996), Kiwanis (Atlanta chpt.), Phi Alpha Theta, Pi Kappa Delta, Alpha Psi Omega, Kappa Delta Pi, Pi Lambda Theta, Phi Delta Kappa, Delta Kappa Gamma. Baptist. Office: Kennesaw State Coll Office of the President PO Box 444 Marietta GA 30061-0444

SIEGEL, CAROLE ETHEL, mathematician; b. N.Y., Sept. 29, 1936; d. David and Helen (Mayer) Schore; m. Bertram Siegel, Aug. 18, 1957; children: Sharon, David. BA in Math., NYU, 1957, MS in Math., 1959, PhD in Math., 1963. With computer dept. Atomic Energy Commn., 1957-59; rsch. asst. Courant Inst. of Math. Sci., 1959-63; rsch. scientist dept. of engring. NYU, N.Y.C., 1963-64; rsch. math. Info. Scis. Div. Rockland Rsch. Inst., Orangeburg, N.Y., 1965-74; head Epidemiology and Health Svcs. Rsch. Lab Stat. Scis., Epidemiology Divsn./Nathan S. Kline Inst. Rsch., Orangeburg, N.Y., 1974—; rsch. prof. dept. psychiatry NYU, 1987—; dep. dir. WHO Collaborating Ctr., Nathan S. Kline Inst., 1987—; grant reviewer NIHM, 1988—; co-prin. investigator Ctr. for Study of Issues in Public Mental Health, NIMH, 1993-95, prin. investigator, dir., 1995—. Editor: (with S. Fischer) Psychiatric Records in Mental Health Care, 1981; contbr. articles to profl. jours. Recipient grants NIMH, 1993—, 88-91, Nat. Ctr. for Health Svcs. Rsch., 1979-82, Nat. Inst. Alcohol Abuse, 1978-82. Mem. Assn. for Health Svcs. Rsch., Am. Soc. Clin. Pharmacology and Therapeutics, Assn. Women in Math., Am. Statis. Assn. Avocations: pottery, gardening, cooking. Office: Nathan S Kline Inst Orangeburg NY 10962

SIEGEL, CHARLES, lawyer, investment banking and brokerage executive; b. N.Y.C., June 6, 1944; s. Edward and Ann (Aronson) S.; m. Francine Marie Prioli, Sept. 26, 1970; children—David Aaron, Stefanie Joy. B.S. in Econs., U. Pa., 1965; J.D., Boston U., 1968. Bar: N.Y. 1969, U.S. Dist. Ct. (so. and ea. dists.) N.Y. 1976, U.S. Ct. Appeals (2nd cir.) 1975, U.S. Ct. Appeals (8th cir.) 1978, U.S. Supreme Ct. 1979. Asst. arbitration dir. N.Y. Stock Exchange, Inc., N.Y.C., 1968-72, arbitrator, 1979—; v.p., asst. sec., asst. legal counsel Blyth Eastman Dillon & Co. Inc., N.Y.C., 1972-80; sr. v.p., spl. counsel E.F. Hutton & Co. Inc., N.Y.C., 1980-86; assoc. dir. Bear, Stearns, & Co. Inc., N.Y.C., 1986-88; sr. v.p., sr. assoc. gen. counsel PaineWebber Inc., N.Y.C., 1988-94, Kelley Drye & Warren, N.Y.C., 1995—; arbitrator N.Y. Futures Exchange Inc., N.Y.C., 1981—; lectr. Securities Industry Assn., N.Y.C., 1985, 86. Mem. ABA. Office: 101 Park Ave New York NY 10178

SIEGEL, DAVID BURTON, lawyer; b. N.Y.C., Mar. 22, 1949; s. Henry and Ruth (Rosenzweig) S.; m. Barbara Joan Brown, Aug. 6, 1972; children: Jeffrey Spencer, Carolyn Rose, Laura Ellen. AB, Columbia Coll., 1971; JD, NYU, 1974. Assoc. atty. Kelley Drye & Warren, N.Y.C., 1974-77; corp. counsel W.R. Grace & Co., N.Y.C., 1977-87, asst. gen. counsel, 1987-91; assoc. gen. counsel W.R. Grace & Co., Boca Raton, Fla., 1991-93; v.p., dep. gen. counsel W.R. Grace & Co., Boca Raton, 1993—. Mem. Econ. Coun. Palm Beach County, Fla., 1993—; mem. bd. dirs. Edn. Partnership of Palm Beach County, 1994—, treas., 1995—. Home: 5896 NW 23rd Way Boca Raton FL 33496 Office: WR Grace & Co One Town Center Rd Boca Raton FL 33486

SIEGEL, DAVID DONALD, law educator; b. Bklyn., Oct. 18, 1931; s. Harry Wilbur and Ida Claire (Scharaga) S.; m. Rosemarie Ann Duffy, Dec. 21, 1969; children: Sheela Nell, Rachel Ann. B.A., CUNY, 1953; J.D., St. John's U., 1958; LL.M., NYU, 1964. Bar: N.Y. 1958. Law sec. to chief judge N.Y. Ct. Appeals, 1958-59; practiced law N.Y.C., 1960-62; asst. prof. law St. John's U., 1962-65, asso. prof., 1965-67, prof., 1967-72, vis. prof., 1972-84, McNiece prof., 1984-90; prof. Albany Law Sch., 1972-84, disting. prof., 1990—; vis. prof. NYU, 1967-70, 84-85, 88-89, SUNY, Buffalo, 1971-72, Cornell U., 1978, Hofstra U., 1980, Albany Law Sch., 1984-90; adv., cons. on procedure Am. Arbitration Assn.; mem. N.Y. adv. com. on civil practice, 1979—, chmn., 1979-81. Author: New York Practice, 1978, 2d edit., 1991, Conflict of Laws in a Nutshell, 1982, 2d edit., 1994, Practising Law Inst. Monograph on Fed. Jurisdiction and Practice, ann. commentaries N.Y. civil practice McKinney's Consolidated Laws and fed. jurisdiction and practice U.S. Code Annotated and Federal Rules Decisions; editor: N.Y. State Law Digest, 1977—, Siegel's Practice Rev., 1993—; draftsman Appellate Division Handbook, 1979, Court of Appeals Handbook, 1981, 2d edit., 1991. Served with U.S. Army, 1953-55. Mem. Am. Law Inst., ABA, N.Y. State Bar Assn., Assn. Bar City N.Y. Jewish. Office: Albany Law Sch 80 New Scotland Ave Albany NY 12208-3434

SIEGEL, FREDERIC RICHARD, geology educator; b. Chelsea, Mass., Feb. 8, 1932; s. Louis and Eva (Minsky) S.; m. Felisa Matilde Puszkin, Mar. 3, 1962; children—Gabriela Davina, Galia Dinah. BA, Harvard U., 1954; MS, U. Kans., 1958, PhD, 1961. Prof. titular Universidad Nacional de Tucuman, Argentina, 1961-63; head geochemistry div. Kans. Geol. Survey, Lawrence, 1963-65; assoc. prof. geochemistry George Washington U., Washington, 1965-69, prof., 1969—, dir. geochemistry program, 1965—, chmn. dept. geology, 1976-86; tech. cons. UN Devel. program, Havana, Cuba, 1980. Author: Applied Geochemistry, 1974, Geoquimica Aplicada, 1992, Natural and Anthropogenic Hazards in Development Planning, 1996; editor: Review of Research on Modern Problems in Geochemistry, 1979. Served with U.S. Army, 1954-56; ETO. Recipient Erasmus Haworth award Dept. Geology, U. Kans., 1958; Fulbright prof., 1970, Best Paper award Energy Minerals div. Am. Assn. Petroleum Geologists, 1989. Mem. Assn. Exploration Geochemists (councillor 1988-95), Soc. Econ. Paleontology and Mineralogists, Geochem. Soc., Internat. Assn. Geochemists and Cosmochemists, Soc. Mining Engrs., Inc. (editor geochemistry divsn. 1989-90), Soc. Environ. Geochemistry and Health. Jewish. Home: 4353 Yuma St NW Washington DC 20016-2027 Office: George Washington U 2029 G St NW Washington DC 20006-4211

SIEGEL, GEORGE HENRY, international business development consultant; b. Bklyn., Oct. 8, 1926; s. Samuel S. and Sara Siegel; m. Lenore D. Greenberg, Oct. 28, 1951; children: Arthur B., Ellen S. BEE, CCNY, 1948; M.S. in Indsl. Engring, NYU, 1951. Registered profl. engr., N.Y. From engr. to gen. mgr. Gen. Electric Corp., Syracuse, Utica and Binghamton, N.Y., 1951-74; v.p., gen. mgr. flight systems div. Bendix Corp., Detroit, 1974-77, chief tech. officer, 1977-79, v.p., gen. mgr. diesel engine controls, 1979-82; v.p., group exec. Bendix Automation Co., Cleve., 1983-84; v.p. tech. Allied-Signal Internat., Morristown, N.J., 1984-90; v.p. Volt Tech. Svcs. Co., N.Y.C., 1991-93; pres. Point North Assocs., Inc., Madison, N.J., 1990—; invited guest lectr. UCLA, 1960-63. Bd. visitors Oakland U., Rochester, Mich., 1977-83. Served with AUS, 1944-46. Mem. IEEE (sr., life, sect. chmn. 1965), Soc. Automotive Engrs. Office: Point North Assocs Inc PO Box 907 Madison NJ 07940-0907

SIEGEL, HERBERT BERNARD, certified professional management consultant; b. N.Y.C., Mar. 10, 1934; s. Jacob and Clara Dora (Goldgeier) S.; m. Joan Miriam Goodkin, Nov. 6, 1955; children—Jeffry Roy, Lori Robin, Amy Hope, Jonathan Stuart. Degree, N.Y. U., 1959, postgrad. in bus., 1960-63; postgrad. in bus., Harvard U., 1975; PhD candidate, Columbia Pacific U., 1995. With William Iselin & Co., Inc., N.Y.C., 1957-67; treas. Bates Mfg. Co., Inc., N.Y.C., 1968; pres. Emle Industries, Inc., N.Y.C., 1968-72; fed. trustee Interstate Stores, Inc., N.Y.C., 1973-78; pres. Nat. Silver Co., N.Y.C., 1973-78, F.B. Rogers Silver Co., N.Y.C., 1979-82; pres., chief exec. officer Quaker City Steel Co., 1980-86, Seal-Kap Packaging Co., N.Y.C., 1980-90, J. Ramsey Reese, Inc., Tarrytown, N.Y., 1980-87; exec. v.p. Deerhill Devel. Corp., 1980-87, Columbia Profl. Baseball Club, Inc., 1980-87; pres., chief exec. officer J.R. Reese Enterprises, Ltd., 1989-90, New Swissco, Inc., 1991; pres. T.P.C.C.-Brandon, Inc., 1991—; prin. officer Whitestone Cons. Group, Ltd., 1991—; trustee Dime Savs. Bank of Williamsburg, N.Y.C.; thesis examiner Grad. Sch. Banking, Rutgers U., 1963-64; lectr. Grad. Sch. Mgmt. and Orgn., Yale U.; bd. dirs. N.Y. Pacific Exch. Ltd., Silvergull Industries Inc. Author: A Trustee's View of Chapter Ten, 1981, Tomorrow's America, Made Today in the U.S.A., 1993, The Masquerade of Cost Cutting, 1995, The Entropy of Government Deficits, 1995. Bd. dirs. United Cerebral Palsy, Nassau, N.Y. Served with AUS, 1955-57. Mem. Am. Mgmt. Assn., Am. Bankruptcy Inst., N.Y. Acad. Sci., NYU Alumni Club, Turnaround Mgmt. Assn., Prime Raters Fin. Club (pres.), Am. Mensa Soc., Am. Cons. League. Office: 515 E Bay Dr Long Beach NY 11561-2409

SIEGEL, HERBERT JAY, communications executive; b. Phila., May 7, 1928; s. Jacob and Fritzi (Stern) S.; m. Ann F. Levy, June 29, 1950; children: John C., William D. BA in Journalism, Lehigh U., 1950. Sec., dir. Official Films, Inc., N.Y.C., 1950-55; v.p., dir. Bev-Rich Products, Inc., Phila., 1955-56, Westley Industries, Inc., Cleve., 1955-58, Phila. Ice Hockey Club, Inc., 1955-60; chmn. bd. Fort Pitt Industries, Inc., Pitts., 1956-58, Seeburg Corp., 1958-60, Centlivre Brewing Corp., Ft. Wayne, Ind., 1959-61, Baldwin-Montrose Chem. Co., 1960-67; chmn. United TV, Inc., 1982—, chief exec. officer, 1983—; pres. Gen. Artists Corp., 1963-65, chmn., 1960-63; chmn. bd., pres. Chris-Craft Industries, Inc., 1968—; dir. Baldwin Rubber Co., Pontiac, Mich., Mono-Sol Corp., Gary, Inc., Piper Aircraft Corp., 1971-77; Warner Communications, Inc., 1984-89; chmn. bd., pres. BHC Communications Inc., 1977—, United TV Inc, 1982—; bd. dirs. Paramount Pictures, 1963-64. Bd. dirs. Phoenix House, 1978-81, United TV, Inc., 1981—; bd. advisors Vets. Bedside Network, 1980—; v.p. Friars Nat. Assn. Found. 1980—; trustee Lehigh U., Blair Acad., 1985. Club: Friars. Office: Chris-Craft Industries Inc 767 5th Ave Fl 46 New York NY 10153

SIEGEL, HERBERT S., physiologist, immunologist; b. Mt. Vernon, N.Y., Aug. 29, 1926; s. David and Regina (Eisner) S.; m. Rhea Hilda Spiro, Feb. 1, 1948; children: Alan, Charles Ira, Lisa Frances. BS, Pa. State U., 1950, MS, 1957, PhD, 1959. Owner, mgr. Windcrest Farm, Plumsteadville, Pa., 1950-55; asst. prof. Va. Poly. Inst., Blacksburg, 1958-62, assoc. prof., 1962-64; rsch. physiologist USDA, Athens, Ga., 1964-84; grad. rsch. asst. Pa. State U., Univ. Park, 1955-58, dept. head Dept. Poultry Sci., 1984-91, prof., 1991—; chair sci. adv. bd. Embrex Corp., Raleigh, N.C., 1988-94; EEO counselor USDA, Athens, 1973-77. Contbr. chpts. to books. With USN, 1944-46, PTO. Fulbright-Hays grantee Fulbright Found., Wageningen, The Netherlands, 1980; recipient Gordon Meml medal British Poultry Sci. Soc., 1994. Fellow AAAS, Poultry Sci. Assn. (editor-in-chief Poultry Sci. 1981-86, 95—, Poultry Sci. Rsch. award 1961); mem. Am. Soc. Zoologists, Soc. Exptl. Biology and Medicine, N.Y. Acad. Sci. Democrat. Jewish. Achievements include discovery of role of stress in immunosuppression in birds, production of acth-like material from leukocytes in birds. Office: Dept Poultry Sci 206 Henning Bldg University Park PA 16802

SIEGEL, HOWARD JEROME, lawyer; b. Chgo., July 29, 1942; s. Leonard and Idele (Lehrner) S.; m. Diane L. Gerber; children: Sari D., Allison J., James G. BS, U. Ill., 1963; JD, Northwestern U., 1966. Bar: Ill. 1966, U.S. dist. Ct. (no. dist.) Ill. 1967. Assoc., Ancel, Stonesifer & Glink, Chgo., 1966-70; ptnr. Goldstine & Siegel, Summit, Ill., 1970-75; sole practice, Chgo., 1975-77; pres. Wexler, Siegel & Shaw, Ltd., Chgo., 1978-82; ptnr. Keck, Mahin & Cate, Chgo., 1982-95, Neal Gerber & Eisenberg, Chgo., 1995—; dir. various corps. Mem. ABA, Chgo. Bar Assn., Ill. Bar Assn., Internat. Council Shopping Ctrs., Urban Land Inst., Chgo. Real.Estate Bd. Clubs: Standard (Chgo.); Ravisloe Country (Homewood, Ill.). Office: Neal Gerber & Eisenberg 2 N LaSalle St Ste 2100 Chicago IL 60602

SIEGEL, IRA T., publishing executive; b. N.Y.C., Sept. 23, 1944; s. David Aaron and Rose (Minsky) S.; m. Sharon Ruth Sacks, Sept. 5, 1965. BS, NYU, 1965; MBA, L.I. U., 1968. Bus. mgr. Buttenheim Pub. Co., N.Y.C., 1965-72; corp. v.p. rsch. Cahners Pub. Co. div. Reed Pub. USA, Boston, 1972-86; pres., COO R.R. Bowker Pub. Co. div. Reed Pub. USA, New Providence, N.J., 1986-91; pres. Martindale-Hubbell div. Reed Pub. USA, New Providence, N.J., 1990-91, Reed Reference Pub. (includes R.R. Bowker Co., Martindale-Hubbell, Nat. Register Pub. Co., The Salesman's Guide, Marquis Who's Who), New Providence, N.J., 1991-95; pres., CEO Lexis-Nexis, Dayton, Ohio, 1995—. Mem. Am. Mktg. Assn., Info. Industry Assn. Office: Lexis-Nexis PO Box 933 Dayton OH 45401

SIEGEL, JACK MORTON, retired biotechnology company executive; b. Sioux City, Iowa, June 11, 1922; s. Harry and Rose (Perlman) S.; m. Betty Virginia Collins, Feb. 22, 1946 (dec. Feb. 1986); children: Jennifer L. Mastricola, Marjorie G., Thomas A.; m. Dolores E. Williams Kinert, Dec. 20, 1991. BS in Chemistry, UCLA, 1944; PhD in Chemistry, Washington U., St. Louis, 1950. Chemist The Clinton Labs., Oak Ridge, Tenn., 1944-46; asst. prof. chemistry U. Ark. Sch. Medicine, Little Rock, 1950-55; chemist, v.p. P-L Biochems. Inc., Milw., 1955-82; v.p., gen. mgr. Pharmacia P-L Biochems. Inc., Milw., 1982-87, pres., 1987-89. Contbr. articles to profl. jours. Mem. AAAS, Am. Chem. Soc. Democrat. Jewish.

SIEGEL, JEFFREY NORTON, lawyer; b. N.Y.C., Nov. 27, 1942; s. George Siegel and Rose (Friedman) Gerber; m. Judith Sharon Chused, June 11, 1966; children: Daniel, Linda. AB, Brown U., 1964; LLB, Harvard U., 1967. Bar: N.Y. 1968. Assoc., ptnr. Golenbock & Barell, N.Y.C., 1967-89; ptnr. Whitman & Ransom, N.Y.C., 1990-93, Shack & Siegel, P.C., N.Y.C., 1993—. Mem. bus. com. The Jewish Mus. Mem. ABA, Assn. Bar City N.Y. (com. securities regulation 1987-90, com. profl. responsibility 1979-84), Phi Beta Kappa. Home: 220 E 72d St New York NY 10021 Office: Shack & Siegel PC 530 5th Ave New York NY 10036-5101

SIEGEL, JEFFREY ROY, lawyer; b. Stuttgart, Germany, Jan. 16, 1957; s. Herbert B. and Joan M. (Goodkin) S.; m. Marilyn E. Seipp Siegel, Aug. 5, 1990; 1 child, Kenneth George. BA in Politics, Princeton U., 1979; JD, U. San Francisco, 1983. Clk. Colo. Ct. Appeals, Denver, 1984-85; assoc. Gibbons, Lees and Schaefer, Walnut Creek, Calif., 1985; PTNR. Gill & Siegel PC, Agana, Guam, 1985-89; pvt. practice San Ramon, Calif., 1990—; cons. Whitestone Group, N.Y.C., 1994—. Mem. State Bar Calif., Colo. Bar Assn., Assn. Trial Lawyers Am., Calif. Trial Lawyers Assn. Democrat. Jewish. Avocations: pvt. pilot, actor. Office: 2817 Crow Canyon Rd Ste 203 San Ramon CA 94583-1639

SIEGEL, JOEL STEVEN, television news correspondent; b. Los Angeles, July 7, 1943; s. Robert and Libby (Kantor) S.; m. Jane Kessler, Nov. 21, 1976 (dec. 1982); m. Melissa Nina De Mayo, Aug. 27, 1985 (div.). BA, UCLA, 1965, postgrad., 1966-67. Copywriter, producer Carson & Roberts Advt., Los Angeles, 1967-72; freelance writer Rolling Stone mag., Los Angeles Times, others, 1967-77; news anchorman Sta. KMET-FM, Los Angeles, 1972; corr. Sta. WCBS-TV, N.Y.C., 1972-76; corr., film critic Sta. WABC-TV, N.Y.C., 1976—, Good Morning America, N.Y.C., 1980—. Author: (Broadway mus.) The First, 1981 (Tony award nomination 1981). Dir. voter registration drive SCLC/Dr. Martin Luther King, Macon, Ga., 1965; joke writer Robert F. Kennedy, 1968. Served with USAR, 1967-73. Recipient 5 Emmy awards, numerous nominations Nat. Acad. TV Arts and Scis. (N.Y. chpt.), Freedom award B'nai Brith/Anti-Defamation League, 1976. Mem. AFTRA, Dramatists Guild, Drama Desk, Gilda's Club (founding pres.). Democrat. Jewish. Office: Good Morning Am 147 Columbus Ave New York NY 10023-5900

SIEGEL, LAURENCE GORDON, conductor; b. N.Y.C., July 23, 1931; s. Jacob and Esther (Gordon) S.; m. Luz M. Morales, Oct. 15, 1959; 1 child, Carla. BA, CCNY, 1953; MusM, New Eng. Conservatory Music, 1955. Worked with Boris Goldovsky and Leonard Bernstein Berkshire Music Ctr.; Dr. Fritz Stiedry; condr. Orquesta Sinfonica del Salvador; Symphony of the Air, N.Y.C.; condr. Orquesta Sinfonica de Las Palmas, Spain, Manila Met. Philharm. Orch. and Opera Assn., Teatro Sperimentale di Spoleto (Italy), Belgrade (Yugoslavia) Symphony, Filharmonica de Stat Oradea (Romania), Honolulu Orch., Shreveport (La.) Festival Orch., Alexandria (Va.) Symphony, Jacksonville (Fla.) Symphony and Opera Co., 1975-85, Conn. Grand Opera Co.; music dir., condr. Puccini Festival Orch., Italy, Italy, 1984; condr. Orch. of the Radio Assn. Italiana, Milan, 1985-96; music dir. North Miami Beach (Fla.) Symphony, 1976—; recorded with various record labels including Audio Team, Miller Internat., Intercord Klassiche Discothek, CTA Records Co. Ltd., Golden Master Series, Stradivari Records, Germany, Pilz Records, Germany, Madacy, Can., Delta, Germany; cons. Miami Internat. Music Competition; music dir., condr. Festival of Continents, Key West, Fla., 1990; chief condr. Osaka (Japan) Opera, 1990; music dir. Panam. Sinfonica, Miami, 1991—; guest condr. Kensington Symphony, Calif., Orch. Sinfonia de Sao Paulo, Orch. Sinfonia de Paraguay, Asuncion, R.I.A. Milano Orch., Italy, 1994, 95. Condr. numerous operas including The Impressario, Cosi Fan Tutte, La Perchole, Don Pasquale, Faust, I Pagliacci, Samson and Dalila, Madame Butterfly, Tosca, La Boheme, Elisir D. Amore, Hansel and Gretl, La Traviata, Fledermaus, Otello, Rigoletto, Il Trovatore, Carmen, Ernani, Merry Widow, Lucia di Lammermoor, Grafin Mariza; condr. albums Tschaikovsky with the New Philharm. Orch. London, Mozart Symphony 41, recs. with London Philharm., London Festival Orch., Royal Philharm. Recipient numerous citations and medals Country of Italy; named hon. Dr. of Music, London, Paris, Knight of Templar Order of Germany.

SIEGEL, LLOYD HARVEY, architect, real estate developer, consultant; b. N.Y.C., Nov. 27, 1928; s. Saul M. and Lillian (Bell) S.; m. Margot Kopsidas Phillips, Oct. 25, 1987. BArch., Princeton U., 1949; MArch., MIT, 1953. Registered architect, N.Y., N.J., Conn., Ohio, Ill., Mich. Designer Skidmore, Owings & Merrill, then I. M. Pei & Assocs., then Antonin Raymond, N.Y.C., 1955-60; assoc. Kelly & Gruzen, N.Y.C., 1960-66; dep. health services adminstr. City of N.Y., 1966-70; dep. exec. dir. health and hosps. governing commn. Cook County, Chgo., 1970-76; prin. L.H.S. Cons. in Health Planning, Facility Design & Mgmt., Washington, 1976—, Siegel & Schroeder, P.C., Chgo., 1983-87; dir. Office Architecture & Engring., VA, Washington, 1987-94; dir. Facilities Quality Office VA, Washington, 1994—; prin. Yacht Harbor Devel. Co., South Haven, Mich., 1983-88, Siegel & Schroeder Developers Inc., Chgo., 1984-88; mem. adv. coms. HEW; mem. pub. adv. panels GSA; mem. adv. com. Legislature State of Ill.; mem. fellowship evaluation com. AIA-Am. Hosp. Assn.; mem. tech. adv. com. to Northeastern Ill. Planning Commn.; chmn. Com. on Architecture for Health, 1984. Author: Hidden Asset? Interstitial Space, A Critical Evaluation, 1987; photography in permanent collections Met. Mus. Art, N.Y.C., Mus. Modern Art, N.Y.C., others; prin. works include N.Y. World's Fair Spanish Pavillion, N.Y.C. (N.Y. chpt. AIA award 1964), Williams Meml. Residence, Flushing, N.Y. (Queens C. of C. award 1964), Hebrew Home for Aged, Riverdale, N.Y. (Bronx C. of C. award 1966). Fulbright fellow Università di Roma, 1954, Politecnico di Milano, 1955. Fellow AIA; mem. Urban Land Inst., The Arts Club, Univ. Club. Avocations: micology, microphagy, oenology. Home: 3133 Connecticut Ave NW Washington DC 20008-5147 Office: VA 810 Vermont Ave NW Washington DC 20420-0001

SIEGEL, LOUIS PENDLETON, forest products executive; b. Richmond, Va., Nov. 6, 1942; s. John Boschen Jr. and Francis Beale (Tyler) S.; m. Nancy Dicks Blanton, Apr. 10, 1974 (dec. July 1976); m. Nancy Northon, June 26, 1982; children: Kathryn Tyler. AB in Econs., Dartmouth Coll., 1967. Asst. cashier, security researcher First Nat. Citibank, N.Y.C., 1967-71; v.p. security rsch. Drexel Burnham Lambert, N.Y.C., 1971-79; with Potlatch Corp., San Francisco, 1979—, sr. v.p. fin. and adminstrn., 1989, group v.p. wood products and corp. planning, 1989-92, group v.p. pulp and paperboard and corp. planning, 1992-93, exec. v.p. pulp-based ops. and corp. planning, 1993-94, pres., COO, 1994—; bd. dirs. San Francisco Fed. Corp. Pres., bd. dir. Bay Area Sci. Fair, San Francisco, 1989-90; bd. dirs. Bay Area Coun. With USCG, 1964-65. Republican. Episcopalian. Avocations: golf, tennis, fishing. Office: Potlatch Corp 1 Maritime Plz San Francisco CA 94111-3404

SIEGEL, MARC MONROE, television and film producer, writer, director; b. N.Y.C., Dec. 8, 1916; s. Isaac and Annie N. (Natelson) S.; m. Anne Dorothy Fishman, Sept. 8, 1940; 1 son, Peter Kieve. B.A., Washington Sq. Coll., 1936; M.A., N.Y. U. Sch. Edn., 1938. Free-lance mag. writer, especially for: New Yorker mag, 1948-50; writer: Eternal Light radio series, NBC, N.Y.C., 1950-60; writer-dir-producer: Directions, ABC-TV, N.Y.C., 1961-78; exec. producer chief writer: Heritage: Civilization and the Jews, WNET, N.Y.C., 1978-84; author: feature screenplays A Child is Crying, 1961, The Young Adventurers, 1963; ABC News Bicentennial spls. Rendezvous With Freedom, 1973, The Right to Believe, 1975, The Will to Be Free, 1976; ABC News feature The Panama Canal, 1977 (Writers Guild award); (Recipient numerous awards, including: Edinburgh Film Festival award 1948, Venice Film Festival award 1962, Cannes Film Festival award 1964, Eternal Light award Jewish Theol. Sem. Am. 1969). Served with USAAF, 1943-45. Peabody award, 1979, 84; Gabriel award Nat. Assn. Catholic Broadcasters, 1979; Emmy award, 1984, Christopher award, 1984; also several awards Freedoms Found. Mem. Nat. Acad. TV Arts and Scis., Writers Guild Am. East (council 1972-73, 78-79, 84-88, awards 1959, 73, 78, 85, Jablow Meml. award 1988), Dirs. Guild Am. Democrat. Home: 75 Central Park W New York NY 10023-6011

SIEGEL, MARTIN JAY, lawyer, investment advisor; b. N.Y.C., Apr. 12, 1942; s. Barney and Ruth (Baer) S. BA in Econs., Mich. State U., 1963; JD, Bklyn. Law Sch., 1966; MBA in Fin., Fordham U., 1980. Served to col. U.S. Army, 1966—, commd. 2d lt., 1966; advanced through grades to col., 1991, ret., 1990; fin. advisor, pvt. practice law, N.Y.C., 1971—. Col. USAR, 1990—. Office: 150 Broadway Rm 1400 New York NY 10038-4401

SIEGEL, MARVIN, newspaper editor; b. N.Y.C., June 23, 1935; s. Murray and Belle (Diamond) S.; 1 child, Joshua Murray. BA, U. Mich., 1957. Reporter The Record, Hackensack, N.J., 1957-59; free-lance writer Western Europe, 1960-62; reporter Fairchild Publs., N.Y.C., 1962-63; editor The World Telegram, N.Y.C., 1963-66; copy editor The N.Y. Times, 1966-67, asst. met. editor, 1967-76, founding editor Weekend sect., 1976-82; founding editor World of N.Y., 1982-86; founding editor Edn. Life The N.Y. Times, 1986, dep. editor Week in Rev., 1987, culture news editor, 1988-92, dep. editor Book Rev., 1992-95; asst. to mng. editor, 1995—. Co-author: The World of New York, 1985, The New York Times: Great Lives of the 20th Century, 1988; editor: The Seven Deadly Sins, 1994. Pfc. U.S. Army. Jewish. Office: NY Times Co 229 W 43d St New York NY 10036-3913

SIEGEL, MICHAEL ELLIOT, nuclear medicine physician, educator; b. N.Y.C., May 13, 1942; s. Benjamin and Rose (Gilbert) S.; m. Marsha Rose Snower, Mar. 20, 1966; children: Herrick Jove, Meridith Ann. AB, Cornell U., 1964; MD, Chgo. Med. Sch., 1968. Diplomate Nat. Bd. Med. Examiners. Intern Cedars-Sinai Med. Ctr., L.A., 1968-69; resident in radiology, 1969-70; NIH fellow in radiology Temple U. Med. Ctr., Phila., 1970-71; NIH fellow in nuclear medicine Johns Hopkins U. Sch. Medicine, Balt., 1971-73, asst. prof. radiology, 1972-76; assoc. prof. radiology, medicine U. So. Calif., L.A., 1976—; prof. radiology, 1989—, dir. divsn. nuclear medicine, 1982—; dir. Sch. Nuclear Medicine, L.A. County-U. So. Calif. Med. Ctr., 1976—; dir. divsn. nuclear medicine Kenneth Norris Cancer Hosp. and Rsch. Ctr., L.A., 1983—; dir. dept. nuclear medicine Orthopaedic Hosp., L.A., 1981—, Intercommunity Hosp., Covina, Calif., 1981—, U. So. Calif. Univ. Hosp., L.A., 1993—; cons. dept. nuclear medicine Rancho Los Amigos Hosp., Downey, Calif., 1976—. Author: Textbook of Nuclear Medicine, 1978, Vascular Surgery, 1983, 88, and numerous others textbooks; editor: Nuclear Cardiology, 1981, Vascular Disease: Nuclear Medicine, 1983. Mem. Maple Ctr., Beverly Hills. Served as maj. USAF, 1974-76. Recipient Outstanding Alumnus award Chgo. Med. Sch., 1991. Fellow Am. Coll. Nuclear Medicine (sci. investigator 1974, 76, nominations com. 1980, program com. 1983, bd. trustees 1993, disting. fellow, 1993, bd. reps., 1993—); mem. Soc. Nuclear Medicine (sci. exhbn. com. 1978-79, program com. 1979-80, Silver medal 1975), Calif. Med. Assn. (sci. adv. bd. 1987—), Radiol. Soc. N.Am., Soc. Nuclear Magnetic Resonance Imaging, Alpha Omega Alpha. Lodge: Friars So. Calif. Research on devel. of nuclear medicine techniques to: evaluate cardiovascular disease and diagnose and treat cancer, clinical utilization of video digital displays in nuclear medicine development; inventor pneumatic radiologic pressure system. Office: U So Calif Med Ctr PO Box 693 1200 N State St Los Angeles CA 90033

SIEGEL, NATHANIEL HAROLD, sociology educator; b. Bklyn., May 17, 1929; s. Victor and Yetta (Kogel) S.; m. Annabelle Replansky, Mar. 3, 1958; children—Anthony, Jennifer. A.B., Bklyn. Coll., 1950; A.M., N.Y.U., 1952, Ph.D., 1956. Asst. prof. sociology Columbia, 1956-59; sociologist Hillside Hosp., Queens, N.Y., 1958-63; assoc. dir. behavioral research N.Y.C. Dept. Health, 1963-64; chief social sci. tng. sect. NIMH, 1964-67, cons., 1970—; prof. sociology Queens Coll., 1967-79, chmn. dept., 1967-70, v.p., dean faculty, 1970-74, provost, 1974-77, acting pres., 1977-78; sr. v.p. acad. affairs SUNY Purchase, 1979-94; prof. sociology SUNY, 1979—. Served with M.C. AUS, 1950-51. Home: 8 Birchfield Rd Larchmont NY 10538-1505 Office: SUNY Dept Sociology Purchase NY 10577

SIEGEL, NED LAWRENCE, real estate developer; b. Newark, Sept. 26, 1951; s. Howard and Esther (Facher) S.; m. Stephanie Moak, Aug. 7, 1976; children: Justin, Joshua, Jillian. BA, U. Conn., 1973; JD, Dickinson Sch. Law, 1976. Law clk. U.S. Dist. Ct., Camden, N.J., 1976-77; assoc. Kimmelman, Wolff & Samson, Roseland, N.J., 1977-78; v.p. Howard Siegel Cos., Manalapan, N.J., 1978-80; pres. The Weingarten-Siegel Group, Manalapan, N.J., 1980-88, Weingarten Siegel Group of Fla., Inc., Boca Raton, Fla., 1985-91, Weingarten, Siegel, Fletcher Group, La Mesa, Calif., 1985-91, The Siegel Schoor Orgn. Fla., INc., Boca Raton, 1991—; pres. SGS Communities Inc., Manalapan, N.J., Boca Raton, 1992—. Bd. govs. Solomon Schechter Sch., West Orange, N.J., 1986-88; mem. bd. adv. Pine Crest Sch. at Boca Raton, 1989-93, mem. bd. dirs. 1992—; active Nat. Jewish Coalition, 1995—; mem. task force City of Boca Raton Affordable Housing, 1995—. Named Bldr. of the Yr., N.J. Shore Bldrs. Assn., 1986. Mem. Fla. Atlantic Bldrs. Assn., N.J. Bldrs. Assn., N.J. Shore Bldrs. Assn. (v.p. 1986-88), Urban Land Inst., N.J. Bar Assn. Republican. Jewish. Avocations: tennis, sailing. Office: 1800 Corporate Blvd NW Ste 300 Boca Raton FL 33431-7336

SIEGEL, NORMAN JOSEPH, pediatrician, educator; b. Houston, Mar. 8, 1943; m. Rise Joan Ross, Dec. 24, 1967; children: Andrew, Karen. BA, Tulane U., 1964; MA, U. Tex. Med. Br., Galveston, 1968, MD, 1968. Intern, then resident Yale-New Haven Hosp., 1968-70; fellow Sch. Medicine, Yale U., New Haven, 1970-72, asst. prof. pediatrics and medicine, 1972-76, assoc. prof., 1976-82, prof., 1982—, vice chmn. pediatrics, 1979—; acting chmn. pediatrics Yale U., 1995—. Contbr. articles to profl. jours., chpts. to books. Grantee NIH, Am. Heart Assn., Hood Found. Mem. Am. Pediatric Soc. (sec.-treas. 1993—), Am. Soc. Pediatric Nephrology (pres. 1988-89), Nat. Kidney Found. (chmn. com. on pediatric nephrology and urology 1987-91, grantee, scientific adv. com. 1988-91), Soc. Pediatric Rsch. (membership sec. 1979-85), Nat. Bd. Med. Examiners (pediatric test com. 1993-95), Phi Beta Kappa, Mu Delta. Office: Yale U Sch Medicine Dept Pediatrics 333 Cedar St PO Box 208064 New Haven CT 06520-8064

SIEGEL, PAUL BARTON, petroleum company executive, lawyer; b. Miami, Jan. 27, 1946; m. Ann Jarrett, Jan. 11, 1970; children—Michael, Allison. B.S. in Bus. Adminstrn., U. Fla., 1968; J.D., Okla. City U., 1974. Bar: Tex. 1975, U.S. Dist. Ct. (so. dist.) Tex. 1978, U.S. Supreme Ct. 1979. Atty. Panhandle Eastern Corp., Houston, 1974-78; gen. counsel BS&B, Inc., Houston, 1978-79; atty. Pennzoil Co., Houston, 1979-81, v.p.-legal, 1981-86, sr. v.p., 1986—; dir. Jiffy Lube Internat., Balt. Mem. Tex. Bar Assn.,

Houston Bar Assn., Phi Delta Phi. Clubs: Texas, Athletic (Houston), Houstonian Club. Office: Pennzoil Co PO Box 2967 Houston TX 77252-2967

SIEGEL, RICHARD DAVID, lawyer, former government official; b. Lewistown, Pa., Oct. 13, 1939; s. Robert and Pearl Eleanor (Nieman) S.; m. Marjorie Esther Greenwald, Mar. 13, 1966; children—Andrew, Jonathan, Michele. B.A., U. Pa., 1960; J.D., Harvard U., 1963. Bar: Pa., D.C., U.S. Supreme Ct. Staff writer Phila. Inquirer, 1964-66; spl. asst. U.S. Rep. Richard Schweiker, Washington, 1966-69; legis. counsel U.S. Senator Richard Schweiker, Washington, 1969-71; assoc. minority counsel Senate Com. on Labor and Human Resources, Washington, 1971-73; sole practice Washington, 1978-79, mem. various firms, 1973-78, 80-81; dep. asst. sec. for natural resources and environment USDA, Washington, 1981-87; pvt. practice, Washington, 1987—. Contbr. articles to profl. jours. Treas. Com. for Senator Schweiker, Washington, 1974; mem. nat. coun. Am. Israel Pub. Affairs Com., Washington, 1974-77; v.p. Tifereth Israel Congregation, Washington, 1980-82, 93—; sec.-treas. North Am.-Israel Hort. Found., 1987-95. With USCGR, 1963-64. Mem. ABA, FBA, Pa. Bar Assn., Assn. Former Senate Aides. Republican. Jewish. Home: 3141 Aberfoyle Pl NW Washington DC 20015-2325 Office: 1400 16th St NW Washington DC 20036-2220

SIEGEL, ROBERT, heat transfer engineer; b. Cleve., July 10, 1927; s. Morris and Mollie (Binder) S.; m. Elaine Jane Jaffe, July 19, 1951; children: Stephen, Lawrence. BS, Case Inst. Tech., 1950, MS, 1951; ScD, MIT, 1953. Heat transfer engr. GE, Schenectady, N.Y., 1953-54; heat transfer analyst Knolls Atomic Power Lab., Schenectady, 1954-55; rsch. scientist NASA Lewis Rsch. Ctr., Cleve., 1955—; adj. prof. U. Toledo, 1981, 85, 95, adj. prof. mech. engring. U. Akron (Ohio), 1987, adj. prof. mech. engring. Cleve. State U., 1989, 91; mem. adv. coun. U. Akron, 1989—. Author: Thermal Radiation Heat Transfer, 1972, 3d edit., 1992; tech. editor ASME, 1973-83, AIAA, 1986—; author numerous sci. papers. With U.S. Army, 1945-47. Recipient Exceptional Sci. Achievement medal NASA, 1986, Space Act award, 1993. Fellow ASME (Heat Transfer Meml. award 1970), AIAA (Thermophysics award 1993); mem. Sigma Xi, Tau Beta Pi. Jewish. Avocations: ballroom dancing, piano. Home: 3052 Warrington Rd Cleveland OH 44120-2425 Office: NASA Lewis Rsch Ctr 21000 Brookpark Rd Cleveland OH 44135-3127

SIEGEL, ROBERT CHARLES, broadcast journalist; b. N.Y.C., June 26, 1947; s. Joseph and Edith Ruth (Joffe) S.; m. Jane Claudia Schwartz, June 17, 1973; children: Erica Anne, Leah Harriet. BA, Columbia U., 1968, postgrad. sch. journalism, 1969-70. Newscaster Sta. WGLI, Babylon, N.Y., 1968-69; reporter, news dir. Sta. WRVR-FM, N.Y.C., 1971-76; assoc. producer, editor Nat. Pub. Radio, Washington, 1976-78, sr. editor, 1976-79, dir. news and info., 1983-87, host All Things Considered, 1987—; sr. editor Nat. Pub. Radio, London, 1979-83; host Ea. Europe: Breaking with the Past, The Learning Channel, Washington, 1990, Earth Scope, Arlington, Va., 1990-91. Editor: The NPR Interviews. Recipient DuPont-Columbia award Columbia U., 1984. Jewish. Avocations: reading, golf, baseball. Home: 1340 19th Rd S Arlington VA 22202-1637 Office: Nat Pub Radio All Things Considered 635 Massachusetts Ave NW Washington DC 20001-3752

SIEGEL, ROBERT TED, physicist; b. Springfield, Mass., June 10, 1928; s. Charles V.D. and Ida B. Siegel; m. Rebecca Weisberg, June 14, 1951; children: Carol D., Naomi L., Joan E., Jonathan D., Richard M.; m. Wendy P. Kramer. BS, Carnegie-Mellon U., 1948, MS, 1950, DS, 1952. Research assoc. Carnegie Mellon U., 1952-57, asst. prof. physics, 1957-60, assoc. prof., 1960-63; prof. Coll. William and Mary, 1963—, W.F.C. Ferguson prof. physics, 1979—, dean grad. studies, 1965-67, dir. space radiation effects lab., 1967-79. Fellow Am. Phys. Soc.; mem. AAAS, AAUP. Jewish. Office: Coll William and Mary Physics Dept Williamsburg VA 23185

SIEGEL, SAMUEL, metals company executive; b. Elizabeth, N.J., Oct. 30, 1930; s. Morris and Anna (Fader) S.; m. Raenea Kershenbaum, Mar. 29, 1953; children: Daryl Lynn, Annie Roslyn. BBA, CUNY, 1952. CPA, N.Y., Ariz. Cost accountant Seaporcel Metals, Inc., Long Island City, N.Y., 1955-56; asst. to controller Deltown Foods, Inc., Yonkers, N.Y., 1956-57; sr. accountant DeLoitte & Touche, N.Y.C., 1957-61; vice chmn., chief fin. officer, treas., sec., dir. Nucor Corp., Charlotte, N.C., 1961—. Mem. AICPA, Am. Soc. Corp. Secs., Fin. Execs. Inst. Home: 3421 Windbluff Dr Charlotte NC 28277-9850 Office: Nucor Corp 2100 Rexford Rd Charlotte NC 28211-3484

SIEGEL, SARAH ANN, lawyer; b. Providence, Aug. 29, 1956. BA in History cum laude, Brandeis U., 1978; JD, Washington U., St. Louis, 1981. Bar: Mo. 1982, U.S. Dist. Ct. (ea. dist.) Mo. 1983. Assoc. atty. St. Louis, 1982-83; staff atty. Land Clearance for Redevel. Authority, St. Louis, 1983-85, gen. counsel, 1985-88; gen. counsel Econ. Devel. Corp., St. Louis, 1988-90, St. Louis Devel. Corp., 1990-91; spl. counsel for devel. City of St. Louis, 1991-92; assoc. Suelthaus & Walsh, P.C., St. Louis, 1992-95, prin., 1995—. Pres. Central Reform Congregation, St. Louis, 1991-93, v.p., 1989-91, bd. dirs. 1987-89. Mem. ABA, Mo. Bar Assn. (vice chair com. on eminent domain 1990-91, steering com. 1987-89), Women Lawyer's Assn. (bd. dirs. 1985-90, v.p. 1989-90). Avocations: hiking, swimming. Office: Suelthaus & Walsh PC 7733 Forsyth Blvd 12th Fl Saint Louis MO 63105

SIEGEL, SHARON BARBARA, middle school educator; b. Bklyn., Nov. 18, 1942; d. Harold and Constance Ruth (Silberman) Dunayer; m. Murray Harvey Siegel, Aug. 9, 1964; children: Roy, Andrew. BS, SUNY, Cortland, 1964; MEd, Ga. State U., 1977. Cert. Tchr. Ariz., N.Y., Ga. 1st grade tchr. Turin Rd. Sch., Rome, N.Y., 1965-67; elem. sch. tchr. Fulton County Schs., Atlanta, 1975-90; 8th grad. math. tchr. Dodgen Mid. Sch., Marietta, Ga., 1990-92; 4th grade tchr., math. tchr. Four Peaks Elem. Sch., Fountain Hills, Ariz., 1992-94; 7th grade at-risk program tchr. Marietta Mid. Sch., 1994-95; 5th grade math. tchr. Dunleith Elem. Sch., Marietta, 1995—. Mem. NSTA, Nat. Coun. Tchrs. Math., Ga. Coun. Tchrs. Math., Ga. Sci. Tchrs. Assn. Avocation: racewalking. Home: 136 Helmswood Cir Marietta GA 30064-5019 Office: Dunleith Elem. Sch. 120 Saine Dr Marietta GA 30060

SIEGEL, SHELDON C., physician; b. Mpls., Jan. 30, 1922; s. Carl S.; m. Priscilla Rikess, Mar. 3, 1946; children—Linda, Nancy. A.A., Va. Jr. Coll., 1940; B.A., B.S., U. Minn., 1942, M.D., 1945. Intern U. Minn. Hosp., 1946, resident in pediatrics, 1947-48; fellow in pediatric allergy Rochester, N.Y., 1949-50; practice medicine specializing in pediatric allergy and pediatrics St. Paul, 1950-52, San Antonio, 1952-54, Los Angeles, 1954—; clin. instr. pediatrics U. Rochester, 1949-50, U. Minn., 1950-51; asst. prof. pediatrics U. Tex., 1952-54; asst. clin. prof. U. Calif. at Los Angeles Med. Sch., 1955, clin. asso. prof., 1957-62, clin. prof., 1963—, co-chief pediatric allergy clinic, 1957—; mem. staff Harbor Gen. Hosp., Torrance, Calif., Daniel Freeman Hosp., Inglewood, Calif., Centinela Valley Community Hosp., Inglewood, Hawthorne (Calif.) Community Hosp. Editorial bd.: Jour. Allergy, 1973-75; contbr. articles to med. jours. Fellow Am. Acad. Allergy (pres. 1974), Am. Coll. Allergists, Am. Acad. Pediatrics; mem. AMA, Allergy Found. Am. (pres. 1976), Calif., Los Angeles County med. assns., Los Angeles Pediatric Soc., Calif., Los Angeles socs. allergy, Western Pediatric Research Soc., Am. Bd. Med. Specialists, Sigma Xi. Office: 11620 Wilshire Blvd Los Angeles CA 90025-1706

SIEGEL, SID, composer, lyricist; b. Chgo., Jan. 20, 1927; s. Michael and Rose (Wolfson) S.; m. Carrie Patricia Zeigler, May 18, 1952; children: David, Jodi, Mark. BMus in Composition, Roosevelt Coll., Chgo., 1950. Composer-lyricist for local TV shows, nightclub performers and popular songs, also commls. for radio and TV, nightclub shows; composer-lyricist, arranger, condr. for radio and TV commls., films, slide presentations, industry shows.; (Recipient numerous awards for music for commls. and films including Cindy Indsl. Film Producers Am. and Capa Chgo. Audio-Visual Producers Assn.). With USNR, 1945-46. Mem. ASCAP, Am. Fedn. Musicians. Address: 326 Satinwood Ct N Buffalo Grove IL 60089-6611

SIEGEL, STANLEY, lawyer, educator; b. N.Y.C., Mar. 2, 1941; s. David Aaron and Rose (Minsky) S.; m. Karina Haum, July 20, 1986. B.S. summa cum laude, NYU, 1960; J.D. magna cum laude, Harvard U., 1963. Bar: N.Y. 1963, D.C. 1964, Mich. 1970, Calif. 1976; CPA, Md. Atty. Office Sec. of Air Force, 1963-66; asst. prof. law U. Mich., Ann Arbor, 1966-69, assoc. prof., 1969-71, prof., 1971-74; ptnr. Honigman, Miller, Schwartz & Cohn, Detroit, 1974-76; prof. law UCLA, 1976-86; prof. law NYU, 1986—, assoc. dean, 1987-89; vis. prof. Stanford Law Sch., 1973, Ctrl. European U., Budapest, 1993—, U. Konstanz, Germany, 1996; fellow Max-Planck Inst., Hamburg, 1988; cons. reorgn. U.S. Postal Svc., 1969-71; exec. sec. Mich. Law Revision Commn., 1973; mem. bd. examiners AICPA, 1980-83. Author: (with Schulman and Moscow) Michigan Business Corporations, 1979, (with Conard and Knauss) Enterprise Organization, 4th edit., 1987, (with D. Siegel) Accounting and Financial Disclosure: A Guide to Basic Concepts, 1983, (with others) Swiss Company Law, 1996. Served to capt. USAF, 1963-66. Mem. ABA, D.C. Bar Assn., Calif. Bar Assn., Assn. of Bar of City of N.Y., Am. Law Inst., AICPA. Office: NYU Law Sch 40 Washington Sq S New York NY 10012-1005

SIEGEL, THOMAS LOUIS, lawyer; b. N.Y.C., Oct. 7, 1939; s. Jack M. and Helen S. (Simpson) S.; m. Ruth L. Rosenthal, June 23, 1963; children: Peter, Karen. B.A., Rutgers U., 1961; J.D., Cornell U., 1964. Bar: N.Y. 1964, D.C. 1967, Tex. 1982. Atty. advisor Office of Gen. Counsel, FHA, Washington, 1968; assoc. mem. firm Arent, Fox, Kintner, Plotkin & Kahn, Washington, 1968-70; gen. counsel Group Health Assn., Inc., 1970-74; ptnr. Diuguid, Siegel & Kennelly, Washington, 1974-80; gen. counsel, div. fed. law and regulation Am. Hosp. Assn., 1980—; pvt. practice Dallas, 1982—; legal counsel St. Paul Hosp., Dallas; legal cons. div. organizational devel. HEW, 1974-80. Pres. bd. trustees St. Luke's House, Bethesda, Md. Served with USAF, 1965-67. Mem. N.Y. State Bar Assn., Tex. Bar Assn., Bar Assn. D.C., Dallas Bar Assn., Nat. Health Lawyers Assn., Rutgers, Cornell U. alumni assns. Home: 3739 Waldorf Dr Dallas TX 75229-3937 Office: 4100 Mcewen Rd Ste 285 Dallas TX 75244-5100

SIEGELMAN, DON EUGENE, state official; b. Mobil, Ala., Feb. 24, 1946; m. Lori Allen; c. Dana, Joseph. B.A., U. Ala.; J.D., Georgetown U., 1972; postgrad., Oxford U., Eng., 1972-73. Bar: Ala. 1972. Sec. of state State of Ala., Montgomery, 1979-87, atty. gen., 1987-94; lt. gov. State of Ala., 1994—. Office: Office of Lt Gov 11 Union St Montgomery AL 36130*

SIEGENTHALER, WALTER ERNST, internal medicine educator; b. Davos, Switzerland, Dec. 14, 1923; s. Walter and Anna S.; m. Gertrud Siegenthaler, Dec. 31, 1957. MD, U. Zurich (Switzerland), 1948; Dr.h.c., Martin Luther U., Halle, Germany, 1991. Chief resident in internal medicine St. Gallen, Switzerland, 1954-58; prof. internal medicine, chmn. dept. U. Bonn (Fed. Republic Germany), 1969-71; asst. in pathology U. Zurich, 1949-50, asst. in internal medicine, 1950-54, chief resident, 1958-61, lectr., 1961-67, asst. prof., 1967-69, assoc. prof., 1971-91, chmn. dept., dean Med. Sch., 1978-80; pres. Conf. Clinic Dirs., Zurich, 1980-91; pres. 10th Internat. Congress Chemotherapy, 1977; pres. Swiss Rsch. Inst. for Climate and Medicine, 1992—. Author textbooks on differential diagnosis, 17th edit., 1993, on clin. pathophysiology, 7th edit., 1994, on internal medicine, 3d edit., 1992; bd. dirs. numerous nat. and internat. sci. jours.; contbr. articles to profl. jours. Bd. dirs. EMDO Found. Zurich, 1974—, Jung Found., Hamburg, 1982-95, Opo Found., Zurich, 1994—, Swiss Found. for the promotion of young people, 1995—. Col. Swiss Army, 1941-88. Recipient Ernst von Bergmann plaque, 1972, Ludwig Heilmeyer gold medal, 1984. Fellow Infectious Diseases Soc. Am. (corr. 1983); mem. German Soc. Internal Medicine (pres. 1983-84, bd. dirs., hon. mem. 1992), Swiss Soc. Internal Medicine (bd. dirs., hon. mem. 1993), Acad. Naturforscher Leopoldina, Soc. for Progress in Internal Medicine (Cologne; bd. dirs., pres. 1992—), Paul Ehrlich Soc. (pres. 1969-71, 73-75, 75-77, hon. 1994), Rotary. Home: Forsterstrasse 61, CH-8044 Zurich Switzerland Office: Univ Hosp, Rämistrasse 100, CH-8091 Zurich Switzerland

SIEGER, CHARLES, librarian; b. Fountain Hill, Pa., Dec. 9, 1944; s. Charles Franklin and Kathryn (Farny) S.; m. Deborah Day Malone, May 13, 1972; children: C. Alexander, Meredith Kathryn. BA History, Wesleyan U., 1969; student, Duke U., 1969-71; MS Libr. Sci., UNC, 1979. Reference, U.S. Documents libr. Fairleigh Dickinson U., Rutherford, N.J., 1980-83, asst. dir. tech. svcs., 1983-85, assoc. dir., 1985-92, dir., 1992-94; dir. Lyndhurst (N.J.) Free Pub. Libr., 1994—. Contbr. articles to World Book ency., legal jours; contbr. chpts. to books. Coach, v.p., then pres. Lyndhurst Youth Soccer Club; treas. Minolta Suburban Youth Soccer League; mem. parent adv. com. Lyndhurst H.S.; v.p. Lipton Youth Soccer. With U.S. Army, 1966-68, Vietnam. Mem. ALA, Govt. Documents Roundtable, Documents Assn. N.J., Inc. Avocation: soccer. Home: 227 Tontine Ave Lyndhurst NJ 07071-1819 Office: Lyndhurst Free Pub Libr 355 Valley Brook Ave Lyndhurst NJ 07071-1810

SIEGFRIED, DAVID CHARLES, lawyer; b. N.Y.C., Feb. 15, 1942; s. Charles Albert and Marjorie Claire (Young) S.; m. Meri Stephanie Smith; children: Karin Elisabeth, Christine Elise. AB summa cum laude, Princeton U., 1964; JD, Harvard U., 1967. Bar: N.Y. 1970. Assoc. Milbank, Tweed, Hadley & McCloy, N.Y.C., 1968-76, ptnr., 1977-79, 83-85, 88—; resident ptnr. Milbank, Tweed, Hadley & McCloy, Hong Kong and Singapore, 1979-83, 85-88; bd. dirs. PALS; speaker at confs. and seminars. Served to 1st lt. USAR, 1967-74. Mem. ABA, Am. Soc. Internat. Law, Brazilian Am. C. of C. (bd. dirs.), Internat. Bar Assn., N.Y. State Bar Assn., Assn. Bar City N.Y., Millburn-Short Hills Hist. Soc. (v.p.). Congregationalist. Clubs: Princeton (New York), Short Hills (N.J.), Am. (Hong Kong/Singapore), Tanglin (Singapore), Cricket. Avocations: running, tennis, historic reading. Home: 30 Western Dr Short Hills NJ 07078-3230

SIEGFRIED, TOM, newspaper editor. Sci. editor Dallas Morning News. Office: The Dallas Morning News Communications Ctr PO Box 655237 Dallas TX 75265-5237

SIEGLER, THOMAS EDMUND, investment banking executive; b. Bklyn., Oct. 12, 1934; s. John G. and Edna (Trill) S.; m. Mary V., July 7, 1956; children—Christopher, John, Mary, Therese, Ellen, James. B.B.A., St. John's U., 1959; M.B.A., NYU, 1966. Fin. analyst Exxon Corp., N.Y.C., 1952-66; sr. v.p., sec. Donaldson, Lufkin & Jenrette, Inc., N.Y.C., 1966—; arbitrator Nat. Assn. of Securities Dealers, N.Y.C. Mem. Am. Soc. Corp. Secs., Nat. Assn. Securities Dealers. Republican. Roman Catholic. Lodge: K.C. Avocations: cabinetry; running. Home: 39 Wildwood Dr Huntington Station NY 11746-6040 Office: Donaldson Lufkin & Jenrette 277 Park Ave New York NY 10172

SIEGMAN, ANTHONY EDWARD, electrical engineer, educator; b. Detroit, Nov. 23, 1931; s. Orra Leslie and Helen Salome (Winnie) S.; (married). AB summa cum laude, Harvard U., 1952; MS, UCLA, 1954; PhD, Stanford U., 1957. Mem. faculty Stanford (Calif.) U., 1957—, assoc. prof. elec. engring., 1960-65, prof., 1965—; dir. Edward L. Ginzton Lab., 1978-83; cons. Lawrence Livermore Labs., Coherent Inc., GTE; mem. Air Force Sci. Adv. Bd.; vis. prof. Harvard U., 1965. Author: Microwave Solid State Masers, 1964, An Introduction to Lasers and Masers, 1970, Lasers, 1986; contbr. over 200 articles to profl. jours. Recipient Schawlow award Laser Inst. Am., 1991; Guggenheim fellow IBM Rsch. Lab., Zurich, 1969-70; Alexander von Humboldt Found. sr. scientist Max Planck Inst. Quantum Optics, Garching, Fed. Republic Germany, 1984-85. Fellow AAAS, IEEE (W.R.G. Baker award 1971, J.J. Ebers award 1977), Am. Phys. Soc., Laser Inst. Am., Optical Soc. Am. (R.W. Wood prize 1980), IEEE Laser Electro-Optics Soc. (Quantum Electronics award 1989), Am. Acad. Arts and Scis.; mem. NAS, NAE, AAUP, Phi Beta Kappa, Sigma Xi. Patentee microwave and optical devices and lasers, including the unstable optical resonator. Office: Stanford U Ginzton Lab Mc 4085 Stanford CA 94305-4055

SIEHL, RICHARD W., lawyer; b. Dayton, Ohio, Sept. 12, 1952. BA magna cum laude, Miami U., 1974; JD, U. Ill., 1977. Bar: Ohio 1977, Fla. 1979, W. Va. 1987. Asst. prosecuting atty. Franklin County, 1977-78; minority counsel Ohio House Reps., 1979-80; dep. dir. Ohio Dept. Adminstrv. Svcs., 1980-82; ptnr. Baker & Hostetler, Columbus, Ohio; chmn. Firmwide Healthcare Practice Group. Mem. ABA, Columbus Bar Assn. (chmn. Health law com.), Am. Acad. Hosp. Attys., Nat. Health Lawyers Assn., Soc. Ohio Hosp. Attys., Phi Beta Kappa, Phi Kappa Phi, Phi Delta Phi. Office: Baker & Hostetler 65 E State St Ste 2100 Columbus OH 43215*

SIEK, RAINER, broadcast executive. Pres. CBS Enterprises, N.Y.C. Office: CBS Enterprises 51 W 52d St New York NY 10019*

SIEKERT, ROBERT GEORGE, neurologist; b. Milw., July 23, 1924; s. Hugo Paul and Elisa (Kraus) S.; m. Mary Jane Evans, Feb. 17, 1951; children: Robert G. Jr., John E., Friedrich A.P. BS, Northwestern U., 1945, MS, 1947, MD, 1948. Cert. Am. Bd. Psychiatry and Neurology. Instr. anatomy U. Pa., Phila., 1948-49; fellow neurology Mayo Found., Rochester, Minn., 1950-54; cons. Mayo Clinic, Rochester, 1954-91, head neurology sect., 1966-76, bd. govs., 1973-80, prof. neurology med. sch., 1969—; chmn. Internat. Stroke Conf. Am. Heart Assn., 1976-80. Editor Mayo Clinic Procs., 1982-86; cons. editor Jour. Stroke, 1992—; contbr. articles to profl. jours. Trustee Mayo Found., Rochester, 1973-81. Served to lt. j.g. M.C., USNR, 1950-52. Recipient Disting. Achievement award Am. Heart Assn., 1984, Merit award, 1989, Robert G. Siekert Young Investigator award Am. Heart Assn., 1986. Fellow Am. Coll. Physicians; mem. Am. Neurol. Assn., Northwestern U. Med. Sch. Alumni Assn. (Service award 1983), Swiss Neurol. Soc. (corr.), Alpha Omega Alpha. Avocation: philately. Office: Mayo Clinic 200 1st St SW Rochester MN 55905-0001

SIEKMAN, THOMAS CLEMENT, lawyer; b. Somerville, Mass., Sept. 22, 1941; s. Aloysius C. and Estelle M. (Forte) S.; m. Claire Dorgan, Oct. 15, 1966; children: Michael T., James T., Amy K. BS in Engring., Merrimack Coll., 1963; JD, Villanova U., 1966. Bar: Mass. 1966, U.S. Dist. Ct. Mass. 1969. Patent atty. Bethlehem (Pa.) Steel, 1966-68, Mohawk Data Scis., Stoneham, Mass., 1968-72, Chittick, Thompson & Pfund, Boston, Mass., 1972-73; from patent atty. to v.p. and gen. counsel Digital Equipment Corp., Maynard, Mass., 1973—; bd. dirs. N.E. chpt. Am. Corp. Coun. Assn., Ashland, Mass., Associated Industries Mass., Boston, N.E. Legal Found., Boston; mem. legal quality coun. Conf. Bd. Trustees Mass. Trustee Mass. Taxpayers Found.; mem. New Eng. Legal Found. Mem. ABA, Am. Soc. Corp. Secs., Internat. Bar Assn., Law Coun. Mfrs.' Alliance for Productivity & Innovation. Avocations: squash, skiing. Home: 73 Edgewater Dr Needham MA 02192-2745 Office: Digital Equipment Corp 111 Powdermill Rd Maynard MA 01754-1482

SIEKMANN, DONALD CHARLES, accountant; b. St. Louis, July 2, 1938; s. Elmer Charles and Mabel Louise (Blue) S.; m. Linda Lee Knowles, Sept. 10, 1966; 1 child, Brian Charles. BS, Washington U., St. Louis, 1960. CPA, Ohio, Ga. Regional mng. ptnr. Arthur Andersen & Co., Cin., 1960—. Columnist Cin. Enquirer, 1983-86, Gannett News Services, 1983-86; editor "Tax Clinic" column Tax Advisor mag., 1974-75. Mem. bd. Cin. Zool. Soc., 1985-88; officer, bd. dirs. Cin. Found. for Pub. TV, 1984-88, Cin. Symphony Orch., 1973-85, Cin. Ballet Co., 1973-88, Cin. Theatrical Assn., Jewish Hosp., 1993—, Cin. Assn. for Performing Arts, 1992—, Cin. United Way, 1992—, Cin. Pk. Bd. Found., 1995—. Mem. AICPA, Ohio Soc. CPAs, Cin. Country Club (trustee 1983-88), Optimists Club (pres. Queen City chpt. 1986). Lutheran. Club: Cin. Country (trustee 1983-88). Home: 5495 Waring Dr Cincinnati OH 45243-3933 Office: Arthur Andersen & Co 425 Walnut St Ste 1500 Cincinnati OH 45202-3916

SIELICKI-KORCZAK, BORIS ZDZISLAW, political educator, investigative consultant; b. Wilno, Lithuania, Poland, Feb. 11, 1939; came to U.S., 1980; s. Wiltold and Antonina (Arciszewski) Sielicki-Korczak; m. Barbara Maria Kaniewski, May 29, 1971; children: Robert, Sandra. MSC, Warsaw U., 1964, Kunstindustriskole, Copenhagen, 1971; PhD, Basel (Switzerland) U., 1973. Pres. Impolex Ltd., Copenhagen, 1970-79; field operative Europe CIA, 1983-90; pres., educator Anti-Soviet Rsch. Ctr., McLean, Va., 1981-84; export dir. Worldwide Investment Ltd., Arlington, Va., 1985-87; pres. Amexim Internat. Co. Ltd., Arlington, 1986-89, BK & Assocs., Arlington, 1990—, Boris S. de Korczak, Inc., Fairfax Station, Va.; pres. R.R. Internat. Ltd., Copenhagen, 1983-89; mng. dir. Securitas Inc., Arlington, 1986-87; multiple appearance on U.S. and fgn. TV shows as expert on terrorism, USSR and Russian intelligence and its ops. Author: A Man From Atlantis, 1976; designer anti-drug poster. Dir. Nat. Lyric Opera Co., Washington, 1981-91. Republican. Avocations: chess, classic music, travel, art, history. Office: PO Box 7153 Fairfax Station VA 22039

SIELOFF, DEBRA ANN, educational administrator, consultant; b. Mt. Clemens, Mich.. BA in Journalism, Oakland U., 1990; postgrad., U. Ariz. Instrnl. sys. designer Chrysler Corp., Detroit, 1978-80, Boeing Vertol, Phila., 1980-82; engring. stds. analyst E.I. DuPont Biomed. Engring. Divsn., Wilmington, Del., 1982-83; computer sys. job performance aid designer Dayco Corp. Internat., Ohio, 1983-84; mng. editor Arabians Mag., Mich., 1984-85; midsize market configuration mgr. GM, Mich., 1985-92; tech. awareness tng. mgr. Ford-UAW Nat. Tng. Ctr., Mich., 1992-93; edn. program mgr. Biosphere 2, Oracle, Ariz., 1993—; dir. One Interactive Prodns., Ariz., 1994—; mem. adv. bd. Tucson Resource Ctr. for Environ. Edn., Tucson Children's Mus., 1994, 95; mem. curriculum rev. com. Ariz. Riparian Coun., Phoenix, 1993; nat. edn. advisor Environ. Health Found., Ariz., 1994—. Recipient Wildlife Artist award Cranbrook Mus. of Natural History, 1975. Mem. NSTA, ASCD, Internat. Assn. Bus. Communicators (renaissance awards chairperson 1992-93), Sierra Club. Home: 1460 E Grimaldi Pl Tucson AZ 85737-3436 Office: Sieloff & Sokol Inc 10450 N La Canada Dr Ste 155 Oro Valley AZ 85737

SIEMENS, TERRANCE LEE, patent agent; b. Waterloo, Iowa, May 4, 1938; s. Curtis Wieben and Vera Mae (Heitman) S.; m. Caroline Vera Camille Runge, 1958 (div. 1973); children: Emillee, Douglas, Lynn, William, Thomas; m. Suzanne Collins; 1 child, Mark Collins Gregory. BSME, Iowa State U., 1962; MS, U. Ill., 1972. Rsch. engr. Deere & Co., Moline, Ill., 1960-70; primary examiner U.S. Patent Office, Washington, 1973-86; pres. Siemens Patent Svcs., Fairfax, Va., 1987—; expert witness in field, 1993—. Served in U.S. Army, 1958-60. Mem. Lions (pres. Crystal City club 1990—). Office: Siemens Patent Svcs 703 23rd St S Arlington VA 22202-2419

SIEMER, DEANNE CLEMENCE, lawyer; b. Buffalo, Dec. 25, 1940; d. Edward D. and Dorothy J. (Helsdon) S.; m. Howard P. Willens; 1 child, Jason L. BA, George Washington U., 1962; LLB, Harvard U., 1968. Bar: N.Y. 1968, D.C. 1969, Md. 1972, Trust Ter. 1976. Economist Office of Mgmt. and Budget, Washington, 1964-67; assoc., then ptnr. Wilmer, Cutler & Pickering, Washington, 1968-90; ptnr. Pillsbury, Madison & Sutro, Washington, 1990-95; mng. dir. Wilsie Co., Saipan, M.P., 1995—; gen. counsel U.S. Dept. of Def., Washington, 1977-79; spl. asst. to sec. U.S. Dept. of Energy, Washington, 1979-80. Author: Tangible Evidence, 1984, 3d edit., 1996, Understanding Modern Ethical Standards, 1985, Manual on Litigation Support Databases, 1986, supplement, 1992. Mem. Lawyers Com. for Civil Rights, Washington, 1973—; mediator D.C. Superior Ct., Washington, 1986—, U.S. Ct. Appeals, Washington, 1988—; chair Nat. Inst. Trial Advocacy, Am. Law Inst., 1995—. Recipient Citation Air Force Assn., 1977, Dist. Pub. Service medal Sec. of Def., 1979, Commendation Pres. of U.S. 1981. Mem. ABA, ATLA, Am. Law Inst., D.C. Bar Assn., No. Marianas Bar Assn., Womens Bar Assn. Episcopalian. Office: Wilsic Co Macaranas Bldg 1st Fl PO Box 909 Saipan MP 96950

SIEMER, FRED HAROLD, securities analyst; b. Mt. Vernon, N.Y., Apr. 3, 1937; s. Fred Henry and Doris Sophie (Peymann) S.; m. Barbara Jean Behrmann, May 20, 1960 (div. 1980); children: Carolyn Doris Baird, Charles Frederick, Janet Ann Bruno; m. Mary Brittain Brown, Aug. 20, 1981 (dec. Sept. 1992). BA in Chemistry, Colgate U., Hamilton, N.Y., 1958; MBA, Fairleigh Dickinson U., Rutherford, N.J., 1970. Cert. fin. analyst. Mgr. rsch. planning Allied Chem. Corp., Morristown, N.J., 1962-69; mgr. econ. evaluation BASF Corp., Parsippany, N.J., 1969-72; chems. analyst Prudential Ins. Co., Newark, 1972-74; v.p. rsch. F.Eberstadt & Co., Inc., N.Y.C., 1974-80, Smith Barney Harris Upham, N.Y.C., 1980-85; pres. Siemer & Co., N.Y.C., 1985-93, F. H. Siemer & Co., Inc., N.Y.C., 1993—. Editor: Chemical Research For Wall St.; contbr. articles to profl. jours. With U.S. Army, 1959-62. Mem. Am. Chem. Soc., N.Y. Soc. Securities Analysts, Assn. for Investment Mgmt. and Rsch., Chem. Analysts of N.Y. and Chem. Specialists of N.Y., Chem. Mktg. Rsch. Assn., Chem. Mktg. Rsch. and Econs. Grp., Soc. de Chemie Indsl. Avocations: reading, walking, tennis, music. Office: F H Siemer & CoInc 500 E 83rd St New York NY 10028-7201

SIEMER, PAUL JENNINGS, public relations executive; b. St. Louis, Jan. 24, 1946; s. Robert Vincent and Pauline Mary (Nece) S.; m. Susan MacDonald Arnott, Aug. 26, 1967. Student, U. Notre Dame, 1964-67. Reporter South Bend Tribune, Ind., 1967-69; reporter St. Louis Globe-Democrat, 1969-76; account exec. Fleishman-Hillard Inc., St. Louis, 1976-79, v.p., sr. ptnr., 1979-84, exec. v.p., sr. ptnr., 1984-95; ptnr. Stolberg & Siemer Inc., St. Louis, 1995—. Mem. Pub. Relations Soc. Am. Roman Catholic. Club: St. Louis Press. Home: 2961 Hatherly Dr Saint Louis MO 63121-4551 Office: Stolberg & Siemer Inc 1608 Menard Saint Louis MO 63104

SIENER, WILLIAM HAROLD, museum director, historian, consultant; b. Silver Creek, N.Y., Feb. 24, 1945; s. Harold Edwin and Christian (Dovesmith) S.; m. Estelle Minervino, Dec. 27, 1968; children: Alison Louise, Christian Dovesmith, Geoffrey David. AB, U. Rochester, 1967; MAT, U. Chgo., 1970; MA, U. Southampton, Eng., 1973; PhD, College William & Mary, 1982. Cert. social studies tchr., N.Y. Tchr. Cen. YMCA High Sch., Chgo., 1968-71; dir. youth svcs. City of Niagara Falls (N.Y.) Youth Bd., 1973; historian Gloucester County (Va.) Hist. Bicentennial Com., 1976; exec. dir. Wyo. Hist. and Geol. Soc., Wilkes-Barre, Pa., 1976-82; curator of history Rochester (N.Y.) Mus. and Sci. Ctr., 1982-86; exec. dir. Buffalo and Erie County (N.Y.) Hist. Soc., 1986—; curator various gallery exhibits, 1976—; mem. adv. bds. Pa. State Hist. Records, 1982, Documentary Heritage Program, Buffalo, 1986-92; adj. assoc. prof. dept. History Buffalo State Coll., 1987—; historian County of Erie, Buffalo, 1988—; cons. Arts Devel. Svcs., Buffalo, 1983, OAS, The Bahamas, 1984, 85, St. Lucia, 1985, 89; mem. Buffalo Preservation Bd., 1986-91; speaker N.Y. Speakers in the Humanities program N.Y. Coun. Humanities, 1992—. Author: (brochure) Silent Sentinel of the Shallow Seas, 1988; (catalog) The Lake Erie Shore: Views from Across the Border; co-author: (exhibit catolog) Children and Their Samplers, 1790-1850, 1983; co-editor: (manuscript guide) A Guide to Gloucester County Virginia, Historical Manuscripts, 1650-1865, 1976.; book and exhibit reviewer profl. jours., 1981—. Active Buffalo Preservation Bd., 1986-91, Leadership Buffalo, 1991; clk. of session Westminster Presbyn. Ch., Buffalo, 1991-92, Choir of Men & Boys St. Paul's Episc. Cathedral, Buffalo, 1993—; del. People to People Citizen Amb. Program Exchange to Russia, 1993; mem. adv. bd. Shakespeare in Delaware Park, Inc., Buffalo, 1993—; trustee Cmty. Music Sch., Buffalo, 1993—; mem. N.Y. Commr. of Edn.'s Task Force on the Future of Mus. in N.Y. State, 1994—. Mem. Am. Assn. Mus. (panel mem. 1985), Mid-Atlantic Assn. Mus. (chmn. internat. com. 1987-88), Am. Assn. for State and Local History, Nat. Trust for Hist. Preservation, Inst. Early Am. History and Culture (assoc.), Mid-Atlantic Assn. Mus's (vice-chmn. small mus. com. 1981-82, panel mem. 1982), Rotary. Democrat. Avocations: travel, camping, swimming, music, photography. Home: 264 Middlesex Rd Buffalo NY 14216-3118 Office: Buffalo/Erie County Hist Soc 25 Nottingham Ct Buffalo NY 14216-3119

SIEPI, CESARE, opera singer; b. Milan, Italy, Feb. 10, 1923. Operatic debut in Rigoletto, Schio, 1941, Il Nabucco, LaScala Opera, Milan, 1946, Don Carlo, Met. Opera, N.Y.C., 1950; soloist debut in, Carnegie Hall, N.Y.C., 1951; sang in Mozart and Verdi requiems, Edinburgh Festival, Albert Hall, London; leading bass at, Salzburg Festival, LaScala, Milan; appeared in: play Bravo Giovanni, 1962; appeared: play Vienna Staatsoper; made many opera recordings for, London Records. (Winner Nat. Singing Competition, Florence 1941, recipient Italy's Orfeo award 1956). Operatic debut, Rigoletto, Schio, at age of 18. Home: 12095 Brookfield Club Dr Roswell GA 30075-1261 Office: c/o SA Gorlinsky Ltd, 33 Dover St, London W1X 4NJ, England

SIERLES, FREDERICK STEPHEN, psychiatrist, educator; b. Bklyn., Nov. 9, 1942; s. Samuel and Elizabeth (Meiselman) S.; m. Laurene Harriet Cohn, Oct. 25, 1970 (div. Aug. 1990); children: Hannah Beth, Joshua Caleb. AB, Columbia U., 1963; MD, Chgo. Med. Sch., 1967. Diplomate Am. Bd. Psychiatry and Neurology. Intern Cook County Hosp., Chgo., 1967-68; resident in psychiatry Mt. Sinai Hosp., N.Y.C., 1968-69, Chgo. Med. Sch., 1969-71, chief resident, 1970-71; staff psychiatrist U.S. Reynolds Army Hosp., Ft. Sill, Okla., 1971-73; assoc. attending psychiatrist Mt. Sinai Hosp., Chgo., 1973-74; instr. psychiatry Chgo. Med. Sch., North Chicago, 1973-74, dir. undergrad. edn. in psychiatry, 1974-94, asst. prof., 1974-78, assoc. prof., 1978-88, prof., Finch U. Health Scis, Chgo. Med. Sch., 1988—, vice chmn., 1990-94, acting chmn., 1994-95, chmn., 1995—, chmn. ednl. affairs com., 1983-85, 86—, chmn. univ. tenure com. 1983-84, 88-94; cons. psychiatry Cook County Hosp., 1974-79, St. Mary of Nazareth Hosp., 1979-84, Great Lakes Naval Hosp., 1987-90, Jackson Park Hosp., 1987-89, Mt. Sinai Hosp., 1988—; chief Mental Health Clinic, North Chicago VA Hosp., 1982-85, chief psychiatry svc., 1983-85. Author: (with others) General Hospital Psychiatry, 1985, Behavioral Science for the Boreds, 1987, rev. 2d edit., 1989, rev. 3rd edit., 1993; editor: Clinical Behavioral Science, 1982, Behavioral Science for Medical Students, 1992; contbr. articles to profl. jours. Coach Glenview (Ill.) Youth Baseball, 1987-89, mgr., 1990 (age 10-12 Glenview World Series winner 1990), Glenview Tennis Club, 1986-90 (3.5 Men's Doubles League winner 1989-90). Maj., M.C., U.S. Army, 1971-73. Recipient Ganser Meml. award Mt. Sinai Hosp., 1970, Nancy C. Roeske award, 1991, Lawrence R. Medoff award, 1993; named Prof. of Yr. Chgo. Med. Sch., 1977, 80, 83, Disting. Alumnus, 1993; N.Y. State Regents scholar, 1959-63; NIMH grantee, 1974-83, Chgo. Med. Sch. grantee, 1974-83. Fellow Am. Psychiat. Assn. (coun. edn. & career devel. 1993-95); mem. Am. Coll. Psychiatrists, Ill. Psychiat. Soc. (fellowship com. 1985—), Columbia Coll. Alumni Secondary Schs. Com., Assn. Dirs. Med. Student Edn. in Psychiatry (exec. council 1985—, chmn. program com. 1987-88, treas. 1989-91, pres. elect 1991-93, pres. 1993-95, immediate past pres. 1995—), Alliance for Clin. Edn., Assn. of Chmn. of Depts. of Psychiatry (Chgo. consortium for psychiatric rsch. 1994—, sec. 1996—), Sigma Xi, Alpha Omega Alpha, Phi Epsilon Pi. Office: Finch U Health Sci Chgo Med Sch 3333 Green Bay Rd North Chicago IL 60064-3037

SIERRA, ROBERTO, composer, music educator; b. Vega Baja, P.R., Oct. 9, 1953. Grad., P.R. Conservatory of Music, U. P.R., 1976; postgrad., Royal Coll. Music, London, U. London, 1976-78, Inst. Sonology, Utrecht, The Netherlands, 1978; studied with Gyorgy Ligeti, Hamberg (Germany) Hochschule for Music, 1979-82. Asst. dir. cultural activities dept. U. P.R., 1983-85, dir., 1985-86, dean of studies, 1986-87; chancellor P.R. Conservatory of Music, 1987—; prof. composition Cornell U., Ithaca, N.Y., 1992—; composer-in-residence Milw. Symphony Orch., 1989-92. Compositions include: (orchestral) Jubilo, 1985, Cuatro ensayos orquestales, 1986, Glosas for piano and orch., 1987, Descargo, 1988, Sasima, 1990; (chamber) Tiempo Muerto for string quartet, 1978, Salsa on the C String for cello and piano, 1981, Seis piezas fáciles for two violins, 1982, Bongo-O for percussion, 1982, Salsa for wind quintet, 1983, Cinco bocetos for clarinet, 1984, Concierto Nocturnal for harsichord, flute, clarinet, oboe, violin and cello, 1985, Memorias Tropicales for string quartet, 1985, El sueño de Antonia for clarinet and percussion, 1985, Toccata y Lamento for guitar, 1987, Essays for wind quintet, 1987, Mano a Mano for two percussionists, 1987, Introducción y Descarga for piano, brass quintet and percussion, 1988, Tributo for harp, flute, clarinet and string quartet, 1988; (piano) Descarga en sol, 1981; (stage) El Mensajero de Plata for chamber opera, 1984, El Comtemplado for ballet, 1987; (harpsichord) Tres Miniaturas, 1982, Con Salsa, 1984; (vocal) Cantos populares for chorus, 1983, Doña Rosita, 1985, Invocaciones, 1986, Glosa a la sombra, 1987; also, Entre terceras for 2 synthesizers and computer, 1988. Office: Conservatorio de Musica de PR Apt 41227, Minillas Station Santurce San Juan PR 00940 also: care Sandra Elm 411 W 21st St New York NY 10011-2950

SIERRA, RUBEN ANGEL GARCIA, professional baseball player; b. Rio Piedras, P.R., Oct. 6, 1965. Grad. high sch., Rio Piedras, P.R. Baseball player Tex. Rangers, 1982-92, Oakland Athletics, 1992-95, N.Y. Yankees, 1995—. Named Am. League Player of Yr., Sporting News, 1989, recipient Silver Slugger award, 1989; named to All-Star team, 1989, 91-92, 94; Am. League RBI Leader, 1989. Office: N.Y. Yankees E 161st St and River Ave Bronx NY 10451*

SIESS, CHESTER PAUL, civil engineering educator; b. Alexandria, La., July 28, 1916; s. Leo C. and Adele (Liebreich) S.; m. Helen Kranson, Oct. 5, 1941; 1 dau., Judith Ann. B.S., La. State U., 1936; M.S., U. Ill., 1939, Ph.D., 1948. Party chief La. Hwy. Commn., 1936-37; research asst. U. Ill., 1937-39; soil engr. Chgo. Subway Project, 1939-41; engr., draftsman N.Y.C. R.R. Co., 1941; mem. faculty U. Ill., 1941—, prof. civil engring., 1955-78, emeritus, head dept. civil engring., 1973-78; mem. adv. com. on reactor safeguards Nuclear Regulatory Commn., 1968-92, chmn., 1972. Recipient award Concrete Reinforcing Steel Inst., 1956, Alumni Honor award for disting. service in engring. U. Ill., 1985, Disting. Service award NRC, 1987; named to Engring. Hall of Distinction, La. State U., 1979. Mem. ASCE (hon. mem., Rsch. prize 1956, Howard medal 1968, Reese award 1970), Nat. Acad. Engring., Am. Concrete Inst. (pres. 1974—, Wason medal 1949, Turner medal 1964, hon. mem.), Reinforced Concrete Rsch. coun. (chmn. 1968-80, Baose award 1974), Internat. Assn. Bridge and Structural Engring., Sigma Xi, Tau Beta Pi, Phi Kappa Phi, Omicron Delta Kappa, Gamma Alpha, Chi Epsilon (chap. hon., nat. hon.). Research in reinforced and prestressed concrete structures and hwy. bridges. Home: 401 Burwash Dr Savoy IL 61874-9573 Office: Newmark Lab 205 N Mathews Ave Urbana IL 61801-2350

SIEVERS, ROBERT H., wholesale distributing company executive; b. San Francisco, Nov. 2, 1941; s. Howard H. and Minnie A. (Sommers) S.; m. Maureen; children: Kirk Robert, Allison Jill, Julie Paige, Jennifer Lori. B.A. in Finance, Calif. State U., 1968. C.P.A., Calif. Audit mgr. Hurdman and Cranston, San Francisco, 1966-76; treas. Falstaff Brewing Corp., San Francisco, 1976-77, also dir.; v.p. fin. Capital Film Labs., Washington, 1977-81; also v.p. fin. Forman Bros. Inc., and Forman Distbg. Co. of Va., Inc. Wholesale Distbrs., 1981—. Mem. AICPA, Calif. Soc. CPAs, D.C. Inst. CPAs. Home: 5522 Southwick St Bethesda MD 20817-3544 Office: 4235 Sheriff Rd NE Washington DC 20019-3736

SIFFERT, ROBERT SPENCER, orthopedic surgeon; b. N.Y.C., June 16, 1918; s. Oscar and Sadye (Rusoff) S.; m. Miriam Sand, June 29, 1941; children: Joan, John. AB in Biology with honors, NYU, 1939, MD, 1943. Diplomate Am. Bd. Orthop. Surgery, Nat. Bd. Med. Examiners. Intern Kings County Hosp., Bklyn., 1943; resident in orthop. surgery Mt. Sinai Hosp., N.Y.C., 1946-49, fellow in pathology, 1949-52, mem. staff, 1949—, dir. orthop. surgery, orthop. surgeon in chief, 1960-86, Lasker/Siffert Disting. Svc. prof., 1986—; pvt. practice N.Y.C., 1949—; dir. dept. orthops. City Hosp., Elmhurst, 1965-86; sr. orthop. cons. N.Y.C. Dept. Health, 1952-60; attending orthop. surgeon Blythedale Children's Hosp., Valhalla, N.Y., 1960-86, cons., 1986-90; prof., chmn. dept. orthops. Mt. Sinai Sch. Medicine, 1966-86, Dr. Robert K. Lippman prof., 1983-86, acting chmn., 1993-94. Contbr. over 100 articles to profl. jours. Mem. adv. bd. CARE-MEDICO, 1972-83, bd. dirs., 1981-83, chmn., 1981-83; bd. dirs. CARE, 1983-90; adv. bd. Orthopaedics Overseas, 1981-93; bd. dirs., mem. profl. adv. com. Easter Seal Soc. for Crippled Children and Adults, 1st v.p., 1977-79. Capt. USAAF, 1944-46, CBI. Decorated 4 Battle Stars; recipient annual award medicine N.Y. Pub. Health Assn., 1958, annual award medicine N.Y. Philanthropic League, 1959, Richman award for humanism in medicine Mt. Sinai Sch. Medicine, 1989. Fellow ACS, APHA; mem. Am. Orthop. Assn., Am. Acad. Orthop. Surgery (chmn. com. on care of handicapped child), Assn. Bone and Joint Surgeons, Internat. Soc. Orthop. Surgery and Traumatology, Internat. Skeletal Soc., Orthop. Rsch. Soc., N.Y. Acad. Medicine (fellow orthop. sect. 1952, sec. 1962-63, chmn. 1963-64), N.Y. State Med. Soc. (chmn. orthop. sect. 1967-68), Century Assn. (N.Y.C.), Phi Beta Kappa, Alpha Omega Alpha. Office: 955 5th Ave New York NY 10021-1738

SIFNEOS, PETER EMANUEL, psychiatrist; b. Greece, Oct. 22, 1920; came to U.S., 1941, naturalized, 1944; s. Demitrios Z. and Mary E. (Lucas) S.; divorced; children: Ann L., Peter G., Jean C. B.Sc., Sorbonne, 1940; M.D., Harvard U., 1946. Diplomate: Am. Bd. Psychiatry. Intern Boston City Hosp., 1946-47; resident in psychiatry McLean Hosp., Belmont, Mass., 1950-52; chief resident Mass. Gen. Hosp., Boston, 1952-53; mem. staff, chief psychiat. clinic Mass. Gen. Hosp., 1954-68; fellow Harvard U. Sch. Public Health, 1953-54; mem. faculty Harvard U. Med. Sch., 1952—, prof. psychiatry, 1973-91, prof. emeritus, 1991—; staff, assoc. dir. psychiatry dept. Beth Israel Hosp., Boston, 1968-94. Author: Ascent from Chaos, 1964, Short-Term Psychotherapy and Emotional Crisis, 1972, Short-Term Dynamic Psychotherapy and Emotional Crisis, 1972, Short-Term Dynamic P)sychotherapy Evaluation and Technique, 1979, 2d edit., 1987, Short-Term Anxiety Provking Psychotherapy, 1992; editor-in-chief Psychotherapy and Psychosomatics, 1974-91; contbr. 121 articles to profl. jours. Served with AUS, 1944-46, 47-50. Fellow Am. Psychiat. Assn. (life); mem. AMA, Internat. Fedn. Med. Psychotherapy (v.p. 1976-88, bd. dirs. 1988-94), Am. Psychosomatic Soc., Boston Psychoanalytic Soc. (life), Hellenic Psychosomatic Soc. (hon.), Italian Psychosomatic Soc. (hon.). Democrat. Home and Office: 59 Common St Belmont MA 02178-3022 *The principles which helped me most have been a belief in good education, a fierce sense of non-conformity, a strong sense of independence, an admiration of creativity and new ideas, a love of writing, teaching, reading, classic music, traveling to lecture and conduct workshops, seminars all over North and South America and Europe, swimming, and luck in being healthy.*

SIFTON, CHARLES PROCTOR, federal judge; b. N.Y.C., Mar. 18, 1935; s. Paul F. and Claire G. S.; m. Susan Scott Rowland, May 20, 1986; children: Samuel, Tobias, John. A.B., Harvard U., 1957; LL.B., Columbia U., 1961. Bar: N.Y. 1961. Assoc. Cadwalader, Wickersham & Taft, 1961-62, 64-66; staff atty. U.S. Senate Fgn. Rels. Com., 1962-63; asst. U.S. atty. N.Y.C., 1966-69; ptnr. LeBoeuf, Lamb, Leiby and MacRae, N.Y.C., 1969-77; judge U.S. Dist. Ct. (ea. dist.) N.Y., Bklyn., 1977—, chief judge, 1995—. Mem. Bar Assn. City of N.Y. Office: US Dist Ct US Courthouse 225 Cadman Plz E Brooklyn NY 11201-1818*

SIFTON, DAVID WHITTIER, magazine editor; b. N.Y.C., Sept. 12, 1940; s. David William and Dorothy (Whittier) S. B.A., Trinity Coll., Hartford, Conn., 1962; M.A., Stanford U., 1967. Editor Inside Edn., N.Y. State Edn. Dept., 1968-70; adminstrv. editor Med. Econs., Oradell, N.J., 1970-72; editor Drug Topics, Oradell, 1972-75; editor in chief Current Prescribing, Oradell, 1975-78, RN mag., Oradell, 1978-83; dir. spl. editorial projects Med. Econs. Co., 1983-90; mgr. PDR Devel., Oradell, 1990—; founder Physicians' Desk Reference on CD-ROM, PDR's Drug Interactions and Side Effects Index, PDR's Indications Index, Pocket PDR (handheld electronic database), The PDR Family Guide to Prescription Drugs, The PDR Family Guide to Women's Health, The PDR Family Guide to Nutrition and Health, The PDR Family Guide to Lifelong Health. Served to 1st lt. USAF, 1963-66. Decorated Air Force Commendation medal; grantee Ford Found., 1967. Mem. Am. Bus. Press (chmn. editorial com. 1975-76). Republican. Episcopalian. Office: Med Econs Co Inc 5 Paragon Dr Montvale NJ 07645-1725

SIFTON, ELISABETH, book publisher; b. N.Y.C., Jan. 13, 1939; d. Reinhold and Ursula (Keppel-Compton) Niebuhr; m. Charles P. Sifton, 1962 (div. 1984); children: Peter Samuel, Charles Tobias, John Paul Gustav; m. Fritz R. Stern, 1996. B.A. magna cum laude, Radcliffe Coll., Cambridge, Mass., 1960; postgrad., U. Paris, 1960-61. Asst. to dep. asst. sec. of state U.S. Dept. of State, Washington, 1961-62; editorial asst., assoc. editor, editor, sr. editor Frederick A. Praeger Pubs., N.Y.C., 1962-68; editor, sr. editor, editor-in-chief The Viking Press, N.Y.C., 1969-83; v.p., pub. Elisabeth Sifton Books, Viking Penguin, N.Y.C., 1984-87; exec. v.p. Alfred A. Knopf, Inc., N.Y.C., 1987-92; sr. v.p. Farrar, Straus & Giroux, 1993—; pub. Hill & Wang, 1993—. Fulbright fellow, 1960-61. Democrat. Episcopalian. Home: 15 Claremont Ave New York NY 10027-6814 Office: Farrar Straus & Giroux 19 Union Sq W New York NY 10003-3307

SIGAL, ISRAEL MICHAEL, mathematics educator; b. Kiev, Ukraine, Aug. 31, 1945; came to U.S., 1978; s. Moshe I. and Eva (Guz) S.; m. Brenda Lynn Tipper; children: Alexander, Daniel. BA, Gorky (Russia) U., 1968; PhD, Tel-Aviv U., 1976. Postdoctoral fellow Swiss Inst. Tech., Zürich, Switzerland, 1976-78; asst. prof. Princeton (N.J.) U., 1978-81; R.H. Revson sr. scientist Weizmann Inst., Rehovot, Israel, 1981-85; prof. U. Calif., Irvine, 1984-90, U. Toronto, Ont., Can., 1985—; invited spkr. various confs. in field including invited talk at Internat. Conf. Mathematicians, Kyoto, 1990; Jeffrey-Williams Lectureship, Can. Math. Soc., 1992. Editor Revs. Math. Physics, 1991—, Internat. Rsch. Notices, 1991—; contbr. articles to profl. and sci. publs. I.W. Killam Rsch. fellow I.W. Killam Found., 1989-91; recipient John L. Synge Award Royal Soc. Can., 1993. Fellow Royal Soc. Can. Office: U Toronto Dept Math, 100 St George St, Toronto, ON Canada M5S 3G3

SIGAL, MICHAEL STEPHEN, lawyer; b. Chgo., July 9, 1942; s. Carl I. and Evelyn (Wallack) S.; m. Kass M. Flaherty, May 16, 1971; 1 child, Sarah Caroline. BS, U. Wis.-Madison, 1964; JD, U. Chgo., 1967. Bar: Ill. 1967, U.S. Dist. Ct. (no. dist.) Ill. 1967. Assoc. firm Sidley & Austin and predecessor firm, Chgo., 1967-73, ptnr., 1973—. Mem. U. Chgo. Law Rev., 1965. Bd. dirs. EMRE Diagnostic Services, Inc., affiliate Michael Reese Hosp., Chgo., 1982-91, The Mary Meyer Sch., Chgo., 1986-87. Mem. ABA, Chgo. Bar Assn., Phi Beta Kappa, Phi Kappa Phi, Phi Eta Sigma. Jewish. Clubs: Law, Monroe (Chgo.); Mill Creek Hunt (bd. dirs. 1992—, Wadsworth, Ill.). Home: 2180 Wilmot Rd Deerfield IL 60015-1556 Office: Sidley & Austin 1 First Nat Plz Chicago IL 60603

SIGALL, HAROLD FRED, psychology educator; b. N.Y.C., June 29, 1943; s. Walter and Regine (Goldenberg) S.; m. Brenda Ann Alpert, Aug. 8, 1965; children: Elana, Jennifer, Emily. BS, CUNY, 1964; PhD, U. Tex., 1968. Asst. prof. psychology U. Rochester, N.Y., 1968-72; assoc. prof. U. Md., College Park, 1972-78, prof., 1978—, dir. grad. program in social psychology; consulting editor Journal of Applied Social psychology, 1992—; cons. social research and decision making to numerous orgns., lectr. Smithsonian Inst., Washington, 1984, 85. Editor Personality and Social Psychology Bull., 1977-81; contbr. numerous articles to profl. jours. Bd. dirs. Columbia (Md.) Jewish Congregation, 1985-87, Howard County (Md.) Jewish Cmty. Sch., Columbia, 1986-87; mem. Human Rights Commn., Howard County, 1994—. NDEA fellow, 1967-68, Danforth Found. fellow, 1970-71. Fellow Am. Psychol. Assn., Am. Psychol. Soc.; mem. Soc. Exptl. Social Psychology. Home: 5060 Castlemoor Dr Columbia MD 21044-1454 Office: U of Md Dept Psychology College Park MD 20742

SIGALOW, STEVEN E., lawyer; b. Akron, Ohio, May 12, 1950. BA, Ohio State U., 1972; JD, Case Western Reserve U., 1975. Bar: Ohio 1975. Ptnr. Jones, Day, Reavis & Pogue, Cleve. Mem. Phi Beta Kappa, Order of Coif. Office: Jones Day Reavis & Pogue 901 Lakeside Ave Cleveland OH 44114*

SIGBAND, NORMAN BRUCE, management communication educator; b. Chgo., June 27, 1920; s. Max and Bessie S.; m. Joan C. Lyons, Aug. 3, 1944; children: Robin, Shelley, Betsy. BA, U. Chgo., 1940, MA, 1941, PhD, 1954; LHD (hon.), DePaul U., 1986. Asst. prof. bus. communication De Paul U., 1946-50, assoc. prof., 1950-54, prof., 1954-65; prof. mgmt. communication U. So. Calif., 1965—, chmn. dept. mktg., 1970-72; assoc. dean U. So. Calif. (Sch. Bus.), 1975-80, Disting. prof. emeritus, 1989—; Disting. Centennial lectr. U. Tex., Austin, 1986; cons. to industry; speaker, condr. workshops, seminars in field; Scholar in Residence, Va. Commonwealth U., 1987, DePaul U., 1988; Disting. emeritus prof. U. So. Calif., 1989.. Author books including: Practical Communication for Everyday Use, 25th edit., 1954, Effective Report Writing for Business, Industry and Government, 1960, Communication for Management, 1970, Communicacion Para Directivos, 1972, Management Communication for Decision Making, 1972, Communication for Management and Business, 1976, Communication for Managers, 6th edit., 1994, Communicating in Business, 1987, 3d edit., 1989, Patient-Pharmacist Consultation: A Communication Skills Approach, 1993, Communication for Pharmacists and Other Health Professionals, 1995, 2d edit., 1996; movies include: Communication Barriers and Gateways, 2d edit., 1993, Listening: A Key to Problem Solving (award winnter), 2d edit., 1993, The Grapevine, The Power of a Minute, 1992; gen. editor books including: Harcourt Brace Jovanovich Bus. series; contbr. numerous articles to profl. jours., mags. Served to capt. AUS, 1942-46, ETO. Decorated Bronze Star; recipient Excellence in Teaching award U. So. Calif., 1975, Dean's award, 1972, Outstanding Educator award, 1973, Disting. Emeritus award, 1989. Fellow Am. Bus. Communication Assn. (pres. 1964-65); mem. Internat. Communication Assn., Acad. Mgmt., Anti-Defamation League, Hadassah Assocs., Blue Key, Phi Kappa Phi, Alpha Kappa Psi, Beta Gamma Sigma. Democrat. Jewish. Home: 3109 Dona Susana Dr Studio City CA 91604-4355 Office: U So Calif Health Sci Campus 1985 Zonal Ave Los Angeles CA 90033-1058

SIGEL, MARSHALL ELLIOT, financial consultant; b. Hartford, Conn., Nov. 25, 1941; s. Paul and Bessie (Somer) S.; m. Sybil R. Miller, Nov. 23, 1995. BS in Econs., U. Pa., 1963; JD, U. Miami, 1982, LLM in Taxation, 1983. Exec. v.p. Advo-System div. KMS Industries, Inc., Hartford, 1963-69, pres., 1969-72; pres. Ad-Type Corp., Hartford, 1963-69, Ad-Lists, Inc., Hartford, 1963-69; fin. cons. Hartford, 1972-83, Boca Raton, Fla., 1987—; pvt. practice law, 1983-87. Bd. dirs. Wharton Sch. Club of South Fla.; mem. citizen's bd. U. Miami. Mem. FOPA, World Pres.' Orgn., citizens bd. U. Miami, Boca Grove Club, 100 Club of So. Palm Beach County. Home and Office: PO Box 273408 Boca Raton FL 33427-3408

SIGETY, CHARLES BIRGE, health care supply manufacturing company executive; b. N.Y.C., Sept. 30, 1952; s. Charles Edward and Katharine Kinne (Snell) S.; m. Elizabeth Ross Pennington, Nov. 27, 1976; children: Austin Douglas, Katharine Colyer, Alexander Birge. BA in English Lit., Bates Coll., 1975. Lic. nursing home adminstr. Adminstr. in tng. Florence Nightingale Nursing Home, N.Y.C., 1972, asst. dir. facility ops., 1975, dir. facility ops., 1975-78, assoc. adminstr., 1978-81, exec. dir., 1981-82; pres., CEO Profl. Med. Products, Inc., Greenwood, S.C., 1982-96; dir. Upper Savannah Internat. Trade Assn., Greenwood, 1993-94, pres., 1993; prin. Bison Investments, Inc., 1996—; mem. Liberty Mutual Ins. Cos. S.C. Adv. Bd., 1986-96; mem. Nations Bank's S.C. Adv. Bd., 1984-96; bd. dirs. Profl. Med. Products, Inc.; mem. County Bank Adv. Bd., Greenwood, 1981; vice chmn. Upper Savannah Bus. Group on Health Care, Greenwood, 1982-87; mem. S.C. Bus. Roundtable for The Initiative for Work Force Excellence, Columbia, 1988-92; dir., mem. exec. com. OSTEO Am., Inc., 1993—; bd. dir. Help for Incontinent People, 1993-96. Bd. visitors Med. U. S.C., 1988. Mem. Young Pres. Orgn., Am. Coll. of Health Care Adminstrs., Health Industry Mfrs. Assn. (official rep. 1982-96), Upper Savannah Internat. Trade Assn. (pres. 1993). Republican. Presbyterian. Avocations: hunting, sailing, woodworking. Office: Bison Investments Inc No 236 3225 S MacDill Ave Tampa FL 33629

SIGETY, CHARLES EDWARD, lawyer, family business consultant; b. N.Y.C., Oct. 10, 1922; s. Charles and Anna (Toth) S.; m. Katharine K. Snell, July 17, 1948; children: Charles, Katharine, Robert, Cornelius, Elizabeth. BS, Columbia U., 1944; MBA, Harvard U., 1947; LLB, Yale U., 1951; LHD (hon.), Cazenovia Coll., 1994. Bar: N.Y. 1952, D.C. 1958. With Bankers Trust Co., 1939-42; instr. adminstrv. engring. Pratt Inst., 1948; instr. econs. Yale U., 1948-50; vis. lectr. acctg. Sch. Gen. Studies Columbia U., N.Y.C., 1948-50, 52; rapporteur com. fed. taxation for U.S. coun. Internat. C. of C., 1952-53; asst. to com. fed. taxation Am. Inst. Accts., 1950-53; with Compton Advt. Agy., N.Y.C., 1954; vis. lectr. law Yale U., 1952; pvt. practice law N.Y.C., 1952-67; pres., dir. Video Vittles, Inc., N.Y.C., 1953-67; dep. commr. FHA, 1955-57; of counsel Javits and Javits, 1959-60; 1st asst. atty. gen. N.Y., 1958-59; dir., mem. exec. com. Gotham Bank, N.Y.C., 1961-63; dir. N.Y. State Housing Fin. Agy., 1962-63; chmn. Met. Ski Slopes, Inc., N.Y.C., 1962-65; pres., exec. adminstr. Florence Nightingale Health Ctr., N.Y.C., 1965-85; chmn. bd. Profl. Med. Products, Inc., Greenwood, S.C., 1982-96; dir. Schaerer AG, Wabern, Switzerland, 1982-88; professorial lectr. Sch. Architecture, Pratt Inst., N.Y.C., 1962-66; mem. Sigety Assocs., cons. in housing mortgage financing and urban renewal, 1957-67; ho. cons. Govt. of Peru, 1956; mem. missions to Hungary, Poland, Fed. Republic Germany, Malta, Czechoslovakia, Russia, Israel, Overseas Pvt. Investment Corp., 1990-92; owner, operator Peppermill Farms, Pipersville, Pa., 1956—. Bd. dirs., sec., v.p., treas. Nat. Coun. Health Ctrs., 1969-85; bd. dirs. Am.-Hungarian Found., 1974-76, Pritikin Rsch. Found., 1991—, Stratford Arms Condo Assn., 1992-93, Global LEadership Inst., 1993—; trustee Cazenovia (N.Y.) Coll., 1981-95; del. White House Conf. on Aging, 1971, White House Conf. on Mgmt. Tng. and Market Econs. Edn. in Ctrl. and Ea. Europe, 1991; bd. visitors Lander Coll., U. S.C., Greenwood, 1982-84; mem. fin. com. World Games, Santa Clara, 1981, London, 1985, Karlsruhe, 1989, The Hague, 1993, Confrerie des Chevaliers du Tastevin, Confrerie de la Chaine des Rotisseurs, Wine and Food Soc., Wednesday 10. Recipient President's medal Cazenovia Coll., 1990; Baker scholar Harvard U., 1947. Mem. Harvard Bus. Sch. Assn. (exec. coun. 1966-69, area chmn. 1967-69), Townsend Harris Alumni Assn. (bd. dirs. 1993—), Yale Club (N.Y.C.), Harvard Bus. Sch. Club (N.Y.C., pres. 1964-65, chmn. 1965-66, bd. dirs. 1964-70), Harvard Club (N.Y.C.), Met. Club (Washington), Alpha Kappa Psi, Phi Delta Phi. Presbyterian. Home: 3600 S Ocean Blvd Boca Raton FL 33432 Office: 1760 3d Ave New York NY 10029

SIGGINS, JACK ARTHUR, librarian; b. Arp, Tex., July 11, 1938; s. Wilbur McCulla and Dayle Marie (Hensley) S.; m. Maureen Ellen Sullivan, Sept. 1, 1984. B.A., Princeton U., 1960; postgrad. law, U. Va., 1961-62; M.A., Am. U., 1967, U. Chgo., 1969. Research analyst Library of Congress, Washington, 1965-66; Librarian Far Eastern Library, U. Chgo., 1968-70; head East Asia Coll. U. Md., College Park, 1970-75, asst. dir. libraries, 1975-

77, assoc. dir. libraries, 1977-82; dep. univ. librarian Yale U., New Haven, 1982-92; pvt. practice orgnl. cons. New Haven, 1993-94; univ. libr. George Washington U., Washington, 1995—; cons. Boston Coll. 1994, U. Mo., 1994, Harvard U., 1994, Nat. Libr. of Australia, 1993, Ctrl. Mich. U., 1993, Tulane U., 1993; advisor Md. Dept. Edn., Balt., 1978-82; mem. adv. com. Sch. Libr. Sci. So. Conn. State U., New Haven, 1981-88; vis. com. Princeton U. Libr., 1987—. Contbr. articles to profl. jours. Served with U.S. Army, 1961-64, Japan. Far Eastern Studies fellow Ford Found., 1966; Title II fellow U. Chgo., 1967-70; fellow Davenport Coll., Yale U., 1983-92. Mem. ALA (univ. libr. standards com. 1985-88), Beta Phi Mu. Club: Princeton (N.Y.C.). Office: George Washington U Gelman Libr Washington DC 20052

SIGHOLTZ, SARA O'MEARA, nonprofit organization executive; b. Knoxville, Tenn.; m. Robert Sigholtz; children: John; stepchildren: Taryn, Whitney. Attended, Briarcliff Jr. Coll.; BA, The Sorbonne, Paris; D (hon.), Endicott Coll. Co-founder, chmn. bd., CEO CHILDHELP USA/Internat. (formerly Children's Village USA), Scottsdale, Ariz., 1974—. Bd. dirs. Internat. Soc. Prevention Child Abuse and Neglect, Children to Children, Inc.; hon. com. mem. Learning Disabilities Found., Inc.; mem. Mayor's adv. bd., Defense for Children Internat., Nat. Soc. Prevention Cruelty to Children, World Affairs Coun.; adv. bd. mem. Ednl. Film Co.; bd. dirs. Internat. Alliance on Child Abuse and Neglect; sustaining mem. Spastic Children's League, past pres.; mem., past recording sec. Assistance League So. Calif. Recipient Cross of Merit, Knightly Order of St. Brigitte, 1967, Victor M. Carter Diamond award Japan-Am. Soc., 1970, Dame Cross of Merit of Order of St. John of Denmark, 1980, Official Seal of 34th Gov. Calif., 1981, Woman of Achievement award Career Guild, 1982, Women Making History award Nat. Fedn. Bus. Profl. Women's Clubs, 1983, Disting. Am. award for svc., 1984, Humanitarian award Nat. Frat. Eagles, 1984, Nat. Recognition award outstanding leadership Am. Heritage Found., 1986, Notable Am. award svc. to Calif., 1986, Dove of Peace award Pacific Southwest and Ctrl. Pacific Regions B'nai B'rith, 1987, Paul Harris fellow award Rotary Found., 1989, Love and Help the Children award, 1990, Presdl. award, 1990, Hubert Humphrey award Touchdown Club Washington, 1994, numerous others. Mem. SAG, AFTRA, Victory Awards (exec. com.), Am. Biographical Inst. (nat. bd. advisors), Alpha Delta Kappa (hon.). Office: Childhelp USA 15757 N 78th St Scottsdale AZ 85260

SIGINER, DENNIS AYDENIZ, mechanical engineering educator, researcher; b. Ankara, Turkey, July 10, 1943; came to U.S., 1976; s. Kazim Siginer and Emine Turkoz; m. Julya Yalcin, Nov. 25, 1994. BS, MS with honors, Tech. U. Istanbul, 1966, ScD, 1971; PhD, U. Minn., 1982. Rsch. assoc. U. Minn., Mpls., 1976-80; asst. prof. U. Ala., Tuscaloosa, 1981-83; assoc. prof. Auburn (Ala.) U., 1984-92, prof. mech. engring., 1992—; organizer, chmn. several internat. and nat. confs.; invited speaker to several countries, fgn. and nat. instns., internat. and nat. meetings; reviewer NSF, Internat. Sci. Found., Jour. Non-Newtonian Fluid Mechanics, Jour. Engring. Sci., Rheologica Acta, Jour. Fluids and Structures, Jour. Fluids Engring., Jour. Heat Transfer, Jour. Dynamic Systems Measurement and Ctrl., Jour. Applied Mechanics, book revs. for pubs. Editor 11 books on devels. in non-Newtonian flows, electrorheol. fluids and fluid mechanics phenomena in microgravity; editor procs. of 1st East-West Conf. on advances in structured and heterogeneous continua, Moscow, 1993; author 4 books; contbr. more than 110 articles to profl. jours. Summer faculty fellow NASA, 1991, 92. Fellow ASME (organizer, editor procs. Symposium on Applications and Devels. Non-Netonian Flows 1995, Symposium on Rheology and Fluid Mechanics Nonlinear Materials 1996, svc. award 1993, 95), Sci. and Tech. Rsch. Coun. Turkey; mem. Am. Soc. Engring. Edn. (rsch. award 1992), Soc. Rheology, Am. Acad. Mechanics, Am. Inst. Physics, Soc. Engring. Sci., N.Y. Acad. Scis., Sigma Xi, Pi Tau Sigma (hon.). Home: 3809 Flintwood Ln Opelika AL 36801-7613 Office: Auburn U Dept Mech Engring Auburn AL 36849-5341

SIGLER, ANDREW CLARK, forest products company executive; b. Bklyn., Sept. 25, 1931; s. Andrew J. and Eleanor (Nicholas) S.; m. Margaret Romefelt, June 16, 1956; children: Andrew Clark, Patricia, Elizabeth. A.B., Dartmouth, 1953; M.B.A., Amos Tuck Sch., 1956. With Champion Papers Co., Hamilton, Ohio, 1957-72, corp. exec. v.p., 1972-74, pres., CEO, 1974-79, chmn., CEO, 1979—; pres. Champion Papers div. Champion Internat. Corp., 1972, exec. v.p., dir. parent co., 1972-74, pres., chief exec. officer, Stamford, Conn., 1974-79, chmn. bd., chief exec. officer, 1979—; dir. Bristol-Myers Squibb Co., Chem. Bank, Gen. Electric Co. Trustee Dartmouth Coll. Served from 2d lt. to 1st lt. USMCR, 1953-55. Office: Champion Internat Corp 1 Champion Plz Stamford CT 06921-0001*

SIGLER, HOLLIS, artist, educator; b. Gary, Ind., Mar. 2, 1948. Studied in Florence, Italy, 1968-69; BFA, Moore Coll. Art, 1970, DFA (hon.), 1994; MFA, Sch. Art Inst. Chgo., 1973. Mem. faculty Columbia Coll., Chgo., 1978—, instr. painting and drawing, 1984—. One-woman shows Akron (Ohio) Art Mus., 1986, S.W. Craft Ctr., San Antonio, 1989, Nat. Mus. Women Arts, Washington, 1991, 93, Printworks Gallery, Chgo., 1991, 93, Priebe Art Gallery, U. Wis., Oshkosh, 1992, Susan Cummins Gallery, Mill Valley, Calif., 1992, 94, Steven Scott Gallery, Balt., 1993, 94, Hartman Ctr. Gallery, Bradley U., Peoria, Ill., 1994, Mus. Contemporary Art, Chgo., 1994, Suburban Fine Arts Ctr., Highland Park, Ill., 1994, Lakeview Mus. Arts and Sci., Peoria, 1994, Decordova Mus. and Sculpture Park, Lincoln, Mass., 1994; exhibited in group shows Whitney Mus. Art Art, N.Y.C., 1981, Walker Art Mus., Mpls., 1982, Mus. Modern Art, N.Y.C., 1984, Corcoran Gallery Art, Washington, 1985; represented in permanent collections Mus. Contemporary Art, Chgo., Indpls. Mus. Art, Seattle Art Mus., Madison Art Ctr., High Mus. Art, Atlanta, also others. Recipient cash award Southwestern Ctr. for Contemporary Art, Winston-Salem, N.C., 1987, Childe Hassam purchase award AAAL, 1988; grantee Ill. Arts Coun., 1986, Nat. Endowment for Arts, 1987. Office: Columbia Coll 600 S Michigan Ave Chicago IL 60605

SIGLER, JAY ADRIAN, political scientist, educator; b. Paterson, N.J., June 21, 1933; s. Benjamin and Lucille (Pakula) S.; m. Janet Barndt, May 5, 1984; children: Niall, Ian. B.A. with honors, Rutgers U., 1954, J.D. (Law Alumni scholar), 1957, M.A. (fellow), 1960, Ph.D., 1962. Asst. prof. polit. sci. Kent (Ohio) State U., 1961-63, U. Vt., Burlington, 1963-64; instr. dept. polit. sci. Rutgers U., Camden, N.J., 1960-61; asso. prof. Rutgers U., 1965-70, prof., 1970-73, Disting. prof. polit. sci., chmn. dept., 1973—; dir. Grad. Program in Public Policy, 1979—; dir. Forum for Policy Rsch. and Pub. Svc. Rutgers U., Camden, N.J., 1995—; assoc. dean Grad. Program in Public Policy, 1970-71. Author: An Introduction to the Legal System, 1968, Double Jeopardy, 1969, The Conservative Tradition in American Thought, 1969, Courts and Public Policy, 1970, El Pensamento Conservador en los Estados Unidos, 1971, Contemporary American Government, 1972, The Performance of American Government, 1972, American Rights Policies, 1975, The Legal Sources of Public Policy, 1977, Understanding Criminal Law, 1981, Minority Rights, 1983, International Handbook of Race and Race Relations, 1987, Interactive Compliance, 1988, Corporate Lawbreaking and Interactive Compliance, 1991; contbr. articles to profl. jours. Mcpl. chmn. Democratic Party, Haddonfield, N.J., 1968-70; mem. Camden County Dem. Com., 1968-71. Served with U.S. Army, 1957-58. Recipient Lindback award for disting. teaching, 1981; Rutgers Research fellow, 1973-74; Eagleton fellow, 1978-79; Am. Polit. Sci. Assn. Project 87 fellow, 1979; Nat. Endowment for Humanities summer fellow, 1979; Warren Sussman Disting. Teaching award, 1995. Mem. AAUP, Law and Soc. Assn., Policy Studies Orgn., Nat. Assn. Schs. Public Affairs and Adminstrn., Am. Polit. Sci. Assn. Club: Rutgers Faculty. Home: PO Box 1932 Edgartown MA 02539-1932 Office: Rutgers U Grad Program Pub Policy 311 N 5th St Camden NJ 08102-1205 *The contemplation of the limits of a life, of the mixture of luck and planning for more luck, is a source of balance and calm. Discovering that a few persons mean more than any things is the hard and painful part.*

SIGLER, LEROY WALTER, banker, lawyer, entrepreneur; b. Racine, Wis., Aug. 3, 1926; s. LeRoy I. and Ruth Ann (Wacynski) S.; m. Joanne I. Nash, June 20, 1947 (dec. Jan. 7, 1966); m. Sylvia L. Schmidt, Sept. 20, 1969; children: Suzanne Sigler Herbster, Cynthia Sigler Whittaker, Lee Scott, Robb Nash, Paul Grant. B.B.A., U. Wis., 1952, J.D., 1952. Bar: Wis. 1952, Ohio 1967. Corp. counsel, asst. sec. J.W. Butler Paper Co., 1952-66, Butler Paper Co., 1952-66; asst. mgr. law dept. Nekoosa Edwards Paper Co., 1952-66; asst. sec., gen. counsel Seilon, Inc., 1966-68, v.p., sec., gen. counsel, 1968-70, pres., gen. counsel, dir., 1970-79; pres., gen. counsel, dir. Bancorp. Leasing, 1973-79, Thomson Internat. Co., Thomson Veracruz S.A., Thomson-Poole, Inc., Inmobilaria Elda S.A., 1971-79, Air-Way Sanitizor, Inc., 1972-79; various positions including pres., vice chmn., dir., sec., gen. counsel Nev. Nat. Bank, 1969-76; v.p., sec. gen., counsel, dir. Nev. Nat. Bancorp., 1969-76; sec., gen. counsel Lamb Enterprises, Inc., Lamb Communications, Inc., 1970-79; chmn., dir. Greenwood's Bancorp., Inc., 1976-81; pres., dir. Nekoosa Port Edwards Bancorp., Inc., 1979—, Nekoosa Port Edwards State Bank, 1980-95; chmn., CEO, dir. Nekoosa Port Edwards State Bank, 195—; bd. dirs. Gross Common Carrier, Inc., Opollo, Lou-Ques Corp., Broadline Leasing, Freightline; pres., dir. Nekoosa Port Edwards Investment, Inc., 1994—; sec., treas. Riverview Health Care Found., Inc., 1996. Chmn. fund drive South Wood County United Fund; co-chmn. Community Planning Commn.; pres. Port Edwards Water Utility, Tri City Airways, Village of Port Edwards;pres., dir. Riverview Hosp., Riverview Manor; dir. Tri City Health Care, Inc., Advanced Med. Equipment, Inc.; chmn. South Wood County Airport Commn.; mem. parish council, fin. com., treas. Sacred Heart Ch., sec., bd. dirs. Sacred Heart Parish Found., Inc., Riverview Health Care Found., 1995; chmn. Nekoosa Bus. Council, 1981-82; chmn. Nekoosa Indsl. Devel., 1983-86. Served with AUS, 1945-47. Mem. Wisconsin Rapids C. of C. (dir. 1960-66, 81-83, Spl. Citizen award 1964), Tri-City Bar Assn. (pres.), 7th Circuit Bar Assn. (v.p.), Toastmasters Club (v.p.), Phi Delta Phi. Lodges: Elk (exalted ruler, trustee); Rotary. Home: PO Box 86 Nekoosa WI 54457-0086 Office: 405 Market St Nekoosa WI 54457-1125 *Play all games possible. Play by the rules. Play to win.*

SIGLER, LOIS OLIVER, home economics educator; b. Piney Flats, Tenn., Sept. 8, 1923; d. Willie Campbell and Lillie (Brown) Oliver; m. William Virgil Sigler Jr., Aug. 25, 1962; 1 child, William Oliver. BS, East Tenn. State U., 1944; MS, U. Tenn., 1952; postgrad., Memphis State U., U. Tenn. Home econs. tchr. Buchanan (Va.) pub. schs., 1944-46; area supr. home econs. edn. and sch. lunch prog. State Dept. Edn., Commonwealth of Va., 1946-54; asst. nat. advisor Future Homemakers of Am./New Homemakers of Am., HEW, Washington, 1954-56; nat. advisor Future Homemakers of Am./New Homemakers of Am., HEW, 1956-63; family living coord. Ohio State Dept. and Columbus (Ohio) Pub. Schs., Columbus Met. Housing Authority, 1963; tchr. Millington (Tenn.) High Sch., 1966-92; ret., 1992. Mem. Tenn. Tchrs. Study Coun., 1986-87, Pres. Kennedy's Food for Peace Coun., Pres. Eisenhower's Adv. Com. on Youth Fitness. Named Tenn. Home Econs. Tchr. of Yr., 1975, Woman of Yr., 1991, Twentieth Century award for achievement, 1991. Mem. NEA, Am. Home Econs. Assn., Tenn. Home Econs. Assn., Am. Voc. Assn., Tenn. Voc. Assn., Nat. Voc. Home Econs. Tchrs. Assn., Tenn. Voc. Home Econs. Tchrs. Assn. (hon. 1992, past sec.-treas., Outstanding Svc. award 1986), W. Tenn. Home Econs. Edn. Assn. (past sec.), Tenn. Edn. Assn. (bd. dirs. 1977-80), W. Tenn. Edn. Assn., Shelby County Edn. Assn. (past sch. rep.), Greater Memphis State U., Inc., Future Homemakers Am. (nat. hon. 1956, state hon. 1991, master advisor award 1988, advisor mentor 1991), Omicron Nu, Pi Lambda Theta. Home: 4785 Rolling Meadows Dr Memphis TN 38128-4868

SIGLER, PAUL BENJAMIN, molecular biology educator, protein crystallographer; b. Richmond, Va., Feb. 19, 1934; s. George and Florence (Kaminsky) S.; m. Althea Jo Martin, Oct. 2, 1958; children—Jennifer, Michele, Jonathan, Deborah, Rebecca. A.B. in Chemistry summa cum laude, Princeton U., 1955; M.D., Columbia U., 1959; Ph.D. in Biochemistry, Cambridge U., 1967. Intern and resident dept. medicine Columbia-Presbyn. Med. Ctr., N.Y.C., 1959-61; research assoc. NIAMD, 1961-63, staff Lab. Molecular Biology, 1963-64; vis. fellow MRC Lab. Molecular Biology, Cambridge, Eng., 1964-67; assoc. prof. biophysics U. Chgo., 1967-73, prof. biophysics and theoretical biology, 1973-84, prof. biochemistry and molecular biology, 1984-88; prof. molecular biophysics and biochemistry Yale U., New Haven, 1989—; investigator Howard Hughes Med. Inst., 1989—. Served with USPHS, 1961-64. Recipient Research Career Devel. award USPHS, 1971-75; Guggenheim fellow, 1974; Katzir fellow, 1975. Fellow Am. Acad. Arts and Scis.; mem. NAS, Am. Crystallographic Assn. Jewish. Avocations: painting; bicycling. Office: Yale U HHMI 154BCMM 295 Congress Ave New Haven CT 06519-1418

SIGMON, DANIEL RAY, foundation administrator; b. Orangeburg, S.C., Sept. 15, 1949; s. Carment Ray and Freida Marion (Stoudenmire) S.; m. Cheryl Mahaffey, Dec. 31, 1976; children: Ashley W. Truluck, Elizabeth Wakefield, Caroline Christine. BE, U. S.C., 1971, MA, 1992. Tchr. Calhoun County Sch. Dist., St. Matthews, S.C., 1971-72; hist. sites supt. S.C. Dept. Parks, Recreation & Tourism, Columbia, S.C., 1972-73; staff historian S.C. Dept. Parks, Recreation & Tourism, 1973-85; exec. dir. Hist. Camden (S.C.), 1985-87; dir. Alexander Homesite & History Mus., Charlotte, N.C., 1987-88; exec. dir. Hist. Columbia Found., Columbia, 1988—. Author: Huntington Beach State Park; A Visitor's Guide, 1984, Hampton Plantation; Visitor's Guide, 1983; editor: A Guide to Historic Sites in Camden, S.C., 1985. Mem. Columbia Action Coun., 1989—, Cultural Coun. Richland and Lexington County, Columbia, 1989—; bd. dirs. Sunrise Found., 1992—; mem. county commn. Palmetto Project Discovery '92, 1991-92. Mem. Nat. Trust Hist. Preservation, Am. Assn. State and Local History, S.C. Confedn. Local Hist. Socs. (exec. coun. 1991—), S.C. Fedn. Mus. (pres. 1994-96), Palmetto Trust Hist. Preservation (exec. com. 1991—). Methodist. Avocations: gardening, backpacking, canoeing, camping, traveling. Office: Hist Columbia Found 1601 Richland St Columbia SC 29201-2633

SIGMON, JOYCE ELIZABETH, professional society administrator; b. Stanley, N.C., Oct. 4, 1935; d. Rome Alfred and Pearl Elizabeth (Beal) S. BS, U. N.C., 1971; MA, Loyola U., 1980. Cert. dental asst., assn. exec. Dental asst. Dr. Paul A. Stroup, Jr., Charlotte, N.C., 1953-63; instr. Wayne Tech. Inst., Goldsboro, N.C., 1963-65, Ctrl. Piedmont Community Coll., Charlotte, 1965-69; dir. Dental Assisting Edn. ADA, Chgo., 1971-85, asst. sec. Coun. Prosthetics Svcs., 1985-87, mgr. Office Quality Assurance, 1987-80, exec. dir. Aux., 1990-92; dir. adminstrv. activities Am. Acad. of Implant Dentistry, Chgo., 1993—; exec. sec. Am. Bd. of Oral Implantology/Implant Dentistry, 1993—. Deacon 4th Presbyn. Ch., 1973-75, elder 1975-77, 88-91, trustee, 1991-94; moderator Presbyn. Women in 4th Ch., 1987-91. Mem. Am. Soc. Assn. Execs., Chgo. Soc. Assn. Execs. (chair CAE com. 1991-92), Am. Dental Assts. Assn., N.C. Dental Assn. (pres. 1968-69), Charlotte Dental Assts. Soc. Presbyterian. Home: 260 E Chestnut St Chicago IL 60611-2423 Office: Am Acad Implant Dentistry 211 E Chicago Ave Chicago IL 60611-2616

SIGMOND, CAROL ANN, lawyer; b. Phila., Jan. 9, 1951; d. Irwin and Mary Florence (Vollmer) S. BA, Grinnell Coll., 1972; JD, Cath. U., 1975. Bar: Va. 1975, D.C. 1980, Md. 1988, N.Y. 1990, U.S. Dist. Ct. (ea. dist.) Va. 1975, U.S. Dist. Ct. (so. and ea. dist.) N.Y. 1991, U.S. Ct. Appeals (4th cir.) 1976, U.S. Ct. Appeals (fed. cir.) 1987. Asst. gen. counsel Washington Met. Area Transit Authority, 1978-85; acting assoc. gen. counsel for appeals and gen. law, 1985-86; assoc. Patterson, Belknap, Webb & Tyler, Washington, 1986-89, Berman, Paley, Goldstein & Kannry, N.Y.C., 1991-93; prin. Law Offices of Carol A. Sigmond, N.Y.C., 1993—; Mem. Women's Nat. Dem. Club. Mem. ABA, D.C. Bar Assn., Arlington County Bar Assn., Va. State Bar Assn., Md. State Bar Assn. Democrat. Mem. LDS. Avocations: piano, bridge.

SIGMOND, RICHARD BRIAN, lawyer; b. Phila., Dec. 7, 1944; s. Joseph and Jean (Nissman) S.; children: Michael, Catherine, Alina; m. Susan Helen Peteraf, Dec. 24, 1984. BS, Phila. Coll. Textiles & Sci., 1966; JD, Temple U., 1969. Bar: Pa. 1969, U.S. Supreme Ct. 1973, U.S. Dist. Ct. (ea. dist.) Pa. 1975, U.S. Ct. Appeals (3d cir.) 1975, N.Y. 1982, D.C. 1995. Atty. Pub. Defender Assn., Phila., 1969-70; ptnr. Meranze, Katz, Spear & Wilderman, Phila., 1970-84; sr. ptnr. Spear, Wilderman, Sigmond, Borish & Endy, Phila., 1985-89, Sagot, Jennings & Sigmond, Phila., 1989—; chmn., bd. dirs. Gatehouse Phila., 1972-83; lectr. Pvt. Industry Coun., Phila., 1985—, labor studies div., Pa. State U., 1978-82, 85-86. Mem. ABA (labor law com., litigation com.), AFL-CIO (lawyers coordinating com.), Pa. Bar Assn. (labor law com.), Phila. Bar Assn. (labor com.), Phi Alpha Delta. Avocations: sailing, writing. Office: Penn Mutual Towers 16th Fl 510 Walnut St Philadelphia PA 19106

SIGMOND, ROBERT M., medical economist; b. Seattle, June 18, 1920; s. Harry and Alice (Gottfeld) S.; m. Barbara, June 29, 1941; children: Alison, Laurence. B.A., Pa. State Coll., 1941, M.A., 1942. Research asso. Gov.'s Commn. on Hosp. Facilities, Standards and Orgn., Phila., 1945-46, Hosp. Council Phila., 1946-50; asst. to v.p. Albert Einstein Med. Center, Phila., 1950-55; exec. v.p. for planning Albert Einstein Med. Center, 1968-70, exec. v.p., 1971-75, recipient trustee medal, 1975; dir. fiscal studies Nat. Commn. Financing of Hosp. Care, Chgo., 1952-54; exec. dir. Hosp. Coun. Western Pa., Pitts., 1955-64, Hosp. Planning Assn., Allegheny County, Pitts., 1964-68; dir. Cmty. Programs for Affordable Health Care, Chgo., 1981-85; cons. Blue Cross Assn. and Blue Cross of Greater Phila., 1976-77; adviser on hosp. affairs Blue Cross Blue Shield Assn., Chgo., 1977-96; sr. cons. Health Alliance Pa., 1995—; scholar-in-residence Sch. Bus. Adminstrn. Temple U., 1985—; past adj. prof. Robert F. Wagner Grad. Sch. of Pub. Policy, chmn. nat. steering com. hosp. cmty. benefit stds. program NYU, 1988-94; past adv. panel on cost effectiveness Congl. Office of Tech. Assessment; past cons. com. cmty. health care coun. on med. svcs. AMA, Social Security Adminstrn., Pa. Gov.'s Hosp. Study Commns., USPHS, OEO, Pitts. Found., U. Mich. Study of Hosp. and Med. Econs., hosp. utilization project Calif. Dept. Health; expert Office Asst. Sec. of Health HEW. Author: Methods of Making Experimental Inferences 2d edit, 1945; (with Thomas Kinser) The Hospital-Blue Cross Plan Relationship, 1976; numerous monographs for profl. jours. Chmn. nat. adv. com. Johnson Found. Community Hosp. Med. Staff Group Practice Program; trustee Dorothy Rider Pool Health Care Trust, Allentown, Pa., Integrated Mental Health Inc., Rochester, N.Y. Recipient 1st C. Rufus Rorem award, 1986, Disting. Svc. award Ohio State U., 1995; Edwin L. Crosby fellow Nuffield Provincial Hosps. Trust, London, 1976. Fellow Am. Pub. Health Assn. (mem. editorial bd. jour.); mem. Am. Hosp. Assn. (hon.), Am. Coll. Healthcare Execs. (Dean Conley award 1969), Forum for Healthcare Planning (award of merit 1984), Soc. Hosp. Planning (Corning award 1981), Internat. Hosp. Fedn., Hosp. Assn. Pa.(Disting. Svc. award 1992), Boondocks Med. Soc. Home: 2912 Carlton House 1801 John F Kennedy Blvd Philadelphia PA 19103-1731

SIGMUND, PAUL EUGENE, political science educator; b. Phila., Jan. 14, 1929; s. Paul Eugene and Marie (Ramsey) S.; m. Barbara Rowena Boggs, Jan. 25, 1964 (dec. 1990); children—Paul Eugene, David, Stephen. AB, Georgetown U., 1950; AB Fulbright scholar, U. Durham, Eng., 1950-51; M.A., Harvard, 1954, Ph.D., 1959; postgrad., U. Paris, France, U. Heidelberg, U. Cologne, Germany, 1955-56. Teaching fellow Harvard, 1953-55, 58-59, instr., 1959-63; assoc. prof. politics Princeton, 1963-70, prof. politics, 1970—. Author: Nicholas of Cusa and Medieval Political Thought, 1963, (with Reinhold Niebuhr) The Democratic Experience, 1969, Natural Law in Political Thought, 1971, 81, The Overthrow of Allende and the Politics of Chile, 1977, Multinationals in Latin America: The Politics of Nationalization, 1980, Liberation Theology at the Crossroads: Democracy or Revolution?, 1990, paperback, 92, The United States and Democracy in Chile, 1993; editor: The Ideologies of the Developing Nations, 1963, 67, 72, Models of Political Change in Latin America, 1970, (with Pedro Aspe) The Political Economy of Income Distribution in Mexico, 1983, Poder, Sociedad y Estado en USA, 1985; assoc. editor: World Politics; translator: The Military and the State in Latin America (A. Rouquié), 1987, St. Thomas Aquinas, On Politics and Ethics, 1988, Nicholas of Cusa, The Catholic Concordance, 1991, 95. Served to 1st lt. USAF, 1956-57. Mem. Am. Polit. Sci. Assn., Latin Am. Studies Assn., Phi Beta Kappa. Home: 8 Evelyn Pl Princeton NJ 08540-3818

SIGNER, ETHAN ROYAL, biotechnology executive; b. Bklyn., Apr. 3, 1937; s. Isador and Elca (Rothstein) S.; m. Laura Karp; 1 child, Jasper K.; children by previous marriage: Kira R., Rachel L. BS, Yale U., 1958; PhD, MIT, 1963. Postdoctoral fellow Med. Rsch. Coun. Lab. Molecular Biology, Cambridge, Eng., 1962-64, Institut Pasteur, Paris, 1964-66; asst. prof. microbiology MIT, Cambridge, 1966-68, assoc. prof. microbiology, 1968-72; vis. prof. genetics Harvard Med. Sch., Boston, 1986-87; prof. biology MIT, Cambridge, 1972—; CEO Pharm. Peptides Inc., Cambridge, 1994—; mem. sci. adv. bd. Plant Resources Venture Fund, Boston, 1981-89, Safer, Inc., Wellesley, Mass., 1987-90, Angenics, Inc., Cambridge, 1981-88; Philips disting. visitor Haverford Coll., 1978; disting. Martin vis. lectr. microbiology U. Calif., San Francisco, 1982; vis. prof. biochemistry U. Paris, 1992, 93; co-founder Pharm. Peptides, Inc., 1994, CEO, 1994—. Co-author: The Genie in the Computer, 1982; assoc. editor Virology, 1969-76; contbr. sci. articles to profl. jours. Marion and Jasper Whiting Found. fellow, 1988, NATO, Am. Cancer Soc., Jane Coffin Childs Fund fellow, 1962-66; Rsch. fellow NIH, NSF, Am. Cancer Soc., U.S. Dept. Energy, U.S. Agr., 1966—; recipient Career Devel. award USPHS, 1969-72, Tchg. award MIT Grad. Student Coun., 1976, Charles E. Reed Faculty Initiatives award, 1990. Mem. AAAS, Am. Soc. Microbiology, Genetics Soc. Am., Internat. Soc. Plant Molecular Biology, Am. Soc. Plant Physiologists, Internat. Soc. Molecular Plant-Microbe Interactions, N.Y. Acad. Scis. Office: Pharm Peptides Inc 1 Hampshire St Cambridge MA 02139-1572

SIGNORILE, VINCENT ANTHONY, lawyer; b. Jersey City, Mar. 22, 1959; s. Ralph R. and Rita (DeRosa) S. BS, St. Peter's Coll., Jersey City, 1981; JD, Seton Hall U., 1985. Bar: N.J. 1985, Pa. 1985. Aide Jersey City Mcpl. Coun., 1980-81, Office of Mayor, City of Jersey City, 1981; law clk. Corp. Counsel Jersey City, 1981-85; law sec. Superior Ct. N.J. for Hudson County, Jersey City, 1985-86; assoc. atty. Jersey City, 1986-89; ptnr. Signorile & Saminski, Jersey City, 1989—. Mem. Hudson County Dem. Com., 1977-81, Jersey City Environ. Com., 1989-93, Jersey City Planning Bd. Com., 1991-93, Jersey City Ins. Fund Com., 1989-93; co-chmn. Hudson County Columbus Parade, 1984-85; elected to Mcpl. Coun. Jersey City, 1989-93. Mem. ABA, N.J. Bar Assn., Pa. Bar Assn., Hudson County Bar Assn. (treas. Young Lawyer's Assn. 1987-88, scholar 1984-85), Assn. Trial Lawyers Am. Roman Catholic. Home: 1691 John F Kennedy Blvd Jersey City NJ 07305-1841 Office: Signorile & Saminski 309 Baldwin Ave Jersey City NJ 07306-1711

SIGUA, GILBERT C., environmental specialist; b. San Pablo, Isabela, Philippines, Oct. 14, 1957; s. Basilio M. and Angelina C. (Castaneda) S.; m. Celia F. Avellanoza, Aug. 20, 1983; children: Gerald Christian, Christine Gicelle. BS in Agr. cum laude, Ctrl. Luzon State U., Nueva Ecija, Philippines, 1978; MS in Soil Chemistry, U. Ark., 1983; PhD in Environ. Soil Chemistry, La. State U., 1990. Cert. profl. soil scientist. Instr. Ctrl. Luzon State U., Nueva Ecija, 1978-83, asst. prof., 1983-86; rsch. asst. La. State U., Baton Rouge, 1986-90, postdoctoral rsch. assoc., 1990-92; rsch. soil scientist Agrl. Rsch. Svc.-USDA, Beltsville, Md., 1992-94; environ. specialist St. Johns River Water Mgmt. Dist., Palatka, Fla., 1994—. Contbr. articles to profl. jours. Pub. rels. officer Filipino-Am. Student Assn., La. State U., 1987-88. Recipient Agrl. Rsch. Svc./USDA Spl. Rsch. Achievement award, 1993; U.S. AID grantee, 1981-83; Rotary Found. fellow, 1986-90. Mem. Soil Sci. Soc. Am., Agronomy Soc. Am., Am. Registry of Cert. Profl. in Agronomy, Crops and Soils, Estuarine Rsch. Fedn., Gamma Sigma Delta. Roman Catholic. Achievements include rsch. for developing comprehensive soil and water-based mgmt. strategies for revegetation and productivity improvement of degraded wetlands; managed and supervised lab and field experiments on the degradation, movement and fate of pesticides and other agri-chemicals in the soil, surface water and groundwater; coordinate estuarine water and sediments quality monitoring and assessment programs for Indian River Lagoon, Florida. Home: 3531 NW 65th Ln Gainesville FL 32653-8824 Office: St Johns River Water Mgmt Environ Scis Divsn PO Box 1429 Palatka FL 32178-1429

SIGUION-REYNA, LEONARDO, lawyer, business executive; b. Dagupan City, The Philippines, Apr. 18, 1921; s. Lamberto and Felisa (Tiongson) S.; m. Armida Ponce-Enrilie, Nov. 24, 1951; children: Monica, Leonardo, Carlos. LLB, U. Santo Tomas, Manila, 1946-48. Bar: Philippines, 1948. Sr. ptnr. Siguion Reyna, Montecillo, and Ongsiako, Makati Metro Manila; chmn. bd. Phimco Industries, Inc., Manila, Sandvick Philippines, Inc., Electrolux Mktg. Corp., Autocorp Group, Inc., Philippine Global Comm., Inc.; pres. Electronic Tele. Systems Industries, Inc., Philippines, Inc., Manila Meml. Park Cemetary, Inc., Valmora Investment & Mgmt. Corp.; dir. ABBC (Phils) Inc., BA Fin. Corp., Inc., Crismida Realty Corp., Dole Philippines, Inc., Electrolux Philippines, Inc., Filflex Indsl. & Mfg. Corp., Goodyear Philippines, Inc., Indsl. Realties, Inc., Investment & Capital Corp. of the Philippines, Proton Pilipinas, Inc.,Philippine Refining Co., Inc., Rizal Comml. Banking Corp., Unilever (Phil) Inc. Mem. Philippine Bar Assn., Casino Español de Manila. Roman Catholic. CLubs: Manila Yacht, Manila Polo, Rotary. Home: 7 Tangile Rd/North Forbes, Makati Manila The Philippines

SIGULER, GEORGE WILLIAM, financial services executive; b. Cleve., Apr. 26, 1947; s. John Frederick and Helen Alice (Popp) S.; m. Pamela Ann Mallon, Oct. 31, 1981; children: George William Jr., Emily Ann, Charles Arthur, Mary Elizabeth. AB, Amherst Coll., 1970; MBA, Harvard U., 1972. Ptnr. Harvard Mgmt. Co., Boston, 1974-83; chief of staff HHS, Washington, 1983-84; exec. v.p. Monarch Capital Corp., Springfield, Mass., 1984-87; vice chmn. bd. Monarch Capital Corp., Springfield, 1987-91; pres. Associated Capital Investor, San Francisco, 1990-91; mng. dir. Mitchell Hutchins Instl. Investors, Inc., N.Y.C., 1991-95; founder Siguler Guff & Co., 1995—; assoc. treas. Harvard U., 1973-88; bd. dirs. Bus. Mortgage Investors, Venture Lending and Leasing, Inc., Russia Ptnrs., L.P., Allied Capital Corp., Washington, Nova Care, King of Prussia, Pa., Healthcare Capital, Inc., Great Neck, N.Y. Mem. vis. com. Harvard U. Med. Sch., Boston, 1986—; mem. nat. adv. com. on community health resources HHS, Washington, 1985-90; trustee Perkins Sch. for Blind, Watertown, Mass., 1976-83, New Eng. Aquarium, 1989-91. Recipient Disting. Svc. award HHS, 1984. Republican. Presbyterian. Office: Siguler Guff & Co 630 5th Ave New York NY 10111

SIGURDSSON, HARALDUR, oceanography educator, researcher; b. Stykkisholmur, Snaefellsnes, Iceland, May 31, 1939; came to U.S., 1974; s. Sigurdur and Anna (Oddsdottir) Steinthorsson; m. Jean Marie Bloom; children: Bergljot, Ashildur. BSc in Geology, Queen's U., Belfast, Northern Ireland, 1965; PhD in Geology, Durham (Eng.) U., 1970. Geologist Univ. Rsch. Inst., Reykjavik, Iceland, 1965-67; volcanologist U. West Indies, St. Augustine, Trinidad and Tobago, 1970-74; assoc. prof. oceanography U. R.I., Kingston, 1974-80, prof., 1980—; cons. U.S. State Dept., 1979, 84, 86. Editor Bull. Volcanology; assoc. editor Jour. Geophys. Rsch.; contbr. over 130 articles to profl. jours. including Nat. History mag. Recipient Excellence award U. R.I., 1993; 20 rsch. grants NSF, 5 rsch. grants Nat. Geog. Soc., 4 rsch. grants NASA, also grantee Iceland Rsch. Coun. Fellow Icelandic Acad. Sci., Explorers Club; mem. Am. Geophys. Union, Internat. Assn. Volcanology and Chemistry of Earth's Interior, Glaciological Soc. Iceland. Avocations: sailing, mountaineering, art. Office: U RI Oceanography Dept S Ferry Rd Narragansett RI 02882-1197

SIH, CHARLES JOHN, pharmaceutical chemistry educator; b. Shanghai, China, Sept. 11, 1933; s. Paul Kwang-Tsien and Teresa (Dong) S.; m. Catherine Elizabeth Hsu, July 11, 1959; children—Shirley, Gilbert, Ronald. A.B. in Biology, Caroll Coll., 1953; M.S. in Bacteriology, Mont. State Coll., 1955; Ph.D. in Bacteriology, U. Wis., 1958. Sr. research microbial biochemist Squibb Inst. for Med. Research, New Brunswick, N.J., 1958-60; mem. faculty U. Wis.-Madison, 1960—, Frederick B. Power prof. pharm. chemistry, 1978, Hilldare prof., 1987—. Recipient 1st Ernest Volwiler award, 1977; Roussel prize, 1980, Am. Pharm. Assoc. award 1987. Mem. Am. Chem. Soc., Soc. Am. Biol. Chemists, Acad. Pharm. Scis., Soc. Am. Microbiologists. Home: 6322 Landfall Dr Madison WI 53705-4309

SIHLER, WILLIAM WOODING, finance educator; b. Seattle, Nov. 17, 1937; s. William and Helen Alice (Wooding) S.; m. Mary Elizabeth Unwin, Aug. 21, 1963; children: Edward Wooding, Jennifer Mary. A.B. summa cum laude in Govt. (Sheldon traveling fellow), Harvard U., 1959, MBA with high distinction, 1962, DBA, 1965. Instr., asst. prof. Harvard U. Bus. Sch., 1964-67; asso. prof. Darden Grad. Bus. Sch., U. Va., Charlottesville, 1967-72; prof. Darden Grad. Bus. Sch., U. Va., 1972-76, A.J. Morris prof., 1976-84; R.E. Trzcinski prof., 1984—, dir. D.B.A. Program, 1971-73, assoc. dean acad. affairs, 1972-77; exec. dir. BAFT/Ctr. for Internat. Banking Studies, 1977-91; bd. dirs. Curtiss-Wright Corp.; pres. Southeastern Cons. Group, Ltd. Co-author: Financial Management: Text and Cases, 2d edit., 1991, The Troubled Money Business, 1992, Financial Service Organizations: Cases in Strategic Management, 1993, Cases in Applied Corporate Finance, 1994; editor: Classics in Commercial Bank Lending, vol. 1, 1981, vol. 2, 1985; contbr. articles to mgmt. publs. and anthologies of readings. Class sec. Harvard M.B.A. Class, 1962, Case Western Res. U., mem. vis. com. Sch. Mgmt., 1976-86, bd. overseers, 1980-86. Recipient DeL. K. Jay prize Harvard U., Disting. Prof. award U. Va. Alumni Assn., 1982; C.J. Bonaparte scholar Harvard U. Mem. Fin. Mgmt. Assn., Am. Econ. Assn., Am. Fin. Assn., Eastern Fin. Assn., Univ. Club (N.Y.C.), Harvard Club (N.Y.C.), Phi Beta Kappa, Beta Gamma Sigma. Home: 202 Sturbridge Rd Charlottesville VA 22901-2116 Office: PO Box 6550 Charlottesville VA 22906-6550

SIIMESTÖ, ORVO KALERVO, financial executive; b. Helsinki, Finland, Aug. 3, 1943; s. Idor and Ilma (Hukka) S.; m. Marja-Liisa Vehviläinen, May 30, 1964; children: Satu Kristiina, Katja Maarit. MBA, Helsinki Sch. Bus. Adminstrn., 1969. Dir. fin. Kone Oy, Hyvinkää, Finland, 1975-83; v.p. fin. Oy Wilhelm Schauman AB, Helsinki, 1983-88, A. Ahlstrom Corp., Helsinki, 1988—. Avocations: sailing, cross-country skiing, volleyball. Office: A Ahlstrom Corp, Eteläesplanadi 14, 00130 Helsinki Finland

SIIROLA, JEFFREY JOHN, chemical engineer; b. Patuxent River, Md., July 17, 1945; s. Arthur Raymond and Nancy Ellen (Harris) S.; m. Sharon Ann Atwood, Apr. 24, 1971; childen: John Daniel, Jennifer Ann. BS in Chem. Engring., U. Utah, 1967; PhD, U. Wis., 1970. Rsch. fellow Eastman Chem. Co., Kingsport, Tenn., 1972--; trustee CACHE Corp., Austin, Tex., 1983--. Co-author: Process Synthesis, 1973. Active Kingsport C. of C. Recycling, 1988—, Appalachian tr. maintenance Eastman Hiking Club, Kingsport, 1973—. With U.S. Army, 1970-72. Mem. AIChE (A.E. Marshall award 1967, Computing Practice award 1991, CAST divsn. programming chair 1988—), Nat. Acad. Engring., Accreditation Bd. for Engring. and Tech., Am. Chem. Soc., Am. Soc. for Engring. Edn., Am. Assn. for Artificial Intelligence. Achievements include development of the AIDES chem. process flowsheet invention procedure. Home: 2517 Wildwood Dr Kingsport TN 37660-4748 Office: Eastman Chem Co PO Box 1972 Kingsport TN 37662-5150

SIKER, EPHRAIM S., anesthesiologist; b. Port Chester, N.Y., Mar. 24, 1926; s. Samuel S. and Adele (Weiser) S.; m. m . Eileen Mary Bohnel, Aug. 5, 1951; children—Kathleen Ellen, Jeffrey Stephen, David Allan, Paul William, Richard Francis. Student, Duke U., 1943-45; M.D., N.Y.U., 1949. Diplomate: Am. Bd. Anesthesiology (dir. 1971—, sec.-treas. 1974-82, pres. 1982-83) Nat. Bd. Med. Examiners. Intern Grasslands Hosp., Valhalla, N.Y., 1949-50, resident in anesthesia, 1950; resident dept. anesthesiology Mercy Hosp., Pitts., 1952-53; assoc. dir. dept. Mercy Hosp., 1955-62, chmn., 1962-92; practice medicine, specializing in anesthesiology Pitts., 1954—; pres. Pitts. Anesthesia Assocs., Ltd., 1967-89; dir. anesthesia services Central Med. Ctr., Pitts., 1973-89; courtesy staff St. Clair Meml. Hosp., Pitts., 1954-89, St. Margaret Meml. Hosp., 1962—; clin. prof. dept. anesthesiology U. Pitts. Sch. Medicine, 1968—; mem. exec. com. Am. Bd. Med. Spltys., 1978-81; Exch. cons. Welsh Nat. Sch. Medicine, Cardiff, 1955-56; mem. Pa. Gov.'s Commn. on Profl. Liability Ins., 1968-70; mem. adv. panel U.S. Pharmacopeia, 1970-76; mem. Am. acupuncture anesthesia study group of Nat. Acad. Scis. to Peoples Republic China, 1974; mem. adv. com. on splty. and geog. distbn. of physicians Inst. Medicine, Nat. Acad. Scis., 1974-76; trustee Ednl. Coun. for Fgn. Med. Grads., 1980-82, Mercy Hosp. Found., 1983-95; bd. dirs., sec. Anesthesia Patient Safety Foun., 1985-89, mem. exec. com., 1985-92, exec. dir., 1992—. Author: (with F.F. Foldes) Narcotics and Narcotic Antagonists, 1964; sect. on narcotic: (with F.F. Foldes) numerous other publs. in med. lit. Ency. Brittanica. Served to lt. M.C. USNR, 1950-52. USPHS postdoctoral research fellow, 1954; hon. fellow faculty anaesthetists Royal Coll. Surgeons, Eng., 1974; hon. fellow faculty anesthetists Coll. Medicine South Africa, 1983; recipient Hippocratic award Mercy Hosp., 1982. Fellow Royal Coll. Surgeons Ireland, Faculty Anaesthetists (hon. 1988); mem. Am. Soc. Anesthesiologists (pres. 1973—, bd. dirs. Disting. Svc. award 1984), AMA (alt. del. 1962), Pa. Med. Soc., Allegheny County Med. Soc., Pa. Soc. Anesthesiologists (pres. 1965, Disting. Svc. award 1986), Royal Soc. Medicine (Eng.), Pitts. Acad. Medicine, Am. Coll. Anesthesiologists (bd. govs. 1969-71), World Fedn. Anesthesiologists (chmn. exec. com. 1980-84, v.p. 1984-88), Assn. Anesthesia Program Dirs. (pres. 1987-89). Developed Siker Laryngoscope, 1956. Home: 185 Crestvue Manor Dr Pittsburgh PA 15228-1814 Office: 1400 Locust St Pittsburgh PA 15219-5166 *If you have to tell someone who you are, then you probably aren't. People are measured by more than their deeds, and such estimations are frequently made on the basis of their inter-personal relationships. While achievement and effort usually bear a linear relationship to each other, the impact that the achiever has on society depends upon the impact he makes on individuals.*

SIKES, ALFRED CALVIN, communications executive; b. Cape Girardeau, Mo., Dec. 16, 1939; s. William Kendall and Marcia (Weber) S.; m. Martha Pagenkopf, Aug. 19, 1961; chldren: Deborah Sue, Christine Louise, Marcia Cay. AB, Westminster Coll., 1961; LLB, U. Mo., 1964. Asst. atty. gen. Senator John Danforth, State of Mo., Jefferson City, 1970-72; campaign mgr. Bond. for Gov. Com., Jefferson City, 1972; dir., gov.-elect transition staff Bond for Gov. Com., Jefferson City, 1972; dir. dept. community and consumer affairs State of Mo., Jefferson City, 1973-76; exec. v.p. Mahaffey Enterprises, Springfield, Mo., 1977-78; pres., CEO Sikes & Assocs., Springfield, Mo., 1978-86; asst. sec. nat. telecom. and info. adminstrn. U.S. Dept. Commerce, Washington, 1986-89; chmn. FCC, Washington, 1989-93; v.p., group head new media and tech. The Hearst Corp., N.Y.C., 1993—. contbr. articles to profl. jours. Pres. Springfield Coun. Chs., 1984. Recipient Alumni Achievement award Westminster Coll., 1987. Mem. Mo. Bar Assn., Orgn. Mo. Jaycees (pres. 1968-69), U.S. Jaycees (v.p. 1969-70), Orgn. Internat. Jaycees (legal counsel 1971-72). Republican. Methodist. Avocations: fishing, hunting, skiing, sailing. Home: 1140 5th Ave # 14B New York NY 10128-0806

SIKORA, JAMES ROBERT, educational business consultant; b. Sacramento, July 8, 1945; s. George Robert and Marian Frances (Fears) S.; m. Marie Lynore Nyarady, June 22, 1968. BEE, U. Santa Clara, 1967; postgrad., U. Calif.-Santa Cruz, 1979--. Electronic engr. GTE-Sylvania, Santa Cruz, 1967-69; systems analyst GTE-Sylvania, 1969-71; sr. support analyst GTE-Sylvania, Mt. View, Calif., 1971-73; bus. systems coordinator Santa Clara County Office Edn., San Jose, Calif., 1973-76; dir. dist. payroll, personnel svcs. Santa Clara County Office Edn., 1976-85, dir. dist. bus. svcs., 1985-95; self-employed sch. bus. cons. Omniserve, Ben Lomond, Calif., 1995—; cons. records mgmt. County Santa Clara, San Jose, 1982; vice-chmn. Edn. Mandated Cost Network Exec. Bd., 1991-95; mem. Schs. Fin. Svcs. subcom. 1987-94. Author, co-editor Howdy Rowdy Memorial, 1979. Friend San Jose/Cleveland Ballet; patron Santa Cruz County Symphony; sponsor Dixieland Monterey; patrons cir. Monterey Bay Aquarium, Long Marine Lab.; dir. cir. San Jose Repertory Theater; fellow Cabrillo Music Festival; active Ctr. Photog. Arts, Napa Valley Wine Libr. Assn., Silver Chancellor's Cir., U. Calif. Santa Cruz, Team Shakespeare, Shakespeare Santa Cruz, Omni Found. Mem. Pub. Agy. Risk Mgmt. Assn., Am. Diabetes Assn., Calif. Assn. Sch. Bus. Ofcls. (subsect. pres. 1984-85, sect. bd. dirs. 1987-93, sect. pres. 1991-92, state bd. dirs. 1991-92, state legis. com. 1989—, state strategic planning com. 1994), Norwegian Elkhound Assn. (pres. 1977-79), Wine Investigation for Novices and Oenephiles, Amnesty Internat., Calif. Trout, Calif. State Parks Found., Am. Dog Owners Assn., Sierra Club (life). Libertarian. Roman Catholic. Avocations: photography, travel, gardening, fishing, snorkelling. Home and Office: 400 Coon Heights Rd Ben Lomond CA 95005-9711

SIKORA, RICHARD INNES, philosophy educator; b. Boston, July 6, 1927; s. Frank E. and Frances (Small) S.; m. Dorothy Daniel, Apr. 25, 1953; 1 child, Anne. A.B. in Philosophy cum laude, Harvard U., 1950; Ph.D. in Philosophy, U. Calif.-Berkeley, 1962. Instr. U. Oreg., Eugene, 1959-60; vis. asst. prof. Whitman Coll., Walla Walla, Wash., 1960-61; asst prof. philosophy U. B.C., Vancouver, Can., 1964-76; asso. prof. U. B.C., 1976-82, prof., 1982—. Editor: (with others) Obligations to Future Generations, 1978; contbr. articles to profl. jours. Served with USCG, 1945-46. Can. Council grantee, 1981-82. Mem. Am. Philosophy Assn., Can. Philosophy Assn. Avocations: classical music; art collecting. Home: 2307 Perkins Ln W Seattle WA 98199 Office: U BC Dept Philosphy, 204-2075 Westbrook Mall, Vancouver, BC Canada V6T 1Z2

SIKORA, SALLY MARIE, nursing administrator; b. Atlantic City, Aug. 9, 1949; d. R. Joseph and Julia G. (Myers) Wimberg; m. Paul A. Sikora, Aug. 15, 1970; children: Andrew Joseph, Paul A. II. ASN, Atlantic C.C., Mays Landing, N.J., 1971; BSN, Stockton State Coll., Pomona, N.J., 1990; MSN, LaSalle U., Phila., 1995. CCRN; cert. instr. ACLS, pediat. ACLS, neonatal ACLS, EMT, BLS trainer. Charge nurse surg. unit Atlantic City Med. Ctr., 1971; head nurse Senator Nursing Home, Atlantic City, 1972; ICU/Critical Care Unit staff and head nurse William Kessler Meml. Hosp., Hammonton, N.J., 1972-80, adminstrv. supr., 1980-82; adminstrv. supr. Atlantic City Med. Ctr., Atlantic Pomona, N.J., 1982-85; critical care mgr. Atlantic City Med. Ctr., Pomona, 1985-90, dir. edn., 1990-91; adminstrv. dir. nursing Shore Meml. Hosp., Somers Point, N.J., 1991—; adj. prof. nursing Atlantic County C.C., 1995—, Cumberland County C.C., 1996; bd. mem. So. N.J. Perinatal Coop., Camden, 1993; lectr., cons. cmty. orgns. and hosps.; establisher Coastal Critical Care Consortium N.J., first free-standing cardiac catheterization lab. without surg. back-up in State N.J.; sch. lectr. elem. and H.S., Pleasantville, N.J.; opened 1st hosp. based detoxifaction unit for outpatient svcs., 1995. Vol. ARC, Pleasantville, N.J., 1980's. Recipient Citation of Merit United Way, Atlantic County, N.J., 1993-94, Pres.'s award for excellence, Atlanticare award. Mem. ANA, Am. Heart Assn. (mgr. tng. ctr. 1990-91), N.J. State Nurses Assn., Assn. Med./Surg. Nurses, So. N.J. Perinatal Cooperative (bd. dirs. 1993—). Republican. Roman Catholic. Avocations: reading, golf. Home: 4 Maple Branch Ct Port Republic NJ 08241-9784 Office: Shore Meml Hosp New York Ave Somers Point NJ 08224

SIKORA, STEPHEN THEODORE, publisher; b. Ukiah, Calif., Sept. 17, 1943; s. John Paul and Florence Anholm (Smith) S.; m. Kathleen Faye Hagemeyer, Aug. 5, 1967 (div. Aug. 1987); children: Benjamin, Anna. BA, U. Calif., Berkeley, 1966; MA, San Francisco State U., 1974. Tchr. Nevada County Sch. Dist., North San Juan, Calif., 1969-71; carpenter, contractor pvt. practice, Calif., 1974-82; publisher pvt. practice, Albany, Calif., 1982—. Editor/publisher (mag.) The Letter Exchange, 1982—. Sgt. U.S. Army, 1966-68. Mem. Phi Beta Kappa. Avocations: homeric Greek studies, bicycling. Office: The Letter Exch PO Box 6218 Albany CA 94706

SIKOROVSKY, EUGENE FRANK, retired lawyer; b. Jackson, Mich., Nov. 27, 1927; s. Frank Joseph and Betty Dorothy (Malik) S.; m. Patricia O'Byrne, July 11, 1953; children: Paul, Charles, Catherine, Elizabeth, Emily. BSEE, U. Mich., 1948; LLB, Harvard U., 1951. Bar: N.Y. 1952, Va. 1970, Ill. 1978. Assoc. predecessor firms Cahill, Gordon & Reindel, 1954-63, ptnr., 1964-68; v.p., gen. counsel, dir. Reynolds Metals Co., Richmond, Va., 1969-76; gen. counsel Gould Inc., Rolling Meadows, Ill., 1977-79; v.p. Gould Inc., 1977-81; dep. gen. counsel Bell & Howell Co., Skokie, Ill., 1981-83; v.p. Bell & Howell Co., Chgo., 1983-88, gen. counsel, 1983-92, sec., 1984-92, sr. v.p., dir., 1988-92. Served to lt. USNR, 1951-54. Mem. Ill. State Bar Assn., Tau Beta Pi, Eta Kappa Nu, Phi Eta Sigma, Phi Delta Theta. Episcopalian. Home: 720 Grandview Ln Lake Forest IL 60045-3953

SIKORSKI, JAMES ALAN, research chemist; b. Stevens Point, Wis., Nov. 9, 1948; s. John Paul and Florence Lucille (Wierzba) S.; m. Jeanne Delaney, Apr. 15, 1968 (div. 1975); 1 child, Christine René; m. Georgina Weber, Nov. 19, 1977. BS, Northeast La. State Coll., 1970; MS, Purdue U., 1976, PhD, 1981. With Monsanto Agrl. Co., St. Louis, 1976-91, sci. fellow, 1987-91; sci. fellow Monsanto Corp. Rsch., St. Louis, 1991-93; sci. fellow med. chem. G.D. Searle R&D, St. Louis, 1994—; instr. organic chemistry St. Louis C.C., 1977-78; adj. prof. biochemistry Ctrl. Meth. Coll., 1995—; invited spkr. tech. presentations and seminars. Contbr. chpts. to books, rev. articles, symposia-in-print and articles to profl. jours.; patentee and co-patentee in field. Mem. AAAS, Am. Chem. Soc., Internat. Soc. Heterocyclic Chemistry, Sigma Xi. Avocations: hiking, canoeing, skiing, photography, snorkeling. Office: GD Searle R&D 700 Chesterfield Pky N Saint Louis MO 63198

SILAK, CATHY R., judge; b. Astoria, N.Y., May 25, 1950; d. Michael John and Rose Marie (Janor) S.; m. Nicholas G. Miller, Aug. 9, 1980; 3 children. BA, NYU, 1971; M in City Planning, Harvard U., 1973; JD, U. Calif., 1976. Bar: Calif. 1977, U.S. Dist. Ct. (no. dist.) Calif. 1977, D.C. 1979, U.S. Ct. Appeals (D.C. cir.) 1979, U.S. Dist. Ct. (so. dist.) N.Y. 1980, Idaho 1983, U.S. Dist. Ct. Idaho 1983, U.S. Ct. Appeals (2nd cir.) 1983, U.S. Ct. Appeals (9th cir.) 1985. Law clk. to Hon. William W. Schwarzer U.S. Dist. Ct. (no dist.), Calif., 1976-77; pvt. practice San Francisco, 1977-79, Washington, 1979-80; asst. U.S. atty. So. Dist. of N.Y., 1980-83; spl. asst. U.S. atty. Dist. of Idaho, 1983-84; pvt. practice Boise, Idaho, 1984-90; judge Idaho Ct. Appeals, 1990-93; justice Idaho Supreme Ct., Boise, 1993—; assoc. gen. counsel Morrison Knudsen Corp., 1989-90; mem. fairness com. Idaho Supreme Ct. and Gov.'s Task Force on Alternative Dispute Resolution; instr. and lectr. in field. Assoc. note and comment editor Calif. Law Rev., 1975-76. Land use planner Mass. Dept. Natural Resources, 1973; founder Idaho Coalition for Adult Literacy; bd. dirs. Literacy Lab., Inc. Recipient Jouce Stein award Boise YWCA, 1992, Women Helping Women award Soroptimist, Boise, 1993. Fellow Idaho Law Found (ann., lectr.); mem. ABA (nat. conf. state trial judges jud. adminstrn. divsn.), Nat. Assn. Women Judges, Idaho State Bar (corp./securities sect., instr.). Office: PO Box 83720 Boise ID 83720-0002

SILAKOSKI, ANTHONY FRANK, utility company executive; b. N.J., Dec. 19, 1952; s. Anthony John and Jeanette Silakoski; m. Linda G. Pinkava, Aug. 9, 1974; children: Kristin, Ryan. BSME, BS in Aerospace Engring., U.S. Naval Acad., 1974; MBA, John Carroll U., 1984. Registered profl. engr., Ohio. Commd. ensign USN, 1974, advanced through grades to lt., 1978; served on USS Andrew Jackson Groton, Conn., 1975-78; served on USS Birmingham Norfolk, Va., 1978-79; resigned now capt. Res. USN, 1979—; ops. engr. Cleve. Electric Illumination Co., 1979-81, dir. tng., 1981-86, gen. supervising engr., 1986—; mgr. Ind. Safety Engring., 1988-95, ombudsman, 1996—. With USNR, 1991-96. Mem. ASME, IEEE, Naval Submarine League, Naval Acad. Alumni Assn., NRA (life). Republican. Roman Catholic. Office: Cleve Electric Illuminating Co PO Box 140E Perry OH 44081-0140

SILANO, ROBERT ANTHONY, editor, defense analyst, educator; b. Bklyn., Sept. 10, 1942; s. Ralph Henry and Charlotte Tecla (Borst) S. BA, Cathedral Coll., 1964; postgrad., New Sch., 1965-66, U. Louvain, 1971-72, U. Kent, Canterbury, 1972-74. Tchr. Bd. of Coop. Ednl. Svcs., Patchogue, N.Y., 1964-65; instr. U.S. Army Spl. Warfare Sch., Ft. Bragg, N.C., 1967-69; rsch. scientist Human Scis. Rsch., Inc., Saigon, Vietnam, 1969-71; plans officer Hdqrs. Dept. of the Army, Washington, 1975-77; R&D coord. Army Materiel Systems Analysis Agy., Aberdeen Proving Ground, Md., 1977-79; rsch. scientist Mission Rsch. Corp., Washington, 1979-80; staff mem. Office of the Sec. of Def., Washington, 1980-81; exec. dir. Coun. on Econs. and Nat. Security, Washington, 1982-85; faculty mem. Inst. of Higher Def. Studies Nat. Def. U., Washington, 1986-92; editor Joint Force Quar. Nat. Def. U., 1992—; lectr. U. Saigon, 1969-70, Georgetown U., Washington, 1985; cons. U.S. Synthetic Fuels Corp., Washington, 1982, Human Sci. Rsch., Inc., Saigon, 1972. Bd. dirs. The Thomas More Soc. of Am., Washington, 1984-88; dep. dir. of planning Commn. on the Bicentennial of the U.S. Constn., Washington, 1986; mem. ABA Working Group on Chem. Weapons, Washington, 1984. Capt. U.S. Army, 1966-69, 75-79, 80-81. Mem. Internat. Inst. for Strategic Studies (London). Republican. Roman Catholic. Avocations: collecting modern first editions and Indosinica. Office: Nat Def U Fort Lesley J NcNair Washington DC 20319-5066

SILAS, CECIL JESSE, retired petroleum company executive; b. Miami, Fla., Apr. 15, 1932; s. David Edward and Hilda Videll (Carver) S.; m. Theodosea Hejda, Nov. 27, 1965; children: Karla, Peter, Michael, James. BSChemE, Ga. Inst. Tech., Atlanta, 1953. With Phillips Petroleum Co., Bartlesville, Okla., 1953-94; pres. Europe-Africa, Brussels and London Phillips Petroleum Co., 1968-74; mng. dir. natural resource group Europe/Africa Phillips Petroleum Co., London, 1974-76; v.p. gas and gas liquids div. natural resources group Phillips Petroleum Co., Bartlesville, 1976-78, sr. v.p. natural resources group, 1978-80, exec. v.p. exploration and prodn., minerals, gas and gas liquids, 1980-82, pres., chief operating officer, 1982-85, chmn., CEO, 1985-94; bd. dirs. Milliken & Co., Ascent Entertainment. Bd. dirs. Jr. Achievement, Reader's digest Assocs., Inc., bd. dirs. of Halliburton Co. COMSAT Corp, Boys/Girls Clubs Am., Atlanta, Frank Phillips Found., Bartlesville, Okla.; parton councillor Atlantic Coun. of the U.S.; bd. dirs. Ethics Resource Ctr., Inc., Okla. Found. for Excellence; trustee Frank Phillips Found.; active Trilateral Commn. Served to 1st lt. Chem. Corps, AUS, 1954-56. Decorated comdr. Order St. Olaf (Norway); inducted into Ga. Inst. Tech. Athletic Hall of Fame, 1959, recipient Former Scholar-Athlete Total Person award, 1988; inducted into Okla. Bus. Hall of Fame, 1989; named CEO of Yr., Internat. TV Assn., 1987. Mem. Conf. Bd., Am. Petroleum Inst., U.S. C. of C. (past chmn. bd. dirs.), Bartlesville Area C. of C., Okla. State C. of C. and Industry, 25 Yr. Club, Phi Delta Theta. Avocations: fishing, golf, hunting. Office: PO Box 2127 Bartlesville OK 74005-2127

SILBAJORIS, FRANK RIMVYDAS, Slavic languages educator; b. Kretinga, Lithuania, Jan. 6, 1926; came to U.S., 1949; s. Pranas and Elzbieta (Bagdonaviciute) S.; m. Milda Zamzickaite, Aug. 31, 1955; children: Victoria, Alex. BA, Antioch Coll., 1953; MA, Columbia U., 1955; PhD, Columbia U., 1962; D Philology (hon.), Latvian Acad. Scis., Riga, 1991. Instr. to asst. prof. Oberlin Coll., Ohio, 1957-63; assoc. prof. Ohio State U., Columbus, 1963-67, prof. Slavic langs., 1967-91, chmn. dept., 1986-89, prof. emeritus, 1992—; cons. NEH, 1978-79, exchange fellow, USSR, 1977-79; dir. NEH summer seminars, 1975, 77, 83, 84, 86, 88. Author: Russian Versification: The Theories of Trediakovskij, Lomonosov and Kantemir, 1968, Perfection of Exile: Fourteen Contemporary Lithuanian Writers, 1970, Tolstoy's Aesthetics and His Art, 1991, War and Peace. Tolstoy's Mirror of the World, 1995; editor: The Architecture of Reading, 1976, Mind Against the Wall, 1983; contbr. articles to profl. jours. Cons., lectr., organizer cultural events Lithuanian-Am. Community Orgn., 1949—. Antioch Coll. scholar, 1950-53; fellow John Hay Whitney Found., 1953-54, Ford Found., 1954-56, Woodrow Wilson Ctr., 1984, IREX, USSR, 1963-64. Mem. Inst. Lithuanian Studies (pres. 1977-82), Assn. Advancement Baltic Studies (pres. 1973-74), Am. Assn. Tchrs. Slavic and East European Langs., Am. Assn. Advancement Slavic Studies, Assn. Russian-Am. Scholars. Avocations: photography; bicycling; swimming; travel. Home: 4082 Ruxton Ln Columbus OH 43220-4046 Office: Ohio State U Dept Slavic Langs Columbus OH 43210

SILBAUGH, PRESTON NORWOOD, lawyer, consultant; b. Stockton, Calif., Jan. 15, 1918; s. Herbert A. and Della Mae (Masten) S.; m. Maria Sarah Arriola; children: Judith Ann Freed, Gloria Stypinski, Ximena Carey Braun, Carol Lee Morgan. A.B. in Philosophy, U. Wash., 1940; J.D., Stanford U., 1953. Bar: Calif. With Lockheed Aircraft Corp., 1941-44, Pan Am. World Airways, 1944, Office Civilian Personnel, War Dept., 1944-45; engaged in ins. and real estate in Calif., 1945-54; mem. faculty Stanford Law Sch., 1954-59, assoc. prof. law, 1956-59, assoc. dean, 1956-59; chief dep. savs. and loan commr. for Calif., 1959-61, bus. and commerce adminstr., dir. investment, savs. and loan commr., mem. gov.'s cabinet, 1961-63; dir. Chile-Calif. Aid Program, Sacramento and Santiago, 1963-65; chmn. bd. Beverly Hills Savs. & Loan Assn., Calif., 1965-84; bd. dirs. Wickes Cos., Inc.; chmn. bd., pres. Simon Bolivar Fund, San Diego, Calneva Land and Cattle Co., San Diego; of counsel firm Miller, Boyko & Bell, San Diego. Author: The Economics of Personal Insurance, 1958; also articles. Mem. pres.'s real estate adv. com. U. Calif., 1966—; mem. Beverly Hills Pub. Bldg. Adv. Com., 1970—. Served with USMCR, 1942-43. Mem. ABA, San Diego County Bar Assn., Soc. Internat. Devel., Inter-Am. Savs. and Loan Union, Internat. Union Building Socs., U. Wash., Stanford, Calif. Aggie alumni assns., Order of Coif, Phi Alpha Delta. Clubs: Commonwealth (San Francisco), Town Hall (Los Angeles). Home: Costanera Sur, Zapallar Chile also: 14500 Johnson Rd Red Bluff CA 96080-9281

SILBER, JOHN ROBERT, academic administrator; b. San Antonio, Aug. 15, 1926; s. Paul G. and Jewell (Joslin) S.; m. Kathryn Underwood, July 12, 1947; children: David Joslin, Mary Rachel, Judith Karen, Kathryn Alexandra, Martha Claire, Laura Ruth, Caroline Jocasta. B.A. summa cum laude, Trinity U., 1947; postgrad., Northwestern U., summer 1944, Yale Div. Sch., 1947-48, U. Tex. Sch. Law, 1948-49; M.A., Yale, 1952, Ph.D., 1956; L.H.D., Kalamazoo Coll., 1970; many others, many others. Instr. dept. philosophy Yale U., 1952-55; asst. prof. U. Tex., Austin, 1955-59, asso. prof., 1959-62, prof. philosophy, 1962-70, chmn. dept. philosophy, 1962-67, Univ. prof. arts and letters, 1967-70, chmn. (Comparative Studies Program), 1967, dean (Coll. Arts and Scis.), 1967-70; Univ. prof., prof. philosophy and law Boston U., 1971—, pres., 1971—; vis. prof. U. Bonn, 1960; fellow Kings Coll. U. London, 1963-64; bd. dirs. N.E. Savs. Bank. Author: The Ethical Significance of Kant's Religion, 1960, Straight Shooting: What's Wrong With America and How to Fix It, 1989; editor: Religion Within the Limits of Reason Alone, 1960, Works in Continental Philosophy, 1967—; assoc. editor: Kant-Studien, 1968—; Contbr. to profl. jours. Chmn. Tex. Soc. to Abolish Capital Punishment, 1960-69; mem. Nat. Commn. United Meth. Higher Edn., 1974-77; exec. bd. Nat. Humanities Inst., 1975-78; trustee Coll. St. Scholastica, 1973-85, U. Denver, 1985-89, WGBH Ednl. Found., 1971—, Adelphi U., 1989—; bd. visitors Air U., 1974-80; bd. dirs. Greater Boston coun. Boy Scouts Am., 1981-93, v.p. fin., 1981-93, Silver Beaver award,

1989; mem. Nat. Humanities Faculty, 1968-73, Nat. Captioning Inst., 1985—; bd. advisors Matchette Found., 1971—; mem. Nat. Bipartisan Commn. on Ctrl. Am., 1983-84, Presdl. Adv. Bd. Radio Broadcasting to Cuba, 1985-92; adv. bd. Schurman Libr. of Am. Hist., Ruprecht-Karl U., Heidelberg, 1986—, Jamestown Found., 1989—; mem. def. policy bd. U.S. Dept. Def., 1987-90; mem. internat. coun.advisors Inst. for Humanities at Salado, 1988—; bd. dirs. New Eng. Holocaust Meml. Com., 1989—, Brit. Inst. of U.S., 1989—; Dem. gubernatorial candidate of Mass., 1990; v.p. U.S. Strategic Inst.; bd. dirs. Americans for Med. Progress, 1992—, chmn., 1994—; bd. advisors Nat. Assn. Scholars. Recipient E. Harris Harbison award for disting. tchg. Danforth Found., 1966, Wilbur Lucius Cross medal Yale Grad. Sch., 1971, Outstanding Civilian Svc. medal U.S. Army, 1985, Disting. Pub. Svc. award Anti-Defamation League of B'nai B'rith, 1989, Horatio Alger award, 1992, Am.-Swiss Friendship award, 1991, Israel Peace medal, 1985, Chrenmedaille U. Heidelberg, 1986, White House Small Bus. award for entrepreneurial excellence, 1986, Cross of Paideia, Greek Orthodox Archdiocese of North and South Am.; Fulbright rsch. fellow Germany, 1959-60; Guggenheim fellow Eng., 1963-64; decorated with Knight Comdr.'s Cross with Star of Order of Merit Fed. Republic of Germany, 1983; commandeur Nat. Order of Arts and Letters (France), 1985. Fellow Royal Soc. Arts; mem. Am. Philos. Assn., Am. Soc. Polit. and Legal Philosophy, Royal Inst. Philosophy, Am. Assn. Higher Edn., Nat. Assn. Ind. Colls. and Univs. (dir. 1976-81), Phi Beta Kappa. Office: Boston U 147 Bay State Rd Boston MA 02215-1708

SILBER, JUDY G., dermatologist; b. Newark, July 26, 1953. MD, SUNY, Bklyn., 1978. Intern Brookdale Med. Ctr., Bklyn., 1978-79; resident in dermatology Kings County Hosp., Bklyn., 1979-82; pvt. practice dermatology; affiliated with Meadowlands Med. Ctr., Secaucus, N.J. Fellow Am. Acad. Dermatology; mem. AMA, N.J. Med. Soc. Office: 992 Clifton Ave Clifton NJ 07013-3502

SILBER, NORMAN JULES, lawyer; b. Tampa, Fla., Apr. 18, 1945; s. Abe and Mildred (Hirsch) S.; m. Linda Geraldine Hirsch, June 10, 1979; 1 child, Michael Hirsch. BA, Tulane U., 1967, JD, 1969; postgrad. in bus. adminstrn. NYU, 1970-72. Bar: Fla. 1970, U.S. Dist. Ct. (so. dist. Fla.) 1975, U.S. Tax Ct. 1975, U.S. Ct. Appeals (5th cir.) 1975, U.S. Ct. Appeals (11th cir.) 1981. With legal dept. Fiduciary Trust Co. N.Y., N.Y.C., 1969-72, asst. trust officer, 1971-72; exec. v.p. I.R.E. Fin. Corp., Miami, Fla., 1972-76; mng. atty. Norman J. Silber, P.A., Miami, 1973-85; ptnr. McDermott, Will & Emery, 1985—. Mem. ABA, Fla. Bar (chmn. 11th jud. cir. grievance com. I 1982-84). Republican. Jewish. Home: 1232 Palermo Ave Miami FL 33134-6327 Office: McDermott Will & Emery 201 S Biscayne Blvd Miami FL 33131-4332

SILBER, WILLIAM LEO, finance educator; b. Yonkers, N.Y., Nov. 26, 1942; s. Joseph F. and Pauline (Rothstein) S.; m. Lillian Frank, Jan. 26, 1964; children: Jonathan Mark, Daniel Jay, Tammy Beth. BA, Yeshiva Coll., 1963; MA, Princeton U., 1966, PhD, 1966. Sr. economist Pres.'s Coun. of Econ. Advisors, Washington, 1970-71; prof. NYU, 1966-90; sr. v.p. Lehman Bros., Kuhn, Loeb, N.Y.C., 1983-84; Gitlow prof. of fin. NYU, 1990—; mem. Commodity Exch., N.Y.C., 1984—, N.Y. Mercantile Exch, 1986-90, N.Y. Cotton Exch., 1987—, N.Y. Stock Exch. Options Divsn., 1984-87; cons. Standard & Poors Corp., N.Y.C., 1986-95, Odyssey Ptnrs., N.Y.C., 1988—, U.S. Senate Budget Com., Washington, 1975; advisor Fed. Res. Bank, N.Y.C., 1978-80, 90—. Author: Principles of Money, Banking and Finance, 1973, 9th rev. edit., 1996, Money, 1970, 4th rev. edit., 1977, Portfolio Behavior, 1970; editor: Financial Options, 1990; assoc. editor Rev. of Econ. and Stats. jour., 1973-94. Trustee Sch. of Bus., Yeshiva U., N.Y.C., 1987—; investment com. Social Sci. Rsch. Coun., N.Y.C., 1980-83; econ. adv. coun. Fed. Res. Bank N.Y., 1990. Mem. Am. Econ. Assn., Am. Fin. Assn. Avocation: collecting antique phonographs. Home: 1048 E 9th St Brooklyn NY 11230-4108 Office: NYU 44 W 4th St New York NY 10012-1126

SILBERBERG, DONALD H., neurologist; b. Washington, Mar. 2, 1934; s. William Aaron and Leslie Frances (Stone) S.; m. Marilyn Alice Damsky, June 7, 1959; children: Mark, Alan. MD, U. Mich., 1958; MA (hon.), U. Pa., 1971. Intern Mt. Sinai Hosp., N.Y.C., 1958-59; clin. assoc. in neurology NIH, Bethesda, Md., 1959-61; Fulbright scholar Nat. Hosp., London, 1961-62; NINDB spl. fellow in neuro-ophthalmology Washington U., St. Louis, 1962-63; assoc. neurology U. Pa., 1963-65, asst. prof., 1965-67, assoc. prof., 1967-71, prof., 1971-73, acting chmn. dept., 1973-74, prof., vice chmn. neurology, 1974-82, chmn., 1982-94, assoc. dean internat. programs, 1994—; active staff U. Pa. Med. Ctr., Phila.; cons. Children's Hosp., Phila.; pres., CEO Betasteron Found., Inc., 1994—. Contbr. articles to profl. jours., abstracts, chpts. in books. Recipient grants in study of multiple sclerosis. Mem. Am. Acad. Neurology, Am. Assn. Neuropathologists, Am. Neurol. Assn., Am. Soc. Neurochemistry, Assn. Rsch. in Nervous and Mental Diseases, Coll. Physicians Phila., Internat. Brain Rsch. Orgn., Internat. Soc. Devel. Neurosci., Internat. Soc. Neurochemistry, John Morgan Soc. U. Pa. (pres. 1974-75), N.Y. Acad. Scis., Nat. Multiple Sclerosis Soc. (rsch. programs adv. bd.), Assn. Univ. Profs. Neurology (pres.-elect 1993), Phila. Neurol. Soc. (pres. 1978-79), Soc. Neurosci., World Fedn. Neurology (co-chair rsch. group on organziation & delivery of neurol. care, pres. rsch. group assn., Inc.), Alpha Omega Alpha. Office: U Pa Med Ctr Dept Neurology 3400 Spruce St Philadelphia PA 19104

SILBERBERG, MICHAEL COUSINS, lawyer; b. N.Y.C., July 26, 1940; s. Samuel and Sophie (Cousins) S.; m. Paula Baller, Aug. 17, 1965 (div. 1983); children: Dana, Sara. AB, Colgate U., 1962; JD, U. Chgo., 1965. Bar: N.Y. 1966, D.C. 1966, U.S. Ct. Appeals (2d cir.) 1972, U.S. Supreme Ct. 1975. Trial atty. civil rights div. U.S. Dept. Justice, Washington, 1966-68; asst. U.S. atty. U.S. Dist. Ct. (so. dist.) N.Y., N.Y.C., 1968-71; assoc. Golenbock & Barell, N.Y.C., 1971-75, ptnr., 1976-89; ptnr. Morvillo, Abramowitz, Grand, Iason & Silberberg, P.C., N.Y.C., 1989—. Author: Civil Practice in the Southern District of New York, 1995. 1st. lt. JAGC, U.S. Army, 1969-70. Home: 160 W 66th St New York NY 10023 Office: Morvillo Abramowitz et al Iason & Silberberg PC 565 5th Ave New York NY 10017-2413

SILBERBERG, RICHARD HOWARD, lawyer; b. N.Y.C., Feb. 20, 1951. BA, U. Wis., 1972; JD, NYU, 1975. Bar: N.Y. 1976, U.S. Dist. Ct. (so. and ea. dists.) N.Y., 1976, U.S. Ct. Appeals (2d cir.) 1982, U.S. Ct. Appeals (3d cir.) 1991, U.S. Ct. Internat. Trade 1983, U.S. Supreme Ct. 1994, U.S. Ct. Appeals (11th cir.) 1996. Assoc. Delson & Gordon, N.Y.C., 1975-83, ptnr., 1983-87; ptnr. Dorsey & Whitney, N.Y.C., 1988—, mng. ptnr., 1994—; mem. panel arbitrators U.S. Dist. Ct. for Ea. Dist. N.Y., 1987—; mem. panel mediators U.S. Dist. Ct. for So. Dist. N.Y., 1992—; trustee Lawyers Com. for Civil Rights Under Law, 1992—. Mng. editor NYU Jour. Internat. Law and Politics, 1974-75. Mem. Am. Arbitration Assn. (panel of arbitrators and mediators 1988—). Office: Dorsey & Whitney 350 Park Ave New York NY 10022-6022

SILBERG, JAY ELIOT, lawyer; b. N.Y.C., Apr. 5, 1941; s. Arnold and Lillian (Liberman) S.; m. Ruth Vogel, June 22, 1975; children: Eric, Karen, Joanne. BA cum laude, Amherst Coll., 1963; LLB, Harvard U., 1966. Bar: N.J. 1966, U.S. Dist. Ct. N.J. 1966, U.S. Ct. Appeals (D.C. cir.) 1970, U.S. Ct. Appeals (7th cir.) 1982, U.S. Supreme Ct. 1983, U.S. Ct. Appeals (6th cir.) 1986. Atty. Office Gen. Counsel AEC, Washington, 1966-69; assoc. Shaw, Pittman, Potts & Trowbridge, Washington, 1969-72, ptnr., 1973—. Mem. Assn. of Bar of City of N.Y. (chmn. nuclear tech. and law com. 1988-91). Republican. Jewish. Home: 6109 Neilwood Dr North Bethesda MD 20852-3706 Office: Shaw Pittman Potts & Trowbridge 2300 N St NW Washington DC 20037-1122

SILBERGELD, ARTHUR F., lawyer; b. St. Louis, June 1, 1942; s. David and Sabina (Silbergeld) S.; m. Carol Ann Schwartz, May 1, 1970; children: Diana Lauren, Julia Kay. BA, U. Mich., 1968; M City Planning, U. Pa., 1971; JD, Temple U., 1975. Bar: N.Y. 1976, Calif. 1978, D.C. 1983, U.S. Ct. Appeals (2d, 9th and D.C. cirs.). Assoc. Vladeck, Elias, Vladeck & Lewis, N.Y.C., 1975-77; field atty. NLRB, Los Angeles, 1977-78; ptnr., head employment law practice group McKenna, Conner & Cuneo, L.A., 1978-89; ptnr., head labor and employment law practice group Graham & James, L.A., 1990-96; labor ptnr. Sonnenschein, Nath & Rosenthal, L.A., 1996—; instr. extension divsn. UCLA, 1981-89. Author: Doing Business in California: An Employment Law Handbook, 2d edit. 1996, Advising California Employers, 1990, 91, 93, 94, 95 supplements; contbr. numerous articles to profl. jours. Founding mem. L.A. Mus. Contemporary Art; mem. Mus. Modern Art, N.Y., Art Inst. Chgo.; bd. dirs. Bay Cities unit Am. Cancer Soc., Calif., 1981-85, Jewish Family Svc. L.A., 1981-85, So. Calif. Employment Round Table, 1990-96. Mem. ABA (com. on devel. law under NLRA 1975—), L.A. County Bar Assn. (exec. bd. labor law sect. 1984—). Office: Sonnenschein Nath & Rosenthal 601 S Figueroa St Flr 15 Los Angeles CA 90017

SILBERGELD, ELLEN KOVNER, environmental epidemiologist and toxicologist; b. Washington, July 29, 1945; d. Joseph and Mary (Gion) Kovner; m. Alan Mark Silbergeld, 1969; children: Sophia, Nicholas. AB, Vassar Coll., 1967; PhD, Johns Hopkins U., 1972. Kennedy fellow Johns Hopkins Med. Sch., Balt., 1974-75; scientist NIH, Bethesda, Md., 1975-81; chief toxics scientist Environ. Def. Fund, Washington, 1982-90; prof. epidemiology, toxicology and pharmacology U.Md., Balt., 1990—, affil. prof. environ. law, 1990—; adj. prof. Johns Hopkins Med. Insts., 1990—; guest scientist NIH, 1982-84; mem. sci. adv. bd. EPA, 1983-89, 94—, Dept. Energy, 1994-95; mem. bd. on environ. sci. and toxicology NAS-NRC, 1983-89; mem. com. geosci. environment and resources, 1994—; mem. bd. sci. counselors Nat. Inst. Environ. Health Scis., 1987-93; cons. Oil and CHem. Atomic Workers, 1970, NSF, 1974-75, OECD, 1987—. Mem. editl. bd. Neurotoxicology, 1981-86, Neurobehavioral Toxicology, 1979-87, Am. Jour. Indsl. Medicine, 1980—, Hazardous Waste, 1985—, Archives Environ. Health, 1986—; mem. editl. bd. Environ. Rsch., 1983—, editor-in-chief, 1994—; contbr. articles to profl. jours. Mem. Homewood Friends Meeting. Recipient Wolman award Md. Pub. Health Assn., 1991, Barsky award APHA, 1992, Md. Gov. Excellence citation, 1990, 93; Fulbright fellow, London, 1967, Woodrow Wilson and Danforth fellow, 1967; NAS exch. fellow, Yugoslavia, 1976; MacArthur Found. fellow, 1993; Baldwin scholar Coll. Notre Dame. Mem. AAAS, Am. Soc. Pharmacology and Exptl. Therapeutics, Soc. for Occupational and Environ. Health (sec.-treas. 1983-85, pres. 1987-89), Soc. Toxicology, Soc. for Neurosci., Am. Pub. Health Assn., Collegium Ramazzini, Phi Beta Kappa. Office: U Md Med Sch Dept Epid Prev Medicine Howard Hall 104 Baltimore MD 21201

SILBERGELD, SAM, psychiatrist; b. Wengrov, Poland, Mar. 1, 1918; came to U.S., 1923; s. Hyman and Frieda (Orenstein) S.; m. Mae Ann Driscoll, June 22, 1952; children: Sandra Sue, Daniel Lance, Janet Joy, Nancy Ann. AA, Blackburn Coll., 1938; BS, U. Chgo., 1939; PhD in Chemistry, U. Ill., 1943; MD, Duke U., 1955. Cert. specialist in psychiatry, Md. Instr. biochemistry Mayo Found., Rochester, Minn., 1942-44; instr., asst. prof. chemistry U. Ill., Chgo., 1945-46, 46-52; med. officer U.S. Pub. Health Svcs., Bethesda, Md., 1956-88; staff asst. to dir. Div. Biologic Standards, NIH, Bethesda, 1956-59; rsch. grants specialist Div. Gen. Med. Sci., NIH, Bethesda, 1959-60; chief gen. clin. rsch. NIH, Bethesda, 1960-64; various rsch. positions NIMH, Md., 1964-81; staff psychiatrist, adminstr. geriatric program St. Elizabeth Hosp., Washington, 1981-87; staff psychiatrist Sheppard & Enoch Pratt Hosp., Balt., 1988-89; clin. prof. dept. psychiatry Uniformed Svcs. of the Health Scis. Sch. of Medicine, Bethesda, 1982—; adj. prof. U. Md., College Park, 1979-87, part-time instr., 1992—. Contbr. numerous articles to profl. jours. Mem. vis. com. in scis. Blackburn Coll., Carlinville, Ill., 1986, trustee, 1987—; ad hoc mem. Eagle Scout Review Bd., Bethesda, 1987—; chmn. Boy Scout Troop Com., Kensington, Md., 1973-80. Rsch. grantee Dept. Psychiatry Stanford Sch. Medicine, 1966-67; recipient Leadership Citation Blackburn U., 1989, Editors Choice award for Outstanding Achievement in Poetry, 1996. Mem. AMA, AAAS, Am. Chem. Soc., Am. Psychiat. Assn., Am. Psychosomatic Soc., N.Y. Acad. Scis., Md. Psychiat. Soc. (mem. quality revue com., peer revue com. 1991—). Avocations: mountaineering, tennis, ping pong, basketball. Home: Box 377 10704 Clermont Ave Garrett Park MD 20896

SILBERMAN, ALAN HARVEY, lawyer; b. Chgo., Oct. 22, 1940; s. Milton J. and Mollie E. (Hymanson) S.; m. Margaret Judith Auslander, Nov. 17, 1968; children: Elena, Mark. BA with distinction, Northwestern U., 1961; LLB, Yale U., 1964. Bar: Ill., 1964, U.S. Dist. Ct. (no. dist.) Ill., 1966, U.S. Ct. Appeals (7th cir.) 1970, (5th and 9th cir.) 1977, (D.C. cir.) 1979, (4th cir.) 1980, (11th cir.) 1981, (3rd cir.) 1982, (8th and 10th cirs.) 1993, U.S. Supreme Ct. 1978. Law clk. U.S. Dist. Ct., Chgo., 1964-66; assoc. Sonnenschein Nath & Rosenthal, Chgo., 1964-71, ptnr., 1972—; mem. antitrust adv. bd. Bur. Nat. Affairs, Washington, 1985—; mem. Ill. Atty. Gen. Franchise Adv. Bd., 1996—. Contbr. articles to profl. jours. Bd. dirs., v.p., sec. Camp Ramah in Wisc., Inc., Chgo., 1966-86, pres., 1986-94; bd. dirs. Nat. Ramah Commn., Inc. of Jewish Theol. Sem. Am., N.Y.C., 1970—, v.p., 1986-94, pres., 1994—. Mem. Ill. State Bar Assn. (chmn. antitrust sect. 1975-76), ABA (chmn. antitrust sect. FTC com. 1981-83, chmn. nat. insts. 1983-85, mem. coun. antitrust sect. 1985-88, fin. officer, 1988-90, sect. del. ho. of dels. 1990-92, chair elect 1992-93, chair 1993-94). Home: 430 Oakdale Ave Glencoe IL 60022-2113 Office: Sonnenschein Nath 233 S Wacker Dr Ste 8000 Chicago IL 60606-6404

SILBERMAN, CHARLES ELIOT, magazine editor, author; b. Des Moines, Jan. 31, 1925; s. Seppy I. and Cel (Levy) S.; m. Arlene Propper, Sept. 12, 1948; children—David, Richard, Jeffrey, Steven. A.B., Columbia, 1946, postgrad. in econs, 1946-49; L.H.D. (hon.), Kenyon Coll., 1972. Tutor econs. Coll. City N.Y., 1946-48; instr. econs. Columbia, 1948-53, lectr. econs., 1955-66; asso. editor Fortune mag., 1953-60, mem. bd. editors, 1961-71; dir. Study Law and Justice, 1972-79, dir. The Study of Jewish Life, 1979-85; Mem. joint commn. on juvenile justice standards Am. Bar Assn.; dir. Carnegie Corp. Study Edn. Educators, 1966-69. Co-author: Markets of the Sixties, 1960; author: Crisis in Black and White, 1964, The Myths of Automation, 1966, Crisis in the Classroom, 1970, The Open Classroom Reader, 1973, Criminal Violence, Criminal Justice, 1978, A Certain People, 1985; contbr. to various publs. Bd. dirs. Found. for Informed Med. Decision Making, West End Synagogue; bd. govs. Reconstructionist Rabbinical Coll.; mem. exec. bd. N.Y. chpt. Am. Jewish Com. Lt. (j.g.) USNR, 1943-46. Field Found. fellow, 1971-72. Fellow Nat. Assn. Bus. Economists. Home and Office: 10 W 66th St New York NY 10023-6206 Home (winter): 1629 Pelican Cove Rd #BA134 Sarasota FL 34231

SILBERMAN, CURT C., lawyer; b. Wuerzburg, Fed. Republic Germany; came to U.S., 1938, naturalized, 1944; s. Adolf and Ida (Rosenbusch) S.; m. Else Kleemann, 1935. Student, U. Berlin, U. Munich; JD summa cum laude, Wuerzburg U., 1931, Rutgers U., 1947. Bar: N.J. 1948, U.S. Supreme Ct., 1957. Pvt. practice internat. pvt. law, Florham Park, N.J., 1948—; counsel to Arnold R. Kent, Florham Park; lectr. internat. pvt. law, 1954, 81, 82, 87, 91, 95; prin. guest lectr. at Univ.'s 400th anniversary U. Wuerzburg, 1982. Pres., Am. Fedn. Jews from Cen. Europe, N.Y., 1962-86, chmn. bd., 1986—; pres. Jewish Philanthropic Fund of 1933, Inc., N.Y., 1971-87, chmn. bd. 1987—; trustee Leo Baeck Inst., N.Y., 1962—, N.Y. Found. Nursing Homes, Inc.; hon. trustee Jewish Family Svc. of Metro-West, N.J.; co-chmn. Coun. Jews from Germany, 1974—; chmn. Rsch. Found. for Jewish Immigration Inc. N.Y.; bd. dir. Conf. on Jewish Material Claims Against Germany. Recipient Golden Doctoral Diploma U. Wuerzburg Law faculty, 1982, Festschrift dedicated to him by Am. Fedn. Jews from Cen. Europe in N.Y., 1969, recipient Pub. Svc. medal. Mem. N.J. Bar Assn. (chmn. com. comparative jurisprudence 1966-73, chmn. com. internat. trade 1974-78), Essex County Bar Assn., German-Am. Lawyers Assn., German-Am. C. of C., Am. Coun. on Germany, Internat. Biographical Dictionary of Cen. European Emigrés (adv. bd.) Contbr. articles to legal jours.; lectr. on polit. edn. and contemporary Jewish history.

SILBERMAN, ENRIQUE, physics researcher and administrator; b. Buenos Aires, Dec. 9, 1921; came to U.S., 1966; m. 1949; 2 children. PhD in Engring., U. Buenos Aires, 1945. Investigator physics Argentina Atomic Energy Commn., Buenos Aires, 1953-58; head dept. Arg AEC, 1958-63; prof. U. Buenos Aires, 1963-66; prof. physics Fisk U., Nashville, 1966—; dir. photonic materials and devices NASA Ctr., 1992—; guest prof. U. Notre Dame, 1963; cons. Arg Nat. Coun. Sci. Rsch., 1964; vis. prof. Vanderbilt U., 1967—. Mem. AAAS, Am. Assn. Physics Tchrs., Am. Phys. Soc., Arg Physics Assn. Office: Fisk U Dept Physics Nashville TN 37208-3051*

SILBERMAN, H. LEE, public relations executive; b. Newark, Apr. 26, 1919; s. Louis and Anna (Horel) S.; m. Ruth Irene Rapp, June 5, 1948; children: Richard Lyle, Gregory Alan, Todd Walter. B.A., U. Wis., 1940. Radio continuity writer Radio Sta. WTAQ, Green Bay, Wis., 1940-41; reporter Bayonne (N.J.) Times, 1941-42; sales exec. War Assets Adminstrn., Chgo., 1946-47; copy editor Acme Newspictures, Chgo., 1947; reporter, editorial writer Wichita (Kans.) Eagle, 1948-55; reporter Wall St. Jour., N.Y.C., 1955-57; banking editor Wall St. Jour., 1957-68; 1st v.p., dir. corporate relations Shearson-Hamill & Co., N.Y.C., 1968-74; N.Y. corr. Economist of London, 1966-72; contbg. editor Finance mag., 1970-74, editor in chief, 1974-76; v.p., dir. Fin. Services Group, Carl Boyir & Assos., Inc., N.Y.C., 1976-78, sr. v.p., 1978-80, exec. v.p., 1981-86; sr. counselor Hill & Knowlton, Inc., N.Y.C., 1986-93, sr. v.p., 1993-96, sr. mng. dir., 1996—. Contbr. articles to profl. jours. Served to capt. C.E. AUS, 1942-46. Recipient Loeb Mag. award U. Conn., 1965; Loeb Achievement award for distinguished writing on fin. Gerald M. Loeb Found., 1968. Mem. Soc. Profl. Journalists, Soc. Silurians, N.Y. Fin. Writers Assn., Deadline Club N.Y., Overseas Press Club, Zeta Beta Tau. Republican. Home: 80 Miller Rd Morristown NJ 07960-5237

SILBERMAN, IRWIN ALAN, public health physician; b. Newport News, Va., Sept. 1, 1932; s. Henry and Toby (Weiss) S.; m. Lynne Sussman, Feb. 1954 (div. 1961); children: Denise, Donn; m. Mitsue Fukuyama, May 1964 (div. 1984); children: Daniel, Dean, Dana; m. Andrea Z. George, Nov. 1993. BA, U. Calif., Berkeley, 1953; MD, U. Calif., San Francisco, 1956; MS, U. No. Colo., 1980. Intern L.A. County Harbor Gen. Hosp., Torrance, Calif., 1956-57; resident ob-gyn. Harbor/UCLA Med. Ctr., Torrance, 1957-61; commd. USAF, 1961, advanced through grades to col., 1973; staff obstetrician-gynecologist Tachikawa (Japan) Air Base, 1963-65; chief ob-gyn. Mather Air Force Base, Sacramento, 1965-66; chief aeromed. services Yokota Air Base, Tokyo, 1966-68; dir. base med. services Itazuke Air Base, Fukuoka, Japan, 1968-70, Kirtland Air Force Base, Albuquerque, 1970-72; chief hosp. services USAF Hosp. Davis-Monthan, Tucson, 1972-81; ret. USAF, 1981; med. dir. CIGNA Healthplan of Fla., Tampa, 1981-83; chief women's clinic H.C. Hudson Comprehensive Health Ctr., L.A., 1983-85; dir. maternal health and family planning programs Los Angeles County Dept. Health Svcs., L.A., 1985-91, dir. family health programs, maternal and child health, 1991—; mil. cons. to surgeon-gen. USAF, 1980-81; bd. dirs. L.A. Regional Family Planning Coun.; pres. Perinatal Adv. Coun. of L.A. Comtys., 1993-94. Chmn. health profls. adv. com. March of Dimes, Los Angeles, 1988; camp physician Boy Scouts Nat. Jamboree, Fort Hill, Va., 1985. Recipient Meritorious Service medal, USAF, 1972, 81, Air Force Commendation medal, 1980, Air medal, 1969. Fellow Am. Coll. Obstetricians and Gynecologists, Am. Coll. Physician Execs., Am. Coll. Preventive Medicine; mem. APHA, Am. Acad. Med. Dirs., So. Calif. Pub. Health Assn. Avocations: skiing, photography. Home: 3716 Beverly Ridge Dr Sherman Oaks CA 91423-4509 Office: LA County Dept Health Svcs 241 N Figueroa St Los Angeles CA 90012-2693

SILBERMAN, JAMES HENRY, editor, publisher; b. Boston, Mar. 21, 1927; s. Henry R. and Dorothy (Conrad) S.; m. Selma Shapiro, Aug. 26, 1986; children by previous marriage: Michael, Ellen. AB, Harvard U., 1950. Asst. to pub. Writer, Inc., 1950-51; asst. to advt. mgr. Little, Brown & Co., 1951-53; publicity dir. Dial Press, Inc., 1953-55, editor, 1954-55, exec. editor, 1955-59, v.p., editor-in-chief, 1959-63; editor The Dial, 1959-62; sr. editor Random House, Inc., N.Y.C., 1963-65, exec. editor, 1965-66, exec. editor, v.p., 1966-68, v.p., editor in chief, 1968-76, also pub., 1975-76; pres., editor-in-chief Summit Books div. Simon & Schuster, 1976-91; v.p., sr. editor Little Brown & Co., N.Y.C., 1991—; judge First Novel, Am. Book Awards, 1982; mem. adv. com. George Polk Meml. Awards, 1980—. Served as pfc. AUS, World War II. Mem. PEN, Assn. Am. Pubs. (Freedom to Read com. 1971-80, Freedom to Pub. com. 1982), Book Table, Pubs. Lunch Club, Corp. of Yaddo (bd. dirs. 1987—, exec. com. 1989—). Clubs: Harvard (N.Y.C.); Century Assn. Home: 315 E 70th St New York NY 10021-8657 Office: Little Brown & Co Inc 1271 Avenue Of The Americas New York NY 10020

SILBERMAN, JOHN ALAN, lawyer; b. Balt., Sept. 20, 1951; s. Ronnie A. and Dovera (Gogel) S. BA, Northwestern U., 1973; JD, Harvard U., 1976. Bar: N.Y. 1977, U.S. Dist. Ct. (so. and ea. dists.) N.Y. 1977. Assoc. Paul, Weiss, Rifkind, Wharton & Garrison, N.Y.C., 1976-84, ptnr., 1985—. Bd. dirs. Coun. on Econ. Priorities, N.Y.C., 1986-90, Young Audiences, N.Y.C., 1988-90. Office: Paul Weiss Rifkind Wharton & Garrison 1285 Avenue Of The Americas New York NY 10019-6028*

SILBERMAN, LAURENCE HIRSCH, federal judge; b. York, Pa., Oct. 12, 1935; s. William and Anna (Hirsch) S.; m. Rosalie G. Gaull, Apr. 28, 1957; children: Robert Stephen, Katherine DeBoer Balaban, Anne Gaull. AB, Dartmouth Coll., 1957; LLB, Harvard U., 1961. Bar: Hawaii 1962, D.C. 1973. Assoc. Moore, Torkildson & Rice and Quinn & Moore, Honolulu, 1961-64; ptnr. Moore, Silberman & Schulze, Honolulu, 1964-67; atty. appellate div. gen. counsel's office NLRB, Washington, 1967-69; solicitor of labor U.S. Dept. Labor, Washington, 1969-70, undersec. labor, 1970-73; ptnr. Steptoe & Johnson, Washington, 1973-74; dep. atty. gen. U.S. Washington, 1974-75; ambassador to Yugoslavia, 1975-77; mng. ptnr. Morrison & Foerster, Washington, 1978-79, 83-85; exec. v.p. Crocker Nat. Bank, San Francisco, 1979-83; judge U.S. Ct. Appeals (D.C. cir.), Washington, 1985—; lectr. labor law and legis. U. Hawaii, 1962-63; adj. prof. adminstrv. law Georgetown U., Washington, 1987-94, NYU, 1995—; Pres.' spl. envoy on ILO affairs, 1976; mem. gen. adv. com. on Arms Control and Disarmament, 1981-85; mem. Def. Policy Bd., 1981-85; vice chmn. State Dept.'s Commn. on Security and Econ. Assistance, 1983-84. Bd. dirs. Com. on Present Danger, 1978-85, Inst. for Ednl. Affairs, 1981-85; vice chmn. adv. council on gen. govt. Rep. Nat. Com., 1977-80. Served with AUS, 1957-58. Am. Enterprise Inst. sr. fellow, 1977-78, vis. fellow 1978-85. Mem. U.S. Jud. Conf. Com. on Ct. Adminstrn. and Case Mgmt., Coun. on Fgn. Rels.

SILBERMAN, ROBERT A. S., lawyer; b. Lebanon, Pa., Mar. 4, 1945; s. Henry T. and Genevieve (Mensh) S.; m. Nancy D. Netzer, Nov. 10, 1974. BA, Yale U., 1967; JD, Harvard U., 1970. Bar: Mass. 1970, Pa. 1984. Assoc. Csaplar & Bok, Boston, 1970-78, ptnr., 1978-90; ptnr. Gaston & Snow, Boston, 1990-91, Edwards & Angell, Boston, 1991—. Mem. citizens rev. com. United Way Massachusetts Bay, Boston, 1981-89; dir. All Newton (Mass.) Music Sch., 1994—, v.p., 1995-96, pres. 1996—. Mem. ABA (vice chmn. health law com. sect. bus. law 1992-95, chmn., 1995—), Internat. Bar Assn., Boston Bar Assn., Nat. Health Lawyers Assn., Phi Beta Kappa. Office: Edwards & Angell 101 Federal St Boston MA 02110-1800

SILBERMAN, ROSALIE GAULL, government official; b. Jackson, Miss., Mar. 31, 1937; d. Samuel and Alice (Berkowitz) Gaull; m. Laurence H. Silberman, Apr. 28, 1957; children: Katherine, Anne, Robert. BA, Smith Coll., 1958. Tchr., 1967-72; with Natl. Adv. Coun. on Edn. of Disadvantaged Children, 1973-75; bd. dirs. Widening Horizons, 1973-75; dir. comm., press sec. Sen. Robert Packwood, 1977-79; exec. dir., sec., treas. New Coalition for Econ. and Social Change, 1981-83; dir. pub. rels. San Francisco Conservatory of Music, 1982-83; spl. asst. Commr. Mimi Weyforth Dawson FCC, 1983-84; with EEOC, 1984-86, vice chmn., 1986-94, commr., 1994-95; exec. dir. Office of Compliance, Libr. Congress, Washington, 1995—. Office: Office Compliance Rm LA 200 Washington DC 20540-1999

SILBERSACK, MARK LOUIS, lawyer; b. Cin., Dec. 27, 1946; s. Joseph Leo and Rhoda Marie (Hinkler) S.; m. Ruth Ann Schwallie, Sept. 7, 1985. AB, Boston Coll., 1968; JD, U. Chgo., 1971. Bar: Ohio 1971, U.S. Dist. Ct. (so. dist.) Ohio 1973, U.S. Ct. Appeals (6th cir.) 1974, U.S. Supreme Ct. 1975. Atty. Dinsmore & Shohl, Cin., 1971—; lectr. Ohio CLE Inst., Columbus, 1981-91. Co-author: Managed Care: The PPO Experience, 1990, Information Sharing Among Health Care Providers, 1994. V.p. Cin. Cmty. Chest, 1985-89, Ohio United Way, Columbus, 1989-94, chmn. bd. dirs., 1994—; pres. Hyde Park Neighborhood Coun., Cin., 1989-91, Hyde Park Ctr. for Older Adults, 1989-91; mem. Cin. Bd. Health, 1991—, chmn., 1995—. Mem. ABA, Ohio State Bar Assn., Cin. Bar Assn., Fed. Bar Assn., Bankers Club, Hyde Park Golf And County Club. Republican. Roman Catholic. Avocations: reading, travel, theater. Home: 3465 Forestoak Ct Cincinnati OH 45208-1842 Office: Dinsmore & Shohl 1900 Chemed Ctr 255 E 5th St Cincinnati OH 45202-4700

SILBERSTEIN, ALAN MARK, financial services executive; b. Munich, Dec. 22, 1947; came to U.S., 1949; s. Leon and Rose (Rosenblatt) S.; m. Carol Krongold, Aug. 30, 1970; children: Eric, Adam, Meredith. BS in Engring., Columbia U., 1969; MBA, Harvard U., 1972. Design engr. Ford

Motor Co., Dearborn, Mich., 1969-70; budget analyst N.Y.C. Bur. of Budget, 1972-74; various positions Chem. Bank, N.Y.C., 1974-88, exec. v.p., head Consumer Banking Group, 1990-92; exec. v.p. and dir. of retail banking Midlantic Corp., Edison, N.J., 1992-95; CEO claims divsn. Travelers/Aetna Property Casualty Corp., Hartford, Conn., 1995—; bd. dirs. N.Y. Switch Corp., 1990-92, Cirrus System, Inc., 1991. Trustee Tenafly Bd. Edn., N.J., 1983-86, Yeshiva U. Sy Syms Sch. Bus., 1989—; mem. consumer adv. coun. Fed. Res. Bd., 1989-91; bd. dirs. N.Y. State Tree Consortium Inc., 1990-92; mem. exec. Bergen County N.J. Boy Scouts Am., 1992—, exec. v.p. fin., 1995. Mem. Am. Bankers Assn. (chmn. retail banking exec. com. 1992—), Harvard Bus. Sch. Club N.Y. (sec. 1981-85, bd. dirs. 1982-83, 85-88). Office: Travelers Ins One Travelers Sq Hartford CT 06183

SILBERSTEIN, DIANE, publishing executive. Publisher The New Yorker, 1995—. Office: Advance Publ Inc 20 W 43rd St New York NY 10036*

SILBEY, JOEL HENRY, history educator; b. Bklyn., Aug. 16, 1933; s. Sidney and Estelle (Mintzer) S.; m. Rosemary Johnson, Aug. 13, 1959; children: Victoria, David. BA, Bklyn. Coll., 1955; MA, U. Iowa, 1956, PhD, 1963. Asst. prof. San Francisco State Coll., 1960-64, U. Md., College Park, 1965-66; asst. prof. Am. History Cornell U., Ithaca, N.Y., 1966-67, assoc. prof., 1967-68, prof., 1968-86, Pres. White prof. history, 1986—; vis. asst. prof. history U. Pitts., 1964-65. Author: The Shrine of Party, 1967, The Transformation of American Politics, 1968, A Respectable Minority: The Democratic Party in the Civil War Era, 1977, The Partisan Imperative: The Dynamics of American Politics before the Civil War, 1985, The American Political Nation, 1838-1893, 1991; editor: (with others) Voters, Parties and Elections, 1972, American Political Behavior, 1984, The History of American Electoral Behavior, 1978; editor-in-chief: Encyclopedia of the American legislative System, 1993; editorial cons. numerous publs.; contbr. numerous articles to profl. jours. Am. Philos. Soc. fellow, 1969-70; NSF fellow, 1970-74; NEH fellow, 1980-81; vis. fellow Ctr. for Advanced Study in the Behavioral Scis., 1985-86; vis. scholar Russell Sage Found., 1988-89; John Simon Guggenheim Meml. fellow, 1989-90. Mem. Am. Hist. Assn. (program com. 1977), Orgn. Am. Historians (chmn. program com. 1983), So. Hist. Assn., Social Sci. History Assn. (co-chmn. membership com., mem. exec. com). Home: 105 Judd Falls Rd Ithaca NY 14850-2715 Office: Cornell U 452 Mcgraw Hall Ithaca NY 14853-4601

SILBEY, ROBERT JAMES, chemistry educator, researcher, consultant; b. N.Y.C., Oct. 19, 1940; s. Sidney Richard and Estelle (Mintzer) S.; m. Susan Sorkin, June 24, 1962; children: Jessica, Anna. BS, CUNY Bklyn. Coll., 1961; PhD, U. Chgo., 1965. Asst. prof. MIT, Cambridge, 1966-76, prof., 1976—, chmn. dept. chemistry; vis. prof. U. Utrecht, The Netherlands, 1972-73, U. Grenoble, France, 1983; cons. Exxon Rsch., Clinton, N.J., 1984—. Author: Physical Chemistry, 1991; editor: Conjugated Polymers, 1991; contbr. articles to profl. jours. Recipient Alexander von Humboldt Found. Sr. Scientist award, 1989, Max Planck award, 1992; Alfred P. Sloan fellow, 1968, John S. Guggenheim fellow, 1972; Dreyfus Found. Tchr.-Scholar grantee, 1969. Fellow AAAS, Am. Acad. Arts and Scis., Am. Phys. Soc. Avocations: swimming, sailing. Office: MIT Dept Chemistry 77 Massachusetts Ave Cambridge MA 02139-4301

SILBIGER, MARTIN L., dean; b. Mar. 17, 1938; m. Ruth Steele, June 4, 1957; children: Martin Lawrence, Jr., Eve Michelle, Jonathan Steele, Holly Christine, Wendy Elizabeth. AB, U. Pa., 1958; MD, Western Res. U., 1962; MBA, U. South Fla., 1989. Diplomate Nat. Bd. Med. Examiners, Am. Bd. Radiology, Am. Bd. Nuclear Medicine. Intern, resident U. Hosps. of Cleve./ The Johns Hopkins Hosp. of Balt., 1963-66; radiologist Tampa Gen. Hosp., 1968-85, co-dir. dept. radiology, 1977-84, chief of staff, 1978-80; assoc. prof. dept. radiology U. So. Fla. Coll. Medicine, 1973-82, chmn., assoc. prof. dept. radiology, 1982-83, chmn., prof. dept. radiology, 1983—; interim dean Sch. of Medicine U. South Fla., 1995—; radiologist Meml. Hosp., 1975-85; cons. physician, med. staff Shriners Hosp. for Crippled Children, Tampa Unit, 1986—, Med. Staff, U. South Fla. Psychiat. Ctr., 1987—; radiology cons. Tampa Gen. Hosp., 1986—, Tampa Vets. Adminstrn. Hosp., 1975—; dir. dept. radiology H. Lee Moffitt Cancer Ctr. and Rsch. Inst., 1986-90; numerous coll. and med. coms. Contbr. numerous articles to profl. jours. and pubis. With NIH, 1966-68. Fellow Am. Coll. Radiology; mem. Am. Cancer Soc., Am. Coll. Radiology, Assn. Am. Med. Colls., Assn. Univ. Radiologists, Fla. Med. Assn., fla. Radiol. Soc., Fla. West Coast Radiol. Soc. (pres. 1977), Hillsborough County Med. Assn., N.Am. Soc. for Cardiac Imaging, Soc. of Chmn. of Acad. Radiology Depts., Soc. Magnetic Resonance, Southeastern Angiographic Soc., So. Med. Assn., So. Radiol. Conf. Office: Univ South Fla Sch of Medicine 12901 Bruce B Downs Blvd Tampa FL 33612-4799

SILCOTT, JAMES, principal; b. Balt., Sept. 15, 1956; s. Thomas Braden and Janet Ann (Kreis) S.; m. Mary Beth Wirth, Sept. 6, 1980; children: Lauren, Bethany, Thomas. BS, Ohio State U., 1979, MA, 1985; postgrad., U. Dayton, 1992—. Cert. secondary English supr., elem. prin., middle sch. prin., secondary prin., asst. supt. Tchr. Bishop Watterson High Sch., Columbus, Ohio, 1979-89, chair drama dept., 1983-89, dir. activities, 1988-89; prin., tchr. Latin St. Timothy elem. sch., Columbus, 1989—; initiator student council, sch. newspaper, sch. recycling program St. Timothy Sch., Columbus, Japanese intern program, 1990, middle sch. leadership tng. program; tchr., adv. com. Columbus State C. C., 1991—; mem. Diocesan com. rewrite teacher supervision standards, 1992, Diocesan com. for tchr. lay-off provisions, 1993; espeaker in field. Contbr. articles to newspapers. Vol. Charity Newsies, Columbus,1990—; mem. fin. com. St. Timothy Parish. Recipient Nat. Sch. Excellence award U.S. Dept. Edn., Washington, 1989. Mem. Prin. Assn. Catholic Elem. Sch. (treas. 1990-92, exec. bd. 1990—), Phi Lambda Theta. Democrat. Roman Catholic. Avocations: swimming, poetry, drama, cycling. Home: 431 Village Dr Columbus OH 43214-2829 Office: St Timothy Sch 1070 Thomas Ln Columbus OH 43220-5047

SILEN, WILLIAM, physician, surgery educator; b. San Francisco, Sept. 13, 1927; s. Dave and Rose (Miller) S.; m. Ruth Heppner, July 13, 1947; children: Stephen, Deborah, Mark. BA, U. Calif., Berkeley, 1946; MD, U. Calif., San Francisco, 1949; MA (hon.), Harvard U., 1966. Diplomate Am. Bd. Surgery. Intern U. Calif., San Francisco, 1949-50, asst. resident gen. surgery, 1950-56, chief resident gen. surgery, 1956-57; asst. chief surgery Denver VA Hosp., 1957-59, chief surgery, 1959-60; asst. chief surgery San Francisco Gen. Hosp., 1960-61, chief surgery, 1961-66; surgeon-in-chief Beth Israel Hosp., Boston, 1966-94; instr. surgery, asst. prof. surgery U. Colo. Med. Sch., Denver, 1957-60; asst. prof. then assoc. prof. surgery U. Calif. Sch. Medicine, San Francisco, 1960-66; prof. surgery Harvard Med. Sch., Boston, 1966—, Johnson and Johnson prof. surgery, 1966-94; dir. Harvard Digestive Diseases Ctr. NIH, Bethesda, Md., 1984-94. Author: Cope's Early Diagnosis of the Acute Abdomen, 1995, Conservative Management of Breast Cancer, 1983, Atlas of Techniques in Breast Surgery, 1995. With USAF, 1950-52. Mem. AMA, ACS, Soc. Univ. Surgeons, H.C. Naffziger Surg. Soc., Phi Beta Kappa. Avocation: bonsai cultivation. Office: Beth Israel Hosp 330 Brookline Ave Boston MA 02215-5400

SILER, EUGENE EDWARD, JR., federal judge; b. Williamsburg, Ky., Oct. 19, 1936; s. Eugene Edward and Lowell (Jones) S.; m. Christy Dyanne Minnich, Oct. 18, 1969; children—Eugene Edward, Adam Troy. B.A. cum laude, Vanderbilt U., 1958; LL.B., U. Va., 1963; LL.M., Georgetown U., 1964. Bar: Ky. 1963, Va. 1963, D.C. 1963. Individual practice law Williamsburg, 1964-65; atty. Whitley County, Ky., 1965-70; U.S. atty. Eastern Dist. Ky., Lexington, 1970-75; judge U.S. Dist. Ct., Eastern and Western Dists., Ky., 1975-91; chief judge Eastern Dist., Ky., 1984-91; judge U.S. Ct. Appeals (6th cir.), 1991—. Campaign co-chmn. Congressman Tim L. Carter, 1966, 5th Congl. Dist.; campaign co-chmn. U.S. Senator J.S. Cooper, 1966; trustee Cumberland Coll., Williamsburg, 1965-73, 80-88; 1st v.p. Ky. Bapt. Convention, 1986-87; bd. dirs. Bapt. Healthcare Systems Inc., 1990—. Served with USN, 1958-60, with Res. 1960-83. E. Barrett Prettyman fellow, 1963-64; recipient medal Freedom's Found., 1968. Mem. FBA, Ky. Bar Assn. (Judge of Yr. award 1992), D.C. Bar Assn., Va. State Bar. Republican. Baptist. Home: PO Box 129 Williamsburg KY 40769-0129 Office: US Ct Appeals 1380 W 5th St, ste.200 London KY 40741-1615

SILER, WALTER ORLANDO, JR., retired business executive; b. Atascadero, Calif., May 21, 1920; s. Walter Orlando and Hylda Ruth Martyn (Jackson) S.; m. Carolyn Louise Townsend, 1978; children by previous marriage: Robert Eugene, Barbara Ellen, Susan Jane,Donald Walter, David Brian. B.S., U. So. Calif., 1941. C.P.A., Calif. Partner Arthur Andersen & Co. (C.P.A.'s), Phoenix, 1958-61; pres., treas., dir. Bargain City, U.S.A., Inc., Phila., 1962; treas., dir. Getty Oil Co., Los Angeles, 1963-67; v.p. Getty Oil Co., 1966-67, asst. controller, 1968-70; controller Fluor Corp., Los Angeles, 1970-72; gen. mgr. Saudi Arabian ops. Whittaker Corp., 1972-73; bus. mgr. Northrop Aircraft Div., Taif, Saudi Arabia, 1973-74; v.p. fin. Fluor Arabia Ltd., Dhahran, Saudi Arabia, 1974-77; mgr. accounting The Ralph M. Parsons Co., Pasadena, Calif., 1977-78; v.p., treas., sec. Parsons Constructors Inc., Pasadena, 1978-85; treas., dir. Mission Corp., 1963-68; treas. Mission Devel. Co., 1963-67; dir. Skelly Oil Co., 1963-68. Served to maj. USAAF, 1941-46. Mem. AICPA, Fin. Execs. Inst. (bd. dirs. L.A. chpt. 1990-93), Calif. Soc. CPAs, Univ. Club of Pasadena (bd. govs. 1990-91), Town Hall Calif. (L.A.), Sigma Nu, Phi Kappa Phi, Beta Gamma Sigma, Beta Alpha Psi. Republican. Home: 703 N Stoneman Ave Apt G Alhambra CA 91801-1410

SILER-KHODR, THERESA MARIE, biochemistry educator; b. Pomona, Calif., June 17, 1947; d. Joseph Horace and Anna Marie (Ary) Siler; m. Gabriel Shukri, Jan. 26, 1974; children: Tanya Ann Khodr, Christina Emilie Knodr, Zeina Gabriella Khodr. BA in Chemistry, Immaculate Heart Coll., L.A., 1968; Phd in Biochemistry, U. Hawaii, 1971. Cert. profl. chemist, Am. Chem. Soc. Nuclear medicine technician St. Vincent's Hosp., L.A., 1968; NIH predoctoral fellow dept biochemistry and biophysics U. Hawaii, Honolulu, 1968-70, predoctoral Ford Found. fellow, 1970, postdoctoral Ford Found. fellow dept. anatomy andreproductive biology, 1971; chief adenohypophyseal hormone sect. InterSci. Inst., L.A., 1972; asst. rsch. biologist dept. reproductive medicine U. Calif., San Diego, 1972-74; asst. prof. dept. ob-gyn. Am. Univ. Beirut Hosp., 1974-76; with U. Tex. Health Sci. Ctr., San Antonio, 1976—, assoc. prof. dept. ob-gyn., 1979-86, prof., 1986—, dir. clin. endocrine infertility lab.; participant preceptor tng. programs including AID program for Internat. Edn. in Gynecology and Obstetrics, Dept. Ob-Gyn., Am. Univ. Beirut Hosp., 1974-76, Reproductive Endocrinology Fellowship Program, Health Sci. Ctr., U. Tex., 1987—; cons. rev. bd. for NIH Intramural Grants, S.W. Biomed. Rsch. Found., 1985-87; extramural reviewer Med. Rsch. Coun. Can., 1985, 86, 87, NICHD, 1985, NSF, 1981; presenter profl. confs. including XI World Congress of Gynecology and Obstetrics, West Berlin, 1985, 1stInternat. Meeting on Human Fetal Membranes, London, Ont., Can., 1986. Contbg. author: Radioimmunoassay Methods, 1971, Biorhythym in Human Reproduction, 1973, Advances in the Biosciences 15, 1975, Physiology and Pathophysiology of Reproduction, 1979, Clinics in Perinatology, 1983, Neonatal and Fetal Medicine, 1989, others; contbr. numerous articles to profl. publs.; mem. editorial bd. Jour. Endocrinological Investigation, 1978-83, Endocrinology, 1987—; ad hoc reviewer Obstetrics and Gynecology, 1982, Psychoneuroendocrinology, 1983, 84, 85, Neuroendocrinology, 1985,86, Placenta, 1987,88. Recipient Wyeth award The Pacific Coast Fertility Soc., 1972, 79, 80, Purdue Frederick Pres.'s award Congress for Am. Coll. Ob-Gyn., 1972, 1st prize Armed Forces Congress of Ob-Gyn., 1971; rsch. grantee Syntex Labs., U. Tex. Health Sci. Ctr., 1980-85, WHO, Am. U. Beirut Hosp., 1975-76, co-investigator, preceptor or cons. many other rsch. grants. Mem. AAAS, NIH (mem. reproductive endocrinology study sect. 1986-89, 90, 93-94, rsch. grantee 1980, 84, 82-86, 88-92), The Endocrine Soc. (chair fetal and neonatal endocrinology session of 65th soc. session 1983, mem. women's caucus), Soc. for Study of Reprodn., Soc. for Gynecologic Investigation, Am. Endocrine Soc., Assn. Profs. of Gynecology and Obstetrics, U. Tex. Health Sci. Ctr. Women's Faculty Assn., Sigma Xi. Office: Univ Tex Health Sci Ctr 7703 Floyd Curl Dr San Antonio TX 78284-6200

SILETS, HARVEY MARVIN, lawyer; b. Chgo., Aug. 25, 1931; s. Joseph Lazarus and Sylvia (Dubner) S.; m. Elaine L. Gordon, June 25, 1961; children: Hayden Leigh, Jonathan Lazarus (dec.), Alexandra Rose. BS cum laude, DePaul U., 1952; JD (Frederick Leicke scholar), U. Mich., 1955. Bar: Ill. 1955, U.S. Dist. Ct. (no. dist.) Ill. 1955, N.Y. 1956, U.S. Tax Ct. 1957, U.S. Ct. Mil. Appeals 1957, U.S. Ct. Appeals (7th cir.) 1958, U.S. Supreme Ct. 1959, U.S. Ct. Appeals (6th cir.) 1965, U.S. Ct. Appeals (2d cir.) 1971, U.S. Ct. Appeals (5th cir.) 1972, U.S. Ct. Appeals (11th cir.). Assoc. Paul, Weiss, Rifkind, Wharton & Garrison, N.Y.C., 1955-56; asst. atty. U.S. Dist. Ct. (no. dist.) Ill., 1958-60; chief tax atty. U.S. atty. No. Dist. Ill., Chgo., 1960-62; ptnr. Harris, Burman & Silets, Chgo., 1962-79, Silets & Martin, Ltd., Chgo., 1979-92; asst. advance tng. program IRS, U. Mich., 1952-53; law lectr. advance fed. taxation John Marshall Law Sch., 1962-66; adj. prof. taxation Chgo.-Kent Coll. Law, 1985—; gen. counsel Nat. Treasury Employees Union, 1968-92; mem. adv. com. tax litigation U.S. Dept. Justice, 1979-82; mem. Tax Reform Com., State of Ill., 1982-83; mem. Speedy Trial Act Planning Group U.S. Dist. Ct. (no. dist.) Ill., 1976-79; mem. civil justice reform act adv. com. U.S. Dist. Ct. (no. dist.) Ill., 1991-94; lectr. in field. Contbr. articles to profl. jours. Trustee Latin Sch., Chgo., 1970-76; active Chgo. Crime Commn., 1975-93, Govv.'s Commn. Reform Tax Laws, Ill., 1982-83. With AUS, 1956-58. Fellow Am. Coll. Trial Lawyers (chmn. com. on fed. rules of criminal procedure 1982-91, fed. rules of evidence com. 1988-93, mem. judiciary com., Upstate Ill. com. chmn. 1990-91), Am. Coll. Tax Counsel, Internat. Acad. Trial Lawyers; mem. ABA (active various coms.), Bar Assn. 7th Fed. Cir. (chmn. com. criminal law and procedure 1972-82, bd. govs. 1983-86, sec. 1986-88, v.p. 1989-90, pres. 1990-91), Fed. Bar Assn. (bd. dirs. 1971—, pres. 1977-78, v.p. 1976-77, sec. 1975-76, treas. 1974-75, active various coms.), Chgo. Bar Assn. (tax com. 1958-66, com. devel. law 1966-72, 78—, com. fed. taxation 1968—, com. evaluation candidates 1978-80, exec. com. tax sect. 1994—), Am. Bd. Criminal Def. Lawyers, Chgo. Soc. Trial Lawyers, Decalogue Soc. Lawyers, Bar Assn. N.Y. City, Nat. Assn. Criminal Def. Lawyers, Standard Club, Cliff Dwellers Club, Chgo. Club, Phi Alpha delta, Pi Gamma Mu. Office: Katten Muchin & Zavis 525 W Monroe St Ste 1600 Chicago IL 60661-3629

SILFEN, DAVID M., investment banker; b. N.Y.C., Nov. 30, 1945; s. Herman and Esther (Weiss) S.; m. Lyn Gordon, June 12, 1971; 1 son, Adam. B.A., U. Pa., 1966; M.B.A., Columbia U., 1968. Assoc. Goldman Sachs & Co., N.Y.C., 1968-74, v.p., 1974-78, ptnr., 1978—. Office: Goldman Sachs & Co 1 New York Plaza New York NY 10004*

SILFVAST, WILLIAM T., laser physics educator, consultant; b. Salt Lake City, June 7, 1937; s. Andrew William and Dorothy Phyllis (Hobba) S.; m. Susan Carol Denton, Sept. 19, 1959; children: Scott William, Robert Denton, Stacey Marie. BS in Physics, BS in Math., U. Utah, 1961, PhD in Physics, 1965. Rsch. assoc. U. Utah, Salt Lake City, 1965-66; NATO postdoctoral fellow Oxford (Eng.) U., 1966-67; mem. tech. staff Bell Labs., Holmdel, N.J., 1967-82; Guggenheim fellow Stanford (Calif.) U., 1982-83; disting. mem. tech. staff AT&T Bell Labs., Holmdel, 1983-89; prof. physics and elec. engring. U. Cen. Fla., Orlando, 1990-94, chair dept. physics, 1994—. Contbr. numerous articles to sci. jours.; numerous patents relating to lasers. Trustee 1st Presbyn. Ch., Matawan, N.J., 1979-82, 88-89; chmn. bd. trustees Monmouth County Arts Coun., Red Bank, N.J., 1987-88. Fellow IEEE (assoc. editor IEEE Jour. Quantum Elecs. 1986-91), Optical Soc. Am. (chmn. tech. coun. 1988-89), Am. Phys. Soc. Avocations: writing, golf, tennis, skiing, automobile restoration. Office: U Cen Fla CREOL PO Box 162700 Orlando FL 32816-2700

SILHAVY, THOMAS JOSEPH, molecular biology educator; b. Wauseon, Ohio, Jan. 13, 1948; s. W.J. and Helen (Batdorf) S.; Daileen K. Stutzman, June 27, 1969; children—Marc Thomas, Ned Thomas. B.S. in Pharmacy, Ferris State Coll., 1971; A.M. in Biochemistry, Harvard U., 1974, Ph.D. in Biochemistry, 1975; D.S., Ferris State Coll, 1982. Instr. Harvard U. Med Sch., Boston, 1978-79; head genetics sect. Nat. Cancer Inst., Frederick, MD., 1979-81, dir. genetics, 1981-84; instr. Advanced Bacterial Genetics, Cold Spring Harbor, N.Y., 1981-85; prof. molecular biology Princeton U., 1984—. Co-author: Experiments with Gene Fusions, 1984, The Power of Bacterial Genetics: A Literature-based Course, 1992; contbr. over 100 articles to profl. jours. Patentee in field. Recipient Advanced Tech. Achievement award Litton, 1982, Wellcom vis. professorship in microbiol. scis., 1990, Pres.'s award for disting. teaching, 1993; Jane Coffin Childs fellow, 1975-77, Med. Rsch. Found. fellow, 1978-79. Fellow Am. Soc. Microbiology, Am. Acad. Microbiology; mem. AAAS, Am. Soc. Biol. Chemists, Am. Soc. Cell Biology. Home: 22 Van Doren Way Belle Mead NJ 08502-5508 Office: Princeton U Dept Molecular Biology Princeton NJ 08544

SILIPIGNI, ALFREDO, opera conductor; b. Atlantic City, Apr. 9, 1931; s. Alfredo and Elisabeth (Calhoun) S.; m. Gloria Rose DiBenedetto, Apr. 11, 1953; children: Marisa, Elisabetta Luisa, Afredo Roberto. Student, Westminster Choir Coll., 1948, Juilliard Sch. Music, 1953; HHD (hon.), Kean Coll. N.J., 1978. Prin. condr., gen. dir., artistic dir. N.J. State Opera, Newark, 1965—, founder Young Artist Program, 1969—; guest lectr. Glassboro (N.J.) State Coll. Carnegie Hall debut with NBC Symphony Orch., 1956; condr. NBC Symphony, Boston, Bklyn. and Conn. operas, Newark Symphony; guest condr. Vienna State Opera, 1976, Grand Liceo di Barcelona, Spain, 1976, London, 1977, also numerous cos. Eng., Venezuela, France, Italy, Mex. and Can. with frequent appearances at L'Opera de Montreal; made recs. fo Zaza by Leoncavallo, "Adriana Lecouvrer" by Cilea; prin. guest condr. and advisor Bellas Artes, Mex., 1993-94. Recipient Centennial medal St. Peter's Coll., 1972, Disting. Svc. to Culture award City of San Remo, Columbia Found. award, Boys Town of Italy award, Music award N.J. Edn. Assn., 1988. Office: NJ State Opera 50 Park Pl 10th Fl Newark NJ 07102-2400

SILJAK, DRAGOSLAV D., engineering educator; b. Belgrade, Yugoslavia, Sept. 10, 1933; came to U.S. 1964, naturalized; s. Dobrilo T. and Ljubica Z. (Zivanovic) S.; m. Dragana T. Todorovic, Sept. 28, 1967; children—Ana, Matija. BSEE, U. Belgrade, 1958, MSEE, 1961, ScD, 1963. Docent prof. U. Belgrade, 1963-64; assoc. prof. U. Santa Clara, Calif., 1964-70; prof. engring. U. Santa Clara, 1970-84, B. and M. Swig Univ. chair, 1984—. Author: Nonlinear Systems, 1969, Large Scale Systems, 1978, Decentralized Control of Complex Systems, 1991. Disting. prof. Fulbright Found., 1984. Fellow IEEE; mem. Serbian Acad. Scis. and Arts (hon.). Mem. Christian Ch. Office: U Santa Clara The Alemeda Santa Clara CA 95053

SILK, ELEANA S., librarian; b. Detroit, Aug. 10, 1951; d. John and Helen (Kavenski) S. BS in Zoology, Mich. State U., 1972; BS in Geology, George Washington U., 1979; MDiv, St. Vladimir's Sem., 1986, MA in Religious Edn., 1988; MLS, Columbia U., 1989. Asst. libr. St. Vladimir's Sem., Crestwood, N.Y., 1985-90, libr., 1990—; mem. history and archives commn., bicentennial commn. Orthodox Ch. in Am., Syosset, N.Y., 1989—. Editor: The Legacy of St. Vladimir, 1989; contbr. articles to religious jours. Mem. ALA, N.Y. Area Theol. Libr. Assn., Oral History Assn., Fellowship Orthodox Stewards, Orthodox Theol. Soc. Am., Federated Russian Orthodox Clubs (chpt. pres. 1978-80, gov. 1981-82). Office: St Vladimir's Sem 575 Scarsdale Rd Tuckahoe NY 10707-1659

SILK, FREDERICK C.Z., financial consultant; b. Pretoria, Transvaal, South Africa, July 29, 1934; arrived in Canada, 1964; s. Frederick Charles and Edythe D'Olier (Ziervogel) S.; m. Margaret Colbourne, May 12, 1962; children: Michael, Alison, Jennifer. BS, Rhodes U., Grahamstown, Republic South Africa, 1954; cert. acctg. theory, U. Witwatersrand, Johannesburg, Republic South Africa, 1957. Acct., cons. Deloitte, Plender, Haskins & Sells, Johannesburg, London and N.Y.C., 1954-64; mgmt. cons. P.S. Ross & Ptnrs., Montreal, Que, Can., 1964-68; v.p. fin. and adminstrn. J&P Coats (Can.) Ltd., Montreal, 1968-74; treas. Standard Brands, Ltd., Montreal, 1974-75; asst. treas. Standard Brands, Inc., N.Y.C., 1975-78; treas. Harlequin Enterprises, Ltd., Toronto, Ont., Can., 1978-82; v.p., treas. Nabisco Brands, Ltd., Toronto, 1982-95; pvt. treas. cons. Toronto, 1995—. Fellow Inst. Chartered Accts. (Eng., Wales), Inst. Chartered Accts. (South Africa), Fin. Execs. Inst. Avocations: music, choral music, Gilbert and Sullivan operettas. Office: Ste 418, 80 Front St E, Toronto, ON Canada M5E 1T4

SILK, GEORGE, photographer; b. Levin, New Zealand, Nov. 17, 1916; s. Arthur and Constance (Naylor) S.; m. Margery G. Schieber, Nov. 28, 1947; children—Stuart, Georgiana B., Shelley G. Ed., New Zealand schs. With photographic store in New Zealand, 1935-39; ofcl. photographer Australian Inf. Forces in Middle East, 1940-42, New Guinea, 1942-43; photographer Life mag., 1943-73; corr. in Life mag., ETO, 1944-45, PTO, 1945, China, 1946, N.Y.C., 1947-73; free lance photographer, 1973—. Pictures in color sect. 1959 annual Ency. Brit.; photographs in Fine Arts exhibit, 1962, 63. Recipient gold medal Art Dirs. Club, 1961; Photographer of Year award Ency. Brit., 1960; Am. Soc. Mag. Photographers Meml. award, 1962; Photographer of Year awards Nat. Press Photographers Assn., U. Mo., World Book, 1960, 62, 63, 64; Brehm Meml. award Rochester Inst. Tech., 1966. Home: Owenoke Park Westport CT 06880-6851

SILK, THOMAS, lawyer; b. Beaver, Pa., Dec. 12, 1937; s. Thomas and Alice Genevieve (Beck) S.; 1 child, Nicole Amory. AB, U. Calif.-Berkeley, 1959, LLB, 1963. Bar: Calif. 1964, U.S. Dist. Ct. (no. dist.) Calif. 1964, U.S. Ct. Appeals (D.C., 2-10th cirs.) 1966-68, U.S. Supreme Ct. 1967. Appellate atty. tax div. U.S. Dept. Justice, Washington, 1964-66; spl. asst. to asst. atty. gen. tax div., 1966-68; assoc. Brobeck, Phleger & Harrison, San Francisco, 1968-71; founder, sr. ptnr. Silk, Adler & Colvin, San Francisco, 1972—; adj. prof. Sch. Law, U. Calif., Berkeley; dir. comparative nonprofit law project of Asia Asia Found., 1995; trustee Jenifer Artman Found., Ctr. Citin Initiatives, St. Francis Found.; author; lectr. tax-exempt orgns., nonprofit corps., charitable estate planning. Office: Silk Adler & Colvin 235 Montgomery St San Francisco CA 94104-2902

SILKENAT, JAMES ROBERT, lawyer; b. Salina, Kans., Aug. 2, 1947; s. Ernest E. and Mildred R. (Iman) S.; children: David Andrew, Katherine Anne. BA, Drury Coll., 1969; JD, U. Chgo., 1972; LLM, NYU, 1978. Bar: N.Y. 1973, D.C. 1980. Assoc. Cravath, Swaine & Moore, N.Y.C., 1972-80; counsel Internat. Fin. Corp., Washington, 1980-86; ptnr. Morgan, Lewis & Bockius, N.Y.C., 1986-89, Morrison & Foerster, N.Y.C., 1989-92, Winthrop, Stimson, Putnam & Roberts, N.Y.C., 1992—; chmn. Council N.Y. Law Assocs., 1978-79, Lawyers Com. Internat. Human Rights, 1978-80. Editor ABA Guide to Fng. Law Firms, Moscow Conf. on Law Bilateral Econ. Rels., ABA Guide to Internat. Bus. Negotiations; contbr. over 70 articles on law and pub. policy to profl. jours. Served to capt. U.S. Army, 1972-73. Fellow NEH, 1977, U.S. Dept. State, 1981. Fellow Am. Bar Found.; mem. ABA (chmn. internat. law and practice sect. 1989-90, chmn. sect. officer's conf. 1990-92, mem. ho. of dels. 1989—, bd. govs. 1994—). Office: Winthrop Stimson Putnam & Roberts One Battery Park Plz New York NY 10004

SILKETT, ROBERT TILLSON, food business consultant; b. Columbia, Mo., Nov. 12, 1929; s. Ross Jacob and Marion Dorchester (Tillson) S.; m. Sally Forrest Lash, Dec. 23, 1954; children—Robert Tillson, Elizabeth L. B.A., Duke U., 1951; M.B.A. with distinction, Wharton Grad. Sch., U. Pa., 1956. With mktg. dept. Anderson Clayton Co., 1956-58; with Gen. Foods Corp., 1958-78, group exec. corp. mktg. and sales, 1976-78; chmn. bd., chief exec. officer Reckitt & Colman N.A., Rochester, N.Y., also R.T. French Co., 1978-86; exec. v.p., dir. Curtice-Burns Foods, Rochester, 1986-90; owner, pres. The RTS Group, Rochester, 1990—. Past bd. dirs. Rochester United Way, Rochester Mus.; mem. exec. bd. Wharton Grad. Sch., Rochester council Boy Scouts Am. Served to lt. USNR, 1951-54. Mem. Wharton Grad. Sch. Alumni Assn. (past chmn.), Beta Gamma Sigma. Republican. Episcopalian. Clubs: Rochester Country, Wilton Riding (past pres.); Wharton M.B.A. (N.Y.C.) (past dir.), Mid Ocean (Bermuda), Key Largo Anglers, Card Sound (Key Largo).

SILLARS, MALCOLM OSGOOD, communication educator; b. Union City, N.J., Feb. 12, 1928; s. Malcolm Osgood and Dorothy Edna (Browning) S.; m. Charlotte Jane Grimm, June 1, 1948; children—Paul Louis, Bruce Malcolm, Alan Leslie. B.A., U. Redlands, 1948, M.A., 1949; Ph.D., U. Iowa, 1955. Asst. prof. communication Iowa State U., Ames, 1949-53; asst. prof. Calif. State U., Los Angeles, 1954-56; prof., dean Calif. State U., Northridge, 1956-71; pres. Calif. State U., 1969-70; prof. U. Mass., Amherst, 1971-74; prof. communication U. Utah, Salt Lake City, 1974—; dean humanities U. Utah, 1974-81. Author: Speech: Content and Communications, 6th edit., 1991, Argumentation and Critical Decision Making, 4th edit., 1996, Messages, Meanings, and Culture, 1991; contbr. articles to profl. jours. Recipient Silver Beaver award Boy Scouts Am. Mem. Speech Communication Assn. (pres.), Western Speech Communication Assn. (pres.), AAUP, ACLU. Democrat. Home: 3508 Eastoaks Dr Salt Lake City UT 84124-3811 Office: U Utah Dept Communication Salt Lake City UT 84112

SILLECK, HARRY GARRISON, lawyer; b. Putnam Valley, N.Y., Mar. 19, 1921; s. Harry Garrison and Bertha May (Barrett) S.; m. June Baird, Mar. 4,

1977. B.A., Union Coll., 1940; LL.B., Columbia U., 1943. Bar: N.Y. 1944, U.S. Supreme Ct. 1966, U.S. Ct. Appeals (2d cir.) 1966 (6th cir.) 1976. Assoc. Dorr Hand Whittaker & Watson, N.Y.C., 1945-55, ptnr., 1955-63; ptnr. Mudge Rose Guthrie Alexander & Ferdon, N.Y.C., 1963-86, chmn., 1978-85. Served to 1st lt. AC, U.S. Army, 1943-45, ETO. Mem. Phi Beta Kappa. Home: 131 E 69th St New York NY 10021-5158

SILLIMAN, RICHARD GEORGE, retired lawyer, retired farm machinery company executive; b. Elgin, Ill., Aug. 11, 1922; s. Charles B. and Mabel Ellen (Winegar) S.; m. Mary L. Yost, June 12, 1945; children—Martha Jane, Charles R. B.A. in History, Cornell Coll., Mt. Vernon, Iowa, 1946; J.D., Northwestern U., 1949. Bar: Ill. 1949. Atty. various U.S. agys., Chgo., 1949-52; atty., asst. sec. Elgin Nat. Watch Co., Ill., 1952-59, sec., gen. atty., 1959-62; asst. gen. counsel Deere & Co., Moline, Ill., 1962-75, assoc. gen. counsel, 1975-82, sec., assoc. gen. counsel, 1982-87. Mem. editorial bd. Ill. Law Rev., 1948-49. Contbr. articles to profl. jours. Past pres., hon. dir. Quad-City Symphony Orch., Moline and Davenport, Iowa, 1968-87; bd. dirs., trustee Upper Rock Island County YMCA, Moline, 1965-87; bd. dirs. Police-Fire Commn., Elgin, 1957-61; bd. dirs., sec. Elgin YMCA, 1955. Served with USN, 1943-46. Mem. ABA, Ill. State Bar Assn. (past chmn. com. on corp. law dept.), Short Hills Country Club (Moline), Union League (Chgo.). Avocations: golf, music, sailing. Home: 4817 6th Street Ct East Moline IL 61244-4274

SILLIN, LELAN FLOR, JR., retired utility executive; b. Tampa, Fla., Apr. 19, 1918; s. Lelan Flor and Ruth (Berry) S.; m. Joan Outhwaite, Sept. 26, 1942; children: Lelan Flor, John Outhwaite, Andrew Borden, William Berry. AB with distinction, U. Mich., 1940, JD, 1942; LLD (hon.), Wesleyan U., 1969. Bar: N.Y. 1946. With Gould & Wilkie, N.Y.C., 1945-51; with Central Hudson Gas & Electric Corp., Poughkeepsie, N.Y., 1951-68, v.p., asst. gen. mgr., 1955-60, pres., 1960-68, chief exec. officer, 1964-67, also trustee; pres. Northeast Utilities, Hartford, Conn., 1968-70, chmn. bd., 1970-83, chief exec. officer, chmn. bd., 1968-83, also trustee; chmn. bd. Conn. Yankee Atomic Power Co., 1971-83, Northeast Energy, 1970-83; former chmn., dir. Fuel Cell User Group; bd. dirs. Waterbury Rep & Am.; past chmn. nat. power survey exec. adv. com. FPC, 1965-72; dir. Inst. Nuclear Power Ops., 1979-85, chmn., 1982-84; chmn. utility nuc. power oversight task com., 1986. Former mem. steering com. Nat. Urban Coalition; former mem. Pres.'s Adv. Com. Environ. Quality; former bd. dirs. Nat. Office Social Responsibility, New Eng. Council; trustee emeritus Edwin Gould Found. for Children, Woodrow Wilson Nat. Fellowship Found., New Eng. Natural Resources Ctr.; trustee emeritus Wesleyan U., former vice-chmn. bd. trustees; past mem. adv. com. White House Conf. on Balanced Nat. Growth and Econ. Devel.; past mem. Pub. Com. on Mental Health; former mem. Am. Arbitration Assn.; former bd. dirs. Conn. Bus. and Industry Assn.; trustee emeritus Vassar Bros. Hosp., Poughkeepsie. Served to capt. USMCR, 1942-45. Recipient Raymond E. Baldwin medal Wesleyan U., 1986, Oliver Townsend award Atomic Indsl. Forum, 1986. Former mem. Conf. Bd. (sr.). Clubs: Hartford; Dauntless (Essex, Conn.); Century Association, University (N.Y.C.). Office: NE Utilities Millstone Nuclear Power Sta Tng Ctr Box 128 Waterford CT 06385

SILLMAN, ARNOLD JOEL, physiologist, educator; b. N.Y.C., Oct. 10, 1940; s. Philip and Anne L. (Pearlman) S.; m. Jean Fletcher Van Keuren, Sept. 26, 1969; children—Andrea Jose, Diana Van Keuren. A.B., U. Calif.-Los Angeles, 1963, M.A., 1965, Ph.D., 1968. Asst. prof. U. Calif.-Los Angeles, 1969-73, Davis, 1975-78, assoc. prof., 1978-85, prof. 1985—; asst. prof. U. Pitts., 1973-75. Contbr. articles to profl. jours. USPHS trainee, UCLA, 1966-67; fellow NSF, 1967-68, Fight for Sight, Inc., 1968-69. Mem. Am. Physiol. Soc., Soc. Gen. Physiologists, Am. Soc. Zoologists, Assn. Research in Vision and Ophthalmology, AAAS, N.Y. Acad. Sci. Jewish. Home: 1140 Los Robles St Davis CA 95616-4927 Office: U Calif Sect Neurobiology Physiology & Behavior Divsn Biol Scis Davis CA 95616

SILLS, DAVID LAWRENCE, retired sociologist; b. N.Y.C., Aug. 24, 1920; s. R. Malcolm and Charlotte Noyes (Babcock) S.; m. Yole Laura Granata, Feb. 18, 1948; 1 son, Gregory Lawrence. BA, Dartmouth Coll., 1942; MA, Yale U., 1948; PhD, Columbia U., 1956. Research analyst pub. opinion and sociol. research div. Allied Occupation of Japan, 1947-50; research asso. Bur. Applied Social Research Columbia U., 1952-61, acting dir., 1961-62, dir. research, 1962; expert UN Tech. Assistance Orgn., Bombay, India, 1960-61; editor Crowell Collier and Macmillan, N.Y.C., 1962-67; assoc. dir. demographic div. Population Council, N.Y.C., 1968-70; dir. Population Council, 1970-72; exec. assoc. Social Sci. Research Council, N.Y.C., 1973-88, exec. assoc. emeritus, 1988—; fellow Ctr. for Advanced Study in Behavioral Scis., Stanford, Calif., 1967-68; vis. scholar Russell Sage Found., 1973. Editor: International Encyclopedia of the Social Sciences, 17 vols., 1968; editor (with Robert K. Merton): Social Science Quotations: Who Said What, Where and When, 1992. Served with U.S. Army, 1942-46. Mem. Am. Assn. Pub. Opinion Rsch., Am. Sociol. Assn., Sociol. Rsch. Assn. Democrat. Episcopalian. Home: Box 303 Norwalk CT 06850

SILLS, HILARY H., public relations executive; b. Chgo., Feb. 24, 1947. Cert. in EEC Studies, U. Brussels, 1968; BA in History, Hollins Coll., 1969. With staff of William Whitehurst U.S. Ho. Reps.; with The Daily Bond Buyer, GE; dir. energy and environment Govt. Rsch. Corp., 1975-87; v.p. Govt. Rsch. Group, 1988-89; sr. cons. Pub. Affairs Comm. Mgmt., 1987-88; v.p. Hill & Knowlton, 1989-91; sr. prin. Capitoline Internat. Group, 1991—. former contbg. editor Economist Intelligence Unit. Mem. Women in Govt. Rels. Office: Capitoline Internat Group Ltd 1615 L St NW # 1150 Washington DC 20036-5610

SILLS, NANCY MINTZ, lawyer; b. N.Y.C., Nov. 3, 1941; d. Samuel and Selma (Kahn) Mintz; m. Stephen J. Sills, Apr. 17, 1966; children: Eric Howard, Ronnie Lynne. BA, U. Wis., 1962; JD cum laude, Albany Law Sch., 1976. Bar: N.Y. 1977, U.S. Dist. Ct. (no. dist.) N.Y. 1977, U.S. Tax Ct. 1984. Asst. editor fin. news Newsweek mag., N.Y.C., 1962-65; staff writer, reporter Forbes mag., N.Y.C., 1965; research assoc. pub. relations Eastern Airlines, N.Y.C., 1965-67; asst. editor Harper & Row, N.Y.C., 1968-69; freelance writer, editor N.Y.C. and Albany, N.Y., 1967-70; confidential law sec. N.Y. State Supreme Ct., Albany, 1976-79; assoc. Whiteman, Osterman & Hanna, Albany, 1979-81, Martin, Noonan, Hislop, Troue & Shudt, Albany, 1981-83; ptnr. Martin, Shudt, Wallace & Sills, Albany, 1984; of counsel Krolick and DeGraff, Albany, 1984-89; ptnr. Hodgson, Russ, Andrews, Woods & Goodyear, Albany, 1990-91; pvt. practice Albany, 1991—; of counsel Lemery & Reid, Albany and Glens Falls, N.Y., 1993-94; asst. counsel N.Y. State Senate, 1983-88; cons. The Ayco Corp., 1975; bd. dirs. Albany Law Sch. Estate Planning Inst., 1980-86. Editor: Reforming American Education, 1969, Up From Poverty, 1968; researcher The Negro Revolution in America, 1963; contbr. articles to mags. Bd. dirs. Jewish Philanthropies Endowment, 1983-86, United Jewish Fedn. N.E. N.Y. Endowment Fund, 1992—, Daus. Sarah Found., 1994—, Albany Jewish Cmty. Ctr., 1984-87; mem. Guilderland (N.Y.) Conservation Adv. Coun., 1993—; planned giving tech. adv. com. Albany Law Sch., 1991-95, chmn., 1992-95; mem. regional cabinet State of Israel Bonds Devel. Corp. for Israel, 1991-92. Mem. ABA, N.Y. State Bar Assn., Albany County Bar Assn., Warren County Bar Assn., Estate Planning Coun. Ea. N.Y., Womens Aux. Albany County Med. Soc., Capital Dist. Trial Lawyers Assn., Capital Dist. Women's Bar Assn., Phi Beta Kappa, Sigma Epsilon Sigma. Republican. Home: 16 Hiawatha Dr Guilderland NY 12084-9526 Office: 126 State St Albany NY 12207-1637

SILVA, BENEDICTO ALVES DE CASTRO, surgeon, educator; b. Salvador, Bahia, Brazil, June 26, 1927; s. Octacílio Alves de Castro and Nathercia Crusoé Silva; m. Maria Guanaes, Dec. 20, 1958; children: Catia Maria, Marta Maria, Gloria Maria. Degree, Bahia U., Salvador, 1952. Asst. prof. faculty odontology Bahia U., 1962-72, adj. prof. faculty odontology, 1972—, maxillar buco surgeon, 1962—; maxillar buco surgeon Santa Izabel Hosp., Salvador, 1953-72, Hosp. Martagão Gesteira, Salvador, 1958-60; coord. Bahia Oral Cancer Ctr., Salvador, 1988—; coord. Oncology Ctr.-Mouth-Bahia, Salvador, 1988—. Author: Patients of High Risk, 1988; contbr. chpt. to book: Phamacology, 1980. Pres. Bahia Dental Coun., Salvador, 1981-85. Officer Brazilian Army, 1944-45. Mem. Brit. Assn. Oral Maxillar Surgery (assoc.), Bahia Dental Acad., Pierre Fuchard Acad. (medal 1990), Minas Gerais Dental Acad. (medal 1990), Brazilian Soc. Cancer, European Sch. Oncology, Bahia Acad. Odontology (pres. 1985—). Home: Padre Daniel Lisboa # 5-A, 40 285-560 Salvador Brazil Office: Med Ctr Graça, Humberton de Campos St # 11, 40150 Salvador Brazil

SILVA, ERNEST R., visual arts educator, artist. BFA, U. R.I., 1971; MFA, Tyler Sch. Art, 1974. Instr. U. R.I., Kingston, 1977-79; lectr. dept. visual arts U. Calif. San Diego, La Jolla, 1979-87, prof. dept. visual arts, 1987—; represented by Jan Baum Gallery, L.A., Lenore Gray Gallery, Providence, R.I., Porter Randall Gallery, La Jolla; bd. dirs. Installation Gallery, San Diego, mem. arts adv. bd., 1992—, exec. com., 1993—; lectr. Phila. Coll. Art, 1973, U. R.I., 1974, 84, 91, RISD, 1977, Tyler Sch. Art, Elkins Park, Pa., 1979, U. Calif. Irvine, 1981, Southwestern Coll., Chula Vista, 1982, San Diego State U., 1985, Nat. Soc. Arts and Letters, Washington, 1986, Friends of Jung, San Diego, 1991. One-person exhbns. include Inst. Contemporary Art, Boston, 1972, Artists Space, N.Y.C., 1975, Anyart Contemporary Art Ctr., Providence, R.I., 1976, Lenore Gray Gallery, Providence, 1978, 79, 92, Roy Boyd Gallery, L.A., 1982, 84, 87, Quint Gallery, San Diego, 1982, 83, 86, Jan Baum Gallery, L.A., 1989, 91, Tuttle Gallery, McDonogh, Md., 1990, Porter Randall Gallery, La Jolla, 1994, many others; group exhbns. include Mus. Phila. Civic Ctr., 1973, Cheltenham (Pa.) Art Ctr., 1973, Pratt Graphic Ctr., N.Y.C., 1975, Corcoran Art Gallery, Washington, 1975, Ft. Worth Art Mus., 1976, Baker Gallery, La Jolla, 1980, Ind. Contemporary Exhbns., L.A., 1982, Navy Pier, Chgo., 1983, 84, 85, Roy Boyd Gallery, Chgo., 1983, 85, 86, Heckscher Mus. Art, Huntington, N.Y., 1984, Indpls. Mus. Art, 1984, Forum Internat. Kunstmesse, Zurich, Switzerland, 1984, Nat. History Mus., San Diego, 1985, Visual Arts Ctr. Alaska, Anchorage, 1985, San Francisco Airport Mus., 1985, Sonrisa Gallery, L.A., 1985, Alaska State Mus., Juneau, 1986, Foire Internat. De L'Art Contemporain, Nice, France, 1986, Lyceum Theatre, San Diego, 1987, Installation Gallery, San Diego, 1986, 87, 88, Chgo. Internat. Art Exposition, 1987,L.A. Convention Ctr., 1987, Cmty. Arts, San Francisco, 1989, 90, Annex Gallery, La Jolla, 1990, Bill Bace Gallery, N.Y.C., 1991, David Lewinson Gallery, Del Mar, Calif., 1991, Southwestern Coll. Art, Chula Vista, Calif., 1992, Boehm Gallery Palomar Coll, San Marcos, Calif., 1993, Porter Randall Gallery, La Jolla, 1992, numerous others; represented in permanent collections Fogg Art Mus. Harvard U., Cambridge, Mass., Grand Rapids (Mich.) Art Mus., La Jolla Mus. Contemporary Art, Laguna Mus. Art, De Saisset Mus. U. Santa Clara, Newport Harbor Art Mus., Newport Beach, Calif., Mus. Contemporary Art, San Diego, La Jolla, San Jose Mus. Art, San Diego Mus. Art; subject reviews, articles, 1974—. Office: U Calif San Diego Visual Arts 0327 La Jolla CA 92093

SILVA, EUGENE JOSEPH, lawyer; b. Gloucester, Mass., May 23, 1942; s. Edward Joseph and Rose (Lebre) S.; m. Nancy Blue-Pearson, Jan. 8, 1972; children: Eugene Joseph II, Michael Joseph. BS with honors, Maine Maritime Acad., 1964; JD, U. Notre Dame, 1972. Bar: Calif. 1972, U.S. Dist. Ct. (so. and cen. dists.) Calif. 1972, Tex. 1977, U.S. Dist. Ct. (so. and ea. dists.) Tex. 1978, U.S. Ct. Appeals (5th, 2d and 11th cirs.) 1978, U.S. Supreme Ct. 1981; lic. Master Mariner. Assoc. Luce, Forward, Hamilton & Scripps, San Diego, 1972-77; assoc. Vinson & Elkins, Houston, 1977-79, ptnr., 1980—. Bd. dirs. Cabrillo Festival Inc., San Diego, 1974-77, San Jose Clinic, Inc., 1990—, pres. 1993-95; bd. dirs. Portuguese Heritage Scholarship Found. Decorated knight Equestrian Order of Holy Sepulchre of Jerusalem; recipient Outstanding Alumni award Maine Maritime Acad., 1990. Mem. Houston Bar Assn., Calif. Bar Assn., Tex. Bar Assn., Internat. Bar Assn., Grays Inn U. Notre Dame Sch. Law (pres. 1970-72), Southeastern Admiralty Law Inst., Maritime Law Assn. U.S. (proctor in admiralty 1974—), Portuguese Union Calif. (bd. dirs. 1973-74), Portuguese Am. League San Diego (pres. 1974-75), Portuguese Am. Leadership Coun. U.S., Asia-Pacific Lawyers Assn., Notre Dame Club (pres. San Diego chpt. 1976-77), Houston Yacht Club, Houston Ctr. Club, The Naval Club (London). Roman Catholic. Home: 8 Smithdale Estates Dr Houston TX 77024-6600 Office: Vinson & Elkins 2500 First City Tower 1001 Fannin St Houston TX 77002

SILVA, FELIPE, former tobacco company executive; b. Cienfuegos, Cuba, Feb. 27, 1919; came to U.S., 1960, naturalized, 1968; s. Felipe and Hortensia (Cardenas) S.; m. Dolores Alvarez, Feb. 3, 1945; children: Ana, Felipe Rafael, Maria Dolores, Lourdes. Student, U. Mich., 1936-38; D. Law, U. Havana, 1942, Public Acct., 1943. Pres. Tabacalera Cubana S.A., 1949-60; spl. sales rep. ACC div. Am. Tobacco Co., St. Petersburg, Fla., 1960-62; mgr. P.R. br. ACC div. Am. Tobacco Co., San Juan, 1963-67; export mgr. Am. Tobacco Co. div. Am. Brands, Inc., N.Y.C., 1968-78; pres. Am. Cigar div. Am. Brands, Inc., 1979-80, pres., chief exec. officer Am. Cigar div., 1981-83, chmn., chief exec. officer cigar div., 1983-84. Mem. U. Mich. Alumni Assn. Roman Catholic. Lodge: Rotary. Home: 600 Grapetree Dr Apt 7bs Miami FL 33149-2703

SILVA, JOANNA KONTAXIS, dietitian; b. Psari Trifilias, Greece, Nov. 19, 1940; came to U.S., 1967; d. George Demetrios and Sophia George (Naisopoulos) Kontaxis; m. Michael Andrew Silva, Oct. 4, 1969; children: Mark Alexander, Paul Richard. BA, Harokopios Coll., Kalithea, Athens, Greece; BS, U. Calif., Berkeley. Chief clin. dietitian A.H.E.P.A. Hosp., Salonika, Greece, 1961-67; clin. dietitian Providence Hosp., Oakland, Calif., 1967-92; renal dietitian B.M.A. Berkeley Dialysis Unit, 1990—; cons. dietitain Calif. Hosp., Oakland, 1976-81, C.D.C. Dialysis Unit, Vallejo, Calif., 1993—, C.A.P.D. Dietitien for Total Renal Care, Walnut Creek, Calif., 1992—. Mem. Am. Dietetic Assn. (registered), Bay Area Dietetic Assn. (hospitality chmn. 1979-87), Calif. Dietetic Assn., Daus. of Penelope (pres. 1990-92). Greek Orthodox. Avocations: swimming, Greek dancing, reading, gardening, traveling. Home: 4 Rita Way Orinda CA 94563-4132 Office: BMA Dialysis 3017 Telegraph Ave Berkeley CA 94705-2013

SILVA, JOHN PHILIP COSTA, newspaper editor; b. Providence, Jan. 19, 1951; s. Silvano Costa and Florence Josephine (Russo) S.; m. Deborah Helen Radovsky, May 8, 1977; children: Daniel David, Matthew Philip. BA in Journalism, U. R.I., 1973. Staff writer Providence Jour.-Bull., 1973-79; staff writer Miami (Fla.) News, 1979-81, asst. city editor, 1981-82; spl. corr. The Wall St. Jour., Miami, 1980-81; city editor Lexington (Ky.) Herald-Leader, 1982-84; night city editor L.A. Herald Examiner, 1984-85, assignment editor, 1985-87; asst. mng. editor Ariz. Daily Star, Tucson, 1987—. Recipient 1st place for spot news UPI Newspapers New Eng., 1977. Mem. Nat. Assn. Hispanic Journalists, Investigative Reporters and Editors Assn. Avocations: writing historical research, computer technology. Home: 9433 N Albatross Dr Tucson AZ 85742 Office: Ariz Daily Star 4850 S Park Ave Tucson AZ 85714-1637

SILVA, JOSEPH DONALD, English language educator; b. Lowell, Mass., Jan. 19, 1935; s. Joseph Maria and Edna (Talbot) S.; m. Lucy Niles, June 22, 1957; children: Joseph Alden, Maria Margriet, Paul Frederic, Amanda Elizabeth. BA, U. N.H., 1957, MA, 1965. Instr. U. N.H., Durham, 1963-66, asst. prof., 1966-72, assoc. prof., 1972-85, prof., 1985—; chmn. N.E. Regional Conf. on English, 1977-79. Author: A Bibliography on the Madeira Islands, 1987. Pastor New Castle (N.H.) Congl. Ch., 1967—; moderator Rockingham (N.H.) Assn. United Ch. of Christ, 1987-89. 1st lt. U.S. Army, 1958. Mem. AAUP (chmn. Durham chpt. 1983-84), Nat. Coun. Tchrs. English, Conf. Coll. Composition and Communication. Avocations: travel, photography, hiking, swimming, gardening. Home: 55 Main St New Castle NH 03854-0132

SILVA, SYLVIA ANNE, educational program director; b. Las Vegas, Nev., Dec. 11, 1937; d. Enrique A. Silva and Faustina Flores; m. Peter Paul Lopez, 1954 (div. 1976); children: Peter John, Marie Anne, Henry Matthew, Vincent Martin, Renee Marie. BA in Social Welfare cum laude, Calif. State U., Chico, 1973, BA in Spanish, 1973, MA in Edn., 1981; EdD, U. San Francisco, 1991. Migrant edn. community aide, 1968-70; case aide counselor Mental Retardation Service, Chico, Calif., 1970-72, elem. sch. tchr., 1973-75; instr., lectr. Calif. State U., Chico, 1975-91, adminstrv. fellow, 1982-83; coordinator Upward Bound project, Chico, 1976-80, dir. student affirmative action, 1980-86; dir. ednl. equity svcs. programs, 1986-89, dir. univ. outreach programs, univ. ednl. equity officer, 1991-95; assoc. vice provost for student affairs, dean of students Ariz. State U., West Phoenix, 1995—; lectr. cross-cultural awareness for counseling program Laverne U., 1984-90; past mem. adv. bd. Western Assn. Ednl. Opportunity Programs; keynote spkr., workshop presenter in field; cons. workshop for county sch. tchrs. and adminstrs., 1990-91; past mem. adv. bd. Ednl. Equity Svcs.; cons. on early childhood edn. Orcut Sch. Dist., Santa Monica, Calif., 1976; instr. Calif. C.C., 1988—; participant Nat. Assn. Student Svc. Profls. Symposium for Women Preparing to Become Sr. Student Affairs Officers. Chmn. student affirmative action adv. bd. Calif. Acad. Partnership Program; co-founder Hispanic Profl. Group; past mem. community adv. bd. Upward Bound; cons. Mendocino Nat. Forest, 1991. Recipient Steve Holman award Western Assn. Ednl. Opportunity, 1988, Outstanding Latina Alumni recognition award Calif. State U., 1992. Mem. Am. Assn. for Higher Edn. (Hispanic caucus), Nat. Assn. Student Affairs Pers., Nat. Assn. for Women in Edn., Hispanic Assn. for Comty. and Edn. (bd. dirs., past pres.), S.E. Asian Student Assn., Ariz. Hispanic C. of C., Phi Delta Kappa, Lambda Theta Nu (founding advisor). Democrat. Roman Catholic. Home: # 26 8225 N Central Ave Phoenix AZ 85020

SILVEIRA, AUGUSTINE, JR., chemistry educator; b. Mattapoisett, Mass., July 17, 1934; s. Augustine and Mildred (Lewis) S.; m. Beverly Ann Washburn, Aug. 20, 1960; children: Linda Ann, Karen Louise. BS, U. Mass., Dartmouth, 1957, ScD (hon.), 1975; PhD., U. Mass., Amherst, 1962. Research chemist Acushnet Process Co., Mass., 1957-58; instr. U. Mass., 1960-62; asst. prof. Rutgers U., 1962-63; assoc. prof. SUNY, Oswego, 1963-64, prof., 1964-67, prof., chmn. dept. chemistry, 1967—, disting. teaching prof., 1976—; Am. Council on Edn. fellow U. Calif., Irvine, 1969-70, vis. prof., 1976-77, 83-84, 91; vis. prof. Calif. State U., Long Beach, 1976-77; cons. to edn. and industry; guest lectr.; evaluator SUNY Grad. Programs, 1968—, Patent Policy Bd., 1971; mem. commn. higher edn. Middle States Assn., 1971—; mem. alumni adv. council U. Mass., 1971-75; mem. N.Y. State Bd. Optometry, 1981-91. Contbr. articles to profl. jours. Recipient N.Y. State/United Univ. Professions Excellence award, 1990; named to Fairhaven H.S. Hall of Fame Lifetime Achievement award; SUNY faculty exch. scholar, 1981—; SUNY rsch. grantee. Fellow Am. Inst. Chemists; mem. AAUP (v.p. 1965-66), Am. Chem. Soc. (dist. rep., Syracuse sect. award 1988), Sigma Xi (pres. 1972-73, 78-79), Delta Kappa Phi, Alpha Kappa Phi, Phi Kappa Phi. Home: 88 Co Rt 24 PO Box 98 Minetto NY 13115-0098 Office: SUNY Oswego Chemistry Dept Oswego NY 13126

SILVEIRA, MILTON ANTHONY, aerospace engineering executive; b. Mattapoisett, Mass., May 4, 1929; s. Antone and Carolinda (Avila) S.; children: Leland R., Douglas S., Carolyn M., Robert S.; m. B. Jane Rogers, June 20, 1992. BS, U. Vt., 1951, MS, 1961, PhD (hon.), 1977; postgrad., U. Va., Va. Poly Inst., U. Houston. Research intern Langley AFB, Hampton, Va., 1951; chief engring. U.S. Army, St. Louis, 1951-54; engring. officer 8th U.S. Army, Korea; acting head loads br. NASA, Hampton, 1955-63; project mgr. Manned Spacecraft Ctr. NASA, Houston, 1963-67, various engring. positions, dep. mgr. orbiter project Johnson Space Ctr., 1967-81; asst. to dep. adminstr. NASA, Washington, 1981-83, chief engr., 1983-86; v.p. advance requirements and analysis, Washington ops. Ford Aerospace and Communications Corp., Arlington, Va., 1987-90; pres. SEL, McLean, Va., 1990—. Mem. AIAA. Home: 7213 Evans Mill Rd Mc Lean VA 22101-3420 Office: SEL PO Box 843 Mc Lean VA 22101-0843

SILVER, BARNARD JOSEPH STEWART, mechanical engineer, consultant; b. Salt Lake City, Mar. 9, 1933; s. Harold Farnes and Madelyn Cannon (Stewart) S.; m. Cherry Bushman, Aug. 12, 1963; children: Madelyn Stewart Palmer, Cannon Farnes, Brenda Picketts Call. BS in Mech. Engring., MIT, 1957; MS in Engring. Mechanics, Stanford U., 1958; grad. Advanced Mgmt. Program, Harvard U., 1977. Registered profl. engr., Colo. Engr. aircraft nuclear propulsion div. Gen. Electric Co., Evandale, Ohio, 1957; engr. Silver Engring. Works, Denver, 1959-66, mgr. sales and tech. svcs., 1966-71; chief engr. Union Sugar div. Consol. Foods Co., Santa Maria, Calif., 1971-74; directeur du complexe SODESUCRE, Abidjan, Côte d'Ivoire, 1974-76; supt. engring. and maintenance U and I, Inc., Moses Lake, Wash., 1976-79; pres. Silver Enterprises, Moses Lake, 1971-88, Silver Energy Systems Corp., Moses Lake, 1980—, Salt Lake, 1990— ; pres., gen. mgr. Silver Chief Corp., 1983—; pres. Silver Corp., 1984-86, 93—; chmn. bd. Silver Pubs., Inc., 1986-87, 89—; chmn. bd. Agronomics Internat., McLean, Va., 1994—; v.p. Barnard J. Stewart Cousins Land Co., 1987-88, 92—; dir. Isle Piquant Sugar Found., 1993-94; mem. steering com. World Botanical Inst., 1993—; instr. engring. Big Bend C.C., 1980-81. Explorer adviser Boy Scouts Am., 1965-66, 89-90, chmn. cub pack com., 1968-74, 94—, chmn. scout troop com., 1968-74, vice chmn. Columbia Basin Dist., 1986-87; pres. Silver Found., 1971-84, v.p., 1984—; ednl. counselor MIT, 1971-89; pres. Chief Moses Jr. H.S. Parent Tchr. Student Assn., 1978-79; missionary Ch. of Jesus Christ of Latter-day Saints, Can., 1953-55, West Africa, 1988, Côte d'Ivoire, 1988-89, Zaire, 1989, Holladay North Stake, 1991, dist. pres. No. B.C., No. Alberta, Yukon and N.W. Ters., 1955; stake high counselor, Santa Maria, Calif., 1971-72, Moses Lake, Wash., 1977-79; presiding elder Côte d'Ivoire, 1974-76, 88; 2d counselor Moses Lake Stake Presidency, 1980-88; bd. dirs. Columbia Basin Allied Arts, 1986-88; mem. Health Sci. Coun. U. Utah, 1991—; mem. Sunday sch. gen. bd. Ch. of Jesus Christ of Latter-Day Saints, 1991-93, com. for mems. with disabilities, 1992-93, choice adv. bd., 1993—; emergency preparedness dir. Holladay North Stake, 1993—. Served with Ordnance Corps, U.S. Army, 1958-59. Decorated chevalier Ordre National (Republic of Côte d'Ivoire). Mem. ASME, Assn. Energy Engrs., AAAS, Am. Soc. Sugar Beet Technologists, Internat. Soc. Sugar Cane Technologists, Am. Soc. Sugar Cane Technologists, Environ. Engrs. & Mgrs. Inst., Sugar Industry Technicians, Nat. Fedn. Ind. Bus.; Utah State Hist. Soc. (life), Mormon Hist. Assn., G.P. Chowder and Marching Soc., Western Hist. Assn., Sons of Utah Pioneers, Univ. Archeol. Soc. (life), Kiwanis, Cannon-Hinckley Study Group, Sigma Xi (life, sec., treas. Utah chpt. 1994—), Pi Tau Sigma, Sigma Chi, Alpha Phi Omega. Republican. Mormon. Home: 4391 Carol Jane Dr Salt Lake City UT 84124-3601 Office: Silver Energy Systems Corp 13184 Rd 3 NE Bldg 1 Ste B Moses Lake WA 98837 also: Silver Enterprises 4391 South 2275 E Carol Jane Dr Salt Lake City UT 84124-3601 also: Silver Publishers Inc PO Box 17755 Salt Lake City UT 84117-0755 also: Silver Chief Corp 1433 S Skyline Dr Moses Lake WA 98837-2417 also: Agronomics Internat 6928 Butternut Ct Mc Lean VA 22101-1506 also: Silver Pubs Inc 2275 E Carol Jane Dr Salt Lake City UT 84124-3601

SILVER, BRIAN QUAYLE, broadcast journalist, musician, educator; b. Denver, Sept. 8, 1942; s. Harold Farnes and Madelyn Cannon (Stewart) S.; m. Shubha Sankaran, Dec. 4, 1988; adopted children: Laila Benazir Robinson, Ganapathi Ramdas Sankaran. BA, Harvard Coll., 1964; postgrad., Sch. Oriental and African Studies U. London, 1969-70; PhD., U. Chgo., 1980. Asst. prof. Urdu U. Minn., 1971-74; assoc. prof. Urdu & Indo-Muslim studies Harvard U., 1974-83; dir. internat. house, asst. dean study abroad Duke U., 1983-86; exec. dir. Internat. Music Assocs., Washington, 1982—; chief, Urdu svc. Voice of Am., Washington, 1986—; dir. internat. exchange programs Pan Orient Arts Found., Manchester, N.H., 1968—, exec. dir., 1994—; bd. dirs. Archive Rsch. Ctr. Ethnomusicology, New Delhi, India, 1993—; South Asia coun. Assn. Asian Studies, Ann Arbor, Mich., 1983-86; lectr. music U. Va., Charlottesville, 1995. Sitar performance in India, Pakistan, Bangladesh, Morocco, England, Canada and U.S., 1966—; contbr. numerous publs. on South Asian Music and Urdu Lit. Dir. Durham Chpt. UNICEF, 1984-86. Named Khansahib, All-Pakistan Music Conf., Lahore, 1988; recipient Gold medal, 1989; Fulbright grantee Inst. Internat. Edn., India, 1964-66, grantee in aid D.C. Commn. for Arts and Humanities/Nat. Endowment for the Arts, 1991-92; Ford fellow Am. Coun. Learned Socs., England, Pakistan, India, 1969-71, Am. Inst. Indian Studies, India, 1982-83. Mem. Soc. Ethnomusicology (New England chpt. v.p. 1978-80), Assn. Asian Music, Internat. Coun. Tradition Mus., Asia Soc., Assn. Asian Studies, Folklore Soc. Greater Washington. Avocations: cooking, gardening, films, travel. Home: 1730 C St NE Washington DC 20002-6661 Office: Internat Music Assoc PO Box 15526 Washington DC 20003-0526

SILVER, CHARLES MORTON, communications company executive; b. New Haven, Sept. 22, 1929; s. Sam and Rose (Fischman) S.; m. Rose Charek, Mar. 27, 1960; children—Ronni Ellen, Suzanne Paula, Steven Mitchell. B.S., U Conn., 1954. With Arthur Andersen & Co., N.Y.C., 1954-61, ITT, N.Y.C., 1961-88; ret. as v.p. and assoc. treas. ITT, 1988. Served with U.S. Army, 1947-48, 50-51. Mem. AICPA, Roxbury Swim and Tennis Club. Home: 51 Akbar Rd Stamford CT 06902-1401 also: PO Box 420275 Summerland Key FL 33042-0275

SILVER, DANIEL B., lawyer; b. Phila., Aug. 14, 1941; s. Samuel and Marjorie (Euster) S.; m. Sybil F. Michelson, Jan. 20, 1963; children—Abigail Ruth, Rachel Ann, Alexander Joseph. A.B., U. Calif., Berkeley, 1961; M.A., Harvard U., 1965, Ph.D., 1967, LL.B., 1968. Bar: D.C. 1968, U.S. Ct.

Appeals (D.C. cir.) 1975, U.S. Supreme Ct. 1975. Assoc. Cleary, Gottlieb, Steen & Hamilton, Washington, 1968-70, 73-76, Brussels, Belgium, 1973-76, ptnr., Washington, 1976-78, 81-83, 85—, Brussels, 1983-85; gen. counsel NSA, Washington, 1978-79, CIA, Washington, 1979-81; adj. prof. Georgetown U. Law Ctr., 1981-83, 89-92, 94; disting. vis. from prac., 1993. Trustee The Textile Mus. Recipient Exceptional Civilian Service award NSA, 1979; Disting. Intelligence medal CIA, 1981. Mem. ABA (sects. antitrust law, pub. contract law, internat. law), Security Affairs Support Assn. (gen. counsel 1982-91), Coun. Fgn. Rels. Democrat. Jewish. Author: (with P. Fabrega) Illness and Shamanistic Curing in Zinacantan, 1975. Office: 1752 N St NW Washington DC 20036-2806

SILVER, DAVID, financial executive, lawyer; b. N.Y.C., Jan. 27, 1931; s. Sol and Fannie (Stein) S.; m. Meryl Young, Sept. 14, 1952 (dec.); children: Daniel, Matthew, Joshua; m. Ann Schwartz, June 4, 1993. B.A., CCNY, 1953; LL.B. cum laude, Harvard U., 1958. Bar: N.Y. 1958, D.C. 1979. Pvt. practice law N.Y.C., 1960-61; spl. counsel SEC, Washington, 1961-65; gen. counsel Investors Planning Corp., N.Y.C., 1965-66; asst. counsel Investment Co. Inst., Washington, 1966-69, gen. counsel, 1969-77, pres., 1977-91; cons. securities regulation Govt. of India, 1964; pres. ICI Mut. Ins. Co., 1987—; lectr. Law Sch., Boston U., 1995—. Served with U.S. Army, 1953-55. Mem. Fed. Bar Assn. (exec. council securities com., past chmn. investment co. com.). Home: 9410 Brooke Dr Bethesda MD 20817-2110 Office: ICI Mutual Insur 1401 H St NW Washington DC 20005

SILVER, DAVID MAYER, former university official; b. West Pittston, Pa., July 16, 1915; s. Morris Jacob and Flora (Mayer) S.; m. Anita Rose Cohen, May 10, 1942; children: Gregory, Terence. AB magna cum laude, Butler U., 1937; AM, U. Ill., 1938, PhD, 1940; LittD (hon.), Butler U., 1990. Mem. faculty Butler U., 1940-85, prof. history, 1954-85, dean Coll. Liberal Arts and Scis., 1963-83, assoc. v.p. grad. studies and research, 1983-85; cons.-evaluator North Ctrl. Assn., 1974-85, mem. commn. higher edn., 1981-85. Author: Lincoln's Supreme Court, 1956, also articles. Pres. Indpls. Bd. Pub. Safety, 1956-63; mem. youth study com. Ohio Valley Council of Hebrew Congregations, 1963-65; Research dir. Ind. Democratic Central Com., 1944; Dem. nominee Ind. Legislature, 1944; Dem. candidate for Indpls. City Council, 1955; Bd. dirs. Indpls. Jewish Social Services, 1953-56. Recipient medal Butler U. Alumni Assn., 1987; U. Ill. scholar history, 1938, fellow, 1938-40; Butler U. faculty fellow, 1950-51. Mem. AAUP, Am. Hist. Assn., Orgn. Am. Historians, Supreme Ct. Hist. Soc., Ind. Hist. Soc., Ind. Conf. Acad. Deans (chmn. 1972), Ind. CLU, B'nai B'rith, Phi Beta Kappa, Phi Kappa Phi, Phi Eta Sigma, Sigma Alpha Mu. Jewish (bd. dirs., pres. Indpls. Hebrew congregation). Club: Broadmoor Country. Home: 8230 N Illinois St Indianapolis IN 46260-2943 *I have learned throughout my life that one succeeds the most when you respect those you deal with - just do the right thing, follow high moral and ethical standards, respect your fellow human beings, be optimistic, and success will come!.*

SILVER, DONALD, surgeon, educator; b. N.Y.C., Oct. 19, 1929; s. Herman and Cecilia (Meyer) S.; m. Helen Elizabeth Harnden, Aug. 9, 1958; children: Elizabeth Tyler, Donald Meyer, Stephanie Davies, William Paige. AB, Duke U., 1950, BS in Medicine, MD, 1955. Diplomate Am. Bd. Surgery, Am. Bd. Gen. Vascular Surgery, Am. Bd. Thoracic Surgery. Intern Duke Med. Ctr., 1955-56, asst. resident, 1958-63, resident, 1963-64; mem. faculty Duke Med. Sch., 1964-75, prof. surgery, 1972-75; cons. Watts Hosp., Durham, 1965-75, VA Hosp., Durham, 1970-75; chief surgery VA Hosp., 1968-70; prof. surgery, chmn. dept. U. Mo. VA Med. Ctr., Columbia, 1975—; cons. Harry S. Truman Hosp., Columbia, 1975—; mem. bd. sci. advisers Cancer Research Center, Columbia, 1975—; mem. surg. study sect. A NIH. Contbr. articles to med. jours., chpts. to books; editorial bds.; Jour. Vascular Surgery, Postgrad. Gen. Surgery, Vascular Surgery. Served with USAF, 1956-58. James IV Surg. traveler, 1977. Fellow ACS (gov. 1994—), Deryl Hart Soc.; mem. AMA, AAAS, Mo. Med. Assn., Boone County Med. Soc., Internat. Cardiovascular Soc., Soc. Univ. Surgeons, Am. Heart Assn. (Mo. affiliate rsch. com.), Soc. Surgery Alimentary Tract, Assn. Acad. Surgery, So. Thoracic Surg. Assn., Internat. Soc. Surgery, Soc. Vascular Surgery, Am. Assn. Thoracic Surgery, Am. Surg. Assn., Ctrl. Surg. Assn. (pres.-elect 1990-91, pres. 1991-92), Western Surg. Assn., Midwestern Vascular Surg. Soc. (pres. 1984-85), Ctrl. Surg. Assn. Found. (treas. 1992-93, wd v.p. 1993-94, 1st v.p. 1994-95, pres. 1995—). Home: 1050 Covered Bridge Rd Columbia MO 65203-9569 Office: U Mo Med Ctr Dept Surgery # M580 Columbia MO 65212

SILVER, GEORGE ALBERT, physician, educator; b. Phila., Dec. 23, 1913; s. Morris M. and Sara (Tutelman) S.; m. Mitzi Blieden, June 5, 1937; children—James David, Jane, Judith Ellen. B.A., U. Pa., Phila., 1934; M.D., Jefferson Med. Coll., Phila., 1938; M.P.H., Johns Hopkins U., Balt., 1948; M.A. (hon.), Yale U., New Haven, 1969. Diplomate Am. Bd. Preventive Medicine. Asst. demonstrator Jefferson Med. Coll., Phila., 1939-42; health officer Balt. City Health Dept., 1948-51; asst. prof. Johns Hopkins U., Balt., 1948-51; chief div. social medicine Montefiore Hosp., N.Y.C., 1951-65; assoc. prof. health adminstrn. Columbia U., N.Y.C., 1952-59; prof. social medicine Albert Einstein Coll. Medicine, N.Y.C., 1959-65; dep. asst. sec. health and sci. affairs HEW, Washington, 1965-68; health exec. Nat. Urban Coalition, Washington, 1968-71; prof. pub. health Yale U., New Haven, 1969-84, emeritus prof. pub. health, 1984—; chair com. on health policy Fedn. Am. Scientists. Author: Family Medical Care, 1963, Spy in the House of Medicine, 1974, Child Health: America's Future, 1978; contbg. editor Am. Jour. Pub. Health. Served to maj. M.C., U.S. Army, 1942-46. Recipient Superior Svc. award HEW, 1966; named to Soc. of Scholars, Johns Hopkins U., 1993; fellow Branford Coll., Yale U. Fellow APHA (assoc. editor jour. 1993—), Nat. Acad. Social Ins., N.Y. Acad. Medicine, Inst. Medicine; mem. NAS (sr.), Elizabethan Club, Sigma Xi. Democrat. Jewish. Home: 590 Ellsworth Ave New Haven CT 06511-1636 Office: Yale U 89 Trumbull St New Haven CT 06511-3723

SILVER, HARRY R., lawyer; b. Phila., Aug. 8, 1946; s. Jerome Benjamin Silver and Josephine Sandler (Steinberg) Furr; m. Jessica Dunsay, Nov. 23, 1972; children: Gregory, Alexander. BA, Temple U., 1968; JD, Columbia U., 1971. Bar: N.Y. 1972, D.C. 1973, U.S. Dist. Ct. D.C., U.S. Ct. Claims, U.S. Ct. Appeals (1st, 4th, 5th, 7th, 8th, 9th, 10th, fed. and D.C. cirs.), U.S. Supreme Ct. Law clk. to presiding justice U.S. Ct. Appeals (2d cir.), N.Y.C., 1971-72; assoc. Arent, Fox, Kintner, Plotkin & Kahn, Washington, 1972-74; atty. U.S. Dept. Justice, Washington, 1974-77, U.S. Dept. Energy, Washington, 1977-78; assoc. Akin, Gump, Strauss, Hauer & Feld, Washington, 1978-81, ptnr., 1981-88; ptnr. Oppenheimer, Wolff & Donelly, Washington, 1988-91, Davis Wright Tremaine, Washington, 1991-94, Ober, Kaler, Grimes & Shriver, Washington, 1994—. Mem. ABA, Fed. Bar Assn. Avocations: running, music, travel. Home: 6829 Wilson Ln Bethesda MD 20817-4948 Office: Ober Kaler Grimes & Shriver 1401 H St NW Ste 500 Washington DC 20005-2110

SILVER, HORACE WARD MARTIN TAVARES, composer, pianist; b. Norwalk, Conn., Sept. 2, 1928; s. John and Gertrude (Edmounds) S. Ed. pub. schs., Norwalk. Pres. Ecaroh Music, Inc., N.Y.C., from 1955. Leader, Horace Silver Quintet, 1955—; Composer: Senor Blues, 1956, Doodlin', 1956, The Preacher, 1956, Nica's Dream, 1956, Lonely Woman, 1956, Home Cookin', 1956, Enchantment, 1956, Cookin' at the Continental, 1957, Moon Rays, 1957, Soulville, 1957, Sister Sadie, 1959, Come on Home, 1959, Peace, 1959, Finger Poppin, 1959, Blowin' the Blues Away, 1959, Strollin', 1960, Filthy McNasty, 1961, The Tokyo Blues, 1962, Silver's Serenade, 1963, Song For My Father, 1965, 89, Que Pasa, 1965; albums include Six Pieces of Silver, 1956, 86, Horace Silver and the Jazz Messengers, 1985, Serenade to a Soul Sister, 1986, The Best of Horace Silver, 1988, Volume 2, 1989, Horace Silver Trio, 1989, Song for my Father, 1989, The Cape Verdean Blues, 1989, Doin the Thing, 1989, Silver's Blues, 1989, Horace-Scope, 1990, It's Got To Be Funky, 1993. Recipient Budweiser Mus. Excellence award, 1958, Silver Record award Blue Note Records, 1959, Citizen Call Entertainment award, 1960. Mem. A.S.C.A.P., Am. Fedn. Musicians. also: Blue Note Records 810 7th Ave Fl 4 New York NY 10019-5818

SILVER, JOAN MICKLIN, film director, screenwriter; b. Omaha, May 24, 1935; d. Maurice David and Doris (Shoshone) Micklin; m. Raphael D. Silver, June 28, 1956; children: Dina, Marisa, Claudia. BA, Sarah Lawrence Coll., 1956. Writer, dir. (movies) Hester Street, 1975 (Writers Guild best screenplay nomination), Chilly Scenes of Winter, 1981, (TV film PBS) Bernice Bobs Her Hair starring Shelly Du Vall, 1975; dir. (TV films HBO) Finnegan, Begin Again with Robert Preston and Mary Tyler Moore, Parole Board, A Private Matter with Sissy Spacek and Aidan Quinn, (TV film Showtime) In The Presence of Mine Enemies, 1996, (films) Between the Lines, 1976, Crossing Delancey with Amy Irving, 1988, Loverboy, 1989, Stepkids, 1991; dir. stage plays and musicals including Album, Maybe I'm Doing It Wrong, Off-Broaday prodn. A...My Name is Alice; prod. On The Yard, (radio) Great Jewish Stories from Eastern Europe and Beyond, 1995. Office: Silverfilm Prodns Inc 510 Park Ave New York NY 10022-1105

SILVER, JOEL, producer. Film producer: The Warriors, 1979, Xanadu, 1980, 48 Hours, 1982, Jekyll & Hyde...Together Again, 1982, Streets of Fire, 1984, Brewster's Millions, 1985, Weird Science, 1985, Commando, 1985, Jumpin' Jack Flash, 1986, Lethal Weapon, 1986, Predator, 1987, Action Jackson, 1988, Die Hard, 1988, Lethal Weapon 2, 1989, Roadhouse, 1989, Ford Fairlane, 1990, Die Hard 2, 1990, Predator 2, 1990, Hudson Hawk, 1991, Ricochet, 1991, The Last Boy Scout, 1991, Lethal Weapon 3, 1992, Demolition Man, 1993, Richie Rich, 1994, Demon Knight, 1994. Office: Silver Pictures 4000 Warner Blvd Burbank CA 91522-0001

SILVER, JONATHAN MOSES, investment management executive; b. Cleve., Sept. 3, 1957; s. Daniel Jeremy and Adele Francis (Zeidman) S.; m. Melissa Moss, 1995. BA with honors, Harvard U., 1979; C.E.P., Inst. Polit. Studies, Paris, 1980; postgrad. Grad. Inst. Internat. Studies, U. Geneva, 1981-82. Asst. to exec. v.p. Manpower Demonstration Rsch. Corp., N.Y.C., 1980-81; asst. polit. dir. John Glenn Presdl. Campaign, Washington, 1983-84; assoc. Mckinsey and Co., N.Y.C., 1984-88; COO Tucker Comm., Inc., Cross River, N.Y., 1988-90; exec. v.p. John Blair Comm. Inc., N.Y.C., 1990-91; COO, mng. dir. Tiger Mgmt. Inc., N.Y.C., 1991-92; asst. dep. sec. U.S. Dept. Commerce, Washington, 1992-94, counselor to the sec. of the interior, 1994-95; gen. ptnr. Commonwealth Holdings, Inc., Washington, 1995—, Millennium Capital, 1996—; ptnr. HS Ptnrs., n.Y.C., 1993—; trustee Jonathan M. Silver Found., N.Y.C., 1993—; vis. com. grad. faculty The New Sch. Bd.; bd. dirs. Am. Forests, The Vol. Consulting Group, Veritas Found. Pub. Allies, First Mexico Pvt. Capital Fund. Harvard Coll. fellow, Cambridge, Mass., 1975-78, John Harvard fellow, 1979, Rotary grad. fellow, Paris, 1979, Fulbright grad. fellow, Swiss Univ. Exchange Grant, 1982. Jewish. Home: 3027 N St NW Washington DC 20007 Office: Commonwealth Holdings INc Ste 500 805 15th St Ste 500 Washington DC 20005

SILVER, LAWRENCE ALAN, marketing executive; b. New Haven, Sept. 5, 1943; s. Herman B. and Marcia (Azersky) S.; m. Deena Rae Rosenberg, Feb. 26, 1967; children: Cheryl Ann, Elyse Stephanie, Marc Aaron. BJ, Boston U., 1965, MS, 1966. Reporter New Haven Register, 1958-66; dir. pub. rels. Spear & Staff, Inc., Babson Park, Mass., 1966-70; pres. Silver Assocs. Pub. Rels. & Advt., Holliston, Mass., 1971-82; pres. RJ Communication, Inc., St. Petersburg, Fla., 1982—; sr. v.p., dir. mktg. Raymond James & Assocs., Inc., St. Petersburg, 1982—; v.p. investor rels. Raymond James Fin., Inc., St. Petersburg, 1983—; chmn. Raymond James Fin. Mktg. Com., St. Petersburg, 1984—; coord. quality svcs. Raymond James Fin., St. Petersburg, 1989—; instr. journalism Framingham (Mass.) State Coll., 1974-80. Mem. Holliston Bylaw Study Com., 1978-82, U. Tampa Ctr. Quality Steering Com., 1993-95; founding pres. Temple Beth Torah, Holliston, 1972-73; bd. dirs. Temple Ahavat Shalom Men's Club, Palm Harbor, 1983-84; trustee Temple Ahavat Shalom, 1985-86, Am. Stage Theatre, St. Petersburg, 1994-96; pres. Temple Ahavat Shalom Brotherhood, 1985-86; founding bd. dirs. Jewish Cmty. Ctr. Greater Framingham, 1969-72; mem. Fla. Edn. and Industry Coalition, 1988-95, St. Petersburg Jr. Coll. Cmty. Outreach program, 1988-89; mem. Fla. Sch. Adv. Coun., 1990-93; mem. adv. coun. Clearwater Jr. League, 1993-94, sch. adv. coun. Tarpon Springs H.S., 1988-93. With U.S. Army, 1967-69. Mem. Securities Industry Assn. (Pub. Rels. Advt. Roundtable 1986-90, Mktg. Roundtable 1988—, sales and mktg. com. 1991—, editor Marketshare 1994—), Boston U. Nat. Alumni Coun. Assoc. editor Venture Capital Jour., 1978-82. Home: 90 Greenhaven Cir Oldsmar FL 34677-4842 Office: Raymond James & Assocs 880 Carillon Pky Saint Petersburg FL 33716

SILVER, LEONARD J., insurance and risk management company executive; b. Philadelphia, Sept. 19, 1927; s. Jacob and Mollie (Milgram) S.; m. Eva Penny Parris, Nov. 20, 1949; children: Jill Denise Silverstein, Brian B. CPCU, cert. risk mgmt. assoc. Pres. Ins. Offices of Leonard J. Silver, Inc., Phila., 1948-58, Am. Excess Co., Phila., 1953-58; pres. 1st Risk Mgmt. Co., Jenkintown, Pa., 1958—, San Juan, P.R., 1963-94; Pres. legal div. First Risk Mgmt., 1991—. With U.S. Army, 1947-48, Korea. Mem. Soc. Risk Mgmt. Cons. (bd. dirs. 1990-91), Ins. Cons. Soc. (founding mem., sec. 1969-70, v.p. 1970-71, pres. 1971-72, bd. dirs.), Ins. Inst. P.R., Am. Inst. Property and Liability Underwriters. Avocations: photography, sailing. Home: 213 Glenwood Rd Elkins Park PA 19027-3522 Office: 1st Risk Mgmt 636 Old York Rd Ste 220 Jenkintown PA 19046-2858

SILVER, LINDA, guidance director, educational consultant; b. N.Y.C., Jan. 11, 1954; d. Victor Paul and Mina (Levin) Berk; children: Brooke, Joshua. BA in Spanish and Secondary Edn., Hofstra U., 1976; MS in Guidance and Counseling, Nova U., 1979. Cert. guidance counselor grades K-12, Spanish tchr. grades 7-12. Spanish tchr. Ponus Ridge Middle Sch., Norwalk, Conn., 1976-77, West Hollywood (Fla.) Pvt. Sch., 1977-79; guidance counselor Collins Elem., Dania, Fla., 1979-89; adult edn. tchr. GED-Off Campus, Ft. Lauderdale, Fla., 1989-90; guidance dir. Bethune Elem., Hollywood, 1989—; family counselor Family Counseling Ctr., Hollywood, 1990-94; ednl. cons. Maimonides Community Sch., Hollywood, 1992—; workshop leader and presenter in field. Named Broward County Elem. Counselor of Yr., Broward Counseling Assn., Ft. Lauderdale, 1990, Fla. Elem. Counselor of Yr., Fla. Sch. Counselors Assn., Orlando, 1992. Mem. ACA, Am. Sch. Counselor Assn., Fla. Sch. Counselors Assn., Broward County Counselors Assn., Fla. Counseling Assn., Exec. Bd. Elem. Counselors (co-chairperson 1992—), Exec. Bd. Maimonides Community Sch. (bd. mem. 1992—), Maimonides Community (chairperson edn. com. 1992—), Hofstra U. South Fla. Alumni Assn. (pres. 1985), Delta Kappa Gamma, Phi Delta Kappa, Sigma Delta Phi. Avocations: gourmet cooking, reading, golfing, collect miniatures. Home: 2010 N 47th Ave Hollywood FL 33021-4128 Office: Bethune Elem 2400 Meade St Hollywood FL 33020-1246

SILVER, MALCOLM DAVID, pathologist, educator; b. Adelaide, South Australia, Apr. 29, 1933; s. Eric Bertram and Stella Louisa (Riley) S.; m. Meredith May Galloway, Jan. 19, 1957; children: Stuart Faulkner, Claire Eleanor, Caryl Louise. M.D., U. Adelaide; Ph.D., McGill U. Diplomate: Am. Bd. Pathology. Resident med. officer Royal Adelaide Hosp., 1957-58; resident in pathology Royal Victoria Hosp.-Pathol. Inst., McGill U., Montreal, Que., Can., 1958-63; research fellow dept. exptl. pathology John Curtin Sch. Med. Research, Australian Nat. U., Canberra, 1963-65; asst. prof. pathology U. Toronto, 1965-68, assoc. prof., 1968-74, prof., 1974—, chmn. dept. pathology, 1985-95; staff pathologist Toronto Gen. Hosp., 1965-72, sr. staff pathologist, 1972-79; prof., chmn. dept. pathology U. Western Ont., London, Ont., Can., 1979-85; chief pathology Univ. Hosp., London, 1979-85; pathologist in chief Toronto Gen. Hosp., 1985-89; pathologist in chief The Toronto Hosp. (Toronto Gen. and Toronto Western Divs.), 1989-91, sr. staff pathologist, 1991—. Edtl. bd. Jour. Cardiovascular Pathology, Modern Pathology, Jour. Long-Term Effects of Med. Implants; contbr. articles to profl. jours. Fellow Royal Coll. Pathologists of Australia, Royal Coll. Physicians and Surgeons Can.; mem. Can. Assn. Pathologists (chmn. membership com. 1975-77), Ont. Assn. Pathologists, Am. Soc. Investigative Pathology, Internat. Acad. Pathology, Can. Med. Assn., Ont. Med. Assn., Can. Cardiovascular Soc., Am. Heart Assn., AAAS. Office: U Toronto Dept Pathology, 100 College St, Toronto, ON Canada M5G 1L5

SILVER, MARY WILCOX, oceanography educator; b. San Francisco, July 13, 1941; d. Philip E. and Mary C. (Kartes) Wilcox; children: Monica, Joel. BA in Zoology, U. Calif., Berkeley, 1963; PhD in Oceanography, U. Calif., La Jolla, 1971. Asst. prof. biology San Francisco State U., 1971-72; prof. marine sci. U. Calif., Santa Cruz, 1972—, chmn. dept., 1992-95. Contbr. numerous articles on biol. oceanography to profl. jours. Grantee NSF, 1979—; recipient Bigelow medal, 1992. Mem. AAAS, Am. Soc. Limnology and Oceanography, Am. Phycological Soc. Office: U Calif Dept Marine Sci Santa Cruz CA 95064

SILVER, MICHAEL, school superintendent; b. Landsberg, Germany, Jan. 30, 1948; came to U.S., 1949; s. Norman and Esther Silver; m. Beverley Ann Moss, May 16, 1971; children: Sabina, Joseph. AB, Washington U., 1970, MEd, 1973, PhD, 1982. Cert. supt. Mo., Wash. Tchr. Normandy Sch. Dist., St. Louis, 1970-72; tchr. Parkway Sch. Dist., St. Louis, 1972-75, asst. prin., 1976-79, adminstrv. asst., 1979-83, asst. to supt., 1983-84, asst. supt., 1984-86; supt. South Ctrl. Sch. Dist., Seattle, 1986—; bd. dirs. Cities in Schs., Seattle; mem. adv. bd. Sta. KCTS, Seattle, 1990—; vis. exec. Seattle U. Sch. Edn., 1995. Author: Values Education, 1976, Facing Issues of Life and Death, 1976. Pres. SeaTac Task Force, Seattle, 1989; bd. dirs. Anti-Defamation League, Seattle, 1987—; mem. City of Tukwila (Wash.) 2000 Com., 1988-90. Recipient A Plus award Wash. Coun. Econ. Edn., 1992; named Exec. Educator, 100 Exec. Educator Mag., 1985, 1996 Associate for Inst. for Ednl. Inquiry Leadership Program; I/D/E/A fellow Charles F. Kettering Found., 1978, 88, Title VI fellow Washington U., 1971-73. Mem. ASCD, Am. Assn. Sch. Adminstrs., Wash. Assn. Sch. Adminstrs. (met. chpt., pres. 1989-90), King County Supts. (chmn. adv. com. 1989-90, 95-96), Southcenter Rotary Club (Paul Harris fellow 1994), Southwest King County C. of C., Phi Delta Kappa. Home: 14127 SE 50th St Bellevue WA 98006-3409 Office: South Central SD 406 4640 S 144th St Seattle WA 98168-4134

SILVER, MORRIS, economist, educator; b. N.Y.C., July 9, 1931; s. Julius and Lilly S.; m. Sondra P. Hartman, Jan. 26, 1958; children: Gerald David, Ronald Alan. B.A., CCNY, 1958; Ph.D. (Earhart Found. fellow, Ford Found. fellow), Columbia U., 1964. Mem. faculty City Coll. CUNY, 1964—, assoc. prof. econs., 1968—, prof., 1972—, chmn. dept., 1969-95; research asso. Nat. Bur. Econ. Research, 1967-71; cons crime deterrence and offender career Hudson Inst., 1974, Nat. Center for Health Services Research, 1970—. Author: (with R.D. Auster) The State as a Firm, 1979, Affluence, Altruism, and Atrophy: The Decline of Welfare States, 1980, Prophets and Markets: The Political Economy of Ancient Israel, 1983, Enterprise and the Scope of the Firm, 1984, Economic Structures of the Ancient Near East, 1985, Foundations of Economic Justice, 1989, Taking Ancient Mythology Economically, 1992, Economic Structures of Antiquity, 1995. Served with AUS, 1953-55. Mem. Am. Econ. Assn. Jewish. Office: Dept Econs City Coll 133 D St New York NY 10031

SILVER, NEIL MARVIN, manufacturing executive; b. Bklyn., June 2, 1928; s. Jack and Rose (Eisenberg) S.; m. Leah Rebecca Coffman Silver, Sept. 4, 1949; children: Pamela Sue, Carole Beth. Student, U. Mich., 1945-46, 48-49; BS, Ind. U., 1951. Asst. mgr. Wolvering Parking Co., Lansing, Mich., 1951-54; treas. Capitol Parking Co., Indpls., 1955-60; controller, asst. to pres. Eberhart Steel Products, Inc., Mishawaka Tool & Die, Inc., Ind., 1961-63; PRES. Allied Quality Products, Inc., Mishawaka, Ind., 1964-67; treas. Allied Screw Products, Inc., Mishawaka, Ind., 1968-88, chmn., sec., 1989—. Bd. dirs. Ind. State Anti-Defamation League, 1955-57; bd. dirs., treas., pres., chmn. Fin. Commn., Family and Children's Ctr., Inc., Mishawaka, Ind., 1957-77; bd. dirs., treas. Family Svc. Assn. St. Joseph County, Ind., 1955-57. With U.S. Army, 1946-48. Mem. AIAA, Soc. Mfg. Engrs., SAE Internat., Internat. Computing Soc., ASM Internat., B'nai B'rith. Avocations: photography, travel. Office: Allied Screw Products Inc PO Box 543 815 E Lincolnway Ave Mishawaka IN 46546-0543

SILVER, PAUL ALLEN, lawyer; b. Providence, Mar. 1, 1950; s. Caroll M. and Gail (Arkin) S.; m. Katherine C. Haspel, June 22, 1975; children: Andrew Haspel, Nathaniel Haspel. AB, Harvard U., 1972; JD, Boston U., 1975. Bar: R.I. 1975, U.S. Dist. Ct. R.I. 1975, Mass. 1985. Assoc. firm Hinckley, Allen, Salisbury & Parsons, Providence, 1975-81; ptnr. Hinckley, Allen & Snyder, Providence, 1981—; faculty MS in Taxation Program, Bryant Coll., North Smithfield, R.I., 1982. Author: Cheap Eats, 1972, 2d edit., 73, 3d edit., 75. Bd. dirs. Travelers Aid Soc. of R.I., Providence, 1983-89, 95—; pres., 1986-89; bd. dirs. Ronald McDonald House, 1987-95, Camp Ruggles, 1991—; bd. trustees Providence Athenaeum, 1995—; active Planned Giving Coun. of R.I. Mem. ABA, R.I. Bar Assn., Estate Planning Coun. of R.I., Moses Brown Sch. Alumni Assn. (bd. dirs. 1984—), Internat. Assn. Fin. Planning (bd. dirs. R.I. chpt. 1986-95). Jewish. Avocations: finance, business. Home: 310 Olney St Providence RI 02906-2326 Office: Hinckley Allen & Snyder 1500 Fleet Ctr Providence RI 02903

SILVER, PAUL ROBERT, marketing executive, consultant; b. Balt., Mar. 15, 1931; s. Harry and Frieda (Rosengarten) S.; m. Natalie Nessa Nechamkin, May 17, 1957; children; Geri Ellen, Steven Marc, Lawrence Alan. BA, U. Md., 1949; BS, U. Balt., 1958; postgrad., Eckerd Coll., 1984. Pres., CEO Sterling Prodns. Inc., Balt., 1950-51; advt. mgr. Hecht Co., Washington, 1951-53; pres., CEO Artists & Models, Inc., Washington and Balt., 1974-76, The Charles Agy. Inc., Washington and Balt., 1955-80, The Golden Triangle Agy., Clearwater, Fla., 1980-82; COO Bridgman Assocs. Inc., Annapolis, Md., 1985-86; dir. promotions Internat. Beverage Expn., Washington, 1986; pres., CEO Prasco Inc., Seminole, Fla., 1982—; CEO Drakeford & Drakeford Mktg., 1995—; cons. Lewis and Ptnrs., Inc., San Francisco, Corp. Vision, Inc., L.A., Computer Response, Inc., Balt., Themes and Schemes, Inc., Dunedin, Fla., San Diego, 1984—, J&B Mgmt. Co., 1991, Alberee Products, Inc., 1992; v.p. Coupon Am., Bel Air, Md., 1987-88; dir. mktg. Miles Homes, Inc., Cheshire, Conn., 1993; CEO Universal Industries, Inc., 1994—; ptnr. Drakeford & Drakeford, PA, 1995—. Active in Radio Free Asia, 1972, Pinellas County Heart Savers, Clearwater, 1981; campaign mgr. for candidates for Balt. City Coun., U.S. Senate and U.S. Congress, 1968, 88, Fla. Commr. Agr., 1990. With U.S. Army, 1953-55, 72. Democrat. Jewish. Avocations: writing, art. Office: Prasco Inc PO Box 24461 Tampa FL 33623-4461

SILVER, R. PHILIP, metal products executive; b. 1942. Grad., U. Mo., 1967. With Amour & Co., Atlanta, 1967-68, Boise Cascade Corp., Idaho, 1968-75; exec. v.p. Fla. Gas Co., Orlando, Fla., 1975-80; pres. Continental Can, Norwalk, Conn., 1980-87; pres., treas. Silgan Corp., Stamford, Conn., 1987-93; chmn bd. dirs., co-chief exec. officer Silgan Corp, Stamford, Conn., 1993—. Office: Silgan Corp 4 Landmark Sq Stamford CT 06901-2502*

SILVER, RALPH DAVID, distilling company director; b. Chgo., Apr. 19, 1924; s. Morris J. and Amelia (Abrams) S.; m. Lois Reich, Feb. 4, 1951; children: Jay, Cappy. B.S., U. Chgo., 1943; postgrad., Northwestern U., 1946-48; J.D., DePaul U., 1952. Bar: Ill. bar 1952. Staff accountant David Himmelblau & Co. (C.P.A.'s), 1946-48; internal revenue agt. U.S. Dept. Treasury, 1948-51; practice in Chgo., 1952-55; atty. Lawrence J. West, 1952-55; fin. cons., bd. dirs. Barton Inc., Chgo., 1955-92; bd. dirs. Stone Fin. Corp., Stone Fin. II Corp., 1992-95; arbitrator N.Y. State Exch., Cir. Ct. of Cook County, Ill., Nat. Assn. Securities Dealers. Bd. dirs., pres. Ralph and Lois Silver Found. Lt. (j.g.) USNR, 1943-46. Mem. ABA, Chgo. Bar Assn., AICPA. Club: Green Acres Country. Home: 1124 Old Elm Ln Glencoe IL 60022-1235

SILVER, RICHARD TOBIAS, physician, educator; b. Jan. 18, 1929; m. Barbara Silver; 1 son, Adam Bennett. Diploma, A.B., Cornell U., 1950, M.D., 1953. Diplomate: Nat. Bd. Med. Examiners, Am. Bd. Internal Medicine, Am. Bd. Clin. Oncology. Intern N.Y. Hosp.-Cornell Med. Ctr., N.Y.C., 1953-54, asst. resident in medicine, 1956-57, resident in hematology, 1957-58; clin. assoc. gen. medicine br. Nat. Cancer Inst., NIH, Bethesda, Md., 1954-56; asst. in medicine Cornell U. Med. Coll., N.Y.C., 1956-58, instr. medicine, 1958-62, clin. asst. prof., 1962-67, clin. assoc. prof., 1967-73, clin. prof., 1973—; pres. N.Y. State Soc. Med. Oncologists and Hematologists, 1991—; asst. attending physician N.Y. Hosp., 1964-67, assoc. attending physician, 1967-73, attending physician, 1973—; asst. vis. physician 2d Cornell Med. div. Bellevue Hosp., N.Y.C., 1963-66; vis. Fulbright prof. U. Bahia Sch. Medicine, Brazil, 1958-59; vis. prof. Hershey Hosp.-Pa. State Hosp., 1976, Mayo Clinic, 1977, Upstate Med. Ctr., Binghamton, N.Y., 1977, Med. Coll. Va., 1979, Med. Sch. Colubia U., 1982, N.J. Coll. Medicine, New Brunswick, 1983, Meml. Med. Ctr. U. Ga., 1984, 86; invited lectr. Med. Coll. Shanghai and Chengchow, 1979, VIII Brazilian Hematology Congress, Salvador, 1981, 14th Internat. Congress Chemotherapy, Kyoto, Japan, 1985, XI Brazilian Congress of Cancerology, Florianoplis, Santa Catarina, 1987, 2d Internat. Conf. CML, Bologna, Italy, 1992; mem. rev. bd. NIH, Nat. Cancer Inst.; cons. Cancer Chemotherapy Investigative Rev. Bd., 1980, clin. trials com., 1979-81; mem. Cornell U. COuncil, 1987—. Author: Morphology of the Blood and Marrow in Clinical Practice, 1970; co-author: (with R.D. Lauper, C.I. Jarowski) A Synopsis of Cancer Chemotherapy, 1977, ed edit., 1987; editor, contbr.: Topics in Cancer, 1982; contbr. chpts. to books and articles to profl. jours., to nat. and internat. profl. confs., seminars and workshops in medicine. Fellow ACP; mem. N.Y. State Soc. Med. Hematologists and Oncologists (pres. 1991—), Cornell U. Med. Coll. Alumni Assn. (pres. 1973-76, sr. advisor 1976—), Am. Soc. Clin. Oncology, Internat. Soc. Hematology, Am. Soc. Hematology, N.Y. Soc. Study of Blood, N.Y. County Med. Soc., N.Y. State Med. Soc. Oncologists and Hematologists (pres. 1991-93), Harvey Soc., Am. Fedn. Clin. Rsch., Am. Assn. Cancer Rsch., Explorers Club (bd. dirs., chmn. sci. adv. com. 1987), Sigma Xi. Office: NY Hosp Cornell Med Ctr 525 E 68th St New York NY 10021-4873 also: 1440 York Ave New York NY 10021-2577

SILVER, RON, actor, director; b. N.Y.C., July 2, 1946; s. Irving Roy and May (Zimelman) S.; m. Lynne Miller, Dec. 24, 1975. BA, U. Buffalo; MA, St. John's U./Chinese Culture, Yangmingshan, Taiwan; student, Yale Law Sch., 1991. Appeared in (stage prodns.) Kaspar, Public Insult, 1971, El Grande de Coca-Cola, 1972, 75, Lotta, 1973, More Than You Deserve, 1973, Awake and Sing, 1976, Angel City, 1977, In the Boom Boom Room, 1979, Gorilla, 1983, Friends, 1983-84, Hurly Burly, 1984-85, Social Security, 1986, Hunting Cockroaches, 1987, Speed-the-Plow (Tony and Drama Desk awards), 1988, 92, Broken Glass, 1994, (films) Tunnelvision, 1976, Semi-Tough, 1977, Silent Rage, 1982, Best Friends, 1982, Lovesick, 1982, The Entity, Silkwood, 1983, The Goodbye People, 1984, Garbo Talks, 1984, Eat and Run, 1985, Enemies a Love Story, 1989, Blue Steel, 1990, Reversal of Fortune, 1990, Married to It, 1992, Time Cop, 1994, Girl 6, 1996, The Arrival, 1996; (TV) Rhoda, 1976-78, The Mac Davis Show, 1976, The Billionaire Boys Club (Emmy nomination), 1986, Hill Street Blues, Wiseguy, 1988, Fellow Traveller, 1990, Forgotten Prisoners: From the Amnesty Files, 1991, Blindside, 1992, Lifepod (also dir.), 1993, The Good Policeman (also exec. producer), 1994, A Woman of Independent Means, 1995, Almost Golden, 1995, Kissinger and Nixon, 1995, Chicago Hope, 1996. Recipient Israel Cultural award. Mem. AFTRA, SAG, Actors' Equity Assn. (pres.), Actors Studio, Actors Fund (trustee), Acad. Motion Picture Arts and Scis., The Creative Coalition (founder, pres.), Coun. on Fgn. Rels., Coun. Woodrow Wilson Internat. Ctr. for Scholars, Nat. Acad. TV Arts and Scis. Office: care David Seltzer Addi- Wechsler 955 S Carillo Dr 3d Fl Los Angeles CA 90048 also: Actors Equity Assn 165 W 46th St New York NY 10036-2501

SILVER, SAMUEL MANUEL, rabbi, author; b. Wilmington, Del., June 7, 1912; s. Adolph David and Adela (Hacker) S.; m. Elaine Shapiro, Feb. 9, 1953; children: Lee, Joshua, Barry, Noah, Daniel. B.A., U. Del., 1933; M.H.L., Hebrew Union Coll., 1940, D.D., 1965. Ordained rabbi, 1940; dir. Hillel Found., U. Md., 1940-42; asst. rabbi in Cleve., 1946-52; rabbi Temple Sinai, Stamford, Conn., 1959-77, Jewish Community Center of Lee County, Cape Coral, Fla., 1977-79, Temple Sinai of South Palm Beach County, Fla., 1979-95; rabbi emeritus Temple Sinai, Delray Beach, Fla., 1995—; Sec. Temple of Understanding, Greenwich, Conn., 1969; v.p. Stamford-Darien Council of Chs. and Synagogues; exec. bd. Fellowship in Prayer, 1970—; pres. Rabbinical Assn. South Palm Beach County, 1980-82. Author: (with Rabbi M.M. Applebaum) Sermonettes for Young People, 1964, How To Enjoy This Moment, 1967, Explaining Judaism to Jews and Christians, 1971, When You Speak English You Often Speak Hebrew, 1973, Mixed Marriage Between Jew and Christian, 1977, Speak to the Children of Israel, 1977, What Happiness Is, 1995; editor: Am. Judaism, 1952-59, The Quotable Am. Rabbis, 1967; columnist Nat. Jewish Post, 1955—. Served as chaplain AUS, 1942-46. Mem. Central Conf. Am. Rabbis (nat. exec. bd. 1954-56), Jewish War Vets (chaplain 1966-70), Assn. Jewish Chaplains U.S. (pres. 1959-62), Stamford-Darien Ministers League (pres. 1961-62), Zionist Orgn. Am. (pres. Southeast region 1984—), Alpha Epsilon Pi. Home and Office: 2309 NW 66 Dr Boca Raton FL 33496-3602 *The greatest of all miracles is that we need not be tomorrow what we are today but that we can improve if we make use of the potential implanted within us by God.*

SILVER, SHEILA JANE, composer, music educator; b. Seattle, Oct. 3, 1946; d. Robert Eugene and Fannie (Horowitz) S.; m. John Feldman, Dec. 11, 1988. BA, U. Calif., Berkeley, 1968; postgrad., Hochschule fur Musik, Stuttgart, Fed. Republic Germany, 1969-71; MFA, Brandeis U., 1972, PhD, 1974. Assoc. prof. music SUNY, Stony Brook, 1979—; mem. Barlow Found. commn., 1996. Composer classical works for orch., string orch., opera, chamber orch., string quartet, various instruments, also vocal and choral compositions and feature film scores. Radcliffe Inst. fellow, 1977-78, Koussevitzky fellow, 1972, Nat. Endowment for the Arts Composer fellow, 1995; recipient Composer award Am. Inst. and Acad. Arts and Letters, 1986, Prix de Rome, Am. Acad. in Rome, 1978-79, CARY Trust Recording award, 1995; winner Nat. Composers' Competition, Internat. Soc. Contemporary Music, 1981-82, competition Indpls. Symphony Orch., 1977, IV Internat. Wettbewerb fur Komponistinnen, 1976. Mem. Fellows of Am. Acad., Am. Music Ctr., N.Y. Women Composers, Rockefeller Found. Jewish. Home and Office: 68-37 Dartmouth St Forest Hills NY 11375-5046

SILVER, SHELDON, state legislator, lawyer; b. N.Y.C., Feb. 13, 1944; s. Nathan and Frieda (Bearman) S.; m. Rosa Mandelkern, June 25, 1967; children: Edward, Janine, Michelle, Esther. BA, Yeshiva U., 1965; JD, Bklyn. Coll., 1968. Bar: N.Y. 1969, U.S. Dist. Ct. (so. and ea. dists.) N.Y. 1970. Assoc. Schechter & Schwartz, N.Y.C., 1968-71; law sec. to Judge Francis Pecora N.Y.C., 1971-76; ptnr. Agri, Bilder & Silver, N.Y.C., 1976-81; pvt. practice N.Y.C., 1981—; mem. N.Y. State Assembly, 1977—, chmn. ways and means com., 1992, speaker, 1994. Vice pres. Bialystoker Synagogue, Young Israel Synagogue. Named Man of Yr., Harry S. Truman Dem. Club, 1977, United Jewish Appeals, 1983, also others. Democrat. Office: 270 Broadway Ste 1800 New York NY 10007-2306

SILVER, SHELLY ANDREA, media artist; b. N.Y.C., July 16, 1957; d. Reuben and Anita (Kuriloff) S. BA, BFA, Cornell U., 1980. program fellow Japan/U.S. Friendship Commn. Artist Exch., 1994, Deutscher Akademischer Austauschdienst Berliner Kunstlerprogramm, 1992; vis. prof. Deutsche Film und Fernsehakademie, 1992; vis. artist Art Inst. Chgo., 1991; adjunct prof. Tisch Sch. of the Arts, N.Y.C., 1996; freelance editor Sesame St., Frontline, Saturday Night Live, HBO, MTV, Showtime, others. Represented in exhbns. including The New Mus., N.Y.C., 1987, The Mus. of Modern Art, 1991, 95, The N.Y. Film Festival (video sect.), 1994, The Mus. of Kyoto, Japan, 1994, The London Film Festival, 1991, Internat. Ctr. Photography, N.Y.C.,. Japan Found. Film & Video grantee, 1995, N.Y. State Coun. Arts Project grantee, 1987, 89, 95, Checkerboard Found. grantee, 1990, Media Bur. Finishing Funds grantee; fellow U.S./Japan Artists Exch., 1993, Nat. Endowment Arts, 1989, 91, N.Y. Found. Arts, 1986, 91. Home and Office: 22 Catherine St Apt 6 New York NY 10038

SILVERBERG, DAVID S., financial consultant; b. Oelwein, Iowa, Mar. 3, 1936; s. Harold and Rose (Fishman) S.; m. Mary Ellen Silverberg, July 20, 1988; children: Laura, Sara, Stanley. Student, U. Minn., 1954-57; LUTC, Life Underwriter Coll., Sioux City, Iowa, 1976; CFP, Coll. Fin. Planning, Denver, 1979. With U.S. Army, 1963-68; fin. cons. Smith Barney, Sioux City, 1978—; instr. Western Iowa Tech. Coll., Sioux City, 1980-87, Inst. of Banking, Sioux City, 1990. Pres. Sioux City Jewish Fedn., 1991-94; v.p. Sioux City Jewish Cemetery Assn., 1990—; bd. dirs. Job Tng. Partnership Act, Sioux City, 1990—. Recipient Young Leadership award Sioux City Jewish Fedn., 1984. mem. Internat. Assn. Fin. Planners, Landmark Lodge AF&AM, Scottish Rite (32nd degree), Shriners, Sioux City Country Club. Avocations: golf, fish. Home: 26 W 45th St Sioux City IA 51104-1002 Office: Smith Barney 600 4th St Sioux City IA 51101-1744

SILVERBERG, LEWIS HENRY, management consultant; b. L.A., Nov. 1, 1934; s. Milton Henry and Marjorie Vella (Coates) S.; m. Amelia Francis Backstrom, June 9, 1959 (div. 1979); children: Stephen, Richard, Donna; m. Alice Ellen Deakins, Mar. 9, 1979. BA, Pomona Coll., 1955; JD, UCLA, 1958. Bar: Calif. 1959, U.S. Supreme Ct. 1966. Pvt. practice San Diego, 1959-89; exec. v.p., dir. Liquor Barn, Inc., San Diego, 1989-93; bus. cons. San Diego, 1993—; referee Calif. inheritance tax and probate, 1972-88. Trustee San Diego Zool. Soc.; active various pub., charitable and ednl. orgns. Republican. Office: First Virtual Holding Ste 300 11975 El Camino Real San Diego CA 92130 Office: Ste 300 11975 El Camino Real San Diego CA 92130-2543

SILVERBERG, MICHAEL JOEL, lawyer; b. Rochester, N.Y., Aug. 12, 1932; s. Goodman and Minnie (Krovetz) S.; m. Charlotte Goldman, June 19, 1955; children: Mark, Daniel. BA, U. Rochester, 1954; JD, Columbia U., 1957. Bar: N.Y. 1958, U.S. Dist. Ct. (so. dist.) N.Y. 1965, U.S. Dist. Ct. (ea. dist.) N.Y. 1990, U.S. Ct. Appeals (2d cir.) 1975, U.S. Supreme Ct. 1967. Instr. Columbia U. Law Sch., N.Y.C., 1957-58; assoc. Phillips, Nizer, Benjamin, Krim & Ballon, N.Y.C., 1960-67, ptnr., 1967—; bd. dirs. AMI/FAMI, N.Y. Mem. exec. bd. N.Y. chpt. Am. Jewish Com. Fulbright scholar U. Strasbourg, France, 1958-59. Mem. ABA, N.Y. State Bar Assn. (com. on internat. litigation), Assn. Bar City N.Y. Home: 205 W End Ave New York NY 10023-4804 Office: Phillips Nizer Benjamin Krim & Ballon LLP 666 Fifth Ave New York NY 10103-0084

SILVERBERG, ROBERT, author; b. N.Y.C., 1935; s. Michael and Helen (Baim) S.; m. Barbara Brown, 1956; m. Karen Haber, 1987. B.A., Columbia U., 1956. Author: novels Thorns, 1967, The Masks of Time, 1968, Hawksbill Station, 1968, Nightwings, 1969, To Live Again, 1969, Tower of Glass, 1970, The World Inside, 1971, Son of Man, 1971, A Time of Changes, 1971, Dying Inside, 1972, The Book of Skulls, 1972, Born with the Dead, 1974, Shadrach in the Furnace, 1976, Lord Valentine's Castle, 1980, Majipoor Chronicles, 1982, Lord of Darkness, 1983, Valentine Pontifex, 1983, Gilgamesh the King, 1984, Tom O'Bedlam, 1985, Star of Gypsies, 1986, At Winter's End, 1988, To the Land of the Living, 1989, The New Springtime, 1990, (with Isaac Asimov) Nightfall, 1990, The Face of the Waters, 1991, (with Isaac Asimov) The Ugly Little Boy, 1992, Kingdoms of the Wall, 1993, (with Isaac Asimov) The Positronic Man, 1993, Hot Sky at Midnight, 1994, Mountains of Majipoor, 1995, Starborne, 1996; non-fiction The Face of the Lost Cities and Vanished Civilizations, 1962, The Great Wall of China, 1965, The Old Ones: Indians of the American Southwest, 1965, Scientists and Scoundrels: A Book of Hoaxes, 1965, The Auk, the Dodo and the Oryx, 1966, The Morning of Mankind: Prehistoric Man in Europe, 1967, Mound Builders of Ancient America: The Archaeology of a Myth, 1968, If I Forget Thee, O Jerusalem: American Jews and the State of Israel, 1970, The Pueblo Revolt, 1970, The Realm of Prester John, 1971. Recipient Hugo award World Sci. Fiction Conv., 1956, 69, 87, 90; Nebula award Sci. Fiction Writers Am., 1970, 72, 75, 86. Mem. Sci. Fiction Writers Am. (pres. 1967-68). Address: PO Box 13160 Oakland CA 94661-0160

SILVERBERG, STUART OWEN, obstetrician, gynecologist; b. Denver, Oct. 14, 1931; s. Edward M. and Sara (Morris) S.; BA, U. Colo., 1952, MD, 1955; m. Joan E. Snyderman, June 19, 1954 (div. Apr. 1970); children: Debra Sue Owen, Eric Owen, Alan Kent; m. 2d, Kay Ellen Conklin, Oct. 18, 1970 (div. Apr. 1982); 1 son, Cris S.; m. 3d, Sandra Kay Miller, Jan., 1983. Intern Women's Hosp. Phila., 1955-56; resident Kings County Hosp., Bklyn., 1958-62; practice medicine specializing in obstetrics and gynecology, Denver, 1962—; mem. staff Rose Med. Ctr., N. Suburban Med. Ctr., U. Hosp., St. Anthony Hosp.; med. exec. bd., chmn. dept. obstetrics and gynecology, 1976-77, 86-87, dir. Laser Ctr., 1994-95; clin. instr. U. Colo. Sch. Medicine, Denver, 1962-72, asst. clin. prof., 1972-88, assoc. clin. prof., 1989—, dir. gynecol. endoscopy and laser surgery, 1988-90; v.p. Productos Alimenticos, La Ponderosa, S.A.; dir., chmn. bd. Wicker Works Video Prodns., Inc., 1983-91; cons. Ft. Logan Mental Health Ctr., Denver, 1964-70; mem. Gov.'s Panel Mental Retardation, 1966; med. adv. bd. Colo. Planned Parenthood, 1966-68, Am. Med. Ctr., Spivak, Colo., 1967-70. Mem. Colo. Emergency Resources Bd., Denver, 1965—. Served to maj. AUS, 1956-58; Germany. Diplomate Am. Bd. Obstetrics and Gynecology, Am. Bd. Laser Surgery. Fellow Am. Coll. Obstetricians and Gynecologists, Am. Soc. Laser Medicine and Surgery, ACS; mem. Am. Internat. fertility socs., Colo. Gynecologists and Obstetricians Soc., Hellman Obstet. and Gynecol. Soc., Colo. Med. Soc. (bd. dirs. 1987-95, speaker of the house 1989-95), Clear Creek Valley Med. Soc. (trustee 1978, 80, 87, 93—, pres. 1995), Phi Sigma Delta, Flying Physicians Assn., Aircraft Owners and Pilots Assn., Nu Sigma Nu, Alpha Epsilon Delta. Jewish. Mem. editorial rev. bd. Colo. Women's Mag.; editor in chief First Image, Physicians Video Jour., 1984-86. Office: 8300 N Alcott St Ste 301 Westminster CO 80030

SILVERMAN, AL, editor; b. Lynn, Mass., Apr. 12, 1926; s. Henry and Minnie (Damsky) S.; m. Rosa Magaro, Sept. 9, 1951; children: Thomas, Brian, Matthew. B.S., Boston U., 1949, Litt.D., 1986. Assoc. editor Sport mag., 1951-52; sports editor True mag., 1952-54; asst. editor Argosy mag., 1954-55; free-lance mag. writer, contbr. Saturday Evening Post, Coronet, Pageant, This Week, Am. Weekly, Am. Heritage, Saturday Review, others, 1955-60; editor-in-chief Saga mag., Impact mag., Sport Library, Sport mag., 1960-72; exec. v.p., editorial dir. Book-of-the-Month Club, 1972—, pres., chief operating officer, 1981—, chmn., chief exec. office, 1985-88; v.p., contbg. editor Viking Penguin, 1989-92, sr. v.p., pub., editor in chief, 1992—; sr. v.p., editor-at-large Viking Penguin, N.Y.C., 1994—. Author: Warren Spahn, 1961, Best from Sport, 1961, (with Phil Rizzuto) The Miracle New York Yankees, 1962, The World of Sport, 1962, Mickey Mantle, Master Yankee, 1963, World Series Heroes, 1964, (with Paul Hornung) Football and the Single Man, 1965, The Specialist in Pro Football, 1966, Sports Titans of the 20th Century, 1968, (with Frank Robinson) My Life is Baseball, 1968, More Sport Titans of the 20th Century, 1969, Joe DiMaggio, The Golden Year, 1969, I Am Third, (with Gale Sayers), 1970, Foster and Laurie, 1974; editor: The Book of the Month, 1986; co-editor: The 20th Century Treasury of Sports, 1992. Mem. Authors Guild. Home: 15 Woods Way White Plains NY 10605-5446 Office: Penguin US 375 Hudson St New York NY 10014-3658

SILVERMAN, ALAN H., lawyer; b. N.Y.C., Feb. 18, 1954; s. Melvin H. and Florence (Green) S.; m. Gretchen E. Freeman, May 25, 1986; children: Willa C.F., Gordon H.F. BA summa cum laude, Hamilton Coll., 1976; MBA, U. Pa., 1980, JD, 1980. Bar: N.Y. 1981, U.S. Dist. Ct. (so. and ea. dist.) N.Y. 1981, U.S. Ct. Internat. Trade 1981, D.C. 1986, U.S. Supreme Ct. 1990. Assoc. Hughes, Hubbard & Reed, N.Y.C., 1980-84; asst. counsel Newsweek, Inc., N.Y.C., 1984-86; v.p., gen. counsel, sec., dir. adminstrn. Post-Newsweek Cable, Phoenix, 1986—. Contbr. articles to profl. jours. Mem. prevention adv. com. Gov. Pa. Justice Commn., 1975-79; bd. dirs. Lawyers' Alliance for N.Y., 1982-85, N.Y. Lawyers Pub. Interest, 1983-85, Nat. Assn. JD-MBA Profls., 1983-85, Bus. Vols. for Arts, Inc., Phoenix, 1989-93, Ariz. Vol. Lawyers for the Arts, Inc., 1994—; mem. Maricopa County Citizens Jud. Adv. Coun., 1990-93. Mem. ABA, Assn. of Bar of City of N.Y., D.C. Bar Assn., Phi Beta Kappa. Home: 5222 N 34th Pl Phoenix AZ 85018-1521 Office: Post-Newsweek Cable 4742 N 24th St Ste 270 Phoenix AZ 85016-4860

SILVERMAN, ALBERT A., retired lawyer, manufacturing company executive; b. Copenhagen, Oct. 14, 1908; came to U.S., 1909, naturalized, 1921; s. Louis and Anna (Mendelsohn) S.; m. Gertrude Adelman, 1929 (div. 1934); 1 child, Violet (Mrs. Robert Blumenthal); m. Florence Cohen, Aug. 5, 1939 (dec. 1966); m. Francie Seifert, Oct. 1, 1975. Student, Northwestern U., 1929-34; AA, Cen. YMCA Coll., Chgo., 1936; JD, Loyola U., Chgo., 1940. Bar: Ill. 1940, Wis. 1959, U.S. Supreme Ct. 1960. With Cen. Republic Bank & Trust Co., Chgo., 1926-32; sec.-treas. Cen.-Ill. Co., 1932-42; corp. atty., sec. Republic Drill & Tool Co., 1942-44; asst. to treas. Hansen Glove Corp., Milw., 1944-45; v.p. Vilter Mfg. Corp., Milw., 1945-49, pres., 1949-88, 89-92, chmn., chief exec. officer, 1970-92, chmn. emeritus, 1992—; bd. dirs., pres. Vilter Found., Inc.; mem. coun. Marquette U. Engring. Sch., 1974-95, assoc., 1995—. Council, Med. Coll. Wis.; former bd. dirs. Milw. Housing Assistance Corp.; bd. dirs. Albert J. and Flora H. Ellinger Found., 1974—. Named Man of Yr. Milw. chpt. Unico Nat., 1967; recipient Francis J. Rooney-St. Thomas More award Loyola U. Law Sch., Chgo., 1974, Community Relations award Milw. police chief, 1974, Antonio R. Rizzuto Gold Medal award Unico Nat., Community Svc. award, VFW, 1989, award Wis. Reg. Bd. NCCJ, 1989; honored by VFW for community svc., 1988. Mem. ABA, ASHRAE, Wis. Bar Assn., Milw. Bar Assn., Chgo. Bar Assn., Am. Zool Soc., Loyola U. Alumni Assn. (hon.), Milw. Athletic Club, Wis. Club, Univ. Club of Milw., Tripoli Country Club, Milw. Athletic Club, Milw. Press Club (Knight of Bohemia award 1979, Headliner award 1981, NCJJ award 1989), Masons (past master Milw. Harmony Lodge 1961, 32 deg.), Shriners, Beta Gamma Sigma (hon.). Jewish. Office: 2405 W Dean Rd River Hills WI 53217-2008 *As we go through life, we experience good and bad times, tragedies and happiness, successes and failures. Sometimes we are even handed lemons. Problems are opportunities, and with lemons one can make lemonade.*

SILVERMAN, ALBERT JACK, psychiatrist, educator; b. Montreal, Que., Can., Jan. 27, 1925; came to U.S., 1950, naturalized, 1955; s. Norman and Molly (Cohen) S.; m. Halina Weinthal, June 22, 1947; children: Barry Evan, Marcy Lynn. B.Sc., McGill U., 1947, M.D., C.M., 1949; grad., Washington Psychoanalytic Inst., 1964. Diplomate: Am. Bd. Psychiatry and Neurology. Intern Jewish Gen. Hosp., Montreal, 1949-50; resident psychiatry Colo. U. Med. Center, 1950-53, instr., 1953; from assoc. to assoc. prof. psychiatry Duke Med. Center, 1953-63; prof. psychiatry, chmn. dept. Rutgers U. Med. Sch., 1964-70; prof. psychiatry U. Mich. Med. Sch., Ann Arbor, 1970-90, prof. emeritus, 1990—; chmn. dept. U. Mich. Med. Sch., 1970-81; cons. Dept. of Def., 1974—; mem. biol. scis. tng. rev. com. NIMH, 1964-69, chmn., 1968-69, mem. rsch. scientist devel. award com., 1970-75, chmn., 1973-75, mem. merit rev. bd. in behavioral scis. VA, 1975-78, chmn., 1976-78, mem. small grants awards com., 1985-89; bd. mgrs. N.J. Neuropsychiat. Inst., 1965-69; trustee N.J. Fund Rsch. and Devel. Nervous and Mental Diseases, 1965-67; bd. dirs. N.J. Mental Health Assn., 1964-69; mem. behavioral sci. com. Nat. Bd. Med. Examiners, 1978-82, chmn., 1984-87, mem. comprehensive com., 1986-93, task force for nervous system, 1989-91; chmn. task force on Cons. Liaison Psychiat., 1991-92. Cons. editor: Psychophysiology, 1970-74, Psychosomatic Medicine, 1972-87; Contbr. articles in field. Served as capt. M.C. USAF, 1955-57. Fellow Am. Coll. Psychiatry (charter), Am. Psychiat. Assn. (chmn. coun. on med. edn. 1970-75, chair task force on DSM III ednl. materials 1979-81), Am. Acad. Psychoanalysis, Am. Coll. Neuropsychopharmacology; mem. Am. Psychosomatic Soc. (coun. 1964-68, 70-74, pres. 1976-77, vis. scholar com. 1992-96, co-chair program com. 1992-93), N.J. Psychoanalytic Soc. (trustee 1968-70), Assn. Rsch. Nervous and Mental Diseases, N.J. Neuropsychiat. Assn. (coun. 1966-69), Group Advancement Psychiatry (chmn. com. psychopathology 1968-74), Soc. Psychophys. Rsch., Soc. Biol. Psychiatry, Mich. Psychiat. Soc. (coun. 1975-77). Home: 19 Regent Dr Ann Arbor MI 48104-1738 Office: Mental Health Rsch Inst 205 Zina Pitcher Pl Ann Arbor MI 48109-0720

SILVERMAN, ALVIN MICHAELS, public relations consultant; b. Louisville, 1912; s. Alvin and May (Michaels) S.; m. Phyllis Israel, Nov. 22, 1936; children: Lora (Mrs. A. Gene Samburg), Jane (Mrs. Carl Culos). Student, Adelbert Coll., Western Res. U., 1930-32. With Cleve. Plain Dealer, 1930-65, beginning as sportswriter, successively schs. editor, city hall reporter, state house corr., Columbus, editorial columnist, day city editor, 1930-57, chief Washington bur., 1957-65; pres., chief exec. officer Pearl-Silverman Agy. (pub. relations consultants), Washington, 1965—; dir. Tiffin Amusement Co., Ellet Co., Bklyn. Devel. Corp. Author: The American Newspaper, 1965. Trustee Ctr. to Protect Workers' Rights. Mem. White House Corrs. Assn., Ohio Legis. Corrs. Assn., D.C. Friends of Ireland, Press Club of Ohio, Woodmont Country Club, Gridiron Club, Fed. City Club, Sigma Delta Chi, Zeta Beta Tau. Home: 4100 Cathedral Ave NW Washington DC 20016-3584 Office: 1125 17th St NW Washington DC 20036-4707

SILVERMAN, ARNOLD, physician; b. N.Y.C., Feb. 15, 1933; s. Sol and Gertrude (Cohen) S.; m. Bonnie J. Fenson, Aug. 28, 1955; children: Jeffrey R., Paul A., David E. B.A., U. Colo., 1954, M.A., 1957, M.D., 1961. Diplomate: Am. Bd. Pediatrics. Intern Colo. Gen. Hosp., Denver, 1961-62; resident in pediatrics U. Minn. Hosp., Mpls., 1962-64; fellow in pediatric gastroenterology U. Colo. Med. Center, Denver, 1964-65; mem. faculty U. Colo. Med. Center, 1965—, assoc. prof. pediatrics, 1975-80; prof. U. Colo. Med. Ctr. (Health Sci. Ctr.), 1980-93, prof. emeritus, 1994—; dir. grad. edn. Denver Children's Hosp., 1967-75, chief gastroenterology svc., 1967-75; dir. pediat. svc. Denver Gen. Hosp., 1975-92; cons. Surgeon Gen. Fitzsimons Army Med. Hosp., 1976-95; mem. Nat. Commn. Digestive Diseases, 1979-80. Author: (with C.C. Roy and D. Alagille) Pediatric Clinic Gastroenterology, 4th edit., 1995. Mem. Am. Acad. Pediatrics, Am. Gastroenterology Assn., Am. Pediatric Soc., Am. Gastroenterology Assn., N.Am. Soc. Pediatric Gastroenterology, Am. Assn. Study Liver Disease, Denver Med. Soc., Alpha Omega Alpha. Jewish. Home: 3335 S Newport St Denver CO 80224-2823

SILVERMAN, ARNOLD BARRY, lawyer; b. Sept. 1, 1937; s. Frank and Lillian Lena (Linder) S.; m. Susan L. Levin, Aug. 7, 1960; children: Michael Eric, Lee Oren. B Enging. Sci., Johns Hopkins U., 1959; LLB cum laude, U. Pitts., 1962. Bar: U.S. Dist. Ct. (we. dist.) Pa. 1963, Pa. 1964, U.S. Patent and Trademark Office 1965, U.S. Supreme Ct. 1967, Can. Patent Office 1968, U.S. Ct. Claims 1975, U.S. Ct. Appeals (3d cir.) 1982, U.S. Ct. Appeals (fed. cir.) 1985. Patent atty. Alcoa, New Kensington, Pa., 1962-67, 68-74, sr. patent atty., 1972-76; ptnr. Price and Silverman, Pitts., 1967-68; v.p., gen. patent counsel Joy Mfg. Co., Pitts., 1976-80; ptnr. Murray Silverman & Keck, Pitts., 1980-81, Buell, Blenko, Ziesenheim & Beck, Pitts., 1984; ptnr. intellectual property sect. Eckert, Seamans, Cherin & Mellott, Pitts., 1984—, chmn., 1992—; spl. asst. atty. gen. State of W.Va., 1985—; spl. counsel patents U. Pitts., 1975—; spkr. on patents, trademarks, copyright, computer law; nat. panel of arbiters Am. Arbitration Assn., 1987—; chair Info. Tech. Practice Group, 1995—. Contbr. articles to profl. jours. on intellectual property, computer and pub. law. Mem. Churchill CSC (Pa.), 1967-90, chmn., 1975-90; mem. Pitts. law com. Anti-Defamation League, 1981—, regional adv. bd., 1982—, ch-chmn. Pitts. region ann. dinner, 1983, mem. chmn. by-laws com., 1983; bd. govs. Slippery Rock U. Found., 1985-91; Pitts. steering com. MIT Enterprise Forum, 1986-87. With U.S. Army, 1963-64. Recipient Am. Spirit Honor medal, Ft. Knox, 1963,. Mem. ABA, ASME, Allegheny County Bar Assn. (chmn. pub. rels. com. 1978-80, vice-chmn. intellectual property sect. 1981-83), Pitts. Patent Law Assn. (chmn. pub. rels. com., 1968-69, chmn. patent laws com., 1970-72, chmn. nominating com., 1973, chmn. legis. action com., 1972-75, bd. mgrs. 1974-88, newsletter editor 1974-88, sec.-treas. 1976-84, v.p. 1984-85, pres. 1985-86, pub. rels. com. 1994-95, program com. 1995—), Am. Intellectual Property Law Assn. (membership com. 1985-88, mem. pub. rels. com. 1994—), U.S. Trademark Assn. (chmn. task force on advt. agys. 1981, membership com. 1987-89), D.C. Bar Assn., Pa. Bar Assn., Assn. Corp. Patent Counsel (emeritus 1980—), Nat. Assn. Coll. and Univ. Attys., Am. Chem. Soc., Licensing Execs. Soc. (co-chair Pitts. 1994—), Brit. Inst. Chartered Patent Agts. (fgn. mem.), Johns Hopkins U. Alumni Assn. (chmn. publicity com. 1963-66, exec. com. 1966-87, v.p. 1969-70, pres. 1971-72, nat. alumni coun. 1989-92), U. Pitts. Gen. Alumni Assn., U. Pitts. Law Alumni Assn. (bd. dirs. 1992—), Robert Bruce Assn. Law Fellows (life), Golden Panthers, Stratford Cmty. Assn. (v.p. 1966-67, gov. 1966-70, pres. 1967-68), Mensa (fellow, lawyers in Mensa 1978—, nat. assoc. counsel patents and trademarks copyrights 1980-82, inventors' spl. interest group 1980-86), Intertel (treas. Pitts. Forum 1983—), Duquesne Club, Order of Coif, Tau Epsilon Rho, Psi Chi. Republican. Jewish. Home: 2019 High Point Dr Murrysville PA 15668-8515 Office: 600 Grant St Ste 42 Pittsburgh PA 15219-2703 *Welcome challenge and perform all tasks with enthusiasm, in a moral manner and to the very best of your ability.*

SILVERMAN, ARTHUR CHARLES, lawyer; b. Lewiston, Maine, June 13, 1938; s. Louis A. and Frances Edith (Brownstone) S.; BS in Elec. Engring., BS in Indsl. Mgmt., MIT, 1961; JD, Columbia U., 1964; m. Donna Linda Zolov, June 18, 1961; children: Leonard Stephen, Daniel Edward. Bar: N.Y. 1965, U.S. Supreme Ct. 1971. Engr., engring. asst. Gen. Electric Co., Pittsfield, Mass. and Phila., 1958-62; assoc. Baer & Marks, N.Y.C., 1965-68; assoc. Golenbock and Barell, N.Y.C., 1968-72, ptnr., 1972-89, Reid & Priest, N.Y.C., 1989—. Sec. Lehrer McGovern Bovis, Inc. 1979—, Bovis Inc., 1988—, dir. 1996—, treas., trustee Ramaz Sch., 1977-84, vice chmn., 1984-85, 86-88, chmn., 1988-92, hon. chmn., 1992—; bd. govs. MIT Hillel Found., 1979-84; mem. bd. Jewish Edn. of City of N.Y., 1981-84; mem. exec. com. Nat. Jewish Ctr. for Learning and Leadership, 1984-90. Mem. IEEE, ABA, NSPE, N.Y. State Bar Assn., Fed. Bar Council, Assn. Bar City N.Y., N.Y. Soc. Architects, Internat. Bar Assn., Inter-Pacific Bar Assn., Constrn. Mgmt. Inst., Bldg. Futures Coun., Masons. Republican. Home: 200 E 74th St New York NY 10021-3618 Office: Reid & Priest LLP 40 W 57th St New York NY 10019-4001

SILVERMAN, BRUCE GARY, advertising executive; b. N.Y.C., Feb. 16, 1945; s. Edward E. and Lillian (Brill) S.; children: Jennifer, Matthew; m. Nancy Cole, 1996. BA, Adelphi U., 1965; JD, Albany Law Sch., 1967. Sr. v.p., exec. creative dir. Ogilvy & Mather Inc., N.Y.C., 1967-80; exec. v.p., exec. creative dir. Bozell & Jacobs Inc., Dallas, 1981-83, Batten, Barton, Durstine & Osborn Inc., L.A., 1984-85; exec. v.p., creative dir. Asher/Gould Advt. Inc., L.A., 1986-89, pres., chief creative officer, 1989-95, pres., COO, 1996—. V.p., bd. dirs. Los Angeles Children's Mus., 1984-88; chmn. Resource Devel. com. Starbright Pavillion Found., 1993. Mem. Acad. TV Arts and Scis. Home: 3168 Dona Mema Pl Studio City CA 91604-4264

Office: Asher/Gould Advt Inc 5900 Wilshire Blvd Los Angeles CA 90036-5013

SILVERMAN, BURTON PHILIP, artist; b. Bklyn., June 11, 1928; s. Morris Daniel and Anne (Firstenberg) S.; m. Claire Guss, June 12, 1969; children: Robert Arthur, Karen Lila. BA, Columbia Coll., 1949. Freelance illustrator Life, Fortune, Esquire, Time, Newsweek, Sports Illus., New York, The New Yorkers mags., 1959—; instr. Sch. Visual Arts, N.Y.C., 1964-67. Co-author: Abel, 1968, A Portfolio of Drawings, 1968; author: Painting People, 1977, Breaking the Rules of Watercolor, 1983; contbr. articles and drawings to profl. jours.; one-man exhbns. include Davis Gallery, N.Y.C, 1956, 58, 62, Kenmore Galleries, Phila., 1963, 67, 70, FAR Gallery, N.Y.C., 1965, 70, 75, 77, Genesis Gallery, N.Y.C., 1979, Sindin Galleries, N.Y.C., 1983, Capricorn Galleries, Bethesda, Md., 1979, 91, Gallery 52, South Orange, N.J., 1967, 70, 77, Harbor Gallery, L.I., 1971, 74, U. Utah, 1967, Doll and Richards, Boston, 1980, Grand Central Galleries, N.Y.C., 1988, Cudahy's Gallery, N.Y.C., 1990, Joseph Keifer, Inc., N.Y.C., 1993, Gerold Wooderlich & Co., N.Y.C., 1996, Merrill Gallery, Denver, 1996; group exhbns. include Butler Inst. Am. Art, Youngstown, Ohio, 1954-71, 74, 76, 79, 88, 90, 93, NAD, N.Y.C., 1958-96, Am. Watercolor Soc., N.Y.C., 1978-82, 84-87, 89-91, 95-96, Pa. Acad. Fine Art, 1949, New Britain (Conn.) Mus. Am. Art, 1964, Wadsworth Atheneum, Hartford, Conn., 1961, Am. Acad. Arts and Letters, 1967, 74, 76, 79, N.Y. Hist. Soc., 1976, Pa. State Mus. Art, Portsmouth (Va.) Mus. Art, 1976, 79-80, 82 (Purchase prize, 1979, 82), Mexico City Mus. Art, 1990, Nat. Portrait Gallery, Washington, 1993, Hofstra Mus., N.Y.C., 1993, South Bend (Ind.) Mus. Art, 1994, Old Forge (N.Y.) Mus. and Gallery, 1994. With AUS, 1951-53. Named to Hall of Fame, Soc. of Illustrators, N.Y., 1990, Pastel Soc. Am., 1992. Mem. NAD (numerous awards and prizes including Joseph Isidor Gold medal 1992, Ranger Purchase prize 1962, 84, Benjamin Altman figure prize 1969), Am. Watercolor Soc. (numerous awards and prizes including Gold medal 1979, Silver medal 1984, 95, annuals). Home and Studio: 324 W 71st St New York NY 10023-3502 *In art I am wary of things too facile, or appealing. My painting is rooted in a realist tradition that is equally concerned with objective facts and subjective realities. It is a visual language that allows me to explore the tensions and ambiguities engendered by this dual aspect of human experience. Art is my life and my life is in my art.*

SILVERMAN, DAVID ALAN, screenwriter, television story consultant; b. Whittier, Calif., Jan. 18, 1952; s. Sol Robert and Jeanne Delores (Weiser) S. Student, George Washington U., 1969; BA in Psychology with honors, Stanford U., 1974; MA in Cinema, U. So. Calif., 1978. Story cons. TV show Alice, 1982-85; contbg. writer TV shows Mork & Mindy, 1979, The Jeffersons, 1979-80, What's Happening Now, 1985, ALF, 1986; story editor TV show One Day At A Time, 1981-82; staff writer TV show New Love American Style, 1985-86; story cons. TV show 9 to 5, 1987; screenwriter De Laurentis Entertainment Group, 1987—; story analyst Am. Internat. Pictures, Los Angeles, 1979. Writer: (TV pilots) Jr. Exec., 1984, For Better Or Worse, 1985, (screenplay) Stepping Out, 1987. Mem. Writers Guild Am., ASCAP, U. So. Calif. Alumni Assn. (Cinema Circulus), Stanford Alumni Assn. Democrat. Home: 1230 Casa Del Rey Dr La Habra CA 90631-8330 Office: care Fox Broadcasting Co PO Box 900 Beverly Hills CA 90213-0900*

SILVERMAN, FRED, television producer; b. N.Y.C., 1937. Student, Syracuse U.; M in TV and Theatre Arts, Ohio State U. With Sta. WGN-TV, Chgo.; then Sta. WPIX-TV, N.Y.C.; then dir. daytime programs CBS-TV, N.Y.C., v.p. programs, 1970-75; pres. ABC Entertainment, N.Y.C., 1975-78; pres., chief exec. officer NBC-TV, N.Y.C., 1978; now pres. Fred Silverman Co., L.A.; co-founder Pierce/Silverman TV Prodn. Co., 1989. Exec. producer TV series Perry Mason Movies, Matlock, In the Heat of the Night, Jake and the Fatman, Father Dowling Mysteries, Diagnosis Murder Starring Dick Van Dyck.

SILVERMAN, FREDERIC NOAH, physician; b. Syracuse, N.Y., June 6, 1914; s. Max and Sophia S.; m. Carolyn R. Weber, Jan. 14, 1945. A.B., Syracuse U., 1935, M.D., 1939. Intern Yale U., 1939-40; resident in pediatrics Johns Hopkins U., Balt., 1940-41; fellow in pediatric pathology Columbia U., N.Y.C., 1941-42; in pediatric radiology Babies Hosp., N.Y.C., 1945-47; dir. dept. radiology Children's Hosp., Cin., 1947-75; asst. prof. to prof. radiology and pediatrics U. Cin., 1947-76; prof. clin. radiology and pediatrics Stanford (Calif.) U., 1976-79, emeritus, 1979—; ad hoc cons. HEW, NAS. Chief editor Caffey's Pediatric X-Ray Diagnosis, 1978—; mem. editorial bd. pediatric and radiol. jours.; contbr. articles to profl. jours. With AUS, 1942-46, South West Pacific area. Decorated Combat Med. Badge; recipient medal Centre Antoine Béclère, Paris, 1981, Gold medal Assn. Univ. Radiologists, 1993. Mem. Am. Acad. Pediatrics, Am. Pediatric Soc., Soc. Pediatric Research (past v.p.), Soc. for Pediatric Radiology (past pres., Gold medal 1988); hon. mem. Am. Roentgen Ray Soc., European Soc. Pediatric Radiology, Spanish Radiology Soc., El Salvador Pediatrics Soc., Chilean Radiol. Soc., regional radiol. socs. Home: 850 Webster St Apt 735 Palo Alto CA 94301-2838 Office: Dept Radiology Stanford U Med Center Stanford CA 94305

SILVERMAN, GEORGE ALAN, broadcasting executive; b. Boston, Aug. 27, 1946; s. Sam and Ann S.; m. Sunnie Gozansky, Sept. 1, 1968; children—Rebecca, Marjorie, Jennifer. B.B.A. in Mktg, U. Miami, Fla., 1969. Gen. sales mgr. CBS, Sta. WEEI-FM, Boston, 1972-75; pres. Sunshine Group Broadcasting, Portland, Maine, 1977—; instr. mktg. Husson Coll., Bangor, Maine. Bd. dirs. Greater Portland Landmarks, Gulf of Marine Aquarium, 1979-80; mem. Greater Portland Arts Council; bd. dirs. Multiple Sclerosis Soc. Mem. Greater Portland Radio Broadcasters Assn. (past pres.), New Eng. Broadcast Assn., Maine Assn. Broadcasters. Home: 98 Carroll St Portland ME 04102-3526 Office: Sunshine Group Broadcasting 1555 Islington St Portsmouth NH 03801-4215

SILVERMAN, HARVEY FOX, engineering educator, dean. BS with Honors in Engring., Trinity Coll., 1965, BSE, 1966; ScM, Brown U., 1968, PhD, 1971. Rsch. assoc. Gerber Sci. Instrument Co., Hartford, Conn., 1964-66; various rsch. and mgmt. positions T.J. Watson Rsch. Ctr. IBM, Yorktown Heights, N.Y., 1970-80; prof. engring. Brown U., Providence, R.I., 1980-91, dir. undergrad. engring. program, 1988-90, dean engring., 1991—; cons. submarine signal divsn. Raytheon Co., Portsmouth, R.I., 1968. Contbr. articles to profl. jours. Trustee Trinity Coll., Hartford, Conn. Grantee IBM, 1981-85, Analog Devices, 1982-87, Lockheed-Martin, 1984-86, AMP, 1984-85, Tektronix, 1985, US West, 1988, NSF, 1982-96. Achievements include research in networks of processing nodes, each of which has a high-speed RISC host coupled to a large, reconfigurable system, time-varying speech analysis, talker independent connected-speech recognition algorithms and systems, microphone-array systems and non-linear opimization. Home: 50 Cindyann Dr East Greenwich RI 02818 Office: Brown U Divsn Engring 182 Hope St Providence RI 02912

SILVERMAN, HENRY JACOB, history educator; b. New Haven, Feb. 22, 1934; s. Morris Samuel and Ethel (Ullman) S.; m. Ann Beryl Snyder, Apr. 12, 1957; children—Edwin Stodel, Emily Davies. B.A. (Univ. scholar), Yale U., 1955, M.A., 1956; M.A. (Ford Found. fellow); postgrad., Stanford U., 1959-60; Ph.D., U. Pa., 1963. Fgn. service officer Dept. States, 1961-63; bibliographer Am. history Library of Congress, Washington, 1963-64; asst. prof. Am. thought and lang. Mich. State U., East Lansing, 1964-68, assoc. prof., 1968-71, prof., 1971-89, prof. history, 1988—, chmn. dept. Am. thought and lang., 1977-87, sec. for acad. governance, 1989-95; chmn. dept. history Mich. State U., 1995—. Author: American Radical Thought, 1970. Fulbright scholar, Munich, 1956-57; Danforth Found. Assoc., 1969-73; Nat. Endowment for Humanities/U. Iowa grantee, 1979. Mem. AAUP (mem. exec. bd. Mich. State U. chpt. 1975-77), ACLU (mem. Laxing exec. bd., 1975-78, v.p. 1991—, Mich. exec. bd. 1993—), Am. Hist. Assn., Am. Studies Assn., Orgn. Am. Historians. Home: 1099 Woodwind Trl Haslett MI 48840-8978 Office: Mich State U Dept History East Lansing MI 48823

SILVERMAN, HENRY RICHARD, diversified business executive, lawyer; b. N.Y.C., Aug. 2, 1940; s. Herbert Robert and Roslyn (Moskowitz) S.; m. Susan H. Herson, June 13, 1965 (div. Jan. 1977); children: Robin Lynn, Deborah Leigh; m. Nancy Ann Kraner, Jan. 22, 1978; 1 child, Catherine Anne. Grad. cum laude, Hackley Sch., Tarrytown, N.Y., 1957; B.A. with honors, Williams Coll., 1961; LL.B., U. Pa., 1964; postgrad. in corp. fin. and taxation, NYU, 1965. Bar: N.Y. 1965, U.S. Tax Ct. 1965, U.S. Ct. Appeals (2d cir.) 1965. Practice law, 1965-66; with White, Weld & Co., beginning 1966; then gen. ptnr. Oppenheimer & Co., until 1970; pres., chief exec. officer ITI Corp., 1970-72; founder, pres. Trans-York Securities Corp., 1972; exec. v.p., chmn. exec. com. Ladenburg, Thalmann & Co., 1973; pres., chief exec. officer Vavasseur Am. Ltd., subs. U.K. mcht. bank, 1974-75; gen. ptnr. Brisbane Ptnrs., 1976-77; prin. various investment groups, 1977—, Silverman Energy Co., N.Y.C., 1977—, NBC Channel 20, Springfield, Ill., 1977-83, ABC Channel 9, Syracuse, N.Y., 1977-81; prin., dir. Delta Queen Steamboat Co., New Orleans, 1977-86; also prin. outdoor advt., music pub., motion picture prodn., radio broadcasting & hardware mfg. cos.; pres., chief exec. officer Reliance Capital Corp., subs. Reliance Group Holdings, Inc., N.Y.C., 1982—; sr. v.p. bus. devel. Reliance Group Holdings, Inc., N.Y.C., 1982-90; chmn., chief exec. officer Days Inns Am., Inc., Atlanta, 1984-89; also dir.; pres., chief exec. officer Telemundo Group, Inc., N.Y.C., 1986-90; gen. ptnr. Blackstone Group, N.Y.C., 1990-91; chmn., CEO HFS Inc., N.Y.C., 1990—. Bd. dirs. N.Y. Univ. Hosp., N.Y.C., 1987—. Served to lt. USNR, 1965-73. Republican. Jewish. Club: Harmonie (N.Y.C.). Avocation: tennis. Office: 712 Fifth Ave 41st Flr New York NY 10019

SILVERMAN, HERBERT R., corporate financial executive; b. N.Y.C., June 10, 1914; s. Jacob and Minnie (Stein) S.; m. Roslyn Moskowitz, Dec. 17, 1933 (dec. Dec. 1965); children: Karen Silverman Mayers, Henry; m. Nadia Gray, Oct. 17, 1967 (dec. June 1994). BS, NYU, 1932; JD, St. Lawrence U., 1935. Bar: N.Y. bar 1935. Organizer, pres. Centaur Credit Corp. (merged with James Talcott, Inc. of N.Y.), 1945; v.p. James Talcott, Inc., 1944-46, exec. v.p., 1956-58, dir., 1956-75, pres., 1958-64, chmn. bd., chief exec. officer, 1961-73; chmn., chief exec. officer Talcott Nat. Corp., 1968-73, also chmn. exec. com., dir., 1968-75; pres. Nat. Comml. Fin. Conf., 1948-52, chmn., 1952-58; bd. dir. Baer-Am. Banking Corp., Partners Fund, Inc., Selected Sectors Fund, Inc.; sr. advisor Bank Julius Baer; adj. prof. fin. NYU Coll. Bus. and Pub. Adminstrn., 1973—; trustee med. ctr., vice chmn. bd. NYU. Named Man of Yr. banking and finance Phi Alpha Kappa; recipient Golden Medallion for humanitarian services B'nai B'rith, Albert Gallatin award NYU, 1978. Mem. ABA, N.Y. Bar Assn., N.Y. Univ. Alumni Fedn. (pres. 1958-60), Phi Alpha Kappa, Iota Theta. Clubs: Harmonie (N.Y.C.); Navesink Country (Middletown, N.J.); N.Y. Univ. (past pres.). Home: 150 Central Park S New York NY 10019-1566

SILVERMAN, HUGH J., philosophy educator; b. Boston, Aug. 17, 1945; s. Leslie and Eleanore (Riffin) S.; m. L. Theresa Watkins, June 22, 1968 (div. Apr. 1983); children: Claire Christine, H. Christopher; m. Gertrude Postl, Sept. 1, 1987. BA, Lehigh U., 1966, MA, 1967; postgrad., U. Paris, 1968, 71-72; PhD, Stanford U., 1973. Lectr. Stanford U., Calif., 1973-74; asst. prof. SUNY, Stony Brook, 1974-79, assoc. prof., 1979-83, prof. philosophy and comparative lit., 1983—; vis. sr. lectr. U. Warwick, Coventry, Eng., 1980, U. Nice, France, 1980, 81; vis. prof. Duquesne U., Pitts., 1978, NYU, 1978-80, 85-86, U. Leeds, Eng., 1988, U. Torino, Italy, 1989, U. Vienna, Austria, 1993, U. Nice, France, 1994; co-dir. Internat. Philos. Seminar, Alto Adige, Italy, 1991—. Author: Inscriptions: Between Phenomenology and Structuralism, 1987, Textualities: Between Hermeneutics and Deconstruction, 1994; editor: Piaget, Philosophy and the Human Sciences, 1980, Philosophy and Non-Philosophy since Merleau-Ponty, 1988, Derrida and Deconstruction, 1989, Postmodernism - Philosophy and the Arts, 1990, Gadamer and Hermeneutics, 1991, Writing the Politics of Difference, 1991, Questioning Foundations: Truth/Subjectivity/Culture, 1993; co-editor: Jean-Paul Sartre: Contemporary Approaches to His Philosophy, 1980, Continental Philosophy in America, 1983, Hermeneutics and Deconstruction, 1985, Descriptions, 1985, Critical and Dialectical Phenomenology, 1987, Horizons of Continental Philosophy, 1987, Postmodernism and Continental Philosophy, 1988, The Textual Sublime: Deconstruction and its Differences, 1990, Merleau-Ponty: Texts and Dialogues, 1992, Textualität der Philosophie-Philosophie und Literatur, 1994; series editor: Routledge Continental Philosophy series, 1986—; co-editor: Humanities Press Contemporary Studies in Philosophy and the Human Sciences series, 1989—, assoc. editor, 1979-89; Humanities Press Series in Philosophy and Literary Theory, 1989—, SUNY Press Contemporary Studies in Philosophy and Literature, 1988—; Bull. for Rsch. in Humanities, 1983-84; mem. editorial bd. Rsch. in Phenomenology, 1981—, Rev. of Existential Psychology and Psychiatry, 1979—; translator: Consciousness and the Acquistion of Language, 1973; contbr. numerous articles to profl. jours. Fulbright-French Govt. and Alliance Francaise fellow, Paris, 1971-72; faculty rsch. fellow SUNY-Stony Brook, 1977, 78, 81; rsch. fellow Am. Coun. Learned Socs., 1981-82; Experienced Faculty Travel fellowship, 1985, 88, 93; recipient MLA travel grant (Brazil), 1993, N.Y. Coun. for Humanities grant, 1976-77, SUNY Chancellor's award for excellence in teaching, 1977. Mem. Soc. Phenomenology and Existential Philosophy (exec. co-dir. 1980-86), Internat. Assn. Philosophy and Lit. (exec. com. 1976—, exec. sec. 1979-87, exec. dir. 1987—), Brit. Soc. Phenomenology (exec. com. 1980—), Merleau-Ponty Circle (chmn. publs. com. 1978—), Heidegger Conf., Am. Soc. Aesthetics, Am. Philos. Assn. (program adv. com. 1986-89, lectures publs. and rsch. com. 1991-94). Home: 105 Bleeker St Prt Jefferson NY 11777-1232 Office: Dept Philosophy Suny Stony Brook NY 11794

SILVERMAN, IRA NORTON, news producer; b. Bklyn., May 17, 1935; s. Joseph and Mildred (Axelrod) S.; m. Elizabeth Parsons Aspray, June 16, 1979; children by previous marriage: Gary, Bruce; stepchildren: Elizabeth, Aime, Alison. AB, Columbia U., 1957. Newspaper, mag. and book editor, 1957-67; producer, writer NBC News, 1967-79; sr. producer spl. projects NBC Nightly News, Washington, 1979-95; contbr. and editl. cons. The New Yorkers, 1995—. Co-author: The Pleasant Avenue Connection, 1976. Recipient Nat. Headliner award, 1977, 78, 81, 87, Alfred I. DuPont-Columbia U. award, 1983-84, 85-86, Emmy award for news and documentary, 1985, 87, award Overseas Press Club Am., 1987, 90, George Polk award L.I. U., 1988, Excellence in TV award Channels mag., 1990, George Foster Peabody award U. Ga., 1991, Citation for Excellence Overseas Press Club, 1992. Avocation: climbing. Office: NBC News 4001 Nebraska Ave NW Washington DC 20016-2733

SILVERMAN, JEFFREY STUART, manufacturing executive; b. N.Y.C., Nov. 25, 1945; s. Harry T. and Roberta S.; m. Pamela Silverman (div.); children: Jason S., Amanda P.; m. Joy Silverman (div.); children: Evan M., Jessica Jaye; m. Lisa Tarnopol, Aug. 1995. BS in Fin., L.I. U., 1967. Mem. N.Y. Stock Exchange, 1968-72; pres. Basil Cable, N.Y.C., 1975-82, Silba Enterprises, N.Y.C., 1975-82; chmn. bd. dirs., CEO Ply-Gem Industries, N.Y.C., 1982—. Office: Ply-Gem Industries Inc 777 3rd Ave Fl 30 New York NY 10017-1401

SILVERMAN, JONATHAN, actor; b. L.A., Aug. 5, 1966; s. Hillel Emanuel and Devora (Halaban) S. Student, U. So. Calif. Appearences include (films) Girls Just Want to Have Fun, 1985, Brighton Beach Memoirs, 1986, Caddyshack II, 1988, Stealing Home, 1988, Weekend at Bernie's, 1989, Class Action, 1991, Little Sister, 1992, Age Isn't Everything, 1992, Weekend at Bernie's II, 1993, Little Big League, 1994, Teresa's Tattoo, 1994, Two Guys Talking About Two Girls, 1994; (TV movies) Traveling Man, 1989, For Richer, For Poorer, 1992, Broadway Bound, 1992, 12:01, 1993, Hands That See, 1994; (TV series) Gimme a Break!, 1985-87, The Single Guy, 1995—; (plays) Brighton Beach Memoirs, Biloxi Blues, Broadway Bound (Helen Hays award 1988), The Illusion (Drama Lounge award 1990), Pay or Play (Drama League award), Sticks and Stones, 1994. Co-founder Artists for a Free South Africa, L.A., 1989—. Mem. Young Artists United (hon. N.Y. and L.A. chpt. 1990, 91).

SILVERMAN, JOSEPH, chemistry educator, scientist; b. N.Y.C., Nov. 5, 1922; s. Jakob and Mary (Chechick) S.; m. Joan Aline Jacks, Jan. 14, 1951; children: Joshua Henry, David Avrom. B.A., Bklyn. Coll., 1944; A.M., Columbia U., 1948, Ph.D., 1951. Head research dept. Walter Kidde (nuclear labs.), Garden City, N.Y., 1952-54; v.p., tech. dir. RAI Research Corp., L.I. City, N.Y., 1954-59; assoc. prof. chemistry State U. N.Y., Stony Brook, 1959-60; prof. dept. materials and nuclear engring. U. Md., College Park, 1960-92, prof. emeritus, 1992—; cons. Danish AEC, Indsl. Research Inst., Japan, Boris Kidric Inst., Yugoslavia, Bechtel Co., GPU Nuclear Corp., GE, IAEA, Vienna; disting. vis. prof. Tokyo U., 1974; gen. chmn. 2d Internat. Meeting on Radiation Processing, Miami, Fla., 1978, 3d Tokyo, 1980, hon. chmn. 6th, Ottawa, 1987; trustee Washington Inst. Values in Pub. Policy, 1981-87. Editor Internat. Jour. Applied Radiation and Isotopes, 1973-78, Internat. Jour. Radiation Engring., 1970-73, Trans. 1st Internat. Meetings on Radiation Processing, 1977, 3d edit., 1981; mem. editorial adv. bd. Radiation Physics and Chemistry, 1978-95. Served with AUS, 1944-46. Recipient Founders award 6th Internat. Mtg. on Radiation Processing, 1987, Centennial medal U. Md. Coll. Engring., 1994; Rsch. fellow Brookhaven Nat. Lab., 1949-51; Guggenheim fellow, 1966-67. Fellow Nordic Soc. Radiation Chemistry and Tech., Am. Phys. Soc., Am. Nuclear Soc. (Radiation Industry award 1975); mem. Am. Chem. Soc., Sigma Xi. Home: 320 Sisson St Silver Spring MD 20902-3156 Office: U Md Dept Materials and Nuclear College Park MD 20742-2115

SILVERMAN, JOSEPH HILLEL, mathematics educator; b. N.Y.C., Mar. 27, 1955; s. Harry and Shirley (Seiner) S.; m. Susan Leslie Greenhaus, June 13, 1976; children: Deborah, Daniel, Jonathan. ScB, Brown U., 1977; MA, Harvard U., 1979, PhD, 1982. Moore instr. MIT, Cambridge, 1982-86; assoc. prof. Boston U., 1986-88; assoc. prof. math. Brown U., Providence, 1988-91, prof., 1991—. Author: Arithmetic of Elliptic Curves, 1986; editor: Arithmetic Geometry, 1987, Rational Points on Elliptic Curves, 1992, Advanced Topics in Arithmetic of Elliptic Curves, 1995. Fellow NSF, 1983-86, Sloan fellow Sloan Found., 1987. Mem. Am. Math. Soc. Avocation: bridge. Office: Brown U Dept Math 79 Waterman St Providence RI 02912-9079

SILVERMAN, KENNETH EUGENE, English educator, writer; b. N.Y.C., Feb. 5, 1936; s. Gustave and Bessie (Goldberg) S.; children: Willa Zahava, Ethan Leigh. B.A., Columbia U., 1956, M.A., 1958, Ph.D., 1964. Instr. English U. Wyo., Laramie, 1958-59; preceptor in English Columbia U., N.Y.C., 1962-64; prof. English, co-dir. The Biography Seminar NYU, N.Y.C., 1964—; adv. council Inst. Early Am. History and Culture 1984-87. Author: Timothy Dwight, 1969, A Cultural History of the American Revolution, 1976, The Life and Times of Cotton Mather, 1984, Edgar A. Poe: Mournful and Never-ending Remembrance, 1991; editor: anthology Colonial American Poetry, 1968; compiler: Selected Letters of Cotton Mather, 1976; mem. editorial bd.: Early Am Lit., 1969-72, 77-80, William and Mary Quar., 1984-87, Am. Lit. 1987-90. Recipient Bancroft prize in Am. history, 1985, Pulitzer Prize for biography, 1985, Edgar Allan Poe award Mystery Writers Am., 1992; grantee Bicentennial award NEH, 1972-74, Am. Philos. Soc., 1986, Am. Coun. Learned Socs., 1986; Guggenheim fellow, 1989-90. Mem. MLA (chmn. Early Am. lit. group 1975), Soc. Am. Historians, Am. Antiquarian Soc., PEN Am. Ctr., Authors Guild, Soc. Am. Magicians,. Jewish. Office: NYU Dept English 19 University Pl New York NY 10003-4501

SILVERMAN, LEONARD M., university dean, electrical engineering educator. B.S., Columbia U., 1962, M.S., 1963, Ph.D., 1966. Prof. elec. engring. U. So. Calif., Los Angeles, dean sch. engring. Mem. Nat. Acad. Engring. Office: U So Calif Sch Engring University Pk Los Angeles CA 90089-1450

SILVERMAN, MARYLIN A., advertising agency executive; b. N.Y.C., Mar. 15, 1941; d. Morris George and Sophie (Betesh) Adler; m. Joseph Elias Silverman, May 30, 1965; children: Lisa, Jennifer. BA, Ind. U.-Bloomington, 1962; student Baruch Grad. Sch. Bus., CUNY, 1963-65. Research analyst Compton Advt., N.Y.C., 1962-63; account research supr. Foote, Cone & Belding, N.Y.C., 1963-68; self-employed market research cons., N.Y.C., 1968-78; research group head Ogilvy & Mather, Inc., N.Y.C., 1978-82; sr. v.p., assoc. research dir. Backer Spielvogel Bates, Inc., N.Y.C., 1982-88, exec. dir. strategic planning and internat. rsch., 1989-91, exec. v.p. strategic planning Bates Worldwide, 1991—; cons. Am. Assn. Advt. Agys., Boys Clubs Am., N.Y.C.; bd. dirs. Women at Risk. Co-author: Marketing Review, 1980. Mem. exec. council Washington Sq. Park Council, 1969-74; mem. exec. bd. Friends Sem. PTA, N.Y.C., 1980-82, Advt. Rsch. Found., Children's Research Council Devel. Com. Mem. Am. Mktg. Assn. (chair Effie awards), Women in Communications, Am. Assn. Advt. Agys. (research com.), Grenwich Ho. Potters and Sculptors Assn. Office: Bates Worldwide 405 Lexington Ave New York NY 10174-0094

SILVERMAN, MELVIN, medical research administrator; b. Montreal, Que., Can., Jan. 4, 1940. BSc, McGill U., 1960, MD, CM, 1964. Rotating intern Montreal Gen. Hosp., 1964-65, resident, 1968-69; resident Bellevue Hosp., N.Y.C., 1965-66; assoc. rsch. scientist dept. medicine NYU, 1966-68; Med. Rsch. Coun. Centennial fellow McGill U. Med. Clinic Montreal Gen. Hosp., 1969-71; asst. prof. dept. medicine McGill U., 1970-71; asst. physician Montreal Gen. Hosp., 1970-71; staff physician nephrology Toronto Gen. Hosp., Ont., Can., 1971-84; asst. prof. to assoc. prof. medicine U. Toronto, 1971-84, assoc. prof. physics, 1975-81, prof. medicine and physics, 1981—; dir. trihosp. Nephrology Svc., Toronto Gen. Hosp., Mt. Sinai Hosp. and women's Coll. Hosp., 1984-90, sr. staff physician, 1990—; dir. MRC Group Membrane Biology, dept. medicine U. Toronto, 1987—, subspecialty tng. program, 1990-91, dir. Inst. Med. Sci., 1991—, dir. MD/PhD program, 1983—; mem. sci. coun. Kidney Found. Can., 1977-85, 94—, Med. Rsch. Coun. Can., 1984-89, 96—, Alta. Heritage Found. Med. Rsch., 1994—. Recipient J. Francis Meml. prize in medicine, 1964, Starr medal, 1974, William Goldie prize, 1975, Trillium award, 1990, Dept. Med. Rsch. award U. Toronto, 1993; numerous grants from various orgns., 1972—. Fellow Royal Coll. Physicians Can.; mem. Am. Soc. Clin. Investigator, Am. Physiol. Soc., Am. Soc. Nephrology, Am. Biophys. Soc., N.Y. Acad. Sci. Office: U Toronto Dept Medicine, Med Sci Bld Rm 7207, Toronto, ON Canada M5S 1A8

SILVERMAN, MERVYN F., health science association administrator, consultant. BS cum laude, Washington and Lee U., 1960; MD, Tulane U., 1964; MPH, Harvard U., 1969. Diplomate Am. Bd. Preventive Medicine. Physician Peace Corps, Thailand, 1965-67; regional med. dir. East Asia and the Pacific Peace Corps, Washington, 1967-68; spl. asst. to commr. FDA, Washington, 1969-70, dir. Office of Consumer Affairs, 1970-72; dir. health Wichita (Kans.)-Sedgwick County Dept. Cmty. Health, 1972-77; med. dir. Planned Parenthood Kans., Wichita, 1976-77; dir. health Dept. Health, San Francisco, 1977-85; health care cons. Mervyn F. Silverman & Assocs., Inc., 1985—; dir. AIDS health svcs. program Robert Wood Johnson Found., 1986-92; nat. spokesperson Am. Found. for AIDS Rsch., 1986-96, pres., also bd. dirs.; resident physician Sta. KPIX-TV, San Francisco, 1979-85; dir., prodr., host weekly health program Sta. KMPX Radio, 1980-82; sr. tech. advisor Acad. Ednl. Devel.-AIDSCOM, 1990-92; advisor to pres. Pan Am. AIDS Found., 1991-93, advisor to mayor of San Juan, Puerto Rico, 1991-93; former med. advisor to bd. dirs. Golden Gate chpt. ARC, San Francisco; past vice chmn. Adv. Health Coun., State of Calif.; former assoc. clin. prof. Wichita State U.; assoc. clin. prof. U. Hawaii; adj. assoc. prof. Sch. Pub. Health and Tropical Medicine Tulane U.; adj. prof. Inst. Health Policy Studies, Sch. Medicine, U. Calif., San Francisco; mem. nat. adv. coun. Harvard AIDS Inst.; spkr., presenter in field. Author: (with others) Humanistic Perspectives in Medical Ethics, 1972, What to Do About AIDS, 1986, AIDS and Patient Management: Legal, Ethical and Social Issues, 1986, AIDS: Facts and Issues, 1986, AIDS in Children, Adolescents and Heterosexual Adults: An Interdisciplinary Approach to Prevention, 1988, others; contbg. and consulting editor Modern Medicine Publs., Mpls., 1970-75; contbg. editor Healthline, 1983-85; contbr. articles to profl. jours. Bd. dirs., vice-chmn. U.S.-China Ednl. Inst. Recipient Award for Courageous Leadership, San Francisco Found., Award of Excellence, KAIROS Support for Care Givers, Civic Achievement award Bay Area Non-Partisan Alliance; Wear Found. fellow Wichita State U.; adj. scholar Kans. Newman Coll. Mem. APHA, AMA, Calif. Med. Assn., San Francisco Med. Soc., Omicron Delta Kappa, Delta Omega. Address: 119 Frederick St San Francisco CA 94117

SILVERMAN, MICHAEL, manufacturing company executive; b. Poland, May 9, 1913; arrived in U.S., 1920; m. Frances Setnor, Aug. 26, 1945; children: Leslie, Evan. Cutting rm. mgr. Rockland (Mass) Sportswear, 1938-58; owner Garmet Cutting Svc., Brockton, Mass., 1958-70; cons. Boston, 1970-73; cutting rm. mgr. Recent Mfg., 1973-85. Author: The New Breakthrough in Plaid Cutting, 1990, Marker Making Manual, 1955; inventor plaid matching device. Avocations: playing in poker tournament, gag writing (New Yorker, Jay Leno show).

SILVERMAN, MOSES, lawyer; b. Bklyn., Mar. 3, 1948; s. Bernard and Anne Silverman; m. Betty B. Robbins, Jan. 19, 1980; children: Benjamin, Rachel. AB, Colby Coll., 1969; JD, NYU, 1973. Bar: N.Y. 1974, U.S. Dist. Ct. (so. and ea. dists.) N.Y. 1974, U.S. Ct. Appeals (2d cir.) 1974, U.S. Ct. Appeals (D.C. cir.) 1977, U.S. Supreme Ct. 1977, D.C. 1982, U.S. Ct. Appeals (fed. cir.) 1985, U.S. Ct. Appeals (11th cir.), 1986 . Assoc. Paul, Weiss, Rifkind, Wharton & Garrison, N.Y.C., 1973-81, ptnr., 1981—. Vol. U.S. Peace Corps., Istanbul, Turkey, 1969-70. Mem. ABA, Assn. of Bar of City of N.Y. Home: 7 Gracie Square New York NY 10028 Office: Paul Weiss Rifkind Wharton & Garrison 1285 Avenue Of The Americas New York NY 10019-6028

SILVERMAN, PAUL HYMAN, parasitologist, former university official; b. Mpls., Oct. 8, 1924; s. Adolph and Libbie (Idlekope) S.; m. Nancy Josephs, May 20, 1945; children: Daniel Joseph, Claire. Student, U. Minn., 1942-43, 46-47; BS, Roosevelt U., 1949; MS in Biology, Northwestern U., 1951; PhD in Parasitology, U. Liverpool, Eng., 1955, DSc, 1968. Rsch. fellow Malaria Rsch. Sta., Hebrew U., Israel, 1951-53; rsch. fellow dept. entomology and parasitology Sch. Tropical Medicine, U. Liverpool, 1953-56; sr. sci. officer dept. parasitology Moredun Inst., Edinburgh, Scotland, 1956-59; head dept. immunoparasitology Allen & Hanbury, Ltd., Ware, Eng., 1960-62; prof. zoology and vet. pathology and hygiene U. Ill., Urbana, 1963-72, chmn., head dept. zoology, 1963-68; sr. staff mem. Ctr. for Zoonoses Rsch., 1964; prof. biology, head divsn. natural scis. Colo. Women's Coll., Denver, 1970-71; prof., chmn. dept. biology, v.p., assoc. provost for rsch. U. N.Mex., 1972-77; provost for rsch. and grad. studies Ctrl. Adminstrn. SUNY, Albany, 1977-79, pres. Rsch. Found., 1979-80; pres. U. Maine, Orono, 1980-84; fellow biol. and med. divsn. Lawrence Berkeley Lab. U. Calif., Berkeley, 1984-86; acting head biomed. divsn. Lawrence Berkeley Lab. Lawrence Berkeley Lab., Berkeley, 1986-87; adj. prof. med. parasitology Sch. Pub. Health U. Calif., Berkeley, 1986, assoc. lab. dir. for life scis., dir Donner Lab., 1987-90, dir. systemwide biotech. rsch. and edn. program, 1989-90; dir. Beckman's Scientific Affairs, Fullerton, Calif., 1990-93; assoc. chancellor Ctr. for Health Scis., adj. prof. medicine U. Calif., Irvine, 1993—; cons., Commn. Colls. and Univs., North Central Assn. Colls. and Secondary Schs., 1964—; chmn. Commn. on Instns. Higher Edn., 1974-76; Fulbright prof. zoology Australian Nat. U., Canberra, 1969; adjoint prof. biology U. Colo., Boulder, 1970-72; examiner for Western Assn. Schs. and Colls., Accrediting Commn. for Sr. Colls. and Univs., Calif., 1972—; mem. bd. Nat. Council on Post-secondary Accreditation, Washington, 1975-77; faculty apointee Sandia Corp., Dept. Energy, Albuquerque, 1974-81; project dir. research in malaria immunology and vaccination AID, 1965-76; project dir. research in Helminth immunity USPHS, NIH, 1964-72; sr. cons. to Ministry Edn. and Culture, Brasilia, Brazil, 1975—; cons. to U.S. Senator George Mitchell, Maine; adv. on malaria immunology WHO, Geneva, 1967; bd. dirs. Inhalation Toxicology Research Inst., Lovelace Biomed. and Environ. Research Inst., Albuquerque, 1977-84; mem. N.Y. State Gov.'s High Tech. Opportunities Task Force; chmn. research and rev. com. N.Y. State Sci. and Tech. Found.; mem. pres.'s council New Eng. Land Grant Univs.; mem. policies and issues com. Nat. Assn. State Univs. and Land Grant Colls.; bd. advs. Lovelace-Bataan Med. Center, Albuquerque, 1974-77; adv. com. U.S. Army Command and Gen. Staff Coll., Ft. Leavenworth, Kans., 1983-84. Contbr. articles to profl. jours. Chmn. Maine Gov.'s Econ. Devel. Conf.; chmn. research rev. com. N.Y. State Sci. and Tech. Found. Fellow Royal Soc. Tropical Medicine and Hygiene, N.Mex. Acad. Sci.; mem. AAAS, Am. Soc. Parasitologists, Am. Soc. Tropical Medicine and Hygiene, Am. Soc. Immunologists, Brit. Soc. Parasitology (coun.), Brit. Soc. Immunologists, Soc. Gen. Microbiology, Soc. Protozoologists, Am. Soc. Zoologists, Human Genome Orgn., Am. Inst. Biol. Scis., N.Y. Acad. Scis., N.Y. Soc. Tropical Medicine, World Acad. Art and Sci., B'nai B'rith, Sigma Xi, Phi Kappa Phi. Office: Univ Calif 501 Administration Bldg Irvine CA 92717

SILVERMAN, PERRY RAYNARD, lawyer, consultant; b. N.Y.C., Nov. 5, 1950; s. Harry and Mary Sheila (Diamond) S.; m. Ruth Klarin, Oct. 7, 1979; children: Aaron, Rachel. BA, SUNY, Albany, 1971; JD, Boston U., 1974; MA, Ohio State U., 1981. Bar: N.Y. 1975, Ohio 1976, U.S. Dist. Ct. (so. dist.) Ohio 1977, U.S. Dist. Ct. (no. ist.) Ohio 1978, U.S. Ct. Claims 1977, U.S. Supreme Ct. 1978. Rsch. assoc. Polimetrics Lab. Ohio State U., Columbus, 1974-75, rsch. assoc. Behavioral Scis. Lab., 1974-76; asst. atty. gen. Ohio Atty. Gen.'s Office, Columbus, 1976-84; prin. Perry R. Silverman Co., LPA, Columbus, 1984—; spl. counsel Atty. Gen. of Ohio, 1984-95; adj. prof. Capital U., Columbus, 1978, 82; cons. Survey Rsch. Assocs., Columbus, 1975-77. Trustee, Congregatoin Beth Tikvah, Worthington, Ohio, 1992-94. Mem. ATLA, Ohio State Bar Assn., Columbus Bar Assn., Ohio Assn. Trial Lawyers, Nat. Assn. Retail Collection Agys. (v.p. 1995—). Office: Perry R Silverman Co LPA 8351 N High St Columbus OH 43235-1440

SILVERMAN, RICHARD BRUCE, chemist, biochemist, educator; b. Phila., May 12, 1946; s. Philip and S. Ruth (Simon) S.; m. Barbara Jean Kesner, Jan. 9, 1983; children: Matthew, Margaret, Philip. BS, Pa. State U., 1968; MA, Harvard U., 1972, PhD, 1974. Postdoctoral fellow Brandeis U., Waltham, Mass., 1974-76; asst. prof. Northwestern U., Evanston, Ill., 1976-82, assoc. prof., 1982-86, prof., 1986—, Arthur Andersen Tchg. and rsch. prof., 1996—, mem. Inst. for Neurosci., 1990—; cons. Procter and Gamble Co., Cin., 1984, Abbott Labs, North Chicago, 1987, Searle R&D, St. Louis, 1988-90, DuPont, 1991, Dow, 1991, Leytig, Voit & Mayer law offices, 1992—, DowElanco, 1993-95, G.D. Searle, 1995—, Affymax, 1995; mem. adv. panel NIH, Bethesda, Md., 1981, 83, 85, 87-91; expert analyst CHEMTRACTS. Mem. editorial bd. Jour. Enzyme Inhibition, 1988—, Archivies Biochemistry and Biophysics, 1993—, Jour. Medicinal Chemistry, 1995—, Archiv der Pharmazie-Pharmaceutical and Medicinal Chemistry, 1995—; contbr. articles to profl. jours.; patentee in field. Served with U.S. Army, 1969-71. Mem. adv. bd. Ill. Math. and Sci. Acad., 1988. Recipient Career Devel. award USPHS, 1982-87; DuPont Young Faculty fellow, 1976, Alfred P. Sloan Found. fellow, 1981-85; grantee various govt. and pvt. insts., 1976—. Fellow AAAS, Am. Inst. Chemists; mem. Am. Chem. Soc. (nat. elected nominating com. div. biol. chemistry, treas. divsn. biol. chemistry 1993—), Am. Soc. Biochem. Molecular Biology. Avocations: tennis, family interactions. Office: Northwestern U Dept Chemistry 2145 Sheridan Rd Evanston IL 60208-3113

SILVERMAN, ROBERT JOSEPH, lawyer; b. Mpls., Apr. 4, 1942; s. Maurice and Toby (Goldstein) S.; 1 child, Adam Graham-Silverman; m. Suzanne M. Brown; 1 child, Thomas B. BA, U. Minn., 1964, JD, 1967. Bar: Minn. 1967. Assoc. Dorsey & Whitney, Mpls., 1967-72, ptnr., 1972—; lectr. William Mitchell Coll. Law, St. Paul, 1977-78, Hamline Law Sch., St. Paul, 1990—, Minn. Continuing Legal Edn., Mpls, 1985—. Bd. dirs. Courage Ctr., Golden Valley, Minn., 1978-84, 85-95, v.p., 1983-86, pres., 1988-89. With USAR, 1967-73. Mem. ABA, Minn. Bar Assn., Hennepin County Bar Assn. Jewish. Office: Dorsey & Whitney 220 S 6th St Minneapolis MN 55402-4502

SILVERMAN, SAMUEL JOSHUA, lawyer; b. Odessa, Russia, Sept. 25, 1908; came to U.S., 1913; s. Benjamin and Ida (Kagarlitzky) S.; m. Claire Gfroerer, Aug. 21, 1941. Student, NYU, 1925; A.B., Columbia U., 1928, LL.B., 1930. Bar: N.Y. With firm Gilman & Unger, 1930-32, Engelhard, Pollak, Pitcher, Stern & Clarke, 1932-35; asst. corp. counsel N.Y.C., 1938-40; partner firm Paul, Weiss, Rifkind, Wharton & Garrison, N.Y.C., 1946-62; of counsel Paul, Weiss, Rifkind, Wharton & Garrison, 1985—; assoc. justice N.Y. Supreme Ct., 1963-66, 71-75; surrogate N.Y. County, 1967-70; assoc. justice appellate div. N.Y. Supreme Ct., 1976-84, spl. master appellate div., 1st dept., 1985-90, mem., spl. counsel, disciplinary com. 1st judicial dept., 1986—, chmn. and chmn. emeritus adv. com. on judicial ethics, 1987—; lectr. Nat. Coll. State Trial Judges, Boulder, Colo., 1966. Bd. dirs. Univ. Settlement, N.Y.C., 1960-74. Fellow Am. Coll. Trial Lawyers; mem. Assn. Bar City N.Y., Am. Law Inst. Democrat. Home: 210 E 68th St New York NY 10021-6047 Office: 1285 Avenue Of The Americas New York NY 10019-6028

SILVERMAN, STANLEY WAYNE, chemical company executive; b. Phila., June 18, 1947; s. Sidney and Ruth (Epstein) S.; m. Ellen J. Seligsohn, June 10, 1970; children: Robert, Eric. BSChemE, Drexel U., 1969, MBA, 1974; postgrad., Harvard U., 1989. Process engr. Atlantic Richfield Co., Phila., 1969-71, PQ Corp., Phila., 1971-74; mgr. oper. planning PQ Corp., Valley Forge, Pa., 1974-76, product mgr., 1976-80, mktg. mgr., 1980-82; nat. sales mgr. PQ Corp., Valley Forge, 1982-84; pres. Nat. Silicates Ltd. subs. PQ Corp., Toronto, Ont., Can., 1984-87; pres. ind. chem. group PQ Corp., Valley Forge, 1987-90, exec. v.p., chief oper. officer, 1990—. Mem. Am. Chem. Soc., Chem. Mktg. Rsch. Assn., Drexel U. Coll. Engring. Adv. Coun., World Affairs Coun. Greater Valley Forge and Phila. Avocations: sailing, jogging, polit. sci. Office: PQ Corp 1200 Swedesford Rd Berwyn PA 19312-1071*

SILVERMAN, STEPHEN MEREDITH, journalist, screenwriter, producer; b. L.A., Nov. 22, 1951; s. Raymond and Shirley (Garfein) S. BA, U. Calif., Irvine, 1973; MS, Columbia U., 1975. Editor-in-chief Coast Mag., L.A., 1975-77; chief entertainment writer N.Y. Post, 1977-88; film critic New Woman Mag., 1986-88; editor-in-chief Hollywood Mag., L.A., 1989-90; adj. prof. Hunter Coll., N.Y.C., 1978, Marymount Manhattan, 1979, Columbia U., 1995—; juror Internat. film festivals, Berlin, Edinburgh, 1991. Author: Public Spectacles, 1981, The Fox That Got Away: The Last Days of the Zanuck Dynasty, 1988, David Lean, 1989, Where There's A Will: Who Inherited What and Why, 1991, Dancing on the Ceiling: Stanley Donen and His Movies, 1996; TV scriptwriter: Hot On the Trail: The Search for Love, Sex and Romance in the Old West and the New, TBS, 1993. Avocation: global exploring. Office: 30 Lincoln Center Plz New York NY 10023-6922

SILVERMAN, SYDEL FINFER, anthropologist; b. Chgo., May 20, 1933; d. Joseph and Elizabeth (Bassman) Finfer; m. Mel Silverman, Dec. 27, 1953 (wid. Sept. 1966); children: Eve Rachel, Julie Beth; m. Eric R. Wolf, Mar. 18, 1972. MA, U. Chgo., 1957; PhD, Columbia U., 1963. From lectr. to prof. anthropology Queens Coll., CUNY, Flushing, 1963-75; prof., exec. officer PhD program anthropology Grad. Sch. CUNY, N.Y.C., 1975-86, acting dean of Grad. Sch., 1982-83; pres. Wenner-Gren Found. for Anthropol. Rsch., N.Y.C., 1987—; bd. dirs. Social Sci. Rsch. Coun., N.Y.C., 1984-87. Author: Three Bells of Civilization, 1975; editor: Totems and Teachers, 1981, Inquiry and Debate in the Human Sciences, 1992, Preserving the Anthropological Record, 1995; contbr. articles to profl. jours. Recipient fellowship Am. Coun. Learned Socs., 1986, NEH, 1973-74, NIH, 1960-63, NSF, 1959; grantee Am. Phil. Soc., 1985. Jewish. Office: Wenner-Gren Found 220 Fifth Ave New York NY 10001-7708

SILVERN, LEONARD CHARLES, retired engineering executive; b. N.Y.C., May 20, 1919; s. Ralph and Augusta (Thaler) S.; m. Gloria Marantz, June 1948 (div. Jan. 1968); 1 child, Ronald; m. Elisabeth Beeny, Aug. 1969 (div. Oct. 1972); m. Gwen Taylor, Nov. 1985. BS in Physics, L.I. U., 1946; MA, Columbia U., 1948, EdD, 1952. Registered profl. consulting engr., Calif. Tng. supr. U.S. Dept. Navy, N.Y.C., 1939-49; tng. dir. exec. dept. N.Y. Div. Safety, Albany, 1949-55; resident engring. psychologist Lincoln Lab. MIT for Rand Corp., Lexington, 1955-56; engr., dir. edn., tng., rsch. labs. Hughes Aircraft Co., Culver City, Calif., 1956-62; dir. human performance engring. lab., cons. engring. psychologist to v.p. tech. Northrop Norair, Hawthorne, Calif., 1962-64; prin. sci., v.p., pres. Edn. and Tng. Cons. Co., L.A., 1964-96, Sedona, Ariz., 1980, pres. Systems Engring. Labs. div., 1980-96; cons. hdqrs. Air Tng. Command USAF, Randolph AFB, Tex., 1964-68, Electronic Industries Assn., Washington, 1963-69, Edn. R and D Ctr., U. Hawaii, 1970-74, Ctr. Vocat. and Tech. Edn., Ohio State U., 1972-73, Coun. for Exceptional Children, 1973-74, Canadore Coll. Applied Arts and Tech., Ont., Can., 1974-76, Centro Nacional de Productividad, Mexico City, 1973-75, N.S. Dept. Edn., Halifax, 1975-79, Aeronutronic Ford-Ford Motor Co., 1975-76, Nat. Tng. Systems Inc., 1976-81, Nfld. Pub. Svc. Commn., 1978, Legis. Affairs Office USDA, 1980, Rocky Point Techs., 1986; adj. prof. edn., pub. adminstrn. U. So. Calif. Grad. Sch., 1957-65; vis. prof. computer scis. U. Calif. Extension Div., L.A., 1963-72. Dist. ops. officer, disaster communications svc. L.A. County Sheriff's Dept., 1973-75, dist. communications officer, 1975-76; bd. dirs. SEARCH, 1976—; mem. adv. com. West Sedona Community Plan of Yavapai County, 1986-88; councilman City of Sedona, 1988-92; rep. COCOPAI, 1988-89; vol. earth team Soil Conservation Svc., U.S. Dept Agr., 1989-92; Verde Resource Assn., 1988-90, Group on Water Logistics, 1989-90; chair publs. com. Ariz. Rural Recycling Conf., 1990. With USN, 1944-46. Mem. IEEE (sr.), APA, Am. Radio Relay League (life), Nat. Solid Waste Mgmt. Symposium (chmn. publs. com. 1988-89), Ariz. Rural Recycling Conf. (chair publs. com. 1990), Friendship Vets. Fire Engine Co. (hon.), Soc. Wireless Pioneers (life), Quarter Century Wireless Assn. (life), Sierra Club (treas. Sedona-Verde Valley Group 1991-93), Assn. Bldg. Coms., Vox Pop (chmn. bd. dirs. Sedona, 1983-93, dir. 1993-95), Nat. Parks and Conservation Assn., Wilderness Soc., Ariz. Ctr. Law in Pub. Interest, Old Old Timers Club. Contbg. editor Ednl. Tech., 1968-73, 81-85; reviewer ACM Computing Revs., 1962-92. Contbr. numerous articles to profl. jours. Office: PO Box 2085 Sedona AZ 86339-2085

SILVERS, EILEEN S., lawyer; b. N.Y.C., Sept. 21, 1948; d. Sidney and Ethel Lynne (Starobin) Swertloff; m. Richard J. Bronstein; children: Steven Jay, Sharron Roth. BA magna cum laude, SUNY-Buffalo, 1970; JD, Columbia U., 1975. Bar: N.Y. 1977, U.S. Tax Ct. 1981, U.S. Ct. Claims 1983, D.C., 1984. Assoc., Paul, Weiss, Rifkind, Wharton & Garrison, N.Y.C., 1975-83, ptnr., 1983-94; v.p. taxes Bristol-Myers Squibb Co., N.Y.C., 1994—. Mem. ABA (tax sect. mem. of coms. on Fgn. Activities of U.S. Taxpayers and U.S. Activities of Foreigners and Tax Treaties 1986—), N.Y. State Bar Assn. (chmn. personal income com. tax sect. 1983-85 , exec. com. 1982-85, 1990-91), D.C. Bar Assn. Home: 20 Mountain Peak Rd Chappaqua NY 10514-2110 Office: Bristol-Myers Squibb Co 345 Park Ave New York NY 10154-0004

SILVERS, GERALD THOMAS, publishing executive; b. Cin., Aug. 26, 1937; s. Steve Allen and Tina Mae (Roberts) S.; m. Ann Gregory Woodward, July 25, 1964. BA, U. Ky., 1960. Asst. research svcs. mgr. Cin. Enquirer, 1963-72, research svcs. dir., 1972-74, research dir., 1974-90, v.p. mktg. svcs., 1990-94, v.p. market devel., 1994—. Mem. Ky. Devel. Coun., Lexington, 1986—; trustee Neediest Kids of All, 1991—. 1st lt. U.S. Army, 1960-62. Recipient Thomas H. Copeland award of merit, 1991. Mem. U. Ky. Alumni Assn. Cin. Chpt. (pres. 1985), Newspaper Research Council (pres. 1985,86), Internat. Newspaper Market Assn., Am. Mktg. Assn. Presbyterian. Home: 229 Watch Hill Rd Covington KY 41011-1822 Office: Cin Enquirer 312 Elm St Cincinnati OH 45202-2739

SILVERS, ROBERT BENJAMIN, editor; b. Mineola, N.Y., Dec. 31, 1929; s. James J. and Rose (Roden) S. A.B., U. Chgo., 1947; grad., Ecole des Sci. Politiques, Paris, France, 1956. Press sec. to Gov. Bowles of Conn., 1950; mem. editorial bd. Paris Rev., 1954—; assoc. editor Harper's mag., 1959-63; co-founder, co-editor N.Y. Rev. Books, 1963—. Editor: Writing in America, 1960, Hidden Histories of Science, 1995; co-editor: The First Anthology: 30 Years of The New York Review of Books 1963-93; translator: La Gangrene, 1961; mem. editorial com. Rivista dei Libri, Italy, 1991—. Bd. dirs. Am. Ditchley Found., 1993—. With AUS, 1952-53. Named Chevalier de l'Ordre Nat. du Merite, France, 1988—. Mem. Coun. Fgn. Rels., Am. Acad. Arts and Scis., Century Assn. Club (N.Y.C.), Coffee House Club (N.Y.C.). Office: NY Rev of Books 250 W 57th St New York NY 10107

SILVERS, SALLY, choreographer, performing company executive; b. Greeneville, Tenn., June 19, 1952; d. Herbert Ralston and Sara Elizabeth (Buchanan) S.; life ptnr. Bruce Erroll Andrews. BA in Dance and Polit. Sci., Antioch Coll., 1975. Artistic dir. Sally Silvers & Dancers, N.Y.C., 1980—; mem. faculty Leicester Poly., 1986, 87, 89, summer choreography project Bennington Coll., 1988-92, Chisenhale Dance Space, London, 1989, 91, Am. Dance Festival, Durham, N.C., 1990, 92; guest tchr. European Dance Devel. Ctr., Arnhem, The Netherlands, 1992—. Choreographer: Politics of the Body Microscope of Conduct, 1980, Social Movement, 1981, Connective Tissue, 1981, Less Time You Know Praxis, 1981, Don't No Do And This, 1981, Lack of Entrepreneurial Thrift, 1982, Celluloid Sally and Mr. E, 1982, Mutate, 1982, Being Red Enough, 1982, Disgusting, 1982, Bedtime at the Reformatory, 1982, Eat the Rich, 1982, They Can't Get It in the Shopping Cart, 1982, Blazing Forceps, 1982, And Find Out Why, 1983, Tips for Totalizers, 1983, Choose Your Weapons, 1984, And Find Out Why, 1984, Extend the Wish for Entire, 1985, No Best Better Way, 1985, Every All Which is Not Us, 1986, Swaps Ego Say So, 1986, Be Careful Now, You Know Sugar Melts in Water, 1987, Fact Confected, 1987, Both, Both, 1987, Tizzy Boost, 1988, Moebius, 1988, Whatever Ever, 1989, Get Tough, Sports and Divertissement, 1989, Flap, 1989, Swan's Crayon, 1989, Fanfare Tripwire, 1990, Harry Meets Sally, 1990, Along the Skid Mark of Recorded History, 1990, Matinee Double-You, 1991, Grand Guignol, 1991, Dash Dash Slang Plural Plus, 1992, The Bubble Cut, 1992, Vigilant Corsage, 1992, Oops Fact, 1992, Small Room, 1993, Exwhyzee, 1993, Elegy, 1993, Now That It Is Now, 1994, Give Em Enough Rope, 1994, Swoon Noir, 1994, Radio Rouge, 1995, Braceletizing, 1995, Hush Comet, 1995, Bite the Pillow, 1995 and others; filmmaker: Little Lieutenant, 1993 (Silver award), N.Y. Dance on Camera Festival; co-author: Resurgant New Writings By Women, 1992; contbr. articles to profl. jours. Grantee Nat. Endowment Arts, 1987, 89, 90, 91, Jerome Found., 1993, Meet the Composer N.Y. Found. for the Arts, 1995; Guggenheim Found. fellow, 1988. Mem. Segue Found. (bd. dirs. Segue Performance Space 1992—). Avocations: reading, writing, art events, costume design. Home: 303 E 8th St Apt 4F New York NY 10009-5212

SILVERS, WILLYS KENT, geneticist; b. N.Y.C., Jan. 12, 1929; s. Lewis Julian and Miriam Elizabeth (Rosenzweig) S.; m. Abigail M. Adams, Sept. 29, 1956; children: Deborah Elizabeth, Willys Kent. BA, Johns Hopkins U., 1950; PhD, U. Chgo., 1954. Assoc. staff scientist Jackson Lab., Bar Harbor, Maine, 1956-57; assoc. mem. Wistar Inst., Phila., 1957-65; mem. faculty U. Pa. Med. Sch., 1965—, prof. genetics, 1967—; mem. allergy and immunology study sect. NIH, 1962-66, adv. bd. primate rsch. ctrs., 1968-71, com. cancer immunobiology Nat. Cancer Inst., 1974-78, bd. sci. overseers Jackson Lab., Bar Harbor, 1980-89. Author: The Immunobiology of Transplantation, 1971, The Coat Colors of Mice: A Model for Mammalian Gene Action and Interaction, 1979; mem. editorial bd. Transplantation, 1963-71, Jour. Exptl. Zoology, 1965-70, 81-86, Jour. Immunology, 1973-77, Jour. Reticuloendothelial Soc., 1974-77; contbr. articles to profl. jours. Mem. Am. Genetic Assn. (coun. 1980-83, pres. 1983). Home: 210 Millcreek Rd Ardmore PA 19003-1506 Office: U Pa Dept Genetics Sch Medicine Philadelphia PA 19104

SILVERSTEIN, ARTHUR MATTHEW, ophthalmic immunologist, educator, historian; b. N.Y.C., Aug. 6, 1928; s. Sol and Beatrice (Pearl) S.; m. Frances Swimmer, 1950; children—Alison, Mark, Judith. A.B., Ohio State U., 1948, M.Sc., 1951; Ph.D., Rensselaer Poly. Inst., 1954; D.Sc. (hon.), U. Granada, Spain, 1986. Research asst. Sloan Kettering Inst., N.Y.C., 1948-49; biochemist N.Y. Health Research Lab., N.Y.C., 1949-52; sr. biochemist N.Y. Health Research Lab., Albany, 1952-54; chief immunobiology Armed Forces Inst. Pathology, Washington, 1956-64; assoc. prof. Johns Hopkins Sch. Medicine, Balt., 1964-67; prof. Johns Hopkins Sch. Medicine, 1967-89, prof. emeritus, 1989—; cons. NIH, 1963-77. Author: Pure Politics and Impure Science: The Swine Flu Affair, 1981, A History of Immunology, 1989; mem. editorial bd. various sci. jours.; contbr. articles to profl. jours. Served to 1st lt. U.S. Army, 1954-56. Recipient Doyne Meml. medal Oxford Ophthal. Congress, Eng., 1974, Endowed Professorship Ind. Order Odd Fellows, 1964-89; Congl. Sci. fellow Fedn. Am. Socs. Exptl. Biology, 1975-76. Mem. AAAS, Am. Assn. Immunologists, Brit. Soc. Immunology, Assn. Research in Vision and Ophthalmology (trustee 1984-87, pres. 1988), Phi Beta Kappa, Sigma Xi. Home: 2011 Skyline Rd Baltimore MD 21204-6442 Office: Johns Hopkins Inst History Medicine 1900 E Monument St Baltimore MD 21205-2113

SILVERSTEIN, BARBARA ANN, conductor, artistic director; b. Phila., July 24, 1947; d. Charles and Selma (Brenner) S.; m. Bernard J. Taylor II, Aug. 19, 1978. Student Bennington Coll., 1965-67; B.Mus., Phila. Coll. Performing Arts, 1970. Assoc. music dir. Suburban Opera Co., Chester, Pa., 1967-75; asst. condr. Toledo Opera Assn., 1975-76; asst. condr., coach Curtis Inst. Music, Phila., 1973-77; asst. condr. Phila. Lyric Opera, 1971-74, Des Moines Opera Festival, Indianola, Iowa, 1974-78; music dir., condr. Savoy Co., Phila., 1977-80, Miss. Opera, Jackson, 1979-82; artistic dir., condr. Pa. Opera Theater, Phila., 1976-93; guest condr. Anchorage Opera, 1982, Opera Del., Wilmington, 1981, 83, Utah Festival Opera Co., 1993—, Lyric Opera of Kansas City, 1995—. Recipient Alumni award U. of Arts, 1989, Wash. H.S., 1991, Greater Phila. Mem. Am. Fedn. Musicians, Music Fund Soc., Pa. Council on the Arts (adv. panel 1987-90) OPERA Am. (bd. dirs. 1987-93, exec. com. 1988-93) . Jewish. Avocations: scuba diving; reading.

SILVERSTEIN, FRED HOWARD, lawyer; b. Chester, Pa., Nov. 4, 1951; s. Norman H. and Miriam R. (Rogol) S.; m. Denise Bleich; children: Allison Joy, Chad Michael. BA, U. Md., 1973; JD, U. Balt., 1975. Law clk. Ct. Appeals Md., Annapolis, 1975-76; assoc. Law Offices of Bernard Goldberg, Ellicott City, Md., 1976-82; asst. pub. defender Pub. Defender's Office, State of Md., Ellicott City, 1976-90; pvt. practice Ellicott City, 1982-94; mng. ptnr. Law Offices of Fred Howard Silverstein, Ellicott City, 1995—; head transition team Clk. of Ct., Ellicott City 1992. Mem. Greengate Cmty. Assn., Balt., 1994. Mem. ABA, Md. State Bar Assn., Howard Bar Assn. (bd. dirs. 1988-92, sec.-treas. 1986-95, pres.-elect), D.C. Bar Assn., Harvard County Bar Assn. (pres. 1995-96), Omicron Delta Kappa, Alpha Kappa Delta, Pi Sigma Alpha. Avocations: basketball, exercise. Home: 2109 Sugarcone Rd Baltimore MD 21209 Office: Law Offices of F H Silverstein 8355 Court Ave Ellicott City MD 21043

SILVERSTEIN, HOWARD ALAN, investment banker; b. N.Y.C., Dec. 31, 1947; s. Samuel and Eleanor Lucille (Lehder) S.; m. Judith R. Goldstein, Aug. 17, 1969 (div. Sept. 1987); children: Rebecca Jill, Kathryn Elizabeth; m. Ruthann Mary Pritchard, Feb. 6, 1988 (div. Aug. 1990); m. Patricia Bleznak, Jan. 24, 1993. B.S. magna cum laude, U. Pa., 1969; postgrad., London Sch. Econs., 1969-70; M.B.A. with high distinction, Harvard U., 1972. With Goldman, Sachs & Co., N.Y.C., 1972—, v.p. investment banking div., 1976-80, gen. ptnr., 1980-94; ltd. ptnr., sr. dir., 1994—; co-head Fin. Instns. Group, N.Y.C., 1987-92, head, 1992-94; past bd. dirs. Hook-SupeRx Inc., Cin., PSWW, Inc., Salt Lake City, Trinity Paper and Plastics Corp., N.Y.C., Underwriters Re Corp., Woodland Hills, Calif.; mem. task force on conceptual framework for fin. acctg. and reporting Fin. Acctg. Stds. Bd., 1978-81; trustee Beth Israel Med. Ctr., N.Y.C., 1995—. Mem. exec. bd. undergrad. divsn. Wharton Sch. U. Pa., Phila., 1995—. Thouron British-Am. exchange fellow, 1969; Loeb Rhoades fellow, 1971; Baker scholar, 1972. Mem. Old Oaks Country Club, India House Club, Beta Gamma Sigma. Office: Goldman Sachs & Co 85 Broad St New York NY 10004-2434

SILVERSTEIN, JOSEPH HARRY, musician; b. Detroit, Mar. 21, 1932; s. Bernard and Ida (Katz) S.; m. Adrienne Shufro, Apr. 27; children—Bernice, Deborah, Marc. Student Curtis Inst. Music, 1945-50; hon. doctoral degrees Tufts U., 1971, Rhode Island U., 1980, Boston Coll., 1981, New Eng. Conservatory, 1986. Violinist, Houston Symphony Orch., Phila. Orch.; concertmaster Denver Symphony Orch., Boston Symphony Orch.; formerly chmn. string dept. New Eng. Conservatory Music; also chmn. faculty Berkshire Music Sch.; mem. faculty Boston U. Sch. Music, Yale U. Sch. Music; music dir. Boston Symphony Chamber Players, Boston U. Symphony Orch., Chautauqua (N.Y.) Instn., 1987—; interim music dir. Toledo Symphony Orch.; prin. guest condr. Balt. Symphony Orch., 1981; condr. Utah Symphony; mus. dir. Worcester Orch., Mass., until 1987. Recipient Silver medal Queen Elizabeth of Belgium Internat. contest, 1959, Naumberg found. award, 1960; named one of ten outstanding young men, Boston C. of C., 1962. Fellow Am. Acad. Arts and Scis. Office: care Utah Symphony Orch 123 W South Temple Salt Lake City UT 84101-1403

SILVERSTEIN, LINDA LEE, secondary school educator; b. Riverside, Calif., July 1, 1953; d. John Conrad and Libbie Lola (Slovak) Woodard; m. Jerry Silverstein, Mar. 24, 1983. BS in Secondary Sci. Edn., Ohio State U., 1976, BS in Zoology, 1976, MA in Ednl. Adminstrn., 1992. Cert. tchr., Ohio; cert. prin., adminstr., Ohio. Tchr. Hilliard (Ohio) City Schs., 1978—; lectr. Dimensions of Learning, Hilliard, 1993-95; edn. vol. Ohio Wildlife Ctr., Dublin, 1985—. Co-author: Human Growth: Guide to a Healthier Your, 1992. Grantee Ohio Dept. Edn., 1994-95; named Martha Holden Jennings scholar Ohio State U., 1983, Tchr. Leader Ctrl. Ohio Regional Profl. Devel. Ctr., 1992-93. Mem. ASCD, Nature Conservancy, Phi Delta Kappa. Republican. Presbyterian. Avocations: gardening, traveling, skiing, volunteering. Home: 93 Garden Rd Columbus OH 43214-2131

SILVERSTEIN, LOUIS, art director, designer, editor; b. Bklyn., Oct. 10, 1919; s. Hyman and Yetta (Brodsky) S.; m. Helen Abby Becker, May 23, 1951; children: Jamie Richard (dec.), Anne Leith. B.F.A., Pratt Inst., Bkyln., 1940; M.A. credit, Inst. of Design, Chgo., 1948-50. Art. dir. Denhard & Stewart Advt., N.Y.C., 1942-43, 46-47; art. dir. Amerika (Russian lang. mag. distbn. USSR), Dept. State Publs., N.Y.C., 1947-48; promotion art dir. N.Y. Times, N.Y.C., 1952-67, corporate art dir., 1967-85, asst. mng. editor, 1969-85; cons. art director N.Y.C., 1985—; designer, cons. various newspapers, mags., U.S. and fgn. lectr. Am. Press Inst., Reston, Va., 1978-85; tchr. Sch. Visual Arts, N.Y.C., 1958-59; lectr. in field; bd. dirs. Am. Inst. Graphic Arts, N.Y.C., 1958-59, Soc. Publ. Designers, 1976-78; cons. Toronto Star, 1988—; founder Louis Silverstein Design Assn.; lectr. Ctr. Ind.

Journalism, Prague, Czechoslovakia, 1991. Co-author: America's Taste, 1961; editor, art dir.: The Earth Times, 1993—, exec. editor, 1994—; exhibited in group shows and galleries, 1951—, Am. Fedn. Arts, 1963, USIA Exhbn., USSR, 1964; designer film strips Am. Fedn. Labor, 1950-52; one-man shows include Cooper Union, 1988, U. Montreal, 1988, Walker Art Ctr., Mpls.; author: Newspaper Design for the Times, 1989; design cons.: The Hill, 1994—, The American, 1996. Served with USAF, 1943-46. Recipient Spl. Gold award N.Y. Times Op-Ed Page, N.Y. Arts Dirs. Club, 1972, Hall of Fame, 1984, Gold Medal Lifetime Achievement award Soc. Publ. Designers, N.Y.C., 1984, Am. Inst. Graphic Arts Design Leadership award, Spl. medal for best design of Am. publs., 1989, Pulitzer prize nominee, 1984, 94, numerous awards Art Dir. Clubs, other profl. groups. Mem. Alliance Graphique Internationale, N.Y. Art Dirs. Club (bd. dirs. 1978-80, 82-84, 86—), Soc. Newspaper Design, Am. Abstract Artists. Jewish. Avocations: tennis; amateur poker. Home: 36 Highland Rd Southampton NY 11968-3612

SILVERSTEIN, MICHAEL ALAN, judge; b. Providence, Sept. 28, 1933; s. Barney and Pearl (Israel) S.; m. Phyllis J. Feer, Sept. 6, 1969; 1 child, Marc R. AB, Brown U., 1956; JD, Boston U., 1959. Bar: R.I., U.S. Dist. Ct. R.I., U.S. Ct. Appeals (1st cir.). Assoc. Higgins & Silverstein, Woonsocket, R.I., 1959-67, ptnr., 1967-89; mng. ptnr. Hinckley, Allen, Snyder & Comen, Providence, Boston, 1989-93; justice R.I. Superior Ct., Providence, 1994—. Bd. dirs., past chmn. Woonsocket Indsl. Devel. Corp., 1967—; trustee Roger Williams U., Bristol, R.I., 1982—. Mem. ABA (corp. banking and bus. law sect.), R.I. Bar Assn., Comml. Law League Am., Assn. Comml. Fin. Attys. Home: 28 Kennedy Blvd Lincoln RI 02865-3602 Office: Rhode Island Superior Ct Licht Judicial Ctr 250 Benefit St Providence RI 02903

SILVERSTEIN, RICHARD, advertising agency executive. Grad., Parsons Sch. of Design. Prin., co-creative dir. Goodby, Silverstein & Ptnrs., San Francisco, 1983—. Office: Goodby Silverstein & Ptnrs 921 Front St San Francisco CA 94111-1426

SILVERSTEIN, SAMUEL CHARLES, cellular biology and physiology educator, researcher; b. N.Y.C., Feb. 11, 1937; s. Paul Robert and Jeanette (Kamen) S.; m. Jo Ann Kleinman, Apr. 2, 1967; children: David Paul, Jennifer Kate. A.B., Dartmouth Coll., 1958; M.D., Albert Einstein Coll. Medicine, 1963. Intern in medicine U. Colo. Med. Center, 1963-64; postdoctoral fellow dept. cell biology Rockefeller U., 1964-67, asst. prof. cellular physiology and immunology, 1968-71, assoc. prof., physician, 1972—; John Dalton prof. physiology Columbia U. Coll. Physicians and Surgeons, N.Y.C., 1983—, chmn. dept., 1983—; asst. resident in medicine Mass. Gen. Hosp., Boston, 1967-68; established investigator Am. Heart Assn., 1972-77; mem. sci. adv. com. Cancer Rsch. Fund of Damon Runyon-Walter Winchell Found., 1975-79, bd. dirs., 1990—; mem. sci. adv. com. N.Y. Blood Ctr.; cons. Nat. Inst. Gen. Med. Scis., 1985-89, Am. Heart Assn., 1986-89; mem. coun. Am. Soc. Cell Biology, 1988-92; chmn. Gordon Conf. Lysosomes, 1982; founder, dir. Columbia U. Summer Rsch. Program for Sci. Tchrs.; bd. dirs. Rsch. Am.; cons. Nat. Inst. Allergy and Infectious Diseases, 1977-78, mem. adv. coun., dir., 1995—. Editor: Transport of Macromolecules in Cellular Systems, 1979; chmn. editl. bd. Jour. Cell Biology, 1979-82, editor, 1978-89. Helen Hay Whitney fellow, 1964-67, John Simon Guggenheim fellow, 1995; recipient John Oliver LaGorce medal Nat. Geog. Soc., 1967, Marie Bonazinga Rsch. award Soc. Leukocyte Biology, 1984, Disting. Alumnus award Albert Einstein Coll. Medicine, 1987. Fellow AAAS, Am. Soc. Microbiology; mem. Am. Soc. Cell Biology, Am. Soc. Clin. Investigation, Am. Assn. Immunologists, Infectious Diseases Soc. Am., Sm. Soc. Biol. Chemists, Am. Physiol. Soc., Assn. Am. Physicians, Practitioners Soc. N.Y., Fedn. Am. Socs. for Exptl. Biology (bd. dirs. 1991—, v.p. 1993-94, pres. 1994-95, chmn. Pub. Affairs adv. coun. 1995-96). Clubs: Am. Alpine (dir. 1963-64, 69-74), Explorers. Achievements include research and numerous publications in field of virology, cell biology, immunology, science policy and mountaineering. Home: 110 Riverside Dr New York NY 10024-3715 Office: Columbia U Coll Physicians & Surgeons 630 W 168th St New York NY 10032-3702

SILVERSTEIN, SHELBY (SHEL SILVERSTEIN), author, cartoonist, composer, folksinger; b. Chgo., 1932; 1 daughter. Former corr., cartoonist Stars and Stripes, Pacific area; now cartoonist, writer Playboy Mag., Chgo., 1956—. Author: (books) Now Here's My Plan, 1960, Lafcadio, the Lion Who Shot Back, 1963, Uncle Shelby's ABZ Book, 1961, Giraffe and a Half, The Giving Tree, 1964, A Playboy's Teevee Jeebies, 1963, More Playboy's Teevee Jeebies, 1965, L'Arbe Au Grand Coeur, 1973, Now Here's My Plan, 1976, Uncle Shelby's Zoo: Don't Bump the Glump, Where the Sidewalk Ends, 1974, The Missing Piece, 1976, The Missing Piece Meets the Big O, 1981, A Light in the Attic, 1981; co-author: Things Change, 1988, The Best American Short Plays 1992-1993: The Theatre Annual Since 1937, 1993; (drawings) Different Dances, 1979, Who Wants a Cheap Rhinoceros, 1964, Uncle Shelby's ABZ, 1985; plays: The Lady or the Tiger, 1981; composer: Comin' After Jinny, Boa Constrictor, A Boy Named Sue, One's On the Way, The Unicorn, So Good to So Bad, Yes, Mr. Rogers, Conch Train Robbery, Freakin' at the Freakers Ball, Where the Side Walk Ends; albums include: Dirty Feet, 1968, Ned Kelly, 1970, Freakin' at the Freakers' Ball, 1972, Sloppy Seconds, 1972, Dr. Hook, 1972, Bobby Bare Sings Lullabys, Legends and Lies, 1973, Drain My Brain, 1980; appeared in film: Who is Harry Kellerman and Why is He Saying Those Terrible Things About Me?, 1971. AUS Japan, Korea, 1950s. Office: Harper Collins Pubs Inc 10 E 53rd St New York NY 10022-5244*

SILVERSTONE, DAVID, advertising executive; b. N.Y.C., Sept. 21, 1932; s. Max and Rose (Orleans) S.; m. Caroline A. Hill, June 14, 1963; children: Eva Hilary, Joshua David. Grad., Queens Coll., 1954; postgrad., Columbia U., Baruch Sch., UCLA. Sr. research analyst McCann-Erickson Inc., N.Y.C., 1956-63, mgr. media research, 1963-68, v.p., dir. mktg., Dataplan, 1968, supr. mktg. devel., 1972-74, mgr. mktg. planning and research, 1974-77, dir. research, 1977-80, sr. v.p., dir. mktg. planning, 1981—; founder, dir. Media Info. Svcs., 1969-72; mem. Advt. Agy. Rsch. Dirs. Coun., 1977-82; mem. Queens Coll. Corp. Adv. Bd., 1986—, adj. prof., 1990—. Author: (with D.E. Sexton, Jr.) Understanding the Computer, Marketing Managers Handbook, 1973. Bd. dirs. United Way of Larchmont, 1974-77, Castle Gallery Coll. of New Rochelle, 1984-92; mem. adv. coun. Sch. Gen. Studies, Columbia U., 1991—. Developer of pioneer system for defining television marketing areas (1968), measuring consumer need states (1975), consumer language of product benefits (1978), global studies of business to business marketing (1981), consumer products (1988), and global brand tracking systems (1989-90). Home: 22 Glenn Rd Larchmont NY 10538-1543

SILVERSTONE, HARRIS J., chemistry educator; b. N.Y.C., Sept. 18, 1939; s. Sidney M. and Estelle (Cohen) S.; m. Ruth C. Federman, 1960; children: Robert, Aron, Nancy, Murray. AB, Harvard U., 1960; PhD, Calif. Inst. Tech., 1964. Asst. prof. Johns Hopkins U., Balt., 1965-68, assoc. prof., 1968-71, prof., 1971—. Contbr. articles to profl. jours. NSF Postdoctoral fellow Yale U., 1964. Mem. Am. Phys. Soc., Am. Chem. Soc., Internat. Soc. Theoretical Chem. Physics. Office: Johns Hopkins U 3400 N Charles St Baltimore MD 21218-2608

SILVERSTONE, LEON MARTIN, cariologist, neuroscientist, educator, researcher; b. London, May 21, 1939; came to U.S., 1976; s. Jack Stanley and Sadie (Osen) S.; m. Susan Petyan, Dec. 20, 1964; children: Samantha, Frances, Mark. Student, Queen Mary Coll., London, 1958-59; L.D.S., U. Leeds, U.K., 1963, B.Ch.D., 1964, D.D.Sc., 1971; L.D.S., Royal Coll. Surgeons, Eng., 1964; Ph.D., U. Bristol, Eng., 1967; postgrad., U. London, 1969-76. House surgeon Leeds Dental Hosp., Eng., 1963-64; research fellow Med. Research Council Unit, Bristol Dental Sch., 1964-67; lectr. in dental surgery U. Bristol, 1967-68; sr. lectr. child dental health Med. Coll., Royal London Hosp., 1969-75, reader in preventive and pediat. dentistry, 1975-76; cons. Royal London Hosp., 1973-76; vis. Lasby prof. Dental Sch. U. Minn., Mpls., 1974-75; prof., head div. cariology Dows Inst. Dental Research, Coll. Dentistry, U. Iowa, Iowa City, 1976-82; assoc. dean for research Dental Sch. U. Colo. Health Scis. Ctr., Denver, 1982-89; dir. Oral Scis. Research Inst. U. Colo. Health Scis. Ctr., 1986-89; biomed. cons., 1990; v.p. R & D The Synaptic Corp., La Jolla, Calif., 1990-95; dir. R&D BioSciences Systems, Inc., LaJolla, Calif., 1995—; vis. Nicholasyen prof. U. Oslo, 1972; cons. Pan Am. Health Orgn., 1973-85, dental rsch. Va, 1978-85; mem. study sect. and program adv. com. NIH-Nat. Inst. Dental Rsch., 1976-84, chmn. subcom. on dental caries, 1982-83, chmn. program adv. com., 1983-84. Mem. editorial bd. Caries Rsch., 1976-86; contbr. chpts. to books, articles in field to profl. publs. Recipient A.B. Bofors prize in child dental health, 1971, ORCA-ROLEX rsch. prize, 1973, Disting. award in child dental health, 1981; NIH/Nat. Inst. Dental Rsch. grantee, 1976-89. Mem. European Orgn. Caries Research (mem. bd., sci. councillor 1971-83, pres. 1977-79), Internat. Assn. Dental Research (pres. cariology group 1982-83, Disting. Scientist award 1984), Am. Assn. Dental Research (pres. cariology group chpt. 1982-83, chmn. publs. com. 1985-86), Brit. Dental Assn., Internat. Assn. Dentistry for Children (exec. com. 1972-79, jour. editor 1971-79), AAAS, Soc. Exptl. Biology and Medicine, Space Medicine Com., AAUP, Am. Acad. Pedodontics, Omega Kappa Upsilon, Sigma Xi. Office: PO Box 1362 La Jolla CA 92038-1362

SILVERTHORNE, MICHAEL JAMES, classics educator; b. Bristol, Eng., Dec. 20, 1941; emigrated to Can., 1966; s. Frederick J. and Freda (Fox) S.; m. Ann Frances O'Malley, Aug. 6, 1966; children: Christopher, Stephen, Katherine. B.A., Oxford U., 1964, B.Litt., 1966, M.A., 1967, D.Phil., 1973. Lectr. McGill U., Montreal, 1966-68; asst. prof. McGill U., 1968-74, assoc. prof. dept. classics, 1974—, chmn. dept., 1981-86, 88-91, 94—. Can. Council fellow, 1969-73; Social Sci. and Humanities Research Council Can. grantee, 1980-83, 92-95. Mem. Classical Assn. Can. (sec. 1991-95), Conf. Social and Polit. Thought. Office: McGill U Classics Dept, 855 Sherbrooke St W, Montreal, PQ Canada H3A 2T7

SILVESTRI, ALAN ANTHONY, film composer; b. N.Y.C., Mar. 26, 1950; s. Louis and Elizabeth (Clarke) S.; m. Sandra Dee Shue; children: Alexandra, Joseph, James. PhD in Music (hon.), Berklee Coll. Music, Boston, 1995. Film scores include The Doberman Gang, 1972, The Amazing Dobermans, Las Vegas Lady, 1976, Romancing the Stone, 1984, Par ou t'es rentre? On t'as vu sortir, 1984, Fandango, 1984, Cat's Eye, 1984, Back to the Future, 1985 (Grammy award nominations best instrumental composition and best album of original score for a motion picutre, 1985), Summer Rental, 1985, Clan of the Cave Bear, 1986, The Delta Force, 1986, American Anthem, 1986, Flight of the Navigator, 1986, No Mercy, 1986, Critical Condition, 1987, Outrageous Fortune, 1987, Predator, 1987, Overboard, 1987, Who Framed Roger Rabbit?, 1988 (Grammy award nominations best instrumental composition and best album of original score for a motion picutre, 1988), My Stepmother Is an Alien, 1988, Mac and Me, 1988, She's Out of Control, 1989, Downtown, 1989, The Abyss, 1989, Back to the Future II, 1989, Back to the Future III, 1990, Young Guns II, 1990, Predator II, 1990, Soapdish, 1991, Dutch, 1991, Ricohet, 1991, Shattered, 1991, Father of the Bride, 1991, Ferngully: The Last Rainforest, 1992, Death Becomes Her, 1992, Stop! Or My Mom Will Shoot, 1992, The Bodyguard, 1992, Cop and a Half, 1993, Sidekicks, 1993, Super Mario Bros., 1993, Judgment Night, 1993, Grumpy Old Men, 1993, Clean Slate, 1994, I Love Trouble, 1994, Blown Away, 1994, Forrest Gump, 1994 (Academy award nomination best original score 1994, Grammy award nomination best instrumental performance 1994, Golden Globe award nomination best original score 1994), Richie Rich, 1994, The Quick and the Dead, 1994; TV themes include CHiPs, 1978-83, Manimal, 1983. Recipient ACE award Nat. Acad. Cable Programming for Tales from the Crypt - All Through the House, 1990, Saturn award Acad. Arts and Sci. for fantasy and horror film, 1987. Mem. Nat. Acad. Recording Arts and Scis., Acad. Motion Picture Arts and Scis.

SILVESTRI, ROBERT, electric company executive; b. New Haven, Nov. 9, 1954; s. Danny and Helen (Turek) S.; m. Debra Ann Summa, Oct. 4, 1980; 1 child, Jason Dante. BS, Fairfield (Conn.) U., 1976; MS, U. New Haven, 1986. Cert. electroplater finisher; cert. lab. dir. Lectr., rschr. Yale U., New Haven, 1976; sr. chemist Mitchell-Bradford Internat., Milford, Conn., 1977-81; dir. C.A.L., Inc., Hamden, Conn., 1981-89; supr. environ. reporting and support svcs. United Illuminating, New Haven, 1989-90, mgr. environ. licensing and regulatory affairs, 1990-94, mgr. environ. ops. and safety, 1994—; chair Bus. Recycling Coun., New Haven, 1990-94; lectr. Middlesex C.C., Middletown, Conn., 1992-95; dir. Bus. Environ. Coun., Bristol, Conn., 1993-95; mem. adv. coms. Conn. Dept. Environ. Protection, 1989—. Co-author community planning report; contbg. author: Connecticut's Environment, 1995. Mem. State of Conn. Environ. Permitting Task Force, Hartford, 1992-94; lobbyist United Illuminating, New Haven, 1991—; dir. Eli Whitney Mus., 1994—. Recipient Keynote Speaker award Conn. Forum of Regulated Environ. Profls., 1991, cert. of merit for bus. recycling Conn. Dept. Environ. Protection, 1991, Green Ribbon award Greater New Haven C. of C., 1991. Mem. Am. Electroplaters' Soc., Am. Chem. Soc., Am. Indsl. Hygiene Assn., Air and Waste Mgmt. Assn. (dir. 1993—), Electric Coun. New Eng., Conn. Bus. and Industry Assn. (steering com. 1995—), Civitan (dir. New Eng. dist. 1992-95). Avocations: woodworking, music, antique automobiles. Home: 1140 Mount Carmel Ave Hamden CT 06518-1610 Office: United Illuminating 157 Church St New Haven CT 06510-2100

SILVESTRO, CLEMENT MARIO, museum director, historian; b. New Haven, Sept. 7, 1924; s. Joseph and Rose (Griego) S.; m. Betty C. Mack, June 26, 1950; 1 dau., Elizabeth J. Silvestro Casner. B.S., Central Conn. State Coll., 1949; M.S., U. Wis., 1951; Ph.D., 1959. Asst. to dir. Wis. Hist. Soc., 1956-57; dir. Am. Assn. State and Local History, 1957-64; editor History News, 1957-64; assoc. dir. Chgo. Hist. Soc., 1964-65, dir., 1965-74, sec., 1970-74; dir. Mus. of Our Nat. Heritage, Lexington, Mass., 1974-92; Mem. exec. com. Am. Assn. Museums, 1965-71, v.p., 1966-71; vis. lectr. Northeastern U., 1983-85. Co-author: A Decade of Collecting: Maps, 1985. Mem. Chgo. Archtl. and Landmark Com., 1968-74; mem. Ill. Historic Sites Adv. Council, 1970-74, U.S. ICOM, Nat. Com., 1970-74; chmn. Pres.'s Adv. Council on Historic Preservation, 1974-77; mem. adv. bd. Eleutherian Mills-Hagley Found., 1973-76; U.S. rep. to UNESCO Internat. Adv. Com. to Safeguard City of Venice, 1975; trustee U.S. Capitol Hist. Soc.; trustee, pres. Fruitlands Mus., 1982-85. Served with USAAF, 1943-45. Decorated Air medal with oak leaf clusters. Mem. Am. Assn. Mus., Orgn. Am Historians (chmn. hist. sites com. 1973-78), Chgo. Hist. Soc., Colonial Soc. Mass., Bostonian Soc., Mass. Hist. Soc. (resident), Union Club Boston, Masons. Home: PO Box 119 Hancock ME 04640

SILVEY, ANITA LYNNE, editor; b. Bridgeport, Conn., Sept. 3, 1947; d. John Oscar and Juanita Lucille (McKitrick) S.; m. Bill Clark, 1988. BS in Edn., Ind. U., 1965-69; MA in Comm. Arts, U. Wis., 1970. Editorial asst. children's book dept. Little Brown and Co., Boston, 1970-71; asst. editor Horn Book Mag., Boston, 1971-75; mng. editor, founder New Boston Rev., 1975-76; mktg. mgr. children's books, libr. svcs. mgr. trade divsn. Houghton Mifflin, Boston, 1976-84; editor-in-chief Horn Book Mag., Boston, 1985-95; v.p., pub. Children's Books Houghton Mifflin Co., Boston, 1995—. Editor: Children's Books and Their Creators, 1995; contbr. articles to profl. jours. Named one of 70 Women Who Have Made a Difference, Women's Nat. Book Assn., 1987. Mem. ALA (chmn. children's librs., Laura Ingalls Wilder award 1987-89), Internat. Reading Assn. (mem. IRA Book award com. 1985-87), Assn. Am. Pubs. (libr. com.), New England Round Table (chmn. 1978-79). Office: Horn Book Mag 11 Beacon St Boston MA 02108-3002

SILVEY, JAMES L., religious publisher. Exec. dir. Baptist Pub. House Baptist Missionary Assn. of Am., Texarkana, Tex. Office: Bapt Missionary Assoc Am Publications Dept 311 Main St Texarkana TX 75501-5604

SILVIA, DAVID ALAN, insurance broker; b. Taunton, Mass., Mar. 5, 1953; s. Edward J. and Loretta (Sousa) S.; m. Janet E. McMahon, Apr. 16, 1988 (div. Jan. 1996); 1 child, David. BA, Roger Williams U., 1975. Sales rep. New England Brass, Taunton, Mass., 1976-81; ins. agt. Prudential Ins., Raynham, Mass., 1981-82; owner, ptnr. CS Assocs., North Attleboro, Mass., 1982-86; broker Fin. Mktg. Assocs., North Dighton, Mass., 1986—. Sec., treas. United Meth. Mens Club, Taunton, 1994, pres., 1995—. Independent. Office: Fin Mktg Assocs 495 Somerset Ave North Dighton MA 02764

SILVIA, JOHN EDWIN, economist; b. Providence, Sept. 22, 1948. BA in Econs. magna cum laude, Northeastern U., 1971, PhD in Econs., 1980. MA in Econs., Brown U., 1973. Rsch. asst. Boston Mcpl. Rsch. Bur., 1969-70; cons. Mass. Pub. Finance Project, 1973; assoc. tech. staff Mitre Corp., Bedford, Mass., 1974-75; instr. econ. St. Anselm's Coll., Manchester, N.H., 1977-79; asst. prof. Ind. U., Indpls., 1979-82; econ. rsch. officer Harris Bank, Chgo., 1982-83; sr. v.p., chief economist Kemper Fin. Svcs., Chgo., 1983—. Contbr. articles to mags., newspapers including Wall Street Jour. Mem. Am. Econ. Assn., Am. Fin. Assn., Nat. Assn. Bus. Economists (bd. dirs.), Chgo. Assn. Bus. Economists (past sec./treas., pres.), Fed. Reserve and Pub. Securities Assn. (econ. adv. com.), Blue Chip Survey. Home: 913 Turnbridge Cir Naperville IL 60540-8343 Office: Zurich Kemper Investments 120 S La Salle St Chicago IL 60603-3402

SILVIUS, DONALD JOE, educational consultant; b. Kingman, Kans., July 30, 1932; s. Henry Edgar and Gladys Mae (Beaty) S.; m. Jean Anne Able, Aug. 30, 1951; children: Laurie Dawn Silvius Gustin, Steven Craig, Jonathan Mark, Brian James. Student So. Calif. Coll., 1949-52; AA, Bakersfield Coll., 1962; BA, Fresno State Coll., 1963, MA, 1968. Radio/TV announcer, musician, music arranger and copyist, life ins. underwriter, other positions, 1953-62; jr. high sch. English tchr., elem. and jr. high counselor, child welfare, attendance and guidance supr., supr. pupil personnel svcs. Standard Sch. Dist., Oildale, Calif., 1963-92; ret. 1992; edn., guidance and computer cons., 1992—; tchr. counseling/guidance and spl. edn. various colls. Pres. North of the River Sanitation Dist. Recipient Standard PTA-Hon. Service award, Bakersfield "Up With People" Appreciation award, Golden Apple Service award Standard Sch. Dist. Tchrs. Assn., Innovations award Calif. Tchrs. Assn., Hon. Service award Kern chpt. Calif. Assn. Sch. Psychologists, Outstanding Ednl. Leader award West Kern chpt. Assn. Calif. Sch. Adminstrs., 1977-78, 7th Dist. PTA-Silver Service award, Continuing Service award Highland-Wingland PTA, Outstanding Community Service for Developmentally Disabled award. Mem. NEA, Calif. Tchrs. Assn., North of the River C. of C., Calif. Assn. Supervision of Child Welfare and Attendance, Assn. Calif. Sch. Adminstrs., Am. Assn. Curriculum Devel., Am. Assn. Counseling and Devel., ACES, ASCD, AMECD, ARVIC, Mental Health Assn. (Calif. exec. bd.), Assn. Kern County, Mensa, PTA, Calif. Assn. Counseling and Devel., Calif. Assn. for Counseling Edn. & Supervision, Calif. Assn. for Adult Devel. & Aging, Calif. Assn. for Measurement & Evaluation in Counseling, Calif. Assn. for Relig. Values & Issues in Counseling, Oildale Lions Club, Phi Delta Kappa

SILVOSO, JOSEPH ANTON, accounting educator; b. Benld, Ill., Sept. 15, 1917; s. Biagio and Camilla (Audo) S.; m. Wilda Lucille Miller, Nov. 16, 1942; children: Joseph A., Gerald R. EdB, Ill. State U., 1941; AM, U. Mo., 1947, PhD, 1951. CPA, Mo., Kans. Instr. U. Mo., 1947-48, 50-51; asst. U. Ill., 1948-49; staff acct/ Deloitte Touche (and predecessor, CPAs), Kansas City, Mo., 1951-55; ednl. dir. Deloitte Touche (and predecessor, CPAs), Detroit, 1956; assoc. prof. accountancy U. Mo., Columbia, 1955-58, prof., 1958-88, prof. emeritus, 1988—, sesquicentennial prof. accountancy, 1990—, KPMG Peat Marwick prof. profl. acctg., 1978-88, chmn. dept. accountancy, 1964-75; dir. Sch. Accountancy, 1975-79; cons. in field, 1956-94. Author: Auditing, 1965, Illustrative Auditing, 1965, Audit Case, 1966. Chmn. Joint Adv. Council Accounting, 1962-64. Served with USAAF, 1942-45. Recipient Shutz Teaching award U. Mo., 1985; Fedn. Sch. Accountancy Faculty Award of Merit renamed FSA Joseph A. Silvoso Faculty Award of Merit in his honor, 1989; established chairs in the sch. of accountancy, specifically the KPMG Peat Marwick/Joseph A. Silvoso Disting. prof., 1992, The Price Waterhouse/Joseph A. Silvoso Disting. prof., 1993, The Joseph A. Silvoso Disting. dir., 1993, The Arthur Andersen/Joseph A. Silvoso Disting. prof., 1994. Mem. Am. Acct. Assn. (chmn. membership com. Mo. 1956-58, nat. chmn. acctg. careers com. 1961-63, sec. treas. 1971-73, pres. 1980-81), AICPA (hon., contbg. editor jour. 1958-61, editorial bd. 1970-72, mem. coun. 1981-86, bd. dirs. 1983-86, Outstanding Acctg./ Educator award 1986, Disting. Svc. award 1986, nominations com. 1988-89), Mo. Soc. CPAs (chmn. acctg. careers com. 1966-67, dir., sec. ednl. found. 1968-70, bd. dirs. 1983-86, Max Myers Disting. Svc. award 1984), Ctrl. States Conf. CPAs (treas. 1975, sec. 1976, v.p. 1977, pres. 1978), Fedn. Schs. Accountancy (dir. 1977-78, v.p. 1981-82, pres. 1982-83), Nat. Assn. Accts., Inst. Internal Auditors, Fin. Exec. Inst., Midwest Econs. Assn., Delta Sigma Pi, Beta Gamma Sigma, Alpha Pi Zeta, Beta Alpha Psi (named Nat. Acad. Acct. of Yr. 1977). Methodist. Avocations: exercise, reading, gardening. Home: 818 Greenwood Ct Columbia MO 65203-2841 Office: U Mo 312 Sch Accountancy Columbia MO 65211

SIM, CRAIG STEPHEN, investment banker; b. Bklyn., Apr. 23, 1942; s. William Henry Craig and Lenore (Overton) S.; m. Susan Hart; children: Brandon Craig William, Stephanie Brooke. BA, Gettysburg Coll., 1965. Account exec. Francis I. duPont & Co., N.Y.C., 1969-72; v.p. E.F. Hutton & Co., N.Y.C., 1972-75; sr. v.p. Donaldson, Lufkin & Jenrette, N.Y.C., 1975-83; exec. v.p. Shearson Am. Express, N.Y.C., 1983-84; mng. dir. Donaldson, Lufkin & Jenrette, N.Y.C., 1984—. Served to capt. USMC, 1965-69. Mem. Bond Club N.Y. (gov. 19779-80, 84-85, 90-93), Lawrence Beach Club, The Leash, India House, St. Andrew's Soc. (N.Y.C.), L.I. Wyandanch Club, Seawanhaka Corinthian Yacht Club, Army and Navy Club (Washington). Office: Donaldson Lufkin & Jenrette Securities Corp 140 Broadway Fl 34 New York NY 10005-1101

SIM, ROBERT WILSON, accountant; b. Three Rivers, Quebec, Can., June 10, 1944; came to U.S., 1955; s. James Wilson and Winnifred May (Stephenson) S.; m. Maureen Ann McCune, Mar. 28, 1970; children: Patricia Marie, Catherine Ann, Jennifer May. BSBA, U. Fla., 1966. CPA, Fla., Mo. Staff acct. Arnold and Co., Sarasota, Fla., 1964-66; audit supr. Ernst and Ernst, Atlanta, 1968-74; audit mgr. Tornwall, Lang and Lee, St. Petersburg, Fla., 1974-76; ptnr. Grant Thornton, St. Petersburg, Fla., 1976-80, Kansas City, Mo., 1980-85, Miami/Ft. Lauderdale, Fla., 1985-90; owner, practitioner Robert W. Sim, CPA, Hollywood, Fla., 1990—. Treas. Mental Health Assn. Pinellas County, Inc., St. Petersburg, 1976-80; sec./treas. Suncoast Rotary Club St. Petersburg, 1976-80; organizer Chinese/Am. Soc. Kansas City, 1983-85. With U.S. Army, 1966-68. Recipient Cert. of Appreciation, St. Petersburg C. of C., 1975, Univ. Fla., 1992; plaque CPA Club Miami, 1990, Youth Orch. Fla., 1992. Mem. Fla. Inst. CPAs (chmn. com. on Univ. Fla. Acctg. Conf. 1993), Women in Distress of Broward County, Inc. (fund raising com. 1992, vol. cons. 1975-80), Miami Fin. Group. Republican. Presbyterian. Avocations: golf, travel/camping, weight lifting, car buff, spectator sports. Office: Robert W Sim CPA 6565 Taft St Ste 211 Hollywood FL 33024-4000

SIMA, ANDERS ADOLPH FREDRIK, neuropathologist, neurosciences researcher; b. Jönköping, Sweden, Dec. 3, 1943; came to the U.S., 1990; s. Karl Jonas Simon and Svea Gunhild (Nilsson) S.; m. Elisabeth Charlotte Hackl, Oct. 26, 1968; children: Patricia, Alexander, Vanessa. BS, U. Vienna, Austria, 1967; MD, U. Göteborg, Sweden, 1973, PhD, 1974. Asst. prof. pathology U. Goteborg, Sweden, 1973-83; asst. prof. pathology U. Toronto, Ont., 1978-81, assoc. prof. pathology, 1981-82; assoc. prof. pathology U. Manitoba, Winnipeg, 1982-85, prof. pathology, 1985-90, dir. Diabetes Rsch. Ctr., 1988-90; prof. pathology U. Mich., Ann Arbor, 1990—, prof. internal medicine, 1991—; dir. neuropathology core MADRC Mich. Alzheimer Disease Rsch. Ctr., Ann Arbor, 1992—; hon. prof. neurosci. Med. Univ., Shanghai, China, 1988; cons. Pfizer, Inc., N.Y.C., 1987—, FDA, Washington, 1988—, Miles Pharm. Inc., West Haven, Conn. 1990—; mem. internat. adv. bd. Hoffman La Roche, Basel, Switzerland, 1992—. Editl. bd. mem. for 8 nat. and internat. jours.; contbr. over 250 articles to profl. jours. Recipient Chinese Acad.'s award for Sci. Achievement, 1981, Acad. Achievement award Toku Med. Soc., Sendai, Japan, 1985, Gold medal Consiglio Nat. delle Ricerche, Rome, 1987; Diabetes Rsch. grantee NIH, Bethesda, Md., 1991, 92, Dementia Related grantee NIH, Bethesda, Md., 1994, Ednl. Tng. grantee Pfizer, Inc., N.Y.C., 1994. Fellow Royal Coll. Physicians (Can.); mem. Royal Coll. Physicians and Surgeons Can., Internat. Study Group on Diabetes in Animals, Am. Assn. Pathologist, Juvenile Diabetes Found. (hon. chmn. 1984, Appreciation award 1984, Spl. Achievement award 1989). Achievements include major contributions to the pathogenesis of diabetic neuropathy; description of genetically linked senile dementias. Avocations: international civic history, medical history, visual arts, linguistics. Office: Univ Mich Box 0580 1331 E Ann St Ann Arbor MI 48109

SIMAAN, MARWAN A., electrical engineering educator; b. July 23, 1946; m. Rita Simaan. MSEE, U. Pitts., 1970; PhD in Elec. Engring., U. Ill., 1972. Registered profl. engr., Pa. Rsch. engr. Shell Devel. Co., Houston, 1974-76; assoc. prof. elec. engring. U. Pitts., 1976-85, prof., 1985-89, Bell of Pa./Bell Atlantic prof., 1989—, chmn. dept. elec. engring., 1991—; cons. Gulf Rsch. and Tech., Pitts., 1979-85, ALCOA, Pitts., 1986-89. Editor: Vertical Seismic Profiles, 1984, Two-dimensional Transforms, 1985, Artificial Intelligence in Petroleum Exploration, 1989, Expert Systems in Exploration, 1991, (series) Advances in Geophysical Signal Processing; co-editor jour.

Multidimensional Systems and Signal Processing; contbr. over 200 articles on signal processing and control to profl. jours. Grantee NSF, ONR, Ben Franklin, Gulf, ALCOA; recipient Outstanding ECE Alumnus U. Ill. Fellow IEEE (Best Paper award 1985); mem. Soc. Exploration Geophysics, Am. Assn. Artificial Intelligence, Eta Kappa Nu, Sigma Xi (Best Paper award ALCOA chpt. 1988). Achievements include patent in application of signal processing technology in aluminum manufacturing. Office: Univ Pitts Dept Elec Engring Pittsburgh PA 15261

SIMANDLE, JEROME B., federal judge; b. Binghamton, N.Y., Apr. 29, 1949; s. Paul R. Sr. and Mary F. Simandle; married; children: Roy C., Liza Jane. BSE magna cum laude, Princeton U., 1971; JD, U. Pa., 1976; diploma in Social Scis., U. Stockholm, 1974-75. Bar: Pa. 1977, N.J. 1978. Law clk. to Hon. John F. Gerry U.S. Dist. Ct., N.J., 1976-78; asst. U.S. atty. Dist. N.J., 1978-83; U.S. magistrate judge U.S. Dist. Ct., N.J., 1983-92, judge, 1992—; mem. lawyers adv. com. U.S. Dist. Ct. N.J., 1984-95; ct. adminstrn. case mgmt. com. Jud. Conf. U.S., 1991—. Internat. grad. fellow Rotary Found., 1974-75. Fellow Am. Bar Found.; mem. ABA, N.J. Bar Assn., Camden Inn of Ct. (master 1987—, program chmn. 1990-93). Office: US Dist Ct US Courthouse One John F Gerry Plz Camden NJ 08101-0888

SIMARD, RODNEY, literature and communications educator, media consultant; b. Ft. Smith, Ark., June 18, 1952; s. Houston H. and Dorothy (Turner) S. BA, U. Memphis, 1974; MA, Miss. State U., 1976; PhD, U. Ala., 1982. Instr. lit. Birmingham-So. Coll., 1981-82; instr. lit. and communications Calif. State U., Bakersfield, 1982-86; asst. prof. lit. Calif. State U., San Bernardino, 1986-92, assoc. prof., coord. Am. Studies program, 1992—. Author: Postmodern Drama, 1984, The Whole Writer's Catalog: An Introduction to Advanced Composition, 1992; gen. editor series American Indian Studies, 1989-93, Studies in American Indian Literatures, 1993; assoc. editor Furniture Methods and Materials, 1973-74; editor Black Warrior Review, 1979-80, Showtime, 1983-84, Tribal Discourse: Proceedings of the Symposium on the Status of American Indians in the CSU; cons. editor Elan, 1988-89; faculty editor Pacific Review, 1988-89; contbg. editor The Variorum Edition of the Poetry of John Donne, 1982-88; contbr. articles to profl. jours., anthologies, other publs. Tribal mem. Cherokee Nation of Okla.; bd. dirs., v.p., mem. profl. adv. coun. Riverside (Calif.) and San Bernardino County Am. Indian Ctr. Mem. MLA, Inland Area Native Am. Assn. (adv. coun., cons. editor assn. newsletter), NAACP, ACLU, Gay Am. Indians, Sigma Tau Delta, Phi Gamma Delta. Office: Calif State U Dept English San Bernardino CA 92407

SIMBRO, WILLIAM CHARLES, journalist; b. Eldon, Iowa, Mar. 9, 1933; s. Elmer Leroy and Miriam Edna (Sheldon) S.; m. Shirley Jo Taylor Hunt, Jan. 18, 1976 (div. Apr. 1990); children: Robert Paul, David William. BA, William Penn Coll., 1956; MDiv, Garrett-Evang. Theol. Sem., 1961; postgrad., U. Iowa, 1958-59, 65-66. Ordained to ministry Meth. Ch., 1962. Pastor Ainsworth (Iowa) Meth. Ch., 1960-64, Coralville (Iowa) Meth. Ch., 1964-66; reporter Cedar Rapids (Iowa) Gazette, 1966-67; chief Cedar Rapids bur. The Des Moines Register, 1967-76, religion writer, 1976—; cons. Rockefeller Found., N.Y.C., 1980. Contbr. articles to profl. jours. Bd. dirs. Moingona coun. Girl Scouts U.S., 1994—. Recipient Faith and Freedom award Religious Heritage Am., 1980. Mem. Religion Newswriters Assn. (treas. 1980-82, Supple Meml. award 1978). Avocations: power walking, traveling, radio reading to the blind. Office: The Des Moines Register 715 Locust St Des Moines IA 50309-3724

SIMBURG, EARL JOSEPH, psychiatrist, psychoanalyst; b. Vonda, Sask., Can., Mar. 21, 1915; came to U.S., 1941; s. Joseph E. and Liza (Yurovsky) S.; m. Virginia Ronan, Feb. 10, 1958; children by previous marriage: Arthur, Melvyn, Sharon. Cert. medicine, U. Sask., Saskatoon, 1935; MDCM, McGill U., Montreal, Que., Can., 1938; grad., San Francisco Psychoanal. Inst., 1959. Diplomate Am. Bd. Psychiatry and Neurology. Intern Royal Victoria Hosp., Montreal, 1938-39; sr. physician Brandon (Can.) Hosp. Mental Diseases, 1939-41; resident Grace New Haven Hosp., 1941-43; pvt. practice psychiatry and psychoanalysis Berkeley, Calif., 1947—; mem. faculty San Francisco Psychoanalytic Inst.; instr. psychiatry Yale U., New Haven, 1941-43, U. Calif., San Francisco, 1949-59; cons. Calif. Dept. Health, Berkeley, 1975-76; pres. med. staff Herrick Hosp. and Health Ctr., 1985; active med. staff Alta-Bates Med. Ctr., Earl J. Simburg lectr.; bd. dirs. Alta-Bates Found.; mem. del. People to People Program to China, 1995. Contbr. articles to profl. jours. and chpts. to books. Served to major M.C. USAF, 1943-47. Earl J. Simburg Lecture given annually in his honor, Alta-Bates Med. Ctr. Fellow Am. Psychiat. Assn. (life), AAAS (life), APSNA (life); mem. AMA, Am. Psychoanalytic Assn. (life, cert.), Calif. Med. Assn., Alameda Contra Costa County Med. Assn., Am. Geriatrics Soc., Am. Assn. for Geriatric Psychiatry, Internat. Psychiat. Assn., Internat. Psychologic Assn. Avocation: tennis. Office: 1500 E Medical Ctr Dr Berkeley CA 94704-2633 *Personal philosophy: Development continues throughout our lives. Any realization of this on going process is rewarding. Any benefit to self and others expresses this development and materialize these rewards.*

SIMCHES, SEYMOUR OLIVER, language educator; b. Boston, Sept. 22, 1919; s. Meyer and Rebecca (Nadell) S.; m. Marcia Harriet Goldberg, Sept. 13, 1953; children: Judith Ellen, Jonathan David. AB, Boston U., 1941; MA, Harvard U., 1942, PhD, 1950. Tchg. fellow Romance langs. Harvard U., 1947-50, resident tutor Adams Ho., 1947-53, mem. upper-commons rm. Adams Ho., 1995—, instr., 1950-53; asst. prof. Amherst Coll., 1953-54; mem. faculty Tufts U., 1954-90, chmn. dept. Romance langs., 1958-70, John Wade prof. modern langs., 1962-90, John Wade prof. emeritus, 1990—, co-founder, bd. dirs. Tufts Exptl. Coll., 1964-68; dir. Tufts Coll. Within, 1971-74, Ctr. for European Studies, 1978-83; founding dir. Tufts European Ctr., 1983—; mem. Mass. Adv. Com. on Fgn. Langs., 1961—; cons. U.S. Office Edn., 1964; dir. Fgn. Lang. Insts., NDEA, 1960-62, 65; mem. bd. examiners advanced placement Coll. Entrance Exam. Bd., 1968—; mem. Mass. Adv. Bd. on Non-Traditional Edn. Author: (with H.H. Golden) Modern French Literature and Language: A Bibliography of Homage Studies, 1956, Modern Iberian Literature and Language: A Bibliography of Homage Studies, 1958, Modern Italian Literature and Language: A Bibliography of Homage Studies, 1958, Le Romantisme et le Gout Esthetique du XVIIIième Siecle, 1964, The Theatre of Jacinto Grau, The Mythic Quest in Ionesco's Plays. Served with USAAF, 1942-46. Decorated Medaille Aero., chevalier officier and commandeur Palmes Academiques (France).; Sheldon traveling fellow Harvard, 1949. Mem. MLA, AAUP, Am. Assn. Tchrs. of French (pres. Boston chpt. 1958-60), Renaissance Soc. Am., New England MLA (chmn. Ea. Mass. chpt. 1955-56), N.E. Conf. Fgn. Lang. Tchrs. (vice chmn. 1964-65), Phi Beta Kappa, Phi Sigma Iota (hon.). Home: 5 Burbank Rd Medford MA 02155-2928

SIMCOX, CRAIG DENNIS, aeronautical engineer; b. Iowa Falls, Iowa, Sept. 18, 1939; s. Clair Mock and Alice Mae (Shane) S.; m. Molly A. H. Simcox, Aug. 4, 1961; 1 child, Vichi Rae Simcox Smokoff. BS in Aero. Engring., Iowa State U., 1962; MS in Aero. and Astro., Stanford U., 1965; PhD, Purdue U., 1969; postgrad., Columbia U., 1981. Research scientist Ames Research Ctr., NASA, Moffett Field, Calif., 1962-65; instr., cons. Purdue U., West Lafayette, Ind., 1965-68; research mgr. Boeing Comml. Airplanes Co., Renton, Wash., 1969-75; lab. mgr. Boeing Comml. Airplanes Co., Seattle, 1975-85; chief engr. Boeing Comml. Airplanes Co., Everett, Wash., 1985-90; dir. customer svcs. Boeing Comml. Airplanes Co., Seattle, 1990—; chmn. numerous nat. and internat. confs. Assoc. editor Tech. Periodic Jur. Aircraft, 1978-87; contbr. articles to profl. jours. V.p. Somerset Assn., Bellevue, Wash., 1978-80; v.p. civic affairs Boeing Mgmt. Assn., Seattle, 1986-88; pres. Eidelweiss Assn., Bellevue, Wash., 1991-92. Fellow AIAA (chmn. 1976-77, dep. dir. 1978-84, sec. aircraft design tech. com. 1988-91). Mem. Christian Ch. Avocations: skiing, golf, photography, music, boating. Home: 4640 132nd Ave SE Bellevue WA 98006-2131 Office: Boeing Comml Airplanes Co PO Box 3707 Seattle WA 98124-2207

SIME, DONALD RAE, business administration educator; b. Los Angeles, July 20, 1926; s. Chester I. and Gaynal (Ramage) S.; m. Patricia Evelyn Hawes, Sept. 4, 1949; children: Julia, Paul, Jill. B.A., Pepperdine Coll., 1949, MA, 1951; BD, Princeton Sem., 1954; PhD, U. Chgo., 1962. Prof. religion Harding Grad. Sch. Harding Coll., 1954-66; prof. dept. religion and psychology Pepperdine Coll., 1966-68, chmn. dept. bus. adminstrn., 1968-69; dean Sch. Bus. and Mgmt. Pepperdine U., 1969-78, v.p., 1973-81, prof., 1978-96; cons. orgnl. devel., affirmative action programs Webco, Page Group, Los Angeles Cons. Group, Conceptual Consultants. Contbr. articles to bus. and religious publs. Served with USNR, 1944-46. Home: 20166 Village 20 Camarillo CA 93012-7506

SIMECKA, BETTY JEAN, convention and visitors bureau executive; b. Topeka, Apr. 15, 1935; d. William Bryan and Regina Marie (Rezac) S.; m. Alex Pappas, Jan. 15, 1956 (div. Apr. 1983); 1 child, Alex William. Student, Butler County Community Coll., 1983-85. Freelance writer and photographer L.A., also St. Marys, Kans., 1969-77; co-owner Creative Enterprises, El Dorado, Kans., 1977-83; coord. excursions into history Butler County Community Coll., El Dorado, 1983-84; dir. Hutchinson (Kans.) Conv. & Visitors Bur., 1984-85; dir. mktg. div. Exec. Mgmt., Inc., Wichita, 1985-87; exec. dir. Topeka Conv. and Visitors Bur., 1987-91, pres., CEO, 1991-96; pres., chmn. Internat. Connections, Inc., 1996—; dir. promotion El Dorado Thunderboat Races, 1977-78. Contbr. articles to jours. and mags.; columnist St. Marys Star, 1973-79. Pres. El Dorado Art Assn., 1984; chmn. Santa Fe Trail Bike Assn., Kans., 1988-90; co-dir. St. Marys Summer Track Festival, 1973-81; chmn. spl. events Mulvane Art Mus., 1990, sec., 1991-92; membership chmn., 1993-94, bd. dirs., 1995-96; bd. dirs. Topeka Civic Theater, 1991-96, co-chmn. spl. events, 1992; Kans. chmn. Russian Festival Com., 1992-93; vice-chmn. Kans. Film Commn., 1993-94, chmn., 1994; bd. dirs. Kans. Expoctr. Adv. Bd.; pres. Kans. Internat. Mus., 1994-96. Recipient Kans. Gov.'s Tourism award, 1993, Disting. Svc. award City of Topeka, 1995, Hist. Ward Meade Disting. award 1995; named Kansan of Yr., 1995, Sales and Mktg. Exec. of Yr., 1995, Woman of Distinction, Internat. Soroptimists, 1996. Mem. Nat. Tour Assn., Sales and Mktg. execs. (bd. dirs. 1991-92), Internat. Assn. Conv. and Visitors Burs. (co-chmn. rural tourism com. 1994), Am. Soc. Assn. Execs., Travel Industry Assn. Kans. (membership chmn. 1988-89, sec. 1990, pres. 1991-92, Outstanding Merit award 1994), St. Marys C. of C. (pres. 1975), I-70 (v.p. 1989, pres. 1990), Optimists (social sec. Topeka chpt. 1988-89). Republican. Methodist. Avocations: writing, painting, photography, masters track. Holder Nat. AAU record for 100-yard dash, 1974.

SIMERAL, WILLIAM GOODRICH, retired chemical company executive; b. Portland, Oreg., May 22, 1926; s. Claire Cornelius and Geneva B. (Goodrich) S.; m. Elizabeth Louise Ross, June 25, 1949; children: Linda Simeral McGregor, Karen Simeral Schousen, William Goodrich Jr., John David. B.S. in Physics, Franklin and Marshall Coll., Lancaster, Pa., 1948; Ph.D. in Physics, U. Mich., 1953. With E.I. duPont de Nemours and Co., Inc., 1953-87; v.p., gen. mgr. plastics dept. E.I. duPont de Nemours and Co., Inc., Wilmington, Del., 1974-76; v.p., gen. mgr. plastic products and resins dept. E.I. duPont de Nemours and Co., Inc., 1976-77, sr. v.p., dir., mem. exec. com., 1977-81, exec. v.p., dir., mem. exec. com., 1981-87; vice chmn. bd., chief operating officer Conoco Inc., 1984-85. Trustee Franklin and Marshall Coll., 1977—, chmn. bd., 1991-94; trustee, bd. dirs. Wilmington Med. Ctr., 1978-93, chmn. bd., 1982-86; bd. dirs. YMCA Wilmington and New Castle County, 1978-81. Mem. Chem. Mfrs. Assn. (vice chmn. bd. 1980-81, chmn. exec. com. 1981-82, chmn. bd. 1982-83), Am. Phys. Soc., Phi Beta Kappa, Sigma Xi, Wilmington Country Club, Quail Creek Country Club, The Club Pelican Bay.

SIMEROTH, DEAN CONRAD, chemical engineer; b. Marysville, Calif., Mar. 21, 1946; s. Raphael Conrad and Mary Beatrice (Watson) S.; m. Phyllis Deborah Minakowski, Feb. 7, 1971 (div. Nov. 1994); 1 child, Brian Conrad. BS in Chem. Engring., U. Calif., Davis, 1968. From air pollution specialist to chief engr. evaluation br. Calif. Air Resources Bd., Sacramento, 1969-87; chief criteria pollutant br. Calif. Air Resources Bd., 1987—. Served in U.S. Army, 1969-71, Korea. Mem. AIChE, Air Waste Mgmt. Assn., Kiwanis (treas. Woodland, Calif. chpt. 1988—). Democrat. Roman Catholic. Avocations: hunting, fishing, tennis, history. Office: Calif Air Resources Bd PO Box 2815 2020 L St Sacramento CA 95812

SIMES, DIMITRI KONSTANTIN, international affairs expert and educator; b. Moscow, Oct. 17, 1947; came to U.S., 1973; s. Konstantin M. and Dina (Kaminsky) S.; m. Anastasia Ryurikov, May 27, 1993. MA, Moscow State U., 1969. Sr. research fellow Ctr. for Strategic and Internat. Studies, Washington, 1973-76, dir. Soviet studies, 1976-80; prof. Soviet studies, exec. dir. Soviet and East European research program Sch. Advanced Internat. Studies, Johns Hopkins U., Washington, 1980-83, lectr., 1983-90; sr. assoc. Carnegie Endowment for Internat. Peace, Washington, 1983-94; pres. Nixon Ctr. for Peace and Freedom, Washington, 1994—; vis. prof. polit. sci. U. Calif., Berkeley, 1982; adj. prof. govt. Columbia U., N.Y.C., 1985, 92; cons. CBS News, N.Y.C., 1985-87, NBC News, 1986—; commentators Voice of Am., 1990—. Author: Detente and Conflict: Soviet Succession: Leadership in Transition, 1978; columnist: Christian Sci. Monitor, Boston, 1983-87, L.A. Times Syndicate, 1987-89, Newsday, 1991—; contbr. articles to newspapers and jours. Vice chmn. Fund for Democracy and Devel. Mem. Coun. on Fgn. Rels. Office: Nixon Ctr Peace and Freedom 1620 I St NW Ste 900 Washington DC 20006-4005

SIMIC, CHARLES, English language educator, poet; b. Beograd, Yugoslavia, May 9, 1938; came to U.S., 1954, naturalized, 1971; s. George and Helen (Matijevich) S.; m. Helen Dubin, Oct. 1964; children: Anna, Philip. BA, NYU, 1967. Editl. asst. Aperture, Quar. of Photography, N.Y.C., 1966-69; prof. English Calif. State U., Hayward, 1970-73, U. N.H., Durham, 1973—; vis. tchr. Boston U., spring 1975, Columbia U., fall 1979. Author: poems What the Grass Says, 1967, Somewhere Among us a Stone is Taking Notes, 1969, Dismantling the Silence, 1971, White, 1972, Return to a Place Lit by a Glass of Milk, 1974, Biography and a Lament, 1976, Charon's Cosmology, 1977, Classic Ballroom Dances, 1980, Austerities, 1982, Weather Forecast for Utopia and Vicinity, 1983, Selected Poems, 1985, Unending Blues, 1986, The World Doesn't End, 1989 (Pulitzer Prize for poetry 1990), The Book of Gods and Devils, 1990, Hotel Insomnia, 1992, A Wedding in Hell, 1994; prose The Uncertain Certainty, 1985, Wonderful Words, Silent Truth, 1990, The Unemployed Fortune Teller; translator, editor: (with C.W. Truesdale) poems Fire Gardens, 1970, (with Mark Strand) Another Republic, 1976, (with others) Selected Poems of Tomaz Salamun, 1987, RollCall of Mirrors, 1987; translator: Four Modern Yugoslav Poets, 1970, (with P. Kastmiler) Atlantis, 1983; contbr. poems to mags. and anthologies. With U.S. Army, 1961-63. Recipient PEN Internat. award for translation, 1970, 80, Edgar Allan Poe award Am. Acad. Poets, 1975, Nat. Inst. Arts and Letters and AAAL award, 1976, Harriet Monroe poetry award U. Chgo., 1980, DiCastignola award Poetry Soc. Am., 1980, Pulitzer prize for poetry, 1990; Guggenheim fellow, 1972-73; Nat. Endowment for Arts fellow, 1974-75, 79-80; Fulbright Travelling fellow, 1982, Ingram Merrill fellow, 1983-84; Mac Arthur fellow, 1984-89. Mem. Am. Acad. Arts and Letters. Home: PO Box 192 Strafford NH 03884-0192 Office: U NH Dept English PO Box 192 Strafford NH 03884-0192

SIMIEN, CLYDE RAY, lawyer; b. Opelousas, La., Jan. 9, 1960; s. Vincent Jr. and Mercedes Simien; m. Margo St. Julien. BSBA, U. Southwestern La., 1982; postgrad., La. State U., 1985; JD, So. U. La., 1986. Bar: La. 1986. Counselor spl. svcs. dept. U. Southwestern La., 1982-84; law clerk Hon. Ron Gomez, House of Reps., La., 1984, Bur. Legis., Senate, La., 1984-85, L.D. Sledge, Atty.-at-law, 1985-86, Sixteenth Judicial Dist. Ct., 1986—; ptnr. Simien & Miniex, Attys.-at-law, Lafayette, La., 1987—; asst. adj. prof. criminal justice Coll. of Arts and Humanities, U. Southwestern La.; asst. dist. atty. Parishes of St. Martin, Iberia, and St. Mary. Mem. ABA, La. Trial Lawyers Assn., La. State Bar Assn., Am. Trial Lawyers Assn., La. Soc. Ind. Accountants, Nat. Soc. Pub. Accountants, Nat. Dist. Attys. Assn., U. Southwestern La. Debate Team, U. Southwestern La. Alumni Assn. Office: Simien & Miniex APLC 104 Rue Iberville Lafayette LA 70508-3102

SIMINI, JOSEPH PETER, accountant, financial consultant, author, former educator; b. Buffalo, Feb. 15, 1921; s. Paul and Ida (Moro) S.; BS, St. Bonaventure U., 1940, BBA, 1949; MBA, U. Calif.-Berkeley, 1957; DBA, Western Colo. U., 1981; m. Marcelline McDermott, Oct. 4, 1968. Insp. naval material Bur. Ordnance, Buffalo and Rochester, N.Y., 1941-44; mgr. Paul Simini Bakery, Buffalo, 1946-48; internal auditor DiGiorgio (Fruit) Corp., San Francisco, 1950-51; tax accountant Price Waterhouse & Co., San Francisco, 1953; sr. accountant Richard L. Hanlin, C.P.A., San Francisco, 1953-54; prof. accounting U. San Francisco, 1954-79, emeritus prof., 1983—; mem. rev. bd. Calif. Bd. Accountancy, 1964-68. Mem. council com. Boy Scouts Am., Buffalo, San Francisco, 1942-65, Scouters Key, San Francisco council; bd. dirs. Nat. Italian Am. Found., Washington, 1979-85. Served to ensign USNR, 1944-46. Recipient Bacon-McLaughlin medal St. Bonaventure U., 1940, Laurel Key, 1940; Outstanding Tchr. award Coll. Bus. Adminstrn., U. San Francisco, 1973; Disting. Tchr. award U. San Francisco, 1975, Joseph Peter Simini award, 1977. Crown Zellerbach Found. fellow, 1968-69; Gold Medal Associazione Piemontese nel Mondo, Turin, Italy, 1984; decorated Knight Order of Merit, Republic of Italy, 1982. CPA, Calif. Mem. Am. Inst. C.P.A.s, Calif. Soc. C.P.A.s (past chmn. ednl. standards, student relations com. San Francisco chpt.), Inst. of Mgmt. Accts. (past pres. San Francisco chpt.), Am. Acctg. Assn., Am. Mgmt. Assn. (lectr. 1968-78), Delta Sigma Pi (past pres. San Francisco alumni club), Beta Gamma Sigma. Roman Catholic. Clubs: Serra (past pres. Golden Gate chpt.), Il Cenacolo (past pres.), Toastmasters (past pres. Magic Word). Lodges: K.C., Rotary (past pres. Daly City). Author: Accounting Made Simple, 1967, 2d rev. edit., 1987, Cost Accounting Concepts for Nonfinancial Executives, 1976, Become Wealthy! Using Tax Savings and Real Estate Investments, 1982, Balance Sheet Basics for the Nonfinancial Managers, 1989, Petals of the Rose, 1990, How to Become Financially Independent, 1996. Tech. editor, Accounting Essentials, 1972. Patentee Dial-A-Trig and Verbum Est card game. Home: 977 Duncan St San Francisco CA 94131-1800 Office: PO Box 31420 San Francisco CA 94131-0420 *Personal philosophy: You can succeed! but you must program yourself for success and know what you want.*

SIMIS, THEODORE LUCKEY, investment banker, information technology executive; b. N.Y.C., June 17, 1924; s. Theodore William Ernest and Helen (Luckey) S.; m. Laura Cushman Ingraham, Sept. 8, 1946; children—Nancy Simis Ricca, Theodore Steven, Karen Simis Woods, June Simis Sobocinski. B.S., NYU, 1950, M.B.A., 1952. With Bell System, 1941-79; various positions to officer level with N.Y. Telephone Co., N.J. Telephone Co., and AT&T; v.p. Warner Amex Cable Co., 1980-81; sr. v.p. E.F. Hutton, Sarasota, Fla., 1982-87; vice chmn., bd. dirs. XMX Corp., Burlington, Mass., 1986—; pres. Pvt. Transatlantic Telecommunication System Inc., McLean, Va., 1987-89; chmn. Value Added Network System, Inc., Sarasota, Fla., 1990-91; dir. Liebenzell Mission, Schooleys Mountain, N.J.; vis. Nieman fellow Harvard U., 1977. Mem. Republican Nat. Com., 1981—. 1st lt. U.S. Army, 1942-53, ETO. Mem. N.Y. Acad. Scis., U.S. C. of C., NYU Club. Lutheran. Home: 6025 Manasota Key Rd Englewood FL 34223-9245

SIMITIS, SPIROS, legal educator; b. Athens, Greece, Oct. 19, 1934; s. George and Fanny (Christopoulo) S.; m. Ilse Grubrich, Aug. 3, 1963. JD, U. Marburg, Fed. Republic Germany, 1956. Assoc. prof. U. Frankfurt, Fed. Republic Germany, 1963; prof. U. Frankfurt, 1969, U. Giessen, Fed. Republic Germany, 1964-69; vis. prof. London Sch. Econs., U. Calif. - Berkeley, 1976, U. Pa., 1980, U. Strasbourg, France, 1987-88, Paris, 1990—, Yale U., New Haven, Conn., 1981—; sec. gen. Internat. Civil Status Commn., 1966-80; chmn. Data Protection Experts Com. of the Coun. of Europe, Strasbourg, 1982-86, Hesse Data Protect commr., 1975-91; mem. rsch. coun. European Univ. Inst. Contbr. numerous articles to legal pubis. Mem. German Lawyers Assn. (bd. dirs. 1970-82), German Coun. Pvt. Internat. Law. Office: Johann Wolfgang Goethe U, Senckenberganlage 31 Postfach, 111932 60054 Frankfurt Germany

SIMKIN, PETER ANTHONY, physician, educator; b. Morgantown, W.Va., Nov. 22, 1935; s. William Edward and Ruth Helen (Commons) S.; m. Penelope Hart Payson, Aug. 9, 1958; children—Andrew, Caroline, Mary, Elizabeth. B.A., Swarthmore Coll., 1957; M.D., U. Pa., 1961. Intern N.C. Meml. Hosp., Chapel Hill, 1961-62; resident N.C. Meml. Hosp., 1962-63, Univ. Hosps. Cleve., 1965-66; fellow in medicine U. Wash., Seattle, 1966-69; asst. prof. U. Wash., 1969-74, asso. prof., 1974-84, prof., 1984—. Mem. editorial bd.: Arthritis and Rheumatism, 1981-85, BIMR Rheumatology, 1980-84; contbr. articles to profl. jours. Bd. dirs. Wash. chpt. Arthritis Found., 1974-90, chmn. med. and sci. com., 1974-78. Served with U.S. Army, 1963-65. Fellow Am. Coll. Rheumatology; mem. Western Soc. Clin. Research, Am. Fedn. Clin. Investigation, Orthopaedic Research Soc. Quaker. Office: Rheumatology 356428 U Wash Seattle WA 98195-6420

SIMKO, HELEN MARY, school library media specialist; b. Trenton, N.J., Feb. 25, 1950; d. Matthew John and Helen Catherine Harbach; m. Thomas F. Simko, Oct. 13, 1973; children: Jesse Matthew, Ian Christopher. BS in Home Econs. Edn., Immaculata Coll., 1972; postgrad. Home Econs. Design, Drexl U., 1972; MLS, So. Conn. State U., 1993, 6th Yr. Degree in Ednl. Founds., 1996. Cert. tchr. Conn. libr. media specialist (provl.) Conn. Substitute tchr. Pub. Schs. of Litchfield, Sch. Dist. #6, Litchfield, Conn., 1981-89; spl. edn. asst. Ctr. Elem. Sch., Litchfield, 1989-93, Litchfield Intermediate Sch., 1993; sch. libr. media specialist Burr Elem. Sch., Hartford, Conn., 1993-94, Swift Jr. H.S., Oakville, Conn., 1994—; mem. student handbook revision com. Ctr. Sch., Litchfield, 1992-93, mission statement revision com., 1992-93, faculty adv. com., 1992-93; mem. Litchfield adv. com. on Quality Edn. and Diversity, 1994; mem. libr. media selection policy revision com. Watertown Bd. Edn., 1994; mem. tech. planning com. Watertown Pub. Schs., 1995—. Active mem. Civic Family Svcs., Litchfield, 1983-89, LWV, Litchfield, 1986-89. Mem. ALA, ASCD, Conn. Edn. Media Assn. (bd. dirs., mem. co-chair), Am. Assn. Sch. Librs., Kappa Omicron Phi, Beta Phi Mu. Roman Catholic. Avocations: sewing, cooking, reading, skiing, tennis. Home: 45 Baldwin Hill Rd Litchfield CT 06759-3305

SIMKO, JAN, English and foreign language, literature educator; b. Zlaté Moravce, Slovakia, Oct. 30, 1920; came to U.S., 1967; s. Simon Simko and Terezia Simkova; m. Libusa Safarikova, Dec. 20, 1950 (div. 1970); children: Jan, Vladimir (dec.). Diploma in English, U. Bratislava, 1942, Diploma in German, 1943, PhD in English, 1944; MPhil in English, U. London, 1967. Tchr. English and German various bus. schs., 1942-45; asst. depts. English and German U. Bratislava, 1945-46; instr. English Econom U., 1946-47; mem. faculty U. Bratislava, 1950-68, from asst. prof. to assoc. prof. English, 1957-68; prof. English Rio Grande Coll., Ohio, 1968-75; instr. Shakespeare Georgetown U., 1982-84; vis. prof. English, scholar-in-residence W.Va. U., Parkersburg, 1989-90; instr. Slovak, Fgn. Svc. Inst., Washington, 1974, 96, fed. govt., 1989, 91, IMF & World Bank, 1994-95; external examiner critical langs. program Kent (Ohio) State U., 1974-91; feature writer Voice of Am., 1983-94, 96; numerous lectureships. Author: 3 English textbooks, 2 bilingual dictionaries, 1 linguistics monograph, numerous linguistics and literature articles, editor: Lectures in the Circle of Modern Philology, 2 vols., 1965-66; chief consulting editor: textbooks of Slovak and Czech, 1993—; contbg. editor: The Review, 1995—. With inf. Czecho-Slovak Army, 1946. Brit. Coun. grantee, 1947-49; Folger Shakespeare Libr./U.S. Dept. State, 1967-68; Internat. Rsch. and Exch. Bd. grantee, 1982, others. Mem. MLA, Slovak Studies Assn., Soc. for Scis. and Arts, Met. Opera Guild, Shakespeare Theater Guild, Nat. Symphony Orch. Assn. Roman Catholic. Avocations: classical music, opera, theatre, fine arts, hiking, swimming. Home: 1356 E Capitol St NE Washington DC 20003-1533

SIMMEL, MARIANNE LENORE, graphic designer; b. Jena, Germany; d. Hans E. and Else R. (Rapp) S. A.B., Smith Coll., 1943; A.M., Harvard U., 1945, Ph.D., 1949. Diplomate Am. Bd. Examiners Profl. Psychology. Intern psychology Worchester (Mass.) State Hosp., 1943; research asst. Neurol. Lab., Boston Dispensary, Tufts Coll. Med. Sch., Boston, 1943-45; instr. psychology Cambridge (Mass.) Jr. Coll., 1945-46; vol. asst. neurol. unit Childrens Hosp., Harvard Med. Sch., 1945-46; instr. psychology Hofstra Coll., 1946-48; vis. lectr. dept. psychology Wellesley Coll., 1948-49; from instr. to clin. assoc. prof. psychology dept. psychiatry Coll. Medicine, U. Ill., 1950-58; psychophysiologist, head psychol. lab. Ill. State Psychopathic Inst., Chgo., 1952-58; asst. dir. Ill. State Psychopathic Inst., 1952-55; vis. lectr. med. psychology Duke Med. Sch., 1958-59; spl. research fellow USPHS, NIMH, 1959-61, 69-70; asst. psychologist in neurosurgery Mass. Gen. Hosp., 1959-61, from 63; research assoc. dept. psychology Brandeis U., 1959-61, from assoc. prof. to prof., 1963-78, adj. prof., from 1978, prof. emeritus psychology, 1987—; research assoc. in neurology Mt. Sinai Hosp., N.Y.C., 1961-67; now graphic designer. Contbr. articles to profl. jours.; Editor: The Reach of Mind: Essays in Memory of Kurt Goldstein, 1968. Recipient Research award Am. Rehab. Counseling Assn., 1964. Fellow Am. Psychol. Assn.; mem. Eastern Psychol. Assn., Psychonomic Soc., AAUP, Am. Soc. Aesthetics, Phi Beta Kappa, Sigma Xi. Home: PO Box 562 North Eastham MA 02651-0562 *Methodology is the last refuge of a sterile mind.*

SIMMERMON, JAMES EVERETT, credit bureau executive; b. Arnold, Pa., Mar. 23, 1926; s. Joseph C. and Melba J. (McGeary) S.; m. Lois Bowden, Apr. 19, 1952; children: James, Thomas, John, Lisa, William. BS in Bus. Adminstrn, Ashland (Ohio) U., 1949. Chmn. Collection Service Ctr., New Kensington, Pa., 1955—; mem. adv. bd. Associated Credit Bus., Houston, 1965-73, bd. dirs., 1984—; bd. dirs. Consumer Credit Counseling Svc. of Western Pa., 1975—; vice chmn. Citizens Gen. Enterprises Inc., 1986—. Trustee Ashland (Ohio) U., 1986—; bd. dirs. Citzens Gen. Hosp., New Kensington, Pa., 1972—. With USNR, 1944-46. Mem. Rotary Club of Fox Chapel (past dist. gov. dist. 7300, 1982-83, Oakmont Country Club, Green Valley Country Club. Home: 302 Fox Chapel Rd Apt 316 Pittsburgh PA 15238-2337

SIMMONDS, JAMES GORDON, mathematician, educator; b. Washington, July 26, 1935; s. James H. and Elisabeth (Welch) S.; m. Monique van den Eynde; children: Robin, Katherine. S.B. in Aero. Engring, MIT, 1958, S.M., 1958, Ph.D. in Math, 1965. Aerospace technologist NASA, Langley AFB, 1958; prof. applied math. U. Va., Charlottesville, 1966—. Contbr. articles to sci. jours. Served with USAF, 1959-62. NATO fellow, 1972; NSF grantee, 1972—. Mem. Math. Assn. Am., Am. Soc. Mechanics, ASME, Soc. for Natural Philosophy, Delta Psi. Home: 2116 Morris Rd Charlottesville VA 22903-1723 Office: U Va Inst Applied Math and Mech Thornton Hall Charlottesville VA 22903-2442

SIMMONDS, RAE NICHOLS, musician, composer, educator; b. Lynn, Mass., Feb. 25, 1919; d. Raymond Edward and Abbie Iola (Spinney) Nichols; m. Carter Fillebrown, Jr., June 27, 1941 (div. May 15, 1971); children: Douglas C. (dec.), Richard A., Mary L., Donald E.; m. Ronald John Simmonds, Oct. 9, 1971 (dec. Nov. 1995). AA, Westbrook Coll., Portland, Maine, 1981; B in Music Performance summa cum laude, U. Maine, 1984; MS in Edn., U. So. Maine, 1989; PhD, Walden U., 1994. Founder, dir. Studio of Music/Children's Studio of Drama, Portsmouth, N.H., 1964-71, Studio of Music, Bromley, Eng., 1971-73, Bromley Children's Theatre, 1971-73, Oughterard Children's Theatre, County Galway, Ireland, 1973-74, Studio of Music, Portland, Maine, 1977—; resident playwright Children's Theatre of Maine, Portland, 1979-81; organist/choir dir. Stevens Ave. Congl. Ch., Portland, 1987-95; field faculty advisor Norwich U., Montpelier, Vt., 1995; field advisor grad. program Vt. Coll., Norwich U., 1995; cons./educator mus. tng. for disabled vets. VA, Portsmouth, N.H., 1966-69; show pianist and organist, mainland U.S.A., 1939-59, Hawaii, 1959-62, Rae Nichols Trio, 1962—. Author/composer children's musical: Shamrock Road, 1980 (Blue Stocking award 1980), Glooscap, 1980; author/composer original scripts and music: Cinderella, If I Were a Princess, Beauty and the Beast, Baba Yaga - A Russian Folk Tale, The Journey - Musical Bible Story, The Perfect Gift - A Christmas Legend; original stories set to music include: Heidi, A Little Princess, Tom Sawyer, Jungle Book, Treasure Island; compositions include: London Jazz Suite, Bitter Suite, Jazz Suite for Trio, Sea Dream, Easter (chorale), others. Recipient Am. Theatre Wing Svc. award, 1944, Pease AFB Svc. Club award, 1967, Bumpus award Westbrook Coll., 1980; Nat. Endowment for Arts grantee, 1969-70; Women's Lit. scholar, 1980, Westbrook scholar, 1980-81, Nason scholar, 1983; Kelaniya U. (Colombo, Sri Lanka) rsch. fellow, 1985-86. Mem. ASCAP, Musicians Assn. of Hawaii, Internat. League Women Composers, Music Tchrs. of Maine, Am. Guild of Organists, Music Tchrs. Nat. Assn., Internat. Alliance for Women in Music, Doctorate Assn. N.Y. Educators, Inc., Delta Omicron, Phi Kappa Phi. Democrat. Episcopalian. Avocations: travel, philately. Home: Back Bay Tower 401 Cumberland Ave Apt 1004 Portland ME 04101-2875

SIMMONS, ADELE SMITH, foundation president, former educator; b. Lake Forest, Ill., June 21, 1941; d. Hermon Dunlap and Ellen T. (Thorne) Smith; m. John L. Simmons; children—Ian, Erica, Kevin. BA in Social Studies with honors, Radcliffe Coll., 1963; PhD, Oxford U., Eng., 1969; LHD (hon.), Lake Forest Coll., 1976, Amherst Coll., 1977, Franklin Pierce Coll., 1978, U. Mass., 1978, Alverno Coll., 1982, Marlboro Coll., 1987, Smith Coll., 1988, Mt. Holyoke Coll., 1989, Am. U., 1992, Tufts U., 1994. Asst. prof. Tufts U., Boston, 1969-72; dean Jackson Coll., Medford, Mass., 1970-72; asst. prof. history, dean student affairs Princeton U., N.J., 1972-77; pres. Hampshire Coll., Amherst, Mass., 1977-89, John D. and Catherine T. MacArthur Found., Chgo., 1989—; bd. dirs. Marsh & McLennan, N.Y.C., 1st Chgo. Corp./NBD, Synergos, Union of Concerned Scientists; cons. Ford. Found., Stockholm Internat. Peace Rsch. Inst., Radcliffe Coll.; former corr. in Mauritius and Tunisia for N.Y. Times, The Economist; high level adv. bd. UN, 1993—. Co-author: (with Freeman, Dunkle, Blau) Exploitation from 9 to 5: Twentieth Century Fund Task Force Report on Working Women, 1975; author: Modern Mauritius, 1982; contbr. articles on edn. and pub. policy in The N.Y. Times, Christian Sci. Monitor, The Bulletin of Atomic Scientist, Harper's, The Atlantic Monthly and others. Commr. Pres.'s Commn. on World Hunger, Washington, 1978-80, Pres.'s Commn. on Environ. Quality, 1991-92; mem. Commn. Global Governance; trustee Carnegie Found. for Advancement Teaching, 1978-86; chair Mayor Richard Daily's Youth Devel. Task Force, 1993-95. Fellow Am. Acad. Arts and Scis.; mem. Phi Beta Kappa. Office: MacArthur Found 140 S Dearborn St Ste 1100 Chicago IL 60603-5202

SIMMONS, ALAN JAY, electrical engineer, consultant; b. N.Y.C., Oct. 14, 1924; s. George and Cherry (Danzig) S.; m. Mary Marcella Bachhuber, April 12, 1947; children, G. David, Peter A., Michael A.; Philip E., Paul I. BS in Physics and Chemistry, Harvard U., 1945; MSEE, MIT, 1948; PhDEE, U. Md., 1957. Electronic scientist Naval Rsch. Lab., Washington, 1948-57; dir. rsch. TRG Inc., Boston, 1957-65; div. mgr. TRG div. Control Data Corp., Boston, 1965-71; group leader MIT Lincoln Lab., Lexington, 1971-87; cons. Winchester, Mass., 1987—. Contbr. articles to profl. jours.; patentee in field. Mem. Town Dem. Com., Winchester, Mass., 1963. Lt. (j.g.) USN, 1943-46. Fellow IEEE (life); mem. AAAS (life), Antennas and Propagation Soc. (pres. 1986). Avocations: gardening, hiking, tennis, travel. Home and Office: PO Box 207 Center Sandwich NH 03227-0207

SIMMONS, ALAN JOHN, philosophy educator; b. Dover, N.J., May 4, 1950; s. Alan Gleason and Jessie May (Ahrens) S.; m. Jean Claire Dreyfus, Mar. 26, 1969 (div. Aug. 1982); 1 child, Shawn Kathleen Simmons; m. Nancy Ellen Schauber, May 30, 1987. AB summa cum laude, Princeton U., 1972; MA, Cornell U., 1975, PhD, 1977. Asst. prof. philosophy U. Va., Charlottesville, 1976-81, assoc. prof. philosophy, 1981-89, prof. philosophy, 1989—; vis. asst. prof. philosophy Johns Hopkins U., Balt., 1981; cons. FBI, Quantico, Va., 1982-88; vis. Prof. Philosophy U. Hawaii, Manoa, 1990. Author: Moral Principles and Political Obligations, 1979, The Lockean Theory of Rights, 1992, On the Edge of Anarchy, 1993; editor: International Ethics, 1985, Punishment, 1995; contbr. articles to profl. jours.; editor Philosophy and Pub. Affairs, 1982—. NEH fellow, 1987-88. Mem. Am. Soc. Polit. Legal Philosophy, N. Am. Soc. Social Philosophy (exec. bd. 1983-84), Va. Philosophical Assn., Am. Philosophical Assn., Phi Beta Kappa, Ctr. Advanced Studies. Office: U Va Dept Philosophy 521 Cabell Hall Charlottesville VA 22903-3125

SIMMONS, BILL, newsman; b. Little Rock, Ark., Sept. 23, 1941; s. William F. and Pauline (Hollenberger) S.; m. Jane, Dec. 27, 1962; children: Theodosia Jane, William Tobias. Newsman AP, Little Rock, Ark., 1962-90, chief of bur., 1990—. Author (short stories) Hunter, Negro; also poems. Named Journalist of Yr., U. Ark., Little Rock, 1983. Home: 13803 Alexander Rd Alexander AR 72002-1509 Office: AP Ste 100 10802 Executive Center Dr Little Rock AR 72211-4377

SIMMONS, CAROLINE THOMPSON, civic worker; b. Denver, Aug. 22, 1910; d. Huston and Caroline Margaret (Cordes) Thompson; m. John Farr Simmons, Nov. 11, 1936; children: John Farr (dec.), Huston T., Malcolm M. (dec.). AB, Bryn Mawr Coll., 1931; MA (hon.), Amherst Coll. Chmn. women's com. Corcoran Gallery Art, 1965-66; vice chmn. women's com. Smithsonian Assos., 1969-71; pres. Decatur House Council, 1963-71; mem. bd. Nat. Theatre, 1979-80; trustee Washington Opera, 1955-65; bd. dirs. Fgn. Student Svc. Coun., 1956-79; mem. Washington Home Bd., 1955-60; bd. dirs. Smithsonian Friends of Music, 1977-79; commr. Nat. Mus. Am. Art, 1979-89; mem. Folger com. Folger Shakespeare Libr., 1979-86, trustee emeritus, 1986—; mem. Washington bd. Am. Mus. in Britain, 1970-93; bd. dirs. Found. Preservation of Historic Georgetown, 1975-89; trustee Marpat Found., 1987—, Amherst Coll., 1979-81, Dacor-Bacon House Found., Phillips Collection, 1990—, Georgetown Presbyn. Ch., 1989-91; v.p. internat. coun. Mus. Modern Art, N.Y.C., 1964-90, emeritus trustee; bd. dirs. Alliance Francaise. Recipient award for eminent svc. Folger Shakespeare Libr., 1986. Mem. Soc. Women Geographers, Sulgrave Club, Chevy Chase Club. Address: 1508 Dumbarton Rock Ct NW Washington DC 20007-3048

SIMMONS, CHARLES, author; b. N.Y.C., Aug. 17, 1924; s. Charles and Mary (Landrigan) S.; m. Helen Elizabeth Fitzgerald, Feb. 8, 1947 (div.); children: Deirdre, Maud; m. Nancy Nicholas, Sept. 17, 1977 (div.). A.B., Columbia U., 1948. Picture editor Unicorn Press, N.Y.C., 1948-51; mem. staff N.Y. Times, 1951-84, asst. book rev. editor, 1963-84; exec. editor Memories mag., 1988-90; editor-at-large Travel Holiday, 1991-93; contbg. editor Penthouse, 1991-92; author/editor Wordworks, 1993-96; vis. writer Am. Acad. in Rome, 1981; regents' lectr. U. Calif. at Santa Barbara, 1981; adj. prof. Sch. Arts, Columbia U., 1981. Author: Powdered Eggs, 1964 (William Faulkner award notable 1st novel), An Old Fashioned Darling, 1971, Wrinkles, 1978, The Belles Lettres Papers, 1987, also stories, articles, lit. criticism: editor (with Nona Balakian) The Creative Present: Notes on Contemporary American Fiction, 1963, (with Alexander Coleman) All There Is to Know: Readings from the Illustrious 11th Edition of Encyclopedia Britannica, 1994. Served with AUS, 1943-46. Home: 221 W 82nd St New York NY 10024-5406

SIMMONS, CLYDE, professional football player; b. Lanes, S.C., Aug. 4, 1964. Student, Western Carolina. Former defensive end Phila. Eagles, 1986-94; with Ariz. Cardinals, 1994—. Named NFL All-Pro team defensive end, The Sporting News, 1991. Played in Pro Bowl, 1991, 92. Office: Ariz Cardinals PO Box 888 Phoenix AZ 85001-0888

SIMMONS, DEIDRE WARNER, performing company executive; b. Easton, Pa., May 11, 1955; d. Francis Joseph and Irene Carol (Burd) Mooney; m. Robert D. Jacobson, June 27, 1981 (div. Mar. 1989); m. William Richard Simmons, Aug. 18, 1990; children: Caitlin Dawn, Abigail Patricia, Samantha Irene. BA in Music, Montclair State Coll., 1978. Music tchr. Warren Hills Regional Sch., Washington, N.J., 1978-80; devel. dir. N.J. Shakespeare Festival, Madison, 1981-83; dir. contbns. Parent Found., Lancaster, Pa., 1983-86; exec. dir. Fulton Opera House, Lancaster, 1986—, capital campaign counsel, 1990-95; mem. adv. bd. Mellon Bank. Vice chmn. bd. dirs. Ind. Eye, Lancaster, 1986-89; mem. adv. com. Lancaster Cultural Coun., 1988—. Mem. Theatre Communications Group, League Hist. Theatres. Avocations: piano, singing. Office: Fulton Opera House 12 N Prince St PO Box 1865 Lancaster PA 17603

SIMMONS, DIANA A., elementary education educator; b. San Diego, Dec. 26, 1936; m. Lewis A. Simmons, Sept. 2, 1957; children: Lisa Simmons Hansen, Marcia Simmons Westfall, Jeffrey. BA, W.Va. Wesleyan Coll., 1975, MAT, 1977. Classroom tchr. Main St. Sch., Buckhannon, W.Va., 1975-78, B-U Intermediate Sch., Buckhannon, 1978—. Mem. AAUW (v.p., pres. 1992-94), Delta Kappa Gamma. Home: 50 Boggess St Buckhannon WV 26201-2145

SIMMONS, EDWIN HOWARD, marine corps officer, historian; b. Paulsboro, N.J., Aug. 25, 1921; s. Edwin Lonsdale and Nettie Emma (Vankirk) S.; m. Frances Bliss, Apr. 25, 1962; children: Edwin Howard, Clarke Vankirk, Bliss, Courtney. B.A., Lehigh U., 1942; M.A., Ohio State U., 1955; postgrad., Amphibious Warfare Sch., 1949-50, Nat. War Coll., 1966-67. Commd. 2d lt. USMC, 1942, advanced through grades to brig. gen., 1967; asst. prof. NROTC, Ohio State U., 1952-55; with Hdqrs. Marine Corps, 1955- 59; naval attache Dominican Republic, 1959-60; with Hdqrs. Marine Corps and Joint Staff, 1962-65, 3d Marine Div., 1965-66, 1st Marine Div., Vietnam, 1970-71; dep. fiscal dir. Marine Corps, 1967-70; dir. Marine Corps history and museums USMC Hdqrs., Arlington, Va., 1971-95, dir. emeritus, 1996—; pres. Am. Mil. Inst., 1979; v.p. U.S. Commn. Mil. History, 1979-83; exec. v.p. Marine Corps Hist. Found., 1979—; pres. Coun. Am. Mil. Past, 1991-95. Author: The United States Marines, 1974, Marines, 1987; Mng. editor: Marine Corps Gazette, 1946-49; sr. editor: Publs. Group, Marine Corps Schs., 1960-61; Contbr. to numerous books, encys., mags., jours. and annuals. Decorated D.S.M., Silver Star, Legion of Merit with two gold stars, Bronze Star with gold star, Meritorious Service medal, Navy Commendation medal, Purple Heart; knight Nat. Order of Vietnam, Vietnamese Cross of Gallantry with 2 palms and silver star; recipient Centennial Disting. Grad. medallion Ohio State U., 1970. Fellow Co. Mil. Historians; mem. Am. Soc. Mil. Comptrollers (nat. v.p. 1967-69, pres. 1969-70), Nat. War Coll. Alumni Assn. (v.p. 1969-70, 74-75), Phi Beta Kappa, Omicron Delta Kappa, Phi Sigma Kappa. Home: 9020 Charles Augustine Dr Alexandria VA 22308-2822 Office: USMC Mus MC Hist Ctr Navy Yard Bldg 160 Washington DC 20374-0580

SIMMONS, ELROY, JR., retired utility executive; b. Johnstown, Pa., Sept. 23, 1928; s. Elroy and Hazel Maria (Shomo) S. BS in Bus. Adminstrn., U. Pitts., 1951. With Pa. Electric Co., Johnstown, 1953, system treasury asst., 1969-71, system coordinator, treasury services, 1971-74, asst. treas., 1974-79, sec., treas., 1979-90; ret., 1990. Bd. dirs. Community Arts Ctr. of Cambria County, 1987-95. With CIC, U.S. Army, 1951-53. Mem. Pa. Electric Assn. (customer relations com. 1965-69), Nat. Corp. Cash Mgmt. Assn., Nat. Assn. Accts., Nat. Assn. Corp. Treas. Republican. Methodist. Home: 1023 Hillside Trl Johnstown PA 15905-1234

SIMMONS, EMORY G., mycologist; b. Ind., Apr. 12, 1920. AB, Wabash Coll., 1941; AM, DePauw U., 1946; PhD in Botany, U. Mich., 1950; DSc in Microbiology (hon.), Kasetsant U., Thailand, 1988. Instr. bacteriology & botany DePauw U., Greencastle, Ind., 1946-47; asst. prof. botany Dartmouth Coll., Hanover, N.H., 1950-53; mycologist U.S. Army Natick Labs., 1953-58, head mycology lab., 1958-74; prin. investor Devel. Ctr. Cult Collection of Fungi, 1974-77; prof. botany U. Mass., Amherst, 1974-77, prof. microbiology, 1977-87, ret., 1987; rsch. assoc. Wabash Coll., Crawfordsville, Ind., 1987—; chmn. adv. com. fungi Am. Type Cult Collection; U.S. rep. Expert Group on Fungus Taxonomy, Orgn. Econ. Coop. & Devel.; rsch. fellow Sec. Army, Thailand Indonesia, 1968-69; adj. prof. U. R.I., 1972-74; mem. exec. bd. U.S. Fedn. Cult Collections, 1974-76, pres., 1976-78; pres., chmn. bd. dirs. Second Internat. Mycology Congress Inc., 1975-78; mem. adv. com. cult collections UN Environ. Program/UNESCO/Internat. Cell Rsch. Orgn., 1977—. Mem AAAS, Mycological Soc. Am. (sec- treas. 1963-65, v.p. 1966, pres. 1968, Disting. Mycologist award 1990), Brit. Mycological Soc., Internat. Assn. Plant Taxonomists. Achievements include research in taxonomic mycology, taxonomy of Fungi imperfecti, taxonomy and cultural characteristics of Ascomycetes. Office: 717 Thornwood Rd Crawfordsville IN 47933-2760

SIMMONS, GENE, musician; b. Haifa, Israel, Aug. 25, 1949; came to U.S., 1958, naturalized, 1963; A.B.A., Sullivan Coll., SUNY, 1970; B.A., Richmond Coll., CUNY, 1972. Singer, songwriter, actor, 1970—; founder, 1973 thereafter mem. group Kiss. Albums include: Alive, 1975, Kiss-The Originals, 1976, Destroyer, 1976, Rock & Roll Over, 1976, Love Gun, 1977, Alive II, 1977, Double Platinum, 1978, Gene Simmons, 1978, Dynasty, 1979, Unmasked, 1980, Music From the Elder, 1981, Creatures of the Night, 1982, Lick It Up, 1983, Animalize, 1984, Kiss, 1974, Hotter Than Hell, 1974, Dressed to Kill, 1975, Beth, 1976, I Was Made for Lovin' You, 1979, Asylum, 1985, Crazy Nights, 1987, Hot In The Shade, 1989, Smashes, Thrashes and Hits, 1989, Revenge, 1992; film appearance in Kiss-Attack of the Phantom, 1978, Runaway, 1984-85. Winner 16 Gold Record Albums, 12 Platinum Record Albums, 2 Gold Single Records. Mem. Am. Fedn. Musicians, AFTRA, ASCAP. Inventor of Axe bass guitar, 1980. Office: care Polygram Records Inc Worldwide Pla 825 8th Ave New York NY 10019-7416 *Listen to everyone around you, but do only what you believe.*

SIMMONS, GEORGE FINLAY, mathematics educator; b. Austin, Tex., Mar. 3, 1925; s. George Finlay and Armede Victoria (Hatcher) S.; m. Hope Bridgeford, Sept. 11, 1954; 1 child, Nancy Bingham. BS, Caltech, 1946; MS, U. Chgo., 1948; PhD, Yale U., 1957. Instr. U. Chgo., 1947-50, U. Maine, Orono, 1950-52, Yale U., New Haven, 1952-56; asst. prof. U. R.I., Kingston, 1956-58, Williams College, Williamstown, Mass., 1958-62; assoc. prof. math. Colo. Coll., Colorado Springs, 1962-65, prof., 1965-90, prof. emeritus, 1990—. Author: Introduction Topology and Modern Analysis, 1962, Differential Equations, 1972, 2d edit., 1991, Precalculus Mathematics in a Nutshell, 1981, Calculus with Analytic Geometry, 1985, 2d edit., 1995, Calculus Gems: Brief Lives and Memorable Mathematics, 1992. Mem. Math. Assn. Am. Avocations: travel, cooking, trout fishing, billiards. Home: 1401 Wood Ave Colorado Springs CO 80907-7348 Office: Colorado College Dept Math Colorado Springs CO 80903

SIMMONS, HARDWICK, investment banker; b. Balt., June 8, 1940; s. Edward Ball and Margaret (Hardwick) S.; m. Sarah Bradlee Dolan, Sept. 9, 1962; children—Elizabeth, Huntington, Benjamin. B.A., Harvard U., 1962, M.B.A., 1966. With Shearson Lehman Bros. Inc., 1966—; regional officer Shearson Lehman Bros. Inc., New Eng., 1972-75; vice chmn., dir. Shearson Lehman Hutton Inc. (formerly Shearson Lehman Bros. Inc.), N.Y.C., 1975-90; chief exec. officer Prudential Securities Inc., N.Y.C., 1990—; dir. Chgo. Bd. Options Exchange. Served with USMCR, 1959-60. Mem. Bond Club N.Y.C. Republican. Office: Prudential Securities 1 Seaport Plz New York NY 10038-3526*

SIMMONS, HARRIS H., banker; b. Salt Lake City, June 25, 1954; s. Roy William and Elizabeth (Ellison) S. BA in Econs., U. Utah, 1977; MBA, Harvard U., 1980. Comml. loan officer Allied Bancshares, Houston, 1980-81; asst. v.p. Zions Bancorp, Salt Lake City, 1981, fin. v.p., 1981-82; sr. v.p. fin. Zions Utah Bancorp, Salt Lake City, 1982-83, exec. v.p., sec., treas., 1984-86, pres., 1986—; pres. Zions Mortgage Co., 1987—; CEO Zions Bancorp, Salt Lake City, 1990—; pres., CEO Zions 1st Nat. Bank, 1990—; bd. dirs. Questar, Inc., Salt Lake City, Entrada Industries, Inc., Salt Lake City, Keystone Comm., Salt Lake City, Simmons Family, Inc., Salt Lake City, Zions 1st Nat. Bank, Salt Lake City, Nat. Bank Ariz., Tucson, Nev. State Bank, Las Vegas. Bd. dirs. United Way, Salt Lake City, 1983-89; bd. dirs. Utah Symphony, 1986—, vice chmn., 1990-95, chmn., 1995—; trustee Salt Lake City C.C., 1993—; v.p. fin. Great Salt Lake coun. Boy Scouts Am., 1991-95; co-chair Greater Salt Lake Shelter-the-Homeless Com., 1986-89, v.p., 1989—. Mem. Utah Bankers Assn. (bd.dirs. 1987-92, chmn. 1990-91), Salt Lake Area C. of C. (bd. dirs. 1991-94), Phi Beta Kappa. Mormon. Office: Zions Bancorp 1380 Kennecott Building Bldg Salt Lake City UT 84133-1102

SIMMONS, JAMES CHARLES, lawyer; b. N.Y.C., June 5, 1935; s. James Knight and Helen (Bielefeld) S.; m. Carolyn Ann Edwards, June 12, 1957; children: James M., Shawn M. Dzielawa. BSMetE, Lehigh U., 1957; JD, Duquesne U., 1965. Bar: Pa. 1965, U.S. Dist. Ct. (we. dist.) Pa. 1965, U.S. Ct. Appeals (3rd cir.) 1965, U.S. Ct. Appeals (fed. cir.) 1977. Metall. engr. Crucible Steel Co. Am., Midland, Pa., 1957-66; contract adminstr. Nuclear Materials & Equipment Corp., Apollo, Pa., 1966-67; patent atty. Bausch & Lomb, Rochester, N.Y., 1967-69; asst. gen. patent counsel Air Products and Chem., Inc., Allentown, Pa., 1969-94; sr. atty. Ratner & Prestia, Valley Forge, Pa., 1994—. Mem. ABA, Am. Intellectual Property Law Assn. (sec. 1993), Pa. Bar Assn., Phila. Intellectual Property Law Assn., Bar Assn. Lehigh County. Office: Ratner & Prestia PO Box 980 500 N Gulph Rd Valley Forge PA 19482

SIMMONS, JAMES F., textiles executive; b. 1944. BA, Ga. Inst. Tech., 1966, MA, 1967. With Celanese Fibers Mktg. Co., Charlotte, N.C., 1968-90, Celanese Tech. Fibers, Chgo., 1968-90, Hoechst Celanese Textile Fibers Group, N.Y.C., 1968-90; v.p., gen. mgr. Hoechst Celanese Chem. Group, Dallas, 1990—. Office: Hoechst Celanese Chem Group 2300 Archdale Dr Charlotte NC 28210*

SIMMONS, J(AMES) GERALD, management consultant; b. Atlanta, Sept. 17, 1929; s. Joseph D. and Nell (Ray) S. BBA, U. Miami, 1956; student advanced mgmt. program, Harvard U., 1969. With IBM Corp., 1956-71; dir. mktg. Data Processing divsn. IBM, White Plains, N.Y., 1969-71; v.p., gen. mgr. dept. and splty. store divsn. Revlon Inc., N.Y.C., 1971-73; v.p. mktg. Wiltek Inc., Norwalk, Conn., 1973-76; pres. Handy HRM Corp., N.Y.C., 1976—. With U.S. Army, 1951-54. Mem. Greenwich (Conn.) Country Club. Avocations: tennis, squash, golf. Office: Handy HRM Corp 250 Park Ave New York NY 10177

SIMMONS, JEAN, actress; b. London, Jan. 31, 1929; d. Charles and Winifred Ada (Lovel) S.; m. Stewart Granger, Dec. 20, 1950 (div. June 1960); 1 dau., Tracy; m. Richard Brooks, Nov. 1, 1960; 1 dau., Kate. Ed., Orange Hill Sch., Burnt Oak, London. Motion picture actress, appearing in English and Am. films including Great Expectations, 1946, Black Narcissus, 1947, Hamlet, 1948 (Acad. award nomination), Adam and Evelyn, 1949, The Actress, 1953, Young Bess, 1953, Guys and Dolls, 1956, The Big Country, 1958, Home Before Dark, 1958, Spartacus, 1960, Elmer Gantry, 1960, The Grass Is Greener, 1960, All the Way Home, 1963, Rough Night in Jericho, 1967, Divorce American Style, 1967, The Happy Ending, 1969 (Acad. award nomination), The Dawning, 1989; also theatre appearance A Little Night Music, Phila. and on tour, 1974; appeared in: TV mini-series The Dain Curse, 1978, A Small Killing, 1981, Valley of the Dolls, 1981, The Thornbirds, 1983 (Emmy award), North and South, 1985, North and South Book II, 1986; TV film: December Flower, 1987, The Legend of Lost Loves, 1988, Great Expectations, 1989; guest TV series Murder She Wrote, 1989, In the Heat of the Night, 1993; TV series Dark Shadows, 1991. Office: care Geoffrey Barr 9400 Readcrest Dr Beverly Hills CA 90210-2552 Office: Susan Smith & Assocs 121 N San Vicente Blvd Beverly Hills CA 90211-2303*

SIMMONS, JEAN ELIZABETH MARGARET (MRS. GLEN R. SIMMONS), chemistry educator; b. Cleve., Jan. 20, 1914; d. Frank Charles and Sarah Anne (Johnston) Saurwein; m. Glen R. Simmons, Nov. 14, 1935; children: Sally Anne, (Frank) Charles, James Fraser. B.A., Western Reserve U., 1933; Ph.D. (Stieglitz fellow 1935-37), U. Chgo., 1938. Faculty Barat Coll., Lake Forest, Ill., 1938-58; prof., chmn. dept. chemistry Barat Coll., 1948-58; faculty Upsala Coll., East Orange, N.J., 1959—; prof. Upsala Coll., 1963-84, prof. emeritus, 1984—, chmn. dept. chemistry, 1965-71, 74, 76-81, chmn. sci. curriculum study, Luth. Ch. Am. grantee, 1965-68, chmn. div. natural scis. and maths., 1965-69, asst. to pres., 1968-73, 78-86; Coordinator basic scis. Evang. Hosp. Sch. Nursing, Chgo., 1943-46; lectr. sci. topics; participant various White House Confs. Contbr. articles to publs. in field. Troop leader Girl Scouts U.S.A., Wheaton, Ill., 1952-58, neighborhood chmn., 1956-57, dist. chmn., DuPage County, 1958; chmn. U. Chgo. Alumni Fund Dr., Wheaton, 1957, 58, Princeton, N.J., 1964, 65; mem. nursing adv. com. East Orange (N.J.) Gen. Hosp., 1963-73; pres. Virginia Gildersleeve Internat. Fund, 1975-81, bd. dirs., 1969-83, chmn. nominating com., 1985-87, oral history com., 1981, hon. mem., 1996. Recipient Lindback Found. award for disting. teaching, 1964; vis. fellow Princeton U., 1977. Fellow Am. Inst. Chemists, AAAS (council 1969-71); mem. Am. Chem. Soc., AAUW (br. treas. 1960-62, chmn. sci. topic 1963-65, state v.p. program 1964, nat. sci. topic implementation chmn. 1965, 66, state dir. 1967-68, 71-72, state pres. 1968-70, 50 Yr. Cert. 1989), Fedn. Orgns. Profl. Women (nat. pres. 1974-75), Internat. Fedn. Univ. Women (alt. del. for U.S. at conf. 1968, 77, 83, del. conf. 1974, ofcl. observer UN Conf. Vienna 1979, Nairobi 1981, convenor membership com. 1980-84, adv. bd. 1980—, oral history com. 1990), AAUP (charter, past chpt. pres.), Phi Beta Kappa (pres. North Jersey alumni assn. 1973-74), Sigma Xi, Sigma Delta Epsilon (nat. pres. 1970-71, dir. 1972-78, edn. liaison 1978-87, chmn. nom. 1986-87, hon., award sci. edn. 1989). Episcopalian. Home: 40 Balsam Ln Princeton NJ 08540-5327

SIMMONS, JESSE DOYLE, minister, educator; b. South Boston, Va., Sept. 3, 1926; s. Heyward Benjamin and Elizabeth (Smith) S.; m. Lois Virginia Ingram, Oct. 12, 1947; children: Nova Lee Norman, Debra S. Sturkie, Virginia S. Miller, Jesse D. Jr. BTh, Holmes Theol. Sem, Greenville, S.C., 1954, B Sacred Lit., 1977; DD (hon.), Holmes Theol. Sem., Greenville, S.C., 1970; EdB, Wade Hampton Coll., Florence, S.C., 1956; DRE (hon.), Agape Christian U., 1994. Ordained to ministry Internat. Pentecostal Holiness Ch., 1952. Evangelist Internat. Pentecostal Holiness Ch., Lake City, S.C., 1950-54; pastor Internat. Pentecostal Holiness Ch., Columbia, S.C., 1954-75; dir. world missions and evangelism S.C. conf. Internat. Pentecostal Holiness Ch., 1975-82; supt. S.C. Conf. Internat. Pentecostal Holiness Ch., Lake City, 1982-85; asst. gen. supt., dir. evangelism, ch. loan fund, dept. armed forces Internat. Pentecostal Holiness Ch., Oklahoma City, 1985-89; vice chmn., dir. world missions dept. chaplains' ministries Internat. Pentecostal Holiness Ch. of S.C. Conf., Oklahoma City, 1989-93; chmn. bd. trustees Holmes Coll. of the Bible, 1979—; gen. exec. bd. Gen. Bd. Adminstrn. Internat. Pentecostal Holiness Ch., Oklahoma City, 1985—; mem. bd. adminstrn. Nat. Assn. Evangelicals, Wheaton, Ill., 1990—, Pentecostal Fellowship N.Am., 1990—. Exec. editor Witnes, 1985-89, Worldorama, 1989—, Keynotes, 1989—. State constable, S.C., 1976; notary publ., S.C., 1982; trustee Holmes Coll. Bible, Greenville, S.C., 1979—. With

U.S. Army, 1944-46, PTO. Mem. Am. Legion. Republican. Home: 8117 W Willow Creek Blvd Oklahoma City OK 73162-2018 Office: Pentecostal Holiness Ch PO Box 12609 Oklahoma City OK 73157-2609 *While much of society place great emphasis on self, independence and personal fulfillment, we would do well to remember that a fulfilled life is a life lived out for others, interdependent and challenging others to fulfillment.*

SIMMONS, JOHN DEREK, investment banker; b. Essex, Eng., July 17, 1931; came to U.S., 1952; s. Simon Leonard and Eve (Smart) S.; m. Rosalind Wellish, Mar. 5, 1961; children: Peter Lawrence, Sharon Leslie. BS, Columbia, 1956; MBA, Rutgers U., 1959; postgrad. NYU, 1959-62.Chief cost acct. Airborne Accessories, Hillside, N.J., 1952-57; sr. cost analyst Curtiss-Wright Corp., Wood Ridge, N.J., 1957; sr. fin. analyst internat. group Ford Motor Co., Jersey City, N.J., 1958-60; rsch. assoc. Nat. Assn. Accts., N.Y.C., 1960-64; asst. to v.p. fin. Air Reduction Co., Inc., 1965-67; mgr. corp. planning Anaconda Wire & Cable Co., N.Y.C., 1968; ind. fin. cons., 1968-71; assoc. cons. Rogers, Slade and Hill, Inc., N.Y.C., 1969-71; v.p., security analyst, economist Moore & Schley, Cameron & Co. (name now changed to Fourteen Rsch. Corp.), 1972-81; v.p., security analyst Merrill Lynch Capital Markets, N.Y.C., 1981-88; security analyst Arnhold and S. Bleichroeder, Inc., N.Y.C., 1988-89; v.p., security analyst, corp. fin. specialist Smith Barney, Harris Upham & Co., Inc., N.Y.C., 1989-90; sr. cons. Carl Byoir & Assocs., N.Y.C., 1991-94; assoc. mng. dir. Commonwealth Assocs., N.Y.C., 1994-95; mng. dir. State St. Capital Markets Corp., N.Y.C., 1996—; lectr. profl. socs. and confs.; lectr. econs., mgmt., polit. sci. Rutgers U., 1957-64. Contbr. articles on econs. of underdeveloped nations, polit. sci., mgmt., fin. to U.S. and fgn. publs. Served to 1st lt. Brit. Army, 1950-52. Granted personal coat of Arms By Queen Elizabeth II: manorial Lord of Ash., Suffolk, Eng. Mem. Am. Econ. Assn., Royal Econ. Soc., N.Y. Soc. Security Analysts, Knight Templar Sovereign Mil. Order of Temple of Jerusalem. Home: 360 E 72nd St New York NY 10021-4753 Office: State St Capital Markets Corp 17 State St New York NY 10004

SIMMONS, JOSEPH JACOB, III, federal commissioner; b. Muskogee, Okla., Mar. 26, 1925; s. Jacob, Jr. and Eva (Flowers) S.; m. Bernice Elizabeth Miller, Jan. 30, 1947; children: Jacob IV, Mary Agnes, Bernice, Jacolyn, Eva Frances. Student, U. Detroit, 1942-44, 46-47; B.S. in Geol. Engring., St. Louis U., 1949; LLD (hon.), Madonna U., 1991. Registered profl. engr., Okla. V.p., sec.-treas., geologist Simmons Royalty Co., Muskogee, 1949-61; regional oil and gas mobilization specialist U.S. Dept. of the Interior, Battle Creek, Mich., 1961-62; domestic petroleum production specialist Office of Oil and Gas U.S. Dept. of the Interior, Washington, 1962-66, asst. dir. Office of Oil and Gas, 1966-68, dep. adminstr. Oil Import Adminstrn., 1968-69, adminstr. Oil Import Adminstrn., 1969-70, Under Sec., 1983-84; v.p. govt. relations Amerada Hess Corp., N.Y.C., 1970-82; commr. ICC, Washington; vice chmn. ICC, 1986, 89, 93; mem. fuel oil mktg. adv. com. Dept. Energy, 1978-82; commr. Pres.'s Commn. on Exec. Exchange, 1970-81; commr. Statue of Liberty Ellis Island Commn., 1983-88, bd. dirs. Found., 1984-86 ; mem. NAS Bd. of Earth Scis. and Resources, 1984—; mem. adv. bd. Dept. of Interior Outer Continental Shelf, 1984—. Youth dir. NAACP, 1950-55; candidate Okla. Ho. of Reps., 1956, City Council, 1956; trustee Madonna Coll., Livonia, Mich., 1969-76, Morehouse Sch. Medicine, Atlanta, 1990—. Served with USAAF, 1944-46. Recipient Alumni Merit award St. Louis U., 1968, Spl. Act of Service award Dept. Interior, 1963, Outstanding Performance award, 1968, Disting. Service award, 1970. Mem. Am. Assn. Petroleum Geologists (Pub. Service award 1984), Soc. Petroleum Engrs., AIME. Office: ICC 12th Constitution Ave NE Washington DC 20423-0001*

SIMMONS, JOSEPH THOMAS, accountant, educator; b. Forest Lake, Minn., Jan. 23, 1936; s. Roland Thomas and Erma (Rabe) S.; m. Winola Ann Zwald, Aug. 18, 1962 (div.); children: Thomas E, Kevin M. BS in Bus. and Econs., Morningside Coll., 1964; MBA, U. S.D., 1965; PhD in Bus., U. Nebr., 1974. CPA, S.D. Prof. acctg. and fin. U. S.D., Vermillion, 1966-69, 75—, dir. Sch. Bus., 1975—; prof. U. Nebr., Lincoln, 1969-71, U. Man., Winnipeg, Can., 1971-75; prin. Simmons and Assocs. Mgmt. Cons., Rapid City, S.D., 1981—; pvt. practice acctg. Rapid City, 1982—; pres. Simmons Profl. Fin. Planning, Vermillion, 1983—; bd. dirs. Powerhouse Computers, Sioux Falls, N.D., v.p. fin., 1992-93; bd. dirs. MDU Resources Inc., Bismarck, N.D., RE/spec, Rapid City, Gro-Tech, Rapid City, Dairlean Inc., Sioux Falls; vis. prof. U. Warsaw, Poland, 1994. Served with U.S. Army, 1958-60. Mem. AICPA, Am. Acctg. Assn., Fin. Mgmt. Assn., S.D. Soc. CPA's. Republican. Methodist. Home and Office: Ponderosa Acres Lot 2 Burbank SD 57010-9731

SIMMONS, LAWRENCE WILLIAM, health care company executive; b. Omaha, May 7, 1947; s. Albin Pachola and Leella Clarice (Franklin) S.; m. Leanna Carol McGee, Nov. 3, 1968; children: Scott, Anthony. Assoc. Gen. Studies, U. Nebr., 1977, B Gen. Studies, 1978. Pharm. sales rep. 3M Pharms., Omaha, 1972-83; dist. sales mgr. 3M Pharms., Chgo., 1983-89; regional sales mgr. midwest region 3M Pharms., St. Paul, 1989-92; group bus. mgr. pharm. and personal care 3M Pharms., Mexico City, 1992-95; group bus. dir. 3M Mexico/Div. V Health Care, 1995—; cluster mem. Xavier U., New Orleans, 1987—; minority outreach rep. 3M, St. Paul, 1987—. With U.S. Army, 1968-71, Vietnam. Mem. Kappa Alpha Psi (polemarch 1981-83, best chpt. award 1983). Office: 7525 Currell Blvd Woodbury MN 55125

SIMMONS, LEE HOWARD, book publishing company executive; b. N.Y.C., Aug. 17, 1935; s. Lee H. and Frances (Goodell) S.; m. Barbara E. Beck, Sept. 6, 1961; children: Christopher, Elizabeth. A.B., Duke U., 1958; M.A., NYU, 1960. Sales mgr. The Orion Press, N.Y.C., 1959-60; advt. mgr. Doubleday & Co., N.Y.C., 1960-61; account exec. Franklin Spier, N.Y.C., 1961-68, v.p., 1968-78, pres., 1978-86; exec. v.p., assoc. pub. Arbor House Pub. Co., N.Y.C., 1986-88; pres. Lee Simmons Assocs. Inc., Port Washington, N.Y., 1988—; chmn. Oblivion Press, N.Y.C., 1977-82, N.Y. is Book Country, N.Y.C., 1986-87. Treas. Port Washington Estates Assn., 1975-78. Episcopalian. Home: 40 Richards Rd Port Washington NY 11050-3416 Office: Lee Simmons Assocs Inc 4 Boylston St Port Washington NY 11050

SIMMONS, MARCIA ANN, reporter; b. Topeka, Kans., Oct. 29, 1954; d. William Eugene Simmons and Ruth Mae (Engle) Shaw; m. George Z. Guzowski, Mar. 20, 1982 (dec. Nov. 1987); children: Kevin King, Stefan Guzowski, William Lindstedt. BA, U. N.Mex., 1977. Anchor, reporter KUNM Radio, Albuquerque, 1975-76; anchor reporter KNWZ Radio, Albuquerque, 1976-77, KOAT-TV, Albuquerque, 1981-88, KOA, Denver, 1991—; reporter, editor Old Town Times, Albuquerque, 1976; assignments editor, anchor KGGM-TV, Albuquerque, 1977-81; reporter KOB-TV, Albuquerque, 1990; media advisor N.Mex. Games, Albuquerque, 1988. Writer, reporter Nativity Newspaper, Broomfield, Colo., 1994. Bd. dirs. Gov.'s Task Force on Developmentally Disabled, Santa Fe, N.Mex., 1988-89, N.Mex. Animal Humane Assn., Albuquerque, 1986; media advisor Bob Schwartz for Dist. Atty. Campaign, Albuquerque, 1988. Recipient Nat. Gavel award ABA, 1982, Reporting award AP, 1985. Mem. Am. Women in Radio and TV. Democrat. Roman Catholic. Avocations: skiing, writing, camping, reading. Home: 1162 Clubhouse Dr Broomfield CO 80020-1240

SIMMONS, MARVIN GENE, geophysics educator; b. Dallas, May 15, 1929; s. Burt H. and Mable (Marshall) S.; divorced; children—Jon Eric, Debra Lynn, Sandra Kay, Pamela Jean. B.S., Tex. Agrl. and Mech. Coll., 1949; M.S., So. Methodist U., 1958; Ph.D., Harvard U., 1962. Petroleum engr. Humble Oil Co., 1949-51; propr. gravel business, 1953-58; asst. prof. So. Meth. U., 1962-65; prof. geophysics MIT, 1965-89, prof. emeritus, 1989—; prin. Hager-Richter Geoscience Inc., 1989—; Cons. NASA, 1965-72; chief scientist NASA (Manned Spacecraft Center), Houston, 1969-71; cons. on siting of nuclear facilities; sec. Internat. Heat Flow Com., 1967-71; chmn. com. drilling for sci. purposes Nat. Acad. Scis., 1965; Mem. geophysics panel NSF. Served with USAF, 1951-53. NSF postdoctoral fellow, 1961-62. Fellow Geol. Soc. Am., Am. Geophys. Union; mem. ASTM (com. C-18 on dimension stone 1986—), Boston Geol. Soc. (pres. 1967-68), Soc. Exploration Geophysicists, Sigma Xi, Tau Beta Pi. Research on physical properties of materials, lunar exploration, marine geophysics, temperature of earth, regional geophysics, engineering geology and geophysics. Home: 180 N Policy St Salem NH 03079-1916 Office: 8 Industrial Way Unit D10 Salem NH 03079-2837

SIMMONS, MERLE EDWIN, foreign language educator; b. Kansas City, Kans., Sept. 27, 1918; s. Walter Earl and Mabel Sophronia (Shoemaker) S.; m. Concepcion Rojas, Sept. 8, 1948; children: Martha Irene, Mary Alice Simmons Roberts. AB, U. Kans., 1939, MA, 1941; teaching fellow, Harvard U., 1946-47; PhD, U. Mich., 1952. Mem. faculty Ind. U., Bloomington, 1942—; prof. Spanish Ind. U., 1962-83, prof. emeritus, 1983—, dir. grad. studies dept. Spanish and Portuguese, 1967-76, chmn. dept., 1976-81. Author: The Mexican Corrido, 1957, A Bibliography of the Romance and Related Forms in Spanish America, 1963, Folklore Bibliography for 1974, 1977, for 1975, 1979, for 1976, 1981, Santiago F. Puglia, An Early Philadelphia Propagandist for Spanish American Independence, 1977, U.S. Political Ideas in Spanish America Before 1830: A Bibliographical Study, 1977, Los escritos de Juan Pablo Viscardo y Guzmán, 1983, Obra completa de Juan Pablo Viscardo y Guzmán, 1988, La Revolución Norteamericana y la Independencia de Hispanoamérica, 1992, also articles. Decorated Gran Oficial of the Order of the Sun (Peru); grantee Am. Philos. Soc., 1955, 76; grantee Am. Coun. Learned Socs., 1962. Mem. AAUP, Am. Folklore Soc., Am. Assn. Tchrs. Spanish and Portuguese, Conf. Latin Am. History, MLA, Midwest MLA, Midwest Assn. Latin Am. Studies, Nat. Acad. History of Venezuela (corr.), Phi Beta Kappa, Phi Sigma Iota. Home: 4233 Saratoga Dr Bloomington IN 47408-3196 Office: Ind U Ballantine Hall # 857 Bloomington IN 47405

SIMMONS, MICHAEL ANTHONY, dean; m. Margaret Clare Martindale; children: Kristen Ann, Jeffrey Michael, Jennifer Clare Roe, Jason Davis. AB cum laude, Harvard Coll., 1963, MD, 1967. Diplomate Am. Bd. Pediatrics, Am. Bd. Neonatal-Perinatal Medicine. Intern Harriet Lane Svc., Johns Hopkins Hosp., Balt., 1967-68, asst. resident, 1968-69, sr. asst. resident, 1969; chief resident Dept. Pediatrics, U. Colo. Med. Ctr., Denver, 1971-72, rsch. fellow in perinatal medicine, 1972-74, clin. instr. in pediatrics, 1974-77, assoc. prof. pediatrics, 1977; assoc. prof. pediatrics and obstetrics Johns Hopkins U. Sch. Medicine, Balt., 1977-83; prof., chmn. dept. pediatrics U. Utah Sch. of Medicine, Salt Lake City, 1983-94; prof. pediatrics, dean U. N.C. at Chapel Hill Sch. Medicine, 1994—; adj. prof. dept. obstetrics and gynecology U. Utah Sch. of Medicine, Salt Lake City, 1984-94; co-dir. newborn svcs. U. Colo. Med. Ctr., Denver, 1974-77, Johns Hopkins Hosp., 1977-83; mem. staff Denver Gen. Hosp., 1976-77, Denver Children's Hosp., 1976-77; vice chmn. clin. affairs dept. pediatrics Johns Hopkins Hosp., 1981-83; chief of pediatrics U. Utah Med. Ctr., Salt Lake, City, 1983-94; med. dir. Primary Children's Med. Ctr., 1983-94; bd. dirs. Triangle Univs. Licensing Consortium, U. N.C. Hosps. Contbr. numerous articles to profl. jours. Fellow Am. Acad. of Pediatrics (excellence in pediatric rsch. com. 1991—, coun. on govt. affairs 1992—); mem. Perinatal Rsch. Soc. (coun. 1982-84, pres.-elect 1985-87, pres. 1989), Western Soc. for Pediatric Rsch. (coun. 1985-86, pres.-elect 1987, pres. 1988), Soc. for Pediatric Rsch., Am. Bd. Pediatrics (sub-bd. of neonatal-perinatal medicine 1983-89, chmn. 1984-88). Office: U NC Sch of Medicine Chapel Hill NC 27514

SIMMONS, MIRIAM QUINN, state legislator; b. Jackson, Miss., Mar. 28, 1928; d. Charles Buford and Viola (Hamill) Quinn; m. Willie Wronal Simmons, July 10, 1952; children: Dick, Sue, Wronal. BS, Miss. U. for Women, 1949. Tchr. Columbia (Miss.) City Schs., 1949-51, 53-54, literacy coord., 1986-87; home demonstration agt. Coop. Extension Svc., Bay Springs, Miss., 1951-52; tchr. Marion County Schs., Columbia, 1952-53, 54-55, Columbia Tng. Sch., 1961-63, Columbia Acad., 1970-73; rep. Miss. Ho. of Reps., Jackson, 1988—; adv. bd. Magnolia Fed. Bank for Savs; trustee State Inst. Higher Learning, Jackson, 1972-84; dir. Miss. Authority for Ednl. TV, Jackson, 1976-88. Named Marion County Outstanding Citizen Columbia Jr. Aux., 1981. Mem. Miss. Fedn. Women's Clubs, Bus. and Profl. Women's Club, Hilltop Garden Club, Delta Kappa Gamma. Democrat. Methodist. Home: 45 Old Highway 98 E Columbia MS 39429-8172

SIMMONS, PETER, law and urban planning educator; b. N.Y.C., July 19, 1931; s. Michael L. and Mary A. S.; m. Ruth J. Tanfield, Jan. 28, 1951; children: Sam, Lizzard. A.B., U. Calif., Berkeley, 1953, LL.B., 1956; postgrad. (Alvord fellow), U. Wis., 1956-58. Prof. SUNY, Buffalo, 1963-67; mem. faculty Ohio State U., 1967-75, U. Ill., 1972, Case Western Res. U., 1974-75; prof. law and urban planning Rutgers U. Coll. Law, Newark, 1975—, dean, 1975-93; university prof. Rutgers U., 1993—. Contbr. articles to profl. jours. Mem. Ohio Housing Commn., 1972-74; commr. Ohio Reclamation Rev. Bd., 1974-75; chmn. N.J. Criminal Disposition Commn., 1983-84; mem. N.J. Law Revision Commn., 1987—. Mem. Am. Planning Assn., Urban Land Inst., Am. Law Inst., AAUP (nat. council 1973-75). Office: Rutgers U Law Sch 15 Washington St Newark NJ 07102-3105

SIMMONS, RALPH OLIVER, physics educator; b. Kensington, Kans., Feb. 19, 1928; s. Fred Charles and Cornelia (Douglass) S.; m. Janet Lee Lull, Aug. 31, 1952; children: Katherine Ann, Bradley Alan, Jill Christine, Joy Diane. B.A., U. Kans., 1950; B.A. (Rhodes scholar), Oxford U., 1953; Ph.D., U. Ill., 1957. Research assoc. U. Ill., Urbana, 1957-59, faculty physics, 1959—, assoc. prof., 1961-65, prof. physics, 1965—, head physics dept., 1970-86; vis. scientist Ctr. for Study Nuclear Energy, Mol, Belgium, 1965; mem. governing bd. Internat. Symposia on Thermal Expansion, 1970-88; cons. Argonne Nat. Lab., 1978-86, Los Alamos Nat. Lab., 1983-84; chmn. Office of Phys. Scis., NRC, 1978-81; mem. Assembly of Math. and Phys. Scis., 1978-81, Geophysics Rsch. Bd., 1978-81; trustee Argonne Univs. Assn., 1979-83. Mem. internat. adv. bd.: Jour. Physics C (Solid State Physics), 1971-76; mem. editorial bd.: Physical Review B, 1978-81. Recipient Sr. U.S. Scientist Rsch. award Alexander von Humboldt Found., 1992; sr. postdoctoral fellow NSF, 1965. Fellow Am. Phys. Soc. (vice chmn., chmn. divsn. solid state physics 1975-77, coun. 1988), AAAS (chmn. sect. B Physics 1985-86); mem. Am. Crystallographic Assn., Am. Assn. Physics Tchrs., Phi Beta Kappa, Sigma Xi, Pi Mu Epsilon. Research on atomic defects in solids, neutron and x-ray scattering, quantum solids, molecular crystals, crystal dynamics, radiation damage. Home: 1005 Foothill Dr Champaign IL 61821-5622

SIMMONS, RAYMOND HEDELIUS, JR., lawyer; b. Salinas, Calif., May 27, 1958; s. Raymond Hedelius and Antoinette (Lynch) S. BA magna cum laude, U. Calif., San Diego, 1979; JD magna cum laude, U. Calif., San Francisco, 1982. Bar: Calif. 1982, U.S. Dist. Ct. (no. dist.) Calif. 1982, Ga. 1987. Assoc. Farella, Braun & Martel, San Francisco, 1982-85; atty., v.p. Barnett-Range Corp., Atlanta, 1985-86; counsel Nationwide Capital Corp. subs. HomeFed. Bank, Atlanta, 1986, HomeFed. Bank, San Diego, 1987-90; gen. counsel, sr. v.p., sec. ITT Fed. Bank, San Francisco, 1990-95; also ITT Residential Capital Corp., ITT Residential Capital Servicing Corp., San Francisco. Mem. ABA, Calif. Bar Assn., Ga. Bar Assn., Calif. Scholarship Fedn. (life), Order of Coif, Thurston Soc.

SIMMONS, RICHARD DE LACEY, mass media executive; b. Cambridge, Mass., Dec. 30, 1934; s. Ernest J. and Winifred (McNamara) S.; m. Mary DeWitt Bleecker, May 20, 1961; children: Christopher DeWitt, Robin Bleecker. Grad., 1951; AB, Harvard Coll., 1955; LLB, Columbia U., 1958. Bar: N.Y. 1959. V.p., gen. counsel Dun & Bradstreet Corp., N.Y.C., 1969-73, exec. v.p., 1976-79, vice chmn., 1979-81; pres. Moody's Investors Svc., N.Y.C., 1973-75, Dun & Bradstreet, Inc., N.Y.C., 1975; pres., chief oper. officer Washington Post Co., Washington, 1981-91; pres. Internat. Herald Tribune, Paris, 1989-96; bd. dirs. Washington Post Co., J.P. Morgan & Co., Inc., Morgan Guaranty Trust Co. N.Y., Union Pacific Corp., Yankee Pub., Inc.; mem. equity adv. bd. GE Investment Corp. Mem. coun. White Burkett Miller Ctr. Pub. Affairs, U. Va. Office: 105 N Washington St Ste 202 Alexandria VA 22314

SIMMONS, RICHARD P., steel company executive; b. 1931; married. Grad., MIT, 1953. With Titanium Metals Corp. Am., 1957-59, Republic Steel, 1959-68; with Allegheny Ludlum Steel Corp., Pitts., 1960—, chief exec. officer, 1980—, chmn., 1986—; also dir. Allegheny Ludlum Corp. (formerly Allegheny Ludlum Steel Corp.), Pitts., formerly also pres. Office: 1000 6th Ppg Pl Pittsburgh PA 15222*

SIMMONS, ROBERT RUHL, state legislator, educator; b. N.Y.C., Feb. 11, 1943; s. Charles Herbert Jr. and Roxane Page (Ruhl) S.; m. Edith Heidi Paffard, June 22, 1974; children: Jane Adams, Robert Waldo Ruhl. BA, Haverford Coll., 1965; MPA, Harvard U., 1979. Ops. officer CIA, Washington, 1969-79; legis. asst. U.S. Senator John H. Chafee, Washington, 1979-81; staff dir. intelligence com. U.S. Senate, Washington, 1981-85; vis. lectr. Yale U., New Haven, Conn., 1985—; mem. Conn. Gen. Assembly, Hartford, 1991—. Contbr. articles to profl. jours. Col. U.S. Army Res. Decorated Bronze Star with 1 oak leaf cluster, Army Commendation medal with 1 oak leaf cluster, Vietnam Svc. medal with four campaign stars, Nat. Def. medal, Army Res. Achievement medal. Episcopalian. Avocations: Chinese art, forestry. Home: 268 N Main St Stonington CT 06378-2910 Office: Legislative Office Bldg The Capital Ste 4200 Hartford CT 06106

SIMMONS, ROY, JR., university athletic coach. Head coach lacrosse team Syracuse U. Orangemen, 1971—. Coached team to Divsn. IA Lacrosse Championship, 1983, 88-90, 93. Office: Syracuse Univ Manley Field House Syracuse NY 13244-5020*

SIMMONS, ROY WILLIAM, banker; b. Portland, Oreg., Jan. 24, 1916; s. Henry Clay and Ida (Mudd) S.; m. Elizabeth Ellison, Oct. 28, 1938; children—Julia Simmons Watkins, Matthew R., Laurence E., Elizabeth Jane Simmons Hoke, Harris H., David E. Asst. cashier First Nat. Bank Layton, Utah, 1944-49; Utah bank commr., 1949-51; exec. v.p. Bank of Utah, Ogden, 1951-53; pres. Lockhart Co., Salt Lake City, 1953-64, Zion's First Nat. Bank, Salt Lake City, 1964-81; chmn. bd. Zion's First Nat. Bank, 1965—; chmn., CEO Zion's Bancorp, 1965-91, chmn. bd., 1991—; chmn. bd. Zion's Savs. & Loan Assn., 1961-69; pres. Lockhart Co., 1964-87; bd. dirs. Beneficial Life Ins. Co., Mountain Fuel Supply Co., Ellison Ranching Co. Chmn. Utah Bus. Devel. Corp., 1969-80; Mem. Utah State Bd. Regents, 1969-81. Mem. Salt Lake City C. of C. (treas. 1964-65), Sigma Pi. Republican. Mem. Ch. of Jesus Christ of Latter Day Saints. Home: 817 E Crestwood Rd Kaysville UT 84037-1712 Office: Zions Bancorp 1000 Kennecott Bldg Salt Lake City UT 84133

SIMMONS, RUSSELL, recording industry executive; b. Hollis, N.Y., 1957; s. Daniel S. Attended, CCNY. Co-founder, owener Def Jam Records, N.Y.C., 1985—; owner Rush Artist Mgmt.; chmn. Rush Comms.; owner 6 record labels. Co-prodr. films Krush Groove, 1985, Tougher Than Leather, 1988; dir. music videos; HBO appearance Russell Simmons Def Comedy Jam; mgmt. co. represents Public Enemy, LL Cool J, others. Office: Def Jam Records 652 Broadway New York NY 10012-2316*

SIMMONS, RUTH DORIS, women's health nurse, educator; b. Bklyn., July 30, 1942; d. Stanley George and Doris Louise (Beckert) S. LPN, Glen Cove (N.Y.) Community, 1964; AD, SUNY, Farmingdale, 1976; BS in Profl. Arts in Edn., St. Joseph's Coll., 1994. Nurse labor/delivery unit Syosset (N.Y.) Hosp., 1964-66; staff nurse ob./gyn. and pediatrics unit Glen Cove Community Hosp., 1966-76; staff nurse labor, delivery, postpartum units Mercy Hosp., Scranton, Pa., 1976—, also asst. childbirth edn. classes. Home: RR 2 Box 2770 Factoryville PA 18419-9658

SIMMONS, S. DALLAS, university president; b. Ahoskie, N.C., Jan. 28, 1940; s. Yvonne Martin; m. Mary A. Simmons, Feb. 10, 1963; children: S. Dallas Jr., Kristie Lynn. BS, N.C. Cen. U., 1962, MS, 1967; PhD, Duke U., 1977. Asst. prof. bus. adminstrn. N.C. Cen. U., Durham, 1967-71, asst. to chancellor, 1971-77, vice chancellor for univ. relations, 1977-81; pres. St. Paul's Coll., Lawrenceville, Va., 1981-85, Va. Union Univ., Richmond, 1985—; faculty cons. IBM, Research Triangle Park, N.C., 1968-71; cons. for edn. devel. officers Nat. Lab. for Higher Edn., Durham, 1972-73; staff asst. to Pres., White House Advance Office, Washington, 1975-76; univ. fed. liaison officer Moton Coll. Service Bur., Washington, 1972-80; mem. competency testing commn. N.C. Bd. Edn., 1977-81; bd. dirs., mem. loan com., mem. planning com. Pace Am. Bank, Lawrenceville, 1984-85. Bd. dirs. N.C. Mus. Life and Sci., Durham, 1972-75, Volunteer Services Bur, Inc., Durham, 1972-77, Va. Poly. Inst. and State U., 1982-83; mem. Durham Civic/Conv. Ctr. Commn., 1972-73, U.S./Zululand Ednl. Found., 1985; trustee, mem. exec. and pers. com. N.C. Cen. U., 1983-85; active various coms. United Negro Coll. Fund; mem. exec. bd. John B. McLendon Found., Inc., 1985. Named one of Outstanding Young Men Am., 1972, Citizen of Yr. Omega Psi Phi, 1983-84, Bus. Assoc. of Yr. Am. Bus. Women's Assn., 1984. Mem. Assn. Episc. Colls. (pres.-elect), Cen. Intercollegiate Athletic Assn. (exec. com. 1981—, bd. dirs. 1981—), Nat. Assn. for Equal Opportunity in Higher Edn. (bd. dirs., chmn. leadership awards com. 1984-85), Am. Mgmt. Assn., Data Processing Mgmt. Assn. (cen. Carolina chpt.), Am. Assn. Sch. Adminstrs., Am. Assn. Univ. Adminstrs., Kappa Alpha Psi (Kappa of Month Dec. 1981), Sigma Pi Phi (alpha beta boulé). African Methodist Episcopalian. Club: Downtown. Lodges: Masons (32 degree), Shriners, Kiwanis, Optimists. Home: 1200 W Graham Rd Richmond VA 23220-1409 Office: Va Union U 1500 N Lombardy St Richmond VA 23220-1711

SIMMONS, SHARON DIANNE, elementary education educator; b. Woodruff, S.C., Apr. 5, 1961; d. James Madison and Lucy Nell (Carlton) Crow; m. Wayne Roy Simmons, Mar. 29, 1986; children: Zachary, Luke. BA in Elem. Edn., U. S.C., 1983, M of Elem. Edn., 1987. Tchr. 3d grade M.S. Bailey Elem. Sch., Clinton, S.C., 1984-85, tchr. 4th grade, 1985-86; tchr. 5th grade Eastside Elem. Sch., Clinton, S.C., 1986-88, tchr. 4th & 5th grades, 1988-90, 91-92, tchr. 5th grade, 1990-91, tchr. 4th grade, 1993-95, tchr. 3rd grade, 1995—; pilot tchr. authentic assessment Eastside Elem. Sch., 1992—, mem. sch. libr. com., 1993—, tchr. chair 4th grade, 1993-94, tchr. grad. course authentic assessment, 1996. Pres. libr. coun. Spartanburg-Woodruff (S.C.) Br. Libr., 1993-95. Recipient Ambassador award The Edn. Ctr., 1993-94. Mem. S.C. Math. Tchrs. Assn., Sch. Improvement Coun. Baptist. Avocations: piano, cross stitch, travel, sports, reading. Home: 651 Parsons Rd Woodruff SC 29388-8700 Office: Eastside Elem Sch 103 Old Colony Rd Clinton SC 29325-9317

SIMMONS, SYLVIA LEJUNE, public affairs specialist, author, publisher; b. Washington, Mar. 22, 1946; d. Thomas Jr. and Jessie Mae Solomon; m. Joseph Milton Marshall, Nov. 3, 1969 (div. Oct. 1973); 1 child, Lauren Denise Warner; m. Lloyd R. Simmons, Aug. 1974; 1 child, Lloyd Desmond. Student, Prince George C.C., 1977-80, 93—. Sec. OMB, Washington, 1970-75, 82-83, Dept. Commerce, Washington, 1975-77, Dept. HUD, Washington, 1977-79, U.S. Trade Rep., Washington, 1980-82; pub. affairs specialist Pennsylvania Ave. Devel. Corp., Washington, 1982—; chair Gardening on the Ave., Pennsylvania Ave. Devel. Corp., Washington, 1989-91, chair pub. use com., 1989—; chair Kid-a-Rama, 1992-93, Children's Book Fair, 192-94; spkr. in field. Author, pub.: (poems) Feelings Collection, 1993. Mem. U.S. Bicentennial Commn. Com., Washington, 1987-92; mem., chair subcom. for logistics Mayor's Task Force Group for Spl. Events, 1985—; mem., exec. sec. Nat. Cherry Blossom Festival Com., 1992—, scholarship com. 1994-95, v.p. cmty. devel., 1995—; mem., corr. sec. Bob Marley Soccer Com., 1990—, events coord., gen. mgr., 1995—; mem., vice chair Internat. Friendship Day Festival Com., 1990—; mem. U.S. World Cup Soccer Com., 1992-94; mem. Jamaican Embassy's JamFest '30 Com., 1992-94. Recipient various certs. of appreciation, other awards. Mem. NAFE. Avocations: record collecting, cooking, preparing for theme parties.

SIMMONS, TED CONRAD, writer; b. Seattle, Sept. 1, 1916; s. Conrad and Clara Evelyn (Beaudry) S.; m. Dorothy Pauline Maltese, June 1, 1942; children: lynn, Juliet. Student U. Wash., 1938-41, UCLA and Los Angeles State U., 1952-54, Oxford (Eng.) U., 1980. Drama critic Seattle Daily Times, 1942; indsl. writer, reporter-editor L.A. Daily News, 1948-51; contbr. Steel, Western Metals, Western Industry, 1951—; past poetry dir. Watts Writers Workshop; instr. Westside Poetry Center; asst. dir. Pacific Coast Writers Conf., Calif. State Coll. Los Angeles. Served with USAAF, 1942-46. Author: (poetry) Deadended, 1966; (novel) Middlearth, 1975; (drama) Greenhouse, 1977, Durable Chaucer, 1978, Rabelais and other plays, 1980, Dickeybird, 1981 (nominated TCG Plays-in-Progress award 1985), Alice and Eve, 1983, Deja Vu, Deja Vu, 1986, The Box, 1987, Ingrid Superstar, 1988, Three Quarks for Mr. Marks, 1989, Ingrid: Skier on the Slopes of Stromboli, 1990, A Midsummer's Hamlet, 1991, Hamlet Nintendo, After Hours, Dueling Banjoes, Viva el Presidente, Climate of the Sun, 1992, Nude Descending Jacob's Ladder, 1993, Almost an Opera, 1994, Landscape with Inverted Tree and Fred Astaire Dancing, 1995, O.J. Othello, Fast Track; writer short story, radio verse; book reviewer Los Angeles Times; contbr. poetry to The Am. Poet, Prairie Wings, Antioch Rev., Year Two Anthology; editor: Venice Poetry Company Presents, 1972. Grantee Art Commn. King County, 1993.

SIMMONS, VAUGHAN PIPPEN, medical consultant; b. Balt., Nov. 19, 1922; s. Harry S. and Sarah Jane (Pippen) S.; m. Marguerite Carolyn Massino, Dec. 27, 1947 (dec. 1990); children: Malynda Sarah, Jefferson

Vaughan. Student, Ill. Inst. Tech., 1943-44; B.S., U. Chgo., 1947, M.D., 1949. Diplomate Am. Bd. Life Ins. Medicine. From instr. to asst. prof. Marquette U. Sch. Medicine, Milw., 1950-56; asst. med. dir. Northwestern Mut. Life Ins. Co., Milw., 1956-60; med. dir. Fidelity Mut. Life Ins. Co., Phila., 1961-73, v.p., 1968-73; v.p., med. dir. Colonial Penn Life Ins. Co., Phila., 1973-84; vis. lectr. ins. medicine Temple U. Sch. Medicine, Phila., 1966-84; asst. prof. anatomy Jefferson Med. Coll., Phila., 1977-88, hon. asst. prof. anatomy, 1988—. Patentee in field (3); contbr. articles to profl. jours. Mem. ofcl. bd. St. Luke United Methodist Ch., Bryn Mawr, Pa., 1963-83, chmn. commn. membership and evangelism, 1963-71, trustee, 1968-83. Served with M.C., U.S. Army, 1943-45, as lt. (j.g.) USNR, 1952-54; Korea. Fellow Coll. Physicians Phila. (chmn. pub. health sect. 1967-68, ins. medicine sect. 1970-72, planning com. 1981-82, adv. bd. Francis C. Wood Inst. History of Medicine 1984-88), Milw. Acad. Medicine, Am. Geriatrics Soc., N.Y. Acad. Medicine; mem. Am. Acad. Ins. Medicine (founding editor Ins. Medicine 1969-71, exec. coun. 1970-72, publs. com. 1967-75), Am. Life Ins. Assn. (sec. med. sect. 1974-77), Pa. Hist. Soc., Am. Assn. Automotive Medicine (dir. 1980-83), Am. Legion, Sigma Xi, Alpha Kappa Kappa. Clubs: Union League (bd. dirs. 1982-85, v.p. 1985-86), Sketch (Phila.). Avocations: photography, amateur radio, drawing, painting, med rsch. and writing. Home: 4665 S Landings Dr Fort Myers FL 33919-4683

SIMMONS, VIRGINIA GILL, educational administrator; b. Gauley Bridge, W.Va., Feb. 14, 1942; d. David Herman and Margaret Josephine (Cameron) Gill; m. James Edward Simmons, Dec. 21, 1962; children: Melissa Marie, Cameron David. BS, W.Va. State U., 1964; MS, Marshall U., Huntington, W.Va., 1969; PhD, Kent (Ohio) State U., 1984. Elem. tchr. Kanawha and Pocahontas County Schs., 1964-67; tchr. mentally retarded Pocahontas County Schs., Marlinton, W.Va., 1967-69; tchr. gifted Kanawha County Schs., Charleston, W.Va., 1974-79, 81-84; cmty. edn. coord. Kanawah County Schs., Charleston, W.Va., 1986-88, spl. edn. specialist, 1984-86; teaching fellow Kent State U., 1979-81; dean evaluation and tng. Governor's Cabinet on Children and Families, Charleston, 1991-93; state coord. gifted W.Va. Dept. Edn., Charleston, 1988-93, state coord. of gov.'s schs., 1993—; adj. prof. Marshall U., Huntington, 1974-85, Kent State U., 1979-83, Coll. Grad. Studies Inst., W.Va., 1984—; cons. on gifted; bd. mem., reader Nat. Rsch. Ctr. on Gifted and Talented, 1991. Editor, writer: Inside, 1987 (Gov.'s award), Expanded Learning Opportunities, 1989-92; editor: Building Your Own Railroad Tracks, 1991. Cand., Dem. Party, Kanawha County, 1974; lobbyist Women's Orgn., W.Va. Legis., 1973-79; chairperson Gov.'s Hwy. Safety Leaders, 1985—; dir. Russia and W.Va.: A Partnership for Exch. Found., Inc., 1993—. Kent State U. Ednl. Rsch. fellow, 1982-83. Mem. ASCD, Fedn. Women's Clubs (pres., state officer), Phi Delta Kappa. Methodist. Office: West Virginia Dept Edn Bldg 6 Rm 362 Charleston WV 25305

SIMMONS, WILLIAM, physicist, aerospace research executive; b. Chgo., Apr. 24, 1932; s. Walter Garfield and Edna Dean (Winch) S.; m. Barbara Millet Haury, Oct. 4, 1954; children: Sheryl Lee, Cynthia Jane, Shelly Jean. BA in Physics, Carleton Coll., 1953; MS in Physics, U. Ill., 1955, PhD in Physics, 1960. Mem. tech. staff Space Tech. Labs., Redondo Beach, Calif., 1960-62; sr. rsch. scientist Gen. Tech., Torrance, Calif., 1962; sr. rsch. scientist TRW, Redondo Beach, 1962-71, dir. rsch., 1984-89, chief engr. spl. projects assigned to Lawrence Livermore (Calif.) Labs., 1989-92; engring. mgr. Lawrence Livermore Labs., 1972-84, rsch. reviewer, 1985-89; prof. engring. UCLA, 1968-72; tech. panel mem. U. Calif., Berkeley, 1985; tech. reviewer Dept. Energy, Washington, 1986—, mem. rev. com., 1987—. Editor, reviewer 2 books, 1982, 83; contbr. numerous articles to profl. jours. 10 patents in electro-optics devices. Named Disting. Engring. Prof. of Yr. UCLA, 1972, one of Top 100 Innovators in U.S.A, Sci. Digest, 1986; George F. Baker Found. scholar Carleton Coll., 1949-53. Mem. IEEE (sr., gen. chmn. symposia 1988, 89, Simon Ramo Major medal 1987), Laser Inst. Am., Laser Engring. and Optical Soc., Am. Phys. Soc., Soc. of Photographic and Instrumentation Engrs., U.S. Chess Club, Phi Beta Kappa, Sigma Xi. Republican. Avocations: chess, table tennis, bridge. Office: Systems Solutions 1621 W 25th St Ste 231 San Pedro CA 90732-4300

SIMMONS SMITH, MONA JEAN (MONICA SIMMONS SMITH), special education educator, writer; b. Sharon, Pa., Sept. 23, 1952; d. James Pearman and Michaelina (Votino) Simmons; children: Manley Taylor Smith, Rachael Christina Smith. BS, Ga. Coll., 1973; MEd, U. Ga., 1975, postgrad. Cert. tchr. T-5 learning disorders, hosp.-homebound edn., T-5 multi-physically handicapped edn., Ga. Tchr. Clayton County Bd. of Edn., Jonesboro, Ga., 1973-74; fellow/instr. U. Ga., Athens, 1974-75, instr., 1978-80; tchr. self-contained learning disabilities Cobb County Bd. of Edn., Marietta, Ga., 1976-78; ednl. coord. Physicians and Surgeons Hosp., Atlanta, 1981-83, Parkway Regional Hosp., Atlanta, 1984-89; hosp. homebound tchr. DeKalb County Bd. of Edn., Atlanta, 1980-86; mktg. mgr. Atlanta, 1987-88; ednl. cons. 1977-80; mem. psycho ednl. testing Ednl. Evaluations, Atlanta, 1976-80; ednl. cons. Comprehensive Care Corp., Atlanta; field based rschr. Prep Sch., Hilton Head, S.C., 1993; lectr. in field. Mem. Atlanta Ballet Guild (life), 1988—; vol. North Arts Ctr. Docent, 1989-91. U. Ga. teaching assistantship, 1976. Mem. Coun. for Exceptional Children (divsn. Children Learning Disabilities), Reynolds Plantation Club, Phi Delta Kappa. Avocations: snow skiing, fishing, travel, dancing, water skiing. Home: 4804 Calais Ct Marietta GA 30067

SIMMS, CHARLES AVERILL, environmental management company executive; b. Hundred, W.Va., Apr. 12, 1937; s. Charles R. and Ada Faith (Devine) S.; m. Linda Magalis, June 24, 1961; children: Brian M., Eric C. BSBA, W.Va. U., 1959. Cert. internal auditor, Md. Jr. acct. Potomac Edison Co., Hagerstown, Md., 1960-61; internal auditor Potomac Edison Co., Hagerstown, 1961-66, supr. internal audits, 1966-69; constrn. audit mgr. Eastalco Aluminum Co., Frederick, Md., 1969-71, gen. acctg. mgr., 1971-73, exec. asst. to pres., 1973-74; contr. Teledyne Nat., Cockeysville, Md., 1974-77, dir. fin. and adminstrn., Northridge, Calif., 1977-79, v.p. ops., Timonium, Md., 1979-83; pres. Nat. Ecology, Inc., Timonium, 1983-89; pres., chief exec. officer Rescon Inc., Balt., 1989-93; chmn. exec. com., bd. dirs. Am. Ecology Corp., Houston, 1984-94. 1st lt. U.S. Army, 1959-67. Mem. Solid Waste Assn. N.Am., Shriners (Cumberland, Md.). Republican. Home: 3241 Sharp Rd Glenwood MD 21738 Office: Md Environ Svc 10320 York Rd Cockeysville Hunt Valley MD 21030

SIMMS, ELLENESE BROOKS, civic leader, retired school system administrator; b. New Orleans, Sept. 10, 1939; d. Annias and Ellen (Lyons) Brooks; m. Clarence Joseph Simms, June 16, 1960 (div. June 1967); 1 child, Stacy René; m. Melvin Simms, Apr. 27, 1968; 1 adopted child, Darrell Dean; 1 child, Christel Melvanesia. BA, Dillard U., 1962; MEd, Loyola U., New Orleans, 1976. Elem. tchr. New Orleans Pub. Schs., 1962-76, prin. Helen S. Edwards Elem. Sch., 1976-86, prin. Robert Russa Moton Elem. Sch., 1986-92, adminstr. for consol. programs, 1992-94; mem. ednl. task force La. Dept. Edn., 1975-76; sec.-treas. Golden Svcs. Inc., exec. dir., 1990—; pres. Profl. Assn. Creative Educators, ednl. cons., 1982—; coord. Orleans Parish schs. area So. Assn. Colls. and Schs., 1982-93; designer, implementer year round sch. pilot project Orleans Parish Schs., 1989-92; mem. internat. curriculum devel. seminar in Cameroon, U. New Orleans, 1983. Mem. Brechtel Park Adv. Bd., 1984-94, Mayor's Algiers Task Force Com., 1984-85; mem. ednl. cmty. adv. bd. Fla./Desire, 1977-94; founder, v.p. Holly Park Civic Assn., pres., 1973-76; co-founder, past sec. Algiers-Gretna br. NAACP, 1990; co-chmn. Citizens Adv. Com. for minority Participation, 1989; commr. Regional Transit Authority, 1991-95, chmn. bd. commrs., 1991-94; founder Greater New Orleans Regional Transit Task Force, 1990, Transit Task Force for Civil Rights, 1993; bd. dirs. Health Edn. Authority of Wis., 1994—. Recipient area chmn. citation New Orleans Sickle Cell Anemia Found., Inc., 1979, Leadership and Svc. award La. Assn. Sch. Execs., 1982, Outstanding Educator award Negro Bus. and Profl. Women's Club New Orleans, 1988, Outstanding Svc. award Prins. Assn. New Orleans Pub. Schs., 1992, New Orleans City Coun., 1992, Woman of Distinction award Austin Met. Bus. Resource Ctr., 1993, Gov.'s award State of La., 1994, cert. of appreciation Nat. Coun. Negro Women, 1994; also others. Mem. Am. Pub. Transit Assn. (v.p. human resources 1992-94, co-chmn. diversity coun. 1992-95; mem. transti 2000 comm. oversight com. 1992), Nat. Assn. for Yr. Round edn. (bd. dirs. 1991-94), Ind. Women's Orgn., La. PTA (hon. state life), Delta Sigma Theta (life, Vol. Svc. award New Orleans Alumnae chpt. 1977). Baptist. Avocations: cooking, crafts. Home: 3701 Mansfield Ave New Orleans LA 70131-5625

SIMMS, FRANCES BELL, elementary education educator; b. Salisbury, N.C., July 29, 1936; d. William Taft and Anne Elmira (Sink) Bell; m. Howard Homer Simms, June 24, 1966 (dec. Oct. 1993); 1 child, Shannon Lara. AB in English, U. N.C., 1958; MEd, U. Fla., 1962; postgrad., Boston U., 1963—, U. Va.; Queen's Coll., Cambridge, U.K. Playroom attendant dept. neurology Children's Hosp., Boston, 1958-60; reading clinician Mills Ctr., Inc., Ft. Lauderdale, Fla., 1960-61; reading/lang. arts tchr. Arlington (Va.) Pub. Schs., 1962—; adv. bd. mem. ad hoc com. Edn. Tech., Arlington, 1965-67; reading instr. Va. Poly. Inst. and State U., Arlington, 1974; prodr., dir. Barcroft Newsbag-CATV, Arlington, 1982—; chair self-study Elem. Sch., Arlington, 1987, 93; adv. bd. Reading is Fundamental of No. Va., Arlington, 1988—. Lay leader, choir mem. Cherrydale Meth. Ch., Arlington, 1976—; laborer Christmas in April, Arlington, 1990—; tutor, vol. instr. Henderson Hall Marine Corps, Arlington, 1990—; organizer, instr. Better Beginnings, Arlington, 1994—. Recipient Literacy award, Margaret McNamara award Reading is Fundamental of No. Va., 1994-95. Mem. Va. State Reading Assn. (mem. conf. coms.), Arlington Edn. Assn. (contbg. editor newsletter 1967-69), Greater Washington Reading Coun. (com. chairperson 1962—, Tchr. of Yr. 1995-96), Delta Kappa Gamma (Alpha Omicron former news writer, v.p., program chairperson, news editor). Avocations: water color, singing in choir, writing poetry, journal keeping, traveling, producing children's musicals. Home: 6110 23rd St N Arlington VA 22205-3414

SIMMS, GLENDA PATRICIA, association administrator; b. St. Elizabeth, Jamaica, Jan. 25, 1939; d. Hubert and Myrtle (Dennis) Thompson; m. Ralph Kirkland, Nov. 11, 1992; children: Michelle Lois, Emil Alf, Shaun Alene. Tchr. diploma, Bethlehem Tchr's. Coll., 1960; BEd, U. Alberta, 1974, MEd, 1976, PhD, 1985; LLD (hon.), U. Manitoba, 1994. Assoc. prof. Sask. Indian Federated Coll., Regina, 1980-85; supr. Intercultural Edn. Regina Pub. Sch. Bd., 1985-87; assoc. prof. Nipissing U. Coll., North Bay, Ont., 1987-90; pres. Can. Adv. Coun. on Status of Women, Ottawa, Ont., 1990—. Contbr. articles to profl. jours.; spkr. in field. Recipient Citation for Citizenship, 1988, Nat. award Can. Coun. Multicultural and Intercultural Edn., 1990, InterAmicus Human Rights award McGill U., 1992, Ryerson Polytech. Inst. Fellowship award, 1993, Pres.'s award Internat. Assn. Bus. Communicators, 1994, Can. Black Achievement award, 1995; named to North Bay Human Rights Hall of Fame, 1991. Mem. Nat. Orgn. Immigrant and Visible Minority Women of Can. (founder), Congress of Black Women of Can. (past pres.), Fedn. Med. Women in Can. (hon.). Avocations: reading, travel. Home: 209 Twyford St, Ottawa, ON Canada

SIMMS, LILLIAN MILLER, nursing educator; b. Detroit, Apr. 13, 1930; d. John Jacob and Mary Agnes (Knight) Miller; m. Richard James Simms, Feb. 2, 1952; children: Richard James Jr., Frederick William, Andrew Michael. BSN, U. Mich., 1952, MSN, 1966, PhD in Ednl. Gerontology, 1977. Program dir., assoc. prof. nursing health svcs. adminstrn. U. Mich., Ann Arbor, 1977-82, interim assoc. dir. nursing, asst. dean clin. affairs, 1981-82, assoc. prof. nursing adminstrn. and health gerontology, 1982-90, assoc. prof. nursing, 1990—; prof. emeritus, 1995; spkr., presenter in field; mem. spl. study sect. NIH, 1986; mem. adv. com., panel of judges for inquiry and practice of nursing svc. adminstr. Intra and Interdisciplinary Inviational Conf., 1990; series editor Delmar Pubs., Inc., 1991-93; mem. med. delegation People to People Citizen Amb. Program, Australia and New Zealand, 1982, People's Republic of China, Hong Kong and Korea, 1989; dir. China project that developed acad. relationships with schs. of nursing in People's Republic of China, 1991-94. Developer nursing concept of work excitement; co-author: Administracion de Servicios de Enfermeria, 1986, A Guide to Redesigning Nursing Practice Patterns, 1992, The Professional Practice of Nursing Administration, 2d edit., 1994; contbr. numerous articles to profl. publs.; reviewer for various publs. in field. Bd. dirs. Domino House Sr. Ctr., Ann Arbor, 1990—. Recipient Excellence in Nursing Edn. award Rho chpt. Sigma Theta Tau, 1995; grantee U. Mich., 1983-84, 84-87, 87-88, Presdl. Initiatives, 1990-92, W.K. Kellogg Found., 1991-93. Fellow Am. Acad. Nursing; mem. ANA, Am. Orgn. Nurse Execs., Midwest Nursing Rsch. Soc., Coun. on Grad. Edn. for Adminstrn. in Nursing (sec. 1986-88, chair publs. com. 1988-89), U. Mich. Nursing Alumni Assn., Sigma Theta Tau. Avocations: reading, gardening, international travel. Home: 1329 Wines Dr Ann Arbor MI 48103-2543 Office: U Mich Sch Nursing 400 N Ingalls St Rm 2174 Ann Arbor MI 48109-0482

SIMMS, LOWELLE, synod executive; b. Sterling, Colo., June 16, 1931; s. Griffin L. and Irene O. (Geer) S.; m. Lois A. Streeter, Aug. 8, 1959. BA, Park Coll., 1953; MDiv, Union Theol. Sem., 1956. Ordained min. Presbyn. Ch., 1956. Pastor East Trenton Presbyn. Ch., Trenton, N.J., 1957-61, Calvary Presbyn. Ch., Phila., 1961-66; min. of mission First, North, Westminster Chs., Kalamazoo, Mich., 1966-69; assoc. exec. Presbytery of Sccoto Valley, Columbus, Ohio, 1969-80; administr. interims Presbytery and Synods Presbyterian Ch., 1980-83; synod exec. Synod of the Covenant, Columbus. Avocation: photography. Office: Synod of the Covenant 6172 Bush Blvd Ste 3000 Columbus OH 43229

SIMMS, MARIA ESTER, health services administrator; b. Bahia Blanca, Argentina; came to U.S., 1963; d. Jose and Esther (Guays) Barberio Esandi; m. Michael Simms, July 15, 1973 (Aug. 1993); children: Michelle Bonnie Lee Carla, Michael London Valentine, Matthew Brandon. Degree medicine, Facultad del Centenario, Rosario, Argentina, 1962; Physician Asst. Cert. (hon.), U. So. Calif., 1977. Medical diplomate. Pres. Midtown Svcs. Inc., L.A., 1973—. Chmn. bd. Am.'s Film Inst., Washington; chmn. bd. trustees World Film Inst. Nominated chairwoman of bd. trustees World Film Inst. Fellow Am. Acad. Physicians' Assts.; mem. Bus. for Law Enforcement (northeast divsn.), Physicians for Social Responsibility, Mercy Crusade Inc., Internat. Found. for Survival Rsch., Noetic Scis. Soc., Inst. Noetic Scis., So. Calif. Alliance for Survival, Supreme Emblem Club of U.S., Order Eastern Star, Flying Samaritans, Shriners. Avocations: coin collecting, designing, writing, oil painting, flying.

SIMMS, MARIA KAY, publishing and computer services executive; b. Princeton, Ill., Nov. 18, 1940; d. Frank B. and Anna (Haurberg) S.; m. Neil F. Michelsen, Oct. 2, 1987 (dec. 1990); children: Shannon Sullivan Stillings, Molly A. Sullivan, Elizabeth Maria Jossick. BFA, Ill. Wesleyan U., 1962. Cert. cons. profl. astrologer; ordained min. L.A. Cmty. Ch. of Religious Sci. Elder priestess Covenant of the Goddess; art tchr. elem. and jr. high pub. schs., Dundee, Northbrook, Ill., 1962-65; high sch. art tchr. Danbury, Conn., 1975-76; self employed gallery painter various cities, 1962-77, free-lance comml. illustrator, 1972-74, 86-87; shop, gallery, café owner Conn., 1976-79; art dir. ACS Pubs., Inc., San Diego, Calif., 1987-90; pres. Astro Comm. Svcs., Inc. (formerly ACS Pubs.), San Diego, 1990—; conf. lectr. United Astrology Congress, 1986, 89, 92, 95, Am. Fedn. Astrologers Internat. Conv., 1982, 84, 86, 88, 90, 92, 94, 96. Author: Twelve Wings of the Eagle, 1988, Dial Detective, 1989; co-author: Search for the Christmas Star, 1989, Circle of the Cosmic Muse, 1994, Your Magical Child, 1994, Future Signs, 1996; contbr. numerous articles to mags. High priestee Cir. of the Cosmic Muse; elder priestess Covenant of the Goddess, 2d officer Calafia Local Coun. Recipient numerous art awards. Mem. Nat. Assn. Women Bus. Owners, Nat. Coun. Geocosmic Rsch. Inc. (dir., pubs. dir. 1981-92, editor jour. 1984-92), Am. Fedn. Astrologers, Internat. Soc. Astrol. Rsch., New Age Pubs. Assn. Office: Astro Comm Svcs Inc 5521 Ruffin Rd San Diego CA 92123-1314

SIMMS, PHILLIP, sports commentator, former professional football player; b. Lebanon, Ky., Nov. 3, 1956. Student, Morehead State U. Quarterback N.Y. Giants, NFL, 1979-94; sports commentator ESPN, Prime Time Monday, 1994—. Named to Pro Bowl Team, 1985, 86, 93; recipient Pro Bowl Player of Game award, 1986, MVP award Super Bowl XXI, 1987. Appeared on NFL Championship Team, 1986. Office: ESPN ESPN Plz Bristol CT 06010

SIMMS, THOMAS HASKELL, chief of police; b. Yuma, Ariz., Sept. 3, 1945; s. Jessie Lee and Mary Elizabeth (Servos) S.; divorced; m. Ginny Lee David, Mar. 26, 1988; children: Thomas Haskell Jr., Julie Marie. BA, St. Mary's Coll., Moraga, Calif., 198l; MA, Calif. Poly., Pomona, 1991. Officer Mountain View (Calif.) Police Dept., 1972-76; police sgt. East Bay Parks, Oakland, Calif., 1976-79; police lt. Town of Moraga, Calif., 1979-84, chief police, 1984-87; chief police City of Piedmont, Calif., 1987-91; chief of police City of Roseville, Calif., 1991—. Bd. dirs. Piedmont coun. Boy Scouts Am., 1988-89. Maj. U.S. Army, 1967-7l, Vietnam. Mem. Calif. Chiefs Police Assn., Calif. Peace Officers Assn., Rotary, Kiwanis (pres. Moraga 1982-83, Kiwanian of Yr. award 1983). Presbyterian. Avocations: hiking, photography, travel, golf. Office: Roseville Police Dept 311 Vernon St Roseville CA 95678-2634

SIMNAD, MASSOUD T., engineering educator; b. Teheran, Iran, Mar. 11, 1920; came to U.S., 1948; s. Reza an Ferhunde (Magari) S.; m. Lenora Virginia Brown, May 28, 1954; childrne: Jeffrey, Virginia. BS, London U., 1942; PhD, U. Cambridge, Eng., 1946. Rsch. fellow U. Cambridge, 1945-48; postdoctoral fellow Carnegie-Mellow U., Pitts., 1949-50, mem. faculty, 1950-56; with Gen. Atomics, San Diego, 1956-81; adj. prof., cons. in engring. U. Calif., San Diego, 1981—; vis. prof. MIT, Cambridge, 1962-63; mem. tech. coms. U.S. Dept. Energy, 1970—; cons. in field. Author papers, monographs in field; patentee in field. Fellow Am. Nuc. Soc., Am. Soc. Metals, AAAs; mem. AIAA, NAE, Electrochem. Soc., Inst. Global Conflict and Cooperation, World Affairs Coun., UN Club, Sierra Club. Avocations: art, music, gardening, sports, travel. Home: 6120 La Flecha Rd PO Box 1806 Rancho Santa Fe CA 92093 Office: U Calif Mail Code R-011 La Jolla CA 92093

SIMOKAITIS, FRANK JOSEPH, air force officer, lawyer; b. St. Louis, Dec. 12, 1922; s. Frank and Constance (Ladish) S.; m. Mary Jane Feeny; children: Frank, Peggy, Mary. Student, Washington U., St. Louis, 1945-47; LL.B., St. Louis U., 1950, J.D., 1970. Bar: U.S. Supreme Ct. U.S 1950, Mo. 1950, also other fed. cts. 1950. Commd. 2d lt. USAAF, 1943; advanced through grades to maj. gen. USAF, 1973; plans and ops. officer Hdqrs. Pacific Air Force, 1960-63; staff officer Hdqrs. USAF, Washington, 1963-69; exec. asst. to sec. air force Hdqrs. USAF, 1969-73; comdt. Air Force Inst. Tech., 1973-78; dir. Dept. Def. affairs Hdqrs. NASA, Washington, 1978-83, cons., 1983—. Bd. dirs. Dayton chpt. ARC, Greater Miami chpt., arbitrator Better Bus. Bur. Decorated D.S.M., Legion of Merit, Air medal with 4 oak leaf clusters, Air Force Commendation medal. Mem. Miami Air Force Assn. (bd. dirs.), Navy League (v.p. U.S. Miami coun.), Bolling AFB Officers Club. Home: 3100 S Manchester St Falls Church VA 22044-2711

SIMON, ALBERT, physicist, engineer, educator; b. N.Y.C., Dec. 27, 1924; s. Emanuel D. and Sarah (Leitner) S.; m. Harriet E. Rubinstein, Aug. 17, 1947 (dec. June 1970); children: Richard, Janet, David; m. Rita Shiffman, June 11, 1972. B.S., CCNY, 1947; Ph.D., U. Rochester, 1950. Registered profl. engr., N.Y. State. Physicist Oak Ridge Nat. Lab., 1950-54, asso. dir. neutron physics div., 1954-61; head plasma physics div. Gen. Atomic Co., San Diego, 1961-66; prof. dept. mech. engring. U. Rochester, N.Y., 1966—; prof. physics U. Rochester, 1968—, chmn. dept. mech. engring., 1977-84; mem. Inst. for Advanced Study, Princeton, 1974-75; sr. vis. fellow U.K. Sci. Research Council, Oxford U., 1975. Author: An Introduction to Thermonuclear Research, 1959; contbr. to: Ency. Americana, 1964, 74; Editor: Advances in Plasma Physics, 1967—. With USN, 1944-46. Recipient Univ. Mentor award, 1988-89; John Simon Guggenheim fellow, 1964-65. Fellow Am. Phys. Soc. (chmn. plasma physics div. 1963-64); mem. ASME, ASEE (chmn. nuclear engring. div. 1985-86). Home: 263 Ashley Dr Rochester NY 14620-3327

SIMON, ARTHUR, pharmacologist, research laboratory executive; b. Bklyn., June 1, 1942; s. Harry and Ann S.; m. Sandra Goldberg, July 10, 1966; children—Brett David, Kira Denise. B.S. in Biology, Phila. Coll. Pharmacy and Sci., 1965; M.S. cum laude, Fairleigh Dickinson U., 1969; Ph.D. in Pharmacology (NIH fellow), U. Cin., 1972. Lab. technician La Wall and Harrisson Research Lab., Phila., 1962-63; research asst. toxicology dept. Wyeth Labs., Paoli, Pa., 1965-66; research assoc. pharmacology dept. Warner Lambert Research Inst., Morris Plains, N.J., 1966-69; research investigator Squibb Inst. for Med. Research, Princeton, N.J., 1972-74; sr. cardiovascular pharmacologist USV Pharm. Corp., Tuckahoe, N.Y., 1974-76; dir. cardiovascular clin. research Bristol Myers Co. Internat. Div., 1974-82; pres., chief exec. officer Research Testing Labs., Inc., Great Neck, N.Y., 1982—. Mem. Dermal Clin. Evaluation Soc., Drug Info. Assn., Assocs. Clin. Pharmacologist, Regulatory Affairs Profl. Soc., Internat. Assn. Dental Rsch., Am. Assn. Dental Rsch. Home: 52 Tamarack Ln Pomona NY 10970-2012 Office: Rsch Testing Labs Inc 255 Great Neck Rd Great Neck NY 11021-3314

SIMON, BARRY PHILIP, lawyer; b. Paterson, N.J., Nov. 22, 1942; s. Alfred Louis and Rhoda (Tapper) S.; m. Hinda Bookstaber, Feb. 9, 1964; children: Alan, John, Eric. BA, Princeton U., 1964; LLB, Yale U., 1967. Bar: N.Y. 1965, Tex. 1986. Assoc. atty. Hughes Hubbard & Reed, N.Y.C., 1967-69, Sullivan & Cromwell, N.Y.C., 1969-72, Shea & Gould, N.Y.C., 1972-73; v.p., gen. counsel Teleprompter Corp., N.Y.C., 1973-82; v.p., sec., gen. counsel Continental Airlines, L.A. and Houston, 1982-86; v.p. in-charge internat. div. Continental Airlines, Houston, 1987-90; sr. v.p. legal affairs, gen. counsel, sec. Continental Airlines, 1990-92; sr. v.p. Tex. Air Corp., 1986-87; sr. v.p. legal affairs, gen. counsel, sec. Ea. Airlines, Miami, 1987-90; exec. v.p., gen. counsel GAF Corp., Wayne, N.J., 1993—. Mem. copyright com. Nat. Cable TV Assn., Washington, 1974-76, mem. utilities com., 1973-82. Recipient Class of 1888 Lit. prize Princeton U., 1961. Mem. Montclair Golf Club, Houston Racquet Club. Home: 2003 Dunstan Houston TX 77005

SIMON, BERNECE KERN, social work educator; b. Denver, Nov. 27, 1914; d. Maurice Meyer and Jennie (Bloch) Kern; m. Marvin L. Simon, Feb. 26, 1939; 1 dau., Anne Elizabeth. B.A., U. Chgo., 1936, M.A., 1942. Social worker Jewish Children's Bur. Chgo., 1938-40, U. Chgo. Hosps. and Clinics, 1940-44; mem. faculty U. Chgo., 1944-81, instr., 1944-48, asst. prof., 1948-60, prof. social casework, 1960—, Samuel Deutsch prof. Sch. Social Service Adminstrn., 1960-81, emeritus, 1981—. Mem. bd. editors 17th Edit. Ency. Social Work, 1975-77, Social Svc. Rev., 1975—; bd. editors: Social Work, 1978-82, book rev. editor, 1982-87; cons. editor Journal of Social Work Education, 1991—; contbr. articles to profl. jours., book chpts., monographs. Mem. Council Social Work Edn. (mem. nat. bd., sec. 1972-74), Nat. Assn. Social Workers, Acad. Cert. Social Workers, Nat. Acads. Practice: Social Work. Office: U Chgo Sch of Social Svc Adminstrn 969 E 60th St Chicago IL 60637

SIMON, CARLY, singer, composer, author; b. N.Y.C., June 25, 1945; d. Richard S.; m. James Taylor, 1972 (div. 1983); children: Sarah Maria, Benjamin Simon; m. James Hart, Dec. 23, 1987. Studied with Pete Seeger. Singer, composer, rec. artist, 1971—. Appeared in film No Nukes, 1980; albums include Carly Simon, 1971, Anticipation, 1972, No Secrets, 1973, Hotcakes, 1974, Playing Possum, 1975, The Best of Carly Simon, 1975, Another Passenger, 1976, Boys in the Trees, 1978, Spy, 1979, Come Upstairs, 1980, Torch, 1981, Hello Big Man, 1983, Spoiled Girl, 1985, Coming Around Again, 1987, Greatest Hits Live, 1988, My Romance, 1990, Have You Seen Me Lately?, 1990, Carly Simon, This Is My Life, 1992, Letters Never Sent, 1994; single records: Nobody Does It Better, 1977, Let the River Run, 1988 (Academy award best original song, 1989), (with Frank Sinatra) In the Wee Small Hours of the Morning, 1993; recipient Grammy award as best new artist 1971; TV appearance: Carly in Concert: My Romance, 1990; author: Amy the Dancing Bear, 1988, The Boy of the Bells, 1990, The Fisherman's Song, 1991, The Nightime Chauffeur, 1993; created opera Romulus Hunt, 1993.

SIMON, CATHY JENSEN, architect; b. L.A., Sept. 30, 1943; d. Bernard Everett and Bitten Hanne (Smith) S.; m. Michael Palmer, Nov. 23, 1972; 1 child, Sarah Marina. B.A. Wellesley Coll., 1965; M. Arch., Harvard U., 1969. Registered architect, Calif. 1974, N.Y. 1988, Mass. 1988, Colo. 1995, Ariz. 1996. Architect Cambridge 7 Assocs., Mass., 1968-69, Building Systems Devel., San Francisco, 1970-72, Mackinlay Winnacker McNeil, Oakland, Calif., 1973-74; prin. Marquis Assocs., San Francisco, 1974-85; prin. Simon Martin-Vegue Winkelstein Moris, 1985—; sr. lectr. architecture U. Calif., Berkeley, 1982-85, vis. lectr., 1973-82; teaching coordinator Women's Sch. Planning and Arch., Santa Cruz, Calif., 1976; speaker ALA Nat. Conv., 1992, Les Grandes Bibliotheques de L'Avenin, Paris, 1991. Prin. works include Yerba Buena Gardens Retail and Entertainment Complex, San Francisco, Mus. N.Mex. Master Plan, Santa Fe, San Francisco Ballet Pavilion, Lick Wilmerding High Sch. Master Plan, San Francisco, Bothell Br. Campus, Bothell, Wash., San Francisco New Main Libr., Oceanside Water Pollution Control Project, San Francisco, Newport Beach (Calif.) Ctrl. Libr.,

Coll. 8 U. Calif., Santa Cruz, Olin Humanities Bldg. Bard Coll., N.Y., San Francisco Day Sch., Fremont (Calif.) Main Libr., Peter J. Shields Libr. U. Calif., Davis, Elena Baskin Visual Art Studios U. Calif., Santa Cruz, Primate Discovery Ctr., San Francisco Zoo, Braun Music Ctr., Stanford U. The Premier, La Jolla Colony, La Jolla, Calif. Mem. exec. com. San Francisco Mus. Modern Art; active Leadership Commn. Design Industry; mem. tech. assistance com., San Francisco Redevel. Agy., San Francisco, 1982—; mem. adv. panel Calif. Bd. Archtl. Examiners; bd. dirs. Golden Gate Nat. Park Assn. Recipient Calif. Preservation award Chambord Apartments, 1984, Adaptive Re-use award Engr. Offices, Am. Soc. Interior Designer, 1982, Commodore Sloat Sch. Honor award Nat. Sch. Bds. Assocs., 1980, Marcus Foster Mid. Sch. Honor award East Bay AIA, 1980; NEA grantee 1983. Mem. Orgn. Women Architects (founding 1972), San Francisco chpt. AIA, AIA (jury mem. nat. honor awards 1980, Los Angeles chpt. awards jury 1984). Home: 265 Jersey St San Francisco CA 94114-3822 Office: Simon Martin-Vegue Winkelstein Moris 501 2nd St # 701 San Francisco CA 94107-1431

SIMON, DAVID, principal. Dean Manhattan Sch. Music, 1970-79; prin. Balt. Sch. Arts. Recipient Blue Ribbon Sch. Award 1990-91. Office: Balt Sch for Arts 712 Cathedral St Baltimore MD 21201-5210

SIMON, DAVID F., lawyer; b. El Paso, Tex., Apr. 14, 1953; s. Maurice and Susan (Bendekovits) S.; m. Deborah Hart, Mar. 1, 1980; children: Alison Mallory, Joshua Alan, Rebecca Elizabeth, Nathaniel Cody. BS magna cum laude, U. Buffalo, 1974; JD cum laude, U. Pa., 1977. Bar: Pa. 1977, N.J. 1978. Law clk. to presiding judge Phila. Ct. Common Pleas, 1977-79; assoc. Wolf, Block, Schorr & Solis-Cohen, Phila., 1979-85, ptnr., 1985-90; sr. v.p., chief legal officer U.S. Healthcare, Inc., Blue Bell, Pa., 1990—; mem. adv. coun. Pa. Dept. Conservation and Natural Resources, 1996—; Pa. Judicial Nominating Commr., Montgomery County, 1995—. Mem. Phila. Bar Assn. (mem. exec. com. young lawyers sect. 1983-85, chmn. computer law com. 1984-85), Pa. Bar Assn. (chmn. in-house counsel com. 1993-94), Pa. Bar Inst. (bd. dirs. 1992-96). Avocations: photography, electronics. Home: PO Box 551 Gwynedd Valley PA 19437-0551 Office: US Healthcare Inc PO Box 1180 Blue Bell PA 19422-0020

SIMON, DONALD JOHN, financial planner, insurance and investment broker; b. Chgo., July 16, 1947; s. Nicholas J. and Alice R. (Vaughan) S.; 1 child, Joshua K. BSBA, Oglethorpe U., 1969. CFP, CLU. Sales rep. D. W. Shaw, Inc., Berlin, N.J., 1969-74; owner Simon Fin. Co., Greenbelt, Md., 1975—. Bd. dirs. Orphans Found. of Am., Washington, 1994—. Mem. Nat. Assn. Life Underwriters. Avocations: music, tennis. Home: 12600 Eastbourne Dr Silver Spring MD 20904-2041

SIMON, DORIS MARIE TYLER, nurse; b. Akron, Ohio, Jan. 24, 1932; d. Gabriel James and Nannie Eliza (Harris) Tyler; m. Matthew Hamilton Simon, Apr. 20, 1952; children: Matthew Derek, Denise Nanette, Gayle Machele, Doris Elizabeth. ADN, El Paso (Tex.) Coll. Media, 1969, El Paso Community Coll., 1976; BSPA in Health Care Adminstrn., St. Joseph's Coll., North Windham, Maine, 1991. RN, Tex. Med. asst. Dr. Melvin Farris, Akron, 1962-63, Dr. Samuel Watt, Akron, 1967-68, Drs. May, Fox and Buchwald, El Paso, 1972-76; head nurse, home dialysis and transplant coord. Hotel Dieu Med. Ctr., El Paso, 1977-87; nurse mgr., transplant coord. Providence Meml. Hosp., El Paso, 1987-94, nurse clinician neurology, 1994-96; transplant coord. Sierra Med. Ctr., El Paso, 1996—; med. asst. instr. Bryman Sch. Med. Assts., El Paso, 1970-72. Youth choir dir. Ft. Sill, Okla., 1964-67; choir dir. Ft. Sill area and Ft. Bliss, Tex., 1964-74; instr. in piano and music theory, Ft. Sill, 1964-67; leader Ft. Sill coun. Girl Scouts U.S., 1965-67; instr. Sch. for Handicapped, Lawton, Okla., 1965-67; nephrology nurse del. to People's Republic China Citizen Amb. Program, People to People Internat., 1988, to Russia and the Baltics Citizen Amb. Group Project Asst. Healthcare, 1992. Recipient Molly Pitcher award U.S. Army, 1963-67, Martin Luther King Jr. Share a Dream Svc. award, 1993, Delta Sigma Theta Outstanding Profl. of 1993 award; named One of 12 Outstanding Personalities of El Paso El Paso Times, 1993. Mem. ANA, Am. Med. Assts. Assn., Am. Nephrology Nurses Assn., Les Charmantes (Akron) (pres./sec. 1950-52), Links Inc. (pres. El Paso chpt. 1992—), Interclub Coun. (pres. 1992—), Donor Awareness Coalition 1992—. Baptist. Avocations: piano, organ, singing, sewing, bowling. Home: 8909 Parkland Dr El Paso TX 79925-4012 Office: Transplant Dept Sierra Med Ctr 1625 Medical Center Dr El Paso TX 79902

SIMON, ECKEHARD (PETER), foreign language educator; b. Schneidemühl, Germany, Jan. 5, 1939; came to U.S., 1955, naturalized, 1960; s. Herbert and Doris (Keiler) S.; m. Eileen Higginbottom, Dec. 19, 1959; children: Anders, Conrad (dec.), Matthew, Frederick. A.B., Columbia U., 1960; A.M., Harvard U., 1961, Ph.D., 1964. Instr., German Harvard U., Cambridge, Mass., 1964-65; asst. prof. Harvard U., 1965-69, asso. prof., 1969-71, prof., 1971—, head tutor and lang. coordinator, 1965-76, chmn. dept. German, 1976-82, 85-86, chmn. com. on medieval studies, 1992-95. Author: Neidhart von Reuental: Geschichte der Forschung und Bibliographie, 1968, Neidhart von Reuental, 1975, The Türkenkalender (1454) Attributed to Gutenberg and the Strasbourg Lunation Tracts, 1988; editor: The Theatre of Medieval Europe, New Research in Early Drama, 1991; mem. editorial adv. bd.: Dictionary of the Middle Ages, 1982-89; contbr. articles to profl. jours. Woodrow Wilson fellow, 1960-61; NEH Younger Scholar fellow, 1968-69; research fellow, 1977-78; Guggenheim fellow, 1968-69; Fulbright fellow U. Cologne, 1983. Mem. MLA, Am. Assn. Tchrs. German, Medieval Acad. Am. (asst. editor Speculum 1981-94, book review editor 1994—). Home: 11 Hayes Ave Lexington MA 02173-3521 Office: Harvard U Boylston Hall Cambridge MA 02138-6531

SIMON, ERIC JACOB, neurochemist, educator; b. Wiesbaden, Germany, June 2, 1924; came to U.S., 1938, naturalized, 1945; s. Joseph and Paula (Meyer) S.; m. Irene M. Ronis, Aug. 9, 1947; children: Martin A., Faye Ruth, Lawrence D. BS, Case Inst. Tech., Cleve., 1944; M.S., U. Chgo., 1947, Ph.D., 1951; hon. doctorate, U. René Descartes, Paris, 1982. Postdoctoral trainee in biochemistry Columbia U. Coll. Physicians and Surgeons, 1951-53; lectr. in chemistry CCNY, 1952-59; research assoc. Cornell U. Med. Coll., 1953-59; asst. prof. medicine NYU Med. Center, 1959-64, assoc. prof. exptl. medicine, 1964-72, prof. exptl. medicine, 1972-80, prof. psychiatry and pharmacology, 1980—; Harry Williams Meml. lectr. Dept. Pharmacology Emory U., Atlanta, 1986; mem. initial rev. com. Nat. Inst. Drug Abuse, 1976-80, chmn. 1979-80, mem. Nat. Adv. Coun. on Drug Abuse, 1989-92; Sterling-Winthrop lectr. Albany Med. Coll., 1977; vis. prof. Coll. de France, Paris, 1990. Trustee Teaneck (N.J.) Bd. Edn., 1975-79. Served with U.S. Army, 1944-46. Recipient Rsch. Pace Setter award Nat. Inst. Drug Abuse, 1977, Louis and Bert Freedman Found. award N.Y. Acad. Scis., 1980, Nathan B. Eddy Meml. award Com. on Problems of Drug Dependence, Lexington, Ky., 1983, Alumni Profl. Achievement award U. Chgo., 1986; Health Rsch. Coun. N.Y.C. career scientist, 1959-75. Fellow AAAS, N.Y. Acad. Scis. (trustee 1986-89); mem. Am. Soc. Biol. Chemists, Am. Soc. Neurochemistry, Am. Soc. Pharmacology, Internat. Soc. Neurochemistry, Am. Chem. Soc., Sigma Xi. Lodge: B'nai B'rith. Research, publs. on opiate receptors, endorphins, biochemistry of analgesic action, vitamin E metabolism, acyl-coenzyme A synthesis. Office: 550 1st Ave New York NY 10016-6481

SIMON, EVELYN, lawyer; b. N.Y.C., May 13, 1943; d. Joseph and Adele (Holzschlag) Berkman; m. Frederick Simon, Aug. 18, 1963; children: Amy Jocelyn, Marcie Ann. AB in Physics, Barnard Coll., 1963; MS in Physics, U. Pitts., 1964; JD, Wayne State U., 1978; LLB, Monash U., Melbourne, Australia, 1980. Bar: Mich. 1980, Victoria (Australia) 1981. Supr. engring. Chrysler Corp., Detroit, 1964-72; edn. and profl. mgr. Engring. Soc. Detroit, 1972-78; solicitor Arthur Robinson & Co., Melbourne, 1980-81; sr. atty. Ford Motor Co., Detroit, 1981-89; assoc. gen. counsel Sheller-Globe Corp., Detroit, 1989-90; v.p. planning, gen. counsel United Techs. Automotive Inc., Dearborn, Mich., 1991-94, v.p. bus. devel. and legal affairs, 1995—. Mem. ABA, Mich. Bar Assn. Home: 1787 Alexander Bloomfield Hills MI 48302 Office: United Tecs Automotive Inc 5200 Auto Club Dr Dearborn MI 48126-4212

SIMON, GARY LEONARD, internist, educator; b. Bklyn., Dec. 18, 1946; s. Bernard and Dorothy (Ligeti) S.; m. Vicki Thiessen, Aug. 29, 1970; children: Jason, Jessica. BS, U. Md., 1968; PhD, U. Wis., 1972; MD, U. Md., 1975. Diplomate Am. Bd. Internal Medicine, Am. Bd. Infectious Diseases. Asst. prof. dept. medicine George Washington U., Washington, 1980-84, assoc. prof., 1984-89, assoc. chmn. medicine, 1984—, prof., 1989—, dir. divsn. infectious diseases, 1993—; cons. on AIDS Assn. Am. Med. Coll., Washington, 1990—. Contbr. articles to profl. jours. on AIDS and infectious diseases. Fellow Am. Coll. Physicians, Infectious Disease Soc. Am.; mem. Am. Soc. Microbiology, Assn. Program Dirs. in Internal Medicine. Office: George Washington U 2150 Pennsylvania Ave NW Washington DC 20037-2396

SIMON, HAROLD, radiologist; b. Trenton, N.J., May 13, 1930; s. John and Rae B. (Gilinsky) S.; m. Jane L. Ludwig, Feb. 25, 1956; children—Steven Gregg, John Gregory. M.D., Duke U., 1955. Diplomate Am. Bd. Radiology, Am. Bd. Nuclear Medicine. Intern U.S. Naval Hosp., Chelsea, Mass., 1955-56; med. officer U.S. Navy, Newport, R.I., 1956-58; resident in radiology Mass. Gen. Hosp., Boston, 1958-61, Oak Ridge Inst. Nuclear Medicine, 1959; instr. radiology Med. Sch., Tufts U., Boston, 1961-63; clin. asst. prof. radiology Med. Sch., Tufts U., 1965, assoc. clin. prof., 1971-77, clin. prof. radiology, 1977—; practice medicine specializing in radiology and nuclear medicine Newton Lower Falls, Mass., 1963—; mem. staff Newton Wellesley Hosp., Newton, Mass.; assoc. chief radiology Newton Wellesley Hosp., 1977—, radiologist-in-chief, 1987-95; dir. Sch. nuclear Med. Tech.; bd. dirs. Grove Bank for Savs.; bd. dirs., mem. CRC com., mem. audit. com. Grove Bank, chmn. audit com. 1995-96; bd. dirs., treas. Newell Physicians, Inc., 1986-93; bd. overseers Newell Health Corp. Contbr. articles to med. jours. Served with USNR, 1955-58. Fellow Am. Coll. Radiology; mem. Radiol. Soc. N.Am., Am. Roentgen Ray Soc., New Eng. Roentgen Ray Soc., Mass. Med. Soc. (mem. ins. com.), Mass. Radiology Soc., Pinebrook Country Club (pres. 1982-85), Belmont Country Club, Presdl. Country Club, Phi Beta Kappa, Phi Eta Sigma. Home: 252 Atlantic Ave Palm Beach FL 33480

SIMON, HERBERT, professional basketball team executive; b. Bronx. Grad., CCNY. With Albert Frankel Co., Indpls., 1959; co-founder Melvin Simon and Assocs., Inc., Indpls., 1959—, pres., 1973—; owner Ind. Pacers (Nat. Basketball Assn.), Indpls., 1983—. Office: Ind Pacers Market Sq Arena 300 E Market St Indianapolis IN 46204-2603*

SIMON, HERBERT A(LEXANDER), social scientist; b. Milwaukee, Wisc., June 15, 1916; s. Arthur and Edna (Merkel) S.; m. Dorothea Pye, Dec. 25, 1937; children: Katherine S. Frank, Peter Arthur, Barbara. AB, U. Chgo., 1936, PhD, 1943, LLD (hon.), 1964; DSc (hon.), Case Inst. Tech., 1963, Yale U., 1963, Marquette U., 1981, Columbia U., 1983, Gustavus Adolphus U., 1984, Mich. Tech. U., 1988, Carnegie-Mellon U., 1990; Fil. Dr. (hon.), Lund U., Sweden, 1968; LLD (hon.), McGill U., Montreal, Que., Can., 1970, U. Mich., 1978, U. Pitts., 1979, U. Paul Valery, France, 1984, Harvard U., 1990; Dr. Econ. Sci. (hon.), Erasmus U. Rotterdam, Netherlands, 1973, Duquesne U., 1988; DSc (hon.), LHD (hon.), Ill. Inst. Tech., 1988; D in Polit. Sci. (hon.), U. Pavia, Italy, 1988; D in Psychology (hon.), U. Rome, 1993. Rsch. asst. U. Chgo., 1936-38; staff mem. Internat. City Mgrs.' Assn.; also asst. editor Pub. Mgmt. and Municipal Year Book, 1938-39; dir. adminstrv. measurement studies Bur. Pub. Adminstrn., U. Calif., 1939-42; asst. prof. polit. sci. Ill. Inst. Tech., 1942-45, assoc. prof., 1945-47, prof., 1947-49; also chmn. dept. polit. and social sci., 1946-49; prof. adminstrn. and psychology Carnegie Mellon U., Pitts., 1949-65, Richard King Mellon univ. prof. computer scis. and psychology, 1965—; head dept. indsl. mgmt. Carnegie Mellon U., 1949-60; assoc. dean Grad. Sch. Indsl. Adminstrn., 1957-73, trustee, 1972-93; emeritus trustee, 1993—; cons. to Internat. City Mgrs. Assn., 1942-49, U.S. Bur. Budget, 1946-49, U.S. Census Bur., 1947, Cowles Found. for Research in Econs., 1947-60; cons. and acting dir. Mgmt. Engring. br. Econ. Cooperation Adminstrn., 1948; Ford Distinguished lectr. N.Y. U., 1959; Vanuxem lectr. Princeton, 1961; William James lectr. Harvard, 1963, Sigma Xi lectr., 1964, 76-78, 86; Harris lectr. Northwestern U., 1967; Karl Taylor Compton lectr. MIT, 1968; Wolfgang Koehler lectr. Dartmouth, 1975; Katz-Newcomb lectr. U. Mich., 1976; Carl Hovland lectr. Yale, 1976; Ueno lectr., Tokyo, 1977; Gaither lectr. U. Calif., Berkeley, 1980; Camp lectr. Stanford U., 1982; Gannon lectr. Fordham U., 1982; Oates vis. fellow Princeton U., 1982; Marschak lectr. UCLA, 1983; Auguste Comte lectr. London Sch. Econs., 1987; Lee Kuan Yew lectr. U. Singapore, 1989, Hitchcock lectr. U. Calif., Berkeley, 1990, lectr. U. Roma Sapienza, 1993, Mattioli lectr. Bocconi U., Milan, 1993; hon. prof. Tianjin (China) U., 1980, Beijing (China) U., 1986; hon. research scientist Inst. Psychology, Chinese Acad. Scis., 1985; chmn. bd. dirs. Social Sci. Research Council, 1961-65; chmn. div. behavioral scis. NRC, 1968-70; mem. President's Sci. Adv. Com., 1968-72; trustee Carnegie Inst., Pitts., 1987-93, hon. trustee, 1993—; cons. bus. and govtl. orgns. Author or co-author books relating to field, including Administrative Behavior, 1947, 3d edit., 1976, Public Administration, 1950, with new Introduction, 1992, Models of Man, 1956, rev. edit., 1991, Organizations, 1958, with new Introduction, 1993, New Science of Management Decision, 1960, rev. edit., 1977, The Shape of Automation, 1965, The Sciences of the Artificial, 1968, 2d edit., 1981, 3d edit., 1996, Human Problem Solving, 1972, Skew Distributions and Business Firm Sizes, 1976, Models of Discovery, 1977, Models of Thought, Vol. I, 1979, Vol. II, 1989, Models of Bounded Rationality, Vols. I and II, 1982, Vol. III, 1996, Reason in Human Affairs, 1983, Protocol Analysis, 1984, with new Introduction, 1993, Scientific Discovery, 1987, Models of My Life, 1991. Chmn. Pa. Gov.'s Milk Inquiry Com., 1964-65. Recipient Adminstrs. award Am. Coll. Hosp. Adminstrs., 1957, Alfred Nobel Mem. prize in econ. scis., 1978, Dow-Jones award, 1983, scholarly contbns. award Acad. Mgmt., 1983, Nat. Medal Sci., 1986, Pender award U. Pa., 1987, Fiorino d'Oro City of Florence, Italy, 1988, Am. Psychol. Found. Gold medal, 1988, award for excellence in the scis. Gov. of Pa., 1990, rsch. excellence award Internat. Joint Conf. Artificial Intelligence, 1995. Fellow AAAS, AP (disting. sci. contbn. award 1969, lifetime contbn. award 1993), Am. Assn. Artificial Intelligence, Am. Econ. Assn. (disting. Ely lectr. 1977), Econometric Soc., Am. Psychol. Soc. (William James fellow), Am. Sociol. Soc., Inst. Mgmt. Scis. (life, v.p. 1954, Von Neumann theory award 1988), Brit. Psychol. Assn. (hon.); mem. IEEE (hon.), Jewish Acad. Arts and Scis., Am. Polit. Sci. Assn. (James Madison award 1984), Am. Soc. Pub. Adminstrn. (hon. Frederick Mosher award 1974, Dwight Waldo award 1995), Assn. Computing Machinery (A.M. Turing award 1975), NAS (com. on sci. and pub. policy 1967-69, 82-90, chmn. com. air quality control 1974, chmn. com. behavioral scis. NSF 1975-76, coun., 1978-81, 83-86, chmn. com. scholarly com. with PRC, 1987-93, co-chmn. com. behavioral sci. in prevention of nuclear war 1986-90), Cognitive Sci. Soc., Soc. Exptl. Psychologists, Am. Philos. Soc., Royal Soc. Letters (Lund; fgn. mem.), Orgnl. Sci. Soc. (Japan, hon.), Yugoslav Acad. Scis. (fgn.), Chinese Acad. Sci. (fgn.), Indonesian Economists Assn. (hon.), Univ. Club Pitts., Phi Beta Kappa, Sigma Xi (Proctor prize 1980). Democrat. Unitarian. Office: Carnegie Mellon U Dept Psychology Schenley Park Pittsburgh PA 15213

SIMON, H(UEY) PAUL, lawyer; b. Lafayette, La., Oct. 19, 1923; s. Jules and Ida (Rogere) S.; m. Carolyn Perkins, Aug. 6, 1949; 1 child, John Clark. B.S., U. Southwestern La., 1943; J.D., Tulane U., 1947. Bar: La. 1947; CPA, La. 1947. Pvt. practice New Orleans, 1947—; asst. prof. advanced acctg. and taxation U. Southwestern La., 1944-45; staff acct. Haskins & Sells (now Deloitte & Touche), New Orleans, 1945-53, prin., 1953-57; ptnr. Deutsch, Kerrigan & Stiles, 1957-79; sr. founding ptnr. law firm Simon, Peragine, Smith & Redfearn, 1979—; mem. bd. adv. editors Tulane Law Rev., 1992—; mem. New Orleans Bd. Trade. Author: Community Property and Liability for Funeral Expenses of Deceased Spouse, 1946, Income Tax Deductibility of Attorney's Fees in Action in Boundary, 1946, Fair Labor Standards Act and Employee's Waiver of Liquidated Damages, 1946, Louisiana Income Tax Law, 1956, Changes Effected by the Louisiana Trust Code, 1965, Gifts to Minors and the Parent's Obligation of Support, 1968; coauthor: Deductions—Business or Hobby, 1975, Role of Attorney in IRS Tax Return Examination, 1978; assoc. editor: The Louisiana CPA, 1956-60; mem. bd. editors Tulane Law Rev., 1945-46, adv. bd. editors, 1992—; estates, gifts and trusts editor The Tax Times, 1986-87. Bd. dirs., mem. fin. com. World Trade Ctr., 1985-86; mem. New Orleans Met. Crime Commn., Coun. for a Better La., New Orleans Met. Area Com., Bur. Govtl. Rsch., Pub. Affairs Rsch. Coun.; co-chmn. NYU Tax Conf., New Orleans, 1976; mem. dean's coun. Tulane U. Law Sch. Fellow Am. Coll. Tax Counsel; mem. ABA (com. ct. procedure tax sect. 1958—), AICPA, La. Bar Assn. (com. on legis. and adminstrv. practice 1966-70), New Orleans Bar Assn., Internat. Bar Assn. (com. on securities issues and trading 1970-88), Am. Judicature Soc., Soc. La. CPAs, New Orleans Assn. Notaries, Tulane U. Alumni Assn., New Orleans C. of C. (coun. 1952-66), Tulane Tax Inst. (program com. 1960—), Internat. House (bd. dirs. 1976-79, 82-85), Internat. Platform Assn., City Energy Club, Press Club, New Orleans Country Club, Phi Delta Phi (past pres. New Orleans chpt.), Sigma Pi Alpha. Roman Catholic. Home: 6075 Canal Blvd New Orleans LA 70124-2936 Office: 30th Fl Energy Ctr New Orleans LA 70163 *Developing and maintaining consistency and constancy in feeling and showing genuine respect towards others nourish and stimulate an individual to become day by day a better person. Whether alone or in the presence of others, one who daily abides by the guidance and rules he would advocate to others invariably finds the greatest reward of all—true respect for one's self.*

SIMON, JACK AARON, geologist, former state official; b. Champaign, Ill., June 17, 1919; s. Abraham and Lenore (Levy) S. B.A., U. Ill., 1941, M.S., 1946; postgrad., Northwestern U., 1947-49, D.Sc. (hon.), 1981. Tech. and research asst. Ill. State Geol. Survey, Urbana, 1937-42; asst. to assoc. geologist Ill. State Geol. Survey, 1945-53, geologist, head, coal sect., 1953-67, prin. geologist, 1967-74, asst. chief, 1973-74, chief, 1974-81, prin. scientist, 1981-83; occasional cons.; asso. prof. dept. metallurgy and mining engring. U. Ill., 1967-74, prof., 1974-77, 80-85, adj. prof. dept. geology, 1979-86. Served with F.A. AUS, 1942-43, F.A., USAAF, 1943-45. Decorated Air Medal with 4 oak leaf clusters; recipient Disting. Svc. award So. Ill. U., Edwardsville, 1982, Coal Day award So. Ill. U., Carbondale, 1982, Alumni Achievement award U. Ill. dept. geology, 1994. Fellow AAAS (sect. E chmn. 1980), Geol. Soc. Am. (chmn. coal geology div. 1962-63, Gilbert H. Cady award 1975, mem. council and exec. com. 1979-81); mem. Am. Assn. Petroleum Geologists (ea. sect. Gordon M. Wood Jr. Meml. award 1991), AIME (chmn. Midwest coal sect. 1966, Percy W. Nicholls award 1981), Am. Inst. Profl. Geologists (v.p. 1973), Am. Mining Congress, Assn. Am. State Geologists (hon.), Ill. Mining Inst. (hon. life; exec. sec.-treas. 1963-68, v.p. 1980-81, pres. 1981-82), Ill. Soc. Coal Preparation Engrs. and Chemists, Ill. Geol. Soc., Ill. Acad. Sci., Soc. Econ. Geologists (councillor 1982-84), B'nai Brith, Sigma Xi. Club: Exchange (Urbana) (pres. 1969). Home: 502 W Oregon St Urbana IL 61801-4044

SIMON, JACQUELINE ALBERT, political scientist, journalist; b. N.Y.C.; d. Louis and Rose (Axelroad) Albert; m. Pierre Simon; children: Lisette, Orville. BA cum laude, NYU, MA, 1972, PhD, 1977. Adj. asst. prof. Southampton Coll., 1977-79; mng. editor Point of Contact, N.Y.C., 1975-76; assoc. editor, U.S. bur. chief Politique Internationale, Paris, 1979—; sr. resident scholar Inst. French Studies, NYU, 1980—, asst. prof. govt., 1982-83; assoc. Inst. on the Media for War and Peace; frequent appearances French TV and radio. Contbg. editor Harper's, 1984-92; contbr. numerous articles to French mags., revs., books on internat. affairs. Bd. dirs. Fresh Air Fund, 1984—. Mem. Women's Fgn. Policy Group, Overseas Press Club (bd. govs.), Phi Beta Kappa. Home: 988 5th Ave New York NY 10021-0143

SIMON, JAMES LOWELL, lawyer; b. Princeton, Ill., Nov. 8, 1944; s. K. Lowell and Elizabeth Ann (Unholz) S.; children: Heather Lyn, Brandon James. Student, U. Ill., 1962-63, JD with honors, 1975; BSEE magna cum laude, Bradley U., 1967. Bar: Fla. 1975, U.S. Dist. Ct. (mid. dist.) Fla. 1976, U.S. Ct. Appeals (11th cir.) 1981, U.S. Patent Office 1983. Engr. Pan Am. World Airways, Cape Kennedy, Fla., 1967-68; assoc. Akerman, Senterfitt & Eidson, Orlando, Fla., 1975-80; ptnr. Bogin, Munns, Munns & Simon, Orlando, 1980-87, Holland & Knight, 1987—. With Seminole County Sch. Adv. Coun., Fla., 1981-88, chmn., 1982, 83; with Forest City Local Sch. Adv. Com., Altamonte Springs, Fla., 1981-84, Code Enforcement Bd., Altamonte Springs, 1983-84, Cen. Bus. Dist. Study com., Altamonte Springs, 1983-85, Rep. Coun. of '76, Seminole County, 1982-87; mem. Seminole County Libr. Adv. Bd., 1989-92, sec., 1990, pres., 1991, Seminole County Citizens for Quality Edn., 1990-92; mem. Seminole County Sch. Dist. Strategic Planning Com., 1991—, Class '91 Leadership Orlando; bd. dirs. Found. for Seminole County Pub. Schs., Inc., 1992-95, chmn., 1993-94; bd. dirs. Greater Seminole C. of C., 1993. Capt. USAF, 1968-72. Mem. ABA, Orange County Bar Assn. (jud. rels. com. 1982-83, fee arbitration com. 1983—), Greater Orlando C. of C., Seminole County Bar Assn. (sec. trial lawyers sect. 1993-94), Phi Kappa Phi, Tau Beta Pi, Sigma Tau, Eta Kappa Nu. Republican. Mormon. Home: 620 Longmeadow Cir Longwood FL 32779-2632 Office: Holland & Knight 200 S Orange Ave Ste 2600 PO Box 1526 Orlando FL 32802

SIMON, JEANNE HURLEY, federal commissioner; m. Paul Simon; 2 children. BA, Barat Coll.; JD, Northwestern U. Legis. analyst Nat. Adv. Coun. Women's Ednl. Programs; mem. Ill. Gen. Assembly; chair Nat. Commn. Librs. and Info. Sci., Washington, 1993—; cons. women's initiative Am. Assn. Ret. Persons, Nat. Security Archive, Emeritus Found.; mem. adv. com. White Ho. Conf. Libr. and Info. Svcs., 1979. Mem. ALA, AAUW, LWV, Ill. Bar Assn., Women's Bar Assn., D.C. Bar Assn., Chgo. Bar Assn. Office: Nat Comm on Libraries 1110 Vermont Ave NW Ste 820 Washington DC 20005-3522

SIMON, JEWEL WOODARD, artist; b. Houston, July 28, 1911; d. Chester Arthur and Rachel (Williams) Woodard; m. Edward Lloyd Simon, Feb. 19, 1939 (dec. Sept. 1984); children: Edward Lloyd Jr., Margaret Jewel Simon Summerour. AB summa cum laude, Atlanta U., 1931; BFA, Atlanta Coll. of Art, 1967. Head math. dept. Jack Yates High Sch., Houston, 1931-39; lectr. in field. One-woman shows at Clark Coll., 1973, Carver Mus., 1974, Huntsville Mus., 1979, Internat. Soc. Artists, 1979, Ariel Gallery, Soho, N.Y., 1990, 91; exhibited in group shows at Ringling Mus., Sarasota, Fla., Atlanta U. Gallery, Du Sable Mus., Chgo., Carver Mus., Tuskegee; sculpture "The Tusi Princess" exhibited in Art U.S.A. 58, N.Y., "Paula-Paulina" exhibited in Internat. Artists Show, N.Y.; numerous others; author: (poems) Flight-Preoccupation with Death, Life and Life Eternal, 1990. Chair, vice-chair, emeritus deaconess bd. First Congl. Ch., Atlanta, chmn. social club, 1948; v.p. bd. dirs. Nat. Girls Clubs; pres. E. R. Carter Elem. Sch. PTA, Atlanta, 1946, Jack & Jill Nat. Projects, Atlanta. Recipient Arts Svc. award Phoenix Arts and Theater Co., 1978, Bronze Jubilee award, 1981, James Weldon Johnson award in art, 1977, Golden Poets award, 1985-92, Golden Poet award, 1990, 91, Golden Seal award Nat. Assn. Chiefs of Police, 1994, Editors Choice award, Nat. Libr. Poetry, 1994. Mem. Alpha Kappa Alpha (Golden Girl award, Gold Dove Heritage award 1979). Home: 67 Ashby St SW Atlanta GA 30314-3737

SIMON, JIMMY LOUIS, pediatrician, educator; b. San Francisco, Dec. 27, 1930; s. Sylvain L. and Hilda H. (Netter) S.; m. Marilyn S. Wachter, June 21, 1953; children: Kent, Nancy. A.B., U. Calif.-Berkeley, 1952; M.D., U. Calif.-Berkeley, San Francisco, 1955. Diplomate Am. Bd. Pediatrics. Intern U. Calif., San Francisco, 1955-56; resident Grace-New Haven Hosp., 1956-57; sr. asst. resident Boston Children's Hosp., 1957-58; instr., asst. prof. pediatrics U. Okla., Oklahoma City, 1960-64; asso. prof. U. Tex. Med. Br., Galveston, 1966-72; prof. pediatrics U. Tex. Med. Br., 1972-74; prof., chmn. pediatrics Bowman Gray Sch. Medicine, Wake Forest U., Winston-Salem, N.C., 1974-96; prof., chmn. emeritus pediatric Bowman Gray Sch. Medicine Wake Forest U., Winston-Salem, N.C., 1996—. Served with USAF, 1958-60. Mem. Am. Pediatric Soc., Am. Acad. Pediatrics, So. Soc. Pediatric Rsch., Am. Bd. Pediatrics, Ambulatory Pediatric Assn., Alpha Omega Alpha. Office: Bowman Gray Sch Med Dept Pediatrics Medical Center Blvd Winston Salem NC 27157

SIMON, JOANNA, singer; b. N.Y.C., Oct. 20, 1940; d. Richard Leo and Andrea S.; m. Gerald R. Walker, Dec. 4, 1976. B.A., Sarah Lawrence Coll. Appeared with maj. opera cos. in U.S. and Europe, including cos. of, Washington, Seattle, Balt., Phila.; mem., N.Y.C. Opera, appeared with: Salzburg (Austria) Festival, and Teatro Colon, Buenos Aires, Argentina, regular appearances as guest soloist with maj. U.S. orchs., including N.Y. Philharmonic, Chgo. Symphony, Boston Symphony, Phila. Orch. Office: care NYC Opera New York State Theatre 20 Lincoln Ctr New York NY 10023

SIMON, JOHN BERN, lawyer; b. Cleve., Aug. 8, 1942; s. Seymour Frank and Roslyn (Schultz) S.; children: Lindsey Helaine, Douglas Banning. BS, U. Wis., 1964; JD, DePaul U., 1967. Bar: Ill. 1967. Asst. U.S. atty. U.S. Justice Dept., Chgo., 1967-70, dep. chief civil div., 1970-71, chief civil div., 1971-74; spl. counsel to dir. Ill. Dept. Pub. Aid, Chgo., 1974-75; legal cons. to Commn. on Rev. of Nat. Policy Toward Gambling, Chgo., 1975-76; ptnr. firm Friedman & Koven, 1975-85, mem. exec. com., 1983-85; ptnr. firm

Jenner & Block, 1986—; spl. cons. to adminstr. DEA Dept. Justice, 1976-77; counsel to Gov.'s Revenue Study Commn. on Legalized Gambling, 1977-78; spl. counsel Ill. Racing Bd., 1979-80; lectr. tng. seminars and confs.; instr. U.S. Atty. Gen.'s Advocacy Inst., Washington, 1974; lectr. Nat. Conf. Organized Crime, Washington, 1975, Dade County Inst. Organized Crime, Ft. Lauderdale, Fla., 1976; faculty Cornell Inst. Organized Crime, Ithaca, N.Y., 1976, judge Miner Moot Ct. competition Northwestern U., 1971-73; mem. law coun. DePaul U., 1974-83, pres. law alumni bd., 1984-85, chmn., 1975-79; adj. prof. DePaul U. Coll. Law, 1977, 81; faculty Practising Law Inst., Chgo., 1984. Contbr. articles to profl. jours. Bd. dirs. Cmty. Film Workshop of Chgo., 1977-90; bd. dirs. Friends of Glencoe Parks, 1977-78, sec., 1978-79; mem. nominating com. Glencoe Sch. Bd., 1978-81, chmn. rules com., 1980-81; pres. Glencoe Hist. Soc., 1979-82; mem. Glencoe Zoning Bd. Appeals, Zoning Commn., Sign Bd. Appeals, 1981-86, chmn., 1984-86; mem. Ill. Inaugural Com., 1979, 83, 87, 95; bd. dirs., mem. exec. con. Chgo. World's Fair Authority, 1983-85; mem. Chancery divsn. task force Spl. Commn. on Adminstrn. of Justice in Cook County, 1985—; trustee De Paul U., 1990, chair phys. plant and property com., 1992-94, vice chair, 1995—; commr. Ill. Racing Bd., 1990—; gen. trustee Lincoln Acad. Ill., 1993—. Recipient Bankcroft-Whitney Am. Jurisprudence award, 1965, 66, Judge Learned Hand Human Rels. award Am. Jewish Com., 1994. Mem. ABA (com. on liaison with the judiciary 1983-95), Fed. Bar Assn. (fed. civil procedure com. 1979—, chmn. 1985-86, bd. mgrs. 1987-89, chmn. house com. 1989-90, treas. 1990-91, 2d v.p. 1991-92, 1st v.p. 1992-93, pres. 1993-94), Ill. Police Assn., Ill. Sheriffs Assn., U.S. Treasury Agts. Assn., DePaul U. Alumni Assn. (pres. 1985-87, chmn. spl. gifts com. campaign, chmn. Simon Commn. 1989-91, nat. chair for ann. giving 1991-94), Std. Club. Office: Jenner & Block One IBM Plz Chicago IL 60611

SIMON, JOHN GERALD, law educator; b. N.Y.C., Sept. 19, 1928; s. Robert Alfred and Madeleine (Marshall) S.; m. Claire Aloise Bising, June 14, 1958; 1 son, John Kirby (dec.). Grad., Ethical Culture Schs., 1946; AB, Harvard U., 1950; LLB, Yale U., 1953; LLD (hon.), Ind. U., 1989. Bar: N.Y. 1953. Asst. to gen. counsel Office Sec. Army, 1956-58; with firm Paul, Weiss, Rifkind, Wharton & Garrison, N.Y.C., 1958-62; mem. faculty Yale Law Sch., 1962—, prof. law, 1967-76, Augustus Lines prof. law, 1976—, dep. dean, 1985-90, acting dean, 1991; dir., co-chmn. program on non-profit orgns. Yale U., 1977-88. Author: (with Powers and Gunnemann) The Ethical Investor, 1972. Pres. Taconic Found., 1967—; trustee, sec. Potomac Inst., 1961-93; mem. grad. bd. Harvard Crimson, 1950—; chmn. bd. dirs. Coop. Assistance Fund, 1970-76, vice chmn., 1977—; mem. governing coun. Rockefeller Archives Ctr., 1982-86; trustee The Found. Ctr., 1983-92. 1st lt. U.S. Army, 1953-56. Recipient Certificate of Achievement Dept. Army, 1956. Mem. Phi Beta Kappa. Office: Yale U Law Sch New Haven CT 06520

SIMON, JOHN IVAN, film and drama critic; b. Subotica, Yugoslavia, May 12, 1925; came to U.S., 1941; s. Joseph and Margaret (Reves) Simmon. AB, Harvard U., 1946, AM, 1948, PhD, 1959. Teaching fellow Harvard U., Cambridge, Mass., 1950-53; instr. U. Wash., 1953-54, MIT, Cambridge, 1954-55; asst. prof. Bard Coll., Annandale-on-Hudson, N.Y., 1957-59; assoc. editor Mid-Century Book Soc., 1959-61; drama critic The Hudson Rev., 1960-80, Theatre Arts Mag., 1962, Sta. WNET-TV, 1963, Commonweal, 1967-68; drama and film critic The New Leader, 1962-73, 75-77, cultural critic, 1974—; drama critic New York mag., 1968-75, 77—, film critic, 1975-77; film critic Esquire mag., 1973-75, Nat. Rev., 1978—; lang. critic Esquire mag., 1977-79; guest prof. U. Pitts.; lectr. in field. Author: Acid Test, 1963, Private Screenings, 1967, Movies into Film, 1971, Ingmar Bergman Directs, 1972, Uneasy Stages, 1976, Singularities, 1976, Paradigms Lost: Reflections on Literacy and its Decline, 1980, Reverse Angle: A Decade of American Films, 1982, Something to Declare: Twelve Years of Films from Abroad, 1983, The Sheep from the Goats: Selected Literary Essays, 1989; editor: Film 67/68, (with Richard Schickel) Fourteen for Now, 1969. With USAF, 1944-45. Recipient George Polk Meml. award in film criticism, 1968, George Jean Nathan award for dramatic criticism, 1969-70, Lit. award AAAL, 1976; Fulbright fellow U. Paris, 1949-50. Mem. PEN, N.Y. Drama Critics Circle, N.Y. Film Critics Circle. Office: New York Mag 755 2nd Ave New York NY 10017-5906

SIMON, JOHN P., lawyer; b. Chgo., Feb. 5, 1953. AB summa cum laude, UCLA, 1973, JD, 1976. Bar: Calif. 1976, Ill. 1983. Ptnr. Sidley & Austin, Chgo. Office: Sidley & Austin 1 First Nat Plz Chicago IL 60603*

SIMON, JOHN ROGER, lawyer; b. Los Angeles, Sept. 16, 1939; s. Abram Robert and Roserna (Finsterwald) S.; m. Mary Ellen Bartlett; children: David, Gregory, Whitney, Andrew, Kate. B.S., U. Calif.-Berkeley, 1961, LL.B., 1964. Bar: Calif. 1965, U.S. Dist. Ct. (cen. dist.) Calif. 1965. Assoc. Keatinge and Sterling, Los Angeles, 1964-65; sole practice, Palm Springs, Calif., 1965-66; assoc. Schlesinger, Schlecht & McCullough, Palm Springs, 1966-68, Fine & Pope, Los Angeles, 1968-70, Cox, Castle & Nicholson, Los Angeles, 1970-72; ptnr. Cox, Castle & Nicholson, Los Angeles and Newport Beach, Calif., 1973-86; ptnr. Sheppard, Mullin, Richter & Hampton, Newport Beach, 1986—. Mem. Pacific Club. Contbr. articles to legal jours. Office: Sheppard Mullin Richter Hampton 4695 Macarthur Ct Fl 7 Newport Beach CA 92660-1882

SIMON, JOSEPH PATRICK, food services executive; b. Phila., Nov. 9, 1932; s. Joseph Patrick and Elizabeth Gertrude (McLaughlin) S.; m. Vera Cornelia Steiner, Sept. 15, 1956; children: Joseph Walter, Walter Joseph, Leslie Vera, Ernest William. B.S., Cornell U., 1955. With Slater Systems, 1955-59; with ARA Services, Inc., Phila., 1959-72; regional v.p. ARA Services, Inc., 1964-66, area v.p., 1966-68, group v.p. and sr. v.p., 1968-70, pres. community and school food service div., 1970-71, gen. mgr., pres. internat. ops., 1971-72; v.p., gen. mgr. airline services div. Dobbs Houses Inc., Memphis, 1972-73; group v.p. Service Systems Corp., Buffalo, 1973-79; pres. Service Systems Corp., 1980-85, also nat. dir.; group v.p. P.J. Schmitt subs. Loblaw Ltd., 1984, sr. v.p., 1985-88, also bd. dirs., 1986, 87. Dist. chmn. Detroit United Fund, 1966-67, Nat. Alliance of Businessmen, 1969; mem. adv. bd. McComb Jr. Coll.; mem. council Cornell U., 1980-83; chmn. bd. Sheehan Emergency Hosp., Buffalo, 1984-85; trustee D'Youville Coll.; bd. dirs. United Fund, Buffalo, 1981-82, CODE Inc., 1986-87. Served as 1st lt. U.S. Army, 1955-56. Mem. Assn. Food Svc. Mgmt. (dir.), Nat. Automatic Merchandising Assn. (dir.), Buffalo C. of C. (dir. 1982-84), Cornell Hotel Soc. Mich. (pres.), Memphis Athletic Club, Detroit Athletic Club, Buffalo Club, Park County Club, The Meadows Country Club, Zeta Psi. Episcopalian. Home: 4422 Whisperwood Sarasota FL 34235-6924

SIMON, KAREN JORDAN, retail executive; b. Bridgeport, Conn., Feb. 11, 1953; d. John Francis and Mary (Kirlik) J.; m. James Lawrence Simon, Aug. 12, 1977. BA, So. Conn. U., 1974. Asst. buyer Gimbels Dept. Store, Bridgeport, Conn., 1970-77; buyer Foremost Div./McKesson June Foods Co., Secaucus, N.J., 1977-79; gen. mgr. Charrette Corp., Woburn, Mass., 1979-80; dir. purchasing Cumberland Farms Inc., Canton, Mass., 1980-88; corp. v.p. Dairy Mart Inc., Enfield, Conn., 1988-90; sr. v.p. Circle K Corp., Phoenix, 1990-92; pres., CEO FISCO Farm and Home Stores, Stockton, Calif., 1993—. Bd. dirs. Future Farmers Am., 1994—. Mem. Nat. Assn. Convenience Stores (exec. coun. 1990-92), Ariz. Retailers Assn. (bd. dirs. 1991-92). Office: FISCO 4554 Qantas Ln Ste 1 Stockton CA 95206-4919

SIMON, KARLA WEBER, law educator; b. New Haven, May 30, 1947; d. Frederick Tyler and Irene Marianne (Schoening) S.; m. Leon E. Irish. BA, Western Coll., Oxford, Ohio, 1969; JD, Duke U., 1972; LLM in Taxation, NYU, 1976. Bar: N.C. 1972, U.S. Dist. Ct. (mid. dist.) N.C. 1973, U.S. Ct. Appeals (4th cir.) 1974, U.S. Supreme Ct. 1991. Ptnr. Hobbet & Simon, Durham, N.C., 1972-76; rsch. fellow Yale U. Law Sch., New Haven, 1976-78; asst. prof., assoc. prof. Seton Hall U. Sch. Law, Newark, 1978-84; prof. U. San Diego Sch. Law, 1984-89, coord. L.A. grad. tax program, 1984-88; prof. Cath. U. Am. Sch. Law, Washington, 1989—; instr. U. Fla. Coll. Law, Gainesville, 1975; adj. asst. prof. Yeshiva U. Benjamin Cardozo Sch. Law, N.Y.C., 1977-78; vis. prof. UCLA Sch. Law, 1982-84; vis. fellow Yale Law Sch., 1993-95; cons. O'Melveny & Myers, Washington, 1988-93; exec. dir. Am. Tax Policy Inst., Washington, 1990-92; pres., CEO Internat. Ctr. for Non-for-Profit Law, 1992—. Mem. ABA (vice chmn. spl. project com. sect. taxation 1994-95, tax procedure com. sect. adminstrv. law 1989-94), Am. Coll. Tax Counsel, Am. Law Inst. Democrat. Avocations: running, collecting art and antiques. Home: 1410 Hopkins St NW Washington DC 20036 Office: Cath U Am Sch Law 3600 John McCormack Rd NE Washington DC 20064-0001

SIMON, KENNETH MARK, lawyer; b. Pitts., Apr. 25, 1952; s. Harvey and Jean (Busis) S.; m. Janet Hahn, June 24, 1979; children: Eliza, Jessica, Zachary. BA, U. Pitts., 1974; JD, Georgetown U., 1977. Bar: D.C. 1977. Assoc. Dickstein, Shapiro & Morin, Washington, 1977-85, ptnr., 1985—; mem. exec. com. Dickstein, Shapiro & Morin, Washington, 1992—; sec. Ocean State Power, Burrillville, R.I., 1989—. Gen. counsel Conservation Internat., Washington, 1988-93. Mem. Fed. Energy Bar (com. on cogeneration and ind. power, vice-chmn. 1989-90, chmn. 1990-91), D.C. Bar Assn. (sect. on environment, energy and natural resources energy com., chmn. energy com. 1988-90), Electric Generation Assn. (gen. counsel 1992-95). Democrat. Office: Dickstein Shapiro Morin 2101 L St NW Washington DC 20037-1526

SIMON, LEE WILL, astronomer; b. Evanston, Ill., Feb. 18, 1940; s. Clarence Turkle and Dorothy Elizabeth (Will) S.; m. Mary Jo Welsh, Feb. 19, 1966; children: John, Dan, Steve. B.A., Northwestern U., 1962, M.S., 1964, Ph.D. in Astronomy, 1972. Staff astronomer, program supr. Adler Planetarium, Chgo., 1969-77; dir. Morrison Planetarium, Calif. Acad. Scis., San Francisco, 1977-83, astronomer, 1983-84. Mem. Am. Astron. Soc., Sigma Xi. Roman Catholic. Home and Office: 245 San Marin Dr Novato CA 94945-1220

SIMON, LEONARD SAMUEL, banker; b. N.Y.C., Oct. 28, 1936; s. Nathaniel and Lena (Pasternack) S.; m. Marion Appel, Sept. 1, 1957; children: Andrew, Jonathan. B.S., MIT, 1958; M.S., Columbia U., 1959, Ph.D., 1963. Mem. faculty Grad. Sch. Mgmt., U. Rochester, 1962-79, prof., 1974-79; v.p. Community Savs. Bank, Rochester, N.Y., 1969-74; sr. v.p. Community Savs. Bank, 1974-77, exec. v.p., 1977-83; exec. v.p. Rochester Community Sav. Bank, 1983-84, chmn., chief exec. officer, 1984—; chmn., CEO, pres. RSCB Fin., Inc., 1995—; chmn. Telephone Computing Svc. Corp., 1974-79; trustee Tchrs. Ins. Annuity Assn. Editor-in-chief, founding editor: Interfaces, 1970-76; Author books and articles in field. Past chmn. Rochester-Monroe County chpt. ARC, Rochester Area Ednl. TV Assn., Career Devel. Svcs. of Rochester; past trustee Ctr. for Govt. Rsch.; mem. Urban Policy Conf., Brookings Instn., 1972-73, 64th Am. Assembly. Ford Found. grantee, 1964; recipient MIT Corp. Leadership award, 1987. Mem. Community Bankers Assn. N.Y. State (bd. dirs.), Savs. and Community Bankers Am., Genesee Valley Club, Beta Gamma Sigma. Office: Rochester Community Savs Bank 235 Main St E Rochester NY 14604-2103

SIMON, LOTHAR, publishing company executive; b. Wuppertal, Germany, Sept. 17, 1938; came to U.S., 1961, naturalized, 1973; s. Fritz and Erna (Backhaus) S.; m. Jeannine Rechtman, Oct. 30, 1964; 1 child, Charles. Mgr. book dept. Franz Bader Book Shop and Globe Book Shop, Washington, 1961-66; sales mgr. Humanities Press Inc., N.Y.C., 1966-73; pres. Longman Inc., N.Y.C., 1973-81; pub. cons., 1981-82; pres., chief exec. officer Sheridan House, Inc., Dobbs Ferry, N.Y., 1982—. Mem. Assn. Am. Pubs. Democrat. Club: Town (Scarsdale, N.Y.). Office: Sheridan House Inc 145 Palisade St Dobbs Ferry NY 10522-1617

SIMON, MARILYN WEINTRAUB, art educator, sculptor; b. Chgo., Aug. 25, 1927; d. William and Caroline Mabel (Bergman) Weintraub; m. Walter E. Simon, Mar. 19, 1950 (dec. Sept. 1990); children: Nina Fay Simon-Rosenthal, Jacob Aaron, Maurine Joy Simon Rubinstein, Linda Gay Simon Shapiro. PhB, U. Chgo., 1947; MEd, Temple U., 1969. Cert. tchr., Pa. Bd. sec. Delaware Valley Smelting Corp., Bristol, Pa., 1957-89; art tchr. Calumet Sch. Dist., Ill., 1951-53; art tchr., chmn. elem. art program Cheltenham (Pa.) Sch. Dist., 1969—; real estate agt., Tullytown, Pa.; speaker in field; devel. dir., exec. bd. Art Forms, Manayunk, Pa. One woman show Hahn Gallery, Phila., 1985; permanent exhibits Elkins Park (Pa.) Libr., Univ. Hosp., Cleve.; also represented in med. offices, private collections; author publs. on using art reproductions in edn. Chmn. Phila. chpt. U. Chgo. Alumni Fund Assn., 1978-84. Recipient numerous art awards including 1st prize Doylestown Art League, 1986-87, Best Sculpture award Mummers's Mus. Phila., 1987, Juror's award Cheltenham Art Ctr., 1987-88, 3d prize Abington Art Ctr., 1988, 1st prize for sculpture Art Assn. of Harrisburg, 1989. Mem. Nat. Art Edn. Assn., Pa. Art Educators Assn. (regional rep. 1988-89, Outstanding Art Educator of Yr. award 1987), Oil Pastel Assn. N.Y.C. (invited mem.). Democrat. Jewish. Office: PO Box 29722 Elkins Park PA 19027-0922

SIMON, MARK, architect; b. N.Y.C., Sept. 5, 1946; s. Sidney Simon and Joan (Lewisohn) Crowell; m. Penelope Bellamy, June 22, 1980; children: Jessica Rabe, Thomas Jefferson. BA, Brandeis U., 1968; MArch, Yale U., 1972. Registered architect, N.Y., N.J., Mass., Conn., R.I., Md., Va. Drafter Lewis Assocs., New Haven, 1972-73, Warren Platner Architects, New Haven, 1973-74; project mgr. Chas. W. Moore Assocs., Essex, Conn., 1974-75; project mgr. Moore Grover Harper, Essex, Conn., 1975-78, ptnr., 1978-84; ptnr. Centerbrook Architects, Essex, Conn., 1984—; vis. critic Carnegie Mellon U., Pitts., 1979, Yale U., New Haven, 1979-82, 85-87, N.C. State U., Raleigh, 1982-83, U. Md., 1989-90, Harvard U., 1990. Contbr. articles to profl. jours.; work included in Centerbrook Reinventing American Archiecture (Michael J. Crosbie), 1993, Centerbrook, Book II (Andrea Oppenheimer Dean), 1996. Recipient Record House award Archtl. Record, 1978, 79, 85, award Am. Wood Coun., 1983, 86, 90, 93, Builder's Choice award Builder mag., 1985, 87,90, Product Design award Inst. Bus. Designers, 1993; 40 under 40 honoree Interiors Mag., 1986; named Emerging Voice, N.Y. Archtl. League, 1986, Top 100 List of U.S. Architects, Archtl. Digest, 1991. Fellow AIA (chmn. com. on design 1986, Jour. Drawing award 1982, Design award 1982, 2 gold awards L.I. chpt., 1984, VA design award 1994, New Eng. Regional Coun. design awards 1980, 86, 90, Brick in Architecture award 1995); mem. Conn. Soc. Architects (bd. dirs. 1985-86, Honor award, 1978, 82, 88, 89, 90, 95, Unbuilt Projects Honor award 1990, 92). Office: Centerbrook Architects & Planners PO Box 955 Essex CT 06426

SIMON, MARTIN STANLEY, commodity marketing company executive, economist; b. St. Louis, Sept. 6, 1926; s. Elmer Ellis and Bessye Marion (Werner) S.; m. Rita Edith Scheinhorn, June 18, 1950; children: Deborah, Richard. B.B.A., CCNY, 1949; M.A., NYU, 1953. Econ. statistician Indsl. Commodity Corp, N.Y.C., 1949-52; agrl. econ. statistician Dept. Agr., Washington, 1952-58; commodity analyst Connell Rice & Sugar Co., Inc., Westfield, N.J., 1958-62, asst. to pres., 1962-67, v.p., 1967-74; sr. v.p. Connell Rice & Sugar Co., Inc. (now The Connell Co.), Westfield, N.J., 1974—; cons. AID, Jamaica, 1963; mem. Rice Insp. Industry Adv. Com., Washington, 1971-72; adv. U.S. Del. to UN FAO Intergovtl. Meetings on Rice, 1981. Served with U.S. Army, 1944-46, ETO. Recipient Class of 1920 award for merit in econ. stats. CCNY, 1949. Mem. Am. Econ. Assn., Rice Millers Assn. (chmn. legis. options working group 1984-86, govt. programs com. 1986-87, chmn. PL480 subcom. 1988-90). Nat. Economists Club. Office: The Connell Co 45 Cardinal Dr Westfield NJ 07090-1019

SIMON, MARVIN KENNETH, electrical engineer, consultant; b. N.Y.C., Sept. 10, 1939; s. Sidney and Belle (Cone) S.; m. Anita Joyce Sauerhof; children: Brette, Jeffrey. BEE, CCNY, 1960; MSEE, Princeton U., 1961; PhD, NYU, 1966. Mem. tech. staff Bell Telephone Labs., Holmdel, N.J., 1961-63, 66-68; sr. rsch. engr. Jet Propulsion Lab., Pasadena, Calif., 1968—; adj. prof. Calif. Inst. Tech., Pasadena, 1986-87, 88-90. Author: Telecommunications Systems Engineering, 1973, Phase-Locked Loops and Their Application, 1978, reprinted, 1991, Spread Spectrum Communications, Vols. I, II, III, 1984, Introduction to Trellis--Coded Modulation with Application, 1990, Digital Communication Techniques, Vol. I: Signal Design and Detection, 1994, Spread Spectrum Communications Handbook, 1994, Mobile Communications Handbook, 1995; also numerous articles; patentee in field. Recipient NASA Exptl. Svc. medal, 1979, NASA Exptl. Engring. Achievement medal, 1995. Fellow IEEE (Bicentennial medal 1984), Inst. for Advancement Engring. Avocation: computer games. Office: Jet Propulsion Lab Mail Stop 238-343 4800 Oak Grove Dr Pasadena CA 91109-8001

SIMON, MELVIN, real estate developer, professional basketball executive; b. Oct. 21, 1926; s. Max and Mae Simon; m. Bren Burns, Sept. 14, 1972; children: Deborah, Cynthia, Tamme, David, Max. Bs in Acctg., CCNY, 1949, M in Bus., Real Estate, 1983; PhD (hon.), Butler U., 1986, Ind. U., 1991. Leasing sgt. Albert Frankel Co., Indpls., 1955-60; pres. Melvin Simon & Assocs., Indpls., 1960-73, chmn. bd., 1973—; co-owner Ind. Pacers, Indpls., 1983—; mem. adv. bd. Wharton's Real Estate, Phila., 1986—. Mem. adv. bd. dean's council Ind. U., Bloomington; bd. dirs. United Cerebral Palsy, Indpls., Muscular Dystrophy Assn., Indpls., Jewish Welfare Found., Indpls.; trustee Urban Land Inst., Internat. Council Shopping Ctrs. Recipient Horatio Alger award Boy's Club Indpls., 1986; named Man of Yr., Jewish Welfare Found., 1980. Democrat. Jewish.

SIMON, MICHAEL ALEXANDER, photographer, educator; b. Budapest, Hungary, June 20, 1936; came to U.S., 1957, naturalized, 1962; s. Miklos and Magda (Schreiber) Stern; m. Carol Susan Winters, Jan. 21, 1961; children: Amy Catherine, Nicholas Andrew. Student, Budapest Tech. U., 1954-56, Pa. State U., 1957-58; MFA in Photography, Rochester Inst. Tech., 1986. Propr. Michael Simon Studio, N.Y.C., 1966-68; mem. faculty Beloit (Wis.) Coll., 1968—, asst. prof. dept. art, 1971-76, chmn. dept. art and art history, 1984—, assoc. prof., 1976-85, prof., 1985—; curator photography Theodore Lyman Wright Art Center, 1980—. Free-lance photographer, 1958-66, artist-in-residence, Nat. Park Service, Mus. Div., Harpers Ferry, W.Va., 1971, vis. artist, U. Del., Newark, 1974, Sch. of Art Inst. Chgo., 1978; numerous one-man shows of photography, 1964—, latest being, Wright Art Center, Beloit, 1977, 78, Mpls. Inst. Arts, 1979, U. Rochester, 1985; group shows include, Gallery 38A, Beloit Coll., 1974, U. Iowa, Iowa City, 1975, Columbia Coll. Gallery, Chgo., 1975, Mpls. Inst. Arts, 1976, Evanston (Ill.) Art Center, 1978, Purdue U., Lafayette, Ind., 1978, Kohler Art Center, Sheboygan, Wis., 1979, Madison Art Ctr., (Wis.), 1983; represented in permanent collections, Mus. Modern Art, N.Y.C., U. Kans., Lawrence, Mpls. Inst. Arts, Sheldon Meml. Art Gallery, Lincoln, Nebr.; Author: (with Dennis Moore) First Lessons in Black and White Photography, 1978; contbr. numerous articles on Hungarian photography to profl. publs. Wis. Arts Bd. fellow, 1980; Nat. Endowment for Arts grantee, 1980; Mellon Fund. grantee, 1977. Mem. Soc. for Photog. Edn. (chmn. nat. bd. 1979-81, chmn. Midwest region 1973-76), Szechenyi Soc. of Hungary. Research on history of Hungarian photography, the photographic snapshot. Office: Beloit Coll Dept Art Beloit WI 53511

SIMON, MICHAEL PAUL, general contractor, realtor; b. Madison, Wis., Sept. 23, 1941; s. Michael Francis and Ferne Doris (DeBower) S.; m. Sharon Lee Hackbart, Aug. 31, 1963; children: René M., Michael V. BS in Bldg. Constrn., Bradley U., 1964. Designer, estimator Michael F. Simon Builders, Inc., Waunakee, Wis., 1964-67, v.p., 1967-73, pres., 1973—. Commentator St. John's Cath. Ch., Waunakee, 1975-93. Named Bus. Man of Yr., Waunakee C. of C., 1980, One of Top Dane County Execs., Madison Mag. Poll, 1994. Mem. Nat. Assn. Home Builders (bd. dirs. 1985—), Wis. Builders Assn. (bd. dirs. 1980-85, membership chair 1981), Madison Area Builders Assn. (pres. 1980, chair arbitration com. 1992-94, Builder of Yr. 1980), Waunakee Rotary. Roman Catholic. Avocations: boating, golf, travel.

SIMON, MORDECAI, religious association administrator, clergyman; b. St. Louis, July 19, 1925; s. Abraham M. and Rose (Solomon) S.; m. Maxine R. Abrams, July 4, 1954; children: Ora, Eve, Avrom. BA, St. Louis U., 1947; MA, Washington U., St. Louis, 1952; MHL, Rabbi, Jewish Theol. Sem. Am., N.Y.C., 1952, DD (hon.), 1977. Ordained rabbi, 1952. Rabbi in Mpls., 1952-56, Waterloo, Iowa, 1956-63; exec. dir. Chgo. Bd. Rabbis, 1963-80, exec. v.p., 1980-95, exec. v.p. emeritus, 1995—; nat. chaplain Jewish War Vets., 1977-78. Host: (weekly program) What's Nu?, Sta. WGN-TV, 1973-92. Mem. Jewish Cmty. Rels. Coun., Jewish United Fund; mem. nat. coun. Joint Distbn. Com., Religious Leaders Com. With AUS, 1943-46. Recipient citation Jewish War Vets., 1967, Boy Scouts Am., 1966, 74, 88, Chgo. chpt. Am. Jewish Congress, 1973, Chgo. Conf. Jewish Women's Orgns., 1973, Chgo. Bd. Rabbis, 1973, Rabbinical Svc. award of Appreciation, Jewish Theol. Sem. Am., 1988, Raoul Wallenberg Humanitarian award, 1989, citation and commendation Ill. Ho. Reps., 1995; Rabbi Mordecai Simon Day proclaimed by Gov. James Edgar, State of Ill., 1995. Mem. Rabbinical Assembly, Coun. Religious Leaders Met. Chgo. Home: 621 County Line Rd Highland Park IL 60035-5220 Office: 1 S Franklin St Chicago IL 60606-4609

SIMON, NEIL, playwright, television writer; b. N.Y.C., July 4, 1927; s. Irving and Mamie Simon; m. Joan Balm, Sept. 30, 1953 (dec.); m. Marsha Mason, 1973 (div.); m. Diane Lander, 1987. Student, NYU, 1946; LLD (hon.), Hofstra U., 1981, Williams Coll., 1984. Author materials for Tamiment (Pa.) revues, 1952-53; author: (with brother Danny) sketches Catch a Star, 1955, (with brother Danny) for New Faces of '56; book for musicals Little Me, 1962, Sweet Charity, 1966 (Evening Standard Drama award 1967), Promises, Promises, 1968 (Tony award nomination 1969), They're Playing Our Song, 1979, Little Me (Tony award nomination 1963 version, rev. version), 1982, The Goodbye Girl, 1993; plays include Come Blow Your Horn, 1961, Barefoot in the Park, 1963 (Tony award nomination 1963), The Odd Couple, 1965 (Tony award 1965), The Star-Spangled Girl, 1966, Plaza Suite, 1968 (Tony award nomination 1968), Last of the Red Hot Lovers, 1969 (Tony award nomination 1970), The Gingerbread Lady, 1970, The Prisoner of Second Avenue, 1971 (Tony award nomination 1972), The Sunshine Boys, 1972, The Good Doctor, 1973, God's Favorite, 1974, California Suite, 1976, Chapter Two, 1977, I Ought to be in Pictures, 1980, Fools, 1981, Brighton Beach Memoirs, 1983, Biloxi Blues, 1985 (Tony award for Best Playwright 1985, Best Play 1985), The Odd Couple (female version), 1985, Broadway Bound, 1986 (Tony award nomination 1987), Rumors, 1988, Lost in Yonkers, 1991 (Pulitzer Prize for drama 1991, Tony award Best Play 1991), Jake's Women, 1992, Laughter on the 23rd Floor, 1993, London Suite, 1995; wrote screenplays adapted from own plays: Barefoot in the Park, 1967, The Odd Couple, 1968, Plaza Suite, 1971, Last of the Red Hot Lovers, 1972, The Prisoner of Second Avenue, 1975, The Sunshine Boys, 1975, California Suite, 1978, Chapter Two, 1979, Only When I Laugh (adapted from play The Gingerbread Lady), 1981, I Ought to be in Pictures, 1982, Brighton Beach Memoirs, 1986, Biloxi Blues, 1988, Broadway Bound, 1992 (TV motion picture), Lost in Yonkers, 1993, (TV motion picture) Jake's Women, 1996; other screenplays include After the Fox, 1966, The Out-of-Towners, 1970, The Heartbreak Kid, 1973, Murder by Death, 1976, The Goodbye Girl, 1977, The Cheap Detective, 1978, Seems Like Old Times, 1980, Max Dugan Returns, 1983, The Lonely Guy (adaptation), 1984, The Sluggers Wife, 1984, The Marrying Man, 1991; other motion pictures based on his stage plays: Come Blow Your Horn, 1963, Sweet Charity, 1969, The Star-Spangled Girl, 1971; wrote for TV shows: The Phil Silvers Arrow Show, 1958, The Tallulah Bankhead Show, 1951, The Sid Caesar Show, 1956-57 (Emmy award 1956-57), Phil Silvers Show, 1958-59 (Emmy award 1958-59), Garry Moore Show, 1959-60; also NBC spl. The Trouble with People, 1972. Served to cpl. USAAF, 1945-46. Recipient Sam S. Shubert award 1968, Writers Guild screen awards, 1968, 70, 75, Writers Guild Laurel award, 1979. Mem. Dramatists Guild, Writers Guild Am. (Laurel award 1979, screen awards 1968, 70, 75). Address: care A DaSilva 502 Park Ave New York NY 10022-1108

SIMON, PAUL, musician, composer; b. Newark, Oct. 13, 1941; s. Louis and Belle S.; m. Peggy Harper (div.); 1 son, Harper; m. Carrie Fisher (div.); m. Edie Brickell, 1992; 1 child, Adrian Edward. B.A., Queens Coll.; postgrad., Bklyn. Law Sch. With music group Simon and Garfunkel, 1964-71; soloist, 1972—; songs recorded with Garfunkel include Mrs. Robinson (Grammy award), The Boxer, Bridge Over Troubled Water (Grammy award); albums with Garfunkel include Wednesday Morning 3 A.M, 1964, Sounds of Silence, 1966, Parsley, Sage, Rosemary and Thyme, 1966, The Graduate (soundtrack), 1968 (Grammy award), Bookends, 1968, Bridge over Troubled Waters, 1970 (Grammy award), Simon and Garfunkel's Greatest Hits, 1972, Concert in the Park, 1982; solo albums include Paul Simon, 1972, There Goes Rhymin' Simon, 1973, Live Rhymin', 1975, Still Crazy After All These Years, 1975 (Grammy award), Greatest Hits, Etc., 1977, One-Trick Pony, 1980, Hearts and Bones, 1983, Graceland, 1986 (Grammy award 1986, 87), Negotiations and Love Songs 1971-86, 1989, Paul Simon: Solo, 1990, The Rhythm of the Saints, 1990, 1964-93, 1993; concerts include Central Park, 1991, Born at the Right Time tour, Johannesburg, South Africa, 1992, series with Art Garfunkel, Paramount, 1993; appeared in films Annie Hall, 1977, One-Trick Pony, 1980; appeared in Showtime prodn. Paul Simon's Graceland: The African Concert, 1987; author: At the Zoo, 1991. Recipient Emmy award for Paul Simon Spl., NBC-TV, 1977; inducted into the Rock & Roll Hall of Fame, 1990.

SIMON, PAUL, senator, educator, author; b. Eugene, Oreg., Nov. 29, 1928; s. Martin Paul and Ruth (Troemel) S.; m. Jeanne Hurley, Apr. 21, 1960;

children: Sheila, Martin. Student, U. Oreg., 1945-46, Dana Coll., Blair, Nebr., 1946-48; 39 hon. doctorates. Pub. Troy (Ill.) Tribune and 14 other So. Ill. weeklies., 1948-66; mem. Ill. Ho. of Reps., 1955-63, Ill. Senate, 1963-69; lt. gov. Ill., 1969-73; fellow John F. Kennedy Sch. Govt., Harvard U., 1972-73; founded pub. affairs reporting program Sangamon State U., Springfield, Ill., 1972-73; mem. 94th-98th Congresses from 22d and 24th Dists. 94th-98th Congresses from 24th and 22d Dists. Ill., Ill., 1975-85; U.S. Senator from Ill., 1985-96; U.S. presdl. candidate, 1987-88. Author: Lovejoy: Martyr to Freedom, 1964, Lincoln's Preparation for Greatness, 1965, A Hungry World, 1966, You Want to Change the World, So Change It, 1971, The Tongue-Tied American, 1980, The Once and Future Democrats, 1982, The Glass House, Politics and Morality in The Nation's Capitol, 1984, Beginnings, 1986, Let's Put America Back to Work, 1986, Winners and Losers, 1989; (with Jeanne Hurley Simon) Protestant-Catholic Marriages Can Succeed, 1967; (with Arthur Simon) The Politics of World Hunger, 1973, Advice and Consent, 1992, Freedom's Champion: Elijah Lovejoy, 1994. With CIC, AUS, 1951-53. Recipient Am. Polit. Sci. Assn. award, 1957; named Best Legislator by Ind. Voters of Ill., 7 times. Mem. Luth. Human Rels. Assn., Am. Legion, VFW, NAACP, Urban League. Democrat. Lutheran. Office: US Senate 462 Dirksen Senate Bldg Washington DC 20510*

SIMON, PETER E., publishing executive; b. Bklyn., June 29, 1953. BA in English, CCNY, 1971; MA in Libr. Sci., Columbia U., 1980. Database mgr. R.R. Bowker, N.Y.C., 1982-84; v.p. R.R. Bowker/Reed Reference Pubs., 1984-93; sr. v.p. Reed Reference Pub., New Providence, N.J., 1993-95, exec. v.p., 1995—. Mem. ABA (assoc.), Info. Industry Assn. (bd. dirs.), Book Industry Study Group, Phi Beta Kappa.

SIMON, RALPH E., electronics executive; b. Passaic, N.J., Oct. 20, 1930; s. Paul and Sophie (Epstein) S.; m. Elena Schiffman, June 22, 1952; children: Richard L., David P., Michael A. BA, Princeton U., 1952; PhD, Cornell U., 1959. Mem. tech. staff RCA Labs., Princeton, N.J., 1958-67, dir., 1967-69; mgr. RCA Electronic Components, Lancaster, Pa., 1969-75; v.p. RCA Solid State Div., Lancaster, Pa., 1975-80; v.p. optoelectronics div. Gen. Instrument Corp., Palo Alto, Calif., 1980-84; pres. Lytel Inc., Somerville, N.J., 1984-87; pres., CEO QT Optoelectronics, Sunnyvale, Calif., 1989—; dir. Xsirius Scientific, Inc., Marina Del Rey, Calif., 1988-91, Applied Electron Corp., Santa Clara, Calif., 1987—. pres., mem. Lawrence Twp. Bd. Edn., Lawrenceville, N.J., 1964-69, Community Action Orgn., 1967-69. Recipient UK Zworykin prize IEEE, 1973. Office: QT Optoelectronics 610 N Mary Ave Sunnyvale CA 94086-2906

SIMON, ROBERT G., lawyer; b. N.Y.C., Feb. 21, 1927; s. Monroe and Claire S. S.; m. Norma Plavnick, Dec. 18, 1949; children: Mark A., Susan. BA, Cornell U., 1947; LLB, JD, Georgetown U., 1950; LLM, NYU, 1961. Bar: D.C. 1950, N.Y. 1951, U.S. Supreme Ct. 1955. Assoc. firms in N.Y.C., 1950-52; legal sec. to judge U.S. Dist. Ct. So. Dist. N.Y., 1953-58; assoc. Jaffe & Wachtell, N.Y.C., 1958-61; legal adv. TV series The Verdict Is Yours, 1958-60; successively dir. bus. affairs, v.p., sr. v.p., mgr. bus. affairs dept. McCann-Erickson, Inc., N.Y.C., 1961-80; sr. broadcast atty. The Interpublic Group of Cos., N.Y.C., 1980-95; adj. faculty Manhattan Community Coll., 1967, Baruch Coll., 1968, CCNY, 1968, New Sch. Social Research, 1972-73; speaker in field. Author: (with Norma Simon) Choosing a College Major: The Social Sciences, 1981; contbr. articles to profl. jours. Dem.-Liberal candidate for county clk. Westchester County, N.Y., 1952; chmn. Narcotics Guidance Coun., Pelham, N.Y., 1973; mem. Nat. Media Coun. on Disability, 1986-90; bd. dirs., gen. counsel Nat. Challenge Com. on Disability, 1986-88; mem. adv. bd. The Caption Ctr. WGBH Found., 1987—. With USAAF, 1944-46. Mem. NATAS (chpt. gov. 1972-85, treas. 1976-81, 1st v.p. 1981-83, pres. 1983-85, nat. trustee 1981-85), N.Y. County Lawyers Assn. (com. on comms. and entertainment law 1990-94), Am. Assn. Advt. Agys. (com. on broadcast adminstrn. policy 1985-93). Home: 2 Garden Pl Pelham NY 10803-3207

SIMON, ROGER, newspaper columnist, author; b. Chgo., Mar. 29, 1948; s. Sheldon and Pauline (Odess) S.; m. Marcia Kramer, May 15, 1977. BA, U. Ill., 1970. Reporter City News Bur. Chgo., 1970; columnist Waukegan News-Sun, Ill., 1970-72, Chgo. Sun-Times, 1972-84, Balt. Sun, 1984—; work syndicated by Creators Syndicate; columnist Regardie's mag., Washington, 1986-91; nationally syndicated columnist Balt. Sun, Balt., 1984—. Author: Simon Says: The Best of Roger Simon, 1985, Road Show, 1990; contbr. freelance articles to Playboy mag., TV Guide, N.Y. Times Review of Books. Recipient Page One award Chgo. Newspaper Guild, 1972, 74, 75, 77, 78, 79, 82, 1st place award for public service UPI, 1974, 80, 82, 83, Silver Gavel award ABA, 1975, 76, 79, Nat. Merit award Assn. Trial Lawyers Am., 1975, 76, Disting. Reporter award Inland Daily Press Assn., 1975, 1st place award for column AP, 1976, 77, 78, 80, 95, Peter Lisagor award, 1980, 82, 83, Distinguished Writing award for commentary Am. Soc. Newspaper Editors, 1984, 86, 2nd place, 1993, Washington-Balt. Newspaper Guild award, 1986, 87, 92, Front Page award for commentary Washington-Balt. Newspaper Guild, 1986, 87, 92, Nat. Headliner award for outstanding column, 1987, 89, 2nd place, 1992, Best Column award Md. chpt. Soc. Profl. Journalists, 1991, 92, 95, 2nd Place Humor award SOc. Newspaper Columnists, 1995; work included in Best Newspaper Writing 1984, 86, 93. Mem. U. Ill. Alumni Assn., Pres.' Council. Office: Baltimore Sun 1627 K St NW Washington DC 20006-1702

SIMON, ROGER LICHTENBERG, writer; b. N.Y.C., Nov. 22, 1943; s. Norman and Ruth Elaine (Lichtenberg) S.; m. Dyanne Asimow, June 10, 1965 (div. May 1981); children: Raphael, Jesse. BA, Dartmouth U., 1964; MFA, Yale U., 1970. U.S. rep. Internat. Mystery Writers meetings in Mex., Italy, Spain and USSR. Author: Heir, 1968, The Mama Tass Manifesto, 1970, Wild Turkey, 1973, The Big Fix, 1974 (Mystery Writers of Am. Spl. award, John Creasy award of Crime Writers Gt. Britain), Peking Duck, 1978, California Roll, 1985, The Straight Man, 1986, Raising the Dead, 1988 (1st detective novel pub. in Soviet Union); screenwriter (films) The Big Fix, 1979, Bustin' Loose, 1980, My Man Adam, 1985, Enemies: A Love Story, 1988 (nominated Acad. award 1990), (with Paul Mazurksy) Scenes From a Mall, 1991. Mem. Internat. Assn. Crime Writers (1st N.Am. pres.), Writers Guild Am. (past bd. dirs.) PEN Ctr. USA West (pres.). *

SIMON, RONALD I., financial consultant; b. Cairo, Nov. 4, 1938; came to U.S., 1942; s. David and Helene (Zilkha) S.; m. Anne Faith Hartman, June 19, 1960; children: Cheryl, Eric, Daniel. BA, Harvard U., 1960; MA, Columbia U., 1962, PhD, 1968. V.p. Harpers Internat., N.Y.C., 1959-62; fin. analyst Amerace Corp., N.Y.C., 1965-66; v.p. Am. Foresight Inc., Phila., 1966-67; asst. to pres. Avco Corp., Greenwich, Conn., 1967-70; exec. v.p. Avco Community Developers Inc., La Jolla, Calif., 1970-73; pres. Ronald I. Simon Inc., La Jolla, 1973—, Delta Data Systems Corp., Phila., 1980-81; exec. v.p. Towner Petroleum Corp., Houston, 1983-85; mng. dir., chief fin. officer The Henley Group Inc., La Jolla, 1986-90; pvt. practice fin. cons. La Jolla, 1990—; chmn. Sonant Corp., San Diego; bd. dirs. Softnet Corp., Chgo., Citadel Corp., L.A. Bd. dirs. San Diego Opera Co., 1988-90; bd. dirs. Univ. Art Gallery U. Calif., San Diego. Ford Found. fellow, 1963-65; recipient Ann. award Nat. Comml. Fin. Conf., 1963. Office: 1020 Prospect St Ste 410C La Jolla CA 92037-4148

SIMON, SEYMOUR, lawyer, former state supreme court justice; b. Chgo., Aug. 10, 1915; s. Ben and Gertrude (Rusky) S.; m. Roslyn Schultz Biel, May 26, 1954; children: John B., Nancy Simon Cooper, Anthony Biel. B.S., Northwestern U., 1935, J.D., 1938; LL.D. (hon.), John Marshall Law Sch., 1982, North Park Coll., 1986, Northwestern U., 1987. Bar: Ill. 1938. Spl. atty. Dept. Justice, 1938-42; practice law Chgo., 1946-74; judge Ill. Appellate Ct., Chgo., 1974-80; presiding justice Ill. Appellate Ct. (1st Dist., 3d Div.), 1977, 79; justice Ill. Supreme Ct., 1980-88; ptnr. Rudnick & Wolfe, Chgo., 1988—; former chmn. Ill. Low-Level Radioactive Waste Disposal Facility Siting Commn.; former dir. Nat. Gen. Corp., Bantam Books, Grosset & Dunlap, Inc., Gt. Am. Ins. Corp. Mem. Cook County Bd. Commrs., 1961-66, pres., 1962-66; pres. Cook County Forest Preserve Dist., 1962-66; mem. Pub. Bldg. Commn., City Chgo., 1962-67; Alderman 40th ward, Chgo., 1955-61, 67-74; Democratic ward committeeman, 1960-74; bd. dirs. Schwab Rehab. Hosp., 1961-71, Swedish Covenant Hosp., 1969-75. Served with USNR, 1942-45. Decorated Legion of Merit; recipient 9th Ann. Pub. Svc. award Tau Epsilon Rho, 1963, Hubert L. Will award Am. Vets. Com., 1983, award of merit Decalogue Soc. Lawyers, 1986, Judge Learned Hand award Am. Jewish Com., 1994, Frances Feinberg Meml. Crown award Associated Talmud Torahs of Chgo., 1995; named to Sr. Citizen's Hall of Fame, City of Chgo., 1989, Hall of Fame Jewish Comty. Ctrs. Chgo., 1989. Mem. ABA, Ill. Bar Assn., Chgo. Bar Assn., Chgo. Hist. Soc., Decalogue Soc. Lawyers (Merit award 1986), Izaak Walton League, Chgo. Hort. Soc., Comml. Club Chgo., Standard Club, Variety Club, Order of Coif; Phi Beta Kappa, Phi Beta Kappa Assocs. Home: 1555 N Astor St Chicago IL 60610-1673 Office: Rudnick & Wolfe Ste 1800 203 N La Salle St Chicago IL 60601-1210

SIMON, SHARRON LOUISE, emergency department administrator; b. Mishwaka, Ind., June 30, 1940; d. Irvin LeRoy Kindig and Mary Madeline (Good) Charlson. ADN, Purdue U., 1974; postgrad., Valparaiso U., 1984-86; BS in Health Arts, Coll. St. Francis, 1989; postgrad., U. Colo., 1990—. SCLS, CEN. Head nurse emergency svcs. The Meth. Hosp. Southlake Campus, Merrillville, Ind., The Meth. Hosp. Northlake Campus, Gary, Ind., 1975-80; asst. to dir. emergency svcs. The Meth. Hosp. Northlake and Southlake Campus, Gary, Ind., 1980, dir. emergency svcs., 1981; dir. Emergency Svcs., Valparaiso, Ind., 1981—; cons. Porter Emergency Physician Assocs., Valparaiso, 1985-92, exec. conf. coord., 1995—; speaker in field. Contbr. articles to profl. jours. Leader Girls Scouts Am., Chesterton, Ind., 1967-73, co-dir. Girls Scouts Am. Day Camp, 1971, dir., 1972. Mem. Nat. Assn. Ambulatory Care, NAFE, Emergency Nurses Assn. Avocations: sculpting, photography. Office: Porter Meml Hosp 814 Laporte Ave Valparaiso IN 46383-5860

SIMON, SHEILA SANDRA, special education educator, administrator; b. N.Y.C., July 24, 1940; d. Leo and Frances (Wexler) Brown; children: Steven Marc, Scott Irwin, Sean Eric, Rebecca Shane. BA in Psychology, Lehman Coll., Bronx, 1974; MS in Spl. Edn., Coll. New Rochelle, N.Y., 1978; MS in Counseling, Loyola Marymount Coll., L.A., 1992; postgrad., UCLA, 1993—. Elem. tchr. spl. edn. N.Y.C. Pub. Schs., Bronx, 1974-79; tchr. spl. edn. Lincoln Spl. Sch., Palm Desert, Calif., 1979-83; tchr., chair dept. spl. edn. Mt. Vernon Jr. H.S. L.A. Unified Sch. Dist., 1983-86, resource specialist Revere Jr. H.S., 1986-91, outreach cons. Manual Arts H.S., 1991-94; exec. dir. spl. edn. commn. L.A. Unified Schs., 1994—. Mem. Los Angeles County Multicultural Collaborative, 1994, Los Angeles County Hate Crime Network, L.A. Roundtable for Children. Recipient Outstanding Sch. Svc. award Revere PTA, L.A., 1988. Mem. Coun. for Exceptional Children, Calif. Assn. of Resource Specialists, Calif. Assn. Counseling and Devel., Calif. Sch. Counselors, Kappa Delta Pi, Delta Kappa Gamma. Avocations: camping, music, travel, painting in oil and watercolor. Office: LA Unified Sch Dist Spl Edn Commn 450 N Grand Ave # H256 Los Angeles CA 90012-2100

SIMON, SHELDON WEISS, political science educator; b. St. Paul, Jan. 31, 1937; s. Blair S. and Jennie M. (Dim) S.; m. Charlann Lilwin Scheid, Apr. 27, 1962; 1 child, Alex Russell. BA summa cum laude, U. Minn., 1958, PhD, 1964; MPA, Princeton U., 1960; postgrad., U. Geneva, 1962-63. Asst. prof., then prof. U. Ky., 1966-75; prof. polit. sci. Ariz. State U., 1975—, chmn. dept., 1975-79, dir. Ctr. Asian Studies, 1980-88; vis. prof. George Washington U., 1965, U. B.C., Can., 1972-73, 79-80, Carleton U., 1976, Monterey Inst. Internat. Studies, 1991, 96, Am. Grad. Sch. Internat. Mgmt., 1991-92; cons. USIA Rsch. Analysis Corp., Am. Enterprise Inst. Pub. Policy Rsch., Hoover Instn., Orkand Corp., Nat. Bur. Asian Rsch. Author: Asian Neutralism and U.S. Policy, 1975, The ASEAN States and Regional Security, 1982, The Future of Asian-Pacific Security Collaboration, 1988; editor: The Military and Security in the Third World, 1978, East Asian Security in the Post-Cold War Era, 1993; also others; contbr. articles to profl. jours., chpts. to books. Mem. Com. Fgn. Relations, Phoenix, 1976—; bd. dirs. Phoenix Little Theater, 1976-79. Grantee Am. Enterprise Inst., 1974, Earhart Found., 1979, 81, 92, 84, 88, U.S. Inst. Peace, 1994-96; Hoover Instn. fellow, 1980, 85. Mem. Am. Polit. Sci. Assn., Assn. Asian Studies, Internat. Studies Assn. (profl. ethics com. 1987-91, v.p. 1991-93), Asia Soc. (contemporary affairs com. 1987—), U.S. Coun. for Asia-Pacific Security, Phi Beta Kappa. Democrat. Jewish. Avocations: acting, singing, tennis. Home: 5630 S Rocky Point Rd Tempe AZ 85283-2134 Office: Ariz State U Polit Sci Dept Tempe AZ 85287

SIMON, STEVE, public relations executive. CEO S&S Pub. Rels., Inc. Office: S & S Public Relations Inc 400 Skokie Blvd Ste 200 Northbrook IL 60062-7902*

SIMON, WILLIAM, biomathematician, educator; b. Pitts., May 27, 1929; m. Maxine Check, June 27, 1965; children: Robert, Steven, Alan. B.S. in Physics, Carnegie Inst. Tech., 1950; M.A. in Applied Physics, Harvard U., 1952, Ph.D., 1958. Staff physicist Comstock & Wescott, Inc. (cons. engrs.), Cambridge, Mass., 1951-53; head instruments sect. Spencer Kennedy Lab., Boston, 1953-57; sr. systems engr. Nat. Radio Co., Malden, Mass., 1957-59; chief physicist Image Instruments, Inc., Newton Lower Falls, Mass., 1959-60; mem. staff M.I.T. Lincoln Lab. and Center for Computer Tech. in Biomed. Scis., 1961-64; research assn. dept. physiology, dir. biomed. tech. cons. group Harvard U. Med. Sch., 1964-68; assn. prof., head div. biomath. U. Rochester Sch. Medicine and Dentistry, 1968-77, prof., head div. biomath., 1977-82, prof. biophysics, 1982—, prof. med. info., 1989; vis. assoc. prof. dept. elec. engring. MIT, 1974-75. Author: Mathematical Techniques for Physiology and Medicine, 1972, Mathematical Techniques for Biology and Medicine, 1977; contbr. articles to profl. jours. Office: U Rochester Box BPHYS Rochester NY 14642

SIMON, WILLIAM EDWARD, investment banker, former secretary of treasury; b. Paterson, N.J., Nov. 27, 1927; m. Carol Girard, Sept. 9, 1950; children: William Edward Jr., John Peter, Mary Beth Simon Streep, Carol Leigh Simon Porges, Aimee Simon Bloom, Julie Ann Simon Munro, Johanna Katrina. BA in Govt. and Law, Lafayette Coll., 1952, LLD (hon.), 1973; other hon. degrees include LLD, Pepperdine U., 1975, Manhattanville Coll., 1978, Washington U., 1980, Boston U., 1980, Washington Coll., 1984, Rider Coll., 1984, Seton Hall U., 1984, Fairleigh Dickinson U., 1984, Rutgers U., 1985, U. Rochester, 1985; D of Civil Law, Jacksonville U., 1976; Scriptural Degree, Israel Torah Rsch. Inst., Jerusalem, 1976; Doctor Philosophiae honoris causa, Tel Aviv U., 1976; DSc, New Eng. Coll., 1977; HHD, Springfield U., 1986; D of Econs., Hanyang U., Seoul, Republic of Korea, 1988. With Union Securities Co., N.Y.C., 1952-57, asst. v.p., mgr. mcpl. trading dept., 1955-57; v.p. Weeden & Co., N.Y.C., 1957-64; joined Salomon Bros. & Hutzler, N.Y.C., 1964; sr. ptnr., mem. exec. com. Salomon Bros., N.Y.C., 1964-73; dep. sec. Dept. Treasury, Washington, 1973-74; adminstr. Fed. Energy Office, Washington, 1973-74; sec. of the treasury, 1974-77; sr. cons. Booz Allen & Hamilton Inc., 1977-79; sr. advisor Blyth Eastman Dillon & Co. Inc., 1977-80; dep. chmn. Olayan Investments Co. Establishment, 1980-82; chmn. Crescent Diversified Ltd., 1980-82, Wesray Corp., 1981-86, Wesray Capital Corp., 1984-86; chmn. emeritus Wesray Corp., Wesray Capital Corp., 1987; currently chmn., pres. William E. Simon & Sons, Morristown, N.J.; co-chmn. WSGP Internat. Inc., L.A.; chmn. William E. Simon Found., Inc.; bd. dirs. Pompano Pk. Realty, Inc., Castleton, Inc.; former cons. W.R. Grace & Co., Brazilinvest, Allstate Ins. Co., Calvin Bullock Ltd., Johnson & Johnson; mem. pub. rev. bd. Arthur Andersen & Co.; past chmn. World Trade Bancorp.; lectr. numerous schs. including Harvard Bus. Sch., U. Mich., Georgetown U., Boston U., U. Chgo., Columbia U., Lafayette Coll., U. Notre Dame, Oxford U., USAF Acad., U.S. Mil. Acad., L.I. U., Washington U., St. Louis, Princeton U., Erasmus U., Rotterdam, The Netherlands, U. Rochester, Susquehanna U., Fairleigh Dickerson U.; lectr. confs., round tables, panels, corps., mem. adv. bd. Classics of Liberty Libr., Corp. for Devel. and Commerce, The Papers of Albert Gallatin. Author: A Time for Truth, 1978, A Time For Action, 1980; mem. editorial adv. bd. Gryphon Editions Inc., The Washington Times. Pres. John M. Olin Found., Richard Nixon Presdl. Libr. and Birthplace Found.; chmn. investment com. USAF Acad., USAF Acad. Academic Devel. Fund; former pres. and treas. U.S. Olympic Com., now mem. bd. adminstrs., fin. com.; mem. budget and fin. com., trustee Heritage Found.; trustee The Animal Med. Ctr., Nat. Investors Hall of Fame, Boston U.; hon. trustee Adelphi U., Newark Boys Chorus Sch.; trustee emeritus Lafayette Coll.; trustee, mem. investment com., mem. exec. adv. coun., trustee Simon Sch., U. Rochester; chmn. bd. trustees U.S. Olympic Found.; bd. dirs. Sequoia Inst., World Cup '94 Organizing Com., Kissinger Assocs., Nat. Football Found. and Hall of Fame Inc., dir. emeritus, Cath. Big Bros., Citizens Against Govt. Waste, Space Studies Inst., Boys Harbor Inc., Internat. Found. for Edn. and Self Help, Citizens Network for Fgn. Affairs, Atlantic Coun. of U.S., Target; bd. dirs., co-chmn. endowment com. Covenant House; hon. dir. The Gerald R. Ford Found.; bd. advisors Cath. League for Religious and Civil Rights; mem. nat. coun. trustees Freedoms Found. at Valley Forge; mem. adv. bd. Jesse Owens Found., sec./treas.; mem. bd. overseers Hoover Instn. on War, Revolution and Peace, Stanford U., Exec. Coun. on Fgn. Diplomacy; mem. adv. bd. Am. rep. Pacific Security Rsch. Inst., Sydney, Australia, U. So. Calif. Sch. Bus. Adminstrn., Nat. Ethnic Coalition of Orgns.; trustee Newark Acad., mem. nominating com.; mem. adv. bd., life mem. S.A.I.L., Inc.-Am. Tall Ship Syndicate, Pvt. Sector Initiatives Found., Women's Sports Found., U.S. Assn. Blind Athletes, Caths. Committed to Support the Pope, The Acton Inst., Ctr. for Internat. Mgmt. Edn., U. Dallas, Ctr. for Christianity and the Common Good; mem. nat. adv. bd. Sudden Infant Death Syndrome Alliance; hon. bd. govs. Tel Aviv U.; bd. dirs. U. Limerick Found.; mem. bd. advisors William J. Casey chair geopolit. studies John M. Ashbrook Ctr. Pub. Affairs; mem. fed. adv. bd. Commn. for Preservation of Treasury Bldg.; mem. Inaugural adv. bd. Gene Autry Western Heritage Mus.; mem. adv. coun. Consumer Alert; mem. internat. adv. coun. Internat. Ctr. for the Disabled; mem. com. Cardinal's Com. of the Laity; bd. govs. Hugh O'Brian Youth Fedn.; bd. govs., mem. fin., investment coms., spl. com. on hosp. environ., mem. internat. adv. bd. N.Y. Hosp.; bd. govs. Ronald Reagan Presdl. Found.; mem. Amb. John D. J. Moore Scholarship Fund, Univ. Coll., Dublin, Ireland, Pres.'s Com. on Arts and Humanities; mem. com. for restoration John B. Kelly Jr. Meml. Boathouse; mem. vis. com. Marine Scis. Rsch. Ctr., SUNY, Stony Brook; mem. internat. councillors Ctr. for Strategic and Internat. Studies; mem. hon. com. Women's Econ. Round Table; mem. exec. com. The Bretton Woods Com.; mem. policy coun. The Tax Found.; mem. of coun. Templeton Coll.; prin. Coun. for Excellence in Govt.; mem. exec. coun. Daytop Village, Inc.; mem. nat. steering com. Jefferson Energy Found.; mem. internat. com. Miles Jesu Internat. Com. for Human Dignity; mem. nat. planning bd. Morality in Media Inc.; mem. chmn.'s coun. Nat. Coun. on Alcoholism and Drug Dependence Inc.; mem. diplomatic coun. People to People Sports Com. Inc.; hon. chmn. Inst. Ednl. Affairs; hon. chmn. fund raising campaign Morris Ctr. YMCA; hon. co-chmn. Liberty Pk. Found., Suffolk County Vietnam Vets. Meml. Commn., U.S. Fitness Acad. Campaign, Nat. Fitness Found.; mem. adv. coun. William J. Donovan Meml. Found. Inc. Served with inf. U.S. Army, 1946-48. Decorated Order of the Nile (Egypt); recipient Investment Bankers Assn. Am. award, 1970, Small Bus. Adminstrn. citation, 1971, 2d ann. Youth Services award Wall St. div. B'nai B'rith, 1971, Outstanding Service to His Country award Port Authority N.Y., 1973, Merit award Securities Industry Assn., 1973, Outstanding Citizen of N.J. award Advt. Club N.J., 1974, Financial World award, 1974, Good Scout award Boy Scouts Am., 1974, Exec. Govt. award OIC Govt. Relations Service, 1974, Outstanding Citizen of Yr. award, 1974, U.S. Indsl. Payroll Savs. award, 1974, Civic Leadership award Am. Jewish Com., 1975, Dean's citation Am. U., 1975, Trustees medal Fairleigh Dickinson U., 1975, Gold medal Nat. Inst. Social Scis., 1975, Am. Eagle award Nat. Invest in Am. Coun., 1975, Achievement award Newark Acad. Alumni Assn., 1975, Bicentennial award U.S. Citizen's Congress, 1975, Young Americans For Freedom citation, 1975, Am. Inst. for Pub. Service award, 1976, Bus. in Pub. Affairs award C. of C. of Md., 1976, Flame of Truth award Fund for Higher Edn. in Israel, 1976, Disting. Achievements award Money Marketers of NYU, 1976, Pa. Soc. medal, 1976, NYU Coll. Bus. and Pub. Adminstrn. medal, 1976, Govt. Service award Pub. Relations Soc. Am., 1976, Carnauba Palm award S.C. Johnson and Son Inc., 1976, proclamation Pub. Relations Soc. Am., 1976, Pres.'s award for outstanding achievement, 1976, Econ. Forum citation Chapman Coll., 1977, Alexander Hamilton award Dept. Treasury, 1977, Am. Legion award, 1977, Brotherhood award NCCJ, 1977, Outstanding Achievement award Freedoms Found. at Valley Forge, 1978, Order of Anthony Wayne citation Valley Forge Mil. Acad. and Jr. Coll., 1978, Disting. Patriot award SAR, 1979, George Washington Kidd award Lafayette Coll. Alumni Assn., 1979, George Washington Honor medal Valley Forge Freedom Found., 1979, Eastside Conservative Club, 1980, Service Above Self award, Easton Rotary Club, 1980, Charles Edison Meml. award, Leadership award Columbia Bus. Sch., 1982, Cath. Big Bros. of Yr. award Lotus Club, 1982, Hall of Fame award Tri-County Scholarship, 1983, Disting. Service award The Liberty Bowl, 1983, Jesse Owens Internat. Amateur Athletic award, 1984, Reed K. Swenson Leadership award Nat. Jr. Coll. Athletic Assn., 1984, Gov.'s Com. on Scholastic Achievement award, 1985, Golden Medallion award Internat. Swimming Hall of Fame, 1985, Internat. Exec. of Yr. award Am. Grad. Sch. Internat. Mgmt., 1985, Humanitarian award Am. Sportscaster Assn., 1985, Man of Yr. award Morristown Rotary Club, 1986, Disting. Citizen award Greater N.Y. council Boy Scouts Am., 1986, Sportsman of Yr. award All-Am. Collegiate Golf Found., 1986, Golden Plate award Am. Acad. Achievement, 1986, Societe d'Honneur award Lafayette Coll., 1986, Kriendler award Marine Corps Sch., 1986, Reunion Alumni Achievement award Newark Acad., 1986, Disting. Service award Cons. Engrs. Council N.J., 1987, Charles McCaffree award Coll. Swimming Coaches Assn. Am. Inc., 1987, Covenant House award, 1988, 1st Ann. award Mid-Atlantic Legal Found., 1988, Pres.'s medal Adelphi U., 1989, Entrepreneur of Yr. award Henry Bloch Sch. Bus. and Pub. Adminstrn., U. Mo., Kansas City, 1989, Jesse Owens Internat. award U.S. Olympic Com., 1990, Ellis Island Medal of Honor award, 1990, Club of Champions Gold medal Cath. Youth Orgn. of Archdiocese N.Y., 1991; named to l'Ordre Olympique by le Comité Internat. Olympique, 1987, U.S. Olympic Com. Hall of Fame, 1991. Mem. Coun. on Fgn. Rels., The Soc. of Friendly Sons of St. Patrick, Pilgrims of U.S., Nat. Fedn. State high Sch. Assns. (chmn. bd. emeritus), Mont Pelerin Soc., Asia Soc. (former trustee), Explorers Club (bd. dirs. 1994), Assn. N.J. Rifle and Pistol Club, Am. Assn. Master Knights of Sovereign Milit. Order of Malta (exec. com.), Villa Taverna Soc. Clubs: Alfalfa (Washington); Balboa Bay (Calif.); Maidstone Inc., Sheriff's Jury Inc., Links, Brook Forum, N.Y. Yacht, Bond of N.Y., Mcpl. Bond of N.Y., N.Y. Athletic (N.Y.C., Man of Yr. 1984); Commonwealth of Calif. (San Francisco); Lyford Cay (Nassau, Bahamas); Mendham Valley Gun (N.J.); Country Club of Colo. (Colorado Springs); Gulf Stream Golf (Fla.); Rolling Rock (Ligonier, Pa.); Waialae Country, Oahu Country (Honolulu); Maui Country; Morris County Golf (N.J.); Robert Trent Jones Internat. Golf (founding bd. dirs.). Numerous scholarships and endowments established. Office: William E Simon & Sons Inc PO Box 1913 Morristown NJ 07960-7301*

SIMON, WILLIAM LEONARD, film and television writer and producer, author; b. Washington, Dec. 3, 1930; s. Isaac B. and Marjorie (Felsteiner) S.; m. Arynne Lucy Abeles, Sept. 18, 1966; 1 child, Victoria Marie; 1 stepson, Sheldon M. Bermont. BEE, Cornell U., 1954; MA in Ednl. Psychology, Golden State U., 1982, PhD in Communications, 1983. Writer features and TV movies, documentary and indsl. films, TV programs, 1958—; lectr. George Washington U., Washington, 1968-70; juror Coun. on Ntontheatrical Events Film Festival, 1975-90, Cindy Festival Blue Ribbon Panel, 1985—; jury, chmn., bd. dirs. CINE film festival, 1990—. Writer over 600 produced works for motion pictures and TV, including (screenplays) Fair Woman Without Discretion, Majorca, Swindle, A Touch of Love, (teleplays and documentaries) From Information to Wisdom, Flight of Freedom II, Missing You, (home video) Star of India Sea, Combat Vietnam series; writer, producer The Star of India: Setting Sail; author: Profit from Experience-The Story of Transformation Management, (best seller), 1995; co-author: Beyond the Numbers, 1996. Pres. Foggy Bottom Citizens Assn., 1963-65, mem. exec. bd., 1965-69; v.p. Shakespeare Summer Festival, 1966-67, trustee, 1965-70; mem. interview com. Cornell U., 1987-88. Lt. USN, 1954-58. Recipient 12 Golden Eagle awards Cine Film Festival, gold medal N.Y. Internat. Festival, gold medal Freedoms Found., IFPA Gold Cindy; awards Berlin, Belgrade and Venice film Festivals, numerous others. Mem. Nat. Acad. TV Arts and Scis. (gov. D.C. chpt. 1970-73), Writers Guild Am., Am. Film Inst., Internat. Documentary Assn., Rotary (bd. dirs., program chmn.), Eta Kappa Nu (chpt. pres. 1953-54), Tau Beta Pi. Republican. Avocations: crew member square-rigged brig Pilgrim, San Diego Museum ship Star of India, tennis. Home: 6151 Paseo Delicias PO Box 2048 Rancho Santa Fe CA 92067-2048

SIMONDS, CHARLES FREDERICK, artist; b. N.Y.C., Nov. 14, 1945; s. Robert and Anita I. (Bell) S. BA, U. Calif., Berkeley, 1967; MFA, Rutgers U., 1969. One man shows include Ctr. nat. d'Art contemporain, Paris, 1975, Mus. Modern Art, N.Y.C., 1976, Westfälischer Kunstverein, Munster, 1978, Mus. Ludwig, Cologne, 1979, Mus. Contemporary Art, Chgo., 1981, Phoenix (Ariz.) Mus. Art, 1982, Brooks Meml. Art Gallery, Memphis, 1982, Solomon R. Guggenheim Mus., N.Y., 1983, Leo Castelli Gallery, N.Y., 1984, Architekturmuseum, Bâle, 1985, Corcoran Gallery Art, Washington, 1988, Fundació "la Caixa," Barcelona, 1994, Galerie nat. Jeu Paume, Paris,

1994; exhibited in group shows Whitney Mus. Am. Art, N.Y., 1975, 77, Mus. d'Art moderne Ville de Paris, 1975, Stedelijk Mus., Amsterdam, 1978, Mus. Modern Art, N.Y., 1979, Hayward Gallery, London, 1980, Tate Gallery, London, 1983, Solomon R. Guggenheim Mus., N.Y., 1985, 87, 89; works included in publs. including Artforum, 1980, Art/Cahier, 1977, Sprache im Technischen Zeitalter, 1978, Art in America, 1983, Images and Issues, 1982, ARTnews, 1978, Beaux Arts, 1986. Fellow Am. Acad. Rome. Home: 26 E 22d St New York NY 10010

SIMONDS, JOHN EDWARD, newspaper editor; b. Boston, July 4, 1935; s. Alvin E. and Ruth Angeline (Rankin) S.; m. Rose B. Muller, Nov. 16, 1968; children—Maximillian P., Malia G.; children by previous marriage—Rachel F., John B. B.A., Bowdoin Coll., 1957. Reporter Daily Tribune, Seymour, Ind., 1957-58, UPI, Columbus, Ohio, 1958-60; reporter, asst. city editor Providence Jour. Bull., 1960-65, Washington Evening Star, 1965-66; corr. Gannett News Svc., Washington, 1966-75; mng. editor Honolulu Star Bull., 1975-80, exec. editor, 1980-87, sr. editor, editorial page editor, 1987-93; exec. Hawaii Newspaper Agy., Honolulu, 1993—. Served with U.S. Army, 1958. Mem. Am. Soc. Newspaper Editors, AP Mng. Editors, Soc. Profl. Journalists, Nat. Conf. Editorial Writers. Home: 5316 Nehu Pl Honolulu HI 96821-1941 Office: Hawaii Newspaper Agy 605 Kapiolani Blvd Honolulu HI 96813-5129

SIMONDS, JOHN ORMSBEE, landscape architect; b. Jamestown, N.D., Mar. 11, 1913; s. Guy Wallace and Marguerite Lois (Ormsbee) S.; m. Marjorie C. Todd, May 1, 1943; children: Taye Anne, John Todd, Polly Jean, Leslie Brook. BS, Mich. State U., 1935, DSc hon.; MLandscape Architecture (Eugene Dodd medal), Harvard U., 1939. Landscape architect Mich. Dept. Parks, 1935-36; ptnr. Simonds and Simonds, Pitts., 1939-70, Collins, Simonds and Simonds, Washington, 1952-70; ptnr. The Environ. Planning and Design Partnership, Pitts., also Miami Lakes, 1970-82, emeritus, 1983—; cons. Dept. Pks., Collier County, Fla., 1986-90, Land and Nature Trust, Lexington, Ky., 1987-92, SW Fla. Water Mgmt. Dist., 1987-89; lectr., vis. critic urban and regional planning Carnegie-Mellon U., 1955-67; vis. critic Grad. Sch. Planning, also Sch. Architecture, Yale, 1961-62; Cons. Chgo. Cen. Area Com., 1962, Allegheny County Dept. Regional Pks., 1961-74; U.S. cons. community planning Inter-Am. Housing and Planning Ctr., Bogota, Colombia, 1960-61; mem. jury Am. Acad. Rome, 1963, 65, 66, 69; mem. Nat. Adv. Com. on Hwy. Beautification; chmn. panel on pks. and open space White House Conf. on Natural Beauty; mem. Interprofl. Commn. on Environ. Design, Joint Com. on Nat. Capital; mem. urban hwy. adv. bd. U.S. Bur. Pub. Rds., 1965-68; mem. landscape architecture adv. panel U.S. C.E., 1968-71, Pres.'s Task Force on Resources and Environ., 1968-70; mem. design adv. panel Operation Breakthrough, HUD, 1970-71; mem. Mid-Atlantic regional adv. bd. Nat. Park Svc., 1976-78; assoc. trustee U. Pa., 1962-66, mem. bd. fine arts, 1962-66; chmn. joint com. planning Carnegie-Mellon U. and U. Pitts., 1959-60; overseer's vis. com. Harvard Grad. Sch. Design, 1962-68, exec. coun. alumni assn., 1960-63; adv. com. Sch. Design, N.C. State U., 1965-67; mem. Fla. Gov.'s Task Force on Natural Resources, 1979-80, Chgo. Bot. Garden 25th Anniversary, 1991, keynote address, 1991, Internat. Fedn. Landscape Architects, Seoul, Korea, 1992; speaker keynote address Internat. Congress Urban Green, Geneva, 1986. Author: Landscape Architecture, the Shaping of Man's Natural Environment, 1961, rev. edit., 1983, Earthscape, a Manual of Environmental Planning, 1978, revised edit. 1986, Garden Cities 21, Creating a Livable Urban Environment, 1994; editor: Virginia's Common Wealth, 1965, The Freeway in the City, 1968; contbr. sect. on urban design Ency. Architecture, 1990, sect. on landscape architecture Ency. Urban Planning, 1980. Maj. works include master plans for Chgo. Bot. Garden, (with others) Mellon Sq., Pitts., (with others) Miami Lakes New Town, Va. I-66 Corridor, Fairfax and Arlington counties, Va., Pelican Bay Community, Fla., Weston New Town, Fla. Bd. dirs. Hubbard Ednl. Trust, 1974—; bd. govs. Pitts. Plan for Arts. Recipient citation Top Men of Year Engring. News-Record, 1973; Charles L. Hutchinson medal Chgo. Hort. Soc., John R. Bracken medal Dept. Landscape Architecture, Pa. State U., 1985, Sigma Lambda Alpha award Coun. Educators in Landscape Architecture, 1979. Fellow Am. Soc. Landscape Architects (mem. exec. com. 1959-67, pres. 1963-65, pres. Found. 1966-68, recipient medal 1973), Royal Soc. Arts (Gt. Britain); mem. NAD (assoc.), Archtl. League N.Y., Royal Town Planning Inst. (hon. corr.); hon. assoc. Pa. chpt. AIA, Harvard-Yale-Princeton Club. Presbyterian (ruling elder). Home: 17 Penhurst Rd Pittsburgh PA 15202-1023 Office: The Loft 17 Penhurst Rd Pittsburgh PA 15202 *Perhaps the most important lesson in life is to learn to address oneself with intensity to each person, object and event. One may be with friends without awareness of either friend or friendship, live with family as an almost stranger, partake of food and drink without savor, pass burgeoning tree, splashing stream, or splendid view without appreciation . . . unless one learns to address all powers of perception-first consciously, and then by habit, to the subject at hand. Only thus may each experience be made rich and rewarding, and life, the sum of experience, be lived to the full.*

SIMONDS, MARSHALL, lawyer; b. Boston, Sept. 17, 1930; s. Sidney Lawrence and Evelyn (Peterson) S.; m. Katharine Blewett, May 9, 1969; children: Robert Bradley, Joshua Lawrence. BA, Princeton U., 1952; LLB, Harvard U., 1955. Bar: Mass. 1955. Since practiced in Boston; ptnr. Goodwin, Procter & Hoar, Boston, 1965—; counsel Mass. Crime Commn., 1963-65; spl. asst. atty. gen. Commonwealth of Mass., 1964-66; dir. Dynatech Corp., 1960-85, Data Packaging Corp., 1972-79; trustee Middlesex Instn. Savs., 1974-79. Moderator of Carlisle, Mass., 1967—; trustee Trustees for Reservations, 1972-78; bd. dirs. South Boston Neighborhood House, 1972-78. Served with USMCR, 1955. Fellow Am. Coll. Trial Lawyers, Am. Bar Found., Mass. Bar Found.; mem. ABA, Mass. Bar Assn., Boston Bar Assn. (coun. 1980-82), New Eng. Legal Found. (dir.), Franklin Flaschner Jud. Inst. (acad. com.), Am. Kennel Club (del.), Labrador Retriever Club (bd. dirs.), Harvard Club (Boston), Orthopedic Found. for Animals (bd. dirs.). Address: Bliss Hill Rd Morrisville VT 05661

SIMONDS, PEGGY MUÑOZ, writer, lecturer, retired literature educator; b. New Rochelle, N.Y., Feb. 29, 1928; d. Francisco Javier Muñoz and Julia Pinckney Dunham; m. Roger Tyrrell Simonds, Nov. 21, 1956; children: Robin Pinckney, Martha Muñoz. BA in English, U. Del., 1949; MA in Creative Writing/Latin Am. Studies, U. of the Americas, Mexico City, 1956; PhD in Lit. and History of Art, Am. U., 1975. Journalist, arts critic Mexico City, 1949-55; tchr. English U. of the Ams., Mexico City, 1953-55; lectr. Greek drama Norfolk (Conn.) Music Sch. of Yale U., summer 1955; tchr. English Montgomery (Md.) Coll., 1966-88, prof. emerita, 1988—; ind. scholar, 1988—; lectr. and presenter in field. Author: Myth, Emblem, and Music in Shakespeare's "Cymbeline": An Iconographic Reconstruction, 1992, A Critical Guide to Iconographic Research in English Renaissance Literature, 1995; contbr. numerous articles to profl. jours. Recipient U. Del. Press award, 1990; NEH fellow, 1982. Mem. Assn. Lit. Scholars and Critics, Shakespeare Assn. Am., Internat. Shakespeare Assn., Renaissance Soc. Am., Southeastern Renaissance Soc., South Ctrl. Renaissance Soc., Internat. Soc. for Classical Tradition, Internat. Soc. for Emblem Studies, Internat. Assn. for Neo-Latin Studies, Phi Kappa Phi. Home and Office: 5406 Beech Ave Bethesda MD 20814

SIMONDS, STEPHEN PAIGE, former state legislator; b. Franconia, N.H., Nov. 25, 1924; s. Stephen Moses and Gertrude Martha (Jesseman) S.; m. Judith Cole, Sept. 13, 1952; children: Scott, Mark, Laura, Jane. BA, U. N.H., 1948; MA in Social Svcs. Adminstrn., U. Chgo., 1953. Caseworker N.H. Dept. Pub. Welfare, Woodsville, 1950-51; dist. supr. N.H. Dept. Pub. Welfare, Conway and Woodsville, 1953-56; field supr. Conn. Dept. Welfare, Hartford, 1958-60; dir. social welfare Maine Dept. Health and Welfare, Augusta, 1960-67; commr. Assitance Payments Adminstrn. HEW, Washington, 1967-69; commr. Cmty. Svcs. Adminstrn. HEW, Washington, 1969-71; founder, dir. Human Svcs. Devel. Inst., U. So. Maine, Portland, 1971-86, dir. Office Internat. Programs, 1986-92; mem. Maine Ho. of Reps., Augusta, 1990-94, mem. human resources com., edn. com. Past pres. World Affairs Coun. of Maine, Cmty. Counseling Ctr. Recipient Disting. Svc. award World Affairs Coun. Maine, 1991; Fulbright scholar, Eng., 1957-58. Mem. Ptnrs. of Ams., Chinese and Am. Friendship Assn. (a founder). Democrat. Avocations: flying, boating, canoeing, gardening. Home: 18 Brentwood Rd Cape Elizabeth ME 04107-2210

SIMONDS, TIMOTHY RAY, lawyer; b. Chattanooga, June 9, 1964; s. W. Ray and Patricia Ann (Brown) S.; m. Cynthia Dawn Rider, Dec. 4, 1993; children: Austin R. Ware, Ashley P. Malone. BS in Polit. Sci., U. Tenn., Chattanooga, 1986; JD, U. Tenn., Knoxville, 1989. Bar: Tenn. 1989, U.S. Dist. Ct. (ea. and mid. dists.) Tenn. 1989, U.S. Ct. Appeals (6th, 11th and fed. cirs.) 1989. Litigation atty. Baker, Donelson, Bearman & Caldwell, Chattanooga, 1989—. Contbr. articles to profl. publs. Election inspector Hamilton County, Tenn., 1994. Mem. ABA, ATLA, Tenn. Bar Assn., Chattanooga Bar Assn. (profl. ethics lectr. 1991-94, mem. com. 1994). Avocations: tennis, boating, book collecting, reading. Office: Baker Donelson Bearman 1800 Republic Ctr 633 Chestnut St Chattanooga TN 37450-0001

SIMONE, ALBERT JOSEPH, academic administrator; b. Boston, Dec. 16, 1935; s. Edward and Mary (DiGiovanni) S.; m. Carolie Roberta Menko, Nov. 7, 1959; children: Edward, Karen, Debra, Laura. BA, Tufts U., 1957; PhD, MIT, 1962. Lectr. Coll. Bus. Adminstrn., Northeastern U., Boston, 1958-59; instr. econs. MIT and Tufts U., Boston, 1959-60; asst. prof. Northeastern U., Tufts U., 1960-63; assoc. prof. Coll. Bus. Adminstrn. Boston Coll., 1963-66, prof., dir. quantitative mgmt. program Coll. Bus. Adminstrn., 1966-68; prof., head dept. quantitative analysis Coll. Bus. Adminstrn. U. Cin., 1968-72, dean Coll. Bus. Adminstrn., 1972-83; v.p. acad. affairs U. Hawaii, Honolulu, 1983-84, acting pres., 1984-85; pres. U. Hawaii System, Honolulu, 1985-92; chancellor U. Hawaii at Manoa, 1985-92; pres. Rochester (N.Y.) Inst. Tech., 1992—; served on, chaired numerous univ. coms.; program chmn. 1970 Nat. Conf. of Am. Prodn. and Inventory Control Soc.; mem. accreditation com. Am. Assembly Collegiate Schs. Bus., 1978-83, visits to U. Ky., Carnegie-Mellon U., 1982; session chmn. various profl. confs.; cons. statis. forecasting, prodn. scheduling and sample design models various cos. including Cin. Gas & Electric Co., Cin. Milacron, Kroger Co.; econ. and mgmt. cons. Atty. Gen.'s Office, State of Mass.; mem. council econ. advisors to Gov., Commonwealth of Mass. Author: Matematica Finita Con Aplicaciones A Las Ciencias Administrativas, 1969, Foundations of Contemporary Mathematics with Applications in the Social and Management Sciences, 1967, Probability: An Introduction with Applications, 1967; (with L. Kattsoff) Finite Mathematics with Applications in the Social and Management Sciences, 1965, (with R. Wessel and E. Willett) Statistics as Applied to Economics and Business, 1965; also articles. Bd. dirs. Greater Rochester Visitors Assn., Inc., Marine Midland Bank, N.A., Rochester/So. Region, United Way of Greater Rochester, Vis. Nurse Svc. of Rochester and Monroe County, Inc., High Tech. of Rochester, Greater Rochester Metro C. of C., Indsl. Mgmt. Coun.; chmn. United Way Vol. Resources Divsn. Steering Com.; trustee George Eastman House; corp. mem. Hillside Children's Ctr. Fellow of grad. sch. U. Cin.; named Prof. of Yr., Delta Sigma Pi, Alpha Theta chpt., U. Cin., 1972. Fellow Am. Inst. Decision Scis. (v.p. publs. 1969-70, v.p. and student liaison 1972, pres. 1974-75, founding editor and editor-in-chief jour. 1970-72, Disting. Svc. award 1972); mem. Acad. Mgmt., Am. Econ. Assn., Am. Inst. Indsl. Engrs., Am. Prodn. and Inventory Control Soc., Am. Statis. Assn., Assn. Computing Machinery, Decision Scis. Inst., Univs. Rsch. Assn., Assn. of Ind. Tech. Univs., The Conf. Bd. RIT Rsch. Corp. (chmn., bd. dirs.), Nat. Commn. for Coop. Edn., N.Y. Commn. for Ind. Coll. and Univs., Rochester Area Coll. Consortium, Econometric Soc., Fin. Execs. Inst., Inst. Mgmt. Sci., Ops. Rsch. Soc. Am., Phi Beta Kappa, Phi Kappa Phi, Beta Gamma Sigma. Office: RIT George Eastman Bldg Two Lomb Meml Dr Rochester NY 14623-5604

SIMONE, JOSEPH R., lawyer; b. N.Y.C., Jan. 7, 1949; m. Virginia E. Simone, May 29, 1971; children: Jacquelyn, Robert. BA cum laude, Queens Coll., 1971; LLM in Taxation, NYU, 1977; JD cum laude, Fordham U., 1974. Bar: N.Y. 1975, U.S. Dist. Ct. (so. dist.) N.Y. 1975, U.S. Ct. Appeals (2d cir.) 1975. Ptnr. Patterson, Belknap, Webb & Tyler, N.Y.C., 1982-88, Schulte, Roth & Zabel, N.Y.C., 1988—. Author: (textbooks) Pension Answer Book, 5th edit., 1990, Essential Facts: Pension and Profit-sharing Plans, 1996; editl. advisor Jour. of Pension Planning. Mem. Am. Arbitration Assn. (panel on multiemployer pension plans, employee benefits law adv. com, co-chair symposium employee benefits), Phi Beta Kappa. Office: Schulte Roth & Zabel 900 3rd Ave New York NY 10022-4728

SIMONES, MARIE DOLOROSA, parochial school educator, nun; b. Dubuque, Iowa, Feb. 21, 1926; d. Joseph P. and Florence Julia (Hagge) S. AB, Loretto Heights Coll., 1948; MA, Notre Dame U., 1967. Joined Sisters of Loretto, Roman Cath. Ch., 1948. Tchr. St. Ann Sch., St. Louis, 1951-55, Arlington, Va., 1955-61; tchr. St. Augustine Sch., Lebanon, Ky., 1961-63, St. Paul the Apostle Sch., St. Louis, 1963-67, St. Vincent de Paul Sch., Denver, 1967—. Mem. Nat. Coun. Social Studies, Archaeological Inst. Avocations: travel, stamps, foreign dolls.

SIMONET, JOHN THOMAS, banker; b. Stillwater, Minn., Aug. 11, 1926; s. Joseph S. and Helen (Martin) S.; m. Helen Kennedy, Sept. 8, 1951; children: William T., Joseph K., Mary, Michelle, Anne. B.B.A., U. Minn., 1948, LL.B., 1951. With First Nat. Bank, St. Paul, 1951-72; cashier First Nat. Bank, 1958-60, v.p., 1960-71; exec. v.p. First Trust Co., St. Paul, 1972-74; pres. First Trust Co., 1974-85, chief adminstrv. officer, 1974-81, chief exec. officer, 1981-85, ret., 1985; asst. treas. Port Authority St. Paul, 1966-71; bd. dirs. First Trust, St. Paul, Carondelet Life Care Corp., Donovan Cos. Inc., Mairs and Power Funds, Inc. Mem. lay adv. bd. exec. com. St. Joseph's Hosp., St. Paul, 1965-70, trustee, 1971-82, chmn. bd. trustees, 1976-79; pres. adv. bd. Catholic Social Service St. Paul, 1968-70; chmn. Archbishop's Appeal Com., 1970; exec. bd. dirs. St. Paul Council Arts and Scis., 1967-69; trustee St. Paul Sem., 1969-92, Tozer Found., 1981—; bd. dirs. United Way, St. Paul, 1976-82, pres., 1980-81; mem. governing bd. St. Paul Found., 1979-85; bd. dirs. Mairs and Power Growth Fund, Mairs and Power Income Fund, 1992—. Served with USNR, 1944-46, 53-55.

SIMONETT, JOHN E., state supreme court justice; b. Mankato, Minn., July 12, 1924; m. Doris Bogut; 6 children. BA, St. John's U., 1948; LLB, U. Minn., 1951. Pvt. practice law Little Falls, Minn., 1951-80; assoc. justice Supreme Ct. of Minn., St. Paul, 1980-94; ret., 1994. Office: 1700 Metropolitan Ctr 333 S 7th St Minneapolis MN 55402

SIMON-GILLO, JEHANNE E., physicist; b. Liege, Belgium, Mar. 27, 1963; came to U.S., 1967; d. Nicolas Victor and Noelle Marie (Van Den Peereboom) Simon; m. Andrew James Gillo, June 9, 1990. BS, Juniata Coll., 1985; PhD, Tex. A&M U., 1991. Postdoctoral work Los Alamos (N.Mex.) Nat. Lab., 1991-94, staff mem., physicist, 1994—. Mem. Am. Chem. Soc., Am. Phys. Soc. Republican. Roman Catholic. Achievements include work on E814, NA44, PHENIX experiments; exptl. physicist studying relativistic heavy-ion collisions, specifically low PT phenomena and deuteron forumation. Office: Los Alamos Nat Lab H846 LANL Los Alamos NM 87545

SIMONIAN, JOHN S., lawyer; s. Samuel and Mary Simonian. BA, U. R.I.; JD, Boston U. Bar: R.I., U.S. Dist. Ct. R.I. state rep. R.I. Ho. of Reps., Providence, 1991—, dep. majority leader, 1993—, chmn. commn. on criminal justice, 1993—, mem. house com. on fin., 1993—, joint com. on veteran's affairs, 1991—. Democrat. Apostolic. Home: 70 Preston Dr Cranston RI 02910-1825

SIMONIAN, SIMON JOHN, surgeon, scientist, educator; b. Antioch, French Ter., Apr. 20, 1932; came to U.S., 1965, naturalized, 1976.; s. John Simon and Marie Cecile (Tomboulian) S.; m. Arpi Ani Yeghiayan, July 11, 1965; children: Leonard Armen, Charles Haig, Andrew Hovig. MD, U. London, 1957; BA in Animal Physiology, St. Edmund Hall, U. Oxford, Eng., 1964; MA in Animal Physiology, U. Oxford, Eng., 1969; MSc in nutrition, immunology & genetics, Harvard U., 1967, ScD in nutrition, immunology & genetics, 1969. Diplomate Am. Bd. Surgery. Rsch. asst. immunology unit Lister Inst. Preventive Medicine, Elstree, Essex, U.K., 1952; intern in medicine Univ. Coll. Hosp., London, 1957; intern in surgery Edinburgh (Scotland) Royal Infirmary, 1957-58, resident in surgery, 1961-62; clin. clk. Nat. Hosp. & Inst. of Neurology, 1958; resident Edinburgh Western Gen. Hosp., 1958-59, City Hosp., Edinburgh, Birmingham Accident and Burns Hosp., U. Birmingham, Eng., 1959-60; demonstrator dept. anatomy Edinburgh U., 1960-61; rsch. fellow in pathology Lab. Chem. Pathology Harvard U., Boston, 1965-68; trainee NIH Harvard U., 1967; instr. immunology Harvard Med. Sch., Boston, 1966-70; instr., assoc. in surgery Harvard Med. Sch., 1968-70, surg. dir. course on transplantation, biology and medicine, 1968-70; vis. prof. Harvard Med. Sch., Mass. Gen. Hosp., Brigham and Womens Hosp., New Eng. Deaconess Hosp., 1982; dir. transplantation immunology unit, asst. in surgery Brigham and Womens Hosp., Boston, 1968-70; resident in surgery Boston City Hosp., 1970-74; attending surgeon in transplantation and gen. surgery services U. Chgo. Med. Ctr., 1974-77; asst. prof. surgery, mem. com. immunology U. Chgo., 1974-77; head div. renal transplantation Hahnemann U. Sch. Medicine and Hosp., 1978-87, prof. surgery, 1978-88, chmn. Transplantation Com., 1983-88, chmn. quality assurance of surgery com., 1986-88; dept. surgery coord. with joint commn. for accreditation of hosps. Hahnemann U. Sch. Medicine, 1986; chief and chmn. dept. surgery St. John Hosp. and Med. Ctr., Detroit, 1988-89, chmn. credentials com. of surgery and oper. rm. com., 1988-89, assoc. v.p. for med. affairs, 1989-90; pres., CEO Vein Inst. of Met. Washington, Inc., 1990—; assoc. Fairfax Hosp., Falls Church, Va., 1990-92, active faculty, 1992—; guest lectr., 1994; clin. assoc. prof. surgery Georgetown U. Sch. Medicine, Washington, 1992—; lectr. in field; vis. prof. Vanderbilt U., 1968, Cedars-Sinai Med. Ctr. UCLA, 1977, Addenbroke's Hosp., Cambridge U., 1977, Karolinska Inst., 1977, Huddinge Hosp. U. Stockholm, 1977, Med. Coll. Pa. and Hosp., 1980, 81, 85, Grad. Hosp. U. Pa., 1981, 85, U. Athens, 1981, U. Coll. Hosp., U. London, 1981, VA Hosp., Tufts U., 1982, Nat. Acad. Scis., Yerevan, Republic Armenia, 1995; cons. Michael Reese Hosp., Chgo., 1976-77, cons. in gen. surgery City of Phila., 1986-88, cons. in vascular surgery Coll. Podiatry, Phila., 1986-88, chief med. team support for U.S. Presdl. visits to Detroit, 1988, 89; vis. surgeon Inst. Vein Disease, Mich., 1989-90; vis. scientist Argonne (Ill.) Nat. Lab., 1969, 74-77; guest lectr., panelist 8th Internat. Congress of Nephrology, Athens, Greece, 1981, 1st Congress Internat. Soc. Edn. and Rsch. in Vascular Disease, San Diego, bd. dirs. 1992, 4th Internat. Dialogue Transition to Global Soc., U. Md., College Park, 1995; chmn. session 5th Armenian Med. World Congress, Paris, 1992, 11th World Congress Internat. Union of Phlebology, Montreal, 1992, 22d World Congress Inernat. Soc. for Cardiovasc. Surgery, Kyoto, Japan, 1995, 6th Annual Congress N. Am. Soc. of Phlebology, Lake Buena Vista, Fla., 1993, sec., bd. dirs. Woodstock, Inc., 1992-93; eminent scholar, external assessor U. Zambia, Lusaka, 1994; chmn. panel, session chmn., panel co-chmn., guest lectr., panelist 17th World Congress Internat. Union Angiology, London, 1995; chmn. panel, adv. bd. 12th World Congress Union Internat. Phlebologie, London, 1995; chmn. panel 1996 N. Am. Soc. Phlebology Ann. Congress, San Diego. Cuthor: Manual of Vascular Access Procedures, 1987; cons. to editorial bd. dateline: Issues in Transplantation, 1985-87; mem. editorial bd. Phila. Medicine, 1988, Transplantation Proc., 1987—, Jour. Transplantation Abstracts, 1968-70; reviewer New England Jour. Medicine, 1993—, Jour. Am. Med. Assn., 1993, Jour. Oncology and Dermatologic Surgery, 1993; contbr. articles to profl. jours. and books; appeared in med. movie Giving. Co-founder Armenian Youth Soc., Eng., 1953, pres. 1953-54; Armenian Studies Program U. Chgo., 1975; bd. govs. Friends Sch., London, 1964-65; Mass. del., co-founder Armenian Assembly, Washington, 1970-74; trustee, fellow co-founder Entry into Manhood of Armenian Youth at Age 13, 1981; co-founder Armenian Am. Health Assn. of Greater Washington, 1992, mem. pharms. com. 1992—, chmn. nominating com., 1993; mem. Am. Friends of St. Edmund Hall, U. Oxford, 1992—, U.S. Campaign for St. Edmund Hall, 1995—, Rep. Presdl. Task Force; mem. St. Mary's Armenian Apostolic Ch., Washington, guest preacher, 1994, 95, 96; mem. Am. Friends Am. U. Armenia, Yerevan, 1994; bd. dirs. Arlington (Va.) Symphony Orch., 1992; mem. regional com. U.S. Campaign for Univ. Oxford, 1993; bd. dirs. First Western Found., Inc., 1994; active amphitheatre endowment fund Boston City Hosp., 1994. Nairn scholar, 1949-52; Middlesex scholar, 1952-57; recipient Suckling prize, 1956, Brit. Med. Research Council award, 1962-64, Alt prize, 1973, Thompson award, 1974-77, Johnson award, 1975-77, Presdl. Medal of Merit, 1982, Kabakjian award Armenian Student Assn. Am., 1986; named outstanding new citizen of Citizenship Coun. of Met. Chgo. and Dept. Justice, Washington, 1976-77, Jonathan E. Rhoads ann. orator, 1984; co-endowed The John and Marie J. Simonian Award, St. Nerces Sem., 1981, John R. Pfeifer, MD, Rsch. Award, Providence Hosp., Southfield, Mich., 1992; endowed the Dennis Knight prize Royal Acad. Music, London, 1991; endowed The Marie J. Simonian Prize, Georgetown U. Med. Sch., 1991 (prize com. 1991—); established The John N.D. Kelly Prize in Med. Studies St. Edmund Hall, U. Oxford, 1992, The Simon J. and Arpi A. Simonian Prize for scholastic excellence for doctoral candidates, Harvard U., 1992; recognized for philanthropy to Hahnemann U. by placques in med. sch. and hosp. lobbies., Simon and Arpi Simonian room Sch. of Humanities and Scis. U. Yerevan, Armenia, 1994, plaque in Cyrus Vesuna Auditorium and Conf. Ctr., Fairfax Hosp., Falls Church, Va., 1995; grantee U.S. Govt., industry cos., founds. Fellow Royal Coll. Surgeons Edinburgh, ACS (Phila., Mich. and Washington chpts.), Phila. Acad. Surgery (Jonathan E. Rhoads ann. orator 1984—, Samuel D. Gross prize com. 1988, councillor 1988); mem. AAAS, AMA (mem. jour. rev. 1993), AAUP, Royal Coll. Surgeons of Eng., Royal Coll. Physicians of London Licentiates, Nat. Assn. Armenian Studies and Rsch. (rep. Midatlantic region 1994—), Armenian Gen. Benevolent Union (pres.' club 1990—), Knights of Vartan, Am. Armenian Med. Assn. (co-founder 1972, treas. 1972-74), Brit. Med. Assn., Immunology Club Boston, Cancer Rsch. Assn. Boston, Physicians for Social Responsibility, Am. Pub. Health Assn., Assn. for Study of Med. Edn., Armenian Med. and Dental Assn. Greater Phila. (co-founder 1983, pres. 1983-85, Outreach award 1986), Assn. Acad. Surgery, Transplantation Soc. (mem. membership com. 1980-82), Am. Fedn. Clin. Rsch., N.Y. Acad. Scis., Am. Soc. Transplant Surgeons (co-founding mem. 1974, chmn. immunosuppression study com. 1974-77, membership com. 1985-87), Am. Venous Forum, Assn. of Ill. Transplant Surgeons, Chgo. Assn. Immunologists, Chgo. Soc. Gastroenterology, Phila. Acad. Scis. (co-chmn. membership com. 1980-88, guest lectr. 1982), Greater Delaware Valley Soc. Transplant Surgeons (councillor 1978-80, 85-88, pres. elect 1980-82, pres. 1982-85), Phila. County Med. Soc. (rep. City Ctr. br. 1981-83, pres. 1984, bd. dirs. 1985-87, chmn. long range planning com. 1986-88), Pa. Med. Soc., Samuel Hahnemann SurAm. Technion Soc., Am. Soc. Artificial Internal Organs, European Soc. Organ Transplant, Oxford and Cambridge Soc. of Phila. and Washington, Internat. Cardiovascular Soc. (N.Am. chpt.), N. Am. Soc. Phlebology (curriculum devel. projects com. 1992—, faculty 1993-95), End Stage Renal Disease Network 24 (mem. med. rev. bd. 1980-82, 86-87), Am. Coll. Physician Execs., Detroit Acad. Surgery, Detroit Surgical Assn., Transplantation Soc. Mich., Organ Procurement Agy. Mich. (adv. bd. 1988-89), Wayne County Med. Soc., Mich. State Med. Soc., Fairfax County Med. Soc., Med. Soc. Va., Met. Vascular Conf., Soc. Brigham Surg. Alumni, Greater Washington Telecomm. Assn. (pres.'s club 1994), Chesapeake Vascular Soc., Oxford Soc. Washington, Harvard Club (Phila. and Washington), Med. Club (Phila.), U. Chgo. Club (Washington), Langley Hill Freinds Meeting, Sigma Xi. Mem. Soc. of Friends. Achievement includes bilateral ling reimplantation, reversal of renal allograft rejection, prevention and tretment of massive gastroduidenal hemrrhage from hemorrhagic gastritie, co-dicovery essential aminoacids phenylalanine and tryptophan assistance in the lyophiizationof the smallpox vaccine, rsch. advantages and disadvantages and prevention of splenectomy in renal transplant recipients. Office: 3301 Woodburn Rd Annandale VA 22003-1229

SIMONICH, SANDRA SUE, elementary education educator; b. Moline, Ill., Aug. 8, 1942; d. Kenneth Fred and Vurl Barbara (Nicely) Liedtke; m. Doyle Alton Oliver, July 9, 1960 (div. Apr. 1982); children: Cassandra Ann Oliver Phillips; m. Joseph Donald Simonich, Mar. 11, 1983. BS, Augustana Coll., 1974; MS, Western Ill. U., 1984. With Bank of Silvis, Ill., 1960; with farm implement John Deere Harvester, East Moline; with parts depot John Deere, East Moline, 1960-68; tchr. Millikin Sch., Geneseo, Ill., 1974-76, S.W. Sch., Geneseo, 1976—; Program initiator Raindows-Counseling for Children with a Loss of Some Kind, 1990, Family Math Program, 1994—; officer IMPACT, elem. coord., 1990—. Mem. Ill. Reading Coun., Rock Island, Ill., 1980—, Jr. Women's Club-Geneseo, 1988; pres. PTA, 1992-94, life mem. Avocations: aerobics, tennis, boating, skiing. Home: 203 Longview Dr Geneseo IL 61254-9113

SIMONNARD, MICHEL ANDRÉ, manufacturing executive; b. Amiens, France, Mar. 25, 1933; came to U.S., 1988; s. Marcel and Marthe (Catoire) S.; m. Axelle Note, May 26, 1988; 1 child, Alexia. Diploma in Engring., Ecole Polytechnique, Paris, 1956; MS, MIT, 1959. Cons. engr. SEMA-METRA, Paris, 1959-62; divisional dir. GRACE, Paris, 1963-65; mng. dir. aluminum sales PECHINEY GROUP, Paris, 1966-67, mng. dir. Cebal div., 1968-74, mng. dir. Ugine Aciers div., 1975-76, group v.p. nuclear fuel and spl. products div., 1977-82, group v.p. internat. trade div., 1981-84, sr. v.p. human resources and communications depts., 1985-86, exec. v.p. supervising human resources and regional affairs, 1987; exec. v.p. supervising Turbine Components div., gen. del. N.Am. Pechiney Group, Greenwich, Conn., 1988-95.

SIMONS, ALBERT, JR., lawyer; b. Charleston, S.C., Nov. 20, 1918; s. Albert and Harriet Porcher (Stoney) S.; m. Caroline Pinckney Mitchell, June 18, 1948; children: Albert III, Julian Mitchell, Cotesworth Pinckney, Caroline Pinckney. A.B., Princeton U., 1940; LL.B., Yale U., 1947. Bar: S.C. 1947, U.S. Dist Ct. (ea. and we. dists.) S.C. 1948, U.S. Ct. Appeals (4th cir.) 1948, U.S. Supreme Ct 1960. Sole practice Charleston, 1948—; assoc. Sinkler & Gibbs, Charleston, 1948; ptnr. Sinkler Gibbs & Simons, Charleston, 1949-87, Sinkler & Boyd, Charleston, 1987—; bd. dirs. Cen. R.R. Co. of S.C. Mem. City Coun., Charleston, 1954-59; mem. Charleston County Bd. of Assessment Control, 1965-82; bd. dirs. S.C. Mcpl. Coun., Legal Aid Soc., Family Agy., Charleston Libr. Soc. Maj. AUS, 1941-46. Decorated Bronze Star medal. Fellow Am. Coll. Probate Counsel; mem. Am., S.C., Charleston County bar assns., St. Cecilia Soc., S.C. Soc., Soc. of Cin., Soc. Colonial Wars, St. Georges Soc., Carolina Art Assn. (former dir.), S.C. Hist. Soc. (past dir.), Charleston Library Soc. (trustee), Hibernian Soc., Princeton Alumni Assn. of S.C. (past pres.), Masons (Charleston), Rotary (Charleston), Carolina Yacht Club (Charleston), Charlleston Club, St. John's Hunting Club at Pooshee Plantation (Berkley County), Alpha Tau Omega, Phi Delta Phi. Episcopalian. Home: Apt 207 1 King St Charleston SC 29401-2719 Office: 160 E Bay St Charleston SC 29401-2120

SIMONS, ALBERT, III, lawyer; b. Charleston, S.C., Nov. 22, 1950; s. Albert Jr. and Caroline Pinckney (Mitchell) S.; m. Theodora Bonnell Wilbur, Jan. 28, 1970; 1 child, Albert IV. BA, U. Va., 1972, JD, 1976. Bar: S.C. 1977, N.Y. 1978. Assoc. Brown, Wood, Ivey, Mitchell & Petty (now Brown & Wood), N.Y.C., 1977-84; ptnr. Orrick, Herrington & Sutcliffe, N.Y.C., 1984—. Mem. S.C. Bar Assn., N.Y. State Bar Assn. Office: Orrick Herrington & Sutcliffe 666 Fifth Ave New York NY 10013-0001

SIMONS, BARRY THOMAS, lawyer; b. Lynn, Mass., Dec. 14, 1946; s. Emanuel Isador and Betty (Darish) S.; m. Laurie Jean Louder, May 5, 1985; children: Britton Eugene, Brett Jacob. BS in Govt., Am. Univ., 1968; JD, NYU, 1971. Bar: Calif. 1971, U.S. Dist. Ct. (ctrl. dist.) Calif. 1972, U.S. Ct. Appeals (9th cir.) 1972, U.S. Supreme Ct. 1978, U.S. Dist. Ct. (so. and no. dists.) Calif. 1979. Pvt. practice Laguna Beach, Calif., 1971—. Editor (law rev.) N.Y. Law Forum, 1971. Apptd. mem. gen. plan revision com. and local coastal task force City of Laguna Beach, 1980. Mem. Orange County Bar Assn. (bd. dirs. 1981), Newport/Harbor Bar Assn. (bd. dirs. 1979), South Orange County Bar Assn. (pres. 1986, bd. dirs. 1980-95), Calif. Attys. for Criminal Justice (chair misdemeanor com. 1995), Nat. Assn. Criminal Def. Attys., Nat. Coll. D.U.I. Def. (founding mem.). Office: 260 St Anns Dr Laguna Beach CA 92651

SIMONS, CHARLES EARL, JR., federal judge; b. Johnston, S.C., Aug. 17, 1916; s. Charles Earl Sr. and Frances (Rhoden) S.; m. Jean Knapp, Oct. 18, 1941 (dec. 1991); children: Charles Earl III, Paul Knapp, Richard Brewster, Jean Brewster Smith; m. Gail Shaw, Feb. 27, 1993. AB, U. S.C., 1937, LLB cum laude, 1939. Bar: S.C. 1939. Ptnr. Lybrand & Simons, Aiken, S.C., 1939-50, Thurmond, Lybrand and Simons, Aiken, 1950-54, Lybrand, Simons & Rich, Aiken, 1950-54, 1954-64; mem. S.C. Ho. of Reps., 1942, 47-48, 61-64; mem. ways and means com., 1947-48, 61-64; judge U.S. Dist. Ct. S.C., Aiken, 1964—, chief judge, 1980-86; sr. status U.S. Dist. Ct., 1987—; mem. S.C. Constl. Revision Com., 1948, Bd. Discipline and Grievance, S.C. Bar, 1958-61, Ethics Adv. Panel, 1981-87; jud. rep. 4th cir. Jud. Conf. U.S., 1973-79; chmn. subcom. on fed. jurisdiction of Com. on Ct. Adminstrn., 1986-87. Mem. Chief Met. Dist. Judges Conf., 1980-89, chmn., 1986-89; bd. dirs. S.C. Athletic Hall of Fame; mem. Jud. Conf. Commn. on Jud. Br., 1988-92. With USN, World War II. Recipient Algernon Sidney Sullivan award, 1937, 64. Mem ABA, S.C. Bar Assn. (com. mem.), Am. Law Inst., Am. Legion, U. S.C. Alumni Assn. (past pres. 1964), S.C. Golf Assn., Aiken Bus. Men's Club (past pres.), Palmetto Golf Club (pres. 1994—), Rotary. Baptist. Home: PO Box 2185 Aiken SC 29802-2185 Office: US Dist Ct SC Charles E Simons Jr Fed Courthouse PO Box 2185 Aiken SC 29802-2185

SIMONS, DOLPH COLLINS, JR., newspaper publisher; b. Lawrence, Kans., Mar. 11, 1930; s. Dolph Collins and Marie (Nelson) S.; m. Pamela Counseller, Feb. 7, 1952; children: Pamela, Linda, Dolph Collins, Dan. A.B., U. Kans., 1951; LL.D. (hon.), Colby Coll., 1972. Reporter Lawrence Jour.-World, 1953, asso. pub., 1957, pub., 1962—, editor, 1978—, pres., 1969—; reporter The Times, London, 1956, Johannesburg (South Africa) Star, 1958; pres. World Co.; mgr. WorldWest; bd. dirs. Commerce Bancshares, Kansas City, Mo.; mem. Pulitzer Awards Jury, 1977, 78, 80, 81. Trustee, past pres. William Allen White Found.; trustee Midwest Rsch. Inst., Menninger Found., Nat. Parks and Conservation Assn., The Kans. Nature Conservancy; former mem. governing bd. Children's Mercy Hosp., Kansas City, Mo.; trustee, chmn. U. Kans. Endowment Assn.; past bd. dirs. Greater Kansas City Community Found. Served to capt. USMRC, 1951-53. Recipient Elijah Parish Lovejoy award, 1972; Fred Ellsworth award for significant service to U. Kans., 1976; Disting. Service citation, 1980. Mem. Newspaper Advt. Bur. (past dir.), Am. Soc. Newspaper Editors, Inland Daily Press Assn. (past dir.), Kans. Press Assn. (past pres., dir.), AP (past dir.), Am. Newspaper Pubs. Assn. (past dir., past nat. sec.), Lawrence C. of C. (past pres., dir.), U. Kans. Alumni Assn. (past pres., dir.), Sigma Delta Chi, Phi Delta Theta. Republican. Episcopalian. Clubs: Lawrence Country, Kansas City Country, Kansas City River. Lodges: Masons, Rotary. Home: 2425 Vermont St Lawrence KS 66046-4761 Office: 609 New Hampshire St Lawrence KS 66044-2243

SIMONS, DONA, artist; b. Bryn Athyn, Pa., Aug. 10, 1953; d. Keneth Alden and Reta Isabel (Evens) S.; m. John Louis Vigo, May 17, 1986. Student, Phila. Coll. Art, 1974, Moore Coll. Art, 1976, Pa. Acad. Fine Arts, 1977-79. Represented by Sylvia Schmidt Gallery, New Orleans. One-woman shows include Frank Tanzer Gallery, Boston, 1975, The Curacao Mus., Netherlands Antilles, 1991, The Curacao Seaquarium, Netherlands Antilles, 1991, Sylvia Schmidt Gallery, New Orleans, 1992, 93, 95, 96; exhibited in group shows a t Berg Gallery, Jenkintown, Pa., 1973, United Artisans Gallery, Chalfont, Pa., 1974, 75, Arthur Roger Gallery, New Orleans, La., 1980, Arts Coun., New Orleans C. of C., 1980, Acad. Gallery, New Orleans Acad. Fine Arts, La., 1982, Am. Italian Renaissance Found., New Orleans, 1985, Found. Prince Pierre de Monaco, Monaco, 1985, The Rittenhouse Galleries, Phila., 1993, 94; commn. portrait of Manuel Piar, Curacao, Netherlands Antilles, 1990. Office: Sylvia Schmidt Gallery 400 Julia St # A New Orleans LA 70130-3606

SIMONS, ELIZABETH R(EIMAN), biochemist, educator; b. Vienna, Austria, Sept. 1, 1929; came to U.S., 1941, naturalized, 1948; d. William and Erna Engle (Weisselberg) Reiman; B.Ch.E., Cooper Union, N.Y.C., 1950; M.S., Yale U., 1951, Ph.D., 1954; m. Harold Lee Simons, Aug. 12, 1951; children—Leslie Ann Mulert, Robert David. Research chemist Tech. Operations, Arlington, Mass., 1953-54; instr. chemistry Wellesley (Mass.) Coll., 1954-57; rsch. asst. Children's Hosp. Med. Center and Cancer Rsch. Found., Boston, 1957-59, rsch. assoc. pathology, 1959-62; research assoc. Harvard Med. Sch., 1962-66, lectr. biol. chemistry, 1966-72; tutor biochemical scis. Harvard Coll., 1971-94 (ret.); assoc. prof. biochemistry Boston U., 1972-78, prof., 1978—. Contbr. articles to profl. jours. Grantee in field. Mem. AAAS, Am. Chem. Soc., Am. Heart Assn., Am. Soc. Biol. Chemists, Am. Soc. Cell Biology, Am. Soc. Hematology, Assn. Women in Sci., Biophys. Soc., Internat. Soc. Thrombosis and Hemostasis, N.Y. Acad. Sci., Sigma Xi. Office: Boston U Sch Medicine 80 E Concord St Roxbury MA 02118-2307

SIMONS, GALE GENE, nuclear engineering educator, university administrator; b. Kingman, Kans., Sept. 25, 1939; s. Robert Earl and Laura V. (Swartz) S.; m. Barbara Irene Rinkel, July 2, 1966; 1 child, Curtis Dean. BS, Kans. State U., 1962, MS, 1964, PhD, 1968. Engr. Argonne Nat. Lab., Idaho Falls, Idaho, 1968-77, mgr. fast source reactor, head exptl. support group, 1972-77; prof. nuclear engring. Kans. State U., Manhattan, 1977—, assoc. dean for rsch., dir. rsch. coun. Coll. Engring., 1988—, bd. dirs. Rsch. Found., 1988—. Presdl. lectr., 1983—, career counselor, 1984—; cons. to pvt. and fed. agys., 1983—; bd. dirs. Kans. Tech. Enterprise Corp., Topeka; com. mem. Kans. Gov.'s Energy Policy Com., Topeka, 1992—; numerous presentations in field; reviewer proposals fed. agys. Contbr. over 100 articles to sci. jours.; patentee radiation dosimeter. Expert witness State of Kans., Topeka, 1986. Fellow AEC, 1964-67; numerous grants from fed. agys., 1979—. Mem. AAAS, IEEE, Am. Nuclear Soc., Health Physics Soc., Am. Soc. for Engring. Edn., Masons, Rotary, Phi Kappa Phi, Tau Beta Pi, Pi Mu Epsilon. Home: 2395 Grandview Ter Manhattan KS 66502-3729 Office: Kans State U Durland Hall Rm 148 Manhattan KS 66506-5103

SIMONS, HELEN, school psychologist, psychotherapist; b. Chgo., Feb. 13, 1930; d. Leo and Sarah (Shrayer) Pomper; m. Broudy Simons, May 20, 1956 (May 1972); children: Larry, Sheri. BA in Biol., Lake Forest Coll., 1951; MA in Clin. Psychology, Roosevelt U., 1972; D of Psychology, Ill. Sch. Profl. Psychology, 1980. Intern Cook County Hosp., Chgo., 1979-80; pvt. practice psychotherapist Chgo., 1980—; sch. psychologist Chgo. Bd. Edn., 1974-79, 80—. Contbr. articles on psychotherapy of A.D.D. and P.T.S.D. children to profl. jours. Mem. APA, Internat. Coun. Psychologists, Nat. Sch. Psychologists Assn., Midwestern Psychol. Assn., Mental Health Assn. Ill., Ill. Psychol. Assn., Ill. Sch. Psychologists Assn., Chgo. Psychol. Assn., Internat. Coun. of Psychologists, Chgo. Sch. Psychol. Assn. Avocations: music, dancing, reading. Home: 6145 N Sheridan Rd Apt 29D Chicago IL 60660-2883 Office: Brennemann Sch 4251 N Clarendon Ave Chicago IL 60613-1523

SIMONS, LAWRENCE BROOK, lawyer; b. N.Y.C., Oct. 19, 1924; s. Harry A. and Marion B. (Brook) S.; m. Annalou Kadin, Aug. 24, 1947; children: Barbara Flexner, Kenneth. Student, Duke U., 1941-43, 46-47; JD, Columbia U., 1949. Bar: N.Y. 1949, D.C. 1984, U.S. Dist. Ct. (so. dist.) N.Y. 1949, U.S. Supreme Ct. 1987. Assoc. Spring & Eastman, N.Y.C., 1949-53; v.p., gen. mgr. Caribe Knitting Mills, San Juan, P.R., 1953-58; pres. LBS Constrn. Co. Inc., S.I., N.Y., 1958-77; asst. sec. housing FHA commn. HUD, Washington, 1977-81; ptnr. Powell, Goldstein, Frazier & Murphy, Washington, 1981—; mem. Task Force on Quality of Life, Dept. of Def., 1995. Trustee Bayley Seton Hosp., S.I., 1981-90, NHP Found., Inc., 1991—; chmn. bd. dirs. N.Y. State Urban Devel. Corp., 1975-77, Nat. Housing Conf., 1981—, Pa. Ave. Devel. Corp., 1981-87; mem. Nat. Housing Task Force, 1988, Nat. Housing Trust, 1990—; trustee Affordable Housing Found., 1990-92, Ctr. for Democracy, 1990-96; pres. Ctr. for Housing Policy, 1992-96, bd. dirs., 1996—. With U.S. Army, 1943-46, ETO. Named Man of Yr. Nat. Housing Conf., Washington, 1985. Mem. ABA, Nat. Assn. Home Builders, Richmond County C. of C., Army Navy C. of C., Sea Pines Country Club, Lambda Alpha. Democrat. Jewish. Avocation: golf. Home: 5610 Wisconsin Ave Bethesda MD 20815-4415 Office: Powell Goldstein Frazier Murphy 1001 Pennsylvania Ave NW Washington DC 20004-2505

SIMONS, LEWIS MARTIN, journalist; b. Paterson, N.J., Jan. 9, 1939; s. Abram and Goldie (Fleisher) S.; m. Carol Lenore Seiderman, Feb. 7, 1965; children: Justine, Rebecca, Adam P.D. BA, NYU, 1962; MS, Columbia U., 1964. Corr. AP, Kuala Lumpur, Singapore, Saigon, Denver, 1965-70, Washington Post, Bangkok, New Delhi, 1971-82; bur. chief Knight-Ridder Newspapers, Tokyo, 1982-95; fgn. policy corr. Time mag., 1996—. Author: Worth Dying For, 1987. With USMC, 1962-64. Recipient Grand prize and Investigative Reporting award Am. Newspaper Guild, 1981, Citation for Excellence, Overseas Press Club Am., 1983, Jessie Meriton White award Friends World Coll., 1986, Investigative Reporters and Editors award U. Mo., 1986, Award of Excellence, World Affairs Coun., 1984, 86, 89, 92, Pulitzer Prize, 1986, George Polk award, 1985, Malcolm S. Forbes award Overseas Press Club Am., 1986, 92, Gerald Loeb award UCLA, 1993; Edward R. Murrow fellow Coun. of Fgn. Rels., 1970-71. Mem. Fgn. Corrs. Club Japan (bd. dirs. 1991-92, pres., 1993-94). Office: Time mag 1050 Connecticut Ave NW Washington DC 20036

SIMONS, LORETTA NICOLE, clinical consultant; b. Phila., Aug. 23, 1969; d. Lewis Ronald and Loretta Marie (Traviglini) S. Student, Harcum Jr. Coll., 1987-88; BA in Psychology, Newmann Coll., 1991; MS in Exptl. Psychology, St. Joseph's U., 1994; postgrad., Temple U., 1994—. Pre-sch. tchr. Seedlings Learning Ctr., Radnor, Pa., 1987-89; aftercare program tchr. Children's Garden, St. David's, Pa., 1989-90; data asst., rsch. assoc./asst. U. Pa./Treatment Rsch. Ctr., 1990; data mgmt. super. Treatment Rsch. Ctr., Phila., 1990-91; drug and alcohol counselor Diagnostic Rehab. Ctr., Phila., 1991-92; clin. therapist, educator Inst. for Learning, Phila., 1992—, clin. dir., 1995—; clin. cons. Diagnostic Rehab. Ctr., Phila., 1992—; instr. Temple U., 1995; rsch. asst. vol. Diagnostic Rehab. Ctr., 1995. Mem. APA (student mem.), Psi Chi, Sigma Xi. Avocations: volunteer work with HIV patients, art shows/demonstrations, exercise, traveling. Home: 6602 Morris Park Rd Philadelphia PA 19151

SIMONS, LYNN OSBORN, state education official; b. Havre, Mont., June 1, 1934; d. Robert Blair and Dorothy (Briggs) Osborn; BA, U. Colo., 1956; postgrad. U. Wyo., 1958-60; m. John Powell Simons, Jan. 19, 1957; children: Clayton Osborn, William Blair. Tchr., Midvale (Utah) Jr. High Sch., 1956-57, Sweetwater County Sch. Dist. 1, Rock Springs, Wyo., 1957-58, U. Wyo., Laramie, 1959-61, Natrona County Sch. Dist. 1, Casper, Wyo., 1963-64; credit mgr. Gallery 323, Casper, 1972-77; Wyo. state supt. public instrn., Cheyenne, 1979-91; sec.'s regional rep. region VIII U.S. Dept. Edn., Denver, 1993—; mem. State Bds. Charities and Reform, Land Commrs., Farm Loan, 1979-91; mem. State Commns. Capitol Bldg., Liquor, 1979-91; Ex-officio mem. bd. trustees U. Wyo., 1979-91; ex-officio mem. Wyo. Community Coll. Commn., 1979-91; mem. steering com. Edn. Commn. of the States, 1988-90; mem. State Bd. Edn., 1971-77, chmn., 1976-77; advisor Nat. Trust for Hist. Preservation, 1980-86. Bd. dirs. Denver Fed. Exec. Bd., 1995—. Mem. LWV (pres. 1970-71). Democrat. Episcopalian. Office: US Dept Edn 1244 Speer Blvd Ste 310 Denver CO 80204-3582

SIMONS, RICHARD DUNCAN, judge; b. Niagara Falls, N.Y., Mar. 23, 1927; s. William Taylor and Sybil Irene (Swick) S.; m. Muriel (Penny) E. Genung, June 9, 1951 (dec. 1992); m. Esther (Esi) Turkington Tremblay, May 21, 1994; children: Ross T., Scott R., Kathryn E., Linda A. A.B., Colgate U., 1949; LL.B., U. Mich., 1952; LLD (hon.), Albany Law Sch., 1983. Bar: N.Y. 1952. Pvt. practice law Rome, N.Y., 1952-63; asst. corp. counsel City of Rome, 1955-58, corp. counsel, 1960-63; justice 5th jud. dist. N.Y. Supreme Ct., 1964-83, assoc. justice appellate div. 3d dept., 1971-72, assoc. justice appellate div. 4th dept., 1973-82; assoc. judge N.Y. Ct. Appeals, 1983—, acting chief judge, 1992-93; mem. Law Sch. Admission Svcs., Bar Passage Study Com. Editorial staff: N.Y. Pattern Jury Instructions, 1979-83. Chmn. Republican City Com., 1958-62; vice chmn. Oneida County Rep. Com., 1958-62; bd. mgrs. Rome Hosp. and Murphy Meml. Hosp., 1953. Served with USN, World War II. NEH fellow U. Va. Law Sch., 1979. Fellow Am. Bar Found., N.Y. State Bar Found.; mem. ABA, N.Y. State Bar Assn., Oneida County Bar Assn., Rome Bar Assn., Am. Law Inst., Inst. Jud. Adminstrn. Home: 1410 N George St Rome NY 13440-2704 Office: NY Ct Appeals Hall 20 Eagle St Albany NY 12207-1004

SIMONS, STEPHEN, mathematics educator, researcher; b. London, Aug. 11, 1938; came to U.S., 1965; s. Jack Isidore Simons and Ethel Esther (Littman) Harris; m. Jacqueline Mania Berchadsky, Aug. 13, 1963; 1 son, Mark. BA, Cambridge U., Eng., 1959, PhD, 1962. Instr. U. B.C., Vancouver, Can., 1962-63; asst. prof. U. BC., Vancouver, Can., 1964-65; asst. prof. U. Calif., Santa Barbara, 1965-67, assoc. prof., 1967-73, prof., 1973—, chmn. dept., 1975-77, 88-89; trustee Math. Scis. Rsch. Inst., Berkeley, Calif., 1988-94. Peterhouse rsch. fellow, Cambridge U., 1963-64. Mem. Am. Math. Soc., The Inst. Mgmt. Scis. Office: Univ Calif Dept Math Santa Barbara CA 93106

SIMONSEN, RICHARD SEVERIN, retired aerospace engineer; b. Hollywood, Calif., Nov. 25, 1932; s. Irving P. and Margaret M. (Knox) S.; m. Marilynn Joy Johnson, June 1, 1955; children: Lynda G. Sheasley, Richard R. BS in Engring., UCLA, 1955; postgrad., Harvard U., 1984, U. Calif., Davis, 1980. Engr. Marquardt Aircraft Co., Van Nuys, Calif., 1955-56; engr., program mgr. Aerojet Gen. Corp., Sacramento, 1959-62, mgr. test ops., 1962-78, dir. product and environ. assurance, 1978-80, v.p., gen. mgr. propulsion divsn., 1980-86, pres. solid propulsion co., 1986-90, pres. propulsion co., 1990-93, corp. exec. v.p., 1993-95, ret., 1995. Pres. Sta. KVIE-TV, PBS, Sacremento, 1992-93, bd. dirs. 1987-93; v.p. fin. Boy Scouts Am. for Northern Calif., 1996. Named Engring. Alumnus of Yr. UCLA, 1993. Mem. Soc. Logistics Engrs. AIAA, Assn. U.S. Army, USAF Assn., mem. Boy's Scout of Am., 1996. Republican. Avocations: skiing, hunting, fishing, outdoor activities. Home: 101 Swift River Dr Folsom CA 95630-1521

SIMONSON, BRUCE MILLER, geologist, educator; b. Washington, May 13, 1950; s. Roy Walter and Susan (Miller) S.; m. Sue Mareske, June 28, 1974; children: Joseph Walter, Sonja Anne, Maya Beth. BA with high honors, Wesleyan U., Middletown, Conn., 1972; PhD, Johns Hopkins U., 1982. Field mapper Nat. Geog. Inst., Honduras, 1973-74; instr. dept. geology Oberlin (Ohio) Coll., 1979-81, asst. prof., 1982-85, assoc. prof., 1985-88, prof., 1989—, chmn. dept. geology, 1986-89, 93—; adj. faculty Case We. Res. U., Cleve., 1983—; vis. scientist Geol. Survey, We. Australia, summers, 1985-87, 89, 93; tchr. U.S. Geol. Survey, Reston, Va., 1985; vis. prof. U.S. Geol. Survey, Denver, Colo., 1992-93. Contbr. articles to profl. jours. Grantee Nat. Geog. Soc., 1986-89, 93-94, 96—, NSF, 1977-79, 84, 91-94, Rsch. Corp., 1983, Petroleum Rsch. Fund, 1982-84. Mem. Geol. Soc. Am., Geol. Soc. Australia, Internat. Assn. Sedimentologists, No. Ohio Geol. Soc., Soc. for Sedimentary Geology (sec. Gt. Lakes sect. 1986-90), Sigma Xi. Office: Oberlin Coll Dept Geology Oberlin OH 44074-1044

SIMONSON, DAVID C., retired newspaper association executive; b. N.Y.C., May 9, 1927; s. Simon and Rebecca (Coolman) S.; m. Lois E. Sneider, Nov. 1, 1952; children: Peter, Eric, John Frederick. BA, Hamilton Coll., 1948; postgrad., U. Vt., 1949, Art Student League of N.Y., 1949. Copywriter Forwell & Mart Advt., N.Y.C., 1949-50; reporter, editor Croton-Cortlandt News, Croton, N.Y., 1950-52; gen. mgr. Colony Publs., N.Y.C., 1952-54; editor, mgr. County Press Newspapers, Croton, 1955-59; promotion dir. Amcrete Corp., Peekskill, N.Y., 1959-60; various positions in mgmt. Patent Trader, Mt. Kisco, N.Y., 1960-72, pub., 1972-77; pres./pub. Pioneer Press Newspapers, Wilmette, Ill., 1977-86; exec. v.p., chief exec. officer Nat. Newspaper Assn., Washington, 1987-92; retired, 1992; bd. dirs. Christian Herald Assn., Chappaqua, N.Y.; lectr. Medill Sch. Journalism, Meridian House, U.S.A., numerous state press assns.; media cons.; seminar leader Eastern Europe for World Press Freedom Com.; cons. to Slovenian publs. for U.S. Info. Agy., 1993-94, cons. to Slovakian publs. for U.S. Info. Agy., 1995; cons. to African publs. for UNESCO, 1955; participant Freedom Forum Roundtables. Chmn. planning bd. Town of Croton-on-Hudson, N.Y., 1962-67, trustee, 1967, mayor, 1969. With USNR, 1945-46. Mem. Suburban Newspapers Am. (pres. 1984-85, bd. dirs. 1980-84), Ill. Press Assn (bd. dirs. 1980-84, 1st v.p. 1986), N.Y. Press Assn. (bd. dirs. 1966-76, 1st v.p. 1976), Nat. Newspaper Assn. (bd. dirs. 1985-86), Cook County Pubs. Assn. (pres. 1983-84). Avocations: painting, cartooning. Home: 1805 28th St S Arlington VA 22202-1536

SIMONSON, JOHN ALEXANDER, banking executive; b. Port Huron, Mich., July 22, 1945; s. Fred Alexander and Harriet (Woolfolk) S.; m. Juleen Marie Sheridan, June 18, 1971 (div. 1991); children: Laura E., Anne M. AB, U. Mich., 1967; MBA, Mich. State U., 1968. Exec. v.p., treas. Key Corp., Inc., Cleve., 1992—. Home: 225 Westwind Dr Apt 49 Avon Lake OH 44012-2420 Office: Soc Nat Bank 127 Paul St Cleveland OH 44146-4602

SIMONSON, LEE STUART, broadcast company executive; b. Balt., July 3, 1948; s. Theodore and Sara (Silver) S.; m. Nancy Paula Levin, Mar. 25, 1973; children: Laura Todd, Michael Theodore. BA, U. Md., 1970. Acct. exec. WGMS-AM-FM (subs. RKO Gen.), Washington, 1971-73, retail sales mgr., 1973-76; sales mgr. WFYR-FM (subs. RKO Gen.), Chgo., 1976-80; v.p., gen. mgr. WRKS-FM (subs. RKO Gen.), N.Y.C., 1980-84, WOR-AM (subs. RKO Gen.), N.Y.C., 1984-88; vice chmn., COO, owner radio stas. Broadcasting Ptnrs., Inc., N.Y.C., 1988-95; co-chmn. Broadcasting Ptnrs., L.L.C., N.Y.C., 1995—. Bd. dirs. N.Y.C. chpt. March of Dimes, 1982—, IRTS Found., 1995—. With USAR, 1970-76. Jewish. Avocations: baseball, reading, tennis, symphony, films.

SIMONSON, MARGARET, newspaper publishing executive. V.p. employee rels. Chgo. Tribune. Office: Chgo Tribune Co 435 N Michigan Ave Chicago IL 60611-4001

SIMONSON, TED, principal. Prin. Los Gatos (Calif.) High Sch. Recipient Blue Ribbon Sch. award, 1990-91. Office: Los Gatos High Sch 20 High School Ct Los Gatos CA 95032-6917

SIMONT, MARC, artist; b. Paris, France, Nov. 23, 1915; came to U.S., 1927, naturalized, 1936; s. Josep and Dolors (Basté) S.; m. Sara Dalton, Apr. 7, 1945; 1 son, Marc Dalton. Attended, Academie Julian, Academie Ranson, André Lhote Sch., all Paris, 1932-35, NAD, N.Y.C., 1936. Asst. to Ezra Winter on Jefferson Wing mural Library of Congress, 1940; author, illustrator 9 children's books, 1939—; illustrator 80 books; author, illustrator: Opera Soufflé, 1950, Polly's Oats, 1951, The Lovely Summer, 1952, (with Red Smith) How to Get to First Base, 1952, Mimi, 1955, The Plumber Out of the Sea, 1955, The Contest at Paca, 1959, How Come Elephants?, 1965, Afternoon in Spain, 1965, A Childs' Eye View of the World, 1972; translator, illustrator The Lieutenant Colonel and The Gypsy, 1971; translator Ibrahim, 1989. Recipient Caldecott honor, 1950, Caldecott award, 1957, citation merit Soc. Illustrators, 1965; Tiffany Found. fellow, 1937. Mem. Am. Vets. Com., Authors Guild. Home: 336 Town St West Cornwall CT 06796-1304

SIMONTACCHI, CAROL NADINE, nutritionist, retail store executive; b. Bellingham, Wash., July 6, 1947; d. Ralph Eugene and Sylvia Arletta (Tyler) Walmer; m. Bob Simontacchi, Oct. 3, 1981; children: Caryl Anne, Bobbie Anne, Melissa Anne, Laurie Anne. BS in Health and Human Svcs., Columbia Pacific U., 1996, postgrad., 1996—. Cert. nutritionist, Wash. CEO The Health Haus, Inc., Vancouver, Wash., 1985—; host radio program Back to the Beginning, Vancouver, 1990—. Author: Your Fat is Not Your Fault, 1994, The Sun Rise Book: Living Beyond Depression, 1996, The Attention! Book, Living Beyond ADHD, 1996. Mem. Soc. Cert. Nutritionists (pres. bd. 1992-93), Nat. Nutritional Foods Assn. (chair edn. com., N.W. region legis. chair 1991—). Republican. Christian Ch. Office: The Health Haus Inc 101 E 8th St Ste 250 Vancouver WA 98660-3294

SIMONTON, ROBERT BENNET, lawyer; b. N.Y.C., Feb. 23, 1933; s. Theodore E. and Beulah H. (Hulsebus) S.; m. Tanya Wood, Aug. 24, 1957; children: Sheri, Robert B. Jr., Scott S. Student Amherst Coll., 1950-52; BS in Engring., Columbia U., 1954; LLB, Syracuse U., 1959. Bar: N.Y. 1959. Patent agt., atty. Theodore E. Simonton, Cazenovia, N.Y., 1956-60; assoc. Hancock, Dorr, Ryan and Shove, Syracuse, N.Y., 1960-64; staff atty. Bristol-Myers Co., Syracuse, 1967, counsel, 1967-71, v.p., counsel Bristol Labs., 1971-74; v.p., sec., gen. counsel Crouse Hinds Co., Syracuse, 1974-75; staff atty. Sterling Drug Inc., N.Y.C., 1975-78, sec., asst. gen. counsel, 1978-88; small bus. cons., 1988—; adj. prof. U. Bridgeport (Conn.) Law Sch., 1988-90; trustee Syracuse Savs. Bank, 1973-76. Bd. govs. Citizens' Found., Syracuse, 1969-70; bd. dirs. Urban League of Syracuse, 1967-72, pres., 1967-71, chmn., 1971-72; bd. visitors Syracuse U. Coll. Law, 1968—; bd. dirs. Graham Windham, also sec., 1986-88, Goodwill Industries Coastal Empire, 1992—, treas., 1993-95; treas. Landings Assn. Inc., 1994-96; bd. trustees Manlius Pub. Hill Sch., 1962-75, chmn., 1971-74. Served with U.S. Army, 1954-56. Recipient Justinian Honor Soc. award Syracuse U. Coll. Law, 1959.

SIMOPOULOS, ARTEMIS PANAGEOTIS, physician, educator; b. Kampos-Avias, Greece, Apr. 3, 1933; came to U.S. 1949, naturalized 1955; d. Panageotis L. and Nena P. (Konteas) S.; m. Alan Lee Pinkerson, Jan. 10, 1957; children: Daphne, Lee, Alexandra. B.A., Barnard Coll., 1952; M.D., Boston U., 1956. Diplomate Am. Bd. Pediatrics. Pediatric intern Kings County Hosp., Bklyn., 1956-57; resident Kings County Hosp., 1957-58; fellow in hematology Children's Hosp., Washington, 1960-61, asst. chief resident in pediatrics, 1961-62, mem. acad. staff, 1962-67, assoc. staff in pediatric nursery service, 1967-71; spl. lectr. pediatrics Ewha Woman's U. Sch. Medicine, Seoul, Korea, 1958-59; asst. prof. pediatrics George Washington U. Sch. Medicine, 1962-67, clin. asst. prof., 1967-71; dir. nurseries George Washington U. Hosp., 1965-67; staff pediatrician Nat. Heart and Lung Inst., NIH, 1968-71, cons. endocrinology br., 1971-78; with div. med. scis. Nat. Acad. Scis., NRC, Washington, 1971-74; exec. sec. Nat. Acad. Scis., NRC, 1974-76, exec. dir. bd. maternal, child and family health research, 1974-76; cons. to dir. Nat. Inst. Child Health and Human Devel., NIH, Bethesda, Md, 1976-77; chief devel. biology and nutrition br., ctrs. for research for mothers and children Nat. Inst. Child Health and Human Devel., NIH, 1977; vice chmn. and exec. sec. nutrition coordinating com. NIH, 1977-78; cons. nutrition and health to spl. asst. to the Pres. for Consumer Affairs The White House, Washington, 1978-81; chmn. nutrition coordinating com. office of the dir. NIH, 1978-86; dir. divsn. nutritional sci. Internat. Life Sci. Inst. Rsch. Found., Washington, 1986-88; dir. Ctr. for Genetics, Nutrition and Health, Washington, 1989-90, pres., 1990—; co-chmn., exec. sec. joint subcom. Human Nutrition Rsch., Office Sci. and

Tech. Policy, Exec. Office of the Pres., 1979-83; vis. prof. Harokopio U., Athens, 1994-95. Editor World Rev. Nutrition and Dietetics, 1989—; contbg. editor Nutrition Revs., 1979—; mem. editorial bd. Jour. Nutrition, Growth, and Cancer, 1982—, Internat. Jour. Vitamin and Nutrition Research, 1986—, n=3 News, 1986-90, Annals Nutrition and Metabolism, 1991—, Food Revs. Internat., 1994—; cons. editor Nutrition Research, 1983—, Annals Internal Medicine, 1984—, Jour. AMA, 1985—, Food Reviews Internat., 1994—; contbr. articles in endocrinology, genetics, nutrition and fitness, omega-3 fatty acids, and obesity to profl. jours. Recipient 1st Presdl. award for studies in field of obesity and weight control Columbia-Presbyn. Med. Ctr., 1993, Outstanding Achievement award promoting nutrition and fitness and positive health Greek Govt., 1992; NIH grantee, 1960-61. Fellow Am. Acad. Pediatrics, Am. Coll. Nutrition; mem. Soc. Pediatric Rsch., Endocrine Soc., Maternity Ctr. Assn. (rsch. adv. com.), Am. Pediatric Soc., Am. Inst. Nutrition, Am. Soc. Clin. Nutrition, Am. Assn. for World Health (v.p. 1981-90, asst. treas. 1981-90, nat. chmn. for World Health Day 1982—, vice chmn. bd. 1991-92, chmn. pgm. com. 1993—, bd. dirs. 1993—), D.C. Med. Soc., N.Am. Assn. for Study Obesity, Internat. Life Scis. Inst. (trustee 1982-88, exec. com. 1982-85, trustee Nutrition Found. 1985-87), Internat. Soc. Study of Fatty Acids and Lipids (sec., treas. 1991-94, 95—). Greek Orthodox. Home: 4330 Klingle St NW Washington DC 20016-3577 Office: Ctr Genetics Nutrition and Health 2001 S St NW Ste 530 Washington DC 20009-1125

SIMOWITZ, LEE H., lawyer; b. Augusta, Ga., Sept. 7, 1946. BA cum laude, Harvard U., 1968; JD, Yale U., 1972. Bar: D.C. 1973. Law clk. to Hon. Harold H. Greene, chief judge Superior Ct., Washington, 1972-73; asst. to dir. bur. consumer protection FTC, Washington, 1975-76; atty.-adviser Calvin J. Collier, chmn. FTC, 1976-77; ptnr. Baker & Hostetler, Washington. Mem. ABA (antiturst law sect., public utility law sect.), D.C. Bar. Office: Baker & Hostetler 1050 Connecticut Ave NW Washington DC 20036-5303*

SIMPICH, WILLIAM MORRIS, public affairs consultant; b. Washington, Sept. 24, 1924; s. Frederick and Margaret (Edwards) S.; m. Margaret Pearson Hunter, Sept. 9, 1950; children: William Morris, Margaret Edwards, John Hunter, Joseph Pearson. Student, George Washington U., 1942-43; BS, U.S. Naval Acad., 1946. Assoc. Ivy Lee & T.J. Ross (name later changed to T.J. Ross & Assocs., Inc.), N.Y.C., 1949-51, 54-63, v.p., 1964, sec., treas., 1965-84, sr. v.p., 1977-84, ret. as exec. v.p., 1984, also bd. dirs. With U.S. Navy, 1946-49, 51-53. Episcopalian. Home: 1021 Church Rd Lusby MD 20657-2636

SIMPKINS, CHARLES, Olympic athlete, track and field. Olympic triple jumper Barcelona, Spain, 1992. Recipient Triple Jump Silver medal Olympics, Barcelona, 1992. Address: 1311 Greenland Dr Murfreesboro TN 37130-2768

SIMPKINS, HENRY, medical educator. BS in Chemistry, U. London, 1964, PhD in Biophys. and Molecular Biology, 1967; MD, U. Miami, 1975. Rsch. biologist U. Calif., San Deigo, 1967-69; head lab. molecular biology and biophys. Lady Davis Inst. Med. Rsch. of Jewish Gen. Hosp., Montreal, Can., 1969-75; asst. prof. dept. biochemistry U. Montreal, 1970-73, assoc. prof., 1973-75; resident U. Colo. Med. Ctr., Denver, 1975-78, instr. dept. pathology, 1976-78, asst. prof. dept. pathology, 1976-77, assoc. prof. dept. pathology, 1977-78; assoc. prof. dept. pathology U. Calif., Irvine, 1978-81, prof. dept. pathology, 1981-85; prof. pathology SUNY, N.Y.C., 1985-91; prof., chmn. dept. pathology and lab. medicine Temple U. Med. Sch., Phila., 1991—; head divsns. chem. pathology and hematopathology U. Calif., Irvine, 1978-81, head disvn. hematopathology, 1981-83, head divsn. hematopathology.blood bank, 1983-85, acting chmn. dept. pathology, 1984; cons. hematopathology Long Beach VA Hosp., 1979-85; dir. dept. pathology and lab. medicine U. Hosp. S.I., N.Y., 1985-91; presenter in field. Contbr. articles to profl. jours. Postdoctoral fellow King's Coll., London, 1964-67, U. Calif., San Diego, 1967-69; Ministry Edn. State scholar, Gt. Britain, 1961-64, Sci. Rsch. Coun. scholar, Gt. Britain, 1964-67; Can. MEd. Rsch. Coun. scholar, 1970-75. Mem. Am. Soc. Clin. Pathologists, Am. Assn. Blood Banks, Am. Soc. Hematology, Coll. Am. Pathologists, Internat. Acad. Pathology, The Pluto Club. Office: Temple U Sch Medicine Dept Pathology and Lab Med Philadelphia PA 19140

SIMPLOT, JOHN R., agribusiness executive; b. Dubuque, Iowa, Jan. 4, 1909; m. Esther Becker; children: Richard, Don, Scott, Gay Simplot Otter. Founder, chmn. J.R. Simplot Co., Boise, Idaho, 1941—; bd. dirs. Micron Technology, First Security Corp., Continental Life and Accident Co., Morrison-Knudsen, Inc. Former chmn. bd. trustees Coll. Idaho. Avocations: skiing, horseback riding, hunting, fishing. Pioneer in commercial frozen french fries. Office: J R Simplot Co PO Box 27 1 Capitol Ctr Boise ID 83707*

SIMPSON, A. W. B., law educator; b. 1931. Fellow Oxford U., Eng., 1955-72; prof. U. Kent, Canterbury, Eng., 1972-84, U. Chgo., 1984-87, U. Mich., Ann Arbor, 1987—. Office: U Mich Law Sch 625 S State St Ann Arbor MI 48109-1215

SIMPSON, ALAN KOOI, senator; b. Cody, Wyo., Sept. 2, 1931; s. Milward Lee and Lorna (Kooi) S.; m. Ann Schroll, June 21, 1954; children—William Lloyd, Colin Mackenzie, Susan Lorna. BS, U. Wyo., 1954, JD, 1958; LLD (hon.), Calif. Western Sch. of Law, 1983, Colo. Coll., 1986, Notre Dame U., 1987; JD (hon.), Am. U., 1989. Bar: Wyo. 1958, U.S. Supreme Ct. 1964. Asst. atty. gen. State of Wyo., 1959; city atty. City of Cody, 1959-69; partner firm Simpson, Kepler, and Simpson, Cody, Wyo., 1959-78; mem. Wyo. Ho. of Reps., 1964-77, majority whip, 1973-75, majority floor leader, 1975-77, speaker pro tem, 1977; legis. participant Eagleton Inst. Politics, Rutgers U., 1971; mem. U.S. Senate from Wyo., 1978—, asst. majority leader, 1985-87, asst. minority leader, 1987-95, chmn. vets. affairs com., chmn. fin. subcom. on Social Security and Family Policy, chmn. subcom. on immigration and refugee policy; mem. Sen. Rep. Policy Com. Spec. Com. on Aging; guest lectr. London exchange program Regent's Coll., London, 1987. Formerly v.p., trustee N.W. C.C., Powell, Wyo., 1968-76; trustee Buffalo Bill Hist. Ctr., Cody, Grand Teton Music Festival; del. Nat. Triennial Episcopal Ch. Conv., 1973, 76. With U.S. Army, 1954-56. Recipient Nat. Assn. Land Grant Colls. Centennial Alum award U. Wyo., 1987, Lifetime Svc. award Vietnam Vets. Am., 1993. Mem. Wyo. Bar Assn., Park County Bar Assn., Fifth Jud. Dist. Bar Assn., Am. Bar Assn., Assn. Trial Lawyers Am., U. Wyo. Alumni Assn. (pres. 1962, 63, Disting. Alumnus award 1985), VFW (life), Am. Legion, Amvets. (Silver Helmet award). Lodges: Eagles, Elks, Masons (33 deg.), Shriners, Rotary (pres. local club 1972-73). Office: US Senate 105 Dirksen Senate Bldg Washington DC 20510-5002*

SIMPSON, ALLYSON BILICH, lawyer; b. Pasadena, Calif., Feb. 5, 1951; d. John Joseph and Barbaran Rita (Bessolo) Bilich; m. Roland Gilbert Simpson, Aug. 11, 1979; children: Megan Elise, Erin Marie, Brian Patrick. BS, U. So. Calif., L.A., 1973, JD, 1976. Bar: Calif. 1976. Staff atty. Gen. Telephone Co., Thousand Oaks, Calif., 1978-79; group staff atty., dir. legis. compliance Pacific Mut. Life Ins. Co., Newport Beach, Calif., 1980-86; corp. counsel and sec. Amicare Ins. Co., Beverly Hills, Calif., 1986; assoc. Leboeuf, Lamb, Leiby & MacRae, L.A., 1986-87; from assoc. to ptnr. Musick, Peeler & Garrett, L.A., 1988-94; ptnr. Sonnenschein Nath & Rosenthal, L.A., 1994-95; sr. v.p., sec., gen. counsel Fremont Pacific Ins. Group, Glendale, Calif., 1995—; vis. pro. bus. law U. So. Calif., L.A., 1981. Trustee St. Anne's Maternity Home Found., L.A., 1991—; bd. dirs. St. Anne's Maternity Home, L.A., 1993—. Mem. Western Pension & Benefits Conf., Conf. of Ins. Counsel. Republican. Roman Catholic. Avocations: music, reading, family. Office: Fremont Pacific Ins Group 500 N Brand Blvd Glendale CA 91203

SIMPSON, ANDREA LYNN, energy communications executive; b. Altadena, Calif., Feb. 10, 1948; d. Kenneth James and Barbara Faries Simpson; m. John R. Myrdal, Dec. 13, 1986; 1 child, Christopher Ryan Myrdal. BA, U. So. Calif., 1969, MS, 1983; postgrad. U. Colo., Boulder Sch. Bank Mktg., 1977. Asst. cashier United Calif. Bank, L.A., 1969-73; asst. v.p. mktg. 1st Hawaiian Bank, Honolulu, 1973-78; v.p. corp. comm. BHP Hawaii, Inc. (formerly Pacific Resources, Inc.), Honolulu, 1978—. Bd. dirs. Arts Coun. Hawaii, 1977-81, Hawaii Heart Assn., 1978-83, Coun. Pacific Girl Scouts U.S., 1982-85, Child and Family Svcs., 1984-86, Honolulu Symphony Soc., 1985-91, Sta. KHPR Hawaii Pub. Radio, 1988-92, Kapiolani Found., 1990-95, Hanahauoli Sch., 1991—; bd. dirs., 2nd. v.p. Girl Scout Coun. Hawaii, 1994—; trustee Hawaii Loa Coll., 1984-86, Kapiolani Women's and Children's Hosp., 1988—, Hawaii Sch. For Girls at LaPietra, 1989-91, Kapiolani Med. Ctr. at Pali Momi, 1994—; commr. Hawaii State Commn. on Status of Women, 1985-87, State Sesquecentennial of Pub. Schs. Commn., 1990-91; bd. dirs. Hawaii Strategic Devel. Corp., 1991—, Hawaii Children's Mus., 1994—, Pacific Asian Affairs Coun., 1994—, Girl Scout Coun. Hawaii, 1994—; adv. dir. Hawaii Kids at Work, 1991—, Hawaii Mothers Against Drunk Driving, 1992—. Named Panhellenic Woman of Yr. Hawaii, 1979, Outstanding Woman in Bus. Hawaii YWCA, 1980, Outstanding Young Woman of Hawaii Girl Scouts Coun. of the Pacific, 1985, 86, Hawaii Legis., 1980. Mem. Am. Mktg. Assn., Pub. Rels. Soc. Am. (bd. dirs. Honolulu chpt. 1984-86, Silver Anvil award 1984, Pub. Rels. Profl. Yr. 1991), Pub. Utilities Communicators Assn. (Communicator of Yr. 1984), Honolulu Advt. Fedn. (Advt. Woman of Yr. 1984), U. So. Calif. Alumni Assn. (bd. dirs. Hawaii 1981-83), Outrigger Canoe Club, Pacific Club, Kaneohe Yacht Club, Rotary (pub. rels. chmn. 1988—, Honolulu chpt.), Alpha Phi (past pres., dir. Hawaii), Hawaii Jaycees (Outstanding Young Person of Hawaii 1978). Office: BHP Hawaii Inc 733 Bishop St Ste 2700 Honolulu HI 96813-4022

SIMPSON, BERYL BRINTNALL, botany educator; b. Dallas, Apr. 28, 1942; d. Edward Everett and Barbara Frances (Brintnall) S.; children: Jonathan, Meghan. AB, Radcliffe Coll., 1964; MA, Harvard U., 1968, PhD, 1968. Rsch. fellow Arnold Arboretum/Gray Herbarium, Cambridge, Mass., 1969-71; curator Smithsonian Instn., Washington, 1971-78; prof. U. Tex., Austin, 1978—; chmn. U.S. Com. to IUBS, 1985-88; co-pres. Internat. Congress Systematic and Evolutionary Biology, 1980-85. Author: Economic Botany, 1994; editor: Mesquite, 1977; contbr. over 100 articles and notes to profl. jours. Recipient Greenman award Mo. Bot. Garden, 1970. Fellow AAAS, Am. Acad. Arts and Sci.; mem. Soc. for Study Evolution (coun. 1975-80, pres. 1985-86), Bot. Soc. Am. (prs. 1990-91, Merit award 1992), Bot. Soc. Washington (v.p. 1975), Am. Soc. Plant Tazonomists (pres. 1994, Cooley award), Am. Inst. Biol. Scis. (bd. dirs. 1993-95), U.S.-Mex. Found. for Sci. (bd. govs.). Office: Dept Botany BIO 308 U Tex Austin TX 78713

SIMPSON, BOB G., quality assurance professional; b. DeWitt, Ark., Feb. 20, 1932; s. Fearmon Lambert Simpson and Myrtle Elsie (Lowrance) Simpson Palmer. BS in Physics., U. Ctrl. Ark., 1962. Quality/reliabilty engr. Motorola Inc., Phoenix, 1963-70; reliability engr. Motorola Inc., Mesa, Ariz., 1973-74; component engr. Control Data Corp., Tucson, 1971-73; mgr. quality assurance Engineered Sys. Inc., Tempe, 1976-90, supr. of quality assurance, 1991—. With USN, 1951-55; with AEC Contractor, 1957-59. Mem. Ch. of God Internat.

SIMPSON, CAROLE ESTELLE, broadcast journalist; b. Chgo., Dec. 7, 1940; d. Lytle Ray and Doretha Viola (Wilbon) S.; m. James Edward Marshall, Sept. 3, 1966; children: Mallika Joy, Adam. BA in Journalism, U. Mich., 1962; postgrad., U. Iowa, 1964-65. News reporter WCFL Radio, Chgo., 1965-68; reporter/anchorwoman WBBM Radio, Chgo., 1968-70; TV news reporter WMAQ-TV, Chgo., 1970-74; NBC news network corr. Midwest Bur., transferred to Washington, from 1974; anchorwoman World News Saturday, Washington, 1988-93, World News Sunday, Washington, 1993—; instr. journalism Tuskegee Inst., Ala., 1962-64; faculty Medill Sch. Journalism, Northwestern U., 1972-74; moderator 1992 Town Mtg. Presdl. Debate. Recipient med. journalism award AMA, Emmy award, Dupont award, Milestone in Broadcasting award Nat. Commn. on Working Women, Disting. Journalist award U. Mo., Star award Am. Women in Radio and TV, Journalist of Yr. award Nat. Assn. Black Journalists, 1992; named Outstanding Woman in Comm., YWCA Met. Chgo., 1974; named to U. Iowa Comm. Hall of Fame; established several coll. scholarships for women and minorities in broadcast journalism. Mem. Internat. Women's Media Found. (bd. of RFK Journalism awards), NAS (mem. of bd. of children and families), Radio TV News Dirs. Found. (trustee), Radio-TV Corrs. Assn. Washington. Office: ABC News Washington Bureau 1717 DeSales St NW Washington DC 20036

SIMPSON, CHARLES EDMOND, crop science educator; b. Winters, Tex., Aug. 19, 1940; s. Robert Charles and Rosalie Helen Simpson; m. Lynann Kruse, Aug. 29, 1964; children: Melissa E. Heatley, Shay L. BS in Agrl. Edn., Tex. A&M U., 1963, MS in Plant Breeding, 1966, PhD in Plant Breeding, 1967. From asst. prof. to assoc. prof. Tex. Agrl. Exptl. Sta., Tex. A&M U., Stephenville, 1967-84, prof., 1984—. Contbr. 8 chpts. to books, numerous articles to profl. jours. Fellow Am. Peanut Rsch. and Edn. Soc. (pres. 1991-92); mem. Am. Soc. Agronomy, Am. Phytopathol. Soc., Coun. on Agrl. Sci. & Tech. Diversity, Crop Sci. Soc. Am. (Frank N. Meyer medal 1993). Lutheran. Avocation: peanut germplasm preservation and collection. Office: Tex A&M U Tex Agrl Exptl Sta PO Box 292 Stephenville TX 76401

SIMPSON, CHARLES R., III, judge; b. Cleve., July 8, 1945; s. Charles Ralph and Anne Marie (Markel) S.; married; 3 children. BA, U. Louisville, 1967, JD, 1970. Bar: Ky. 1970, U.S. Dist. Ct. (we. dist.) Ky. 1971, U.S. Cir. Ct. (6th cir.) 1985. With Rubin, Trautwein & Mays, Louisville, 1971-75, Levin, Yussman & Simpson, Louisville, 1975-77; judge U.S. Dist. Ct. (we. dist.) Ky., Louisville, 1986—; pvt. practice Louisville, 1977-86; part-time staff counsel Jefferson County Judge/Exec., 1978-84; adminstr. Jefferson County Alcoholic Beverage Control, 1983-84; city clk. City of Rolling Fields, 1985-86. Roman Catholic. Office: We Dist Ct Ky 247 US Courthouse 601 W Broadway Louisville KY 40202*

SIMPSON, CURTIS CHAPMAN, III, lawyer; b. Leonia, N.J., Apr. 19, 1952; s. Curtis Chapman Simpson Jr. and Marguerite (Johnson) Host; m. Joy D.; children: Ashley Blake, Curtis Chapman. BA, George Washington U., 1977; JD, Calif. Western U., 1980. Bar: Calif. 1981, U.S. Dist. Ct. (cen. dist.) Calif. 1983, U.S. Ct. Claims 1991. Pres. Curtis C. Simpson, III, P.C., Santa Barbara, Calif., 1981-84; assoc. Schurmer & Drane, Santa Barbara, 1984-90; prin. Curtis Simpson Law Firm, Santa Barbara, Oxnard, Calif., 1991—; ct.-appointed arbitrator superior cts. Santa Barbara County, Ventura County, San Luis Obispo County, all Calif., 1991—. Contbr. to profl. jours. Co-chmn. youth group leader Montecito YMCA, 1992; bd. dirs. Montecito Ednl. Found., 1993—; co-pres. Montecito Ednl. Found., 1994—. Mem. Assn. Trial Lawyers Am., Consumer Attys. Calif. (cert. recognition 1991—), State Bar Calif., Santa Barbara County Bar Assn., Ventura County Bar Assn., Hon. Order Ky. Cols., Coral Casino Beach and Cabana Club. Episcopalian. Office: Curtis Simpson Law Firm 120 E De La Guerra St Santa Barbara CA 93101-2226

SIMPSON, DANIEL H., ambassador; b. Wheeling, W.Va., July 9, 1939; married; 4 children. BA, Yale U., 1961; cert. in African studies, Northwestern U., 1973. Joined Fgn. Svc., U.S. Dept. State, Washington, 1966—, staff asst. Bur. Security and Consular Affairs, 1966-67, speech writer for asst. sec. state for African affairs, 1968, desk officer for Rhodesia, Botswana, Lesotho, and Swaziland, 1973-74; tng. officer USIA, Washington, 1967-68; polit., econ. and consular officer Am. Embassy, Bujumbura, Burundi, 1968-70; polit. officer Am. Embassy, Pretoria, Republic South Africa, 1970-72; dep. chief mission Am. Embassy, Beirut, until 1989; amb. to Cen. African Republic, Bangui, 1989-93; dep. comdr. Army War Coll., Carlisle, Pa., 1993-94; ambassador to Somalia Mogadishu, 1994-95; ambasador to Zaire Kinshasa, 1995—. Home and Office: Am Embassy Kinshasa Unit 31550 APO AE 09828

SIMPSON, DANIEL REID, lawyer; b. Glen Alpine, N.C., Feb. 20, 1927; s. James R. and Margaret Ethel (Newton) S.; m. Mary Alice Leonard, Feb. 25, 1930; children: Mary Simpson Beyer, Ethel B. Simpson Todd, James R. II. BS, Wake Forest U., 1949, LLB, 1951. Bar: N.C. 1951, U.S. Dist. Ct. (we. dist.) N.C. 1951, U.S. Ct. Appeals (4th and 5th cirs.) 1980. Dir. First Union Nat. Bank, Morganton, N.C. Mem. N.C. Ho. of Reps., 1959-65; now mem. N.C. Senate, mem. N.C. Joint Legis. Edn. Oversight Com.; mem. oversight com. N.C. Dept. of Corrections; hon. mem. bd. dirs. N.C. Restaurant Assns.; del. Rep. Nat. Conv., 1968, 76, mem. N.C. Rep. Exec. Com. Served with AUS, 1943-45, PTO. Mem. N.C. Bar Assn., Burke County Bar Assn. Baptist. Club: Masons. Home: Box 2358 Nebo NC 28761 Office: Simpson Aycock PA 204 E Mcdowell St Morganton NC 28655-3545 also: PO Box 1329 Morganton NC 28680-1329 *When you get off your knees, leave your troubles on the floor. No mistake was ever corrected by worrying about it.*

SIMPSON, DAVID WILLIAM, artist, educator; b. Pasadena, Calif., Jan. 20, 1928; s. Frederick and Mary Adeline (White) S.; m. Dolores D. Debus, July 30, 1954; 1 stepchild, Gregory C. Vose; 1 child, Lisa C. B.F.A., Calif. Sch. Fine Arts, 1956; M.A., San Francisco State Coll., 1958. Instr. art Am. River Jr. Coll., Sacramento, 1958-60, Contra Costa Jr. Coll., San Pablo, Calif., 1960-65; prof. art U. Calif., Berkeley, 1967-91, prof. emeritus, 1991—. Exhibited in one-man shows including Robert Elkon Gallery, N.Y.C., 1961, 63, 64, San Francisco Mus. Art, 1967, Henri Gallery, Washington, 1968, Oakland Mus., 1978, Modernism, San Francisco, 1980-81, 84, 86, Sheldon Meml. Art Gallery, Lincoln, Nebr., 1990, Mincher/Wilcox Gallery, San Francisco, 1991, 92, 93, Angles Gallery, Santa Monica, Calif., 1991, 92, 94, Bemis Found., Omaha, Nebr., 1991, Anthony Ralph Gallery, N.Y.C., 1992, John Berggruen Gallery, San Francisco, 1994, Charlotte Jackson Fine Art, Santa Fe, 1995, Laguna Art Mus., Laguna Beach, Calif., 1995; group shows include Mus. Modern Art, N.Y.C., 1963, Carnegie Internat., Pitts., 1961-62, 66-67, L.A. Mus. Art, 1964, U. Ill., 1969, Expo '70, Osaka, Japan, 1970, Josly Art Mus., Omaha, 1970, John Berggruen Gallery, San Francisco, 1979, Janus Gallery, L.A., 1980, Gallery Show, Tokyo, 1984, Koplin Gallery, L.A., 1987, Angles Gallery, Santa Monica, 1988, 90, John Good Gallery, N.Y., 1992, John Berggruen Gallery, San Francisco, 1993, Cheryl Haines Gallery, San Francisco, 1996; represented in permanent collections including Phila. Mus. Art, Nat. Collection Fine Arts, Washington, Seattle Art Mus., La Jolla (Calif.) Mus. Art, Mus. Modern Art, N.Y.C., San Francisco Mus. Art, Oakland (Calif.) Mus., Panza Collection, Italy, Laguna Art Mus., Laguna Beach, Calif., Univ. Art Mus., Berkeley, Calif., Museo Cantonale d'Arte Lugano, Switzerland. Home: 565 Vistamont St Berkeley CA 94708 Office: U Calif Art Dept Berkeley CA 94720

SIMPSON, DENNIS DWAYNE, psychologist, educator; b. Lubbock, Tex., Nov. 9, 1943; s. Homer Arnold and Georgie Lee (Barrett) S.; m. Sherry Ann Johnson, Aug. 20, 1965; children: Jason Renn, Jeffrey Todd, Jennifer Lynn. BA, U. Tex., 1966; PhD, Tex. Christian U., 1970. Asst. prof. psychology Tex. Christian U., Ft. Worth, 1970-74, assoc. prof., 1974-79, prof., 1979-82, dir., prof., 1989—, S.B. Sells prof. psychology, 1992—; dir., prof. Tex. A&M U., College Station, 1982-89; sci. adv. bd. NIDA Rsch. Ctrs., Washington, 1992—; adv. bd. Nat. Drug Treatment Evaluation Studies, Washington, 1992—; expert advisor U.S. Acctg. Office, Health and Human Svcs., others; cons. WHO, fgn. govts. regarding drug rsch. Mem. editl. bd. Am. Jour of Drug and Alcohol Abuse, 1992, Internat. Jour. of the Addictions, 1995, Substance Use and Misuse; contbr. over 150 articles to profl. jours.; author 5 books. Recipient Disting. Rsch. Achievement award Tex. Commn. on Alcohol and Drug Abuse, 1987; recipient numerous grants. Mem. APA, Am. Psychol. Soc., Am. Evaluation Assn., Soc. of Psychologists in Addictive Behaviors, Southwestern Psychol. Assn., Sigma Xi. Achievements include research emphasis on the process of treatment service delivery in relation client attributes and how they related to retention rates, relapse, posttreatment outcomes; research on drug use in the workplace, other areas. Office: Tex Christian U Inst Behavioral Rsch PO Box 298740 Fort Worth TX 76129

SIMPSON, ELIZABETH ANN, reading and language arts educator; b. Collins, Miss., Oct. 20, 1940; d. Clyde C. and Edna L. (Lewis) McRaney; m. Arthur Thomas Simpson, Dec. 15, 1962; children: Lisa Bukovnik, Art, Cindy Simpson-Scharff, Sheri Lucas. BS, U. So. Miss., 1978, MEd, 1982. Tchr. Biloxi (Miss.) Pub. Schs., 1978—; conv. presenter Miss. Coun. Tchrs. of English, Jackson, 1992. Leader Girl Scouts Am., San Antonio, 1970, Biloxi, 1975; Sunday sch. tchr. Episcopal Ch. of the Redeemer, Biloxi, 1978. Fellow South Miss. Writing Project, 1991, 92. Mem. Internat. Reading Assn., Nat. Coun. Tchrs. of English, Nat. Coun. Tchrs. of Math., Miss. Reading Assn. (sec. Gulf Coast chpt. 1986), Phi Delta Kappa, Phi Kappa Phi. Home: 347 Saint Mary Blvd Biloxi MS 39531-3419 Office: Beauvoir Elem Sch 2003 Lawrence St Biloxi MS 39531-4106

SIMPSON, FREDERICK JAMES, retired research administrator; b. Regina, Sask., Can., June 8, 1922; s. Ralph James and Lillian Mary (Anderson) S.; m. Margaret Christine Simpson, May 28, 1947; children: Christine Louise, Steven James, Leslie Coleen, Ralph Edwin, David Glen. B.Sc., U. Alta., Can., 1944, M.Sc. in Agr., 1946; Ph.D. in Bacteriology, U. Wis., 1952. With Nat. Research Council Can., 1946-84; asst. dir. Atlantic Research Lab., Halifax, N.S., 1970-73; dir. Atlantic Research Lab., 1973-84; sci. cons., 1985-90; vis. scientist U. Ill., Urbana, 1955-56, vis. prof., 1964; mem. exec. council Atlantic Provinces Interuniv. Com. on Scis., 1976-79, chmn., 1981-84; pres. Fed. Inst. Mgmt., Halifax, 1981-82. Contbr. numerous articles to profl. jours. Decorated Queen's Silver Anniversary medal. Fellow Royal Soc. of Arts (London); mem. Can. Soc. Microbiologists (hon., sec.-treas. 1969-70, v.p. 1971-72, pres. 1972-73), Nova Scotian Inst. Sci. (v.p. 1975-76, pres. 1977-78), Internat. Phycological Soc., Aquaculture Assn. Can., Sigma Xi. Mem. United Ch. of Canada.

SIMPSON, GEORGE TRUE, surgeon, educator; b. Aurora, Colo., Apr. 29, 1943; s. George True and Meryle Flora (Moore) S.; m. Sharon Louise Mason, Mar. 9, 1944; children: Amber-Louise Elizabeth, George True III. BA in History, LaSierra U., 1969; MD, Loma Linda U., 1973, MPH, 1975. Diplomate Am. Bd. Otolaryngology, Am. Bd. Laser Surgery, Nat. Bd. Med. Examiners. Surgery resident U. Ala. Hosp. & Clinics, Birmingham, 1973-75; surgeon Kalabo Hosp., Zambia, 1975; otolaryngology resident UCLA Head/Neck Surgery, L.A., 1975-78; pediatric otolaryngology fellow Children's Hosp, Boston, 1978-79; assoc. prof., acting chair Boston (Mass.) U., 1979-90; dir. dept. otolaryngology Boston (Mass.) City Hosp., 1979-90; otolaryngologist-in-chief U. Hosp., Boston, 1984-90; chmn. dept. otolaryngology SUNY, Buffalo, 1991—, Sisters of Charity Hosp., Buffalo, 1991—; pres. U. Head/Neck Surgery, Buffalo, 1991—; cons. Ministry Pub. Health, State of Kuwait, 1976, MIT, Cambridge, 1979—, Gillette Corp., Boston, 1984-90; pres. Boston City Hosp. Med. Staff, 1983, 85; bd. dirs. Voice Found. Sci. Adv., Phila.; chmn. otolaryngology sect. 10 Internat. Congress on Lasers in medicine and Surgery, Taipei, Taiwan, 1989; examiner Am. Bd. Otolaryngology, Chgo., 1992, 93, 94. Author: Lasers in Otolaryngology, 1985; author, editor: Textbook of General Medicine, 1987; editor: Lasers in Otolaryngology: OTOL Clinics of N.Am., 1990; contbr. articles to profl. jours. With U.S. Army, 1964-66. Recipient Caring Physician award Mass. Nursing Assn., Mass. Med. Assn., 1989. Fellow ACS, Am. Acad. Otolaryngology-Head/Neck Surgery (Honor award 1987), Am. Acad. Pediatrics, Am. Soc. Head/Neck Surgery, Am. Bronche-osophagological, Am. Acad. Facial Plastic and Reconstructive Surgery, Am. Acad. Cosmetic Surgery, Royal Soc. Medicine, Am. Bd. Laser Surgery; mem. Am. Assn. Acad. Depts. Otolaryngology, Assn. for Rsch. in Otolaryngology, Soc. Univ. Otolaryngologist, Internat. Soc. for History Otolaryngology (sec./treas. 1984-87, v.p. 1987—), Buffalo Otolaryngology Soc., Buffalo Canoe Club, Buffalo Club, Orchard Park Country Club. Avocations: medical history, personal computing, music, running, boating.

SIMPSON, H. RICHARD (DICK SIMPSON), retailer; b. Akron, Ohio, Oct. 10, 1930; s. Bert M. and Violet K. (Mathias) S.; m. Joan Rose Marshall, Mar. 22, 1970; children—Carla Sue, Barry Nelson, Richard Drew, Catherine, Irene Elizabeth, Student, U. Akron, 1949-50; B.S., U. Md., 1955. Mgr. Tex. Gen. Motors Corp., Detroit, 1959-62; pres. Friendly Pontiac, Friendly Toyota, Derrick Chrysler, Simpson Oil Corp., Corp. S., Dick Tiger Homes, Austin, 1962-85. Served to lt. col. USAF, 1953-75; Korea. Decorated D.F.C., Air Medal. Mem. Soc. Automotive Engrs., Res. Officers Assn. Methodist. Clubs: Horseshoe Bay Yacht, Horseshoe Bay Country. Lodges: Rotary, Masons. Home: PO Box 8186 Marble Falls TX 78657-9206

SIMPSON, JOAN YÉ VONNE, accountant, educator, business owner; b. Fairfield, Ill., Dec. 7, 1952; d. Harold M. and Pauline (Trailor) Reeder; children from previous marriage: Tammy Ann, James Edward; m. Roy E. Simpson, Dec. 28, 1990. AS, Vol. State Community Coll., 1984; postgrad., Am. Inst. Bankers, 1987; Austin Peay STate U. Owner Springfield Bookkeeping Svcs., 1978-82; jr. audit staff mem. Duane M. Brown, Springfield, Tenn., 1985-86; ops. supt. Joint Indsl. Techs., Portland, Tenn., 1986-88; tchr. Nashville State Tech. Inst., 1982-93; owner J.B.S. Bookkeeping and Mgmt., 1989—; pres. The Driver Leasing Co., Inc., 1992—, Carousel Creations Co., Inc., 1990—; speaker Women's Bus. Ownership Conf., Home and Minister's Inst. Copyrights rsch.: bus. devel. home based and home bound. Active Girl Scouts U.S. Gamma Beta Phi. Home: 2735 Browning Branch Rd Bethpage TN 37022-4523

SIMPSON, JOANNE MALKUS, meteorologist; b. Boston, Mar. 23, 1923; d. Russell and Virginia (Vaughan) Gerould; m. Robert H. Simpson, Jan. 6, 1965; children by previous marriage: David Starr Malkus, Steven Willem Malkus, Karen Elizabeth Malkus. B.S., U. Chgo., 1943, M.S., 1945, Ph.D., 1949; D.Sc. (hon.), SUNY, Albany, 1991. Instr. physics and meteorology Ill. Inst. Tech., 1946-49, asst. prof., 1949-51; meteorologist Woods Hole Oceanographic Instn., 1951-61; prof. meteorology UCLA, 1961-65; dir. exptl. meteorology lab. NOAA, Dept. Commerce, Washington, 1965-74; prof. environ. scis. U. Va., Charlottesville, 1974-76; W.W. Corcoran prof. environ. scis. U. Va., 1976-81; head Severe Storms br. Goddard Lab. Atmospheres, NASA, Greenbelt, Md., 1981-88, chief scientist for meteorology, 1988—; Goddard sr. fellow, earth scis. dir. Goddard Space Flight Ctr., NASA, 1988—; project scientist tropical rainfall measuring mission, 1986—; mem. Bd. on Atmospheric Scis. and Climate, NRC/NAS, 1990-93, Bd. on Geophys. and Environ. Data, 1993—. Author: (with Herbert Riehl) Cloud Structure and Distributions Over the Tropical Pacific Ocean; assoc. editor: Revs. Geophysics and Space Physics, 1964-72, 75-77; contbr. articles to profl. jours. Mem. Fla. Gov.'s Environ. Coordinating Coun., 1971-74. Recipient Disting. Authorship award NOAA, 1969, Silver medal Dept. Commerce, 1967, Gold medal, 1972, Vincent J. Schaefer award Weather Modification Assn., 1979, Cmty. Headliner award Women in Comm., 1973, Profl. Achievement award U. Chgo. Alumni Assn., 1975, 92, Lifetime Achievement award Women in Sci. Engring., 1990, Exceptional Sci. Achievement award NASA, 1982, William Nordberg award NASA, 1994; named Woman of Yr. L.A. Times, 1963; Guggenheim fellow, 1954-55, Goddard Sr. fellow, 1988—. Fellow Am. Meterol. Soc. (hon., coun. 1975-77, 79-81, exec. com. 1977, 79-81, commr. sci. and tech. activities 1982-88, pres.-elect 1988, pres. 1989, publs. commr. 1992—, Meisinger award 1962, Rossby Rsch. medal 1983, Charles Franklin Brooks award 1992), Am. Geophys. Union, NAE Oceanography Soc.; mem. Cosmos Club, Phi Beta Kappa, Sigma Xi. Home: 540 N St SW Washington DC 20024-4557 Office: NASA Goddard Space Flight Ctr Earth Scis Dir Greenbelt MD 20771

SIMPSON, JOE LEIGH, obstetrics and gynecology educator; b. Birmingham, Ala., Apr. 4, 1943; s. Robert S. and Winnie (Leigh) S.; m. Sandra A. Carson, May 6, 1978; children: Scott, Reid. MD, Duke U., 1968. Diplomate Am. Bd. Ob-Gyn, Am. Bd. Med. Genetics. Fellow in ob-gyn Cornell Med. Coll., N.Y.C., 1968-73; clin. assoc. N.Y. Blood Ctr., N.Y.C., 1969-73; asst. clin. prof. ob-gyn U. Tex., San Antonio, 1973-75; assoc. prof., head ob-gyn Northwestern U. Med. Sch., Chgo., 1975-79, prof. ob-gyn, 1979-86; Faculty prof. chmn. dept. ob-gyn U. Tenn., Memphis, 1986-94; Ernst W. Bertner chmn. and prof. dept. ob-gyn., prof. dept. molecular and human genetics Baylor Coll. of Medicine, Houston, 1994—; mem. genetics grant rev. and adv. bd. HHS, 1979-82; mem. clin. rsch. panel March of Dimes, 1986-94, chmn. adv. panel reproductive hazards, 1988-92; mem. accreditation coun. grad. med. edn. Residency Rev. Com. Med. Genetics, 1993—. Author: Disorders of Sexual Development, 1976; author: (with others) Genetics in Obstetrics and Gynecology, 1982, 2d edit., 1992, Obstetrics: Normal and Problem Pregnancies, 1986, 2d edit., 1991; co-editor: Genetic Diseases in Pregnancy, 1981, Material Serum Screening for Fetal Genetic Disorders, 1992, Essentials of Prenatal Diagnosis, 1993; contbr. numerous articles to profl. jours. and chpts. to books. Maj. U.S. Army, 1973-75. Recipient numerous awards Nat. Insts. Child Health and Devel., March of Dimes, Wyeth-Ayerest pub. recognition award Assn. Profs. Ob-Gyn, 1992. Fellow Am. Coll. Obstetricians and Gynecologists (chmn. genetics subcom. 1981-84); mem. Am. Gynecol. and Obstet. Soc., Am. Fertility Soc. (bd. dirs. 1984-87, pres. 1993-94), Soc. Gynecologic Investigation (mem. coun., Pres.'s Achievement award 1986), Soc. Advancement Contraception (bd. dirs. 1988—, treas. 1992—), Am. Soc. Human Genetics (mem. program com. 1988-91).

SIMPSON, JOHN ALEXANDER, physicist; b. Portland, Oreg., Nov. 3, 1916; s. John A. and Janet (Br) S.; m. Elizabeth Alice Hilts, Nov. 30, 1946 (div. Sept. 1977); children: Mary Ann, John Alexander; m. Elizabeth Scott Johnson, Aug. 23, 1980. A.B., Reed Coll., 1940, D.Sc. (hon.), 1981; M.S., NYU, 1942, Ph.D., 1943. Research assoc. OSRD, 1941-42; sci. group leader Manhattan Project, 1943-46; instr. U. Chgo., 1945-47, asst. prof., 1947-49, assoc. prof., 1949-54, chmn. com. on biophysics, 1951; prof. physics, dept. physics and Fermi Inst. Nuclear Studies, 1954- 68, Edward L. Ryerson Disting. Service prof. physics, 1968-74, Arthur H. Compton Disting. Service prof. physics, 1974-87, Arthur H. Compton Disting. prof. emeritus, 1987—; also dir. Enrico Fermi Inst., 1973-78; Mem. Internat. Com. IGY; chmn. bd. Ednl. Found. Nuclear Sci.; mem. tech. panel cosmic rays NRC; mem. Internat. Commn. Cosmic Radiation, 1962—; mem. astronomy missions bd. NASA, 1968; vis. assoc. physics Calif. Inst. Tech.; vis. scholar U. Calif., Berkeley.; founder Lab. Astrophysics and Space Research in Enrico Fermi Inst., 1962, Space Sci. Working Group, Washington, 1982. Bd. overseers, vis. com. astronomy Harvard; mem. Pres. Ford's Sci. Adv. Group on Sci. Problems, 1975-76; life trustee Adler Planetarium, 1977—. Recipient medal for exceptional sci. achievement NASA, Quantrell award for excellence in teaching, Gagarin medal Nat. Soviet Socialists Rep. Acad. of Scis., Cospar award UN Com. on Space Rsch., 1990; fellow Ctr. Policy Study, U. Chgo., Guggenheim fellow, 1972, 84-85; Nora and Edward Ryerson lectr., 1986; A. H. Compton Centennial lectr., 1992. Fellow Am. Acad. Arts and Scis., Am. Geophys. Union (Parker lectr. 1992), Am. Phys. Soc. (chmn. cosmic physics div. 1970-71); mem. NAS (mem. space sci. bd., Henryk Arctowski medal and premium 1993), Am. Philosophical Soc. (elected 1996), Internat. Union Pure and Applied Physics (pres. cosmic ray commn. 1963-67), Atomic Scientists Chgo. (chmn. 1945-46, bd. bull. 1945—, pres. bull. bd. sponsors 1993—), Am. Astron. Soc. (Bruno Rossi prize 1991), Internat. Acad. Astronautics, Smithsonian Inst. (Martin Marietta chair in history of space sci. 1987-88, Glennan, Webb, Seamans Group 1986—), Phi Beta Kappa, Sigma Xi. Achievements include research in nuclear radiation and instrumentation, also origin of cosmic radiation, solar physics, magnetospheric physics, high energy astrophys. problems, and acceleration and isotopic and elemental composition of charged particles in space; prin. investigator for 33 expts. in earth satellites and deep space probes, also 1st probes to Mercury, Mars, Jupiter and Saturn, fly by at Venus, 9 planetary encounters, comet dust expts. on the 2 Vega spacecraft to Halley's comet, 1986; Ulysses space craft experiments over poles of the sun, 1990—, Pioneer 10 space craft outside solar system. Office: Fermi Inst 5630 S Ellis Ave Chicago IL 60637-1433

SIMPSON, JOHN M., lawyer; b. Ponca City, Okla., Sept. 26, 1950. AB, Harvard U., 1972; JD, Columbia U., 1978. Bar: D.C. 1979, N.C. 1988. Mem. Fulbright & Jaworski L.L.P., Washington. Office: Fulbright & Jaworski LLP Market Square 801 Pennsylvania Ave NW Washington DC 20004-2604

SIMPSON, JOHN MATHES, newspaper editor; b. Madison, Wis., Jan. 7, 1948; s. Robert C. and Mary (Mathes) S.; m. Carol Flaker, July 2, 1977; children: Kate, Alexis. BA, SUNY, Binghamton, 1969. Reporter, editor Sun-Bulletin, Binghamton, 1970-76; mng. editor Ithaca (N.Y.) Jour., 1976-78; mng. editor, exec. editor Pacific Daily News, Agana, Guam, 1978-83; internat. mng. editor USA Today, Washington, 1984-86, 88—, spl. projects mng. editor, 1986-87; dir. corp. projects Gannett Internat., Washington, 1987-88. Dir. World Press Freedom Com. Mem. Am. Soc. Newspaper Editors, Inter Am. Press Assn. (bd. dirs.), World Press Fedn. Com., World Editors Forum Adv. Com., Nat. Press Club. Office: USA Today Internat 1000 Wilson Blvd Arlington VA 22209-3901

SIMPSON, JOHN NOEL, health care administrator; b. Durham, N.C., Feb. 27, 1936; s. William Hays and Lucile (McNab) S.; A.B., Duke U., 1957; M.H.A., Med. Coll. Va., 1959; m. Virginia Marshall, June 27, 1959; children: John Noel, William M. Asst. adminstr. Riverside Health Sys., Newport News, Va., 1962-65, assoc. adminstr., 1965-70; assoc. adminstr. Richmond (Va.) Meml. Hosp., 1970-74, sr. v.p., adminstr., 1974-77, exec. v.p., 1977-80, pres., 1980-85; pres. Health Corp. Va., 1985—; preceptor Sch. Health Adminstrn., Duke U. and Med. Coll. Va., Washington U., St. Louis; bd. dirs. Sun Health, Inc./Sun Alliance, 1979-92, vice chmn., 1984, chmn., 1985-87; vice-chmn. Med./Bus. Coalition, 1981-83; participant Leadership Met. Richmond; bd. dirs. Ctrl. Va. Health Sys. Agy., 1980-84, Richmond chpt. ARC, 1980-83; mem. Va. Bd. Med. Assistance, 1980-84; mem. joint subcom. studying Va.'s med. malpractice laws divsn. legal svcs. Gen. Assembly of Comm. of Va., 1984; chmn. Va. Health Network, 1989-91; chmn. Hanover Bus. Coun., 1994-95; mem. Gov.'s Regional Econ. Devel. Adv. Coun., 1994-95. Served with Med. Service Corps, U.S. Army, 1959-62. Fellow Am. Coll. Healthcare Execs. (Council of Regents 1976-82, Edgar C. Hayhow award 1976, bd. govs. 1990-94, regents award sr. exec. level 1995); mem. Am. Hosp. Assn. (chmn. RPBIII 1994—, del. 1989-93, mem. bd. trustees 1994—, Va. Hosp. Assn. (dir. 1974—, chmn.-elect, chmn. 1984-85), Va. Ins. Reciprocal (chmn. 1977-79), Met. Richmond C. of C. (bd. dirs.). Republican. Presbyterian. Home: 9127 Carterham Rd Richmond VA 23229-7752 Office: Health Corp of Va 1300 Westwood Ave Richmond VA 23227-4612

SIMPSON, JOHN WISTAR, energy consultant, former manufacturing company executive; b. Glenn Springs, S.C., Sept. 25, 1914; s. Richard Caspar and Mary (Berkeley) S.; m. Esther Slattery, Jan. 17, 1948; children: John Wistar, Carter B., Patricia A., Barbara J. Student, Wofford Coll., 1932-33, DSc, 1972; BS, U.S. Naval Acad., 1937; MS, U. Pitts., 1941; DSc (hon.), Seton Hill Coll., 1970. With Westinghouse Electric Corp., 1937-77; mgr. Navy and Marine switchboard engring., switchgear div., on leave as mgr. nuclear engring. Daniels pile group, Oak Ridge Nat. Lab., successively as Westinghouse Electric Corp. (Bettis Atomic Power div.), 1949-58; v.p. Westinghouse Electric Corp.; gen. mgr. Westinghouse Electric Corp. (Bettis atomic power lab.), 1958-59, v.p., gen. mgr. atomic power divs., 1959-62, v.p. engring. and research, 1962-63, v.p. electric utility group, 1963-69, pres. power systems, corp. exec. v.p., dir., 1971-77; chmn. bd. Internat. Energy Assocs. Ltd., 1976-80; pres. Simpson Bus. Services, Inc., 1980-86; v.p. Sea Pines Assocs., Hilton Head Island, S.C., 1989-91, also bd. dirs., 1987-91; bd. dirs. Sea Pines Real Estate Cos., Hilton Head Island, S.C., 1987-91; pvt. energy cons.; mem. adv. bd. Lawrence Livermore Nat. Lab. Fusion, 1975-88; mem. Naval Tech. Mission to Japan, 1945; del. 1st Internat. Conf. on Peaceful Uses Atomic Energy, Geneva, Switzerland, 1955, Conf. on Peaceful Uses Atomic Energy (2d Internat. Conf.), 1958; chmn. Atomic Indsl. Forum, 1974-75; mem. energy research adv. bd. Dept. Energy, 1981-83; chmn. com. on outlook for fusion hybrid and tritium breeding fusion reactors NRC; mem. sci. adv. bd. Notre Dame, 1974-86. Author: Nuclear Power from Underseas to Outer Space, 1994. Mem. governing bd. Nat. Coun. Chs., 1979-81; trustee Seton Hall Coll., 1969-76, Point Park Coll., 1973—, Wofford Coll., 1973-87. Recipient Navy cert. of merit for civilian svc. in World War II, Gold medal for advancement of rsch. Am. Soc. Metals, Disting. Alumnus award U. Pitts. Fellow IEEE (Edison medal 1971), ASME (hon. mem., George Westinghouse Gold medal 1975), Am. Nuclear Soc. (pres. 1973); mem. Nat. Acad. Engring., Franklin Inst. (Newcomen Gold medal), Rolling Rock Club (Ligonier, Pa.), Melrose Club, Bear Creek Golf Club, Sea Pines Club (Hilton Head, S.C.). Home and Office: 36 E Beach Lagoon Rd Hilton Head Island SC 29928-5714 *The guiding principles of my career have been to work in an area I considered to be of major importance, to have the most competent people working for me, to know enough technically that I could properly evaluate performance and, as far as possible, always make my position clear to all.*

SIMPSON, JULIETTE RICH, elementary educator; b. Bainbridge, Ga., Jan. 9, 1944; d. Robert Lloyd Jr. and Juliette (Lane) Rich; m. Ralph Felward Simpson, Aug. 13, 1966; children: Juliette, Elena. AB in Elem. Edn., Wesleyan Coll., 1966. 2d grade tchr. Bibb County Sch. System, Macon, Ga., 1966-69; title I tchr. Tift County Sch. System, Tifton, Ga., 1974-77, 3d grade tchr., 1977—; mem. sci. curriculum writing com. Tift County Bd. Edn., Tifton, 1989-90, mem. lang. arts curriculum writing com., 1990-91, mem. social studies curriculum writing com., 1991-92. Alt. del. Nat. Rep. Conv., Atlanta, 1992; mem. State Rep. Com., 1994—; 8th dist. Phil Gramm leadership chmn.; chmn. Tift County Rep. Party, 1994-96; co-pres. Tifton Cir. Bar Assn., 1990-91; active Annie Belle Clark Sch. PTO; v.p. Tifton Choral Soc., 1994-96. Mem. Profl. Assn. Ga. Educators, Internat. Reading Assn., Tift County Found. for Ednl. Excellence (Outstanding Tchr. award), Ga. Coun. for Social Scis., Dogwood Garden Club. Presbyterian. Home: 1020 N College Ave Tifton GA 31794-3942 Office: Annie Belle Clark Sch 506 W 12th St Tifton GA 31794-3930

SIMPSON, LAVADA CRAIN, nurse; b. Hollis, Ark., Mar. 5, 1938; d. Raymond Leslie and Lucy Viola (Davis) Crain; m. Cecil Edward Simpson, Dec. 20, 1958; children: Gregory Kent, Randall Scott, Lavada Suzanne. Diploma, Bapt. Meml. Hosp., 1958. RN, Ark. Staff nurse Desha County Hosp., Dumas, Ark., 1958-66, dir. nursing, 1959; staff nurse McGehee (Ark.) Desha County Hosp., 1967; sch. nurse Delta Sch. Dist., Rohwer, Ark., 1969-77, 86—; home health nurse McGehee Hosp. Home Health, 1986—; sch. nurse Tillar (Ark.) Sch. Dist., 1987-89; mem. Desha County Pub. Health Adv. Bd., 1973-78. Bd. dirs. Am. Cancer Soc., Desha County, 1980—. Mem. Delta Warrior Booster Club (v.p. 1969-92). Democrat. Baptist. Avocations: crafts, camping, traveling. Home: PO Box 502 Mc Gehee AR 71654-0502 Office: McGehee Hosp Home Health PO Box 351 Mc Gehee AR 71654-0351

SIMPSON, LOUIS A., insurance company executive; b. Chgo., Dec. 23, 1936; s. Irving and Lillian (Rubin) S.; m. Margaret Rowley, Dec. 16, 1959; children: Irving, Kenneth, Edward. Student, Northwestern U., 1954-55; BA, Ohio Wesleyan U., 1958; AM, Princeton U., 1960. Instr. econs. Princeton U., 1961-62; assoc., ptnr. Stein Roe & Farnham, Chgo., 1962-69; v.p. Shareholders Mgmt., Los Angeles, 1969-70; sr. v.p., exec. v.p., pres. Western Asset Mgmt., Los Angeles, 1970-79; vice chmn. bd. Geico Corp., Washington, 1979-93, pres., chief exec. officer capital ops., 1993—; bd. dirs. Potomac Capital Investment, Salomon, Inc., Potomac Electric Power, Pacific Am. Income Shares, Western Asset Trust, Thompson PBE, Cohr Inc. Mem. endowments com. Ohio Wesleyan U.; regent Loyola Marymount U., L.A. Woodrow Wilson fellow, 1958. Mem. Washington Soc. Ins. Analysts (bd. dirs. 1981-84), L.A. Soc. Fin. Analysts, Calif. Club, L.A. Country Club, Arts Club Chgo., Chevy Chase Club, Met. Club. Episcopalian. Office: Geico Corp 1 Geico Plz Washington DC 20076

SIMPSON, LOUIS ASTON MARANTZ, English educator, author; b. Jamaica, W.I., Mar. 27, 1923; s. Aston and Rosalind (Marantz) S.; m. Jeanne Claire Rogers, 1949 (div. 1954); 1 child, Louis Matthew; m. Dorothy Mildred Roochvarg, 1955 (div. 1979); children: Anne Borovoi, Anthony Rolf; m. Miriam Butensky Bachner, 1985. Higher schs. certificate, Munro Coll., Jamaica, 1939; B.S., Columbia U., 1948, A.M., 1950, Ph.D., 1959; D.H.L., Eastern Mich. U., 1977; DLitt, Hampden Sydney Coll., 1990. Editor Bobbs-Merrill Pub. Co., N.Y.C., 1950-55; instr. Columbia U., 1955-59; prof. English U. Calif., Berkeley, 1959-67; prof. English SUNY, Stony Brook, 1967-91, Disting. prof., 1991—. Author: (poems) The Arrivistes, 1949, Good News of Death, 1955, A Dream of Governors, 1959, At the End of the Open Road, 1963 (Pulitzer prize for poetry 1964), Selected Poems, 1965, Adventures of the Letter I, 1971, Searching for the Ox, 1976, Caviare at the Funeral, 1980, The Best Hour of the Night, 1983, People Live Here: Selected Poems 1949-83, 1983, Collected Poems, 1988, In the Room We Share, 1990, Wei Wei and Other Friends, 1990, Jamaica Poems, 1993, There You Are, 1995, (prose) Riverside Drive, 1962, James Hogg: A Critical Study, 1962, North of Jamaica, 1972, Three on the Tower: The Lives and Works of Ezra Pound, T.S. Eliot and William Carlos Williams, 1975, A Revolution in Taste: Studies of Dylan Thomas, Allen Ginsberg, Sylvia Plath and Robert Lowell, 1978, A Company of Poets, 1981, The Character of the Poet, 1986, Selected Prose, 1989, Ships Going into the Blue, 1994, The King My Father's Wreck, 1995; editor: The New Poets of England and America, 1957, An Introduction to Poetry, 1967. Served with AUS, 1943-45. Decorated Purple Heart, Bronze Star with oak leaf cluster; Hudson Rev. fellow, 1957, Guggenheim fellow, 1962, 70; Am. Coun. Learned Socs. grantee, 1963; recipient Prix de Rome, 1957, Millay award, 1960, Distinguished Alumnus award Columbia U., 1960, medal for excellence Columbia U., 1965; American Acad. of Arts and Letters award in literature, 1976; Centenary medal Inst. of Jamaica, 1980, Jewish Book Coun. award for poetry, 1981, Elmer Holmes Bobst award, 1987. Fellow Am. Acad. in Rome. Home: 186 Old Field Rd Setauket NY 11733-1636

SIMPSON, MADELINE LOUISA, psychologist; b. Norfolk, Va., June 22, 1923; d. David Edward and Zenobia Eleanor (Ross) S. BA, Fisk U., 1944; MS, Boston U., 1951; MA, The New Sch., 1967; PhD, U. Md., 1981; MPA, Va. Commonwealth U., 1985. Psychologist, N.Y. Practitioner Norfolk County Dept. Pub. Welfare, Portsmouth, Va., 1946-51, N.Y.C. Dept. Hosps. and the Hosp. for Joint Diseases, 1951-56; founder, dir. Centre d'Etudes Sociales, Port-au-Prince, Haiti, 1959-61; social work practitioner and supr. Child Welfare Agy., N.Y.C., 1961-68; asst. prof. psycyhol. Del. State Coll., Dover, 1969-71; assoc. prof. psychol. Cheyney (Pa.) State Coll., 1972-75, 78; asst. prof. psychol. Longwood Coll., Farmville, Va., 1979-85; assoc prof. St. Paul's Coll., Lawrenceville, Va., 1985-90. Mem. local human rights com. Va. Dept. Mental Health, Mental Retardation and Substance Abuse Svcs., Piedmont Geriatric Hosp., Burkeville, Va., 1983-89, recipient Cert. of Recognition, 1988. Mem. Gold Circle Club of Am. Psychol. Assn., Delta Sigma Theta (life).

SIMPSON, MARY MICHAEL, priest, psychotherapist; b. Evansville, Ind., Dec. 1; d. Link Wilson and Mary Garrett (Price) S. B.A., B.S., Tex. Women's U., 1946; grad. N.Y. Tng. Sch. for Deaconesses, 1949; grad., Westchester Inst. Tng. in Psychoanalysis and Psychotherapy, 1976; S.T.M., Gen. Theol. Sem., 1982. Missionary Holy Cross Mission, Bolahun, Liberia, 1950-52; mem. Order of St. Helena, 1952—; acad. head Margaret Hall Sch., Versailles, Ky., 1958-61; sister in charge Convent of St. Helena, Bolahan, 1962-67, novice dir., 1968-74; pastoral counselor on staff Cathedral St. John the Divine, N.Y.C., 1974-87, canon residentiary, canon counselor, 1977-87, hon. canon, 1988—; ordained priest Episcopal Ch., 1977; cons. psychotherapist Union Theol. Sem., 1980-83; dir. Cathedral Counseling Service, 1975-87; priest-in-charge St. John's Ch. Wilmot, New Rochelle, N.Y., 1987-88; pvt. practice psycholanalyst, 1974—; Bd. dirs. Westchester Inst. Tng. in Psychoanalysis and Psychotherapy, 1982-84; trustee Council on Internat. and Pub. Affairs, 1983-87; interim pastor St. Michael's Ch., Manhattan, 1992-94; cons. Diocese of N.Y., 1992—. Mem. Nat. Assn. Advancement of Psychoanalysis, N.Y. State Assn. Practicing Psychotherapists, N.Y. Soc. Clin. Psychologists. Author: The Ordination of Women in the American Episcopal Church: the Present Situation, 1981; contbg. author: Yes to Women Priests, 1978. Home and Office: 151 E 31st St Apt 8H New York NY 10016-9502

SIMPSON, MICHAEL, metals service center executive; b. Albany, N.Y., Dec. 10, 1938; s. John McLaren Simpson and Constance (Hasler) Ames; B.A., U. Mich., 1965, M.B.A., 1966; m. Barbara Ann Bodtke, Jan. 5, 1963; children: Leslie Simpson Wikstrom, Elizabeth McLaren. Product mgr. Armour & Co., Chgo., 1966-68; with A. M. Castle & Co., Franklin Park, Ill., 1968—, pres. Hy-Alloy Steels Co. div., 1974-79, v.p. Midwestern region, 1977-79, chmn. bd., 1979—, dir., 1972—. Trustee, Rush-Presbyterian St. Luke's Med. Ctr., Chgo., 1978—, exec. com., 1980—, vice-chmn., 1991—; trustee Oldfields Sch., Glencoe, Md., 1982-87, 95—. Served in USMC, 1957-58. Mem. Steel Service Center Inst. (chmn. exec. com. 1982-84, bd. dirs. 1981-94). Republican. Episcopalian. Clubs: Shore Acres; Onwentsia; Racquet of Chicago. Office: A M Castle & Co 3400 Wolf Rd Franklin Park IL 60131-1319

SIMPSON, MICHAEL KEVIN, academic administrator, political science educator; b. Bellafonte, Pa., Apr. 22, 1949; s. Robert Paul and Helen Elisabeth (Popso) S.; m. Carol Anne Martin, June 27, 1970; children: Jennifer Lyn, Robert Manton. BA, Fordham Coll., 1970; MA, Tufts U., 1974, MA in Law and Diplomacy, 1976, PhD, 1976; MBA, Syracuse U., 1983. Instr. Newbury Jr. Coll., Boston, 1976-77; asst. prof. then prof. polit. sci. Utica (N.Y.) Coll. of Syracuse U., 1976—, v.p., 1987-88, pres., 1988—; Fulbright lectr. Univ. Nancy II, France, 1981-82; vis. prof. Syracuse U. Program in Strasbourg, 1981-82, 85-87; resident dir. Internat. Programs, Strasbourg, 1985-87; trustee Savs. Bank of Utica. Contbr. articles to profl. jours. Mem. exec. com. Land of Oneidas coun. Boy Scouts Am., 1991; bd. dirs. United Way of Greater Utica, 1987, mem. campaign cabinet, mem. exec. com.; mem. Leadership Coun., N.E./Midwest Inst., 1989; chmn. Health and Hosp. Coun., 1989-90; mem. joint hosp. bd. Mohawk Valley Network; dir. ministers and missionaries benefit bd. Am. Bapt. Chs., 1995. Decorated Def. Meritorious Svc. medal; recipient Grad. Alumni award Syracuse U. Sch. Mgmt., 1983, Disting. Teaching award Utica Coll., 1983, Silver Beaver award Boy Scouts Am.; Paul Harris fellow Rotary Internat. Mem. Internat. Studies Assn., Naval Res. Assn., Rotary (bd. dirs. Utica club 1988—, v.p. 1991-92, pres., 1992), Phi Beta Kappa. Democrat. Home: 22 Ironwood Rd New Hartford NY 13413-3904 Office: Syracuse U Utica Coll 1600 Burrstone Rd Utica NY 13502-4857

SIMPSON, MICHAEL MARCIAL, science specialist, consultant; b. Honolulu, Sept. 24, 1954; s. Marcial Tolentino and Beatrice (Martin) S. AB in Biol. Scis., U. Calif., Berkeley, 1976; MS in Biol. Scis., U. San Francisco, 1977; MS in Energy and Resources, U. Calif., Berkeley, 1979; PhD in Environ. Scis. and Engring., UCLA, 1986. Assoc. researcher NASA, Moffett Field, Calif., 1973; radio program host, producer Sta. KUSF-FM, San Francisco, 1976-78; rsch. asst. Lawrence Berkeley Lab., Berkeley, Calif., 1977-79; rsch. assoc. UCLA/U.S. Dept. Energy, 1979-81; congl. fellow, environ. health U.S. Congress, Washington, 1981-82; head, biomed. policy sect. and specialist in life scis. U.S. Congl. Rsch. Svc., Washington, 1982—; adv. bd. Banbury Ctr., Cold Spring Harbor, N.Y., 1985—; adj. faculty The Washington Ctr., 1992—. Contbr. articles to profl. jours. Values clarification educator, Alexandria, Va., 1985—. Fellow AAAS (Named Congl. Sci. fellow 1981-82); mem. Washington Acad. Sci., Library of Congress Profl. Assn., UCLA in Washington (exec. steering com. 1986-92). Avocations: photography, bicycle touring, short story writing, travel. Office: US Congl Rsch Svc CRS-SPR-LM413 Washington DC 20540-7490

SIMPSON, MURRAY, engineer, consultant; b. N.Y.C., July 27, 1921; s. George and Sonia (Vernov) S.; m. Ethel Gladstein, June 29, 1947; children: Anne Simpson Everett, David, Mindy, Jonathan. BEE, CCNY, 1942; MEE, Polytech. Inst. of N.Y., 1952. Engr. Internat. Tel.&Tel., N.Y.C., 1942-44; sr. engr. Raytheon Co., Waltham, Mass., 1946-48; sect. mgr. Fairchild Guided Missles div., Farmingdale, N.Y., 1948-50; v.p. Maxson Elec. Co., N.Y.C., 1950-62; pres. SEDCO Systems Inc. subs. Raytheon Co., Melville, N.Y., 1963-86; cons. M. Simpson Assocs., West Hempstead, N.Y., 1986—; former chmn. bd. dirs. Radyne Corp. Contbr. articles to profl. jours. former bd. dirs. United Way of L.I., N.Y., 1984-87. Served to lt. (j.g.) USNR, 1944-46, PTO. Fellow IEEE (chmn. L.I. sect. 1963-64); mem. Anchorage Yacht Club, Inverrary Country Club. Clubs: Anchorage Yacht, Inverrary Country. Avocations: boating, skiing, golf, tennis. *Don't be afraid to take risk in the hope of great reward and satisfaction. The worst that could happen is that you may fail. A much greater loss is that you never tried and perhaps missed the great opportunity of your life.*

SIMPSON, O. J. (ORENTHAL JAMES SIMPSON), former professional football player, actor, sports commentator; b. San Francisco, July 9, 1947; s. Jimmie and Eunice (Durton) S.; m. Marguerite Whitley, June 24, 1967 (div.); children: Arnelle, Jason; m. Nicole Brown, 1985 (div. 1992); children: Sydney, Justin. Student, U. So. Calif.; grad., City Coll. San Francisco. Halfback Buffalo Bills, 1969-78, San Francisco 49'ers, 1978-79; sports commentator ABC Sports, 1979-86; analyst ABC Monday Night Football broadcasts, 1984-1985; co-host NBC Sports NFL Live. Motion picture appearances include The Towering Inferno, 1974, The Cassandra Crossing, 1977, Killer Force, 1976, Capricorn One, 1978, Firepower, 1979, Hambone & Hillie, 1984, The Naked Gun, 1988, The Naked Gun 2 1/2: The Smell of Fear, 1991, The Naked Gun 33 1/3: The Final Insult, 1994; TV films include A Killing Affair, 1977, Goldie and the Boxer, 1979, The Golden Moment: An Olympic Love Story, 1980, Student Exchange, Cocaine and Blue Eyes; co-host "NFL" Live on NBC, 1990—; author: I Want to Tell You, 1995. Recipient Heisman trophy N.Y. Downtown Athletic Club, 1968; voted Coll. Player of Decade ABC Sports, 1970; named to Am. Football League All-Star Team, 1970, ProBowl Team, 1972, 73, 74, 75, 76; named Nat. Football League Player of Decade Pro Football Monthly, 1979; inducted into Pro Football Hall of Fame, 1985; mem. world record 440 yard relay team (38.6 seconds), 1967; former record holder for most yards rushing gained in a season, most yards rushing gained in a game.

SIMPSON, OCLERIS C., agricultural research administrator; b. Normangee, Tex., Sept. 10, 1939. BS, Prairie View A&M U., 1960; MS, Iowa State U., 1962; PhD in Animal Sci., U. Nebr., 1965. Assoc. prof. Ft. Valley State Coll., Ga., 1965-69; rsch. instr. Med. Coll. Ga., 1970-71; rsch. assoc. meharry Med. Coll., Nashville, 1972-74; rsch. coord. Ft. Valley State Coll., Ga., 1974-78; rsch. dir. Prairie View A&M U., 1973-83, asst. dir. planning and evaluation, 1983; dean rsch. and ext., rsch. dir. and ext. adminstr. Langston (Okla.) U., 1983—. Mem. U.S. Investment Team China, Joint Coun. Food and Agr. Sci., 1890 Land-Grant Colls. and Univs., Internat. Sci. and Edn. Coun. (tech. assistance sub-com.). Office: Langston U Agrl Rsch & Extention PO Box 730 Langston OK 73050-0730 Office: Langston U PO Box 730 Langston OK 73050*

SIMPSON, PAMELA HEMENWAY, art historian, educator; b. Omaha, Sept. 8, 1946; d. Myrle E. and Leone K. (Cook) Hemenway; m. Henry H. Simpson III, Apr. 4, 1970; 1 child, Peter Stuart Hay. BA, Gettysburg Coll., 1968; MA, U. Mo., 1970; PhD, U. Del., 1974. Instr. art history Pa. State Extension Campus, Media, 1973, Washington and Lee U., Lexington, Va., 1973-74; asst. prof. Washington and Lee U., Lexington, 1974-79, assoc. prof., 1979-85, prof. art history, 1985—, Ernest Williams prof., 1993, chair art dept., 1987—, assoc. dean of coll., 1981-86; chair co-edn. steering com. Washington and Lee Univ., Lexington, 1984-86; cons., head county survey Va. Hist. Landmarks Commn., Richmond, 1977-81. Author: Architecture of Historic Lexington, 1977 (Am. Assn. for State and Local History award 1977); book reviewer Women's Art Jour., columnist, 1990—; contbr. articles to profl. jours. Officer Rockbridge Hist. Soc., Lexington, 1980—, Rockbridge Valley Nat. Orgn. for Women, Rockbridge County, Va., 1984—, Historic Lexington (Va.) Found., 1987—; founder, officer Rockbridge Area Coalition Against Sexual Assault, Lexington, 1990—. Recipient Outstanding Faculty award State Coun. of Higher Edn., State of Va., 1995; grantee Nat. Endowment for Arts, 1974, NEH, 1975, 77, Glenn, Washington and Lee U., 1980-81, 91; NEH Summer Inst. scholar, 1989; Hagley-Winterthur Mus. fellow, 1991. Mem. Southeastern Soc. Archtl. Historians (bd. dirs. 1990-94, v.p. 1993-94, pres. 1994-95), Soc. Archtl. Historians, Coll. Art Assn., Vernacular Architecture Forum (bd. dirs. 1982-84, 2d v.p. 1988-91), southeastern Coll. Art Conf. (pres. 1986-90, 2d v.p. 1994—, editor rev. 1979-82). Democrat. Episcopalian. Avocations: painting, reading mysteries. Office: Washington & Lee Univ Dupont Hall Lexington VA 24450

SIMPSON, RICHARD ALLAN, electrical engineer, radar astronomy researcher; b. Portsmouth, N.H., June 25, 1945; m. Ann M. Reisenauer, 1991. BS, MIT, 1967; MS, Stanford U., 1969, PhD in Elec. Engring., 1973—. Rsch. assoc. Stanford U., 1973-76, sr. rsch. assoc. radar astronomy, 1976—; vis. rsch assoc. Arecibo Obs., 1975-76, 78. Mem. AAAS, IEEE, Am. Astron. Soc., Am. Geophys. Union, Union Radio Scientifique Internationale. *

SIMPSON, RICHARD KENDALL, JR., surgeon, physician, researcher; b. Atlanta, Sept. 10, 1953; s. Richard Kendall and Juliet Hodges (Rowsey) S.; m. Martha Anne Baucom, Sept. 22, 1984. BA, Coker Coll., 1975; PhD, Med. U. S.C., 1980, MD, 1982; postgrad. Warnborough Coll., Oxford, Eng., 1974. Diplomate Nat. Bd. Med. Examiners, Am. Bd. Neurosurgery. Teaching asst. dept. physiology Med. U. S.C., Charleston, 1976-80, research assoc., 1980-83, intern neurology, 1982-83; resident neurosurgery dept. neurosurgery Baylor Coll. Medicine, Houston, 1983-89, asst. prof., 1989-94, assoc. prof. dept. neurosurgery, anesthesiology and physical medicine and rehab., 1995—; chief neurology sect. VA Med. Ctr., 1991—. Author: Peripheral Nerve Fiber Group and Spinal Corp Pathway Contributions to the Somatosensory Evoked Potential, 1980. Recipient Clin. Neurology Rsch. award, 1983, Physician Recognition award, 1986, Mayfield award, 1989, Minora Suzuki award, 1989, Young Alumni award, 1990, William H. Sweet award, 1994; ACS scholar, 1986; ACS Faculty fellow, 1994, Watson fellow Coker Coll., 1974, Baylor Coll. of Medicine Master Tchr. fellowship. Mem. AMA, Am. Pain Soc., Am. Acad. Clin. Neurophysiology, Am. Acad. Pain Med., Tex. Med. Found., Soc. Neurosci., Houston Neurol. Soc., Sigma Xi, Alpha Omega Alpha. Soc. Episcopalian. Home: 14314 River Forest Dr Houston TX 77079-7417 Office: Baylor Coll Med Dept Neurosurgery 1 Baylor Plz Houston TX 77030-3411

SIMPSON, RICHARD LEE, sociologist, educator; b. Washington, Feb. 2, 1929; s. Donald Dake and Lottie (Lee) S.; m. Ida Ann Harper, July 10, 1955; children: Robert Donald, Frank Daniel. A.B., U. N.C., 1950, Ph.D., 1956; M.A., Cornell U., 1952. Instr. Pa. State U., University Park, 1956-57; asst. prof. sociology Northwestern U., Evanston, Ill., 1957-58; asst. prof. U. N. C., Chapel Hill, 1958-61, assoc. prof. sociology, 1961-65; prof. U. N. C., Chapel Hill, 1965-80, Kenan prof. sociology, 1980—; acting dir. Inst. Research Social Sci., Chapel Hill, 1966-67. Author numerous research papers, articles and book chpts. in field; editor: Social Forces, 1969-72, 83—; co-editor Research in Sociology of Work, 1981—. Mem. Am. Sociol. Assn., So. Sociol. Soc. (pres. 1971-72), Sociol. Research Assn. Methodist. Home: 604 Brookview Dr Chapel Hill NC 27514-1406 Office: Univ NC Dept Sociology Cb 3210 Hamilton Hall Chapel Hill NC 27599

SIMPSON, ROBERT EDWARD, economist, consultant; b. Chgo., July 7, 1917; s. James Albert and Mabel Grace (Farrell) S.; m. Anna Margareta Nelson, May 22, 1954; children: Karen Anne, Heather Margot, John Frederick II. A.B., Amherst Coll., 1938; student, Nat. Inst. Pub. Affairs, 1939; M.A., George Washington U., 1964. Student U.S. Central Statis. Bd., 1938-39; economist U.S. Nat. Resources Com., 1939-40; personnel work Office Sec. of War, 1941; economist civilian supply div. WPB, 1941-42; econ., adminstrv. work Nat. Housing Adminstrn., 1946-47; asst. dir. European div., later dept. asst. dir. for econ. affairs Office Internat. Trade U.S. Dept. Commerce, 1947-53; dir. Office Econ. Affairs, Bur. Fgn. Commerce, 1953-61, Office Regional Econs., Bur. Internat. Commerce, 1961-70, Office Internat. Comml. Relations, 1970-73; counsellor for econ. and comml. affairs Am. Embassy, Canberra, Australia, 1973-77; dir. Office Country Affairs, U.S. Dept. Commerce, Washington, 1978-79; cons. economist, 1980—; mem. pub. adv. com. Met. Washington Council of Govts., 1987-88; assigned Nat. War Coll., Washington, 1961-62. Mem. U.S. dels. to various internat. confs., 1948-79; bd. examiners for U.S. Fgn. Svc.; mem. gov. bd. Common Cause, Md., 1985-88, v.p. 1987-88; v.p. Montgomery County Civic Fedn., 1985—; mem. Montgomery County Econ. Adv. Coun., 1989—; treas. Montgomery County Citizens PAC, 1993—. Comdr. USNR, 1942-46, PTO, ETO. Decorated Bronze Star. Mem. Nat. Economists Club, Phi Beta Kappa, Delta Tau Delta, Kappa Theta. Office: PO Box 386 Glen Echo MD 20812-0386

SIMPSON, ROBERT GLENN, lawyer; b. Seattle, June 27, 1932; s. Harold Vernon and Anna Rondeau (McCabe) S.; m. Josephine Anne Heald, June 7, 1959; children: Jenifer Jane, Thomas Glenn, Mary Elizabeth. BS, U. Oreg., 1954; LLB, Willamette U., 1959. Bar: Oreg. 1959. Assoc. William B. Adams Law Office, Portland, Oreg., 1959-67; ptnr. Adams McLaughlin & Simpson, Portland, 1967-70, Schwabe Williamson & Wyatt, Portland, 1970—. Trustee, sec. Legacy Good Samaritan Hosp. & Med. Ctr., Portland, 1983-89, mem. cmty. bd., 1989—; trustee, chancellor Epsicopal Diocese of Oreg., Portland, 1988—. Mem. Oreg. State Bar (exec. com. health law sect. 1987-90), Am. Acad. Hosp. Attys. (program com. 1987-88), Oreg. Acad. Hosp. Attys. (pres. 1977-78, legis. com. 1989), Multnomah Athletic Club, Univ. Club, City Club. Home: 13345 SW Iron Mountain Blvd Portland OR 97219-9306 Office: Schwabe Williamson & Wyatt 1211 SW 5th Ave Ste 1800 Portland OR 97204-3713

SIMPSON, R(OBERT) SMITH, author, retired diplomat; b. Arlington County, Va., Nov. 9, 1906; s. Hendree Paine and Edith Lydia (Smith) S.; m. Henriette S. Lanniée, Nov. 7, 1934; children: Margaret Lanniée Simpson Maurin-Stunkard, Zélia Tinsley. B.S., U. Va., 1927, M.S., 1928; LL.B., Cornell U., 1931; postgrad., Columbia U., 1931-32. Spl. labor adviser, exec. NRA, 1933-34; trade. assn. exec., adminstrv. agt. Asphalt, Shingle and Roofing Code Authority, 1934-35; instr., then asst. prof. bus. law U. Pa., 1935-44; spl. adviser Pa. Unemployment Relief and Assistance Commn., co-drafter Pa. Unemployment Compensation Act, 1936; adviser N.J. Civil Service Commn., 1939; adv. unemployment compensation and relief joint Pa. State Commn., 1939-42; asst. dir. fgn. div. recruitment and manning orgn. War Shipping Adminstrn., 1942-43; with Dept. State, 1943-62, 65-66; fgn. svc. officer, 1944-62; consul gen. Mozambique, 1954-57; adv. African affairs Dept. Labor, 1958-60, dir. office country programs, 1960-61; dep. examiner bd. fgn. service examiners Dept. State, 1961-62, cons., 1965-66; lectr. Georgetown U., 1973, research prof. diplomacy, 1974-77; del. and/or mem. numerous nat. and internat. meetings; founding mem., bd. dirs. Inst. Study Diplomacy, Georgetown U., Washington, 1978-94, emeritus founding mem., 1995—. Author: Anatomy of the State Department, 1967, The Crisis in American Diplomacy, 1980, Some Perspectives on the Study of Diplomacy, 1986, Education in Diplomacy, 1987; editor: Belgium in Transition, 1946, Resources and Needs of American Diplomacy, 1968; Instruction in Diplomacy: The Liberal Arts Approach, 1972. Annual diplomacy debate named in his honor Univ. Va. Mem. Am. Fgn. Svc. Assn., Consular Officers Assn., Assn. for Diplomatic Studies and Tng., Inst. for Study of Diplomacy (Georgetown U., founding, bd. dirs.), Jefferson Lit. and Debating Soc. (U. Va., assoc.), Raven Soc., Phi Beta Kappa, Phi Sigma Kappa. Presbyterian. Address: 250 Pantops Mountain Rd #41 Charlottesville VA 22911-8680 *I can remember standing on a slope of the Arlington National Cemetery as a teenager one Christmas Day, down apiece from the broken mast of the battleship Maine and, as I laid a wreath on the grave of an ancestor, vowing to do whatever I could the rest of my life for good will and peace among men. From that day, this has been my consuming objective. The broken mast of the Maine has been a kind of compass needle by which my private and diplomatic life has been guided.*

SIMPSON, RUSSELL GORDON, lawyer, mayor, counselor to not-for-profit organizations; b. Springfield, Mass., May 22, 1927; s. Archer Roberts and Maude Ethel (Gordon) S.; m. Bickley S. Flower, Sept. 11, 1954; children: Barbara G., Elisabeth Pires-Fernandes, Helen Blair. B.A., Yale U., 1951; J.D., Boston U., 1956; postgrad., Parker Sch. Internat. Law, 1962. Bar: Mass. 1956, U.S. Dist. Ct. (fed. dist.) Mass. 1957, U.S. Ct. Appeals (2d cir.) 1958, U.S. Supreme Ct. 1980. Advt. mgr. Burden Bryant Co., Springfield, 1951-53; assoc. Goodwin, Procter & Hoar, Boston, 1956-64, ptnr., 1965-87, of counsel, 1987—; sr. advisor to pres. World Learning, Inc., Brattleboro, Vt., 1988-89, exec. v.p., 189-90, sr. v.p., 1990-91, trustee, 1991—, exec. com., 1994—; counselor to not-for-profit orgns., 1991—. Author: The Lawyer's Basic Corporate Practice Manual, 1971, rev. edit., 1978, 84, 87. Mayor Jupiter Island, Fla., 1993—; hon. consul New Eng. of Bolivia, 1958-82, mem. spl. com. to revise Mass. Corrupt Practices Act, 1961-62; trustee Save the Children Fedn., Westport, Conn., 1995—; dir., mem. exec. com. Cmty. Found. Palm Beach and Martin Counties, West palm Beach, Fla., 1994—. Named Outstanding Young Man of Greater Boston, 1963. Fellow Am. Bar Found., Mass. Bar Found.; mem. Mass. Bar Assn. (chmn. banking and bus. law sect. 1980-83, bd. dels., exec. com. 1983-87, v.p. 1985-87), ABA (corp. banking and bus. law sect., com. on law firms, co-chmn. com. on law firm governance, panel on corp. law edl. programs). Home: 101 Harbor Way Box 1106 Hobe Sound FL 33475

SIMPSON, STEVEN QUINTON, physician, researcher; b. Miami, Okla., Aug. 17, 1957; s. Dallas James and Carolyn Sue (Moberly) S.; m. Pamela Janette Nicklaus, May 20, 1989; children: Nathan Edward, Andrew Dallas. BS, Baker U., 1979; MD, U. Kans., 1983. Diplomate Am. Bd. Internal Medicine, Am. Bd. Pulmonary Disease, Am. Bd. Critical Care Medicine; cert. Nat. Inst. Occupational Safety and Health. Intern in internal medicine Kans. U. Med. Ctr., Kansas City, 1983-84, resident in internal medicine, 1984-86; fellow in pulmonary and critical care medicine Rush-Presbyn. St. Luke's Med. Ctr., Chgo., 1986-89, instr. medicine Divsn. Pulmonary and Critical Care Medicine, 1986-89, asst. prof. Divsn. Pulmonary and Critical Care Medicine, 1989-90; asst. prof. Divsn. Pulmonary and Critical Care Medicine U. N.Mex., 1990—; attending physician Rush-Presbyn. St. Luke's Med. Ctr., Chgo., 1989-90, U. N.Mex. Hosp., Albuquerque, 1990—; adj. scientist Inhalation Toxicology Rsch. Inst., Lovelace Biomed. and Environ. Rsch. Inst., Albuquerque, 1991—; consulting physician Miner's Colfax Med. Ctr., Raton, N.Mex., 1990—, dir. Cardiopulmonary Outreach Program and Black Lung Clinic, 1992-95; attending physician Albuquerque VA Med. Ctr., 1992—, dir. med. ICU, 1993—; presenter 19th Ann. Am. Thoracic Soc. Lung Disease Symposium, N.Mex., 1991, 94, 96, program chair, 1996, U. N.Mex., 1993, Soc. of Critical Care Medicine, 1994. Author: (with others) The Physiologic and Pathologic Effects of Cytokines, 1990; contbr. articles to profl. jours. Grantee Chgo. Lung Assn., 1989-91, Am. Lung Assn., 1991-93, Miner's Colfax Med. Ctr., 1992—, N.Mex. Dept. Health, 1993-94. Mem. AAAS, ACP (Cecile Lehman Mayer Rsch. award finalist 1988, 92, Alfred Soffer Rsch. award 1992, DuPont Young Investigator award 1993), Am. Coll. Chest Physicians, Am. Thoracic Soc. (sec.-treas. N.Mex. chpt. 1994-95, pres. 1995-96), Am. Fedn. for Clin. Rsch., N.Y. Acad. Scis., Soc. Critical Care Medicine, Blue Key Nat. Honor Soc., Alpha Delta Sigma. Avocations: writing prose, guitar, hiking. Office: U N Mex Dept Med Pulmonary Divsn 2211 Lomas Blvd NE # 5-acc Albuquerque NM 87106-2745

SIMPSON, THOMAS WILLIAM, physician; b. Winston-Salem, N.C., Jan. 24, 1918; s. Thomas William Sr. and Sara Elizabeth (McGee) S.; m. Doris McElroy Cullings, June 2, 1941; children: Lucia Elisabeth Simpson Shen. BS with honors, Southwestern (Rhodes), 1940; MD, John Hopkins, 1943. Diplomate Am. Bd. Internal Medicine. Med. resident Vets. Adminstrn., Columbia, S.C., 1947-49; med. faculty Wake Forest Univ., Winston-Salem, N.C., 1949-66; med. officer Panama Canal Zone, Coco Solo, 1966-67; med. faculty U. Hawaii, Honolulu, 1967-70; med. faculty Johns Hopkins U., Balt., 1970-83, faculty emeritus, 1983—; health dir. Va. Health Dept.; chief med. cons. U. Hawaii, Okinawa, 1967-70; trop med. cons. DOD, 1967-70; resident coord. Johns Hopkins CMRT, Calcutta, India, 1970-72, acting dir., 1973-74. Author: (with others) Hunter's Tropical Medicine, 1984; contbr. articles to profl. jours. Oral fluid therapy cholera, Johns Hopkins U., 1971-72, health status migrant workers, Del Marva, 1983-85. Lt. USN, 1943-47. Recipient Commendation N.C. Health Dept., 1966, Va. Mental Hygiene Dept. 1988. Fellow ACP (coms.), Royal Soc. Tropical Medicine and Hygiene; mem. Am. Ornithologists Union, Am. Soc. Tropical Medicine and Hygiene (coms.). Democrat. Presbyterian. Achievements include incrimination of pigs as important amplifying host of Japanese encephalitis, restoration of Okinawan health care system after WW2, crucial early field trial of oral fluid therapy for cholera in West Bengal, improvement of health care for Haitian and Hispanic migrant farm workers. Office: Johns Hopkins Instn 615 N Wolfe St Baltimore MD 21205

SIMPSON, VINSON RALEIGH, manufacturing company executive; b. Chgo., Aug. 9, 1928; s. Vinson Raleigh and Elsie (Passeger) S.; m. Elizabeth Caroline Matte, Sept. 9, 1950; children: Kathleen Simpson Jackson, Nancy Simpson Ignacio, James Morgan. S.B. in Chem. Engring, Mass. Inst. Tech., 1950; M.B.A., Ind. U., 1955. With Trane Co., LaCrosse, Wis., 1950-75, mgr. mktg. services, 1957-64, mgr. dealer devel., 1964-66; mng. dir. Trane Ltd., Edinburgh, Scotland, 1966; v.p. internat. Trane Co., LaCrosse, Wis., 1967, exec. v.p., 1968-70; exec. v.p., gen. mgr. comml. air conditioning div., 1970-73, pres., 1973-75; pres. Simpson and Co., La Crosse, 1975-76; pres., chief operating officer Marathon Electric Mfg. Corp., Wausau, Wis., 1976-80; chmn., pres., chief exec. officer Marion Body Works, Inc., Wis., 1980-93, chmn., 1993—; bd. dirs. Clintonville Area Found. Regional chmn. edn. coun. MIT; trustee Northland Coll.; bd. dirs., v.p. Fox Valley Tech. Coll. Found.; past pres. bd. dirs. Wausau Area Jr. Achievement; mem. Marion Minutemen, Adv. Team, U. Wis. Served with USAF, 1951-53. Decorated Korean War Commendation ribbon. Mem. Fire Apparatus Mfrs., Nat. Truck Equipment Assn., Am. Legion, Kappa Kappa Sigma, Alpha Tau Omega, Beta Gamma Sigma (mem. dirs. table). Congregationalist. Lodges: Masons, Shriners, Jesters, Rotary (past pres. Marion club, Paul Harris fellow). Avocations: running, handball, snorkeling, water skiing, cross country skiing. Home: 171 Fairway Dr Clintonville WI 54929-1071 Office: Marion Body Works Inc 211 W Ramsdell PO Box 500 Marion WI 54950-0500

SIMPSON, WILLIAM ARTHUR, insurance company executive; b. Oakland, Calif., Feb. 2, 1939; s. Arthur Earl and Pauline (Mikalasic) S.; m. Nancy Ellen Simpson, Mar. 31, 1962; children—Sharon Elizabeth, Shelley Pauline. B.S., U. Calif.-Berkeley, 1961; postgrad. Exec. Mgmt. Program, Columbia U. C.L.U. V.p. mktg. Countrywide Life, L.A., 1973-76; v.p. agy. Occidental Life of Calif., L.A., 1976-79; pres., CEO Vol. State Life, Chattanooga, 1979-83; exec. v.p. Transam. Occidental Life Ins. Co., L.A., 1983-86, pres., 1986-88, pres., CEO, COO, 1988-90, also bd. dirs.; dir. USLIFE Corp., N.Y.C., 1990—; pres., CEO All Am. Life Ins. Co., Pasadena, Calif., 1990-94, USLIFE Life Ins. div. USLIFE Corp., 1994; pres., CEO USLIFE Corp., 1995—, mem. Office of Chmn., 1995—. Pres. Chattanooga coun. Boy Scouts Am., 1982, bd. dirs., L.A., 1983, v.p., 1983-85, vice-chmn L.A. area, 1989, chmn., 1989; pres. bd. councillors L.A. County Am. Cancer Soc.; trustee Verdugo Hills Hosp. Found. 1st lt. U.S. Army, 1961-64. Mem. Am. Soc. CLUs, Life Ins. Mktg. and Rsch. Assn. (bd. dirs. 1986-89). Republican. Presbyterian. Lodge: Rotary. Avocations: golf; skiing. Office: USLIFE Corp 125 Maiden Ln New York NY 10038

SIMPSON, WILLIAM KELLY, curator, Egyptologist, educator; b. N.Y.C., Jan. 3, 1928; s. Kenneth Farrand and Helen L.K. (Porter) S.; m. Marilyn E. Milton, June 19, 1953; children: Laura Krickerbacker Simpson Thorn, Abby Rockefeller Simpson Mydland. BA, Yale U., 1947, MA, 1948, PhD, 1954. Asst. in Egyptian art Met. Mus. Art, 1948-54; rsch. fellow Center Middle East Studies, Harvard U., 1957-58; mem. faculty Yale U., New Haven, 1958—; prof. Egyptology Yale U., 1965—, chmn. dept. Near Eastern langs., 1966-69; curator Egyptian and ancient Near Eastern art Mus. Fine Arts, Boston, 1970-86; ltd. partner Kin and Co., 1967-69; ltd. ptnr. Venrock, 1970—; dir. editor of papers Penn-Yale Archaeol. Expdn. to Egypt, 1960—; mem. adv. council fgn. currency program Smithsonian Instn., 1966-69. Author: Papyrus Reisner I-Records of a Building Project, 1963, Hekanefer and the Dynastic Material from Toshka, 1963, Papyrus Reisner II-Accounts of the Dockyard Workshop, 1965, Papyrus Reisner III: Records of a Building Project in the Early Twelfth Dynasty, 1969, The Terrace of the Great God at Abydos, 1974, The Mastabas of Qar and Idu, 1976, The Offering Chapel of Sekhem-ankh-ptah, 1976, The Offering Chapel of Kayemnofret in the Museum of Fine Arts Boston, 1992, The Inscribed Material from the Pennsylvania-Yale Excavations at Abydos, 1995, (with others) The Ancient Near East, A History, 1971, The Literature of Ancient Egypt, 1972, The Mastaba of Queen Mersyankh III, 1994. Trustee Am. Sch. Classical Studies, Athens, Am. U. in Cairo; mem. internat. council Mus. Modern Art, N.Y.C.; pres. Wrexham Found., 1965-67. Fulbright fellow Egypt, 1955-57; Guggenheim fellow, 1965. Mem. Am. Oriental Soc., Am. Philos. Soc., Archaeol. Inst. Am., Internat. Assn. Egyptologists, Egypt Exploration Soc., Soc. française d'egyptologie, German Archaeol. Inst., Foundation egyptologique Reine Elisabeth. Clubs: Century (N.Y.C.), Met. Opera (N.Y.C.), University (N.Y.C.), Union (N.Y.C.), River (N.Y.C.); Union Boat (Boston); Bedford (N.Y.); Golf and Tennis. Home: 129 Katonah Woods Rd Katonah NY 10536-9532

SIMPSON, WILLIAM STEWART, retired psychiatrist, sex therapist; b. Edmonton, Alta., Can., Apr. 11, 1924; came to U.S., 1950, naturalized, 1963; s. William Edward And Ethel Lillian (Stewart) S.; m. Eleanor Elizabeth Whitbread, June 17, 1950; children—David Kenneth, Ian Stewart, James William, Bert Edward. B.Sc., U. Alta., 1946, M.D., 1948. Diplomate Am. Bd. Psychiatry and Neurology, Am. Bd. Sexology. Rotating intern U. Alta. Hosp., 1948-49, resident in internal medicine, 1949-50; resident in psychiatry Topeka State Hosp., 1950-53, cons., 1967-68, asst. sect. chief, 1953-54, clin. dir., 1954-59, 68-72; fellow Menninger Sch. Psychiatry, Topeka, 1950-53; sect. chief C.F. Menninger Meml. Hosp., 1959-66, dir. edn., 1963-66; assoc. dir. Menninger Sch. Psychiatry, 1966-68; dir. field services Menninger Found., 1972-74, sr. staff psychiatrist adult outpatient dept., 1977-84, assoc. dir. adult outpatient dept., 1984-88; dir. Ctr. for Sexual Health, 1986-92; dir. Psychopharmacotherapy Clinic Menninger Clinic, 1989-90; chief psychiatry service, residency tng. program Topeka VA Hosp., 1974-77; dir. Midwest Impotence Ctr., Kansas City, Mo., 1988-91; mem. faculty Menninger Sch. Psychiatry, 1953-92, Ann. Seminar Inst. on Alcoholism, U. Wis., 1973-74; guest lectr. sex therapy Chinese Med. Assn., Rep. of China, 1985, Med. Sch. Tokai (Japan) U., 1985, dept. psychology U. Warsaw, Poland, 1987; cons. Osawatomie State Hosp., 1954-68, Colmery-O'Neill VA Hosp., 1983-92; mem. staff Stormont-Vail Hosp., Topeka, St. Francis Hosp., Topeka, Kans. Rehab. Hosp., Topeka, 1988-92; cons. in sex therapy Colmery-O'Neill VA Hosp., Topeka, 1983-92. Assoc. editor Bull. Menninger Clinic, 1963-70; cons. editor Jour. Med. Aspects of Human Sexuality, 1991-92. Bd. dirs. Topeka Civic Symphony Soc., 1953-55, Topeka People to People Council, 1963-66; ruling elder local Presbyn. ch., 1960—; mem. Kans. Citizens' Adv. Com. on Alcoholism, 1973-78; co-founder Topeka affiliate Nat. Council on Alcoholism, 1964, pres., bd. dirs., 1964, bd. dirs. N.Y.C., 1967, v.p., 1971-73, pres., 1973-75, mem. exec. com., 1967. Recipient Bronze Key award, Topeka affiliate Nat. Council on Alcoholism; 1972, Silver Key award, 1975, Outstanding Achievement award U. Alta. Med. Alumni Assn., 1975. Fellow Am. Psychiat. Assn. (life); mem. Topeka Inst. Psychoanalysis (cert.), Am. Assn. Sex Educators, Counselors and Therapists (cert. sex therapist, sex educator, supr.), Am. Psychoanalytic Assn. (cert.), AMA, Kans. Psychiat. Soc., Kans. Med. Soc., Shawnee County Med. Soc., Topeka Psychoanalytic Soc., Menninger Sch. Psychiatry Alumni Assn. (pres. 1979-80), Soc. for Sci. Study of Sex, Soc. for Sex Therapy and Research, Am. Assn. Sex Educators, Counselors and Therapists, Phi Delta Theta (Phi of Yr. award Kansas Beta chpt. 1964). Democrat. Presbyterian. Club: Saturday Night Literary (pres. 1990-91). Lodge: Rotary. Avocations: reading, classical music, photography, masters swimming. Home: 834 SW Buchanan St Topeka KS 66606-1428

SIMS, ARMITA B., principal. Prin. Beeber Mid. Sch., Phila. Office: Beeber Middle Sch 59th & Malvern Ave Philadelphia PA 19131

SIMS, BENNETT JONES, minister, educator; b. Greenfield, Mass., Aug. 9, 1920; s. Lewis Raymond and Sarah Cosette (Jones) S.; children: Laura (Mrs. John P. Boucher), Grayson, David. AB, Baker U., 1943, LHD (hon.), 1985; postgrad., Princeton Theol. Sem., 1946-47; B.D., Va. Theol. Sem., 1949, D.D., 1966; D.D., U. of South, 1972; Merrill fellow, Harvard U., 1964-65; postgrad., Cath. U., 1969-71. Ordained to ministry Episc. Ch. as deacon, 1949, priest, 1950. Rector Ch. of Redeemer, Balt., 1951-64; dir. continuing edn. Va. Theol. Sem., 1966-72; bishop of Atlanta, 1972-83; vis. prof. theology Emory U., Atlanta, 1980-88, pres. Inst. for Servant Leadership, 1988—; priest-in-charge St. Alban's Ch., Tokyo, 1962, 69. Trustee U. of South. With USNR, 1943-46. Named Young Man of Yr. Balt. C. of C., 1953; Disting. Alumnus of Yr., Baker U., 1972. Office: Inst Servant Leadership Hendersonville NC 28793

SIMS, DAVID BRYSON, JR., engineer; b. Memphis, Aug. 12, 1947; s. David Bryson and Ruth (Gnuse) S.; m. Carole Braddock, Nov. 21, 1970; children: Jennifer Braddock, David Bryson III. BSChemE, U. Tenn., 1969; MS Mech. Engring., U. Memphis, 1972, MS Civil Engring., 1974. Registered profl. engr., Ga., Mi., Va., Kans., N.C., Tenn., S.C., La., Ohio, Ind., Fla., Md. Engr. DuPont, Memphis, 1969-73; cons. engr. Elles, Reaves, Fanning & Oakley, Memphis, 1973-75; engr. W.R. Grace, Memphis, 1975-79; engring. mgr. W.R. Grace, Wilmington, N.C., 1979-85; prin. David Sims & Assocs., Wilmington, 1985—; trustee Cape Fear Acad., Wilmington, 1987-92; part-time instr. Cape Fear C.C., Wilmington, 1981-86. Bd. dirs., pres. Bradley Creek Boatominium, Wilmington, 1990—. Mem. NSPE, ASHRAE, AIChE (sec. 1972, pres. 1973), Nat. Fire Protection Assn. Republican. Presbyterian. Home: 2721 Shandy Ln Wilmington NC 28409-2042 Office: David Sims & Assocs 108 N Kerr Ave Ste K-1 Wilmington NC 28405-3444

SIMS, DOUGLAS D., bank executive; b. 1946. Grad., U. Ill., Urbana, 1968. With St. Louis Bank for Cooperatives, St. Louis, 1969-74; v.p. Ctrl. Bank for Coops., 1974-78; pres. St. Louis Bank for Coops., 1978-84; exec. v.p. Farm Credit Banks of St. Louis, 1984-86, pres., 1986-88; pres. Nat. Bank for Cooperatives, Englewood, Colo., 1988-93; CEO CoBank, Englewood, 1994—. Office: CoBank 5500 S Quebec St Englewood CO 80111-1914

SIMS, EDWARD HOWELL, editor, publisher; b. Orangeburg, S.C., May 29, 1923; s. Hugo Sheridan and Jesse Lucile (Howell) S.; m. Frances Dell Hartt, Jan. 5, 1946; m. Martha Lurene Bass, July 18, 1960; children—Edward H., Robert; m. Bente Thorlund Christensen, Oct. 4, 1969; children—Edward Christian, Frederik. A.B., Wofford Coll., 1943; postgrad., Emory U., 1946-47. Mng. editor Orangeburg Times and Democrat, 1946, editor, 1952—; Washington corr., founder Washington bur. for number S.C. dailies, 1947; dir. Sims Pub. Co., Orangeburg. Columnist: Looking South From Washington, 1948—; Washington Bur. chief: Editor's Copy syndicate, 1950-52; editor-pub., 1952—; radio news analyst: The News Of The Week In Washington, 1951—; Author: American Aces, 1958, Greatest Fighter Missions, 1962, The Fighter Pilots, 1967, Fighter Tactics 1914-70, 1972, Aces Over the Oceans, 1987; contbr. articles to publs. White House corr. covering Pres."s confs., 1948—; mem. Senate and House press galleries, 1947—; Am. consul Munich, Germany, 1963-65; cons. Exec. Office of White House, 1966-67; consul gen. Zurich, 1992; apptd. mem. Commn. to Preserve Am. Heritage Abroad, 1987. Served to 1st lt. USAF, World War II. Recipient Young Man of the Year award S.C. Jr. C. of C., 1959. Mem. White House Corrs. Assn., Am. Legion, V.F.W. Methodist. Clubs: Rotary, Nat. Press; Metropolitan (Washington); R.A.F. (London). Home: 3803 Pin Oaks St Sarasota FL 34232-1241 also: PO Box 400 Fairview NC 28730-0400 Office: PO Box 532 Orangeburg SC 29116-0532

SIMS, EVERETT MARTIN, publishing company executive; b. Morristown, N.J., June 27, 1920; s. Walter Leonard and Amy Ethel (Coleman) S. B.A., Drew U., Madison, N.J., 1941; M.A., Harvard U., 1947. Dir. project planning div. Prentice-Hall, Inc., Englewood Cliffs, N.J., 1950-60; asst. v.p. Prentice-Hall, Inc., 1956-60; with Harcourt Brace Jovanovich, Inc., N.Y.C., 1960-82; v.p. Harcourt Brace Jovanovich, Inc., 1970-80, sr. v.p., 1980-82; dir. coll. dept., 1970-82; pres. Media Systems Corp., 1974-77, chmn., 1977-81; pres. Telamon Enterprises, Inc., 1982—. Served with USAAF, 1942-45;

Served with USAF, 1950-51, ETO. Decorated Air medal Croix de Guerre, (France). Home and Office: 180 Sebonac Rd Southampton NY 11968-2727

SIMS, EZRA, composer; b. Birmingham, Ala., Jan. 16, 1928; s. Ezra G. and Kathryn W. (Wallace) S. BA, Birmingham So. Coll., 1947; postgrad., Birmingham Conservatory Music, 1945-48; MusB in Composition, Yale U. Sch. Music, 1952; MA in Composition, Mills Coll., 1956. Librarian Harvard Music Library, Cambridge, Mass., 1958-62, 65-74; music dir. New Eng. Dinosaur Dance Theatre, Boston, 1968-78; instr. theory New Eng. Conservatory Music, Boston, 1976-78; instr. microtonal theory Mozarteum, Salzburg, 1992-93; freelance composer Cambridge, 1974—; dir. Dinosaur Annex Music Ensemble, Cambridge, pres. 1977-81; guest composer 23d Ann. Contemporary Music Festival, Ill. Wesleyan U., 1977; lectr. various colls. including Warwick U., Cleve. Inst. Music, Internat. Christian U., Westport Friends of Music, Schlumberger-Doll Rsch., Webster U., Mozarteum, Northwestern U., Hochschule für Musik, Hamburg. Composer over 100 works, predominantly microtonal music for various mediums including Chamber Cantata on Chinese Poems, 1954, Mass, 1955, Two Folk Songs, 1958, String Quartet, 1959, Sieben-Spencer Lieder, 1960, Sonate Concertanti, 1961, Third Quartet, 1962, Buchlein for Lyon, 1962, Cantata III, 1963, Octet for Strings, 1964, In Memoriam Alice Hawthorne, 1967, Antimatter: Three Dances for Toby, 1968, A Frank Overture: Four Dented Interludes and Coda, 1969, Pastorale, 1970, Clement Wenceslaus Lothaire Nepomucene, Prince Mettermich (1773-1859), In Memoriam, 1970, Real Toads, 1970, Interlope, 1971, Tango Variations, 1971, Museum Piece, 1972, Where the Wild Things Are, 1973, String Quartet #2 1962, 1974, After Lyle or Untitled, 1975, When the Angels Blow Their Trumpets, 1976, Celebration of Dead Ladies, 1976, Elegie-nach Rilke, 1976, Collage XIII, 1977, Aeneas on the Saxophone, 1977, Come Away, 1978, Midorigaoka, 1978, 5 Songs, 1979, -And, As I Was Saying..., 1979, Two for One, 1980, Sextet, 1981, All Done From Memory, 1980, Phenomena, 1981, Solo After Sextet, 1981, Quartet, 1982, Pictures for an Institution, 1983, Tune and Variations, 1983, Brief Elegies, 1983, String Quartet #4, 1984, The Conversions, 1985, Wedding Winds, 1986, Quintet, 1987, Chase, 1987, Solo in four movements, 1987, AEDM in memoriam, 1988, Flight, 1989, Night Piece: IN Girum Imus nocte et Consuminur Igni, 1989, Concert Piece, 1990, Duo, 1992, Invocation, 1992, Stanzas, 1995; contbr. articles to profl. jours. Served as pvt. U.S. Army, 1952-54. Recipient Composers Forum award, 1959, Koussevitzky Found. commn., 1983, Am. Acad. Arts and Letters award, 1985; grantee Cambridge Arts Coun., 1975, 76, Martha Baird Rockefeller Found., 1977; fellow Guggenheim Found., 1962, Nat. Endowment for Arts, 1976, 78, Mass. Artists Found., 1979, Fulbright Sr. Scholar, 1992. Mem. Am. Composers Alliance, Broadcast Music, Inc. Home and Office: 1168 Massachusetts Ave Cambridge MA 02138-5205

SIMS, HENRY P., management educator. Prof. mgmt. U. Md., College Park. Author: The Thinking Organization: Dynamics of Organizational Social Cognition, 1986, Super Leadership: Leading Others to Lead Themselves, 1989, The New Leadership Paradigm: Social Learning and Cognition in Organizations, 1992, Business Without Bosses: How Self-Managing Teams Are Building High-Performance Companies, 1993, Company of Heroes: Unleashing the Power of Self Leadership, 1996. Office: U Md Dept Mgmt College Park MD 20742-0001

SIMS, HUNTER W., JR., lawyer; b. Richmond, Va., Oct. 21, 1944. BS, U. Va., 1967; JD, U. Richmond, 1971. Bar: Va. 1971. Law clk. to Hon. Walter E. Hoffman U.S. Dist. Ct. (ea. dist.), Va., 1971-72; asst. U.S. atty. State of Va. (ea. dist), 1972-75; ptnr. Kaufman & Canoles P.C., Norfolk, Va. Mem. ABA, Va. Bar Assn. (bd. govs. construction law sect. 1982-85, bd. govs. antitrust sect. 1989-92, bd. dirs. 1990-92), Va. State Bar, Fed. Bar Assn., Va. Beach Bar Assn., Am. Inns of Ct., Norfolk/Portsmouth Bar Assn. (sec. 1981-86), Omicron Delta Kappa, Phi Delta Phi, McNeill Law Soc. Office: Kaufman & Canoles PC PO Box 3037 1 Commercial Place Norfolk VA 23514-3037

SIMS, J. TAYLOR, academic administrator. Acting pres. Cleve. State U., sr. v.p. Office: Cleveland State University Office of Development E 24th and Euclid Ave Cleveland OH 44115

SIMS, JAMES HYLBERT, English educator, former university administrator; b. Orlando, Fla., Oct. 29, 1924; s. James W. and Anna L. (Hylbert) S.; m. Ruth Elizabeth Gray, Jan. 3, 1944; children: James W., Timothy C., Suzannah C., C. Andrew, John M. BA in English, History and Psychology, U. Fla., 1949, MA in English, 1950, PhD in English Lit., 1959. Lic. comml. pilot FAA. Instr. English Tenn. Temple Coll., 1950-51; pres., instr. English Tri-State Bapt. Coll., Evansville, Ind., 1951-54; instr. English U. Fla., Gainesville, 1955-57, 58-59; prof. English, chmn. dept. Tift Coll., Forsyth, Ga., 1959-61, Austin Peay State U., Clarksville, Tenn., 1961-66; prof. U. Okla., Norman, 1966-76; prof. English and dean Coll. Liberal Arts U. So. Miss., Hattiesburg, 1976-82, v.p. acad. affairs, 1982-89, Disting. prof. English, v.p. emeritus for Acad. affairs, 1989—; Clyde Kilby lectr. Wheaton (Ill.) Coll., 1991-92, Charles G. Smith lectr. in English Baylor U., 1994. Author: Biblical Allusions in Shakespeare's Comedies, 1960, The Bible in Milton's Epics, 1962, Dramatic Uses of Biblical Allusions in Marlowe and Shakespeare, 1966, Milton and Scriptural Tradition: The Bible Into Poetry, 1984, A Comparative Literary Study of Daniel and Revelation: Shaping the End, 1995; contbr. chpts. to books; contbr. numerous articles on lit. criticism, comparative lit. and lit. history to scholarly jours.; assoc. editor: Seventeenth-Century News, 1968—. Bd. dirs. Baptist Faith Missions, Internat. Bd. Jewish Missions. Served with USN, 1943-46. Fellow Southeastern Inst. Medieval and Renaissance Studies, 1965-66, NEH, summer 1974, NEH-Huntington Libr., 1973, 78-79; recipient Regents' Superior Tchg. award U. Okla., 1968. Mem. MLA, Milton Soc. Am. (pres. 1976), South Atlantic MLA, South Ctrl. MLA, South Ctrl. Renaissance Conf. (pres. 1983), Conf. Christianity and Lit. (chmn. South Ctrl. 1981-82, 87-88, nat. pres. 1990-92), Rotary (Paul Harris fellow). Democrat. Baptist. Home: 3103 Delwood Dr Hattiesburg MS 39401-7214 Office: U So Miss English Dept Hattiesburg MS 39406

SIMS, JAMES LARRY, hospital administrator, healthcare consultant; b. Birmingham, Ala., Feb. 16, 1936; s. James Alexander and Elsie Lee (Coleman) S.; m. Sandra Anne Hanzel, July 25, 1981. AB, Birmingham Southern, 1958; cert., U. Ala., 1970. Diplomate Am. Acad. Med. Adminstrs. Sgt. USAF res. Fellow Am. Acad. Med. Adminstrs., Royal Soc. Health, Am. Coll. Healthcare Execs.; mem. Fla. Hosp. Personnel Dirs. Assn. (pres. 1964-65), South Fla. Hosp. Personnel Dirs. Assn. (pres. 1967-68), Fla. Hosp. Pub. Rels. Assn. (pres. 1970-71), South Fla. Pub. Rels. Coun. (pres. 1963-64). Democrat. Methodist. Home: Flying S Ranch PO Box 7825 Las Cruces NM 88006

SIMS, JANETTE ELIZABETH LOWMAN, educational director; b. Lincolnton, N.C., July 21, 1934; d. Lee Hobson and Myrtle Elizabeth (Travis) Lowman; m. Mickey Ray Sims, Feb. 2, 1951; children: Carol Lee Sims Walden, Rickey Ray. BS, Lenoir-Rhyne Coll., 1968; MAT, U. N.C., 1973; EdD, U. N.C., Greensboro, 1989. N.C. "G" tchg. cert; cert. devel. edn. specialist. Quality control supr. Kiser Roth Hosiery, Inc., Maiden, N.C., 1959-63; 9th grade phys. sci. and math. tchr. Cherryville (N.C.) Jr. H.S., 1968; phys. sci., chemistry and astronomy tchr. Maiden (N.C.) H.S., 1968-75; dir. studies lab. coord. Catawba Valley C.C., Hickory, N.C., 1975-79; physics, chemistry, math. and computer sci. instr. Catawba Valley C.C., Hickory, 1979-90, dir. developmental studies and learning assistance ctr., 1990—; trustee Catawba County Assn. for Spl. Edn., Conover, 1978-79, Catawba Valley Found., Hickory, 1993—, chair, 1996; apprentice program instr. Meredith/Burda Corp., Newton, N.C., 1979-88; chairperson N.C. Math. Assn. Two-Yr. Colls. Devel. Math. Com., N.C., 1991-93. Coun. mem., choir mem., tchr. Faith Luth. Ch., Conover, 1980—. Mem. NEA, N.C. Assn. Educators (local unit pres.), Nat. Assn. Developmental Educators, N.C. Assn. Developmental Educators (regional chair 1990), Atlantic Assn. Physics Tchrs. (chair nominations com. 1992), Am. Legion Aux., Delta Kappa Gamma. Avocations: golfing, sewing, cooking. Home: 300 Parlier Ave Conover NC 28613-9312 Office: Catawba Valley CC 2550 Us Highway 70 SE Hickory NC 28602-8302

SIMS, JOE, lawyer; b. Phoenix, Sept. 29, 1944; s. Joe and Pauline Jane (Saunders) S.; m. Robin Ann Reed, Jan. 30, 1965; 1 child, Shannon Dane. BS in Fin., Ariz. State U., 1967, JD, 1970. Bar: Ariz. 1970, U.S. Supreme Ct. 1975, D.C 1978. Trial atty. antitrust div. Dept. Justice, Washington, 1970-73; spl. asst. to asst. atty. gen., 1973-75; dep. asst. atty. gen. for policy planning and legislation, 1975-77, dep. asst. atty. gen. for regulatory matters and fgn. commerce, 1977-78; mem. firm Jones, Day, Reavis & Pogue, Washington, 1978-79; ptnr. Jones, Day, Reavis & Pogue, 1979—; resident fellow Am. Enterprise Inst. for Pub. Policy Rsch., Washington, 1978-79, vis. fellow, 1979-81; prin. Coun. for Excellence in Govt. Contbr. various articles to prof. jours. Mem. ABA (chmn. antitrust law sect. one com. 1987-90, bus. law sect. antitrust law com. 1988-91, antitrust law civil practice and procedure com. 1990-91), Am. Law Inst., D.C. Bar Assn., City Club Washington, Tournament Players Club (Potomac, Md.), Firestone Country Club (Akron, Ohio), Collecton River Plantation (Hilton Head Island, S.C.). Republican. Home: 10100 New London Dr Potomac MD 20854-4849 Office: Jones Day Reavis & Pogue 1450 G St NW Ste 600 Washington DC 20005-2001

SIMS, JOHN WILLIAM, lawyer; b. Vicksburg, Miss., Mar. 25, 1917; s. John Ernest and Helen Ross (Moore) S.; m. Marie Elise Hebert, Sept. 28, 1940; 1 dau., Helen Moore. B.A., Tulane U., 1937, LL.B., 1939. Bar: La. 1939. Of counsel Phelps Dunbar; mem. permanent adv. bd.-planning com. Admiralty Law Inst., Tulane U., New Orleans, 1966—, chmn., 1985-91, adj. prof. law, 1981-95. Assoc. editor Am. Maritime Cases, 1974-96; mem. editl. bd. Lloyd's Maritime and Comml. Law Quar., 1984-92; mem. bd. adv. editors Tulane Law Rev., 1985-93, Maritime Advisor-Ct. Case Digest, 1985—; contbr. articles to profl. jours. Trustee Gulf South Rsch. Inst., 1965-68, Children's Hosp., 1975-78; bd. dirs. Coun. for Better La., Bur. Govt. Rsch., 1973-84, USCG Found., 1986-91, La. World Expn., Inc., 1980-84, World Trade Ctr., 1985—; bd. dirs., v.p. New Orleans Opera Assn., 1974-93; mem. men's adv. bd. Christian Woman's Exch. Lt USCGR, 1942-45. Named Rex, King of Carnival Mardi Gras, New Orleans, 1981; recipient Disting. Pub. Service award Dept. Transp. U.S. Coast Guard, 1985. Fellow Am. Coll. Trial Lawyers; mem. Am., La. (past sec.-treas.), New Orleans Bar assns., Maritime Law Assn. U.S. (2d v.p. 1976-78, 1st v.p. 1978-80, pres. 1980-82, com. Supreme Ct. admiralty rules 1963-69, com. limitation of liability 1963—, com. Comite Maritime Internat. 1965-80, com. uniformity admiralty law 1975-92, com. liquified natural gas transp. 1978-80, del. Comite Maritime Internat. conv. N.Y.C. 1965, Rio de Janeiro, 1977, Montreal, 1981, adv. cons. Hamburg 1974, titular mem. Comite Maritime Internat. 1979—, del. Comite Maritime Internat. Lisbon Conv., 1985), SAR, Soc. Colonial Wars, Order of Coif, Phi Beta Kappa, Omicron Delta Kappa, Phi Delta Theta, Phi Delta Phi. Clubs: Boston, Louisiana. Office: Texaco Ctr 400 Poydras St Fl 30 New Orleans LA 70130-3245

SIMS, KATHY LOU BUSEY, deputy chief of police; b. Pensacola, Fla., Oct. 11, 1954; d. Nick and Bessie Lois (Allen) Busey; m. Thomas Clyde Sims, Feb. 10, 1971 (div. 1976). Cert. in automobile mechanics, Falkner State Coll., Fayetteville, N.C., 1977; student, Troy State U., Pensacola, 1981-82, Pensacola Jr. Coll., 1987-88. Cashier Winn-Dixie Supermarket, Pensacola, 1971-72; mgr. Taco House Restaurant, Pensacola, 1972-73; bartender Bros. and Sisters, Pensacola, 1973-75, Stop & Shop, Pensacola, 1974-76; carpenter Waylon Constrn. Co., Fayetteville, N.C., 1978-79; officer Dept. Def. Police, Naval Air Sta. Pensacola, Fla., 1980-88, asst. chief police, 1989-91, deputy chief of police, 1991-96, collateral duty chief investigator, 1991-93; relocation counselor PAS Pensacola Family Svc. Ctr., 1996—; equal employment cons. Naval Air Sta., Pensacola, 1989—; speaker, law enforcement instr. on crisis intervention, spouse and child abuse, domestic violence, sexual battery, sexual assault, and self esteem, 1990—, trainer for rape response; crisis intervention & critical incident intervention specialist, 1980—, victims advocate & rape crisis intervention specialist, 1989—; facilitator Rape Survivor's Support Group, 1995—; starter rape survivor's support group, Pensacola, 1995—; rape victims adv. Lakeview Ctr., 1994—, rape survivors crisis counselor (vol.), 1994—, sexual assault victim's intervention specialist, 1992—, crisis intervention specialist, 1984—. Vol. Allie Yniestra Elem. Sch., 1989-93; rape victim advocate, Lakeview, 1992-95; sexual assault victim's intervention specialist, 1992—, crisis intervention specialist, 1984—; facilitator Rpae Survivor's Support Group, Pensacola, 1995—. With U.S. Army, 1976-79. Recipient livesaving award ARC, Pensacola, 1985, Disting. Svc. award Fla. Coun. Crime and Delinquency, 1993, Woman of Yr., 1992. Mem. NAFE, MADD (critical incident stress debriefing team mem.). Democrat. Baptist. Office: Naval Air Sta Pensacola FL 32508

SIMS, KAY ELLEN, critical care nurse; b. Tacoma Park, Md., Oct. 31, 1949; d. Paul Frederick and Shirley Eileen Smith; divorced; 1 child, Steffanie Gayle. Diploma, Johns Hopkins Sch. Nursing, 1970; BSN, Union U., 1991; MSN, U. Tenn., 1993. RN, Tenn., Md.; cert. critical care; cert. continuing educator and staff devel. Staff nurse Washington Adventist Hosp., Takcoma Park; instr. Bapt. Hosp. Sch. Nursing, Memphis; staff and head nurse Bapt. Meml. Hosp., Memphis, staff devel. instr. cardiovascular intensive care unit and telemetry, 1980-94; edn. specialist, 1994—. Mem. AACN (regional advisor, chpt. pres., newsletter editor, seminar spkr.), Soc. Critical Care Medicine, Sigma Theta Tau, Alpha Chi. Methodist. Office: Bapt Meml Hosp 899 Madison Ave Memphis TN 38103-3405

SIMS, KEITH, professional football player; b. Balt., June 17, 1967. BS in Indsl. Tech., Iowa State U. Guard Miami Dolphins, 1990—; player AFC Championship Game, 1992. Named to Pro Bowl Team, 1993. Office: Miami Dolphins 2269 NE 199th St Miami FL 33180

SIMS, KENT OTWAY, economist; b. Chickasha, Okla., Nov. 2, 1940; s. Jesse Otway and Mable Vela (Bear) S.; m. Jeanette McCollum, June 9, 1961; children: Marketa, Adam. B.A., U. Colo., 1963, Ph.D., 1966. registered investment advisor. Economist Urban Renewal Authority, Denver, 1965-66, U.S. Dept. State mission to Pakistan, 1966-69; economist Fed. Res. Bank of San Francisco, 1969-71, asst. v.p., 1971-72, v.p., dir. research, 1972-74, sr. v.p., 1974-82, exec. v.p., chief fin. officer, 1982-85; fin. advisor, investment mgr., mgmt. cons. Theodore R. Seton, 1985-86; ptnr. C&K Partnership, 1987-89; pres. Her Equal Share, Inc., 1986-89, San Francisco Econ. Devel. Corp., 1988-91; dir. econ. planning and devel. Mayor's Office, San Francisco, 1992-93, San Francisco Redevel. Agy., 1993—. Bd. govs. Econ. Lit. Coun. Calif., Long Beach, 1983-88; trustee Strybing Arboretum Soc. Golden Gate Park, San Francisco, 1993—; bd. dirs. Jewish Community Mus., San Francisco, 1986-93, Design Coun. San Francisco Bay Area, 1989-90, Career Resources Devel. Ctr., 1991-92; adv. bd. St. Lukes Hosp., San Francisco, 1988—. Mem. Am. Econs. Assn., Nat. Audubon Soc. Am. Clubs: Sierra.

SIMS, KONSTANZE OLEVIA, social worker; b. Dallas, Dec. 20, 1944; d. Kenneth Winn and Odie Lee (Wells) S. Student, U. Dallas, 1963-64; BA, U. Tex., Arlington, 1968; MEd, U. North Tex., 1972. Sec. Stillman Coll. Regional Campaign Fund, Dallas, 1969; employment interviewer Zale Corp., Dallas, 1969-71; sch. counselor Bishop Dunne High Sch, Dallas, 1973-78; dir. guidance Notre Dame High Sch., Wichita Falls, Tex., 1978-81; taxpayer svc. rep. IRS, Dallas, 1981-83, acct. analyst, 1983-88; freelance Dallas, 1989-90; social worker Tex. Dept. Human Svcs., Dallas, 1991—. Reader, North Tex. Taping & Radio for the Blind, Dallas, 1991—; mem. choir St. Peter the Apostle Cath. Ch.; mem. Whale Adoption Project; mem. Union Chorale. Mem. AAUW, Am. Counseling Assn., Nat. Specialty Merchandising Assn., Am. Multicultural Counseling Assn., Am. Bible Tchrs. Assn., Tex. Counseling Assn., Tex. Multicultural Counseling Assn., Assn. Rsch. and Enlightenment, Inc., Assn. for Spiritual, Ethical, and Religious Values in Counseling, U. Tex Arlington Alumni Assn., U. North Tex. Alumni Assn. Avocations: reading, crossword puzzles, singing. Office: Tex Dept Human Svcs 4533 Ross Ave Dallas TX 75204-8417

SIMS, PAUL KIBLER, geologist; b. Newton, Ill., Sept. 8, 1918; s. Dorris Lee and Vere (Kibler) S.; m. Dolores Carsell Thomas, Sept. 15, 1940; children: Thomas Courtney, Charlotte Ann. AB, U. Ill., 1940, MS, 1942; PhD, Princeton, 1950. Spl. asst. geologist Ill. Geol. Survey, 1942-43; geologist U.S. Geol. Survey, 1943-61; prof. geology, dir. Minn. Geol. survey U. Minn., 1961-73; research geologist U.S. Geol. Survey, 1973-95, rsch. geologist emeritus, 1995—; pres. Econ. Geology Pub. Co., 1979—; Bd. dirs. North Star Research and Devel. Inst., Mpls., 1966-73. Co-editor: Geology of Minnesota, 1972, 75th anniversary vo.. Economic Geology, 1981. Adviser Minn. Outdoor Recreation Resources Commn., 1963-67. Served with USNR, 1943-46. Recipient Meritorious Service award U.S. Dept. Interior, 1984; Goldich medal Inst. on Lake Superior Geology, 1985, Disting. Svc. award U.S. Dept. Interior, 1991. Fellow Geol. Soc. Am., Soc. Econ. Geologists (councilor 1965-68, pres. 1975, Ralph W. Marsden award medal 1989); mem. Internat. Assn. on Genesis of Ore Deposits, Internat. Union Geol. Sci. (subcom. Precambrian stratigraphy, sec. 1976-84), Assn. Am. State Geologists (hon.), Colo. Sci. Soc. (hon.). Research geology metalliferous ore deposits Colo., Minn., Wis., N.J., Ariz., Wash., Wyo., also early evolution earth's crust in N. Am. Home: 1315 Overhill Rd Golden CO 80401-4238 *Hard work and diligence can cover for a lot of deficincies.*

SIMS, RICHARD LEE, hospital administrator; b. Columbus, Ohio, Jan. 6, 1929; s. Dorwin Delos and Christine Anna (Hanstein) S.; m. Marilyn Lou Atkinson, June 2, 1951; children: John Christopher, Steven Paul. B.S., Ohio State U., 1951. Pres. Doctors Hosp. Found., Columbus; preceptor faculty Ohio State U. Coll. Health Care Adminstrn.; past chmn. hosp. council Franklin County; ret., 1995; past chmn. Hosp. Shared Svc. Inc.; chmn. Found. Osteo Health Svcs., 1989-93. Past pres. Franklin County chpt. ARC; past chmn. 1st Comty. Village Bd.; past chmn. governing bd. 1st Comty. Ch. With Med. Svc. AUS, 1953-56; maj. Ohio N.G., 1956-74. Recipient Distinguished Service award Columbus Jr. C. of C., 1960-63. Fellow Am. Coll. Healthcare Execs., Am. Coll. Osteo. Healthcare Execs.; mem. Am. Osteo. Hosp. Assn. (chmn. 1988), Ohio Trade Assn. Execs. (past pres.), Ohio Hosp. Assn. (past chmn. bd.), Ohio Osteo. Hosp. Assn. (past pres.), Am. Legion (past post comdr.), Sigma Chi. Clubs: University, Rotary (pres. 1978-79), Columbus. Home: 1180 Kenbrook Hills Dr Columbus OH 43220-4941

SIMS, ROBERT BARRY, lawyer; b. N.Y.C., Aug. 20, 1942; s. Irving Zach and Laura (Levine) S.; m. Roberta Jane Donner, Nov. 17, 1973; children: Alexandra Lauren, Andrew Michael, Amanda Morgan. AB, Franklin and Marshall Coll., 1964; JD, George Washington U., 1967; MBA, NYU, 1969. Bar: N.Y. 1968, D.C. 1969, Conn. 1980, Tex. 1995, U.S. Dist. Ct. D.C. 1969, U.S. Dist. Ct. (so. and ea. dists.) N.Y. 1970, U.S. Dist. Ct. Conn. 1978, U.S. Ct. Appeals (2d and D.C. cirs.) 1969, U.S. Ct. Claims 1977, U.S. Ct. Customs and Patent Appeals 1978, U.S. Supreme Ct. 1979, U.S. Ct. Internat. Trade 1981. Assoc. firm Cahill, Gordon & Reindel, N.Y.C., 1967-69, Whitman & Ransom, N.Y.C., 1969-72; asst. counsel Gen. Signal Corp., N.Y.C., Stamford, Conn., 1972-76; v.p., sec., gen. counsel Raymark Corp. (formerly Raybestos-Manhattan, Inc.), Trumbull, Conn., 1976-82; assoc. gen. counsel Lever Bros. Co., N.Y.C., 1983; asst. to pres., corp. counsel Math. Applications Group, Inc., Elmsford, N.Y., 1984; sr. v.p., sec., gen. counsel Summagraphics Corp., Seymour, Conn., 1984—. Mem. ABA, N.Y. State Bar Assn., Assn. Bar City N.Y., D.C. Bar Assn., Conn. Bar Assn., Coporate Bar Assn. Office: Summagraphics Corp 8500 Cameron Rd Austin TX 78754

SIMS, ROBERT BELL, professional society administrator, public affairs official, newspaper publisher; b. Alamo, Tenn., Nov. 26, 1934; s. Robert Leslie and Lucille (Bell) S.; m. Patricia June Lytton, June 25, 1961; children—Jacqueline, James, Carolyn, William. B.A., Union U., Jackson, Tenn., 1956; postgrad., U. Sydney, Australia, 1957; M.A. in Polit. Sci., U. Wis., Madison, 1971, M.A. in Journalism, 1971; Grad., Nat. War Coll. Reporter Jackson Sun, Tenn., 1955-56; dir. pub. relations Union U., Jackson, 1958; commd. ensign USN, 1958, served to capt., 1984; spl. asst. to Pres., dir. pub. affairs NSC, Washington, 1982-83; spl. asst. to Pres., dep. press sec. for fgn. affairs The White House, Washington, 1983-85; asst. sec. def. pub. affairs Dept. of Def., Washington, 1985-87; v.p. communications Nat. Geographic Soc., Washington, 1987-89, sr. v.p., 1989—; owner, pub. The Crockett Times, Alamo, Tenn., 1974—. Author: Pentagon Reporters, 1983. Mem. bd. visitors U. Tenn. Coll. Arts and Scis., 1992—; bd. dirs. Mag. Pubs. Assn., 1992—, Travel Industry Assn., 1992—. Decorated Legion of Merit; Rotary Internat. Found. fellow, 1957; recipient Disting. Service award Union U., 1985. Mem. Sigma Delta Chi. Republican. Lodge: Masons. Home: 2701 O St NW Washington DC 20007 Office: Nat Geog Soc Washington DC 20036

SIMS, WILLIAM RILEY, design and facility management educator, consultant; b. Gulfport, Miss., Dec. 17, 1938; s. William Riley and Hallie Pauline (Mills) S.; m. Jean Lee Booth, June 17, 1962; 1 child, Hallie Jean. B.Arch., U. N.Mex., 1963; M.Arch., M.C.P., U. Pa., 1965; Ph.D., MIT, 1973. Cert. facility mgr. Internat. Facility Mgmt. Assn., 1993. Planner, urban designer Phila. City Planning Commn., 1964; planner, urban designer Wallace McHarg Assocs., Phila., 1965; lectr. dep. city and regional planning U. Calif., Berkeley, 1966-68; asst. prof. dept. urban planning U. Wash., Seattle, 1970-73; assoc. prof. dept. city and regional planning Ohio State U., Columbus, 1973-80; prof., chmn. dept. design and environ. analysis Cornell U., Ithaca, N.Y., 1980—, co-dir. Internat. Facility Mgmt. program, 1989-93; co-dir. Workplace Studies Program, 1993—; cons. Columbus, Ohio, 1978-80; prin. Orbit-II Study, Ithaca, 1984—, Becker-Sims Assocs. (formerly Facility Rsch. Assocs.), Ithaca, 1984—. Author: Neighborhoods, 1975, Managing the Reinvented Workplace, 1996; (with others) Taos Adobes, 1965; editor (jour.) Design Guidelines from Post Occupancy Evaluation, 1980; contbr. articles to profl. jours.; mem. publs. bd. Jour. Interior Design Edn. and Research, 1986-89. Trustee Columbus Landmarks Found., 1978-80; mem. bldgs. and properties com. Cornell U. Trustees. Fulbright scholar U.S. Inst. Internat. Edn., Norway, 1965-66; Mellon faculty fellow U. Wash., 1969, Ford faculty fellow Ohio State U., 1974. Mem. ASTM (chmn. assessing bldg. performance 1988-92), Internat. Facility Mgrs. Assn. (bd. dirs. 1984-87, cert. and accreditation task forces 1989—), Environ. Design Rsch. Assn., Assn. for Study of Man and Environ. Rels. (editl. bd. 1978-86), Am. Assn. Housing Educators (editl. bd. 1978-85). Home: 735 Ridge Rd Lansing NY 14882-8805 Office: Cornell U Dept Design & Environ Analysis Ithaca NY 14853-4401

SIMS, WILSON, lawyer; b. Nashville, Dec. 24, 1924; s. Cecil and Grace (Wilson) S.; m. Linda Bell, Aug. 12, 1948; children: Linda Rickman, Suzanne, Wilson. B.A., U. N.C., 1946; J.D., Vanderbilt U., 1948. Bar: Tenn. 1948. Since practiced in Nashville; ptnr. Bass, Berry & Sims, 1948—; gen. counsel, dir. Baird Ward Printing Co., Tenn., 1950-76, Southeastern Capital Corp., 1955-60, Martha White Foods, Synercon Corp., 1968-76, Forrest Life Ins. Co., 1970-75, Charter Co., 1983-84, The Bailey Co., Kenworth of Tenn., Inc. Chmn. Tenn. Commn. for Human Devel., 1970, Tenn. Commn. on Continuing Legal Edn., 1986-90; mem. Tenn. Gen. Assembly, 1959; bd. dirs. Nashville YMCA, United Cerebal Palsy, Kidney Found., Matthew 25, McKendree Village; trustee Meharry Med. Coll., Webb Sch., Bell Buckle, Tenn.; adv. bd. Jr. League; mem. bd. visitors U. N.C. 1st lt. USMCR, 1942-45, 50-52. Fellow Am. Bar Found. (life), Nashville Bar Found.; mem. ABA, Tenn. Bar Assn. (past speaker ho. of dels., past pres.), Nashville Bar Assn. (past pres., dir., Pub. Svc. award), Tenn. Bar Found. (past chmn.), Am. Judicature Soc., Am. Acad. Polit. Sci., Vanderbilt U. Law Alumni Assn. (past pres., Disting. Alumnus award), Nashville C. of C. (2 terms bd. govs.), Belle Meade Country (bd. dirs.), Wade Hampton Golf Club. Methodist. Home: 22 Foxhall Close Nashville TN 37215-1862 Office: Bass Berry & Sims 2700 First Am Ctr Nashville TN 37238

SIMSON, GARY JOSEPH, legal educator; b. Newark, Mar. 18, 1950; s. Marvin and Mildred (Silberg) S.; m. Rosalind Slivka, Aug. 15, 1971; children: Nathaniel, Jennie Anne. BA, Yale Coll., 1971; JD, Yale U., 1974. Bar: Conn. 1974, N.Y. 1980. Law clk. to judge U.S. Ct. Appeals 2d Cir., 1974-75; asst. prof. law, U. Tex., 1975-77, prof. law, 1977-80; vis. prof. law Cornell U., Ithaca, N.Y., 1979-80, prof. law, 1980—; vis. prof. law U. Calif., Berkeley, 1986; chair adv. bd. law casebook series Carolina Acad. Press. Author: Issues and Perspectives in Conflict of Laws, 1985, 2d edit., 1991. Mem. ABA, ACLU, Phi Beta Kappa. Contbr. articles to legal publs. Office: Cornell U Law Sch Myron Taylor Hall Ithaca NY 14853

SIMSON, JO ANNE, anatomy and cell biology educator; b. Chgo., Nov. 19, 1936; d. Kenneth Brown and Helen Marjorie (Pascoe) Valentine; m. Arnold Simson, June 1961 (div.); 1 child, Maria; m. Michael Smith, Nov. 10, 1971 (div.); children: Elizabeth Smith, Briana Smith. BA, Kalamazoo Coll., 1959; MS, U. Mich., 1961; PhD, SUNY, Syracuse, 1969. Postdoctoral fellow Temple U. Health Sci. Ctr., Phila., 1968-70; asst. prof. Med. U. S.C., Charleston, 1970-76, assoc. prof., 1976-83, prof. anatomy and cell biology, 1983—; featured in Smithsonian exhibit, Sci. in Am. Life, 1994—. Contbr. articles to profl. jours.; author short stories and poems. Active adult edn. Unitarian Ch., Charleston, 1973-75, social action, 1990-92. Grantee NSF, 1959-60, NIH, 1966-67, 72-87, 91-95. Mem. Am. Assn. Anatomists, Am. Soc. Cell Biology, Histochem. Soc. (sec. 1979-82, exec. com. 1985-89),

Fogarty Internat. Fellowship Bioctr. (Basel, Switzerland, 1987-88), Amnesty Internat. (newsletter editor Group 168 1982-86), Phi Beta Kappa. Home: 1760 Pittsford Cir Charleston SC 29412-4110 Office: Med U SC Anatomy 171 Ashley Ave Charleston SC 29425-0001 *In the end, it is only what a person has created and given to the rest of the world that endures.*

SIMUNICH, MARY ELIZABETH HEDRICK (MRS. WILLIAM A. SIMUNICH), public relations executive; b. Chgo.; d. Tubman Keene and Mary (McCamish) Hedrick; m. William A. Simunich, Dec. 6, 1941. Student Phoenix Coll., 1967-69, Met. Bus. Coll., 1938-40. Exec. sec. sales mgr. Sta. KPHO radio, 1950-53; exec. sec. mgr. Sta. KPHO-TV, 1953-54; account exec. Tom Rippey & Assos., 1955-56; pub. rels. dir. Phoenix Symphony, 1956-62; co-founder, v.p. Paul J. Hughes Pub. Rels., Inc., 1960-65; owner Mary Simunich Pub. Rels., Phoenix, 1966-77; pub. rels. dir. Walter O. Boswell Meml. Hosp., Sun City, Ariz., 1969-85; pub. rels. cons., 1985—; pres. DARCI PR, Phoenix, 1994—, Cityscape, Inc. (formerly Citynet, Inc.), 1994—; instr. pub. rels. Phoenix Coll. Evening Sch., 1973-78. Bd. dirs. Anytown, Ariz., 1969-72; founder, sec. Friends Am. Geriatrics, 1977-86. Named Phoenix Advt. Woman of Year, Phoenix Jr. Advt. Club, 1962; recipient award Blue Cross, 1963; 1st Pl. award Ariz. Press Women, 1966. Mem. NAFE, Women in Comm., Internat. Assn. Bus. Communicators (pres. Ariz. chpt. 1970-71, dir.), Pub. Rels. Soc. Am. (sec., dir. 1976-78), Am. Soc. Hosp. Pub. Rels. (dir. Ariz. chpt. 1976-78), Nat., Ariz. Press Women. Home: 4133 N 34th Pl Phoenix AZ 85018-4771 Office: DARCI Group 2425 E Camelback Ste 450 Phoenix AZ 85016-4236

SINAI, ALLEN LEO, economist, educator; b. Detroit, Apr. 4, 1939; s. Joseph and Betty Paula (Feinberg) S.; m. Lee Davis Etsten, June 23, 1963; children: Lauren Beth, Todd Michael. AB, U. Mich., 1961; MA, Northwestern U., 1966, PhD, 1969. Asst. prof. to assoc. prof. econs. U. Ill.-Chgo., 1966-75; chmn. fin. info. group, chief fin. economist Data Resources, Lexington, Mass., 1971-83; chief economist, mng. dir. Lehman Bros. and Shearson Lehman Bros. Inc., N.Y.C., 1983-87; chief economist, exec. v.p. The Boston Co. Inc., 1988-93; pres., CEO The Boston Co. Econ. Advisors Inc., Boston and N.Y.C., 1988-93, Econ. Advisors, Inc., 1993—; mng. dir., chief global economist Lehman Bros., N.Y.C., 1993—, chief global economist, dir. global econs.; cons. Laural Cons., Lexington and Evanston, Ill., 1966; vis. assoc. prof. econs. and fin. MIT, Cambridge, 1975-77; adj. prof. econs. Boston U., 1977-78, 81-83, NYU, 1984-88; adj. prof. econs. and fin. Lemberg Sch., Brandeis U., 1988—; vis. faculty Sloan Sch., MIT, 1989-91. Contbr. articles to profl. jours. and books. Mem. reducing the fed. budget deficit task force Roosevelt Ctr., Washington, 1984; bd. govs. Com. on Developing Am. Capitalism, 1984—, chmn., 1990-95; bd. economists Time Mag., 1991—. Recipient Alumnus Merit award Northwestern U., 1985. Mem. Am. Econ. Assn., Econometric Soc., Ea. Econs. Assn. (v.p. 1988-89, pres. 1990-91, Otto Eckstein prize 1988, fellow 1994), Western Econ. Assn. (exec. com.), Econometric Soc., Nat. Assn. Bus. Econs. Jewish. Avocations: tennis; skiing. Home: 16 Holmes Rd Lexington MA 02173-1917 Office: Econ Advisors Inc 260 Franklin St Fl 15 Boston MA 02110-3112

SINATRA, FRANK (FRANCIS ALBERT SINATRA), singer, actor; b. Hoboken, N.J., Dec. 12, 1915; s. Anthony and Natalie (Garaventi) S.; m. Nancy Barbato, Feb. 4, 1939 (div.); children: Nancy, Frank Wayne, Christine; m. Ava Gardner (div.); m. Mia Farrow, 1966 (div.); m. Barbara Marx, 1976. Student, Demarest High Sch., Hoboken, Drake Inst.; hon. doctorate, Stevens Inst. Tech., Hoboken, 1985. Sang with sch. band and helped form sch. glee club; worked after sch. on news truck of Jersey Observer; copy boy on graduation with sports div. covering coll. sports events (won first prize on Maj. Bowes Amateur Hour, touring with co. for 3 months); sustaining programs on 4 radio stas. and in Rustic Cabin, N.J., toured with Harry James Band, then Tommy Dorsey's, solo night club and concert appearances; starred on radio program Lucky Strike Hit Parade; appeared in motion pictures From Here to Eternity (Acad. award as best supporting actor 1953), Las Vegas Nights, 1946, Ship Ahoy, 1942, Miracle of the Bells, 1948, Kissing Bandit, 1949, Take Me Out to the Ball Game, 1949, Higher and Higher, 1942, Step Lively, 1944, Anchors Aweigh, 1945, It Happened in Brooklyn, 1947, Guys and Dolls, 1956, Not as a Stranger, 1955, The Tender Trap, 1955, The Man With the Golden Arm, 1955, Johnny Concho, 1956, The Pride and the Passion, 1957, Pal Joey, 1957, Some Came Running, 1959, Never So Few, 1960, Can-Can, 1960, Oceans 11, 1960, Pepe, 1960, The Devil at 4 O'Clock, 1961, The Manchurian Candidate, 1962, Come Blow Your Horn, 1963, Robin and the Seven Hoods, 1963, None But the Brave, 1964, Assault on a Queen, 1965, Von Ryan's Express, 1966, Tony Rome, 1966, Lady in Cement, 1967, The Detective, 1968, Dirty Dingus McGee, 1970, Who Framed Roger Rabbit (voice), 1988; actor, producer motion picture The First Deadly Sin, 1980, TV movie Contract on Cherry Street, 1977; hit songs include Night and Day, 1943, Nancy, 1945, Young at Heart, 1954, Love and Marriage, 1955, The Tender Trap, 1955, How Little We Know, 1956, Chicago, 1957, All the Way, 1957, High Hopes, 1959, It Was a Very Good Year, 1965, Strangers in the Night, 1966, My Way, 1969, (with Nancy Sinatra) Somethin Stupid, 1969; albums include Songs for Swingin' Lovers, 1956, Come Dance With Me, 1959, Come Fly With Me, 1962, September of My Years (Grammy award for best album), 1965, Moonlight 1966, Greatest Hits, 1968, My Way, 1969, Greatest Hits, Volume 2, 1970, L.A. is My Lady, 1984, The Very Good Years, 1991, Where Are You, 1992, The World We Knew, Duets, 1993, Duets II, 1994, You Make Me Feel So Young, 1995, Hello, Young Lovers, 1996; (with Bing Crosby) All the Best, 1995; (with Luciano Pavarotti) Live in Concert, 1995; (with Tommy Dorsey Orch.) There Are Such Things, 1996; author: A Man and His Art, 1990. Recipient Spl. Oscar award Acad. Motion Picture Arts and Scis., 1945, Sylvania TV award, 1959, Grammy awards for album of yr., 1959, 65, 66, best vocalist, 1959, 65, 66, rec. of yr., 1966, Peabody and Emmy awards, 1965, Jean Hersholt award Acad. Motion Picture Arts and Scis., 1971, Golden Apple award as male star of yr. Hollywood Women's Press Club, 1977, Humanitarian award Variety Clubs Internat., 1980, Cross of Sci. and the Arts, Austria, 1984, Presdl. Medal of Freedom, 1985, Kennedy Ctr. honor, 1986, Life Achievement award NAACP, 1987, Grammy Lifetime Achievement award, 1994. Club: Friars (abbot). Office: care Thomas Cassidy Inc 366 Horseshoe Dr Basalt CO 81621-9104 also: care Sinatra Enterprises 9100 Wilshire Blvd # 455 Beverly Hills CA 90212-3415*

SINAY, HERSHEL DAVID, publisher; b. Chgo., Mar. 15, 1938; s. Irving Paul and Gertrude (Drucker) S. BA, U. So. Calif., 1960. Telecommunications and Cinema account exec. Wall St. Jour., L.A., 1961-63; account exec. R.J. Friedman Assocs., L.A., 1963-66; dir. sales Performing Arts Mag., L.A., 1966-72; pub. East, West Network, L.A., 1972-79, 85-87; pres., pub. Calif. Bus. Mag., L.A., 1979-85; pub., editor-in-chief Ranch & Coast Mag., DelMar, Calif., 1987-88; pub. Am. Film Mag., L.A., 1988-91; pres., owner Project Mktg. Custom Publ. Specialists Pubs. of the Am. Film Inst. Life Achievement Award Annual, 1991—; Pubs. of Am. Cinema Editors Tribute Program, 1993—. Included in Billboard Music awards Tribute Book, 1993, 1st Ann. Thurgood Marshall Lifetime Achievement award Tribute Book, NAACP Legal Def. and Ednl. Fund, 1993; recipient 32 Maggie awards Western Pub. Assn., 1979-93. Mem. Am. Film Inst., L.A. Advt. Club. Avocations: yachting, jogging, gardening. Office: 810 S Hauser Blvd Los Angeles CA 90036-4726

SINAY, JOSEPH, retail executive; b. Chgo., Dec. 5, 1920; s. Hyman and Ella S.; m. Ruth Milman, Mar. 7, 1961; 1 dau., Elise Sinay Spilker. Student, Herzl Jr. Coll., 1939. Gen. mgr. Fanchon & Marco Theatres, Los Angeles, 1943-54; v.p., founder Interstate United, Chgo., 1953-56; partner Josam Investment Co., Los Angeles, 1956—; chmn. bd., pres., chief exec. officer R B Industries Inc., L.A., 1956-89, now cons. Bd. dirs. Am. Acad. Dramatic Arts; pres. Variety Clubs Internat., 1985-87; gen. chmn. United Jewish Welfare L.A., 1976; pres. We. region Am. Friends Hebrew U., 1980; Calif. fin. chmn. Muskie for Pres., 1972; trustee Idyllwild Arts Found., 1968-73; bd. dirs. Constl. Rights Found., 1973-78. Mem. Nat. Home Furnishing Assn. Jewish. Office: Josam Investment Co 1801 Century Park E Los Angeles CA 90067-2302

SINCERO, ARCADIO PACQUIAO, engineering educator; b. Antipolo, Tuburan, Cebu, The Philippines, Nov. 13, 1938; came to U.S., 1973; s. Santiago Encarguiz Sincero and Guadiosa Lipar Pacquiao; m. Gregoria Managase Alivio, Nov. 16, 1969; children: Roscoe, Arcadio Jr. BSChemE, Cebu Inst. Tech., 1965; ME, Asian Inst. Tech., Bangkok, 1968; DSc in Environ. Engring., George Washington U., 1987. Registered profl. engr., Md., Pa. Assoc. prof. civil and chem. engring. Cebu Inst. Tech., 1969-72; assoc. prof. Inst. Tech. Far Ea. U., the Philippines, 1972-73; planner critical path method Consolidated Engring. Co., Balt., 1973-74; pub. works engr. City of Balt., 1974-75; pub. health engr. State of Md., Balt., 1975-78, water resources engr., 1978-79, chief permits divsn., 1979-88; assoc. prof. civil engring. Morgan State U., Balt., 1988—. Author: (with G. A. Sincero) Environmental Engineering: A Design Approach, 1996; contbr. articles to profl. jours. Mem. ASCE, AIChE, AAUP, Am. Soc. Engring. Edn., Asian Soc. Environ. Protection, Water Environment Fedn. Achievements include research in environmental engineering, water quality, treatment of water by reverse osmosis for removal of organic chemicals, pollution engineering. Office: Morgan State U Dept Civil Engring Baltimore MD 21239

SINCLAIR, ALASTAIR JAMES, geology educator; b. Hamilton, Ont., Can., Aug. 1, 1935; s. Burton Leslie and Grace (Isherwood) S.; m. Elizabeth Mary Sylvia Hill, June 13, 1964; children: Alison Trevena, Fiona Tamsin. BS, U. Toronto, 1957, MS, 1958; PhD, U. B.C., 1964. Asst. prof. U. Wash., Seattle, 1962-64; asst. prof. U. B.C., Vancouver, 1964-68, assoc. prof., 1968-74, prof., 1974—, head dept. geol. scis., 1985-90, dir. Geol. Engring., 1979-80, 81-82, 92—; pres. Sinclair Cons. Ltd., Vancouver, 1980—; bd. dirs. FSS Internat., Vancouver. Contbr. numerous articles to profl. jours. Killam Sr. fellow, 1990-91. Fellow Geol. Assn. Can. (treas. mineral deposits divsn. 1978-89), Soc. Econ. Geologists; mem. Assn. Profl. Engrs. B.C., Internat. Assn. Math. Geologists, Assn. Exploration Geochemists (councillor 1992-96), Can. Inst. Mining, Metallurgy and Petroleum (life, Robert Elver award 1991), Geol. Soc. Brazil (hon. mem. sci.-tech. commn. geochemistry 1982), Brazilian Geochem. Soc. (hon. 1987). Avocations: classical music, skiing. Home: 2972 W 44th Ave, Vancouver, BC Canada V6N 3K4 Office: U BC, Dept Geological Sciences, Vancouver, BC Canada V6T 1Z4

SINCLAIR, CAROLE, publisher, editor, author; b. Haddonfield, N.J., May 13, 1942; d. Earl Walter and Ruth (Sinclair) Dunham; 1 child, Wendy. Student, U. Florence, Italy, 1963; BA in Polit. Sci., Bucknell U, 1964. Advt. copywriter BBD&O Advertising, N.Y.C., 1966-67; sales promotion mgr. Macmillan Pub. Co., N.Y.C., 1967-71; mktg. mgr. Doubleday & Co., Inc., N.Y.C., 1972-74, promotion dir., 1974-76, advt. mgr., sales and promotion, chmn. mktg. com., 1976-80; v.p. mktg., editorial dir. Davis Pubs., N.Y.C., 1980-83; founder, pub., editorial dir., sr. v.p. Sylvia Porter's Personal Fin. Mag., N.Y.C., 1983-90; pres. The Sylvia Porter Orgn., Inc., N.Y.C., 1980-91; founder, pres. Sinclair Media Inc., N.Y.C., 1990—; mktg. dir. Denver Pub. Inst., summers 1975-78; lectr. Columbia U. Bus. Sch. and Sch. of Journalism, 1976; host nationally syndicated TV show, Sylvia Porter's Money Tips, syndicated daily radio show, Sylvia Porter's Personal Fin. Report, audio cassette series on fin. topics. Author: Keys for Women Starting and Owning a Business, 1991, Keys to Women's Basic Professional Needs, 1991, When Women Retire, 1992; contbg. editor Pushcart Prize, 1977; contbr. The Business of Publishing, 1980. Renaissance Art Program fellow, Florence, Italy, 1963; White House intern, 1962. Mem. Women's Forum, Intercorp. Communications Group, Mag. Pubs.' Assn., Advt. Women in N.Y., Spence Sch. Parent's League. Presbyterian. Club: Pubs. Lunch. Avocation: boating.

SINCLAIR, DAISY, advertising executive, casting director; b. Perth Amboy, N.J., Mar. 22, 1941; d. James Patrick and Margaret Mary (McAniff) Nieland; m. James Pratt Sinclair, May 25, 1978; children: Duncan, Gibbons. BA, Caldwell Coll., 1962. Jr. copywriter Young & Rubican, N.Y.C., 1962-64; various positions in casting dept. Ogilvy & Mather, N.Y.C., 1964-90, sr. v.p., dir. casting, 1990—. Mem. Am. Assn. Advt. (talent agt. com. 1972—), Drama League N.Y. (3d v.p. 1982—), The Knickerbocker Greys (v.p.), Edgartown Yacht Club, Chapaquoit Yacht Club, The Tuxedo Club. Republican. Episcopalian. Avocations: opera, theater, sailing, skiing. Home: 4 E 95th St New York NY 10128-0705 Office: Ogilvy & Mather Advt Worldwide Plz 309 W 49th St New York NY 10019-7316

SINCLAIR, DORIS PAULA GIMMESON, nurse, educational administrator; b. Troy, Ohio, Dec. 5, 1932; d. Dwight Paul and Florence Mable (Oller) Gimmeson; m. Robert A. Sinclair, Sr., May 16, 1956; children: Elizabeth Ann Sinclair Biggan, Robert A., Mary Ruth, Sinclair Lonnerghan. Cert., Trinity U., San Antonio, 1955; diploma Baptist Meml. Hosp. Sch. Nursing, 1955; BSN cum laude, Incarnate Word Coll., San Antonio, 1968; MSN, U. Tex.-San Antonio, 1974. RN, Tex. Office nurse for pvt. practitioner, San Antonio, 1955-57, 59-62; staff nurse Bapt. Meml. Hosp., San Antonio, 1957-59, 63-64; instr. maternal child care nursing Bapt. Meml. Hosp. Sch. Nursing, San Antonio, 1962-63, 68-71, instr. clin. nursing, 1964-66; asst. dir. Bapt. Meml. Hosp. System Sch. Nursing, San Antonio, 1971-72, acting dir., 1972-74, dir., 1974-86, retired, 1986-87, pub. sch. nurse, 1987-88; dir. Bapt. Meml. Hosp. System Sch. Profl. Nursing, San Antonio, 1988-95, ret.; mem. Bd. Vocat. Nurse Examiners, State of Tex., Austin, 1978-81; accreditation visitor So. Assn. Colls. and Schs., 1981-82; mem. coordinating bd., nursing edn. adv. com., Tex. Coll. and Univ. System, Austin, 1982-83. Coord., Explorer Scout Post 634, San Antonio, 1983-86; adv. bd. nurse career program Chicago Health Policy Devel., Inc., San Antonio, 1983-86. Recipient Nurse of Yr. award Baptist Meml. Hosp. System, 1973, Exec. of Yr. award Profl. Secs. Internat., 1994. Mem. Nat. League Nursing (accreditation visitor 1982-86, alt. accreditation bd. rev. 1991-93), Tex. League Nursing, Am. Hosp. Assn. Assembly Hosp. Schs. Nursing (nominating com. 1976-78, program com. 1979-80, chmn. program com. 1980-81), Council Deans and Dirs. of Schs. of Profl. Nursing for State of Tex. (chairperson 1978-79), Tex. Higher Edn. Co-ordinating Bd. (nursing adv. com. 1989-90), Am. Hosp. Assn. Inst. for Hosp. Clin. Nursing Edn. (gov. coun. 1990-92), Bapt. Meml. Hosp. System Sch. Nursing Alumni Assn., Sigma Theta Tau. Methodist. Clubs: San Antonio Coll. Faculty Wives, Ladies Oriental Shrine N. Am., Bapt. Meml. Hosp. System Lamplighter Assn. Avocations: gourmet cooking; ceramics; swimming.

SINCLAIR, GLENN BRUCE, mechanical engineering educator, researcher; b. Auckland, New Zealand, Mar. 7, 1946; came to U.S., 1969; s. Alan John and Piri (Vincent) S.; m. Della Jane Sutton, Dec. 23, 1972; children—Heidi Lee, Heather Ann, Hillary Colleen, Christopher Alan. B.Sc., U. Auckland, 1967, B.E., 1969; Ph.D., Calif. Inst. Tech., 1972. J. Willard Gibbs instr. mech. engring. Yale U., New Haven, 1972-74; lectr. U. Auckland, 1974-77; asst. prof. Carnegie-Mellon U., Pitts., 1977-80, assoc. prof., 1980-82, prof., 1982—, head, 1986-92; vis. prof. Cambridge U., Eng., 1981; research scientist Dept. Sci. and Indsl. Research, Wellington, New Zealand, 1968-69; summer prof. Pratt & Whitney, Hartford, Conn., 1978, Aircraft Corp., West Palm Beach, Fla., 1979; cons. in field. Contbr. articles to profl. jours. Fulbright scholar, 1969-72. Mem. Am. Acad. Mechanics. Office: Carnegie-Mellon Univ Dept Mech Engring 5000 Forbes Ave Pittsburgh PA 15213-3890

SINCLAIR, JAMES BURTON, plant pathology educator, consultant; b. Chgo., Dec. 21, 1927; s. James Lawrence Sinclair and Helen Marie (Thompson) Owens. BSc, Lawrence U., 1951; PhD, U. Wis., 1955. Grad. rsch. asst. U. Wis., Madison, 1951-55, grad. rsch. assoc., 1955-56; from asst. prof. to assoc. prof. La. State U., Baton Rouge, 1956-65, prof., 1965-68, adminstrv. asst. to chancellor, 1966-68; prof. U. Ill., Urbana, 1968—, dir. nat. soybean rsch. lab., 1992—. Co-author: Basic Plant Pathology Methods, 1985, Principles of Seed Pathology, 1987, Anatomy and Physiology of Diseased Plants, 1991; contbr. articles to profl. jours. Sgt. U.S. Army, 1946-47. Recipient Soybean Rsch. Recognition award Am. Soybean Assn., 1983, Prodn. Rsch. award, 1989, Paul A. Funk award, 1984, Disting. Svc. award USDA, 1988, Disting. Svc. award Phytopathol. Soc. (north ctrl. divsn.), 1991, Rsch. award Land of Lincoln Soybean Assn., 1992. Fellow Am. Phytopathol. Soc., Nat. Acad. of Scis./India; mem. Ill. Crop Improvement Assn. (hon.), Rotary (chmn. internat. com. Savoy chpt. 1990-91, v.p. 1991-93, pres. 1993-94). Home: 408 Arbours Dr Savoy IL 61874-9752 Office: U Ill Dept Plant Pathology 1102 S Goodwin Ave Urbana IL 61801-4730

SINCLAIR, JOSEPH SAMUELS, broadcasting company executive, retail merchant; b. Narragansett, R.I., June 14, 1922; s. James and Bertha (Samuels) S.; m. Betty Virginia Hintz, Feb. 16, 1946 (dec. 1968); children: Sherry Murr, Lani Patricia, Jodie Carol; m. Rosalyn K. Dwares, Oct. 24, 1969; children: Sara Ellen Sinclair, Steven Dwares. Student, Williams Coll., 1940-41; BS, U.S. Naval Acad., 1945; DBA (hon.), Johnson and Wales Coll., 1976. Asst. to program mgr. Sta. WJAR-TV, Providence, 1949-57, mgr., 1957-60; dir. Outlet Co., 1955-58, mem. exec. com., 1958-60, v.p., 1960, pres., 1960-68, chmn. bd. dirs., 1968-84; pres. Sinclair Communications, Sinclair Assn., Sinclair Ventures, Providence, 1984—. Mem. pres.'s coun. Providence Coll.; trustee R.I. Coun. Econ. Edn., U. R.I. Found.; mem. adv. bd. Salve Regina Coll.; mem. Wheeler Sch. bd., Providence. Lt. (j.g.) 1945-47, lt. USNR, 1950-52. Decorated Italian Star Solidarity; recipient R.I. Advt. Silver medal, 1968. Mem. Navy League R.I., Naval War Coll. Found., Nat. Assn. Broadcasters (bd. dirs.), TV Pioneers, Internat. Radio and TV Soc., World Bus. Coun., Nat. Broadcasters Club, R.I. Assn. Broadcasters (v.p.), R.I. Commodores (adm.), R.I. 100 Club (pres.), Wellington Country Club, Sports Car Am. Club, Wellington Club, Point Judith Country Club, Dunes Club, Aurora Club, Palm Beach Polo and Country Club. Home and Office: 170 Westminster St Providence RI 02903-2101

SINCLAIR, JULIE MOORES WILLIAMS, consulting law librarian; b. Montgomery, Ala., May 2, 1954; d. Benjamin Buford and Marilyn Moores (Simpson) Williams; m. Winfield James Sinclair, Dec. 16, 1978. BA, U. of South, 1976; MLS, U. Ala., Tuscaloosa, 1977; JD, Washington U., St. Louis, 1987. Bar: Ala. 1989, U.S. Dist. Ct. (no. dist.) Ala. 1989. Serials libr. Ala. Dept. Archives and History, Montgomery, 1977; cataloguing libr. Ala. Pub. Libr. Svc., Montgomery, 1978; league libr. Ala. League Municipalities, Montgomery, 1978-84; asst. libr. Mo. Ct. Appeals, St. Louis, 1984-86, law clk., 1987-88; cons. Law Libr. Cons., Birmingham, Ala., 1988—. Contbr. numerous articles to profl. jours. Mem. exec. com. Jefferson County Women's Polit. Caucus, 1988—. Mem. Ala. Bar Assn., Ala. Libr. Assn., Am. Assn. Law Librs., Law Libr. Assn. Ala. (charter, v.p. 1992-93, pres. 1993-94), Ala. Fedn. Bus. and Profl. Women (sec. 1993-94, 2d v.p. 1994-95, 1st v.p. 1995-96), Order of Gownsmen, Phi Alpha Theta. Episcopalian. Avocations: travel and sightseeing, reading, attending theatre, especially Shakespeare. Office: Law Libr Cons 956 Montclair Rd Ste 218 Birmingham AL 35213-1215

SINCLAIR, KENT, law educator; b. San Diego, July 8, 1946; s. Kent and Ruth Melva (Wilson) S.; m. Kathryn Spining; children: K. Scott, Keith A. AB, U. Calif., 1968, JD, 1971. Bar: Calif. 1972, U.S. Dist. Ct. (so. dist.) N.Y. 1972, U.S. Ct. Appeals (2d cir.) 1972, N.Y. 1973, Va. 1986, U.S. Supreme Ct. 1990. Law clk. to judge James Browning U.S. Ct. Appeals 9th Cir., San Francisco, 1971-72; chief staff atty. U.S. Ct. Appeals 9th Cir., 1972; atty. Shearman & Sterling, N.Y.C., 1972-77; judge-magistrate U.S. Dist. Ct. So. Dist., N.Y.C., 1977-83; prof. law U. Va., Charlottesville, Va., 1983-89; prof. law, assoc. dean U. Va., 1989-93; spl. master U.S. Dist. Ct. SDN.Y., 1983-88; dep. spl. master Supreme Ct. U.S., 1989—; reporter decisions Supreme Ct. Va., Richmond, 1985—; dir. Va. Judges Inst., Charlottesville, 1984—. Author: Federal Civil Practice, 1992, Virginia Civil Procedure, 1993, Practice Before Federal Magistrates, 1984, Moore's Federal Practice, 1984, The Trial Handbook, 1989. Edn. dir. Va. State Bar, 1983-89, mem. Mem. Am. Law Inst., Va. Bar Assn. Avocation: computers. Office: U Va Sch Law 580 Massie Rd Charlottesville VA 22903-1738*

SINCLAIR, ROLF MALCOLM, physicist; b. N.Y.C., Aug. 15, 1929; s. Nathan and Elizabeth (Stout) S.; m. Margaret Lee Andrews, June 13, 1959 (div. 1978); children: Elizabeth Ann, Andrew Caisley; m. Allyn J. Miner, July 29, 1991. B.S., Calif. Inst. Tech., 1949; M.A. (Reade scholar), Rice U., 1951, Ph.D. (Inst. fellow), 1954. Physicist, Westinghouse Research Labs., 1953-56; vis. scientist U. Hamburg, Germany, 1956-57, U. Paris, 1957-58, U.K. Atomic Energy Authority, Culham Lab., Eng., 1965-66; research physicist Princeton U., 1958-69; program dir. NSF, Washington, 1969—; mem. Solstice Project, 1978-91; NSF rep. U.S. Solar Eclipse Expdn. to India, 1980, Amundsen-Scott South Pole Sta., 1995; Disting. vis. prof. N.Mex. State U., 1985; vis. prof. No. Ariz. U., 1986; vis. sci. Los Alamos Nat. Lab., 1988-89, guest scientist, 1989—; cons. to industry, 1960-69. Fellow Am. Phys. Soc. (panel pub. affairs 1976-77, nominating com. 1988-90), AAAS (sec. physics sect. 1972—, mem. coun. 1972-73, nominating com. 1982-83), Sigma Xi. Research and publs. on physics, archaeoastronomy, tech. and instrumentation. Home: 7508 Tarrytown Rd Chevy Chase MD 20815-6027 Office: Nat Sci Found Physics Divsn 4201 Wilson Blvd Arlington VA 22230-0001

SINCLAIR, SARA VORIS, health facility administrator, nurse; b. Kansas City, Mo., Apr. 13, 1942; d. Franklin Defenbaugh and Inez Estelle (Figenbaum) Voris; m. James W. Sinclair, June 13, 1964; children: Thomas James, Elizabeth Kathleen, Joan Sara. BSN, UCLA, 1965. RN, Utah; lic. health care facility adminstr.; cert. health care adminstr. Staff nurse UCLA Med. Ctr. Hosp., 1964-65; charge nurse Boulder (Colo.) Meml. Hosp., 1966, Boulder (Colo.) Manor Nursing Home, 1974-75, Four Seasons Nursing Home, Joliet, Ill., 1975-76; dir. nursing Home Health Agy of Olympia Fields, Joliet, Ill., 1977-79; dir. nursing Sunshine Terr. Found., Inc., Logan, Utah, 1980, asst. adminstr., 1980-81, adminstr., 1981-93; dir. divsn. health systems improvement Utah Dept. Health, Salt Lake City, 1993—; mem. long term care profl. and tech. adv. com. Joint Commn. on Accreditation Healthcare Orgns., Chgo., 1987-91, chmn., 1990-91; adj. lectr. Utah State U., 1991-93; mem. adj. clin. faculty Weber State U., Ogden, Utah; moderator radio program Healthwise Sta. KUSU-FM, 1985-93; spkr. Nat. Coun. Aging, 1993, Alzheimer's Disease Assn. Ann. Conf., 1993; del. White House Conf. on Aging, 1995; chmn. Utah Dept. of Health's Ethics, Instnl. Rev. Bd. Com., 1995—, Utah Dept. Health Risk Mgmt. Com., 1995—; exec. com. Utah Long Term Care Coalition, 1995; presenter in field. Contbg. author: Associate Degree Nursing and The Nursing Home, 1988. Mem. dean's adv. coun. Coll. Bus. Utah State U., Logan, 1989-91, mem. presdl. search com., 1991-92; chmn., co-founder Cache Comty. Health Coun., Logan, 1985; chmn. bd. Hospice of Cache Valley, Logan, 1986; mem. Utah State Adv. Coun. on Aging, 1986-93; apptd. chmn. Utah Health Facilities Com., 1989-91; chmn. Bear River Dist. Adv. Coun. on Aging, 1989-91; chmn. health and human svcs. subcom. Cache 2010, 1992-93. Recipient Disting. Svc. award Utah State U., 1989. Fellow Am. Coll. Health Care Adminstrs. (presenter 1992-93, 95, presenter 1996 ann. convocation New Orleans, v.p. Utah chpt. 1992-94, convocation and edn. coms. 1992-93, region IX vice gov. 1994-96); mem. Am. Healthcare Assn. (non-proprietary v.p. 1986-87, region v.p. 1987-89, presenter workshop conv. 1990-93, presenter ann. convocation 1995, exec. com. 1993), Utah Health Care Assn. (pres. 1983-85, treas. 1991-93, Disting. Svc. award 1991), Utah Gerontol. Soc. (bd. dirs. 1992-93, 95—, chmn. nominating com. 1993-94, chmn. ann. conf. 1996, pres.-elect 1996), Cache C. of C. (pres. 1991), Logan Bus. and Profl. Women's Club (pres. 1989, Woman of Achievement award 1982, Woman of Yr. 1982), Rotary (Logan chpt., chair comty. svc. com. 1989-90). Avocations: walking, reading. Office: Utah Dept Health Div Health Sys Improvement 288 N 1460 W Salt Lake City UT 84114-2851 also: PO Box 142851 Salt Lake City UT 84114-2851

SINCLAIR, VIRGIL LEE, JR., judge, writer; b. Canton, Ohio, Nov. 10, 1951; s. Virgil Lee and Thelma Irene (Dunlap) S.; children: Kelly, Shannon; m. Janet Brahler Sinclair. BA, Kent State U., 1973; JD, U. Akron, 1976; postgrad. Case Western Res. U., 1979. Adminstr. Stark County Prosecutor's Office, Canton, 1974-76; mem. faculty Walsh Coll., Canton, 1976-78; asst. pros. atty. Stark County, Canton, 1976-77; ptnr. Amerman Burt Jones Co. LPA, Canton, 1976-91, Buckingham, Doolittle and Burroughs Co., L.P.A., Canton, 1991-95; judge Stark County Common Pleas Ct., 1995—; legal adviser Mayor's Office, City of North Canton, Ohio, 1978-79; referee Stark County Family Ct., Canton, 1981, Canton Mcpl. Ct., 1991—; spl. referee Canton Mcpl. Ct., 1985-86. Author: Law Enforcement Officers' Guide to Juvenile Law, 1975, Lay Manual of Juvenile Law, 1976; editor U. Akron Law Rev.; contbr. to Ohio Family Law, 1983, also articles to profl. jours. Mem. North Canton Planning Comm., 1979-82; bd. mgrs. North Canton YMCA, 1976—, Camp Tippecanoe, Ohio, 1981—; profl. adviser Parents Without Partners, 1980—; spl. dep. Stark County Sheriff Dept., 1983—; trustee Palace Theatre Assn., Canton, 1982—. Recipient Disting. Service award U.S. Jaycees, 1984. Mem. ABA, Ohio Bar Assn., Stark County Bar Assn. (lectr. 1984), Ohio Trial Lawyers Assn., Assn. Trial Lawyers Am., Nat. Dist. Attys. Assn., Delta Theta Phi (bailiff 1976; nat. key winner 1975-76), Jaycees. Republican. Methodist. Lodge: Elks, Eagles, Masons.

SINCLAIR, WARREN KEITH, radiation biophysicist, organization executive, consultant; b. Dunedin, New Zealand, Mar. 9, 1924; came to U.S., 1954; naturalized, 1959; s. Ernest W. and Jessie E. (Craig) S.; m. Elizabeth J. Edwards, Mar. 19, 1948; children: Bruce W., Roslyn E. Munn. BSc, U. Otago, New Zealand, 1944, MSc, 1945; PhD, U. London, 1950. Cert. Am. Bd. Health Physics. Radiol. physicist U. Otago, 1945-47; radiol. physicist U. London Royal Marsden Hosp., 1947-54; chmn. dept. physics, prof. U. Tex.

M.D. Anderson Hosp., 1954-60; sr. biophysicist Argonne (Ill.) Nat. Lab., 1960-85, div. dir., 1970-74, assoc. lab. dir., 1974-81; prof. radiation biology U. Chgo., 1964-85, prof. emeritus, 1985—; mem. Internat. Commn. on Radiation Units and Measurements, 1969-85, Internat. Commn. on Radiol. Protection, 1977—; alt. del. UN Sci. Com. on Effects of Atomic Radiation, 1979—; mem. Nat. Coun. on Radiation Protection and Measurements, 1967-91, hon. mem., pres., 1991—; L.S. Taylor lectr. Nat. Council on Radiation Protection and Measurements, 1993; H. M. Parker lectr. Battelle Found.; mem. expert panel WHO; sec. gen. 5th internat. Congress Radiation Rsch., 1974; chmn. bd. on radiation effects NAS-NRC, 1992—; cons. in field. Author: Radiation Research: Biomedical, Chemical and Physical Perspectives, 1975; Contbr. numerous articles to profl. jours., also chpts. to books. Served with N.Z. Army, 1942-43. Nat. New Zealand scholar, 1942-45. Fellow Inst. Physics; mem. Am. Assn. Physicists in Medicine (pres. 1961-62, Coolidge award 1986), Nat. Coun. on Radiation Protection and Measurements (pres. 1977-91, pres. emeritus 1991—), Radiation Rsch. Soc. (coun. 1964-67, pres. 1978-79, Failla award 1987), Brit. Inst. Radiology (coun. 1953-54), Internat. Assn. Radiation Rsch. (coun. 1966-70, 76-83), Radiol. Soc. N.Am., Biophys. Soc., Soc. Nuclear Medicine, Bioelectromagnetics Soc., Health Physics Soc., Soc. Risk Analysis, Hosp. Physicists Assn., Innominates Club (Chgo.), Cosmos Club (Washington). Home: 2900 Ascott Ln Olney MD 20832-2626 Office: 7910 Woodmont Ave Ste 800 Bethesda MD 20814-3015

SINCLAIR, WILLIAM DONALD, church official, fundraising consultant, political activist; b. L.A., Dec. 27, 1924; s. Arthur Livingston and Lillian May (Holt) S.; m. Barbara Jean Hughes, Aug. 9, 1952; children: Paul Scott, Victoria Sharon. BA cum laude, St. Martin's Coll., Olympia, Wash., 1975; postgrad. Emory U., 1978-79. Commd. 2d lt. USAAF, 1944, advanced through grades to col., USAF, 1970; served as pilot and navigator in Italy, Korea, Vietnam and Japan; ret., 1975; bus. adminstr. First United Methodist Ch., Colorado Springs, Colo., 1976-85; bus. adminstr. Village Seven Presbyn. Ch., 1985-87; bus. adminstr. Sunrise United Meth. Ch., 1987-89; vice-chmn. council fin. and adminstrn. Rocky Mountain conf. United Meth. Ch., U.S.A., 1979-83. Bd. dirs. Chins-Up Colorado Springs, 1983—; chmn. bd. dirs. Pikes Peak Performing Arts Ctr., 1985-92; pres. Pioneers Mus. Found., 1985—; Rep. candidate for Colo. State Chmn., 1992-93. Decorated Legion of Merit with oak leaf cluster, D.F.C., Air medal with 6 oak leaf cluster, Dept. Def. Meritorious Service medal, Vietnam Cross of Gallantry with Palms. Fellow Nat. Assn. Ch. Bus. Adminstrs. (nat. dir., regional v.p., v.p. 1983-85, pres. 1985-87; Ch. Bus. Adminstr. of Yr. award 1983, inducted hall of fame 1995), Colo. Assn. Ch. Bus. Adminstrs. (past pres.), United Meth., Assn. Ch. Bus. Admins. Adminstrs. (nat. sec. 1978-81), Christian Ministries Mgmt. Assn. (dir. 1983-85), USAF Acad. Athletic Assn. Clubs: Colorado Springs Country, Garden of the Gods, Met. (Denver), Winter Night Club. Lodge: Rotary (pres. Downtown Colorado Springs club 1985-86), Order of Daedalians. Home: 3007 Chelton Dr Colorado Springs CO 80909-1008 *Ten words of two letters each, spoken by a black clergyman during the civil rights crusade of the 60s, are my guide to the future: "If it is to be, it is up to me." Only with this in mind can change occur.*

SINCOFF, MICHAEL Z., human resources and marketing professional; b. Washington, D.C., June 28, 1943; s. Murray P. and Anna F. (Jaffe) S. m. Kathleen M. Dunham, Oct. 9, 1983. BA, U. Md., 1964, MA, 1966; PhD, Purdue U., 1969. Instr. U. Tenn., Knoxville, 1968; asst. prof. Ohio U., Athens, 1969-74, dir. Ctr. for Comm. Studies, 1969-76, assoc. prof., 1974-76; vis. prof. U. Minn., St. Paul, 1974; dir. personnel devel. Celanese Corp., N.Y., 1976-79; dir. employee comm. Hoechst-Celanese formerly The Mead Corp., Dayton, Ohio, 1979-81; dir. edn., tng. The Mead Corp., Dayton, Ohio, 1981-83; assoc. dean Sch. of Bus. Adminstrn. Georgetown U., Washington, 1983-84; v.p. human resources ADVO-System, Inc. now ADVO, Inc., Hartford, 1984-87; v.p. human resources, corp. officer DIMAC Direct Inc., St. Louis, 1987-88; sr. v.p. human resources and adminstrn., sr. corp. officer DIMAC Corp. (parent of DIMAC Direct Inc.), St. Louis, 1988—; also sec., asst. treas. DIMAC Corp. (parent of DIMAC Direct, Inc.), St. Louis, 1988—. Author, editor human resources sect. Am. Mgmt. Assn. Mgmt. Handbook, 3d edit., 1994; author approximately 50 books and articles; mem. edtl. adv. bd. Jour. Applied Comm. Rsch., 1991—. Life mem. Internat. Comm. Assn. (bus. mgr.-exec. sec. 1969-73, fin. com. 1982-85); mem. Am. Mgmt. Assn. (human resources coun. 1990—), Direct Mktg. Assn., Printing Industries of Am. (employer resources group 1989—).

SINDELAR, WILLIAM FRANCIS, surgeon, researcher; b. Cleve., Mar. 13, 1945; s. William Frank and Josephine Ann (Storkan) S.; m. Aleta Beth Merkel, May 8, 1982 (div. July 7, 1987). A.B., Western Res. U., 1967; M.A., Case Western Res. U., 1968, Ph.D., 1970, M.D., 1971. Diplomate Am. Bd. Surgery. Instr. Marine Biol. Lab., Woods Hole, Mass., 1966-67; fellow in biology Western Res. U., Cleve., 1966-67; fellow in surgery Johns Hopkins U., Balt., 1971-73; clin. assoc. Nat. Cancer Inst., Bethesda, Md., 1973-75, sr. investigator, 1977—; fellow in surgery U. Md., Balt., 1975-77, cons. in surgery, 1980-91. Contbr. articles to profl. jours., chpts. to books. NSF grantee; NIH grantee; recipient President's Scholar award Western Res. U., 1967, Thwing Throphy Leadership award Western Res. U., 1967, J.D. Lane Research award USPHS Profl. Assn., 1983, Brian Bednarz Lectureship Worcester Meml. Hosp., 1983, Curts Lectureship Dartmouth Med. Sch., 1990. Fellow ACS, Internat. Coll. Surgeons; mem. AAAS, Am. Assn. Cancer Research, Am. Fedn. for Clin. Rsch., Am. Pancreatic Assn., Am. Radium Soc., Am. Soc. Cell Biology, Am. Soc. Clin. Oncology, Am. Soc. for Microbiology, Assn. Acad. Surgery, Assn. Mil. Surgeons of U.S., Commn. Officers Assn. of USPHS, Internat. Assn. Pancreatology, Internat. Hepatobiliary Pancreatic Assn., Internat. Photodynamic Assn., Johns Hopkins Med. and Surg. Assn., N.Y. Acad. Scis., Pancreas Club, Res. Officers Assn. of U.S., Soc. Surgery of Alimentary Tract, Soc. Surg. Oncology, Soc. Univ. Surgeons, Southeastern Surg. Congress, So. Assn. for Oncology, So. Med. Assn., Univ. Md. Surg. Soc., Phi Beta Kappa, Alpha Omega Alpha, Omicron Delta Kappa, Pi Delta Epsilon, Phi Rho Sigma. Republican. Roman Catholic. Home: 8009 York Rd Baltimore MD 21204-7025 Office: NIH Nat Cancer Inst Surgery Br Bethesda MD 20892

SINDEN, HARRY, professional hockey team executive; b. Collins Bay, Ont., Can., Sept. 14, 1932; m. Eleanor Sinden; children: Nancy, Carol, Dawn, Julie. Player Hull-Ottawa Eastern Pro League hockey team; player-coach Kingston team, from 1961; coach numerous teams Central League, until 1967; coach Boston Bruins, Nat. Hockey League team, 1966-70, mng. dir., from 1972, now pres., gen. mgr., alt. gov.; TV hockey commentator, 1970-72; coach Team Can., 1973, Stanley Cup team, 1970. Office: Boston Bruins 150 Causeway St Boston MA 02114-1310

SINDLINGER, VERNE E., bishop. Bishop Lincoln Trails Synod, Indpls. Office: Presbyterian Church USA 1100 W 42nd St Indianapolis IN 46208-3345

SINDONI, ELIO, physics educator; b. Merate, Como, Italy, Nov. 1, 1937; s. Adolfo and Amalia (Tocco) S. Laurea in Physics, U. Milan, 1961, PhD in Nuclear Physics, 1966. Asst. U. Milan, 1961-66, assoc. prof., 1967-90; prof. U. Udine, Italy, 1990-91, prof. gen. physics, 1991—; postdoctoral fellow Princeton (N.J.) U., 1969-70; prof. environ. sci. U. Milan, 1991—; sci. sec. internat. Sch. Plasma Physics, Piero Caldirola, Milan-Varenna, Italy, 1971-84, pres., dir., 1984—; organizer, chmn. various internat. meetings on plasma physics, nuclear fusion and fission, environ. relationships between sci., philosophy, theology, art and ethics. Author: Electromagnetismo I and II, 1976, Il Fuoco. Mem. Italian Phys. Soc., Am. Phys. Soc. Roman Catholic. Avocation: classical music. Home: Via Della Sila 15, 20131 Milan Italy Office: U Milan Dept Physics/Environ Scis, Via L Emanueli 15, 20126 Milan Italy

SINEATH, TIMOTHY WAYNE, library educator, university dean; b. Jacksonville, Fla., May 21, 1940; s. Holcombe Asbury and Christine Marcel (Cook) S.; m. Patricia Ann Greenwood, June 8, 1962; children: Philip Greenwood, Paul Byron. B.A., Fla. State U., 1962, M.S., 1963; Ph.D. (Higher Edn. Act fellow), U. Ill., 1970. Reference librarian U. Ga., 1963-64, catalog librarian, 1964-66; acad. coordinator continuing edn. in library sci. U. Ill., 1966-68; asst. prof. library sci. Simmons Coll., 1970-74, coordinator doctoral program, 1974-77; prof., dean Coll. Libr. Sci. and Info. Sci. U. Ky., Lexington, 1977-87, prof., 1987—; cons. to libraries, schs., chs., industry; mem. Lexington (Ky.) Public Library Bd., 1978—. Author profl. reports; contbr. articles on library and info. sci., gen. info. mgmt., organizational and small group behavior to profl. jours. Mem. ALA, Am. Soc. Info. Sci., Assn. for Libr. and Info. Sci. Edn. (pres. 1993). Episcopalian. Home: 3418 Bay Leaf Dr Lexington KY 40502-3804 Office: U Ky MI King Bldg Lexington KY 40508-1557

SINEGAL, JAMES D., variety store wholesale business executive; b. 1936. With Fed-Mart Corp., 1954-77, exec. v.p.; v.p. Builders Enporium, 1977-78; exec. v.p. Price Co., 1978-79; with Sinegal/Chamberlin & Assocs., 1979-83; pres., chief oper. officer Costco Wholesale Corp., 1983—, chief exec. officer, 1988—, bd. dirs. Office: Costco Wholesale Corp 10809 120th Ave NE Kirkland WA 98033-5024*

SINEX, FRANCIS MAROTT, biochemist, educator; b. Indpls., Jan. 11, 1923; s. Francis Herr and Helen Myrtilla (Marott) S.; m. Virginia Hofer, 1948 (dec.); 1 dau., Katherine; m. Joan S. Martin, May 19, 1951; children—Ellen Jane, Margaret Ann. A.B., DePauw U., 1944; M.A., Ind. U., 1946; Ph.D., Harvard, 1950. Exec. officer biochemistry div., med. dept. Brookhaven Nat. Lab., Upton, N.Y., 1952-57; chmn. dept. biochemistry Boston U. Sch. Medicine, 1957-77; co-dir. Gerontology Center, 1974-77, head bio-med. gerontology sect., 1977—. Pres. Eastern Mass. Alzheimer Disease and Related Disorders Soc., 1980-89. Fellow Gerontol. Soc. (pres. 1969-70); mem. Soc. Biol. Chemists. Home: T8 60 Glen Rd Brookline MA 02146 Office: 80 E Concord St Boston MA 02118-2307

SINFELT, JOHN HENRY, chemist; b. Munson, Pa., Feb. 18, 1931; s. Henry Gustave and June Lillian (McDonald) S.; m. Muriel Jean Vadersen, July 14, 1956; 1 son, Klaus Herbert. B.S., Pa. State U., 1951; Ph.D., U. Ill., 1954, D.Sc. (hon.), 1981. Research engr. Exxon Research Engring. Co., Linden, N.J., 1954-57; sr. research engr. Exxon Research Engring. Co., 1957-62, research assoc., 1962-68, sr. research assoc., 1968-72, sci. advisor, 1972-79, sr. sci. advisor, 1979-96, sr. sci. advisor emeritus, 1996—; vis. prof. chem. engring. U. Minn., 1969; Lacey lectr. Calif. Inst. Tech., 1973; Reilly lectr. U. Notre Dame, 1974; Frontiers in Chemistry lectr. Case Western Res. U., Cleve., 1978; Matthew Van Winkle lectr. U. Tex., 1979; Francois Gault lectr. catalysis Coun. Europe Rsch. Group Catalysis, 1980; Mobay lectr. in chemistry U. Pitts., 1980; disting. vis. lectr. in chemistry, U. Tex., 1981; Robert Welch Found. lectr. Confs. on Chem. Rsch., 1981; Camille and Henry Dreyfus lectr. UCLA, 1982; Edward Clark Lee Meml. lectr. U. Chgo., 1983; Dow disting. lectr. in chemistry Mich. State U., 1984; Arthur D. Little lectr. Northeastern U., 1985; VOllmer W. Fries lectr. Rensselaer Poly. Inst., 1986; disting. lectr. Ctr. Chem. Physics U. Fla., 1988; David M. Mason lectr. Stanford U., 1995, cons. prof. dept. chem. engring., 1996—. Contbr. articles to sci. jours. Recipient Dickson prize Carnegie-Mellon U., 1977, Internat. prize for new materials Am. Phys. Soc., 1978, Nat. medal of Sci., 1979, Perkin medal in chemistry Soc. Chem. Industry, 1984, Disting. Alumnus award Pa. State U., 1985; named to N.J. Inventors Hall of Fame, 1991. Fellow AIChE (Alpha Chi Sigma award 1971, Profl. Progress award 1975), Am. Acad. Arts and Scis., Am. Inst. Chemists (Chem. Pioneer award 1981, Gold medal 1984); mem. NAS (award for indsl. application of sci. 1996), NAE, Am. Chem. Soc. (Carothers lectr. Del. sect. 1982, Petroleum Chemistry award 1976, Murphree award 1986), Catalysis Soc. (Emmett award 1973), Am. Philos. Soc. Methodist. Achievements include introduction and development of concept of bimetallic clusters as catalysts; invention of polymetallic cluster catalysts used commercially in petroleum reforming. Office: Exxon Research Engineering Co Clinton Township Rte 22 E Annandale NJ 08801

SING, ROBERT FONG, physician; b. Camden, N.J., May 29, 1953; s. William Fong and Elizabeth (Maxwell) S.; m. Lauren McNamee, May 11, 1991. BS in Biology, Ursinus Coll., 1975; DO, Coll. Osteo. Medicine, Surgery, 1978. Intern, then resident Met. Hosp., Phila., 1978-80; dir. Emergency Dept. Springfield (Pa.) Hosp., 1984—; dir. sports medicine Sports Sci. Ctr., 1987—; med. dir. Emergency Ambulance Svcs., Inc., 1994-95; owner J. Enright Jewelers, Inc., Swarthmore, Pa., 1995—; owner, pres. Finish Line Sports, Inc., Phila., 1988-94; owner J. Enright Jewelers, Inc. Swarthmore, Pa.; sch. and team physician Springfield Sch. Dist., 1989, Rose Tree-Media (Pa.) Sch. Dist., 1987; chief med. officer Kent Profl. Bicyling Tour of China, 1995, U.S. Olympic Cycling Trials, 1996. Author: Dynamics of the Javelin Throw, 1984. Med. dir. Springfield Ambulance Corp., 1988—. Named to Athletic Hall of Fame, 1985. Fellow Am. Coll. Emergency Physicians, Am. Coll. Sports Medicine, Am. Coll. Osteo. Emergency Physicians. Avocations: track and field, classical music, bicycling. Home: 1274 Gradyville Rd Glen Mills PA 19342-9614 Office: Springfield Hosp 190 W Sproul Rd Springfield PA 19064-2027

SING, WILLIAM BENDER, lawyer; b. Houston, Oct. 16, 1947; s. William Bender Sr. and Alice Irene (Detmers) S.; m. Doris Anne Spradley, Sept. 1, 1967; children: Erin Elaine, Emily Elizabeth. BS cum laude, U. Houston, 1968, JD magna cum laude, 1971. Bar: Tex. 1971. Assoc. Fulbright & Jaworski, LLP, Houston, 1973-80, ptnr., 1980—. Elder, trustee St. Andrew's Presbyn. Ch., Houston; past pres., bd. dirs. St. Andrew's Presbyn. Sch., Houston; past pres. Houston C.C. Place Civic Assn. 1st lt. U.S. Army, 1971-73. Mem. ABA, Tex. Bar Assn., Houston Bar Assn., Order of the Barons Law Honor Soc., Phi Delta Phi, Phi Kappa Phi, Omicron Delta Epsilon. Presbyterian. Avocation: reading history and literature. Office: Fulbright & Jaworski LLP 1301 Mckinney St Houston TX 77010

SINGEL, MARK STEPHEN, state official; b. Johnstown, Pa., Sept. 12, 1953; s. Stephen and Jean Ann (Mertle) S.; m. Jacqueline Lynn Schonek; children: Allyson Jean, Jonathan Albert, Christopher Mark. BA, Pa. State U., 1974, postgrad., 1975; postgrad., George Washington U., 1979. Legis. intern Pa. Ho. of Reps., 1972-73; legis. asst. to U.S. Rep. Helen S. Meyner, 1975; adminstrv. asst. to U.S. Rep. Helen S. Mayner, 1976-79, to U.S. Rep. Peter A. Peyser, 1979; U.S. senator from Pa., 1980-87; lt. gov. State of Pa., 1987—, acting gov., 1993; Chmn. Pa. Energy Office, Pa. Emergency Mgmt. Coun., Pa. Heritage Affairs Commn.; mem. Pa. Econ. Devel. Partnership Bd.; trustee Pa. State U.; mem. Nat. Gov.'s Task Force on Hazardous Materials; mem. adv. bd. U. Pitts.-Johnstown, Indiana U. of Pa.; bd. dirs. Johnstown Flood Mus. Recipient Man of Yr. award Archdiocese of Pitts. Byzantine Rite, 1982, Community Achievement award Johnstown Lodge 214 Order Italian Sons and Daughters Am., 1986, Disting. Svc. award Pa. Industries for Blind and Handicapped, 1988, Humanitarian award Chapel of Four Chaplains, Valley Forge, 1990. Mem. adv. bd. U. Pitts.-Johnstown, Indiana U. of Pa.; bd. dirs. Johnstown Flood Mus. Recipient Man of Yr. award Archdiocese of Pitts. Byzantine Rite, 1982. Mem. Cambria County Young Dems., Travelers Protective Assn., Johnstown Sportsmen's Assn., Greek Catholic Union, Elks, Pi Kappa Phi (alumni bd. dirs.), Phi Kappa Phi, Omciron Delta Kappa. Democrat. Office: Office of Lt Gov 200 Main Capitol Building Harrisburg PA 17120-0022*

SINGER, ALLEN MORRIS, lawyer; b. Mpls., Dec. 30, 1923; s. William and Ida (Simenstein) S. JD, U. Chgo., 1948; LLM, Harvard U., 1958. Bar: Ill. 1948, Calif. 1949. Sole practice, 1950-55, 59—; v.p., sec., gen. counsel Am. Bldg. Maintenance Industries, San Francisco, 1969-85; assoc. prof. law U. Oreg., 1955-59; lectr. law Stanford, 1960-62; of counsel Cooper, White & Cooper, San Francisco, 1970—. Contbr. articles to profl. jours. Mem. U. Chgo. Nat. Alumni Cabinet, 1978-80. Served as 2d lt., USAAF, 1943-45. Mem. ABA, San Francisco Bar Assn., Calif. Bar Assn., Am. Arbitration Assn. (nat. panel of arbitrators). Home: 1070 Green St Apt 703 San Francisco CA 94133-3677 Office: Cooper White & Cooper 201 California St Fl 17 San Francisco CA 94111-5019

SINGER, ARMAND EDWARDS, foreign language educator; b. Detroit, Nov. 30, 1914; s. Elvin Satori Singer and Fredericka Elizabeth (Edwards) Singer Goetz; m. Mary Rebecca White, Aug. 8, 1940; 1 child, Fredericka Ann Hill. A.B., Amherst Coll., 1935; M.A., Duke U., 1939, Ph.D., 1944; diploma, U. Paris, 1939; postgrad., Ind. U., summer 1964. Teaching fellow in sci. Amherst Coll., 1935-36; instr. French and Spanish, part-time Duke, 1938-40; teaching fellow Romance langs. W.Va. U., Morgantown, 1940-41, instr., 1941-47, asst. prof., 1947-55, assoc. prof., 1955-60, prof., 1960-80, prof. emeritus, 1980—, chmn. program for humanities, 1963-72, chmn. dept. integrated studies, 1963, acting chmn. dept. religion and program for humanities, 1973, dir. ann. colloquium on modern lit., 1976-80, 85-86, 96. Author: A Bibliography of the Don Juan Theme: Versions and Criticism, 1954, The Don Juan Theme, Versions and Criticism: An Annotated Bibliography, 1965, Paul Bourget, 1975, The Don Juan Theme: A Bibliography of Versions, Analogues, Uses, and Adaptations, 1993, The Armand E. Singer Tibet, 1809-1975, 1995, (with J.F. Stasny) Anthology of Readings: Humanities I, 1966, Anthology of Readings: Humanities II, 1967; editor: (with Jürgen E. Schlunk) Martin Walser: International Perspectives, 1987; editor W.Va. U. Philol. Papers, 1948-50, 53-55, editor-in-chief, 1951-52, 55—, 1001 Horny Limericks by Ward Marden, 1996; editor, contbr. Essays on the Literature of Mountaineering, 1982; contbr. numerous articles to profl. and philatelic jours. Bd. dirs. Community Concert Assn., Morgantown, 1959-60, Humanities Found. W.Va., 1981-87. Recipient 4th Ann. Humanities award W.Va. Humanities Coun., 1990. Mem. MLA (internat. bibliography com. 1956-59, nat. del. assembly 1975-78), So. Atlantic MLA (exec. com. 1971-74), Am. Assn. Tchrs. Spanish and Portuguese, Am. Philatelic Soc., Nepal and Tibet Philatelic Study Circle, Nepal Philatelic Soc., Collectors Club of N.Y., Phi Beta Kappa. Republican. Home: 248 Grandview Ave Morgantown WV 26505-6925 *In an age of deteriorating standards, I want to be counted among those educators who stand against the tide. We ask too little of others, we ask too little of ourselves; others ask too little of us. When we constantly encounter shoddy construction, shoddy merchandise, shoddy performances, shoddy ethics, shoddy education, we may be tempted to forswear our standards. But through our hands pass tomorrow's leaders. As teachers we must help stop this erosion of our national pride. If we fail, make no mistake: it could well destroy us all.*

SINGER, ARTHUR LOUIS, JR., foundation executive; b. Scranton, Pa., Feb. 14, 1929; s. Arthur and Isabel S.; m. Joan Cristal, July 26, 1952; children—Arthur, Philip, Charles. A.B., Williams Coll., 1950; M.B.A., U. Mich., 1952. Adminstr. Mass. Inst. Tech., 1955-63; exec. asso. (Carnegie Corp.), N.Y.C., 1963-66; pres. Edn. Devel. Center, Newton, Mass., 1966-68; v.p. Alfred P. Sloan Found., N.Y.C., 1968-94, cons., 1994—. Served to lt. (j.g.) USNR, 1952-55. Home: 23 Owenoke Park Westport CT 06880-6834 Office: 630 5th Ave Ste 2550 New York NY 10111-0001

SINGER, CECILE DORIS, state legislator. BA, Queens Coll. Past rep. Spl. Svcs. for Children, N.Y.C.; past exec. dir. N.Y. State Assembly Social Svcs. and Judiciary Coms., Joint Legis. Com. on Corps., Authorities and Commns.; past pub. rep. Yonkers (N.Y.) Emergency Control Bd.; past coord. Westchester County Assembly Dels.; past chief of staff for dep. minority leader; mem. N.Y. State Assembly, Albany, 1988—, leadership sec. Rep. Conf., mem. assembly children & families com., mem. various other coms.; bd. dirs. Hudson Valley Bank; past rep. Temp. Commn. to Revise Social Svcs. Law; mem. Presdl. Commn. on Privacy Conf., N.Y. State Senate Transp. Conf.; mem. task force on substance abuse Am. Legis. Exch. Coun., task force on econ. devel., crime victims' rights, hosp. crisis, women's issues, com. on mass transit; sec. Rep. Conf. Nat. Adv. Panel Child Care Action Campaign; dir. Hudson Valley Bank; chmn. Westchester County Commn. on Pub. Financing of Campaigns; chmn. Lower Hudson Valley Adv. Com. N.Y. State Divsn. for Women. Mem. adv. bd. Legal Awareness for Women, Big Bros. and Big Sisters, Westchester C.C. Found., Westchester 2000 Rsch., Womens Adv. Bd. Westchester County; mem. task force on certiorari Westchester County Sch. Bds. Assn.; sch. and cmty. chmn. Yonkers PTA; bd. dirs. Yonkers Gen. Hosp., Yonkers chpt. United Jewish Appeal. Recipient Jenkins Meml. award, Nat. PTA award; inducted Women's Hall of Fame, 1996, Sr. Citizens Hall of Fame, 1996. Mem. Mental Health Assn. (bd. dirs., mem. nominating and pub. affairs coms. Westchester County chpt.), Rotary. Home: 117 Cliffside Dr Yonkers NY 10710-3144 Office: 21 Scarsdale Rd Yonkers NY 10707

SINGER, CRAIG, broker, consultant, investor; b. N.Y.C., Aug. 13, 1947; s. Albert and Dorothy (Blackman) S.; m. Ellen Rappaport, Aug. 31, 1969; children: Chad Adam, Cara Danielle. BS, Cornell U., 1969; JD, Columbia U., 1972. Bar: N.Y. 1973. Exec. Continental Wingate Co., Inc., N.Y.C., 1972-74; exec. v.p. Integrated Resources, Inc., N.Y.C., 1974-87; chmn. bd. Integrated Resources Housing Corp., Integrated Funding, Inc., Resources Funding Corp., AIM Capital Mgmt. Corp., 1983-87; cons., investor, broker, Bedford Corners, N.Y., 1988—; pres. Westminster Fin. Group, Inc., 1989—. Former dir. Assn. Govt. Assisted Housing, Inc., 1976-84; former mem. exec. com. Coalition for Low and Moderate Income Housing; former mem. edn. adv. bd. Bur. Nat. Affairs Housing and Devel. Reporter. Home and Office: 148 Meeting House Rd RFD 4 Bedford Corners NY 10549

SINGER, DANIEL MORRIS, lawyer; b. Bklyn., Oct. 10, 1930; s. Samuel W. and Fannie G. (Sabloff) S.; m. Maxine Frank, June 15, 1952; children: Amy E., Ellen R., David B., Stephanie F. BA with honors, Swarthmore Coll., 1951; LLB, Yale U., 1954. Bar: N.Y. 1956, U.S. Dist. Ct. D.C. 1957, U.S. Ct. Appeals (D.C. cir.) 1957, U.S. Supreme Ct., 1959. Motions clk. U.S. Ct. Appeals D.C. Cir., 1956-57, law clk. to Judge George T. Washington, 1957-58; assoc. Fried, Frank, Harris, Shriver & Jacobson, Washington, 1958-64, ptnr., 1965-87, counsel, 1987—; arbitrator complex comml. case and constrn. nat. panels; mediator US Dist. Ct., Washington; vol. atty. Lawyers Com. for Civil Rights Under Law, 1965, 66; mem. exec. com. Washington Lawyers Com. for Civil Rights Under Law, 1973—; bd. mgrs. Swarthmore Coll., 1987-91. Bd. dirs., sec.-treas. Nat. Com. Tithing in Investment, 1964-65; dir. sec.-treas. Council for a Livable World, 1962-64; mem. gov. council, exec. com. Am. Jewish Congress, 1986—, v.p. 1988-92; dir. Am. Soc. for the Protection of Nature in Israel, 1986—. With Signal Corps, U.S. Army, 1954-56. Mem. ABA, D.C. Bar. Home: 5410 39th St NW Washington DC 20015-2902 Office: Fried Frank Harris Shriver 1001 Pennsylvania Ave NW Ste 800 Washington DC 20004-2505

SINGER, DAVID MICHAEL, marketing and public relations company executive; b. Bklyn., N.Y., Feb. 11, 1957; s. Seymour Allena and Ellen Sybil (Pavnick) S.; m. Panela Rae Silton, July 20, 1986; 1 child, Max!. BA in History, NYU, 1978; MA in Communications, Syracuse U., 1979; MA in Media, New Sch. Social Research, 1983; JD, Yeshiva U., 1981. Cons. pub. rels. Burson-Marsteller, N.Y.C., 1979-81, The Haas Group, N.Y.C., 1981-84, Braff & Co., N.Y.C., 1987-89; pub., editor-in-chief Lodestone Pub., N.Y.C., 1984-87; chief oper. officer Pentagon Ltd., N.Y.C., 1989-91; v.p. pub. rels. Braff & Co., N.Y.C., 1991-92; v.p. G.S. Schwartz & Co., N.Y.C., 1993—; lectr. evening div. NYU, 1982—; dir. media rels. Braff & Co. Contbr. articles and poems to profl. and consumer jours. and mags. Pres. Jewish Cultural Found., N.Y.C., 1976. Named Mem. of Yr., N.Y. State Kiwanis, 1976, Outstanding Young Man of Am., Jaycees, 1977; recipient Cert. Recognition Am. Film Inst., 1982, ANDY Design award Advt. Club N.Y., 1983, Proclamation Bklyn. Borough Pres., 1987. Mem. Alpha Epsilon Pi (Bro. of Yr. 1976). Avocations: baseball, politics, ping-pong, films, theater.

SINGER, DONALD IVAN, architect; b. Trenton, N.J., Feb. 20, 1938; s. Harold William and Beatrice (Lavine) S.; m. Elaine Ruth Segall, Aug. 23, 1959; children: Lauren Elizabeth, Susan Meredith. BArch, U. Fla., 1960; MS in Architecture, Columbia U., 1961. Registered architect, Fla. Draftsman Charles Reed, Jr. Architect, Hollywood, Fla., 1961-62; pvt. practice architecture Ft. Lauderdale, 1964—; mem. design adv. bd. Formica Corp., N.Y.C., 1977-82, design critique com. Dade County Aviation Authority, Miami, Fla., 1987-89. Prin. works include office bldg. R.J. Pavlik Corp. Hdqrs., 1980 (honor award Fla. Assn. AIA 1981), City Pk. Urban Pla. and Garage, Ft. Lauderdale, Fla., 1982 (honor award Fla. Assn. AIA 1983), office bldg. Fire Prevention Bur., 1987 (honor award Fla. Assn. AIA 1987), prototype sch. Forest Glen Middle Sch., 1989 (Fla. Concrete Assn. award 1990). Pres. Downtown Coun., Ft. Lauderdale, 1980-81; trustee Mus. Art, Ft. Lauderdale, 1980-85; vice chmn. Riverwalk Com., Ft. Lauderdale, 1989-91; chmn. Art-in-Pub. Places Com., Broward County, Fla., 1990-91; chmn. Design Broward, 1994-95. With USAF, 1961-62. Recipient Morretti award Broward Cultural Affairs Coun., 1983, Leadership award, 1995, Disting. Alumni award U. Fla. Sch. Architecture, 1991. Fellow AIA; mem. Fla. Assn. AIA (honor award for design 1984, chmn. conf. com. 1986-87, chmn. design awards com. 1988-89). Republican. Jewish. Avocation: photography. Office: 13 W Las Olas Blvd Fort Lauderdale FL 33301-1823 *We all wish for those moments during which our thoughts focus to a unity and we know something complete and of total simplicity. Architecture has the potential to afford those moments.*

SINGER, ELEANOR, sociologist, editor; b. Vienna, Austria, Mar. 4, 1930; came to U.S., 1938; d. Alfons and Anna (Troedl) Schwarzbart; m. Alan Gerard Singer, Sept. 8, 1949; children: Emily Ann, Lawrence Alexander. BA, Queens Coll., 1951; PhD, Columbia U., 1966. Asst. editor Am.

Scholar, Williamsburg, Va., 1951-52; editor Tchrs. Coll. Press, N.Y.C., 1952-56, Dryden-Holt, N.Y.C., 1956-57; rsch. assoc., sr. rsch. assoc., sr. rsch. scholar Columbia U., N.Y.C., 1966-94; rsch. scientist Inst. for Social Rsch. U. Mich., Ann Arbor, 1994—; editor Pub. Opinion Quar., N.Y.C., 1975-86. Author: (with Carol Weiss) The Reporting of Social Science in the Mass Media, 1988, (with Phyllis Endreny) Reporting On Risk, 1993; editor: (with Herbert H. Hyman) Readings in Reference Group Theory and Research, 1968, (with Stanley Presser) Survey Research Methods: A Reader, 1989; contbr. articles to profl. jours. Mem. Am. Assn. Pub. Opinion Research (pres. N.Y.C. chpt. 1983-84, pres. 1987-88), Am. Sociol. Assn., Am. Statis. Assn. Office: U Mich Inst Social Rsch Box 1248 Ann Arbor MI 48106

SINGER, FREDERICK RAPHAEL, medical researcher, educator; b. St. Louis, June 27, 1939; s. Meyer and Lee (Minkle) S.; m. Sandra Joy Barnes, Aug. 16, 1964; children: Stefanie, Jeffrey. Student UCLA, 1956-59; BS, U. Calif.-Berkeley, 1960; MD, U. Calif.-San Francisco, 1963. Diplomate Am. Bd. Internal Medicine, Am. Bd. Endocrinology and Metabolism. Intern UCLA Affiliated Hosp., 1963-64; resident VA Hosp., Los Angeles, 1964-65, 68-69; instr. in medicine Harvard U., Boston, 1971-72; asst. prof. medicine UCLA, 1972-73; asst. prof. medicine U. So. Calif., L.A., 1973-74, assoc. prof., 1974-78, prof., 1978-89, prof. orthopaedic surgery, 1980-89; dir. Bone Ctr. Cedars-Sinai Med. Ctr., L.A., 1989-92; prof. medicine, UCLA, 1989-92, clin. prof. medicine, 1993—; dir. Osteoporosis/Metabolic Bone Disease program St. Johns Hosp. and Health Ctr., Santa Monica, 1992—; dir. Skeletal Biology Lab, John Wayne Cancer Inst., Santa Monica, 1992—; mem. endocrine and metabolic drug adv. com. FDA, USPHS, Bethesda, Md., 1983-87. Author: Paget's Disease of Bone, 1977. Contbr. numerous articles, revs. to profl. jours. Vice chmn. community adv. com. Univ. High Sch., L.A., 1984. Served as capt. USAF, 1965-67. Calif. State scholar, 1956-60; clin. investigator VA, 1971-73. Mem. Endocrine Soc., Am. Soc. Clin. Investigation, Am. Soc. Bone and Mineral Research (chmn. pub. affairs 1981-86, coun. 1987, pres.-elect 1989, pres. 1990), Paget's Disease Found. (chmn. bd. dirs. 1990—). Office: John Wayne Cancer Inst 2200 Santa Monica Blvd Santa Monica CA 90404-2301

SINGER, GARY JAMES, lawyer; b. L.A., Oct. 8, 1952; s. Stanley Merle and Ernestine Alice (Brandstatter) S.; m. Melanie Carol Rabin, Mar. 19, 1978; children: Brian, Kimberly, Andrew. BA, U. Calif., Irvine, 1974; JD, Loyola U., 1977. Bar: Calif. 1977, U.S. Dist. Ct. (fed. dist.) 1978. Assoc. O'Melveny & Myers, L.A., Newport Beach, Calif., 1977-84; ptnr. O'Melveny & Myers, 1985—; bd. dirs. Irvine Barclay Theatre. Avocations: golf, skiing, reading. Office: O'Melveny & Myers 610 Newport Ctr Dr Ste 1700 Newport Beach CA 92660-6419

SINGER, GERALD MICHAEL, lawyer, educator, author, arbitrator and mediator; b. Mpls., Sept. 9, 1920; s. Charles and Rachael Caroline (Feldman) S.; m. Lillian Kaplan, July 10, 1944; children: Barbara Ellen, Alan Mark. JD, Loyola U., L.A., 1968. Bar: Calif. 1969, U.S. Dist. Ct. Calif. (so dist.) 1969, U.S. Ct. Appeals (9th cir.) 1969, U.S. Supreme Ct. 1972. Pres. Bigg of Calif., Inc., 1948-69; pvt. practice, Encino, Calif., 1969—; adj. prof. law Loyola U., 1975-85, 92; judge pro tem Calif. Superior Ct., 1973—, arbitrator, 1976—; judge pro tem Calif. Mcpl. Ct., 1973—; arbitrator, mediator, 1988—; sr. panel mem. AAA Comml. Arbitrators, L.A., Internat. Arbitration World Ct., The Hague; lectr. to various law schs., bar assns. and legal groups, 1976—. Author: How To Go Directly Into Solo Law Practice (Without Missing a Meal), 1976, rev. edit. as How To Go Directly Into Your Own Computerized Solo Law Practice Without Missing a Meal (Or a Byte), 1986, updated, 1989, rev. edit. as How To Go Directly Into, and Manage, Your Own Solo Law Practice (Without Missing a Meal), 1993, 100 page supplement, 1994. Mem. Com. To Elect Ricard Nixon, Com. to Reelect Richard Nixon, Com. to Elect and Reelect Ronald Reagan, L.A. Staff sgt. Signal Corps, U.S. Army and USAAF, 1942-46. Mem. Am. Arbitration Assn. (arbitrator 1973—). Republican. Avocations: golf, sailing, horseback riding, photography, videography. Office: NPO 271 Box 555 38-180 Del Webb Blvd Palm Desert CA 92211

SINGER, HENRY A., behavioral scientist, institute director; b. Mt. Vernon, N.Y., Apr. 13, 1919; s. A.D. and Evelyn (Zierler) S.; m. Rosina Scimonelli, Jan. 7, 1944 (dec. Jan. 1991); children: Victoria, David Anthony. BS, Columbia U., 1942; MA, NYU, 1947, PhD (Rockefeller fellow 1947-48), 1950, PhD, 1973. Instr. Human Rels. Ctr. NYU, 1948-50; assoc. prof. SUNY, Fredonia, 1950-51; adviser U.S. Mission to Philippines, 1951-54; cons. Conn. Edn. Assn., 1954-56; dir. edn. Hilton Hotel Corp., 1956-58; cons. Conn. Assn. Mental Health, 1958-59; dir. edn. Remington Rand div. Sperry Rand, 1959-62; exec. dir. Soc. Advancement Mgmt., 1963-66; higher edn. officer CUNY, 1966-68; exec. dir. Human Resources Inst. Inc., Westport, Conn., 1969—; with Diebold Inst. Pub. Policy Studies, N.Y.C., 1981-87; exec. asst. Am. Nobel Com., N.Y.C., Conn., 1947-50, vice chmn., 1981-66, exec. officer, 1986-92, hon. chair, 1992—; vis. prof. Cornell U., 1949-83, U. Philippines, 1952-53, NYU, 1960-62, CUNY, 1962-63, Columbia U., 1963-64, Western Conn. U., 1964-70, U. Tehran, 1975, 77, Empire State Coll., SUNY, 1981; vis. prin. lectr. Hong Kong Poly., 1976-78, U. Hong Kong, 1992; sr. dir. Experience Compression Lab., Barnum Internat., 1960-93. Editor: Connecticut Teacher, 1954-56, Connecticut Mental Health News, 1958-59, Advanced Management, 1959-66; Contbr. articles to U.S. and internat. publs. vis. expert AID mission, Spain, 1962, Internat. Human Resources, Tehran, Iran, 1965, 75, 77; assoc. dir. engring. mgmt. workshops Columbia U., 1963-66; vis. lectr. Asian Inst. for Mgmt., 1977; bd. dirs. Conn. Assn. Mental Health, 1960-62, Mohonk Home for Boys, Westport, Conn., 1981—, NYU Alumni Coun., 1990—. Recipient award Council Internat. Progress in Mgmt., 1963; Rockefeller fellow, 1948-49. Fellow Am. Soc. Applied Anthropology, Hong Kong Psych. Soc., Internat. Acad. Counseling and Psychotherapy; Mem. APA (life). Clubs: Overseas Press (gov.), Columbia U., Princeton (N.Y.C.); Fgn. Corres. (Hong Kong). Home: 1617 Bayhouse Ct Apt 219 Sarasota FL 34231-6728 Office: One Morningside Dr N Westport CT 06880-5051 *Perhaps life teaches us that relating successfully to others is the one sure road to survival in an increasingly crowded environment. One measurement of this successful human relationship is the degree to which one human being is able to inconvenience himself for another.*

SINGER, IRVING, philosophy educator; b. N.Y.C., Dec. 24, 1925; s. Isidore and Nettie (Stromer) S.; m. Josephine Fisk, June 10, 1949; children—Anne, Margaret, Emily, Benjamin. AB summa cum laude, Harvard U., 1948, MA, 1949, PhD, 1952. Instr. philosophy Cornell U., 1953-56; asst. prof. U. Mich., 1956-59; vis. lectr. Johns Hopkins U., 1957-58; mem. faculty M.I.T., 1958—, prof. philosophy, 1969—. Author: Santayana's Aesthetics, 1957, The Nature of Love: Plato to Luther, 1966, rev. edit., 1984, The Goals of Human Sexuality, 1973, Mozart and Beethoven, 1977, The Nature of Love: Courtly and Romantic, 1984, The Nature of Love: The Modern World, 1987, Meaning in Life: The Creation of Value, 1992, The Pursuit of Love, 1994. Served with AUS, 1944-46. Fellow Guggenheim Found., 1965, Rockefeller Found., 1970, Bollingen Found., 1966; grantee Am. Council Learned Socs., 1966; Fulbright fellow, 1955. Mem. Am. Philos. Assn., Am. Soc. Aesthetics. Office: MIT Rm 20E210A Cambridge MA 02139

SINGER, JOEL DAVID, political science educator; b. Bklyn., Dec. 7, 1925; s. Morris L. and Anne (Newman) S.; m. C. Diane Macaulay, Apr., 1990; children: Kathryn Louise, Eleanor Anne. BA, Duke U., 1946; LLD (hon.), Northwestern U., 1983; PhD, NYU, 1956. Instr. NYU, 1954-55, Vassar Coll., 1955-57; vis. fellow social relations Harvard U., 1957-58; vis. asst. prof. U. Mich., Ann Arbor, 1958-60; sr. scientist Mental Health Research Inst. U. Mich., 1960-82, assoc. prof., 1964-65, prof. polit. sci., 1965—, coordinator World Politics Program, 1969-75, 81-90; vis. prof. U. Oslo and Inst. Social Research, 1963-64, 90, Carnegie Endowment Internat. Peace and Grd. Inst. Internat. Studies, Geneva, 1967-68, Zuma and U. Mannheim (W. Ger.), 1976, Grad. Inst. Internat. Studies, Geneva, 1983-84; cons. in field; U. Groningen, The Netherlands, 1991. Author: Financing International Organization: The United Nations Budget Process, 1961, Deterrence, Arms Control and Disarmament: Toward a Synthesis in National Security Policy, 1962, rev. 1984, (with Melvin Small) The Wages of War, 1816-1965: A Statistical Handbook, 1972, (with Susan Jones) Beyond Conjecture in International Politics: Abstracts of Data Based Research, 1972, (with Dorothy La Barr) The Study of International Politics: A Guide to Sources for the Student, Teacher and Researcher, 1976, Correlates of War I and II, 1979, 80, (with Melvin Small) Resort to Arms: International and Civil War, 1816-1980, 1982, Models, Methods, and Progress: A Peace Research Odyssey, 1990, (with Paul Diehl) Measuring the Correlates of War; monographs; contbr. articles to profl. jours.; mem. editorial bd. ABC: Polit. Sci. and Govt., 1968-84, Polit. Sci. Reviewer, 1971—, Conflict Mgmt. and Peace Sci., 1978—, Etudes Polemologigues, 1978—, Internat. Studies Quar., 1989—, Jour. Conflict Resolution, 1989—, Internat. Interactions, 1989—. With USNR, 1943-66. Ford fellow, 1956; Ford grantee, 1957-58; Phoenix Meml. Fund grantee, 1959,, 1981-82; Fulbright scholar, 1963-64; Carnegie Corp. research grantee, 1963-67; NSF grantee, 1967-76, 1986-89, 1992-94; Guggenheim grantee, 1978-79. Mem. Am. Polit. Sci. Assn. (Helen Dwight Reid award com. 1967, 95, chmn. Woodrow Wilson award com., chmn. nominating com. 1970), Internat. Polit. Sci. Assn. (chmn. conflict and peace rsch. com. 1974—), World Assn. Internat. Rels., Internat. Soc. Polit. Psychology, Internat. Soc. Rsch. on Aggression, Social Sci. History Assn., Peace Sci. Soc., Internat. Peace Rsch. Assn. (pres. 1972-73), Consortium on Peace Rsch., Edn. and Devel., AAAS, Fedn. Am. Scientists (nat. coun. 1991-95), Union Concerned Scientists, Arms Control Assn., Internat. Studies Assn. (pres. 1985-86), Com. Nat. Security, Am. Com. on East-West Accord, World Federalist Assn. Office: U Mich Dept Polit Sci Ann Arbor MI 48109 *As a researcher, teacher, consultant and activist, my goal has been to bring rigorous scientific methods to bear on the causes of war question, and to encourage the integration of ethical concern and hard evidence.*

SINGER, KURT DEUTSCH, news commentator, author, publisher; b. Vienna, Austria, Aug. 10, 1911; came to U.S., 1940, naturalized, 1951; s. Ignaz Deutsch and Irene (Singer) S.; m. Hilda Tradelius, Dec. 23, 1932 (div. 1954); children: Marian Alice Birgit, Kenneth Walt; m. Jane Sherrod, Apr. 9, 1955 (dec. Jan. 1985); m. Katherine Han, Apr. 8, 1989. Student, U. Zürich, Switzerland, 1930, Labor Coll., Stockholm, Sweden, 1936; Ph.D., Div. Coll. Metaphysics, Indpls., 1951. Escaped to Sweden, 1934; founder Ossietzky Com. (successful in release Ossietzky from concentration camp); corr. Swedish mag. Folket i Bild, 1935-40; founder Niemöller Com.; pub. biography Göring in Eng. (confiscated in Sweden), 1940; co-founder pro-Allied newspaper Trots Allt, 1939; corr. Swedish newspapers in, U.S., 1940; editor News Background, 1942; lectr. U. Minn., U. Kans., U. Wis., 1945-49; radio commentator WKAT, 1950; corr. N.Am. Newspaper Alliance, N.Y.C., 1953—; pres. Singer Media Corp., 1987—; dir. Oceanic Press Service, San Clemente, Calif. Author, editor: underground weekly Mitteilungsblätter, Berlin, Germany, 1933; author: The Coming War, 1934, (biog.) Carl von Ossietzky, 1936 (Nobel Peace prize), Germany's Secret Service in Central America, 1943, Spies and Saboteurs in Argentina, 1943, Duel for the Northland, 1943, White Book of the Church of Norway, 1944, Spies and Traitors of World War II, 1945, Who are the Communists in America, 1948, 3000 Years of Espionage, 1951, World's Greatest Women Spies, 1952, Kippie the Cow; juvenile, 1952, Gentlemen Spies, 1953, The Man in the Trojan Horse, 1954, World's Best Spy Stories, 1954, Charles Laughton Story; adapted TV, motion pictures, 1954, Spy Stories and Asia, 1955, More Spy Stories, 1955, My Greatest Crime Story, 1956, My Most Famous Case, 1957, The Danny Kaye Saga; My Strangest Case, 1958, Spy Omnibus, 1959, Spies for Democracy, 1960, Crime Omnibus Spies Who Changed History, 1961, Hemmingway-Life and Death of a Giant, 1961, True Adventures in Crime, Dr. Albert Schweitzer, Medical Missionary, 1962, Lyndon Baines Johnson-Man of Reason, 1964, Ho-i-man; juveniles, 1965; Kurt Singer's Ghost Omnibus, 1965; juvenile Kurt Singer's Horror Omnibus; The World's Greatest Stories of the Occult, The Unearthly, 1965, Mata Hari-Goddess of Sin, 1965, Lyndon Johnson-From Kennedy to Vietnam, 1966, Weird Tales Anthology, 1966, I Can't Sleep at Night, 1966, Weird Tales of Supernatural, 1967, Tales of Terror, 1967, Famous Short Stories, 1967, Folktales of the South Pacific, 1967, Tales of The Uncanny, 1968, Gothic Reader, 1968, Bloch and Bradbury, 1969, Folktales of Mexico, 1969, Tales of the Unknown, 1970, The House in the Valley, 1970, Hablan Los Artistas, 1970, Tales of the Macabre, 1971, Three Thousand Years of Espionage, 1971, El Mundo de Hoy, 1971, Cuentos Fantasticos del Mas, 1971, Aldous Huxley, El Camino al Infierno, 1971, Ghouls and Ghosts, 1972, The Unearthly, 1972, The Gothic Reader, 1972, Satanic Omnibus, 1973, The Plague of the Living Dead, 1973, Gothic Horror Omnibus, 1974, Dictionary of Household Hints and Help, 1974, Supernatural, 1974, They are Possessed, 1976, True Adventures into the Unknown, 1980, I Spied-And Survived, 1980, Great Adventures in Crime, 1982, The Oblong Box, 1982, Shriek, 1984, First Target Book of Horror, 1984, 2d, 1984, 3d, 1985, 4th, 1985, Solve A Crime, 1994, The Ultimate Quiz Book, 1994, The Complete Guide to Career Advancement, 1994, The Sex Quiz Book, 1994, The Marriage Quiz Book, The Psychology Quiz Book, The Teenage Quiz Book, Success Secrets, 1995, Conozcase Mejor y Triunfe, 1995, The Joy of Practical Parenting, 1995; editor: UN Calendar, 1959-58; contbr. articles to newspapers, popular mags., U.S., fgn. countries, all his books and papers in Boston U. Library-Spl. Collections. Mem. UN Speakers Research Com., UN Children's Emergency Fund, Menninger Found. Mem. Nat. Geog. Soc., Smithsonian Assos., Internat. Platform Assn. (v.p.), United Sch. Assemblies (pres.). Address: Singer Media Corp Seaview Business Pk 1030 Calle Cordillera # 106 San Clemente CA 92673-6234 *In the sunset years of my life, I feel stronger than ever that the most important contribution one makes in a lifetime is to plant as many seeds as possible with many people, and perhaps many countries. Who knows where the seeds of ideas survive and expand?.*

SINGER, MARCUS GEORGE, philosopher, educator; b. N.Y.C., Jan. 4, 1926; s. David Emanuel and Esther (Kobre) S.; m. Blanche Ladenson, Aug. 10, 1947; children: Karen Beth, Debra Ann. A.B., U. Ill., 1948; Ph.D. (Susan Linn Sage fellow), Cornell U., 1952. Asst. in philosophy Cornell U., Ithaca, N.Y., 1948-49; instr. philosophy Cornell U., 1951-52; instr. philosophy U. Wis.-Madison, 1952-55, asst. prof., 1955-59, assoc. prof., 1959-63, prof. philosophy, 1963-92, prof. emeritus, 1992—, chmn. dept. philosophy, 1963-68; chmn. philosophy dept. U. Wis. Center System, 1964-66; dir. pub. lectr. series Royal Inst. Philosophy, London, 1984-85; vis. fellow Birkbeck Coll., U. London, 1962-63; research assoc. U. Calif.-Berkeley, 1969; vis. Cowling prof. philosophy Carleton Coll., Northfield, Minn., 1972; vis. prof. humanities U. Fla., Gainesville, 1975; vis. fellow U. Warwick, 1977, 84-85; vis. Francis M. Bernardin disting. prof. humanities U. Mo., Kansas City, 1979; hon. research fellow Birkbeck Coll., U. London, 1984-85; acad. visitor London Sch. Econs., U. London, 1984-85. Author: Generalization in Ethics, 2d edit., 1971, Verallgemeinerung in der Ethik, 1975; editor: Morals and Values, 1977, American Philosophy, 1986, Reason, Reality, and Speculative Philosophy, 1996; contbr. Essays in Moral Philosophy, 1958, Ency. of Philosophy, 1967, Law and Philosophy, 1970, Skepticism and Moral Principles, 1973, Morals and Values, 1977, Acad. Am. Ency., 1982, 84, 89, World Book Ency., 1984, 86, Gewirth's Ethical Rationalism, 1984, Morality and Universality, 1985, American Philosophy, 1986, New Directions in Ethics, 1986, The Handbook of Western Philosophy, 1988, Applying Philosophy, 1988, Moral Philosophy: Historical and Contemporary Essays, 1989, Key Themes in Philosophy, 1990, Essays on Henry Sidgwick, 1992, Ency. of Ethics, 1992, A History of Western Ethics, 1992, Ethics, 1993, Cambridge Dictionary of Philosophy, 1995, Biographical Dictionary of Twentieth Century Philosophers, 1996; co-editor: Introductory Readings in Philosophy, 2d edit., 1974, Reason and the Common Good, 1963, Belief, Knowledge and Truth, 1970, Legislative Intent and other Essays on Law, Politics and Morality, 1993. Served with USAAF, 1944-45. Am. Philos. Assn. Western Div. fellow, 1956-57; Summer Research grant Social Sci. Research Council, 1958; Guggenheim fellow, 1962-63; Inst. for Research in Humanities fellow U. Wis., 1984. Mem. Am. Philos. Assn. (v.p. Western divsn. 1984-85, pres. Ctrl. divsn. 1985-86, bd. officers 1991-94), Royal Inst. Philosophy, AAUP, Aristotelian Soc., Mind Assn., Wis. Acad. Scis., Arts and Letters, Sidgwick Soc. (exec. dir.), Phi Beta Kappa, Phi Kappa Phi. Home: 5021 Regent St Madison WI 53705-4745

SINGER, MARKUS MORTON, retired trade association executive; b. N.Y.C., Dec. 20, 1917; s. Isadore and Nettie (Stromer) S.; m. Phyllis Berger, June 26, 1945; children—Fredric L., Robert B. B.C.S., NYU, 1939; postgrad., George Washington U., 1951-55. With Nat. Food Brokers Assn., Washington, 1946—, v.p., 1961-65, exec. v.p., 1965-71, pres., 1972-83, pres. emeritus, 1983—, acting pres., chief exec. officer, 1987-88; lifetime hon. trustee Nat. Food Brokers Assn. Edn. and Tng. Found. Served with AUS, 1942-45. Recipient Pres.'s award as Man of Yr. Can. Food Brokers Assn., 1976. Mem. European Food Brokers Assn. (hon. life), Frozen Food Industry Disting. Order of Zerocrats. Jewish.

SINGER, MAXINE FRANK, biochemist, think tank executive; b. N.Y.C., Feb. 15, 1931; d. Hyman S. and Henrietta (Perlowitz) Frank; m. Daniel Morris Singer, June 15, 1952; children: Amy Elizabeth, Ellen Ruth, David Byrd, Stephanie Frank. AB, Swarthmore Coll., 1952, DSc (hon.), 1978; PhD, Yale U., 1957; DSc (hon.), Wesleyan U., 1977, Swarthmore Coll., 1978, U.Md.-Baltimore County, 1985, Cedar Crest Coll., 1986, CUNY, 1988, Brandeis U., 1988, Radcliffe Coll., 1990, Williams Coll., 1990, Franklin and Marshall Coll., 1991, George Washington U., 1991, NYU, 1992, Lehigh U., 1992, Dartmouth Coll., 1993, Yale U., 1994, Harvard U., 1994; PhD honiris causa, Weizmann Inst. Sci., 1995. USPHS postdoctoral fellow NIH, Bethesda, Md., 1956-58; rsch. chemist biochemistry NIH, 1958-74; head sect. on nucleic acid enzymology Nat. Cancer Inst., 1974-79; chief Lab. of Biochemistry, Nat. Cancer Inst., 1979-87, rsch. chemist, 1987-88; pres. Carnegie Inst. Washington, 1988—; Regents vis. lectr. U. Calif., Berkeley, 1981; bd. dirs. Johnson & Johnson; mem. sci. coun. Internat. Inst. Genetics and Biophysics, Naples, Italy, 1982-86; Chulabhorn Rsch. Inst. (adv. bd. 1990—). Mem. editorial bd. Jour. Biol. Chemistry, 1968-74, Sci. mag., 1972-82; chmn. editorial bd. Procs. of NAS, 1985-88; author (with Paul Berg) 2 books on molecular biology; contbr. articles to scholarly jours. Trustee Wesleyan U., Middletown, Conn., 1972-75, Yale Corp., New Haven, 1975-90; bd. govs. Weizmann Inst. Sci., Rehovot, Israel, 1978—; bd. dirs. Whitehead Inst., 1985-94; chmn. Smithsonian Coun., 1992-93. Recipient award for achievement in biol. scis. Washington Acad. Scis., 1969, award for rsch. in biol. scis. Yale Sci. and Engring. Assn., 1974, Superior Svc. Honor award HEW, 1975, Dirs. award NIH, 1977, Disting. Svc. medal HHS, 1983, Presdl. Disting. Exec. Rank award, 1987, U.S. Disting. Exec. Rank award, 1987, Mory's Cup Bd. Govs. Mory's Assn., 1991, Wilbur Lucius Cross Medal for Honor Yale Grad. Sch. Assn., 1991, Nat. Medal Sci. NSF, 1992, Pub. Svc. award NIH Alumni Assn., 1995. Fellow Am. Acad. Arts and Scis.; mem. NAS (coun. 1982-85, com. sci., engring and pub. policy 1989-91), AAAS (Sci. Freedom and Responsibility award 1982), Am. Soc. Biol. Chemists, Am. Soc. Microbiologists, Am. Chem. Soc., Am. Philos. Soc., Inst. Medicine of NAS, Pontifical Acad. of Scis, Human Genome Orgn., N.Y. Acad. Scis. Home: 5410 39th St NW Washington DC 20015-2902 Office: Carnegie Inst Washington 1530 P St NW Washington DC 20005-1910

SINGER, NORMAN A., diplomat; b. Milw., Oct. 5, 1938; s. August S. and Lucille (Stachowski) S.; m. Dietlind Schmidt, May 15, 1964; children—Daniela, Dirk. B.A. in Polit. Sci., Sophia U., 1967, M.A. in Internat. Relations, 1970; M.A. in Mgmt., Syracuse U., 1976. Joined U.S. Fgn. Service, 1962; consul, chief consular services Am. Consulate Gen., Jerusalem, 1976-79; dir. Office of field support U.S. Dept. State, Washington, 1979-82; consul gen., prin. officer Am. Consulate Gen., Edinburgh, Scotland, 1982—; the dean Consular Corps of Edinburgh-Leith, 1984—. Served with U.S. Army, 1959-61. Recipient Meritorious Honor award U.S. Ambassador, Bonn, 1973; Superior Honor award Asst. Sec. for Near Eastern Affairs, 1979; Silver Cross of Orthodox Palestine Soc., Archimandrite of Jerusalem, 1979; Superior Honor award Asst. Sec. for European Affaris, 1984. Mem. English Speaking Union (bd. dirs. Scottish Nat. Com. 1982—), Am. European Community Assn. (bd. dirs. 1984—), Brit. Inst. Mgmt., Edinburgh-Leith Petroleum Club, Am. C. of C. in Scotland (adv. bd.). Roman Catholic. Clubs: New, Scottish Arts, Bruntsfield Links Golfing Soc. (Edinburgh). Avocations: golf; squash; gardening; traveling. Home: 3604 S 15th Pl Milwaukee WI 53221-1612 Office: Am Consulate Gen, 3 Regent Terr, Edinburgh Scotland EH7 5BW

SINGER, NORMAN H., lawyer; b. N.Y.C., Apr. 14, 1945. AB, St. Lawrence U., 1967; JD, Washington & Lee U., 1970. Bar: Va. 1971, D.C. 1974. Ptnr. Keck, Mahin & Cate, Washington; teaching asst. Sch. Law Washington & Lee U., 1969-70. Mem. ABA, Va. Bar Assn., D.C. Bar, Va. State Bar, Bar Assn. D.C., Va. Trial Lawyers Assn. Office: Keck Mahin & Cate 1201 New York Ave NW PH Washington DC 20005-3919*

SINGER, NORMAN SOL, food products executive, inventor; b. Phila., Dec. 10, 1937; s. Herman and Thelma (Scheinberg) S.; m. Anne Goldstein, Aug. 23, 1959; children: Amy Debra, Judith Ellen. BS, Rutgers U., 1961. Sr. lab. technician Bur. Biological Rsch., New Brunswick, N.J., 1960-61; food scientist Thomas J. Lipton, Inc., Englewood Cliffs, N.J., 1961-68; rsch. dir. McCain Foods, Florenceville, Can., 1968-70; sr. scientist John Labatt Ltd., London, Ontario, Can., 1970-84; fellow/dir. exploration The NutraSweet Co., Deerfield, Ill., 1984-94; pres. Ideas Workshop Cons., Inc., Highland Park, Ill., 1994—; co-founder, CEO Sous Chef Culinary Supply, Inc., Highland Park, Ill., 1994—. Patentee in field. Recipient Outstanding Am. Inventor award Intellectual Property Owners Found., Washington, 1989. Mem. Inst. Food Technology, Product Devel. and Mgmt. Assn., Chgo. Horticultural Soc., Sigma Xi. Avocations: gourmet cooking, carving bone and antler, collecting amerind carvings, bicycling. Home: 40 Ridge Rd Highland Park IL 60035-4337 Office: Sous Chef Culinary Supply Highland Park IL 60035

SINGER, PAUL MEYER, lawyer; b. Pitts., May 20, 1943; s. Sidney Morris and Doris (Lyttle) S.; m. Laurie Stern, 1989. BS in Bus., U. Minn., 1965; JD, U. Pitts., 1968; LLM, Harvard U., 1970. Law clk. to presiding justice Pa. Supreme Ct., Pitts., 1970-71; atty. Am. Express Credit Corp., N.Y.C., 1971-73; ptnr. Reed, Smith, Shaw & McClay, Pitts., 1973—. Fellow Am. Coll. Bankruptcy; mem. Harvard-Yale-Princeton Club, Duquesne Club. Office: Reed Smith Shaw & McClay 435 6th Ave Pittsburgh PA 15219-1809

SINGER, PHILIP C., environmental engineer, educator; b. Bklyn., Sept. 6, 1942; married Ellen Becker, 1965; children: Naomi, Elizabeth, Robert, Jennifer. BCE, Cooepr Union, 1963; MS, Northwestern U., 1965; SM, Harvard U., 1965, PhD, 1969. Asst. prof. civil engring. U. Notre Dame, 1969-73; assoc. prof. engring. sci. and engring. U. N.C., Chapel Hill, 1973-78, prof., 1978—, dir. water resources engring. program, 1979—. Mem. ASCE, Mat. Acad. Engring., Am. Chem. Soc., Am. Water Works Assn., Water Environment Fedn., Assn. Environ. Engring. Profs., Internat. Ozone Assn. Office: Univ North Carolina Dept Enviro & Eng Sciences Chapel Hill NC 27599*

SINGER, PHYLLIS, editor; b. Newark, May 22, 1947; d. Carl N. and Marion (Heller) S.; children: James, Daniel. B.S., Boston U., 1969. Mgr. print and broadcast traffic F. William Free & Co., advt., N.Y.C., 1969-70; researcher, reporter, editor L.I. Comml. Rev., Syosset, N.Y., 1970-72; with Newsday, L.I., 1972—, asst. editor, then sr. editor viewpoints, asst. mng. editor, N.Y. Newsday, 1985-95, now asst. mng. editor features; mem. bd. Newspaper Features Council. Mem. Am. Assn. Sunday and Feature Editors. Office: Newsday Inc 235 Pinelawn Rd Melville NY 11747-4226

SINGER, ROBERT NORMAN, motor behavior educator; b. Bklyn., Sept. 27, 1936; s. Abraham and Ann (Norman) S.; m. Beverly; children: Richard, Bonni Jill. BS, Bklyn. Coll., 1961; MS, Pa. State U., 1962; PhD, Ohio State U., 1964. Instr. phys. edn. Ohio State U., Columbus, 1963-64, asst. prof., 1964-65; asst. prof. Ill. State U., Normal, 1965-67, dir. motor learning lab., 1965-69, assoc. prof., 1968-69, asst. dean Coll. Applied Sci. and Tech., 1967-69; assoc. prof., dir. motor learning lab. Mich. State U., East Lansing, 1969-70; prof. Fla. State U., Tallahassee, 1970-87, dir. motor learning lab., 1970-72, dir. div. human performance, 1972-75, dir. Motor Behavior Ctr., 1975-87; chair dept. of exercise and sport scis. U. Fla., Gainesville, 1987—; lectr. in N.Am., S.Am., Africa, Australia, Asia and Europe; cons. in field. Author: Motor Learning and Human Performance, 1968, rev. edit., 1975, 80, Coaching, Athletics and Psychology, 1972, Physical Education, 1972, Teaching Physical Education, 1974, rev. edit., 1980, Laboratory and Field Experiments in Motor Learning, 1975, Myths and Truths in Sports Psychology, 1975, The Learning of Motor Skills, 1982, Sustaining Motivation in Sport, 1984, Peak Performance, 1986; editor: Readings in Motor Learning, 1972, The Psychomotor Domain, 1972, Foundations of Physical Education, 1976, Completed Research in Health, Physical Education and Recreation, 1968-74, Handbook of Research on Sport Psychology, 1993; mem. editl. bd. Rsch. Quar., 1968-81, Jour. Motor Behavior, 1968-81, Jour. Sport and Exercise Psychology, 1979-92, The Sport Psychologist, 1986-94, The Internat. Jour. Sport Psychology, 1977-88, Jour. Applied Sport Psychology, 1987-95; reviewer numerous jours.; contbr. articles to numerous anthologies and profl. jours. Served with U.S. Army, 1955-58. Recipient Disting. Alumnus award Bklyn. Coll., 1989. Mem. AAHPERD, APA (pres. divsn. of exercise and sport psychology 1995—), Am. Acad. Kinesiology and Phys. Edn. (pres. 1995-96), Internat. Soc. Sport Psychology (prex. 1985-89, 90-93), Am. Ednl. Rsch. Assn., N.Am. Soc. Sport Psychology and Phys. Activity. Home: 6305 NW 56th Ln Gainesville FL 32653-3116 Office: U Fla

100 Florida Gym Gainesville FL 32611 *I have always enjoyed my activities and have looked forward to new challenges and horizons. Intrinsic motivational values have guided my involvement in various endeavors, and the outcomes have been extremely rewarding.*

SINGER, SAMUEL L(OEWENBERG), journalist; b. Phila., May 2, 1911; s. Benjamin and Hattie May (Loewenberg) S.; m. Betty Janet Levi, June 12, 1939; children—Ruth Babette, Samuel Lawrence, Robert Benjamin. B.S. in Journalism, Temple U., 1934. Mem. staff Phila. Inquirer, 1934-81, music editor, 1955-81, emeritus, 1981—, public service editor, 1973-81; tchr. undergrad. journalism course Temple U., 1946—, tchr. music criticism, 1965-70, adj. prof. journalism, 1973—; tchr. theatre and music reviewing Main Line Sch. Night, 1994—. Condr. radio program This Week's Music, 1961-72; author: Reviewing the Performing Arts, 1973. Organist Congregation Temple Judea, 1933-41, Phila. Ethical Soc., 1942-56, Main Line Reform Temple, 1951-55, Beth Israel, Phila., 1956-65, Coatesville, Pa., 1966-88, Zion Evang. Luth. Ch., 1956-82, St. Matthew's Evang. Luth. Ch., 1972-82, IHS Episcopal Ch., Drexel Hill, Pa, 1984—. Served with USNR, 1943-45. Named Outstanding 1934 Journalism Alumnus, Temple U., 1988. Mem. Am. Guild Organists (editor Phila. chpt. publ. Crescendo 1971-76), Newspaper Guild, Phila. Press Assn., Mus. Fund Soc. Phila., Music Critics Assn., Phila. Mus. Art, Phila. Orch. Assn., Sigma Delta Chi (life). Home: 1431 Greywall Ln Wynnewood PA 19096-3811 *Never do anything you can't tell your children.*

SINGER, SARAH BETH, poet; b. N.Y.C., July 4, 1915; d. Samuel and Rose (Dunetz) White; m. Leon Eugene Singer, Nov. 23, 1938; children: Jack, Rachel. B.A., NYU, 1934; postgrad., New Sch. Social Research, 1961-63. Tchr. creative writing Hillside Hosp., Queens, N.Y., 1964-75, Samuel Field YMHA, Queens, 1980-82. Author: Magic Casements, 1957, After the Beginning, 1975, Of Love and Shoes, 1987, The Gathering, 1992, contbr. poetry to anthologies, poetry mags. and quars. including: Am. Women Poets, 1976, Yearbook Am. Poetry, 1981, The Best of 1980, 81, Filtered Images, 1992, the Croton Rev., The Lyric, Bitterroot, Judaism, Encore, The Jewish Frontier, Yankee, Hartford Courant, Poet Lore, N.Y.Times, Christian Sci. Monitor, Voices Internat., The Round Table, Orphic Lute, Brussels Sprout, Poetry and Medicine Column Jour. AMA, The Shakespeare Newsletter, Midstream (N.Y.C. Jewish Rev.), The Penwoman; cons. editor Poet Lore, 1975-81. Recipient Stephen Vincent Benet award Poet Lore, 1968, 71, Dellbrook award Shenandoah Valley Acad. Lit. and Dellbrook-Shenandoah Coll. Writers' Conf., 1978, 79, C.W. Post Poetry award, 1979-80, award for best poem Lyric quar., 1981, biennial award for achievement in poetry Seattle br. Nat League Penwomen, 1988; award for traditional poetry Wash. Poets Assn., 1989, crit. of merit Muse mag.,1990, Editor's Choice award for Haiku Brussels Sprout, 1992, poem chosen for Met. Bus. Poetry Project, Seattle, 1992; poem Upon My Demise translated into Russian, recorded 1st rpize Marj McAllister award Voices Internat. 1993. Mem. PEN, Poets and Writers, Nat. League Am. Penwomen (poetry chmn. L.I. br. 1957-87, publicity chmn. 1990, sec. Seattle br. 1990, pres. 1992-94, v.p. 1994—, publicity chmn. State of Wash. 1992—, Marion Doyle Meml. award 1976, 1st prize nat. peotry contet 1976, Drama award 1977, Poetry award 1977, 1st prize modern rhymed poetry 1978, Lectr. award 1980, Sonnet award Alexandria br. 1980, 81, Catherine Cushman Leach award 1982; poetry award Phoenix br. 1983, Pasadena br. 1984, Alexandria br. 1985, 1st prize award Portland br. 1990, structured verse award Spokane br. 1992, Della Crowder Miller Meml. Petrarchan Sonnet award 1994, Honorable Mention Anita Marie Boggs Meml. award 1994, Owl award and Ann. award for achievement in poetry Seattle br. 1994, Poet's Choice award Portland br. 1995, 2d prize Internat. Poetry Contest, Palomar br., 1996), Poetry Soc. Am. (v.p. 1974-78, exec. dir. L.I., 1979-83, James Joyce award 1972, Consuelo Ford award 1973, Gustav Davidson award 1974, 1st prize award 1975, Celia Wagner award 1976). Address: 2360 43rd Ave E Apt 415 Seattle WA 98112-2703 *As a poet, I have sought never to compromise my standards as to what constitutes poetry, despite fads that come and go. My goal has been to achieve whatever perfection I can in my work, and to preserve enough humility to realize that the best is never good enough. My life has truly been enriched by vision and aspiration. As a poet, the important thing for me is to create something moving and beautiful. Publication is a welcome by-product, but in itself, is not the goal for which I strive.*

SINGER, S(IEGFRIED) FRED, geophysicist, educator; b. Vienna, Austria, Sept. 27, 1924; came to U.S., 1940, naturalized, 1944; s. Joseph B. and Anne (Kelman) S.; m. Candace Carolyn Crandall, 1990. B.E.E., Ohio State U., 1943, D.Sc. (hon.), 1970; A.M., Princeton, 1944, Ph.D. in Physics, 1948. Instr. physics Princeton, 1943-44; physicist, applied physics lab. Johns Hopkins, 1946-50; sci. liaison officer Office Naval Research, Am. embassy, London, 1950-53; asso. prof. physics U. Md., College Park, 1953-59; prof. U. Md., 1959-62; dir. Nat. Weather Satellite Center, Dept. Commerce, 1962-64; dean Sch. Environ. and Planetary Scis., U. Miami, 1964-67; dep. asst. sec. for water quality and research Dept. Interior, Washington, 1967-70; dep. asst. adminstr. EPA, Washington, 1970-71; prof. environ. scis. U. Va., Charlottesville, 1971-87; chief scientist U.S. Dept. Transp., Washington, 1987-89; pres. Sci. and Environ. Policy Project, 1989—; vis. rsch. prof. Jet Propulsion Lab., Calif. Inst. Tech., 1961-62; Fed. Exec. fellow Brookings Instn., 1971; vis. Sid Richardson prof. J.B. Johnson Sch., U. Tex., 1978; sr. fellow Heritage Found., 1982-83; vis. eminent scholar George Mason U., 1984-86, disting. rsch. prof., 1994—; head sci. evaluation group astronautics and space exploration com. U.S. Ho. of Reps., 1958; cons. U.S. Treasury Dept., GAO, Office Tech. Assessment, U.S. Congress; mem. bd. Nat. Com. on Am. Fgn. Policy; mem. White House Panel on U.S.-Brazil Sci. and Tech. Exch., 1987; guest scholar Nat Air and Space Mus., Smithsonian Instn., 1991, Woodrow Wilson Internat. Ctr. for Scholars, 1991, Hoover Instn., 1992; disting. rsch. rpof. Inst. for Space Sci. and Tech., Gainesville, Fla., 1989—; bd. dirs. AMREP Corp., Patent Enforcement Fund, Inc. Author: Geophysical Research with Artificial Earth Satellites, 1956, Manned Laboratories in Space, 1970, Global Effects of Environmental Pollution, 1970, Is There an Optimum Level of Population, 1971, The Changing Global Environment, 1975, Arid Zone Development: Potentialities and Problems, 1977, The Economic Effects of Demographic Changes, 1977, Energy, 1979, Price of World Oil, 1983, Free Market Energy, 1984, Global Climate Change, 1990, Origins of The Universe, 1990, The Ocean in Human Affairs, 1990, The Greenhouse Debate Continued, 1992; sci. adv. com. Dept State 1981; vice chmn. Nat. Adv. Com. Oceans and Atmosphere, 1981-86; contbr. articles on space, energy, environment and population problems to profl. publs. Served with USNR, 1944-46. Recipient Presdl. commendation, 1958, gold medal for exceptional service Dept. Commerce, 1965; named Outstanding Young Man U.S. Jr. C. of C., 1959. Fellow AAAS (com. coun. affairs 1970), AIAA, Am. Geophys. Union, Am. Phys. Soc.; mem. Internat. Acad. Astronautics, European Acad. for Environ. Affairs, Pan Am. Med. Assn. (pres. sect. on environ. health scis. 1973—), Cosmos Club (Washington), Colonnade Club (Charlottesville). Office: 4084 University Dr Ste 101 Fairfax VA 22030-6803

SINGER, SUZANNE FRIED, editor; b. N.Y.C., July 9, 1935; d. Maurice Aaron and Augusta G. (Ginsberg) Fried; m. Max Singer, Feb. 12, 1959; children: Saul, Alexander, Daniel, Benjamin. BA with honors, Swarthmore Coll., 1956; MA, Columbia U., 1958. Program asst. NSF, Washington, 1958-60; assoc. editor Bibl. Archaeology Rev., Washington, 1979-84, mng. editor, 1984-96, exec. editor, 1996—; mng. editor Bibl. Rev., Washington, 1985-94, exec. editor, 1994—; mng. editor Moment, Washington, 1990—. Mem. Am. Schs. Oriental Rsch., Soc. Bibl. Lit. Jewish. Office: Bibl Archaeology Soc 4710 41st St NW Washington DC 20016-1700

SINGER, THOMAS ERIC, industrial company executive; b. Vienna, Austria, Mar. 6, 1926; came to U.S., 1938, naturalized, 1944; s. Henry and Berthe (dePokroi) S.; m. Ellen Colt, Dec. 20, 1952; children: Dominique, Mary F., Carlyle, Henry, Ellen. BA, George Washington U., 1950; MA, Harvard Coll., 1952. Fgn. affairs officer State Dept., 1952-55; export mgr. Polaroid Corp., Cambridge, Mass., 1955-58; with Gillette Co., 1958-79, exec. v.p., 1971-79; sr. v.p. Ingalls Assocs., Boston, 1979-81; chmn. Pontara Ltd., 1981-86; pres. Sontek Industries, 1983-84; prin. Thomas Singer and Daus., Boston, 1986—; bd. dirs. Galaxy Cheese Co. Trustee Faulkner Hosp., Boston; corporator Babson Coll., Wellesley, Mass., Childrens Mus., Boston; mem. Mayor's Com. for Cultural Affairs. With U.S. Army, 1944-46. Named hon. consul of Peru in Boston, 1969. Mem. Algonquin Club, Harvard Club (N.Y.C.), Essex County Club (Manchester, Mass.). Home: PO Box 362 Ipswich MA 01938-0362 Office: Thomas Singer and Daus 180 Beacon St Boston MA 02116-1401

SINGER, THOMAS KENYON, international business consultant, farmer; b. Wilson, N.Y., Jan. 30, 1932; s. Harold Thomas and Grace (Kenyon) S.; m. Jacqueline Germain Moulin, June 8, 1957; children: Marc Andre, Vivianne Grace Singer Scott, Claire Anne, Michelle Moulin Singer Ross, Gail Kenyon Singer Watson. BS in Econs., U. Pa., 1954. Dir. mktg. Europe Kaiser Aluminum & Chem. Corp., London, 1965-67; v.p. Kaiser LeNickel subs., Oakland, Calif., 1967-73, div. mgr., 1973-75; v.p. govt. relations Kaiser Aluminum & Chem. Corp., Washington, 1975-81; corp. v.p. Kaiser Aluminum & Chem. Corp., Oakland, Calif., 1977-86; pres. Kaiser Internat. Corp., Oakland, Calif., 1982-86, also dir.; dir., pres. IBA, Inc. Capt. USAF, 1955-57, Casablanca, Morocco. Mem. French-Am. C. of C. Republican. Episcopalian. Clubs: Army and Navy (Washington). Home: 6627 Hummingbird Ln Box 210 Appleton NY 14008

SINGER-MAGDOFF, LAURA JOAN SILVER (MRS. SAMUEL MAGDOFF), psychotherapist; b. N.Y.C., Mar. 21, 1917; d. Max David and Minnie (Stabsky) Silver; m. Edward I. Plotkin, 1938 (dec. 1945); 1 child, JoAnn Melanie; m. Arthur I. Singer, 1948 (div. 1962); m. Samuel Magdoff, Dec. 23, 1963. Student, NYU, 1936-38, U. Minn., 1938-39; BS, MA, Columbia U., 1946, EdD, 1961. Diplomate Am. Bd. Sexology; cert. sex educator, therapist Am. Assn. Sex Educators, Counselors and Therapists. Nursery and elem. sch. tchr., dir. Bronxville, N.Y., 1943-45; tchr. Cherry Lawn Sch., Darien, Conn., 1943-44, Columbia Grammar Sch., 1951-53, N.Y. Children's Colony, 1953-54; psychotherapist, marital, family counselor Community Guidance Service, N.Y.C., 1958-91; pvt. practice, 1958—; founder, pres. Save A Marriage, Inc., 1974—; pres. Interpersonal Devel. Inst., Inc., 1983, co-producer Gleam Prodns., 1989; adj. prof. Tchrs. Coll., Columbia U., 1961-74; vis. faculty New Sch. for Social Research; faculty Am. Assn. for Psychoanalysis and psychotherapy; psychotherapist TV series Living Together; past mem. exec. bd. Sex Info. and Edn. Coun. of U.S., Cmty. Sec. Info.; adviser bd. trustees Nat. Accreditation Assn. for Psychoanalysis, Inc.; supr. dept. psychology CUNY, 1994-96. Co-author: (with Barbara L. Stern) Stages the Crises that Shape Your Marriage, 1980; (with JoAnn Magdoff) Sexual Relations and Therapeutic Practice; author: (with others) Human Sexuality, 1988, Family Therapy Collection: Aspen, 1989; cons. editor Jour. Sex and Marital Therapy; former mem. adv. bd. Jour. Marriage and Family Counselors; former mem. editorial bd. Jour. Divorce; co-producer (documentary film) Door of Hope, 1991. Fellow Am. Inst. Psychotherapy and Psychoanalysis, Am. Assn. Marriage and Family Therapists (past pres., supr.), Am. Orthopsychiat. Assn., Soc. Sci. Study Sex, Am. Acad. Clin. Sexologists (clin. fellow); mem. World Fedn. Mental Health, N.Y. Soc. Clin. Psychologists (past editor Newsletter, mem. exec. bd.), Am. Family Therapy Assn. (charter), Am. Psychol. Assn., Am. Soc. Psychologists in Pvt. Practice, Assn. Applied Psychoanalysis, Nat. Council Family Relations. Address: 1 Lincoln Plz New York NY 10023-7129

SINGH, JYOTI SHANKAR, political organization director; b. Pathalgaon, India, Apr. 15, 1935; came to U.S., 1972; s. Brijnath Kumar and Tirthmani (Singh) S.; m. Maria Luz Molares, 1962; children: Anil, Rajeev, Ajit. BA, Banaras U., India, 1952, MA, 1954, LLB, 1955; MA, NYU, 1979; D (honoris causa), Internat. Inst. Integration, Bolivia, 1980. Assoc. sec. coordinating secretariat Leiden, The Netherlands, 1960-61, sec. gen. coordinating secretariat, 1961-64; programme cons. Internat. Youth Centre, New Delhi, 1965-66; sec. gen. World Assembly of Youth, Brussels, 1966-72; liaison officer Fund for Population Activities UN, N.Y.C., 1972-73, asst. exec. sec. World Population Yr., 1973-74, dep. chief info. and pub. affairs, 1975-80, chief info. and external rels., 1980-85, dir. info. and external rels., 1986-90; dir. tech. and evaluation div. UN Population Fund, N.Y.C., 1990-95; dep. exec. dir. UN Population Fund, 1995-96, exec. dir. program, 1995—; hon. prof. Cen. Am. U., Managua, Nicaragua, 1975; exec. coord. UN Internat. Conf. on Population, 1982-84; exec. coord. Internat. Conf. on Population and Devel., 1992-94; chmn. The Earth Times, 1995—. Author: A New International Economic Order, 1977; editor: World Population Policies, 1979; editor-in-chief Populi, 1980-90. Mem. Soc. for Internat. Devel. Home: 10 Waterside Plz Apt 26D New York NY 10010-2606 Office: The Earth Times 205 E 42d Ste 1316 New York NY 10017

SINGH, KRISHNA PAL, mechanical engineer; b. Patna, India, May 1, 1947; s. Balmiki Singh and Ram Rati Devi; m. Martha J. Trimble, May 18, 1974; children: Amy, Kris. BSME, BIT Sindri, India, 1967; MSME, U. Pa., 1969, PhD, 1972. Registered profl. engr., Pa., Mich. Prin. engr. Joseph Oat Corp., Camden, N.J., 1971-74, chief engr., 1974-79, v.p. engring., 1979-86; pres., CEO Holtec Internat., Cherry Hill, N.J., 1986—. Co-author: Mechanical Design of Heat Exchangers and Pressure Vessel Components, 1984; contbr. to profl. publs. Fellow ASME; mem. AICE, AM. Nuclear Soc., Thermal Exchangers Mfg. Assn. (vibration com.). Achievements include patents for heat exchanger for withstanding cycle changes in temperature and radioactive fuel cell storage rack. Office: Holtec Internat 2060 Fairfax Ave Cherry Hill NJ 08003-1612

SINGH, MANMOHAN, orthopedic surgeon, educator; b. Patiala, Punjab, India, Oct. 5, 1940; came to U.S., 1969; s. Ajmer and Kartar (Kaur) S.; m. Manjit Anand, Jan. 1, 1974; children: Kirpal, Gurmeet. MB, BS, Govt. Med. Coll., Patiala, 1964; MSurgery, Panjab U., Chandigarh, India, 1968. Diplomate Am. Bd. Orthopaedic Surgery. Rsch. fellow Inst. Internat. Edn., Chgo., 1969-74; resident in orthopedic surgery Michael Reese Hosp. and Med. Ctr., Chgo., 1974-78, mem. attending staff, dir. orthopedic rsch., 1979-94; fellow in orthopedic oncology Mayo Clinic and Mayo Found., Rochester, Minn., 1979-80; assoc. prof. U. Ill., Chgo., 1996—; pvt. practice, Chgo.; mem. vis. faculty Mayo Grad. Sch., Rochester, 1969. Developer x-ray method (Singh Index) and bone density method (Radius Index) for diagnosis of osteoporosis. Fulbright travel grantee, 1968. Fellow Am. Acad. Orthop. Surgeons, Am. Orthop. Foot and Ankle Soc.; mem. Orthop. Rsch. Soc., Am. Soc. for Bone and Mineral Rsch., Internat. Bone and Mineral Soc. Democrat. Sikh. Avocations: stamp collecting, photography, tennis. Office: 443 E 31st St Chicago IL 60616-4051

SINGH, RAJENDRA, mechanical engineering educator; b. Dhampur, India, Feb. 13, 1950; came to U.S., 1973; s. Raghubir and Ishwar (Kali) S.; m. Veena Ghungesh, June 24, 1979; children: Rohit, Arun. BS with honors, Birla Inst., 1971; MS, U. Roorkee, India, 1973; PhD, Purdue U., 1975. Grad. instr. Purdue U., West Layfayette, Ind., 1973-75; sr. engr. Carrier Corp., Syracuse, N.Y., 1975-79; asst. prof. Ohio State U., Columbus, 1979-83, assoc. prof., 1983-87, prof., 1987—; adj. lectr. Syracuse (N.Y.) U., 1977-79; bd. dirs. Nat. Conf. Fluid Power, Milw., Inst. of Noise Control Engring.; gen. chmn. Nat. Noise Conf., Columbus, 1985; leader of U.S. delegation to India-U.S.A. Symposium on Vibration and Noise Engring., 1996; vis. prof. U. Calif., Berkeley, 1987-88; cons., lectr. in field. Contbr. articles to profl. jours. Recipient Gold medal U. Roorkee, 1973, R. H. Kohr Rsch. award Purdue U., 1975, Excellence in Teaching award Inst. Noise Control Engring., 1989, George Westinghouse award Am. Soc. Engring. Edn., 1993, rsch. awards Ohio State U., 1983, 87, 91, 96. Fellow ASME, Acoustical Soc. Am.; mem. Soc. for Exptl. Mechanics, Inst. Noise Control Engring., Am. Soc. Engring. Edn. (George Westinghouse award 1993). Achievements include patent for rolling door; development of new analytical and experimental techniques in machine dynamics, acoustics, vibration and fluid control. Home: 4772 Belfield Ct Dublin OH 43017-2592 Office: Ohio State U 206 W 18th Ave Columbus OH 43210-1107

SINGHAL, AVINASH CHANDRA, engineering administrator, educator; b. Aligarh, India, Nov. 4, 1941; s. Shiam Sunder and Pushpa Lata (Jindal) S.; m. Uma Rani Sharma, Sept. 5, 1967; children: Ritu Chanchal, Anita, Neil Raj. BSc, Agra U., India, 1957; BSc with honors in Engring., St. Andrews U., Dundee, Scotland, 1959, BSC in Engring. with honors, 1960; MS, MIT, 1961, CE, 1962, ScD, 1964. Registered profl. engr., N.Y., Que., Ariz. Rsch. engr. Kaman Aircraft, Burlington, Mass., 1964-65; prof. Laval U., Quebec, Can., 1965-69; asst. program mgr. TRW, Redondo Beach, Calif., 1969-71; mgr. GE, Phila., 1971-72; mgr. tech. svcs. Engrs. India Ltd., New Delhi, 1972-74; project engr. Weidlinger Assocs., N.Y.C., 1974-77; prof. Ariz. State U., Tempe, 1977—; dir. Cen. Bldg. Rsch. Inst., 1992-93; dir. Earthquake Rsch. Lab., Tempe, 1978-89; grad. coord. structural engring. Ariz. State U., Tempe, 1991-92, senator acad. senate, 1995-98, chmn. governance grievance, 1995-96; cons. McDonnell Aircraft Corp., St. Louis, 1977-78, Sperry Corp., 1979-80, McDonnell Douglas Helicopter Co., 1990-91, Ariz. Nuc. Power Plant, 1991-92; reviewer of proposals NSF, Washington, 1980-91, CSIR, India, 1990-93; U.S. del. U.S./China Workshop on Arch Dams, Beijing, 1987, Can. del. Shell Structures, USSR, 1964; session chmn. Fifth Internat. Conf. on Soil Dynamics and Earthquake Engring., Karlsruhe, Fed. Republic of Germany, 1991; rsch. prof. Nat. Cen. U. Taiwan, Republic of China, 1990; vis. prof. U. Melbourne, Australia, 1983-84, U. Auckland, New Zealand, 1983-84; nodal dir. wood substitute rsch. program, India, 1992-93. Mem. editl. bd. Soil Dynamics and Earthquake Engring., 1991—, Advances in Earthquake Engring., 1995—; reviewer Jour. Psychol. Reports, Perceptual and Motor Skills; contbr. Nuclear Waste Storage, 1986, (proc. publ.) Earthquake Behavior of Buried Pipelines, 1989, Wood Substitute: A National Priority, 1992, System Flexibility and Reflected Pressures, 1993, Simulation of Blast Pressures on Flexible Panels, 1994; editor: Seismic Performance of Pipelines & Storage Tanks, 1985, Recent Advances in Lifeline Earthquake Engineering, 1987, Seismic Ground Motions Response, Repair and Instrumentation of Pipes and Bridges, 1992; contbr. articles to Jour. Performance of Constructed Facilities, ASCE, Jour. Computers and Structures, Jour. ASME, Jour. Aerospace Engring. ASCE; reviewer, bd. editors Jour. Earthquake Engring. and Structural Dynamics, Structural Engring. Papers Jour. ASCE. Chmn. bd. dirs. India Assn. Greater Phoenix, 1985-86; pres. India Assn. Greater boston, 1964-65; v.p., treas. Dobson Ranch Homeowners Assn., Mesa, Ariz., 1988-91; founding mem. Asian Am. Assn. Ariz., Phoenix, 1987-89; founding mem., pres. Asian Am. Faculty Assn., Ariz. State U., Tempe, 1986-88; cons. UN Devel. Program New Delhi, 1991-92. McLintock fellow MIT, 1960, Carnegie fellow MIT, 1960-63, fellow Royal Astron. Soc., London, 1961-64, rsch. fellow Kobe U., Japan, 1990; Denninson scholar Instn. Civil Engrs., London, 1959; Henry Adams Rsch. medal Structural Engrs., London, 1972; grantee Can. Def. Rsch. Bd., 1966-69, NSF, 1978-82, Engring. Found., 1978-79, U.S. Army Corps Engrs., 1984-86, U.S. Dept. Interior, 1986-88, Office Naval Rsch., 1994; recipient 1st prize bridge bldg. Instn. Strucural Engrs., Merit award Inst. Engrs., India. Fellow ASCE, Ctrl. Bldg. Rsch. Inst. (chmn. mgmt. coun., chmn. APEX com.), N.Y. Acad. Scis., Sigma Xi, Tau Beta Pi, Chi Epsilon. Achievements include research in computer engineering, blast effects on structures, in lifeline engineering, earthquake strengthening of deteriorated arch dams, steel and concrete buildings, bridges, building materials, non-linear finite element dynamics and engineering mechanics. Home: 2631 S El Marino Mesa AZ 85202-7302 Office: Ariz State U Dept Civil Engring 5306 Tempe AZ 85287-5306 *Service to mankind and love for the family and friends is the key to success and happiness.*

SINGHAL, KISHORE, engineering administrator; b. Allahabad, India, Dec. 28, 1944; came to U.S., 1966; s. Jagdish Chandra and Pushpa Lata (Mital) S.; m. Kumud Agrawal, Aug. 17, 1973; children: Monica, Nina. B Tech. with honors, Indian Inst. Tech., Kharagpur, 1966; MS, Columbia U., 1967, ScD in Engring., 1970. Postdoctoral fellow U. Waterloo, Ont., Can., 1970-71, lectr., 1972, asst. prof., 1973-77, assoc. prof., 1977-83, prof., 1983-88, adj. prof., 1988—, assoc. chmn. grad. studies in systems design, 1977-83; cons., then vis. mem. staff AT&T Bell Labs., Murray Hill, N.J., 1984-85; supr. AT&T Bell Labs., Allentown, Pa., 1985—; cons. Bell No., Ottawa, Ont., 1972-82. Author: Computer Aided Circuit Design, 1983 (transl. into Russian, Chinese and Pharsi), 2d edit., 1993; editor: Analog Circuit Design, 1987. Higgins fellow Columbia U., 1966, Boese fellow, 1967. Fellow IEEE. Avocations: reading, hiking. Office: AT&T Bell Labs 1247 S Cedar Crest Blvd Allentown PA 18103-6201

SINGHVI, SURENDRA SINGH, finance and strategy consultant; b. Jodhpur, Rajasthan, India, Jan. 16, 1942; came to U.S., 1962, naturalized 1986; s. Rang Raj and Ugam Kanwar (Surana) S.; m. Sushila Bhandari, July 7, 1965; children: Seema, Sandeep. B in Commerce, Rajasthan U., 1961; MBA, Atlanta U., 1963; PhD, Columbia U., 1967. CPA, Cert. Mgmt. Acct. Asst. prof. fin. Miami U., Oxford, Ohio, 1967-69, assoc. prof., 1969-70; adj. prof. fin., 1970-95; fin. mgr. ARMCO Inc., Middletown, Ohio, 1970-79, asst. treas., 1979-83, gen. fin. mgr., 1983-86; v.p. and treas. Edison Bros. Stores, Inc., St. Louis, 1986-90; pres. Singhvi & Assocs., Inc., Dayton, Ohio, 1990—; bd. dirs. Columbia Indsl. Sales Corp., Hauer Music Co., Oasis Property Inc. Author: Planning for Capital Investment, 1980; co-editor: Frontiers of Financial Management, 4th edit., 1984, Global Finance 2000-A Handbook of Strategy and Organization (The Conference Board), 1996; contbr. over 90 articles to profl. jours. Recipient Chancellor's Gold medal Rajasthan U. Mem. Planning Forum, Inst. Mgmt. Accts. (Bayer Silver medal 1978), Fin. Execs. Inst., Rotary (dir. internat. program Middletown chpt. 1973-86, Dayton chpt. 1995—), India Club (pres. Dayton chpt. 1980). Avocations: swimming, bridge, traveling, photography, writing. Home: 439 Ridge Line Ct Dayton OH 45458 Office: Singhvi and Assocs Inc 515 Windsor Park Dayton OH 45459

SINGLE, RICHARD WAYNE, SR., lawyer; b. Balt., June 17, 1938; s. William and Lillian (Griffin) S.; m. Emily K. Kaffl, Nov. 4, 1962; children: Richard W. Jr., Stacey Lyn. AB, U. Md., 1959, JD, 1961. Bar: Md. 1961, U.S. Dist. Ct. Md. 1961, U.S. Supreme Ct. 1978. Staff atty. Legal Aid Bur. Balt., 1962-64; house counsel Gen. Automatic Prodns. Corp., Balt., 1964-67; resident counsel Nat. Industries, Inc., Odenton, Md., 1967-69; asst. counsel McCormick & Co., Inc., Hunt Valley, Md., 1969-72, asst. sec., asst. counsel, 1972-75, asst. sec., assoc. gen. counsel, 1975-82, div. gen. counsel, v.p., 1983-86, gen counsel, v.p., sec., 1986-96, v.p. govt. affairs, sec., 1996—, also bd. dirs.; bd. dirs. McCormick Can., Inc., London, Ont., Can., McCormick de Mexico, Mexico City, Helix Health System, Balt. Trustee Franklin Sq. Hosp., Balt., 1986—. Mem. ABA, Md. Bar Assn. Republican. Avocation: boating. Office: McCormick & Co Inc PO Box 6000 18 Loveton Cir Sparks MD 21152-6000

SINGLEHURST, DONA GEISENHEYNER, horse farm owner; b. Tacoma, June 19, 1928; d. Herbert Russell and Rose Evelyn (Rubish) Geisenheyner; m. Thomas G. Singlehurst, May 16, 1959 (dec.); 1 child, Suanna Singlehurst. BA in Psychology, Whitman Coll., 1950. With pub. rels. and advt. staff Lane Wells, L.A., 1950-52; staff mem. in charge new bus. Bishop Trust Co., Honolulu, 1953-58; mgr. Town & Country Stables, Honolulu, 1958-62; co-owner, v.p. pub. rels. Carol & Mary, Ltd., Honolulu, 1964-84; owner Stanhope Farms, Waialua, Hawaii, 1969—; internat. dressage judge, sport horse breeding judge Am. Horse Shows Assn.; sr. judge Can. Dressage Fedn. Chmn. ways and means com. The Outdoor Cir., Hawaii, 1958-64, life mem.; pres. emeritus Morris Animal Found., Englewood, Colo., 1988—, pres., 1984-88; bd. dirs., pres. Delta Soc., Renton, Wash., 1994—; mem. Jr. League of Honolulu. Recipient Best Friends award Honolulu Vet. Soc., 1986, Spl. Recognition award Am. Animal Hosp. Assn., 1988, Recognition award Am. Vet. Med. Assn. Mem. NAFE, Hawaii Horse Show Assn. (Harry Hutaff award 1985, past pres., bd. dirs.), Hawaii Combined Tng. Assn. (past pres. bd. dirs.), Calif. Dressage Soc., U.S. Dressage Fedn., U.S. Equestrian Team (area chmn. 1981-85), Hawaiian Humane Soc. (life), U.S. Pony Clubs (dist. commr. 1970-75, nat. examiner 1970-75), Pacific Club, Outrigger Canoe Club. Republican. Episcopalian. Avocations: music, travel. Home and Office: Stanhope Farms Waialua HI 96791

SINGLETARY, JAMES, JR., principal; b. Buffalo, Jan. 24, 1947; m. Carolyn Price, July 24, 1971; children: Arien, Craig, Brandon, Evan. Cert. sheet metal, Erie C.C., Buffalo, 1974; BS, SUNY, Buffalo, 1990; MS, Canisius Coll., 1993. Cert. tchr. permanent, 1988, sch. adminstr. and supr., 1993. Sheet metal worker Buffalo Sheets Metal, 1970-77; customer engr. IBM, Buffalo, 1977-83; sheet metal worker, drafting tchr. Buffalo Pub. Schs., 1983-93; acting asst. prin., asst. prin. Seneca Vocat. H.S., Buffalo, 1993—; 2d v.p. bd. dirs. Rev. Marvin W. Robinson Cmty. Ctr., Inc. Adv. coun. mem. SUNY and Buffalo Vocat. Tech. Edn. Coun., 1988-91. With USN, 1964-70. Mem. Am. Edn. Rsch. Assn., Am. Fedn. Sch. Adminstrs., N.Y. State Fedn. Suprs. and Adminstrs., Vocat. Tech. Guild Buffalo, Buffalo Coun. Suprs. and Adminstrs., Buffalo State Coll. Alumni Assn., Phi Delta Kappa, Canisius Coll. Alumni Assn. Avocations: bowling, tennis, roller skating. Home: 273 Humboldt Pky Buffalo NY 14208-1044 Office: Seneca Vocat HS 666 E Delavan Ave Buffalo NY 14215-3014

SINGLETARY, MICHAEL, retired professional football player; b. Houston, Oct. 9, 1958; m. Kim Singletary; children: Kristin, Matthew. BA in Mgmt., Baylor U., 1981. Middle linebacker Chgo. Bears, 1981-93. Named Defensive MVP, season 1985; named to Pro Bowl team, 1983-91, Sporting News All-Pro team, 1984-89, 91, Sporting News Coll. All-Am.

team, 1980. mem. NFL Super Bowl Championship Team, 1985. Office: Chgo Bears Halas Hall 250 Washington Rd Lake Forest IL 60045-2499

SINGLETARY, OTIS ARNOLD, JR., university president emeritus; b. Gulfport, Miss., Oct. 31, 1921; s. Otis Arnold and May Charlotte (Walker) S.; m. Gloria Walton, June 6, 1944; children: Bonnie, Scot, Kendall Ann. B.A., Millsaps Coll., 1947; M.A., La State U., 1949, Ph.D., 1954. Mem. faculty U. Tex., Austin, 1954-61, prof. history, 1960-61, assoc. dean Sch. Arts and Scis., 1956-59, asst. to pres., 1960-61; chancellor U. N.C., Greensboro, 1961-66; v.p. Am. Council on Edn., Washington, 1966-68; on leave as dir. Job Corps, OEO, Washington, 1964-65; exec. vice chancellor acad. affairs U. Tex. System, 1968-69; pres. U. Ky., Lexington, 1969-87, prof. emeritus, 1987—; bd. dirs. Howell Corp. Author: Negro Militia and the Reconstruction, 1957, The Mexican War, 1960; editor: American Universities and Colleges, 1968. Regional chmn. Woodrow Wilson Nat. Fellowship Found., 1959-61; chmn. N.C. Rhodes Scholarship Com., 1964-66; chmn. Ky. Rhodes Scholarship Com., 1970-71, 73-74, 77, 80-81, 84-86; mem. So. Regional Edn. Bd., 1969—; chmn. dept. Army history adv. com., 1972-80; bd. visitors Air U., Maxwell AFB, 1973-76. Served with USNR, 1943-46, 51-54. Recipient Scarborough Teaching Excellence award U. Tex., 1958, Students Assn. Teaching Excellence award, 1958, 59; Carnegie Corp. grantee, 1961. Mem. Am. Hist. Assn., So. Hist. Assn., Am. Mil. Inst. (Moncado Book Fund award 1954), Am. Assn. Higher Edn. (dir. 1969—), Phi Beta Kappa (senator 1977-94, v.p. 1985-88, pres. 1988-91), Phi Alpha Theta, Omicron Delta Kappa, Pi Kappa Alpha. Democrat. Methodist. Office: U of Ky 104 King Library N Lexington KY 40506

SINGLETERRY, GARY LEE, investment banker; b. Seattle, May 10, 1948; s. Richard W. and Anita J. (Fowler) S.; m. Mary Beth Burfeind, Nov. 29, 1969; children: Douglas, Laura. AB, Harvard U., 1970; MBA, Stanford U., 1974. Assoc. Morgan Stanley & Co., N.Y.C., 1974-79, Wm Sword & Co., Princeton, N.J., 1979-80; v.p. Thomson, McKinnon & Co., N.Y.C., 1981-82; mng. dir. Dean Witter Reynolds, N.Y.C., 1983-85, Prudential-Bache Securities, N.Y.C., 1985-91; pres. Singleterry & Co., Parsippany, N.J., 1991—. Mem. FNMA Nat. Adv. Coun., 1991. Republican. Office: Singleterry & Co 4 Campus Dr Parsippany NJ 07054-4401

SINGLETON, ALBERT OLIN, III, physician; b. Galesburg, Ill., Feb. 16, 1946; s. Albert Olin Jr. and Eliz Joan (Anderson) S.; m. Ann Terrell, Mar. 30, 1975; children: Terrell Albert Olin IV, Caroline, Sidney Elizabeth. BA in English, U. Tex., 1969; MD, U. Tex., Galveston, 1973. bd. cert. Gen. Psychiatry, 1981, Geriatric Psychiatry, 1994. Gen. psychiatry intern, resident U. Tex. Med. Branch, 1973-76, child and adolescent psychiatry fellow, 1976-78; instr. U. Tex. Med. Br., Galveston, 1978—, Colo. Health Sci. Ctr., Denver, 1993—; pres. Titus Harris Clinic, Galveston, 1982-93; asst. chief psychiatry, asst. chief med. staff Colo. Mental Health Inst., Pueblo, 1994-95, chief med. staff, chief psychiatry, 1995—, med. dir., 1996—, dir. med. student edn., 1996—; bd. dirs. Gulf Health Network, Galveston, 1991-93. Chmn. bd. Ctr. for Transp. and Commerce, Galveston, 1990-92; S.W. region dir. AAPRCO, Washington, 1992—. Mem. Galveston County Med. Soc. (pres. 1993). Episcopalian. Office: 2989 Broadmoor Valley Rd Colorado Springs CO 80906-4467

SINGLETON, DONALD EDWARD, journalist; b. Morristown, N.J., Nov. 8, 1936; s. Edward Leslie and Charlotte (Angerbauer) S.; m. Maureen Ann McNiff, Aug. 8, 1959 (div. 1977); children: Nancy Ann, Mark Aram, Jill Susan. Student, Fairleigh Dickinson U., 1955-58. Reporter Dover (N.J.) Advance, 1959-61, Morristown Daily Record, 1961-63, Newark Eve. News, 1963-64; feature reporter-writer N.Y. Daily News, 1964—. Organizer Com. to Save Church Sq. Park, Hoboken, N.J.; vice chmn. Hoboken Environment Com.; mem. due process com. ACLU., Mem. bd. edn., City of Hoboken, 1974-77. Recipient Pub. Service award N.Y. Council Civic Affairs, 1967; President's Distinguished Service award N.Y.C. Council, 1969; Newspaper award merit Women's Press Club N.Y.C., 1970, 79; citation VFW, 1970; Heywood Broun Meml. award Am. Newspaper Guild, 1970; Silver medal for pub. service journalism N.Y. chpt. Pub. Relations Soc. Am., 1970; certificate merit Am. Bar Assn., 1971; Page One award Newspaper Guild N.Y., 1970; Feature award Newspaper Reporters Assn. N.Y., 1972; Consistent Excellence award Uniformed Firefighters Assn., 1991. Mem. Am. Newspaper Guild. Club: Press (N.Y.C.). Home: 366 Ogden Ave Jersey City NJ 07307-1115 Office: 220 E 42nd St New York NY 10017-5806 *In reporting, I try very hard to avoid gathering facts in such a way as to fulfill a preconception. I also attempt to force myself to review constantly my opinions about my subjects, and to keep my mind as open as possible. In writing, I try to ask myself the following questions regularly: "Is this what I really believe? Or am I simply writing this way because I believe that this is what some other person or group would like me to write?" Unless I can answer the first question in the affirmative, and the second in the negative, I am not satisfied with a particular story.*

SINGLETON, GREGORY RAY, dean; b. Lexington, Tenn., Sept. 25, 1961; s. Bobby Ray and Shirley Aileen (Flowers) S. AS, Jackson State C.C., 1979; BS, Memphis State U., 1985, MS, 1994. Cert. elem. edn., Tenn. Ednl. and leadership cons. Kappa Alpha, Lexington, Va., 1985-86; ednl. instr. Memphis City Schs., 1986-87; coord. fraternity/sorority affairs Memphis State U., 1987-94; asst. dean of students Purdue U., West Lafayette, Ind., 1994—. Vol. Crisis Ctr. Greater Lafayette, Ind., 1994; pres. young alumni coun. Memphis State U., 1992, v.p., 1991; chmn. speakers' bur. Memphis in May, 1992, 93; bd. dirs. United Cerebral Palsy Mid-South, Inc., Memphis, 1993-94; regional advisor BACCHUS and Gamma Peer Edn. Network, Denver, 1991—. Named one of Outstanding Young Men Am. U.S. Jaycees, 1984; recipient Outstanding Advisor award Southeastern Interfraternity Conf., 1992, Southeastern Panhellenic Conf., 1990. Mem. Assn. Fraternity Advisors (exec. v.p. 1994-95), Nat. Assn. Student Pers. Adminstrs., Nat. Assn. Campus Activities, Kappa Alpha, Omicron Delta Kappa (pres. Memphis alumni chpt. 1989). Democrat. Avocations: tennis, golf, community service. Home: 1193 Anthrop Dr Apt 2 West Lafayette IN 47906-1884 Office: Purdue U 1096 Schleman Hall Rm 250 West Lafayette IN 47907-1096

SINGLETON, HARRY MICHAEL, lawyer; b. Meadville, Pa., Apr. 10, 1949; s. Getdins T. and Rose Ann (Fucci) S.; children: Harry M. Jr., Leah Rose DiFucci. B.A., Johns Hopkins U., 1971; J.D., Yale U., 1974. Bar: D.C. 1975, U.S. Dist. Ct. D.C. 1975, U.S. Ct. Appeals (D.C. cir.) 1975, U.S. Ct. Mil. Appeals 1975, Pa. 1976. Assoc. Houston & Gardner, Washington, 1974-75, Covington & Burling, Washington, 1976-77; atty. FTC, Washington, 1975-76; dep. minority counsel Com. on D.C./U.S. Ho. of Reps., Washington, 1977-79, minority chief counsel, staff dir., 1979-81; dep. asst. sec. U.S. Dept. Commerce, Washington, 1981-82; asst. sec. U.S. Dept. Edn., Washington, 1982-86; pres. Harry M. Singleton & Assocs., Washington, 1986-91; pvt. practice law Washington, 1991—; legis. cons. Am. Enterprise Inst., Washington, 1975. Pres. bd. trustees Barney Neighborhood House, Washington, 1978-80; corp. bd. dirs. Children's Hosp. Nat. Med. Ctr., Washington, 1984-88; mem. D.C. Rep. State Com., 1991—, Rep. Nat. Com., 1992—, R.N.C. exec. coun., 1993-95. Mem. Rep. Nat. Lawyers Assn. (bd. dirs. D.C. chpt. 1990-91), Coun. of 100 Black Reps. (bd. dirs. 1991-92), D.C. Black Rep. Coun. (chmn. 1992-93), Rep. Nat. African-Am. Coun. (nat. chmn. 1993—), D.C. Rep. Nat. African-Am. Coun. (chmn. 1993—), Rep. Nat. Hispanic Assembly Washington, Lions. Republican. Presbyterian. Office: 2300 M St NW Ste 800 Washington DC 20037-1434

SINGLETON, HENRY EARL, industrialist; b. Haslet, Tex., Nov. 27, 1916; s. John Bartholomew and Victoria (Flores) S.; m. Caroline A. Wood, Nov. 30, 1942; children: Christina, John, William, James, Diana. S.B., S.M., Mass. Inst. Tech., 1940, Sc.D., 1950. V.p. Litton Industries, Inc., Beverly Hills, Calif., 1954-60; CEO Teledyne Inc., Los Angeles, 1960-86; chmn. Teledyne Inc., 1960-91, Singleton Group, Beverly Hills, Calif., 1988—; chmn. exec. com. Teledyne, Inc., L.A., 1991—. Office: 335 N Maple Dr Ste 177 Beverly Hills CA 90210-3858

SINGLETON, JAMES KEITH, federal judge; b. Oakland, Calif., Jan. 27, 1939; s. James K. and Irene Elisabeth (Lilly) S.; m. Sandra Claire Hoskins, Oct. 15, 1966; children: Matthew David, Michael Keith. Student, U. Santa Clara, 1957-58; AB in Polit. Sci., U. Calif., Berkeley, 1961, LLB, 1964. Bar: Calif. 1965, Alaska, 1965. Assoc. Delaney Wiles Moore and Hayes, Anchorage, 1963, 65-68, Law Offices Roger Cremo, Anchorage, 1968-70; judge Alaska Superior Ct., Anchorage, 1970-80, Alaska Ct. Appeals, Anchorage, 1980-90; judge U.S. Dist. Ct. for Alaska, Anchorage, 1990-95, chief judge, 1995—; chmn. Alaska Local Boundary Commn., Anchorage, 1966-69. Chmn. 3d Dist. Rep. Com., Anchorage, 1969-70. Mem. ABA, Alaska Bar Assn., Phi Delta Phi, Tau Kappa Epsilon. Office: US Dist Ct 222 W 7th Ave Unit 41 Anchorage AK 99513-7504

SINGLETON, JOHN, director, screenwriter; b. L.A., Jan. 6, 1968; s. Danny Singleton and Sheila Ward. BA, U. So. Calif., 1990. Writer, dir. Boyz N the Hood, 1991 (Acad. award nominee Best Dir. and Best Screenplay 1992); writer, dir., prodr. Poetic Justice, 1993, Higher Learning, 1995; dir., prodr., screenwriter Michael Jackson's Remember the Time video, 1992. First African-American and youngest person to be nominated for an Academy Award for Best Director. Office: Creative Artists Agy 9830 Wilshire Blvd Beverly Hills CA 90212-1804 also: New Deal Prodns 10202 Washington Blvd Culver City CA 90232-3119

SINGLETON, JOHN KNOX, hospital administrator; b. Atlanta, July 9, 1948; married. BA, U. N.C., 1970; MA, Duke U., 1973. Adminstrv. asst. U. Hosp., Cleve., 1970-71; sr. adminstrv. asst. Guy's Hosp., London, 1973-75; asst. dir. Milton S. Hershey Med. Ctr., Hershey, Pa., 1975-76, assoc. dir., 1976-78, dir., 1978-83; exec. v.p. Fairfax Hosp., Falls Church, Va., 1983-85; pres. Inova Health Systems, Inc., Springfield, Va., 1985—. Office: Inova Health System 8001 Braddock Springfield VA 22151-2215*

SINGLETON, JOHN VIRGIL, JR., retired federal judge, lawyer; b. Kaufman, Tex., Mar. 20, 1918; s. John Virgil Sr. and Jennie (Shelton) S.; m. Jane Guilford Tully, Apr. 18, 1953 (dec. Apr. 1991); m. Sylvia Gregg, May 13, 1991. BA, U. Tex., LLB, 1942. Bar: Tex. 1942. Assoc., gen. counsel Houston Harris County Ship Channel Navigation Dist. Fulbright, Crooker, Freeman & Bates, 1946-54; ptnr. Bates, Riggs & Singleton, 1954-56, Bell & Singleton, 1957-61, Barrow, Bland, Rehmet & Singleton, 1962-66; judge U.S. Dist. Ct. (so. dist.) Tex., 1966-92, chief judge, 1979-88, sr. judge, 1988-92; pres. Houston Jr. Bar Assn., 1952-53; co-chmn. 5th cir. dist. judges divsn. Jud. Conf., 1969, chmn., 1970, rep. from 5th cir. Jud Conf. U.S., 1980-83, also chmn. legis. com.; mem. Fifth Cir. Jud. Coun., 1984—; bd. dirs. TransAmerican Waste Industries, Inc. Mem. Tex. Depository Bd., 1963-66; co-chmn. Harris County Lyndon B. Johnson for Pres. Com., 1960-61; del.-at-large Dem. Nat. Conv., 1956, 60, 64; regional coord. 7-state area Dem. Nat. Com., Lyndon B. Johnson-Hubert Humphrey Campaign for Pres., 1964; mem. exec. com., Tex. Dem. Com., 1962-65, chmn. fin. com. 1964-66; former bd. dirs. Houston Speech and Hearing Ctr.; trustee Houston Legal Found., Retina Rsch. Found.; mem. chancellor's coun. U. Tex.; mem. exec. com. Lombardi Awards Trophy; mem. tex. Longhorn Edn. Found.; sponsor Found. for Tex. Excellence; oversight com. renovation Meml. Park Golf Course, 1995. Named to Waxahachie High Sch. Hall of Fame. Mem. ABA (liaison rep. to spl. com. evaluation disciplinary enforcement, litigation sect. ad hoc com. on tng. for spl. masters, jury comprehension com.), Fed. Judges Assn. (bd. dirs. 1974—, mem. exec. com.), Houston Bar Assn. (v.p. 1956-57, editor Houston Lawyer 1954-55, chmn. unauthorized practice law com. 1961-62), Tex. Bar Found. (charter mem. fellows), Tex. Bar Assn. (dist. dir.), State Bar Tex. (adminstrn. justice com., chmn. unauthorized practice of law com., 1961-62, chmn. grievance com. 22d dist. 1965-66, bd. dirs. 1966, fed. jud. liaison to state bd. dirs. 1984-85, pres. state bar task force Thurgood Marshall Sch. Law, 1986—, charter mem. fellows Tex. Bar Found.), U. Tex. Ex-Students Assn. (life mem., pres. Houston chpt. 1961-62, mem. exec. com., chmn. scholarship com., at large mem. 1969-80), Rotary, Cowboys (foreman, straw boss), Am. Judicature Soc., Order of Coif (Houston chpt. 1989—), Delta Tau Delta (pres. 1940-41), Phi Alpha Delta, Lakeside Country Club (Houston, past sec., bd. dirs.). Episcopalian. Office: 314 N Post Oak Ln Houston TX 77024

SINGLETON, LAVERNA, community health nurse; b. Friend, Nebr., Nov. 14, 1940; d. Lester and Frances Anna M. (O'Dea) S. Diploma, St. Elizabeth Hosp., Lincoln, Nebr., 1961; BAAS, Midwestern State U., Wichita Falls, Tex., 1988, MA in Pub. Adminstrn., 1990. Quality control coord. Bethania Regional Health Care Ctr., Wichita Falls, head nurse, orthopedics, 1969-77, asst. dir. nursing, 1977-90; regional rev. mgr. Tex. Peer Rev. Orgn., Tex. Med. Found., Dallas, 1991-93; quality mgmt. mgr. Vis. Nurse Assn. Tex., Dallas, 1993—. Mem. NLN, Tex. League Nursing, Tex. Orgn. Nurse Execs., Pi Sigma Alpha.

SINGLETON, MARVIN AYERS, otolaryngologist, senator; b. Baytown, Tex., Oct. 7, 1939; s. Henry Marvin and Mary Ruth (Mitchell) S.; B.A., U. of the South, 1962; M.D., U. Tenn., 1966. Intern, City of Memphis Hosps., 1966-67; resident in surgery Highland Alameda City Hosp., Oakland, Calif., 1967-68, resident in otolaryngology U. Tenn. Hosp., Memphis, 1968-71; Am. Acad. Otolaryngology and Ophthalmology fellow in otolaryngic pathology Armed Forces Inst. Pathology, Washington, 1971; fellow in otologic surgery U. Colo. at Gallup (N.Mex.) Indian Med. Center, 1972; practice medicine specializing in otolaryngology and allergies, Joplin, Mo., 1972—; founder, operator Home and Farm Investments, Joplin, 1975—, staff mem. Freeman Hosp., St. John's Hosp., Joplin, Oakhill Hosp.; cons. in otolaryngology Parsons (Kans.) State Hosp. and Tng. Center, Mo. Crippled Children's Service, Santa Fe R.R.; pres. Ozark Mfg. Co., Inc., Joplin. Mem. Internat. Arabian Racing Bd., 1983-88; mem. Mo. State Senate, 1990—, chmn. Senate Rep. Caucus; del. Rep. Nat. Conv., 1988, 92. Served with USNG, 1966-72. Diplomate Am. Bd. Otolaryngology. Fellow A.C.S., Am. Acad. Otolaryngologic Allergy, (past pres.), Am. Assn. Clin. Immunology and Allergy; mem. AMA (Mo. del.), Mo. State, So., Jasper County med. assns., Council of Otolaryngology, Mo. State Allergy Assn., Ear, Nose and Throat Soc. Mo. (past pres.), Joplin C. of C., Masons (32 degree), Sigma Alpha Epsilon, Phi Theta Kappa, Phi Chi. Methodist. Club: Elks. Contbr. articles to profl. jours. Home: 4476 Five Mile Rd Seneca MO 64856 Office: 114 W 32nd St Joplin MO 64804-3651

SINGLETON, PHILIP ARTHUR, corporate executive; b. Detroit, May 2, 1914; m. Eleanor A. DeVilbiss, Aug. 16, 1941; children: Kimberley P., Janet D., John R.M., Tobias T. (dec.). BSME magna cum laude, U. Mich., 1935; cert., Harvard U. Bus. Sch., 1940; LL.B., Yale U., 1941, J.D., 1946. Bar: Conn. 1941, U.S. Supreme Ct 1946; enrolled Inns of Ct., London, Middle Temple, 1952-55; registered profl. engr. With Monsanto Chem. Co. (and asso. cos.), 1940-55; successively at Merrimac div., Everett, Mass.; asst. to pres. of Monsanto Co., Washington; exec. v.p. Nealco-Monsanto Co., Everett; asst. dir. fgn. dept. Monsanto Co., St. Louis, 1949-50; mng. dir. Monsanto Chems., Ltd., London, Eng., 1956; asst. to pres., sec. exec. com. Monsanto Chems. Co., St. Louis, 1956; dir., mem. exec. com. Forth Chems., Ltd., Scotland; dir. Monsanto Chems., India, Bombay, Monsanto Chem., Australia, Tororo Exploration Syndicate, Uganda, Monsanto Boussois S/A, Paris, Casco A/B, Stockholm, S.I.C.E., Milan, S.I.D.A.C. S/A, Brussels, 1951; exec. v.p. Prophy-lactic Brush Co., Florence, Mass., 1951-56; pres., dir. Prophy-lactic Brush Co., 1957-66; v.p. Vistron Corp.; pres. Pro Brush and Prolon Dinnerware divs., 1957-68; with Warner-Lambert Pharm. Co., Morris Plains, N.J., 1956-63, also sr. v.p. parent firm, 1960-63; with responsibility for indsl. divs. including Md. Glass Corp., Balt., Gulfport Glass Corp., Miss., Nepera Chem. Co.,, Harriman, N.Y.; chmn. chief exec. officer Singleton Assocs. Internat., Amherst, Mass., 1967-90; chmn. bd. Hoodfoam Industries, Inc., Marblehead, Mass., 1968-72; chmn. bd., dir. Mazzucchelli, Inc., N.Y.C., 1968-71; chmn., chief exec. officer Plastics Industry Adv. Services, Far East Trading and Tech.; pres. Environ. Research Services, High Arctic Tech. Services, 1986-94; ret., 1994; dir., mem. audit com., div. policy com. Mass. Mut. Life Ins. Co.; dir. Keuffel & Esser Co., Morristown, N.J., Davis Cos. Inc., Denver, Hood Enterprises Inc., Marblehead, Mass., Deerfield Plastics Co., South Deerfield, Mass., Barry Wright Corp., Watertown, Mass., Hardigg Industries Inc., South Deerfield, Mass., Howard Mfg. Co., Littleton, Colo., Amtel, Inc., Koehring Co., Compo Industries Inc., Davis Cos., Denver, Towle Mfg. Co., Courier Corp.; dir., mem. compensation com. and employee benefit com. Hershey Foods Corp., Pa.; chmn., dir., mem. audit com. Werner & Pfleiderer Corp.; mem. Park St. Investment Trust, Boston.; mem. regional appeals bd. War Manpower Commn., 1943-45; employer mem. U.S. delegation ILO, Geneva, Switzerland, 1953-54; pres. Plastics Industry Adv. Services, Amherst, Mass., 1968-83; chmn., chief exec. officer Polar Technology Services-High Arctic and Antarctica. Mem. nat. adv. council Hampshire Coll., Amherst; mem. corp. Northeastern U., Boston., Boston Mus. Sci.; mem. Park St. Ptnrs., 1982—; founding bd. dirs. Plastics Edn. Found. Mem. NAM (dir. 1961-63), Am. Chem. Soc., Soc. Plastics Industry (dir.-at-large 1962-64, v.p. 1965-66, pres., dir. 1967-69), Pilgrims Soc., Soc. Chem. Industry London, U.S. C. of C. London (dir. 1953-56), Internat. C. of C. (overseas investment com., Paris 1953-55), Am. Brush Mfrs. Assn. (dir., pres.), Asso. Industries Mass. (v.p. 1963-65, dir. 1966—), Explorers Club, Union Club (Boston), Royal Thames Yacht Club (London), Cruising Club Am., Edarmoc Club (Detroit), Rotary (Amherst club), Beta Gamma Sigma (hon.), Phi Kappa Psi, Tau Beta Pi (nat. officer, pres. Mich. chpt., editor Council Bull.), Phi Eta Sigma. Republican. Presbyterian. Clubs: Comml., Mchts., Union (Boston); Five Islands Yacht (Maine); Ends of the Earth, Philippics, Royal Cruising, Royal Thames Yacht (London); Intrepids, Travellers Century (Calif.); Beefeaters; Plastics Pioneers (N.Y.); Michigamua, Vulcans (Ann Arbor, Mich.). Home: 332 Spencer Dr Amherst MA 01002 Office: 1072 S East St Amherst MA 01002-3075

SINGLETON, SAMUEL WINSTON, physician, pharmaceutical company executive; b. Blackpool, Eng., Nov. 17, 1928; came to U.S., 1953, naturalized, 1955; s. Samuel Smith and Jessica Constance M. (Knights) S.; m. Sheila Yolande C. Kershaw, Aug. 23, 1953; 1 child, Diane Jane. M.B., Ch.B., U. Manchester, 1952. Diplomate: Am. Bd. Pediatrics. Intern Chester, Pa., 1953-54; pediatric resident Oakland, Calif., 1956-58; assoc. physician, dir. clin. investigation, med. dir., v.p. Burroughs Wellcome Co., Research Triangle Park, N.C., 1960-89; asst. clin. prof. pediatrics Duke U., Durham, N.C., 1972-90; dir. B.W. Fund. Served with M.C. USNR, 1954-60. Home: 429 Tranquility Rd Moneta VA 24121

SINGLETON, WILLIAM DEAN, former newspaper publisher; b. Graham, Tex., Aug. 1, 1951; s. William Hyde and Florence E. (Myrick) S.; m. Adrienne Casale, Dec. 31, 1983; children: William Dean II, Susan Paige, Adam Nicholas. Student, Tyler (Tex.) Jr. Coll., El Centro Coll., Dallas, U. Tex., Arlington. Various positions with The Dallas Morning News, Tyler Morning Telegraph, Wichita Falls Record News, and others, 1966-78; various positions with Albritton Communications Co., 1976-78, pres. newspaper div., 1978-83; pres. Gloucester County Times, Inc., 1983-85; pres. MediaNews Group, Inc., 1985-88, vice chmn., pres., CEO, 1988—; chmn., pres. The Houston Post, 1988-95. Mem. Salvation Army, Am. Heart Assn. of Ft. Bend County. Mem. Newspaper Assn. Am. (bd. govs.), So. Newspapers Assn., New Eng. Newspaper Assn., N.J. Press Assn., Tex. Daily Newspaper Assn., Greater Houston Partnership Assn. Baptist.

SINGLETON-WOOD, ALLAN JAMES, communications executive; b. Newport, Monmouthshire, Eng., Feb. 13, 1933; emigrated to Can., 1968; s. Charles James and Violet Anne (Bond) S.-W.; m. Joan Davies, June 23, 1956; children: Ceri, Glendon. Student, London U., 1949-51. TV and radio musical dir., 1953-57, TV producer, 1957-61; freelance producer for BBC, 1962-64; indsl. advt. mgr. Western Mail, Cardiff, Wales, 1964; advt. dir. Voice of Brit. Industry Mags., London, 1966; mktg. services exec. The Sun and The People, I.P.C. Newspapers, London, 1966-68; mktg. services mgr. Fin. Post, Toronto, Ont., Can., 1969-71; research mgr. Fin. Post, 1971-76, nat. sales mgr., 1976-77; pub. Fin. Post Mag., 1978-79, dir. advt. sales Fin. Post Div., 1980-83; pub. Small Bus. Mag., 1983-87; v.p. pub. Bedford House Ltd., Toronto, Ont., Can., 1987-88; pub. Small Bus. mag., v.p. CB Media Ltd., Toronto, 1988—; v.p. pub. Can. Bus. and Small Bus. mags., Who's Who in Can. Bus., Who's Who in Can. Fin., 1989—; corp. pub., gen. mgr. Sentry Comm., Willowdale, Ont., 1991-92; group pub. Bus. Publs. divsn. MacLean Hunter Ltd., Toronto, Ont., 1992-93; pres. Can. Productivity divsn. CB Media Ltd., Toronto, 1994—; pres., CEO Singleton-Wood Comm. Inc., Toronto, 1996—; lectr. at various univs.; cons. in field; pres., founder Can. Info. Productivity Awards, 1994—. Composer: contemporary music including title theme of Swing High, BBC nat. network series, 1953-57. Mem. Anglican Ch. Office: CB Media Ltd, 777 Bay St, Toronto, ON Canada M5W 1A7

SINGLEY, JOHN EDWARD, JR., environmental scientist, consultant; b. Wildwood, N.J., July 31, 1924; s. John Edward Singley and Dorothy Mae (Pfrommer) S.; m. Virginia H. Ragsdale, Mar. 17, 1950; children: Gladys, Ann, Margaret, Patricia. B.S., Ga. Inst. Tech, 1950; M.S., Ga. Inst. Tech., 1952; Ph.D., U. Fla., 1966. Chemist Redstone Arsenal, Huntsville, Ala., 1950-51; dir. tech. services Tenn. Corp., College Park, Ga., 1951-64; lectr. chemistry Ga. State U., Atlanta, 1954-64, assoc. prof., 1964-67; prof. environ. engring. sci. U. Fla., Gainesville, 1967-90, prof. emeritus, 1990—; dir. TREEO Ctr., Gainesville, 1978-86; v.p. James M. Montgomery, Cons. Engrs., Inc., Gainesville, 1984-93, Montgomery Watson Cons. Engrs. Inc., Gainesville, 1993—; sr. v.p. Environ. Scis. Engring. Inc., Gainesville, 1977-84; prin. Water and Air Rsch., Gainesville, 1970-77. Patentee in field of polymers. Mem. Fulton County Rep. Exec. Com., 1962-64; trustee Water for People, 1990-92. With USN, 1943-45. Recipient Donald R. Boyd award Met. Water Agys., 1992. Fellow Am. Inst. Chemists, Inst. Water and Environ. Mgmt.; mem. Am. Water Works Assn. (hon., life, bd. dirs. 1984-87, exec. com. 1986-87, 89-93, v.p. 1989-90, pres.-elect 1990-91, pres. 1991-92, Fuller award 1974, rsch. award 1983, Abel Wolmon award of excellence 1995, Disting. Pub. Svc. award 1995), Fla. Water and Pollution Control Operators Assn. (Flanigan award 1979), Nat. Lime Assn. (Recognition award), Internat. Water Supply Assn., Nat. Assn. Corrosion Engrs., Internat. Ozone Assn. (bd. dirs. 1985-93). Presbyterian. Club: Gainesville, Civitan (pres. 1972, lt. gov. Fla. dist. 1973-76). Home: 1719 NW 23rd Blvd Gainesville FL 32605-3082 Office: Montgomery Watson Cons Engrs Inc 1020 NW 23rd Ave Ste D Gainesville FL 32609-3460

SINGLEY, MARK ELDRIDGE, agricultural engineering educator; b. Delano, Pa., Jan. 25, 1921; s. Maurice and Clara (Rhodes) S.; m. Janet Twichell, Oct. 3, 1942; children: Donald Heath, Frances Marvin, Jeremy Mark, Paul Victor. BS, Pa. State U., 1942; MS, Rutgers U., 1949. Adminstrv. asst. UNRRA, 1946; prof. II biol. and agrl. engring. Rutgers U., New Brunswick, N.J., 1947-87; chmn. dept. Rutgers U., 1961-71; v.p. rsch. and devel. Bedminster Bioconversion Corp., Haddonfield, N.J., 1987—; bd. dirs. Agriplane. Chmn. Hillsborough Twp., Somerset County (N.J.) Planning Bd., 1956-73; pres. Hillsborough Twp. (N.J.) Democratic Club, 1979-80, Agrl. Mus. State of N.J., 1983—, pres. bd. trustee, 1984-89. With USNR, 1942-46. Named Prof. of Yr. Cook Coll., 1985. Fellow AAAS (sect. com. O), Am. Soc. Agrl. Engrs. (chmn. North Atlantic region 1966, bd. dir. 1973-75, Massey-Ferguson medal 1987); mem. Am. Forage and Grassland Council (bd. dir. 1966-69). Home and Office: 335 Amwell Rd Belle Mead NJ 08502-1203

SINGSTOCK, DAVID JOHN, military officer; b. Oshkosh, Wis., July 19, 1940; s. Arnold William and Viola Rufine (Gerdener) S.; children: Susan, Brian, Elissa, Timothy. BS with distinction, Maine Maritime Acad., 1964; student, U.S. Merchant Marine Acad., 1959-62; BSBA with distinction, George Washington U., 1973, MS, 1975. Lic. profl. marine engr. Commd. ensign USN, 1964, advanced through grades to comdr., 1984, various sea assignments including combat duty in Vietnam, 1964-69; engr. officer USS Harold J. Ellison USN, Norfolk, Va., 1969-71, ADP fin. mgr. Cinclantflt, 1971-73; planning and quality assurance officer supr. shipbuilding USN, Portsmouth, Va., 1973-76; prodn./repair officer supr. shipbuilding USN, Bath, Maine, 1976-79; ship maintenance mgr. chief naval ops. USN, Washington, 1980-83, dir. fleet modernization program space/naval warfare systems command, 1983-86, program mgr. USS Stark restoration naval sea systems command, 1986-88, tech. dir. dep. asst. sec. Navy for internat. programs, 1988-93; sr. tech. advisor Royal Saudi Naval Forces Ops. Desert Shield and Desert Storm, 1990-91; sr. naval tech. mem. to sec. of Def. chartered delegation of sr. U.S. ofcls., Saudi Arabia, 1991; retired U.S. Navy, 1993. Asst. scoutmaster Boy Scouts Am., Dumfries, Va., 1985-90; coach Youth Soccer, Maine, Va., 1976-84; active local property owners civic orgns., Va., Maine, 1970—; instr. ARC, Seattle, 1967-68. Decorated Navy Commendation medal, Navy Achievement medal, Vietnamese Cross of Gallantry, Meritorious Svc. Medal, Joint Svc. Commendation medal, Bronze Star, Purple Heart; recipient Cert. of Appreciation and Gratitude, Comdr. of Saudi Arabian Armed Forces. Mem. Am. Soc. Naval Engrs. (dep. com. chmn., speaker 1988), Nat. Contract Mgmt. Assn. (cert. contracts mgr.), Ret. Officers Assn., Nat. Eagle Scout Assn., Mason (32 degree), Scottish Rite, Shriner. Presbyterian. Avocations: sailing, jogging, camping, golf, music. Home: 1125 Portner Rd Alexandria VA 22314-1314 Office: Vitro Corp Ste 200 1919 S Eads St Ste 200 Arlington VA 22202

SINHA, RAMESH CHANDRA, plant pathologist; b. Bareilly, India, Feb. 10, 1934; s. Bhawani Prasada and Ram Pyari; m. Indu Bala Sinha; children:

Sanjeev, Sangita. BS, Bareilly Coll., 1953; MS, Lucknow (India) U., 1956; PhD, London U., 1960, DSc, 1975. Exptl. officer Rothamster Exptl. Sta., Harpenden, 1959-60; research assoc. U. Ill., Urbana, 1960-65; research scientist Agriculture Can., Ottawa, Ont., Can., 1965—, prin. research sci., 1965—. Contbr. articles in field. Fellow Royal Soc. Can.; mem. Can. Phytopathol. Soc., Indian Phytopathol. Soc. Avocations: badminton, golfing, bridge. Home: 21 Barran St, Nepean, ON Canada K2J 1G3 Office: Plant Rsch Centre, K W Neatby Bldg, Agric Canada, Ottawa, ON Canada K1A 0C6

SINICROPI, ANTHONY VINCENT, industrial relations and human resources educator; b. Olean, N.Y., Mar. 30, 1931; s. Anthony and Christina Maria (LaBella) S.; m. Margaret Frances Michienzi, June 16, 1956; children—Stephen, Christine, Angela, Anthony J., Annette, Joseph. B.A. in Econs. cum laude, St. Bonaventure Coll., 1956; M.I.L.R., Cornell U., 1958; Ph.D., U. Iowa, 1968. Instr. St. Bonaventure Coll., Olean, N.Y., 1958-60; asst. prof. Gannon Coll., Erie, Pa., 1960-63; John F. Murray prof dept. indsl. relations and human resources U. Iowa, Iowa City, 1963-93, John F. Murray prof. emeritus, 1993—, ombudsperson, 1985-89; labor arbritrator, Washington, 1963—. Co-author: Evidence in Arbitration, 1982, Remedies in Arbitration, 1983, Management Rights in Arbitration, 1986; contbr. numerous articles to profl. jours. Served with USAF, 1951-53. Mem. Indsl. Relations Research Assn., Soc. Profls. in Dispute Resolution (pres. 1979), Nat. Acad. Arbitrators (bd. govs. 1983—, v.p. 1983-91, pres. 1991-92). Avocation: music.

SININING, VICENTE C., education educator; b. Escalante, Philippines, May 15, 1968; s. Fortunato V. and Aida (Cabatania) S. BS in Chem. Engring., St. Augustine Coll., Philippines, 1988; BS in Computer Sci. with honors, Internat. U., Independence, Mo., 1991. Programmer/sys. analyst Portfolio Computer Sys., Philippines; faculty Internat. U., Philippines, 1991-92; tchr. Brownsville (Tex.) Ind. Sch. Dist., 1992, Mt. Bachelor Acad., Prineville, Oreg., 1993-94; vis. lectr. Mt. Carmel Coll., Escalante, Philippines, 1994—; founder, exec. dir. INFOSYS; lectr./rschr. in field; cons./moderator The Carmelite Ember. Contbr. articles to profl. jours.; author: The Study of Human Behavior: An Integrated Approach, 1994; editor The Technoscope, The Eagle. Founder/dir. TRACEASKI Prodn. (non-profit orgn.). Avocations: reading, photography, painting, singing, making short films.

SINISE, GARY, actor, director; b. 1955. co-founder, artistic dir. Steppenwolf Theatre, Chgo. Appeared in (plays) The Indian Wants The Bronx, 1977, Getting Out, 1980 (Joseph Jefferson award), Of Mice And Men, 1980, Loose Ends, 1982, True West, 1983 (also dir., Obie award best dir. 1982-83), Balm in Gilead, 1984, Streamers, 1985, The Caretaker, 1986, Grapes of Wrath, 1990 (Tony award and Drama Desk), (TV films) The Final Days, 1989, My Name is Bill W., 1989, The Stand, 1994; (dir. theatrical films) Miles from Home, 1988, Of Mice and Men, 1991 (also actor); (actor) Jack The Bear, 1991, A Midnight Clear, 1991, Forrest Gump, 1994, The Quick and the Dead, 1995, Apollo 13, 1995; various TV appearances including Crime Story (also dir.), Hunter, True West, Grapes of Wrath; dir. (plays) Frank's Wild Years, Action, The Miss Firecracker Contest, Waiting for the Parade, Tracers, Orphans, Landscape of the Body, 1984, (TV tapes) thirtysomething, 1989, China Beach, 1991. Office: care CAA 9830 Wilshire Blvd Beverly Hills CA 90212-1804 Office: Licker & Ozurovich 2029 Century Park E # 500 Los Angeles CA 90067

SINK, JOHN DAVIS, leadership consultant, scientist; b. Homer City, Pa., Dec. 19, 1934; s. Aaron Tinsman and Louella Bell (Davis) S.; m. Nancy Lee Hile, Nov. 9, 1956 (dec. Aug. 1961); 1 child, Lou Ann. (dec.); m. Claire Kaye Huschka, June 13, 1964 (div. Feb. 1987); children: Kara Joan, Karl John; m. Sharon Ferrando Padden, July 15, 1989; 1 child, Lisa Michelle Padden. BS in Animal/Vet. Sci., Pa. State U., 1956, MS in Biophysics/Animal Sci., 1960, PhD in Biochemistry/Animal Sci., 1962; EdD in Higher Edn., U. Pitts., 1986. Administrv. officer, exec. asst. to sec. agr. State of Pa., Harrisburg, 1962; prof., group leader dept. food, dairy and animal sci. Inst. Policy Rsch. and Evaluation, Pa. State U., University Park, 1962-79; pres. Collegian, Inc., 1971-72; joint planning and evaluation staff officer Sci. and Edn. Adminstrn., U.S. Dept. Agr., Washington, 1979-80; prof., chmn. intercoll. program food sci. and nutrition, interdivisional program agrl. biochemistry and div. animal and vet. scis. W.Va. U., Morgantown, 1980-85; pres., CEO Pa. State U.-Uniontown, 1985-92; pres. Sink, Padden & Assocs., Atlanta, 1992—; dir. S.W. Inst., Uniontown, 1989-92; gen. mgr. Cavert Wire Co., Inc., Atlanta, 1993—; exec. asst., naval rep. to gov. and adj. gen. State W.Va., Charleston, 1981-84; cons. Allied Mills, Inc., Am. Air Lines, Am. Home Foods, Inc., Apollo Analytical Labs., Armour Food Co., Atlas Chem. Industries, others. Mem. nat. adv. bd. Am. Security Council, 1981—; mem. nat. adv. council Nat. Commn. Higher Edn. Issues, 1980-82; bd. dirs. W.Va. Cattleman's Assn., 1981-83, W.Va. Poultry Assn., 1980-83, Pembroke Welsh Corgi Club Am., 1980-83, Penn State Stockmen's Club, 1969-71, Greater Uniontown Indsl. Fund, 1986-91, Fayette County Econ. Devel. Council, 1985-93, Westmoreland-Fayette coun. Boy Scouts Am., 1986-91, Westmoreland-Fayette Hist. Soc., 1986-91, Fayette County Soil Conservation Dist., 1990-93, Pa. Youth Found., 1989-93, Fayette County Coop. Extension Bd., 1992-93, Pa. Masonic Found., 1993; pastor Sardis United Meth. Ch., Atlanta, 1995—. Capt. USNR, 1956-86, ret. Decorated Army commendation medal; recipient Nat. Merit Trophy award Nat. Block and Bridle Club, 1956; W.Va. Disting. Achievement medal; Disting. Leadership award Am. Security Council Found., 1983. Pa. Meat Packers Assn. scholar, 1958-62; hon. fellow in biochemistry U. Wis., 1965-65; NSF postdoctoral fellow, 1964-65; Darbaker prize Pa. Acad. Sci., 1967. Fellow AAAS, Am. Inst. Chemists, Inst. Food Technologists; mem. Am. Meat Sci. Assn. (pres. 1974-75), Pa. Air N.G. Armory (trustee 1968-80), Pa. Acad. Sci., U.S. Naval Inst., Naval Res. Assn., Navy League U.S., Res. Officers Assn., Armed Forces Communications and Electronics Assn., Acad. Polit. Sci. (world affairs coun. Pitts. chpt.), Am. Assn. Higher Edn., Am. Assn. Univ. Adminstrs., Am. Chem. Soc., Biophys. Soc., Am. Soc. Animal Sci., Inst. Food Technologists, Soc. Rsch. Adminstrs., Am. Cancer Soc. (bd. dirs. 1988-91), Greater Uniontown C. of C. (bd. dirs. 1989-93), Greater Connellsville C. of C. (pres., bd. dirs. 1989-91), North Fayette C. of C. (bd. dirs. 1986-89), Mon Valley Tri-State Network, Inc. (chmn. bd. dirs. 1989-92), Rotary (sec. State Coll. 1969-71, Paul Harris fellow 1991), Elks, Internat. Assn. of Turtles, Consistory, Shriners, Masons, Alpha Zeta, Omicron Delta Kappa, Gamma Sigma Delta, Sigma Xi, Phi Lambda Upsilon, Gamma Alpha, Phi Tau Sigma, Phi Sigma, Phi Delta Kappa, Pi Sigma Phi. Democrat. Author: The Control of Metabolism, 1974, Citizen Extraordinarire, 1993; contbr. numerous articles to profl. publs. Home: 2726 Phillips Dr Marietta GA 30064-4224 Office: PO Box 43264 Atlanta GA 30336-0264

SINKFORD, JEANNE CRAIG, dentist, educator; b. Washington, Jan. 30, 1933; d. Richard E. and Geneva (Jefferson) Craig; m. Stanley M. Sinkford, Dec. 8, 1951; children: Dianne Sylvia, Janet Lynn, Stanley M. III. BS, Howard U., 1953, MS, 1962, DDS, 1958, PhD, 1963; DSc (hon.), Georgetown U., 1978; DSc (Hon.), U. Med. and Dentistry of N.J., 1992. Instr. prosthodontics Sch. Dentistry Howard U., Washington, 1958-60, mem. faculty dentistry, 1964—, rsch. coord., co-chmn. dept. restorative dentistry, assoc. dean, 1968-75, dean, 1975-91, prof. Prosthodontics Grad. Sch., 1977-91; dean emeritus, prof. Sch. Dentistry Howard U.; spl. asst. Am. Assn. Dental Schs., 1991-93, dir. office women and minority affairs, 1993—; instr. rsch. and crown and bridge Northwestern U. Sch. Dentistry, 1963-64; cons. prosthodontics and rsch. VA Hosp., Washington, 1965—; resident Children's Hosp. Nat. Med. Ctr., 1974-75; cons. St. Elizabeth's Hosp.; mem. attending staff Freedman's Hosp., Washington, 1964—; adv. bd. D.C. Gen. Hosp., 1975—; mem. Nat. Adv. Dental Rsch. Coun., Nat. Bd. Dental Examiners; mem. ad hoc adv. panel Tuskegee Syphilis Study for HEW; sponsor D.C. Pub. Health Apprentice Program; mem. adv. coun. to dir. NIH; adv. com. NIH/NIDR/NIA Aging Rsch. Coun.; mem. dental devices classification panel FDA; mem. select panel for promotion child health, 1979-80; mem. spl. med. adv. group VA; bd. overseers U. Pa. Dental Sch., Boston U. Dental Sch.; bd. advs. U. Pitts. Dental Sch.; mem. anat. rev. bd. for D.C. NRC Gov. Bd.; cons. Food and Drug Adminstrn.; Nat. Adv. Rsch. Coun., 1993—; active Nat. Rsch. Coun. Governing Bd. Mem. editorial rev. bd. Jour. Am. Coll. Dentists, 1988—. Adv. bd. United Negro Coll. Fund, Robert Wood Johnson Health Policy Fellowships; mem. Mayor's Block Grant Adv. Com., 1982; mem. parents' coun. Sidwell Friends, 1983; mem. adv. bd. D.C., mem. Women's Health Task Force, NIH; bd. dirs. Girl Scouts U.S.A., 1993—. Louise C. Ball fellow grad. tng., 1960-63. Fellow Am. Coll. Dentists (sec.-treas. Wash. met. sect.), Internat. Coll. Dentists (award of merit); mem. ADA (chmn. appeal bd. coun. on dental edn. 1975-82), Am. Soc. for Geriatric Dentistry (bd. dirs.), Internat. Assn. Dental Research, Dist. Dental Soc., Am. Inst. Oral Biology, North Portal Civic League, Inst. Grad. Dentists (trustee), So. Conf. Dental Deans (chmn.), Wash. Coun. Adminstrv. Women, Assn. Am. Women Dentists, Am. Pedodontic Soc., Am. Prosthodontic Soc., Fed. Prosthodontic Orgn., Nat. Dental Assn., Inst. Medicine (coun.), Am. Soc. Dentistry for Children, N.Y. Acad. Scis., Smithsonian Assocs., Dean's Coun., Proctor and Gamble, Golden Key Honor Soc., Links Inc., Sigma Xi (pres.), Phi Beta Kappa, Omicron Kappa Upsilon, Psi Chi, Beta Kappa Chi. Address: 1765 Verbena St NW Washington DC 20012-1048

SINKLAR, ROBERT, insurance company executive. Chmn., pres., CEO Minn. Mutual Life Ins. Co., St. Paul. Office: Minn Mutual Life Ins Co 400 Robert St N Saint Paul MN 55101*

SINKO, CHRISTOPHER MICHAEL, scientist; b. Englewood, N.J., July 19, 1962; s. Patsy John and Patricia Lou (Anderson) S.; m. Angela Carole Small, Aug. 5, 1984. BS in Chem. Engring., Rutgers U., 1984; MS in Pharmaceutics, U. Mich., 1986, DPhil in Pharmaceutics, 1989. Scientist The Upjohn Co., Kalamazoo, 1989-91; rsch. scientist Pfizer, Inc., Groton, Conn., 1991-93, sr. rsch. scientist, 1993-95, sr. rsch. investigator, 1995—; lectr. U. Mich. Coll. Pharmacy, Ann Arbor, 1990. Contbr. articles to profl. jours. Pharmaceutical Mfrs. Assn. fellow, 1987; recipient North Jersey Sect. Rsch. award AICE, 1984. Mem. Am. Assn. Pharm. Scientists. Achievements include identification and definition of physical aging mechanisms in glassy polymers, flow testing technique which is now routinely used to characterize the flowability of pharmaceutical formulations during product development. Office: Pfizer Ctrl Rsch Eastern Point Rd Groton CT 06340

SINNER, GEORGE ALBERT, former state governor, farmer, corporate executive; b. Fargo, N.D., May 29, 1928; s. Albert and Katherine (Wild) S.; m. Elizabeth Jane Baute, Aug. 10, 1951; children: Robert, George, Elizabeth, Martha, Paula, Mary Jo, Jim, Jerry, Joe, Eric. BA in Philosophy, St. Johns U., St. Cloud, Minn., 1950. Farmer Sinner Bros. and Bresnahan, Casselton, N.D., 1952-93; mem. N.D. Senate, 1962-66; mem. N.D. Ho. of Reps., 1982-84, chmn. fin. and tax com., 1983; gov. State of N.D., Bismarck, 1985-93; v.p. pub. & govt. affairs Am. Crystal Sugar Co., Moorhead, Minn., 1990—; U.S. del. Inter-Am. Food and Agr. Conf., 1966; founder, chmn. N.D. Crops Coun., Fargo, 1978-83; chmn. No. Crops Inst. Coun., Fargo, 1980-83; mem. Interstate Oil Compact Commn., 1986-88; chmn. Am. Energy Assurance Coun., 1987-89; presdl. appointee to Adv. Commn. on Govtl. Rels., 1989-92. Candidate for U.S. Congress, 1964; chmn., bd. dirs. S.E. Region Mental Health and Retardation Clinic, Fargo, 1964-66; mem. N.D. Bd. Higher Edn., Bismarck, 1966-75, chmn., 1970, Broadcasting Coun., 1968-73; co-founder bd. dirs. Tri-Coll. Univ. Bd., Fargo, N.D., and Moorhead, Minn., 1970-84; del. N.D. Constl. Conv., Bismarck, 1972; mem. Casselton Planning and Zoning Commn., 1982-85. With N.D. N.G., 1950-51. Recipient Rotary Diversified Farming award, 1960, Outstanding Farming award N.D. State U., 1964, L.B. Hartz Profl. Achievement award Moorhead (Minn.) State U., 1980, EPA Nat. Wetlands award, 1992, Nat. Ducks Unltd. Wetlands Conservation award, 1992; named Nat. Water Statesman of Yr., 1992, Doctor of Law, St. John's U., 1992, Doctor of Humanities, N.D. State U., 1993. Mem. Nat. Gov.'s Assn. (chmn. com. agr. 1987-89, chmn. com. energy and environment, lead gov. out-of-state sales tax collection), Western Govs. Assn. (chmn. 1989-90, lead gov., mem. water pollution com. 1985-93, chmn. 1989-90), N.D. Cattle Feeders' Assn. (farm prodn.), Red River Valley Sugarbeet Growers Assn. (pres. bd. dirs. 1975-79), Greater N.D. Assn. (bd. dirs. 1981), N.D. Farm Bur. (farm prodn.), N.D. Wheat Producers (farm prodn.), N.D. Crop Improvement Assn. (farm prodn.), N.D. Stockmen's Assn. (farm prodn.), Am. Soybean Assn. (farm prodn.), N.D. Barley Coun. (farm prodn.), N.D. Farmers Union (farm prodn.), Am. Legion. Avocations: family, tennis, basketball, hockey, softball, reading. Office: 101 3rd St N Moorhead MN 56560-1952

SINNINGER, DWIGHT VIRGIL, research engineer; b. Bourbon, Ind., Dec. 29, 1901; s. Norman E. and Myra (Huff) S.; student Armour Inst., 1928, U. Chgo., 1942, Northwestern U., 1943; m. Coyla Annetta Annis, Mar. 1, 1929; m. Charlotte M. Lenz, Jan. 21, 1983. Registered profl. engr., Ill. Electronics rsch. engr. Johnson Labs., Chgo., 1935-42; chief engr. Pathfinder Radio Corp., 1943-44, Rowe Engring. Corp., 1945-48, Hupp Electronics Co. div. Hupp Corp., 1948-61; dir. rsch. Pioneer Electric & Research Corp., Forest Park, Ill., 1961-65, Senn Custom, Inc., Forest Park and San Antonio, 1967—. Patentee in field. Mem. IEEE. Address: PO Box 982 Kerrville TX 78029-0982

SINNOTT, JOHN PATRICK, lawyer, educator; b. Bklyn., Aug. 17, 1931; s. John Patrick and Elizabeth Muriel (Zinkand) S.; m. Rose Marie Yuppa, May 30, 1959; children: James Alexander, Jessica Michelle. BS, U.S. Naval Acad., 1953; MS, U.S. Air Force Inst. Tech., 1956; JD, No. Ky. U., 1960. Bar: Ohio 1961, N.Y. 1963, U.S. Patent Office 1963, N.J. 1970, U.S. Supreme Ct. 1977. Assoc. Brumbaugh, Graves, Donohue & Raymond, N.Y.C., 1961-63; patent atty. Bell Tel. Labs., Murray Hill, N.J., 1963-64; patent atty. Schlumberger Ltd., N.Y.C., 1964-71; asst. chief patent counsel Babcock & Wilcox, N.Y.C., 1971-79; chief patent and trademark counsel Am. Standard Inc., N.Y.C., 1979-92; of counsel Morgan & Finnegan, N.Y.C., 1992—; adj. lectr. N.J. Inst. Tech., Newark, 1974-89; adj. prof. Seton Hall U. Sch. Law, Newark, 1989—. Author: World Patent Law and Practice, Vols. 2-20, 1993; A Practical Guide to Document Authentication, 5th edit. 1996, Counterfeit Goods Suppression, 1993; also numerous articles. Bd. dirs. New Providence Community Swimming Pool (N.J.), 1970; mem. local Selective Service Bd., Plainfield, N.J., 1971. Lt. comdr. USAF, 1953-61, col. AUS (ret.), 1991. Decorated Legion of Merit Nat. Def. Svc. medal, Meritorious Svc. medal, Res. Comp. Achievement medal, Armed Forces Res. medal. Mem. N.Y. Patent Law Assn. (bd. dirs. 1974-82), N.J. Patent Law Assn. (com. chmn. 1981-82). Republican. Roman Catholic. Clubs: Squadron A (N.Y.C.); Cosmos. Home: Two Blackburn Pl Summit NJ 07901 Office: Morgan & Finnegan 345 Park Ave New York NY 10154-0004

SINNOTT, WILLIAM MICHAEL, social studies educator; b. Jersey City, Mar. 6, 1948; s. Myles and Agnes Bridget (Ryan) S.; m. Louise Rosemary DeStefano, Dec. 27, 1969; children: Daria, Jessica, Carrie Ann. BA cum laude, Bloomfield Coll., 1970; MA, NYU, 1971; MAT, Fairleigh Dickinson U., 1974. Cert. tchr. social studies K-12, N.J. Permanent substitute tchr. Jersey City Bd. of Edn., 1971-73; tchr. mid. sch. social studies New Providence (N.J.) Bd. of Edn., 1973-89; tchr. U.S. history and anthropology New Providence H.S., 1989—; asst. track coach New Providence H.S., 1976-82, head coach boys track, 1983—. Mem. 11th N.J. Vols., Warren County, 1994, Oxford (N.J.) Hist. Soc., 1994, Friends of Shippen Manor, Oxford, 1994. Recipient Scholar's Tchr. award Star-Ledger, 1994; named Boys Track Coach of Yr., Star-Ledger, 1994, The Courier-News, 1987, 94, Mountain Valley Conf. Track Coaches Assn., 1992, 93, 94, N.J. Track mag., 1994. Mem. NEA, Nat. Coun. for Social Studies, Nat. Fedn. Interscholastic Coaches, N.J. State Coaches Assn. Roman Catholic. Avocations: Civil War re-enactment, travel, track. Home: 15 Lincoln Ave Oxford NJ 07863-3056 Office: New Providence HS 35 Pioneer Dr New Providence NJ 07974-1515

SINOR, DENIS, Orientalist, educator; b. Kolozsvar, Hungary, Apr. 17, 1916; s. Miklos and Marguerite (Weitzenfeld) S.; m. Eugenia Trinajstic; children: Christophe (dec.), Sophie. BA, U. Budapest, 1938; MA, Cambridge (Eng.) U., 1948; doctorate (hon.), U. Szeged, Hungary, 1971. Attache Centre National de la Recherche Scientifique, Paris, 1939-48; univ. lectr. Altaic studies Cambridge U., 1948-62; prof. Uralic and Altaic studies and history Ind. U., Bloomington, 1962-81, disting. prof. Uralic and Altaic studies and history, 1975-86, disting. prof. emeritus Uralic and Altaic studies and history, 1986—, chmn. dept. Uralic and Altaic studies, 1963-1981, dir. Lang. and Area Ctr., 1963-88, dir. Asian studies program, 1965-67, dir. Asian Studies Rsch. Inst., 1967-79, dir. Rsch. Inst. for Inner Asian Studies, 1979-1981, 85-86; Sec. gen. Permanent Internat. Altaistic Conf., 1960—; rsch. project dir. U.S. Office Edn., 1969-70; sec. Internat. Union Orientalists, 1954-64; vis. prof. Institut Nat. des Langues et Civilizations Orientales, Paris, spring 1974; scholar-in-residence Rockefeller Found. Study Ctr., Bellagio, 1975; vice chmn. UNESCO Commn. for History Civilization Cen. Asia, 1981—, mem. consultative com. UNESCO Silk Rd. Project, 1990—; summer seminar dir. NEH, 1988. Author: Orientalism and History, 1954, History of Hungary, 1959, Introduction a l'ètude de l'Eurasie Centrale, 1963, Aspects of Altaic Civilization, 1963, Inner Asia, 1968, Inner Asia and Its Contacts with Medieval Europe, 1977, Tanulmányok, 1982, Essays in Comparative Altaic Linguistics, 1990; editor, contbr.: Modern Hungary, 1977, Studies in Finno-Ugric Linguistics, 1977, Uralic Languages, 1988, Essays on Uzbek History, Culture and Languages, 1993, Cambridge History of Early Inner Asia, Hanbook of Uralic Studies, Jour. Asian History, Ind. U. Uralic and Altaic Series; mem. Am. editl. rev. bd. Britannica-Hungarica. Served with Forces Françaises de l'Intérieur, 1943-44; with French Army, 1944-45. NEH grantee, 1981, 87, 88; recipient Jubilee prize U. Budapest, 1938, Barczi Geza Meml. medal, 1981, Gold medal Permanent Internat. Altaistic Conf., 1982, Arminius Vambery Meml. medal, 1983, The Thomas Hart Benton Mural Medallion, Hungarian Order of Star, 1986; Am. Philos. Soc. Research grantee, 1963; Am. Council Learned Soc. research grantee, 1962; Guggenheim fellow, 1968-69, 1981-82. Fellow Körösi Csoma Soc. (hon.); mem. Royal Asiatic Soc. (hon. sec. 1954-64, Denis Sinor medal for Inner Asian Studies named in his honor 1992), Am. Oriental Soc. (pres. Midwest br. 1968-70, nat. pres. 1975-76), Assn. Asian Studies, Am. Hist. Soc., Soc. Asiatique (hon.), Tibet Soc. (pres. 1969-74), Mongolia Soc. (pres. 1987-94), Hungarian Acad. Scis. (hon.), Acad. Europaea (fgn.), Deutsche Morgenlandische Gesellschaft, Suomalais-Ugrilaisen Seura (hon. corr.), Soc. Uralo-Altaica (v.p. 1964-94, hon.), Internat. Union Oriental and Asian Studies (v.p. 1993—), Cosmos Club Washington, Explorers Club N.Y.C., United Oxford and Cambridge Club London. Home: 5581 E Lampkins Ridge Rd Bloomington IN 47401-8674 Office: Indiana U Dept Ctrl Eurasian Studies Goodbody Hall Bloomington IN 47405

SINOR, HOWARD EARL, JR., lawyer; b. New Orleans, Sept. 6, 1949; s. Howard E. and Beverly M. (Bourgeois) S.; m. Terran Ann Woodward, June 10, 1972; children: Sally, Vera Sue, Sarah, Sadie. BA with hons., U. New Orleans, 1971; JD cum laude, Harvard U., 1975. Bar: La. 1975, U.S. Supreme Ct. 1983, U.S. Ct. Appeals (5th and 11th cir.), U.S. Dist. Ct. (ea., middle, we.) Dist. La. Assoc. Jones, Walker, Waechter, Poitevent, Carrere & Denegre, New Orleans, 1975-80; sr. ptnr. Jones, Walker, Waechter, Poitevent, Carrere & Denegre, 1980—. Contbg. author: La. Appellate Practice Handbook, 1990, 93; editor: CLE Manual of Recent Developments, 1985, 2d edit., 1986; contbr. articles to profl. jours. Recipient Pres.'s award, La. State Bar Assn., 1987. Fellow La. Bar Found.; mem. ABA, Fed. Bar Assn., New Orleans Bar Assn., La. State Bar Assn. (chmn. antitrust sect. 1987-89). Avocations: golf, hiking, cross-country skiing. Office: Jones Walker Waechter Poitevent Carrere & Denegre 201 Saint Charles Ave New Orleans LA 70170-1000

SINSHEIMER, ROBERT LOUIS, retired university chancellor and educator; b. Washington, Feb. 5, 1920; s. Allen S. and Rose (Davidson) S.; m. Flora Joan Hirsch, Aug. 8, 1943 (div. 1972); children: Lois June (Mrs. Wickstrom), Kathy Jean (Mrs. Vandagriff), Roger Allen; m. Kathleen Mae Reynolds, Sept. 10, 1972 (div. 1980); m. Karen Current, Aug. 1, 1981. S.B., MIT, 1941, M.S., 1942, Ph.D., 1948. Staff mem. radiation lab. MIT, Cambridge, 1942-46; assoc. prof. biophysics, physics dept. Iowa State Coll., Ames, 1949-55; prof. Iowa State Coll., 1955-57; prof. biophysics Calif. Inst. Tech., Pasadena, 1957-77; chmn. div. biology Calif. Inst. Tech., 1968-77; chancellor U. Calif., Santa Cruz, 1977-87, chancellor emeritus, 1987—; prof. U. Calif., Santa Barbara, 1988-90, prof. emeritus, 1990—. Editor: Jour. Molecular Biology, 1959-67, Ann. Rev. Biochemistry, 1966-72. Named Calif. Scientist of Year, 1968; recipient N.W. Beijerinck-Virologie medal Netherlands Acad. Sci., 1969. Fellow Am. Acad. Arts and Scis.; mem. Am. Soc. Biol. Chemists, Biophys. soc. (pres. 1970), AAAS, Nat. Acad. Scis. (mem. council 1970-73, chmn. bd. editors Proc. 1972-80), Inst. Medicine. Achievements include discovery of single-stranded DNA, circular DNA; co-investigator in first in vitro replication of infective DNA. Office: Univ of Calif Dept Biol Sci Santa Barbara CA 93106

SINSHEIMER, WARREN JACK, lawyer; b. N.Y.C., May 22, 1927; s. Jerome William and Elizabeth (Berch) S.; m. Florence Dubin, Mar. 30, 1950; children: Linda Ruth, Ralph David, Alan Jay, Michael Neal. Student, Ind. U., 1943-47; JD cum laude, N.Y. Law Sch., 1950; LLM, NYU, 1957; MPhil, Columbia U., 1977. Bar: N.Y. bar 1950. Ptnr. Sinsheimer, Sinsheimer & Dubin, N.Y.C., 1950-78, Satterlee & Stephens, N.Y.C., 1978-86, Patterson, Belknap, Webb & Tyler, N.Y.C., 1986-91; counsel Patterson Belknap Webb & Tyler, N.Y.C., 1991-96; pres., bd. dirs. Neighborhood Bagel Corp., 1994—; pres. Plessey, Inc., N.Y.C., 1956-70, chmn., CEO, 1970-89; dir. oversees ops. and devel. The Plessey Co., Ltd., Illford, Essex, Eng., 1969-70, dep. chief exec., dir., 1976-89; dir. Plessey, Inc.; pres., chief exec. dir. The Neighborhood Bagel Corp. Chmn. Com. of 68, 1964-67; Mem Westchester County Republican Com., 1956-73; chmn. Nat. Scranton for Pres. Com., 1964; mem. N.Y. State Assembly, 1965-66; Bd. visitors Wassaic State Sch., 1962-64. Served with USNR, 1944-45; with USAF, 1950-52. Mem. ABA, Assn. Bar City N.Y., Am. Digital Radio Soc. (pres. 1994), Jerusalem Shalom Hartman Inst. (bd. dirs. 1991—), Torch and Scroll, Century Club (Purchase, N.Y.), Zeta Beta Tau. Jewish. Home: 22 Murray Hill Rd Scarsdale NY 10583-2828 Office: Westchester/Putnam Legal Svcs 4 Cromwell Pl White Plains NY 10601

SINTON, PETER, newspaper editor, journalist. Bus./fin. editor The San Francisco Chronicle, sr. bus. writer, 1995—. Office: Chronicle Pub Co 901 Mission St San Francisco CA 94103-2905

SINTROS, JAMES LEE, management consultant, arbitrator; b. Lowell, Mass., May 20, 1947; s. Constantine James and Martha Lou (Sawyer) S.; m. Effegenia Liakos, June 27, 1971 (div. Feb. 1993); 1 child, Sarah Gillian; m. Barbara Anne Kendall, Dec. 26, 1993. BS, U. Mass., Lowell, 1970; JD, Suffolk U., 1974. Cert. registered arbitrator. Cons., Andover, Mass., 1974—; sr. cons. Cassidy & Assocs., Washington, 1985-95; clk. West of Ireland Edn. Fund, Inc., N.Y.C. and Galway, Ireland, 1990—; dir. Mass. Ctr. for S.I.D.S., 1989—; clk., dir. S.I.D.S. Outreach Found., Inc., Mass., 1991—; exec. dir. Internat. Ednl. and Med. Alliance New Eng., Inc., Mass., 1989—; exec. dir., treas. Joseph W. Stilwell Inst. Found., Ltd., Chongqing, China, 1989—; v.p., dir. G.T.N.Y. Found., Inc., N.Y.C., 1991-95; pres., treas., clk., bd. dirs. Global Brokers Internat. Ltd., Dublin, Ireland, 1993—; pres., treas., bd. dirs. Multinat. Bus. Devel. Coalition, Ltd., Hong Kong, 1990—; internat. cons. Suffolk U., Boston, 1992—; spl. asst. to pres. New Eng. Coll. Optometry, Boston, 1992-96; automobile racer in U.S. and abroad, 1965-82. Bd. dirs., vice chair Young Audiences of Mass., 1979-82; bd. dirs. Boston Classical Orch., 1985-89, Critical Langs. and Area Studies Consortium, 1990-93; corporator Merrimack Valley Cmty. Found., Inc.; treas. Am.- Ireland Ednl. Found., N.Y.C., Dublin, Ireland, 1995—. Mem. Am. Registry Arbitrators. Home: Brickend Farm 134 Boston Rd Chelmsford MA 01824-3965 Office: 93 Main St Andover MA 01810-3840

SINTZ, EDWARD FRANCIS, librarian; b. New Trenton, Ind., Feb. 6, 1924; s. John and Edith E. (Rudicil) S.; m. Donna Norris, Apr. 12, 1952; children—Ann Kristin, Lesley Elizabeth, Julie Melinda. B.A., U. Kans., 1950; M.A. in L.S, U. Denver, 1954; M.S. in Pub. Adminstrn, U. Mo., 1965. With Kansas City (Mo.) Pub. Library, 1954-66, asst. dir., 1964-66; asso. librarian St. Louis Pub. Library, 1966-68; dir. pub. libraries Miami, Fla., 1968-89, ret.; instr. Washington U., St. Louis, 1966-67; library surveys for Mo. State Library, 1967-68; library bldg. cons., 1965—. Editor: Mo. Library Assn. Quar, 1956-58. Served with USAAF, 1942-45. Mem. ALA, Fla. Library Assn. (pres. 1975-76), Southeastern Library Assn. Club: Kiwanian. Home: 7105 Lakeside Dr Charlotte NC 28215

SION, MAURICE, mathematics educator; b. Skopje, Yugoslavia, Oct. 17, 1928; came to Can., 1960; s. Max and Sarah (Alalouf) S.; m. Emilie Grace Chisholm, Sept. 15, 1957; children—Crispin, Sarah, Dirk. B.A., NYU, 1947, M.A., 1948; Ph.D., U. Calif.-Berkeley, 1951. Mathematician Nat. Bur. Standards, Washington, 1951-52; instr. U. Calif.-Berkeley, 1952-53; mem. Inst. for Advanced Study, Princeton, N.J., 1955-57, 62; asst. prof. U. Calif.-Berkeley, 1957-60; asst. prof. U. B.C., Vancouver, 1960, assoc. prof., 1961, prof., 1964-89, prof. emeritus, 1989—, head math. dept., 1984-86; dir. Quadra Inst. Math., Vancouver, 1970-89, prof. emeritus, 1989—. Author: Introduction to Methods of Real Analysis, 1969; Theory Semi Group Valued Measures, 1973. Contbr. articles to profl. jours. Served with U.S. Army, 1953-55. Mem. Am. Math. Soc., Can. Math. Soc. (v.p. 1972-74). Office: U BC, Dept Math, Vancouver, BC Canada V6T 1Z2

SIOUI, RICHARD HENRY, chemical engineer; b. Bklyn., Sept. 25, 1937; s. Joseph Fernand and Ellen Annette (Johnson) S.; m. Mary Ann Kapinos,

July 21, 1962; children: Kathleen, Thomas, Daniel, Rebecca, Linda, Michelle. BS, Northeastern U., 1964; PhD, U. Mass., 1968. Sr. rsch. engr. Norton Co., Superabrasives div., Worcester, Mass., 1968-71, rsch. supr., 1971-78, tech. mgr., 1978-83, rsch. dir., 1983-87, dir. of tech., 1987—. Com. chmn. Boy Scouts Am. Troop 178, Holden, Mass., 1981-86. With USAF, 1955-59. Recipient Outstanding Engring. Alumnus award U. Mass., 1995. Mem. AIChE, Am. Indian Sci. and Engring. Sci., Diamond Wheel Mfrs. Inst. (stds, safety and health com.). Achievements include patents relative to the manufacture and composition of abrasive products in which diamond or cubic boron nitride is the abrasive. Home: 22 Streeter Rd Hubbardston MA 01452-1433 Office: Norton Co 1 New Bond St Worcester MA 01606-2614

SIPER, CYNTHIA DAWN, special education educator; b. Bklyn., Apr. 16, 1965; d. Joel S. and Diana M. (Kessler) Rosenblatt; m. Alan Siper, Apr. 9, 1989; children: Rebecca Ruth, Daniel Louis. BS in Edn., SUNY, Plattsburgh, 1988; MEd, SUNY, New Paltz, 1992. Cert. K-12 spl. edn. tchr., N-6 elem. edn. tchr., N.Y. Tchr. spl. edn. Valley Cen. Sch. Dist., Montgomery, N.Y., 1988-90, Middletown (N.Y.) Enlarged City Sch. Dist., 1990—; spl. edn. tchr. rep. Coun. on Spl. Edn., Middletown, 1990—. Mem. Coun. for Exceptional Children, Middletown Tchrs. Assn., Kappa Delta Pi. Avocation: collecting Disneyana.

SIPES, JAMES LAMOYNE, landscape architect, educator; b. Elizabethtown, Ky., Jan. 28, 1957; s. William L. and Betty Jean (Miller) S.; m. Kimberly A. Blevins, Feb. 5, 1983; children: Matthew, Sara, Ally. BS in Landscape Architecture, U. Ky., 1982; M in Landscape Architecture, Iowa State U., 1984. Registered landscape architect, Tex. Teaching asst. U. Ky., Lexington, 1981-82; planning intern Lexington-Fayette Govt., 1982-83; teaching asst. Iowa State U., Ames, 1983-84; landscape architect Nat. Park Svc., Gunnison, Colo., 1984-85, Schrickel, Rollins Assocs., Arlington, Tex., 1985-88, U.S. Forest Svc., Dillon, Mont., 1989; computer graphic cons. Video Perspectives, Inc., Louisville, 1990; lectr. U. Idaho, Moscow, 1989-93; assoc. prof. landscape architecture Wash. State U., Pullman, 1988-94, U. Okla., Norman, 1995—; cons. Computer Graphics and Simulations, Salt Lake City, 1993-94; mem. adv. bd. Cmty. Childcare Ctr., Pullman, 1992—. Computer editor Landscape Architecture Mag., Washington, 1994—; producer Animated World, PBS, 1994—; contbr. articles to profl. jours. Mem. Pullman Civic Trust, 1993-94. Recipient Cert. of Appreciation, Soil Conservation Svc., 1992, Cert. of Appreciation, U.S. Forest Svc., 1990. Mem. Am. Soc. Landscape Architects (Honor award 1984, 94, Tex. Design award 1992), Coun. Educators in Landscape Architecture, Nat. Computer Graphics Assn., Pacific N.W. Recreation Consortium, Gamma Sigma Delta, Phi Kappa Phi. Avocations: sports, art, reading, technology. Office: U Okla Landscape Architecture Dept Landscape Architecture Norman OK 73019

SIPES, KAREN KAY, newspaper editor; b. Higginsville, Mo., Jan. 8, 1947; d. Walter John and Katherine Marie (McLelland) Heins; m. Joel Rodney Sipes, Sept. 24, 1971; 1 child, Lesley Katherine. BS in Edn., Ctrl. Mo. State U., 1970. Reporter/news editor Newton Kansan, 1973-76; sports writer Capital-Jour., Topeka, 1976-83, spl. sects. editor, 1983-85, editl. page editor, 1985-92, mng. editor/features, 1992—. Co-chair Mayor's Commn. on Literacy, Topeka, 1996—; mem. Act Against Violence Com., Topeka, 1995—. Mem. Ctrl. Mo. State U. Alumni Assn. (bd. dirs. 1996—). Avocations: music, gardening, art. Office: The Capital-Journal 616 SE Jefferson Topeka KS 66607

SIPFLE, DAVID ARTHUR, philosophy educator; b. Pekin, Ill., Aug. 29, 1932; s. Karl Edward and Louis Adele (Hinners) S.; m. Mary-Alice Slauson, Sept. 4, 1954; children: Ann Littlefield (dec.), Gail Elizabeth. BA in Math., Philosophy magna cum laude, Carleton Coll., 1953; MA, Yale U., 1955, PhD, 1958. Instr. philosophy Robert Coll., Istanbul, Turkey, 1957-58, Am. Coll. for Girls, Istanbul, 1957-60; asst. prof. Carleton Coll., Northfield, Minn., 1960-67, assoc. prof., 1967-70, chmn. dept., 1968-71, 89-92, prof., 1970-92, William H. Laird prof. philosophy and liberal arts, 1992—; vis. fellow Wolfson Coll., Cambridge U., 1975-76. Translator: (with Mary-Alice Sipfle) Emile Meyerson, The Relativistic Deduction: Epistemological Implications of the Theory of Relativity, 1985, Explanation in the Sciences, 1991; contbr. articles to profl. jours. NEH Younger Humanist fellow, Nice, France, 1971-72, NSF Sci. Faculty fellow, Cambridge, Eng., 1975-76; Carleton Coll. Faculty Devel. grantee, 1981-83, 86-87. Mem. Am. Philos. Assn., Metaphysical Soc. Am., Philosophy of Sci. Assn., History of Sci. Soc. Avocation: cross country skiing. Office: Carleton Coll 1 N Coll St Northfield MN 55057

SIPIORA, LEONARD PAUL, retired museum director; b. Lawrence, Mass., Sept. 1, 1934; s. Walter and Agnes S.; m. Sandra Joyce Coon, 1962; children—Alexandra, Erika. A.B. cum laude, U. Mich., 1955, M.A., 1956. Dir. museums City of El Paso, Tex., 1967-90; ret.; co-founder, pres. El Paso Arts Council, 1969-71; sec.-treas. El Paso Council Internat. Visitors, 1968-71; trustee El Paso Mus. Art; bd. dirs. Tex. Com. Humanities, Assn. Southwestern Humanities Council; adv. bd. S.W. Arts Found. Bd. dirs. Community Concert Assn. El Paso, El Paso Symphony Orch., El Paso Hist. Soc. Mem. Assn. Mus. Dirs., Mountain Plains Mus. Assn. (pres. 1978-79), Tex. Assn. Museums (pres. 1977-79), Knights of Malta (decorated Grand Cross), Prior of Tex., Kappa Pi. Republican. Lutheran. Home: 1012 Blanchard Ave El Paso TX 79902-2727

SIPPEL, WILLIAM LEROY, lawyer; b. Fond du Lac, Wis., Aug. 14, 1948; s. Alfonse Aloysious and Virginia Laura (Weber) S.; m. Barbara Jean Brost, Aug. 23, 1970; children: Katharine Jean, David William. BA, U. Wis., JD. Bar: Wis. 1974, U.S. Dist. Ct. (we. dist.) Wis. 1974, Minn. 1981, U.S. Dist. Ct. Minn. 1981, U.S. Ct. Appeals (10th cir.) 1984, U.S. Ct. Appeals (8th cir.) 1985. Research assoc. dept. agrl. econs. U. Wis., Madison, 1974-75; counsel monopolies and comml. law subcom. Ho. Judiciary Com., Washington, 1975-80; spl. asst. to asst. gen. antitrust div. U.S. Dept. of Justice, Washington, 1980-81; from assoc. to ptnr. Doherty, Rumble & Butler, Mpls. and St. Paul, Minn., 1981—. Co-author: The Antitrust Health Care Handbook, 1988. Mem. program com. Minn. World Trade Assn., Mpls., St. Paul, 1985-86, bd. dirs., 1986, Minn. With USAF, 1971-77. Mem. ABA (vice chmn. ins. industry com. 1990-91), Minn. Bar Assn. (co-chmn. antitrust sect. 1986-88, internat. law sect. coun. 1986-89, treas. 1989-90, sec. 1990-91, vice chmn. 1995-96, chmn. 1996-97), Minn. Med. Alley Assn. (co-chmn. internat. bus. com. 1990-95, Hennepin County Office Internat. Trade (bd. dirs. 1988-93), Phi Beta Kappa. Roman Catholic. Avocations: computers, reading. Home: 1448 Pinewood Dr Saint Paul MN 55125-2063 Office: Doherty Rumble & Butler PA 2800 Minnesota World Trade Ctr Saint Paul MN 55101

SIPPLE, JOHN HARRISON, physician; b. July 1, 1930. BA, Cornell U., 1952; MD, Cornell Med. Coll., 1955. Diplomate Am. Bd. Internal Medicine, Pulmonary Disease. Intern Upstate Med. Ctr./SUNY, 1955-56, resident, 1956-59; fellow Johns Hopkins Hosp., Balt., 1961-62; clin. prof. medicine SUNY Health Sci. Ctr., Syracuse; attending phys. Crouse Irving Meml. Hosp., 1962—, State Univ. Hosp.; cons. Syracuse VA Med. Ctr., Syracuse State Sch., 1962-78; med. dir. Onondaga C.C. Respiratory Therapy Tech. Cert. Program, 1976-78; cons. physician Comm. on the Handicapped, Jamesville-Dewitt Sch. Dist., 1975-77; cons. Cayuga Health Ctr., 1977-78, Laurentian Med. Group, 1976-77, others; mem. exec. com. Univ. Hosp., 1993—; mem. critical care com. Clancy Irving Meml. Hosp., 1993—. Contbr. articles to profl. jours. and publs. Vol. physician Empire State Games, 1984, 87; mem.-at-large med. bd. Univ. Hosp., 1994-96, others. Fellow Am. Coll. Physicians (program chmn. 1977, mem. coun. of N.Y. state chpt. 1986-93, gov.-elect upstate N.Y. 1988, gov. 1989-93, mem. med. informatics com. 1992-93), Am. Coll. Chest Physicians; mem. Am. Fedn. Clin. Rsch., AMA, Med. Soc. State of N.Y., Onondaga County Med. Soc., Heart Assn. of Upstate N.Y., Trudeau Soc. (mem. chmn. 1971), Am. Thoracic Soc.

SIPPO, ARTHUR CARMINE, occupational medicine physician; b. Jan. 30, 1953; s. Carmine Constantine and Mildred Angela (Musto) S.; m. Katherine Velma Sager, Jan. 87, 1987; children: Sean, Tiffany, Courtney. BS in Chemistry magna cum laude, St. Peter's Coll., Jersey City, 1974; MD, Vanderbilt U., 1978; MPH, Johns Hopkins U., 1983. Diplomate Am. Bd. Preventive Medicine. Commd. 2d lt. U.S. Army, 1978, advanced through grades to lt. col., 1992; intern in ob-gyn. Walter Reed Army Med. Ctr., 1978-79; 1st brigade surgeon 101st Airborne Div., Ft. Campbell, Ky., 1979-81; resident in aerospace medicine USAF Sch. Aerospace Medicine, Brooks AFB, Tex., 1981-83; dir. biodynamics rsch. div. U.S. Army Aeromed. Rsch. Lab., Ft. Rucker, Ala., 1983-86; exch. officer RAF Inst. Aviation Medicine, Farnborough, Hants., Eng., 1986-90; ret., 1990; occupational medicine physicians Occupational Care Cons., Holland, Ohio, 1990-92; comdr. 145th M.A.S.H., Camp Perry, Ohio, 1992-94; dep. comdr. for clin. svcs. 112th Med. Brigade Ohio Army Nat. Guard, Columbus, 1994-95; asst. state surgeon Ohio Army N.G., Columbus, 1995—; med. dir. Libbey Glass, Inc., Toledo, 1990—, Clyde (Ohio) divsn. Whirlpool Corp., 1990—; mem. aerospace cons. adv. panel U.S. Army Surgeon Gen.'s Office. Author: Arthropometic Considerations of the U.S. Army, 1988. Mem. Ohio N.G., 1990—. Master Am. Coll. Occup. and Environ. Medicine; fellow Am. Coll. Preventive Medicine, Aerospace Med. Assn.; mem. Soc. U.S. Army Flight Surgeons, Am. Coll. Emergency Physicians, Fellowship Cath. Scholars. Roman Catholic. Avocations: theology, philosophy, Biblical studies, patristics, paleontology. Office: Occupational Care Cons 6855 Spring Valley Dr Ste 160 Holland OH 43528-9374

SIQUELAND, EINAR, psychology educator; b. Glasgow, Mont., Nov. 15, 1932; s. Harald and Anna Lydia (Dristersen) S.; m. Marian McGrail, Dec. 1960 (div. May 1970); children: Lynne Ruth, Beth Ann; m. Jillian E.A. Godfree, June 29, 1973. BA, Pacific Luth. U., 1954; MS, U. Wash., 1962, PhD, 1963. Rsch. assoc. pharmacology U. Wash., Seattle, 1958-59; clin. intern psychology VA Mental Hygiene Clinic, Seattle, 1960-61; asst. prof. dept. psychology Brown U., Providence, 1965-69, assoc. prof., 1969-88, prof., 1988—; rsch. scientist dept. Pediatrics Women's and Infants' Hosp., Providence, 1975—. Contbr. articles to profl. jours., chpts. to books. With U.S. Army, 1956-58, Korea. Predoctoral fellow USPHS, 1961-63, postdoctoral fellow, 1963-65. Mem. AAUP, APA, Am. Psychol. Soc., Soc. Rsch. in Child Devel., Sigma Xi. Office: Brown U Dept Psychology PO Box 1853 Providence RI 02912-1853

SIRI, WILLIAM E., physicist; b. Phila., Jan. 2, 1919; s. Emil Mark and Caroline (Schaedel) S.; m. Margaret Jean Brandenburg, Dec. 3, 1949; children: Margaret Lynn, Ann Kathryn. B.Sc., U. Chgo., 1942; postgrad. in physics, U. Calif.-Berkeley, 1947-50. Licensed profl. engr., Calif. Research engr. Baldwin-Lima-Hamilton Corp., 1943; physicist Manhattan Project Lawrence-Berkeley Lab., U. Calif., Berkeley, 1943-45, prin. investigator biophysics and research, 1945-74, mgr. energy analysis program, 1974-81, sr. scientist emeritus, 1981—; cons. energy and environment, 1982—; lectr. U. Calif. Summer Inst., 1962-72; vis. scientist Nat. Cancer Inst., 1970; exec. v.p. Am. Mt. Everest Expdn., Inc.; field leader U. Calif. Peruvian Expdns., 1950-52; leader Calif. Himalayan Expdn., 1954; field leader Internat. Physiol. Expdn. to Antarctica, 1957; dep. leader Am. Mt. Everest Expdn., 1963. Author: Nuclear Radiations and Isotopic Tracers, 1949, papers on energy systems analyses, biophys. research, conservation and mountaineering. Pres. Save San Francisco Bay Assn., 1968-88; bd. dirs. Sierra Club Found., 1964-78; gov. gen. Mountain Medicine Inst., 1988—; vice chmn. The Bay Inst., 1985—; bd. dirs. San Francisco Bay-Delta Preservation Assn., 1987—, treas., 1987—. Lt. (j.g.) USNR, 1950-59. Co-recipient Hubbard medal Nat. Geog. Soc., 1963, Elsa Kent Kane medal Phila. Geog. Soc., 1963, Sol Feinstone Environ. award, 1977, Environ. award East Bay Regional Park Dist., 1984. Mem. Am. Phys. Soc., Biophys. Soc., Am. Assn. Physicists in Medicine, Sigma Xi. Democrat. Lutheran. Clubs: Sierra (dir. 1955-74, pres. 1964-66, William Colby award 1975, John Muir award 1994), American Alpine (v.p.), Explorers (certificate of merit 1964). Home: 1015 Leneve Pl El Cerrito CA 94530-2751

SIRICA, ALPHONSE EUGENE, pathology educator; b. Waterbury, Conn., Jan. 16, 1944; s. Alphonse Eugene and Elena Virginia (Mascolo) S.; m. Annette Marie Murray, June 9, 1984; children: Gabrielle Theresa, Nicholas Steven. MS, Fordham U., 1968; PhD in Biomed. Sci., U. Conn., 1977. Asst. prof. U. Wis., Madison, 1979-84; assoc. prof. Med. Coll. Va., Va. Commonwealth U., Richmond, 1984-90, prof. of pathology, 1990—, divsn. chair exptl. pathology, 1992—; regular mem. sci. adv. com. on carcinogenesis and nutrition Am. Cancer Soc., Atlanta, 1989-92, metabolic pathology study sect., NIH, Bethesda, 1991-95. Editor, author: The Pathobiology of Neoplasia, 1989, The Role of Cell Types in Hepatocarcinogenesis, 1992, Cellular and Molecular Pathogenesis, 1996; co-editor, author: Biliary and Pancreatic Ductal Epithelia: Pathobiology and Pathophysiology, 1996; mem. editl. bd. Pathobiology, 1990—, Hepatology, 1991-94; rev. bd. In Vitro Cellular and Devel. Biology, 1987—; contbr. rsch. papers to Am. Jour. Pathology, Cancer Rsch., others. Mem. AAAS, Am. Soc. Cell Biology, Am. Assn. Cancer Rsch. (chmn. Va. state legis. com. 1992-95), Soc. for In Vitro Biology, Assn.Clin. Scientist, Am. Soc. Investigative Pathology (chair program com. 1994-96), Am. Assn. Study Liver Diseases, N.Y. Acad. Scis., Soc. Exptl. Biology and Medicine, Hans Popper Hepatopathology Soc., Soc. Toxicology. Democrat. Roman Catholic. Achievements include development of collagen gel-nylon mesh system for culturing hepatocytes; first establishment and characterization of hyperplastic bile ductular epithelial cells in culture; research in hepato and biliary carcinogenesis, pathobiology of hepatocyte and biliary epithelial cells. Office: Med Coll Va Va Commonwealth U PO Box 980297 Richmond VA 23298-0297

SIRIGNANO, WILLIAM ALFONSO, aerospace and mechanical engineer, educator; b. Bronx, N.Y., Apr. 14, 1938; s. Anthony P. and Lucy (Caruso) S.; m. Lynn Haisfield, Nov. 26, 1977; children: Monica Ann, Jacqueline Hope, Justin Anthony. B.Aero.Engring., Rensselaer Poly. Inst., 1959; Ph.D., Princeton U., 1964. Mem. research staff Guggenheim Labs., aerospace, mech. scis. dept. Princeton U., 1964-67, asst. prof. aerospace and mech. scis., 1967-69, assoc. prof., 1969-73, prof., 1973-79, dept. dir. grad. studies, 1974-78; George Tallman Ladd prof., head dept. mech. engring. Carnegie-Mellon U., 1979-85; dean Sch. Engring., U. Calif.-Irvine, 1985-94; cons. indsutry and govt., 1966—; lectr. and cons. NATO adv. group on aero. rsch. and devel., 1967, 75, 80; chmn. nat. and internat. tech. congs.; chmn. acad. adv. coun. Indsl. Rsch. Inst., 1985-88; mem. space sci. applications adv. com. NASA, 1985-90, chmn. combustion sci. microgravity disciplinary working group, 1987-90; chmn. com. on microgravity rsch. space studies bd. NRC, 1991-94. Assoc. editor: Combustion Sci. and Tech., 1969-70; assoc. tech. editor Jour. Heat Transfer, 1986-92; contbr. articles to nat. and internat. profl. jours., also rsch. monographs. United Aircraft research fellow, 1973-74; Disting. Alumni Rsch. award U. Calif. Irvine, 1992. Fellow AIAA (Pendray Aerospace Lit. award 1991, Propellants and Combustion award 1992), ASME (Freeman scholar 1992), IDERS (v.p. 1991-95, pres. 1995—, Oppenheim award 1993), AAAS; mem. Combustion Inst. (treas. internat. orgn., chmn. ea. sect.), Soc. Indsl. and Applied Math., Orange County Engring. Coun. (Excellence award 1994), Am. Electronics Assn. (recognition 1994). Office: U Calif Sch Engring S 3202 Engring Gateway Irvine CA 92717

SIRIS, ETHEL SILVERMAN, endocrinologist; b. Clifton, N.J., Aug. 21, 1945; s. Irving A. and Gertrude (Gollop) Silverman; m. Samuel G. Siris, June 2, 1971; children: Benjamin A., Sara A. AB in Biology magna cum laude, Radcliffe Coll. Harvard U., 1963-67; MD, Columbia U. Coll. Physicians and Surgeons, 1967-71. Nat. Bd. of Medical Examiners, Diplomate Am Bd. Internal Medicine, Diplomate Am. Bd. Internal Medicine, Certification in Endocrinology and Metabolism. Intern, asst. resident dept. medicine Presbyn. Hosp., N.Y.C., 1971-74, asst. attending physician, 1977-84, assoc. attending physician, 1984-91, attending physician, 1991—; NIH guest worker Reproduction Rsch. Br. Nat. Inst. Child Health and Human Devel., NIH, 1974-75, NIH rsch. fellow, 1975-76; fellow in Endocrinology Columbia U. Coll. of Physicians & Surgeons and Presbyn. Hosp., N.Y.C., 1976-77; bd. dirs. the Paget Found. for Paget's Disease of Bone and Related Disorders;; bd. trustees Nat. Osteoporosis Found.; mem. instl. rev. bd. Columbia-Presbyn. Med. Ctr., assoc. program dir. Irving Ctr. Clin. Rsch.,, 1990-95, dir. programs in osteoporosis Ctr. for Women's Health, 1993—; asst. prof. dept. medicine Columbia U., 1977-84, assoc. prof. clin. medicine, 1984-91, prof. clin. medicine, 1991—, course dir. phys. diagnosis dept. medicine, 1985—; mem. endocrinologic and metabolic drugs adv. com. FDA, 1992-95. Contbr. numerous articles to profl. jours. Upjohn award Columbia U. Coll. of Physicians and Surgeons, 1971, Mary Putnam Jacobi award for Clin. Rsch., 1979, Rsch. award The Paget's Disease Fdn., 1986, 87. Am. Soc. for Bone and Mineral Rsch., Endocrine Soc., Am. Assn. of Clin. Endocrinologists, Phi Beta Kappa, Alpha Omega Alpha. Home: 60 Prescott St Demarest NJ 07627-1420 Office: Dept Medicine Columbia U Coll Physicians & Surgeons 630 W 168th St New York NY 10032-3702

SIRIWARDANE, RANJANI VINITA, chemist; b. Matale, Sri Lanka, May 30, 1955; d. Buddhipriya and Kumari Wijesundera; m. Hema Jayalath Siriwardane, Feb. 10, 1977; children: Nishani Marcia, Emil Nuwan. BS Chemistry, U. Sri Lanka, 1977; MS Chemistry, Va. Poly. Inst. and State U., 1979, PhD Chemistry, 1981. Rsch. assoc. W. Va. U., Morgantown, 1981-84, rsch. asst. prof., 1987-88; rsch. fellow U.S. Dept. Energy, Morgantown, 1984-87, rsch. chemist, 1988—; lectr. in field. Contbr. articles to profl. jours. and publs.; patentee in field. Recipient award for Acad. Excellence in Grad. Studies, Atlantic Richfield Co., 1981. Mem. Am. Chem. Soc., Sigma Xi, Phi Kappa Phi, Phi Lambda. Office: US Dept Energy METC Collins Ferry Rd Morgantown WV 26505

SIRKIN, JOEL H., lawyer; b. Pitts., Jan. 7, 1946; s. Sidney and Marion (Wolkin) S.; m. Karen Sargent, Aug. 7, 1977; children: Alex S., Jacob O. BA magna cum laude, Johns Hopkins U., 1967; JD cum laude, Harvard U., 1972. Bar: Mass. 1972. Prin. Cambridge (Mass.) Pilot Sch., 1970-71; staff atty. Cambridge-Somerville Legal Services, 1972-74; sr. ptnr. Hale & Dorr, Boston, 1974—. Author: Public School Law. Dir. Mass. Children's Lobby, Boston, 1980-84; mem. fin. com. Town of Wayland, Mass., 1993-96. Mem. Phi Beta Kappa. Avocations: gardening, tennis, golf. Home: 10 Wildwood Rd Wayland MA 01778-2122 Office: Hale & Dorr 60 State St Boston MA 02109-1803

SIROIS, CHARLES, communications executive; b. Chicoutimi, Que., Can., May 22, 1954; children: Françoise-Charles, Marie-Hélène. Founder Nat. Telesys. Ltd., Nat. Pagette Ltd., Montreal, 1986-88; chmn., CEO BCE Mobile Comms., Inc., Montreal, 1988-90, Teleglobe, Inc., Teleglobe Can., Inc., Montreal, 1992-94, Telesystem Fin. Corp., Montreal, 1990—, Nat. Telesystem Ltd., Montreal, 1990—; chmn. Microcell Telecomms., Inc.; bd. dirs. Hydro-Québec, Radiomutuel, Inc., École nat. de l'humour; mem. Fed. Adv. Coun. on the Info. Hwy., Global Info. Infrastructure Commn., Univ. du Québec á Montréal, chmn. fundraising campaign, 1994—. Co-author: The Medium and the Muse, 1995. Mem. Order of Can. (hon.). Office: Telesys Ltd, 1000 de la Gauchetière St W 25th Fl, Montreal, PQ Canada H3B 4W5 also: Teleglobe Inc/Teleglobe Can Inc, 1000 de la Gauchetière St W 24th Fl, Montreal, PQ Canada H3B 4X5

SIROIS, GERARD, pharmacy educator; b. Andreville, Kamouraska, Que., Can., Dec. 5, 1934; s. Paul-Etienne and Marie-Anna (Caron) S.; children: Nathalie, Stephane. B.Pharm., U. Montreal, 1960; M.S., Purdue U., 1962, Ph.D., 1965. Lic. pharmacist, Que. Asst. prof. pharmacy U. Montreal, 1965-71, assoc. prof., 1971-76, prof., 1976—, pres. Ethic Com. for Health, 1984—. Grantee Med. Research Council Can., 1974-79; grantee Ministere d'Education du Que., 1972-74. Mem. Am. Pharm. Assn., Assn. Faculties of Pharmacy of Can., Am. Assn. Pharm. Scientists, Can. Soc. Hosp. Pharmacists, Sigma Xi. Roman Catholic. Home: 6352 Matte St, Montreal-Nord, PQ Canada H1G 2E8 Office: U Montreal Faculte Pharmacie, 2900 Blvd Edouard Montpetit, Montreal, PQ Canada H3C 3J7

SIRONEN, LYNN JANE, secondary school educator; b. London, Dec. 15, 1951; came to U.S., 1953; d. Harold Walter and Jane Adele Markham; m. Jan Steven Sironen, June 5, 1971; children: Karen, Christina, Steven. BA in Elem. Edn., U. R.I., 1973, MA in Sci. Edn., 1986. Elem. tchr. North Kingstown (R.I.) Schs., 1973, 75, substitute tchr., 1974, 80, computer tchr., 1985-86, tchr. sci., 1986—; tchr. sci. Westerly (R.I.) Schs., 1981, The Wheeler Sch., Providence, 1981-82; grad. asst. U. R.I., Kingston, 1982-84, part-time instr., 1987. Mem., vice comdr., exec. bd. North Kingstown Ambulance Corps, 1975-87; pres. North Kingstown Band Parents, 1992-94. Mem. Nat. Sci. Tchrs. Assn., NEA of North Kingstown (sec. 1994-96), North Kingstown Bus. and Profl. Women's Club (treas. 1993-94) Rotary (Tchr. of Month 1993). Episcopalian. Home: PO Box 152 North Kingstown RI 02852-0152 Office: North Kingstown High School 150 Fairway Dr North Kingstown RI 02852-6202

SIROTKIN, PHILLIP LEONARD, educational administrator; b. Moline, Ill., Aug. 2, 1923; s. Alexander and Molly (Berghaus) S.; m. Cecille Sylvia Gussack, May 1, 1945; children—Steven Marc, Laurie Anne. B.A. (McGregor Found. scholar), Wayne State U., 1945; M.A., U. Chgo., 1947, Ph.D. (Walgreen Found. scholar, Carnegie fellow), 1951. Lectr. U. Chgo., 1949-50; instr. Wellesley Coll., 1950-52, asst. prof. polit. sci., 1953-57; asso. dir. Western Interstate Commn. Higher Edn., Boulder, Colo., 1957-60; exec. asst. to dir. Calif. Dept. Mental Hygiene, Sacramento, 1960-63; asst. dir. NIMH, 1964-66, asso. dir., 1967-71, cons., 1971-73; exec. v.p., acad. v.p. State U. N.Y. at Albany, 1971-76; exec. dir. Western Interstate Commn. Higher Edn., Boulder, Colo., 1976-90, sr. adviser, 1990—; sr. adviser Midwestern Legis. Higher Edn. Steering Com., Boulder, Colo., 1990-91; sr. cons. Midwestern Higher Edn. Commn., 1991—; bd. dirs. Boulder County Mental Health Ctr., 1992—; mem. ovesight commn. Hispanic Agenda, Larasa, 1992—; cons. Nebr. Post-Secondary Edn. Commn., 1994; mem. nat. adv. com. Soc. Coll. and Univ. Planning, 1976, adv. panel, rev. state system higher edn. in N.D., 1986, gov.'s com. on bi-state med. edn. plan for N.D. and S.D., 1988-90, Edn. Commn. States' Nat. Task Force for Minority Achievement in Higher Edn., 1989-91; cons. Bur. Health Manpower Edn., NIH, 1972-74, Nat. Ctr. Health Svcs. Rsch., 1975-85; spl. cons. AID, 1963-64; case writer Resources for the Future, 1954-55; mem. 1st U.S. Mission on Mental Health to USSR, 1967. Author: The Echo Park Dam Controversy and Upper Colorado River Development, 1959. Bd. dirs. Council Social Work Edn., 1959-60. Served to 1st lt. AUS, 1943-46. Recipient Superior Service award HEW, 1967; Wellesley Coll. Faculty Research award, 1956. Home: 299 Green Rock Dr Boulder CO 80302-4745 Office: PO Drawer P Boulder CO 80302

SIS, PETER, illustrator, children's book author, artist, filmmaker; b. Brno, Czech Republic, May 11, 1949; came to U.S., 1982, naturalized, 1988; s. Vladimir and Alena (Petrvalska) S.; m. Terry Ann Lajtha, Oct. 23, 1990; children: Madeleine, Matej. BA, Acad. Fine Arts, Prague, Czech Republic, 1968, MA, 1974. Author, illustrator: Rainbow Rhino, 1987, Waving, 1988, Going Up, 1989, Beach Ball, 1990, Follow the Dream, 1991, An Ocean World, 1992, A Small, Tall Tale from the Far Far North, 1992, Komodo!, 1993, The Three Golden Keys, 1994, Starry Messenger, 1996; illustrator: Fairy Tales of the Brothers Grimm, 2 vols., 1976, 77, Hexe Lakritze and Buchstabenkonig, 1977, Zizkov Romances, 1978, Hexe Lakritze and Rhino Rhinoceros, 1979, Poetry, 1980, Baltic Fairy Tales, 1981, Little Singer, 1982, Bean Boy, 1983, Stories to solve, 1984, Whipping Boy, 1985 (Newberry medal 1987), Oaf, 1986, Three Yellow Dogs, 1986, Higgledy Piggledy, 1986, Jed and the Space Bandits, 1987, After Midnight, 1987, City Lights, 1987, Scarebird, 1988, Alphabet Soup, 1988, Halloween, 1989, The Ghost in the Noonday Sun, 1989, The Midnight Horse, 1990, More Stories to Solve, 1991, Rumpelstiltskin, 1993, The Dragons Are Singing Tonight, 1993, Still More Stories to Solve, 1994, The 13th Floor, 1995, Monday's Troll, 1996; filmmaker: (TV series) Hexe Lakritze, 1982, (short films) Mimikry, 1975, Island for 6,000 Alarm Clocks, 1977, Heads, 1979 (Golden Bear award Berlin Film Festival 1980), Players, 1981 (Grand Prix Toronto Film Festival 1981), You Gotta Serve Somebody, 1983 (CINE Golden Eagle award 1983), Aesop's Fables, 1984, Twelve Months, 1985; artist one man shows include Gallery Martinska, Gallery Nerudova, Gallery Rubin, Prague, 1977-79, Gallery Klostermauer, St. Gallen, 1975, Gallery Ploem, Delft, 1977, Gallery Vista Nova, Zurich, 1980, Gallery Medici, London, 1981, Sch. Art U. Ohio, Athens, 1990. Recipient Best Illustrated Book award N.Y. Times, 1988, 90, 92, 93, 94, gold medal Soc. Illustrators, 1993, silver medal, 1993, 94, Horn Book Honor Book award Boston Globe, 1993, 94. Home: 252 Lafayette St Apt 5E New York NY 10012-4064 Office: care Greenwillow Books 1350 Avenue Of The Americas New York NY 10019-4702

SIS, RAYMOND FRANCIS, veterinarian, educator; b. Munden, Kans., July 22, 1931; s. Frank J. and Edvie (Shimanek) S.; m. Janice L. Murphy, Aug. 31, 1953; children: Susan, Valerie, Mark, Michael, Amy. B.S., Kans. State U., 1953, D.V.M., 1957; M.S., Iowa State U., 1962, Ph.D., 1965. Clinician Blue Cross Animal Hosp., Albuquerque, 1957; asst. prof. small animal surgery Iowa State U., Ames, 1964-66; assoc. prof. anatomy Tex. A&M U., College Station, 1966-68, prof., 1968—, head dept. vet. anatomy, 1968-83. Served with USAF, 1957-61; mem. Res., 1961-91. Mem. Am. Vet. Med. Assn., Tex. Vet. Med. Assn. (dir. 1970-75), Tex. Assn. Lab Animal Sci. (pres. 1973), Am. Assn. Vet Anatomists (sec.-treas. 1973, pres. 1975), World Assn. Vet Anatomists, Am. Assn. Vet. Clinicians, Brazos Valley Vet. Med. Assn. (pres. 1971), Tex. Acad. Vet. Practice (v.p. 1973), Internat. Assn. for

Aquatic Animal Medicine (bd. dirs. 1984-86, pres. 1991-92), World Aquaculture Soc., The Crustacean Soc., Tex. Aquaculture Assn., U.S. Aquaculture Soc., Serra Club (pres. 1985-86), Blue Key, Sigma Xi, Phi Zeta (exec. councilman 1969), Alpha Zeta, Phi Kappa Phi, Phi Sigma, Gamma Sigma Delta, Alpha Gamma Rho (adviser 1962-65, 77-85, pres. 1953, pres. alumni assn. 1976-83). Lodges: K.C. (trustee 1969, pres. 1968), Lions. Home: 2519 Willow Bend Dr Bryan TX 77802-2461 Office: Tex A&M U Dept Anatomy College Station TX 77843

SISCHY, INGRID BARBARA, magazine editor, art critic; b. Johannesburg, Republic of South Africa, Mar. 2, 1952; came to U.S., 1967; d. Benjamin and Claire S. BS, Sarah Lawrence Coll., 1973; PhD (hon.), Moore Coll. Art, 1987. Assoc. editor Print Collector's Newsletter, N.Y.C., 1974-77; dir. Printed Matter, N.Y.C., 1977-78; curatorial intern Mus. Modern Art, N.Y.C., 1978-79; editor ArtForum Mag., N.Y.C., 1979-88; editor-in-chief Interview, N.Y.C., 1989—. Office: Interview Magazine 575 Broadway Fl 5 New York NY 10012-3230

SISCO, JOSEPH JOHN, management consultant, corporation director, educator, government official; b. Chgo., Oct. 31, 1919; m. Jean Churchill Head, Mar. 26, 1946; children: Carol Bolton, Jane Murdock. Student, Morton Jr. Coll., 1937-39; A.B. magna cum laude, Knox Coll., 1941; M.A., U. Chgo., 1947, Ph.D., 1950. Newspaper reporter, 1936-40; with City News Bur., Chgo., 1937; high sch. tchr., 1941, govt. service, 1950-51; staff Dept. State, 1951-76; successivley fgn. affairs officer, specialist internat. orgnl. affairs, officer-in charge Gen. Assembly, Security Council affairs, fgn. service officer, officer-in-charge UN polit. affairs, 1951-58; dep. dir. Office UN Polit. and Security Affairs, 1958-60, dir., 1960-63; dep. asst. sec. Bur. Internat. Orgn. Affairs, 1963-65, asst. sec. state internat. orgn. affairs, 1965-69; asst. sec. state Near East-South Asia, 1969-74; under sec. state for polit. affairs, 1974-76; pres. Am. U., Washington, 1976-80; chancellor Am. U., 1980-81; ptnr. Sisco Assocs. (mgmt. cons.), Washington, 1981—; bd. dirs. Raytheon Govt. Svcs., Inc., Tenneco InterPublic Group Inc., Braun Govt.; mem. U.S. delegation UN Collective Measures Com., 1952, U.S. delegations to UN Gen. Assembly, 1952-68; U.S. del. Spl. UN Gen. Assembly, session of Mid East, 1967; exec. officer, 1954=57; polit. adviser U.S. delegation Internat. Atomic Energy Agy., 1959; lectr. Fgn. Svc. Inst. Contbr. articles on internat. orgn., fgn. affairs to publs. Served as 1st lt., inf. AUS, 1941-45. Recipient Top Ten Career Service award Civil Service League, 1966, Rockefeller pub. service award, 1971; Silver Helmet Peace award Am. Vets. Com., 1973. Clubs: Cosmos (Washington), Internat. (Washington). Home: 2517 Massachusetts Ave NW Washington DC 20008-2823 Office: 1250 24th St NW Washington DC 20037-1124

SISISKY, NORMAN, congressman, soft drink bottler; b. Balt., June 9, 1927; m. Rhoda Brown, June 12, 1949; children: Mark B., Terry R., Richard L., Stuart J. BS in Bus. Adminstrn., Va. Commonwealth U., 1949; LLD (hon.), Va. State U. Pres., owner Pepsi-Cola Bottling Co. of Petersburg, Inc.; pres., dir. Lee Distbg. Co., Inc., Petersburg, Rhonor Corp., Petersburg; pres. Belfield Land, Inc., Petersburg; mem. Va. Gen. Assembly, Richmond, 1974-82, 98th-104th Congresses from 4th Va. dist., Washington, 1983—; mem. Ho. nat. security com., ranking mem. mil. readiness subcom., subcom. mil. procurement, panel on morale, welfare & recreation, Ho. small bus. com., subcom. procurement, exports & bus. opportunities; dir. Bank of Va., Richmond; vice-chair defense and security com. North Atlantic Assembly. Pres. Appomattox Indls. Devel. Corp.; bd. visitors Va. State U.; commr. Petersburg Hosp. Authority; trustee Va. State Coll. Found.; bd. dirs. Southside Va. Emergency Crew and Community Resource Devel. Bd. Served with USN 1945-46. Recipient Nat. Security Leadership award, Peace Through Stregnth Victory award, Douglas MacArthur award, Watchdog Treasury award, Thomas Jefferson award, 1994 Achievement award Va. Jaycees, Spirit of Enterprise U.S. C. of C., Small Bus. award Nat. Fedn. Ind. Bus. Mem. Nat. Soft Drink Assn. (chmn. bd. 1981-82), Petersburg C. of C. (v.p.). Democrat. Jewish. Club: Moose. Office: US Ho of Reps 2371 Rayburn Bldg Washington DC 20515-0005*

SISK, DANIEL ARTHUR, lawyer; b. Albuquerque, July 12, 1927; s. Arthur Henry and Myrl (Hope) S.; m. Katharine Banning, Nov. 27, 1954; children: John, Sarah, Thomas. B.A., Stanford U., 1950, J.D., 1954. Bar: N.Mex. 1955, Calif. 1954. Ptnr. firm Modrall, Sperling, Roehl, Harris & Sisk, Albuquerque, 1954-70, 71—; justice N.Mex. Supreme Ct., Santa Fe, 1970; chmn. bd. Sunwest Fin. Svcs., Inc., Albuquerque, 1975-90. Pres. Legal Aid Soc., Albuquerque, 1960-61; trustee Sandia Sch., 1968-72, Albuquerque Acad., 1971-73, A.T. & S.F. Meml. Hosps., Topeka, 1966-82; bd. dirs. N.Mex. Sch. Banking Found., 1981-85. Served with USNR, 1945-46, PTO; to capt. USMCR, 1951-52, Korea. Mem. N.Mex. Bar Assn., Albuquerque Bar Assn. (dir. 1962-63), ABA, State Bar Calif. Presbyn. (elder). Office: Sunwest Bldg 500 4th St NW # 2168 Albuquerque NM 87102-2183

SISK, MARK SEAN, priest, seminary dean, religious educator; b. Takoma Park, Md., Aug. 18, 1942; s. Robert James and Alma Irene (Davis) S.; m. Karen Lynn Womack, Aug. 31, 1963; children: Michael A., Heather K., Bronwyn E. BS, U. Md., 1964; MDiv, Gen. Theolog. Sem., 1967, DD, 1985. Asst. Christ Ch., New Brunswick, N.J., 1967-70; assoc. Christ Ch., Bronxville, N.Y., 1970-73; rector St. John's Ch., Kingston, N.Y., 1973-77; archdeacon Diocese of N.Y., N.Y.C., 1977-84; dean, pres. Seabury-Western Theol. Sem., Evanston, Ill., 1984—; sec. Coun. Episc. Sem. Deans, 1984-85; mem. task force for recruitment, tng. and deployment of black clergy, 1986-87. Pres. Anglican Theol. Review. Active Coun. for Devel. Ministry, 1988-93, exec. com., 1991-94. Named Hon. Canon Cathedral of St. John the Divine, N.Y.C., 1977. Mem. Soc. Bibl. Lit., Assn. Chgo. Theol. Schs. (pres. 1990-91), Soc. St. Francis (third order). Home: 625 Garrett Pl Evanston IL 60201-2903 Office: Seabury-Western Theol Sem 2122 Sheridan Rd Evanston IL 60201-2938

SISK, ROBERT JOSEPH, lawyer; b. Hartford, Conn., Nov. 8, 1928; s. David and Pearl S.; m. Kathryn L. Norton, Mar. 27, 1955 (dec. Mar. 1967); m. Xenia Dahlberg, May 16, 1968 (div. 1993); children: Julie N., Robert J., Jr., Kathryn L. Tucker, Laura A., Philip A., John H.; m. Sandra L. Clark, June 17, 1995. AB, Dartmouth Coll., 1950; LLB, Yale U., 1956. Bar: N.Y. 1957. Assoc. Hughes Hubbard & Reed, N.Y.C., 1956-63, ptnr., 1964—, chmn., 1994—; bd. dirs. Allied Artists Pictures Corp., 1969-75, Allied Art Industries, 1976-79, Allen-Bradley Co., 1973-85; chmn. planning and program com. 2nd Cir. Jud. Conf. Served to lt. (j.g.) USN, 1950-53; Korea. Fellow Am. Coll. Trial Lawyers; mem. Assn. Bar of City of N.Y., Century Assn. (N.Y.), Yale Club (N.Y.C.), Nisi Prius (N.Y.C.), Round Hill Club (Greenwich, Conn.), Riverside Yacht Club (Greenwich). Democrat. Avocations: sailing; tennis; skiing. Home: 23 Meadow Rd Deer Park Greenwich CT 06830 Office: Hughes Hubbard & Reed 1 Battery Park Plz New York NY 10004-1405

SISKAR, JOHN FREDERICK, art educator; b. Kenmore, N.Y., May 27, 1957; s. Robert Michael and Marion Rose (Stuff) S.; m. Susan Schuessler, June 25, 1982; children: John William, Benjamin Mark. BS in art edn. cum laude, Buffalo State Coll., 1982; EdM, U. Buffalo, 1988, postgrad., 1991—. Curriculum cons. Arts Coun. Chautauqua County, Jamestown, N.Y., 1987; cons., writer N.Y. State Edn. Dept., Albany, 1987, trainer, 1987-90; instr. State U., Fredonia, N.Y., 1993; art educator Fredonia H.S., 1983-93, dir. art, 1988-93; curriculum cons. Burchfield-Penney Arts Cen., Buffalo, N.Y., 1994—; instr. art edn. dept. Buffalo State Coll., 1993—; art educator Chautauqua County Sch. Bd. Assoc., Fredonia, 1986—; portfolio adj. N.Y. State Summer Sch. for Arts, Albany, 1993—. Editor, cons. curriculum guide Western N.Y. Arch. & Design, 1994—; coord. Billboard Design, 1987-88. Coord. of division Northern Chautauqua Soccer Assn., Dunkirk, N.Y., 1993; team coach, 1989-93, team coach Dunkirk Fredonia Soccer League, Fredonia, 1992; vol. Fredonia Preservation Soc., 1989-92. Recipient summer profl. grant Fredonia Cen. Schs., 1992, curriculum devel. grant, 1984, 86, 87, 88, 90, 92. Mem. Assn. Supervision and Curriculum Devel., N.Y. State Art Tchrs. Assn. (chair of mgmt. plan, coord. of student exhibits 1982—), N.Y. State Art Tchrs. Assn. One Western (v.p., pres.-elect, pres. 1983—, editorial adv. bd. mem. 1987-90), Nat. Art Edn. Assn., Fredonia Tchrs. Assn. (newsletter graphics editor 1983-93). Office: Buffalo State Coll Art Edn Dept 1300 Elmwood Ave Buffalo NY 14222-1004

SISKE, ROGER CHARLES, lawyer; b. Starkville, Miss., Mar. 2, 1944; s. Lester L. and Helen (Cagan) S.; m. Regina Markunas, May 31, 1969; children: Kelly, Jennifer, Kimberly. BS in Fin., Ohio State U., 1966; JD magna cum laude, U. Mich., 1969. Bar: Ill. 1969. Assoc. Sonnenschein Nath & Rosenthal, Chgo., 1969-78, ptnr., 1978—, chmn. nat. employee benefits and exec. compensation dept. Past chmn., sec. coun. employee benefits Ill. State Bar Assn. Served to capt. U.S. Army, 1970-71. Decorated Bronze Star. Mem. ABA (past chmn. tax sect. employee benefits com., past chmn. joint com. on employee benefits and exec. compensation and bus. law sect., employee benefits and exec. compensation com.), Chgo. Bar Assn. (past chmn. employee benefits com., mem. exec. council of tax com.), Order of Coif (editor law review). Republican. Office: Sonnenschein Nath Rosenthal 233 S Wacker Dr Ste 8000 Chicago IL 60606-6404

SISKEL, GENE (EUGENE KAL SISKEL), film critic; b. Chgo., Jan. 26, 1946; s. Nathan W. and Ida (Kalis) S.; m. Marlene Iglitzen, 1980; children: Kate Adi, Callie Gray. BA, Yale U., 1967; postgrad., Dept. Def. Info. Sch., 1968; PhD of Letters (hon.), Ill. Coll., 1989. Fellow Coro Found., 1968; film critic Chgo. Tribune, 1969—, CBS This Morning, 1990—, WBBM-TV, Chgo., 1974—. Host. Nightwatch, Sta. WTTW-TV, 1979-80 (Emmy award 1979); co-host (with Roger Ebert) Sneak Previews, Sta. WTTW-TV and PBS Network, 1975-82 (Emmy award 1980), At the Movies, syndicated TV, 1982-86, Siskel & Ebert, syndicated TV, 1986—; author: (with Ebert) The Future of the Movies, 1991. Mem. Arts Club Chgo. Office: care Chgo Tribune PO Box 25340 Chicago IL 60625-0340

SISKIN, CARYL F., women's health primary care nurse practitioner; b. Louisville, June 2, 1939; d. Ralph E. and Esther Marian (Binder) Flumbaum; m. Michael Baggish, 1960 (div. 1983); children: Jeffrey Steven Baggish, Mindy Ann Baggish, Cindy Beth Baggish, Stuart Harrison Baggish; m. Robert S. Siskin, 1985. Diploma, St. Anthony Hosp. Sch. Nursing, 1960; student, Nazareth Coll., Johns Hopkins U.; BSN summa cum laude, U. Hartford, 1980. Cert. NCC, ob-gyn NP. Head nurse Womens Clinic Johns Hopkins Hosp., Balt.; clin. instr., ob-gyn. dept. Mt. Sinai Hosp., Hartford, Conn.; mem. internat. health care team S.E. Asia U.S. AID, 1973-74; ob-gyn. N.P. collaborative practice George Bacall, M.D., Hartford, 1984-90; pvt. practice Bloomfield, Conn., 1990-94. Vol. local soup kitchen; co-founder Rebekah's House, West Palm Beach, Fla. Mem. ANA, Nurses Assn. of Am. Coll. Ob-Gyn., Am. Acad. Nurse Practitioners, Assn. Reproductive Health Profls., Am. Fertility Soc., Jewish Arts Found., Temple Israel Sisterhood, Sigma Theta Tau (1st pres. Iota Upsilon chpt.). Home: 13677 Rivoli Dr Palm Beach Gardens FL 33410

SISKIN, EDWARD JOSEPH, engineering and construction company executive; b. Bklyn., Apr. 30, 1941; s. Haskell and Sylvia (Steckler) S.; m. Patricia Ann Moore, June 26, 1965 (div. Apr. 1990); children: Candice P. Howard, Cristin Jo; m. Jean Elizabeth Bowen, Dec. 17, 1994. BSEE, U. Pa., 1963; cert., Bettis Reactor Engring. Sch., West Mifflin, Pa., 1965; postgrad., George Washington U., 1963-67. Registered profl. engr., Pa., Mass., N.Y., N.J., Ill., Fla., W.Va., Ind., S.C., Tex., La., Nebr., Calif., Ala. Engr. U.S. AEC, Washington, 1963-67; field office mgr. U.S. AEC, Pitts., 1967-70, Groton, Conn., 1970-77; project mgr. Stone & Webster Engring. Corp., Boston, 1977-78, asst. engring. mgr., 1978-79; engring. mgr. Stone & Webster Engring. Corp., N.Y.C., 1979-83, v.p. & mgr., 1984-86; sr. v.p. & mgr. Stone & Webster Engring. Corp., Cherry Hill, N.J., 1987-88; exec. v.p. Stone & Webster Engring. Corp., Cherry Hill, 1988-90; dir. Stone & Webster Engring. Corp., Boston, 1985-90; gen. mgr. Superconducting Supercollider Lab., Dallas, 1990-94; pres. Enerjoin Svcs., Inc., 1994—; mem. adv. com. Inst. of Nuclear Power Ops., Atlanta, 1987-90, adv. bd. Ctr. for Chem. Plant Safety, N.Y.C., 1988-90. Bd. dirs. PenJerDel Coun., Phila., 1987-90. Lt. USN, 1963-69. Sr. mem. IEEE; mem. Am. Nuclear Soc., Am. Philatelic Soc. (State College, Pa.). Office: PO Box 17 Haddonfield NJ 08033-0016

SISKIND, ARTHUR, lawyer, director; b. N.Y., Oct. 11, 1938; s. William and Sylvia (Schuman) S.; m. Mary Ann Silverman, Nov. 10, 1962; children: Laura, Julie, Kenneth. BA in Liberal Arts, Cornell U., 1960, LLB with distinction, 1962. Ptnr. Squadron, Ellenoff, Plesent & Lehrer, N.Y., 1970-91; sr. exec. v.p., group gen. counsel, mem. exec. com., dir. The News Corp. Ltd., N.Y., 1991—. Dir. Brit. Sky Broadcasting Group, PLC, Star TV Ltd. Active Cornell Law Sch. Adv. Coun. Capt. U.S. Army, 1963-65. Mem. ABA, City Bar Assn., Cornell Club. Office: The News Corp Ltd 1211 Ave of the Americas New York NY 10036

SISKIND, DONALD HENRY, lawyer; b. Providence, Dec. 25, 1937; s. Samuel and Sadie (Wasserman) S.; m. Beth Mohel, July 15, 1962; children: Steven M., Edward M. BS, U. Pa., 1959; LLB, Columbia U., 1962. Bar: Mass. 1962, N.Y. 1963. Assoc. Marshall Bratter Greene Allison & Tucker, N.Y.C., 1962-69, ptnr., 1969-82; ptnr. Rosenman & Colin, N.Y.C., 1982—; bd. dirs. Chgo. Title Ins. Co.; chmn. various seminars Practicing Law Inst., 1974—; vis. lectr. Columbia U. Sch. Law, 1993—; mem. adv. bd. Wharton Real Estate Ctr. Mem. adv. bd. Real Estate Fin. Jour.; contbr. articles to profl. jours. Pres. Greenville Community Coun., 1974-76; pres. bd. edn. Union Free Sch. Dist., Scarsdale, N.Y., 1978-81. Mem. ABA, Am. Coll. Real Estate Lawyers (pres.-elect), Anglo Am. Real Property Isnt., N.Y. State Bar Assn., Assn. of Bar of City of N.Y., Phi Alpha Psi. Home: 876 Park Ave New York NY 10021-1832 Office: Rosenman & Colin 575 Madison Ave New York NY 10022-2511

SISKIND, RALPH WALTER, lawyer; b. Washington, May 29, 1949; m. Linda Paula Friedman. BS, Case Inst. Tech., 1971; MS, U. Pa., 1973; JD, Temple U., 1977. Bar: Pa. 1977, U.S. Dist. Ct. (ea. dist.) Pa. 1977. Engr. Westinghouse Electric Corp., Phila., 1971-74, Standard Pressed Steel, Jenkintown, Pa., 1974, U.S. Mint, Phila., 1975-78; atty. U.S. EPA, Phila., 1978-85; assoc. Blank, Rome, Comisky & McCauley, Phila., 1985-90; ptnr. Wolf, Block, Schorr & Solis-Cohen, Phila., 1990—. Co-author quar. articles Jour. Environ. Regulation, 1991-95; contbr. articles to profl. jours. Office: Wolf Block Schorr 12 Fl Packard Bldg SE Corner 15 & Chestnut Sts Philadelphia PA 19102-2678

SISKO, MARIE FERRARIS, fund raising executive; b. N.Y.C.; BA, Queens Coll., 1975; postgrad. Adelphi U., 1976; divorced; children: Warren Joseph, Robert Edward. Pers. dir. Daypac Inc., 1969-70; sales asst. Ponder & Best, 1971-73; sales adminstr. Ampacet Corp., 1973-75; mktg. rep. Better Bus. Bur., 1975-77; ast. dir. Leukemia Soc. Am., 1978-82; campaign dir. Ketchum, Inc., 1982-85; dir. maj. gifts Seton Hall U., 1985-88; program dir. Brakeley, John Price Jones, 1988-93; fund raising cons., 1990—. Mem. Nat. Soc. Fund Raising Execs., Queens Coll. Alumni Assn. (pres. Ace chpt. 1977-79). Lutheran. Home: 32 Center Dr Flushing NY 11357-1005

SISLER, HARRY HALL, chemist, educator; b. Ironton, Ohio, Mar. 13, 1917; s. Harry C. and Minta A. (Hall) S.; m. Helen E. Shaver, June 29, 1940; children: Elizabeth A., David F., Raymond K., Susan C.; m. Hannelore L. Wass, Apr. 13, 1978. BSc, Ohio State U., 1936; MSc, U. Ill., 1937, PhD, 1939; Doctorate honoris causa, U. Poznan, Poland, 1977. Instr. Chgo. City Colls., 1939-41; from instr. to assoc. prof. chemistry U. Kans., Lawrence, 1941-46; from asst. prof. to prof. chemistry Ohio State U., Columbus, 1946-56; Arthur and Ruth Sloan vis. prof. chemistry Harvard, fall, 1962-63; prof., chmn. dept. chemistry U. Fla., Gainesville, 1956-68; dean Coll. Arts and Scis. U. Fla., 1968-70, exec. v.p., 1970-73, dean grad. sch., 1973-79, Disting. Svc. prof. chemistry, 1979—; indsl. cons. W.R. Grace & Co., Martin Marietta Aerospace, Naval Ordnance Lab., TVA; chemistry adv. panel, also vis. scientists panel NSF, 1959-62; cons. USAF Acad., Battelle Meml. Inst., chmn. interinstl. com. nuclear research, Fla., 1958-64; mem. Fla. Nuclear Devel. Commn. Teaching Sci. and Math., 1958; chemistry adv. panel Oak Ridge Nat. Lab., 1965-69; dir. sponsored rsch. U. Fla., 1976-79. Author: Electronic Structure, Properties, and the Periodic Law, 2d edit, 1973, Starlight-A Book of Poems, 1976, Of Outer and Inner Space—A Book of Poems, 1981, Earth, Air, Fire and Water-A Book of Poems, 1989, (with others) Gen. Chemistry—A Systematic Approach, 2d edit, 1959, Coll. Chemistry—A Systematic Approach, 4th edit, 1980, Essentials of Chemistry, 2d edit, 1959, A Systematic Laboratory Course in Chemistry, 1950, Essentials of Experimental Chemistry, 2d edit, 1959, Semimicro Qualitative Analysis, 1958, rev. edit., 1965, Comprehensive Inorganic Chemistry, Vol. V, 1956, Chemistry in Non-Aqueous Solvents, 1961, The Chloramination Reaction, 1977, Dying-Facing the Facts, 1988, Inorganic Reactions and Methods, Vol. 7, 1988, Encyclopedia of Inorganic Chemistry, Vol. 5, Nitrogen: Inorganic Chemistry, 1994.; cons. editor: (with others) Dowden, Hutchinson & Ross, 1971-78; series editor: (with others) Phys. and Inorganic Textbook Series, Reinhold Pub. Corp, 1958-70; contbr. (with others) articles to profl. jours. Decorated Royal Order North Star(Sweden); Named Outstanding Chemist in South, Am. Chem. Soc., 1969, Outstanding Chemist in Southeast, Am. Chem. Soc., 1960, James Flack Norris award Am. Chem. Soc., 1979; recipient Outstanding Centennial Achievement award Ohio State U., 1970. Mem. Am. Chem. Soc. (nat. chmn. div. chem. edn. 1957-58, exec. com. 1957-60, bd. publ. Jour. Chem. Edn. 1956-58), Phi Beta Kappa, Sigma Xi, Phi Delta Kappa, Phi Lambda Upsilon, Phi Kappa Phi, Alpha Chi Sigma. Methodist. Patentee in field. Home: 6014 NW 54th Way Gainesville FL 32653-3265

SISLER, WILLIAM PHILIP, publishing executive; b. Yonkers, N.Y., May 4, 1947; s. William Andrew and Doris Elizabeth (Krasko) S.; m. Elaine Herg, Aug. 23, 1969; 1 child, Jonathan William. BA magna cum laude, Canisius Coll., 1969; PhD, Johns Hopkins U., 1977, M in Adminstrv. Sci., 1983. Asst. then assoc., sr. humanities editor Johns Hopkins U. Press, Balt., 1973-83; exec. editor Oxford U. Press, N.Y.C., 1983-86, v.p., exec. editor humanities and social scis., 1987-90; dir. Harvard U. Press, Cambridge, Mass., 1990—. Johns Hopkins U. fellow, 1969-73. Mem. Century Assn., Harvard Club of N.Y.C. Roman Catholic. Office: Harvard U Press 79 Garden St Cambridge MA 02138-1423

SISLEY, BECKY LYNN, physical education educator; b. Seattle, May 10, 1939; d. Leslie James and Blanche (Howe) S.; m. Jerry Newcomb, 1994. BA, U. Wash., 1961; MSPE, U. N.C., 1964, EdD, 1973. Tchr. Lake Washington High Sch., Kirkland, Wash., 1961-62; instr. U. Wis., Madison, 1963-65, U. Oreg., Eugene, 1965-68; prof. phys. edn. U. Oreg., 1968—, women's athletic dir., 1973-79, head undergrad. studies in phys. edn., 1985-92. Co-author: Softball for Girls, 1971; contbr. articles to profl. jours. Admitted to Hall of Fame, N.W. Women's Sports Found., Seattle, 1981, Honor award, N.W. Dist. Assn. for Health, Phys. Edn., Recreation and Dance, 1988, State of Oreg. Sports Hall of Fame, 1993; recipient Honor award Nat. Assn. for Girls and Women in Sports, 1995; U.S. record holder Age 50-54 Triple Jump, Javelin, High Jump, Age 55-50 Javelin, Pole Vault; world record holder Age 55-59 Pole Vault. Mem. AAHPERD, Oreg. Alliance Health, Phys. Edn., Recreation and Dance (hon. life mem.), Western Soc. for Phys. Edn. of Coll. Women (exec. bd. 1982-85), Oreg. High Sch. Coaches Assn., Nat. Softball Coaches Acad., N.W. Coll. Women's Sports Assn. (pres. 1977-78), Oreg. Women's Sports Leadership Network (dir. 1987—), Phi Epsilon Kappa, others. Office: University of Oregon Phys Activity & Recreation Svcs Eugene OR 97403

SISLEY, G. WILLIAM, lawyer; b. Morristown, N.J., Feb. 25, 1944; s. George William and Dorothy (Woods) S.; m. Doris Mortenson, Feb. 3, 1979; children: Amanda, Andrew. A.B., Princeton U., 1966; J.D., NYU, 1969. Bar: N.J. 1970, N.Y. 1970, Conn. 1983. Legal sec. Superior Ct. N.J., 1969-70; assoc. Pitney, Hardin & Kipp, Newark, 1970-74; corp. atty., counsel to bus. equipment group SCM Corp., N.Y.C., 1974-78; asst. gen. counsel The Continental Group Inc., Stamford, Conn., 1978-85, corp. sec., 1980-85; ptnr. Davidson, Dawson & Clark, New Canaan, Conn., 1986-89; of counsel Winthrop, Stimson, Putnam & Roberts, Stamford, Conn., 1989-91, ptnr., 1991—. Mem. Am. Soc. Corp. Secs., Corp. Transfer Agt. Assn., Westchester-Fairfield County Corp. Counsel Assn., Assn. of Bar of City of N.Y. Clubs: Princeton (N.Y.C.); Innis Arden Golf (Old Greenwich, Conn.). Home: 26 Keofferam Rd Old Greenwich CT 06870-2127 Office: Wintrop Stimson et al 695 E Main St Stamford CT 06904-6760

SISLEY, NINA MAE, physician, public health officer; b. Jacksonville, Fla., Aug. 19, 1924; d. Leonard Percy and Verna (Martin) S.; m. George W. Fischer, May 16, 1962 (dec. 1990). BA, Tex. State Coll. for Women, 1944; MD, U. Tex., Galveston, 1950; MPH, U. Mich., 1963. Intern City of Detroit Receiving Hosp., 1950-51; resident in gen. practice St. Mary's Infirmary, Galveston, Tex., 1951-52; sch. physician Galveston Ind. Sch. Dist., 1953-56; dir. med. svcs. San Antonio Health Dept., 1960-63, acting dir., 1963-64; resident in pub. health Tex. Dept. Pub. Health, San Antonio, 1963-65; dir. community health svcs. Corpus Christi-Nueces County (Tex.) Health Dept., 1964-67; dir. Corpus Christi-Nueces County (Tex.) Dept. Pub. Health, 1987—; dir. Tb control region 5 Tex. Dept. Health, Corpus Christi, 1967-73; dir. pub. health region 11 Tex. Dept. Health, Rosenberg, 1978-87; chief chronic illness control City of Houston Health Dept., 1973-78; lectr. Incarnate Word Coll., San Antonio, 1963-64; adj. prof. U. Tex. Sch. Pub. Health, Houston, 1980—; guest lectr. Corpus Christi State U., 1987—; pvt. practice Galveston, Stockdale, Hereford and Borger, Tex., 1952-59; mem. adv. bd. Koch Refinery. Bd. dirs. Coastal Bend chpt. ARC, Corpus Christi, 1990-94, United Way-Coastal Bend, Coastal Bend Coalition on AIDS, 1988-94, Coastal Bend chpt. Am. Diabetes Assn., 1990—; mem. Nuences County Child Fatality Rev. Com. Fellow Am. Coll. Preventive Medicine; mem. AMA, APHA, Tex. Med. Assn., Nuences County Med. Soc. (pres.-elect 1996—), Tex. Assn. Pub. Health Physicians (pres. 1991-92), Tex. Pub. Health Assn. Episcopalian. Avocations: fishing, crossword puzzles, raising African violets. Home: 62 Rock Creek Dr Corpus Christi TX 78412-4214 Office: Corpus Christi-Nueces County Dept Health 1702 Horne Rd Corpus Christi TX 78416-1902

SISMAN, ELAINE ROCHELLE, musicology educator; b. N.Y.C., Jan. 20, 1952; d. Irving and Margot (Weintraub) S.; m. Martin Fridson, June 14, 1981; children: Arielle, Daniel. AB, Cornell U., 1972; MFA, Princeton U., 1974, PhD, 1978. Instr. music history U. Mich., Ann Arbor, 1976-79, asst. prof., 1979-82; asst. prof. Columbia U., N.Y.C., 1982-90, assoc. prof., 1990-94, prof., 1995—; vis. prof. Harvard U., 1996. Author: Haydn and the Classical Variation, 1993, Mozart's "Jupiter" Symphony, 1993; assoc. editor: 19th Century Music, Beethoven Forum; also articles; co-editor; Beethoven Forum. Recipient Gt. Tchr. award Columbia U., 1992, Alexander Hamilton medal Columbia U., 1994; fellow NEH, 1981-82; travel grantee Am. Coun. Learned Socs. Mem. Am. Musicological Soc. (pres. Greater N.Y. chpt. 1982-84, bd. dirs. 1992-94, Einstein award 1983, mem. editl. Jour. of AMS), Am. Brahms Soc. (bd. dirs. 1993—), Soc. Fellows in Humanities Columbia U. (chmn. 1992-94). Office: Columbia U Dept Music 703 Dodge New York NY 10027

SISSEL, GEORGE ALLEN, manufacturing executive; b. Chgo., July 30, 1936; s. William Wortl. and Hannah Ruth (Harlan) S.; m. Mary Ruth Runsvold, Oct. 5, 1968; children: Jenifer Ruth, Gregory Allen. B.S. in Elec. Engring., U. Colo., 1958; J.D. cum laude, U. Minn., 1966. Bar: Colo. 1966, Ind. 1973, U.S. Supreme Ct. 1981. Assoc. Sherman & Howard, Denver, 1966-70; with Ball Corp., Muncie, Ind., 1970—; assoc. gen. counsel Ball Corp., 1974-78, gen. counsel, 1978-95, corp. sec., 1980-95, v.p., 1981-87, sr. v.p., 1987-95; acting pres., CEO Ball Corp., Muncie, 1994-95, bd. dirs., pres., CEO, 1995—, chmn. bd., 1996—; bd. advisors First Chgo. Equity Capital, 1995—; bd. dirs. First Merchants Bank. Assoc. editor: U. Minn. Law Rev., 1965-66. Served with USN, 1958-63. Mem. ABA, Con. Mfrs. Inst. (bd. dirs., chmn.), Nat. Assn. Mfrs. (bd. dirs.), Am. Soc. Corp. Secs., Colo. Bar Assn., Ind. Bar Assn., Ind. C. of C. (bd. dirs.), Order of Coif, MIT Soc. Sr. Execs., (bd. govs. 1987-95), Sigma Chi, Sigma Tau, Eta Kappa Nu. Methodist. Lodge: Rotary. Home: 2600 W Berwyn Rd Muncie IN 47304-5115 Office: Ball Corp 345 S High St Muncie IN 47305-2326

SISSOM, LEIGHTON ESTEN, engineering educator, dean, consultant; b. Manchester, Tenn., Aug. 26, 1934; s. Willie Esten and Bertha Sarah (Davis) S.; m. Evelyn Janelle Lee, June 13, 1953; children: Terry Lee, Denny Leighton. B.S., Middle Tenn. State Coll., 1956; B.S. in Mech. Engring., Tenn. Technol. U., 1962; M.S. in Mech. Engring., Ga. Inst. Tech., 1964, Ph.D., 1965. Diplomate Nat. Acad. Forensic Engrs.; registered profl. engr., Tenn. Draftsman Westinghouse Electric Corp., Tullahoma, 1953-57; mech. designer ARO, Inc., Tullahoma, 1957-58; instr. mech. engring. Tenn. Technol. U., Cookeville, 1958-62, chmn. dept. mech. engring., 1965-79, dean engring., 1979—, dean of engring. emeritus, 1988—; prin. cons. Sissom & Assocs., Cookeville, Tenn., 1962—; bd. dirs. Accreditation Bd. Engring. and Tech., N.Y.C., 1978-86, treas., 1982-86. Author: (with Donald R. Pitts) Elements of Transport Phenomena, 1972, Heat Transfer, 1977, 1,000 Solved Problems in Heat Transfer, 1991; contbr. An Attorney's Guide to Engineering, 1986; contbr. articles to various publs. Fellow ASME (sr. v.p. 1982-86, gov. 1986-88, Golden medallion), Am. Soc. Engring. Edn. (bd. dirs. 1984-87, pres. 1991-92), Accreditation Bd. Engring. and Tech.; mem. NSPE, Soc. Automotive Engrs., Nat. Engring. Deans Coun. (chmn. 1984-87), Order of the Engr. (chmn. bd. govs. 1994-96), Tau Beta Pi (v.p. 1986-89, councillor 1986-89). Home and Office: 1151 Shipley Church Rd Cookeville TN 38501-7730

SISSON, JEAN CRALLE, middle school educator; b. Village, Va., Nov. 16, 1941; d. Willard Andrew and Carolyn (Headley) Cralle; m. James B. Sisson, June 20, 1964 (div. Oct. 1994); 1 child, Kimberly Carol. BS in Elem. Edn., Longwood Coll., 1964; MA in Adminstrn. and Supervision, Va. Commonwealth U., 1979. Tchr. 2nd grade Tappahannock (Va.) Elem. Sch., 1964-67; tchr. 2nd and 4th grades Farnham (Va.) Elem. Sch., 1967-71; tchr. 6th grade Callao (Va.) Elem. Sch., 1971-81; tchr. 6th and 7th grades Northumberland Mid. Sch., Heathsville, Va., 1981—; sr. mem. Supt. Adv. Com., Heathsville, 1986-93. Author: My Survival, 1994; author of children's books, short stories and poetry. Lifetime mem. Gibeon Bapt. Ch., Village, Va., 1942—. Mem. NEA, ASCD, Aerobics & Fitness Assn. Am., Va. Mid. Sch. Assn., Exercise Safety Assn., Nat. Coun. of English Tchrs., Nat. Wildlife Fedn. Republican. Avocations: aerobics, writing, reading, cooking, archeology. Home: RR 1 Box 39A Callao VA 22435-9706 Office: Northumberland Mid Sch PO Box 100 Heathsville VA 22473-0100

SISSON, RAY L., dean; b. Pueblo, Colo., Apr. 24, 1934; s. William Franklin and Lillie Mae (Hall) S.; m. Dixie Lee McConnell, Oct. 5, 1952; children: Mark Lynn, Bryan Keith, Tammy Sue Ann. BSEE, U. Colo., 1960; MSEE, Colo. State U., 1966; AA, Pueblo Coll., 1958; EdD, U. No. Colo., 1973. Electronic technician TV Svcs. Co., Pueblo, 1958, Sid's Appliance Ctr., Tucson; from instr. engring. to asst. prof. So. Colo. State Coll., Pueblo, 1960-63, assoc. prof., 1963-76, engring., electronics dept. head, 1968-70; dean Sch. Applied Sci. and Engring. Tech. U. So. Colo., Pueblo, 1973-84, prof., 1976—, interim dean Coll. Engring. and Sci., 1984-85, dean Coll. Applied Sci. and Engring. Tech., 1985—; cons. Escuela Superior Politecnica del Litoral, Ecuador, 1979-82, SUNY, Alfred, Farmingdale, 1982, Moorhead U., 1985, N.Mex. Highlands U., 1985, 90, Kans. State U., Salina, 1994. Bd. dirs. Colo. Transp. Inst., 1993—; exec. dir. So. Colo. Bus. and Tech. Ctr., 1994—. Recipient James H. McGraw award Am. Soc. Engring. Edn., 1990; NSF grantee, 1964, 65, 67, 68, 80-83. Mem. IEEE, ABET (tech. accreditation commn. 1990—, chmn. definition com. 1991, vice chmn. tech. accreditation commn., 1993—), Am. Soc. Engring. Edn. (active, spectrum com. 1989-90, chmn. definition com. 1991, fellow 1993), Engring. Tech. Leadership Inst. (founding mem., bd. dirs. 1983-88, chmn. 1984-85), Profl. Engrs. Colo. (So. chpt., assoc. mem., chair young engrs. 1969, scholarship, edn. com. 1969, chair state scholarship com. 1968), Phi Delta Kappa, Eta Kappa Nu, Tau Alpha Pi. Home: 403 Starlite Dr Pueblo CO 81005-2685 Office: U So Colo 2200 Bonforte Blvd Pueblo CO 81001-4901

SISSON, ROBERT F., photographer, writer, lecturer, educator; b. Glen Ridge, N.J., May 30, 1923; s. Horace R. and Frances A. S.; m. Patricia Matthews, Oct. 15, 1978; 1 son by previous marriage, Robert F.H.; 1 stepson, James A. Matthews. With Nat. Geographic Soc., Washington, 1942-88, chief nat. sci. photographer, 1981-88; free-lance photographer, 1988—; lectr. in field; mem. nature staff Sarastoa Mag., 1989; owner Macro/Nature Workshops, Englewood, Fla. Photographer one-man shows, Nat. Geog. Soc., Washington, 1974, Washington Press Club, 1976, Berkshire (Mass.) Mus., 1976, Brooks Inst., Santa Barbara, Calif., 1980, U. Miami, 1993, Sea Ctr., Santa Barbara, Calif., 1993, Corcoran Gallery of Art's Spl. World Tour, 1988, permanent collections, Mus. Art, N.Y.C. Recipient 1st prize for color photograph White House News Photographers Assn., 1961; recipient Canadian Natural Sci. award, 1967, Louis Schmidt award, 1991. Fellow Biol. Photographers Assn.; mem. Biol. Photog. Assn. (awards for color prints 1967), Nat. Audubon Soc., Nat. Geog. Soc., Nat. Wildlife Fedn., Soc. Photog. Scientists and Engrs., N.Y. Acad. Scis., Sigma Delta Chi. Office: Macro/Nature Photography PO Box 1649 Englewood FL 34295-1649 *The true wonders of the natural world gave me inspiration and a challenge. My cameras and I are privileged to share images of this world with all people.*

SISSON, VIRGINIA BAKER, geology educator; b. Boston, Apr. 8, 1957; d. Thomas Kingsford and Edith Virginia (Arnold) S.; m. William Bronson Maze, Oct. 14, 1989. AB, Bryn Mawr Coll., 1979; MA, Princeton U., 1981, PhD, 1985. Rsch. assoc. Princeton (N.J.) U., 1985-86; rsch. assoc. Rice U., Houston, 1986-87, lectr., 1987-92, asst. prof. geology, 1992—; cons. U.S. Geol. Survey, Anchorage, 1984-95. Contbr. more than 20 articles to sci. publs. Rsch. grantee, NSF, Houston and Calif., 1988, Houston and Scotland, 1990, Alaska, 1990, Venezuela, 1990, Alaska, 1993. Mem. Assn. Women Geologists, Am. Women in Sci., Am. Geophys. Union, Geol. Soc. Am., Mineral Soc. of Am., Mineral Assn. Can. Avocations: pilot, cross-country skiing, soccer, recorder playing. Home: 4118 Lanark Ln Houston TX 77025-1115 Office: Rice U Dept Geology and Geophys 6100 South Main St Houston TX 77251

SISTO, ELENA, artist, educator; b. Boston, Jan. 11, 1952; d. Fernando Jr. and Grace Sisto; m. John David Kirkpatrick. BA, Brown U., 1975; grad., N.Y. Studio Sch., 1977; postgrad., Yale U., Norfolk, Conn., 1975, Skowhegan (Maine) Sch., 1976. Gallery artist Vanderwoude Tanabaum, N.Y.C., 1983-89; gallery artist Damon Brandt Gallery, N.Y.C., 1989-91, Germans Van Eck, N.Y.C., 1991—; tchr. Bates Coll., Maine, 1986, Colby Coll., Maine, 1986, SUNY-Purchase, 1988, R.I. Sch. Design, Providence, 1987—, N.Y. Studio Sch., N.Y.C., 1987—, Bard Coll., summer, 1990, Columbia U., N.Y.C. Exhibited in one-man shows at David Beitzel Gallery, 1995; represented in various pub. and pvt. collections. Fellow Skowhegan Sch., 1970, Yale Norfolk, 1975, NEA, 1983, 89-90, Millary Colony, 1987, Handhollow Found., 1995.

SISTO, FERNANDO, mechanical engineering educator; b. La Coruña, Spain, Aug. 2, 1924; s. Fernando Cartelle and Clara (Reiss) S.; m. Grace Jeanette Wexler, June 27, 1946; children: Jane Caroll, Ellen Gail, Todd Frederic. Student, NYU, 1940-43; BS, U.S. Naval Acad., 1946; ScD, MIT, 1952; M Engring. (hon.), Stevens Inst. Tech., 1962. Registered profl. engr., N.J. Commd. ensign USN, 1946, service in the Pacific, ret., 1949; propulsion div. chief Curtiss-Wright Research, Clifton, N.J., 1952-58; prof. mech. engring. Stevens Inst. Tech., Hoboken, N.J., 1959—, chmn. dept., 1966-79, George Meade Bond prof., 1978—, dean of the grad. sch., 1993-94; bd. dirs., trustee Am. Capital Mut. Funds, Houston, 1960—, chmn. bd., 1992-95; co-chmn. merged bd. Van Kampen Am. Capital, 1995—; bd. dirs. Dynalysis of Princeton; cons. UN Devel. Program at Nat. Aero. Lab., Bangalore, India, 1978. Co-author: (textbook) A Modern Course in Aeroelasticity, 1978, 3d edit., 1995. Lt. USN, 1943-49. R.C. DuPont fellow MIT, 1951-52. Fellow ASME; mem. Adirondack Mountain Club. Avocations: skiing, tennis, woodworking, sculling. Office: Stevens Inst Tech Dept Mech Engring Hoboken NJ 07030-5991

SITEMAN, ALVIN JEROME, banker; b. St. Louis, Mar. 23, 1928; s. Philip L. and Bertha (Newman) S.; m. Ruth Levinsohn, June 22, 1952; children: Estelle, Nancy, Joanne, Suzanne. BS in engring. adminstrn., MIT, 1948. Pres., bd. dirs. Flash Oil Corp., St. Louis, 1950—, The Siteman Orgn. Inc., St. Louis, 1960—, Site Oil Co. Mo., St. Louis, 1970—; vice chmn. Mark Twain Bancshares Inc., St. Louis, 1979-86, chmn., 1987—, also bd. dirs.; bd. dirs. Insituform Tech., Inc., Memphis, Tenn. Trustee, commr. St. Louis Art Mus., 1984—; trustee, mem. exec. com. Washington U., 1985-93, Jewish Hosp. St. Louis, 1985-95; Barnes-Jewish Hosp., 1996—. Republican. Avocations: fishing, hunting, golf, flying. Office: The Siteman Orgn Inc 50 S Bemiston Ave Saint Louis MO 63105-3306

SITES, JAMES PHILIP, lawyer, consul; b. Detroit, Sept. 17, 1948; s. James Neil and Inger Marie (Krogh) S.; m. Barbara Teresa Mazurek, Apr. 9, 1978; children: Philip Erling, Teresa Elizabeth. Student, U. Oslo, Norway, 1968-69; BA, Haverford Coll., 1970; JD, Georgetown U., 1973, ML in Taxation, 1979. Bar: Md. 1973, D.C. 1974, U.S. Supreme Ct. 1978, Mont. 1984, U.S. Tax Ct. 1984, U.S. Dist. Ct. Mont. 1984, U.S. Ct. Appeals (9th cir.) 1988. Law clk. to judge James C. Morton, Jr. Ct. Spl. Appeals Md., Annapolis, 1974-75; law clk. to judge Orman W. Ketcham Superior Ct. D.C., Washington, 1975-76; gen. atty. U.S. Immigration & Naturalization Svc., Washington, 1976-77; trial atty. tax div. U.S. Dept. Justice, Washington, 1977-84; ptnr. Crowley, Haughey, Hanson, Toole & Dietrich, Billings, Mont., 1984—; consul for Govt. of Norway State of Mont., Billings, 1987—; instr. Norwegian Ea. Mont. Coll., 1987-88, Sons of Norway, 1989—; v.p. Scandinavian Studies Assn., 1989—; bd. dirs. Billings Com. on Fgn. Rels., 1988—; mem. Mont. Coun. for Internat. Visitors, The Norsemen's Fedn. Chair local exec. bd. Mont. State U., Billings, 1993—. U. Oslo scholar, 1969; recipient Peace Rsch. award Haverford Coll., 1970. Mem. Md. State Bar Assn., Mont. State Bar (co-chmn. com. on income and property taxes 1987-91, chair tax and probate sect. 1991-92, chair tax litigation subcom. 1992—), D.C. Bar Assn., Am. Immigration Lawyers Assn., Norwegian-Am. C. of C., Hilands Golf Club, Kenwood Golf and Country Club, Billings Stamp Club, Elks, Masons. Avocations: philately, sports card collecting, hiking, Nordic skiing. Office: Crowley Haughey Hanson Toole & Dietrich Consulate for Norway 490 N 31st St Billings MT 59101-1256

SITES, JOHN MILTON, mathematics educator, computer consultant; b. Balt., June 28, 1966; s. John Edward and Nancy Christine (Kamynskie) S. BS in Math. cum laude, Allentown Coll., Center Valley, Pa., 1992, postgrad., 1995—. With Harmes & Assocs., Balt., 1983, 84; internat. arrival bag handler State Aviation Bd., Balt., 1984-86; customer svc. agt. United Airlines, Allentown, 1986-87, Henson Airlines, various locations, 1987-88; tutor Northampton C.C., Bethlehem, Pa., 1988-89, Allentown Coll., Center Valley, 1990-91; supr. ground svcs. Continental Express Airlines, Allentown, 1988-90; sr. chief operator Allentown Coll. Acad. Computing Ctr., Center Valley, 1990-92; computer sci. coord. Sacred Heart Sch., Bethlehem, 1992—; paraprofl. for disadvantaged, at-risk & handicapped students Career Inst. Tech., Easton, Pa., 1992—; computer cons. and planner Bangor (Pa.) Area Sr. H.S., 1992—, Wilson H.S., Easton, 1992—, Easton H.S., 1992—; group supr. Pvt. Industry Coun. Career Awareness Program, 1993-94; adj. math. faculty mem. Northampton C.C., Bethlehem, Pa., 1993-94. Contbr. articles to profl. jours. Activity aide United Cerebral Palsy, Bethlehem, 1987-88. Mem. Math. Assn. Am. (v.p. 1991), Pa. Coun. Tchrs. Math. Christian Ch. Avocations; model railroading, photography, antiques, computer hardware and software evaluation. Home: 3843 Suncrest Ln Bethlehem PA 18017-3485 Office: Career Inst of Tech 5335 Kesslersville Rd Easton PA 18040-6720

SITKOFF, THEODORE, public management executive; b. Phila., Jan. 25, 1932. BS in Econs., U. Pa., 1953, Masters of Govt. Adminstr., 1955. Acct. Commonwealth of Pa., 1955-59, comptr. dept. pub. welfare, 1959-61, dir. accounts gov.'s office of adminstrn., 1961-64; mem. hdqs. staff Pub. Adminstrn. Svc., McLean, Va., 1964-69, v.p., 1973-77, pres., 1977—, CEO; fin. dir. Fed. Land Devel. Authority Govt. of Malaysia and UN Exec. Corp., 1970-72; founder Ctr. Privatization. Office: Public Administration Service 8301 Greensboro Dr Ste 420 Mc Lean VA 22102-3603*

SITOMER, SHEILA MARIE, television producer, director; b. Hartford, Conn., Aug. 25, 1951; d. George W. and Mary E. (Chaponis) Bowe; m. Daniel J. Sitomer, Aug. 25, 1985. BA, Smith Coll., 1973. Field producer, dir. Good Morning Am., ABC-TV, N.Y.C., 1981-86; field producer Evening Magazine, WWOR-TV, KDKA-TV, Secaucus, Pitts., N.J., Pa., 1978-79, 88; supervising producer The Reporters, Fox Broadcasting, N.Y.C., 1988; producer Inside Edition, King World Prodns., N.Y.C., 1988-95; co-exec. prodr. Inside Edition and Am. Jour., 1995—. Vol. Nathaniel Witherell Nursing Home, Greenwich, Conn., 1988—. Recipient 3 Emmies, New England chpt. TV Acad. Arts & Scis., 1975-78, 2 Emmys, N.Y. chpt. TV Acad. Arts & Scis., 1979, 89, recipient first prize Internat. Film & TV Festival N.Y., 1988, No. N.J. Press Club award, 1988. Mem. Dirs. Guild Am., Actors Equity Assn. Office: Inside Edition 402 E 76th St New York NY 10021-3104

SITRICK, JAMES BAKER, lawyer; b. Davenport, Iowa, Feb. 21, 1935; s. Philip and Miriam (Baker) S.; m. Anne H.M. Helmers, Aug. 21, 1971; children: James Baker Jr., Margaret A., Catherine Baker. BA, U. Wis., 1957; LLM, Yale U., 1960. Bar: N.Y. 1961. Spl. asst. to asst. sec. treasury for internat. taxation U.S. Treasury, Washington, 1965-67; ptnr. Courdert Bros., N.Y.C., 1975—; chmn. exec. com. Coudert Bros., N.Y.C., 1982-93, sr. ptnr., 1993—; mem. mgmt. com. Ctrl. Suiker Maatschappij, The Netherlands, 1984—; lectr. numerous confs. and orgns. Contbr. articles to profl. jours. Mem. Coun. on Fgn. Rels.; chmn. Glyndebourne Opera Assn. Am., Benjamin Franklin Found. for Bibliotuque Nat., Paris, English Chamber Orch. Soc. Am.; mem. bd. overseers faculty arts and scis. NYU; trustee French Inst. Alliance-Francais, Folger Shakespeare Libr. Washington; vice-chmn. Coun. for U.S. and Italy; chmn. coun. fellows, dir. roundtable Pierpont Morgan Libr. 1st lt. U.S. Army, 1960-61. Frick Collection fellow. Mem. Grolier Club, Century Assn., Knickerbocker Club, Racquet and Tennis Club, Meadow Club. Office: Coudert Bros 1114 Avenue Of The Americas New York NY 10036-7703

SITRICK, MICHAEL STEVEN, communications executive; b. Davenport, Iowa, June 8, 1947; s. J. Herman and Marcia B. (Bofman) S.; m. Nancy Elaine Eiseman, July 1, 1969; children: Julie, Sheri, Alison. BS in Bus. Adminstrn. and Journalism, U. Md., 1969. Coordinator press services Western Electric, Chgo., 1969-70; asst. dir. program services City of Chgo., 1970-72; asst. v.p. Selz, Seabolt & Assocs., Chgo., 1972-74; dir. communications and pub. affairs Nat. Can Corp., Chgo., 1974-81; dir. communications Wickes Cos., Inc., San Diego, 1981-82; v.p. communications Wickes Cos., Inc., Santa Monica, Calif., 1982-84, sr. v.p. communications, 1984-89; chmn., chief exec. officer Sitrick and Co., L.A. and N.Y.C., 1989—. Office: Sitrick and Co 1875 Century Park E Ste 950 Los Angeles CA 90067-2510

SITTER, JOHN EDWARD, English literature educator; b. Cumberland, Md., Jan. 4, 1944; s. Vivian S. Snider; m. Deborah Ayer, June 19, 1971; children: Zachary, Amelia, Benjamin. AB, Harvard U., 1966; PhD, U. Minn., 1969. Asst. prof. English U. Mass., Amherst, 1969-75, assoc. prof. English, 1975-80; prof. English Emory U., Atlanta, 1980-85, Dobbs prof. English, 1985-93, Charles Howard Candler prof., 1993—, chmn. dept. English, 1994—; vis. lectr. U. Kent, Canterbury, Eng., 1974-75. Author: The Poetry of Pope's "Dunciad", 1971, Literary Loneliness, 1982 (Gottschalk prize 1982), Arguments of Augustan Wit, 1991; editor: The Eighteenth Century Poets, 2 Vols., 1990-91; contbr. articles to profl. jours. Nat. Def. Edn. Act fellow U. Minn., 1966-69, Nat. Humanities Ctr fellow, 1978-79. Mem. Am. Assn. Univ. Profs., Modern Language Assn., Am. Soc. 18th Century Studies. Office: Emory U Dept Of English Atlanta GA 30322

SITTON, CLAUDE FOX, newspaper editor; b. Emory, Ga., Dec. 4, 1925; s. Claude B. and Pauline (Fox) S.; m. Eva McLaurin Whetstone, June 5, 1953; children: Lea Sitton, Clinton, Suzanna Sitton Greene, McLaurin. A.B., Emory U., 1949, L.H.D., 1984. Reporter Internat. News Service, 1949-50; with U.P., 1950-55; writer-editor U.P., N.Y.C., 1952-55; information officer USIA, 1955-57; mem. staff N.Y. Times, 1957-68, nat. news dir., 1964-68; editorial dir. The News and Observer Pub. Co., Raleigh, N.C., 1968-90; dir. The News and Observer Pub. Co., 1969-90, v.p., 1970-90; editor News and Observer, 1970-90; sr. lectr. Emory U., Atlanta, 1991-94; active Pulitzer Prize Bd., 1985-94, chmn., 1992-93; bd. counselors Oxford Coll. Emory U., 1993—. Lay mem. Commn. on Evaluation of Disciplinary Enforcement, Ga. Supreme Ct., 1995—; mem. Ga. First Amendment Found. Bd., 1994—. With USNR, 1943-46; PTO. Recipient Pulitzer prize for commentary, 1983. Mem. Am. Soc. Newspaper Editors (dir. 1977-83). Home: PO Box 1326 Oxford GA 30267-1326

SIVCO, DEBORAH LEE, research materials scientist; b. Somerville, N.J., Dec. 21, 1957. BA in chem. edn., Rutgers Univ., 1980; MS in material sci., Stevens Inst., 1988. III-V processing tech. Laser Diode Labs, New Brunswick, N.J., 1980-81; with Bell Labs.-Lucent Technologist, Murray Hill, N.J., 1981—. Recipient Newcomb Cleveland prize AAAS, 1993-94, Electronics Letters premium Instn. Elec. Engrs. U.K., 1995. Office: AT&T Bell Labs 600 Mountain Ave New Providence NJ 07974

SIVE, DAVID, lawyer; b. Bklyn., Sept. 22, 1922; s. Abraham Leon and Rebecca (Schwartz) S.; m. Mary Robinson, July 23, 1948; children: Rebecca, Helen, Alfred, Walter, Theodore. A.B., Bklyn. Coll., 1943; LL.B., Columbia U., 1948. Bar: N.Y. 1948, U.S. Supreme Ct. 1964. Partner Sive, Paget & Riesel, and predecessors, N.Y.C., 1957—; prof. Pace U. Law Sch., White Plains, N.Y., 1995—; adj. prof. law Columbia Law Sch. and other law schs., 1965—; short term sr. Fulbright scholar, 1994. Author: (with Reed Rowley) Rowley on Partnerships, 1959; contbr. articles to law revs. Dem. candidate for N.Y. State Supreme Ct., 1965; trustee Natural Resources Def. Coun., Inc., 1969-93. With U.S. Army, 1943-45. Decorated Purple Heart and oak leaf cluster. Mem. Am., N.Y. State (Root/Stimson award for pub. service 1977) bar assns., Assn. of Bar of City of N.Y. (mem. exec. com. 1972-76, chmn. environ. law com. 1971-75), Am. Law Inst., Sierra Club (chmn. Atlantic chpt. 1968-69, nat. dir. 1968-69). Home: Millbrook Rd Margaretville NY 12455 Office: Pace Univ Law Sch 78 N Broadway White Plains NY 10603-9999 also: c/o Sive Paget & Riesel 460 Park Ave New York NY 10022

SIVE, REBECCA ANNE, public affairs company executive; b. N.Y.C., Jan. 29, 1950; d. David and Mary (Robinson) S.; m. Clark Steven Tomashefsky, June 18, 1972. BA, Carleton Coll., 1972; MA in Am. History, U. Ill., Chgo., 1975. Asst. to chmn. of pres.' task force on vocations Carleton Coll., Northfield, Minn., 1972; asst. to acquisitions librarian Am. Hosp. Assn., Chgo., 1973; rsch. asst. Jane Addams Hull House, Chgo., 1974; instr. Loop Coll., Chgo., 1975, Columbia Coll., Chgo., 1975-76; cons. Am. Jewish Com., Chgo., 1975, Ctr. for Urban Affairs, Northwestern U., Evanston, Ill., 1977, Ill. Consultation on Ethnicity in Edn., 1976, MLA, 1977; dir. Ill. Women's History Project, 1975-76; founder, exec. dir. Midwest Women's Ctr., Chgo., 1977-81; exec. dir. Playboy Found., 1981-84; v.p. pub. affairs/pub. rels. Playboy Video Corp., 1985; v.p. pub. affairs Playboy Enterprises, Inc., Chgo., 1985-86; pres. The Sive Group, Inc., Chgo., 1986—; guest speaker various ednl. orgns., 1972—; instr. Roosevelt U., Chgo., 1977-78; dir. spl. projects Inst. on Pluralism and Group Identity, Am. Jewish Com., Chgo., 1975-77; cons. Nat. Women's Polit. Caucus, 1978-80; bd. dirs. NOVA Health Systems, Woodlawn Community Devel. Corp.; trainer Midwest Acad.; mem. adv. bd. urban studies program Associated Colls. Midwest; proposal reviewer NEH. Contbr. articles to profl. jours. Commr. Chgo. Park Dist., 1986-88; mem. steering com. Ill. Commn. on Human Rels., 1976; mem. structure com. Nat. Women's Agenda Coalition, 1976-77; del.-at-large Nat. Women's conf., 1977; mem. Ill. Gov.'s Com. on Displaced Homemakers, 1979-81, Ill. Human Rights Com., 1980-87, Ill. coordinating com., Internat Womens Yr.; coord. Ill. Bicentennial Photog. Exhbn., 1977; mem. Ill. Employment and Tng. Coun.; mem. employment com. Ill. Com. on Status of Women; bd. dirs. Nat. Abortion Rights Action League and NARAL Found., Ill. div. ACLU, Midwest Women's Ctr. Recipient award for outstanding community leadership YWCA Met. Chgo., 1979, award for outstanding community leadership Chgo. Jaycees, 1988. Home: 3529 N Marshfield Ave Chicago IL 60657-1224 Office: The Sive Group 359 W Chicago Ave Ste 201 Chicago IL 60610-3025

SIVERD, ROBERT JOSEPH, lawyer; b. Newark, July 27, 1948; s. Clifford David and Elizabeth Ann (Klink) S.; m. Bonita Marie Shulock, Jan. 8, 1972; children: Robert J. Jr., Veronica Leigh. AB in French, Georgetown U., 1970; JD, 1973; postgrad. LaSorbonne, Paris, 1969. Bar: N.Y. 1974, U.S. Dist. Ct. (so. and ea. dists.) N.Y. 1974, U.S. Ct. Appeals (2nd cir.) 1974, U.S. Supreme Ct. 1980, U.S. Dist. Ct. (ea. dist.) Pa. 1984, U.S. Ct. Appeals (3rd cir.) 1984, (6th cir.) 1985, Ohio 1991, Ky. 1992. Assoc. Donovan Leisure Newton & Irvine, N.Y.C., 1973-83; staff v.p., litigation counsel Am. Fin. Group, Inc., Greenwich, Conn., 1983-86, v.p. litigation counsel, 1986-87, v.p. assoc. gen. counsel, Cin., 1987-92; sr. v.p., gen. counsel and sec. Gen. Cable Corp., 1992-94, exec. v.p., gen. counsel and sec., 1994—. Mem. ABA, Cin. Bar Assn., Assn. of Bar of City of N.Y., Ky. Bar Assn. Republican. Office: Gen Cable Corp 4 Tesseneer Dr Newport KY 41076-9753

SIVERSON, RANDOLPH MARTIN, political science educator; b. Los Angeles, July 29, 1940; s. Clifford Martin and Lorene (Sanders) S.; m. Mary Suzanne Strayer, Dec. 31, 1966; children: Andrew, Erica, Courtney. AB, San Francisco State U., 1962, MA, 1965; PhD, Stanford U., 1969. Lectr. polit. sci. Stanford U., Calif., 1967; asst. prof. U. Calif., Riverside, 1967-70; asst. prof. U. Calif., Davis, 1970-75, assoc. prof., 1975-81, prof., 1981—; Fulbright lectr. El Colegio de Mexico, Mexico City, 1974-75; vis. prof. Naval Postgrad. Sch., Monterey, Calif., 1980. Co-author: The Diffusion of War, 1991; editor: (with others) Change in the International System, 1980; editor Internat. Interactions, 1984-91; mem. editorial bd. Am. Polit. Sci. Rev., 1989-91. Mem. Internat. Studies Assn., Am. Polit. Sci. Assn., Western Polit. Sci. Assn. (pres. 1991), Midwest Polit. Sci. Assn. Roman Catholic. Office: U Calif Davis Dept Polit Sci Davis CA 95616

SIVIN, NATHAN, historian, educator; b. May 11, 1931; m. Carole Delmore. BS in Humanities and Sci., MIT, 1958; MA in History of Sci., Harvard U., 1960, PhD in History of Sci., 1966. Prof. Chinese history and history of sci., dept. history and sociology of sci. U. Pa., Phila., 1977—, acting chmn. dept., 1989; vis. lectr., Singapore U., 1962; vis. prof. Rsch. Inst. Humanistic Studies, Kyoto, Japan, 67-68, 71-72, 74, 79-80; vis. scientist Sinologisch Inst., Leiden, The Netherlands, Cambridge U., Eng., People's Republic China; vis. assoc., dir. Needham Rsch. Inst., Cambridge, 1987—; advisor Acad. Traditional Chinese Medicine, Beijing; numerous lectures and colloquia in Europe, Asia, N.Am. Author: (monograph) Chinese Alchemy: Preliminary Studies, 1968, Chinese trans. 1973, Cosmos and Computation in Early Chinese Mathematical Astronomy, 1969, Traditional Medicine in Contemporary China, 1987, Science in Ancient China: Researches and Reflections, 1995, Medicine, Philosophy and Religion in Ancient China: Researches and Reflections, 1995; author with others, editor or co-editor: Chinese Science, 1973, Science and Technology in East Asia, 1977, Astronomy in Contemporary China, 1979, Science and Civilisation in China, Vol.5, 1980, Science and Medicine in Twentieth-Century China, 1989, The Contemporary Atlas of China, 1989, Science in Ancient China, 1995, Medicine, Philosophy and Religion in Ancient China, 1995; also numerous articles for profl. jours., essays, prefaces to books, book revs.; editor, pub. Chinese Science, 1973-92; mem. editorial bd. U. Pa. Press, 1980-83, numerous jours.; gen. editor: (monograph series) Science, Medicine and Technology in East Asia, 3 Vol. MIT E. Asian Sci. Series, 6 vol.; adv. editor Tech. and Culture, 1973—. Mem. adminstrv. bd. Chinese Cultural and Community Ctr., Phila., 1983-84. Guggenheim fellow, 1971-72; Japan Soc. Promotion of Sci. rsch. fellow, 1979-80; grantee NSF, 1968-70, 79-81, Ford Found., 1970, Nat. Libr. Medicine NIH, 1976, IBM Corp., 1985, Nat. Program Advanced Study and Rsch. China, Com. Scholarly Communication with People's Republic China, 1986-87. Fellow Am. Acad. Arts and Scis.; mem. Am. Soc. for Study of Religion (exec. com. 1982-83, v.p. 1993—), Soc. for Studies Chinese Religion (bd. dirs., exec. coun. 1986-89), T'ang Studies Soc. (bd. dirs. 1986—), Internat. Soc. for History East Asian Sci., Tech. and Medicine (pres. 1990-93), Chinese Acad. Scis. (hon. prof. 1989—), Franklin Inn Club (pres. 1995), Acad. Internat. D'histoire des Scis. Home: 8125 Roanoke St Philadelphia PA 19118-3949 Office: U Pa Dept History & Sociology Sciences Philadelphia PA 19104-3325

SIVOLELLA, JOHN JOSEPH, lawyer; b. Springfield, N.J., Jan. 12, 1964; s. William and Dolores Ann (Purdue) S.; m. Eileen Karen Haws, Aug. 8, 1992. BA with high honors, Rutgers Coll., 1987; MPA, Princeton U., 1991; JD, NYU, 1992. Bar: N.J. 1992, U.S. Dist. Ct. N.J. 1992. Intern U.S. Dept. of State, Tegucigalpa, Honduras, 1989, U.S. Atty.'s Office, Newark, 1990; rsch. asst. Dean Oscar Chase NYU Law Sch., N.Y.C., 1990, 91; summer assoc. Steptoe & Johnson, Washington, 1991; jud. clk. to Justice Stewart G. Pollock Supreme Ct. of N.J., Morristown, N.J., 1992-93; assoc. Wilentz, Goldman & Spitzer, Woodbridge, N.J., 1993; asst. counsel Gov. Christine Todd Whitman, Trenton, N.J., 1994—; mem. bd. of adjustment City of Summit, 1996-97. Editor Annual Survey of Am. Law, 1990-91. Named Henry Rutgers Scholar, Rutgers U., 1987; Garden State Grad. fellow N.J. Dept. Higher Edn., 1988. Mem. N.J. State Bar Assn., Princeton Grad. Alumni Assn., Rutgers Alumni Assn., NYU Law Alumni Assn., Phi Beta Kappa, Phi Alpha Theta, Phi Sigma Iota. Republican. Roman Catholic. Avocations: athletics, travel, Spanish. Home: 204 Woodland Ave Summit NJ 07901 Office: Office of Counsel to Gov CN 001 Trenton NJ 08625

SIX, FRED N., state supreme court justice; b. Independence, Mo., Apr. 20, 1929. AB, U. Kans., 1951, JD with honors, 1956; LLM in Judicial Process, U. Va., 1990. Bar: Kans. 1956. Asst. atty. gen. State of Kans., 1957-58; pvt. practice Lawrence, Kans., 1958-87; judge Kans. Ct. Appeals, 1987-88; justice Kans. Supreme Ct., Topeka, 1988—; editor-in-chief U. Kans. Law Review, 1955-56; lectr. on law Washburn U. Sch. Law, 1957-58, U. Kans., 1975-76. Maj. USMC, 1951-53; USMCR, 1957-62. Recipient Disting. Alumnus award U. Kans. Sch. Law, 1994. Fellow Am. Bar Found. (chmn. Kans. chpt. 1983-87); mem. ABA (jud. adminstrn. divsn.), Internat. Law Assn. (Am. br.), Am. Judicature Soc., Kans. Bar Assn., Kans. Bar Found., Kans. Law Soc. (pres. 1970-72), Kans. Inn of Ct. (pres. 1993-94), Order of Coif, Phi Delta Phi. Office: Kans Supreme Ct 301 SW 10th Ave Topeka KS 66612-1507

SIZEMORE, CAROLYN LEE, nuclear medicine technologist; b. Indpls., July 22, 1945; d. Alonzo Chester and Elsie Louise Marie (Osterman) Armstrong; m. Jessie S. Sizemore Sr., June 9, 1966; 1 child, Jessie S. Jr. AA in

Nuclear Medicine, Prince George's Community Coll, Largo, Md., 1981; BA in Bus. Adminstrn., Trinity Coll., 1988. Registered technologist (nuclear medicine); cert. nuclear medicine technologist, Md.; lic. nuclear med. technologist. Nuclear med. technologist Washington Hosp. Ctr., 1981-88; chief technologist, mem. com. Capitol Hill Hosp., Washington, 1988-91; chief technologist, asst. radiation safety officer Nat. Hosp. Med. Ctr., Arlington, Va., 1991—; mem. Am. Registry of Radiologic Technologists Nuclear Medicine Exam. Com., 1990-93. Contbr. articles to profl. jours. Mem. com. Medlantic Rsch. Found., Washington, 1989-93; sec. Crestview Area Citizens Assn., 1994-95. Mem. Va. Soc. Radiol. Technologists, Potomac Dist. Soc. Radiol. Technologists, Med. Soc. Radiol. Technologsts, Med. Soc. Nuclear Medicine Technologists, Soc. Nuclear Medicine (chmn. membership 1983-85, sec. 1985-87, 88-89, co-editor Isotopics 1991, editor Isotopics 1992-96, nominating com. 1995-96), Nuclear Medicine Adv. Bd., Am. Legion Aux. (exec. com. 1975-76), Internat. Platform Assn., Crestview Area Citizens Assn. (sec. 1994-95). Republican. Lutheran. Avocations: various crafts, reading, aerobics, weight lifting. Home: 6700 Danford Dr Clinton MD 20735-4019

SIZEMORE, HERMAN MASON, JR., newspaper executive; b. Halifax, Va., Apr. 15, 1941; s. Herman Mason and Hazel (Johnson) S.; m. Connie Catterton, June 22, 1963; children: Jill, Jennifer. AB in History, Coll. William and Mary, 1963; postgrad., U. Mo., 1965; MBA, U. Wash., 1985. Reporter Norfolk (Va.) Ledger-Star, summers 1961, 62, 63; copy editor Seattle Times, 1965-70, copy-desk chief, 1970-75, asst. mng. editor, 1975-77, mng. editor, 1977-81, prodn. dir., 1981-83, asst. gen. mgr., 1984, v.p., gen. mgr., 1985, pres., chief operating officer, 1985—; vis. instr. Sch. Comms. U. Wash., 1972-78; bd. dirs. Times Comms. Co., Walla Walla Union-Bull, Inc., Yakima Herald-Republic, Times Community Newspapers, Inc., Northwestern Mut. Life Ins. Co., 1993—, mem. policyowner examining com., 1985, chmn., 1986. Bd. dirs. Ctrl. Puget Sound Campfire Coun., 1985-91, pres., 1989-90; bd. dirs. Ptnrs. in Pub. Edn., 1987-88, United Way of King County, 1994—, Downtown Seattle Assn.; adv. coun. Puget Sound Blood Ctr. and Program; adv. bd. USO-Puget Sound Area. Named Seattle Newsmaker of Tomorrow, 1978. Mem. AP Mng. Editors, Soc. Profl. Journalists, Pacific N.W. Newspaper Assn., Allied Daily Newspapers Washington (bd. dirs.), Coll. William and Mary Alumni Assn. (bd. dirs.), Greater Seattle C. of C., U. Wash. Exec. MBA Alumni Assn. (pres. 1988, bd. dirs.), Wash. Athletic Club, Rainier Club, Rotary. Methodist. Office: Seattle Times PO Box 70 Seattle WA 98111-0070

SIZEMORE, NICKY LEE, computer scientist; b. N.Y.C., Feb. 13, 1946; s. Ralph Lee and Edith Ann (Wangler) S.; m. Frauke Julika Hoffmann, Oct. 31, 1974; 1 child, Jennifer Lee Sizemore; 1 stepchild, Mark Anthony Miracle. BS in Computer Sci., SUNY, 1989. Sgt. first class U.S. Army, 1964-68, 70-86; computer operator UNIVAC, Washington, 1968-69, programmer, 1969-70; programmer/analyst Ultra Systems, Inc., Sierra Vista, Ariz., 1986-87; computer scientist Comarco, Inc., Sierra Vista, 1987-92, ARC, Profl. Svcs. Group, Sierra Vista, 1992-93, Computer Scis. Corp., Ft. Huachuca, Ariz., 1994; sr. cons. Inference Corp., 1995; subject matter expert Northrop Grumman Corp., 1996; sr. info. sys. engr. Harris Corp., Sierra Vista, Ariz., 1996—; speaker numerous confs., seminars, symposia. Mem. AIAA (mem. artificial intelligence standard com.), Computer Soc. IEEE, Am. Assn. for Artificial Intelligence (co-dir. workshop on verification, validation, and test of knowledge-based sys. 1988), Assn. for Computing Machinery, Armed Forces Comms.-Electronics Assn., Am. Def. Preparedness Assn. Avocations: chess, jogging/aerobics, karate. Home: 880 E Charles Dr Sierra Vista AZ 85635-1611 Office: Harris Tech Svcs Corp 101 E Wilcox Dr Sierra Vista AZ 85635

SIZEMORE, ROBERT DENNIS, school counselor, educational administrator; b. Indpls., July 30, 1943; s. George R. and Thelma L. (Lagle) S.; m. Leslie Ann, June 14, 1969; children: Christopher J., Kelly Ann. BS in Edn., Ind. U., 1967; MS in Secondary Edn., U. Bridgeport, 1972; cert., Portland State U., 1987. Cert. secondary tchr. and counselor, Oreg. Tchr. Marseilles (Ill.) Jr. High, 1967-69, Greenwich (Conn.) High Sch., 1969-76, Oregon City (Oreg.) High Sch., 1976-77; tchr., counselor, adminstr., asst. prin. curriculum Reynolds High Sch., Portland, Oreg., 1977—; presenter Nat. Coun. Social Studies Conventions; mem. high sch. reform network N.W. Regional Ednl. Lab.; officer Congress of Oreg. Sch. Adminstrs.-Oreg. Assn. Secondary Sch. Adminstrs., 1995-97; cons. in field; adj. staff Lewis and Clark Coll. Mem. ASCD, NEA, AACD, Nat. Assn. Secondary Sch. Prins., Congress Oreg. Sch. Adminstrs. (conv. presenter). Office: 1698 SW Cherry Park Rd Troutdale OR 97060-1481

SIZEMORE, WILLIAM CHRISTIAN, academic administrator; b. South Boston, Va., June 19, 1938; s. Herman Mason and Hazel (Johnson) S.; m. Anne Catherine Mills, June 24, 1961; children: Robert C., Richard M., Edward S. BA, U. Richmond, 1960; BD, Southeastern Bapt. Theol. Sem., Wake Forest, N.C., 1963; MLS, U. N.C., 1964; MLS (advanced), Fla. State U., 1971, PhD, 1973; postgrad., Harvard U., 1989. Library asst. U. N.C., Chapel Hill, 1963-64; assoc. librarian, instr. grad. research Southeastern Bapt. Theol. Sem., 1964-66; librarian, assoc. prof. South Ga. Coll., Douglas, 1966-71, acad. dean, prof., 1971-80, dean coll., prof., 1980-83, acting pres., 1982-83; pres. Alderson-Broaddus Coll., Philippi, W.Va., 1983-94, William Jewell Coll., Liberty, Mo., 1994—; cons. Continental R&D, Shawnee Mission, Kans., 1987-92, So. Assn. Colls. and Schs., Atlanta, 1977, S.C. Commn. on Higher Edn., Columbia, 1975-76, State Coun. Higher Edn. for Va., Richmond, 1969-70, Software Valley Corp., 1989-94. Contbr. articles to profl. jours. Mem. Barbour County Devel. Authority, Philippi, 1984-94, Barbour County Emergency Food and Shelter Bd., 1985-94, Barbour County Extension Com., 1990-94; mem. exec. coun. Yellow Pine area Boy Scouts Am., Valdosta, 1974-76; pres. Satilla Librarians Ednl. Coun., Douglas, 1969-71; lectr., workshop leader on Bible studies various orgns., 1966—; mem. bd. advisors Swatow Kakwang Profl. Acad., Peoples Republic China; pres. bd. dirs. W.Va. Intercollegiate Athletic Conf., 1985-86, coun. of pres. Nat. Assn. Intercollegiate Athletics; bd. dirs., mem. exec. com. Broaddus Hosp., Philippi, 1983-94; chmn. W.Va. Productive Industry Efforts Found., 1989-92; mem. mktg. com. W.Va. Life Scis. Park Found., 1989-94, Gov.'s Partnership for Progress, 1989-94; mem. adv. panel W.Va. Rural Health Initiative, 1991-94; mem. gov. bd., bd. dirs. W.Va. Alliance of Hosps., 1991-94; mem. bd. dirs. Clay-Platte Econ. Devel. Coun., 1996—, Kansas City chpt. Am. Red Cross, 1996—. Joseph Ruzicka scholar N.C. Library Assn., 1963; recipient Douglas Pilot Club Edn. award, 1981. Mem. ALA, Am. Assn. for Higher Edn., Am. Assn. Univ. Adminstrs., Nat. Coun. Instrnl. Adminstrs., W.Va. Assn. Coll. and Univ. Pres. (exec. com., v.p., pres. 1992), Mountain State Assn. Colls., W.Va. Found. for Ind. Colls. (dir. 1983-84, v.p. 1988-92), Mo. Colls. Fund, Barbour County C. of C. (bd. dirs. 1988-94, v.p. 1988-90, pres. 1990-92, chmn. bd. 1992-94), Liberty Area C. of C. (bd. dirs. 1995—), Kansas City Club, Univ. Club. Democrat. Baptist. Avocations: woodworking, gardening. Home: 510 E Mississippi St Liberty MO 64068-1518 Office: William Jewell Coll Office of Pres 500 College Hl Liberty MO 64068-1843

SIZEMORE, WILLIAM HOWARD, JR., newspaper editor; b. South Boston, Va., Dec. 8, 1948; s. W. Howard and Genevieve T. (Walton) S.; m. Mary K. Lamont, Jan. 29, 1972; children: Justin, Jennifer, Julie. BA in Philosophy, Coll. William and Mary, 1971. Editor The Clarksville (Va.) Times, 1972-75; reporter The Roanoke (Va.) Times, 1975-76, The Times-Herald, Newport News, Va., 1976-81; editor, pub. The York Town Crier, Yorktown, Va., 1981-88; copy editor The Ledger-Star, Norfolk, Va., 1982-89, news editor, 1989-95; writer, editor The Virginian-Pilot, Norfolk, Va., 1995—. Recipient various Excellence in Writing and Layout awards Va. Press Assn., 1972-95. Avocations: tennis, music, bicycling, camping. Home: 107 Azalea Dr Yorktown VA 23692-4645 Office: Virginian-Pilot/Ledger-Star 150 W Brambleton Ave Norfolk VA 23510-2018

SIZER, IRWIN WHITING, biochemistry educator; b. Bridgewater, Mass., Apr. 4, 1910; s. Ralph Waldo Emerson and Annie Jenkins (Scott) S.; m. Helen Whitcomb, June 23, 1935; 1 child, Meredith Ann (Mrs. Twomey). A.B., Brown U., 1931, Sc.D. (hon.), 1971; Ph.D., Rutgers U., 1935. Teaching fellow Rutgers U., 1931-35; dir. oyster pest control investigation for N.J. U.S. Bur. Fisheries, 1935; instr. MIT, Cambridge, 1935-39; asst. prof. MIT, 1939-42, asso. prof. physiology, 1942-56, prof. biochemistry, 1956—, exec. officer biology, 1954-55, acting head biol. dept., 1955-56, head biol. dept., 1956-67, dean Grad. Sch., 1967-75, cons. resource devel., 1975-85; pres. Whitaker Health Sci. Fund, Inc., 1974-84; cons. in resource devel. MIT, 1992-95; bd. dirs. Boston Fed. Savs. Bank, Lexington, Mass.; cons. in biochemistry to pharm. industry Ford Found., 1990-95; dir. Biol. Scis. Curriculum Study. Contbr. sci. papers, enzymology, biochemistry to profl. jours.; mem. adv. bd. Tech. Rev. Trustee, bd. govs. Rutgers U.; trustee Boston Biomed. Research Inst.; corp. mem. Lesley Coll.; trustee Mus. of Sci., Theobold Smith Research Inst. Honored byIrwin Sizer award for acad. innovation, 1975—; named hon. mem. MIT Class of 1924, hon. mem. MIT Alumni Assn. Fellow Am. Acad. Arts and Sci., Am. Inst. Chemists; mem. Am. Physiol. Soc., Am. Soc. Zoologists, Am. Soc. Biol. Chemists, Am. Chem. Soc., Sigma Xi (pres. Mass. Inst. Tech. 1958-59), Phi Beta Kappa (hon. mem.), Delta Omega. Home: 52 Dartmouth Ct Bedford MA 01730-2908

SIZER, PHILLIP SPELMAN, consultant, retired oil field services executive; b. Whittier, Calif., Apr. 11, 1926; s. Frank Milton and Helen Louise (Saylor) S.; m. Evelyn Sue Jones, Aug. 16, 1952; children: Phillip Spelman, Ves Warner. BME, So. Meth. U., 1948. Registered profl. engr., Tex. With Otis Engring. Corp., Dallas, 1948-91; project engr. Otis Engring. Corp., 1958-62, chief devel. engr., 1962-70, v.p. R & D, 1970-73, v.p. engring. and rsch., 1973-76, sr. v.p., tech. dir., 1977-91, bd. dirs., 1975-91; pres. Sizer Engring. Inc., 1992—; bd. dirs. DHV Internat., Inc.; cons. in field; mem. exec. com. Offshore Tech. Conf., 1976-79. Patentee in field. Mem. U. Tex. Mech. Engring. Dept. Vis. Com., 1977-83. Named to Hall of Achievement Coll. Engring., U. Tex., Arlington, 1983. Fellow ASME (chmn. exec. com. petroleum divsn. 1974-75, SPEE-1 chmn. main com. 1981-88, Engr. of Yr. award North Tex. sect. 1971, centennial medal 1980, OILDROP award petroleum divsn. 1982, Dedicated Svc. award 1985, Silver Patent award 1990); mem. Soc. Petroleum Engrs., S.W. Rsch. Inst. (trustee 1982—), Petroleum Engrs., Club of Dallas, Rotary Internat., Kappa Sigma, Tau Beta Pi, Kappa Mu Epsilon. Home: 14127 Tanglewood Dr Dallas TX 75234-3851

SIZER, THEODORE R., education educator; b. New Haven, June 23, 1932; m. Nancy Faust. BA in English Lit., Yale U., 1953; MAT in Social Studies, Harvard U., 1957, Phd in Edn. and Am. History, 1961; PedD (hon.), Lawrence U., 1969; LittD (hon.), Union Coll., 1972; LLD (hon.), Conn. Coll., 1984; LHD (hon.), Williams Coll., 1984; MA ad eundem, Brown U., 1985; LHD (hon.), Lowell U., 1985, Dartmouth Coll., 1985, Lafayette Coll., 1991; Webster U., 1992, Ind. U., 1993, Mt. Holyoke Coll., 1993, U. Maine, 1993. English and math. tchr. Roxbury Latin Sch., Boston, 1955-56; history and geography tchr. Melbourne (Australia) Grammar Sch., 1958; asst. prof. edn., dir. MA in tchrs. program Harvard U., Cambridge, Mass., 1961-64; dean grad. sch. edn. Harvard U., Cambridge, 1964-72; headmaster, instr. in history Phillips Acad., Andover, Mass., 1972-81; chmn. A Study of High Schs., 1981-84; chmn. edn. dept. Brown U., Providence, 1984-89, Walter H. Annenberg prof. edn., 1993-94; dir. Annenberg Inst. Sch. Reform, 1994—; vis. prof. U. Brisol, U.K., 1971, Brown U., Providence, spring 1983. Author: Secondary Schools at the Turn of the Century, 1964, The Age of the Academies, 1964, Religion and Public Education, 1967, (with Nancy F. Sizer) Moral Education: Five Lectures, 1970, Places for Learning, Places for Joy: Speculations on American School Reform, 1972, Horace's Compromise: The Dilemma of the American High School, 1984, rev. edit., 1985, Horace's School: Redesigning the American High School, 1992. Capt. U.S. Army, 1953-55. Named Guggenheim fellow, 1971; recipient citations Am. Fedn. Tchrs., Nat. Assn. Secondary Sch. Prins., Phillips Exeter Acad., Boston C. of C., Andover C. of C., Lehigh U. Edn. Alumni, 1991, Nat. Assn. Coll. Admissions Counsellors, 1991, Anthony Wayne award Wayne State U., 1981, Gold medal for excellence in undergrad. teaching CASE, 1988, Tchrs. Coll. medal Tchrs. Coll., Columbia U., 1991, Harold W. McGraw prize in edn., 1991, James Bryant Conant award Edn. Commn. States, 1992, Disting. Svc. award Coun. Chief State Sch. Officers, 1992, Coun. Am. Private Edn., 1993, Nat. Award Distinction U. Pa., 1993. Office: Brown Univ Coalition of Essential Schs PO Box 1969 Providence RI 02912-1969

SJOBERG, DONALD, bishop. Formerly bishop Western Can. Synod Lutheran Ch. in Am.-Can.; pres. Evangel. Luth. Ch. in Can., Winnipeg, Man., 1986—, Can. Council of Churches, 1988—. Office: Evang Luth Ch, 1512 St James St, Winnipeg, MB Canada R3H 0L2

SJOERDSMA, ALBERT, research institute executive; b. Lansing, Ill., Aug. 31, 1924; s. Sam and Agnes S.; m. Fern E. MacAllister, Dec. 2, 1950; children—Leslie, Ann, Albert, Britt. Ph.B., U. Chgo., 1944, B.S., 1945, Ph.D., 1948, M.D., 1949. Research asst. U. Chgo., 1947-49, NIH postdoctoral research fellow, 1950; intern U. Mich. Hosp., Ann Arbor, 1949-50; resident physician Michael Reese Hosp., Chgo., 1951; resident in internal medicine USPHS Hosp., Balt., 1951-53; sr. investigator, chief exptl. therapeutics br. Nat. Heart and Lung Inst., Bethesda, Md., 1953-71; v.p. Merrell Internat. Co., Strasbourg, France, 1971-78; v.p. pharm. research and devel. Richardson-Merrell Inc., 1978-81; v.p. pharm. research Merrell Dow Pharms., Cin., 1981-83; pres. Merrell Dow Research Inst., Cin., 1983-89; pres. emeritus Merrell Dow Research Inst., Cin., 1989-94; vis. spl. fellow Gen. Hosp., Malmo, Sweden, 1959-60; spl. lectr. George Washington U., 1959-71; Anton Julius Carlson lectr. U. Chgo., 1984; hon. chmn. 2d World Conf. on Clin. Pharmacology and Therapeutics, Washington, 1983; clin. prof. medicine U. Cin. Med. Ctr., 1986-91. Mem. AAAS (Theobold Smith award med. scis. 1958), Am. Soc. Pharm. and Exptl. Therapeutics (Harry Gold award in clin. pharmacology 1977, Exptl. Therapeutics award 1990), Am. Soc. Clin. Pharmacology and Therapeutics (Oscar B. Hunter Meml. award in therapeutics 1981), Internat. Soc. Hypertension, Coun. High Blood Pressure Rsch., Am. Heart Assn., Am. Fedn. Clin. Rsch., Am. Soc. Clin. Investigation, Am. Soc. Exptl. Biology and Medicine, Assn. Am. Physicians, Am. Coll. Neuropsychopharmacology. Home and Office: 263 N Dogwood Trail Kitty Hawk NC 27949

SJOLANDER, GARY WALFRED, physicist; b. Bagley, Minn., Dec. 5, 1942; s. Tage Walfred and Evelyn Mildred (Kaehn) S.; m. Joann Lorraine Tressler, June 18, 1966; 1 child, Toby Ryan. BS in Physics, U. Minn., 1970, MS in Physics, 1974, PhD in Physics, 1975. Rsch. assoc. U. Minn., Mpls., 1975-76; rsch. scientist Johns Hopkins U., Balt., 1977-78, sr. physicist, 1978-82; sr. engr. Westinghouse Electric Corp., Annapolis, Md., 1982-85; sr. staff engr. Lockheed Martin Astronautics, Denver, 1985-95; engring. scientist data techs. divsn. TRW, Aurora, Colo., 1996—; pres. Cypress Improvement Assn., Inc., Severna Park, Md., 1984-85; advisor Inroads/Denver, Inc., 1986-88. Author numerous articles in field. With USAF, 1960-64. Mem. AIAA, Internat. Soc. for Optical Engring., Am. Geophys. Union, The Planetary Soc. Lutheran. Avocations: tennis, motorcycling, wooden-ship models, piano, woodworking. Home: 811 W Kettle Ave Littleton CO 80120-4443

SJOSTRAND, FRITIOF STIG, biologist, educator; b. Stockholm, Sweden, Nov. 5, 1912; s. Nils Johan and Dagmar (Hansen) S.; m. Marta Bruhn-Fahraeus, Mar. 24, 1941 (dec. June 1954); 1 child, Rutger; m. Ebba Gyllenkrok, Mar. 28, 1955; 1 child, Johan; m. Birgitta Petterson, Jan. 23, 1969; 1 child, Peter. M.D., Karolinska Institutet, Stockholm, 1941, Ph.D., 1945; Ph.D. (hon.), U. Siena, 1974, North-East Hill U., Shillon, India, 1989. Asst. prof. anatomy Karolinska Institutet, 1945-48, assoc. prof., 1949-59, prof. histology, 1960-61; research assoc. MIT, 1947-48; vis. prof. UCLA, 1959, prof. zoology, 1960-82, prof. emeritus molecular biology, 1982—. Author: Über die Eigenfluoreszenz Tierischer Gewebe Mit Besonderer Berücksichtigung der Sägetierniere, 1944, Electron Microscopy of Cells and Tissues, Vol. I, 1967, Deducing Function from Structure, Vols. I and II, 1990; also numerous articles. Decorated North Star Orden Sweden; recipient Jubilee award Swedish Med. Soc., 1959, Anders Retzius gold medal, 1967; Paul Ehrlich-Ludwig Darmstaedter prize, 1971. Fellow Royal Micros. Soc. (hon., London), Am. Acad. Arts and Scis.; mem. Electron Microscopy Soc. Am. (hon., Disting. Scientist award 1992), Japan Electron Microscopy Soc. (hon.), Scandinavian Electron Microscopy Soc. (hon.). Achievements include development technique for high resolution electron microscopy of cells, fluorescence microspectrography; inventor ultramicrotome.

SJØVOLD, TORSTEIN, osteologist, educator; b. Norway, Nov. 5, 1946; arrived in Sweden, 1971; s. Thorleif and Aase Fredrikke (Bay) S.; m. Anne Marie Bergby, Jan. 7, 1970 (div. Feb. 1980); children: Thorbjørn, Erik; m.Rose-Marie Birgitta Axelsson, July 11, 1981; children: Hannah Kristine, Henrik William. PhD, Stockholm U., 1977. Rsch. asst. Stockholm U., 1974-77, assoc. prof. pro-temp, 1977-78, assoc. prof., 1978-79, prof., 1979—; mem. rsch. team for the study of Tyrolean Ice man, 1991—; head Osteological Rsch. Lab., Stockholm U., Solna, Sweden, 1977—, assoc. dean faculty of humanities, 1984-87, head dept. archaeology, 1978-83. Author: OSSA 4, Supplement 1, 1977, Frost and Found, Natural History, 1993; contbr. articles to profl. jours. Mem. Anthrop. Soc. of Croatia (hon.), The Order of Internat. Fellowship, Norwegian Acad. of Sci., 1993. Home: Kuskbostaden, Ulriksdal Royal Castle, S-17071 Solna Sweden Office: Osteol Rsch Lab Stockholm U, Ulriksdal Royal Castle, S-17071 Solna Sweden

SKADDEN, DONALD HARVEY, professional society executive, accounting educator; b. Danville, Ill., Jan. 26, 1925; s. Harvey Frank and Lois Mary (Strawbridge) S.; m. Barbara Ann Meade, June 16, 1946 (dec.); children: John D., David H.; m. Karin Matson, Mar. 18, 1985. BS, U. Ill., 1948, MS, 1949, PhD, 1955. CPA, Ill. Asst. prof. acctg. U. Ill., Urbana, 1955-58, assoc. prof., 1958-61, prof., 1961-73, assoc. dean Coll. Commerce and Bus. Adminstrn., 1969-71; sr. acct. Haskins & Sells, 1957-58; Arthur Young prof. accounting U. Mich., Ann Arbor, 1973-87, chmn. acctg. faculty, 1976-79, assoc. dean for acad. affairs, 1979-87; v.p. taxation AICPA, 1987-92; exec. dir. Am. Tax Policy Inst., 1992—; dir. Paton Acctg. Ctr., 1976-79; mem. Fin. Acctg. Stds. Adv. Commn., 1980-84, ABA Commn. on Taxpayer Compliance, 1984-88; mem. commrs. adv. group IRS, 1990-91; active Nat. Conf. Lawyers and CPAs, 1993—. Author: Federal Income Tax: Student Workbook, 1965; Co-author: Principles of Federal Income Taxation; Editor: The Illinois CPA, 1964-66; editorial bd.: The Tax Adviser, 1969-74, The Accounting Review, 1973-75. Alderman, City of Urbana, 1961-69, mayor, 1969. With AUS, 1943-46, ETO. Decorated Combat Inf. badge. Mem. Am. Inst. CPA's (exec. com. of fed. tax div. 1979-82, council 1980-83), Ill. Soc. CPA's (bd. dirs. 1966-68, chair in accountancy 1968-73), Am. Acctg. Assn. (pres. 1979-80), Am. Taxation Assn. (pres. 1977-78), Urbana Assn. Commerce and Industry (bd. dirs. 1970-73), Beta Gamma Sigma, Phi Kappa Phi, Beta Alpha Psi. Methodist. Home: 3112 Chipping Wedge Ct Sanford NC 27330-8336

SKAFF, ANDREW JOSEPH, lawyer, public utilities, energy and transportation executive; b. Sioux Falls, S.D., Aug. 30, 1945; s. Andrew Joseph and Alice Maxine (Skaff) S.; m. Lois Carol Phillips, Oct. 4, 1971; children—Amy Phillips, Julie Phillips. B.S. in Bus. Adminstrn, Miami U., Oxford, Ohio, 1967; J.D., U. Toledo, 1970. Bar: Calif. 1971, U.S. Supreme Ct. 1974. Prin., sr. counsel Calif. Public Utilities Commn., 1977; gen. counsel Delta Calif. Industries, Oakland, 1977-82; sec. Delta Calif. Industries, 1978-82; mem. Silver Rosen, Fischer & Stecher, San Francisco, 1982-84; sr. ptnr. Skaff and Anderson, San Francisco, 1984-90; pvt. practice Law Office of Andrew J. Skaff, 1990-95; ptnr. Knox Ricksen, Oakland, 1995—; officer Delta Calif. Industries and subs. Contbr. articles to legal jours.; contbg. mem. law rev. U. Toledo, 1970. Mem. Calif. Bar Assn., Conf. Calif. Pub. Utilities Counsel, Calif. Cogeneration Coun., Assn. Transp. Practitioners, Alameda County Bar Assn. Office: Lake Merritt Plz 1999 Harrison St 17th Fl Oakland CA 94612-3517

SKAFF, JOSEPH JOHN, state agency administrator, retired army officer; b. Charleston, W.Va., June 13, 1930; s. Michael Joseph and Zahia S.; m. Maree A. Fleming, Aug. 4, 1957; children: Joseph M., Lynn M. Johnson, Gregory M., Nancy E. Kochman. B.S., U.S. Mil Acad., 1955; M.S., George Washington U., 1968. Commd. 2d lt. U.S. Army, 1955; commanded 1/27 FA battalion, 1968-69; advanced through grades to maj. gen.; dep. dir. internat. negotiations U.S. Army Joint Chiefs of Staff, Washington, 1979-81; mem. staff and faculty U.S. Mil. Acad., 1972-76; also dep. commr. U.S. del. Standing Consultative Commn., Geneva, 1979-81; dep. dir. ops. readiness and moblzn. Hdqrs. Dept. Army, Washington, 1981-83; dep. comdr./chief staff U.S. Army in Japan, 1982-84; dep. commdg. gen., commdg. gen. 1st U.S. Army, Fort Devens, Mass., 1985-89, adj. gen. W.Va., 1989-95; sec. mil. affairs and pub. safety W.Va., 1989—. Decorated D.S.M., Def. Superior Svc. medal, Legion of Merit, Bronze Star, Air medal, others. Mem. Assn. Grads. U.S. Mil. Acad., Assn. U.S. Army, Arty. Assn., Adj. Gens. Assn. U.S., Nat. Guard Assn. U.S., Officers Christian Fellowship, Fellowship Christian Athletes. Eastern Orthodox.

SKAGGS, ARLINE DOTSON, elementary school educator; b. Houston, Sept. 10, 1935; d. Gordon Alonzo and Fannie Mae (O'Kelley) Dotson; m. May 24, 1958 (div. Dec. 1969); children: Fred Mack, Ray Gordon. BS, U. Houston, 1957. Recreation leader VA Hosp., Houston, 1957-59; 4th and 5th grade tchr. Houston Ind. Sch. Dist., 1967-91; ret., 1991—; sponsor Number Sense, 1975-87, Sci. Fair, 1984-85. Auditor PTA, 1985, 87, 88; treas. Mt. Olive Luth. Sch. PTO, 1967-68; pres. Gulfgate Lioness Club, 1966-67; mem. Delphian Soc., 1965, Ch. of Houston Bread Distbn. program, 1990-91; treas. Houston Night Chpt. Women's Aglow, 1982; tchr. Children's Ch., 1972, 83, 84; prayer ptnr. Trinity Broadcasting Network, 1989-90, Christian Broadcasting Network, 1982-83; Braves scorekeeper Braes Bayou Little League, 1969-71; mem. United Way Funding Com., Salvation Army, Star of Hope & United Svcs. Orgn., 1974-76. Winning sponsor Citywide Math. Competition, Houston Ind. Sch. Dist., 1982, N.E. Area Math. Competition, 1976, 78, 79, 81, 82, 83, Lockhart Math. Contest, 1987. Mem. NEA (del. 1974), Houston Tchrs. Assn. (sch. rep. 1968-77, exec. bd. 1972-74, dir. N.E. area 1972-74, by-laws chmn. 1976), Tex. State Tchrs. Assn. (life, del. convs. 1968-75). Avocations: reading, grandparenting, travel. Home: 4437 Vivian St Bellaire TX 77401-5630

SKAGGS, BEBE REBECCA PATTEN, college dean, clergywoman; b. Berkeley, Calif., Jan. 30, 1950; d. Carl Thomas and Bebe (Harrison) P. BS in Bible, Patten Coll., 1969; BA in Philosophy, Holy Names Coll., 1970; MA in Bibl. Studies New Testament, Wheaton Coll., 1972; PhD in Bibl. Studies New Testament, Drew U., 1976; MA in Philosophy, Dominican Sch. Philosophy & Theology, 1990; postgrad., U. Calif., Berkeley, 1991-92. Ordained to ministry Christian Evang. Ch., 1963. Co-pastor Christian Cathedral, Christian Evang. Chs. Am., Inc., 1964—; assoc. prof. Patten Coll., Oakland, Calif., 1975-82, dean, 1977—, prof. N.T., 1982—; presenter in field. Author: Before the Times, 1980, The World of the Early Church, 1990; contbg. author: Internat. Standard Bibl. Ency., rev. edit., 1983. Active Wheaton Coll. Symphony, 1971-72, Drew U. Ensemble, 1971-75, Young Artists Symphony, N.J., 1972-75, Somerset Hill Symphony, N.J., 1973-74, Peninsula Symphony, 1977, 80-81, Madison Chamber Trio, N.J., 1973-75. Named one of Outstanding Young Women of Am., 1976, 77, 80-81, 82; St. Olaf's Coll. fellow, 1990. Mem. AAUP, Am. Acad. Religion, Soc. Bibl. Lit., Internat. Biographical Assn., Christian Evang. Chs. of Am., Inc. (bd. dirs. 1964—), Christian Assn. for Student Affairs, Assn. for Christians in Student Devel., Inst. for Bibl. Rsch., Phi Delta Kappa.

SKAGGS, DAVID E., congressman; b. Cin., Feb. 22, 1943; s. Charles and Juanita Skaggs; m. Laura Locher, Jan. 3, 1987; 1 child, Matthew; stepchildren: Clare, Will. BA in Philosophy, Wesleyan U., 1964; student law, U. Va., 1964-65; LLB, Yale U., 1967. Bar: N.Y. 1968, Colo. 1971. Assoc. Newcomer & Douglass, Boulder, Colo., 1971-74, 77-78; chief of staff Congressman Tim Wirth, Washington, 1975-77; ptnr. Skaggs, Stone & Sheehy, Boulder, 1978-86; mem. 100th-104th Congresses from 2d Colo. dist., Washington, 1987—; mem. Appropriations com., subcoms. Commerce and Justice, Interior; mem. Ho. Permanent Select Com. on Intelligence; chmn. Dem. Study Group; mem. Colo. Ho. of Reps., Denver, 1980-86; minority leader, 1982-85. Former bd. dirs. Rocky Mountain Planned Parenthood, Mental Health Assn. Colo., Boulder County United Way, Boulder Civic Opera. Served to capt. USMC, 1968-71, Vietnam; maj. USMCR, 1971-77. Mem. Colo. Bar Assn., Boulder County Bar Assn., Boulder C. of C. Democrat. Congregationalist. Office: US House of Reps 1124 Longworth Bldg Washington DC 20515-0602 also: 9101 Harlan St Unit 130 Westminster CO 80030-2925

SKAGGS, L. SAM, retail company executive; b. 1922; married. With Am. Stores Co., Salt Lake City, 1945—, chmn. bd., chief exec. officer, 1962-89, chmn., 1989—, also bd. dirs.; chmn. Sav-On Drugs, Anaheim, Calif., bd. dirs. Served with USAAF, 1942-45. Office: Am Stores Co 709 E South Temple Salt Lake City UT 84102-1205

SKAGGS, RICHARD WAYNE, agricultural engineering educator; b. Grayson, Ky., Aug. 20, 1942; s. Daniel M. and Gertrude (Adkins) S.; m. Judy Ann Kuhn, Aug. 25, 1962; children: Rebecca Diane Skaggs Ramsey,

Steven Glen. BS in Agr. Engring., U. Ky., 1964, MS in Agr. Engring., 1966; PhD, Purdue U., 1970. Registered profl. engr., N.C. Grad. asst. U. Ky., Lexington, 1964-66; grad. instr. in rsch. Purdue U., West Lafaytte, Ind., 1966-70; asst. prof. agrl. engring. N.C. State U., Raleigh, 1970-74, assoc. prof., 1974-79, prof., 1979-84, William Neal Reynolds prof., 1984—, disting. univ. prof., 1991—; cons. on drainage U.S. Aid, Egypt, 1989—; cons., lectr. on water mgmt., India, 1992, Malaysia, 1993, 95, New Zealand, 1993. Contbr. over 240 articles on water mgmt. and hydrology to profl. jours. Recipient Outstanding Young Scientist award N.C. State U. chpt. Sigma Xi, 1978; Alumni Rsch. award N.C. State U. Alumni Assn., 1983, Alumni Disting. Profl. award for grad. tchg., 1991, Alexander Q. Holladay Award for Excellence, N.C. State U., 1994, Superior Svc. award USDA, 1986, 90; named to Drainage Hall of Fame, Ohio State U., 1984, Engring. Hall of Distinction, U. Ky., 1994; named Outstanding Alumnus Agrl. Engr., U. Ky., 1985. Fellow Am. Soc. Agrl. Engrs. (chmn. nat. drainage symposium com. 1976, mem. nominating com. 1979, 95-96, Hancor Soil and Water Engring. award 1986, bd. dirs. 1992-94, John Deere Gold medal 1993); mem. NRC (com. on wetland characterization), NAE. Avocations: basketball, golf, reading. Home: 2824 Sandia Dr Raleigh NC 27607-3150 Office: NC State U Dept Biol-Agrl Eng PO Box 7625 Raleigh NC 27695-7625

SKAGGS, RICKY, country musician; b. Ky., July 18, 1954; s. Hobert and Dorothy S.; m. Sharon White, 1981; 4 children. First profl. job, age 15, playing mandolin with Ralph Stanley group Clinch Mountain Boys; subsequently with Country Gentlemen, J.D. Crowe and New South; then formed own group Boone Creek; joined Emmylou Harris backup group Hot Band, 1977; played with The Whites; joined Grand Ole Opry, 1982; albums include Waitin' for the Sun to Shine, 1981, Highways and Heartaches, Don't Cheat in Our Hometown, Country Boy, 1984, Favorite Country Songs, Live in London, Love's Gonna Get Ya!, Comin' Home To Stay, 1988, Kentucky Thunder, 1989, My Father's Son, 1991, Super Hits, 1993, Solid Ground. Recipient Horizon award for best newcomer Country Music Assn., male vocalist of yr. award, 1982, best instrumental group award, 1983, 84, 85, 6 Country Music Assn. awards including Entertainer of Yr. award, 1985, Vocal Event of Yr. award, 1991, Grammy award for best country instrumental, 1984, 85, 86, Grammy award for best country vocal collaboration, 1992, 6 Acad. of Country Music awards, MusicDove award Gospel Music Assn., Playboy Reader's Poll Best Country Instrumental Performance, 1989, Eng.'s Country Music Round Up Most Popualr Internat. Male, 1986-87, Edison award, 1987, 50th Anniversary award USO, 1989, various awards Music City News, Cash Box, Radio and Records; named Christian Country Artist of Yr. Gospel Voice Mag., 1993, Musician of Yr. award Christian Country Music Assn., 1994. Office: 54 Music Sq E Ste 301 Nashville TN 37203-4315

SKAGGS, SANFORD MERLE, lawyer; b. Berkeley, Calif., Oct. 24, 1939; s. Sherman G. and Barbara Jewel (Stinson) S.; m. Sharon Ann Barnes, Sept. 3, 1976; children: Stephen, Paula Ferry, Barbara Gallagher, Darren Peterson. B.A., U. Calif.-Berkeley, 1961, J.D., 1964. Bar: Calif. 1965. Atty. Pacific Gas and Electric Co., San Francisco, 1964-73; gen. counsel Pacific Gas Transmission Co., San Francisco, 1973-75; ptnr. Van Voorhis & Skaggs, Walnut Creek, Calif., 1975-85, McCutchen, Doyle, Brown & Enersen, San Francisco and Walnut Creek, 1985—; mem.Calif. Law Revision Commn., 1990—, chmn. 1993; dir. John Muir Med. Ctr., 1996—. Councilman City of Walnut Creek, 1972-78, mayor 1974-75, 76-77; bd. dirs. East Bay Mcpl. Utility Dist., 1978-90, pres., 1982-90; dir. Calif. Symphony, 1992—; trustee Contra Costa County Law Libr., 1978—. Mem. Calif. State Bar Assn., Contra Costa County Bar Assn., Urban Land Inst., Lambda Alpha, Alpha Delta Phi, Phi Delta Phi. Republican. Office: McCutchen Doyle Brown & Enersen PO Box V 1331 N California Blvd Walnut Creek CA 94596

SKAGGS, WAYNE GERARD, financial services company executive; b. Bonneterre, Mo., Dec. 12, 1929; s. Jasper Pinkney and Lattie May (Duren) S.; m. Hana Kaneko, June 1, 1952; children: Robert Kenneth, Melody Jane, Joy Elizabeth. Student, Mo. Inst. Acctg. and Law, 1947-48, U. Mo., Columbia, 1954-55. With Advantage Capital Corp. (formerly Am. Capital Corp.), Houston, 1955—; pres., chief oper. officer Mktg. Group of Cos., Houston, 1976-80; corp. v.p., cons. Mktg. Group of Cos., 1972-90. Served with USAF, 1950-54, Korea. Mem. Nat. Assn. Securities Dealers (nat. vice chmn. 1977, dist. chmn. 1972), Nat. Bus. Conduct (gov., chmn. 1976), Investment Co. Inst. Republican. Presbyterian. Club: Optimists (pres. club 1966, life mem.). Home: PO Box 726 Wimberley TX 78676-0726

SKAL, DEBRA LYNN, lawyer; b. Dayton, Ohio, Oct. 2, 1958; d. Lawrence and Anne Bernice (Cunix) S. BS with high distinction, Ind. U., 1986; JD, Duke U., 1989. Bar: Ga. 1989. Assoc. Powell, Goldstein, Frazer & Murphy, Atlanta, 1989—. Exec. editor: Alaska Law Rev., 1987-89. Mem. Lupus Found. Am., Atlanta, 1992—; coun. mem. Yes!Atlanta, 1990—; mem. Sjogren's Found., Port Washington, N.Y., 1992—. Mem. ABA, State Bar Assn. Ga., Atlanta Bar Assn., Beta Gamma Sigma. Office: Powell Goldstein Frazer & Murphy 191 Peachtree St NE 16th Fl Atlanta GA 30303

SKALA, GARY DENNIS, electric and gas utilities executive management consultant; b. Bay Shore, N.Y, Oct. 15, 1946; s. Harry A. and Emily Skala. BS in Mgmt. Engring., Rensselaer Polytech. Inst., 1969; MA in Psychology, Hofstra U., 1972; postgrad., Chgo. Theol. Sem., 1996. Engr. L.I. Lighting Co., Hicksville, N.Y., 1969-71; labor rels. coord. L.I. Lighting Co., 1971-73; mgmt. cons. Gilbert/Commonwealth, N.Y.C., 1973-74; sr. mgmt. cons. Booz, Allen & Hamilton, San Francisco, 1974-78; mgr. utility cons. A.T. Kearney, Chgo., 1978-81; mng. cons. Cresap, div. Towers Perrin, Chgo., 1981-85; pres. Gary D. Skala & Assocs. Mgmt. Cons., Chgo., 1985—; lectr. on utility bus. issues Edison Electric Inst., Utility Exec. Mgmt. Com., Internat. Maintenance Conf., Assn. Rural Electric Coops., Inst. Indsl. Engrs.; subcontracting cons. Arthur D. Little Inc., Liberty Cons. Group, Ernst & Young, Cresap, A.T. Kearney, Towers Perrin, Michael Paris Assocs. Ltd., Planmetrics. Contbr. articles to profl. jours. Trustee, strategic planning com. Samaritan Inst. for Religious Studies; mem. bd. Ordained Ministry of Great Lakes Dist. of Universal Fellowship Met. Cmty. Chs.; vice moderator bd. dirs. Good Shepherd Parish Met. Cmty. Ch. of Chgo; vol. The Night Ministry of Chgo. Mem. Inst. Indsl. Engrs. (sr. mem. utility div. 1978—, charter), Am. Inst. Indsl. Engrs. (chmn. Midwest chpt. utility div. 1980-81). Avocations: managing the Jerry Lee Lewis Archives, Jason D. Williams Archives.

SKALAGARD, HANS MARTIN, artist; b. Skuo, Faroe Islands, Feb. 7, 1924; s. Ole Johannes and Hanna Elisa (Fredriksen) S.; came to U.S., 1942, naturalized, 1955. Pupil Anton Otto Fisher, 1947; m. Mignon Diana Haack Haegland, Mar. 31, 1955; 1 child, Karen Solveig Sikes. Joined U.S. Mcht. Marine, 1942, advanced through grades to chief mate, 1945, ret., 1965; owner, operator Skalagard Sq., Rigger Art Gallery, Carmel, 1966—; libr. Mayo Hays O'Donnel Libr., Monterey, Calif., 1971-73; painter U.S. Naval Heritage series, 1973—; exhibited in numerous one-man shows including Palace Legion of Honor, San Francisco, 1960, J.F. Howland, 1963-65, Fairmont Hotel, San Francisco, 1963, Galerie de Tours, 1969, 72-73, Pebble Beach Gallery, 1968, Laguna Beach (Calif.) Gallery, 1969, Arden Gallery, Atlanta, 1970, Gilbert Gallery, San Francisco, Maritine Mus. of Monterey, Calif., 1993, Rigger Art Gallery, Carmel, Calif., Stanton Ctr., Monterey, 1993, St. Francis Yacht Club, San Francisco, 1995, Monterey Nat. Mus., 1993; group shows: Am. Artists, Eugene, Oreg., Robert Louis Stevenson Exhibit, Carmel Valley Gallery, Biarritz and Paris, France, David Findley Galleries, N.Y.C. and Faroe Island, Europe, Martime Mus., Calif, 1993, 94, 95, Pacific Coast Lumber Schooners, 1994, numerous others; represented in permanent collections; Naval Post Grad. Sch. and Libr., Allen Knight Maritime Mus., Salvation Army Bldg., Monterey, Calif., Robert Louis Stevenson Sch., Pebble Beach, Anenberg Art Galleries, Chestlibrook Ltd., Skalagard Art Gallery, Carmel, 1984; work represented in numerous boosk including Modern Masters of Marine Art, 1993; profiled in profl. jours.; lectr. Bd. dirs. Allen Knight Maritime Mus., 1973—, mem. adv. and acquisition coms., 1973-77; founder Skalagard Square Rigger Gallery; chairperson Mayor's Choice Exhibit Carmel, Calif., 1995; co founder Carmel Gallery Alliance. Recipient Silver medal Tommaso Campanella Internat. Acad. Arts, Letters and Scis., Rome, 1970, Gold medal, 1972, Gold medal and hon. life membership Academia Italia dell Arti e del Honoro, 1980, Gold medal for artistic merit Academia d'Italia. Mem. Navy League (bd. dir. Monterey), Internat. Platform Assn., Sons of Norway (cultural dir. 1974-75, 76-77). Subject of cover and article Palette Talk, 1980, Compass mag., 1980. Home: 25197 Canyon Dr Carmel CA 93923-8329 Office: PO Box 6611 Carmel CA 93921-6611 also: Dolores At 5th St Carmel CA 93921

SKALAK, RICHARD, engineering mechanics educator, researcher; b. N.Y.C., Feb. 5, 1923; s. Rudolph and Anna (Tuma) S.; m. Anna Lesta Allison, Jan. 24, 1953; children: Steven Leslie, Thomas Cooper, Martha Jean, Barbara Anne. BS, Columbia U., 1943, CE, 1946, PhD, 1954; MD (hon.), Gothenburg U., Sweden, 1990. Instr. civil engring. Columbia U., N.Y.C., 1948-54, asst. prof., 1954-60, assoc. prof., 1960-64, prof., 1964-77, James Kip Finch prof. engring. mechanics, 1977-88, emeritus, 1988—, dir. Bioengring. Inst., 1978-88; prof. bioengring. U. Calif., San Diego, 1988—, dir. Inst. for Mechs. and Materials, 1992—; Hunter lectr. Clemson U., 1994; mem. panel Gov.'s Conf. on Sci. and Engring., R&D, 1989-90. Contbr. articles to sci. jours. Bd. dirs. Biotech. Inst., Gothenburg, Sweden, 1978—; mem. adv. bd. Ctr. for Biomed. Engring., N.Y.C., 1994—. Recipient Great Tchr. award Columbia Coll. Soc. of Older Grads., 1972, Merit medal Czechoslovakian Acad. Scis., 1990. Fellow AAAS, ASME (Centennial medal 1980, Melville medal 1990, editor jour. 1984), Am. Acad. Mechanics, Soc. Engring. Sci., Am. Inst. Med. and Biol. Engring. (founding); mem. NAE, Soc. Rheology, Am. Heart Assn., Microcirculatory Soc., Internat. Soc. Biorheology (Poiseuille medal 1989), Biomed. Engring. Soc. (Alza medal 1983), Cardiovascular System Dynamics Soc., Am. Soc. for Engring. Edn., Tau Beta Pi, Sigma Xi. Democrat. Presbyterian. Home: 8916 Montrose Way San Diego CA 92122 Office: U Calif San Diego Ames Dept Bioengring La Jolla CA 92093-0412

SKALKA, ANNA MARIE, molecular biologist, virologist; b. N.Y.C., July 2, 1938. AB, Adelphi U., 1959; PhD in Microbiology, NYU, 1964. Am. Cancer Soc. fellow molecular biology genetics rsch. unit Carnegie Inst., 1964-66, fellow, 1966-69; asst. mem. dept. cell biology lab. molecular and biochemical genetics Roche Inst. Molecular Biology, 1969-71, assoc. mem., 1971-76, mem., 1976-80, head, 1980—; now dir. Inst. Cancer Rsch., Phila.; adj. prof. microbiology, Sch. Medicine, U. Pa., 1973—, Rockefeller U., 1975. Mem. AAAS, Am. Soc. Microbiology, Am. Soc. Biol. Chem., Assn. Women Sci., Sigma Xi. Achievements include research in the structure and function of DNA, host and viral functions in the synthesis of viral DNA and RNA, phage DNA as a vehicle for the amplification and study of eukaryotic genes, molecular biology of avian retroviruses. Office: Inst for Cancer Rsch Fox Chase Cancer Ctr 7701 Burholme Ave Philadelphia PA 19111-2412

SKALKA, HAROLD WALTER, ophthalmologist, educator; b. N.Y.C., Aug. 22, 1941; s. Jack and Sylvia Skalka; m. Barbara Jean Herbert, Oct. 2, 1965; children: Jennifer, Gretchen, Kirsten. AB with distinction, Cornell U., 1962; MD, NYU, 1966. Intern Greenwich (Conn.) Hosp., 1966-67; resident in ophthalmology Bellevue Hosp., Univ. Hosp., Manhattan VA Hosp., 1967-70; fellow in retinal physiology and ultrasonography, 1970-71; cons. in ophthalmology St. Jude's Hosp., Montgomery, Ala., 1971-73; asst. prof. ophthalmology U. Ala., Birmingham, 1973-75, assoc. prof., 1975-80, prof., 1980-81, assoc. prof. dept. medicine, 1980—, prof., chmn. combined program in ophthalmology, 1981—; acting chmn. combined program ophthalmology U. Ala., 1974-76; ophthalmologist Lowndes County Bd. Health Community Health Project, 1972. Contbr. articles to Am. Jour. Ophthalmology, Eye, Ear, Nose and Throat Monthly, Annals of Ophthalmology, Ophthalmic Surgery, Jour. Clin. Ultrasound, Jour. Pediatric Ophthalmology and Strabismus, The Lancet, AMA Archives of Ophthalmology, Jour. So. Med. Assn., Acta Ophthalmologica, Metabolic and Pediatric Ophthalmology, Applied Radiology, British Jour. Ophthalmology, Blood, Neuro-Ophthalmology; editorial bd.: Ala. Jour. Med. Sci. Major USAFMC, 1971-73. Mem. AAAS, AMA, ACS, SIDUO, Ala. Sight Conservation Assn., Ala. Conservancy, Ala. Wildlife Fedn., Eye Bank Bd., Am. Acad. Ophthalmology, Am. Inst. Ultrasound in Medicine, Internat. Soc. for Clin. Electrophysiology of Vision, Internat. Soc. on Metabolic Eye Disease, Assn. for Rsch. in Vision and Ophthalmology, AAUP, Am. Intraocular Implant Soc., Am. Assn. Ophthalmology, Pan Am. Assn. Ophthalmology, So. Med. Assn., Rsch. to Prevent Blindness, Ala. Acad. Ophthalmology, Ala. Med. Assn., Jefferson County Med. Soc., Contact Lens Assn. Ophthalmologists, Ala. Ultrasound Soc., Royal Soc. Medicine, N.Y. Acad. Scis., Am. Soc. Standardized Ophthalmic Echography (charter exec. bd. mem.), Am. Coll. Nutrition. Office: Eye Found Hosp U Ala 700 18th St S Ste 300 Birmingham AL 35233-1856

SKALKO, RICHARD GALLANT, anatomist, educator; b. Providence, Apr. 10, 1936; s. Francis Charles and Emilie Margaret (Gallant) S.; m. Louise Marie Luchetti (div. 1982); m. Priscilla Ann Brown, 1985; children—Patricia, Margaret, Christine. A.B., Providence Coll., 1957; M.S., St. John's U., 1959; Ph.D., U. Fla., 1963. Instr. anatomy Cornell U. Med. Coll., 1963-66, asst. prof., 1966-67; asst. prof. anatomy La. State U. Med. Ctr., New Orleans, 1967-69, assoc. prof., 1969-70; dir. Embryology Lab., Birth Defects Inst., N.Y. State Health Dept., Albany, 1970-77; assoc. prof. anatomy and toxicology Albany Med. Coll., 1970-76, prof., 1976-77; prof. anatomy and cell biology East Tenn. State U. Coll. Medicine, Johnson City, 1977—, chmn. dept., 1977—; mem. sci. adv. bd. NCTR, FDA, 1976-79; vis. prof. Institut fur Toxikologie und Embryonalpharmakologie, Freie U., Berlin, 1978; mem. human embryology and devel. study sect., NIH, 1990-94. Mem. Am. Assn. Anatomists, Teratology Soc., Soc. Devel. Biology, European Teratology Soc., Soc. Toxicology. Democrat. Roman Catholic. Author: Basic Concepts in Teratology, 1985; editor: Heredity and Society, 1973; Congenital Defects, 1974. Home: 3302 Pine Timbers Dr Johnson City TN 37604-1404 Office: East Tenn State U Coll Medicine Dept Anatomy and Cell Biology Johnson City TN 37614-0582

SKALL, GREGG P., lawyer; b El Paso, Tex., Mar. 28, 1944; s. Ben Milton and Lottie (Berger) S.; m. Monte Kaye Leake, June 27, 1971; 1 child, Brandon Cornell. BS, Ohio State U., 1966; JD, U. Cin., 1969. Bar: Ohio 1969, D.C. 1971, D.C. Dist. Ct. 1971, U.S. Dist. Ct. (no. dist.) Ohio 1972, D.C. Ct. Appeals 1971, U.S. Supreme Ct. 1978. Atty. gen. State of Ohio, Cleve., summer 1967; intern U.S. Dept. Justice, div. Civil Rights, Washington, summer 1968; tax law specialist IRS, Washington, 1969; gen. atty. FCC, Washington, 1970-72; ptnr. Garber, Simon, Haiman, Gutfeld, Werthiemer & Friedman, Cleve., 1972-75; acting gen. counsel Office Telecommunications Policy Exec. Office of the Pres. of the U.S., Washington, 1975-78; chief counsel Nat. Telecommunications and Info. Adminstrn., Washington, 1978-80; ptnr. Blum, Nash & Railsback, Washington, 1980-84, Baker & Hostetler, Washington, 1984-92, Pepper & Corazzini LLP, Washington, 1992—; professorial lectr. telecomms. law and regulatory policy George Washington U., Washington, 1978-80; mem. adv. bd. Pike & Fischer Radio Regulation, 1991—; comms. counsel to Minn., Calif. and Nev. Broadcasters Assns., 1990—. Co-author: The Broadcaster's Survival Guide: A Handbook of FCC Rules and Regulations for Radio and TV Stations, 1988; contbr. articles to law jours. Mem. Fed. Bar Assn. (chmn. regulated industries com. 1979-81), ABA, Fed. Communications Bar Assn., Minn. Broadcasters Assn., Calif. Broadcasters Assn. Lodge: Masons. Office: Pepper & Corazzini 200 Montgomery Bldg 1776 K St NW Washington DC 20006-2304

SKALLA, JOHN LIONELL, insurance agent; b. Marysville, Kans., July 25, 1933; s. Ernest John and Charlotte Violet (Ricker) S.; m. Allene Davison, Aug. 17, 1957; children: Camille, Johnette. BA, U. Nebr., 1957. CLU, ChFC. Agt. Conn. Mut. Life Ins. Co., Lincoln, Nebr., 1957-61; gen. agt. Conn. Mut. Life Ins. Co., Des Moines, 1961-69, Houston, 1969—; bd. dirs., mem. strategy and ops. com. Conn. Mut. Life Ins., Hartford, chmn. adv. com. Conn. Mut. Gen. Agts., 1989; nat. bd. dirs. Gen. Agts. and Mgrs. Conf., Washington; bd. dirs. Univ. of Houston Sch. of Ins. and Fin. Svcs. Contbr. articles to profl. jours. Trustee U. Nebr. Found. Bd., Lincoln; gen. chmn. Vice Lombardi Award Dinner, Houston, 1978; past pres. Whitehall Club, Houston; bd. dirs. Am. Cancer Soc., Houston; trustee Goodwill Industries, Houston; mem. Houston Bus. and Estate Planning Coun., Houston Estate and Fin. Forum. Recipient Mgr. of Yr. award Houston Gen. Agts. and Mgrs. Assn., 1995. Mem. Nat. Assn. Life Underwriters (Nat. Quality awards 1962-95), Million Dollar Round Table, Am. Soc. CLU and ChFC (Woody Woodson award 1993, Hall of Fame 1993), Tex. Assn. Life Underwriters, Houston Assn. Life Underwriters, Houston Estate and Fin. Forum, Rotary, Houston Bus. & Estate Planning Coun. Republican. Episcopalian. Avocations: travel, reading, writing, speaking. Office: John L Skalla & Assocs 4265 San Felipe 7th Fl Houston TX 77027

SKAMBIS, CHRISTOPHER CHARLES, JR., lawyer; b. Painesville, Ohio, Jan. 21, 1953; s. Christopher Charles and Anne (haritos) S.; m. Susan Elaine Adrianson, Dec. 18, 1976; children: Adrianne Elaine, Christopher Roy. Student, U. Pa., 1970-72; BA, U. Conn., 1972-74; JD, Ohio State U. Coll. Law, Columbus, 1975-78. Bar: Fla. 1978, Fla. Supreme Ct., 1978, U.S. Dist. Ct. (ctrl. dist.), 1979, U.S. Ct. Appeals (5th and 11th cir.) 1981, U.S. Supreme Ct. 1989. Assoc. VandenBerg, Gay & Burke, Orlando, Fla., 1978-81, ptnr., 1982; ptnr. VandenBurg, Gay, Burke, Wilson & Arkin, Orlando, Fla., 1982-85, Foley & Lardner, Orlando, Fla., 1985—; mem. Orange County Bar Assn., Orlando, Fla., 1978, Fla. Bar 9D Grievance Commn., Orlando, Fla., 1989; arbitrator Fla. Bar 9th Cir. Fee Arbitration Commn., Orlando, Fla., 1987; co-chair Federal and State Trial Practice Co., Orlando, Fla., 1992—. Mem. Am. Judicature Soc., ABA. Avocations: amateur ham radio operator, little league, coalition for homeless. Office: Foley & Lardner PO Box 2193 111 N Orange Ave Ste 1800 Orlando FL 32802-2193 Office: 111 N Orange Ave Se 900 Orlando FL 32801*

SKARR, MICHAEL W., state agency administrator. B in Mech. Engring., Marquette U.; MBA, Lewis U.; cert. in mgmt. arts, Aurora U. Mem. Ill. State Bd. Edn., Springfield, 1991-93, chairperson, 1993—; mem. Joint Edn. Com., Ill.; past mem. Naperville Dist. 203 Bd. Edn., chmn. regulatory process com. Past chmn. Will County United Way Campaign; past pres., mem. exec. bd. Rainbow Coun. Boy Scouts Am.; past bd. dirs. Rialto Square Theatre Corp.

SKATES, RONALD LOUIS, computer manufacturing executive; b. Kansas City, Mo., Sept. 25, 1941; s. Raymond and Suzanne (Lispi) S.; m. Mary Austin; children: Melissa, Elizabeth. AB cum laude, Harvard U., 1963, MBA, 1965. Acct. Price Waterhouse, Boston, audit ptnr., 1976-86; sr. v.p. fin. and adminstrn. Data Gen. Corp., Westboro, Mass., 1986-88, dir., exec. v.p., chief oper. officer, 1988-89; pres., CEO Mass. Gen. Hosp., Boston, 1990—, overseer, 1992—. Overseer Mus. Fine Arts, 1989. Mem. AICPA, Mass. Soc. CPAs. Office: Data Gen Corp 3400 Computer Dr Westborough MA 01580-0001*

SKED, MARIE JOSEPHINE, financial service owner, nurse; b. Stroudsburg, Pa., June 15, 1935; d. Newell Walter and Marjorie Frances (Keegan) Felton; m. Henry Daniel Kehr, Sept. 25, 1955 (div. Dec. 1972); children: Wendy Carol, John Francis, Newell Walter; m. Ogden Stanley Sked, Mar. 10, 1973. Student, Temple U., 1953-55; AAS in Nursing, Mercer County C.C., 1970; postgrad., Stockton State Coll., 1973-74. RN, Pa. LPN, emergency rm. and float nurse Zurbrugg Meml. Hosp., Riverside, N.J., 1964-67; LPN, staff nurse State of N.J. E.R. Johnstone Rsch. for Mentally Retarded, Bordentown, 1967-70, head nurse, 1970-71; asst. oper. rm. supr. Hamilton Hosp., Trenton, N.J., 1971-76; pvt. scrub nurse Dr. Ralph Ellis, Trenton, 1977-78; owner Income Tax Svc., Newfoundland, Pa., 1985—. Sec.-treas. Panther Lake Homeowner's Assn., 1984-94; mem. Pa. Hist. Mus. Commn. State of N.J. scholar, 1968. Mem. AARP (instr. for income tax vols. 1985—). Avocations: downhill skiing, bowling, reading, gardening, volunteer tax service. Home: Pine Grove Rd PO Box 216 Newfoundland PA 18445

SKEEN, JOSEPH RICHARD, congressman; b. Roswell, N.Mex., June 30, 1927; s. Thomas Dudley and Ilah (Adamson) S.; m. Mary Helen Jones, Nov. 17, 1945; children: Mary Elisa, Mikell Lee. B.S., Tex. A&M U., 1950. Soil and water engr. Ramah Navajo and Zuni Indians, 1951; rancher Lincoln County, N.Mex., 1952—; mem. N.Mex. Senate, 1960-70, 97th-103rd Congresses from 2nd N.Mex. dist., Washington, D.C., 1981—; mem. appropriations com., subcom. agr., chmn. appropriations com., subcom. def., mem. subcom. interior. Chmn. N.Mex. Republican Party, 1963-66. Served with USN, 1945-46; Served with USAFR, 1949-52. Mem. Nat. Woolgrowers Assn., Nat. Cattle Growers Assn., N.Mex. Woolgrowers Assn., N.Mex. Cattle Growers Assn., N.Mex. Farm and Livestock Bur. Republican. Club: Elks. Office: House of Representatives Washington DC 20515

SKEES, WILLIAM LEONARD, JR., lawyer; b. Indpls., Jan. 26, 1947; s. William Leonard and Marian Catherine (Fagan) S.; children: Kristina Suzanne, Elizabeth Ann; m. Dena Kay Wynalda, July 23, 1983; children: Catherine Fagan, William Leonard III (dec.), Samuel Jackson. BA, Ball State U., 1969; JD, Ind. U., 1971. Bar: Ind. 1971, Ky. 1981. Law clk. U.S. Dist. Ct. (no. dist.), Fort Wayne, Ind., 1971-72; assoc. Ice, Miller Donadio & Ryan, Indpls., 1972-80; mem. Brown, Todd & Heyburn, P.L.L.C, Louisville, 1981—. Contbr. articles to jours. in field. Mem. bd. visitors Ind. U. Sch. Law, 1975-91; bd. dirs., past pres. The Louisville Housing Partnership, 1978—, Stage One, Louisville Children's Theatre, pres., 1990-91; bd. dirs. Ky. Chpt. Nat. SIDS Found. Recipient Disting. Citizen award Mayor of Louisville, 1983, Cert. Merit Bd. Aldermen, Louisville, 1984, Cert. Appreciation Fiscal Ct., Louisville, 1986. Mem. ABA, Ky. Bar Assn., Ind. Bar Assn., Louisville Bar Assn., Nat. Assn. Bond Lawyers. Office: Brown Todd & Heyburn 3200 Providian Center Louisville KY 40202-2873

SKEETE, F. HERBERT, bishop; b. N.Y.C., Mar. 22, 1930; s. Ernest A. and Elma I. (Ramsey) S.; m. Shirley C. Hunte, Oct. 4, 1952; children—Michael H., Mark C. BA, Bklyn. Coll., 1959; MDiv, Drew U., 1962, D in Ministry, 1975; STM, N.Y. Theol. Sem., 1970; DHL(hon.), Philander Smith Coll., 1983, Jewish Theol. Sem. N.Y., 1986; DD, Ea. Bapt. Theol. Sem., 1986. Ordained to ministry United Meth. Ch., 1961; pastor Union United Meth. Ch., South Ozone Park, N.Y.C., 1960-67, N.Y.C. Mission Soc., 1967-68, Salem United Meth. Ch., Harlem, N.Y.C., 1968-80; bishop Phila. area United Meth. Ch., Valley Forge, Pa., 1980-88, Boston area, 1988—. Office: United Methodist Ctr care Beverly Abbotte PO Box 277 Winthrop ME 04364

SKEFF, KELLEY MICHAEL, health facility administrator; b. Center, Colo., 1944. MD, U. Chgo., 1970. Diplomate Am. Bd. Internal Medicine. Intern Harbor Gen. Hosp., Torrance, Calif., 1970-71; resident in internal medicine U. Colo. Med. Ctr., Denver, 1974-75; resident in internal medicine Stanford (Calif.) U. Hosps., 1975-76, fellow in internal medicine, 1976; program dir. Stanford U. Recipient Alpha Omega Alpha award Assocs. Am. Med. Coll., 1994. Office: Stanford U Dept Med 300 Pasteur Dr Palo Alto CA 94305-2203*

SKELLY, THOMAS FRANCIS, manufacturing company executive; b. Boston, Jan. 19, 1934; s. Michael Gerard and Katherine Agnes (Kelly) S.; m. Patricia A. Limerick, Sept. 6, 1958; children—Thomas Francis, John M., Peter G., Matthew M. B.S., Northeastern U., 1956; M.B.A., Babson Coll., 1966. Mgr. Peat, Marwick, Mitchell & Co. (C.P.A.'s), Boston, 1957-67; with Gillette Co., Boston, 1967—; controller Gillette Co., 1973—, v.p., 1979-80, sr. v.p. fin., 1980—; mng. dir. Gillette Overseas Fin. Corp. N.V., Netherlands Antilles; dir. Neworld Bank, Boston. Bd. dirs. nat. coun. Northeastern U., bd. trustees; bd. dirs. Nat. Fgn. Trade Coun. Capt. AUS, 1957-59. Home: 54 Magnolia Dr Westwood MA 02090-3215 Office: Gillette Co Prudential Tower Bldg Boston MA 02199

SKELOS, DEAN G., senator; b. Rockville Center, N.Y.; m. Gail Skelos; 1 child, Adam. BA in History, Washington Coll., 1970; JD, Forham U., 1975. State assemblyman N.Y., 1981-82; senator N.Y. State Senate, 1984; dep. majority leader; chmn. standing com. on aging N.Y. State Senate, 1984-94, Majority Task Force on Aging in 21st Century, 1987-92, co-chmn. legislative task force on demographic rsch. and reapportionment, mem. majority task force on religious desecration and bigotry, mem. legis. commn. on sci. and tech., mem. majority task force on def. spending, chmn. task force on econ. recovery and job devel., mem. numerous coms. Mem. fact-finding mission to Israel Jewish Community Rels. Coun.; former mem. Coun. of Nat. Inst. on Aging. Recipient Torch of Liberty award B'nai B'rith. Mem. Elks, Sons of Italy, Kiwanis, Order of AHEPA. Office: Legislative Office Bldg 609 Albany NY 12247 also: 55 Front St Rockville Centre NY 11570-4007

SKELTON, BYRON GEORGE, federal judge; b. Florence, Tex., Sept. 1, 1905; s. Clarence Edgar and Avis (Bowmer) S.; m. Ruth Alice Thomas, Nov. 28, 1931; children: Sue, Sandra. Student, Baylor U., 1923-24; AB, U. Tex., 1927, MA, 1928, LLB, 1931. Bar: Tex. 1931, Circuit Ct. Appeals 1937, U.S. Supreme Ct. 1946, FCC 1950, Tax Ct. U.S 1952, U.S. Treasury Dept 1952, ICC 1953. Practice of law Temple, Tex., 1931-66; partner Saulsbury & Skelton, 1934-42, Saulsbury, Skelton, Everton, Bowmer & Courtney, 1944-

55, Skelton, Bowmer & Courtney, 1955-66; judge U.S. Ct. Claims, Washington, 1966-77; sr. fed. judge U.S. Ct. Claims, 1977-82, U.S. Ct. Appeals (fed. cir.), Washington, 1982—; county atty., Bell County, Tex., 1934-38; spl. asst. U.S. amb. to Argentina, 1942-45; city atty., Temple, 1945-60; dir. First Nat. Bank of Temple. Dem. nat. committeeman for Tex., 1956-64; del. Dem. Nat. Conv., 1948, 56, 60, 64; del. Tex. Dem. Conv., 1946, 48, 50, 52, 54, 56, 58, 60, 62, 64, vice chmn., 1948, 58; chmn. Dem. Adv. Coun. of Tex., 1955-57; former pres. Temple YMCA; pres. Temple Indsl. Found., 1966. Appointed Ky. Col. and Adm. in Tex. Navy, 1959; recipient Legion of Honor DeMolay, 1980, Temple Outstanding Citizen award, 1984. Mem. ABA, State Bar Tex., Bell-Lampasas and Mills Counties Bar Assn. (past pres.), Am. Law Inst., Am. Judicature Soc., Temple C. of C. (past pres., dir.), Ex-Students' Assn. U. Tex. (past pres., mem. exec.coun.), Gen. Soc. Mayflower Descs., Masons (past worshipful master), Shriners, Kiwanis (past pres.), Phi Beta Kappa, Pi Sigma Alpha, Sigma Delta Pi, Delta Theta Phi. Democrat. Methodist. Home: 1101 Dakota Dr Temple TX 76504-4905 Office: US Ct Appeals 305 Fed Bldg Temple TX 76501

SKELTON, DIANN CLEVENGER, elementary education educator; b. Kennett, Mo., Nov. 26, 1956; d. Opie O'Neal and D. Charlenene (Duke) C.; m. Jason Skelton. BSEd in Early Childhood Edn., Ark. State U., 1978, MSEd in Spl. Edn., 1979, MSEd in Early Childhood Edn., 1989. Spl. edn. tchr. Blytheville (Ark.) Pub. Sch., 1978-82; tchr. early childhood edn. Hayti (Mo.) Pub. Schs., 1982-86, tchr. kindergarten, 1986-91, tchr. 2d grade, 1991—. Mem. Mo. State Tchrs. Assn., Assn. Supervision and Curriculum Devel., Beta Sigma Phi, Kappa Delta Pi, Delta Kappa Gamma. Republican. Baptist. Avocations: cross stitch, sporting events, Am. Kennel Club registered Dobermans. Office: Hayti Pub Schs 500 N 4th St Hayti MO 63851-1116

SKELTON, DON RICHARD, consulting actuary, retired insurance company executive; b. Des Moines, Dec. 9, 1931; s. Donald Harold and Wanda Mae (Johnson) S.; m. Barbara Joan Harris (dec. 1962); children: David, Janet; m. Alyce Mae Washington, May 15, 1964 (div. 1979); children: Laura, Lisa, James; m. Patricia Ann Matroni, July 10, 1981. BSBA, Drake U., 1953. Actuarial trainee Monarch Life Ins. Co., Springfield, Mass., 1953-57, mgr. group ins. dept., 1957-58, asst. actuary, 1958-64, group pension actuary, 1964-67, asst. v.p., group actuary, 1967, v.p. R & D, 1967-83; v.p. Monarch Capital Corp., Springfield, Mass., 1980-91; sr. v.p. Monarch Life Ins. Co., Springfield, 1988-91; v.p. Monarch Fin. Svcs., Inc., 1989-91; pres., chief exec. officer First Variable Life Ins. Co., 1985-87, 91, also bd. dirs., ret., 1992; cons. actuary Longmeadow, Mass., 1992—. Mem. budget com. Pioneer Valley United Way, Springfield, 1964-69, chmn. 1969-70. Fellow Soc. Actuaries, Life Office Mgmt. Assn.; mem. Coll. Life Underwriters. Republican. Clubs: Hartford (Conn.) Actuaries; Boston Actuaries. Avocations: golf, sailing, physical fitness. Home: 8 Althea Dr Longmeadow MA 01106-1707

SKELTON, DOROTHY GENEVA SIMMONS (MRS. JOHN WILLIAM SKELTON), art educator; b. Woodland, Calif.; d. Jack Elijah and Helen Anna (Siebe) Simmons; BA, U. Calif., 1940, MA, 1943; m. John William Skelton, July 16, 1941. Sr. rsch. analyst War Dept., Gen. Staff, M.I. Div. G-2, Pentagon, Washington, 1944-45; vol. rschr. monuments, fine arts and archives sect. Restitution Br., Office Mil. Govt. for Hesse, Wiesbaden, German, 1947-48; vol. art tchr. German children in Bad Nauheim, Germany, 1947-48; art educator, lectr. Dayton (Ohio) Art Inst., 1955; art educator Lincoln Sch., Dayton, 1956-60; instr. art and art edn. U. Va. Sch. Continuing Edn., Charlottesville, 1962-75; rschr. genealogy, exhibited in group shows, Calif., Colo., Ohio, Washington and Va.; represented in permanent collections Madison Hall, Charlottesville, Madison (Va.) Ctr. Recipient Hon. Black Belt Karate Sch. of Culpeper, Va., 1992. Vol. art cons.; bd. dirs. Va. Rappahannock-Rapidan Vol. Emergency Med. Svcs. Coun., 1978—. Mem. Nat. League Am. Pen Women, AAUW, Am. Assn. Museums, Coll. Art Assn. Am., Inst. for Study of Art in Edn., Dayton Soc. Painters and Sculptors, Nat. Soc. Arts and Letters (life), Va. Mus. Fine Arts, Cal. Alumni Assn., Air Force Officers Wives Club. Republican. Methodist. Clubs: Army Navy Country. Chief collaborator: John Skelton of Georgia, 1969; author: The Squire Simmons Family, 1746-1986, 1986. Address: Lotos Lakes Brightwood VA 22715

SKELTON, DOUGLAS H., architect; b. Cottage Grove, Oreg., Apr. 17, 1939; s. Harry Edward and Mary Jane (Caldwell) S.; m. Bonita L. Baker, June 17, 1961; children: Paul D., Cynthia J., Justin D. Student, Oreg. State U., 1957-59; degree in architecture, U. Oreg., 1963. Registered architect, Oreg. Draftsman Payne & Struble Architecture, Medford, Oreg., 1965-66; intern architect Wayne Struble Architect, Medford, Oreg., 1966-70, assoc., 1973-78; project architect William Seibert Architect, Medford, Oreg., 1970-73; ptnr. Struble & Skelton Architects, Medford, Oreg., 1978-83; owner Douglas Skelton Architect, Medford, Oreg., 1983-89; ptnr. Skelton, Straus & Seibert Architects, Medford, Oreg., 1989—; mem. law rev. com. State Bd. Architects, Oreg., 1991. Design bldg. renovation (911 Mag. award 1991, Excellence in Sch. Architecture AS&U mag. 1987). Chmn. Hist. and Archtl. Rev. Commn., City of Jacksonville, 1992—; bd. dirs. Rogue Valley Christian Ch., 1994. Recipient Outstanding Sch. Bldg. award Am. Sch. and Univ. mag., 1987. Mem. AIA (v.p. So. Oreg. chpt. 1972, pres. 1973), Architects Coun. Oreg. (del., treas. 1989), Medford/Jackson C. of C. (devel. com. 1992—), Rotary (bd. dirs. Jacksonville/Applegate chpt. 1994). Avocations: camping, fishing, boating, bicycling, cross-country skiing. Office: Skelton Straus & Seibert 26 Hawthorne St Medford OR 97504-7114

SKELTON, GORDON WILLIAM, data processing executive, educator; b. Vicksburg, Miss., Oct. 31, 1949; s. Alan Gordon and Martha Hope (Butcher) S.; m. Sandra Lea Champion, May 1974 (div. 1981); m. Janet Elaine Johnson, Feb. 14, 1986; 1 stepchild, Brian Quarles. BA, McMurry Coll., 1974; MA, U. So. Miss., 1975, postgrad., 1975-77, MS, 1987; postgrad., U. South Africa, 1994—. Cert. in data processing. Systems analyst Criminal Justice Planning Commn., Jackson, Miss., 1978-80; cord. Miss. Statis. Analysis Ctr., Jackson, 1980-83; data processing mgr. Dept. Adminstrn. Fed.-State Programs, Jackson, 1983-84; mgr. pub. tech. So. Ctr. Rsch. and Innovation, Hattiesburg, Miss., 1985-87; internal cons. Sec. of State, State of Miss., Jackson, 1987; system support mgr. CENTEC, Jackson, 1987-88; instr. dept. computer sci. Belhaven Coll., Jackson, 1988—; v.p. info. svcs. Miss. Valley Title Ins. Co., Jackson, 1988—. Author: (with others) Trends in Ergonomics/Human Factors, 1986. Treas. Singles and Doubles Sunday Sch. Class, Jackson, 1989, 91. With U.S. Army, 1970-73, Vietnam. Recipient Cert. of Appreciation, U.S. Dept. Justice/Bur. Justice Stats., 1982. Mem. IEEE Computer Soc., Data Processing Mgmt. Assn. (chpt. pres. 1991, 92, program chair 1990), Assn. Computing Machinery, Am. Soc. Quality Control. Presbyterian. Avocations: gardening, collecting baseball cards, collecting Civil War relics. Office: Miss Valley Title Ins Co 315 Tombigbee St Jackson MS 39201-4605

SKELTON, ISAAC NEWTON, IV (IKE SKELTON), congressman; b. Lexington, Mo., Dec. 20, 1931; s. Isaac Newton and Carolyn (Boone) S.; m. Susan B. Anding, July 22, 1961; children: Ike, Jim, Page. AB, U. Mo., 1953, LLB, 1956. Bar: Mo. 1956. Pvt. practice Lexington; pros. atty. Lafayette County, Mo., 1957-60; spl. asst. atty. gen. State of Mo., 1961-63; mem. Mo. Senate from 28th dist., 1971-76; mem. 95th-104th Congresses from 4th Mo. Dist., 1977—, ranking minority mem. nat. security subcom. on mil. procurement. Active Boy Scouts Am. Mem. Phi Beta Kappa, Sigma Chi. Democrat. Mem. Christian Ch. Clubs: Masons, Shriners, Elks. Home: 1814 Franklin St Lexington MO 64067-1708 Office: US Ho of Reps 2227 Rayburn House Bldg Washington DC 20515*

SKELTON, JOHN EDWARD, computer technology consultant; b. Amarillo, Tex., May 10, 1934; s. Floyd Wayne and Lucille Annabelle (Padduck) S.; m. Katherine Dow, Mar. 22, 1959; children: Laura Ann, Jeanette Kay, Jeffrey Edward. BA, U. Denver, 1956, MA, 1962, PhD, 1971. Mathematician U.S. Naval Ordnance Lab., Corona, Calif., 1956-59; various sales support and mktg. positions Burroughs Corp., Denver, Detroit, Pasadena, Calif., 1959-67; asst. prof. U. Denver, 1967-74; dir. Computer Ctr., U. Minn., Duluth, 1974-85; prof., dir. computing svcs. Oreg. State U., Corvallis, 1985-94; computer tech. cons., Corvallis, 1995—; cons. World Bank, China, 1988, Educom Cons. Group, 1985. Author: Introduction to the Basic Language, 1971; co-auhtor: Who Runs the Computer, 1975; also articles. Mem. Assn. for Computing Machinery (pres. Rocky Mountain chpt. 1971, faculty advisor U. Minn. 1980-82, peer rev. team 3 regions 1981-90), Assn. for Spl. Interest Group on Univ. Computing (bd. dirs. 1987-91), Rotary (dist. youth exch. com. 1991—), Sigma Xi (chpt. pres. 1983-84), Phi Kappa Phi (chpt. pres. 1989-90). Episcopalian. Avocations: travel, photography, hiking.

SKELTON, RED (RICHARD SKELTON), comedian, artist; b. Vincennes, Ind., July 18, 1913; s. Joseph and Ida (Mae) S.; m. Edna Marie Stillwell, June 1932 (div. 1940, dec.); m. 2d, Georgia Maureen Davis, Mar. 1945 (dec.); children: Valentina Maureen Alonso, Richard Freeman (dec.); m. 3d, Lothian Toland, Oct., 1973. HHD, Ball State U., 1986. Began acting career at age of 10 yrs.; successively with a tent show, a minstrel show, on a show boat, a clown in Hagenbeck & Wallace Circus, on burlesque in the Midwest, Walkathon contests (as master of ceremonies); appeared at Loew's Montreal Theatre in vaudeville (developed the doughnut dunking pantomime), 1936; made Broadway debut, June 1937; first motion picture appearance in Having a Wonderful Time, 1939; has since appeared in Flight Command, 1940, The People vs. Dr. Kildare, 1941, Dr. Kildare's Wedding Day, 1941, Lady Be Good, 1941, Whistling in the Dark, 1941, Whistling in Dixie, 1942, Maisie Gets Her Man, 1942, Panama Hattie, 1942, Ship Ahoy, 1942, I Dood It, 1943, Whistling in Brooklyn, 1943, DuBarry Was A Lady, 1943, Thousands Cheer, 1943, Bathing Beauty, 1944, Ziedfield Follies, 1946, The Show Off, 1946, Merton of the Movies, 1947, The Fuller Brush Man, 1948, A Southern Yankee, 1948, Neptune's Daughter, 1949, The Yellow Cab Man, 1950, Three Little Words, 1950, Watch the Birdie, 1950, The Fuller Brush Girl, 1950, Dutchess of Idaho, 1950, Excuse My Dust, 1950, Texas Carnival, 1951, Lovely to Look At, 1952, The Clown, 1952, Halfa Hero, 1953, The Great Diamond Robbery, 1953, Susan Slept Here, 1954, Around the World in 80 Days, 1956, Public Pigeon Number One, 1957, Ocean's Eleven, 1960, Those Magnificent Men in Their Flying Machines, 1965, Eighteen Again, 1988; had first own radio program, 1937, Red Skelton's Scrpabook of Satire, 1942; The Red Skelton Show on TV, 1951-71; nightclub performer, also writer and composer for radio, TV, movies; entertained service men World War II and Korea as pvt. in F.A.; artist original oil paintings and hand sketched linens. Bd. dirs. Red Skelton Needy Children's Fund. Recipient AMVETS Silver Helmet Americanism award, 1969, Freedom's Found. award, 1970, Nat. Comdrs. award Am. Legion, 1970; winner 3 Emmy awards, Golden Globe award, 1978, Ann. Achievement award SAG, 1987, Am. Comedy Hall of Fame award, 1993, Gourgas Gold medal Masonic Order, 1995. Address: PO Box 390190 Anza CA 92539-0190

SKELTON, W. DOUGLAS, dean. Dean Mercer U. Sch. Med., Macon, Ga., 1995—. Office: Mercer Univ Sch of Medicine Office of the Provost 1400 Coleman Ave Macon GA 31207-1000 Office: Mercer Univ Sch Medicine 1550 College St Macon GA 31207*

SKENE, G(EORGE) NEIL, publisher, lawyer; b. Jackson, Miss., Aug. 29, 1951; s. George Neil and Louise (Pate) S.; m. Madelyn Miller, Aug. 4, 1984; children: Christopher, Jennifer, Katherine. BA, Vanderbilt U., 1973; JD, Mercer U., 1977. Bar: Fla. 1978. Intern Macon (Ga.) Telegraph & News, 1968-70; reporter Tampa (Fla.) Times, 1973-74; reporter St. Petersburg (Fla.) Times, 1977-78, asst. city editor, 1978-80; capital bur. chief St. Petersburg (Fla.) Times, Tallahassee, 1980-84; editor Evening Ind., St. Petersburg, 1984-86; exec. editor Congl. Quar. Inc., Washington, 1986-89, pres., editor, pub., 1990—; bd. dirs. Times Pub. Co., St. Petersburg. Mem. bd. visitors Law Sch. Mercer U., Macon, Ga., 1986-94; trustee Poynter Inst. for Media Studies, St. Petersburg, 1988—; mem. bd. advisors Grad. Sch. Journalism U. Calif., Berkeley, 1991-96. Mem. Fla. Bar Assn. Office: Congressional Quarterly Inc 1414 22nd St NW Washington DC 20037

SKENE, NEIL, publishing executive. Office: Congressional Quarterly Svc 1414 22nd St NW Washington DC 20037-1003

SKERRITT, TOM, actor; b. Detroit, Aug. 25, 1933. Student, Wayne State U. Films: War Hunt, 1962, One Man's Way, 1964, Those Calloways, 1964, M*A*S*H, 1970, WIld Rovers, 1972, Fuzz, 1972, Big Bad Mama, 1974, Thieves Like Us, 1974, The Devil's Rain, 1975, The Turning Point, 1977, Up In Smoke, 1978, Alien, 1979, Ice Castles, 1979, Silence of the North, 1981, A Dangerous Summer, 1981, Savage Harvest, 1981, Fighting Back, 1982, The Dead Zone, 1983, Top Gun, 1986, Space Camp, 1987, The Big Town, 1987, Wisdom, 1987, Opposing Force, 1987, Maid to Order, 1987, Poltergeist III, 1988, Steel Magnolias, 1989, Big Man On Campus, 1990, The Rookie, 1991, Blue Movie Blue, 1991, Poison Ivy, 1991, A River Runs Through It, 1992; TV shows: Ryan's Four, 1983, On The Edge, 1987, Cheers, 1987-88, Picket Fences, 1992— (Emmy award Outstanding Lead Actor in a Drama Series, 1993); TV movies: The Bird Man, The Last Day, Maneaters Are Loose!, Calendar Girl Murders, Miles to Go, True Believer, Parent Trap II, A Touch of Scandal, Poker Alice, Nightmare At Bitter Creek, Moving Target, The Heist, Red King White Knight, The China Lake Murders, Child of the Night, In Sickness and In Health, Getting Up and Going Home. Office: Guttman Assocs 118 S Beverly Dr Beverly Hills CA 90212-3003

SKERRY, PHILIP JOHN, English educator; b. Boston, May 6, 1944; s. Angelina (Creilson) S.; m. Amy Simon, June 15, 1968; children: Jessica Blythe, Ethan Amadeus. BA in English, U. Mass., 1966; MA in English, Case Western Res. U., 1968; PhD, Indiana U. of Pa., 1975. Instr. English Lakeland Community Coll., Mentor, Ohio, 1968-69, prof., 1973—, chmn. dept., 1991-93; assoc. prof. Tarrant County Jr. Coll., Hurst, Tex., 1971-73; project dir. Early English Composition Assessment Program Ohio Bd. Regents, Columbus, 1985-92; participant Dir. Guild Am. summer sem., 1988, 92. Host TV talk show Western Res. Connection, 1980-86; contbg. author: Superman at 50: The Persistence of a Legend, 1987, Beyond the Stars IV, 1993, Beyond the Stars V, 1996; contbr. articles to profl. jours. Chmn. Jump Rope for your Heart program Am. Heart Assn., Cleve., 1980-83, mem. adv. com., 1984; trustee, pres. Sussex Community Assn., Shaker Heights, Ohio, 1982; mem. adv. com. N.E. Ohio Assn. for Children with Learning Disabilities, 1975-76; bd. dirs. Shaker Heights Youth Ctr., 1991-92. Grantee NEH, 1983, Martha Holden Jennings Found., 1991-92; Humanities scholar Ohio Program for the Humanities, 1983—. Mem. NEA, Nat. Coun. Tchrs. English, Popular Culture Assn. Democrat. Avocations: collecting movies, coffee roasting. Home: 3655 Sutherland Rd Shaker Heights OH 44122-5134 Office: Lakeland Cmty Coll 7700 Clocktower Dr Kirtland OH 44094-5198

SKEWES-COX, BENNET, accountant, educator; b. Valparaiso, Chile, Dec. 12, 1918; came to U.S., 1919, naturalized, 1943; s. Vernon and Edith Page (Smith) S-C.; B.A., U. Calif., Berkeley, 1940; M.A., Georgetown U., 1947; B.B.A., Golden Gate Coll., 1953; m. Mary Osborne Craig, Aug. 31, 1946; children: Anita Page McCann, Pamela Skewes-Cox Anderson, Amy Osborne Skewes-Cox (Mrs. Robert Twiss). Asst. to press officer Am. Embassy, Santiago, Chile, 1941-43; state exec. dir. United World Federalists of Calif., 1948-50; pvt. practice acctg., San Francisco, 1953—; asst. prof. internat. relations San Francisco State U., 1960-62; grad. researcher Stanford (Calif.) U., 1962-63, Georgetown U., Washington, 1963-65; pres. Acad. World Studies, San Francisco, 1969—; sec. Alpha Delta Phi Bldg. Co., San Francisco, 1957—; lectr. in field. Mem. Democratic state central com. Calif., 1958-60, fgn. policy chmn. Calif. Dem. Council, 1959-61, treas. Marin County Dem. Central Com., 1956-62; founder, 1st. chmn. Calif. Council for UN Univ., 1976—; compiler World Knowledge Bank; bd. dirs. Research on Abolition of War; treas. Marin Citizens for Energy Planning. Served as lt. (j.g.), USNR, 1943-46. Mem. Assn. for World Edn. (internat. council 1975—), Am. Soc. Internat. Law, Am. Polit. Sci. Assn., San Francisco Com. Fgn. Relations, Am. Acctg. Assn., Calif. State Univ. Profs., AAUP, Nat. Soc. Public Accts., Fedn. Am. Scientists, UN Assn., Internat. Polit. Sci. Assn. World Federalists Assn., World Govt. Orgns. Coalition (treas.). Clubs: University, Commonwealth of Calif., Lagunitas Country. Author: The Manifold Meanings of Peace, 1964; The United Nations from League to Government, 1965; Peace, Truce or War, 1967. Office: Acad World Studies 2806 Van Ness Ave San Francisco CA 94109-1426

SKIBINSKI, OLGA, artist, art conservator; b. Bucharest, Romania, Sept. 15, 1939; came to U.S., 1986; d. Alois Skibinski and Marina Barbulescu; divorced; 1 child, Stefan. BA, Fine Arts Coll., 1963; diploma in art conservation, Nat. Mus. Art, 1967. Sr. art conservator Nat. Mus. Art, Bucharest, 1964-86; freelance artist and art conservator N.Y.C., 1986—; lectr. on art conservation. One woman shows at Orizont Gallery, Bucharest, Romania, 1978, Mus. Fine Arts, Craiova, Romania, 1981, Simeza Gallery, Bucharest, 1984, Romanian Cultural Ctr., N.Y.C., 1993; contbr. articles to art mags. Mem. Internat. Inst. for Conservation London, Am. Inst. for Conservation, West Side Art Coalition, Ward-Nasse Gallery. Republican. Avocation: classical music. Home: 78-12 35th Ave Apt 4A Jackson Heights NY 11372

SKIBITZKE, HERBERT ERNST, JR., hydrologist; b. Benton Harbor, Mich., Mar. 30, 1921; s. Herbert Ernst and Jennie (Richie) S.; m. Eva Hegel, Mar. 22, 1943; 1 child, Herbert William (dec.). Student, Ariz. State U., 1947; Hon. ScD, U. Ariz., 1988. Registered profl. engr., 11 states; registered profl. land surveyor, Ariz.; registered ground water hydrologist. Mathematician U.S. Geol. Survey, Phoenix, 1948-54, rsch. hydrologist, 1954-76; pres., sr. hydrologist Hydro Data, Inc., Tempe, Ariz., 1976-85; cons. Skibitzke Engrs. & Assocs., Phoenix, 1986-90; co-founder, pres., sr. hydrologist Hydro Analysis, Inc., Tempe, 1990—; co-founder, instr. Sch. Hydrology, U. Ariz., Tucson, 1960-64; adv. bd. Sch. Hydrology, Tarleton State U., Stephensville, Tex., 1986-90, Am. Inst. Hydrology, Mpls., 1989—. Contbr. articles to profl. jours., chpts. to books. Lt. USN, 1943-46. Recipient Lifetime Svc. awards, U. Ariz. Fellow ASCE; mem. Am. Inst. Hydrology (C.V. Theis award 1991), Assn. Ground Water Scientists and Engrs., Geol. Soc. Washington, Nat. Water Well Assn. Achievements include development of first computer (electric analog) applied to GW studies; patent on electronic flowmeter for U.S. Geol. Survey; pioneered development/application of remote sensing techniques to collect information on water resources; methods to analyze contaminant movement in ground water systems; development of state of the art analytical methods for hydrologic occurrences. Office: Hydro-Analysis Inc PO Box 27334 Tempe AZ 85285-7334

SKIDD, THOMAS PATRICK, JR., lawyer; b. Norwalk, Conn., July 2, 1936; s. Thomas Patrick and Anne (Sims) S.; m. Judith Chase Roberts, Sept. 10, 1960; children: Suanne C., Sherry E., Thomas Patrick III, Jody E. BA in Econs., Georgetown U., 1958; LLB, Yale U., 1961. Bar: Conn. 1961, U.S. Supreme Ct. 1963. Ptnr. Cummings & Lockwood, Stamford, Conn., 1961—; bd. dirs., mem. exec. com. Conn. Attys. Title Ins. Co., Rocky Hill, Conn. Mem. Conn. Bar Assn. (real estate sect.), Stamford-Norwalk Regional Bar Assn., Roton Point Club (Rowayton, Conn.). Roman Catholic. Avocation: phonograph record collector. Office: Cummings & Lockwood 4 Stamford Plz 107 Elm St Stamford CT 06904-0120

SKIDDELL, ELLIOT LEWIS, rabbi; b. Chelsea, Mass., Mar. 3, 1951; s. Jack and Evelyn (Starr) S.; m. Julie F. Goldberg, May 27, 1979; children: Sarit, Elanit. BA, U. Mass., 1974; MA, Temple U., 1979. Ordained rabbi, 1980. Rabbi Temple Beth El, Newark, Del., 1977-80; asst. rabbi Har Zion Temple, Penn Valley, Pa., 1980-82; rabbi Ramat Shalom Synogogue, Plantation, Fla., 1982—; placement dir. Reconstructionist Rabbinical Assn., Wyncote, Pa., 1985—; pres. Jewish Nat. Fund Broward and Palm Beach, 1987-89, North Broward Bd. Rabbis, Ft. Lauderdale, 1986-87, Reconstructionist Rabbinical Assn., 1980-82. Co-editor booklet: Mordecai Kaplan Centennial Resource Booklet, 1981. Bd. dirs. Jewish Fedn. Greater Ft. Lauderdale, 1986-89. Office: 11301 W Broward Blvd Fort Lauderdale FL 33325-2521 *I believe that the most important task facing us today is the creation of community and a sense of belonging to a community. For our own sake and for future generations, the sense of belonging to something larger than ourselves needs to be instilled.*

SKIDMORE, DONALD EARL, JR., government official; b. Tacoma, Apr. 27, 1944; s. Donald E. and Ingeborg (Johnsrud) S.; BSc, Evangel Coll., 1968. With Dept. Social and Health Svcs., State of Wash., Yakima, 1967-74; quality rev. specialist Social Security Adminstrn., Seattle, 1974-76, program analyst, Balt., 1976-79, Seattle, 1979-81, quality assurance officer, mgr. Satellite office, Spokane, Wash., 1981-84, program analyst, Seattle, 1984-90, mgmt. analyst, 1990—. Pres., bd. dirs. Compton Court Condo Assn., 1980-81; v.p., trustee Norwood Village, 1987-90; vice chair ops. subcom., mem. citizen's adv. com. METRO, 1987-89; mem. citizen's adv. com. land use planning, Bellevue, Wash., 1988-90. Grad. Bellevue Police Citizen's Acad., 1992. Office: 2201 6th Ave Ste 510B M/S 55 Seattle WA 98121-1836

SKIDMORE, HOWARD FRANKLYN, public relations counsel; b. Bklyn., Sept. 24, 1917; s. William F. and Mae (White) S.; m. Zaza Irina O'Hara, Dec. 4, 1943; children: Joel Michael, Susan Irina. Student, Coll. City N.Y., 1938-39. Editorial staff N.Y. Herald Tribune, 1937-42, 45-47; asst. to dir. pub. relations C. & O. Ry., N.Y.C., 1948; exec. asst. to v.p. passenger traffic, pub. relations, advt. C. & O. Ry., Cleve., 1949-53; dir. pub. relations C. & O. Ry., 1954-59, spl. asst. to chmn. bd., 1954-77, dir. pub. relations and passenger traffic, 1959-63; v.p. C. & O. Ry., also B. & O. Ry., 1963-77, Western Md. Ry., 1973-77, Chessie System, Inc., 1974-77; pres. Howard Skidmore Co., Inc., Cleve., 1977-83. Trustee Cleve. Music Sch. Settlement, 1958—. Served with USNR, 1942-45. Mem. Soc. Silurians, R.R. Pub. Relations Assn. (pres. 1958), Pub. Relations Soc. Am., Soc. Profl. Journalists. Clubs: Nat. Press (Washington); Carmel Valley Racquet; Canterbury Golf (Cleve.). Home: 26360 Monte Verde St Carmel CA 93923-9233

SKIDMORE, JAMES ALBERT, JR., management, computer technology and engineering services company executive; b. Newark, June 30, 1932; s. James A. and Frances W. (Barker) S.; m. Peggy Ann Young, July 10, 1954; children: Jacqueline Sue Skidmore, James Albert III. BA, Muhlenberg Coll., 1954. Customer sales rep. N.J. Bell Telephone Co., Newark, 1957-65, then dist. sales mgr., div. mktg. mgr.; asst. to pres. for pub. affairs Pepsi Co., Inc., N.Y.C., 1966-69; asst. to Pres. of U.S., 1968-69; v.p. Handy Assoc., N.Y.C., 1969-70, pres., 1971-72; pres., CEO Sci. Mgmt. Corp., Basking Ridge, N.J., 1972—, chmn. bd. dir. Newark Brush Co., 1974-79; bd. dirs. Franklin State Bank, Somerset, N.J., Franklin Bancorp, United Jersey Banks, United Jersey Bank Franklin State exec. com. UJB Fin., 1985-93, Blue Cross & Blue Shield N.J., Inc., Enterprise Holding Co., Inc.; trustee Blue Cross of N.J., 1983—; dir. Coca Cola, N.Y., 1980-85, Mariner Communications, 1983-85; mem., chmn. mktg. com. Seton Hall Commn., 1987; mem. dean's adv. coun. Rutgers U. Grad. Sch. Mgmt., 1989; trustee Pub. Affairs Rsch. Inst. N.J., 1989; lectr. U. Amsterdam (The Netherlands), 1967, U. Toronto (Ont., Can.), U. Helsinki (Finland), 1967, Tokyo U. Mem. Nat. Council on Crime and Delinquency, 1965-66; mem. Nat. Commn. on Youth Employment, 1966-67; state chmn. N.J. Nat. Found. March of Dimes, 1966-73; mem. exec. bd. Watchung Area council Boy Scouts Am., 1972-77, dir. NE region, 1983-90; mem. Citizen's Adv. Bd. on Youth Opportunity 1969-75; state chmn. United Citizens for Nixon-Agnew, N.J., 1968; bd. govs. Alpha Tau Omega Found., 1967-73; bd. dirs. Muhlenberg Coll., Allentown, Pa., 1980-92, N.E. region Boy Scouts Am., 1983—. Recipient Disting. Citizens award Boy Scouts Am., 1983, Private Sector Initiative award Pres. Reagan, 1985. Trustee Brick Twp. Hosp., Inc., Brick Town, N.J., 1976-80; bd. dirs. Am. Christmas Trains and Trucks, chmn., 1966; pres. Project Concern, San Diego,1966-78. Served to capt. USMC, 1954-57. Decorated Order of St. John (Eng.); recipient Internat. Understanding award, Brussels, 1966, Disting. Service award, St. Paul, 1966, Freedom Found. George Washington Medal of Honor award, 1965, Outstanding Achievement in Life award Muhlenberg Coll. Alumni, 1966, Ambassador award U.S. Jaycees, 1977, Trinidad and Tobago award Prime Minister of Ireland, 1970 Human Relations award Soc. Advancement of Mgmt., 1982; Statesman award N.J. Jaycees, 1983; Disting. Citizens award Boy Scouts Am., 1983; inducted into U.S. Jaycees Hall of Leadership, 1983. Mem. N.J. State C. of C. (bd. dirs.), Muhlenberg Coll. Alumni Assn., Alpha Tau Omega. Clubs: Sky N.Y.C., Baltusrol Golf, Longboat Key. Guest columnist Rotary Internat. mag., 1966-68, Kiwanis mag., 1966-68, Japan Times on Community Responsibility and Leadership, 1965-67. Home: 177 Sutton Dr Berkeley Heights NJ 07922-2512 also: 1465 Gulf of Mexico Dr Longboat Key FL 34228-3401 Office: Sci Mgmt Corp 721 Us Highway 202 Bridgewater NJ 08807-1760 also: 641 Ocean Sea Girt NJ 08750

SKIDMORE, LINDA CAROL, science and engineering program administrator, consultant; b. Salisbury, Md., July 15, 1948; d. David Donaldson Skidmore Sr. and Mabel Frances Matthews Shockley; m. Charles Raymond Dix, Sept. 13, 1969 (div. Dec. 1991); 1 child, Larisa-Rose. BA, Loyola Coll., Balt., 1972; MEd, Salisbury (Md.) State Coll., 1982. Advanced profl. Md. State Dept. Edn. Tchr. secondary schs. Balt., 1972-73; tchr. James M. Bennett Sr. High Sch., Salisbury, 1973-77, coord. English dept., 1978-81; adminstrv. asst. Commn. Human Resources Nat. Rsch. Coun., Washington, 1981-82; adminstrv. assoc. Office Sci. Engring. Pers. Nat. Rsch. Coun.,

Washington, 1982-84, adminstrv. officer, 1984-87, program officer, 1987-90, study dir., 1990-94; dir. com. on women in sci. and engring., 1994—; instr. English Salisbury State Coll., 1979; cons. leadership tng. program for women Md. State Tchrs. Assn., Balt., 1978-81, Anne Arundel County Pub. Schs., Annapolis, Md., 1982-90; prin. investigator Engring. Personnel Data Needs in the 1990's, Edn. and Employment Engrs., Minorities Sci. and Engring., Women Sci. and Engring.; staff officer Com. on the Internat. Exch. and Movement Engrs., Com. Engring. Labor-Market Adjustments, Com. on Scientists and Engrs. in Fed. Govt.; panel on gender differences in the career outcomes of PhD scientists and engrs.; presenter Computer Math. Sci. Fair, 1990—; lectr. in field. Editor: Women: Their Underrepresentation and Career Differentials in Science and Engineering, 1987, Minorities: Their Underrepresentation and Career Differentials in Science and Engineering, 1987, On Time to the Doctorate, 1989, (with Alan K. Campbell) Recruitment, Retention and Utilization of Federal Scientists and Engineers, 1990, (with Marsha Lakes Matyas) Science and Engineering Programs: On Target for Women?, 1992, Women Scientists and Engineers Employed in Industry: Why So Few?, 1994; author: Women and Minorities in Science and Engineering, 1989; contbr. articles to profl. jours. Original appointee Wicomico County Commn. Women, 1977-81; Sunday sch. tchr. Severna Park, Md. United Meth. Ch., 1985-91; mem. Heartfriends, 1987—, co-chmn., 1989-90. Recipient cert. of Appreciation Wicomico County Bd. Edn., 1980; named Outstanding Young Woman Wicomico County Jaycees, 1977. Mem. AAAS, AAUW (chair women's issues Severna Park, Md. br. 1990-92, 1st v.p. 1992-95), Am. Assn. Higher Edn., Assn. for Women in Sci., Commn. on Profls. in Sci. and Tech., Fedn. Orgns. for Profl. Women, Nat. Coun. for Rsch. on Women, N.Y. Acad. Scis., Scho. Sci. and Math. Assn., Am. Ednl. Rsch. Assn. (spl. interest group on women and edn.), Nat. Coalition for Women and Girls in Edn., Women in Engring. Program Adv. Network, Women in Tech. Internat., Am. Legion Aux., Nat. Mus. Women Arts (charter), Md. State Tchrs. Assn. (chair women's caucus 1977-78, human rights com. 1979-81, meritorious svc. 1978, 80), Wicomico County Edn. Assn. (pres. 1978-79), Sigma Delta Epsilon. Democrat. Avocations: cross-stitching, writing poetry, reading historical novels, sailing. Home: 912 Winsap Ct Baltimore MD 21227 Office: NRC Office Sci and Engring Pers Rm TJ 2011 2101 Constitution Ave NW Washington DC 20418

SKIDMORE, REX AUSTIN, social work educator; b. Salt Lake City, Dec. 31, 1914; s. Charles H. and Louise (Wangsgaard) S.; m. Knell Spencer, Aug. 31, 1939; children: Lee Spencer, Larry Rex. BA, U. Utah, 1938, MA, 1939; PhD, U. Pa., 1941; PhD (hon.), U. Utah, 1996. Instr. sociology U. Pa., 1940-41, Utah State Agrl. Coll., Logan, 1941-42; spl. agt. FBI, Miami, Fla., San Francisco, San Antonio, 1943-45; dir. bur. student counsel U. Utah, 1947-57, asso. prof., 1947-50, prof., 1950-85, dean Grad. Sch. Social Work, 1956-75. Author: Mormon Recreation: Theory and Practice, 1941, Building Your Marriage, 1951, 3d edit., 1964, Marriage Consulting, 1956, Introduction to Social Work, 1964, 6th edit., 1994, Introduction to Mental Health, 1979, Social Work Administration, 1983, 3d edit., 1995; contbr. articles to sociol. jours. Chmn. Western Mental Health Council, Western Interstate Commn. Higher Edn., 1964-65; mem. Nat. Adv. Council Nat. Manpower and Tng. Recipient Disting. Svc. award Cmty. Svc. Coun., NASW, 1975, Utah Conf. on Human Svcs., 1976, U. Utah Prof. Emeritus Svc. award, 1994. Mem. Coun. on Social Work Edn., Phi Kappa Phi, Pi Kappa Alpha, Pi Gamma Mu. Mem. Ch. of Jesus Christ Latter-Day Saints. Home: 1444 S 20th E Salt Lake City UT 84108 *A significant idea for successful living is knowing that: Loving is the central ingredient in human relationships; and the essence of loving is giving, not getting.*

SKIGEN, PATRICIA SUE, lawyer; b. Springfield, Mass., June 16, 1942; d. David P. and Gertrude H. (Hirschhaut) S.; m. Irwin J. Sugarman, May 1973 (div. Nov. 1994); 1 child, Alexander David. BA with distinction, Cornell U., 1964; LLB, Yale U., 1968. Bar: N.Y. 1968, U.S. Dist. Ct. (so. dist.) N.Y. 1969. Law clk. Anderson, Mori & Rabinowitz, Tokyo, 1966-67; assoc. Rosenman Colin Kaye Petschek Freund & Emil, N.Y.C., 1968-70; assoc. Willkie Farr & Gallagher, N.Y.C., 1970-75, ptnr., 1977-95; v.p., co-chair corp. fin. group legal dept. Chase Manhattan Bank, N.Y.C., 1995—; dep. supt., gen. counsel N.Y. State Banking Dept., N.Y.C., 1975-77, 1st dep. supt. banks, 1977; adj. prof. Benjamin Cardozo Law Sch. Yeshiva U., 1979. Contbr. articles to profl. jours. Cornell U. Dean's scholar, 1960-64, Regent's scholar, 1960-64, Yale Law Sch. scholar, 1964-68. Mem. ABA (corp. banking and bus. law sect.), Assn. of Bar of City of N.Y. (chmn. com. banking 1991-94, long range planning com. 1994—, audit com. 1995—), Phi Beta Kappa, Phi Kappa Phi. Office: Chase Manhattan Bank 270 Park Ave New York NY 10081

SKILBECK, CAROL LYNN MARIE, elementary educator and small business owner; b. Seymour, Ind., May 1, 1953; d. Harry Charles and Barbara Josephine (Knue) S.; div.; 1 child, Michael Charles. Postgrad., U. Cin., 1977, No. Ky. U., 1985-86, Northern Ky. U. Cert. tchr., Ohio. Sec. Procter & Gamble, Cin., 1971-76; classified typist The Cin. Enquirer, Cin., 1976; tchr. St. Aloysius Sch., Cin., 1977-79, St. William Sch., Cin., 1979-82; legal sec. County Dept. Human Svcs., Cin., 1982-86; tchr. St. Jude Sch., Cin., 1986-91; educator, owner CLS Tutoring Svcs., Cin., 1991—; photographer Interstate Studio and Am. Sch. Pictures, 1994—; tchr. St. Martin Gifted Program, Cin., 1992-93, Oak Hills Schs. Community Edn., Cin., 1990—, Super Saturday Gifted Program, Cin., 1990—; adult leader antidrug program Just Say No, Cin., 1989-92. Author: Study Skills Workshop, 1993; writer, dir. Christmas play, 1993. Vol. interior designer for homeless shelter St. Joseph's Carpenter Shop, Cin., 1990; mem. LaSalle PTA, 1993—; vol. Habitat for Humanity. Mem. Nat. Tchrs. Assn. Democrat. Roman Catholic. Avocations: writing, jazz/tap dance, community theatre, interior decorating, aerobics instructor. Home and Office: 3801 Dina Ter Cincinnati OH 45211-6527

SKILES, JAMES JEAN, electrical and computer engineering educator; b. St Louis, Oct. 16, 1928; s. Coy Emerson and Vernetta Beatrice (Maples) S.; m. Deloris Audrey McKenney, Sept. 4, 1948; children: Steven, Randall, Jeffrey. BSEE, Washington U., St. Louis, 1948; MS, U. Mo.-Rolla, 1951; PhD, U. Wis., 1954. Registered profl. engr., Wis. Engr. Union Electric Co., St. Louis, 1948-49; instr. U. Mo.-Rolla, 1949-51; prof. elec. engring. U. Wis., Madison, 1954-89, prof. emeritus, 1989—, chmn. Dept. Elec. Engring., 1967-72, dir. Univ. Industry Rsch. program, 1972-75, dir. Energy Rsch. Ctr., 1975-95; cons. in field. Contbr. articles to profl. jours. Mem. Monona Grove Dist. Schs. Bd., Wis., 1961-69; mem. adv. com. Wis. Energy Office, Madison, 1979-80, Wis. Pub. Service Commn., 1980-81. Recipient Wis. Electric Utilities Professorship in Energy Engring. U. Wis., 1975-89; recipient Benjamin Smith Reynolds Teaching award, 1980, Kiekhofer Teaching award, 1955, Acad of Elec. Engring. award U. Mo.-Rolla, 1982. Mem. IEEE (sr.), Am. Soc. Engring. Edn. Home: 8099 Coray Ln Verona WI 53593-9073 Office: Univ of Wisconsin Dept Elec & Computer Engring 1415 Engineering Dr Madison WI 53706-1691

SKILES, PAUL, church administrator. Dir. Communications Division of the Church of the Nazarene, Kansas City, Mo.; ret. Office: Church of the Nazarene 6401 Paseo Blvd Kansas City MO 64131-1213

SKILLERN, FRANK FLETCHER, law educator; b. Sept. 26, 1942; s. Will T. and Vera Catherine (Ryberg) S.; m. Susan Schlaefer, Sept. 3, 1966; children: Nathan Edward, Leah Catherine. AB, U. Chgo., 1964; JD, U. Denver, 1966; LLM, U. Mich., 1969. Bar: Colo. 1967, Tex. 1978. Pvt. practice law Denver, 1967; gen. atty. Maritime Adminstrn., Washington, 1967-68; asst. prof. law Ohio No. U., 1969-71; asst. prof. law Tex. Tech U., Lubbock, 1971-73, assoc. prof. law, 1973-75, prof. law, 1975—; vis. prof. U. Tex. Law Sch., summer 1979, U. Ark. Law Sch., 1979-80, U. Tulsa Coll. Law, 1981-82; cons. and speaker in field. Author: Environmental Protection: The Legal Framework, 1981, 2d edit. published as Environmental Protection Handbook, 1995, Regulation of Water and Sewer Utilities, 1989, Texas Water Law, Vol. I, 1988, rev. edit., 1992, Vol. II, 1991; contbr. chpts. to Powell on Real Property, Zoning and Land Use Controls, others; author cong. procs. and numerous articles. Mem. ABA (mem. publs. com. Sect. Natural Resources Law 1984—, vice chair internat. environ. law com. Sect. Natural Resources Law 1987). Office: Tex Tech U Sch Law PO Box 40004 Lubbock TX 79409-0004

SKILLICORN, JUDY PETTIBONE, gifted/talented education coordinator; b. Cleve., June 16, 1943; d. C. Arthur and Dorothy Laura (Parratt) Pettibone; m. Robert Charles Skillicorn, Aug. 21, 1965; children: Jodie Lynn, Brian Jeffrey, Jennifer Laura. BS in Edn., Ohio State U., 1965; MEd, Cleve. State U., 1988. 6th grade tchr. Windermer Sch., Upper Arlington, Ohio, 1965-68; pvt. tutor, 1968-71; adminstr. Westshore Montessori Sch., Elyria, Lorain & Amherst, Ohio, 1981; ch. educator First Congl. Ch., Elyria, 1982-84, St. Peters United Ch. of Christ, Amherst, Ohio, 1984; tchr. gifted Clearview Local Schs., Lorain, 1985-90; coord. gifted Lorain County Bd. Edn., Elyria, 1990—, planning dir. county-wide sch. creative & performing arts; founder Arts Advocacy of Lorain County, 1994, pres. 1996; founder Arts Connected Tchg. pilot program in 4 sch. dists., 1995-96. Author: Young Authors Handbook, 1991, 92, 93, 94, 95, 96. Chairperson tickets Elyria 150th Bicentennial Celebration; pageant dir. Ch. Medieval Feast, Elyria, 1988-91; chmn. diaconate First Congl. Ch., Elyria, 1990-93; mem. com. Lorain County Beautiful, Seventh Generation, 1995—. Recipient Partnership in Edn. for Young Authors Program grades K-6 Nat. Assn. Coll. Stores, Oberlin, 1993-96, for Writers conf. Program grades 7-9, 1993-96; Jennings scholar tchr. Martha Holden Jennings Found., 1990-91. Mem. Writing Tchrs. Network (publ. com. 1991-93), North Ctrl. Consortium for Gifted (treas., v.p. 1991-93), Lorain County Elem. Sch. Adminstrs. (sec.-treas. 1993, v.p. 1993-94, pres. 1994-95), Consortium Ohio Coords. for Gifted, Ohio Assn. Gifted Children, Chautauqua Lit. Soc., Internat. Network for Visual and Performing Arts Schs., Phi Delta Kappa. Avocations: reading including children's literature, travel, attending plays, arts actvities and concerts, gardening. Office: Lorain County Office Edn 1885 Lake Ave Elyria OH 44035-2551

SKILLIN, EDWARD SIMEON, magazine publisher; b. N.Y.C., Jan. 23, 1904; s. Edward Simeon and Geraldine Madeleine (Fearons) S.; m. Jane Anne Edwards, Jan. 27, 1945; children: Edward John, Elizabeth Ann Skillin Flanagan, Arthur Paul, Susan Geraldine Skillin Thuvanuti, Mary Jane Skillin Davis. Grad., Phillips Acad., Andover, Mass., 1921; AB, Williams Coll., 1925; MA, Columbia U., 1933; LHD (hon.), St. Benedict's Coll., Atchison, Kans., 1954, Fordham U., 1974; LLD, St. Vincent's Coll., Latrobe, Pa., 1959, St. Francis Xavier U., Antigonish, N.S., Can., 1966, Stonehill Coll., 1979. With ednl. dept. Henry Holt & Co., N.Y.C., 1925-32; mem. staff Commonweal Found., N.Y.C., 1933-38, editor, 1938-67, pub., 1967—. Editor: The Commonweal Reader, 1949. Recipient Centennial citation St. John's U., Collegeville, Minn., 1957, St. Francis de Sales award Cath. Press Assn., 1987, Pax Christi award St. John's U., 1990. Mem. Cath. Commn. on Intellectual and Cultural Affairs, Phi Beta Kappa, Phi Gamma Delta. Office: Commonweal Found 15 Dutch St New York NY 10038-3719 *Grateful for many things: faith, family, the influence of 3 friends, good health, and 60 years with a socially-minded Christian journal of opinion.*

SKILLING, DAVID VAN DIEST, manufacturing executive; b. St. Louis, Sept. 16, 1933; s. David Miller Jr. and Eloise Margaret (van Diest) S.; m. Barbara Jo Chaney, Aug. 4, 1956; children: Kimberly Alice, Mark Chaney. BS, Colo. Coll., 1955; MBA, Pepperdine U., 1977. With TRW, Inc., Los Angeles, 1970-83, Cleve., 1983-93, Orange, Calif., 1993—; dir. mktg. energy group TRW, Los Angeles, 1978-83, v.p. planning and devel., indsl. and energy sector, 1983-86, v.p. corp. planning and devel., 1987-89, exec. v.p., gen. mgr. infosystems and svcs., 1989—; bd. dirs. Lamson & Sessions, Cleve. Bd. dirs. ISI, 1995—; trustee The Colo. Coll., 1994—. Mem. NAM (bd. dirs. 1988-93), Assn. for Corp. Growth, Calif. Bus. Roundtable (exec. com. 1994—), Orange County C. of C. (bd. dirs. 1993—). Republican. Office: TRW Inc 505 City Pkwy W Orange CA 92608

SKILLING, JOHN BOWER, structural and civil engineer; b. L.A., Oct. 8, 1921; s. Harold C. and Helen M. (Bower) S.; m. Mary Jane Stender, May 1, 1943; children: William, Susan, Ann. B.S., U. Wash., 1947. Design engr. W.H. Witt Co., Seattle, 1947-52; partner successor firm Worthington, Skilling, Helle and Jackson, Seattle, 1959-67, Skilling, Helle, Christiansen, Robertson, Seattle, 1967-82; chmn., CEO successor firm Skilling Ward Rogers Barkshire, Inc., Seattle, 1983-87; chmn. Skilling Ward Magnusson Barkshire, Inc. and successor firm, Seattle, 1987—; mem. Bldg. Research Adv. Bd. Mem. Seattle Found. Fellow ASCE; mem. NAE, Am. Concrete Inst., Internat. Assn. Shell Structures, Structural Engrs. Assn. Wash., AIA (hon.), Am. Inst. Steel Constrn., Wash. Athletic Club, Seattle Tennis Club, Broadmoor Golf Club, Lampda Alpha. Clubs: 101; Dean's, Pres.'s (Univ. Wash.). Home: 539 Mcgilvra Blvd E Seattle WA 98112-5047 Office: Skilling Ward Magnusson Barkshire Inc 1301 5th Ave Ste 3200 Seattle WA 98101-2603

SKILLING, RAYMOND INWOOD, lawyer; b. Enniskillen, U.K., July 14, 1939; s. Dane and Elizabeth (Burleigh) S.; m. Alice Mae Welsh, Aug. 14, 1982; 1 child by previous marriage, Keith A. F. LLB, Queen's U., Belfast, U.K., 1961; JD, U. Chgo., 1962. Solicitor English Supreme Ct. 1966. Bar: Ill 1974. Assoc. Clifford-Turner (now Clifford Chance), London, 1963-69, ptnr., 1969-76; exec. v.p., chief counsel Aon Corp. (and predecessor cos.), Chgo., 1976—; bd. dirs. Aon Corp. (and predecessor cos.). Commonwealth fellow, U. Chgo., 1961-62, Bigelow teaching fellow U. Chgo. Law Sch., 1962-63; Fulbright scholar U.S. Ednl. Commn., London, 1961-63; recipient McKane medal Queen's U., Belfast, 1961. Mem. ABA, Ill. Bar Assn., Chgo. Bar Assn., The Casino Chgo., Chgo. Club, Econ. Club Chgo., Racquet Club Chgo., The Carlton Club London. Office: Aon Corp 123 N Wacker Dr Chicago IL 60606-1700

SKILLING, THOMAS ETHELBERT, III, meteorologist, meteorology educator; b. Pitts., Feb. 20, 1952; s. Elizabeth Clarke. Student, U. Wis., 1970-74; Dr. Humanities (hon.), Lewis U., Romeoville, Ill., 1995. Meteorologist Sta. WKKD-AM-FM, Aurora, Ill., 1967-70, Sta. WLXT-TV, Aurora, 1969-70, Sta. WKOW-TV, Madison, Wis., 1970-74, Sta. WTSO, Madison, 1970-74, Sta. WTLV-TV, Jacksonville, Fla., 1974-75, Sta. WITI-TV, Milw., 1975-78, Sta. WAUK, Waukesha, Wis., 1976-77, Sta. WGN-TV, Chgo., 1978—; weather forecaster Wis. Farm Broadcast Network, Madison, 1970-74; weather cons. Piper, Jaffray & Hopwood, Madison, 1972-74; instr. meteorology Columbia Coll., Chgo., 1982-92, Adler Planetarium, Chgo., 1985-86. Vol. Chgo. chpt. Muscular Dystrophy Assn. Recipient Emmy award for "It Sounded Like a Freight Train," 1991, "The Cosmic Challenge," 1994; Peter Lisagor awards for weather spls. aired on WGN, 1991, 93. Fellow Am. Meteorol. Soc. (v.p. Chgo. chpt. 1985-86, TV Seal of Approval), Nat. Weather Assn., Soc. Profl. Journalists, Chgo. Acad. TV Arts and Scis. Avocations: hiking, cross country skiing. Home: 6033 N Sheridan Rd Apt 31C Chicago IL 60660-3022 Office: Sta WGN-TV 2501 W Bradley Pl Chicago IL 60618-4701

SKILLINGSTAD, CONSTANCE YVONNE, social services administrator, educator; b. Portland, Oreg., Nov. 18, 1944; d. Irving Elmer and Beulah Ruby (Aleckson) Erickson; m. David W. Skillingstad, Jan. 12, 1968 (div. Mar. 1981); children: Michael, Brian. BA in Sociology, U. Minn., 1966; MBA, U. St. Thomas, St. Paul, 1982. Cert. vol. adminstr.; lic. social worker. Social worker Rock County Welfare Dept., Luverne, Minn., 1966-68; social worker Hennepin County Social Svcs., Mpls., 1968-70, vol. coord., 1970-78; vol. coord. St. Joseph's Home for Children, Mpls., 1978-89, mgr. community resources, 1989-94; exec. dir. Mpls. Crisis Nursery, 1994—; mem. community faculty Met. State U., St. Paul and Mpls., 1982—; faculty U. St. Thomas Ctr. for Non Profit Mgmt., 1990—; trainer, mem. adv. commn. Mpls. Vol. Ctr., 1978-90, cons., 1980—, chmn. Contbr. articles to Jour. Vol. Adminstrn. Mem. adv. bd. Mothers Against Drunk Driving, Minn., 1986-88; vice chmn., chmn. adminstrv. coun., lay leader Hobart United Meth. Ch.; lay rep. to Minn. Ann. Conf. of Meth. Chs., 1989-92; active Park Ave United Meth. Ch., 1992—. Named one of Oustanding Young Women Am., 1974, Woman od Distinction Mpls. St. Paul Mag./KARE-TV, 1995. Mem. Minn. Assn. Vol. Dirs. (pres. 1975, sec., ethics chmn. 1987—), Assn. for Vol. Adminstrn. (v.p. regional affairs 1985-87, mem. assessment panel 1986—, coord. nat. tng. team, cert. process for vol. adminstrs. 1988-92, profl. devel. chair 1990-92), Minn. Social Svcs. Assn. (pres. 1981, Disting. Svc. award 1987). Mem. Dem.-Farmer-Labor Party. Methodist. Avocations: bridge, volleyball, accordian, traveling, reading. Office: Mpls Crisis Nursery 4255 3rd Ave S Minneapolis MN 55409-2105

SKILLMAN, THOMAS GRANT, endocrinology consultant, former educator; b. Cin., Jan. 7, 1925; s. Harold Grant and Faustina (Jobes) S.; m. Elizabeth Louise McClellan, Sept. 6, 1947; children: Linda, Barbara. B.S., Baldwin-Wallace Coll., 1946; M.D., U. Cin., 1949. Intern Cin. Gen. Hosp., 1949-50, resident, 1952-54; instr. medicine U. Cin., 1952-57; asst. prof. medicine Ohio State U., Columbus, 1957-61; dir. endocrinology and metabolism Coll. Medicine Ohio State U., 1967-74, Ralph Kurtz prof. endocrinology, 1974-81, prof. emeritus, 1981—, cons. to v.p. med. affairs, 1981—; asso. prof. medicine Creighton U., Omaha, 1961-67. Editor: Case Studies in Endocrinology, 1971; Contbr. numerous articles to med. jours. Served with USNR, 1943-45; 1950-52, Korea. Recipient Golden Apple award Student Am. Med. Assn., 1966. Mem. Am. Diabetes Assn., Central Soc. Clin. Investigation, Am. Fedn. for Clin. Research, Alpha Omega Alpha. Club: Ohio State Golf (Columbus). Home: 4179 Stoneroot Dr Hilliard OH 43026-3023 Office: Ohio State U Hosps Meiling Hall # 200G Columbus OH 43210

SKILLMAN, WILLIAM ALFRED, consulting engineering executive; b. Lakehurst, N.J., Jan. 22, 1928; s. Wilbur Newton and Greta Alfreda (Ekman) S.; m. Anne Marie Cavender, Sept. 19, 1948; children—Thomas R., Gregory A., Karen L. B.S. in Engring. Physics, Lehigh U., 1952; M.S. in Physics, U. Rochester, 1954. Assoc. engr. Westinghouse Electric Corp., Balt., 1954-56, engr., 1956-58, sr. engr., 1958-61, supervisory engr., 1961-64, advisory engr., 1964-73, sr. adv. engr., 1973-85, cons. engr., 1986-93, cons. electronic systems group, 1993—. Author: Radar Calculations Using the TI-59 Programmable Calculator, 1983; author: (with others) Radar Handbook, 2d edit., 1990. Patentee in field. Served with USN, 1946-48. Fellow IEEE (life); mem. Aerospace and Electronic Sys. Soc. (Pioneer award 1995), Phi Beta Kappa. Republican. Methodist. Avocations: photography; canoeing; hiking; programming. Home and Office: 605 Forest View Rd Linthicum Heights MD 21090-2819

SKILLRUD, HAROLD CLAYTON, minister; b. St. Cloud, Minn., June 29, 1928; s. Harold and Amanda Skillrud; m. Lois Dickhart, June 8, 1951; children: David, Janet, John. BA magna cum laude, Gustavus Adolphus Coll., 1950; MDiv magna cum laude, Augustana Theol. Sem., Rock Island, Ill., 1954; STM, Luth. Sch. Theology, Chgo., 1969; DD (hon.), Augustana Coll., 1978, Newberry Coll., 1988. Ordained to ministry Evang. Luth. Ch. in Am., 1954. Supply pastor Saron Luth. Ch., Big Lake, Minn., 1950-51; mem. staff 1st Luth. Ch., Rock Island, Ill., 1951-52; intern, organizer new mission Faith Luth. Ch., Syosset, N.Y., 1952-53; sr. pastor St. John's Luth. Ch., Bloomington, Ill., 1954-79, Luth. Ch. of the Redeemer, Atlanta, 1979-87; bishop Southeastern Synod Evang. Luth. Ch. in Am., Atlanta, 1987-95, regional rep. bd. pensions, 1995—; del. to various convs. Luth. Ch. in Am., Luth. World Fedn. in Helsinki, 1963, mem. bd. publ., 1976-84, pastor-evangelist Evang. Outreach Emphasis program, 1977-79, mem. exec. bd. Ill. synod, 1977-79, pres. bd. publ., 1980-84, leader stewardship cluster Southeastern synod, 1983, mem. exec. bd. Southeastern synod, 1984-87; mem. exec. coun., Luth. Ch. in Am., 1984-87; mem. task force on new ch. design Commn. on New Luth. Ch., task force on ch. pub. house, 1985; del. constituting conv. Evang. Luth. Ch. in Am., 1987, del. assemblies Evang. Luth. Ch. in Am., 1989, 91, 93, 95; mem. commn. on clergy confidentiality Luth. Coun. in USA, 1987; co-chair USA Luth.- Roman Cath. Dialogue; mem. Task Force on Theol. Edn. Author: LSTC: Decade of Decision, 1969; co-editor Scripture and Tradition, Lutherans and Catholics in Dialogue, 1995; mem. edtl. bd. Partners mag., 1978-80; contbr. articles and sermons to religious jours. Former bd. dirs. Augustana Theol. Sem.; bd. dirs. Augustana Coll., 1969-77, chmn. bd., 1976-77; bd. dirs. Kessler Reformation Collection, Newberry Coll., Luth. World Relief, Augsburg Fortress; chmn. bd. dirs. Luth. Sch. Theology, Chgo., 1962-69; mem. Leadership Atlanta, 1980-81, United Way, Atlanta, 1980-81; mem. Bishop's Commn. on Econ. Justice, 1985-86; pres. bd. dirs. Atlanta Samaritan House, 1986-87. Recipient Alumni award Luth. Sch. Theology, Chgo., 1976, award Leadership Atlanta, 1981, The Rev. John Bachman award, Luth. Theol. Sem., Columbia, S.C., 1996. Mem. Luth. Sch. Theology Alumni Assn. (pres. 1975-77), Conf. of Bishops, Kiwanis (pres. Midtown chpt. 1984-85). Avocations: travel, photography. Home: 368 E Wesley Rd NE Atlanta GA 30305-3824

SKILTON, JOHN SINGLETON, lawyer; b. Washington, Apr. 13, 1944; s. Robert Henry and Margaret (Neisser) S.; m. Carmen Fisher, Jan. 28, 1967; children: Laura Anne, Susan Elizabeth, Robert John. BA, U. Wis., 1966, JD, 1969. Bar: Wis. Supreme Ct. 1969, U.S. Dist. Ct. (ea. and we. dists.) Wis. 1969, U.S. Ct. Appeals (7th cir.) 1969, U.S. Supreme Ct. 1989. Law clk. 7th Cir. Ct. Appeals, Milw., 1969-70; assoc. Foley & Lardner, Milw., 1970-77; ptnr. Foley & Lardner, Madison, Wis., 1977—. Bd. visitors U. Wis. Law Sch., Madison, 1982-90, chmn., 1988-89; chair Wis. Fed. Nominating Commn., 1994; mem. Gov.'s Task Force on Bus. Ct., 1994-95. Fellow Am. Bar Found., Am. Coll. Trial Lawyers; mem. Am. Law Inst., Am. Acad. Appellate Lawyers, 7th Cir. Bar Assn. (pres. 1985-86, chmn. 7th cir. adv. com. on rules 1994—), State Bar Wis. (pres. 1995-96, Pres.'s award of excellence 1989), Western Dist. Wis. Bar Assn. (pres. 1992-93), Western Dist. Adv. Group (chmn. 1991), James E. Doyle Am. Inn of Ct. (coun. 1992-94), Am. Inns of Ct. Found. (trustee 1995—), U. Wis. Law Alumni Assn. (bd. dirs. 1991—, pres. 1993-95). Home: 8 N Prospect Ave Madison WI 53705-3936 Office: Foley & Lardner 150 E Gilman St Madison WI 53703-2808

SKINNER, ALASTAIR, accountant; b. Hamilton, Ont., Can., Apr. 4, 1936; s. Allistair and Isabelle (Drysdale) S.; m. Patricia Skinner; children: Lisa, Iain, James, Graeme. CA, Queens U., Kingston, Ont., Can., 1959; MBA, Harvard U., 1963. Cert. mgmt. cons. Served to maj. Can. Army Res., 1954-71; nat. mng. ptnr. MacGillivray & Co. (name now Doane Raymond), 1977-83; ptnr.-in-charge Toronto (Ont.) Office, Spicer MacGillivray (name now Doane Raymond), 1984-86, 88-91; ptnr. Doane Raymond, Toronto, 1991—. Co-author: profl. manuals. Fellow Inst. Chartered Accts. of Ont. (pres. 1983-84), Soc. Mgmt. Accts. of Can. (bd. dirs.); mem. Inst. Mgmt. Cons. of Ont., Can. Tax Found. (bd. govs.), Pub. Accts. Coun. Ont. Club: Albany (Toronto), Devil's Glen Country Club. Avocations: skiing, bridge. Office: Doane Raymond Ste 1900, Royal Bank Plz, Box 55 S Tower, Toronto, ON Canada M5J 2P9

SKINNER, ANDREW CHARLES, history educator, religious writer; b. Durango, Colo., Apr. 25, 1951; s. Charles La Verne and Julia Magdalena (Schunk) S.; m. Janet Corbridge, Mar. 22, 1974; children: Cheryl Lyn, Charles Lon, Kelli Ann, Mark Andrew, Holly, Suzanne. BA with disting., U. Colo., 1975; MA with disting., Iliff Sch. of Theology, Denver, 1978; ThM, Harvard U., 1980; PhD, U. Denver, 1986. Group mgr. May Co. Dept. Store, Denver, 1980-83; assoc. studio dir. Talking Books Pub. Co., Denver, 1984-88; instr. history Metro. State Coll., Denver, 1984-88; prof. history Ricks Coll., Rexburg, Utah, 1988-92; prof. ancient scripture Brigham Young U., Provo, Utah, 1992—; vis. instr. ancient scripture Brigham Young U., Provo, Utah, 1987; vis. prof. Jerusalem Ctr. for Nr. Eastern Studies, Israel; cons. Univ. Without Walls, Loretto Heights Coll., Denver, 1985-88; mem. editorial staff Dead Sea Scrolls, publ. bd. Israel Antiquities Authority. Author chpts. numerous books and encyclopaedia articles; co-author: Jerusalem-The Eternal City. Bishop Mormon Ch., Denver, 1986-88; varsity scout leader Teton Parks coun. Boy Scouts Am., Rexburg, 1988-89; host Internat. Scholars Conf. on Holocaust and the Chs., 1995. Mil. history fellow U.S. Mil. Acad., 1989. Mem. Am. Hist. Assn., Soc. Bibl. Lit., Mormon History Assn., Phi Theta Kappa, Phi Alpha Theta. Mem. LDS Ch. Office: Brigham Young U Dept Ancient Scripture JSB 270-M Provo UT 84602

SKINNER, BRIAN JOHN, geologist, educator; b. Wallaroo, South Australia, Dec. 15, 1928; came to U.S., 1958, naturalized, 1963; s. Joshua Henry and Joyce Barbara Lloyd (Prince) S.; m. Helen Catherine Wild, Oct. 9, 1954; children: Adrienne Wild, Stephanie Wild, Thalassa Wild. B.Sc., U. Adelaide, Australia, 1950; A.M., Harvard U., 1952, Ph.D., 1955. Lectr. U. Adelaide, 1955-58; research geologist U.S. Geol. Survey, 1958-62, chief br. exptl. geochemistry and mineralogy, 1962-66; prof. geology and geophysics, chmn. dept. Yale U., New Haven, 1966-73; Eugene Higgins prof. Yale U., 1972—; Hugh Exton McKinstry Meml. lectr. Harvard U., 1978; Alex L. du Toit lectr. Combined Socs. South Africa, 1979; Cecil H. and Ida Green lectr. U. B.C., 1983; Thayer Lindsley Meml. lectr. Soc. Econ. Geologists, 1983; Soc. Econ. Geologists Overseas lectr., 1985; Hoffman lectr. Harvard U., 1986, Joubin-James lectr. U. Toronto, 1987; mem. exec. com. divsn. earth scis. NRC, 1966-69; chmn. com. mineral resources and the environ. Nat. Acad. Scis.-NRC, 1973-75; mem. Lunar Sample Analysis Planning Team, 1968-70, Lunar Sci. Rev. Bd., 1971-72, U.S. Nat. Com. for Geochemistry, 1966-67, U.S. Nat. Com. for Geology, 1973-77, 85-93, chmn., 1987-93, chmn. bd. earth scis. NRC, 1987-88, earth scis. and resources, 1989-90; mem. bd. Internat. Geol. Correlation Program, UNESCO-IUGS, 1985-89, 90-96, chmn., 1986-89; cons. Office Sci. and Tech. Policy, 197-80, NSF, 1977-82; dir. Econ. Geology Pub. Co.; chmn. governing bd. Am. Jour. Sci., 1972—. Author: Earth Resources, 1969, 77, 86, Man and the Ocean, 1973, Physical Geology, 1974, 77, 87, Rocks and Rock Minerals, 1979, The New Iron Age Ahead, 1987, Resources and World Development, 1987, The Dynamic Earth, 1989, 92, 95, The Blue Planet, 1995; editor: Econ. Geology, 1969—, Oxford Univ. Press Monographs in Geological Sciences, 1979—; editl. bd. Am. Scientist, 1974-90, chmn., 1987-90. Trustee Hopkins Grammar Sch., 1978-83. Recipient Disting. Contbns. award Assn. Earth Sci. Editors, 1979, Silver medal Soc. Econ. Geologists, 1981, Neil Miner award Nat. Assn. Geology Tchrs., 1995; Guggenheim fellow, 1970. Fellow Geol. Soc. Am. (councillor 1976-78, chmn. spl. publs. com. 1980-81, chmn. com. on coms. 1983, pres. 1985); mem. Geochem. Soc. (pres. 1972-73), Conn. Acad. Sci. and Engring. (div. chmn. 1978-80, council 1982-87), Soc. Econ. Geologists (pres. 1995). Home: PO Box 894 Woodbury CT 06798-0894

SKINNER, CHARLES SCOFIELD, technology management service executive, consultant, mechanical engineer; b. Cleve., Feb. 10, 1940; s. Harry Harrison and Margaret Charlotte (Scofield) S.; m. Nancy Lee Cleveland, Sept. 20, 1974; children: Jeffrey Charles, Melinda Lee. MME, Cornell U., 1969; MBA, Case Western Res. U., 1979; BSME, Cornell U., 1963; postgrad., MIT, 1972, Stanford U., 1977, Harvard U., 1982. Registered profl. engr., N.Y., Ohio. Mfg. engr. GM, Detroit, 1963-64; market researcher Exxon Corp., N.Y.C., 1964-65; sr. ptnr. Booz-Allen & Hamilton, Inc., N.Y.C., 1970-85; pres., CEO Strategic Technology Inc., Cleve., 1985—; cons. Booz-Allen & Hamilton, Inc., 1970-85, Strategic Tech., Inc., 1985—, also bd. dirs.; cons. First Pacific Networks, Inc., Sunnyvale, Calif., 1988-89. Author: CIM Implementation Planning Guide, 1988, (with others) The Management of Productivity, 1986; contbr. numerous articles to profl. jours. Fundraiser Culver (Ind.) Ednl. Found., 1969-92, Cornell U., Ithaca, N.Y., 1975—, Old Trail Sch., Akron, Ohio, 1988—, Univ. Sch., Shaker Hts., Ohio, 1991—. Capt. U.S. Army, 1965-68. Decorated Air medal with 23 oak leaf clusters, Vietnam Campaign medal with device, Aviator medal, Vietnam Service medal, Exxon Corp. grantee, 1968-69. Mem. Soc. Mfg. Engrs. (chmn. mfg. and learning divsn., tech. coun. 1982-83), Culver Legion (life), Cornell Club of N.Y., Mid-Day Club, Cornell Club of N.E. Ohio (treas. 1993), Sigma Chi (treas. 1962-63), SAR, We. Res. Soc., Scabbard and Blade (hon.), Phoebus (hon.), Masons, Shriners, Vietnam Vets. Am., VFW. Avocations: squash, golf, piloting. Office: Strategic Tech Inc 24200 Chagrin Blvd Cleveland OH 44122

SKINNER, DAVID BERNT, surgeon, educator; b. Joliet, Ill., Apr. 28, 1935; s. James Madden and Bertha Elinor (Tapper) S.; m. May Elinor Tischer, Aug. 25, 1956; children: Linda Elinor, Kristin Anne, Carise Berntine, Margaret Leigh. B.A. with high honors, U. Rochester, N.Y., 1958, Sc.D. (hon.), 1980; M.D. cum laude, Yale U., 1959; MD (hon.), U. Lund, 1994, Technishe U. Munich, 1995. Diplomate: Am. Bd. Surgery (dir. 1974-80), Am. Bd. Thoracic Surgery. Intern, then resident in surgery Mass. Gen. Hosp., Boston, 1959-65; sr. registrar in thoracic surgery Frenchay Hosp., Bristol, Eng., 1963-64; teaching fellow Harvard U. Med. Sch., 1965; from asst. prof. surgery to prof. Johns Hopkins U. Med. Sch., also surgeon Johns Hopkins Hosp., 1968-72; Dallas B. Phemister prof. surgery, chmn. dept. U. Chgo. Hosps. and Clinics, 1972-87; prof. surgery Cornell U., 1987—; pres., CEO N.Y. Hosp., 1987—; dir. Omnis Surg. Inc., 1984-85, Churchill Livingston, 1990-93, Lab. Corp. Am.; mem. Pres.' Biomed. Rsch. Panel, 1975-76. Author: Atlas of Esophageal Surgery, 1991; author: (with others) Gastroesophageal Reflux and Hiatal Hernia, 1972, Management of Esophageal Diseases, 1988; editor: Surgical Practice Illustrated, 1988-95; editor Current Topics in Surg. Rsch., 1969-71, Jour. Surg. Rsch., 1972-83; co-editor: Surg. Treatment of Digestive Disease, 1985, Esophageal Disorders, 1985, Reconstructive Surgery of the Gastrointestinal Tract, 1985, Primary Motility Disorders of the Esophagus, 1991; mem. editl. bd. Jour. Thoracic and Cardiovascular Surgery, Annals of Surgery; contbr. profl. jours., chpts. in books. Elder Fourth Presbyn. Ch., Chgo., 1976-87, clk. of session, 1978-82, 84-87; bd. visitors Cornell U. Med. Coll., 1980-87. Served to maj. M.C. USAF, 1966-68. Decorated Chevalier Nat. Order of Merit (France); John and Mary Markle scholar acad. medicine, 1969-74. Fellow ACS; mem. AMA, Internat. Surg. Group, Am., Western, So. Surg. Assns., Soc. Univ. Surgeons (pres. 1978-79), Am. Soc. Artificial Internal Organs (pres. 1977), Soc. Surg. Chmn. (pres. 1980-82), Am. Assn. Thoracic Surgery (coun. 1981-86, pres.-elect 1995-96), Soc. Vascular Surgery, Soc. Thoracic Surgery, Soc. Pelvic Surgeons, Soc. Surgery Alimentary Tract, Soc. Internat. de Chirurgie, Collegium Internat. de Chirurgie Digestivae, Am. Coll. Chest Physicians, Ctrl. Surg. Soc., Internat. Soc. Diseases Esophagus (pres. 1992-95), Assn. Acad. Surgery, Halsted Soc., Soc. Clin. Surgery (pres. 1986-88), Phi Beta Kappa, Alpha Omega Alpha. Clubs: Quadrangle (Chgo.); Cosmos (Washington); University (N.Y.C.); River (N.Y.C.). Home: 79 E 79th St New York NY 10021-0202 Office: Soc NY Hosp Office Pres 525 E 68th St New York NY 10021-4873

SKINNER, G(EORGE) WILLIAM, anthropologist, educator; b. Oakland, Calif., Feb. 14, 1925; s. John James and Eunice (Engle) S.; m. Carol Bagger, Mar. 25, 1951 (div. Jan. 1970); children: Geoffrey Crane, James Lauriston, Mark Williamson, Jeremy Burr; m. Susan Mann, Apr. 26, 1980; 1 dau., Alison Jane. Student, Deep Springs (Calif.) Coll., 1942-43; B.A. with distinction in Far Eastern Studies, Cornell U., Ithaca, N.Y., 1947, Ph.D. in Cultural Anthropology, 1954. Field dir. Cornell U. S.E. Asia program, also Cornell Research Center, Bangkok, Thailand, 1951-55; rsch. assoc. in Indonesia, 1956-58; asso. prof., then prof. anthropology Cornell U., Ithaca, N.Y., 1960-65; asst. prof. sociology Columbia, 1958-60; sr. specialist in residence East-West Ctr. Honolulu, 1965-66; prof. anthropology Stanford, 1966-89; Barbara Kimball Browning prof. humanities and scis., 1987-89; prof. anthropology U. Calif., Davis, 1990—; vis. prof. U. Pa., 1977, Duke U., spring 1978, Keio U., Tokyo, spring 1985, fall 1988, U. Calif.-San Diego, fall 1986; field rsch. China, 1949-50, 77, S.E. ASia, 1950-51, Thailand, 1951-53, 54-55, Java and Borneo, 1956-58, Japan, 1985, 88, 95; mem. joint com. on contemporary China Social Sci. Research Coun.-Am. Acad. Learned Socs., 1961-65, 80-81, internat. com. on Chinese studies, 1963-64, mem. joint com. on Chinese studies, 1981-83; mem. subcom. rsch. Chinese Soc. Social Sci. Rsch. Coun., 1961-70, chmn., 1963-70; dir. program on East Asian Local Systems, 1969-71; dir. Chinese Soc. Bibliography Project, 1964-73; assoc. dir. Cornell China Program, 1961-63; dir. London-Cornell Project Social Rsch., 1962-65; mem. com. on scholarly communication with People's Republic of China, Nat. Acad. Scis., 1966-70, mem. social scis. and humanities panel, 1982-83; mem. adv. com. Ctr. for Chinese Rsch. Materials, Assn. Rsch. Libraries, 1967-70; mem. policy and planning com. China in Time and Space, 1993—. Author: Chinese Society in Thailand, 1957, Leadership and Power in the Chinese Community of Thailand, 1958; also articles; Editor: The Social Sciences and Thailand, 1956, Local, Ethnic and National Loyalties in Village Indonesia, 1959, Modern Chinese Society: An Analytical Bibliography, 3 vols, 1973, (with Mark Elvin) The Chinese City Between Two Worlds, 1974, (with A. Thomas Kirsch) Change and Persistence in Thai Society, 1975, The City in Late Imperial China, 1977, The Study of Chinese Society, 1979. Served to ensign USNR, 1943-46. Fellow Center for Advanced Study in Behavioral Scis., 1969-70; Guggenheim fellow, 1969; NIMH spl. fellow, 1970. Mem. NAS, AAAS, Am. Anthrop. Assn., Am. Sociol. Assn., Assn. Asian Studies (bd. dirs. 1962-65, chmn. nominating com. 1967-68, pres. 1983-84), Soc. for Cultural Anthropology, Internat. Union for Sci. Study of Population, Social Sci. History Assn., Am. Ethnol. Soc., Population Assn. Am., Siam Soc., Soc. Qing Studies, Soc. Econ. Anthropology, Phi Beta Kappa, Sigma Xi. Office: Dept Anthropology U Calif Davis CA 95616

SKINNER, HARRY BRYANT, orthopaedic surgery educator; b. Cleve., Oct. 13, 1943; s. Harry Bryant and Marion (Eastlick) S. BS, Alfred U., 1965; MS, PhD, U. Calif., Berkeley, 1970; MD, Med. U. S.C., 1975. Asst. prof. Youngstown (Ohio) State U., 1970-71; postdoctoral research assoc. Clemson (S.C.) U., 1971-72; lectr. Calif. State U., Sacramento, 1977-79; asst./assoc. prof. Tulane U., New Orleans, 1979-82; assoc. prof. orthopaedic surgery U. Calif., San Francisco, 1983-86, prof., 1986-94; prof. mech. engring. U. Calif., Berkeley, 1993—; chair grad. group U. Calif., Berkeley and San Francisco; prof., chmn. dept. orthopedic surgery U. Calif., Irvine, 1994—, prof. mech. and aerospace engring. Engring. Sch., 1995—; adj. asst./assoc. prof. Sch. Engring., Tulane U., New Orleans, 1979-82; dir. rehab. research and devel. VA Med. Ctr., San Francisco, 1983—. Mem. editorial bd. Orthopaedics jour., 1984-88, guest editor, 1985, Jour. Biomed. Materials Research, 1983—; contbr. articles to profl. jours. Grantee NIH, 1978-84, Nat. Inst. Dental Rsch., 1978-84, VA, 1978—, Schleider Found., 1980-82, Am. Fedn. Aging Rsch., 1986-89. Fellow ACS, Am. Acad. Orthopaedic Surgeons; mem. Orthopaedic Rsch. Soc., Soc. for Biomaterials (charter), Am. Orthopaedic Assn., The Hip Soc., Sigma Xi. Office: U Calif Dept Orthopaedic Surgery 29A 101 City Dr S Orange CA 92668

SKINNER, JAMES LAURISTON, chemist, educator; b. Ithaca, N.Y., Aug. 17, 1953; s. G. William and Carol (Bagger) S.; m. Wendy Moore, May 31, 1986; children: Colin Andrew, Duncan Geoffrey. AB, U. Calif., Santa Cruz, 1975; PhD, Harvard U., 1979. Rsch. assoc. Stanford (Calif.) U., 1980-81; from asst. prof. to prof. chemistry Columbia U., N.Y.C., 1981-90; Hirschfelder prof. chemistry U. Wis., Madison, 1990—; vis. scientist Inst. Theol. Physics U. Calif., Santa Barbara, 1987; vis. prof. physics U. Jos. Fourier, Grenoble, France, 1987. Contbr. articles to profl. jours. Recipient Fresenius award Phi Lambda Upsilon, 1989, Camille and Henry Dreyfus Tchr.-Scholar award, 1984, NSF Presdl. Young Investigator award, 1984, Humboldt Sr. Scientist award, 1993; NSF grad fellow, 1975, NSF postdoctoral fellow, 1980, Alfred P. Sloan Found. fellow, 1984, Guggenheim fellow, 1993. Mem. AAAS, Am. Chem. Soc., Am. Phys. Soc. Achievements include fundamental research in condensed phase theoretical chemistry. Office: U Wis Dept Chemistry Theoretical Chem Inst 1101 University Ave Madison WI 53706-1322

SKINNER, KNUTE RUMSEY, poet, English educator; b. St. Louis, Apr. 25, 1929; s. George Rumsey and Lidi (Skjoldvig) S.; m. Jeanne Pratt; 1953; divorced 1954; 1 child, Frank; m. Linda Kuhn, Mar. 30, 1961 (div. Sept. 1977); children: Dunstan, Morgan; m. Edna Kiel, Mar. 25, 1978. Student, Culver-Stockton Coll., 1947-49; B.A., U. No. Colo., 1951; M.A., Middlebury Coll., 1954; Ph.D., U. Iowa, 1958. Instr. English U. Iowa, Iowa City, 1955-56, 57-58, 60-61; asst. prof. English Okla. Coll. for Women, 1961-62; lectr. creative writing Western Wash. U., Bellingham, 1962-71; asso. prof. English Western Wash. U., 1971-73, prof. English, 1973—; pres. Signpost Press Inc., nonprofit corp., 1983-95. Author: Stranger with a Watch, 1965, A Close Sky Over Killaspuglonane, 1968, 75, In Dinosaur Country, 1969, The Sorcerers: A Laotian Tale, 1972, Hearing of the Hard Times, 1981, The Flame Room, 1983, Selected Poems, 1985, Learning to Spell "Zucchini," 1988, The Bears and Other Poems, 1991, What Trudy Knows and Other Poems, 1994; editor: Bellingham Rev., 1977-83, 93-95; contbr. poetry, short stories to anthologies, textbooks, periodicals. Nat. Endowment for the Arts fellow, 1975. Mem. Am. Conf. Irish Studies, Wash. Poets Assn. Office: Western Washington U HU 323 Bellingham WA 98225-9055

SKINNER, NANCY JO, municipal recreation executive; b. Ogallala, Nebr., Nov. 5, 1956; d. Dale Warren Skinner and Beverly Jane (Fister) Berry. AA, Platte Community Coll., 1977; BS, U. Ariz., 1981; MBA, U. Phoenix, 1990; diploma, Nat. Exec. Devel. Sch., 1992. Cert. leisure profl. Sports specialist YWCA, Tucson, 1981, asst. dir. summer day camp, 1981, dir. health, phys. edn. and recreation, 1981-82; sr. recreation specialist Pima County Parks and Recreation Dept., Tucson, 1983, recreation program coord., 1983-90; recreation coord. III Phoenix Parks, Recreation and Libr. Dept., 1990-94, recreation supr., 1994—; labor mgmt. quality of work life rep. Pima County Govt., 1987; dist. coord. Atlantic Richfield Co. Jesse Owens Games, Tucson, 1986-89; adv. Pima County Health Dept. Better Health Through Self Awareness, 1982-83. Dir. tournament Sportsman Fund-Send a Kid to Camp, Tucson, 1984, 85, 86; mem. labor mgmt. quality of working life com. Pima County Govt., 1987; dist. coord. Nat. Health Screening Coun., Tucson, 1982-85; event coord. Tucson Women's Commn. Saguaro Classic, 1984; com. mem. United Way, Tucson, 1982-83; panelist Quality Conf. City of Phoenix, 1992. Musco/APRf Grad. scholar; recipient City of Phoenix Excellence award, 1994. Mem. Nat. Recreation and Parks Assn., Ariz. Parks and Recreation Assn. (cert., treas. dist. IV 1987, pres. 1988, 89, state treas. 1990, pub. rels. chair 1993, Tenderfoot award 1984, co-chair state conf. ednl. program com. 1995), Delta Psi Kappa. Democrat. Methodist. Avocations: music, reading, travel, tennis, golf. Office: Phoenix Pks Recreation & Libr Dept 3901 W Glendale Ave Phoenix AZ 85051-8132

SKINNER, PATRICIA MORAG, state legislator; b. Glasgow, Scotland, Dec. 3, 1932; d. John Stuart and Frances Charlotte (Swann) Robertson; m. Robert A. Skinner, Dec. 28, 1957; children: Robin Ann, Pamela. BA, NYU, 1953. Mdse. trainee Lord & Taylor, N.Y.C., 1955-59; adminstrv. asst. Atlantic Products, N.Y.C., 1954-59; newspaper corr. Salem Observer, N.H., 1964-84; mem. N.H. Ho. of Reps., 1973-94, chmn. labor, human resources and rehab. com., 1975-86, House Edn. Com., 1987, chmn., 1989-94, exec. com. Nat. Conf. State Legislatures, 1987-90; chmn. N.H. Adv. Council Unemployment Compensation, 1984-94. Bd. dirs. chmn. Castle Jr. Coll., 1975, chmn. bd., 1988—; v.p. bd. Swift Water council Girl Scouts U.S., v.p. 1987-92; mem. chmn. coun. N.H. Voc-Tech. Coll., Nashua, 1978-83; trustee Nesmith Library, Windham, N.H., 1982—, chmn. bd. trustees, 1994. Mem. N.H. Fedn. Women's Clubs (parliamentarian, legis chmn. 1984—), N.H. Fedn. Republican Women's Clubs (pres. 1979-82). Christian Scientist. Club: Windham Woman's (pres. 1981-83). Lodge: Order Eastern Star.

SKINNER, PETER GRAEME, publishing executive, lawyer; b. London, Ont., Can., July 27, 1944; came to U.S., 1952; s. George Woodley and Marjorie Grace S. A.B., Princeton U., 1966; J.D., Columbia U., 1970, M.B.A., 1970. Bar: N.Y. 1971. Assoc. Patterson, Belknap, Webb & Tyler, N.Y.C., 1970-77; ptnr. Patterson, Belknap, Webb & Tyler, 1977-85; sr. v.p., gen. counsel, sec. Dow Jones & Co., N.Y.C., 1985-95; pres. Dow Jones TV, N.Y.C., 1995—. Mem. ABA, N.Y. State Bar Assn., Assn. Bar City N.Y. Office: Dow Jones & Co Inc 200 Liberty St New York NY 10281-1003*

SKINNER, SAMUEL KNOX, utilities executive, lawyer; b. Chgo., June 10, 1938; s. Vernon Orlo and Imelda Jane (Curran) S.; m. Mary Jacobs, 1989; children: Thomas, Steven, Jane. B.S., U. Ill., 1960; J.D., DePaul U., 1966. Bar: Ill. 1966. Asst. U.S. atty. No. Dist. Ill., Chgo., 1968-74, 1st asst. U.S. atty., 1974-75, U.S. atty., 1975-77; ptnr. Sidley & Austin, Chgo., 1977-89; chmn. Regional Transp. Authority, Chgo., 1984; U.S. sec. of transp., 1989-91; chief of staff White House, Washington, 1991-92; gen. chmn. Republican Nat. Com., Washington, 1992-93; pres. Commonwealth Edison Co., Chgo. Chmn. Ill. Capitol Devel. Bd., 1977-84. Served as 1st lt. U.S. Army, 1960-61. Mem. ABA, Ill. Bar Assn., Chgo. Bar Assn., Chgo. Club, Shoreacres Club. Republican. Presbyterian. Office: Commonwealth Edison Co 1 1st Nat Plz Chicago IL 60603*

SKINNER, STANLEY THAYER, utility company executive, lawyer; b. Fort Smith, Ark., Aug. 18, 1937; s. John Willard and Irma Lee (Peters) S.; m. Margaret Olsen, Aug. 16, 1957; children—Steven Kent, Ronald Kevin. B.A. with honors, San Diego State U., 1960; M.A., U. Calif., Berkeley, 1961, J.D., 1964. Bar: Supreme Ct. Calif. bar 1965, U.S. Circuit Ct. Appeals for 9th Circuit bar 1965, 10th Circuit bar 1966. Atty. Pacific Gas and Electric Co., San Francisco, 1964-73; sr. counsel Pacific Gas and Electric Co., 1973, treas., 1974-76, v.p. fin., 1976, sr. v.p., 1977, exec. v.p., 1978-86, exec. v.p., chief fin. officer, 1982-85, vice chmn. bd., 1986-91, pres., chief oper. officer, 1991-94; pres., CEO Pacific Gas and Electric Co., San Francisco, 1994—, also chmn. bd. dirs.; chmn. bd. dirs., CEO Pacific Gas and Electric Co., 1995—; bd. dirs. Fed. Res. Bank of San Francisco, Pacific Gas Transmission Co. Bd. dirs. United Way of Bay Area, campaign chmn., 1992; trustee, former chmn. bd. dirs. Golden Gate U.; bd. dirs. Bay Area chpt. ARC, Bay Area Coun., Bay Area Econ. Forum. Mem. Calif. State Bar Assn., Calif. State C. of C. (bd. dirs.), San Francisco C. of C. (bd. dirs.), Bus. Coun., Bay Area Coun., Bus. Roundtable, Moraga Country Club. Republican. Presbyterian. Office: Pacific Gas & Electric Co 77 Beale St San Francisco CA 94105-1814

SKINNER, THOMAS, broadcasting and film executive; b. Poughkeepsie, N.Y., Aug. 17, 1934; s. Clarence F. and Frances D. S.; m. Elizabeth Burroughs, June 22, 1957; children: Kristin Jon, Karin Anne, Erik Lloyd. BS, SUNY, Fredonia, 1956; MA, U. Mich., 1957, PhD, 1962. Instr. speech U. Mich., 1960; assoc. prof., exec. producer dept. broadcasting San Diego State U., 1961-66; asst. mgr. Sta. WITF-TV, Hershey, Pa., 1966-70; v.p. Sta. WQED-TV, Pitts., 1970-72; exec. v.p., COO QED Communications Inc. (WQED-TV, WQED-FM, Pittsburgh mag., WQEX-TV), 1972-93; founder, pres., exec. prodr. Windrush Assocs., 1993—. Exec. prodr. spls. and series including (for PBS) Nat. Geog. spls. Planet Earth, The Infinite Voyage, Conserving Am., (for TBS) Pirate Tales, (for A&E) Floating Palaces, Calif. and the Dream Seekers, (for Discovery) Battleship. Recipient award as exec. prodr. DuPont Columbia, 1979, Oscar award as dir. Acad. Motion Picture Arts and Scis., 1967, Emmy award as exec. prodr. Nat. Acad. TV Arts and Scis., 1979, 83-84, 86-87, Peabody award as exec. prodr., 1980, 86. Episcopalian. Address: PO Box 446 Suttons Bay MI 49682-0446

SKINNER, WALTER JAY, federal judge; b. Washington, Sept. 12, 1927; s. Frederick Snowden and Mary Waterman (Comstock) S.; m. Sylvia Henderson, Aug. 12, 1950; 4 children. A.B., Harvard, 1948; J.D., 1952. Bar: Mass. 1952, U.S. Dist. Ct. 1954. Assoc. firm Gaston, Snow, Rice & Boyd, Boston, 1952-57; pvt. practice law Scituate, Mass., 1957-63; asst. dist. atty. Plymouth County, 1957-63; town counsel Scituate, 1957-63; asst. atty. gen., chief Criminal Div., Commonwealth of Mass., 1963-65; mem. firm Wardwell, Allen, McLaughlin & Skinner, Boston, 1965-74; judge U.S. Dist. Ct. of Mass., 1974—; sr. status, 1992—. Bd. dirs. Douglas A. Thom Clinic, 1966-70. Mem. ABA, Mass. Bar Assn., Boston Bar Assn., City Club, Eight O'Clock Club (Newton, Mass.). Office: US Dist Ct US Courthouse 90 Devonshire St Rm 1503 Boston MA 02109

SKINNER, WICKHAM, business administration educator; b. Cin., Feb. 20, 1924; s. Charles Wickham and Ruth (Hargrave) S.; m. Alice Sturges Blackmer, May 18, 1946; children: Polly Gay (Mrs. David Light), Charles Barry. B.Engring., Yale U., 1944; M.B.A., Harvard U., 1948, D.B.A., 1961. Chem. engr. Manhattan project at Los Alamos, 1946-48; with Honeywell Corp., 1948-58, asst. sec., 1957-58; mem. faculty Harvard Grad. Sch. Bus. Adminstrn., 1960-86, prof., 1967-74, James E. Robison prof. bus. adminstrn., 1974-86, asso. dean, 1974-77, dir. div. internat. activities, 1967-70; tchr. Pakistan, France, Vietnam, Australia, Singapore, Turkey, Tunisia, Ital; bd. dirs. Wilevco Corp., Helix Tech. Corp., Somerset Industries, Bath Iron Works. Author: American Industry in Developing Economies, 1968, Manufacturing in Corporate Strategy, 1977, Manufacturing: The Formidable Competitive Weapon, 1985; also articles. Mem. spl. coms. Weston (Mass.) Sch. Com., 1962-64, 64-68; acad. adv. Bunting Inst., Work-in-Am. Inst.; mem. planning com., Wayzata, Minn., 1955-56; pres. Eastern Acad. Mgmt., 1968-69; Candidate for mayor, Wayzata, 1955; bd. dirs. Fla. Philharmonic Orch., 1956-58; bd. dirs. Nat. Resources Council Maine, 1986-93, pres. 1989-92; class agt. Yale Alumni Fund, 1944-69; trustee, treas. Urbana (Ohio) U., 1960-70; trustee Babson Coll., 1981-85, Mass. Audubon Soc., 1983-84; mem. Mfg. Studies Bd. NAS, 1979-84, chmn. 1987-89; bd. dirs. Farnsworth Mus., Rockland, Maine, 1990—, v.p., 1991-94, pres., 1994—. Served with AUS, 1944-46. Recipient McKinsey prize Harvard Bus. Rev., 1986. Fellow Acad. Mgmt.; mem. Ops Mgmt. Assn. (bd. dirs. 1987—). Mem. Swedenborgian Ch. Home: PO Box 282B Saint George ME 04857-9998 Office: Harvard U Bus Sch Soldiers Field Rd Boston MA 02163

SKIPP, TRACY JOHN, academic advisor, counselor; b. Bourne, Mass., Feb. 10, 1966; s. Herbert Bucklin and Nanette Marie (Fisher) S.; m. Karyn Shayann Brennan, Nov. 24, 1986; children: Tracy John Jr., Brennan Ross Anthony, Megan Shaylynn. Paralegal grad., Albuquerque Career Inst., 1989; B cum laude Univ. Studies, U. N.Mex., 1995. Med. asst. pvt. psychiat. practice, Albuquerque, 1987-89; owner Skipp's Legal Support Resources, Albuquerque, 1990-95; academic advisor, counselor U. N.Mex., Albuquerque, 1996—. Co-author, illustrator: The Gift of the Apple, The Birth of a Star. Active Secular Franciscan Order, 1996; sustaining mem. Rep. Nat. Com., Washington, 1988—; rep. gen. honors coun., internat. affairs coun. Associated Stuents U. N.Mex., co-chmn. U. N.Mex. Vol. Svc. Coalition; med. missionary to Mex. St. Mark's United Meth. Ch. of El Paso; participant in 1996 Rolex Awards for Enterprise. Named Man of the Yr., Am. Biog. Inst., 1995; L.B. Reeder scholar, 1992-95, Fulbright scholar Dudley Wynn Honors Ctr., 1996. Fellow Internat. Bio. Assn.(Internat. Order of Merit Award, 1994); assoc. Am. Bio. Inst. (dep. gov., 1994—); mem. Internat. Platform Assn., Am. Freedom Coalition, Nat. Notary Assn., Legal Assts. N.Mex., Nat. Fedn. Paralegal Assn., N.Mex. Acad. Sci., Blue Key, Phi Beta Delta, Phi Delta Kappa. Republican. Roman Catholic. Avocations: reading, making art, writing hypertext software for Macintosh. Office: U New Mex Bachelor Univ Studies Program U Coll Albuquerque NM 87123-1456

SKIPPER, NATHAN RICHARD, JR., lawyer; b. Wilmington, N.C., May 29, 1934; s. Nathan Richard and Mary Dell (Sidbury) S.; m. Barbara Lynn Renton, Sept. 5, 1959 (div. June 1978); children: Nathan Richard III, Valerie Lynne; m. Karen Marie Haughton, Sept. 26, 1987. AB, Duke U., 1956, JD, 1962; AAS, Oakland Community Coll., 1980. Bar: N.Y. 1963, U.S. Dist. Ct. (so. dist.) N.Y. 1964, Mich. 1971, U.S. Dist. Ct. (ea. dist.) Mich. 1979, N.C. 1991. Assoc. Cravath, Swaine & Moore, N.Y.C., 1962-70; counsel financings Ford Motor Co., Dearborn, Mich., 1970-78; gen. counsel, sec. Volkswagen Am., Inc., Troy, Mich., 1978-89, consulting counsel, 1989-91; assoc. Ward and Smith, P.A., New Bern, N.C., 1990-93, ptnr., 1994—. Served to capt. USAF, 1956-59, USAFR, 1962-75. Mem. ABA, SAR, N.C. Bar Assn., Ea. Carolina Yacht Club, Phi Delta Phi. Avocations: photography, boating, tennis. Home: 1108 Country Club Dr New Bern NC 28562-7102

SKIPTUNIS, RAYMOND J., computer science company executive; b. Hazleton, Pa., 1943. CEO, CFO Digital Solutions Inc., South Plainfield, N.J. Mem. Am. Payroll Assn. Office: Digital Solutions Inc 4041 F Hadley Rd South Plainfield NJ 07080*

SKIRNICK, ROBERT ANDREW, lawyer; b. Chgo., Apr. 23, 1938; s. Andrew and Stella (Sanders) S.; children: Rebecca, David; m. Maria Ann Castellano, Oct. 4, 1974; 1 child, Gabriella. BA, Roosevelt U., 1961; JD, U. Chgo., 1966. Bar: U.S. Dist. Ct. (no. dist.) Ill. 1966, U.S. Ct. Appeals (7th cir.) 1968, U.S. Supreme Ct. 1970, U.S. Ct. Appeals (5th and 9th cirs.) 1982, N.Y. 1982, U.S. Ct. Appeals (3d cir.) 1983, U.S. Dist. Ct. (ea. dist.) Mich. 1988, (so. dist. and ea. dist.) N.Y. 1989, U.S. Ct. Appeals (2nd cir.) 1990, U.S. Dist. Ct. (no. dist.) Calif. 1992, U.S. Ct. Appeals (11th Cir.) 1992, U.S. Dist. Ct. (so. dist.) Tex. 1992, U.S. Dist. Ct. Ariz. 1993. Atty. office gen. counsel honors program HEW, Washington, 1966-68; ptnr. Fortes, Eiger, Epstein & Skirnick, Chgo., 1975-77, Much, Shelist, Freed, Chgo., 1977-79, Wolf, Popper, Ross, Wolf & Jones, N.Y.C., 1979-87, Kaplan, Kilsheimer & Foley, N.Y.C., 1988-89, Wechsler, Skirnick, Harwood, Halebian & Feffer, N.Y.C., 1989-95, Lovell & Skirnick, LLP, N.Y.C., 1995—; instr. NYU, 1979-80; cons. Nat. Legal Aid and Def. Assn., Chgo., 1968-69; spl. asst. atty. gen. Ill. Atty Gen. Office, Chgo., 1972-73; spl. antitrust counsel State of Conn., 1976-77; mem. adv. bd. Small Bus. Legal Def. Commn., San Francisco, 1982—; lectr. Practicing Law Inst., N.Y.C., 1986-87; spl. master So. Dist. N.Y., 1988-91. Author: (with others) Federal Subject Matter Jurisdiction of U.S. District Courts, Federal Civil Practice, 1974, Antitrust Class Actions-Twenty Years Under Rule 23, 1986, The State Court Class Action-A Potpourri of Difference in the ABA Forum, Summer 1985; contbg. author: Multiparty Bargaining in Class Actions, Attourneys' Practice Guide to Negotiations, 2d edit., 1996; bd. editors Ill. Bar Antitrust Newsletter, 1969-73' topic & articles editor Jour. Forum Com. on Franchising, 1981-86. Atty. Office Gen. Counsel Honors Program, U.S. Dept. HEW, 1966-68; chmn. Ill. Legis. Com. Antitrust Section Ill. Bar., 1970-71; Topic and Articles Editor, Jour. Forum Com. on Franchising, 1981-86; mem., bd. dirs., Nat. Assn. for Pub. Interest Law fellowships, Washington, 1991—, v.p., 1994—. Mem. ABA (co-chair securities law subcom., litigation sect. 1987, com. on futures regulation, forum com. on franchising), ATLA, Fed. Bar Coun. (com. on second cir cts. 1983-86), N.Y. State Bar Assn. (class action com.), N.Y. State Trial Lawyers Assn., Ill. Bar Assn. (chmn. antitrust sect. Ill. legis. com. 1970-71), Nat. Assn. for Pub. Interest Law Fellowships (mem. exec. com., mem. selection com., mem. investment and fin. com., bd. dirs. 1991—, v.p. 1994—), Navy League of U.S. (N.Y. coun., jour. com. 1995—), Plandome Country Club. Office: Lovell & Skirnick 63 Wall St New York NY 10005

SKLANSKY, JACK, electrical and computer engineering educator, researcher; b. N.Y.C., Nov. 15, 1928; s. Abraham and Clara S.; m. Gloria Joy Weiss, Dec. 24, 1957; children: David Alan, Mark Steven, Jeffrey Paul. BEE, CCNY, 1950; MSEE, Purdue U., 1952; D in Engring. Sci., Columbia U., 1955. Research engr. RCA Labs., Princeton, N.J., 1955-65; mgr. Nat. Cash Register Co., Dayton, Ohio, 1965-66; prof. elec. and computer engring. U. Calif., Irvine, 1966—; pres. Scanicon Corp., Irvine, 1980-89. Author: (with others) Pattern Classifiers and Trainable Machines, 1981; editor: Pattern Recognition, 1973, (with others) Biomedical Images and Computers, 1982; editor-in-chief: Machine Vision and Applications, 1987. Recipient best paper award Jour. Pattern Recognition, 1977; rsch. grantee NIH, 1971-84, Army Rsch. Office, 1984-91, NSF, 1992—, Office of Naval

Rsch., 1995—. Fellow IEEE, Internat. Assn. for Pattern Recognition; mem. ACM. Office: U Calif Dept Elec & Computer Engring Irvine CA 92717

SKLAR, ALEXANDER, electric company executive, educator; b. N.Y.C., May 18, 1915; s. David and Bessie (Wolf) S.; student Cooper Union, N.Y.C., 1932-35; M.B.A., Fla. Atlantic U., 1976; m. Hilda Rae Gevarter, Oct. 27, 1940; 1 dau., Carolyn Mae (Mrs. Louis M. Taff). Chief engr. Aerovox Corp., New Bedford, Mass., 1933-39; mgr. mfg., engring. Indsl. Condenser Corp., Chgo., 1939-44; owner Capacitron, Inc., 1944-48; exec. v.p. Jefferson Electric Co., Bellwood, Ill., 1948-65; v.p., gen. mgr. electro-mech. div. Essex Internat., Detroit, 1965-67; adviser, dir. various corp., 1968—; vis. prof. mgmt. Fla. Atlantic U., Boca Raton, 1971-92; ret. 1993; lectr. profl. mgmt. U. Calif. at Los Angeles, Harvard Grad. Sch. Bus. Adminstrn., U. Ill. Mem. Acad. Internat. Bus., Soc. Automotive Engrs. Address: 4100 Galt Ocean Dr Fort Lauderdale FL 33308-6002

SKLAR, DORIS ROSLYN, conference planning executive; b. N.Y.C., Feb. 15, 1936; d. Philip and Anna (Donn) S. BA, Hunter Coll., 1957. Sec. GE Co., N.Y.C., 1957-69; exec. sec. Behavioral Sci. Applications, Inc., N.Y.C., 1969-72; conf. planning specialist GE Co., N.Y.C., 1972-76, conf. planning cons., 1976-82, mgr. conf. planning, 1982-96; pres. Sklar Worldwide Meeting Mgmt., N.Y.C., 1996—; adj. asst. prof. mgmt. inst. Sch. Continuing Edn., NYU, 1988-91; speaker in field. Contbr. articles to profl. publs. Recipient Pacesetter award Hospitality and Mktg. Assn. Internat., 1995. Mem. Profl. Conv. Mgmt. Assn., Meeting Profls. Internat., Acad. Women Achievers, Internat. Assn. Conf. Ctrs. (pres.'s coun. 1992—). Avocations: public speaking, ballet.

SKLAR, KATHRYN KISH, historian, educator; b. Columbus, Ohio, Dec. 26, 1939; d. William Edward and Elizabeth Sue (Rhodes) Kish; m. Robert A. Sklar, 1958 (div. 1978); children: Leonard Scott, Susan Rebecca Sklar Friedman; m. Thomas L. Dublin, Apr. 30, 1988. B.A. magna cum laude, Radcliffe Coll., 1965; Ph.D., U. Mich., 1969. Asst. prof., lectr. U. Mich., Ann Arbor, 1969-74; assoc. prof. history UCLA, 1974-81, prof., 1981-88, chmn. com. to administer program in women's studies Coll. Letters and Sci., 1974-81; Disting. Prof. history SUNY, Binghamton, 1988—; Pulitzer juror in history, 1976; fellow Newberry Libr. Family and Community History Seminar, 1973; NEH cons. in women's studies U. Utah, 1977-79, Santa Clara U., 1978-80, Roosevelt U., 1980-82; hist. cons. AAUW; active Calif. Coun. for Humanities, 1981-85, N.Y. Coun. for Humanities, 1992—. Author: Catharine Beecher: A Study in American Domesticity, 1973 (Berkshire prize 1974); editor: Catharine Beecher: A Treatise on Domestic Economy, 1977, Harriet Beecher Stowe: Uncle Tom's Cabin, or Life Among the Lowly: The Minister's Wooing, Oldtown Folks, 1981, Notes of Sixty Years: The Autobiography of Florence Kelley, 1849-1926, 1984, (with Thomas Dublin) Women and Power in American History: A Reader (2 vols.), 1991, (with Linda Kerber and Alice Kessler-Harris) U.S. History as Women's History: New Feminist Essays, 1995; co-editor: The Social Survey Movement in Historical Perspective, 1992, Florence Kelley and the Nation's Work: The Rise of Women's Political Culture, 1830-1900, 1995; mem. editl. bd. Jour. Women's History, 1987—, Women's History Rev., 1990—, Jour. Am. History, 1978-81; contbr. chpts. to books. Fellow Woodrow Wilson Found., 1965-67, Danforth Found., 1967-69, Radcliffe Inst., 1973-74, Nat. Humanities Inst., 1975-76, Rockefeller Found. Humanities, 1981-82, Woodrow Wilson Internat. Ctr. for Scholars, 1982, 1992-93, Guggenheim Found., 1984, Ctr. Advanced Study Behavioral and Social Scis., Stanford U., 1987-88, AAUW, 1990-91; Daniels fellow Am. Antiquarian Soc., 1976, NEH fellow Newberry Library, 1982-83; Ford Found. faculty rsch. grantee, 1973-74; grantee NEH, 1976-78, UCLA Coun. for Internat. and Comparative Studies, 1983. Mem. Am. Hist. Assn. (chmn. com. on women historians 1980-83, v.p. Pacific Coast br. 1986-87, pres. 1987-88), Orgn. Am. Historians (exec. bd. 1983-86, Merle Curti award com. 1978-79, lectr. 1982—), Am. Studies Assn. (coun. mem.-at-large 1978-80), Berkshire Conf. Women Historians, Am. Antiquarian Soc., Phi Beta Kappa. Avocation: photography. Office: SUNY Dept History Binghamton NY 13902

SKLAR, LOUISE MARGARET, service executive; b. L.A., Aug. 12, 1934; d. Samuel Baldwin Smith and Judith LeRoy (Boughton) Nelson; m. Edwynn Edgar Schroeder, Mar. 20, 1955 (div. July 1975); children: Neil Nelson, Leslie Louise Schroeder Grandclaudon, Samuel George; m. Martin Sklar, Oct. 17, 1983. Student, U. So. Calif., 1952-54, UCLA, 1977-79. Acct. Valentine Assocs., Northridge, Calif., 1976-78, programmer, 1978-79; contr. Western Monetary, Encino, Calif., 1979-81; pres. Automated Computer Composition, Chatsworth, Calif., 1984—. Mem. Am. Contract Bridge League (bd. govs. 1993—, mem. nat. charity com. 1982, mem. nat. goodwill com. 1994—), Assn. Los Angeles County Bridge Units (bd. dirs. 1990—, sec. 1984-86), DAR, Conn. Soc. Genealogists, Ky. Hist. Soc., So. Calif. Asistance League, Heart of Am. Geneal. Soc., Chatsworth C. of C., Greater L.A. Zoo Assn., Zeta Tau Alpha. Republican. Avocations: tournament bridge, travel. Office: Automated Computer Composition Inc 21356 Nordhoff St Chatsworth CA 91311-5818

SKLAR, MORTY E., publisher, editor; b. Sunnyside, N.Y., Nov. 28, 1935; s. Jack and Selma (Ehrlich) S.; m. Shelley Joy Sterling, Aug. 17, 1981 (div. 1983); m. Marcela B. Bruno, June 7, 1993; children: Patricio Bruno, Marcos Bruno. BA in English, U. Iowa, 1972. Founding editor, pub. The Spirit That Moves Us Press, Jackson Heights, N.Y., 1974—. Author: The Night We Stood Up For Our Rights, 1977; editor: The Casting of Bells, 1983 (Jaroslav Seifert, Nobel prize 1984). Founder (with others) Phoenix House, N.Y.C., 1966; active Increase the Peace Vol. Corps., N.Y.C., 1992—. With U.S. Army, 1954-56. Mem. PEN, Acad. Am. Poets, Small Press Ctr. Democrat. Jewish. Avocations: photography, reading. Office: The Spirit That Moves Us Press PO Box 720820-WW Jackson Heights NY 11372

SKLAR, RICHARD LAWRENCE, political science educator; b. N.Y.C., Mar. 22, 1930; s. Kalman and Sophie (Laub) S.; m. Eva Molineux, July 14, 1962; children: Judith Anne, Katherine Elizabeth. A.B., U. Utah, 1952; M.A., Princeton U., 1957, Ph.D., 1961; mem. faculty; UCLA. mem. fgn. area fellowship program Africa Nat. Com., 1970-73; Simon vis. prof. U. Manchester, Eng., 1975; Fulbright vis. prof. U. Zimbabwe, 1984; Lester Martin fellow Harry S. Truman Rsch. Inst., Hebrew U. Jerusalem, 1979; fellow Africa Inst. South Africa, 1994—. Mem. faculty Brandeis U., U. Ibadan, Nigeria, U. Zambia; SUNY-Stony Brook; UCLA, now prof. emeritus polit. sci.; mem. fgn. area fellowship program Africa Nat. Com., 1970-73; Simon vis. prof. U. Manchester, Eng., 1975, Fulbright vis. prof. U. Zimbabwe, 1984; Lester Martin fellow Harry S. Truman Rsch. Inst., Hebrew U. Jerusalem, 1979; fellow Africa Inst. of South Africa, 1994—. Author: Nigerian Political Parties: Power in an Emergent African Nation, 1963, Corporate Power in an African State, 1975; co-author: Postimperialism: International Capitalism and Development, 1987, African Politics and Problems in Development, 1991; contbr. articles to profl. jours. Served with U.S. Army, 1952-54. Rockefeller Found. grantee, 1967. Mem. Am. Polit. Sci. Assn., African Studies Assn. (dir. 1976-78, 80-83, v.p. 1980-81, pres. 1981-82), AAUP (pres. Calif. Conf. 1980-81). Home: 1951 Holmby Ave Los Angeles CA 90025-5905

SKLAREN, CARY STEWART, lawyer; b. Bklyn., Sept. 26, 1943; s. Jules Joseph and Florence (Somber) S.; m. Linda Genero, May 25, 1972; children: Robyn Alison, Adam William. BA, NYU, 1964; JD, Fordham U., 1967. Bar: N.Y. 1969, Mich. 1980. Assoc. product liability counsel Bristol-Myers Co., N.Y.C., 1969-79; sr. atty. Ford Mtr. Co., Dearborn, Mich., 1979-81; asst. gen. counsel Am. Mtrs. Corp., Southfield, Mich., 1981-84; ptnr. Herzfeld & Rubin, P.C., N.Y.C., 1984—. Contbr. articles to profl. jours.; author: (with others) Practical Products Liability, 1988, Products Liability, 1989. Capt. U.S. Army, 1967-69. Mem. ABA, Assn. Bar City of N.Y. Home: 851 President St Brooklyn NY 11215-1405 Office: Herzfeld & Rubin PC 40 Wall St New York NY 10005

SKLAREW, ROBERT JAY, biomedical research educator, consultant; b. N.Y.C., Nov. 25, 1941; s. Arthur and Jeanette (Laven) S.; m. Toby Willner, July 15, 1970; children: David Michael, Gary Richard. BA in Zoology, Cornell U., 1963; MS, NYU, 1965, PhD in Biology, 1970. Assoc. rsch. scientist Sch. of Medicine NYU, N.Y.C., 1965-70, rsch. scientist Sch. of Medicine, 1971-73, sr. rsch. scientist Sch. of Medicine, 1973-79; rsch. asst. prof. pathology Sch. of Medicine Goldwater Meml. Hosp., N.Y.C., 1979-87, rsch. assoc. prof. pathology Sch. of Medicine, 1987-88, dir. cytokinetics and imaging lab. NYU Rsch. Svc., 1980-88; prof. cell biology, anatomy and medicine N.Y. Med. Coll., Valhalla, 1988—; rsch. assoc. dept. pathology Lenox Hill Hosp., N.Y.C., 1981-88; pres., CEO R.J. Sklarew Imaging Assoc., Inc., Larchmont, N.Y., 1990—; chmn. consensus panel for diagnostic cancer imaging Nat. Cancer Inst., 1994. Author: Microscopic Imaging of Steroid Receptors, 1990; sr. author: Cytometry, Jour. Histochem. Cytochem., Cancer, Exptl. Cell Rsch. Mem. Beth Emeth Synagogue, Larchmont, 1974—; group leader Boy Scouts Am., Larchmont, 1978-80. Grantee Am. Cancer Soc., Nat. Cancer Inst./NIH Conc. for Tobacco Rsch., R.J. Reynolds Industries Found., NYU; recipient Shannon award Nat. Cancer Inst., 1991. Mem. AAAS, Cell Kinetics Soc. (sec. 1983-85, 85-87, v.p. 1987-88, pres. 1988-89, chmn. nominations 1991, 93), N.Y. Acad. Sci., Soc. for Analytic Cytology, Soc. for Cell Biology, Tissue Culture Assn., Union Concerned Scientists, Kappa Delta Rho. Democrat. Achievements include development of methodology, algorithms and Receptogram analytic software for application of microscopic imaging in medical research and in pathodiagnosis of cancer, imaging methods for simultaneous densitometry and autoradiographic analysis; research in diagnostic imaging of steroid receptors, oncogenes and DNA ploidy in cancer, proliferative patterns and cell cycle kinetics of human solid tumors. Home: 8 Vine Rd Larchmont NY 10538-1247 Office: NY Med Coll Cancer Rsch Inst 100 Grasslands Rd Elmsford NY 10523-1110

SKLARIN, ANN H., artist; b. N.Y.C., May 21, 1933; d. Sidney and Revera (Myers) Hirsch; m. Burton S. Sklarin, June 29, 1960; children: Laurie Sklarin Ember, Richard, Peter. BA in Art History, Wellesley Coll., 1955; MA in Secondary Art Edn., Columbia U., 1956. Art tchr. jr. high sch. N.Y.C. Sch. System, 1956-61, chmn. art. dept. jr. high sch., 1957-61. One-woman shows include Long Beach (N.Y.) Libr., 1973, Silvermine Guild Ctr. Arts, New Canaan, Conn., 1986, Long Beach Mus. Art, 1986, Discovery Art Gallery, Glen Cove, N.Y., 1987—; exhibited in juried shows at Nassau C.C., Garden City, N.Y., 1970, Nassau County (N.Y.) John F. Kennedy Ctr. Performing Arts, 1970 (1st Pl. award 1970), Long Beach Art Assn., 1970 (1st Pl. award 1970), Gregory Mus., 1973-74, L.I. Arts 76, Hempstead, N.Y., 1976, 5 Towns Music and Art Found., Woodmere, N.Y., 1980 (1st Pl. award 1981, Honorable Mention award 1981), 83 (3d Pl. award 1983), 85, Long Beach Art Assn. and Long Beach Mus. Art, 1982 (1st Pl. award 1982), 84, 85 (3d Pl. award 1985), Silvermine Guild Arts, 1984 (Richardson-Vicks Inc. award 1985), 87 (Pepperidge Farm Inc. award 1987), Long Beach Mus. Art, 1985 (Best in Show-Grumbacher award 1985), Heckscher Mus., Huntington, N.Y., 1985, 87, Fine Arts Mus. L.I., Hempstead, 1985, 91, Long Beach Art League and Long Beach Mus. Art, 1986 (2d Pl. award 1986), Wunsch Arts Ctr., Glen Cove, 1986, 87, Smithtown Twp. Arts Coun., St. James, 1989 (Honorable Mention award 1989); exhibited in group shows at Hewlett-Woodmere Libr., 1969, B.J. Spoke Gallery, Port Washington, N.Y., 1985, Shirley Scott Gallery, Southampton, N.Y., 1986, Smithtown Twp. Arts Coun., St. James, N.Y., 1988, 90, N.Y. Inst. Tech., Old Westbury, N.Y., 1989, Dowling Coll., Oakdale, N.Y., 1990, Discovery Art Gallery, 1992, 93, 94, 95, Silvermine Guild Arts Ctr., 1992, Sound Shore Gallery, Stamford, Conn., 1993, Krasdale Foods Gallery, N.Y.C., 1993. Mem. exec. bd. 5 Towns Music & Art Found., 1960—, pres., 1971-74. Mem. Silvermine Guild Artists, Discovery Gallery (artist mem.). Avocations: tennis, jogging, hiking, traveling, reading. Studio: 501 Broadway Lawrence NY 11559-2501

SKLARIN, BURTON S., endocrinologist; b. N.Y.C., Feb. 28, 1932; s. Louis and Molla (Beiser) S.; m. Ann Hirsch, June 29, 1960; children: Laurie, Richard, Peter. A.B., NYU, 1953, M.D., 1957. Diplomate: Am. Bd. Internal Medicine, Am. Bd. Endocrinology and Metabolism. Intern Bellevue Hosp., N.Y.C., 1957-58, resident, 1958-61, asst. vis. clin. physician, 1961—; practice medicine specializing in endocrinology Lawrence, N.Y., 1961—; chief endocrinology St. John's Episcopal Hosp., 1961—, pres. med. staff, 1978-80, also chmn. med. exec. com.; asst. prof. clin. medicine NYU, 1961—, asst. in medicine Univ. Hosp., 1961; endocrinologist, staff physician L.I. Jewish Hosp.; cons. Franklin Gen Hosp. Contbr. articles on endocrinology to profl. publs. Vice pres. bd. trustees Woodmere Acad. Fellow ACP, Am. Coll. Endocrinology, N.Y. Acad. Medicine, Soc. Nuclear Medicine; mem. Nassau County Med. Soc., N.Y. Diabetes Assn., Endocrine Soc., Rockaway Med. Soc. (past pres.), Am. Assn. Clin. Endocrinologists. Home and Office: 501 Broadway Lawrence NY 11559-2501

SKLAROV, DIANE MARIE, nursing administrator, emergency care nurse; b. Chgo., July 18, 1957; d. Edward and Anna Maria (Linehan) S. BSN, Duke U., 1978; MS in Nursing, U. Tex., Houston, 1984. RN, N.C., Tex., Fla.; cert. ACLS provider, trauma nurse core curriculum instr. Staff nurse emergency dept., asst. head nurse Charlotte (N.C.) Meml. Hosp. and Med. Ctr.; staff nurse emergency dept. Hermann Hosp., Houston; mgr. patient care emergency dept. North Miami (Fla.) Med. Ctr.-Parkway Med. Ctr.; adminstrv. ladm, dir. emergency/endoscopy svcs. Miami Heart Inst., Miami Beach, Fla.; adv. com. EMS MDCC. Contbg. author: Trauma Nursing: The Art and Science, 1993. Bd. dirs. Chaminade-Madonna Coll. Prep. Named to Alumni Hall of Fame, Chaminade-Madonna, 1994. Mem. Emergency Nurses Assn. (cert., bd. dirs. Dade-Broward chpt.), Sigma Theta Tau, Kappa Alpha Theta.

SKLARSKY, CHARLES B., lawyer; b. Chgo., June 13, 1946; s. Morris and Sadie (Brenner) S.; m. Elizabeth Ann Hardzinski, Dec. 28, 1973; children: Jacob Daniel, Katherine Gabrielle, Jessica Leah. AB, Harvard U., 1968; JD, U. Wis., 1973. Bar: Wis. 1973, Ill. 1973, U.S. Dist. Ct. (no. dist.) Ill. 1973, U.S. Ct. Appeals (7th cir.) 1978, U.S. Ct. Appeals (2nd cir.) 1986. Asst. states atty. Cook County, Chgo., 1973-78; asst. U.S. atty. U.S. Dist. Ct. (no. dist.) Ill., Chgo., 1978-86; ptnr. Jenner & Block, Chgo., 1986—. Mem. ABA, Chgo. Bar Assn. Office: Jenner & Block 1 E Ibm Plz Chicago IL 60611*

SKLENAR, HERBERT ANTHONY, industrial products manufacturing company executive; b. Omaha, June 7, 1931; s. Michael Joseph and Alice Madeline (Spicka) S.; m. Eleanor Lydia Vincenz, Sept. 15, 1956; children: Susan A., Patricia I. BSBA summa cum laude, U. Omaha, 1952; MBA, Harvard U., 1954. CPA, W.Va. V.p., comptr. Parkersburg-Aetna Corp., W.Va., 1956-63; v.p., dir. Marmac Corp, Parkersburg, 1963-66; mgr. fin. control Boise-Cascade Corp., Idaho, 1966-67; exec. v.p. fin. and adminstrn., sec. Cudahy Co., Phoenix, 1967-72; chmn. bd. dirs., CEO Vulcan Materials Co., Birmingham, Ala., 1972—; bd. dirs. Amsouth Bancorp., Birmingham, Protective Life Corp., Birmingham., Temple-Inland, Inc., Diboll, Tex. Author: (with others) The Automatic Factory: A Critical Examination, 1955. Trustee So. Rsch. Inst., Leadership Birmingham, Leadership Ala.; chmn. bd. trustees Birmingham-So. Coll. Recipient Alumni Achievement award U. Nebr.-Omaha, 1977, cert. merit W.Va. Soc. CPAs, Elizah Watts Sells award AICPA, 1965, Brotherhood award NCCJ, 1993. Mem. Shoal Creek Club, Birmingham Country Club, The Club, Univ. Club N.Y.C., Chgo. Club, Delta Sigma Pi (Leadership award 1952), Omicron Delta Kappa, Phi Kappa Phi, Phi Eta Sigma. Republican. Presbyterian. Home: 2809 Shook Hill Cir Birmingham AL 35223-2618 Office: Vulcan Materials Co 1 Metroplex Dr Birmingham AL 35209-6805

SKLENS, THOMAS, insurance executive. Pres. Sedgwick of N.Y. Office: 1290 6th Ave Lobby 6 New York NY 10104

SKODON, EMIL MARK, diplomat; b. Chgo., Nov. 25, 1953; s. Emil John and Anne (Soltes) S.; m. Dorothea Shaffer, Mar. 6, 1982; children: Catherine Marie, Christine Louise. BA, U. Chgo., 1975, MBA, 1976. Consular officer U.S. Embassy, Bridgetown, Barbados, 1977-79; econ. officer U.S. Embassy, East Berlin, Germany, 1979-81, Office of So. African Affairs, Dept. State, Washington, 1982-84; econ. officer U.S. Embassy, Vienna, Austria, 1984-88, Kuwait City, Kuwait, 1989-91; dep. chief mission U.S. Embassy, Singapore, 1995—; consul gen. U.S. Consulate Gen., Perth, Australia, 1991-94. Mem. Nat. Trust for Hist. Preservation. Avocations: visiting historic sites, good food, spending time with family. Office: US Embassy, 30 Hill St, Singapore 179360, Singapore also: US Embassy Singapore Psc 470 # Dcm FPO AP 96534-0470

SKOGLUND, ELIZABETH RUTH, marriage, child and family counselor; b. Chgo., June 17, 1937; d. Ragnar Emmanuel and Elizabeth Alvera (Benson) S. BA, UCLA, 1959; MA, Pasadena Coll., 1969. Cert. tchr., Calif.; cert. marriage, family and child counselor, Calif. Tchr. Marlborough Sch., Los Angeles, 1959-61; tchr., counselor Glendale (Calif.) High Sch., 1961-72; pvt. practice family counseling Burbank, Calif., 1972—. Author: over 20 books including It's OK to Be a Woman Again, 1988, Making Bad Times Good, 1991, Safety Zones, 1991, Harold's Dog Horace is Scared of the Dark, 1992, The Welcoming Hearth, 1993, Amma: The Life and Words of Amy Carmichael, 1994. Mem. Calif. Assn. Marriage and Family Therapists, Simon Wiesenthal Ctr. Republican. Avocations: photography, miniatures, cooking.

SKOGLUND, JOHN C., former professional football team executive. Former treas., chmn. bd., bd. dirs. Minn. Vikings Ventures, Inc.; chmn. Minn. Vikings Football Club; chmn. bd., pres. Skoglund Comms., Inc., Duluth, Minn. Office: Minn Vikings 9520 Viking Dr Eden Prairie MN 55344-3825*

SKOGMAN, DALE R., bishop. Bishop No. Great Lakes Synod, Marquette, Mich. Address: Evangelical Lutheran Church 1029 N 3rd St Marquette MI 49855-3509

SKOL, MICHAEL, financial consultant; b. Chgo., Oct. 15, 1942; s. Ted and Rebecca (Williams) S.; m. Claudia Serwer, Sept. 29, 1973. BA, Yale U., 1964. U.S. fgn. svc. officer Dept. State, 1965-96; polit. officer U.S. Embassy, Buenos Aires, 1966-67, Saigon, Viet Nam, 1968-70; desk officer Dept. State, Washington, 1970-72; comml. attache U.S. Embassy, Santo Domingo, Dominican Republic, 1972-75; econ. comml. officer U.S. Consulate Gen., Naples, Italy, 1975-76; comml. attache U.S. Embassy, Rome, 1976-78; polit. counselor U.S. Embassy, San Jose, Costa Rica, 1978-82; dep. dir. policy planning Inter-Am. Affairs Bur. Dept. State, Washington, 1982-85; dep. chief of mission U.S. Embassy, Bogota, Colombia, 1985-87; dir. Andean affairs Dept. State, Washington, 1987-88; dep. asst. sec. state for S. Am. U.S. Dept. of State, Washington, 1988-90; amb. U.S. Embassy, Caracas, Venezuela, 1990-93; prin. dep. asst. sec. for Latin Am./Caribbean Dept. State, Washington, 1993-96; sr. v.p. Diplomatic Resolutions, Inc., Washington, 1996—. Mem. Yale Club of Colombia, Yale Club of Venezuela, Yale Club of Washington, Yale Club of N.Y. Home: 3033 Cleveland Ave NW Washington DC 20008-3532 Office: 1420 16th St NW Washington DC 20036

SKOLAS, JOHN ARGYLE, lawyer; b. Westby, Wis., June 18, 1952; s. Argyle Carlyle and Ardys Margaret (Trygestad) S.; m. Joan Larson, Apr. 21, 1979. BA, Luther Coll., 1974; JD, U. Wis., 1977; MBA, Harvard U., 1988. Bar: Wis. 1977, Minn. 1977; CPA, Iowa. Tax specialist Coopers & Lybrand, Mpls., 1977-78; assoc. Johns, Flaherty & Gillette, LaCrosse, Wis., 1979-80; assoc. to ptnr. Muchin, Muchin, Bendix & Skolas, Manitowoc, Wis., 1980-86; v.p., legal counsel N.Am. THORN EMI Inc., Boston, 1988-91; pres., corp. officer the Ams. THORN EMI Inc., Boston, Wilmington, Del., 1992—. Dir. Planned Parenthood, Manitowoc, 1984-86; deacon Faith Luth. Ch., Valders, Wis., 1984-86, St. Paul Luth. Ch., Arlington, Mass., 1991-92. Mem. Minn. Bar Assn., Wis. Bar Assn. Avocations: running, drawing, reading, travel. Office: Thorn EMI N Am Holdings 2751 Centerville Rd Ste 205 Wilmington DE 19808-1627*

SKOLER, DANIEL LAWRENCE, lawyer, judge, educator; b. Newark, Jan. 15, 1929; s. Arthur Emil and Marian June (Bardack) S.; m. Shirley Weiss, Sept. 20, 1953; children—Glen David, Michael James, Deborah. Student Rutgers U., 1945-47, U. Chgo., 1947-49; J.D. cum laude, Harvard U., 1952. Bar: N.Y. 1953, Ill. 1963, D.C. 1968. Assoc. Willkie Farr Gallagher Walton & Fitzgibbon, N.Y.C., 1955-59; staff atty. U.S. Industries, Inc., N.Y.C., 1959-61; asst. dir. Am. Judicature Soc., Chgo., 1961-62; exec. dir. Nat. Council Juvenile Ct. Judges, Chgo., 1962-65; dir. Commn. on Correctional Facilities and Services ABA, 1971-75, Commn. on Mentally Disabled, Washington, 1976-77; dir. public service activities ABA, 1977-80; dir. office law enforcement assistance Law Enforcement Assistance Adminstrn., Dept. Justice, Washington, 1965-71; vis. fellow Nat. Inst. Law Enforcement and Criminal Justice, 1975-76; chmn. Trademark and Appeal Bd., Dept. Commerce, Washington, 1982-84, dep. asst. commr. for Trademarks, 1984-86 ; dep. assoc. commr. Hearings and Appeals, Social Security Adminstrn., Washington, 1980-82; adj. prof. Georgetown U., George Washington U., American U., D.C. Law Sch., Washington & Lee Law Sch.; mem. Commn. on Accreditation for Corrections, 1974-78, chmn., 1976-77. Dir. Edn. and training Fed. Jud. Ctr., 1986-91. Fellow Nat. Acad. Public Adminstrn.; mem. ABA Commn. on Legal Problems of the Elderly, 1981-86; assoc. commr. hearings and appeals Social Security Adminstrn., 1991-95; bd. dir. ABA sect. Individual Rights & Responsibilities and Govt. Lawyers Divsn.; bd. dir. Nat. Ctr. on Children and the Law; mem. U.S. Adminstrv. Conf. Author: Organizing the Non System: Government Structuring of Criminal Justice Services, 1977. Home: 7036 Buxton Ter Bethesda MD 20817-4404 Office: Social Security Administration 5107 Leesburg Pike Falls Church VA 22041-3234

SKOLER, LOUIS, architect, educator; b. Utica, N.Y., Apr. 5, 1920; s. Harry and Etta (Mitkoff) S.; m. Celia Rebecca Stern, 1952; children: Elisa Anne, Harry Jay. BArch, Cornell U., 1951. Maj. designer Sargent, Webster, Crenshaw & Folley, Syracuse, N.Y., 1951-59; design critic Cornell U., Ithaca, N.Y., 1956-57; pvt. practice architecture, Syracuse, 1956-69; faculty, Sch. Architecture Syracuse (N.Y.) U., 1959-92, prof. emeritus, 1990—; head of Masters in Architecture I Program, 1980-82, head undergrad. program, 1989-90, architecture programs abroad, London, 1977, Scandinavia, 1985, Japan, 1988; ptnr. Architects Partnership, Syracuse, 1969-71; pres. Skoler & Lee Architects, P.C., Syracuse, 1971-89; lectr. Nanjing Inst. Tech., China, 1986; arbitrator Am. Arbitration Assn., 1980—. Named Best in Residential Design, Design-in-Steel, 1968-69. Mem. AIA. Home: 213 Scottholm Ter Syracuse NY 13224-1737 *A guiding principle over many years of teaching and practice, is the interrelationship of theory and work-of idea and circumstance, of imagination and the forces generated by day to day life.*

SKOLFIELD, MELISSA T., government official; b. New Orleans, June 25, 1958; m. Frank W. Curtis. BA in Econ. and Behavioral Sci., Rice U., 1980; MA in Pub. Affairs, George Washington U., 1986. Account exec. McDaniel & Tate Pub. Rels., Houston, 1981-84; press sec. Rep. Michael Andrews of Tex., 1985-87; press sec. Senator Dale Bumpers of Ark., 1987-93; dep. asst. sec. for pub. affairs for policy and strategy Dept. Health and Human Svcs., Washington, 1993-95, asst. sec. pub. affairs, 1995—. Press asst. Dem. Nat. Com., Dem. Nat. Conv., 1988, Clinton Pres. Campaign, Dem. Nat. Com., 1992. Mem. Senate Press Secs. Assn. (pres.), Assn. Dem. Press Assts., Pub. Rels. Soc. Am. Office: Dept Health & Human Svcs 200 Indendence Ave SW Washington DC 20201

SKOLNICK, MALCOLM HARRIS, biophysics researcher, educator, patent lawyer, mediator; b. Salt Lake City, Aug. 11, 1935; s. Max Cantor and Charlotte Sylvia (Letman) S.; m. Lois Marlene Ray, Sept. 1, 1959; children: Michael, David, Sara, Jonathan. BS in Physics (with honors), U. Utah, 1956; MS in Physics, Cornell U., 1959, PhD in Theoretical Nuclear Physics, 1963; JD, U. Houston, 1986. chmn. health care tech. study sect. Nat. Ctr. Health Svcs. Rsch. HHS, 1975-79; editl. assocs. Cts., Health Sci. and Law, Washington, 1989-93; bd. dirs. Medquest Svcs., Inc., Biodyne, Inc. Staff scientist Elem. Sci. Study, Watertown, Mass., 1962-63; mem. Inst. for Advanced Study, Princeton, N.J., 1963-64; instr. Physics Dept. MIT, Cambridge, Mass., 1964-65; staff scientist dir. Edn. Devel. Ctr., Watertown, 1965-67; assoc. prof. physics Physics Dept. SUNY, Stony Brook, 1967-70; assoc. prof. dir. comm. Health Sci. Ctr. SUNY, Stony Brook, 1968-71; prof. biophysics grad. sch. biomed. sci. U. Tex. Health Sci. Ctr., Houston, 1971-94, prof. biomedical comm., 1971-83, prof. health svcs. rsch., 1988-95, dir. neurophysiology rsch. ctr., 1985-91; prof. tech. and health law U. Tex. Sch. Pub. Health, 1994—; dir. office tech. mgmt. U. Tex. Health Sci. Ctr., Houston, 1991-96; chmn. healt care tech. study sect. Nat. Ctr. Health Svcs. Rsch. HHS, 1975-79; editorial assoc. Cts., Health Sci. and Law, Washington, 1989-93; bd. dirs. Medquest, Inc. Patentee in field; contbr. numerous articles to profl. jours. With USNR, 1953-61, hon. discharge. Recipient Silver Beaver award Boy Scouts Am., 1978; Ford Found. scholar, U. Utah, 1952; rsch. grantee Nat. Inst. for Drug Abuse. Mem. ABA, IEEE, Soc. Neurosci., Licensing Exec. Soc., Am. Intellectual Property Law Assn., Tex. Tech. Transfer Assn. (bd. dirs.), Houston Intellectual Property Law Assn., Houston Soc. Engring. in Medicine and Biology (bd. dirs.), Am. Soc. Law and Medicine, S.W. Assn. Biotech. Cos. (bd. dirs.), Soc. Accident Reconstrn., Tex. Empowerment Network (pres., bd. dirs.), Assoc. Univ. Tech. Mgrs. Office: Univ Tex Health Sci Ctr Sch Pub Health Rm 342 Box 20186 Houston TX 77225

SKOLNICK, MARK HENRY, research geneticist, medical biophysics educator; b. Temple, Tex., Jan. 28, 1946; married, 1970; 2 children. BA, U. Calif., Berkeley, 1968; PhD in Genetics, Stanford U., 1975. Asst. rsch. prof. U. Utah, Salt Lake City, 1974-76, asst. prof. med. biophysics and computers, 1976—, adj. asst. prof. biology, 1978—; mem. Internat. Union Sci. Study of Population, 1976—; dir. divsn. health Utah State Dept Social Svc., 1977—; mem. nat. cancer inst. NIH, 1978—. NIH rsch. grantee, 1974-81, 76-80, 77-80, 79—; pub. health grantee, 1976-81. Mem. Am. Soc. Human Genetics. Office: U Utah 50 N Medical Dr Salt Lake City UT 84132-0001*

SKOLNIK, BARNET DAVID, entrepreneur; b. N.Y.C., Feb. 8, 1941; s. Jack and Edythe (Savitz) S.; children: Sarah, Deborah, Daniel, Joseph, Benjamin, Rebecca. AB in Am. Govt. cum laude, Harvard U., 1962, LLB, 1965. Bar: D.C. 1966, Md. 1984, Maine 1991. Atty. criminal div. U.S. Dept. Justice, Washington, 1966-68; asst. U.S. atty. for Dist. Md., Balt., 1968-78; chief public corruption unit U.S. Atty.'s Office, Balt., 1973-78; pvt. practice law Washington, 1978-83, 89-91, Balt., 1983-89, Portland, Maine, 1991-94; entrepreneur Maine, 1994—; tchr., lectr. on trial practice, white collar criminality, public corruption. Recipient Spl. Achievement award Dept. Justice, 1972, 74, Spl. Commendation for Outstanding Svc., Dept. Justice, 1978, Younger Fed. Lawyer award Fed. Bar Assn., 1974, Atty. Gen.'s Disting. Service award, 1974, Legal award Assn. Fed. Investigators, 1977. Home and Office: 12 Hunts Point Rd Cape Elizabeth ME 04107-2903

SKOLNIK, MERRILL I., electrical engineer; b. Balt., Nov. 6, 1927; s. Samuel and Mary (Baker) S.; m. Judith Magid, June 4, 1950; children: Norma Jean, Martin Allen, Julia Anne, Ellen Charlotte. BEng, Johns Hopkins U., 1947, MSEng, 1949, DEng, 1951. Research scientist Johns Hopkins U., Balt., 1947-54; vis. prof. Johns Hopkins U., 1973-74; engring. specialist Sylvania Electric, Boston, 1954; staff mem. MIT Lincoln Lab., Lexington, Mass., 1954-59; research mgr. Electronic Communications, Timonium, Md., 1959-64, Inst. Def. Analyses, Arlington, Va., 1964-65; supr. radar div. Naval Research Lab., Washington, 1965-96, radar sys. cons., 1996—; mem. bd. visitors Duke U. Engring. Sch., Durham, N.C., 1976-93; disting. vis. sci. Jet Propulsion Lab., 1990-92; mem. Md. Gov.'s Exec. Adv. Com., 1993-95. Author: Introduction to Radar Systems, 1962, 2d edit., 1980, Radar Handbook, 1970, 2d edit., 1990; editor: Radar Applications, 1988. Recipient Heinrich Hertz premium Instn. Electronic and Radio Engrs., London, 1964, Disting. Civilian Service award U.S. Navy, 1982; Meritorious Exec. award Sr. Exec. Service, 1986; Disting. Alumnus award Johns Hopkins U., 1979; named to Soc. of Scholars, Johns Hopkins U., 1975. Fellow IEEE (editor Proceedings 1986-89, Harry Diamond award 1983, Centennial medal 1984); mem. Nat. Acad. Engring. Home: 8123 McDonogh Rd Baltimore MD 21208-1005 Office: Naval Rsch Lab Washington DC 20375

SKOLNIKOFF, EUGENE B., political science educator; b. Phila., Aug. 29, 1928; s. Benjamin H. and Betty (Turoff) S.; m. Winifred S. Weinstein, Sept. 15, 1957; children: David, Matthew, Jessica. B.S., M.I.T., 1950, M.S., 1950, Ph.D., 1965; B.A., Oxford (Eng.) U., 1952, M.A., 1955. Registered profl. engr. Rsch. asst. in elec. engring. Uppsala U., Sweden, 1950; prof. polit. sci. M.I.T., 1965—, chmn. polit. sci. dept., 1970-74; dir. Center for Internat. Studies, 1972-87; vis. rsch. prof. Carnegie Endowment for Internat. Peace, Geneva, 1969-70; vis. fellow Balliol Coll., U. Oxford, 1989; systems analyst Inst. for Def. Analyses, Washington, 1957-58; mem. White House staff Office Spl. Asst. to Pres. for Sci. and Tech., Washington, 1958-63; adj. prof. Fletcher Sch. Law and Diplomacy, Tufts U., Medford, Mass., 1965-72; sr. cons. White House Office of Sci. and Tech. Policy, 1977-81, also vice chmn. adv. com. on sci., tech. and devel.; mem. policy rev. com. on nat. low-level nuclear waste mgmt., 1980-86; cons. Dept. State, Office of Tech. Assessment, AID, OECD, Resources for the Future, Am. Soc. Internat. Law, Ford Found., Inst. Def. Analyses; chmn., pres. Sci. and Public Policy Studies Group, 1967-73; mem. Internat. Council Sci. Policy Studies; Montague Burton vis. prof. U. Edinburgh, 1977. Author: Science, Technology and American Foreign Policy, 1967, International Imperatives of Technology, 1972, The Elusive Transformation: Science, Technology, and the Evolution of International Politics, 1993; co-editor: World Eco-Crisis, 1972, Visions of Apocalypse, End or Rebirth?, 1985; contbr. articles to publs.; chmn. editorial bd. Pub. Sci., 1971-75; mem. editorial bd. Tech. Rev., 1976-78, Social Studies of Sci., 1970-75, Internat. Orgn., 1974-80. Trustee German Marshall Fund, 1979-87, chmn., 1980-86; trustee UN Rsch. Inst. for Social Devel., 1979-85; bd. dirs. Saco Def., 1984-86; mem. Overseas Devel. Coun.; mem. U.S. del. UN Commn. for Social Devel., 1979; mem. State Dept. Adv. Com. on Sci. and Tech., 1987—. Served with U.S. Army Security Agy., 1955-57. Rhodes scholar, 1950-52; Rockefeller Found. fellow, 1963-65; decorated Comdr.'s Cross Fed. Republic Germany, Order of Rising Sun, Golden Rays, Neck Ribbon, Japan. Fellow Am. Acad. Arts and Scis. (councillor 1973-77), AAAS (sec. sect. K 1967-69, mem. com. on sci. and pub. policy 1973-74, com. on sci., engring. and pub. policy 1984-89); mem. UN Assn., Am. Coun. on Germany, Fedn. Am. Scientists, (coun. 1981-85), Coun. Fgn. Rels., Am. Assn. Rhodes Scholars, Soc. for Internat. Devel., Soc. for Social Studies of Sci., Sigma Xi, Tau Beta Pi, Eta Kappa Nu. Patentee hybrid circuits. Home: 3 Chandler St Lexington MA 02173-3601 Office: MIT E51-263A 77 Massachusetts Ave Cambridge MA 02139-4307

SKOLOVSKY, ZADEL, concert pianist, educator; b. Vancouver, B.C., Can.; came to U.S., 1923, naturalized, 1929; s. Max and Kate (Jones) S.; m. Alice Maffett Glass, July 29, 1947 (div. 1953). Diploma, Curtis Inst. Music, 1937; studied piano with, Isabelle Vengerova and Leopold Godowsky; conducting with, Fritz Reiner and Pierre Monteux; violin with, Edwin Bachmann. Prof. music Ind. U., 1975-87, prof. emeritus, 1987—; juror NYU Internat. Tchaikovsky Piano Competition, 1978, 3d Latin Am. Teresa Carreno Piano Competition, Caracas, Venezuela, 1978, U. Md. Internat. Piano Competition, 1981, Joanna Hodges Internat. Piano Competition, Palm Desert, Calif., 1983; tchr. master classes; concert tour of U.S., S. Am. and Far East, 1989-90. Debut at Town Hall as winner of the Walter W. Naumburg award, 1939; appearances in recitals in Carnegie Hall, N.Y.C., 1939—, ann. concert tours U.S.A. and Can., 1939—, biennial tours Europe, Israel, S.Am., Far East, also condr. master classes, 1986—; soloist with N.Y. Philharmonic Symphony Orch.; soloist under condrs. Dimitri Mitropoulos, Charles Munch, Leonard Bernstein, Lorin Maazel, Erich Leinsdorf, Jan Kubelik, Paul Kletzki, Arthur Rodzinski, Paul Paray; appeared as a soloist Lewishohn Stadium, N.Y. and Robin Hood Dell, Phila., under condrs. Vladimir Golschmann, Pierre Monteux, Alexander Smallens; soloist with NBC Orch., Nat. Orch. Assn., Phila. Orch., Nat. Orch., Washington, San Francisco Symphony, Israel Philharmonic, Residentie Orch. at The Hague, L'Orchestre Nat. de Belgique, B.B.C. Scottish Orch., orchs. of Luxembourg, Lisbon, Portugal, Hilversum Radio, Holland, Paris, London, Ravinia, Chgo., N.Y.C.; also appeared on TV; first performance Second Piano Concerto by Prokofieff with N.Y. Philharmonic Orch. under Charles Munch, 1948; world premier Concerto No. 4 of Darius Milhaud with Boston Symphony, 1950; 1st extensive European tour, 1953; appeared with Residency Orch. of the Hague, 2d tour, appeared as soloist with Israel Philharmonic Orch. at opening concert World Festival Music, 1954, appeared in Mexico, 1965, European tour, Eng., Holland, Scandinavia, Belgium, 1965-66, 67, recital, Queen Elizabeth Hall, London, Eng., 1971, 73, recitals, B.C., 1975; concert tour of, S. Am., 1978, U.S., Can. and Europe, 1981-82, Can., 1991; 1st concert tour of Far East, 1983; mus. films for TV., recorded for Columbia Masterworks Records, Philips Records; transcontinental Can. tour, 1991, U.S.A, 1991; annual concert tours U.S.A., Can., Europe, 1992-93. Recipient prizes from Nat. Fedn. Music Clubs, 1943, Nat. Music League, 1940, Robin Hood Dell Young Am. Artists award 1943; recipient Walter W. Naumburg award, 1939. Democrat. Jewish. Club: Lotos (N.Y.C.). Avocations: tennis, chess, literature, theater.

SKOM, JOSEPH HARRY, medical educator; b. Aurora, Ill.; m. Edith Rosen Skom, June 27, 1948; children: Harriet Meyer, Roler. Intern Johns Hopkins Hosp., Balt., 1952-53; resident in medicine U. Chgo. Clinics, 1953-55, rsch. fellow in medicine, 1955-56; instr. in medicine U. Chgo., 1956-57; instr., assoc. in medicine Northwestern U., Chgo., 1957-66, asst. prof. medicine, 1966-73, assoc. prof. medicine, 1973-85, prof. clin. medicine, 1985—. Author: (with others) Obstetrics & Gynecology, 1978, Treatment of Juvenilee Diabetics, 1980; contbr. articles to profl. jours. Chmn. Com. on Preservation Adolescents; mem. Joint Commn. on Accreditation of Health Care Orgns., 1989—. With U.S. Army, 1943-46. U. Geneva faculty fellow 1969. Fellow ACP; mem. AMA (chmn. com. drug abuse 1973-85, pres. No. Ill. and Greater Chgo. chpt. 1973-75, exec. com. coun. sci. affairs 1980-90), Am. Diabetes Assn. (past pres. No. Ill. chpt., bd. dirs.), Ill. Med. Soc. (pres. 1976-77). Avocations: biolgraphy, history, tennis, golfing, bridge, music. Office: Assocs in Internal Medicine 211 E Chicago Ave Chicago IL 60611*

SKOMAL, EDWARD NELSON, aerospace company executive, consultant; b. Kansas City, Mo., Apr. 15, 1926; s. Edward Albert and Ruth (Bangs) S.; m. Elizabeth Birkbeck, Mar. 4, 1951; children: Susan Beth, Catherine Anne, Margaret Elaine; m. Joan Kerner, Apr. 9, 1988. BA, Rice U., Houston, 1947, MA, 1949. Engr., Socony Rsch. Labs., Dallas, 1949-51; asst. sect. head Nat. Bur. Standards, Washington, 1951-56; project engr. Sylvania Research Lab., Palo Alto, Calif., 1956-59; mgr. applications engring., chief applications engr. Motorola Solid State Systems Div., Phoenix, 1959-63; dir. communications dept. Aerospace Corp., El Segundo, Calif., 1963-86, ret., 1986; mem. Presdl. Joint Tech. Adv. Com. on Electromagnetic Compatibility, Washington, 1965-70, 71-75. Author: Man Made Radio Noise, 1978, Automatic Vehicle Location Systems, 1980; Measuring the Radio Frequency Environment, 1985; contbr. articles to profl. jours. Patentee in field of radio systems, solid state devices, radar cross sect. reduction of ballistic rentry vehicles and solid state microwave components. Elder Presbyn. Ch., Redlands, Calif. Served with USN, 1944-6. Fellow IEEE (life, chmn. tech. adv. com. 1982-86, chmn. tech. com. electromagnetic environments 1976-82, standards com. 1980—, nat. com. standards coordinating com. on definitions 1986—, Richard A. Stoddart award 1980, cert. of Achievement 1971, Paper of Yr. award 1970); mem. IEEE Electromagnetic Soc. (life), Am. Phys. Soc., Internat. Union Radio Scientists, Sigma Xi. Republican. Presbyterian. Home: 1831 Valle Vista Dr Redlands CA 92373-7246

SKOMOROWSKY, PETER P., accounting company executive, lawyer; b. Leipzig, Germany, Nov. 14, 1932. Home: 25 E 86th St New York NY 10028-0553 Office: care Grant Thornton 605 3rd Ave New York NY 10158

SKONIECZKA, RICHARD GERALD, retired police chief, coroner; b. Erie, Pa., Jan. 16, 1932; s. Alois Frank and Margaret (Kloor) S.; m. Marilyn Ann Hultman, Oct. 13, 1951 (dec. Oct. 1986); children: Cheryl, Sandra, Carrie, Richard Jr.; m. Angela Marie Stanton, Dec. 1987; stepchildren: Michael Stanton, Donald Stanton. Switchman, crane operator Hammermill Paper Co., Erie, 1955-57; patrolman Bur. of Police, Erie, 1957-62, detective sgt., 1962-72, dep. chief patrol, 1972-80, chief of police, 1980-88; chief dep. coroner Erie, 1988-93, retired 1993. Office: 2110 E 42nd St Erie PA 16510

SKOOG, DONALD PAUL, retired physician, educator; b. Sioux City, Iowa, Sept. 29, 1931; m. Mary Ann Bunn, 1955; children: Robert Eugene, David Alan (dec.), Kristin Marie. BA magna cum laude, Midland Lutheran Coll., Fremont, Nebr., 1953; MD cum laude, U. Nebr., 1958; DSci (hon.), Midland Luth. Coll., 1993. Diplomate Am. Bd. Pathology. Intern, then resident in pathology Bishop Clarkson Meml. Hosp., Omaha, 1958-62; resident in pathology Parkland Meml. Hosp., Dallas, 1962-63; fellow in pathology U. Tex. Southwestern Med. Sch., Dallas, 1962-63; practice medicine specializing in pathology Omaha, 1963-92; pathologist Bishop Clarkson Meml. Hosp., 1963-88, chmn. dept. pathology, 1978-80, dir. dept., 1986-87, chmn. med. edn. com., 1978-83, sec.-treas. med. staff, 1982-87; prof. pathology and microbiology U. Nebr. Med. Sch., 1977-93, mem. dean's faculty adv. coun., 1977-79, mem. grad. and continuing edn. com., 1980-85, mem. council for affiliated instns., 1981-83, mem. admissions com. 1986-91, sr. cons. pathology and microbiology, 1993—; assoc. med. dir. ARC Blood Svcs., Midwest region, Omaha, 1988, med. dir./dir. 1989-91, dir./prin. officer, 1991-92, mem. computer systems selection com., 1991; med. affairs com. ARC Blood Svcs., Washington, 1991-92; bd. dirs., exec. com. Health Planning Coun. of the Midlands, 1975-77; mem. exec. com., chmn. loan com. Nebr. Med. Edn. Fund, 1983-91, sec., treas., 1984-91. Mem. editorial bd. Lab. Medicine, 1979—; contbr. articles to med. jours. Councilman Luther Meml. Luth. Ch., Omaha, 1966-72, 87-91, vice chmn., 1969-72; trustee Midland Luth. Coll., 1968-87, chmn., 1973-75. Recipient Alumni Achievement award Midland Luth. Coll., 1972, Disting. Svc. award Sch. of Allied Health Program, U. Nebr. Med. Ctr., 1990. Fellow Am. Soc. Clin. Pathologists (hematology profl. self-assessment com. 1972, 75,78, adv. coun. 1972-78, chmn. coun. hematology 1978-81, editor Hematology Check Sample 1983-88, Disting. Svc. award Commn. on Continuing Edn. 1985, mem. bd. censors 1987-89, mem. nat. meeting activities com. 1989-92, chmn. 1990-92, Israel Davidsohn disting. svc. award 1993), Coll. Am. Pathologists (hematology resource com. 1981-86, vice chmn. 1982-85); mem. AMA, Am. Assn. Blood Banks, Nebr. Assn. Pathologists, Nebr. Med. Assn., Met. Omaha Med. Soc. (coun. on grievances and profl. ethics 1983-91), Midland Luth. Coll. Alumni Assn. (pres. 1969-70), Alpha Omega Alpha (pres. U. Nebr. chpt. 1976-77, counsellor 1984-90). Home: 706 S 96th St Omaha NE 68114-4918

SKOOG, FOLKE KARL, botany educator; b. Fjärås, Sweden, July 15, 1908; came to U.S., 1925, naturalized, 1935; s. Karl Gustav and Sigrid (Person) S.; m. Birgit Anna Lisa Bergner, Jan. 31, 1947; 1 dau., Karin. BS, Calif. Inst. Tech., 1932, PhD, 1936; PhD (hon.), U. Lund, Sweden, 1956; DSc (hon.), U. Ill., 1980; DAgr. Sci., U. Pisa, Italy, 1991, Swedish U. Agrl. Scis., Uppsala, 1991. Teaching asst., research fellow biology Calif. Inst. Tech., 1934-36; NRC fellow U. Calif., Berkeley, 1936-37, summer 1938; instr., tutor biology Harvard U., 1937-41, research assoc., 1941; assoc., assoc. prof. biology Johns Hopkins U., 1941-44; chemist Q.M.C.; also tech. rep. U.S. Army ETO, 1944-46; asso. prof. botany U. Wis.-Madison, 1947-49, prof., from 1949, C. Leonard Huskins prof. botany, now emeritus.; vis. physiologist Pineapple Research Inst., U. Hawaii, 1938-39; assoc. physiologist NIH, USPHS, 1943; vis. lectr. Washington U., 1946, Swedish U. Agrl. Scis., Ultuna, 1952; v.p. physiol. sect. Internat. Bot. Congress, Paris, 1954, Edinburgh, 1964, Leningrad, 1975. Editor: Plant Growth Substances, 1951, 80; contbr. articles to profl. jours. Track and field mem. Swedish Olympic Team, 1932. Recipient cert. of merit Bot. Soc. Am., 1956, Nat. Medal of Sci., U.S., 1991, Cosimo Ridolfi medal, 1991, John Ericsson medal, 1992. Mem. NAS, Bot. Soc. Am. (chmn. physiol. sect. 1954-55), Am. Soc. Plant Physiologists (v.p. 1952-53, pres. 1957-58, Stephen Hales award 1954, Reid Barnes life mem. award 1970), Soc. Devel. Biology (pres. 1971), Am. Soc. Gen. Physiologists (v.p. 1955-57, pres. 1957-58), Internat. Plant Growth Substances Assn. (hon. life mem., v.p. 1976-79, pres. 1979-82), Am. Soc. Biol. Chemists, Am. Acad. Arts and Scis., Deutsche Akademie der Naturforscher Leopoldina, Swedish Royal Acad. Scis., Tissue Culture Assn. (hon. life mem. 1991, Life Achievement award 1992), Russian Soc. Plant Physiologists (hon. life mem.). Achievements include patents in field. Home: 2820 Marshall Ct Madison WI 53705-2270 Office: U Wis Dept Botany Madison WI 53706

SKOOG, GERALD DUANE, science educator; b. Sioux City, Iowa, Feb. 27, 1936; s. Paul and Mary Ann Skoog; m. Elizabeth Ann Lee, Dec. 28, 1962; children: Jeffrey, John, Sarah. B.S., U. Nebr., 1958; M.A., U. No. Iowa, 1963; Ed.D., U. Nebr., 1969. Tchr. various schs., Nebr., Ill., 1958-69; instr. U. Nebr., Lincoln, summer 1969; asst. prof. curriculum and instrn. Tex. Tech U., Lubbock, 1969-72, assoc. prof., coordinator program, 1972-74, assoc. prof., chmn. secondary edn., 1976-80, prof., chmn. secondary edn., 1980-90, prof., chmn. curriculum and instrn., 1990—; pres. faculty senate Tex. Tech U., 1986-87; vis. prof. Western Ill. U., summer 1972; lectr. in field; participant, facilitator numerous workshops; cons. Contbr. numerous articles to profl. jours., also reviewer articles and papers; co-author secondary sch. science textbooks. Bd. dirs. Gloria Dei Luth. Ch., Lubbock, 1971-74, 92-93; bd. dirs. Luth. Coun. Cmty. Action, 1970-71, Good Neighbor Ministry, 1982-84; leader Boy Scouts Am., 1978-79; foster parent Luth. Social Svcs. Tex.; bd. dirs. Triangle Coalition for Sci. and Tech., 1986-95. Recipient Pres.'s Faculty Achievement award Tex. Tech. U., 1986, Disting. Leadership award, 1996. Mem. Nat. Sci. Tchrs. Assn. (life, bd. dirs. 1977-79, pres. 1985-86, various coms., Disting. Svc. to Sci. Edn. award 1994), Nat. Assn. Rsch. Sci. Teaching, Assn. Edn. Tchrs. Sci., Assn. Supervision and Curriculum Devel., Nat. Sci. Suprs. Assn., Sci. Tchrs. Assn. Tex. (hon. mem., past pres.), Nat. Assn. Biology Tchrs., Tex. Assn. Tchr. Edn. (com. 1981-82), Soc. Study Edn., Phi Delta Kappa. Home: 3214 67th St Lubbock TX 79413-6206 Office: Tex Tech U Coll Edn Lubbock TX 79409

SKOOG, WILLIAM ARTHUR, former oncologist; b. Culver City, Calif., Apr. 10, 1925; s. John Lundeen and Allis Rose (Gatz) S.; m. Ann Douglas, Sept. 17, 1949; children: Karen, William Arthur, James Douglas, Allison. AA, UCLA, 1944; BA with gt. distinction, Stanford U., 1946, MD, 1949. Intern in medicine Stanford Hosp., San Francisco, 1948-49, asst. resident medicine, 1949-50; asst. resident medicine N.Y. Hosp., N.Y.C., 1950-51; sr. resident medicine Wadsworth VA Hosp., Los Angeles, 1951, attending specialist internal medicine, 1962-68; practice medicine specializing in internal medicine, Los Altos, Calif., 1959-61; pvt. practice hematology and oncology Calif. Oncologic and Surg. Med. Group, Inc., Santa Monica, Calif., 1971-72; pvt. practice med. oncology, San Bernardino, Calif., 1972-94; assoc. staff Palo Alto-Stanford (Calif.) Hosp. Center, 1959-61, U. Calif. Med. Center, San Francisco, 1959-61; asso. attending physician U. Calif. at Los Angeles Hosp. and Clinics, 1961-78; vis. physician internal medicine Harbor Gen. Hosp., Torrance, Calif., 1962-65, attending physician, 1965-71; cons. chemistry Clin. Lab., UCLA Hosp., 1963-68; affiliate cons. staff St. John's Hosp., Santa Monica, Calif., 1967-71, courtesy staff, 1971-72; courtesy attending med. staff Santa Monica Hosp., 1967-72; staff physician St. Bernardine (Calif.) Hosp., 1972-94, hon. staff, 1994—; staff physician San Bernardino Cmty. Hosp., 1972-90, courtesy staff, 1990-94; chief sect. oncology San Bernardino County Hosp., 1972-76; cons. staff Redlands (Calif.) Cmty. Hosp., 1972-83, courtesy staff, 1983-94, hon. staff, 1994—; asst. in medicine Cornell Med. Coll., N.Y.C., 1950-51; jr. rsch. physician UCLA Atomic Energy Project, 1954-55; instr. medicine, asst. rsch. physician dept. medicine UCLA Med. Center, 1955-56, asst. prof. medicine, asst. rsch. physician, 1956-59; clin. asso. hematology VA Center, Los Angeles, 1956-59; co-dir. metabolic rsch. unit UCLA Center for Health Scis., 1955-59, 61-65; co-dir. Health Scis. Clin. Rsch. Ctr., 1965-68, dir., 1968-72; clin. instr. medicine Stanford, 1959-61; asst. clin. prof. medicine, assoc. rsch. physician U. Calif. Med. Center, San Francisco, 1959-61; lectr. medicine UCLA Sch. Medicine, 1961-62, assoc. prof. medicine, 1962-73, assoc. clin. prof. medicine, 1973—. Served with USNR, 1943-46, lt. M.C., 1951-53. Fellow ACP; mem. Am., Calif. med. assns., So. Calif. Acad. Clin. Oncology, Western Soc. Clin. Research, Am. Fedn. Clin. Research, Los Angeles Acad. Medicine, San Bernardino County Med. Soc., Am. Soc. Clin. Oncology, Am. Soc. Internal Medicine, Calif. Soc. Internal Medicine, Inland Soc. Internal Medicine, Phi Beta Kappa, Alpha Omega Alpha, Sigma Xi, Alpha Kappa Kappa. Episcopalian (vestryman 1965-70). Club: Redlands Country. Contbr. articles to profl. jours. Home: 1119 Kimberly Pl Redlands CA 92373-6786

SKOPIL, OTTO RICHARD, JR., federal judge; b. Portland, Oreg., June 3, 1919; s. Otto Richard and Freda Martha (Boetticher) S.; m. Janet Rae Lundy, July 27, 1956; children: Otto Richard III, Casey Robert, Shannon Ida, Molly Jo. BA in Econs., Willamette U., 1941, LLB, 1946, LLD (hon.), 1983. Bar: Oreg. 1946, IRS, U.S. Treasury Dept., U.S. Dist. Ct. Oreg., U.S. Ct. Appeals (9th cir.), U.S. Supreme Ct. 1946. Assoc. Skopil & Skopil, 1946-51; ptnr. Williams, Skopil, Miller & Beck (and predecessors), Salem, Oreg., 1951-72; judge U.S. Dist. Ct., Portland, 1972-79; chief judge U.S. Dist. Ct., 1976-79; judge U.S. Ct. Appeals (9th cir.), Portland, 1979—; chmn. com. adminstrn. of fed. magistrate sys. U.S. Jud. Conf., 1980-86; co-founder Oreg. chpt. Am. Leadership Forum; chmn. 9th cir. Jud. Coun. Magistrates Adv. Com., 1988-91; chmn. U.S. Jud. Conf. Long Range Planning Com., 1990-95. Hi-Y adviser Salem YMCA, 1951-52; appeal agt. SSS, Marion County (Oreg.) Draft Bd., 1953-66; master of ceremonies 1st Gov.'s Prayer Breakfast for State Oreg., 1959; mem. citizens adv. com., City of Salem, 1970-71; chmn. Gov.'s Com. on Staffing Mental Instns., 1969-70; pres., bd. dirs. Marion County Tb and Health Assn., 1958-61; bd. dirs. Willamette Valley Camp Fire Girls, 1946-56, Internat. Christian Leadership, 1959, Fed. Jud. Ctr., 1979; trustee Willamette U., 1969-71; elder Mt. Park Ch., 1979-81. Served to lt. USNR, 1942-46. Recipient Oreg. Legal Citizen of Yr. award, 1986, Disting. Alumni award Willamette U. Sch. Law, 1988. Mem. ABA, Oreg. Bar Assn. (bd. govs.), Marion County Bar Assn., Am. Judicature Soc., Oreg. Assn. Def. Counsel (dir.), Def. Research Inst., Assn. Ins. Attys. U.S. and Can. (Oreg. rep. 1970), Internat. Soc. Barristers, Prayer Breakfast Movement (fellowship council). Clubs: Salem, Exchange (pres. 1947), Illahe Hills Country (pres., dir. 1964-67). Office: US Ct Appeals 232 Pioneer Courthouse 555 SW Yamhill St Portland OR 97204-1336

SKORTON, DAVID JAN, university official, physician, educator, researcher; b. Milw., Nov. 22, 1949; s. Samuel and Pauline (Millstein) S.; 1 child, Joshua Samuel. BA, Northwestern U., 1970; MD, Northwestern U., Chgo., 1974. Diplomate Nat. Bd. Med. Examiners, Am. Bd. Internal Medicine, Am. Bd. Cardiovascular Disease. Resident UCLA, 1974-77, fellow in cardiology, 1977-80, chief resident in medicine, 1978-79, adj. asst. prof., 1978-80; instr. medicine U. Iowa, Iowa City, 1980-81, asst. prof., 1981-84, asst. prof. elec. and computer engring., 1982-84, assoc. prof. medicine and elec. and computer engring., 1984-88, prof., 1988—; acting dir., then dir. div. gen. internal medicine U. Iowa Coll. Medicine, 1985-89, assoc. chmn. for clinical programs, 1989-92, v.p. for rsch., 1992—; dir. echocardiology lab. VA Med. Ctr., Iowa City, 1980-89; mem. internat. and coop. projects study sect. NIH, 1988-92, chmn., 1990-92; lectr. in field numerous sci. sessions, nat. and internat. meetings; manuscript reviewer maj. jours. in field. Editor: Cardiac Imaging and Image Processing, 1986, Cardiac Imaing, 1990, 2d edit., 1996; mem. editl. bd. Am Jour. Cardiac Imaging, Am. Jour. Noninvasive Cardiology, Echocardiography, Circulation, 1986-88, Jour. Am. Coll. Cardiology, 1989-93, Jour. Am. Soc. Echocardiography, 1990-91, Internat. Jour. Cardiac Imaging, Ultrasonic Imaging, Cardiovascular Imaging (Italy), Clin. Cardiology, 1988-93; sect. editor Jour. Am. Soc. Echocardiography; contbr. numerous articles and sci. abstracts to profl. jours., chpts. to books. Regents' scholar UCLA, 1967-68; named Intern-of-Yr., UCLA, 1975; recipient Rsch. Assoc. Career Devel. award VA, Iowa City, 1981-84, Rsch. Career Devel. award Nat. Heart Lung & Blood Inst., Iowa City, 1984-89. Fellow ACP (governing coun. Iowa 1983-85), Am. Coll. Cardiology (chmn. computer applications com. 1984-90, gov. Iowa sect. 1987-90, trustee 1991-96), Am. Heart Assn., Am. Physiol. Soc.; mem. AAAS, Am. Soc. Echocardiography (bd. dirs. 1983-86), Am. Inst. Ultrasound in Medicine (bd. govs. 1986-89), Am. Fedn. for Clin. Rsch., Assn. Univ. Cardiologists, Internat. Soc. for Adult Congenital Cardiac Disease, Soc. Magnetic Resonance Imaging, Soc. Magnetic Resonance in Medicine. Jewish. Office: U Iowa VP for Rsch 201 Gilmore Hall Iowa City IA 52242-1320

SKOTAK, ROBERT F., film production company executive; b. Dearborn, Mich.. Visual effects artist Hollywood, Calif., 1976—; co-founder, pres., visual effects dir. 4-Ward Prodns., Inc., L.A., 1989—. Visual effects artist, designer, supr. (films) Battle Beyond the Stars, Escape from New York, To Be or Not To Be, Strange Invaders, Forbidden World (Top Honor in visual effects French Film Festival 1982), Aliens (Am. and Brit. Acad. award 1986), The Abyss, 1989, (with 4-Ward Prodns.) Tremors, Darkman, 1989, Clifford, True Identity, Cast A Deadly Spell, Terminator 2, (Am. and British Acad. award, Saturn award Acad. of Sci. Fiction 1991), Batman Returns (Am. and British Academy award nominations), 1992, Honey, I Blew Up the Baby, 1992, Dracula, 1992, Heart and Souls, 1993, Fatal Instinct, 1993, No Escape, 1994; visual effects artist, designer, supr., co-prodn. designer (films) Galaxy of Terror, Creature (Acad. Sci. Fiction Best Visual Effects nomination 1984); author: Alien Worlds, 1978; universal filmscript series: This Island Earth, 1990; pub. Fantascene Mag., 1975-78. Mem. Writers Guild Am., Acad. Motion Picture Arts & Scis. Office: 4-Ward Prodns Inc 2801 Hyperion Ave # 104 Los Angeles CA 90027-2571

SKOTHEIM, ROBERT ALLEN, museum administrator; b. Seattle, Jan. 31, 1933; s. Sivert O. and Marjorie F. (Allen) S.; m. Nadine Vail, June 14, 1953; children—Marjorie, Kris, Julia. BA, U. Wash., 1955, MA, 1958, PhD, 1962; LLD (hon.), Hobart and William Smith Colls., Geneva, N.Y., 1975; LittD (hon.), Whitman Coll., 1988; LHD (hon.), Coll. Idaho, 1988, Occidental Coll., 1989, Ill. Wesleyan U., 1990; DFA (hon.), Willamette U., 1989. Prof. history U. Wash., 1962-63; prof. history Wayne State U., Detroit, 1963-66; prof. UCLA, 1966-67, U. Colo., Boulder, 1967-72; provost, dean faculty Hobart and William Smith Colls., 1972-75; pres. Whitman Coll., Walla Walla, Wash., 1975-88, Huntington Libr., Art Collections & Bot. Gardens, San Marino, Calif., 1988—. Author: American Intellectual Histories and Historians, 1966, Totalitarianism and American Social Thought, 1971; Editor: The Historian and the Climate of Opinion, 1969; co-editor: American Social Thought: Sources and Interpretations, 2 vols, 1972. Guggenheim fellow, 1967-68. Mem. Phi Beta Kappa (hon.). Office: Huntington Library Art Collections & Bot Gardens 1151 Oxford Rd San Marino CA 91108-1299

SKOV, ARLIE MASON, petroleum engineer, consultant; b. Perry, Okla., Sept. 21, 1928; s. Arnold and Mary (Mason) S.; m. Luella Luticia Sloan, July 31, 1951; children: Gregory Morgan, Jeffrey Markham, Tamara Kay. BS in Petroleum Engring., U. Okla., 1956; postgrad., U. Va., 1966. Engr. Sohio Petroleum Co., Pauls Valley, Okla., 1957-58; staff engr. Sohio Petroleum Co., Oklahoma City, 1958-65, mgr. spl. projects, 1966-75, asst. mgr. engring.,

1975-76; mgr. prodn. planning BP Alaska Inc., San Francisco, 1977-80; project advisor Sohio Gas Pipeline Co., San Francisco, 1980-81; mgr. new tech. devel. Sohio Petroleum Co., San Francisco, 1981-83; dir. prodn. tech. Sohio Petroleum Co. and Standard Oil Prodn., Dallas, 1983-88; sr. cons. BP Exploration, Inc., Houston, 1989-92; owner Arlie M. Skov, Inc. Petroleum Consulting, Houston, 1993—. Recipient Disting. Svc. award Okla. Petroleum Coun. 1973. Mem. AIME (bd. dirs. 1977-79, trustee 1990-92, 95-97) Soc. Petroleum Engrs. (bd. dirs. 1972-74, exec. com. 1990-92, pres. 1991, Disting. mem.). Avocations: reading, travel. Office: A M Skov Inc 1155 Dairy Ashford Ste 216 Houston TX 77079-3012

SKOVE, THOMAS MALCOLM, retired manufacturing company financial executive; b. Cleve., June 27, 1925; s. Thomas Malcolm and Ethel C. (Rush) S.; m. Helen Busing, June 12, 1948; children: Margaret, Thomas, Richard, Marcie, Douglas. B.S., Bucknell U., 1949. Controller, treas. Cleve. Twist Drill Co., 1949-68; treas. Acme-Cleve. Corp., 1968-81, dep. treas., 1981-86, treas., 1986-88. Councilman, City of Aurora, Ohio, 1977-83; chmn. Aurora Meml. Library Trust, 1984-89. Served with USN, 1943-46. Mem. Sugar Mill Country Club (pres. 1993-94). Republican. Home: 209 Bromely Cir New Smyrna Beach FL 32168-2006

SKOWRON, TADEUSZ ADAM, physician; b. Czestochowa, Poland, Dec. 17, 1950; came to U.S., 1976; s. Stanislaw and Genowefa (Widera) S.; m. Elizabeth Sliwowska, Feb. 17, 1990; children: Sebastian Adam, Annette Kira. MD, Med. Acad., Lodz, Poland, 1975. House physician Bklyn.-Cumberland Med. Ctr., 1979-80, fellow in neurology, 1981-83; resident in medicine Marshall U. Sch. Medicine, Huntington, W.Va., 1983-86, instr., 1986-87; pvt. practice, Bridgeport, Conn., 1987—; clin. specialist II, State Sch., Newark, 1981; advisor Congress Med. Polonia, Czestochowa, 1990—. Mem. Polish cultural events com. Sacred Heart U., Fairfield, Conn., 1990—. Mem. ACP, AMA, AAAS, N.Y. Acad. Scis. Home: 47 Mcquillan Ave Stratford CT 06497-4626 Office: 50 Ridgefield Ave Ste 317 Bridgeport CT 06610-3106

SKOWRONSKI, VINCENT PAUL, concert violinist, recording artist, executive producer, producer classical recordings; b. Kenosha, Wis., Jan. 22, 1944. MusB, Northwestern U., 1966, MusM, 1968. V.p. Eberley-Skowronski, Inc., Evanston, Ill., 1973-92; internat. dir. mktg. and pub. rels. Vincent Skowronski: Producer of Classical Recordings, Evanston, 1993—; internat. broker rare instruments Strings & Things, Evanston, 1973-92; owner Vincent Skowronski: Fine Violins, Evanston, 1993—; internat. dir. mktg. and pub. rels. EB-SKO Prodns., Evanston, 1978-92; dir. media comm. E-S Mgmt., Evanston, 1985-92; instr. violin Northwestern U., 1969-71; asst. prof. violin U. Wyo., 1971-72; pvt. violin tchr., chamber music coach, lectr., master classes. Solo violinist debut Chgo. Youth Orch., 1959; soloist Chgo. Civic Orch., 1968, guest solo artist Am. Artist Gala, Nat. Puerto Rican TV, 1960; solo guest artist Young Am. Musicians Sta. WKAR-TV Mich. State U., 1966, N.Am. premiere R. Nanes' Rhapsody Pathetique for violin and orch., Chgo. Cultural Ctr., 1994, Beijing, 1994, DePaul U. Ctr., Chgo., 1994, Skowronski in Recital: 20 Years Remembered, Northwestern U., Evanston, Ill., 1994, IV Internat. Tchaikovsky Competition Commemorative Recital-Moscow Remembered: 1970-95, Evanston, Ill., 1995; featured solo artist Artist Showcase, Sta. WGN-TV Chgo., 1966-71; featured soloist Honors Concert-Northwestern U., 1966, guest solo artist A.M. Am., Sta. ABC-TV, 1977—; numerous concerts and recitals in Europe, Cen.Am., Mex. and U.S.; solo guest artist radio appearances include Continental Bank Concerts, Sta. WFMT-FM Chgo., 1983, 85-86, 88, 90, United Airlines Presents, Live!, Sta. WFMT-FM Chgo., Schumann, 1986, Szymanowski, 1987, Bloch, 1988, Saint-Saens, 1989, Grieg, 1991, Excursions in Music: The Artistry of Vincent P. Skowronski, Sta. KQED-FM San Francisco, 1979, Skowronski: Musical Giant, Interlake Profiles, Sta. WFMT-FM Chgo., 1980, Skowronski at 50: A Birthday Celebration Sta. WNIB-FM, Chgo., 1994; guest solo artist, producer, annotator Separate but Equal, 1976, All Brahms, 1977; solo artist, exec. producer, annotator Gentleman Gypsy, 1978, Strauss and Szymanowski, 1979, Franck and Szymanowski, 1982, Skowronski Alone, 1995; producer, annotator Opera Lady I, 1978, Eberley Sings Strauss, 1980, American Girl, 1983, Opera Lady II, 1984; guest performances numerous TV stas. Bd. dirs. Chgo. Youth Orch., 1973-77, v.p., 1974-77; artistic cons. Classical and Protege Symphony Orchs., Chgo., 1994—; adjudicator ice skating shows and competitions Wilmette (Ill.) Park Dist., 1985-89; guest panelist classical performance-career forum Sch. of Music, Northwestern U., Evanston, 1992, 94; guest cons. career symposium Edwin G. Foreman High Sch., Chgo., 1989; mem. mayor's founding com. Evanston Arts Coun., 1974-75. Recipient Roy Harris award Inter-Am. U., San German, P.R., 1960, award Am. Fedn. Musicians, 1961, award Soc. Am. Musicians, 1961, McCormick Found. award Chgo. Tribune, 1965, Wade Fetzer award for excellence in performance Northwestern U., 1966, award Crescendo Musical Club, 1967; selected as one of 7 violinists chosen to represent U.S. in IV Internat. Tachaikovsky Competition, Moscow, 1970. Mem. Sigma Nu, Internat. Platform Assn.

SKRAMSTAD, HAROLD KENNETH, JR., museum administrator, consultant; b. Washington, June 3, 1941; s. Harold K. and Sarah (Shroat) S.; m. Susan Chappelear, Dec. 28, 1963; children: Robert, Elizabeth. AB, George Washington U., 1963, PhD, 1971. Asst. dir. Am. studies program Smithsonian Instn., Washington, 1969-71, spl. asst. to dir. Nat. Mus. Am. History, 1971, chief spl. projects Nat. Mus. Am. History, chief exhibit programs Nat. Mus. Am. History, 1971-74; dir. Chgo. Hist. Soc., 1974-80; pres. Henry Ford Mus. and Greenfield Village, Dearborn, Mich., 1981—; mem. Nat. Coun. on Humanities, 1994; mem. mus. mgmt. adv. com. J. Paul Getty Trust, L.A., 1984-90. Chmn. bd. Met. Detroit Conv. and Visitors Bur., 1993, chmn., mem. exec. com., 1985—; trustee Coll. Art and Design, Detroit, 1981—; mem. Mich. Travel Commn., 1989—. Recipient Charles Frankel prize Nat. Endowment for the Humanities, 1992. Mem. Am. Assn. Mus. (v.p. 1984-88, accreditation commn. 1982, ethics commn. 1992-93), Smithsonian Instn. Nat. Air and Space Mus. (pub. programming adv. com. 1990—), Nat. Coun. on the Humanitites, 1994, Greater Detroit and Windsor Japan-Am. Soc. (bd. dirs. 1989—), Detroit Club, Cosmos Club (Washington). Home: Stone Mill 20900 Oakwood Blvd Dearborn MI 48124 Office: Henry Ford Mus Greenfield Village Dearborn MI 48124

SKRATEK, SYLVIA PAULETTE, mediator, arbitrator, dispute systems designer; b. Detroit, Dec. 23, 1950; d. William Joseph and Helen (Meskauskas) S.; m. John Wayne Gullion, Dec. 21,1984. BS, Wayne State U., 1971; MLS, Western Mich. U., 1976; PhD, U. Mich., 1985. Media specialist Jackson (Mich.) Pub. Schs., 1971-79; contract specialist Jackson County Edn. Assn., 1976-79; field rep. Mich. Edn. Assn., E.Lansing, 1979-81; contract adminstr. Wash. Edn. Assn., Federal Way, 1981-85, regional coord., 1985-88, program adminstr., from 1988; dir. mediation svcs. Conflict Mgmt. Inst., Lake Oswego, Ore., 1986-87; exec. dir. N.W. Ctr. for Conciliation, 1987-88; served in Wash. State Senate, 1990-94; tng. cons. City of Seattle, 1986—; trustee Group Health Coop. of Puget Sound, Wash., 1984-87; sole proprietor Skratek & Assocs., 1980—; pres. Resolutions Internat., 1990—; v.p. Mediation Rsch. and Edn. Project, Inc., 1990—. Contbr. articles to legal jours. Mem. Soc. for Profls. in Dispute Resolution, Indsl. Rels. Rsch. Assn. Avocations: swimming, piano, Asian cooking, cross country skiing.

SKREBNESKI, VICTOR, photographer; b. Chgo., Dec. 17, 1929; s. Joseph and Anna (Casper) S. Student, Art Inst. Chgo., 1945, Inst. Design, 1947. Propr. Skrebneski Studio, Chgo., 1956—. Author: Skrebneski, 1969, The Human Form, 1973, Skrebneski Portraits: A Matter of Record, 1978. Exhbns. include Charles Cowles Gallery, N.Y.C., 1992. Bd. dirs. Chgo. Internat. Film Festival. Recipient award Art Directors Soc., 1958-75. Mem. Dirs. Guild Am., Soc. Photographers in Communications. Club: Arts (Chgo.). Address: 1350 N La Salle Dr Chicago IL 60610-1911*

SKRETNY, WILLIAM MARION, federal judge; b. Buffalo, Mar. 8, 1945; s. William S. and Rita E. (Wyroski) S.; m. Carol Ann Mergenhagen; children: Brian Alexander, Brooke Ann, Nina Clare. AB, Canisius Coll., 1966; JD, Howard U., 1969; LLM, Northwestern U., 1972. Bar: Ill. 1969, U.S. Dist. Ct. (no. dist) Ill. 1969, N.Y. 1972, U.S. Ct. Appeals (7th cir.) 1972, U.S. Dist. Ct. (we. dist.) N.Y. 1973, U.S. Ct. Appeals (2d cir.) 1976, U.S. Supreme Ct. 1980. Asst. U.S. atty. Office of U.S. Atty. No. Dist. Ill., Chgo., 1971-73; asst. U.S. atty. Office of U.S. Atty. We. Dist. N.Y., Buffalo, 1973-81, 1st asst., 1975-81; gen. ptnr. Duke, Holzman, Yaeger & Radlin, Buffalo, 1981-83; 1st dep. dist. atty. Office Dist. Atty Erie County, Buffalo, 1983-88; assoc. Gross, Shuman, Brizdle and Gillfillan, PC, Buffalo, 1988; of counsel Cox, Barrell, Buffalo, 1989-90; judge U.S. Dist. Ct. (we. dist.) N.Y., Buffalo, 1990—; task force atty. tng. Office U.S. Atty Gen., 1978; spl. counsel U.S. Atty Gen.'s Advocacy Inst., 1979; staff atty. Office Spl. Prosecutor, Dept. Justice, Washington, 1980; faculty advisor Nat. Coll. D.A.s, Houston, 1987; lectr. Northwestern U., Chgo., 1980; mem. jud. com. on security, space and facilities Erie and N.Y.State Bar Assns., 1994. Contbr. articles to profl. jours. Bd. dirs. Sudden Infant Death Found. We. N.Y., 1979, Cerebral Palsy Foun. We. N.Y., 1985; co-v.p. PTA Harlem Rd. Sch., 1982; chmn. major corps. divsn. Studio Arena Theatre, Buffalo, 1982; chmn. Polish Culture, Canisius Coll., 1985, trustee, 1989; regional chmn. Cath. Charities Appeal, 1986-87. Scholar Howard U., 1966; fellow Ford Found., 1969; named Citizen of Yr. Am Pol Eagle Newspaper, 1977, 90, Disting. Grad. Nat. Cath. Edn. Assn. Dept. Elem. Sch., 1991, Disting. Alumnus Canisius Coll., 1993. Mem. ABA, Fed. Bar Assn., Fed. Judges Assn., Western N.Y. Trial Lawyers Assn., Thomas More Legal Soc. (pres. 1980), Advocates Soc. Western N.Y., Erie County Bar Assn., Chgo. Bar Assn., Canisius Coll. Alumni Assn. (pres. 1989), Di Gamma, Phi Alpha Delta. Republican. Roman Catholic. Office: US District Court 68 Court St Rm 507 Buffalo NY 14202-3406

SKROMME, LAWRENCE H., consulting agricultural engineer; b. Roland, Iowa, Aug. 26, 1913; s. Austin G. and Ingeborg B. (Holmedal) S.; m. Margaret Elizabeth Gleason, June 24, 1939; children: Cherlyn Sue Granrose, Inga Jean Hill, Karen Ann Sequino. B.S. with honors, Iowa State U., Ames, 1937. Registered profl. engr., Pa. Design and test engr. Goodyear Tire and Rubber Co., Akron, Ohio, 1937-41; project engr., asst. chief engr. Harry Ferguson Inc., Detroit, 1941-51; chief engr. Sperry New Holland div. Sperry Corp., New Holland, Pa., 1951-61, v.p. engrng., 1961-78; cons. agrl. engr. Lancaster, Pa., 1978—; mem. adv. bd. U.S. Congress Com. on Sci. and Tech., 1989—; cons. AID, World Bank, others, 1978-85, Saudi Arabia, 1985-86. Patentee; contbr. articles to profl. jours. Rsch. adv. com. U.S. Dept. Agr., Washington, 1964-68; gov.'s com. agr. and land preservation Gov. of Pa., 1965-69; bd. dirs. awards com. Engrs. Joint Coun., N.Y.C., 1967-75; dir., v.p., pres. Farm and Home Found. Lancaster County, 1968—; Lancaster County Agrl. Land Preservation Bd., 1978—, sec.-treas. 1989—. Mem. Am. Soc. Agrl. Engrs. (gold medal 1974, v.p. 1952-55, pres. 1959-60, fellow 1965—), NAE (peer and membership com. 1978—), Nat. Soc. Profl. Engrs., Internat. Assn. Agrl. Engrs. (v.p. 1974-79, pres. farm machine div.), Am. Soc. Engring. Edn., Phi Kappa Phi, Alpha Zeta, Tau Beta Pi. Republican. Methodist. Avocations: collecting old tools and antiques.

SKROWACZEWSKI, STANISLAW, conductor, composer; b. Lwow, Poland, Oct. 3, 1923; came to U.S., 1960; s. Pawel and Zofia (Karszniewicz) S.; m. Krystyna Jarosz, Sept. 6, 1956; children: Anna, Paul, Nicholas. Diploma faculty philosophy, U. Lwow, 1945; diploma faculties composition and conducting, Acad. Music Lwow, 1945, Conservatory at Krakow, Poland, 1946; L.H.D., Hamline U., 1963, Macalester Coll., 1972; L.H.D. hon. doctorate, U. Minn. Guest condr. in Europe, S.A., U.S., 1947—; Composer, 1931—, pianist, 1928—, violinist, 1934—, condr., 1939—; permanent condr., music dir. Wroclaw (Poland) Philharmonic, 1946-47, Katowice (Poland) Nat. Philharmonic, 1949-54, Krakow Philharmonic, 1955-56, Warsaw Nat. Philharmonic Orch., 1957-59, Minnesota Orch., 1960-79; prin. condr., mus. adviser Halle Orch., Manchester, Eng., 1984-91; musical advisor St. Paul Chamber Orchestra, 1986-87; first symphony and overture for orch. written at age 8, played by Lwow Philharm. Orch., 1931. Composer: 4 symphonies Prelude and Fugue for Orchestra (conducted first performance Paris), 1948, Overture, 1947 (2d prize Szymanowski Concours, Warsaw 1947); Cantiques des Cantiques, 1951, String Quartet, 1953 (2d Prize Internat. Concours Composers, Belgium 1953), Suite Symphonique, 1954 (first prize, gold medal Composers Competition Moscow 1957), Music at Night, 1954, Ricercari Notturni, 1978 (3d prize Kennedy Center Friedheim Competition, Washington), Concerti for Clarinet and Orch., 1980, Violin Concerto, 1985, Concerto for Orch., 1985, Fanfare for Orch., 1987, Sextett for Oboe, Violin, Viola, Orchestra, 1980, String Trio for Violin, Viola, 1990, Triple Concerto for Violin, Clarinet, Piano, Orchestra, 1992, Fantasie per Tre (Flute, Oboe, Cello), 1993, Chamber Concerto, 1993, Passacaglia Immaginaria for Orch., 1995; also music for theatre, motion pictures, songs and piano sonatas, English horn concerto; rec. by Mercury, Columbia, RCA Victor, Vox, EMI, Angel. Recipient nat. prize for artistic activity Poland, 1953; First prize Santa Cecilia Internat. Concours for Condrs., Rome, 1956. Mem. Union Polish Composers, Internat. Soc. Modern Music, Nat. Assn. Am. Composers-Condrs., Am. Music Center. Office: Orch Hall 1111 Nicollet Mall Minneapolis MN 55403-2406

SKUBE, MICHAEL, journalist, critic; b. Springfield, Ill.; 1 child, Noah. Degree in polit. sci., La. State U. Former tchr. math and sci. La.; formerly with U.S. Customs Svc., Miami, Fla.; book reviewer Miami Herald, from 1974; Raleigh (N.C.) bur. chief Winston-Salem (N.C.) Jour., 1978-82; editorial writer The News and Observer, Raleigh, 1982-86, became book editor, 1986; now book editor Atlanta Jour. and Constn., 1987—. Recipient Pulitzer Prize for criticism, 1989, Disting. Writing award for commentary and column writing Am. Soc. Newspaper Editors, 1989, 1st Pl. award for columns N.C. Press Assn. Office: Atlanta Jour and Constn 72 Marietta St NW Atlanta GA 30303-2804

SKUDLARSKI, PAWEL, physicist; b. Warsaw, Poland, Sept. 30, 1963; came to U.S., 1989; s. Krzysztof and Wiktoria (Górowicz) S.; m. Beata Agnieszka, July 20, 1966; 1 child, Ola Monica. MS in Physics, U. Warsaw, 1986; PhD in Physics, U. Mo., 1993. Postdoctoral fellow Yale U., New Haven, Conn., 1993—. Contbr. articles to profl. jours. Avocations: skiing, snow boarding, wind surfing. Office: Yale Univ 333 Cedar Fitkin B New Haven CT 06510

SKULINA, THOMAS RAYMOND, lawyer; b. Cleve., Sept. 14, 1933; s. John J. and Mary B. (Vesely) S. AB, John Carroll U., 1955; JD, Case Western Res. U., 1959, LLM, 1962. Bar: Ohio 1959, U.S. Supreme Ct. 1964, ICC 1965. Ptnr. Skulina & Stringer, Cleve., 1967-72, Riemer Oberdank & Skulina, Cleve., 1978-81, Skulina, Fillo, Walters & Negrelli, 1981-86, Skulina & McKeon, Cleve., 1986-90, Skulina & Hill, Cleve., 1990—; atty. Penn Cen. Transp. Co., Cleve., 1960-65, asst. gen. atty., 1965-78, trial counsel, 1965-76; with Consol. Rail Corp., 1976-78; tchr. comml. law Practicing Law Inst., N.Y.C., 1970; practicing arbitrator Am. Arbitration Assn., Fed. Mediation and Conciliation Svc., 1990—; arbitrator Mcpl. Securities Rulemaking Bd., 1994—, N.Y. Stock Exch., 1995—, NASD, 1996—. Contbr. articles to legal jours. Income tax and fed. fund coord. City of Warrensville Heights, Ohio, 1970-77; spl. counsel City of North Olmstead, Ohio, 1971-75, spl. counsel to Ohio Atty. Gen., 1983-93, Cleve. Charter Rev. Commn., 1988; pres. Civil Svc. Commn., Cleve., 1977-86, referee, 1986—; fact-finder State Employees Rels. Bd., Ohio, 1986—. With U.S. Army, 1959. Mem. ABA (R.R. and motor carrier com. 1988—, jr. chmn. 1989—), Soc. Profls. in Dispute Resolution, Cleve. Bar Assn. (grievance com. 1987-93, chmn. 1989-90, trustee 1993—), Ohio Bar Assn. (bd. govs. litigation sect. 1986—, negligence law com. 1989—, ethics and profl. responsibility com. 1990—), Fed. Bar Assn., Ohio Trial Lawyers Assn., Am. Arbitration Assn. (labor panel 1988—), Nat. Assn. R.R. Trial Counsel, Internat. Assn. Law and Sci., Pub. Sector Labor Rels. Assn., Indsl. Rels. Rsch. Assn. Democrat. Roman Catholic. Home: 3162 W 165th St Cleveland OH 44111-1016 Office: Skulina & Hill 24803 Detroit Rd Cleveland OH 44145-2512

SKUMMER, MARY ANNE, hearing impaired educator, coordinator; b. Chgo., Jan. 11, 1951; d. Joseph Frank and Marie Jane (Babiarz) S. BS in Biology, Loyola U., 1973, EdD Curriculum and Instruction, 1990; MA Edn. of Hearing Impaired, Northwestern U., 1975; MA EMH, Roosvelt U., 1982. Cert. tchr. deaf and hard of hearing, Ill., educable mentally handicapped, Ill., gen. supervisory, Ill. Cons. for hearing impaired State of N.D., Bismarck, 1975-76; educator Dept. Mental Health and Devel. Disabilities, Park Forest, Ill., 1976-92; spl. needs coord. State of Ill. DMHDD, Park Forest, 1992—; adj. faculty mem. Prairie State Coll., Chgo. Heights, Ill., 1984—; expert witness Deaf and Hard of Hearing, Robert W. Karr & Assocs., Chgo., 1992-93. Extraordinary minister, mem. parish coun. St. Mary's Ch., Park Forest, Ill. Fellow Am. Biographical Inst., 1995. Democrat. Roman Catholic. Avocations: gardening, stamp collecting. Home: 3612 213th St Matteson IL 60443-2511 Office: State of Ill DMHDD 114 N Orchard Dr Park Forest IL 60466-1200

SKUPINSKI, BOGDAN KAZIMIERZ, artist; b. Poland, July 16, 1942; came to U.S., 1971, naturalized, 1976; s. Kazimierz Stanislaw and Jrena Lucja (Kanar) S. BA, Acad. Fine Arts, Krakow, Poland, 1969, MA, 1971; cert., Ecole Nationale Superieure de Beaux Arts, Paris, 1971. Pres. Bogdan & Assoc., N.Y.C. Graphic artist: painting Proclamation, 1968, Escape, 1968, Return, 1969, Good Journey, (permanent collection N.J. State Mus., 1971, The Stable, (permanent collection Library of Congress), 1971, Nouvel Ordre, 1970 (annual prize Ministry of Cultural Affairs of France), Gare du Nord, 1970 (award Commn. Fine Arts. Paris), anti-war themes, 1969-76; life and work of John F. Kennedy and Albert Michelson, 1969-76. Recipient Grand Prix, Nat. Salon Young Artists, 1968, People's Choice award 2d Nat. Graphic Rev., Karkow, 1969, ann. Bartoczek and Babrowski award Polish Ministry Art and Culture, 1970, lst prize for prints and drawings Nat. Conn. Acad. Exhbn., Hartford, 1971, medal Internat. Exhbn. Graphic Art, Frechen, Fed. Republic Germany, 1976, Presdl. Medal of Merit, 1990; fellow Ecole Nat. Superieure Beaux Arts. Fellow Pratt Inst.; mem. NAD (Cannon prize for graphics 1971), Kosciuszko Found., Rep. Presdl. Task Force. Roman Catholic. Home: Cathedral Sta PO Box 849 215 W 104th St New York NY 10025-4230

SKUPSKY, STANLEY, laser scientist. Group leader theory and computation lab. laser energetics U. Rochester, N.Y. Recipient award for Excellence in Plasma Physics Rsch. Am. Physical Soc., 1993. Office: U Rochester Lab for Laser Energetics Rochester NY 14627

SKURKA, KATHLEEN, sculptor, educator; b. Pitts., Pa., Jan. 23, 1947; d. Cornelius Albert and Ruby Nell (Spencer) S. BFA, U. Ala., Tuscaloosa, 1969, MA, 1970, MFA, 1971. Asst. prof. art Ala. State U., Montgomery, 1971—; pottery instr. Montgomery Sch. Fine Arts, 1989-90, Armory Learning Arts Ctr., Montgomery, 1990—. Exhibited sculpture in one-person exhbn. Other-Worldly Creatures and Forms, 1988, Sculpture in Black and White, 1989, Odd Icons, 1992, Ala. City Invitational, 1992, 93, El Dorado Gallery, Colorado Springs, Colo., 1992, Gallery La Luz, N.Mex., 1992, South Bend (Ind.) Regional Mus. Art, 1992, Catskill Arts Soc., Hurleyville, N.Y., 1992, Jacksonville (Ala.) State U., 1994. Recipient 1st pl. award and Best Media ward Roswell Fine Arts LEague, N.MEx. Ministrue Art Soc., 1992, Ala. Originality award, 1993, 3d pl. award Women Artists Exhbn., Ala., 1993. Mem. Internat. Sculpture Ctr., Ala. Craftsman Assn., Artifice Rex, Women's Caucus Art. Roman Catholic. Home: PO Box 6085 Montgomery AL 36106-0085

SKURLA, LAURUS See **LAURUS**

SKUTT, THOMAS JAMES, insurance company executive; b. Omaha, Nov. 1, 1930; s. Vestor Joseph and Angela (Anderson) S.; m. Jeanne Cecille Plunkett, Sept. 3, 1955; children: Mary Elizabeth Sutton, Kimberly Ann Davis, Thomas V.J. BA, Yale U., 1952; LLB, Creighton U., 1957; postgrad., Harvard U., 1979. Ptnr. Spire, Morrow & Skutt, Omaha, 1961-69; with Mut. of Omaha, 1969—, exec. v.p., sec., 1980-81, vice chmn. bd. dirs., 1981-84, 1st vice chmn. bd. dirs., chief exec. officer, 1984-86; chmn. bd. dirs., chief exec. officer Mutual of Omaha Ins. Co., 1986-96; chmn. bd. dirs., chief exec. officer United of Omaha subs. Mut. of Omaha, 1986-96; chmn. bd. dirs. United Mutual of Omaha Life Ins. Co., 1996—; chmn. bd., dir. United of Omaha Life Ins. Co., 1996—; bd. dirs. United of Omaha, Mut. Omaha Ins. Co., Companion Life Ins. Co., United World Life Ins. Co. Past pres., selected Citizen of Yr., Mid-Am. Coun. Boy Scouts Am., 1987, 89, 93.mem. exec. bd. 1980—; mem. consultation com. SAC, Omaha, 1984; bd. dirs. Omaha Zool. Soc., 1978—, pres., 1987-88, past. bd. dirs.; gen. chmn. campaign United Way of Midlands, 1979-80, bd. dirs., 1981—; bd. dirs. Creighton U., Omaha, 1983—. Recipient Humanitarian award Nat. Conf. Christians and Jews, 1992. Mem. Greater Omaha C. of C. (bd. dirs. 1979—, chmn. 1983, past chmn.), Mpls. Club, Yale Club N.Y.C., Knights of Ak-Sar-Ben (bd. govs. 1985, King XCVI 1992). Republican. Roman Catholic. Avocations: golf, tennis. Home: 400 N 62nd St Omaha NE 68132-1955 Office: Mut Omaha Ins Co 10250 Regency Cir Ste 175 Omaha NE 68114

SKVARLA, LUCYANN M., college official; b. Kingston, Pa., Jan. 15, 1959; d. John T. and Sophie H. (Turel) S. AS, Lackawanna Jr. Coll., Wilkes-Barre, Pa., 1978; BS, King's Coll., Wilkes-Barre, 1992. Cert. profl. sec. Sec. King's Coll., Wilkes-Barre, 1978, sec./adminstrv. asst., 1978-87, asst. for instnl. rsch., 1987—; part-time instr. non-credit workshops King's Coll., 1994—; part-time instr. McCann Sch. Bus., Wyoming, Pa., 1989-91. Lector St. Hedwig's Ch., Kingston, Pa., 1983-92. Mem. Assn. for Instnl. Rsch. (participant in inst. at No. Ky. U. 1993), N.E. Assn. for Instnl. Rsch., Delta Mu Delta, Delta Epsilon Sigma, Alpha Sigma Lambda. Avocations: country line dancing, bowling, plastic canvas needlepoint, crocheting. Office: Kings Coll 133 N River St Wilkes Barre PA 18711

SKVORECKY, JOSEF VACLAV, English literature educator, novelist; b. Nachod, Czechoslovakia, Sept. 27, 1924; arrived Can., 1969; s. Josef Karel and Anna (Kurazova) S.; m. Zdenka Josefa Salivarova, Mar. 30, 1958. Ph.D., Charles U., Czechoslovakia, 1951; LHD (hon.), SUNY, 1986; postgrad., Masaryk U., 1991, U. Calgary, 1992, U. Toronto, 1992. Vis. lectr. U. Toronto, Ont., Can., 1969-70; writer-in-residence U. Toronto, 1970-71, assoc. prof., 1971-75, prof. English, 1975-90; prof. emeritus, 1990—; lectr. on lit. topics Voice of Am., 1973—; adv. to Pres. Vaclav Havel, 1990. Editor: Sixty Eight Publ. Corp., Toronto, 1972—; author: The End of the Nylon Age, 1967, Republic of Whores, 1969, The Miracle Game, 1972, The End of Lieutenant Boruvka, 1975, The Swell Season, 1975, The Bass Saxophone, 1979, The Cowards, 1980, The Return of Lieutenant Boruvka, 1980, The Engineer of Human Souls, 1984, Miss Silver's Past, 1985, Dvorak in Love, 1986, The Bride from Texas, 1992; short story collections: The Menorah, 1964, The Life of High society, 1965, The Mournful Demeanor of Lieutenant Boruvka, 1966, A Babylonian Story, 1967, The Bitter World, 1969, Sins for Father Knox, 1973, Oh, My Papa! 1972; plays: The New Men and Women CBC Radio 1977, God in Your House, 1980 (1st prize Multicultural Theatre Festival Hamilton 1980); films: The Tank Battalion, 1991, The Swell Season, 1994; essays: Reading Detecive Stories, 1965, They-Which Is We, 1968, All the Bright Young Men and Women, 1972, Working Overtime, 1979, Talkin' Moscow Blues, 1989. Decorated Order of the White Lion; apptd. mem. Order of Can., 1992; Recipient Neustadt Internat. prize for lit., U. Okla., 1980, Gov. Gen. Can.'s award, 1985, lit. prize Echoing Green Found., 1990; Guggenheim fellow, 1980. Fellow Royal Soc. Can.; mem. Can. Writers' Union, Authors' League Am., Crime Writers Can., Mystery Writers Am., The Internat. PEN Club, Can. br. Czechoslovak Nat. Assn. Can. (mem. Presidium), Coun. Free Czechoslovakia (mem. Presidium), Order of Can. Progressive Conservative. Roman Catholic. Avocation: swing music. Home: 487 Sackville St, Toronto, ON Canada M4X 1T6

SKWAR, DONALD R., newspaper editor. Exec. sports editor Boston Globe. Office: Boston Globe 135 Morrissey Blvd Boston MA 02107

SKWIERSKY, PAUL, accountant; b. N.Y.C., Aug. 14, 1925; s. Abraham and Dora (Rainer) S.; m. Gloria Evelyn Lederman, Dec. 27, 1947; children: Janet S., Denise C. Skwiersky Cohen. BS, NYU, 1948. CPA, N.Y., N.J. Mng. ptnr. Benjamin Nadel & Co., N.Y.C., 1942-87, Skwiersky, Alpert & Bressler, N.Y.C., 1987—; bd. dirs. Philip & Janice Levin Found., North Plainfield, N.J., Darcy Found., Inc., N.Y.C., 1980-87, Levin Mgmt. Corp., North Plainfield, Allstate Constrn. Corp., North Plainfield; panelist, arbitrator Am. Arbitration Assn., N.Y.C. Dir. Birchwood Park Civic Assn., Syosset, N.Y., 1962. Sgt. U.S. Army, 1943-46. Mem. Fiber Producers Credit Assn., Textile Distbrs. Assn., Inc., N.Y. Credit & Fin. Mgmt. Assn., N.Y. State Soc. CPAs, Masons (master 1977-79), Fountains of Palm Beach Country Club. Avocations: reading, travel, golf. Office: Skwiersky Alpert Bressler 462 7th Ave New York NY 10018-7606

SKY, ALISON, artist, designer; b. N.Y.C.. BFA, Adelphi U., 1967; student, Art Students League, 1967-69, Columbia U. Co-founder, v.p. Sculpture in the Environ./SITE, N.Y.C., 1969-91; co-founder, prin. SITE Projects, N.Y.C., 1970-91; adj. faculty mem. Parsons Sch. Design, N.Y.C., 1994-95, Cooper Union, N.Y.C., 1995; vis. artist Purchase Coll., SUNY, 1994-95; artist-in-residence Urban Glass, 1995; lectr. in field. Exhbns. include The Venice Biennale, 1975, The Pompidou Ctr. and Louvre, Paris, 1975, The Mus. Modern Art, N.Y.C., 1979, 84, Ronald Feldman Fine Arts, N.Y.C., 1980, 83, The Wadsworth Atheneum, Hartford, Conn., 1980, The Va. Mus. Fine Arts, Richmond, Va., 1980, Neuer Berliner Kunstverein,

1982, Castello Sforzesco, Sala Viscontea, 1983, Victoria and Albert Mus., London, 1984, Nat. Mus. Modern Art, Tokyo, 1985-86, The Triennale di Milano, Italy, 1985, Whitney Mus. Am. Art, N.Y.C., 1985-86, Grey Art Gallery, N.Y.C., 1987-88, Documenta 8, Kassel, Germany, 1987, Am. Craft Mus., N.Y.C., 1996; permanent collections include, Smithsonian Instns., Washington, Mus. Modern Art, N.Y.C., Avery Libr., Columbia U., N.Y.C., Formica Corp., N.J., GSA, Pharr, Tex.; projects include BEST Products, 1979-84, Williwear Ltd., N.Y.C. and London, 1982-89, SITE Studio, 1984, The Mus. Borough of Bklyn., N.Y.C., 1985, Laurie Mallet House Memories, N.Y.C., 1986, Hwy. 86, Vancouver, Can., 1986, Pershing Sq., L.A., 1986, MTV Sets, N.Y.C., 1988, SWATCH, N.Y.C. and Zurich, Switzerland, 1988-90, Rockplex, Music Complex, Universal City, Calif., 1989, Peace Garden, Washington, 1989, NASA Exhibit, Sevilla, Spain, 1990, N.Y.C. Pub. Libr., 1990, Franz Mayer, Munich, 1991, Robert Lehman Gallery, 1996; author: (series of Books) ON SITE, 1971-76, Unbuilt America, 1976; pub. numerous books on art, 1971-76. Artery Arts finalist, Boston, 1994-95, RTA Arts-in-Transit finalist, Cleve., 1994, Pub. Art Commn. finalist, Cleve., 1994; Design fellow NEA, 1984, 90, Pollock-Krasner Found. fellow, 1991, Fulbright Indo-Am. fellow, 1992. Fellow Am. Acad. Rome. Studio: 60 Greene St New York NY 10012-4301

SKYLSTAD, WILLIAM S., bishop; b. Omak, Wash., Mar. 2, 1934; s. Stephen Martin and Reneldes Elizzbeth (Danzl) S. Student, Pontifical Coll., Josephinum, Worthington, Ohio; M.Ed., Gonzaga U. Ordained priest Roman Catholic Ch., 1960; asst. pastor Pullman, Wash., 1960-62; tchr. Mater Cleri Sem., 1961-68, rector, 1968-74; pastor Assumption Parish, Spokane, 1974-76; chancellor Diocese of Spokane, 1976-77; ordained bishop, 1977; bishop of Yakima, Wash., 1977-90, Spokane, Wash., 1990—. Office: Diocese of Spokane PO Box 1453 1023 W Riverside Ave Spokane WA 99201-1103 Home: 1025 W Cleveland Ave Spokane WA 99205-3320*

SKYLV, GRETHE KROGH, rheumatologist, anthropologist; b. Copenhagen, Denmark, May 31, 1938; d. Aage Krogh and Herdis Fischer (Lindeskov) Christoffersen; m. Axel Skylv, Jan. 12, 1962 (div. Feb. 1994); children: Lise, Kirsten, Mikael; m. Klaus Bruhn Jensen, Oct. 15, 1994. MD, U. Copenhagen, 1967, MA in Anthropology, 1990. Resident various hosps., Copenhagen, 1967-79; pvt. practice Hillerod, Denmark, 1979-84; dept. head Rehab. Ctr. for Torture Victims, Copenhagen, 1985-92; cons. Danish Red Cross, 1993—; rsch. scholar on cross-cultural interpersonal comm. Faculty of Humanities, U. Copenhagen, 1994—; cons. Orgn. for Manual Therapy, Denmark, 1985—, Internat. Rehab. Medicine Assn., 1991—, various Danish treatment ctrs. for torture victims & refugees, 1993—; com. mem. North-South issues Univ.-wide rsch.; mem. interdisciplinary rsch. groups comm. med. contexts, 1994—; bd. dirs. Network for Interdisciplinary Qualitative Rsch., Denmark, 1989—. Guest editor: Danish Soc. for Anthropology Soc. Jour., 1988-89; contbr. articles to profl. jours. Recipient Honorary award Cranio-Facial Pain Ctr. 1990. Fellow European Assn. Social Anthropologists, Danish Med. Assn. (bd. for ethnic minorities 1996—), Danish Manual Therapy Orgn., Danish Assn. for Rheumatology, Danish Assn. Internal Medicine, Danish Soc. for Social Anthropology, Physicians for Human Rights. Avocation: black belt in jujitsu. Home: Mosesvinget 54, DK-2400 Copenhagen Denmark

SLAATTÈ, HOWARD ALEXANDER, minister, philosophy educator; b. Evanston, Ill., Oct. 18, 1919; s. Iver T. and Esther (Larsen) S.; m. Mildred Gegenheimer, June 20, 1951; children: Elaine Slaatte Tran, Mark, Paul. A.A., Kendall Coll., 1940; B.A. cum laude, U. N.D., 1942; B.D. cum laude, Drew U., 1945, Ph.D., 1956; Drew fellow, Mansfield Coll., Oxford (Eng.) U., 1949-50. Ordained to ministry Meth. Ch. as elder, 1943 Pastor Detroit Conf. United Meth. Ch., 1950-65; assoc. prof. systematic theology Temple U., 1956-60; vis. prof., prof. philosophy and religion McMurry Coll. (now named McMurry U.), 1960-65; prof. dept. philosophy Marshall U., Huntington, W.Va., 1965-89, prof. emeritus, 1989—, chmn. dept., 1966-81, mem. grad. council, 1970-73, mem. research bd., 1974-76, mem. acad. standards and policy com., 1975-77, research grantee, 1976, 77; mem. bd. Campus Christian Center, 1973-75; prof. ethics St. Leo (Fla.) Coll., 1993; lectr. Traverse City (Mich.) State Hosp., 1966-71, Am. Ontoanalytical Assn. internat. conf., Acapulco, Mex., 1970, World Congress Logotherapy, San Diego, 1980, other orgns.; mem. W.Va. Conf., United Meth. Ch., 1965-85. Author: Time and Its End, 1962, Fire in the Brand, 1963, The Pertinence of the Paradox, 1968, The Paradox of Existentialist Theology, 1971, Modern Science and the Human Condition, 1974, The Arminian Arm of Theology, 1977, The Dogma of Immaculate Perception, 1979, Discovering Your Real Self, 1980, The Seven Ecumenical Councils, 1980, The Creativity of Consciousness, 1983, Contemporary Philosophies of Religion, 1986, Time, Existence and Destiny, 1988, Critical Survey of Ethics, 1988; co-author: The Philosophy of Martin Heidegger, 1983, Religious Issues in Contemporary Philosophy, 1988, Our Cultural Cancer and Its Cure, 1995, A Re-Appraisal of Kierkegaard, 1995; contbr. Analecta Frankliana, 1981; gen. editor: (series) Contemporary Existentialism; contbr. to theol. and philos. jours. Mem. W.Va. Conf. United Meth. Ch., 1966—; bd. dirs. Inst. for Advanced Philos. Research, 1979-90; chmn. bd. dirs. Salvation Army of Huntington, W. Va. Recipient Outstanding Educators of Am. award, 1975, Profl. Excellence award Faculty Merit Fedn., State of W.Va., 1986; named to Honorable Order of Ky. Colonels, W.Va. Ambassador of Good Will; named Internat. Man of Yr., 1993; NSF fellow, 1965, Benedum Found. rsch. grantee, 1970, NSF rsch.-grantee, 1965, 71. Mem. W.Va. Philos. Assn. (pres., 1966-67, 83-84), Am. Philos. Assn., AAUP, Am. Acad. Religion. Home: 14123 Oak Knoll St Spring Hill FL 34609-3157 *Most knowledge is relative, a balanced existential position with empirical implications, except for the divine Absolute encountered by faith in existence. The revealed principles opened up thereby, especially the ultimacy of sacrifical love (Agape), give basis and motivation for vital morality and a healthy culture. True freedom springs from commitment to these principles.*

SLABY, LILLIAN FRANCES, home finance counselor, real estate professional; b. Cleve., June 9, 1931; d. Bismarck Otto and Marie Theresa (Emo) Newman; m. Jack Glenn Slaby, Sept. 22, 1951; children: Lonna, Jan, Jeffrey, James, Jack. Student, Dyke Coll., 1949-50. Lic. realtor, Ohio. Home fin. counselor, real estate assoc. HGM Hilltop, Rocky River, Ohio, 1978-88, Realty One, Westlake, Ohio, 1988-91; with Riveredge Realty, Rocky River, Ohio, 1993—. Mem. Internat. Graphoanalysis Soc. (cert.), World Assn. of Document Examiners. Roman Catholic. Avocations: landscaping design, fashion design. Home: 5106 NW 16th Pl Gainesville FL 32605-3302 Office: Riveredge Realty Detroit Rd Rocky River OH 44116

SLACK, DONALD CARL, agricultural engineer, educator; b. Cody, Wyo., June 25, 1942; s. Clarence Ralbon and Clara May (Beightol) S.; m. Marion Arline Kimball, Dec. 19, 1964; children: Jonel Marie, Jennifer Michelle. BS in Agrl. Engring., U. Wyo., 1965; MS in Agrl. Engring., U. Ky., 1968, PhD in Agrl. Engring., 1975. Registered profl. engr., Ky., Ariz. Asst. civil engr. City of Los Angeles, 1965; research specialist U. Ky., Lexington, 1966-70; agrl. engring. advisor U. Ky., Tha Phra, Thailand, 1970-73; research asst. U. Ky., Lexington, 1973-75; from asst. prof. to assoc. prof. agrl. engring. U. Minn., St. Paul, 1975-84; prof. U. Ariz., Tucson, 1984—, head dept. agrl. and biosystems engring., 1991—; tech. advisor Ariz. Dept. Water Resources, Phoenix, 1985—; cons. Winrock Internat., Morrilton, Ark., 1984, Water Mgmt. Synthesis II, Logan, Utah, 1985, Desert Agrl. Tech. Systems, Tucson, 1985—, Portek Hermosillo, Mex., 1989—, World Bank, Washington, 1992—; dep. program support mgr. Rsch. Irrigation Support Project for Asia and the Near East, Arlington, Va., 1987-94. Contbr. articles to profl. jours. Fellow ASCE (Outstanding Jour. Paper award 1988); mem. Am. Soc. Agrl. Engrs. (Ariz. sect. Engr. of Yr. 1993), Am. Geophys. Union, Am. Soc. Agronomy, Soil Sci. Soc. Am., Am. Soc. Engring. Edn., SAR, Brotherhood of Knights of the Vine (master knight), Sigma Xi, Tau Beta Pi, Alpha Epsilon, Gamma Sigma Delta. Democrat. Lutheran. Achievements include 3 patents pending; developer of infrared based irrigation scheduling device. Avocations: hunting, camping, hiking, model railroading. Home: 9230 E Visco Pl Tucson AZ 85710-3167 Office: U Ariz Agrl Biosystems Engrin Tucson AZ 85721 *Personal philosophy: Don't take yourself too seriously and don't take anyone else too seriously either.*

SLACK, EDWARD DORSEY, III, financial systems professional, consultant; b. Fairmont, W.Va., June 2, 1942; s. Edward Dorsey Jr. and Margaret Elaine (Higgs) S.; m. Donna Jean Carter, Oct. 19, 1944; children: Ted, Robyn. BS in Indsl. Engring., W.Va. U., 1965, postgrad., 1965-66. Registered profl. engr., W.Va. Assoc. systems and procedures analyst Westinghouse Atomic Power divs., Pitts., 1966-69; systems and procedures analyst Westinghouse Nuclear Energy Systems, Pitts., 1969-72, sr. systems analyst, 1972-75, mgr. payroll and fin. systems, 1975-77; mgr. standard ledger conversion Westinghouse Energy Systems, Pitts., 1977, mgr. fin. systems and control, 1978-90, mgr. fin. systems and standard ledger, 1990-91, mgr. payroll, cost and fin. systems control, 1991-94; data processing analyst & decision support coord. Braddock (Pa.) Med. Ctr., 1995—; developer computer programs; designer fin. systems computer modules. Developer computer programs; designer and installer computer modules. Mem. NSPE, W.Va. Soc. Profl. Engrs. Avocations: walking, jogging, basketball, spectator sports, sports cards. Home: 179 Autumn Dr Trafford PA 15085-1448 Office: Braddock Med Ctr 400 Holland Ave Braddock PA 15064

SLACK, FRANCES SPIVEY, maternal, women's health and medical, surgical nurse; b. Ouachita Parish, La., Mar. 2, 1947; d. Jack Shelton and Ethel Mae (Thompson) Spivey; m. Roosevelt Slack, Jr., Feb. 4, 1966; children: Rodney J., Shannon N. Student, Gramblin U., 1965-66; BA, NE La. U., 1980, BSN, 1985. RN, La. Staff nurse No. La. Dialysis Ctr., Monroe, St. Francis Med. Ctr., Monroe; charge nurse labor and delivery room Glenwood Med. Ctr., West Monroe, La.; charge nurse med.-surg. unit E.A. Conway Hosp., Monroe; dir. nursing svc. Ridgecrest Nursing Home, West Monroe, La.

SLACK, LEWIS, organization administrator; b. Phila., Apr. 15, 1924; s. Lewis and Martha (Fitzgerald) S.; m. Sarah Hunt Wyman, Dec. 29, 1948; children—Elizabeth Wyman, Susan Towne, Christopher Morgan. S.B., Harvard U., 1944; Ph.D., Washington U., St. Louis, 1950. Physicist U.S. Naval Research Lab., 1950-54; assoc. prof. physics George Washington U., Washington, 1954-57; prof. physics George Washington U., 1957-62, acting head physics dept., 1957-60; asst. exec. sec. div. phys. scis. Nat. Acad. Scis.-NRC, Washington, 1962-67; sec. com. nuclear sci. NRC, 1962-67, mem. commn. human resources, 1974-78; dir. ednl. programs Am. Inst. Physics, N.Y.C., 1967-87; cons. Gen. Atomics div. Gen. Dynamics Corp., La Jolla, Calif., summers, 1959, 60; chmn. phys. scis. Am. exhibit Internat. Conf. Peaceful Uses Atomic Energy, Geneva, Switzerland, 1958; mem. Sci. Manpower Commn., 1968-87, pres., 1974-75, treas., 1976; mem. U.S. nat. com. Internat. Union for Pure and Applied Physics, 1972-78, sec., 1974-78; Mem. adv. com. Physics Today, 1963-67, chmn., 1967. Mem. Bruce Mus., Greenwich, Conn. (collections com., edn. com., exhbns. com., 1988-95). With USNR, 1943-46. Fellow Washington Acad. Scis., AAAS (mem. council 1971-72, 76-78); mem. Am. Phys. Soc., Am. Assn. Physics Tchrs. Episcopalian. Research beta ray and gamma ray spectroscopy. Home: 2104 Tadley Dr Chapel Hill NC 27514-2109

SLADE, BERNARD, playwright; b. St. Catharines, Ont., Can., May 2, 1930; s. Frederick and Bessie (Walbourne) Newbound; m. Jill Florence Hancock, July 25, 1953; children: Laurel, Christopher. Ed., Caernarvon Grammar Sch. Eng. Actor: Garden Ctr. Theatre, Vineland, Ont., Crest Theatre, Toronto, CBC-TV, Citadel Theatre, Edmonton, Alta.; screenwriter of over 20 hour TV plays for CBC, CBS, ABC, NBC, 1957—; writer/creator (TV series) Love on a Rooftop, The Patridge Family, The Flying Nun, The Girl with Something Extra, Bridget Loves Bernie; story editor, writer 15 episodes of TV series Bewitched; writer/creator (plays) A Very Close Family, 1962, Same Time Next Year (Drama Desk award 1975, Tony award nomination 1975), Tribute, 1978, Romantic Comedy, 1979, Special Occasions, 1981, Fatal Attraction, 1984, Return Engagements, 1986, Sweet William, 1987, An Act of the Imagination, 1987, I Remember You, 1991, You Say Tomatoes, 1993, Everytime I See You, 1994, Same Time, Another Year; feature films: Same Time, Next Year, 1977, Tribute, 1978, Romantic Comedy, 1979. Recipient Acad. award nomination Motion Picture Arts and Scis., 1978. Mem. Dramatists Guild Am., Writers Guild Am. (award nomination), Acad. Motion Picture Arts and Scis. (Acad. award nomination 1978), Soc. Authors and Artists (France). Avocation: tennis. Office: care Jack Hutto Agy 405 W 23rd St New York NY 10011-1404 *I am a prisoner of a childhood dream: to write for the theatre. The fulfillment of that dream has lived up to all my expectations. I believe the theatre should be a celebration of the human condition and that the artist's job is to remind us of all that is good about ourselves. I feel privileged to be given a platform for my particular vision of life, and, whether my plays succeed or fail, I am always grateful for the use of the hall.*

SLADE, BERNARD NEWTON, electronics company executive; b. Sioux City, Iowa, Dec. 21, 1923; s. William Charles and Katherine Gertrude Slotsky; m. Margot Friedlein, Aug. 18, 1946; children: Steven P., Eric J. BSEE, U. Wis., 1948; MS, Stevens Inst. Tech., 1954. Devel. engr. tube div. RCA, Harrison, N.J., 1948-55; devel. engr. RCA Labs., Princeton, N.J., 1955-56; mgr. tech. program IBM, Poughkeepsie, N.Y., 1956-60; mgr. product ops. IBM, Hopewell Junction, N.Y., 1960-64; mgr. mfg. tech. IBM World Trade Corp., Armonk, N.Y., 1964-65; corp. dir. of mfg. tech. IBM Corp., Armonk, 1965-84; sr. cons. Arthur D. Little, Inc., Cambridge, Mass., 1984-86, Gemini Cons., Morristown, N.J., 1986-93; founder and v.p. Yieldup Internat. Corp., 1993—; bd. dirs. V3 Semicondr. Corp. Co-author: Winning the Productivity Race, 1985; author: Compressing the Product Development Cycle, 1992; contbr. numerous articles to tech. jours.; patentee in field; contbg. author: Transistors, 1956, Handbook of Semiconductor Electronics, 1962. 2d lt. AUS, 1943-46. Mem. IEEE (sr.), Sigma Xi. Home: 12 Merry Hill Rd Poughkeepsie NY 12603-3214 Office: Yieldup Internat Corp 117 Easy St Mountain View CA 94043

SLADE, GERALD JACK, publishing company executive; b. Utica, N.Y., May 24, 1919; s. John H. and Sada (Jacobson) S.; m. Dorothy Casler, Oct. 24, 1942; children—John, Carolyn, David. B.A. summa cum laude, Colgate U., 1941; M.B.A., Harvard, 1943. Chmn. bd., pres., chief exec. officer Western Pub. Co., Racine, Wis.; dir. Mattel, Inc., Wells-Gardner Electronics Corp., 1st Nat. Bank of Racine, Joseph Schlitz Brewing Co.; Past pres. Nat. Assn. Electronic Organ Mfrs. Mem. Phi Beta Kappa, Kappa Delta Rho. Home: 3352 SE Fairway W Stuart FL 34997-6030

SLADE, JOHN DANTON, lobbyist, radio talk show host; b. Balt., Apr. 5, 1939; s. Eldon and Marie (Smith) S.; m. Dale Iris Walden, Mar. 14, 1964 (dec. Dec. 1965); 1 child, Kenyatta Conrad; m. Deborah Faye Douglas, Dec. 11, 1987. BA in Sociology, Morgan State U., 1964; MA in Sociology, CUNY, 1966. Mgmt. trainee IBM, N.Y.C., 1966-69; producer, dir. WBAL-TV, Balt., 1969-71, WGBH-TV, Boston, 1971-73, KPIX-TV, San Francisco, 1973-75; announcer KEST Radio, San Francisco, 1975-76; gen. mgr. Channel 8 Access TV, San Francisco, 1975-79; owner Swansbriar Plantation, Cumberland, Va., 1979-85; asst. prof. military sci., dept. chmn. Howard U., Bowie State U., Georgetown U., Washington, 1985-88; acting chief Nat. Guard Bur., Washington, 1988-92; exec. dir. Assn. Reserve Minority Svc. Members, Inc., Washington, 1992—; talk show host WOL Radio, Washington; bd. dirs. Meridian Distributors, St. Thomas, V.I.; guest lectr. Stanford (Calif.) U., Northeastern U., Boston, Morgan State Coll., Balt., Merritt Coll., Oakland, Calif., U. Mass., Amherst; mem. spl. com. San Francisco Chronicle; mem. Balt. Community Rels. Commn.; mem. N.G. Drug Reduction Bd., 1990-91. Author: Last Testament of an American, 1993, Flight of an Angel, 1993, The Founding and Ascendancy of Iota Phi Theta, 1994; Man-Made (Guide to Single Mothers Raising Black Boys Alone), 1994; film producer Breaking the Chains of Bondage, 1972. Lt. col. U.S. Army, 1985-92. Recipient Roy Wilkens Renown Svc. award, 1991, Award of Honor, NAACP, Balt., Community Svc. award Les Hommes Civic and Social Club, Hampton, Va., 1991. Mem. Iota Phi Theta (founding mem., bus. mgr. 1963-64). Republican. Office: ARMS 1401 Madison St NW Washington DC 20011-6805

SLADE, LLEWELLYN EUGENE, lawyer, engineer; b. Carroll, Iowa, May 1, 1911; s. Llewellyn and Mary (Veach) S.; m. Jane England Dickinson, June 8, 1945 (dec. Dec. 1992); 1 child, Yvonne Slade Tidd. B.S. in Elec. Engring., Iowa State U., 1938, M.S., 1942; J.D., Drake U., 1951. Registered profl. engr., Iowa. Rsch. engr. Iowa State U. Ext. Svc., 1938-40; With Iowa Power & Light Co., Des Moines, 1940-68; exec. v.p. ops., dir. Iowa Power & Light Co., 1964-68; cons. Nebr. Public Power Dist. nuclear project; pvt. practice as exec. counsellor, atty., profl. engr., 1968—; fed. ct. bankruptcy trustee, Solid Waste Com. City of Des Moines; past mgmt. adv. and dir. Wright Tree Service Cos.; mem. panel arbitrators U.S. Fed. Mediation and Conciliation Service, Iowa Pub. Employees Relations Bd. Former chmn., trustee Des Moines Metro Transit Authority. Mem. Fed., Am., Iowa, Polk County bar assns., Iowa Engring. Soc. (Anson Marston award for outstanding svc. 1957, Outstanding Svc. award 1987), Nat. Soc. Profl. Engrs. Engrs. Club Des Moines, Atomic Indsl. Forum, Greater Des Moines C. of C., Iowa Arboretum (bd. dirs.), Des Moines Club, Men's Garden Club of Am., Masons (32 deg.), Shriners, Rotary. Lutheran. Home: 5833 Pleasant Dr Des Moines IA 50312-1211

SLADE, ROY, artist, college president, museum director; b. Cardiff, U.K., July 14, 1933; came to U.S., 1967, naturalized, 1975; s. David Trevor and Millicent (Stone) S. N.D.D., Cardiff Coll. Art, 1954; A.T.D., U. Wales, 1954; D of Arts, Art Inst. So. Calif., 1994. Tchr. art and crafts Heolgam High Sch., Wales, 1956-60; lectr. art Clarendon Coll., Nottingham, Eng., 1960-64; sr. lectr. fine art Leeds Coll. Art, Eng., 1964-67; prof. painting Corcoran Sch. Art, Washington, 1967-68, assoc. dean, 1969-70, dean, 1970-77; dir. Corcoran Gallery of Art, Washington, 1972-77; pres., dir. Cranbrook Acad. Art, Bloomfield Hills, Mich., 1977-94; sr. lectr. Leeds Coll. Art, Eng. 1968-69; vis. Boston Mus. Fine Arts, 1970. Exhibited one-man shows Howard Roberts Gallery, Cardiff, Wales, 1958, New Art Ctr., London, 1960, U. Birmingham, 1964, 69, Herbert Art Gallery and Mus., Coventry, 1964, Va. State Art League, 1967, Mus. of Arts and Crafts, Columbus, Ga., 1968, Jefferson Place Gallery, Washington, 1968, 70, 72, 73, Park Sq. Gallery, Leeds, 1969, St. Mary's Coll., Md., 1971, Guelph U., Ont., Can., 1971, Hood Coll., 1974, Pyramid Gallery, Washington, 1976, Robert Kidd Gallery, 1981, 92, Herman Miller, Inc., Mich., 1985; group shows in U.K., Washington, Can.; represented in permanent collections Arts Council Gt. Brit., Contemporary Art Soc., Nuffield Found., Ministry of Works, Eng., Brit. Embassy, Washington, Brit. Overseas Airways Corp., U. Birmingham, Wakefield City Art Gallery, Clarendon Coll., Cadbury Bros., Ltd., Eng., Lord Ogmore, Local Edn. Authorities. Mem. D.C. Commn. on Arts.; bd. dirs. Artists for Environment Found., Nat. Assn. Schs. Art; chmn. Nat. Council Art Adminstrs., 1981. Served with Brit. Army, 1954-56. Decorated knight 1st class Order of White Rose (Finland), Royal Order of Polar Star (Sweden); recipient award Welsh Soc., Phila., 1974, Gov.'s Arts Orgn. award, 1988; Fulbright scholar, 1967-68. Mem. Nat. Soc. Lit. and Arts, AIA (hon. Detroit chpt.), Assn. Art Mus. Dirs. (hon.). Home: PO Box 48 Harsens Island MI 48028-0048

SLADE, THOMAS BOG, III, lawyer, investment banker; b. Balt., June 22, 1931; s. Thomas Bog Jr. and Blanche Evangeline (Hall) S.; m. Sunya Johanna Bowen, July 25, 1959 (div. 1976); children: Sunya Kirsten, DeWitt Bowen, Vivian Watson; m. Mary Stewart Bolton, Apr. 3, 1976. BA, U. Va., 1953, LLB, 1954. Bar: Fla. 1956, U.S. Supreme Ct. 1966. Assoc. Patterson, Freeman, Richardson & Watson, Jacksonville, Fla., 1956-61; ptnr. Freeman, Richardson, Watson, Slade, McCarthy & Kelly, Jacksonville, 1961-80; pvt. practice Jacksonville, 1980-81; ptnr. Foley & Lardner, Jacksonville, 1981-92; sr. v.p. Gardnyr Michael Capital, Inc., Jacksonville, 1992—. Served to 1st lt., U.S. Army, 1954-56. Mem. Fla. Bar (bd. govs. 1966-69, pres. young lawyers sect. 1967-68), Nat. Assn. Bond Lawyers, Jacksonville Bar Assn., Club at World Trade Ctr. (N.Y.C.), Fla Yacht Club, Univ. Club of Jacksonville. Office: Gardnyr Michael Capital Inc 2764 Vernon Terrace Ste B1 Jacksonville FL 32205

SLADEK, LYLE VIRGIL, mathematician, educator; b. Pukwana, S.D., Oct. 13, 1923; s. Charles Frank and Emma Margaret (Swanson) S.; m. Patricia Knotts, Sept. 12, 1948; children: Susan, Ann, Laura, Karen. B.S., S.D. State U., 1948; M.A., U. S.D., 1949, Stanford U., 1963; Ph.D., UCLA, 1970. Tchr. high sch. Mitchell, S.D., 1950-56; asst. prof. math. Black Hills State Coll., S.D., 1957-62; prof. math. Calif. Luth. Univ., Thousand Oaks, 1963-94, prof. emeritus, 1994—; lectr. in field. Contbr. short stories, poems to mags. and newspapers. Pres. congregation Our Savior's Lutheran Ch., Spearfish, S.D., 1961. Served as officer U.S. Army, 1943-46, PTO, ETO. Shell Merit fellow, 1956; NSF fellow, 1956-57, 62-63; recipient Meritorious Achievement award edn. S.D. Mines and Tech., 1957; Fulbright-Hays lectr. Bahamas, 1980-81. Mem. Math. Assn. Am., Blue Key, Pi Kappa Delta, Phi Delta Kappa. Home: 3243 Pioneer St Thousand Oaks CA 91360-2730 *I learned from my parents during the dust bowl years that adversity often can be overcome through patience and determination, and that problems provide challenges that add spice to life. I have sought to return full measure to society for all the opportunities and joys of life that have come my way.*

SLADEK, RONALD JOHN, physics educator; b. Chgo., Sept. 19, 1926; s. James Joseph and Rose (Vachulka) S.; m. Jeanne T. McFadden, Sept. 19, 1953; children—Linda, James, Frances, Stephen, Rosemarie, Edward. Ph.B., U. Chgo., 1947, S.B., 1949, S.M., 1950, Ph.D. (AEC fellow), 1954. Research physicist Westinghouse Research Labs., Pitts., 1953-60, fellow scientist, 1960-61; assoc. prof. physics Purdue U., West Lafayette, Ind., 1961-66, prof., 1966-91, prof. physics emeritus, 1992—, acting head dept. physics, 1969-71, assoc. dean sci., 1974-87; vis. scientist Sci. Center, N.Am. Rockwell Corp., Thousand Oaks, Calif., summer 1967; sabbatical scientist Xerox Research Center, Palo Alto, Calif., 1976-77. Contbr. articles to profl. jours. With USNR, 1945-46. Fellow Am. Phys. Soc. Home: 963 Ridgeview Dr Reno NV 89511-8506

SLAGLE, JACOB WINEBRENNER, JR., food products executive; b. Balt., Jan. 18, 1945; s. Jacob Winebrenner and Anna Dorothea (Vernon-Williams) S.; m. Sharon Carol Muth, Nov. 18, 1973 (div. 1982); children: Alexander, Dylan; m. Nina Kathleen Tou, May 20, 1994. Student, U. Ariz., 1963-65; BA in Sociology, U. Md., 1969; diploma, Broadcasting Inst. Md., Balt., 1975. Claims adjuster Govt. Employees Ins. Co., Towson, Md., 1969-71; exec. Slagle & Slagle, Inc., Balt., 1971-81, pres., 1981-92; pres. Denzer's Food Products, Balt., 1992—; bd. dirs. H.S.A., Inc., Marietta, Ga., 1992, 93; freelance writer for various nespapers and mags.; monthly columnist Jake About Town, Balt. Chronicle, 1989-93; mem. bd. advisors Broadcasting Inst. Md., 1990-93. Contbg. author: Baltimore: A Living Renaissance, 1981; contbg. writer Food Distbn. Mag., 1994—. Bd. dirs. Hist. Balt. Soc., 1979—, v.p., 1989—; bd. dirs. Intervention with Pact, Balt., 1982-89; pres. Hanover House Condominium Assn., Balt., 1983—; arbitrator BBB Greater Md., Balt., 1983-91; mem. Greater Balt. Com. Leadership Group, 1996. Mem. Homebuilders Assn. Md. (bd. dirs. remodelers coun. 1989-93, Remodeling Assoc. of Yr. 1992), Md. Splty. Foods Assn. (bd. dirs. 1994—, sec. 1995, pres. 1996), Balt. Blues Soc. (bd. dirs. 1992—, sec. 1995—), Rotary (bd. dirs. Balt. 1992-94).

SLAGLE, JAMES ROBERT, computer science educator; b. Bklyn., 1934; married; 5 children. BS summa cum laude, St. John's U., 1955; MS in Math., MIT, 1957, PhD in Math., 1961. Staff mathematician Lincoln Lab. MIT, 1955-63; group leader Lawrence Livermore Radiation Lab. U. Calif., Livermore, 1963-67; chief heuristics lab. divsn. computer rsch. and tech. NIH, Bethesda, Md., 1967-74; chief computer sci. lab. comm. scis. divsn. Naval Rsch. Lab., Washington, 1974-81, spl. asst., 1981-84; Disting. prof. computer sci. U. Minn., Mpls., 1984—; mem. faculty dept. elec. engring. MIT, 1962-63; mem. faculty dept. computer sci. and elec. engring. U. Calif., Berkeley, 1964-67; mem. faculty dept. computer sci. Johns Hopkins U., 1967-74; cons. in field. Author: Artificial Intelligence: The Heuristic Programming Approach, 1971. Contbr. articles to profl. jours. Named one of Ten Outstanding Young Men of Am., U.S. Jaycees, 1969; recipient Outstanding Handicapped Fed. Employee of Yr. award, 1979; Mary P. Oenslager Career Achievement award, Recording for the Blind, 1982. Fellow AAAS, IEEE, Am. Assn. Artificial Intelligence; mem. Computer Soc. of IEEE. Office: U Minn Computer Sci Dept 4-192 EE/Csi Bldg 200 Union St SE Minneapolis MN 55455-0154

SLAGLE, LARRY B., human resources specialist; b. Templeton, Pa., Dec. 17, 1934; s. William Harry and Luella (Armstrong) S. AB, Wabash Coll., 1956; postgrad., Am. U., 1967-71. Dep. adminstr. for mgmt. and budget USDA Animal & Plant Health Inspection Svc., Washington, 1978-88, assoc. adminstr., 1988-90; dir. pers. USDA, Washington, 1990-94; pvt. practice human resources and orgnl. cons., 1994—; bd. dirs. Fgn. Aid Through Edn. With U.S. Army, 1957-59, Korea. Named Meritorious Exec. President Reagan, 1985, President Bush, 1991. Avocation: cycling. Home and Office: 208 6th St SE Washington DC 20003-1134

SLAGLE, ROBERT LEE, II, elementary and secondary education educator; b. Carlisle, Pa., Oct. 16, 1962; s. Robert Lee and Hilda Carolyn (Jones) S.; m. Cynthia Jean Phifer, Feb. 8, 1992; children: Robert Lee III, Theodore

Calvin George. BA in Bus. and Acctg., Gettysburg Coll., 1984; MA in Adminstrn., George Washington U., 1988; MA in Edn., Beaver Coll., 1994. Cert. tchr. elem. and secondary social studies, Pa. Engr. officer U.S. Army, Ft. Belvoir, Eustis, Va., 1984-88; ptnr., constrn. mgr. Triple S Quality Builders, Mechanicsburg, Pa., 1988-90; constrn. dir. Rite Aid Corp., Harrisburg, Pa., 1989-92; tchr. Colonial Sch. Dist., Plymouth Meeting, Pa., 1992—; coach Plymouth (Pa.) Whitemarsh H.S. Football, 1991—, Plymouth (Pa.)-Whitemarsh H.S. Weight Lifting, 1991—, Whitemarsh (Pa.) Twp. Big League Baseball, 1992—. Lay reader St. Mary's Episcopal Ch., Andorra-Phila., Pa., 1992—. Capt. U.S. Army Corps of Engrs., 1984-88. Decorated Army Commendation medal U.S. Army Dept. Def., 1985, Meritorious Svc. medal U.S. Army Dept. Def., 1988. Mem. ASCD, Nat. Coun. Tchrs. Math., Colonial Edn. Assn. Republican. Avocations: carpentry, weight training and conditioning, hunting, outdoor recreation, American history and politics. Home: 4033 Center Ave Lafayette Hill PA 19444-1425

SLAIBY, THEODORE GEORGE, aeronautical engineer, consultant; b. Washington, Conn., Apr. 12, 1929; s. George and Afifi (Buzaid) S.; m. Margaret Sullivan, June 29, 1957; children: Peter E., Jeffrey M., Barbara E. BS in Aero. Engring., Rensselaer Poly. Inst., 1950. Engr. tech. and rsch. group Pratt & Whitney Aircraft Engines, East Hartford, Conn., 1950-56, asst. project engr., tech. and rsch. group, 1956-60, devel. engr., advanced engines, 1960-67, mgr. new project devel. programs, 1967-76, dir. design & analytical engring., 1976-81, v.p. product integrity, 1981-83, v.p. engring., 1983-87, ret., 1987; engring. cons. United Techs. Corp., Hartford, Conn., 1987—; cons. to various engring. cos. Author or co-author numerous tech. papers, 1958-70; patentee in field. Avocations: farming, hunting, fishing, history, language study. Home: 251 Spring St Manchester CT 06040-6640

SLAIN, JOHN JOSEPH, legal educator; b. Jan. 21, 1927. A.B., Providence Coll., 1952; LL.B., NYU, 1955. Bar: N.Y. 1956. Assoc. Cravath, Swaine & Moore, 1955-60; v.p., gen. counsel AIM Cos., Inc., 1961-66, dir., 1964-71; assoc. prof. law Ind. U.-Indpls., 1965-70; prof. law Ohio State U., Columbus, 1970-77, NYU, N.Y.C., 1977—. Dir., treas. Indpls. Legal Services Orgn., 1966-71; dir. Ohio Catholic Charities, 1975-77. Republican. Episcopalian. Office: NYU Law Sch 40 Washington Sq S New York NY 10012-1005

SLAKEY, LINDA LOUISE, biochemistry educator; b. Oakland, Calif., Jan. 2, 1939; d. William Henry and Georgia Evelyn Slakey. BS, Siena Heights Coll., 1962; PhD, U. Mich., 1967; postgrad., U. Wis., 1970-73. Elem. sch. tchr. Saint Edmund's Sch., Oak Park, Ill., 1958-61; tchr. Resurrection H.S., Lansing, Mich., 1962-63; instr. in chemistry St. Dominic's Coll., St. Charles, Ill., 1967-69; rsch. assoc. Argonne (Ill.) Nat. Libr., 1969-70; project assoc., dept. physiol. chemistry U. Wis., Madison, 1970-73; asst. prof. dept. biochemistry U. Mass., Amherst, 1973-79, assoc. prof., 1979-87, prof., 1987—, head dept. biochemistry and molecular biology, 1986-91, dean Coll. Natural Scis. and Math., 1993—; adv. com. arteriosclerosis and hypertension Nat. Heart & Lung and Blood Inst., Washington, 1978-81, mem. rev. com. B, 1981-87; vis. scientist Clin. Rsch. Ctr, Harrow, Eng., 1984-85. Contbr. articles to profl. jours. NSF predoctoral fellow U. Mich., 1963-67, NIH spl. fellow, 1970-73. Fellow Am. Heart Assn. (established investigator 1977-82), Arteriosclerosis Soc. of Am. Heart Assn.; mem. Am. Soc. Cell Biology, Am. Soc. for Biochemistry and Molecular Biology, Sigma Xi, Sigma Delta Epsilon. Office: U Mass Coll Natural Sci & Math 722 Lederle Tower B Amherst MA 01003

SLANE, HENRY PINDELL, broadcasting executive; b. Peoria, Ill., Dec. 29, 1920; s. Carl P. and Frances (Pindell) S.; children by previous marriage: John, Elizabeth Jean, Henry Pindell, Barbara. A.B., Yale U., 1943. Became pub. Peoria Newspapers, Inc., Peoria Broadcasting Co.; now pres. Peoria Jour. Star, Inc.; pres. PJS Publs., Inc. (Sew News, Shooting Times and Rotor & Wing, Profitable Crafts Merchandising and Crafts mags.). Served with USNR, 1943-46. Mem. Am. Soc. Newspaper Editors, Chi Psi, Sigma Delta Chi. Clubs: Peoria Country, Creve Coeur (Ill.) Country, Sturgeon Bay (Wis.). Home: 5188 N Prospect Rd Peoria IL 61614-5354 Office: Peoria Jour Star Inc 1 News Plz Peoria IL 61643-0001

SLANSKY, JERRY WILLIAM, investment company executive; b. Chgo., Mar. 8, 1947; s. Elmer Edward and Florence Anna (Kosobud) S.; m. Marlene Jean Cannella, Jan. 29, 1950; children: Brett Matthew, Blake Adam. BA, Elmhurst Coll., 1969; MA, No. Ill. U., 1971. Mktg. rep. Bantam Book Co., Chgo., 1972-73, Charles Levy Circulating Co., Chgo., 1973-76; account exec. Merrill Lynch, Chgo., 1976-77; account exec. Oppenheimer & Co., Inc., Chgo., 1977—, asst. v.p., 1978, v.p., 1979, sr. v.p., 1981, mng. dir., 1986, ptnr., 1986—. Bd. dirs. Lake Geneva (Wis.) Beach Assn., 1987—, Glen Ellyn Youth Ctr., Glenbard West H.S. Mem. Nat. Assn. Securities Dealers (arbitrator 1988—), N.Y. Stock Exch., Chgo. Bd. Options, Am. Arbitration. Assn, Omaha C. of C. Presbyterian. Avocations: swimming, water skiing, golf. Office: Oppenheimer & Co Inc 311 S Wacker Dr Chicago IL 60606-6618

SLAPPEY, STERLING GREENE, writer, journalist, researcher; b. Ft. Valley, Ga., June 18, 1917; s. Jenkins Sterling and Elma Louise (Greene) S.; m. Margaret Byne Sellers, Jan. 13, 1945; children—Margaret, Charles. Student, Ala. Poly. Inst. (now Auburn U.), 1937, 38, U. Ga., Atlanta, 1938-39. Reporter Atlanta Georgian & Sunday Am., 1938-39, Atlanta Constn., 1940, 41, 45, 46, AP, Atlanta, London, Moscow, 1947-59; specialist in racial affairs U.S. News & World Report, 1960-62; Central European bur. chief Los Angeles Times, based in Bonn, West Germany, 1963-66; sr. editor Nation's Bus., Washington, 1966-78; dir. Future of Bus. Program; dir. public affairs Georgetown U. Center for Strategic and Internat. Studies, Washington, 1978-84, supr. spl. events, 1984-88; columnist Washingtonian Mag., 1971-74; free-lance writer various publs.; sec. Iberian Imports Inc., Alexandria, 1969-78; pres. Alexandria Bath and Linen Co., 1978-84. Author: novel Exodus of the Damned, 1968, Pioneers of American Business, 1973, Future of Business, 1980. Served with AUS, 1941-45. Mem. Overseas Writers, Landmarks Soc., White House Corrs. Assn., State Dept. Corrs. Assn., Friends Kennedy Center, Assn. for Preservation Va. Antiquities, Smithsonian Assos., Alexandria Assembly, Nat. Trust Historic Preservation, Am. Acad. Polit. Sci., Acad. Social and Polit. Sci., Phi Delta Theta, Internat. Club (Washington). Home: 205 Princess St Alexandria VA 22314-2326

SLASH (SAUL HUDSON), guitarist; b. Stoke-on-Trent, Eng., July 23, 1965; s. Anthony and Ola Hudson; m. Renée Suran, Oct. 10, 1992. Guitarist Guns n' Roses, 1985—. Albums: (with Guns N' Roses) Live Like a Suicide, 1986, Appetite for Destruction, 1987, GN'R Lies, 1988, Use Your Illusion I, 1991, Use Your Illusion II, 1991, The Spaghetti Incident?, 1993, (with Slash's Snakepit) It's Five O'Clock Somewhere, 1995; worked as guitarist with Iggy Pop, Bob Dylan, Michael Jackson, Lenny Kravitz.

SLATE, FLOYD OWEN, chemist, materials scientist, civil engineer, educator, researcher; b. Carroll County, Ind., July 26, 1920; s. Ora George and Gladys Marie (Miller) S.; m. Margaret Mary Magley, Oct. 14, 1939; children: Sally Lee Slate McEnteer, Sandra Kay Slate Miller, Rex Owen. B.S., Purdue U., 1941, M.S., 1942, Ph.D., 1944. Chemist Manhattan Project, N.Y.C., Oak Ridge and Decatur, Ill., 1944-46; asst. prof. civil engring. Purdue U., Lafayette, Ind., 1946-49; v.p., dir. Geotechnics & Resources Inc., White Plains, N.Y., 1959-63; prof. engring. materials Cornell U., Ithaca, N.Y., 1949-87; prof. emeritus, 1987; internat. lectr., cons. concrete, low-cost housing. Author books, research papers on concrete, low-cost housing, soil stabilization, 1944—. Recipient Excellence in Teaching award Cornell U., 1976, sr. fellow East-West Center, 1976, NSF research grantee, 1960-86. Fellow Am. Concrete Inst. (hon., Wason Research medal 1957, 65, 74, 86, Anderson award 1983), Am. Inst. Chemists; mem. ASCE, ASTM, Am. Chem. Soc. Research on internal structure of concrete vs. properties, chemistry applied to engring. problems, and low-cost housing for developing countries. Home: 255 The Esplanade N Apt 306 Venice FL 34285-1518 Office: Hollister Hall Cornell U Ithaca NY 14853 *Think positively and be optimistic. Be considerate of others, try to help others, and enjoy life.*

SLATE, JOE HUTSON, psychologist, educator; b. Hartselle, Ala., Sept. 21, 1930; s. Murphy Edmund and Marie (Hutson) S.; m. Rachel Holladay, July 1, 1950; children: Marc Allan, John David, James Daryl. B.S., Athens Coll., 1960; M.A., U. Ala., 1965, Ph.D., 1970. Mem. faculty Athens (Ala.) State Coll., 1965-92, prof. psychology, 1974-92, chmn. behavioral scis., 1974-92; pvt. practice psychology Athens, 1970-92, Hartselle, 1992—; v.p. Slate Security Systems, Hartselle, Ala., 1984—. Author: Psychic Phenomena, 1988, Self-Empowerment, 1991, Psychic Empowerment, 1995, Psychic Empowerment for Health and Fitness, 1996. Named hon. prof. Montevallo U., 1973, prof. emeritus Athens State, Coll., 1992. Mem. APA, Am. Soc. Clin. Hypnosis, Inst. Parapsychol. Rsch. (founder), Coun. for Nat. Register Health Svc. Providers in Psychology, NEA, Ala. Edn. Assn., Delta Tau Delta, Phi Delta Kappa, Kappa Delta Pi. Home and Office: 1807 Highway 31 NW Hartselle AL 35640-4442

SLATE, JOHN BUTLER, biomedical engineer; b. Schenectady, N.Y., Sept. 27, 1953; s. Herbert Butler and Violet (Perugi) S. BSEE, U. Wis., 1975, MEE, 1977, PhDEE, 1980. Spl. fellow of cardiovascular surgery U. Ala., Birmingham, 1980-81, dept. biomed. research engr., 1981-82; microbiology fellow, 1981-82; sr. research engr. IMED Corp., San Diego, 1982-83, sr. research scientist, 1983-86; sci. dir. Pacesetter Infusion Ltd. (dba MiniMed Technologies), Sylmar, Calif., 1986-87; v.p. tech. MiniMed Technologies, Sylmar, Calif., 1987-91; v.p. R & D Siemens Infusion Systems, Sylmar, Calif., 1991-93; v.p. tech. devel. Via Med., San Diego, 1993-94; pres. Slate Engring., San Diego, 1994—. Mem. IEEE (IEE Ayrton award), Biomed. Engring. Soc., Sigma Xi. Office: Slate Engring 3914 Kendall St San Diego CA 92109

SLATE, MARTIN IRA, pension benefit executive. Grad., Harvard U., 1967; JD, Yale U., 1970; LLM in Taxation, Georgetown U., 1988. Dir. field svcs. EEOC, 1980-81; dir. ERISA program IRS, 1986-92; exec. dir. Pension Benefit Guaranty Corp., 1993—; adj. prof. in taxation Georgetown Law Ctr., 1988-92. Contbr. articles to profl. publs. Mem. Phi Beta Kappa. Office: Pension Benefit Guar Corp 1200 K St NW Washington DC 20005

SLATE, WILLIAM KENNETH, II, international dispute resolution association executive; b. Winston-Salem, N.C., Jan. 17, 1943; s. William Kenneth Slate and Elsie (Corrine) Runge; m. Sheryl Ruth Barker, Nov. 25, 1979; 1 child, Eliza Hayes. BA, Wake Forest U., 1965; JD, U. Richmond, 1968; postgrad., Oxford U., 1974, Harvard U., 1984; MBA, U. Pa., 1990. Bar: Va. 1968, U.S. Ct. Appeals (4th cir.) 1972, U.S. Ct. Appeals (3d cir.) 1984, U.S. Supreme Ct. 1975. Atty. FBI, U.S. Justice Dept., Washington, 1968-70; adminstr. The Hustings Ct., Richmond, Va., 1970-72, U.S. Ct. Appeals (4th cir.), Richmond, 1972-84; cir. exec. 3d Jud. Cir. U.S., Phila., 1984-87; CEO Va. State Bar, 1987-88; dir. Congressionally Chartered Fed. Cts. Study Com., 1988-90; cons. Supreme Ct. of U.S., 1991-92; founder, pres. Justice Rsch. Inst., Phila. and Washington, 1990-94; pres. Am. Arbitration Assn., 1994—; founder Nat. Conf. Appellate Ct. Adminstrs., Washington, 1973; founder, bd. dirs. Council for Ct. Excellence, Washington, 1982-87; mem. Chief Justice Task Force on Fed. Rule Making, Washington, 1979; mem. governing bd. Va. State Bar, 1980-84. Contbr. articles and book revs. to profl. jours. Founder Richmond, Va. Audubon Soc., 1972; pres. Region XII Episcopal Diocese of Va., Richmond, 1975-78; mem. adv. bd. Wake Forest U., Winston-Salem, Chowan Coll., Murfreesboro, N.C., Inst. for Ct. Mgmt. Mem. ABA, Richmond Bar Assn. (mem. exec. com. 1992-94), Am. Judicature Soc. (exec. com. 1984-87, treas. 1986-87, v.p. 1988-90), Va. State Bar for Young Lawyers (pres. 1975-76). Avocations: birding, opera music, reading. Home: 750 S 2nd St Philadelphia PA 19147-3427 Office: Am Arbitration Assn 140 W 51st St New York NY 10020-1203

SLATER, CATHRYN BUFORD, federal agency administrator; married; 5 children. BSE in English with honors, U. Ark., 1969, MA in English with high honors, 1972; postgrad., Duke U., 1990. Spl. asst., liaison natural & cultural resources State Ark., Little Rock, 1984-88; state hist. preservation officer, dir. Ark. Hist. Preservation Program, Little Rock, 1988—; lectr. English dept. U. Ark., Little Rock, 1975-84, 88—. Bd. dirs. Nat. Conf. State Hist. Preservation Officers, 1990-94, exec. com., 1992-94, chmn. critical issues com., 1992-94, sec., 1993-95; bd. dirs. Shelter Battered Women, Pulaski County, Ark., Ctrl. H.S. Parent Tchr. Student Assn., Little Rock, Pulaski Heights United Meth. Ch. Mem. Nat. Pks. & Conservation Assn., Nature Conservancy, Nat. Trust Hist. Preservation, Sierra Club, Wilderness Soc., Audubon Soc. Avocations: reading, hiking, canoeing, camping, backpacking. Address: 38 River Ridge Cir Little Rock AR 72207*

SLATER, CHARLES JAMES, construction company executive; b. Munich, Feb. 16, 1949; s. Robert Marsh and Mary Elizabeth (James) S.; m. Pamela S. Senning, Sept. 17, 1974 (div. Apr. 1992); children: Mary Katherine, Robert Charles; m. Kristie J. Alexander, May 11, 1992. BA in Polit. Sci., U. Tenn., 1974. Safety mgr. Daniel Internat. Co., Kingsport, Tenn., 1981-83; safety and med. mgr. Daniel Internat. Co., Georgetown, S.C., 1983-84; risk mgmt. mgr. Yeargin Inc., Kingsport, 1985-88, Omaha, 1990; resident engr. Yeargin Inc., Frankfort, Ind., 1991, Florence, S.C., 1991; safety and risk mgmt. dir. Harbert-Yeargin Inc., Greenville, S.C., 1992—; bd. advisors Assoc. Bldrs. and Contractors/Nat. Safety Coun., Washington, 1993—. Pres. Tenn. Vol. Firefighters Assn., Sullivan County, 1987-89, Kingsport Area Safety Coun., 1989. Mem. Am. Inst. Constructors (chpt. pres. 1993-94), Am. Soc. Safety Engrs., Nat. Safety Mgmt. Soc., Constrn. Industry Coop. Alliance (instr. 1992), Safety Dirs. League (charter), Constrn. Specifications Inst. Episcopalian. Avocations: golf, chess, reading, cinematography. Home: PO Box 6021 Greenville SC 29606-6021 Office: Raytheon Engrs & Constructo PO Box 6508 Greenville SC 29606-6508

SLATER, CHRISTIAN, actor; b. N.Y.C., Aug. 18, 1969; s. Michael Hawkins and Mary Jo Slater. Appearences include (theatre) The Music Man, 1980, Between Daylight and Boonville, 1980, Copperfield, 1981, Macbeth, 1982, Merlin, 1983, Landscape of the Body, 1984, Dry Land, 1986, (TV movies) Living Proof: The Hank Williams Jr. Story, 1983, Desperate for Love, 1989, (films) The Legend of Billy Jean, 1985, The Name of the Rose, 1986, Tucker: The Man and His Dream, 1988, Gleaming the Cube, 1989, Heathers, 1989, Beyond the Stars, 1989, The Wizard, 1989, Tales from the Darkside: The Movie, 1989, Young Guns II, 1990, Pump Up the Volume, 1990, Robin Hood: Prince of Thieves, 1991, Mobsters, 1991, Star Trek VI: The Undiscovered Country, 1991, Kuffs, 1992, Ferngully...The Last Rainforest (voice), 1992, Where the Day Takes You, 1992, Untamed Heart, 1993, True Romance, 1993, Jimmy Hollywood, 1994, Interview with the Vampire, 1994, Murder in the First, 1995, Bed of Roses, 1995. Office: Creative Artists Agy care Rich Kurtzman 9830 Wilshire Blvd Beverly Hills CA 90212

SLATER, DORIS ERNESTINE WILKE, business executive; b. Oakes, N.D.; d. Arthur Waldemar and Anna Mary (Dill) Wilke; m. Lawrence Bert Slater, June 4, 1930 (dec., 1960). Grad. high sch. Sec. to circulation mgr. Mpls. Daily Star, 1928-30; promotion activities Lions Internat. in U.S., Can., Cuba, 1930-48; exec. sec. parade and spl. events com. Inaugural Com., 1948-49; exec. sec. Nat. Capital Sesquicentennial Commn., 1949-50, Capitol Hill Assos., Inc., 1951, Pres.'s Cup Regatta, 1951; adminstrv. asst. Nat. Assn. Food Chains, 1951-60; v.p., sec.-treas. John A. Logan Assos., Inc., Washington, 1960—; v.p., sec.-treas. Logan, Seaman, Slater, Inc., 1962—; mng. dir. Western Hemisphere, Internat. Assn. Chain Stores, 1964—. With pub. relations div. Boston Met. chpt. ARC, 1941-42; mem. Nat. Cherry Blossom Festival Com., 1949—; mem. Inaugural Ball Com., 1953, 57, 65. Methodist. Lion. Home and Office: 2500 Wisconsin Ave NW Washington DC 20007-4501

SLATER, GEORGE RICHARD, retired banker; b. Indpls., Feb. 13, 1924; s. George Greenleaf and Chloe (Shoemaker) S.; m. Mary Catherine Brown; children: George Greenleaf, Kathleen Slater Hamar, John Goodwill, Frederick Richard. BS, Purdue U., 1946, MS, 1957, PhD, 1963. Chief economist Allis-Chalmers Mfg. Co., Milw., 1957-60; v.p. Citizens Nat. Bank of Decatur (Ill.), 1960-64; sr. v.p., group exec. Met. Group, Harris Trust & Savs. Bank, Chgo., 1964-76; pres., chief exec. officer Marine Bank, N.A., Milw., 1976-83; chmn., chief exec. officer Marine Corp. (now Banc One Wis. Corp.), Milw., 1978-89; vice-chmn. Banc One Corp., Columbus, Ohio, 1988-89, ret., 1989; adv. coun. J.L. Kellogg Grad. Sch. Mgmt. Northwestern U.; bd. dirs. Marcus Corp., John's Island Club. 1st lt. F.A. U.S. Army, 1943-46. Episcopalian. Home: John's Island 275 Coconut Palm Rd Vero Beach FL 32963-3708 *Man has the obligation to his fellow man to strive for productivity, excellence and harmony.*

SLATER, HELEN RACHEL, actress; b. N.Y.C., Dec. 15, 1963; d. Gerald and Alice Joan (Chrin) S. Stage appearances include Responsible Parties, 1985, Almost Romance, 1987; films: Supergirl, 1984, The Legend of Billie Jean, 1985, Ruthless People, 1986, The Secret of My Success, 1987, Sticky Fingers, 1988, Happy Together, 1989, City Slickers, 1991, Lassie, 1994; TV appearances include (series) Capital News, 1990, (movies) Chantilly Lace, 1993, 12:01, 1993. Office: Innovative Artists 1999 Ave of Stars/Ste 2850 Los Angeles CA 90211*

SLATER, JAMES MUNRO, radiation oncologist; b. Salt Lake City, Jan. 7, 1929; s. Donald Munro and Leone Forestine (Fehr) S.; m. JoAnn Strout, Dec. 28, 1948; children: James, Julie, Jan, Jerry, Jon. B.S. in Physics, U. Utah, Utah State U., 1954; M.D., Loma Linda U., 1963. Diplomate: Am. Bd. Radiology. Intern Latter Day Saints Hosp., Salt Lake City, 1963-64; resident in radiology Latter Day Saints Hosp., 1964-65; resident in radiotherapy Loma Linda U. Med. Ctr., White Meml. Med. Center, Los Angeles; fellow in radiotherapy Loma Linda U. Med. Ctr., White Meml. Med. Center, 1967-68, U. Tex.-M.D. Anderson Hosp. and Tumor Inst., Houston, 1968-69; mem. faculty Loma Linda (Calif.) U., 1975—, prof. radiology, 1979—, chmn. radiation scis. dept., 1979-89, dir. nuclear medicine, 1970—, dir. radiation oncology, 1975-79, chmn. dept. radiation oncology, 1990—, dir. Cancer Inst., 1993—, exec. v.p. Med. Ctr., 1994—; treas. med. ctr., 1995—; treas. Med. Ctr., 1995—; co-dir. cmty. radiology oncology program L.A. County-U. So. Calif. Comprehensive Cancer Ctr., 1978-83; mem. cancer adv. coun. State of Calif., 1980-85; clin. prof. U. So. Calif., 1982—; founding mem. Proton Therapy Coop. Group, 1985—, chmn. 1987-91; cons. charged particle therapy program Lawrence Berkeley Lab., 1986-94; cons. R&D monoclonal antibodies Hybritech Inc., 1985-94, bd. dirs., 1985-94; cons. Berkeley lab., 1986-94; mem. panel cons. Internat. Atomic Energy Agy. UNA 1994—; cons. Sci. Applications Internat. Corp., 1979, 89-91. Bd. dirs. Am. Cancer Soc., San Bernardino/Riverside, 1976—, exec. com., 1976—; pres. Inland Empire chpt., 1981-83. NIH fellow, 1968-69; recipient exhbn. awards Radiol. Soc. N.Am., 1973, exhbn. awards European Assn. Radiology, 1975, exhbn. awards Am. Soc. Therapeutic Radiologists, 1978, Alumnus of Yr. award, 1993, 94. Fellow Am. Coll. Radiology; mem. AMA, ACS (liaison mem. to commn. on cancer 1976-84), Am. Radium Soc., Am. Soc. Clin. Oncology, Am. Soc. Therapeutics Radiologists, Assn. Univ. Radiologists, Calif. Med. Assn., Calif. Radiol. Soc., Gilbert H. Fletcher Soc. (pres. 1981-82), Loma Linda U. Med. Sch. Alumni Assn., Radiol. Soc. N.Am., Bernardino County Med Soc., Soc. Chairmen Of Acad. Radiation Oncology Programs, Alpha Omega Alpha. Achievements include development of world's first proton accelerator system for treating patients with cancer and some benign diseases in a hospital environment; development of world's first computer assisted radiation treatment planning system utilizing patient's digitized anatomic images with overlying radiation distribution images. Home: 1210 W Highland Ave Redlands CA 92373-6659 Office: Loma Linda U Radiation Medicine Loma Linda CA 92350

SLATER, JILL SHERRY, lawyer; b. N.Y.C., Apr. 8, 1943. BA with distinction and honors, Cornell U., 1964; JD cum laude, Harvard U., 1968. Bar: Mass. 1968, Calif. 1971, U.S. Dist. Ct. (cen. dist.) Calif. 1971, U.S. Ct. Appeals (9th cir.) 1974, U.S. Dist. Ct. (so. dist.) Calif. 1977, U.S. Dist. Ct. (ea. dist.) Calif. 1984, U.S. Dist. Ct. (no. dist) Calif. 1985, U.S. Ct. Appeals (Fed. cir.) 1982, U.S. Supreme Ct. 1986, N.Y. 1988. Atty. Boston Redevel. Authority, 1968-70; from assoc. to ptnr. Latham & Watkins, N.Y.C., 1970—. Woodrow Wilson fellow, 1964. Mem. ABA., Phi Beta Kappa. Office: Latham & Watkins Ste 1000 885 Third Ave New York NY 10022-4802

SLATER, JOAN ELIZABETH, English educator; b. Paterson, N.J., Aug. 27, 1947; d. Anthony Joseph and Emma (Liguori) Nicola; m. Francis Graham Slater, Nov. 16, 1974; children: David, Kristin, Kylie. BA in English, Montclair State Coll., 1968, MA in English, 1971. Cert. English, speech and theater arts tchr., N.J., Tex. Tchr. Anthony Wayne Jr. High Sch., Wayne, N.J., 1968-70, Wayne Valley High Sch., Wayne, N.J., 1970-74, Strack Intermediate Sch., Klein, Tex., 1987—; cons. Tex. Assessment Acad. Skills, Houston Post Newspaper, 1994—; adv. bd. Tex. Edn. Assn., winter 1993; sch. dist. rep. Southern Assn. Colls. and Schs., 1993; editor, advisor Pawprints Lit. Mag., 1989—. Co-author: Klein Curriculum for the Gifted and Talented, 1992-93. Com. chairperson Klein After-Prom Extravaganza, 1994-95; parent supporter Challenge Soccer Club, Klein, 1993—; mem. Rep. Nat. Com., Washington, 1994—; mem. Klein H.S. Girls Soccer Team Bd., 1995-96. Mem. North Harris County Coun. Tchrs. English (sec. 1992-95), Klein Edn. Assn., Nat. Coun. Tchrs. English, Tex. Mid. Sch. Assn., Internat. Reading Assn., Greater Houston Area Reading Coun., Nat. Charity League. Avocations: aerobics, interior decorating, reading. Home: 6018 Spring Oak Holw Spring TX 77379-8833 Office: Strack Intermediate Sch 18027 Kuykendahl Rd Klein TX 77379-8116

SLATER, JOHN BLACKWELL, landscape architect; b. Kansas City, Mo., Mar. 20, 1943; s. Marcus Bedford and Helen (Butler) S.; m. Sue Stallings, June 22, 1968; 1 child, Alice Butler. B in Landscape Architecture, Syracuse U., 1965; student, SUNY, Syracuse U. Registered landscape architect, Md., N.Y., Va. Landscape architect A.E. Bye Assocs., Cos Cob, Conn., 1969-71, The Rouse Co., Columbia, Md., 1971-74, Slater Assocs., Columbia, 1974—; mem. bd. examiners of landscape architects State of Md., 1993—. Prin. works include design Sully Plantation Hist. Park, Oakland Mills Courtyard, Benjamin Banneker Hist. Park, Port Deposit Hist. Restoration of Streetscape, Columbia Town Ctr. Park, S.I. Mall Expansion. Lt. USN, 1966-69. Fellow Am. Soc. Landscape Architects (trustee 1981-87, v.p. 1987-88, awards Md. chpt. 1979, 89, 90), Howard County Assn. Landscape Architects (pres. 1991), Rotary (pres. Columbia Town Ctr. club). Avocations: sailing, gardening, photography. Home: 4993 Dalton Dr Columbia MD 21045-1805 Office: Slater Assocs Inc 5560 Sterrett Pl Ste 302 Columbia MD 21044-2616

SLATER, JOHN GREENLEAF, financial consultant; b. Milw., Mar. 25, 1935; s. Thomas McIndoe and Margaret Mary (McAnarney) S.; m. Colleen Mary Conway, July 19, 1958; children: James C., John T., Ann E. Borngesser. BS in Econs, Marquette U., 1958, MA, 1960. With First Wis. Nat. Bank, Milw., 1960-69; with First Wis. Nat. Bank, Madison, 1969-79, exec. v.p., dir., 1973-79; sr. v.p. Fifth Third Bank, Cin., 1979-82; pres., chief exec. officer Slater Carley Group, Inc., Cin., 1982-85; exec. v.p., bd. dirs. E. W. Buschman Co., Cin., 1985-94; pres., CEO Diamond Machine Co., Inc., Cin., 1994-96; pvt. practice Cin., 1996—; bd. dirs. Bhat Industries, CinTech Inc. Mem. Madison Adv. Com. Drug Abuse, 1970-71; mem. long-range planning com. Edgewood High Sch., Madison, 1972-75; mem. long-range planning task force OKI Regional Planning Commn., 1980-81; bd. dirs. First Offenders Sch., 1975-79. Mem. Wis. Bus. Economists Assn. (pres. 1973), Nat. Assn. Bus. Economists, Cin. Inst. for Small Enterprise, Fin. Execs. Inst., Nat. Venture Capital Assn., Conveyer Equipment Mfrs. Assn., Cin. New Bus. Devel. Council (chair 1989), Phi Gamma Mu. Roman Catholic. Home and Office: 3748 Fallentree Ln Cincinnati OH 45236-1036

SLATER, JONATHAN E., director. Dir. Shady Hill Sch., Cambridge, Mass. Office: Shady Hill Sch 178 Coolidge Hl Cambridge MA 02138-5520

SLATER, JOSEPH ELLIOTT, educational institute administrator; b. Salt Lake City, Aug. 17, 1922; m. Annelore Kremser, Dec. 20, 1947; children: Bonnie Karen Hurst, Sandra Marian Slater. BA with honors, U. Calif.-Berkeley, 1943, postgrad., 1943; LLB with honors, Colo. Coll.; PhD (hon.), U. Denver, U. N.H., Kung Hee, Korea. Teaching asst., reader U. Calif.-Berkeley, 1942-43; dep. U.S. sec. Allied Control Council, Berlin, Germany, 1945-48; UN planning staff Dept. State, Washington, 1949; sec.-gen. Allied High Commn. for Germany, Bonn, 1949-52; exec. sec., U.S. spl. rep. in Europe, U.S. sec. to U.S. del. to NATO and OEEC, Paris, France, 1952-53; chief economist Creole Petroleum Corp. (Standard Oil Co. N.J.), Caracas, Venezuela, 1954-57; mem. and dir. internat. affairs program Ford Found., 1957-68, study dir. spl. com. to establish policies and programs, 1961-62; asst. mng. dir. Devel. Loan Fund, Washington, 1960-61; dep. asst. sec. state for edn. and cultural affairs, 1961-62; pres. Salk Inst., LaJolla, Calif., 1967-72, hon. trustee, pres. emeritus; pres., CEO trustee Aspen Inst. for Humanistic Studies, 1969-86, pres. emeritus, trustee, sr. fellow, 1986—; chmn. John J. McCloy Internat. Ctr., 1986—; pres. Anderson Found., N.Y.C., 1969-72; adv. bd. Volvo Internat.; dir. Volvo N.Am. Sec. Pres.'s Com. on Fgn. Assistance (Draper Com.), 1959; del. Atlantic Conf., 1959;

mem. devel. assistance panel Pres.'s Sci. Adv. Com., 1960-61; cons. Dept. State, 1961-68; founder, dir., bd. dirs. Creole Found., 1956-57; trustee Carnegie Hall Corp., 1960-86, Asia Soc., 1971-86, Am. Coun. on Germany, 1971-86; mem. vis. com., dept. philosophy MIT, 1971-83; trustee Acad. for Ednl. Devel., Internat. Council Ednl. Devel., John J. McCloy Fund; bd. dirs. Eisenhower Exchange Fellowships, Internat. Inst. Environ. Devel., Ctr. for Pub. Resources. Served to lt. USNR, 1943-46; mil. govt. planning officer London, Paris, Berlin; trustee Lovelace Med. Found., 1993—. Decorated Order of Merit Fed. Republic Germany). Mem. NAS (mem. pres.'s cir.), Inst. Strategic Studies (London), Coun. Fgn. Rels., Ctr. for Inter-Am. Rels., Am. Acad. Arts & Scis., Am. Coun. for Jean Monnet Studies (dir.), Inst. for East-West Dynamics (dir.), N.Y. Acad. Scis., Phi Beta Kappa. Clubs: Century Assn. (N.Y.C.), Mid-Atlantic (N.Y.C.). Home: 870 Union Plz New York NY 10017

SLATER, KRISTIE, construction company executive; b. Rock Springs, Wyo., Nov. 14, 1957; d. Fredrick Earl and Shirley Joan (McWilliams) Alexander; m. C. James Slater, May 11, 1992. A in Bus. Adminstrn., Salt Lake City Coll., 1978. EMT, Wyo. Cost engr., material coord. Project Constrn. Corp., LaBarge, Wyo., 1985; cost engr., scheduler Flour Daniel Constrn. Co., Salt Lake City, 1985-86, Bibby Edible Oils, Liverpool, Eng., 1986-87; cost engr., safety technician Sunvic, Inc./I.S.T.S., Inc., Augusta, Ga., 1987-88; cost engr. Brown & Root, Inc., Ashdown, Ark., 1988-89, Wickliffe, Ky., 1989; sr. cost engr. Brown & Root, Inc., Pasadena, Tex., 1989-90, LaPorte, Tex., 1990-91; project controls mgr. Yeargin Inc., Thousand Oaks, Calif., 1991-92; corp. controls mgr. Suitt Constrn. Co., Greenville, S.C., 1993-95. Pres. 4-H State Coun., Laramie, Wyo., 1976; mem. com. Houston Livestock Show and Rodeo. Mem. LDS Ch. Avocations: horseback riding, reading, golf.

SLATER, LEONARD, writer, editor; b. N.Y.C., July 15, 1920; s. Max and Jean (Lenobel) S.; m. Betty Moorsteen, 1946; children: Amy, Lucy. BA in Polit. Sci., U. Mich., 1941. Reporter, writer, White House and Pentagon NBC News, Washington, 1941-44; corr. Washington bur., White House and Pentagon Time mag., 1945-47; corr. Eastern Europe and Middle East Newsweek mag., N.Y.C.; assoc. editor, bur. chief Newsweek mag., Los Angeles, 1947-58; sr. editor, columnist McCalls' mag., N.Y. and Europe, 1958-64; free-lance writer, editor, 1964—. Author: Aly, 1965, The Pledge, 1970; contbr. articles to mags. Mem. Authors League of Am. Home: 4370 Arista Dr San Diego CA 92103-1029 also: Binicalaf Minorca, Balearic Islands Spain

SLATER, MARILEE HEBERT, theatre administrator, producer, director, consultant; b. Laredo, Tex., Feb. 25, 1949; d. Minos Joseph and Eulalie (Fisher) Hebert; m. Stewart E. Slater, Dec. 3, 1972 (div. July 1978). BA, Baylor U., 1970, MA, 1972. Cert. secondary sch. tchr., Tex. Actress, dir., assoc. producer Everyman Players, Ky. and La., 1972-80; community rels. dir. Actors Theatre of Louisville, 1973-74, dir. children's theatre, lunchtime & cabaret theatre, 1974-76, dir., apprentice intern program, 1974-77, new play festivals coord., 1979-81, mgr. internat. touring, 1980—, assoc. dir., 1981—; guest dir. Louisville Children's Theatre, 1978; grants panelist Ky. Arts Coun., La. Arts Coun.; conf. lectr. Ky. Arts Coun., Va. Arts Commn., Southeastern Theatre Conf., S.W. Theatre Conf., So. Arts Fedn. Author: (play) Hey Diddle Diddle!, 1976. Pres. Ky. Citizens for Arts, 1985-86, 90-91; co-chmn. subcom. on arts Edn. Workforce, 1990-93; grad. Leadership Louisville, 1989, bd. dirs., 1992—; vice-chmn. Focus Louisville, 1994-96; chmn. Louisville Downtown Mgmt. Dist., 1996; mem. Downtown Devel. Implementation com., Louisville, 1991-93; Louisville Forum adv. coun., 1995-96; bd. dirs. Louisville Ctrl. Area, 1996; pres. Park IV Condo Assn., 1989-91, sec. Main St. Assn., 1992-96; staging dir., cons. Walnut St. Bapt. Ch., 1980—. Bingham fellow, 1995-96; recipient Ky. Commonwealth award 1996. Democrat. Baptist. Avocations: photography, travel, hiking, music. Office: Actors Theatre Louisville 316 W Main St Louisville KY 40202-4218

SLATER, OLIVER EUGENE, bishop; b. Sibley, La., Sept. 10, 1906; s. Oliver Thornwell and Mattie (Kennon) S.; m. Eva B Richardson, Nov. 25, 1931; children: Susan Slater Edenborough, Stewart Eugene. AB, So. Meth. U., 1930, BD, 1932, LLD (hon.), 1964; DD (hon.), McMurray Coll., 1951; LHD, Southwestern Coll., Winfield, Kans., 1961; LLD, Baker U., 1962. Ordained to ministry Meth. Ch., 1932. Pastor Rochelle, Tex., 1932-33, Menard, Tex., 1933-36, Ozona, Tex., 1936-42, San Antonio, 1942-44, Houston, 1944-50; pastor Polk St. Ch., Amarillo, Tex., 1950-60; consecrated bishop, 1960; bishop Kans. area Meth. Ch., 1960-64, Kans. area Meth. Ch., San Antonio-N.W. Tex. area, 1964-68, San Antonio area United Meth. Ch., 1968-76; bishop-in-residence Perkins Sch. Theology, So. Meth. U., 1976-80, bishop in residence emeritus, 1980—; Mem. jurisdictional confs. Meth. Ch., 1948, 56, 60, gen. confs., 1956, 60, pres. gen. bd. edn. (now of United Meth. Ch.), 1964-72; mem. commn. on archives and history United Meth. Ch., 1968-76, mem. interboard com. on enlistment for ch. occupations, 1968-72; pres. designate Council Bishops, 1971-72, pres., 1972-73. Author: (autobiography) Oliver's Travels, One Bishop's Journey, 1988. Chmn. Commn. on Archives, 1972-76; Trustee So. Meth. U., 1960-76, vice chmn. trustees, 1973-76; trustee Southwestern U.; mem. bd. Global Ministries, 1972-76. Recipient Disting. Alumnus award So. Meth. U., 1975.

SLATER, RODNEY E., federal administrator; b. Tutwyler, Miss., Feb. 23, 1955; m. Cassandra Wilkins; 1 child. BS, Ea. Mich. U., 1977; JD, U. Ark., 1980. Asst. atty. gen. State of Ark., 1980-82; spl. asst. for community and minority affairs Gov. of Ark., 1983-85, exec. asst. for econ. and community programs, 1985-87; dir. intergovernmental rels. Ark. State U., 1987-93; adminstr. fed. hwy. adminstrn. Dept. Transp., Washington, 1993—; mem. Ark. State Hwy. and Transp. Commn., 1987-93, chair, 1992-93; dep. campaign mgr., sr. traveling advisor Clinton for Pres. Campaign, 1992; dep. to chair Clinton/Gore Transition Team, 1992-93. Ark. liaison Martin Luther King, Jr. Fed. Holiday Commn., 1983-87; mem. Ark. Sesquicentennial Commn., 1986. Mem. Ark. Bar Assn. (sec.-treas. 1989-93), W. Harold Flowers Law Soc. (pres. 1985-92). Office: Fed Hwy Adminstrn 400 7th St SW Rm 4218 Washington DC 20590-0001

SLATER, SHELLEY, document and training manager; b. Ogden, Utah, June 26, 1959; d. Lynn Russell and Darlene (Allen) Slater; m. Dale Thomas Hansen, Jan. 26, 1977 (div. Feb. 1979); 1 child, Thomas Arthur; m. Eugene Allan DuVall, Mar. 8, 1981 (div. Dec. 1985); 1 child, Gregory Allan; m. Steven Blake Allender, June 9, 1990 (div. May 1993). BBA cum laude, Regis U., 1992, postgrad., 1992—. Installation, repair technician MT Bell, Clearfield, Utah, 1977-81; ctrl. office technician MT Bell, Salt Lake City, 1981-83, engring. specialist, 1983-86; engring. specialist U.S. West Comm., Englewood, Colo., 1986-93; network analyst, documentation and tng. mgr. Time Warner Comm., Englewood, Colo., 1993—; bus. cons. Jr. Achievement, Denver, 1988-89. Day capt. AZTEC Denver Mus. of Natural History, 1992; loaned exec. Mile High United Way, 1993. Mem. Soc. of Cable Telecomms. Engrs. (v.p. Rocky Mt. chpt.). Democrat. Avocations: snow skiing, biking, softball, golf. Home: 9618 S Cordova Dr Highlands Ranch CO 80126-3788 Office: Time Warner Comm 160 Inverness Dr W Englewood CO 80112-5001

SLATER, THOMAS GLASCOCK, JR., lawyer; b. Washington, Mar. 15, 1944; s. Thomas G. and Hylton R. S.; m. Kathryn Holden, June 18, 1966; children: Thomas Glascock, Tacie Holden, Andrew Fletcher. B.A., Va. Mil. Inst., 1966; LL.B., U. Va., 1969. Bar: Va. 1969, U.S. Dist. Ct. (ea. dist.) Va. 1970, U.S. Dist Ct. (we. dist.) Va. 1979, U.S. Ct. Appeals (4th cir.) 1975, U.S. Ct. Appeals D.C. 1980, U.S. Supreme Ct. 1981. Assoc. Hunton & Williams, Richmond, Va., 1969-76, ptnr., 1976—; lectr. Pres. VMI Found. Fellow ABA, Va. Law Found.; mem. 4th Cir. Jud. Conf., Va. Bar Assn., Va. State Bar Coun. (exec. com.), D.C. Bar Assn., Richmond Bar Assn. (pres. 1989-90), Va. Mil. Inst. Alumni Assn. (past pres.). Office: Hunton & Williams Riverfrnt Plaza East Tower 951 E Byrd St Richmond VA 23219-4040

SLATKIN, LEONARD EDWARD, conductor, music director, pianist; b. L.A., Sept. 1, 1944; s. Felix Slatkin and Eleanor Aller; m. Linda Hohenfeld, Mar. 29, 1986. Began violin study, 1947; piano study with, Victor Aller and Selma Cramer, 1955; composition study with, Castelnuovo-Tedesco, 1958; viola study with, Sol Schoenbach, 1959; conducting study with, Felix Slatkin, Amerigo Marino and Ingolf Dahl; student, Ind. U., 1962, L.A. City Coll., 1963, Juilliard Sch.; student (Irving Berlin fellow in musical direction), beginning 1964; student of, Jean Morel and Walter Susskind. Founder, music dir., condr. St. Louis Symphony Youth Orch., 1969—, mus. advisor, 1979-80; mus. dir., condr. St. Louis Symphony Orch., 1979-96; mus. dir. Nat. Symphony Orch., Washington, 1996—; current mgmt. ICM Artist, Ltd., Harold Holt, Ltd., Konzertdirektion/Schmidt. Conducting debut as asst. condr., Youth Symphony of N.Y., Carnegie Hall, 1966; asst. condr., Juilliard Opera Theater and Dance Dept., 1967, St. Louis Symphony Orch., 1968-71, assoc. condr., 1971-74; guest conductor Concertgebouw, Royal Danish Orch., Tivoli, English Chamber Orch., BBC Manchester, London Philarmonic, London Synphony Orch., Philarmonia Orch., Nat. Orch. Paris, Stockholm, Oslo, Goetborg, Scottish Nat. Orch., NHK Tokyo, Israel, Berlin, Vienna State Opera, Lyric Opera Chgo., Stuttgart Opera and throughout the world; debut with Chgo. Symphony Orch., 1974, N.Y. Philharmonic, 1974, Phila. Orch., 1974, European debut with Royal Philharmonic Orch., 1974, debut with USSR orchs., 1976-77, Tokyo debut, 1986, Met. Opera debut, 1991; prin. guest condr. Minn. Orch., beginning 1974; summer artistic dir., 1979-89, music dir., New Orleans Philharmonic Symphony Orch., 1977-78, artistic dir. Great Woods, 1990; artistic adminstr. Blossom, 1991; composer: The Raven, Dialogue for Two Cellos and Orchestra, (string quartets) Extensions 1, 2, 3, 4; numerous recordings for RCA, Angel EMI, Vox. Telarc, Philips, Warner Bros. and others. Recipient 2 Grammy awards for Prokofiev Symphony No. 5 with St. Louis Symphony Orch. Nat. Acad. Rec. Arts and Scis., 1985, Declaration of Honor in Silver Austrian Govt., 1986, 5 Honorary Doctorates. Mem. Nat. Acad. Rec. Arts and Scis. (Chgo. chpt. bd. govs.). Office: St Louis Symphony Orch Powell Symphony Hall 718 N Grand Blvd Saint Louis MO 63103-1011 also: National Symphony Orchestra John F Kennedy Ctr Washington DC 20566

SLATKIN, MURRAY, paint sundry distribution executive; b. N.Y.C., June 6, 1905; s. Hyman Noah and Rose (Goldman) S.; m. Lillian Selsky, June 19, 1938; children—Joan, Robert. A.B., Johns Hopkins U., 1925; J.D., U. Md., 1929. Bar: Md. With Felmor Corp., Balt., 1925-38, pres., 1938-92; pres. Nat. Paint Distbrs., Des Plaines, Ill., 1966-68; Chmn. bd. dirs. Felmor Corp., Balt., 1992. Hon. v.p. Zionist Orgn. Am., 1980—. Recipient 1st Judge Sobeloff award, 1973. Mem. Screen Actors Guild, Am. Fedn., T.V. & Radio Artists. Democrat. Jewish. Lodge: B'nai B'rith (Man of Yr. award Menorah lodge 1969, hon. pres. 1982—). Office: Felmor Corp 2020 Hollins Ferry Rd Baltimore MD 21230-1607

SLATKIN, NORA, government official; b. Glen Cove, N.Y., May 5, 1955; d. Carl L. and Muriel (Breen) S.; m. Deral Willis, July 4, 1982; stepchildren: Nick, Lisa, Kelly. BA in Internat. Rels., Lehigh U., 1977; MS in Fgn. Svc., Georgetown U., 1979. Def. analyst Congl. Budget Office, Washington, 1977-84; mem. profl. staff House Armed Svcs. Com., Washington, 1984-93; asst. Sec. of Navy for rsch., devel., acquisition Washington, 1994—; exec. dir. CIA, Washington, 1995—; spl. asst. to under sec. of def. for acquistion Office Sec. Def., Washington, 1993. Grad. fellow Nat. Security Coun. Dept. State CIA. Mem. Phi Beta Kappa. Avocation: boating. Home: 36 Chesapeake Lndg Annapolis MD 21403-2615 Office: Asst Sec Navy Rsch Devel Acquisition 1000 Navy Pentagon Washington DC 20350-1000*

SLATTER, JOHN GREGORY, research scientist; b. Guelph, Ont., Can., Feb. 7, 1955; came to U.S., 1988; s. Wallace Osborne Conway and Nancy Dalzel (Hanna) S.; m. Vandana Khare, July 23, 1988. BSc in Biology and Chemistry with honors, Lakehead U., Thunder Bay, Ont., 1977; MSc in Pharm. Scis., U. B.C., Vancouver, Can., 1983, BSc in Pharm. Scis., 1988, PhD in Pharm. Scis., 1988. Lic. pharmacist, B.C. Postdoctoral fellow U. Wash., Seattle, 1988-90; rsch. scientist Upjohn Co., Kalamazoo, 1990-94, sr. scientist, 1994—. Contbr. articles to profl. jours. including Drug Metabolism and Disposition, Chem. Rsch. in Toxicology, Xenobiotica. U. B.C. grad. fellow, 1983. Mem. Am. Chem. Soc., Internat. Soc. for Study Xenobiotics, Kalamazoo Over-30 Hockey Assn. (2d v.p. 1992-94). Achievements include co-discovery of structure of transport form of methyl isocyanate in biological systems; research in toxic symptoms of survivors of the Bhopal Industrial Accident. Home: 3041 Hunters Hill Kalamazoo MI 49004 Office: Upjohn Co Drug Metabolism Rsch Portage Rd Kalamazoo MI 49007

SLATTERY, CHARLES WILBUR, biochemistry educator; b. La Junta, Colo., Nov. 18, 1937; s. Robert Ernest Slattery and Virgie Belle (Chamberlain) Tobin; m. Arline Sylvia Reile, June 15, 1958; children: Scott Charles, Coleen Kay. BA, Union Coll., 1959; MS, U. Nebr., 1961, PhD, 1965. Instr. chemistry Union Coll., Lincoln, Nebr., 1961-63; asst. prof., assoc. prof. chemistry Atlantic Union Coll., South Lancaster, Mass., 1963-68; rsch. assoc. biophysics MIT, Cambridge, 1967-70; asst. prof., then prof. biochemistry Loma Linda U., Calif., 1970-80, prof. biochemistry-pediatrics, 1980—, chmn. dept., 1983—; vis. prof. U. So. Calif., L.A., 1978-79. Contbr. articles to profl. jours. NIH grantee, 1979-82, 86-89, Am. Heart Assn. (Calif.), 1981-83, 83-84. Mem. AAAS, Am. Chem. Soc. (biochemistry div.), Am. Dairy Sci. Assn., Am. Heart Assn. Thrombosis Coun., N.Y. Acad. Scis., The Protein Soc., Am. Soc. Biochemistry and Molecular Biology. Internat. Soc. for Rsch. on Human Milk and Lactation, Sigma Xi. Office: Loma Linda U Sch of Medicine Dept of Biochemistry Loma Linda CA 92350

SLATTERY, EDWARD J., bishop; b. Chgo., Aug. 11, 1940. Student, St. Mary of the Lake Sem., Mundelein, Ill., Loyola U., Chgo. Ordained priest Roman Cath. Ch., 1966. Ordained priest Chgo., 1966; v.p. Cath. Ch. Ext. Soc., 1971-76, pres., 1976-94; ordained bishop Diocese of Tulsa, 1994—. Office: Diocese of Tulsa Chancery Office PO Box 2009 Tulsa OK 74101*

SLATTERY, JAMES JOSEPH (JOE SLATTERY), actor; b. Memphis, Feb. 7, 1922; s. James Joseph and Katie May (Carlin) S.; m. Mary Margaret Costello, May 23, 1944 (dec. Aug. 1987); children: James Joseph, John P., Ann, Mary, Nancy; m. Marilyn Daus, Sept. 16, 1989. A.B., Hendrix Coll., Conway, Ark., 1947. pres. Am. Fedn. TV and Radio Artists, 1976-79; dir. Bank No. Ill., Glenview, Ill. Actor. Served with USAAF, 1942-46; to lt. col. USAF (ret.). Recipient Disting. Grad. award Hendrix Coll., 1986. Mem. Screen Actors Guild. Roman Catholic. Address: 5 The Court Of Bayview Northbrook IL 60062-3201

SLATTERY, JAMES LEE, lawyer; b. N.Y.C., Apr. 6, 1939; s. John Joseph and Grace (Lee) S.; m. Noel Kingsland Cockcroft, June 4, 1963; children: James Spencer, Jared T. BS, NYU, 1962; JD, Washington & Lee U., 1968. Bar: R.I. 1968, Pa. 1981, Fla. 1994. Assoc. Tillinghast, Collins & Graham, Providence, 1968-71; assoc. gen. counsel Itek Corp., Lexington, Mass., 1971-75; gen. counsel Lukens Steel Co., Coatsville, Pa., 1975-85; sr. v.p., sec., gen. counsel Paradyne Corp., Largo, Fla., 1985—. Pres. Amherst (N.H.) Reps., 1974; bd. dirs. Chester County (Pa.) Airport Authority, West Chester, 1980-85; bd. trustees Fla. Orch., 1992—. Lt. USNR, 1962-65. Mem. R.I. Bar Assn., Pa. Bar Assn., Fla. Bar Assn., Dunedin (Fla.) Boat Club, Treasure Island (Fla.) Yacht Club. Episcopalian. Avocations: tennis, sailing. Office: Paradyne Corp 8550 Ulmerton Rd E Largo FL 34641-3842

SLATTERY, JILL SHERIDAN, lawyer; b. East Orange, N.J., Apr. 4, 1943; d. Sanford and Melba Edith (Clark) Sheridan; m. William C. Slattery, Sept. 25, 1965; children: William S., Meaghan J. BSN, U. Pa., 1965; MS, Boston U., 1967; JD cum laude, Seton Hall U., 1979. Bar: N.J. 1980, U.S. Dist. Ct. N.J. 1980, U.S. Ct. Appeals (3d cir.) 1980, N.Y. 1990. Asst. prof. Rutgers U., Newark, 1974-76; law clk. to judge Hon. Robert Muir Morris County, Morristown, N.J., 1979-80; ptnr. Nardino & Slattery, Montclair, N.J., 1980-83, Agostini, Copeland & Slattery, Verona, N.J., 1990-93, Agostini & Slattery, Verona, 1993—; pvt. practice Montclair, 1983-90; mem. faculty, lectr. at nursing colls., N.J., 1980—; chair Essex County Jud. Apointment Com., 1990—; chair V-C dist. ethics com. N.J. Supreme Ct., 1992-95. Author, editor textbook: Maternal Child Nutrition, 1979. Mem. Essex County Dem. Orgn., Millburn, N.J., 1976—; bd. dirs. Ctr. for Family Studies, Springfield, N.J., 1994—; bd. dirs., pres. Millburn-Short Hills Scholastic Boosters, 1987-94; mem. ethics com. The Hospice, Inc. Named Woman of Yr., Millburn-Short Hills Bus. and Profl. Women's Club, 1985. Mem. Am. Assn. Nurse Attys., N.J. State Bar Assn., Essex County Bar Assn. (trustee). Avocation: travel. Office: Agostini & Slattery 25 Pompton Ave Verona NJ 07044-2915

SLATTERY, PAUL FRANCIS, physicist, educator; b. Hartford, Conn., July 21, 1940; s. James Francis and Katherine (Ahearn) S.; m. Jean Frances Breitenbach, Aug. 29, 1964; 1 child, Ryan Lahey. BS in Physics magna cum laude, U. Notre Dame, 1962; MS in Physics, Yale U., 1963, PhD in Physics, 1967. Rsch. assoc., AEC postdoctoral fellow U. Rochester, N.Y., 1967-69, asst. prof., 1969-73, assoc. prof., 1973-78, prof., 1978—, chmn. dept. physics and astronomy, 1986—; vis. prof. Stanford Linear Accelerator Ctr., Stanford U., 1978; sci. spokesman Expt. 706 Fermi Nat. Accelerator Lab., Batavia, Ill., 1981—, guest scientist, 1992-94; prin. investigator U.S. DOE, 1976—, spokesman for prin. investigators, 1980-87; regional rep. Fermi Nat. Accelerator Lab.; bd. overseers Univs. Rsch. Assn., Inc., Washington, 1989-95, chmn. physics com., 1991-95. Contbr. numerous articles on high energy physics to profl. jours. Raycroft Walsh scholar United Aircraft Corp., 1958-62; NASA predoctoral grantee Yale U., 1963-66; Sterling fellow Yale U., 1966, Guggenheim Meml.Found. fellow, 1992-93. Fellow Am. Phys. Soc.; mem. Fermilab Users Orgn. (exec. com. 1976-77). Office: U Rochester Dept Physics & Astronomy Rochester NY 14627

SLAUGH, LYNN H., chemist. With Shell Devel. Co., Houston. Author 132 patents; inventor two indsl. processes; contbr. articles to profl. jours. Recipient Indsl. Chemistry award Am. Chem. Soc., 1995. Office: Shell Chem Comp PO Box 1380 Houston TX 77251-1380

SLAUGHTER, ALEXANDER HOKE, lawyer; b. Charlottesville, Va., Nov. 24, 1937; s. Edward Ratliff and Mary (Hoke) S.; m. Virginia Borah, 1964 (div.); 1 child, David A.; m. Mary Peeples, 1971. BA, Yale U., 1960; LLB, U. Va., 1963. Episcopalian. Home: 1410 Pump House Dr Richmond VA 23221-3915 Office: McGuire Woods Battle & Boothe LLP One James Ctr 901 E Cary St Richmond VA 23219-4030

SLAUGHTER, EDWARD RATLIFF, JR., lawyer; b. Raleigh, N.C., Sept. 15, 1931; s. Edward Ratliff and Mary McBee (Hoke) S.; m. Anne Limbosch, July 25, 1957; children: Anne-Marie, Hoke, Bryan. A.B., Princeton U., 1953; postgrad. (Rotary Found. fellow), U. Brussels, 1955-56; LL.B., U. Va., 1959. Bar: Va. 1959, D.C. 1981. Assoc. firm McGuire, Woods & Battle (now McGuire, Woods, Battle & Boothe) and predecessors, Charlottesville, Va., 1959-64; ptnr. McGuire, Woods & Battle and predecessors, 1964-79, head dept. litigation, 1964-79; spl. asst. for litigation to atty. gen. U.S., 1979-81; ptnr. firm Whitman & Ransom, Washington, 1981-84; prin. Slaughter & Redinger, P.C., Charlottesville, 1984-95, Slaughter, Izakowitz, Clarke & Nunley, P.C., 1995-96, Woods, Rogers & Hazlegrove, P.L.C., 1996—; vis. lectr. trial advocacy U. Va., 1970-77, Va. procedure, 1986-91; disting. lectr. U. Tunis, 1996. Chmn. Albemarle County (Va.) Dem. Com., 1969-73; pres. Charlottesville-Albemarle United Way, 1972; commr. accounts Albemarle County, 1986—; trustee Lime Kiln Arts, Inc., 1992—. Served with USNR, 1953-55. Fellow Am. Bar Found., Am. Coll. Trial Lawyers; mem. Am. Bar Assn., D.C. Bar, Charlottesville-Albemarle Bar Assn. (pres. 1976-77), Va. Bar Assn. (pres. 1978), Va. State Bar (bd. govs. internat. practice sect. 1992—), Va. Trial Lawyers Assn., Thomas Jefferson Inn Ct. (pres. 1995-96). Club: Boar's Head Sports, Farmington Country. Home: 111 Falcon Dr Charlottesville VA 22901-2035 Office: Woods Rogers & Hazlegrove PLC PO Box 2964 250 W Main St Ste 300 Charlottesville VA 22902-2964

SLAUGHTER, FRANK GILL, author, physician; b. Washington, Feb. 25, 1908; s. Stephen Lucius and Sallie Nicholson (Gill) S.; m. Jane Mundy, June 10, 1933; children: Frank G., Randolph M. A.B., Duke U., 1926; M.D., Johns Hopkins U., 1930; L.H.D., Jacksonville U., 1975. Diplomate Am. Bd. Surgery. Intern, asst. resident and resident surgeon Jefferson Hosp., Roanoke, Va., 1930-34; practice medicine specializing in surgery Jacksonville, Fla., 1934-42; ret., 1946; lectr. W. Colston Leigh, Inc., N.Y.C., 1947-49. Author: That None Should Die, 1941, Spencer Brade, M.D, 1942, Air Surgeon, 1942, Battle Surgeon, 1944, A Touch of Glory, 1945, In a Dark Garden, 1946, The New Science of Surgery, 1946, The Golden Isle, 1947, Sangaree, 1948, Medicine for Moderns, 1948, Divine Mistress, 1949, The Stubborn Heart, 1950, Immortal Magyar, 1950, Fort Everglades, 1951, The Road to Bithynia, 1951, East Side General, 1952, The Galileans, 1953, Storm Haven, 1953, The Song of Ruth, Apalachee Gold, 1954, The Healer, Flight from Natchez, 1955, The Scarlet Cord, 1956, The Warrior, 1956, Sword and Scalpel, 1957, The Mapmaker, 1957, Daybreak, 1958, The Thorn of Arimathea, 1958, The Crown and the Cross, 1959, Lorena, 1959, The Land and the Promise, 1960, Pilgrims in Paradise, 1960, Epidemic, 1961, The Curse of Jezebel, 1961, David: Warrior and King, 1962, Tomorrow's Miracle, 1962, Devil's Harvest, 1963, Upon This Rock, 1963, A Savage Place, 1964, The Purple Quest, 1965, Constantine: The Miracle of the Flaming Cross, 1965, Surgeon, U.S.A, 1966, God's Warrior, 1967, Doctor's Wives, 1967, The Sins of Herod, 1968, Surgeon's Choice, 1969, Countdown, 1970, Code Five, 1971, Convention M.D, 1972, Women in White, 1974, Stonewall Brigade, 1975, Plague Ship, 1976, Devil's Gamble, 1977, The Passionate Rebel, 1979, Gospel Fever, 1980, Doctor's Daughters, 1981, Doctors At Risk, 1983, No Greater Love, 1984, Transplant, 1987. Served from maj. to lt. col. M.C., U.S. Army, 1942-46. Fellow ACS. Presbyterian (elder). Home: PO Box 14 Jacksonville FL 32210-0014

SLAUGHTER, JOHN BROOKS, university administrator; b. Topeka, Mar. 16, 1934; s. Reuben Brooks and Dora (Reeves) S.; m. Ida Bernice Johnson, Aug. 31, 1956; children: John Brooks, Jacqueline Michelle. Student, Washburn U., 1951-53; BSEE, Kans. State U., 1956, DSc (hon.), 1988; MS in Engring., UCLA, 1961; PhD in Engring. Scis, U. Calif., San Diego, 1971; D Engring. (hon.), Rensselaer Poly. Inst., 1981; DSc (hon.), U. So. Calif., 1981, Tuskegee Inst., 1981, U. Md., 1982, U. Notre Dame, 1982, U. Miami, 1983, U. Mass., 1983, Tex. So. U., 1984, U. Toledo, 1985, U. Ill., 1986, SUNY, 1986; LHD (hon.), Bowie State Coll., 1987; DSc (hon.), Morehouse Coll., 1988, Kans. State U., 1988; LLD (hon.), U. Pacific, 1989; DSc (hon.), Pomona Coll., 1989; LHD (hon.), Alfred U., 1991, Calif. Luth. U., 1991, Washburn U., 1992. Registered profl. engr., Wash. Electronics engr. Gen. Dynamics Convair, San Diego, 1956-60; with Naval Electronics Lab. Center, San Diego, 1960-75, div. head, 1965-71, dept. head, 1971-75; dir. applied physics lab. U. Wash., 1975-77; asst. dir. NSF, Washington, 1977-79; dir. NSF, 1980-82; acad. v.p., provost Wash. State U., 1979-80; chancellor U. Md., College Park, 1982-88; pres. Occidental Coll., Los Angeles, 1988—; bd. dirs., vice chmn. San Diego Transit Corp., 1968-75; mem. com. on minorities in engring. Nat. Rsch. Coun., 1976-79; mem. Commn. on Pre-Coll. Edn. in Math., Sci. and Tech. Nat. Sci. Bd., 1982-83; bd. dirs. Monsanto Co., ARCO, Avery Dennison Corp., IBM, Northrop Grumman Corp.; chmn. advancement com. Music Ctr. of L.A. County, 1989-93. Editor: Jour. Computers and Elec. Engring, 1972—. Bd. dirs. San Diego Urban League, 1962-66, pres., 1964-66; mem. Pres.'s Com. on Nat. Medal Sci., 1979-80; trustee Rensselaer Poly. Inst., 1982; chmn. Pres.'s Com. Nat. Collegiate Athletic Assn., 1986-88; bd. govs. Town Hall of Calif., 1990; bd. dirs. L.A. World Affairs Coun., 1990. Recipient Engring. Disting. Alumnus of Yr. award UCLA, 1978, UCLA medal, 1989, Roger Revelle award U. Calif.-San Diego, 1991, Disting. Svc. award NSF, 1979, Svc. in Engring. award Kans. State U., 1981, Disting. Alumnus of Yr. award U. Calif.-San Diego, 1982; Naval Electronics Lab. Ctr. fellow, 1969-70; elected to Topeka High Sch. Hall of Fame, 1983, Hall of Fame of Am. Soc. Engring. Edn., 1993; named Kansan of Yr. by Kans. Native Sons and Daus., 1994. Fellow IEEE (chmn. com. on minority affairs 1976-80), Am. Acad. Arts and Scis.; mem. NAE, Nat. Collegiate Athletic Assn. (chmn. pres. commn.), Am. Soc. for Engring. Edn. (inducted into Hall of Fame 1993), Phi Beta Kappa (hon.), Tau Beta Phi, Eta Kappa Nu. Office: Occidental Coll 1600 Campus Rd Los Angeles CA 90041-3384

SLAUGHTER, LOUISE MCINTOSH, congresswoman; b. Harlan County, Ky., Aug. 14, 1929; d. Oscar Lewis and Grace (Byers) McIntosh; m. Robert Slaughter, 1956; children: Megan Rae, Amy Louise, Emily Robin. BS, U. Ky., 1951, MS, 1953. Bacteriologist Ky. Dept. Health, Louisville, 1951-52, U. Ky., 1952-53; market researcher Procter & Gamble, Cin., 1953-56; mem. staff Office of the Lt. Gov. N.Y., Albany, 1978-82; state rep. N.Y. Gen. Assembly, Albany, 1983-86; mem. 100th-103rd Congresses from 30th (now 28th) N.Y. dist., Washington, D.C., 1987—; mem. Ho. Govt. Reform and Oversight com., Ho. Budget com. Del. Dem. Nat. Conv., 1972, 76, 80, 88, 92; mem. Monroe County Pure Water Adminstrn. Bd., Nat. Ctr. for Policy Alternatives Adv. Bd., League of Women Voters, Nat. Women's Polit. Caucus. Office: US Ho of Reps Office of House Mems 2347 Rayburn Bldg Washington DC 20515-0005

SLAUGHTER-DEFOE, DIANA TRESA, education educator; b. Chgo., Oct. 28, 1941; d. John Ison and Gwendolyn Malva (Armstead) S.; m. Michael Defoe (div.). BA, U. Chgo., 1962, MA, 1964, PhD, 1968. Instr. dept. psychiatry Howard U., Washington, 1967-68; rsch. asso., asst. prof.

Yale U. Child Study Ctr., New Haven, 1968-70; asst. prof. dept. behavioral scis. and edn. U. Chgo., 1970-77; assoc. prof. edn. and African Am. studies and Ctr. for Urban Affairs and Policy Rsch. Northwestern U., Evanston, Ill., 1977-90, prof., 1990—; mem. nat. adv. bd. Fed. Ctr. for Child Abuse & Neglect, 1979-82, coord. Human Devel. and Social Policy Program, 1994—; mem. nat. adv. bd. Learning Rsch. and Devel. Ctr. U. Pitts., Ednl. Rsch. & Devel. Ctr., U. Tex., Austin; chmn., dir. public policy program com. Chgo. Black Child Devel. Inst., 1982-84; dir. Ill. Infant Mental Health Com., 1982-83; mem. res. adv. bd. Chgo. Urban League, 1986—. Fellow APA (mem. divsn. ethnic and minority affairs, com. on children, youth & families, bd. sci. affairs 1995—, mem. editl. bd. Child Devel., 1995—, Disting. Contbn. to Rsch. in Pub. Policy award 1993); mem. Soc. for Rsch. in Child Devel. (governing coun. 1981-87), Am. Ednl. Rsch. Assn., Assn. Black Psychologists, Nat. Head Start (mem. R & E adv. bd.), Nat. Acad. Scis. (com. on child devel. and publ. policy, 1987-93), Delta Sigma Theta. Contbr. articles to profl. jours. Home: 835 Ridge Ave Evanston IL 60202-1776 Office: 2115 N Campus Dr Evanston IL 60208-0002

SLAVENS, THOMAS PAUL, library science educator; b. Cincinnati, Iowa, Nov. 12, 1928; s. William Blaine and Rhoda (Bowen) S.; m. Cora Pearl Hart, July 9, 1950; 1 son, Mark Thomas. B.A., Phillips U., 1951; M.Div., Union Theol. Sem., 1954; M.A., U. Minn., 1962; Ph.D., U. Mich., 1965. Ordained to ministry Christian Ch., 1953. Pastor First Christian Ch., Sac City, Iowa, 1953-56, Sioux Falls, S.D., 1956-60; librarian Divinity Sch., Drake U., Des Moines, 1960-64; teaching fellow Sch. Info., U. Mich., Ann Arbor, 1964-65; instr. U. Mich., Ann Arbor, 1965-66, asst. prof., 1966-69, assoc. prof., 1969-77, prof., 1977—; vis. prof. U. Coll. of Wales, 1978, 80, 93; vis. scholar U. Oxford, Eng., 1980; adv. bd. Marcel Dekker Inc., N.Y.C., 1982—; cons. Nutrition Planning Abstracts-UN, N.Y.C., 1977-79. Author-editor: Library Problems in the Humanities, 1981, (with John F. Wilson) Research Guide to Religious Studies, 1982, (with W. Eugene Kleinbauer) Research Guide to History of Western Art, 1982, (with Terrence Tice) Research Guide to Philosophy, 1983, Theological Libraries at Oxford, 1984, (with James Pruett) Research Guide to Musicology, 1985, The Literary Adviser, 1985, A Great Library through Gifts, 1986, The Retrieval of Information, 1989, Number One in the U.S.A.: Records and Wins in Sports, Entertainment, Business, and Science, 1988, 2d edit., 1990, Doors to God, 1990, Sources of Information for Historical Research, 1994, Introduction to Systematic Theology, 1992, Reference Interviews Questions and Materials, 3d edit., 1994. Served with U.S. Army, 1946-48. Recipient Warner Rice Faculty award U. Mich., 1975; H.W. Wilson fellow, 1960; Lilly Endowment fellow Am. Theol. Library Assn., 1963. Mem. ALA (chmn. coms. 1964—), Assn. Libr. and Info. Sci. Edn. (pres. 1972), Beta Phi Mu. Home: 3745 Tremont Ln Ann Arbor MI 48105-3022 Office: University of Michigan School of Information 550 E University Ave Ann Arbor MI 48109-1092

SLAVICH, DENIS MICHAEL, engineering and construction company executive; b. San Francisco, June 1, 1940; s. Francis Luke and Betsy Florence (Carpenter) S.; m. Michele Christine Meyer, June 15, 1963 (div. July 1, 1979) 1 child: Samantha Nicole; m. Debbie Teh-Yan Chao, Nov. 22, 1980; children: David Francis, Destinie Florence. BSEE, U. Calif., Berkeley, 1964; MBA, U. Pitts., 1967; PhD, MIT, 1971. Elec. engr. Douglas Aircraft, Santa Monica, Calif., 1964-65, Hughes Aircraft, Culver City, Calif., 1965-66; prof. Boston U., 1969-71, Stanford U., Palo Alto, Calif., 1984; sr. v.p. Bechtel Group, Inc., San Francisco, 1971-91; v.p. Fluor Daniel, Inc., Irvine, Calif., 1991-95; exec. v.p., CFO Morrison Knudsen Corp., Boise, 1995—. Contbr. articles to profl. jours. Mem. Am. Fin. Assn., Nat. Assn. Bus. Econs., U. Calif. Engring. Alumni Soc., San Francisco C. of C. (bd. dirs. 1987-89), Olympic Club, Pacific Union Club, Beta Gamma Sigma. Avocations: golf; hiking. Office: Morrison Knudsen Corp PO Box 73 Boise ID 83729

SLAVICK, ANN LILLIAN, art educator; b. Chgo., Sept. 29, 1933; d. Irving and Goldie (Bernstein) Friedman; m. Lester Irwin Slavick, Nov. 21, 1954 (div. Mar. 1987); children: Jack, Rachel. BFA, Sch. of Art Inst. of Chgo., 1973, MA in Art History, Theory, Criticism, 1991. Dir. art gallery South Shore Commn., Chgo., 1963-67; tchr. painting, drawing, crafts Halfway House, Chgo., 1972-73; tchr. studio art Conant H.S., Hoffman Estates, Ill., 1973-74; tchr. art history and studio arts New Trier H.S., Winnetka and Northfield, Ill., 1974-80; tchr. 20th century art history New Trier Adult Edn. Program, Winnetka, 1980-81; tchr. art adult edn. program H.S. Dist. 113, Highland Park, Ill., 1980-81; rschr., writer Art History Notes McDougall-Littel Pub., Evanston, Ill., 1984-85; tchr. art and art history Highland Park and Deerfield (Ill.) H.S., 1980—; tchr. art history Coll. of Lake County, Grayslake, Ill., 1986-88; faculty chair for visual arts Focus on the Arts, Highland Park H.S., 1981-85, faculty coord. Focus on the Arts, 1987—. One woman show Bernal Gallery, 1979, U. Ill., Chgo., 1983, Ann Brierly Gallery, Winnetka, 1984; exhibited paintings, drawings, prints and constrns. throughout Chgo. area; work represented by Art Rental and Sales Gallery, Art Inst. Chgo., 1960-87, Bernal Gallery, 1978-82; group shows at Bernal Gallery; work in pvt. collections in Ill., N.Y., Calif., Ariz., Ohio. Recipient Outstanding Svc. in Art Edn. award Ea. Ill. U., 1992, Mayors award for contbn. to the arts, Highland Park, 1995. Mem. Nat. Art Edn. Assn., Ill. Art Edn. Assn. Avocations: cooking, reading, theatre. Home: 5057 N Sheridan Rd Chicago IL 60640-3127 Office: Highland Park High Sch 433 Vine Ave Highland Park IL 60035-2044

SLAVIN, ALEXANDRA NADAL, artistic director, educator; b. Port-au-Prince, Haiti, Oct. 26, 1943; came to U.S., 1946; d. Pierre E. and Marie Therese (Clerié) Nadal; m. Eugene Slavin, Dec. 24, 1967; 1 child, Nicholas V. Grad. high sch., Chgo. Dancer Ballet Russe de Monte Carlo, N.Y.C., 1960-61, Chgo. Opera Ballet and N.Y.C. Opera Ballet, 1961-64, Am. Ballet Theatre, N.Y.C., 1965-66, Ballet de Monte Carlo, 1966-67, The Royal Winnipeg (Can.) Ballet, 1967-72; artistic dir. Ballet Austin, Tex., 1972-89; owner, dir. The Slavin Nadal Sch. Ballet, Austin, 1989—. Recipient Achievement in the Arts award Austin chpt. YWCA, 1987. Roman Catholic. Avocation: gardening. Office: Slavin-Nadal Sch Ballet 5521 Burnet Rd Austin TX 78756-1603

SLAVIN, ARLENE, artist; b. N.Y.C., Oct. 26, 1942; d. Louis and Sally (Bryck) Eisenberg; m. Neal Slavin, May 24, 1964 (div. 1979); m. Eric Bregman, Sept. 21, 1980; 1 child, Ethan. BFA, Cooper Union for the Advancement of Sci. and Art, 1964; MFA, Pratt Inst., 1967. One woman exhbns. include Fischbach Gallery, N.Y., 1973,74, Brooke Alexander Gallery, N.Y., 1976, Alexander Milliken Gallery, N.Y.C., 1979, 80, 81, 83, U. Colo., 1981, Pratt Inst., N.Y.C., 1981, Am. Embassy, Belgrad, Yugoslavia, 1984, Heckscher Mus., Huntington, N.Y., 1987, Katherine Rich Perlow Gallery, 1988, Chauncey Gallery, Princeton, N.J., 1990, The Gallery Benjamin N. Cardoza Sch. Law, 1991, Norton Ctr. for Arts, Danville, Ky., 1992, Kavesh Gallery, Ketchum, Idaho, 1993; exhibited in group shows at Bass Mus. Art, Fla., Whitney Museum of Art, 1973, The Contempory Arts Center, Cinn., Oh., 1974, Indianapolis Museum of Art, 1974, Madison (Wis.) Art Ctr., Santa Barbara (Calif.) Mus., Winnipeg (Can.) Art Gallery, Gensler Assocs., San Francisco, 1986, Eliane Benson Gallery, Bridgehampton, N.Y., 1987, 89, 91, 93, City of N.Y. Parks and Recreation Central Park, N.Y.C. 1989, Benton Gallery, Southampton, N.Y., 1991, Parish Mus., Southampton, 1991, Michele Miller Fine Art, 1993 ; executed murals N.Y. Aquarium, Bklyn., 1982, Pub. Art Fund, N.Y.C., 1983, Albert Einstein Sch. of Medicine, Bronx, N.Y., 1983, Hudson River Mus., Yonkers, N.Y., 1983, Bellevue Hosp. Ctr., N.Y.C., 1986; represented in permanent collections at Met. Mus. of Art, N.Y.C, Bklyn. Mus., Fogg Art Mus., Cambridge, Mass., Hudson River Mus., Yonkers, N.Y., Hecksler Mus., Huntington, N.Y., Cin. Art Mus., Readers' Digest, Pleasantville, N.Y., Guild Hall, East Hampton, N.Y., Allen Meml. Art Mus., Oberlin, Ohio, Norton Mus., Palm Beach, Fla., Portland (Oreg.) Mus., Orlando (Fla.) Mus. Art, Neuburger Mus., Purchase, N.Y.; commd. work iron gates Cathedral St. John the Divine, N.Y.C., 1988, 55' steel fence Henry St Settlement, N.Y., 1992, metal work stairway De Soto Sch., N.Y. Sch. Art, 1994-95. Grantee Nat. Endowment for Arts, 1977-78, Threshold Found., 1991. Home and Studio: 119 E 18th St New York NY 10003-2107

SLAVIN, CRAIG STEVEN, management and franchising consultant; b. Tucson, Sept. 7, 1951; s. Sidney and Eileen (Gilbert) S.; m. Carol Lynn Haft, Aug. 30, 1982; children: Carly Blair, Samantha Illyna. Student, U. Ariz., 1969073, U. Balt., 1978. Dir. franchising and sales Evelyn Wood Reading Dynamics, Walnut Creek, Calif., 1974-75; dir. franchising Pasquale Food Co., Birmingham, Ala., 1975-77; exec. v.p. Franchise Concepts, Flossmoor, Ill., 1977-80; pres. Franchise Architects, Chgo., 1980-88; mng. dir. franchise practice Arthur Andersen & Co., Chgo., 1988-91; chmn. Franchise Architects, Riverwoods, Ill., 1991—; founder, bd. dirs. Franchise Broadcast Network, Riverwoods, 1991—. Author: Complete Guide to Self-Employment in Franchising, 1991, Franchising for the Growing Company, 1993, AMACON, The Franchising Handbook; creator of Franchise Success System. Mem. ABA (faculty), Am. Arbitration Assn., Internat. Franchise Assn., Nat. Assn. Info. Suppliers, Water Quality Assn., Inst. Mgmt. Cons., Coun. Franchise Suppliers (adv. bd. dirs.), Nat. Restaurant Assn. Avocations: golf, chess, saltwater fish. Home and Office: The Franchise Architects 3 Metawa Ln Deerfield IL 60015-3551

SLAVIN, NEAL, photographer; b. Bklyn., Aug. 19, 1941; s. Harry and Ida (Pomerantz) S.; 1 child, Olivia Frederica Annika. B.F.A., Cooper Union, 1963. Graphic designer Macmillan Pub. Co., 1965; instr. photographer Cooper Union, Sch. Visual Arts, Queens Coll., Manhattanville Coll.; ptnr. Slavin/Schaffer Films. One-man shows Royal Ont. (Can.) Mus., Toronto, 1976, Light Gallery, N.Y.C., 1976, Center for Creative Photography, Tucson, 1976, Wadsworth Atheneum, Hartford, 1976, Internat. Ctr. Photography, N.Y.C., 1986, Nat. Mus. Photography, Film and TV, Bradford, Eng., 1986; group shows include Galerie Zabriskie, Paris, 1977, Chgo. Center for Contemporary Photography, 1978, Nat. Mus. Photography, Eng., 1984; represented in permanent collections Met. Mus. Art, N.Y.C., Mus. Modern Art, N.Y.C., Mus. of Photography, Rochester, N.Y., Centre National de la Photographie, Paris; retrospective exhbns. Ctr. for Creative Photography, Tucson, Exch. Nat. Bank, Chgo., Palais de Tokyo, Paris; photog. books include Portugal, 1971, When Two or More are Gathered Together, 1976, Britons, 1986. Recipient Augustus Saint Gaudens award Cooper Union Sch. Art and Architecture, 1988; Fulbright grantee, 1968, Nat. Endowment Arts grantee, 1972. Mem. Am. Soc. Mag. Photographers (Corp. Photographer of Yr. 1986), Dirs. Guild of Am. Address: 62 Greene St New York NY 10012-4346 *Nothing in my life has been worth anything unless it has had risk.*

SLAVIN, RAYMOND GRANAM, allergist, immunologist; b. Cleve., June 29, 1930; s. Philip and Dinah (Baskind) S.; m. Alberta Cohrt, June 10, 1953; children: Philip, Stuart, David, Linda. A.B., U. Mich., 1952; M.D., St. Louis U., 1956; M.S., Northwestern U., 1963. Diplomate: Am. Bd. Internal Medicine, Am. Bd. Allergy and Immunology (treas.). Intern U. Mich. Hosp., Ann Arbor, 1956-57; resident St. Louis U. Hosp., 1959-61; fellow in allergy and immunology Northwestern U. Med. Sch., 1961-64; asst. prof. internal medicine and microbiology St. Louis U., 1965-70, assoc., 1970-73, prof., 1973—, dir. div. allergy and immunology, 1965—; mem. NIH study sect., 1985-89; cons. U.S. Army M.C. Contbr. numerous articles to med. publs.; editorial bd.: Jour. Allergy and Clin. Immunology, 1975-81, Tice Practice Medicine, 1973-84, Jour. Club of Allergy, 1978-80. Chmn. bd. Asthma and Allergy Found. Am., 1985-88. With M.C., U.S. Army, 1957-59. Grantee NIH, 1967-70, 84—, Nat. Inst. Occpl. Safety and Health, 1974-80. Fellow ACP, Am. Acad. Allergy and Immunology (exec. bd., historian, pres. 1983-84); mem. Am. Assn. Immunologists, Central Soc. Clin. Research, AAAS. Democrat. Jewish. Home: 631 E Polo Dr Saint Louis MO 63105-2629 Office: 1402 S Grand Blvd Saint Louis MO 63104-1004

SLAVIN, SIMON, social administration educator; b. N.Y.C., Jan. 20, 1916; s. Isadore and Mary (Sushansky) S.; m. Jeannette Rose Littinsky, Jan. 16, 1938; children: Rayna (Mrs. Robert Epstein dec.), Vicky Jane, Johanna. B.S. in Social Sci, CCNY, 1937; M.A., Columbia U., 1938, Ed.D., 1953. Regional supr. United Service Orgn. Jewish Welfare Bd., Chgo., 1945-46; exec. dir. YM-YWHA, Mt. Vernon, N.Y., 1946-53; exec. sec. div. recreation and group work and sect. on services to handicapped Welfare and Health Council of N.Y.C., 1953-54; exec. dir. Ednl. Alliance, N.Y.C., 1954-60; asso. prof. social work Columbia U., 1960-63; prof., 1963-68, chmn. community orgn. area, 1960-66, chmn. advanced programs, 1966-67; Simon Sr. Research fellow U. Manchester, Eng., 1967-68; dean Sch. Social Adminstrn., Temple U., 1968-78, prof., 1978-80, prof., founding dean emeritus, 1983—; chmn. regional adv. com. Region III Dept. Pub. Welfare, Phila., 1972-74; instr. Adelphi Coll., 1955-58, N.Y. U., 1956-57, Chgo. U., 1958-59; cons. N.Y.C. Commr. of Drug Addiction Services. Author, co-editor: Leadership in Social Administration, 1980; editor: Social Administration: The Management of Social Services, 1978, Applying Computers in Social Service and Mental Health Agencies, 1983, An Introduction to Human Services Management, 1985, Managing Finances, Personnel and Information in Human Services, 1985; contbr. chpts. to Migration and Social Welfare, 1971, Evaluation of Social Intervention, 1972, A Design for Social Work Practice, 1974, Social Work Futures, 1983, Educating Managers of Nonprofit Organizations, 1988; editor in chief Adminstrn. in Social Work, 1977-92; book series editor Haworth Press, 1990—; also numerous articles to profl. jours. Mem. personnel adv. com. Nat. Urban League, 1964-66. Recipient Assn. for Community Orgn. and Social Adminstrn. Outstanding Life Achievement award, 1993. Home: Kimball Fams 235 Walker St Lenox MA 01240

SLAVITT, DAVID WALTON, retired lawyer; b. Chgo., Mar. 15, 1931; s. Isaac and Fay (Goldstein) S.; m. Roberta Chelnek, July 26, 1953; children: Steven, Denise, Howard. B.S., UCLA, 1952, J.D., 1955. Bar: Calif. 1956; C.P.A., Calif. Since practiced in Los Angeles; pres. Slavitt & Borofsky (P.C.), 1969-87; moderator continuing edn. programs. Author articles in field. Served with USNR, 1955. Mem. Am. Assn. Atty.-C.P.A.s (pres. 1964), ABA, State Bar Calif., Calif. Assn. Atty.-C.P.A.s (pres. 1963), Beverly Hills Bar Assn. (vice chmn. continuing edn. of bar 1970, asst. chmn. law practice mgmt. com. 1973).

SLAVITT, EARL BENTON, lawyer; b. Chgo., Sept. 12, 1939; s. Harold Hal and Rose (Hoffman) S.; m. Amy Lerner, July 12, 1987; 1 child, Gabriel Harrel; children from previous marriage: Andrew Miller, Lesley Deborah. BS in Econs., U. Pa., 1961, JD, 1964. Bar: Ill. 1964, U.S. Dist. Ct. (no. dist.) Ill. 1964, U.S. Supreme Ct. 1971. Assoc. Wisch, Crane & Kravets, Chgo., 1964-67, Ressman & Tishler, Chgo., 1967-69; assoc., then ptnr. Levy & Erens, Chgo., 1969-78; ptnr. Tash & Slavitt, Chgo., 1978-81, Katten Muchin & Zavis, Chgo., 1981—. Contbr. articles to profl. jours.; author poems and plays. Vol. Hospice of Ill. Masonic Med. Ctr., Chgo., 1987-89, Pro bono Advocates, 1989, Chgo. Ho., 1991 (recipient Outstanding Vol. award), Lawyers for the Creative Arts, Bus. Vols. for the Arts, 1992—; bd. dirs. Playwrights Ctr., Chgo., 1987, Jewish Reconstructionist Congregation, Chgo., 1978, 91, 92, Legal Clinic for the Disabled, 1993—, pres., 1995—, Sarah's Circle, 1994—. Mem. Ill. State Bar Assn. (mem. real estate com. 1976, recipient Pro Bono Cert. Accomplishment 1994), Chgo. Bar Assn. (mem. real estate com. 1976, real estate fin. com. 1982), Chgo. Coun. Lawyers (mem. jud. selection com. 1969), Lawyers in Mensa (bd. govs. 1983). Democrat. Jewish. Office: Katten Muchin & Zavis 525 W Monroe St Ste 1600 Chicago IL 60661-3693

SLAVKIN, HAROLD C., biologist; b. Chgo., Mar. 20, 1938; m. Lois S. Slavkin; children: Mark D., Todd P. BA (hon.), U. So. Calif., 1961, DDS (hon.), 1965; Doctorate (hon.), Georgetown U., 1990. Mem. faculty grad. program in cellular and molecular biology U. So. Calif., L.A., 1968—, mem. faculty gerontology inst., 1969, prof. sch. dentistry, 1974—, chmn. grad. program in craniofacial molecular biology, 1975-85; dir. Ctr. for Craniofacial Molecular Biology, L.A., 1989-95; George & Mary Lou Boone prof. craniofacial molecular biology U. So. Calif. Sch. Dentistry, L.A., 1989-95; dir. Nat. Inst. Dental Rsch., NIH, Bethesda, Md., 1995—; vis. prof. Israel Inst. Tech., Haifa, 1987-88; cons. U.S. News and World Report, 1985-95, L.A. Edn. Partnership, 1983-95, Torstar Books, Inc., 1985-95. Contbr. articles to profl. jours. Mem. sci. adv. bd. Calif. Mus. Sci. and Tech., 1985-95. Rsch. scholar U. Coll. London, 1980. Mem. AAAS, Am. Assn. Anatomists, Am. Inst. Biol. Scis., Am. Soc. for Cell Biology, Am. Assn. for Dental Rsch. (pres. 1993-94), N.Y. Acad. Scis., Inst. Medicine of NAS, Los Angeles County Art Mus. Assocs. Office: Nat Inst Dental Rsch Bldg 31C Rm 2C34 NIH 9000 Rockville Pike Bethesda MD 20892

SLAY, A(NGELA) MICHELE, fundraiser; b. Geneva, Ala., May 1, 1967; d. Robert Huey and Annie Mavis (Ausley) S. BS in Pub. Adminstr., Samford U., 1989; M of Pub. Adminstr., U. Ala., 1991. Project asst. Muscular Dystrophy Assn., Birmingham; asst. project dir. Ala. Pub. TV, Birmingham; devel. mgr. Ala. Symphony Orch., Birmingham; campaign assoc. United Way of Ctrl. Ala., Birmingham, 1993—. Mem. Shelby County Econ. Devel. Coun., Inverness, Ala., 1993—; internship Ala. Rep. Party, Birmingham, 1989. Mem. Nat. Soc. of Fund Raising Execs., Am. Soc. of Pub. Adminstrs., North Shelby County C. of C., Gamma Sigma Sigma (nat. pres. 1993-95, nat. sec. 1991-93, dist. dir. 1989-91, Nat. Sister of the Yr. 1989), Pi Alpha Alpha (chpt. pres. 1995—). Republican. Southern Bapist. Avocations: reading, cooking, swimming, traveling, volunteering. Home: 306 Woodmere Ln Birmingham AL 35226 Office: United Way of Ctrl Ala 3600 8th Ave S Birmingham AL 35222

SLAY-BARBER, DORIS A., educational consultant; b. San Antonio, Sept. 22, 1952; d. Harold and Lottie (Pieniazek) Brietzke; m. H. Gene Barber, June 27, 1987; children: G. L. Slay, Gary, Mike. BA, St. Mary's U., 1974; MEd, Trinity U., 1984. Cert. elem. tchr., Tex. Cons. computer software Edn. Svc. Ctr.; tchr., coord. gifted/talented program East Central Ind. Sch. Dist., San Antonio; ednl. cons. Edn. Svc. Ctr. Region 20, San Antonio. Mem. ASCD, Bus. and Profl. Womens Club Inc. of San Antonio, Phi Delta Kappa.

SLAYDEN, JAMES BRAGDON, retired department store executive; b. Seattle, Sept. 28, 1924; s. Philip Lee and Ruth Alwin (Bragdon) S.; m. Barbara Marie McBride, May 7, 1955; children: Tracy Anne, James Bragdon. B.A., U. Wash., 1948; M.B.A., U. So. Calif., 1949. Buyer Frederick & Nelson (dept. store), Seattle, 1949-59; div. mdse. mgr. Frederick & Nelson (dept. store), 1959-65; gen. mgr. Bullocks Westwood, Los Angeles, 1965-69; exec. v.p., gen. mdse. mgr. May D&F Co. dept. store, Denver, 1969-72; pres., CEO J. W. Robinson dept. store, L.A., 1972-78; exec. v.p. ops. Marshall Field & Co., Chgo., 1978-80; lectr. mktg. U. So. Calif., 1985-93. Active United Crusade United Way, L.A., 1973-78, Chgo. Heart Assn., 1978-79; chmn. Pvt. Industry Coun., 1982-95; cons. Internat. Exec. Svc. Corps., 1987—. With U.S. Army, 1943-45. Mem. Phi Kappa Psi. Republican. Christian Scientist. Home: 37 Mela Ln Palos Verdes Peninsula CA 90275-5086

SLAYMAKER, GENE ARTHUR, public relations executive; b. Kenton, Ohio, Sept. 15, 1928; s. Edwin Paul and Anne Elizabeth (Grable) S.; divorced; children: Jill Brook, Scott Wood, Leslie Beth; m. Julie Ann Graff, Feb. 3, 1979; 1 adopted child, Peter Fredric Bannon II; stepchildren: Jennifer Elizabeth Nash, David Frank Nash. B.A. in Radio Journalism, Ohio State U. Announcer, reporter WLWC-TV, Columbus, Ohio, 1951-52; anchor, reporter WKBN-AM-FM-TV, Youngstown, Ohio, 1952-56, KYW-TV, Cleve., 1956-60; editor news Sta. WFBM-AM-FM-TV, Indpls., 1960-68; dir. news, sports, pub. affairs WTLC-FM and WTUX-AM, Indpls., 1976-92; community rels. liaison Marion County Pros. Atty. Office, Indpls., 1993; pres., founder Slaymaker and Assocs., Indpls., 1969—. Past bd. dirs. Park-Tudor Father's Assn.; mem. Meridian Kessler Neighborhood Assn., pres., 1968-69. Recipient Disting. Service award (2). Mem. Ind. AP Broadcasters Assn. (awards), UPI (awards), Nat. Fedn. Press Women, Soc. Profl. Journalists (awards Ind. chpt., bd. dirs., chpt. pres. 1991-92, Radio-TV News Dirs. Assn. (region bd. dirs. 1987-91), Indpls. Press Club, Women's Press Club Ind. Democrat. Clubs: Nat. Headliners, Unity. Avocations: writing; painting; singing; gardening; tennis. Home: 5161 NW Washington Blvd Indianapolis IN 46205-1071 Office: Slaymaker Assoc 5161 NW Washington Blvd Indianapolis IN 46205*

SLAYMAKER, H. OLAV, geography educator; b. Swansea, Wales, Jan. 31, 1939; came to Can., 1968; s. Arthur J. and Astri H. (Breen) S.; m. Margaret A. Rapson, Apr. 8, 1967; children—Karen M., Paul O., Sarah J., Heidi R. BA, King's Coll., Cambridge, Eng., 1961; AM, Harvard U., 1963; PhD, Cambridge U., 1968. Asst. lectr. U. Coll. Wales, Aberystwyth, 1964-66; lectr. U. Coll. Wales, 1966-68; asst. prof. geography U.B.C., Vancouver, Can., 1968-70, assoc. prof., 1970-81, prof., 1981—, head dept., 1982—, assoc. v.p. rsch.; cons. water quality br. Inland Waters, Vancouver, 1976—. Editor: Mountain Geomorphology, 1972, Field Experiments, 1978, High Mountains, 1981, Extreme Landforming Events, 1983, Geomorphology and Land Managment, 1986, Erosion Budgets and Their Hydrologic Basis, 1986, Canada's Gold Environments, 1993, Steepland Geomorphology, 1995. Senate mem. Vancouver Sch. Theology, 1973-75; bd. dirs. Regent Coll., Vancouver, 1975-78, U. B.C., 1984-87. Research grantee Natural Sci. and Engring. Research Council, Ottawa, Ont., Can., 1968—. Mem. Can. Assn. Geographers (pres. 1991-92), Am. Geophys. Union, Internat. Geog. Union (commn. chmn., sec., chmn. Can. nat. com. 1984-88), Internat. Assn. Geomorphologists (v.p. 1993—), Faculty Club (Vancouver). Anglican. Avocations: mountain hiking; philately. Office: Univ BC Dept Geography, 1984 West Mall, Vancouver, BC Canada V6T 1Z2

SLAYMAN, CAROLYN WALCH, geneticist, educator; b. Portland, Maine, Mar. 11, 1937; d. John Weston and Ruth Dyer (Sanborn) Walch; m. Clifford L. Slayman; children—Andrew, Rachel. B.A. with highest honors, Swarthmore Coll., 1958; Ph.D., Rockefeller U., 1963; D.Sc. (hon.), Bowdoin Coll., 1985. Instr., then asst. prof. Case Western Res. U., Cleve., 1967; from asst. prof. to prof. genetics Yale U. Sch. Medicine, New Haven, 1967—, Sterling prof. genetics, 1991—, chmn. dept. genetics, 1984-95, dep. dean for acad. and sci. affairs, 1995—; chmn. genetic basis of disease rev. commn. NIH, 1981-85, nat. adv. gen. med. scis. coun., 1989-93; bd. dirs. J. Weston Walch Pub., Portland, Maine, The Perkin-Elmer Corp.; mem. sci. rev. bd. Howard Hughes Med. Inst., 1992—. Mem. editorial bd. Jour. Biol. Chemistry, 1989-94; contbr. articles to sci. jours. Trustee Foote Sch., New Haven, Conn., 1983-89, Hopkins Sch., New Haven, 1988-93; bd. overseers Bowdoin Coll., Brunswick, Maine, 1976-88, trustee, 1988—. Recipient Deborah Morton award Westbrook Coll., 1986. Mem. Am. Soc. Biol. Chemists, Genetics Soc. Am., Soc. Gen. Physiologists, Am. Soc. Microbiology, Phi Beta Kappa. Office: Yale U Sch Medicine Dept Genetics 333 Cedar St New Haven CT 06510-3206

SLAYMAN, CLIFFORD LEROY, JR., biophysicist, educator; b. Mt. Vernon, Ohio, July 7, 1936; s. Clifford Leroy and Ethel May (Stantz) S.; m. Carolyn Ruth Walch, Dec. 26, 1959; children: Andrew Lowell, Rachel Whitehouse. AB, Kenyon Coll., 1958; PhD, Rockefeller Inst., 1963; DSc (hon.), Kenyon Coll, 1991. NSF fellow Cambridge (Eng.) U., 1963-64; asst. prof. Western Res. U., Cleve., 1964-67; from asst. prof. to prof. physiology Yale U., New Haven, 1967—; mem panel on pre-doctoral fellowships NSF, Washington, 1969-71; DOE-DOA-NSF panel on Plant Sci. Ctrs., Washington, 1988. Editor: Electrogenic Ion Pumps, 1982; contbr. articles to profl. jours. and revs.; editorial bd. Bio Sci. Jour., 1985-88, Jour. Membrane Biology, 1982—. Mem. Hamden (Conn.) Neighborhood Preservation Com., 1980-82. Grantee NIH, 1964-91, NSF, 1979-82, DOE, 1985—. Mem. AAAS, Am. Physiol. Soc., Am. Soc. Plant Physiologists, N.Y. Acad. Scis., Soc. Gen. Physiologists, Conn. Acad. Scis. Avocations: antique house restoration, conservation, nature watching. Office: Yale Sch Medicine 333 Cedar St New Haven CT 06510-3206

SLAYTON, GUS, foundaiton administrator; b. Pocahontas, Ark., Jan. 20, 1937; s. Alvin M. and Eula Inis (Milam) S.; m. Ruth Virginia Furr, May 27, 1961 (dec. Nov. 1989). B.A., U. Md., College Park, 1973. Served as enlisted man U.S. Army, 1957-63, commd. 2d lt., 1963, advanced through grades to lt. col., 1978; various operational and research and devel. assignments, including The Pentagon, 1974-78, ret., 1980; exec. dir. Assn. of Old Crows, Alexandria, Va., 1980-92, AOC Ednl. Found., 1992—. Decorated Legion of Merit (2), Bronze Star (2). Republican. Avocation: real estate investment. Home: 25165 Elk Lick Rd Chantilly VA 22021-4267

SLAYTON, JOHN ARTHUR, electric motor manufacturing executive; b. St. Joseph, Mo., Aug. 12, 1918; s. Ernest Roy and Cora Belle (Hutchison) S.; m. Elizabeth Van Horn Duerr, Aug. 15, 1942; children: Richard, Elizabeth, Jane, James, Robert, Sarah, Mary. B.S., U. Mo., 1940. Salesman Burroughs Co., Chgo., 1940-42; acct. Standard Brands, Green Bay, Wis., 1945-48; exec. v.p. Marathon Electric, Wausau, Wis., 1948-88, pres., vice chmn., 1988—. Pres. C. of C. Found., Wausau, 1981-89, Woodson YMCA Found., 1977—; bd. dirs. Wausau Hosp. Ctr., 1976-82, North Ctrl. Mental Health Found., 1980-85, Wausau Area Vol. Exch., 1983-89, Wasau Health Found., 1975—; pres., bd. dirs. Grant Theatre Found., 1985—; bd. dirs., treas. Lehigh Yawkey Woodson Art Mus., 1985—, pres., 1996—; trstuee, elder 1st Presbyn. Ch., 1960-65. Served in USN, 1942-44. Recipient Citation of Merit U. Mo., Columbia, 1976,W ausau Disting. Community Service award, 1983, Wis. Gov.'s award, 1986; Paul Harris fellow, 1977. Mem. Wausau Area C. of C. (pres., dir. 1977-81). Republican. Clubs: Wausau Country (pres., dir. 1958-61), Wausau, YMCA (pres., dir. 1961-67). Lodge: Rotary (pres., dir.

1960-63). Home: 1804 Town Line Rd Wausau WI 54403-9119 Office: Marathon Electric 100 W Randolph St Wausau WI 54401-2569

SLAYTON, WILLIAM LAREW, planning consultant, former government official; b. Topeka, Dec. 2, 1916; s. Clarence Harvey and Mary (Larew) S.; m. Mary Prichard, Aug. 30, 1941; children: Mary Elizabeth Slayton Campbell, Barbara Slayton Shelton. Student, U. Omaha, 1937-39; A.B., U. Chgo., 1940, M.A., 1942; D.H.L. (hon.), Clarkson Coll. Tech., 1965. Polit. sec. Alderman Paul H. Douglas, Chgo., 1940-42; planning analyst Milw. Planning Commn., 1944-45, 46-47; municipal reference librarian Milw., 1947-48; asso. dir. Urban Redevel. Study, Chgo., 1948-50; field rep. div. slum clearance and urban redevel. HHFA, Washington, 1950; dir. redevel. Nat. Assn. Housing and Redevel. Ofcls., Washington, 1950-55; v.p. planning, redevel. Webb & Knapp, Inc., Washington, 1955-60; planning partner I.M. Pei & Partners, N.Y.C., 1956-61; commr. Urban Renewal Adminstrn., HHFA, HUD, Washington, 1961-66; dir. Urban Policy Center, Urban Am., Inc., Washington, 1966; exec. v.p. Urban Am., Inc., 1966-69, pres., 1969; exec. v.p. AIA, Washington, 1969-77, AIA Found., 1970-77; mem. bd. AIA Corp., 1970-77; vice chmn. AIA Research Corp., 1973-77; chmn. urban devel. advisory com. HUD, 1967-68; mem. U.S. del. Econ. Commn. for Europe, 1970; dep. asst. sec. of state for fgn. bldgs., 1978-83; cons. Nat. Assn. Housing and Redevel. Ofcls., 1983-87, Am. Planning Assn., 1987—. Bd. dirs. Met. Washington Ear, 1995—. With USNR, 1945-46. Recipient gold medal Royal Instn. Chartered Surveyors, Great Britain, 1965, Justin Herman award Nat. Assn. Housing and Redevel. Ofcls., 1994. Mem. Potomac Inst. (dir.), AIA (hon.), Am. Planning Assn., Am. Inst. Cert. Planners.

SLECHTA, ROBERT FRANK, biologist, educator; b. N.Y.C., June 4, 1928; s. Frank C. and Helen (Pospisil) S.; m. Betty S. Youngren, May 16, 1953; 1 son, Marc William. A.B., Clark U., 1949, M.A., 1951; postgrad., Columbia, 1951-52; Ph.D., Boston U., 1955. Research asst. Worcester Found., Shrewsbury, Mass., 1952-53; biologist U.S. Army Med. Nutrition Lab., Denver, 1953-55; instr., research asso. Tufts U., 1955-58; mem. faculty Boston U., 1958—, prof. biology, 1965-91, prof. emeritus, 1991—, assoc. dean Grad. Sch., 1967-78. Author: (with M. Hawthorne and E. Blaustein) Laboratory Manual for General Biology, 1965; also articles and book revs. Mem. Boston Zool. Soc. (dir. 1967-78, trustee 1978-79), Am. Inst. Biol. Scis., AAAS, Microcirculation Soc., Am. Soc. Zoologists, Soc. Study Reprodn., Sigma Xi. Research on limb regeneration in urodeles, starvation in prisoners of war, human factors in aircraft seating, effects on progestational compounds on reprodn. (early work on contraceptive pill), quantitative studies of blood flow in living microscopic vessels in mammals and amphibians. Home: 101 Wilson Rd Bedford MA 01730-1320 Office: Boston U Biology Dept 2 Cummington St Boston MA 02215-2425

SLEDGE, CLEMENT BLOUNT, orthopedic surgeon, educator; b. Ada, Okla., Nov. 1, 1930; s. John B. and Mollie D. (Blount) S.; m. Georgia Kurrus, Apr. 13, 1957; children—Margaret, John, Matthew, Claire. M.D., Yale U., 1955; M.A. (hon.), Harvard U., 1970; ScD (hon.), U. The South, 1987. Diplomate: Am. Bd. Orthopedic Surgery. Intern Barnes Hosp., St. Louis, 1955-56; resident in orthopedic surgery Harvard U., 1960-63; fellow in orthopedic pathology Armed Forces Inst. Pathology, 1963; vis. scientist Strangeways Research Lab., Cambridge (Eng.) U., 1963-66; asst. prof. orthopedic surgery Harvard U., 1963-67, asso. prof., 1967-70, prof., 1970—, chmn. dept., 1970—; chmn. dept. orthopedic surgery Brigham and Women's Hosp. Editor: Textbook of Rheumatology, 1981, 85, 89, 93; contbr. more than 100 articles to sci. jours. Active Arthritis Found.; chmn. Nat. Arthritis Adv. Bd., 1978-80. Served with M.C. USNR, 1956-58. Fellow Med. Found. Boston, 1963-66; Gebbie research fellow, 1968; NIH grantee, 1967—. Mem. Am. Acad. Orthopedic Surgeons (pres. 1985-86), Orthopedic Rsch. Soc. (pres. 1978-80), Am. Rheumatism Assn., Inst. of Medicine, Nat. Acad. Sci., Interurban Orthopedic Club, The Hip Soc. (pres. 1985). Episcopalian. Office: Brigham and Women's Hosp 75 Francis St Boston MA 02115

SLEDGE, JAMES SCOTT, judge; b. Gadsden, Ala., July 20, 1947; s. L. Lee and Kathryn (Privott) S.; m. Joan Nichols, Dec. 27, 1969; children: Joanna Scott, Dorothy Privott. BA, Auburn U., 1969; JD, U. Ala., 1974, postgrad., 1989. Bar: Ala. 1974, U.S. Ct. Appeals (5th cir.) 1975, U.S. Ct. Appeals (11th cir.) 1981. Ptnr. Inzer, Suttle, Swann & Stivender, P.A., Gadsden, 1974-91; mcpl. judge, Gadsden, 1975-91; judge U.S. Bankruptcy Ct. No. Dist. Ala., 1991—; instr. U. Ala., Gadsden, 1975-77, Gadsden State Community Coll., 1989-90. Lay minister, vestryman Holy Comforter Episc. Ch., Gadsden, 1976—; mem. Ala. Coun. on the Arts, 1994—; incorporator Episc. Day Sch., Gadsden, 1976, Kyle Home for Devel. Disadvantaged, Gadsden, 1979; bd. dirs. Salvation Army, 1984-91, Etowah County Health Dept., 1975-91, Episc. Day Sch., 1992—, Gadsden Symphony, 1993—; mem. Ala. Dem. Exec. Com., 1990-91, Etowah County Dem. Exec. Com., 1984-91; county coordinator U.S. Senator Howell Heflin, Etowah County, Ala., 1978, 84, 90; founder Gadsden Cultural Arts Found., 1983, chmn., 1986-91. Capt. U.S. Army, 1969-71, Vietnam. Decorated Bronze Star, Legion of Honor (Vietnam); recipient Governor's award for art Ala. Coun. of the Arts, 1993. Mem. Ala. State Bar (charter mem. bankruptcy sect., vice chmn. 1984, regional liaison bankruptcy bench and bar 1984), Gadsden-Etowah C. of C. (gen. counsel, v.p., bd. dirs. 1986-93), Phi Kappa Phi, Phi Eta Sigma. Lodge: Kiwanis (bd. dirs. 1981-84). Home: 435 Turrentine Ave Gadsden AL 35901-4059

SLEED, JOEL, newspaper editor; b. N.Y.C., Jan. 29, 1929; m. MaryLou Kalwara, Nov. 15, 1983; children: Jodie Parenti, Jill, Jeffrey, Kristin Kalwara, Karen Hepler. Travel editor The Star-Ledger, Newark, N.J.; travel columnist Newhouse News Svc., N.Y.C. Office: Newhouse News Svc 140 E 45th St New York NY 10017-3144 also: Star-Ledger Star-Ledger Plz Newark NJ 07102

SLEICHER, CHARLES ALBERT, chemical engineer; b. Albany, N.Y., Aug. 15, 1924; s. Charles Albert and Beatrice Eugena (Cole) S.; m. Janis Jorgensen, Sept. 5, 1953; children—Jeffrey Mark, Gretchen Gail. B.S., Brown U., 1946; M.S., M.I.T., 1949; Ph.D., U. Mich., 1955. Asst. dir. M.I.T. Sch. Chem. Engring.; Practice Bangor, Maine, 1949-51; research engr. Shell Devel. Co., Emeryville, Calif., 1955-59; assoc. prof. chem. engring. U. Wash., Seattle, 1960-66, prof., 1966-92, prof. emeritus, 1993—, dept. chmn., 1977-89; cons. Westinghouse-Hanford Co.; profl. photographer, 1994—. Contbr. articles on extraction, heat transfer, fluid mechanics, pesticide transport to profl. jours. Served with USN, 1943-47. NSF postdoctoral fellow, 1959-60; SEED grantee, 1973-74; research grantee NSF; research grantee Chevron Research Corp.; research grantee Am. Chem. Soc. Fellow AIChE (program awards coms.); mem. AAAS, Am. Chem. Soc., Sigma Xi. Chem. reactor design patentee. Home: 5002 Harold Pl NE Seattle WA 98105-2809 Office: U Wash Dept Chem Engring Box 351750 Seattle WA 98105

SLEIGH, SYLVIA, artist, educator; b. Llandudno, North Wales; came to U.S., 1961; d. John Harold and Katherine Amy (Miller) S.; m. Lawrence Alloway, June 28, 1954. Student, Sch. Art, Brighton, Sussex, Eng., 1932-36; diploma, U. London Extra-Mural Dept., 1947. Vis. asst. prof. SUNY-Stony Brook, 1978; instr. New Sch. Social Research, N.Y.C., 1974-77, 78-80; Edith Kreeger Wolf disting. prof. Northwestern U., Evanston, Ill., 1977; vis. artist Baldwin Seminar Oberlin Coll., Ohio, 1982, New Sch. Social Rsch., N.Y.C. One person shows include Bennington (Vt.) Coll., 1963, Soho 20 Art Gallery, N.Y.C., 1974, 76, 80, 82, A.I.R. Gallery, N.Y.C., 1974, 76, 78, Ohio State U., Columbus, 1976, Matrix, Wadsworth Atheneum, Hartford, Conn., 1976, Marianne Deson Gallery, Chgo., 1990, G.W. Einstein, Inc., N.Y.C., 1980, 83, 85, U. Mo., Saint Louis, 1981, Zaks Gallery, Chgo., 1985, 95, Milw. Art Mus., Butler Inst., Youngstown, Ohio, 1990, Stiebel Modern, N.Y.C., 1992, 94, Gallery 609, Denver, Canton (Ohio) Art Inst.; exhibited in group shows Newhouse Gallery, S.I., N.Y., Stamford (Conn.) Mus., 1985, Albany (N.Y.) Inst. Art, Cin. Art Mus., New Orleans Mus. Art, Denver Art Mus., Pa. Acad. Fine Arts, 1989, Calsten Art Gallery, Stevens Point, Wis., 1993, Rutgers U., New Brunswick, 1996, Stiebel Modern, N.Y.C., 1994, Soho 20, N.Y.C., 1993, Katzen Brown Gallery, N.Y.C., 1989, Zaks Gallery, Chgo., 1986,. Panelist Creative Artists Pub. Service Program, N.Y.C., 1976. Nat. Endowment for Arts grantee, 1982, Pollock-Krasner Found. grantee, 1985. Home: 330 W 20th St New York NY 10011-3302

SLEIGHT, ARTHUR WILLIAM, chemist; b. Ballston Spa, N.Y., Apr. 1, 1939; s. Hollis Decker and Elizabeth (Smith) S.; AB, Hamilton Coll., 1960; PhD, U. Conn., 1963; m. Betty F. Hilberg, Apr. 19, 1963; children: Jeffrey William, Jeannette Anne, Jason Arthur. Faculty, U. Stockholm, Sweden, 1963-64; with E.I. du Pont de Nemours & Co., Inc., Wilmington, Del., 1965-89, rsch. mgr. solid state/catalytic chemistry, 1981-89; Harris Chair prof. materials sci. Oreg. State U., Corvallis, 1989—; adj. prof. U. Del., 1978-89. Mem. Presdl. Commn. Superconductivity, 1989. Recipient Phila. chpt. Am. Inst.. Chemists award, 1988, Gold Medal award Nat. Assn. Sci. Tech. and Soc., 1994. Mem. Am. Chem. Soc. (award Del. sect. 1978). Editor Materials Rsch. Bull., 1994—; editorial bd. Inorganic Chemistry Rev., 1979—, Jour. Catalysis, 1986—, Applied Catalysis, 1987—, Solid State Scis., 1987—, Chemistry of Materials, 1988—, Materials Chemistry and Physics, 1988—, Jour. of Solid State Chemistry, 1988—; patentee in field; contbr. articles to profl. jours. Home: PO Box 907 Philomath OR 97370-0907 Office: Oreg State U Dept Chemistry Gilbert 153 Corvallis OR 97331-4003

SLEMON, GORDON RICHARD, electrical engineering educator; b. Bowmanville, Ont., Can., Aug. 15, 1924; s. Milton Everitt and Selena (Johns) S.; m. Margaret Jean Matheson, July 9, 1949; children: Sally, Stephen, Mark, Jane. B.A.Sc., U. Toronto, 1946, M.A.Sc., 1948; D.I.C., Imperial Coll. Sci., London (Eng.) U., 1951, Ph.D., 1952; D of Engring. (hon.), Meml. U. Nfld., 1994. Asst. prof. elec. engring. N.S. Tech. Coll., Can., 1953-55; assoc. prof. U. Toronto, Ont., Can., 1955-63, prof., 1964-90, chmn. dept. elec. engring., 1966-76, dean of faculty of applied sci. and engring., 1979-86, prof. emeritus, 1990—; Colombo plan adviser, India, 1963-64; pres. Elec. Engring. Consociates, 1976-79; bd. dirs. Inverpower Controls Ltd., MettNet Ltd. Author: (with J.M. Ham) Scientific Basis of Electrical Engineering, Magnetoelectric Devices, (with A. Straughen) Electric Machinery; (with S.B. Dewan, A. Straughen) Power Semiconductor Drives, Electric Machines and Drives; contbr. articles to profl. jours. Chmn. Innovations Found., 1980-93, vice chmn., 1993—; chmn. Microelectronics Devel. Ctr., 1983-88. Recipient excellence in teaching award Western Electric, 1965, Can. Centennial medal, 1967, Ross medal, 1978, 83, Gold medal Jugoslav Union of Nikola Tesla Socs., Engring. Alumni medal, Educator of Yr. award Can. Engrs., 1992, Hall of Distinction award U. Toronto, 1992. Fellow Can. Acad. Engring., Engring. Inst. Can., Instn. Elec. Engrs. (hon. fellow 1995), Officer of Order of Can. 1995, IEEE (Centennial medal 1984, Nikola Tesla award); mem. Am. Soc. Engring. Edn., others. Patentee in field. Home: 40 Chatfield Dr, Don Mills, ON Canada Office: U Toronto, Faculty Applied Sci and Engring, Toronto, ON Canada

SLEPIAN, DAVID, mathematician, communications engineer; b. Pitts., June 30, 1923; s. Joseph and Rose Grace (Myerson) S.; m. Janice Dorothea Berek, Apr. 18, 1950; children: Steven Louis, Don Joseph, Anne Maria. Student, U. Mich., 1941-43; MA, Harvard U., 1947, PhD, 1949; postdoctoral studies, Cambridge U., Eng., 1949, Sorbonne, Paris, 1950. With AT&T Bell Labs., Murray Hill, N.J., 1950-82, head math. studies dept., 1970-82; prof. elec. engring. U. Hawaii, Honolulu, 1970-81; McKay prof. elec. engring. U. Calif., Berkeley, 1957-58, Regents lectr., 1977. Editor, author: Development of Information Theory, 1973; contbr. articles to profl. jours.; patentee in field. Served with U.S. Army, 1943-46, ETO. Von Neumann lectr. Soc. for Indsl. and Applied Math., 1982; Parker fellow in physics Harvard U., 1949-50. Fellow IEEE (editor Procs. 1969-70, Alexander Graham Bell award 1981), AAAS, Inst. Math. Stats.; mem. NAS, NAE, Am. Acad. Arts and Scis. Avocations: music, travel, languages. Home: 212 Summit Ave Summit NJ 07901-2966

SLEPIAN, PAUL, mathematician, educator; b. Boston, Mar. 26, 1923; s. Philip and Ida (Goldstein) S.; children—Laura, Jean. S.B., Mass. Inst. Tech., 1950; Ph.D., Brown U., 1956. Mathematician Hughes Aircraft Co., 1956-60; assoc. prof. math. U. Ariz., 1960-62; assoc. prof. Rensselaer Poly. Inst., Troy, N.Y., 1962-65; prof. math. Rensselaer Poly. Inst., 1965-69; prof., chmn. dept. math. Bucknell U., Lewisburg, Pa., 1969-70; prof. math. Howard U., Washington, 1970—; summer vis. staff mem. Los Alamos Sci. Lab., 1976, 78, 79. Mem. Am. Math. Soc., Soc. Indsl. and Applied Math., Math. Assn. Am. Home: 1331 W 40th St Baltimore MD 21211-1728

SLESNICK, WILLIAM ELLIS, mathematician, educator; b. Oklahoma City, Feb. 24, 1925; s. Isaac Ralph and Adele (Miller) S. B.S., U.S. Naval Acad., 1945; B.A., U. Okla., 1948; B.A. (Rhodes scholar), Oxford (Eng.) U., 1950, M.A., 1954; A.M., Harvard, 1952; A.M. (hon.), Dartmouth, 1972. Math. master St. Paul's Sch., Concord, N.H., 1952-62; vis. instr. Dartmouth Coll., 1958-59, mem. faculty, 1062-94, prof. math., 1971-94; prof. emeritus, 1994—; asst. dir. ednl. uses Kiewit Computation Center, 1966-69; mem. N.H. Rhodes Scholar Selection Com.; mem. advanced placement exam. com. math. Coll. Entrance Exam. Bd., 1967-71; mem. Nat. Humanities Faculty, 1972—. Co-author: 12 math. textbooks including (with R.H. Crowell) Calculus With Analytic Geometry, 1968. Active Boy Scouts Am., 1937—, attache world bur., 1955, 67, coun. exec. bd., 1964—, dist. chmn., 1974-76; mem. nat. com. Order of Arrow, 1965—, mem. internat. com., 1974-93; mem. Nat. Jewish Com. Scouting, 1973—, internat. ambassador, 1993—; mem. assembly of overseers Mary Hitchcock Meml. Hosp., Hanover; trustee Lawrence L. Lee Mus., Hanover-Norwich Youth Fund, New Hampton (N.H.) Sch., 1975-81; mem. selection com. Okla. Found. for Excellence, 1986-91. With USN, 1942-47. Recipient Vigil Honor, 1948, Nat. Disting. Svc. award Order of Arrow, 1967, Silver Beaver award Boy Scouts Am., 1967, Silver Antelope award, 1972, Disting. Svc. award Daniel Webster Coll., 1994, Wendell C. Badger award Dartmouth Coll., 1978, Disting. Eagle Scout award, 1979, Shofar award, 1979, Silver Buffalo award, 1990, Presidential medal Dartmouth Coll., 1991. Mem. Nat. Council Tchrs. Math., Math. Assn. Am., Assn. Tchrs. Math. in New Eng., Assn. Am. Rhodes Scholars, Phi Beta Kappa (chpt. pres. 1974-77), Phi Eta Sigma, Pi Mu Epsilon, Alpha Phi Omega. Home: 306 Kendal at Hanover 80 Lyme Rd Hanover NH 03755-1218

SLETTEBAK, ARNE, astronomer, educator; b. Free City of Danzig, Aug. 8, 1925; came to U.S., 1927, naturalized, 1932; s. Nicolai and Valerie (Janczak) S.; m. Constance Pixler, Aug. 28, 1949; children: Marcia Diane, John Andrew. B.S. in Physics, U. Chgo., 1945, Ph.D. in Astronomy, 1949. Mem. faculty Ohio State U., Columbus, 1949—, prof. astronomy, 1959-94, chmn. dept. astronomy, 1962-78, prof. emeritus, 1994—; dir. Perkins Obs., Delaware, Ohio, 1959-78, mem. steering com. Earth Sci. Curriculum Project, 1965-68; mem. NRC Commn. on Astronomy adv. to Office Naval Research, 1963-65, chmn., 1965-66; mem. adv. panel for astronomy NSF, 1968-71; Fulbright lectr., vis. prof. U. Vienna, 1974-75, 81, 91; vis. prof. U. Louis Pasteur, Strasbourg, 1991; mem. nat. screening com. grad. study grants Fulbright Com., 1987-89. Fulbright rsch. fellow Hamburg, Fed. Republic Germany, 1955-56, Japan Soc. for Promotion Sci. fellow, 1988. Mem. Assn. Univs. for Research Astronomy (dir. 1961-79, chmn. sci. com. 1970-73), Am. Astron. Soc. (coun. 1964-67), Internat. Astron. Union (v.p. commn. 45, 1976-79, pres. 1979-82, chmn. working group on Be stars, 1982-85), Sigma Xi. Home: 601 Seabury Dr Worthington OH 43085-3557 Office: Ohio State U Dept Astronomy Columbus OH 43210

SLETTEN, JOHN ROBERT, construction company executive; b. Gt. Falls, Mont., Sept. 19, 1932; s. John and Hedvig Marie (Finstad) S.; m. Patricia Gail Thomas, Dec. 16, 1962; children: Leighanne, Kristen Gail, Erik John. BS in Archtl. Engring., Mont. State U., 1956. Estimator Sletten Constrn. Co., Gt. Falls, 1956-63; v.p., area mgr. Sletten Constrn. Co., Las Vegas, Nev., 1963-65; pres., chief exec. officer Sletten Constrn. Co., Gt. Falls, 1969—; bd. dirs. 1st Banks, Gt. Falls, Blue Cross-Blue Shield, Helena, Mont. Chmn. Gt. Falls Mil. Affairs Com., 1985; pres. President's Cir., Mont. State U., Bozeman, 1986; trustee Mont. Hist. Soc., Helena, 1987. with USMC, 1950-52. Mem. Mont. Contractors Assn. (bd. dirs. 1969-75, pres. 1974), Mont. C. of C. (chmn. 1984), Pachyderm Club, Rotary (bd. dirs. Gt. Falls), Elks. Republican. Lutheran. Avocations: skiing, fishing, hunting. Office: Sletten Inc 1000 25th St N PO Box 2467 Great Falls MT 59403-2467

SLEWITZKE, CONNIE LEE, retired army officer; b. Mosinee, Wis., Apr. 15, 1931; d. Leo Thomas and Amelia Marie (Hoffman) S. BSN, U. Md., Balt., 1971; MA in Counseling and Guidance, St. Mary's U., San Antonio, 1976. Commd. 1st lt. U.S. Army, 1957, advanced through grades to brig. gen., 1987; ret., 1987; chief dept. nursing Letterman Army Med. Ctr. U.S. Army, San Francisco, 1978-80; asst. chief nurse Army Nurse Corps U.S. Army, Washington, 1980-83; chief brigadier gen. U.S. Army, 1983-87; mem. Va. Adv. Com. on Women Vets. Contbr. articles to profl. jours. Decorated D.S.M., Legion of Merit, Bronze Star medal. Mem. ANA, Va. Nurses Assn., Alumni Assn. U.S. Army War Coll., Assn. U.S. Army, Women in Mil. Svc. for Am. Found. (v.p.), Am. Assn. for History of Nursing, Sigma Theta Tau. Avocations: photography; travel; music.

SLICHTER, CHARLES PENCE, physicist, educator; b. Ithaca, N.Y., Jan. 21, 1924; s. Sumner Huber and Ada (Pence) S.; m. Gertrude Thayer Almy, Aug. 23, 1952 (div. Sept. 1977); children: Sumner Pence, William Almy, Jacob Huber, Ann Thayer; m. Anne FitzGerald, June 7, 1980; children—Daniel Huber, David Pence. AB, Harvard U., 1946, MA, 1947, PhD, 1949. Research asst. Underwater Explosives Research Lab., Woods Hole, Mass., 1943-46; mem. faculty U. Ill., Urbana, 1949—, prof. physics, 1955—, prof. Ctr. for Advanced Study, 1968—, prof. chemistry, 1986—; Morris Loeb lectr. Harvard U., 1961; dir. Polaroid Co.; mem. Pres.'s Sci. Adv. Com., 1964-69, Com. on Nat. Medal Sci., 1969-74, Nat. Sci. Bd., 1975-84, Pres.'s Com. Sci. and Tech., 1976. Author: Principles of Magnetic Resonance, 1963, 3d edit., 1989; Contbr. articles to profl. jours. Former trustee, mem. corp. Woods Hole Oceanog. Instn.; mem. Harvard Corp., 1970-95. Recipient Langmuir award Am. Phys. Soc., 1969, Buckley prize, 1996; Alfred P. Sloan fellow, 1955-61. Fellow AAAS, Am. Physical Soc.; mem. NAS (Comstock prize 1993), Am. Acad. Arts and Scis., Am. Philos. Soc., Internat. Soc. Magnetic Resonance (pres. 1987-90, Trienniel prize 1986). Home: 61 Chestnut Ct Champaign IL 61821-7121

SLICK, GRACE WING, singer; b. Chgo., Oct. 30, 1939; d. Ivan W. and Virginia (Barnett) Wing; m. Gerald Robert Slick, Aug. 26, 1961 (div. 1970); 1 dau., China; m. Skip Johnson, Nov. 29, 1976. Student, Finch Coll., 1957-58, U. Miami, Fla., 1958-59. Singer with, Great Society, 1965-66, Jefferson Airplane, 1966-72, Jefferson Starship, 1974—; solo albums include: Manhole, 1974, The Best of the Great Society, Dreams, 1980, Welcome to the Wrecking Ball, 1981, Software, 1984; albums with Jefferson Starship include: Surrealistic Pillow, 1967, Earth, 1978, Modern Times, 1980, Winds of Change, 1982, Blows against the Empire, 1988, DragonFly, 1988, Freedom at Point Zero, 1979, Nuclear Furniture, Red Octopus, 1975, Jefferson Airplane, 1989, Gold, 1991, Jefferson Airplane Loves You, 1992, Jefferson Starship at their Best, 1993; albums with Starship included Knee Deep in the Hoopla, 1985, No Protection, 1987, Love Among The Cannibals, 1989, Greatest Hits (Ten Years and Change), 1991.

SLIDER, MARGARET ELIZABETH, elementary education educator; b. Spanish Fork, Utah, Nov. 27, 1945; d. Ira Elmo and Aurelia May (Peterson) Johnson; m. Richard Keith Slider, Oct. 25, 1968; children: Thomas Richard, Christopher Alan. AA, Chaffey Coll., 1966; BA, Calif. State U., San Bernardino, 1968, MEd in English as Second Lang., 1993. Cert. elem. tchr., Calif. Tchr. Colton (Calif.) Unified Sch. Dist., 1968—; lead sci. tchr. McKinley Sch., 1994—; mem. kindergarten assessment com. Colton Joint Unified Sch. Dist., Colton, 1988-90, dist. math. curriculum com., 1992-94; trainer Calif. State Dept. Edn. Early Intervention for Sch. Success, 1993—, demonstrator on-site classroom, 1994. Treas. McKinley Sch. PTA, Colton, 1989-91. Mem. NEA, ASCD, AAUW, Calif. Tchrs. Assn., Calif. Elem. Edn. Assn., Calif. Assn. of Tchrs. of English to Students of Other Langs., Calif. Mathematics Coun., Assn. Colton Educators, Pi Lambda Theta. Avocations: needlework, reading, bicycling. Home: 1628 Waterford Ave Redlands CA 92374-3967 Office: Colton Unified Sch Dist 1212 Valencia Dr Colton CA 92324-1731

SLIEPCEVICH, CEDOMIR M., engineering educator; b. Anaconda, Mont., Oct. 4, 1920; s. Maksim and Jovanka (Lubibratich) S.; m. Cleo L. Whorton, Oct. 21, 1955. BS, U. Mich., 1941, MS, 1942, PhD, 1948. Assoc. prof. dept. chem. and metall. engring. U. Mich., 1946-55; prof., chmn. Sch. Chem. Engring.; also assoc. dean Coll. Engring., U. Okla., 1955-62, George Lynn Cross Rsch. prof., 1963-91, Robert W. Hughes Centennial prof. engring., 1989-91, prof. emeritus, 1991—; pres. Univ. Engrs., Inc., 1965-78, Univ. Technologists, Inc., 1977—; cons. chem. engr. Author numerous tech. papers. Recipient Curtis W. McGraw Research award, 1958; Ipatieff award, 1959; George Westinghouse award, 1964; Sesquicentennial award U. Mich., 1967; Okla. Outstanding Scientist award, 1975; Disting. Service citation U. Okla., 1975; William H. Walker award, 1978; Gas Industry Research award 1986; named Okla. Profl. Engr. of Yr., 1973, Nat. Profl. Engr. of Year, 1974; inducted into Okla. Hall Fame, 1974. Fellow Am. Inst. Chem. Engrs.; mem. Nat. Acad. Engrs., U. Okla. Coll. Engring. Disting. Grads. Soc. (1st hon. mem.). Home: RR 1 Box 41-b1 Washington OK 73093-9801

SLIFKA, ALFRED A., oil corporation executive; b. Boston, June 3, 1932; s. Abraham and Sonya S.; m. Gilda Koritz; children: Adam, Jennifer, Eric. Grad. high sch., Boston, 1949. Pres., dir., co-owner Global Petroleum Corp., Waltham, Mass., CEO; bd. dirs. New England Fuel Inst., 1974—, Better Home Heat Coun., Petroleum Inst. Rsch. Found., N.Y.C.; past bd. dirs. U.S. Trust Co., Boston. Contbr. articles to profl. jours. vice chmn. Hebrew Rehab. Ctr., Boston; trustee Combined Jewish Philanthropies, Boston; bd. dirs. Griffith Consumers Co., Cheverly, Md. With U.S. Army. Mem. N.Y. Merc. Exch., Pine Brook Country Club (past gov. 1985-89). Avocations: jogging, golf, tennis. Office: Global Petroleum Corp 800 South St Waltham MA 02154-1439*

SLIFKIN, LAWRENCE MYER, physics educator; b. Bluefield, W.Va., Sept. 29, 1925; s. Isaac L. and Eva (Baden) S.; m. Miriam Kresses, July 4, 1948; children: Anne, Rebecca, Merle, Naomi. BA, NYU, 1947; PhD, Princeton U., 1950. Rsch. assoc., rsch. asst. prof. U. Ill., Urbana, 1950-54; asst prof. U. Minn., Mpls., 1954-55; asst. prof., then prof. physics U. N.C., Chapel Hill, 1955-91, Bowman Gray prof., 1979-82, Alumni Disting. prof., 1983-91, prof. emeritus, 1991—; liaison sci. U.S. Office Naval Rsch., London, 1969-70; collaborateur étranger, CEN-Saclay, France, 1975-76. Editor: (with J. H. Crawford): Point Defects in Solids, vol. I, 1972, vol. II, 1975; contbr. more than 125 articles to profl. jours. and books. With U.S. Army, 1944-46, PTO. Fellow Am. Phys. Soc. (exec. com. div. condensed matter physics 1978-80, Jesse Beams award rsch. excellence S.E. Sect. 1977), Soc. Photographic Scientists and Engrs.; mem. Am. Assn. Physics Tchrs. Democrat. Jewish. Avocations: music, travel, reading, swimming, grandfathering. Home: 313 Burlage Cir Chapel Hill NC 27514-2703 Office: U NC-Chapel Hill Cb 3255 Phillips Hall Chapel Hill NC 27599

SLIGER, HERBERT JACQUEMIN, JR., lawyer; b. Urbana, Ill., Nov. 21, 1948; s. Herbert Jacquemin and Marina (Mantia) S.; m. June 5, 1971 (div. June 8, 1992); children: Lauren Christine, Matthew Ryan, Nicholas Adam, Claire Nicole, Adam Gregory. BS in Fin., U. Ill., 1970; JD, U. Ariz., 1974. Bar: Ariz. 1974, Ill. 1975, U.S. Supreme Ct. 1983, Okla. 1984, U.S. Ct. Appeals (7th cir.) 1980, U.S. Tax Ct. 1980; CPA, Okla. Lawyer Charles W. Phillips Law Offices, Harrisburg, Ill., 1974-75; trust counsel Magna Trust Co., F/K/A Millikin Nat. Bank, Decatur, Ill., 1976-80, First of America Trust Co., Springfield, Ill., 1980-83; mgr. employee benefits trust dept. First Interstate Bank of Okla., NA, Oklahoma City, 1983-89; v.p., pension counsel Star Bank, NA, Cin., Cin., 1989-90; asst. gen. counsel Bank One Ariz. Corp., Phoenix, 1990-95; asst. gen. counsel, nat. practice group head Banc One Corp., Columbus, Ohio, 1995—; co-chmn. Nat. Conf. Lawyers and Corp. Fiduciaries, 1992-94. Contbr. articles to profl. jours. Mem. ABA (sect. bus. law, banking law com., trust and investment svcs. subcom. 1991—, sect. real property, probate and trust law 1974—, fiduciary income taxation subcom. 1994—, fiduciary environ. problems com. 1993—, section of taxation, employee benefits com. 1991—), State Bar of Ariz., Okla. Bar Assn., Am. Bankers Assn. (chmn. trust counsel com. 1992-94, mem. and head of fiduciary law dept. Nat./Grad. Trust Sch. Bd. of Faculty Advisors 1994-95, faculty mem. teaching "fiduciary duties under ERISA" Nat. Employee Benefit Trust Sch. 1994—, spokesman Environ. Risk Task Force 1994-95, mem. trust and investment divsn. exec. com. 1992-94, mini-adv. bd. chairperson trusts and estates 1995—). Roman Catholic. Avocations: phys. fitness, original print collecting. Home: 158 Sheffield Dr Gahanna OH 43230 Office: Bank One Corp 100 E Broad St Columbus OH 43271

SLIKER, TODD RICHARD, accountant, lawyer; b. Rochester, N.Y., Feb. 9, 1936; s. Harold Garland and Marion Ethel (Caps) S.; BS with honors (Ford Found. scholar), U. Wis., 1955; PhD, Cornell U., 1962; MBA, Harvard, 1970; JD, U. Denver, 1982; m. Gretchen Paula Zeiter, Dec. 27, 1963; children: Cynthia Garland, Kathryn Clifton. Bar: Colo. 1983. With

Clevite Corp., Cleve., 1962-68, head applied physics sect., 1965-68; asst. to pres. Granville-Phillips Co., Boulder, Colo., 1970; v.p., gen. mgr. McDowell Electronics, Inc., Metuchen, N.J., 1970-71; pres. C.A. Compton, Inc., mfrs. audio-visual equipment, Boulder, 1971-77; chief acct. C&S Inc., Englewood, Colo., 1977-80, v.p., 1980-82; sole practice law, Boulder, 1983-88; mgmt. real estate, 1972—. Del., Colo. Rep. Assembly, 1974, 76; Rep. dist. fin. coordinator, 1974-75; precinct committeeman, 1974-86, 92-94; chmn. Boulder County Rep. 1200 Club, 1975-79; mem. Colo. Rep. State Cen. Com., 1977-81, asst. treas., 1979-87; sect. corr. Harvard U., 1981—. Served to 1st lt. USAF, 1955-57. Recipient paper award vehicular communication group IEEE, 1966. Lic. real estate salesman, securities salesman; CPA, Colo. Mem. Colo. Soc. CPAs (govt. relations task force 1983-86), Colo. Bar Assn. (publs. com. 1982-84), Am. Phys. Soc., Optical Soc. Am. (referee Jour.), Colo. Harvard Bus. Sch. Club, Hist. Boulder Club, Rotary, Sigma Xi, Phi Kappa Phi, Theta Chi, Beta Alpha Psi. Contbr. articles to profl. jours. Patentee in field. Home: 12500 Oxford Rd Longmont CO 80501-8436 *Personal philosophy: The good will last.*

SLINGER, MICHAEL JEFFERY, law library director; b. Pitts., Apr. 12, 1956; s. Maurice and Mary Helen (Kengerski) S.; m. Cheryl Blaney, Apr. 19, 1980; children: Rebecca, Sarah. BA, U. Pitts., 1978; M Librianship, U. S.C., 1979; JD, Duquesne U., 1984. Reference libr. Duquesne U. Sch. Law, Pitts., 1983-84; rsch. libr. U. Notre Dame (Ind.) Sch. Law, 1984-85, head rsch. svcs., 1985-86, assoc. dir. pub. svcs., 1986-90; law libr. dir., assoc. prof. law Suffolk U. Sch. Law, Boston, 1990-93, law libr. dir., prof. law, 1994-95; law libr. dir., prof. law Cleve. State U., 1995—. Contbr. articles to profl. jours., chpt. to book. Mem. ABA, ALA, Am. Assn. Law Librs., Am. Assn. Law Schs. (exec. bd. sect. on law librs. 1993-94), New Eng. Law Libr. Consortium (treas. 1992-95), Ohio Regional Assn. Law Librs. (v.p. 1987-88, pres. 1988-89, Pres. award 1989). Avocations: reading, sports, family. Office: Cleveland-Marshall Coll Law Bartunek Law Libr 1801 Euclid Ave Cleveland OH 44115-2403

SLIPSKI, RONALD EDWARD, lawyer, educator; b. Youngstown, Ohio, May 27, 1953; s. Margaret Alice (Seman) Reno; m. Geralyn Balchak, May 17, 1980; children: Jana Veronica, Marek Joseph, Lukas Balchak, Adrian Matthew. BA, Youngstown State U., 1975, MA, 1976; JD, U. Akron, 1979. Bar: Ohio 1979, U.S. Dist. Ct. (no. dist.) Ohio 1981, U.S. Ct. Appeals (6th cir.) 1985. Law clk. Ohio Ct. Appeals 7th Appellate Dist., Youngstown, 1980-81; sr. ptnr. Green, Haines, Sgambati, Murphy & Macala Co., LPA, Youngstown, 1981—; instr. mgmt. and history dept. Youngstown State U., 1980—. Mem. ABA, Nat. Orgn. Social Security Claimant's Reps, Ohio State Bar Assn., Mahoning County Bar Assn., Mahoning-Trumbull Counties Acad. Trial Lawyers, Ohio Acad. Trial Lawyers, Am. Soc. for Legal History, Phi Kappa Phi.

SLIVE, SEYMOUR, museum director, fine arts educator; b. Chgo., Sept. 15, 1920; s. Daniel and Sonia (Rapoport) S.; m. Zoya Gregorevna Sandomirsky, June 29, 1946; children: Katherine, Alexander, Sarah. AB, U. Chgo., 1943, PhD, 1952; MA (hon.), Harvard U., 1958, Oxford (Eng.) U., 1972. Instr. fine arts Oberlin (Ohio) Coll., 1950-51; chmn. art dept. Pomona (Calif.) Coll., 1952-54; mem. faculty Harvard U., Cambridge, Mass., 1954—, prof. fine arts, 1961—, Gleason prof. fine arts, 1973-91, Gleason prof. fine arts emeritus, 1991—, chmn. dept. fine arts, 1968-71, dir. Fogg Art Mus., 1975-82; Elizabeth and John Moors Cabot dir. emeritus Harvard art museums, 1982; exchange prof. Leningrad (USSR) U., 1961; Ryerson lectr. Yale U., 1962; Slade prof. Oxford (Eng.) U., 1972-73. Author: Rembrandt and His Critics, 1630-1730, 1953, The Rembrandt Bible, 1959, Catalogue of the Paintings of Frans Hals, 1962, Drawings of Rembrandt, 1965, (with Jakob Rosenberg and E.H. ter Kuile) Dutch Art and Architecture 1600-1800, 2nd edit., 1978, Rembrandt's Drawings, 1965, Frans Hals, 3 vols., 1970-74, Jacob van Ruisdael, 1981, Frans Hals, 1989, Dutch Painting: 1600-1800, 1995. Trustee Solomon R. Guggenheim Found., 1978—, Norton Simon Mus., 1989-91; bd. dirs. Burlington mag. Found., 1987—. Lt. (j.g.) USNR, 1943-46, PTO. Decorated officer Order Orange Nassau Netherlands, 1962; Fulbright fellow Netherlands, 1951-52; Guggenheim fellow, 1956-57, 78-79; Fulbright research scholar Utrecht (Netherlands) U., 1959-60. Fellow Am. Acad. Arts and Scis.; mem. Karel van Mander Soc. (hon.), Coll. Art Assn. (dir. 1958-62, 65-69), Renaissance Soc., Dutch Soc. Scis. (fgn. mem.), Brit. Acad. (corr. fellow). Office: Harvard U Sackler Art Museum Cambridge MA 02138

SLOAN, ALLAN HERBERT, journalist; b. Bklyn., Nov. 27, 1944; s. Samuel and Doris (Shanblott) S.; m. Nancy Nolan, June 29, 1969; children: Sharon R., Susan M., Dena A. BA, Bklyn. Coll., 1966; MS, Columbia U., 1967. Reporter Charlotte (N.C.) Observer, 1968-72, Detroit Free Press, 1972-79; assoc. staff writer Forbes Mag., N.Y.C., 1979-81; writer Money Mag., N.Y.C., 1982-84; sr. editor Forbes Mag., N.Y.C., 1984-88; columnist N.Y. Newsday, N.Y.C., 1989-95; Wall St. editor Newsweek Mag., N.Y.C., 1995—. Author: Three Plus One Equals Billions: The Bendix-Martin Marietta War, 1982. Recipient Loeb award for fin. journalism Loeb Found., 1974, 84, 91, 93, Hancock award for fin. journalism Hancock Found., 1992. Jewish. Office: Newsweek 257 W 57th St New York NY 10019-1802

SLOAN, DAVID EDWARD, retired corporate executive; b. Winnipeg, Man., Can., Mar. 29, 1922; s. David and Annie Maud (Gorvin) S.; m. Kathleen Lowry Craig, Dec. 26, 1947; children: Pamela Jane, John David, Kathleen Anne. B.Commerce, U. Man., 1942. With Monarch Life Assurance Co., Winnipeg, 1946-47; with Can. Pacific Ltd., 1947-88, treas., 1969-88; pres. and chief exec. officer Can. Pacific Securities Ltd., 1985-88; mem. adv. com. Can. Pension Plan, Can. Govt., 1967-76, chmn., 1974-76. Lt. Royal Can. Army Service Corps, 1942-45. Mem. Fin. Exec. Inst. Can. (past pres. Montreal chpt.), Toronto Soc. Fin. Analysts, Soc. Internat. Treas. (internat. chmn. 1985-86, mem. coun. advisors 1978-87), Assn. Investment Mgmt. and Rsch., U. Man. Alumni Assn., The Toronto Hunt Club. Mem. United Ch. Can. Home: 316 Rosemary Rd, Toronto, ON Canada M5P 3E3

SLOAN, DAVID W., lawyer; b. Rahway, N.J., June 23, 1941; s. Harper Allen and Margaret (Walker) S.; m. Margaret J. Neville, Oct. 23, 1965; children: Matthew A., John S. AB, Princeton U., 1963; MS, Stanford U., 1965; JD, Harvard U., 1970. Bar: Calif. 1971, Ohio 1973. Assoc. Brobeck, Phleger & Harrison, San Francisco, 1970-73; assoc. and ptnr. Burke, Haber & Berick, Cleve., 1973-83; ptnr. Jones, Day, Reavis & Pogue, Cleve., 1983—; adj. prof. law Case Western Reserve U., 1975. Vol. Peace Corps., Turkey, 1965-67; sr. warden St. Paul's Episcopal Ch., Cleveland Heights. Mem. ABA (former council mem. sect. on science and technology), Ohio Bar Assn., Cleve. Bar Assn., Computer Law Assn., Sigma Xi, Alzheimer's Assn. (former trustee and v.p.). Office: Jones Day Reavis & Pogue North Point 901 Lakeside Ave E Cleveland OH 44114-1116

SLOAN, EARLE DENDY, JR., chemical engineering educator; b. Seneca, S.C., Apr. 23, 1944; s. Earle Dendy and Sarah (Bellotte) S.; m. Marjorie Nilson, Sept. 7, 1968; children: Earle Dendy III, John Mark. BSChemE, Clemson U., 1965, MSChemE, 1972, PhD in Chem. Engring., 1974. Engr. Du Pont, Chattanooga, 1965-66, Seaford, Del., 1966-67; cons. Du Pont, Parkersburg, W.Va., 1967-68; sr. engr. Du Pont, Camden, S.C., 1968-70; postdoctoral fellow Rice U., 1975; prof. chem. engring. Colo. Sch. Mines, Golden, 1976—, Gaylord and Phyllis Weaver dist. prof. chem. engring., 1992—; pres. faculty senate Colo. Sch. Mines, 1989-90; Tokyo Electric Power Co. chair Keio U., Japan, 1996. Author: Clathrate Hydrates of Natural Gases, 1990; chmn. pub. bd. Chem. Engring. Edn., 1990—. Scoutmaster local Cub Scouts, 1978-81; elder Presbyn. Ch., Golden, Colo., 1977-79, 92-94. Fellow AIChE (chmn. area Ia thermodynamics and transport 1990-93); mem. Am. Soc. for Engring. Edn. (chmn. ednl. rsch. methods divsn. 1983-85, chmn. chem. engring. divsn.), Am. Chem. Soc., Soc. Petroleum Engrs. (Disting. Lectr. 1996—). Avocations: long distance running, piano, philosophy. Home: 2121 Washington Ave Golden CO 80401-2374

SLOAN, FRANK ALLEN, economics educator; b. Greensboro, N.C., Aug. 15, 1942; s. Harry Benjamin and Edith (Vortreflich) S.; m. Paula Jane Rackoff, June 22, 1969; children: Elyse Valerie, Richard Matthew. A.B., Oberlin Coll., 1964; Ph.D., Harvard U., 1969. Research economist Rand Corp., Santa Monica, Calif., 1968-71; asst. prof. econs. U. Fla., Gainesville, 1971-73, assoc. prof., 1973-76; prof. econs. Vanderbilt U., Nashville, 1976-84; Centennial prof. econs. Vanderbilt U., 1984-93, chmn. dept., 1986-89; J. Alexander McMahon Prof. econs. Duke University, Durham, NC, 1993—; dir. Health Policy Ctr. Vanderbilt U. Inst. Pub. Policy Studies, 1976—; mem. Inst. Medicine, Washington, 1982—, dist. medicine coun., 1990—; mem. Nat. Coun. Health Care Tech., Washington, 1979-81, Nat. Allergy and Infectious Disease Council, Washington, 1971-74; cons. adv. coun. Social Security, Washington, 1983. Co-author: Private Physicians and Public Programs, 1978, Hospital Labor Markets, 1980, Insurance, Regulation and Hospital Costs, 1980, Uncompensated Hospital Care: Rights and Responsibilities, 1986, Insuring Medical Malpractice, 1991. Mem. Am. Econ. Assn., So. Econ. Assn., Western Econ. Assn. Home: 109 Millbrae Ln Chapel Hill NC 27514 Office: Duke University Ctr for Health Policy PO Box 90253 Durham NC 27708

SLOAN, FRANK KEENAN, lawyer, writer; b. Johnson City, Tenn., Oct. 11, 1921; s. Z. Frank and Maria Pearl (Witten) S.; m. Helen Rhett Yobs, Feb. 23, 1946 (dec. 1978); children: Richard O., Lewis W., Christine McC., Frank Keenan; m. Alice E. Hamburger, June 22, 1979; children: Carl Francis, Alline Elizabeth. BA, U. S.C., 1943, LLB, JD, 1948. Bar: S.C. 1948. With firm Cooper & Gary, Columbia, S.C., 1948-62; dep. asst. sec. Dept. Def., Washington, 1962-65; S.E. regional dir. OEO, Atlanta, 1965-67; sole practice law Columbia, 1967-77, 87—; chief dep. atty. gen. State of S.C., Columbia, 1977-87; from instr. to assoc. prof. law U. S.C., 1954-62; syndicated columnist, Columbia, 1989-94. Author: (with J.F. Flanagan) S.C. Rules of Civil Procedure; contbr. articles to legal jours. Exec. dir., sec. S.C. Dem. Party, 1960-62, county atty., county exec., Richland County, S.C., 1970-72. Served with USN, 1943-46, 51-52; capt. Res. (ret.). Mem. Mil. Order of World Wars, Rotary (Columbia club), Forest Lake Club (Columbia), Phi Beta Kappa. Democrat. Lutheran. Home: 3320 Devereaux Rd Columbia SC 29205-1919

SLOAN, HUGH WALTER, JR., automotive industry executive; b. Princeton, N.J., Nov. 1, 1940; s. Hugh Walter and Elizabeth (Johnson) S.; m. Deborah Louise Murray, Feb. 20, 1971; children: Melissa, Peter, Jennifer, William. A.B. in History with honors, Princeton U., 1963. Staff asst. to Pres. U.S., White House, Washington, 1969-71; treas. Pres. Nixon's Reelection Campaign, Washington, 1971; spl. asst. to pres. Budd Co., Troy, Mich., 1973-74, exec. asst. internat., 1974-77, mgr. corp. mktg., 1977-79; pres., gen. mgr. Budd Can. Inc., Kitchener, Ont., 1979-85; pres. automotive The Woodbridge Group, Troy, Mich., 1985—; bd. dirs. Woodbridge Foam Corp., Cartex Corp., Mfrs. Life Ins. Co., Schneider Corp. Trustee Princeton U.; bd. dirs. The Cmty. House, Jr. Achievement of Can. Lt. USNR, 1963-65. Recipient Outstanding Bus. Leader award Wilfrid Laurier U., 1987. Mem. World Pres. Orgn., Automotive Parts Mfrs. Assn. (past chmn.), Automotive Market Rsch. Coun. (past pres.), Bloomfield Hills (Mich.) Country Club. Republican. Office: Woodbridge Group 2500 Meijer Dr Troy MI 48084-7146

SLOAN, JEANETTE PASIN, artist; b. Chgo., Mar. 18, 1946; d. Antonio and Anna (Baggio) Pasin; children: Eugene Blakely, Anna Jeanette. BFA, Marymount Coll., Tarrytown, N.Y., 1967; MFA, U. Chgo., 1969. Exhibited in one-woman shows G.W. Einstein Gallery, N.Y.C., 1977-85, Landfall Press Gallery, Chgo., N.Y.C., 1978, 87, Frumkin & Struve Gallery, Chgo., 1981, Roger Ransay Gallery, Chgo., 1987, 89, 92, Adams-Middleton Gallery, Dallas, 1987, Tatischeff Gallery, Santa Monica, Calif., 1989, Steven Scott Gallery, Balt., 1989, Butters Gallery, Portland, Oreg., 1989, 91, 94, 96, Tatischeff Gallery, N.Y.C., 1995, Ouarter Editions, N.Y.C., 1995, Elliot Smith Gallery, St. Louis, 1994, Peltz Gallery, Milw., 1994-95; represented in permanent collections Art Mus. Chgo., Cleve. Mus. Art, Ill. State Mus., Indpls. Mus. Art, Canton (Ohio) Art Inst., Ball State Bus., Mpls., Inst. Art, Fogg Mus. Harvard U., Yale U. Art Gallery, Snite Mus. U. Notre Dame, Met. Mus. Art, N.Y.C., Herbert F. Johnson Mus. Cornell U., Ithaca, N.Y.; exhibited in group shows. Studio: 535 Keystone Ave River Forest IL 60305-1611

SLOAN, JERRY (GERALD EUGENE SLOAN), professional basketball coach; b. Mar. 28, 1942; m. Bobbye; 3 children: Kathy, Brian, Holly. Student, Evansville Coll., Evansville, Ind. Professional basketball player, Baltimore, 1965-66, Chicago Bulls, NBA, 1966-76; head coach Chicago Bulls, 1979-82; scout Utah Jazz, NBA, Salt Lake City, 1983-84, asst. coach, 1984-88, head coach, 1988—; player 2 NBA All-Star games; named to NBA All-Defensive First Team, 1969, 72, 74, 75. Office: care Utah Jazz Delta Ctr 301 West South Temple Salt Lake City UT 84101-1105*

SLOAN, O. TEMPLE, JR., automotive equipment executive; b. Sanford, N.C., Feb. 21, 1939; s. Orris Temple and Thelma (Hamilton) S.; m. Carol Carson; children: C. Carson Henline, O. Temple Sloan III, Mark H. Sloan. BA in Bus. Adminstrn., Duke U., 1961. Founder, pres. Gen. Parts Inc., Raleigh, N.C., 1961—; now chmn. Gen. Parts Inc., Raleigh; chmn. bd. dirs. Highwoods Properties Inc., Raleigh; bd. dirs. So. Equipment Co., Raleigh, CARQUEST Corp., Tarrytown, N.Y., Al Smith Buick Inc. Recipient Automotive Edn. Rep. award Northwood Inst., 1977, Silver Beaver award Boy Scouts Am., Dist. Award of Merit, Disting. Eagle award Boy Scouts Am. Trustee Boys & Girls Homes N.C., Lake Waccamaw, 1973—, Glenaire Retirement Ctr., Raleigh, 1985—; adv. bd. Salvation Army, Raleigh, 1973-87, chmn., 1976-77; exec. bd., v.p., treas. Occoneechee council Boy Scouts Am., 1967—; bd. visitors Peace Coll., Raleigh, 1985-87, trustee, 1987—, vice chmn.; trustee St. Andrew's Presbyn. Coll., 1990—; bd. dirs. Rex Hosp. Found., 1989-90; elder Presbyn. Ch. Mem. Automotive Warehouse Distbrs. Assn. Inc. (dir. 1969—, chmn. 1976-77, scholarship award 1977, Automotive Man of Yr. award 1989), The Fifty Group (bd. dirs. 1983-88, pres. 1986-87), Greater Raleigh C. of C. (bd. dirs. 1989-91). Republican. Club: Carolina Country (Raleigh). Avocations: fishing, hunting, ranching. Home: 5528 Knightdale Eagle Rock Rd Knightdale NC 27545-8416 Office: Gen Parts Inc PO Box 26006 Raleigh NC 27611-6006*

SLOAN, REBA FAYE, dietitian, consultant; b. South Bend, Ind., Feb. 5, 1955; d. Kenneth and Ruby Faye (Long) Lewis; m. Gilbert Kevin Sloan, May 22, 1976. BS, Harding U., 1976; MPH, Loma Linda U., 1989; Cert. Tng. in Child/Adolescent Obesity, U. Calif., San Francisco. Registered dietitian; lic. dietitian and nutritionist; cert. advanced clin. tng. adolescent obesity. Dietetic intern Vanderbilt U. Med. Ctr., Nashville, 1978, rsch. dietitian, 1979-80; therapeutic dietitian Bapt. Hosp., Nashville, 1981-85; staff dietitian Nautilus Total Fitness Ctrs., Nashville, 1983-86; cons. dietitian Nashville Met. Govt., 1986-95, Bapt. Hosp. Ctr. for Health Promotion, Nashville, 1987-91, Parkwest Eating Disorder Clinic, Nashville, 1989-91; pvt. practice, 1992—; adj. prof. Vanderbilt U., 1995; nutrition cons. The Nashville Striders, 1979-81; cons. nutritionist; mem. Vanderbilt U. Eating Disorder Com. Vol. Belmont Ch. Ministries, Nashville, 1981—; speaker Am. Heart Assn., Nashville, 1990—. Recipient cert. of appreciation Am. Heart Assn., 1990; Leaders fellow YMCA. Mem. Am. Dietetic Assn., Sports and Cardiovascular Nutritionists, Cons. Nutritionists, Am. Coll. Sports Medicine, Am. Running and Fitness Assn., Nashville Dist. Dietetic Assn. (contbr. diet manual 1984), Nat. Assn. for Chrisian Recovery, Alpha Chi. Avocations: travel, running, fitness, reading. Home: 1817 Shackleford Rd Nashville TN 37215-3525 Office: 121 21st Ave N Ste 208 Nashville TN 37203-5213

SLOAN, RICHARD, artist; b. Chgo., Dec. 11, 1935; s. Samuel Theodore and Lelia (Beach) S.; m. Arlene Florence Miller, Aug. 11, 1962 (dec. June 1994). Attended, Am. Acad. Art, 1951-53. Advt. illustrator; staff artist Lincoln Park Zoo., Chgo.; master wildlife artist Leigh Yawkey Woodson Art Mus., 1994. Exhbns. include Explorer's Hall Nat. Geographic Soc., Brit. Mus. Natural History, Royal Scottish Acad., Carnegie Mus., Calif. Acad. Scis., Boston Mus. Sci., Am. Mus. Natural History, Nat. Collection Fine Art Smithsonian Inst., Washington, 1979, Leigh Yawkey Woodson Art Mus. (13 exhbns., 1979—), Beijing Mus. Natural History, 1987; Roger Tory Peterson Inst. Natural History nat. mus. tour, 1993, James Ford Bell Mus. Nat. History, U. Minn., 1994; spl. guest artist 1st Vancouver Internat. Wildlife Art Show, 1994; permanent collections Smithsonian Inst., Leigh Yawkey Woodson Art Mus., Ill. State Mus.; pvt. collections throughout world; contbr. Nat. Wildlife Stamp Program, World Wildlife Fund, international stamps; paintings featured Nat. and Internat. Wildlife Mag., U.S. Art, Wildlife Art News, Ariz. Wildlife Mag., numerous others; artist, illustrator Encyc. Brit., 1963, (book) Raptors of Arizona, 1994. Recipient Award of Excellence Cin. Mus. Nat. History, 1984, Award of Merit Anchorage Audubon Soc., 1985. Mem. Soc. Animal Artists (award of excellence 1990). Home: 10451 SE Jupiter Narrows Dr Hobe Sound FL 33455

SLOANE, BEVERLY LEBOV, writer, consultant; b. N.Y.C., May 26, 1936; d. Benjamin S. and Anne (Weinberg) LeBov; m. Robert Malcolm Sloane, Sept. 27, 1959; 1 child, Alison Lori Sloane Gaylin. AB, Vassar Coll., 1958; MA, Claremont Grad. Sch., 1975, doctoral study, 1975-76; cert. in exec. mgmt., UCLA Grad. Sch. Mgmt., 1982, grad. exec. mgmt. program., UCLA 1982; grad. intensive bioethics course Kennedy Inst. Ethics, Georgetown U., 1987, advanced bioethics course, 1988; grad. sem. in Health Care Ethics, U. Wash. Sch. Medicine, Seattle, summer 1988-90, 94; grad. Summer Bioethics Inst. Loyola Marymount U., summer, 1990; grad. Annual Summer Inst. on Teaching or Writing, Columbia Tchrs. Coll., summer 1990; grad. Annual Summer Inst. on Advanced Teaching of Writing, summer, 1993, Annual Inst. Pub. Health and Human Rights, Harvard U. Sch. Pub. Health, 1994, grad. profl. pub. course Stanford U., 1982, grad. exec. refresher course profl. pub. Stanford U., 1994; cert. Exec. Mgmt. Inst. in Health Care, U. So. Calif., 1995, cert. advanced exec. program Grad. Sch. Mgmt. UCLA, 1995; cert. in ethics corps tng. program, Josephson Inst. of Ethics, 1991, cert.; ethics fellow Loma Linda U. Med. Ctr., 1989; cert. clin. intensive biomedical ethics, Loma Linda U. Med. Ctr., 1989. Circulation libr. Harvard Med. Libr., Boston, 1958-59; social worker Conn. State Welfare, New Haven, 1960-61; tchr. English, Hebrew Day Sch., New Haven, 1961-64; instr. creative writing and English lit. Monmouth Coll., West Long Branch, N.J., 1967-69; freelance writer, Arcadia, Calif., 1970—; v.p. council grad. students, Claremont Grad. sch., 1971-72, adj. dir. Writing Ctr. Speaker Series Claremont Grad. Sch., 1993—, spkr., 1996; mem. adv. com. tech. and profl. writing Dept. English, Calif. State U., Long Beach, 1980-82; mem. adv. bd. Calif. Health Rev., 1982-83; mem. Foothill Health Dist. Adv. Coun. L.A. County Dept. Health Svcs., 1987-93, pres., 1989-91, immediate past pres., 1991-92. Ann. Key Mem. award, 1990. Author: From Vassar to Kitchen, 1967, A Guide to Health Facilities: Personnel and Management, 1971, 2nd edit. 1977, 3d edit., 1992. Mem. pub. relations bd. Monmouth County Mental Health Assn., 1968-69; chmn. creative writing group Calif. Inst. Tech. Woman's Club, 1975-79; mem. ethics com., human subjects protection com. Jewish Home for the Aging, Reseda, Calif., 1994—, Santa Teresita Hosp., 1994—; mem. task force edn. and cultural activities, City of Duarte, 1987-88; mem. strategic planning task force com., campaign com. for pre-eminence Claremont Grad. Sch., 1986-87, mem. alumni coun., 1993—, bd. dirs., governing bd. alumni assn., 1993—, mem. alumni coun., mem. steering com. annual alumni day 1994—, mem. alumni awards com., 1994—, mem. alumni events com., 1994—, mem. vol. devel. com., 1994—; Vassar Coll. Class rep. to Alumnae Assn. Fall Coun. Meeting, 1989,, class corr. Vassar Coll. Quarterly Alumnae Mag., 1993—; co-chmn. Vassar Christmas Showcase New Haven Vassar Club, 1965-66, rep. to Vassar Coll. Alumnae Assn. Fall Coun. Meeting, 1965-66; co-chmn. Vassar Club So. Calif. Annual Book Fair, 1970-71; chmn. creative writing group Yale U. Newcomers, 1965-66, dir. creative writing group Yale U. Women's Orgn., 1966-67; grad. AMA Ann. Health Reporting Conf., 1992, 93; mem. exec. program network UCLA Grad. Sch. Mgmt., 1987—; trustee Ctr. for Improvement of Child Caring, 1981-83; mem. League Crippled Children, 1982—, bd. dirs., 1988-91, treas. for gen. meetings, 1990-91, chair hostesses com., 1988-89, pub. rels. com., 1990-91; bd. dirs. L.A. Commn. on Assaults Against Women, 1983-84; v.p. Temple Beth David, 1983-86; mem. cmty. rels. com. Jewish Fedn. Council Greater L.A., 1985-87; del. Task Force on Minorities in Newspaper Bus., 1987-89; cmty. rep. County Health Ctrs. Network Tobacco Control Program, 1991. Recipient cert. of appreciation City of Duarte, 1988, County of L.A., 1988; Coro Found. fellow, 1979; named Calif. Communicator of Achievement, Woman of Yr. Calif. Press Women, Am. Med. Writers Assn. (pres. Pacific Southwest chpt. 1987-89, dir. 1980-93, Pacific S.W. del. to nat. bd. 1980-87, 89-91, chmn. various conv. coms., chmn. nat. book awards trade category 1982-83, chmn. Nat. Conv. Networking Luncheon 1983, 84, chmn. freelance and pub. relations coms. Nat. Midyr. Conf. 1983-84, workshop leader ann. conf. 1984-87, 90-92, 95—, nat. chmn. freelance sect. 1984-85, gen. chmn. 1985, Asilomar Western Regional Conf., gen. chmn. 1985, workshop leader 1985, program co-chmn. 1987, speaker 1985, 88-89, program co-chmn. 1989, nat. exec. bd. dirs. 1985-86, nat. adminstr. sects. 1985-86, pres.-elect Pacific S.W. chpt. 1985-87, pres. 1987-89, immediate past pres. 1989-91, bd. dirs., 1991-93, moderator gen. session nat. conf. 1987, chair gen. session nat. conf., 1986-87, chair Walter C. Alvarez Meml. Found. award 1986-87, Appreciation award for outstanding leadership 1989, named to Workshop Leaders Honor Roll 1991); mem. Women in Comm. (dir. 1980-82, 89-90, v.p. cmty. affairs 1981-82, N.E. area rep. 1980-81, chmn. awards banquet 1982, sem. leader, speaker ann. nat. profl. conf., 1985, program adv. com. L.A. chpt. 1987, v.p. activities 1989-90, chmn. L.A. chpt. 1st ann. Agnes Underwood Freedom of Info. Awards Banquet 1982, recognition award 1983, nominating com. 1982, 83, com. Women of the Press Awards luncheon 1988, Women in Comm. awards luncheon 1988), Am. Assn. for Higher Edn., AAUW (legis. chmn. Arcadia br. 1976-77, books and plays chmn. Arcadia br. 1973-74, creative writing chmn. 1969-70, 1st v.p. program dir. 1975-76, networking chmn. 1981-82, chmn. task force promoting individual liberties 1987-88, named Woman of Yr., Woman of Achievement award 1986, cert. of appreciation 1987), Coll. English Assn., APHA, Am. Soc. Law, Medicine and Ethics, Calif. Press Women (v.p. programs L.A. chpt. 1982-85, pres. 1985-87, state pres. 1987-89, past immediate past state pres. 1989-91, chmn. state speakers bur. 1989—, del nat. bd. 1989—, moderator ann. spring conv., 1990, 92, chmn. nominating com. 1990-91, Calif. lit. dir. 1990-92, dir. state lit. com. 1990-92, dir. family literacy day Calif., 1990, Cert. of Appreciation, 1991, named Calif. Communicator of Achievement 1992), AAUP, Internat. Comm. Assn., N.Y. Acad. Scis., Ind. Writers So. Calif. (bd. dirs. 1989-90, dir. Specialized Groups 1989-90, dir. at large 1989-90, bd. dirs. corp. 1988-89, dir. Speech Writing Group, 1991-92), Hastings Ctr., AAAS, Nat. Fedn. Press Women, (bd. dirs. 1987-93, nat. co-chmn. task force recruitment of minorities 1987-89, del. 1987-89, nat. dir. of speakers bur. 1989-93, editor of speakers bur. directory 1991, cert. of appreciation, 1991, 93, Plenary of Past Pres. state 1989—, workshop leader-speaker ann. nat. conf. 1990, chair state women of achievement com. 1986-87, editor Speakers Bur. Addendum Directory, 1992, editor Speakers Bur. Directory 1991, 92, named 1st runner up Nat. Communicator of Achievement 1992), AAUW (chpt. Woman of Achievement award 1986, chmn. task force promoting individual liberties 1987-88, speaker 1987, Cert. of Appreciation 1987, Woman of Achievement-Woman of Yr. 1986), Internat. Assn. Bus. Communicators, Soc. for Tech. Comm. (workshop leader, 1985, 86), Kennedy Inst. Ethics, Soc. Health and Human Values, Assoc. Writing Programs, Authors Guild. Clubs: Women's City (Pasadena), Claremont Colls. Faculty House, Pasadena Athletic, Town Hall of Calif. (vice chair cmty. affairs sect. 1982-87, speaker 1986, faculty-instr. Exec. Breakfast Inst. 1985-86, mem. study sect. coun. 1986-88), Authors Guild. Lodge: Rotary (chair Duarte Rotary mag. 1988-89, mem. dist. friendship exch. com. 1988-89, mem. internat. svc. com. 1989-90, info. svc. com. 1989-90) Home and Office: 1301 N Santa Anita Ave Arcadia CA 91006-2419

SLOANE, CARL STUART, business educator, management consultant; b. N.Y.C., Feb. 9, 1937; s. George and Dorothy (Cohen) S.; m. Toby Tattlebaum, Dec. 27, 1958; children: Lisa Beth, Amy Rachel, Todd Cowan. BA, Harvard U., 1958, MBA, 1960. Asst. to pres. Revlon, Inc., N.Y.C., 1960-62; mgmt. cons. Harbridge House, Inc., Boston, 1962-69 ; exec. v.p., treas. Temple, Barker & Sloane, Inc., Lexington, Mass., 1970-78, pres., CEO, 1978-90, chmn., CEO, 1990-91; prof. bus. adminstrn. Harvard Grad. Sch. Bus. Adminstrn., 1991—; mem. policyholders' examining com. N.W. Mut. Life Ins. Co.; mem. bus. adv. com. Transp. Ctr., Northwestern U., 1984-91; mem. adv. com. Ctr. for Sci. and Internat. Affairs, Kennedy Sch. Govt., Harvard U., 1984—; bd. dirs. Am. Pres. Co.'s Ltd., Oakland, Calif., 1983-90, Moore McCormack Resources Inc., Stamford, Conn., 1976-88, Leaseway Transp., Inc., 1993-95, Ionics, Inc., 1995—, Sapient Corp., 1995—. Bd. dirs. Harvard-Radcliffe Hillel, Cambridge, Mass., 1987—, chmn., 1994—; bd. dir., trustee Beth Israel Hosp., Boston, 1993—; nat. fund chmn. Harvard U. Bus. Sch., 1987-89, also vis. com. Mem. Assn. Mgmt. Cons. Firms (chmn. 1984-86), Harvard U. Bus. Sch. Alumni Assn. (v.p. 1989, pres. 1989-91), Boston Yacht Club (Marblehead). Home: Sargent Rd Marblehead MA 01945-3744 Office: Harvard Bus Sch Soldiers Field Boston MA 02163

SLOANE, HARVEY I., public health officer. BA, Yale U., 1958; MD, Case Western Res. U., 1963. Intern Cleve. Clinic, 1964; physician Appalachian Health Program USPHS, Ky., 1964-66; founder, project dir. Park Du Valle Neighborhood Health Ctr., Louisville, 1967-72; mayor Louisville, 1973-77, 81-85; county judge exec. County of Jefferson, Louisville, 1986-90; pres., co-founder Health Care for Am. and Health Care for Am. Policy Inst., Washington, 1991-93; pres. Leukemia Soc. Am. Rsch. Found., Washington, 1993-94; project dir. health professions tng. and devel. Nat. Assn. Cmty.

Health Ctrs., Washington, 1994-95; acting commr. D.C. Commn. Pub. Health, 1995—; dir. Rural Ky. Housing Found., 1979-81; vis. scholar health care policy rsch. George Washington U., 1990-91, adj. assoc. prof. health care scis., 1993—; vol. physician AMA's Physician Exch. Program, Vietnam, 1966. Chair Easter Seal Campaign, Ky., 1982, 83; active Action for Clean Air, Louisville, 1968-73, Louisville/Jefferson County Pollution Control Bd., 1969-73. Mem. AMA, 20th Century Fund (bd. dirs.), NAACP, Leukemia Soc. Am. (bd. dirs.), Partnership for Prevention (bd. dirs.). Office: DC Commn Public Health 1660 G St NW Washington DC 20001

SLOANE, MARSHALL M., banker; b. Somerville, Mass., 1926; s. Jacob and Rose (Jacobson) S.; m. Barbara Gluck, Mar. 7, 1954; children—Barry Richard, Jonathan Gary, Linda Ruth. Chmn. bd., CEO, founder Century Bank and Trust Co., Somerville, Mass., 1969—; chmn. bd., pres. Century Bancorp Inc., Somerville, 1972—, Sloane Furniture Co., 1952-68. Chmn. bd. visitors Boston U.; bd. trustees Boston U.; exec. bd. Boy Scouts Am., trustee Nat. Mus. Boy Scouts Am.; trustee Catholic Found. of the Archdiocese of Boston, Boston Regional Office Cath. Charities; active Mass. Gen. Hosp. Coun., Corp. Ptnrs. Health Care Sys., Inc., Corp. Perkins Sch. for Blind. Served with USN. Recipient Good Scout award Greater Boston Council Boy Scouts Am., 1983, Shofar award Nat. Jewish Relationships Council Boy Scouts Am., 1984, Mortimer Schiff award Jewish Relationships Com. Boy Scouts Am., Commendation from Nat. Baptist Relationships Boy Scouts Am., 1985, Silver Beaver award Boy Scouts Am., 1979, Silver Antelope award, 1983, Silver Buffalo award, 1988, Allah-O-Akbar award Nat. Islamic Com. on Scouting, 1985, Theo. Storer award for svc. to Boston community, 1986, Israeli Peace medal, 1987, St. George medal Nat. Cath. Community, BSA, 1990, Bus. and Profl. award Religious Heritage, 1991, Sword of Hope award Am. Cancer Soc., 1992; named Baden Powell inductee World scout Found. Boy Scouts Am., 1989; decorated Knight of St. Gregory The Great by Pope John Paul II, 1994. Mem. Mass. Bankers Assn., Exec. Club, Algonquin Club, Pinebrook Club, Masons. Jewish. Office: Century Bancorp Inc 400 Mystic Ave Medford MA 02155-6316

SLOANE, NEIL JAMES ALEXANDER, mathematician, researcher; b. Beaumaris, Wales, Oct. 10, 1939; came to U.S., 1961; s. Charles Ronald and Jessie (Robinson) S.; m. Susanna Stevens Cuyler, Mar. 8, 1980. BA with honors, U. Melbourne, Australia, 1959, BEE, 1960; MS, Cornell U., 1964, PhD, 1967. Asst. prof. Cornell U., Ithaca, N.Y., 1967-69; mem. tech. staff ATT Bell Labs., Murray Hill, N.J., 1969—. Author: Handbook of Integer Sequences, 1973; co-author: (with F.J. MacWilliams) Theory of Error-Correcting Codes, 1977, (with J.H. Conway) Sphere-Packings, Lattices and Groups, 1988, 2d edit., 1993, (with A.D. Wyner) Claude Elwood Shannon: Collected Papers, 1993, (with S. Plouffe) Encyclopedia of Integer Sequences, 1995. Fellow IEEE (editor in chief Trans. Info. Theory jour. 1978-80); mem. Math. Assn. Am. (Chauvenet prize 1979, Earle Raymond Hedrick lectr. 1984), Am. Math. Soc. Avocation: rock climbing. Office: AT&T Bell Labs 600 Mountain Ave Rm 2c-376 New Providence NJ 07974-2008

SLOANE, ROBERT MALCOLM, healthcare consultant; b. Boston, Feb. 11, 1933; s. Alvin and Florence (Goldberg) S.; m. Beverly LeBov, Sept. 27, 1959; 1 dau., Alison. A.B., Brown U., 1954; M.S., Columbia U., 1958. Adminstrv. resident Mt. Auburn Hosp., Cambridge, Mass., 1957-58; med. adminstr. AT&T, N.Y.C., 1959-60; asst. dir. Yale New Haven Hosp., 1961-67; assoc. adminstr. Monmouth Med. Center, Long Branch, N.J., 1967-69; adminstr. City of Hope Nat. Med. Center, Duarte, Calif., 1969-80; pres. Los Angeles Orthopedic Hosp., Los Angeles Orthopedic Found., 1980-86; pres., CEO Anaheim (Calif.) Meml. Hosp., 1986-94; pres. Vol. Hosp. Am. West, Inc., L.A., 1990-95; healthcare cons. Arcadia, Calif., 1996—; mem. faculty Columbia U. Sch. Medicine, 1958-59, Yale U. Sch. Medicine, 1963-67, Quinnipac Coll., 1963-67, Pasadena City Coll., 1972-73, Calif. Inst. Tech., 1973-85, U. So. Calif., 1976-79, clin. prof. 1987—, UCLA, 1985-87; chmn. bd. Health Data Net, 1971-73; bd. dirs. Intervalley Health Plan, 1995—; pres. Anaheim (Calif.) Meml. Hosp., 1986-94, Anaheim Meml. Devel. Found., 1986-94. Author: (with B. L. Sloane) A Guide to Health Facilities: Personnel and Management, 1971, 3d edit., 1992; mem. editorial and adv. bd. Health Devices, 1972-90; contbr. articles to hosp. jours. Bd. dirs. Health Systems Agy. Los Angeles County, 1977-78; bd. dirs. Calif. Hosp. Polit. Action Com., 1979-87, vice chmn., 1980-83, chmn., 1983-85. Served to lt. (j.g.) USNR, 1954-56. Fellow Am. Coll. Hosp. Adminstrs. (regent 1989-93, nominations com. 1994—); mem. Am. Hosp. Assn., Hosp Coun. So. Calif. (bd. dirs., sec. 1982, treas. 1983, chmn. elect 1984, chmn. 1985, past chmn. 1986, 89), Calif. Hosp. Assn. (bd. dirs. exec. com. 1984-86, 89), Anaheim C. of C. (bd. dirs. 1994). Home: 1301 N Santa Anita Ave Arcadia CA 91006-2419 Office: 150 N Santa Anita Ste 300 Arcadia CA 91006

SLOANE, THOMAS O., speech educator; b. West Frankfort, Ill., July 12, 1929; s. Thomas Orville and Blanche (Morris) S.; m. Barbara Lee Lewis, Nov. 1, 1952; children—Elizabeth Alison, David Lewis, Emily. B.A., So. Ill. U., 1951, M.A., 1952; Ph.D., Northwestern U., 1960. Instr. English, Washington and Lee U., 1958-60; asst. prof. speech U. Ill., 1960-65, assoc. prof., 1965-70, assoc. head dept., 1967-68, asst. dean liberal arts and scis., 1966-67; prof. rhetoric, chmn. rhetoric dept. U. Calif., Berkeley, 1970-92, pres.'s chair, 1987-90; dir. Nat. Endowment Humanities Summer Seminar for Coll. Tchrs., 1979. Editor: The Oral Study of Literature, 1966, The Passions of the Minde in Generall (Thomas Wright), 1971, (with Raymond B. Waddington) The Rhetoric of Renaissance Poetry, 1974, (with Joanna H. Maclay) Interpretation, 1972; Donne, Milton and the End of Humanist Rhetoric, 1985; contbr. articles to profl. jours. Served to lt. USNR, 1952-55. Faculty research fellow, 1964; U. Ill. instructional devel. awardee, 1965; Henry H. Huntington Library research awardee, 1967; U. Calif. humanities research fellow, 1974; Guggenheim fellow, 1981-82. Mem. MLA, Renaissance Soc. Am., Speech Communications Assn. Office: U Calif Berkeley CA 94720

SLOCOMB, PAUL D., lawyer; b. Seattle, July 9, 1945. BS, U. Wash., 1967; JD, Harvard U., 1972. Bar: Ill. 1972. Ptnr. Baker & McKenzie, Chgo. Office: Baker & McKenzie 1 Prudential Plz 130 E Randolph St Chicago IL 60601

SLOCOMBE, DOUGLAS, cinematographer; b. London, Eng., Feb. 10, 1913. Cinematographer: (films) (with Wilkie Cooper) The Big Blockade, 1942, (with Ernest Palmer) For Those in Peril, 1944, The Girl on the Canal, 1947, The Loves of Joanna Godden, 1947, Another Shore, 1948, (with Jack Parker) The Captive Heart, 1948, It Always Rains on Sunday, 1949, Kind Hearts and Coronets, 1949, Saraband, 1949, Cage of Gold, 1950, Dance Hall, 1950, (with J. Saeholme) Hue and Cry, 1950, A Run for Your Money, 1950, The Lavender Hill Mob, 1951, Crash of Silence, 1952, His Excellency, 1952, The Man in the White Suit, 1952, The Titfield Thunderbolt, 1953, Lease of Life, 1954, The Love Lottery, 1954, The Light Touch, 1955, Decision Against Time, 1957, Panic in the Parlour, 1957, The Smallest Show on Earth, 1957, All at Sea, 1958, Davy, 1958, Tread Softly Stranger, 1959, The Boy Who Stole a Million, 1960, Circus of Horrors, 1960, The Mark, 1961, Scream of Fear, 1961, Freud, 1962, The L-Shaped Room, 1962, Wonderful to Be Young!, 1962, Guns at Batasi, 1964, The Servant, 1964 (British Academy award best cinematography 1964), The Third Secret, 1964, A High Wind in Jamaica, 1965, The Blue Max, 1966, Promise Her Anything, 1966, Fathom, 1967, The Fearless Vampire Killer; or, Pardon Me but Your Teeth Are in My Neck, 1967, Robbery, 1967, Boom!, 1968, The Lion in Winter, 1968, The Italian Job, 1969, The Buttercup Chain, 1971, Murphy's War, 1971, The Music Lovers, 1971, Travels with My Aunt, 1972 (Academy award nomination best cinematography 1972), Jesus Christ, Superstar, 1973, The Destructors, 1974, The Great Gatsby, 1974 (British Academy award best cinematography 1974), Hedda, 1975, The Maids, 1975, Rollerball, 1975, That Lucky Touch, 1975, The Bawdy Adventures of Tom Jones, 1976, Nasty Habits, 1976, The Sailor Who Fell from Grace with the Sea, 1976, Julia, 1977 (Academy award nomination best cinematography 1977, British Academy award best cinematography 1977), Close Encounters of the Third Kind, 1977, Caravans, 1978, Lost and Found, 1979, The Lady Vanishes, 1980, Nijinsky, 1980, (with Paul Beeson) Raiders of the Lost Ark, 1981 (Academy award nomination best cinematography 1981), Never Say Never Again, 1983, The Pirates of Penzance, 1983, Indiana Jones and the Temple of Doom, 1984, Water, 1985, Lady Jane, 1986, (with Beeson and Robert Stevens) Indiana Jones and the Last Crusade, 1989, (TV movie) The Corn Is Green, 1979; dir. photography: (films) Dead of the Night, 1945, Ludwig II, 1954, Heaven and Earth, 1956; photographer: (TV movie) Love Among the Ruins, 1975, (documentary) Lights Out in Europe. Address: 24 Hereford Sq, London SW7, England Office: London Mgt. 235/241 Regent St, London WR1 7AG, England

SLOCOMBE, WALTER BECKER, government official, lawyer; b. Albuquerque, Sept. 23, 1941; m. Ellen Seidman; children: Sarah Cody, Merrin Hayes, Benjamin William. B.A., Princeton U., 1963; postgrad., Balliol Coll., Oxford U., 1963-65; LL.B., Harvard U., 1968. Bar: D.C. 1970. Law clk. Justice Abe Fortas, U.S. Supreme Ct., 1968-69; mem. Nat. Security Council staff, 1969-70; rsch. assoc. Internat. Inst. Strategic Studies, London, 1970-71; mem. firm Caplin and Drysdale, Washington, 1971-76, 81-93; ptnr. Caplin and Drysdale, 1974-76, 81-93; dep. under-sec. for policy planning U.S. Dept. Def., Washington, 1979-81, prin. dep. under-sec., 1993-94, under-sec. of def. for policy, 1994—; prin. dep. asst. sec. for internat. security affairs, dir. Def. Dept. SALT Task Force, Dept. Def., Washington, 1977-79. Rhodes scholar, 1963-65. Mem. Council Fgn. Relations, Internat. Inst. Strategic Studies, Am. Bar Assn., ACLU. Democrat. Office: The Pentagon PDUSD(P) Rm 4E808 Washington DC 20301-2000

SLOCUM, DONALD WARREN, chemist; m. Laurel Hopper, 1990; children from previous marriage: Warren, Matthew. BS in Chemistry, BA in English, U. Rochester; PhD in Chemistry, NYU, 1963. Postdoctoral rsch. assoc. Duke U., Durham, N.C., 1963-64; asst. prof. chemistry Carnegie Inst. Tech., Pitts., 1964-65; from asst. to assoc. prof. chemistry So. Ill. U., Carbondale, 1965-72; prof. So. Ill. U., 1972-81, adj. prof., 1981-84; program dir. chem. dynamics sect., chemistry div. NSF, Washington, 1984-85; program leader div. ednl. programs, sr. scientist chem. tech. div. Argonne (Ill.) Nat. Lab., 1985-90; head dept. chemistry Western Ky. U., Bowling Green, 1990-95, prof. chemistry, 1995—; Co-editor: Advances in Chemistry Series of Am. Chem. Soc., vol. 230, 1992, Methane and Alkane Activation (Plenum), 1996; contbr. over 60 articles to profl. jours., chpts. to books. Co-editor: Advances in Chemistry Series of Am. Chem. Soc., Vol. 230, 1992, Methane and Alkane Activation (Plenum), 1995; contbr. over 60 articles to profl. jours., chpts. to books. Mem. Am. Chem. Soc. (sec. gen. elect catalysis and surface sci. secretariat 1992, sec. gen. 1993, organic divsn. rep. to catalysis and surface sci. secretariat, 1993—, co-chmn. symposium, San Diego, 1994), Chem. Soc. Gt. Britain, Catalysis Soc., Sigma Xi. Avocations: music, literature, sports. Office: Western Ky U Dept Chemistry Bowling Green KY 42101

SLOCUM, ELIZABETH, newspaper editor; b. Boston, Mar. 21, 1947; d. William and Elizabeth (Dowell) Dulligan; m. James Jackson Slocum, Nov. 21, 1969. B.S. in Journalism, U. Mo., Columbia, 1969. Reporter So. Illinoisan, Carbondale, 1969; reporter, copy editor North Shore Pub. Co., Milw., 1970-72; reporter, copy editor Milw. Jour., 1972-77, asst. mag. editor, 1972-79, mag. editor, 1979-86, Features/Lifestyle editor, 1986-92, Features editor, 1993, asst. mng. editor Features, 1994—; editor-in-residence So. Ill. U., Carbondale, 1980, U. Wis, Eau Claire, Wis., 1982, U. So. Fla., Jacksonville, 1983; bd. dirs. Nat. Editorial Bd. for Sunday Mags., N.Y.C., 1983-86. Mem. TEMPO, Milw., 1983—. Recipient best mag. story award Milw. Press Club, 1978, Penney-Mo. award for best Lifestyle sect., 1991. Mem. Milw. Press Club (pres. 1979), Sigma Delta Chi (treas. Milw. chpt. 1977). Avocations: skiing, hiking. Office: Milw Jour/Features PO Box 661 Milwaukee WI 53201-0661

SLOCUM, GEORGE SIGMAN, energy company executive; b. East Orange, N.J., Sept. 9, 1940. B.A., Cornell U., 1962, M.B.A., 1967. Mgmt. trainee Richardson-Merrell, Inc., 1962; v.p. Citibank N.A., 1967-78; v.p. fin. Transco Energy Co., Houston, 1978-80, sr. v.p., 1980-81, exec. v.p., CFO, dir., 1981-84, pres., COO, dir., 1984-87, pres., CEO, dir., 1987-92. Bd. dirs. Houston Hospice, Soc. for Performing Arts, Houston; trustee Boy Scouts Am., Cornell U.; mem. alumni adv. coun. Cornell U. Grad. Sch. Mgmt. Served with U.S. Army, 1963-65. Mem. Am. Gas Assn., Nat. Petroleum Coun. Avocation: tennis. Home: 10776 Bridlewood St Houston TX 77024-5413 Office: Cayuga Lake Farm 3533 R and 90 Aurora NY 13026

SLOCUM, R.C., university athletic coach. Asst. football coach Tex. A&M U. Aggies, 1972-80, 82-89, U. So. Calif., 1981; head football coach Tex. A&M U. Aggies, 1989—. Office: Texas A&M Univ College Station TX 77843-1228

SLOCUMB, HEATHCLIFF, professional baseball player; b. Jamaica, N.Y., June 7, 1966. Grad. H.S., Flushing, N.Y. With Chgo. Cubs, 1991-93, Cleve. Indians, 1993; pitcher Phila. Phillies, 1994—. Selected to N.L All-Star Team, 1995. Office: Phila Phillies PO Box 7575 Philadelphia PA 19101*

SLOGOFF, STEPHEN, anesthesiologist, educator; b. Phila., PA, July 7, 1942; s. Israel and Lillian (Rittenberg) S.; m. Barbara Anita Gershman, June 2, 1963; children: Michele, Deborah. AB in Biology, Franklin and Marshall Coll., 1964; MD, Jefferson Med. Coll., 1967. Diplomate Am. Bd. Med. Examiners, Am. Bd. Anesthesiology (jr. assoc. examiner 1977-80, sr. assoc. examiner 1980-81, bd. dirs. 1981-93, pres. 1989-90, joint coun. on in-tng. exams, vice chmn. 1983-86, chmn. 1986-92). Intern Harrisburg (Pa.) Hosp., 1967-68; resident in anesthesiology Jefferson Med. Coll. Hosp., 1968-71; chief anesthesia sect. U.S. Army, Brooke Army Med. Ctr., Fort Sam Houston, Tex., 1971-74; staff anesthesiologist Baylor Coll. Medicne, Houston, 1974-75; attending cardiovascular anesthesiologist U. Tex. Health Sci. Ctr., Houston, 1974-93, clin. asst. prof., 1977-81, clin. assoc. prof., 1981-85, clin. prof., 1985-93; prof., chmn. dept. anesthesiology Loyola U., Chgo., 1993—; chmn. rsch com., co-dir. rsch. labs Tex. Heart Inst., Houston, 1990-93. Contbr. articles to profl. jours. Mem. Am. Soc. Anesthesiologists, Alpha Omega Alpha. Avocations: tennis,jogging. Office: Loyola U Med Ctr Dept Anesthesia 2160 S 1st Ave Maywood IL 60153-3304

SLOMANSON, LLOYD HOWARD, architect, musician; b. N.Y.C., July 31, 1928; s. Albert Jerome and Dorothea (Jacobson) S.; m. Joan Barbara Kanel; children: Peter, Eric. BArch, Syracuse U., 1949. Registered architect, 18 states including N.Y. and N.J.; NCARB; registered profl. planner, N.J.; registered interior designer, Tex. Archtl. draftsman Rich & Conn Architects, Bklyn., 1949-50; project architect Fordyce & Hamby/Raymond Loewy, N.Y.C., 1951-53; project architect, assoc. ptnr. Serge P. Petroff, Architect, N.Y.C., 1953-58; project dir. Robert W. Hegardt, Architect, N.Y.C., 1959-60; project architect, ptnr. Fordyce & Hamby Assocs., N.Y.C., 1960-67; ptnr. Fordyce, Hamby & Kennerly, N.Y.C., 1967-69, Hamby, Kennerly & Slomanson, N.Y.C., 1969-72, Kennerly, Slomanson & Smith, N.Y.C., 1972-81; mng. ptnr. Slomanson, Smith & Barresi, N.Y.C., 1981—; arbitrator Am. Arbitration Assn., N.Y.C. Author articles. Served with U.S. Army, 1950-51. Recipient 1st prize for design S.I. C. of C., 1967, 84. Mem. AIA, N.Y. Soc. Architects (Store of Yr. award 1985, Design award 1993), N.Y. State Assn. Architects, Bldg. Ofcls. Conf. Am., Univ. Club, The Players. Avocations: playing music with a big band, photography. Office: Slomanson Smith & Barresi 65 Bleecker St New York NY 10012-2420

SLOMANSON, WILLIAM REED, law educator, legal writer; b. Johnstown, Pa., May 1, 1945; s. Aaron Jacob and Mary Jane (Reed) S.; m. Anna Maria Valladolid, June 24, 1972; children: Lorena, Michael, Paul, Christina. BA, U. Pitts., 1967; JD, Calif. Western U., 1974; LLM, Columbia U., N.Y.C., 1975. Bar: Calif. 1975. Assoc. Booth, Mitchel, Strange & Smith, L.A., 1975-77; prof. law Western State U., San Diego and Fullerton, Calif., 1977-95; prof. Thomas Jefferson Sch. of Law, 1996—; judge Provisional Dist. World Ct., L.A., 1990—; mem. bd. advisors San Diego C.C. Dist., 1989—. Author: (reference book) International Business Bibliography, 1989, (textbooks) Fundamental Perspectives on International Law, 1990, 2nd edit., 1995, California Civil Procedure, 1991, California Civil Procedure in a Nutshell, 1992, (practitioner's treatise) The Choice Between State and Federal Courts in California, 1994, supplement, 1996. Lt. USN, 1967-71, Vietnam. Mem. Am. Soc. Internat. Law (chair, editor newsletter on UN decade of internat. law), San Diego County Bar Assn. (co-chair internat. law sect. 1988-92). Office: Western State U 2121 San Diego Ave San Diego CA 92110-2905

SLONAKER, CELESTER LEE, principal; b. Richmond, Va., Sept. 13, 1943; s. Troy Kent and Betty Lee (Ferguson) S.; m. Carol Preston Laws, Aug. 1, 1970; children: Allen Terrell, Sarah Lindsey. B Music Edn., Va. Commonwealth U., Richmond, 1965, MA, 1972. Music tchr. Chesterfield County (Va.)-Elem. and High Sch., 1965-71; asst. prin. Chesterfield County-Crestwood, 1971-75, prin., 1975-81; prin. Chesterfield County-Greenfield, 1981-90, Chesterfield County-Woolridge, 1990-92; dir. elem. edn. Instrn. Div. Ctr., Richmond, 1992—; organist/choirmaster Meth. Ch., Richmond, 1962-69, St. Andrew's Episcopal Ch., Richmond, 1969—; cellist Richmond Community Orch., 1955-73. Group leader Community Orgns., Richmond, 1970-85; chmn. sch. bd. Episcopal Parochial Sch., Richmond, 1975-85; bd. mem. Richmond Ballet, 1983-89. Recipient Sch. Community award County Coun. PTA, Chesterfield County, 1983. Mem. ASCD, Nat. Assn. Elem. Prins., Va. Assn. Elem. Prins., Chesterfield Assn. Elem. Prins. (pres. 1985). Avocations: antiques, gardening, music. Office: Instrn Div Ctr 2318 Mcrae Rd Richmond VA 23235-3028

SLONAKER, NORMAN DALE, lawyer; b. Havre, Mont., Sept. 16, 1940; s. Frederick and Agnes (Monson) S.; m. Helen Bogumil, Aug. 29, 1964. BS, U. Wash., Seattle, 1962; LLM, Harvard U., 1965. Bar: N.Y. 1966. Assoc. Brown & Wood, N.Y.C., 1965-72, ptnr., 1973—. Office: Brown & Wood 1 World Trade Ctr New York NY 10048-0202

SLONE, R. WAYNE, utility company executive; b. 1935. Pres., chief exec. officer, chmn. bd. CILCO (Ctrl. Ill. Light Co.), Peoria, Ill. Office: CILCO 300 Liberty St Peoria IL 61602-1400*

SLONE, RONALD RICH, academic consultant; b. Cin., July 1, 1943; s. Roy E. and Myrtle I. (Stephens) S.; m. Marilyn Norma Hornemann, Mar. 14, 1982. BSBA, Miami (Ohio) U., 1965; MBA, U. Cin., 1966. Isntr. bus. Ind. State U., Terre Haute, 1966-69; asst., assoc. dir. accreditation Am. Assembly Collegiate Schs. Bus., St. Louis, 1969-73, dir. accreditation, 1976-83; cons. Fla. Bd. Regents, Tallahassee, 1983-84; dir. rsch. and planning Coll. Bus. Coll. Bus. Boise (Idaho) State U., 1984-92; pres. Strategic Directions, Boise, 1993—. Mem. Beta Gamma Sigma (mng. dir. 1973-78). Presbyterian. Avocations: classic cars, gardening, reading. Home and Office: 330 Fall Dr Boise ID 83706-4820

SLONECKER, CHARLES EDWARD, anatomist, medical educator, author; b. Gig Harbor, Wash., Nov. 30, 1938; s. William Mead and Helen Spencer (Henderson) S.; m. Jan Hunter, June 24, 1961; children—David Charles, Derron Scott, John Patrick. Student, Olympic Coll., 1957-58; student in Sci., U. Wash., 1958-60, DDS, 1965, PhD in Biol. Structure, 1967. Sci. asst. in pathology U. Bern, Switzerland, 1967-68; asst. prof. U. B.C., Vancouver, Canada, 1968-71, assoc. prof., 1971-76, prof., 1976, head of anatomy, 1981-92, dir. ceremonies and univ. rels., 1989—. Advisor Community Unit YMCA, Vancouver, 1981-92; group com. chmn. Boy Scouts, Can., 1976-82. Served with U.S. Army, 1956-61. Recipient Award of Merit Am. Acad. Dental Medicine, 1965; recipient Award of Merit Wash. State Dental Assn., 1965, Dennis P. Duskin Meml. award U. Wash., 1965, Master Tchr. award, Cert. of Merit U. B.C., 1975-76. Fellow Am. Coll. Dentists; mem. Am. Assn. Anatomists (Centennial Gold medal 1987, program sec. 1982-90, v.p. 1991-93, pres. 1994), Can. Assn. U. Tchrs., Sigma Xi (pres. U. B.C. 1981-82, 88-89), Omicron Kappa Upsilon (chpt. sec.), U. B.C. Faculty Club. Anglican. Home: 6007 Dunbar St, Vancouver, BC Canada V6N 1W8 Office: Univ BC, 6251 Cecil Green Park Rd, Vancouver, BC Canada V6T 1W5

SLONIM, ARNOLD ROBERT, biochemist, physiologist; b. Springfield, Mass., Feb. 15, 1926; s. Sam and Esther (Kantor) S.; married, 1951; 3 children; m. 1984. BS, Tufts Coll., 1947; AM, Boston U., 1948; PhD, Johns Hopkins U., 1953. Rsch. asst. nutrition Sterling-Winthrop Rsch. Inst., Rensselaer, N.Y., 1948-49; rsch. asst. pharmacology George Washington U. Med. Sch., Washington, 1949-50; rsch. asst., jr. instr. biology Johns Hopkins U., Balt., 1950-53; rsch. assoc. chemotherapy Children's Cancer Rsch. Found. Harvard U., Boston, 1953-54; head chem. lab. Lynn (Mass.) Hosp., 1955-56; various positions including chief applied ecology, supervisory rsch. biologist, physiologist & biochemist, phys. sci. adminstr., biotech. mgr. Aerospace Med. Rsch. Lab., Wright-Patterson AFB, Ohio, 1956-86; cons., pres. ARSLO Assocs., Columbus, Ohio, 1987—; lectr. Mass. Sch. Physiotherapy, Boston, 1955-56, Antioch U., 1984-85; mem. internat. bioastronautics com. Internat. Astronautical Fedn., 1966—; mem. environ. carcinogens program Internat. Agy. for Rsch. on Cancer/WHO, Paris, 1981—. Mem. com. on biol. handbooks Fedn. Am. Socs. for Exptl. Biology, 1966-71; mem. editorial bd. Aerospace Medicine, 1967-71; contbr. articles to profl. jours. Served with USN, 1944-46. Mem. Aerospace Med. Assn., Am. Soc. Biochemistry and Molecular Biology, Am. Physiol. Soc., N.Y. Acad. Sci., Internat. Acad. Aviation and Space Medicine, Sigma Xi, Masons, Scottish Rite, Shriners. Office: 630 Cranfield Pl Columbus OH 43213-3407

SLONINA, KATHERINE LEE, insurance consultant; b. Chgo., Apr. 14, 1951; d. Henry Rudulph and Patricia June (Gnoske) S.; m. Frank A. Ventresco, July 1973 (div. Jan. 1990). MBA, Roosevelt U., 1993. With Zurich-Am. Ins. Co., Schaumburg, Ill., 1970-82; mgr. tech. svcs. Harco Nat. Ins. Co., Schaumburg, 1982-87; product analyst, product cons., sr. product cons. CNA Ins. Co., Chgo., 1987—. Dir. blood drives, United Way campaigns, Chgo. and Schaumburg; vol. reading instr. Project Literacy U.S., Elk Grove Village, Ill., 1990—; vol. Spl. Olympics, Clearbrook Ctr., Rolling Meadows, Ill., 1987, 88, piano instr., 1991—; poll watcher, election judge Ind. Voters of Ill., Chgo. Mem. Nat. Assn. Ins. Women (cert., Ill. state dir. 1988-90, Ill. state legis. chair 1986-87), Ins. Women of Suburban Chgo. (bd. dirs. 1984-87, pres. 1987-88). Avocations: needlework, gardening, bicycling. Home: 1020 Florida Ln Elk Grove Village IL 60007-2928 Office: CNA Ins Cos 333 S Wabash Ave Chicago IL 60604-4107

SLORP, JOHN S., academic administrator; b. Hartford, Conn., Dec. 5, 1936. Student, Ocean Coll., Calif., 1956, Taft Coll., Calif., 1961; BFA Painting, Calif. Coll. Arts and Crafts, 1963, MFA Painting, 1965. Grad. tchr. U. N.D., Grand Forks, 1964; in house designer Nat. Canner's Assn., Berkeley, Calif., 1965; mem. faculty Md. Inst. Coll. Art, Balt., 1965-82; chair Found. Studies Md. Inst. Coll. Art, 1972-78; mem. faculty Emma Lake program U. Sask., Can., 1967-68, 70; selection, planning group for Polish Posters Smithsonian Instn., Md. Inst. Coll. Art, Warsaw, Poland, 1977; planner, initiator visual arts facility, curriculum Balt. High Sch. Arts, 1979-81; adjudicator Arts Recognition and Talent Search, Princeton, N.J., 1980-82; mem. Commn. Accredation Nat. Assn. Schs. Art and Design, 1985-88; pres. Memphis Coll. Art, 1982-90, Mpls. Coll. Art and Design, 1990—; com. Advanced Placement Studio Art Ednl. Testing Svc., Princeton, N.J., 1975-82; chair Assn. Memphis Area Colls. and Univs., 1986-88. Prodr. film A Romance of Calligraphy; calligrapher various brochures, manuscripts, album covers, children's books. Mem. Hotel adv. com. City of Memphis and Shelby County Convention Hotel, 1982; adv. bd. Memphis Design Ctr.; bd. trustees Opera Memphis, 1985—, ART Today Memphis Brooks Mus., 1988—. Avocations: painting, calligraphy, computer graphics. Office: Mpls Coll Art Design Office of President 2501 Stevens Ave Minneapolis MN 55404-4347

SLOSBERG, MIKE, advertising executive; b. Phila., Aug. 29, 1934; s. Sam. M. and Florence (Frank) S.; m. Joan Shidler, Aug. 29, 1957 (div. 1984); children: Sydney Ellen, Robert Morton; m. Janet Cohn, June 10, 1987. BSBA, U. Denver, 1960. Copy writer Young & Rubicam, Inc., N.Y.C., 1960-65, v.p. creative supr., 1965-69, sr. v.p., assoc. creative dir., 1971-78; v.p. creative dir. Young & Rubicam, Inc., Los Angeles, 1969-71; pres. Wunderman, Rocotta & Kline, N.Y.C., 1978-83; exec. v.p., exec. creative dir. Marsteller, Inc., N.Y.C., 1983-84; exec. v.p., exec. creative dir. Bozell Jacobs, Kenyon & Eckhardt, N.Y.C., 1984-86, pres. direct mktg. div., 1986-87; exec. creative dir. Bronner Slosberg Humphrey, Boston, 1987—. Author: The August Strangers, 1978. Mem. Direct Mktg. Assn., Boston Advt. Club, New Eng. Direct Mktg. Assn., The One Club, Direct Mktg. Idea Exchange, Friars Club, N.Y. Athletic Club. Avocations: writing novels, skiing. Office: Bronner Slosberg Humphrey Prudential Tower 800 Boylston St Boston MA 02199

SLOTIN, RONALD DAVID, state legislator; b. Atlanta, Jan. 24, 1963; s. Theodore Herbert and Peggy Ann (Schaffer) S. BBA, U. Ga., 1985. Mem. Ga. State Senate, Atlanta, rules com., mem. health and human svcs. com. Office: 304 Legislative Office Bui Atlanta GA 30334

SLOTKIN, RICHARD SIDNEY, American studies educator, writer; b. Bklyn., Nov. 8, 1942; s. Herman and Roselyn B. (Seplowitz) S.; m. Iris F. Shupack, June 23, 1963; 1 child, Joel Elliot. B.A., Bklyn. Coll., 1963; Ph.D., Brown U., 1967; M.A. (hon.), Wesleyan U., Middletown, Conn., 1976. Mem. faculty Wesleyan U., 1966—, prof. English, 1976—, Olin prof., 1982—, chmn. dept. Am. studies, 1976—. Author: Regeneration Through Violence: The Mythology of the American Frontier, 1600-1860, 1973 (Albert Beveridge award Am. Hist. Assn.), (with J.K. Folsom) So Dreadfull a Judgement: Puritan Responses to King Philip's War, 1675-1677, 1978, The Crater: A Novel of the Civil War, 1980, The Fatal Environment: The Myth of the Frontier in the Age of Industrialization, 1800-1890, The Return of Henry Starr, 1988, Gunfighter Nation: The Myth of the Frontier in Twentieth Century America, 1992 (National Book award nominee, 1993); and articles. Fellow Center Humanities; fellow Wesleyan U., 1969-70, 74-75, 80—; fellow NEH, 1973-74, Rockefeller Found., 1976-77; recipient Don D. Walker prize AQ; lit. award Little Big Horn Assocs., 1986. Fellow Soc. Am. Historians; mem. MLA, AAUP, PEN, Am. Film Inst., Am. Studies Assn. (Mary Turpie prize for tchg. and program-bldg. 1995), Am. Hist. Assn., Orgn. Am. Historians, Western History Assn., Authors Guild, Western Writers Assn. Jewish. Office: Wesleyan Univ English Dept Middletown CT 06459

SLOTKIN, TODD JAMES, holding company executive, venture capitalist; b. Detroit, Mar. 19, 1953; s. Hugo Slotkin and Babette Walsey Okin; m. Judy Scavone, Jan. 30, 1988; children: Matthew Hugo, William Joseph, Thomas Samuel, Peter Benjamin. BS, Cornell U., 1974, MBA, 1975. With Citicorp, 1975-92, sr. credit officer, 1984-92, head divsn. corp. fin., 1988-90, sr. mng. dir., 1990-92; sr. v.p. MacAndrews & Forbes Holdings, Inc., N.Y.C., 1992—. Mem. exec. com. United Jewish Appeal, N.Y.C., 1989—. Home: 876 Park Ave Apt 11 N New York NY 10021-1832 Office: MacAndrews & Forbes Holding 35 E 62nd St New York NY 10021-8016

SLOTNICK, MORTIMER H., artist; b. N.Y.C., Nov. 7, 1920; s. Max S. and Sarah B. S.; m. Phyllis June Gluckin, July 26, 1953; children: Debra Jan, Mark Stuart. B.S.S., CCNY, 1942; M.A., Tchrs. Coll., Columbia U., 1942. Tchr. visual arts, public schs. New Rochelle, N.Y., 1946-64; supr. arts and humanities City Sch. Dist., 1964-72; prin. Davis Elem. Sch., 1972-84; adj. prof. art CCNY, 1964-72; prof. art Coll. New Rochelle, N.Y., 1972-78; adj. prof. edn. Pace U., 1988-93. One-man shows include Ada Ahrtz Galleries, N.Y.C., 1959, Westport (Conn.) Art Gallery, 1986, New Rochelle Coun. on the Arts, 1989; exhibited in group shows Nat. Acad. N.Y., World Trade Ctr., N.Y.C., Lever House, N.Y.C., Am. Artists Profl. League, Nat. Arts Club, Salmagundi Club; represented in permanent collections Nat. Mus. Am. Art, Smithsonian Instn., New Britain Mus. Am. Art, Johnson Mus. Art Cornell U., Nat. Archives, Washington, Truman Home, Independence, Mo., F.D.R. Mus., Hyde Park, N.Y.; also pvt. and corp. collections; works published in Artists of Am. Calendar. Mem. City Art Commn. New Rochelle, 1977-80. Served with AUS, 1942-46, ETO, PTO. Mem. N.Y. Artists Equity Assn., Allied Artists Am., Am. Artists Profl. League, Coll. Art Assn., Nat. Assn. Humanities Edn., Art. Pub., Am. Artists Group, Bernard Picture Co., McLeery-Cumming Co., Donald Art. Co., Scafa-Tornabene Art Publ., A. B. Franklin Gallery, Internet, Masons. Club: Masons. Home: 43 Amherst Dr New Rochelle NY 10804-1814 *An artist must respect the totality of his art. His work must express his integrity, his honesty and his wish to communicate with the viewer. It must strive toward the sublime. Anything less is unworthy of being called art.*

SLOVIK, SANDRA LEE, art educator; b. Elizabeth, N.J., Mar. 22, 1943; d. Edward Stanley and Frances (Garbus) S. BA, Newark State Coll., 1965, MA, 1970. Cert. art tchr. Art tchr. Holmdel (N.J.) Twp. Bd. Edn., 1965—; computer art in-sv. tng. Holmdel Bd. Edn., 1990; computer art workshop Madison (N.J.) Bd. Edn., 1991. Charter supporter, mem. Statue of Liberty/Ellis Island Found., 1976—; charter supporter Sheriffs' Assn. N.J., 1993—; mem. PTA, Holmdel, 1965—. Recipient Curriculum award N.J. ASCD, 1992; grantee Holmdel Bd. Edn., 1989, 90, N.J. Bus., Industry, Sci., Edn. Consortium, 1990. Mem. NEA, Nat. Art Edn., Assn., N.J. Art Educators Assn., N.J. Edn. Assn., Monmouth County Edn. Assn., Holmdel Twp. Edn. Assn. (sr. bldg. rep. 1977-79). Avocations: travel, sports. Office: Village Sch 67 McCampbell Rd Holmdel NJ 07733-2231

SLOVIK, THOMAS BERNARD, sales executive; b. Reading, Pa., Nov. 9, 1946; s. Frank Joseph and Stella Mary (Jankowski) S.; m. Lynn Louise Merkel, Sept. 20, 1975; m. Lynn Louise Merkel, Sept. 20, 1975; 1 child, Shay Lynn. Student, Pa. State U., 1965-66, U. Pitts., 1980-81; BS, Calif. Coast U., 1986. Draftsman Gilbert Assocs., Inc., Reading, Pa., 1965-69; salesman U. Machinery Co., Reading, Pa., 1969-79; v.p. sales Universal Machinery Co., Reading, Pa., 1982-86; sales mgr. Lectromelt Corp., Pitts., 1979-82; v.p. Nat. Industry USA, Inc., Hampton, Va., 1986-91; sales mgr. ABB-Spl. Transformers, St. Louis, 1991—. Contbr. articles to profl. jours. Pres. Grafton-Tabb (Va.) Youth Football, 1990; coord. St. Alban Youth Basketball, Grover, Mo., 1991—. With USAR, 1964-70. Mem. AIME (mem.electric furnace conf. com. 1980—, mfr.'s rep.), Adminstrv. Mgmt. Soc. (cert. adminstrv. mgr.). Lutheran. Avocations: coaching youth basketball, golf, travel. Home: 2312 Forest Leaf Pky Ballwin MO 63011-1867

SLOVIKOWSKI, GERALD JUDE, manufacturing company executive; b. N.Y.C., Feb. 9, 1949; s. Felix J. and Wilhelmina S. BS in Mech. Engring. with honors, Pratt Inst., Bklyn., 1970; MBA magna cum laude, Wagner Coll., N.Y.C., 1975. Registered profl. engr., N.J. Project engr. Mobil Oil Corp., N.Y.C., 1970-72; project mgr. Am. Home Products, N.Y.C., 1972-74; ops. mgr. Continental Oil Corp., Houston, 1974-75, bus. devel. mgr., 1975-77; v.p. and gen. mgr. Herman, Sommer & Assocs., Newark, 1977-80; exec. v.p. and gen. mgr. Engineered Products Co., Inc., Oldbridge, N.J., 1980—; bd. dirs. Urban Assocs., Holmdel, N.J., Engineered Products Co., Perth Amboy, N.J., GS Indsl. Co., N.J.; prof. bus. adminstrn. Middlesex Coll., Edison, N.J., 1981—. Cons. Woodbridge Twp. Econ. Devel. Council, Woodbridge, N.J., 1980. Recipient Cons. Engrs. award N.Y. Cons. Engring. Assn., 1970, Dow Jones Fin. award Dow Jones Wall Street Jour., 1975. Mem. ASME, Am. Nuclear Soc. (assoc.), Am. Inst. Chem. Engrs. (assoc.), Tau Beta Pi, Pi Tau Sigma, Delta Mu Delta, Pi Mu Epsilon. Home: 29 Buchannan Way Flemington NJ 08822-3205

SLOVIN, BRUCE, diversified holding company executive; b. N.Y.C., 1935. BA, Cornell U., 1957; JD, Harvard U. Law Sch., 1960. Pvt. practice N.Y.C., 1960-64; with Kane Miller Corp., 1964-74, Hanson Industries, Inc., 1974-80; with MacAndrews & Forbes Group, Inc., N.Y.C., 1980—, now pres., dir.; pres., dir. MacAndrews & Forbes Holdings, Inc. (parent), Wilmington, Del.; pres., chief operating officer, dir. Revlon Group, Inc. (subs.), N.Y.C.; chmn. exec. com. Revlon, Inc. (subs.), N.Y.C.; dir. Oak Hill Sportswear Corp., Gulf Resources & Chem. Corp., Moore Med. Corp., Four Star Internat. Inc. Office: Revlon Group 555 SW 12th Ave Pompano Beach FL 33069-3531 also: Revlon Group Inc 35 E 62nd St New York NY 10021-8016 Office: MacAndrews & Forbes 36 E 62nd St New York NY 10021-8005*

SLOVITER, DOLORES KORMAN, federal judge; b. Phila., Sept. 5, 1932; d. David and Tillie Korman; m. Henry A. Sloviter, Apr. 3, 1969; 1 dau., Vikki Amanda. AB in Econs. with distinction, Temple U., 1953, LHD (hon.), 1986; LLB magna cum laude, U. Pa., 1956; LLD (hon.), The Dickinson Sch. Law, 1984, U. Richmond, 1992; LL.D. (hon.), Widener U., 1994. Bar: Pa. 1957. Assoc., then ptnr. Dilworth, Paxson, Kalish, Kohn & Levy, Phila., 1956-69; mem. firm Harold E. Kohn (P.A.), Phila., 1969-72; assoc. prof., then prof. law Temple U. Law Sch., Phila., 1972-79; judge U.S. Ct. Appeals (3d cir.), Phila., 1979—, chief judge, 1991—; mem. bd. overseers U. Pa. Law Sch. Mem. S.E. region Pa. Gov.'s Conf. on Aging, 1976-79, Com. of 70, 1976-79; trustee Jewish Publ. Soc. Am., 1983-89; Jud. Conf. U.S. com. Bicentennial Constn., 1987-90, com. on Rules of Practice and Procedure, 1990-93. Recipient Juliette Low medal Girl Scouts Greater Phila., Inc., 1990, Honor award Girls High Alumnae Assn., 1991, Jud. award Pa. Bar Assn., 1994, U. Pa. James Wilson award, 1996, Temple U. Cert. of Honor award, 1996; Disting. Fulbright scholar, Chile, 1990. Mem. ABA, Fed. Bar Assn., Fed. Judges Assn., Am. Law Inst., Nat. Assn. Women Judges, Am. Judicature Soc. (bd. dirs. 1990-95), Phila. Bar Assn. (gov. 1976-78), Order of Coif (pres. U. Pa. chpt. 1975-77), Phi Beta Kappa. Office: US Ct Appeals 18614 US Courthouse 601 Market St Philadelphia PA 19106-1510

SLOVITER, HENRY ALLAN, medical educator; b. Phila., June 16, 1914; s. Samuel and Rose (Seltzer) S.; m. Dolores Korman, Apr. 3, 1969. A.B., Temple U., 1935, A.M., 1936; Ph.D., U. Pa., 1942, M.D., 1949. Chemist, U.S. Naval Base, Phila., 1936-45; intern Hosp. U. Pa., 1949-50; research fellow U. Pa. Sch. Medicine, 1945-49, asst. prof., 1952-56, asso. prof., 1956-68, prof., 1968—; vis. scientist biochemistry dept. Tokyo U.; U.S. project officer USPHS Fogarty Internat. Center program Inst. for Biology, Belgrade, Yugoslavia, 1971, 74; vis. prof. Academia Sinica, China, 1983; rsch. scientist Tokyo Met. Inst. Med. Rsch., 1984; vis. lectr. King Edward Meml. Hosp., Bombay, 1990. Contbr. articles profl. jours. Am. Cancer Soc. fellow Nat. Int. Med. Rsch., London, 1950-52; Coll. de France endocrinology dept. rsch. fellow Paris, 1952; sr. internat. fellow USPHS Fogarty Internat. Ctr., St. Mary's Hosp. Med. Sch., London, 1978; recipient glycerine rsch. award, 1954; exch. scholar Tokyo U., 1963, USSR, 1965, 71, India, 1967; recipient alumni award Temple U., 1992. Fellow AAAS; mem. Internat. Soc. Neurochemistry, Am. Soc. Biol. Chemists, Internat. Soc. Blood Transfusion, Am. Physiol. Soc., Belgian Soc. for Anesthesia and Reanimation (hon.), Hungarian Soc. Hematology and Blood Transfusion. Home: 310 S Front St Philadelphia PA 19106-4310 Office: U Pa Sch Medicine Philadelphia PA 19104

SLOVUT, GORDON, reporter. Health and science reporter The Mpls. Star Tribune, Minn. Office: Mpls. Star Tribune 425 Portland Ave Minneapolis MN 55488-0001

SLOWIK, RICHARD ANDREW, air force officer; b. Detroit, Sept. 9, 1939; s. Louis Stanley and Mary Jean (Zaucha) S. BS, USAF Acad., 1963; BS in Bus. Adminstrn., No. Mich. U., 1967; LLB, LaSalle Extension U., 1969; MBA, Fla. Tech. U., 1972; MS in Adminstrn., Ga. Coll., 1979; MA, Georgetown U., 1983; postgrad. cert., Va. Polytech. Inst. and State U., 1986. Commd. 1st lt. U.S. Air Force, 1963, advanced through grades to lt. col.; pilot Craig AFB, Ala., 1963-64, Sawyer AFB, Mich., 1964-68; forward air contr. Pacific Air Forces, South Vietnam, 1968-69; pilot SAC, McCoy AFB, Fla., 1969-71; asst. prof. aerospace studies Va. Poly. Inst. and State U., Blacksburg, 1972-76; br. chief current ops. br. Robins AFB, Ga., 1976-80; asst. dep. chief ops. group Hdqrs. Air Force, Pentagon, Washington, 1980-82; Western Hemisphere and Pacific Area desk officer Nat. Mil. Command Center, Pentagon, Washington, 1982-83; mil. rep. Ops. Ctr., Dept. State, Washington, 1983-85; ops. officer 97th Bombardment Wing, Blytheville AFB, Ark., 1985-87, chief base ops. and trg. div., 97th Combat Support Group, Blytheville AFB, 1987-88, chief airfield mgmt. div. Eaker AFB, Ark., 1988-91, free-lance writer, 1991—. Group ops. officer CAP, Marquette, Mich., 1967-68, Orlando, Fla., 1970-72, sr. programs officer, Blacksburg, 1972-76, Warner Robins, Ga., 1976-80, wing plans and programs officer, Washington, 1980—. Decorated Defense Meritorious Service Medal, 10 Air medals, 3 Air Force Meritorious Service medals, 2 Commendation medals, Cross of Gallantry with Palm, Presdl. Legion of Merit, others; recipient Presdl. Legion of Merit, Presdl. Medal of Merit (3), Presdl. Achievement award (3). Mem. Acad. of Mgmt., Air Force Assn., Cato Inst., Heritage Found., Mil. Order World Wars, Am. Def. Preparedness Assn., Am. Security Council, Order of Daedalians. Roman Catholic. Home and Office: 1708 N Broadway St Blytheville AR 72315-1313

SLOYAN, GERARD STEPHEN, religious studies educator, priest; b. N.Y.C., Dec. 13, 1919; s. Jerome James and Marie (Kelley) S. A.B., Seton Hall U., 1940; S.T.L., Cath. U. Am., 1944, Ph.D., 1948; DLitt, Seton Hall U., 1984; HHD, St. Ambrose U., 1995. Ordained priest Roman Cath. Ch., 1944. Asst. pastor in Trenton, Maple Shade, N.J., 1947-50; mem. faculty Cath. U. Am., Washington, 1950-67, chmn. dept. religion, 1957-67; prof. N.T. studies Temple U., Phila., 1967-90, chmn. dept. religion, 1970-74, 84-86; vis. prof. Cath. U. Am., Washington, 1992—, Iowa State U., 1995. English editor: N.T., The New American Bible, 1970; author: Jesus on Trial: Development of the Passion Narratives, 1973, Commentary on the New Lectionary, 1975, Is Christ the End of the Law?, 1978, Jesus in Focus, 1983, 2d edit., 1993, The Jesus Tradition, 1986, John: "Interpretation" Commentary, 1988, Jesus, Redeemer and Divine Word, 1989, What Are They Saying About John?, 1991, Walking in the Truth: 1, 2, and 3 John, 1995, The Crucifixion of Jesus, History, Myth, Faith, 1995. Recipient Pro Ecclesia et Pontifice medal, 1970, Johannes Quasten medal Cath U. Am., 1985, Michael Mathis award Notre Dame Ctr. Pastoral Liturgy, 1994. Mem. AAUP, Cath. Bibl. Assn., Soc. Bibl. Lit., Cath. Theol. Soc. Am. (John Courtney Murray award 1981, pres. 1993-94), Coll. Theology Soc. (pres. 1964-66), Liturg. Conf. (pres. 1962-64, v.p. 1970-71, 75-88, chmn. bd. dirs. 1980-88), N.Am. Acad. Liturgy (Berakah award 1986). Democrat.

SLOYAN, PATRICK JOSEPH, journalist; b. Stamford, Conn., Jan. 11, 1937; s. James Joseph and Annamae (O'Brien) S.; m. Phyllis Hampton, Nov. 19, 1960; children: Nora, Amy, Patrick, John. BS, U. Md., 1963. Reporter Albany (N.Y.) Times-Union, 1957-58, Balt. News Post, 1958-60, United Press Internat., Washington, 1960-69, Hearst News Svc., Washington, 1969-74; reporter Newsday, Washington, 1974-81, bur. chief, 1986-88, sr. corr., 1988—; bur. chief Newsday, London, 1981-86; chmn. Fund for Investigative Journalism, Washington, 1987—. With U.S. Army, 1955-57. Recipient Best Writing award Am. Soc. Newspaper Editors, 1982, War Reporting award George Polk Awards, 1992, Pulitzer Prize for internat. reporting, 1992. Mem. Gridiron Club. Roman Catholic. Avocations: swimming, tennis, gardening. Home: 17115 Simpson Circle Paeonian Springs VA 22129-9701 Office: Newsday 1730 Pennsylvania Ave NW Washington DC 20006

SLUDIKOFF, STANLEY ROBERT, publisher, writer; b. Bronx, N.Y., July 17, 1935; s. Harry and Lillie (Elberger) S.; m. Ann Paula Blumberg, June 30, 1972; children: Lisa Beth, Jaime Dawn, Bonnie Joy. B.Arch., Pratt Inst., 1957; grad. student, U. So. Calif., 1960-62. Lic. architect, real estate broker. Project planner Robert E. Alexander, F.A.I.A. & Assos., Los Angeles, 1965-66, Daniel, Mann, Johnson & Mendenhall (City and Regional Planning Cons.), Los Angeles, 1967-70; pres., publisher Gambling Times Inc., also Two Worlds Mgmt., Inc., Los Angeles, 1971—; v.p. Prima Quality Farms, Inc., P.R.; chmn. Creative Games, Inc., 1992—; pres. Las Vegas TV Weekley, also Postal West, Las Vegas, 1975-79; founder Stanley Roberts Sch. Winning Blackjack, 1976; instr. city and regional planning program U. So. Calif., 1960-63. Author: (under pen name Stanley Roberts) Winning Blackjack, 1971, How to Win at Weekend Blackjack, 1973, Gambling Times Guide to Blackjack, 1983; author: The Beginner's Guide to Winning Blackjack, 1983, According to Gambling Times: The Rules of Casino Games, 1983, The Casino Gourmet, 6 vols., 1984, Casinos of the Caribbean, 1984; also monthly column, 1977—; inventor Daily Digit lottery game; patentee in field. Mem. Destination 90 Forum, Citizens Planning Group, San Fernando Valley, Calif., 1966-67, Rebuild L.A. land use com., 1992—. Served to lt. col. U.S. Army, now Res. ret. Recipient commendation from mayor Los Angeles for work on model cities funding, 1968. Mem. AIA, Am. Planning Assn., Am. Inst. Cert. Planners, Internat. Casino Assn. (sec. 1980—), Res. Officers Assn. (life), Mensa (life). Home: 17147 Vintage St Northridge CA 91325-1653 Office: 16140 Valerio St # B Van Nuys CA 91406-2916 *The challenge of being alive lies in the development of one's maximum potential. To do less is to fly in the face of the gifts of creation, to shorten the aspect of one's life and to deny the fullness of existence. "The weakness of the flesh" prevents anyone's full development from reaching fruition but the personal and societal loss lies in giving up too soon, before we have fully tested our limits.*

SLUSHER, KIMBERLY GOODE, researcher; b. Benham, Ky., Oct. 4, 1960; d. Herschel James and Nevelyn Faye (Hayes) Goode; m. Joe Allan Slusher, May 1, 1985; 1 child, Tarah Rene. BS in Agr., Ea. Ky. U., 1982; MS in Agr., U. Tenn., 1989. Rsch. asst. U. Tenn., Knoxville, 1983-89; info. analyst Oak Ridge (Tenn.) Nat. Lab., 1989—, tchr., cons. sci. honors program, 1993. Author: (army study) Drinking Water Contamination Study, 1995; contbr. chpt.: Teratogens: Chemicals Which Cause Birth Defects, 1993. Methodist. Avocations: gardening, piano. Office: Biomed & Environ Info Analysis Sect 1060 Commerce Park Dr Oak Ridge TN 37830-8026

SLUSSER, WILLIAM PETER, investment banker; b. Oakland, Calif., June 20, 1929; s. Eugene and Thelma (Donovan) S.; m. Joanne Eleanor Briggs, June 20, 1953; children: Kathleen E., Martin E., Wendelin M., Caroline E., Sarah A. BA cum laude, Stanford U., 1951; MBA, Harvard U., 1953. Mgr. spl. situations dept. Dean Witter & Co., N.Y.C., 1955-60; partner, sr. v.p. in charge corp. fin. dept., 1960-75, also dir.; mem. exec. com. Shields & Co.; co-mgr. investment banking div., sr. v.p. Paine Webber Inc., 1975-80; mng. dir., head merger and aquisitions dept. Paine Webber, Inc., N.Y.C., 1980-88; pres. Slusser Assocs., Inc., N.Y.C., 1988—; underwriter or fin. cons. Square D. Co., Times Mirror Co., Ashland Oil, Inc., Ga. Pacific, TRW, Inc., Avon Products, TransAm. Realty Investors, Atex, Inc. subs. Eastman Kodak Co., Perini Corp., Downey Savs. & Loan, Booth Newspapers, Inc., Holly Hill Lumber Co., Stanhome, Inc., Santee Portland Cement Co., Grow Group, Crown Cork & Seal Co., Dr. Pepper Co. of So. Calif., Cap Gemini Sogeti, Ltd., London, De La Rue, P.L.C., London, VNU Inc., Haarlem, Netherlands, Bertelsmann Pub. Co., Fed. Republic Germany, ADT Ltd., London, Bank of Guam, Houghton Mifflin Co., Orion Research, Inc., Pacific Holding Co., also vice chmn., 1969-73; bd. dirs. Ampex Corp., ADT Ltd., Buffalo Color Corp.; founder original Stockholder Assoc. Mortgage Cos. Lectr. to profl. assns. Mem. Ends of the Earth; bd. fin. advisors Columbia U. Bus. Sch., Calif. Senate Commn. on Local Govt. Investments, mem. Calif. Senate commn. on corp. governance. Served to 1st lt. USAF, 1953-55. Mem. Investment Assn. N.Y., Soc. Calif. Pioneers, Alpha Delta Phi (exec. council 1956-62, treas. 1961). Clubs: Knickerbocker, Downtown, Stanford Assocs., Harvard (N.Y.C.); Lawrence Beach, Stanford of N.Y. Author numerous articles; contbr.; Handbook of Mergers, Acquisitions and Buyouts, The Mergers & Acquisitions Handbook. Home: 901 Lexington Ave New York NY 10021-5902 also: Slusser Ranch Windsor CA 95492 Office: Slusser Assocs Inc 1 Citicorp Ctr 153 E 53rd St Rm 5100 New York NY 10022-4611

SLUTSKY, KENNETH JOEL, lawyer; b. N.Y.C., Sept. 18, 1953; s. Clement and June (Gross) S.; m. Nancy Ellen Goldfarb, Jan. 15, 1978; children: Rachel, Jason, Jenna. BA, Columbia U., 1975; JD, Harvard U., 1978. Bar: N.J. 1978, U.S. Dist. Ct. N.J. 1978. Assoc. Lowenstein, Sandler, Brochin, Kohl, Fisher & Boylan, Roseland, N.J., 1978-83; mem. firm Lowenstein, Sandler, Kohl, Fisher & Boylan, P.A., Roseland, N.J., 1984—. Mem. met. N.J. chpt. Am. Jewish Com., Millburn, Jewish Family Svc. Metrowest N.J., Florham Park. Mem. ABA, N.J. Bar Assn. Home: 2 Hampton Ct N Caldwell NJ 07006-4701 Office: Lowenstein Sandler Kohl Fisher & Boylan PA 65 Livingston Ave Roseland NJ 07068-1725

SLUTSKY, LORIE ANN, foundation executive; b. N.Y.C., Jan. 5, 1953; d. Edward and Adele (Moskowitz) S. BA, Colgate U., 1975; MA in Urban Policy and Analysis, New Sch. for Social Rsch., N.Y.C., 1977. Program officer N.Y. Cmty. Trust, N.Y.C., 1977-83, v.p., 1983-87, exec. v.p., 1987-89, pres., CEO, 1990—; former mem. and chmn. bd. Coun. on Founds., Inc., Washington, 1986-95. Trustee, chmn. budget com. Colgate U., Hamilton, N.Y., 1989—; vice chmn., bd. dirs. Found. Ctr., N.Y.C., United Way, N.Y.C. Office: NY Community Trust 2 Park Ave New York NY 10016-5603

SLY, MARILYNN JANE, elementary education educator; b. Des Moines, Aug. 16, 1963; d. Loren Eugene and Barbara Jean (Grob) Meggison; stepchildren: Julie Michelle, Nicholas Burton; m. Gary Lee Sly, July 26, 1986; 1 child, Shelby Barbara. BS, Iowa State U., 1985; MEd, U. Nev., 1991. Dist. mgr. Westmark Property Mgmt., Des Moines, 1985-86; substitute tchr. Des Moines Pub. Schs., 1986-87, elem. tchr., 1991—; policy change clk. Am. Mutual Life, Des Moines, 1987-88; chpt. 1 tchr. Clark County Schs., Las Vegas, 1988-91; dir., sec., treas. Sunbelt Investments, Ltd., West Des Moines, 1991—, Meggison Real Estate, Inc., West Des Moines, 1991—, Meggison Devl., Inc., West Des Moines, 1991—. Contbr. articles to profl. jours. Recipient Communicator award Miss Iowa USA, 1985. Mem. NEA, Iowa State Edn. Assn., Des Moines Edn. Assn., Internat. Reading Assn., Ctrl. Iowa Reading Coun., Alpha Omicron Pi. Episcopalian. Avocations: children's literature, needlework, reading, travel, investments. Office: Des Moines Pub Schs 710 College Ave Des Moines IA 50314-2844

SLY, RIDGE MICHAEL, physician, educator; b. Seattle, Nov. 3, 1933; s. Ridge Joseph and Eva Jean (Ruddell) S.; m. Ann Turner Jennings, June 12, 1957; children—Teresa Ann, Cynthia Marie. A.B., Kenyon Coll., 1956; M.D., Washington U., St. Louis, 1960. Diplomate Am. Bd. Pediatrics, Am. Sub-Bd. Pediatric Allergy, Am. Bd. Allergy and Immunology. Intern, resident in pediatrics St. Louis Children's Hosp, 1960-62; chief resident in pediatrics U. Ky. Med. Ctr., Lexington, 1962-63; fellow in allergy and immunology UCLA Med. Ctr., 1965-67; asst. prof., assoc. prof., prof. pediatrics La. State U. Med. Ctr., New Orleans, 1967-78; dir. allergy and immunology Children's Nat. Med. Ctr., Washington, 1978—; prof. pediatrics George Washington U., Washington, 1978—. Author: Textbook of Pediatric Allergy, 1985; mem. editl. bd. Annals of Allergy, Asthma, & Immunology, 1982—, Jour. Asthma, 1982-93, Clin. Revs. in Allergy, 1982—, Pediat. Asthma, Allergy, & Immunology, 1987—; assoc. editor Annals of Allergy, Asthma, & Immunology, 1989-90, editor, 1990—; contbr. articles to profl. jours. Served to capt. USAF, 1963-65. Recipient La. plaque Am. Lung Assn. of La., 1978. Fellow Am. Acad. Allergy, Asthma & Immunology (chmn. com. on drugs 1981-87), Am. Acad. Pediats. (sect. on allergy com. 1972-75), Am. Coll. Allergy, Asthma, and Immunology (Disting. Fellow award 1993); mem. Am. Thoracic Soc., Assn. for Care of Asthma (pres. 1980-81, dir. postgrad. courses 1980—, Peshkin Meml. award 1983), Am. Med. Writer's Assn., Coun. Biology Editors, Phi Beta Kappa. Republican. Baptist. Avocations: music (organ, piano). Office: Children's Nat Med Ctr 111 Michigan Ave NW Washington DC 20010-2970

SLY, WILLIAM S., biochemist, educator; b. East St. Louis, Ill., Oct. 19, 1932. MD, St. Louis U., 1957. Intern, asst. resident Ward Med Barnes Hosp., St. Louis, 1957-59; clin. assoc. nat. heart inst. NIH, Bethesda, Md., 1959-63, rsch. biochemist, 1959-63; dir. divsn. med. genetics, dept. medicine and pediatrics, sch. medicine Washington U., 1964-84, from asst. prof. to prof. medicine, 1964-78, from asst. prof. to prof. pediatrics, 1967-78, prof. pediatrics, medicine and genetics, 1978-84; prof. biochemistry, chmn. E. A. Doisy dept. biochemistry, prof. pediatrics sch. med. St. Louis U., 1984—; vis. physician Nat. Heart Inst., 1961-63, pediatric genetics clinic U. Wis., Madison, 1963-64; Am. Cancer Soc. fellow lab. enzymol Nat. Ctr. Sci. Rsch., Gif-sur-Yvette, France, 1963, dept. biochemistry and genetics U. Wis., 1963-64; attending physician St. Louis County Hosp., Mo., 1964-84; asst. physician Barnes Hosp., St. Louis, 1964-84, St. Louis Children's Hosp., 1967-84; genetics cons. Homer G. Philips Hosp., St. Louis, 1969-81; mem. genetics study sect. divsn. rsch. grants NIH, 1971-75; mem. active staff Cardinal Glennon Children's Hosp., St. Louis, 1984—; mem. med. adv. bd. Howard Hughes Med. Inst., 1989-92. Recipient Merit award NIH, 1988; named Passano Found. laureate, 1991; Travelling fellow Royal Soc. Medicine, 1973. Mem. NAS, AMA, AAAS, Am. Soc. Human Genetics (mem. steering com. human cell biology program 1971-73, com. genetic counseling 1972-76), Am. Soc. Clin. Investigation, Am. Chem. Soc., Genetics Soc. Am., Am. Soc. Microbiology, Soc. Pediatric Rsch., Sigma Xi. Achievements include research in biochemical regulation, enveloped viruses as membrane probes in human diseases, lysosomal enzyme replacement in storage diseases, somatic cell genetics. Office: St Louis U Med Sch Dept Biochemistry 1402 S Grand Blvd Saint Louis MO 63104-1004

SLYE, LEONARD FRANKLIN See ROGERS, ROY

SMAGORINSKY, JOSEPH, meteorologist; b. N.Y.C., Jan. 29, 1924; s. Nathan and Dinah (Azaroff) S.; m. Margaret Knoepfel, May 29, 1948; children: Anne, Peter, Teresa, Julia, Frederick. BS, NYU, 1947, MS, 1948, PhD, 1953; ScD (hon.), U. Munich, 1972. Research asst., instr. meteorology N.Y. U., 1946-48; with U.S. Weather Bur., 1948-50, 53-65, chief gen. circulation research sect., 1955-63; meteorologist Inst. Advanced Study, Princeton, N.J., 1950-53; acting dir. Inst. Atmospheric Scis. Environ. Scis. Services Adminstrn., Washington, 1965-66; dir. Geophys. Fluid Dynamics Lab. Environ. Scis. Services Adminstrn.-NOAA, Washington and Princeton, 1964-83; cons., 1983—; vice chmn. U.S. Com. Global Atmospheric Research Program, Nat. Acad. Sci., 1967-73, 80-87, officer, 1974-77, mem. climate bd., 1978-87, chmn. com. on internat. climate programs, 1979, bd. internat. orgns. and programs, 1979-83, chmn. climate research com., 1981-87; chmn. joint organizing com. Global Atmospheric Research Program, Internat. Council Sci. Unions/World Meteorol. Orgn., 1976-80, officer, 1967-80; chmn. Joint Sci. Com. World Climate Research Program, 1980-81; chmn. climate coordinating forum Internat. Council Sci. Unions, 1980-84; vis. lectr. with rank of prof. Princeton U., 1968-83, vis. sr. fellow, 1983—; Sigmx Xi nat. lectr., 1983-85; Brittingham vis. prof. U. Wis., 1986. Contbr. to profl. publns. 1st lt. USAAF, 1943-46. Decorated Air medal; recipient Gold medal Dept. Commerce, 1966, award for sci. research and achievement Environ. Sci. Services Adminstrn., 1970, U.S. Presdl. award, 1980, Buys Ballot Gold medal Royal Netherlands Acad. Arts and Scis., 1973, IMO prize and

Gold medal World Meteorol. Orgn., 1974. Fellow AAAS, Am. Meteorol. Soc. (hon. mem., councilor 1974-77, assoc. editor jour. 1965-74, Meisinger award 1967, Wexler Meml. lectr. 1969, Carl-Gustaf Rossby Research Gold medal 1972, Cleveland Abbe award for disting. service to atmospheric sci. 1980, pres. 1986, Charles Franklin Brooks award 1991); mem. Royal Meteorol. Soc. (hon., Symons Meml. lectr. 1963, Symons Meml. gold medal 1981). Home: 21 Duffield Pl Princeton NJ 08540-2605

SMAILI, AHMAD, mechanical engineering educator; b. Gaza, Lebanon, Nov. 4, 1955; came to U.S., 1976; s. Abdulkarim and Fatme (Mourad) S.; m. Maha Hazime, Aug. 10, 1989; children: Layla, Ali. BS, Tenn. Technol. U., 1979, MS, 1981, PhD, 1986. Asst. prof. Miss. State U., Starkville, 1987-91; asst. prof. Tenn. Technol. U., Cookeville, 1991-95, assoc. prof., 1995—; cons. Waste Policy Inst., Washington, 1992, U. Tenn. Space Inst., Tullahoma, 1993-94, Marine Gears, Greenville, Miss., 1990-91, Geka Thermal Sys., Atlanta, 1994—. Contbr. articles to profl. jours. Co-chmn. Cookeville Refugee Support Com., 1993—. Named Outstanding Faculty Mem., Student Assn. of Miss. State U., 1989. Mem. ASME (faculty advisor), Am. Soc. Engring. Edn., Pi Tau Sigma (Purple Shaft Trophy 1989, 90), N.Y. Acad. Scis., Tau Beta Pi. Muslim. Achievements include introduction for the first time the concept of "Robomechs" parallel-drive linkage arms for multi-function task applications. Avocations: Karate (2d degree black belt), travel, soccer. Home: 799 W Oak Dr Apt D-1 Cookeville TN 38501 Office: Tenn Technol U W 10th St Box 5014 Cookeville TN 38505

SMALBACH, BARBARA SCHILLER, foreign language educator; b. N.Y.C., Feb. 18, 1942; d. Sylvan Bertram and Frances (Siegel) Schiller; m. Mervyn Stockman, Nov. 21, 1962 (div. Jan. 1965); m. David H. Smalbach, Aug. 29, 1969. BA Adelphi U., 1963, MA 1968. Tchr. fgn. langs. Long Beach Pub. Sch. System, N.Y., 1963-64; teaching fellow dept. fgn. langs. Queens Coll., Flushing, N.Y., 1964-65; tchr. fgn. langs. Farmingdale Pub. Sch. System, N.Y., 1966—. Mem. Rockville Centre BiCentennial Festival Com., 1975-76; founder, pres. Friends of Rockville Centre Pub. Library, 1980-82; founder, co-chmn. Hist. Homes Tour, 1980-84; co-chmn. Rockville Centre Anniversary Celebration, 1983; pres. Mus. of The Village of Rockville Centre, 1985-87, Rockville Centre Village historian, 1986—; treas. Assn. of Nassau County Hist. Orgns., 1984—. Mem. NE Conf. on Teaching Fgn. Langs., AAUW (N.Y. state div. br. council rep. 1987, Div. Com. on Pub. Support for Pub. Ed., Dist. VI, 1984-87; Div. Com. Br. Council, Dist. VI, 1982-84; Nassau County Br. Pres., 1980-82; L.I. Women of Achievement award 1980, co-founder and co-chair excellence & equality for women & girls conf. 1989-94, edn. area rep. 1987-89, 91-92, state nominations com. 1986-87, state membership v.p. 1989-91, assoc. com. (LAF) 1990-91, co-founder and chair L.I. AAUW Day, 1983-86, Area Coordinator Project WIPE, 1984-88, co-creator and co-developer of anti-censorship workshops); Delta Kappa Gamma, Sigma Delta Pi. Republican. Jewish. Club: Tam O'Shanter (Brookville, N.Y.); Gleneagles (Delray Beach, Fla.). Avocations: travel, golf, reading. Home: 10 Allen Rd Rockville Centre NY 11570-1201

SMALDONE, EDWARD MICHAEL, composer; b. Wantagh, N.Y., Nov. 19, 1956; m. Karen Ajamian, Aug. 5, 1979; children: Laura, Gregory, Julia. BA in Music, Queens Coll., 1978, MA in Music, 1980; PhD in Music, CUNY, 1986. Lectr. SUNY, Purchase, 1986-90; adj. asst. prof. Hofstra U., Hempstead, N.Y., 1988-90; vis. asst. prof. New Sch. for Social Rsch., N.Y.C., 1988; adminstrv. dir. Speculum Musicae, N.Y.C., 1988-89; artistic dir. Sounds for the Left Bank, Rego Park, N.Y., 1985-92; asst. prof. Copland Sch. of Music, CUNY, Flushing, 1990—; composer in residence N.Y.C. Pub. Schs., 1994, 95; Carlisle Project Choreographer and Composer Collaboration Commn., 1994. Composer: Two String Quartets, 1980, 86, Dialogue for orch., 1987, Double Duo (flute, clarinet, violin, cello), 1987, Transformational Etudes (solo piano), 1990, Rhapsody for piano and orch., 1992, Suite for violin and piano, 1993. Recipient Standard award ASCAP, 1986—, Creative Incentive award CUNY Rsch. Found., 1992, 95; residency fellow Yaddo Corp., 1986, 87, Composer's fellow Charles Ives Ctr. for Am. Music, 1990, residency fellow MacDowell Colony, 1994, Goddard Lieberson fellow Am. Acad. Arts and Letters, 1993; prize winner Percussive Arts Soc., 1994. Home: 228 Manhasset Ave Manhasset NY 11030-2220 Office: Copland Sch of Music Queens College Flushing NY 11030

SMALE, JOHN GRAY, diversified industry executive; b. Listowel, Ont., Can., Aug. 1, 1927; s. Peter John and Vera Gladys (Gray) S.; m. Phyllis Anne Weaver, Sept. 2, 1950; children: John Gray, Catherine Anne, Lisa Beth, Peter McKee. BS, Miami U., Oxford, Ohio, 1949, LLD (hon.), 1979; LLD (hon.), Kenyon Coll., Gambier, Ohio, 1974; DSc (hon.), DePauw U., 1983; DCL (hon.), St. Augustine's Coll., 1985; LLD (hon.), Xavier U., 1986. With Vick Chem. Co., 1949-50, Bio-Rsch., Inc., N.Y.C., 1950-52; pres. Procter & Gamble Co., 1974-86, chief exec., 1981-90, chmn. bd., 1986-90; dir. General Motors Corp., Detroit, 1992-95, chmn. of exec. com. of bd., 1996—; chmn. exec. com. Gen. Motors Corp., Detroit, 1996—; also bd. dirs. General Motors Corp., Detroit; bd. dirs. Gen. Motors Corp. Bd. govs. Nature Conservancy; emeritus trustee Kenyon Coll. With USNR, 1945-46. Mem. Bus. Coun., Comml. Club, Queen City Club, Cin. Country Club. Office: GM PO Box 599 Cincinnati OH 45201-0599

SMALES, FRED BENSON, corporate executive; b. Keokuk, Iowa, Oct. 7, 1914; s. Fred B. and Mary Alice (Warwick) S.; m. Constance Brennan, Dec. 11, 1965; children: Fred Benson III, Catherine (Mrs. Jonathan Christensen); children by previous marriage: Patricia (Mrs. Murray Pilkington), Nancy (Mrs. Bruce Clark). Student public schs., Los Angeles. With Champion Internat., Inc., 1933-68, successively San Francisco mgr., 1938-44, Los Angeles, Western div. mgr., 1944-55, v.p. Western sales div., 1955-65, v.p., regional dir., 1965-68; pres. Lewers & Cooke, Inc. div. Champion Internat., Inc., Honolulu, 1966-68; chmn. Securities of Am., Inc., 1968-70; chmn., dir. Hawaiian Cement Co., 1970-84; pres. Transpacific Cons., 1984-94, Plywood Hawaii, 1995—. Trustee Hawaii-Pacific U., Hawaii Maritime Ctr. Recipient Disting. Citizen award Nat. Govs. Assn., 1986. Mem. C. of C. Hawaii (past chmn.), So. Calif. Yachting Assn. (sr. staff commodore), Balboa Yacht Club (Newport Beach, Calif, sr. staff commodore), Transpacific Yacht (bd. dirs.), Waikiki Yacht (staff commodore), Pacific Club (past pres.), Royal Hawaiian Ocean Racing (vice commodore), Sequoia Yacht Club (Redwood City, Calif., sr. staff commodore). Home: 46-422 Hulupala Pl Kaneohe HI 96744-4243 Office: 1062 Kokowaera Pl Honolulu HI 96819

SMALKIN, FREDERIC N., federal judge. BA, Johns Hopkins U., 1968; JD, U. Maryland, 1971. Atty. office of judge advocate gen. Dept. Army, 1972-74, asst. to gen. counsel, 1974-76; pvt. practice Monkton, Md., 1976; magistrate U.S. Dist. Ct. Md., Balt., 1976-86, judge, 1986—; lectr. comml. law U. Md., Balt., 1978—, SMH bar rev., Balt., 1985-86, 93-95, BRI/Modern Bar Rev. Course, Inc., Balt., 1980-81; panel spkr. on Utilization of Magistrates at the 1985 fourth cir., Jud. Conf. Capt. U.S. Army, 1968-76, lt. col. CAP (USAF Auxiliary). Mem. Fed. Bar Assn., Order of Coif, Phi Beta Kappa. Office: US Dist Ct 101 W Lombard St Baltimore MD 21201-2626

SMALL, ALDEN THOMAS, judge; b. Columbia, S.C., Oct. 4, 1943; s. Alden Killin and Shirley Edna (Eldridge) S.; m. Judy Jo Worley, June 25, 1966; children—Benjamin, Jane. AB, Duke U., 1965; JD, Wake Forest U., 1969. Bar: N.C. 1969. Asst. v.p. First Union Corp., Greensboro, N.C., 1969-72; assoc. dir., gen. counsel Community Enterprise Devel. Corp. Alaska, Anchorage, 1972-73, v.p., assoc. gen. counsel, First Union Corp., Raleigh, N.C., 1973-82; judge U.S. Bankruptcy Ct. (ea. dist.) N.C., 1982—, chief judge, 1992—; bd. govs. Nat. Conf. of Bankruptcy Judges, 1987-90; adj. prof. law Campbell U. Sch. Law, 1980-82; bd. dirs. Am. Bankruptcy Inst., 1989-95; chmn. Nat. Conf. Bankruptcy Judges Ednl. Endowment, 1993-94; mem. long range planning com. U.S. Judicial Conf., 1992—; mem. faculty Nat. Comml. Lending Sch., 1981-82; cons. Nat. Coalition for Bankruptcy Reform, 1981-82. Contributing editor Norton Bankruptcy Law and Practice. Mem. ABA, Am. Bankers Assn. (bankruptcy task force 1980-82), N.C. Bankers Assn. (bank counsel com. 1980-82), N.C. Bar Assn. (bankruptcy council), Kappa Sigma, Phi Alpha Delta. Republican. Office: US Bankruptcy Ct PO Box 2747 Raleigh NC 27602-2747

SMALL, DONALD MACFARLAND, biophysics educator, gastroenterologist; b. Newton, Mass., Sept. 15, 1931; s. Grace (MacFarland) S.; m. Elisabeth Chan, July 8, 1957 (div. 1979); children: Geoffrey, Philip; m. Kathryn Ross, July 26, 1986; 1 child, Samuel. BA, Occidental Coll., 1954; MA (hon.), Oxford (Eng.) U., 1964; MD, UCLA, 1960. Intern, asst. resident in medicine Mass. Meml. Hosps., Boston, 1960-62; sr. resident Boston City Hosp., 1962-63, vis. physician med. svcs., 1965—; asst. prof. medicine Boston U. Sch. Medicine, 1968-69, assoc. prof. medicine and biochemistry, 1969-73, prof., 1973—, prof. biophysics, chmn. dept., 1989—, dir. Biophysics Inst., 1972—; spl. tng. in phys. chemistry of lipids Inst. Pasteur, Paris, 1963-65; mem. adv. bd. Gladstone Found Labs., San Francisco, 1980—, Liver Ctr., U. Colo., Denver, 1985—; George Lyman Duff Meml. lectr. Coun. Arteriosclerosis, Am. Heart Assn., 1986; cons. Nat. Inst. Arthritis and Metabolic Diseases, NIH, 1968-72, mem. task force Nat. Heart, Lung and Blood Inst., 1990; also others. Author, editor: Physical Chemistry of Lipids, 1986; mem. editl. bd. Gastroenterology, 1967-74, Arteriosclerosis, 1980—, Jour. Biol. Chemistry, Current Opinions in Structural Biology, 1990; subeditor: Jour. Lipid Rsch., 1974-78, editor, 1979-83; editor: (with R. Havel) Advances in Lipid Rsch., 1989—; mem. internat. bd. editors Jour. Nutritional Biochemistry, 1989—; contbr. articles and revs. to profl. jours.; author: (with A. Adams) The Healthy Meateaters Cookbook, 1991. Bd. dirs. Franconia (N.H.) Ski Racing Club, 1974-77. Recipient Eppinger prize IV Internat. Congress on Liver Disease, 1976, Disting. Achievment award Modern Medicine, 1978, UCLA Sch. Medicine Alumni Assn., 1988; Marshall scholar Magdalen Coll., Oxford, 1956-58, Aesculapian scholar UCLA, 1958-60, Markle scholar, 1966-70; also others. Mem. AAAS, Am. Heart Assn. (fellow coun. arteriosclerosis, chmn. program com. 1988-90, chmn. coun. 1992-94), Am. Assn. Physicians, Am. Soc. Biol. Chemists, Biophys. Soc., Am. Soc. Clin. Investigation, Am. Gastroent. Assn. (Ann. Disting. Achievement award 1972), Am. Oil Chemists Soc., Am. Fedn. Clin. Rsch., Am. Chem. Soc., Mass. Med. Soc., Suffolk Dist. Med. Soc., Phi Beta Kappa, Alpha Omega Alpha, Sigma Xi. Achievements include patent on method for making meat products having a reduced saturate fat and cholesterol content. Office: Boston U Sch Medicine Dept Biophysics 80 E Concord St Roxbury MA 02118-2307

SMALL, ELISABETH CHAN, psychiatrist, educator; b. Beijing, July 11, 1934; came to U.S., 1937; d. Stanley Hong and Lily Luella (Lum) Chan; m. Donald M. Small, July 8, 1957 (div. 1980); children Geoffrey Brooks, Philip Willard Stanley; m. H. Sidney Robinson, Jan. 12, 1991. Student, Immaculate Heart Coll., Los Angeles, 1951-52; BA in Polit. Sci., UCLA, 1955, MD, 1960. Intern Newton-Wellesley Hosp., Mass., 1960-61; asst. dir. for venereal diseases Mass. Dept. Pub. Health, 1961-63; resident in psychiatry Boston State Hosp., Mattapan, Mass., 1965-66; resident in psychiatry Tufts New Eng. Med. Ctr. Hosps., 1966-69, psychiat. cons. dept. gynecology, 1973-75; asst. clin. prof. psychiatry Sch. Medicine Tufts U., 1973-75, assoc. clin. prof., 1975-82, asst. clin. prof. ob-gyn, 1977-80, assoc. clin. prof. ob-gyn, 1980-82; assoc. prof. psychiatry, ob-gyn U. Nev. Sch. Med., Reno, 1982-85; practice psychiatry specializing in psychological effects of bodily changes on women, 1969—; clin. prof. psychiatry U. Nev. Sch. Medicine, Reno, 1985-86, prof. psychiatry, 1986-95, clin. assoc. prof. ob-gyn, 1985-88, emeritus prof. psychiatry and behavioral scis., 1995—; mem. staff Tufts New Eng. Med. Ctr. Hosps., 1977-82, St. Margaret's Hosps., Boston, 1977-82, Washoe Med. Ctr., Reno, Sparks (Nev.) Family Hosp., Truckee Meadows Hosp., Reno, St. Mary's Hosp., Reno; chief psychiatry svc. Reno VA Med. Ctr., 1989-94; lectr. various univs., 1961—; cons. in psychiatry; mem. psychiatry adv. panel Hosp. Satellite Network; mem. office external peer rev. NIMH, HEW; psychiat. cons. to Boston Redevelopment Authority on Relocation of Chinese Families of South Cove Area, 1968-70; mem. New Eng. Med. Ctr. Hosps. Cancer Ctr. Com., 1979-80, Pain Control Com., 1981-82, Tufts Univ. Sch. Medicine Reproductive System Curriculum Com., 1975-82. Mem. editorial bd. Psychiat. Update Am. (Psychiat. Assn. ann. rev.), 1983-85; reviewer Psychosomatics and Hosp. Community Psychiatry, New Eng. Jour. of Medicine, Am. Jour. of Psychiatry Psychosomatic Medicine; contbr. articles to profl. jours. Immaculate Heart Coll. scholar, 1951-52; Mira Hershey scholar UCLA, 1955; fellow Radcliffe Inst., 1967-70. Mem. AMA, Am. Psychiat. Assn. (rep. to sect. com. AAAS, chmn. ad hoc com. Asian-Am. Psychiatrists 1975, task force 1975-77, task force cost effectiveness in consultation 1984—, caucus chmn. 1981-82, sci. program com. 1982-88, courses subcom. chmn. sci. program com. 1986-88), Nev. Psychiat. Assn., Assn. for Acad. Psychiatry (fellowship com. 1982), Washoe County Med. Assn., Nev. Med. Soc., Am. Coll.Psychiatrists (sci. program com. 1989-96). Avocations: snow skiing, culinary arts. Home: 602 Alley Oop Reno NV 89509-3668 Office: 475 Hill St Reno NV 89501

SMALL, ERWIN, veterinarian, educator; b. Boston, Nov. 28, 1924. Cert., Vt. State Sch. Agr., 1943; BS, U. Ill., 1955, DVM, 1957, MS, 1965. Diplomate: Am. Coll. Vet. Internal Medicine, Am. Coll. Vet. Dermatology. Intern Angell Meml. Animal Hosp., Boston, 1957-58; with U. Ill. Coll. Vet. Medicine, Urbana, 1958-92; prof. vet. clin. medicine U. Ill. Coll. Vet. Medicine, 1968-92, assoc. dean alumni and public affairs, chief of medicine, 1970-84, asst. dept. chmn., 1989-92; prof. emeritus, assoc. dean alumni and pub. affairs U. Ill. Coll. Vet. Medicine, Urbana, 1992—. Contbr. articles to profl. jours. Served with USMC, 1944-46, 50-51, PTO. Recipient Nat. Gamma award Ohio State U., 1971, Ill. State VMA Svc. award, 1973, Nat. Zeta award Auburn U., 1974, Bustad Companion Animal Veterinarian award, 1993, Disting. Svc. award U. Ill. Alumni Assn., 1995; named Outstanding Tchr., Nordens Labs., 1967, Outstanding Educator, 1973, Outstanding Faculty Mem., Dad's Assn. U. Ill., 1990, Veterinarian of Yr., Mass. Soc. for Prevention Cruelty to Animals, 1993. Fellow Am. Coll. Vet. Pharmacology and Therapeutics; mem. Am. Vet. Med. Assn. (chmn. coun. edn. 1981-82, chmn. program com. 1983-87, Pres.'s award 1992), Am. Animal Hosp. Assn. (award 1983, Midwest Region Svc. award 1989), Am. Coll. Vet. Dermatology (pres.), Internat. Vet. Symposia (pres.), Am. Assn. Vet. Clinics (pres., Faculty Achievement award 1992), Ill. Vet. Med. Polit. Action Com. (past chmn.), Am. Legion, VFW, Moose, Omega Tau Sigma (pres. 1971-79), Phi Zeta, Gamma Sigma Delta. Republican. Jewish. Home: 58 E Daniel St A-4 Champaign IL 61820-5921 Office: Vet Med Adminstrn U Ill Coll Vet Medicine Urbana IL 61801

SMALL, GEORGE LEROY, geographer, educator; b. Malden, Mass., Mar. 27, 1924; s. George Arthur and Alice Mildred (Weston) S.; m. Geraldine H. Koepke, July 4, 1970; 1 dau., Elizabeth Mary. B.A., Brown U., 1950; M.I.A., Columbia U., 1952, Ph.D., 1968. French tchr. pvt. schs. Ariz., 1955-62; instr. geography Hunter Coll., 1964-68; asso. prof. geography Coll. S.I., CUNY, 1968—; cons. problems of whaling to environ. groups. Author: The Blue Whale, 1971. Served with U.S. Army, 1942-46. Recipient Nat. Book award, 1972; Rotary Found. fellow, 1952-53. Mem. Assn. Am. Geographers. Office: CUNY Coll Staten Is New York NY 10301

SMALL, HAMISH, chemist; b. Newtown Crommelin, North Ireland, Oct. 5, 1929; s. Johnston and Jean (Wilson) S.; m. Beryl Maureen Burley, Mar. 27, 1954; children: Deborah Jane, Claire Leslie. BS, Queens U., Belfast, Northern Ireland, 1949; MS, Queens U., Belfast, Northern Irelend, 1953. Chemist U.S. Atomic Energy Authority, Harwell, England, 1949-55; rsch. scientist Dow Chem. Co., Midland, Mich., 1955-83; chemist ind. rsch. and consulting, 1983—. Author: Ion Chromatography, 1990; patentee in field; contbr. 30 articles to profl. jours. Recipient Albert F. Sperry award Instrument Soc. Am., 1978, A.O. Beckman award, 1983, Herbert H. Dow Gold Medal Dow Chem. Co., 1983, Stephen Dal Nogare award, 1984, Am. Chem. Soc. award in Chromatography, 1991. Mem. Am. Chem. Soc. Avocations: painting, sketching, music, walking. Home: 4176 Oxford Dr Leland MI 49654-9716

SMALL, JEFFREY, lawyer, law educator; b. N.Y.C., Oct. 11, 1941; s. I Maxwell and Norma Small; children: Lara, David. AB, Cornell U., 1963; JD, NYU, 1966. Bar: N.Y. 1967. Assoc. in law U. Calif., N.Y.C., 1968; assoc. adj. prof. law NYU, N.Y.C., 1978—; assoc. Davis, Polk & Wardwell, N.Y.C., 1966-76, ptnr., 1976—. Fulbright scholar, Madrid, 1967. Office: Davis Polk & Wardwell 450 Lexington Ave New York NY 10017-3911*

SMALL, JENNIFER JEAN, writer, journalist; b. Chgo., Dec. 16, 1951; d. Len Howard and Jean Alice (Shaver) S. BA in Comparative Lit., Sarah Lawrence Coll., 1974. Wire filer, radio copy editor, features writers UPI, San Francisco, 1974-76; reporter statehouse bur. UPI, Montpelier, Vt., 1976-78; from Washington corr. to editorial dir. Small Newspaper Group, 1979-88, v.p., bd. dirs., 1979-89; freelance writer The Daily Jour., Kankakee, Ill., 1971-74, 78-79, The Aspen (Colo.) Times, summer 1973, The People's Almanac, 1974, UPI Paris bur., fall 1978, Small Newspaper Group, Paris, fall, 1978, The Illini Daily News, U. Ill., 1980; writer UPI articles for Atlanta Jour. and Constn., Boston Herald Am., Boston Globe, Cin. Post, Christian Sci. Monitor, Hartford Courant, L.A. Times, Miami Herald, NASA Current News, Pitts. Press, Providence Jour., Stars and Stripes, Star-Ledger (Newark), Washington Post; fiction contbr. Bread Loaf Writer's Conf. Middleberry Coll., 1989, 90. Bd. deacons Georgetown Presbyn. Ch., 1989-90, The Phillips Contemporaries Steering Com., The Phillips Collection, 1993-94; alumnae trustee Sarah Lawrence Coll., 1990-94; mem. arts and media com. Threshold Found., 1991, 92; bd. dirs. Organizing for Devel., an Internat. Inst., Washington, 1994-95. Recipient 1st pl. Investigative News award Nat. Newspaper Assn., 1987, citation for Best Consumer Journalism Nat. Press Club, 1986, 2d pl. Best Series award Calif./Nev. UPI Newspaper Contest, 1986, 2d pl. Investigative Reporting award Ill. UPI Newspaper Contest, 1986, 1st pl. award, 1985, Peter Lisagor award for Exemplary Journalism nominee, Chgo. Headline Club, 1986, Spl. Svc. award for Journalistic Excellence Ill. Valley Area C. of C., 1984, Livingston Awards for Young Journalists finalist, 1985. Mem. Washington Area Alumnae Assn. Sarah Lawrence Coll. (chair 1988-90). Avocations: the arts, preserving indigenous cultures, walking, swimming, enjoying nature. Office: 1155 Connecticut Ave NW Ste 500 Washington DC 20036-4306

SMALL, JONATHAN ANDREW, lawyer; b. N.Y.C., Dec. 26, 1942; s. Milton and Teresa Markell (Joseph) S.; m. Cornelia Mendenhall, June 8, 1969; children: Anne, Katherine. BA, Brown U., 1964; student, U. Paris, 1962-63; LLB, Harvard U., 1967; MA, Fletcher Sch. of Law and Diplomacy, 1968; LLM, NYU, 1974. Bar: N.Y. 1967. VISTA vol. Washington and Cambridge, Mass., 1968; law clk. to judge U.S. Ct. Appeals (2d cir.), 1968-69; assoc. Debevoise & Plimpton, N.Y.C., 1969-75, ptnr., 1976—; cons. Spl. Task Force on N.Y. State Taxation, 1976. Trustee Brearley Sch., 1985-95; bd. dirs. Nonprofit Coordinating Com. of N.Y., 1985—, Muscular Dystrophy Assn., 1986-88. Mem. ABA, N.Y. State Bar Assn. (chmn. tax sect. com. exempt orgns. 1980-82, co-chmn., 1995), Assn. Bar City N.Y., Nonprofit Forum, Phi Beta Kappa. Home: 60 E End Ave New York NY 10028 Office: Debevoise & Plimpton 875 3rd Ave New York NY 10022-6225

SMALL, KENNETH ALAN, economics educator; b. Sodus, N.Y., Feb. 9, 1945; s. Cyril Galloway and Gertrude Estelle (Andrews) S.; m. Adair Bowman, June 8, 1968; 1 child, Gretchen Lenore. BA, BS, U. Rochester, 1968; MA, U. Calif., Berkeley, 1972, PhD, 1976. Asst. prof. Princeton (N.J.) U., 1976-83; rsch. assoc. Brookings Inst., Washington, 1978-79; assoc. prof. U. Calif., Irvine, 1983-86, prof. econs., 1986—, assoc. dean social sci., 1986-92, chmn. econs., 1992-95; vis. prof. Harvard U., Cambridge, Mass., 1991-92; cons. N.Y. State Legislature, Albany, 1982-83, Rand Corp., Santa Monica, Calif., 1985-86, ECO N.W., Eugene, Oreg., 1987—, World Bank, Washington, 1990—, Port Authority of N.Y. and N.J., 1994, Nat. Coop. Highway Rsch. Program, 1992-94; mem. study com. on urban transp. congestion pricing NRC, 1992-94, mem. highway cost allocation rev. com., 1995-96. Co-author: Futures for a Declining City, 1981, Urban Decline, 1982, Road Work, 1989; author: Urban Transportation Economics, 1992; co-editor: Urban Studies, Glasgow, Scotland, 1992—, Kluwer Acad. Publs. book series, Dordrecht, The Netherlands, 1993—; assoc. editor Regional Sci. and Urban Econs., Amsterdam, The Netherlands, 1987—; editl. bd. mem. Jour. Urban Econs., San Diego, 1989—, Transportation, Dordrecht, 1993—, Jour. Transport Econs. and Policy, Bath, U.K., 1995—. Grantee NSF, 1977-87, Inst. Transp. Studies U. Calif., 1984-89, Haynes Found., 1987-88, U.S. and Calif. Depts. Transp., 1988-94, Nat. Coop. Highway Rsch. Program, 1995-96. Mem. Am. Econ. Assn. (com. on status of women in econs. profession 1995—), Econometric Soc., Transp. Rsch. Bd., Royal Econ. Soc., Regional Sci. Assn., Am. Real Estate and Urban Econs. Assn. Office: Univ Calif Dept Econs Irvine CA 92717

SMALL, LAWRENCE FARNSWORTH, history educator; b. Bangor, Maine, Dec. 30, 1925; s. Irving Wheelock and Geneva May (Turner) S.; m. Elfie Joan Ames, Aug. 9, 1947; children: Kathleen Ann, Linda Jean, Lawrence Farnsworth, Daniel Irving (dec.). BD, Bangor Theol. Sem., 1948; BA, U. Maine, 1948, MA, 1951; PhD, Harvard U., 1955, LHD (hon.), 1991. Ordained to ministry Congregational Ch., 1950; minister Paramus (N.J.) Congl. Ch., 1955-59; asso. prof. history Rocky Mountain Coll., Billings, Mont., 1959-61; prof. Rocky Mountain Coll., 1975-90, dean of Coll., 1961-65, acting pres., 1965-66, pres., 1966-75; chmn. Mont. commn. Higher Edn. Facilities Act, 1965-75; exec. dir. Mont. Assn. Chs., 1984-90. Author: Montana Passage, A Century of Politics on the Yellowstone, Journey with the Law, The Life of Judge William J. Jameson; editor: Religion in Montana, Pathways to the Present, vols. I and II. Pres. Yellowstone County Council Chs., 1968-70; treas. Mont. Conf., United Ch. of Christ, 1970-73; chmn. bd. dirs. Western Independent Colls. Found.; bd. dirs. Community Concert Assn., Yellowstone County Mental Health Assn., Billings Citizens for Community Devel., Billings United Fund; trustee Billings Deaconess Hosp.; chmn. bd. dirs. Inst. for Peace Studies, Mont. Mem. Phi Beta Kappa, Phi Kappa Phi. Club: Kiwanis (pres. Billings, lt. gov.). Home: 7320 Sumatra Pl # 4 Billings MT 59106-2526 *One does not have to be great to embrace great ideas, but having done so, one's life will be changed for the better.*

SMALL, LAWRENCE M., financial organization executive; b. 1941. BS, Brown U., 1963; JD (hon.), Morehouse Coll. Vice chmn. bd., chmn. exec. com., dir. Citicorp, N.Y.C., 1964-91; pres., COO Fed. Nat. Mortgage Assn., 1991—; bd. dirs. Chubb Corp., Marriott Internat. Trustee emeritus Brown U.; trustee Morehouse Coll., Atlanta, 1973—, N.Y.U. Med. Ctr.; bd. dirs. Spanish Repertory Theatre; mem. U.S. Holocaust Meml. Coun. Office: Fed Nat Mortgage Assn 3900 Wisconsin Ave NW Washington DC 20016-2806

SMALL, MARSHALL LEE, lawyer; b. Kansas City, Mo., Sept. 8, 1927; s. Phillip and Lillian (Mendelsohn) S.; m. Mary Rogell, June 27, 1954; children: Daniel, Elizabeth. B.A., Stanford U., 1949, J.D., 1951. Bar: Mo. 1951, Calif. 1955, N.Y. 1990. Law clk. to Justice William O. Douglas U.S. Supreme Ct., Washington, 1951-52; assoc. Morrison & Foerster, San Francisco, 1954-60, ptnr., 1961-92, sr. of counsel, 1993—; reporter corp. governance project Am. Law Inst., 1982-92. 1st lt. U.S. Army, 1952-54. Mem. ABA (com. corp. laws 1975-82), Phi Beta Kappa, Order of Coif. Office: Morrison & Foerster 345 California St San Francisco CA 94104-2635

SMALL, MELVIN, history educator; b. N.Y.C., Mar. 14, 1939; s. Herman Z. and Ann (Ashkinazy) S.; m. Sarajane Miller, Oct. 23, 1958; children: Michael, Mark. BA, Dartmouth Coll., 1960; MA, U. Mich., 1961, PhD, 1965. Asst. prof. history Wayne State U., Detroit, 1965-68, assoc. prof., 1968-76, prof., 1976—, chmn. dept. history, 1979-86; vis. prof. U. Mich., Ann Arbor, 1968, Marygrove Coll., Detroit, 1971, Aarhus (Denmark) U., 1972-74, 83, Windsor (Ont., Can.) U., 1977-78. Author: Was War Necessary, 1980, Johnson, Nixon and the Doves, 1988, Covering Dissent, 1994, Democracy and Diplomacy, 1996; co-author: Wages of War, 1972, Resort to Arms, 1982; editor: Public Opinion and Historians, 1970; co-editor: International War, 1986, Appeasing Fascism, 1991, Give Peace a Chance, 1992; mem. editl. bd. Internat. Interactions, 1987-91, Peace and Change, 1989—; restaurant critic Detroit Metro Times, 1982-95; history book reviewer Detroit Free Press, 1988—. Mem. hon. bd. Swords into Plowshares Mus., 1992—. Recipient Disting. Faculty award Mich. Assn. Governing Bds., 1993; Am. Coun. Learned Socs. fellow, 1969; Stanford Ctr. for Advanced Study fellow, 1969-70; grantee Am. Coun. Learned Socs., 1983, Johnson Libr., 1982, 88, Can. Govt., 1987. Mem. Coun. on Peace Rsch. in History (nat. coun. 1986-90, pres. 1990-92), Am. Hist. Assn., Atlantic Coun. (acad. assoc.), Orgn. Am. Historians, Soc. for Historians of Am. Fgn. Rels. (Warren Kuehl prize 1989). Home: 1815 Northwood Blvd Royal Oak MI 48073-3919 Office: Wayne State U Dept History 3119 Fab Detroit MI 48202

SMALL, MELVIN D., physician, educator; b. Somerville, Mass., May 22, 1925; s. Sidney J. and Ida (Gelbsman) S.; m. Judith Nogee, Dec. 23, 1962; children: Michael Dorian, Michele. AB, U. Wis., 1953; MD, Duke U. Sch. Medicine, 1959; studied under Dr. Gregory Pincus, Worcester Found. Exptl. Biol. and Medicine, 1950-53; studied under Prof. Brian Abel-Smith, London Sch. Econs, 1986-90. Lic. physician, Fla., Md., D.C., Va. Intern Georgetown U. Med. Ctr., Washington, 1959-60, resident, 1960-61; chief gastrointestinal rsch. Georgetown U. Med. Ctr., 1961-64, instr. medicine, 1961-66, asst. prof. medicine, 1966-67, asst. clin. prof. medicine, 1967-81, 93—; chief gastroenterology sect. Georgetown divsn. D.C. Gen. Hosp., 1964-68; cons. Children's Hosp., Washington, 1962-66; active staff Fairfax (Va.) Hosp., 1961-73, Commonwealth Drs. Hosp., Fairfax, 1969-74, Arlington (Va.) Hosp., 1961-85, Circle Terr. Hosp., Alexandria, 1965-85, Mt. Vernon Hosp., Alexandria, 1976-85; hon. staff mem. Alexandria Hosp., 1985-89,

92—; attending physician D.C. Gen. Hosp., 1961-68, Georgetown U. Hosp., 1961-81, 93—, Mt. Sinai Hosp., Miami Beach, Fla., 1992—; chief animal experimentation Cancer rsch. under Dr. Sidney Farber Children's Med. Ctr., Boston, 1948-50; rsch. asst. Boston U. Sch. Medicine, 1956-57; chmn. dept. medicine Alexandria Hosp., 1964-85; founder, chmn., No. Va. Consortium for Continuing Med. Edn., 1974-86, chmn. emeritus, 1986; lectr. in field. Author publs. in field. Trustee Jefferson Meml. Hosp., 1965-74, mem. founding group, 1965, chmn. pharmacy com., 1965-76, co-chmn. tissue com., 1965-74; nominated candidate for Palm Beach (Fla.) Town Coun. Rsch. fellow under Norman Zamcheck Mallory Inst. Pathology, Boston, 1953-59, Gastroenterology rsch. under Franz Ingelfinger, Evans Meml. Hosp., Boston, AEC, 1951-53. Mem. AMA, Am. Coll. Gastroenterology, ACP, Am. Gastroent. Assn., Am. Inst. Nutrition, Am. Physiol. Soc., Am. Soc. Gastrointestinal Endoscopy, D.C. Med. Soc., Med. Soc. Va. (chmn. commn. on continuing med. edn. 1978-81), Alexandria Med. Soc. (v.p. 1979-80), Royal Soc. Medicine. Home: 2335 S Ocean Blvd 2A Palm Beach FL 33480

SMALL, MICHAEL, composer; b. 1939. Scores include (films) Out of It, 1969, Puzzle of a Downfall Child, 1970, Jenny, 1970, The Revoltionary, 1970, The Sporting Club, 1971, Klute, 1971, Child's Play, 1972, Dealing: Or the Berkeley-to-Boston Forty-Brick Lost-Bag Blues, 1972, Love and Pain and the Whole Damned Thing, 1973, The Parallax View, 1974, The Drowning Pool, 1975, The Stepford Wives, 1975, Night Moves, 1975, Marathon Man, 1976, Audrey Rose, 1977, Girlfriends, 1978, The Driver, 1978, Comes a Horseman, 1978, Going in Style, 1979, Those Lips, Those Eyes, 1980, The Postman Always Rings Twice, 1981, Continental Divide, 1981, Rollover, 1981, The Star Chamber, 1983, Kidco, 1984, Firstborn, 1984, Target, 1985, Dream Lover, 1986, Brighton Beach Memoirs, 1986, Black Widow, 1987, Orphans, 1987, Jaws the Revenge, 1987, 1969, 1988, See You in the Morning, 1989, Mountains of the Moon, 1990, Mobsters, 1991, Consenting Adults, 1992, Wagons East!, 1994, (documentaries) Pumping Iron, 1977, American Dream, 1989, (TV movies) The Boy Who Drank Too Much, 1980, The Lathe of Heaven, 1980, Chiefs, 1983, Nobody's Child, 1986, Queen, 1993. Office: Marks and Vangelos Mgt 19301 Ventura Blvd Ste 206 Tarzana CA 91356-3041

SMALL, NATALIE SETTIMELLI, pediatric mental health counselor; b. Quincy, Mass., June 2, 1933; d. Joseph Peter and Edmea Natalie (Bagnaschi) Settimelli; m. Parker Adams Small, Jr., Aug. 26, 1956; children: Parker Adams III, Peter McMichael, Carla Edmea. BA, Tufts U., 1955; MA, EdS, U. Fla., 1976; PhD, 1987. Cert. child life specialist. Pediatric counselor U. Fla. Coll. Medicine, Gainesville, 1976-80; pediatric counselor Shands Hosp.-U. Fla., Gainesville, 1980-87, supr. child life dept. patient and family resources, 1987—; adminstrv. liaison for self-dir. work teams, mem. faculty Ctr. for Coop. Learning for Health and Sci. Edn., Gainesville, 1988—, assoc. dir., 1996; cons. and lectr. in field. Author: Parents Know Best, 1991; co-author team packs series for teaching at risk adolescent health edn. and coop. learning. Bd. dirs. Ronald McDonald House, Gainesville, 1980—, mem. exec. com., 1991—; bd. dirs. Gainesville Assn. Creative Arts, 1994—; mem. health prof. adv. com. March of Dimes, Gainesville, 1986—, HIV prevention planning partnership, 1995. Boston Stewart Club scholar, Florence, Italy, 1955; grantee Jessie Ball Du Pont Fund, 1978, Children's Miracle Network, 1990, 92, 93, 94, 95; recipient Caring and Sharing award Ronald McDonald House, 1995. Mem. ACA, Nat. Bd. Cert. Counselors, Am. Assn. Mental Health Counselors, Assn. for the Care of Children's Health, Fla. Assn. Child Life Profls., Child Life Coun. Roman Catholic. Avocations: traveling, reading, swimming. Home: 3454 NW 12th Ave Gainesville FL 32605-4811 Office: Shands Hosp Patient and Family Resources PO Box 100306 Gainesville FL 32610

SMALL, PARKER ADAMS, JR., pediatrician, educator; b. Cin., July 5, 1932; s. Parker Adams and Grace (McMichael) S.; m. Natalie Settimelli, Aug. 26, 1956; children: Parker Adams, Peter McMichael, Carla Edmea. Student, Tufts U., 1950-53; MD, U. Cin., 1957. Med. intern Pa. Hosp., Phila., 1957-58; research assoc. Nat. Heart Inst. NIH, Washington, 1958-60; research fellow St. Mary's Hosp., London, Eng., 1960-61; sr. surgeon NIMH, Washington, 1961-66; prof. immunology and med. microbiology U. Fla., 1966-95, chmn. dept., 1966-75, prof. pediatrics, 1979—, prof. pathology, 1995—; dir. Ctr. for Coop. Learning for Health Sci. Edn., U. Fla., 1988—; vis. prof. U. Lausanne, Switzerland, 1972, U. Lagos, Nigeria, 1982, Al Hada Hosp., Saudi Arabia, 1983; vis. scholar Assn. Am. Med. Colls., Washington, 1973; assoc. life scis. panel Nat. Acad. Scis., 1981-88, co-chmn., 1982-83; bd. dirs. biol. scis. curriculum study Biol. Sci. Curriculum Study, 1984-90, exec. bd., 1987-90; mem. edn. adv. com. Nat. Fund Med. Edn., 1984-87; mem. study com. Nat. Bd. Med. Examiners, 1983-85, mem. nat. vaccine adv. com., 1987-91, chmn. subcom. on new vaccines, 1987-91; cons. in field. Creator patient oriented problem solving system/POPS, for teaching immunology and coop. learning to med. students and Team Packs for teaching K-12 & college students health edn. and coop. learning; editor: The Secretory Immunologic System, 1971; mem. editorial bd. Infection and Immunity, 1974-76, Jour. Med. Edn., 1978-80; cons. editor Microbios, Cytobios; contbr. articles to profl. jours. Sec., treas. Oakmont, Md., 1964-65, mayor, 1965-66; chmn. Citizens for Pub. Schs. Gainesville, Fla., 1969-70. With USPHS, 1958-60, 61-66. Named Tchr. of Yr. U. Fla. Coll. Medicine, 1978-79, Disting. Lectr. AMA, 1986; recipient Presdl. medallion U. Fla., 1987, Nat. Basic Sci. Disting. Teaching award Alpha Omega Alpha, 1993, Jacob Ehrenzeller award, 1995; NIH spl. fellow, 1960-61, rsch. grantee, 1966—, U. Fla. Tchr./Scholar and commencement spkr., 1987; invited lectr. Assn. Am. Med. Colls., 1992. Mem. AAAS, Am. Assn. Immunologists (edn. com. 1983-86), Physicians for Social Responsibility, Fla. Med. Assn., Phi Beta Kappa, Sigma Xi, Theta Delta Chi. Home: 3454 NW 12th Ave Gainesville FL 32605-4811 Office: U Fla Coll Med PO Box 100275 Gainesville FL 32610-0275

SMALL, RALPH MILTON, publisher, clergyman; b. Richland Center, Wis., Oct. 26, 1917; s. John Marion and Jessie Angeline (Rowe) S.; m. Patricia Courson Small, June 11, 1977; children—Gregory, Randall. B.A. cum laude, Cin. Bible Sem., 1939, postgrad, 1939-41; postgrad, U. Cin., 1941, Clarion State Tchrs. Coll., 1941, Lincoln Christian Coll., 1947; D.D., Pacific Christian Coll., 1971. Ordained to ministry Ch. of Christ, 1939. Minister Antioch Ch. of Christ, Hoopeston, Ill., 1939-63; Bible Sch. cons. Standard Publ. Co., Cin., 1963; weekly columnist The Lookout, 1964-69, dir. dept. ch. growth, 1964-70; editor Seek, 1970, exec. editor, 1970, v.p., publisher, 1971-86; sr. adults min. Clovernook Christian Ch., Cin., 1992—; cons. Standard Pub. Co. Moderator: The Living Word, WDAN-TV, 1954-59. Trustee Milligan Coll., chmn., 1990-91; nat. chmn. Milligan Coll. Capital Funds Campaign, 1989-91; dir. Nat. Christian Edn. Conv., 1965-86; bd. dirs. Fellowship, Inc., Muscular Dystrophy, Danville, Ill.; sec. bd. advisers Directory of Ministry, Christian Chs./Chs. of Christ, 1973-83; sec. bd. dirs. Christian Ch. Found. for the Handicapped, Knoxville, Tenn., 1981—. Chaplain AUS, 1945. Mem. Delta Aleph Tau. Home: 207 W Sequoya Trl Greensburg IN 47240-8302

SMALL, RICHARD DAVID, research scientist; b. Syracuse, N.Y., Jan. 6, 1945; s. Sydney Morton Small and Gertrude (Burman) Goldberg; m. Tsipora Meirson, Dec. 11, 1977; children: Eileen Lara, Carrie Ayala, Sharon Yael. BS, Rutgers U., 1967, MS, 1968, MPhil., 1969, PhD, 1971. Instr. Rutgers U., New Brunswick, N.J., 1970-71; sr. lectr. Technion, Haifa, Israel, 1971-78; rsch. scientist, dir. for thermal scis. Pacific-Sierra Rsch. Corp., L.A., 1979-94; pres. Eastwind Rsch. Corp., Westlake Village, CA, 1994—; vis. asst. prof. U. Calif., L.A., 1977-79; vis. scholar U. Calif., 1979-81, San Francisco State U., 1994——; lectr. various univs. and confs.; adv. com. City Savs. and Loan Assn., 1985; mem. adv. and rev. coms. NAS, other sci. orgns. Author: 1 book; contbr. more than 100 tech. articles; reviewer profl. jours., confs. and symposia. With Israeli Army, 1977. Recipient Rothschild Fund. prize, 1974; NDEA fellow, 1967-70; N.J. Soc. Profl. Engrs. scholar, 1967. Mem. AAAS, AIAA, Sigma Xi. Jewish. Achievements include developing model for environ. impact of Kuwait oil fires; rsch. on smoke prodn. from global nuclear exchs. was focal point in nuclear winter debate; developed series of theoretical models of large fires. Office: Eastwind Rsch Corp PO Box 13081 Long Beach CA 90803-8081

SMALL, RICHARD DONALD, travel company executive; b. West Orange, N.J., May 24, 1929; s. Joseph George and Elizabeth (McGarry) S.; A.B. cum laude, U. Notre Dame, 1951; m. Arlene P. Small; children: Colleen P., Richard Donald, Joseph W., Mark G., Brian P. With Union-Camp Corp., N.Y.C., Chgo., 1952-62; pres. Alumni Holidays, Inc., 1962—, AHI Internat. Corp., 1962—, All Horizons, Inc., 1982—; chmn. AHI, Inc., 1982-89; bd. dirs. French Cruise Lines, Des Plaines, Ill., Russian Cruise Lines. Recipient Munich Ptnr. award, 1989. Mem. Univ. Club (Chgo., bd. dirs. Alumni Campus Abroad, 1994). Home: 190 N Sheridan Rd Lake Forest IL 60045-2429 also: 2202 Wailea Elua Wailea Maui HI 96753 Office: 1st National Bank Bldg 701 Lee St Des Plaines IL 60016-4539

SMALL, S(AUL) MOUCHLY, psychiatrist, educator; b. N.Y.C., Oct. 11, 1913; s. Joseph and Esther (Mouchly) S.; m. Sophie Scholl, June 13, 1937; children: Susan Steinhart, Laurie Block, Jonathan, Cynthia McDonald. BS, CCNY, 1933; MD cum laude, Cornell U., 1937. Diplomate Am. Bd. Psychiatry and Neurology. Instr. psychiatry Cornell Med. Coll., N.Y.C., 1940-43; lectr. psychiatry Columbia U., N.Y.C., 1948-51; adj. and assoc. attending psychiatrist Mt. Sinai Hosp., N.Y.C., 1946-51; prof., chmn. dept. psychiatry SUNY, Buffalo, 1951-78; prof. emeritus dept. psychiatry SUNY, 1978—; dir. psychiatry Meyer Meml. Hosp., Buffalo, 1951-78; attending psychiatrist Erie County Med. Ctr., Buffalo, 1951—, Buffalo Gen. Hosp., 1963—; chief psychiatric cons. VA Hosp., Buffalo, 1952—; neuropsychiat. cons. Surgeon Gen. U.S. Army, Washington, 1947-70; cons. U.S. DOD, Washington, 1966—; mem. N.Y. State Bd. Profl. Med. Conduct, Albany, 1985—; emeritus dir. Am. Bd. Psychiatry and Neurology, 1986—. Co-author textbook: Handbook of Psychiatry, 1943; contbr. articles to profl. jours., chpts. to books. Acting dir. Erie County Mental Health Bd., Buffalo, then mem. bd. dirs.; pres. Muscular Dystrophy Assn., N.Y.C., 1980-89, bd. dirs., chmn. exec. com., 1989—, pres. emeritus, 1989—. Fellow Am. Psychiat. Assn. (Disting. Svc. citation 1978, Psychiatrist of Yr. award 1975), Am. Coll. Psychiatrists (Bowis gold medal 1975), Am. Coll. Psychoanalysts, Am. Assn. Social Psychiatry; mem. AMA, N.Y. Acad. Medicine. Avocations: photography, swimming. Home: 75 Oakbrook Dr # G Buffalo NY 14221-2560 Office: Erie County Med Ctr K-Annex Bldg 462 Grider St Buffalo NY 14215-3075

SMALL, WILLIAM ANDREW, mathematics educator; b. Cobleskill, N.Y., Oct. 16, 1914; s. James Arner and Lois (Patterson) S.; children: Lois (Mrs. Paul Gindling). James (dec.). B.S., U.S. Naval Acad., 1936; A.B., U. Rochester, 1950, M.A., 1952, Ph.D., 1958. Commd. ensign U.S. Navy, 1936, advanced through grades to lt. comdr., 1944; comdt. cadets, instr. DeVeaux Sch., Niagara Falls, N.Y., 1945-48; instr. U. Rochester, 1951-55; Alfred (N.Y.) U., 1955-56; asst. prof. math. Grinnell (Iowa) Coll., 1956-58, assoc. prof., chmn. dept., 1958-60; prof. math. Tenn. Tech. U., 1960-62, State Univ. Coll., Geneseo, N.Y., 1962-85; chmn. dept. math. State Univ. Coll., 1962-78; prof. emeritus, disting. service prof. SUNY, 1985—; Fulbright-Hays lectr. math. Aleppo U., Syrian Arab Republic, 1964-65. Contbr. articles to profl. jours. Mem. Math. Assn. Am., U.S. Naval Inst., Mil. Order World Wars, Ret. Officers Assn., Seneca Army Depot Officers Club, Am. Legion, Rotary (pres. Geneseo club 1990-91), Phi Beta Kappa. Episcopalian. Home: 28 Court St PO Box 367 Geneseo NY 14454-0367

SMALL, WILLIAM EDWIN, JR., association executive; b. Jackson, Mich., Jan. 18, 1937; s. William Edwin and Lena Louisa (Hunt) S.; m. Ruth Ann Toombs, Mar. 28, 1959; children: Suzanne Marie, William Edwin III, Bryan Anthony. AS, Jackson C.C., 1959; BS in Geology, Mich. State U., 1961, MA in Journalism, 1964. Reporter Sci. Svc., Washington, 1961-62; writer sci. U. Chgo., 1963-64; sci. info. officer Pa. State U., State College, 1964-66; corr. McGraw-Hill, Washington, 1966-69; staff com. pub. works U.S. Senate, 1969; founding editor Biomed. News, 1969-71; dir. pub. info. Nat. Bur. Standards, Washington, 1972-76; editor Am. Pharmacy Jour., 1979-82; dir. media and info. svcs. AMA, Washington, 1982-86; exec. dir. Nat. Found. Infectious Diseases, Washington, 1986-91, Assn. Biotech. Cos., 1991-93; CEO, Bioconfs. Internat., Bethesda, Md., 1993-95, WESmall & Assocs., Assn. Execs., Louisa, Va., 1995—; owner recreation resort Small Country, Louisa, 1976—. Author: Third Pollution, 1971. With Security Agy., AUS, 1955-59. Recipient Superior Accomplishment award U.S. Dept. Commerce, 1974. Fellow AAAS; life mem. Nat. Assn. Sci. Writers. Office: PO Box 343 Louisa VA 23093-0343

SMALLEY, ARTHUR LOUIS, JR., engineering and construction company executive; b. Houston, Jan. 25, 1921; s. Arthur L. and Ebby (Curry) S.; m. Ruth Evelyn Britton, Mar. 18, 1946; children: Arthur Louis III, Tom Edward. BSChemE, U. Tex., Austin, 1942. Registered profl. engr., Tex. Dir. engrng. Celanese Chem. Co., Houston, 1964-72; mktg. exec. Fish Engring. Co., Houston, 1972-74; pres. Matthew Hall & Co., Inc., Houston, 1974-87; cons. Davy McKee Corp., Houston, 1987-95; exec. v.p. Offshore Gas Devels. Ltd., San Marino, Calif., 1995—; dir. Walter Internat., 1991. Life mem. Houston Livestock and Rodeo; mem. Engring. Found. Adv. Coun. U. Tex. Recipient Silver Beaver award Boy Scouts Am., 1963; named Disting. Engrng. Grad., U. Tex., 1987. Mem. Am. Inst. Chem. Engrs., Am. Petroleum Inst., Pres. Assn., Petroleum Club (Houston), Chemists Club of N.Y., Oriental Club (London), Houston Club, Traveler's Century Club, Rotary. Republican. Episcopalian. Mem. internat. adv. bd. Ency. Chem. Processing and Design. Home: 438 Hunterwood Dr Houston TX 77024-6936 Office: 7887 Katy Freeway Houston TX 77024

SMALLEY, CHRISTOPHER JOSEPH, pharmaceutical company professional; b. Phila., June 26, 1953; s. Charles Wilfred and Verna May (Coulter) S.; m. Maria Visniskie, Aug. 9, 1974; children: Christa Maria, Mark Charles, Lora Loray. BS, Phila. Coll. Pharmacy and Sci., 1976; MBA, Temple U., 1982; PhD, LaSalle U., 1991. Mfg. pharmacist supr. McNeil Labs., Fort Washington, Pa., 1976-77; mfg. pharmacist group supr. McNeil Consumer Products Co., 1978-79, mfg. pharmacist mgr., 1980-85; tech. svcs. mgr. Janssen Pharmaceutica, 1985-88, plant mgr., 1988-94; quality assurance dir. Sanofi rsch. divsn. Sanofi Winthrop Pharm. Rsch., Malvern, Pa., 1994—. Mem. Rep. Nat. Com., 1979—. With USNR Med. Corps, 1986-95, with USAF, 1995—. Mem. Am. Pharm. Assn., Assn. Mil. Surgeons of U.S., Am. Assn. Pharm. Scientists, Internat. Soc. Pharm. Engrs., Aerospace Med. Assn., Am. Acad. Med. Adminstrs., Assn. Med. Svc. Corps Officers, Pa. Pharm. Assn., Inst. Enivron. Scis., Eastern Assn. GMP Trainers, Parenteral Drug Assn. (chmn. tng. com.), Pharm. Mfrs. Assn. (prodn. sect.), Phila. Pharm. Forum, USN Inst., NRA, Kappa Psi. Presbyterian. Home: 421 Drayton Rd Oreland PA 19075-2010 Office: 9 Great Valley Pkwy Malvern PA 19355

SMALLEY, DAVID VINCENT, lawyer; b. N.Y.C., Mar. 27, 1935; s. Vincent R. and Ethel A. (Sullivan) S.; m. Patricia Doyle Tolles, Nov. 28, 1964; children—Brian W., Gregory T. B.A., Hamilton Coll.; LL.B., Harvard U. Bar: N.Y. 1960. Assoc. Debevoise & Plimpton, N.Y.C., 1959-67, ptnr., 1968—. Mem. ABA, Assn. of Bar of City of N.Y. Home: 14 E 90th St New York NY 10128-0671 Office: Debevoise & Plimpton 875 3rd Ave New York NY 10022-6225

SMALLEY, EUGENE BYRON, plant pathology educator, forest pathologist, mycologist; b. L.A., July 11, 1926; s. Guy Byron and Lena Ernestina S.; m. Gladys Louise Doerksen, Feb. 5, 1954 (div. 1974): children: Daniel B., Lisa L., Sara C., Anthony B., Andrew J.; m. Joan Alice Potter, June 4, 1978. BS, UCLA, 1949; MS, U. Calif., Berkeley, 1953, PhD, 1957. Rsch. asst. plant pathology U. Calif., Berkeley, 1953-57; asst. prof. plant pathology U. Wis., Madison, 1957-64, assoc. prof., 1964-69, prof., 1969-94, prof. emeritus, 1994—, acting chair dept. plant pathology, 1988-89; mem. exec. com. Ctr. Environ. Toxicology, 1967—; rsch. advisor Elm Rsch. Inst., Harrisville, N.H., 1974—, Pitney Bowes Elms Across Europe, 1979—; U.S. advisor EEC Dutch Elm Disease Program, 1979; lectr. Gordon Rsch. Conf., 1967, 86. Contbr. articles to profl. jours.; patentee in field. Mem. com. NRC, 1982-83. With USN, 1944-46. Recipient numerous rsch. grants, B.Y. Morrison Meml. Lectr. award USDA/ARS, 1995. Mem. AAAS, Am. Phytopath. Soc., Wis. Arborists Assn. (hon.), Mycological Soc. Am., Sigma Xi, Gamma Sigma Delta. Democrat. Episcopalian. Home: 2831 Pleasant View Hts Cottage Grove WI 53527-9517 Office: U Wis Dept Plant Pathology 1630 Linden Dr Madison WI 53706-1520

SMALLEY, RICHARD ERRETT, chemistry and physics educator, researcher; b. Akron, Ohio, June 6, 1943; s. Frank Dudley and Virginia (Rhoads) S.; m. Judith Grace Sampierj, May 4, 1968; (div. July, 1979); 1 child, Chad; m. Mary Lynn Chapieski, July 10, 1980 (div. Nov., 1994). BS in Chemistry, U. Mich., 1965; MA in Chemistry, Princeton U., 1971, PhD in Chemistry, 1973; Doctor Honoris causa, Univ. Liege, Belgium, 1991; DSc (hon.), U. Chgo., 1995. Assoc. The James Franck Inst., Chgo., 1973-76; asst. prof. William Marsh Rice U., Houston, 1976-80, prof., 1981-82, Gene & Norman Hackerman prof. chemistry, 1982—; prof. Dept. Physics Rice U., Houston, 1990—; chmn. Rice Quantum Inst., Houston, 1986—. Contbr. numerous articles to profl. jours. Recipient Franklin medal, Franklin Inst., Phila., 1996. Fellow Am. Phys. Soc. (divsn. chem. physics, Irving Langmuir prize 1991, Internat. New Materials prize 1992); mem. AAAS, NAS, Am. Chem. Soc. (divsn. phys. chemistry, William H. Nichols medal 1993, S.W. regional award 1992, Harrison Howe award Rochester sect. 1994, Madison Marshall award North Ala. sect. 1995), Materials Rsch. Soc., Am. Acad. Arts and Scis., Sigma Xi. Office: Rice U Ctr Nanoscale Sci & Tech Mail Stop 100 PO Box 1892 Houston TX 77251-1892

SMALLEY, ROBERT MANNING, government official; b. Los Angeles, Nov. 14, 1925; s. William Denny and Helen (McConnell) S.; m. Lois Louisa Williamson, Nov. 28, 1948 (div.) m. Rosemary Sumner, Jan. 4, 1957; children—Leslie Estelle, David Christian. Student, UCLA, 1946-48. Radio news editor Mut. Radio Broadcasting System, Los Angeles, 1950-55; mgr. Agrl. Info. Inc., Sacramento, Calif., 1957-59; with Whitaker & Baxter, San Francisco, 1956-57, 59-61; sec. Mayor, San Francisco, 1961-63; asst. dir. pub. relations Republican Nat. Com., 1964; press sec. Republican vice presdl. candidate William E. Miller, 1964; dir. pub. relations Republican Nat. Com., 1965; v.p. Whitaker & Baxter, San Francisco, 1966-68; asst. press sec. Republican vice presdl. candidate Spiro Agnew, 1968; spl. asst. Sec. Commerce, Washington, 1969-72; adminstrv. asst. U.S. Senator Robert P. Griffin, Washington, 1972-73; dir. corp. affairs Potomac Electric Power Co., Washington, 1973-75; U.S. rep. devel. assistance com. O.E.C.D., Paris, France, 1975-77; spl. asst. U.S. Senator Robert P. Griffin, Washington, 1977-78; asst. to campaign mgr. Reagan for Pres. Com., Washington, 1979; sr. advisor mgmt. communications IBM, 1979-82; dep. asst. sec. of state pub. affairs Dept. of State, Washington, 1982-87, U.S. amb. to Kingdom of Lesotho, 1987-89; lectr. in pub. policy The Kendig Group, Columbia Artists Mgmt., Inc., N.Y.C., 1990—; sr. cons. Capitoline/MS & L, Washington. Served with USN, 1944-46, PTO. Episcopalian. Office: PO Box 823 Arlington VA 22216-0823

SMALLEY, WILLIAM EDWARD, bishop; b. New Brunswick, N.J., Apr. 8, 1940; s. August Harold and Emma May (Gleason) S.; m. Carole A. Kuhns, Sept. 12, 1964; children: Michelle Lynn, Jennifer Ann. BA in Sociology, Lehigh U., 1962; MDiv, Episcopal Theol. Sch., 1965; MeD, Temple U., 1970; D of Ministry, Wesley Theol. Sem., 1987. Ordained to ministry Episcopal Ch., 1965, bishop, 1989. Vicar St. Peter's Episcopal Ch., Plymouth, Pa., 1965-67, St. Martin-in-the-Fields Ch., Nuangola, Pa., 1965-67; rector All Saints' Episcopal Ch., Lehighton, Pa., 1967-75; fed. program adminstr. Lehighton Area Schs., 1970-72; rector Episcopal Ministry of Unity, Palmerton, Pa., 1975-80; bishop Episcopal Diocese Kans., Topeka, 1989—. Pres. Gaithersburg (Md.) Pastoral Counseling Inc., 1986-89; bd. dirs. Washington Pastoral Counseling, 1988-89; chmn. Turner House Inc., Kansas City, Kans., 1989—, Episcopal Social Svcs., Wichita, Kans., 1989—; bd. dirs. Christ Ch. Hosp., Topeka, 1989—, St. Francis Acad., Atchison, Kans., 1989—; v.p. Province VII, The Episcopal Ch., 1993-95, pres. Province VII, 1995—; pres. Province VII Hosp of Bishops; mem. Ch. Devel. Bd.; chair Presiding Bishop's Coun. Advice; mem. joint nominating com. for Presiding Bishop. Mem. Omicron Delta Kappa. Democrat. Avocations: gardening, swimming, cross-stitching, reading.

SMALLMAN, BEVERLEY N., biology educator; b. Port Perry, Ont., Can., Dec. 11, 1913; s. Richard Benjamin and Ethel May (Doubt) S.; m. Hazel Mayne, Dec. 11, 1937 (dec. 1962); 1 child, Sylvia Gail; m. Florence Hazel Cook, July 27, 1965. B.A., Queens U., Kingston, Ont., 1936; M.Sc., Western U. Ont., Can., 1938; Ph.D., U. Edinburgh, Scotland, 1941; LL.D.(hon.), Trent U., Ont., 1982. Mem. staff Stored Grain Insect Investigations Bd. of Grain Commnrs., Winnipeg, 1941-45; officer-in-charge Stored Products Lab., Agrl. Can., Winnipeg, 1945-50; head entomol. sect. rsch. inst. Agrl. Can., London, 1950-57; chief entomol., rsch. dir. entomology, plant pathology Agrl. Can., Ottawa, 1957-63; prof., head dept. biology Queens U., Kingston, Ont., Can., 1963-73, prof. biology, 1973-78, prof. emeritus biology, 1979—; vis. scientist Nat. Inst. Med. Rsch., London, Eng., 1954-56, CSIRO Labs., Brisbane, Australia, 1970-71, 76; apiary insp. Province of Ont., 1981-91; cons., lectr. in field. Prin. author: Agricultural Science in Canada, 1970, Queen's Biology, 1992; co-author: Good Bye Bugs, 1983. Contbr. articles to profl. jours. Fellow Royal Soc. Can.; mem. Entomol. Soc. Can., Zool. Soc. Can., Entomol. Soc. Man. (founding pres. 1945), Entomol. Soc. Ont. Avocations: Mini-farming; beekeeping; writing popular science reviews. Home: RR 2, Yarker, ON Canada K0K 3N0

SMALLWOOD, FRANKLIN, political science educator; b. Ridgewood, N.J., June 24, 1927; s. J. William and Carolyn (Linkroum) S.; m. Ann Logie, Sept. 8, 1951; children: Susan, Sandra, David, Donald. A.B., Dartmouth Coll., 1951, A.M. (hon.), 1968; M.P.A., Harvard U., 1953, Ph.D., 1958. With AEC, 1953-57; asst. to pres. Dartmouth Coll., 1957-59, mem. faculty, 1959-92, prof. govt., 1967-92, Nelson A. Rockefeller prof. govt. emeritus, 1992—; U. Vt., Burlington, 1989—; chmn. city planning and urban studies program Dartmouth Coll., 1965-72, chmn. social sci. div., 1968-72, asso. dean faculty, 1968-72, acting dean, 1972, v.p. student affairs, 1975-77, chmn. policy studies program, 1977-83, dir. Nelson A. Rockefeller Center for Social Scis., 1983-86; chmn. Vt. Gov.'s Commn. Higher Edn., 1973-80, Vt. Adv. Commn. on Intergovtl. Relations, 1985-86, Vt. Legis Apportionment Bd., 1990—; fenceviewer Norwich, Vt., 1976-90. Author: Metro Toronto: A Decade Later, 1963, Greater London: The Politics of Metropolitan Reform, 1965, Free and Independent, 1976, The Politics of Policy Implementation, 1980, The Other Candidates, 1983. Mem. Vt. Senate, 1973-75; trustee Vt. State Colls., 1967-73, chmn., 1973. Served with AUS, 1945-46. Recipient Superior Achievement award AEC, 1957, Dartmouth Presdl. Leadership medal, 1991; fellow Inst. Pub. Adminstrn., 1960; Dartmouth Coll. Faculty fellow, 1962-63; Nuffield Coll. (Oxford U.), vis. fellow, 1981, 86-87. Mem. Am. Soc. Pub. Adminstrn., Phi Beta Kappa. Office: 38 Northshore Dr Burlington VT 05401-1259

SMALLY, DONALD JAY, consulting engineering executive; b. Cleve., 1922; s. Daniel James and Alice (Rohrheimer) S.; m. Ruth Janet Glasser, July 8, 1944; children: Alan Jon, Leonard Arthur. B.M.E., U. Cin., 1949. Prodn. engr. N. Ransohoff, Inc., Cin., 1949-50; chief engr. Mosby Engring. Assocs., Sarasota, Fla., 1952-55; prin. Smally, Wellford & Nalven, Inc., Sarasota, 1956-91; mem. tech. adv. com. Manatee Community Coll., Sarasota, 1965-90; mem. adv. com. Vocat.-Tech. High Sch., Sarasota, 1968-80. V.p. Sarasota YMCA, 1968-71, Sarasota Opera Assn., 1975-88, pres., 1988-89; chmn. Sarasota Vol. Talent Pool, 1973-76; sec.-treas. Civitan Found., 1965-79; bd. dirs. Suncoast Heart Assn., 1976; mem. Fla. Coordinating Coun. for Vocat. and Adult Edn., 1984-95, chmn., 1987-88; chmn. Sarasota Hist. Preservation Bd., 1988-91; pres. Sarasota County Rd. Improvement Task Force, 1990-93; mem. Sarasota County Pub. Sch. Found., 1990-95, chmn., 1990-91; v.p. Hist. Soc. Sarasota, 1990-91, Children's Haven and Adult Ctr. Bd., 1983—, pres., 1991-94; pres. John Ringling Ctr. Found., 1991—; mem. Plymouth Harbor Bd., 1994—. Recipient Good Citizenship award SAR, 1975, Disting. Alumni award U. Cin. Engring. Coll., 1985, Outstanding Svc. award Myakna Chpt. Fla. Engring. Soc., 1993; named Citizen of Yr. Sarasota Civitan Club, 1975, Engr. of Yr. Sarasota-Manatee Engrs. Soc., 1976. Fellow Am. Cons. Engrs. Council (treas. 1980-82), Fla. Engring. Soc. (pres. Sarasota-Manatee chpt. 1956-58); mem. Sarasota County C. of C. (past dir., v.p. 1983), Cons. Engrs. Council Fla. (pres. 1968), Fla. Soc. Profl. Land Surveyors (chpt. pres. 1973), Am. Water Works Resources Assn. (pres. Fla. Soc. 1981), Sarasota-Manatee Engring. Soc.

SMARANDACHE, FLORENTIN, mathematics researcher, writer; b. Balcesti-Vilcea, Romania, Dec. 10, 1954; came to U.S., 1990; s. Gheorghe and Maria (Mitroiescu) S.; m. Eleonora Niculescu; children: Mihai-Liviu, Silviu-Gabriel. MS, U. Craiova, 1979; postgrad., Ariz. State U., 1991. Mathematician I.U.G., Craiova, Romania, 1979-81; math. prof. Romanian Coll., 1981-82, 1984-86, 1988; math. tchr. Coop. Ministry, Morocco, 1982-84; French tutor pvt. practice, Turkey, 1988-90; software engr. Honeywell, Phoenix, 1990-95; prof. math. Pima C.C., Tucson, 1995—. Author: Nonpoems, 1990, Only Problems, Not Solutions, 1991, numerous other books; contbr. articles to profl. jours. Mem. U.S. Math. Assn., Romania Math. Assn., Zentralblatt fur Math. (reviewer). Achievements include development of Smarandache function, numbers, quotients, double factorials, consecutive sequence, reverse sequence, mirror sequence, destructive sequence, symmetric sequence, permutable sequence, consecutive sieve, prime base, cubic base, square base, class of paradoxes, multi-structure and multispace, paradoxist geometry, anti-geometry, inconsistent systems of axioms. Home: 2456 S Rose Peak Dr Tucson AZ 85710-7413

SMARDON, RICHARD CLAY, landscape architecture and environmental studies educator; b. Burlington, Vt., May 13, 1948; s. Philip Albert and Louise Gertrude (Peters) S.; m. Anne Marie Graveline, Aug. 19, 1973; children: Regina Elizabeth, Andrea May. BS cum laude, U. Mass., 1970, MLA, 1973; PhD in Environ. Planning, U. Calif., Berkeley, 1982. Environ. planner, landscape architect Wallace, Floyd, Ellenzweig, Inc., Cambridge, Mass., 1972-73; assoc. planner Exec. Office Environ. Affairs, State of Mass., Boston, 1973-75; environ. impact assessment specialist USDA extension svc. Oreg. State U., Corvallis, 1975-76; landscape architect USDA Pacific S.W. Forest and Range Expt. Sta., Berkeley, 1977; rsch. landscape architect U. Calif., Berkeley, 1977-79; prof. landscape architecture, sr. rsch. assoc. SUNY Coll. Environ. Sci. and Forestry, Syracuse, 1979-86, prof. environ. studies, 1987—, dir. Inst. for Environ. Policy and Planning, 1987-95; co-dir. Gt. Lakes Rsch. Consortium, Syracuse, 1986-96; guest lectr. numerous univs.; adj. asst. prof. U. Mass., Amherst, 1974-75; Sea Grant trainee Inst. for Urban and Regional Devel., Berkeley, 1976; condr., presenter numerous seminars and workshops; cons. to numerous orgns.; mem. com. on environ. design and landscape Transp. Rsch. Bd.-NAS, 1985-95; mem. tech. adv. bd. Wetlands Rsch., Inc., Chgo., 1985; mem. adv. bd. Wetlands Fund, N.Y., 1985; v.p. Integrated Site Inc., Syracuse. Co-editor: Our National Landscape, 1979, spl. issue Coastal Zone Mgmt. Jour., 1982, The Future of Wetlands, 1983, Foundations for Visual Project Analysis, 1986, The Legal Landscape, 1993, Protecting Floodplain Resources, 1995; mem. editl. bd. Northeastern Environ. Sci. Jour., 1981, Landscape and Urban Planning, 1991; contbr. over 100 articles to profl. jours. Bd. dirs. Sackets Harbor Area Hist. Preservation Found., Watertown, N.Y., 1984-90; pres. Save the County, Inc., Fayetteville, N.Y., 1986-88; apptd. to Great Lakes (N.Y.) Adv. Commn., chmn., 1993. Recipient Beatrice Farrand award U. Calif., 1979, Am. Soc. Landscape Architects award, 1972, Pub. Svc. award in edn., 1990, Progressive Architecture mag. award 1992, Pres.'s Pub. Svc. award 1994. Mem. AAAS, Am. Land Resource Assn. (charter), Internat. Assn. for Impact Assessment, Coastal Soc., Alpha Zeta (life), Sigma Lambda Alpha. Avocations: folk guitar, hiking, skiing, travel. Office: SUNY Inst Environ Policy Planning Syracuse NY 13210 Office: Integrated Site Inc 886 E Brighton Ave Syracuse NY 13205-2538

SMARG, RICHARD MICHAEL, employee benefits consultant, insurance specialist; b. Orange, N.J., July 25, 1952; s. Nicholas and Dorothy Smarg; m. Lynda E. Broms, Oct. 18, 1975; 1 child, Daniel. BS in Econs., U. N.H., 1974. CLU, ChFC. With New Eng. Mut. Life Ins. Co., Manchester, N.H., 1975-78; assoc. Baldwin & Clarke Cos., Bedford, N.H., 1978-88; founder, pres. N.H. Retirement & Ins. Cons., Bedford, 1988—, Fla. Retirement & Ins. Cons., Naples, 1988—; instr. Am. Coll., Bryn Mawr, Pa., 1985—; speaker in field. Contbr. articles to profl. jours. Mem. Estate Planning Coun., Fla., Million Dollar Round Table (life, state coord. 1987-91), Rotary Internat. (Paul Harris fellow 1991), English-Speaking Union (v.p. Naples, Fla.). Republican. Episcopalian. Avocations: golf, running, photography, travel, sports cars. Office: Fla Retirement & Ins Consultants Ste 215 4001 N Tamiami Trail Naples FL 33940

SMARR, LARRY LEE, science administrator, educator, astrophysicist; b. Columbia, Mo., Oct. 16, 1948; s. Robert L. Jr. and Jane (Crampton) S.; m. Janet Levarie, June 3, 1973; children: Joseph Robert, Benjamin Lee. BA, MS, U. Mo., 1970; MS, Stanford U., 1972; PhD, U. Tex., 1975. Rsch. asst. in physics U. Tex., Austin, 1972-74; lectr. dept. astrophys. sci. Princeton U., 1974-75; rsch. assoc. Princeton U. Obs., 1975-76; rsch. affiliate dept. physics Yale U., New Haven, Conn., 1978-79; asst. prof. astronomy dept. U. Ill., Urbana, 1979-81, asst. prof. physics dept., 1980-81, assoc. prof. astronomy and physics dept., 1981-85, prof. astronomy and physics dept., 1985—; dir. Nat. Ctr. for Supercomputing Applications, Champaign, Ill., 1985—; cons. Lawrence Livermore Nat. Lab., Calif., 1976—, Los Alamos (New Nex.) Nat. Lab., 1983—; mem. Commn. on Phys. Sci., Math. and Resources, NRC, Washington, 1987-90, commn. on Geoscience, Environ. and Resources, 1990—, adv. panel on Basic Rsch. in the 90's Office Tech. Assesment, 1990—. Editor: Sources of Gravitational Radiation, 1979; mem. editoral bd. Science mag., 1986-90; contbr. over 50 sci. articles to jours. in field. Co-founder, co-dir. Ill. Alliance to Prevent Nuclear War, Champaign, 1981-84. Recipient Fahrney medal Franklin Inst., Phila., 1990; NSF fellow Stanford U., 1970-73, Woodrow Wilson fellow, 1970-71, Lane Scholar U. Tex., Austin, 1972-73, jr. fellow Harvard U., 1976-79, Alfred P. Sloan fellow, 1980-84. Fellow Am. Phys. Soc.; mem. AAAS, Am. Astron. Soc., Govt. Rsch. Roundtable U. Ind. Avocations: marine aquarium, gardening. Office: NCSA at UIUC 605 E Springfield Ave Champaign IL 61820-5518

SMART, ALLEN RICH, II, lawyer; b. Chgo., July 3, 1934; s. Jackson W. Smart and Dorothy (Byrnes) Bowles. Student, Deerfield Acad., 1949-52; AB magna cum laude, Princeton U., 1956; LLB, Harvard U., 1961. Bar: Ill. 1961. Assoc. Bell Boyd & Lloyd, Chgo., 1961-69, ptnr., 1970-91, of counsel, 1992—. Bd. dirs. Rec. for Blind, Inc., Chgo., 1984-95, vice-chmn., 1987-90; co-chmn. zoning com. Old Town Triangle Assn., Chgo., 1987-94; bd. dirs. Lawrence Hall Sch. for Boys, 1965-70, Old Masters Soc., Art Inst., 1987—; governing mem. Orchestral Assn. Lt. USNR, 1956-58. Mem. ABA, Ill. Bar Assn., Chgo. Bar Assn., Infant Welfare Soc. Chgo. (bd. dirs. 1971-95, pres. 1982-86), Friends of the Parks Chgo. (bd. dirs. 1986—), Renaissance Soc. Chgo. (bd. dirs. 1988—), University (bd. dirs. 1986-89), Arts, Legal, Law, Economic clubs of Chgo. Home: 1732 N North Park Ave Chicago IL 60614-5710 Office: Bell Boyd & Lloyd 3200 Three First Nat Pl Chicago IL 60602

SMART, CHARLES RICH, retired surgeon; b. Ogden, Utah, Nov. 7, 1926; s. Junius Hatch and Avon (Rich) S.; m. Dorothea Jean Cannon Sharp, Dec. 23, 1952; children—Thomas, Edward, Christopher, Angela, Cynthia, David. B.S. with honors, U. Utah, 1945; M.D. with honors, Temple U., 1955. Intern Los Angeles County Hosp., 1955-56; resident Hosp. U. Pa., Phila., 1956-61; asst. prof. surgery in residence UCLA, 1963-66; assoc. prof. surgery Coll. Medicine, U. Utah, 1966-69, cancer coordinator, 1967-69, clin. assoc. prof. surgery, 1969-75, clin. prof. surgery, 1975-85; mem. staff, chief of surgery Latter-day Saints Hosp., 1974-84; chmn. SEER Group Nat. Cancer Inst., 1976-78, chief community oncology and rehab. br., 1985-86, chief early detection br., 1987-92; ret., 1992; dir. Rocky Mountain Coop. Tumor Registry, 1969-85; bd. dirs. Am. Cancer Soc., 1976-79. Contbr. research articles to med. jours. Fellow ACS; mem. Utah Med. Assn., AMA, Pan-Pacific Surg. Soc., Bay Surg. Soc., Los Angeles Surg. Soc., Salt Lake Surg. Soc., Internat. Soc. Chemotherapists, Am. Assn. Cancer Edn., Am. Soc. Clin. Oncology, Soc. Head and Neck Surgeons, Am. Soc. Surg. Oncologists, Alpha Omega Alpha. Republican. Mormon. Home: 1262 Chandler Dr Salt Lake City UT 84103-4240

SMART, JACKSON WYMAN, JR., business executive; b. Chgo., Aug. 27, 1930; s. Jackson Wyman and Dorothy (Byrnes) S.; m. Suzanne Tobey, July 6, 1957; 1 son, Jackson W. III. B.B.A., U. Mich., 1952; M.B.A., Harvard, 1954. With First Nat. Bank Chgo., 1956-64; exec. v.p. comml. banking Bank of Commonwealth, Detroit, 1964-69; pres., dir. MSP Industries Corp. (subsidiary W.R. Grace & Co. 1972), Center Line, Mich., 1969-71, pres., CEO, 1971-75; chmn., pres., treas., dir. The Delos Internat. Group, Inc. (subs. Automatic Data Processing Inc. 1976), Princeton, N.J., 1975-77; chmn., pres., CEO, dir. Central Nat. Bank (merged with Exch. Nat. Bank, Chgo. 1982), Chgo., 1977-82; chmn. fin. com. Exch. Internat. Corp., Chgo., 1982-83; chmn. exec. com. Thomas Industries, Inc., Louisville, Ky., 1983-87; chmn., CEO, dir. MSP Communications, Inc., Chgo., 1988—; bd. dirs. Fed. Express Corp., Memphis, chmn. fin. com., 1976-78; bd. dirs. Goldman Sachs Funds Group, N.Y.C.; chmn. Terminal Data Corp., Moorpark, Calif., 1992-94 (merger Banctec 1994); bd. dirs. 1st Commonwealth Inc., Chgo., 1988—, chmn. exec. com., 1996—; bd. dirs. Inroads Capital Ptnrs. Bd. dirs. Evanston (Ill.) Hosp., Hadley Sch. Blind, Winnetka, Ill., chmn. 1987-89. Mem. Chief Execs. Orgn., Birmingham Club (Mich.), Athletic Club, Comml. Club, Econ. Club, Univ. Club, Hundred Club of Cook County, Chgo. Club, Indian Hill Club, Ocean Club of Fla. (Ocean Ridge), Country Club of Fla. (Golf), Coral Beach and Tennis Club (Bermuda), Old Elm Club (Highland Park, Ill.). Office: 1 Northfield Plz Northfield IL 60093-1251

SMART, JACOB EDWARD, management consultant; b. Ridgeland, S.C., May 31, 1909; s. William Edward and Alma (Nettles) S.; m. Elizabeth Gohmert, Feb. 20, 1932 (div. 1946); children—Joan Elizabeth, Jacklyn Cabell, William Edward, Rosemary. Student, Marion Mil. Inst., 1926-27; B.S., U.S. Mil. Acad., 1931; student, Nat. War Coll., 1949-50. Commd. lt. USAF, 1931, advanced through grades to gen., 1963; served various posts U.S. and Europe, 1931-55; asst. vice chief of staff USAF, Washington, 1955-59; comdr. (12th Air Force), Waco, Texas, 1959-60; vice comdr. tactical air command Langley AFB, 1960-61; comdr. 5th Air Force and U.S. Forces in Japan, Japan, 1961-63, Cinc. Pacific Air Forces, 1963-64; dep. comdr. in chief (Hdqrs. U.S. European Command), 1964-66; ret., 1966; spl. asst. to adminstr. NASA, 1966-67, asst. adminstr. for policy, 1967-68; asst. adminstr. for Dept. Def. and inter-agy. affairs, 1968-73; v.p. Earth Satellite Corp., Washington, 1973-75; cons., 1975—. Decorated D.S.C., D.S.M. with 4 oak leaf clusters, Legion of Merit, D.F.C., Air medal with 3 oak leaf clusters, Purple Heart, Commendation Ribbon; hon. comdr. Order Brit. Empire; Order of Service Merit 1st class Korea; Medal of Cloud and Banner with Grand Cordon China; comdr. Legion of Honor France; Order of Sacred Treasures Japan). Mem. Assn. Grads. U.S. Mil. Acad., Air Force Assn. Home: PO Box Y Ridgeland SC 29936-0925

SMART, L(OUIS) EDWIN, JR., business executive, lawyer; b. Columbus, Ohio, Nov. 17, 1923; s. Louis Edwin and Esther (Guthery) S.; m. Virginia Alice Knouff, Mar. 1, 1944 (div. 1958); children: Cynthia Stephanie, Douglas Edwin; m. Jeanie A. Milone, Aug. 29, 1964; 1 child, Dana Gregory. AB magna cum laude, Harvard U., 1947, JD magna cum laude, 1949. Bar: N.Y. 1950. Assoc. firm Hughes, Hubbard & Ewing, N.Y.C., 1949-56; ptnr. firm Hughes Hubbard & Reed, N.Y.C., 1957-64, counsel, 1989—; pres. Bendix Internat.; dir. Bendix Corp. (and fgn. subs.), 1964-67; sr. v.p. external affairs Trans World Airlines, Inc., 1967-71, sr. v.p. corp. affairs, 1971-75, vice chmn., 1976, chmn. bd., chief exec. officer, 1977-78, chmn. bd., 1979-85; chmn. bd., chief exec. officer Transworld Corp. (name now Flagstar Cos., Inc.), 1978-87, chmn. exec. com., 1987-89, also bd. dirs.; chmn. bd. Hilton Internat. Co., 1978-86; of counsel Hughes Hubbard & Reed, N.Y.C., 1989—; bd. dirs. Continental Corp., Sonat Inc., Flagstar Cos., Inc., Flagstar Corp. Editor Harvard Law Rev., 1947-48. Lt. USNR, 1943-46. Mem. ABA, N.Y. County Lawyers Assn., Harvard Club, Marco Polo Club, Phi Beta Kappa, Sigma Alpha Epsilon. Office: Hughes Hubbard & Reed 1 Battery Park Plz New York NY 10004-1405

SMART, MARRIOTT WIECKHOFF, research librarian consultant; b. Memphis, Aug. 26, 1935; d. Gerhard Emil and Beatrice (Flanegan) Wieckhoff; m. John A. Smart, May 9, 1959; children: Denise, Holly. B.S. in Geology, U. Tex.-Austin, 1957; M.L.S., U. Pitts., 1976. Geophysicist Mobil Corp., New Orleans, 1957-59; geologist Hanson Oil Co., Roswell, N.Mex., 1959-62; info. specialist Gulf Corp., Pitts., 1977-79, library mgr., Denver, 1979-84, library cons. team, Pitts., 1984; supr. Library-Info. Ctr., Amoco Minerals Co., Englewood, Colo., 1984; dir. Library-Info. Ctr., Cyprus Minerals Co., 1985-92; cons. Ask Marriott, Littleton, Colo., 1992—. Choir mem. Grace Presbyn. Ch., Littleton, 1979—. Mem. Spl. Libraries Assn. (bull. bus. mgr. 1982, treas. petroleum and energy divsn. 1984-86, chmn. petroleum and energy divsn. 1987-88, pres. Rocky Mountain chpt. 1991-92), Colo. Info. Profls. Network, Women in Mining, Alpha Chi Omega. Home: 3337 E Easter Pl Littleton CO 80122-1910

SMART, PAUL M., utility company executive, lawyer; b. Middleport, Ohio, Jan. 6, 1929. A.B. summa cum laude, Capital U., 1952; J.D. summa cum laude, Ohio State U., 1953. Bar: Ohio 1953. Ptnr. Fuller & Henry, Toledo, 1959-84; v.p. Toledo Edison Co., 1974-78, sr. v.p., gen. counsel corp. devel., 1984-85, pres., chief oper. officer, 1985-88, vice-chmn., 1988—, also dir.; past exec. v.p. Centerior Energy Corp., Cleve., vice chmn., 1989—. Fellow Ohio State Bar Found.; mem. Am. Bar Found., Order of Coif, Phi Delta Phi. *

SMART, STEPHEN BRUCE, JR., business and government executive; b. N.Y.C., Feb. 7, 1923; s. Stephen Bruce and Beatrice (Cobb) S.; m. Edith Minturn Merrill, Sept. 10, 1949; children: Edith Minturn Smart Moore, William Candler, Charlotte Merrill Smart Rogan, Priscilla Smart Schwarzenbach. Student, Milton Acad.; A.B. cum laude, Harvard U., 1945; S.M., MIT, 1947. Sales engr. Permutit Co., N.Y., 1947-51; various sales, gen. mgmt. positions Continental Group, Inc. (formerly Continental Can Co.), N.Y.C., 1953-85, v.p. Central metal div., 1962-65, v.p. marketing and corporate planning, 1965-67, v.p., asst. gen. mgr. paper operations, 1967-69, group v.p. paper operations, 1969-71, exec. v.p. paper operations, 1971-73, vice chmn. bd., 1973-75, pres., 1975-85, chmn., chief exec. officer, 1981-85; undersec. for internat. trade Dept. Commerce, Washington, 1985-88; cons. Dept. State, Washington, 1988-89; sr. fellow World Resources Inst., Washington, 1988-95; bd. dirs. World Resources Inst,. Inform Inc. Editor: Beyond Compliance: A New Industry View of the Environment, 1992. 1st lt. AUS, 1943-46; C.E., 1951-53. Mem. Coun. Fgn. Rels., The Bus. Coun., Sigma Xi. Clubs: Pequot Yacht, Tennis (Middleburg, Va.). Home and Office: 20561 Trappe Rd Upperville VA 22176-9708

SMARTSCHAN, GLENN FRED, educational administrator; b. Allentown, Pa., Dec. 11, 1946; s. Fred Gotfred and Joyce Isabel (Hensinger) S.; m. Linda Susan Bastinelli, Mar. 18. 1972; children: Erin Joy, Lauren Nicole. BS in Edn., Kutztown State Coll., 1968; MS in Edn., Temple U., 1972; EdD in Ednl. Adminstrn., Lehigh U., 1979. Cert. tchr. history and comprehensive social studies, secondary prin., supt., Pa. Tchr. 8th grade social studies South Mountain Jr. High Sch., Allentown Sch. Dist., 1968-76, adminstrv. asst. to prin. Raub Jr. High Sch., 1976-78, prin., 1978-80, dist. dir. curriculum, 1980-84, asst. to supt. for curriculum and community services, 1984-86; supt. of schs. Brandywine Heights Area Sch. Dist., Topton, Pa., 1986-90; supt. of sch. Mt. Lebanon Sch. Dist., Pitts., 1990—; adj. prof. Cedar Crest Coll., 1986-88; chief exec. officer Ednl. Dynamics Cons., Assoc. Cambridge Group, 1993; assoc. The Cambridge Group, 1993—; speaker, cons. on alternative edn., scope and sequence devel., criterion referenced testing; strategic planning bd. dirs. Alternative House Inc., Bethlehem, Pa., 1976-81, chairperson program com., 1977-78, v.p., 1979, pres., 1980; mem. adv. com. Lehigh County (Pa.) Hist. Mus., 1980-86; bd. dirs. Girls' Club Allentown, 1983-86, v.p., 1985. Mem. Assn. Supervision and Curriculum Devel., Pa. Assn. Supervision and Curriculum Devel. (exec. com., registrar eastern regional meeting, v.p. Eastern region, pres. Eastern region 1988), Am. Assn. Sch. Adminstrs., Pa. Assn. Sch. Adminstrs., Pa. Sch. Bds. Assn., Alumni Coun. Lehigh U. (pres. 1986), Phi Delta Kappa, Fleetwood Club, Rotary (charter mem. Allentown club, exec. com. 1985), Dormont-Mt. Lebanon Club. Roman Catholic. Home: One Spalding Cir Pittsburgh PA 15228 Office: Mt Lebanon Sch Dist 7 Horseman Dr Pittsburgh PA 15228-1128

SMATHERS, FRANK, JR., banker, horticulturist; b. Atlantic City, July 17, 1909; s. Frank and Lura (Jones) S.; m. Mary Belle Wall, Mar. 27, 1935; children: Lowry, Pamela Smathers MacCorquodale, Ann Smathers Prescott, Lura Smathers Bergh. Student, U. N.C., 1928-30; LLB, U. Miami, 1933; student, Grad. Sch. Banking, Rutgers U., 1939-42. Bar: Fla. 1933. Asst. state atty. State of Fla., 1934-35; asst. trust officer Miami Beach (Fla.) 1st Nat. Bank, 1936-39, v.p., trust officer, dir., 1936-56, asst. pres., trust officer, 1956-57, pres., 1957-67, chmn., 1966-74; chmn. bd. United Nat. Bank, Miami, 1964-74; chmn. Coral Gables 1st Nat. Bank, 1966-74, United Bancshares, 1966-73, Security Exch. Bank, West Palm Beach, Fla., 1970-73; vice chmn. United Nat. Bank, Dadeland, 1968-74; chmn. United Nat. Bank, Westland, Fla., 1972-74; pres., chief exec. officer United 1st Fla. Banks, Inc., 1973-74; chmn., chief exec. officer Flagship Banks Inc., 1974-75. Pres. Fedn. Econ. Concern, Dade County, Fla.; vice chmn. Assn. Governing Bds. Colls. and Univs.; trustee U. Miami, Rutgers U., Grad. Sch. Banking, St. Francis Hosp., Miami Beach., Fairchild Tropical Garden; bd. dirs. Fla. Coun. 100. With U.S. Army, 1928, 42-43; with Office Price Adminstrn., Washington, 1944-45. Mem. Iron Arrow Hon. Soc., SAR, Metropolitan Club (Washington), Indian Creek Country Club, Coral Reef Yacht Club, Yale Club (N.Y.C.), Royal and Ancient Golf Club, Pine Valley Golf Club, Delta Kappa Epsilon. Methodist. Home: 11511 SW 57th Ave Miami FL 33156-5002

SMATHERS, JAMES BURTON, medical physicist, educator; b. Prairie du Chien, Wis., Aug. 26, 1935; s. James Levi and Irma Marie (Stindt) S.; m. Sylvia Lee Rath, Apr. 20, 1957; children—Kristine Kay, Kathryn Ann, James Scott, Ernest Kent. B.Nuclear Enging., N.C. State Coll., 1957, M.S., 1959; Ph.D., U. Md., 1967. Diplomate Am. Bd. Radiology, Am. Bd. Med. Physics, Am. Bd. Medical Physics; cert. in radiation oncology physics; registered profl. engr., D.C., Tex., Calif. Research engr. Atomics Internat., Canoga Park, Calif., 1959, Walter Reed Army Inst. Research, Washington, 1961-67; prof. nuclear engring. Tex. A. and M. U., College Station, 1967-80; prof., head bioengring. Tex. A. and M. U., 1976-80; prof., head med. physics, dept. radiation oncology UCLA, 1980—; cons. U.S. Army, Dept. Energy, also pvt.; industry. Served with U.S. Army, 1959-61. Recipient Excellence in Teaching award Gen. Dynamics, 1971; Excellence in Research award Tex. A. and M. U. Former Students Assn., 1976. Mem. Am. Nuclear Soc., Health Physics Soc., Am. Assn. Physcists in Medicine, Am. Soc. Engring. Edn. (Outstanding Tchr. award in nuclear engring. div. 1972), Radiation Research Soc., Nat. Soc. Profl. Engrs., Calif. Soc. Profl. Engrs., Sigma Xi, Sigma Pi Sigma, Phi Kappa Phi. Home: 18229 Minnehaha St Northridge CA 91326-3427 Office: UCLA Dept Radiation Oncology B265 200 UCLA Med Plz Los Angeles CA 90095

SMEAL, CAROLYN A., community health nurse, educator; b. Guilford, N.Y., Jan. 30, 1930; d. Charles C. and Margaret C. (Wilson) Bloom; m. William C. Smeal, May 28, 1949; children: Dale, Sandra Smeal Barlow, Stacey (dec.), William M. Diploma, Millard Fillmore Hosp., Buffalo, 1950; BS, SUNY, Buffalo, 1967. Cert. community health nurse, sch. nurse-tchr. Staff nurse in oper. rm., emergency rm. Niagara Falls (N.Y.) Meml. Med. Ctr.; staff nurse Niagara Falls Air Base; sch. nurse tchr. Bd. Edn., Niagara Falls; community health nurse Niagara County Health Dept., Niagara Falls; retired, 1995. Bd. dirs. Ctr. for Young Parents, Cerebral Palsy Recreation Group. Mem. Assn. for Retarded Children (bd. dirs., past pres.). Home: 710 Chilton Ave Niagara Falls NY 14301-1008

SMEAL, PAUL LESTER, retired horticulture educator; b. Clearfield, Pa., June 11, 1932; s. Walter Vernon and Agatha (Cowder) S.; m. Gladys Matilda Smeal, July 17, 1954; children: Lester Alan, Gwen Hope, Tracy Gay. BS, Pa. State U., 1954; MS, U. Md., 1958, PhD, 1961. Asst. prof. horticulture Va. Poly. Inst. and State U., Blacksburg, 1960-61, assoc. prof., 1961-67, prof., 1967-92, prof. emeritus, 1993—; pres. faculty senate Va. Poly. Inst. and State U., 1984-86. Advisor Alpha Zeta, 1984-86. Recipient Quill and Trowel Comm. award Garden Writers Assn. Am., 1986, 87, Disting. Svc. award Nat. Assn. Country Agrl. Agts., 1987, L.C. Chadwick Teaching award Am. Assn. Nurserymen, 1988, Nursery Ext. award Am. Assn. Nurserymen, 1990. Fellow Am. Soc. Hort. Sci. (mem. pub. affairs com. 1979-82, chmn. ad hoc com 1984-86, pres. so. region 1978-79, sec.-treas. 1989—, others, Carl S. Bittner Extension award 1984, Henry M. Covington Extension award 1991); mem. Internat. Plant Propagator's Soc. (chmn. rsch. com. ea. region 1987-90, bd. dirs. 1991, 2d v.p. 1991, v.p. 1992, pres. 1993), Va. Nurserymen's Assn. (hon.). Republican. Lutheran. Home: 1107 Kentwood Dr Blacksburg VA 24060-5656

SMEDINGHOFF, THOMAS J., lawyer; b. Chgo., July 15, 1951; s. John A. and Dorothy M.; m. Mary Beth Smedinghoff. BA in Math., Knox Coll., 1973; JD, U. Mich., 1978. Bar: Ill. 1978, U.S. Dist. Ct. (no. dist.) Ill. 1978. Assoc. McBride, Baker & Coles and predecessor McBride & Baker, Chgo., 1978-84, ptnr., 1985—. adj. prof. computer law John Marshall Law Sch., Chgo.; chair Ill. Commn. on Electronic Commerce and Crime, 1996—. Office: McBride Baker & Coles 500 W Madison St Ste 40 Chicago IL 60661-2511

SMEDLEY, LAWRENCE THOMAS, retired organization executive; b. Lorain, Ohio, Sept. 2, 1929; s. Robert E. and Gerda Sofia (Johnson) S.; m. Carmen Nancy Suarez, June 29, 1962; children: Lorraine, Robert, Lawrence, Richard. BA, Bowling Green State U., 1952; MA, U. Mich., 1957; PhD, Am. U., 1972. Analyst Social Security dept. AFL-CIO, Washington, 1962-65, asst. dir. dept., 1965-73, assoc. dir. dept. occupation safety-health-social security, 1973-88; exec. dir. Nat. Coun. Sr. Citizens, Inc., Washington, 1988-96; former mem. numerous presdl. task forces and coms. on older Ams. and disabled; mem. planning and adv. coms. White House Conf. on Aging, 1971, 81; former mem. adv. coun. on employee welfare and pension plans Dept. Labor, also former mem. spl. task force examining policies relating to asset reversions from over-funded pension plans. Co-chmn. Leadership Coun. Aging Orgns., Washington, 1988-95; mem. exec. bd. Com. for Nat. Health Ins., WAshington, 1989—; mem. policy conv. White House Conf. on Aging, 1995. With M.I., U.S. Army, 1952-55, Korea. Recipient Disting. Svc. award Commn. on Accreditation of Facilities of Rehab., 1975, Dedicated Svc. award White House Conf. on Handicapped, 1977, award of honor Industry-Labor Coun., 1981, Outstanding Svc. award Pres.'s Com. on Employment of Handicapped, 1987. Democrat. Lutheran. Home: 1616 Winding Waye Ln Silver Spring MD 20902-1456 Office: Nat Council of Senior Citizens 1331 F St NW Washington DC 20004-1107

SMEDS, EDWARD WILLIAM, food company executive; b. Chgo., Feb. 15, 1936; s. Sigvard A. and Ida S.; m. Alice J. Lawler, Jan. 26, 1957; children—Ellen R., Brad W. BS, Carthage Coll., 1957; MS, U. Ill., 1959; grad. advanced mgmt. program, Harvard U., 1977. With Borg Warner Corp., 1958-61; with Kraft Foods div. Kraft Inc., 1961-75, v.p., dir. personnel, ops. group, 1976-78, v.p. human resources, 1978-79, sr. v.p. human resources, 1979-80, sr. v.p. fin. and adminstrn., 1980-84; pres. Kraft Asia Pacific, 1984-88; chmn. Kraft Foods Ltd., Australia, 1984-88; pres. Kraft Ltd. Can., 1988-89; sr. v.p. ops. and logistics Kraft Gen. Foods, Glenview, Ill., 1990-93; pres. customer svc. and ops. Kraft Gen. Foods, Northfield, Ill., 1993—. Trustee Carthage Coll., Cornerstone Found. Mem. Global Bus. Mgmt. Coun., Econ. Club of Chgo., Chgo. Coun. on Fgn. Rels., Sunset Ridge Country Club, Club at Pelican Bay. Home: 10 Regentwood Rd Northfield IL 60093-2728 also: 6814 Pelican Bay Blvd Naples FL 33963-8218 Office: Kraft Gen Foods 3 Lakes Dr Northfield IL 60093

SMEDSRUD, MILTON E., health association executive, consultant; b. Battle Lake, Minn., Mar. 23, 1932; s. Sivert E. and Sophie (Larson) S.; m. Birgitte Y. Villiamsen, Feb. 18, 1956; children: Gregory, Jeffrey. Student, Moorhead (Minn.) State U., 1950-51. Pres., owner Smedsrud Inc., 1969; founder, chmn., CEO, Communicating for Agr., Fergus Falls, Minn., 1972—, Communicating for Seniors, Fergus Falls, 1986—, Communicating for Health Consumers, Fergus Falls, 1990—; founder CA Internat. Exch. Program, Fergus Falls, 1985—; owner Smedsrud Farms, Battle Lake, 1988—. 1st lt. USAF, 1952-56. Democrat. Lutheran. Avocations: fishing, travel. Home: RR 1 Box 60A Battle Lake MN 56515-9734 Office: 112 E Lincoln Ave Fergus Falls MN 56537-2217

SMEE, JOHN, church administrator. Dir. Missionary Ministries of the Church of the Namzarene, Kansas City, Mo. Office: Church of the Nazarene 6401 Paseo Blvd Kansas City MO 64131-1213

SMEETON, THOMAS ROONEY, governmental affairs consultant; b. Evanston, Ill., Sept. 26, 1934; s. Cecil Brooks, Jr. and Florence Mary (Rooney).; m. Susan Diane Tollefson, Feb. 23, 1963; children: Sean, Timothy, Shannon, Brendan, Colin. BS in History, Marquette U., 1958; postgrad., U. Notre Dame, 1958-59; grad., Armed Forces Staff Coll., 1972. Intellience officer U.S. CIA, Langley, Va., 1962-73; vp., gen. mgr. Nowicki Fla. Devel. Corp., Ft. Lauderdale, 1973-75; cons. spl. projects com. on fgn. affairs U.S. House Reps., Washington, 1975-86, minority counsel permanent select com. on intelligence, 1986-92, minority staff dir. Iran/Contra com., 1987-88, exec. dir. Rep. policy com., 1993-94; adminstr., chief investigator House Judiciary Com., Washington, D.C., 1995-96; govtl. affairs cons., 1996—. Contbg. author: (with Hyde) For Every Idle Silence, 1985. With U.S. Army, 1959-62. Recipient Agy. Seal medallion CIA, 1993. Mem. Notre Dame Club Washington (vice chmn. 1982-84), Am. Legion. Republican. Roman Catholic. Avocation: golf. Home and Office: 9414 Wallingford Dr Burke VA 22015-1733

SMEGAL, THOMAS FRANK, JR., lawyer; b. Eveleth, Minn., June 15, 1935; s. Thomas Frank and Genevieve (Andreachi) S.; m. Susan Jane Stanton, May 28, 1966; children: Thomas Frank, Elizabeth Jane. BS in Chem. Enging., Mich. Technol. U., 1957; JD, George Washington U., 1961. Bar: Va. 1961, D.C. 1961, Calif. 1964, U.S. Supreme Ct. 1976. Patent examiner U.S. Patent Office, Washington, 1957-61; staff patent atty. Shell Devel. Co., San Francisco, 1962-65; patent atty. Townsend and Townsend, San Francisco, 1965-91, mng. ptnr., 1974-89; sr. ptnr. Graham and James, San Francisco, 1992—; mem. U.S. del. to Paris Conv. for Protection of Indsl. Property. Pres. bd. dirs. Legal Aid Soc. San Francisco, 1982-84, Youth Law

Ctr., 1973-84; bd. dirs. Nat. Ctr. for Youth Law, 1978-84, San Francisco Lawyers Com. for Urban Affairs, 1972—, Legal Svcs. for Children, 1980-88; presdl. nom., Legal Svcs. Corp., 1984-90, 93—. Capt. Chem. Corps, U.S. Army, 1961-62. Recipient St. Thomas More award, 1982. Mem. Ct. of Appeals for Federal Ct. (adv. com. 1992—), ABA (chmn. PTC sect. 1990-91, ho. of dels. 1988—, mem. standing com. Legal Aid and Indigent Defendants, 1991-94, chair sect. officer conf., 1992-94, mem. bd. govs., 1994—), Nat. Coun. Intellectual Property Law Assn. (chmn. 1989), Nat. Inventors Hall Fame (pres. 1988), Calif. Bar Assn. (v.p. bd. govs. 1986-87), Am. Patent Law Assn. (pres. 1986), Internat. Assn. Intellectual Property Lawyers (pres. 1995—), Bar Assn. San Francisco (pres. 1978), Patent Law Assn. San Francisco (pres. 1974). Republican. Roman Catholic. Clubs: World Trade, Olympic, Golden Gate Breakfast (San Francisco); Claremont (Berkeley). Contbr. articles to publs. in field. Office: Graham & James 1 Maritime Plz Ste 300 Alco San Francisco CA 94111-3404

SMELSER, NEIL JOSEPH, sociologist; b. Kahoka, Mo., July 22, 1930; s. Joseph Nelson and Susie Marie (Hess) S.; m. Helen Thelma Margolis, June 10, 1954 (div. 1965); children: Eric Jonathan, Tina Rachel; m. Sharin Fateley, Dec. 20, 1967; children: Joseph Neil, Sarah Joanne. B.A., Harvard U., 1952, Ph.D., 1958; B.A., Magdalen Coll., Oxford U., Eng., 1954; M.A., Magdalen Coll., Oxford U., 1959; grad., San Francisco Psychoanalytic Inst., 1971. Mem. faculty U. Calif., Berkeley, 1958-94, prof. sociology, 1962—, asst. chancellor ednl. devel., 1966-68; assoc. dir. Inst. of Internat. Studies, Berkeley, 1969-73, 80-89; Univ. prof. sociology U. Calif., Berkeley, 1972-94; prof. emeritus, 1994—; dir. edn. abroad program for U. Calif., Berkeley, 1977-79, spl. advisor Office of Pres., 1993-94, dir. Ctr. for Advanced Study in Behavioral Scis., 1994—; bd. dirs. Found. Fund for Rsch. in Psychiatry, 1967-70; bd. dirs. Social Sci. Rsch. Coun., 1968-71, chmn., 1971-73, mem. com. econ. growth, 1961-65; trustee Ctr. for Advanced Study in Behavioral Scis., 1980-86, 87-93, chmn., 1984-86; trustee Russell Sage Found., 1990—; mem. subcom. humanism Am. Bd. Internal Medicine, 1981-85, 89-90, mem. adv. com., 1992—, chmn. adv. com., 1995—; chmn. sociology panel Behavioral and Social Scis. survey NAS and Social Sci. Rsch. Coun., 1967-69; mem. com. on basic rsch. in behavioral and social scis. NRC, 1980-89, chmn., 1984-86, co-chmn., 1986-89. Author: (with T. Parsons) Economy and Society, 1956, Social Change in the Industrial Revolution, 1959, Theory of Collective Behavior, 1962, The Sociology of Economic Life, 1963, 2d edit., 1975, Essays in Sociological Explanation, 1968, Sociological Theory: A Contemporary View, 1971, Comparative Methods in the Social Sciences, 1976, (with Robin Content) The Changing Academic Market, 1980, Sociology, 1981, 2d edit., 1984, 3d edit. 1987, 4th edit. 1991, 5th edit., 1995, Social Paralysis and Social Change, 1991, Effective Committee Service, 1993, Sociology, 1994; editor: (with W.T. Smelser) Personality and Social Systems, 1963, 2d edit., 1971, (with S.M. Lipset) Social Structure and Mobility in Economic Development, 1966, Sociology, 1967, 2d edit., 1973, (with James Davis) Sociology: A Survey Report, 1969, Karl Marx on Society and Social Change, 1973, (with Gabriel Almond) Public Higher Education in California, 1974, (with Erik Erikson) Themes of Work and Love in Adulthood, 1980, (with Jeffrey Alexander et al) The Micro-Macro Link, 1987, Handbook of Sociology, 1988, (with Hans Haferkamp) Social Change and Modernity, 1992, (with Richard Munch) Theory of Culture, 1992, (with Richard Swedberg) The Handbook of Economic Sociology, 1994; editor Am. Sociol. Rev., 1962-65, 89-90; adv. editor Am. Jour. Sociology, 1960-62. Rhodes scholar, 1952-54; jr. fellow Soc. Fellows, Harvard U., 1955-58; fellow Russell Sage Found., 1989-90. Mem. Am. Sociol. Assn. (coun. 1962-65, 67-70, exec. com. 1963-65, pres. elect 1995-96, pres. 1996-97), Pacific Sociol. Assn., Internat. Sociol. Assn. (exec. com. 1986-94, v.p. 1990-94), Am. Acad. Arts and Scis. (hon.), Am. Philos. Soc. (hon.), Nat. Acad. of Scis. (hon.). Home: 890 Robb Rd Palo Alto CA 94306-3729

SMELT, RONALD, retired aircraft company executive; b. Houghtonle Spring, Durham, Eng., Dec. 4, 1913; came to U.S., 1948, naturalized, 1955; s. Henry Wilson and Florence (Bradburn) S.; m. Marie Anita Collings, Nov. 2, 1940 (dec. May 1964); 1 son, David; m. Jean Stuart, Jan. 15, 1965. B.A., King's Coll., Cambridge (Eng.) U., 1935, M.A., 1939; Ph.D., Stanford, 1961. With Royal Aircraft Establishment, 1935-48, chief high speed flight, 1940-45, chief guided weapons dept., 1945-48; dep. chief aeroballistic research dept. USN Ordnance Lab., 1948-50; chief gas dynamics facility ARO, Inc., Tullahoma, Tenn., 1950-57; dir. research and devel. Lockheed Aircraft Corp. (missile systems div.), Sunnyvale, Calif., 1958-59; mgr. Lockheed Aircraft Corp. (Discoverer Satellite system), 1959-60, chief scientist, 1960-62, v.p., gen. mgr. space programs div., 1962-63, v.p., chief scientist, 1963-78; Guggenheim lectr. Internat. Congress Aero. Sci., 1978; Mem. com. on space vehicle aerodynamics NASA, 1965-66, chmn. research adv. com. on space vehicles, 1966-73, chmn. research and tech. adv. council, 1973-77; chmn. tech. adv. bd. Dept. Transp., 1970-74; mem. engring. adv. com. Stanford U., 1988-89; adv. com. NASA-Stanford Ctr. for Turbulence Rsch. Fellow Cambridge Philos. Soc., Royal Aero. Soc. (London), Am. Astronautical Soc., AIAA (hon.; dir.-at-large 1966-68, pres. 1969, 70); mem. Nat. Acad. Engring.. Home: 7250 Driver Valley Rd Oakland OR 97462-9679

SMELTZ, EDWARD J., engineer; b. Willard, Ohio, Nov. 26, 1952; s. Harold Munroe and Marvel Arneta (Swander) S.; m. Mary Ruth Huffman, Oct. 15, 1977; children: Keith, Jeremy, Kendra. BA in Physics, Otterbein Coll., 1975. Assembly line worker Midwest Inds., Willard, Ohio, 1972-76; telephone maintenance CXS Corp., Willard, Ohio, 1976-82; technician Motorola, Ft. Worth, 1982-84, board test engr., 1984-87, system adminstr., 1987-90, 94—, lead engr. Fastco lab., 1990-94, system designer, 1984—. Active Cmty. Cleanup, Recycling, Ft. Worth, 1992-94, Watauga, Tex., 1986-92,. Mem. IEEE, Nat. Model Railroading Assn. Avocations: bible study, model trains, computer programming, wood carving, reading.

SMELTZER, DEBRA JEAN, botanist; b. Camden, Ark., Oct. 13, 1953; d. William Dewey and Frankie Jean (Braswell) S.; m. James Richard Ziesler, Sept. 1, 1984. Cert. in interior design, Bauder Fashion Coll., Arlington, Tex., 1973; BA in Botany, U. Tex., 1985. Biol. rsch. asst. U.S. Dept. Interior, Everglades Nat. Park, Fla., 1980; biologist, surveyor Great Lakes Dredge and Dock, Miami Beach, Fla., 1981-82, 1984; biologist, surveyor, drafter Great Lakes Dredge and Dock, Port Everglades, Fla., 1984; biologist, lab. tech. J.B. Reark and Assocs., Miami, 1982-84; fisheries biologist Kathryn Chandler and Assocs., Alexandria, Va., 1981-84; pres. Greensleeves, Inc., Miami and San Juan, P.R., 1985—, San Juan, P.R., 1991-95; v.p. G.D.S., Inc., Miami, 1995—; bd. govs. Nat. Coun. for Interior Hort. Cert., Columbus, Ohio, 1989-92; licensee Interior Landscape Internat. Corp., Dade, Monroe, Caribbean, 1990-92. Active Fairchild Tropical Gardens, Miami, Ch. of the Little Flower. Recipient Best Project award Interiorscape Mag., 1989, State Award of Excellence Fla. Nurserymen and Growers Assn., 1989. Mem. Associated Landscape Contractors Am. (award of Distinction 1989, 91, 92 [2], Grand award 1990), South Fla. Interior Landscape Assn. (ednl. com. 1987-89, bd. dirs. 1986-87, author newsletter articles 1986-89, founder 1986), South Fla. Hort. Soc., Inc., South Fla. Tex. Execs., Coral Gables C. of C. (trustee coun.). Democrat. Avocations: water skiing, snow skiing, scuba diving, photography. Office: Greensleeves Inc 9774 SW 60th St Miami FL 33173-1421

SMERCINA, CHARLES JOSEPH, mayor, accountant; b. Cleve., Sept. 18, 1932; s. Edward Steven and Barbara Rose (Vincik) S.; m. Dorothy Rita Pazdernik, May 9, 1953; children: Cynthia Bomeli Smercina, David. ABA in Acctg., Fenn Coll.; ABA in Mgmt., BBA in Acctg., Cleve. State U.; postgrad., Kent State U., Case Western Res. U., Youngstown (Ohio) State U. CPA, Ohio. Chmn. CSC, Solon, 1956-66; councilman City of Solon, Ohio, 1966-68, vice mayor, 1966-67, income tax adminstr., 1968-73, mayor, 1974-75, 78-87; cons. taxation, mcpl. fin. various Ohio communities, 1970—; lectr. polit.. sci., corp. fin. Case Western Res. U. Mem. Am. Soc. Pub. Adminstrs., Mayors Assn. Ohio, Cuyahoga County Mayors and City Mgrs. Assn., Mcpl. Fin. Officers Am., Nat. League of Cities, Nat. Soc. Pub. Accts., Ohio Assn. Pub. Safety Dirs., Ohio Assn. Tax Adminstrs. (past pres.), Ohio Mcpl. League, Water Pollution Control Fedn., Solon C. of C., VFW, Council on Human Relations, Ohio Nature Conservancy, Nat. Arbor Day Found. Democrat. Roman Catholic. Lodges: Rotary, KC. Home: 5075 Brainard Rd Cleveland OH 44139-1101

SMERDON, ERNEST THOMAS, academic administrator; b. Ritchey, Mo., Jan. 19, 1930; s. John Erle and Ada (Davidson) S.; m. Joanne Duck, June 9, 1951; children: Thomas, Katherine, Gary. BS in Engring., U. Mo., 1951, MS in Engring., 1956, PhD in Engring., 1959. Registered profl. engr., Ariz. Chmn. dept. agrl. engring. U. Fla., Gainesville, 1968-74, asst. dean for rsch., 1974-76; vice chancellor for acad. affairs U. Tex. System, Austin, 1976-82; dir. Ctr. for Rsch. in Water Resources U. Tex., 1982-88; dean Coll. Engring. and Mines U. Ariz., Tucson, 1988-92; vice provost, dean Engring U. Ariz., 1992—; mem. bd. sci. and tech. for internat. devel. NRC, Washington, 1990-94. Editor: Managing Water Related Conflicts: The Engineer's Role, 1989. Mem. Ariz. Gov.'s Sci. and Tech. Coun., Tucson, 1989—; bd. dirs. Greater Tucson Econ. Coun., Tucson, 1990-95. Recipient Disting. Svc. in Engring. award U. Mo., 1982. Fellow AAAS, ASCE (hon. mem., Outstanding Svc. award irrigation and drainage divsn. 1988, Royce Tipton award 1989), NAE (peer com. 1986-90, acad. adv. bd. 1989-95, tech. policy options co. 1990-91), Am. Soc. Agrl. Engrs., Am. Water Resources Assn. (Icko Iben award 1989), Am. Soc. Engring. Edn. (chmn., bd. dirs. engring. dean's coun.), Am. Geophys. Union, Univ. Coun. on Water Resources, Ariz. Soc. Profl. Engrs. (Engr. of Yr. award 1990), Sigma Xi, Phi Kappa Phi, Tau Beta Pi, Pi Mu Epsilon. Avocations: hiking, golf, scuba diving, painting. Office: University of Arizona Engineering Experiment Sta Tucson AZ 85721

SMERNOFF, RICHARD LOUIS, oil company executive; b. N.Y.C., July 26, 1941; s. George Stephen and Anna Theresa (Dutoit) S.; m. Agnes Elizabeth Neubauer, Sept. 27, 1969; children—Richard Louis Jr., Christopher Max. B.B.A., CCNY, 1966. CPA, N.Y. Asst. to controller F. Levy Levy & Co., N.Y.C., 1967-70; audit supr. Coopers & Lybrand, N.Y.C., 1970-74; dir. fin. controls Internat. Paper Co., N.Y.C., 1974-78; sr. v.p. Amerada Hess Corp., Woodbridge, N.J., 1978-91; pres. Am. Ultramar, Tarrytown, N.Y., 1991-92; fin. officer Datascope Corp., Montvale, N.J., 1992-94; fin. dir. Lasmo Plc, London, 1994—. Mem. AICPA. Republican. Roman Catholic. Avocations: golf, fishing. Home: 3 Trevor Sq Knightsbridge, London SW7 1DT, England Office: 100 Liverpool St, London EC2M 2BB, England

SMETANKA, MARY JANE, reporter. Education and learning reporter Minn. Star Tribune, Mpls. Office: Mpls. Star Tribune 425 Portland Ave Minneapolis MN 55488-0001

SMETHERAM, HERBERT EDWIN, government official; b. Seattle, Sept. 9, 1934; s. Francis Edwin and Grace Elizabeth (Warner) S.; m. Beverly Joan Heckert, Sept. 7, 1963; children: Alice, Helen, Charles. BA, U. Wash., 1956; diploma, Naval Intelligence Sch., 1962; MA, U. Md., 1971; diploma in Swedish, U.S. Fgn. Svc. Inst., 1978; MBA, Rollins Coll., 1991. Ensign USN, 1956, advanced through grades to capt., 1976; comdr. USS Lind (DD-703), 1971-73; attache to Sweden USN, Stockholm, 1978-81; comdr. Naval Adminstrn. Command, Orlando, Fla., 1981-84; ret. USN, 1984; strategic planner electronics, info. and missiles group Martin Marietta Corp., Orlando, 1985-93; exec. dir. re-use com. Naval Tng. Ctr., Orlando, 1993—, mem. retention com., 1991-93. Mem. ARC Ctrl. Fla.; mem. steering com. U.S. Congressman McCollum for Re-election; mem. U.S. Senator Hawkins Naval Acad. Nominating Com., Orlando, 1982-86, Fla. Gov.'s Def. Reinvestment Task Force, 1992-93; mem. Ctrl. Fla. coun. USO, Orlando, 1981-93, pres., 1991-93. Decorated Royal Order of North Star (Sweden). Mem. AIAA, SAR, Electronics Industry Assn. (requirements com. 1985-93), Nat. Assn. Installation Developers (southeast regional dir. 1996—), Ret. Officers Assn., Navy League, Fla. Tennis Assn., Army Navy Country Club, Orlando Tennis Ctr., Royal Tennis Club Stockholm, Delta Kappa Epsilon. Republican. Episcopalian. Avocation: tennis. Home: 3985 Lake Mira Dr Orlando FL 32817-1643

SMETHURST, E(DWARD) WILLIAM, JR., brokerage house executive; b. Newark, Apr. 15, 1930; s. Edward William and Helen Lea (Wiener) S.; m. Ludlow Bixby, June 30, 953; children: James, Andrew, Katherine. AB, Amherst Coll., 1952; MBA, Harvard U., 1958. Credit analyst Chase Manhattan Bank, N.Y.C., 1958-60; mgr. securities Irwin Mgmt. Co., Columbus, Ind., 1961-64; ptnr. Wertheim & Co., N.Y.C., 1965-79; sr. v.p. Cyrus J. Lawrence Inc., N.Y.C., 1980-87; mng. dir. Wertheim Schroder & Co. Inc., N.Y.C., 1988-95; pres., chief investment officer Schroder Wertheim Investment Svcs., N.Y.C., 1990—; chmn., trustee Wertheim Series Trust, N.Y.C.; chmn. Ctr. Redevel. Corp., South Hadley, Mass., 1988—. Trustee Mount Holyoke Coll., South Hadley, Mass., 1982—. Lt. USN, 1952-55. Episcopalian. Home: 861 Bingham Rd Ridgewood NJ 07450-2111 Office: Wertheim Schroder & Co Inc 787 7th Ave New York NY 10019-6018

SMETHURST, ROBERT GUY, lawyer; b. Calgary, Alta., Can., May 28, 1929; s. Herbert Guy and Muriel (Wilson) S.; m. Carol Ann Higgins; children from previous marriage: Linda Anne, David Guy. Student, U. B.C., 1946-47; LL.B., U. Man., 1952. Bar: Man. 1953, created Queen's counsel 1968. Practice in Winnipeg, 1954-87; partner firm D'Arcy and Deacon (formerly D'Arcy, Irving, Haig & Smethurst), 1965-87; exec. dir. B.C. br. Can. Bar Assn., 1987—; commr. Uniform Law Conf., 1964-86, pres., 1978-79; counsel Man. Pub. Utility Bd., 1968-69; Mem. Man. Law Reform Com., 1971-80; pres. Victorian Order Nurses Can., 1976-79. Mem. Can. Bar Assn. (pres. Man. br. 1971-73), Man. Bar Assn. (pres. 1969-70), Can. Bar Ins. Assn. (pres. 1983-85), Phi Delta Theta. Office: 845 Cambie St 10th flr, Vancouver, BC Canada V6B 5T3

SMIDDY, JOSEPH CHARLES, retired college chancellor; b. Jellico, Tenn., June 20, 1920; s. Joseph F. and Sara Nan (Tye) S.; m. Reba Graham, Sept. 6, 1985; children—Joseph F., Elizabeth Lee. BA, Lincoln Meml. U., 1948, LHD, 1970; MA, Peabody Coll., 1952; LLD, U. Richmond, 1975; LHD, Coll. William and Mary, 1986; DAm, Cumberland Coll., 1993. Tchr. Jonesville High Sch., 1948-51, prin., 1951-52; sec.-treas. Powell Valley Oil Co., Big Stone Gap, Va., 1952-53; prof. biology Clinch Valley Coll., U. Va., Wise, 1953-56; dean Clinch Valley Coll., U. Va., 1956-57, dir., 1957-68, chancellor, 1968-85, chancellor emeritus, 1985—; mem. Charter Day Award Emory and Henry Coll., 1980, Commonwealth Day awrd James Madison U., 1985. Folk music performer, collector and composer. Trustee Bapt. Sem. at Richmond, Va. Served with AUS, 1942-45, PTO. Recipient Laurel Leaves award Appalachian Consortium, 1995, Kanto Ednl. award Wise County, 1995. Mem. Baptist Gen. Assn. Va. (pres. 1974—). Clubs: Masons, Shriners, Kiwanis. Home: Ridgefield Acres Wise VA 24293 Office: PO Box 3160 Wise VA 24293-3160

SMIETANA, WALTER, educational research director; b. New Bedford, Mass., Nov. 8, 1922; s. Stanislaw and Frances (Wojtal) S. AB in Edn., U. Mich., 1948; MS, Boston U., 1956, EdD, 1965; ScD (hon.), U. Mass., Dartmouth, 1975. Cert. tchr., Mich. Tchr. sci. and math. Somerset (Mass.) Pub. Schs., 1948-65; prof. edn. Elmhurst (Ill.) Coll., 1965-69; prof. edn. Alliance Coll., Cambridge Springs, Pa., 1969-87, chmn. divsn. social sci., pres., 1971-72; dir. rsch. SYLLAGENES, New Bedford, 1987—; liaison Study of Undergrad. Experience in Am., Carnegie Found. for Advancement of Teaching, Alliance Coll., 1984; participant Pa. Dept. Edn. ETS, Tchr. Cert. Test Devel., 1986-87; develop and accredite new tchr. edn. programs, state, regional and nat. levels, 1965-87; develop and evaluate year abroad and exch. programs Alliance Coll./Jagiellonian U., Cracow, Poland in coop. with U.S. Office Edn., 1969-85. Chmn. city com. Rep. Party, New Bedford, 1953-58; mem. citizens adv. com. Heritage State Park, New Bedford, 1989-93; chmn. bd. trustees Inst. Tech., New Bedford, 1963-64; chmn. adv. com. The Rsch. Found., New Bedford, 1962-64. Recipient Cert. of Merit for non-English Lang. Resources Rsch., Yeshiva U., 1981; U.S. Office Edn./ERIC grantee, 1969. Mem. World Future Soc., Inst. for Global Ethics, Nat. Space Soc., Inst. Noetic Scis., Libr. of Congress Assocs. (charter mem.). Republican. Roman Catholic. Avocations: astronomy, photography.

SMILES, RONALD, management educator; b. Sunderland, Eng., June 15, 1933; s. Andrew and Margaret (Turns) S.; m. Evelyn Lorraine Webster, Apr. 12, 1959 (div. June 1981); children: Tracy Lynn, Scott Webster, Wendy Louise; m. Linda Janet Miller, June 23, 1990. Assoc. in Bus. Adminstrn., U. Pa., 1968; BSBA, Phila. Coll. Textiles & Sci., 1969; PhD, Calif. Western U., 1977; MA, U. Tex., Arlington, 1985, PhD, 1987. V.p. Liquid Dynamics Corp., Southampton, Pa., 1968-71; pres., gen. mgr. Internat. Election Systems Corp., Burlington, N.J., 1971-76; plant mgr. Rack Engring. Co., Connellsville, Pa., 1977-80; v.p. Ft. Worth (Tex.) Houdaille, 1980-85; chmn. grad. sch. bus. Dallas Bapt. U., 1987-92, prof., 1987—, assoc. dean, 1996—. Author: Impact on Legislation of Competition in the Voting Machine Industry, 1978, A Study of Japanese Targeting Practices and U.S. Machine Tool Industry Responses, 1985, Occupational Accident Statistics: An Evaluation of Injury and Illness Incidence Rates, 1987. Mem. Burlington County (N.J.) Selective Svc. Bd., 1974-76. Served with Royal Arty., 1951-53. Mem. Greater Connellsville C. of C. (v.p. 1979-80), Night Watch Honor Soc., Sigma Kappa Phi, Alpha Delta Epsilon (award 1968). Home: 2818 Timber Hill Dr Grapevine TX 76051-6432 Office: Dallas Bapt Univ Off Dean Coll Bus Dallas TX 75211

SMILEY, D. E., petroleum company executive. JD, La. State U., 1955. Former ptnr. Sartain, McCollister & Smiley, Baton Rouge, La.; with law dept. Exxon Corp., New Orleans, 1961-66, mgr. Washington office, 1966-78, v.p. Washington office, 1978—. Office: Exxon Corp Washington Office 2001 Pennsylvania Ave NW # 300 Washington DC 20006-1850

SMILEY, JANE GRAVES, author, educator; b. L.A., Sept. 26, 1949; d. James La Verne and Frances Nuelle (Graves) S.; m. John Whiston, Sept. 4, 1970 (div.); m. William Silag, May 1, 1978 (div.); children: Phoebe Silag, Lucy Silag; m. Stephen Mark Mortensen, July 25, 1987; 1 child, Axel James Mortensen. BA, Vassar Coll., 1971; MFA, U. Iowa, 1976, MA, 1978, PhD, 1978. Asst. prof. Iowa State U., Ames, 1981-84, assoc. prof., 1984-89, prof., 1989-90, Disting. prof., 1992—; vis. asst. prof. U. Iowa, Iowa City, 1981, 87. Author: (fiction) Barn Blind, 1980, At Paradise Gate, 1981 (Friends of American Writers prize 1981), Duplicate Keys, 1984, The Age of Grief, 1987 (Nat. Book Critics Cirle award nomination 1987), The Greenlanders, 1988, Ordinary Love and Goodwill, 1989, A Thousand Acres, 1991 (Pulitzer Prize for fiction 1992, Nat. Book Critics Cirle award 1992, Midland Authors award 1992, Amb. award 1992, Heartland prize 1992), Moo: A Novel, 1995; (non-fiction) Catskill Crafts: Artisans of the Catskill Mountains, 1987. Grantee Fulbright U.S. Govt., Iceland, 1976-77, NEA, 1978, 87; recipient O. Henry award, 1982, 85, 88. Mem. Author's Guild, Screenwriters Guild. Avocations: cooking, swimming, playing piano, quilting. Office: Iowa State U Dept English 201 Ross Ames IA 50011-1401*

SMILEY, LINDA CASE, financial planner; b. Harrisburg, Pa., Sept. 10, 1958; d. Paul Willis and Olive Blanche Case; m. Edward Barton Smiley, Oct. 20, 1984; children: Danielle Elizabeth, Michelle Lynn, Noelle Elise. Student, Albright Coll., 1975-76; AA, Harrisburg (Pa.) Area C.C., 1982; BS, Elizabethtown Coll., 1989; postgrad., Lebanon Valley Coll., 1993—. CFP. Clk. Pa. Pub. Utility Commn., Harrisburg, 1977-81; nuclear chemistry tech. GPU Nuclear Corp., Middletown, Pa., 1981-89; registered rep. John Hancock, Boston, 1989-90; dist. rep. Luth. Brotherhood, Mpls., 1990-95; fin. planner Nationwide Ins. Co., Cleona, Pa., 1996—. Mem. AAUW, Nat. Assn. Fraternal Ins. Counselors, Nat. Assn. Life Underwriters, Million Dollar Round Table. Republican. Lutheran. Avocations: ballet, piano, aerobics. Home: 276 Kokomo Ave Hummelstown PA 17036-1118 Office: Nationwide Ins Co Cleona PA

SMILEY, LOGAN HENRY, journalist, public concern consulant; b. Atlanta, Feb. 1, 1926; s. Logan Smiley and Gladys (McCullum) Butcher. BA in Cinema, U. So. Calif., 1950; MS in Journalism, U. Calif., L.A., 1953. Pub. rels. dir. L.A. Open Golf Tournament, 1953-54; producer, dir., co-founder Bishop's Co., Westwood, Calif., 1953-55; producer ABC-TV, Hollywood, Calif., 1957-58; asst. producer Marlon Brando Prodns., Paramount Pictures, Hollywood, Calif., 1957-58, Paris, 1959-60; cons. L.A. C. of C., 1953-56, United Artists Corp., L.A., 1958-60, Russell Birdwell, Pub. Rels., N.Y.C. and London, 1960-64; pres. Pub. Concern Films, Ft. Lauderdale, Fla., 1990—, Nat. Comm. Assocs., Miami, also Jalapa, Mex., 1948—. Writer, columnist San Antonio Light, 1948-50; editor Art Direction Mag., 1968-70, Group Travel Mag., 1970-71; editor, assoc. pub. CLIO Mag., 1968-74, Musical Am. Mag., 1964-66; editor, designer New Spirit Mag. of Social Svc., 1978-80. Mem. Fla. press corps Jimmy Carter for Pres., Atlanta, 1976; chmn. So. Fla. Jerry Brown for Pres., Miami, 1992. With USNR, 1943-45. Recipient Barnett Peace prize Southwestern U., 1944, scholarship S.W. State Tchrs. Coll., 1943, 1st place award Tex. Secondary Sch. System, 1943. Democrat. Avocations: art and book collector, journal/diary writing. Home: 18301 NE 11th Ave Miami FL 33179-4606 Office: Nat Comms Assn PO Box 600495 Miami FL 33164-0220

SMILEY, MARILYNN JEAN, musicologist; b. Columbia City, Ind., June 5, 1932; d. Orla Raymond and Mary Jane (Bailey) S. BS (State scholar), Ball State U., 1954; MusM, Northwestern U., 1958; cert., Ecoles d'Art Americaines, Fontainebleau, France, 1959; Ph.D. (Grad. scholar, Delta Kampa Gamma scholar), U. Ill., 1970. Public sch. music tchr. Logansport, Ind., 1954-61; faculty music dept. SUNY-Oswego, 1961—, Disting. Teaching prof., 1974—, chmn. dept., 1976-81; presenter papers at confs. Contbr. articles to profl. jours. Bd. dirs. Oswego Opera Theatre, 1978—, Oswego Orch. Soc., 1978—, Penfield Libr. Assocs., 1985—. SUNY Research Found. fellow, summers 1971, 72, 74. Mem. AAUW (br. coun. rep. dist. III, N.Y. State div. 1986-88, br. coun. coord. N.Y. State div. 1988-90, pres. Oswego br. 1984-86, N.Y. divsn. area interest rep. cultural interests 1990-92, grantee 1984, N.Y. divsn. diversity dir. 1993—), NEH (rsch. grantee 1990-91), Am. Musicological Soc. (chmn. N.Y. chpt. 1975-77, chpt. rep. to AMS Coun. 1993—, bd. dirs. N.Y. State-St. Lawrence chpt. 1993—), Medieval Acad. Am., Music Libr. Assn., Coll. Music Soc., Renaissance Soc. Am., Sonneck Soc. Am., Oswego County Hist. Soc., Heritage Found. of Oswego, Delta Kappa Gamma, Phi Delta Kappa, Delta Phi Alpha, Pi Kappa Lambda, Sigma Alpha Iota, Sigma Tau Delta, Kappa Delta Pi. Methodist. Office: SUNY Dept Music Oswego NY 13126

SMILEY, RICHARD WAYNE, research center administrator, researcher; b. Paso Robles, Calif., Aug. 17, 1943; s. Cecil Wallace and Elenore Louise (Hamm) S.; m. Marilyn Lois Wenning, June 24, 1967; 1 child, Shawn Elizabeth. BSc in Soil Sci., Calif. State Poly. U., San Luis Obispo, 1965; MSc in Soils, Wash. State U., 1969, PhD in Plant Pathology, 1972. Asst. soil scientist Agrl. Rsch. Svc., USDA, Pullman, Wash., 1966-69; rsch. asst. dept. plant pathology Wash. State U., Pullman, 1969-72; soil microbiologist Commonwealth Sci. and Indsl. Rsch. Orgn., Adelaide, Australia, 1972-73; rsch. assoc. dept. plant pathology Cornell U., Ithaca, N.Y., 1973-74, asst. prof., 1975-80, assoc. prof., 1980-85; supt. Columbia Basin Agr. Rsch. Ctr., prof. Oreg. State U., Pendleton, 1985—; vis. scientist Plant Rsch. Inst., Victoria Dept. Agr., Melbourne, Australia, 1982-83. Author: Compendium of Turfgrass Diseases, 1983, 2d edit., 1992; contbr. more than 200 articles to profl. jours.; author slide set illustrating diseases of turfgrasses. Postdoctoral fellow NATO, 1972. Fellow Am. Phytopath. Soc. (sr. editor APS Press 1984-87, editor-in-chief 1987-91); mem. Am. Soc. Agronomy, Internat. Turfgrass Soc., Am. Sod Producers Assn. (hon. life), Coun. Agrl. Sci. and Tech., Rotary (pres. Pendleton chpt. 1991-92, Paul Harris fellow 1993). Achievements include discovery of the etiology of a serious disease of turfgrasses, which led to a redefinition of studies and disease processes in turfgrasses. Office: Oreg State U Columbia Basin Agr Rsch Ctr PO Box 370 Pendleton OR 97801-0370

SMILEY, ROBERT HERSCHEL, university dean; b. Scottsbluff, Nebr., Mar. 17, 1943; s. Eldridge Herschel and Lucile Agnes (Kolterman) S., m. Sandra P. Mason (div. 1975); children: Peter, Michael, Robin; m. JoAnn Charlene Cannon, June 3, 1978; 1 child, Matthew. BS, UCLA, 1966, MS, 1969; PhD, Stanford U., 1973. Sr. aerospace engr. Martin Marietta Co., Littleton, Colo., 1966-67; mem. tech. staff, engr. Hughes Aircraft Co., Culver City, Calif., 1967-69; prof. econs. and policy, assoc. dean Grad. Sch. Mgmt. Cornell U., Ithaca, N.Y., 1973-89; dean, prof. mgmt. Grad. Sch. Mgmt. U. Calif., Davis, 1989—; econ. cons. IBM, GM, Amex, SBA, Air Transport Assn., others; mem. rsch. adv. bd. NFIB, 1988—, policy adv. com. Ctr. for Coops., Davis, 1989—, adv. bd. Tech. Devel. Ctr., Davis, 1990—. Editor Sinergie, 1984—, Small Bus. Econs., 1988—; mem. editorial bd. Comstock's Mag., 1989—; contbr. articles to econs. and mgmt. jours. Bd. dirs. Sacramento Valley Forum, 1990—, Japan-Am. Conf., Sacramento, 1991—; chair sponsors com. Access '91, Sacramento, 1991; bd. govs. Capitol Club. SBA grantee, DOE grantee. Mem. Am. Econs. Assn., European Assn. for Rsch., Western Econs. Assn., Beta Gamma Sigma, Capitol Club. Avocations: skiing, tennis, swimming, biking. Office: U Calif-Davis Dept Grad Sch Mgmt Davis CA 95616-8609

SMILEY, ROBERT WILLIAM, industrial engineer; b. Phila., Oct. 18, 1919; s. Albert James and Laura Emma (Hoiler) S.; children from previous marriage: Robert, James, Lauralee, Mary; m. Gloria Morais, Jun. 30, 1990; stepchildren: Deborah, Sheila, Vicki, James, Sonja, Michelle. Certificate in Indsl. Engring, Gen. Motors Inst., 1942; student, U. Rochester, 1948;

student mgmt. program for execs., U. Pitts. Grad. Sch. Bus., 1968; student, San Jose State Coll., 1969; BSBA, Coll. Notre Dame, Belmont, Calif., 1972, MBA, 1974. Registered profl. engr., Calif. With A.S. Hamilton (cons. engrs.), Rochester, N.Y., 1946-48; commd. lt. comdr. USN, 1952, advanced through grades to comdr., 1960; engaged in tech. contract mgmt. (Poseidon/Polaris and Terrier Missile Programs), 1952-64; officer in charge (Polaris Missile Facility Pacific), Bremerton, Wash., 1964-66; resigned, 1966; mgr. product assurance Missile Systems div. Lockheed Missiles and Space Co., Sunnyvale, Calif., 1966-72; mgr. materiel Missile Systems div. Lockheed Missiles and Space Co., 1972-77; mgr. product assurance McDonnell Douglas Astronautics, 1977-78; dir. product assurance Aerojet Tactical Systems, Sacramento, 1978-83; dir. quality assurance Aerojet Solid Propulsion Co., Sacramento, 1984-92, Tahoe Surg. Instruments, Inc., 1992—; frequent guest lectr. at colls. on quality control and reliability; chmn. Polaris/Minuteman/Pershing Missile Nondestruct Test Com., 1958-64; quality control cons. Dragon Missile Program, U.S. Army, 1971. Contbr. articles to sci. jours., chpt. to Reliability Handbook, 1966, Reliability Engineering and Management, 1988. Docent Calif. State Railroad and Mus., 1994—; chmn. sec. chpt. svc. Corps Retired Exec., 1992, dist. mgr., 1995. With USNR, 1942-46, 51-52; now capt. ret. Recipient letters of Commendation for work on Polaris/Poseidon Sec. of Navy, 1960, certificate of Honor Soc. for Nondestructive Testing, 1966. Fellow Am. Soc. Quality Control (chmn. San Francisco sect. 1969-70, exec. bd. 1966—, chmn. reliability divsn. 1971, 81, nat. v.p. 1984-85; mem. SCORE (chmn. Sacramento chpt. 1993—), Aircraft Industries Assn. (chmn. quality assurance com.), Navy League, AAAS, Am. Mgmt. Assn. Home and Office: 9144 Green Ravine Ln Fair Oaks CA 95628-4110 *A man can consider himself successful only if he leaves the world better than he found it partly through his efforts.*

SMILEY, ROBERT WILLIAM, JR., investment banker; b. Lansing, Mich., Nov. 17, 1943; s. Robert William Sr. and Rebecca Lee (Flint) S. AB in Econs., Stanford U., 1970; postgrad., San Fernando Valley Coll. Law, 1973-75; MBA in Corp. Fin., City U. Los Angeles, 1979; LLB, LaSalle U., 1982. Bar: Calif. 1984. Sr. v.p. mktg. Actuarial Systems Inc., San Jose, Calif., 1972-73; founder, chmn. Benefit Systems Inc., L.A., and SE Nev., 1973-84, Brentwood Square Savs. and Loan, Los Angeles, 1982-84; chmn., CEO The Benefit Capital Cos. Inc., L.A. and S.E. Nev., 1984—; lectr. U. Calif. Extension, Los Angeles and Berkeley, 1977—; instr. Am. Coll. Life Underwriters. Editor, contbg. author: Employee Stock Ownership Plans: Business Planning, Implementation, Law and Taxation, 1989—; contbg. author: The Handbook of Employee Benefits, 1984, 4th edit., 1996; contbr. articles to profl. jours. Mem. nat. adv. coun., trustee Reason Found., Santa Monica, Calif., 1983-91; bd. dirs. Nat. Ctr. for Employee Ownership, Oakland, Calif. With USN, 1961-64, Vietnam. Recipient Spl. Achievement award Pres.' Commn. on Pension Policy, 1984. Fellow Life Mgmt. Inst.; mem. Employee Stock Ownership Plan Assn. (founder, pres., bd. dirs., lifetime dir.), Assn. for Corp. Growth, Western and SW Pension Confs., Nat. Assn. Bus. Economists, ABA, Calif. Bar Assn. Office: The Benefit Capital Cos Inc PO Box 542 Logandale NV 89021-0542

SMILLIE, THOMSON JOHN, opera producer; b. Glasgow, Scotland, Sept. 29, 1942; s. John Baird and Mary (Thomson) S.; m. Anne Ivy Pringle, July 14, 1965; children: Jane, Jonathan, Julia, David. MA, Glasgow U., 1963. Dir. pub. rels. Scottish Opera, 1966-78; artistic dir. Wexford Festival, Ireland, 1973-78; gen. mgr. Opera Co., Boston, 1978-80; gen. dir. Ky. Opera, Louisville, 1981—. Contbr. articles to various publs. Avocations: reading, collecting antiques. Home: 4701 Kitty Hawk Way Louisville KY 40207-1752

SMIRNI, ALLAN DESMOND, lawyer; b. N.Y.C., Aug. 27, 1939; s. Donald W. and Ruby M. (King) S.; 1 child, Amie Joy. BA, CUNY, 1960; JD, U. Calif., Berkeley, 1971. Bar: Calif. 1972, U.S. Dist. Ct. (no. dist.) Calif. 1972, U.S. Ct. Appeals (9th cir.) 1972. Assoc. Brobeck, Phleger & Harrison, San Francisco, 1971-74; asst. gen. counsel Envirotech Corp., Menlo Park, Calif., 1975-81; chief counsel sec. Televideo Systems, Inc., Sunnyvale, Calif., 1982-86; v.p., gen. counsel, sec. Memorex Corp., Santa Clara, Calif., 1987-89, Pyramid Tech. Corp., San Jose, Calif., 1989—. Adv. bd. dirs. Social Advocates for Youth, Cupertino, Calif., 1985—. Capt. USAF, 1961-67. Mem. Am. Corp. Counsel Assn., Am. Soc. Corp. Secs., Charles Houston Bar Assn. Roman Catholic. Avocations: reading, walking, movies, theatre. Home: 1363 Lennox Way Sunnyvale CA 94087-3129 Office: Pyramid Tech Corp 3860 N 1st St San Jose CA 95134-1702

SMIRNIOTIS, PANAGIOTIS GEORGE, chemical engineering educator; b. Egion, Greece, May 28; came to U.S., 1989; s. George and Efthalia (Gana) S. BS, U. Patras (Greece), 1989; PhD, SUNY, Buffalo, 1994. Rsch. assoc. Aluminium of Greece, Greece, 1987; rsch. asst. chem. engring. dept. U. Patras, Patras, 1987-89; tchg. asst., rsch. asst. chem. engring. dept. U. SUNY, Buffalo, 1989-94; prof. engring. U. Cin., Cin., 1994—. Contbr. 22 articles to profl. jours. Mem. AIChE, Air & Waste Mgmt. Assn., Am. Chem. Soc., Soc. Petroleum Engrs. Avocations: volleyball, swimming, dancing. Office: U Cin Dept Chem Engring 697 Rhodes Hall Cincinnati OH 45221-0171

SMISKO, NICHOLAS RICHARD, bishop, educator; b. Perth Amboy, N.J., Feb. 23, 1936; s. Andrew and Anna (Totin) S. BTh, Christ the Saviour Sem., 1959; BA, U. Youngstown, 1961; Lic. in Theology, Halki (Greece) Sch. Theology, 1965. Ordained priest Carpatho-Russian Orthodox Greek Cath. Ch., 1959. Pastorate Sts. Peter and Paul Ch., Windber, Pa., 1959-62; prefect of discipline Christ the Saviour Sem., Johnstown, Pa., 1963-65; pastor Sts. Peter and Paul Ch., Homer City, Pa., 1965-71, St. Michael's Ch., Clymer, Pa., 1971-72; pastorate St. Nicholas Ch., N.Y.C., 1972-77; abbot Monastery of the Annunciation, Tuxedo Park, N.Y., 1978-83; bishop of Amissos Carpatho-Russian Orthodox Diocese, 1983—; mem. del. Ecumenical Patriarchate World Coun. Chs. 6th Gen. Assembly, Vancouver, B.C., Can.; mem. standing conf. Canonical Orthodox Bishops in Ams.; active Orthodox-Cath. Consultation of Hierarchs. Mem. Halki Alumni Assn. Am., Christ the Saviour Sem. Alumni Assn., Am. Soc. Constantinople. Home and Office: 312 Garfield St Johnstown PA 15906

SMISKO, RICHARD G. See NICHOLAS

SMIT, HANS, law educator, academic administrator, lawyer; b. Amsterdam, Netherlands, Aug. 13, 1927; came to U.S. 1952; s. Eylard Albertus and Trijntje (de Jong) S.; m. Beverly M. Gershgol, Aug. 1, 1954; children: Robert Hugh, Marion Tina. LLB with highest honors, U. Amsterdam, 1946, JD with highest honors, 1949; AM, Columbia U., 1953, LLB with highest honors, 1958; D. (hon.), U. Paris I, 1991. Bar: Supreme Ct. Netherlands 1946, N.Y. 1974. Ptnr. Bodenhausen, Blackstone, Rueb, Bloemsma & Smit, The Hague, 1952-58; assoc. Sullivan & Cromwell, N.Y.C., 1958-60; mem. faculty law Columbia U., N.Y.C., 1960—, assoc. prof., 1960-62, prof., 1962—, Stanley H. Fuld prof. law, 1978—; dir. Parker Sch. Fgn. and Comparative Law; vis. prof. U. Paris, Sorbonne-Pantheon, 1975-76, 89-90, 92-94; dir. Project on Internat. Proc., Columbia U.; reporter U.S. Com. on Internat. Rules Jud. Procedure, 1960-67; bd. dirs. Project on European Legal Inst., 1968, Leyden-Amsterdam-Columbia Summer Program in Am. Law; cons. internat. comml. transactions, internat. litig.; arbitrator ICC and AAA. Author: International Co-operation in Litigation, 1963, (with others) Elements of Civil Procedure, 5th edit., 1985, International Law, 3d edit., 1993, (with Pechota) World Arbitration Reporter, 1986, (with Herzog) The Law of the European Community, 1978; editor-in-chief Am. Rev. of International. Arbitration. Mem. All-Dutch Waterpolo team 1946-48, All-Am. Waterpolo team, AAU, 1954. Knight Order of Netherlands Lion, 1987. Mem. ABA, Internat. Bar Assn., Am. Fgn. Law Assn., Assn. of Bar of City of N.Y., Am. Soc. Internat. Law, German-Am. Lawyers' Assn., Internat. Assn. Jurists of U.S.A.-Italy, Internat. Acad. Comparative Law, Royal Dutch Soc. Arts and Scis. (assoc.), Am. Arbitration Assn., Internat. C. of C. Home: 351 Riverside Dr New York NY 10025-2739 Office: Columbia U Sch Law 435 W 116th St New York NY 10027-7201

SMITH, A. ROBERT, editor, author; b. York, Pa., Feb. 13, 1925; s. Arthur R. and Inez (Dunnick) S.; m. Yvonne Franklin, 1945 (div. 1965); 1 child, Dana C.; m. Elizabeth McDowell Morgan, 1967 (div. 1988); children: Philip S. Morgan IV, Edward A. M. Morgan, Elizabeth A. Morgan; m. Jane Dreifus, 1993. BS, Juniata Coll., 1950; postgrad., George Washington U., 1950. Reporter Huntingdon (Pa.) Daily News, 1947, Evening Star, Washington, 1950; Washington corr. Eugene (Oreg.) Register-Guard, 1951-78, Portland Oregonian, 1952-72, King Broadcasting, 1976-78; assoc. editor Virginian-Pilot, Norfolk, 1978-83; editor Venture Inward, Assn. Rsch. and Enlightenment mag., Virginia Beach, Va., 1984—. Author: The Tiger in the Senate, 1962, Hugh Lynn Cayce: About My Father's Business, 1988; co-author: (with Eric Sevareid and Fred J. Maroon) Washington: Magnificent Capital, 1965, (with James V. Giles) An American Rape, 1975. With USNR, 1943-46, PTO. Office: ARE 67th And Atlantic Ave Virginia Beach VA 23451

SMITH, AARON, health researcher, clinical psychologist; b. Boston, Nov. 3, 1930; s. Harry and Anne (Gilgoff) S.; m. Sept. 7, 1952 (div.); children—Naomi E., Jeffrey O., David G., Andrew H.; m. D. Sharon Casey, Jan. 7, 1972. A.B., Brown U., 1952; Ph.D., U. Ill., 1958. Co-dir., Northeast Psychol. Clinic, Phila., 1959-75; dir. research Haverford State Hosp., Pa., 1962-73, asst. hosp. dir., 1973-75; assoc. rsch. prof. U. Nev., Reno, 1975—; dir. rsch VA Med. Ctr., Reno, 1975—; exec. dir. Sierra Biomedical Rsch. Corp., 1989—; chmn. Nev. Legislature Mental Health Task Force, Carson City, 1978; sci. adviser Gov.'s Com. on Radiation Effects, Carson City, 1979-82. Co-author: Anti-depressant Drug Studies 1956-66, 1969; Medications and Emotional Illness, 1976; co-editor: Goal Attainment Sealing: Application, Theory, and Measurement, 1994; contbr. chpts. to books and articles to profl. jours. Grantee Squibb Inst. Med. Research, 1965-69, NIMH, 1965-69, Smith Kline & French Labs., 1968-69, VA Health Services Research, 1976-93. Mem. Am. Psychol. Assn., Western Psychol. Assn., Gerontol. Soc. Am., Assn. Health Svcs. Rsch. Home: 12790 Roseview Ln Reno NV 89511-8671 Office: VA Med Ctr 1000 Locust St Reno NV 89520-0102

SMITH, ADA L., state legislator; b. Amherst County, Va., Apr. 18, 1945; d. Thomas and Lillian Smith. Grad., CUNY. Dep. clk. N.Y.C.; state senator N.Y. Legislature, Albany, 1988—; mem. various coms. N.Y. Legislature, ranking corp. commn. and authorities, 1994, minority whip; mem. Senate Dem. Task Force Women's Issues, Senate Dem. Task Force Financing Affordable Housing, Senate Dem. Task Force Child Care 2000, Sen. Dem. Task Force Affirmative Action and Econ. Devel., Senate Dem. Task Force Primary Health Care, Senate Minority Puerto Rican and Hispanic Task Force; chair Senate Minority Task Force on Privatization of Kennedy and Laguardia Airports. Trustee, life dir. Coll. Fund Baruch Coll. Recipient Outstanding Alumni award Baruch Coll. Mem. African Am. Clergy and Elected Ofcls., Inc. (treas.), N.Y. Assn. of State Black and Puerto Rican Legislators (vice chair), Baruch Coll. Alumni Assn. (pres., Disting. Svc. award, Outstanding Achievement award). Home: 67 Manhattan Ave Brooklyn NY 11206-3156 Office: NY State Senate Rm 304 Legis Office Bldg Albany NY 12247 also: Queens Dist Office 116-43 Sutphin Blvd Jamaica NY 11436

SMITH, ADAM See GOODMAN, GEORGE JEROME WALDO

SMITH, ADRIAN DEVAUN, architect; b. Chgo., Aug. 19, 1944; s. Alfred D. and Hazel (Davis) S.; m. Nancy L. Smith, Aug. 17, 1968; children: Katherine, Jason. Student, Tex. A&M U., 1962-66; B.Arch., U. Ill., Chgo., 1969. Registered architect Ill., Ohio, N.J., N.Y., Mass., Iowa, Md., Conn., D.C., Fla., Ind., Mo., R.I., Tex. Design ptnr. Skidmore, Owings, & Merrill, Chgo., 1967—, ptnr., 1980—, CEO, 1994—; vis. faculty Sch. Architecture, U. Ill., Chgo., 1984; chmn. Senator Richard A. Newhouse Bldg. Competition Jury, 1982, U. Ill. Sch. Archtl. Alumni Assn., AIA Jury on Inst. Honors; chmn. Skidmore Owings Merrill Found.; mem. Chgo. Ctrl. Area; recipient U. Ill. Alumni Achievement award. cons. and lectr. in field. Designer numerous projects including Jin Mao Tower (World's Tallest Mixed-Use Project), Shanghai, China, Banco de Occidente, Guatemala City (CCAIA Interior Architecture award 1981, NAIA Honor award 1982), Three 1st Nat. Bank Chgo. (CCAIA Lighting Soc. award 1984), United Gulf Bank, Manama, Bahrain (Progressive Architecture award 1984, CCAIA Disting. Bldg. award 1988, NAIA Honor award 1988, CCAIA Disting. Detail Honor award 1989), 222 N. LaSalle, Chgo. (Disting Bldg. award CCAIA 1988), Art Inst. Chgo. 2d Fl. Galleries (CCAIA Disting. Bldg. award 1987), Rowes Wharf, Boston (Build Am. award 1988, Build Mass. award 1989, ULI award 1989, PCI Profl. Design award 1989, CCAIA Hon. award 1990, Nat. AIA Honor award 1994), AT&T Corp. Ctr., Chgo. (recipient Gold Metal Ill. Ind. Masonry award), NBC Tower (Chgo. Sun Times Bldg. of Yr. award 1989, CCAIA Disting. Bldg. award 1990, PCI Design award 1989), 75 State St., Boston (Archtl. Woodwork Inst. award 1989, Nat. Comml. Builder's Coun. Merit award 1990, Bldg. Stone Inst. Tucker Archtl. award 1990), Arthur Anderson Training Ctr. (Masonry award 1988), St. Charles, Ill., USG Hdqs., Chgo., Heller Internat. Tower, Chgo., designer numerous other fgn. projects including: Monterey Cultural Ctr., Mex., 1978; hdqrs. Banco de Occidente, Guatemala City, 1978 (AIA Nat. Honor award, Bus. Interior Design award Guatemala 1981, CCAIA Interior Architecture award 1982, NAIA Honor award), Canary Wharf Fin. Ctr., London, Eng., 1988, 10 Ludgate (CCAIA 1994 Honor award), 100 Ludgate, London, 1992, Aramco Hdqs. Dhahrain Saudi Arabia, Shanghai China, 1994; contbr. articles to profl jours.; subject numerous publs. in architecture. Mem. com. Task Force for New City Plan, Chgo., Light Up Chgo., Cen. Area Com. Task Force, Chgo.; chmn. Senator Richard A. Newhouse Bldg. Competition Jury, 1982, Progressive Architecture Design Jury, 1985. Fellow AIA (mem. Young Architects Award Design Jury, 1987, Mich. Jury 1988, Disting. Bldg. award 1990), Royal Inst. Brit. Architects, Archtl. Registration Coun. U.K., Nat. Coun. Archtl. Registration Bds., Architecture Soc. of Art Inst. Chgo., Chgo. Arch. Found. (bd. dirs.), Chgo. Archtl. Club, Urban Land Inst. (bd. dirs.), University Club, Arts Club. Home: 1100 W Summerfield Dr Lake Forest IL 60045-1545 Office: Skidmore Owings & Merrill 224 S Michigan Ave Ste 1000 Chicago IL 60604-2507

SMITH, AL FREDERICK, professional football player; b. Los Angeles, Calif., Nov. 26, 1964. Student, Calif. State Polytech., Pomona; BS in Sociology, Utah State, 1987. Linebacker Houston Oilers, 1987—. Played in Pro Bowl, 1991-92. Office: Houston Oilers 6910 Fannin St Fl 3 Houston TX 77030-3806

SMITH, ALAN JAY, computer science educator, consultant; b. N.Y.C., Apr. 10, 1949; s. Harry and Elsie (Mark) S. SB, MIT, 1971; MS, Stanford (Calif.) U., 1973, PhD in Computer Sci., 1974. From asst. prof. to full prof. U. Calif., Berkeley, 1974—; assoc. editor ACM Trans. on Computers Systems, 1982-93; vice-chmn. elec. engring. & computer sci. dept. U. Calif., Berkeley, 1982-84; nat. lectr. ACM, 1985-86; mem. editorial bd. Jour. Microprocessors and Microsystems, 1988—; subject area editor Jour. Parallel and Distbn. Computing, 1989—; mem. IFIP working group 7.3. Fellow IEEE (disting. visitor 1986-87); mem. Assn. for Computing Machinery (chmn. spl. interest group on computer architecture 1991-93, chmn. spl. interest group on ops. systems 1983-87, bd. dirs. spl. interest group on performance evaluation 1985-89, bd. dirs. spl. interest group on computer architecture 1993—), Computer Measurement Group. Office: U Calif Dept of Computer Sci Berkeley CA 94720

SMITH, ALAN W., JR., management consultant; b. Pensacola, Fla., Nov. 16, 1943; s. Alan W. and Eleanor C. (Handy) S.; m. Mary Arthur, June 12, 1965 (div. May 1978); children: Alison, Andrew; m. Patricia A. Waterfield, May 26, 1979; children: Amy, Cary. AB, Harvard U., 1965. Personnel rep. John Hancock, Boston, 1966-68; cons. Cole & Assocs. Inc., Boston, 1968-72; exec. v.p. Cole Surveys Inc., Boston, 1972-79; v.p. The Wyatt Co., San Francisco, 1979—. Contbr. articles to profl. jours. Mem. Am. Compensation Assn., Western Pension Conf. Avocations: music, photography. Office: The Wyatt Co 601 13th St NW Ste 1000 Washington DC 20005-3807*

SMITH, ALBERT ALOYSIUS, JR., electrical engineer, consultant; b. Yonkers, N.Y., Dec. 2, 1935; s. Albert Aloysius and Jean Mary (Misiewicz) S.; B.S.E.E., Milw. Sch. Engring., 1961; M.S.E.E., N.Y.U., 1964; m. Rosemarie Tricarelli, Apr. 4, 1964 (dec. 1982); children—Denise, Matthew. Staff engr. Adler/Westrex, New Rochelle, N.Y., 1961-64; adv. engr. IBM, Kingston, N.Y., 1964-78, sr. engr., Poughkeepsie, N.Y., 1978-85, Kingston, N.Y., 1985-91; cons., 1991—. Com. chmn. Woodstock Boy Scout Troup 34, 1978-79; com. chmn. Woodstock Cub Pack 34, 1976-78. Served with USN, 1953-56. Recipient Outstanding Alumnus award Milw. Sch. Engring., 1981. Invention Achievement awards IBM, 1979, 90, Div. award, 1981. Fellow IEEE (tech. com. on electromagnetic environments, assoc. editor Trans. on EMC); mem. Am. Nat. Standards Com. Roman Catholic. Author: Coupling of External Electromagnetic Fields to Transmission Lines, 1977; Measuring the Radio Frequency Environment, 1985. Home: 11 Streamside Ter Woodstock NY 12498-1521

SMITH, ALBERT CHARLES, biologist, educator; b. Springfield, Mass., Apr. 5, 1906; s. Henry Joseph and Jeanette Rose (Machol) S.; m. Nina Grönstrand, June 15, 1935; children: Katherine (Mrs. L. J. Campbell), Michael Alexis; m. Emma van Ginneken, Aug. 1, 1966. AB, Columbia U., 1926, PhD, 1933. Asst. curator N.Y. Bot. Garden, 1928-31, asso. curator, 1931-40; curator herbarium Arnold Arboretum of Harvard U., 1940-48; curator div. phanerogams U.S. Nat. Mus., Smithsonian Instn., 1948-56; program dir. systematic biology NSF, 1956-58; dir. Mus. of Natural History, Smithsonian Instn., 1958-62, asst. sec., 1962-63; prof. botany, dir. research U. Hawaii, Honolulu, 1963-65; Gerrit Parmile Wilder prof. botany U. Hawaii, 1965-70, prof. emeritus, 1970—; Ray Ethan Torrey prof. botany U. Mass., Amherst, 1970-76; prof. emeritus U. Mass., 1976—; editorial cons. Nat. Tropical Bot. Garden, Hawaii, 1977-91; bot. expdns., Colombia, Peru, Brazil, Brit. Guiana, Fiji, West Indies, 1926-69; del. Internat. Bot. Congresses, Amsterdam, 1935, Stockholm, 1950; v.p. systematic sect., Montreal, 1959, Internat. Zool. Congress, London, 1958; pres. Am. Soc. Plant Taxonomists, 1955, Bot. Soc. Washington, 1962, Biol. Soc. Washington, 1962-64, Hawaiian Bot. Soc., 1967. Author: Flora Vitiensis Nova: a New Flora of Fiji, Vol. I, 1979, Vol. II, 1981, Vol. III, 1985, Vol. IV, 1988, Vol. V, 1991; also tech. articles; Editor: Brittonia, 1935-40, Jour. Arnold Arboretum, 1941-48, Sargentia, 1942-48, Allertonia, 1977-88; editorial com.: International Code Botanical Nomenclature, 1954-64. Recipient Robert Allerton award for excellence in tropical botany, 1979, Asa Gray award Am. Soc. Plant Taxonomists, 1992, Charles Reed Bishop medal, 1995; Bishop Mus. fellow Yale U., 1933-34, Guggenheim fellow, 1946-47. Fellow Am. Acad. Arts and Scis.; mem. NAS, Bot. Soc. Am. (Merit award 1970), Assn. Tropical Biology (pres. 1967-68), Internat. Assn. Plant Taxonomy (v.p. 1959-64), Fiji Soc. (hon.), Washington Biologists' Field Club (pres. 1962-64). Home: 2474 Aha Aina Pl Honolulu HI 96821-1048

SMITH, ALEXANDER JOHN COURT, insurance executive; b. Glasgow, Scotland, Apr. 13, 1934; s. John Court and Mary Walker (Anderson) S.; m. Margaret Gillespie, Oct. 15, 1968. Student, Scottish schs. Actuarial trainee Scottish Mut. Ins. Co., Glasgow, 1957; asst. actuary Zurich Life Ins. Co., Toronto, Can., 1958-61; from actuary to exec. v.p. William M. Mercer Ltd., Toronto, 1961-74; pres. William M. Mercer, Inc., Toronto, 1974-82; sr. v.p., dir. Marsh & McLennan, Inc., N.Y.C., 1974-78; group v.p. Marsh & McLennan Cos. Cons. and Fin. Svcs. Group, N.Y.C., 1982-84, pres., 1984-85; vice chmn. Marsh & McLennan Cos., N.Y.C., 1984-86, pres., 1986-92, chmn., CEO, 1992—. Trustee The Putnam Funds, 1986—, Cen. Park Conservancy, 1988—, Carnegie Hall Soc., 1992—. Fellow Faculty Actuaries Edinburgh, Can. Inst. Actuaries, Conf. Cons. Actuaries; mem. Soc. Actuaries (assoc.), Am. Acad. Actuaries, Internat. Congress Actuaries, Internat. Assn. Cons. Actuaries, Racquet and Tennis Club, Royal Can. Yacht Club, Apawamis Club, Caledonian Club, Blind Brook Club Inc. Home: 630 Park Ave New York NY 10021-6544 Office: Marsh & McLennan Cos Inc 1166 Ave of the Americas New York NY 10036-2708

SMITH, ALEXANDER WYLY, JR., lawyer; b. Atlanta, June 9, 1923; s. Alexander Wyly and Laura (Payne) S.; m. Betty Rawson Haverty, Aug. 31, 1946; children—Elizabeth Smith Crew, Clarence Haverty, Laura Smith Brown, James Haverty, Edward Kendrick, Anthony Marion, William Rawson. Grad., Marist Sch., 1941; student, Holy Cross Coll., 1941-42; B.B.A., U. Ga., 1947, LL.B. cum laude, 1949. Bar: Ga. 1948. Practiced in Atlanta, 1948—; ptnr. Smith, Gambrell & Russell and predecessor, 1949-94; ret., 1994. Bd. dirs. Our Lady of Perpetual Help Free Cancer Home; bd. dirs., planning and devel. coun. Cath. Archdiocese Atlanta, Marist Sch., Atlanta, John and Mary Franklin Found. Served with USAAF, 1943-46. Mem. Ga. Bar Assn., Atlanta Bar Assn., Phi Delta Phi, Chi Phi, Piedmont Driving Club Atlanta, Peachtree Golf Club Atlanta (pres. 1989-91). Clubs: Piedmont Driving (Atlanta), Peachtree Golf (Atlanta) (pres. 1989-91). Home: 158 W Wesley Rd NW Atlanta GA 30305-3523 Office: 300 Promenade II 1230 Peachtree St NE Atlanta GA 30309-3575

SMITH, ALEXIS, artist, educator; b. L.A., Aug. 24, 1949; d. Dayrel Driver and Lucille Lloyd (Doak) Smith; m. Scott Grieger, June 11, 1990. BA in Art, U. Calif., Irvine, 1970. Teaching position Calif. Inst. Arts, 1975, 96; teaching position U. Calif., Irvine, 1976, San Diego, 1977-78; teaching position UCLA, 1979-82, 85-88, Skowhegan (Maine) Sch. Painting and Sculpture, 1990, So. Meth. U., 1993; vis. artist and lectr. in field. One person exhbns. include Whitney Mus. Am. Art, N.Y.C., 1975, Nicholas Wilder Gallery, L.A., 1977, Holly Solomon Gallery, N.Y.C., 1977, 78, 79, 81, Walker Art Ctr., Mpls., 1986, Bklyn. Mus., 1987-88, Margo Leavin Gallery, L.A., 1982, 85, 88, 90, 93, 94, 95, Retrospective Whitney Mus. Am. Art, N.Y.C., 1991, MOCA, L.A., 1991-92, Gerald Peters Gallery, Dallas, 1995; exhibited in group shows at Pasadena (Calif.) Mus. Modern Art, Whitney Mus. Am. Art, Musee d'art Moderne, Paris, Inst. Contemporary Art, Boston, Contemporary Arts Mus., Houston, Hirshhorn Mus. and Sculpture Garden, Washington, Mus. Contemporary Art, Chgo., Los Angeles County Mus. Art, UCLA, Getty Ctr for History of Art and Humanities, Santa Monica, Calif., others; numerous commns. including The Stuart Collection U. Calif., San Diego, terazzo floor designs for L.A. Conv. Ctr. Expansion Project; subject of numerous articles. Trustee Beyond Baroque Lit. Arts Ctr., 1990-95; bd. govs. Skowhegan Sch., 1990-93; mem. artist adv. coun. L.A. Mus. Contemporary Art, 1979—. Recipient New Talent award Los Angeles County Mus. Art, 1974; Nat. Endowment for the Arts grantee, 1976, 87. Office: Margo Leavin Gallery 812 N Robertson Blvd Los Angeles CA 90069

SMITH, ALFRED EUGENE, educational administrator; b. Birmingham, Ala., Nov. 23, 1952; s. Elves Joe Japher and Lucinda (Banks) S.; m. Sharon Lenette Murray, Mar. 2, 1973; children: Amaya Ytesia, Adric Romell. AD, Rutherford Coll., 1972; BS, Dallas Bapt. U., 1985; MEd, East Tex. State U., 1992. Tchr. Lobias Murray Christian Acad., Dallas, 1984-91, adminstr., 1991—. Avocations: painting, horseback riding, computers. Office: Lobias Murray Christian Acad 330 E Ann Arbor Ave Dallas TX 75216-6717

SMITH, ALFRED GOUD, anthropologist, educator; b. The Hague, Netherlands, Aug. 20, 1921; s. William G. and Joan (Wraslouski) S.; m. Britta Helen Bonazzi, May 30, 1946. A.B. (Simon Mandlebaum scholar, Am. Council Learned Socs. fellow in Oriental Langs.), U. Mich., 1943; postgrad., Princeton U., Yale U., 1943; M.A., U. Wis., 1947, Ph.D., 1956. Far East analyst OSS and Dept. State, Washington, 1944-46; asst., instr. philosophy and anthropology U. Wis., 1946-50; supr. linguistics, Pacific area specialist Trust Ter. Pacific Islands and Dept. Interior, Micronesia and Washington, 1950-53; asst. prof. anthropology Antioch Coll., Yellow Springs, Ohio, 1953-56; asst. prof., asso. prof. anthropology Emory U., Atlanta, 1956-62; asso. prof., prof. anthropology, community service and pub. affairs. U. Oreg., Eugene, 1962-73; dir. Center for Communication Research, U. Tex., Austin, 1973-78; prof. anthropology Ctr. Communication Research Sch. Communication, U. Tex., 1973—; cons. Ga. Dept. Pub. Health, 1956-60, Peace Corps, 1965-69, Job Corps, 1968-70, USIA, 1972-79, 82; U.S. State Dept. specialist, Mex., 1978; cons. on problems of communication and anthropology to state and fed. agys., industry, museums, instns. of higher learning; staff mem. AID Communication Seminars, 1966-81; lectr. in field, Eng., Mex. and Can. Author: Communication and Culture, 1966, Cognitive Styles in Law Schools, 1979; mem. editl. bd. Communication and Info. Scis., Info. and Behavior, Progress in Communication Scis.; contbr. articles to profl. jours., chpts. to books; further reprintings and revs. Served to 1st lt. AUS, 1942-45. Fellow Am. Anthrop. Assn., AAAS; mem. Internat. Communication Assn. (pres. 1973-74, dir.), Sigma Xi, Alpha Kappa Delta, Phi Kappa Phi. Club: Town and Gown. Home: 1801 Lavaca St Austin TX 78701-1304 Office: U Tex Coll Communication Austin TX 78712

SMITH, ALLIE MAITLAND, university dean; b. Lumberton, N.C., June 9, 1934; s. Allie McCoy and Emma Hattie (Wright) S.; m. Sarah Louise Whitlock, June 16, 1957; children: Sara Leianne, Hollis Duval, Meredith Lorren. BME with honors, N.C. State U., Raleigh, 1956, MS, 1961, PhD, 1966. Assoc. engr. Martin Co., Balt., 1956-57; devel. engr. Western Electric Co., 1957-60; mem. tech. staff Bell Tel. Labs., Burlington, N.C., 1960-62; instr., then asst. prof. extension N.C. State U., 1958-62; rsch. project engr. Rsch. Triangle Inst., Durham, N.C., 1962-66; rsch. supr. Sverdrup/ARO,

Inc., Arnold Air Force Sta., Tenn., 1966-79; adj. prof. U. Tenn., Tullahoma, 1967-79; prof. mech. engring., dean Sch. Engring. U. Miss., 1979—; bd. dirs., mem. scholarship bd. Miss. Mineral Resources Inst.; exec. chmn. 14th conf. Southeastern Conf. on Theoretical and Applied Mechanics, mem. exec. com. 13th through 16th confs., mem. ops. com. and policy com., 1990-96, session chair, 1994; mem. organizing com., internat. sci. adv. bd., plenary session presiding officer Internat. Conf. on Hydrosci. and Engring., 1993, 95. Author: Fundamentals of Silicon Integrated Device Technology, Vol. I: Oxidation, Diffusion and Epitaxy, 1967, also articles, revs.; editor: Radiative Transfer and Thermal Control, 1976, Thermophysics of Spacecraft and Outer Planet Entry Probes, 1977, Fundamentals and Applications of Radiation Heat Transfer, 1987, Developments in Theoretical and Applied Mechanics, Vol. XIV, 1988, Radiation Heat Transfer: Fundamentals and Applications, 1990, Fundamentals of Radiation Heat Transfer, 1991, Radiative Heat Transfer: Theory and Applications, 1993, Solution Methods for and Application of Radiative Heat Transfer in Participating Media, 1996. Fellow ASME (mem. aerospace heat transfer com. 1975—), AIAA (chmn. thermophysics tech. com. 1975-77, chmn. terrestrial energy sys. tech. com. 1979-81, chmn. confs. 1975, 79, assoc. editor jour. 1975-77, 86—, mem. nat. publ. com. 1979-83, Nat. Thermophysics award 1978, Hermann Oberth award 1984-85, Space Shuttle Flag Challenger plaque 1984, supernumerary dir. Ala.-Miss. sect. 1994—); mem. AAUP, NSPE (pres. N.E. Miss. chpt. 1990-91), Am. Soc. Engring. Edn. (host Nat. Engring. Deans' Inst. 1991), N.Y. Acad. Scis., Rotary, Sigma Xi, Phi Kappa Phi, Tau Beta Pi, Pi Tau Sigma, Upsilon Pi Epsilon, Sigma Pi (scholar 1955), Order of the Engr., Rotary Club. Achievements include discovery of anomalous refraction maxima phenomenon. Home: PO Box 1857 University MS 38677-1857 Office: U Miss 101 Carrier Hall University MS 38677

SMITH, ALLISON LONDON, English language educator, real estate developer; b. Kansas City, Mo., Dec. 1, 1942; d. William Jay Sr. and Emily Ann (Allison) L.; m. Bruce Mitchell Smith, June 5, 1965; children: Travis Mitchell, Chase London. BS, U. Mo., 1964, postgrad., 1992-93; postgrad., S.W. Mo. State U., 1966-68. Educator Overland Park Sch. System, Shawnee Mission, Kans., 1964-66, West Plains Sch. System, West Plains, Mo., 1967-72; legal aid R. Jack Garrett, Atty. at Law, West Plains, Mo., 1972-74; province collegiate dir. Gamma Phi Beta, Mo./Kans., 1974-77; legal aid Howell County Prosecuting Atty., West Plains, Mo., 1978-80; educator Southwest Mo. State Univ., West Plains, Mo., 1981--; v.p. Southern Hills Ctr., Ltd., West Plains, 1979--; sec. treas, K & S Devel., Ltd., Harrison, Ark., 1982--. Pres. Ozark Med. Ctr. Aux., 1971; sec., treas. Country Club Bd. Dirs., 1975; choreographer People's Park Players and H.S. Prodns., 1975—; bd. govs. S.W. Mo. State U., 1995—. Named Outstanding Young Women Am., 1970; recipient svc. award Gamma Phi Beta, Denver, 1982; Fanfare for Fifty Theta Kappa Phi, Columbia, Mo., 1980. Mem. Nat. Assn. Tchrs. Coll. English, Nat. Soc. Legal Secs., DAR, PEO Sisterhood, Jefferson Club U. Mo., Gamma Phi Beta, Phi Delta Theta Mothers Club. Republican. Episcopalian. Home: 8064 County Road 5010 West Plains MO 65775-5071 Office: SW Mo State U Central Hall 128 Garfield Ave West Plains MO 65775-2715

SMITH, ALMA DAVIS, elementary education educator; b. Washington, June 27, 1951; d. Wyatt Deeble and Martha Elizabeth (Lingenfelter) Davis; m. Perry James Smith, Jan. 1, 1979; children: Lauren, Hunter. BS, James Madison U., 1973; MEd, U. Va., 1978. Cert. elem. tchr. and prin., Va. Tchr. Robert E. Lee Elem. Sch., Spotsylvania, Va., 1973-79, Conehurst Elem. Sch., Salem, Va., 1979, Hopkins Rd. Elem. Sch., Richmond, Va., 1980-87; tchr. Reams Rd. Elem. Sch., Richmond, Va., 1987-95, asst. prin. summer sch., 1990; tchr. Crestwood Elem. Sch., Richmond, Va., 1995—. Bd. mem. PTA, 1994-95, life mem., 1995. Mem. NEA, Spotsylvania Edn. Assn. (numerous chair positions), Chesterfield Edn. Assn. Home: 2811 Ellesmere Dr Midlothian VA 23113-3800

SMITH, ANDERSON DODD, psychologist; b. Richmond, Va., May 3, 1944; s. John Edward and Nancy (Dodd) S.; B.A., Washington and Lee U., Lexington, Va., 1966; M.A., U. Va., 1969, Ph.D. in Exptl. Psychology (Francis DuPont fellow), 1970; m. Glenna Ellen Bevell, Aug. 13, 1966; children—Nancy Taylor, Leigh-Ellen Anderson. Research and teaching asst. U. Va., 1966-70; mem. faculty Ga. Inst. Tech., Atlanta, 1970—, prof. psychology, 1980-86, dir. psychology, 1986—; affiliate scientist Yerkes Regional Primate Ctr.; adj. prof. Ga. State U. Vice chmn. Atlanta Neighborhood Planning Unit; bd. dirs. Northside Shepard's Ctr., North Atlanta Teen Ctr.; vestryman St. Anne's Episcopal Ch., Atlanta; pres. St. Anne's Terr. Retirement, Inc. Recipient Outstanding Tchr. award Ga. Inst. Tech., 1975; Monie Ferst Sustained Research award Sigma Xi, 1982; grantee NIH, 1972—, NIMH, 1978-79, 80-81. Fellow Am. Psychol. Assn. (chmn. program and edn. coms. div. 20), Gerontol. Soc.; mem. Psychonomic Soc., Southeastern Psychol. Assn., Sigma Xi (coll. nat. lectrs. 1987—), Phi Kappa Phi (past chpt. pres.). Asso. editor: Aging in the 1980's, 1980; editor psychol. scis. Jour. Gerontology, 1980-86. Contbr. articles to profl. publs. Home: 3009 Rockingham Dr NW Atlanta GA 30327-1232 Office: Sch Psychology Ga Inst Tech Atlanta GA 30332

SMITH, ANDREW J., chemicals executive; b. 1941. Grad., Concordia Coll., 1963. With E.I. Du Pont de Nemours & Co., Gregory, Tex., 1965-76, Consolidated Thermoplastics, Dallas, 1976-84; with Rexene Corp., Dallas, 1984-91, CEO, 1992—; with Itex Enterprises Inc., Dallas, 1991-92. Office: Rexene Corp 5005 Lyndon B Johnson Fwy Dallas TX 75244-6119*

SMITH, ANDREW VAUGHN, telephone company executive; b. Roseburg, Oreg., July 17, 1924; s. Andrew Britt and Ella Mae (Vaughn) S.; m. Dorothy LaVonne Crabtree, Apr. 25, 1943; children: Janet L., James A. B.S. in Elec. Engring, Oreg. State U., 1950. Registered profl. engr., Oreg. With Pacific N.W. Bell Tel. Co., 1951-88; asst. v.p. ops. Pacific N.W. Bell Tel. Co., Seattle, 1965, v.p. ops., 1970-78; v.p., gen. mgr. Pacific N.W. Bell Tel. Co., Portland, Oreg., 1965-70; pres. Pacific N.W. Bell Tel. Co., Seattle, 1978-88; pres. ops. U.S. West Communications, 1988-89; exec. v.p. U.S. West Inc., 1989; pres. Telephone Pioneers of Am., 1989-90; ret. U.S. West Inc., 1989; bd. dirs. Univar Corp., Seattle, Cascade Natural Gas, Seattle, Airborne Freight Corp., Seattle Prime Source, Pennsouken, N.J. Hon. trustee Oreg. State U. Found.; trustee U. Wash. Grad. Sch. Bus., 1985, chmn. bd. trustees, 1984-85; gen. chmn. United Way of King County, 1980-81; mem. Wash. State Investment Com., Olympia, 1989-92; mem. bd. regents U. Wash., 1989-95. With USNR, 1943-46. Mem. Seattle C. of C. (chmn. 1985-86). Mem. Wash. Athletic Club (pres. 1982-83), Seattle Yacht Club, Rainier Club, Overlake Golf and Country Club, Multnomah Club (Portland), Columbia Tower Club (Seattle), Desert Island Country Club (Palm Desert, Calif.), The Palm Springs (Calif.) Club. Episcopalian. Office: 1600 Bell Plz Rm 1802 Seattle WA 98191

SMITH, ANN C., nursing educator; b. Weehawken, N.J., Aug. 11, 1937; d. John Aloysius Smith and Ruth Dorothea-Louise Wiese. Diploma, Bellevue Schs. of Nursing, N.Y.C., 1959; BS, MA, NYU, 1966, 68; MA, New Sch. for Social Rsch., N.Y.C., 1982; MSN, CUNY, 1988. Gerontol. nurse practitioner, N.Y. Prof. Bronx (N.Y.) Community College/CUNY. Capt. USAR Nurse Corp, 1959-63. Mem. ANA, Nat. League Nursing, N.Y. State Nurses Assn., N.Y. State Coalition Nurse Practitioners, Sigma Theta Tau.

SMITH, ANNA DEAVERE, actress, playwright; b. Balt., Sept. 18, 1950; d. Deavere Young and Anna (Young) S. BA, Beaver Coll., Pa., 1971, hon. doctorate; MFA, Am. Conservatory Theatre, 1976; hon. doctorate, U. N.C. Ann O'Day Maples prof. arts and drama Stanford U. Playwright, performer one-woman shows On the Road: A Search for American Character, 1983, Aye, Aye, Aye, I'm Integrated, 1984, Piano, 1991 (Drama-Logue award), Fires in the Mirros, 1992 (Obie award 1992, Drama Desk award 1992), Twilight: Los Angeles 1992 (Obie award, 2 Tony award nominations, Drama Critics Cir. spl. citation, Outer Critics Cir. award, Drama Desk award, Audelco award, Beverly Hills, Hollywood NAACP theatre awards); writer libretto for Judith Jamison, performer Hymn, 1993; other appearances include (state) Horatio, 1974, Alma, the Ghost of Spring Street, 1975, Mother Courage, 1980, Tartuffe, 1983, (TV) All My Children, 1983, (films) Soup for One, 1982, Dave, 1993, Philadelphia, 1993, The American President, 1995. Named One of Women of Yr., Glamour mag., 1993; fellow Bunting Inst., Radcliffe Coll. Office: 1676 Dolores St San Francisco CA 94110 also: Stanford Univ Dept of Drama Memorial Hall Stanford CA 94305

SMITH, ANNA NICOLE, model; b. Mexia, Tex.; 1 child, Daniel; m. J. Howard Marshall II, Jun. 27, 1994 (dec.). Model for Guess? jeans. Appeared in films Naked Gun 33 1/3: The Final Insult, 1994, The Hudsucker Proxy, 1994; cover model Playboy, 1992 (Playmate of the Yr. 1994).

SMITH, ANNIE LEE NORTHERN, school system administrator; b. Houston, Dec. 27, 1932; d. Lee Fletcher and Christine (Johnson) Williams; stepfather Leamer Williams; m. Louis Northern, Dec. 23, 1956 (dec. 1965); 1 son, Eric V.; m. 2d Jules Smith, Jan 28, 1967. B.S., Tex. So. U., 1954, M.Ed., 1959, postgrad., 1978, Tex. A & M U., 1988; CSD (hon.) Guadalupe Coll., San Antonio, 1988; cert. mid-mgmt., 1959. Tchr. Stone Crest Nursery Sch., Houston, 1954-57, Cypress Fairbanks Ind. Sch. Dist. (Tex.), 1957-59, Houston Ind. Sch. Dist., 1959-75; instructional coordinator, 1975-77, prin., 1977—; staff dir., Houston Ind. Sch. Dist., 1990-94; ret. 1994. instr. Nat. Bapt. Pub. Bd., Nashville; speaker in field. Active Houston YWCA; reporter, announcer, youth coord., pulpit com., St. John Bapt. Ch., 1977—. Recipient Outstanding Performance award Houston Ind. Sch. Dist., 1974, Merit award, 1978, Cert. Appreciation City of Houston, 1986, State of Tex., 1986, Achievement award Spinal Health Edn., Outstanding Leadership award Lovett Sch., Svc. award H.A.S.A., 1994, Elrod Sch. H.L.S.D., 1994, Johnson Washington Family, 1994, Leadership award St.John Bapt. Ch. Youth Dept., Houston, 1994, Women of Distinction award Houston Women's Dist. Task Force, 1994, Black Togetherness award A.O.I.P., 1995, Key to City award, City of Miami, Fla., 1995, others. Mem. NEA, NAACP, HAABSE, Nat. Coun. Negro Women, Nat. Coun. Black Educators, Parent Tchrs. Orgn., Houston Tchrs. Assn., Houston Prins. Assn., Tex. State Tchrs. Assn., Tex. Elem. Sch. Tchrs. Assn., Nat. Women of Achievement (pres. 1961—, reg. dir. 1991—, service award, 1993), Am. Legion Aux., Mamie Charity Club (youth sponsor, reporter, sec., Outstanding Leadership award 1976), Sigma Gamma Rho (service award 1976-80, Outstanding Educator award 1980, appreciation award 1994, spl. recognition cert. 1995), Eta Phi Beta (achievement award 1993). Address: 2922 S Peach Hollow Cir Pearland TX 77584-2032 Office: 11544 S Gessner Dr Houston TX 77071-2210

SMITH, APOLLO MILTON OLIN, retired aerodynamics engineer; b. Columbia Mo., July 2, 1911; s. Orsino Cecil and Blanche Alice (Whitaker) S.; m. Elisabeth Caroline Krost, Dec. 5, 1943; children: Tove Anne, Gerard Nicholas, Kathleen Roberta. BS in Mech. Engring., Calif. Inst. Tech., 1936, MS, 1937, MS in Aero. Engring., 1938; DSc (hon.), U. Colo., 1975. Asst. chief aerodynamicist Douglas Aircraft Co., El Segundo, Calif., 1938-42, 1944-48, supr. design rsch., 1948-54; supr. aerodynamic rsch. McDonnell Douglas Corp., Long Beach, Calif., 1954-69; chief engr. Aerojet Engring. Corp., Pasadena, Calif., 1942-44; chief aerodynamics engr. rsch. McDonnell Douglas Corp., Long Beach, 1969-75; adj. prof. UCLA, 1975-80; cons. aerodyn. engr., San Marino, Calif., 1975-86. Author: (with others) Analysis of Turbulent Boundary Layers, 1974, contbr. over 65 tech. papers. Recipient Robert H. Goddard award Am. Rocket Soc., 1954, Engring. Achievement award Douglas Aircraft Co., 1958, Casey Baldwin award Can. Aeros. and Space Inst., 1971, Fluids Engring. award ASME, 1985. Fellow AIAA (hon.); Wright Bros. lectr. 1974); mem. NAE. Home: 2245 Ashbourne Dr San Marino CA 91108-2304

SMITH, ARTHUR, radio and television producer, composer; b. Clinton, S.C., Apr. 1, 1921; s. Clayton Seymour and Viola (Fields) S.; m. Dorothy Byars, Apr. 12, 1941; children: Arthur Reginald, Constance (Mrs. Wiley Brown), Robert Clayton. Grad. high sch. Rec. artist RCA Victor, 1936-38; band leader, composer Sta. WSPA, Spartanburg, S.C., 1938-41, Sta. WBT, Charlotte, N.C., 1941-43; band leader, composer, producer CBS Radio, WBT, WBTV, Charlotte, 1945-70; producer WSOC-TV Cox Broadcasting Co., Charlotte, 1970—; dir. Hardware Mut. Ins. Co., Am. Bank & Trust Co., Meat Centers; pres. Clay Music Corp., Charlotte, 1960-76; owner Arthur Smith Studios, Charlotte, 1961—; v.p. CMH Records, L.A.; founder Arthur Smith King Mackerel Tournament, Myrtle Beach, S.C., 1976, Arthur Smith Kingfish, Dolphin, Wahoo Tournament of the Palm Beaches (Fla.), 1983. Prin.: The Arthur Smith Show, 1971-76; composer: numerous compositions, including Guitar Boogie, 1946; also rec. artist: more than 100 albums for MGM, DOT, Monument and Starday, numerous compositions, including Dueling Banjos, 1973 (BMI Song of Year 1973); composer: (with Clay Smith) sound track of film Death Driver, 1975, Dark Sunday, 1976; musical score for Living Legend and Lady Grey-Superstar, 1979; co-host with Clay Smith of syndicated radio show "The Arthur Smith Sportsman Journal". Bd. dirs. Charlotte Sch. of Arts, Am. Heart Assn., Marine Sci. Coun.; trustee, dir. Gardner Webb Coll.; trustrr Boys Home N.C.; founder, chmn. Arthur Smith Bluefish Tournament of N.Y.; chmn. Alzheimer's Assn. Served with USN, 1943-45. Named Bapt. Layman of Yr. Southeastern Sem. Louisville, 1969; named to N.C. Broadcasters Hall of Fame, 1990; recipient Religion Emphasis award Am. Legion, 1971, S.C. Tourism award State of S.C., 1979, Cine Golden Eagle award for film The Hawk and John McNeely, 1980, Lung Assn. award, 1993. Mem. Am. Fedn. Musicians (dir. local 342, pres. local 342 1943-76), AFTRA, Salt Water Anglers Tournament Soc. (founder, chmn. bd.), U.S. Sportsfishing Assn. (chmn. 1985). Democrat. Clubs: Masons, Shriners, Kiwanis, Charlotte City, Red Fez. Home: 7224 Sardis Rd Charlotte NC 28270-6062 Office: Arthur Smith Studios 100 Smithfield Dr Charlotte NC 28270-6543 *To me, success is not a destination - it's a journey. Integrity is not a business principle - it's a matter of right or wrong. Whatever I shall achieve in this world I owe to complete trust in, and commitment to God through Christ, a loving and understanding wife and family and loyal associates.*

SMITH, ARTHUR B(EVERLY), JR., lawyer; b. Abilene, Tex., Sept. 11, 1944; s. Arthur B. and Florence B. (Baker) S.; children: Arthur C., Sarah R. BS, Cornell U., 1966; JD, U. Chgo., 1969. Bar: Ill. 1969, N.Y. 1976. Assoc. Vedder, Price, Kaufman & Kammholz, Chgo., 1969-74; asst. prof. labor law N.Y. State Sch. Indsl. and Labor Rls., Cornell U., 1975-77; ptnr. Vedder, Price, Kaufman & Kammholz, Chgo., 1977-86; founding mem. Murphy, Smith & Polk, Chgo., 1986—; guest. lectr. Northwestern U. Grad. Sch. Mgmt., 1979, Sch. Law, spring 1980; mem. hearing bd. Ill. Atty. Registration and Disciplinary Commn. Recipient award for highest degree of dedication and excellence in teaching N.Y. State Sch. Indsl. and Labor Relations, Cornell U., 1977. Mem. ABA (co-chmn. com. on devel. law under Nat. Labor Relations Act, Sect. Labor Rels. Law 1976-77), N.Y. State Bar Assn., Phi Eta Sigma, Phi Kappa Phi. Presbyterian. Clubs: Chgo. Athletic Assn., Monroe (Chgo.). Author: Employment Discrimination Law Cases and Materials, 4th edit., 1994; Construction Labor Relations, 1984, supplement, 1993; co-editor-in-chief: 1976 Annual Supplement to Morris, The Developing Labor Law, 1977; asst. editor: The Developing Labor Law, 3d edit., 1992; contbr. articles to profl. jours. Office: Murphy Smith & Polk 2 First National Plz Fl 25 Chicago IL 60603

SMITH, ARTHUR JOHN STEWART, physicist, educator; b. Victoria, B.C., Can., June 28, 1938; s. James Stewart and Lillian May (Geernaert) S.; m. Norma Ruth Askeland, May 20, 1966; children: Peter James, Ian Alexander. B.A., U. B.C., 1959, M.Sc., 1961; Ph.D., Princeton U., 1966. Postdoctoral fellow Deutsches Electronen-Synchrotron, Hamburg, W. Germany, 1966-67; mem. faculty dept. physics Princeton U., 1967—, prof., 1978—, Class of 1909 prof., 1992—, assoc. chmn. dept., 1979-83, chmn. dept. physics, 1990—; vis. scientist Brookhaven Nat. Lab., 1967—, Fermilab, 1974—, Superconducting Supercollider Lab., 1990-94. Assoc. editor Phys. Rev. Letters, 1986-89; contbr. articles to profl. jours. Fellow Am. Phys. Soc. (chmn. divsn. of particles and fields 1991). Achievements include research on experimental high-energy particle physics; kaon decays and quark structure of hadrons. Home: 4 Ober Rd Princeton NJ 08540-4918 Office: PO Box 708 Princeton NJ 08544-0708

SMITH, ARTHUR KITTREDGE, JR., academic administrator, political science educator; b. Derry, N.H., Aug. 15, 1937; s. Arthur Kittredge and Rena Belle (Roberts) S.; m. June Mary Dahar, Nov. 28, 1959; children: Arthur, Valerie, Meredith. B.S., U.S. Naval Acad., 1959; M.A., U. N.H., 1966; Ph.D., Cornell U., 1970. Vis. prof. El Colegio de Mexico, Mexico City, 1968-69; asst. prof. polit. sci. SUNY-Binghamton, 1970-74, assoc. prof., 1974-84, prof., 1984-88, provost for grad. studies and research, 1976-83, v.p. for adminstrn., 1982-88; prof. govt. and internat. studies U. S.C., Columbia, 1988-91, exec. v.p. for acad. affairs, provost, 1988-90, 91, interim pres., 1990-91; pres., prof. polit. sci. U. Utah, Salt Lake City, 1991—. Author: (with Claude E. Welch, Jr.) Military Role and Rule: Perspectives on Civil-Military Relations, 1975; contbr. articles to profl. jours. Active Am. Stores Co., First Security Corp. Served with USN, 1959-65. Lehman fellow, 1966-69, NDEA fellow, 1969-70. Mem. Am. Polit. Sci. Assn., L.Am. Studies Assn., Inter-Univ. Sem. on Armed Forces and Soc., Am. Coun. on Edn., World Affairs Coun. (pres. Binghamton chpt. 1976-76), Phi Beta Kappa, Pi Sigma Alpha, Omicron Delta Kappa, Phi Delta Kappa, Beta Gamma Sigma, Phi Kappa Phi. Home: 1480 Military Way Salt Lake City UT 84103-4455 Office: U Utah Office of the Pres 203 Park Building Bldg Salt Lake City UT 84112-1201

SMITH, BAKER ARMSTRONG, management executive, lawyer; b. Brunswick, Ga., Oct. 3, 1947; s. William Armstrong and Priscilla (Baker) S.; m. Deborah Elizabeth Ellis, Nov. 13, 1982; children: Ellis Armstrong, Elizabeth Anne, Everett Baker, Emery Manning. BS, U.S. Naval Acad., 1969; MBA, Northeastern U., 1975; JD cum laude, Suffolk U., 1977; LLM in Labor, Georgetown U., 1981. Bar: Ga. 1977, D.C. 1978, U.S. Supreme Ct. 1980; cert. turnaround profl., 1994. Commd. ensign U.S. Navy, 1969, advanced through grades to lt., 1974; exec. dir., founder The Center on Nat. Labor Policy, Inc., North Springfield, Va., 1977-81; asst. to sec., dir. labor relations U.S. Dept. HUD, Washington, 1981-83; exec. v.p. U.S. Bus. and Indsl. Council, Nashville, 1983-84; pres. Am. Quality Builders, Inc., Nashville, 1984-86; v.p. Hopeman Bros., Inc., Waynesboro, Va., 1986-88; ptnr. Morris, Anderson, Atlanta, 1988—; sec., founder U.S. Constitutional Rights Legal Def. Fund, Inc., Atlanta, 1983—; trustee Leadership Inst., Springfield, Va., 1978—; dir. Turnaround Mgmt. Assn., 1994—; sec., treas. Assn. Cert. Turnaround Profls., Boston, 1995—; mem. Coun. for Nat. Policy, Washington, 1981—, Civil Rights Reviewing Authority U.S. Dept. Edn., Washington, 1984-88; transition team leader Office of the Pres.-Elect of the U.S., NLRB, Occupational Safety and Health Review Commn., Fed. Mediation and Conciliation Service, Nat. Mediation Bd., Fed. Labor Relations Authority, Washington, 1980-81; instr. law, faculty sec. No. Va. Law Sch., Alexandria, Va., 1980-83; instr. law D.C. Law Sch., Washington, 1978-80. Contbg. author: Mandate for Leadership, 1981; contbr. articles to profl. jours. Served to lt. USN, 1969-74. Mem. St. George's House, Windsor Castle (assoc.), ABA (Nat. Law Day chmn. 1976-77, Silver Key award 1977), Phila. Soc., U.S. Supreme Ct. Hist. Soc., Federalist Soc., Joseph Story Soc., Beta Gamma Sigma, Phi Delta Phi (pres. 1989-91). Republican. Presbyterian. Club: Capitol Hill (Washington), Piedmont (Winston-Salem). Home: 3360 E Terrell Branch Ct Marietta GA 30067-5164

SMITH, BARBARA ANN, elementary education educator; b. Peoria, Ill., Dec. 21, 1933; d. Gerald Clyde and Kathryn Jane Smith. BS, Taylor U., Ft. Wayne, Ind., 1959; MS, St. Francis Coll., Ft. Wayne, 1967. Tchr. freshman phys. edn. Taylor U., 1957-58; tchr. James H. Smart Sch., Ft. Wayne, 1959-67, Southwick Elem. Sch., Ft. Wayne, 1967-95, Meadowbrook Elem., 1995—; chair Young Authors, Ft. Wayne, 1990-92; chair Coalition of Essential Schs., Ft. Wayne, 1992-94; mem. coun. Region 8 Dept. Edn., Ind., 1992-94; chairperson Performance Based Assessment Climate Com., 1992-94; facilitator Ind. 2000, 1993-95; chair Parent/Staff Adv. Coun., Ft. Wayne, 1994-95; title I Home/Sch. Coord., 1995. Campaign worker Rick Hawks for Congress, Ft. Wayne, 1990. Recipient various teaching awards. Mem. NEA, Ind. Profls., Internat. Reading Assn. (sec. 1993-94, Fort Wayne chpt. Elem. Tchr. of Yr. 1993), East Allen Tchrs., Ind. State Tchrs. Assn. Republican. Avocations: reading, travel, western line dancing, aerobics, biking. Home: 2803 Cherokee Run New Haven IN 46774-2917

SMITH, BARBARA ANNE, healthcare management company consultant; b. N.Y.C., Oct. 10, 1941; d. John Allen and Lelia Maria (De Silva) Santoro; m. Joseph Newton Smith, Feb. 5, 1961 (div. Sept. 1984); children: J. Michael, Robert Lawrence. Student, Oceanside/Carlsbad Coll. Real estate agt. Routh Robbins, Inc., Washington, 1973-75; gen. mgr. Mall Shops, Inc., Kansas City, Kans., 1975-80; regional mgr. FAO Schwarz, N.Y.C., 1980-84; clin. adminstr. North Denver Med. Ctr., Thornton, Colo., 1984-88; adminstrv. dir. Country Side Ambulatory Surgery Ctr., Leesburg, Va., 1989-91; pres. SCS Healthcare Mgmt. Inc., Washington, 1991—; bd. dirs. Franz Carl Weber Internat., Geneva, 1982-84. Pres. Am. Women Chile, 1968; v.p. Oak Park Assn., Kansas City, 1977-78, pres., 1978-79; vol. Visitor Info. and Assn. Reception Ctr. program Smithsonian Instn., Washington. Mem. NAFE, Network Colo., Profl. Bus. Women Assn., Med. Group Mgmt. Assn., Federated Ambulatory Surgery Assn.

SMITH, BARBARA BARNARD, music educator; b. Ventura, Calif., June 10, 1920; d. Fred W. and Grace (Hobson) S. B.A., Pomona Coll., 1942; Mus.M., U. Rochester, 1943, performer's cert., 1944. Mem. faculty piano and theory Eastman Sch. Music, U. Rochester, 1943-49; mem. faculty U. Hawaii, Honolulu, 1949—; assoc. prof. music U. Hawaii, 1953-62, prof., 1962-82, prof. emeritus, 1982—; sr. fellow East-West Center, 1973; lectr., recitals in Hawaiian and Asian music, U.S., Europe and Asia, 1956—; field researcher Asia, 1956, 60, 66, 71, 80, Micronesia, 1963, 70, 87, 88, 90, 91, Solomon Islands, 1976. Author publs. on ethnomusicology. Mem. Internat. Soc. Music Edn., Internat. Musicol. Soc., Am. Musicol. Soc., Soc. Ethnomusicology, Internat. Coun. for Traditional Music, Asia Soc., Am. Mus. Instrument Soc., Coll. Music Soc., Soc. for Asian Music, Music Educators Nat. Conf., Pacific Sci. Assn., Assn. for Chinese Music Rsch., Phi Beta Kappa, Mu Phi Epsilon. Home: 581 Kamoku St Apt 2004 Honolulu HI 96826-5210

SMITH, BARBARA JEAN, lawyer; b. Washington, Jan. 9, 1947; d. Harry Wallace and Jean (Fraser) S.; m. Philip R. Chall, July 13, 1991; children: Brian C.S. Brown, Craig F.S. Brown, Amy E. Chall, Carrie A. Chall. BA, Old Dominion Coll., 1968; MBA, Pepperdine U., 1974; JD, Case Western Res. U., 1977. Bar: Ohio 1977. Assoc. Squire, Sanders & Dempsey, Cleve., 1977-88, ptnr., 1988-93; shareholder McDonald, Hopkins, Burke & Haber Co., L.P.A., Cleve., 1993—. Bd. editors Health Law Jour. of Ohio, 1989-95; contbr. articles to health jours. and periodicals. Trustee Urban Community Sch., Cleve., 1984-86. Mem. Ohio Women's Bar Assn. (pres. 1994-95), Cleve. Bar Assn. (trustee 1992-95, chair health law sect. 1991-92, Appreciation award 1989, 91), Nat. Health Lawyers Assn., Am. Acad. Hosp. Attys., Ohio State Bar Assn. (health law com. 1991—), Soc. Ohio Hosp. Attys. Democrat. Mem. United Ch. of Christ. Avocations: reading, hiking. Home: 220 Grey Fox Run Chagrin Falls OH 44022-3398 Office: McDonald Hopkins Burke & Haber 2100 Bank One Ctr 600 Superior Ave E Cleveland OH 44114-2908

SMITH, BARBARA MARTIN, art educator; b. St. Louis, Feb. 3, 1945; d. Charles Landon and Mary Louise (Nolker) Martin; m. Timothy Van Gorder Smith, Nov. 27, 1976; children: Brian Eliot, Marjorie Van Gorder. BA, Lawrence U., 1967; MFA, So. Ill. U., 1975. Cert. tchr., Mo. Art instr. Horton Watkins High Sch., Ladue, Mo., 1968-76; leader Experiment in Internat. Living, Brattleboro, Vt., 1974; art tchr. Michigan City (Ind.) Ctr. for the Arts, 1979-80, Cleve. Mus. of Art, 1981-83; art instr. Villa Duchesne, St. Louis, 1986—; edn. dir. Dunes Art Found., Michigan City, 1979; co-chmn. Internat. Wives Group, Cleve. Coun. on World Affairs, 1982-84; bd. dirs. Webster Groves (Mo.) Sch. Found., 1992. Exhibited in shows at Art Inst. of Chgo., 1979, So. Ill. U. Alumnae Exhibit, 1982, Focus Fiber, Cleve. Mus. of Art, 1982, Nova, Wearable Art, Kuban Gallery, Cleve., 1983, Drawings & Prints, St. Louis Artist's Guild, 1986. Recipient Grad. Fellowship Ann. Grad. award So. Ill. U., 1975; named Artist in Residence/ Artist in Schs. Ind. Arts Commn./NEA, 1978-79; named to Honors Seminar for Advancement of Art Edn., R.I. Sch. of Design, 1988, Mem. Art Edn. Delegation to Japan, 1992. Mem. Nat. Art Edn. Assn., Internat. Soc. for Edn. through Art, St. Louis Art Mus., St. Louis Artist Guild. Home: 135 Jefferson Rd Webster Grv MO 63119-2934 Office: Villa Duchesne Oak Hill Sch 801 S Spoede Rd Des Peres MO 63131-2606

SMITH, BARNARD ELLIOT, management educator; b. Mpls., May 6, 1926; s. Sheldon Strong and Jessie (Gould) S.; m. Betty Lou Strohschein, Aug. 28, 1949; children: Carolyn Louise, Eileen Elizabeth. B.S. in Mech. Engring. with distinction, U. Minn., 1949, M.S., 1950; Ph.D., Stanford U., 1961; M.A. (hon.), Dartmouth Coll., 1971. Asst. prof. mech. engring. U. N.D., 1950-51; mfg. specialist A.O. Smith Co., Milw., 1951-54; asst. prof. indsl. engring. Oreg. State Coll., 1954-58, Stanford U., 1958-61; asso. prof. mgmt. Sloan Sch. Mgmt., MIT, 1961-68; prof. mgmt. Indian Inst. Mgmt., Calcutta, 1965-68; prof. engring. Thayer Sch. Engring. Dartmouth Coll., 1968-71; dean Stuart Sch. Mgmt. and Finance, Ill. Inst. Tech., 1971-75, prof. mgmt., 1975-80; David M. French disting. prof. mgmt. U. Mich., Flint, 1980-89, emeritus, 1989; pres. Vineyards of the Acad., 1989, The Acad. of

Wine of Oreg. Inc., 1993—; cons. in field. Served with USNR, 1944-46. Mem. Phi Tau Sigma, Beta Gamma Sigma. Home: 18200 Highway 238 Grants Pass OR 97527-8631

SMITH, BARRY DAVID, obstetrician-gynecologist, educator; b. Suffern, N.Y., July 3, 1938; s. Alexander N. and Beatrice (Morris) S.; m. Maryann Blair, Oct. 11, 1963; children: Gillian, Adam. AB, Dartmouth Coll., 1959; MD, Cornell U., 1962. Diplomate Am. Bd. Ob-Gyn. Resident in ob-gyn N.Y. Hosp. Cornell U. Med. Ctr., N.Y.C., 1963-67, chief resident, instr., 1967-68; staff obstetrician/gynecologist Mary Hitchcock Meml. Hosp., Hanover, N.H., 1970—; asst. prof. Dartmouth Coll., Hanover, 1970-78, assoc. prof., 1979—; chief sect. ob-gyn. Hitchcock Clinic, 1977-95, bd. govs., 1975-85, bd. dirs., 1980-86; chief sect. ob-gyn. Dartmouth Med. Ctr., 1977—, chmn. dept. ob-gyn., 1992-95, vice chair dept., 1995—. Treas., pres. Norwich (Vt.) Recreation and Conservation Council, 1975-77. Served to comdr. USNR. Fellow Am. Coll. Ob-gyn. (v.p. N.H. sect. 1991-94, pres. 1994—, chair N.H. sect. 1994—), Am. Fertility Soc., Am. Soc. Colposcopy. Avocations: skiing, tennis, sailing. Office: Dartmouth Hitchcock Clinic 1 Medical Center Dr Lebanon NH 03756-0001

SMITH, BARRY MERTON, financial planner, consultant; b. Dunedin, Fla., Oct. 18, 1943; s. Ollie Morris and Leila Elizabeth (Crisman) S.; m. Susan Gay Stewart, Aug. 13, 1977; children: Jason, Justin, Joshua. Student, U. Fla., 1961-65, St. Petersburg Jr. Coll., 1963; BS in Agr., U. Fla., 1971; postgrad., U. Ctrl. Fla., 1980-83. CFP. Loan svc. rep. Columbia (S.C.) Bank for Coops., 1972; v.p. Apopka (Fla.) Growers Supply Inc., 1972-78, V-J Growers Supply Inc., Apopka, 1978-81, Estimation, Inc., Timonium, Md., 1981, Benbow Industries, Apopka, 1982; ptnr. Billy H. Wells and Assocs., Sanford, Fla., 1982-85; dist. mgr. The Equitable Life of N.Y., Orlando, Fla., 1982-85; v.p. CFS Securities Corp., Longwood, Fla., 1985-90, pres., CEO, 1991—. Capt. U.S. Army, 1966-70, Vietnam. Mem. Internat. Assn. for Fin. Planners (bd. dirs. ctrl. Fla. chpt. 1989-91), Inst. CFPs, Fla. Foliage Assn. (bd. dirs. 1978, treas. 1979-80, Sertoma Club (v.p. 1978-79). Avocations: jogging, baseball. Office: CFG Securities Corp 2180 State Road 434 W Ste 1150 Longwood FL 32779-5041

SMITH, BERNADETTE YVONNE, pediatrician; b. Upper Sandusky, Ohio, June 18, 1968; d. David Earl and Patricia Jo (Rall) S. BS in Zoology, Ohio State U., 1990, MD, 1995. Rsch. asst. divsn. bone marrow transplant Ohio State U., Columbus, 1987; rsch. asst. pediatric br. NCI, NIH, Bethesda, Md., 1988; rsch. ass. divsn. radiobiology Ohio State U., 1988, rsch. asst. dept. zoology, 1990; rsch. asst. dept. neonatology Columbus Children's Hosp., Columbus, 1991; rsch. scientist lab. of immunoregulation NIAID, NIH, Bethesda, 1992-93; pediatric resident Baylor Med. Ctr./Tex. Children's Hosp., Houston, 1995—. Author various abstracts, 1993-94. Ohio State U. acad. scholar, 1990-94, Samuel J. Roessler Meml. Med. rsch. scholar Ohio State U., 1991, Howard Hughes Med. Inst. rsch. scholar, 1992-93, fellow, 1993-95. Mem. AMA, AAAS, N.Y. Acad. Sci., Landacre Rsch. Honor Soc., Ohio State U. Alumni Assn., Am. Med. Women's Assn., Ohio State Med. Assn. Avocations: reading, mountain biking, roller-blading, golf, tennis. Office: Baylor Med Ctr Tex Children's Hosp Houston TX 77030

SMITH, BERNALD STEPHEN, retired airline pilot, aviation consultant; b. Long Beach, Calif., Dec. 24, 1926; s. Donald Albert and Bernice Merrill (Stephens) S.; m. Marilyn Mae Spence, July 22, 1949; children: Lorraine Ann Smith Foute, Evelyn Donice Smith DeRoos, Mark Stephen, Diane April (dec.). Student, U. Calif., Berkeley, 1944-45, 50-51. Cert. airline transport pilot, flight engr., FAA. Capt. Transocean Air Lines, Oakland (Calif.) and Tokyo, 1951-53, Hartford, Conn., 1954-55; 1st officer United Air Lines, Seattle, 1955, San Francisco, 1956-68; tng. capt. United Air Lines, Denver and San Francisco, 1961-68; capt. United Air Lines, San Francisco, 1968-86, 2d officer, 1986-93, ret., 1993; founder, v.p. AviaAm., Palo Alto, Calif., 1970-72, AviaInternat., Palo Alto, 1972-74; cons. Caproni Vizzola, Milan, 1972-84; prin., cons. Internat. Aviation Cons. and Investments, Fremont, Calif., 1985—; instr. aviation Ohlone Coll., Fremont, 1976; founder Pacific Soaring Coun.; founder, trustee AirSailing, Inc., 1970—, Soaring Safety Found., 1985—. Author/editor: American Soaring Handbook, 1975, 80; contbr. articles to profl. jours. Trustee Nat. Soaring Mus., 1975—, pres. 1975-78; active RTCA, SSA del., 1992—, FAI del., 1996. Comdr. USNR. Fellow Internat. GPS Svc. for Geodynamics; mem. AIAA (pub. bd. 1977-94), Soaring Soc. Am. (pres. 1969-70, chmn. pub. bd. 1971-84, chmn. ins. com. 1975-93, bd. dirs. 1963—, Warren Eaton Meml. Trophy 1977, Exceptional Svc. award 1970, 75, 82, 88, 91, named to Hall of Fame 1984), Soc. Automotive Engring., Nat. Aero. Assn., Exptl. Aircraft Assn., Aircraft Owners and Pilots Assn., Airline Pilots Assn., Seaplane Pilots Assn., Orgn. Scientifique et Technique Internat. du Vol a Voile (bd. dirs., U.S. del. 1981—), Fedn. Aeronatique Internat. (Paul Tissandier Diplome 1992, Lilienthal medal 1993, Highest Soaring award, U.S. del. 1991—), Commn. de Vol a Voile (U.S. del. 1970-71, 78, 85—, v.p. 1988-96), U. Calif. Alumni Assn. (life), Inst. Navigation, Civil GPS Svc. Interface Com. Democrat. Methodist. Office: Internat Aviation Cons Investments PO Box 3075 Fremont CA 94539-0307

SMITH, BERNARD JOSEPH CONNOLLY, civil engineer; b. Elizabeth, N.J., Mar. 11, 1930; s. Bernard Joseph and Julia Susan (Connolly) S.; BS, U. Notre Dame, 1951; BS in Civil Engring., Tex. A&M U., 1957; MBA in Fin., U. Calif.-Berkeley, 1976; m. Josephine Kerley, Dec. 20, 1971; children: Julia Susan Alice, Teresa Mary Josephine, Anne Marie Kathleen. Asst. Bernard J. Smith, cons. engr. office, Dallas, 1947-57; hydraulic engr. C.E., U.S. Army, San Francisco, 1957-59, St. Paul dist., 1959-60, Kansas City (Mo.) dist., 1960-63, Sacramento dist., 1963-65; engr. Fed. Energy Regulatory Commn., San Francisco Regional Office, 1965—. Served with U.S. Army, 1952-54. Registered profl. engr., Calif., Mo.; lic. real estate broker, Calif. Mem. ASCE (sec. power div. San Francisco sect. 1969), Soc. Am. Mil. Engrs. (treas. Kansas City post 1962), Res. Officers Assn. (chpt. pres. 1973). Club: Commonwealth of Calif. Home: 247 28th Ave San Francisco CA 94121-1001 Office: Fed Energy Regulatory Commn 901 Market St San Francisco CA 94103-1729

SMITH, BERT KRUGER, mental health services professional, consultant; b. Wichita Falls, Tex., Nov. 18, 1915; d. Sam and Fania (Feldman) Kruger; m. Sidney Stewart Smith, Jan. 19, 1936; children: Sheldon Stuart, Jared Burt (dec.), Randy Smith Huke. BJ, U. Mo., 1936; MA, U. Tex., 1949; DHL (hon.), U. Mo., 1985. Soc. and entertainment editor Wichita Falls Post, 1936-37; freelance writer Juneau, Alaska, 1937; assoc. pub. Coleman Daily Dem. Voice, 1950-51; assoc. editor Jr. Coll. Jour., Austin, Tex., 1952-55; spl. cons., exec. Hogg Found. for Mental Health, Austin, 1952—; chmn. bd. Austin Groups for the Elderly, 1985—. Author: No Language But A Cry, 1964, Your Non-Learning Child, 1968, A Teaspoon of Honey, 1970, Insights for Uptights, 1970, Aging in America, 1973, The Pursuit of Dignity, 1977, Looking Forward, 1983; contbr. numerous articles to profl. jours. Bert Kruger Smith professorship Sch. Social Work U. Tex., 1982; recipient Disting. Svc. award City of Austin, 1988, Cert. of Appreciation, Tex. Dept. Human Svcs., 1989, Ann Bert Smith award Sr.'s Respite Svc., 1989, S.W. Found. Founders' Spirit award, 1990, Tex. Leadership award Ann. Tex. Joint Conf. on Aging, 1992, Tex. Leadership award Tex. Dept. on Aging, 1992; named to Tex. Women's Hall of Fame, 1988. Mem. Women in Comm. (Lifetime Achievement award 1994), Am. Fedn. for Aging Rsch., Adult Svc. Coun. (bd. dirs. 1970—, Family Elder Care Guardian Angel award 1996), Family Eldercare (bd. dirs. 1979—), Authors Guild, Nat. Assn. Sci. Writers, Hadassah, B'nai B'rith Women, Delta Kappa Gamma (hon). Jewish. Avocations: walking, reading. Home: 5818 Westslope Dr Austin TX 78731-3633 Office: Hogg Found Mental Health PO Box 7998 Austin TX 78713-7998 also: U Tex Austin Austin TX 78713

SMITH, BETTY, writer, nonprofit foundation executive; b. Bonham, Tex., Sept. 16; d. Sim and Gertrude (Dearing) S. Student, Stephens Coll.; BJ, U. Tex. Women's editor Daily Texan; pres. Hope Assocs. Corp., N.Y.C., 1948-50; pres., owner Betty Smith Assocs., N.Y.C., 1950—. Author: A Matter of Heart, 1969. Pres. Melchior Heldentenor Found., N.Y.C., 1987—, Gerda Lissner Found., 1994—; v.p. Herman Lissner Found., 1990—. Mem. Author's Guild. Home: 322 E 55th St New York NY 10022-4157 Office: c/o Lissner Found 135 E 55th St New York NY 10022-4049

SMITH, BETTY DENNY, county official, administrator, fashion executive; b. Centralia, Ill., Nov. 12, 1932; d. Otto and Ferne Elizabeth (Beier) Hasenfuss; m. Peter S. Smith, Dec. 5, 1964; children: Carla Kip, Bruce Kimball. Student, U. Ill., 1950-52; student, L.A. City Coll., 1953-57, UCLA, 1965, U. San Francisco, 1982-84. Freelance fashion coordinator L.A., N.Y.C., 1953-58; tchr. fashion Rita LeRoy Internat. Studios, 1959-60; mgr. Mo Nadler Fashion, L.A., 1961-64; showroom dir. Jean of Calif. Fashions, L.A., 1965—; freelance polit. book reviewer for community newspapers, 1961-62; staff writer Valley Citizen News, 1963. Bd. dirs. Pet Assistance Found., 1969-76; founder, pres., dir. Vol. Services to Animals L.A., 1972-76; mem. County Com. To Discuss Animals in Rsch., 1973-74; mem. blue ribbon com. on animal control L.A. County, 1973-74; dir. L.A. County Animal Care and Control, 1976-82; mem. Calif. Animal Health Technician Exam. Com., 1975-82, chmn., 1979; bd. dirs. L.A. Soc. for Prevention Cruelty to Animals, 1984-94, Calif. Coun. Companion Animal Advocates, 1993—; dir. West Coast Regional Office, Am. Humane Assn., 1988—; CFO Coalition for Pet Population Control, 1987-92; mem. Calif. Rep. Cen. Com., 1964-72, mem. exec. com., 1971-73; mem. L.A. County Rep. Cen. Com., 1964-70, mem. exec. com., 1966-70; chmn. 29th Congl. Cen. Com., 1969-70; sec. 28th Senatorial Cen. Com., 1967-68, 45th Assembly Dist. Cen. Com., 1965-68; mem. speakers bur. George Murphy for U.S. Senate, 1970; campaign mgr. Los Angeles County for Spencer Williams for Atty. Gen., 1966; mem. adv. com. Moorpark Coll., 1988—; mem. adv. bd. Wishbone Prodn., 1995—. Mem. Internat. Platform Assn., Mannequins Assn. (bd. dirs. 1967-68), Motion Picture and TV Industry Assn. (govt. rels. and pub. affairs com. 1992—), Lawyer's Wives San Gabriel Valley (bd. dirs. 1971-74, pres. 1972-73), L.A. Athletic Club, Town Hall. Home: 1766 Bluffhill Dr Monterey Park CA 91754

SMITH, BETTY FAYE, textile chemist; b. Magnolia, Ark., June 29, 1930; d. Carl Excel and Nannie (Nall) S. B.S., U. Ark., 1951; M.S., U. Tenn., 1957; Ph.D., U. Minn., 1960, 65. Home agt. Ark. Agrl. Extension Service, 1951-56; mem. faculty Cornell U., 1965-70, assoc. prof. textiles, 1965-70, chmn. dept., 1968-69; prof. textiles, chmn. dept. U. Md., 1970-91, prof. textiles, 1991-92; prof. materials engring., 1992—. Author papers in field. Fellow Textile Inst.; mem. Fiber Soc., Am. Chem. Soc., Am. Assn. Textile Chemists and Colorists, Soc. Dyers and Colourists, AAUP, Sigma Xi, Omicron Nu, Phi Upsilon Omicron, Iota Sigma Pi. Democrat. Methodist. Home: 9216 St Andrews Pl College Park MD 20740-3937 Office: Univ Md Dept Matls & Nuclear Engring Rm 2100 Marie Mount College Park MD 20742

SMITH, BRADLEY YOULE, lawyer; b. N.Y.C., Feb. 11, 1948; s. Bradley and Christine (Brown) S.; m. Anne Barre, Dec. 31, 1986; children: Bradley McLaren, Andrew Robert, Lauren Barre, Timothy James, Lynden Eleanor, Christina McLaren. BA in History cum laude, Yale U., 1970; JD, NYU, 1974. Bar: N.Y. 1975, U.S. Dist. Ct. (so. dist.) N.Y. 1975, U.S. Ct. Appeals (2d cir.) 1975. With Davis Polk & Wardwell, N.Y.C., 1974—, ptnr., 1980—. Trustee Royal Coll. Surgeons Found., Inc. Mem. ABA (chmn. subcom. secured transactions 1983-87, moderator and panelist com. banking law and uniform comml. code), Am. Law Inst., N.Y. State Bar Assn. (mem. banking law com.). Office: Davis Polk & Wardwell 450 Lexington Ave New York NY 10017-3911

SMITH, BRENDA JOYCE, author, editor, social studies educator; b. Washington, Jan. 2, 1946; d. William Eugene and Marjorie (Williams) Young; m. Duane Milton Smith, Aug. 4, 1978. BA in History and Govt. cum laude, Ohio U., 1968, postgrad. in Am. and European History, 1972. Tchr. Jr. High Sch., Lancaster, Ohio, 1968-69, Reynoldsburg (Ohio) Mid. Sch. and High Sch., 1970-71; grad. teaching asst. Ohio U., Athens, 1969-70, 71-72; polit. speech writer Legis. Reference Bur., Columbus, Ohio, 1972-74; pub. rels. writer Josephinum Coll., Columbus, 1976-78; social studies editor Merrill Pub. Co., Columbus, 1979-91; freelance author/editor social studies Columbus, 1991—. Project editor: Human Heritage: A World History, 1985, 89, World History: The Human Experience, 1992; author: The Collapse of the Soviet Union, 1994, Egypt of the Pharaohs, 1995; writer-editor African Am. history series, 5th grade; writer of 3 Am. history books. Del. 1st U.S.-Russia Joint Conf. on Edn., 1994. Mem. Nat. Coun. Social Studies, Ohio Coun. Social Studies, Freelance Editl. Assn. Office: 3710 Harborough Dr Gahanna OH 43230-4037

SMITH, BRENDA MARIE, vocational home economics educator; b. Winchester, Tenn., May 28, 1957; d. William Ralph and Mary Elizabeth (Wynne) Hall; m. Kevin Wayne Smith, Mar. 30, 1980; children: Jessica, Andrea. BS in Edn., S.W. Mo. State U., 1979, MS in Edn., 1989. Cert. tchr., home economist, Mo. Tchr. vocat. home econs., advisor Koshkonong (Mo.) Schs., 1979-80, Ava (Mo.) R-1 Sch. Dist., 1980-83, West Plains (Mo.) R-7 Schs., 1983—; advisor Future Homemakers Am., 1979—; adj. faculty S.W. Bapt. U., Mountain View (Mo.) Ctr., 1992-93; mem. WPHS Better Edn. Techniques Team, West Plains, 1987—; mem. adv. bd. Step One Teen Parenting Program, West Plains, 1992—; mem. adv. bd. home econs. dept. S.W. Mo. State U., Springfield, 1983—. Sec. bd. dirs. Friendship Circle Presch., West Plains, 1989-91, chair bd. dirs., 1991-92. Mem. Future Homemakers Am. Alumni Assn., Mo. Home Econs. Tchrs. Assn. (bd. dirs. 1987—, treas. 1989-93, pres.-elect 1993-94, pres. 1994-95), Am. Vocat. Assn., Mo. Vocat. Assn., Am. Home Econs. Assn. (sec. dist. E 1982-83, cert. home economist), Mo. Home Econs. Assn., Mo. State Tchrs. Assn., Cmty. Tchrs. Assn. (pres. 1989-90, 92-93), Bus. and Profl. Women. Methodist. Avocations: collecting antiques, sewing, camping, tennis, golf. Home: 702 Shuttee St West Plains MO 65775-2916 Office: West Plains Sr High 602 E Olden St West Plains MO 65775-3334

SMITH, BRIAN RAY DOUGLAS, ; b. Victoria, B.C., July 7, 1934; s. Douglas Edgar and E. Eleanor (Parfitt) S.; m. Barbara; children: Claire E, Christopher C. BA, U. B.C., 1956, LLB, 1960; MA, Queen's U., 1960. Min. edn. B.C., 1979-82, min. energy, mines, and petroleum resources, 1982-83, atty. gen., 1983-88; chmn. Can. Nat. Rlwy., 1989—; bd. dirs. Internat. Comml. Arbitration Ctr., Vancouver, B.C., Ballet B.C., Tennis Can.; mem. Vancouver Bd. of Trade. Mayor Oak Bay, B.C., 1974-79; bd. dirs. Ballet B.C., Tennis Can., Vancouver Bd. Trade. Mem. Union Club, Victoria C. of C., Vancouver Lawn and Tennis Club, Victoria Golf Club.

SMITH, BRIAN WILLIAM, lawyer, former government official; b. N.Y.C., Feb. 3, 1947; s. William Francis and Dorothy Edwina (Vogel) S.; m. Donna Jean Holverson, Apr. 24, 1976; children: Mark Holverson, Lauren Elizabeth. BA, St. John's U., N.Y.C., 1968, JD, 1971; MS, Columbia U., 1981. Bar: N.Y. 1972, D.C. 1975, U.S. Dist. Ct. (ea. and so. dists.) N.Y. 1975, U.S. Supreme Ct. 1976, U.S. Dist. Ct. D.C. 1986. Atty. Am. Express Co., N.Y.C., 1970-73, CIT Fin. Corp., N.Y.C., 1973-74; assoc. counsel, mng. atty. Interbank Card Assn. (named changed to Master Card Internat., Inc.), N.Y.C., 1974-75, sr. v.p., corp. sec., gen. counsel, 1975-82; chief counsel Compt. of Currency, Washington, 1982-84; ptnr. Stroock & Stroock & Lavan, Washington, 1984-92, mng. ptnr., 1986-92; ptnr. Mayer, Brown & Platt, Washington and N.Y.C., 1992—; lectr. fin. industry. Editor: Bank Investment Products Deskbook, 1995; spkr. in field. Capt., USAR, 1970-78. Mem. ABA, N.Y. State Bar Assn., D.C. Bar Assn., Assn. Bar City N.Y., Fed. Bar Assn., N.Y. Athletic Club, Met. Club N.Y. Home: 35 W Lenox St Chevy Chase MD 20815-4208 Office: Mayer Brown & Platt 2000 Pennsylvania Ave NW Washington DC 20006-1812

SMITH, BRICE REYNOLDS, JR., retired engineering company executive; b. St. Louis; s. Brice Reynolds and Frances Matilda (Cook) S.; m. Jane Medart; children: Brice Reynolds III, Victoria D. Smith Trauscht, Hollis M. Smith Norman, Karen C. Smith Branom, Todd E. BCE, U. Mo., Columbia, 1951; MCE, MIT, 1952; Cert. advanced mgmt. program, Harvard U., Hawaii, 1961. Registered profl. engr., D.C., Fla., Kans., Md., Mass., Mich., Mo., N.D., Ohio, Oreg., Tenn., Va., N.C., N.Y. Resident engr. Sverdrup & Parcel, St. Louis, 1954-59, asst. to v.p. fgn. ops., 1959-64, treas., 1964-69, v.p., treas., 1970-75; exec. v.p. Sverdrup Corp., St. Louis, 1976-81, pres., 1982-94, CEO, 1986-94, also chmn. bd. dirs.; ret., 1994; dir. Boatmen's Trust Co., St. Louis; bd. dirs. Convention Plaza Redevel. Corp., St. Louis. Bd. dirs. Civic Progress, Inc., Greater St. Louis campaign United Way; bd. dirs. Arts and Edn. Coun. Greater St. Louis, St. Louis Area coun. Boy Scouts Am., Hawthorn Found., Mo., Mo. Hist. Soc., Constrn. Industry Pres. Forum. 1st lt. USAF, 1952-54. Recipient Mo. Honor award for Disting. Service to Engring., U. Mo., 1979; Levee Stone award, Downtown St. Louis, Inc., 1982. Fellow Am. Cons. Engrs. Coun.; mem. ASCE, NSPE, Mo. Soc. Profl. Engrs., Cons. Engrs. Coun. Mo. (past pres.), The Moles, Newcomen Soc. U.S., Bellerive Country Club, Log Cabin Club, St. Louis Club.

SMITH, BRUCE, professional football player; b. Norfolk, Va., June 18, 1963. Student, Va. Tech. U. With Buffalo Bills, 1985—; player Super Bowl XXV, 1990, XXVI, 1991, XXVII, 1992, XXVIII, 1993. Recipient Outland trophy, 1984; named to Pro-Bowl, 1987-90, 92, 93, Sporting News All-Pro team, 1987-88, 90. Office: Buffalo Bills 1 Bills Drive Orchard Park NY 14127-2296

SMITH, BRUCE DAVID, archaeologist; b. Iowa City, Iowa, Mar. 24, 1946; s. Goldwin Albert and Emily C. (Bateman) S.; m. Martha Mary Johnson, Sept. 22, 1973; children: David Vernon, Jonathan Oliver. B.A., U. Mich., 1968, M.A., 1971, Ph.D., 1973. Mem. faculty Loyola U., Chgo., 1973-74, U. Ga., Athens, 1974-77; curator N.Am. archaeology Nat. Mus. Natural History, Smithsonian Instn., Washington, 1977—, sr. scientist, dir. archaeobiology program, 1991—, spl. asst. to dir., 1983, asst. dir., 1986; mem. anthropology rev. panel NSF, 1982-83. Author: Mississippian Patterns of Animal Exploitation, 1975, Prehistoric Patterns of Human Behavior, 1978, Mississippian Settlement Patterns, 1978, Mississippian Emergence, 1990, Rivers of Change, 1992, Emergence of Agriculture, 1994, Mississippian Households and Communities, 1995. Horace H. Rackham prize fellow, 1971-73, Smithsonian Instn. Regents Pub. fellow, 1987; recipient James Henry Breasted prize Am. Hist. Assn., 1995. Mem. Soc. Am. Archaeology (sec. 1985-89, pres. 1993-95), Southeastern Archaeol. Conf. (pres. 1982-84). Home: 2202 Whiteoaks Dr Alexandria VA 22306-2458 Office: Smithsonian Instn Nat Mus Natural History Dept Anthropology Washington DC 20560

SMITH, BRUCE R., English language educator; b. Jackson, Miss., Mar. 21, 1946. Student, U. Birmingham, England, 1966-67; BA magna cum laude in English with honors, Tulane U., 1968; MA, U. Rochester, 1971, PhD with distinction, 1973. From asst. prof. to assoc. prof. English Georgetown U., Washington, 1972-87, prof., 1987—; faculty Bread Loaf Sch. English, Middlebury Coll., 1994—. Author: Ancient Scripts and Modern Experience on the English Stage 1500-1700, 1988, Homosexual Desire in Shakespeare's England: A Cultural Poetics, 1991, Roasting the Swan of Avon: Shakespeare's Redoubtable Enemies and Dubious Friends, 1994; edit. bd. Shakespeare Quar., 1995—; contbr. chpts. to books, articles to profl. jours. Summer grantee Georgetown U. Acad. Rsch., 1976, 84, 87, 89, 91, 92; grantee Intercultural Curriculum Devel., 1982, Agecroft Assn., 1991; Mellon fellow Hungtington Libr., 1996; jr. fellow Folger Inst., 1979-85, fellow, 1990; ACLS fellow, 1979-80; NEH fellow, 1987-88; Va. Found. Humanites fellow, 1989. Mem. Shakespeare Assn. Am. (pres. 1994-95). Office: Georgetown U Dept English Washington DC 20057

SMITH, BYRON OWEN, lawyer; b. Mitchell, S.D., July 28, 1916; s. Frank B. and Elizabeth (Klosterman) S.; m. Jean Knox Harris, Dec. 20, 1938; children: Sheryl S. (Mrs. Kenneth P. King), Laird W., Ryland R., Ford R. A.B., Stanford, 1937, J.D., 1940. Bar: Calif. 1940. Assoc. Stephens, Jones, Inch & LaFever, L.A., 1940-41; ptnr. Stephens, Jones, LaFever & Smith, L.A., 1945-77; ptnr. Adams, Duque & Hazeltine, L.A., 1977-95, of counsel, 1995—. Served to comdr. USNR, 1942-45, 51. Fellow Am. Coll. Trust and Estate Counsel; me. Calif. State Club Assn. (dir., pres. 1974), So. Calif. Golf Assn. (dir. 1966-71), Annandale Golf Club (dir. 1963-66, pres. 1966), Eldorado Country Club (sec., dir. 1970-72), Calif. Club, Phi Delta Phi, Alpha Delta Phi. Home: 1 S Orange Grove Blvd Pasadena CA 91105-1782 Office: Adams Duque & Hazeltine 777 S Figueroa St Los Angeles CA 90017-5800

SMITH, C. KENNETH, corporate executive; b. Brackenridge, Pa., Feb. 1, 1918; s. Clarence H. and Mary (Ferguson) S.; m. AnnaBell Amlin. Degree in bus., U. Pitts., 1942. Mng. ptnr. Ernst & Young, CPAs, Columbus, Ohio, 1964-78; fin. dir., mem. mayor's cabinet City of Columbus, 1983; mng. dir. Fairoaks Internat., 1978—; profl. outside dir. various corps.; guest lectr. Ohio State U. Mem. exec. com. Nat. Football Found. and Hall Fame, Columbus Sports Arena Task Force; co-founder, past chmn. Greater Columbus Arts Coun.; advisor Columbus Found.; bd. govs. Westerville Fund, chmn., 1984-87; mem. Forward Columbus Com.; bd. dirs. Devel. Com. Greater Columbus, Quality Edn. Com., Columbus Zool Park, Columbus Jr. Achievement, Nat. Jr. Achievement; mem. Otterbein Coll. Theatre Adv. Bd.; trustee Columbus Symphony Orch., gen. chmn. symphony grand ball, 1975; trustee Franklin U., 1970—, chmn. bd.; adv. bd. Kenyon Rev., Kenyon Coll.; co-founder, trustee Columbus Leadership Program. Named One of 10 Top Men in Columbus, Columbus Citizen Jour., 1971; named in Columbus Dispatch Blue Chip Profile, 1977; named to Hon. Order Ky. Cols. Mem. AICPA, Am. Acad. Arts and Scis., Am. Mgmt. Assn. (pres.'s coun.), Am. Acctg. Assn., Columbus Soc. Fin. Analysts, Nat. Assn. Corp. Dirs., Columbus Assn. Performing Arts (pres., chmn. bd. 1970-72, chmn. profl. theatre com.), Columbus Mus. Art, Columbus Civic Ballet, Nat. Audubon Soc., Am. Forestry Assn., Am. Tree Farm Sys., Nature Conservancy, Ohio Hist. Soc., Columbus Area C. of C. (chmn. bd. 1968-70, Man of Yr. award 1979), Ohio C. of C. (dir. 1974). Conglist. Clubs: Mason (32 deg., Shriner), Rotarian (dir. 1976—, pres. 1978-79), Columbus (dir. 1968-74), Columbus Country, Royal Commonwealth (London), Torch (pres. 1979-80), Athletic (Columbus); Zanesfield Rod and Gun, Maennerchor, U. Pitts. Alumni Assn., Ohio State U. Alumni Assn. (life); Faculty (Ohio State U.), Presidents (Ohio State U.); Press of Ohio, Ohio Commodore. Home and Office: Fairoaks Farm Westerville OH 43081-9580 *To live life to the fullest, to love and be loved, to pursue knowledge and wisdom, to achieve goals, then set new ones, to be blessed with good health, to be at peace with God and man. This be my prayer.*

SMITH, C. LEMOYNE, publishing company executive; b. Atkins, Ark., Sept. 15, 1934; s. Cecil Garland and Salena Bell (Wilson) S.; m. Selma Jean Tucker, May 23, 1964; 1 child, Jennifer Lee. B.S., Ark. Tech. U., 1956; M.Ed., U. Ark., 1958. Tchr. pub. schs., Little Rock, 1956-58; instr. bus. adminstrn. Ark. Tech. U., Russellville, 1958-60; sales rep. South-Western Pub. Co., Cin., 1960-67, editorial staff, 1967-82, pres., chief exec. officer, 1982-90, chmn., 1990-91, ret., 1991. Bd. dirs. Cin. Council on World Affairs, 1983—. Mem. Am. Vocat. Assn., Nat. Bus. Edn. Assn., Delta Pi Epsilon. Republican. Methodist. Avocations: bridge; travel. Office: South-Western Pub Co 5101 Madison Rd Cincinnati OH 45227-1427

SMITH, C. THOMAS, JR., hospital administrator; b. Little Rock, Apr. 10, 1938; s. Carl Thomas and Mary Elizabeth (Singleton) S.; m. Martha Nell Fincher, June 24, 1961; children: Laura, Adam. BA, Baylor U., 1960; MBA, U. Chgo., 1962; DSc (hon.), U. Bridgeport, 1986; DHL (hon.), Quinnipiac Coll., 1988. Asst. to chmn. dept. psychology Baylor U., Waco, Tex., 1959-60; adminstrv. extern Ark. Bapt. Med. Ctr., Little Rock, summer 1958, acting personnel dir., summer 1960; adminstrv. extern Bapt. Meml. Hosp., Memphis, summer 1959, adminstrv. resident, 1961-62, adminstrv. asst., 1962-63, adminstrv. assoc., 1963-67; assoc. dir. U. Minn. Hosp., Mpls., 1967-71; coordinator health scis. planning U. Minn., Mpls., 1969-71; assoc. exec. dir. Herny Ford. Hosp., Detroit, 1971-74, v.p., exec. dir., 1974-77, trustee, 1974-77; pres. Yale-New Hosp., 1977—, trustee, 1978—; pres. Yale-New Haven Health Svcs. Corp., 1983—, also bd. dirs.; lectr. health care adminstrn. U. Minn., 1969-71; lectr. dept. epidemiology and pub. health Sch. Medicine, Yale U., 1977—; lectr. Sch. Orgn. and Mgmt., Yale U., 1979—; preceptor grad. programs in hosp. and health care adminstrn. Yale U., 1977—; speaker in field; trustee Nat. Com. Quality Health Care, 1978—, Hosp. Rsch and Ednl. Trust, 1987—; bd. dirs. Hosp. Rsch. and Devel., Inc., 1983-89; bd. dirs., exec. com. Vol. Hosps. Am., Inc., 1983—; U.S. del. King Edward's Hosp. Fund for London, 1983-88; mem. coun. on health care tech. Inst. Medicine, NAS, 1986-88; bd. dirs. Vol. Hosps. Am. of So. New Eng., 1985—, Vol. Hosps. Am. Enterprises, 1988—; bd. dirs. Genetech, Inc., New Haven Savs. Bank. Mem. editorial bds. Jour. Med. Edn., 1974-78, Health Care Mgmt. Rev., 1982—, Health Services Research, 1984-88. Bd. dirs. United Way Greater New Haven, 1984-89, campaign chmn., 1986; bd. dirs. Sci. Pk. Devel. Corp., New Haven, 1983—; trustee U. Bridgeport, 1987-89. Mem. Am. Hosp. Assn. (trustee 1987—, chmn. elect 1990), Assn. Am. Med. Colls. (adminstrv. bd. council teaching hosps. 1982-86, chmn. 1986), Am. Coll. Healthcare Execs., Conn. Hosp. Assn. (trustee 1982-86), Quinnipiack Club, New Haven Country Club, Woodbridge Country Club. Congregationalist. Home: 17703 Cedar Creek Canyon Dr Dallas TX 75252-4969 Office: Yale-New Haven Hosp 20 York St New Haven CT 06510-3220

SMITH, CAREY DANIEL, undersea warfare technologist, acoustician; b. Kenedy, Tex., July 10, 1932; s. Ernest Edwin and Nancy Margaret (Willoughby) S.; m. Fannie Belle Walker, Sept. 18, 1954; children: Daniel Carey, Bryan Owen, Ernest Price, Sara Elizabeth Babyak. BS in Math. and Physics, U. Tex., 1959. Rsch. physicist Def. Rsch. Lab./U. Tex., Austin, 1958-64; electro-acoustic engr. Bur. Ships, Washington, 1964-66; dir. sonar tech. office Naval Sea Sys. Command, Washington, 1966-79, dir. Undersea Warfare Tech. Office, 1979-86; sr. cons. U.S. Navy/Sec. of Def., Washington, 1987—; fgn. liaison specialist in undersea warfare as collatoral duty USN, 1966-86; chmn. sonar tech. panel Tech. Coop. Program of multiple allied nations, 1972-86; tech. advisor undersea warfare div. Am. Def. Preparedness Assn., 1976-86. Chair deacons McLean (Va.) Bapt. Ch., 1988-89; chair Band Parents, McLean H.S., 1979-80, chair Sports Boosters, 1977-78. With USN, 1951-56. Decorated Legion of Honor (France); recipient Disting. Civilian Svc. award Sec. Navy, 1979, also Brit., Can., French, Japanese, and New Zealand navies commendations, 1985-86. Fellow Acoustical Soc. Am. Achievements include development of numerous advanced, innovative techniques incorporated in fleet sonar, torpedo, mine, countermeasure, acoustic communications, underwater combat control/ocean environmental acoustic systems; color display for high resolution sonars. Home and Office: 1638 Dinneen Dr Mc Lean VA 22101-4646

SMITH, CARL BERNARD, education educator, writer; b. Dayton, Ohio, Feb. 29, 1932; s. Carl R. and Elizabeth Ann (Lefeld) S.; m. Virginia Lee Cope, Aug. 30, 1958; children—Madonna, Anthony, Regina, Marla. B.A., U. Dayton, 1954; M.A., Miami U., Oxford, Ohio, 1961; Ph.D., Case Western Res. U., 1967. Tchr., Cathedral Latin High Sch., Cleve., 1954-57; customer corr. E.F. MacDonald Co., Dayton, 1958-59; tchr. Kettering (Ohio) High Sch., 1959-61; editor Reardon Baer Pub. Co., Cleve., 1961-62; tchr./researcher Case Western Res. U., Cleve., 1962-65, Cleve. Pub. Schs., 1966-67; asst. prof. edn. Ind. U., Bloomington, 1967-69, assoc. prof., 1970-72, prof., 1973—; dir. ERIC Ctr., 1988—, Family Literacy Ctr., 1990—; pres. Grayson Bernard Pub. Co., 1988—, Am. Family Learning Corp., 1996—. Pres. Bd. Edn., St. Charles Sch., Bloomington, 1976-80. Recipient Sch. Bell award NEA, 1967. Mem. Internat. Reading Assn., Nat. Council Tchrs. of English, Assn. Supervision and Curriculum Devel., Am. Ednl. Research Assn., Phi Delta Kappa. Republican. Roman Catholic. Author: Reading Instruction through Diagnostic Teaching, (Pi Lambda Theta Best Book in Edn. award, 1972; Getting People To Read, 1978; sr. author: Series r, 1983, New View, 1993; Teaching Reading and Writing Together, 1984, Connect! Getting Your Kids to Talk to You, 1994, Word History A Resource Book, 1995. Home: 401 Serena Ln Bloomington IN 47401-9226 Office: Sch Edn Ind U ERIC Clearinghouse Smith Rsch Ctr Bloomington IN 47405

SMITH, CARL RICHARD, association executive, former air force officer; b. New Holland, Pa., Dec. 20, 1933; s. Lemmon Lloyd and Martha Marie (Grabill) S.; m. Mariana Roth, June 15, 1956; children: Timothy Carl, Jeffry Francis, Desi Marie. B.S. in Econs., Franklin and Marshall Coll., Lancaster, Pa., 1955; M.S. in Bus. Adminstrn., George Washington U., 1966. Commd. 2d lt. U.S. Air Force, 1955, advanced through grades to lt. gen., 1986; served in Vietnam and Belgium; assigned Hdqrs. USAF, Washington, 1966-70, 76-78, 86-91; mil. asst. to sec. def., 1978-83; assigned comdr. Lackland AFB, Tex., 1983-86; asst. vice chief of staff Hdqrs. USAF, 1986-91, ret., 1991; exec. v.p. Armed Forces Benefit Assn., Alexandria, Va., 1991—. Decorated Def. D.S.M. with oak leaf cluster, Air Force D.S.M., Legion of Merit with oak leaf cluster, D.F.C., Bronze Star, Meritorious Service medal, Air medal with 2 oak leaf clusters, Air Force Commendation medal. Mem. Air Force Assn., Lambda Chi Alpha. Methodist. Home: 2345 S Queen St Arlington VA 22202-1550 Office: Armed Forces Benefit Assn 909 N Washington St Alexandria VA 22314-1555

SMITH, CARLTON MYLES, military officer; b. Sacramento, Sept. 21, 1920; s. Carl Walter and Minnie Clamina (Friberg) S.; m. Phyllis Lee Routzahn, Nov. 2, 1947; children: Fredrick Benjamin Brown, Brian Webb Smith, Randal Lee Smith, Dennis Stuart Smith. BA, U. Calif., Berkeley, 1946. Joined USAF, 1942, advanced through ranks to lt. col.; various intelligence assignments to chief Advanced Intelligence Courses Br./Def. Intelligency Agy., retired, 1972. Co-author: Stonyford Pedigree, 1988; compiler Genealogist's Historiograph. 1986, (computer program) Genealogist's Historiograph, 1988. Decorated Air medal, WWII, Bronze Star, Meritorious Svc. medal. Mem. Calif. State Geneal. Alliance (pres. 1985-87), Nat. Geneal. Soc. (Merit award 1985), 303d Bomb Group Assn. (mem. chmn. 1991-96). Avocations: geneal. and hist. rsch., travel, writing. Home: 12700-54 Red Maple Cir Sonora CA 95370-5269 *Success in life comes to some in the form of fame, an ego trip. True success and complete self-satisfaction comes to all whose fame stems from service to others, an excursion for the improvement of mankind.*

SMITH, CAROLE DIANNE, legal editor, writer; b. Seattle, June 12, 1945; d. Glaude Francis and Elaine Claire (Finkenstein) S.; m. Stephen Bruce Presser, June 18, 1968 (div. June 1987); children: David Carter, Elisabeth Catherine. AB cum laude, Harvard U., Radcliffe Coll., 1968; JD, Georgetown U., 1974. Bar: Pa. 1974. Law clk. to Hon. Judith Jamison Phila., 1974-75; assoc. Gratz, Tate, Spiegel, Ervin & Ruthrouff, Phila., 1975-76; freelance editor, writer Evanston, Ill., 1983-87; editor Ill. Inst. Tech., Chgo., 1987-88; mng. editor LawLetters, Inc., Chgo., 1988-89; editor ABA, Chgo., 1989-95; product devel. dir. Gt. Lakes Divsn. Lawyers Coop. Pub., Deerfield, Ill., 1995—. Author Jour. Legal Medicine, 1975, Selling and the Law: Advertising and Promotion, 1987; (under pseudonym Sarah Toast) 61 childrens' books, 1994-96; editor The Brief, 1990-95, Criminal Justice, 1989-90, 92-95 (Gen. Excellence award Soc. Nat. Assn. Pubs. 1990, Feature Article award-bronze Soc. Nat. Assn. Pubs. 1994), Franchise Law Jour., 1995; mem. editl. bd. The Brief, ABA Tort and Ins. Practice Sect., 1995—. Dir. Radcliffe Club of Chgo., 1990-93; mem. parents council Latin Sch. Chgo., 1995—. Mem. ABA, Chgo.-Lincoln Inn of Ct. Office: Lawyers Coop Pub 155 Pfingsten Rd Deerfield IL 60015

SMITH, CARTER BLAKEMORE, broadcaster; b. San Francisco, Jan. 1, 1937; s. Donald V. and Charlotte M. (Nichols) S.; children: Carter Blakemore, Clayton M. AA, City Coll. San Francisco, 1958; BA, San Francisco State U., 1960; postgrad. N.Y. Inst. Finance, 1969-70; Assoc. in Fin. PLanning, Coll. for Fin. Planning, 1984. Announcer, Sta. KBLF, Red Bluff, Calif., 1954-56; personality Sta. KRE-KRE FM, Berkeley, Calif., 1958-63, Sta. KSFO, San Francisco, 1963-72, Sta. KNBR, San Francisco, 1972-83, Sta. KSFO, San Francisco, 1983-86, Sta. KFRC, San Francisco, 1986-91, 93-94, Sta. KABL, San Francisco, 1996—; mem. faculty radio-TV dept. San Francisco State U., 1960-61. Mem. adv. bd. Little Jim Club Children's Hosp., 1968-71; bd. dirs. Marin County Humane Soc., 1968-73, San Francisco Zool. Soc., 1980-90; trustee Family Svc. Agy. Marin, 1976-85; mem. alumni bd. Lowell High Sch. Recipient award San Francisco Press Club, 1965; named one of Outstanding Young Men in Am. U.S. Jaycees, 1972. Mem. Amateur Radio Relay League (life), Quarter Century Wireless Assn., Alpha Epsilon Rho.

SMITH, CARY CHRISTOPHER, artist; b. Ponce, P.R., Oct. 1, 1955; s. Roger William and Headley Hall (Mills) S.; m. Virginia Vernon Knowles, Nov. 26, 1977; children: Emily Hall, Hayley Knowles. Student, Sir John Cass Art Sch., London, Eng., 1976; BFA, Syracuse U., 1977. One-man shows include Port Washington (N.Y.) Pub. Libr., 1980, Julian Pretto Gallery, N.Y.C., 1987, Koury Wingate Gallery, N.Y.C., 1988, 90, Galerie Six Friedrich, Munich, Germany, 1989, Lawrence Oliver Gallery, Phila., 1989, Ezra and Cecil Zilkha Gallery, Wesleyan U., Middletown, Conn., 1989, Linda Cathcart Gallery, Santa Monica, Calif., 1991, Rubin Spangle Gallery, N.Y.C., 1992, Roger Ramsay Gallery, Chgo., 1993, Salvatore Ala Gallery, N.Y.C., 1994, Galerie Jorg Paal, Munich, 1995; exhibited in group shows at Stux Gallery, Boston, 1987, White Columns, N.Y.C., 1987, Mission West, N.Y.C., 1987, A.L.G.O. Gallery, N.Y.C., 1987, Postmasters Gallery, N.Y.C., 1988, Jacob Javits Ctr., N.Y.C., 1988, Koury Wingate Gallery, N.Y.C., 1988, 89, 90, Wolff Gallery, N.Y.C., 1988, Whitney Mus. Am. Art, N.Y.C., 1989, 91, 93, Rastovski Gallery, N.Y.C., 1989, Marc Richards Gallery, Santa Monica, 1990, Vrej Baghoomian Gallery, N.Y.C., 1990, Marilyn Pearl Gallery, N.Y.C., 1991, Fay Gold Gallery, Atlanta, 1991, Wadsworth Atheneum, Hartford, Conn., 1992, 96, Rubin Spangle Gallery, N.Y.C., 1992, Salvatore Ala Gallery, N.Y.C., 1993, 94, Pamela Archincloss Gallery, N.Y.C., 1995, Galerie Jorg Paal, Munich, 1996; represented in permanent collections Whitney Mus. Am. Art, N.Y.C., Bklyn. (N.Y.) Mus., Osaka (Japan) Mus., Wadsworth Ateneum, Hartford, New Britain (Conn.) Mus. Am. Art. Recipient Conn. Commn. on the Arts grant for painting, 1983, 86, Art in Pub. Spaces award Conn. Commn. on the Arts, 1985, Nat. Endowment for the Arts Fellowship in Painting, 1991-92, Pollock Krasner grant for painting, 1993. Home: 426 Main St Farmington CT 06032

SMITH, CATHY DAWN, administrator; b. Northampton, Pa., Feb. 6, 1954; d. Russell W. and Edna (Kleckner) Seidel; m. Ronald James Smith, Nov. 1, 1975; 1 child, Ronald James Jr. Grad. high sch., Slatington, Pa. Fiscal asst. Ctr. for Humanistic Change, Inc., Bath, Pa., 1985—. Sec. Parkland Sch. dist. Drug Free Schs. Bd., Orefield, Pa., 1989—; mem. comty. action com. Alert-Partnership for a Drug Free Valley, Lehigh Valley, Pa., 1992-94; program coord. Parkland Alliance for Youth, Pa., 1977-85; explorer advisor Explorers Officer Assn., 1994—; mem. Minsi Trails coun. Boy Scouts Am., 1976—; 1st v.p. Catasauqua Suburban North YMCA, 1993. Mem. Chapel of Four Chaplains, Lehigh Valley Kennel Club. Democrat. mem. United Ch. Christ. Avocations: crafts, cooking, baking, sports. Office: Ctr for Humanistic Change Inc 7574 Beth Bath Pike Bath PA 18014-8967

SMITH, CECE, venture capitalist; b. Washington, Nov. 16, 1944; d. Linn Charles and Grace Inez (Walker) S.; m. John Ford Lacy, Apr. 22, 1978. B.B.A., U. Mich., 1966; M.L.A., So. Meth. U., 1974. C.P.A., Tex. Staff accountant Arthur Young & Co. (C.P.A.s), Boston, 1966-68; staff accountant, then asst. to controller Wyly Corp., Dallas, 1969-72; controller, treas. sub. Univ. Computing Co., Dallas, 1972-74; controller Steak and Ale Restaurants Am., Inc., Dallas, 1974-76; v.p. fin. Steak and Ale Restaurants Am., Inc., 1976-80, exec. v.p., 1980-81; exec. v.p. Pearle Health Services, Inc.,, 1981-84, pres. Primacare div., 1984-86; gen. ptnr. Phillips-Smith Specialty Retail Group, 1986—; pres. Le Sportsac Dallas, Inc., 1981-87; bd. dirs. Henry Silverman Jewelers, Inc., Cheers, Inc., Lil Things, Inc., Hot Topic, Inc.; chmn. Fed. Res. Bank of Dallas, 1994—. Former co-chmn. pres.'s rsch. coun. U. Tex. S.W. Med. Ctr. Dallas; mem. vis. com. U. Mich. Grad. Sch. Bus.; former exec. bd. So. Meth. U. Cox Sch. Bus.; former v.p., bd. dirs. Jr. Achievement Dallas, past pres. Charter 100; past treas. Dallas Assembly; former bd. dirs. Taco Villa, Inc., BizMart, Inc., A Pea in the Pod, Inc. Mem. Tex. Soc. CPAs (former dir.). Home: 3710 Shenandoah Dallas TX 75205-2121 Office: 5080 Spectrum Dr Ste 700 W Dallas TX 75248-4658

SMITH, CHARLES, federal agency administrator; married; 3 children. BA in Psychology, Albright Coll. With Social Security Adminstrn., 1961-66, U.S. Dept. Labor, 1966—; regional adminstr. Office of Asst. Sec. Adminstrn. & Mgmt. U.S. Dept. Labor, N.Y., regional adminstr. Labor Mgmt. Adminstrn., area adminstr. Office of Labor Mgmt. Stds.; dep. asst. sec. Office of Am. Workplace U.S. Dept. Labor, Washington. Office: US Dept Labor Am Workplace Office 200 Constitution Ave NW Washington DC 20210

SMITH, CHARLES CONARD, refractory company executive; b. Mexico, Mo., Feb. 10, 1936; s. Charles Adelbert and Waldine (Barnes) S.; m. Constance Nagel, Oct. 6, 1962; children: Stewart Ashley, Graham Prior. BS in Ceramic Engring., Iowa State U., 1958; MBA, Stanford U., 1962. Process engr. Kaiser Refractory divsn. Kaiser Aluminum, Moss Landing, Calif., 1962-65; materials mgr. Kaiser Refractory divsn. Kaiser Aluminum, Mexico, Mo., 1965-67; divsn. planning Kaiser Refractory divsn. Kaiser Aluminum, Oakland, Calif., 1967-69; v.p., gen. mgr. Kaiser Refractories Argentina, Buenos Aires, 1969-74; with divsn. planning Kaiser Refractories divsn. Kaiser Aluminum, Oakland, 1974-77, mktg. mgr., 1977-80, gen. mgr. mfg., 1980-82, v.p., gen. mgr. refractories divsn., 1982-85; chmn., pres., CEO Nat. Refractories and Mineral Corp., Livermore, Calif., 1985—. Patentee in refractory field. Lt. USNR, 1958-60. Mem. Refractories Inst. (past chmn., exec. com.). Republican. Avocations: fishing, biking, kite flying, photography, music. Home: 63 Lincoln Ave Piedmont CA 94611-3830

SMITH, CHARLES E., protective services official; b. Memphis; married; 3 children. B of Personnel Adminstrn. Firefighter Memphis Fire Dept., 1975-79, lt., 1979-84, capt., 1984-87, dist. chief fire fighting, 1987-91, divsn. chief tng., 1991-92, dir. fire svcs., 1992—; apptd. commr. Tenn. Commn. Fire Fighting Personnel Stds. & Edn. Bd. dirs. Cath. Charities, Inc., Fire Mus. Memphis. Mem. Nat. Inst. Urban Search & Rescue, NAt. Fire Protection Assn., Tenn. Fire Chiefs (bd. dirs.), Alliance for Fire and Emergency Mgmt. (stds. cabinet). Roman Catholic. Office: Office of Dir Fire Svcs 65 S Front St Memphis TN 38103

SMITH, CHARLES EDWIN, computer science educator, consultant; b. Columbia, Mo., Apr. 15, 1950; s. William Walter and Nelletha Pearl (Lavendar) S.; m. Mary L. Davis, July 27, 1991. AA, Edison C.C., Ft. Myers, Fla., 1971; BS, Troy State U., 1979; MA, Webster U., St. Louis, 1989. Cert. computing profl. Enlisted USAF, Tyndall AFB, Fla., 1975-79; advanced through grades to maj. USAF; commd. 2d lt. USAF, Scott AFB, Ill., 1979; maj. USAFR, 1989—; adj. instr. Manatee C.C., Venice, Fla., 1989-90, Edison C.C., Punta Gorda, Fla., 1989-92; prof. computer sci. Edison C.C., 1992—; cons. Charles E. Smith Consulting, North Port, Fla., 1989-91. Assoc. mem. Charlotte County Econs. Devel. Coun., Port Charlotte, Fla., 1992—. Mem. Fla. Assn. C.C.s, Bass Anglers Sportsman's Soc., N.Am. Fishing Club. Republican. Avocations: reading, fishing, boating. Office: Edison C C 2511 Vasco St Punta Gorda FL 33950-2807

SMITH, CHARLES HADDON, geoscientist, consultant; b. Dartmouth, N.S., Can., Sept. 3, 1926; s. Albion Benson and Dora Pauline (McGill) S.; m. Mary Gertrude Saint, Sept. 5, 1949; children: Charles Douglas, Richard David, Alan Michael, Timothy McGill. B.Sc. and Diploma in Engring, Dalhousie U., Can., 1946, M.Sc. in Geology, 1948; M.S., Yale U., 1951, Ph.D. in Econ. Geology, 1952. Instr. Dalhousie U., Halifax, N.S., 1946-48; geologist Cerro de Pasco Copper Corp., Morococha, Peru, 1949, Geol. Survey of Can., Ottawa, Ont., 1952-64; chief petrological scis. div. Geol. Survey of Can., 1964-67, chief crustal geology div., 1967-68; sci. adviser Sci. Council Can., Ottawa, 1968-70; dir. planning Dept. Energy Mines and Resources, Ottawa, 1970-71; asst. dep. minister sci. and tech. Dept. Energy Mines and Resources, 1971-75, sr. asst. dep. minister, 1975-81; pres. Charles H. Smith Cons., 1982-94; mem. adv. coun. dept. geology and geophysics Princeton U., 1967-76; sci. advisor Can. Commn. for UNESCO, 1983-89; exec. dir. Can. Nat. Com./World Energy Conf., 1983-90; bd. govs. Can. Inst. Radiation Safety, 1983-86; hon. mem. Energy Coun. Can., 1991—; coord. 150th anniversary Geol. Survey Can., 1990-93. Mem. editl. bd. Am. Jour. Sci., 1967-72, Mineralium Deposita, 1968-83, Jour. Petrology, 1966-70, Econ. Geology, 1966-70; contbr. articles to profl. jours. Fellow Royal Soc. Can. (fgn. sec. 1986-90), Mineral. Soc. Am., Soc. Econ. Geologists (v.p. N.Am. 1968-70); mem. Can. Inst. Mining and Metallurgy (life mem., v.p. 1982-84), Assn. Profl. Engrs. Ont., Geol. Assn. Can., Can. Geosci. Coun. (pres. 1984), Rotary.

SMITH, CHARLES HENRY, JR., industrial executive; b. Cleve., July 28, 1920; s. Charles H. and Florence (Reno) S.; m. Rhea Day, Sept. 18, 1943 (dec. Jan. 1990); children: Charles Henry, Deborah Rhea Smith Potantus, Hudson Day; m. Florence M. Johnson, Mar. 9, 1991. B.S., Mass. Inst. Tech., 1942. Pres., dir. Steel Improvement & Forge Co. (name changed to Sifco Industries, Inc.), Cleve., 1943-70; chmn., chief exec. officer Steel Improvement & Forge Co. (name changed to Sifco Industries, Inc.), 1970-83, chmn., 1970—; pres. Can. Steel Improvement, Etobicoke, Ont., 1951-54; chmn. bd. Sifco Custom Machining Inc., Mpls., Sifco Selective Plating Inc., Cleve., Sifco Bearing Inc., Avon, Ohio, 1970-88; chmn., consultative coun. Sifco do Brazil, Sao Paulo, 1959-81; chmn. Sifco Turbine Component Svcs., Tampa, Fla.; dir. Sifco Turbine Components Ltd., Cork, Ireland; adv. com. bd. dirs. New Eng. Mut. Life Ins. Co., 1973-77; dir. Bharat Forge Co. Ltd., Poona, India, Aikoh Sifco Co. Ltd., Tokyo, 1970-83, Industrias Kaiser Argentina, 1958-63; mem. Com. on Manpower Resources for Nat. Security, 1953-54; U.S. employer del. Internat. Labor Conf., Geneva, 1956, 75-92, Buenos Aires, 1961; mem. adv. coun. U.S.-Japanese econ. rels. U.S. State Dept., 1970-75; dir., mem. com. experts study relationship between multinat. corps. and social policy ILO, mem. governing body, 1975-78; dir. U.S.-USSR Econ. and Trade Coun., 1975; chmn. U.S. sect. Brazil-U.S. Bus. Coun., 1976-77. Trustee Cleve. YMCA; chmn. bd. mgrs. Addison br., chmn. internat. adv. com. Center Internat. Mgmt. Studies, chmn., 1982-88; bd. dirs. YMCA of the U.S.A., 1983-88, chmn. internat. com.; vice chmn. No. Ohio Rep. Fin. Com.; chmn. No. Ohio Rep. Small Bus. Com., 1956, Partners of Alliance for Ohio, 1969-72; trustee Defiance Coll., 1958-74, St. Alexis Hosp., 1960-70, Booth Meml. Hosp., 1964-74, Judson Park; trustee Ednl. Research Council Am., 1976-86, chmn., 1978-86; pres. bd. trustees Forging Industry Edn. and Research Found., 1961-65; bd. dirs. Nat. Endowment for Democracy, 1983-91; adv. bd. Salvation Army. Named One of Ten Outstanding Young Men Am., 1955. Mem. Forging Industry Assn. (dir. 1954-55, pres. 1956-58), Young Pres.'s Orgn. (chmn. Cleve. chpt. 1956-57), U.S. C. of C. (dir. 1967-81, v.p. 1970-73, treas. 1973-74, chmn. bd. 1974-75, chmn. exec. com. 1975-76), The Ocean Club Fla. (Ocean Ridge), Union Club (Cleve.), Shaker Heights Country Club (dir.), Pine Lake Trout Club, Burning Tree Club (Bethesda, Md.), Va. Hot Springs Golf and Tennis Club, Pepper Pike Club, La Mirador (Mt. Pelerin, Switzerland), Delray Dunes Golf and Tennis Club (Boynton Beach, Fla.). Home: 4565 S Lake Dr Boynton Beach FL 33436-5904 also: 3885-1 Lander Rd Chagrin Falls OH 44022-1368 also: North Ridge Hot Springs VA 24445

SMITH, CHARLES ISAAC, geology educator; b. Hearne, Tex., Feb. 9, 1931; s. Walter Lee and Nellie Lucille (Clearwater) S.; m. Anita Lou Howell, Aug. 22, 1961; children: Lanita Maylene, James Emmett, Timothy Stephen, Sheila Nell. B.S., Baylor U., 1952; M.A., La. State U., 1955; Ph.D., U. Mich., 1966. Geologist Shell Devel. Co., Houston, 1955-60, 62-65; prof. geology U. Mich., Ann Arbor, 1965-77, chmn. dept., 1970-77; prof. geology U. Tex., Arlington, 1977-93, prof. emeritus, 1994—, chmn. dept., 1977-89, cons. geologist, 1993—. Author research papers. Mem. Geol. Soc. Am., Am. Assn. Petroleum Geologists, Am. Inst. Profl. Geologists (cert.). Home: 207 Fletcher Dr Del Rio TX 78840-3051 Office: Univ Tex Dept Geology Arlington TX 76019

SMITH, CHARLES KENT, family medicine educator; b. Des Moines, June 30, 1938; s. Herman Joseph and Elizabeth (Opinham) S.; m. Patricia Hughes Moore, Sept. 1977; children: Laurence, Eleanor, Andrew, Matthew. BA, Northwestern U., 1960, MD, 1963, MS, 1964. Diplomate Am. Bd. Internal Medicine, Am. Bd. Family Practice. Rotating intern U. Mich. Hosp., Ann Arbor, 1963-64, asst. resident medicine, 1967-68; sr. rsch. fellow in medicine (endocrinology) U. Wash. Hosp., Seattle, 1968-70, resident dept. psychiatry, 1970-72, attending staff, 1972-85; instr. dept. internal medicine U. Wash., 1970-71, from instr., asst. prof. to assoc. prof. dept. family medicine, 1971-81, prof., 1981-85, acting chmn. dept., 1976, vice chmn. dept., 1977-85, affiliate Diabetes Rsch. Ctr., 1980-85; prof., chmn. dept. family and community medicine Ea. Va. Med. Sch., Norfolk, 1985-88, mem. dean's coun. chmn. and allied coms., mem. minority affairs coms., 1985-88; prof., chmn. dept. family medicine Case Western Res. U., Cleve., 1988—, Dorothy Jones Weatherhead prof. dept. family medicine, 1992—, acting vice dean Sch. Medicine, 1995-96; mem. com. on med. edn., med. coun. and allied coms. U. Hosps. Cleve., 1988—, chmn. com. med. edn., 1992—, dir. family medicine dept.; gen. practice, locum tenens, Wrangell, Alaska, May.-June, 1970; attending staff Children's Orthopedic Hosp., Seattle, 1972-85, Med. Ctr. Hosps., Norfolk, 1985-88, Children's Hosp. of King's Daughters, Norfolk, 1986-88; cons. family mediation panel Family Ct., Superior Ct. King County, Wash., 1976-80; co-presenter 6th Internat. Workshop/Seminar Life Planning Ctr., Practice and Edn. Primary Care Medicine, Jichi Med. Sch., Japan, 1983; vis. prof. Hunan Med. Sch., Changsha, Peoples Republic China, 1984; grant reviewer HHS, Health Resources Adminstrn., Bur. Health Professions, others. Author numerous abstracts, proc., book revs., articles in profl. jours.; reviewer Jour. Family Pactice, 1977-90, books Jour. AMA, 1977—. Capt. USAF, 1963-65. Royal Soc. Medicine U.K. travelling fellow, 1974; grantee prin. investigator Spl. Project Family Medicine, 78-61, U. Wash., 1981-86, Ea. Va. Med. Sch., 1986-89, 87-90, 88-91, Case Western U., 1988-94. Fellow ACP, Am. Acad. Family Physicians (mem. chpts. in Wash. Va., Ohio, others; mem. Soc. Tchrs. Family Medicine (constn. and by-laws com. 1982-84), Assn. Depts. Family Medicine (treas. 1988—), N.Am. Primary Care Rsch. Group (mem. exec. steering com., sec. 1977-80, co-chmn. 7th ann. meeting 1979), Am. Psychiat. Assn. Home: 2857 Litchfield Rd Cleveland OH 44120-1736 Office: Case Western Res U Dept Family Medicine 10900 Euclid Ave Cleveland OH 44106-4950

SMITH, CHARLES OLIVER, engineer; b. Clinton, Mass., May 28, 1920; s. Oliver E. and Flora (Small) S.; m. Mary J. Boyle, Feb. 9, 1946; children: Mary J., Charles M., John P., Susan M., Peter G., Robert A., Katherine M. BS in Mech. Engring., Worcester Poly. Inst., 1941; SM, MIT, 1947, ScD in Metallurgy, 1951. Instr. mech. engring. Worcester Poly. Inst., 1941-43; instr., then asst. prof. Mass. Inst. Tech., 1946-51; research engr. Alcoa Research Lab., 1951-55, Oak Ridge Nat. Lab, 1955-65; prof. engring. U. Detroit, 1965-76, U. Nebr., 1976-81, Rose-Hulman Inst. Tech., 1981-86. Author: Product Liability: Are You Vulnerable?, Nuclear Reactor Materials, Science of Engineering Materials, Introduction to Reliability in Design; also numerous papers on materials, design, product liability, engring. edn. Served with USNR, 1943-46. Recipient St. George award Boy Scouts Am. Fellow ASME (Triodyne Safety award 1992, Machine Design award, 1993), Am. Soc. Engring. Edn. (Fred Merryfield award 1981); mem. AIME, Am. Soc. Metals, Sigma Xi, Tau Beta Pi, Pi Tau Sigma, Phi Kappa Theta. Home: 1920 College Ave Terre Haute IN 47803-4035

SMITH, CHARLES PAUL, newspaper publisher; b. Hartford, Conn., Nov. 1, 1926; s. Thomas S. and Kathryn (Klingler) S.; m. Carolyn Calkins, Feb. 12, 1966; children: Charles, Timothy. BS, U.S. Naval Acad., 1947. Commd. ensign USN, 1947, advanced through grades to lt., line officer, 1947-58, resigned; mgr. Container Corp. Am., Phila., 1958-66, Chattanooga, 1966-68; pub. Daily Intelligencer, Doylestown, Pa., 1968—. Roman Catholic. Office: Calkins Newspapers Inc 333 N Broad St Doylestown PA 18901-3407

SMITH, CHARLES RAYMOND, JR., lawyer; b. Wilkes-Barre, Pa., Apr. 4, 1948; s. Charles Raymond and Dorothy (Huminik) S.; m. Laura Anne Vassamillet, June 16, 1984; children: Emilie Rose, Madeleine Anne. BS magna cum laude, Syracuse U., 1970; JD cum laude, U. Pitts., 1974. Bar: Pa. 1974. Acct. Arthur Andersen & Co., Pitts., 1970-71; atty. Kirkpatrick & Lockhart, Pitts., 1974—. Chmn. bd. dirs. Greater Pitts. Conv. and Visitors Bur., 1988-90. Mem. ABA, Pitts. Tax Club, Allegheny Country Club, Edgeworth Club, Duquesne Club, Order of Coif. Avocations: golf, travel. Home: 130 Woodland Rd Sewickley PA 15143-1125 Office: Kirkpatrick & Lockhart 1500 Oliver Building Bldg Pittsburgh PA 15222-2312

SMITH, CHARLES THOMAS, retired dentist, educator; b. San Diego, Mar. 22, 1914; s. Sydney Alexander and Lydia Ellen (Hoff) S.; m. Ruth Anita Anderson, May 20, 1935 (dec. Jan. 1979); children: Charlyn Ruth, Charles Thomas; m. Mary Lou Sessums, July 21, 1979. A.B., Pacific Union Coll., 1935; D.D.S., Coll. Phys. and Surg., 1940; LL.H., Loma Linda U. Sch. of Dentistry, 1971. Tchr. Glendale Union Acad., 1935-36; pvt. practice dentistry San Diego, 1940-53; dean-elect Sch. Dentistry, Loma Linda U., 1959-60, dean, 1960-71, dean emeritus, 1971; prof. emeritus Loma Linda U., 1973—; program coordinator div. Physicians and Health Profession Edn., NIH, 1971-73; prof. dept. community dentistry U. Tex. at San Antonio, 1973-83, acting dean student affairs Dental Sch., 1975-76, assoc. dean for acad. affairs, 1976-77, acting chmn. dept. community dentistry, 1977-83; Cons. dental facilities rev. com. USPHS, 1964-69; mem. grants and allocations com. Am. Found. for Dental Health, 1973-80. Dir. Paradise Valley Sanitarium and Hosp., 1947-59, San Diego Union Acad., 1947-53; founder San Diego Children's Dental Health Center; exhibit chmn. Pacific Coast Dental Conf., 1957; pres. Am. Cancer Soc., 1950; trustee Loma Linda U., 1976-90. Served as maj. AUS Dental Corps, 1953-55. Fellow Am. Coll. Dentists (vice chmn. So. Calif. chpt. 1967-68, chmn. 1968-69), Internat. Coll. Dentists; mem. So. Calif. Dental Assn. (chmn. council on dental edn. 1963-68, treas. 1967-71), San Diego County Dental Soc. (pres. 1949), Am. Acad. Dental Practice Adminstrn., Western Dental Deans Assn. (chmn. 1960-67), Western Deans and Dental Examiners (v.p. 1969—, pres. 1970), Am. Assn. Dental Schs. (mem. exec. com., v.p. council deans 1971), Acad. Dentistry Internat. (v.p. 1985-89, treas. 1985-89, chmn. awards com. 1989-90, assoc. chmn., 1986—), Nat. Assn. Seventh Day Adventists, Am. Acad. Periodontology, Acad. Dentistry Internationale, Delta Sigma Delta, Tau Kappa Omega, Omicron Kappa Upsilon. Home: 34-895 Surrey Way Thousand Palms CA 92276-4121

SMITH, CHARLES WILLIAM, social sciences educator, sociologist; b. Providence; s. Joseph and Clara (Loitman) S.; m. Rita Cope, Sept. 3, 1963; children: Abigail Cope, Jonathan Cope. AB, Wesleyan U., 1960; MA, Brandeis U., 1966, PhD in Sociology, 1966. Instr. sociology Simmons Coll., Boston, 1964-65; from lectr. to assoc. prof. Queens Coll., Flushing, N.Y., 1965-71, from assoc. to prof. sociology, 1979—; grad. faculty Grad. Ctr.

CUNY, 1986—; vis. scholar Nuffield Coll., Oxford, Eng., 1979-80, Wesleyan U., Middletown, Conn., 1987-88; chair dept. sociology Queens Coll., Flushing, 1988-91, acting dean of faculty social sci., 1991-92, dean faculty social sci., 1992—; cons. auctions, 1986—. Author: The Mind of the Market: A Study of Stock Market Philosophies, Their Uses and Implications, 1981, Critique of Sociological Reasoning: An Essay in Philosophic Sociology, 1982, Auctions: The Social Construction of Values, 1989; editor Jour. for Theory of Social Behavior, 1983—. Bd. dirs., pres. Cmty. Action Program of White Plains, N.Y., 1974-79; bd. trustees, v.p. Temple Israel Ctr. of White Plains, 1975-94; class agt., alumni activities Wesleyan U., Middletown, Conn., 1960—. Recipient FIPSE award Dept. Edn., 1993-96, Ford Found. Diversity grant, 1990-93. Office: Queens Coll CUNY 65-30 Kissena Blvd Flushing NY 11367-1575

SMITH, CHARLES WILLIAM, engineering educator; b. Christiansburg, Va., Jan. 1, 1926; s. Robert Floyd and Ollie (Surface) S.; m. Doris Graham Burton, Sept. 9, 1950; children: Terry Jane Kelley, David Bryan. BSCE, Va. Poly. Inst., 1947, MS in Applied Mechanics, 1949. Registered profl. engr., Va. Isntr. Va. Poly. Inst. and State U., Blacksburg, 1947-48, asst. prof., 1949-52, assoc. prof., 1953-57, prof. engring., 1958-81, alumni disting. prof., 1982-92, alumni disting. prof. emeritus, 1992—; advanced grad. engring. tng. program GE Co., Lynchburg, Va., 1962; grad. tng. program Western Elec.-Bell Labs., Winston-Salem, N.C., 1963, 64; bd. dirs. Local Water Authority, Blacksburg, 1975—. Author: (with others) Experimental Techniques in Fracture Mechanics, Vol. 2, 1973, Inelastic Behavior of Composite Materials, 1975, Mechanics of Fracture, Vol. 6, 1981, Handbook of Experimental Stress Analysis, 1986, Experimental Techniques in Fracture, Vol. 3, 1993; editor: Fracture Mechanics, Vol. 11, co-editor, Vol. 17; regional editor: Jour. of Theoretical and Applied Fracture Mechanics, 1984—; guest editor: (jour.) Optics and Lasers in Engineering, 1991; contbr. articles to profl. jours. Recipient Scientific Achievement award NASA Langley Rsch. Ctr., 1986, Dan H. Pletta award for engring. educator of yr. Va. Consortium Engring. Schs., 1991. Fellow Soc. Experimental Mechanics (numerous coms., M.M. Frocht award for oustanding educator in experimental mechanics 1983, William M. Murray medal for contbns. to experimental mechanics, 1993, B.J. Lazan award for rsch. in experimental mechanics, 1995), Am. Acad. Mechanics; mem. ASTM, ASME, NSPE (many coms. 1950-70), Am. Soc. Engring. Edn. (chmn. nominating com. 1971), Soc. Engring. Sci. (organizing com. 1977-81 annual meetings co-chmn. 1984), Internat. Assn. Structural Mechanics in Reactor Tech. Methodist. Achievements include development of refined merger of optical methods to measure stress intensity factor distributions in three dimensional cracked bodies in nuclear, missile and aircraft industries. Office: Va Poly Inst and State Univ ESM-VPISU-0219 Blacksburg VA 24061

SMITH, CHARLES WILSON, JR., university dean; b. Ft. Lauderdale, Fla., Apr. 15, 1949; m. Constance Killen; children: Thaddeus, Cameron, Amber, Isaac, Jordan, Rachael. MD, U. N.C., 1974, BS, 1979. Diplomate Am. Bd. Family Practice (bd. dirs., com. mem., treas., pres. 1991-92). Resident in psychiatry U. N.C. Meml. Hosp., 1974-75, resident in family practice, 1975-78; pvt. practice, Muscatine, Ia., 1978-79; asst. prof. Wright State U., 1979-83, assoc. prof., 1983-86; chief of family medicine sch. of primary med. care U. Ala., Huntsville, 1986-87, assoc. dean clin. affairs, 1986-87, acting dean, 1986; assoc. dean U. Ala. Sch. of Medicine, Huntsville, 1986-89; exec. assoc. dean for clin. affairs U. Ark. for Med. Scis., Little Rock, 1989—, prof. family and community medicine, 1989—, exec. dir. faculty practice plan, 1991—; dir. family practice residency program Miami Valley Hosp., Dayton, Ohio, 1979-86. Co-author: Family Practice Desk Reference, 2d edit., 1995; editor Primary Care Currents, 1985—; dep. editor Am. Family Physician, 1987—; contbr. numerous articles to profl. jours. Bd. dirs. Nicholas J. Pisacano Found., 1990—. Mem. AMA, Am. Acad. Family Physicians (editor mag.), Ark. Acad. Family Physicians, Ark. Med. Assn., Pulaski County Med. Soc. Home: 4 Chelsea Rd Little Rock AR 72212-3723 Office: U Ark for Med Scis 4301 W Markham St # 719 Little Rock AR 72205-7101

SMITH, CHARLES Z., state supreme court justice; b. Lakeland, Fla., Feb. 23, 1927; s. John R. and Eva (Love) S.; m. Eleanor Jane Martinez, Aug. 20, 1955; children: Carlos M., Michael O., Stephen P., Felica L. BS, Temple U., 1952; JD, U. Wash., 1955. Bar: Wash. 1955. Law clk. Wash. Supreme Ct., Olympia, 1955-56; dep. pros. atty., asst. chief criminal div. King County, Seattle, 1956-60; ptnr. Bianchi, Smith & Tobin, Seattle, 1960-61; spl. asst. to atty. gen. criminal div. U.S. Dept. Justice, Washington, 1961-64; judge criminal dept. Seattle Mcpl. Ct., 1965-66; judge Superior Ct. King County, 1966-73; former assoc. dean, prof. law U. Wash., 1973; now justice Wash. Supreme Ct., Olympia. Mem. adv. bd. NAACP, Seattle Urban League, Wash. State Literacy Coun., Boys Club, Wash. Citizens for Migrant Affairs, Medina Children's Svc., Children's Home Soc. Wash., Seattle Better Bus. Bur., Seattle Foundation, Seattle Symphony Orch., Seattle Opera Assn., Community Svc. Ctr. for Deaf and Hard of Hearing, Seattle U., Seattle Sexual Assault Ctr., Seattle Psychoanalytic Inst., The Little Sch., Linfield Coll., Japanese Am. Citizens League, Kawabe Meml. Hous, Puget Counseling Ctr, Am. Cancer Soc., Hutchinson Cancer Rsch. Ctr., Robert Chinn Found.; pres. Am. Bapt. Chs. U.S.A., 1976-77, lt. col. ret. USMCR. Mem. ABA, Am. Judicature Soc., Washington Bar Assn., Seattle-King County Bar Assn., Order of Coif., Phi Alpha Delta, Alpha Phi Alpha. Office: Wash Supreme Ct Temple of Justice PO Box 40929 Olympia WA 98504

SMITH, CHARLOTTE REED, retired music educator; b. Eubank, Ky., Sept. 15, 1921; d. Joseph Lumpkin and Cornelia Elizabeth (Spenser) Reed; m. Walter Lindsay Smith, Aug. 24, 1949; children—Walter Lindsay IV, Elizabeth Reed. B.A. in Music, Tift Coll., 1941; M.A. in Mus. Theory, Eastman Sch. of Music, 1946; postgrad. Juilliard Sch., 1949. Asst. prof. theory Okla. Bapt. U., 1944-45, Washburn U., 1946-48; prof. music Furman U., Greenville, S.C., 1948-92; chmn. dept. music, 1987-92. Editor: Seven Penitential Psalms with Two Laudate Psalms, 1983; author: Manual of Sixteenth-Century Contrapuntal Style, 1989. Mem. Internat. Musicological Soc., Am. Musicological Soc., Soc. for Music Theory, AAUP (sec.-treas. Furman chpt. 1984-85), Nat. Fedn. Music Clubs, Pi Kappa Lambda. Republican. Baptist.

SMITH, CHESTER, broadcasting executive; b. Wade, Okla., Mar. 29, 1930; s. Louis L. and Effie (Brown) S.; m. Naomi L. Crenshaw, July 19, 1959; children: Lauri, Lorna, Roxanne. Country western performer on Capitol records, TV and radio, 1947-61; owner, mgr. Sta. KLOC, Ceres-Modesto, Calif., 1963-81, Sta. KCBA-TV, Salinas-Monterey, Calif., 1981—; owner, gen. ptnr. Sta. KCSO-TV, Modesto-Stockton-Sacramento, Sta. KCVU-TV, Paradise-Chico-Redding, Calif., 1986—, Sta.; co-owner Sta. KBVU-TV, Eureka, Calif., 1990—; owner Sta. KNSO-TV, Merced-Fresno, KDS TV, Chico, Calif. Mem. Calif. Broadcasters Assn. Republican. Mem. Christian Ch. original rec. Wait A Little Longer Please Jesus; inducted Country Music Hall of Fame, Nashville, 1955, inductee Western Swing Hall of Fame, Sacramento, 1988.

SMITH, CHESTER LEO, lawyer; b. Kansas City, Mo., Jan. 23, 1922; s. Chester Leo and Alameda Mariposa (West) S.; m. Ann Smith; 1 dau., Blithe. BA, U. Chgo., 1942; JD, Harvard U., 1948. Bar: Ill. 1949, Calif. 1951. Asst. to v.p. Cuneo Press, Chgo., 1948-49; individual practice Los Angeles, 1951-87, ret., 1987. Author: Midway 4 June, 1942, 1962, (plays) My Empress Eva Darling, The Last Execution, Images of Che, Cross-Examination at Auschwitz; editor: (Wu Han): The Dismissal of Hai Jui, 1968; contbr. stories to, Collier's, Am. Legion mag. Served to 1st lt. Air Corps, USMCR, 1942-45, Okinawa, Borneo. Decorated Air medal (3). Mem. State Bar Calif. Address: PO Box 49590 Los Angeles CA 90049-0590

SMITH, CHRISTINE, pharmaceutical executive; b. Bronx, N.Y., Oct. 28, 1958; d. Frank and Virginia (Widmer) Michalchuk. AA, Suffolk County C.C., Farmingvale, N.Y., 1978, AS, 1979; BA, SUNY, Stony Brook, 1980. Cert. dental asst., N.Y. Purchasing agt. Ctrl. Dental Supply Co., Hempstead, N.Y., 1981-82; sales mgr. Capital Credit Corp., Hempstead, N.Y., 1982-83; pharm. rep. Bristol Myers, Evansville, Ind., 1983-91, Syntex Labs., Palo Alto, Calif., 1991-93, Abbott Labs., Abbott Park, Ill., 1993—; pres. The Image Consultants, Huntington, N.Y., 1989-91. Mem. Tai-Zen Acad. Self-Def., U.S. Karate Studios. Roman Catholic. Avocations: creative writing, consulting to business persons, reading. Office: Abbott Labs 1 Abbott Park Rd Abbott Park IL 60064-3500

SMITH, CHRISTOPHER HENRY, congressman; b. Rahway, N.J., Mar. 4, 1953; s. Bernard Henry and Katherine Joan (Hall) S.; m. Marie Hahn, July 2, 1977; children: Melissa, Christopher, Michael Jonathan, Elyse. Student, Worcester Coll., Eng., 1973-74; B.A. in Bus. Adminstrn., Trenton State Coll., 1975. Exec. dir. N.J. Right to Life Com., 1976-77; dir. instl. sales Leisure Unltd. Inc., Woodbridge, N.J., 1978-80; mem. 97th-104th Congresses from 4th N.J. dist., Washington, D.C., 1981—; chmn. internat. rels. subcom. on internat. ops. and human rights 97th-104th Congresses from 4th N.J. dist., mem. vets. affairs com., chmn. Helsinki com.; U.S. rep. to UN internat. conf. immunizing world's children. Active human rights movements Romania, China, USSR, Vietnam. Named Legislator of Yr. VFW, Legislator of Yr. Internat. Assn. Chiropractors, Legislator of Yr. KC, 1989; recipient Leader for Peace award Peace Corps. Mem. Nat. Fedn. Ind. Bus. Republican. Roman Catholic. Office: 2370 Rayburn Ho Office Bldg Washington DC 20515*

SMITH, CHUCK, religious organization leader. Pres. Alliance for Life. Office: 109 Oakscresent Fort McMurray AL*

SMITH, CLAIR S., JR., oil industry executive. With Lion Oil, El Dorado, Ark., 1954-70; CEO P & O Falco, Bossier City, La., 1970-84; with Enron Oil, Houston, 1984-87; pres. C. S. SmithEnterprises, Shreveport, La., 1982—; chmn. bd. S & D Falco, Inc., Shreveport, La., 1989—. Office: S & D Falco Inc 950 Wells Island Rd Shreveport LA 71107-5504*

SMITH, CLAIR SCOTT, III, petroleum company executive; b. 1963. Pres., CEO Enron Oil Corp., Midland, Tex., 1984-90, S & D Falco Inc., Shreveport, La., 1990—. Office: S & D Falco Inc 950 Wells Island Rd Shreveport LA 71107-5504*

SMITH, CLARA JEAN, retired nursing home administrator; b. Berwick, Pa., Aug. 31, 1932; d. Barton Fredrick and Evelyn Miriam (Bomboy) Hough; RN, Williamsport (Pa.) Hosp., 1953; B.S. in Nursing Edn., Wilkes Coll., Wilkes-Barre, Pa., 1960; M.S. in Edn., Temple U., Phila., 1969; m. Robert W. Smith, June 7, 1958. From staff nurse to dir. nursing Retreat State Hosp., Hunlock Creek, Pa., 1953-80; dir. long term care facility Danville (Pa.) State Hosp., 1980-82; ret., 1982; dir. accrediatation coordination and quality assurance Nursing Home Adminstrs., 1980—; speaker, instr. in field. Author tng. and ednl. programs. Mem. Pa. State Employees Retirement Assn. (pres. Luzerne/Columbia County chpt., regional v.p. northeastern Pa.), Williamsport Hosp. Sch. Nursing Alumni, Sunshine Club, Town Hill Hobby Group, Town Hill Over 50 Group. Methodist. Home: PO Box 999 Berwick PA 18603-0699

SMITH, CLARK ROBINSON, lawyer; b. Chgo., Feb. 17, 1938; s. Carlton Robinson and Theda Clark (Peters) S.; m. Trina Helen Hendershot, Jan. 20, 1962; children: Clark Carlton, Luke Owen. BS in Econs., U. Pa., 1961; LLB, U. Wis., 1965. Bar: Mass. 1966, U.S. Surpeme Ct. 1976, U.S. Dist. Ct. Mass. 1976, U.S. Tax Ct. 1976. From law clk. to assoc. Johnson Clapp Ives & King, Boston, 1965-67; pvt. practice Boston, 1972—; bd. dirs., acting chair Zoning Bd. Appeals, Wenham, Mass., 1982-94; bd. dirs. Menasha Corp., Neenah, Wis., Beverly (Mass.) Nat. Bank. Trustee Beverly Regional YMCA, 1984—; bd. dirs. North Country Sch., Lake Placid, N.Y., 1988-95, Menasha Corp. Found., Neenah, 1994; chmn. bd. Theda C. Smith Found., Neenah, 1980—, United Way Cen. North Shore, Beverly, 1993-94. Fellow Mass. Bar Found. (mem. com., county advisor 1990—); mem. ABA, Mass. Bar Assn., Boston Bar Assn. (coms., vol. civil case appts. 1976—), Boston Bar Found. (life, endowment advisor 1990—). Republican. Episcopalian. Avocations: golfing, tennis, skiing. Home: 11 Dodges Row Wenham MA 01984-1601 Office: Ste 1900 101 Federal St Boston MA 02110

SMITH, CLIFFORD LEE, clergyman; b. Barberton, Ohio, Feb. 27, 1945; s. Howard Donald and Alpha Louisa (McCaman) S.; m. Paulette Joan Wall, Sept. 28, 1963; 1 child, Christina Marie. BA, Ky. Christian Coll., Grayson, 1972, BTh, 1973, MMin, 1987. Ordained to ministry Ch. of Christ, 1972. Minister Allentown Ch. of Christ, Wheelersburg, Ohio, 1969-71, Bradford Ch. of Christ, Pomery, Ohio, 1971-75, First Christian Ch., Havre de Grace, Md., 1976-87; pres. Eastern Christian Coll., Bel Air, Md., 1988-92, trustee, 1977-88; clergyman The Christian Ch. at Arnold, Md., 1992—; pres. Ea. Christian Coll., Bel Air, Md., 1988-92; v.p. Eastern Christian Conv., N.E. U.S., 1990; 1st v.p. Mid-Atlantic Christian Ch. Evangelism, 1980-85. Republican. Avocations: fishing, hunting, reading. Home and Office: PO Box 9683 Arnold MD 21012-0683

SMITH, CLIFFORD NEAL, business educator, writer; b. Wakita, Okla., May 30, 1923; s. Jesse Newton and Inez Lane (Jones) S.; m. Anna Piszczan-Czaja, Sept. 3, 1951; children: Helen Inez Smith Barrette. BS, Okla. State U., 1943; AM, U. Chgo., 1948; postgrad. Columbia U., 1960. Selector, U.S. Displaced Persons Commn., Washington and Munich, Germany, 1948-51; auditor Phillips Petroleum Co., Caracas, Venezuela, 1951-58; planning analyst Mobil Internat. Oil Co., N.Y.C., 1960, 65-66, Mobil Oil A.G., Deutschland, Hamburg, Germany, 1961-63; asst. to v.p. for Germany, Mobil Inner Europe, Inc., Geneva, 1963-65; asst. prof. No. Ill. U. Sch. Bus., DeKalb, 1966-69, part-time prof. internat. bus., 1970—; owner Westland Publs.; lectr. in field. Author: Federal Land Series, vol. 1, 1972, vol. 2, 1973, vol. 3, 1980, vol. 4, part 1, 1982, vol. 4, part 2, 1986, Encyclopedia of German-American Genealogical Research, American Genealogical Resources in German Archives, 1977, numerous monographs in German-Am., Brit.-Am., French-Am. geneal. research series, German and Central European Emigration Series; contbg. editor Nat. Geog. Soc. Quar., Geneal. jour. (Utah); contbr. articles to profl. jours. Mem. at large exec. com. Friends Com. on Nat. Legis., 1968-75; mem. regional exec. com. Am. Friends Service Com., 1969-76; v.p. Riverside Dem., N.Y.C., 1959-61; precinct committeeman, 1984—; mem. Ariz. State Central Com. of Dem. Party, 1984—; sec. Dem. Cen. Com. of Cochise County. Recipient Distinguished Service medal Ill. Geneal. Soc., 1973, award for outstanding service to sci. genealogy Am. Soc. Genealogists, 1973; court appointed arbitrator for civil cases, 1992. Fellow Geneal. Soc. of Utah; mem. S.R., SAR, Soc. Descs. Colonial Clergy, Soc. Advancement Mgmt., Ill. Genealogic Soc. (dir. 1968-69), Phi Eta Sigma, Beta Alpha Psi, Sigma Iota Epsilon. Mem. Soc. of Friends. Club: American of Hamburg (v.p. 1962-63); contbr. articles to profl. jours. Address: PO Box 117 Mc Neal AZ 85617-0117

SMITH, CLIFFORD VAUGHN, JR., academic administrator; b. Washington, Nov. 29, 1931; s. Clifford Vaughn and Jean (Murray) S.; m. Nina Marie Smith, Aug. 22, 1953; children: Sharon, Debra, Patricia. BSCE, State U. Iowa, 1954; MS Engring., Johns Hopkins U., 1960, PhD, 1966; PhD (hon.), Tuskegee U., 1991. V.p. Oreg. State U., Corvallis, 1978-81, spl. asst. to chancellor, dir. Council Adv. Sci. and Engring. Edn., 1983-85, dir. Radiation Ctr., 1985-86; exec. engr. Bechtel Nat. Inc., Oak Ridge, Tenn., 1981-83; chancellor U. Wis., Milw., 1986-90; pres. GE Fund, Fairfield, Conn., 1990—; bd. dirs. Astronautics Corp. Am., Milw.; cons. NSF, Washington, 1985—, Envirodyne Engrs., St. Louis, 1985—; mem. radiation adv. com. to sci. adv. bd. U.S. EPA, Washington, 1984—; adv. com. nuclear waste U.S. Nuclear Regulatory Commn., 1988-90; EHR adv. com. NSF, 1991—; steering com. human resources devel. for tech. industry simulation UNESCO, 1992—; mem. Nat. Bd. Fund for Improvement Postsecondary Edn., U.S. Dept. Edn., 1993—. Bd. dirs. Milw. County Research Park, 1987—, Greater Milw. Com., 1987—, Columbia Hosp. Health System Inc., Milw., 1987—; at-large gov. Am. Heart Assn., Milw., 1987—; trustee Inst. Internat. Edn., 1992—; bd. assocs. Gallaudet Univ., 1993—. Recipient Gold medal for exceptional service EPA, 1973; named Eminent Engr., Tau Beta Pi, 1979; hon. faculty mem. Blue Key Nat. Honor Fraternity, 1980. Mem. ASCE, NSPE, Am. Soc. Engring. Edn., Am. Nuclear Soc., Phi Kappa Phi. Roman Catholic. Club: Univ. (Milw.). Avocations: reading historical novels, travel. Home: 12 Valley View Rd Newtown CT 06470-1922 Office: GE Found 3135 Easton Tpke Fairfield CT 06431-0002

SMITH, CLODUS RAY, academic administrator; b. Blanchard, Okla., May 15, 1928; s. William Thomas and Rachel (Hale) S.; m. Pauline R. Chaat; children: Martha Lynn, William Paul, Paula Diane. Assoc. degree, Cameron State Coll., 1948; BS in Agrl. Edn., Okla. A & M Coll., 1950; MS in Vocat. Edn., Okla. State U., 1955; EdD in Vocat. Edn., Cornell U., 1960. Grad. asst. Cornell U., 1957-59; asst. prof. U. Md., 1959-62, assoc. prof., 1962-63, dir. Summer Sch., 1963-72, adminstrv. dean, 1972-73; spl. asst. to pres. Cleve. State U., 1973-74, v.p. for univ. rels., 1974-83; pres. Rio Grande Coll. and Rio Grande Community Coll., Ohio, 1983-86, Lake Erie Coll., Painesville, Ohio, 1986-92, Okla. Ind. Coll. Found., Oklahoma City, 1993—, Okla. Assn. Ind. Colls. and Univs., 1993—; cons. NEA, Naval Weapons Lab., Dehlgren, Va.; researcher Personal and Profl. Satisfactions; contract investigator Nat. Endowment for Humanities; dir. Human Resources and Community Devel., Prince George's County, Md. Author: Planning and Paying for College, 1958, Rural Recreation for Profit, 1971, A Strategy for University Relations, 1975, State Relations for the 1980 Decade, 1982. Amb. Natural Resources, Ohio, 1984, chmn. dept.; founder N.Am. Assn. of Summer Schs., 1979. Recipient Rsch. award Nat. Project in Agrl. Communications, 1959, Edn. award Prince George's C. of C., 1971. Mem. Am. Assn. U. Adminstrs., Am. Assn. for Higher Edn., Nat. Soc. for Study Edn., Coun. for Support and Advancement Edn., Am. Alumni Coun., Al Koran Hunter's Club, Shriners. Methodist. Avocations: hunting, fishing. Home: 6617 115th St Oklahoma City OK 73162 Office: Okla Ind Coll Found 114 E Sheridan Ave Ste 101 Oklahoma City OK 73104-2418

SMITH, CLYDE CURRY, historian, educator; b. Hamilton, Ohio, Dec. 16, 1929; s. Charles Clyde and Mabel Ethel Ola (Curry) S.; m. Ellen Marie Gormsen, June 13, 1953; children: Harald Clyde, Karen Margaret Evans. BA in Physics cum laude and MS, Miami U., Oxford, Ohio, 1951; BDiv, U. Chgo., 1954, MA, 1961, PhD, 1968. Ordained to ministry Christian Ch. (Disciples of Christ), 1954. Exec. asst. to dean Disciples Div. House, Chgo., 1956-57; lectr. in O.T., Univ. Coll. U. Chgo., 1957; asst. prof. St. John's Coll. U. Manitoba, Winnipeg, Can., 1958-63; instr. Brandeis U., Waltham, Mass., 1963-65; prof. ancient history and religions U. Wis., River Falls, 1965-90, prof. emeritus, 1990—; vis. prof. religious studies Culver-Stockton Coll., Canton, Mo., 1990, U. Newcastle-upon-Tyne, Eng., 1992-94; vis. lectr. div., Edge Hill Coll. of Edn., Ormskirk, Eng., 1970-71; postdoctoral fellow Johns Hopkins U., Balt., 1977; NEH fellow-in-residence U. Calif., Santa Barbara, 1978-79; vis. rsch. fellow, lectr. religious studies U. Aberdeen, Scotland, 1980, 85-86. Contbr. articles to prof. publs. Mem. Pierce County Hist. Assn., River Falls, 1965—, Wis. Dems., 1965—, Dem. Nat. Com., 1983—; charter mem. Sci. Mus. of Minn., St. Paul, 1973—; founding mem. River Falls Cmty. Arts Base, 1996—. Recipient Gov.'s Spl. award State of Wis., 1990, several grants. Mem. Assn. Ancient Historians, Can. Soc. Ch. History (founder, treas. 1960-63), N.Am. Patristic Soc., Can. Soc. for Mesopotamian Studies, Soc. for Promotion Roman Studies of London, Hellenic Soc. London, Brit. Sch. Archaeology in Iraq, Brit. Inst. Archaeology in Ankara, Oriental Inst. U. Chgo., Phi Beta Kappa. Democrat. Avocations: outerspace, battleships, dinosaurs. Home: 939 W Maple St River Falls WI 54022-2055 *We can begin thought with the assumption that there is a world which knows neither origin nor end but which includes us; we can conclude with the affirmations that there was a "when" whatever is was not, and that whatever is will with time cease to be. Our concern then can be to enhance value and empower others, especially those who follow.*

SMITH, CLYDE R., counselor educator; b. Donaldson, Ark., June 15, 1933; s. Clyde Raymond Smith and Annie Pearl (Burnett) Cypert; m. Jannis Lowery, July 31, 1952; 1 child, Renee Lowery. BS, Ark. State U., 1957; MEd, U. Mo., 1958; EdD, U. Tenn., Knoxville, 1969. Employment placement counselor Mo. Bur. for the Blind, Kansas City, Mo., 1958-60; counselor Presbyn. Guidance Ctr., Rhodes U., Memphis, 1960-67; assoc. prof. edn. Bradley U., Peoria, Ill., 1969—; vocat. cons. Social Security Adminstrn. Bur. Hearings and Appeals, Memphis, 1963-69, Peoria, 1969-78. Contbr. articles to profl. jours. Bd dirs. Peoria Hts. Sch. Dist. 325, 1974-76, Children's Home Assn. Ill., Peoria, 1978-80. Recipient Jefferson award Am. Inst. for Pub. Svc., 1978, Tom Connor award C. of C., Peoria, 1978, Others award Salvation Army, 1984. Mem. Am. Counseling Assn. (life), Nat. Career Devel. Assn., Peoria Lions (life, pres. 1975-76, bd. dirs. 1978-81, 85-91, dep. dist. gov. 1982-83, zone chmn. 1983-84, Melvin Jones fellow). Republican. Presbyterian. Avocations: reading, music, hiking, collecting old movies. Home: 1511 W Callender Ave Peoria IL 61606-1615 Office: Bradley U 306 Westlake Hall Peoria IL 61625

SMITH, CORLIES MORGAN, publishing executive; b. Phila., Mar. 31, 1929; s. Charles Ross and Mary Howard (Stewart) S.; m. Sheila de Peyster Carey, June 17, 1950; children: Mark, Nicholas, Peter, Baylies, Timothy. BA, Yale U., 1951. Assoc. editor J.B. Lippincott Co., Phila., 1955-62; sr. editor The Viking Press, N.Y.C., 1962-83; editorial dir. Ticknor & Fields, N.Y.C., 1984-89; editor in chief Harcourt Brace & Co., N.Y.C., 1990-94, editorial con., 1995—. Home and Office: 1435 Lexington Ave New York NY 10128-1625

SMITH, CORNELIA MARSCHALL, biology educator, retired; b. Llano, Tex., Oct. 15, 1895; d. Ernst and Lucie (Meusebach) Marschall; m. Charles G. Smith, Sept. 9, 1926 (wid. Aug. 1967). BA in Pre-Med/Biology, Baylor U., 1918; MA in Biology, U. Chgo., 1925; PhD in Biology, Johns Hopkins, 1928. Prof. biology Waco (Tex.) High Sch., 1918-25; prof. botany Baylor U., Waco, 1928-30, asst. prof. biology, 1930-35, chmn. biology dept., 1940-67, dir. Strecker Mus., 1940-67; chmn. biology dept. John B. Stetson U., DeLand, Fla., 1935-40; sec. treas. Tex. Bd. Examiners of Basic Scis., 1960-67; v.p. Tex. Acad. Sci., 1954, treas. 1944-46. Editor: Spencer's Proverb Lore, 1970; author: Browning's Proverb Lore, 1989, A Monograph: The Artist Pen Browning, 1993, A Monograph: The Physical Browning, 1981. Recipient Herbert H. Reynolds award Baylor U., Waco, 1991; Cornelia M. Smith Professorship in Biology initiated 1980, Cornelia Marschall Smith Day of Celebration, 1992; named Minnie Piper Prof. of Yr., 1965. Mem. Mortar Bd. (hon.), Baylor Round Table, Beta Beta Beta, Omicron Delta Kappa (hon.), Sigma Xi. Democrat. Baptist. Avocations: attending symphony performances, hosting social parties, going to work daily. Home: 801 James Ave Waco TX 76706-1472 Office: Armstrong Browning Libr PO Box 97152 Waco TX 76798

SMITH, CRAIG RICHARDS, manufacturing executive; b. Los Angeles, June 2, 1940; s. Max Boley and Dorcas (Richards) S.; m. Diann Kuhni, June 2, 1960; children: Bradley, Sharee, Tracy, Cindy, Kristen, Michelle. BS in Physics, Brigham Young U., 1962, MBA, 1965. V.p. ops. WER Indsl. div. Emerson Electric, Grand Island, N.Y., 1972-76; v.p., gen. mgr. Carborundum Bonded Abrasives Div., Buffalo, 1976-70; v.p., div. mgr. Raymark Corp., Trumbull, Conn., 1980-85, now bd. dirs.; pres., chief exec. officer Raytech Corp., Shelton, 1985—, also bd. dirs. Republican. Mormon. Avocations: running, golf, tennis, basketball. Office: Raytech Corp 1 Corporate Dr Ste 512 Shelton CT 06484-6211

SMITH, CULLEN, lawyer; b. Waco, Tex., May 31, 1925; s. Curtis Cullen and Elizabeth (Brient) S.; m. Laura Risher Dossett, Mar. 6, 1948; children: Sallie Chesnutt Smith Wright, Alethea Risher Smith Gilbert, Elizabeth Brient Smith. Student, Emory U., 1943-44, Duke U., 1944; B.B.A., Baylor U., 1948, J.D., 1950. Bar: Tex. 1950. Ptnr. firm Smith, McIlheran & Smith, Weslaco, Tex., 1950-53, Naman, Howell, Smith & Lee (P.C.), Waco, 1953—; lectr. law Baylor U. Sch. Law, 1964-72. Contbr. articles to legal publs. Mem. standing com. Episcopal Diocese of Tex., 1960-63, 74-75; trustee Episcopal Theol. Sem. of S.W., 1962-67; mem. Waco City Coun., 1983-86; chmn. bd. Vanguard Sch., 1975; bd. dirs. G.H. Pape Found., 1993-94; bd. dirs., vice chmn. Tex. Ctr. for Legal Ethics and Professionalism, 1994—. 1st lt. USMCR, 1943-46. Named One of 5 Outstanding Young Texans Tex. Jr. C. of C., 1957, Baylor Lawyer of Yr., 1980. Fellow Am. Bar Found., Tex. Bar Found. (chmn. bd. 1973-74), fellow Coll. of Law Practice Mgmt.; mem. ABA (chmn. standing com. econs. law practice 1965-69, chmn. spl. com. on law book pub. practices 1970-72, chmn. gen. practice sect. 1973-74, mem. ho. of dels. 1974-81), Am. Law Firm Assn. (chmn. 1989-90), Waco-McLennan County Bar Assn. (pres. 1956-57), Mont. Bar Assn. (hon.), State Bar Tex. (pres. jr. bar 1957-58, chmn. profl. econs. com. 1959-61, chmn. spl. com. on revision Tex. Canons Ethics 1969-71, dir. 1971-74, pres. 1978-79), Baylor U. Law Alumni Assn. (pres. 1962-63), Order of Coif, Delta Sigma Phi, Phi Delta Phi. Clubs: Ridgewood Country (pres. 1965), Hedonia (pres. 1957). Lodge: Rotary. Avocation: photography. Home: Oak Grove Farm 447 Meandering Way China Spring TX 76633-2905 Office: Naman Howell Smith & Lee PC Tex Ctr PO Box 1470 Waco TX 76703-1470

SMITH, CURTIS JOHNSTON, government executive; b. Honolulu, Jan. 7, 1947; s. Robert Johnston and Sara Adelaide (Marshall) S.; m. Susan Helen Manell, June 17, 1967; 1 dau., Morgan Lynn. BA, Calif. Luth. Coll., Thousand Oaks, 1969; MA, Ohio State U., 1972, PhD, 1975. Legis. asst.

Office of Pers. Mgmt., Washington, 1977-80, spl. asst. to assoc. dir. for compensation, 1980-82, dep. asst. dir. for pay and benefits policy, 1982-84, sr. examiner office mgmt. and budget, 1984-85, policy advisor to dir., 1985-86, assoc. dir. for career entry and employee devel., 1986-89, assoc. dir. ret., ins., 1989-94; dir. Office Exec. Resources and dir. Fed. Exec. Inst., Charlottesville, Va., 1994—; mem. Nat. Accountancy Pub. Adminstrs. panel on pub. svc. Assn. Va. Health Policy Ctr. Mem. Am. Soc. Pub. Adminstrn., Internat. Personnel Mgmt. Assn., Trout Unlimited (No. Va.). Avocations: fishing, golf, bicycling. Office: Fed Exec Inst Office Exec Resources 1301 Emmet St N Charlottesville VA 22903-4872

SMITH, CYNTHIA MARIE, mathematics educator; b. Titusville, Fla., Mar. 3, 1965; d. Earl Edson and Diana Lynn (Smith) Smith; m. Bret Michael Sewell, May 16, 1987 (div. Dec. 1990); m. Vincent Anthony Miller, Dec. 18, 1993. BS in Math., Howard Payne U., Brownwood, Tex., 1987; MA in Math., U. North Tex., 1992. Part-time instr. U. North Tex., Denton, 1990-92; tchr. math. Edinburg (Tex.) H.S., 1992; part-time instr. U. Tex.-Pan Am., Edinburg, 1992, instr. math., 1992—; part-time instr. South Tex. C.C., McAllen, 1994, curriculum cons., 1994—; math. cons. St. Joseph Cath. Sch., Edinburg, 1994—; Tex. pre-engring. program instr., Edinburg, 1994; tchr. trainer Pittman Elem. Sch., Raymondville, Tex., 1994, Elsa (Tex.) Mid. Sch., 1994, Chapa Primary Sch., LaJoya, Tex., 1994. Author: The Eulerian Functions of Cyclic Groups, Dihedral Groups and P-groups, 1992. Mem. Nat. Coun. Tchrs. Math., Rio Grande Valley Coun. Tchrs. Math. Republican. Roman Catholic. Avocations: skiing, hiking, painting. Home: 2073 Scenic Dr 1B Lancaster OH 43130 Office: Univ of Texas-Pan American Math/Computer Sci Dept Edinburg TX 78539

SMITH, DALLAS R., federal official; b. Bolton, N.C., Oct. 1, 1942; s. John William and Bonnie Arlene (Jacobs) S.; m. Shirley Ann Turner, Apr. 10, 1966; 2 children. BS, N.C. Agrl. and Tech. U., 1965; postgrad., U. Md., 1968-69. Agrl. ext. agent N.C. ext. svc. tobacco and peanuts divsn. agrl. stabilization and conservation svc. Dept. Agr., 1965-68, cotton mktg. specialist, 1969-75, chief peanut br., 1976-77, dep. dir., 1977-85, dir., 1985-93; dep. under sec. internat. affairs and commodity programs office of sec. Dept. Agr., Washington, 1993—; now dep. under sec. farm and foreign agrl. srvs. Dept. Agrl. Active Patuxent River 4-H Ctr. Sgt. U.S. Army, res. Nat. 4-H fellow. Presbyterian. Avocations: woodworking, tennis. Office: Dept of Agrl Farm & Foreign Agrl Srvs Rm 205E 14th & Independence Ave SW Washington DC 20250-0002*

SMITH, DANIEL CLIFFORD, lawyer; b. Cin., Aug. 9, 1936; s. Clifford John and Vivian Aileen (Stone) S.; m. Carroll Cunningham; children—Edward, Andrew, Scott. B.S., Ariz. State U., 1960; postgrad. George Washington U., 1961-62; J.D., Am. U., 1965. Bar: D.C. 1965, U.S. Ct. Appeals (D.C. cir.) 1966, U.S. Ct. Appeals (Fed. cir), U.S. Dist. Ct. D.C. 1966, Va. 1967, U.S. Supreme Ct. 1969, U.S. Ct. Appeals (4th cir., 5th cir., 7th cir., 9th cir., 11th cir.), U.S. Ct. Claims, U.S. Ct. Customs and Patent Appeals, U.S. Tax Ct. Assoc. Alpern & Feissner, Washington, 1963-66; atty. FTC, Washington, 1966-70; ptnr. Arent, Fox, Kintner, Plotkin & Kahn, Washington, 1970-93, Canfield & Smith, Washington, 1993—. Pres., dir. Country Pl. Citizens Assn., Inc., 1974-77; bd. dirs. Sea Watch Condominium, Ocean City, Md., 1978—, treas., 1982-86, pres. 1986—; active Supreme Ct. Hist. Soc., Friends Nat. Zoo, Smithsonian Inst. Assocs., Ariz. State Soc. Served with USMC. Mem. D.C. Bar Assn. (dir. 1974-76, chmn. consumer protection com. 1972-74, chmn. D.C. affairs sect. 1975-76), Va. State Bar Assn., ABA (antitrust law sect, FTC com.), Fed. Bar Assn., Assn. Trial Lawyers Am., Direct Selling Assn. (lawyers council), Ariz. State U. Alumni Assn., Delta Theta Phi. Clubs: Rotary (pres. 1987-88), Optimist (pres. 1972-73), Country Glen, Internat. Town and Country (dir. 1969-73), Masons. Contbr. articles to legal jours. Office: Canfield & Smith Fed Bar Bldg 1815 H St NW Ste 1001 Washington DC 20006-3604

SMITH, DANIEL R., bank holding company executive; b. 1934. With First of Am. Bank-Mich., 1955-82, sr. v.p., 1971-77, pres., then pres., chief exec. officer, 1977-82; with First of Am. Bank Corp., Kalamazoo, 1982—, pres., 1982-85, chmn. bd., chief exec. officer, 1985-96, also bd. dirs.; retired, 1996. Capt. USAR, 1955-64. Office: First of Am Bank Corp 211 S Rose St Kalamazoo MI 49007-4706

SMITH, DANIEL TIMOTHY, lawyer; b. Denver, July 20, 1948; s. Harold Kennedy and Dorothy (Gannon) S. BA, Duke U., 1970; JD, U. Denver, 1973. Bar: Colo. 1973, U.S. Dist. Ct. Colo. 1973, U.S. Ct. Appeals (10th cir.), U.S. Supreme Ct. 1979, U.S. Ct. Claims 1979. Dep. dist. atty. Denver Dist. Atty. Office, 1973-74; spl. asst. atty. gen. Colo. Atty. Gen.'s Office, Denver, 1973-74; asst. U.S. atty. Dist. of Colo., Denver, 1974-76; ptnr. Wiggins & Smith P.C., Denver, 1977-87; pvt. practice Denver, 1987—. Chmn. fundraising Am. Cancer Soc., Denver., 1992-93; mem. golf com. Am. Heart Assn., Denver, 1988—. Mem. ABA, Colo. Criminal Def. Bar (sec. 1979-81). Avocation: golf. Office: 430 E 7th Ave # 200 Denver CO 80203

SMITH, DATUS CLIFFORD, JR., former foundation executive, publisher; b. Jackson, Mich., May 3, 1907; s. Datus Clifford and Marion (Houston) S.; m. Dorothy Hunt, Aug. 29, 1931 (dec. 1973); children: Sandra, Karen. B.S., Princeton U., 1929, M.A. (hon.), 1958. Grad. mgr. student employment Princeton U., 1929-30; editor Princeton Alumni Weekly, 1931-40; editor Princeton U. Press, 1941-53, dir. sec., 1942-53; assoc. prof. Princeton U., 1943-47, prof., 1947-53; pres. Franklin Book Programs, 1052-67; v.p. JDR 3d Fund, 1967-73; asso. John D. Rockefeller 3d, 1967-73; coordinator Japan philanthropy project Council on Founds., 1974-75; cons. Asia Soc., Nat. Endowment for Humanities, Hazen Found., Am. Council Learned Socs., Assn. Am. Pubs., Indo-U.S. Subcom. Edn. and Culture; past chmn. Found. Internat. Group; Bowker lectr. N.Y. Pub. Library, 1958; adv. council Ctr. for Book, Library of Congress; past pres. Assn. Am. Univ. Presses; dir. Am. Book Pub. Council.; Past chmn. editorial com. Pub. Opinion Quar.; vis. com. Harvard Press; Nat. Book Com.; trustee Center Applied Linguistics, Japan Center Internat. Exchange, Mason Early Edn. Found.; hon. life trustee Asia Soc., 1983—; trustee JDR 3d Fund, Haskins Labs.; pres. U.S. Bd. on Books for Young People, 1981-84. Author: Land and People of Indonesia, 1961, 83, Guide to Book Publishing, 1966, 68, 94, Economics of Book Publishing in Developing Countries, 1976; contbr. to Fgn. Affairs, Atlantic Monthly, Scholarly Pub., Internat. Ency. Book Pub., Ency. Asian History; project dir., Publishers Weekly; mng. editor Meadow Lark. Trustee, pres. U.S. Com. for UNICEF, 1977-79, vice chmn., 1979-81; past mem. U.S. nat. commn. UNESCO; sec. Meadow Lakes Forum; mem. Dem. County com., Mercer County. Decorated Order of Homayoun Iran; recipient Disting. Svc. award Assn. Am. Univ. Presses, 1975, Princeton in Asia award 1989, Helenka Pantaleoni award UNICEF, 1989, Asalaksen Internat. Publ. award, 1991; named to Pub. Hall of Fame, 1985. Mem. PEN, Am. Ctr. Home: 708 Meadow Lks Hightstown NJ 08520 Office: US Com for UNICEF 331 E 38th St New York NY 10016-2772

SMITH, DAVID BROOKS, federal judge; b. 1951. BA, Franklin and Marshall Coll., 1973; JD, Dickinson Sch. Law, 1976. Pvt. practice Jubelirer, Carothers, Krier, Halpern & Smith, Altoona, Pa., 1976-84; judge Ct. Common Pleas of Blair County, Pa., 1984-88, U.S. Dist. Ct. (we. dist.) Pa., 1988—; asst. dist. atty. Blair County, part-time, 1981-83, dist. atty. part-time, 1983-84; instr. Pa. State U., Altoona campus, 1977-87, St. Francis Coll., 1986—; adv. com. on criminal rules U.S. Jud. Conf., 1993—. Trustee St. Francis Coll. Mem. Pa. Bar Assn., Am. Judicature Soc., Pa. Soc., Amen Corner, Blair County Game, Fish and Forestry Assn., Fed. Judges Assn. (bd. dirs. 1993—), Masons, Pi Gamma Mu. Office: US Courthouse 7th And Grant St Rm 936 Pittsburgh PA 15219

SMITH, DAVID BRUCE, lawyer; b. Moline, Ill., May 9, 1948; s. Neal Schriever and Barbara Jean (Harris) S.; m. Yvonne Bess Smith, May 27, 1972; children: Neal, Stephanie. BSME, U. Iowa, 1970; JD, U. Tex., 1973. Bar: Tex. 1973, Wis. 1975. Patent examiner U.S. Patent and Trademark Office, Washington, 1973-74; atty. Nilles & Kirby S.C., Milw., 1974-76, Globe-Union, Inc., Milw., 1976-77, Michael Best & Friedrich, Milw., 1978—. Pres. Milw. County coun. Boy Scouts Am., Milw., 1994-95. Mem. ABA, State Bar Wis., Wis. Intellectual Property Law Assn., Ozaukee Country Club, Milw. Club. Office: Michael Best & Friedrich 100 E Wisconsin Ave Milwaukee WI 53202-4107

SMITH, DAVID C., dean; b. LaPorte, Ind., June 10, 1932; m. Betty Irene Rule; children: Pauline, Earl. BA, No. Iowa U., 1954, MA, 1958; PhD, Northwestern U., 1966. Cert. sch. adminstrn., psychology, ednl. psychology. Tchr., prin. Cresco (Iowa) Pub. Schs., 1954-56; prin. Decorah (Iowa) Community Sch. Dist., 1957-58, dir. elem. edn., 1958-60; tchr. child growth Luther Coll., Decorah, 1960 summer; assoc. prof. Coll. Edn. Mich. State U., East Lansing, 1966-70; assoc. dean Coll. Edn. No. Ill. U., DeKalb, 1970-72; area coord. Coll. Edn. U. Ark., Fayetteville, 1972-76; dean sch. edn. U. Mont., Missoula, 1976-78; dean Coll. Edn. U. Fla., Gainesville, 1978-94; cons. Assn. Am. Schs., Sao Paulo, Brazil, 1984, Am. Cmty. Sch., Aman, Jordan, 1987, Colegio Maya, Guatemala City, Guatemala, 1988, Trinidad, 1995; chmn. Edn. Stds. Commn. State of Fla., 1980-88. Editor: Essential Knowledge for Beginning Educators, 1983; assoc. editor Jour. of Tchr. Edn., 1990; contbr. articles to profl. jours. Mem. Gov.'s Profl. Tchr. Task Force, State of Fla., 1985, Comprehensive System of Personnel Devel. Oversight Com., State of Fla., 1986; resolution of commendation Fla. Cabinet for Leadership and Svc., State of Fla., 1988. Recipient Alumni Achievement award U. No. Iowa, Cedar Falls, 1984, Resolution of Commendation award Fla. Cabinet for Leadership and Svc., State of Fla., 1988, Recognition award Fla. Coun. of Economic Edn., 1989. Mem. Assn. for Advancement of Internat. Edn. (bd. dirs. 1979—, treas.), Fla. Assn. Colls. for Tchr. Edn. (pres. 1981, 92), Am. Assn. Colls. for Tchr. Edn. (pres. 1984), Nat. Assn. Secondary Sch. Prins. (adv. bd. dirs., com. sch.-coll. rels. 1983-86), Am. Coun. on Edn. (bd. dirs. 1985), Nat. Coun. for Accreditation Tchr. Edn. (bd. examiners 1988-91), So. Regional Consortium Colls. Edn. (pres.-elect 1990, pres. 1991, adv. coun. state reps. 1993, Edward C. Pomeroy Outstanding Contbn. to Edn. award 1992, Edn. Stds. Commn. 1993-94), Profl. Archers Assn. Home: 8612 SW 1st Pl Gainesville FL 32607-1486 Office: U Fla Coll Edn 174 Normal Hall Gainesville FL 32611-2053

SMITH, DAVID CLARK, research scientist; b. Owensboro, Ky., Feb. 8, 1937; s. Robert Emmitt and Mary Margaret (Flaherty) S.; m. Kathleen Sue Kohne, June 27, 1964; children: Christine, Jennifer, Paula. BSME, U. Dayton, 1959; MS, Northwestern U., 1961, PhD, 1964; postgrad. 1964. Rsch. scientist United Technologies Research Ctr., East Hartford, Conn., 1965-67, sr. rsch. scientist, 1967-68, prin. scientist, 1968-80, mgr. exptl. optics, 1980-82, mgr. optical physics, 1982-91, cons. DCS Assoc., 1992—, Conn. Tech. Assocs., 1992—. Author: (with G. Bekefi) Principles of Laser Plasmas, 1976. Contbr. articles to profl. jours. Patentee in field. Chmn. Youth and Family Resource Ctr. Commn., 1979-84; bd. dirs. Glastonbury A Better Chance, Conn., 1970-78; mem. Glastonbury Energy Com., 1979-83; tutor YMCA Read to Succeed Literacy; vol. Habitat for Humanity. Named Man of Yr., Friends of Glastonbury Youth, 1984; recipient Outstanding Svc. award, 1985, Glastonbury, Conn., United Technologies Outstanding Svc. award., 1987. Mem. IEEE, Am. Phys. Soc., AAAS, Sigma Xi. Democrat. Roman Catholic. Avocations: tennis; sailing. Home: 44 Candlelight Dr Glastonbury CT 06033-2537 Office: DCS Assoc PO Box 157 East Glastonbury CT 06025-0157

SMITH, DAVID DOYLE, management consultant, consulting engineer; b. Newport, Tenn., Aug. 17, 1956; s. Doyle E. and Lena Maude (Clemmons) S.; m. Judith Ann Craig, Nov. 1, 1991; 1 child, Adam Gabriel; stepchildren: Christine, James. BSEE, U. Tenn., 1981. Registered profl. engr., Tenn., Ga. Engring. apprentice E.I. DuPont, Brevard, N.C., 1976; field engr. IBM Corp., Knoxville, Tenn., 1977-79; rsch. asst. Office of Naval Rsch. U. Tenn., Knoxville, 1980-81; systems test engr. Tex. Instruments, Inc., Johnson City, Tenn., 1981-82, product engr., 1982-83, product mgr., 1983-87; missile design engr., supr. Tex. Instruments, Inc., Lewisville, Tex., 1987-89; sr. systems engr. U.S. Data Corp., Richardson, Tex., 1989-90; lead cons. Keane, Inc., Atlanta, 1991-94; mgr., mgmt. cons. Ernst & Young LLP, Atlanta, 1994—; lectr. Tech. Inst., 1983-86; developer RTU Sys. for oil and gas, water, and electric utilities, 1990-92. Co-author profl. papers. Mem. IEEE, NSPE, Am. Prodn. and Inventory Control Socs. Avocations: archaeology, writing. Home: 1080 Allenbrook Ln Roswell GA 30075-2983 Office: Ernst & Young LLP 600 Peachtree St Atlanta GA 30308-2215

SMITH, DAVID ELVIN, physician; b. Bakersfield, Calif., Feb. 7, 1939; s. Elvin W. and Dorothy (McGinnis) S.; m. Millicent Buxton; children: Julia, Suzanne, Christopher Buxton-Smith, Sabree Hill. Intern San Francisco Gen. Hosp., 1965; fellow pharmacology and toxicology U. Calif., San Francisco, 1965-67, assoc. clin. prof. occupational medicine, clin. toxicology, 1967—, dir. psychopharmacology study group, 1966-70; practice specializing in toxicology/addiction medicine San Francisco, 1965—; physician Presbyn. Alcoholic Clinic, 1965-67, Contra Cost Alcoholic Clinic, 1965-67; dir. alcohol and drug abuse screening unit San Francisco Gen. Hosp., 1967-68; co-dir. Calif. drug abuse info. project U. Calif. Med. Ctr., 1967-72; founder, med. dir. Haight-Ashbury Free Med. Clinic, San Francisco, 1967—; rsch. dir. Merritt Peralta Chem. Dependency Hosp., Oakland, Calif., 1984—; chmn. Nat. Drug Abuse Conf., 1977; mem. Calif. Gov.'s Commn. on Narcotics and Drug Abuse, 1977—; nat. health adviser to former U.S. Pres. Jimmy Carter; mem. Pres. Clinton's Health Care Task Force on Addiction and Nat. Health Reform, 1993; with Office Drug Abuse Policy, White House Task Force Physicians for Drug Abuse Prevention; dir. Benzodiazepine Rsch. and Tng. Project, Substance Abuse and Sexual Concerns Project, PCP Rsch. and Tng. Project; cons. numerous fed. drug abuse agys. Author: Love Needs Care, 1970, The New Social Drug: Cultural, Medical and Legal Perspectives on Marijuana, 1971, The Free Clnic: Community Approaches to Health Care and Drug Abuse, 1971, Treating the Cocaine Abuser, 1985, The Benzodiazepines: Current Standard Medical Practice, 1986, Physicians' Guide to Drug Abuse, 1987; co-author: It's So Good, Don't Even Try it Once: Heroin in Perspective, 1972, Uppers and Downers, 1973, Drugs in the Classroom, 1973, Barbiturate Use and Abuse, 1977, A Multicultural View of Drug Abuse, 1978, Amphetamine Use, Misuse and Abuse, 1979, PCP: Problems and Prevention, 1981, Sexological Aspects of Substance Use and Abuse, Treatment of the Cocaine Abuser, 1985, The Haight Ashbury Free Medical Clinic: Still Free After All These Years, Drug Free: Alternatives to Drug Abuse, 1987, Treatment of Opiate Dependence, Designer Drugs, 1988, Treatment of Cocaine Dependence, 1988, Treatment of Opiate Dependence, 1988, The New Drugs, 1989, Crack and Ice in the Era of Smokeable Drugs, 1992, others; also drug edn. films; founder, editor Jour. Psychedelic Drugs (now Jour. Psychoactive Drugs), 1967—; contbr. over 300 articles to profl. jours. Mem. Physicians for Prevention White House Office Drug Abuse Policy, 1995; pres. Youth Projects, Inc.; founder, chmn. bd., pres. Nat. Free Clin. Coun., 1968-72. Recipient Rsch. award Borden Found., 1964, AMA Rsch. award, 1977, Cmty. Svc. award U. Calif.-San Francisco, 1974, Calif. State Drug Abuse Treatment award, 1984, Vernelle Fox Drug Abuse Treatment award, 1985, UCLA Sidney Cohen Addiction Medicine award, 1989, U. Calif. San Francisco medal of honor, 1995; named one of Best Doctors in U.S., 1995. Mem. AMA (alt. del.), CMA (alt. del.), Am. Soc. on Addiction Medicine (bd. dirs., pres. 1995), San Francisco Med. Soc., Am. Pub. Health Assn., Calif. Soc. on Addiction Medicine (pres., bd. dirs.), Am. Soc. Addiction Medicine, Sigma Xi, Phi Beta Kappa. Methodist. Home: 289 Frederick St San Francisco CA 94117-4051 Office: Hight Ashbury Free Clinics 612 Clayton St San Francisco CA 94117-1911

SMITH, DAVID ENGLISH, physician, educator; b. San Francisco, June 9, 1920; s. David English and Myrtle (Goodin) S.; m. Margaret Elizabeth Bronson, June 9, 1948; children: Ann English Smith Elbert, David Bronson, Mary Margaret. A.B., Central Coll. Mo., 1941; M.D. cum laude, Washington U., St. Louis, 1944. Intern, resident pathology Barnes Hosp., St. Louis, 1944-46; instr. pathology Washington U. Med. Sch., 1948-51, asst. prof., 1951-54, asst. head dept., 1953-54, assoc. prof., 1954-55; prof. pathology U. Va. Sch. Medicine, 1955-73, chmn. dept., 1958-73; dir. div. U. Va. Sch. Medicine (Cancer Studies), 1972-73; prof. pathology Northwestern U. Sch. Medicine, 1974-75, U. Pa. Sch. Medicine, 1976-80; prof. pathology Tulane U. Sch. Medicine, 1980-85, assoc. dean, 1980-85; prof. pathology U. Tex. Med. Br., 1986—; assoc. dir. Am. Bd. Med. Spltys., 1974-75; v.p., sec., dir. undergrad. evaluation Nat. Bd. Med. Examiners, 1975-80; trustee Am. Bd. Pathology, 1966-73, v.p., 1973; mem. Nat. Bd. Med. Examiners, chmn. pathology test com., 1966-72; chmn. test com. Ednl. Commn. for Fgn. Med. Grads., 1979-91. Editor: Survey of Pathology in Medicine and Surgery, 1966-70; contbr. articles to profl. publs. Pres. Va. div. Am. Cancer Soc., 1967-69. Served from 1st lt. to capt. M.C. AUS, 1946-48. Mem. Va. Soc. Pathology (pres. 1960), Am. Assn. Pathologists, Internat. Acad. Pathology (council 1956-59, pres. 1964-65), Am. Soc. Clin. Pathologists (co-dir. self assessment program 1970-75), AMA, Am. Assn. Neuropathologists, AAAS, Sigma Xi, Alpha Omega Alpha, Phi Beta Pi, Alpha Epsilon Delta. Home: 59 Colony Park Cir Galveston TX 77551-1737

SMITH, DAVID EUGENE, business administration educator; b. Boise, Idaho, Dec. 14, 1941; s. Roy Arthur and Anna Margaret (Fries) S.; m. Patricia Stroy, Aug. 4, 1973; 1 child, Zachary Adam. BS in Applied Stats., San Francisco State Coll., 1964, MS in Mgmt. Sci., 1966; MBA, PhD in Bus. Adminstrn., U. Santa Clara, 1969. Asst. to dir. mgmt ctr. Grad. Sch. Bus., U. Santa Clara, Calif., 1966-69, lectr. mktg., 1968; asst. prof. bus. adminstrn. Mktg./Quantitative Studies Dept., San Jose State U., Calif., 1969-71, assoc. prof. bus. adminstrn., 1971-76, prof. bus. adminstrn., 1976—, chmn. dept., 1986-89. Author: Quantitative Business Analysis, 1977, Internat. Edit., 1979, 1982; contbr. articles to profl. jours. Mem. INFORMS, Phi Kappa Phi, Beta Gamma Sigma. Republican. Avocations: tennis, fishing, skiing. Home: 22448 Tim Tam Ct Los Gatos CA 95030-8521 Office: San Jose State U Mktg/MIS/Decision Scis One Washington Sq San Jose CA 95192

SMITH, DAVID GILBERT, political science educator; b. Norman, Okla., Oct. 10, 1926; s. Gilbert Harmer and Virginia (Haizlip) S.; m. Carlota Shipman (div. 1967); m. 2d, Eleanor Cowan; children: Alison Claire, Joel Anthony; stepchildren: Laura Gergen, Stan Gergen. BA, U. Okla., 1948, MA, 1950; PhD, Johns Hopkins U., 1953. Instr. polit. sci. Swarthmore (Pa.) Coll., 1953-55, asst. prof. polit. sci., 1957, prof., 1967—, Centennial prof., 1977-87, Richter prof. polit. sci., 1987-92, chmn., 1970-87, prof. emeritus, 1992—; asst. prof. polit. sci. Stanford U., Palo Alto, Calif., 1956-57; cons. HEW, NAS, NRC, Ford Found. Author: (with J. Roland Pennock) Political Science: An Introduction, 1965, The Convention and the Constitution, 1965, 2d edit., 1987, Paying for Medicare, 1992; also articles. Chmn. ACLU, Delaware County, Pa., 1965-70, Health and Welfare Coun., Delaware County, 1970-73; v.p. Delaware Valley HMO, Concordville, Pa., 1978-81; pres. Media (Pa.) Child Guidance, 1980-82; bd. dirs. Friends Life Care at Home, 1992—. Sgt. U.S. Army, 1945-46. Mem. Am. Soc. for Polit. and Legal Philosophy, Phi Beta Kappa. Democrat. Presbyterian. Home: 448 S Jackson St Media PA 19063-3716

SMITH, DAVID JEDDIE, American literature educator; b. Portsmouth, Va., Dec. 19, 1942; s. Ralph Gearld and Catherine Mary (Cornwell) S.; m. Deloras Mae Weaver, Mar. 31, 1966; children: David Jeddie, Lael Cornwell, Mary Catherine. BA, U. Va., 1965; MA, So. Ill. U., 1969; PhD, Ohio U., 1976. Staff creative writing Bennington (Vt.) Coll. summer prog., 1980-87; instr. English We. Mich. U., Kalamazoo, 1973-74; asst. prof. English Cottey Coll., Nevada, Mo., 1974-75; assoc. prof. English U. Utah, Salt Lake City, 1976-80; vis. prof. English SUNY, Binghamton, 1980-81; assoc. prof. English U. Fla., Gainesville, 1981-82; prof. Am. it. Va. Commonwealth U., Richmond, 1982-89; prof. Am. Lit. La. State U., 1990—; lectr. in field; cons. in field. Author: Local Assays, 1985, The Roundhouse Voices: Selected and new Poems, 1985, The Morrow Anthology of Younger American Poets, 1985, Gray Soldiers, 1984, Southern Delights, 1984, In the House of the Judge, 1983, The Pure Clear Word: Essays on the Poetry of James Wright, 1982, Onliness, 1981, Homage to Edgar Allan Poe, 1981, Cuba Night, 1990, Night Pleasures: New and Selected Poems, 1992, Fate's Kite: Poems 1991-1995, 1995, others; editor New Va. Rev., 1987, The Back Doors: A Poetry Mag., Southern Rev., 1990; contbr. articles to profl. jours. Recipient Va. Prize in Poetry, 1988, Prairie Schooner poetry prize, 1980, Portland Rev. poetry prize, 1979, Sou'wester poetry prize, 1973, others; Guggenheim fellow, 1981, Lyndhurst fellow, 1987, 88, 89, others. Mem. MLA, Poetry Soc. Am., Poetry Soc. Va., PEN, Nat. Book Critics Cir., Assoc. Writing Progs., Writers in Va. (bd. dirs.), So. Modern Lang. Assn., Modern Lang. Assn., Acad. Am. Poets. Office: La State U So Rev 43 Allen Hall Baton Rouge LA 70803

SMITH, DAVID JOHN, physicist, educator; b. Melbourne, Australia, Oct. 10, 1948; arrived in U.S., 1984; s. Arthur and Agnes Frances S.; m. Gwenneth Paula Bland, Sept. 18, 1971 (div. 1992); children: Heather F., Marion J. BSc with honors, U. Melbourne, Australia, 1970, PhD, 1978, DSc, 1988. Post-doctoral rsch. asst. Cavendish Lab. U. Cambridge, Eng., 1976-78, sr. rsch. assoc., 1979-84; assoc. prof. Ariz. State U., Tempe, 1984-87, prof., 1987—; dir. Cambridge U. High Resolution Electron Microscope, 1979-84, NSF Ctr. for High Resolution Electron Microscopy, Tempe, 1991—. Author 7 chpts. in books; editor 10 conf. procs.; contbr. over 200 articles to profl. jours. Recipient Faculty Achievement award Burlington Resources Found., 1990. Fellow Inst. Physics (U.K., Charles Vernon Boys prize 1985); mem. Royal Micros. Soc. (U.K.), Am. Phys. Soc., Material Rsch. Soc., Microscopy Soc. Am. Office: Ariz State U Ctr Solid State Sci Tempe AZ 85287

SMITH, DAVID JOHN, JR., plastic surgeon; b. Indpls., Feb. 20, 1947; s. David John and Carolyn (Culp) S.; m. Nancy Loonsten, June 7, 1975; children: Matthew, Peter, Hadley. BA, Wesleyan U., 1969; MD, Ind. U., 1973. Diplomate Am. Bd. Plastic Surgery. Resident Emory U.-Grady Hosp., Atlanta, 1973-78; resident Ind. U. Med. Ctr., Indpls., 1978-80; Christine Kleinert fellow in hand surgery, 1979; asst. prof. surgery Ind. U. Sch. Medicine, 1980-84; assoc. prof. of surgery Wayne State U. Sch. Medicine, 1984-87; assoc. prof. plastic surgery, surgery sect. head U. Mich. Med. Ctr., Ann Arbor, 1987-92, prof. surgery sect. head, 1992—; mem. Residency Rev. Com. for Plastic Surgery, 1992, vice chmn., 1994, chmn. 1996—. Mem. editl. bd. Jour. of Surg. Rsch., 1989-95, Annals of Plastic Surgery, 1992—, assoc. editor, 1994, Yearbook of Hand Surgery, 1989—; guest reviewer Surgery, 1988—, Plastic and Reconstructive Surgery, 1988—; contbr. articles to profl. jours. Recipient numerous grants. Fellow ACS (many coms.), Soc. Univ. Surgeons, Am. Assn. Plastic Surgeons, Am. Surg. Assn., Am. Bd. Plastic Surgeons, Assn. for Acad. Surgery, Western Surg. Assn., Ctrl. Surg. Assn., Am. Soc. for Surgery of the Hand, Am. Soc. Plastic and Reconstructive Surgeons, Plastic Surgery Ednl. Found. (bd. dirs. 1988—, treas. 1994, v.p., pres.-elec., other coms.), Plastic Surgery Rsch. Coun., Am. Burn Assn., Am. Burn Life Support Nat. Faculty, Am. Assn. for Hand Surgeons (pres. 1994). Home: 769 Heatherway St Ann Arbor MI 48104-2731 Office: U Mich Med Ctr 2130 Taubman Health Ctr 1500 E Medical Center Dr Ann Arbor MI 48109-0340

SMITH, DAVID JULIAN, educational consultant; b. Boston, Apr. 24, 1944; s. Julian John and Anita Regina (Goldman) S.; m. Suzanne Marilla Shaw, June 18, 1966. AB, Harvard U., 1966; MAT, Reed Coll., 1967. Cert. elem. tchr., Mass., Hawaii, Oreg. 10th grade tchr. Punahou Sch., Honolulu, 1967-69; 7th, 9th grades tchr. U. Hawaii Lab. Sch., Honolulu, 1969-70; 7th grade head tchr. Shady Hill Sch., Cambridge, Mass., 1970-92; pvt. practice ednl. cons. Cambridge, 1992—. Author: Mapping the World By Heart, 1992, Abigail's Atlas, 1992, Making Maps from Memory, 1989; contbr. articles to profl. jours. Bd. dirs. Cambridge Mental Health Assn., 1991—, Cambridge Ctr. for Adult Edn., 1988—; active Cambridge Civic Assn. Mem. Nat. Coun. for Social Studies, Nat. Coun. for Geog. Edn., Assn. Am. Geographers, Inst. British Geographers. Office: Mapping the World by Heart 4 Blanchard Rd Cambridge MA 02138-1009

SMITH, DAVID KING, newspaper publishing executive; b. L.A., Oct. 12, 1963; s. Michael David and Dorothy Margaret (Mason) S.; m. Kirstin Andrea Gustafson, June 22, 1991; children: Zachary David, Jacob Alexander. BA, UCLA, 1987. Salesperson, advt. exec. Call. Newspaper Svc., 1989-91; leadership cons. Phi Gamma Delta Internat. Fraternity, Lexington, Ky. 1987-89. Republican. Episcopalian. Avocations: fishing, church fellowship, motivational tapes, reading, child-rearing. Office: San Diego Commerce 110 W C St # 811 San Diego CA 92101

SMITH, DAVID KINGMAN, retired oil company executive, consultant; b. Malone, N.Y., June 5, 1928; s. Ernest DeAlton and Louisa Kingman (Bolster) S.; m. Lois Louise Wing, June 13, 1959; children: Mara Louise, David Andrew. BS in Engring., Princeton U., 1952. Registered profl. engr., Tex. Civil engr., supt. Raymont Internat. Inc., N.Y.C., 1952-55, asst. v.p., 1970-71, v.p., 1971-74; group v.p. Raymont Internat. Inc., Houston, 1974-80; mgr. Raymond-Brown and Root, Maracaibo, Venezuela, 1955-70; sr. engring. assoc. Exxon Prodn. Rsch. Co., Houston, 1980-81, supr., 1982-95; cons. project mgmt., 1995—. Pres. Yorkshire Civic Assn., Houston, 1979-80, trustee, 1985—. With U.S. Army, 1946-48, PTO. Mem. ASCE, NSPE, Soc. Petroleum Engrs. (continuing edn. com. Gulf Coast chmn. 1989-93, treas. 1987-88, nat. continuing edn. com. 1991-93, dir. Gulf Coast sect. 1994-95), Tex. Soc. Profl. Engrs., Men's Garden Club Houston, Am. Legion, Princeton Alumni Assn. (dir. Houston sect.), Cen Ners In square dance club (pres.

1996). Republican. Methodist. Avocations: photography, gardening, tennis, golf, square dancing. Home: 611 W Forest Dr Houston TX 77079

SMITH, DAVID LEE, newspaper editor; b. Shelby, Ohio, Apr. 4, 1939; s. Ferris Francis and Rita Ann (Metzger) S.; m. Betty Stewart Walker, Sept. 10, 1960; children: Stacie Lynn, Stefanie Linn, David Lee, II (dec.). Student, Pontifical Coll. Josephinum, Worthington, Ohio, 1953-56, Ohio State U., Mansfield, 1961. Sports writer Mansfield News-Jour., 1960-61; sports editor Ashland (Ohio) Times-Gazette, 1961-63, Miami (Fla.) News, 1963-67, Ft. Lauderdale (Fla.) News, 1967-70, Boston Globe, 1970-78, Washington Star, 1978-81; dep. mng. editor, exec. sports editor Dallas Morning News, 1981—; condr. seminars. Bd. dirs. Doak Walker Nat. Running Back Award, The Dallas Athletic Club, GTE-SMU Athletic Forum. Served with USMC, 1957-60. Mem. AP Sports Editors Assn. (1st pres. 1974-75), Baseball Writers Assn. (Red Smith award for major contbns. to sports journalism 1990), Football Writers Assn., Golf Writers Assn., Dallas Athletic Club (pres.). Roman Catholic. Home: 5723 Berkshire Ln Dallas TX 75209-2401 Office: Dallas Morning News Communications Center Dallas TX 75265

SMITH, DAVID LYLE, art educator; b. Harpersfield, N.Y., June 6, 1926; s. Thomas Howard and Grace Louisa (Vedder) S.; m. Alyce Louise Oosterhouse, June 6, 1952; children: C Matthew, Markalan, Elizabeth, Leigh, Stuart. BD in Design, U. Mich., 1951, MA in Edn., 1953; DPhil, Mich. State U., 1966. Graphic artist Ednl. TV Program U. Mich., Ann Arbor, 1952-53; tchr. art C.W. Otto Jr. H.S., Lansing, Mich., 1955-63; tchr. elem. art. Lansing Pub. Schs., 1963-67; assoc. prof. Dept. Art and Design U. Wis., Stevens Point, 1967-96; retired, 1996. Exhbnx. include U. Wis. Stevens Point Faculty Show, 1974-76, 87, 90-93, 95, Packages-Carlsten Art Gallery, 1978, 79, New Visions Gallery, Marshfield, Wis., 1989, 92, 95, Milw. Art Mus., 1992, U. Colo. Mountainside Art Guild & Fiske Planetarium, 1992, 93, 94, N.Mex., Art League, 1993, 94, Alexander House, Port Edwards, Wis., 1993, 95, Ann. Carnegie Art Ctr. Nat. Exhbn., North Tonawanda, N.Y., 1993, L.I. Arts Coun., Freeposrt, N.Y., 1994, others; accepted in nat. juried art competitions, 15 in 1993, 49 in 1994, 22 in 1995, 9 in 1996; one-man shows include Lincoln Ctr., Stevens Point, Wis., 1989, 93, others.; two-man shows (with Richard Schneider) Alexander House 1993; also Ctr. for Visual Arts 1996; three person show Brown County Libr. 1996. Mem. Nat. Art Edn. Assn., Wis. Art Edn. Assn. (bd. dirs., higher edn. rep. 1978-82), NEA, Wis. Edn. Ass. Coun., Assn. U. Wis. Profls. (sec. 1993-96), Wis. Alliance for Arts Edn. Republican. Presbyterian. Avocations: sketching, gardening, traveling. Home: 4242 Janick Cir N Stevens Point WI 54481-2511

SMITH, DAVID MARTYN, forestry educator; b. Bryan, Tex., Mar. 10, 1921; s. John Blackmer and Doris (Clark) S.; m. Catherine Van Aken, June 16, 1951; children: Ellen, Nancy. B.S., U. R.I., 1941; postgrad., NYU, 1942; M.F., Yale U., 1946, Ph.D., 1950; D.Sc. (hon.), Bates Coll., 1986, U. R.I., 1993. Instr. Sch. Forestry and Environ. Studies, Yale U., 1946-47, 48-51, asst. prof., 1951-57, asst. dean, 1953-58, assoc. prof., 1957-63; prof. Yale U., 1963-90, Morris K. Jesup prof. silviculture, 1967-90, Morris K. Jesup prof. emeritus, 1990—; cons. Baskahegan Co.; vis. prof. U. Munich, 1981; mem. Conn. Forestry Practices Bd., 1991—; pres., bd. dirs. Connwood Foresters, Inc. Author: Practice of Silviculture, 1962, 86. Capt. Weather Svc., USAAF, 1942-45. Fellow Soc. Am. Foresters (Disting. Svc. New Eng. sect. award 1969, 93); mem. Am. Forestry Assn. (Disting. Svc. award 1990), Nat. Acad. Forest Scis. Mex. (corr.), Ecol. Soc. Am., Conn. Forest and Park Assn. (dir.), Sigma Xi, Phi Kappa Phi. Mem. United Ch. of Christ. Home: 55 Woodlawn St Hamden CT 06517-1338 Office: 360 Prospect St New Haven CT 06511-2104

SMITH, DAVID RYAN, museum director; b. Ft. Worth, Apr. 23, 1952; s. David Earnest and Helen Virginia (Armstrong) S.; m. Peggy Lou Bennett, Mar. 9, 1974; children: Jennifer Renee, Kenneth Ryan. BS in Am. Studies, Harding U., 1974; MA in History, U. Tex., 1979. Dir. Star of the Republic Mus., Washington, Tex., 1977-87, Panhandle-Plains Hist. Mus., Canyon, Tex., 1987-91; exec. dir. Tex. Energy Mus., Beaumont, Tex., 1992—; field reviewer Inst. Mus. Svcs., Wash., 1985—. Chmn. Tex. Antiquities Com., 1990-92; mem. Summerlee Commn. on Tex. History, 1989-92. Bd. dirs. Edison Pla. Mus., Beaumont, Beaumont Conv. and Visitors Bur.; mem. cmty. adv. coun. Mobil Refinery; chmn. Beaumont History Conf. Named Outstanding Alumnus Harding U., 1987. Mem. Am. Assn. Mus. (surveyor mus. assessment program), Tex. State Hist. Assn., Tex. Assn. Mus. (coun. 1979-81, 84-86), Cen. Tex. Mus. Assn. (chmn. 1979-81, 84-86), S.E. Tex. Mus. Assn. (treas. 1995—), Rotary. Mem. Ch. of Christ. Avocations: backpacking, canoeing, tennis, running. Home: 9265 Meadowbend Dr Beaumont TX 77706-3829 Office: Tex Energy Mus 600 Main St Beaumont TX 77701-3305

SMITH, DAVID SHIVERICK, lawyer, former ambassador; b. Omaha, Jan. 25, 1918; s. Floyd Monroe and Anna (Shiverick) S.; m. June Noble, Dec. 8, 1945 (div. 1968); children:Noble, David Shiverick, Jeremy T., Bradford D.; m. Mary Edson, Feb. 14, 1972. Degre Superieur, Sorbonne, Paris, 1938; B.A. magna cum laude, Dartmouth Coll., 1939; J.D., Columbia U., 1942. Bar: N.Y. 1942, Conn. 1950, D.C. 1954. Asso. Breed, Abbott & Morgan, N.Y.C., 1946-48; legal dept. ABC, N.Y.C., 1948-50; partner Chapman, Bryson, Walsh & O'Connell, N.Y.C. and Washington, 1950-54; spl. asst. to undersec. Dept. State, Washington, 1954; asst. sec. Air Force, 1954-59; dir. internat. fellows program Columbia U., 1959-75, coordinator internat. studies, 1960-75, asso. dean sch. internat. affairs, 1960-74; cons. AEC, 1959-60; partner Baker & McKenzie (and predecessor), N.Y.C. and Washington, 1960-75, Martin & Smith (and predecessors), Washington, 1975-76, 77-88; ambassador to Sweden, 1976-77; dir. United Svcs. Life Ins. Corp., Internat. Bank, USLICO Corp., Liberian Svcs., Inc.; mem. Coun. Fgn. Rels.; dir. Fgn. Policy Assn.; mem. adv. coun. Sch. Advanced Intenat. Studies, Johns Hopkins U., 1962—; pres., dir. Ctr. for Inter-Am. Rels., N.Y.C., 1969-74. Adv. and contbg. editor: Jour. Internat. Affairs, 1960-74; editor: The Next Asia, 1969, Prospects for Latin America, 1970, Concerns in World Affairs, 1973, From War to Peace, 1974. Chmn. bd. George Olmsted Found., 1977—; active in past various charitable orgns. Lt. USNR, 1942-54; PTO; col. USAFR, 1955-75. Decorated Purple Heart. Mem. ABA, Am. Soc. Internat. Law, Am. Fgn. Law Assn., N.Y. State Bar Assn., Conn. Bar Assn., Fed. Bar Assn. (v.p. for N.Y., N.J. and Conn.), Pilgrims of U.S., France-Am. Soc., English Speaking Union, Asia Soc., Coun. on Foreign Rels., Hudson Inst., Washington Inst. Fgn. Affairs, Coun. Fgn. Rels., Coun. Am. Ambs. (bd. dirs., sec.), Soc. Mayflower Descs., Brook Club (N.Y.C.), Met. Club (Washington), Chevy Chase Club, Bathing Corp. of Southampton (N.Y.), Meadow Club (Southampton), Bath and Tennis Club, Everglades Club (Palm Beach), The Crocodiles, Old Guard Soc. Palm Beach Golfers, Phi Beta Kappa. Home: 525 S Flagler Dr Apt 20-c West Palm Beach FL 33401-5922

SMITH, DAVID STUART, anesthesiology educator, physician; b. Detroit, May 29, 1946; s. Philip and Eleanor (Bishop) S.; m. Suzanne Wanda Zeleznik, Aug. 17, 1969; children: Katherine Michele, Lisa Anne. BA, Oakland U.; MD, Med. Coll. Wis., 1975, PhD, 1975. Intern Dept. of Medicine, Med. Coll. Wis., Milw., 1975-76; resident Dept. Anesthesia, U. Pa., Phila., 1976-78, fellow, 1978-80; dir., div. of neuroanesthesia Hosp. U. Pa., Phila., 1982—, attending anesthesiologist, 1980—; asst. prof. U. Pa., Phila., 1980-89, assoc. prof., 1989—; editorial bd. Jour. Neurosurgical Anesthesia, N.Y.C., 1987—. Co-editor: Anesthesia and Neurosurgery, 3d edit., 1994; author and co-author of numerous sci. papers, revs., and book chpts. Sr. fellow, Nat. Rsch. Svc. award, Phila., 1985-87. Fellow Coll. Physicians Phila.; mem. Am. Soc. Anesthesiologists, Soc. Neurosurg. Anesthesia and Critical Care (sec., treas. 1987-89, v.p. 1989-90, pres. elect 1990-91, pres. 1991-92), Assn. U. Anesthetists, Internat. Soc. Cerebral Blood Flow and Metabolism, Internat. Soc. Neurochemistry. Jewish. Office: Hosp U Pa Dept Anesthesia 3400 Spruce St Philadelphia PA 19104

SMITH, DAVID THORNTON, lawyer, educator; b. Pawtucket, R.I., Dec. 11, 1935; s. Herbert Jeffers and Harriet Amelia (Thornton) S.; m. Sandra June Gustavson, Dec. 20, 1958; children—David T., Douglas A., Daniel H. B.A., Yale U., 1957; J.D. cum laude, Boston U., 1960. Bar: Mass. 1961, U.S. Supreme Ct. 1964. Instr. law Ind. U., Bloomington, 1960-62; asst. prof. law Duquesne U., Pitts., 1962-63, Case Western Res. U., Cleve., 1963-65; asso. prof. Case Western Res. U., 1965-68; asso. prof. law U. Fla., Gainesville, 1968-69; prof. U. Fla., 1969—; lectr. Fla. Bankers Assn., Fla. Trust Sch., 1973—. Author: (with M. Sussman and J. Cates) The Family and Inheritance, 1970, Florida Probate Code Manual, 1975. Mem. Am. Bar Assn., Mass. Bar Assn., Am. Law Inst., Am. Judicature Soc., AAUP (past pres. U. Fla. chpt.), Fla. Blue Key, Selden Soc., Omicron Delta Kappa, Phi Alpha Delta. Lutheran. Home: 6405 NW 18th Ave Gainesville FL 32605-3209 Office: Univ Fla Coll Of Law Gainesville FL 32611

SMITH, DAVID TODD, publishing company executive; b. Stamford, Conn., Nov. 19, 1953; arrived in Can., 1956; m. Margaret Beryl Starke, Dec. 30, 1978; children: Erik Joseph, Maximilian Peter Starke. BBA in Fin. and Econs., Wilfrid Laurier U., Waterloo, Ont., Can., 1976; MBA in Fin., McMaster U., Hamilton, Ont., 1978. Cert. gen. acct., Ont. Fin. analyst Economical Mut. Ins. Co., Kitchener, Ont., 1976-78; portfolio mgr. Mcht. Trust Co., Toronto, Ont., 1978-80; treasury officer Harlequin Enterprises Ltd., Toronto, 1980-82, asst. treas., 1982-89; treas. Torstar Corp., Toronto, 1989—. Office: Torstar Corp, 1 Yonge St, Toronto, ON Canada M5E 1P9

SMITH, DAVID WALDO EDWARD, pathology and gerontology educator, physician; b. Fargo, N.D., Apr. 3, 1934; s. Waldo Edward and Martha (Althaus) S.; m. Diane Leigh Walker, June 18, 1960. BA, Swarthmore Coll., 1956; MD, Yale U., 1960. Intern, asst. resident, research fellow pathology Yale U. Med. Sch., 1960-62; research assoc. lab. molecular biology Nat. Inst. Arthritis and Metabolic Diseases, 1962-64, investigator lab. exptl. pathology, 1964-67; assoc. prof. pathology and microbiology Ind. U. Med. Sch., 1967-69; prof. pathology Northwestern U. Med. Sch., 1969—, dir. Ctr. on Aging, 1988—; Guest investigator Internat. Lab. Genetics and Biophysics, Naples, Italy, 1969; mem. ad hoc biochemistry study sect. NIH, 1974-75, mem. pathobiol. chemistry study sect., 1975-79, cons., 1982; sabbatical leave NIH, 1986-87; chmn. NIH Conf. on Gender and Longevity: Why Do Women Live Longer Than Men?, 1987. Author: Human Longevity, 1993, also research papers, chpts. in books.; editorial bd. Yale Jour. Biology and Medicine, 1957-60. Sr. surgeon USPHS, 1958-67. Recipient Career Devel. award NIH, 1968-69. Mem. AAAS, Am. Soc.for Investigative Pathology, Am. Soc. for Biochem. and Molecular Biology, Gerontol. Soc. Am., Sigma Xi, Alpha Omega Alpha. Home: 1212 N Lake Shore Dr Apt 33an Chicago IL 60610-2362 Office: Northwestern U Med Sch Dept Pathology 303 E Chicago Ave Chicago IL 60611-3008

SMITH, DAVID WAYNE, psychologist; b. Ind., Apr. 16, 1927; s. Lowell Wayne and Ruth Elizabeth (Westphal) S.; m. Marcene B. Leever, Oct. 20, 1948; children: David Wayne, Laurreen Lea. B.S., Purdue U., 1949; M.S., Ind. U., 1953, Ph.D., 1955. Prof. rehab., dir. Rehab. Center; asso. dean, later asst. v.p. acad. affairs Ariz. Health Scis. Center, U. Ariz., Tucson, 1955-80; research prof. rehab., adj. prof. medicine, cons. in research S.W. Arthritis Center, Coll. Medicine, 1980-87; prof. rehab. and rheumatology, dept. medicine U. Ariz., 1987—, also dir. disability assessment program; pres. allied health professions sect. Nat. Arthritis Found.; bd. dirs. Nat. Arthritis Found. (S.W. chpt.); nat. vice chmn. bd. dirs.; mem. NIH Nat. Arthritis Adv. Bd., 1977-84; also chmn. subcom. community programs and rehab.; mem. staff Ariz. Legislature Health Welfare, 1972-73; Mem. Gov.'s Council Dept. Econ. Security, 1978-85; pres., bd. dirs. Tucson Assn. for Blind, 1974-86; chmn. Gov.'s Council on Blind and Visually Impaired, 1987—; active Gov.'s Coun. on Arthritis and Musculoskeletal Disease, 1987—. Author: Worksamples; contbr. chpts. to books and articles to profl. jours. Recipient Gov.'s awards for leadership in rehab., 1966, 69, 72, 73; awards for sci. and vol. services Nat. Arthritis Found., 1973, 75; 1st nat. Addie Thomas award Nat. Arthritis Found., 1983, Benson award, 1989, Govt. Affairs award, 1989; Arthritis Found. fellow, 1983. Mem. Am. Psychol. Assn. (div. 17 counseling psychology), Assn. Schs. Allied Health Professions, Nat. Rehab. Assn., Ariz. Psychol. Assn. Home: 5765 N Camino Real Tucson AZ 85718-4213 Office: U Ariz Arizona Health Scis Ctr Tucson AZ 85724

SMITH, DAVID YARNELL, financial consultant; b. Chattanooga, Apr. 9, 1963; s. Eugene Scott and Johnathan (Yarnell) S.; m. Donna Kathryn Swisher, July 1, 1989. BS in Bus. Adminstrn. with honors, U. Tenn., 1985; MBA, Ga. State U., 1989. Comml. banking officer, comml. bus. devel. coord., then asst. v.p. and asst. mgr. Trust Co. Bank, Atlanta, 1985-89; asst. v.p. Bank of Am., Nat. Trust & Savings Assn., Atlanta, 1989-91; fin. cons., mgr. Petty & Landis, CPAs, Chattanooga, 1991—. Mem. Omicron Delta Kappa, Alpha Gamma Rho, Delta Sigma Pi. Avocations: golf, hunting. Office: Petty & Landis Krystal Bldg Ste 700 Chattanooga TN 37402

SMITH, DEAN, communications advisor, arbitrator; b. N.Y.C., Aug. 10, 1925; s. Franklin Grant and Anna Lucille (Kranebell) S.; m. Andree Marie Praileur, Aug. 9, 1947; children—David F., Christopher P. Student, NYU, 1945-46, Columbia U., 1946-47, N.Y. Sch. Printing, 1946-47. Editor ShowBill Mag., N.Y.C., 1945-47; news editor Boulder City (Nev.) Daily News, 1947-49; owner, pub., editor Tucson Sun-News, N.Y.C., 1949-51; dir. radio and TV news Sta. WBEN/WBEN-TV, Buffalo, 1951-53; dir. pub. svc. and promotion Indpls. Times, Buffalo, 1953-56; v.p., gen. mgr Kendall Assocs., Inc., N.Y.C., 1956-60; dir. Office Publs. and Info., Commerce Dept., Washington, 1961-70, dir. publs. div., 1970; asst. dir. Nat. Tech. Info. Svc., Springfield, Va., 1971-81, dir. office of market devel., 1982-83; assoc. dir. NTIS, Springfield, Va., 1984-85, self-employed communications advisor, 1986—. Chmn. for fed. mail list policy Vice Pres.'s Com. on Right of Privacy; chmn. presdl. domestic policy rev. work group on fed. acquisition of fgn. tech., 1979; bd. dirs. Commerce Fed. Credit Union. Served with AUS, 1943-45. Decorated Silver Star with oak leaf cluster, Bronze Star, Purple Heart with oak leaf cluster; recipient award Ariz. Newspaper Assn., 1950, Ind. Photo Journalism award, 1954. Mem. Am. Arbitration Assn. (panelist), Soc. Mayflower Descendants, Sons of Revolution (treas.), Flagon and Trencher, Soc. for the Descendants of the Colonial Clergy. Democrat. Home and Office: 2325 49th St NW Washington DC 20007-1002

SMITH, DEAN EDWARDS, university basketball coach; b. Emporia, Kans., Feb. 28, 1931; s. Alfred Dillon and Vesta Marie (Edwards) S.; m. Linnea Weblemoe, May 21, 1976; children: Sharon, Sandy, Scott, Kristen, Kelly. B.S. in Math. and Phys. Edn., U. Kans., 1953. Asst. basketball coach U.S. Air Force Acad., 1955-58; asst. basketball coach U. N.C., 1958-61, head basketball coach, 1961—; mem. U.S. and Canadian Basketball Rules Com., 1967-73; U.S. basketball coach Olympics, Montreal, Que., Can., 1976; lectr. basketball clinics, Germany, Italy. Served with USAF, 1954-58. Named Coach of Year Atlantic Coast Conf., 1967, 1968, 1971, 1976, 1977, 79, Nat. Basketball Coach of Year, 1977, Nat. Coach of Yr. U.S. Basketball Writers, 1979, Naismith Basketball Hall of Fame, 1982. Mem. Nat. Assn. Basketball Coaches (Nat. Basketball Coach of Year 1976, dir. 1972—, pres. 1981-82), Fellowship Christian Athletes (dir. 1965-70). Baptist. Office: U NC Office Basketball Coach PO Box 2126 Chapel Hill NC 27515-2126

SMITH, DEBBIE JANE, telecommunications manager; b. Fairfield, Ala., Oct. 21, 1957; d. Samuel Adams and Patsy H. (Walker) S. BA in Bus. Adminstrn., Birmingham So. Coll., 1981; MBA, Samford U., 1984. Keypunch operator Mortgage Corp. of the South, Birmingham, Ala., 1976-77, shipping clk., 1977-78; keypunch operator Ala. Power, Birmingham, 1978-79; white page directory clk. South Ctrl. Bell Telephone Co., Birmingham, 1979-83; dispatch clk. BellSouth Advanced Sys., Birmingham, 1983-87, sys. facility adminstr., 1987, supr. telecomm. adminstrn. ctr., 1987-89; staff mgr.-technical support BellSouth Comm. Sys., Birmingham, 1989-93; mgr. telecomm. sys. BellSouth Telecomm., Birmingham, 1993—. Pre-sch. choir dir. 1st Bapt. Ch. Pelham, Ala., 1992-94, 1st Bapt. Ch. Midfield, Ala., 1982-90, coord., worker children's dept., 1990, mem. fin. com., pers. com., benevolence com., 1982-90. Recipient Nat. Cmty. Leadership and Svc. award U.S. Achievement Acad., Lexington, Ky., 1984. Republican. Home: 123 Stratshire Ln Pelham AL 35124-2711 Office: BellSouth Telecomm 3196 Highway 280 S Rm 206N Birmingham AL 35243-4183

SMITH, DENNIS (EDWARD), publisher, author; b. N.Y.C., Sept. 9, 1940; s. John and Mary (Hogan) S.; m. Patricia Ann Kearney, Aug. 24, 1963 (div. May 1988); children: Brendan, Dennis, Sean, Deirdre and Aislinn (twins). BA, NYU, 1970, MA, 1972. Adj. asst. prof. Coll. New Rochelle, 1973-74; fireman City of N.Y., 1963-80; founder, pub., editor in chief Firehouse Mag., N.Y.C., 1976-89. Author: Report from Engine Co. 82, 1972, Final Fire, 1975, Firehouse, 1977, Dennis Smith's History of American Firefighting, 1978, Glitter and Ash, 1980, The Aran Islands—A Personal Journey, 1980, Steely Blue, 1985, Firefighters, Their lives in Their Own Words, 1988, The Little Fire Engine That Saved the City, 1990. Mem. bd. advisors Boys and Girls Clubs Am., N.Y.C., N.Y.C. Cultural Affairs; bd. dirs. The New York Fire Safety Found.; bd. dirs., chmn. Kips Bay Boys and Girls Club, N.Y.C., N.Y. Acad. Art; bd. dirs., pres. Found. for Health and Safety Am. Firefighters; bd. dirs. Ireland House at NYU. With USAF, 1957-60. Recipient Christopher award for non-fiction, 1973. Mem. Union League Club. Democrat. Roman Catholic. Home and Office: 50 Hidden Cove Ct Southampton NY 11968-1520

SMITH, DENTYE M., library media specialist; b. Atlanta, July 21, 1936; d. William Harry and Gladys Magdalene (Bruce) S. AB, Spelman Coll., 1958; MLM, Ga. State U., 1975. Cert. Libr., media specialist. Tchr. English Atlanta Pub. Schs., 1961-82, supr. tchr., 1968-69, tchr. journalism, 1975-80, libr. media specialist, 1982-94; media specialist West Fulton High Sch., 1982-92, West Fulton Mid. Sch., 1992, Booker T. Washington Comprehensive High Sch., Atlanta, 1992-94; leader jur. gt. books Archer and West Fulton high schs.; coord. Atlanta Pub. Schs. reading cert., program West Fulton H.S.; vol. liaison Atlanta-Fulton Pub. Libr., 1987-94, local arrangements com. Atlanta Libr. Assn., 1990-91; seminar presenter in field; coord. study skills seminars Morris Brown Coll.'s Summer Upward Bound Program, 1993, 94, 95; mem. High Mus. of Art, Atlanta, Atlanta Hist. Soc., Ga. Pub. TV. Contbr. articles to profl. jours. Named to Acad. Hall of Fame, Atlanta Pub. Schs., 1990; recipient Tchr. of Yr. award West Fulton H.S., Atlanta, 1974, acad. achievement incentive program award in media APS, 1990. Mem. ALA, NEA, Nat. Coun. Tchrs. English, Am. Assn. Sch. Librs., Ga. Assn. Educators, Atlanta Assn. Educators, Ga. Libr. Assn., Ga. Libr. Media Assn., Nat. Alumnae Assn. Spelman Coll., Ga. State U. Alumni Assn., Nat. Trust Historic Preservation, Ga. Trust Historic Preservation, Libr. of Congress Assocs., Atlanta Ret. Tchrs. Assn., Atlanta Hist. Assn., Ga. Ret. Tchrs. Assn., Nat. Ret. Tchrs. Assn., The Smithsonian Assocs.

SMITH, DEREK ARMAND, publishing company executive; b. Hamilton, Ont., Can., Sept. 2, 1953; came to U.S., 1981; s. Alastair A.G. and Jessie Mead (Maben) S.; m. Rebecca Oldfield, Oct. 10, 1981; 1 child, Alastair Maben Oldfield. BCom., U. Toronto, 1976. Chartered acct.; CPA, Mass. Staff acct. Office of Auditor Gen., Ottawa, 1976-78; chartered acct. Peat Marwick Thorne, Ottawa, 1978-79; v.p. fin. adminstrn. Can. Dry Bottling Ltd., Kingston, Ont., 1979-81; supervising sr. Peat Marwick, Boston, 1981-82; mgr. corp. reporting Warren, Gorham & Lamont, Inc., Boston, 1981-82; asst. contr. Warren, Gorham & Lamont, Inc., N.Y.C., 1982-84, sr. v.p., CFO, 1988-90; sr. v.p., CFO Penguin Books USA Inc., N.Y.C., 1990—; exec. v.p., 1995—; pres. Trinity Coll. Sch. Fund, Darien, Conn., 1992; gov. Trinity Coll. Sch., Port Hope, Ont., 1992. Trustee John Hart Hunter Endl. Found., N.Y.C., 1992. Mem. Assn. of Chartered Accts. in the U.S. Ltd. (treas. 1990-93, dir. 1989-94, hon. dir. 1994—), Kappa Alpha Soc. (exec. coun., v.p. 1991-93, pres. 1993-95, past pres. 1995—). Episcopalian. Avocations: skiing, sailing, tennis, paddle tennis, golf. Office: Penguin Books USA Inc 375 Hudson St New York NY 10014-3658

SMITH, DERRIN RAY, information systems company executive; b. Columbus, Ohio, Feb. 19, 1955; s. Ray Stanley Smith and Clara (Diddle) Craver; m. Catherine Marie Massey, Aug. 18, 1979; children: Shannon Cathleen, Allison Collette, Micayla Colleen, Nicole Catherine. BS, Regis U., 1981; MBA, U. Phoenix, 1984; PhD, U. Denver, 1991. Test lab. mgr. Ball Aerospace Systems, Ball Corp., Boulder, 1975-84; sr. systems engr. Martin Marietta Info. Systems, Denver, 1984-87; tech. cons. MITRE Fed. R & D Ctr., Colorado Springs, 1988-92; pres. DRS Scis., Inc., Denver, 1992—; nat. program mgr. cable/telephone/full svc. network The Nat. Program Mgr. Time Warner, 1995—; tech. cons. U.S. Space Command--RAPIER, Colorado Springs, 1989-91, Unisys Corp., Greenwood Village, Colo., 1992; adj. prof. CIS dept. Univ. Coll., U. Denver, 1992; secretariat Corp. Planner's Roundtable, St. Louis, 1982-84; speaker in field. Author: Evolving the Mountain; Defense Acquisition Management of Strategic Command and Control System Procurements, 1991; contbr. articles to profl. jours. Res. police officer Federal Heights (Colo.) Police Dept., 1979-82. With USMC, 1978-84. Recipient Outstanding Achievement award Rocky Mountain News, 1981, Reservist of Yr. award Navy League U.S., 1981. Mem. Assn. Former Intelligence Officers (pres. Rocky Mountain chpt.). Roman Catholic. Avocations: martial arts, skiing, sailing, creative writing, mountaineering. Home: 3746 E Easter Cir S Littleton CO 80122-2033 Office: DRS Sciences Inc PO 2091 Littleton CO 80161-2091

SMITH, DOLORES MAXINE PLUNK, dancer, educator; b. Webster City, Iowa, Dec. 22, 1926; d. Herschel Swanson and Kathryn (Wilke) Hassig; m. Del O. Furrey, Aug. 26, 1945 (div. Feb. 1960); children: Bob H. Furrey, Jon B. Furrey, Kathryn E. Furrey; m. Dewey Pechota, 1962 (div. 1963); m. Leon Plunk, 1965 (div. 1966); m. Harold Burdick, 1974 (div. 1977); m. Floyd E. Smith, July 13, 1985. BS in Edn., Black Hills Tchrs. Coll., 1962; MA, Tex. Woman's U., 1964, PhD, 1974. Owner, operator pvt. dance studios, S.D., 1953-62; tchr. rural schs. Rosebud Reservation, S.D., 1945-49; tchr. Mellette County Pub. Schs., White River, S.D., 1958-60, St. Francis Indian Day Sch., 1960-61, Converse County (Wyo.) High Sch., 1961-62; grad. asst. Tex. Woman's U., Denton, 1962-64, 71; asst. prof. dance Sam Houston U., Huntsville, Tex., 1964-65; prof. Ctrl. Mo. State U., Warrensburg, 1965—; judge dance contest Kansas City Dance Theatre Co., 1987, 88, World Dance Assn., 1988, Mo. State Fair, 1989; judge Miss Am. Co-ed Pageants, 1991-93; dir. Dance Partisans Assn., Ctrl. Mo. State U., 1982—, cmty. children's gymnastics program, 1982—, tchr. cmty. dance program, 1988—, dir. show dance team, 1991—; dance coord. Internat. Coun. Health, Phys. Edn., Recreation, Sport and Dance, 1991—; presenter Japanese Asia Dance Events, Malaysia, 1994, Dance Edn. Conf., Mich. State U., 1994. Contbr. articles to profl. jours. Bd. dirs. Kansas City Dance Theatre Co.; dir. Commn. on Dance, 1991-96, co-dir., 1994-96. Coun. for Health, Phys. Edn., Recreation, Sport and Dance scholar, 1995. Mem. Dance Masters Am. (sec. 1985-87, chmn. Mr. and Miss Dance Contest 1985, scholarships com. 1988-90), AAHPERD (honors award cen. dist. chpt., cen. dist. presentor 1991-92, dance chair, coll. chair, dance performance chair 1989-90, v.p. dance edn. 1991-93), Mo. Assn. Health, Phys. Edn., Recreation and Dance (pres. 1972, svc. award), Nat. Dance Assn. (v.p. dance edn. 1991-93, chmn. Heritage luncheon 1968, 78, 87, Heritage award com. 1988-89, mem. ad hoc spl. svcs. com. 1989—, pub. Spotlight 1989-90), Mid-Am. Dance Network (on-site coord. choreographers/dancers workshop 1992, bd. dirs., sec. 1992-94), Mo. Art Coun. Basic Arts Edn. (basic arts edn. task force higher edn.), Dance and Child Internat. (display chair, presider 1991), Asian Pacific Conf. Arts Edn. (presenter 1989), Assn. Supervision and Curriculum Devel., Internat. Congress Health, Phys. Edn. and Recreation Presenters (congress dels. representing dance, presenter 1991, 93), Internat. Phys. Edn. and Sports for Girls and Women, Phys. Edn. and Recreation, Mo. Alliance for Arts Edn. Avocations: raising and showing Belgium and Shire draft horses, draft ponies, donkey, mules, stained glass, cake decorating. Home: 130 SW 400th Rd Warrensburg MO 64093-8109 Office: Ctrl Mo State U Dept Physical Education Warrensburg MO 64093

SMITH, DON EDWARD, school system administrator; b. Kansas City, Mo., Feb. 4, 1950; s. Herbert Thurman and Ella Marie (Meador) S.; m. Alberta Allred, Dec. 26, 1978; children: Don E. Jr., Heather JoDon. BA, Ark. State U., Jonesboro, 1974, BS Edn., 1980, MS Edn., 1986. Cert. sch. adminstr. Tchr. Marked Tree (Ark.) Sch. Dist., 1980-81; tchr./coach Trumann (Ark.) Sch. Dist., 1981-90; supt. Stanford Sch. Dist., Paragould, Ark., 1990-94, Wonderview Sch. Dist., Hattieville, Ark., 1994—. Mem. Regional Leaders, Paragould, 1992—. With USN, 1974-77. Recipient Acad. and Music scholarship, Ark. State U., 1968, 69. Mem. Am. Assn. Sch. Adminstrs., Ark. Assn. Edn. Adminstrs., Ark. Assn. Secondary Adminstrs., Ark. Assn. Sch. Bus. Ofcls., Ark. Rural Edn. Assn., Greene County C. of C. (chmn.-elect edn. com. 1990-94), Masons, Phi Beta Kappa, Kappa Delta Pi. Avocations: fishing, racing cars. Home and Office: Wonderview Sch Dist RR 1 Box 219 Hattieville AR 72063-9719

SMITH, DONALD ARTHUR, mechanical engineer, researcher; b. Hartford, Conn., Apr. 9, 1945; s. Winfred Arthur and Marguerite Elisabeth (Johnson) S.; m. Marianne Carol Taverna, June 17, 1967; 1 child, Adam James. BS in Mech. Engring., U. Hartford, 1968. Rsch. engr. Combustion Engring. Inc., Windsor, Conn., 1968-71; supr. fluid rsch. Combustion Engring. Inc., Windsor, 1971-77, mgr. combustion rsch., 1977-84; dir. R&D Hartford Steam Boiler Inspection & Ins. Co., 1984—; co. rep. Indsl. Rsch. Inst., Washington, 1989—; treas. Am. Flame Rsch. Com., 1983—. Tech. editor: HSB Locomotive, 1990-91. Haddam (Conn.) Planning and Zoning Commn., 1991-95; pres. Sherwood Camp Assn., Haddam, 1971-81. Named Engr. Yr. ASME (Hartford sect.), 1989. Mem. U. Hartford Alumni Bd.,

Lions. Republican. Roman Catholic. Achievements include patents in spray atomizers, burners, ignitors and flame scanning systems for indsl. application. Established Combustion Engring.'s fluid mechanics and combustion rsch. facilities, Hartford Steam Boiler's corp. R&D program. Home: PO Box 95-42 Smith Hill Rd Haddam CT 06438 Office: Hartford Steam Boiler One State St Hartford CT 06102

SMITH, DONALD E., broadcast engineer, manager; b. Salt Lake City, Sept. 10, 1930; s. Thurman A. and Louise (Cardall) S.; B.A. Columbia Coll., Chgo., 1955; B.S.; U. Utah, 1970; postgrad. U. So. Calif., U. Utah, PhD (hon.) Columbia Coll., 1985; m. Helen B. Lacy, 1978. Engr., Iowa State U., (WOI-TV), 1955-56; asst. chief engr. KLRJ-TV, Las Vegas, 1956-60; studio field engr. ABC, Hollywood, Cal., 1960; chief engr. Teletape, Inc., Salt Lake City, 1961; engring. supr. KUER, U. Utah, Salt Lake City, 1962-74, gen. mgr., 1975-85. Freelance cinematographer, 1950—; cons. radio TV (mgmt. engr. and prodn.), 1965—. Mem. Soc. Motion Pictures and TV Engrs., Lambda Chi Alpha. Home: 963 Hollywood Ave Salt Lake City UT 84105-3347

SMITH, DONALD EUGENE, healthcare facility management administrator owner; b. Mishawaka, Ind., Oct. 15, 1936; s. Ernest Hartmann and Lucile Emma (Krumanaker) S.; m. Nancy Mae Jaffke, Sept. 2, 1961; children: Adam, Reid, Lynn. AB, Wabash Coll., 1959; MBA, U. Chgo., 1963. Adminstrv. resident Ind. U. Med. Ctr., 1960-61; assoc. dir. Ind. U. Hosps., 1966-72; pres. Henderson & Smith Corp., Indpls., 1978—; lectr. in health adminstrn. Ind. U., 1965-66, adj. asst. prof. in health adminstrn., 1966-78; ptnr. Covington (Ind.) Manor Health Care Ctr., Carmel (Ind.) Care Ctr., Countryside Manor, Anderson, Ind., Dearborn Enterprises, Lawrenceburg, Ind., Manor House at Riverview, Noblesville, Ind., Rawlins House, Pendleton, Ind., Manor House of Carmel, Ind., Northridge, Crawfordsville, Ind., Power Purchasing, Inc., Greenwood, Ind.; chmn. Ind. State Bd. Registration and Edn. Health Facility Adminstrs., 1969-82. Bd. dirs. Ind. U. Med. Ctr. Fed. Credit Union, 1965-68, Ind. Blue Cross, 1966-71; med. ctr. chmn. United Fund Drive, 1962-65; sec. Carmel (Ind.) Classic, 1979, v.p., 1981, pres., 1982-83; bd. trustees Wabash Coll., 1986—, mem. exec. com., 1986—, chmn. capital campaign drive, 1987-91, mem. long range planning com., 1985; active Hamilton County Rep. Fin. Com., 1990—. Fellow ACHS; mem. Am. Health Care Assn., Ind. Health Care Assn., Wabash Coll. Alumni Assn., U. Chgo. Hosp. Adminstrn. Alumni Assn., Woodland Country Club, Skyline Club. Office: Henderson & Smith Corp 10333 N Meridian St Ste 250 Indianapolis IN 46290-1081

SMITH, DONALD EUGENE, banker; b. Terre Haute, Ind., Nov. 4, 1926; s. Henry P. and Ruth I. (Bius) S.; m. Mary F. Ryan, June 25, 1947; children: Virginia Lee, Sarah Jane. Student, Ind. U., 1945-47, Ind. State U., 1947-48. Pres. Deep Vein Coal Co., Terre Haute, Ind., 1947—; with R.J. Oil Co., Inc., 1948—; pres. Princeton Mining Co., Terre Haute, 1947—, Terre Haute Oil Corp., 1947—; chmn. of bd. Terre Haute 1st Nat. Bank, 1969—; pres., CEO 1st Fin. Corp., Terre Haute, 1969—; pres. Deep Vein Coal Co., R.J. Oil Co., Princeton Mining Co., Terre Haute Oil Co.; bd. dirs. So. Ind. Gas and Electric Co. Trustee Ind. State U.; bd. mgrs. Rose-Hulman Inst. Tech., 1978—; pres. Alliance for Growth and Progress, 1987—; treas. Terre Haute Econ. Devel. Commn., 1981—; mem. Ind. Econ. Devel. Coun. Mem. Terre Haute C. of C. (bd. dirs. 1982—). Club: Country of Terre Haute. Lodge: Elks. Home: 94 Allendale Terre Haute IN 47802-4751 Office: Terre Haute First Nat Bank One First Financial Pla PO Box 540 Terre Haute IN 47807

SMITH, DONALD EVANS, library consultant; b. Shanendoah, Iowa, Dec. 2, 1915; s. William Wesley and Bess Alice (Evans) S.; student Ricks Coll., 1939-40; BA, Hastings Coll., 1946; MLS, U. Wash., 1964. Tchr. English, librarian Tenino (Wash.) High Sch., 1950-51, Rochester (Wash.) High Sch., 1954-59; librarian North Thurston High Sch., Lacey, Wash., 1959-67; head librarian, coord. instructional materials Lakes High Sch., Lakewood Ctr., Wash., 1967-80; library cons., 1980—. Mem. awards com. Wash. Library Commn., 1964-66. With Signal Corps, AUS, 1942-45; to 1st lt., M.I., U.S. Army, 1951-54; to col. Wash. State Guard, 1971-80, now ret. Mem. Wash. Assn. Sch. Librarians (com. chmn.), Clover Park Edn. Assn. (com. chmn. 1970-71), Am. Legion, Phi Delta Kappa (del. nat. confs.). Home and Office: 4530 26th Loop SE Lacey WA 98503-3264

SMITH, DONALD NICKERSON, food service executive; b. Can., Sept. 12, 1940; came to U.S., 1946, naturalized, 1956; s. Fred Raymond and Hazel (Nickerson) S.; m. Beverley Thorell, Dec. 1961 (div.); children: Jeffrey, Stacy, Darby; m. Angela Dangerfield, Mar. 8, 1984. BA, U. Mont., 1962; D in Bus. Adminstrn. (hon.), Upper Iowa U., 1980. Sr. exec. v.p., sr. ops. officer McDonald's Corp., Oak Brook, Ill., 1964-77; pres., chief exec. officer Burger King Corp., Miami, 1977-80; sr. v.p., pres. food svc. div. PepsiCo, Inc., Purchase, N.Y., 1980-83; pres., chief exec. officer Chart House, Inc. (name changed to Diversifoods, Inc.), Itasca, Ill., 1983-85; chmn., chief exec. officer Tenn. Restaurant Co., Itasca, 1985—; chmn., pres., CEO Friendly Holding Corp., Wilbraham, Mass. With USMCR, 1957-65. Named Adman of the Yr., Advt. Age mag., 1979. *

SMITH, DONALD NORBERT, engineering executive; b. Ft. Wayne, Ind., June 12, 1931. BS in Indsl. Mgmt., Ind. U., 1953; Diploma Grad. Sch. Bus., U. N.C., 1960. Asst. mgr. Ann Arbor (Mich.) Rsch. Labs/Burroughs Corp., 1961-64; dir. Indsl. Devel. Divsn. U. Mich., Ann Arbor, 1964-93; assoc. dir.-mfg. systems rsch. Office for Study Auto Transp. U. Mich. Transp. Rsch. Inst., Ann Arbor, 1993—. Co-author: Management Standards for Computers and Numerical Controls, 1977; contbr. articles to profl. jours. Recipient Peace award, Israel, 1967, Mfg. Tech. award ASTME, 1968, Engring. Merit award, San Fernando Valley Engrs. Coun., 1971, Man of Yr. award Great Lakes Chpt. Numerical Control Soc., 1975, Archimedes Engring. award Calif. Soc. Profl. Engrs., Disting. CAD/CAM Achievements award L.A. Coun. Engrs., 1982, Achievement award for promoting Swedish/Am. trade, Kingdom of Sweden, 1983, Tech. Transfer award NASA/Rockwell Internat., 1984. Fellow Soc. Mfg. Engrs. (Indsl. Tech. Mgmt. award 1978, internat. awards com. 1986, 88, 89, Joseph A. Siegel Internat. Svc. award 1988, Pres.'s award Robotics Internat. 1985). Roman Catholic. Avocation: boating. Office: Office Study Automotive Transp 2901 Baxter Rd Ann Arbor MI 48109-2150

SMITH, DORIS CORINNE KEMP, retired nurse; b. Bogalusa, La., Nov. 22, 1919; d. Milton Jones and Maude Maria (Fortenberry) Kemp; m. Joseph William Smith, Oct. 13, 1940 (dec.). BS in Nursing, U. Colo., 1957, MS in Nursing Adminstrn., 1958. RN, Colo. Head nurse Chgo. Bridge & Iron Co., Morgan City, La., 1941-45, Shannon Hosp., San Angelo, Tex., 1945-50; dir. nursing Yoakum County Hosp., Denver City, Tex., 1951-52; hosp. supr. Med. Arts Hosp., Odessa, Tex., 1952-55; dir. insvc. edn. St. Anthony Hosp., Denver, 1961-66; coord. Sch. Vocat. Nursing, Kiamichi Area Vocat.-Tech. Nursing Sch., Wilburton, Okla., 1969-77; supr. non-ambulatory unit Lubbock (Tex.) State Sch., 1978-85, ret., 1985; mem. steering com. Western Interstate Commn. on Higher Edn. for Nurses, Denver, 1963-65; mem. curriculum and materials com. Okla. Bd. Vocat.-Tech. Edn., Stillwater, 1971-76; mem. Invitational Conf. To Plan Nursing for Future, Oklahoma City, 1976-77; mem. survey team to appraise Sch. of Vocat.-Tech. Edn. Schs. for Okla. Dept. Vocat.-Tech. Edn., 1975-76. Author, editor: Survey of Functions Expected of the General Duty Nurse, State of Colorado, 1958; co-editor: Curriculum Guides; contbr. numerous articles to profl. jours. Recipient citation of merit Okla. State U., 1976; named Woman of Yr. Sunrise chpt. Am. Bus. Women's Assn., 1994-95. Mem. AAAS, ANA, AAUW (life), Nat. League for Nursing, Tex. League for Nursing, Tex. Nurses Assn., Dist. 18 Nurses Assn., Tex. Employees Assn. (v.p. 1984-85), U. Colo. Alumni Assn., Am. Bus. Women's Assn. (pres. Lubbock chpt. 1986-87, rec. sec. 1989-90, edn. chair 1994-95, hospitality chair 1995-96), Bus. and Profl. Women's Assn. (sec. 1992-95), Chancellor's Club U. Colo., Pi Lambda Theta (sec. local chpt. 1957-58). Republican. Avocations: gardening, swimming, walking, travel, fishing. Home: 2103 55th St Lubbock TX 79412-2612

SMITH, DORIS VICTORIA, educational agency administrator; b. N.Y.C., July 5, 1937; d. Albin and Victoria (Anderson) Olson; m. Howard R. Smith, Aug. 21, 1960; children: Kurt, Steven, Andrea. BS in Edn., Wagner Coll., 1959; MA in Edn., Kean Coll., 1963, cert., 1980; EdD, Fairleigh Dickinson U., 1984, Nova Southeastern U., 1995. Cert. adminstr., tchr. elem. edn., N.J. Thorough and efficient coord. East Hanover (N.J.) Twp. Sch. Dist., 1977-79; ednl. specialist N.J. State Dept. Edn., Morristown, 1979—, ednl. planner, 1982-87, ednl. mgr., 1987—; pres. N.E. Coalition Ednl. Leaders, Inc.; founding mem. Morris County Curriculum Network. Author: Affirmative Action—Rules and Regulations, 1982, Supervising Early Childhood Programs, 1984. Past pres. bd. trustees Florham Park Libr.; founding mem. Morris Area Tech. Alliance; founding mem., pres. Calvary Nursery Sch.; bd. of trust office N.J. Coun. Edn.; pres. bd. trustees Madison/Chatham Adult Sch.; trustee Morris County Children's Svcs. Tchr. insvc. grantee; recipient Disting. Svc. award N.E. Coalition Ednl. Leaders, 1991, Disting. Svc. award Morris County Prins. and Suprs. Assn., Outstanding Educator award N.J. ASCD, 1995. Mem. N.J. Coun. Edn., N.J. Schoolmasters Assn., Phi Delta Kappa.

SMITH, DOROTHY OTTINGER, jewelry designer, civic leader; b. Indpls.; d. Albert Ellsworth and Leona Aurelia (Waller) Ottinger; student Herron Art Sch. of Purdue U. and Ind. U., 1941-42; m. James Emory Smith, June 25, 1943 (div. 1984); children: Michael Ottinger, Sarah Anne, Theodore Arnold, Lisa Marie. Comml. artist William H. Block Co., Indpls., 1942-43, H.P. Wasson Co., 1943-44; dir. Riverside (Calif.) Art Center, 1963-64; jewelry designer, Riverside, 1970—; numerous design commns. Adviser Riverside chpt. Freedom's Found. of Valley Forge; co-chmn. fund raising com. Riverside Art Ctr. and Mus., 1966-67, bd. dirs. Art Alliance, 1980-81, Art Mus.; mem. Riverside City Hall sculpture selection panel Nat. Endowment Arts, 1974-75; chmn. fund raising benefit Riverside Art Ctr. and Mus., 1973-74, trustee, 1980-84, chmn. permanent collection, 1981-84, co-chmn. fund drive, 1982-84; chmn. Riverside Mcpl. Arts Commn., 1974-76, Silver Anniversary Gala, 1992; juror Riverside Civic Ctr. Purchase Prize Art Show, 1975; mem. pub. bldgs. and grounds subcom., gen. plan citizens com. City of Riverside, 1965-66; mem. Mayor's Commn. on Civic Beauty, Mayor's Commn. on Sister City Sendai, 1965-66; bd. dirs., chmn. spl. events Children's League of Riverside Community Hosp., 1952-53; bd. dirs. Crippled Children's Soc. of Riverside, spl. events chmn., 1952-53; bd. dirs. Jr. League of Riverside, rec. sec., 1960-61; bd. dirs. Nat. Charity League, pres. Riverside chpt., 1965-66; mem. exec. com. of bd. trustees Riverside Arts Found., 1977-91, fund drive chmn., 1978-79, project rev. chmn., 1978-79; juror Gemco Charitable and Scholarship Found., 1977-85; mem. bd. women deacons Calvary Presbyn. Ch., 1978-80, elder, 1989-92; mem. incorporating bd. Inland Empire United Fund for Arts, 1980-81; bd. dirs. Hospice Orgn. Riverside County, 1982-84; Art Awareness chmn. Riverside Arts Found.; mem. Calif. Coun. Humanities, 1982-86. Recipient cert. Riverside City Coun., 1977, plaque Mayor of Riverside, 1977. Mem. Riverside Art Assn. (pres. 1961-63, 1st v.p. 1964-65, 67-68, trustee 1959-70, 80-84, 87-92), Art Alliance of Riverside Art Ctr. and Museum (founder 1964, pres. 1969-70). Recipient Spl. Recognition Riverside Cultural Arts Coun., 1981, Disting. Service plaque Riverside Art Ctr. and Mus., Jr. League Silver Raincross Community Svc. award, 1989, Cert. Appreciation Outstanding Svc. to the Arts Community Riverside Arts Found., 1990. Address: 3979 Chapman Pl Riverside CA 92506-1150

SMITH, DOUGLAS V., manufacturing executive, heavy; b. 1943. BS Mech. Engring., Clemson U.; MS Mech. Engring., U. Ky.; MBA, Harvard Bus. Sch. Pres., CEO, dir. Lufkin (Tex.)Industries, Inc., 1993—. Office: Lufkin Industries Inc 601 S Raguet St Lufkin TX 75904-3951*

SMITH, DUDLEY RENWICK, insurance company executive; b. N.Y.C., June 10, 1937; s. Crosby Tuttle and Vernon (Siems) S.; m. Juliana Buros, Nov. 17, 1962; children: Clayton Tuttle, Bradley Renwick, Gregory Dudley. AB, Dartmouth Coll., 1960. V.p. Fed. Ins. Co., Warren, N.J.; sr. v.p. Chubb & Son Inc., Warren, 1961—; trustee Chubb Found. Home: 55 Montadale Cir Princeton NJ 08540-7619 Office: Chubb & Son Inc 15 Mountain View Rd PO Box 1615 Warren NJ 07061-1615

SMITH, DWIGHT MORRELL, chemistry educator; b. Hudson, N.Y., Oct. 10, 1931; s. Elliott Monroe and Edith Helen (Hall) S.; m. Alice Beverly Bond, Aug. 27, 1955 (dec. 1990); children—Karen Elizabeth, Susan Allison, Jonathan Aaron; m. Elfi Nelson, Dec. 28, 1991. B.A., Central Coll., Pella, Iowa, 1953; Ph.D., Pa. State U., 1957; ScD (hon.), Cen. Coll., 1986; LittD (hon.), U. Denver, 1990. Postdoctoral fellow, instr. Calif. Inst. Tech., 1957-59; sr. chemist Texaco Rsch. Ctr., Beacon, N.Y., 1959-61; asst. prof. chemistry Wesleyan U., Middletown, Conn., 1961-66; assoc. prof. Hope Coll., Holland, Mich., 1966-69, prof., 1969-72; prof. chemistry U. Denver, 1972—, chmn. dept., 1972-83, vice chancellor for acad. affairs, 1983-84, chancellor, 1984-89; pres., bd. trustees Hawaii Loa Coll., Kaneohe, 1990-92; bd. dirs. Aina Inst., Hawaii; mem. Registry for Interim Coll. and Univ. Pres.; mem. adv. bd. Solar Energy Rsch. Inst., 1989-91, Denver Rsch. Inst.; mem. vis. com. Zettlemoyer Ctr. for Surface Studies Lehigh U., 1990—. Editor Revs. on Petroleum Chemistry, 1975-78; contbr. articles to profl. jours.; patentee selective hydrogenation. Chmn. Chs. United for Social Action, Holland, 1968-69; mem. adv. com. Holland Sch. Bd., 1969-70; bd. commrs. Colo. Adv. Tech. Inst., 1984-88, Univ. Senate, United Meth. Ch., Nashville, 1987-88, 91-93; mem. adv. bd. United Way, Inst. Internat. Edn., Japan Am. Soc. Colo., Denver Winter Games Olympics Com.; mem. ch. bds. or consistories Ref. Ch. Am., N.Y., Conn., Mich., United Meth. Ch., Colo. DuPont fellow, 1956-57, NSF fellow Scripps Inst., 1971-72; recipient grants Research Corp., Petroleum Research Fund, NSF, Solar Energy Research Inst. Mem. Am. Chem. Soc. (chmn. Colo. 1976, sec. western Mich. 1970-71, award Colo. sect. 1986), Catalysis Soc., Soc. Applied Spectroscopy, Mile High Club, Pinehurst Country Club, Sigma Xi. Home: 1931 W Sanibel Ct Littleton CO 80120 Office: U Denver Dept Chem Univ Park Denver CO 80208

SMITH, DWIGHT RAYMOND, ecology and wildlife educator, writer; b. Sanders, Idaho, July 28, 1921; s. Andrew Leonard and Effie Elizabeth (Simons) S.; m. Carol Elizabeth Breclaw (dec. 1983); children Alan Dwight (dec.), Sharon Lee Smith Dequine, Gary Robert, Mark Jonathan (dec.). BS in Forestry, U. Idaho, 1949, MS in Wildlife Mgmt., 1951; PhD in Ecology, Utah State U., 1971. Rsch. biologist Idaho Fish and Game Dept., Salmon, 1950-52, area game mgr., 1953-56; range scientist U.S. Forest Svc., Ft. Collins, Colo., 1957-61, wildlife rsch. biologist, 1962-65; asst. prof. Colo. State U., Ft. Collins, 1965-70, assoc. prof., 1971-75, prof., 1975-83, prof. emeritus, 1983—; nature photographer Alan Landsburg Prodns., Hollywood, Calif., 1971; energy cons. CF&I Steel, Pueblo, Colo., 1981. Author: Above Timberline: A Wildlife Biologist's Rocky Mountain Journal, 1981; writer/photographer (film) Research in the Rockies: A Scientist Explores the Alpine, 1973; contbr. articles to profl. jours. Served to 2d lt. (via battlefield comm.) inf. U.S. Army, 1942-45, PTO, ETO. Decorated Bronze Star. Decorated Bronze Star. Rsch. grantee, fellow U.S. Fish and Wildlife Svc., 1949-50, Wildlife Mgmt. Inst., 1950, Nat. Wildlife Fedn., 1954-55. Fellow Explorers Club; mem. Toastmasters (ednl. v.p. local chpt. 1960-62, pres. 1963), Xi Sigma Pi, Sigma Xi, Gamma Sigma Delta, Phi Kappa Phi. Democrat. Roman Catholic. Avocations: photography, piloting, bicycling, skiing, square dancing. Home: 1916 Harmony Dr Fort Collins CO 80525-3442 *Do not be afraid of enthusiasm. You can do nothing effectively without it.*

SMITH, EDGAR BENTON, physician; b. Houston, June 2, 1932; s. Burt Benton and Lela Elizabeth (Grant) S.; m. Francis Elaine Newton, Aug. 1, 1953; children—Sheri Elaine Smith Dinehart, Robin Marie Smith Fredrickson. Student, Rice U., 1950-53; BA, U. Houston, 1956; MD, Baylor U., 1957; diploma clin. medicine of the tropics, U. London, 1967. Intern Walter Reed Gen. Hosp., Washington, 1957-58; resident Brooke Gen. Hosp., Ft. Sam Houston, Tex., 1960-63; asst. prof. dermatology U. Miami Sch. Medicine, 1967-68, Baylor Coll. Medicine, Houston, 1968-71; asso. prof. medicine (dermatology) U. N.Mex. Sch. Medicine, Albuquerque, 1971-75; prof. U. N.Mex. Sch. Medicine, 1975-78; prof., chmn. dept. dermatology U. Tex. Med. Br., Galveston, 1978—. Contbr. articles in field to profl. jours. Served with U.S. Army, 1956-66. Recipient Khatali award U. N.Mex. Sch. Medicine, 1976; Fulbright scholar London Sch. Hygiene and Tropical Medicine, 1966-67; Alfred Stengel travelling scholar ACP, 1967. Mem. AMA, Am. Acad. Dermatology (bd. dirs. 1978-82, pres.-elect 1988, pres. 1989, Sulzberger internat. lectr. 1992), Assn. Profs. Dermatology (sec.-treas. 1979-82), Am. Dermatol. Assn. (bd. dirs. 1994—), Southwestern Dermatol. Soc. (sec. 1974-77, pres. 1978), South Ctrl. Dermatol. Congress (sec.-gen. 1973-76, pres. 1976-81), Tex. Dermatol. Soc. (trustee 1986), So. Med. Assn. (chmn. dermatology sect. 1988), Galveston Arty. Club, Yacht Club, Baker Street Irregulars, Alpha Omega Alpha. Democrat. Methodist. Home: 3017 Ave O Galveston TX 77550 Office: U Tex Med Br Dept Dermatology Galveston TX 77555-0783

SMITH, EDGAR EUGENE, biochemist, university administrator; b. Hollandale, Miss., Aug. 6, 1934; s. Sam and Augusta Lillie (McCoy) S.; m. Inez Oree Wiley, May 27, 1955; children—E. Donald, Anthony R., Stephen S., Gregory S. B.S., Tougaloo Coll., 1955; M.S., Purdue U., 1957, Ph.D., 1960. Rsch. fellow in surgery (biochemistry) Harvard Med. Sch., Boston, 1959-61; rsch. assoc. Harvard Med. Sch., 1961-68; assoc. in surg. rsch. Beth Israel Hosp., Boston, 1959-68; asst. prof. surgery (chemistry) Boston U. Sch. Medicine, 1968-70, assoc. prof. biochemistry, 1970-74; assoc. prof. biochemistry U. Mass. Med. Sch., Worcester, 1974-80, prof. emeritus biochemistry and molecular biology, 1991—; assoc. dean acad. affairs U. Mass. Med. Sch., 1974-77, provost, 1975-83; asst. dean minority affairs, prin. investigator Bur. Health Manpower Spl. Project grant Boston U. Sch. Medicine, 1972-74; v.p. acad. affairs U. Mass. System, 1983-91; v.p. Nellie Mae, 1990-93; acting pres. Tougaloo Coll., 1995—; mem. governing bd. Robert Wood Johnson Health Policy Fellowship Program, Inst. Medicine, NAS, 1978-85. Contbr. writings to sci. publs. Chmn. bd. overseers Sch. Medicine Morehouse Coll.; trustee Tougaloo Coll., Metco Scholarship Fund, Lexington, Mass.; bd. dirs. Dimock Community Health Center, Boston, New Urban League of Greater Boston, So. Edn. Found., 1976-79; chmn. Boston Com. for Nat. Med. Fellowships, Inc. Recipient research career devel. award Nat. Cancer Inst., 1969-74, award for outstanding achievement in biochemistry Nat. Consortium for Black Profl. Devel., 1976, human relations award Mass. Teachers Assn., 1977, health award NAACP, 1977; Robert Wood Johnson Health Policy fellow Inst. Medicine, Nat. Acad. Scis., 1977-78; named Alumnus of Yr. Tougaloo Coll., 1969, Disting. Alumnus Nat. Assn. for Equal Opportunities in Higher Edn., 1979, 92, Old Master Purdue U., 1978. Fellow Am. Inst. Chemists; mem. Am. Soc. Biol. Chemists, Am. Chem. Soc. (div. biol. chemists), AAAS, N.Y. Acad. Scis., Am. Assn. for Cancer Research, Boston Cancer Research Assn., Am. Polit. Sci. Assn., Am. Soc. Biol. Chemists (com. on minorities 1980-83), Josiah Macy, Jr. Found. Scholarship Com. Marine Biol. Lab., Woods Hole, Mass., Sigma Xi, Phi Lambda Upsilon, Alpha Phi Alpha. Home: 81 Hill St Lexington MA 02173-6532

SMITH, EDWARD HERBERT, radiologist, educator; b. N.Y.C., Feb. 18, 1936; s. Nathan Leon and Rebecca Ada (Brodsky) S.; m. Anne Chantler Oliphant, June 27, 1971; children: Peter Chantler, Jeffrey Martin. A.B., Columbia Coll., 1956; M.D., SUNY, 1960. Intern U. Calif. Hosp., San Francisco, 1960-61; resident in internal medicine Montefiore Hosp., N.Y.C., 1961-62; resident in radiology Kings County Hosp. Ctr., Bklyn., 1964-67, radiologist, 1967-69; instr. SUNY-Bklyn., 1967-69; radiologist Children's Hosp. Med. Ctr., Boston, 1969-70, Peter Bent Brigham Hosp., Boston, 1969-80; dir. div. radiology Charles A. Dana Cancer Research Ctr., Boston, 1974-80; instr. Harvard Med. Sch., Boston, 1969-70, asst. prof., 1970-75, assoc. prof., 1975-80, lectr. radiology, 1980—; radiologist U. Mass. Med. Ctr., Worcester, 1980—, prof., chmmn. dept. radiology, 1980—; prof. U. Mass. Med. Sch., Worcester, 1980—; prof. dept. surgery in urology U. Mass. Med. Sch., 1983—; vis. radiologist Rambam Govt. Hosp., Haifa, Israel, 1972; vis. prof. dept. ultrasound U. Copenhagen, Herlev, Denmark, 1977-78, Shanghai Med. Ctr., Peoples Republic China, 1987; cons. Tng. Program in Diagnostic Ultrasound for Physicians and Technologists, Va., 1974-75; reviewer profl. jours. Author: (with others) Abdominal Ultrasound: Static and Dynamic Scanning, 1980; contbr. articles to profl. jours. Fogarty sr. internat. fellow John E. Fogarty Internat. Ctr. for Advanced Study in Health Scis., NIH, Copenhagen, 1977-78. Fellow Am. Coll. Radiology, Soc. Radiologists in Ultrasound (charter); mem. Assn. Univ. Radiologists, Am. Inst. Ultrasound in Medicine, Am. Roentgen Ray Soc., Radiol. Soc. N.Am., New Eng. Soc. Ultrasound in Medicine (charter, pres. 1978-79), New Eng. Roentgen Ray Soc. (pres. 1989-90), Mass. Radiologic Soc. (exec. coun.). Office: U Mass Med Ctr Dept Radiology 55 Lake Ave N Worcester MA 01655-0002 *I have enjoyed a rewarding career in academic medicine but I am extremely concerned with the momentum shifting toward for profit "managed care", medicine will become a business with primary concern with the bottom line and we will lose the "care" in medical care and the American public will be the big loser.*

SMITH, EDWARD JUDE, biologist; b. Serabu, Sierra Leone, Oct. 31, 1961; s. Karimu and Yemah (Brewah) S.; m. Gilceria Estandien Pimentel, Oct. 9, 1991; children: Dehmeh, Ngeindaloh. BSc, U. Sierra Leone, 1984; MSc, Oreg. State U., 1989, PhD, 1991. Rsch. asst. Oreg. State U., Corvallis, Oreg., 1987-91; postdoctoral rsch. assoc. Iowa State U., Ames, 1991-92; asst. prof. Tuskegee (Ala.) U., 1992—. Contbr. articles to profl. jours. Sec. Pace, Auburn, Ala., 1994. Mem. Am. Soc. Genetics, USDA (sec. 1994, pres. 1995). Roman Catholic. Achievements include rsch. on discriminant analysis of selected lines; rsch. on candidate markers for tibial dyschondroplasia; rsch. on an animal model to study the molecular basis for heterosis. Home: 827 Cahaba Dr Auburn AL 36830 Office: Tuskegee U 109 Milbank Hall Tuskegee AL 36088

SMITH, EDWARD K., economist, consultant; b. Buffalo, Apr. 12, 1922; s. Clifford Kershaw and Helen (Baro) S.; m. Mary Alice Pendergast, Dec. 20, 1948; children: Benjamin, Christopher, Loretta Christopher, Katherine Smith Fuscoe, Alice Ryan, Margarita Treuth, James, Daniel. B.A., Hobart Coll., 1946; M.A., U. Buffalo, 1950, Harvard U., 1955; Ph.D., Harvard U., 1960. From asst. to assoc. prof. econs. Boston Coll., 1956-64; dep. asst. sec. U.S. Dept. Commerce, Washington, 1965-68; prof., chmn. dept. econs. Colo. State U., Ft. Collins, 1968-70; v.p. Nat. Bur. Econ. Research, N.Y.C., 1970-77; sr. econ. cons. Brimmer & Co. Inc., Washington, 1977-83; dir. Internat. Banking Ctr., Fla. Internat. U., Miami, 1982, Bur. Ind. Econs., U.S. Dept. Commerce, Washington, 1983; assoc. dir. Bur. Econ. Analysis, 1984-88; cons. economist, 1988—; vis. prof. econs. U. Colo., 1965, Yale U., New Haven, 1971, Fla. Internat. U., Miami, 1982. Author: The Economic State of New England, 1954. Fiscal advisor Lt. Gov. Mass., Boston, 1955; mem. Pres.'s Task Force on Environ., 1966, Pres.'s Task Force on Housing, 1968, Gov. Carey's Task Force on Unemployment, N.Y.C., 1974; trustee St. Mary's Coll., Newburgh, N.Y., 1972-77. Served with U.S. Army, 1943-46. Mem. Am. Econs. Assn., Nat. Assn. Bus. Economists, So. Regional Sci. Assn., Nat. Economists Club (v.p. 1984, bd. dirs. 1985-86). Democrat. Episcopalian.

SMITH, EDWARD PAUL, JR., lawyer; b. Westbury, N.Y., Jan. 13, 1939; s. Edward Paul Sr. and Margaret (Eisenhauer) S.; m. Mary Elizabeth Neagle, Mar. 29, 1980; children: Nora, Edward, Brian, Thomas, Brendan. BA, Coll. of the Holy Cross, 1960; LLB, Columbia U., 1963. Bar: N.Y. 1964, Fla. 1966. Assoc. Chadbourne & Parke, N.Y.C., 1964-75, prin., 1975—; corp. sec. Am. Bur. Metal Statis., N.Y.C., 1978—. Author: Regulation of Employee Benefit Plans, Under Erisa, 1990. Capt. USAF, 1964-67. Mem. N.Y. State Bar Assn., Fla. Bar Assn. Roman Catholic. Home: 36 Avon Rd Bronxville NY 10708-1614 Office: Chadbourne & Parke 30 Rockefeller Plz New York NY 10112

SMITH, EDWARD REAUGH, retired lawyer, cemetery and funeral home consultant; b. Flora, Ill., Sept. 23, 1932; m. Jo Anne Myers, Sept. 10, 1954; children: Mark and Michael (twins), Jillian. BS, Midwestern U., 1953; LLB, So. Meth. U., 1957. Bar: Tex. 1957, U.S. Dist. Ct. (so. dist.) Tex. 1957, U.S. Dist. Ct. (no. dist.) Tex. 1961, U.S. Tax Ct. 1961, U.S. Ct. Appeals (5th cir.) 1971, U.S. Ct. Claims 1971, U.S. Supreme Ct. 1982; CPA, Tex. Atty. Vinson, Elkins, Weems & Searls, Houston, 1957-59, Nelson, McCleskey & Harringer, Lubbock, Tex., 1959-61; pvt. practice Lubbock, 1961-62; ptnr. Smith, Baker, Field & Clifford Inc. (formerly Smith & Baker Inc.), Lubbock, 1962-84; CPA Tex., 1955-92; chmn., CEO Resthaven Funeral Home and Cemetery, Lubbock, 1979-93; cons. Svc. Corp. Internat., Lubbock, 1993—; bd. dirs. Briercroft Savs. Assn., 1962-84, Tex. Cemetery Assn., 1986-87, 90-91; pres., bd. chmn. Resthaven Funeral Home, 1965-69, Resthaven of Lubbock, Inc., 1979-93, Lakeview Meml. Gardens, 1978-86; lectr. profl. meetings on taxes and estate planning; bd. visitors So. Meth. U. Law Sch., 1968-71; chmn. estate planning seminar for women Tex. Tech. Found., 1971; pres. South Plains Trust and Estate Coun., 1963-64, others. Contbr. articles to profl. jours. Mem. Lubbock Planning and Zoning Commn., 1964-65, chmn., 1966, budget divsn. United Fund; co-chmn. profl. divsn. United Way, 1981; tchr., bd. dirs. First Meth. Ch., Lubbock, 1963-88; pres. Haynes Elem. Sch. PTA, 1968-69; past mem. pres.'s adv. bd. Lubbock Christian Coll.; bd. dirs. Tex. Tech. U. Found., 1968-89, sec., 1969-76, vice-chmn., 1976-78, chmn., 1978-81, chmn. fund raising com., 1979-81; bd. dirs. Tex. Tech. U. Med. Sch. Found., 1970-78, vice-chmn., 1972-73, chmn., 1973-74; mem. pres.'s coun. Tex. Tech. U., 1978—; spkr. ann. banquet Flora Acad. Found., Flora H.S., 1991; bd. dirs. Lubbock Symphony Orch., 1996—. Mem. Am. Anthroposophical Soc., Tex. Cemeteries Assn. (hon. life), Alpha Chi. Avocations: mountain trails, research, writing.

SMITH, EDWARD SAMUEL, federal judge; b. Birmingham, Ala., Mar. 27, 1919; s. Joseph Daniel and Sarah Jane (Tatum) S.; m. Innes Adams Comer, May 5, 1942; children: Edward Samuel, Innes Smith Cameron Richards. Student, Ala. Poly. Inst., 1936-38; B.A., U. Va., 1941, J.D., 1947. Bar: Va. 1947, D.C. 1948, Md. 1953. Assoc., then ptnr. firm Blair, Korner, Doyle & Appel, Washington, 1947-54; ptnr. firm Blair, Korner, Doyle & Worth, 1954-61; gen. counsel Nat. Cath. Edn. Assn., 1958-61; chief trial sect., tax. div. Dept. Justice, 1961, asst. for civil trials, dep. asst. atty. gen., 1961-63; ptnr. firm, head tax dept. Piper & Marbury, Balt., 1963-78; mng. ptnr. Piper & Marbury, 1971-74; assoc. judge U.S. Ct. Claims, Washington, 1978-82; judge U.S. Ct. Appeals (Fed. Cir.), Washington, 1982—, sr. circuit judge, 1989—; liaison atty. gen. to Lawyers Com. Civil Rights Under Law, 1963; adj. faculty Cumberland Sch. Law, Samford U., 1992—. Bd. dirs. Roland Park Civic League, Inc., Balt., 1977-78; pres., St. Andrew's Soc. Washington, 1956-58. Served to lt. USNR, 1941-46; to comdr. USNR, Ret. 1968. Mem. ABA (chmn. com. on tax litigation 1977-78), Fed. Bar Assn., Md. State Bar Assn. (chmn. sect. of taxation 1971-72), D.C. Bar Assn., Va. State Bar, Met. Club, Chevy Chase Club, Lawyers Club of Washington, Summit Club (Birmingham), Lambda Chi Alpha. Democrat. Episcopalian. Office: Hugo Black US Courthouse 1729 5th Ave N Birmingham AL 35203-2000 also: US Ct Appeals Fed Crct Nat Cts Bldg 717 Madison Pl NW Washington DC 20439-0001 *The second most important rule of life is that we should never become disillusioned with the Golden Rule when others do not follow it.*•

SMITH, EDWIN ERIC, lawyer; b. Louisville, Sept. 29, 1946; s. Lester Henry and Nancy Joy (Heyman) S.; m. Katharine Case Thomson, Aug. 16, 1969; children: Benjamin Clark, George Lewis, Andrew Laurence. BA, Yale U., 1968; JD, Harvard Law Sch., 1974. Bar: Mass. 1974, U.S. Dist. Ct. Mass. 1974. Assoc. Bingham, Dana & Gould, Boston, 1974-81, ptnr., 1981—; lectr. in field; Mass. commr. on uniform state laws; mem. uniform comml. code articles 5 and 9 drafting com. Lt. USNR, 1969-74. Recipient Achievement Medal USN, 1971. Mem. ABA (chmn. uniform comml. code com. bus. law sect.), Am. Law Inst. (Uniform Comml. Code article 9 study com.), Am. Coll. Comml. Fin. Lawyers (bd. regents), Assn. Comml. Fin. Attys. Home: 4 Chiltern Rd Weston MA 02193-2714 Office: Bingham Dana & Gould 150 Federal St Boston MA 02110-1745

SMITH, EDWIN IDE, medical educator; b. Norfolk, Va., May 13, 1924; s. Charles Carroll and Lila (Ide) S.; m. Matilda Janet Snelling, Mar. 31, 1951; children: Sarah Pinckney Smith Crotty, Susan Ide Smith Thurmond, Charles Carroll III. Student, Harvard Coll., 1942-44, Georgetown U., 1944-46; MD, Johns Hopkins U., 1948. Diplomate Am. Bd. Surgery. Intern Johns Hopkins Hosp., Balt., 1948-49; Halsted fellow in surgery Johns Hopkins Sch. Medicine, Balt., 1949-50; resident Boston Children's Hosp., 1950, 52-53, 55-56, Vanderbilt U. Hosp., Nashville, 1953-55; pvt. practice pediatric surgery Norfolk, Va., 1956-63; assoc. prof. surgery U. Mo. Coll. Medicine, Kansas City, 1963-68, U. Okla. Coll. Medicine, Oklahoma City, 1968-71; prof. surgery U. Okla. Coll. Medicine, 1971-89; prof. surgery U. Tex. S.W. Med. Ctr., Dallas, 1989-94, emeritus prof., 1994—; medical educator emeritus, 1994—; surgeon-in-chief Children's Mercy Hosp., Kansas City, Kans., 1963-68; chief pediatric surgery Children's Hosp. Oklahoma City, 1968-87, U. Tex. S.W. Med. Ctr., Dallas, 1989-92. Contbr. articles to profl. jours., chpts. to books. Mem. hosp. care commn. Am. Acad. Pediatrics, 1973-79; mem. select com. med. tech. Okla. Health Planning Commn., 1981-85; trustee Ctrl. Okla. Ambulance Trust, Oklahoma City, 1976-80. Mem. Am. Burn Assn., ACS, Am. Pediatric Surgery Assn., Am. Surg. Assn., Soc. Surg. Oncology, So. Surg. Assn. Republican. Episcopalian. Avocations: tennis, travel. Office: U Tex SW Med Ctr 5323 Harry Hines Blvd Dallas TX 75235-9031

SMITH, EDWIN O., real estate executive, state legislator; b. Brattleboro, Vt., Sept. 12, 1945; s. Orson G. and Eleanor (Stearns) S.; m. Sharron Holmes, Aug. 21, 1969; children: Dwight H., Jason E. Grad., Northampton (Mass.) Jr. Coll., 1968. With Peerless Ins. Co., Keene, N.H., 1968-70; ind. agt. Colton Ins. Agy., Hinsdale, N.H., 1970-88; real estate broker River Valley Realty Inc., Hinsdale, 1987—; mem. N.H. Ho. of Reps., Concord, 1992—. Asst. majority whip N.H. Ho. of Reps.; trustee, vice chmn. Rescue Inc., Brattleboro, Vt., 1981—; mem. Hinsdale Budget Com., 1971-86, also chmn. Mem. Aircraft Owners and Pilots Assn., Masons, Elks, Lions (pres., dir.). Republican. Home: PO Box 26 764 Brattleboro Rd Hinsdale NH 03451 Office: River Valley Realty Inc 6 Main St Hinsdale NH 03451

SMITH, ELAINE DIANA, foreign service officer; b. Glencoe, Ill., Sept. 15, 1924; d. John Raymond and Elsie (Gelbard) S. BA, Grinnell Coll., 1946; MA, Johns Hopkins U., 1947; PhD, Am. U., 1959. Commd. fgn. service officer U.S. Dept. State, 1947; assigned to Brussels, 1947-50, Tehran, Iran, 1951-53, Wellington, N.Z., 1954-56; assigned to Dept. State, Washington, 1956-60, Ankara, Turkey, 1960-69, Istanbul, Turkey, 1969-72; assigned to Dept. Commerce Exchange, 1972-73; dep. examiner Fgn. Service Bd. Examiners, 1974-75; Turkish desk officer (Dept. State), Washington, 1975-78; consul gen., Izmir, Turkey, 1978—. Author: Origins of the Kemalist Movement, 1919-1923, 1959. Recipient Alumni award Grinnell Coll., 1957. Mem. U.S. Fgn. Svc. Assn., Phi Beta Kappa. Home: The Plaza 800 25th St NW Apt 306 Washington DC 20037-2207

SMITH, ELDON, dean. Dean U. Calgary, Alberta, Can. Office: U Calgary, Faculty Medicine, 3300 Hosp Dr, Calgary, Canada T2N 4N1

SMITH, ELDRED GEE, church leader; b. Lehi, Utah, Jan. 9, 1907; s. Hyrum Gibbs and Martha E. (Gee) S.; m. Jeanne A. Ness, Aug. 17, 1932 (dec. June 1977); children: Miriam Smith Skeen, Eldred Gary, Audrey Gay Smith Vance, Gordon Raynor, Sylvia Dawn Smith Isom; m. Hortense H. Child, May 18, 1978; stepchildren: Carol Jane Child Burdette (dec.), Thomas Robert Child. Employed with sales div. Bennett Glass & Paint Co., Salt Lake City, 6 years; mech. design engr. Remington Arms Co., 2 years; design engr., prodn. equipment design Tenn. Eastman Corp., Oak Ridge, Tenn., 3 years; now presiding patriarch Ch. Jesus Christ of Latter-day Saints. Home: 2942 Devonshire Cir Salt Lake City UT 84108-2526 Office: 47 E South Temple Salt Lake City UT 84150-1005

SMITH, ELDRED REID, library educator; b. Payette, Idaho, June 30, 1931; s. Lawrence E. and Jennie (Reid) S.; m. Judith Ausubel, June 25, 1953; children: Steven, Janet. B.A., U. Calif.-Berkeley, 1956, M.A., 1962; M.L.S., U. So. Calif., 1957. Aquisition reference librarian Long Beach State Coll. Library, 1957-59; reference librarian San Francisco State Coll. Library, 1959-60; bibliographer U. Calif.-Berkeley Library, 1960-65, head search div. acquisition dept., 1966-69, head loan dept., 1969-70, asso. univ. librarian, 1970-72, acting univ. librarian, 1971-72; dir. libraries, also prof. SUNY, Buffalo, 1973-76; univ. librarian U. Minn., 1976-87, prof., 1976-96; lectr. Sch. Library Sci., U. Wash., 1972; bd. dirs. Center for Research Libraries, 1975-77. Author: The Librarian, The Scholar, and the Future of the Research Library, 1990; contbr. articles to libr. jours. Council on Library Resources fellow, 1970. Mem. ALA, Assn. Research Libraries (dir. 1979-85, pres. 1983-84), Assn. Coll. and Research Libraries (pres. 1977-78, dir. 1976-79, com. on academic status 1969-74, chmn. univ. libraries sect. 1974-75). Home: 847 Gelston Pl El Cerrito CA 94530

SMITH, ELISE FIBER, international non-profit development agency administrator; b. Detroit, June 14, 1932; d. Guy and Mildred Geneva (Johnson) Fiber; m. James Frederick Smith, Aug. 11, 1956 (div. 1983); children: Gregory Douglas, Guy Charles. BA, U. Mich., 1954; postgrad., U. Strasbourg, France, 1954-55; MA, Case Western Res. U., 1956. Tchr. U.S. Binat. Ctr., Caracas, Venezuela, 1964-66; instr. English Am. U., 1966-68; prof. lang. faculty Catholic U., Lima, Peru, 1968-70; coord. English lang. and culture program, lang. faculty El Rosario U., Bogota, Colombia, 1971-73; lang. specialist, mem. faculty Am. U., English Lang. Inst., 1975-78; exec. dir. OEF Internat. (name formerly Overseas Edn. Fund), Washington, 1978-89, bd. dirs.; dir. Leadership Program, Winrock Internat. Inst. for Agrl. Devel., 1989—; v.p., bd. dirs. Pvt. Agys. Collaborating Together, N.Y.C., 1983-89; trustee Internat. Devel. Conf., Washington, 1983—, mem. exec. com., 1985-90; mem. hon. com. for Global Crossroads Nat. Assembly, Global Perspectives in Edn., Inc., N.Y.C., 1984, Washington, 1984-92, mem. gen. assembly, 1992; mem. nat. com. Focus on Hunger '84, L.A.; sec. bd. dirs. U.S. Binat. Sch., Bogota, Colombia, 1971-73; ofcl. observer UN Conf. on Status Women, 1980, 85, 95; mem. mental health adv. com. Dept. State, 1974-76; U.S. del. planning seminar integration women in devel. OAS, 1978; participant Women, Law and Devel. Forum; mem. exec. com., co-chair commn. advancement women Interaction (Am. Coun. for Vol. Internat. Action), 1994; bd. dirs. Sudan-Am. Found.; mem. adv. bd. Global Links Devel. Edn., Washington, 1985-86; adv. coun. Global Fund for Women, 1988-93. Co-editor: Toward Internationalism: Readings in Cross-cultural Communication, 1979, 2d edit. 1986. Bd. dirs. Internat. Ctr. Rsch. on Women, 1992—; mem. adv. com. on vol. fgn. aid U.S. AID, 1994—. Rotary Internat. fellow Strasbourg, France, 1954-55; grantee Dept. State, 1975. Mem. Soc. Internat. Devel., Assn. Women in Devel., Soc. Intercultural Edn. Tng. and Rsch., Coalition Women in Internat. Devel. (co-founder 1979, chair 1993—), Pvt. Agys. in Internat. Devel. (co-chmn. 1980-82, pres. 1982-85), Nat. Assn. Fgn. Student Affairs (grantee 1975), U. Mich. Alumni Assn., Women's Fgn. Policy Group. Unitarian. Home: 4701 Connecticut Ave NW Apt 304 Washington DC 20008-5617 Office: Winrock Inst 1611 N Kent St Ste 600 Arlington VA 22209-2111

SMITH, ELIZABETH PATIENCE, oil industry executive, lawyer; b. N.Y.C., June 21, 1949; d. Harry Martin and Frances (Blauvelt) S.; m. Kwan-Lan Mao, Apr. 1, 1989. BA cum laude, Bucknell U., 1971; JD, Georgetown U., 1976. Atty. Texaco Inc., White Plains, N.Y., 1976-84, dir. investor rels., 1984-89, v.p. corp. communications div., investor rels., 1989-92, v.p. investor rels. and shareholder svcs., 1992—. Mem. bd. trustees Marymount Coll., Tarrytown, N.Y.; bd. dirs. Westchester Edn. Coalition, Texaco Found. Mem. Petroleum Investor Rels. Assn., Nat. Investor Rels. Inst., Investor Rels. Assn., N.Y. Bar Assn. Office: Texaco Inc 2000 Westchester Ave White Plains NY 10650-0001

SMITH, ELIZABETH SHELTON, art educator; b. Washington, Feb. 12, 1924; d. Benjamin Warren and Sarah Priscilla (Harrell) Shelton; m. John Edwin Smith, Aug. 16, 1947 (dec. July 1992); children: Shelley Hobson, Dale Henslee, John Edwin Jr.; m. Headley Morris Cox Jr., Dec. 30, 1994. BA in Art, Meredith Coll., 1946; MEd in Supervision and Adminstrn., Clemson U., 1974. Youth dir. St. John's Bapt. Ch., Charlotte, N.C., 1946-47; art tchr. Raleigh (N.C.) Pub. Schs., 1947-49, East Mecklenberg H.S., Charlotte, 1968-69, D. W. Daniel H.S., Central, S.C., 1970-86; art instr. U. S.C., Columbia, 1966-68; adj. prof. Clemson (S.C.) U., 1991-93; artist-in-residence edn. program S.C. Arts Commn., Columbia, 1991—. Exhibited in numerous one and two person shows and in group exhibits, 1946—. Vol. worker, editor newsletter Pickens County Habitat for Humanity, Clemson, 1981—; vol. art tchr. St. Andrew's Elem. Sch., Columbia, 1962-68. Named S.C. Tchr. of Yr., S.C. Dept. Edn. and Ency. Britannica, 1976, Citizen of Yr. Clemson Rotary Club, 1979, Disting. Alumna award Meredith Coll., 1996. Mem. S.C. Art Edn. Assn. (pres. 1978, Lifetime Svc. award 1990, Lifetime Achievement in Art Edn. award 1995), Nat. Art Edn. Assn. (ret. art educator affiliate, pres. 1994, Disting. Svc. award 1995), S.C. Watercolor Soc., Upstate Visual Artists (Best in Show award). Baptist. Avocations: travel, reading, writing, music. Home: 1604 Six Mile Hwy Central SC 29630-9483

SMITH, ELSKE VAN PANHUYS, retired university administrator; b. Monte Carlo, Monaco, Nov. 9, 1929; came to U.S., 1943; d. Johan Abraham AE and Vera (Craven) van Panhuys; m. Henry J. Smith, Sept. 10, 1950 (dec. June 1983); children: Ralph A., Kenneth A. BA, Radcliffe U., 1950, MS, 1951, PhD, 1956. Rsch. assoc. Sacramento Peak Observatory, Sunspot, N.Mex., 1955-62; rsch. fellow Joint Inst. for Lab. Astrophysics, Boulder, Colo., 1962-63; assoc. to prof. U. Md., College Park, 1963-80, asst. provost, 1973-78, asst. vice chancellor, 1978-80; dean, coll. humanities and scis. Va. Commonwealth U., Richmond, 1980-92, interim dir. environ. studies, 1992-95; ret., 1995; cons. NASA, Greenbelt, Md., 1964-76, reviewer, Washington, 1970's, NSF, Washington, 1970's, 86; vis. com. Assn. of Univ.'s for Rsch. in Astronomy, Tucson, 1975-78. Author: (with others) Solar Flares, 1963, Introductory Astronomy and Astrophysics, 1973, 3d edit., 1992; also numerous articles. Mem. various environ. orgns. Rsch. grantee Rsch. Corp., 1956-57, NSF, 1966-69, 90, NIH, 1981-90, NASA, 1974-78; program grantee Va. Found. for Humanities, 1985, NEH, 1987, Assn. Am. Colls., 1987. Fellow AAAS; mem. Am. Astron. Soc. (counselor 1977-80, vis. prof. 1975-78), Internat. Astron. Union (chief U.S. del. 1979, U.S. Nat. com.), Coun. Colls. of Arts and Scis. (bd. dirs. 1989), Phi Beta Kappa. Democrat. Avocations: hiking, travel, environmental issues. Home: PO Box 756 Lee MA 01238

SMITH, ELVIE LAWRENCE, corporate director; b. Eatonia, Sask., Can., Jan. 8, 1926; s. Harry Burton and Laura Mae (Fallow) S.; m. Jacqueline Moy Colleary, Dec. 15, 1956; children: Ronald, Paul, David, Marguerite. BS with great distinction, U. Sask., 1947; MSME, Purdue U., 1949; LLD (hon.), Concordia U., 1983; D in Engring., Carleton U., 1984, Purdue U., 1987. Exptl. engr. Nat. Research Council, Ottawa, Ont., Can., 1949-56; with Pratt & Whitney Can. Inc., 1957—, exec. v.p. ops., 1978-80, pres., CEO, 1980-84, chmn., 1984-94, dir., 1970—. Decorated Order of Can., 1992; recipient Sawyer award ASME, 1986, Gold Medal Polish People's Republic, 1985, Aerospace Leadership award SAE, 1994; named to Can. Aviation Hall of Fame, 1993. Fellow Can. Aeronautics and Space Inst. (McCurty award 1976, C.D. Howe award 1983); mem. Aerospace Industries Assn. Can. (life, chmn. 1982-83), Gatineau Gliding Club. Home: St-Lambert, PQ Canada Office: Pratt & Whitney Can Inc, 1000 Marie Victorin, Longueuil, PQ Canada J4G 1A1

SMITH, ELWIN EARL, mining and oil company executive; b. Ellicottville, N.Y., Sept. 30, 1922; s. Henry B. and Beatrice M. (Spellman) S.; m. Mary Ellen Kirchmaier, Nov. 4, 1944; children: Peter E., Michael E., Timothy E. Student, U. Ala., 1941-43, NYU, 1954, Internat. Program, Harvard Bus. Sch., 1962. Sales engr. Cities Service Oil Co., N.Y.C., 1949-55; gen. sales mgr. Climax Molybdenum Co., N.Y.C., 1955-64; Exec. v.p., dir. Lithium Corp. Am., Gastonia, N.C., 1964-69; pres., chief exec. officer Lithium Corp. Am., 1969-77; v.p., dir. Gulf Resources & Chem. Co., Houston, 1970-77; pres., dir. Asia Lithium Corp., Osaka, Japan, 1970-77; pres. Amax Iron Ore, Greenwich, Conn., 1977-80; corp. v.p., group exec. for indsl. minerals and resources group Amax Iron Ore, 1978-80; exec. v.p. Amax Inc., Greenwich, 1981-82, sr. exec. v.p., 1982-85; prin. Elwin Smith Internat. Sales Engrs., Darien, Conn., 1986—; dir. Essex Chem. Corp., 1983-88, Freeport Mac Mo Ran Copper Co., 1988—, Am. Metal & Coal Co., Greenwich, Ct., Ethanol Corp., Sydney, Australia, First Dynasty Mines, Denver; chmn. Seven Seas Cinema, Stamford, Conn., 1985-95. Served to 1st lt. U.S. Army Paratroopers, 1943-48. Decorated Combat Inf. badge, Bronze Star, sr. parachute badge. Mem. AIME, Am. Petroleum Inst., Am. Chem. Soc., Am. Australian Assn., Japan Soc., Asia Soc., Mining and Petroleum Club of Sydney (Australia), Copper Club N.Y., Weeburn Country Club, Masons. Republican. Home and Office: 7 Tokeneke Trl Darien CT 06820-6126

SMITH, EMIL L., biochemist, consultant; b. N.Y.C., July 5, 1911; s. Abraham and Esther (Lubart) S.; m. Esther Press, Mar. 29, 1934; children—Joseph Donald, Jeffrey Bernard. B.S., Columbia U., 1931, Ph.D., 1936. Instr. biophysics Columbia U., N.Y.C., 1936-38; John Simon Guggenheim fellow Cambridge U., Eng., 1938-39, Yale U., New Haven, 1939-40; fellow Rockefeller Inst., N.Y.C., 1940-42; biophysicist, biochemist E. R. Squibb & Sons, New Brunswick, N.J., 1942-46; assoc. prof. to prof. biochemistry U. Utah, Salt Lake City, 1946-63; prof. biol. chemistry Sch. Medicine UCLA, 1963-79, prof. emeritus, 1979—; cons. NIH, Am. Cancer Soc., Office Naval Research. Author: (with others) Principles of Biochemistry, 7th edit., 1983; also numerous articles. Recipient Stein-Moore award Protein Soc., 1987. Mem. NAS, Am. Acad. Arts and Scis., Am. Philos. Soc., Am. Soc. Biol. Chemists, Am. Chem. Soc., Protein Soc., Acad. Scis. USSR (fgn.). Office: UCLA Sch Medicine Los Angeles CA 90095-1737

SMITH, EMMITT J., III, professional football player; b. Pensacola, Fla., May 15, 1969; s. Emmitt Jr. and Mary Smith. Student, U. Fla. With Dallas Cowboys, 1990—; player Pro-Bowl, 1990-92, NFC Championship game, 1992, 93, Super Bowl XXVII, 1992, Super Bowl XXVIII, 1993; owner Emmitt Inc. Recipient MVP award for season, 1993, MVP award for Super Bowl, 1993; named Running Back, Sporting News Coll. All-Am. team, 1989, Offensive Rookie of Yr., 1990, Running Back, Sporting News NFL All-Pro team, 1992, 93, NFL Player of Yr., Sporting News, 1993; named to Pro-Bowl, 1993, 95. Led NFL in rushing, 1991-93, 95; Led NFL running backs in scoring, 1992, 95. Office: Dallas Cowboys One Cowboys Pky Irving TX 75063•

SMITH, EMORY CLARK, lawyer, financial advisor; b. Denton, Tex., Nov. 2, 1910; s. James Willis and Julia (Miller) S.; 1 child, Cynthia Smith O'Brien. BA, U. North Tex., 1929; MA, U. Tex., 1933; JD, So. Meth. U., 1937; SJD, George Washington U., 1954. Bar: Tex. 1937, Okla. 1937, U.S. Supreme Ct. 1954, U.S. Ct. Mil. Appeals 1955, U.S. Ct. Claims 1956, U.S. Ct. Customs and Patent Appeals 1956. Pvt. practice Oklahoma City, 1937-42; commd. USN, 1942-72, advanced through grades to capt.; chief counsel USN Oceanographic Office U.S. Civil Svc., Washington, 1972-73; cons. anti-trust atty. Foster Assocs., Washington, 1973-84; pvt. practice Washington, 1994; ret., 1995; adj. prof. internat. law Am. U., Washington, 1977-84; energy cons. Foster Assocs., 1973-84; fin. advisor Friday Music Found., Washington, 1988-94; lectr. in field. Author: Law of the Sea, 1954; contbr. articles to profl. jours. Vestryman St. Alban's Ch., Washington, 1957-59, St. Paul's Within the Walls, Rome, 1967-68. Named Disting. Alumnus U. North Tex., 1972. Fellow N.Y. Explorers Club, Fed. Bar Assn., Inter-Am. Bar Assn. (natural resources com. chmn. 1973-76), Masons. Republican. Episcopalian. Avocation: farming. Office: 2118 49th St NW Washington DC 20007

SMITH, EPHRAIM PHILIP, university dean, educator; b. Fall River, Mass., Sept. 19, 1942; s. Jacob Max and Bertha (Horvitz) S.; m. Linda Sue Katz, Sept. 3, 1967; children—Benjamin, Rachel, Leah. B.S., Providence Coll., 1964; M.S., U. Mass., 1965; Ph.D., U. Ill., 1968. Chmn. dept. acctg. U. R.I., Kingston, 1972-73; dean Sch. Bus. Shippensburg State Coll., Pa., 1973-75; dean Coll. Bus. Adminstrn. Cleve. State U., 1975-90; dean Sch. Bus. Adminstrn. and Econ. Calif. State U., Fullerton, 1990—. co-author: Principles of Supervision: FIrst and Second Level Management, 1984, Federal Taxation-Advanced Topics, 1995, Federal Taxation-Basic Principles, 1996, Federal Taxation Comprehensive Topics, 1996; contbr. articles to profl. jours. Mem. Am. Acctg. Assn., Am. Taxation Assn., Am. Inst. for Decision Scis., Fin. Execs. Inst., Beta Gamma Sigma, Beta Alpha Psi. Office: Calif State U Sch Bus Adminstrn and Econ 800 N State College Blvd Fullerton CA 92634-9480

SMITH, ERIC, wholesale distribution executive; b. 1953. Graduate, Ball State U., 1976. With ADIAppliances, Indpls., 1975-96; with Major Video Concepts, Inc., Indpls., 1984—, now v.p. Office: Major Video Concepts Inc 7998 Georgetown Rd Ste 1000 Indianapolis IN 46268-1697•

SMITH, ERIC PARKMAN, retired railroad executive; b. Cambridge, Mass., Mar. 23, 1910; s. B. Farnham and Helen T. (Blanchard) S.; AB, Harvard U., 1932, MBA, 1934. Staff fed. coordinator transp., Washington, 1934; with traffic and operating depts. N.Y. New Haven & Hartford R.R., Boston and New Haven, Conn., 1934-53; with Maine Central R.R., Portland, 1953-82, sec. adv. bd. retirement trust plan, 1958-82, asst. treas., dir. cost analysis, 1970-82, bd. dirs., 1981-82. Trustee parish donations 1st Parish in Concord, Unitarian-Universalist Ch., 1960-96. Mem. New Eng. R.R. Club (hon., pres. 1973-74), Louisa May Alcott Meml. Assn. (dir. 1984—, treas. 1987—), The Thoreau Soc. (dir. 1987-95, treas. 1987-95). Author: Verses on an Icelandic Vacation, 1965, The Church in Concord and its Ministers, 1971, In All That Dwell Below the Skies, 1972; contbr. The Meeting House on the Green, 1985. Home and Office: 35 Academy Ln Concord MA 01742-2431

SMITH, ERNEST E., lawyer, educator; b. Gonzales, Tex., Sept. 8, 1936; s. Ernest Edgar and Sue (Harris) S.; m. Paula Virginia Young; children—Brian, Carter. B.A., So. Methodist U., 1958; LL.B., Harvard U., 1962. Asst. prof. law U. Tex., Austin, 1963-65, assoc. prof., 1965-68, prof., 1968—, dean, 1974-79. Co-author: Probate and Decendents Estates, 1971, Cases and Materials on Oil and Gas, 1972, Texas Oil & Gas Law, 1989, Oil and Gas Law, 1993, International Petroleum Transactions, 1993; bd. editors Oil and Gas Reporter, Dallas, 1982—; contbr. articles to profl. jours. Treas. St. Andrew's Episcopal Sch., Austin, 1981-83; trustee Rocky Mountain Law Found., 1986—, Ea. Mineral Law Found., 1988—. Mem. Federacion Interamericana de Abogados, State Bar Tex. (sec., treas., chmn. oil and gas law sect. 1982—). Methodist. Avocation: Spanish language. Home: 1400 Winsted Ln Austin TX 78703-3852 Office: U Tex Sch Law 727 E 26th St Austin TX 78705-3224•

SMITH, ERNEST KETCHAM, electrical engineer; b. Peking, China, May 31, 1922; (parents Am. citizens); s. Ernest Ketcham and Grace (Goodrich) S.; m. Mary Louise Standish, June 23, 1950; children: Priscilla Varland, Nancy Smith, Cynthia Jackson. BA in Physics, Swarthmore Coll., 1944; MSEE, Cornell U., 1951, Ph.D., 1956. Chief plans and allocations engr. Mut. Broadcasting System, 1946-49; with Nat. Bur. Stds. Ctrl. Radio Propagation Lab., 1951-65; chief ionosphere research sect. Nat. Bur. Standards, Boulder, Colo., 1957-60; div. chief Nat. Bur. Standards, 1960-65; dir. aeronomy lab. Environ. Sci. Services Adminstrn., Boulder, 1965-67; dir. Inst. Telecommunication Scis., 1968, dir. univ. relations, 1968-70; assoc. dir. Inst. Telecommunications Scis. Office of Telecommunications, Boulder, 1970-72, cons., 1972-76; mem. tech. staff Jet Propulsion Lab. Calif. Inst. Tech., Pasadena, 1976-87; adj. prof. dept. Elec. and Computer Engring. U. Colo., Boulder, 1987—; vis. fellow Coop. Inst. Rsch. on Environ. Scis., 1968; assoc. Harvard Coll. Obs., 1965-75; adj. Prof. U. Colo.m 1969-78, 87—; internat. vice-chmn. study group 6, Internat. Radio Consultative Com., 1958-70, chmn. U.S. study group, 1970-76; mem. U.S. nat. com. Internat. Sci. Radio Union, mem.-at-large U.S. nat. com., 1985-88; convenor Boulder Gatekeepers to the Future, 1990-96,. Author: Worldwide Occurrence of Sporadic E, 1957; (with S. Matsushita) Ionospheric Sporadic E, 1962. Contbr. numerous articles to profl. jours. Editor: Electromagnetic Probing of the Upper Atmosphere, 1969; assoc. editor for propagation IEEE Antennas and Propagation Mag., 1989—. Mem. 1st Congl. Ch., moderator elect, 1995, moderator, 1996. Recipient Diplôme d'honneur, Internat. Radio Consultative Com., Internat. Telecom. Union, 1978. Fellow IEEE (fellow com. 1993, 94, 95), AAAS; mem. Am. Geophys. Union, Electromagnetics Acad., Svc. Club, Kiwanis, Univ. Club, Athenaeum Club (Pasadena), Boulder Country Club, Sigma Xi (pres. U. Colo. chpt. 1994-95, v.p. 95-96). Home: 5159 Idylwild Trl Boulder CO 80301-3667 Office: U Colo Dept Elec and Computer Engring Campus Box 425 Boulder CO 80309 *A weakness of many large organizations is that it is difficult for senior administrators to step down after peaking in their 40s. I'm grateful for a crisis at age 50 which resulted in my taking early retirement at age 54 than accepting a more modest job until age 65.*

SMITH, ESTHER THOMAS, editor; b. Jesup, Ga., Mar. 13, 1939; d. Joseph H. and Leslie (McCarthy) Thomas; m. James D. Smith, June 2, 1962; children: Leslie, Amy, James Thomas. BA, Agnes Scott Coll., 1962. Staff writer, Sunday women's editor Atlanta Jour.-Constn., 1961-62; mng. editor Bull. of U. Miami Sch. Medicine, 1965-66; corr. Atlanta Jour.-Constn. and Fla. Times-Union, 1964, 67-68; founding editor Bus. Rev. of Washington, 1978-81; founding editor, gen. mgr. Washington Bus. Jour., 1982; pres., bd. dirs. Tech News, Inc., 1986—, ceo, 1995—; editor-at-large Washington Tech., 1986—, Tech. Transfer Bus. Mag., 1992-95; bd. dirs. MIT Enterprise Forum of Washington/Balt., 1981-82, TechNews, Inc., 1986—; mem. Greater Washington Board of Trade, Internat. Task Force, Women's Forum, Washington, 1981—; mem. No. Va. Bus. Round Table (exec. com.); mem. adv. bd. Va. Math Coalition, 1991-94; bd. trustees Ctr. for Excellence in Edn., 1993—. Mem. Assn. Tech. Bus. Couns. (chmn. bd. advisors 1989-94), Pres.'s Forum, Mid-Atlantic Venture Assn., No. Va. Tech. Coun. (mem. exec. com., bd. dir.), Suburban Maryland High Tech. Coun. Office: 8500 Leesburg Pike Ste 7500 Vienna VA 22182-2409

SMITH, EUGENE WILSON, retired university president and educator; b. Forrest City, Ark., June 10, 1930; s. Milton Saumel and Frank Leslie (Wilson) S.; m. Rebecca Ann Slaughter, May 27, 1956; children: Lucinda Anne, Bradley Eugene. B.A., Ark. State U., 1952; M.Ed., U. Miss., 1955, Ed.D., 1958. Mem. faculty Ark. State U., State University, 1958-92, prof. edn., 1971-92, v.p. adminstrn., 1968-71, dean Grad. Sch., 1971-84, interim pres., 1980, sr. v.p., 1980-84, pres., 1984-92, 94-95; pres. emeritus Ark. State U., State University, 1992—, interim pres., 1994-95; pres. Jonesboro Indsl. Devel. Corp., 1983-94; mem. exec. com. Conf. So. Grad. Schs., 1973-74, Ark. State Coun. on Econ. Edn., 1987-90; pres. Am. South Athletic Conf., 1987-89; dir. Mercantile Bank of Jonesboro, Union Planteus Bank of Northeast Ark. Alderman, City of Jonesboro, 1982-84. Served to 1st lt. AUS, 1952-54,

Korea. W.K. Kellogg Found. rsch. fellow, 1954-58. Mem. Ark. Adv. Council Elem. and Secondary Edn., Jonesboro C. of C. (dir. 1967-69, 80-85, v.p. 1981-82, pres. 1982-83), Phi Kappa Phi, Phi Delta Kappa, Kappa Delta Pi. Club: Rotary (pres. 1974-75). Home: 407 Lynne Ct Jonesboro AR 72401-8807

SMITH, EVERETT G., chemicals executive; b. 1909. Grad., Dartmouth Coll., 1930. With Edgar Ricker & Co., 1930-38; treas. Albert Trostel & Sons Co., Milw., 1938-46, v.p., 1946-51, exec. v.p., 1951-62, pres., treas., 1962—, also chmn. bd. dirs., treas.; pres. Everett Smith Investment Co. Ltd. of Del., Inc., Milw.; v.p. Maysteel Corp., Menomonee Falls, Wis. Office: Albert Trostel & Sons Co 10201 W Lincoln Ave Milwaukee WI 53227-2136*

SMITH, FERN M., judge; b. San Francisco, Nov. 7, 1933. AA, Foothill Coll., 1970; BA, Stanford U., 1972, JD, 1975. Bar: Calif. 1975. m. F. Robert Burrows; children: Susan Morgan, Julie. Assoc. firm Bronson, Bronson & McKinnon, San Francisco, 1975-81, ptnr., 1982-86; judge San Francisco County Superior Ct., 1986-88, U.S. Dist. Ct. for Northern Dist. Calif., 1988—; mem. U.S. Jud. Conf., Adv. Com. Rules of Evidence, 1993—; mem. hiring, mgmt. and pers. coms., active recruiting various law schs. Contbr. articles to legal publ. Apptd. by Chief Justice Malcolm Lucas to the Calif. Jud. Coun.'s Adv. Task Force on Gender Bias in the Cts., 1987-89; bd. visitors Law Sch. Stanford U. Mem. ABA, Queen's Bench, Nat. Assn. Women Judges, Calif. Women Lawyers, Women's Forum West/Internat. Women's Forum, Bar Assn. of San Francisco, Fed. Judges Assn., 9th Cir. Dist. Judges Assn., Am. Judicature Soc., Calif. State Fed. Judicial Coun., Phi Beta Kappa.*

SMITH, FLOYD LESLIE, insurance company executive; b. Silver Creek, N.Y., Nov. 12, 1931; s. Harry Lee and Fanny Diem (Arnold) S.; m. Jane Kathryn Elters, Feb. 18, 1956; children: Keith Arnold, Bruce Erik. A.B., Oberlin Coll., (Ohio), 1953; M.B.A., NYU, 1962. Investment trainee Mut. of N.Y., N.Y.C., 1953-64, dir. investments, 1964-66; asst. v.p. securities investment Mut. of. N.Y., N.Y.C., 1966-69; 2d v.p. securities investment Mut. of N.Y., N.Y.C., 1969-74, v.p. securities investment, 1974-78, sr. v.p., 1978-81, chief investment officer, 1981-83, exec. v.p., chief investment officer, 1983-89; vice chmn., chief investment officer Mut. of N.Y., 1989-91; trustee The Mut. Life Ins. Co. of N.Y., 1988-91; dir. MONY Series Fund, 1983—, Empire Fidelity Investments Life Ins. Co., 1994—; trustee MONY Real Estate Investors, N.Y.C., 1981-90; bd. dirs., chmn. exec. com. Ins. Systems Am., Atlanta, 1974-82. Trustee Friends Sem., N.Y.C., 1975-84, Village of Saltaire, 1984-87; dir. St. Maarten Condo. Assn., Naples, Fla., 1993—; mem. Saltaire (N.Y.) Zoning Bd. Appeals, 1982-84. With Signal Corps, U.S. Army, 1954-56. Mem. Ft. Worth Boat Club, Edgewater Club.

SMITH, FLOYD RODENBACK, retired utilities executive; b. San Francisco, June 25, 1913; s. Floyd M. and Elizabeth (Rodenback) S.; m. Marion LaFrae Blythe, Oct. 5, 1935; children: Marion Katherine Smith White, Virginia Helene. Student, Long Beach (Calif.) Jr. Coll., 1931-33; B.S., N.Mex. State U., 1935; postgrad., Harvard Bus. School, 1962. Registered profl. engr., Tex. With Gulf States Utilities Co., Beaumont, Tex., 1935-78; dir. Gulf States Utilities Co., 1965-78, v.p. Baton Rouge div., 1965-67, v.p. div. ops., 1967-69, exec. v.p., 1969, pres., 1970-73, prin. exec. officer, 1970-78, chmn. bd., prin. exec. officer, 1973-78; pres. S.W. Atomic Energy Assocs., 1971-77; mgmt. cons., 1978-85. Bd. dirs., past chmn. Beaumont chpt. ARC; bd. dirs. Central City Devel. Corp., 1971-81, YMCA, 1980-83; trustee United Appeals, pres., 1975; pres. Tex. Atomic Energy Research Found., 1976-78. Named Disting. Alumnus Engring. Sch., N.Mex. State U., 1977. Mem. Tex. Atomic Energy Rsch. Found. (bd. dirs. 1970-78, pres. 1976-78), Southeastern Elec. Exch. (pres. 1975-76, bd. dirs. 1970-78), Tex. Rsch. League (bd. dirs. 1970-78), Assn. Electric Cos. of Tex. (chmn. 1978-79), Utility Shareholders Assn. of Tex. (chmn. 1986-93), Beaumont C. of C. (bd. dirs. 1970-76). Presbyterian. Clubs: Beaumont Country, Beaumont (bd. dirs. 1974-76), Tower Club. Home: 21 Cheska Hollow Beaumont TX 77706-2750

SMITH, FORREST L., restaurateur; b. Detroit, Feb. 17, 1945; s. Charles LeRoy and Doris Irene (Milliken) S.; children—Dianna Lynn, Christian Lee; m. Kimberly Smith; stepchildren: Blayre Farkas, Sammantha Farkas. Student pub. schs., Ithaca, N.Y. With Ky. Fried Chicken Nat. Mgmt. Co. Inc., asst. mgr., mgr., supr., area mgr., dist. mgr., sr. dist. mgr., regional mgr., 1969-74; exec. v.p., chief operating officer, prin. Lewis Foods Inc., Riverside, Conn., 1974-83. founder, chmn., chief exec. officer, Smith Foods Corp., Greenwich, Conn., 1974—; owner/operator chain McDonald's Restaurants, N.Y.C., 1974—; dir. N.Y. McDonald's owner/operator Advt. Coop., 1981—, mktg. com., 1979—, chmn. pub. relations com., 1982-86, by-laws com., 1981—, security com., 1981—, N.Y. polit. action com., chmn. tri state mktg. com., 1990-91; exec. com. McDonald's Met. Area Owner/Operator Assn. Ronald Ho. Task Force, 1983—; bd. dirs., limited ptnr. Sr. Living Svcs; chmn. Ronald McDonald Children's Charities, N.Y. Chpt.; mem. N.Y. Region ROAB Op. Com.; past bd. dirs. N.Y.C. Bd. Edn.-Coop. Edn.; bd dirs., v.p. Ronald McDonald Ho., N.Y.C. mem. Fathers' Council, Riverside Sch. PTA, Conn., 1981-83; mem. Mayor Koch's N.Y.C. Spl. Anti-Graffiti Task Force, 1981-83; bd. dirs. Vital Vols. for Improvement of 3d Ave and Lexington Ave, 1974-80; bd. dirs., exec. com., fin. com., pub. relations com. We Care About N.Y., 19846; bd. dirs. Grand Ctrl. Partnership, 34th St. Partnership, Citykids, HACER; chmn., founder Smith Children's Charities Found.; co-exec. producer United Negro Coll. Fund/McDonald's concert series; chmn. bd. dirs. spl. projects fundraising com. Boy Scouts Am., 1982-83, bd. dirs. Greater N.Y. council, 1982-83. Recipient Meritious citations from N.Y. Urban League, United Negro College Fund (twice), N.Y. City Bd. Edn. Mem. Five Boroughs McDonald's Owner/Operator Assn. (pres. 1981), Manhattan-Bronx McDonald's Owner/Operator Group (chmn. 1977-78), NAACP (life), Greenwich Village C. of C. (bd. dirs. 1983), N.Y.C. C. of C., Mid-Manhattan C. of C. (bd. dirs. 1979-83), Greenwich Symphony Assn., U.S. Tennis Assn., Eastern Tennis Assn., N.Y. Met. Owner Operators' Assn. Coop. (v.p. bd. dirs.), Nat. Rifle Assn., Airplane Owners and Pilots Assn. Clubs: Sales Exec. (N.Y.C.); Old Greenwich Yacht, Greenwich Racquet, St. Croix Yacht Club, Tamarack County Club, New Yorker Club, N.Y. Athletic Club. Home: 4 Cliffdale Rd Greenwich CT 06831-2944 Office: 254 Mill St Greenwich CT 06830-5808

SMITH, FRANK FORSYTHE, JR., lawyer; b. Crystal City, Tex., June 2, 1942; s. Frank F. and Allyne Y. (Allen) S.; m. Martha S. Strack, Aug. 7, 1965; children: Martha Lee, Amanda L. BA, U. Tex., 1964, JD, 1968; MA, U. Mich., 1965. Bar: Tex. 1968. Assoc., ptnr. Vinson & Elkins, Houston, 1968—. Contbr. articles to profl. jours. Mem. Am. Land Title Assn. Lender's Coun., State Bar of Tex., Am. Coll. Real Estate Lawyers. Office: Vinson & Elkins 3536 First City Tower 1001 Fannin St Houston TX 77002

SMITH, FRANKLIN L., school system administrator; b. Cape Charles, Va., May 26, 1943; s. Frank and Margaret (Dixon) S.; m. Gloria Hall, July 30, 1977; children: Franklin L. Jr., Frederick L., Ericka, Delvin L., Kristy L. BS, Va. State U., 1967, MEd, 1972; EdD, Nova U., 1980. Tchr. health, phys. edn., drivers edn. Petersburg (Va.) Pub. Schs., 1968-72, asst. prin., 1972-74, prin., 1975-82, asst. supt., 1982-85; asst. supt. Dayton (Ohio) Pub. Schs., 1985, interim supt., 1985-86, supt., 1986-91; supt. D.C. Pub. Schs., Washington, 1991—. Bd. dirs. Am. Youth Found.; chmn. membership com., mem. exec. com. of bd. dirs., co-chair AIDS edn. task force Coun. of Great City Schs.; charter mem. nat. exec. coun. Nat. Alumni Bd. Nova U., Ft. Lauderdale, Fla.; bd. dirs. Nat. Conf. Christians & Jews. Recipient Exemplary Leadership award for Region IX State of Ohio, BASA, 1988, Smitty award Miami Valley chpt. Pub. Rels. Soc. Am., 1989; named Ohio Supt. of Yr. Am. Assn. Sch. Adminstrs., 1988. Mem. NAACP (life), Am. Assn. Sch. Adminstrs., Nat. Alliance Black Sch. Adminstrs., Nat. Assn. Elem. Sch. Prins., Nat. Assn. Secondary Sch. Prins., Kappa Alpha Psi (polemarch Petersburg Alumni chpt. 1976-78, achievement award 1987), Phi Delta Kappa, Sigma Pi Phi. Democrat. Baptist. Office: DC Pub Schs 415 12th St NW Washington DC 20004

SMITH, FRANKLIN SUMNER, JR., retired insurance executive; b. Athens, Ga., Jan. 11, 1924; s. Franklin Sumner and Florence (Davis) S.; m. Eleanor Deanne Milligan, Feb. 22, 1947 (dec. Dec. 1982); children: Franklin Sumner III, Katharine Ruth; m. Jane Martin, Apr. 6, 1986. Student, Davidson Coll., 1940-41, Furman U., 1941-42. V.p., sec. Frank S. Smith Co., Inc., Columbia, S.C., 1946-60; resident mgr. Dick & Merle-Smith, N.Y.C., 1961-66; with Colonial Life & Accident Ins. Co., Columbia, 1966-93, vice chmn. bd., 1987-92, pres., CEO, 1992-93; vice chmn. bd. Colonial Cos., Inc., Columbia, 1989-92, pres., CEO, 1992-93, bd. dirs., 1989-94. Mem. Richland County Coun., Columbia, 1965-70, chmn. 1967-69; chmn. bd. trustees Richland Meml. Hosp., 1971-80, 93—; mem. United Way of Midlands, S.C., gen. campaign chmn., 1977, pres., 1979; pres. Greater Columbia C. of C., 1974-75, S.C. C. of C., 1987-88, U. S.C. Ednl. Found., 1992—. Recipient Vol. of Yr. award United Way of S.C., 1977, Humanitarian of Yr. award United Way of Midlands, 1989, Amb. of Yr. award Greater Columbia C. of C., 1991, Humanitarian award Richland Meml. Hosp. Found., 1993, Outstanding Philanthropist award Assn. Fund-raising Execs. (Ctrl. S.C. chpt.), 1994. Mem. Assn. of S.C. Life Ins. Cos. (pres. 1973, 82), S.C. Mcpl. Assn. (pres. 1964-65), Assn. of U.S. Army (pres. Palmetto chpt. 1978-82, Civilian of Yr. award 1983), Pine Tree Hunt Club (pres. 1954-56), The Palmetto Club (pres. 1976-89, chmn. 1990—). Presbyterian. Home: 4720 Wrenwood Ln Columbia SC 29206-4650 Mailing Address: PO Box 61047 Columbia SC 29260

SMITH, FRED DOYLE, nurse; b. Ferris, Tex., Mar. 12, 1930; s. Luther Lee and Willie Lane (Coats) S.; children: Ronald, Patricia, Donald, Stacy, Rhonda. Student, Southwestern Bus. U., Houston, 1950-51; diploma blood gasses analyst, East Tenn. Children's Hosp., Knoxville, 1985; LPN, Tenn. LPN Program, 1983. LPN, Tenn. Respiratory therapy asst. Claiborne County Hosp., Tazewell, Tenn., 1984-87; nurse Clairborne County Nursing Home, Tazewell, 1987, Brakebill Nursing Home, Knoxville, Tenn.; nurse med.-surg. wing East Tenn. Bapt. Hosp., Knoxville, 1988-89; nurse Hancock County Health Dept., Sneedville, Tenn.; respiratory therapy asst. Wariota Health Care Ctr. (formerly Meadowbrook Manor), Maynardville, Tenn., 1987-88, nurse, 1989—. Parent Foster Parent Assn., Tazewell. With USN, 1951-59. Mem. Highlander Club, Hutt River Command. Democrat. Baptist. Avocations: singing, cooking. Home: 485 Cole Rd New Tazewell TN 37825-3007 Office: Wariota Health Care Ctr 215 Richardson Way Maynardville TN 37807-3803

SMITH, FREDA M., minister; b. Pocatello, Idaho, Nov. 22, 1935; s. Alfred Avery and Mary V. (Clark) S. BA in Psychology, Calif. State U., Sacramento, 1974, MA in Psychology, 1989; D of Ministry (hon.), Samaritan Theol. Inst., 1990. Ordained to ministry Universal Fellowship Met. Cmty. Chs., 1973. Pastor Cathedral of Promise, Met. Cmty. Chs., Sacramento, 1972—; instr. Samaritan Theol. Inst., L.A., 1974—; dir. evangelism Universal Fellowship Met. Cmty. Chs., worldwide, 1993—, vice-moderator, bd. elders, 1973-93. Author: Dear Dora/Dangerous Derek, 1970; author video series Homosexuality and the Bible, 1993; author audio series Manna for the Journey, 1988. Chair Sacramento LGB Town Coun., 1992-93; co-chair Calif. Com. for Law Reform, 1971-74. Recipient Eleanor Roosevelt Club award, 1975, Woman in History award for courage Sacramento History Ctr., 1991. Mem. Phi Kappa Phi. Avocations: photography, chess, gold panning, 4 wheeling, reading. Home: 6209 Governor Ln Sacramento CA 95828 Office: River City Met Cmty Chs PO Box 245125 Sacramento CA 95824-5125

SMITH, FREDDYE L(EE), financial planner; b. Oklahoma City, Oct. 16, 1938; d. Frederick Douglass and Leeoshia M. (Harris) Moon; divorced; children: Karyn Smith Cole, Stanford Brandon. BA, Fisk U., 1959; MA, U. Chgo., 1964. CFP, 1984. Tchr. of French Chgo. Bd. Edn., 1961-69, guidance counselor, 1969-80; fin. planner Waddell & Reed, Chgo., 1980—. Contbr. articles to profl. jours. Adv. bd. Cmty. Mental Health Coun., Chgo., 1994—. Named Fin. Planner of Yr., Eta Phi Beta, 1996; honoree Alpha Gamma Pi Sorority. Mem. Internat. Assn. for Cert. Fin. Planners, Internat. Bd. Stds. and Practices for CFP, Zonta Internat., Alpha Gamma Pi, Alpha Kappa Alpha. Mem. Trinity United Ch. Christ. Avocations: interior design, photography. Office: Waddell & Reed 1525 E 53rd St Ste 803 Chicago IL 60615-4530

SMITH, FREDERICK COE, manufacturing executive; b. Ridgewood, N.J., June 3, 1916; s. Frederick Coe and Mary (Steffee) S.; m. Ruth Pfeiffer, Oct. 5, 1940; children: Frederick Coe, Geoffrey, Roger, William, Bart. B.S., Cornell U., 1938; M.B.A., Harvard U., 1940. With Armstrong Cork Co., Lancaster, Pa., 1940-41; with Huffy Corp., Dayton, Ohio, 1946-86; pres., chief exec. officer Huffy Corp., 1961-72, chmn., chief exec. officer, 1972-76, chmn., 1976-78, chmn. exec. com., 1979-86. Chmn. Sinclair C.C. Found.; past chmn. nat. bd. dirs. Planned Parenthood Fedn.; former dir. Internat. Parenthood Fedn.; past chmn. Dayton Found.; trustee emeritus Alan Gutmacher Inst., Ohio United Way; chmn. employment and tng. com. Gov.'s Human Investment Coun. Lt. col. USAAF, 1941-46. Decorated Legion of Merit.

SMITH, FREDERICK ROBERT, JR., social studies educator; b. Lynn, Mass., Sept. 19, 1929; s. Frederick Robert and Margaret Theresa (Donovan) S. m. Mary Patricia Barry, Aug. 28, 1954; children: Brian Patrick, Barry Frederick, Brendan Edmund. A.B., Duke U., 1951; M.Ed., Boston U., 1954; Ph.D., U. Mich., 1960. Tchr. social studies public Jackson, Mich., 1954-58; instr. Eastern Mich. U., 1959, U. Mich., 1959-60; mem. faculty Sch. Edn., Ind. U., Bloomington, 1960-94; prof. Sch. Edn., Ind. U., 1969-94, chmn. social studies edn., 1965-69, chmn. secondary edn. dept., 1969-72, chmn. dept. curriculum and instrn., 1983-84, assoc. dean adminstrn. and devel., 1975-78, dir. external rels., 1991-94; dir. devel. Bloomington campus and annual giving Ind. U. Found., 1984-90; prof. emeritus retired, 1994; vis. prof. U. Wis., summer 1967, U. Hawaii, summer 1972. Co-author: New Strategies and Curriculum in Social Studies, 1969, Secondary Schools in a Changing Society, 1976; co-editor 2 books. Bd. overseers St. Meinrad Coll. and Sem., 1991—, trustee, 1995—. With USAF, 1951-53. Recipient Booklist award Phi Lambda Theta, 1965, 69. Mem. Ind. Coun. Social Studies (pres. 1968-69), Phi Delta Kappa, Kappa Sigma, Phi Kappa Phi. Roman Catholic. Home: 2306 E Edgehill Ct Bloomington IN 47401-6839 Office: Indiana Univ Sch of Edu Rm 3032 Bloomington IN 47405

SMITH, FREDERICK THEODORE, lawyer, educator; b. Jersey City, Apr. 7, 1956; s. George Gilbert and Caroline (Jeter) S. BA, Harvard Coll., 1978; BA, MA, Oxford (Eng.) U., 1980; JD, Harvard U., 1985; MPA, J.F. Kennedy Sch., 1985. Bar: N.J. 1987, U.S. Dist. N.J. 1990. Summer assoc. Lowenstein, Sandler, Kohl, Fisher & Boylan, Newark, 1982, Manatt, Phelps, Rothenber & Tunney, L.A., 1983; intern Office of N.J. Pub. Adv., spring 1985; summer assoc. Kaye, Scholer, Fierman, Hays & Handler, Washington, 1985; jud. clerkship to Hon. David Nelson Fed. Dist. Ct., Boston, 1985-86; assoc. Shearman & Sterling, N.Y.C., 1984, 86-87; assoc. McCarter & English, Newark, 1987-93, ptnr., 1993—; N.J. Bd. Law Examiners, 1990—; hearing officer Essex County, N.J., 1988-91; adj. prof. Seton Hall Law Sch., N.J., 1994—. Editor: New Jersey Law of Product Liability, 1994; mem. editl. bd. N.J. Lawyer, 1993-95. Bd. overseers Gov.'s Schs. N.J., 1994—; trustee St. Peter's Prep. Sch., Jersey City, 1993—. Recipient Rhodes scholarship Oxford U./Rhodes Trust, Eng., 1978-80, Earl Warren scholarship NAACP Legal Def. Fund, 1981. Mem. Harvard Club N.J. (exec. com. 1990—). Home: Apt 3N 264 9th St Jersey City NJ 07302 Office: McCarter and English 4 Gateway Ctr 100 Mulberry Newark NJ 07101-0652

SMITH, FREDERICK WALLACE, transportation company executive; b. Marks, Miss., Aug. 11, 1944; s. Frederick Smith; m. Diane Avis. Grad., Yale U., 1966. Cert. comml. pilot. Owner Ark Aviation, 1969-71; founder, pres. Fed. Express Corp., Memphis, 1971—, chmn. bd., pres, CEO, 1975—. Served with USMC, 1966-70. Office: Fed Express Corp 2005 Corporate Ave PO Box 727 Memphis TN 38132*

SMITH, FREDRICA EMRICH, rheumatologist, internist; b. Princeton, N.J., Apr. 28, 1945; d. Raymond Jay and Carolyn Sarah (Schleicher) Emrich; m. Paul David Smith, June 10, 1967. AB, Bryn Mawr Coll., 1967; MD, Duke U., 1971. Intern, resident U. N.Mex. Affiliated Hosps., 1971-73; fellow U. Va. Hosp., Charlottesville, 1974-75; pvt. practice, Los Alamos, N.Mex., 1975—; chmn. credentials com. Los Alamos Med. Ctr., 1983—, chief staff, 1990; bd. dirs. N.Mex. Physicians Mut. Liability Ins. Co., Albuquerque. Contbr. articles to med. jours. Mem. bass sect. Los Alamos Symphony, 1975—; mem. Los Alamos County Parks and Recreation Bd., 1984-88, 92—, Los Alamos County Med. Indigent Health Care Task Force, 1989—; mem. ops. subcom. Aquatic Ctr., Los Alamos County, 1988—. Fellow ACP, Am. Coll. Rheumatology; mem. N.Mex. Soc. Internal Medicine (pres. 1993—), Friends of Bandelier. Democrat. Avocations: swimming, music, reading, hiking. Office: Los Alamos Med Ctr 3917 West Rd Los Alamos NM 87544-2222

SMITH, G. E. KIDDER, architect, author; b. Birmingham, Ala., Oct. 1, 1913; s. F. Hopkinson and Annie (Kidder) S.; m. Dorothea Fales Wilder, Aug. 22, 1942; children: G.E. Kidder, Hopkinson Kidder. A.B., Princeton U., 1935, M.F.A., 1938; student, Ecole Americaine, Fontainbleau, France, 1935. Registered architect, N.Y., Ala., N.C. Architect Princeton Expdn. to, Antioch, Syria, 1938; designer, site planner, camoufleur with Caribbean Architect-Engr. on Army bases, Caribbean, 1940-42; own archtl. practice, 1946—; lectr. numerous European archtl. socs., also many Am. univs. and museums; archtl. critic Yale U., 1948-49; vis. prof. MIT, 1955-56; guest arch. Archtl. Inst. Japan, 1988. Author: (with P.L. Goodwin) Brazil Builds, 1943, Switzerland Builds, 1950, Italy Builds, 1955, Sweden Builds, 1950, rev. edit., 1957, The New Architecture of Europe, 1961, The New Churches of Europe, 1963, A Pictorial History of Architecture in America, 1976, The Architecture of the United States, 3 vols, 1981, The Beacon Guide to New England Churches, 1989, Looking at Architecture, 1990, Source Book of American Architecture, 1995; also contbr. articles to encys.; exhibits, Stockholm Builds, 1940, Brazil Builds, 1943; installed: Power in the Pacific, USN, 1945 (all at Museum Modern Art, N.Y.C); New Churches of Germany, Goethe House, N.Y.C., and Am. Fedn. Arts, 1957-58, Masterpieces of European Posters (donated), Va. State Mus., Richmond, 1958; Work of Alvar Aalto, Smithsonian Instn., 1965-82, Am.'s Archtl. Heritage for, Smithsonian Instn., 1976, Smithsonian, 1976, photographs in collection, Mus. Modern Art, Met. Mus., N.Y.C. Served to lt. USNR, 1942-46. Recipient Butler prize Princeton, 1938; fellow Am. Scandinavian Found., 1939-40; Guggenheim Found. fellow, 1946-47; President's fellow Brown U., 1949-50; research Fulbright fellow Italy, 1950-51; research Fulbright fellow India, 1965-66; Samuel H. Kress grantee India, 1967; Brunner scholar, 1959-60; Graham Found. for Advanced Study in Arts-Nat. Endowment on Arts joint fellowship, 1967-69; Nat. Endowment Arts fellow, 1974-75; Ford Found. grantee, 1970-71, 75-76; decorated Order So. Cross Brazil; Premio ENIT gold medal Italy; recipient gold medal (archtl. photography) AIA, 1964; E.M. Conover award, 1965; subject of public TV spl., 1976. Fellow AIA, Internat. Inst. Arts and Letters (life; Switzerland); mem. Soc. Archtl. Historians, Assn. Collegiate Schs. of Architecture, Municipal Art Soc. N.Y.C., Coll. Art Assn. Episcopalian. Clubs: Century Assn. (N.Y.C.); Cooperstown Country. Address: 163 E 81st St New York NY 10028-1806

SMITH, G. ELAINE, religious organization executive. Pres. ABC Bd. of Nat. Ministries, Valley Forge, Pa. Office: ABC Board of National Ministries PO Box 851 Valley Forge PA 19482-0851

SMITH, GARDNER WATKINS, physician; b. Boston, July 2, 1931; s. George Van Siclen and Olive (Watkins) S.; m. Susan Elizabeth Whiteford, Sept. 6, 1958; children—Elizabeth Whiteford, Rebecca Tremain, George Van Siclen II. Grad., Phillips Acad., 1949; M.D., Harvard, 1956; A.B., Princeton, 1969. Diplomate: Am. Bd. Surgery, Am. Bd. Thoracic Surgery. Intern Johns Hopkins Hosp., Balt., 1956-57; asst. resident Johns Hopkins Hosp., 1958-59, fellow, 1957-58, asst. in surgery, 1957-59, prof. surgery, 1970—, surgeon, 1970—, dep. dir. dept. surgery, 1978-85; asst. resident U. Va., Charlottesville, 1959-61, resident, 1961-62, asst. in surgery, 1959-63, cardiovascular resident, 1962-63, instr., 1963-65, asst. prof., 1965-68, assoc. prof., 1968-70, surgeon, 1963-70; chief surgery Balt. City Hosp., 1970-79, vis. surgeon, 1979-85; chmn. sect. surg. scis. Johns Hopkins Bayview Med. Ctr., 1985—; cons. Greater Balt. Med. Ctr., 1970-91, Lock Haven VA Hosp., Balt., 1971-92, Walter Reed Army Med. Ctr., 1976-90, Nat. Naval Med. Ctr., 1984-90. Contbr. articles to med. jours. Mem. Soc. U. Surgeons, Am., So. surg. assns., A.C.S., Am. Gastroenterol. Assn., Assn. for Acad. Surgery, Balt. City Med. Soc., Halsted Soc., Med. and Chirurgical Faculty of Md., Soc. Surgery Alimentary Tract, Soc. Vascular Surgery, Internat. Cardiovascular Soc., So. Soc. Clin. Surgeons, Southeastern Surg Congress, So. Assn. Vasular Surgery, Va. Surg. Assn., Cum Laude Soc., Alpha Omega Alpha, Nu Sigma Nu. Home: 1503 Old Orchard Ln Baltimore MD 21204-3654 Office: Johns Hopkins Bayview Med Ctr 4940 Eastern Ave Baltimore MD 21224-2780

SMITH, GEOFFREY ADAMS, special purpose mobile unit manufacturing executive; b. Bay Shore, N.Y., Mar. 17, 1947; s. Ian Morrison and Dorothy Brumbach (Adams) S.; m. Linda Ann Lehmann, July 15, 1972; 1 child, Chad William. BS in Managerial Sci., Lehigh U., 1969. Supr. Roadway Express, South Kearny, N.J., 1969-72; v.p. mktg. Med. Coaches, Inc, Oneonta, N.Y., 1972-76, pres., CEO, 1976—, chmn. bd., 1976; dir. Wilber Nat. Bank, Oneonta, 1996—, Preferred Mut. Ins., New Berlin, N.Y., 1979—; bd. dirs. and v.p. Wilderness Properties Ltd., Oneonta, 1986—; bd. dirs. Moex, Inc., Jefferson, Oreg. Bd. dirs. N.Y. State Dist. Export Council, 1982—; bd. dirs., v.p. Thomas A. Dooley Found., 1984—; trustee A.O. Fox Meml. Hosp. Found., 1984—; adv. com. Oneonta Ctr. for Econ. and Community Devel; advocacy com. Nat. Soccer Hall Fame; coun. mem. citizens bd. Hartwick Coll.; bd. dirs. Future of Oneonta Found., Otsego Orthops. Sports Medicine Found.; mem. N.Y. State Govs. Bus. Adv. Coun. Served with Army N.G., 1969-76. Mem. Greater Oneonta C. of C. (pres., bd. dirs. 1976-82), Am. Legion, Oneonta Country Club (bd. dirs.), Rotary (pres., bd. dirs. Oneonta club 1975-82), Elks. Republican. Methodist. Avocations: racquetball, softball, photography, travelling, golf. Home: Hcr # 862 West Oneonta NY 13861 Office: Medical Coaches Inc PO Box 129 Hemlock Rd Oneonta NY 13820

SMITH, GEOFFREY R.W., lawyer; b. San Francisco, May 26, 1945. AB with honors, Stanford U., 1967, JD, 1970. Bar: Calif. 1971, D.C. 1971. Assoc. gen. counsel Pharm. Mfgs. Assn., 1979-87; ptnr. McDermott, Will & Emery, Washington. Mem. bd. editors Food, Drug and Cosmetic Law Jour., 1987-90. Mem. ABA (mem. bus. law sect. 1970-88, mem. antitrust sect. 1970—, mem. torts and ins. sects. 1978—, mem. adminstrv. law sect. 1975—, mem. food and drug com. 1972—, mem. ad hoc tort reform com. 1988, chmn. subcom. punitive damages 1991, mem. health reform com.), Am. Tort Reform Assn. (chmn. 1987-88, bd. dirs. 1987—), Regulatory Affairs Soc. Office: McDermott Will & Emery 1850 K St NW Washington DC 20006-2213*

SMITH, GEORGE CURTIS, judge; b. Columbus, Ohio, Aug. 8, 1935; s. George B. and Dorothy R. S.; m. Barbara Jean Wood, July 10, 1963; children: Curtis, Geoffrey, Elizabeth Ann. BA, Ohio State U., 1957, JD, 1959. Bar: Ohio 1959, U.S. Dist. Ct. (so. dist.) Ohio 1987. Asst. city atty. City of Columbus, 1959-62; exec. asst. to Mayor of Columbus, 1962-63; asst. atty. gen. State of Ohio, 1964; chief counsel to pros. atty. Franklin County, Ohio, 1965-70, pros. atty., 1971-80; judge Franklin County Mcpl. Ct., Columbus, 1980-85; judge Franklin County Common Pleas Ct., 1985-87; mem. Ohio Supreme Ct. Coun. on Victims Rights, 1988-94; judge in residence Law Sch. U. Cin., 1993; faculty Ohio Jud. Coll., Litigation Practice Inst.; chmn. 1994, Fed. Bench-Bar Conf., 1995; lectr. ABA Anti-Trust Sec., 1995; alumni spkr. law graduation Ohio State U., 1995; pres. Young Rep. Club, 1963, Perry Group, 1996; exec. com. Franklin County Rep. Party, 1971-80; Elder Presbyn. Ch. Recipient Superior Jud. Service award Supreme Ct. Ohio; Resolution of Honor, Columbus Bldg. and Constrn. Trades Coun. Mem. Ohio Pros. Attys. Assn. (pres., Ohio Prosecutor of Yr, Award of Honor, Leadership award), Columbus Bar Assn., Assn. Trial Lawyers Am., Columbus Bar Found., Fed. Bar Assn., Ohio Mcpl. Judges Assn. (v.p. 1983), Columbus Athletic Club (pres., dir.), Lawyers Club of Columbus (pres. 1975), Masons (33d degree), Aladdin Shrine. Presbyterian. Office: 85 Marconi Blvd Columbus OH 43215-2823

SMITH, GEORGE DRURY, publisher, editor, collagist, writer; b. Dayton, Ohio, Mar. 10, 1927; s. Martin Jefferson and Viola (Haas) S.; m. Anne Liard Jennings, Apr. 1967 (div. 1975). A.B. cum laude, Marietta Coll., 1953; Diplome de Phonetique, U. Grenoble, 1950; student, U. Madrid, 1950-51, Heidelberg U., 1951-52, U. Minn., 1953-55, U. Calif.-Berkeley, 1965, UCLA, 1968. Assoc. pub., CFO, Argonaut newspaper, 1972-96; dir. Lambda Point Cons. and Pentacle Group, 1984—. Editor: Beyond Baroque, 1968-80, NewLetters, 1969-75, (book series) NewBooks, 1976-78. Founder, bd. dirs. Beyond Baroque Found., Venice, Calif., 1968-80; mem. Mcpl. Arts Adv. Bd., L.A., 1980-82; chmn. Save Westminster Auditorium Com., Venice, 1977-80; advisor Venice Cultural Ctr. Com., 1981-83. With U.S. Army, 1945-47. Grantee Nat. Endowment for Arts, 1973-80, Calif. Arts Coun., 1977-80, Mcpl. Arts Commn., 1977-80, Coordinating Coun. Lit. Mags., 1974-80.

Mem. Rosicrucians. Democrat. *I believe that if we have faith we can live without fear; that the universe is benevolent if we can love unconditionally; that we can live righteously and prosper if we are honest and seek divine guidance; and that our mission is to enjoy life and strive for beauty.*

SMITH, GEORGE FOSTER, retired aerospace company executive; b. Franklin, Ind., May 9, 1922; s. John Earl and Ruth (Foster) S.; m. Jean Arthur Farnsworth, June 3, 1950; children—David Foster, Craig Farnsworth, Sharon Windsor. B.S. in Physics, Calif. Inst. Tech., 1944, M.S., 1948, Ph.D. magna cum laude (Standard Oil fellow 1949-50), 1952. Founding staff mem. Engring. Research Assos., St. Paul, 1946-48; teaching fellow, resident asso. Calif. Inst. Tech., 1948-52; mem. staff Hughes Research Labs., Malibu, Calif., 1952-87; asso. dir. Hughes Research Labs., 1962-69, dir., 1969-87; v.p. Hughes Aircraft Co., 1965-81, sr. v.p., 1981-87, mem. policy bd., 1966-87; adj. asso. prof. elec. engring. U. So. Calif., 1959-62; cons. Army Sci. Adv. Panel, 1975-78. Contbr. numerous articles to profl. jours. Adv. local Explorer post Boy Scouts Am., 1965-70; bd. mgrs. Westchester YMCA, 1974—, chmn., 1979-81; chmn. trustees Pacific Presbyn. Ch., Los Angeles, 1959-62. Served to lt. (j.g.) USNR, 1944-46. Recipient Disting. Alumnus award Calif. Inst. Tech., 1991. Fellow IEEE (pres. Sorenson fellows 1972-73, Frederick Philips award 1988), Am. Phys. Soc.; mem. AAAS, Caltech Assocs. (bd. dirs. 1990—, pres. 1993-94), Sierra Club, Sigma Xi (chpt. pres. 1957-58), Tau Beta Pi. Achievements include 6 patents in field; directed leading industrial research in electronics, lasers, and electro-optics; conducted first laser range finder experiments. Office: Hughes Aircraft Co Rsch Labs 3011 Malibu Canyon Rd Malibu CA 90265-4737

SMITH, GEORGE JOSEPH, legal assistant; b. Paterson, N.J., Jan. 31, 1951; s. Edward Alfred and Cecelia Angelia (Darms) S.; m. Jean Ann Corry, Mar. 25, 1976 (div. Oct., 1981); m. Margaret Elizabeth Johnson, Dec. 2, 1988; children: Nolan, Jessica. Student, County Coll. of Morris, Dover, N.J., 1970-72; BA in Polit. Sci., Blackburn Coll., Carlinville, Ill., 1972-75. Legal asst. Willkie, Farr & Gallagher, N.Y.C., 1983-86, Sills, Cummis, Zuckerman et al., Newark, 1987-89, Kay, Collyer & Boose, N.Y.C., 1989-92, De Cotiis, Fitzpatrick & Gluck, Trenton, N.J., 1992—. Mem. Nat. Assn. Bond Lawyers. Home: 265 Danforth Ave Jersey City NJ 07305-1942 Office: De Cotiis Fitzpatrick & Gluck 50 W State St 1 State St SQ Trenton NJ 08607-1375

SMITH, GEORGE LEONARD, industrial engineering educator; b. State College, Pa., Sept. 6, 1935; s. George Leonard and Frieda Regina (Droege) S.; m. Patricia Gallagher, Dec. 29, 1962; children: Stephanie Ann, Seana Maureen. BS in Indsl. Engring., Pa. State U., 1957; MS in Indsl. Engring., Lehigh U., 1958, MS in Psychology, 1967; PhD in Indsl. Engring., Okla. State U., 1969. Registered profl. engr., Pa. Asst. prof. Ohio State U., Columbus, 1968-72, assoc. prof., 1972-77, prof. indsl. engring., 1977-95, prof. emeritus, 1995, chmn. dept. indsl. and systems engring., 1982-94, assoc. dean for acad. affairs, 1991-93; arbitrator Fed. Mediation and Conciliation Service, 1970—; vis. Disting. Prof. New U. of Lisbon, Portugal, 1990—. Editor: Human Factors, 1980-83; author: Work Measurement: A Systems Approach, 1978. Pub. mem. Ohio Power Siting Commn., 1970-75. Recipient Disting Teaching award Coll. Engring., Ohio State U., 1982. Fellow Inst. Indsl. Engrs. (Human Factors Soc., div. dir. 1979-81, v.p. edn. rsch. 1988-91, Spl. citation ergonomics divsn.), Soc. for Engring. and Mgmt. Systems (pres. 1996), World Acad. of Productivity Sci.; mem. Am. Soc. Engring. Edn. Democrat. Roman Catholic. Home: 858 Katherines Ridge Ln Columbus OH 43235-3462 Office: 858 Katherine's Ridge Ln Columbus OH 43235-3462

SMITH, GEORGE LESTER, lawyer; b. Ft. Meade, Md., July 14, 1951; s. Dale Ellison and Jane (Sheppard) S.; m. Patricia P. Smith, July 25, 1981; 1 child, Bradford D. BA, Claremont McKenna Coll., 1973; JD, U. Calif., Davis, 1976; LLM, U. Fla., 1987. Bar: Wash. 1980, Calif. 1976; CPA, Calif., Wash. Acct. Touche Ross & Co., San Francisco, 1976-78; assoc. Graham & Dunn, Seattle, 1982-87; ptnr. Foster Pepper & Shefelman, Seattle, 1987—. Capt. JAGC, U.S. Army, 1978-82. Office: 777 108th Ave NE Ste 2250 Bellevue WA 98004-5120

SMITH, GEORGE PATRICK, II, lawyer, educator; b. Wabash, Ind., Sept. 1, 1939; s. George Patrick and Marie Louise (Barrett) S. BS, Ind. U., 1961, JD, 1964; certificate, Hague Acad. Internat. Law, 1965; LLM, Columbia U., 1975. Bar: Ind. 1964, U.S. Supreme Ct. 1968. Kannert teaching fellow Ind. U. Sch. Law, 1964-65; instr. law U. Mich. Sch. Law, 1965-66; practiced in Ind. and Washington, 1965—; legal adviser Fgn. Claims Settlement Commn., Dept. State, Washington, 1966; asst. prof., asst. dean State U. N.Y. at Buffalo Law Sch., 1967-69; vis. asst. prof. law George Washington U., Nat. Law Center, summer 1968; assoc. prof. law U. Ark., 1969-71; spl. counsel EPA, Washington, 1971-74; adj. prof. law Cath. U. Law Sch., Washington, 1973-74, prof., 1977—; adj. prof. law Georgetown U. Law Ctr., 1971-75; assoc. prof. law U. Pitts. Sch. Law, 1975-78; Commonwealth fellow in law, sci. and medicine Yale U., New Haven, 1976-77; vis. prof. law U. Conn., 1977; disting. vis. scholar Kennedy Bioethics Inst., Georgetown U., 1977-81; vis. scholar Cambridge (Eng.) U., summer 1975, spring 1978-79, Hoover Inst. on War, Revolution and Peace Stanford (Calif.) U., summer 1983, Inst. Soc., Ethics and Life Scis., Hastings Ctr., N.Y., 1981, Lilly Rare Books Libr., Ind. U., July 1981, The Kinsey Inst. for Rsch. in Sex, Gender and Reproduction, U. Ind., July 1981, Am. Bar Found., Chgo., 1986, 87, Vatican Libr., Rome, July, 1989; Rockefeller Found. resdl. scholar, Bellagio, Italy, 1980; lectr. Sch. Medicine, Uniformed Svcs. U. Health Scis., Bethesda, Md., 1979-87; cons. environ. legislation Govt. of Greece, 1977; spl. counsel to Gov. Ark. for environ. affairs, 1969-71; cons. Ark. Planning Commn., 1970-71; mem. Ark. Waterway Commn., 1970-71; chmn. Ark. Com. on Environ. Control, 1970-71; mem. com. on hwy. rsch. NRC, NAS, 1971-81; life mem. Ind. U. Found.; univ. fellow Columbia U. Law Sch., 1974-75; fellow Max Planck Inst., Heidelberg, Fed. Republic of Germany, summer 1983; mem. Pres. Reagan's Pvt. Sector Survey on Cost Control, 1982; vis. fellow Clare Hall Cambridge U., 1983-84, summer 87, law, sci. and medicine Hughes Hall, Cambridge (Eng.) U., 1989, also vis. mem. law faculty, Apr.-Aug., 1989; Fulbright vis. prof. U. New South Wales, Syndey, Australia, 1984, vis. prof., vis. fellow Ctr. for Law and Tech., 1987; vis. fellow Inst. Advanced Study, Ind. U., 1985; vis. prof. law U. Notre Dame, 1986; vis. scholar Am. Bar Found., Chgo., 1986, 87; sr. vis. fellow U. Singapore, 1987; vis. fellow McGill U. Ctr. for Medicine, Ethics and Law, Montreal, 1988, Ctr. for Biomed. Ethics U. Va. Health Scis. Ctr., Charlottesville, 1990, Ctr. for Bioethics Monash U., Melbourne, Australia, 1990, Working Ctr. Studies in German and Internat. Med. Malpractice Law Free U. Berlin, 1992; vis. rsch. fellow Ctr. for Advanced Study of Ethics Georgetown U., Washington, 1990-91; rsch. fellow Divinity Sch. Yale U., New Haven, 1991; assoc. Med. Inst. for Law Faculty, Cleve. Clinic Ctr. Creative Thinking in Medicine Cleve. State U., 1991; vis. prof. rsch. U. Auckland Law Faculty, 1991, U. Sydney Law Faculty, 1991, U. Victoria Law Faculty, B.C., Can., 1992, Trinity Coll., 1992, Dublin U., Ireland, 1992, Wolfson Coll. Cambridge U., 1992, Ind. U. Sch. Public and Environ. Affairs, 1992, Queensland U. Faculty Law, Australia, 1993; vis. scholar Ctr. Biomed. Ethics U. Minn. Med. Sch., Mpls., 1991, Ctr. for Socio-Legal Studies Oxford U., July 1992, Princeton (N.J.) Theol. Sem., 1993, Ctr. Med. Ethics Pritzker Sch. Medicine U. Chgo., 1993; vis. fellow Ctr. for Internat. Malpractice Law Free U. Berlin, Jan. 1992, King's Coll. Ctr. for Med. Law and Ethics U. London, June 1992; vis. sr. fellow Ctr. for Study Aging and Human Devel. Duke U. Med. Ctr., 1994; vis. prof. Rsch. U. Otiago, 1994; faculty of law, vis. fellow U. Bioethics Rsch. Ctr., Dunedin, New Zealand, 1994; vis. scholar Poynter Ctr. for Study of Ethics Am. Instns., Ind. U., Bloomington, 1994, law, medicine and ethics Schs. Medicine and Pub. Health Boston U., 1995, Ctr. Law and Health Ind. U., Indpls., 1995. Author: Restricting the Concept of Free Seas, 1980, Legal, Ethical and Social Issues of the Brave New World, 1980, Genetics, Ethics and the Law, 1981, Medical-Legal Aspects of Cryonics, 1983, The New Biology, 1989, Final Choices: Autonomy in Health Care Decisions, 1989, Bioethics and the Law, 1993, Legal and Healthcare Ethics for the Elderly, 1996; contbr. articles to profl. jours. U. Ark. del. Pacem In Maribus Conf., Malta, 1970. Recipient Disting. Alumni award Ind. U. Bd. Trustees, 1985, citation for Path-Breaking Work; establishment of George P. Smith II Disting. Research Professorship, Ind. U., Bloomington, 1986. Mem. ABA (rep. UN Conf. on Human Environ., Stockholm 1972, rep. Law of Sea Conf., UN, N.Y.C. 1976, Switzerland 1979, cons. UNESCO Declaration on the Production of the Protection of the Human Genome, Paris 1995), Nat. Cathedral Assn. Washington, Am. Assn. Bioethics, Am. Law Inst., Soc. Ind. Pioneers, Am. Friends of Cambridge U., Order of St. John Hospitaller, Alpha Kappa Psi, Phi Alpha Delta, Sigma Alpha Epsilon, Order of Omega. Republican. Club: Cosmos (Washington). *Think big, work hard and, above all, have a dream: these are the simple guideposts for a fulfilling life.*

SMITH, GEORGE S., JR., communications financial executive; b. Newark, Dec. 8, 1948; m. Pamela Smith. BS in Acctg., Hiram Scott Coll., Scott's Bluff, Nebr., 1971. Cash mgr. Diamondhead Corp., N.Y.C., 1971-75, Texasgulf Inc., N.Y.C., 1975-77; dir. fin. svcs. Viacom Internat. Inc., N.Y.C., 1977-79, dir. fin. planning, 1979-81, controller radio div., 1981-83, v.p. fin. and adminstrn. broadcast group, 1983-85, v.p., controller, 1985-87, sr. v.p., chief fin. officer Viacom Inc., 1987—. Mem. Broadcast Fin. Mgmt. Assn., Fin. Execs. Inst. Office: Viacom Inc 1515 Broadway New York NY 10036

SMITH, GEORGE THORNEWELL, retired state supreme court justice; b. Camilla, Ga., Oct. 15, 1916; s. George C. and Rosa (Gray) S.; m. Eloise Taylor, Sept. 1, 1943 (dec.). Grad., Abraham Baldwin Agrl. Coll., 1940; LLB, U. Ga., 1948. Bar: Ga. 1947. Assoc. Cain & Smith, Cairo, Ga., 1947-71; city atty. Cairo, 1949-58; atty. Grady County, 1950-59; solicitor Cairo City Ct., 1951-59; mem. Ga. Ho. of Reps., 1959-67, speaker of the house, 1963-67; lt. gov. State of Ga., 1967-71; city atty. East Point, Ga., 1973-76; judge Ga. Ct. Appeals, 1976-81; justice Ga. Supreme Ct., Atlanta, 1981-91, presiding justice, 1990-91; of counsel Barnes, Browning Tanksley and Casurella, Marietta, Ga., 1992—; past mem. exec. com. Nat. Conf. Appellate Judges; vice chmn. Nat. Conf. Lt. Govs. Trustee Nat. Arthritis Found. Lt. comdr. USN, 1940-45. Only person in the state's history to serve in an elective capacity in all 3 brs. of govt. Mem. State Bar Ga., Cobb County Bar Assn., Lawyers Club Atlanta, Am. Legion, VFW, Moose, Kiwanis. Avocations: hunting, bowling, golf. Office: Barnes Browning Tanksley and Casurella 166 Anderson St Ste 225 Marietta GA 30060-1984

SMITH, GEORGE WOLFRAM, physicist, educator; b. Des Plaines, Ill., Sept. 19, 1932; s. Murray Sawyer and Alice Lucile (Wolfram) S.; m. Mary Lee Sackett, Sept. 7, 1956; children—Dean, Grant. B.A., Knox Coll., 1954; M.A., Rice U., 1956, Ph.D., 1958. Welch Found. fellow Rice U., 1958-59; sr. rsch. physicist GM, Warren, Mich., 1959-76; dept. rsch. scientist GM, 1976-81, sr. staff rsch. scientist, 1981-87, prin. rsch. scientist, 1987—; lectr. physics and astronomy Cranbrook Inst. Sci., Bloomfield Hills, Mich., 1963-87, mem. sci. adv. com., 1989—; instr. Lawrence Inst. Tech., 1963-65; vice chmn. Gordon Rsch. Conf. on Orientational Disorder in Crystals, 1976, chmn., 1978; co-chmn. Internat. Symposium on Particulate Carbon, 1980; mem. rev. com. Liquid Crystal Inst., Kent (Ohio) State U., 1984-85; mem. adv. com. Conf. on Electrorheological Fluids, 1991, 93; mem. adv. bd. NSF Sci. and Tech. Ctr. for Advanced Liquid Crystalline Optical Materials, 1996—. Co-editor: Particulate Carbon: Formation During Combustion, 1981; editl. cons. Ency. Applied Physics, 1988—; contbr. Handbook of Chemistry and Physics; contbr. articles to sci. and tech. jours.; patentee on temperature measuring device, liquid crystal device tech., dielectric heating, graphite fiber growth, polymer-dispersed liquid crystals. Mem. Mich. Regtl. Civil War Roundtable, 1965—, pres., 1971-72. Recipient Knox Coll. Achievement award 1977, John M. Campbell Research award, 1980, Charles L. McCuen Achievement award, Gen. Motors, 1985. Fellow Am. Phys. Soc. (com. on applications of physics 1988-91, chmn. 1991, chmn. com. on tutorials 1991, mem. Pake Prize Com. 1993-94); mem. Soc. Info. Display (program com. 1990-93), Phi Beta Kappa, Sigma Xi (chpt. pres. 1980-81), Phi Delta Theta, Alpha Delta. Home: 1882 Melbourne St Birmingham MI 48009-1163 Office: GM Rsch and Devel Ctr Physics and Phys Chem Dept Warren MI 48090-9055

SMITH, GERARD PETER, neuroscientist; b. Phila., Mar. 24, 1935; s. Stanley Alward and Agnes Marie (McLarney) S.; m. Barbara McInnis, May 12, 1962; children: Christopher, Mark, Hilary, Maura. BS, St. Joseph's U., Phila., 1956; MD, U. Pa., 1960. Intern, resident N.Y. Hosp., 1960-62; asst. prof. physiology U. Pa. Sch. Medicine, Phila., 1964-68; from asst. to assoc. prof. Cornell U., N.Y.C., 1968—, prof. psychiatry (behavioral neurosci.), 1973—; vis. prof. MIT, 1973-74, Rockefeller U., 1979-80; adj. prof., 1982-86; cons. NIH; Curt Richter lectr. Johns Hopkins U., 1976; Leon lectr. U. Pa., 1990, Stellar lectr. U. Pa., 1993; Rushton lectr. Fla. State U., 1992, Merck, Sharpe, and Dohm prof. neurosci. U. Flinder, Australia, 1992; dir. Eating Disorders Inst., N.Y. Hosp.-Cornell Med. Ctr., 1984-88. Recipient Rsch. Scientist USPHS, 1982; NIH grantee. Mem. AAAS, Am. Physiol. Soc., Soc. for Neurosci., Ea. Psychol. Assn., Am. Assn. for Rsch. in Nervous and Mental Disease, Endocrine Soc., Soc. Biol. Psychiatry, Soc. for Study Ingestive Behavior (pres.), Internat. Behavioral Neurosci. Soc. (pres.), Alpha Omega Alpha, Alpha Sigma Nu. Office: EW Bourne Behavioral Rsch Lab NY Hosp Cornell Med Ctr 21 Bloomingdale Rd White Plains NY 10605-1504

SMITH, GLEE SIDNEY, JR., lawyer; b. Rozel, Kans., Apr. 29, 1921; s. Glee S. and Bernice M. (Augustine) S.; m. Geraldine B. Buhler, Dec. 14, 1943; children: Glee S., Stephen B., Susan K. AB, U. Kans., 1943, JD, 1947. Bar: Kans. 1947, U.S. Dist. Ct. 1951, U.S. Supreme Ct. 1973, U.S. Ct. Mil. Appeals 1988. Ptnr. Smith, Burnett & Larson, Larned, Kans., 1947—; of counsel Barber, Emerson et. al., Lawrence, Kans., 1992—, Kans. state senator, 1957-73, pres. Senate, 1965-73; mem. Kans. Bd. Regents, 1975-83, pres., 1976; bd. govs. Kans. U. Law Soc., 1967—; mem. Kans. Jud. Coun., 1963-65; county atty. Pawnee County, 1949-53; mem. bd. edn. Larned, 1951-63; Kans. commr. Nat. Conf. Commn. on Uniform State Laws, 1963—. Bd. dirs. Nat. Legal Svcs. Corp., 1975-79. Served to 1st lt. U.S. Army, 1943-45. Recipient Disting. Svc. award, U. Kans. Law Sch., 1976; Disting. Svc. citation U. Kans., 1984. Fellow Am. Coll. Probate Counsel, Am. Bar Found.; mem. ABA (bd. of govs. 1987-90, chmn. ops. com. 1989-90, exec. com. 1989-90, chmn. task force on solo and small firm practitioner 1990-91, chmn. com. on solo and small firm practitioners 1992-94, chmn. task force on applying fed. legis. to congress 1994-96), Kans. Bar Assn. (del. to ABA ho. of dels. 1982-92, bd. govs. 1982-92, leadership award 1973, medal of Distinction 1993), Southwest Kans. Bar Assn., Am. Judicature Soc. Republican. Presbyterian. Clubs: Kiwanis, Masons. Home: 115 E 9th St Apt 5 Larned KS 67550-2647 Home: 4313 Quail Pointe Rd Lawrence KS 66047-1966

SMITH, GLENN STANLEY, electrical engineering educator; b. Salem, Mass., June 1, 1945; s. Stanley Ernest and Florence Estelle (Chaney) S.; m. Linda Lee Holmquist, Aug. 4, 1968; children: Geoffrey Douglas, Eleanor Leigh. BS, Tufts U., 1967; MS, Harvard U., 1968, PhD, 1972. Postdoctoral rsch. fellow Harvard U., Cambridge, Mass., 1972-75; rsch. assoc., lectr. Northeastern U., Boston, 1973-75; asst. prof. elec. engring. Ga. Inst. Tech., Atlanta, 1975-79, assoc. prof., 1979-84, prof., 1984-89, Regents' prof., 1989—. Co-author: Antennas in Matter, 1981; assoc. editor Radio Sci., 1983-87. Fellow IEEE (editorial bd. IEEE Press 1988-91); mem. Internat. Union Radio Sci. Home: 2518 Hazelwood Dr NE Atlanta GA 30345-2145 Office: Sch Elec Engring Ga Inst Tech Atlanta GA 30332

SMITH, G(ODFREY) T(AYLOR), academic administrator; b. Newton, Miss., Nov. 12, 1935; s. Taylor and Edna (Blanton) S.; m. Joni Eaton, Sept. 1, 1956; children: Paul Brian, Sherry Lynn. BA, Coll. of Wooster, 1956; MPA with distinction, Cornell U., 1960; LLD (hon.), Bethany Coll., 1979. Asso. dir. devel. Cornell U., 1960-62; dir. devel. Coll. Wooster, 1962-66, v.p., 1966-77; pres. Chapman U., Orange, Calif., 1977-88, pres. emeritus, 1988—; lectr. in field. Contbr. numerous articles on coll. mgmt. to profl. publs. Bd. dirs. Wayne County (Ohio) Indsl. Devel. Corp., 1966-72, World Affairs Coun. Orange Coun., Calif., 1978-89, Orange County chpt. NCCJ, 1979-86, Orange County coun. Boy Scouts Am., 1980-85, Coun. Ind. Colls., 1985-87; bd. dirs. div. higher edn. Christian Ch. (Disciples of Christ), 1980-86, chmn., 1984-86; bd. dirs., mem. exec. com. Ind. Colls. So. Calif., 1979-88, pres., 1981-82; mem. exec. com. Assn. Ind. Calif. Colls. and Univs., 1980-88, treas., 1982-87. Recipient Steuben Apple award for Tchg. Excellence, Coun. for Advancement and Support of Edn., 1984, Disting. Alumnus award Coll. of Wooster, 1991, Faith and Reason award Christian Ch. (Disciples of Christ), 1993; Smith Hall dedicated at Chapman U., 1988; Alfred P. Sloan fellow Cornell U., 1960. Presbyterian. Home: 2200 Lupine Dr Ashland OR 97520-3642 *If we treat people as they are, they will stay as they are. But if we treat them for what they might be and might become, they will become those better selves.*

SMITH, GOFF, industrial equipment manufacturing executive; b. Jackson, Tenn., Oct. 7, 1916; s. Fred Thomas and Mabel (Goff) S.; m. Nancy Dall, Nov. 28, 1942 (dec. 1972); children: Goff Thomas, Susan Knight; m. Harriet Schneider Oliver, June 23, 1973. BSE, U. Mich., 1938, MBA, 1939; MS, MIT, 1953. Trainee Bucyrus Erie, South Milwaukee, Wis., 1939-40; mem. sales staff Amsted Industries, Chgo. and N.Y.C., 1946-55; subsidiary pres. Amsted Industries, Chgo., 1955-60, v.p., 1960-69, pres., dir., 1969-74, pres., CEO, dir., 1974-80, chmn., 1980-82. Pres. Village of Winnetka, Ill., 1967-69; pres., bd. dirs. United Way Chgo., 1976-85; bd. dirs. Rehab. Inst., Chgo., Chgo. Theol. Sem., Presbyn. Home, Evanston, Ill.; trustee Sigma Chi Found. Maj. U.S. Army, 1940-46. Sloan Fellow MIT, 1952-53. Republican. Avocations: hunting, fishing, golf.

SMITH, GORDON E., religious organization executive. Exec. dir. ABC Ministers & Miss. Benefit Bd., Valley Forge, Pa. Office: ABC Ministers & Miss Benefit Bd PO Box 851 Valley Forge PA 19482-0851

SMITH, GORDON H., civil engineer; b. N.Y.C., Mar. 17, 1936; s. Henry and Theodora (Augenstern) S.; m. Norma Kaplan, Feb. 28, 1960; children: Randy Smith Aberg, Robin Smith Kolstad. BS in Engring., Yale U., 1957. Registered profl. engr., Mich., N.Y. V.p., chief engr. Albro Metal Products Corp., N.Y.C., 1957-69, pres., 1969-75; pres. Gordon H. Smith Corp., N.Y.C., 1975—. Contbr. articles to Archtl. Record, Progressive Arch., ASTM, Chgo. High Rise Com. Mem. NSPE, ASTM, ASCE, AIA (Inst. Honors 1994), Nat. Assn. Archtl. Metal Mfrs. (v.p., prs., bd. dirs.), Archtl. Aluminum Mfrs. Assn. (v.p., bd. dirs.), Nat. Assn. Miscellaneous, Ornamental and Archtl. Metal Mfrs. (bd. dirs.), Constrn. Specifications Inst. Office: Gordon H Smith Corp 200 Madison Ave New York NY 10016-3903

SMITH, GORDON HOWELL, lawyer; b. Syracuse, N.Y., Oct. 26, 1915; s. Lewis P. and Maud (Mixer) S.; m. Eunice Hale, June 28,1947; children: Lewis Peter, Susan S. Rizk, Catherine S. Maxson, Maud S. Daudon. B.A., Princeton U., 1932-36; LL.B., Yale U., 1939. Bar: N.Y. 1939, Ill. 1946. Asso. Lord, Day & Lord, N.Y.C., 1939-41, Gardner, Carton & Douglas, Chgo., 1946-51; partner Mackenzie, Smith & Michell, Syracuse, 1951-53; partner Gardner, Carton & Douglas, 1954-57, 60-85, of counsel, 1986—; sec., dir. Smith-Corona, Inc., 1951-54, v.p., Syracuse, 1957-60. Bd. dirs. Rehab. Inst. Chgo., chmn., 1974-78, 83-86; bd. dirs. United Way Met. Chgo., 1962-85. Served to lt. comdr. USNR, 1941-46. Mem. Am. Soc. Corporate Secs., Am., Ill., Chgo. bar assns. Clubs: Comml., Law, Econ., Legal, Chgo., Old Elm (Chgo.). Home: 1302 N Green Bay Rd Lake Forest IL 60045-1108 Office: 321 N Clark St Ste 3400 Chicago IL 60610-4714

SMITH, GORDON PAUL, management consulting company executive; b. Salem, Mass., Dec. 25, 1916; s. Gordon and May (Vaughan) S.; m. Daphne Miller, Nov. 23, 1943 (div. 1968); m. Ramona Chamberlain, Sept. 27, 1969; children: Randall B., Roderick F. B.S. in Econs, U. Mass., 1947; M.S. in Govt. Mgmt, U. Denver (Sloan fellow), 1948; postgrad. in polit. sci, NYU, 1948-50; DHL (hon.), Monterey Inst. Internat. Studies, 1994. Economist Tax Found., Inc., N.Y.C., 1948-50; with Booz, Allen & Hamilton, 1951-70; partner Booz, Allen & Hamilton, San Francisco, 1959-62, v.p., 1962-67, mng. pntr. Western U.S., 1968-70; partner Harrod, Williams and Smith (real estate devel.), San Francisco, 1962-69; state dir. fin. State of Calif., 1967-68; pres. Gordon Paul Smith & Co., Mgmt. Cons., 1968—; pres., chief exec. officer Golconda Corp., 1972-74, chmn. bd., 1974-85; pres. Cermetek Corp., 1978-80; bd. dirs., exec. com. First Calif. Co., 1970-72, Groman Corp., 1976-85; bd. dirs. Madison Venture Capital Corp.; adviser task force def. procurement and contracting Hoover Commn., 1954-55; spl. asst. to pres. Republic Aviation Corp., 1954-55; cons., Hawaii, 1960-61, Alaska, 1963; cons. Wash. Hwy. Adminstrn., 1964, also 10 states and fed. agys., 1951-70, Am. Baseball League and Calif. Angels, 1960-62; bd. dirs. Monterey Coll. Law; chmn. Ft. Ord Econ. Devel. Adv. Group, 1991; chmn. Coalition on Rsch. and Edn., 1993—; bd. dirs. Monterey Bay Futures Project; over 750 TV, radio and speaking appearances on econs., mgmt. and public issues. Author articles on govt., econs. and edn. Mem. 24 bds. and commns. State of Calif., 1967-72; mem. Calif. Select Com. on Master Plan for Edn., 1971-73; mem. alumni council U. Mass., 1950-54, bd. dirs. alumni assn., 1964-70; bd. dirs. Alumni Assn. Mt. Hermon Prep. Sch., 1963; bd. dirs. Stanford Med. Ctr., 1960-62, pres., chmn., 1962-66; chmn. West Coast Cancer Found., 1976-87, Coalition Rsch. and Edn., 1993—; trustee, chmn. Monterey Inst. Internat. Studies, 1978-92; trustee Northfield Mt. Hermon Sch., 1983-93, Robert Louis Stevenson Sch., 1993—; mem. devel. council Community Hosp. of Monterey Peninsula, 1983—; bd. dirs. Friends of the Performing Arts, 1985—; bd. dirs. Monterey County Symphony Orch., 1991—, Monterey Bay Futures Project, 1992—. Served to 1st lt., cav. AUS, 1943-46, ETO. Recipient spl. commendation Hoover Commn., 1955, Alumni of Yr. award U. Mass., 1963, Trustee of Yr. award Monterey-Peninsula, 1991, Monterey-Peninsula Outstanding Citizen of Yr. award, 1992, Laura Bride Powers Heritage award, 1991, U.S. Congl. award, 1992, Calif. Senate and Assembly Outstanding Citizen award, 1992, Wisdom award of honor Wisdom Soc., 1992; permanent Gordon Paul Smith Disting. Chair for Internat. Studies established at Monterey Inst. Internat. Studies; Gordon Paul Smith Scholarship Fund named in his honor Northfield Mt. Hermon Sch.; named to Honorable Order of Ky. Cols. Mem. Monterey History and Art Assn. (bd. dirs. 1987-92, pres. 1985-87, chmn. 1987-92, hon. lifetime dir. 1992—), The Stanton Ctr. Heritage Ctr. (chmn. 1987-92, chmn. emeritus 1992—), Salvation Army (bd. dirs., chmn. hon. cabinet), Monterey Peninsula Mus. Art, Carmel Valley (Calif.) Country Club, Monterey Peninsula Country Club, Old Capitol Club. Home: 253 Del Mesa Carmel CA 93923 *If the quest for personal success is only for an accumulation of prestige, power or wealth, then personal failure will be assured. Genuine personal success can surely be found, however, through a significant and lasting contribution toward helping the progress of others and raising the human worth. This is the true mark of leadership.*

SMITH, GORDON ROSS, retired English language educator; b. Monmouth County, N.J., May 23, 1917; s. Mortimer Dickerson and Elizabeth Clara (Ross) S.; m. Jane Pakenham, Aug. 29, 1948; children: Gordon Ross, Corinna Pakenham. B.S., Columbia U., 1948, M.A., 1949; Ph.D., Pa. State U., 1956. Instr. English, Waynesburg (Pa.) Coll., 1949-50; instr. English, Pa. State U., 1950-56, asst. prof., 1956-59, assoc. prof., 1959-63, prof., 1963-66; Folger Shakespeare Library fellow, 1958; Fulbright lectr. Royal U. Malta, 1962-63; prof. English, Temple U., Phila., 1966-84, prof. emeritus, 1984—. Author: A Classified Shakespeare Bibliography, 1936-58, 1963, Essays on Shakespeare, 1965; cons. editor: Jour. History of Ideas; editorial bd.: Film Forum Rev, Columbia U., 1948-49; contbr. articles to scholarly jours. Democratic party committeeman, State College, Pa., 1952-56. Served with AUS, 1943-46. Mem. Shakespeare Assn. Am., Pa. Hist. Soc., Huguenot Hist. Soc., Du Bois Assn. (pres. 1983-84 v.p. 1980-83, 85-89), Geneal. Soc. Pa., Pilgrim Soc., Internat. Shakespeare Assn. Home: 232 Dock Dr Lansdale PA 19446-6234

SMITH, GRANT WARREN, II, university administrator, physical sciences educator; b. Kansas City, Mo., Jan. 21, 1941; m. Constance M. Krambeer, 1962; 1 child, Grant Warren III. BA, Grinnell Coll., 1962; PhD, Cornell U., 1966, postgrad., 1967. Asst. prof. chemistry Cornell U., Ithaca, N.Y., 1966-68, vis. prof., Am. Council on Edn. fellow, 1973-74; assoc. prof. U. Alaska, Fairbanks, 1968-77, prof., 1977-78, head dept. chemistry and chem. engring., 1968-73, acting head dept. gen. sci., 1972-73; pres. univ. assembly U. Alaska System, 1976-77; prof. phys. scis., dean Sch. Scis. and Techs. U. Houston, Clear Lake, 1979-84; prof. chemistry Southeastern La. U., Hammond, 1984-95, honors prof. arts and scis., 1995—, v.p. for acad. affairs, 1984-86, pres., 1986—. Bd. dirs. Houston Area Research Ctr., 1982-83; violinist, pres. exec. bd. Clear Lake Symphony, 1980-84. NIH fellow, 1963-66, DuPont fellow, 1967. Fellow Royal Soc. Chemistry (London, chartered chemist), Explorers Club; mem. Am. Assn. Higher Edn., Am. Assn. Univ. Adminstrs. (bd. dirs. 1982-85, 86-88, v.p. 1988-90), AAAS, Am. Chem. Soc., Internat. Assn. Univ. Pres., Soc. Econ. Botany, Am. Soc. Pharmacognosy, Ethnopharmacology Soc., Soc. of Ethnobiology, Nat. Speleological Soc., Am. Spelean History Assn., Arctic Inst. N.Am., Hammond C. of C. (bd. dirs. 1988-90), Rotary, Sigma Xi, Phi Kappa Phi, Beta Gamma Sigma, Phi Eta Sigma. Office: Southeastern La U # 942 Hammond LA 70402

SMITH, GREGORY ALLGIRE, academic director; b. Washington, Mar. 31, 1951; s. Donald Eugene and Mary Elizabeth (Reichert) S.; m. Susan Elizabeth Watts, Oct. 31, 1980; 1 child, David Joseph Smith-Watts. BA, The Johns Hopkins U., 1972; MA, Williams Coll., Williamstown, Mass., 1974. Adminstrv. asst. Washington Project for the Arts, 1975; intern Walker Art Ctr., Mpls., 1975-76; asst. devel. officer The Sci. Mus. of Minn., St. Paul, 1977; asst. dir. Akron (Ohio) Art Inst., 1977-80; asst. to dir. Toledo Mus.

Art, 1980-82, asst. dir. adminstrn., 1982-86; exec. v.p. Internat. Exhbns. Found., Washington, 1986-87; dir. The Telfair Mus. Art, Savannah, Ga., 1987-94, Art Acad. of Cin., 1994—. Mem. Am. Assn. Mus. (surveyor mus. assessment program 1988—), Assn. Art Mus. Adminstrs. (founder 1984-85), Ohio Found. on the Arts (v.p. 1981-83, trustee 1981-84), Coll. Art Assn., Univ. Club, Rotary. Avocations: collecting arts & crafts movement objects, repairing old houses, landscape design. Home: 2533 Erie Ave Cincinnato OH 45208 Office: Art Acad of Cin 1125 Saint Gregory St Cincinnati OH 45202-1734

SMITH, GREGORY SCOTT, medical researcher, educator; b. Troy, N.Y., Mar. 22, 1955; s. Oney Percy and Gloria Ann (Tetrault) S.; m. Carol Lee Brown, Nov. 15, 1980. BS in Biology, LeMoyne Coll., 1977; MS in Physiology, U. Tex. Houston, 1989, PhD in Physiology, 1993. From rsch. asst. to rsch. assoc. Surgery U. Tex. Med. Sch., Houston, 1979-90, postdoctoral fellow Pathology, 1993-94, asst. prof. surgery and pathology, 1994—. Contbr. chpts. in books and articles to profl. jours. Head usher Braeburn Presbyn. Ch., Houston, 1987—; judge Houston Sci. and Engring. Fair, 1993—. Mem. Am. Physiol. Soc., Gastroenterology Rsch. Group, Am. Gastroenterology Assn. Republican. Avocations: woodworking, fishing, cooking.

SMITH, GREGORY WHITE, writer; b. Ithaca, N.Y., Oct. 4, 1951; s. William R. and Kathryn (White) S. BA, Colby Coll., 1973; JD, Harvard U., 1977, MEd, 1980. Bar: Mass., 1980. Fellow Thomas J. Watson, 1973-74; pres. Woodward/White, Inc.; overseer Colby Coll.; mem. bd. trustees Columbus Acad. Author: (with Steven Naifeh) Moving Up in Style, 1980, Gene Davis, 1981, How to Make Love to a Woman, 1982, What Every Client Needs to Know About Using a Lawyer, 1982, The Bargain Hunter's Guide to Art Collecting, 1982, Why Can't Men Open Up?: Overcoming Men's Fear of Intimacy, 1984, The Mormon Murders: A True Story of Greed, Forgery, Deceit, and Death, 1988, Jackson Pollock: An American Saga, 1989 (Nat. Book award nomination for nonfiction 1990, Pulitzer Prize for biography 1991), Final Justice: The True Story of the Richest Man Ever Tried for Murder, 1993, A Stranger in the Family: A True Story of Murder, Madness, and Unconditional Love, 1995; editor: (with Naifeh) The Best Lawyers in America, The Best Doctors in America. Office: Woodward/White 129 1st Ave Aiken SC 29801-4862*

SMITH, GRIFFIN, JR., lawyer; b. Fayetteville, Ark., June 29, 1941; s. Griffin and Mildred (Cross) S.; m. Mary Elizabeth Routh, Sept. 1, 1979. BA in History, Rice U., 1963; MA in Polit. Sci., Columbia U., 1965; postgrad. in philosophy, Oxford U., 1966; JD, U. Tex., 1969. Bar: Tex. 1969, U.S. Dist. Ct. (ea., we., no. and so. dists.) Tex. 1969, Ark. 1981, U.S. Dist. Ct. (ea. and we. dists.) Ark.1981. Spl. asst. to Senator Fulbright U.S. Senate, Washington, 1968-69; atty. estate and gift tax div. IRS, Houston, 1970; rsch. dir. Tex. gubernatorial campaign Paul Eggers, 1970; chief counsel constl. amendments com. Tex. Senate, 1971, chief counsel drug law reform com., 1971-73; editor natural areas survey Lyndon B. Johnson Sch. Pub. Affairs U. Tex., Austin, 1973-77; speech writer Pres. of U.S., 1977-78; ptnr. Smith & Nixon (formerly Smith, Smith, Nixon & Duke), Little Rock, 1984—. Author: A Consumer Viewpoint on State Taxation, 1971, Marijuana in Texas, 1972, The Best of Texas Monthly, 1978, Texas Monthly's Political Reader, 1978, 80, Journey into China, 1982, Forgotten Texas: A Wilderness Portfolio, 1983, The Great State of Texas, 1985; sr. editor Tex. Monthly mag., 1973-77, now contbg. editor: travel editor Ark. Democrat; contbr. articles to Nat. Geog. Saturday Rev., Atlantic Monthly, and others. Woodrow Wilson fellow, 1964. Mem. State Bar Tex., Ark. Bar Assn., Tex. Inst. Letters (award for best work of journalism in Tex. 1974, 76). Democrat. Episcopalian. Office: Smith & Nixon 1955 Union Nat Bank Bldg Little Rock AR 72201

SMITH, GROVER CLEVELAND, English language educator; b. Atlanta, Sept. 6, 1923; s. Grover C. and Lillian Julia (McDaniel) S.; m. Phyllis Jean Snyder, June 19, 1948 (div. 1965); children: Alice Elizabeth, Charles Grover; m. Dulcie Barbara Soper, Dec. 29, 1965; children: Stephen Kenneth, Julia Margaret. BA with honors, Columbia U., 1944, MA, 1945, Ph.D. (Alexander M. Proudfit fellow), 1950. Instr. English Rutgers U., 1946-48, Yale U., 1948-52; instr. English Duke U., 1952-55, asst. prof., 1955-61, asso. prof., 1961-66, prof., 1966-93; prof. emeritus, 1993—; mem. summer faculty CUNY, 1946, 47, 48, Columbia U., 1963, 64, NYU, 1963, Wake Forest U., 1966, vis. lectr., 1963, 64. Author: T.S. Eliot's Poetry and Plays: A Study in Sources and Meaning, 1956 (Poetry Chapbook award), Archibald MacLeish, 1971, Ford Madox Ford, 1972, The Waste Land, 1983, T.S. Eliot and the Use of Memory, 1996; editor: Josiah Royce's Seminar, 1913-1914: As Recorded in the Notebooks of Harry T. Costello, 1963, Letters of Aldous Huxley, 1969. Mem. Christian Gauss Award com., 1973-75. With U.S. Army, 1943. Guggenheim fellow, 1958; Am. Philos. Soc. grantee, 1965; Am. Learned Socs. grantee, 1965; Nat. Endowment Humanities grantee, 1979; fellow, 1980. Mem. T.S. Eliot Soc. (bd. dirs. 1986-94, v.p. 1986-88, editor News and Notes, 1987-88, 90-91, pres. 1989-91), Am. Lit. Assn. (rep. to coun. of Am. Author Socs. 1990-91), Nat. Assn. Scholars. Office: Duke U Dept English PO Box 90015 Durham NC 27708-0015

SMITH, GUY LINCOLN, IV, strategic communications company executive; b. New Orleans, Mar. 16, 1949; s. Guy Lincoln III and Laura Louise (Orr) S.; m. Marjorie Russell, June 19, 1971; children: Abigail, Guy Lincoln V, Laura. Student, Bowling Green State U., 1967-68, U. Tenn., 1968-70, Am. U., 1971, U.S. Dept. Agrl. Grad. Sch., Washington, 1971. Reporter, asst. city editor The Knoxville Jour., 1967-70; dir. info. Appalachian Regional Commn., Washington, 1970-72; dir. info., press sec. to mayor City of Knoxville, 1972-76; mgr. corp. affairs Miller Brewing Co., Milw., 1976-79; v.p. corp. affairs The Seven-Up Co., St. Louis, 1979-84, Philip Morris U.S.A., N.Y.C., 1984-88; v.p. corp. affairs Philip Morris Cos. Inc., N.Y.C., 1989-91, pub. Philip Morris Mag., 1986-91; COO Hill and Knowlton, Inc., N.Y.C., 1991-93; chmn. Smith Worldwide, Inc., N.Y.C., 1993—; mem. pvt. sect. com. on pub. rels. USIA. Bd. dirs. Barrier Island Trust, Tallahassee, Fla., 1991—, AmeriCares, Inc. Recipient Excellence in News Writing award William Randolph Hearst Found., 1969, Achievement award Puerto Rican Family Inst., 1988; named confrere Sovereign Military Order of St. John of Jerusalem, of Rhodes, and of Malta, 1986, Outstanding Pub. Rels.-Pub. Affairs Exec. of Yr. Gallagher Report, 1988. Mem. Nat. Press Club, Kappa Alpha. Roman Catholic. Office: 171 Madison Ave New York NY 10016-5110

SMITH, HALLETT DARIUS, retired English literature educator; b. Chattanooga, Aug. 15, 1907; s. Charles Wilson and Elizabeth Russell (Atkinson) S.; m. Mary Elizabeth Earl, Dec. 30, 1931; children—Diana Russell Smith Gordon, Hallett Earl. A.B., U. Colo., 1928, L.H.D., 1968; Ph.D., Yale U., 1934. Instr. English Williams Coll., Williamstown, Mass., 1931-36, asst. prof., 1937-40, assoc. prof., 1940-45, prof., 1946-49; prof. Calif. Inst. Tech., Pasadena, 1949-75, chmn. div. humanities, 1949-70; Guggenheim fellow, 1947-48; vis. prof. Columbia U., summer 1949; sr. research asso. Huntington Library, 1970—; Henry W. and Albert A. Berg prof. Eng. lit. N.Y. U., spring 1977; vis. prof. U. B.C., Spring 1980; Mem. Commn. English. Author: The Golden Hind, 1942, The Critical Reader, 1949, Elizabethan Poetry, 1951, Renaissance England, 1956, Twentieth Century Interpretations of The Tempest, 1970, Shakespeare's Romances, 1972, The Tension of the Lyre: Poetry in Shakespeare's Sonnets, 1981; contbr. articles to ednl. jours. Trustee Am. Univs. Field Staff, Poly. Sch.; mem. adv. com. Guggenheim Found. Recipient Poetry Chapbook prize Poetry Soc. Am., 1952; Phi Beta Kappa vis. scholar, 1959-60. Fellow Am. Acad. Arts and Scis.; mem. Modern Lang. Assn. Am., Phi Beta Kappa (senator at large). Home: Bradbury Oaks Rm 200 1763 Royal Oaks Dr Duarte CA 91010-1970

SMITH, HAMILTON OTHANEL, molecular biologist, educator; b. N.Y.C., N.Y., Aug. 23, 1931; s. Bunnie Othanel and Tommie Harkey S.; m. Elizabeth Anne Bolton, May 25, 1957; children: Joel, Barry, Dirk, Bryan, Kirsten. Student, U. Ill., 1948-50; A.B. in Math, U. Calif., Berkeley, 1952; M.D., Johns Hopkins U., 1956. Intern Barnes Hosp., St. Louis, 1956-57; resident in medicine Henry Ford Hosp., Detroit, 1959-62; USPHS fellow dept. human genetics U. Mich., Ann Arbor, 1962-64; rsch. assoc. U. Mich., 1964-67; asst. prof. molecular biology and genetics Sch. Medicine Johns Hopkins U., Balt., 1967-69; assoc. prof. Johns Hopkins U., 1969-73, prof., 1973—; asso. Inst. für Molekularbologie der U. Zurich, Switzerland, 1975-76; assoc. Rsch. Inst. Molecular Pathology, Vienna, 1990-91. Contbr. articles to profl. jours. Served to lt. M.C. USNR, 1957-59. Recipient Nobel Prize in medicine, 1978; Guggenheim fellow, 1975-76. Mem. Am. Soc. Microbiology, AAAS, Am. Soc. Biol. Chemists, Nat. Acad. Sci. Office: Johns Hopkins U Sch Med Dept Molecular Genetics 725 N Wolfe St Baltimore MD 21205-2105

SMITH, HARMON LEE, JR., clergyman, moral theology educator; b. Ellisville, Miss., Aug. 23, 1930; s. Harmon Lee Sr. and Mary (O'Donnell) S.; children: Pamela Lee, Amy Joanna, Harmon Lee III. AB, Millsaps Coll., 1952; BD, Duke U., 1955, PhD, 1962. Ordain to priest Episcopal Ch., 1972. Asst. dean Duke U. Divinity Sch., Durham, N.C., 1959-65, asst. prof. Christian ethics, 1962-68, assoc. prof. moral theology, 1968-73, prof. moral theology, 1973—, prof. community and family medicine, 1974—; cons. med. ethics; vis. prof. U. N.C., 1964, 70, 72, U. Edinburgh, Scotland, 1969, U. Windsor, Ont., 1974. Author books on Christian theology, ethics and med. ethics; sr. editor Social Science and Medicine, 1973-89; contbr. articles on Christian ethics to various publs. Lilly Found. fellow, 1960; Gurney Harris Kearns Found. fellow, 1961; Nat. Humanities Ctr. fellow, 1982-83. Mem. Am. Assn. Theol. Schs., Am. Soc. Christian Ethics, Am. Acad. Religion, Soc. for Religion in Higher Edn., Soc. Health and Human Values. Home: 3510 Randolph Rd Durham NC 27705-5347 Office: Duke U The Divinity Sch Durham NC 27706

SMITH, HAROLD B., manufacturing executive; b. Chgo., Apr. 7, 1933; s. Harold Byron and Pauline (Hart) S. Grad., Choate Sch., 1951; B.S., Princeton U., 1955; M.B.A., Northwestern U., 1957. With Ill. Tool Works, Inc., Chgo., 1954—; exec. v.p. Ill. Tool Works, Inc., 1968-72, pres., 1972-81, vice chmn., 1981, chmn. exec. com., 1982—, also bd. dirs.; bd. dirs. W.W. Grainger, Inc., No. Trust Corp.; trustee Northwestern Mut. Life Ins. Co. Mem. Rep. Nat. Com., 1976—; chmn. Ill. Rep. Com., 1993—; del. Rep. Nat. Conv., 1964, 76, 88, 92; bd. dirs. Adler Planetarium, Boys and Girls Clubs Am., Northwestern U., Rush-Presbyn.-St. Luke's Med. Ctr., Newberry Libr. Clubs: Chicago, Commercial, Commonwealth, Economic, Northwestern, Princeton (Chgo.). Office: Ill Tool Works Inc 3600 W Lake Ave Glenview IL 60025-1215

SMITH, HAROLD CHARLES, private pension fund executive; b. N.Y.C., Jan. 11, 1934; s. Harold Elmore and Hedwig Agnes (Gronke) S. BA cum laude with honors, Ursinus Coll., 1955, DD (hon.), 1993; MBA, NYU, 1958; M in Div., Union Theol. Sem., N.Y.C., 1958. DD Ursinus Coll., 1993. CFA; ordanined minister United Ch. of Christ, 1959. Vice pres. YMCA Retirement Fund, Inc., N.Y.C., 1958-69, portfolio mgr., 1960—, assoc. sec., 1969-77, v.p., 1977-80, exec. v.p., 1980-82, pres. elect, 1982-83, pres., 1983—; pastor 1st E&R Ch., Bridgeport, Conn., 1958-88, Unity Hill United Ch. of Christ, 1988—; assoc. prof. bus. and fin. L.I. U., 1969-71; trustee Bank Mart, Bridgeport, Conn., 1983-91; bd. dirs. Y Mut. Ins. Co., treas. 1988—, United Ch. Residencies, 1962-65. Trustee YWCA Greater Bridgeport, 1975-79, Pension Funds United Ch. of Christ, 1968—, Springfield Coll. (Mass.), 1983—; bd. dirs. YMCA Greater N.Y., 1983—, Bridgeport Area Found., 1989—, Ursinus Coll., Pa., 1994—, Coun. of Chs. of Greater Bridgeport, 1995-96. Mem. N.Y. Soc. Security Analysts, Am. Econs. Assn., Fin. Analysts Fedn., World and Trade Club, Mcht's Club, Masons, Marco Polo Club, Order Eastern Star. Author: Getting it All Together for Retirement, 1977. Office: YMCA Retirement 225 Broadway New York NY 10007-3001 *It is a great privilege to serve and to be a part of organizations dedicated to making life and this world better.*

SMITH, HAROLD CHARLES, biochemistry educator, academic administrator; b. Münich, Germany, Feb. 5, 1954; came to U.S., 1966; s. Harold Charles Sr. and Gisela (Pointer) S.; m. Jenny Marie Lyverse, Aug. 21, 1976; children: Charles, Owen, Hanna Marie, Sammy Jay. BS, Purdue U., 1975, MS, 1978; MA, SUNY, Buffalo, 1980, PhD, 1982. Postdoctoral assoc. dept. biochemistry SUNY, Buffalo, 1982-83; postdoctoral assoc. dept. pharmacology Baylor Coll. Medicine, Houston, 1983-85, postdoctoral fellow dept. genetics, 1983-85, rsch. assoc. dept. biochemistry, 1985-86; assoc. prof. U. Rochester, N.Y., 1986—; dir. grad. studies dept. pathology U. Rochester, 1993—. Contbr. articles to profl. jours.; mem. editl. bd. Molecular and Cellular Biochemistry. Rsch. grantee Office of Naval Res., 1989-92, NIH, 1992-99, Coun. for Tobacco Rsch., 1993-96. Mem. Am. Heart Assn., N.Y. Acad. Sci., RNA Soc., Sigma Xi (Rsch. award 1981). Lutheran. Achievements include first to propose hypothesis for apoB mRNA editing (The Mooring Sequence Hypothesis) and demonstrate the tripartite cis-acting elements for editing site recognition and the role of multiple proteins, as an editosome, in the editing activity; first to demonstrate in vitro DNA replication in nuclear matrix presentations. Home: 1056 Farnsworth Rd S Rochester NY 14623 Office: Univ Rochester Dept Pathology 601 Elmwood Ave Rochester NY 14642

SMITH, H(AROLD) LAWRENCE, lawyer; b. Evergreen Park, Ill., June 27, 1932; s. Harold Lawrence and Lorna Catherine (White) S.; m. Madonna Jeanne Koehl, June 9, 1956 (div. 1968); children: Lawrence Kirby, Sandra Michele, Madonna Clare Galloway; m. Nancy Leigh Baum, May 2, 1970 (dec.); m. Louise Fredericka Jeffrey, Nov. 2, 1984 (div. 1994). BS, U.S. Naval Acad., 1956; JD, John Marshall Law Sch., 1965. Bar: Ill. 1965, Mich. 1986, U.S. Dist. Ct. (no. dist.) Ill. 1965, U.S. Ct. Appeals (7th cir.) 1967, U.S. Ct. of Customs and Patent Appeals, 1976, U.S. Ct. Appeals (fed. cir.) 1982, U.S. Patent and Trademark Office 1968. Tech. asst. Langner, Parry, Card & Langner, Chgo., 1961-65, assoc., 1965-69; patent atty. Borg-Warner Corp., Chgo., 1970-74; sr. patent atty. Continental Can Co., Inc., Chgo. and Oak Brook, Ill., 1974-82, asst. gen. counsel, Stamford, Conn., 1982-86; ptnr. Varnum, Riddering, Schmidt & Howlett, Grand Rapids, Mich., 1986—; adj. prof. patent law Cooley Law Sch., 1991—. Served to lt. USN, 1956-61. Mem. Intellectual Property Law Assn. Chgo., Chartered Inst. Patent Agts. (London), World Affairs Coun. of Western Mich. (dir. 1996—). Club: Peninsular. Office: Varnum Riddering Schmidt & Howlett Bridgewater Pl PO Box 352 Grand Rapids MI 49501-0352

SMITH, HARRY DELANO, educational administrator; b. Florence, Ala., June 10, 1954; s. Cornelius Everett and Nadine (Olive) S.; m. Wanda Joy Skipworth, Nov. 23, 1978; children: Benjamin Delano, Rebekah Joy. BS, U. North Ala., 1975, MA, 1977, EdS, 1983; EdD, U. Ala., Tuscaloosa, 1989. Cert. class AA supr.-prin., Ala. Exec. dir. Christian Student Ctr., Florence, 1980-83; head dept. math. Mars Hill Bible Sch., Florence, 1983-87; tchr. math. and physics Muscle Shoals (Ala.) High Sch., 1975-80, asst. prin., 1987-88, prin., 1989—; farmer, Killen, Ala., 1974-80; tchr. summer sch. Sheffield (Ala.) High Sch., 1977-78; dir. scholars program Muscle Shoals Schs., 1987-88; asst. prin. Avalon Mid. Sch., Muscle Shoals, 1987-88, prin., 1988-89; math. cons. Cartersville (Ga.) City Schs., 1991-92; curriculum cons. Eufaula (Ala.) High Sch., 1991-92; co-chmn. Ala. Learner Outcomes Com., Montgomery, 1991-92; dist. judge All-State Acad. Team, Athens, Ala., 1991-92; coach Ala. Mathcounts team NSPE, Birmingham, 1985. Dir. music and edn. Shoals Ch. of Christ, 1992. Named Outstanding Young Educator, No. Dist. Ala. Jaycees, 1987; Beeson fellow Samford U., 1987. Mem. ASCD, Nat. Assn. Secondary Sch. Prins., Am. Assn. Sch. Adminstrs., Ala. Coun. Sch. Adminstrs. and Suprs., Ala. Assn. Secondary Sch. Prins., Kappa Delta Pi, Phi Kappa Phi. Avocations: travel, stamp collecting, reading, bowling. Home: 1403 Brookford Pl Muscle Shoals AL 35661-2670 Office: Muscle Shoals High Sch 100 E Trojan Dr Muscle Shoals AL 35661-3173

SMITH, HARRY LEE, laboratory technician, chemist; b. Panama City, Fla., Oct. 19, 1936; s. Sanders and Pearl Jane (Williams) S. AA, Gulf Coast Coll., 1968; BS, U. Fla., Gainesville, 1971. Lab tech. St. Joe Paper Co., Port Saint Joe, Fla., 1955—; supt. St. Joe Stevedoring Co., Fla., 1985—; pres. St. Joe Papermakers Fed. Credit Union, Fla., 1968—; pres. Local 1713, St. Joe, Fla., 1992—. E3 U.S. Army, 1959-65. Mem. Mason, Scottish Rite. Home: PO Box 394 Port Saint Joe FL 32456-0394 Office: St Joe Papermakers Credit Union PO Box 236 Port Saint Joe FL 32456-0236

SMITH, HARVEY, social science research administrator. Dir. Social Sci. Rsch. Inst. No. Ill. U., De Kalb, Ill. Office: No Ill U Social Sci Rsch Inst De Kalb IL 60115*

SMITH, HARVEY ALVIN, mathematics educator, consultant; b. Easton, Pa., Jan. 30, 1932; s. William Augustus and Ruth Carolyn (Krauth) S.; m. Ruth Wismer Kolb, Aug. 27, 1955; children: Deirdre Lynn, Kirsten Nadine, Brinton Averill. B.S., Lehigh U., 1952; M.S., U. Pa., 1955, A.M., 1958, Ph.D., 1964. Asst. prof. math Drexel U., 1960-65; mem. tech. staff Inst. Def. Analyses, Arlington, Va., 1965-66; assoc. prof. math Oakland U., 1966-68; ops. research scientist Exec. Office of Pres., Washington, 1968-70; prof. math. Oakland U., 1970-77; prof. Ariz. State U., Tempe, 1977—; cons. Inst. Def. Analyses, 1967-69, Exec. Office Pres., 1967-73, U.S. Arms Control and Disarmament Agy, 1973-79, Los Alamos Nat. Lab. Author: Mathematical Foundation of Systems Analysis, 1969. NSF fellow, 1964-65; recipient Meritorious Service award Exec. Office of Pres., 1970. Mem. Soc. Indsl. and Applied Math., Am. Math. Soc., AAAS, Sigma Xi. Home: 18 E Concorda Dr Tempe AZ 85282-3517 Office: Ariz State U Dept Math Tempe AZ 85287

SMITH, HEDRICK LAURENCE, journalist, television comentator, author, lecturer; b. Kilmacolm, Scotland, July 9, 1933; s. Sterling L. and Phebe (Hedrick) S.; m. Ann Bickford, June 29, 1957 (div. Dec. 1985); children: Laurel Ann, Jennifer Laurence, Sterling Scott, Lesley Roberts; m. Susan Zox, Mar. 7, 1987. Grad., Choate Sch., 1951; BA, Williams Coll., 1955, LittD (hon.), 1975; postgrad. (Fulbright scholar), Balliol Coll., Oxford, Eng., 1955-56; LittD (hon.), Wittenburg U., 1985, N.H. Coll., 1991; LHD (hon.), Columbia Coll., 1992; LittD (hon.), Amherst Coll., 1992; LHD (hon.), U. S.C., 1992. With U.P.I., Memphis, Nashville, Atlanta, 1959-62; with N.Y. Times, 1962-88, Washington and S.E., 1962-63; with Vietnam, 1963-64; Middle East corr. N.Y. Times, Cairo, U.A.R., 1964-66; diplomatic news corr. N.Y. Times, Washington, 1962-64, 66-71; Moscow Bur. chief N.Y. Times, 1971-74, dep. nat. editor, 1975-76, Washington Bur. chief, 1976-79, chief Washington corr., 1980-85; Washington correspondent N.Y. Times mag., 1987-88; vis. journalist Am. Enterprise Inst., 1985-87; fellow Fgn. Policy Inst., Johns Hopkins U. Sch Advanced Internat. Studies, 1989—; panelist Washington Week in Rev., PBS, 1969—. Author: The Russians, 1975 (Overseas Press Club award 1976), The Power Game: How Washington Works, 1988, The New Russians, 1990 (Overseas Press Club citation 1991), Rethinking America, 1995; co-author: The Pentagon Papers, 1972, Reagan the Man, the President, 1981, Beyond Reagan: The Politics of Upheaval, 1986, Seven Days That Shook the World, 1991; TV documentaries Star Wars, 1985, Moscow Jews, 1986, Space Bridge, Chernobyl: Three Mile Island, 1987, 4-part Power Game series, PBS, 1989, Countdown to White House: The Bush Transition, 1989, 4-part series Inside Gorbachev's USSR, 1990 (George Polk award Gold Baton awarrd Columbia-Du Pont), Guns, Tanks and Gorbachev, 1991, Soviets, 1991 (George Peabody award), 4-part series PBS, Challenge to America, 1994, Across the River pub. TV program, 1995, The People and the Power Game, 1996 (Hillman award). Mem. Pulitzer prize team N.Y. Times, pub. svc. Pentagon Papers Series, 1972; trustee Williams Coll., 1982—. With USAF, 1956-59. Recipient Pulitzer prize for internat. reporting from Soviet Union and Ea. Europe, 1974; Nieman fellow Harvard U., 1969-70. Mem. Gridiron Club, Phi Beta Kappa.

SMITH, HENRY CHARLES, III, symphony orchestra conductor; b. Phila., Jan. 31, 1931; s. Henry Charles Jr. and Gertrude Ruth (Downs) S.; m. Mary Jane Dressner, Sept. 3, 1955; children—Katherine Anne, Pamela Jane, Henry Charles IV. BA, U. Pa., 1952; artist diploma, Curtis Inst. Music, Phila., 1955. Solo trombonist Phila. Orch., 1955-67; condr. Rochester (Minn.) Symphony Orch., 1967-68; assoc. prof. music Ind. U., Bloomington, 1968-71; resident condr., ednl. dir. Minn. Orch., Mpls., 1971-88; prof. music U. Tex., Austin, 1988-89, Frank C. Erwin Centennial Prof. of Opera, 1988-89; music dir. S.D. Symphony, Sioux Falls, 1989—; prof. Ariz. State U., Tempe, 1989-93, prof. emeritus, 1993—; vis. prof. U. Tex., Austin, 1987-88; founding mem. Phila. Brass Ensemble, 1956—. Composer 5 books of solos for trombone including Solos for the Trombone Player, 1963, Hear Us As We Pray, 1963, First Solos for the Trombone Player, 1972, Easy Duets for Winds, 1972; editor 14 books 20th century symphonies lit. Served to 1st lt. AUS, 1952-54. Recipient 3 Grammy nominations, 1967, 76, 1 Grammy award for best chamber music rec. with Phila. Brass Ensemble, 1969. Mem. Internat. Trombone Assn. (dir.), Am. Symphony Orch. League, Music Educators Nat. Conf., Am. Guild Organists, Am. Fedn. Musicians, Tubist Universal Brotherhood Assn., Acacia Fraternity. Republican. Congregationalist. Home: 8032 Pennsylvania Rd Bloomington MN 55438

SMITH, HENRY CLAY, retired psychology educator; b. Catonsville, Md., May 9, 1913; s. Harry C. and Lovell (Figgins) S.; m. Nancy Woollcott, Aug. 27, 1938; children—David Barton, Woollcott Keston, Barbara Sunderland. A.B. magna cum laude, St. John's Coll., Annapolis, Md., 1934; Ph.D., Johns Hopkins U., 1939. Instr. psychology U. Vt., Burlington, 1940-43; dir. tng. and research Western Electric Co., Balt., 1943-45; asso. prof. Knox Coll., Galesburg, Ill., 1945-46; asso. prof. psychology, chmn. dept. Hamilton Coll., Clinton, N.Y., 1946-49; prof. psychology Mich. State U., East Lansing, from 1949; ret., 1983; Fulbright research fellow, Italy, 1955-56; cons. prof. Waseda U., Tokyo, 1960. Author: Sensitivity Training, 2d edit, 1973, Personality Development, 2d edit, 1974; co-author: Social Perception, 1968, Psychology of Industrial Behavior, 3d edit, 1972, Ten Keys to Understanding People, 1987. Fellow APA; mem. Phi Beta Kappa. Home: PO Box 3086 West Tisbury MA 02575-3086

SMITH, HERALD ALVIN, JR., transportation executive; b. Beaconsfield, Iowa, Dec. 23, 1923; s. Herald Alvin and Iva Viola (Briggeman) S.; m. Miriam Gayle Armstrong, Oct. 5, 1946; children: Sharon Konchar, John, Susan Johnson, Jim. Student, U. Iowa, 1942-43, Coe Coll., Cedar Rapids, Iowa, 1944-45. Pres., chmn. bd. CRST, Inc., Cedar Rapids, 1955-77, chmn. bd., chief exec. officer, 1977-83; chmn. bd. CRST Internat., Inc., Cedar Rapids, 1983—; chmn. bd., pres. Crest Microfilm, Inc., Cedar Rapids, 1980—. Mem. Gov.'s Blue Ribbon Task Force on Transp., Iowa, 1982; trustee Regional Transit Authority, Cedar Rapids, 1967-78; campaign mgr. United Way, 1973-74; bd. dirs. CMC Colls. Associated, 1979, Cornell Coll., Mt. Vernon, Iowa, 1979-87, Four Oaks Treatment Ctr., 1986—. Mem. Am. Trucking Assn., Inc. (interstate carriers conf. 1st v.p. 1980-81, pres. 1981-82, chmn. 1982-83), Iowa Motor Truck Assn. (pres., chmn. bd. 1978-79, exec. bd. 1979—). Avocations: tennis, sailing, running a resort. Office: CRST Internat Inc 3930 16th Ave SW Cedar Rapids IA 52404-2332

SMITH, HILARY CRANWELL BOWEN, investment banker; b. Balt., Nov. 1, 1937; s. Henry Bowen and Clayton (Cranwell) S.; m. Janet Simmons, June 9, 1962. BA, Colgate U., 1960; MBA, U. Va., 1967. V.p. Goldman, Sachs & Co., N.Y.C., 1969-74, E. F. Hutton & Co., N.Y.C., 1974-77; sr. v.p. Blyth Eastman Dillon, N.Y.C., 1977-79; mng. dir. Salomon Bros., N.Y.C., 1979-90, Dillon, Read & Co., Inc., N.Y.C., 1990—. Lt. USN, 1960-63. Office: Dillon Read & Co Inc 535 Madison Ave Fl 15 New York NY 10022-4212

SMITH, HOKE LAFOLLETTE, university president; b. Galesburg, Ill., May 7, 1931; s. Claude Hoke and Bernice (LaFollette) S.; m. Barbara E. Walvoord, June 30, 1979; children by previous marriage: Kevin, Kerry, Amy, Glen. B.A. (Harold fellow), Knox Coll., 1953; M.A., U. Va., 1954; Ph.D. (fellow 1958), Emory U., 1958; hon. degree, Sung Kyun Kwan U., Korea, 1993, Knox Coll., 1995. Asst. prof. polit. sci. Hiram Coll., Ohio, 1958-64; assoc. prof. polit. sci. Hiram Coll., 1964-67; asst. to pres., prof. polit. sci. Drake U., Des Moines, Iowa, Md., 1967-70; chmn. interim governing com. Drake U., 1971-72, v.p. acad. adminstrn., 1970-79; pres. Towson (Md.) State U., 1979—; mem. univ. adv. council Life Ins. Council Am., 1969-71. Chmn. exec. com. Coun. Econ. Edn., Md., Towson, 1979—; bd. dirs. Balt. Coun. on Fgn. Rels.; chmn. Very Spl. Arts of Md. With U.S. Army, 1954-56. Recipient Eileen Tosney award Am. Assn. Univ Administrs., 1991; Congl. fellow Am. Polit. Sci. Assn., 1964-65. Mem. Am. Assn. State Colls. and Univs. (bd. dirs. 1984-88, bd. dirs. found., 1985-87, chmn. elect. 1985-86, chmn. 1986-87), Am. Coun. Edn. (bd. dirs., exec. com. 1988-94, chmn. elect 1991-92, chmn. 1992-93, past chmn. 1993-94), Am. Assn. Higher Edn., Soc. for Coll. and Univ. Planning (bd. dirs. 1986-88), Balt. C. of C. (adv. coun.), Phi Beta Kappa, Phi Kappa Phi, Omicron Delta Kappa, Delta Sigma Rho, Gamma Gamma, Pi Sigma Alpha. Office: Towson State U Office Pres Baltimore MD 21204

SMITH, HOWARD, film editor. Editor: (films) Live a Little, Steal a Lot, 1975, Mackintosh & T.J., 1975, Tex, 1982, Twilight Zone-The Movie ("Terror at 20,000 Feet"), 1983, (with David Garfield and Suzanne Petit) Sylvester, 1985, (with David Bretherton) Baby-Secret of the Lost Legend, 1985, At Close Range, 1986, Near Dark, 1987, (with Sonya Sones Tramer) River's Edge, 1987, The Abyss, 1989, Big Man on Campus, 1989, (with Joel Goodman and Conrad Buff) After Dark, My Sweet, 1990, Point Break, 1991, Glengarry Glen Ross, 1992, The Saint of Fort Washington, 1993, Two Bits,

1994, (TV movies) Flying Blind, 1990. Office: care Lawrence Mirisch The Mirisch Agency 10100 Santa Monica Blvd Ste 700 Los Angeles CA 90067-4011

SMITH, HOWARD MCQUEEN, librarian; b. Charlotte, N.C., July 25, 1919; s. Daniel Holt and Pearl Elizabeth (Truitt) S.; m. Elaine Betty Wiefel, June 27, 1949; children: Leslie, Steven Holt. B.A., U. Va., 1941; A.B. in L.S, U. Mich., 1946, M. Pub. Adminstrn., 1947. Reference asst. Enoch Pratt Free Library, Balt., 1947-49; coordinator library activities Richmond (Va.) Area Univ. Center, 1949-50; exec. asst. to dir. Enoch Pratt Free Library, 1950-53, head films dept., 1953-55; personnel officer Free Library Phila., 1955-59; city librarian Richmond Pub. Library, 1959-84. Served to lt. (s.g.) USNR, 1942-46. Mem. ALA.

SMITH, HOWARD ROSS, economics educator, academic administrator, researcher, consultant; b. Des Moines, July 6, 1917; s. John Truman and Miriam Sylvia (Ross) S.; m. Gwendolyn Thomas Collins, Feb. 20, 1943; children—David, Janet, Richard. A.B., Simpson Coll., 1938; M.A., La. State U., 1940, Ph.D., 1945. Instr. La. State U., Baton Rouge, 1940-43; economist War Prodn. Bd., Washington, 1943-46; assoc. prof. U. Ga., Athens, 1946-49, prof., 1949—, dept. head, 1963-76. Author: Economic History of U.S., 1955, Government and Business, 1958, Democracy and Public Interest, 1960, The Capitalist Imperative, 1975, Management, 1980. Rockefeller Found. fellow, 1948-49; recipient Ford Found. award, Egypt, 1961-63; Fulbright award, Columbia, 1973. Mem. Acad. Mgmt. Democrat. Presbyterian. Home: 382 Westview Dr Athens GA 30606-4636 Office: Univ Ga Athens GA 30602

SMITH, HOWARD RUSSELL, manufacturing company executive; b. Clark County, Ohio, Aug. 15, 1914; s. Lewis Hoskins and Eula (Elder) S.; m. Jeanne Rogers, June 27, 1942; children: Stewart Russell, Douglas Howard, Jeanne Ellen Smith James. A.B., Pomona Coll., 1936. Security analyst Kidder, Peabody & Co., N.Y.C., 1936-37; economist ILO, Geneva, 1937-40; asst. to pres. Blue Diamond Corp., Los Angeles, 1940-46; pres., dir. Avery Dennison Corp., Pasadena, Calif., 1946-75, chmn. bd., 1975-84, chmn. exec. com., 1984-95; dir. emeritus, 1995—; chmn. bd. Kinsmith Fin. Corp., San Marino, Calif., 1979—. Bd. dirs., past pres., chmn. Los Angeles Philharm. Assn.; chmn. emeritus, bd. trustees Pomona Coll., Claremont, Calif.; past chmn. bd. Children's Hosp. Los Angeles, Community TV of So. Calif. (Sta. KCET), Los Angeles. With USNR, 1943-46. Home: 1458 Hillcrest Ave Pasadena CA 91106-4503 Office: Avery Dennison Corp 150 N Orange Grove Blvd Pasadena CA 91103-3534

SMITH, IAN CORMACK PALMER, biophysicist; b. Winnipeg, Man., Can., Sept. 23, 1939; s. Cormack and Grace Mary S.; m. Eva Gunilla Landvik, Mar. 27, 1965; children: Brittmarie, Cormack, Duncan, Roderick. BS, U. Man., 1961, MS, 1962; PhD, Cambridge U., England, 1965; Filosophie Doktor (hon.), U. Stockholm, 1986; DSc (hon.), U. Winnipeg, 1990; Diploma Tech. (hon.), Red River Coll., 1996. Fellow Stanford U., 1965-66; mem. rsch. staff Bell Tel. Labs., Murray Hill, N.J., 1966-67; rsch. officer divsn. biol. scis. NRC, Ottawa, 1967-87, dir. gen., 1987-91; dir.-gen. Inst. Biodiagnostics, Winnipeg, 1992—; adj. prof. chemistry and biochemistry Carleton U., 1973-90, U. Ottawa, 1976-92; adj. prof. chemistry, physics and anatomy U. Man., 1992—; adj. prof. biophysics U. Ill., Chgo., 1974-80; allied scientist Ottawa Civic Hosp., 1985—, Ottawa Gen. Hosp., 1989—, Ont. Cancer Found., 1989-91, St. Boniface Hosp., 1992—, Health Scis. Ctr., 1993—, Econ. Tech. Innovation Coun., Man., 1994—, exec. com., 1995—, Man. Health Rsch. Coun., 1995—. Contbr. chps. to books, articles in field to profl. jours. Recipient Barringer award Can. Spectroscopy Soc., 1979, Herzberg award, 1986, Organon Teknika award Can. Soc. Clin. Chemists, 1987, Sr. Scientist award Sigma Xi, 1995. Fellow Chem. Inst. Can. (Merck award 1978, Labatt award 1984), Royal Soc. Can. (Flavelle medal 1996), Soc. Magnetic Resonance Medicine (exec. com. 1989-94); mem. Internat. Coun. Sci. Unions (gen. com. 1993—), Am. Chem. Soc., Biophys. Soc., Can. Biochem. Soc. (Ayerst award 1978), Biophys. Soc. Can. (pres. 1992-94), Internat. Union Pure and Applied Biophysics (coun. 1993—), U. Man. Alumni Assn. (bd. dirs. 1993—). Office: Inst Biodiagnostics, Winnipeg, MB Canada R3B 1Y6

SMITH, ILEENE A., book editor; b. N.Y.C., Jan. 21, 1953; d. Norman and Jeanne (Jaffe) S.; m. Howard A. Sobel, June 3, 1979; children: Nathaniel Jacob, Rebecca Julia. BA, Brandeis U., Waltham, Mass., 1975; MA, Columbia U., 1978. Editorial asst. Atheneum Publishers, N.Y.C., 1979-82; sr. editor Summit Books, N.Y.C., 1982-91, lit. editor, 1991-92; edit. cons. The Elie Wiesel Found. for Humanity, 1993—; editl. cons. Marsalis on Music; cons. editor Paris Rev., N.Y., 1987—. Author introductory scripts for Met. Opera Telecasts, 1987-93. Jerusalem fellow, 1987; recipient Tony Godwin Meml. award, 1982, PEN/Roger Klein award for editl. excellence, 1988, Contbg. to Prodn. of Aida cert. NATAS, 1990.

SMITH, IVAN HURON, architect; b. Danville, Ind., Jan. 25, 1907; s. Calvin Wesley and Irma (Huron) S.; m. Sara Butler, Aug. 18, 1972; 1 child by previous marriage, Norma Smith Benton. Student, Ga. Inst. Tech., 1926; B.Arch., U. Fla., 1929. With Ivan H. Smith (architect), 1936-41; partner Reynolds, Smith & Hills (architects and engrs.), Jacksonville, Fla., 1941-70; chmn. bd. emeritus Reynolds, Smith & Hills (Architects, Engrs., Planners, Inc.), Jacksonville, Tampa, Orlando, Merritt Island and Ft. Lauderdale, Fla., 1971-77; sec. Jacksonville Bldg. Code Adv. Bd., 1951-68; mem. Duval County Govt. Study Commn., 1966-67; chmn. Jacksonville Constrn. Trades Qualification Bd., 1971. Important works include City Hall, Jacksonville, Duval County Ct. House, Jacksonville, Baptist Hosp, Jacksonville, Engring. Bldg, Nuclear Sci. Bldg, Fla. Field Stadium at, U. Fla.; dormitories Council Bldg, Jacksonville U.; fed. bldgs., Jacksonville, Gainesville, Fla., So. Bell Telephone bldgs; Internat. Airport, Tampa, Fla.; (with Edward Durell Stone) Fla. State Capitol Center. Mem. council Jacksonville U., 1958-76; pres. Jacksonville Humane Soc., 1956-59; bd. dirs. Jacksonville-Duval Safety Council. Served with USNR, 1943-45. Recipient U. Fla. Disting. Alumnus award, 1981, Jacksonville U. Order of the Dolphin, 1985; Paul Harris fellow, 1980. Fellow AIA (Outstanding Service award Fla. region 1965, chpt. pres. 1942, 56); mem. Fla. Assn. Architects (dir. 1957, Gold medal 1981), Jacksonville C. of C. (dir. 1957-59), Beta Theta Pi, Phi Kappa Phi, Sigma Tau. Clubs: Gargoyle (U. Fla.); River (Jacksonville), Univ. (Jacksonville), San Jose Country (Jacksonville), Epping Forest Yacht (Jacksonville), Rotary (Jacksonville, Paul Harris fellow 1980). Home: 6000 San Jose Blvd # 201 Jacksonville FL 32217-2381 Office: 4651 Salisbury Rd Jacksonville FL 32256-6107

SMITH, J. BRIAN, advertising executive, public affairs consultant, campaign management firm executive; b. Boston, Jan. 25, 1950; s. Leonard Francis and Rose Geraldine (McDonald) S.; children: Maris, Daniel, Brian, Michael. BA, Loyola Coll., 1971. Chief writer domestic affairs Rep. Nat. Com., Washington, 1971-72; press sec.to John J. Rhodes of Ariz. U.S. Ho. Minority Leader, Washington, 1973-76; pres. Smith & Harroff, Inc., Washington, 1976. Contbr. numerous articles to profl. jours., popular mags; scriptwriter documentary films; polit. commentator for many TV, radio programs. Bd. dirs. Alexandria (Va.) Country Day Sch., 1989-94. Mem. Am. Assn. Polit. Cons. Roman Catholic. Office: Smith & Harroff Inc 99 Canal Center Plz Ste 200 Alexandria VA 22314-1595

SMITH, J. E. GENE, electric power industry executive. V. chmn. Ala. Electric Coop., Andalusia, Ala.; CEO Florida Electric Coop Assoc., De Funiak Springs, FL. Office: Florida Electric Coop Assoc. 1350 West Baldwin De Funiak Springs FL 32433*

SMITH, J. KELLUM, JR., foundation executive, lawyer; b. N.Y.C., June 18, 1927; s. James Kellum and Elizabeth Dexter (Walker) S.; m. Sarah Tod Lohmann, July 22, 1950 (div. 1993); children: Alison Andrews, Timothy Kellum, Jennifer Harlow, Christopher Lohmann; m. Angela Marina Brown, Feb. 3, 1995. Grad., Phillips Exeter Acad., 1945; A.B. magna cum laude, Amherst Coll., 1950; LL.B., Harvard, 1953. Bar: N.Y. 1955. Assoc. Lord, Day & Lord, N.Y.C., 1953-59; asst. sec. John Simon Guggenheim Meml. Found., 1960-62; mem. staff Rockefeller Found., 1962-74, asst. sec., 1963-64, sec., 1964-74; v.p., sec. Andrew W. Mellon Found., N.Y.C., 1974-89, sr. fellow, 1989-92; sr. advisor, 1992—. Trustee Nat. Sculpture Soc., 1955-71, Nat. Ins. Archtl. Edn., 1961-69, St. Bernard's Sch., N.Y.C., 1968-78, Found. for Child Devel., 1968-74; trustee Brearley Sch., N.Y.C., 1964-80, pres., 1973-78; trustee Am. Acad. in Rome, 1964-95, treas., 1965-66, 2d v.p., 1968-72, 84-88, sec., 1973-84, 89-95. With USAAF, 1945-46. Mem. Phi Beta Kappa. Club: Century Association (N.Y.C.). Home: 550 Number 37 Rd Saranac NY 12981-2956 Office: Mellon Found 140 E 62nd St New York NY 10021-8142

SMITH, J. ROY, education educator; b. Washington, Ga., Sept. 13, 1936; s. James Roy and Nellie Irene (Mansfield) S. BA, Mercer U., 1956; postgrad., Brown U., 1957; cert., Oxford U., Eng., 1963. Tchr. City of Cranston, R.I., 1957-59; with Charleston County, Charleston, S.C., 1962-64, 76-79; tchr. Fulton County, Fairburn, Ga., 1965-76, Berkeley County, Moncks Corner, S.C., 1979-94. Lt. (j.g.) USN, 1959-62. Charleston Area Writing Project fellow; recipient English Speaking Union scholarship Oxford U., 1963; Newspaper Fund of the Wall Street Jour. fellow. Mem. SAR (sec./treas. S.C. Soc. 1977-78), Soc. Second War with Great Britain, Sons and Daus. of Pilgrims (gov. Ga. br. 1976, hon. gov. 1976—), S.C. Hist. Soc., Ga. Hist. Soc., Kappa Phi Kappa (registered tour guide, lectr.). Home and Office: 110 Coming St Charleston SC 29403-6103

SMITH, J. STEVEN, electric power industry executive. MBA, Ind. U., 1977. Asst. dir. Ind. Statewide Assn. Rural Electric Coops., 1974-77; with Hoosier Energy Rural Electric Coop., Bloomington, Ind., 1977—, sr. v.p., 1991, now pres., CEO. Office: Hoosier Energy Rural Elec Coop PO Box 908 Bloomington IN 47402*

SMITH, J. W., dean. Exec. dean N.D. State U., Bottineau. Office: ND State U Bottineau Office Exec Dean Bottineau ND 58318

SMITH, JACK, food service executive. Prtn. Smith Realty, Grundy, Va., 1955—; chmn. K-VA-T Food Stores, Grundy, Va. Office: K-VA-T Food Stores 329 N Main St Grundy VA 24614*

SMITH, JACK PRESCOTT, journalist; b. Paris, Apr. 25, 1945; s. Howard Kingsbury and Benedicte (Traberg) S.; divorced; 1 child, Alexander Kingsbury. BA in History, Carnegie-Mellon U., 1971, Oxford (Eng.) U., 1974. Writer-producer Sta. WIIC-TV News, Pitts., 1969-70; producer-reporter Sta. WLS-TV News, Chgo., 1974-76; fgn. corr. ABC-TV News, Paris, 1976-80; corr. ABC-TV News, Washington, 1980—. Served with inf. U.S. Army, 1964-67. Decorated Purple Heart, Army Commendation medal; recipient citation for best mag. reporting in fgn. affairs Overseas Press Club, 1967. Office: ABC News 1717 Desales St NW Washington DC 20036-4401

SMITH, JACKIE, former professional football player. Student, Northwestern Louisiana State U. With St. Louis Cardinals, 1963-77, Dallas Cowboys, 1978. NFL Hall of Fame, 1994. Retired as the leading receiver among tightends. Office: care Pro Football Hall of Fame 2121 George Halas Dr NW Canton OH 44708-2630

SMITH, JAMES A., lawyer; b. Akron, Ohio, June 11, 1930; s. Barton H. and Myrna S. (Young) S.; m. Melda I. Perry, Jan. 17, 1959; children: Hugh, Sarah Louise. AB, Western Res. U., 1952; postgrad., Columbia U., 1954-56, LLB, 1961; postgrad., Yale U., 1956-58. Bar: Ohio 1961, U.S. Dist. Ct. (no. dist.) Ohio 1963, U.S. Ct. Appeals (6th cir.) 1973, U.S. Supreme Ct. 1974, U.S. Ct. Appeals (11th cir.) 1983, U.S. Ct. Appeals (D.C. cir.) 1984. Assoc. Squire, Sanders and Dempsey, Cleve., 1961-70, ptnr., 1970-91, counsel, 1991-96; mem. spl. adv. com. Nat. Conf. Commrs. on Uniform State Laws, 1972-74. Trustee Chagrin Falls Community Park, 1968-78, Greater Cleve. Neighborhood Ctrs. Assn., 1973-78, Legal Aid Soc. Cleve., 1977-80, Cleve. Inst. Music, 1994—; mem. Charter Rev. Commn., Chagrin Falls, 1966. Lt. (j.g.) USNR, 1952-54. Fellow Am. Coll. Trial Lawyers; mem. ABA, Ohio Bar Assn., Cleve. Bar Assn. (trustee 1988-92), U.S. Ct. Appeals for 6th Cir. Jud. Conf. (life), Ohio Ct. Appeals for 8th Jud. Dist. Conf. (life), Am. Inns of Ct. (master of bench), Ct. of Nisi Prius (clk. 1975-76, judge 1994-95), Phi Beta Kappa, Omicron Delta Kappa, Delta Sigma Rho. Democrat.

SMITH, JAMES BARRY, lawyer; b. N.Y.C., Feb. 28, 1947; s. Irving and Vera (Donaghy) S.; m. Kathleen O'Connor, May 28, 1977; childen: Jennifer, Kelly. BA in Econs., Colgate U., 1968; JD, Boston U., 1974. Assoc. McDermott, Will & Emery, Chgo., 1974-78; assoc. Coffield, Ungaretti & Harris, Chgo., 1978-80, ptnr., 1980—, head real estate dept., 1988—. Lt. U.S. Navy, 1968-70. Mem. Chgo. Bar Assn., Chgo. Mortgage Atty. Assn. Avocations: sports, reading, travel. Office: Coffield Ungaretti & Harris 3500 Three First Nat Pla Chicago IL 60602

SMITH, JAMES C., telecommunications industry executive. V.p. The Ohio Bell Tele. Co., Cleve., 1992—. Office: The Ohio Bell Tel Co 45 Erieview Plz Cleveland OH 44114-1814*

SMITH, JAMES EDWARD, newspaper company executive; b. N.Y.C., June 26, 1945; s. James Edward and Loretta Anne (Johnston) S.; m. Beverly Lynn Jermyn, Feb. 23, 1980; children: Allison Bridget, Cori Patricia. BA, State U. N.Y., 1969; MA, Cornell U., 1973, PhD, 1976. Asst. prof. Sociology, U. Miami, Coral Gables, Fla., 1973-80; research mgr. News & Sun-Sentinel Co., Ft. Lauderdale, Fla., 1980—; v.p. mktg., v.p./dir. mktg. and promotion Ft. Lauderdale Sun Sentinel, 1991—; bd. dirs. Newspaper Research Council Des Moines. Contbr. articles to profl. jours. Mem. Syndicated Research Task Force, N.Y.C., 1987-, Future Advt. Task Force on Mktg. Data, N.Y.C., 1986-87; pres. Econ. Forum Broward, 1982-85; research chmn. Broward Tourist Devel. Council, 1984--; research cons. Discovery Ctr., Ft. Lauderdale, 1988. Recipient Gavel award Am. Bar Assn., 1981. Mem. Leadership Broward (Best Group 1986), Leadership Broward Alumni. Home: 9321 NW 10th Ct Fort Lauderdale FL 33322-4929 Office: News & Sun-Sentinel Co 200 E Las Olas Blvd Fort Lauderdale FL 33301-2293

SMITH, J(AMES) E(VERETT) KEITH, psychologist, educator; b. Royal, Iowa, Apr. 30, 1928; s. James H. and Naomi Dorothy (James) S.; m. Greta Standish, Sept. 10, 1949. B.S. in Math, Iowa State U., 1949; A.M. in Psychology, U. Mich., 1952, Ph.D., 1954. Staff psychologist Mass. Inst. Tech., Lincoln Lab., Cambridge, Mass., 1954-64; research psychologist Mental Health Research Inst., Ann Arbor, Mich., 1964-67; prof. psychology U. Mich., Ann Arbor, 1964—; prof. statistics U. Mich., 1977—, chmn. dept. psychology, 1971-76; lectr. Brandeis U., 1960. Cons. editor Psychol. Bull., 1967-70; editor Jour. Math. Psychology, 1971-74. Mem. Commn. on Human Factors, NRC, 1980-82. hon. Research fellow Univ. Coll., London, 1972; mem. rev. panels NSF, 1972-74, Nat. Inst. Gen. Med. Sci., 1967-71; vis. scholar Beijing U., 1985; chmn. spl. study sect. NIH, 1985. Fellow Am. Psychol. Assn.; mem. Am. Statis. Assn., Psychometric Soc., Inst. Math. Statis., Sigma Xi, Phi Kappa Phi, Pi Mu Epsilon, Delta Upsilon. Home: 1160 Heatherway St Ann Arbor MI 48104-2838

SMITH, JAMES GILBERT, electrical engineer; b. Benton, Ill., May 1, 1930; s. Jesse and Ruby Frances S.; m. Barbara Ann Smothers, July 29, 1955; 1 child, Julie. B.S. in Elec. Enging, U. Mo., Rolla, 1957, M.S., 1959, Ph.D., 1967. Instr., then asst. prof. U. Mo., Rolla, 1958-66; mem. faculty So. Ill. U., Carbondale, 1966-93, prof. elec. enging., 1972-93, chmn. dept. elec. scis. and systems enging., 1971-80, prof. emeritus, 1993—. Served with AUS, 1951-53, Korea. Decorated Bronze Star. Faculty fellow NSF, 1961. Mem. Rotary (Paul Harris fellow 1988). Office: So Ill U Coll Engring Carbondale IL 62901

SMITH, JAMES JOHN, physiologist; b. St. Paul, Jan. 28, 1914; s. James W. and Catherine (Welsch) S.; m. Mariellen Schumacher, Mar. 17, 1945 (dec.); children: Philip W., Lucy G. Shaker, Paul R., Gregory K. M.D., St. Louis U., 1937; Ph.D., Northwestern U., 1946. Intern St. Paul-Ramsey Med. Ctr., 1937-38; fellow in pathology Cook County Hosp., Chgo., 1938-39; Koesler research fellow in physiology Northwestern U., Chgo., 1939-41; dean Stritch Sch. Med., Loyola U., 1946-50, assoc. prof. physiology, 1946-50; chief edn. div., dept. medicine and surgery VA, 1950-52; prof., dir. dept. physiology Med. Coll. Wis., Milw., 1952-79; prof. physiology and medicine Med. Coll. Wis., 1979—; dir. human performance lab. and dep. dir. Cardiopulmonary Rehab. Ctr. VA Med. Ctr., Milw., 1978—; assoc. clin. prof. George Washington U. 1950-52 Fulbright research prof. U. Heidelberg, Physiology Inst., Germany, 1959-60; medico-legal cons. on retirement policy for high stress professions. Author textbooks on circulatory physiology, numerous articles in field. Decorated Legion of Merit; recipient Disting. Service award Med. Coll. Wis., 1982. Mem. Soc. Exptl. Biology, Am. Physiol. Soc., Am. Gerontol. Assn., Sigma Xi. Roman Catholic. Researcher in aviation medicine, U.S. Air Force, 1941-46. Home: 11050 W Maple Ln Milwaukee WI 53225-4428 Office: 8701 W Watertown Plank Rd Milwaukee WI 53226-3548

SMITH, JAMES LAWRENCE, research physicist; b. Detroit, Sept. 3, 1943; s. William Leo and Marjorie Marie (Underwood) S.; m. Carol Ann Adam, Mar. 27, 1965; children: David Adam, William Leo. BS, Wayne State U., 1965; PhD, Brown U., 1974. Mem. staff Los Alamos (N.Mex.) Nat. Lab., 1973-82, fellow, 1982-86, dir. ctr. materials sci., 1986-87, fellow, 1987—; chief scientist Superconductivity Tech. Ctr., 1988-95; co-editor Philos. Mag., 1990-95; editor Philos. Mag. B., 1995—. Contbr. articles to profl. jours. Recipient E.O. Lawrence award, 1986, Disting. Alumni award Wayne State U., 1993. Fellow Am. Phys. Soc. (internat. prize for new materials 1990); mem. AAAS, Materials Rsch. Soc., Minerals Metals Materials Soc., Am. Crystallographic Assn. Achievements include patents for design of magnetic field and high-strength conductors. Office: Los Alamos Nat Lab Superconductivity Tech Ctr Mail Stop K763 Los Alamos NM 87545

SMITH, JAMES LOUIS, III, lawyer; b. Fort Worth, Tex., Mar. 21, 1943; s. James Louis Jr. and Ellen Vickers (Smedley) S.; m. Jane Benton, Mar. 25, 1965 (div. Oct. 1982); children: Rebecca, Sarah; m. Sandra Howell, Dec. 29, 1984; stepchildren: Kristen, Mason. BA cum laude with distinction, Dartmouth Coll., 1965; JD, Duke U., 1968. Bar: Ga. Assoc. Sutherland, Asbill & Brennan, Atlanta, 1968-74, ptnr., 1974-82; shareholder Trotter Smith & Jacobs, Atlanta, 1983-92; ptnr. Troutman Sanders, Atlanta, 1992—. Contbr. articles profl. jours.; mng. editor Duke Law Jour. Chmn. legal divsn. United Way, 1989, fundraiser, mem. allocation com. homeless and hungry, 1991, 92; co-chmn. pledge fulfillment com. YES! Atlanta Coun., 1991-92; mem. adv. com. Atlanta Vols. Lawyers Found.; mem. Assn. Corp. Growth, Northwest Presbyn. Ch. Mem. ABA (fed. securities law com. 1933 act registration statements subcom., ptnrships and unicorp. bus. orgns. com. bus. law sect.), State Bar Ga. (chmn. corp. and banking law sect., chmn. gen. ptnrship and limited ptnrship law revision coms. corp. sect. 1982-91, chmn. subcom. Ga. bus. corp. code rev. com. 1987-89, exec. com. corp. and banking law sect. 1982-91, lectr. ann. corp. and banking law inst. 1983, 87-88, 90-91, 93), Atlanta Bar (lectr. ann. corp. bus. seminar 1983, 88, advanced securities seminar 1989, 94), Practicing Law Inst. (lectr. securities fillings 1994-95), Order of Coif. Presbyterian. Avocations: canoeing, hiking, tennis, jogging, travel. Office: Troutman Sanders 600 Peachtree St NE Atlanta GA 30308-2216

SMITH, JAMES MORTON, museum administrator, historian; b. Bernie, Mo., May 28, 1919; BEd, So. Ill. U., 1941; MA, U. Okla., 1946; PhD, Cornell U., 1951; DHL (hon.), Widener U., 1984; m. Kathryn Hegler, Jan. 5, 1945; children: Melissa Jane, James Morton. Editor, Inst. Early Am. History and Culture, Williamsburg, Va., 1955-66; prof. history Cornell U., Ithaca, N.Y., 1966-70, U. Del., Newark, 1976-90; dir. State Hist. Soc. Wis., Madison, 1970-76, Henry Francis DuPont Winterthur (Del.) Mus., 1976-84. Lt. USCGR, 1943-45. Mem. Assn. Art Mus. Dirs., Am. Assn. Museums, Am. Hist. Assn., Orgn. Am. Historians, Am. Assn. State and Local History, Soc. Historians of Early Am. Republic. Author: Freedom's Fetters, 1956, Liberty and Justice, 1958, Seventeenth-Century America, 1959, George Washington: A Profile, 1969, The Constitution, 1971, Politics and Society in American History, 1973, The Republic of Letters, 1995. Home: 120 Sharpless Dr Elkton MD 21921-2073

SMITH, JAMES OSCAR (JIMMY SMITH), jazz organist; b. Norristown, Pa., Dec. 8, 1928; s. James and Grace Elizabeth (Weldon) S.; m. Edna Joy Goins, Mar. 31, 1957; children: James Oscar, Jia Charlene. Student, Ornstein Sch. Music, Phila., 1946-49. Jazz organist, 1951—; owner, dir. Edmy Music Pub. Co., 1962—, Trieste Builders Co., 1962—, Jay Cec Corp., 1962—; appeared at Antibes (Frances) Jazz Festival, 1962, Complain-de-Tour Jazz Festival, Belgium, 1963. composer, performer background music film Where the Spies Are, 1965; composer music film La Metamorphose de Clopertes, 1965; performed with Art Blakey, Stanley Turrentine, Jackie McLean, Hank Mobley, others; composer numerous organ pieces; compiler organ books; numerous recordings including The Sermon, A Walk on the Wild Side, Got My Mojo Working, Slaughter On Tenth Avenue, Bluesette, House Party, 1985, Plays the Blues, 1988, Midnight Special, 1989, Best Of, 1991, Fourmost, 1991, Sum Serious Blues, 1993. Recipient downbeat Mag's. Reader and Critics award, 1962, 63, 64; also downbeat Mag's. Reader's Poll, 1989. Mem. Broadcast Music Inc., AFTRA, NAACP, Nat. Acad. Recording Arts and Scis. Lodge: Masons. Office: care Abby Hoffer 22312 E 48th St New York NY 10017-1538 Office: care CEMA 1750 Vine St Los Angeles CA 90028-5247

SMITH, JAMES PATRICK, economist; b. Bklyn., Aug. 3, 1943; s. James P. and Winefred (Harrison) S.; m. Sandra Berry, Oct. 25, 1983; children: Gillian Claire, Lauren Teresa. B.S., Fordham U., 1965; Ph.D., U. Chgo., 1972. Research assoc. Nat. Bur. Econ. Research, N.Y.C., 1972-74; sr. economist Rand Corp., Santa Monica, Calif., 1974—, dir. of research labor and population, 1977—. bd. mem. Occupational Safety and Health Standards State Calif. Editor: Female Labor Supply, 1980; bd. editors Am. Econ. Rev., 1980-83; author articles in field. Recipient Merit award NIH, 1995—. Mem. NIA (steering com., health and retirement survey), Nat. Adv. Bd. Poverty Inst. Mem. Am. Econ. Assn., Phi Beta Kappa. Office: RAND PO Box 2138 Santa Monica CA 90407-2138

SMITH, JAMES ROLAND, state legislator; b. Aiken, S.C., Feb. 26, 1933; s. Walter Daniel and Maebell Smith; m. Peggy Cato, Mar. 3, 1953; children: Garry R., Todd D., Caroline M. Student, Oral Roberts Univ., U. S.C., So. Meth. U.; DDiv, Universal Bible Inst., 1975. Rural postal carrier U.S. Postal Svc., Warrenville, S.C., 1969-88; min. Aiken, S.C., 1965—; legislator S.C. Ho. of Reps., Columbia, 1989—. Dir. Beech Island (S.C.) Rural Water Dist., 1973-83; bd. dirs. Aiken County Bd. Edn., 1983-88. Mem. Am. Legion (post 153), Midland Valley C. of C., Midland Valley Lions Club, Graniteville (S.C.) Exch. Club, Beech Island Agriculture Club, Jackson Agriculture Club. Republican. Avocation: family. Home: PO Drawer D Langley SC 29834 Office: SC Ho of Reps 416 Beatty Rd Bldg B Columbia SC 29210-4620

SMITH, JAMES TODD See LL COOL J

SMITH, JAMES WALKER, lawyer; b. S.I., N.Y., May 11, 1957; s. James Patrick and Ann Catherine (Sullivan) S.; m. Erin Patricia Murphy, Aug. 15, 1982; children: Patrick James, Daniel Timothy, Meghan Kathleen, James John. BA magna cum laude, Fordham U., 1979, JD, 1982; LLM, NYU, 1988. BAr: N.Y. 1983, N.J. 1984, Pa. 1993, U.S. Supreme Ct. 1994. Assoc. Mendes & Mount, N.Y.C., 1982, Costello Shea & Gaffney, N.Y.C., 1982-86; ptnr. Anderson Kill Olick & Oshinsky P.C., N.Y.C., 1986—; arbitrator N.Y.C. (N.Y.) Civil Ct., 1987-89; faculty chairperson hosp. law Fordham Law Sch., N.Y.C., 1989-93; mediator U.S. Dist. Ct. (so. dist.) N.Y., N.Y.C., 1992—. Author: Hospital Liability, 1985—; editor-in-chief: New York Practice Guide, 1993—; contbg. editor Medical Malpractice Law and Strategy, 1993—; bd. editors Fordham Urban Law Jour., 1981-82. Mem. N.Y. County Lawyer's Assn. (com. on tort law 1993-95), Assn. of the Bar of the City of N.Y. (com. on tort law 1990-92, com. on state cts. 1994—). Roman Catholic. Avocations: golf, coaching youth basketball. Home: 28 Rokeby Pl Staten Island NY 10310 Office: Anderson Kill Olick & Oshinsky 1251 Avenue of the Americas New York NY 10020

SMITH, JAMES WARREN, pathologist, microbiologist, parasitologist; b. Logan, Utah, July 5, 1934; s. Kenneth Warren and Nina Lou (Sykes) S.; m. Nancy Chesterman, July 19, 1958; children: Warren, Scott. BS, U. Iowa, 1956, MD, 1959. Diplomate Am. Bd. Pathology. Intern, Colo. Gen. Hosp., Denver, 1959-60; resident U. Iowa Hosps., Iowa City, 1960-65; asst. prof. pathology U. Vt., Burlington, 1967-70; prof. pathology Ind. U., Indpls., 1970—, chmn. dept. pathology and lab. med., 1992—. Contbr. articles to profl. jours. Served to lt. comdr. USN, 1965-67. Recipient Oustanding Contbrn. to Clin. Microbiology award South Central Assn. Clin. Microbiology, 1977. Fellow Coll. Am. Pathologists (chmn. microbiology resource com. 1981-85), Infectious Disease Soc. Am., Am. Soc. Investigative

Pathology, Royal Soc. Tropical Medicine and Hygiene, AMA, Am. Soc. Clin. Pathology, Am. Soc. Microbiology, Am. Soc. Tropical Medicine and Hygiene, U.S.-Can. Acad. Pathology, Assn. Pathology Chairs, Binford Dammin Soc. Infectious Disease Pathologists. Soc. Protozoologists Office: Ind Univ Med Ctr 635 Barnhill Dr Rm 128A Indianapolis IN 46202-5120

SMITH, JANE FARWELL, civic worker; b. Chgo.; d. John Charles and Jessie Greene (Delaware) Farwell; m. Wakelee R. Smith, Feb. 7, 1929; children—Diana Jane Smith Gauss, Carol Louise Smith Anderson. Student, U. Chgo., 1925-28. Pres. Infant Soc. Chgo., Beverly Hills (Ill.) Center, 1949; chmn. Am. heritage com. DAR, Ill., 1963-65; Am. heritage com. nat. vice chmn. DAR, 1965-68, Insignia chmn., Ill., 1966, Ill. treas., 1966-68, mem. nat. Americanism and manual for citizenship com., 1968, Ill. regent, 1969-71; mem. U.S.A. Bicentennial Commn., DAR, 1971-74; nat. corr. sec. gen. DAR, 1971-74, 1st. v.p. gen., 1974-75, pres. gen., 1975-77, hon. life pres. gen., 1977-81, mem. long range planning commn., 1988-93; trustee U.S. Capitol Hist. Soc., 1976-82; pres. 4th Div. Ex-Regents Club, 1981-82. Mem. Kate Duncan Sch. Bd., Grant, Ala., 1975-86, Tamassee Sch. Bd., Tamassee, S.C., 1975-77. Recipient Gold medal of appreciation Ill. chpt. S.A.R., 1970, resolution of congratulation Senate of 80th Assembly of State of Ill., 1977. Mem. Nat. Gavel Soc. (life), DAR (pres. exec. club 1983-85, pres. nat. officers' club 1986-88), DAR Museum (life), Daus. Colonial Wars, Nat. Soc. New Eng. Women, Alden Kindred Am., Colonial Dames Am., Daus. Am. Colonists, Daus. Founders and Patriots, Nat. Soc. Women Desc. Ancient and Hon. Arty. Co., Am. Nat. Soc. Old Plymouth Colony Descs., Soc. Mayflower Descs., Colonial Daus. 17th Century, Hereditary Order of First Families of Mass., Colonial Wars Nat. Soc., New. Eng. Women. Episcopalian. Home: 851 W Heather Ln Milwaukee WI 53217-2107

SMITH, JANE FLORENCE, elementary school educator; b. Little Falls, N.Y., Nov. 26, 1947; d. Cecil Charles and Florence Louise (Pierce) Harrad; m. James Reuben Smith, July 16, 1983. AA, Dutchess C.C., Poughkeepsie, N.Y., 1967; BS, Oneonta State Coll., 1970. Cert. tchr. (permanent or life) nursery-6, 7-9 English, N.Y. 6th grade tchr. Dolgeville (N.Y.) Ctrl. Sch., 1970—; Cims math. coord. Dolgeville Ctrl. Sch., 1984—. Chmn. trustees Hoyer Hill Cemetery (historic landmark), 1983—. Mem. DAR (regent 1977-83, registrar 1987— Henderson chpt.), Nat. Coun. Tchrs. of Math. Republican. Methodist. Avocations: antiques, stamp collecting, gardening. Home: Park Rd PO Box 7 Van Hornesville NY 13475 Office: Dolgeville Ctrl Sch Slawson St Extension Dolgeville NY 13329

SMITH, JANE WARDELL, historian, philanthropist, entrepreneur; b. Detroit, Aug. 9, 1943; d. John Slater and Lucille Maude (Hoskins) Beck; m. marshall Smith, Oct. 31, 1964 (div. 1972); children: Aaron Wardell, Gerald Allen. Student, Detroit Bus. Coll., Cass Sch. Tech. Exec. sec. Wayne County Cir. Ct. 7th Dist., 1968-72, Wayne County Friend of Ct., Detroit, 1968-72; with exec. mgmt. City Detroit Pers. Dept., 1972-79; fin. analyst City of Detroit, 1979-82, Merlite Industries, N.Y.C., 1994—; salesperson Mason Shoe Co., Chippewa Falls, 1968-72; fin. analyst A. J. Valenci, Salem, W.Va., 1968-72; examiner Mich. State Dept., Detroit, 1972-79. Critic various consumer groups. Vol. Richard Austin polit. campaign, Grand River, Mich., 1975, John Conters polit. campaign, Livernois, Mich., 1980; mem. Mayor's Com. for Human Resources, Detroit, 1979; active local drama and theater clubs, Detroit, 1980—, local Bapt. Ch., 1984—. Recipient numerous awards, honors and achievements. Democrat. Avocations: swimming, bicycling, tennis, dance, roller skating.

SMITH, JANET MARIE, professional sports team executive; b. Jackson, Miss., Dec. 13, 1957; d. Thomas Henry and Nellie Brown (Smith) S. BArch, Miss. State U., 1981; MA in Urban Planning, CCNY, 1984. Draftsman Thomas H. Smith and Assocs. Architects, Jackson, 1979; mktg. coord. The Eggers Group, P.C. Architects and Planners, N.Y.C., 1980; program assoc. Ptnrs. for Livable Places, Washington, 1980-82; coord. asst. Lance Jay Brown, Architect and Urban Planner, N.Y.C., 1983-84; coord. architecture and design Battery Park City Authority, N.Y.C., 1982-84; pres., chief exec. officer Pershing Sq. Mgmt. Assn., L.A., 1985-89; v.p. stadium planning and devel. Balt. Orioles Oriole Park at Camden Yard, 1989-94; v.p. sports facilities Turner Properties, Atlanta, 1994—; v.p. planning and devel. Atlanta Braves, Braves, 1994—; bd. dirs. Assn. Collegiate Schs. Architecture, Washington, 1979-82, Assn. Student Chpts. AIA, Washington, 1979-82. Guest editor: Urban Design Internat., 1985; assoc. editor: Crit, 1979-82; contbr. articles to profl. jours. Named Disting. Grad., Nat. Assn. State Univs. and Land Grant Colls., 1988, One of Outstanding Young Women of Am., 1982; recipient Spirit of Miss. award, Sta. WLBT, Jackson, 1987. Mem. AIA (assoc.), Urban Land Inst. Democrat. Episcopalian. Office: Turner Properties Inc 1 CNN Center Ste 275 Atlanta GA 30303

SMITH, JANICE SELF, family nurse practitioner; b. Marietta, Ga., Nov. 8, 1942; d. Robert Dewey and Dovia Evelyn (Seay) Self; m. Charles William Smith, Nov. 9, 1963; children: Scott, Stephanie, Suzanne. Diploma, Piedmont Hosp. Sch. Nursing, 1963; Cert. Family Nurse Practitioner, Ga. State U., 1981; BSN, West Ga. Coll., 1994. RN, Ga.; cert. family nurse practitioner, Ga. Staff nurse Gordon Hosp., Calhoun, Ga., 1963-69; pub. health nurse Gordon County Health Dept., Calhoun, Ga., 1977-80; family nurse practitioner Gordon Primary Care Unit, Calhoun, Ga., 1982—; rep. health dept. Child ABuse Coun., Calhoun, 1986; led effort to implement Good Touch-Bad Touch program, Calhoun, 1986. Chmn. pub. edn. Am. Cancer Soc., Calhoun, 1971, bd. chmn., 1973, chmn. patient svcs., 1974-79; sec. commn. on missions 1st United Meth. Ch., Calhoun, 1994. Named Gord County Vol. of the Yr., 1979; Ingram scholar West Ga. Coll., 1994. Mem. ANA, Ga. Pub. Health Assn. (sec. nursing sect. 1994-95, vice chair nursing sect. 1995-96, chair nursing sect. 1996—), Ga. Nurses Assn. (treas. 1995-96), Nurses Honor Soc. West Ga. Coll. Methodist. Avocations: travel, reading, attending a variety of musical performances and plays. Home: 141 Derby Ln Calhoun GA 30701-2023 Office: Gordon County Health Dept 310 N River St Calhoun GA 30701

SMITH, JEAN KENNEDY, ambassador; b. Brookline, Mass., Feb. 20, 1928; d. Joseph P. and Rose Kennedy; m. Stephen E. Smith (dec.); 4 children. BA, Manhattanville Coll. Founder, dir., chair Very Spl. Arts, 1974—; amb. to Ireland Dublin, 1993—. Author: (with George Plimpton) Chronicles of Courage, 1993; contbr. articles on the disabled to profl. jours. Trustee Joseph P. Kennedy, Jr. Found., 1964—, John F. Kennedy Ctr. Performing Arts. Recipient Sec.'s award Dept. Vets. Affairs, Vol. of Yr. award People-to-People Com. Handicapped, Margaret Mead Humanitarian award Coun. Cerebral Palsy Auxs., Jefferson award Am. Inst. Pub. Svc., Spirit of Achievement award Yeshiva U., Humanitarian award Capital Children's Mus. Address: Am Embassy, 42 Elgin Rd, Ballsbridge Dublin Ireland*

SMITH, JEAN WEBB (MRS. WILLIAM FRENCH SMITH), civic worker; b. L.A.; d. James Ellwood and Violet (Hughes) Webb; B.A. summa cum laude, Stanford U., 1940; m. George William Vaughan, Mar. 14, 1942 (dec. Sept. 1963); children: George William, Merry; m. William French Smith, Nov. 6, 1964. Mem. Nat. Vol. Svc. Adv. Coun. (ACTION), 1973-76, vice chmn., 1974-76; dir. Beneficial Standard Corp., 1976-85. bd. dirs. Cmty. TV So. Calif., 1979-93; mem. Calif. Arts Commn., 1971-74, vice chmn., 1973-74; bd. dirs. The Founders, Music Ctr., L.A., 1971-74; bd. dirs. costume coun. L.A. County Mus. Art, 1971-73; bd. dirs. United Way, Inc., 1973-80, Hosp. Good Samaritan, 1973-80, L.A. chpt. NCCJ, 1977-80, Nat. Symphony Orch., 1980-85, L.A. World Affairs Coun., 1990, L.A. chpt. ARC, 1994-95; bd. fellows Claremont Univ. Ctr. and Grad. Sch., 1987—; bd. dirs. Hosp. Good Samaritan, 1973-80; mem. exec. com., 1975-80; mem. nat. bd. dirs. Boys' Clubs Am., 1977-80; mem. adv. bd. Salvation Army, 1979—; bd. overseers The Hoover Instn. on War, Revolution and Peace, 1989-94; mem. President's Commn. on White House Fellowships, 1980-90, Nat. Coun. on the Humanities, 1987-90; bd. govs. Calif. Cmty. Found., 1990—; bd. regents Children's Hosp. L.A., 1993—. Named Woman of Yr. for cmty. svc. L.A. Times, 1958; recipient Citizens of Yr. award Boys Clubs Greater L.A., 1982, Life Achievement award Boy Scouts Am., L.A. coun., 1985. Mem. Jr. League of L.A. (pres. 1954-55, Spirit of Volunteerism award 1996), Assn. Jr. Leagues of Am. (dir. Region XII, 1956-58, pres. 1958-60), Phi Beta Kappa, Kappa Kappa Gamma. Home: 11718 Wetherby Ln Los Angeles CA 90077-1348

SMITH, J(EFFERSON) VERNE, state senator, business executive; b. Greer, S.C., Jan. 15, 1925; s. Jefferson Verne and Lillian (Farley) S.; m. Jean Myers, Nov. 27, 1947; children: Jefferson Verne III, Carole Jean Olmert. Student, Presbyn. Coll., Clinton, S.C., 1942-43; LHD (hon.), Med. U. S.C., 1990. Pres. The Tire Exch.; senator State of S.C., Columbia; chmn. senate labor, commerce & industry com., legis. study com. on alcohol & drug abuse; vice chmn. med. affairs com., health care planning and oversight com.; vice chmn. fin. com., rules com. gen. com., others; bd. dirs. So. Nat. S.C., Greer. Chmn. bd. commrs. Comm. on Pub. Works, Greer, 1969-72; mem. steering com. S.C. Dem. Party; past chmn. Greenville County Dem. Party; bd. govs. Shriners Hosp. for Crippled Children; bd. commrs. Cedar Springs Inst. for Deaf and Blind; bd. dirs. Peace Ctr. for the Performing Arts, 1989. Named Legislator of Yr. S.C. Autism Soc., 1987-88, S.C. Health Care Assn., 1990, S.C. Hosp. Assn., 1991, Outstanding Senator of Yr. S.C. Sch. Bd. Assn., 1992; recipient plaque for svc. to North Greenville County Travelers Rest City Coun., 1992; J. Verne Smith award named in his honor S.C. Assn. Residential Care Homes, 1989; recipient Meritorious medal S.C. Mil. Dept., 1992; Verne Smith Week declared City of Greer, 1992; Verne Smith Libr. & Tech. Resource Ctr. named in his honor Greenville Tech. Coll., 1992; named Am. Legion Legislator of the Yr., Senate, 1994, Legislator of Yr., S.C. Assn. of Children's Home and Family Svcs., 1994; recipient Meritorious Svc. award Govs. Sch. for the Arts, 1994, Order of Palmetto, 1995. Mem. Masons, Scottish Rite, Shriners, Kappa Alpha. Democrat. Presbyterian. Avocations: reading, walking. Office: SC Senate PO Box 142 Columbia SC 29202-0142

SMITH, JEFFREY ALAN, occupational medicine physician, toxicologist; b. Plainfield, N.J., Dec. 13, 1953; s. John Oliver and Regina Delores (Rudnicki) S. BSChemE with high honors, N.C. State U., 1974; MD with honors, U. N.C., 1979; MS in Toxicology, W.Va. U., 1990. Environ. engr. U.S. EPA, Durham, N.C., 1974-75; mem. staff, cons. PEDCo Environ., Inc., Durham, 1975-80; dir. environ. health PEDCo Environ., Inc., Cin., 1981-82; intern New Hanover Meml. Hosp., Wilmington, N.C., 1980-81; ind. contractor various urgent care ctrs. Cin., 1982-84; dir. Marion (Ohio) Correctional Inst., F.C. Smith Clinic, Inc., 1984-88; resident W.Va. U., Morgantown, 1988-91; med. officer Nat. Inst. Occupational Safety and Health, Morgantown, 1991; dir. occupational medicine Concord (N.C.) Family Medicine/Monroe Urgent Care, 1991-95. Co-author: Environmental Assessment of the Domestic Industries, 1976, Dioxins, 1980. Mem. Am. Coll. Occupation and Environ. Medicine, Am. Conf. Govt. Indsl. Hygienists, Am. Coll. Physician Execs., N.C. Med. Soc., So. Med. Assn., Phi Kappa Phi, Alpha Omega Alpha. Avocations: book collecting, philately, mountain climbing, white water canoeing. Home: 1511 Lake Dr Monroe NC 28112-9415

SMITH, JEFFREY ALLEN, lawyer; b. Cleve., Feb. 2, 1944; s. William R. and Esther Mae Smith; m. Ruth Ann Sweeton, June 10, 1967; children: Amy Esther, Adam Minor. AB, Clark U., 1966; JD, Boston U., 1969. Bar: Maine 1971, U.S. Dist. Ct. Maine 1971, U.S. Supreme Ct. 1980. Clk. to judge Maine Probate Ct., 1970; assoc. Law Offices of Harold J. Shapiro, Gardiner, Maine, 1971-73; ptnr. Smith Stein Bernotavicz & Orbeton, Hallowell, Richmond & Bath and predecessor firms Smith & Stein, and Smith Stein & Bernotavicz, Hallowell, Richmond, Hallowell, Maine, 1973-85, mng. ptnr., 1980-84, Smith & Assoc. P.A., Hallowell, 1985—, assoc. Douglas F. Jennings, 1993—; instr. trusts and estates and legal writing Beal Bus. Coll., Brunswick, Maine, 1981-82. Mem., Monmouth (Maine) Planning Bd., 1978-85; cubmaster Pine Tree council Boy Scouts Am., 1982-85; Vista vol. Alaska Legal Services, 1969-70. Mem. ABA, Maine Bar Assn., Kennebec County Bar Assn., Assn. Trial Lawyers Am., Maine Trial Lawyers Assn. (bd. govs. 1986—), Maine Organic Farmers and Gardeners Assn., bd. trustees Theater at Monmouth, bd. dir. Monmouth Cmty. Players. Democrat. Methodist (lay leader 1978—). Author: Santa's Will, 1978, Santa's Codicil, 1979, Letter to Smith Stein & Bernotavicz From Santa, 1982, contbr. articles to publs. Home: Blue Heron Farm Town F Rd Monmouth ME 04259 Office: PO Box 351 144 Water Hallowell ME 04347-0351

SMITH, JEFFREY E., historian, educator; b. Columbus, Ohio, July 5, 1956; s. George Edward and Anna Marie (Fisher) S.; m. Kristine Runberg, Aug. 15, 1987; 1 child, Lucy Kathryn. BA, Mount Union Coll., Alliance, Ohio, 1978; MFA, Syracuse U., 1981; PhD, U. Akron, 1991. Dir. Summit County Hist. Soc., Akron, Ohio, 1981-90; exec. dir. St. Louis Merc. Libr., St. Louis, 1990-94; instr. Washington U., St. Louis, 1992—; pres. Janus Applied History Group, St. Louis, 1994—; adj. prof. U. Akron, 1984-86. Contbr. articles to profl. jours. Mem. Am. Assn. for State and Local History (Award of Merit 1987), Ohio Assn. Hist. Socs. and Mus. (various award 1984-90), Orgn. Am. Historians, Ohio Mus. Assn. (sec., trustee), Hower House Mus. (bd. dirs.). Office: Janus Applied History Group 3920 Cleveland Ave Saint Louis MO 63110

SMITH, JEFFREY EARL, management consulting executive; b. Dunkirk, N.Y., June 15, 1958; s. Earl Redmond and Ruth Aliene (Crawford) S.; m. Ellen Lori Pichney, Feb. 9, 1992; children: Daniel Edward, Benjamin Michael. BS in Civil Engring., Worcester (Mass.) Poly. Inst., 1981; BA in Physics, Coll. of the Holy Cross, 1981; MBA, U. Md., 1995. From ops. engr. to info. ctr. mgr. Dresser Atlas, Houston, 1981-83; divsnl. info. sys. mgr. Dresser Industries, 1983-86; solution team mgr. AT&T Info. Sys., Houston, 1986; sr. mgmt. cons. Gemini Cons. Co., Morristown, N.J., 1986-89; prin., regional dir. Gen. Elec. Cons. Svcs., Phila., 1990-91; pres., mng. dir. Knowledge Cons. Co., Rockville, 1989-95; sr. mgmt. cons. IBM Cons. Group, Chgo., 1995—. Home: Knowledge Consulting Co 7440 Damascus Rd Laytonsville MD 20882 Office: IBM Cons Group 1 IBM Plz 6th Fl Dept PJE Chicago IL 60611

SMITH, JEFFREY GREENWOOD, industry executive, retired army officer; b. Ft. Sam Houston, Tex., Oct. 14, 1921; s. Henry Joseph Moody and Gladys Adrienne (Haile) S.; m. Dorothy Jane Holland, June 2, 1948; children: Meredith B. Exnicios, Jennifer H. Meyer, Jeffrey Greenwood, Tracy E. McDonald, Melissa A. Deutsch, Ashley A. Pollock. B.S. in Civil Engring, Va. Mil. Inst., 1943; M.S. in Mech. Engring, Johns Hopkins U., 1949; M.A. in Internat. Affairs, George Washington U., 1964. Commd. 2d lt. U.S. Army, 1944, advanced through grades to lt. gen., 1975; service in CBI, Korea, Germany and Vietnam; comdr. 2d Inf. Div., Korea, 1971-73; dep. chief staff ops. Hdqrs. Army Forces Command, Ft. McPherson, Ga., 1973-74; chief staff Hdqrs. Army Forces Command, 1974-75; comdr. 1st U.S. Army, Ft. Meade, Md., 1975-79; ret., 1979; dir. govt. rels. Ethyl Corp., Washington, 1980—, v.p. govt. rels., 1992—, ret., 1994. Decorated D.S.M., Silver Star, Legion of Merit with 3 oak leaf clusters, D.F.C., Bronze Star with V device and 2 oak leaf clusters, Air medal with 12 oak leaf clusters, Army Commendation medal with oak leaf cluster, Purple Heart with oak leaf cluster, Combat Inf. badge (2); breast Order Yun Hui Republic China; Order Security Merit Korea; Gallantry Cross with silver and gold stars (Vietnam) Army Distinguished Service Order. Mem. Assn. U.S. Army, Mil. Order Carabao, Kappa Alpha. Clubs: Army and Navy. Home: 3000 Sevor Ln Alexandria VA 22309-2221

SMITH, JEFFREY K., publishing executive; b. Cleve., June 25, 1948; s. James D. and Inez (Hobson) S.; m. Mary Frances Smith, Dec. 29, 1971; children: Gwynneth F., Colin J., Douglas F. Student, U. Edinburgh, Scotland, 1968-69; BA, Duke U., 1970; MA, U. Wis., 1971. Editor Fed. Register, Washington, 1971-73; sales rep. Harper and Row, Cleve., 1974-76; acquisitions editor Harper and Row, N.Y.C., 1976-77; acquisitions editor Kluwer Acad. Pubs., The Hague, The Netherlands, 1977-81; acquisitions editor Kluwer Acad. Pubs., Boston, 1981-83, v.p., 1983—; pres. Kluwer Acad. Pubs., 1996—; also bd. dirs. Kluwer Acad. Pubs., Boston. Office: Kluwer Acad Pubs 101 Philip Dr Norwell MA 02061-1615

SMITH, JEFFREY L. (THE FRUGAL GOURMET), cook, writer; b. Seattle, Jan. 22, 1939; s. Emely S.; m. Patricia M. Dailey, 1964; children: Jason, Channing. BA, U. Puget Sound, 1962, DHL (hon.), 1987; MDiv, Drew U., 1965, DDiv (hon.), 1993. Ordained to ministry United Meth. Ch., 1965. Served Meth. chs. Hartsdale, N.Y., rural, Wash.; chaplain, asst. prof. religion U. Puget Sound, Tacoma, Wash., 1966-72; founder The Chaplain's Pantry, Tacoma, 1972-83; host Seattle Today TV program The Frugal Gourmet (formerly Cooking Fish Creatively), 1973-77; host PBS program The Frugal Gourmet, 1983—. Author: The Frugal Gourmet, 1984, The Frugal Gourmet Cooks with Wine, 1986, The Frugal Gourmet Cooks American, 1987, The Frugal Gourmet Cooks Three Ancient Cuisines: China, Greece and Rome, 1989, The Frugal Gourmet on Our Immigrant Ancestors: Recipes You Should Have Gotten From Your Grandmother, 1990, The Frugal Gourmet's Culinary Handbook, 1991, The Frugal Gourmet Celebrates Christmas, 1991, The Frugal Gourmet Whole Family Cookbook, 1992, The Frugal Gourmet Cooks Italian: Recipes from the New and Old World Simplified for the American Kitchen, 1993, The Frugal Gourmet Keeps the Feast: Past, Present and Future, 1995. Recipient Daytime Emmy nominations (5), Best of the West Edn. TV award Western Ednl. Network, 1986. Office: The Frugal Gourmet Inc 88 Virginia St Unit 2 Seattle WA 98101-1047

SMITH, JEFFREY MICHAEL, lawyer; b. Mpls., July 9, 1947; s. Philip and Gertrude E. (Miller) S.; 1 son, Brandon Michael. BA summa cum laude, U. Minn., 1970; student U. Malaya, 1967-68; JD magna cum laude, U. Minn., 1973. Bar: Ga. 1973. Assoc. Powell, Goldstein, Frazier & Murphy, 1973-76; ptnr. Rogers & Hardin, 1976-79; ptnr. Bondurant, Stephenson & Smith, 1979-85, Arnall, Golden & Gregory, 1985-92, Katz, Smith & Cohen, 1992—; vis. lectr. Duke U., 1976-77, 79-80, 89-93; adj. prof. Emory U., 1976-79, 81-82; lectr. Vanderbilt U., 1977-82. Co-author: Preventing Legal Malpractice, 1996, Legal Malpractice, 1996. Bd. visitors U. Minn. Law Sch., 1976-82. Mem. ABA (vice chmn. com. profl. officers and dirs. liability law, 1979-83, chmn. 1983-84, vice chmn. com. profl. liability 1980-82, mem. standing com. lawyer's profl. liability 1981-85, chmn. 1985-87, standing com. lawyer competency 1993-95), State Bar of Ga. (chmn. profl. liability and ins. com. 1978-89, trustee Inst. of Continuing Legal Edn. in Ga. 1979-80), Order of Coif, Phi Beta Kappa. Home: 145 15th St NE Apt 811 Atlanta GA 30309-3559 Office: Katz Smith & Cohen Ivy Place 2d Fl 3423 Piedmont Rd NE Atlanta GA 30305-1754

SMITH, JEFFREY P., supermarket chain executive; b. 1950. Student, Utah State U., 1968-70. With Smith's Food and Drug Ctrs., Salt Lake City, 1970—, pres., COO, 1984-88, chmn., CEO, 1988—, also bd. dirs. Office: Smith's Food & Drug Ctrs Inc 1550 S Redwood Rd Salt Lake City UT 84104-5105*

SMITH, JEFFRY ALAN, health administrator, physician, consultant; b. L.A., Dec. 8, 1943; s. Stanley W. and Marjorie E. S.; m. Jo Anne Hague. BA in Philosophy, UCLA, 1967, MPH, 1972; BA in Biology, Calif. State U., Northridge, 1971; MD, UACJ, 1977. Diplomate Am. Bd. Family Practice. Resident in family practice WAH, Takoma Park, Md., NIH, Bethesda, Md., Walter Reed Army Hosp., Washington, Children's Hosp. Nat. Med. Ctr., Washington, 1977-80; occupational physician Nev. Test Site, U.S. Dept. Energy, Las Vegas, 1981-82; dir. occupational medicine and environ. health Pacific Missile Test Ctr., Point Mugu, Calif., 1982-84; dist. health officer State Hawaii Dept. Health, Kauai, 1984-86; asst. dir. health County of Riverside (Calif.) Dept. Health, 1986-87; regional med. dir. Calif. Forensic Med. Group, Monterey, Calif., 1987-94; med. dir. Cmty. Human Svcs., Monterey, Calif., 1987-94, Colstrip (Mont.) Med. Ctr., 1994—. Fellow Am. Acad. Family Physicians; mem. AMA, Am. Occupational Medicine Assn., Flying Physicians, Am. Pub. Health Assn. Avocations: pvt. pilot. Office: PO Box 1907 Colstrip MT 59323

SMITH, JEROME HAZEN, pathologist; b. Omaha, Oct. 9, 1936; s. Hazen Dow and Helen Kellogg (Hewitt) S.; m. Marilyn Kay Stauber, 1961; children: Nathaniel, Kathryn Hewitt, Andrew Kellogg. B.S. in Medicine, U. Nebr., 1960, M.D., 1963, M.S. in Anatomy, 1962; M.Sc. Hygiene in Tropical Pub. Health, Harvard U., 1969. Diplomate: Am. Bd. Pathology. Rotating intern Mpls.-Hennepin County Gen. Hosp., 1963-64; from jr. asst. resident in pathology to chief resident in clin. pathology Peter Bent Brigham Hosp., Boston, 1964-72, assoc. pathologist, 1973; from rsch. fellow in pathology to instr. Harvard U. Med. Sch., Boston, 1964-73; pathologist, head dept. Inst. Med. Evangelique, Kimpese, Congo, 1968; chief autopsy svcs. Inst.Tropical Medicine, Hosp. Mama Yemo, Fomeco, Kinshasa, Zaire, 1973-74; med. dir. anatomic pathology Inst. Tropical Medicine, Hosp. Mama Yemo, Fomeco, Kinshasa, Zaire, 1974; asst. prof. anatomic pathology U. Ariz. Med. Sch., Tucson; dir. anatomic pathology and microbiology Tucson VA Hosp., 1975-76; mem. faculty U. Tex. Med. Br., Galveston, 1976-84, 90—, prof. pathology, 1979-84, 90—, dir. autopsy service, 1977-84, dir. clin. parasitology lab., 1977-81, 90-94, dir. pathology edn., 1993-95, prof. grad. sch., 1980-84, 90—, adj. prof. pathology, 1989-90; cons. Shriners Burn Inst., Galveston, 1980-84, 90-91; prof pathology and lab. medicine Tex. A&M U. Coll. Medicine, College Station, 1984-88; pres. Birch Tree, Inc., 1995—. Contbr. numerous articles to med. jours. Comdr. M.C. USNR, 1969-71. Recipient Avalon tuition award, 1961; NSF fellow, 1959; Poynter fellow, 1960; USPHS trainee, 1961, 68-69. MEm. NRA (life), Am. Soc. Clin. Pathologists, U.S.-Can. Acad. Pathologists, Am. Soc. Parasitologists, N.Y. Acad. Scis., Tex. Med. Assn., Tex. Soc. Pathologists, Tex. Soc. Infectious Diseases, Galveston County Med. Soc., Am. Soc. Tropical Medicine and Hygiene, Houston Soc. Clin. Pathologists (Harlan Spjut award 1995), Houston Safari Club (bd. dirs. 1994—), Sigma Xi. Republican. Home: 2706 Wilmington Dr Dickinson TX 77539-4664 Office: U Tex Med Br Dept Pathology Galveston TX 77550 *Your only lasting investment is in your fellow men. Your only certain investment is in God.*

SMITH, JERRY EDWIN, federal judge; b. Del Rio, Tex., Nov. 7, 1946; s. Lemuel Edwin and Ruth Irene (Henderson) S.; m. Mary Jane Blackburn, June 4, 1977; children: Clark, Ruth Ann, J.J. BA, Yale U., 1969, JD, 1972. Bar: Tex. 1972. Law clk. to judge U.S. Dist. Ct. (no. dist.) Tex., Lubbock, 1972-73; assoc. then ptnr. Fulbright & Jaworski, Houston, 1973-84; city atty. City of Houston, 1984-88; cir. judge U.S. Ct. Appeals (5th cir.), Houston, 1988—. Chmn. Harris County Rep. Party, Houston, 1977-78; committeeman State Rep. Exec. Com., Tex., 1976-88. Mem. State Bar Tex., Houston Bar Assn. Methodist. Home: PO Box 130608 Houston TX 77219-0608 Office: US Ct Appeals 12621 US Courthouse 515 Rusk St Houston TX 77002-2698

SMITH, JESSE GRAHAM, JR., dermatologist, educator; b. Winston-Salem, N.C., Nov. 22, 1928; s. Jesse Graham and Pauline Field (Griffith) S.; m. Dorothy Jean Butler, Dec. 28, 1950; children: Jesse Graham, Cynthia Lynn, Grant Butler. B.S., Duke U., 1962, M.D., 1951. Diplomate: Am. Bd. Dermatology (dir. 1974-83, pres. 1980-81). Intern VA Hosp., Chamblee, Ga., 1951-52; resident in dermatology Duke U., 1954-56, assoc. prof. dermatology, 1960-62, prof., 1962-67; resident U. Miami, 1956-57, asst. prof., 1957-60; prof. dermatology Med. Coll. Ga., 1967-91, chmn. dept. dermatology, 1967-91, acting chmn. dept. pathology, 1973-75, acting v.p. devel., 1984-85; chief staff Talmadge Meml. Hosp., Augusta, Ga., 1970-72; prof. dermatology, chief div. of dermatology U. South Ala., Mobile, 1991—; mem. advisory council Nat. Inst. Arthritis, 1975-79. Editorial bd. Archives of Dermatology, 1963-72, Jour. Investigative Dermatology, 1966-67, Jour. AMA, 1974-80; editorial bd. So. Med. Jour., 1976—, assoc. editor, 1991-92, editor, 1992—; editor Jour. Am. Acad. Dermatology, 1978-88; contbr. chpts. to books, articles to profl. jours. Served with USPHS, 1952-54. Recipient Disting. Alumnus award Duke U. 1981. Fellow ACP, Royal Soc. Medicine; mem. Am. Acad. Dermatology (hon., dir. 1971-74, 78-88, pres.-elect 1988-89, pres. 1989-90), Can. Dermatol. Assn. (hon.), Am. Dermatol. Assn. (sec. 1976-81, pres. 1981-82), Soc. Investigative Dermatology (dir. 1964-69, pres. 1979-80), S.E. Dermatol. Assn. (sec. 1970-71, pres. 1975-76), Ga. Soc. Dermatology (pres. 1979-80), So. Med. Assn. (chmn. sect. dermatology 1981-84), Assn. Profs. Dermatology (dir. 1976-77, 80-82, pres. 1984-86), Med. Rsch. Found. Ga. (bd. dirs. 1967-91, pres. 1974-75), Alpha Omega Alpha. Home: 4272 Bitand Spur # 4 Mobile AL 36608 Office: USAMC 3401 Medical Park Dr Ste 103 Mobile AL 36693-3318

SMITH, JO ANNE, writer, retired educator; b. Mpls., Mar. 18, 1930; d. Robert Bradburn and Virginia Mae S. BA, U. Minn., 1951, MA, 1957. Wire and sports editor Rhinelander (Wis.) Daily News, 1951-52; staff corr., night mgr. UPI, Mpls., 1952-56; interim instr. U. N.C., Chapel Hill, 1957-58; instr. U. Fla., Gainesville, 1959-65; asst. prof. journalism, communications U. Fla., 1965-68, assoc. prof., 1968-76, prof., 1976-88, disting. lectr., 1977. Author: JM409 Casebook and Study Guide, 1976, Mass Communications Law Casebook, 1979, 3d edit., 1985. Active, Friends of Libr., Alachua County Humane Soc. Recipient outstanding Prof. award Fla. Blue Key, 1976; Danforth assoc., 1976-85. Mem. Women in Communications, Assn. Edn. in Journalism, Phi Beta Kappa, Kappa Tau Alpha. Democrat. Unitarian. Home: 208 NW 21st Ter Gainesville FL 32603-1732

SMITH, JOAN PETERSEN, nursing administrator, educator; b. Aurora, Nebr., Apr. 4, 1943; d. Ardean Leroy and Leone Eleanor (Ketterer) Petersen; m. Tyrone Wilson Smith, Aug. 15, 1979; 1 child, Steven. BSN, Boston U., 1967; MPA, Roosevelt U., 1977. Dir. ambulatory nursing Michael Reese Hosp., Chgo., 1978-80; v.p. patient care svcs. Marin Gen. Hosp., Greenbrae, Calif., 1980-84, Alta Bates Hosp., Berkeley, Calif., 1984-86; assoc. dir. health and hosp. sys., dir. nursing Santa Clara Valley Med. Ctr., San Jose, Calif., 1986—; asst. clin. prof. U. Calif. Sch. Nursing, San Francisco, 1985—. Recipient Tribute to Women in Industry award YWCA Santa Clara Valley, 1995; mgmt. fellow Nat. Assn. Pub. Hosps., 1991. Mem. Am. Orgn. Nurse Execs., Calif. Orgn. Nurse Execs., Sigma Theta Tau. Home: 1944 Melvin Rd Oakland CA 94602-2027 Office: Santa Clara Valley Med Ctr 751 S Bascom Ave San Jose CA 95128-2604

SMITH, JOE, recording industry executive. Pres. Capitol EMI Music Inc., L.A. Office: Capitol EMI Music Inc 1750 Vine St Los Angeles CA 90028-5247

SMITH, JOE DORSEY, JR., retired newspaper executive; b. Selma, La., Apr. 6, 1922; s. Joe Dorsey and Louise (Lindsay) S.; m. Margaret Jane Wilson, Nov. 20, 1943; 1 child, Lawrence Dorsey. B.A., La. Coll. Pineville, 1939-43. Gen. mgr. Alexandria Daily Town Talk, La., 1958—; pub. Alexandria Daily Town Talk, 1965—; pres. McCormick & Co., Inc., 1968—, chmn., 1990-96. Served with USAF, 1942-45. Mem. Newspaper Assn. Am. Democrat. Episcopalian. Clubs: Alexandria Golf and Country, Boston, New Orleans. Home: 2734 Georges Ln Alexandria LA 71301-4721 Office: Ste 1003 Hibernia Bldg 934 3d St Alexandria VA 71301

SMITH, JOE MAUK, chemical engineer, educator; b. Sterling, Colo., Feb. 14, 1916; s. Harold Rockwell and Mary Calista (Mauk) S.; m. Essie Johnstone McCutcheon, Dec. 23, 1943; children—Rebecca K., Marsha Mauk. B.S., Calif. Inst. Tech., 1937; Ph.D., Mass. Inst. Tech., 1943. Chem. engr. Texas Co., Standard Oil Co. of Calif., 1937-41; instr. chem. engring. Mass. Inst. Tech., 1943; asst. prof. chem. engring. U. Md., 1945; prof. chem. engring. Purdue U., 1945-56; dean Coll. Tech., U. N.H., 1956-57; prof. chem. engring. Northwestern U., 1957-59, Walter P. Murphy prof. chem. engring., 1959-61; prof. engring. U. Calif., 1961—, chmn. dept. chem. engring., 1964-72; hon. prof. chem. engring. U. Buenos Aires, Argentina, 1964—; Fulbright lectr., Eng., Italy, Spain, 1965, Argentina, 1963, 65, Ecuador, 1970, Brazil 1990; Mudaliar Meml. lectr. U. Madras, India, 1967; UNESCO cons., Venezuela, 1972-82; spl. vis. professorship Yokohama Nat. U., Japan, 1991. Author: Introduction to Chemical Engineering Thermodynamics, 1949, 4th edit, 1986, Chemical Engineering Kinetics, 1956, 3d edit., 1981. Guggenheim research award for study in Holland; also Fulbright award, 1953-54. Mem. Am. Chem. Soc., Am. Inst. Chem. Engrs. (Walker award 1960, Wilhelm award 1977, Lewis award 1984), Nat. Acad. Engring., Sigma Xi, Tau Beta Pi.

SMITH, JOEY SPAULS, mental health nurse, biofeedback therapist, bodyworker, hypnotist; b. Washington, Oct. 9, 1944; d. Walter Jr. and Marian (Och) Spauls; children: Kelly, Sean. BSN, Med. Coll. Va., 1966; MA in Edn., U. Nebr., Lincoln, 1975. RNC, ANA; cert. psychiat. and mental health nurse; cert. massage practitioner , cert. hypnotist, cert. biofeedback therapist. Staff nurse Booth Meml. Hosp., Omaha, 1969-71; asst. house supr. Nebr. Meth. Hosp., Omaha, 1971-72; head nurse, clin. instr. U. Calif., Davis, 1976-78; staff nurse Atascadero State Hosp., Calif. Dept. Mental Health, 1978-79; nurse instr. psychiat. technician Atascadero State Hosp., 1979-84, insvc. tng. coord., 1984-86; nursing coord. chem. dependency recovery program French Hosp. Med. Ctr., San Luis Obispo, Calif., 1986-87; relief house supr. San Luis Obispo County Gen. Hosp., 1982-88; regional program assoc. statewide nursing program Consortium Calif. Sate U., 1986-88; nurse instr., health svcs. staff devel. coord. Calif. Men's Colony, Dept. Corrections, San Luis Obispo, 1987-92; pvt. practice San Luis Obispo, Calif., 1990—; clin. instr. nursing divsn. Cuesta Coll., 1988—; relief house supr. San Luis Obispo County Gen. Hosp., 1982-88, regional program assoc. statewide nursing program Consortium Calif. State U., 1986-88. 1st lt. U.S. Army Nurse Corps., 1965-67. Mem. Assn. Applied Psychophysiology and Biofeedback, Am. Holistic Nurses Assn., Consol. Assn. Nurses in Substance Abuse (cert. chem. dependency nurse), Biofeedback Cert. Inst. Am. (cert. biofeedback therapist, cert. stress mgr., stress mgmt. edn.), Alpha Sigma Chi, Phi Delta Gamma. Home: 1321 Cavalier Ln San Luis Obispo CA 93405-4905 Office: PO Box 4823 San Luis Obispo CA 93403-4823

SMITH, JOHN BREWSTER, dean library sciences, director; b. Bryan, Tex., June 26, 1937; s. Elmer Gillam and Sara Roland (Lull) S.; m. Ida Hawa, Dec. 28, 1963; children: Susan Helen, Rona Esther. B.A., Tex. A & M U., 1960; M.S., Columbia U., 1963, cert. advanced librarianship, 1984, DLS, 1991. Asst. law librarian Columbia U., N.Y.C., 1963-66; asst. library dir. for pub. services Tex. A & M U., College Station, 1966-69, dir. libraries, 1969-74; dir. libraries, dean library scis. SUNY, Stony Brook, 1974—. Named Librarian of Year Tex. Library Assn., 1972. Mem. ALA, N.Y. Libr. Assn., State U. N.Y. Librs. Assn., L.I. Archives Conf. Home: 121 Gnarled Hollow Rd East Setauket NY 11733-1959 Office: SUNY Stony Brook Librs F Melville Jr Meml Libr Stony Brook NY 11794

SMITH, JOHN EDWIN, philosophy educator; b. Bklyn., May 27, 1921; s. Joseph Robert and Florence Grace (Dunn) S.; m. Marilyn Blanche Schulhof, Aug. 25, 1951; children: Robin Dunn, Diana Edwards. AB, Columbia U., 1942, PhD, 1948; BD, Union Theol. Sem., N.Y.C., 1945; MA, Yale U., 1959; LL.D., U. Notre Dame, 1964. Instr. religion and philosophy Vassar Coll., 1945-46; instr., then asst. prof. Barnard Coll., 1946-52; mem. faculty Yale U., 1952—, prof. philosophy, 1959—, chmn. dept., 1961—, Clark prof. philosophy, 1972-91, Clark prof. philosophy emeritus, 1991—; vis. prof. Union Theol. Sem., 1959, U. Mich., 1958; guest prof. U. Heidelberg, Germany, 1955-56; Fagothey chair of philosophy U. Santa Clara, 1984, vis. prof. Boston Coll., 1992; Dudleian lectr. Harvard, 1960; lectr. Am. Week, U. Munich, Germany, 1961; Suarez lectr. Fordham U., 1963; pub. lectr. King's College, Univ. London, 1965; Aquinas lectr. Marquette U., 1967; Warfield lectr. Princeton Theol. Sem., 1970; Fulbright lectr. Kyoto U., Japan, 1971; Sprunt lectr. Union Theol. Sem., Va., 1973; Mead-Swing lectr. Oberlin Coll., 1975; H. Richard Niebuhr lectr. Elmhurst Coll., Ill., 1977; Merrick lectr. Ohio Wesleyan U., 1977; Roy Wood Sellars lectr. Bucknell U., 1978; O'Hara lectr. U. Notre Dame, 1984; Hooker disting. vis. prof. Mc Master U., 1985; mem. adv. com. Nat. Humanities Inst., New Haven, 1974, dir., 1977—. Author: Royce's Social Infinite, 1950, Value Convictions and Higher Education, 1958, Reason and God, 1961, The Spirit of American Philosophy, 1963, The Philosophy of Religion, 1965, Religion and Empiricism, 1967, Experience and God, 1968, Themes in American Philosophy, 1970, Contemporary American Philosophy, 1970, The Analogy of Experience, 1973, Purpose and Thought: The Meaning of Pragmatism, 1978, America's Philosophical Vision, 1992, Jonathan Edwards, Puritan, Preacher, Philosopher, 1992, Quasi-Religions: Humanism, Marxism, Nationalism, 1994; translator: (R. Kroner): Kant's Weltanschauung, 1956; editor: (Jonathan Edwards): Religious Affections, Vol. 2, 1959; gen. editor, Yale edit.: Works of Jonathan Edwards; Editorial bd.: Monist, 1962—, Jour. Religious Studies, Philosophy East and West, Jour. Chinese Philosophy, The Personalist Forum, Jour. Faith and Philosophy, Jour. Speculative Philosophy. Named Hon. Alumnus, Harvard Div. Sch., 1960; recipient Herbert W. Schneider award Soc. for Advancement of Am. Philosophy, 1990, Founder's medal Metaphys. Soc. Am., 1996; Am. Coun. Learned Socs. fellow, 1964-65. Mem. Culinary Inst. Am. (dir. New Haven affiliate), Am. Philos. Assn. (v.p. 1980, pres. 1981), Am. Theol. Soc. (pres. 1967-68), Metaphys. Soc. Am. (pres. 1970-71, founder's medal, 1996), Hegel Soc. Am. (pres. 1971), Charles S. Peirce Soc. (pres. 1992). Home: 300 Ridgewood Ave Hamden CT 06517-1428 Office: PO Box 201562 New Haven CT 06520-1562

SMITH, JOHN FRANCIS, materials science educator; b. Kansas City, Kans., May 9, 1923; s. Peter Francis and Johanna Teresa (Spandle) S.; m. Evelyn Ann Ross, Sept. 1, 1947; children—Mark Francis, Letitia Ann Smith Harder. BA with distinction, U. Mo.-Kansas City, 1948; PhD, Iowa State U., 1953. Grad. asst. Iowa State U., Ames, 1948-53; faculty and research scientist Iowa State U., Ames, 1953-88; dept. chmn., div. chief Ames Lab. Iowa State U., Ames, 1966-70; cons. Tex. Instruments, Inc., Dallas and Attleboro, Mass., 1958-63, Argonne Nat. Lab., Ill., 1964-70, Iowa Hwy. Commn., Ames, Los Alamos Nat. Lab., N.Mex., 1984-88, bur. standards Nat. Inst. Standards and Tech., Gaithersburg, Md., 1988-91, Sandia Nat. Lab., Albuquerque, N.M., 1991-92, ASM Internat., Cleve., 1992—. Patentee ultrasonic determination of texture in metal sheet and plate, lead-free soldier; author: Phase Diagrams of Binary Vanadium Alloys; Hellcats Over the Philippine Deep; co-author: Thorium: Preparation and Properties, 1975; editor: Calculation of Phase Diagrams and Thermochemistry of Alloy Phases, 1978; editor Jour. Phase Equilibria; contbr. articles to profl. publs. Mem. former comdr. Ames-Boone Squad CAP, 1970-75. With USN, 1942-46, PTO, comdr. USNR, 1946-64. Decorated Air medal with star; Disting. Svc. award Civil Air Patrol, Maxwell AFB, Ala., 1979; Faculty Citation Iowa State Alumni Assn., Ames, 1977. Fellow Am. Inst. Chemists, ASM (chmn. Des Moines chpt. 1966); mem. AIME, Materials Research Soc., Alpha Sigma Mu (trustee 1984-86). Roman Catholic. Clubs: Silent Knights, Inc. (trustee 1980—), Exptl. Aircraft Assn. Avocation: flying. Home: RR 5 Box 343 Ames IA 50010-9520 Office: Iowa State U Ames Lab 122 Metallurgy Ames IA 50010

SMITH, JOHN FRANCIS, JR., automobile company executive; b. Worcester, Mass., Apr. 6, 1938; s. John Francis and Eleanor C. (Sullivan) S.; children: Brian, Kevin; m. Lydia G. Sigrist, Aug. 27, 1988; 1 stepchild, Nicola. B.B.A., U. Mass., 1960; M.B.A., Boston U., 1965. Fisher Body div. mgr. Gen. Motors Corp., Framingham, Mass., 1961-73; asst. treas Gen. Motors Corp., N.Y.C., 1973-80; comptroller Gen. Motors Corp., Detroit, 1980-81, dir. worldwide product planning, 1981-84; pres., gen. mgr. Gen. Motors Can., Oshawa, Ont., Can., 1984-85; exec. v.p. Gen. Motors Europe, Glattbrugg, Switzerland, 1986-87, pres., 1987-88; exec. v.p. internat. ops. Gen. Motors Corp., Detroit, 1988-90; vice chmn. internat. ops. Gen. Motors Corp., 1990, bd. dirs., mem. fin. com., 1990—, pres., COO, 1992—; CEO, pres., 1992-95; chmn. bd. Gen. Motors Corp., Detroit, 1996—; pres.'s coun. Global Strategy Bd.; bd. dirs. EDS, Hughes Electronics Corp., Gen. Motors Acceptance Corp.; mem. Bus. Roundtable Policy Com.; mem. U.S. Japan Bus. Coun., Am. Soc. Corp. Execs.; mem. Bd. of Detroit Renaissance; bus. coun. Meml. Sloan-Kettering Cancer Ctr.; bd. dirs. Procter & Gamble Co. Mem. chancellor's exec. com. U. Mass., dir.; trustee United Way S.E. Mich., New Am. Revolution, Boston U. Mem. Am. Soc. Corp. Execs., Am. Auto Mfrs. Assn. (bd. dirs.), Econ. Club Detroit (bd. dirs.), Beta Gamma Sigma (pres.), Dirs. Table. Roman Catholic. Office: GM 3044 W Grand Blvd Detroit MI 48202-3091

SMITH, JOHN FRANCIS, III, lawyer; b. White Plains, N.Y., Sept. 24, 1941; s. John Francis and Mary Dake (Mairs) S.; m. Susan Brown; children: John, Stephen, Peter. AB, Princeton U., 1963; LLB, Yale U., 1970. Bar: Pa. 1970, U.S. Supreme Ct. 1985. Assoc. Dilworth, Paxson, Kalish & Kauffman, Phila., 1970-75, ptnr., 1975-86, sr. ptnr., 1986-91; sr. litigation ptnr. Reed Smith Shaw & McClay, Phila., 1991—, mem. exec. com., 1993—. Mem. exec. com. Employment Discrimination Referral Project, 1971-74; pres. Society Hill Civic Assn., 1975-76, Phila. Chamber Ensemble, 1977-80; bd. govs. Pa. Economy League (ea. divsn.), 1983—, sec. 1995—; vice chair Health Care Task Force, 1993—; bd. dirs. World Affairs Council Phila., 1983-87, chmn. bd. dirs. program com., 1986-87; Burn Found., 1987—; moderator Main Line Unitarian Ch., 1986-89; founder and pres. Found. for Individual Responsibility and Social Trust (FIRST), 1995—. Served to lt. (j.g.) USNR, 1963-67; Vietnam. Mem. ABA, Phila. Bar Assn., Yale Law Sch. Alumni Assn. (exec. com. 1982-88, sec. 1987-88). Club: Princeton (Phila.). Office: Reed Smith Shaw & McClay 2500 One Liberty Pl Philadelphia PA 19103

SMITH, JOHN GELSTON, lawyer; b. Chgo., Aug. 10, 1923; s. Fred G. and Ferne (Keiser) S.; m. JoAnn Stanton, Aug. 17, 1944; children: Carey S., JoAnne G. B.S., U. Notre Dame, 1949, LL.B., 1950. Bar: Ill. 1950. Assoc. Lord, Bissell & Brook, Chgo., 1950-54, 57, ptnr., 1958-90, of counsel, 1990—; asst. atty. gen. State of Ill., Springfield, 1954-56; bd. dirs. Lloyd's of London Press, Inc.; lectr. ins. law Northwestern U., Evanston, 1952, 56-57; chmn. 1st Non-Profit Ins. Co., 1991-93. Chmn. Gov.'s Transition Task Force, Ill. Dept. Ins., Springfield, 1969; chmn. Gov.'s Adv. Bd. Ill. Dept. Ins., 1969-73; atty.-in-fact Underwriters at Lloyd's, London, 1974-88; adv. com. William J. Campbell Library of U.S. Cts., Chgo., 1963-87; trustee Lake Bluff (Ill.) Village Bd., 1965-69. Served to 1st lt. USAAF, 1942-45. Home: 382 Ravine Park Dr Lake Forest IL 60045-1341 Office: Lord Bissell & Brook 115 S La Salle St Chicago IL 60603-3801

SMITH, JOHN JAMES, JR., environmental engineering consultant; b. Franklin, N.J., Dec. 6, 1936; s. John James Smith and Estelle Mary (Gurka) Cook; m. Sondra Lanphear, Dec. 19, 1956; 1 child, James H. BS in Chemistry, U. Fla., 1967. Dir. consulting svcs., v.p. Black, Crow & Eidsness, Gainesville, Fla., 1968-77; divsn. mgr., v.p. water & wastewater CH2M Hill, Gainesville, 1977-78, regional mgr., sr. v.p. water & wastewater, 1978-90, dist. mgr., sr. v.p. Envrinon. Engring. Lab., 1990-93; pres. Quality Analytical Labs. CH2M Hill Ltd., Gainesville, 1994-95; dir., sr. v.p. Gulf Coast Chem. & Petrochem. Program CH2M Hill, Gainesville, 1996—; bd. dirs. N. Fla. Tech. Innovation Corp., N.E. Fla. Ednl. Delivery Sys.; chmn. U. Fla. Engring. Adv. Coun., 1994-96. Author conf. proc.; contbr. articles to profl. jours. Bd. dirs. Fla. Arts Celebration, Coun. on Econ. Outreach, Ctr. Performing Arts. With USAF. Mem. Am. Chem. Soc., Am. Water Works Assn. (nat. chmn. water quality monitoring com., trustee Fla. sect. 1979-82, chmn. Fla. sect. 1985-86, George Warren Fuller award 1988), Fla. Inst. Cons. Engrs., Fla. Chem. Industry Coun., Internat. Assn. Water Pollution Rsch., Water Pollution Control Fedn., Rotary, Sigma Xi. Achievements include development, design and research in numerous water and wastewater systems and facilities. Office: CH2M Hill PO Box 147009 3011 SW Williston Rd Gainesville FL 32614

SMITH, JOHN JOSEPH, lawyer; b. Pitts., Nov. 14, 1911; s. John J. and Alta Ethel (McGrady) S.; m. Ruth Lee Snavely, July 11, 1942; children: John Joseph Jr., Robert William. AB, Birmingham So. Coll., 1931; AM, U. Va., 1932, postgrad. in Econs., 1932-34; JD, U. Ala., 1937. Bar: Ala. 1937, U.S. Dist. Ct. (no. dist.) Ala. 1940, U.S. Supreme Ct. 1945, U.S. Ct. Appeals (5th cir.) 1950. Assoc. Murphy, Hanna & Woodall, Birmingham, Ala., 1937; asst. prof. U. Va., Charlottesville, 1937-39; office solicitor U.S. Dept. Labor, Washington, 1939-42; enforcement atty. Office of Price Adminstrn., Atlanta, 1942-43; legal counsel Bechtel-McCone Corp., Birmingham, 1943-46; pvt. practice Birmingham, 1946—. Author: Selected Principles of the Law of Contracts, Sales and Negotiable Instruments, 1938. Founder, commr. Homewood (Ala.) Joy Open Baseball League, 1958-72, dir., 1972-90; gov's staff Ala., 1963-71; chmn. Homewood Citizens Action Com. Against Annexation; life mem. Ala. Sheriffs' Boys and Girls Ranches Builders Club. Recipient Youth Service award Pop Warner Conf., Phila., 1961, Clifford Crow Meml. Community Service award, Shades Valley Civitan Club, Homewood, 1981; received key to City of Homewood, 1982, 88. Mem. ABA, Ala. Bar Assn., Birmingham Bar Assn. (ethics com., unlawful practice of law com., fee arbitration com., econs. of law com., acct.'s liaison com., meml. com.), Order of Coif (founder Farrah Order of Jurisprudence, pres. 1937, alumni organizer U. Ala. Sch. Law chpt., pres. 1969-73, life historian). Methodist. Clubs: The Club (Homewood); City Salesmen's (Birmingham) (Man of Yr. award 1986). Lodges: Masons (life mem., master 1956-57, chmn. legal adv. com. for grand lodge), KT, Shriners, Royal Order Scotland, Scottish Rite (So. jurisdiction). Home: 1506 Primrose Pl Birmingham AL 35209-5426 Office: Smith & Smith Marathon Bldg 618 38th St S Birmingham AL 35222-2414

SMITH, JOHN JOSEPH, JR., textile company executive, educator; b. Fall River, Mass., Feb. 11, 1913; s. John J. and Mabel E. (Reid) S.; m. Mary C. Moson, Aug. 8, 1936; children—Nancy S. (Mrs. John Lee Lesher, Jr.), Robert J. B.S. in Chem. Engring., Tufts U., 1935. With Johnson & Johnson subsidiary Chicopee Mfg. Corp., New Brunswick, N.J., 1935—; pres. Chicopee Mfg. Corp., 1959—, chmn., 1971-74; with Chicopee Mills, Inc., N.Y.C., 1959—; pres. Chicopee Mills, Inc., 1960—, chmn., 1971-75; dir. Johnson & Johnson, New Brunswick, 1961-74, mem. exec. com., 1966-74; chmn. Chicopee Cuyk Holland, Devro Moodiesburn Scotland; prof. Fla. Atlantic U., Boca Raton, adj. prof., 1976-82. Mem. Am. Assn. Tech. Colorists and Chemists, Am. Chem. Soc., Gulf Stream Golf Club, The Little Club, Delray Beach (Fla.) Club, The Misguamicut Club, Watch Hill (R.I.) Yacht Club. Home: 1225 S Ocean Blvd Delray Beach FL 33483

SMITH, JOHN LEE, JR., minister, former association administrator; b. Fairfax, Ala., Dec. 11, 1920; s. John Lee and Mae Celia (Smith) S.; m. Vivian Herrington, Aug. 15, 1942; children—Vicky Smith Davis, Joan Smith Wimberly, Jennifer Lee Smith Ruscilli. A.B., Samford U., 1950; student, New Orleans Bapt. Theol. Sem., 1950-51, 53; D.D., Ohio Christian Coll., 1967, Birmingham Bapt. Bible Coll., 1979; postgrad., Auburn U., 1956, Baylor U., 1972-73; LL.D., Nat. Christian U., 1974. Owner Smith's Grocery Co., Montgomery, Ala., 1945-47; ordained minister Bapt. Ch., 1947; pastor Dolomite Bapt. Ch., Birmingham, Ala., 1947-50, Elim Bapt. Ch., Brewton, Ala., 1950-51; pastor 1st Bapt. Ch., Tallapoosa, Ga., 1951-52, Villa Rica, Ga., 1952-54, Fairfax, Ala., 1954-57; pastor West End Bapt. Ch., Birmingham, 1957-59, 88-94, Dalraida Bapt. Ch., Montgomery, 1959-66, 83-86, 1st Bapt. Ch., Demopolis, Ala., 1966-69; assoc. exec. dir. Ala. Council Alcohol Problems, Birmingham, 1969-70, exec. dir., 1970-78; exec. dir. Am. Council Alcohol Problems, Washington, 1972-74, sec., 1974-79, v.p., 1979-87; pastor Benton (Ala.) Bapt. Ch., 1987-88, Vinesville (Ala.) Bapt. Ch., 1994—; tchr., dir. Bessemer Bapt. Inst., 1978-83; exec. dir. missions Bessemer Bapt. Assn., 1978-83; tchr. Mercer U. extension, Carrollton, Ga., 1953-54; tchr. Extension div. Samford U., Fairfax, Ala., 1955-57, South Ala. area dir., 1986-87; mem. bd. ministerial edn. Bapt. Ch., 1958-59, Christian Life Comm., 1959-60; pres. Bessemer Ministers Alliance, 1979-81. Contbr. profl. jours. Chmn. Marengo County Cancer Soc., 1967-68, Good News Ala., Jefferson County, 1977-79, Gov.'s Commn. on Pornography, 1970-78, Nat. Temperance and Prohibition Council, 1973-80, Nat. Coordinating Council on Drug Edn., 1972-78, Alcohol Drug Problems Assn. Am., 1972-78; exec. dir. Temperance Edn., Inc., Washington, 1972-74; trustee Internat. Reform Fedn., 1973-74; adv. bd. JCCEO, 1975-82; bd. dirs. Bessemer Rescue Mission, 1978-83, 89-94, Bessemer YMCA, 1978-83; mem. adv. bd. Bessemer Salvation Army, 1978-83. Served to capt. USAAF, 1942-45, ETO. Mem. C. of C., Trident, Phi Kappa Phi. Club: Mason. Home: PO Box 535 Helena AL 35080-0535

SMITH, JOHN LEWIS, III, lawyer; b. Washington, Aug. 8, 1941. BA, Princeton U., 1963; JD, Georgetown U., 1967. Bar: D.C. 1968. Mng. ptnr. Baker & Hostetler, Washington. Mem. D.C. Bar. Office: Baker & Hostetler 1050 Connecticut Ave NW Ste 11 Washington DC 20036-5303*

SMITH, JOHN M., trucking executive; b. 1948. Degree in econs., Cornell Coll., 1971; MBA, Cornell U., 1974. With CRST Internat. Inc., Cedar Rapids, Iowa, 1971—, pres., CEO, 1987—. Named Regional Entrepreneur of the Yr., 1992. Mem. ATA (exec. com.), ITCC. Office: CRST Internat Inc 3960 16th Ave SW Cedar Rapids IA 52404-2332

SMITH, J(OHN) MALCOLM, political science educator; b. Vancouver, B.C., Can., Jan. 24, 1921; (parents Am. citizens); s. George John and Henrietta E. (Smith) S.; m. Connie Grace Shaw, June 2, 1943; children: Sheila C., Nancy L., Patricia L. BA, U. Wash., 1946; MA, Stanford U., 1948, PhD, 1951. Asst. prof. polit. sci. U. Calif., Riverside, 1945-57; instr. polit. sci. Stanford (Calif.) U., 1947-50; instr. pub. law and govt. Columbia U., N.Y.C., 1950-52; organizer World Affairs Coun., L.A., 1952-54; prof. polit. sci. Calif. State U., Hayward, 1965—; cons. Office of Sec. USAF, Washington, 1957-58, Commn. on Civil Rights, Washington, 1958-59; spl. asst. minority whip U.S. Senate, Washington, 1959-61; vis. prof. U. S.D., 1961-62, Ariz. State U., 1962-63; Merrill prof. Utah State U., 1976; mem. Ctr. for Study of Presidency. Co-author: Powers of the President During Crisis, 1961, President and National Security, 1972; contbr. articles to profl. jours. Midshipman USNR, 1940-43; 1st lt. infantry U.S. Army, 1943-45. Grantee Ford Found., 1955-56, John S. Sheppard, 1951-52. Mem. Acad. Polit. Sci., The Supreme Ct. Hist. Soc. Home: 2289 East Ave Hayward CA 94541-5631 Office: Calif State U Dept Polit Sci Hayward CA 94542

SMITH, JOHN MATTHEW, insurance company executive; b. Bklyn., Mar. 21, 1936; s. John Bernard and Mary (Lukas) S.; m. Kathryn Ellen Hurley, May 30, 1959; children—Mary Ellen, Kathryn Ann Jacques, Sarah Jane. B.A., Bklyn. Coll., 1959. With Met. Life Ins. Co., N.Y.C., 1959-68; with Guardian Life Ins. Co., N.Y.C., 1968—, sr. v.p., 1983-94, exec. v.p., 1995—; adj. prof. Coll. Ins., N.Y.C., 1975—; pres. Guardian Investor Svcs. Corp., N.Y.C., 1977—, Baillie Gifford Internat. Fund, N.Y.C., 1990—; exec. v.p. Guardian Ins. & Annuity Co., N.Y.C., 1981—. Served with U.S. Army, 1956-58. Mem. Nat. Assn. Securities Dealers (registered prin.). Democrat. Roman Catholic. Avocations: woodworking; electronics. Office: Guardian Life Ins Co 201 Park Ave S New York NY 10003-1605

SMITH, JOHN MCNEILL, JR., lawyer; b. Rowland, N.C., Apr. 9, 1918; s. John McNeill and Roberta (Andrew) S.; m. Louise Jordan; children: Louise Smith Nichols, Anne Smith Cole, John McNeill III, Eleanor. AB, U. N.C., 1938; LLB, Columbia U., 1941. Bar: N.C. 1941, N.Y. 1942. Assoc. Root Clark Buckner & Ballantine, N.Y.C., 1941, Smith Wharton & Jordan, Greensboro, N.C., 1945-48; ptnr. Smith Wharton Sapp & Moore and successor firm: Smith Helms Mulliss & Moore, Greensboro, 1948—; vis. prof. U. N.C. Law Sch., Chapel Hill, 1964-65; faculty Nat. Inst. Trial Advocacy. Author, editor: Equal Protection of the Laws in North Carolina, 1963; contbr. articles to jours in field. Mem. N.C. Ho. of Reps., 1970, N.C. Senate, 1971-78; bd. dirs. Alt. Energy Corp. N.C., 1980-88, N.C. Ctr. for Pub. Policy Rsch., 1980-92; chmn. N.C. State Bd. Ethics, 1980-84; pres. N.C. Vol. Lawyers for the Arts, 1984-89. Served to lt. comdr. USNR, 1941-48. Recipient award NCCJ, 1990; named one of 100 Most Influential Lawyers, Nat. Bar Jour., 1985, 88, 91. Mem. ABA (chmn. ind. rights and responsibilities 1972, mem. ho. dels. 1974, chmn. commn. on mentally disabled 1979, Ctrl. and Ea. European law initiate liaison to Estonia 1992-93), Internat. Bar Assn., N.C. Bar Assn. (chairperson constl. rights and responsibilities 1994—, Liberty Bell award 1990), Greensboro Bar Assn., N.C. Acad. Trial Lawyers, N.C. Assn. Def. Attys., Nat. Acad. Elder Law Attys., Am. Bus. Club (pres. 1968-70). Avocations: concert band, photography, bicycling, tennis. Home: 2501 W Market St Greensboro NC 27403-1519 Office: Smith Helms Mulliss & Moore PO Box 21927 300 N Greene St Ste 1400 Greensboro NC 27401-2167

SMITH, JOHN MICHAEL, lawyer; b. Summit, N.J., Sept. 23, 1959; s. Paul Harry and Mary (Konieczny) S. BA in Polit. Sci., Ursinus Coll., Collegeville, Pa., 1981; JD, Del. Law Sch., Wilmington, 1985; LLM in Environ. Law, George Washington U., Washington, 1995. Bar: Pa. 1985, U.S. Ct. Military Appeals 1986. Asst. staff judge adv. 4th Combat Support Group, Seymour Johnson AFB, N.C., 1986-87, 343d Combat Support Group, Eielson AFB, AK, 1987-88; area def. counsel USAF Judiciary, Eielson AFB, AK, 1988-90; asst. staff judge adv. Headquarters 7th Air Force, Osan AFB, Rep. of Korea, 1990-91; dep. staff judge adv. 438th Airlift Wing, McGuire AFB, N.J., 1991-94, Air Force Legal Svcs. Agy. Environ. Law & Litigation Divsn., Arlington, Va., 1995—; Mem. Pa. Bar Assn., 1985-88. Recipient Air Force Commendation medal USAF, 1987, 90, 91, Air Force Achievement medal USAF, 1992, Air Force Meritorious Svc. medal, 1995. Roman Catholic. Avocations: racquetball, computers, bicycling. Home: Apt 203 1201 Braddock Pl Alexandria VA 22314 Office: AFLSA/JACE Ste 629 1501 Wilson Blvd Arlington VA 22209-2403

SMITH, JOHN STANLEY, lawyer, mediator; b. Albany, N.Y., Nov. 15, 1946; s. Robert Stanley Smith and Sylvia Rose Murgia Neary; m. Diane Marie Doucette, July 9, 1947 (div. 1995); children: Jon Jeffrey, James Michael, Brian Matthew, Melissa Marie. BA, St. Bernardine of Siena Coll., Loudonville, N.Y., 1968; JD, U. Balt., 1986. Bar: Md. 1986, U.S. Dist. Ct. Md. 1987, D.C. 1988. Commd. U.S. Army, 1968, advanced through grades to lt. col.; comdr. assault helicopter platoon U.S. Army, Vietnam, 1970-71; comdr. A Btry 3d Bn. 38th Field Artillery U.S. Army, Ft. Sill, Okla., 1972-74; comdr. 132 Assault Support Helicopter Co. U.S. Army, Hunter Airfield, 1975, ops. officer 145th Aviation Bn., 1976-78; divsn. artillery aviation officer 25th Divsn. Artillery U.S. Army, Schofield Barracks, 1979-80; dep. dir. Directorate of Res. Forces, Ft. Meade, Md., 1981-82; dep. chief Unit Tng. Br. First U.S. Army, 1982-84; divsn. chief Concepts Analysis Agy., Bethesda, Md., 1984-87; exec. officer war plans Dept. of Army, Washington, 1987-90; ptnr. Dziennik & Smith, Glen Burnie, Balt., 1990-92; v.p., gen. counsel Academy Title Group, Glen Burnie, 1992-93; pvt. practice Glen Burnie, 1992—; owner Smith Mediation Svcs., Glen Burnie, 1992—; pres. Lorimar Title Corp., Glen Bunnie, 1995—. Author: Mid Range Forces Study 88-92, 1985, Mid Range Forces Study 90-94, 1986, Mid Range Forces Study 90-97, 1987. Bd. dirs. No. Anne Arundel County Rep. Club, 1994-95. Decorated Legion of Merit, Bronze Star, Air Medal, Purple Heart. Mem. ABA, Md. Bar Assn., Anne Arundel County Bar Assn., Balt. City Bar Assn., Acad. Family Mediators, No. Anne Arundel County C. of C. (pres. 1996). Roman Catholic. Avocations: running, bowling, basketball, hiking, camping. Office: 5 Crain Hwy N Glen Burnie MD 21061-3516

SMITH, JOHN STUART, lawyer; b. Rochester, N.Y., Sept. 4, 1943; s. Cecil Y. and Helen M. (Van Patten) S.; m. Nancy Schauman, Aug. 28, 1965; children—Kristan, Debra Barton. A.B. magna cum laude, Harvard U., 1965, LL.B. cum laude, 1968. Bar: N.Y. 1968, D.C. 1968, U.S. dist. ct. (we. dist.) N.Y. 1969, U.S. dist. ct. (so. dist.) N.Y. 1973, U.S. dist. ct. (no. dist.) N.Y. 1977, U.S. dist. ct. (no. dist.) Tex. 1980, U.S. Ct. Apls. (5th cir.) 1971, (2d cir.) 1972, (9th cir.) 1980, U.S. Sup. Ct. 1978. Assoc. Nixon, Hargrave, Devans & Doyle, Rochester, N.Y., 1968-74, mem., 1975—. Bd. dirs. Rochester Chamber Orch., 1970-75, Geva Theater, 1988. Mem. ABA, N.Y. State Bar Assn. (past chmn. criminal procedure subcom. antitrust sect.), Monroe County Bar Assn. Office: PO Box 1051 1 Clinton Sq Rochester NY 14603 also: 1 Thomas Cir NW Washington DC 20005-5802 also: # 702 1026 16th St NW Apt 702 Washington DC 20036-5712

SMITH, JOHN WILSON, III, newspaper editor, columnist, statistician; b. Pottsville, Pa., June 2, 1935; s. John Wilson II and Hannah (Morris) S.; m. Jean Ann Longenecker, Nov. 21, 1973; children: Jeffrey W., Jennifer L., Jodi A. BA in History magna cum laude, Franklin & Marshall Coll., 1957; MA in Journalism, Syracuse U., 1959. Sports writer Reading (Pa.) Eagle, 1958-81, sports editor, 1981-82; news editor, columnist Reading Eagle/Times, 1983-87, religion editor, columnist, 1988—; copy chief Reading Eagle, 1987—; statistician Ea. Pa. Football Conf., Hazleton, 1981—, Dist. 11, Allentown, Pa., 1984—; moderator Reading Bapt. Assn., 1966-68. Pres. Western Berks Jr. Baseball League, West Lawn, Pa., 1993—; sports ofcl. Pa. Interscholastic Athletic Assn., Mechanicsburg, 1955-95. Named to Pa. Am. Legion Sports Hall of Fame, 1972, St. Clair, Pa. Oldtimers Sports Hall of Fame, 1993. Mem. Religion Newswriters Assn., Phi Beta Kappa, Sigma Delta Chi. Am. Bapt. Avocation: youth baseball administrator and coach. Home: 1121 Whitfield Blvd West Lawn PA 19609 Office: Reading Eagle Times PO Box 582 Reading PA 19603

SMITH, JONATHAN DAVID, medical educator; b. Cleve., Jan. 10, 1955. BS, U. Calif., Santa Cruz, 1978; PhD, Harvard U., 1984. Postdoctoral Lab. Biochem. Genetics and Metabolism The Rockefeller U., N.Y.C., 1984-89, asst. prof., 1989—. Contbr. articles to profl. jours. Recipient Nat. Rsch. Svc. award NIH, 1985-87, Program Project award, 1995—. Mem. AAAS, Am. Heart Assn. (Investigatorship award N.Y.C. affiliate 1989-92, Grant-in-Aid 1989-92, 92-95, Established Investigator 1994—). Achievements include identification of genes that regulate atherosclerosis; development of animal models useful for testing therapies to proevent atherosclerosis; characterization of novel functions of apolopoprotein E which are relevant to Alzheimer's disease, cardiovascular disease and longevity. Office: The Rockefeller U 1230 Park Ave New York NY 10021

SMITH, JOSEF RILEY, internist; b. Council Bluffs, Iowa, Oct. 1, 1926; s. George William Smith and Margaret (Wood) Hill; divorced; children: Sarah L. Kratz, David L., Mary E. Loeb, John R., Ruthann P. Sherrier, Mark A.; m. Susan Frances Irwin, Feb. 9, 1973; 1 child, Christopher I. Student, Tulane U., 1944-46; BM, Northwestern U., 1950, MD, 1951; MSEE, Marquette U., 1964. Diplomate Am. Bd. Internal Medicine. Instr. internal medicine U. Miss. Med. Sch., Jackson, 1956-59; asst. prof. Marquette U. Med. Sch., Milw., 1959-63; from assoc. prof. to full prof. U. Mich. Med. Sch., Ann Arbor, 1963-72; physician Youngstown (Ohio) Hosp., 1972-79, Group Health Med. Assn., Tucson, 1979-84, Assocs. in Internal Medicine, Tucson, 1985-87; pvt. practice Tucson, 1987—. Co-author: Clinical Cardiopulmonary Physiology, 1960, Textbook of Pulmonary Disease, 1965, 2d rev. edit., 1974; contbr. articles to profl. jours. Controller Mahoning County TB Clinic, Youngstown, 1973-79. Served to lt. USNR, 1952-54. Fellow ACP, Sigma Xi; mem. Ariz. Med. Assn., Pima County Med. Assn., Am. Thoracic Soc., Ariz. Thoracic Soc., Bioengring. Med. Soc. (founder). Avocations: photography, computer programming. Office: 2224 N Craycroft Rd Ste 109 Tucson AZ 85712-2811

SMITH, JOSEPH NEWTON, III, retired architect, educator; b. Jacksonville, Fla., July 4, 1925; s. Joseph Newton, Jr. and Oneal (Kemp) S.; m. Gloria Bevis, Aug. 24, 1946; 1 child, Gordon Kemp. B.S., Ga. Inst. Tech., 1948, B.Arch., 1949. Designer and/or architect archtl. firms in Miami, Fla., 1949-56; propr. Joseph N. Smith, Architect, Miami, 1956-63; partner firm Smith, Polychrone and Wolfcale, Atlanta, 1966-69; gen. cons. architecture, 1969-73; mem. faculty Sch. Architecture, Ga. Inst. Tech., 1963-82, prof. architecture, asst. dir. sch., 1971-77, asst. dean, 1977-82; v.p. interior design Thompson, Ventulett, Steinback and Assocs., Architects and Interior Designers, Atlanta, 1982-88; ptnr. TVS & Assocs. One-man shows: Archtl. Book Show Atlanta, 1987, Connell Gallery, Atlanta, 1992. Served to lt. (j.g.) USNR, 1943-46. Recipient Birch Burdette Long Meml. award Archtl. League N.Y., 1956; award merit S. Atlantic region AIA for Key Biscayne (Fla.) Presbyn. Ch., 1964, for Friendship Center, low income housing Atlanta, 1970; named Honored Artist of Year, Young Women of Arts, 1974. Fellow AIA. Presbyterian. Home: 2466 Ridgewood Rd NW Atlanta GA 30318-1316

SMITH, JOSEPH PHELAN, film company executive; b. N.Y.C.; s. John William and Margaret Mary (Phelan) S.; m. Madelyn Eleanor Davis, Jan. 17, 1942; children: Kevin, Karen, Margaret, Lisa. BS, Columbia U. Former salesman Van Alstyne Noel & Co., N.Y.C.; former salesman RKO Radio Pictures, Inc., Boston, Omaha, div. mgr., Los Angeles, Portland, Oreg., San Francisco, 1938-47; former exec. v.p. Lippert Prodns., Hollywood, Calif.; former v.p., gen. mgr. sales Telepictures, N.Y.C.; founding pres. Cinema Vue Corp.; now pres. Pathe News Inc., N.Y.C., Pathe Pictures Inc., N.Y.C. Served with U.S. Army. Mem. Motion Picture Pioneers, Am. Film Inst., Elks. Republican. Office: Pathe News Inc 270 Madison Ave 5th FL New York NY 10016

SMITH, JOSEPH PHILIP, lawyer; b. Jackson, Tenn., June 14, 1944; s. William Benjamin and Virginia Marie (Carey) S.; m. Deborah J. Smith, Dec. 22, 1972; 1 child, Virginia Louise. BA, U. Miss., 1967, JD, 1975; MEd, U. So. Miss., 1977; postgrad., U. Memphis, 1994—. Bar: Miss. 1975, Tex. 1979, N. Mex. 1991, Colo. 1991, Tenn. 1995, U.S. Dist. Ct. (no. dist.) Miss. 1975, U.S. Dist. Ct. (no. dist.) Tex. 1982, U.S. Dist. Ct. N.Mex. 1993, U.S. Dist. Ct. Colo. 1993, U.S. Ct. Appeals (10th cir.) 1993. Assoc., then ptnr. Byrnes, Myers, Adair, Campbell & Sinex, Houston, 1979-85; pvt. practice Marks, Miss., Memphis, Raton, N.Mex., 1985—. Mem. Archdiocese of Santa Fe Sch. Bd., 1991-92. Capt. USAF, 1967-71. Mem. ABA, Colo. Bar Assn., Miss. Pub. Defender Assn. (treas. 1988-90), Rotary (pres., sec. Marks-Raton club 1985-90). Republican. Roman Catholic. Home: 674 St Augustine Sq Memphis TN 38104

SMITH, JOSEPH SETON, electronics company executive, consultant; b. N.Y.C., July 16, 1925; s. William Thomas and Loretto Agnes (Gorman) S.; m. Marion Susan McManus, June 14, 1952; children: Marion R., Loretto A., Joseph S., John J., Eleanor M., William T., Vincent C., Regina M. BSEE, Iowa State U., 1946; MEE, NYU, 1950, DSc, 1955. Rsch. assoc. prof. NYU, N.Y.C., 1947-55; asst. chief engr. Burroughs Corp., Bklyn., 1955-59; div. mgr. Sperry Rand Corp., Gt. Neck, N.Y., 1959-66; v.p. Litton Industries, Beverly Hills, Calif., 1966-72; sr. v.p. Figgie Internat. Corp., Cleve., 1972-79; pres. J.S. Smith Corp., Cleve., 1979-87; exec. dir. Ctr. for Venture Devel., Cleve., 1983-87; v.p., gen. mgr. CSD Telephonics Corp., Farmingdale, N.Y., 1987-93; v.p. Technology Telephonics Corp., 1993—; bd. dirs. Waterlox Corp., Cleve.; trustee Enterprise Devel. Inc. subs. Case Western Res. U., Cleve.; cons. on creation and growth tech. cos. Contbr. articles on radar, systems integration, instrumentation, and entrepreneurship to profl. jours. Organizer, keynote speaker Cleve. Entrepreneurship Confs., 1984, 85; music dir. Ch. St. Gregory the Great, Cleve. Lt. (j.g.) USN, 1943-46. Fellow IEEE (chmn. N.Y. sect. 1957-58); mem. Hermit Club (Cleve.), Mayfield Country Club (Cleve.), Sigma Xi, Eta Kappa Nu, Pi Mu Epsilon. Home: 4912 Countryside Rd Lyndhurst OH 44124-2515 Office: Telephonics Corp Command Systems Div 815 Broadhollow Rd Farmingdale NY 11735-3904

SMITH, JOY S., pediatric emergency nurse; b. Florence, S.C., Dec. 25, 1939; d. Marion Carl and Christine (Cunningham) Summersett; m. Richard M. Smith, Dec. 23, 1962; children: David C., Christine L. Diploma, McLeod Infirmary Sch. Nursing, Florence, S.C., 1960, McLeod Infirmary Sch. Anesthesia, Florence, 1962; BSN, Wilmington Coll., 1994; postgrad., U. Del. Cert. provider PALS, emergency nurse. Nurse anesthetist St. Lukes and Tex. Children's Hosps., Houston; head nurse Newark (Del). Emergency Ctr.; supr. emergency dept. Sacred Heart Med. Ctr., Chester, Pa.; nurse mgr. Alfred I. duPont Inst., Wilmington, Del. Mem. Emergency Nurses Assn. Office: Alfred I du Pont Inst Wilmington DE 19899

SMITH, JUDITH ANN, academic administrator; b. Springfield, Mo., Jan. 1, 1950; d. Harley Jr. and Barbara Jean (Anderson) Cozad; m. Robert Eugene Smith, July 11, 1969. BS in Edn., S.W. Mo. State U., 1973, MA in English, 1976. Cert. tchr. (life), Mo. Tchr. R-12 Schs., Springfield, 1973-83; program/communications mgr. Performing Arts Ctr. Trust, Tulsa, 1983-84; gen. mgr. Springfield Symphony Assn., 1984-86; assoc. dir. devel., dir. planning giving S.W. Mo. State U., 1986-89, dir. devel. alumni rels., 1989—; dir. Summerscape (gifted program), Springfield, 1980-82; mem. NCAA fiscal integrity com. S.W. Mo. State U., 1994-96. Vol. Springfield Symphony Guild, 1986—; vol. fundraising advisor First Night, Springfield, 1993—; appointee Greene County Hist. Sites Bd., 1994—, chair, 1995-96; bd. dirs. Springfield Area Arts Coun., 1995—, Discovery Ctr. of Springfield, 1994—. Named Outstanding Young Educator Springfield Jaycees, 1976, Mo. Jaycees, 1977. Mem. Coun. for Advancement and Support of Edn. (com. on women and minorities 1988-90, Merit and Excellence awards 1988, 89, 90), Leadership Springfield Alumni Assn., PEO, Rotary, Delta Kappa Gamma (past chpt. officer). Office: SW Mo State U 901 S National Ave Springfield MO 65804-0027

SMITH, JULIA LADD, medical oncologist, hospice physician; b. Rochester, N.Y., July 26, 1951; d. John Herbert and Isabel (Walcott) Ladd; m. Stephen Slade Smith; 1 child. BA, Smith Coll., 1973; MD, N.Y. Med. Coll., 1976. Diplomate Am. Bd. Internal Medicine, Am. Bd. Med. Oncology. Intern in medicine N.Y. Med. Coll., N.Y.C., 1976-77; resident in medicine Rochester Gen. Hosp., 1977-79; internist Genesee Valley Group Health, Rochester, 1979-80; oncology fellow U. Rochester, 1980-82, asst. prof. oncology in medicine sch. medicine & dentistry, 1986—; oncologist Med. Ctr. Clinic, Ltd., Pitts., 1982-83; oncologist, internist Rutgers Community Health Plan, New Brunswick, N.J., 1983-86; med. dir. Genesse Region Home Care Assn./Hospice, Rochester, 1988—. Bd. dirs. Am. Cancer Soc., Monroe County, 1988-92. Nat. Cancer Inst. rsch. grantee, 1993-95. Mem. ACP, Am. Soc. Clin. Oncology, Acad. Hospice Physicians. Unitarian-Universalist. Avocations: sailing, reading, movies, bridge. Address: Genesee Hosp 224 Alexander St Rochester NY 14607

SMITH, JULIAN CLEVELAND, JR., chemical engineering educator; b. Westmount, Que., Can., Mar. 10, 1919; s. Julian Cleveland and Bertha (Alexander) S.; m. Joan Elsen, June 1, 1946; children: Robert Elsen, Diane Louise Smith Brook, Brian Richard. B.Chemistry, Cornell U., 1941, Chem. Engr., 1942. Chem. engr. E. I. duPont de Nemours and Co., Inc., 1942-46; mem. faculty Cornell U., 1946—, prof. chem. engring., 1953-86, prof. emeritus, 1986—, dir. continuing engring. edn., 1965-71; assoc. dir. Cornell U. (Sch. Chem. Engring.), 1973-75, dir., 1975-83; vis. lectr. U. Edinburgh, 1971-72; cons. to govt. and industry, 1947—; UNESCO cons. Universidad de Oriente, Venezuela, 1975. Author: (with W. L. McCabe and P. Harriott) Unit Operations of Chemical Engineering, 1956, 5th edit., 1993, also articles; sect. editor: Perry's Chemical Engineers Handbook, 1963. Fellow Am. Inst. Chem. Engrs.; mem. Am. Chem. Soc., Sigma Xi, Tau Beta Pi, Phi Kappa Phi, Alpha Delta Phi. Clubs: Ithaca Country, Statler (Ithaca). Home: 711 The Pky Ithaca NY 14850-1546

SMITH, JULIAN PAYNE, gynecological oncologist, educator; b. Portsmouth, Ohio, Mar. 23, 1930; s. Emory Farl and Lola Blanche (Payne) S.; m. Eleanore G. Stankunas, June 5, 1954; children: Susan Sharon, Charles Douglas, Geraldine Gigi, David James. Student, U. Mich., 1947-48; BA, Ohio Wesleyan U., 1951; MD, Columbia U., 1955. Diplomate Am. Bd. Ob-Gyn. Intern Univ. Hosps., Cleve., 1955-56; resident in ob/gyn Cornell N.Y. Hosp., 1956-57; resident in ob-gyn Columbia Presbyn. Med. Ctr., N.Y.C., 1957-59; fellow in gynecology-oncology U. Tex., Houston, 1963-66; pvt. practice Portsmouth, 1961-63; prof. U. Tex. System Cancer Center, M.D. Anderson Hosp. and Tumor Inst., Houston, 1973-77; prof. ob-gyn, dir. gynecologic oncology Wayne State U. Med. Sch., Detroit, 1977-83; pvt. practice medicine specializing in gynecologic oncology Southfield, Mich., 1983-86; prof. of ob-gyn Loyola U., Chgo., 1986-88; prof., dir. gynecology oncology Loyola U. Med. Ctr., Maywood, Ill., 1986-88; prof. ob-gyn, dir. gynecologic oncology U. Md. Sch. Medicine, Balt., 1988—. Editor: (with Gravlee) Endometrium, 1977, A Review of the World Literature, 1977, (with Delgado) Management of Complications in Gynecologic Oncology, 1982, (with Hafez) Carcinoma of the Cervix, 1982; contbr. articles to profl. jours. Bd. dirs. Am. Cancer Soc., Wayne County, Mich., 1980-81. Capt. M.C., USAR, 1959-61. Mem. Am. Coll. Ob-Gyn., Am. Radium Soc., Am. Assn. Ob-Gyn., Felix Rutledge Soc. (pres. 1968-70), Am. Gynecol. Soc., Am. Gynecol. and Obstet. Soc., Soc. Gynecol. Oncologists (pres. 1984-85), Soc. Pelvic Surgeons (pres. 1994-95), Mid. Atlantic Gynecol. Oncology Soc. (pres. 1991-92), Med. Ch. Soc. Md. Republican. Methodist. Home: 22 Treadwell Ct Lutherville Timonium MD 21093-3764 Office: U Md Sch Medicine Dept Ob-Gyn 22 S Greene St Baltimore MD 21201-1544

SMITH, JUNE BURLINGAME, English educator; b. Barrington, N.J., June 1, 1935; d. Leslie Grant and Esther (Bellini) Burlingame; m. Gregory Lloyd Smith, July 6, 1963; children: Gilia Cobb Burlingame Smith, Cyrus Comstock. BA, Reed Coll., 1956; MS, Ind. U., 1959; MA, Calif. State U., Dominquez Hills, 1986. Sec. to dean Reed Coll., 1956-57; residence hall supr. Ind. U., 1957-59; buyer Macy's Calif., 1959-63; residence hall supr. U. Wash., 1963, interviewer Tchr. Placement Bur., 1964; music tchr. Chinook Jr. High Sch., Bellevue, Wash., 1964-68; pvt. practice music tchr., 1971-83; gifted grant coord. South Shores/CSUDH Magnet Sch., 1981; tchr. cons. L.A. Unified Sch. Dist., 1981-82; assoc. prof. English L.A. Community Colls., Harbor Coll., Wilmington, Calif., 1989—; sexual harrassment officer Harbor Coll., Wilmington, Calif., 1991-92. Chair Sex Equity Commn., L.A. Unified Sch. Dist., 1988-91; bd. dirs. Harbor Inter Faith Shelter, 1994—. Mem. AAUW (pres. San Pedro, Calif. br. 1989-90, mem. task force Initiative for Equity in Edn. 1991-95), Am. Acad. Poets, Phi Kappa Phi, Delta Kappa. Democrat. Home: 3915 S Carolina St San Pedro CA 90731-7115 Office: LA Community Coll Harbor 1111 Figueroa Pl Wilmington CA 90744-2311

SMITH, KAREN MARIE, middle school educator; b. Jersey City, Sept. 23, 1950; d. George A. and Marie M. (Sahr) Wolfstirn; m. Donald W. Smith, Jan. 8, 1972; children: Susan Marie, Sean Michael. BA, William Paterson. 2nd & 3rd grade tchr. Our Lady Queen of Peace, Maywood, N.J., 1972-77; 6th, 7th, 8th grade tchr. St. Peter's Acad., River Edge, N.J., 1985-94; 6th grade tchr. South Orange (N.J.) Middle Sch., 1994—. Girl scout leader Bergen County, N.J., 1983-94 (named Outstanding leader 1990, Honor pin 1993). Mem. NEA, N.J. Edn. Assn., Nat. Coun. Tchrs. English, Nat. Coun. Tchrs. Math., South Orange/Maplewood Edn. Assn., Irish Dance Tchrs. N.Am. (reg. dir.). Roman Catholic. Avocations: computers, crafts, reading, camping, hiking. Home: 650 Edel Ave Maywood NJ 07607-1529

SMITH, KATHLEEN TENER, bank executive; b. Pitts., Oct. 19, 1943; d. Edward Harrison Jr. and Barbara Elizabeth (McCormick) Tener; m. Roger Davis Smith, May 30, 1970 (dec.); children: Silas Wheelock, Jocelyn Tener, Luke Ewing Taft. BA summa cum laude, Vassar Coll., 1965; MA in Econs., Harvard U., 1968. Rsch. assoc. Harvard U. Grad. Sch. Bus., Cambridge, Mass., 1967-69; assoc. economist Chase Manhattan Bank, N.Y.C., 1969-70, asst. treas., 1971, 2d v.p., 1972, v.p., 1973—, sec. asset liability mgmt. com., 1985-90, treas. Global Bank, 1990-91, divsn. exec. structured investment products, 1991-93, global mktg. and comms. exec. Global Risk Mgmt. Sect., 1993-94; global mktg. and comms. product devel. exec. Chase Global Markets Sect., 1994—. Editor: Commodity Derivatives and Finance, 1996. Trustee Vassar Coll., Poughkeepsie, N.Y., 1979-91, mem. exec. com., 1987-91; mem. subcom. on edn. Chase Manhattan Found., N.Y.C., 1985-90. NSF fellow, 1965-67. Mem. Am. Fin. Assn., Am. Econ. Assn., Fin. Mgmt. Assn., Yale Club. Republican. Episcopalian. Home: 454 State Route 32 N New Paltz NY 12561-3040 Office: Chase Manhattan Bank 1 Chase Manhattan Plz New York NY 10081-1000

SMITH, KATHY ANN, educator, state senator; b. Muncie, Ind., Apr. 10, 1944; d. John Francis and H. Emily (Walter) Wallace; m. George Frederick Smith, June 22, 1979; 1 child, Alison Marie Smith. BS in Edn., Ind. U., 1966; postgrad., Ball State U., 1973. Cert. secondary lang. arts tchr., Ind. English tchr. New Albany (Ind.) Floyd Co. Sch. Corp., 1966—; adj. faculty Ind. U. S.E., New Albany, 1977-84. Ind. State senator Ind. Gen. Assembly, Indpls., 1986—; del. Dem. Nat. Conv., N.Y., 1976-80, San Francisco, 1984, Atlanta, 1988, Ind. Dem. State Conv., Indpls., 1980, 82, 84, 86, 88, 90; mem., del. Dem. Nat. Platform Com., Washington, 1984. Mem. New Albany Floyd County Edn. Assn. (legis. chair 1977-86, exec. com. 1979-86), Ind. State Tchrs. Assn. (chair polit. action com. 1978-81, 83-86), NEA (NEA polit. action com. 1978-81, 83-84), Nat. Coun. Tchrs. of English, Pi Lambda Theta (hon., pres. 1986-88), Psi Iota Xi. Democrat. Avocations: reading, aerobics, skiing, writing. Home: 1214 Beechwood Ave New Albany IN 47150-2521 Office: Ind State Senate State Capital Indianapolis IN 46204

SMITH, KEITH, protective services official. Now fire chief City of Indpls. Office: Fire Dept 50 N Alabama St # 208E Indianapolis IN 46204-3301*

SMITH, KEN, physicist. Exec. dir. Quantum Inst. Rice U. Office: Rice U Quantum Inst PO Box 1892 Houston TX 77251-1892*

SMITH, KEN, landscape architect. BS in landscape architecture, Iowa State U., 1976; M in landscape architecture, Harvard U., 1986. Landscape architect N.Y., Calif., Mass., Iowa. Landscape architect State Conservation Commn. State Iowa, 1979-84, The Office of Peter Walker and Martha Schwartz, Inc., N.Y.C., San Francisco, 1986-89; cons. Dept. Environ. Mgmt. Commonwealth Mass., 1984-86; prin. Martha Schwartz Ken Smith David Meyer, Inc., San Francisco, 1990-92, Ken Smith Landscape Architect, San Francisco, 1992—; adj. prof. CCNY Sch. Architecture Urban Landscape Program, 1992—; temp. asst. prof. Iowa State U. Coll. Design, 1982. Contbr. articles to profl. jours. Ctr. Pub. Architecture fellow Randalls Island Project, N.Y.C., 1994; honorable mention Am. City Design Comp., Architecture Soc. Atlanta, 1994, San Diego Housing Commn., 1992; 1st place award limited design comp. Cumberland Park, Toronto, Ont., 1991, Bridging the Gaps Design Comp. Columbia U. Grad. Sch. Architecture Planning/Preservation and N.Y. Bldg. Arts Forum, 1990; spl. mention Boston Visions Comp. Boston Soc. Archs., 1988. Office: City Coll NY Urban Landscape Arch Program Convent Ave & 138th St New York NY 10031 Office: 80 Warren St Ste 28 New YTork NY 10007

SMITH, KENNETH ALAN, chemical engineer, educator; b. Winthrop, Mass., Nov. 28, 1936; s. James Edward and Alice Gertrude (Walters) S.; m. Ambia Marie Olsson, Oct. 14, 1961; children: Kirsten Heather, Edward Eric, Andrew Ian Beaumont, Thurston Garrett. S.B., MIT, 1958, S.M., 1959, Sc.D., 1962; postgrad., Cambridge (Eng.) U., 1964-65. Asst. prof. chem. engring. MIT, 1961-67, assoc. prof., 1967-71, prof., 1971—, Edwin R. Gilliland prof. chem. engring., 1989—, acting head dept., 1976-77, assoc. provost, 1980-81, assoc. provost, v.p. rsch., 1981-91, dir. Whitaker Coll. Health Sci. and Tech., 1989-91; cons. chem. and oil cos. NSF fellow, 1964-65, Overseas fellow, Churchill Coll., (Eng.), 1993. Mem. Am. Inst. Chem. Engrs., Nat. Acad. Engring., Am. Chem. Soc., AAAS, Sigma Xi, Phi Lambda Upsilon, Tau Beta Pi. Episcopalian. Home: 32 School St Manchester MA 01944-1336 Office: MIT Bldg 66-540 Cambridge MA 02139

SMITH, KENNETH BLOSE, former financial executive; b. Monmouth, Ill., Jan. 29, 1926; s. Elmer Edwin and Florence (Logan) S.; m. Julia M. Stupp, June 17, 1950; children: Donald E., Paul C., Marilyn D. B.S., U. Iowa, 1947. Internal auditor Deere & Co, Moline, Ill., 1947-52; treas. John Deere Chem. Co., Pryor, Okla., 1952-65; fin. mgr. Deere & Co., Moline, Ill., 1965-71, asst. treas., 1971-81, treas., 1981-85. Republican. Lutheran.

SMITH, KENNETH BRYANT, seminary administrator; b. Montclair, N.J., Feb. 19, 1931; m. Gladys Moran; children: Kenneth Bryant Jr., Kourtney Beth, Kristen Bernard. BA, Va. Union U., 1953; postgrad., Drew U., 1953-54; BD, Bethany Theol. Sem., 1960; DD (hon.), Elmhurst Coll., 1971, Shaw U., 1987; D Ps (hon.), Nat. Lewis U., 1981; LittD (hon.), Chgo. State U., 1990; STD, Olivet Coll., 1992. Ordained to ministry United Ch. of Christ, 1960. Assoc. min. Park Manor Congl. Ch., Chgo., 1957-61; min. Trinity United Ch. of Christ, Chgo., 1961-66; min. urban affairs The Community Renewal Soc., 1966-68; sr. min. Ch. of Good Shepherd, Chgo., 1968-84; pres. Chgo. Theol. Sem., U. Chgo., 1984—. Mem. Met. Chgo. YMCA, 1986—, Community Renewal Soc., 1966-68. Office: Chgo Theol Sem 5757 S University Ave Chicago IL 60637-1507

SMITH, KENNETH CARLESS, electrical engineering educator; b. Toronto, May 8, 1932; s. Reginald Thomas and Viola Evelyn (Carless) S.; children—K. David, Kevin A. B.A.Sc., U. Toronto, 1954, M.A.Sc. in Elec. Engring., 1956, Ph.D. in Physics, 1960. Transmission engr. Can. Nat. Telegraphs, Toronto, 1954-55; rsch. engr. U. Toronto at U. Ill., Urbana, 1956-58; asst. prof. elec. engring. U. Ill., Urbana, 1961-64, assoc. prof., 1964-65; asst. prof. elec. engring. U. Toronto, 1960-61, assoc. prof. elec. engring. and computer sci., 1965-70, prof., 1970-81, prof. depts. elec. engring., computer sci., info. studies, 1981—, chmn. dept. elec. engring., 1976-81; pres. Elec. Engring. Consociates Ltd., Toronto, 1974-76; mem. Ont. Task Force on Microelectronic Tech., 1980-81; adv. prof. Shanghai Tiedao U., People's Republic China, 1989—; vis. prof. Hong Kong U. Sci. and Tech., Clearwater Bay, Hong Kong, 1993—; dir. several firms, U.S., Hong Kong and Can.; Author: (with A.S. Sedra) Microelectronic Circuits, 1982, Spanish edit., 1985, Korean edit., 1989, Hebrew edit., 1990, 3d edit., 1991, Greek edit., 1994, Italian edit., 1995, Portuguese edit., 1995, Lab. Explorations, 1991, Additional Problems, 1992, Problems Supplement, 1995; contbr. chpts. to books and articles to profl. jours.; patentee in field. Fellow IEEE, Cirs. and Sys. Soc. (chmn. confs. procedures and planning, publs. coun.), Can. Soc. for Profl. Engrs. (bd. dirs. 1984-93, pres. 1988-91), Internat. Solid State Cir. Conf. (exec. com., awards chmn. 1975—, press chair 1994—). Liberal. Mem. Anglican Ch. Home: 56 Torbrick Rd, Toronto, ON Canada M4J 4Z5 Office: U Toronto Dept Elec and Computer Engring, 10 King's Coll. Rd, Toronto, ON Canada M5S 1A4

SMITH, KENNETH JUDSON, JR., chemist, theoretician, educator; b. Raleigh, N.C., Sept. 4, 1930; s. Kenneth Judson and Irene (Strickland) S.; m. Dorothy Margaret Ratcliffe, Mar. 6, 1953; children: Patricia Lynne Smith Pittman, Pamela Jean. A.B., East Carolina U., 1957; M.A., Duke U., 1959, Ph.D., 1961. Research chemist Chemstrand Research Center, Durham, N.C., 1961-65; sr. research chemist Chemstrand Research Center, 1965-68; asst. prof. polymer research SUNY Coll. Environ. Sci. and Forestry, Syracuse, 1968-70; assoc. prof. SUNY Coll. Environ. Sci. and Forestry, 1970-73, prof., 1973—, asst. dir. Polymer Research Center, 1971-79, acting dir., 1979-83, dir. Organic Materials Sci. Program, 1971-75, chmn. dept. chemistry, 1972-84; vis. prof. Instituto di Chimica Industriale, U. Genoa, Italy, 1979; cons. U.S. Army Materials and Mechanics Rsch. Ctr., Watertown, Mass., 1973-75, cert. of appreciation 1973, NRC, Washington, 1980-87; mem. adv. coun. Syracuse Met. Transp. Coun., 1975-84; mem. adv. bd. confs. in polymer sci. and tech. SUNY, New Paltz, 1977-85; mem. rsch. found. joint com. on procedures SUNY, Albany, 1974-81. Contbr. articles to profl. jours. Served with USMC, 1951-54. Recipient cert. Appreciation U.S. Army Materials and Mechanics Rsch. Ctr., 1973. Mem. AAAS, Am. Chem. Soc. (dir. Syracuse sect. 1977-79, chmn. 1978, councilor 1979-82), Am. Phys. Soc. (com. on internat. freedom of scientists, small coms.), Am. Inst. Chemists, Soc. Plastics Engrs., Math. Assn. Am., N.Y. Acad. Scis., Sigma Xi, Phi Lambda Upsilon, Kappa Delta Pi. Achievements include research on statistical mechanics, mechanical properties and theoretical studies of polymers; rubber elasticity and thermoelasticity; crystallization of networks; structure-property relationships; ultimate properties of fibers. Home: 108 Scottholm Blvd Syracuse NY 13224-1728 Office: Coll Environ Sci and Forestry Suny Syracuse NY 13210

SMITH, KENT ASHTON, scientific and technical information executive; b. Boston, Sept. 3, 1938; s. Kent Wooliscroft and Dorothy Patten Smith; m. Mary Margaret Gaffney; children: Holly L. Smith Volz, Kent W. BA, Hobart Coll., 1960; MBA, Cornell U., 1962; postgrad., Am. U., 1978-79. Mgmt. analyst Office of Sec., HEW, Washington, 1962-65; adminstrv. officer divsn. rsch. facilities and resources NIH, Bethesda, Md., 1965-67, asst. exec. officer divsn. rsch. facilities and resources, 1967-68, exec. offider divsn. rsch. resources, 1968-71, asst. dir. adminstrn. Nat. Libr. Medicine, 1971-78, dep. dir., 1978—; mem. exec. bd. Internat. Coun. Sci. and Tech. Info., Paris, 1983-86, treas., 1986-88, pres.-elect, 1989, pres., 1990-94; treas. Nat. Fed. Abstracting and Info. Sci., Phila., 1986-88, exec. bd., 1985—, pres. elect, 1989, pres., 1990; v.p. U.S. Nat. Com. of UNESCO-PGI, Washington, 1983-85; mem. exec. adv. bd. Fed. Libr. and Info. Ctr. Com., Washington, 1984-89; chmn. exec. com. CENDI-Info. Consortia, Washington, 1985—. Contbr.

articles to profl. jours., chpt. to book: Management of Federally Sponsored Libraries, 1995. Mem. Citizens Com. for Pub. Libr. Montgomery County, Bethesda, 1981-82; fin. dir. Christ Ch., Rockville, Md., 1990-91. Recipient Asst. Sec. for Health Exceptional Achievement award USPHS, 1978. Mem. ASPA (vice chmn. 1971-72), Am. Mgmt. Assn., Am. Soc. Info. Svcs., Med. Libr. Assn., Assn. Rsch. Librs., Assn. Advanced Sci. Episcopalian. Avocations: theater, golf, baseball, bird watching, genealogy. Home: Internat Coun Sci & Tech 17903 Gainford Pl Olney MD 20832 Office: Nat Libr Medicine 8600 Rockville Pike Bethesda MD 20894

SMITH, KENT ELLIOT, lawyer; b. Blair, Nebr., Dec. 11, 1965; s. Richard Adams and Jacqueline Anne (Reeh) S.; m. Steffanie Anne Jordan, Aug. 10, 1991. B Accountancy, U. Miss., 1988, JD, 1991. Assoc. Langston, Langston, Michael & Bowen, Bonneville, Miss., 1991-92; ptnr. Balducci & Smith, Oxford, Miss., 1992-94, Webb, Sanders, Deaton, Balducci, Smith & Faulks, Oxford, 1994—. Mem. Miss. Bar Assn., Ala. Bar Assn., Tenn. Bar Assn., Am. Inns of Ct. (exec. com. 1994-95), Def. Rsch. Inst., Am. Trial Lawyers Assn., ABA. Avocations: golf, hunting, family outings. Office: Webb Sanders Deaton et al PO Box 148 2154 S Lamar Blvd Oxford MS 38655

SMITH, K(ERMIT) WAYNE, computer company executive; b. Newton, N.C., Sept. 15, 1938; s. Harold Robert and Hazel K. (Smith) S.; m. Audrey M. Kennedy, Dec. 19, 1958; 1 son, Stuart W. BA, Wake Forest U., 1960; MA, Princeton U., 1962, PhD, 1964; postgrad., U. So. Calif., 1965; LLD (hon.), Ohio U., 1992. Instr. Princeton U., 1963; asst. prof. econs. and polit. sci. U.S. Mil. Acad., 1963-66; spl. asst. to asst. sec. def. for sys. analysis Washington, 1966-69; program mgr. def. studies RAND Corp., Santa Monica, Calif., 1969-70; dir. program analysis NSC, Washington, 1970-72; group v.p. planning Dart Industries, L.A., 1972-73; group pres. resort devel. group Dart Industries, 1973-76; exec. v.p. Washington Group, Inc., 1976-77; mng. ptnr. Coopers & Lybrand, Washington, 1977-80, group mng. ptnr., 1980-83; chmn., CEO World Book, Inc., 1983-86; prof. Wake Forest U., 1986-88; CEO OCLC Online Computer Libr. Ctr., Inc., Dublin, Ohio, 1989—, also bd. dirs.; sr. cons. Dept. Def., Dept. State, NSC, NASA, Dept. Energy, OMB, GAO; bd. dirs. Excelco Corp., Nat. City Bank, Columbus, Info. Dimensions, Inc. Author: How Much is Enough? Shaping the Defense Program, 1961-69, 1971; contbr. articles to profl. jours. Mem. vis. com. Brookings Instn., Washington, 1971-79; mem. bd. visitors Wake Forest U., 1974-78, 82-90, chmn. bd. visitors, 1976-78, trustee, 1991-95, 96—; mem. bd. visitors Def. Sys. Mgmt. Coll., 1982-85, Lenoir Rhyne Coll., 1988-94, Mershon Ctr. Ohio State U., 1990-92, Columbus Assn. for Performing Arts, 1991-95, U. Pitts. Sch. Libr. and Info. Sci., 1992-95; mem. bd. visitors Bowman Gray Bapt. Hosp. Med. Ctr., 1992-95, chmn. bd. visitors, 1993-95. Danforth fellow, Woodrow Wilson fellow Princeton U., 1962. Mem. ALA, Coun. Fgn. Rels., Internat. Inst. Strategic Studies, Inst. Internat. Edn., Coun. Higher Edn., Am. Assn. Higher Edn., Am. Soc. Info. Sci., Washington Golf and Country Club, Chgo. Club, Lakes Golf and Country Club, Capital Club, PhiBeta Kappa, Omicron Delta Kappa, Kappa Sigma. Methodist. Home: 8530 Preston Mill Ct Dublin OH 43017-9648 Office: Online Computer Libr Ctr Inc 6565 Frantz Rd Dublin OH 43017-5308

SMITH, KERRY CLARK, lawyer; b. Phoenix, July 12, 1935; s. Clark and Fay (Jackson) S.; m. Michael Waterman, 1958; children: Kevin, Ian. AB, Stanford U., 1957, JD, 1962. Bar: Calif. 1963, U.S. Supreme Ct. 1980. Assoc. Chickering & Gregory, San Francisco, 1962-70, ptnr., 1970-81; ptnr. Pettit & Martin, San Francisco, 1981-95, Hovis, Smith, Larson, Stewart, Lipscomb & Cross, San Francisco, 1995—. Mem. editl. bd. Stanford Law Rev., 1961-62. Lt. USN, 1957-60. Mem. ABA (bus. law sect., mem. banking and savs. and loan coms.), Calif. Bar Assn. (bus. law sect.), San Francisco Bar Assn., Orinda County Club, La Quinta Resort Golf Club, San Francisco Univ. Club. Office: Hovis Smith Larson et al 21st Fl 100 Pine St San Francisco CA 94111

SMITH, LAMAR SEELIGSON, congressman; b. San Antonio, Nov. 19, 1947; s. Campbell and Eloise Keith (Seeligson) S.; m. Elizabeth Schaefer, Mar. 20, 1992; children: Nell Selligson, Tobin Wells. BA, Yale U., 1969; JD, So. Meth. U., 1975. Mgmt. intern SBA, Washington, 1969-70; bus. writer The Christian Sci. Monitor, Boston, 1970-72; assoc. Maebius & Duncan, Inc., San Antonio, 1975-76; chmn. Rep. Party of Bexar County, San Antonio, 1978-81; state rep. Dist. 57-F, San Antonio, 1981-82; county commr. Precinct 3 Bexar County, 1982-85; mem. 100th-104th Congresses from 21st Tex. dist., 1987—; mem. budget com., jud. com., subcom. crime and criminal justice; ptnr. Lamar Seeligson Ranch, Premont, Tex., 1975—. Christian Scientist. Office: US Ho of Reps 2443 Rayburn Bldg Washington DC 20515-0005*

SMITH, LANE JEFFREY, automotive journalist, technical consultant; b. Honolulu, May 17, 1954; s. Gerald Hague and JoEllen (Lane) S.; m. Susan Elizabeth Gumm, May 24, 1980; children: Amber Elizabeth, Graham Hague. BS in Journalism, Iowa State U., 1978. Feature editor Car Craft mag. Peterson Pub., L.A., 1979—, tech. editor, sr. editor, editor Hot Rod Mag., 1987-92, exec. editor, 1993—; speaker in field. Avocations: military history, aviation, building and racing high performance automobiles. Home: 18320 Citronia Northridge CA 91325 Office: Hot Rod Mag 6420 Wilshire Blvd Los Angeles CA 90048-5502

SMITH, LANTY L(LOYD), lawyer, business executive; b. Sherrodsville, Ohio, Dec. 11, 1942; s. Lloyd H. and Ellen Ruth (Newell) S.; m. Margaret Hays Chandler, June 11, 1966; children: Abigail Lamoreaux Presson, Margaret Ellen, Amanda Prescott. BS with honors in Math., Wittenberg U., Springfield, Ohio, 1964; LLB with honors, Duke U., 1967. Bar: Ohio 1967. Assoc. Jones, Day, Cockley & Reavis, Cleve., 1967-68, 69-73; ptnr. Jones, Day, Reavis & Pogue, Cleve., 1974-77; exec. v.p., sr. gen. counsel Burlington Industries, Inc., Greensboro, N.C., 1977-86, pres., 1986-88; chmn., chief exec. officer Precision Fabrics Group Inc., Greensboro, 1988—; chmn. The Greenwood Group, Inc., Raleigh, N.C., 1992—; chmn. bd. visitors Duke Univ. Sch. Law; bd. dirs., mem. exec. com. First Union Corp., Masland Corp., PC Press, Inc., Wikoff Color. Bd. govs. Ctr. for Creative Leadership; chmn. Cone Hosp.; mem. exec. com. Greensboro Devel. Corp., Greater Greensboro Found.; trustee Kathleen Price Bryan Family Fund; bd. of visitors N.C. Agrl. & Tech. State U. Mem. ABA, N.C. Inst. Medicine, N.C. Textile Found., Greensboro Rotary. Episcopalian. Home: 1401 Westridge Rd Greensboro NC 27410-2912 Office: 301 N Elm St Fl 6 Greensboro NC 27401-2149

SMITH, LARRY DENNIS, paper mill stores executive; b. Altoona, Pa., Dec. 12, 1954; s. Bernard Robert and Dollie Edith (Nofsker) S. BS in Art Edn., Ind. U. Pa., 1977. Audio artist, 1974—; artist Mail Art Network, 1980—; organizer, curator Manifesto Shnn Archives, East Freedom, Pa., 1982-86; established Patriots of the Am. Revolution Heraldic Register, 1993. Author: Manifesto Shnnalchemy, 1981, In the Wake of the Disaster Machine, 1981; editor: Artcomnet, 1981-87; artist The Labours of Grimnlaek, 1984; one-man shows in Rome, Stockholm, Zurich, Brusque and Helsinki; group show Seoul Internat. Bienale, 1984; editor 150th Anniversary History of Blair County, 1993—. Mem. SAR. Republican. Avocations: genealogical research, rare book collector, gardening. Home: RR1 Box 704-A East Freedom PA 16637-9770 Office: Appleton Papers Inc 100 Paper Mill Rd Roaring Spring PA 16673-1480

SMITH, LAUREN ASHLEY, lawyer, journalist, clergyman, physicist; b. Clinton, Iowa, Nov. 30, 1924; s. William Thomas Roy and Ethel (Cook) S.; m. Barbara Ann Mills, Aug. 22, 1947; children: Christopher A., Laura Nan Smith Pringle, William Thomas Roy II. BS, U. Minn., 1946, JD, 1949; postgrad., U. Chgo., 1943-49; MDiv, McCormick Theol. Sem., 1950; postgrad., U. Iowa, 1992. Bar: Colo. 1957, Iowa 1959, Ill. 1963, Minn. 1983, U.S. Supreme Ct. 1967; ordained to ministry Presbyn. Ch., 1950. Pastor Presbyn. Ch., Fredonia, Kans., 1950-52, Lamar, Colo., 1952-57; pastor Congl. Ch., Clinton, 1975-80; editor The Comml., Pine Bluff, Ark., 1957-58; pvt. practice Clinton, 1959—; internat. conferee Stanley Found., Warrenton, Va., 1963-72; legal observer USSR, 1978; co-sponsor All India Renewable Energy Conf., Bangalore, 1981; law sch. conferee U. Minn., China, 1983; sr. assoc. Molecular Nanotech. Foresight Inst., Palo Alto, Calif. Author: (jurisprudence treatise) Forma Dat Esse Rel, 1975, (monograph) First Strike Option, 1983; co-author: India On to New Horizons, 1989; columnist Crow Call, 1968—; co-editor Press and News of India, 1978-82; pub. Crow Call; pseudonym Christopher Crow, 1981—; editor Asian Econ. Community Jour.; contbr. articles to religious publs. Minister-at-large Presbyn. Ch. U.S.A., Iowa, 1987—, mem. nat. New Spiritual Formation Network; bd. dirs. Iowa divsn. UN Assn. U.S.A., Iowa City, 1970-85; sr. assoc. Molecular Nanotechnology Foresight Inst., Palo Alto, Calif.; Franciscans United Nations Non Govt. Orgn. Mem. Iowa Bar Assn., Ill. Bar Assn., St. Andrews Soc., Clinton County Bar Assn. (pres. 1968, Best in Iowa citation), Clinton Ministerial Assn., Samaritan Health Systems Chaplain Corps., Quaker Internat. Yokefellow, Nat. Network for New Spiritual Formation Presbyn. Ch. USA, Molecular Nanotechnology Foresight Inst. (sr. assoc.), Franciscans Internat.

SMITH, LAWRENCE, insurance executive. Prin. William Mercer, Inc. Office: 400 Renaissance Ctr Detroit MI 48243

SMITH, LAWRENCE J., bishop. Pres., regionary bishop The Liberal Cath. Ch.-Province of the U.S.A., Evergreen Park, Ill. Office: Liberal Cath Ch 9740 S Avers Ave Evergreen Park IL 60642-2946

SMITH, LAWRENCE LEIGHTON, conductor; b. Portland, Oreg., Apr. 8, 1936; s. Lawrence Keller and Bonita Evelyn (Wood) S.; children by previous marriage: Kevin, Laura, Gregory; stepchildren: Kristine, John. B.S. cum laude, Portland State Coll., 1956; grad. magna cum laude, Mannes Coll. Music, N.Y.C., 1959; Ph D (Hon.), Ind. U, 1992; D (hon.), U. Louisville, Ind. State U. Mem. faculty Mannes Coll. Music, 1959-62; prof. piano Boston U., 1963-64; asst. condr. Met. Opera, 1964-67; mem. faculty Curtis Inst., Phila., 1968-69, Calif. Inst. Arts, 1970-72, U. Tex., 1962-63; prin. guest condr. Phoenix Symphony, 1970-73; music dir., condr. Austin (Tex.) Symphony, 1971-72, Oreg. Symphony, Portland, 1973-80; pres., music dir. San Antonio Symphony, 1980-85; music dir., condr. Louisville Orch., 1983-95, condr. laureate, 1995—; faculty mem. Yale U., 1994—; guest condr. N.Y. Philharm., L.A. Philharm., Tulsa Philharm., Winnipeg (Man., Can.) Orch., Minn. Orch., Cin. Symphony, St. Louis Symphony, Moscow Philharm., Tokyo Philharm. Recipient 1st prize Met. Internat. Condrs. competition, 1964, Ditson Condrs. award Columbia U., 1988. Mem. Am. Fedn. Musicians, Mensa. Buddhist.

SMITH, LAWRENCE R., lawyer; b. Oak Park, Ill., Jan. 27, 1948. AB cum laude, Coll. of Holy Cross, 1970; JD, U. Mich., 1973. Bar: Ill. 1973. Ptnr. Querrey & Harrow Ltd., Chgo.; panel Am. Arbitration Assn. Mem. ABA, Am. LAw Assn. (bd. dirs.), Ill. State Bar Assn., Chgo. Bar Assn., Ill. Assn. Def. Trial Counsel (pres. 1988-89), Def. Rsch. Inst. Address: 180 N Stetson Ave Ste 3500 Chicago IL 60601-6710

SMITH, LEE ARTHUR, professional baseball player; b. Jamestown, La., Dec. 4, 1957. Student, Northwestern State U., La. Pitcher Chgo. Cubs, 1975-87, Boston Red Sox, 1987-90, St. Louis Cardinals, 1990-93, N.Y. Yankees, 1993-94; with Balt. Orioles, 1994, Calif. Angels, 1994—. Named Nat. League Fireman of Yr., Sporting News, 1991, 94; holder maj. league record for most consecutive errorless games by pitcher, Nat. League single-season record for most saves; Nat. League Saves Leader, 1983, 91-92; mem. Nat. League All-Star team, 1983, 87, 91-94; named Nat League Co-Fireman of Yr., Sporting News, 1983, 92. Office: Calif Angels 2000 Gene Autry Way Anaheim CA 92806*

SMITH, LEE ELTON, surgery educator, retired military officer; b. Ventura, Calif., July 19, 1937; s. Raymond Elroy and Edith Irene (Jordan) S.; m. Carole Sue Smith; children: Justine Diane, Alexander Loren. BS, U. Calif., Berkeley, 1959; MD, U. Calif., San Francisco, 1962. Diplomate Am. Bd. Surgery, Am. Bd. Colon and Rectal Surgery (pres. 1992-93). Commd. ens. USN, 1960, advanced through grades to capt., 1977; intern U. Utah, Salt Lake City, 1962-63; resident USN, San Diego, Calif., 1966-70; staff surgeon USN, Bremerton, Wash., 1970-72; resident colorectal surgery U. Minn., Mpls., 1972-73; dir. colorectal surgery Nat. Naval Med. Ctr. USN, Bethesda, Md., 1973-82; ret. USN, 1983, Seattle, 1982; prof. surgery George Washington U., Washington, 1983—; clin. prof. surgery Uniformed Svcs. U., Bethesda; pres. Am. Bd. Colon and Rectal Surgery, 1993-94. Editor: Practical Guide to Anorectal Physiology, 1990, 2d edit., 1995; assoc. editor Diseases of the Colon & Rectum, 1984—, Perspectives in Colon and Rectal Surgery, 1989—. Mem. ACS (pres. Met. Washington chpt. 1993-94), Soc. Am. Gastrointestinal Endoscopic Surgeons (pres. 1989-90), Am. Cancer Soc. (v.p. D.C. chpt. 1985—). Home: 1200 N Nash St Apt 518 Arlington VA 22209-3614 Office: Washington Hosp Ctr 110 Irving St Washington DC 20010

SMITH, LEE HERMAN, business executive; b. Ector, Tex., Jan. 7, 1935; s. Lee Herman and Willie Mae (Morrison) S.; m. Eva Landers, Feb. 18, 1960; 1 dau., Diette. B.S. in Math., Tex. A&M U., 1957, Ph.D. in Stats., 1964; M.S. in Engring. Adminstrn., So. Methodist U., 1961. Various engring. positions, 1957-65; asst. prof. Sch. Bus., U. Tex., Arlington, 1965-66, assoc. dean, assoc. prof., 1967-68; exec. planning adviser N.Am. Aviation Co., Los Angeles, summer 1966; prof., chmn. dept. quantitative mgmt. sci. U. Houston, 1969-71; dean faculties, prof. mgmt. sci. U. Tex., Dallas, 1971-72, v.p. acad. affairs, prof. mgmt. sci., 1972-74; pres. S.W. Tex. State U., San Marcos, 1974-81, TRAVELHOST, Inc., 1981-87, 89-93; chief exec. officer Neuro Systems Inc., 1984-85; pres. J & P Petroleum Products, Inc., 1986-87, Standard Life Ins. Co. of Miss., Jackson, 1987-89, Intercontinental Life Ins. Co. of N.J., 1987-89; exec. search cons. Sandhurst Assocs., 1993-94; pres. Voyager Expanded Learning Inc., 1995-96; cons. in field; mem. sci. adv. com. Callier Hearing and Speech Center, Dallas; mem. Am. Assn. State Colls. and Univs. trip to People's Republic of China, 1975, Republic of China, 1976; chmn. bd. Central Tex. Higher Edn. Authority, 1977-78; mem. Gov.'s Higher Edn. Mgmt. Effectiveness Council, 1980-81. Author books, articles, revs. in field. Tex. A & M Coll. Opportunity scholar, 1953-57; Iowa State U. Research Found. fellow, 1961; Gen. Electric Co. fellow, 1962; Ling-Temco-Vought fellow, 1963-64; U. Tex. travel grantee, 1967. Mem. Am. Statis. Assn. (pres. N.Tex. chpt. 1967-68), Ops. Research Soc. Am., Inst. Mgmt. Scis. (program chmn. meetings), Am. Inst. Decision Scis. (v.p. planning and devel. 1970-71, council 1971-72), S. Tex. C. of C., Delta Sigma Pi, Phi Kappa Phi. Home: 2300 Grayson Dr Apt 212 Grapevine TX 76051-7001

SMITH, LEO EMMET, lawyer; b. Chgo., Jan 6, 1927; s. Albert J. and Cecilia G. (Dwyer) S.; m. Rita Gleason, Apr. 14, 1956; children: Mary Cecilia, Gerianne, Kathleen, Leo A., Maureen. JD, DePaul U., 1950. Admitted to Ill. bar, 1950; assoc. with law firm also engaged in pvt. industry, 1950-54; asst. states atty. Cook County, Ill., 1954-57; asst. counsel Traffic Inst., Northwestern U., Evanston, Ill., 1957-60; asst. exec. sec. Comml. Law League Am., Chgo., 1960-61, exec. dir., 1961-83, editor Comml. Law Jour., 1961-89, editor emeritus, 1989—; assoc. Howe & Hutton, Ltd., Chgo., 1985—. Fellow Chgo. Bar Found. (life); mem. Chgo. Bar Assn. (chmn. libr. com. 1983), Am. Acad. Matrimonial Lawyers (exec. dir. 1982-84), World Assn. Lawyers (founding mem. 1975), Am. Soc. Assn. Execs., Chgo. Soc. Assn. Execs., Assn. Econs. Coun., Friends of Northwestern Sta. (spokesperson 1984). Contbr. articles to legal jours. Home: 1104 S Knight Ave Park Ridge IL 60068-4447 Office: Howe & Hutton Ltd 20 N Wacker Dr Chicago IL 60606-2806

SMITH, LEO GILBERT, hospital administrator; b. Oroville, Calif., July 29, 1929; s. Leo Paul and Laura Mae (Hoffschulte) S.; m. Marcia Elise Ernest, Jan. 26, 1952; children: Matthew Paul, Mara Lee, Bridget Mari, Leo Ernest. B.S.C., U. Santa Clara, 1951; M.P.H., U. Calif., 1958. Adminstrv. resident San Diego County Gen. Hosp., 1958-59; asst. hosp. adminstr. Santa Clara Valley Med. Center, 1959-67, adminstr., 1967-76, dir. planning, 1976-77; health care cons., 1977-80; adminstr. Puget Sound Hosp., 1980-82; mgr. Tacoma Family Medicine dept Multicare Med. Ctr., Tacoma, Wash., 1982-86, dir. clinic services, 1986-91; clinic mgr. Providence Factoria Family Healthcare div. Providence Med. Ctr., Seattle, 1992; ret. Bd. dirs. Children's Home Soc. of Calif., chmn. dist. bd., 1969-70; chmn. br. bd. Children's Home Soc. of Wash., 1985. Served in mil. 1952-54. Mem. Cen. Coast Hosp. Conf. (pres. 1970), Hosp. Coun. No. Calif. (dir. 1970-73), Am. Coll. Hosp. Adminstrs., Med. Group Mgrs. Assn., Tacoma Sunrise Rotary (pres. 1982-83, Dist. 5020 Youth Exch. officer 1991—). Home: 7122 Turquoise Dr SW Tacoma WA 98498-6431

SMITH, LEON POLK, artist; b. Chickasha, Okla., May 20, 1906. BA, East Cen. State U., 1934; MA, Columbia U., 1938. Lectr. Brandeis U., 1968; resident artist U. Calif., Davis, 1972; lectr. SUNY-Old Westbury, 1978, Yale U., 1983, East Cen. U., Ada, Okla., 1986. One-man shows include San Francisco Mus. and Rose Mus. Retrospective, 1968, Musèe Nat. d'Art Modern, Georges Pompidou (Beaubourg), Paris, Washburn Gallery, N.Y.C., 1981-82, Nat. Galerie, Berlin, 1983, Burnett Miller Gallery, L.A., 1985, Hoffmann Galerie, Friedberg, Germany, 1987, Venice Biennale, 1987, Cleve. Mus. Art, Inyedian Art Gallery, Lausanne, Switzerland, Schlègl Gallery, Zurich; exhibited in group shows at Haus der Kunst, Munich, 1982, Nat. Gallery, Washington, 1984, Nat. Mus., Berlin, 1984, Wilhelm-Hack-Mus., Ludwigshafen, Germany, 1988, U. Okla. Mus. Art, 1989, Grenoble Mus., France, 1989, Bklyn. Mus., 1995; represented in permanent collections Guggenheim Mus., N.Y.C., Met. Mus. Art, N.Y.C., Mus. Modern Art, N.Y.C., Birmingham Mus. Art, Whitney Mus. Art, N.Y.C., Hirshhorn Mus., Nat. Gallery, Berlin, Peter Ludwig, Vienna, Austria, Nürnberg Kunsthalle, Germany, Wilhelm Hack Mus., Ludwigshafen-an Rhein, Germany, Wiesbaden Mus., Germany, Nurnberg Mus. Art, Germany, Grenoble Mus., France, Wiesbaden Mus. Germany, Bklyn. Mus. Solomon R. Guggenheim fellow, 1943; recipient Hassum Speicher Fund Purchase Exhbn. award Am. Acad. and Inst. Arts and Letters, 1979, Disting. Alumnus award East Ctrl. U., 1986; grantee Nat. Coun. Arts, 1967, Tamarind, 1968, Longview grantee, 1958. Office: 31 Union Sq W Studio 14E New York NY 10003

SMITH, LEONARD BINGLEY, musician; b. Poughkeepsie, N.Y., Sept. 5, 1915; s. Frank Roderick and Ethel (Schubert) S.; m. Helen Gladys Rowe, Apr. 20, 1940 (dec. 1993); 1 dau., Sandra Victoria. Student, N.Y. Mil. Acad., 1930-33, Ernest Williams Sch. Music, 1933-36, NYU, 1936-37, Curtis Inst. Music, 1943-45; H.H.D., Detroit Inst. Tech., 1965. Pres. Accompaniments Unltd., Inc., 1952—. Cornet soloist, Ernest Williams Band, 1933-36, The Goldman Band, summers 1936-42; 1st trumpet, Barrere Little Symphony, 1935-37, Detroit Symphony Orch., 1937-42, Ford Sunday Evening Hour, 1937-42; condr., The Leonard Smith Concert Band, 1945—, Detroit Concert Band, 1945—, U. Detroit Bands, 1949-50, Moslem AAONMS Band, 1945-57, Scandinavian Symphony Orch. of Detroit, 1959-61, guest condr., Indpls. Symphony Orch., 1967; guest condr., soloist, clinician numerous concerts, U.S., Can.; mus. dir. John Philip Sousa documentary for BBC, 1970; Sousa Am. Bicentennial Recorded Collection; record series Gems concert band, Blossom Festival Band; condr. Blossom Festival Concert Band, 1972—; The Indomitable Teddy Roosevelt; producer: Our Am. Heritage in Music, 1970; pres., Bandland, Inc., 1951-61; Author: Treasury of Scales; over 350 pub. compositions; mem. bd. advisors Instrumentalist mag. Chmn. music com. Mich. Civil War Centennial Commn., 1961-64; gov. bd. Mac Award. With USNR, 1942-45. Recipient spl. medal Mich. Polish Legion Am. Vets., Distinguished Service medal Kappa Kappa Psi; Mich. Minuteman Gov.'s award, 1973; Freedom Found. award, 1975; Gen. William Booth award, 1976, Embassy Mich. Tourism award, 1979; named Alumnus of Distinction N.Y. Mil. Acad., 1976. Mem. ASCAP, Philippine Bandsmen's Assn. (hon.), Am. Fedn. Musicians, Internat. Platform Assn., Assn. Concert Bands (pres. 1982-83). Clubs: Masons (33 deg.), Shriners, K.T, Jesters. Office: care Detroit Concert Band Inc 7443 E Butherus Dr Ste 100 Scottsdale AZ 85260-2423

SMITH, LEONARD WARE, lawyer; b. Lancaster, Ky., Jan. 1, 1938; s. William F. and Willie (Ware) S.; m. Carole Irene Binkley, Mar. 18, 1978; 1 stepchild, Gina Harper; children: Rebecca Ann, Andrew Ware. Student, Centre Coll., 1956-57; BA, Eastern Ky. U., 1961; JD, U. Ky., 1968. Bar: Ky. 1969, Tenn. 1988. Pvt. practice law Lancaster, 1969-70; atty. TVA, Knoxville, Tenn., 1970-86; sr. atty. TVA, Knoxville, 1986-92, ret., 1992; city atty. City of Lancaster, 1969-70; bd. dirs., chmn. TVA Employees Credit Union, 1980-84. Bd. govs. Shrine Hosp., Greenville, S.C. Capt., U.S. Army, 1961-66. Mem. Ky. Bar Assn., Masons (32 deg. K.C.C.H.), Scottish Rite, Shriners (Potentate Kerbela Shrine Temple 1989, mem. Imperial Shrine jurisprudence & laws com., imperial rep., 1988—, v.p. South Atlantic Shrine Assn. 1992—). Home and Office: 416 Kendall Rd Knoxville TN 37919-6803

SMITH, LEROY HARRINGTON, JR., mechanical engineer, aerodynamics consultant; b. Balt., Nov. 3, 1928; s. Leroy Harrington and Edna (Marsh) S.; m. Barbara Ann Williams, July 7, 1951; children: Glenn Harrington, Bruce Lyttleton, Cynthia Ann. BS in Engring., Johns Hopkins U., 1949, MS, 1951, Dr. Engring., 1954. Compressor aerodynamacist Gen. Electric Co., Cin., 1954-61, mgr. turbomachinery devel., 1961-68, mgr. compressor & fan design tech., 1968-75, mgr. turbomachinery aerodynamics tech., 1975-92; cons. technologist Turbomachinery Aerodynamics Gen. Electric Co., 1992—. Contbr. articles to ASME Trans.; holder 12 patents. Recipient Perry T. Egbert Jr. awards, 1969, 83, Charles P. Steinmetz award, 1987 Gen. Electric Co. Fellow ASME (Gas Turbine award 1981, 87, R. Tom Sawyer award 1987, Aircraft Engine Tech. award 1993); mem. NAE, Ohio River Launch Club. Office: GE Aircraft Eng Mail Drop A411 1 Neumann Way Cincinnati OH 45215-1915

SMITH, LESLIE E., physical chemist; b. N.Y.C., Jan. 6, 1941. BSc, Case Inst. Tech., 1962; PhD in Chemistry, Cath. U. Am., 1970. Phys. chemist polymers divsn. Nat. Bur. Stds., 1964-66, 69-74, chief polymer stability and stds., 1974-82; chief polymers divsn. Nat. Inst. Stds. & Tech., 1982—. Editor Polymer Commun., 1984—. Mem. AAAS, Am. Chem. Soc. Office: Nat Inst of Stds and Tech Polymers Divsn Bldg 224 Rm A309 Gaithersburg MD 20899

SMITH, LESLIE ROPER, hospital and healthcare administrator; b. Stockton, Calif., June 20, 1928; s. Austin J. and Helen (Roper) S.; m. Edith Sue Fincher, June 22, 1952; children: Melinda Sue, Leslie Erin, Timothy Brian. A.B., U. Pacific, 1951; M.S. in Pub. Adminstrn, U. So. Calif., 1956. Adminstrv. asst. Ranchos Los Amigos Hosp., Downey, Calif., 1953-57; asst. adminstr. Harbor Gen. Hosp., Torrance, Calif., 1957-65; adminstr. Harbor Gen. Hosp., 1966-71; acting regional dir. Los Angeles County Coastal Health Services Region, 1973; pres. San Pedro Peninsula Hosp., San Pedro, Cal., 1974-86; exec. dir. Los Angeles County/U. So. Calif. Med. Center, 1971-73; adminstr. Long Beach (Calif.) Hosp., 1965-66; asso. clin. prof. community medicine and pub. health, also emergency medicine U. So. Calif., 1968-78; instr. U. So. Calif. (Sch. Pub. Adminstrn.), 1968; preceptor hosp. adminstrn. UCLA Sch. Pub. Health, 1964—; chief exec. officer French Hosp. Med. Ctr. and Health Plan, 1986-87; dir. health care services McCormack & Farrow, 1987—; lectr. in field, 1963—; cons. emergency health services HEW, 1970-73; chmn. com. diaster preparedness Hosp. Council So. Calif., 1966-72, sec., 1971—, pres., 1973; mem. Calif. Assembly Com. on Emergency Med. Services, 1970, Calif. Emergency Med. Adv. Com., 1972-75, Los Angeles County Commn. on Emergency Med. Services, 1975-83, Los Angeles Health Planning and Devel. Agy. Commn., 1980-83; bd. dirs. Blue Cross of So. Calif.; mem. hosp. relations com. Blue Cross of Calif.; mem. adv. com. on emergency health services Calif. Dept. Health, 1974-75; bd. dirs., mem. exec. com. Truck Ins. Exchange of Farmers Ins. Group, 1977-82; bd. dirs. Hosp. Council of So. Calif., 1966-76, 81-86, Health Resources Inst., 1985-86; chmn. Preferred Health Network, 1983-86. Mem. goals com., Torrance, 1968—; pres. Silver Spur Little League, Palos Verdes, 1969-70. Served with AUS, 1946-48. Recipient Silver Knight and Gold Knight award Nat. Mgmt. Assn., 1970, 85, Walker Fellowship award, 1976. Fellow Am. Coll. Health Care Execs. (life); mem. Am., Nat. mgmt. assns., Am. Hosp. Assn. (chmn. com. on community emergency health services 1973), Calif. Hosp. Assn. (chmn. com. emergency services 1965-70, trustee 1973-76, bd. dirs. Calif. Ins. Service Group 1980-82), County Suprs. Assn. Calif. (chmn. joint subcom. on emergency care 1970). Presbyn. (elder, trustee). Home: 27 Marseille Laguna Niguel CA 92677

SMITH, LESTER MARTIN, broadcasting executive; b. N.Y.C., Oct. 20, 1919; s. Alexander and Sadie S.; m. Bernice Reitz, Sept. 28, 1962; 1 child, Alexander. B.S. in Bus. Adminstrn, NYU, 1940. Chief exec. officer Alexander Broadcasting Co., radio stas. in, 1954—; gen. partner 700 Investment Co.; past dir. Seattle C. of C.; past chmn. dir. Radio Advt. Bur. Served to maj. U.S. Army, 1942-46. Decorated Bronze Star. Mem. Nat. Assn. Broadcasters (past dir.), Oreg. Assn. Broadcasters (past pres.), Broadcast Pioneers. Clubs: Rotary (Seattle), Rainer (Seattle), Wash. Athletic (Seattle). Address: 700 112th Ave NE Bellevue WA 98004-5106

SMITH, LEVIE DAVID, JR., real estate appraiser, consultant; b. Lakeland, Fla., Oct. 19, 1924; s. Levie David and Grace (Ross) S.; m. Annie

Laurie Hogan, Aug. 29, 1948; children: Nancy, L. David, Judy. BS, Fla. So. Coll., 1947. Salesman Smith & Smith, Realtors, Lakeland, 1947-50; staff appraiser Smith & Son, Appraisers, Lakeland, 1952-72; pres. Levie D. Smith & Assoc., Inc., Lakeland, 1973-95, cons., 1996—; chmn. bd. dirs. First Fed. of Fla., Lakeland, acting pres., 1992-95, dir. emeritus, 1996—; pres. Fla. Assn. Realtors, Orlando, 1970; chmn. Fla. Real Estate Commn., Orlando, 1979. Past trustee Polk Theatre, Inc., pres. 1989, chmn. adv. bd., 1994-95; mem. adv. bd. Imperial Symphony Orch., 1993—; mem. exec. bd. Gulf Ridge Coun. Boy Scouts Am., dist. chmn. 1995—; mem. real estate adv. bd. U. Fla. Lt. USN, 1943-46, 50-52. Recipient Silver Beaver award Gulf Ridge Coun., Boy Scouts Am., 1984. Mem. Am. Inst. Real Estate Appraisers (govt. coun. 1976-83, v.p. 1982-83, SE Meritorious award 1987), Lakeland Rotary Club (pres. 1976-77, Paul Harris fellow, 4 way test award). Presbyterian. Avocations: gardening, camping, fishing. Home: 515 Laurel Ln Lakeland FL 33813-1650 Office: Levie D Smith & Assocs Inc 101 Doris Dr Lakeland FL 33813-1004

SMITH, LEWIS DENNIS, academic administrator; b. Muncie, Ind., Jan. 18, 1938; s. Thurman Lewis and Dorothy Ann (Dennis) S.; m. Suzanne F. Metcalfe; children: Lauren Kay, Raymond Bradley. AB, Ind. U., 1959, PhD, 1963. Asst. biologist Argonne (Ill.) Nat. Lab., 1964-67, assoc. biologist, 1967-69; assoc. prof. Purdue U., West Lafayette, Ind., 1969-73; prof. biology Purdue U., West Lafayette, 1973-87, assoc. head dept. biol. scis., 1979-80, head dept., 1980-87; prof. dept. devel. and cell. U. Calif., Irvine, 1987-94, dean Sch. Biol. Scis., 1987-90, exec. vice chancellor, 1990-94; pres. U. of Nebr., 1994—; instr. embryology Woods Hole (Mass.) Marine Biology Lab., summers 1972, 73, 74, 88, 89; mem. Space Sci. Bd., Washington, 1986-91; chmn. Space Biology and Medicine, Space Sci. Bd., 1986-91; mem. cell biology study sect. NIH, Bethesda, Md., 1971-75; chmn., 1977-79, bd. sci. counselors Nat. Inst. Child Health and Human Devel., 1990-95, chmn. 1992-95; mem. space biology peer rev. bd. AIBS, 1980-85. Guggenheim fellow, 1987. Mem. Am. Soc. Biochemistry and Molecular Biology, AAAS, Internat. Soc. for Devel. Biology, Soc. for Devel. Biology, Am. Soc. Cell Biology. Home: 5930 Norman Rd Lincoln NE 68512-1920 Office: Varner Hall 3835 Holdrege St Lincoln NE 68503-1435

SMITH, LEWIS MOTTER, JR., advertising and direct marketing executive; b. Kansas City, Mo., Nov. 4, 1932; s. Lewis Motter and Virginia (Smith) S.; m. Alice Allen, June 28, 1975; children: Katherine Allen, Patience Allen. Student, Kenyon Coll., 1951-53, Columbia U., 1956-58. Copywriter mail order div. Grolier Soc., Inc., N.Y.C., 1957-59; free lance copywriter Santa Fe, N.M., 1960-61; v.p. creative services Grolier Enterprises Inc., N.Y.C., 1962-67; v.p., creative planning dir. Wunderman, Ricotta & Kline, Inc., N.Y.C., 1968-72; exec. v.p., creative dir., 1972-79; exec. v.p. Young & Rubicam Direct Mktg. Group, 1980; sr. v.p., dir. mktg. Book-of-the-Month Club, Inc., 1980-84, dir., 1981-84; exec. v.p., creative dir. SSC&B: Vos Direct Inc., N.Y.C., 1985-87; pres., dir. creative services Lintas: Direct Inc. (formerly SSC&B: Vos Direct Inc.), N.Y.C., 1987-89; pres. Lew Smith & Assocs., Inc., 1989—. Bd. dirs. Young Concert Artists, Inc., N.Y.C., 1966-67, Harlem Sch. Arts, 1967-68. Served with U.S. Army, 1953-56. Mem. Delta Phi. Episcopalian. Home and Office: 45 Knollwood Rd Rhinebeck NY 12572-2313

SMITH, LEY S., pharmaceutical company executive; b. 1934. BA, U. Western Ont., Can., 1958. With Upjohn Co., Kalamazoo, Mich., 1958—, now pres. & COO. Office: Pharmacia and Upjohn Inc 7000 Portage Rd Kalamazoo MI 49001-0102*

SMITH, LINDA A., congresswoman, former state legislator; d. Vern Smith; children: Sheri, Robi. Office mgr.; former mem. Wash. State Ho. of Reps.; mem. Wash. State Senate; congresswoman, Wash. 3rd Dist. U.S. House Reps., Washington, D.C., 1995—. Republican. Home: 10009 NW Ridgecrest Ave Vancouver WA 98685-5159 Office: 1217 Longworth Washington DC 20515*

SMITH, LIZ (MARY ELIZABETH SMITH), newspaper columnist, broadcast journalist; b. Ft. Worth, Feb. 2, 1923; d. Sloan and Sarah Elizabeth (McCall) S. BJ., U. Tex., 1948. Editor Dell Publns., N.Y.C., 1950-53; assoc. producer CBS Radio, 1953-55, NBC-TV, 1955-59; assoc. on Cholly Knickerbocker newspaper column, N.Y.C., 1959-64; film critic Cosmopolitan mag., 1966; columnist Chgo. Tribune-N.Y. Daily News Syndicate (now Tribune Media Services), 1976-91, New York Newsday, L.A. Times Syndicate, 1991—, Family Circle mag., 1993—; TV commentator WNBC-TV, N.Y.C., 1978-91; commentator Fox-TV, N.Y.C., 1991—; freelance mag. writer, also staff writer Sports Illus. mag.; commentator Gossip Show E! Entertainment, 1993—. Author: The Mother Book, 1978. Office: N Y Newsday 2 Park Ave New York NY 10016-5603 *A career in Journalism? Any career at all? I say learn to type. Read a lot. Keep on keeping on. Work is its own reward and success is loving your work. And remember, never give up. After the Middle Ages comes the Renaissance.*

SMITH, LLOYD, musician; b. Cleve., Dec. 1, 1941; s. Thomas George Russell and Anita May (Speer) S.; m. Rheta R. Naylor, Mar. 30, 1967 (div. Nov. 1994); 1 child, Peter Eldon; m. Nancy R. Bean, June 6, 1995. Mus.B., Curtis Inst. Music, 1965. Tchr. Settlement Music Sch., 1970-72, 92—. Cellist Pitts. Symphony, 1965-67, Phila. Orch., 1967—, asst. prin. cello, 1988—; soloist Indpls. Symphony, 1958, 68, Garden State Philharmonic, 1964, Lansdowne Symphony, 1965, West Jersey Chamber Orch., 1991, Haverford-Bryn Mawr Symphony, 1992; mem. Huntingdon Trio, 1974-93, Wister quartet, 1988—. Alumni rep. Curtis Inst. Music Bd. Trustees, chmn. Parents' Com., 1989-90; bd. dirs. Phila. Youth Orch., 1987-91, Community Out Reach Partnership, 1988-90. Mem. Am. Soc. Ancient Instruments (asst. artistic dir. 1975-77, music dir. 1977-80), Curtis Inst. Music Nat. Alumni Assn. (treas., bd. dirs. 1989-90), 1807 & Friends (bd. dirs. 1994—). Home: 5639 E Wister St Philadelphia PA 19144-1522 Office: 5639 E Wister St Philadelphia PA 19144-1522

SMITH, LLOYD HILTON, independent oil and gas producer; b. Pitts., July 9, 1905; s. Roland Hilton and Jane (Lloyd) S.; m. Jane Clay Zevely, Sept. 7, 1931; children: Camilla; m. Elizabeth Keith Wiess, May 25, 1940; children: Sandra Keith, Sharon Lloyd, Sydney Carothers. Ph.B., Yale U., 1929. Statistician Biggs, Mohrman & Co., N.Y.C., 1932; mgr. New York office Laird & Co., 1933-34; v.p. Argus Research Corp., 1934-35; chmn., dir. Paraffine Oil Corp., 1949-81; past dir. 1st City Nat. Bank Houston, Nat. Rev., Curtiss-Wright Corp., Info. Storage Systems, Falcon Seaboard, Inc. Mem. Houston Mus. Sci.; trustee Pine Manor Coll., 1963-74; past dir. DeBakey Med. Found. Lt. comdr. USNR, 1942-45. Republican. Clubs: Bayou, Ramada (Houston); Everglades, Bath and Tennis (Palm Beach); Racquet and Tennis (N.Y.C.), Brook (N.Y.C.), River (N.Y.C.); Nat. Golf Links of America, Southampton, Meadow. Home: 101 El Vedado Rd Palm Beach FL 33480-4731

SMITH, LLOYD HOLLINGSWORTH, physician; b. Easley, S.C., Mar. 27, 1924; s. Lloyd H. and Phyllis (Page) S.; m. Margaret Constance Avery, Feb. 27, 1954; children—Virginia Constance, Christopher Avery, Rebecca Anne, Charlotte Page, Elizabeth Hollingsworth, Jeffrey Hollingsworth. A.B., Washington and Lee U., 1944, D.Sc., 1969; M.D., Harvard, 1948. Intern, then resident Mass. Gen. Hosp., Boston, 1948-50; chief resident physician Mass. Gen. Hosp., 1955-56; mem. Harvard Soc. Fellows, 1952-54; asst. prof. Harvard Soc. Fellows (Med. Sch.), 1956-63; vis. investigator Karolinska Inst., Stockholm, 1954-55, Oxford (Eng.) U., 1963-64; prof. medicine, chmn. dept. U. Calif. Med. Sch., San Francisco, 1964-85, assoc dean, 1985—; Mem. Pres.'s Sci. Adv. Com., 1970-73. Bd. overseers Harvard, 1974-80. Served to capt., M.C. AUS, 1950-52. Mem. Am. Acad. Arts and Scis., Am. Soc. Clin. Investigation (pres. 1969-70), Western Soc. Clin. Rsch. (pres. 1969-70), Assn. Am. Physicians (pres. 1974-75), Am. Fedn. Clin. Rsch. Spl. research genetic and metabolic diseases. Home: 309 Evergreen Dr Kentfield CA 94904-2709 Office: U Calif San Francisco Med Ctr San Francisco CA 94143

SMITH, LOIS ARLENE, actress, writer; b. Topeka, Nov. 3, 1930; d. William Oren and Carrie D. (Gottshalk) Humbert; m. Wesley Dale Smith, Nov. 5, 1948 (div. 1973); 1 child, Moon Elizabeth. Student, U. Wash., 1948-50; studied with Lee Strasberg, Actor's Studio, N.Y.C., 1955—. guest dir. Juilliard Sch., 1987; Clarence Ross fellow Am. Theater Wing at Eugene O'Neill Theater Ctr., 1983; mem. adv. panel program fund Pub. Broadcasting Service, 1981-82; hon. founder Harold Clurman Theatre Artists Fund, Ctr. for Arts, SUNY-Purchase, 1981. Author: play All There Is, 1982; debut in Time Out for Ginger, 1952; actress Broadway and off-Broadway prodns., 1952—; stage appearances include Theater of the Living Arts, Mark Taper Forum, Long Wharf Theater and Steppenwolf Theater Co.; appears on network and pub. TV programs; stage appearances include, The Young and the Beautiful, 1955, The Glass Menagerie, 1956, Blues for Mr. Charlie, 1964, Orpheus Descending, 1957, Miss Julie, 1966, Uncle Vanya, 1965, 69, The Iceman Cometh, 1973, Harry Outside, 1975, Hillbilly Women, 1979, 81, the Vienna Notes, 1985, The Stick Wife, April Snow, 1987, The Grapes of Wrath, 1988-89, 90, Measure for Measure, Beside Herself, 1989, Escape from Happiness, 1993, Buried Child, 1995-96; films include East of Eden, 1955, Five Easy Pieces, 1970, Next Stop Greenwich Village, 1975, Resurrection, 1980, Green Card, 1990, Fried Green Tomatoes, 1991, Falling Down, 1993, How to Make an American Quilt, 1995, Dead Man Walking, 1995, Life, 1996, Twister, 1996. Named Best Supporting Actress for Five Easy Pieces, Nat. Soc. Film Critics, 1971; recipient Tony nomination for Grapes of Wrath, 1990; named to Filmdom's Famous Fives for East of Eden, Failm Daily mag., 1955. Mem. SAG, AFTRA, Actors Equity Assn., Dramatists Guild, Actors Studio, Ensemble Studio Theater, Steppenwolf Theatre Co. Ensemble, Acad. Motion Picture Arts and Scis.

SMITH, LOIS COLSTON, secondary school educator; b. Edgewater, Ala., Aug. 3, 1919; d. Roy Minnie and Rebecca (Hayes) Colston; children: Linnie Ree Colston Carter, Lois Louise Colston Smith, Jessie Mae Colston Smith, Johnny Colston, Dorothy Dean Colston Cottingham, Lillian Dolly B. Colston Tarver. BS, A&M U., 1939; MA, N.Y.U., 1957. Vocat. Home Econ. Edn. 3rd and 4th grade tchr. Sulligent, Ala., 1957-61; elem. prin. Millport, Ala., 1962-67; 11th grade sci. and social studies tchr. Vernon, Ala., 1967-70; 7th-9th grade gen. and vocat. home econ. tchr. Tuscaloosa, Ala., 1970-80, 7th grade gen. and voca. home econ. tchr., 1980-92; ret., 1995. Chmn. Voters registration, Tuscaloosa, Ala., 1980; troop leader Girl Scouts Am., Tuscaloosa, Ala., 1967-92; mem. bd. dirs. Shelter State Community Coll. Wellness Coun., 1993. Recipient Tombigbee Girl Scout 15 yr. svc. pin, Cert. Appreciation, Valuable Svc. award, Girl Scouts; named Zeta of Yr., Beta Eta Zeta chpt., Stillman Coll., 1983, Golden Cert. of Appreciation and Admiration Ala. A&M U., Huntsville, 1993. Mem. Ala. Edn. Assn., NEA, Order of Eastern Star, Ala. Vocat. Assn., AAUW, Beta Eta Zeta. Democrat. Baptist. Avocations: sewing, cooking, crocheting, fishing, gardening, ceramics, singing. Home: 3238 18th Pl Tuscaloosa AL 35401-4102

SMITH, LONNIE MAX, diversified industries executive; b. Twin Falls, Idaho, July 28, 1944; s. Lonnie E. and Christie (Stuart) S.; m. Cheryl Diane Smith, June 10, 1968; children: Kristen, Maryam, Rebecca, Michael, Catherine. BSEE, Utah State U., 1967; MBA, Harvard U., 1974. Engr., mgr. field services, mgr. tech. services to asst. to v.p. plans and control IBM Corp., San Francisco, Palo Alto, Calif., and White Plains, N.Y., 1967-74; mgr., corp. strategy, then cons. Boston Cons. Group, 1974-76; exec. v.p. Am. Tourister, Inc., Warren, R.I., 1978-81; sr. v.p. corp. planning Hillenbrand Industries, Inc., Batesville, Ind., 1977-78, sr. exec. v.p., 1982—, also bd. dirs.; pres., chmn. bd. Hillenbrand Internat. Sales Corp.; v.p., bd. dirs. Forecorp, Inc., Batesville; bd. dirs. Hillenbrand Investment Adv. Corp., Batesville Casket Co., Batesville Internat. Corp., Hill-rom Co., The Forethought Group, Inc., Hilico Life Inst. Co., Medeco Security Locks, Inc., Salem, Va. Served to 1st lt. U.S. Army, 1969-72. Republican. Mormon. Avocations: tennis, skiing. Office: Hillenbrand Industries Inc 700 State Route 46 E Batesville IN 47006-8928

SMITH, LOREN ALLAN, federal judge; b. Chgo., Ill., Dec. 22, 1944; m. Catherine Yore; children: Loren Jr., Adam. BA in Polit. Sci., Northwestern U., 1966, JD, 1969; LLD (hon.), John Marshall Law Sch., 1995. Bar: Ill. 1970, D.C., U.S. Ct. Mil. Appeals 1973, U.S. Ct. Appeals (D.C. cir.) 1974, U.S. Supreme Ct. 1974, U.S. Ct. Claims, 1985, U.S. Ct. Appeals (fed. cir.) 1986. Gen. atty. FCC, 1973; asst. to spl. counsel to the pres. White House, Washington, 1973-74; spl. asst. U.S. atty. D.C., 1974-75; counsel Reagan for Pres. campaigns, 1976, 80; prof. Del. Law Sch., 1976-84; dep. dir. Office Exec. Br. Mgmt. Presdl. Transition, 1980-81; chmn. Adminstrv. Conf. U.S., 1981-85; appointed judge U.S. Claims Ct., 1985, designated chief judge, 1986—; adj. prof. Internat. Law Sch., 1973-74, Georgetown U. Law Ctr., 1992—, Am. U. Sch. Law, 1994—; past mem. Pres.'s Cabinet Coun. on Legal Policy, Pres.' Cabinet Coun. on Mgmt. and Adminstrn.; chmn. Coun. Ind. Regulatory Atys.; Allen chair U. Richmond Sch. Law, 1996. Contbr. articles to profl. jours. Recipient Presdl. medal Cath. U. Am. Law Sch., 1993, Romanian medal of justice Romanian Min. of Justice, 1995. Republican. Jewish.

SMITH, LORETTA MAE, contracting officer; b. Washington Twp., Pa., May 25, 1939; d. Irvin Calvin and Viola Mary (Deibler) Shambaugh; 1 child, Miriam Estella Smith. B in Humanities, Pa. State U., 1984. Bookkeeper Harrisburg (Pa.) Nat. Bank, 1957-62; contract specialist USN, Mechanicsburg, Pa., 1987—; founder Telecare, Harrisburg, Pa., 1972-82. Active ARC, instr. CPR, 1982—; active Girl Scouts U.S., trainer, 1972—. Recipient Hemlock award Hemlock coun. Girl Scouts U.S., Harrisburg, 1981; Merit scholar Hall Found., 1982. Mem. Nat. Contract Mgmt. Assn., Mensa. Avocations: walking in woods, birding, swimming, making music.

SMITH, LOUIS ADRIAN, lawyer; b. Lansing, Mich., Apr. 22, 1939; s. John Paul and Marjorie (Christmas) S.; m. Karen Emens, Feb. 5, 1966; children: Timothy P., Patrick L., Elizabeth K. BA cum laude, Mich. State U., 1962; JD, U. Mich., 1965; LLD (hon.), Thomas M. Cooley Law Sch., 1980. Bar: Mich. 1974, U.S. Ct. Appeals 1972, U.S. Supreme Ct. 1971. Atty. Fowler & Smith, Lansing, 1965-67, Doyle & Smith, Lansing, 1968-74, Louis A. Smith, Atty., P.C., Traverse City, Mich., 1975-76, Smith, Johnson & Brandt, Attys., P.C., Traverse City, Mich., 1982—; co-founder and bd. dirs. Thomas M. Cooley Law Sch., Lansing, Mich., 1972-94; bd. dirs. Empire Nat. Bank, Traverse City; mem. adv. coun. Univ. Notre Dame (Ind.) Law Sch., 1987—. Bd. trustees Interlochen (Mich.) Arts Acad., 1988. With U.S. Army, 1957-61. Fellow Mich. State Bar Found.; mem. ABA, Fed. Bar Assn., State Bar Mich., Assn. Trial Lawyers, D.C. Bar, Ingham County Bar Assn., Grand Traverse-Leelanau-Antrim County Bar, Am. Judicature Soc., Traverse City Golf and Country Club (pres. 1989), Crystal Downs Country Club, Tournament Players Club at Prestantia, Royal Dornach Scotland. Office: Smith Johnson Brandt 603 Bay St PO Box 705 Traverse City MI 49685

SMITH, LOWELL, dancer; b. Memphis. Mem. Dance Theatre of Harlem, 1977—, prin. dancer, also acting sch. dir.; instr. Memphis Acad. of Ballet, N.Y. Drama Sch. Performances include Swan Lake (Act II), The Four Temperaments, Scheherazade, Holberg Suite, Serenade, Footprints Dress for Red, Equus, Troy Game, Fall River Legen, A Song for Dead Warriors; TV appearances include PBS's Dance in America showing of Streetcar Named Desire, NBC's airing of Giselle; performed at the White House State Dinner, 1981.

SMITH, LUCIUS SKINNER, III, educational foundation administrator; b. Boulder, Colo., July 11, 1919; s. Lucius Skinner Jr. and Georgie Elizabeth (Hoxie) S.; m. Josephine Lamb Butler, 1942 (div. 1963); children: Lucius S. IV (dec.), Suzy Smith Hunt, Alexander Gavin Butler, Alan Bret, Anthony Butler Mason; m. Emilie Jensen, 1964 (div. 1974); m. Maria Katalin Feher, Sept. 27, 1974. BA in Modern European History, U. Calif., Berkeley, 1941. Cons., lobbyist Am. Bar Ctr. and Keogh Act for the Self-Employed, 1955-60; journalist Hearst Corp., Boston, 1970-75; pub. rels. and exec. search Washington and St. Louis, 1976-86; cons. Am. Freedom Train for Am.'s Bicentennial, 1975; adj. gen. Nat. Assn. Atomic Vets., Independence, Mo., 1985-90; pres. Atomic Libr. and Tech. Found., Washington, 1988—. Supported enactment of Radiation-Exposed Vets. Compensation Act, 1988. Naval aviator USMC, 1941-45, PTO, Lt. col. ret. USMC Res. Decorated DFC, Bronze star, Air medal with gold star, Presl. unit citation. Office: 218 N Washington St Du Quoin IL 62832-1769

SMITH, MACON STROTHER, architect; b. Raleigh, N.C., Feb. 24, 1919; s. Junious Walters and Mary Macon (Strother) S.; m. Jeanette Marjorie Williams, Feb. 14, 1944; children: Stephen Williams, Patricia Macon Smith Hoover. BS in Archtl./Aero. Engrng. with honors, N.C. State U., 1941. Registered architect, N.C. Part-time draftsman F. Carter Williams, Architects, Raleigh, 1940-41, project architect, 1946-55, ptnr., 1955-80, v.p., 1980—; draftsman Cooper & Shumaker, Architects, Raleigh, 1945-46; part-time instr. Sch. Design N.C. State U., Raleigh, 1957-58, juror student work; mem. Gov.'s Low Cost Housing Com., Raleigh, 1966-67; chmn. Gov.'s City and County Subcom. Low Cost Housing, 1967-68. Co-designer addition class rm. bldg. project displayed in Nat. Gold Medal Exhbn. Bldg. Arts, Archtl. League N.Y., 1957 (citation South Atlantic AIA). V.p. Raleigh Lions Club, 1965. Lt. comdr. USNR, 1941-45. Recipient 2d prize weathermaker home competition for S. and S.W. U.S.A Carrier Corp., 1953, 2d award Ch. Architecture Guild, 1956. Fellow AIA (dir. South Atlantic regional bd. 1964-71, mem. fellow selection com. 1973-75, chmn. 1975); mem. N.C. chpt. AIA (treas., v.p., pres., dir., 1962-67, mem. com. to establish archtl. sch. at U. N.C. Charlotte 1966-69, adv. com. new sch. 1970-73, Merit award ch. design 1958), N.C. Archtl. Found. (sec.-treas., v.p., pres. 1963-71), Carolina Country Club. Democrat. Presbyterian. Avocations: tennis, golf. Home: 3721 Lassiter Mill Rd Raleigh NC 27609-7042

SMITH, DAME MAGGIE, actress; b. Ilford, Eng., Dec. 28, 1934; d. Nathaniel and Margaret (Hutton) S.; m. Robert Stephens, 1967 (div. 1974); m. Beverley Cross, 1974. Grad., Oxford High Sch. Girls; D.Litt. (hon.), St. Andrews, 1971; DLitt (hon.), Oxford U., 1994. dir. United British Artists, 1982—. Stage and film actress, 1952—; stage appearances include: New Faces, debut N.Y.C., 1956, Share My Lettuce, 1957, The Stepmother, 1958, Rhinoceros, 1960, Strip The Willow, 1960, The Rehearsal, 1961, The Private Ear and The Public Eye, 1962, Mary, Mary, 1961; appearances at Old Vic, 1959-60, Nat. Theatre, London, 1963—; productions at Nat. Theatre include Private Lives, 1972, Othello, Hay Fever, Master Builder, Hedda Gabbler, Much Ado About Nothing, Miss Julie, Black Comedy, Stratford Festival, Ont., Can., 1976, 77, 78, 80, Antony and Cleopatra, Macbeth, Three Sisters, Richard III, Night and Day, London and N.Y.C., 1979-80, Virginia, London, 1981, Way of the World, Chichester Festival, London, 1984-85, Interpreters, London, 1985-86, Lettice and Lovage, 1988, also in N.Y., 1990, The Importance of Being Earnest, 1993, Three Tall Women, 1994; films include Othello, 1966, The Honey Pot, 1967, Oh What a Lovely War, 1968, Hot Millions, 1968, The Prime of Miss Jean Brodie, 1968 (Acad. award for best actress), Love and Pain and The Whole Damn Thing, 1971, Travels With My Aunt, 1972, Murder by Death, 1976, Death on the Nile, 1977, California Suite, 1978 (Acad. award for best supporting actress), Quartet, 1978, Clash of the Titans, 1981, Evil under the Sun, 1981, The Missionary, 1982, A Private Function, 1984 (best actress award Brit. Acad. of Film & TV Arts, 1985), Lily in Love, 1985, A Room With a View, 1985, The Lonely Passion of Judith Hearn, 1987 (Brit. Acad. of Film & TV Arts award, 1989), Paris By Night, 1988, Hook, 1991, Sister Act, 1992, The Secret Garden, 1993, Richard III, 1995, The First Wives Club, 1996; TV films include Memento Mori, 1992, Suddenly Last Summer, 1993 (Lead Actress-Miniseries Emmy nominee, 1993); BBC-TV appearance Bed Among the Lentils, 1988. Recipient Best Actress award Eve. Std., 1962, 70, 82, 85, 94, Best Film Actress award Soc. Film and TV Arts U.K., 1968, Film Critics Guild, 1968, Taomina Gold award, 1985, Antoinette Perry award (Tony), 1990, Shakespeare prize, 1991; decorated Dame Brit. Empire, 1989; named Actress of Yr., Variety Club, 1963, 72, Brit. Acad. Best Screen Actress, 1985; Brit. Film Inst. fellow, 1992, Theater Hall of Fame, 1994. Office: Write on Cue, 15 New Row 3d Fl, London WC2N 4LA, England*

SMITH, M(AHLON) BREWSTER, psychologist, educator; b. Syracuse, N.Y., June 26, 1919; s. Mahlon Ellwood and Blanche Alice (Hinman) S.; m. Jean Dresden Schwartz, June 1942 (div. 1945); m. Deborah Anderson, June, 1947; children: Joshua H., T. Daniel, Rebecca M., J. Torquil. Student, Reed Coll., Portland, Oreg., 1935- 38; A.B., Stanford U., 1939, A.M., 1940; Ph.D., Harvard U., 1947. Rantoul scholar Harvard U., 1940-41; jr. analyst Office Coordinator of Information, U.S. Govt., 1941; Social Sci. Research Council fellow Harvard U., 1946-47; asst. prof. social psychology Harvard U. (Dept. Social Relations), 1947-49; prof. psychology, chmn. dept. Vassar Coll., 1949-52; staff Social Sci. Research Council, 1952-56; prof. psychology NYU, 1956-59; prof. psychology U. Calif. at Berkeley, 1959-68, dir. Inst. Human Devel., 1965-68; prof., chmn. dept. psychology U. Chgo., 1968-70; prof. psychology U. Calif. at Santa Cruz, 1970-88, prof. emeritus, 1988—, vice chancellor social scis., 1970-75; fellow Center Advanced Studies Behavioral Scis., 1964-65; Vice pres. Joint Commn. Mental Illness and Health, 1955-61. Author: Social Psychology and Human Values, 1969, Humanizing Social Psychology, 1974, Values, Self and Society, 1991; co-author: The American Soldier, 1949, Opinions and Personality, 1956; editor: Jour. Social Issues, 1951-55, Jour. Abnormal Soc. Psychology, 1956-61; contbr. articles to profl. jours. Served from pvt. to maj. Adj. Gen. Div. AUS, 1942-46; research officer Information and Edn. div. War Dept., 1943-46; research asso. spl. com. on soldier attitudes Social Sci. Research Council 1946. Decorated Bronze Star medal.; NIMH fellow, 1964-65, NEH fellow, 1975-76; Belding scholar Found. for Child Devel., 1982-83; Gold medal award lifetime contbn. to psychology in pub. interest Am. Psychol. Found., 1992. Fellow AAAS, APA (pres. 1978, Disting. Contbn. to Pub. Interest award 1988, Henry A. Murray award in personality psychology 1993); mem. Soc. Psychol. Study Social Issues (pres. 1959, Kurt Lewin Meml. award 1986), Western Psychol. Assn. (pres. 1986, Lifetime Contbn. award 1996), Psychologists for Social Responsibility (pres. 1987-90), Internat. Soc. Polit. Psychology (Harold Lasswell award 1993), Internat. Assn. Applied Psychology (pres. divsn. polit. psychology 1994—), Cosmos Club (Washington), Phi Beta Kappa, Sigma Xi. Democrat. Home: 316 Escalona Dr Santa Cruz CA 95060-2607

SMITH, MALCOLM BARRY ESTES, philosophy educator, lawyer; b. Houston, Oct. 24, 1939; s. Fairleigh Estes and Norma Barry (McNab) S.; m. Patricia Sweetser; children: Malcolm, Eric. BA, Va. Mil. Inst., 1961; PhD, Cornell U., 1969; JD, U. Calif., Berkeley, 1984. BarL Mass. 1985, U.S. Supreme Ct. 1992. Instr. philosophy Smith Coll., Northampton, Mass., 1967-69, asst. prof. philosophy, 1969-74, assoc. prof., 1974-79, prof., 1979—. Served to capt. USAR, 1964-66. Mem. ABA, Mass. Bar Assn., Am. Philos. Assn. Home: 9 Park St Northampton MA 01060-1236 Office: Smith Coll Dept Philosophy PO Box 839 Northampton MA 01061-0839

SMITH, MALCOLM BERNARD, investment company executive; b. Lynn, Mass., May 27, 1923; s. Philip and Ida (Zenis) S.; m. Betty Booth, June 20, 1948; children: Eric, Daniel. B.A. summa cum laude, Dartmouth Coll., 1944; M.A. in Econs., Harvard U., 1948; hon. degree, New Sch. for Social Rsch., 1995. Sec. Gen. Am. Investors Co., N.Y.C., 1956-57, treas., 1957-59, v.p., 1958-61, pres., 1961-89, vice chmn., 1989—, also bd. dirs. Chmn. fin. com. N.Y. Found., 1973-82, treas., 1979-82, trustee, 1973-89, 91—, chmn. 1982-85; chmn. New Sch. for Social Rsch., N.Y.C., 1985-95, trustee, 1982—, treas., 1982-84, chmn. ednl. policy com., 1984-85, chmn. exec. com., 1985-95; trustee John Simon Guggenheim Meml. Found., 1982-85, chmn. fin. com., 1985-95, Human Rights Watch, 1993—; mng. trustee Permanent Fund of MLA, 1987—; mem. investment com. Fedn. Jewish Philantrophies, N.Y., 1975-96, Phi Beta Kappa Found., 1987—; bd. dirs. Learning Smith, Inc., 1992-93; Cybersmith, Inc., 1994—. With U.S. Army, 1943-46. Mem. AAAS (chmn. investment and fin. com. 1975—), Investment Co. Inst. (bd. govs. 1987-95), Assn. Publicly Traded Investment Funds (bd. dirs. 1970-87, chmn. 1971-79, Coun. on Fgn. Rels., N.Y. Soc. Security Analysts, Phi Beta Kappa Assocs. (adv. com. 1984-93, bd. dirs. 1993—), Phi Beta Kappa. Club: Harvard (bd. mgrs. 1984-86), Century Assn. (N.Y.C.). Home: PO Box 358 Pound Ridge NY 10576-0358 Office: Gen Am Investors Co Inc 450 Lexington Ave New York NY 10017-3911

SMITH, MALCOLM NORMAN, manufacturing company executive; b. Milw., Feb. 25, 1921; s. Samuel H. and Dorothea (Werner) S.; m. Muriel J. Foreman, Feb. 14, 1943; 1 dau., Louise K. BS in Econs, U. Pa., 1942. With Ekco Products Co., Chgo., 1946-50, 56-63; v.p. Ekco Products Co., 1956-63; dir. Platers & Stampers Ltd. (Brit. div. Ekco), London, 1950-56; pres., chief exec. officer, dir. Argus, Inc., Chgo., 1963-68; pres. Malcolm N. Smith & Co., Chgo., 1968-70; adminstrv. v.p., cashier Am. Nat. Bank and Trust Co., Chgo., 1970-75; pres. Macromatic div. Macromatic Inc., 1975-88; pres. Macromatic Divsn. of Milw. Electronics Corp., Chgo., 1988-93, Newmac, Inc., 1994—; profl. lectr. U. Chgo. Grad Sch. Bus., 1968-82; bd. dirs. Acorn Internat. Fund. Bd. dirs. The Acorn Fund. 1st lt. USMCR, 1942-46. Decorated Silver Star. Mem. Friends of Franklin, Inc. (pres. 1992—), Lake Shore Country Club, The Casino, Royal Tennis Ct., Hampton Ct. Palace. Home: 309 Maple Ave Highland Park IL 60035-2056

SMITH, MALCOLM SOMMERVILLE, bass; b. Rockville Centre, N.Y., June 22, 1933; s. Carlton Newell and Margaret (Sommerville) S.; m. Margaret Yauger, Oct. 4, 1975. B.Music Edn., Oberlin Coll., 1957, B.Mus., 1960; M.A. in Ednl. Adminstrn, Columbia Tchrs. Coll., 1958; student, Ind. U. Sch. Music, 1960-62. Dir. choral music, Ramapo Regional High Sch., Wyckoff, N.J., 1958-60; basso, Lyric Opera, Chgo., 1961, 63; bass soloist Russian tour, Robert Shaw Choral, 1962; leading bass, N.Y.C. Opera, 1965-70, Deutsche Oper Am Rhein, Dusseldorf, Germany, 1971—, Vienna State Opera, 1973-74, 86 Met. Opera, Japan Tour, spring 1975, Met. Opera, N.Y.C., 1975-77, Paris Opera, 1978, Barcelona Opera, 1978, Sao Paulo, Brazil, 1978, Mexico City, 1979, 80, Berlin Opera, 1979, 80, Montreal Symphony, 1979, 80, 81, 82, Hamburg Opera, 1981, Köln Opera, 1980, Stuttgart Opera, 1980, Frankfurt Opera, 1980, Rome Opera, 1980, Trieste (Italy) Opera, 1981, Berlin Staatsoper, 1982, 85, Lyric Opera Phila, 1982, Los Angeles Philharm. at Hollywood Bowl, 1984, Mannheim Opera, Fed. Republic Germany, 1986, Turin Opera, Italy, 1986, 88, Bordeaux, France, 1987, Dresden Opera, German Dem. Republic, 1987, Hannover Opera, Fed. Republic Germany, 1987, Staats Oper Berlin Japan Tour, 1987, Polish TV, 1989, Oslo Opera, 1987, Paris Radio, 1988-89, Orange Festival, France, 1988, Penderecki Festival, Krakow, Poland, 1988; maj. soloist Schleswig Holstein Festival, Fed. Republic Germany, 1989, Krakow Philharmonic, Poland, 1988, Maggio Musicale, Florence, Italy,1988, Boston Symphony, Minn., Cin., Houston, Utah, Seattle, Chgo., Phila., Balt. Symphony, 1993, Mexico Nat. Symphony, 1993, Nat. symphonies, also, Cin. Summer Opera, Central City (Colo.) Summer Opera, Festival of two Worlds, Spoleto, Italy., Saratoga Festival, 1985, debut, La Scala, Milan, Italy, 1982, Salzburg Festival, 1986, Athens Festival, 1987, Bordeaux (France) Opera, 1987, Ft. Worth Opera, 1988, Orange Festival, France, 1988, Staatsoper Munich, 1990, Bastille Opera, Paris, 1991, Heidelberg Summer festival, 1991, 92, Brussels Opera, 1992, 93, 94, Opera Nice, France, 1992, Opera Montpelier, France, 1992, Cin. Opera, 1994, Düsseldorf Opera, 1994, tour Japan, 1994, Bregenz (Austria) Festival, 1996, Honolulu Opera, 1996; recorded War and Peace, 1986, Penderecki Requiem, 1990. Served with AUS, 1954-56. Recipient Kämmersanger title Dusseldorf (Germany) Opera, 1996. Congregationalist. Office: care Thea Dispeker Artists Rep 59 E 54th St New York NY 10022-4211 *Hard work and a sense of humor.*

SMITH, MARCIA LYNN ELLISON (MARKY SMITH), psychotherapist; b. Houston, Nov. 23, 1946; d. James Thomas and Eugenia Irene (Adams) E.; m. Thomas Owen, Nov. 28, 1969; children: Angela Michelle, James Randolph, Holly Lynn, John Thomas. BA, Tex. A & I U., 1969; MEd, Houston Bapt. U., 1987. Cert. sch. counselor, secondary tchr., Tex., cert. chemical dependency specialist, cert. compulsory gambling counselor, cert. supervisory cons.; lic. profl. counselor, marriage and family therapist, chemical dependency counselor, psychol. assoc. Tchr. Corpus Christi (Tex.) Ind. Sch. Dist., 1969-75; gymnastics judge U.S. Gymnastics Fedn., Houston, 1975-82; counselor Katy (Tex.) Ind. Sch. Dist., 1987-90; program coord. Adolescent Psychiat. Day Hosp./Intermediate Care Twelve Oaks Hosp., Houston, 1990-91; aftercare coord. Pasadena Gen. Hosp., 1991-93; owner and psychotherapist Tex. Psychotherapy Assocs., Houston, 1993—. Illustrator: Teacher, Teacher, Don't Whip Me, 1955, Exiled Heart, 1965, The Innocent Child, 1982. Pres. Carver-Kemp PTA, Bryan, Tex., 1978; dir. Kingsland Bapt. Ch. Children's Choir, Katy, 1981-86; mem. Century Com. for Excellence in Edn., 1983-84; v.p. Gymnastic Boosters of Houston, 1980-83. Mem. Am. Assn. Counseling and Devel., Tex. Psychol. Assn., Tex. Assn. Counseling and Devel., Assn. Tex. Profl. Educators, Houston Assn. Counseling and Devel., Beta Sigma Phi (sec. 1973), Psi Chi. Republican. Baptist. Avocations: water sports, crafts, piano, flute, reading. Home: 1323 Dominion Dr Katy TX 77450-4309 Office: Tex Psychotherapy Assocs PO Box 631206 Houston TX 77263

SMITH, MARGARET HAMILTON DONALD, physician; b. N.Y.C., Jan. 26, 1915; d. Donald P. and Margaret D. (Warner) S.; m. Morris F. Shaffer, Dec. 28, 1959; 1 child, Charlotte A.; 1 stepchild, Alexander F. B. es lettres, Gymnase de Lausanne, Switzerland, 1933; M.D., Johns Hopkins U., 1939. Diplomate: Am. Bd. Pediatrics. Intern Balt. City Hosp., 1939-40, Johns Hopkins Hosp., Balt., 1940-41; resident in pediatrics U. Hosp., Ann Arbor, Mich., 1941-42; Nat. Rsch. Coun. fellow in animal pathology Rockefeller Inst. Princeton, N.J., 1946-48; faculty Johns Hopkins U., 1943-46; med. dir. Sydenham Hosp., Balt., 1942-45; faculty pediatrics, microbiology, epidemiology Tulane U., New Orleans, 1948-73; prof. pediatrics Tulane U., 1961-73, 80, prof. emeritus, 1980—; dir. Children's Hosp. of Newark, 1975-77; faculty NYU, 1955-59, Coll. Medicine and Dentistry of N.J., 1974-77; staff Ochsner Clinic, 1977-80; mem. microbiology and infectious disease adv. com. Nat. Inst. Allergy and Infectious Diseases, 1975-80; mem. adv. com. on elimination of Tb. Ctrs. for Disease Control, 1987-90; bd. Scientific Counselors, NIH Divsn. Biol. Stds., 1969-72; pediatrician, Hosp. Albert Schweitzer, Haiti, 1958, 80, 85; vis. prof. U. Geneva, Switzerland, 1971. Contbr. chpts. to books, numerous articles in field to profl. jours. Recipient Mead Johnson award Am. Acad. Pediatrics, 1953, Jacobi award Acad. and AMA, 1979, Disting. Physician award Pediatric Infectious Disease Soc., 1989. Mem. Soc. for Pediatric Rsch. (v.p. 1958), Am. Pediatric Soc. (pres. 1976), Am. Acad. Pediatrics, Infectious Diseases Soc. Am., Am. Thoracic Soc., Alpha Omega Alpha. Democrat. Unitarian. Home: 5315 Camp St New Orleans LA 70115-3035 Office: Tulane U Sch Medicine Dept Pediatrics 1430 Tulane Ave New Orleans LA 70112-2699

SMITH, MARGARET PHYLLIS, editor, consultant; b. Plymouth, Pa., Aug. 24, 1925; d. Harold Dewitt and Mae Elmira (Bittenbender) S. AB magna cum laude, Bucknell U., 1946, AM, 1947; postgrad., U. Pa., summer 1951-54. Instr. English Bucknell U., Lewisburg, Pa., 1947-52, asst. prof., 1952-55; personnel asst. RCA Labs., Princeton, N.J., 1955-58, staff writer pub. affairs dept., 1958-76, adminstr. communications, 1976-87; editor spl. projects David Sarnoff Rsch. Ctr. (formerly RCA Labs.), Princeton, 1987-92, contbg. editor, 1992—; mng. editor Vision mag. David Sarnoff Rsch. Ctr., 1987—, editor UPDATE newsletter, 1969—. Editor: 1942-67 Twenty-five Years at RCA Laboratories, 1968. Mem. corp. communications com. United Way, Princeton, 1976-88. Mem. AAUW, N.J. Press Women (publicity dir. 1985-86), Internat. Assn. Bus. Communicators. Episcopalian. Office: David Sarnoff Rsch Ctr 201 Washington Rd Princeton NJ 08540-6449

SMITH, MARGARET TAYLOR, volunteer; b. Roanoke Rapids, N.C., May 31, 1925; d. George Napoleon and Sarah Luella (Waller) T.; m. Sidney William Smith Jr., Aug. 15, 1947; children: Sarah Smith, Sidney William Smith III, Susan Smith, Amy Smith. BA in Sociology, Duke U., 1947. Chair. bd. trustees Kresge Found., Troy, MI, 1985—; chmn. Nat. Coun. for Women's Studies Duke U., N.C.; 1986—, mem. Trinity Bd. Visitors, 1988—; chmn. Radius Corp./Health Care Ctrs. Detroit Med. Ctr., 1989—, also bd. dirs. Recipient the Merrill-Palmer award Wayne State U., Detroit, 1987. Mem. The Village Club, The Econ. Club of Detroit, Pi Beta Phi. Methodist.

SMITH, MARIE EDMONDS, real estate agent, property manager; b. Quapaw, Okla., Oct. 5, 1927; d. Thomas Joseph and Maud Ethel (Douglas) Edmonds; m. Robert Lee Smith, Aug. 14, 1966 (dec. 1983). Grad. vocat. nurse, Hoag Hosp., Costa Mesa, Calif., 1953; BA, So. Calif. Coll., 1955; MS, U. Alaska, 1963. Lic. vocat. nurse, Calif.; cert. sci. tchr., Alaska. Nurse Calif. Dept. Nurses, Costa Mesa, 1952-60; tchr. Alaska Dept. Edn., Aniak and Anchorage, 1955-60; tchr. sci. Garden Grove (Calif.) Sch. Dist., 1960-87; property mgr. Huntington Beach, Calif., 1970—; agent Sterling Realtors, Huntington Beach, 1988—. Author: Ocean Biology, 1969. Bd. dirs., tchr. Harbor Christian Fellowship, Costa Mesa, 1966-83; com. chmn. Garden Grove Unified Sch. Dist. PTA, 1977. NSF grantee, 1960-62. Mem. AAUW, So. Calif. Coll. Alumnae Assn. Republican. Avocations: skin diving, travel. Home: 83ll Reilly Dr Huntington Beach CA 92646 Office: L8153 Brookhurst St Fountain Valley CA 92708

SMITH, MARION PAFFORD, avionics company executive; b. Waycross, Ga., Dec. 12, 1925; s. Rossa Elbert and Lillian Solee (Pafford) S.; m. Esther Pat Davis, Nov. 23, 1952; children: Bryan P., Danton D., Patricia Anne. Student, Okla. State U., 1944, Yale U., 1945; BS in EE, La. State U., 1949; postgrad., U. So. Fla., 1966-70. Engr. Bell Telephone Co., Baton Rouge, 1949-51; mgr. engring. Vitro Labs., Silver Spring, Md., 1952-57; design engring. mgr. dept. design and constrn. flight hand contrs. Space Shuttle and Space Sta. Honeywell Avionics Div., Clearwater, Fla., 1957—; vice chmn., bd. dirs. First Union, Largo, Fla., 1985-93; cons. U.S. Army Mgmt. Engring. Tng. Agy., 1975-79; U.S. Del. Internat. Elec. Tech. Commn., 1965-85, chmn. chief U.S. tech. adviser com. on reliability and maintainability, 1975-85, v.p., exec. com. U.S. nat. com., 1975-84; U.S. del. NATO Quality Conf., 1973; mem. White House Summit Conf. on Inflation, 1975; del. White House Conf. on Handicapped, 1977; mem. nat. adv. coun. on devel. disabilities HEW, 1974-78, Fla. Adv. Coun. on Devel. Ctr. for Persons with Disabilities, 1974-78, Fla. Advocacy, 1983—; mem. devel. coun. Morton Plant Hosp., Clearwater, 1971-74. 1st lt. Signal Corps, AUS, 1944-45, 51-52. Served to 1st lt. Signal Corps AUS, 1944-45, 51-52. Recipient McDonald award Fla. Rehab. Assn., 1968; Bilgore award Citizen of Year Clearwater, Fla., 1969; Outstanding Service award Am. Soc. Quality Control, 1968-69; United Comml. Travelers award Most Outstanding Service Retarded Fla., 1970; named Engr. of Year Fla. W. Coast, 1970; Service to Mankind award Sertoma Clubs, 1977. Fellow IEEE (dir., Nat. Reliability award 1979); mem. Assn. Retarded Citizens USA (pres. 1973-75, nat. govt. affairs chmn. 1975-83), Am. Assn. Mental Deficiency, Nat. Symposium Reliability Quality Control (gen. chmn.), Sigma Chi. Presbyterian elder. Club: Kiwanis (Marion P. Smith award established in his honor). Home: 1884 Oakdale Ln N Clearwater FL 34624-6441 Office: 13350 US Hwy 19 Clearwater FL 34624-7226 *True turning points in life are sometimes difficult to recognize, but for those who have become parents of a handicapped child, particularly a mentally retarded child, then that turning point is easy to recognize. After the difficult period of adjustment, one becomes aware of a realization that all persons have human dignity and worth and can make a contribution to humanity and to society.*

SMITH, MARJORIE AILEEN MATTHEWS, museum director; b. Richmond, Va., Aug. 19, 1918; d. Harry Anderson and Adelia Charlotte (Howland) Matthews; m. Robert Woodrow Smith, July 23, 1945 (dec. Mar. 1992). Pilot lic., Taneytown (Md.) Aviation Svc., 1944, cert. ground sch. instr., 1945. Founder, editor, pub. Spinning Wheel, Taneytown, 1945-63; v.p. Antiques Publs., Inc., Taneytown, 1960-68; pres. Prism Inc., Taneytown, 1968-78; mus. dir. Trapshooting Hall of Fame, Vandalia, Ohio, 1976—, sec., 1993—. Co-author: Handbook of Tomorrow's Antiques, 1954; contbr. articles to profl. publs. Sec. Balt. area coun. Girl Scouts USA, 1950. Named to All-Am. Trapshooting team Sports Afield mag., 1960, 61. Mem. Nat. League Am. Pen Women, Amateur Trapshooting Assn. (life), Am. Contract Bridge League, Internat. Assn. Sports Mus. and Halls of Fame (bd. dirs. 1993-94). Lutheran. Avocations: duplicate bridge, trapshooting, antiques collecting. Office: Trapshooting Hall of Fame 601 W National Rd Vandalia OH 45377-1036

SMITH, MARK HALLARD, architect; b. Detroit, June 28, 1955; s. John Hallard and Barbara Ruth (Hinkle) S.; m. Janee Lynne Batey, July 18, 1981; children: Elizabeth Anne, Jacquelyne Ruth. BS, Ga. Inst. Tech., 1977, MArch, 1979. Registered architect, Fla.; cert. Nat. Coun. Archtl. Registration Bds. Draftsman Kirkland/Ogram Architects, Atlanta, 1979-80; project mgr. Bailey Vrooman Allegret, Atlanta, 1980-81, Rabun Hatch and Dendy, Atlanta, 1981; project architect C. Randolph Wedding & Assocs., St. Petersburg, Fla., 1981-83, Stearman Architects, St. Petersburg, 1983-90, Carl Abbott Arch. FAIA PA, Sarasota, Fla., 1990-94; prin. Smith Architects, Sarasota, 1994—; panelist Ringling Mus. Art, Sarasota, 1991. Asst. editor Centerline, 1990. Chmn. Sarasota Design Conf., 1993-94; mem. steering com. John Ringling Ctr. Found., Sarasota, 1995; pres. Men's Club, St. Michael The Archangel Ch., 1993—. Chmn. Sarasota Design Conf., 1994, 96; mem. steering com. John Ringling Ctr. Found., Sarasota, 1995; pres. Men's Club, St. Michael The Archangel Ch., 1993-96. Mem. AIA (archtl. juror Palm Beach chpt. 1993, pres. Fla. Gulf Coast chpt. 1994-95, Fla. award of excellence 1993, Fla. bd. dirs. 1995—, Fla. Pres. award 1994), Nat. Trust for Hist. Preservation, Tiger Bay Club. Republican. Roman Catholic. Avocation: tennis. Home: 5562 Cape Aqua Dr Sarasota FL 34242-1804 Office: Smith Architects Sarasota FL 34242

SMITH, MARK LEE, architect; b. L.A., Nov. 16, 1957; s. Selma (Moidel) Smith. BA in History of Architecture, UCLA, 1978, MA in Architecture, 1980. Registered architect Calif., Nev., Oreg., Wash., Tenn., Colo. Designer, drafter John B. Ferguson and Assocs., L.A., 1976-83, architect, 1983; pvt. practice architecture L.A., 1984—; mem. Los Angeles County Archtl. Evaluation Bd., 1990—. Contbr. articles to profl. jours. Bd. govs. UCLA John Wooden Ctr., 1978-80. Regents scholar, U. Calif., Berkeley, UCLA, 1975-78; UCLA Grad. Sch. Architecture Rsch. fellow, 1979-80. Mem. AIA (treas. San Fernando Valley chpt. 1986, bd. dirs. 1986—, v.p. 1987, pres. 1988, Design award 1988, 89, 90, 91, chmn. Design awards 1994, bd. dirs. Calif. coun. 1989-94, v.p. 1991-94, chmn. continuing edn. 1991-93, chmn. 1992 conf.), Phi Beta Kappa. Office: 18340 Ventura Blvd Ste 225 Tarzana CA 91356-4234

SMITH, MARKWICK KERN, JR., management consultant; b. N.Y.C., Feb. 14, 1928; s. Markwick Kern and Elizabeth (Morning) S.; m. Martia Reed, Mar. 2, 1951; children—Karen, Rebecca, Mark David, Jennifer. B.S., Mass. Inst. Tech., 1951, Ph.D., 1954; M.F.A., Vt. Coll., 1988. Vice pres., then exec. v.p. Geophys. Service Inc., Dallas, 1962-67, pres., 1967-69; v.p. Tex. Instruments, Dallas, 1967-73; mgmt. cons., author Norwich, Vt., 1973—. Served with USNR, 1946-48. Mem. NAE. Congregationalist. Address: PO Box 189 Main St Norwich VT 05055

SMITH, MARSHALL SAVIDGE, government official, academic dean, educator; b. East Orange, N.J., Sept. 16, 1937; s. Marshall Parsons and Ann Eileen (Zulauf) S.; m. Carol Goodspeed, June 25, 1960 (div. Aug. 1962); m. Louise Nixon Claiborn, Aug. 1964; children: Adam, Jennifer, Matthew, Megan. AB, Harvard U., 1960, EdM, 1963, EdD, 1970. Computer analyst and programmer Raytheon Corp., Andover, Mass., 1959-62; instr., assoc. prof. Harvard U., Cambridge, Mass., 1966-76; asst., assoc. dir. Nat. Inst. Edn., Washington, 1973-76; asst. commr. edn. HEW, Washington, 1976-79, chief of staff to U.S. Dept. Edn. sec., 1980; prof. U. Wis., Madison, 1980-86; prof., dean Sch. Edn. Stanford (Calif.) U., 1986-93; under-sec. edn. U.S. Dept. Edn., 1993—; task force, chmn. Clinton Presdl. Transition Team, 1992-93; chmn. PEW Forum on Ednl. Reform; chmn. bd. internat. com. studies in edn. NAS, 1992-93. Author: The General Inquirer, 1967, Inequality, 1972; contbr. several articles to profl. jours, chpts. to books. Pres. Madison West Hockey Assn., 1982-84. Mem. Am. Ednl. Rsch. Assn. (chmn. orgn. instl. affiliates 1985-86), Cleve. Conf., Nat. Acad. Edn., Cosmos Club. Democrat. Avocation: environmental issues, coaching youth soccer. Home: 900 N Stafford St Apt 1817 Arlington VA 22203-1848 Office: US Dept Edn Under Sec Edn 600 Independence Ave SW Washington DC 20202-0004 Also: Stanford U Edu Dept Stanford CA 94305

SMITH, MARTIN BERNHARD, journalist; b. San Francisco, Apr. 20, 1930; s. John Edgar and Anna Sophie (Thorsen) S.; m. Joan Lovat Muller, Apr. 25, 1953; children: Catherine Joan, Karen Anne. AB, U. Calif., Berkeley, 1952, M Journalism, 1968. Reporter, city editor Modesto (Calif.) Bee, 1957-64; reporter, mng. editor Sacramento Bee, 1964-75; polit. editor, columnist McClatchy Newspapers, Sacramento, 1975-92; ret., 1992. Episcopalian.

SMITH, MARTIN CRUZ, author; b. Reading, Pa., Nov. 3, 1942; s. John and Louisa (Lopez) S.; m. Emily Stanton Arnold, June 15, 1968; children: Ellen, Luisa, Samuel. BA, U. Pa., 1964. Author: Gorky Park, 1981, Stallion Gate, 1986, Polar Star, 1989, Red Square, 1992, Rose, 1996.

SMITH, MARTIN HENRY, pediatrician; b. Gainesville, Ga., Nov. 3, 1921; s. Charles E. and Mamie Mae (Emmett) S.; m. Mary Gillis, Feb. 25, 1950; children: Susan, Margaret, Mary. MD, Emory U., 1945. Diplomate Am. Bd. Pediatrics. Intern City Hosp. System, Winston-Salem, N.C., 1945-46; fellow in infectious diseases Grady Meml. Hosp., Atlanta, 1948-49; resident Henrietta Egleston Hosp., Atlanta, 1949-50, Children's Hosp., Washington, 1950-51; practice medicine, specializing in pediatrics Gainesville, Ga.; ret., 1988; clin. asst. prof. Emory U. Hosp., Atlanta; chief of staff Hall County Hosp., Gainesville, 1965-66; mem. Nat. Vaccine Adv. Commn., 1990—, chmn., 1991. Contbr. articles to profl. jours. Chmn. Nat. Vaccine Adv. Com., 1991—. Capt. M.C., U.S. Army, 1946-48. Fellow Am. Acad. Pediatrics (chpt. chmn. 1966-69, dist. chmn. 1977-83, pres.-elect 1984-85, pres. 1985-86); mem. Hall County Med. Soc. (pres. 1960), Ga. Pediatric Soc. (pres. 1965-66), Med. Assn. Ga., AMA, Alpha Omega Alpha. Episcopalian. Clubs: Chattahoochee Country (Gainesville); Piedmont Driving (Atlanta).

SMITH, MARTIN JAY, advertising and marketing executive; b. N.Y.C., Feb. 1, 1942; s. Nathan and Helen (Schwartz) S.; m. Ellen Susan Chadakoff, Dec. 20, 1964; children: Hilary, Nancy. BA, U. Pitts., 1963. With sta. clearance dept. ABC Radio Network, N.Y.C., 1965-66; asst. account exec. Norman Craig & Kummel, N.Y.C., 1966-67, account exec., 1967-68; account exec. Gotham, Inc., N.Y.C., 1968-72, account supr., 1972-74, v.p., 1974-78, sr. v.p., 1978-80, exec. v.p., 1980-84, vice chmn., 1984—. Sgt. USAR, 1963-69. Mem. Am. Advt. Assn. Am. (mem. mgmt. com. 1987). Avocations: flying, tennis, golf. Home: 920 Park Ave New York NY 10028-0208 Office: Gotham Inc 260 Madison Ave New York NY 10016-2401

SMITH, MARTIN LANE, biomedical researcher; b. Seattle, Mar. 15, 1959; s. Melvin Dale and Rosemary (Nations) S. BA, Austin Coll., 1981; PhD, Emory U., 1990. Assoc. U. Pitts. Sch. Medicine, 1990-93, NIH, Bethesda, Md., 1993—; instr. biology Emory U., Atlanta, 1985-89. Contbr. articles to profl. jours. NIH grantee, 1991-93; recipient Am. Cancer Soc. award, 1992. Mem. AAAS, Am. Assn. Cancer Rsch., Sigma Xi. Avocations: coin collecting, hiking, travel.

SMITH, MARVIN FREDERICK, JR., chemical engineer, consultant; b. Newark, N.J., Oct. 22, 1932; s. Marvin F. and Helen (Marsh) S.; m. Jacqueline Pettit, June 20, 1959; 1 child, Scott C. BSChE, Newark (N.J.) Coll. Engring., 1954. Field engr. E.I. DuPont, Newark, Del., 1954-55, Newport, Del., 1957-59; dir. mfg. and rsch. Bon Ami Co., N.Y.C., 1959-63; sr. rsch. engr. Exxon Rsch. & Engring. Co., Linden, N.J., 1964-68; project head, engring. assoc. Exxon Chem. Co., Linden, N.J., 1968-89; engring. assoc. Exxon Rsch. & Engring. Co., Linden, 1989-92; cons., expert witness Paul, Weiss, Rifkind, Wharton & Garrison, N.Y.C., 1992—. Contbr. articles to profl. jours. including Transactions of Soc. Automotive Engrs. ASTM, Nat. Petroleum Refiners. Assn. Mgr. baseball team Aberdeen Little League, 1978-83; team mgr., dir. basketball league Aberdeen Recreation League, 1978; chmn. tennis com. Strathmore Bath and Tennis Club, Aberdeen, 1980-82. With U.S. Army, 1955-57. Fellow ASTM (chmn. high temperature rheology 1978-91, Appreciation award 1988, Excellence in Symposium Mgmt. award 1990, Merit award 1993); mem. Soc. Automotive Engrs. Achievements include patents for Petroleum Additives and a Shear-Stability Test Device; key innovations in high temperature and low temperature viscometers used by petroleum industry; concept and devel. of novel multigrade motor oils for autos and trucks. Avocation: senior singles competition in national and regional tennis tournaments. Home and Office: 81 Avondale Ln Aberdeen NJ 07747-1239

SMITH, MARY ALICE See ALICE, MARY

SMITH, MARY ELINOR, retired dean, mathematics educator, counselor; b. Louisville, Dec. 18, 1913; d. Harry Robert and Susan Magdalene (Corrigan) S. AA, Sacred Heart Jr. Coll., Louisville, 1933; BA, Nazareth Coll., 1935; postgrad., U. Minn., summers 1937-39; MA, Cath. U. Am., 1951; student NDEA Inst., Mich. State U., 1967-68. Tchr. math. Jefferson County Schs., Medora, Ky., 1935-36; substitute tchr. Louisville Pub. Schs., 1936-37, tchr. math., 1937-44; hosp. staff aide ARC, 1944-45; caseworker Jefferson County Children's Home, Louisville, 1946-48; dean women, lectr. Quincy (Ill.) Coll., 1950-52; dean women, lectr. Cath. U., Washington, 1952-71, assoc. dean counseling and svcs., 1971-79; ret., 1979; scholarship evaluator AAUW, Washington, 1975-79, Youth for Understanding, Washington, 1980-86; conf. lectr. Barry U., Miami Shores, Fla., 1990. Chair Task Force on AIDS, Spalding U., Louisville, 1988-89; bd. trustees Ursuline Campus Schs., Inc., Louisville, 1990-92; mem. St. Francis of Assisi Parish, 1986—. Recipient Cert. of Appreciation, Black Students of Cath. U., 1977, Frank A. Kunz Alumni award Cath. U., 1978, Outstanding Svc. Appreciation award Undergrad. Student Govt., Cath. U., 1978-79, Citation, Nat. Assn. Women Deans, Adminstrs., Counselors, 1979, Citation, Pres. and Bd. Trustees of Cath. U., 1952-79; Mary Elinor Smith Community Svc. award, 1980—, Caritas award Spalding U., 1985. Mem. APA, Women's Overseas Svc. League (treas. 1991-92), Ky. Ch. Myasthenia Gravis Found., Louisville Geneal. Soc. (city/county chair 1989-90), Spalding U. Alumni Assn., Ursuline Acad. Alumnae Assn., Filson Club, Veritas Soc. Democrat. Roman Catholic. Avocations: reading, the arts, writing memories, travel, Elderhostel, genealogy. Home: 2126 Village Dr Apt 2 Louisville KY 40205-1940

SMITH, MARY LEVI, academic administrator; b. Jan. 30, 1936. Pres. Ky. State U., Frankfort. Office: Kentucky State U Office of President Frankfort KY 40601

SMITH, MARY LOU, librarian; b. Huntington, Ind., Mar. 8, 1927; d. Harry Martin and Birtha (Fox) Bowers; m. Donald Eugene Smith, Oct. 2, 1948; children: Larry Wayne, Samuel Lee, Lynn Ellen Smith Worch, Michael Ray. BS in Edn., Huntington Coll., 1971; MS in Edn., Ball State U., 1973, MLS, 1973. Cert. tchr.; cert. libr.; cert. audio visual. Profl. musician Ft. Wayne (Ind.) Civic Symphony, 1942-45, Philharmonic Orch., Ft. Wayne, 1945-57, Civic Symphony, Chgo., 1947-49; owner M.L. Smith Reed Co., Huntington, Ind., 1950-65; libr., audio-visual specialist Huntington Sch. Systems, 1971-75; libr. Huntington Coll., 1975-77, Warsaw (Ind.) High Sch., 1978-85, Pub. Libr., Port Isabel, Tex., 1994-95; area coord. Am. Inst. Fgn. Study, Greenwich, Conn., 1978-85. Head ladies dept. YMCA, Huntington, 1966-70; bd. dirs., sec.-treas. Outdoor Resorts, Port Isabel, 1986-92; swimming instr. ARC, 1966-69; mem. Rosary Sodality, Huntington. Mem. AAUW, Ind. Sch. Libr. Assn. (sec. 1973-75), Ind. Sch. Libr. Assn., Ind. Ret. Tchrs. Assn., Altrusa Internat. (editor Warsaw chpt. 1983-86), Sigma Phi Gamma. Roman Catholic. Avocations: golf, bowling, bridge. Home: 950 S Garcia St Unit 53 Port Isabel TX 78578-4010 Home (summer): 901 Evergreen Ave Huntington IN 46750-4026 Office: Port Isabel Libr 213 N Yturria St Port Isabel TX 78578-4602

SMITH, MARY LOUISE, politics and public affairs consultant; b. Eddyville, Iowa, Oct. 6, 1914; d. Frank and Louise Anna (Jager) Epperson; BA, U. Iowa, 1935; LHD (hon.), Drake U., 1980; LLD (hon.), Grinnell Coll., 1984; m. Elmer Milton Smith, Oct. 7, 1934; children: Robert C., Margaret L., James E. Mem. Eagle Grove (Iowa) Bd. Edn., 1955-60; Republican precinct committeewoman, Eagle Grove, 1960-62, vice-chairwoman, Wright County, Iowa, 1962-63; mem. Rep. Nat. Com., 1964-84, mem. exec. com., 1969-84, mem. conv. reforms com., 1966, vice-chairwoman Steiger com. on conv. reform, 1973, co-chmn. nat. com., 1974, chmn. Com., 1974-77; vice-chairwoman U.S. Commn. on Civil Rights, 1982-83; vice-chairwoman Midwest region Rep. Conf., 1969-71; del. Rep. Nat. Conv., 1968, 72, 76, 80, 84, alt. del., 1964, hon officer, 1988, 92, organized and called to order, 1976; vice-chairwoman Iowa Presdl. campaign, 1964; nat. co-chmn. Physicians Com. for Presdl. Campaign, 1972; co-chairwoman Iowa Com. to Reelect the Pres., 1972; mem. Nat. Commn. on Observance Internat. Women's Year, 1975-77, del. Internat. Women's Yr. Conf., Houston, 1977; vis. fellow Woodrow Wilson Fellowship Found., 1979. Mem. U.S. del. to Extraordinary Session of UNESCO Gen. Conf., Paris, 1973; mem. U.S. del. 15th session population commn. UN Econ. and Social Council, Geneva, 1969; mem. Pres.'s Commn. for Observance of 25th Anniversary of UN, 1970-71; mem. Iowa Commn. for Blind, 1961-63, chairwoman, 1963; mem. Iowa Gov.'s Commn. on Aging, 1962; trustee Robert A. Taft Inst. Govt., 1974-84, Herbert Hoover Presdl. Libr. Assn., Inc., 1979-91. Pres. Eagle Grove Cmty. Chest; bd. dirs. Mental Health Center North Iowa, 1962-63, YWCA of Greater Des Moines, 1983-87, Orchard Place Resdl. Facility for Emotionally Disturbed Children, 1983-88, Learning Channel, cable TV, 1984-87, Iowa Peace Inst., 1985-90, Planned Parenthood of Greater Iowa, 1986-92, U. Iowa Found., 1987—; trustee Drake U., 1990—; bd. dirs. U.S. Inst. Peace, 1990—, Chrysalis Womens Found., 1994—; bd. dirs., nat. co-chair Rep. Mainstream Com.; bd. dirs. Alliance for Arts and Understanding, 1993-96; mem. adv. coun. U. Iowa Hawkeye Fund Women's Program, 1982-87, co-founder Iowa Women's Archives, 1991; chairperson UN Day for Iowa, 1987; polit. communication ctr. conf. U. Okla., 1987; disting. vis. exec. Coll. Bus. Asminstrn. U. Iowa, 1988; co-chmn. select com. on drug abuse City of Des Moines, 1989-90; mem. Des Moines Human Rights Commn., 1995—; hon. chmn. Iowa Student/Parent Mock Election, 1995-96. Named hon. col., mil. staff Gov. Iowa, 1973; Iowa Women's Hall of Fame, 1977; named to Iowa City H.S. Hall of Fame, 1995; recipient Disting. Alumni award U. Iowa, 1984, Hancher Medallion award, 1991; Cristine Wilson medal for equality and justice Iowa Commn. on Status of Women, 1984, Elinor Robson award Coun. for Internat. Understanding, 1992, Pres. award Midwest Archives Conf., 1994; Mary Louise Smith award named in her honor, YWCA, 1988; Mary Louise Smith endowed chair in Women and Politics, Iowa State U., 1995; Brotherhood/Sisterhood award Iowa region NCCJ, 1996. Mem.

Women's Aux. AMA, UN Assn., Nat. Conf. Christians and Jews, Nat. Women's Polit. Caucus (adv. bd. 1978—), PEO, Kappa Alpha Theta. Address: 654 59th St Des Moines IA 50312-1250 *The concept of "giving back" to the community in return for the benefits you have received establishes a sound basis for public service. I also believe that a woman who has achieved any degree of success in any field has an obligation to help other women in their efforts to succeed.*

SMITH, MAURICE EDWARD, lawyer, business consultant; b. Denver, Mar. 30, 1919; s. Edward Daniel and Junie Ardella (Fox) S.; m. Gloria Tanner, June 17, 1944; children: Christine, Kathryn, Carol (dec.), Daniel. Student, Brigham Young U., 1938-40; BS in Commerce, U. Denver, 1942; LLB, Stanford U., 1948. Mem. staff Ralph B. Mayo & Co., Denver, 1949-50; v.p. fin., gen. counsel Husky Oil Co., Cody, Wyo., 1950-61; exec. v.p. Cen. Nat. Ins. Group, Omaha, 1961-65; treas., legal counsel Sunnen Products Co., St. Louis, 1965-69; v.p., treas. Global Marine, Inc., Los Angeles, 1969-78; pvt. bus. cons., 1978—. Mem. Cody City Council, 1955-57. Served with USNR, 1942-45. Mem. Calif. Bar Assn., Kiwanis Club of Provo. Mem. Ch. Jesus Christ of Latter-day Saints. Home: PO Box 327 Provo UT 84603-0327

SMITH, MAURY DRANE, lawyer; b. Samson, Ala., Feb. 2, 1927; s. Abb Jackson and Rose Drane (Sellers) S.; m. Lucile West Martin, Aug. 15, 1953; children: Martha Smith Vandervoort, Sally Smith Legg, Maury D. Smith, Jr. BS, U. Ala., 1950, LLB, JD, 1952. Bar: Ala., 1952; U.S. Dist. Ct. (mid., no. and so. dists.) Ala. 1953; U.S. Ct. Appeals, 1957, U.S. Supreme Ct., 1957. Asst. atty. gen. State of Ala., Montgomery, 1952-55; asst. dist. atty. Montgomery County, 1955-63; ptnr. Balch & Bingham, Montgomery, 1955—; chmn. lawyers adv. com. Mid. Dist. Ala., Montgomery, 1990—; mem. U.S. Ct. of Appeals 11th cir. adv. com. on rules, Montgomery, 1990—, U.S. Dist. Ct. Mid. Dist. civil justice reform act adv. com., Montgomery, 1991—. Pres. Montgomery Area United Way, Ala., 1987; mem. Leadership Montgomery, 1994. Fellow Am. Coll. Trial Lawyers, Am. Bar Found.; mem. Univ. Ala. System (bd. trustees 1991—), Ala. Law Inst. (mem. coun.), ABA (mem. litigation sect.), Montgomery County Bar Assn. (pres. 1976), Montgomery Area C. of C. (pres. 1984), Ala. State Bar (chmn. jud. bldg. task force 1987-94). Avocations: farming, tennis. Home: 2426 Midfield Dr Montgomery AL 36111-1529 Office: Balch & Bingham 2 Dexter Ave PO Box 78 Montgomery AL 36101

SMITH, MERLIN GALE, engineering executive, researcher; b. Germantown, Ky., May 12, 1928; s. Allen Edward and Gladys Myrtle (Kaiser) S.; m. Elinore Klein, Dec. 23, 1955; children: Laurence Robin, Derek Randall, April Rena. B.E.E., U. Cin., 1950; M.E.E., Columbia U., 1957. With IBM, N.Y.C. and Yorktown Heights, N.Y., 1952-92; engring. mgr. large scale integration IBM, Yorktown Heights, 1964-70; research staff mem. IBM, 1970-92; pvt. practice cons., 1992—; bd. govs. Computer Soc., 1970-80, 87-88, sec., 1972-73, v.p., 1975-76, 87-88, pres. 1977-78; bd. dirs. Nat. Computer Conf., 1973-77, chmn., 1975, conf. chmn., 1978. Contbr. articles to profl. jours. Served with Signal Corps AUS, 1951-52. Fellow IEEE (mem. tech. activities bd. 1977-78, 83-84, bd. dirs. 1983-86, exec. v.p. 1985, v.p. tech. activities 1986); mem. Am. Fedn. Info. Processing Socs. (dir. 1977-79, exec. com. 1978-79). Patentee in field. Home and Office: Farnham Point Rd PO Box 215 East Boothbay ME 04544-0215

SMITH, MERRITT ROE, history educator; b. Waverly, N.Y., Nov. 14, 1940; s. Wilson Niles and Mary Eleanor (Fitzgerald) S.; m. Bronwyn M. Mellquist, Aug. 24, 1974. A.B., Georgetown U., 1963; M.A., Pa. State U., 1965, Ph.D., 1971. Asst. prof. history Ohio State U., Columbus, 1970-74, assoc. prof., 1974-78; vis. prof. history and sociology of sci. U. Pa., Phila., 1976; prof. history and tech. program in sci., tech. and soc. M.I.T., Cambridge, 1978—, Metcalfe prof. engring. and the liberal arts, 1989-92, dir. progam in sci., tech. and soc., 1992-96, Leverett and William King Cutten prof., 1993—. Author: Harpers Ferry Armory and the New Technology, 1977, Military Enterprise and Technological Change, 1985, Science, Technology and the Military, 2 vols., 1988, Does Technology Drive History?, 1994; mem. editorial bd. Tech. and Culture, 1973-91, Bus. History Rev., 1978-85, MIT Press, 1986-91. Mem. Mass. Hist. Soc.; trustee Hagley Mus. and Libr., Mus. Am. Textile History, Charles Babbage Inst.; bd. advisors MIT Mus. Recipient Cert. of Commendation Am. Assn. State and Local History, 1978, Disting. Tchg. award Ohio State U., 1978; grantee Ohio State U., 1972, Am. Philos. Soc., 1974, Harvard Bus. Sch., 1974-75, Eleutherian Mills-Hagley Found., 1978-79, Alfred P. Sloan Found., 1994—; Guggenheim fellow, 1983-84, Regents fellow Smithsonian Instn., 1984-85. Mem. AAAS, Am. Acad. Arts and Scis., Soc. History Tech. (mem. exec. council, Dexter Prize com., Da Vinci medal 1994, mus. com., v.p., pres. 1989-91), Orgn. Am. Historians (Frederick Jackson Turner award 1977), Bus. History Conf., Am. Antiquarian Soc., Newcomen Soc. N. Am., Soc. Indsl. Archeology, History Sci. Soc. (Pfizer award 1978), Phi Kappa Phi, Phi Alpha Theta. Home: 17 Longfellow Rd Newton MA 02162-1505 Office: MIT Rm E51-110 Cambridge MA 02139

SMITH, MICHAEL, biochemistry educator; b. Blackpool, Eng., Apr. 26, 1932. BSc, U. Manchester, Eng., 1953, PhD, 1956. Fellow B.C. Rsch. Coun., 1956-60; rsch. assoc. Inst. Enzyme Rsch., U. Wis., 1960-61; head chem. sect. Vancouver Lab. Fisheries Rsch. Bd. Can., 1961-66; med. rsch. assoc. Med. Rsch. Coun. Can., 1966-71, career investigator, 1971—; assoc. prof. biochem. U. B.C., Vancouver, 1966-70, prof., 1970—, Peter Wall disting. prof. biotech., 1994—;, 1993—. Recipient Gairdner Found. Internat. award, 1986, Nobel Prize in Chemistry, 1993. Fellow Chem Inst. Can., Royal Soc. (London), Royal Soc. Can., Royal Soc. Chemistry; mem. Sigma Xi, Order of British Columbia, Companion of the Order of Can. Achievements include rsch. in nucleic acid and nucleotide chemistry and biochemistry using in-vitro mutagenesis gene expression. Home: 2618 Point Grey Rd, Vancouver, BC Canada Office: U BC Biotech Lab, 6174 University Blvd, Vancouver, BC Canada V6T 1Z3

SMITH, MICHAEL, management consultant; b. Hartford, Conn., Nov. 25, 1953; s. Robert Smith and Evelyn (Levine) Lieberman, m. Judy Beth Ludwig, Oct. 21, 1984. BA in Econs., U. Miami, Coral Gables, Fla., 1974; MBA in Fin., George Washington U., 1980. Rsch. analyst gov. ops. com. Senate, Washington, 1976-77; assoc. A.T. Kearney, Inc., Washington, Chgo., 1977-82; dir. mktg. Kwikasair Express, Inc., Mt. Prospect, Ill., 1982-83; dir. acquisitions/product mgr. new bus. devel. Alberto-Culver Co., Melrose Park, Ill., 1983-85; sr. mgr. Ernst & Whinney, Chgo., 1985-89; sr. cons. Buccino & Assocs., Chgo., 1989—. Pres. young leadership div. Jewish United Fund, Chgo., 1987-88; bd. dirs. Jewish Family and Community Svc., Chgo., 1988. Mem. Standard Club. Democrat. Home: 150 Millstone Rd Deerfield IL 60015-4549

SMITH, MICHAEL, retired university chancellor; b. St. Joseph, Mo., Jan. 30, 1941; s. Walton Joseph and Margaret Dorothy (Chubb) S.; m. Connie Stanton, Oct. 27, 1965; children: Jeffrey, Timothy. AD, Mo. Western Community Coll., 1960; BS, N.E. Mo. State U., 1967; PhD, U. Nebr., 1975. Ins. investigator Retail Credit Co., St. Joseph, Mo., 1963-65; instr. Havana (Ill.) High Sch., 1967-68, West Bend (Iowa) High Sch., 1968-70, U. Nebr., 1972-75; asst. prof. English Albany (Ga.) Jr. Coll., 1975-78; chmn. arts and scis., dir. internat. programs U. Minn., Crookston, 1978-80; chief exec. officer, coll. dean N.D. State U., Bottineau, 1980-87; provost, dean of faculty Richard Bland Coll., Coll. William and Mary, 1987-89; chancellor La. State U., Eunice, 1989-95; commr. North Cen. Assn. Colls. and Schs., 1984-87, accreditation cons./evaluator, 1982-87. With U.S. Army, 1960-63.

SMITH, MICHAEL, bishop; b. Oldcastle, Meath, Ireland, June 6, 1940; s. John Smith and Bridie Fagan. Lic. in Philosophy, Lateran U., Rome, 1959, Lic. in Theology, 1963, D in Canon Law, 1966. Ordained priest, 1963. Asst. pastor Diocese of Meath, 1967-68; Clonmellon; chancellor, hosp. chaplain Diocese of Meath, 1968-84, bishop, 1984—; exec. sec. Irish Bishops' Conf., Meath, 1970-84, episcopal sec., 1984—. Avocations: golf, walking. Office: Bishop's House, Dublin Rd, Mullingar Westmeath, Ireland

SMITH, MICHAEL, retail company executive; b. Mpls., Sept. 26, 1960; s. Clayton Daniel and Mary Ann (Tait) S.; m. Diann Link, Sept. 12, 1992. BS, U. Wis., 1983. Circulation planner Lands' End, Dodgeville, Wis., 1983-86; assoc. circulation mgr. Lands' End, Dodgeville, 1986-87, mgr. merchandising rsch., 1987-89, product mgr./mktg. mgr., 1989-90, mng. dir., 1990-91, v.p. Coming Home, 1991-94, pres., CEO, 1994—. Office: Lands End 5 Lands End Ln Dodgeville WI 53595

SMITH, MICHAEL ALEXIS, petroleum geologist; b. Boston, Nov. 8, 1944; s. Albert Charles and Nina (Gronstrand) S.; m. Nancy Laura Wilson, Dec. 19, 1971; 1 child, Christine Lara. B.S., U. Mich., 1966; M.S., U. Kans., 1969; Ph.D., U. Tex., 1975. Marine geologist U.S. Geol. Survey, Washington, 1966-68, petroleum geologist, 1975-81, geochemist, 1976-81; rsch. geochemist Getty Oil Co., Houston, 1981-83, supr. basin evaluation and structural geology, 1983-84; rsch. assoc. Texaco Inc., Houston, 1984-92; chief geologist Geo-Strat, Inc., Houston, 1992—; adj. prof. geology Emory U., Atlanta, 1988-89; geophysicist Minerals Mgmt. Svc., New Orleans, 1994—. Contbr. articles to profl. jours. and books. Fellow Geol. Soc. Am.; mem. Am. Assn. Petroleum Geologists, Am. Geophys. Union, Houston Geol. Soc., Am. Assn. of Stratigraphic Palynologists , Rocky Mountain Assn. Geologists, Soc. Organic Petrology (founding mem.). Avocations: music; running. Research interest: geol. and depositional facies controls on petroleum occurrence; regional source-rock geochemistry and organic petrology; biostratigraphy, paleogeography, and paleoecology. Home: 1123 Shillington Dr Katy TX 77450-4204 Office: Geo-Strat Inc 1718 Triway Ln Houston TX 77043-3346

SMITH, MICHAEL CHARLES, personnel director, human resources specialist; b. DuQuoin, Ill., Apr. 1, 1947; s. Michael Paul and Audrey Elizabeth (Bigham) S.; m. Janelle Ann Hutchings, Apr. 10, 1971; 1 child, Rachel Elizabeth. BS, Murray State U., 1974. Dist. sales mgr. Protective Life Ins. Cos., Murray, Ky., 1973—; employee rels. rep. G.D. Freeman United Coal Co., DuQuoin, 1975-79; dir. personnel and safety Tuck Tape Inc., Carbondale, Ill., 1979-80; supr. personnel GTE Elec. Components and Materials Div., Muncy, Pa., 1980-82; human resources mgr. GTE Elec. Components Div., Williamsport, Pa., 1982-85, Muncy, Pa., 1985-88; human resources mgr. GTE Lighting Spl. Projects, Waldoboro, Maine, 1988-89, GTE Ctrl. Devices, Stanoish, Maine, 1989-92, Keebler Co., Macon, Ga., 1992—; chmn. and organizer State Employment Office for Employer Adv. Council Ill., Carbondale, 1979-80, chairperson Ill. Job Service Adv. Council, 1975; adult edn. instr. Rend Lake Community Coll., Pinckneyville, Ill., 1977-78. Charter pres. Murray State Jaycees, 1972. Served to sgt. USAF, 1967-71. Recipient P. Daniel Coyne Meml. award Maine Safety Coun., 1993; named to Hon. Order Ky. Cols. Mem. Cen. Pa. Safety Assn. Republican. Presbyterian. Lodge: Masons. Avocations: golf, fishing, tennis, reading, family activities. Home: 108 Saddle Run Ct N Macon GA 31210-8612 Office: Keebler Co 2475 Meade Rd Macon GA 31206

SMITH, MICHAEL CORDON, lawyer; b. Boise, July 30, 1954; s. Jay Myrven Jr. and Jena Vee (Cordon) S.; m. Candace Louise Langley, Dec. 10, 1977; children: Angela K., Nicole E., Jeremy L., Melanie D. BS with high honors, Brigham Young U., 1977; JD, UCLA, 1980. Assoc. Johnson & Poulson, L.A., 1980-87, ptnr., 1980-86; pvt. practice Torrance, Calif., 1987-91; judge pro tem L.A. Mcpl. Ct., 1986-94, L.A. Superior Ct., 1991-95, ct. apptd. arbitrator, 1986-91. Mem. Nat. Employment Lawyers Assn., Calif. Employment Lawyers Assn., L.A. County Bar Assn. (vice chair law office mgmt. sect. 1992-94, exec. com. 1985-95, state bar conv. del. 1995), Consumer Attys. Assn. L.A. Republican. Mem. LDS Ch. Avocations: genealogy, computers, audio-visual electronics. Office: Ste # 300 23133 Hawthorne Blvd Torrance CA 90505

SMITH, MICHAEL JAMES, industrial engineering educator; b. Madison, Wis., May 12, 1945; s. James William and Ruth Gladys (Murphy) S.; m. Patricia Ann Bentley, June 22, 1968; children: Megan Colleen, Melissa Maureen. BA, U. Wis., 1968, MA, 1970, PhD, 1973. Rsch. analyst Wis. Dept. Industry Labor, Madison, 1971-74; rsch. psychologist Nat. Inst. for Occupational Safety and Health, USPHS, Cin., 1974-84; prof. U. Wis., Madison, 1984—; owner, prin. M.J. Smith Assocs. Inc., Madison, 1991—. Contbr. articles to profl. jours. Mem. APA, Inst. Indsl. Engrs. (sr.), Human Factors Soc., Assn. Computer Machinery, Am. Soc. Testing and Measurement. Avocation: tennis. Home: 6719 Shamrock Glen Cir Middleton WI 53562-1144 Office: U Wis Dept Indsl Engring Human Factors Rsch Lab 1513 University Ave Madison WI 53706-1539

SMITH, MICHAEL JOSEPH, composer, pianist, lecturer; b. Tiline, Ky., Aug. 13, 1938; s. Marvin Gilford and Bobbie Bell (Vinson) S.; m. Kerstin Alli-Maria Andersson, May 1973; children: Tanja Michaelsdotter, Kassandra Michaelsdotter; m. Wei Wei, 1994; children: Symington Wei, Remington Wei. Student, New Eng. Conservatory Music, Julliard Sch. Pres., bd. dirs. World Music (U.S.A.), Inc., Atlanta, 1993—; composer-in-residence, Ga., 1980, 88-90; lectr., performer Agnes Scott Coll., Atlanta, Bowdoin Coll., Maine, Royal Opera, Stockholm, Ctrl. Conservatory Music, Beijing and Xian, China; rschr. IBM Corp. Scandinavia and Roland Synthesizer Corp., 1986—. Performed 1st European concert tour, 1970; on concert tours of jazz and contemporary ensembles in Western Europe and U.S., from 1972; composer 10 major ballet works, scores for major films and TV projects, 560 works for various ensembles; commns. include Moscow Philharm., Tbilisi Chamber Orch., various European ensembles, ballet cos.; performances include Atlanta Olympics, 1996, Bolshoi Theatre, Moscow, Leningrad U., Royal Swedish Opera, Stockholm, Lincoln Ctr., N.Y.C., Carnegie Hall, N.Y.C., Philharm. Hall, Berlin, stadiums in Shanghai, Guanshou, Yunan and Hong Kong; numerous recs., from 1970. With USN, 1955-59. Mem. Swedish Composers Soc., Internat. Soc. Contemporary Music. Home and Office: PO Box 81107 Conyers GA 30208-9107

SMITH, MICHAEL LEIGH, manufacturing executive; b. Long Beach, Calif., Mar. 17, 1946; s. Donald Earl and Francella Mary (Maxwell) S.; m. Nancy Jeanette Graves, Feb. 22, 1968; children: Michael Leigh II, Teresa Pauline. Student, El Camino Coll., 1965-66, U. Phoenix, 1993—. Dir. material control Pacific Electricord/Leviton, Gardena, Calif., 1972-75; sales engr. Indsl. Molding Corp., Torrance, Calif., 1975-76; dir. mktg. and adminstrn. Credit Bur. of Palm Springs, Calif., 1976-78; sales mgr. Indsl. Molding Corp. divsn. Kaiser Steel, Torrance, Calif., 1978-87; v.p., gen. mgr. Euro-Tec, Inc., Anaheim, Calif., 1987-90; gen. mgr. Husky Injection Molding Systems, Inc., Costa Mesa, Calif., 1990—; speaker, lectr. in field; mem. adv. bd. Modern Plastics, N.Y., 1981; profl. magician Acad. Magical Arts and Scis., Hollywood, Calif., 1970—; mem. task force Am. Plastics Coun., 1991—. Contbr. articles to profl. publs. Mem. Soc. Plastics Industry (officer, bd. dirs. 1983-86, pres. So. Calif. chpt. 1987-89, legis. liaison western sect. 1990-92, bd. dirs. western sect. exec. bd. 1987—, treas. western sect. exec. bd. 1995—). Office: Husky Injection Molding Systems Inc 3505 Cadillac Ave Ste N-4 Costa Mesa CA 92626-1429

SMITH, MICHAEL PETER, social science educator, researcher; b. Dunkirk, N.Y., Aug. 2, 1942; s. Peter Joseph and Rosalie Barbara (Lipka) S.; m. Patricia Anne Lendway, Aug. 21, 1965. BA magna cum laude, St. Michael's Coll., 1964; MA in Polit. Sci., U. Mass., 1966, PhD in Polit. Sci., 1971. Instr., asst. prof. dept. govt. Dartmouth Coll., Hanover, N.H., 1968-71; asst. prof. dept. polit. sci. Boston U., 1971-74; assoc. prof., prof. dept. polit. sci. Tulane U., New Orleans, 1974-86; prof. community studies U. Calif., Davis, 1986—, chmn. dept. applied behavioral scis., 1986-91; vis. prof. pub. policy U. Calif., Berkeley, 1981, city planning U. N.C., Chapel Hill, 1982, city planning U. Calif., Berkeley, 1985; vis. scholar in govt. U. Essex, Eng., 1979; vis. scholar polit. and social sci. U. Cambridge, Eng., 1982; vis. scholar Inst. Urban and Regional Devel., U. Calif., Berkeley, 1990. Author: The City & Social Theory, 1979, City, State and Market, 1988; co-author: Restructuring the City, 1983, California's Changing Faces, 1993; editor: Cities in Transformation, 1984, Breaking Chains, 1991, After Modernism, 1992, Marginal Spaces, 1995, Comparative Urban & Community Research, 1986—; co-editor: The Capitalist City, 1987—, The Bubbling Cauldron, 1995; mem. editl. bd. U. Press Am., 1976—. Mem. Internat. Polit. Sci. Assn., Am. Polit. Sci. Assn., Internat. Sociol. Assn. Research Coms. on Urban & Regional Devel. and Comparative Community Research. Office: Dept Human & Cmty Devel Univ Calif Davis CA 95616

SMITH, MICHAEL TOWNSEND, author, editor, stage director; b. Kansas City, Mo., Oct. 5, 1935; s. Lewis Motter and Dorothy (Pew) S.; m. Carol E. Storke, 1992; children: Julian Bach, Alfred St. John. Student, Yale U., 1953-55. Theatre critic Village Voice, N.Y.C., 1959-68, 1971-74, assoc. editor, 1962-65; curator, judge Obie awards for theatre, 1962-68, 1971-74; playwright mem. Open Theatre, N.Y.C., 1962-66; mgr. Sundance Festival, Upper Black Eddy, Pa., 1966-68; dir. Theatre Genesis, N.Y.C., 1971-74; arts editor Taos (N.Mex.) News, 1977-78; music critic New London (Conn.) Day, 1982-86; instrument maker, adminstr. Zuckermann Harpsichords Inc., 1974-77, 79-85; dir. Boston Early Music Festival and Exhbn., 1983-85; asst. press sec., speechwriter Mayor Edward I. Koch, N.Y.C., 1986-89; mgr. 14th St. Stage Lighting, N.Y.C., 1989-90; lighting dir. The Living Theatre, N.Y.C., 1990-93; music critic Santa Barbara (Calif.) News-Press, 1992; arts editor Santa Barbara Ind., 1992-94; editor Santa Barbara Mag. and Pasadena Mag., 1995—. Author: (fiction) Getting Across, 1962; Near the End, 1965, Automatic Vaudeville, 1970, High Points of Youth, 1986; (poetry) American Baby, 1975, A Sojourn in Paris, 1985; (plays) I Like It, 1961; The Next Thing, 1963, A Dog's Love, 1965, Captain Jack's Revenge, 1970, Country Music, 1971, Double Solitaire, 1973, Prussian Suite, 1973, The Dinner Show, 1974, A Wedding Party, 1974, Cowgirl Ecstasy, 1976, Heavy Pockets, 1981, One Hundred Thousand Songs, 1982, Turnip Family Secrets, 1983, Half Life, 1984, Trouble (as Vernon Oreille), 1987, (with Alfred Brooks) Sameness, 1990, Life Before Death, 1992, Entertaining Vancouver, 1993, Come in Here, 1994; (memoir) Wild Dogs, 1991; translations Life Is Dream, 1978, (with Pascale Cheminee) Agatha, 1985; critical jour. Theatre Jour., 1968, Theatre Trip, 1969; also articles; editor: anthologies Eight Plays from Off-Off-Broadway, 1966, The Best of Off-Off-Broadway, 1969, More Plays from Off-Off-Broadway, 1971. Dir. Lobero Found., The Arts Fund of Santa Barbara. Recipient creative arts citation in theatre Brandeis U., 1965; Obie award, 1971; Rockefeller Found. award, 1976. Address: care Santa Barbara Mag 2064 Alameda Padre Serra Ste 120 Santa Barbara CA 93103

SMITH, MICHAEL W., popular musician. Recipient Best Pop/Contemporary Gospel album Grammy award, 1996. Office: Reunion Records 2908 Poston Ave Nashville TN 37203*

SMITH, MICHELE, lawyer; b. Ogden, Utah, Feb. 12, 1955; d. Max S. and Grace B. (Gerstman) Smith; m. Philip A. Turner, Aug. 25, 1985. BA, SUNY, Buffalo, 1976; JD, U. Chgo., 1979. Law clk. U.S. Ct. Appeals (7th cir.), Chgo., 1979-81; asst. atty. no. dist. U.S. Atty's Office, Chgo., 1981-89; assoc. gen. counsel Navistar Internat. Transportation Corp., Chgo., 1989—. Mem. Am. Corp. Counsel Assn., Phi Beta Kappa. Office: Navistar Internat Transp Corp 455 N Cityfront Plaza Dr Chicago IL 60611-5503

SMITH, MILTON RAY, computer company executive, lawyer; b. Idaho, 1935. AA, Long Beach (Calif.) City Coll., 1958; BS, Portland State U., 1962; MS, Oreg. State U., 1969; JD, Lewis and Clark Coll., 1970. Bar: Oreg. 1970, U.S. Dist. Ct. Oreg. 1970, U.S. Ct. Appeals (9th cir.) 1971, U.S. Supreme Ct. 1973. Tech. writer Northrop Corp., Hawthorne, Calif., 1957-58; engring. writer Tektronix Inc., Beaverton, Oreg., 1958-60, design engr., 1960-63, project engr., 1963-65, program mgr., 1966-70; asst. engring. mgr. Eldorado Electronics, Concord, Calif., 1965-66; ptnr. Acker, Underwood & Smith, Portland, Oreg., 1970-86; chmn., chief exec. officer Floating Point Systems Inc., Beaverton, 1986-88, pres., chief exec. officer, 1991-92, also vice chmn. bd. dirs.; pres., chief exec. officer Thrustmaster Inc., Tigard, Oreg., 1992-94; pres., CEO Zeelan Tech., Inc., Beaverton, Oreg., 1994-95; mgmt. cons., 1995—; CEO, Test Sys. Strategies, Inc., Beaverton, 1992-93; bd. dirs. ThrustMaster, Inc., Beaverton, Distbn. Scis. Corp., Hillsboro, Oreg., Zeelan Tech., Inc., Beaverton. Bd. dirs. Oreg. Bus. Council, Portland, 1986-88; mem. bd. visitors Northwestern Sch. Law, Portland, 1986—. With USN, 1953-56. Mem. Am. Electronics Assn. (exec. com. Oreg. coun. 1987-93, vice chmn. 1994-95, chmn. 1995—), Oreg. State Bar, Founders Club Portland. Republican. Office: 6717 NE 126th St Vancouver WA 98686-3485

SMITH, MORTON EDWARD, ophthalmology educator, dean; b. Balt., Oct. 17, 1934. BS, U. Md., 1956, MD, 1960. Bd. cert. Ophthalmology Bd.; lic. physician Mo., Md., Wis. Rotating intern Denver Gen. Hosp., 1960-61; resident, nat. inst. of neorol. diseases and blindness fellow in opthalmology Washington U. Sch. Medicine-Barnes Hosp., 1961-63; NIH spl. fellow in ophthalmic pathology Armed Forces Inst. of Pathology, Washington, 1964; chief resident, instr. ophthalmology Washington U. Sch. Medicine, St. Louis, 1965-66, instr. ophthalmology, 1966-67, asst. prof. ophthalmology and pathology, 1967-69, assoc. prof. ophthalmology and pathology, 1969-75, prof. ophthalmology and pathology, 1975—, asst. dean, 1978-91, assoc. dean, 1991-96, prof. emeritus, assoc. dean emeritus, 1996—; prof. ophthalmology U. Wis., Madison, 1995—; vis. scholar Eye Inst., Columbia Presbyn. Med. Ctr., N.Y.C., 1966; prof./lectr. Montefiore Hosp., Pitts., 1969, U. Ark., 1970, 77, 80, 82, 84, 86, 88, U. Fla., 1972, 81, U. Tex. and Lackland AFB, San Antonio, 1973, U. Colo., 1974, 82, U. Mo., 1974, 79, 80, 88, So. Ill. U., Springfield, 1974, U. Md., 1975, Montreal (Can.) Gen. Hosp., 1975, U. Wis., 1976, 87, 93, U. Pitts., 1977, 83, 87, U. Iowa, 1977, 87, Cleve. Clinic, 1978, Colo. Ophthalmol. Soc., 1978, Brooke Army Hosp., San Antonio, 1979, Wills Eye Hosp., Phila., 1980, USPHS Hosp., San Francisco, 1981, U. Calif., Davis, 1981, Sinai Hosp., Balt., 1985, 89, 94, U. Calif., San Diego, 1985, Tufts U., Boston, 1985, Cornell U., Ithaca, N.Y., 1988, U. Wash., Seattle, 1990, Brown U., Providence, 1990, Vanderbilt U., Nashville, 1991, Duke U., Durham, N.C., 1992; Chandler lectr. Harvard U., 1988; The Lois A. Young-Thomas Meml. lectr. U. Md., 1991; Braley lectr. U. Iowa, 1993; Havener Meml. lectr. Ohio State, 1994. Editor pathology sect.: Perspectives in Ophthalmology, 1977; mem. editl. bd. Ophthalmic Plastic & Reconstructive Surgery, 1986-90; contbr. articles to profl. jours. With USAR M.C., 1958-66. Scholar U. Md., 1958, 59. Fellow Am. Acad. Ophthalmology (ophthalmic pathology com. 1977-83, chmn. ophthalmic com. 1979-83, Honor award for svc. 1981, Sr. Honor award 1992); mem. AMA, Am. Bd. Ophthalmology (diplomate, bd. dirs. 1992—), Assn. for Rsch. in Vision and Ophthalmology (chmn. sect. pathology ann. meeting 1971), Am. Assn. Ophthalmic Pathologists (pres. 1977-80), Assn. Am. Med. Colls. (group med. edn. 1985—), Mo. Med. Assn., Mo. Ophthalmol. Soc., Verhoeff Soc., Theobald Soc., St. Louis Med. Soc., St. Louis Ophthalmol. Soc., Soc. Med. Coll. Dirs. for Continuing Med. Edn., Alpha Omega Alpha (sec.-treas. Wash. U. chpt. 1993—). Office: U Wis Dept Ophthalmology F4/336 CSC 600 Highland Madison WI 53792-3220

SMITH, MORTON HOWISON, religious organization administrator, educator; b. Roanoke, Va., Dec. 11, 1923; s. James Brookes and Margaret Morton (Howison) S.; m. Lois Virginia Knopf, July 7, 1925; children: Samuel Warfield, Susanne Rochet Margaret. BA, U. Mich., 1947; BD, Columbia Theol. Sem., 1953; ThM, ThD, Free U., Amsterdam, The Netherlands, 1962. Ordained to ministry Presbyn. Ch., 1954. Pastor Springfield-Roller Presbyn. Chs., Carroll County, Md., 1954; prof. bible Belhaven Coll., Jackson, Miss., 1954-63; guest lectr. Westminster Theol. Sem., Phila., 1963-64; prof. Reformed Theol. Sem., Jackson, 1964-79; stated clk. gen. assembly Presbyn. Ch. in Am., Decatur, Ga., 1973-88; prof. systematic theology, dean faculty Greenville Presbyn. Theol. Sem., 1987—; advisor to bd. dirs. Greenville (S.C.) Presbyn. Theol. Sem., 1986—; mem. bd. dirs. Presbyn. Jour., Asheville, N.C., 1965-87; lectr. on theology Republic of So. Africa , June-July, 1988, Riga, Latvia, 1992, Budapest, Hungary, 1994, Prague, Czech Republic, 1994, 95, Trinidad and Tobago, 1995, on mission, Republic of Korea, June-July, 1989. Author: Studies in Southern Presbyterian Theology, 1962, 2d edit. 1987, How Is the Gold Become Dim, 1973, (pamphlet) Reformed Evangelism, 1970, Testimony, 1986, Commentary on the Book of Church Order, 1990, Harmony of the Westminster Confession and Catechisms, 1990, Systematic Theology, 1994; contbr. articles to Reformed Theology in Am., 1985. Trustee Covenant Coll., Lookout Mountain, Tenn., 1982-90. 1st lt. USAAF, 1942-45. Fulbright fellow U.S. Govt., 1958. Mem. N.Am. Presbyn. and Reformed Coun. of Chs. (sec. 1977-92). Avocations: flying, traveling, genealogy. Office: Greenville Presbyn Theol Sem PO Box 9279 Greenville SC 29604-9279

SMITH, MURRAY LIVINGSTONE, advertising executive; b. London, Nov. 21, 1937; came to U.S., 1967; s. Thomas Phillip Livingstone and Agnes Breckenridge (Murray) S.; m. Francoise Henriette Frapport, Jan. 12, 1960 (div. 1968); 1 child, Alexander Livingstone, Gertrude-Mercer Livingstone. BSC with honors in Econs., U. London, 1959, MSC in Econs., 1961. Account exec. Colman, Prentis & Varley, London, 1961-62; mgr. Colman, Prentis & Varley, Athens, Greece, 1962-66; dept. M.D. Colman, Prentis & Varley, Paris, 1966-67; v.p. account supr. Kenyon & Eckhardt, N.Y.C., 1967-72; sr. v.p. Latin Am. Kenyon & Eckhardt, N.Y.C., Sao Paulo, Brazil, 1972-78; exec. v.p. internat. Kenyon & Eckhardt, N.Y.C., 1978-86; pres. internat. Bozell, Jacobs, Kenyon & Eckhardt, N.Y.C., 1986—. Mem. Internat. Advt. Assn. (product service com.), Assn. Am. Advt. Agys. (internat com. mem., 1979-82, 86—). Clubs: Aston Martin Owners, Vintage Sports Car, Bugatti Owners, Ferrari Owners. Avocations: motor sports, archaeology, ornithology, literature. Home: SC 1225 Park Ave New York NY 10128 Office: Bozell Jacobs Kenyon & Eckhardt 40 W 23rd St New York NY 10010-5200*

SMITH, MURRAY THOMAS, transportation company executive; b. Hudson, S.D., 1939; s. Rex D. and Frances M. Smith; m. Diane R. Cramer, Dec. 4, 1959 (div. June 1994); children: Lisa B., Thomas M., Amy R.; m. Donna Thomas Kjonaas, Jan. 1995. V.p. Overland Express Inc., Indpls., 1978-82; v.p. ops. R.T.C. Transp. Inc., Forest Pk., Ga., 1982-83; with Midwest Coast Transport L.P., Sioux Falls, S.D., 1983—, sr. v.p., 1983-84; pres. Midwest Coast Transport L.P., Sioux Falls, S.D., 1984-89, prin., pres., chief exec. officer, 1989—, also bd. dirs.; bd. dirs. Interstate Carrier Conf., Nat. Penslake Logistics Assn. Bd. dirs. Sioux Valley Hosp., 1991—, United Way, Sioux Falls, 1991—. Office: Midwest Coast Transport LP 1600 E Benson Rd Sioux Falls SD 57104-0871

SMITH, MYRON GEORGE, former government official, consultant; b. Terrebonne, Minn., June 9, 1920; s. Adrian G. and Marie E. (Crompe) S.; m. Louise J. Hennessey, May 22, 1944 (div. 1973); children: Michael, Thomas, John, Patricia, Dennis; m. Nguyen Anh My, Aug. 30, 1975; children: Yvette, Bryan. BS in Agrl. Econs. and Soil Sci., U. Minn., 1946. Soil scientist USDA, 1946-50, agrl. ext. advisor, 1950-58; owner No. Ill. Agrl. Svc., 1958-62; with U.S. AID, Dept. State, 1962-84; agrl. sales advisor U.S. AID, Dept. State, India, 1962-66; asst. dir. crop prodn. Vietnam U.S. AID, Dept. State, 1966-70, chief agrl. divsn. Indonesia, 1970-73; assoc. dir. U.S. AID, Dept. State, Vietnam, 1974-75; chief agrl. divsn. Mali U.S. AID, Dept. State, 1976-81, chief agrl. project mgr. West Africa, 1981-84; agrl. cons. U.S. AID, Dept. State, Zaire, 1988-90, Indonesia, 1993-94; assoc. prof. U. Ark., 1985. 1st lt. USAAF, 1941-45. Decorated Purple Heart, Air medal with 6 oak leaf clusters, D.F.C., Am. Campaign medal, WW II Victory medal, European-African-Middle Eastern Campaign medals with 4 oak leaf clusters, Agr. medal 2d class, Vietnam, 1969, Agr. medal 1st class, Vietnam, 1970, Labor medal 1st class, Vietnam, 1970, Economy medal 2d class, Vietnam, 1970. Mem. Am. Fgn. Service Assn. Home: Usaid Box 4 # 8135 APO AP 96520-5000 Office: USAID Box 4 APO AP 96520-8135 *Life's many paths selected and ultimate goals achieved can rarely be perceived in the early career years. Life's many, peripatetic journeys are most interesting and rewarding when self, professional and social self-improvement is pursued continuously and sincerely.*

SMITH, MYRON JOHN, JR., librarian, author; b. Toledo, May 3, 1944; s. Myron John and Marion Oliva (Herbert) S.; 1 son, Myron John III. Student, Coll. Steubenville, 1962; AB, Ashland Coll., 1966; MLS, Western Mich. U., 1967; MA, Shippensburg U., 1969; postgrad., U. Wis., Purdue U.; LittD, Cardinal Newman Coll., 1982. Rsch. librarian G.W. Blunt White Libr., Mystic Seaport, Conn., 1967-68; asst. librarian Western Md. Coll., Westminster, 1969-72; libr. dir. Huntington (Ind.) Pub. Libr., 1972-76; prof. history and libr. sci., dir. librs. Benedum Libr. Salem-Teikyo U.; dir., then assoc. dir. aviation program Salem (W.Va.) Coll., 1976-90; prof. history and libr. sci., libr. dir. Tusculum Coll., Greeneville, Tenn., 1990—; mem. Am. Com. on History 2d World War, Assn. for Bibliography of History. Author: American Naval Bibliography Series, 1972-74, Huntington Centennial Handbook, 1973, The Sophisticated Lady: The Battleship Indiana in World War II, 1973, World War II at Sea: A Bibliography of Sources in English, 1976, (with Robert Webber) Sea Fiction Guide, 1976, The Cloak and Dagger Bibliography, 1976, World War I in the Air, 1977, Air War Chronology 1939-45, 1977, Air War Bibliography Series, 1977—, The Mountain State Battleship: USS West Virginia, 1979, Air War Southeast Asia, 1979, The Soviet Navy, 1941-1978, 1979, The Secret Wars Series, 1980-81, The Soviet Air and Strategic Rocket Forces, 1941-1980, 1981, The Soviet Army, 1941-1980, 1981, Equestrian Studies: The Salem College Guide, 1981, The Cloak and Dagger Fiction Guide: An Annotated Guide to Spy Thrillers, 1981, (with Terry White) 3d edit., 1994, The Mountaineer Battlewagon: USS West Virginia, 1982, The Keystone Battlewagon: USS Pennsylvania, 1983, The Golden State Battlewagon: USS California, 1983, Watergate: A Bibliography, 1983 World War II: Mediterranean and European Theaters, 1984, The United States Navy and Coast Guard, 1946-1983: A Bibliography of English Language Works and 16mm Films, 1984, U.S. Television Network News: A Guide to Sources in English, 1984, Battleships and Battlecruisers, 1884-1984: A Bibliography and Chronology, 1985, Baseball: A Comprehensive Bibliography, 1986, 99th Infantry Division Bibliography, 1986, The Airline Bibliography: The Salem College Guide to Sources on Commercial Aviation, Vol. I, The United States, 1986, Vol. II, Airliners and Foreign Carriers, 1987, Passenger Airliners of the United States, 1926-86: A Pictorial Guide, 1987, rev. edit. through 1991, 1991, 3d rev. edit. through 1995, 1995, Brooklyn/Los Angeles Dodgers: A Bibliography, 1987, American Warplane Bibliography, 1989, Volunteer Battlewagon: The U.S.S. Tennessee (BB-43), 1989; editor: Sports Teams and Players Bibliography Series, 1987, Battle and Leaders Bibliography Series, 1988, 100 Years of Opportunity: A Pictorial History of Salem College, 1888-1988, 1988, Pro Football Bio-Bibliography, 1920-1988, 1989, Pearl Harbor, December 7, 1941: An Annotated Bibliography, 1991, Battles of the Coral Sea and Midway, 1942: A Bibliography, 1991, World War II at Sea, 1974-1989: A Bibliography, 1990, Professional Football: The Official Pro Football Hall of Fame Bibliography, 1993, Baseball: A Comprehensive Bibliography-1st Supplement: 1985-1991, 93, The College Football Bibliography, 1994, Glimpses of Tusculum College: A Pictorial History, 1794-1994, 1994; contbr. articles to various jours. Recipient Nelson Ross award Profl. Football Rsch. Assn., 1993; 1st Am. recipient Richard Franck Gold medal Bibliothek für Zeitgeschichte, Stuttgart, Fed. Rep. Germany, 1981. Mem. ALA, U.S. Naval Inst., U.S. Mil. Inst., U.S. Air Force Found., Assn. Bibliog. of History (pres. 1981-82), Beta Phi Mu, Phi Alpha Theta. Club: Optimist. Office: Tusculum Coll PO Box 5005 Greeneville TN 37743-0001

SMITH, NANCY HOHENDORF, sales and marketing executive; b. Detroit, Jan. 30, 1943; d. Donald Gerald and Lucille Marie (Kopp) Hohendorf; m. Richard Harold Smith, Aug. 21, 1978 (div. Jan. 1984). BA, U. Detroit, 1965; MA, Wayne State U., 1969. Customer rep. Xerox Corp., Detroit, 1965-67; mktg. rep. Univ. Microfilms subs. Xerox Corp., Ann Arbor, Mich., 1967-73, mktg. coord., 1973-74, mgr. dir. mktg., 1975-76; mgr. mktg. Xerox Corp., Can., 1976-77; major account mktg. exec. Xerox Corp., Hartford, Conn., 1978-79, New Haven, Conn., 1979-80; account exec. State of N.Y. Xerox Corp., N.Y.C., 1981; N.Y. region mgr. customer support Xerox Corp., Greenwich, Conn., 1982, N.Y. region sales ops. mgr., 1982; State of Ohio account exec. Xerox Corp., Columbus, 1983; new bus. sales mgr. Xerox Corp., Dayton, Ohio, 1983, major accounts sales mgr., 1984; info. systems sales and support mgr., quality specialist Xerox Corp., Detroit, 1985-87, new product launch mgr., ops. quality mgr., 1988, dist. mktg. mgr., 1989-91, major accounts sales mgr., 1992—. Named to Outstanding Young Women of Am., 1968, Outstanding Bus. Woman, Dayton C. of C., 1984, Women's Inner Circle of Achievement, 1990. Mem. NAFE, Am. Mgmt. Assn., Women's Econ. Club Detroit, Detroit Inst. Arts Founders' Soc., Greater Detroit C. of C. Republican. Roman Catholic. Avocations: interior decorating, reading, music, art. Home: 23308 Reynard Dr Southfield MI 48034-6924 Office: Xerox Corp 300 Galleria Officentre Southfield MI 48034-4700

SMITH, NANCY LYNNE, journalist, real estate agent, public relations consultant; b. San Antonio, July 31, 1947; d. Tillman Louis and Enid Maxine (Woolverton) Brown; m. Allan Roy Jones, Nov. 28, 1969 (div. 1975); 1 dau., Christina Elizabeth Woolverton Jones. BA, So. Meth. U., 1968; postgrad. So. Meth. U., 1969-70, Vanderbilt U., 1964, Ecole Nouvelle de la Suisse Romande, Lausanne, Switzerland, 1962. Tchr. spl. edn. Hot Springs Sch. Dist. (Ark.), 1970-72; reporter, soc. editor Dallas Morning News, 1974-82; soc./celebrity columnist Dallas Times Herald, 1982—; owner, pub. High Soc., Soc. Fax; realtor, Ebby Halliday Realtors; stringer Washington Post, 1978; contbg. editor Ultra mag., Houston, 1981-82, Tex. Woman mag., Dallas, 1979-80, Profl. Woman mag., Dallas, 1979-80; mem. bd. advisors Ultra Mag., 1985—; owner Nancy Smith Pub. Rels. Appeared on TV series Jocelyn's Weekend, Sta. KDFI-TV, 1985. Bd. dirs. TACA arts support orgn., Dallas, 1980—, asst. chmn. custom auction, 1978-83; judge Miss Tex. USA Contest, 1984; bd. dirs. Am. Parkinson Disease Assn. (Dallas chpt.), mem. adv. bd. Cattle Baron's Ball Com., Dallas Symphony Debutante presentations; hon. mem. Dallas Opera Women's Bd., Northwood Inst. Women's Bd., Dallas Symphony League; mem. Friends of Winston Churchill Meml. and Library, Dallas Theatre Ctr. Women's Guild, Childrens' Med. Ctr. Auxiliary; hon. mem. Crystal Charity Ball Com.; mem. Community Council Greater Dallas Community Awareness Goals Com. Impact '88, 1985—; co-chmn. Multiple Sclerosis San Simeon Gala, 1988; celebrity co-chmn. Greer Garson Gala of Hope 1990-91; gala chmn. Greer Garson Gala of Hope for Am. Parkinson's Disease Assn., 1991-93; chmn. gala benefit Northwood U., 1994; co-chmn. star studded stomp Mar. Dimes, 1994; mem. Femmes du Monde spl. activities com., com. Dallas Coun. World Affairs. Mem. Soc. Profl. Journalists (v.p. communications 1978-79), Nat. Press Club, Dallas Press Club, DAR, Daus. of Republic of Tex. (registrar 1972), Dallas So. Memorial Assn., Dallas County Heritage Soc., Dallas Mus. Art League, Dallas Opera Guild. Club: Argyle (sec. 1983-84), The 500 (Dallas), Energy. Home: 6324D Bandera Ave Dallas TX 75225-3614 Office: 8333 Douglas Ste 100 Dallas TX 75225

SMITH, NATHAN MCKAY, library and information sciences educator; b. Wendell, Idaho, Apr. 22, 1935; s. M. Blair and Vaunda H. (Hawkes) S.; m. Joyce A. Carman, July 5, 1953; children: Nathan M., Jeffrey M., Pamela J., Russell A., Kristen E. BS in Secondary Edn., Eastern Oreg. Coll., 1961; MS in Gen. Sci., Oreg. State U., 1965; MLS, Brigham Young U., 1969, PhD in Zoology, 1972. Tchr. sci. Dalles Jr. High Sch., The Dalles, Oreg., 1961-64; asst. sci. librarian Brigham Young U., Provo, Utah, 1968, life sci. librarian, 1970-73; prof. Sch. Library and Info. Sci., Brigham Young U., Provo, Utah, 1973-82, dir., 1982-93, life sci. libr., 1993—; cons. Weber County Library, Ogden, Utah, 1980—; back issues sec. Herpetologists League, 1976-81. Served to sgt. USAF, 1953-57. Yr. scholar NSF Acad., 1964; fellow NDEA Title IV, 1969; recipient research award Assn. Library and Info. Sci. Edn., 1983. Mem. ALA (councilor legis. council), Assn. Library Info. Sci. Edn., Mountain Plains Library Assn., Utah Library Assn. (exec. bd., pres.), N. Am. Soc. Adlerian Psychology, Phi Kappa Phi, Sigma Xi, Beta Phi Mu. Mem. LDS Ch. Home: 1606 Locust Ln Provo UT 84604-2806 Office: Brigham Young U Bean Mus Provo UT 84602

SMITH, NEIL, professional football player; b. New Orleans, Apr. 10, 1966. Student, U. Nebr. Defensive end Kansas City Chiefs, 1988—. Played in Pro Bowl, 1991-93; named defensive lineman The Sporting News All-America team, 1987. Office: Kansas City Chiefs 1 Arrowhead Dr Kansas City MO 64129-1651

SMITH, NICK, congressman, farmer; b. Addison, Mich., Nov. 5, 1934; s. LeGrand John and Blanche (Nichols) S.; m. Bonnalyn Belle Atwood, Jan. 1, 1960; children: Julianna, Bradley, Elizabeth, Stacia. BA, Mich. State U., 1957; MS, U. Del., 1959. Radio & TV farm editor Sta. WDEL, Wilmington, Del., 1957-59; radio editor Sta. KSWD, Wichita Falls, Tex., 1959-60; capt. intelligence USAF, Tex., 1959-61; mem. twp. bd. Somerset Twp., Addison, 1962-68; asst. dep. adminstr. USDA, Washington, 1972-74; state rep. Mich. Ho. of Reps., Lansing, 1978-82; state senator Mich. State Senate, Lansing, 1982-92; mem. 103rd-104th Congresses from 7th Mich. dist., 1993—; chmn. Senate Agrl. Com., 1982-92, Senate Corrections Appropriation Com., 1984-90, Senate Mil. Affairs Com., 1984-90, Senate Fin. Com., 1990-92; mem. agriculturecom., budget com. Leader's Task Force on Economy, 1993—. Del. Am. Assembly on World Population & Hunger, Washington, 1973; nat. del. on U.S.-Soviet Cooperation and Trade, 1991; former trustee Somerset Congl. Ch. Capt. USAF, 1959-61. Fellow Kellogg Found., 1965; named Hon. FFA State Star Farmer, 1987, SCF Conservator of Yr. Hillsdale County, 1988. Mem. Mich. Farm Bur. (bd. dirs.), Jackson C. of C., Mich. State U. Alumni Club, Masons. Republican. Office: US House of Reps 1530 Longworth Hob Washington DC 20515-2207*

SMITH, NOEL WILSON, psychology educator; b. Marion, Ind., Nov. 2, 1933; s. Anthony and Mary Louise (Wilson) S.; m. Marilyn C. Coleman, June 17, 1954; children: Thor and Lance (twins). AB, Ind. U., 1955, PhD, 1962; MA, U. Colo., 1958; 1971-95. Asst. prof. psychology Wis. State U., Platteville, 1962-63; asst. prof. psychology SUNY, Plattsburgh, 1963-66, assoc. prof., 1966-71, prof., 1971-95, prof. emeritus, 1995—. Author: Greek and Interbehavioral Psychology, 1990, rev. edit., 1993, An Analysis of Ice Age Art: Its Psychology and Belief, 1992; co-author: The Science of Psychology: Interbehavioral Survey, 1975; sr. editor: Reassessment in Psychology, 1983; editor: Interbehavioral Psychology newsletter, 1970-77; contbr. articles to profl. jours. Fellow APA; mem. AAUP (pres. SUNY coun. 1980-82), Am. Psychol. Soc., Cheiron Internat. Soc. History of Behavior Sci., Sigma Xi. Home: 7 W Court St Plattsburgh NY 12901-2301 Office: SUNY Dept Psychology Beaumont Hall Plattsburgh NY 12901

SMITH, NORMA JANE, elementary education educator; b. N.Y.C., Aug. 19, 1933; d. Raymond and Thelma (Kavares) Schneider; m. Thomas Edward Smith; children: Robyn, Sharon, Ilene. BA, CUNY, 1955; cert. in art, N.Y. Inst. Tech., 1986; postgrad., L.I. U., 1990. Cert. tchr., N.Y. Tchr. grade 1 Plainedge (N.Y.) Pub. Schs., 1956-59; tchr., reading specialist Half Hollow Hills Schs., Dix Hills, N.Y., 1969-70, tchr. grade 4, 1970-95, tng. and supervision of student tchrs., 1972-93, drama dir., 1982-95, social studies coord., 1982, 83, sci. coord., 1988, 89; instr. in-svc. tchr. edn. courses Half Hollow Hills, 1989, 90, 91; advisor Math Olympiads, Chestnut Hills, 1994-95. Author: The Queen's Mirrors, 1973, Pot Pourri, 1984, Spelling Pizazz, 1992, A Fish Named Willie Blue, 1992. Bd. dirs. San Remo (N.Y.) Civic Assn. Recipient award for 20 yrs. of dedicated svc. to children of Chestnut Hill, Chestnut Hill PTA, 1990. Mem. ASCD, Half Hollow Hills Tchrs. Assn. (rep. 1974-79, newsletter publ. 1996—), Soc. of Children's Book Writers and Illustrators. Avocations: writing, piano, art, theater arts. Home: 17 Acacia Rd Kings Park NY 11754

SMITH, NORMAN CLARK, fund raising consultant; b. Hartford, Conn., Jan. 2, 1917; s. Raymond W. and Elinor (Smith) S. A.B., Middlebury Coll., 1939; postgrad., Hartford Coll. Law, Trinity Coll. Tchr. Loomis Sch., 1945-50, adminstr., tchr., 1952-53, asst. bus. mgr., 1953-55, bus. mgr., 1955-58, controller, 1958-63; treas. Vassar Coll., 1963-64; v.p. devel., planning Emory U., Atlanta, 1964-76; v.p. univ. devel. U. Del., 1976-79. Bd. dirs., past chmn. bd. Nat. Soc. Fund Raising Execs.; past trustee LoomisInst., Watkinson Sch.; past chmn. Ga. Conservancy; past pres. Mashantucket Land Trust of Southeastern Conn.; trustee emeritus, pas pres. Conn. River Mus., Essex; mem. Conn. State Coun. on Environ. Quality, Naval War Coll. Found.; mem. citizens adv. coun. Project Oceanology; trustee Conn. Antiquarian and Landmarks Soc.; former mem. Nat. Exec. Svc. Corps.; pres. Groton Edn. Found. Capt. USNR, 1941-45, 50-52. Decorated Navy Cross. Mem. Chi Psi, Omicron Delta Kappa. Club: Rotary. Home and Office: 161 Pequot Ave Mystic CT 06355-1728

SMITH, NORMAN CUTLER, geologist, business executive, educator; b. Paterson, N.J., Mar. 18, 1915; s. Archibald Nicholas and Ruth (Cutler) S.; m. Dorothy Phyllis Barnes, June 12, 1942; children—Roxanne Lorraine, Lee Cutler. Student, Pennington Prep. Sch., 1930-33, Drew U., 1933-34; AB in Geology and Biology cum laude, Washington and Lee U., 1937; postgrad., Harvard U., 1940-42, U. Okla., 1947. Field geologist Standard Oil Co. Venezuela, 1938-40; teaching fellow Harvard Grad. Sch. Geology, 1941-42; geologist Humble Oil & Refining Co., 1946-49; cons. geologist and photogeol. specialist, 1949-62; exec. dir. Am. Assn. Petroleum Geologists, 1963-72; pres. Resource Devel. Internat., Inc., Atlanta, 1973-88, 1973-88; chmn. bd. and faculty N.C. Center for Creative Retirement U. N.C., Asheville, 1988-93; bd. dirs. Oil Mining Corp., Boulder, Colo., 1990—; founder, 1st pres. Coun. Sci. Socs., Dallas-Ft. Worth area, 1958, chmn bd., 1960; mem. standing com. Nat. Com. on Geology, 1962-72. Author articles, chpts. in books in field. Bd. dirs. Tulsa Sci. Found., 1967; trustee Tulsa Sci. Ctr., 1967-72; mem. Buncombe County Reorgn. Commn.; bd. dirs. Colburn Gem. and Mineral Mus. Served to lt. (s.g.) USNR, 1942-46, PTO. Fellow AAAS, Geol. Soc. Am.; mem. Tulsa Soc. Assn. Execs. (pres. 1968; hon.), Dallas Geol. Soc. (pres. 1958-59, exec. com. 1956-60; hon.), Am. Assn. Petroleum Geologists, Soc. Petroleum Engrs., Soc. Exploration Geophysicists, Coun. Engring. and Sci. Soc. Secs. Home: 105 Windward Dr Asheville NC 28803-9555

SMITH, NORMAN OBED, physical chemist, educator; b. Winnipeg, Man., Can., Jan. 23, 1914; came to U.S., 1950, naturalized, 1958; s. Ernest and Ruth (Kilpatrick) S.; m. Anna Marie O'Connor, July 1, 1944; children: Richard Obed, Graham Michael, Stephen Housley. B.Sc., U. Man., 1935, M.Sc., 1936; Ph.D., NYU, 1939. Teaching fellow NYU, 1936-39; mem. faculty dept. chemistry U. Man., Winnipeg, 1939-50; asst. prof. U. Man., 1946-49, assoc. prof., 1949-50; assoc. prof. Fordham U., N.Y.C., 1950-65; prof. chemistry Fordham U., 1965-84, prof. emeritus, 1984—, chmn. dept., 1974-78; sr. phys. chemist Arthur D. Little, Inc., Cambridge, Mass., 1957; indsl. cons. Author: (with others) The Phase Rule and Its Applications, 1951, Chemical Thermodynamics, A Problems Approach, 1967, Elementary Statistical Thermodynamics, A Problems Approach, 1982; contbr. to: Ency. Brit, 1974. Fellow Chem. Inst. Can.; mem. Am. Chem. Soc., Asso. Can. Coll. Organists, Am. Guild Organists (dir. chpt. 1964-66, 79-82, 91-92), Sigma Xi, Phi Lambda Upsilon. Home: 59 Monrovia Blvd Tuckahoe NY 10707-1023 Office: Fordham U Dept Chemistry New York NY 10458-5198

SMITH, NORMAN RAYMOND, college president; b. Toronto, Ont., Can., Oct. 24, 1946; s. William Raymond and Jeanne (Malin) S.; m. Susan Robinson, Dec. 26, 1981; 1 child, Caroline Robinson. BS, Drexel U., 1969, MBA, 1971; EdD, Harvard U., 1984. Assoc. dean students Drexel U., Phila., 1971-73; dean of students, professor Phila. Coll. Textiles and Sci., 1973-78; asst. dean Harvard Grad. Sch. Edn., Cambridge, Mass., 1978-80, John F. Kennedy Sch. Govt., Harvard U., Cambridge, 1980-84; exec. v.p. Moore Coll. Art, Phila., 1984-87; pres. Wagner Coll., S.I., N.Y., 1988—; dir. Dime Bancorp; assoc. Harvard U. Philosophy of Edn. Rsch. Ctr., Cambridge, 1987—. Author: How to Make The Right Decisions About College, 1993. Chair mayor's cabinet transition search City of Boston, 1983-84; trustee N.Y. Coun. of Ind. Colls. and Univs., 1994—. Lt. U.S. Army, 1969-73. Recipient U. medal Drexel U., 1993, Pres.'s medal NYU, 1994. Mem. Ind. Coll. Fund N.Y. (sec.-treas.), Harvard Club of N.Y.C., Richmond County Country Club. Home: 79 Howard Ave Staten Island NY 10301-4404 Office: Wagner College Office of Pres Staten Island NY 10301

SMITH, NORMAN T., lawyer; b. Akron, Ohio, Nov. 23, 1935; s. Norman and Margaret (Stall) S.; m. Marilyn Deanna Richards, Oct. 1, 1960; children: Brian T., Valerie E., Gregory D. BS, Ohio State U., 1957; MBA, Case Western Res. U., 1959; JD, U. Mich., 1963. Bar: Ohio 1963. Ptnr. Porter, Wright, Morris & Arthur (and predecessor firms), Columbus, Ohio, 1963—; past. exec. dir. Ohio Title Ins. Rating Bur., Columbus, 1972-89; instr. Capital U. Legal Assistant Program, Columbus, 1985—. Sr. warden St. Marks Episcopal Ch., Upper Arlington, Ohio, 1970-73, 85; pres. 412 Sycamore, Inc., Cin., 1983—; mem. bd. edn. Upper Arlington, 1980-83, Bd Zoning Adjustment, Columbus, 1977-85. Recipient Merit award Ohio Legal Ctr. Inst. Fellow Ohio State Bar Found., Columbus Bar Found.; mem. ABA, Ohio State Bar Assn. (coun. dels. 1985-95, chmn. real property bd. govs. 1980-82), Am. Coll. Real Estate Lawyers, Ohio Land Title Assn. (pres. 1976), Columbus Bar Assn., Nat. Conf. Bar Examiners (real property drafting com. multistate bar exam 1988-95), Columbus Athletic Club, Leatherlips Yacht Club (gov. 1970-71). Republican. Episcopalian. Office: Porter Wright Morris & Arthur 41 S High St Columbus OH 43215-6101

SMITH, NUMA LAMAR, JR., lawyer; b. Rock Hill, S.C., Nov. 22, 1915; s. Numa Lamar and Grace (Hanes) S.; m. Mary Catherine Gray, Mar. 24, 1941; children: Patricia Gray, Elizabeth Hanes, Lamar Douglas. A.B., Furman U., 1938; LL.B. with distinction, Duke U., 1941. Bar: N.Y. 1942, D.C. 1946. Assoc. firm White & Case, N.Y.C., 1941-42, Miller & Chevalier, Washington, 1946-49; partner Miller & Chevalier, 1949-83, counsel, 1983—; bd. visitors, 1973-83; sr. fellow Duke U. Law Sch., 1979-80. Assoc. editor: Duke Law Jour, 1940-41. Served with U.S. Army, 1942-46; with Judge Adv. Gen. Corps 1944-46. Recipient Gen. Excellence award Furman U., 1938. Fellow Am. Bar Found.; mem. ABA, D.C. Bar Assn., Am. Law Inst., Duke Law Alumni Assn. (pres. 1967-69), Order of Coif, Met. Club (Washington), Burning Tree Club (Bethesda, Md.), Washington Golf Club (Arlington, Va.), Sigma Alpha Epsilon. Baptist. Home: 7515 Pelican Bay Blvd Naples FL 33963

SMITH, ORIN ROBERT, chemical company executive; b. Newark, Aug. 13, 1935; s. Sydney R. and Gladys Emmett (DeGroff) S.; m. Stephanie M. Bennett-Smith; children: Lindsay, Robin; 1 stepchild, Brendan. BA in Econometrics, Brown U., 1957; MBA in Mgmt., Seton Hall U., 1964; PhD in Econs. (hon.), Centenary Coll., 1991; LLD (hon.), Monmouth Coll., 1994. Various sales and mktg. mgmt. positions Allied Chem. Corp., Morristown, N.J., 1959-69; dir. sales and mktg. Richardson-Merrell Co., Phillipsburg, N.J., 1969-72; with M&T Chems., Greenwich, Conn., 1972-77, pres., 1975-77; with Engelhard Minerals & Chems. Corp., Menlo Park, Edison, N.J., 1977-81, corp. sr. v.p., 1978-81, pres. div. minerals and chems., 1978-81, also bd. dirs., 1979-81, pres., dir. various U.S. subs., 1979-81; exec. v.p., pres. div. minerals and chems. Engelhard Corp., Menlo Park, Edison, 1981-84, bd. dirs., 1981—; pres., CEO, Engelhard Corp., Iselin, N.J., 1984-95, chmn., CEO, 1995—; also bd. dirs.; bd. dirs. Summit Bank Co., The Summit Bancorp, Vulcan Materials Co., La. Land and Exploration Co., NAM, Perkin-Elmer Corp., Ingersoll-Rand Corp., Minorco, Engelhard Corp., Mfrs. Alliance. Trustee N.J. State C. of C., Inst. for Tech. Advancement, Henry R. Kessler Found., Inc.; mem. bd. overseers N.J. Inst. Tech.; trustee Plimoth Plantation; 1st vice chmn. bd. trustees Centenary Coll.; past chmn. Ind. Coll. Fund N.J.; past dir.-at-large U. Maine Pulp and Paper Found. Lt. (j.g.) USN, 1957-59. Mem. Chem. Mfrs. Assn. (past bd. dirs.), Am. Mgmt. Assn. (gen. mgmt. coun.), Econ. Club (N.Y.C.), Union League Club (N.Y.C.), Duxbury Yacht Club, New Bedford Yacht Club, N.Y. Yacht Club. Office: Engelhard Corp 101 Wood Ave S Iselin NJ 08830-2703

SMITH, ORVILLE AUVERNE, physiology educator; b. Nogales, Ariz., June 16, 1927; s. Orville Auverne and Bess (Gill) S.; m. Clara Jean Smith; children—Nanette, Marcella. B.A. in Psychology, U. Ariz., 1949; M.A., Mich. State U., 1950, Ph.D., 1953. Instr. psychology Mich. State U., East Lansing, 1953-54; fellow U. Pa., Phila., 1954-56; trainee dept. physiology and biophysics U. Wash., Seattle, 1956-58, instr. physiology and biophysics, 1958-59, asst. prof., 1959-61, 62-63; asst. dir. Regional Primate Research Ctr., 1962-69, assoc. prof., 1963-67, prof., 1967—; assoc. dir. Regional Primate Research Center, 1969-71, dir., 1971-88. Contbr. articles to profl. jours. Mem. Am. Physiol. Soc., Am. Soc. Primatologists (pres. 1977-79), Internat. Congress Physiol. Scis., Am. Assn. Anatomists, AAAS, Pavlovian Soc. N.Am. (pres. 1977-78), Internat. Primatological Soc., AAUP, Neurosci. Soc. Home: 7521 30th Ave NE Seattle WA 98115-4719 Office: U Wash Regional Primate Research Ctr SJ-50 Seattle WA 98195

SMITH, OZZIE (OSBORNE EARL SMITH), professional baseball player; b. Mobile, Ala., Dec. 26, 1954; m. Denise Jackson, Nov. 1, 1980; children: Osborne Earl Jr., Dustin Cameron. Grad., Calif. State Poly. U., San Luis Obispo. Shortstop San Diego Padres Baseball Club, Nat. League, 1977-82, St. Louis Cardinals Baseball Club, Nat. League, 1982—. Player Nat. League All-Star Team, 1981-92, 94, All-Star Team Sporting News, 1982, 84-87, World Series Championship Team, 1982; recipient Most Valuable Player award Nat. League Championship Series, 1985, Gold Glove award, 1980-92, Silver Slugger award, 1987. Avocations: jazz, word puzzles, backgammon. Office: St Louis Cardinals Busch Meml Stadium 250 Stadium Plz Saint Louis MO 63102-1722

SMITH, PAT EVERETT, chemical company executive; b. San Diego, July 17, 1930; s. Jack and Eva (Coffman) S.; m. Sept. 16, 1961. BS in Chemistry, UCLA, 1954. Chemist Lever Bros., Los Angeles, 1959-64; dir. rsch. and devel. Cee Bee Chem. Co., Los Angeles, 1964-69; material and process engr. Gary Aircraft Corp., San Antonio, 1969-71; v.p., owner Eldorado Chem. Co., San Antonio, 1969—. Inventor U.S. Patent Process for Biochemical Reactions, 1975. Election judge City of Hill Country Village, Tex. 1983. With U.S. Army, 1955-59. Recipient Smalley award Am. Oil Chemists' Soc. 1961. Mem. Nat. Assn. Corrosion Engrs., Am. Soc. Test Methods, Soc. Automotive Engrs., Soc. for the Advancement of Material and Process Engrs., Aircraft Owners and Pilots Assn., Tech. Assn. of Pulp and Paper Engrs., Harp & Shamrock Soc. Avocations: natural science, painting, archaeology, languages, cooking. Office: Eldorado Chem Co PO Box 34837 San Antonio TX 78265-4837

SMITH, PATRICIA ANNE, special education educator; b. West Chester, Pa., Aug. 19, 1967; d. William Richard and Carol Anne (Benn) S. BS in Spl. Edn. cum laude, West Chester U., 1989; postgrad., Immaculata Coll., 1993—. Cert. mentally and physically handicapped tchr., Pa. Learning support tchr. Chester County Intermediate Unit, Downington, Pa., 1989-90, early intervention tchr., 1990-92; autistic support tchr. Coatesville (Pa.) Area Sch. Dist., 1992—, event coord. WOYC workshops, 1993-96; workshop presenter ann. conf. Pa. Assn. of Resources for People with Mental Retardation, Hershey, 1994; presenter info. sessions ann. conf. Del. Valley Assn. for Edn. of Young Children, Phila., 1994, Lions, Downington, Pa., 1992, early childhood conf. Capital Area Assn. for Edn. of Young Children, Harrisburg,

Pa., 1995, vols. Caln Athletic Assn. Challenger League, 1995—; mentor West Chester U., 1995—. Mem. recreation adv. bd. dirs. Assn. for Retarded Citizens, Exton, Pa., 1993—, Daisy Girl Scout Leader, 1995—; vol. tutor Chester County Libr. Adult Literacy Program, 1995—. Recipient Outstanding Svc. award Coatesville Area Parent Coun., 1994, 96, Vol. award Friendship PTA, 1993, 96; grantee Pa. Dept. Edn., 1993, Pa. Early Childhood Edn. Assn. Workshop presenter award, 1993, Coatesville Area Sch. Bd. Recognition award, 1993. Mem. ASCD, Nat. Assn. for the Edn. of Young Children, Autism Soc. Am., Kappa Delta Pi. Republican. Roman Catholic. Home: 501 Clover Mill Rd Exton PA 19341-2505 Office: Friendship Elem Sch 296 Reeceville Rd Coatesville PA 19320

SMITH, PATRICIA GRACE, government official; b. Tuskegee, Ala., Nov. 10, 1947; d. Douglas and Wilhelmina (Griffin) Jones; m. J. Clay Smith, Jr., June 25, 1983; children—Eugene Douglas, Stager Clay, Michelle L., Michael L. B.A. in English, Tuskegee Inst., 1968; postgrad. Auburn U., 1969-71, Harvard U., 1974, George Washington U., 1983; cert. sr. exec. service 1987; exec. mgmt. tng. devel. assignments Dept. Def., 1986, U.S. Senate Commerce Com., 1987. Instr. Tuskegee Institute, Ala., 1969-71; program mgr. Curber Assocs., Washington, 1971-73; dir. placement Nat. Assn. Broadcasters, Washington, 1973-74, dir. pub. affairs, 1974-77; assoc. producer Group W Broadcasting, Balt., 1977, producer, 1977-78; dir. affiliate relations and programming Sheridan Broadcasting Network, Crystal City, Va., 1978-80; dep. dir. policy, assoc. mng. dir. pub. info. and reference svcs., FCC, Washington, 1992-94, acting assoc. mng. dir., pub. info. and reference svcs., 1994; dep. dir. Office Pub. Affairs, 1994—; chief of staff office assoc. adminstr. for comml. space transp., FAA, U.S. Dept. Transp., 1994—. vice chmn. Nat. Conf. Black Lawyers Task Force on Communications, Washington, 1975-87. Mem. D.C. Donor Project, Nat. Kidney Found., Washington, 1984—; trustee, mem. exec. com., nominating com., youth adv. com. Nat. Urban League, 1976-81; mem. communications com. Cancer Coordinating Council, 1977-84; mem. Braintrust Subcom. on Children's Programming, Congl. Black Caucus, 1976—; mem. adv. bd. Black Arts Celebration, 1978-83; mem. NAACP; mem. journalism and communications adv. council Auburn U., 1976-78; mem. Washington Urban League, 1985—; bd. dirs. Black Film Rev., 1989-91; mem D.C. Commn. on Human Rights, 1986-88, chmn. 1988-91; mem. adv. coun. Nat. Insts. Health, 1992—; mem. bd. advisors The Salvation Army, 1993—. Named Outstanding Young Woman of Yr., Washington, 1975, 78; recipient Sustained Superior Performance award FCC, Washington, 1982-94. Mem. Women in Communications, Inc. (mem. nat. adv. com.), Lambda Iota Tau. Club: Broadcasters (bd. dirs. 1976-77). Democrat. Baptist. Avocations: writing, swimming. Home: 4010 16th St NW Washington DC 20011-7002 Office: DOT/OCST 400 7th St SW Rm 5415 Washington DC 20590-0001

SMITH, PATRICK JOHN, editor, writer; b. N.Y.C., Dec. 11, 1932; s. H. Ben and Geraldine (Wilson) S.; m. Elisabeth Munro, Nov. 27, 1964; children: Douglass Munro, Matthew Wilson. Student, Phillips Exeter, 1951; AB, Princeton U., 1955. Freelance writer and critic, 1958-70; editor, pub. The Mus. Newsletter, N.Y.C., 1970-77; pres. Music Critics Assn., Washington, 1977-81; dir. opera mus. theater program NEA, Washington, 1985-89; editor Opera News, N.Y.C., 1989—. Author: The Tenth Muse: A History of the Opera Libretto, 1970, A Year at the Met, 1983. Office: Opera News 70 Lincoln Center Plz New York NY 10023-6548

SMITH, PAUL EDMUND, JR., philosophy and religion educator; b. Northampton, Mass., Feb. 6, 1927; s. Paul Edmund and Mary Jane (Murphy) S.; B.A., U. Mass., 1948; postgrad. Harvard U., 1948-49; M.A., Boston U., 1957; B.D., Columbia Theol. Sem., 1957, M.Div., 1971; postgrad. U. N.C., 1967-68. Instr. Latin and French, Chester (Vt.) High Sch., 1949-53, Loris (S.C.) High Sch., 1953-54; lectr. history U. Ga., Albany, 1957-59; instr. Latin, Rocky Mount (Va.) High Sch., 1959-61; minister Henderson Presbyn. Ch., Albany, 1957-59, Rocky Mount (Va.) Presbyn. Ch., 1959-64; asst. prof. religion Ferrum (Va.) Coll., 1961-68; vis. lectr. history John Tyler C.C., Chester, Va., 1968-69; instr. philosophy and religion Richard Bland Coll., Petersburg, Va., 1968-71, asst. prof., 1971-76, asso. prof., 1976—, chmn. dept., 1971—. Mem. Am. Hist. Assn., Presbytery of the Peaks. Democrat. Presbyterian. Office: Richard Bland Coll Commerce Hall Petersburg VA 23805

SMITH, PAUL FREDERICK, plant physiologist, consultant; b. Copeland, Kans., Dec. 17, 1916; s. Frederick Eugene and Susie Irene (Wikoff) S.; m. Marjorie Haselwood, July 6, 1940; children: Gary Lynn, Carol Jeanne. BS, U. Okla., 1938, MS, 1940; PhD, U. Calif., 1944. Asst. plant physiologist USDA, Salinas, Calif., 1943-45, Orlando, Fla., 1946-50; assoc. physiologist USDA, 1950-55, plant physiologist, 1956-61, prin. physiologist, 1962-71, head physiologist, 1971-75, hort. cons., 1975—. Contbr. chpts. to books and articles to profl. publs. With USN, 1945-46. Fellow Am. Soc. Hort. Sci.; mem. Fla. Hort. Soc. (hon. life, Presdl. Gold medal 1970). Achievements include research in streamlining fertilization practices on citrus thereby avoiding deficiencies and excesses. Home and Office: 2695 Ashville St Orlando FL 32818-9018

SMITH, PAUL J., museum administrator; b. Buffalo; student Art Inst. Buffalo, Sch. Am. Craftsmen, Rochester, N.Y.; DFA (hon.) New Sch. Social Research, 1987. Staff mem. Am. Craft Coun., N.Y.C., 1957—, dir. Am. Craft Mus., 1963-87, dir. emeritus, 1987—; juror numerous exhibitions; lectr. and cons. in field of contemporary crafts and design. Trustee Louis Comfort Tiffany Found., Penland Sch. Crafts; adv. trustee Haystack Mountain Sch. Crafts, Deer Isle, Maine; nat. coun. Atlantic Ctr. for Arts, Inc. Office: PO Box 6735 Yorkville Station New York NY 10128

SMITH, PAUL LETTON, JR., geophysicist; b. Columbia, Mo., Dec. 16, 1932; s. Paul Letton and Helen Marie (Doersam) S.; m. Mary Barbara Noel; children: Patrick, Melody, Timothy, Christopher, Anne. BS in Physics, Carnegie Inst. Tech., 1955, MSEE, 1957, PhD in Elec. Engring., 1960. From instr. to asst. prof. Carnegie Inst. Tech., Pitts., 1955-63; sr. engr. Midwest Rsch. Inst., Kansas City, Mo., 1963-66; from rsch. engr. to sr. scientist and group head Inst. Atmospheric Scis., S.D. Sch. Mines and Tech., Rapid City, 1966-81; vis. prof. McGill U., Montreal, Que., Can., 1969-70; chief scientist Air Weather Svc. USAF, Scott AFB, Ill., 1974-75; dir. Inst. Atmospheric Scis., S.D. Sch. Mines and Tech., Rapid City, 1981—; lectr. Tech. Svc. Corp., Silver Spring, Md., 1972-91; vis. scientist Alberta Rsch. Coun., Edmonton, Can., 1984-85; dir. S.D. Space Grant Consortium, Rapid City, 1991-96; Fulbright lectr. U. Helsinki, 1986. Contbr. over 50 articles to profl. jours. Fellow Am. Meteorol. Soc. (Editor's award 1992); mem. IEEE (sr.), Weather Modification Assn. (Thunderbird award 1995), Sigma Xi. Home: 2107 9th St Rapid City SD 57701-5315

SMITH, PAUL THOMAS, financial services company executive; b. Garden City, N.Y., May 17, 1938; s. Leo Joseph and Martha Duncan (Perine) S.; m. Carole A. Dlugolenski, Sept. 1, 1962; children—Laura Jane, Paul Thomas, Elizabeth Ann, Kathryn Celinda. B.B.A., U. Notre Dame, 1960; M.B.A., Harvard U., 1964. C.P.A., N.Y. chartered fin. analyst. In charge accountant Deloitte & Touche, N.Y.C., 1964-67; from investment analyst to 2d v.p. N.Y. Life Ins. Co., N.Y.C., 1967-78, v.p. investments, 1978-83, v.p., chief equity investment officer, 1983-88, sr. v.p. corp. planning and devel., 1988-91, sr. v.p. venture capital, chief equity investment officer, 1991—. Served to lt. USN, 1960-62. Mem. Inst. Chartered Fin. Analysts, N.Y. Soc. Security Analysts. Club: Cherry Valley. Office: 51 Madison Ave New York NY 10010-1603

SMITH, PAUL TRAYLOR, mayor, former business executive, former army officer; b. Burkesville, Ky., June 22, 1923; s. Samuel Joseph and Bonnie (Ferguson) S.; m. Elizabeth C. Nolte, July 2, 1942; m. Phyllis Jean Corbin, Oct. 11, 1975; children: Gregory L., Douglas B., Paula J. Smith Richardson, Mary K. B.A., U. Md., 1960, M.B.A., 1962. Enlisted in U.S. Army, 1940, advanced through grades to maj. gen., 1975; service in Japan, Ger., Korea, Vietnam; adj. gen. Continental Army Command, 1968-70, comdg. gen. U.S. Army Computer Systems Command, 1973-75; adj. gen. U.S. Army, 1975-77; exec. v.p. Taylorcraft Devel. Corp., Inc., Burkesville, Ky., 1977-82; mayor City of Burkesville, Burkesville, Ky., 1982. Bd. dirs. Lake Cumberland Area Devel. Dist. Inc., Lake Cumberland Housing Agy., Inc.; bd. dirs., mem. exec. com., legis. policy com. Ky. League of Cities, also trustee investemnt pool bd., 1st v.p.; chmn. Lake Area Inspection Svc. Inc.; chmn. bd. dirs. Lake Cumberland Area Devel. Dist., Revolving Loan Fund Com., Lake Cumberland Housing Agy., Burkesville Manor Corp.; trustee Ky. Mcpl. Risk Mgmt. Agy. Decorated D.S.M., Legion of Merit with 2 oak leaf clusters, Bronze Star. Mem. Assn. U.S. Army, Ret. Officers Assn. Address: PO Box 607 Burkesville KY 42717-0607 *Make sure the goals and standards you set for yourself are higher than others might set for you. You are the key to your own success or fortune.*

SMITH, PAUL VERGON, JR., corporate executive, retired oil company executive; b. Lima, Ohio, Apr. 25, 1921; s. Paul Vergon and Aleta Rose (Bowers) S.; m. Alta Fern Chipps, Mar. 2, 1945; children: Douglas, Marsha, Jeffrey, Alison. AB, Miami U., Oxford, Ohio, 1942; MS, U. Ill., 1943, PhD, 1945. With Exxon Research & Engring. Co., 1946-66, 72-86, mgr. pub. affairs, 1972-80, mgr. ednl. and profl. soc. relations, Florham Park, N.J., 1981-86; asst. dir. chem. research Esso Petroleum Co., Abingdon, Eng., 1966-67; dir. chem. research Esso Research S.A., Brussels, 1967-71; mem. adv. bd. Cache, Inc., Austin, Tex., 1979-86; pres. APS Assocs., Westfield, N.J., 1986-90; bd. dirs., treas. Jets, Inc., Alexandria, Va.; dir. CENTCOM, Ltd.; mem. exec. bd. N.J. Bus./Industry/Sci. Edn. Consortium. Patentee in field; contbr. numerous articles to profl. jours., chpts. to books. Bd. dirs. United Way of Union County, N.J., 1980-86; chmn. research adv. council Miami U., 1980-84. Recipient Pres.'s award Am. Assn. Petroleum Geologists, 1955; Spl. award N.J. Sci. Tchrs. Assn., 1985. Mem. AAAS, Am. Chem. Soc. (dir. 1978-86, chmn. bd. 1984-86; Belden award 1984), Am. Soc. Engring. Edn. (dir. 1980-86, v.p. 1980-86), Country Club Naples, Phi Beta Kappa, Sigma Xi, Omicron Delta Kappa, Phi Eta Sigma, Alpha Chi Sigma, Pi Mu Epsilon, Sigma Pi Sigma, Phi Lambda Upsilon. Republican. Methodist.

SMITH, PAUL WINSTON, petroleum geologist; b. Norman, Okla., Dec. 11, 1959; s. Earl Winston and Mona Margaret (Wicker) S.; m. Bridget Ann Bright, Dec. 10, 1983; 1 child, Daniel Winston. BS in Geology, U. Okla., 1982, MS, 1992. Geol. asst. Siskon Corp., Reno, Nev., 1978-80; from geologist to pres. Norex Corp., Norman, 1980-93; sr. geologist Dwight's Energydata, Oklahoma City, 1993—; bd. dirs. Gold Hill Corp., Norman, Norex Corp. Contbg. author: Oklahoma Geologic Survey Symposium on the Viola and Simpson Groups in the Mid Continent, 1995; contbr. articles to profl. jours. Asst. scoutmaster Boy Scouts Am., Norman, 1988-92. Mem. Am. Assn. Petroleum Geologists, Oklahoma City Geol. Soc. (grantee 1991). Avocations: swimming, snow skiing, camping, fishing, hunting. Home: 4304 Upper Lakes Dr Norman OK 73072 Office: Dwights Energydata 4350 Will Rogers Pkwy Oklahoma City OK 73108

SMITH, PETER, chemist, educator, consultant; b. Sale, Cheshire, Eng., Sept. 7, 1924; came to U.S., 1951; s. Peter and Winifred Emma (Jenkins) S.; m. Hilary Joan Hewitt Roe, 1951; children: Helen Andrews Winifred, Eric Peter, Richard Harry, Gillian Carol. B.A. Queens' Coll., Cambridge U., 1946, M.A., 1949, Ph.D., 1953. Jr. sci. officer Royal Aircraft Establishment, Farnborough, Hampshire, Eng., 1943-46; demonstrator chemistry dept. Leeds U., Yorkshire, England, 1950-51; postdoctoral research fellow in chemistry Harvard U., Cambridge, Mass., 1951-54; asst. prof. chemistry Purdue U., West Lafayette, Ind., 1954-59; asst. prof. chemistry Duke U., Durham, N.C., 1959-61, assoc. prof., 1961-70, prof., 1970-95; prof. chemistry emeritus, 1995—. Contbg. author: chem. research jours. Fulbright postdoctoral scholar Fulbright Commn., Harvard U., 1951-53. Mem. Am. Chem. Soc., Royal Soc. Chemistry, Am. Phys. Soc., Sigma Xi, Phi Lambda Upsilon, Alpha Chi Sigma. Home: 2711 Circle Dr Durham NC 27705-5726 Office: Dept Chemistry Paul M Gross Chem Lab PO Box 90346 Durham NC 27708-0346

SMITH, PETER DOUGLAS, dean; b. Lowestoft, England, Aug. 13, 1933; s. William and Gladys Ethel (Lakey) S.; m. E. Gwenda Jones, Nov. 14, 1964 (div.); 1 child, W. Morgan Smith. BA, U. Birmingham, England, 1954; MLitt, U. Durham, England, 1964; MA (hon.), Dartmouth Coll., 1980. Asst. to registrar McMaster U., Hamilton, Can., 1956-58, asst/assoc. dir. extension, 1958-65; asst. to chancellor U. Calif., Santa Cruz, 1965-67, asst. vice chancellor, 1967-69; dir. Hopkins Ctr. Dartmouth Coll., Hanover, N.H., 1969-81, historian of the Dickey Presidency, 1982-87; dean Sch. of the Arts Columbia U., N.Y., 1987—; trustee Vt. Coun. on the Arts, 1983-86, pres. 1985-86. Mem. Century Club. Avocations: acting, letter writing, listening to music. Home: 15 Claremont Ave New York NY 10027 Office: Sch of the Arts Columbia U New York NY 10027

SMITH, PETER HOPKINSON, political scientist, consultant, author; b. Bklyn., Jan. 17, 1940; s. Joseph Hopkinson and Mary Edna (Sullivan) S.; children: Jonathan Yeardley, Peter Hopkinson Jr, Joanna Alexandra. BA, Harvard U., 1961; MA, PhD, Columbia U., 1966. Asst. prof. Dartmouth Coll., Hanover, N.H., 1966-68; from asst. prof. to prof. U. Wis., Madison, 1968-80; prof. MIT, Cambridge, 1980-86; Simón Bolívar prof. L.Am. studies U. Calif., San Diego, 1987—, dir. Ctr. for Iberian and L.Am. studies, 1989—; cons. Ford Found., N.Y.C., 1984—; vis. mem. Inst. for Advanced Study, Princeton, N.J., 1972-73. Author: Politics and Beef in Argentina: Patterns of Conflict and Change, 1969, Argentina and the Failure of Democracy: Conflict among Political Elites, 1904-55, 1974, Labyrinths of Power: Political Recruitment in Twentieth-Century Mexico, 1979, Mexico: The Quest for a U.S. Policy, 1980, Mexico: Neighbor in Transition, 1984; co-author: Modern Latin America, 1984, 89, 92, editor: Statistics, Epistemology, and History, 1984, Drug Policy in the Americas, 1992, The Challenge of Integration: Europe and the Americas, 1993, Talons of the Eagle, 1995; co-editor: New Approaches to Latin Am. History, 1974, The Family in Latin America, 1978; series editor: Latin America in Global Perspective, 1995—; contbr. articles to profl. jours. Guggenheim fellow, 1975-76; disting. Fulbright lectr. Mexico, 1984. Mem. Latin Am. Studies Assn. (pres. 1981), Am. Polit. Sci. Assn., Am. Hist. Assn., Coun. for Internat. Exch. Scholars, Coun. on Fgn. Rels. Office: U Calif Ctr Iberian and LAm Studies 9500 Gilman Dr La Jolla CA 92093-0528

SMITH, PETER JOHN, geographer, educator; b. Rakaia, New Zealand, Sept. 18, 1931; s. Sidney Charles and Ethel May (Pettit) S.; m. Sheana Mary Lee, May 30, 1959; children: Katrina, Hugh. BA, U. New Zealand, 1953, MA, 1954; diploma of town and regional planning (Central Mortgage and Housing Corp. planning fellow), U. Toronto, 1959; Ph.D., U. Edinburgh, Scotland, 1964. Tchr. schs. New Zealand and Gt. Britain, 1951-55; research planner Calgary City Planning Dept., 1956-59; mem. faculty dept. geography U. Alta., Edmonton, Can., 1959-94, prof., 1969-94, chmn. dept., 1967-75, prof. emeritus, 1994—; Planning cons., 1958—. Author: Population and Production: An Introduction to Some Problems in Economic Geography, rev. edit, 1971, The Edmonton-Calgary Corridor, 1978; editor: The Prairie Provinces, 1972, Edmonton: The Emerging Metropolitan Pattern, 1978, Environment and Economy: Essays on the Human Geography of Alberta, 1984, A World of Real Places: Essays in Honor of William C. Wonders, 1990. Recipient certificate of distinction Town Planning Inst. Can., 1959; Social Scis. and Humanities Research Council grantee, 1977, 84; Leave fellow Can. Council, 1970. Mem. Canadian Assn. Geographers (newsletter editor 1969-77, councillor 1966-70, v.p. 1972-73, pres. 1973-74, editor Can. Geographer 1978-84, award for svc. to the profession), Canadian Inst. Planners, Am. Assn. Geographers, Internat. Planning Hist. Soc. (councillor 1993—), Am. Soc. City and Regional Planning History. Home: 64 Marlboro Rd, Edmonton, AB Canada T6J 2C6

SMITH, PETER LANSDOWN, art director. Art dir.: (films) Chapter Two, 1979, Seems Like Old Times, 1980, The Last Married Couple in America, 1980, Paternity, 1981, Night Shift, 1982, Fandango, 1985, Jagged Edge, 1985, Big Trouble, 1986, Star Trek IV: The Voyage Home, 1986, Nadine, 1987, Blind Date, 1987, Tequila Sunrise, 1988, Fat Man and Little Boy, 1989, Groundhog Day, 1993; prodn. designer: (films) Going Berserk, 1983, The New Kids, 1985. Office: care Art Directors Guild 11365 Ventura Blvd Ste 315 Studio City CA 91604-3148

SMITH, PETER WALKER, finance executive; b. Syracuse, N.Y., May 19, 1923; s. Stanley Sherwood and Elizabeth Wilkins (Young) S.; m. Lucile Elizabeth Edson, June 22, 1946; children: Andrew E., Laurie (Mrs. Samuel J. Falzone), Pamela C. (Mrs. Denison W. Schweppe, Jr.), Stanley E. B.Chem. Engring., Rensselaer Poly. Inst., 1947; M.B.A., Harvard U., 1948; LL.B., Cleve. Marshall Law Sch., 1955. Bar: Ohio 1955; Registered profl. engr., Ohio. Div. controller Raytheon Co., Lexington, Mass., 1958-66; v.p. finance, indsl. systems and equipment group Litton Industries Inc., Stamford, Conn., 1966-70; v.p. finance, treas. Copeland Corp., Sidney, Ohio, 1970-74; v.p. fin., treas., dir. Instrumentation Lab. Inc., Lexington, Mass., 1974-78; chief fin. officer, treas. Ionics, Inc., Watertown, Mass., 1978-80; v.p. fin., treas. Data Printer Corp., Malden, Mass., 1980-84, Orion Research Inc., Boston, 1984-87; pvt. practice cons. Concord, Mass., 1987—. Mem. fin. adv. bd., Northeastern U., Boston. Lt. AUS, 1943-46, 50-52. Mem. Fin. Execs. Inst., Am. Prodn. and Inventory Control Soc. (founding), Rensselaer Soc. Engrs., Sigma Xi, Tau Beta Pi. Home and Office: 155 Monument St Concord MA 01742-1808

SMITH, PETER WILLIAM EBBLEWHITE, electrical engineering educator, scientist; b. London, Nov. 3, 1937; m. Jacqueline Marie Mankiewicz, June 18, 1966; children: Christal, Dawn N. BSc, McGill U., Montreal, Que., Can., 1958, MSc, 1961, PhD, 1964. Mem. of staff Can. Marconi Co., Mont., 1958-59; mem. tech. staff Bell Labs., Holmdel, N.J., 1963-83; dist. mgr. Bellcore, Red Bank, N.J., 1984-87, div. mgr., 1989-92; prof. elec. and computer engring. U. Toronto, 1992—; exec. dir. Ont. Laser and Lightwave Rsch. Ctr., 1992-95. Editor-in-chief IEEE Press Progress in Lasers and Electro-Optics Series, 1987-92; editor Optics Letters, 1989-95; contbr. over 200 articles to profl. jours., books and refereed conf. proc. Board dirs. Monmouth Arts Found., Red Bank, 1965-82. Recipient Sr. Scientist award NATO, 1979. Fellow IEEE (Quantum Electronics award 1986), Optical Soc. Am. (bd. dirs., chmn. bd. editors); mem. IEEE Lasers and Electro-Optics Soc. (pres. 1984), Am. Phys. Soc., Can. Assn. Physicists. Achievements include first demonstration of waveguide gas laser, non-linear optical interface; development of hybrid bistable optical devices; 32 patents in field. Office: U Toronto, Dept Elec & Computer Engrin, Toronto, ON Canada M5S 1A4

SMITH, PETER WILSON, symphony orchestra administrator; b. Utica, N.Y., Mar. 15, 1938; s. Stanley W. and Frances (Brown) S.; m. Kay Gardner, 1960 (div. 1972); children: Juliana, Jennifer; m. Lynn Perrott, 1976. B.Mus., U. Mich., 1965. Asst. mgr. Indpls. Symphony, 1966-67; asst. mgr. St. Louis Symphony, 1967-68; exec. dir. Norfolk Symphony, Va., 1968-72; ops. mgr. Buffalo Philharmonic, 1972-74; ops. adminstr. Carnegie Hall Corp., N.Y.C., 1974-76; mng. dir. Ft. Wayne (Ind.) Philharmonic, 1976-85; exec. dir. Grand Rapids (Mich.) Symphony, 1985-95, pres., 1995—. Served to airman 1st class USAF, 1961-64. Mem. Met. Orch. Mgrs. Assn. (pres. 1979-81), Regional Orch. Mgrs. Assn. (v.p. 1987-89), Am. Symphony Orch. League (bd. dirs. 1989-91), Mgrs. Am. Orch. (vice-chmn. 1989-91). Office: Grand Rapids Symphony 169 Louis Campau Promenade Ste 1 Grand Rapids MI 49503

SMITH, PHILIP DANIEL, academic administrator, education educator; b. Dayton, Ohio, Dec. 25, 1933; s. Hubert Edgar and Edith (Parker) S.; m. Marilyn Brown, Nov. 25, 1953; children: Carolyn Smith Valentine, Norman Daniel, Stanley Nathan. BS cum laude, Bob Jones U., 1955; MEd, Miami U., Oxford, Ohio, 1956; EdD, Pa. State U., 1964. Dean coll. arts and sci. Bob Jones U., Greenville, S.C., 1961-65, registrar, 1965-81, prof. edn., 1956—, provost, 1981—; mem. edn. adv. bd. One Touch Systems, Inc., 1995—. cons. for books Beginnings for Christian Schools, English Skills for Christian Schools. Pres. Bob Jones U. Alumni Assn., Greenville, 1970-71; mem. coll. parallel adv. com. Tri-County Tech. Coll., Pendleton, S.C., 1973-86. Mem. Assn. Ednl. Communications and Tech. (life mem.; membership coordinator for profl. assns. 1969-72, vice chair nat. membership com. 1972-73, chair nat. membership com. 1973-75, council del. S.C. chpt. 1972-73, audiovisual instrn. editorial adv. com. 1974-75, del. to Lake Okoboji ednl. media leadership conf. 1972, 74), Assn. Ednl. Communications and Tech. of S.C. (bd. dirs. 1970-75, pres. 1972-73, award for outstanding contbns. and service 1971), Am. Assn. Collegiate Registrars and Admissions Officers, Phi Delta Kappa. Republican. Baptist. Office: Bob Jones U Off of Provost Greenville SC 29614

SMITH, PHILIP EDWARD LAKE, anthropology educator; b. Fortune, Nfld., Can., Aug. 12, 1927; s. George Frederick and Alice Maggie (Lake) S.; m. Fumiko Ikawa, 1959; 1 son, Douglas Philip Edward. B.A., Acadia U., 1948; M.A., Harvard U., 1957, Ph.D., 1962; postgrad., Universite de Bordeaux, 1958-59; D. Litt. (hon.), Meml. U. Nfld., 1976. Lectr. anthropology U. Toronto, Ont., Can., 1961-63; asst. prof. U. Toronto, 1963-65, asso. prof., 1965-66; asso. prof. archaeology Universite de Montreal, 1966-69, prof., 1969—; v.p. Ednl. Found. for Anthropology and the Public, 1981-84. Author: Le Solutreen en France, 1966, Food Production and Its Consequences, 1976, Japanese edit., 1986, Palaeolithic Archaeology in Iran, 1986; co-editor: The Hilly Flanks and Beyond, 1983; fgn. corr. L'Anthropologie (Paris); contbr. articles to profl. jours.; mem. internat. adv. com. Anthropologie et Societies (Que.). Can. Council Research grantee, 1969, 71, 74, 77; Leave grantee, 1970; research grantee, 1983; NRC research grantee, 1967; Soc. Sci. and Humanities Research Council Can. leave grantee, 1981; exchange research visitor to China, 1984. Fellow Royal Soc. Can., Am. Anthrop. Assn.; mem. Internat. Union Prehistoric and Protohistoric Scis. (permanent coun.), Current Anthropology (assoc.), Can. Soc. for Archaeology Abroad (past pres.), Internat. Union Anthrop. and Ethnol. Scis. (interim chmn. Can. del. to permanent coun. 1979-84, dept. chmn. 1981-84), Can. Inst. Baghdad. Archaeol. expdn. dir., Egypt, 1962-63, Iran, 1965, 67, 69, 71, 74, 77; other field work in Mex., U.S.A., France, Iraq, French W. Indies, India, 1954-82. Home: 3955 Ramezay Ave, Montreal, PQ Canada H3Y 3K3 Office: Univ de Montreal, Dept Anthropologie, Montreal, PQ Canada H3C 3J7

SMITH, PHILIP JOHN, industrial and systems engineering educator; b. Bradenton, Fla., July 11, 1953; s. John Fredrick and Valerie Eline (Polk) S. BA in Psychology, U. Mich., 1975, MS in Indsl. and Ops. Engring., 1976, PhD in Psychology and Indsl. Engring., 1979. Lectr. dept. indsl. engring. U. Mich., Ann Arbor, 1979-80, rsch. scientist Ctr. for Ergonomics, 1979-80; asst. prof. dept. indsl. engring. Ohio State U., Columbus, 1980-86, assoc. prof., 1986-92, prof. indsl. and sys. engring., 1992—; cons. Ford, Dearborn, Mich., 1986—, Travellers Ins. Co., Hartford, Conn., 1991—. Co-editor: Challenges in Indexing Electronic Text and Images, 1994; contbr. articles, paper to profl. publs. Mem. IEEE Sys., Man and Cybernetics, Am. Soc. for Info. Sci., Assn. Computing Machinery (spl. interest group for info. retrieval 1992-93), Human Factors Soc. Avocation: dressage. Home: 7197 Calhoun Rd Ostrander OH 43061-9420 Office: Ohio State U Engring Dept 1971 Neil Ave Columbus OH 43210-1210

SMITH, PHILIP JONES, lawyer; b. York, Pa., May 14, 1941; s. Clark S. and Margaret Ann (Jones) S.; m. Ann F. Johnson, Apr. 21, 1973; 1 child, James M. BA cum laude, Williams Coll., 1963; LLB, U. Va., 1966. Bar: Mass. 1967. Assoc. Ropes & Gray, Boston, 1967-76, ptnr., 1976—; lectr. Boston U. Sch. of Law, Boston, 1985—. Contbr. chpts. to books, articles to profl. jours. Bd. dirs., pres. Greater Boston Youth Symphony Orch., Boston, 1978—; bd. dirs., v.p. The Keewaydin Found., Salisbury, Vt., 1980—; bd. dirs., past treas. Project STEP, Boston, 1987-95; overseer, chair facilities com. New Eng. Conservatory, Boston, 1989-95. Fulbright scholar U. Madrid, 1966-67. Mem. ABA, Eastern Yacht Club (sec. 1977-83), N.Y. Yacht Club, Essex County Club, Order of Coif. Home: 35 Harbor Ave Marblehead MA 01945-3636 Office: Ropes & Gray One Internat Pl Boston MA 02110-2624

SMITH, PHILIP LUTHER, molecular geneticist; b. Milan, Ind., Dec. 23, 1956; s. Donald Walter and Evelyn Emma (Vornheder) S.; m. Mary Ann Radike, Feb. 9, 1985; children: Martha Jesse, Philip Benjamin. BS, Purdue U., 1980. Rsch. asst. U. Cin. Coll. of Medicine, Cin., 1981-84; sr. phys. biochemist Med. Coll. of Ohio, Toledo, 1985-89; sr. rsch. molecular geneticist Marion Merrell Dow Rsch. Inst./Hoechst Marion Roussel Inc., Cin., 1990-95; patent info. scientist Hoechst Marion Roussel, Cin., 1996—. Contbr. articles to profl. jours. Mem. AAAS, Am. Radio Amateur Satellite Corp., Am. Chem. Soc., The Prot. Soc., Am. Radio Relay League, Purdue U. Alumni Assn. (life). Roman Catholic. Achievements include rsch. in synthesis, purification and characterization of DNA/RNA oligonucleotides, peptides, proteins and synthetic compounds with a pharmaceutical significance; rsch. in protein chemistry with an emphasis on protein structure and function. Avocations: amateur radio, electronics, volunteer teaching.

SMITH, PHILIP MEEK, science policy consultant, writer; b. Springfield, Ohio, May 18, 1932; s. Clarenc Mitchell S. and Lois Ellen (Meek) Dudley. B.S., Ohio State U., 1954, M.A., 1955; DSc (hon.), N.C. State U.,

1986. Mem. staff U.S. Nat. Com. for Internat. Geophys. Yr., Nat. Acad. Scis., 1957-58; program dir. NSF, 1958-63, dir. ops. U.S. Antarctic Research program, 1964-69, dep. head div. polar programs, 1970-73; chief gen. sci. br. Office Mgmt. and Budget Exec. Office of Pres., 1973-74; exec. asst. to dir. and sci. advisor to pres. NSF, 1974-76; exec. sec. Pres.'s Com. Nat. Medal of Sci., 1974-76; assoc. dir. Office Sci. and Tech. Policy, Exec. Office of Pres., 1976-81; spl. asst. to chmn. Nat. Sci. Bd., 1981; exec. officer NRC-Nat. Acad. Scis., Washington, 1981-94; corp. mem. Woods Hole Oceanographic Instn., 1983-89; pres. Cave Research Found., Yellow Springs, Ohio, 1957-63; chmn. tech. panels Fed. Coordinating Council Sci. and Enging. and Tech., 1976-80; ptnr. McGeary and Smith, Washington, 1995—; bd. Aurora Flight Scis. Corp.; mem. adv. consulting bd. Geophys. Inst., U. Ala., 1994—. Author: (with others) Defrosting Antarctic Secrets, 1962; The Frozen Future, a Prophetic Report from Antarctica, 1973; contbr. numerous articles to profl. jours. Bd. dirs. Washington Project for Arts, 1983-84, Washington Sculptors Group, 1983-84. 1st lt. U.S. Army, 1955-57. Decorated Commendation medal and Antarctic Service medal U.S. Navy, 1957; recipient Meritorious Service medal NSF, 1972. Mem. AAAS, Antarctican Soc., Cosmos Club (Washington), Am. Alpine Club (N.Y.C.), Coun. Excellence Govt. (prin.). Office: McGeary and Smith 464 M St SW Washington DC 20024-2609

SMITH, PHILIP WAYNE, writer, communications company executive; b. Fayetteville, Tenn., Sept. 2, 1945; s. Clyde Wilson and Chastain (Finch) S.; m. Susan Jones, June 22, 1968; 1 child, Alan Wayne. Student, U. So. Miss., 1963-64, Athens Coll., 1964-65, 69-70. Reporter The Huntsville (Ala.) Times, 1964-66, The Elk Valley Times, Fayetteville, 1969-70; edn. reporter The Huntsville Times, 1970-71; Washington corr. The Huntsville Times, Washington, 1971-76; White House corr. Newhouse News Svc., Washington, 1977-80, Pentagon corr., 1981-84; writer Huntsville, 1984—; pres. P.S. Comms., Huntsville, 1994—; pub. rels. cons. Teledyne Brown Enging., Huntsville, 1984—; safety film producer VECO, Inc., Prudhoe Bay, Alaska, 1991. Co-author: Protecting the President, 1985 (Lit. Guild alt. selection 1986); screenwriter Our Land Too, 1987, Chemicals in War, 1989, Security: Everyone's Job, 1990, Face to Face Prospecting, 1992, Investigating Child Abuse, 1992, Lead Generation, 1993, Telephone Prospecting, 1993, Delayed Enlistment Program Management, 1993, Recruiter Sales Presentation, 1994, Duties and Responsibilities of Recruiting Station Commanders, 1994, Training Future Leaders, 1994, Rehabilitative Training Instructor Program, 1994, U.S. Army Program Executive Office for Tactical Missiles, 1995, Training: The Army Advantage, 1995, National Environmental Policy Act Compliance, 1996, Operations of the M21 RSCAAL, 1996. Sgt. USMC, 1966-69, Vietnam. Decorated Navy Achievement medal with combat V; named for Reporting Without Deadline, Ala. Press Assn., 1972, News Feature Writing, Ala. AP, 1975. Mem. Tenn. Screenwriting Assn., VFW. Democrat. Episcopalian. Avocations: tennis, swimming. Home and Office: 8007 Hickory Hill Ln SE Huntsville AL 35802-3252

SMITH, PHILLIP CARL, marine and ship pilot, rancher; b. Wewahitchka, Fla., Aug. 12, 1941; s. Ottis Benjamin and Bessie (Kemp) S.; m. Belle Melancon, Feb. 28, 1966; children: Debra Kay, Phillip Carl Jr. Diploma, Wewahitchka High Sch., 1959. Commd. radar observer, unltd. 1st class pilot lic. for Sabine Waterway and tributaries, Tex. From deckhand to capt. Sabine Towing Co., Groves, Tex., 1959-64; ship pilot, ptnr./owner Sabine Pilots, Groves, Tex., 1965—; rancher Tex., 1979—; rander, owner Red S Ranch, Kirbyville, Tex., 1979—, God's Little Acres Ranch; cons. in field, 1965—; expert witness maritime ct. cases, Beaumont, Tex. Elder LDS Ch., Port Arthur, Tex., 1973—. With U.S. Army, 1962-67. Mem. Masons (32 degree). Avocations: ranching, boating, RV travel, conservation, nature lover. Home: 324 Farm Dr Bridge City TX 77611-2723

SMITH, PHILLIP HARTLEY, steel company executive; b. Sydney, Australia, Jan. 26, 1927; came to U.S., 1950, naturalized, 1960; s. Norman Edward and Elizabeth (Williams) S.; m. Martha Frances Dittrich, June 4, 1955; children: Elizabeth, Thomas, Johanna, Alice, Margaret, Sarah. B.Enging. with 1st class honors in Mining and Metallurgy, U. Sydney, 1950; Metall. Engr., MIT, 1952; diploma indsl. rels., U. Chgo., 1958; LLD, Grove City Coll., 1975. Successively trainee, metallurgist, foreman Indiana Harbor, Ind., Inland Steel Co., 1952-55; successively trainee, metallurgist, dir. purchasing and planning La Salle Steel Co., Hammond, Ind., 1956-64; with Copperweld Corp., Pitts., 1964-77; pres. Copperweld Corp., 1967-77, chmn., 1973-77; pres., chief exec. officer Bekaert Steel Wire Corp., Pitts., 1978-82; mng. ptnr. Hartley Smith & Ptnrs., 1982-84; chmn. Smith, Yuill & Co. Inc., 1984—; bd. dirs. Mitech Labs. Inc., Salem Corp.; adj. prof. bus. Grove City Coll.; vis. dean sr. exec. program Dalian U. Tech., Peoples Republic of China. Patentee in field; editor: Mechanical Working of Steel, 1961; author: Essays in Management, A Guide to Young Managers on the Way Up. Trustee Berea (Ky.) Coll., Wheeling Jesuit U., 1978-85, Grove City Coll.; chmn. Inroads Inc.; chair Sydney U. Found. Cadet officer Australian Mcht. Marine, 1942-43, Royal Australian Fleet Aux., 1943. Recipient Nat. Steelmaking award, 1955, Outstanding Chief Exec. Officer in Steel Industry award Fin. World, 1975; Nuffield scholar, 1949; Fulbright fellow, 1950. Mem. Univ. Club of Chgo., Duquesne Club of Pitts., Fox Chapel Golf Club, Rolling Rock Club (Ligonier, Pa.), Sigma Xi. Home: 102 Haverford Rd Pittsburgh PA 15238-1620

SMITH, PHILLIPS GUY, banker; b. Orange, N.J., Sept. 15, 1946; s. Phillips Upham and Helen Ottilie (Voderberg) S.; m. Ann Dixon Schickhaus, Dec. 29, 1973; children: Guy Dixon, William Schickhaus, Louisa Upham. B in Enging., Stevens Inst. Tech., Hoboken, N.J.; MBA, U. Pa., 1975. Comml. banking rep. The Bank of N.Y., N.Y.C., 1976-78, asst. treas., 1978-79, asst. v.p., 1979-80, v.p., 1980-85, sr. v.p., 1985-93; mng. dir. N.Am. Internat. Strategy Svcs., Inc., N.Y.C., 1993—. Vestryman Ch. of The Heavenly Rest, N.Y.C., 1983-88, treas., 1985-87; trustee Tabor Acad., Marion, Mass., 1987—, treas., 1991—. Lt. USN, 1970-74, Vietnam. Mem. Racquet and Tennis Club, Down Town Assn., Rockaway Hunting Club, Nantucket Yacht Club. Episcopalian. Home: 9 E 94th St New York NY 10128-1911 Office: Internat Strategy Svcs Inc 2 Wall St New York NY 10005-2001

SMITH, PIERCE REILAND, stock brokerage, investment banking executive; b. Bangor, Maine, Oct. 5, 1943; s. Warren Reiland and Pamela Pierce (Morse) S.; m. Carol Kirsten Hynning, May 28, 1968. BS, Yale U., 1966; MBA, Stanford U., 1972. V.p. Comml. Credit Co., Balt., 1973-80, Mellon Bank, Pitts., 1980-82; sr. v.p., treas. Norwest Corp., Mpls., 1982-87; exec. v.p., treas. PaineWebber Inc., N.Y.C., 1987—. Lt. USCG, 1966-70. Avocations: boating, collecting art. Office: PaineWebber Inc 1285 Ave Of The Americas New York NY 10019-6028*

SMITH, PRESTON EARL, corporate executive; b. Canton, S.D., Dec. 17, 1944; s. Eugene Benjamin and Flavia (Ertz) S.; m. Anne Barrington; children: Janine Marie, Stephanie Ann, Flavia Ann. Buyer J.C. Penney's, Dayton, Ohio, 1966-69; with Montgomery County, Dayton, 1969-75; securities profl. GM Corp., Dayton, 1975-88; founder Buckey Radiant Barrier, Dayton, 1988-92, Quantum Internat., Pullayup, Wash., 1992-96, Tech 2000 Inc, Roswell, Ga., 1996—. Inducted into the U.S. Space Found. Hall of Fame, Colo., 1969; nominated to Nat. Space Tech. Hall of Fame NASA, 1995, One of 50 Cos. using NASA Tech. in the U.S., included in NASA Spinoff Book, 1993, 95. Mem. ASTM, Nat. Assn. Radiant Barrier Tech. (v.p., founder), Dayton Engrs. Club (Pres.'s award for excellence as outstanding new mem. 1991). Achievements include working with NASA, development of super insulation in for of Super "Q" Radiant Barrier which stops the basic law of physics, "heat seeks cool", educating about the Super "Q" Radiant Barrier technology to reduce energy consumption throughout the world. Home: 200 Spring Creek Rd Roswell GA 30075 Office: Tech 2000 Inc 200 Spring Creek Rd Roswell GA 30075

SMITH, R. GENE, health facility administrator; b. 1935. V. chmn. Vencor Inc., Louisville, 1985—. Office: Vencor Inc 3600 National City Tower 101 S 5th St Louisville KY 40202*

SMITH, R. GORDON, lawyer; b. Roanoke, Va., May 28, 1938. BA with highest honors, U. Va., 1960; LLB magna cum laude, Harvard Law Sch., 1964. Bar: Va. 1964. Law clk. to judge U.S. Ct. Appeals (5th cir.), 1964-65; ptnr. McGuire, Woods, Battle & Boothe, Richmond, Va.; exec., legislation editor Harvard Law Rev., 1963-64. Fellow Am. Bar Found.; mem. Va. Bar Assn. (pres. 1987-88), Am. Law Inst., Phi Beta Kappa, Omicron Delta Kappa. Office: McGuire Woods 1 James River Plz Richmond VA 23219-3229

SMITH, R. JEFFERY, grain company executive; b. 1950. BA, Boston Coll., 1972; MBA, Cornell U., 1974. Various trading and mgmt. positions Continental Grain, N.Y.C., 1974-87; v.p. trading Ctrl. Soya Co., Ferruzzi Group, Ft. Wayne, Ind., 1987—; pres., COO Ferruzzi Trading USA, Inc., N.Y.C., 1990—. Office: Ferruzzi Trading USA Inc 1114 Avenue Of The Americas New York NY 10036-7703*

SMITH, RALPH ALEXANDER, cultural and educational policy educator; b. Ellwood City, Pa., June 12, 1929; s. J.V. and B. V. S.; m. Christiana M. Kolbe, Nov. 16, 1955. A.B., Columbia Coll., 1954; M.A., Teachers Coll., Columbia U., 1959, Ed.D., 1962. Faculty, art history and arts edn. Kent (Ohio) State U., 1959-61, Wis. State U., Oshkosh, 1961-63, SUNY, New Paltz, 1963-64; faculty edn. and art edn. U. Ill., Urbana-Champaign, 1964—; also prof. cultural and ednl. policy & aesthetic edn. U. Ill.; first Italo DeFrancesca Meml. lectr. Kutztown State U., 1974, Leon Jackman Meml. lectr., Perth, Australia, 1985, Dean's lectr. Coll. Fine Arts and Comm., Brigham Young U., 1985, Dunbar lectr. Millsaps Coll., 1993; disting. vis. prof. Ohio State U., 1987; sr. scholar Coll. Edn. U. Ill., 1991. Author: (with Albert William Levi) Art Education: A Critical Necessity, 1991; founder, editor Jour. Aesthetic Edn., 1966—; editor: Aesthetics and Criticism in Art Education, 1966, Aesthetic Concepts and Education, 1970, Aesthetics and Problems of Education, 1971, Regaining Educational Leadership, 1975, Cultural Literacy and Arts Education, 1991; co-author: Research in the Arts and Aesthetic Education: A Directory of Investigators and Their Fields of Inquiry, 1978, Excellence in Art Education: Ideas and Initiatives, 1987; editor: Discipline-Based Art Education, 1989, The Sense of Art: A Study in Aesthetic Education, 1989, (with Alan Simpson) Aesthetics and Arts Education, 1991, (with Bennett Reimer) The Arts, Education and Aesthetic Knowing, 1992, (with Ronald Berman) Public Policy and the Aesthetic Interest, 1992, General Knowledge and Arts Education, 1994, Excellence II: The Continuing Quest Art Education, 1995. Bd. govs. Inst. Study of Art in Edn.; trustee Nat. Ctr. Study of Art in Edn. With Med. Svc., U.S. Army, 1954-57. Recipient spl. merit recognition Coll. Edn., U. Ill., 1975, Disting. lectr. Studies in Art Edn. award, 1991. Fellow Nat. Art Edn. Assn. (Disting., Manuel Barkan Meml. award 1973); mem. Coun. Policy Studies in Art Edn. (first exec. sec. 1978-82), Ill. Art Edn. Assn. (Disting.). Home: 2909 Heathwood Ct Champaign IL 61821-7659 Office: U Ill 361 Education 1310 S 6th St Champaign IL 61820-6925

SMITH, RALPH LEE, author, musician; b. Phila., Nov. 6, 1927; s. Hugh Harold and Barbara (Schatkin) S.; m. Betty H. Smith, Sept. 1954 (div. Jan. 1963); children: David Bruce, Robert Hugh; m. Mary Louise Hollowell, 1971 (div. 1977); m. Shizuko Maruyama, 1977; 1 child, Lisa Koyuki. BA, Swarthmore Coll., 1951; MEd, U. Va., 1987. Editor Nat. Better Business Bur., N.Y.C., 1954-58; free-lance writer, 1958-73; assoc. prof. Sch. Communications Howard U., 1973-76; telecommunications exec. and cons., 1976-86. Pub. info. dir. Nat. Assn. Home Bldrs. Rsch. Ctr.; folk musician on Appalachian dulcimer; recs. include Dulcimer: Old Time and Traditional Music, 1973, Tunes of the Blue Ridge and Great Smoky Mountains, 1983; author: The Health Hucksters, 1960, At Your Own Risk, 1969, The Wired Nation, 1970, The Story of the Dulcimer, 1986, Smart House: The Coming Revolution in Housing, 1987. Recipient Russell L. Cecil Disting. Med. Writing award Arthritis Found., 1963;,AMA Jour. award, 1965, Nat. Mag. award Columbia U. Grad. Sch. Journalism, 1971, Bus. and Fin. Journalism award U. Mo., 1971; Nelson Poynter fellow in journalism and comms. Yale U., 1972. Home: 1662 Chimney House Rd Reston VA 22090-4302 Office: 400 Prince Georges Blvd Upper Marlboro MD 20772-8731

SMITH, RALPH WESLEY, JR., federal judge; b. Ghent, N.Y., July 16, 1936; s. Ralph Wesley and Kathleen S. (Callahan) S.; m. Nancy Ann Fetzer, Dec. 30, 1961 (div. 1981); children: Mark Owen, Tara Denise, Todd Kendall; m. Barbara Anne Milian, Nov. 8, 1982; stepchildren: Kim Highter, Jeffrey Highter, Eric Highter. Student, Sorbonne, U. Paris, Paris, 1954-55; BA, Yale U., 1956; LLB, Albany Law Sch., 1966. Bar: N.Y. 1966, U.S. Dist. Ct. (no. dist.) N.Y. 1966. Assoc. Hinman, Straub Law Firm, Albany, N.Y., 1966-69; chief asst. dist. atty. Albany County, N.Y., 1969-73, dist. atty., 1974; regional dir. state nursing home investigation Asst. Atty. Gen., Albany, 1975-77; dir. State Organized Crime Task Force, 1978-82; U.S. magistrate judge U.S. Dist. Ct. (no. dist.) N.Y., Albany, 1982—; judge moot ct. Albany Law Sch., 1983—; lectr. N.Y. State Bar Assn., 1985—. Capt. USNR, 1957-82. Mem. Fed. Magistrate Judges Assn., Columbia County Bar Assn., Columbia County Magistrates Assn. Republican. Roman Catholic. Avocations: fishing, bicycling, skiing, sailing, camping. Home: 2375 Route 66 Chatham NY 12037-9717 Office: US Dist Ct 445 Broadway Rm 314 Albany NY 12207-2928

SMITH, RANDY P., metal products executive; b. 1949. MBA, U. Toledo, 1972. CFO, v.p. Automatic Switch Co., Florham Park, N.J., 1993-95; pres. Automatic Switch Co., 1995—. Office: Automatic Switch Co 50-60 Hanover Rd Florham Park NJ 07932-1503*

SMITH, RAY E., church officer; b. Mar. 29, 1932; m. Helen N. Smith; children: Danene, Stephen. Grad., Open Bible Coll., 1953; postgrad., Ea. Mont. U. Lic. Open Bible Standard Chs., 1953, ordained, 1955. Pioneer pastor Open Bible Standard Chs., Billings, Mont., 1953-59; pastor Open Bible Standard Chs., Rapid City, S.D., 1959-67; supt. S.D. dist. Open Bible Standard Chs., 1959-63, supt. Mountain Plains region, 1963-67, pres., 1967-76, 79—, mem. nat. bd. dirs., 1959—; pastor Lighthouse Temple, Eugene, Oreg., 1976-79. Bd. adminstrs. Pentecostal Fellowship N.Am., 1967—; 1st vice chmn. Pentecostal Fellowship of N.Am.; founding dir. Citizens for Better TV, 1975, Coun. for Nat. Righteousness, 1975. Mem. Nat. Assn. Evangelicals (mem. bd. adminstrn. 1967—). Office: Open Bible Standard Chs Inc 2020 Bell Ave Des Moines IA 50315-1096

SMITH, RAYMOND, dancer; b. Edinburgh, Scotland. Grad., Nat. Ballet Sch. Corps de ballet Nat. Ballet Can., 1975-78, 2d soloist, 1978-80, prin. dancer, 1980—; guest artist, Scottish Ballet, Edinburgh, 1983; prin. dancer London Festival Ballet. Appeared in Mad Shadows, 1977, The Sleeping Beauty, 1978, 80-81, Swan Lake, 1978, 83, The Nutcracker, 1978, Les Sylphide, 1978, 80, 81-82, Romeo and Juliet, 1978, La Fille Mal Gardee, 1980-81, Etudes, 1980-81, Song of a Wayfarer, 1980-81, Giselle, 1981-82, Napoli, 1981-82, Don Quixote, 1982, Liebestod, 1982, Sphinx, 1983, Here We Come, 1983, Sylvia, 1983, Onegin, 1984; choreographer roles in Newcomers, 1980, All Night Wonder, 1981, Portrait of Love and Death, 1982, Components, 1984; created roles in works by Patsalas, Kudelka, McFall, Tetley, Forsythe, Alleyne, and Bennathan. Office: National Ballet of Canada, 157 King St E, Toronto, ON Canada M5C 1G9

SMITH, RAYMOND LLOYD, former university president, consultant; b. Vanceboro, Maine, Jan. 25, 1917; s. Ivan and Genevieve (Gatcomb) S.; m. Beatrice Bennett, Dec. 4, 1943; children: Bennett Charles, Martin Lloyd. B.S. cum laude, U. Alaska, 1943; M.S. in Metall. Enging, U. Pa., 1951, Ph.D. in Metall. Enging, 1953; D.Sc. (hon.), Western Mich. U.; LL.D., No. Mich. U.; D.Eng. (hon.), Mich. Technol. U., S.D. Sch. Mines and Tech. Instr. math. U. Alaska, 1946-47, asst. prof. metallurgy, 1948-49; rsch. assoc. dept. metallurgy U. Pa., 1949-53; sr. rsch. metallurgist Franklin Inst. Labs., Phila., 1953; sect. chief metallurgy Franklin Inst. Labs., 1954-56, assoc. dir., 1957, tech. dir., 1958-59; prof., head metall. dept. Mich. Technol. U., Houghton, 1959-64, coord. rsch., 1960-64, pres., 1965-79; pres. Am. Soc. Metals, 1979-80, Houghton (Mich.) Daily Mining Gazette, 1979-81, R. L. Smith, Inc.; Am. Soc. Metals/The Metallurgical Soc. joint disting. lectr. in materials, 1983; mem. indsl. adv. bd. mining enging. dept. Mich. Tech. U.; bd. dirs. Lake Superior & Ishpeming R.R. Contbr. numerous articles to metall. sci. jours.; patentee in field. Bd. dirs. Community Water Co., Green Valley. With AUS, 1943-46. Recipient Distinguished Alumnus award U. Alaska, Clair M. Donovan award Mich. Tech. U., D. Robert Yarnall award U. Pa. Enging. Sch.; Outstanding Service award Air Force ROTC; Rotary Paul Harris fellow. Fellow Metall. Soc., AIME (Henry Krumb meml. lectr. 1981), Am. Soc. for Metals (hon.). mem. Internat. Exec. Svc. Corps., Scabbard and Blade, Blue Key, Tau Beta Pi, Alpha Sigma Mu (hon. lectr. 1982), Alpha Phi Omega, Phi Kappa Phi, Theta Tau. Home: PO Box 726 Green Valley AZ 85622-0726 *A sense of humor is one of the important building blocks for that firm sense of balance so necessary to meet the challenges of life. It's like the seasoning of a chef's masterpiece.*

SMITH, RAYMOND THOMAS, anthropology educator; b. Oldham, Lancashire, Eng., Jan. 12, 1925; s. Harry and Margaret (Mulchrone) S.; m. Flora Alexandrina Tong, June 30, 1954; children: Fenela, Colin, Anthony. B.A., Cambridge (Eng.) U., 1950, M.A., 1951, Ph.D., 1954. Sociol. research officer govt. Brit. Guiana, 1951-54; research fellow U. W.I., 1954-59; prof. sociology U. Ghana, 1959-62; sr. lectr. sociology, prof. anthropology U. West Indies, 1962-66; prof. anthropology U. Chgo., 1966-95, prof. emeritus, 1995—, chmn. dept. anthropology, 1975-81, 84-85, 94-95; vis. prof. U. Calif. - Berkeley, 1957-58, McGill U., Montreal, 1964-65; mem. com. on child devel. research and public policy NRC, 1977-80; dir. Caribbean Consortium Grad. Sch., 1985-86. Author: The Negro Family in British Guiana, 1956, British Guiana, 1962, 2d edit., 1980, Kinship and Class In The West Indies, 1988, The Matrifocal Family, 1996; co-author: Class Differences in American Kinship, 1978; editor: Kinship Ideology and Practice in Latin America, 1984; contbr. articles to profl. jours. Co-investigator urban family life project U. Chgo., 1986-90. Served with RAF, 1943-48. Guggenheim fellow, 1983-84. Fellow Am. Anthrop. Assn.; mem. Assn. Social Anthropologists. Office: Univ Chicago Dept Anthropology 1126 E 59th St Chicago IL 60637-1580

SMITH, RAYMOND VICTOR, paper products manufacturing executive; b. Vancouver, B.C., Can., Apr. 28, 1926; s. Stanley Victor and Kathryn Stewart (Hunter) S.; m. Marilyn Joyce Meldrum, Oct. 17, 1947; children—Vicki, Kathi, Stan. Student, U. B.C., Banff Sch. Advanced Mgmt.; student Advanced Mgmt. Program, Harvard U. Trumpeter Dal Richards Band, 1942; ptnr. Warren McCuish Mens' Clothiers, 1947; sales rep. Vancouver Paper Box, 1949-54; with Home Oil Distbrs., 1954-57; domestic rep. kraft paper and board sales MacMillan Bloedel Ltd., 1957-67; asst. mgr. Kraft Paper & Board Sales, 1961-65; newsprint rep. Powell River-Alberni Sales Corp., Pasadena, Calif., 1965-67; mgr. Powell River-Alberni Sales Corp., Pasadena, 1967-68; mgr. supply control and sales adminstrn. MacMillan Bloedel Ltd., Vancouver, 1968-70, gen. mgr., 1970-71, v.p. mktg. paper and pulp, 1971-73, v.p., gen. mgr. newsprint, 1973-77, group v.p. pulp and paper, 1977-79, sr. v.p. pulp and paper, 1979-80, chief oper. officer, 1980-83, pres., 1980-90, chief exec. officer, 1983-90, chmn. bd., 1991—; bd. dirs. Can. Imperial Bank of Commerce. Served with Can. Army, 1944. Clubs: Capilano Golf and Country, Vancouver. Avocations: music, golf. Office: MacMillan Bloedel Ltd, 925 W Georgia St, Vancouver, BC Canada V6C 3L2

SMITH, RAYMOND W., telecommunications company executive; b. Pitts., 1937. B.S., Carnegie-Mellon U., 1959; M.B.A., U. Pitts., 1967. Dir. budget planning and analysis comptroller dept. AT&T, 1976-77; with Bell of Pa., Phila., 1959-75, 77-85, div. ops. mgr. Western area, 1971-74; asst. v.p. pub. relations Bell of Pa. and Diamond State Telephone, Phila., 1974-75; v.p., gen. mgr. Eastern region Bell of Pa. and Diamond State Tel., Phila., 1977-81, v.p.-regulatory, 1981-83, pres., chief exec. officer, 1983-85; vice chmn., chief fin. officer, dir. parent co. Bell Atlantic Corp., Phila., 1985-88; pres., chief oper. officer Bell Atlantic Corp., 1988; chmn., chief exec. officer Bell Atlantic Corp., Phila., 1989—; bd. dirs. USAir Group, Core States Fin. Corp.; mem. Bus. Roundtable, 1990—; mem. nat. adv. bd. Pvt. Sector Coun., 1990—; mem. James Madison nat. coun. Libr. of Congress, 1990—. Pub. playwright. Vice chmn. Phila. blood donor campaign ARC; mem. bd. advisors Arden Theatre Co., 1991—. With Signal Corps, U.S. Army, 1959-60. Office: Bell Atlantic Corp 1717 Arch St Philadelphia PA 19103-2713

SMITH, REBECCA BEACH, federal judge; b. 1949. BA, Coll. William and Mary, 1971; postgrad., U. Va., 1971-73; JD, Coll. William and Mary, 1979. Assoc. Wilcox & Savage, 1980-85; U.S. magistrate Ea. Dist. Va., 1985-89; dist. judge U.S. Dist. Ct. (ea. dist.) Va., Norfolk, 1989—; exec. editor Law Review, 1978-79. Active Chrysler Mus. Norfolk, Jean Outland Chrysler Libr. Assocs., Va. Opera Assn., Friends of the Zoo, Friends of Norfolk Pub. Libr., Ch. of the Good Shepherd. John Marshall Soc. fellow; recipient Acad. Achievement and Leadership award St. George Tucker Soc.; named one of Outstanding Women of Am., 1979. Mem. ABA, Va. State Bar Assn., Fed. Bar Assn. Supreme Ct. Hist. Soc., Fourth Cir. Judicial Conf., The Harbor Club, Order of Coif., Phi Beta Kappa. Office: US Dist Ct US Courthouse 600 Granby St Ste 358 Norfolk VA 23510-1915*

SMITH, REBECCA JANE, nursing administrator; b. Connersville, Ind., Apr. 4, 1959; d. John Franklin and Catherine Lavon (O'Hara) Caldwell; m. William Roscoe Smith, Aug. 9, 1990; 1 child, Bryon Steven Caldwell. Assocs., Ivy Tech. (Ind. Vocat. Coll.), 1989; postgrad., Ind. U. East, Richmond, 1994—. RN, Ind., LPN, Ind. Nurse on call Kare Ambulance, Cambridge City, Ind., 1984-94; dir. nursing svcs. Landmark Group Home Svcs., Connersville, Ind., 1989-93; asst. DON Lincoln Lodge Nursing Ctr., Connersville, 1989-90, DON, 1990—; mem. Alzheimer's adv. bd. Lincoln Lodge Nursing Ctr., Connersville, 1990—; mem. adv. bd. Connersville Area Vocat. Sch., 1989—, sec. adv. bd., 1991-92, 92-93, 93-94; mem. corp. policy com. Transitional Health Svcs., Louisville, 1994; rschr. Alzheimer's disease George Washington U., 1990—. Bd. dirs. Ind. State Police Alliance, 1988—; active Humor Project, N.Y.C., 1986—, Nat. Arbor Found., Ind. Sheriff's Assn., 1989—, Wayne County Sheriff's Assn., 1988—. Mem. Ind. Nurses Assn., Local DON Club (pres., founder local chpt. 1993—), Continuity of Care Assn. (regional chpt.), Fraternal Order of Police (gold mem.), Local Registered Nurses Club (ways and means com. 1989—). Home: PO Box 517 Milton IN 47357-0517 Office: Lincoln Lodge Health Care 1039 E 5th St Connersville IN 47331-3301

SMITH, REBECCA MCCULLOCH, human relations educator; b. Greensboro, N.C., Feb. 29, 1928; d. David Martin and Virginia Pearl (Woodburn) McCulloch; m. George Clarence Smith Jr., Mar. 30, 1945; 1 child, John Randolph. BS, Woman's Coll., U. N.C., 1947, MS, 1952; PhD, U. N.C., Greensboro, 1967; postgrad., Harvard U., 1989. Tchr. pub. schs., N.C. and S.C., 1947-57; instr. U. N.C., Greensboro, 1958-66, asst. prof. to prof. emeritus human devel. and family studies, 1967-91, adj. prof. emeritus, 1991-94, dir. grad. program, 1975-82; adj. prof. ednl. cons. depts. edn. N.C., S.C., Ind., Ont., Man.; vis. prof. N.W. La. State U., 1965, 67, U. Wash., 1970, Hood Coll., 1976, 86. Named Outstanding Alumna Sch. Home Econs., 1976; recipient Sperry award for service to families N.C. Family Life Coun., 1979. Mem. Nat. Coun. Family Rels. (exec. com. 1974-76, treas. 1987-89, Osborne award 1973), U. N.C. at Greensboro Alumni Assn. (chair membership recruitment com. 1994—). Author: Teaching About Family Relationships, 1975, Klemer's Marriage and Family Relationships, 2d edit., 1975, Resources for Teaching About Family Life Education, 1976, Family Matters: Concepts in Marriage and Personal Relationships, 1982; co-author: History of the School of Human Environmental Sciences: 1892-1992, 1992, assoc. editor Family Relations (Jour. Applied Family and Child Studies), 1980-90; ednl. cons. Current Life Studies, 1977-84. Home: 1212 Ritters Lake Rd Greensboro NC 27406-7816 Office: U NC Dept Human Devel Sch Human Environ Scis Greensboro NC 27412

SMITH, REGINALD BRIAN FURNESS, anesthesiologist, educator; b. Warrington, Eng., Feb. 7, 1931; s. Reginald and Betty (Bell) S.; m. Margarete Groppe, July 18, 1963; children—Corinne, Malcolm. M.B., B.S., U. London, 1955; D.T.M. and H., Liverpool Sch. Tropical Medicine, 1959. Intern Poole Gen. Hosp., Dorset, Eng., 1955-56, Wilson Meml. Hosp., Johnson City, N.Y., 1962-63; resident in anesthesiology Med. Coll. Va., Richmond, 1963-64; resident in anesthesiology U. Pitts., 1964-65, clin. instr., 1965-66; asst. prof., 1969-71, asso. clin. prof., 1971-74, prof., 1974-78, acting chmn. dept. anesthesiology, 1977-78; prof., chmn. dept. U. Tex. Health Sci. Center, San Antonio, 1978—; anesthesiologist in chief hosps. U. Tex. Health Sci. Ctr., 1978—, med. dir. hyperbaric medicine unit Univ. Hosp., 1993—; dir. anesthesiology Eye and Ear Hosp., Pitts., 1971-76; Univ. Hosp.; anesthesiologist in chief Presbyn. Univ. Hosp., Pitts., 1976-78. Contbg. editor: Internat. Ophthalmology Clinics, 1973, Internat. Anesthesiology Clinics, 1983; contbr. articles to profl. jours. Served to capt. Brit. Army, 1957-59. Fellow ACP, Am. Coll. Anesthesiologists, Am. Coll. Chest Physicians; mem. AMA, Internat. Anesthesia Rsch. Soc., Am. Coll. Hyperbaric Physicians, Am. Soc. Anesthesiologists (pres. Western Pa. 1974-75), Tex. Soc. Anesthesiologists, San Antonio Soc. Anesthesiologists (pres. 1990), Tex. Med. Assn., Bexar County Med. Soc. Home: 213 Canada Verde St San Antonio TX 78232-1104 Office: 7703 Floyd Curl Dr San Antonio TX 78284-6200

SMITH, REX WILLIAM, journalist; b. Danville, Ill., Oct. 19, 1952; s. Ralph William and Lillian Grace (Hart) S.; m. Marion Roach, July 15, 1989. BA cum laude, Trinity U., San Antonio, 1974; MS with highest honors, Columbia U., N.Y.C., 1980. Mng. editor Rensselaer (Ind.) Republican newspaper, 1974-75; legis. asst. U.S. Rep. Floyd J. Fithian, Washington, 1975-79; reporter, spl. writer Newsday, L.I., N.Y., 1980-87, chief Albany (N.Y.) bur., 1987-91; editor The Record, Troy, N.Y., 1991-95; mng. editor Times Union, Albany, N.Y., 1995—. Contbr. numerous articles to newspapers and mags. Recipient Community Svc. award Rensselaer C. of C., 1975, Media award World Hunger Fund, 1983, Disting. Svc. medal Soc. Profl. Journalists, 1987, Editorial award Common Cause, 1992, award for disting. community svc. N.Y. State Pubs. Assn., 1994; Rotary fellow, 1979, Pulitzer Travel fellow Columbia U., 1982. Presbyterian. Home: Fox Hollow Lodge Dill Brook Rd Petersburgh NY 12138 Office: Times Union Box 15000 Albany NY 12212

SMITH, RICHARD A., physician, educator; b. Norwalk, Conn., Oct. 13, 1932. BS, Howard U., 1953, MD, 1957; MPH, Columbia U., 1960. Diplomat Am. Bd. Preventive Medicine. Intern USPHS Hosp., Seattle, 1957-58; resident L.A. City Health Dept., 1958-59; epidemiologist Wash. State Health Dept., 1960-61; sr. physician Peace Corps, Lagos, Nigeria, 1961-63; asst. prof. dept. preventive medicine Howard U., Washington, 1963-68; assoc. prof., dir. Medex program Sch. Pub. Health and Cmty. Medicine U. Wash., 1968-72; dir. Medex group John A. Burns Sch. Medicine, U. Hawaii, Honolulu, 1972—; Africa regional med. officer med. program divsn. Peace Corps., 1963-64, dep. dir., 1964-65; exec. mgmt. trainee Office Surgeon Gen., 1965-66, spl. asst. dir. Office Internat. Health, 1966, chief Office Planning, 1967, dep. dir. Office Internat. Health, 1967-68; clin. asst. prof. dept. cmty. and internat. health Sch. Medicine Georgetown U., Washington, 1967-68; advisor, U.S. del. WHO, 1967, 70; mem. Internat. Task Force World Health Manpower, 1970, cons., 1977—; adj. prof. family practice and cmty. health U. Hawaii, Honolulu, 1972—; mem. Nat. Adv. Allied Health Profl. Coun., NIH, 1971; bd. dirs. Am. Inst. Rsch. Fellow Am. Coll. Preventive Medicine; mem. Inst. Medicine-NAS, APHA, Am. Soc. Tropical Medicine and Hygiene. *

SMITH, RICHARD ALAN, publishing and speciality retailing executive; b. Boston, 1924; married. BS, Harvard U., 1946; LLD (hon.), Boston Coll., 1988. With Smith Mgmt. Co., 1947-61; chmn. bd., CEO, Gen. Cinema Corp. (name changed to Harcourt Gen., Inc. 1993), Chestnut Hill, Mass., 1961-91, Neiman Marcus Group, Chestnut Hill, Mass., 1987—; chmn. Harcourt Gen., Inc., Chestnut Hill, 1993—; chmn., CEO, pres. GC Cos., Inc., Chestnut Hill, 1993—; bd. dirs. Liberty Mut. Ins. Co., 1st Nat. Bank of Boston Corp. Office: Harcourt Gen Inc 27 Boylston St Chestnut Hill MA 02167-1719*

SMITH, RICHARD BOWEN, retired national park superintendent; b. Grandville, Mich., Mar. 8, 1938; s. William Jr. and Mary Elizabeth (Bowen) S.; m. Katherine Theresa Short, Sept. 21, 1980. BA in History, Albion Coll., 1960; MA in English, Mich. State U., 1967. Tchr. Grand Rapids (Mich.) Jr. H.S., 1960-66; vol. Peace Corps, Asuncion, Paraguay, 1968-70; ranger Nat. Pk. Svc., Yosemite, Calif., 1971-76; ranger. instr. Nat. Pk. Svc., Grand Canyon, Ariz., 1976-78; ranger, legis. specialist Nat. Pk. Svc., Washington, 1978-80; asst. supt. Nat. Pk. Svc., Everglades, Fla., 1980-83; assoc. regional dir. ops. Nat. Pk. Svc., Phila., 1984-86; supt. Nat. Pk. Svc., Carlsbad Caverns, N.Mex., 1986-88; assoc. regional dir. ops. Nat. Pk. Svc., Santa Fe, 1988-89; assoc. regional dir. resources mgmt. Nat. Park Service, Santa Fe, 1990-94; cons. on protected area mgmt. in L.Am., 1994—; temp. supt. Yellowstone Nat. Pk., 1994—; owner R & K Internat., 1994—. Recipient Meritorious Svc. award Dept. of Interior, 1992. Home: 2 Roadrunner Trl Placitas NM 87043-9424

SMITH, RICHARD C., JR., state agency administrator. Chmn. Ark. State Bd. Edn., Little Rock, 1995—. Office: Bd Edn Office of Chmn Bldg 4 Capitol Mall Little Rock AR 72201-1071

SMITH, RICHARD EMERSON (DICK SMITH), make-up artist; b. Larchmont, N.Y., June 26, 1922; s. Richard Roy and Coral (Brown) S.; m. Jocelyn De Rosa, Jan. 10, 1949; children: Douglas Todd, David Emerson. BA, Yale U., 1944. Pioneer dir. first TV make-up dept. NBC-TV, N.Y.C., 1945-59; make-up dir. David Susskind Prodns., N.Y.C., 1959-61; freelance make-up artist, cons., 1961—; cons., lectr. Yoyogi Animation Sch., Tokyo, 1992—. Credits include Requiem for a Heavyweight, 1962, The World of Henry Orient, 1963, Mark Twain, Tonight!, 1967 (Emmy award 1967), Midnight Cowboy, 1968, Little Big Man, 1969, The Godfather, 1971, The Exorcist, 1973, The Godfather, Part II, 1974, The Sunshine Boys, 1975, Taxi Driver, 1975, Altered States, 1979, Scanners, 1980, Ghost Story, 1981, The Hunger, 1982, Amadeus, 1983 (U.S. Acad. award 1984, Brit. Acad. award 1985), Starman, 1984, Poltergeist III, 1987, Everybody's All-American, 1988, Sweet Home (Japanese film), 1988, Dad, 1989, Death Becomes Her, 1991, Forever Young, 1992; author: The Advanced Professional Make-Up Techniques.

SMITH, RICHARD ERNEST, retired insurance company executive; b. Adrian, Mich., Oct. 29, 1935; s. Albert Forrest and Thelma (Brock) S.; m. Joanne Piplow, Oct. 11, 1955; children: Kathryn, Albert, Sharon, Richard, Heidi. Student, Spring Arbor Coll., 1955. CLU. Mgr. White Hardware, Adrian, 1950-59; dist. mgr. Met. Life, Adrian and Lafayette, Ind., 1959-75; dir. regional Ohio Nat. Life, Cin., 1975-78; agy. v.p. Provident Life, Bismarck, N.D., 1978-86, pres., 1986-90; bd. dirs. Provident Life Ins. Co. Commr. City of Adrian, 1966-71; trustee Medctr. One, Bismarck, 1986—, Bismarck State Coll. Found., 1987-91; bd. dirs. Macinac Straits Hosp., St. Ignace, Mich., 1995—, Bismarck Devel. Assn., 1987-91, Greater Adrian Devel. Assn., 1966-70. Republican. Club: Apple Creek Country (Bismarck). Lodge: Elks. Avocation: travel. Home: N 5072 Epoufette Bay Rd Naubinway MI 49762-9722 Office: Provident Life Ins Co 316 N 5th St Bismarck ND 58501-4030

SMITH, RICHARD GRANT, retired telecommunications executive, electrical engineer; b. Flint, Mich., Jan. 19, 1937; s. Grand Ladd and Pauline Lorain (Lott) S.; m. Carol Ann Treanor, Apr. 18, 1965; children: Scott, Holly, Heather. BSEE, Stanford U., 1958, MSEE, 1959, PhDEE, 1963. Mem. tech. staff Bell Labs., Murray Hill, N.J., 1963-68, supr., 1968-82, dept. head, 1982-87; dir. AT&T Bell Labs., Breinigsville, 1987-93; ret., 1993; ind. cons., 1993—; chmn. CLEOS, 1980. Contbr. chpts. in books. Vice chmn. Bernards Twp. Parks and Recreation, 1976-78. Fellow IEEE (Centennial award 1984), OSA; mem. Phi Beta Kappa, Tau Beta Pi, Theta Delta Chi.

SMITH, RICHARD HOWARD, banker; b. Tulare, Calif., Aug. 27, 1927; s. Howard Charles and Sue Elizabeth (Cheyne) S.; B.A., Principia Coll, 1958; LL.B., LaSalle U., 1975; postgrad. Sch. Banking U. Wash., 1970-72; m. Patricia Ann Howery, Mar. 12, 1950; children—Jeffrey Howard, Holly Lee, Gregory Scott, Deborah Elaine. Prin., Aurora Elementary Sch., Tulare, 1951-53; prin. Desert Sun Sch., Idyllwild, Calif., 1953-55; trust adminstr. trainee Bank of Am., San Diego, 1955-58, asst. trust officer, Ventura, Redlands, Riverside and L.A., 1958-65; asst. trust officer Security Pacific Bank, Fresno, Calif., 1965-68; trust officer, 1968-72, v.p., mgr., 1972-88, Pasadena, 1988—; instr. San Bernardino Valley Coll., 1962—, Fresno City Coll., 1977—. With USN, 1945-46. Mem. Pasadena Bar Assn. Home: 3222 W Dovewood Ln Fresno CA 93711-2125*

SMITH, RICHARD JACKSON, elementary education educator, parental involvement coordinator; b. Mt. Airy, N.C., Feb. 17, 1947; s. Robert Wayne and Ruth (Jackson) S.; m. Sue Monday, Sept. 10, 1971 (dec. Nov. 21, 1981); 1 child, Richard Jackson Jr. BA, U. N.C., 1972; MA, Appalachian State U., 1975; EdD, U. N.C., 1994. Elem. tchr. Surry County Schs., Dobson, N.C., 1967—, parent coord., 1992—; part-time instr. grad. equivalency diploma/adult basic edn. and effective tchr. tng. classes Surry C.C., Dobson, 1988-92; cons. Eckerd Family Youth Alternatives, Inc., 1994—. Local and dist. chmn., state treas. N.C. Polit. Action Com. for Edn., Raleigh, 1976-81; state exec. com. N.C. Dem. Party, Raleigh, 1981-83; trustee, deacon First Bapt. Ch. of Pilot Mountain, 1988—, Sunday sch. dir., 1991—. Mem. ASCD, NEA (congressional lobbying 1976-80), Internat. Reading Assn. (local unit chair 1986—), N.C. Assn. Educators (local, dist. pres. 1979-81, local, dist., state chmn. legis. commn. 1980-81), Pilot Mountain Jaycees (life, charter mem., pres. 1979-80, Officer of Yr. 1978, 79), Geneal. Soc. Rockingham & Stokes Counties, Stokes County Hist. Soc., Sons Confederate Vets. (Stokes County aide de camp 1994—), Masons (32 degree, Scottish Rite, edn. chmn. 1986—, scholarship chmn. 1986—, ambassador 1990—, lodge master 1990, Cert. of Meritorious Svc. 1988). Home: PO Box 433 517 E Main St Pilot Mountain NC 27041 Office: Surry County Schs PO Box 364 Dobson NC 27017

SMITH, RICHARD JOSEPH, history educator; b. Sacramento, Oct. 30, 1944; s. Joseph Benjamin and Margaret Elaine (Stoddard) S.; m. Alice Ellen Weisenberger, July 1, 1967; 1 child, Tyler Stoddard. BA, U. Calif., Davis, 1966, MA, 1968, PhD, 1972. Lectr. Chinese U. Hong Kong, 1972-73, U. Calif., 1972-73; asst. prof. history Rice U., Houston, 1973-78, assoc. prof., 1978-83, prof., 1983—, Minnie Stevens Piper prof., 1987, Sarofim Disting. Teaching prof., 1993—; adj. prof. U. Tex., Austin, 1983—; cons. FBI, CIA, Washington, 1985—, NEH, Washington, 1983—, various mus., Houston, Boston, N.Y.C., 1987—. Author: Mercenaries and Mandarins, 1978, Traditional Chinese Culture, 1978, China's Cultural Heritage, 1983, 2d edit., 1994, Fortune-Tellers and Philosophers, 1991, Robert Hart and China's Early Modernization, 1991, Chinese Almanacs, 1993, Cosmology, Ontology and Human Efficacy, 1993, H.B. Morse: Customs Commissioner and Historian of China, 1995, Chinese Maps, 1996. adj. mem. Houston Mus. Fine Arts, 1986—; guest curator Children's Mus., Houston, 1987-89, 91—; pres. Tex. Found. for China Studies, Houston, 1988-93. Mem. Assn. for Asian Studies (pres. S.W. conf. 1990-91), Asia Soc. (bd. dirs. Houston Ctr. 1976—), Nat. Com. on U.S.-China Rels., Houston-Taipei Soc. (bd. dirs. 1990—), Phi Kappa Phi. Democrat. Avocations: sports, travel, music. Home: 2403 Goldsmith St Houston TX 77030-1813 Office: Rice U Dept History MS-42 6100 Main St Houston TX 77005-1892

SMITH, RICHARD MELVYN, government official; b. Lebanon, Tenn., May 2, 1940; s. Roy D. and V. Ruth (Draper) S.; m. Patti Hawkins, Feb. 29, 1964; 1 child, Douglas. B.S.E.E., Tenn. Technol. U., 1963. Asst. Engr.-in-charge FCC, Phila., 1972, Balt., 1971-72; chief investigations br. FCC, Washington, 1974-77, asst. chief enforcement div., 1977-80, dep. chief Field Ops. Bur., 1981-94, chief Office Engring. and Tech., 1994—. Recipient sr. exec. service award FCC, 1983, 84, 85, 86, 87, 88. Avocations: instrument-rated pvt. pilot. Office: FCC Ste 480 2000 M St NW Washington DC 20554

SMITH, RICHARD MILLS, editor in chief, magazine executive; b. Detroit, Jan. 12, 1946; s. William Steele Smith and Janet (Mills) Morrison; m. Lee Ann Vanderstoep (div.); children: Scott William, Anna Mills; m. Soon-Young Yoon, Oct. 20, 1978; 1 child, Song-Mee. BA summa cum laude, Albion Coll., 1968; postgrad., Columbia U., 1968-69, MS, 1970; LLD (hon.), Albion Coll., 1993. Reporter Associated Press, N.Y., 1969; assoc. editor foreign dept. Newsweek, N.Y., 1970-73, gen. editor nat. affairs dept., 1973-74; editor Asian region, bur. chief Hong Kong Newsweek, Asia, Hong Kong, 1974-77; mng. editor Newsweek Internat., N.Y., 1977-81; asst. mng. editor Newsweek, N.Y.C., 1982, exec. editor, 1983, editor in chief, 1984-91, editor in chief, pres., 1991—. Trustee Albion Coll.; bd. dirs. Cooper-Hewitt Nat. Design Mus., Smithsonian Institution. Recipient Disting. Alumni award Albion Coll., 1974. Mem. Am. Soc. Mag. Editors (mem. exec. com. 1985-88), Mag. Pubs. Assn. (bd. dirs.), Coun. on Fgn. Rels., Century Assn., Phi Beta Kappa. Office: Newsweek Inc 251 W 57th St New York NY 10019-1894

SMITH, RICHARD MULDROW, lawyer; b. Jefferson City, Mo., Sept. 2, 1939; s. Elmer Clyde and Mary (Muldrow) S.; children—Stephen, Michael. J.D., U. Ark., 1963; postgrad. U: Ill., 1963-64. Bar: Ark. 1963, D.C. 1980, U.S. Ct. Appeals (D.C. cir.) 1980, U.S. Supreme Ct. 1980. Asst. prof. U. N.C., Chapel Hill, 1964-67, assoc. prof., 1967-73, prof. 1973-79; spl. counsel FPC, Washington, 1976-77; mem. White House Energy Policy Staff, Washington, 1978-79; dir., Office of Policy Coordination, Dept. of Energy, Washington, 1978-79; ptnr. Mayer, Brown & Platt, Washington, 1979-91; pres. Little Creek Marina Inc., Norfolk, Va., 1992—. Author (with others) North Carolina Uniform Commercial Code Forms Annotated, 2 vols., 1967. Mem. ABA (pub. utility law sect., council mem. 1985-88, chmn. gas com. 1988-89, chmn. publ. com. 1989-91). Home: 4941 Adelia Dr Virginia Beach VA 23455-2227 Office: 4801 Pretty Lake Ave Norfolk VA 23518-2005

SMITH, RICHARD THOMAS, electrical engineer; b. Allentown, Pa., June 15, 1925; s. Raymond Willard and Mary (Rau) S.; m. Naomi Elsie Anthony, May 26, 1956; children: Cynthia Louise, Carol Ann. B.S. with high honors, Lehigh U., 1946, M.S., 1947; Ph.D., Ill. Inst. Tech., 1955. Registered profl. engr., Mass., Okla., Tex., Gt. Britain. Instr., Lehigh U., Bethlehem, Pa., 1947-50; analytical and design engr. Gen. Electric Co., Schenectady, 1952-58; asso. prof. U. Tex., Austin, 1958-61; George Westinghouse prof. elec. engring. Va. Poly. Inst., Blacksburg, 1961-62; project dir. Tracor, Inc., Austin, 1962-64; sr. engr., asst. dir., dir., v.p. Southwest Research Inst., San Antonio, 1964-66; Okla. Gas and Electric prof. elec. engring. U. Okla., Norman, 1966-68; prof. elec. machinery Rensselaer Poly. Inst., Troy, N.Y., 1968-70; NSF fellow U. Colo., 1970; Alcoa&UMR Disting. prof. elec. engring. U. Mo., Rolla, 1970-73; inst. engr., dir. Nondestructive Testing Info. Analysis Center, Southwest Research Inst., San Antonio, 1973-83; cons., 1983—; adj. prof. U. Tex., 1974-83, prof., 1983-87; cons., reviewer numerous cos. Author: Analysis of Electrical Machines, 1982. Recipient Excellence Fund U. Tex., 1959, DuPont Meml. prize Lehigh U., 1946. Fellow AIAA (assoc.), Instn. Elec. Engrs. (Eng.); mem. Am. Soc. Engring. Edn., I.E.E.E. (1st paper prize 1960, 63, sr.), N.Y. Acad. Scis., I.E.E.E. (numerous coms.), Internat. Electrotech. Commn. (adv. group 1971-74), Sigma Xi, Tau Beta Pi, Pi Mu Epsilon, Phi Eta Sigma, Eta Kappa Nu, Phi Kappa Phi. Office: 402 Yosemite Dr San Antonio TX 78232-1251

SMITH, RICHEY, chemical company executive; b. Akron, Ohio, Nov. 11, 1933; s. Thomas William and Martha (Richey) S.; m. Sandra Cosgrave Roe, Nov. 25, 1961; children: Mason Roe, Parker Richey. BS, U. Va., 1956. Asst. to pres. Sun Products Corp., Barberton, Ohio, 1960-64, v.p., 1964-67, gen. mgr., dir., 1967-69; chmn., CEO Sun Products Corp., 1969-76; prin. A.T. Kearney Co., Cleve., 1977-87; chmn., CEO Richey Industries, Inc., Medina, Ohio, 1987—; dir. Jaite Packaging, Inc. Mem. exec. com. Great Trail coun. Boy Scouts Am., 1973-75; chmn. capital funds dr. Summit County Planned Parenthood, 1970-71; trustee Old Trail Sch., Barberton Citizens Hosp., Medina County Arts Coun.; treas. Friends of Metro Park; vestryman St. Paul's Episcopal Ch.; corp. bd. Cleve. Mus. of Art. Mem. Bluecoats, Navy League (pres. Akron coun. 1972-73), Young Pres. Orgn., Portage Country Club (bd. dirs.), Mayflower Club, Sawgrass Club (Fla.) Farmington Club (Charlottesville, Va.), Rotary (trustee Akron Club 1974-75), Chi Psi. Home: 721 Delaware Ave Akron OH 44303-1303 Office: PO Box 928 910 Lake Rd Medina OH 44256-2453

SMITH, RITA SUE, administrator; b. Winter Haven, Fla., Apr. 19, 1954; d. Vernon Harris and Sarah Olive (Williams) S. AA, Polk C.C., 1974; BS in Psychology, Mich. State U., 1976. Childcare worker Wallace Village for Children, Broomfield, Colo., 1980-81; counselor, program supr. Alternatives to Family Violence, Commerce City, Colo., 1981-84; counselor Ending Violence Effectivly, Denver, 1984-86; dir. Women in Crisis, Arvada, Colo., 1986-88; freelance television and film prodn. Ctrl. Fla., 1989-92; dir. Nat. Coalition Against Domestic Violence, Denver, 1992—. Co-author: (manual) Family Violence: The LEgal Response, 1987. Vol. Peace River Spouse Abuse Shelter, Lakeland, Fla., 1989-91, Refuge House, Tallahassee, 1991-92, Adams County (Colo.) Rape Task Force, 1982. Democrat. Avocations: reading, biking, racquetball. Office: Nat Coalition Against Domestic Violence PO Box 18749 Denver CO 80218

SMITH, ROBERT BERNARD, JR., lawyer; b. May 11, 1959; married; two children. BS, Barry U., 1986; JD, U. Miami, Fla., 1989. Bar: Fla. 1989, U.S. Dist. Ct. (so. and mid. dists.) Fla., U.S. Ct. Appeals (5th and 11th cirs.), D.C., D.C. 1993. Law clk. Spence Payne, Masington, Grossman & Needle, P.A., Miami, 1987-88, Holland & Knight, Miami, summer 1988, 89, SEC, Miami, fall 1988; assoc. Holland & Knight, Miami, 1989-90, Ruden, Barnett, McCloskey, Smith, Schuster & Russell, P.A., Miami, 1990-93; prin. Law Offices of Robert B. Smith, P.A., Miami, 1993—; prin. New Wave Beverage Internat. Corp., Global Food Forum, Inc., Hemisphere Indsl. Devel. Holdings, Inc. Mem. D.C. Bar Assn.

SMITH, ROBERT BOULWARE, III, vascular surgeon, educator; b. Atlanta, June 15, 1933; s. Robert Boulware Jr. Smith and Mary Eva (Black) Fanning; m. Florence Chance Limehouse, Aug. 22, 1953; children: Victoria Joanne Smith Harkins, Robert Boulware IV, Brian Scott. MD, Emory U., 1957. Diplomate Am. Bd. Surgery, Am. Bd. Vascular Surgery. Intern in surgery Columbia Presbyn. Hosp., N.Y.C., 1957-58, resident in surgery, 1960-65; asst. prof. surgery Emory U. Sch. Medicine, Atlanta, 1966-69, assoc. prof., 1969-77, prof., 1977—, head gen. vascular surgery, 1984—; chief surg. svc. VA Med. Ctr., Atlanta, 1969-88; assoc. med. dir. Emory U. Hosp., 1993-95, med. dir., 1995—. Contbr. numerous articles, book chpts. to profl. publs.; co-editor: Trauma to the Thorax and Abdomen, 1969, Medical Management of the Surgical Patient, 1982, 3d edit., 1995. Capt. M.C., U.S. Army, 1958-60. Mem. ACS, Am. Surg. Assn., So. Assn. Vascular Surgery (sec. 1986-91, pres. 1992-93), Soc. Vascular Surgery, Assn. VA Surgeons (pres. 1983-84, Disting. Svc. award 1988), Ga. Surg. Soc. (pres. 1992-93), Atlanta Vascular Soc. (pres. 1986-88), Phi Beta Kappa, Alpha Omega Alpha. Republican. United Methodist. Avocation: music, travel. Home: 2701 Coldwater Canyon Dr Tucker GA 30084-2358 Office: The Emory Clinic 1365 Clifton Rd NE Atlanta GA 30307-1013

SMITH, ROBERT BRUCE, college administrator; b. Phila., July 8, 1937; s. Graeme Conlee and Margaret Edith (Moote) S.; m. Eileen Adele Petznick, Aug. 21, 1959; children: Monica, Sara, Douglas. BS, Wheaton (Ill.) Coll., 1958; PhD, U. Calif., Berkeley, 1962. Asst. prof. chemistry U. Nev., Las Vegas, 1961-66, assoc. prof., chmn. dept., 1966-68, prof., dean Coll. Sci., Engring. and Math., 1968-81; v.p. acad. affairs Weber State U., Ogden, Utah, 1981-93, provost, 1993-96; mem. Nev. Bd. Examiners Basic Scis., 1970-75, Nev. Bd. Pharmacy, 1972-77; mem. Commn. on Colls., N.W. Assn. Schs. and Colls., 1985-94, chmn. Commn. on Colls., 1989-94; dir. Am. Assn. State Colls. and Univs. Acad. Leadership Inst., 1986-96. NSF fellow, 1959-61. Mem. AAAS, Am. Assn. Higher Edn., Sigma Xi, Phi Kappa Phi. Home: 2732 Polk Ave Ogden UT 84403-0431 Office: Weber State Univ Off of the Provost 1004 University Cir Ogden UT 84408-1004

SMITH, ROBERT BRUCE, former security consultant, retired army officer; b. De Quincy, La., Apr. 22, 1920; s. Malcolm Monard and Jewell (Perkins) S.; m. Gladys Opal Borel, Feb. 22, 1941; children: Susan, Richard, Bruce. B.J., La. State U., 1941; grad., Command and Gen. Staff Coll., 1951-52, Army War Coll., 1958-59. Commd. 2d lt. U.S. Army, 1941, advanced through grades to maj. gen., 1969; plans and ops. officer 83d Div. Arty., Europe, 1943-45; personnel officer Philippine-Ryukyus Command, Manila, 1947-49; prof. mil. sci. and tactics ROTC, Lanier High Sch., Macon, Ga., 1949-51; chief res. officers sect., procurement br. Dept. Army, 1952-55; chief troop info. Office Chief Info., Dept. Army, 1962-63, dep. chief info., 1968-69; comdg. officer 8th F.A. Bn., 25th Inf. Div., Hawaii, 1955-56; G-1 25th Inf. Div. and U.S. Army Hawaii, Hawaii, 1956-58; mem. staff, faculty Command and Gen. Staff Coll., Fort Leavenworth, Kans., 1959-62; chief Alt. Nat. Mil. Command Center, Fort Ritchie, Md., 1963-64; dep. dir. ops. Office Joint Chiefs of Staff, 1964-65; asst. div. comdr. 7th Inf. Div., Korea, 1965-66; dep. comdt. Army War Coll., Carlisle, Pa., 1966-68; dep. comdg. gen. Ryukyus Islands, 1969-72, 6th U.S. Army, Presidio of San Francisco, 1972-73; ret. active duty, 1973; reporter, news editor Lake Charles (La.), 1946-47; region adminstrv. mgr. Burns Security Service, Oakland, Calif., 1974-76; ptnr. constrn. co. Napa, Calif., 1976-77, Burns Security Service, 1978-81; now ret.; dir. 1st Am. Title Co., Napa, Calif., 1988-92. Trustee Queen of Valley Hosp. Found., 1987-89; mem. Nat. coun. Boy Scouts Am., 1969-70; pres. Silverado Property Owners Assn., Inc., 1990-92. Decorated D.S.M. with oak leaf cluster, Legion of Merit with 2 oak leaf clusters, Bronze Star with oak leaf cluster; inducted into La. State U.'s Manship Sch. of Mass Communication Hall of Fame, 1996. Club: Silverado Country (Napa, Calif.). Home: 350 St Andrews Dr Napa CA 94558-1544

SMITH, ROBERT BURNS, newspaper magazine executive; b. Columbus, Ohio, Feb. 24, 1929; s. Edwin Clyde and Blanche (Burns) S.; m. Marjorie Ann Otten. BS, Ohio State U., 1949. Reporter, then asst. news editor Ohio State Jour., Columbus, 1948-59; with Columbus Dispatch, 1959—, mng. editor, 1968-80; editor-in-chief Living Single mag., 1980-86, Ohio mag., 1980-89; editor Columbus Dispatch, 1989-95, editor-in-chief, 1995—, 1996—; v.p. Dispatch Features, Columbus, 1968—, Dispatch Charities, Columbus, 1990—; bd. dirs. Dispatch Printing Co.; v.p. Ohio Mag. Inc., 1990-95, pres., 1995—; pres. Dispatch Consumer News Svcs., Inc., 1996—. Sec.-treas. James Faulkner Meml. Fund, Columbus, 1967—; trustee Ohio Hist. Soc., 1986—, pres., 1988-95; trustee Dawes Arboretum, 1988-96, Hayes Presdl. Ctr., 1995—; active Ohio Privacy Bd., 1977-81. Mem. Blue Pencil Ohio (v.p. 1969, pres. 1970), AP Ohio (v.p. 1974, pres. 1975), Mag. Pub. Assn., Am. Soc. Mag. Editors, Am. Soc. Newspaper Editors, Regional Pubs. Assn. (bd. dirs. 1986-89), York Temple Country Club, Masons, Rotary, Sigma Delta Chi, Delta Tau Delta. Presbyterian. Home: 1456 Sandalwood Pl Columbus OH 43229-4445 Office: The Columbus Dispatch 34 S 3rd St Columbus OH 43215-4201

SMITH, ROBERT CLINTON, senator; b. Trenton, N.J., Mar. 30, 1941; s. Donald and Margaret (Eldridge) S.; m. Mary Jo Hutchinson, July 2, 1966; children: Jennifer L., Robert Clinton, Jason H. A.A., Trenton Jr. Coll., 1963, B.A., Lafayette Coll., 1965; postgrad., Long Beach State U., 1968-69. Tchr., realtor Wolfeboro, N.H., 1975-85; chmn. Gov. Wentworth Dist. Sch. Bd., 1978-84; mem. 99th-101st Congresses from 1st N.H. dist., 1985-90; U.S. Senator from New Hampshire, 1990—; mem. armed svcs., environ. and pub. works, govt. affairs, ethic com. With USN, 1965-67, Vietnam; with USNR, 1962-65, 67-69. Decorated campaign medal (Republic of Vietnam). Mem. VFW, Am. Legion, NRA, Theta Xi. Republican. Roman Catholic. Office: US Senate 332 Dirksen Senate Ofc Washington DC 20510

SMITH, ROBERT DRAKE, railroad executive; b. Ft. Worth, Oct. 26, 1944; s. Kermit Rudebeck and Lynne Grace (Harris) S. BA with honors, U. Puget Sound, 1966; MBA, U. Pa., 1968. Planning analyst C. & N.W. Ry. Co., Chgo., 1968; supr. program planning C. & N.W. Ry. Co., 1969, mgr. program planning, 1970-73; corp. sec. Chgo. & North Western Transp. Co., 1973-82, v.p., corp. sec., 1982-84, sr. v.p. corp. communications, sec., 1985-86; sr. v.p. investor relations CNW Corp., Chgo., 1986-89; chmn. Aberdeen Ptnrs., Inc., 1990—. Mem. governing bd. Chgo. Symphony Orch.; vol. Juvenile Ct. Cook County, 1970-78. Mem. Am. Soc. Corp. Secs., Assn. Am. R.R.s, Nat. Investor Rels. Inst., N.Y. Soc. Security Analysts, Chgo. Coun. Fgn. Rels., Wharton Sch. Alumni Assn., Assn. for Investment Mgmt. and Rsch., N.Y. Athletic Club, Cliff Dwellers Club, Penn Club (N.Y.C.), Alpha Kappa Psi. Home: 1212 N Lake Shore Dr Apt 26bn Chicago IL 60610-2388

SMITH, ROBERT EARL, space scientist; b. Indpls., Sept. 13, 1923; s. Harold Bennett and Bernice (McCaslin) S.; m. Elizabeth Lee Usak, Jan. 3, 1947 (dec. 1984); children: Stephanie Lee, Robert Michael, Cynthia Ann, Kelly Andrew; m. Lyla Lee Lewellen, July 1, 1988. B.S., Fla. State U., 1959, M.S., 1960; M.S., U. Mich., 1969, Ph.D., 1974. Enlisted U.S. Army Air Force, 1943-44; advanced through grades to maj. U.S. Air Force, 1955; airway traffic controller Berlin, Germany, 1945; staff weather reconnaissance officer 9th Air Force, 1956; ret., 1963; project scientist Atmospheric Cloud Physics Lab.; dep. chief atmospheric scis. div. NASA/Marshall Space Flight Ctr., Ala., 1963-86; sr. scientific cons. Univs. Space Rsch. Assn., Huntsville, Ala., 1986-87; sr. computer cons. Computer Scis. Corp., Huntsville, 1987-89; chief space sci. and applications div. FWG Assocs., Inc., Huntsville, 1989-92; NASA program mgr. Physitron, Inc., Huntsville, 1992-96; sr. computer scientist Computer Scis. Corp., Huntsville, 1996—. Mem. AIAA, Pi Mu Epsilon, Sigma Phi Epsilon. Home: 125 Westbury Dr SW Huntsville AL 35802-1619 Office: NASA/MSFC Huntsville AL 35812

SMITH, ROBERT EVERETT, lawyer; b. N.Y.C., Mar. 15, 1936; s. Arthur L. and Augusta (Cohen) S.; m. Emily Lucille Lehman, July 17, 1960; children: Amy, Karen, Victoria. BA, Dartmouth Coll., 1957; LLB, Harvard U., 1960. Bar: N.Y. 1960, U.S. Dist. Ct. (so. dist.) N.Y. 1962, U.S. Ct. Appeals (2d cir.) 1963, U.S. Supreme Ct. 1967, U.S. Dist. Ct. (ea. dist.) N.Y. 1969, U.S. Ct. Appeals (3d cir.) 1982, U.S. Ct. Appeals (9th cir.) 1988. Assoc. Paul, Weiss, Rifkind, Wharton & Garrison, N.Y.C., 1960-65; from assoc. to ptnr. Baar, Bennett & Fullen, N.Y.C., 1965-74; ptnr. Guggenheimer & Untermyer, N.Y.C., 1974-85; ptnr. Rosenman & Colin LLP, N.Y.C., 1985—, chmn., 1994—. With U.S. Army, 1961-64. Mem. ABA, N.Y. State Bar Assn., Assn. of Bar of City of N.Y., Fed. Bar Coun., N.Y. County Lawyers Assn., Am. Arbitration Assn. (nat. panel arbitrators), The Am. Law Inst. Office: Rosenman & Colin 575 Madison Ave New York NY 10022-2511

SMITH, ROBERT FREEMAN, history educator; b. Little Rock, May 13, 1930; s. Robert Freeman and Emma Martha Gottlieb (Buerkle) S.; m. Alberta Vester, Feb. 1, 1950 (dec. 1985); children: Robin Ann, Robert Freeman III; m. Charlotte Ann Coleman, Sept. 9, 1985. BA, U. Ark., 1951, MA, 1952; PhD, U. Wis., Madison, 1958. Instr. U. Ark., Fayetteville, 1953; asst. prof. Tex. Luth. Coll., Seguin, 1958-62; assoc. prof. U. R.I., Kingston, 1962-66, U. Conn., Storrs, 1966-69; prof. history U. Toledo, 1969-86, disting. univ. prof., 1986—; vis. prof. U. Wis., Madison, 1966-67. Author: The United States and Cuba: Business and Diplomacy 1917-1960, 1961 (Tex. Writers' Roundup award 1961), What Happened in Cuba: A Documentary History of U.S.-Cuban Relations, 1963, The United States and Revolutionary Nationalism in Mexico, 1916-1932, 1973 (Ohio Acad. History award 1973), The Era of Caribbean Intervention, 1890-1930, 1981, The Era of Good Neighbors, Cold Warriors, and Hairshirts, 1930-82, 1983, The Caribbean World and the United States: Mixing Rum & Coca-Cola, 1994; contbr. to numerous publs. Lt. col. 43rd Mil. Police Bn., Ohio Mil. Res. 1st lt. U.S. Army, 1953-55. Knapp fellow in history U. Wis., 1957; Tom L. Evans rsch. fellow Harry S. Truman Libr., Independence, Mo., 1976-77, Mexican Ministry Fgn. Rels. fellow, 1991-92. Mem. Soc. Historians of Am. Fgn. Rels., Soc. Mil. History, U.S. Naval Inst., Ohio Acad. History, So. Hist. Assn., Orgn. Am. Historians, Assn. U.S. Army, State Guard Assn. of U.S., Am. Legion, Masons, Scottish Rite, Shriners, Phi Beta Kappa, Phi Alpha Theta. Episcopalian. Avocation: photography. Home: 4110 Dunkirk Rd Toledo OH 43606-2217 Office: U Toledo Dept History Toledo OH 43606

SMITH, ROBERT G., lawyer, assemblyman, educator; b. Scranton, Pa., Mar. 25, 1947; s. Philip and Ruth (Delmar) S.; m. Ellen Theresa Foster, 1968; children: Karen Elizabeth, Lisa. BA in History, U. Scranton, 1969, MS in Chemistry, 1970; MS in Environ. Sci., Rutgers U., 1973; JD, Seton Hall U., 1981. Bar: N.J. 1981. Sci. tchr. Lourdesmont High Sch., Clark Summit, Pa., 1968-70; environ. health sci. curriculum coordinator Middlesex County Coll., Edison, N.J., 1972-73, adminstrv. asst. to dean sci., 1974-77, instr., 1970-74, asst. prof., 1974-76, assoc. prof., 1976-79, prof. chemistry and environmental sci., 1979-86; law clk. N.J. Dept. Environ. Protection, Trenton, 1980; prin., pvt. practice law Bob Smith and Assocs., Piscataway, N.J., 1981—; zoning bd. atty. City of New Brunswick, N.J., 1993—. Mayor of Piscataway Twp., 1981-86; N.J. assemblyman N.J. 17th Legis. Dist., 1986—, mem. appropriations com. and environ. quality com., assembly select com. on ocean pollution, 1988, assembly energy and hazardous waste com. policy and rules, 1994; parliamentarian Assembly Dem. caucus, 1988-90, chmn. task force on environment, 1987; chmn. Piscataway Dem. Orgn., 1981-90; counsel N.J. State Dem. Platform Com., 1987, 89; chmn. Middlesex County Dem. Orgn., 1991-92; Assembly Dem. Dep. Minority Leader, 1993-95; councilman-at-large Piscataway Twp., 1977-80, pres. council, 1979, v.p., 1978; mem. Middlesex County Transp. Coordinating Com., 1980-86; chmn. Piscataway Environ. Commn., 1971-75; mem. Piscataway Planning Bd., 1981-86, sec., 1975, chmn., 1976; bd. dirs. N.J. Conf. Mayors, 1984-86; mem. tech. adv. com. air pollution Middlesex County Planning Bd., 1973-74; mem. Greenbrook Basin com. Area 208 Mgmt. Planning Program, 1975-76; mem. commr.'s adv. com. N.J. Dept. Environ. Protection, 1972-86; mem. Joyce Kilmer dist. Thomas A. Edison council Boy Scouts Am., 1983-86. Recipient Disting. Citizen award Piscataway Jewish Congregation B'nai Shalom, 1982; named Legis. of Yr. Eden Inst., 1990, Environ Legislator of Yr., N.J. Environ. Fedn.; U. Scranton Presdl. scholar, 1965-69. Mem. Middlesex County Bar Assn. Roman Catholic. Contbg. author Jour. of Air Pollution Control Assn., 1976; contbg. author; Environmental Health Science, 1975; co-editor: New Jersey State Wastewater Treatment Operations Manual, 1979. Office: 216 Stelton Rd Rm 250 Piscataway NJ 08854-3283 also: 44 Stelton Rd Piscataway NJ 08854-2638

SMITH, ROBERT HOUSTON, archeologist, humanities and religious studies educator; b. McAlester, Okla., Feb. 13, 1931; s. Vaughn Hubert and Bobbie Louise (Nelson) S.; m. Geraldine Warshaw, Jan. 26, 1969; 1 child, Vanessa Eleanor. BA, U. Tulsa, 1952; BD, Yale U., 1955, PhD, 1960. Instr. Coll. Wooster, Ohio, 1960-62, asst. prof., 1962-65, assoc. prof., 1965-70, prof., 1970-72, Fox prof. religious studies, 1979-93, chmn. dept., 1981-93, chmn. archaeology program, 1979-93; Grosvenor lectr. Nat. Geographic Soc., Washington, 1985; dir. Coll. Wooster Archeol. Expdn. to Pella, Jordan, 1966-85; cons. on devel. bus. and profl. codes of ethics. Author: Excavations at Khirbet Kufin, 1962, Pella of the Decapolis, vol. 1, 1973, vol. 2, 1989, Patches of Godlight: The Pattern of Thought of C.S. Lewis, 1986, The Passmores in America: A Quaker Family Through Six Generations, 1992; coauthor: Pella in Jordan 1, 1982, Pella in Jordan 2, 1992; lectr. Digging Up the Past, NBC-TV Edn. Exchange series, 1968; contbr. articles to profl. jours. Trustee Am. Ctr. Oriental Research, Amman, Jordan, 1979-85. NEH grantee, 1979-81, Nat. Geographic Soc. grantee, 1979-85; Yale U. fellow Am. Sch. Oriental Research, 1958-59. Mem. Am. Schs. Oriental Research, Soc. Profl. Archaeologists, Soc. Biblical Lit., Archaeological Inst. Am. Democrat. Presbyterian. Avocation: landscape painting. Home: 2900-5 Tice Creek Dr Walnut Creek CA 94595

SMITH, ROBERT HUGH, engineering construction company executive; b. Wichita, Kans., Dec. 29, 1936; s. Richard Lyon and E. Eileen (O'Neal) S.; m. Melinda Louise Fitch, Sept. 26, 1959 (div. Dec. 1969); children: Robert Blake, Thomas Hugh; m. Margaret Anne Moseley, Dec. 11, 1977; 1 child, Steven Richard. BS, Kans. State U., 1959; MS, U. Kansas, 1964, PhD, 1970. Sr. process engr. FMC Corp., Lawrence, Kans., 1959-64; rsch. engr. Phillips Petroleum Co., Bartleville, Okla., 1964-66; group leader Standard Oil of Ohio, Warrenville Heights, Ohio, 1966-67; sr. rsch. assoc., group leader Atlantic Richfield, Plano, Tex., 1970-80; regional mgr., sr. mgr., sales mgr. Fluor Daniel, Houston and Marlton, N.J., 1980-90; v.p., gen. mgr. Badger Design & Construction, Tampa, Fla., 1990-93; exec. v.p., COO The Pritchard Corp., Overland Park, Kans., 1993—. Patentee in the field; contbr. to profl. jours. Adv. bd. dept. chem. enging U. Kans., Lawrence, 1993—. Mem. AIChE (chmn., vice chmn., sec. 1962—, Engr. of Yr. award Dallas 1980, exec. bd. Engr. and Cons. Contracting divsn.), Phi Lambda Upsilon, Sigma Xi. Avocations: tennis, sailing, skiing, reading.

SMITH, ROBERT JOHN, healthcare executive; b. Vancouver, B.C., Can., Oct. 23, 1944; s. Robert Sanford and Gladys (McHardy) S.; m. Agnes Patricia Kelly, Dec. 31, 1970; children: Andrea Lynn, Kelly Anne, Jocelyn Marie. BComm, U. B.C., Can., 1968, MBA, 1971. Exec. dir. The Arthritis Soc., Vancouver, B.C., Can., 1978-80; dep. dir. The Cancer Control Agy., Vancouver, B.C., 1980-88; pres., CEO Lions Gate Hosp., North Vancouver, B.C., 1988-96, Neustar Med. Svcs. Corp., Vancouver, 1996—; bd. dirs. B.C. Health Svcs. Ltd., Vancouver, 1991-94, Western Interprovincial Network, Vancouver, 1993-94. Fellow Can. Coll. Health Svc. Exec., Can. Hosp. Assn. (past chair 1994). Avocations: softball, skiing, hiking. Home: 3220 Del Rio Dr, North Vancouver, BC Canada V7A 4C2 Office: Neustar Med Svcs Corp, Ste 1500, 1188 W Georgia St, Vancouver, BC Canada V6E 4AZ

SMITH, ROBERT JOHN, anthropology educator; b. Essex, Mo., June 27, 1927; s. Will Dan and Fern (Jones) S.; m. Kazuko Sasaki, Aug. 22, 1955. B.A. summa cum laude, U. Minn., 1949; M.A., Cornell U., 1951, Ph.D., 1953. Engaged in cultural anthrop. field research N.S., Can., 1950, Japan, 1951-52, 55, 57-58, Brazil, 1966-67; mem. faculty Cornell U., 1953—, prof. anthropology, 1963-74, Goldwin Smith prof. anthropology, 1974—, chmn. dept. Asian studies, 1961-66, chmn. dept. antropology, 1967-71, 76-82; vis. prof. anthropology U. Ariz., 1971, U. Hawaii, 1978, Nat. Mus. Ethnology, Osaka, Japan, 1982. Author: (with Cornell) Two Japanese Villages, 1956, (with Cornell, Saito and Maeyama) Japanese and Their Descendants in Brazil, 1967; editor: (with Beardsley) Japanese Culture: Its Development and Characteristics, 1962, Social Organization and the Applications of Anthropology, 1974, Ancestor Worship in Contemporary Japan, 1974, Kurusu: The Price of Progress in a Japanese Village, 1951-75, 1978, (with Wiswell) Women of Suye Mura, 1982, Japanese Society: Tradition, Self and the Social Order, 1983, (with K. Smith) Diary of a Japanese Innkeeper's Daughter, 1984. Served with AUS, 1944-46. Tng. grantee Social Sci. Rsch. Coun., Japan, 1951-52; recipient Individual Exch. award to Japan Inst. Internat. Edn., 1957-58; Fulbright lectr. Tokyo Met. U., 1962-63; NSF rsch. grantee, 1965-67; Japan Found. grantee, 1979; awarded Order of the Rising Sun, Govt. of Japan, 1993. Fellow Am. Anthrop. Assn., Assn. for Asian Studies (v.p. 1987-88, pres. 1988-89), Soc. Applied Anthropology (editor jour. Human Orgn. 1961-66). Home: 107 Northview Rd Ithaca NY 14850-6039 Office: Cornell U Dept Anthropology Ithaca NY 14853

SMITH, ROBERT KEITH, information technology analyst; b. Ashland, Ky., Dec. 30, 1955; s. Robert French and Neva Lee (Stapleton) S.; m. Rebecca Slone, July 30, 1994; children: Jonathan Wesley, Robert Charles. BS in Police Adminstrn., Ea. Ky. U., 1977; MS in Sys. Mgmt., U. So. Calif., 1983. Commd. 2d lt., 1977; advanced through grades to lt. col. U.S. Army, 1989; def. mgmt. cons. TRW Sys. Overseas, Inc., Saudi Arabia, 1993-95; sr. info. tech. analyst, project mgr. Columbia Gas. Transmission, Inc., Charleston, W.Va., 1995—. Chmn. First aid com. ARC, San Antonio, 1987-89. With U.S. Army res., 1993—. Mem. Am. Mgmt. Assn., Soc. Logistics Engrs., Inst. Indsl. Engrs., Project Mgmt. Inst. Republican. Baptist. Avocations: music, hunting. Home: 2250 Circle Dr Milton WV 25541-1004 Office: Columbia Gas Transmission PO Box 1273 PO Box 1273 Charleston WV 25325-1273

SMITH, ROBERT KIMMEL, author; b. Bklyn., July 31, 1930; s. Theodore and Sally (Kimmel) S.; m. Claire Medney, Sept. 4, 1954; children: Heidi Medney, Roger Kimmel. Student, CUNY Bklyn. Coll., 1947-48. Copywriter Doyle, Dane, Bernbach Advt., N.Y.C., 1957-61; copy chief Grey Advt., N.Y.C., 1961-63; group head, creative dir. West, Weir, Bartel Advt., N.Y.C., 1964-67; co-owner, creative dir. Boyce, Smith & Toback Advt., N.Y.C., 1967-69; author, playwright Bklyn., 1970—. Author: (novels) Ransom, 1971, Sadie Shapiro's Knitting Book, 1973, Sadie Shapiro in Miami, 1977, Sadie Shapiro, Matchmaker, 1980, Jane's House, 1982; (juveniles) Chocolate Fever, 1972, Jelly Belly, 1981, The War With Grandpa, 1984, Mostly Michael, 1987, Bobby Baseball, 1989, The Squeaky Wheel, 1990; (plays) A Little Singing, A Little Dancing, 1971, A Little Dancing, 1974. Bd. dirs. Prospect Pk. South Assn., Bklyn., 1976-86, pres., 1984-86. With U.S. Army, 1951-53. Recipient Best Book award ALA, 1983, Nene prize Hawaii Libr. Assn., 1984, Children's Book award S.C. Libr., 1984, 86, Tenn. Libr. Assn., 1988, Ga. Libr. Assn., 1989, Ala. Libr. Assn., 1989, Dorothy Canfield Fisher award Vt. Libr. Assn., 1986, Mark Twain award Mo. Libr. Assn., 1987, Golden Sower award Nebr. Libr. Assn., 1987, William Allen White Young Reader's Choice award Kans. Libr. Assn., 1987, Pacific N.W. Libr. Assn., 1987, Young Readers' medal Calif. Libr. Assn., 1990, Knickerbocker award N.Y. State Libr. Assn., 1995. Mem. Authors Guild, Writers Guild, Soc. Children's Book Writers, Eugene O'Neill Theater. Avocations: gardening, reading, cooking, tennis. Address: care Harold Ober Assocs 425 Madison Ave New York NY 10017-1110

SMITH, ROBERT L., principal. Prin. Thomson (Ga.) High Sch. Recipient Blue Ribbon award U.S. Dept. Edn., 1990-91. Office: Thomson High Sch PO Box 1077 Thomson GA 30824-1077

SMITH, ROBERT L., medical research administrator; b. N.Y.C., Mar. 29, 1941; m. Carolee Smith, 1968; children: Jana, Shayna, Marni. BEE, CCNY, 1962; MSEE, NYU, 1966; PhD in Neurosci., Syracuse U., 1973. Devel. engr. Wheeler Lab., Great Neck, N.Y., 1962-64; lectr. elec. engring. CCNY, 1964-66; instr. elec. engring. Syracuse U., 1970-74, from asst. prof. to assoc. prof. sensory rsch., 1974-85, prof. neurosci., 1985—, dir. Inst. Sensory Rsch., 1993—. Assoc. editor Jour. Acoustical Soc. Am., 1986-89. NIH fellow, 1979-84. Fellow Acoustical Soc. Am.; mem. Assn. Rsch. Otolaryngology, Soc. Neurosci., Sigma Xi. Achievements include research in neurophysiology and neural coding in the auditory nervous system; single unit recording from the cochlea, auditory nerve and cochlear nucleus; mathematical modeling of the results and systems analysis of the auditory system; biological engineering. Office: Syracuse U Inst for Sensory Rsch MerrillLn Syracuse NY 13244-5290*

SMITH, ROBERT LEE, agriculturalist; b. Ottawa, Ill., Apr. 2, 1921; s. Charles Emanuel and Helen Beatrice (Cray) S.; m. Lillian Pearl Francisco, 1947 (div. 1969); children: Charles, Jerome (dec.), Rodger, Lawrence, Eileen, Arlene. PhD in Humane Sci. (hon.), Cleo U., 1990. Elder, tchr. Meth. Ch., El Paso, Ill., 1955-67; dir. rsch. Ill. Farmers Union, Springfield, 1963-68; radio officer, pilot search and rescue unit Civil Air Patrol, Woodford County, 1964-69; lectr. U. Ill., Champaign, 1989-90. Contbr. articles to profl. jours. Dir. Ill. Youth Corps, No. Ill., 1965-68; Dem. candidate for state rep. Capt. USAF, 1944-46; with USAFR, 1955-68. Mem. Mensa (life, pres. cen. Ill. chpt. 1980-85, editor 1981-84), Moose. Avocations: writing, bridge, dancing, hiking, reading. Home: 1120 Northwood Dr N Champaign IL 61821-2116

SMITH, ROBERT LEONARD, pastor, religious studies educator; b. San Antonio, Dec. 23, 1924; s. Leonard and Alice Jewel (Horton) S.; m. Ethelyn Hughes, Feb. 8, 1945; children: Robert Leonard, Judy Claire Smith Bynum. BS, Centenary Coll., Shreveport, La., 1947; BDiv, Southwestern Seminary, 1953, MDiv, 1987; DD (hon.), Ouachita U., 1961. Ordained to ministry, Bapt. Ch., 1953. Pastor First Bapt. Ch., Crossett, Ark., 1953-55, Pine Bluff, Ark., 1955-65, Houston, 1965-69, Pompano Beach, Fla., 1969-84; disting. prof. preaching and ch. adminstrn., dean Howard Payne U., Brownwood, Tex., 1984-94; mem. Bapt. Sunday Sch. Bd., Nashville, 1957-65; presented Sermons in Art in 38 states. Author: Successful Chalk-Talk, 1972; author, prodr. (TV series) The Art of Living, 1960-67; contbr. articles to religious jours.; oil and watercolor artist; one man shows include Stetson U., Deland, Fla., 1984, Lighthouse Point Nat. Bank, Fla., 1975, First Nat. Bank, Pompano Beach, Fla., 1976, Citizens Nat. Bank, Brownwood, Tex., 1991, Howard Payne U., Brownwood, 1994; exhibited at Jefferson County Fair, Pine Bluff, Ark., 1964, First Meth. Ch., Pompano Beach, 1974. Mem. Ark. Exec. Bd., Little Rock, 1954-62, Tex. Exec. Bd., Dallas, 1966-80, Fla. Exec. Bd., Jacksonville, 1966-80; trustee Pine Bluff (Ark.) Mental Health Ctr., 1959, Henderson Mental Health Clinic, Ft. Lauderdale, Fla., 1971-75, Stetson U., DeLand, Fla., 1978-82. Mem. Rotary Internat. Avocations: oil and watercolor painting, flying, golf. Home: 3 Quail Creek Rd Brownwood TX 76801-6309 Office: Howard Payne U 1000 Fisk Ave Brownwood TX 76801-2715

SMITH, ROBERT LONDON, commissioner, retired air force officer, political scientist, educator; b. Alexandria, La., Oct. 13, 1919; s. Daniel Charleston and Lillie (Roberts) S.; m. Jewel Busch, Feb. 5, 1949; children: Jewel Diane, Robert London, Karl Busch. B.A., Coll. St. Joseph, 1954; M.A., U. Okla., 1955; Ph.D., Am. U., 1964. Commd. 2d lt. USAAF, 1941; advanced through grades to lt. col. USAF, 1961; various assignments in aircraft engring., command and logistics, 1941-60; rsch. logistics Hdqs. Office Aerospace Rsch., 1960-63; project sci., adminstr. postdoctoral rsch. program, asst. dir. NAS, Hdqs. Office Sci. Rsch., 1963-65; ret., 1965; asso. prof. polit. sci., head dept. eve. classes and corr. study U. Alaska, College, 1966-68, dean Coll. Bus., Econs. and Govt., 1968-70, prof., head dept. polit. sci., 1966-84, prof. emeritus, 1984—; commr. Alaska Dept. Health and Social Services, 1983—; mem. govt. panels and planning groups; dir. Arctic 1st Fed. Savs. & Loan Assn.; corporator Mt. McKinley Mut. Savs. Bank. Author: (with others) Squadron Adminstration, 1951; also publs. on nat. security and nat. def.; Contbr. to: (with others) The United Nations Peace University, 1965. Committeeman Western region Boy Scouts Am., 1968-73; mem. exec. bd. Midnight Sun council, 1973-74, committeeman-at-large nat. council, 1968—; mem. Alaska Gov.'s Employment Commn.; pres. United Service Orgn. Council, Fairbanks, Alaska; mem. active corps execs. SBA. Recipient Silver Beaver award Boy Scouts Am.; named Outstanding Prof. U. Alaska, 1975. Mem. Nat. Acad. Econs. and Polit. Sci., AAAS, Air Force Hist. Found., Nat. Inst. Social and Behavioral Scis., Nat. Inst. U.S. in World Affairs, Am. Polit. Sci. Assn., Assn. U.S. Army (bd. dirs. Polar Bear chpt.), Alaska C. of C. (edn. com.), Pi Gamma Mu, Pi Sigma Alpha. Roman Catholic. Club: Rotary. Home: Smithhaven 100 Goldizen Ave Fairbanks AK 99709-3634 also: Smithport 9994 Salcha Dr Salcha AK 99714-9624 also: Smithawaii Nani Kai Hale 73 N Kihei Rd Apt 607 Kihei HI 96753-8827 also: Costa Vida Unit #920-921, KM 4 456 Carr Apdo Postal 186, Puerto Vallarta Jalisco, Mexico

SMITH, ROBERT LOUIS, construction company executive; b. Parkersburg, W.Va., Apr. 19, 1922; s. Everett Clerc and Janet (Morrison) S.; m. June Irene Odbert, Oct. 25, 1948; children: Peter Clerc, Morrison James, Edna Louise. B.S. in Civil Enging., Lehigh U., 1944. Design engr. Chrysler Corp., 1944-46; engr. Harrison Constrn. Co., Charleston, W.Va., 1946-47; sr. engr. Creole Petroleum Co., Las Piedras, Venezuela, 1947-55; v.p. Rea Constrn. Co., Charlotte, N.C., 1955-64; exec. v.p. Warren Bros. Co., Cambridge, Mass., 1964-68; pres. Warren Bros. Co., 1968-79; also dir.; sr. v.p. Ashland Oil, Inc., Ky., 1974-79; pres. Robert L. Smith & Assos., Lexington, 1979—; pres., dir. Tree Farm Devel. Corp., Cambridge, 1979—; dir. Panastalto (S.A.), Wilder Constrn. Co., Inc., J.H. Shears Sons, Inc. Fellow ASCE; mem. Nat. Asphalt Pavement Assn. (dir.), Phi Beta Kappa, Tau Beta Pi, Sigma Chi. Republican. Unitarian. Home and Office: 140 Worthen Rd Lexington MA 02173-7020

SMITH, ROBERT MASON, university dean; b. Fort Sill, Okla., May 5, 1945; s. Arnold Mason and Lillyan (Scott) S.; m. Ramona Lynne Stukey, June 15, 1968; children: David, Angela. BA, Wichita State U., 1967; MA, Ohio U., 1968; PhD, Temple U., 1976. Debate coach Princeton U. (N.J.), 1971-73, Wichita (Kans.) State U., 1973-87, assoc. dean Coll. Liberal Arts and Scis., 1977-87; dean coll. arts and scis. U. Tenn., Martin, 1987—, dir. Gov. Sch. for Humanities, 1996spl. asst. U.S. Dept. HHS, Washington, 1980-81; cons. in field; chmn. corp. communication bd. Ea. Airlines, Miami, Fla., 1984-86. Mem. State Behavorial Sci. Regulatory Bd., Topeka, 1985-87; trustee Leadership Kans., Topeka, 1986-87; founder, bd. dirs. WestStar Regional Tenn. Leadership Program, 1989—. Recipient Excellence in Tchg. award Coun. for Advancement and Support of Edn., 1984, Crystal Apple award for outstanding tchg., 1995, Nat. Assn. for Cmty. Leadership award for disting. leadership, 1995, Disting. Leadership award Nat. Assn. Cmty. Leadership; HHS fellow, 1980. Mem. Kans. Speech Communication Assn. (Outstanding Coll. Speech Tchr. award 1977, pres. 1978), Assn. for Communication Adminstrn. (pres. 1988), Tenn. Coun. Colls. Arts & Scis. (pres. 1989-90), Tenn. Speech Comm. Assn. (pres. 1993-94), Phi Kappa Phi, Phi Eta Sigma, Beta Theta Pi, Phi Theta Kappa, Rotary. Baptist. Home: 168 Weldon Dr Martin TN 38237-1322 Office: U Tenn Coll Arts & Scis Martin TN 38238

SMITH, ROBERT MCNEIL, university dean; b. Balt., Jan. 14, 1932; s. Walter H. and Clara (Goodwin) S.; m. Bette A. Smith, June 15, 1961; children: David, Andrew, Michele, Denise, Jonathan, Kristen. B.S., U. Md., 1957; M.Ed., U. Ill., 1958, Ed.D., 1962. Asso. prof., research asso. cleft palate research center Sch. Dentistry, U. Pitts., 1963-66; asso. prof. U. Del., 1966-67; prof. spl. edn. Pa. State U., 1967-78, asst. provost, 1974-78; dean Coll. Edn., Va. Poly. Inst. and State U., Blacksburg, 1978-92; cons. in field. Author books, monographs, articles in field, also chpts. in books. Served with AUS, 1953-55. Fellow Am. Council Edn., 1973, U.S. Office Edn., 1961; resident fellow U. Md., 1958. Fellow Am. Assn. Mental Deficiency; mem. Coun. Exceptional Children, Am. Cleft Palate Assn., AAAS, Nat. Assn. Accts., Am. Coll. Sports Medicine, Phi Delta Kappa, Kappa Delta Pi, Iota Lambda Sigma Psi. Home: 3336 Mcever Rd Blacksburg VA 24060-8710 Office: Va Tech 300 War Memorial Hall Blacksburg VA 24061

SMITH, ROBERT MICHAEL, lawyer; b. Boston, Nov. 4, 1940; s. Sydney and Minnie (Appel) S.; m. Catherine Kersey, Apr. 14, 1981 (dec. 1983). AB cum laude, Harvard Coll., 1962; diploma, Centro de Estudos de Espanol, Barcelona, 1963; MA in Internat. Affairs, Columbia U., 1964, MS in Journalism with high honors, 1965; JD, Yale U., 1975. Bar: Calif., N.Y., D.C., U.S. Supreme Ct. Intern in econ. devel. UN, Geneva, 1964; corres. Time Mag., N.Y.C., 1965-66, The N.Y. Times, Washington, 1968-72, 75-76; atty. Heller, Ehrman, White & McAuliffe, San Francisco, 1976-78; spl. asst. Office of Atty. Gen. of U.S., Washington, 1979-80; dir. Office Pub. Affairs U.S. Dept. Justice, Washington, 1979-80; mem. U.S. delegation Internat. Ct. of Justice, The Hague, 1980; asst. U.S. atty. No. Dist. Calif., San Francisco, 1981-82; counsel, sr. counsel to sr. litigation counsel Bank of Am. NT & SA, San Francisco, 1982-86; pvt. practice law San Francisco, 1988—; lectr. FBI Acad., Quantico, Va., 1980, Internat. Bankers Assn. Calif., 1994, Cmty. Bankers No. Calif., 1994, 95; judge Golden Medallion Broadcast Media awards State Bar of Calif., 1985; judge pro tem Mcpl. Ct. City and County of San Francisco, 1989-96. Bd. editors Yale Law Jour., 1974-75; editor Litigation, jour. ABA litigation sect., 1978-81; mem. editl. adv. bd. Bancroft-Whitney, 1991-94; contbr. articles to profl. jours. Bd. dirs. Neighborhood Legal Assistance Found., San Francisco, 1985-87, Nob Hill Assn., San Francisco, 1985-93; bd. dirs., fin. com. St. Francis Found., San Francisco, 1993-94. 1st lt. inf., USAR, 1965-71. Recipient UPI Award for Newswriting, 1958; Harvard Coll. scholar, 1958-62, Fulbright scholar, 1962-63; Columbia U. Internat. fellow, 1964-65. Mem. ABA (corp. counsel com. 1986—, alternative dispute resolution sect. 1994—), Assn. Atty. Mediators (v.p. No. Calif. chpt. 1995), State Bar of Calif. (pub. affairs com. 1982-85, litigation sect. 1990—), Bar Assn. of San Francisco (bench-bar media com. 1985—, alternative dispute resolution com. 1994—), Assn. Bus. Trial Lawyers No. Calif., Assn. of Former U.S. Attys. No. Dist. Calif., Am. Arbitration Assn. (mem. comml. arbitration panel, No. Calif. adv. coun., mediator Am. Arbitration Ctr. for Mediation), Profl. Atty. Mediators, Cmty. Bds. of San Francisco (conciliator), German-Am. C. of C. West U.S., Harvard Club of San Francisco (bd. dirs. 1986-94, pres. 1992-94), Yale Club of San Francisco (bd. dirs. 1989-94), Soc. Profls. in Dispute Resolution (assoc. mem.), Columbia U. Alumni Club of No. Calif. (exec. com. 1978-92). Home: 142 Rue de Courcelles, 75017 Paris France

SMITH, ROBERT MOORS, anesthesiologist; b. Winchester, Mass., Dec. 10, 1912; s. Francis E. and Elsie C. (Davis) S.; m. Margaret Louise Nash, Aug. 7, 1937; children: Jonathan E., Marcia A., Karen E. A.B., Dartmouth Coll., 1934; M.D., Harvard U., 1938. Diplomate: Am. Bd. Anesthesiology. Rotating intern Faulkner Hosp., Jamaica Plain, Mass., 1938-39; asst. in pathology Faulkner Hosp., 1939; intern in surgery Boston City Hosp., 1939-41; gen. practice medicine Cohasset, Mass., 1941-42; anesthesiologist Children's Hosp. Med. Center, Boston, 1946-81; dir. anesthesiology Children's Hosp. Med. Center, 1946-80, pres. staff, 1966-68; assoc. anesthesiologist Peter Bent Brigham Hosp., Boston, 1958-61; assoc. anesthesiologist Boston Lying-In Hosp., 1964-70; instr. anesthesia Harvard Med. Sch., Boston, 1948-63; assoc. in anesthesia Harvard Med. Sch., 1955, asst. clin. prof. anesthesia, 1963-66, assoc. clin. prof., 1966-81, clin. prof. anesthesia, 1976-81, clin. prof. emeritus, 1981—; chief anesthesiology Kennedy Meml. Children's Hosp., 1981-88; anesthesiologist Franciscan Children's Hosp., 1988-94. Bd. dirs. Minuteman council Boy Scouts Am. Served to maj. U.S. Army, 1941-46. Recipient Disting. Svc. award Am. Soc. Anesthesiologists, 1988. Fellow Am. Coll. Anesthesiologists (gov. 1952-58); mem. AMA, Mass. Med. Soc., New Eng. Soc. Anethesiologists (pres. 1966), Mass. Soc. Anesthesiologists (pres. 1955, dir. 1965-68), New Eng. Pediatric Soc., Assn. Univ. Anesthesiologists, Am. Acad. Pediatrics (chmn. com. pediatric anesthesiology 1963-64, 76-77), Royal Acad. Surgeons (Ireland) (hon.), Pan Am. Med. Soc. Home: 4 Leslie Rd Winchester MA 01890-3123

SMITH, ROBERT NELSON, former government official, anesthesiologist; b. Toledo, Apr. 2, 1920; s. Robert Frederick and Amy Laura (Nelson) S.; children: Sandralyn, Sharon, Robert Nelson, Marilyn Anne, Marcia, Elizabeth. Student, U. Mich., 1938-39; BS, U.S. Mil. Acad., 1943; MS, MIT, 1945; MD, U. Nebr., 1952. Diplomate Am. Bd. Anesthesiologists. Commd. capt. USAAF, 1943, resigned, 1948; intern Toledo Hosp., Ohio, 1952-53; resident Toledo Hosp., 1954-57; anesthesiologist KFC Med. Corp., Toledo, 1954-76; asst. sec. def. for health affairs Washington, 1976-78; bd. dirs. Ohio Med. Indemnity Corp., Columbus, 1968-78; mem. anesthetic and life support drugs adv. com. FDA, Dept. HHS, 1986-90; mem. disability adv. coun. SSA, Dept. HHS, 1986-89. Chmn. State Health Planning Council, 1974-76; mem. Statewide Health Coordinating Council, until 1976. Recipient Sec. Def. medal for outstanding pub. service, 1977. Mem. AMA (Ho. of Dels. Resolution of Commendation), Ohio Med. Assn. (pres. 1970, commendation 1977), Am. Soc. Anesthesiology, Inverness Club, Rotary. Club: Inverness (Toledo). Home: 3424 Gallatin Rd Toledo OH 43606-2442

SMITH, ROBERT PEASE, retired physiatrist; b. Burlington, Vt., Apr. 26, 1917; s. Levi Pease and Julia (Pease) S.; m. Caroline Wheelock, July 5, 1947; children: Robert Pease Jr., Cynthia W., Julia Smith Wilson Wheelock, Sarah Smith Neagle, Alexander Wheelock, Elizabeth Huntington. AB, Princeton U., 1939; MD, Harvard U., Boston, 1943; postgrad., Harvard U., 1947. Diplomate Am. Bd. Phys. Medicine and Rehab. Intern Mass. Gen. Hosp., Boston, 1943-44; asst. resident in pathology New Eng. Deaconess Hosp., Boston, 1943; resident in medicine Mary Fletcher Hosp., Burlington; rsch. fellow Harvard Med., Boston, Mass., 1955; dir. Vt. Rehab. Ctr., 1956-66; dir. rehab. Louisville (Ky.) Rehab. Ctr., 1969-72, Gaylord Hosp., New Britain (Conn.) Meml. Hosp., 1972-87, Stamford (Conn.) Rehab. Ctr., 1972-76; dir. physical medicine Stamford (Conn.) Hosp., 1972-76; cons. Lawrence Meml. Hosp., New London, Conn.; dir. rehab. Gaylord Hosp., Wallingford, 1969-72; cons. Norwalk Hosp.; asst. prof. Yale U. Sch. Medicine, 1972-80, N.Y. Med. Coll., 1972-83; staff mem. Jewish Meml. Hosp., Ky., Children's Hosp., Louisville Gen. Hosp., Meth. Evangelical Hosp., VA Hosp, Norton Meml. Infirmary; asst., assoc. prof. Coll. Medicine U. Louisville. Contbr.

articles to med. jours. Capt. M.C., AUS, 1944-46, ETO. Decorated Bronze Star Combat Med. Badge. Fellow ACP, Am. Acad. Phys. Medicine, Am. Congress Rehab. Medicine; mem. Am. Acad. Phys. Med. and Rehab., Am. Congress Med. Rehab. (past pres. ea. sect.), Am. Soc. for Clin. Evoked Potentials, Chittenden County Med. Soc. (life). Congregationalist. Home: Converse Bay Rd RR 2 Box 2506 Charlotte VT 05445

SMITH, ROBERT POWELL, foundation executive, former ambassador; b. Joplin, Mo., Mar. 5, 1929; s. Powell Augusta and Estella (Farris) S.; m. Alice Irene Rountree, Aug. 22, 1953; children: Michael Bryan, Steven Powell, Karen Louise, David Robert. B.A., Tex. Christian U., 1954, M.A., 1955. Fgn. svc. officer Dept. State, 1955-81; press officer Washington, 1955; vice-consul Lahore, West Pakistan, 1956-58; 2d sec. Beirut, Lebanon, 1959-61; consul and prin. officer Enugu, Nigeria, 1962-65; officer-in-charge Ghanaian Affairs, 1966; officer-in-charge Nigerian Affairs, dep. dir. Office West African Affairs, 1967-69; dep. chief of mission, counselor of embassy Pretoria, South Africa, 1970-74; ambassador to Malta, 1974-76, Ghana, 1976-79, Liberia, 1979-81. Pres. Africa Wildlife Leadership Found., 1981-85. Served with USMCR, 1946-49, 50-52. Decorated Air medal.; recipient Meritorious Honor award State Dept., 1967. Mem. Am. Fgn. Service Assn. Baptist.

SMITH, ROBERT RUTHERFORD, university dean, communication educator; b. Buffalo, Nov. 18, 1933; s. Thomas Newlands and Mary Jane (Rutherford) S.; m. Suzanne Louise Stines, June 7, 1958; children: Eric Anthony, Gwendolyn Anne. B.A. cum laude, U. Buffalo, 1955; M.A., Ohio State U., 1956, Ph.D., 1963. Prof. communication, chmn. div. broadcasting and film Sch. Pub. Communication, Boston U., 1961-78; prof., dean. Sch. Communication and Theater Temple U., Phila., 1978-95; cons. Nat. Endowment for Arts, others. Author: poems Participations, 1972; criticism Beyond the Wasteland, 1980; editorTV Quar., 1971, Feedback, 1973-76; contbr. articles to profl. jours. Mem. communication com. Mass. Council Chs., 1971-76. Served with AUS, 1959-61. Mem. Broadcast Edn. Assn. (pres. 1984-85), Speech Communication Assn., Broadcase Pioneers (pres. Phila. 1985-86), Soc. Profl. Journalists (pres. 1983-85), Appalachian Mountain Club (Boston), Delmont Club (pres. 1992-94). Home: 6 Trout Farm Ln Plympton MA 02367 Office: Temple U Sch Communication Philadelphia PA 19122

SMITH, ROBERT SAMUEL, banker, former agricultural finance educator; b. Laconia, N.H., June 16, 1920; s. Samuel W. and Winnifred (Page) S.; m. Mary Morgan, June 20, 1942; children: Patricia, Peggy, Morgan Scott, Sharon, Starlee. BS, Cornell U., 1942, MS, 1950, PhD, 1952. County agrl. agt. Livingston County, Mt. Morris, N.Y., 1942-44, Lewis County, Lowville, N.Y., 1944, Belknap County, Laconia, 1947-49; assoc. prof. edn. Cornell U., Ithaca, N.Y., 1952-54, assoc. prof. farm mgmt., 1954-58, prof. agrl. fin., 1958-77, W.T. Myers prof. agrl. fin., 1977-81; chmn. Tompkins County Trust Co., Ithaca, 1978-92, chmn. emeritus, 1992—; trustee Mut. of N.Y./MONY Fin. Svcs., N.Y.C., 1981-93, emeritus, 1993—; bd. dirs. Challenge Industries, Ithaca, N.Y.; advisor Ministry of Agr., Israel, 1960-61, Agrl. Devel. Bank of Iran, 1968. Contbr. numerous articles to profl. jours. Elder First Presbyn. Ch., Ithaca, 1970; bd. dirs. Am. Agriculturist Found., Ithaca, 1980, East Lawn Cemetery Assn., Ithaca, 1987, Hospicare Found., Ithaca. 1st lt. U.S. Army, 1944-47, ETO. Recipient Tax Edn. award IRS, Buffalo, 1973, Disting. Svc. citation N.Y. State Agrl. Soc., 1982. Mem. Country Club of Ithaca, City Club Ithaca, Phi Kappa Phi, Epsilon Sigma Phi. Republican. Avocations: golf, bridge. Home: 60 Wedgewood Dr Ithaca NY 14850-1063 Office: Tompkins County Trust Co The Commons Ithaca NY 14850

SMITH, ROBERT SELLERS, lawyer; b. Samson, Ala., July 31, 1931; s. Abb Jackson and Rose (Sellers) S.; m. June Claire West, Feb. 2, 1963; children-Robert Sellers, David West, Rosemary True, Adam Douglas. BS, U. Va., 1953, LLB, 1958, LLM, 1990. Bar: Ala. 1959. Asst. counsel spl. com. to investigate campaign expenditures U.S. Ho. of Reps., 1960; counsel U.S. Senate Labor and Pub. Welfare Com., 1961-63; ptnr. firm Smith, Huckaby & Graves (P.A.), Huntsville, 1963-85, Bradley, Arant, Rose & White, Huntsville, 1985-95; ptnr. Foley, Smith & Mahmood, Huntsville, 1995—; instr. econs., Am. econ. history U. Ala., 1963-64; Mem. industry adv. com., select com. small bus. U.S. Senate. Author: West's Tax Law Dictionary and 11 other books; mem. bd. editors Ala. Lawyer, 1994—. Pres. Madison County (Ala.) Legal Aid Soc., 1971-75; pres. North Ala. Estate Planning Council, 1974. Served with U.S. Navy, 1953-57. Mem. ABA, Internat. Bar Assn., Ala. Bar Assn., Huntsville-Madison County Bar Assn. (pres. 1988). Episcopalian. Home: 6004 Macon Ct SE Huntsville AL 35802-1932 Office: Foley Smith & Mahmood 200 W Court Sq Huntsville AL 35801

SMITH, ROBERT VICTOR, university administrator; b. Glendale, N.Y., Feb. 16, 1942; s. Robert Arthur and Marie Marlene (Florence) S. BS in Pharm. Sci., St. John's U., Jamaica, N.Y., 1963; MS in Pharm. Chemistry, U. Mich., 1964, PhD in Pharm. Chemistry, 1968. Asst. prof., then assoc. prof. U. Iowa, Iowa City, 1968-74; assoc. prof., asst. dir. U. Tex., Austin, 1974-77, area coordinator basic pharmaceutics, 1975-76, assoc. dir. Drug Dynamics Inst., 1977-78, dir. Drug Dynamics Inst., Coll. Pharmacy, 1979-85, James E. Bauerle Centennial prof. Coll. Pharmacy, 1983-85; prof., dean Coll. Pharmacy Wash. State U., Pullman, 1985-86, vice provost for research, dean Grad. Sch., 1987—; cons. E. R. Squibb, New Brunswick, N.J., 1979-82, Upjohn Co., Kalamazoo, Mich., 1982-85; external examiner U. Malaysia, Penang, 1981-82; mem. sci. adv. bd. Biodecision Labs., Pitts., 1985-86; Wash. Biotech. Found., 1989-90; mem. noms. com. Coun. Grad. Schs., Washington, 1990-91; accreditation evaluator Northwest Assn. Schs. and Colls., Seattle, 1991—; mem. exec. com. grad. deans African-Am. Inst., N.Y., 1992—. Author: Textbook of Biopharmaceutic Analysis, 1981, Graduate Research: A Guide for Students in the Sciences, 1990, Development and Management of University Research Groups, 1986. Bd. dirs. Wash. Tech. Ctr., 1990-92. Grantee NIH, 1974-83; fellow Acad. Pharm. Scis., 1981, Am. Assn. Pharm. Scientists, 1987; recipient Disting. Alumnus award Coll. Pharmacy U. Mich., 1990, Outstanding Svc. award Wash. State U., Grad. and Profl. Student Assn., 1993. Mem. Am. Assn. Colls. Pharmacy (chmn. research and grad. affairs com. 1983-84), U.S. Pharmacopeia (revision com. 1985-90), Acad. Pharm. Scis. (chmn., vice chmn. 1983-85, 90, Presdl. citation 1985), Wash. Rsch. Found. (bd. dirs. 1989—). Unitarian. Home: 862 Indian Hills Dr Moscow ID 83843 Office: Wash State Univ Grad Sch Pullman WA 99164

SMITH, ROBERT WALTER, food company executive; b. Chgo., Nov. 11, 1937; s. Ernest Gilmer and Anna (Reptik) S.; m. Audrey Mavis Segar, Apr. 20, 1962; children: Melissa Ann, Kathleen Diane, Michael Robert. BS, U. Ariz., 1963. Mgmt. trainee Fleming Cos. Inc., Houston, 1963-64, mgr. store planning, 1964-65; mgr. store planning Fleming Cos. Inc., Austin, 1965-66, Phila., 1966-72; dir. site selection Fleming Cos. Inc., Topeka, 1972-75, dir. store devel., 1975-83; v.p. store devel. Fleming Cos. Inc., Oklahoma City, 1983—, sr. v.p. retail devel., 1993—. Mem. Nat. Assn. Corp. Real Estate Execs., Internat. Coun. Shopping Ctrs. Republican. Lutheran. Office: Fleming Cos Inc Box 26647 6301 Waterford Blvd Oklahoma City OK 73126

SMITH, ROBERT WESTON See WOLFMAN JACK

SMITH, ROBERT WILLIAM, former insurance company executive, lawyer; b. Catskill, N.Y., Apr. 2, 1923; s. Victor and Leda Leone (Cline) S.; m. Inez R. Iuzzolino, Jan. 31, 1976; children: Jeffrey, Timothy, Kathy. BS cum laude, Syracuse U., 1948; JD cum laude, Seton Hall U. Coll. of Law, 1987. Bar: N.J. 1987; accredited pers. exec.; CLU. With Prudential Ins. Co. Am., Newark, 1948-84; sr. v.p. Prudential Ins. Co. Am., 1973-84; mem. adv. council on mgmt. and personnel research (Conf. Bd.), 1975-83, chmn., 1977-78; now ret.; chmn. LOMA Personnel Council, 1971-72; bus. adminstr., City of Newark, 1970. Trustee Coll. of Ins., 1974-83; trustee State Theater of N.J., 1983-92, chmn., 1984-87; cons. Nat. Exec. Svc. Corps, 1988—. Served to lst lt. USAAF, 1942-45. Decorated Air medal with 5 oak leaf clusters. Mem. Beta Gamma Sigma, Alpha Kappa Psi, Sigma Phi Epsilon. Home: 41 Woodbine Rd Florham Park NJ 07932-2647

SMITH, ROBERTA HAWKING, plant physiologist; b. Tulare, Calif., May 3, 1945; d. William Brevard and Freda Lois (Kessler) Hawkins; m. James Willie Smith Jr., Sept. 17, 1968; children: James Willie III, Cristine Lois. BS, U. Calif., Riverside, 1967, MS, 1968, PhD, 1970. Postdoctoral fellow dept. plant sci. Tex. A&M U., College Station, 1972-73, asst. prof. dept. plant sci., 1974-79, assoc. prof. dept. plant sci., 1979-85, prof. dept. soil and crop sci., 1985—; asst. prof. Sam Huston State U., Huntsville, Tex., 1973-74. Editl. bd. In Vitro Cellular and Dev. Biology, 1991-96, Jour. Plant Physiology, 1994—; assoc. editor Jour. Crop Sci., 1995—. Mem. Crop Sci. Soc. Am. (chmn. C-7 divsn. 1990-91), Internat. Crops Rsch. Inst. Semi-Arid Tropics (bd. govs. 1989-95), Faculty of Plant Physiology (chmn. 1987-89), Soc. In Vitro Biology (chmn. plant divsn. 1983-86, pres. 1994-96). Republican. Methodist. Avocations: Western horseback riding, gardening, reading. Home: RR 1 Box 701 Hearne TX 77859-9734 Office: Tex A&M Univ Dept Soil And Sci College Station TX 77843

SMITH, ROBIN DOYLE, judge; b. Oklahoma City, Jan. 23, 1957; s. Travis Ray and Juanita May (Stephens) S. BS, Okla. State U., 1979; JD, Tex. Tech. U., 1981. Bar: Tex. 1982. Asst. city atty. City of Midland, Tex., 1982-83, presiding judge, 1984—; sole practice Midland, 1983-84; bd. dirs. Tex. Mcpl. Cts. Assn., 2 v.p., 1989-90, pres.-elect, 1990-91, pres., 1991-92, bd. tng. ctr., Austin. Contbg. author Tex. Mcpl. Court Procedures Manual, 1988, Tex. Mcpl. Ct. Tng. Ctr. Newsletter, 1987; pub. Tex. Mcpl. Ct. Justice Ct. News, 1987—. Grad. Leadership Midland, 1987. Named one of five outstanding young Texans Tex. Jr. C. of C., 1994.3. Mem. ABA (del. to conf. of spl. ct. judges 1988, 89, 90, 91, 92, 93, 94, 95, exec. com. 1990—, vice chair 1994-95, chair-elect 1995-96), State Bar Tex. (chmn. mcpl. judges sect. 1988-89, state bar coll. 1986—). Republican. Avocations: water sports, scuba diving, sailing, outdoor activities. Home: PO Box 585 Midland TX 79702-0585 Office: City of Midland Tex PO Box 1152 Midland TX 79702-1152

SMITH, RODGER FIELD, financial executive; b. Milw., Jan. 23, 1941; s. Millard Beale and Alice Catherine (Field) S.; m. Sarah Godfrey, June 19, 1964; children: Rodger F. Jr., Scott G., Reid W. BSChemE, U. Wis., 1964, MBA in Fin. with distinction, 1965. V.p. Allis Chalmers, Milw., 1966-76; ptnr. Greenwich (Conn.) Assocs., 1976—; trustee Harbor Funds, Toledo, 1987—; bd. dirs. Arlington Capital, London, 1991. Author articles and spkr. on investing pension funds. Fund raiser United Way, Milw., 1966-76. Mem. U. Wis. Alumni Assn. (nat. bd. dirs. 1994—), Wee Burn Country Club, Bascom Hill Soc., Tau Beta Pi (chmn. trust adv. com. 1986—), Beta Gamma Sigma. Avocations: travel, golf, tennis, coin collecting. Office: Greenwich Assocs Office Park Eight Greenwich CT 06830

SMITH, RODNEY, electronics executive; b. 1941. BSEE, Southampton Coll. Advanced Tech., Eng. Various positions to v.p., gen. mgr. Fairchild Semiconductor Corp., Mountain View, Calif., 1969-83; chmn., pres., CEO Altera Corp., San Jose, Calif., 1983—. Office: Altera Corp 2610 Orchard Pky San Jose CA 95134-2020*

SMITH, ROGER DEAN, pathologist; b. N.Y.C., Oct. 6, 1932; s. Joseph Leslie and Matilda (Feigelson) S.; m. Margaret Helen Smith, Apr. 24, 1957; children—Wade Russell, Craig Andrew, Douglas Dean, Roger Len. A.B., Cornell U., 1954; M.D., N.Y. Med. Coll., 1958. Diplomate Am. Bd. Pathology, Nat. Bd. Med. Examiners (flex test com. 1982-94, chmn. 1983-90, U.S. med. licensing exam. step 3 devel. com. 1992-94, med. licensing exam. step 3 com. 1994—). Asst. prof. dept. pathology U. Ill. Coll. Medicine, Chgo., 1966; cons. renal pathology Presbyn. St. Lukes Hosp., W. Side VA Hosp., Chgo., 1969; asso. prof. dept. pathology U. Ill. Coll. Medicine, Chgo., 1970, dir. ind. study program, asst. dean, 1971-72; Mary M. Emery prof. U. Cin., 1972—, dir. dept. pathology, 1972-90, dir. autopsy svc., 1991—; dir. lab. services U. Cin. Hosp.; mem. test coms. Nat. Bd. Med. Examiners, 1976—. Contbr. research papers to profl. jours. Capt. M.C. U.S. Army, 1959-61. Recipient Hoektoen award Chgo. Pathology Soc.; USPHS pathology research fellow, 1962-66; Am. Cancer Soc. grantee, 1965-68; NIH grantee, 1968-72, 75-79. Mem. Am. Assn. Pathologists (chmn. 1972, pres. 1985-88), Coll. Am. Pathologists (chmn. edn. com. and manpower task force 1983-90), Internat. Acad. Pathology, Am. Assn. Clin. Pathologists, Armed Forces Inst. Pathology (sci. adv. bd. 1989-94). Home: 1319 Dillon Ave Cincinnati OH 45208-4208 Office: U Cin Coll Medicine Dept Pathology Cincinnati OH 45267

SMITH, ROGER WINSTON, political theorist, educator; b. Birmingham, Ala., July 9, 1936; s. Buford Houston and Sarah Louise (Trucks) S.; m. Martha Christin Daniels, Jan. 16, 1960; children—Louisa, David. A.B. magna cum laude, Harvard U., 1958, postgrad. in law, 1958-59; M.A. in Polit. Sci., U. Calif.-Berkeley, 1963, Ph.D. in Polit. Sci., 1971. Teaching assoc. U. Calif.-Berkeley, 1965-66; asst. prof. govt. Coll. William and Mary, Williamsburg, Va., 1967-72, assoc. prof., 1972-80, prof, 1980—; sr. lectr. politics Glasgow (Scotland) U., 1977-78; lectr. N.E.H., 1988; cons. Nelson-Hall Pubs., Chgo.; mem. coun. Inst. Internat. Conf. on the Holocaust and Genocide, Jerusalem; co-founder, v.p. Assn. Genocide Scholars; film cons. Armenian Heritage Project. Co-author, editor: Guilt: Man and Society, 1971; co-author: Genocide and the Modern Age, 1986, Genocide, vol. 2, 1991, Bearing Witness to the Holocaust, 1939-89; contbg. editor Internet on the Holocaust and Genocide; contbr. articles to profl. jours. Served to 1st lt. U.S. Army, 1960-62, Japan. Fellow NSF, 1966, College of William and Mary, 1977. Mem. Am. Polit. Sci. Assn., Human Rights Watch, Cultural Survival. Democrat. Baptist. Avocations: gardening; walking. Home: 102 Lake Dr Williamsburg VA 23185-3113 Office: Coll William and Mary Dept Govt Williamsburg VA 23187

SMITH, RONALD EARL, aircraft design engineer; b. St. Louis, May 22, 1947; s. Lawrence Abner and Judith Evelyn (Roberson) S.; children: Kimberly A., Russell E. BSME, U. Mo., 1970, MS in Mech. and Aerospace Engring., 1971; PDD in Engring. Mgmt., U. Mo., Rolla, 1986; postgrad., Def. Sys. Mgmt. Coll., Ft. Belvoir, Va., 1990. Student coop. engr. McDonnell Douglas, St. Louis, 1966-70, design engr., 1971-90, head design engr., 1990-91; program mgr. MD-12 wing McDonnell Douglas, Long Beach, Calif., 1992; chief sys. engr. McDonnell Douglas, St. Louis, 1992-93, chief engr. F/A-18, 1993—. Editor newsletter Gateway News, 1992; contbr. articles to profl. jours. Team mgr. Creve Coeur Athletic Assn., St. Louis, 1987, team coach, 1986. Fellow AIAA (assoc., com. mem. 1976-86, treas. 1982-83, vice chmn. 1993-94, chmn. 1994-95, Sect. Svc. award 1996); mem. Tau Beta Pi. Avocation: skiing. Home: 14062 Forest Crest Dr Chesterfield MO 63017-3242

SMITH, RONALD EMORY, telecommunications executive; b. Shelburne, N.S., Can., May 26, 1950; s. Edgar Earle and Ida Mae (Porter) S.; children: Stephen, Sarah, Susan. BBA, Acadia U., Wolfville, N.S., 1971. Chartered acct., N.S. Staff acct., mgr. Clarkson Gordon (now Ernst & Young), Halifax, N.S., 1971-78, Toronto, Ont., Can., 1978-80; prin., ptnr. Woods Gordon (now Ernst & Young), Toronto, 1980-87; v.p. fin. and sales Maritime Tel. & Tel., Halifax, 1987—; dir. Maritime Med. Care Inc., Dartmouth, N.S., 1995—; bd. dirs. The Island Telephone Co. Ltd., Charlottetown, P.E.I., Can., MT&T Leasing Inc., Halifax, MT&T Mobility Inc., Halifax. Dir. Coun. for Can. Unity, 1994—; bd. govs. Acadia U., 1994—; chmn. Atlantic Provinces Econ. Coun., Halifax, 1993-95, Grace Hosp. Bd. Trustees, 1989—; pres. Can. Assn. for Cmty. Living, 1989-93, chmn. Min.'s Task Force on Physician Policy Devel., N.S., 1991-93; mem. coun. fin. execs. Conf. Bd. Mem. Fin. Execs. Inst., Can. Inst. Chartered Accts., Inst. Chartered Accts. N.S., Ashburn Golf Club. Roman Catholic. Avocations: golf, hiking, travel. Office: Maritime Tel & Tel Co Ltd, 1505 Barrington St PO Box 880, Halifax, NS Canada B3J 2W3

SMITH, RONALD LYNN, health system executive; b. Algona, Iowa, Sept. 22, 1940; s. Russell Malcom and Helen Lucille (Gridley) S.; m. Jacqueline Sue Yarger, Dec. 23, 1962 (div. Aug. 1981); children: Sheri Rene, Gregory Mark, Brenton Alan; m. Sylvia Jo Grotjan, Dec. 31, 1982; 1 child, Russell Lynn. B.S., Iowa State U., 1962; postgrad., U. S.D., 1963; M.A., U. Iowa, 1965. With Harris Hosp.-Methodist, Ft. Worth, 1967-82, assoc. exec. dir., 1974-76, exec. dir., 1977-82; pres. Harris Meth. Health System, Ft. Worth, 1982—; trustee Am. Healthcare Systems, Nat. Com. for Quality Health Care; mem. adv. coun. Hill-Rom Co., 1991; mem. healthcare exec. adv. coun. IBM, 1991; mem. bd. Tex. Commerce Bank. Trustee Tarrant County United Way, 1977-79, campaign chmn., 1992, chmn. bd. trustees 1993, chmn. bd. dirs., 1994, area-wide svcs. chair, 1988—, self-sufficiency task force; bd. mem. Tex. Rsch. League, 1990—, nat. bd. visitors Tex. Christian U., 1990—; bd. visitors Tex. Wesleyan U., 1995—. Fellow Am. Coll. Hosp. Execs.; mem. Tex. Hosp. Assn. (trustee 1983-87, chmn. 1986-87), Dallas-Ft. Worth Hosp. Coun. (pres. 1981), Ft. Worth C. of C. (bd. dirs. 1992), Rotary. Methodist.

SMITH, ROWLAND JAMES, educational administrator; b. Johannesburg, S. Africa, Aug. 19, 1938; s. John James and Gladys Spencer (Coldrey) S.; m. Catherine Anne Lane, Sept. 22, 1962; children: Russell Claude, Belinda Claire. B.A., U. Natal, 1959, Ph.D., 1967; M.A., Oxford U., Eng., 1967. Lectr. English U. Witwatersrand, Johannesburg, S. Africa, 1963-67; asst. prof. Dalhousie U., Halifax, N.S., Can., 1967-70, assoc. prof. English, 1970-77, prof., 1977-88, McCulloch prof., 1988-94, chmn. English dept., 1977-83, 85-86, dir. Centre for African Studies, 1976-77, asst. dean arts and scis., 1972-74, dean arts and social scis., 1988-93, provost Coll. Arts and Scis., 1988-89, 90-91, 92-93; vis. prof., rsch. assoc. Multidisciplinary Ctr. Can. Studies, U. Rouen, 1994; prof. Wilfrid Laurier U., Waterloo, Ontario, 1994—, v.p. acad., 1994—. Author: Lyric and Polemic: The Literary Personality of Roy Campbell, 1972; editor: Exile and Tradition: Studies in African and Caribbean Literature, 1976, Critical Essays on Nadine Gordimer, 1990. Bd. govs. Halifax Grammar Sch., 1972-74; bd. govs. Neptune Theatre Found., 1977-78; mem. selection com. IODE Meml. Scholarships for N.S., 1969-71, Rhodes Scholarships N.S., 1972-74; mem. edn. com. Victoria Gen. Hosp., 1986-90; dir. publicity and promotion N.S. Rugby Football Union, 1987-89; chair liaison com. edn. dept. N.S. U., 1990-93; mem. book prize jury, Can. Fedn. for Humanities, 1990, regional judge (Can. and the Caribbean) Commonwealth Writers Prize, 1991. Recipient Transvaal Rhodes scholar, 1960; vis. fellow Dalhousie U., 1965-66, vis. scholar Ctr. Canadian Studies U. Western Sydney, Macarthur, New South Wales; Can. Council leave fellow, 1974-75, research grantee, 1977; grantee Social Scis. and Humanities Research Council of Can., 1978, internat. grantee, 1985, grantee Cultural Personalities Exchange program Assn. Canadian Studies in Australia and New Zealand, 1996. Mem. Assn. Can. Univ. Tchrs. English (sec.-treas. 1968-70, profl. concern com. 1979-81), Can. Assn. for Commonwealth Lit. and Lang. Studies (exec. mem. 1989-92, pres. 1995—), Can. Assn. Chmn. English (v.p. 1981-82, pres. 1982-83, exec. mem.-at-large 1985-86), Can. Fedn. Humanities (aid to scholarly publs. com. 1979-85, bd. dirs. 1992-94), MLA (div. chmn. 1984). Office: Wilfrid Laurier U, Office of VP Acad, Waterloo, ON Canada N2L 3C5

SMITH, ROY FORGE, art director, production designer. Art dir.: (films) Far from the Madding Crowd, 1967, The Assassination Bureau, 1969, The Amazing Mr. Blunden, 1972, Yesterday, 1980, The Last Chase, 1981, Mrs. Soffel, 1984; prodn. designer: (films) Monty Python and the Holy Grail, 1974, The House By the Lake, 1976, Jabberwocky, 1977, The Hound of the Baskervilles, 1979, Running, 1979, Funeral Home, 1981, Melanie, 1983, Curtains, 1983, The Believers, 1987, Burnin' Love, 1987, The Kiss, 1988, Bill & Ted's Excellent Adventure, 1989, Teenage Mutant Ninja Turtles, 1990, Teenage Mutant Ninja Turtles II: The Secret of the Ooze, 1991, Warlock, 1991, Teenage Mutant Ninja Turtles III, 1993, Robin Hood: Men in Tights, 1993, The Page Master, 1994, (TV movies) Clown White, 1980, A Deadly Business, 1986, Haunted By Her Past, 1987, The Lost Capone, 1990, (TV series) SCTV, 1983. Office: Sandra Marsh Mgt 9150 Wilshire Blvd Ste 220 Beverly Hills CA 90212-3429

SMITH, ROY JORDAN, religious organization administrator; b. Franklin, N.C., July 7, 1929; s. Sanford Jordan and Pearl Elizabeth (Kinsland) S.; m. Doris Elizabeth Pearce, Dec. 20, 1950; children: Ginger Smith Graves, Roy J. Jr., Tracy M. BA, Wake Forest U., 1952, DD (hon.), 1995; MDiv, Southeastern Bapt. Theol. Sem., Wake Forest, N.C., 1956; DD (hon.), Campbell U., 1981. Ordained to ministry Bapt. State Conv., 1954. Pastor Union Hope Bapt. Ch., Zebulon, N.C., 1954-57, Jersey Bapt. Ch., Lexington, N.C., 1957-62; regional missionary Bapt. State Conv., Sylva, N.C., 1962-67; dir. town and country missions Bapt. State Conv., Raleigh, N.C., 1967-78, assoc. exec. dir., 1978-84, exec. dir., 1984—; cons. on sem. extension, Nashville, 1962-77; cons. on leisure ministry Bapt. Home Mission Bd., Atlanta, 1962-77. Contbr. articles to religious publs. Chaplain Lions Club, Linwood, N.C., 1959-62, Sylva Fire Dept., 1964-67. Mem. Assn. State Exec. Dirs. (pres. 1994-95). Avocations: camping, gardening, fishing, travel. Home: 4746 Wildwood St Raleigh NC 27612 Office: Bapt State Conv PO Box 1107 Cary NC 27512-1107

SMITH, ROY PHILIP, judge; b. S.I., N.Y., Dec. 29, 1933; s. Philip Aloysius and Virginia (Collins) S.; m. Elizabeth Helen Wink, Jan. 23, 1965; children: Matthew P., Jean E. BA, St. Joseph's Coll., Yonkers, N.Y., 1956; JD, Fordham U., 1965. Bar: N.Y. Asst. reg. counsel FAA, N.Y.C., 1966-79; adminstrv. law judge U.S. Dept. Labor, Washington, 1979-83; adminstrv. appeals judge Benefits Rev. Bd., Washington, 1983—, chmn., chief adminstrv. appeals judge, 1988-90; adj. prof. aviation law Dowling Coll., Oakdale, N.Y., 1972-79; adj. prof. transp. law Adelphi U., Garden City, N.Y., 1975-79; vis. prof. Georgetown U. Law Sch., 1989—. With U.S. Army, 1957-59. Mem. Assn. of Bar of City of N.Y. (sec.-treas. aeronautics com. 1978-79), Fed. Adminstrv. Law Judges Conf. (treas. 1983-84, mem. exec. com. 1982-83), Internat. Platform Assn., Friendly Sons of St. Patrick, Edgemoor Club. Avocation: tennis. Home: 6700 Pawtucket Rd Bethesda MD 20817-4836 Office: Benefits Rev Bd 800 K St NW Washington DC 20001-8000

SMITH, RUBY LUCILLE, librarian; b. Nobob, Ky., Sept. 19, 1917; d. James Ira and Myrtie Olive (Crabtree) Jones; AB, Western Ky. State Tchrs. Coll., 1943, MA, 1966; m. Kenneth Cornelius Smith, Dec. 25, 1946; children: Kenneth Cornelius, Corma Ann. Tchr. rural schs., Barren County, Ky., 1941-42; tchr. secondary sch. English, libr. Temple Hill Consol. Sch., Glasgow, Ky., 1943-47, 49-51, 53-56, sch. libr., 1956-83. Sec. Barren County Cancer Soc., 1968-70, Barren County Fair Bd., 1969-70; leader 4-H Club, 1957-72, mem. council Barren County; coord. AARP tax-aide program, 1985—, assoc. dist. dir., 1988—. Trustee Mary Wood Weldon Meml. Libr., 1964—; trustee Barren County Pub. Libr., 1969—, sec., 1969—; instr. 55 Alive Mature Driving AARP, 1993—. Mem. NEA (life), Ky. Edn. Assn., Ky. Sch. Media Assn. (sec. 1970-71), 3d Dist. Libr. Assn. (pres. 1944, 66), Barren County Edn. Assn. (pres. 1960-62, treas. 1979-80), 3d Dist. Ret. Tchrs. Assn. (pres. 1991-92), Ky. Ret. Tchrs Assn. (v.p. 1992-93, pres.-elect 1993, pres. 1994-95), Ky. Audio Visual Assn., Glasgow-Barren County Ret. Tchrs. Assn. (pres. 1984-86, sec. 1989, treas. 1990), Ky. Libr. Trustee Assn. (bd. dirs. 1985—, pres. 1986-88, 93-94, dir. Barren River region 1985—), Barren County Rep. Women's Club, Monroe Assn. Woman's Missionary Union (dir. 1968-72, 79-83 Monroe Assn. Bapts. (libr. dir. 1972-88, sec. 1985—), Ky. Libr. Assn., Delta Kappa Gamma (pres. Delta chpt. 1996—). Home: 54 E Nobob Rd Summer Shade KY 42166-8405

SMITH, RUSSELL FRANCIS, transportation executive; b. Washington, Mar. 26, 1944; s. Raymond Francis and Elma Gloria (Daugherty) S.. Student East Carolina U., 1964, N.C. State U., 1964-65; BS with honors, U. Md.-Coll. Park, 1969, MBA, 1975. Exec. asst. mgr. Hotel Corp. Am. Internat. Inn and Mayflower Hotel, Washington, 1966-68; sr. venture capital cons. Initiative Investing Corp., Washington, 1968-69; pres., gen. mgr. Associated Trades Corp., Washington, 1970-74; cons. in fin., Greenbelt, Md., 1974-76; mng. cons. Bradford Nat. Corp., Washington, 1976-79; v.p. OAO Corp., Washington, 1979-81; ptnr. for fin. evaluation and ops. analysis Blake, Brunell, Lehmann & Co., Washington, 1981-86; v.p. mgmt. services adminstrn. United Airlines Svcs. Corp., Lakewood, Colo., 1986-91, cons. Venture Fund of Washington, 1991—. Chmn. com. on wildlife Prince George Humane Soc., Hyattsville, Md., 1968-71, Soc. for Prevention Cruelty to Animals, Hyattsville. 1971-75. Served with U.S. Army, 1963-66. Decorated Silver Star medal, Bronze Star medal with V device, Purple Heart. Mem. Am. Fin. Assn., Ops. Research Soc. Am., Am. Acctg. Assn., N.Am. Soc. Corp. Planners, Internat. Assn. Math. Modeling, Assn. MBA Execs. (registered investment advisor), Beta Gamma Sigma, Beta Alpha Psi. Republican.

SMITH, RUSSELL JACK, former intelligence official; b. Jackson, Mich., July 4, 1913; s. Lee C. and Georgia L. (Weed) S.; m. Rosemary Thomson, Sept. 5, 1938; children: Stephen M., Scott T., Christopher G. AB, Miami U., Oxford, Ohio, 1937; PhD, Cornell U., 1941. Asst. instr. English Cornell U., 1937-41; instr. English Williams Coll., 1941-45; with OSS, 1945; asst. prof. English Wells Coll., 1946-47; with CIA, 1947-74, mem. bd. nat. estimates, 1957-62, dir. current intelligence, 1962-66, dep. dir. for intelligence, 1966-71; spl. asst. U.S. Embassy, New Delhi, 1971-74; rsch. cons., 1975—; assigned Nat. War Coll., 1951-52, U.S. rep. Brit. Joint Intelligence Com., Far East, Singapore, 1954-56. Author: John Dryden, A Study in Controversy, 1941, The Unknown CIA: My Three Decades with the Agency, 1989, (novels) The Secret War, 1986, The Singapore Chance, 1991, Lodestone, 1993, Whirligig, 1994. Recipient Nat. Civil Svc. League award, 1971, Disting. Intelligence medal CIA, 1974. Mem. Phi Beta Kappa, Phi Delta Theta, Omicron Delta Kappa. Home: 1138 Bellview Rd Mc Lean VA 22102-1104

SMITH, RUSSELL L., film critic; b. Dallas, Nov. 11, 1956. BJ, U. Tex., Arlington, 1983. Pop music critic Dallas Morning News, 1984-89, film critic, 1989—. Recipient First Pl. award criticism Tex. AP Mng. Editors, 1989, awards of merit Gay and Lesbian Assn. Against Defamation, Dallas, 1992, Tex. Lesbian and Gay Journalists Assn., Austin, 1993. Office: Dallas Morning News 508 Young St Dallas TX 75202-4808

SMITH, RUTH LILLIAN SCHLUCHTER, librarian; b. Detroit, Oct. 18, 1917; d. Clayton John and Gertrude Katherine (Kastler) Schluchter; m. Thomas Guilford Smith, Sept. 28, 1946; 1 son, Pemberton, III. AB, Wayne State U., Detroit, 1939; AB in Libr. Sci., U. Mich., Ann Arbor, 1942. Libr. Detroit Pub. Libr., 1942-43; rsch. asst. Moore Sch. Elec. Engring. U. Pa., Phila., 1946-47; libr. Bethesda (Md.) Meth. Ch. Libr., 1955-61; reference libr., chief reader svcs. Inst. Def. Analyses, Arlington, Va., 1961-65, chief unclassified libr. sect., 1965-67, head libr., 1967-75, mgr. tech. info. svcs., 1975-81; dir. office customer svcs. Nat. Tech. Info. Svc., 1981-88, cons., 1988—; leader ch. libr. workshops, 1960—; speaker profl. meetings; founder, chmn. Com. Info. Hang-ups, 1969-86; mem. Depository Libr. Coun. to Pub. Printer, 1975-78, Def. Tech. Info. Ctr. Resource Sharing Adv. Group, 1980-82; chmn. edn. working group Fed. Libr. and Info. Ctr. Com., 1984-88, cons., 1988—. Author: Publicity for a Church Library, 1966, Workshop Planning, 1972, (with Claudia Hannaford) Promotion Planning, 1975, Getting the Books off the Shelves, 1975, rev. edit., 1985, 2nd rev. edit., 1991, Cataloging Made Easy, 1978, rev. edit., 1986, Setting up a Library: How to Begin or Begin Again, 1979, rev. edit., 1987, 2nd rev. edit., 1994, Running a Library, 1982; contbr. articles to library and religious jours. Mem. ALA, Am. Soc. Info. Sci., Ch. and Synagogue Library Assn. (founding mem., life mem., pres. 1967-68), Fedn. Info. Users (v.p. interactive affairs 1973-75), Spl. Libraries Assn. (chmn. aerospace div. 1975-76, chmn. library mgmt. div. 1978-79, chmn. div. cabinet 1980-81, John Cotton Dana award 1979, SLA Fellow award 1987, Hall of Fame award 1988). Republican. Methodist. Home: 5304 Glenwood Rd Bethesda MD 20814-1406

SMITH, SALLYE WRYE, librarian; b. Birmingham, Ala., Nov. 11, 1923; d. William Florin and Margaret (Howard) Wrye; m. Stuart Werner Smith, Sept. 20, 1947 (dec. June 1981); children: Carol Ann, Susan Patricia, Michael Christopher, Julie Lynn, Lori Kathleen. BA, U. Ala., 1945; MA, U. Denver, 1969. Psychometrician U.S. Army, Deshon Gen. Hosp., Butler, Pa., 1945-46, U.S. Vet. Adminstrn. Vocat. Guidance, U. Ala., Tuscaloosa, 1946; clin. psychologist U.S. Army, Walter Reed Gen. Hosp., Washington, 1946-47, U.S. Army, Fitzsimons Gen. Hosp., Denver, 1948, U.S. Vets. Adminstrn., Ft. Logan, Colo., 1948-50; head sci.-engring. libr. U. Denver, Colo., 1969-72; instr., reference libr. Penrose Libr., U. Denver, 1972-80, asst. prof., reference libr., 1980-90, interim dir., 1990-92; vis. prof. U. Denver Grad. Sch. Libr. Info. Mgmt., 1975-77, 83; info. broker Colo. Rschrs., Denver, 1979—; cons., presenter The Indsl. Info. Workshop Inst. de Investigaciones Tecnologicas, Bogota, Colombia, 1979, LIPI-DRI-PDIN workshop on R&D mgmt., Jakarta, Indonesia, 1982; mem. BRS User Adv. Bd., Latham, N.Y., 1983-86. Indexer: Statistical Abstract of Colorado 1976-77, 1977. Recipient Cert. of Recognition, Sigma Xi, U. Denver chpt., 1983. Mem. ALA, Spl. Libr. Assn., Colo. Libr. Assn., Phi Beta Kappa, Beta Phi Mu.

SMITH, SAM PRITZKER, columnist, author; b. Bklyn., Jan. 24, 1948; s. Leon and Betty (Pritzker) S.; m. Kathleen Ellen Rood, Jan. 24, 1976; 1 child, Connor. BBA in Acctg., Pace U., N.Y.C., 1970; MA in Journalism, Ball State U., Muncie, Ind., 1974. Acct. Arthur Young & Co., N.Y.C., 1970-72; reporter Ft. Wayne (Ind.) News Sentinal, Ft. Wayne, 1973-76, States News Svc., Washington, 1976-79; press sec. U.S. Senator Lowell Weicker Jr., 1979; writer/reporter Chgo. Tribune, 1979-90, columnist, 1991—. Author: The Jordan Rules, 1991; Second Coming, 1995; contbr. articles to mags. including Inside Sports, Sport, Basketball Digest. With USAR, 1970-76. Recipient Journalism awards AP, UPI, Sigma Delta Chi; named Ball State U. Journalism Alumnus of Yr. Office: Chicago Tribune 435 N Michigan Ave Chicago IL 60611-4001

SMITH, SAMUEL BOYD, history educator; b. Adams, Tenn., Oct. 23, 1929; s. Carl S. and Annie (Tolleson) S.; m. Martha Sue Fitzsimmons, Dec. 23, 1956; children—David Fitzsimmons, Mark Tolleson, Stephen Boyd. Student, Milligan Coll., 1947-48, U. Tenn., 1948-49, Syracuse U., 1951-52; B.S., Peabody Coll., 1956; M.A., Vanderbilt U., 1960, Ph.D., 1962. Asst. prof. history U. South Fla., 1961-64; state librarian and archivist, chmn. Tenn. Hist. Commn., 1964-69; lectr. history Peabody Coll., 1965-66; assoc. prof. history U. Tenn., 1969-71, prof., editor Andrew Jackson Presdl. Papers, 1972-79; prof. Tenn. State U., Nashville, 1979—. Co-author: This is Tennessee, 1973; Editor and compiler: Tennessee History: A Bibliography, 1974; co-editor: The Papers of Andrew Jackson, vol. I, 1980. Served with USAF, 1951-54. Mem. Orgn. Am. Historians, Am. Hist. Assn., Tenn. Hist. Assn., Shakespeare Club, Rotarian. Democrat. Methodist. Home: 1135 Sewanee Rd Nashville TN 37220-1017 Office: Tenn State Univ History Dept Downtown Campus Nashville TN 37203

SMITH, SAMUEL DAVID, artist, educator; b. Thorndale, Tex., Feb. 11, 1918; s. Otto Frank and Jeanette (Joyce) S.; m. Elizabeth Marie Smith; children: Cezanne, Rembrandt, Michelangelo. Ed. pub. schs. Prof. art U. N.Mex., 1956-84, prof. art emeritus, 1984—. Illustrator: Roots in Adobe, 1967, Cowboy's Christmas Tree, 1956; also: Coronet mag; one man exhbns. include, Corcoran Gallery Art, Washington, 1949, Santa Fe Mus. Art, 1947, Roswell (N.Mex.) Mus. Fine Art, 1953, 64, Goodwell (Okla.) Hist. Mus., 1964, Panhandle Plains Mus., Canyon City, Tex., 1964, Biltomore Galleries, Los Angeles, 1946, First Nat. Bank, Los Alamos, 1968, group exhbns. include, Baker Galleries, Lubbock, Tex., 1964-73, Met. Mus., N.Y.C., 1944, Blue Door Gallery, Taos, N.Mex., 1946-53, Galeria del Sol, Albuquerque, 1968-73, Brandywine Galleries, 1972-73, Watercolor Workshop, Telluride, Colo., 1964; one-man show includes Retrospective Exhbn. U. of N.Mex., Albuquerque, 1986, World War II War Art Exibit, Nat. Bldg. Mus., 1995. Served as combat artist AUS, 1942-45. Hon. life mem. N.Mex. Art League. Mem. Artist Equity Assn. (pres. N.Mex. chpt. 1957-58, 66-67, 70-71), Elks. Gallery: PO Box 2006 Telluride CO 81435-2006

SMITH, SAMUEL HOWARD, academic administrator, plant pathologist; b. Salinas, Calif., Feb. 4, 1940; s. Adrian Reed and Elsa (Jacop) S.; m. Patricia Ann Walter, July 8, 1960; children: Samuel Howard, Linda Marie. BS in Plant Pathology, U. Calif., Berkeley, 1961, PhD, 1964; D (hon.), Nihon U., Tokyo, 1989. NATO fellow Glasshouse Crops Research Inst., Sussex, Eng., 1964-65; asst. prof. plant pathology U. Calif., Berkeley, 1965-69; assoc. prof. Pa. State U., Arendtsville, 1969-71; assoc. prof. Pa. State U., University Park, 1971-74, prof., 1974-85, head dept. plant pathology, 1976-81, dean Coll. Agr., dir. Pa. Agrl. Expt. Sta. and Coop. Extension Service, 1981-85; pres. Wash. State U., 1985—; bd. dirs. Assoc. Weestern Univs.; adv. com. Wash. Sch. Employees Credit Union, 1993-95; mem. adv. com. Battelle Pacific N.W. Lab., 1993—; chair Pacific-10 Conf. CEOs, 1993-94; bd. dirs. All-Nations Alliance for Minority Participation; mem. pres.' commn. NCAA, 1994—, divsn. I chair, 1995-96; chair Pres.'s Commn., 1996—. Bd. dirs. Forward Wash., 1986-95, China Rels. Coun.; mem. Wash. Coun. Internat. Trade, Western Insterstate Commn. Higher Edn.; bd. dirs. Assn. Western Univs., 1993—. Mem. AAAS, Am. Phytopath. Soc., Nat. Assn. State Univs. and Land-Grand Colls. (bd. dirs. 1994—, chair commn. info. tech. 1994—), Gamma Sigma Delta, Alpha Zeta, Epsilon Sigma Phi, Sigma Xi, Omicron Delta Kappa, Golden Key, Pi Kappa Alpha (hon.). Home: 755 NE Campus St Pullman WA 99163-4223 Office: Wash State U French Adminstrn Bldg Pullman WA 99164-1048

SMITH, SAMUEL JOSEPH, soil scientist; b. Montgomery, Ala., July 19, 1939; s. Samuel Alexander and Lucy (Poje) S. BS, Auburn U., 1961; PhD, Iowa State U., 1967. Soil scientist USDA Agrl. Rsch. Svc., Beltsville, Md., 1969-71; soil scientist USDA Agrl. Rsch. Svc., Durant, Okla., 1971-78, soil scientist, rsch. leader, 1978-94; collaborator Soil Sci., 1994—. Contbr. over 120 articles to rsch. publs. in soil and water sci. Roman Catholic. Office: USDA Agrl Rsch Svc PO Box 1430 Durant OK 74702-1430

SMITH, SARAH KIM HUEY, training and development consultant; b. Wichita Falls, Tex., Nov. 5, 1952; d. John Thomas Huey and Dovie Maurine (Nash) Huey Murphy; m. Robert Lynn Smith, Apr. 22, 1982. BA summa cum laude, Midwestern State U., 1975; MA, Tex. Tech U., 1976. Prodn. coord. Tex. Instruments, Inc., Lubbock, Tex., 1976-77, tng. mgr., 1977-80, br. tng. mgr., 1980-82; sr. cons. Action Systems, Inc., Dallas, 1982-84; tng. mgr. Aviall, Inc., Dallas, 1984-86; dist. mgr. Devel. Dimensions Internat., Dallas, 1986-90; v.p. DDI Pitts., 1990-91; v.p., gen. mgr. DDI Can., Toronto, 1991-92; v.p. DDI L.A., 1992—; presentor seminars, papers at convs. Vol. tchr. Operation L.I.F.T. (Literacy Instrn. for Texans), Dallas, 1983-84, Big Bros./Big Sisters, 1988-89; mem. Foster Parents Plan, Amnesty Internat., World Wildlife Fund, People for the Ethical Treatment of Animals. Mem. Am. Soc. Tng. and Devel., Alpha Chi Omega, Alpha Psi Omega. Democrat. Avocations: running, music, reading. Office: DDI 6033 W Century Blvd Ste 340 Los Angeles CA 90045-6410

SMITH, SCOTT, insurance executive. COO Sedgwick Noble Lowndes. Office: 1285 Ave of Americas New York NY 10019

SMITH, SCOTT CLYBOURN, media company executive; b. Evanston, Ill., Sept. 13, 1950; s. E. Sawyer and Jerolanne (Jones) S.; m. Martha Reilly, June 22, 1974; children—Carolyn Baldwin, Thomas Clybourn. B.A., Yale U., 1973; M.Mgmt., Northwestern U., 1976. Comml. banking officer No. Trust Co., Chgo., 1973-77; fin. planning mgr. Tribune Co., Chgo., 1977-79, asst. treas., 1979-81, treas., 1981-82, v.p., treas., 1982-84, v.p. fin., 1984-89, sr. v.p., chief fin. officer, 1989-91, sr. v.p. for devel., 1991-93; pres., CEO, pub. Sun Sentinel Co., Ft. Lauderdale, Fla., 1993—. Bd. dirs. United Way of Broward County, Broward Workshop, Broward C.C. Found., Boys and Girls Club of Broward, Mus. of Discovery and Sci., Econ. Coun. Palm Beach. Episcopalian. Clubs: Glen View (Golf, Ill.), Lauderdale Yacht Club, Fort Lauderdale Country Club. Office: Sun Sentinel 200 E Las Olas Blvd Fort Lauderdale FL 33301-2248

SMITH, SELMA MOIDEL, lawyer, composer; b. Warren, Ohio, Apr. 3, 1919; d. Louis and Mary (Oyer) Moidel; 1 child, Mark Lee. Student U. Calif., 1936-39, U. So. Calif., 1939-41; JD, Pacific Coast U., 1942. Bar: Calif. 1943, U.S. Dist. Ct. 1943, U.S. Supreme Ct. 1958. Gen. practice law; mem. firm Moidel, Moidel, Moidel & Smith. Field dir. civilian adv. com. WAC, 1943; mem. nat. bd. Med. Coll. Pa. (formerly Woman's Med. Coll. Pa.), 1953—, exec. bd., 1976-80, pres., 1980-82, chmn. past pres. com., 1990-92. Decorated La Order del Merito Juan Pablo Duarte (Dominican Republic). Mem. ABA, State Bar Calif. (servicemen's legal aid com., conf. com. on unauthorized practice of medicine, 1964, Disting. Svc. award 1993), L.A. Bar Assn. (psychopathic ct. com., Outstanding Svc. award 1993), L.A. Lawyers Club (pub. defenders com.), Nat. Assn. Women Lawyers (chmn. com. unauthorized practice of law, social commn. UN, regional dir. western states, Hawaii 1949-51, mem. jud. adminstrn. com. 1960, nat. chmn. world peace through law com. 1966-67), League of Ams. (dir.), Inter-Am. Bar Assn., So. Calif. Women Lawyers Assn. (pres. 1947, 48), Women Lawyers Assn. L.A. (chmn. Law Day com. 1966, subject of oral hist. project, 1986), Coun. Bar Assns. L.A. County (charter sec. 1950), Calif. Bus. Women's Coun. (dir. 1951), L.A. Bus. Women's Coun. (pres. 1952), Calif. Pres.'s Coun. (1st v.p.), Nat. Assn. Composers U.S.A. (dir. 1974-79, ann. luncheon chmn. 1975), Nat. Fedn. Music Clubs (nat. vice chmn. for Western region, 1973-78), Calif. Fedn. Music Clubs (state chmn. Am. Music 1971-75, state conv. chmn. 1972), Docents of L.A. Philharm. (v.p. 1973-83, chmn. Latin Am. community rels. 1972-75, press and pub. rels. 1972-75, cons. coord. 1973-75), Assn. Learning in Retirement Orgns. in West (pres. 1993-94, exec. com. 1994-95, Disting. Svc. award 1995), Euterpe Opera Club (v.p. 1974-75, chmn. auditions 1972, chmn. awards 1973-75), ASCAP, Iota Tau Tau (dean L.A., supreme treas.), Plato Soc. of UCLA (Toga editor, 1990-93, sec. 1991-92, chmn. colloquium com. 1992-93, discussion leader UCLA Constitution Bicentennial Project, 1985-87, moderator UCLA extension lecture series 1990, Exceptional Leadership award 1994). Composer of numerous works including Espressivo-Four Piano Pieces (orchestral premiere 1987, performance Nat. Mus. Women in the Arts 1989). Home: 5272 Lindley Ave Encino CA 91316-3518

SMITH, SEYMOUR MASLIN, financial advisor, investment banker; b. Hartford, Conn., Sept. 19, 1941; s. Seymour Ewing and Margaret Ruth (Maslin) S.; m. Anita P. Streeter, Nov. 12, 1966. A.B., Hamilton Coll., 1963; M.B.A., Columbia U., 1970. With Conn. Bank and Trust Co., Hartford, 1970-85, sr. v.p., 1976-80, exec. v.p., treas., 1980-85; pres. Am. Cruise Lines Inc., 1986-87; exec. v.p., chief fin. officer New Eng. Savs. Bank, New London, 1989-93; fin. advisor, investment banker pvt. practice, Essex, Conn., 1993-94; v.p., CFO Patient Edn. Media, Inc. (an affiliate of Time Life, Inc.), 1995—. Trustee Conn. Public Expenditure Council, Conn. State U., 1973-83. Served to lt. USN, 1963-68, Vietnam. Republican. Episcopalian.

SMITH, SHARMAN BRIDGES, state librarian; b. Lambert, Miss., Sept. 2, 1951; d. Gilbert Asa and Vivian Pearl Bridges; m. Gary Walter Smith, Oct. 3, 1975; children: Heather Elisabeth, Millicent Helen. BS, Miss. U. for Women, Columbus, 1972; MLS, George Peabody Coll., Nashville, 1975. Head libr. Clinton (Miss.) Pub. Libr., 1972-74; asst. dir. Lincoln-Lawrence-Franklin Regional Libr., Brookhaven, Miss., 1975-77, dir., 1977-78; info. svcs. mgr. Miss. Libr. Commn., Jackson, 1978-87, asst. dir. libr. ops., 1987-89, dir. libr. svcs. div., 1989-92; state librarian State Libr. of Iowa, Des Moines, 1992—; bd. trustees Bibliog. Ctr. for Rsch., Denver. Office: State Libr Iowa E 12th St Grand Des Moines IA 50319

SMITH, SHARON LENETTE, principal; b. Henderson, Tex., May 20, 1953; d. Lobias and Shirley Mae (Hollis) Murray; m. Alfred Eugene Smith, Mar. 2, 1973; children: Amaya Ytesia, Adric Romell. AA, El Centro Coll., 1973; BS, Dallas Bapt. U., 1984; MEd, East Tex. State U., 1992. Cert. tchr., Tex. Tchr. Lobias Murray Christian Acad., Dallas, 1979-92, prin., 1992—. Avocations: sewing, reading, drawing, crafts, needlepoint.

SMITH, SHARON LOUISE, state official; b. St. Cloud, Minn., Oct. 25, 1950; d. John Val and Jacquelyn Joyce (Heinen) S. BA, Coll. St. Catherine, 1973; MA, Hamline U., 1990; MPA, U. So. Calif., 1993, DPA, 1994. Tng. officer Emergency Mgmt. divsn. State of Minn., St. Paul, 1973-74, disaster planner, 1974-77, response coord., 1977-79, population planner, 1979-80, comm. officer, 1980-82, adminstrv. dir., 1982-91, power plant planner, 1991—. Ides of March scholar, 1991, 92, Friends of Washington Pub. Affairs Ctr. scholar, 1992. Mem. ASPA, Pi Gamma Mu. Avocations: writing, skiiing, travel, volunteer work with the elderly. Home: 1581 Wheelock Ln # 304 Saint Paul MN 55117-5965

SMITH, SHARON PATRICIA, university dean; b. Jersey City, Nov. 6, 1948; d. Vincent C. and Dorothy (Linehan) S. AB, Rutgers U., 1970, MA, 1972, PhD, 1974. Rsch. assoc. Princeton (N.J.) U., 1974-76, vis. sr. rsch. economist, 1988-90; economist Fed. Res. Bank, N.Y.C., 1976-81, sr. economist, 1981-82; dist. mgr. AT&T, N.Y.C. and Piscataway, N.J., 1982-90; prof. mgmt. systems, dean Coll. of Bus. Adminstrn. Fordham U., Bronx, 1990—; vis. assoc. prof. N.Y. State Sch. Indsl. and Labor Rels., Ithaca, N.Y., 1981; adj. assoc. Drew U., Madison, N.J., 1984. Author: Equal Pay in the Public Sector: Fact or Fantasy, 1977, (with Albert Rees) Faculty Retirement in the Arts and Sciences, 1991; contbr. articles to profl. jours. Adv. bd. Archbishop Hughes Inst. on Religion and Culture; adv. com. Security Trader's Assn. Found., Inc. NDEA fellow, 1970-73. Mem. Am. Econ. Assn., N.J. Human Resource Planners Assn., Indsl. Rels. Rsch. Assn., Am. Assn. for Higher Edn., Princeton Club N.Y. Democrat. Roman Catholic. Home: 45 Wellington Ave Short Hills NJ 07078-3307 Office: Fordham U Coll of Bus Adminstrn 101 Thebaud Hall Bronx NY 10458

SMITH, SHARRON WILLIAMS, chemistry educator; b. Ashland, Ky., Apr. 3, 1941; d. James Archie and May (Waggoner) Williams; m. William Owen Smith, Jr., Aug. 16, 1964; children: Leslie Dyan, Kevin Andrew. BA, Transylvania U., 1963; PhD, U. Ky., 1975. Chemist, Procter & Gamble, Cin., 1963-64; tchr. sci. Lexington pub. schs., Ky., 1964-67; chemist NIH, Bethesda, Md., 1974-75; asst. prof. chemistry Hood Coll., Frederick, Md., 1975-81, assoc. prof., 1981-87, prof. 1987—, chair dept. chemistry, physics and astronomy, 1982-86, 95—, acting dean grad. sch. 1989-91, Whitaker prof. Chemistry, 1993—. NDEA fellow, 1967-70, Dissertation Yr. fellow U. Ky., Lexington, 1970-71; grantee Hood Coll. Bd. Assocs., 1981, 85, 91, Beneficial-Hodson faculty fellow Hood Coll., 1984, 92; grantee NSF, 1986. Mem. AAAS, Am. Chem. Soc., Middle Atlantic Assn. Liberal Arts Chemistry Tchrs. (pres. 1984-85). Democrat. Office: Hood Coll Dept Chemistry Frederick MD 21701

SMITH, SHERWOOD DRAUGHON, retired hospital administrator; b. Durham, N.C., Feb. 12, 1925; s. Cody Hood and Eula (Draughon) S.; m. Patricia Ann Collins, Jan. 27, 1952; children—David Cody, Kenneth Heber, Sherwood Allan, Steven Collins, Sarah Amy. B.A., Duke, 1950, M.S., 1952. Asst. adminstr. Hubbard Hosp., Nashville, 1952-54; adminstr. Hubbard Hosp., 1954-56; exec. dir. Lakeland (Fla.) Gen. Hosp., 1956-88, ret., 1988. Bd. dirs., exec. com. Suncoast Health Council; bd. dirs. Blue Cross Fla.; past pres., bd. dirs. Southeastern Hosp. Conf., del., 1968-80; pres. Central Fla. Hosp. Council, 1961-62; mem. Fla. Health Planning Council, 1971—; Mem. Adv. Com. Employment, Lakeland; mem. Polk County Planning Council, 1970—; bishop Ch. of Jesus Christ of Latter-day Saints. Served with AUS, 1942-46. Fellow Am. Coll. Hosps. Adminstrs. (regent dist. III 1970-73); mem. Fla. Hosp. Assn. (pres. 1966, bd. dirs.), Am. Hosp. Assn. (Fla. del. 1967-73, trustee 1974-80, chmn. regional adv. bd.). Club: Rotarian. Home: 1515 Leighton Ave Lakeland FL 33803-2518

SMITH, SHERWOOD HUBBARD, JR., utilities executive; b. Jacksonville, Fla., Sept. 1, 1934; s. Sherwood Hubbard and Catherine Gertrude (Milliken) S.; m. Eva Hackney Hargrave, July 20, 1957; children: Marlin Hamilton, Cameron Hargrave, Eva Hackney. AB, U. N.C., 1956, JD, 1960; D civil laws, St. Augustine's Coll., 1988; LDD, Campbell U., 1990; HHD, Francis Marion Coll., 1990. Bar: N.C. 1960. Assoc. Lassiter, Moore & Van Allen, Charlotte, 1960-62; ptnr. Joyner & Howison, Raleigh, 1963-65; assoc. gen. counsel Carolina Power & Light Co., Raleigh, 1965-70, sr. v.p., gen. counsel, 1971-74, exec. v.p., 1974-76, pres., 1976-92, chmn. bd., 1980—; chmn., CEO, former pres. Carolina Power & Light Co., Raleigh, N.C.; bd. dirs. Global TransPark Found., Inc., Hackney Bros., Inc., No. Telecom Ltd., Northwestern Mut. Life Inst. Co., Springs Industries, Wachovia Corp.; dir. Nuclear Energy Inst., 1994—; pres., dir. Global TransPark Authority; chmn. Am. Nuclear Energy Coun., 1980-83, Edison Electric Inst., 1985-86, Southeastern Elec. Reliability Coun., 1988-90, Nuclear Power Oversight Com., 1990-94. Mem. N.C. Coun. Mgmt. and Devel.; trustee Z Smith Reynolds Found., 1978—, Nat. Humanities Ctr.; bd. dirs. N.C. Citizens for Bus. and Industry, chmn., 1985-86; bd. dirs. Rsch. Triangle Found. of N.C.; mem. com. U.S. World Energy Conf.; bd. dirs. Microelectronics Ctr. of N.C., 1980—; mem. Pres.'s Coun. for Internat. Youth Exch., Kenan Inst. Pvt. Enterprise; trustee Com. Econ. Devel.; mem. Bus. Coun., 1991—, Bus. Roundtable; former bd. trustees, chmn. Rex Hosp. Recipient Nat. Humanitarian award Am. Lung Assn., 1993, Outstanding Leadership award in Mgmt. scis. Am. Soc. Mech. Engrs., 1983, A.E. Finley Disting. Svc. award Greater Raleigh C. of C., 1985. Mem. Elec. Power Rsch. Inst. (bd. dirs. 1984-89), Greater Raleigh C. of C. (pres. 1979), Am. Nuclear Soc., U.S. C. of C. (energy com.), Assn. Edison Illuminating Cos. (pres. 1990-91), Phi Beta Kappa. Home: 408 Drummond Dr Raleigh NC 27609-7006 Office: Carolina Power & Light Co PO Box 1551 411 Fayetteville Street Mall Raleigh NC 27602-1551*

SMITH, SHERYL VELTING, elementary school executive director; b. Grand Rapids, Mich., Apr. 5, 1946; d. Louis and Martha (Kamminga) Velting; children: Laura, Paul. BA in Elem. Edn., Western Mich. U., Kalamazoo, 1968; MA in Adminstrn. and Supr./Edn., Akron U., 1980. Cert. edn. adminstr. and supr. Elem. tchr. Northview Pub. Schs., Grand Rapids, Mich., 1968-69, Ft. Knox (Ky.) Dependent Schs., 1969-70, Dept. of Def., Okinawa, 1970-71, Jefferson County Schs., Louisville, 1971-76, Hudson (Ohio) Local Schs., 1976-80; dir., preschool tchr. The Treehouse Preschool, 1981-83; exec. dir. High Meadows Sch., Roswell, Ga., 1993—; regional conf. bd. Assn. Gifted Children, Akron, Ohio, 1979; chairwomen bd. dirs. Friends of High Meadows, Roswell, Ga., 1990-94; mem. adv. bd. Mt. Pisgah Christian Schs., Alpharetta, Ga., 1991-92; mem. North Fulton Cmty. Found. Bd., 1996—. Avocations: sports, gardening, travel, reading. Office: High Meadows Sch 1055 Willeo Rd Roswell GA 30075-4131

SMITH, SHIRLEY, artist; b. Wichita, Kans., Apr. 17, 1929; d. Harold Marvin and Blanche Carrie (Alexander) S. BFA, Kans. State U., 1951; postgrad., Provincetown (Mass.) Workshop, 1962-66. One woman exhbns. 55 Mercer St. Gallery, N.Y.C., 1973, Wichita Art Mus, 1978, Stamford Mus. and Nature Ctr., Conn., 1987, Aaron Gallery, Washington, 1987, 88, Joan Hodgell Gallery, Sarasota, Fla., 1987; group exhbns. include Chrysler Mus., Provincetown, 1964, The Va. Mus., Richmond, 1970, Whitney Mus. Am. Art, 1971, Colo. Springs Fine Art Ctr., 1972, Everson Mus., Syracuse, N.Y., 1976-80, Nat. Acad. Design, N.Y.C., 1986, One Penn Pla., N.Y.C., 1987, 88, Am. Acad., Inst. Arts and Letters, N.Y.C., 1990, 91; permanent collections Whitney Mus. Am. Art, N.Y.C., U. Calif. Art Mus., Berkeley, Phoenix Art Mus., The Aldrich Mus. Contemporary Art, Ridgefield, Conn., Ulrich Mus., Wichita, Everson Mus., Syracuse, South County Bank collection, St. Louis, Prudential Life Ins., Newark, N.J., King Features Syndicate, N.Y.C., Chase Manhattan Bank Collection, N.Y.C., Senator Nancy Kassabaum Russel Senate Bldg., Washington. Recipient Grumbacher Cash award for mixed media New Eng. Exhibition, Silvermine, Conn., 1967, Acad. Inst. award Am. Acad. Arts and Letters, N.Y.C., 1991. Mem. Artist Equity. Democrat. Presbyterian. Avocation: bike riding. Home: 141 Wooster St New York NY 10012-3163

SMITH, SIBLEY JUDSON, JR., historic site administrator; b. Alexandria, La., June 26, 1955; s. Sibley Judson and Eunice Lee (Raulins) S.; m. Alice Laurie Casey, Nov. 28, 1980; children: Jacob Lee, Casey Raulins. Student, N.E. La. U., 1973-76; BA in History magna cum laude, Christopher Newport Coll., 1985; MA in Am. Studies, Coll. of William and Mary, 1992. Mus. interpreter Colonial Williamsburg (Va.) Found., 1979-87; coord. of interpretation Historic Hudson Valley, Inc., Tarrytown, N.Y., 1987-88; historic site mgr. Philipse Manor Hall State Historic Site, Yonkers, N.Y., 1988-91; exec. dir. Allaire (N.J.) Village, Inc., 1991—. Mem. Alpha Chi, Alpha Psi Omega. Avocations: gardening, theater, movies, mus. Office: Allaire Village Inc PO Box 220 Farmingdale NJ 07727-0220

SMITH, SIDNEY OSLIN, JR., lawyer; b. Gainesville, Ga., Dec. 30, 1923; s. Sidney Oslin and Isabelle Price (Charters) S.; m. Patricia Irwin Horkan, Aug. 4, 1944; children—Charters Smith Wilson, Ellen Smith Andersen, Sidney Oslin III. A.B. cum laude, Harvard Coll., 1947; LL.B. summa cum laude, U. Ga., 1949. Bar: Ga. 1948. Ptnr. Telford, Wayne & Smith, Gainesville, Ga., 1949-62; asst. solicitor Superior Cts., Northeastern Jud. Cir. Ga., 1951-61, judge, 1962-65; judge U.S. Dist. Ct. (no. dist.) Ga., 1965-68, chief judge, 1968-74; ptnr. Alston, Miller & Gaines, Atlanta, 1974-82; ptnr. Alston & Bird, Atlanta, 1982-94, of counsel, 1994—. Chmn. Gainesville Bd. Edn., 1959-62; trustee Brenau Coll., Gainesville, 1974—, chmn., 1976-84; mem. state bd. regents Univ. System of Ga., 1980-87, chmn., 1984-85. Served to capt. U.S. Army, 1943-46, ETO. Fellow ABA, Am. Coll. Trial Lawyers; mem. Am. Law Inst., Am. Judicature Soc., Commerce Club, Chattahoochee Club, Phi Beta Kappa, Phi Kappa Phi, Phi Delta Phi, Phi Delta Theta. Democrat. Episcopalian. Home: 2541 Club Dr Gainesville GA 30506-1769 Office: Alston & Bird 1 Atlantic Ctr 1201 W Peachtree St NW Atlanta GA 30309-3400

SMITH, SIDNEY RUFUS, JR., linguist, educator; b. Greensboro, N.C., Sept. 18, 1931; s. Sidney Rufus and Page (Johnston) S.; m. Vera Pautzsch, Apr. 19, 1969 (div. 1975); children: Stephanie Alice, Eric Brian. B.A., Duke U., 1953; Ph.D., U. N.C., 1965. Asst. prof. U. Conn., Storrs, 1965-66; asst. prof. U. N.C., Chapel Hill, 1966-71, assoc. prof., 1971-79, prof., 1979—, chmn. Germanic langs., 1979-89, 94—, chmn. linguistics, 1981-84. Author numerous articles for profl. publs. Local troop leader Girl Scouts U.S.A. Served to sgt. AUS, 1953-56. Recipient Northeast Conf. Teaching Langs. Stephen Freeman award, 1969. Mem. Linguistic Soc. Am., MLA, Soc. Advancement Scandinavian Study, Am. Assn. Tchrs. German, S. Atlantic MLA, Internat. Brotherhood Magicians. Democrat. Office: U NC Dept Germanic Langs Chapel Hill NC 27599

SMITH, SIDNEY TALBERT, biomedical engineer; b. Decatur, Ill., Oct. 30, 1954; s. Sidney Paulsen and Patricia Louise (Talbert) S.; m. Katherine Louise Wolf, June 24, 1989. BS, Millikin U., 1976; postgrad., Washington U., St. Louis, 1976-78; MBA with honors, Lake Forest (Ill.) Sch. Mgmt., 1985. Rsch. asst. Baxter Travenol, Morton Grove, Ill., 1980-82; devel. engr. Fenwal divsn. Travenol Labs., Round Lake, Ill., 1982-83, sr. devel. engr., 1983-84; prin. engr. Fenwal divsn. Baxter Healthcare, Round Lake, 1984-88; project mgr. biotech. systems Baxter Healthcare, Round Lake, 1988-89; dir.

devel. Applied Immune Scis., Menlo Park, Calif., 1990-91; prin. Smith Engring., Lake Forest, Ill., 1989-96; mgr. container devel. advanced engr. Baxter Healthcare Corp., Deerfield, Ill., 1996—; cons. Safety Diagnostics, Evanston, Ill., 1989-91, Clintec Nutrition, Deerfield, Ill., 1991—, Baxter Healthcare Corp., Deerfield, Ill., 1993—, Teltech Resource Network Corp., Mpls., 1995—. Patentee in field. Mem. Lake Forest/Lake Bluff Running Club (bd. mem. 1995), Vintage Sports Car Drivers Assn., Porsche Club Am. Presbyterian. Avocations: running, racing, mountain climbing, photography. Home: 1326 W Everett Rd Lake Forest IL 60045-2610

SMITH, SIDNEY TED, environmental engineer, consultant; b. Waterloo, Iowa, July 23, 1918; s. Sidney Charles and Maud Katheryn (Fry) S.; m. Dorothy Walton Buckingham, Aug. 17, 1942 (dec. Aug. 1968); children: Karen L. Jones, Sidney Tom, Jonathan Gregg; m. Joyce Lee Smith, June 3, 1972. BS in Mech. Engring., Iowa State U., 1940. Registered profl. engr. Iowa, Kans., Mo., Wyo. Owner Sid Smith & Co., Waterloo, 1946-60; profl. engr. Stanley Engring. Co., Muscatine, Iowa, 1960-62, various orgns., Kansas City, Mo., 1962-68; dir. design and projects Burns & McDonnell, Kansas City, 1968-92; cons. Sargent & Lundy, Chgo., 1993-94, Sega, Inc., Overland Park, Kans., 1994—. Capt. U.S. Army Air Corp., 1941-46. Mem. ASHRAE, NSPR, Nat. Fire Protection Assn., Air and Waste Mgmt. Assn., Am. Legion. Republican. Presbyterian. Achievements include design of first limestone flue gas desulfurization system for 500 MW utility boiler that removed 95% sulfur dioxide; designed first cold side precipitator for 500 MW utility boiler that operated successfully with low sulfur coal flyash. Avocations: golf, fishing, reading. Home: 9713 W 91st Terr Overland Park KS 66212-4861 Office: 15238 Broadmoor Overland Park KS 66223

SMITH, SINJIN, beach volleyball player; b. L.A., May 7, 1957. former pres. Assn. Volleyball Profls.; v.p. Internat. Volleyball Fedn., World Beach Coun. Bd. dirs. Big Bros., U.S. Volleyball Assn. Named Most Successful Player in History, 1996 Olympian. Office: 14707 Mekendree Ave Pacific Palisades CA 90272

SMITH, SPENCER BAILEY, engineering and business educator; b. Ottawa, Ont., Can., Jan. 31, 1927; s. Sidney B. and Etta (Bailey) S.; m. Mildred E. Spidell, Dec. 31, 1954. B.Eng., McGill U., 1949; M.S., Columbia U., 1950, Eng.Sc.D., 1958. Adminstrv. engr. Mergenthaler Linotype Co., N.Y.C., 1953-58; ops. research mgr. Raytheon Co., Newton, Mass., 1958-61; ops research mgr. Montgomery Ward & Co., Chgo., 1961-66; assoc. prof., then prof. Ill. Inst. Tech., 1966—, chmn. dept. indsl. and systems engring., 1971-77, dir. Stuart Sch. Office of Research, 1977-82; tchr. TV courses Nat. Tech. U. Author: Computer-Based Production and Inventory Control, 1989; contbr. articles to profl. jours.; patentee on order quantity calculator, 1964. Vol. cons. on sch. redistricting Elem. Sch. Dist., Evanston, Ill., 1972-74. Research grantee Harris Trust and Savs. Bank, 1968-70, Ill. Law Enforcement Commn., 1972-74, U.S. Army C.E., 1981, Am. Prodn. and Inventory Control Soc., 1980. Mem. Ops. Rsch. Soc. Am., Inst. Mgmt. Sci., Inst. Indsl. Engrs., Am. Statis. Assn., ASME, Am. Prodn. and Inventory Control Soc., Soc. Mfg. Engrs. Presbyterian. Club: University (Chgo.). Home: 2530 Lawndale Ave Evanston IL 60201-1158 Office: Ill Inst Tech 565 W Adams St Chicago IL 60661-3601

SMITH, STAN LEE, biology educator; b. Wolf Lake, Ind., June 8, 1947; s. Donald Ray and Margaret Ellen (Hutsell) S.; m. Beth Ellen Grimme, Aug. 12, 1972; children: Daniel Nathan, Michael David. BS in Biology, Purdue U., 1970, MS in Biology, 1973; PhD in Biology, Northwestern U., 1978. Bacteriologist City-County Bd. Health, Ft. Wayne, Ind., 1972-74; lectr. Northwestern U., Evanston, Ill., 1978-79, NIH postdoctoral fellow, 1979-80; from asst. prof. to assoc. prof. Bowling Green (Ohio) State U., 1980-92, prof., 1992—; reviewer Scott Foresman and Co., Willard Grant Press, Houghton Mifflin Co., Times Mirror Mosby Coll. Publ., West Ednl. Publ., D.C. Heath Co., NSF, McGraw Hill, W.H. Freeman, Prentice Hall. Contbr. articles to Nature, Insect Biochemistry, Jour. Insect Physiology, Molecular and Cellular Endocrinology, Biochem. and Biophys. Rsch. Comms., Experientia. Recipient Nat. Rsch. Svc. award NIH, 1979-81; rsch. grantee NIH, 1984-86, Ohio Bd. Regents Bowling Green State U., 1986-89, Faculty Rsch. Com., 1980-83, 92-93. Mem. AAAS, Am. Soc. Zoologists, Entomol. Soc. Am., Sigma Xi (Outstanding Young Scientist Bowling Green State U. chpt. 1989). Democrat. Achievements include rsch. and discoveries in areas of insect biochemistry and endocrinology, biochemistry and physiology of ecdysteroids and cytochrome P-450 enzyme systems, effects of plant allelochemicals on ecdysteroidogenesis. Office: Bowling Green State U Dept Biol Scis Bowling Green OH 43403

SMITH, STAN VLADIMIR, economist, financial service company executive; b. Rhinelander, Wis., Nov. 16, 1946; s. Valy Zdenek and Sylvia S.; children: Cara, David. BS in Ops. Research, Cornell U., 1968; MBA, U. Chgo., 1972, postgrad., 1973. Lectr. U. Chgo., 1973; economist bd. govs. Fed. Res. System, Washington, 1973-74; staff economist First Nat. Bank of Chgo., 1974; assoc. December Group, Chgo., 1974-77; founding pres. Seaquest Internat., Chgo., 1977-85; mgr., ptnr. Ibbotson Assocs., Chgo., 1981-85; pres. Corp. Fin. Group, Ltd., Chgo., 1981-85; expert econ. witness in field; adj. prof. Coll. Law DePaul U., Chgo. Author: Economic/Hedonic Damages, 1990; founding editor Stocks, Bonds, Bills and Inflation yearbook, 1983; bd. editors Jour. Forensic Economics, 1991—; also contbr. articles in field. Founder, exec. dir. Ctr. for Value of Life, 1996. Fellow Allied Chem., 1967, John McMullen Trust, 1969; grantee Ford Found., 1972, U.S. Fed. Res., 1973. Mem. Am. Econ. Assn., Am. Fin. Assn., Nat. Assn. Forensic Econs., Nat. Acad. Econ. Arbitrators (founder 1989—), Am. Arbitration Assn. (arbitrator), Nat. Futures Assn. (arbitrator), Am. Bd. Forensic Examiners, Alpha delta Phi. Office: Corp Fin Group 1165 N Clark St Ste 650 Chicago IL 60610-2845

SMITH, STANFORD SIDNEY, state treasurer; b. Denver, Oct. 20, 1923; s. Frank Jay and Lelah (Beamer) S.; m. Harriet Holdrege, Feb. 7, 1947; children: Monta Smith Ramirez, Franklin Stanley. Student, Calif. Inst. Tech., 1941-42, Stanford U., 1942-43; BS, U.S. Naval Acad., 1946. Pres. Vebar Livestock Co., Thermopolis, Wyo., 1961-89; mem. Wyo. Senate, 1974-76; pres. Wyo. Wool GrowersAssn., 1976-78; mem. Wyo. Ho. of Reps., Cheyenne, 1978-82; treas. State Wyo., Cheyenne, 1983—; dir. Coun. of State Govts., 1990-92; v.p. Wyo. Wool Growers, dir., 1976-82. County commr. Hot Springs County, Wyo, 1966-74. Lt. USN, 1943-54. Decorated Bronze Star. Mem. Nat. Assn. State Treas. (pres. 1990-91). Republican. Methodist. Office: State of Wyoming State Capital Cheyenne WY 82002

SMITH, STANLEY KENT, economics and demographics educator; b. Peoria, Ill., Oct. 11, 1945; s. Tilman R. and Louella M. (Schertz) S.; m. Rita J. Kandel, Aug. 12, 1967; children: Ian, Rachel. BA with high honors, Goshen Coll., 1967; postgrad., Mich. State U., 1971-72; PhD, U. Mich., 1976. Asst. dir. Mennonite Cen. Com., Cochabamba, Bolivia, 1968-70; teaching fellow Mich. State U., East Lansing, 1971-72; econ. demography trainee U. Mich., Ann Arbor, 1972-76; asst. prof. econs. and demographics U. Fla., Gainesville, 1976-81, assoc. prof., 1981-90, prof., dir. bur. econ. and bus. rsch., 1990—; cons. numerous orgns. including GM, Petroleum Inst. Am., N.Y. Times, 1977—; Fla. rep. Fed.-State Coop. Program for Population Estimates and Projections, 1976—. Contbr. articles to profl. publs. Treas. Alachua County Boys Choir, Gainesville, 1984-86; coach Youth Soccer, Inc., Gainesville, 1985; moderator United Ch., Gainesville, 1988-89. Mem. Am. Econ. Assn., Population Assn. Am., So. Demographic Assn. Avocations: sports, music, travel. Office: Univ Fla Bur Economic & Business Rsch 221 Matherly Hall Gainesville FL 32611-2017

SMITH, STANLEY ROGER, retired professional tennis player; b. Pasadena, Calif., Dec. 14, 1946; s. Charles Kenneth and Rhoda (Widmer) S.; m. Marjory Logan Gengler, Nov. 23, 1974; children: Ramsey Gengler, Trevor Austin, Logan Widmer, Austin Church. B.A., U. So. Calif., 1969; L.H.D., Greenville Coll., 1974, Winthrop Coll., N.C. Profl. tennis player, 1968—; mem. U.S. Davis Cup Team, 1968-79, 81; adviser Pres.'s Council on Phys. Fitness, 1971-75; chmn. Stan Smith Design, Inc.; dir. coaching USTA; cons. Sea Pines Plantations, 1971—, Adidas, Landersheim, France, 1971—, Fischer G.m.b.H., Austria, 1980-86, Prince Adv. Staff, 1986—; bd. dirs. Hilton Head br. Citizens & So. Nat. Bank S.C. Writer: nationally syndicated newspaper column Stan Smith's Tennis Tips, 1971—; Author: Inside Tennis, 1974, Stan Smith's Six Tennis Basics, 1974, The Executive Tennis Diary 1975, 1974, Stan Smith's Guide to Better Tennis, 1975, (with Bob Lutz) Modern Doubles, 1975, It's More Than Just a Game, 1977; also video with Arthur Ashe, Vic Braden: Tennis Our Way. Bd. dirs. Greater Los Angeles Big Bros. Am., 1966-71; hon. tennis chmn. Duke's Children's Classic, 1982—; hon. chmn. Am. Festival Fitness and Sport, 1987. Served with AUS, 1970-72. Decorated D.S.M.; named Martini and Rossi Player of Year, 1971, 72; holder 26 U.S. singles and doubles titles, including U.S. Open singles, 1971, U.S. Open doubles, 1968, 74, 78, 80; ranked number one in U.S. doubles, 1968, 69, 1970, 71, 72, 74; number one in U.S. singles, 1969, 71, 72, 73; winner Wimbledon singles title, 1972, 6 World championship tennis titles in 1973, including; World Championship of Tennis Finals in singles, also; Rothman's World Doubles title; ranked world's number one tennis player, 1972, 73; Lebair Sportsmanship Trophy, 1969; Johnston Sportsmanship Trophy, 1968; champion 35 & Over Cir. Singles and Doubles Championships, 1982, 84, 86; named to U.S. Collegiate Hall of Fame, 1984, to Carolina Tennis Hall of Fame, 1986, to Internat. Hall of Fame, 1987. Mem. Assn. Tennis Profls. (dir. 1972-79, 81-83), Men's Internat. Profl. Tennis Council, Athletes in Action, Beta Theta Pi. Republican. Presbyterian. Clubs: Sea Pines Plantation, Los Angeles Tennis, All England, West Side Tennis, No. Century XXI, Balboa Bay. Office: 1101 Wilson Blvd Ste 1800 Arlington VA 22209-2248 *God has given me certain talents. I feel a great opportunity and responsibility to develop and use these talents to their fullest on and off the tennis courts. I see great potential in our country and especially in our youth today, and I hope to provide some leadership and direction that this youth will need to develop their potential constructively. God has given me a great life so far and I plan to rely on His guidance to take me the rest of the way.**

SMITH, STANTON KINNIE, JR., utility executive, lawyer; b. Rockford, Ill., Feb. 14, 1931; s. Stanton Kinnie and Elizabeth (Brown) S.; m. Mary Beth Sanders, July 11, 1953; children: Stanton E., Kathryn A., Dana. BA, Yale U., 1953; JD, U. Wis., 1956. Bar: Ill. 1956, Mich. 1976. Ptnr. Sidley & Austin, Chgo., 1964-84; vice-chmn., gen. counsel Am. Natural Resources Co., Detroit, 1984-87; sr. v.p. Costal Corp., Houston, 1985-87, also dir.; vice chmn., gen. counsel CMS Energy Corp., 1987-88, pres. 1988-92, vice chmn., 1992-96, also bd. dirs.; sr. counsel Skadden, Arps, Slate, Meagher & Flom; bd. dirs. Clarcor Corp. Trustee Founders Soc., Detroit Inst. Arts, Rockford Coll., Devel. Bd. Yale U., Mich. Opera Theater; bd. advisors U. Wis. Law Sch., Mich. State U., Pub. Utility Inst. Office: CMS Energy Corp 330 Town Center Dr Dearborn MI 48126-2711

SMITH, STEPHANIE MARIE, lawyer; b. Manhattan, Kans., May 15, 1955; d. William C. and Joyce A. (Davis) S. BS in Fgn. Studies (Economics), Georgetown U., 1977; JD, U. Mich., 1980. Bar: Colo. 1980, U.S. Dist. Ct. Colo. 1980, U.S. Ct. Appeals (10th cir.) 1980, (9th cir.) 1995, Ariz. 1985, Nev. 1985, U.S. Dist. Ct. Nev. 1985. Assoc. Fishman & Geman, Denver, 1980-81, Hart & Trinen, Denver, 1982-85; ptnr. Jolley, Urga, Wirth & Woodbury, Las Vegas, Nev., 1985—; lawyer rep. 9th Cir. Jud. Conf., 1994—, chmn. Nev. delegation, 1995. Mem. ABA, Nev. Bar Assn., Am. Bankruptcy Inst., So. Nev. Bankruptcy Lawyers' Assn. Office: Jolley Urga Wirth & Woodbury 300 S 4th St Ste 800 Las Vegas NV 89101-6018

SMITH, STEPHEN ALEXANDER, retail and wholesale food distribution company executive; b. Toronto, Ont., Can., Mar. 1, 1957; s. Alexander and Norma Eileen (McEwan) S.; m. Mary E. Cavasin, June 14, 1980; children: Lauren, Carolyn. B Commerce, U. Toronto, 1979. Chartered acctg., Ont. Acct. Price Waterhouse, Toronto, 1979-84, mgr., 1984-85; mgr. systems and internal control Loblaw Cos. Ltd., Toronto, 1985-86, asst. contr., 1986-87, contr., 1987—, v.p., 1989—, sr. v.p., 1994—. Office: Loblaw Cos Ltd, 22 St Clair Ave E Ste 1500, Toronto, ON Canada M4T 2S8

SMITH, STEPHEN DALE, safety engineer; b. Hamilton, Ohio, Dec. 2, 1951; s. Dale H. and Katherine M. (Schmidt) S.; m. Sabrina Gara Smith, May 29, 1982; 1 child, Corita K. BS, Miami U., Oxford, Ohio, 1975; MS, Ctrl. Mo. State U., Warrensburg, 1979. Driver edn. tchr. Switzerland County Schs., Vevay, Ind., 1975-78; grad. asst. Ctrl. Mo. State U., 1978-79; hwy. safety technician Nat. Hwy. Transp. Safety Adminstrn., U.S. Dept. Transp., Kansas City, Mo., 1979-80; safety advisor GCC Beverages, Boston, 1980-83; safety mgr. GCC Beverages/Pepsi-Cola, Miami, Fla., 1983-84; safety specialist Fed. Express, Parsippany, N.J., 1984-87; sr. safety specialist Fed. Express, Cin., 1987—. Active Boy Scouts Am., Parsippany, also Fairfield, Ohio, 1983—; head usher, trustee, lay liturgist St. Mark's United Meth. Ch., Fairfield, 1989—. Mem. Am. Soc. Safety Engrs. (sec. S.W. Ohio chpt. 1994-95, v.p. 1995-96). Home: 5100 W Scioto Dr Fairfield OH 45014-1563 Office: Fed Express 4675 Cornell Rd Ste 290 Cincinnati OH 45241-2491

SMITH, STEPHEN EDWARD, lawyer; b. Boston, Aug. 5, 1950; s. Sydney and Minnie (Appel) S.; m. Eileen Beth O'Farrell, June 15, 1986; children: Nora, Bennett, Liliana. AB in Polit. Sci., Boston U., 1972; JD, Washington U., St. Louis, 1976. Bar: Ill. 1976, Mass. 1985, U.S. Dist. Ct. (no. dist.) Ill. 1977, U.S. Dist. Ct. (no. dist.) Ind. 1986, U.S. Dist. Ct. Mass. 1987, U.S. Dist. Ct. (so. dist.) Wis. 1987, U.S. Ct. Appeals (7th cir.) 1981. Assoc., ptnr. Brown & Blumtsberg, Chgo., 1976-80; founding ptnr. Cantwell, Smith & Van Daele, Chgo., 1980-84; ptnr. Gottlieb & Schwartz, Chgo., 1984-85; of cousnel Siemon, Larsen & Prudy, Chgo., 1985-90; solo practitioner Chgo., 1990-94; assoc. prof. clin. practice Ill. Inst. Tech. Chgo.-Kent Coll. law, Chgo., 1994-95; of counsel Field Golan & Swiger, Chgo., 1995—; mediator Ctr. for Conflict Resolution, Chgo., 1992—; cmty. adv. coun. WBEZ, Chgo., 1985—; arbitrator NASD, Chgo., 1994—. Past. bd. dirs., past pres. Jane Addams Ctr., Hull House Assn., Chgo. Mem. Am. Arbitration Assn. (comml. and internat. panels), Univ. Club of Chgo. Office: Field Golan & Swiger 21st Floor Three First Nat Plz Chicago IL 60602

SMITH, STEPHEN GRANT, journalist; b. N.Y.C., Mar. 6, 1949; s. John J. and Nora O.S.; m. Sarah Rowbotham Bedell, May 22, 1982; children: R. Kirk Bedell, Elisabeth DeCou Bedell, David Branson Smith. Student, Deerfield Acad.; BA, U. Pa., 1971. City Hall reporter Daily Hampshire Gazette, Northampton, Mass., 1971-73; spl. assignment reporter Albany Times-Union, 1973-74; dep. regional editor Phila. Inquirer, 1974-76; asst. met. editor Boston Globe, 1976-78; sr. editor Horizon Mag., 1978; staff writer Time Mag., 1978-80, sr. editor, 1980-82, Nation editor, 1982-85, acting asst. mng. editor, 1985-86; exec. editor Newsweek Mag., 1986-91; Washington news editor Knight-Ridder newspapers, 1991-94; founding editor Civilization Mag., Washington, 1994—; chmn. publs. com. U. Pa. Chmn. publs. com. U. Pa. Mem. Am. Soc. Mag. Editors, Coun. of Fgn. Rels., World Affairs Coun. Washington, U. Pa. Gen. Alumni Soc. (exec. com.), Fourth Estate Golf Soc., St. Anthony Hall. Clubs: Nat. Press, Brook, Century, Met., Beefsteak. Home (summer): PO Box 183 Little Compton RI 02837-0183 Office: Civilization Magazine 666 Pennsylvania Ave SE Washington DC 20003-4319

SMITH, STEPHEN KENDALL, lawyer; b. Burlington, Vt., May 31, 1941; s. Lester Hurlin and Elizabeth Helen (Mitchell) S.; m. Margaret Anne Weir, Sept. 2, 1967; children: Andrew Kendall, Edward Anthony, Charles Franklin, Charlotte Catherine. AB with distinction, Ind. U., 1964; BA, Oxford U., 1966, MA, 1971; JD, Columbia U., 1972. Bar: Ind. 1972, U.S. Dist. Ct. (so. dist.) Ind. 1972, U.S. Dist. Ct. (no. dist.) Ind. 1978, U.S. Ct. Appeals (7th cir.). Assoc. Barnes, Hickam, Pantzer & Boyd and predecessors, Indpls., 1972-79, ptnr., 1980-81; ptnr. Barnes & Thornburg and predecessors, Indpls., 1981—, co-chair litigatin mgmt. and econs. com., 1991-94, co-chair equality in the law com., 1994—. Contbr. articles to legal jours. Sec. Indpls. Com. on Fgn. Rels., 1978-87, chmn., 1987—. Capt. U.S. Army, 1966-69. Rhodes scholar, 1964. Mem. ABA (litigation sect., jury instrn. project 1983—), Fed. Bar Assn., Ind. Bar Assn., Indpls. Bar Assn., 7th Cir. Bar Assn., SAR (chancellor Ind. Soc. 1985—). Democrat. Presbyterian. Home: 4414 N Meridian St Indianapolis IN 46208-3534 Office: Barnes & Thornburg 11 S Meridian St Ste 1313 Indianapolis IN 46204-3506

SMITH, STEPHEN RANDOLPH, aerospace executive; b. Des Moines, Apr. 17, 1928; s. Norvin Ellis and Helen (Heberling) S.; m. Margaret Anne Graves, Dec. 20, 1950; children: Stephen Randolph Jr., Susan Canning, Sara Kutler, Anne Barrette, Julia Carroll. BSME, Stanford U., 1951, MSME, 1952; MBA Advanced Mgmt. Program, Harvard U., 1974. Registered profl. engr., Calif. Sr. analyst, preliminary design engr. Northrop & Garrett Corps., L.A. and Hawthorne, Calif., 1952-55; propulsion lead design engr. Northrop Corp., Hawthorne, 1955-59; engring. rep. ea. dist. Northrop Corp., Washington, 1959-60; T-38/F-5/F-20 program mgr. Northrop Corp., Hawthorne, 1960-75; v.p. Iran ops. Northrop Corp., Tehran, 1975-78; v.p. advanced projects Northrop Corp., Hawthorne, 1978-83, v.p. engring. and advanced devel., 1983-86, v.p., program mgr. F-20/YF-23A, 1986-88, corp. v.p., gen. mgr. aircraft divsn., 1988-92; cons. tech. mgmt. Palos Verdes, Calif., 1992—; bd. mem. Quarterdeck Ptnrs., Inc., L.A. and Washington, 1992—, NASA Advanced Aeronautics Com., 1984-86; invited lectr. aircraft design USAF Acad., 1983. Author, designer, patentee in field. Bd. dirs. Boy Scouts Am., L.A. coun., 1986—, charter comm. chmn., 1996; pres. Penn Srs., Palos Verdes, Calif., 1996. Sgt. U.S. Army, 1946-48. Recipient Disting. Civilian Svc. medal U.S. Dept. Def., Washington, 1983. Fellow AIAA (chmn. L.A. sect. 1985-86, adv. bd. 1988—, Spl. Citation 1994), Inst. Advancement Engring.; mem. Soc. Automotive Engrs. (chmn. aerotech. 1986-87, honors 1987), Sierra Club, Trailfinders Conservation Coun. (life, coun. chief 1940). Republican. Episcopalian. Avocations: competitive sailing, tennis, backpacking, skiing, running. Home and Office: 2249 Via Guadalana Palos Verdes Estates CA 90274

SMITH, STEVEN ALBERT, philosophy educator; b. What Cheer, Iowa, May 12, 1939; s. Irving James and Mary (Emmons) S.; m. Daryl Goldgraben, Aug. 2, 1970 (div. Mar. 1987); 1 child, David Irving; m. Patricia Adkisson, Aug. 11, 1991. BA, Earlham Coll., 1961; MA, Harvard U., 1963, PhD, 1972. Instr. Claremont (Calif.) McKenna Coll., 1968-72, asst. prof., 1972-75, assoc. prof., 1975-90, full prof. philosophy, 1990—. Author: Satisfaction of Interest and the Concept of Morality, 1974; editor: Ways of Wisdowm, 1983, Everyday Zen, 1989, Nothing Special, 1993, Now Zen, 1995; contbr. articles to profl. jours. Elected bd. mem. Mt. Baldy (Calif.) I&W Assn., 1973-75. Grantee Nat. Endowment for Humanities, 1972. Mem. Am. Philos. Assn., Am. Assn. Philosophy Tchrs., N.Am. Soc. Social Philosophy. Democrat. Quaker. Home: Apt C 914 Redding Way Upland CA 91786-3837 Office: Claremont McKenna Coll 890 Columbia Ave Claremont CA 91711-3901

SMITH, STEVEN COLE, engineering process consultant; b. Idaho Falls, Idaho, Oct. 3, 1952; s. Merrell Cordon and Myrtle Jean (McArthur) S.; m. Gay Lynn Pendleton, May 2, 1975; children: Jennifer, Melinda, Gregory, Aimilee. BS, Brigham Young U., 1977; MS, West Coast U., 1992. Engr. Gen. Dynamics, San Diego, 1978-81, Hughes Aircraft, L.A., 1981-82; cons. CAD/CAM Splty., L.A., 1982-83; system mgr. Solar Turbines, San Diego, 1983-87; mktg. support Evans and Sutherland, Costa Mesa, Calif., 1987-88; mktg. mgr. Computervision, San Diego, 1988—; instr. Southwestern C.C., San Diego, 1986-87. Mem. AIAA. Mormon. Office: Computervision 9805 Scranton Rd Ste 160 San Diego CA 92121-1765

SMITH, STEVEN DELANO, professional basketball player; b. Highland Park, Mich., Mar. 31, 1969. Student, Mich. State U. Guard Miami Heat, 1991-94; with Atlanta Hawks, 1994—. Named Sporting News All-Am. First Team, 1990, 91, NBA All-Rookie Team, 1992, Dream Team II, 1994. Office: Atlanta Hawks South Tower One CNN Ctr Ste 405 Atlanta GA 30303*

SMITH, STEVEN RAY, law educator; b. Spirit Lake, Iowa, July 8, 1946; s. Byrnard L. and Dorothy V. (Fischbeck) S.; m. Lera Baker, June 15, 1975. BA, Buena Vista Coll., 1968; JD, U. Iowa, 1971, MA, 1971. Bar: Iowa 1971, Ky. 1987, Ohio 1992. From asst. to assoc. dean Sch. Law U. Louisville, 1974-81, acting dean, 1974-75, 76, prof. law, 1971-88, assoc. in medicine Med. Sch., 1983-88; dep. dir/ Assn. Am. Law Schs., 1987-88; dean, prof. law Cleve. State U., 1988-96; pres., dean and prof. Calif. Western Sch. of Law, 1996—. Author: Law, Behavior and Mental Health: Policy and Practice, 1987; contbr. chpts. to books, articles to profl. jours. Trustee U. Louisville, 1980-82, SCRIBES, 1993—; chmn. faculty adv. com. Ky. Coun. Higher Edn., 1981-82; pres. Ky. Congress of Senate Faculty Leaders, 1982-84; bd. trustees Am. Bd. Profl. Psychology, 1994—. Recipient Grawemeyer award Innovative Teaching. Metroversity Consortium, 1983, Pres. award Cleve.-Marshall Law Alumni Assn., 1995. Fellow Ohio State Bar Found.; mem. ABA (stds. rev. com. 1991-95, govt. rels. com. 1993-95, joint commn. ABA/Assn. Am. Law Schs. financing of legal edn. 1993-94), APA (pub. mem. ethics com.), Am. Econs. Assn., Assn. Am. Law Schs. (chmn. librs. com., dep. dir. 1987-88, mem. accreditation com. 1993-96, chair accreditation com. 1994-96), Ohio State Bar Assn. (coun. of dels. 1992-96), Order of Coif, City Club of Cleve. (pres. 1994-95). Office: Calif We Sch Law Office of the Pres 225 Cedar St San Diego CA 92101

SMITH, STEVEN SIDNEY, molecular biologist; b. Idaho Falls, Idaho, Feb. 11, 1946; s. Sidney Ervin and Hermie Phyllis (Robertson) S.; m. Nancy Louise Turner, Dec. 20, 1974. BS, U. Idaho, 1968; PhD, UCLA, 1974. Asst. research scientist Beckman Research Inst. City of Hope Nat. Med. Ctr., Duarte, Calif., 1982-84, staff Cancer Ctr., 1983—, asst. research scientist depts. Thoracic Surgery and Molecular Biology, 1985-87, assoc. research scientist, 1987-95; rsch. sci. Beckman Research Inst. City of Hope Nat. Med. Ctr., Duarte, 1995—; rsch. scientist City of Hope Nat. Med. Ctr., 1995—; dir. dept. cell and tumor biology Beckman Research Inst. City of Hope Nat. Med. Ctr., Duarte, Calif., 1990—; Wellcome vis. prof. medicine Okla. State U., 1995-96; cons. Molecular Biosystems Inc., San Diego, 1981-84, Am. Inst. Biol. Scis., Washington, 1994. Contbr. articles to profl. jours. Grantee NIH, 1983-93, Coun. for Tobacco Rsch., 1983-92, March of Dimes, 1988-91, Smokeless Tobacco Rsch. Coun., 1992—, Office of Naval Rsch., 1994—; Swiss Nat. Sci. Found. fellow U. Bern, 1974-77, Scripps Clinic and Rsch. Found., La. Jolla, Calif., 1978-82, NIH fellow Scripps Clinic, 1979-81. Mem. Am. Soc. Cell Biology, Am. Assn. Cancer Rsch., Am. Crystallographic Assn., Am. Chem. Soc., Am. Weightlifting Assn., Phi Beta Kappa. Avocation: backpacking. Office: City of Hope Nat Med Ctr 1500 Duarte Rd Duarte CA 91010-3012

SMITH, STEWART EDWARD, physical chemist; b. Balt., Oct. 5, 1937; s. Ambrose Jefferson and Gladys Ruth (Stewart) S.; children: Nicole Catherine, Stewart Bradford; m. Loretta Inez Moody, Mar. 9, 1994. BS, Howard U., 1960; PhD, Ohio State U., 1969. Chemist Du Pont, Gibbstown, N.J., 1963-64; rsch. chemist Du Pont, Wilmington, Del., 1972-74; tech. svc. rep. Du Pont, Wilmington, 1974-78; rsch. chemist Sun Oil, Marcus Hook, Pa., 1969-71; coal chemist Exxon Rsch. and Engring., Baytown, Tex., 1976-81, group head, 1981-82; relocation coord. Exxon Rsch. and Engring., Clinton, N.J., 1982-84; sr. staff chemist Exxon Rsch. and Engring., Baytown, 1984-86; advisory engr. Westinghouse-Bettis, West Mifflin, Pa., 1986—. Contbr. articles to profl. jours. Mem. jr. high sch. adv. bd., Wilmington, 1975; coach Little League Baseball, Clear Lake City, Tex., 1979. Lt. U.S. Army, 1961-63. Recipient Pres.'s award Howard U. Alumni, Wilmington, 1976. Mem. AAAS, Am. Chem. Soc., Sigma Xi, Kappa Alpha Psi. Avocations: physical fitness, jogging, gourmet cooking. Home: 125 Amberwood Ct Bethel Park PA 15102-2252 Office: Westinghouse Elec Corp PO Box 79 West Mifflin PA 15122-0079

SMITH, S(TEWART) GREGORY, ophthalmologist, inventor, product developer, consultant, author; b. Wyandotte, Mich., Jan. 24, 1953; s. Stewart Gene and Veronica (Latta) S. BA in Econs. with distinction, U. Mich., 1974; MD, Wayne State U., 1978. Diplomate Am. Bd. Ophthalmology, Nat. Bd. Med. Examiners. Intern, Sacred Heart Med. Ctr., Spokane, Wash.,1978; resident in ophthalmology U. Minn., Mpls., 1979-82, fellow cornea and anterior segment surgery, 1982-83; practice medicine specializing in cornea and anterior segment surgery, and ophthalmology Wilmington, Del., 1983—; clin. prof. ophthalmology U. Pa., Hershey Med. Ctr., 1984—; clin. asst. prof. Thomas JeffersonU.; attending surgeon Wills Eye Hosp., Phila., 1984—; mem. sr. faculty 3M Vision Care Dept., Mpls., 1984-90, rsch. cons., 1984, lectr., 1983—, cons. Am. Cyanamid Opthalmic Divsn., 1990-94, Am. Home Product, 1995—; lectr. in field, Korea, Hong Kong, Thailand, Malaysia, Phillipines, France, Spain, Ireland, Portugal, Holland, Denmark, England; cons. Am. Home Products, 1995—. Author: Complications ofIntraocular Lenses and Their Management, 1988; co-author: Vision Without Glasses, 1990, Sight for Life, 1990, Can You Really See Clearly Without Glasses, 1996; contbr. articles to Fly Fisherman Mag. and other profl. publs. Patentee investigational devices and pharmaceutical, tilt control for automotive vehicles. Recipient award for Best Sci. Poster, Contact Lens Assn. of Ophthalmologists, 1980; Best Film award Internat. Congress of Cataract Surgeons, 1985; Grand Prize Am. Soc. Cataract and Refractive Surgeons Film Festival, 1986. Fellow Am. Intraocular Implant Soc., Castroviejo Soc. (Best Paper award 1984), AMA, Eye Bank Assn. Am., Am. Soc. Cataract and Refractive Surgery Internat. Soc. Refractive Surgery, Am. Acad.

Ophthalmology, Assn. for Rsch. and Vision in Ophthalmology, Internat. Intraocular Implant Club, Wills Eye Hosp. Alumni Soc., European Soc. Cataract & Refracture Soc. Avocations: fly fishing, hunting, saxophone, tennis, skiing. Home: Nine Gates Rd Yorklyn DE 19736 Office: 1100 N Grant Ave Wilmington DE 19805-2670

SMITH, STUART A., lawyer; b. N.Y.C., Mar. 16, 1941; s. Sydney S. and Gertrude (Blinder) S.; m. Helaine Levi, Mar. 14, 1982. AB, Columbia Coll., N.Y.C., 1961; LLB, Harvard U., 1964. Bar: N.Y. 1964, U.S. Tax Ct. 1965, U.S. Supreme Ct. 1967, D.C. 1970. Law clk. to chief judge U.S. Tax Ct., Washington, 1964-66; atty. U.S. Dept. Justice Tax Div., Washington, 1966-70; pvt. practice Washington, 1970-73; tax asst. to solicitor gen. U.S. Dept. Justice, Washington, 1973-83; pvt. practice N.Y.C., 1983-91; ptnr. Piper & Marbury LLP, N.Y.C., 1991—. Author: How You Can Get the Most from the New Tax Law, 1982; contbr. articles to law revs. Mem. ABA (chmn. tax sect. subcom.), Assn. of Bar of City of N.Y (fed. taxation com.), Am. Law Inst. (tax adv. group), Univ. Club (N.Y.C., Washington), Harvard Club N.Y.C.), RAC Club (London). Office: Piper & Marbury LLP 53 Wall St New York NY 10005-2899

SMITH, STUART LYON, psychiatrist, corporate executive; b. Montreal, Que., Can., May 7, 1938; s. Moe Samuel and Nettie (Krainer) S.; m. Patricia Ann Springate, Jan. 2, 1964; children: Tanya, Craig. BSc, McGill U., 1958, MD, CM, 1962, diploma in psychiatry, 1967; LLD (hon.), Mt. Allison U., 1992. Intern. Montreal Gen. Hosp., 1962-63, resident in psychiatry, 1963-67; from asst. prof. to assoc. prof. medicine McMaster U., Hamilton, Ont., Can., 1967-75; mem. Ont. Legislature, 1975-82, also leader Ont. Liberal Party, 1976-82, and leader of the opposition, 1977-82; chmn. Sci. Coun. Can., Ottawa, 1982-87; pres. RockCliffe Rsch. and Tech., Inc., 1987—, Philip Utilities Mgmt. Corp., Toronto, Ont., 1994—; sr. v.p. Philip Environment Inc., Toronto, 1994—; bd. dirs. Can. Trade Group Inc.; chmn. Ensyn Techs., Inc., 1990—; vis. prof. psychiatry McMaster U., 1982-93; adj. prof. U. Ottawa, 1986-94; chmn. com. on inquiry on Can. Univ. Edn., 1999-91; chmn. bd. trustees Ottawa Gen. Hosp., 1991-94; chmn. Nat. Roundtable on Environ. and Economy, Ottawa, 1995—. Mem. bd. govs. U. Ottawa, 1989-94. Decorated knight Nat. Order of Merit, France, 1988; McLaughlin travelling fellow, 1964-65. Fellow Royal Coll. Physicians and Surgeons of Can. Jewish.

SMITH, STUART SEABORNE, writer, government official, union official; b. N.Y.C., Jan. 27, 1930; s. Purcell Leonard and Elizabeth (Wright) S.; m. Birte Moeller Jacobsen, Apr. 27, 1956 (div. 1972); children: Stuart Seaborne, Bjarne Moeller; m. Editha Maria Fuchs, Jan. 3, 1973; children: Cornelia Gerda, Melanie Carla. Grad., Lawrenceville (N.J.) Sch., 1948; student, Princeton U., 1948-51, U. Heidelberg, Germany, 1953-54, U. Madrid, Spain, 1954-55, U. Copenhagen, Denmark, 1955-56. Reporter Balt. Sun, 1957-65, fgn. corr. chief Bonn (Germany) bur., 1965-69, corr. Washington Bur., 1969-70; with ABA, 1970-71, Dept. Justice, Washington, 1971—; exec. dir. Capitol Employees Organizing Group, 1979—; pub. Balt. Banner, 1965. Served with AUS, 1951-53. Recipient Spl. award for meritorious svc. Washington-Balt. Newspaper Guild, 1965, meritorious award Dept. Justice, 1985, 87, Sustained Superior Performance award Dept. Justice, 1992, 93. Mem. Am. Fedn. State, County and Mcpl. Employees (pres. coun. 26 1977-80, 87-95, chief steward Local 2830 1975-80, 81-82, pres. 1982—, Meritorious Svc. award Local 2830, 1980). Home: 10522 Tyler Ter Potomac MD 20854-4059 Office: Office of Justice Programs Washington DC 20531 *I believe in honor and democracy and social justice. I further believe that for the most part we are the ignorant slaves of political and philosophical superstitions, but in the end the truth shall set us free.*

SMITH, SUE FRANCES, newspaper editor; b. Lockhart, Tex., July 4, 1940; d. Monroe John Baylor and Myrtle (Krause) Mueck; m. Michael Vogtel Smith, Apr. 20, 1963 (div. July 1977); 1 child, Jordan Meredith. B. Journalism, U. Tex., 1962. Feature writer, photographer Corpus Christi Caller Times, 1962-64; feature writer, editor Chgo. Tribune, 1964-76; features editor Dallas Times Herald, 1976-82; sales assoc. Bumpas Assocs., Dallas, 1982-83; asst. mng. editor for features Denver Post, 1983-84, assoc. editor, 1984-91; asst. mng. editor in charge of Sunday paper Dallas Morning News, 1991-94, asst. mng. editor Lifestyles, 1994-96, dep. mng. editor Lifestyles, 1996—; active Coun. Pres., 1993. Mem. Am. Assn. Sunday and Feature Editors (pres. 1993), Newspaper Features Coun. (bd. dirs., sec., treas.), Tex. Associated Press Mng. Editors (bd. dirs.), Delta Gamma. Home: 6060 Jereme Trl Dallas TX 75252-5130 Office: 508 Young St Dallas TX 75202-4808

SMITH, SUSAN ARLENE, nursing educator; b. Columbia, S.C., Dec. 16, 1953; d. Gibson and Eva Mae (Sharpe) Lawson; m. John Earl Smith, May 14, 1977; 1 child, Nancy Michelle. BSN, U. S.C., 1976, MSN, 1979. RN, S.C.; cert. HIV/AIDS educator ARC. Proofreader, sec. Vogue Press Printing, Columbia, 1972-74; nursing asst. Bapt. Med. Ctr., Columbia, 1974-76, staff nurse obstetrics, 1976-78; staff nurse, program nurse specialist for child health Ctrl. Midlands Health Dist., Columbia, 1978-80; prof. nursing U. S.C., Columbia, 1981-83; staff nurse ob/gyn. surgery Lexington Med. Ctr., West Columbia, S.C., 1981-86; prof. pediatrics nursing and HIV/AIDS edn. Midlands Tech. Coll., Columbia, 1986—; CEO HIV/AIDS ednl./support network Tomorrow's Hope, 1993—; mem. adv. bd. S.C. AIDS Tng. Network, Columbia, 1994—; presenter in field. Co-author: HIV Disease/AIDS: Curriculum for Allied Health Students, 1991; contbr. articles to profl. publs.; author manual in field. Founder, facilitator support group for HIV/AIDS patients, West Columbia, 1992—, HIV/AIDS Care Team, West Columbia, 1992—, HIV/AIDS Peer Edn. Program, Columbia, 1994; mem. nat. AIDS task force So. Bapt. Conv., 1994—; mem. Nat. AIDS Task Force, 1995—; mem. AIDS care team, mem. pers. com., pres. sanctuary choir, Sunday sch. tchr. Trinity Bapt. Ch.; vol. March of Dimes, Arthritis Found.; fundraiser AIDS Walk, 1994; spkr. on health careers Davis Elem. Sch. Named Outstanding Faculty Mem. So. Region Assn. C.C. Trustees, 1993, Tchr. of Yr., Midlands Tech. Coll., 1992, Faculty Mem. of Yr., 1993. Mem. Bapt. Nursing Fellowship (chair nominating com. 1992—), Sigma Theta Tau. Avocations: old movies, crafts, travel, collecting miniatures, writing. Home: 116 Longleaf Dr Cayce SC 29033-1912 Office: Midlands Tech Coll PO Box 2408 Columbia SC 29202-2408

SMITH, SUSAN ELIZABETH, guidance director; b. Phila., Mar. 24, 1950; d. E. Burke Hogue and Janet Coffin Hogue Ebert; m. J. Russell Smith, June 17, 1972 (div. June 1989); 1 child, Drew Russell. BS in Elem. Edn., E. Stroudsburg Coll., 1972; MEd in Counseling, U. Okla., 1974, postgrad., 1976-77; postgrad., Trenton State Coll., 1989-90; EdM in Devel. Disabilities, Rutgers U., 1992, postgrad., 1994—. Cert. elem. tchr., N.C.; cert. elem. tchr., early childhood edn. tchr., guidance and counseling, Okla.; cert. elem. tchr., guidance and counseling, tchr. of handicapped, psychology tchr., supr. instrn., dir. student pers. svcs., N.J. Elem. tchr. Morton Elem. Sch. Onslow County Schs., Jacksonville, N.C., 1971-72; instr. U. Isfahan, Iran, 1974-76; guidance counselor Moore (Okla.) Pub. Schs., 1976-77; counselor Johnstone Tng. Ctr. N.J. Divsn. Devel. Disabilities, Bordentown, 1988-90; spl. edn. tchr. Willingboro (N.J.) Schs., 1990-91; guidance counselor Haledon (N.J.) Pub. Schs., 1991-92; spl. edn. adj. tchr. Gateway Sch., Carteret, N.J., 1991-93; guidance counselor Bloomfield (N.J.) Pub. Schs., 1992-94; dir. guidance Somerville (N.J.) Pub. Schs., 1994-95; adj. prof. in spl. edn. Essex County (N.J.) Coll., 1994; guidance Ft. Lee (N.J.) Schs., 1995—; cons., seminar and workshop presenter on behavior mgmt., parenting skills, and behavior modification techniques; cons. N.J. Fragile X Assn. Author: Motivational Awards for ESL Students, 1993, Parent Contracts to Improve School Behaviors, 1996; contbr. articles to profl. jours. Leader Boy Scouts Am., Oklahoma City, 1983-87, com. chmn., Redmond, Wash., 1987-88. Recipient Rsch. award ERIC/CAPS, 1992, Svc. award N.J. Fragile X Assn., 1993. Mem. ACA, Am. Sch. Counselor Assn. (grantee 1992), N.J. Counseling Assn., N.J. Sch. Counseling Assn., Assn. for Multicultural Counseling and Devel., AAUW, Assn. for Counselor Edn. and Supervision, N.J. Assn. for Counselor Edn. and Supervision, N.J. Prins. and Suprs. Assn., Nat. Assn. Coll. Admissions Counselors (grantee 1995), Alpha Omicron Pi. Episcopalian. Home: 13 Yale St Nutley NJ 07110-3386

SMITH, TAD RANDOLPH, lawyer; b. El Paso, Tex., July 20, 1928; s. Eugene Rufus and Dorothy (Derrick) S.; m. JoAnn Wilson, Aug. 24, 1949; children: Laura Bonsch, Derrick, Cameron Ann Compton. BBA, U. Tex. 1952, LLB, 1951. Bar: Tex. 1951; assoc. firm Kemp, Smith, Duncan & Hammond, P.C., El Paso, 1951, ptnr., 1952-81, CEO, 1975—, shareholder, 1981—; bd. dirs. El Paso Indsl. Devel. Corp. Active United Way of El Paso; chmn. El Paso County Reps., 1958-61, Tex. Rep. State Exec. Com., 1961-62; alt. del. Rep. Nat. Conv., 1952, 62, del., 1964; dir. El Paso Electric Co., 1961-90, State Nat. Bank of El Paso, 1969-90, Petro, Inc., 1987—, The Leavell Co., 1970—; trustee Robert E. and Evelyn McKee Found. 1970-90, Property Trust of America, 1971-91; mem. devel. bd. U. Tex. El Paso, 1973-81, v.p., 1975, chmn. 1976; dinner treas. Nat. Jewish Hosp. and Research Ctr., 1977, chmn. 1978, presenter of honoree, 1985; bd. dirs. Southwestern Children's Home, El Paso, 1959-78, Nat. Conf. Christians and Jews, 1965-76, chmn. 1968-69, adv. dir. 1976—; trustee Hervey Found., 1990—, Lydia Patterson Inst., 1994—. Named Outstanding Young Man El Paso, El Paso Jaycees, 1961; recipient Humanitarian award El Paso chpt. NCCJ, 1983. Fellow Tex. Bar Found.; mem. ABA, Tex. Bar Assn., El Paso Bar Assn. (pres. 1971-72), El Paso C. of C. (dir. 1979-82), Sigma Chi. Republican. Methodist. Home: 1202 Thunderbird Dr El Paso TX 79912-2028 Office: Kemp Smith Duncan & Hammond 2000 State Nat Plz 221 N Kansas St El Paso TX 79901-1443

SMITH, TAMMY SUE, food service management professional; b. Tulsa, Feb. 18, 1961; d. Clyde Earnest and Susan Viola (Deckard) S.; children: Jeffrey Clyde Ray, Brandi Sue-Etta. A in Edn., Claremore Jr. Coll., 1981; BS in Edn., Northeastern State U., 1983, MEd in Counseling, 1991. Cert. food svc. sanitation instr., Ill.; cert. home econs. tchr., Okla., Ill.; cert. counselor, Okla., Ill. Vocat. home econs. tchr. Oilton (Okla.) Pub. Sch., 1983-85; asst. mgr. McDonald's Corp., Tulsa, 1985-86; food svc. supr. Tulsa Job Corp, 1986-88; vocat. home econs. tchr. Foyil (Okla.) Pub. Sch., 1988-90, Ft. Gibson (Okla.) Pub. Sch., 1990-91; food svc. tech. instr. MacMurray Coll., Jacksonville, Ill., 1991—; also project connect coord., food svc. instr. MacMurray Coll. Named one of Outstanding Young Women of Am., 1989. Mem. AAUW, Am. Dietetic Assn., Dietary Mgrs. Assn., Assn. for Female Offenders, Am. Sewing Guild, Am. Vocat. Assn., Am. Correctional Food Svc. Assn., Ill. Vocat. Assn., Ill. Restaurant Assn., Nat. Restaurant Assn., Adult Vocat. Edn. Assn., Correctional Edn. Assn., Nat. Jaycees, Ill. Jaycees, Lincoln Jaycees, Jr. Jaycees (co-leader), Kappa Delta Pi, Rho Theta Sigma. Avocations: sewing, reading, creative cookery, sports fan. Home: 1115 Macon St Lincoln IL 62656-9772 Office: MacMurray Coll c/o Logan Correctional Ctr PO Box 1000 Lincoln IL 62656

SMITH, TAYLOR, professional football team executive; b. Atlanta, GA, May 3, 1953; m. Louise; children: Ryan, Brooks, Rebecca. BBA, U. Ga., 1976. With Atlanta Falcons, Ga., former mem. front office staff, former corp. sec., former exec. v.p.; now pres. Atlanta Falcons, Atlanta, GA. Bd. dirs. Gwinnett Found.; active Falcons Youth Found. Mem. Rotary. Office: Atlanta Falcons 1 Falcon Pl Suwanee GA 30174*

SMITH, TEFFT W., lawyer; b. Evanston, Ill., Nov. 18, 1946. BA, Brown U., 1968; JD, U. Chgo., 1971. Bar: Ill. 1971. Ptnr. Kirkland & Ellis, Chgo. Mem. ABA (litigation sect., antitrust law sect.). Office: Kirkland & Ellis 200 E Randolph St Chicago IL 60601-6436*

SMITH, TERENCE FITZGERALD, television news correspondent; b. Bryn Mawr, Pa., Nov. 18, 1938; s. Walter W. and Catherine M. (Cody) S.; m. Phyllis Ann Charnley, June 20, 1964 (div. 1987); children: Elizabeth Reed, Christopher Wellesly. B.A., U. Notre Dame, 1960. Reporter Stamford (Conn.) Adv., 1960-62, N.Y. (N.Y.C.) Herald Tribune, 1963-65; with N.Y. Times, N.Y.C., 1965-85; fgn. corr. N.Y. Times, Israel, Thailand; Vietnam bur. chief N.Y. Times, 1969-70; diplomatic corr. N.Y. Times, Washington, 1970-72; chief corr. N.Y. Times, Israel, 1972-76; dep. fgn. editor N.Y. Times, 1976-77, chief White House corr., 1978-81, sr. corr. Washington bur., 1981, editor Washington Talk page, 1981-85; Washington corr. CBS Morning News, 1985-86; White House corr. CBS News, Washington, 1986-88; Washington corr. CBS News, 1989-90; sr. corr. CBS Sunday Morning, 1991—; lectr., freelance writer. Mem. Overseas Writers Assn., Washington. Office: CBS News 2020 M St NW Washington DC 20036-3368

SMITH, THELMA TINA HARRIETTE, gallery owner, artist; b. Folkston, Ga., May 5, 1938; d. Harry Charles and Malinda Estelle (Kennison) Causey; m. Billy Wayne Smith, July 23, 1955; children: Sherry Yvonne, Susan Marie, Dennis Wayne, Chris Michael. Student, U. Tex., Arlington, 1968-70; studies with various art instrs. Gen. office worker Superior Ins. Corp., Dallas, 1956-57, Zanes-Ewalt Warehouse, Dallas, 1957-67; bookkeeper Atlas Match Co., Arlington, 1967-68; sr. acct. Automated Refrigerated Air Conditioner Mfg. Corp., Arlington, 1968-70; acct. Conn. Gen. Life Ins. Corp., Dallas, 1972-74; freelance artist Denton, Tex., 1974—; gallery owner, custom framer Tina Smith Studio-Gallery, Mabank, Tex., 1983—. Painting in pub. and pvt. collections in numerous states including N.Y., Fla., Ga. and N.D.; editor Cedar Creek Art Soc. Yearbook, 1983—. Treas. Cedar Creek Art Soc., 1987-88, 89—; mem. com. to establish state endorsed Arts Coun. for Cedar Creek Lake Area, Gun Barrel City, Tex. Recipient numerous watercolor and pastel awards Henderson County Art League, Cedar Creek Art Soc., Cmty. Svc. award Mayor Wilson Tippit, Gun Barrel City, Tex., 1986. Mem. Southwestern Watercolor Soc. (Dallas), Pastel Soc. of the S.W. (Dallas), Cedar Creek Art Soc. (Gun Barrel City) (v.p. 1983-86, treas.), Profl. Picture Framers Assn. Baptist. Avocations: water activities, gardening. Office: Tina Smith Studio-Gallery 139 W Main St Gun Barrel City TX 75147

SMITH, THEODORE W., construction executive; b. 1927. Pres. Dinwiddie Constrn. Co., San Francisco, 1947—. Office: Dinwiddie Constrn Co Crocker Ctr W Tower 275 Battery St Ste 300 San Francisco CA 94111-3330*

SMITH, THOMAS CLAIR, manufacturing company executive; b. Indiana, Pa., Mar. 14, 1925; s. William Bryan and Edna Louise (Thomas) S.; m. Marilyn Louise Globisch, May 29, 1948; children: Claudia Lynn Smith Holtry, Craig Randall. BSME, Pa. State U., 1946; A, Alexander Hamilton Bus. Inst., 1949. Registered profl. engr., Pa. Structural test engr. Chance Vought Aircraft Co., Bridgeport, Conn., 1946-48; test engr. Fed. Mogul Bearings Co., Lancaster, Pa., 1949-51; fuse engr. to mgr. materials Hamilton Watch Co. (name now Hamilton Tech.), Lancaster, Pa., 1952-70; plant mgr. Woodstream Corp., Lititz, Pa., 1970-79, v.p. mktg., 1980—; faculty, coach Lacrosse Franklin and Marshall Coll., Lancaster, 1950-53. Pub. Smith, Bryan, Allison & Morris Geneal. Chart, 1989; author and pub. of 1600 person geneal. chart in Libr. of Congress, 1989; patentee electric watch, 1957, swivel snap, 1975; author Penna Law 110 of 1992 and Pa. Law 22 of 1994/saving ancestral cemeteries. Pres., bd. dirs. Lancaster County Mental Health Assn., 1952-60, Lancaster County Cmty. Svc. Ctr., 1968-78, Am. Cancer Soc., 1968—; bd. dirs. Hearing Conservation Assn., Lancaster, 1955-60, ARC, Lancaster, 1967—, United Way, Lancaster, 1968-72, Ephrata (Pa.) Area Rehab. Ctr., 1986—; mem. All-Am. Lacrosse Team, 1945, Heritage Ctr. Lancaster, 1980—, Ind. County Hist. Soc., 1984—, Greene County Hist. Soc., Waynesburg, Pa., 1985—, Selective Svc. Bd., 1992—; trustee Lancaster Hist. Soc., 1992—, mem., 1983—; judge elections, Lancaster City, 1994—. Recipient Outstanding Svc. award Mental Health Assn., Lancaster, 1961, Edward D. Eshelman award as Humanitarian of Yr., Am. Cancer Soc., Lancaster, 1991; named Boss of Yr. Am. Bus. Womens Assn., 1978, Man of Yr. Am. Cancer Soc., 1984, Tennis Family of Yr., Pa., N.J., Del., 1970. Mem. Order of Crown of Charlemagne in U.S.A. (life), Pa. State U. Alumni Club (life), Pa. Sons of Revolution (bd. dirs., sec. 1990—), Phi Delta Theta (pres. Pa. State U. chpt. 1945), Wheatland Tennis Club (v.p. 1990-94, pres. 1995). Republican. Presbyterian. Club: Lancaster Country (chmn. tennis com. 1960-75). Avocations: genealogy, tennis, skiing. Home: 1420 Quarry Ln Lancaster PA 17603-2426 Office: Woodstream Corp 69 N Locust St Lititz PA 17543-1714 *You only go through this life on earth once. Don't waste that time. Put it to use in helping to make the earth a better place.*

SMITH, THOMAS EUGENE, investment company executive, financial consultant; b. Brown's Summit, N.C., Aug. 23, 1930; s. Howard Cleveland and Annie May (Warren) S.; m. Joan Cretcher Hopkins, Sept. 22, 1948; 1 dau., Vicki Joan. Student, George Washington U., 1948-50, Am. U., 1950-55 (intermittently). Pres., dir. T. Eugene Smith, Inc. investment co. and real estate and fin. cons. co., Falls Church, Va., 1950—; pres. The Potomac Corp., Falls Church, Va., 1960-74; pres., dir. Nat. Bank of Fairfax, Va., 1975-81, dir.; exec. v.p. First & Mchts. Nat. Bank, Richmond, Va., 1981-83; chmn., dir. Decisions and Designs, Inc., McLean, Va., 1983-86; ptnr. Braddock-Ravensworth Ltd. Partnership, 1964—; sec., dir. Port Royal, Inc., 1965—; ptnr. Lee Graham Shopping Ctr., 1969—; chmn., pres., dir. Am. Mobile Home Towns, Inc., holding co., 1969-85; dir., pres. Topsail, Inc., 1983-89; ptnr. Potomac Greens Assn., 1986—; bd. dirs. Growth Fund of Washington, Am. Funds Tax Exempt Series I, Washington Mut. Investors, M.G. Thalheimer Realty Advisors, Inc.; chmn., bd. dirs. River Capital Corp., Alexandria, Va., 1986-89, J. Webb, Inc., 1986—; acting dir., mem. mgmt. com. Alexandria 20/20, 1988-91, acting dir., 1988-89; pres., dir. Pender Marina Holdings, Inc., 1988—, Pender Land Holdings, Inc., 1990—; mem. CSX Realty Adv. Bd., 1992—. Bd. dirs. Wolftrap Found., Washington, 1974-84; trustee Sta. WETA-TV, 1978-86; mem. Nat. Capital Planning Commn., Washington, 1980-83, vice chmn., 1981-83; mem. Va. Hwys. and Transp. Commn., Richmond, 1982-86; trustee Ch. Schs., Diocese of Va., 1983-88; mem. Va. Gov.'s Coun. Econ. Advisors, 1985-94, Met. Washington Airports Authority, 1986-94; chmn. Fairfax County Transp. Commn. for the Future, 1988-89; dir. Air and Space Heritage Coun., 1987-90. Mem. Nat. Assn. Small Bus. Investment Cos. (treas. and bd. dirs. 1962-66), Commonwealth Club (Richmond), Met. Club (Washington). Democrat. Episcopalian. Home: 666 Tintagel Ln Mc Lean VA 22101-1835

SMITH, THOMAS HUNTER, ophthalmologist, ophthalmic plastic and orbital surgeon; b. Silver Creek, Miss., Aug. 10, 1939; s. Hunter and Wincil (Barr) S.; m. Michele Ann Campbell, Feb. 27, 1982; 1 child, Thomas Hunter IV. BA, U. So. Miss., 1961; MD, Tulane U., 1967; BA in Latin Am. Studies, Tex. Christian U., 1987, MA in Latin Am. History, 1995. Diplomate Am. Bd. Ophthalmology. Intern Charity Hosp., New Orleans, 1967-68; resident in ophthalmology Tulane U., New Orleans, 1968-71; dir., sec. bd. dirs. Ophthalmology Assocs., Ft. Worth, 1971—; clin. prof. Tex. Tech. U. Med. Sch., Lubbock, 1979—; bd. examiners Am. Bd. Ophthalmology, 1983-90; guest lectr., invited speaker numerous schs., confs., symposia throughout N.Am., Ctrl. Am., South Am., Europe and India; hon. mem. ophthalmology dept. Santa Casa de São Paulo Med. Sch. Contbr. articles to profl. jours. Cons. ophthalmologist Helen Keller Internat.; deacon South Hills Christian Ch.,. Recipient Tex. Chpt. award Am. Assn. Workers for the Blind, 1978, Recognition award Lions Club Sight & Tissue Found., Cen. Am., 1977-79; named to Alumni Hall of Fame U. So. Miss., 1989. Fellow ACS, Am. Acad. Ophthalmology (bd. counsellors 1995—), Am. Acad. Facial Plastic and Reconstructive Surgery; mem. Tex. Med. Assn. (com. socio-econs.), Pan-Am. Assn. Ophthalmology (adminstr. 1988-93, bd. dirs. 1993—), Internat. Cos. Cryosurgery, Royal Soc. Medicine (affiliate), Tex. Soc. Ophthalmology and Otolaryngology, Peruvian Ophthalmol. Soc. (hon.), Santa Casa De São Paulo (hon. assoc.), Tex. Ophthalmol. Assn. (past mem. exec. coun., treas.), Tex. Med. Assn., Tarrant County Med. Soc., Byron Smith Ex Fellows Assn., Tarrant County Multiple Sclerosis Soc. (past pres.), Tarrant County Assn. for Blind, Tulane Med. Alumni Assn. (bd. dirs.), S.Am. Explorers Club, Colonial Country Club, Petroleum Club Ft. Worth, Sigma Xi, Omicron Delta Kappa. Mem. Disciples of Christ. Avocations: hunting, fishing, flying, world travel. Office: Ophthalmology Assocs 1201 Summit Ave Fort Worth TX 76102-4413

SMITH, THOMAS KENT, radiologist; b. Bowling Green, Ohio, Aug. 21, 1934; s. Robert O. and Roslyn Smith; m. Jaleh Saidi, Feb. 1, 1974; children: Jeffrey, Todd, Mark, Blake, Tyler. BS with high honors, U. Cin., 1957; MD, Case Western Res. U., 1961. Intern Nat. Naval Med. Ctr., Bethesda, Md., 1961-62; resident in radiology VA Med. Ctr., Long Beach, Calif., 1965-69; dir. radiology Harriman Jones Med. Group, Long Beach, 1969-88; fellow in MRI/CT U. Calif., San Francisco, 1988-89; dir. MRI Orange County MRI, Fountain Valley, Calif., 1989-90; chmn. dept. diagnostic imaging Kaiser Permanente Med. Ctr., Honolulu, 1990—; fellow in radiologic pathology Armed Forces Inst. of Pathology, Washington, 1968; mem. adv. bd. Hawaii Permanente Med. Group, Honolulu, 1990—; bd. dirs. Harriman Jones Med. Group, Harriman Jones Assocs.; assoc. clin. prof. radiology U. Hawaii, Honolulu, 1990—; asst. clin. prof. U. Calif., Irvine, 1970-88; clin. instr. U. Calif., San Francisco, 1988-89, asst. clin. prof., 1989—; cons. in radiologic devel. Kaiser Permanente Internat., 1996—. Lt. USN, 1961-65. Mem. Hawaii Radiol. Soc. (pres. 1992-93), Radiol. Soc. N.Am., Am. Coll. Radiology, Internat. Soc. Magnetic Resonance in Medicine, Margulis Soc., Calif. Radiol. Soc., Alpha Omega Alpha. Avocations: fishing, travel, photography. Home: 46-434 Haiku Plantation Dr Kaneohe HI 96744-4207 Office: Kaiser Permanente Med Ctr 3288 Moanalua Rd Honolulu HI 96819

SMITH, THOMAS SHORE, lawyer; b. Rock Springs, Wyo., Dec. 7, 1924; s. Thomas and Anne E. (McTee) S.; m. Jacqueline Emily Krueger, May 25, 1952; children: Carolyn Jane, Karl Thomas, David Shore. BSBA, U. Wyo., 1950, JD, 1959. Bar: U.S. Dist. Ct. Wyo. 1960, U.S. Ct. Appeals (10th cir.) 1960, U.S. Tax Ct. 1969, U.S. Supreme Ct. 1971. Of counsel Smith, Stanfield & Scott, LLC, Laramie, Wyo., 1963—; atty. City of Laramie, 1963-86; instr. mcpl. law U. Wyo., 1987, mem. dean's adv. com. Law Sch.; dir. budget and fin. Govt. of Am. Samoa, 1954-56. Bd. dirs. Bur. Land Mgmt., Rawlins, Wyo., 1984-89, chmn. bd. dirs., 1989; pres. Ivinson Hosp. Found., 1994-95; bd. dirs. U. Wyo. Found., 1991—. Francis Warren scholar, 1958. Mem Wyo. Bar Assn. (pres. 1984-85), Albany County Bar Assn., Western States Bar Conf. (pres. 1985-86), Elks. Republican. Episcopalian. Avocation: golf. Office: Smith Stanfield & Scott LLC PO Box 971 515 E Ivinson Ave Laramie WY 82070-3157

SMITH, THOMAS WINSTON, cotton marketing executive; b. Crosbyton, Tex., Mar. 16, 1935; s. Lance L. and Willie Mae (Little) S.; m. Patricia Mae Zachary, Dec. 13, 1958; children—Janna Olean, Thomas Mark. B.S., Tex. A&M U., 1957; P.M.D., Harvard U., 1964. Various positions Calcot Ltd., Bakersfield, Calif., 1957-77, exec. v.p., pres., 1977—; v.p. Amcot, Inc., Amcot Internat., Inc., Bakersfield, 1977—, also bd. dirs.; pres. Nat. Cotton Coun., Memphis; bd. mgrs. N.Y. Cotton Exchange, N.Y.C. Bd. dir. Greater Bakersfield Meml. Hosp.; mem. pres.'s adv. commn. Calif. State Coll., Bakersfield. Mem. Rotary.

SMITH, THOMAS WOODWARD, cardiologist, educator; b. Akron, Ohio, Mar. 29, 1936; s. Luther David and Beatrice Pearl (Woodward) S.; m. Sherley Louise Goodwin, Sept. 13, 1958; children: Julia Goodwin, Geoffrey Woodward, Allison Lloyd. A.B., Harvard U., 1958, M.D., 1965. Diplomate: Am. Bd. Internal Medicine; Am. Bd. Cardiovascular Diseases. Intern in medicine Mass. Gen. Hosp., Boston, 1965-66, asst. resident in medicine, 1966-67, clin. and research fellow in cardiology, 1967-69, Nat. Heart and Lung Inst. spl. fellow, 1969-71, asst. in medicine, 1969-72, assoc. program dir. myocardial infarction research unit, 1972-74, asst. physician, 1972-77, cons. in medicine, 1977—; asst. prof. medicine Harvard U. Med. Sch., 1971-73, assoc. prof., 1973-79, prof., 1979—; physician Peter Bent Brigham Hosp. (now Brigham and Women's Hosp.), Boston, chief cardiovascular div.; cons. in cardiology Children's Hosp. Med. Ctr. and Sidney Farber Cancer Inst. (now Dana-Farber Cancer Inst.); prof. medicine MIT div. Health Scis. and Tech.; Hall vis. prof., Sydney, Australia, 1977; Sir Henry Hallett Dale vis. prof. Johns Hopkins U. Med. Sch., 1979; Nahum lectr. Yale U. Sch. Medicine, 1979. Reviewer med. jours.; contbr. articles to profl. publs. Mem. Am. Heart Assn. (council clin. cardiology, council basic sci., council on circulation, established investigator 1971-76 Rosenthal award), Am. Fedn. Clin. Research, Paul Dudley White Soc., AAAS, Am. Soc. Pharmacology and Exptl. Therapeutics, Am. Soc. Clin. Investigation, Am. Coll. Cardiology, ACP, Assn. Univ. Cardiologists, Am. Physiol. Soc., Assn. Am. Physicians, Soc. Gen. Physiologists, Alpha Omega Alpha. Home: 128 Wellesley St Weston MA 02193-1555 Office: Brigham and Women's Hosp 75 Francis St Boston MA 02115-6110

SMITH, TOM EUGENE, retail food company executive; b. Salisbury, N.C., May 2, 1942; s. Ralph Eugene and Cora Belle (Ervin) S.; m. Martha Hatley; children: Leigh Ann, Nancy Thompson. AB in Bus. Adminstrn., Catawba Coll., 1964, LLD (hon.), 1986. With Del Monte Sales Co., 1964-67; account mgr. Del Monte Sales Co., Hickory, N.C., 1967-68; sales supr. Del Monte Sales Co., Charlotte, N.C., 1969-70; buyer Food Lion Stores, Inc., Salisbury, 1970-74, v.p. distbn., 1974-77, exec. v.p., 1977-81, pres., 1981—, chief exec. officer, 1986—, also bd. dirs.; chmn. bd., 1990—; chief exec. officer Food Lion Inc., Salisbury, 1986—; bd. dirs. N.C. Nat. Bank (chmn. bd. Salisbury chpt.), N.C. Food Dealers (pres. 1988). Trustee Catawba Coll., 1986—; bd. dirs. United Way, Salisbury, 1975-77. Recipient Martin Luther King Humanitarian award 1987, bronze and silver Chief Exec. Officer of Yr. awards Fin. World Mag., 1988. Mem. Nat. Assn. Retail Grocers, Sales Execs. Club (bd. dirs. 1974-79, pres. 1980), N.C. Food Dealers Assn. (bd. dirs. 1981—, 3d v.p. 1985, 2d v.p. 1986—), Am. Legion, C. of C. (bd. dirs.

1975-77). Republican. Lutheran. Club: Salisbury Country. Lodge: Rotary (bd. dirs. 1975-76). Avocations: traveling. Office: Food Lion Inc PO Box 1330 2110 Executive Dr Salisbury NC 28147-9047*

SMITH, V. KERRY, economics educator; b. Jersey City, Mar. 11, 1945; s. Vincent C. and Dorothy E. (Linehan) S.; m. Pauline Anne Taylor, May 10, 1969; children: Timothy, Shelley. AB, Rutgers U., 1966, PhD, 1970. Asst. prof., then assoc. prof. Bowling Green State U., Ohio, 1969-72; rsch. assoc. Resources for Future, Washington, 1971-73; assoc. prof. SUNY, Binghamton, 1973-75, prof., 1975-78; sr. fellow Resources for Future, Washington, 1976-79; prof. U. N.C., Chapel Hill, 1979-83; Centennial prof. Vanderbilt U., Nashville, 1983-87; Univ. Disting. prof. N.C. State U., 1987-94; Arts and Scis. prof. environ. econs. Duke U., 1994—; adviser energy div. Oak Ridge Nat. Lab., 1978-80, U. N.C. Inst. Environ. Studies, 1980-83; mem. panel NSF, 1981-83, sci. adv. bd. EPA. Author: Monte Carlo Methods, 1973, Technical Change, Relative Prices and Environmental Resource Evaluation, 1974, The costs of Congestion: An Econometric Analysis of Wilderness Recreation, 1976, Structure and Properties of a Wilderness Travel Simulator: An Application to the Spanish Peaks Area, 1976, The Economic Consequences of Air Pollution, 1976, Scarcity and Growth Reconsidered, 1979, (with others) Explorations in Natural Resource Economics, 1982, (with others) Environmental Policy Under Reagan's executive Order, 1984, (with W.H. Desvousges) Measuring Water Quality Benefits, 1986, (with others) Environmental Resources and Applied Welfare Economics, 1988, (with R.J. Kopp) Valuing Natural Assets: The Economics of Natural Resource Damage Assessment, Resources for the Future, 1993, Estimating Economic Values for Nature, 1996; editor Advances in Applied Micro Econs. series; contbr. numerous articles to profl. jours. Guggenheim fellow, 1976; grantee Resources for Future, 1970, 73, 74, 86, Fed. Energy Adminstrn. 1975, N.Y. Sea Grant Inst., 1975, Ford Found., 1976, NSF, 1977, 79, 83, Electric Power Rsch. Inst., 1978, Nat. Oceanic and Atmospheric Adminstrn., 1980, Sloan Found., 1981, 86, EPA, 1983-88, N.C. Sea Grant Program, 1987-93. Russell Sage Found., 1989-91; recipient Frederick V. Waugh medal Am. Agrl. Econ. Assn., 1992. Mem. Am. Econ. Assn., Am. Statis. Assn., Econometric Soc., So. Econ. Assn. (exec. com. 1981-83, 1st v.p. 1987, pres. elect 1988, pres. 1989), Assn. Environ. and Resource Economists (bd. dirs. 1975-79, v.p. 1979-80, chmn. com. 1982-83, pres. 1985-86, Disting. Svc. award 1989).

SMITH, VAN P., airplane engine company executive; b. Oneida, N.Y., Sept. 8, 1928; m. Margaret Ann Kennedy, Nov. 19, 1960; children: Lynn Ann Smith Walters, Mark Charles, Paul Gregory, Susan Colleen, Victor Patrick. AB in Pub. Adminstrn. and Econs., Colgate U., 1950; JD, Georgetown U., 1955; LLD (hon.), Ball State U., 1980; D of Bus. (hon.), Vincennes U., 1985; LLD (hon.), Ind. State U., 1986. Bar: D.C., Ind. Assoc. Warner, Clark & Warner, Muncie, Ind., 1955-56; co-founder, dir. Ontario Corp. of Muncie, 1956-63, sec. then v.p. sales, 1956-63, pres., chief exec. officer, 1963—, also chmn. bd., 1978—; chmn. bd. Ontario Forge Corp., Pyromet Industries Inc., Sherry Labs, Inc., Ontario Devel. Corp., Ontario Systems Corp., W.W. Rich Found., all in Muncie, Ontario Corp. Ltd., U.K., Pyromet Inc., Calif., Ontario Techs., Calif., CDS Engring., Calif., Dulond Toll and Engring. Inc, Fla., and other subs. Ontario Corp.; bd. dirs. N.G. Gilbert Corp., Muncie, Hoosier Motor Club, Indpls., Ind. Bell Telephone Co, Inc., Indpls., Indsl. Trust & Savs. Bank, Muncie, Lilly Indsl. Coatings, Inc., Indpls., Maxon Corp, Muncie, Pub. Service Ind., and other subs. Ontario Corp.; ptnr. Del. Aviation, Smittie's Men's Store, Village Developers, all in Muncie. Rep. mem. Ind. Ho. of Reps., 1960-62; del. Ind. and Nat. Rep. Conv.; pres. Muncie Police & Fire Commn., 1963-66; mem. parochial sch. bd. St. Mary's Sch., Muncie, 1968-70; mem. Ind. Employment Security Bd., 1969-71, Ind. Commn. Higher Edn., 1971—, Nat. Adv. Council SBA, 1982—, Gov.'s Fiscal Policy Adv. Council, 1982—, Ind. Labor & Mgmt. Council, 1983—, Ind. Econ. Devel. Council, 1985—, Presdl. Observation Team Phillipine Nat. election, 1986, Presdl. Trade Mission to several Far Eastern countries, 1984; bd. dirs. Bus.-Industry Polit. Action Com., 1984—; trustee Colgate U., 1985—, La Lumiere Sch., 1983—, Acad. for Community Leadership, 1975—; bd. dirs. Muncie Symphony Assn., 1980-88, pres. 1986-87; pres. Del. County United Way, 1969-70; bd. dirs. Newman Found. Ind., 1969—, Religious Heritage Am. 1986-88; active St. Mary's Cath. Parish, Muncie; mem. Diocese of Lafayette Bishop's Com. 100, 1969-80, pres. 1969-70; bd. regents Cath. U. Am., Washington, 1986-90, trustee 1990—; trustee Interlochen (Mich.) Ctr. for Arts, 1991—. Served 1st lt. USAF, 1951-53. Named one of Outstanding Young Men of Am., Jaycees, 1960; recipient Bus. and Layman award, Religious Heritage Am., 1984, Ind. Cath. Layman award, Faith, Family & Football of Ind., Inc. 1985, Civic Service award, Ind. Assn. Cities and Towns, 1985; invested Knight of Equestrian Order of Holy Sepulchre of Jerusalem, 1986. Mem. ABA, Ind. Bar Assn., Ind. Mfrs. Assn. (chmn. 1978-80, bd. dirs. 1978—), Forging Industry Assn. (pres. 1976-77), Alliance of Metalworking Industries (chmn. 1978-80), U.S. C. of C. (chmn. numerous coms., active panels and councils 1977—), Ind. State C. of C. (exec. com. 1982—), Rotary (past pres.), Meridian Hills Country Club, Theta Chi (pres. Iota chpt. 1950), Delta Theta Phi, Beta Gamma Sigma (hon.), Delta Sigma Pi (hon.). Clubs: Columbia, Skyline (Indpls.); Ind. Soc. of Chgo. Lodges: Rotary (local past pres.), Elks, KC. Home: 805 N Briar Rd Muncie IN 47304-5101 Office: 123 E Adams St Muncie IN 47305-2402

SMITH, VERNON G., education educator, state representative; b. Gary, Ind.. BS, Ind. U., 1966, MS, 1969, EdD, 1978; postgrad., Ind.U.-Purdue U., 1986-90. Tchr. Gary Pub. Schs. Systems, 1966-71, resource tchr., 1971-72; asst. prin. Ivanhoe Sch., Gary, 1972-78; prin. Nobel Sch., Gary, 1978-85, Williams Sch., Gary, 1985-92; part-time counselor edn. div. Ind. U. N.W., Gary, 1967-69, adj. lectr., 1987-92, asst. prof., 1992—; mem. Ind. Ho. of Reps., Indpls., 1990—; columnist Gary Crusader, 1969-71; speaker Devel. Tng. Inst., 1986—. Author: (with D. McClam) Building Bridges Instead of Walls—History of I.U. Dons, Inc., 1979; also articles. Mem. Gary City Coun., 1972-90; precinct committeeman Gary Dem. Com., 1972-92; founder, chmn. Gary City-wide Festival Com.; bd. dirs. N.W. Ind. Urban League; founder, pres. I.U. Dons, Inc.; past pres. Gary Cmty. Mental Health Bd.; v.p. Gary Common Coun., 1982, 85-87, pres., 1976, 83-84, 88; past mem. bd. dirs. Little League World series; founder, past sponsor Youth Ensuring Solidarity, Young Citizens' League; chmn. Ind. Commn. on Status of Black Males, 1992—; mem. Gov.'s Commn. for Drug-Free Ind., 1990—. Recipient citation in edn. Gary NAACP, 1970, Good Govt. award Gary Jaycees, 1977, Outstanding Svc. award Gary Young Dems., 1979, Businessman of Yr. award Gary Downtown Mchts., 1979, Bd. Dirs. Svcs. award Gary Cmty. Health Ctr., 1982, G.O.I.C. Dr. Leon H. Sullivan award, 1982, Gary Jaycees Youth award, 1983, Info Newspaper Outstanding Citizen of N.W. Ind. and Info. Newspaper's Outstanding Educator award, 1984, Post Tribune Blaine Marz Tap award, 1984, Gary Cmty. Sch. Corp. Speech Dept. Recognition award, 1984, Gary Cmty. Mental Health Ctr.'s 10th Yr. Svc. award, 1985, Roosevelt H.S. Exemplary Svc. award, 1985, Gary Crusader 25th Anniversary award, 1986, Purdue U. Ednl. Opportunity Programs Black History Svc. award, 1986, Educator Par Excellence awa4rd Williams Sch., 1987, Black Woman Hall of Fame Found. Success award, 1987, Black Women Hall of Fame Bethune-Tubman-Truth award, 1987, Our Lady of Perpetual Help Ch. Hon. Mem. award, 1987, Gary Educator of Christ Adminstr. Leadership award, 1988, NBC-LEO Appreciation award, 1988, Omega Psi Phi Citizen of Yr., 1989, Omicron Rho chpt. Appreciation award, 1991, Gary Cmty. Schs. Presenters award, 1991, Mr. G.'s Svc. award, 1991, Appreciation award Ind. Assn. Chiefs Police, 1992, Meth. Hosp., 1992, Bros. Keeper, 1992, Svc. award Ind. Assn. Elem. and Mid. Sch. Prins., 1992, I.U. N.W. Alumni Assn. Divsn. of Edn. Disting. Educator award, 1992, N.W. Ind. Black Expo's Sen. Carolyn Mosby Above and Beyond award, 1995. Mem. NAACP (life), Ind. Assn. Sch. Prins., No. Ind. Assn. Black School Educators (founder), Ind. U. N.W. Alumni Assn. (life, Disting. Educator award 1992), Phi Delta Kappa, Omega Psi Phi (life, Omega Man of Yr. award 1974, Citizen of Yr. award 10th dist. 1989, appreciation award Omicrono Rho chpt. 1991). Baptist. Home: PO Box M622 Gary IN 46401-0622 Office: Ind U NW 3400 Broadway Hawthorn #339 Gary IN 46408

SMITH, VERNON LOMAX, economist, researcher; b. Wichita, Kans., Jan. 1, 1927; s. Vernon Chessman and Lula Belle (Lomax) S.; m. Joyce Harkleroad, June 6, 1950 (div. Aug. 1975); m. Carol Breckner, Jan. 1, 1980. BSEE, Calif. Inst. Tech., 1949; MA in Econs., U. Kans., 1952; PhD in Econs., Harvard U., 1955; D of Mgmt. (hon.), Purdue U., 1990. Asst. prof. econs. Purdue U., West Lafayette, Ind., 1955-58, assoc. prof., 1958-61, prof., 1961-65, Krannert prof., 1965-67; prof. Brown U., Providence, 1967-68, U. Mass., Amherst, 1968-75; prof. U. Ariz., Tucson, 1975—, Regents' prof.; Contbr. articles to profl. jours. Fellow Ctr. for Advanced Study in Behavioral Scis., Stanford, Calif., 1972-73; Sherman Fairchild Disting. Scholar Calif. Inst. Tech., Pasadena, 1973-74; adj. scholar CATO Inst., Washington, 1983—. Fellow AAAS, Am. Acad. Arts and Scis., Econometric Soc., Am. Econ. Assn. (Disting. fellow); me. Pvt. Enterprise Edn. Assn. (Adam Smith award), Nat. Acad. Sci. Home: 6020 N Pontatoc Rd Tucson AZ 85719 Office: U Ariz Eion Sci Lab Tucson AZ 85718

SMITH, VERONICA LATTA, real estate corporation officer; b. Wyandotte, Mich., Jan. 13, 1925; d. Jan August and Helena (Hulak) Latta; m. Stewart Gene Smith, Apr. 12, 1952; children: Stewart Gregory, Patrick Allen, Paul Donald, Alison Veronica, Alisa Margaret Lyons, Glenn Laurence. BA in Sociology, U. Mich., 1948, postgrad., 1948. Tchr. Coral Gables (Fla.) Pub. Sch. System, 1949-50; COO Latta Ins. Agy, Wyandotte, 1950-62; treas. L & S Devel. Co., Grosse Ile, Mich., 1963-84; v.p. Regency Devel., Riverview, Mich., 1984—. Active U. Mich. Bd. Regents, 1985-92, regent emeritus, 1993—; mem., pres. Martha Cook Bd. Govs., U. Mich., 1972-78, 76-78; del. Rep. County Conv., Wayne County, Mich., 1988—, Rep. State Conv., Grand Rapids, Mich., 1985, 87, 89, 91, 92, 94, Detroit, 1986, 88, 90, 92; mem. pres. adv. com. Campaign for Mich., 1992—, mem. campaign steering com., 1992—. Mem. Mich. Lawyers Aux. (treas. 1975, chmn. 1976, 77, 78, 79), Nat. Assn. Ins. Women (cert.), Faculty Women's Club U. Mich. (hon.), Radrick Farms Golf Club (Ann Arbor), Pres.'s Club U. Mich., Investment Club (pres. 1976, sec. 1974-75, treas. 1975-76), Alpha Kappa Delta. Home: 22225 Balmoral Dr Grosse Ile MI 48138-1403

SMITH, VINCENT DACOSTA, artist; b. Bklyn., Dec. 12, 1929; s. Beresford Leopold and Louise S.; m. Cynthia I. Linton, July 15, 1972. Student, Art Students League, N.Y.C., 1953, Bklyn. Mus. Sch., 1955-56; B. Profl. Services, Empire State Coll., 1980. Instr. painting and graphics Whitney Mus. Art, N.Y.C., 1967-76; instr. painting Ceda Project, 1978-80; artist in residence Smithsonian Conf. Center, Elkridge, Md., 1967, Cite des Arts Internat., Paris, 1978; participant 2d World Black and African Festival Arts and Culture, Lagos, Nigeria, 1977; commns. include Impressions: Our World Portfolio of Prints, 1974, mural at Boys and Girls High Sch., Bklyn., 1976, mural for Tremont/Crotona Social Svc. Ctr. Human Resources Adminstrn. and CETA Project, N.Y.C., 1980, mural for Oberia D. Dempsey Multi-Svc. Ctr. for Cen. Harlem, Dept. Cultural Affairs, N.Y.C., 1988, 2 murals for 116 St. Sta., N.Y.C. Met. Transit Authority; film tapes and videos include Bernie Casey: Black Dimensions in Contemporary Am. Art, Carnation Co., Los Angeles, 1971, Tee Collins, Barbara Cobb: The First Water, Theatre Eleven, 1977, Robert Fassbinder: The Creative Pulse of Afro-Am. Culture, WTVG, N.J., 1978, Bearden Plays Bearden, Third World Cinema, 1980, Works on Paper, Storefront Mus./Paul Robeson Theatre, Jamaica, N.Y., 1981; host bi-weekly program, discussions with 45 activists WBAI-FM Radio. Illustrator: Folklore Stories from Africa, 1974; exhbns. include Hall of Springs Mus., Saratoga, N.Y., 1970, Contemporary Black Am. Artists, Whitney Mus. Am. Art, N.Y.C., 1971, Two Generations, Newark Mus., 1971, Mus. of Sci. and Industry, Chgo., 1975, Bronx Mus. Art, 1977, Bklyn. Mus., 1979; one-man exhbns. include Lacarda Gallery, N.Y.C., 1967, 68, 70, 73, 75, 77, Paa Ya Paa Gallery, Nairobi, Kenya, 1973, Chemchemi Creative Arts Center, Arusha, Tanzania, 1973, Kibo Art Gallery, Mt. Kilimanjaro, Tanzania, 1973, Portland (Maine) Art Mus., 1974, Reading (Pa.) Public Mus., 1974, Erie (Pa.) Art Center, 1977, Gallery 7, Detroit, 1977; represented in permanent collections, Mus. Modern Art, N.Y.C., Newark Mus., Bklyn. Mus., U. Va. Art Mus.; also subject of TV film; host Vincent Smith Dialogues with Contemporary Artists, Radio Sta. WPAI-FM, 1986-88. Served with U.S. Army, 1948-49. Recipient Thomas B. Clark prize N.A.D., 1974; Winslow and Newton prize Nat. Soc. Painters in Casein and Acrylic, 1978; John Hay Whitney fellow, 1959; Nat. Endowment Arts grantee, 1973; Nat. Inst. Arts and Letters grantee, 1968; Cultural Council Found. grantee, 1971. Mem. Nat. Conf. Artists. Home: 264 E Broadway New York NY 10002-5670 *I have tried to develop three things which I feel are necessary to achieving some success in one's chosen field: a philosophy in which one keeps physically fit, mentally aware and consistent in one's work. Through a belief in the importance of the work one can constantly strive to grow and reach new heights.*

SMITH, VINCENT MILTON, lawyer, designer, consultant; b. Barbourville, Ky., Nov. 21, 1940; s. Virgil Milton and Louis (McGalliard) S.; 1 child, Jessica Todd. BA, Harvard U., 1962; LLB, Yale U., 1965. Bar: N.Y. 1966. Assoc. Breed, Abbott & Morgan, N.Y.C., 1965-70; assoc. Debevoise & Plimpton, N.Y.C., 1970-75, ptnr., 1975-95; CEO Lanf, Winslow & Smith Co., Chatham, N.J., 1995—; mem. adv. bd. Chgo. Title Ins. Co., N.Y.C., 1979—. Trustee Chatham Players, N.J., 1967-77, 87-91, Summit Friends Meeting, Chatham, 1973—, N.J. Shakespeare Festival, Madison, 1975-80, Playwrights Theatre N.J., 1989-91. Mem. ABA, N.Y. State Bar Assn., Assn. of Bar of City of N.Y., Am. Land Title Assn., Urban Land Inst. Mem. Soc. of Friends. Clubs: Harvard, N.Y. Athletic. Office: Debevoise & Plimpton 875 3rd Ave New York NY 10022-6225

SMITH, VIRGIL CLARK, state legislator; b. Detroit, July 4, 1947; s. Virgil Columbus and Eliza (Boyer) S.; m. Evelyn Owens (div.); children: Virgil Kai, Adam Smith; m. Elizabeth Ann Little. BA in polit. sci., Mich. State U., 1969; JD, Wayne State U., 1972. Legal advisor various community groups, Detroit, 1972-73; supervising atty. Wayne County Legal Svcs., Detroit, 1973-74; sr. asst.corp. counsel law dept. City of Detroit, 1974-75; mem. Mich. State Ho. Reps., 1976-88, Mich. State Senate, 1988—; mem. Appropriations Comm. Mem. Nat. Caucus Black State Legislators, Nat. Caucus of State Legistlators, Mich. Legis. Black Caucus (2d chair 1991-92). Democrat. Avocations: golf, swimming, bowling, skiing. Office: State Senate PO Box 30036 Lansing MI 48909-7536 Address: 19316 Norwood St Detroit MI 48234-1820

SMITH, VIRGINIA A., media consultant; b. Washington, Oct. 23, 1962; d. Kenneth Ross and Patricia Marcella (Maher) S. BBA, Va. Commonwealth U., 1986; postgrad., George Washington U., 1994—. Pub. rels. coord. Richmond Comedy Club, Va., 1987-90; media coord. Medalist Sports, Richmond, Va., 1991; event coord. ProServ, Washington, 1992; paralegal Law Resources, Washington, 1993-94; cons. MCI, McLean, Va., 1994—; cons., media rels. Va. Internat. Gold Cup, Middleburg, Va., 1993-94, Project Life Animal Rescue, Washington, 1994, The President's Golf Cup, Washington, 1994. Editor: Tour DuPont Mag., 1991. Vol. Octagon Club, Winchester, Va., 1980-81, Senatorial Campaigns, Richmond, 1988, Washington, 1994. Mem. Smithsonian, Nat. Assn. Female Execs. Republican. Roman Catholic. Avocations: writing, golfing, reading. Home: 116 Stonewall Dr Winchester VA 22602

SMITH, VIRGINIA DODD (MRS. HAVEN SMITH), congresswoman; b. Randolph, Iowa, June 30, 1911; d. Clifton Clark and Erville (Reeves) Dodd; m. Haven N. Smith, Aug. 27, 1931. A.B., U. Nebr., 1936; hon. degree, Nebr. U., 1987, Chadron State Coll., 1988. Nat. pres. Am. Country Life Assn., 1951-54; nat. chmn. Am. Farm Bur. Women, 1954-74; dir. Am. Farm Bur. Fedn., 1954-74, Country Women's Council; world dep. pres. Asso. Country Women of World, 1962-68; mem. Dept. Agr. Nat. Home Econs. Research Adv. Com., 1960-65; bd. dirs. Norwest Bank Cmty. Bd., Property Owners and Residents Bd., Sun Health Corp. Bd., Recreation Ctrs. Sun City West, sec., mem. gov. bd.; bd. dirs. Del Webb Hosp. Mem. Crusade for Freedom European inspection tour, 1958; del. Republican Nat. Conv., 1956, 72; bd. govs. Agrl. Hall of Fame, 1959—; mem. Nat. Livestock and Meat Bd., 1955-58, Nat. Commn. Community Health Services, 1963-66; adv. mem. Nebr. Sch. Bds. Assns., 1949; mem. Nebr. Territorial Centennial Commn., 1953, Gov.'s Commn. Status of Women, 1964-66; chmn. Presdl. Task Force on Rural Devel., 1969-70; mem. appropriations com., ranking minority mem. agrl. appropriations subcom., appropriations subcom. on energy and water devel. 94th-101st Congresses from 3d dist. Nebr.; v.p. Farm Film Found., 1964-74, Good Will ambassador to Switzerland, 1950. Apptd. adm. Nebr. Navy; bd. dirs. Shepherd of the Hills Meth. Ch. Recipient award of Merit, DAR, 1956; Disting. Service award U. Nebr., 1956, 60; award for best pub. address on freedom Freedom Found., 1966; Eyes on Nebr. award Nebr. Optometric Assn., 1970; Internat. Service award Midwest Conf. World Affairs, 1970; Woman of Achievement award Nebr. Bus. and Profl. Women, 1971; selected as 1 of 6 U.S. women Govt. France for 3 week goodwill mission to France, 1969; Outstanding 4H Alumni award Iowa State U., 1973, 74; Watchdog of Treasury award, 1976, 78, 80, 82, 83, 84, 86, 88; Guardian of Small Bus. award, 1976, 78, 80, 82, 84, 86, 88; Nebr. Ak-Sar-Ben award, 1983, Agrl. Achievement, Nebr. U., 1987; named Favorite Community Leader, Sun City West, 1994. Mem. AAUW, Delta Kappa Gamma (state hon. mem.), Beta Sigma Phi (internat. hon. mem.), Chi Omega, PEO (past pres.), Eastern Star. Methodist. Club: Business and Professional Women. Address: 13828 W Terra Vista Dr Sun City West AZ 85375-5432 *As a fifteen-year-old high school valedictorian, I wrote these words in my valedictory message, "There is no excellence without great labor." Almost half a century later, I continue to live by this philosophy.*

SMITH, VIRGINIA WARREN, artist, writer, educator; b. Atlanta, Mar. 7, 1947; d. Ralph Henry and Dorothy Jane (Kubler) S. AB in Philosophy, Ga. State U., 1976, M Visual Art in Art and Photography, 1978. dir. The Upstairs Artspace, Tryon, N.C., 1984-86; mng. editor Art Papers, Atlanta, 1986-88; art critic Atlanta (Ga.) Jour./Constn., Atlanta, 1987-92; adj. faculty Atlanta (Ga.) Coll. Art, 1991—, Ga. State U., Atlanta, 1991—. Author, photographer: Scoring in Heaven: Gravestones and Cemetery Art in the American Sunbelt States, 1991, Alaska: Trail Tails and Eccentric Detours, 1992; exhbns. include High Mus. Art, Atlanta, 1972, 78, 80, 81, 82, 84, 88, 89, Nexus Contemporary Art Ctr., Atlanta, 1986, 87, 91, Sandler Hudson Gallery, Atlanta, 1987, 89, 92, Jackson Fine Art, Atlanta, 1988, 91, 93, Aperture Found., N.Y.C., 1989, MS Found., N.Y.C., 1991, Albany (Ga.) Mus. Art, 1991, Montgomery (Ala.) Mus. Art, 1992, Bernice Steinbaum Gallery, N.Y.C., 1992, Wyndy MoreLead Gallery, New Orleans, 1991, 92, U.S. Info. Agy., Washington, 1994, Chatahouchee Valley Art Mus., Lagrange, Ga., 1994, others; works in permanent collections including Mus. Modern Art, N.Y.C., Mus. Fine Arts, Boston, High Mus. of Art, Atlanta, New Orleans Mus. Art, Harvard U., Rochester Inst. Tech., N.Y., U. N.Mex., Ctr. for Study of So. Culture U. Miss., Oxford, Miss., Columbia (S.C.) Mus. Art and Sci., Ringling Sch. Art, Sarasota, Fla., City of Atlanta, Franklin Furnace, N.Y.C. Bd. mem. Art Papers, Atlanta, 1983-88; adv. bd. memd. Arts Festival Atlanta, Ga., 1990-93. Mem. Coll. Art Assn., Soc. for Photog. Edn., Photography Forum of the High Mus. Art (v.p. 1994-95). Democrat. Avocation: collecting snowdomes. Home and Office: PO Box 1110 Columbus NC 28722

SMITH, VME (VERNA MAE EDOM SMITH), sociology educator, freelance writer, photographer; b. Marshfield, Wis., June 19, 1929; d. Clifton Cedric and Vilia Clarissa (Patefield) Edom; children: Teri Freas, Anthony Thomas. AB in Sociology, U. Mo., 1951; MA in Sociology, George Washington, 1965; PhD in Human Devel., U. Md., 1981. Tchr. Alcohol Safety Action Program Fairfax County, Va., 1973-75; instr. sociology No. Va. C.C., Manassas, 1975-77, asst. prof., 1977-81, assoc. prof., 1981-84, prof., 1984-94, prof. emerita, 1995; coord. coop. edn. No. Va. Community Coll., Manassas, 1983-89; Chancellor's Commonwealth prof. Manassas, 1991-93; freelance writer, editor and photographer, 1965—; co-dir. Clifton C. Edom Truth With a Camera (photography seminars); asst. producer history of photography program Sta. WETA-TV, Washington, 1965; rsch. and prodn. asst., photographer, publs. editor No. Va. Ednl. TV, Sta. WNVT, 1970-7l; cons. migrant div. Md. Dept. Edn., Balt., summer 1977; researcher, photographer Roundabout presch. high sch. series on Am. Values Sta. WNVT, 1970-71. Author, photographer: Middleburg and Nearby, 1986; co-author: Small Town America, 1993; contbr. photography to various works including Visual Impact in Print (Hurley and McDougall), 1971, Looking Forward to a Career in Education (Moses), 1976, Child Growth and Development (Terry, Sorrentino and Flatter), 1979, Photojournalism (Edom), 1976, 80, Migrant Child Welfare, 1977, (Cavenaugh), Caring for Children, 1973 (5 publs. by L.B. Murphy), Dept. Health, Edn. and Welfare, Nat. Geog., 1961, Head Start Newsletter, 1973-74. Mem. ednl. adv. com. Head Start, Warrenton, Va. Recipient Emmy Ohio State Children's Programming award; Fulbright-Hays Rsch. grantee, 1993. Mem. Va. Assn. Coop. Edn. (com. mem.). Democrat.

SMITH, W. STUART, strategic planning director; b. Binghamton, N.Y., May 3, 1943; married. B, Washington & Lee U., 1965; M, Mich. State U., 1967, Va. Commonwealth U., 1974. Adminstrv. resident MUSC Med. Ctr., Charleston, 1973-74, asst. dir., 1974-79, assoc. dir., 1979-83, dir. ops., 1983-87, dir. mktg., 1987-92, exec. dir., 1993-94; dir. strategic planning, 1994—. Mem. S.C. Hosp. Assn. (bd. dirs.). Home: 1304 Horseshoe Bend Mount Pleasant SC 29464 Office: MUSC Med Ctr Med U SC 171 Ashley Ave Charleston SC 29425-0001

SMITH, WALDO GREGORIUS, former government official; b. Bklyn., July 29, 1911; s. John Henry and Margaret (Gregorius) S.; m. Mildred Pearl Prescott, July 30, 1935 (dec. Jan. 1992); 1 dau., Carole Elizabeth Smith Levin. Student CCNY, N.Y., 1928-29; BS in Forestry, Cornell U., 1933. Registered prof. engr., Colo. Forester Forest Svc., U.S. Dept. Agr., Atlanta, 1933-41, Ala. Div. Forestry, Brewton, 1941-42; engr., civil engring. technician Geol. Survey, U.S. Dept. Interior, 1942-71, cartographic technician, 1972-75; chmn. Public Transp. Council, 1975-89; legislator aide to individuals Colo. State Legis. Internship Program, 1987-95. Recipient 40 Yr. Civil Service award pin and scroll; 42 Yr. Govt. Service award plaque. Fellow Am. Congress Surveying and Mapping (life, sec.-treas. Colo. chpt. 1961, program chmn. 1962, reporter 1969, mem. nat. membership devel. com. 1973-74, rep. to Colo. Engring. Council 1976-77); mem. AAAS (emeritus), Denver Fed. Center Profl. Engrs. Group (U.S. Geol. Survey rep. 1973-76, Engr. of Yr. award 1975), Nat. Soc. Profl. Engrs. (pre-coll. guidance com. 1986-91, life 92—), Profl. Engrs. Colo. (chpt. scholarship chmn. 1979—, advt. corr., service award 1983), Cornell U. Alumni Assn. (alumni secondary schs. com. Quadrangle Club), Common Cause, Colo. Engring. Council (chmn. library com. 1970—, spl. rep. Regional Transp. Dist., 1974-75; mem. sci. fair com. 1970-71; rep. ex officio Denver Pub. Library Found. Bd. Trustees 1975-80, mem. historic agreement with Denver Pub. Libr. 1993, Pres.'s Outstanding Service award 1987), Environ. Concerns (chmn. com. 1988—, treas. 1989-91, mem. site specific adv. bd., restoration adv. bd. Rocky Mountain arsenal cleanup 1994—), Fedn. Am. Scientists, Am. Soc. Engring. Edn., People for Am. Way. Contbr. articles to profl. jours. Home: 3821 W 25th Ave Denver CO 80211-4417 *Personal philosophy: A new acronym: T'n'T=Truth and Trust; give posterity a decent break.*

SMITH, WALTER DOUGLAS, retired college president; b. Harriman, Tenn., Nov. 17, 1918; s. Walter Blaine and Jeanetta Mae (Scarborough) S.; m. Rhondda Verle Miller, Apr. 5, 1947; children: Ian Douglas Miller, Walter Henry. B.A., Lincoln Meml. U., Harrogate, Tenn., 1943; M.A., U. Mich., 1947, Ph.D., 1950. Faculty psychology Fla. State U., 1950-59; dean coll., prof. psychology Winthrop Coll., Rock Hill, S.C., 1959-66; v.p. acad. affairs, dean of faculty Winthrop Coll., 1966-68; pres. Salisbury (Md.) State Coll., 1968-70, Francis Marion Coll., Florence, S.C., 1970-83. Served with USNR, 1943-46. Mem. Am. Psychol. Assn. Presbyterian. Home: 609 S Graham St Florence SC 29501-5142

SMITH, WALTER JOSEPH, JR., lawyer, educator; b. N.Y.C., Feb. 23, 1936; s. Walter J. and Florence W. (Watson) S.; m. Felicitas U. Von Zeschau, Oct. 5, 1968; children—Caroline, Alexandria, Christopher. A.B., Hamilton Coll., 1958; LL.B., Columbia U., 1961. Bar: U.S. Ct. Mil. Appeals 1967, U.S. Dist. Ct. (D.C. dist.) 1967, U.S. Ct. Appeals (D.C. cir.) 1967, U.S. Supreme Ct. 1974, U.S. Ct. Claims 1975. Mem. Judge Advocate Gen.'s Office, U.S. Navy, Washington, 1966-68; trial atty., Washington, 1968-75; ptnr. Wilson, Elser, Moskowitz, Edelman & Dicker, Washington, 1975—; mng. ptnr., 1979—; adj. prof. law Antioch Sch. Law, 1981—. Pres. Dogwood Assn., 1982-83. Served to lt. USN, 1962-67. Recipient Pres.'s award Am. Soc. Pharmacy Law, 1984. Mem. ABA, Def. Research Inst., Counsellors, D.C. Bar Assn. Democrat. Roman Catholic. Clubs: Tuckahoe. Author: Insurance Protection in Product Liability. Office: Wilson Elser Moskowitz Edelman & Dicker 5th Fl The Colorado Bldg 1341 G St NW Washington DC 20005-3105

SMITH, WALTER S., JR., federal judge; b. Marlin, Tex., Oct. 26, 1940; s. Walter S. and Mary Elizabeth Smith; children—Debra Elizabeth, Susan Kay. BA, Baylor U., 1964, JD, 1966. Bar: Tex. Assoc. Dunnam & Dunnam, Waco, Tex., 1966-69; ptnr. Wallace & Smith, Waco, 1969-78, Haley & Fulbright, Waco, 1978-80; judge Tex. Dist. Ct., 1980-83; U.S. magistrate U.S. Dist. Ct. (we. dist.) Tex., 1983-84; judge U.S. Dist. Ct. (we. dist.) Tex., Waco, 1984—. Named Outstanding Young Lawyer of Yr., Waco-McLennan County Bar Assn., 1976. Office: US Dist Ct PO Box 1908 Waco TX 76703-1908*

SMITH, WALTER SAGE, environmental engineer, consultant; b. Hammond, Ind., Nov. 12, 1938; s. Reading Barlow and Lois Cora (Riddle) S.; m. Doris Jean Bryson, Oct. 23, 1961 (div. Sept. 1976); children: Cami Stryker Davis, Adam Smith, Kelly A. Stryker, Alex Smith; m. Jacqueline P. Stryker, June 4, 1977. BSChemE, Bucknell U., 1961. Registered profl. engr., N.C., N.J. Engr. Pub. Health Svc. Commn. Corp., Cin., 1961-72; co-owner, pres. Entropy Environmentalists, Inc., Research Triangle Park, N.C., 1972-92, pres., cons., 1974-76; owner, pres. Walter Smith & Assocs., Inc., Cary, N.C., 1993—; v.p. Nutech Corp., Raleigh, N.C., 1974-76, Housing Corp. of the South, Raleigh, 1977-78, Umstead Devel. Corp., Raleigh, 1977-80. Editor (newsletter) Stack Sampling News, Entropy Quarterly. Vice pres. Black Horse Run Homeowners Assn., Raleigh, 1984. Fellow Air and Waste Mgmt. Assn.; mem. Am. Acad. Environ. Engrs. (diplomate 1985), Carolinas Air Pollution Control Assn., Source Evaluation Soc. (founder 1984). Episcopalian. Avocations: swimming, sailing, reading. Home: 6225 Splitrock Trl Apex NC 27502-9778 Office: Walter Smith & Assocs Inc P O Box 117 Cary NC 27511-0117

SMITH, WALTON NAPIER, lawyer; b. Macon, Ga., Feb. 26, 1942; s. Robert Monroe and Marion Rose (Napier) S.; m. Susan Rush Baum, Oct. 10, 1970; children—Rush Hendley, Berkeley Bosman. A.B. cum laude, Dartmouth Coll., 1964; J.D., Harvard U., 1967. Bar: Ga. 1966, D.C. 1972, Ill. 1978, U.S. Supreme Ct. 1971. Counsel, Nat. R.R. Passenger Corp., Washington, 1971-75; assoc. Lord, Bissell & Brook, Washington and Chgo., 1975-79, ptnr., Chgo. and Atlanta, 1980—. Served to capt. JAGC, U.S. Army, 1964-71. Decorated Bronze Star, Army Commendation medal. Mem. ABA, Ill. Bar Assn., State Bar Ga., Nat. Assn. R.R. Trial Counsel. Democrat. Episcopalian. Clubs: Union League (Chgo.); Commerce Club. Office: Lord Bissell & Brook 1201 W Peachtree St NW Atlanta GA 30309-3400

SMITH, WARREN ALLEN, editor, writer; b. Minburn, Iowa, Oct. 27, 1921; s. Harry Clark and Ruth Marion (Miles) S.; BA, U. No. Iowa, 1948; MA, Columbia U., 1949. Chmn. dept. Eng., Bentley Sch., N.Y.C., 1949-54, New Canaan (Conn.) High Sch., 1954-86; founder, pres., chmn. bd. Variety Sound Corp., N.Y.C., 1961-90; pres. Afro-Carib Records, 1971-90, Talent Mgmt., 1982-90, pres. AAA Rec. Studio, 1985-90; founder, pres. Variety Rec. Studio, 1961-95; instr. Columbia U., 1961-62. Pres., Taursa Fund, 1971-73; bd. dirs. 31 Jane Street Corp. Author: Humanists on Humanism: A Directory of Non-Believers or, Who's Who in Hell; book rev. editor The Humanist, 1953-58; editor (jour.) Taking Stock, 1967-93, Pique, 1990-93, Van Rijn's Pad, 1991; contbr. book revs. Libr. Jour.; editl. assoc. Free Inquiry, 1992—; syndicated columnist Manhattan Scene in W.I. newspapers. Treas. Secular Humanist Soc. N.Y., 1988-93; sec. Jane St. Corp., 1995—. With AUS, 1942-46. Recipient Leavey award Freedoms Found. at Valley Forge, 1985. Mem. ASCAP, Coun. Secular Humanism, Mensa, N.Y. Skeptics Soc. (bd. dirs. 1990-94), Internat. Press Inst., Am. Unitarian Assn., Rationalist Press Assn., Conn. Edn. Assn., Asociación Iberoamericana Ético Humanista (hon.), Brit. Humanist Assn., Humanist Book Club (pres. 1957-62), Bertrand Russell Soc. (v.p. 1977-80, bd. dirs. 1973—), Mensa Investment Club (chmn. 1967, 73—). Signer Humanist Manifesto II, 1973. Avocation: teratology. Home and Office: 31 Jane St Apt 10D New York NY 10014-1980

SMITH, WARREN JAMES, optical scientist, consultant, lecturer; b. Rochester, N.Y., Aug. 17, 1922; s. Warren Abrams and Jessica Madelyn (Forshay) S.; m. Mary Helen Geddes, May 18, 1944; children: David Whitney, Barbara Jamie. BS, U. Rochester, 1944; postgrad., U. Calif., Santa Barbara, 1960. Physicist Clinton Engr. Works, Tenn. Eastman Co., Oak Ridge, 1944-46; chief optical engr. Simpson Optical Mfg. Co., Chgo., 1946-59; mgr. optical sect. Raytheon Corp., Santa Barbara, 1959-62; v.p. R & D, Infrared Industries, Santa Barbara, 1962-87; chief scientist Kaiser Electro-Optics, Inc., Carlsbad, Calif., 1987—; lectr. U. Wis., Madison, 1972—, U. Rochester, 1988—, Genesee Computer Ctr., Rochester, 1982-93, Sinclair Optics, 1994—; cons. in field; expert witness. Author: Modern Optical Engineering, 1966, 2d edit., 1990, Modern Lens Design, 1992; editor McGraw-Hill series Optical and Electro-Optical Engineering; also articles. Fellow Optical Soc. Am. (pres. 1980, organizer, chmn. tech. confs.), Soc. Photo-Optical Instrumentation Engrs. (life), Internat. Soc. Optical Engring. (pres. 1983, organizer, chmn. tech. confs., Gold medal 1985, Dirs. award 1992), Sigma Chi. Avocations: tennis, sailing. Home: 1165 Countrywood Ln Vista CA 92083-5334 Office: Kaiser Electro-Optics Inc 2752 Loker Ave W Carlsbad CA 92008-6603

SMITH, WAYMAN FLYNN, III, brewery executive, lawyer; b. St. Louis, June 18, 1940; s. Wayman Flynn and Edythe (Meaux) S.; 1 child, Kymberly Ann. Student, Washington U., St. Louis, 1957-59; B.S., Monmouth Coll., West Long Branch, N.J., 1962; J.D., Howard U., 1965. Bar: Mo. 1966, U.S Dist. Ct. (ea. dist.) Mo. 1966. Dir. conciliation Mo. Commn. on Human Rights, Jefferson City, 1966-69; judge City of St. Louis, 1971-75; mem. Wilson, Smith, McCullin, St. Louis, 1969-80; v.p. corp. affairs Anheuser-Busch Cos., St. Louis, 1980—; dir. Anheuser-Busch, Inc., St. Louis. Mem. bd. alderman City of St. Louis, 1975-87. Named Disting. Alumni, Howard U., 1983, Monmouth Coll., 1983. Mem. ABA, Nat. Bar Assn., Mound City Bar Assn., Bar Assn. Met. St. Louis. Democrat. Episcopalian. Office: Anheuser-Busch Cos 1 Busch Pl Saint Louis MO 63118-1849*

SMITH, WAYNE CALVIN, chemical engineer; b. Beaver, Okla., Mar. 19, 1935; s. Dean C. and Loraine S.; m. Suellyn Joyce Canon, Aug. 18, 1984. BS, Okla. U., 1958, MSChemE, 1964; PhDChemE, Colo. U., 1974. Registered profl. engr., Tex., Okla., Colo.; cert. emergency response specialist. Process engr. Shell Oil Co., Deer Park, Tex., 1958-59; sr. devel. engr. Monsanto, Pensacola, Fla., 1965-66; project leader Phillips Petroleum Co., Bartlesville, Okla., 1967-69; acting chief process control EPA Nat. Enforcement Investigations Ctr., Denver, 1971-78; firm wide mgr. pollution control Dames & Moore, Golden, Colo., 1978-81; regional mgr. Hittman Assocs., Englewood, Colo., 1981-82; pres. Encon Environs Control Svcs., Golden, Colo., 1982-83; chief hazardous waste mgmt. Woodword-Clyde Cons., Englewood, 1983-84; exec. cons. Kellogg Corp., Littleton, Colo., 1984-86; program mgr. Radian Corp., Austin, Tex., 1986-93; prin. engr., office mgr. Tetra Tech, Inc., Oklahoma City, 1993—. Contbr. over 30 articles to profl. jours. Capt. USMC, 1959-62. Scholar Magnolia Petroleum Co., 1956-58; fellow Phillips Petroleum Co., 1962-64, Marathon Oil Co., 1966-67, Gulf Oil Co., 1969-71. Mem. AICE, Am. Arbitration Assn., Water Pollution Control Fedn., Soc. Plastics Engrs., The Greens Country Club, Sigma Xi. Baptist. Avocations: golf, woodworking. Office: Tetra Tech Inc 806 W Curtis Dr Ste I Midwest City OK 73110-3041

SMITH, WAYNE RICHARD, lawyer; b. Petoskey, Mich., Apr. 30, 1934; s. Wayne Anson and Frances Lynetta (Cooper) S.; m. Carrie J. Swanson, June 18, 1959; children: Stephen, Douglas (dec.), Rebecca. AB, U. Mich., 1956, JD, 1959. Bar: Mich. 1959. Asst. atty. gen. State of Mich., 1960-62; pros. atty. Emmet County (Mich.), 1963-68; dist. judge 90th Jud. Dist. Mich., 1969-72; sr. ptnr. Smith & Powers, Petoskey; city atty. City of Petoskey, 1976—; lectr. real estate law U. Mich. Trustee North Central Mich. Coll., 1981—, chmn., 1992—; mem. No. Mich. Cmty. Mental Health Bd., 1972-92, chmn. 1979-81. Mem. ABA, Am. Judicature Soc., Emmet-Charlevoix Bar Assn. (pres. 1967). Presbyterian. Home: 201 Sunset Petoskey MI 49770-0111 Address: PO Box 636 2 Pennsylvania Plz Petoskey MI 49770-0636

SMITH, WENDELL MURRAY, graphic arts control and equipment manufacturing executive; b. Bklyn., May 15, 1935; s. J. Henry and Roberta (Foard) S.; m. Margaret McGregor, Aug. 24, 1957; children: Karen, Wendy, Kimberley, Kathryn, Jennifer. AB, Dartmouth Coll., 1957, MS in Engring., 1958. Devel. engr. Sikorsky Aircraft Co., Stratford, Conn., 1958-60; sales engr., mgr. Barnes Engring. Corp., Stamford, Conn., 1960-65; v.p. mktg. Baldwin-Gegenheimer Corp., Stamford, 1966-70, pres., chief exec. officer, 1971-79; pres. Polestar Corp., Stamford, 1980—; pres., chmn. bd., chief exec. officer Baldwin Tech. Co., Inc., Rowayton, Conn., 1984-95; chmn. Baldwin Tech. Co., Inc., Norwalk, Conn., 1995—; bd. dirs. Globe Ticket and Label Co., Bowne & Co.; trustee Bermuda Biol. Sta. for Rsch. Recipient John L. Kronenberg Industry Leadership award, 1991. Mem. Rsch. and Engring. Coun. (pres.), Graphic Comms. Assn. (bd. dirs., vice chmn.), Soderstrom Soc. of Nat. Assn. Printers and Lithographers, Stamford Ctr. for the Arts (bd. dirs.), Stamford Yacht Club, N.Y. Yacht Club, Royal Bermuda Yacht Club, Mid-Ocean Club. Republican. Methodist. Home: 10 Manor House, Smith's FL07 Bermuda Office: Baldwin Tech Co Inc 65 Rowayton Ave Norwalk CT 06853-1600

SMITH, WENDY L., foundation executive; b. Chgo., Sept. 12, 1950; d. John Arthur and Dolores Mae (Webb) Rothenberger; m. Alan Richard Smith; children: Angela Fuhs, Erica Smith. Ed., Oakton C.C., Des Plaines, Ill., 1986, Mundelein Coll., 1990. Purchasing clk. AIT Industries, Skokie, Ill., 1975-76; purchasing agt. MCC Powers, Skokie, 1976-78; office mgr. Spartan Engring., Skokie, 1978-80, Brunswick Corp., Skokie, 1980—; successively sr. sec., coord. indsl. rels., dir. Brunswick Found., Lake Forest, Ill., 1982-89; pres. Brunswick Found., Lake Forest, 1989—; asst. sec. Brunswick Pub. Charitable Found., Lake Forest, 1989—; mem. adv. com. Found. for Ind. Higher Edn., Stamford, Conn., 1989—, Coun. Better Bus. Burs., Arlington, Va., 1988-90; bd. dirs. Associated Colls. of Ill., 1991—; bd. dirs., mem. trustees com., mem. compensation and benefits com. Donors Forum of Chgo., 1988-93. Bd. dirs. INROADS/Chgo., Inc., 1994—; mem. steering com. Dist. 57 Edn. Found., Mt. Prospect, Ill., 1996—. Recipient Pvt. Sector Initiative Commendation, U.S. Pres., 1987-89. Mem. Donors Forum Chgo. (treas. 1988-91, bd. dirs., mem. exec. com., chairperson audit and fin. com., mem. trustees com. 1992—), Coun. on Founds., Ind. Sector Suburban Contbns. Network (chairperson 1987-89), Women in Philanthropy Corp. Founds. (mem. cmty. rels. com. 1985-87), Chgo. Women in Philanthropy. Avocations: antique restoration, pleasure reading, bowling, golf. Office: Brunswick Found 1 N Field Ct Lake Forest IL 60045-4810

SMITH, WHITNEY BOUSMAN, music and drama critic; b. Cin., May 31, 1956; s. Lawrence Spencer and Ruby Virginia (Bousman) S. BA in Journalism, Ind. U., 1978. Reporter South Bend (Ind.) Tribune, 1977, The Repository, Canton, Ohio, 1978-82; reporter Comml. Appeal, Memphis, 1982—, on spl. assignment in Italy, 1992. Compiler guide to papers of early 20th century Memphis drama critic Hugh Higbee Huhn, 1988. Trombonist Germantown (Tenn.) Symphony Orch., 1987-88. Recipient Community Svc. award League Women Voters, 1980. Office: Comml Appeal 495 Union Ave Memphis TN 38103-3242

SMITH, WILBUR LAZEAR, radiologist, educator; b. Warwick, N.Y., Oct. 11, 1943; s. Wilbur and Betty (Norris) S.; m. Rebecca Rowlands, June 19, 1965; children: Jason, Daniel, Joanna, Noah, Ethan, Jacob. BA, SUNY-Buffalo, 1965, MD, 1969. Diplomate Am. Bd. Radiology, Am. Bd. Pediatrics. Intern, then resident Buffalo Children's Hosp., 1969-71; resident in pediatric radiology Cin. Gen. and Children Hosp., 1971-74; asst. prof. pediatrics and radiology Ind. U., Indpls., 1975-78, assoc. prof., 1978-80, acting dir. pediatric radiology, 1979-80; assoc. prof. U. Iowa, Iowa City, 1980-82, prof., 1982—, dir. med. edn. radiology, 1980-86, vice chmn. dept. radiology, 1986-94, interim head, 1994-96, dir. pediatric radiology, 1980-92. Contbr. articles to profl. jours. Served with USAR, 1969-77. Assoc. editor Gastrointestinal Imaging in Pediatrics, Acad. Radiology, 1992—. Soccer coach Iowa City Kickers, 1980—; mem. equity adv. com. Iowa City Sch. Bd., 1983-87. Recipient Merke Prize Medicine award SUNY, 1968, Wurlitzer Prize Medicine SUNY, 1968. Fellow Am. Acad. Pediatrics, Am. Coll. Radiology; mem. AMA, Iowa Radiol. Soc. (pres. 1987-88), Assn. Univ. Radiologists (pres. 1995-96), Soc. Pediat. Radiology (treas. 1995—). Mem. Soc. Friends. Avocation: photography. Home: 2271 Cae Dr Iowa City IA 52246-4515 Office: U Iowa Dept Radiology Iowa City IA 52242

SMITH, WILBURN JACKSON, JR., retired bank executive; b. Charlotte, N.C., June 13, 1921; s. Wilburn Jackson and Banna (Oswalt) S.; B.S. in Acctg., U. N.C., 1943; postgrad. in comml. banking Rutgers U. Sch. Banking, 1953, postgrad. in investment banking, 1956; m. Terry Mosteller, Jan. 4, 1944; children: Kenneth M., M. Scott (dec.), Wilburn Jackson III, Curtis Todd. With First Union Nat. Bank, Charlotte, 1946-74, exec. v.p., 1960-67, 1st exec. v.p., 1967-74; pres., mng. trustee Cameron-Brown Investment Group, Raleigh, N.C., 1974-78; chmn. loan policy com. N.C. Nat. Bank, Charlotte, 1979-88; bd. dirs. Charter Bancshares, Inc., Houston, Burroughs & Chapin Co. Inc., Myrtle Beach, S.C.; cons. in field. Served with USN, 1943-46. Recipient Citizenship award Charlotte Civitan, 1972. Mem. Robert Morris Assocs. Baptist. Club: Myers Park Country (Charlotte).

SMITH, WILFRED IRVIN, former Canadian government official; b. Port La Tour, Can., May 20, 1919; s. Claude Albert and Deborah (Inglis) S.; m. Joan Eileen Capstick, Nov. 27, 1946; children: Gordon, Heather, Gail. B.A., Acadia U., Wolfville, N.S., Can., 1943, M.A., 1946, D.C.L., 1975; Ph.D., U. Minn., 1968. Lectr. U. Minn., 1948, U. Sask., 1948-50, Carleton U., 1955-60; mem. staff Pub. Archives Can., 1950-84, dir. hist. br., 1964-65, asst., then acting dominion archivist, 1965-70, dominion archivist, 1970-84; mem. Canadian Nat. Library Adv. Bd., Canadian Permanent Com. Geog. Names, Historic Sites and Monuments Bd. Can, Indian Hist. Manuscripts Commn.; former mem. internat. adv. com. documentation, libraries and archives UNESCO. Author: Code Word Canloan, 1992; contbr. articles to profl. jours. Served to maj. Canadian and Brit. armies, 1943-45. Decorated officer Order Can.; recipient Can. decoration, 1958, Centennial medal, 1967, Jubilee medal, 1978, Royal Soc. Can. medal, 1980, Outstanding Achievement award Can. Govt., 1983. Fellow Soc. Am. Archivists (past pres.); hon. life mem. Internat. Council Archives (sec. gen.), Canadian Hist. Assn. (past editor hist. booklets), Assn. Canadian Archivists, Order St. John; mem. Soc. Archivists, Am. Antiquarian Assn., Canadian Heraldry Soc. (hon. v.p.), United Empire Loyalists Assn. (hon. v.p.), Guards Assn., Friends of Can. War Mus. Home: 201-71 Somerset St W, Ottawa, ON Canada K2P 2G2

SMITH, WILL, actor, rapper; b. Phila.; m. Sheree Smith; 1 child, Willard Smith III. Albums (as The Fresh Prince with DJ Jazzy Jeff): And in this Corner..., 1989, Homebase, 1991, Rock the House, 1991 reissue, He's the DJ, I'm the Rapper, 1988; TV series: The Fresh Prince of Bel-Air, 1990—; Movies: Where the Day Takes You, 1992, Made in America, 1993, Six Degrees of Separation, 1993, Bad Boys, 1995. Office: CAA 9830 Wilshire Blvd Beverly Hills CA 90212*

SMITH, WILLIAM BURTON, chemist, educator; b. Muncie, Ind., Dec. 13, 1927; s. Merrill Mark and Felice Hoy (Richardson) S.; m. Marian Louise Roseborough, Aug. 9, 1954; children: Mark W., Frederick D., Mary F. BA, Kalamazoo Coll., 1949; PhD, Brown U., 1954. Research asso. Fla. State U., 1953-54, U. Chgo., 1954-55; asst. prof., then asso. prof. Ohio U., 1955-61; R.A. Welch vis. prof. chemistry Tex. Christian U., 1960-61, prof. chemistry, chmn. dept., 1961-81; Research participant Oak Ridge Inst. Nuclear Studies, 1956—. Author: A Modern Introduction to Organic Chemistry, 1961, Molecular Orbital Methods in Organic Chemistry, 1974, Introduction to Theoretical Organic Chemistry and Molecular Modelling, 1996; also rsch. articles. Recipient Chancellor's award, 1989. Fellow Royal Soc. of Chemistry; mem. Am. Chem. Soc. (Doherty award 1990), Sigma Xi. Home: 3604 Wedghill Way Fort Worth TX 76133-2156

SMITH, WILLIAM CHARLES, lawyer; b. Batavia, N.Y., June 9, 1930; s. William F. and Verna B. (Busmire) S.; m. Lucia P. Pierce, July 10, 1954; children: William Charles, Leonard P., Victoria J. B.A., U. Buffalo, 1952; LL.B., Harvard U., 1955. Bar: Maine 1955, D.C. 1962, Fla. 1995, U.S. Dist. Ct. Maine, 1956, U.S. Tax Ct. 1960, U.S. Ct. Appeals (1st cir.) 1977, U.S. Ct. Claims 1985, U.S. Supreme Ct. 1960. Assoc. Portland, Maine, 1955-57; ptnr. Hutchinson, Pierce, Atwood & Allen, Portland, 1957-59; counsel Office Tax Legis. Counsel, U.S. Treasury Dept., Washington, 1959-61; ptnr. Pierce, Atwood, Scribner, Allen, Smith and Lancaster, Portland, 1961—; exec. com. Fed. Tax Inst., New Eng. Vice chmn. budget com. United Community Services, 1966-68, chmn., 1968-70, nat. budget and consultation com., 1969-71; bd. dirs. Portland Goodwill, Inc., 1967-69, United Way, Inc., 1968-74, 75-80, Portland Widow's Wood Soc., 1962—; trustee Portland Regional Opportunity Program, 1967-68, Freyburg Acad., 1976—, Found. Blood Research, 1979-85. Mem. ABA, Maine Bar Assn., D.C. Bar, Fla. Bar, Cumberland County Bar Assn., Am. Law Inst., Am. Coll. Trust and Estate Counsel, Am. Coll. Tax Counsel. Republican. Unitarian. Clubs: Portland Country, Mid-Ocean (Bermuda); Naples Country (Maine); Meadows Country (Fla.). Home: 392 Spring St Portland ME 04102-3642 Office: Pierce Atwood Scribner Allen Smith & Lancaster One Monument Sq Portland ME 04101-1110

SMITH, WILLIAM HENRY PRESTON, writer, editor, former corporate executive; b. Pleasanton, Tex., Sept. 8, 1924; s. Sidney Newton and Willie Gertrude (Cloyd) S.; m. Frances Dixon, July 1, 1950; children: Juliet, Dixon, David. B.J., U. Tex., 1949. Reporter Dallas Morning News, 1949-52; advt. asst. Dallas Power & Light Co., 1952-55; dir. pub. relations Greater Boston C. of C., 1955-58; with New Eng. Telephone and Telegraph Co., Boston, 1958-86, asst. v.p., 1966-75, corp. sec., 1975-83, dir. pub. relations, 1983-86; free-lance writer Dover, Mass., 1986—. Editor: Bus. Ethics Resource Newsletter. Bd. dirs., v.p. Mass. Soc. for Prevention Cruelty to Children; bd. dirs. Bus. Ethics Found., Urban Dynamics Adv. Coun.; mem. support policies com. United Way Mass; bd. advisors to pres. Andover Newton Theol. Sch. With paratroopers U.S. Army, 1943-46. Decorated Purple Heart. Mem. Am. Soc. Corp. Secs., Friars, Dedham Country and Polo Club, Down Town Club, Wellesley Coll. Club, Friars, Sigma Delta Chi, Delta Kappa Epsilon. Republican. Home and Office: 10 Turtle Ln Dover MA 02030-2053

SMITH, WILLIAM HULSE, forestry and environmental studies educator; b. Trenton, N.J., May 9, 1939; s. Philip Andrews and Marion (Hulse) S.; m. Judith Chapin Pease, July 6, 1963 (div. 1982); children—Scott William, Philip Chapin; m. Deborah Banks Coit, June 17, 1983; 1 child, Tyler Banks. B.S., Rutgers U., 1961, Ph.D., 1965; M.F., Yale U., 1963. Asst. prof. forestry Rutgers U., 1965-66; asst. prof. Yale U., 1966-72, assoc. prof., 1972-75, prof., 1975—, dean, 1981-83, Clifton R. Musser prof. forest biology, 1985—. Author: Tree Pathology, 1970, Air Pollution and Forest Ecosystems, 1981, 2d edit., 1990. Mem. Conn. Siting Council, 1985. NSF grantee, U.S. Dept. Agr. Forest Service grantee. Mem. Soc. Am. Foresters, Am. Phytopath. Soc., Ecol. Soc. Am. Home: 1 Northwinds Dr Ivoryton CT 06442-1261 Office: Sch Forestry and Environ Studies Yale U 370 Prospect St New Haven CT 06511-2104

SMITH, WILLIAM J., lawyer; b. Pitts., Jan. 9, 1941. BSBA, Duquesne U., 1967, JD, 1971. Bar: Pa. 1971. Ptnr. Reed Smith Shaw & McClay, Pitts. Office: Reed Smith Shaw & McClay James H Reed Bldg Mellon Sq 435 6th Ave Pittsburgh PA 15219-1809

SMITH, WILLIAM JAY, author; b. Winnfield, La., Apr. 22, 1918; s. Jay and Georgia (Campster) S.; m. Barbara Howes, Oct. 1, 1947 (div. June 1965); children: David Emerson, Gregory Jay; m. Sonja Haussmann, Sept. 3, 1966. Student, Institut de Touraine, Tours, France, 1938; B.A., Washington U., St. Louis, 1939, M.A., 1941; postgrad., Columbia U., 1946-47; postgrad. Rhodes scholar, Oxford U., 1947-48; postgrad., U. Florence, Italy, 1948-50; Litt.D., New Eng. Coll., 1973. Asst. in French Washington U., 1939-41; instr. English and French Columbia U., 1946-47; lectr. English Williams Coll., 1951, poet in residence, lectr. English, 1959-64, 66-67; Ford Found. fellow Arena Stage, Washington, 1964-65; writer in residence Hollins Coll., 1965-66, prof. English, 1967, 70-80, prof. emeritus, 1980; cons. poetry Libr. of Congress, Washington, 1968-70, hon. cons. in Am. letters, 1970-76; vis. prof., acting chmn., writing divsn. Sch. Arts, Columbia U., 1973, 74-75; mem. staff Salzburg (Austria) Seminar, 1975; mem. jury Nat. Book award, 1962, 70, 75, Neustadt Internat. prize for lit., 1978, Com. of Pegasus Prize for Lit., 1979—; poet in residence Cathedral St. John the Divine, N.Y., 1985-88. Author: Poems, 1947, Celebration at Dark, 1950, Laughing Time, 1955, Poems, 1947-57, Boy Blue's Book of Beasts, 1957, Puptents and Pebbles: A Nonsense ABC, 1959, Typewriter Town, 1960, The Spectra Hoax, 1961, What Did I See, 1962, Ho for a Hat, 1964, (with Louise Bogan) The Golden Journey; Poems for Young People, 1965, The Tin Can and Other Poems, 1966, Poems from France, 1967, If I Had a Boat, 1967, Mr. Smith and Other Nonsense, 1968, New and Selected Poems, 1970, The Streaks of the Tulip, selected criticism, 1972, Poems from Italy, 1973, Venice in the Fog, 1975, The Telephone, 1977, Laughing Time, 1980, The Traveler's Tree, New and Selected Poems, 1980, Army Brat, a Memoir, 1980, A Green Place: Modern Poems, 1982, Plain Talk: Epigrams, Epitaphs, Satires, Nonsense, Occasional Concrete and Quotidian Poems, 1988, Ho for a Hat (rev.), 1989, Collected Poems 1939-1989, 1990, Laughing Time: Collected Nonsense, 1990, Birds and Beasts, 1990, Big and LIttle, 1992 (with Carol Ra) Behind the King's Kitchen: A Roster of Rhyming Riddles, 1992; translator: (with Emanuel Brasil) Brazilian Poetry 1950-80, 1984, (with Ingvar Schousboe) The Pact: My Friendship with Isak Dinesen by Thorkild Bjørnvig, 1983, (with J.S. Holmes) Dutch Interior: Post-War Poetry of the Netherlands and Flanders, 1984, Scirocco by Romualdo Romano, 1951; Poems of a Multimillionaire by Valery Larbaud, 1955, Selected Writings of Jules Laforgue, 1956, Children of the Forest by Elsa Beskow, 1969, Two Plays by Charles Bertin: Christopher Columbus and Don Juan, 1970, The Pirate Book by Lennart Hellsing, 1972, (with Leif Sjöberg) Agadir by Artur Lundkvist, 1979, Moral Tales of Jules Laforgue, 1985, Collected Translations: Italian, French, Spanish, Portuguese, 1985, (with Dana Gioia) Poems from Italy, 1985, (with Leif Sjöberg) Wild Bouquet: Nature Poems by Harry Martinson, 1985, (with Sonja Haussmann Smith) The Madman and the Medusa by Tchicaya U Tam'Si, 1989, Songs of Childhood by Federico Garcia Lorca, 1994; editor: Herrick, 1962, Light Verse and Satires by Witter Bynner, 1978, (with F.D. Reeve) An Arrow in the Wall: Selected Poetry and Prose by Andrei Voznesensky, 1986 (one of 16 Best Books of 1986, N.Y. Times), Life Sentence: Selected Poems of Nina Cassian, 1990. Mem. Vt. Ho. of Reps., 1960-62. Served to lt. USNR, 1941-45. Recipient Alumni citation Washington U., 1963; prize Poetry mag., 1945, 64; Henry Bellamann Major award, 1970; Russell Liones award Nat. Inst. Arts and Letters, 1972; Gold medal Labor Hungary 1978; Golden Rose award New Eng. Poetry Club, 1979, médaille de vermeil French Acad., 1991, Pro Cultura Hungarica medal, Hungary, 1993; Nat. Endowment for Arts fellow, 1972, 95; NEH fellow, 1975, 89; Ingram Merrill fellow, 1982; Camargo Found. fellow, 1986. Mem. Am. Acad. Arts and Letters (v.p. for literature 1986-89), Am. Assn. Rhodes Scholars, Acad. Am. Poets, Authors Guild (council), P.E.N. Club: Century. Home: 63 Luther Shaw Rd Cummington MA 01026-9787 also: 52-56 rue d'Alleray, 75015 Paris France Office: care Harriet Wasserman 137 E 36th St # 19D New York NY 10016-3528

SMITH, WILLIAM JOHN, container manufacturing company executive; b. Cranford, N.J., June 27, 1926; s. William J. and Caroline S. (Gaffney) S.; m. Dolores A. Masson, Nov. 14, 1953; children: Karen Smith Finnell, Judith, William John, John, Steven. B.M.E., Syracuse U., 1950; grad., advanced mgmt. program Harvard U., 1967, Dartmouth Inst., 1976. With Am. Can Co., 1950-82; sr. v.p. tech. and research and devel. Am. Can Co., Greenwich, Conn., 1974-80; chmn. corp. operating com. Am. Can Co., 1979-80, pres. Paper Sector, corp. exec. v.p. Paper Sector, 1980-82; pres., chief exec. officer U.S. Can Co., Oak Brook, Ill., 1983—. Trustee Syracuse U., adv. bd. Coll. Engring. Served with USN, 1943-46. Mem. SAR, Pi Kappa Alpha, Theta Tau. Republican. Roman Catholic. Clubs: Chicago, Carlton (Chgo.), Landmark (Stamford, Conn.). Home: 516 Weed St New Canaan CT 06840-6127 Office: US Can Co 900 Commerce Dr Suite 302 Oak Brook IL 60521

SMITH, WILLIAM K., real estate developer; b. 1944. BA, U. Redlands, 1966; JD, UCLA, 1969. With Mission Viejo (Calif.) Co., 1969—, officer, 1974—, now sr. v.p., gen. counsel. Office: Mission Viejo Co 26137 La Paz Rd Mission Viejo CA 92691

SMITH, WILLIAM LAFAYETTE, JR., lawyer; b. Wills Point, Tex., Nov. 27, 1948; s. William Lafayette and Hazel Estes (Adams) S.; m. Ann Boutwell, June 11, 1970 (dec. 1993); children: Jefferson, Ginger, Amanda, Marcie, Melissa, Winter, Flint, Shannon. BA cum laude, North Tex. State U., 1975; JD, So. Meth. U., 1978. Bar: Tex. 1978, U.S. Dist. Ct. (ea. dist.) Tex. 1983, U.S. Dist. Ct. (no. dist.) Tex. 1989, U.S. Dist. Ct. (we. dist.) Tex. 1990, U.S. Ct. Appeals (5th cir.) 1983, U.S. Supreme Ct. 1990; cert. civil trial lawyer. Pvt. practice Denton, Tex., 1978—. With USN, 1968-71. Mem. Tex. Trial Lawyers Assn. (med. negligence and polit. coms. 1990-91), Assn. Trial Lawyers Am. Democrat. Methodist. Avocations: fishing, aerobatic flying. Home: 285 Fairway Acres Argyle TX 76226 Office: PO Box 149 Argyle TX 76226

SMITH, WILLIAM LEWIS, hotel executive; b. Cleve., Nov. 7, 1925; s. Floyd Holland and Florence (Goebelbecker) S.; m. Dorothy Losch, Aug. 2, 1945; children: Diane, William, Bradley, Tracey. Student, John Carroll U., Kent State U., Darden Sch., U. Va. Cert. hotel adminstr., cert. engring. ops. exec. With Halle Bros. Co., Cleve., 1946-58; with Hilton Hotel Corp., various locations, 1958-89, Statler Hilton, Cleve., 1958-61, Hilton Inn, Tarrytown, N.Y., 1961-63, N.Y. Hilton, N.Y.C., 1963-68, Conrad Hilton Hotel, Chgo., 1968-78, Fontainebleau Hilton, Miami Beach, Fla., 1978-80, Washington Hilton, 1980-84, Chgo. Hilton and Towers, 1984-89; asst. sec. Hilton Hotels Corp., 1971-89; with Bus. Cons. Internat., Barrington, Ill., 1989—;

vis. lect. U. Wis.-Stout, 1974, U. Notre Dame, 1975, 76, U. Houston, 1980, Cornell U., Ithaca, N.Y., 1987. Bd. dirs. Mich. Blvd. Assn., 1968-78, Good Shepherd Manor, Momence, Ill., 1973-89, Maur Hill Prep. Sch., Atchison, Kans., 1973-79, Met. Fair and Expn. Authority Chgo., 1975-78, Chgo. Conv. and Vis. Bur., Chgo. Conv. and Tourism Bur., 1975-78, 84-89, Miami Beach Visitor and Conv. Authority, 1978-80, Burnham Park Planning Bd., 1984-86; mem. Nat. 4-H Service Com., 1969-76, mem. adv. com., 1977-78; mem. adv. bd. Mercy Hosp. and Med. Ctr., Chgo., 1973-78, 84—, Echols Internat. Hotel Schs., Inc., 1984-89; mem. D.C. Bldg. Code Adv. Com., 1981-84, Near South Task Force Chgo. Cen. Area Com., 1984-89; mem. exec. com. Washington Conv. and Visitors Assn., 1981-84; mem. hotel/motel mgmt. adv. bd. Howard U., 1983-84; mem. bus. adv. council Coll. Bus. Administrn., U. Ill., Chgo., 1984-86; mem. steering com. South Side Planning Bd., 1984-89. Served with USNR, 1943-45. Recipient Partner-in-4-H award, 1971; Good Scout award Boy Scouts Am., 1974; Ignatian award, 1975. Mem. Am. Hotel and Motel Assn. (life, exec. engr. com. 1983-89), Washington Hotel Assn. (bd. dirs. 1980-84), Ill. Restaurant Assn. (bd. dirs. 1984-89, chmn. 1989), Hotel-Motel Assn. Ill. (bd. dirs. 1986-89, life). Address: 16 Champlain Rd Barrington IL 60010

SMITH, WILLIAM RANDOLPH, lawyer; b. Houston, July 30, 1928; s. Angie Frank and Bess Patience (Crutchfield) S.; m. Margaret Ann Pickett, Nov. 25, 1950; children: Sherren Bess (dec.), William Randolph Jr., Margaret Moody, David Christian. B.A., So. Meth. U., 1948; LL.B., U. Tex., 1951. Assoc. Vinson & Elkins, Houston, 1951-64, ptnr., 1965-91; dir. Weatherford Internat., Houston, 1979-95, several pvt. corps. Bd. dirs. Meth. Hosp. System, Houston, 1970—; trustee M.D. Anderson Hosp., 1975-92, So. Meth. U., Dallas, 1975-88, Briarwood Sch./Brookwood Community, Houston, 1970—. 1st lt. USAF, 1952-53. Mem. Houston Country Club, Ramada Club (sec. 1978-94). Home: 58 E Broad Oaks Dr Houston TX 77056-1202 Office: Vinson & Elkins 3311 First City Tower 1001 Fannin St Houston TX 77002

SMITH, WILLIAM RANDOLPH (RANDY SMITH), health care management association executive; b. Spartanburg, S.C., July 23, 1948; s. Jesse Edward and Helen (Knox) S.; m. Donna Marie HAwthorne, July 18, 1970; children: Kirstin Leigh, Andrea Marie. BA, Furman U., 1970; MHA, Duke U., 1972. Exec. dir. Riverside Hosp., Wilmington, Del., 1974-79; assoc. exec. dir. Brookwood Med. Ctr., Brimingham, Ala., 1979-81, exec. dir., 1983-85; v.p. ops. Am. Med. Internat., Atlanta, 1981-89; interim chief fin. officer Am. Med. Internat., Beverly Hills, Calif., 1989-90; chief adminstrv. officer Am. Med. Internat., Dallas, 1990, exec. v.p. ops., 1990-95; exec. v.p. Tenet Health Corp, Dallas, 1995—; bd. dirs. EPIC Healthcare Group, Dallas, 1989-92. Bd. dirs. Ala. Symphony Assn., Birmingham, 1985, State of Ala. Ballet, Birmingham, 1983-85. Lt. U.S. Army, 1972-74. Mem. Fedn. Am. Health Systems (bd. dirs. 1989—, pres. 1993, chmn. 1994). Episcopalian. Avocations: skiing, tennis, automobiles. Office: Tenet Healthcare Inc Ste 200 14001 Dallas Pkwy Dallas TX 75240

SMITH, WILLIAM RAY, retired biophysicist, engineer; b. Lyman, Okla., June 26, 1925; s. Harry Wait and Daisy Belle (Hull) S. BA, Bethany Nazarene Coll., 1948; MA, Wichita State U., 1950; PhD, UCLA, 1967. Engr., Beech Aircraft Corp., Wichita, Kans., 1951-53; sr. group engr. McDonnell Aircraft Corp., St. Louis, 1953-60; sr. engr. Lockheed Aircraft Corp., Burbank, Calif., 1961-63; sr. engr. scientist McDonnell Douglas Corp., Long Beach, Calif., 1966-71; mem. tech. staff Rockwell Internat., L.A., 1973-86, CDI Corp.-West, Costa Mesa, Calif., 1986-88, McDonnell Douglas Aircraft Corp., Long Beach, 1988-93; ret., 1993. tchr. math. Pasadena Coll. (now Point Loma Nazarene Coll., San Diego), 1962-66, Glendale Coll., Calif., 1972; asst. prof. math. Mt. St. Mary's Coll., L.A., 1972-73; math. cons. L.A. Union Rescue Mission Bank of Am. Learning Ctr., 1995—; docent Will Rogers State Park Nature Mus., 1995—. Recipient Recognition certificate NASA, 1982. Mem. UCLA Chancellor's Assocs., Internat. Visitors Coun. L.A., Town Hall Calif., Yosemite Assocs., Santa Monica Yacht Club, L.A. World Affairs Coun., Sigma Xi, Pi Mu Epsilon. Republican. Presbyterian. Avocations: sailing, photography, teaching Sunday sch. first grade. Home: 2405 Roscomare Rd Los Angeles CA 90077-1839

SMITH, WILLIAM ROBERT, utility company executive; b. Mount Clemens, Mich., Nov. 11, 1916; s. Robert L. and Elsie (Chamberlain) S.; BS, Detroit Inst. Tech., 1947; postgrad. Detroit Coll. Law, U. Mich. Grad. Sch. Bus. Adminstrn.; children: William R., Laura A. (dec.). Indsl. engr. Detroit Edison Co., 1934-60; mgr. econ. devel. East Ohio Gas Co., Cleve., 1960-80; mgr. nat. accounts Consol. Natural Gas Co., Cleve., 1980-85; dir. mktg. Edison Polymer Innovation Corp. 1985-88; exec. dir. Western Res. Econ. Devel. Coun., 1988—; pres. T.S.T. Corp. Trustee Cleve. Ballet; bd. dirs. Animal Protective League and Humane Soc. Served with USAAF, 1942-45. Registered profl. engr., Mich., Ohio. Fellow Am. Indsl. Devel. Council; Indsl. Devel. Rsch. Coun., Assn. Ohio Commodores, Shaker Heights (Ohio) Country Club, Delta Theta Tau. Presbyterian. Home: 27750 Fairmount Blvd Cleveland OH 44124-4612 Office: Kent State Univ Coll Bus Adminstrn Goodyear Exec Office Kent OH 44242

SMITH, WILLIAM YOUNG, consultant, former air force officer; b. Hot Springs, Ark., Aug. 13, 1925; s. Ray Sammons and Elisabeth Randolph (Young) S.; m. Maria Helene Petschek, May 30, 1957; children: Raymond P., Mark P., Derek P. Student, Washington and Lee U., 1943-44; BS, U.S. Mil. Acad., 1948; MPA, Harvard U., 1954, PhD, 1961; grad., Nat. War Coll., 1965. Commd. 2d lt. USAF, 1948, advanced through grades to gen., 1979; jet fighter pilot Korea, 1951-52; assoc. prof. social scis. U.S. Mil. Acad., 1954-58; mem. staff Pres.' Commn. to Study Mil. Assistance Program, 1959; mem. war plans staff USAF Hdqrs., 1960; staff asst. to Gen. Maxwell Taylor, mil. rep. to Pres. J.F. Kennedy White Ho., 1961-62; mem. staff NSC and staff asst. to chmn. Joint Chiefs of Staff, 1962-64; dep. chief, policy and negotiations, chief war plans Hdqrs. USAF, Europe, 1965-67; comdr. 603d Air Base Wing, Sembach AFB, Fed. Republic Germany, 1967-68; mil. asst. to sec. Air Force, 1968-71; vice comdr., then comdr. Oklahoma City Air Materiel Command, 1971-73; dir. doctrine, concepts and objectives Hdqrs. USAF, 1973-74; dir. policy plans and nat. security affairs Office Asst. Sec. Def. for Internat. Security Affairs, 1974-75; asst. to chmn. Joint Chiefs of Staff, 1975-79; chief of staff SHAPE, Belgium, 1979-81; dep. comdr. in chief U.S. European Command, Stuttgart, Fed. Republic Germany, 1981-83; ret. USAF, 1983; fellow Woodrow Wilson Internat. Ctr. for Scholars, Smithsonian Inst, Washington, 1983-84; pres. Inst. for Def. Analyses, Alexandria, Va., 1985-91, pres. emeritus, 1991—, also trustee; treas., chmn. fin. com., Atlantic Coun.; mem. exec. com., bd. dirs. Nat. Security Archive. Life fellow Met. Mus. Art. Decorated DSM with oak leaf cluster, Air Force DSM with oak leaf cluster, Silver Star, Legion of Merit with oak leaf cluster, DFC, Air medal with 3 oak leaf clusters, Joint Svc. Commendation medal, Purple Heart, Armed Forces Cross in Gold (Fed. Republic Germany), Ordre Nationale de Merite (France), DOD medal for disting. pub. svc. Mem. Nat. Acad. Pub. Adminstrn., Nat. War Coll. Alumni Assn. (pres. 1985-87), West Point Soc. of D.C. (pres. 1987-89), Coun. Fgn. Rels., Cosmos Club. Office: Inst Def Analyses 1801 N Beauregard St Alexandria VA 22311-1733

SMITH, WILLIE TESREAU, JR., retired judge, lawyer; b. Sumter, S.C., Jan. 17, 1920; s. Willie T. and Mary (Moore) S.; student Benedict Coll., 1937-40; AB, Johnson C. Smith U., 1947; LLB, S.C. State Coll., 1954, JD, 1976; m. Anna Marie Clark, June 9, 1955; 1 son, Willie Tesreau, III. Admitted to S.C. bar, 1954; began gen. practice, Greenville, 1954; past exec. dir. Legal Svcs. Agy. Greenville County, Inc.; state family ct. judge 13th Jud. Circuit S.C., 1977-91; ret. 1991. Mem. adv. bd. Greenville Tech. Edn. Ctr. Adult Edn. Program and Para-Legal Program, Greenville Tech. Coll. Found. Bd.; past bd. dirs. Greenville Urban League; past trustee Greenville County Sch. Dist. Served with AUS, 1942-45, USAF, 1949-52. Mem. Am., Nat. (jud. coun.), S.C., Greenville County bar assns., Southeastern Lawyers Assn., Nat. Coun. Juvenile and Family Ct. Judges, Am. Legion, Greater Greenville C. of C. (past dir.), Phillis Wheatley Assn. (dir.), NAACP, Omega Psi Phi, Delta Beta Boule, Sigma Pi Phi. Presbyterian (past chmn. bd. trustees Fairfield-McClelland Presbytery, past moderator Foothills Presbytery). Clubs: Masons, Shriners, Rotary. Home: 601 Jacobs Rd Greenville SC 29605-3318

SMITH, WILLIS ALLEN, retired consultant, former food company executive; b. Balt., Oct. 26, 1919; s. Willis Alfred and Grace Lee (Roberts) S.; m. Joann Cobb, Aug. 29, 1970. Student, Johns Hopkins U., 1937-41, 46-48, Coll. William and Mary, Norfolk, Va., 1941-42. C.P.A., Md., Ohio, N.Y. Clk. Gas & Electric Co., Balt., 1936-41; acct. F. W. Lafrentz & Co., Balt., 1946-51; mgr. F.W. Lafrentz & Co., Salisbury, Md., 1952-53; partner F.W. Lafrentz & Co., Cleve., 1953-62, Main Lafrentz & Co., N.Y.C., 1963-74; comptroller CPC Internat. Inc., Englewood Cliffs, N.J., 1974-81, v.p., 1981-84; mem. bd. Internat. Acctg. Standards Com., 1979-82; lectr. Third Commodity Conf., Chgo., 1973, Internat. Acctg. Conf., N.Y.C., 1977, 10th Corp. Acctg. and Fin. Reporting Inst., Washington, 1979, Audit Mgmt. Conf., N.Y.C., 1982, Auditing and Acctg. Symposium, N.J., 1987. Contbr.: Accountants Handbook, 6th edit., 1981; articles to profl. jours. Served with USNR, 1941-45, PTO. Mem. AICPA (v.p. 1982-83), N.Y. State Soc. CPAs (v.p. 1977-78, Outstanding Svc. award 1983), Fin. Execs. Inst., Inst. Mgmt. Accts., Am. Acctg. Assn., Ridgewood Country Club (N.J.), The Club Pelican Bay, Club at Edgewater, Shriners. Home: Apt 407 792 Willowbrook Dr Naples FL 33963-8536

SMITH, WINTHROP HIRAM, JR., financial services executive; b. N.Y.C., Aug. 5, 1949; s. Winthrop Hiram Sr. and Vivian Gordon (Brown) S.; m. Margaret Dunn, Aug. 7, 1971. BA, Amherst Coll., 1971; MBA, U. Pa., 1974. Investment banker Merrill Lynch, Pierce, Fenner & Smith, N.Y.C., 1974-77, mgr. fin. analysis, 1977-78, mgr. compensation and benefits, 1978-80, dir. human resources, 1980-82; dir. strategic devel. and mktg. Merrill Lynch Capital Markets, N.Y.C., 1982-84, dir. emerging investor svcs., 1984-85; sr. v.p., regional dir. Merrill Lynch, Pierce, Fenner & Smith, N.Y.C., 1985-90, nat. sales dir., 1990-92; exec. v.p., chmn. Merrill Lynch Internat., 1992—. Bd. dirs. Cancer Rsch. Inst., N.Y.C. Ballet; trustee Deerfield Acad.; advisor Outward Bound. Mem. Coun. on Fgn. Rels., Fgn. Policy Assn. (bd. dirs.), Greewich Country Club, Blind Brook Club, F Street Club, The Links. Republican. Episcopalian. Avocations: running, golf, riding, bicycling, skiing. Office: Merrill Lynch Pierce Fenner Smith World Financial Ctr 250 Vesey St New York NY 10281-1308*

SMITH, YVONNE SMART, advertising agency executive; b. Asheville, N.C., June 25, 1947; d. Gardner Ford and Yvonne (Boyd) Smart. BFA, Auburn U., 1969. Asst. art dir. Mademoiselle mag., N.Y.C., 1969-72; art dir. Cargill, Wilson & Acree Advt. div. Doyle Dane Bernbach, Charlotte, N.C., 1972-74; art dir., creative supr. Tracy-Locke Advt., Dallas, 1974-76; v.p., assoc. creative dir., exec. art dir. Chiat/Day Advt., Los Angeles, 1976-85, sr. v.p., assoc. creative dir., Venice, Calif., 1991—; prin. Yvonne Smith, Inc., 1985-91; sr. v.p., assoc. creative dir. Chiat/Day Advt., Venice, N.Y.C., London, Toronto, 1991—; guest lectr. UCLA, 1980-83, Art Ctr. Coll. Design, Los Angeles, 1982; judge advt. awards. Subject of profl. articles. Recipient One Show award N.Y. Art Dirs. Club, 1974-83, Belding awards Los Angeles Advt. Club, 1976-83, Andy awards N.Y. Arts Dirs. Club, 1976-83, Art Dirs. Club award, 1976—, Steven Kelly award, 1983, 84, Clio awards, 1984, CA awards, 1976-84. Mem. Communicating Arts (sec. 1974), Los Angeles Creative Club. Club: N.Y. Jr. League (N.Y.C.). Office: Chiat/Day Advt 320 Hampton Dr Venice CA 90291-2624

SMITH, ZACHARY TAYLOR, II, retired tobacco company executive; b. Mt. Airy, N.C., June 15, 1923; s. Eugene Gray and Leonita (Yates) S. AB in Econs., U. N.C., 1947; LLD (hon.), Wake Forest U., 1989. With R.J. Reynolds Tobacco Co., 1947-85, treas., dir., 1970-85. Trustee, past pres. Z. Smith Reynolds Found.; life trustee Wake Forest U.; bd. dirs. Mary Reynolds Babcock Found.; past bd. dirs. Arts and Scis. Found., U. N.C.; mem. nat. devel. coun. U. N.C.; past bd. dirs. Med. Found. N.C.; mem. nat. devel. coun. U. N.C.; past bd. dirs. Leadership Winston-Salem; past mem. adv. coun. The Carolina Challenge; past chmn. bd. visitors U. N.C. Chapel Hill; past mem. Reynolds Scholarship com., past mem. bd. visitors Wake Forest U.; mem. adv. coun. to hosp., past mem. bd. visitors inst. policy studies and pub. affairs Duke U.; past bd. dirs., N.C. Sch. Arts Found., Devotion Found., N.C. Outward Bound Sch., Small Bus. Devel. Com., Winston-Salem Symphony, Citizens Planning Coun.; past trustee Forsyth Hosp. Authority; past pres., dir. Child Guidance Clinic Forsyth County, YMCA, Red Shield Boy's Clubs; past pres. Z. Smith Reynolds Found., Mary Reynolds Babcock Found.; past chmn. indsl. divsn. Arts Coun. fund drive; past v.p., dir. Arts Coun.; past v.p., dir. Amos Cottage; past bd. visitors Meredith Coll.; past trustee St. Augustine Coll.; past bd. dirs. alumni assn. U. N.C.; vice chmn., dir. Friends of U. N.C.-Greensboro Libr.; co-founder Club Med. Sch. U. N.C., Chapel Hill. Mem. Old Town Club, Rotary. Democrat. Episcopalian. Home: 2548 Forest Dr Winston Salem NC 27104

SMITHBURG, WILLIAM DEAN, food manufacturing company executive; b. Chgo., July 9, 1938; s. Pearl L. and Margaret L. (Savage) S.; children: Susan, Thomas. BS, DePaul U., 1960; MBA, Northwestern U., 1962. With Leo Burnett Co., Chgo., 1961-63, McCann-Erickson, Inc., Chgo., 1963-66; various positions Quaker Oats Co., Chgo., 1966-71, gen. mgr. cereals and mixes divsn., 1971-75, pres. food divsn., 1975-76, exec. v.p. U.S. grocery products, 1976-79, pres., 1979-83, chief exec. officer, 1979—, chmn., 1983—, also bd. dirs. Served with USAR, 1959-60. Roman Catholic. Office: Quaker Oats Co 321 N Clark St Chicago IL 60610-4714

SMITHEE, JOHN TRUE, lawyer, state legislator; b. Amarillo, Tex., Sept. 7, 1951; s. John J. and Mildred B. (True) S.; m. Becky Collins, Aug. 18, 1979; children: Jennifer, Rebecca, John True. BBA, West Tex. State U., Canyon, 1973; JD, Tex. Tech U., 1976. Bar: Tex. 1976, U.S. Supreme Ct., 1983. Atty. Templeton, Smithee, Hayes & Fields, Amarillo, Tex., 1976—; mem. Tex. Ho. of Reps., Austin, 1985—, chmn. ins. com., 1993—. Mem. State Bar Tex., Amarillo Bar Assn. Republican. Home: 2808 Parker St Amarillo TX 79109-3546 Office: Templeton Smithee Hayes & Fields 600 S Tyler St Ste 12075 Amarillo TX 79101-2351

SMITHER, GERTRUDE JACKSON, minister; b. Dallas, Oct. 6, 1937; d. John Nelson and Sallie Bell (Gaston) Jackson; m. Robert Bush Smither Jr., Aug. 20, 1960; children: Robert, Sallie, John, Mary Kate. BA, U. Tex., 1959; MDiv, Episcopal Theol. Sem. S.W., Austin, 1985. Ordained to ministry, Episcopal Ch., 1990. Dir. religious edn. Trinity Episcopal Ch., Galveston, Tex., 1979-83; chaplain U. Tex. Med. Br., Galveston, 1985-92; coord. Diocese Dallas Hosp. Chaplaincy and Canon Chaplain St. Matthew's Cathedral, Dallas, 1992—; asst. St. Luke the Physician Episcopal Ch., Galveston, 1985-92; chaplain William Temple Found., Galveston, 1985-92; chaplain U. Tex. Med. Br., 1985-92; pres. St. Vincent's Episcopal House, Galveston, 1987, 88, 91; chmn. Campus Mins., 1987-91; mem. Coun. Religious Ministry, UTMB, 1985-92. Fellow Coll. of Chaplains Inc. (continuing edn. chair Tex. north region), Galveston Ministerial Assn. (pres. 1991). Home: 7854 Caruth Ct Dallas TX 75225-8132 Office: Saint Matthews Cathedral 5100 Ross Ave Dallas TX 75206-7709

SMITHER, HOWARD ELBERT, musicologist; b. Pittsburg, Kans., Nov. 15, 1925; s. Elbert S. and Ethel (Schwab) S.; m. Doris J. Arvin (div. 1976); children: Thomas A., Jesse N. Woodsmith; m. Ann M. Woodward. AB magna cum laude, spl. honors in music, Hamline U., 1950; MA in musicology, Cornell U., 1952; postgrad., U. Munich, 1953-54; PhD in musicology, Cornell U., 1960. Instr. Oberlin Coll. and Conservatory of Music, Oberlin, Ohio, 1955-57, asst. prof., 1957-60; asst. prof. U. Kans., Lawrence, 1960-63; assoc. prof. Tulane U., New Orleans, 1963-68; assoc. prof. U. N.C., Chapel Hill, 1968-71, prof., 1971-79, dir. grad. studies in music, 1977-79, 83-84, 86-88, James Gordon Hanes prof. humanities in music, 1979-92, James Gordon Hanes prof. emeritus humanities in music, 1992—; John Bird prof. of music U. Wales, Cardiff, 1993-95; Lectr., chmn. panels regional, nat. and internat. meetings, confs., symposiums, 1964-90. Author: A History of the Oratorio, Vol. 1, The Oratorio in the Baroque Era: Italy, Vienna, Paris, 1977 (transl. Italian), Vol. 2, The Oratorio in the Baroque Era: Protestant Germany and England, 1977 (Deems Taylor award ASCAP 1978), The Oratorio in the Classical Era, 1987; editor The Italian Oratorio 1650-1800, Vols. 1-3, 6, 8, 11, 12, 13, 16, 18, 19, 20, 24, 25, 27, 1986-87; editor, translator poems in Alfred Einstein's The Italian Madrigal, 1971; author publs. in periodicals, dictionaries, encys., congress reports, record-jacket notes, abstracts, revs.; music rev. editor Notes, 1967-69; mem. editorial bd. Detroit Monographs in Musicology, 1971-87; chmn. editorial bd. Early Musical Masterworks: Editions and Commentaries, 1978-83; mem. editorial bd. Videodisc Music Series, NEH, 1982-86; editor Oratorios of the Italian Baroque, 1983—. Fellow Cornell U., 1953-54, NEH, Italy, 1972-73, England, 1979-80, Guggenheim, 1984-85; Fulbright sr. rsch. grant in Italy, 1965-66, sr. Fulbright lectr. Moscow State Conservatory, 1990. Mem. Am. Mus. Soc. (chmn. S.E. chpt. 1969-71, mem. coun. 1969-71, 75-77, bd. dirs. 1977-79, pres. 1980-82, del. to Am. Coun. Learned Socs. 1984-88, to Internat. Congress Strasbourg 1982), Music Libr. Assn. (bd. dirs. 1968-70), Sonneck Soc. Avocations: hiking, photography.

SMITHEY, DONALD LEON, airport authority director; b. St. Louis, Aug. 31, 1940; children: Kelly, Jill. Student, St. Ambrose Coll., 1962; BS in Bus. Mgmt., So. Ill. U., 1966; postgrad., U. Mo. Asst. ops. dispatcher Ozark Airlines, 1971-72; transp. analyst Olin Corp., 1972-78, cost acct., 1978-80; commr. St. Louis Regional Airport Authority, 1971-80, chmn., 1974-80, airport dir., 1980-83; asst. dir. Cedar Rapids Mcpl. Airport, 1983-85; dir. adminstrn. Omaha Airport Authority, 1985-87, dep. exec. dir., 1987-89, exec. dir., 1989—. Mem. Am. Assn. Airport Execs. (Great Lakes chpt.), Airports Coun. Internat., Iowa Airport Exec. Assn. (past pres.), Ill. Pub. Airports Assn. (past v.p.), Exptl. Aircraft Assn., Omaha Rotary Club, Masonic Lodge (Bethalto, Ill.), Tangier Shrine (Omaha), Quiet Birdmen Assn., Silver Wings Fraternity. Office: Omaha Airport Authority 4501 Abbott Dr Omaha NE 68110

SMITH-FARNSWORTH, SHARON ANNE, elementary education educator; b. San Francisco, Aug. 6, 1945; d. Donald Franklin and Maxine Anna (Alterman) Steiner; m. Edward Earl Smith III, Nov. 7, 1968 (div. Dec. 1987); 1 child, Edward Earl IV; m. Matthew Lee Farnsworth, Jan. 15, 1988;. BA in History, U. Calif., Berkeley, 1967; cert. in gifted and talented in edn., U. Calif., Riverside, 1986. Cert. elem. tchr., Calif. Tchr. Manhattan Beach (Calif.) City Sch., 1968-78, Moreno Valley (Calif.) Unified Sch. Dist., 1984—. Mem. ASCD, NEA, NAACP, Calif. Leadership Acad., Calif. Tchrs. Assn., Moreno Valley Educators Assn. (rep. 1984-91, v.p. 1991-94), Smithsonian Inst., Phi Sigma Sigma. Republican. Avocations: reading, writing poetry, traveling. Home: 10689 Willow Creek Rd Moreno Valley CA 92557-2953 Office: Badger Springs Mid Sch 24750 Delphinium Ave Moreno Valley CA 92553-5812

SMITH-GOMES, KATHLEEN MARIE, special education educator; b. Mineola, N.Y., June 27, 1963; d. Warren Henry and Mary Cecilia (O'Reilly) Smith; m. Rui Cameira Gomes, July 12, 1986; 1 child, Kayla Elizabeth. BS in Spl. Edn. and Elem. Edn., SUNY, Buffalo, 1985; MS in Spl. Edn. summa cum laude, SUNY, Albany, 1986; cert. in supervision, Kean Coll., 1993, MS in Administrn., 1995. Cert. tchr., N.Y., N.J. Spl. edn. intern Niskayuna H.S., Schenectady, N.Y., 1985, SUNY, Albany, 1986; elem. tchr. St. Hedwig Sch., Elizabeth, N.J., 1986-87; resource/inclusion tchr. Colts Neck (N.J.) Pub. Sch., 1987-88; spl. edn. tchr. Matawan (N.J.) Regional H.S., 1988-89; resource/inclusion tchr. Roselle (N.J.) Pub. Schs., 1989—, acting spl. edn. dept. chair, 1995—, spl. edn. dept. chair, 1995—, mem. curriculum revision team, 1993-94, inclusion pilot program trainer, 1993—, mem. drug and alcohol core team Abraham Clark H.S., 1991—; adminstrv. intern spl. edn. Kean Coll., 1994; advisor AIDS presentation, 1993; presenter Inclusion Workshop CEC Annual Conf., 1995. Advisor Quilts for Kids, Roselle, 1989-90; mem. Fairway Civic Assn., Union Twp., N.J., 1995—. Recipient Vol. award Pres. Bush, 1990; grantee SUNY, 1985-86. Mem. ASCD, N.J. Edn. Assn., Coun. for Exceptional Children, Roselle Edn. Assn. (bldg. rep. 1989—), Phi Delta Kappa (pub. rels. com. 1992—). Republican. Roman Catholic. Avocations: aviculture, sewing, water skiing, boating, gardening. Home: 755 Evergreen Pky Union NJ 07083-8731 Office: Abraham Clark HS 122 E 6th Ave Roselle NJ 07203-2026

SMITH-LEINS, TERRI L., mathematics educator; b. Salina, Kans., Sept. 19, 1950; d. John W. and Myldred M. (Hays) Smith; m. Larry L. Leins, May 26, 1984. BS, Ft. Hays (Kans.) U., 1973, MS, 1976; AA, Stephen Coll., Columbia, Mo., 1970. Math tchr. Scott City (Kans.) Jr. H.S., Howard (Kans.) Schs.; instr. math. Westark C.C., Ft. Smith, Ark. Contbr. articles to profl. jours., chpts. to books. Mem. AADE, ASCD, Nat. Assn. Devel. Edn. (state sec. 1986-88, computer access com. 1980-85), Phi Delta Kappa (Kappan of Yr. 1985), Delta Kappa Gamma (state chairperson women in art 1993-95). Home: PO Box 3446 Fort Smith AR 72913-3446

SMITH-PIERCE, PATRICIA A., speech professional; b. Washington, May 24, 1939; d. Edward Milton and Mary Louise (Reimbold) Anderson; m. Wayne D. Pierce, Mar. 25, 1978. BA, Ohio State U., 1961; MA, U. Utah, 1970; PhD, Wash. State U., 1977. Stewardess Am. Airlines, Chgo., 1962-63; selling supr. The Emporium, San Francisco, 1963-65; buyer Cain-Sloan Co., Nashville, 1967-68; speech coach William Rainey Harper Coll., Palatine, Ill., 1970-76, prof., 1970-95, chmn. speech dept., 1985-92, dir. corp. svcs., 1990-91; prof. emeritus, 1996—; cons. Inst. Mgmt. Devel., Palatine, 1983—; bd. dirs. Ill. Women's Agenda, 1981-87, v.p., 1982-83, pres., 1983-85; bd. dirs. Women in Charge, Chgo., 1987-90; cons. various corp. and govtl. agys.; mem. com. Ill. Commn. on Status of Women, 1983-85; trainer Mex. Am. Legal Def. and Edn. Fund, Leadership Program Chgo., 1986—. Mem. Ill. Minority and Female Bus. Enterprise Coun., 1984-94. Mem. AAUW (1st v.p. state orgn. 1985-87, bd. dirs. 1981-87, nat. trainer 1987—), Human Resources Mgmt. Assn. Chgo., Zonta Internat. Avocations: reading, golf. Office: William Rainey Harper Coll 1200 W Algonquin Rd Palatine IL 60067-7373

SMITHSON, LOWELL LEE, lawyer; b. Kansas City, Mo., Apr. 29, 1930; s. Spurgeon Lee and Lena Louise (Ruddy) S.; m. Rosemary Carol Leitz, Jan. 30, 1960 (div. Sept. 1985); m. Phyllis Galley Westover, June 8, 1986; children: Carol Maria Louise, Katherine Frances Lee. AB in Polit. Sci., U. Mo., 1952, JD, 1954. Bar: Mo. 1954, U.S. Dist. Ct. (we. dist.) Mo. 1955, U.S. Supreme Ct. 1986. Ptnr. Smithson & Smithson, Kansas City, 1956-59; assoc. Spencer, Fane, Britt & Browne, Kansas City, 1959-64, ptnr., 1964—; adj. prof. law U. Mo., Kansas City, 1982. Pres. Kansas City Mental Health Assn., 1963-65; mem. bd. pres. All Souls Unitarian Ch. Kansas City, 1965-67; chmn. com. select dean for law sch. U. Mo., 1983. 1st lt. U.S. Army, 1954-56, Korea. Mem. Kansas City Bar Assn., Lawyers Assn. Kansas City, Assn. Trial Lawyers Am., Western Mo. Def. Lawyers Assn., Fed. Energy Bar Assn., Phi Beta Kappa, Phi Delta Phi. Democrat. Unitarian Ch. Avocations: skiing, reading, tennis, swimming, canoeing. Home: 1215 W 65th St Kansas City MO 64113-1803 Office: Spencer Fane Britt & Browne 1000 Walnut 1400 Commerce Bank Bldg Kansas City MO 64106

SMITH-THOMPSON, PATRICIA ANN, public relations consultant, educator; b. Chgo., June 7, 1933; d. Clarence Richard and Ruth Margaret (Jacobson) Nowack; m. Tyler Thompson, Aug. 1, 1992. Student Cornell U., 1951-52; BA, Centenary Coll., Hackettstown, N.J., 1983. Prodn. asst. Your Hit Parade Batten, Barton, Durstine & Osborne, 1953-54; pvt. practice polit. cons., 1954-66; legal sec., asst. Atty. John C. Cushman, 1966-68; field dep. L.A. County Assessor, 1968-69, pub. info. officer L.A. County Probation Dept., 1969-73; dir. consumer rels. Fireman's Fund, San Francisco, 1973-76; pvt. practice pub. rels. cons., 1976-77; spl. projects officer L.A. County Transp. Commn., 1977-78; tchr. Calif. State U.-Dominguez Hills, 1979-86; editor, writer Jet Propulsion Lab., 1979-80; pub. info. dir. L.A. Bd. Pub. Works, 1980-82; pub. info. cons. City of Pasadena, (Calif.), 1982-84; pub. rels. cons., 1983-90, community rels./Worldport L.A., 1990-92. Contbr. articles to profl. jours. Mem. First United Methodist Ch. Commn. on Missions and Social Concerns, 1983-89; bd. dirs. Depot, 1983-87; mem. devel. com. Pasadena Guidance Clinics, 1984-85. Recipient Pro award L.A. Publicity Club, 1978, Outstanding Achievement award Soc. Consumer Affairs Profls. in Bus., 1976, Disting. Alumni award Centenary Coll., 1992. Mem. Pub. Relations Soc. Am. (accredited mem.; award for consumer program 1977, 2 awards 1984, Joseph Roos Community Service award 1985), Nat. Press Women (pub. relations award 1986), Calif. Press Women (awards 1974, 78, 83, 84, 85, community relations 1stplace winner 1986, 87, 88, 89), Nat. Assn. Mental Health Info. Offices (3 regional awards 1986). Republican.

SMITH-WILLIAMS, CATHY, education educator; b. Richlands, Va., May 18, 1954; d. James Alvin and Doris Janet (Wilson) Smith; 1 child, Erin Amanda; m. Sam Williams. AS, S.W. Va. Community Coll., 1974; BS, Clinch Valley Coll., 1978; MS, Radford U., 1983. Cert. elem. grades 4-7, reading specialist grades K-12, devel. edn. specialist. Chpt. I reading tchr. Russell County Schs., Lebanon, Va., 1978-90; adj. faculty, reading S.W. Va. C.C., Richlands, 1983-87; elem. tchr. Russell County Schs., Lebanon; instr. devel. and basic reading and study skills NE State Tech. C.C., Blountville, Tenn., 1990-93; reading faculty Heartland C.C., Bloomington, Ill., 1993—; open learning coord. Heartland C.C. Mem. Nat. Assn. Devel. Edn., Nat. Assn. Devel. Educators, Ill. Reading Assn., Ill. Assn. Learning Assistance

Profls., Kellogg Inst. Office: Heartland C C 1226 N Towanda Ave Bloomington IL 61701-3424

SMITS, EDWARD JOHN, museum consultant; b. Freeport, N.Y., Dec. 11, 1933; s. Karl M. and Jennie (Spring) S.; m. Ruth K. Hall; children: E. John, Robert K., Theodore R. BA, Hofstra U., 1955; MA, NYU, 1959. Curator Nassau County Hist. Mus., East Meadow, N.Y., 1956-70; dir. mus. svcs. Div. Mus. Svcs. Nassau County, Syosset, N.Y., 1971-92; Nassau County historian, 1985—. Author: Long Island Landmarks, 1970, Creation of Nassau County, 1959, Nassau, Suburbia U.S.A., 1974. Trustee Friends for L.I.'s Heritage, Nassau County Hist. Soc.; trustee, past pres. Levittown Libr. Bd. 1st lt. U.S. Army, 1955-56. Fulbright grantee, 1965; recipient Nassau County disting. svc. award, 1970, alumni disting. svc. award Hofstra U., 1970, H. Sherwood Historic Preservation on L.I. award Soc. for the Preservation of L.I. Antiquities, 1975. Mem. Am. Assn. Mus. Avocations: book collecting, antique toys, golf. Home: 14 Wavy Ln Wantagh NY 11793-1202

SMITS, HELEN LIDA, public adminstrator, physician, educator; b. Long Beach, Calif., Dec. 3, 1936; d. Theodore Richard Smits and Anna Mary Wells; m. Roger LeCompte, Aug. 28, 1976; 1 child, Theodore. BA with honors, Swarthmore Coll., 1958; MA, Yale U., 1961, MD cum laude, 1967. Intern, asst. resident Hosp. U. Pa., 1967-68; fellow Beth Israel Hosp., Boston, 1969-70; chief resident Hosp. U. Pa., 1970-71; chief med. clinic U. Pa., 1971-75; assoc. adminstr. for patient care svcs. U. Pa. Hosp., 1975-77; v.p. med. affairs Community Health Plan Georgetown U., Washington, 1977; dir. health standards and quality bur. Health Care Financing Adminstrn., HHS, Washington, 1977-80; sr. rsch. assoc. The Urban Inst., Washington, 1980-81; assoc. prof. Yale U. Med. Sch., New Haven, 1981-85; assoc. v.p. for health affairs U. Conn. Health Ctr., Farmington, 1985-87; prof. community medicine U. Conn. Sch. Medicine, Farmington, 1985-93; hosp. dir. John Dempsey Hosp., Farmington, 1987-93; dep. adminstr. Health Care Financing Adminstrn., Washington, 1993—; commr. Joint Com. on Accreditation Hosps., Chgo., 1989-93, chair, 1991-92. Contbr. numerous articles to profl. jours. Bd. dirs. The Ivoryton Playhouse Fedn., Inc., 1990-92, The Connecticut River Mus., 1990-93, Hartford Stage, 1990-93; mem. Dem. Town Com., Essex, Conn., 1982-89. Recipient Superior Svc. award HHS, Washington, 1982; Royal Soc. Medicine Found. fellow, London, 1973; Fulbright scholar, 1959-60. Mem. ACP (master, regent 1984-90), Phi Beta Kappa, Alpha Omega Alpha. Episcopalian. Avocations: sailing, cooking, gardening. Home: 81 Main St Ivoryton CT 06442-1032 Office: Health Care Fin Adminstrn 200 Independence Ave SW Washington DC 20201-0004

SMITS, JIMMY, actor; b. N.Y.C., July 9, 1955; two children. Master's degree, Cornell Univ., 1982. Appearances include Off-Broadway prodns., tours with regional theatres; (TV series) Miami Vice, 1984, L.A. Law, 1986-91 (Outstanding Actor in Dramatics Series Emmy award 1990), NYPD Blue, 1994—; (TV movies) Rockabye, 1986, The Highwayman, 1986, Glitz, 1988, The Broken Cord, 1992, Stephen King's The Tommyknockers, 1993; (films) Running Scared, 1986, The Believers, 1987, Old Gringo, 1989, Vital Signs, 1990, Switch, 1991, Gross Misconduct, 1993, My Family, 1995. Avocations: football, basketball, softball, reading. Office: care Marilyn Sherman 1516 S Beverly Dr Apt 304 Los Angeles CA 90035-3059*

SMITTLE, NELSON DEAN, electronics executive; b. Peebles, Ohio, Sept. 19, 1934; s. Nelson John and Alma Katherine (Green) S.; m. Claire Wiggins, May 5, 1973. BS, BFA, U. Cin., 1962, MA, 1971. Commd. 2d lt. U.S. Army, 1962; staff officer U.S. Army Photo Agy. Pentagon, Washington, 1966; detachment comdr. tactical comms. Republic South Vietnam, 1967-68; comdr. 907th communications squadron Rickenbacker AFB, Ohio, 1972; dir. ops. fixed communications Air Combat Command Langley AFB, Va., 1982; dir. info. systems AWACS Saudi Arabia, 1984-85; dep. chief of staff standard systems Air Material Command Wright-Patterson AFB, Ohio, 1985; comdr. engrng. installation divsn. Tinker AFB, Okla., 1988; commn. transferred to USAF, 1970, commd. col., 1988; ret. USAF, Cin., 1991; pres. Falcon Techs., Cin., 1991—; tchr. Princeton City Sch. Dist., Cin., 1992-94; cons. Air War Coll., Air Univ., Maxwell AFB, Ala., 1987—, Defense Systems Mgmt. Coll., Ft. Belvior, Va., 1988—. Author: (books) Army Visual Presentation, 1966 (medal 1966), Famous Movements in Aviation History, 1997. Mem. Batavia (Ohio) City Coun., 1972; pres. Ohio Buckeye Wing Assn., Columbus, 1973; mem. Air Force Policy Coun., Washington, 1978; congl. campaign mgr., 1993; bd. dirs. Cin. Art Club, 1995—. Decorated Commendation medal; recipient Meritorious Svc. medal Dept. Def., 1986, 91. Mem. DAV, Air Force Assn., Res. Officers Assn., Am. Soc. Aviation Artists. Avocations: freelance writer, exhibiting artist, walking, science fiction. Home and Office: Falcon Techs 159 Francisridge Dr Cincinnati OH 45238-6051

SMIY, PAUL R., manufacturing executive, heavy; b. 1923. With Elliott Co, Jeannette, Pa., pres., CEO, 1986-91, chmn., 1991—; also CEO New Elliott Corp., Jeannette, Pa.; asst. chmn. bd. Jeannette (Pa.) Healthpace Corp. Chmn. bd. Jeannette (Pa.) Dist. Meml. Hosp. Office: Elliott Co 901 N 4th St Jeannette PA 15644-1474*

SMOCK, DONALD JOE, governmental liaison, political consultant; b. Ponca City, Okla., Sept. 24, 1964; s. Joe Clellan and Ruth Esther Smock. BA in Polit. Sci., U. Ctrl. Okla., 1991, MA in Urban Affairs, 1993. Founder Smock Polit. Systems, Edmond, Okla., 1990—; rschr. The Nigh Inst. State Govt., Edmond, 1993-94; U. Ctrl. Okla. del. to Ctr. Study of Pres. Symposium, Washington, 1993; govt. liaison Elizey Electric Motor Co., 1994—. Charter founder Ronald Reagan Rep. Ctr., 1989; del. State of Okla. Rep. Presdl. Task Force, 1996; mem. Rep. Presdl. Trust, 1996. Recipient Okla. Rep. Blue Key award, 1984, Presdl. Commn., 1992, Merit cert. Rep. Nat. Com., 1990; named to Ronald Reagon Rep. Ctr. Presdl. Commemorative Honor Roll, 1991; flag dedicated in name Rotunda of U.S. Capitol, 1990. Mem. Tau Kappa Epsilon (Delta Nu colony inductee, chpt. advisor 1990-92, Fraternity for Life inductee, David Crain Leadership award 1986, Ed Howell Leadership award 1988-89, Red Carnation Ball dedicated in name 1989-90, 94, Top Alumnus 1990-91), Pi Sigma Alpha. Republican. Mem. Ch. of Christ. Home: PO Box 6323 Edmond OK 73083-6323

SMOCK, RAYMOND WILLIAM, historian; b. Jeffersonville, Ind., Feb. 8, 1941; s. Richard and Lottie (Paciorek) S.; m. Phyllis Lee Chadwick, Feb. 12, 1961. B.A., Roosevelt U., Chgo., 1966; Ph.D., U. Md., College Park, 1974. Rsch. asst. Md. Constl. Conv., Annapolis, 1967-68; lectr. in history U. Md., College Park, 1968-72; co-editor The Booker T. Washington Papers, 14 vols., 1972-83; pres. Instructional Resources Corp., Lanham, Md., 1976-83; pres. Rsch. Materials Corp., College Park, 1982-83, dir., 1982-85; historian, dir. Office for Bicentennial, U.S. Ho. of Reps., Washington, 1983-89, Office of Historian, U.S. Ho. of Reps., Washington, 1989-95; mem. bd. editorial advisers Md. Historian, College Park, 1971—. Author: A Talent for Detail: The Photographs of Miss Frances Benjamin Johnston 1889-1910, 1974; coeditor: A Guide to Manuscripts in the Presidential Libraries, 1985; editor: Booker T. Washington in Perspective: The Essays of Louis R. Harlan, 1988. Ford Found. fellow, 1970; recipient Philip M. Hamer award Soc. Am. Archivists, 1979. Mem. Nat. Coun. Pub. History, Assn. for Documentary Editing (pres. 1983-84), Orgn. Am. Historians, So. Hist. Assn., Soc. History in Fed. Govt. Avocations: photography; astronomy.

SMOCK, TIMOTHY ROBERT, lawyer; b. Richmond, Ind., June 24, 1951; s. Robert Martin and Thelma Elizabeth (Cozad) S.; m. Martha Caroline Middleton, Apr. 4, 1992; children: Andrew Zoller, Alison Pierce. BA, Wittenberg U., 1973; JD cum laude, Ind. U., 1977. Bar: Ind. 1977, Ariz. 1979, U.S. Dist. Ct. (so. dist.) Ind. 1977, U.S. Dist. Ct. Ariz. 1979, U.S. Ct. Apeals (7th cir.) 1977, U.S. Ct. Appeals (9th cir.) 1979. Jud. clk. Ct. of Appeals of Ind., Indpls., 1977-79; assoc. Lewis and Roca, Phoenix, 1979-82; assoc./shareholder Gallagher & Kennedy, Phoenix, 1982-89; ptnr. Scult, French, Zwillinger & Smock, Phoenix, 1989-94, Smock and Weinberger, Phoenix, 1994—; judge, pro tempore Maricopa County Superior Ct., Phoenix, 1989—; faculty State Bar Course on Professionalism, Ariz. Supreme Ct./State Bar, Phoenix, 1992—; speaker, Continuing Legal Edn., Maricopa County and Ariz. State Bar, 1988—. Mem. ABA, Ariz. Bar Assn., Maricopa Bar Assn., Def. Rsch. Inst. Office: Smock and Weinberger 2700 N Central Ave # 1125 Phoenix AZ 85004

SMOKER, ROY ELLIS, military officer; b. Richmond, Ind., Dec. 7, 1943; s. Vernon Willard and Emma May (Creager) S.; m. Linda Carol Kensinger, Sept. 7, 1969; children: Cheryl Lynn, Deborah June. BA in Econs. and Math., Blackburn Coll., 1965; MA in Econs., U. N.D., 1967; PhD, U. Mo., 1984. Commd. 2d lt. USAF, 1971, advanced through grades to col., 1992, chief rsch. integration Office Productivity and Rsch., 1980-82, sr. mil. estate program analyst Office Sec. Def., 1982-84, sr. logistics analyst, 1984-85, dep. dir., dir. program control Milstar Joint Program Office, 1985-89, chief econ. analysis asst. sec. USAF for fin. mgmt., 1989-90, chief space and strategic def., 1990-91; dir. bus. ops. Title Sys. Program Office Titan Sys. Program Office, 1991-93; comptroller Arnold (Tenn.) Engrng. Devel. Ctr., 1993—. Fin. advisor Alzheimer's Assn., Tullahoma, Tenn., 1993—; chmn. bd. trustees 1st United Meth. Ch., Huntington Beach, Calif., 1987-89. Decorated Joint Svc. Achievement medals, Air Orgnl. Excellence award, and numerous others. Mem. Mo. U. Alumni Assn., Am. Soc. Mil. Comptrollers, Franklin County C. of C. (bd. dirs.).

SMOLANSKY, OLES M., humanities educator; b. Ukraine, USSR, May 2, 1930; came to U.S. 1950; s. Mykola S. and Irene (Plinto) S.; m. Bettie Moretz, Dec. 29, 1966; chidlren: Alexandra, Nicholas. BA, NYU, 1953; MA, Columbia U., 1955, PhD, 1959. Instr. UCLA, 1960-62; asst. prof. Lehigh U., Bethlehem, Pa., 1963-66, assoc. prof., 1966-70, prof., 1970-85, univ. prof., 1985—. Author: The Soviet Union and the Arab East Under Khrushchev, 1974, The USSR and Iraq: The Soviet Quest for Influence, 1991; co-editor: Russia and America: From Rivalry to Reconciliation, 1993, Regional Power Rivalries in the New Eurasia: Russia, Turkey, and Iran, 1995; contbr. articles to profl. jours. Recipient joint fellowship, Rockefeller Found. and Ford Found., N.Y.C., 1962-63, sr. research joint fellowship, Research Inst. on Communist Affairs and Middle East Inst., Columbia U., N.Y.C., 1972-73, research fellowship, Ford Found., N.Y.C., 1980-81. Mem. Internat. Studies Assn., Am. Assn. for Advancement of Slavic Studies (Marshall Shulman award 1992), Middle East Studies Assn., Mid. East Inst. Democrat. Greek-Orthodox. Avocations: music, sports. Home: 3665 Walt Whitman Ln Bethlehem PA 18017-1553 Office: Lehigh U Dept Internat Rels Bethlehem PA 18015

SMOLAR, EDWARD NELSON, physician, consultant; b. Bklyn., Sept. 26, 1943; s. Harry and Diane (Orans) S.; m. Sharon Elaine Wechsler, June 24, 1973; children: Todd Devon, Gregory Fielding. BS in Biol. Scis. with honors, Union Coll., 1964; MD, Albert Einstein Coll. of Medicine, 1968; MBA with honors, Nova U., 1985, MS, 1990. Diplomate Am. Bd. Internal Medicine, Am. Bd. Endocrinology and Metabolism, Am. Bd. Geriatric Medicine, Nat. Bd. Med. Examiners; CLU, ChFC, CFP. Asst. instr. of medicine SUNY, Bklyn., 1973-75; clin. instr. of medicine N.Y. Med. Coll., 1974-79; physician pvt. practice, N.Y., 1975-80; asst. prof. of clin. medicine N.Y. Med. Coll., 1979-80; pvt. practice N.Y.C., 1975-80, Pompano Beach, 1980-84, Ft. Lauderdale, Fla., 1984—; clin. asst. prof. medicine U. Miami, Fla., 1982-89; adj. faculty Friedt Sch. Bus., Nova U., Ft. Lauderdale, Fla., 1987-88;. cons. Profl. Fin. Cons. Palm Beach, Inc., Boca Raton, Fla., 1988—. Contbr. articles to med. jours. Pres. Am. Diabetes Assn., 1980-81, bd. dirs., 1987—; mem. adv. bd. Hospice, Inc., 1985—. Surgeon USPHS, 1968-71, inactive res., 1971—. Fellow ACP, Am. Coll. Angiology, Am. Coll. Endocrinology, N.Y. Acad. Medicine (life), Royal Soc. Health, Royal Soc. Medicine; mem. Am. Acad. Polit. and Social Sci., Endocrine Soc., Am. Acad. Polit. Sci. (life), Assn. Mil. Surgeons U.S. (life), U.S. Naval Inst. (life), Am. Soc. CLUs and ChFCs. Republican. Jewish. Avocations: antique collecting, gourmet food, jazz music, history and nostalgia, hiking. Office: 5601 N Dixie Hwy Fort Lauderdale FL 33334-4148

SMOLENSKY, EUGENE, economics educator; b. Bklyn., Mar. 4, 1932; s. Abraham and Jennie (Miller) S.; m. Natalie Joan Rabinowitz, Aug. 16, 1952; children: Paul, Beth. B.A., Bklyn. Coll., 1952; M.A., Am. U., 1956; Ph.D., U. Pa., 1961. Prof. econs. U. Wis., Madison, 1968-88, chmn. dept., 1978-80, 86-88; dir. Inst. for Research on Poverty, U. Wis., 1980-83; dean Grad. Sch. Pub. Policy U. Calif., Berkeley, 1988—. Author: Public Expenditures, Taxation and the Distribution of Income: The U.S., 1950, 61, 70, 77. Mem. Nat. Acad. Pub. Adminstrn., 1994; mem. com. on child devel. rsch. and pub. policy NAS, Washington, 1982-87, mem. com. on status of women in labor market, 1985-87. With USN, 1952-56. Mem. Am. Econs. Assn. Democrat. Jewish. Avocation: collecting old master etchings and lithographs. Home: 669 Woodmont Ave Berkeley CA 94708-1233 Office: U Calif Dept Pub Policy 2607 Hearst Ave Berkeley CA 94709-1005

SMOLIN, RONALD PHILIP, publisher; b. Phila., Aug. 12, 1941; s. Harry and Frances (Gordon) S. B.A., Pa. State U., 1963. Staff writer Prudential Ins. Co., Newark, 1964-65; pub. info. officer Newark War on Proverty program, 1965-66; dir. publs. N.Y.C. Human Resources Adminstrn., 1966-75; chmn. Beekman Pubs., Inc., N.Y.C., 1973-77; pres. Internat. Ideas Inc., N.Y.C., 1977-85, Am. Investor Info. Services Inc., 1983-89, Trans-Atlantic Publs. Inc., 1985—, Coronet Books Inc., 1986—; pres. Premium PET Kitchen Inc., 1992-95. Address: Coronet Books Inc 311 Bainbridge St Philadelphia PA 19147-1543

SMOLINSKI, EDWARD ALBERT, holding company executive, lawyer, accountant, deacon; b. N.Y.C., Jan. 6, 1928; s. Albert John and Adele (Weber) S.; m. Joan E. Winslow, Nov. 12, 1955; children: Albert, Edward, Linda, Donna. B.S. in Acctg., L.I. U., 1948; M.B.A., NYU, 1950, J.D., 1956. Bar: N.Y. 1957; C.P.A., N.Y.; ordained deacon Roman Cath. Ch., 1977. Acct. various cert. pub. acctg. firms. N.Y.C., 1948-53; acctg. supr. Curtiss Wright Co., Woodridge, N.J., 1953-60; mem. treasury staff Sperry-Rand Corp., Great Neck, N.Y., 1960-62; corp. controller Fairchild Camera and Instrument Co., Syosset, N.Y., 1968-69; v.p., treas., chief fin. officer Grow Group, Inc., N.Y.C., 1969-89; asst. treas./sec. United Indsl. Corp., N.Y.C., 1989—; adj. asst. prof. Hunter Coll., 1989. Bd. dirs. Long Island U.-Bus. Game, N.Y.C., 1977-83, NYU Mgmt. Decision Lab., 1983-88; deacon Diocese of Bklyn., Roman Cath. Ch., 1977—. Mem. AICPA (com. on nat. def. 1963), N.Y. Bar, Fin. Execs. Inst. Roman Catholic. Lodge: Elks. Home: 70-19 Juno St Forest Hills NY 11375-5839 Office: United Indsl Corp 18 E 48th St New York NY 10017-1014

SMOLKER, GARY STEVEN, lawyer; b. L.A., Nov. 5, 1945; s. Paul and Shayndy Charolette (Sirott) S.; m. Alice Graham; children: Terra, Judy, Leah. BS, U. Calif.-Berkeley, 1967; MS, Cornell U., 1968; JD cum laude, Loyola U., L.A., 1973. Bar: Calif. 1973, U.S. Dist. Ct. (cen. dist.) Calif. 1973, U.S. Tax Ct. 1973, U.S. Ct. Appeals (9th cir.) 1973, U.S. Supreme Ct. 1978, U.S. Dist. Ct. (so., ea. and no. dists.) Calif. 1981. Guest researcher Lawrence Radiation Lab., U. Calif., 1967; teaching fellow Sch. Chem. Engring., Cornell U.; mem. tech. staff Hughes Aircraft Co., Culver City, Calif., 1968-70; in advanced mktg. and tech. TRW, Redondo Beach, Calif., 1970-72; sole practice, Beverly Hills, Calif., 1973-89, L.A., 1989—; guest lectr. UCLA Extension, 1973-74, Loyola U. Law Sch., 1979; speaker, panelist in field; adv. Loyola U. Law Sch., 1973—. Contbr. articles to profl. jours.; inventor self-destruct aluminum tungstic oxide films, electrolytic anticompromise process. Mem. Nat. Assn. Real Estate Editors, Calif. State Bar Assn., L.A. County Bar Assn., Beverly Hills Bar Assn. (sr. editor jour. 1978-79, contbg. editor jour. 1980-82, 86-90, editor-in-chief 1984-86, pub. Smolker Letter 1985—). Jewish. Lodge: B'nai B'rith (anti-defamation league). Office: 5777 W Century Blvd Ste 1255 Los Angeles CA 90045-5696

SMOLLA, RODNEY ALAN, lawyer, educator; b. Pueblo, Colo., Mar. 13, 1953; s. Richard Paul and Harriet (Waskowiak) S.; m. Linda A. Malone, Apr. 13, 1979. BA, Yale U., 1975; JD, Duke U., 1978. Bar: Ill. 1979, U.S. Supreme Ct. 1987. Law clk. to presiding judge U.S. Ct. Appeals, Jackson, Miss., 1978-79; assoc. Mayer, Brown & Pratt, Chgo., 1979-80; asst. prof. De Paul U. Sch. Law, Chgo., 1980-81, U. Ill. Coll. Law, 1981-83; prof. U. Ark. Sch. Law, 1983-87; vis. prof. U. Denver Coll. Law, 1987-88; Arthur B. Hanson prof. constl. law Coll. of William and Mary, Williamsburg, Va., 1988—, dir. Inst. Bill of Rights Law, 1988—. Author: Suing the Press: Libel, The Media & Power, 1986 (cert. of merit ABA 1987), Law of Defamation, 1986, Jerry Falwell V. Larry Flynt: The First Amendment on Trial, 1988; (with Banks and Braveman) Constitutional Law: Structure and Rights in Our Federal System, 1991, Free Speech in an Open Society, 1992 (William O. Douglas award 1993), Smolla and Nimmer on Freedom of Speech, 1994, Federal Civil Rights Acts, 1994; editor: A Year in the Life of the Supreme Court, 1995. Fellow, cons. Annenberg Washington Program in Communications, 1987—; project dir. Annenberg Libel Reform Task Force, 1988-89; reporter Bill of Rights Adv. Com. to the Commn. on the Bicentennial of U.S. Constitution, 1989—. Recipient Disting. Prof. of Yr. award U. Ark., 1986. Mem. ABA, Ill. Bar Assn., AAUP (mem. litigation com. 1988—). Home: 119 Richneck Rd Williamsburg VA 23185-3245 Office: William and Mary Sch Law Inst Bill Of Law Williamsburg VA 23187

SMOLTZ, JOHN ANDREW, professional baseball player; b. Warren, Mich., May 15, 1967. With Detroit Tigers, 1985-87; pitcher Atlanta Braves, 1987—; player Nat. League All-Star Game, 1989, 92, 93, 96. Leader in strikeouts in Nat. League, 1992. Office: Atlanta Braves PO Box 4064 Atlanta GA 30302*

SMOOK, MALCOLM ANDREW, chemist, chemical company executive; b. Seattle, Aug. 22, 1924; s. Joseph Murray and Bonnie (Hanson) S.; m. Mary Louise Nominee, Dec. 19, 1945; children—Frances Lynn, Valerie Dale. B.S., U. Calif., Berkeley, 1945; Ph.D. in Organic Chemistry, Ohio State U., 1949. With E. I. duPont de Nemours & Co., Wilmington, Del., 1949—; research supr. E. I. duPont de Nemours & Co., 1952-53, div. head, 1953-57, asst. lab. dir., 1957-60, lab. dir., 1960-63, asst. research dir., 1963-75, gen. lab. dir., 1975-80, mgr. patents and regulatory affairs, 1980-84; cons. Malcolm A. Smook, Inc., 1985—; mem. adv. com. NASA, 1971-76. Contbr. articles to profl. jours. Served to lt. (j.g.) USN, 1943-46. Socony Vacuum fellow, 1948-49. Mem. Am. Chem. Soc., Sigma Xi. Patentee in field (6). Home and Office: 59 Rockford Rd Wilmington DE 19806-1003

SMOOT, E. PHILIP, chemicals executive; b. 1939. Graduate, Long Beach State Coll., 1959. With Lee Smith & Co., Santa Rosa, Calif., 1964-66; v.p. Bell Industries, Inc., Santa Rosa, Calif., 1966-73; with Cirtel, Inc., Irvine, Calif., 1973-74, Electro-Etched Circuits, L.A., 1974-77, Gulton Piezo Co., L.A., 1977-70, Oak Industries, Inc., San Diego, 1979-81; with Park Electrochemical Corp., New Hyde Park, N.Y., 1981—, now exec. v.p.; bd. dirs. New Eng. Laminates Co., Inc., Walden, N.Y. With USAF, 1959-64. Office: Park Electrochem Corp 5 Dakota Dr New Hyde Park NY 11042-1109*

SMOOT, GEORGE FITZGERALD, III, astrophysicist; b. Yukon, Fla., Feb. 20, 1945. BS in math., BS in physics, MIT, 1966, Ph.D. in physics, 1970. Rsch. physicist MIT, 1970; rsch. physicist Univ. Calif., Berkeley, Calif., 1971—, Lawrence Berkeley Lab., 1974—; prof. physics U. Calif., Berkeley, 1993—; team leader, differential microwave radiometer experiment, COBE (Cosmic Background Explorer) satellite. Author: (with Keay Davidson) Wrinkles in Time, 1993. Recipient Space/Missiles Laurels award Aviation Week & Space Technology, 1992, Lawrence Mem. award US Dept of Energy, 1994. Mem. Internat. Astron. Union, Am. Phys. Soc., Am. Astron. Soc., Sigma Xi. Office: Bldg 50-205 LBNL Berkeley CA 94720

SMOOT, HAZEL LAMPKIN, retired piano teacher, poet; b. Kamiah, Idaho, Oct. 17, 1916; d. Albert Chuning and Cora Benson (Buckland) Weaver; m. Daniel Joseph Smoot, Feb. 18, 1939 (div. 1960); children: Daniel Jerome, David Reed. AA, Sacramento City Coll., 1937; student, Linfield Coll., 1938. Contbr. poetry to anthologies published by World of Poetry, also to Vantage Press and The Golden Treasury of Great Poems, Great American Poetry Anthology. Scholar Linfield Coll.; recipient Golden Poetry awards World of Poetry, 1987, 88, 89, Best Poems of 1966 award Nat. Libr. of Poetry, A Sea of Treasures award Nat. Libr. of Poetry. Avocations: poetry, walking, reading, music, singing.

SMOOT, JOSEPH GRADY, university administrator; b. Winter Haven, Fla., May 7, 1932; s. Robert Malcolm and Vera (Eaton) S.; m. Florence Rozell, May 30, 1955 (dec.); m. Irma Jean Kopitzke, June 4, 1959; 1 child, Andrew Christopher. BA, So. Coll., 1955; MA, U. Ky., 1958, PhD, 1964. Tchr., Ky. Secondary Schs., 1955-57; from instr. to assoc. prof. history Columbia Union Coll., Takoma Park, Md., 1960-68, acad. dean, 1965-68; prof. history Andrews U., Berrien Springs, Mich., 1968-84, dean Sch. Grad. Studies, 1968-69, v.p. acad. adminstrn., 1969-76, pres., 1976-84; v.p. for devel. Pittsburg State U., Kans., 1984—; exec. dir. Pitts. State U. Found., 1985—; bd. dirs. 1st State Bank and Trust Co., Pitts., 1994—; founder Pitts. State U. Radio Sta.-KRPS-FM, 1988; commr. North Cen. Assn., 1987-91, cons., evaluator, 1978—; cons. internat. edn; trustee Loma Linda U., 1976-84, U. Ea. Africa, Baraton, Kenya, 1979-84, Hindsdale Hosp., Ill., 1973-84; chmn., bd. trustees Andrews Broadcasting Corp., 1976-84; bd. dirs. Internat. U. Thailand Found., 1987-95, trustee, 1994-95. Contbr. articles to profl. jours; editor: Spottiswoode Soc. Record, 1990—. Active Pitts. Area Festival Assn., 1984-86, bd. dirs. Pitts. United Way, 1987-92, Pitts. C. of C. Found., 1990-93; bd. advisors Pitts. Salvation Army, 1987-92, vice-chmn., 1990-91, chmn., 1991-92; bd. trustees Mt. Carmel Med. Ctr. Found., 1991-95; bd. dirs. S.E. Kans. Symphony Orch., 1995—. Recipient Disting. Pres. award Mich. Coll. Found., 1984. Mem. Inst. Early Am. History and Culture (assoc.), Am. Hist. Assn., So. Hist. Assn., Orgn. Am. Historians, Soc. for Historians of Early Am. Rep., Soc. History of Authorship, Reading & Pub., Phi Alpha Theta. Club: Crestwood Country. Lodge: Rotary (dist. chmn. scholarship com. 1986-88, Paul Harris Fellow) Home: 1809 Heritage Rd Pittsburg KS 66762-3556 Office: Office of V.P. for Development Pittsburg State U Pittsburg KS 66762

SMOOT, LEON DOUGLAS, chemical engineering educator, research director, former university dean; b. Provo, Utah, July 26, 1934; s. Douglas Parley and Jennie (Hallam) S.; m. Marian Bird, Sept. 7, 1953; children: Analee, LaCinda, Michelle, Melinda Lee. BS, Brigham Young U., 1956, B in Engring. Sci., 1957; MS, U. Wash., 1958, PhD, 1960. Registered profl. engr., Utah. Engr. Boeing Corp., Seattle, 1956; teaching and research asst. Brigham Young U., 1954-57; engr. Phillips Petroleum Corp., Arco, Idaho, 1957; engr., cons. Hercules Powder Co., Bacchus, Utah, 1961-63; asst. prof. Brigham Young U., 1960-63; engr. Lockheed Propulsion, Redlands, Calif., 1963-67; vis. asst. prof. Calif. Inst. Tech., 1966-67; asso. prof. to prof. Brigham Young U., 1967—, chmn. dept. chem. engring., 1970-77, dean Coll. Engring. and Tech., 1977-94, dean emeritus, 1994—; dir. Advanced Combustion Engring. Rsch. Ctr., 1986—; expert witness on combustion and explosions; dir. Advanced Combustion Engring. Research Ctr. (NSF), 1986—; cons. Hercules, Thiokol, Lockheed, Teledyne, Atlantic Research Corp., Raytheon, Redd and Redd, Billings Energy, Ford, Bacon & Davis, Jaycor, Intel Com Radiation Tech., Phys. Dynamics, Nat. Soc. Propellants and Explosives, France, DFVLR, West Germany, Martin Marietta, Honeywell, Phillips Petroleum Co., Exxon, Nat. Bur. Standards, Eyring Research Inst., Systems, Sci. and Software., Los Alamos Nat. Lab., others. Author 5 books on coal combustion; contbr. over 200 articles and tech. jours. Mem. adv. coun. U.S. Office of Tech. Assessment. Mem. AIChE, Am. Soc. Engring. Edn., Combustion Inst., Rsch. Soc. Am., Sigma Xi, Tau Beta Pi, Phi Lambda Epsilon. Republican. Mem. LDS Ch. Office: Brigham Young U Advanced Combustion Engring Rsch Ctr 45 Crabtree Tech Bldg Provo UT 84602

SMOOT, OLIVER REED, JR., lawyer, trade association executive; b. San Antonio, Aug. 24, 1940; s. Oliver Reed and Angie Frances (Watters) S.; m. Sandra Lee Curry, July 25, 1964; children: Stephen Reed, Sheryl Anne. BS, MIT, 1962; JD, Georgetown U., 1966. Bar: D.C. 1966, Va. 1967. Computer systems mgr. Inst. for Def. Analyses, Arlington, Va., 1962-69; program mgr., v.p., then exec. v.p. and treas. Computer and Bus. Equipment Mfrs. Assn., Washington, 1969—. Author: (with others) Computers and the Law, 3d edit., 1981; chpt. editor: Toward a Law of Global Communications Networks, 1986. Bd. dirs. Am. Nat. Standards Inst. Mem. ABA (chmn. sci. and tech. sect. 1989-90), Computer Law Assn. (pres. 1990-91), Assn. for Computing Machinery. Methodist. Avocations: alpine skiing, gardening. Office: Computer & Bus Equip Mfrs Assn 1250 I St Ste 200 Washington DC 20005

SMOOT, SKIPI LUNDQUIST, psychologist; b. Aberdeen, Wash., Apr. 10, 1934; d. Warren Duncan and Miriam Stephen (Bishop) Dobbins; m. Harold Richard Lundquist, June 2, 1951 (div. Mar. 1973); children: Kurt Richard, Mark David, Ted Douglas, Blake Donald; m. Edward Lee Smoot, June 14, 1975. BA in Psychology, Coll. of William and Mary, 1978; MA, Pepperdine U., 1980; PhD, Calif. Sch. of Profl. Psychology, San Diego, 1985. Lic. clin. psychologist, Calif.; lic. marriage and family therapist, Calif. Owner, operator McDonald's Restaurants, San Pedro and Torrance, Calif., 1965-76, Williamsburg, Va., 1965-76; psychotherapist Coll. Hosp., Cerritos, Calif., 1979-81, Orange County Child Guidance, Laguna Hills, Calif., 1981-82; psychotherapist Calif. State Police, Costa Mesa, 1982-83, Anaheim, 1983-84; psychologist Orange County Mental Health, Santa Ana, Calif., 1984-85, Psychol. Ctr., Orange and El Toro, Calif., 1985-91; clin. dir. Career Ambitions, Irvine and Laguna Hills, 1991-94, Psychol. Decisions, Irvine-Laguna Hills, Calif., 1991-94; psychol. cons. seminars and workshops for bus., Irvine and Laguna Hills, 1991-94. Mem. APA, Calif. Psychol. Assn., Calif. Assn. Marriage and Family Therapists. Democrat. Avocations: Music, travel, rsch. Office: Psychol Decisions Career Ambitions Unltd 23161 Lake Ctr Dr Ste 124 Lake Forest CA 92630

SMOOT, WENDELL MCMEANS, JR., investment counselor; b. Salt Lake City, Jan. 15, 1921; s. Wendell M. and Rebecca (Clawson) S.; m. Barbara Davis, June 24, 1942; children: Wendell M. III, Margaret, David, John, Mary. B.A., U. Utah, 1942. Gen. ptnr. J.A. Hogle & Co., Salt Lake City, 1945-63, Goodbody & Co., N.Y.C., 1963-70; chmn. Smoot, Miller, Cheney & Co., Salt Lake City, 1971—. Pres. Great Salt Lake council Boy Scouts Am., 1968-70; chmn. Utah State Pioneer Meml. Theatre, 1978-79; pres. Mormon Tabernacle Choir. Served to capt., U.S. Army, 1942-45; ETO. Mem. Fin. Analysts Soc. Republican. Mem. Ch. of Jesus Christ of Latter Day Saints. Club: The Country. Lodge: Rotary.

SMORAL, VINCENT J., electrical engineer; b. Syracuse, N.Y., May 13, 1946; s. Anthony Vincent and Stephanie (Koutin) S.; m. Theresa W. Gut, Aug. 5, 1967; children: Jennifer, Laura, Anne. BSEE, Syracuse U., 1967. Jr. engr. Fed. Systems Div. IBM, Owego, N.Y., 1967-68; adv. engr. logic design IBM, Owego, 1968-80, sr. engr./systems, 1980-90, sr. engr./program mgr., 1990-93; sr. engr. Lockheed Martin Fed. Systems Co., Owego, 1994—. Designer 688 Class Sonar, An/UYS-1 Sigmal Processor, AWACS Computer, 3838 Array Processor, 1968-80; mgr. AN/UYK-43 Computer, AWACS Computer, Rugged Processor, 1990-93; patentee in field. Fellow AIAA (assoc.; mem. nat. computer systems tech. com. 1990-95); mem. IEEE. Democrat. Roman Catholic. Avocations: swimming, sailing, fishing, skiing. Home: 812 Skylane Terr Endwell NY 13760 Office: Lockheed Martin-Fed Systems 1801 State Rte 17C Owego NY 13827

SMOTHERMON, PEGGI STERLING, middle school educator; b. Dallas, Nov. 11, 1948; d. Kiel Sterling and Ann C. (Wolfe) Sterling; m. William C. Smothermon Jr., June 20, 1981; children: Kirsten, Melinda, William III. BA, So. Meth. U., Dallas, 1973; MLA, So. Meth. U., 1978. Tchr. Richardson (Tex.) Ind. Sch. Dist., 1973-90, Coppell (Tex.) Ind. Sch. Dist., 1990-96. J.J. Pearce scholar. Mem. Nat. Coun. Tchrs. Math., NSTA, NEA (faculty rep., membership chmn., sec.), Tex. Tchrs. Assn., Assn. Coppell Educators, Tex. Computer Edn. Assn., Tex. Coun. Tchrs. Math., Kappa Delta Pi. Home: 408 Greenridge Dr Coppell TX 75019-5714

SMOTHERS, DICK, actor, singer; b. Nov. 20, 1939; s. Thomas B. and Ruth Smothers; children: Susan, Dick, Steven, Andrew, Sara, Remick. Student, San Jose State Coll. Night club appearances in Lake Tahoe, Las Vegas and various venues in U.S.; co-star half-hour situation comedy TV Series Smothers Bros. Show, 1965-66, TV show Smothers Bros. Comedy Hour, 1967-69, 70, weekly variety hour The Smothers Bros. Show, NBC-TV, 1975; appeared on Broadway in I Love My Wife, 1978; appeared in TV movie Terror at Alcatraz, 1982, feature film Casino, 1995; starred in Smothers Bros. Spl., 1988.

SMOTHERS, TOM, actor, singer; b. Feb. 2, 1937; s. Thomas B. and Ruth Smothers; children: Tom, Bo, Riley Rose; m. Marcy Carriker, Sept. 9, 1990. Student, San Jose State Coll. owner winery, Kenwood, Calif. Nightclub appearances in Lake Tahoe, Las Vegas, Nev., and various venues in U.S.; co-star TV situation comedy Smothers Brothers Show, 1965-66, Smothers Brothers Comedy Hour, CBS-TV, 1967-69, 70, weekly variety show The Smothers Brothers Show, NBC-TV, 1975; starred in films The Silver Bears, Get To Know Your Rabbit, A Pleasure Doing Business, Another Nice Mess, Serial, There Goes the Bride, Pandemonium, Speed Zone; starred on Broadway in I Love My Wife, 1978-79; appeared in TV movie Terror at Alcatraz, 1982; starred in Smothers Brothers Spl. and Series, 1988-89. Office: Knave Prodns 8489 W 3rd St Los Angeles CA 90048-4147

SMOTHERS, WILLIAM EDGAR, JR., geophysical exploration company executive; b. Shawnee, Okla., July 9, 1928; s. William Edgar and Lena Rivers (Randolph) S.; m. Marilyn Myrtle Cales, Sept. 6, 1952; children: Bill, Susan. BS in Commerce, Okla. State U., 1950. Staff acct. Amoco Prodn. Co., Tulsa, 1953-56; chief internal auditor Seismography Svc. Corp., Tulsa, 1956-63, mgr. tax and auditing, 1964-77, v.p., treas., 1978—. Vice chmn. Tulsa United Way Drive, 1976, chmn., 1977. Capt. U.S. Army, 1951-53. Mem. Am. Mgmt. Assn., Tax Execs. Inst., Nat. Assn. Accts., Systems Mgmt. Assn., Petroleum Club, Tulsa Country Club. Democrat. Presbyterian. Home: 9103 E 38th Pl Tulsa OK 74145-3437 Office: Seismograph Svc Corp PO Box 1590 Tulsa OK 74102

SMOTRICH, DAVID ISADORE, architect; b. Norwich, Conn., Oct. 6, 1933; s. Max Z. and Ida (Babinsky) S.; m. Bernice D. Strachman, Mar. 25, 1956; children—Ross Lawrence, Maura Faye, Hannah. AB, Harvard U., 1955, MArch, 1960. Mem. master planning team Town of Arad, State of Israel, 1961-62; assoc. Platt Assocs. (architects), N.Y.C., 1963-65; gen. partner Smotrich & Platt (architects), N.Y.C., 1965-74, Smotrich Platt & Buttrick, 1975-76, Smotrich & Platt, 1976-85, David Smotrich & Ptnrs., 1985—; Cons. to Jerusalem Master Plan Office, Israel Ministry of Housing, 1967. Mem. planning bd. Town of New Castle, N.Y., 1974-81; mem. exec. bd. Road Rev. League, Bedford, N.Y., 1966-70. Served with AUS, 1955-57. Recipient Bard award, 1969, 85; Archtl. Record award, 1971, 73, 74, 75, 78; Design award HUD, 1980. Mem. AIA (Nat. Honor award 1969, N.Y. State Honor awards 1984, 94, Cmty. Design awards 1991, 93, AIA Coll. of Fellows 1993), Assn. Engrs. and Archs. in Israel, Phi Beta Kappa, Harvard Club (N.Y.C.). Home: 7 Mayberry Close Chappaqua NY 10514-1113 Office: David Smotrich & Ptnrs 443 Park Ave S New York NY 10016

SMOUSE, H(ERVEY) RUSSELL, lawyer; b. Oakland, Md., Aug. 13, 1932; s. Hervey Reed and Vernie (Rush) S.; m. Creta M. Staley, June 15, 1955; children: Kristin Anne, Randall Forsyth, Gregory Russell. AB, Princeton U., 1955; LLB, U. Md., 1958. Bar: Md. 1958, U.S. Tax Ct. 1979, U.S. Ct. Appeals (4th cir.) 1960, U.S. Supreme Ct. 1974. Atty., Atty. Gen.'s Honors Program, Dept. Justice, Washington, 1958-60, asst. U.S. atty. Dist. Md., 1960-62; assoc. Pierson and Pierson, Balt., 1962-64; atty. B.&O. R.R., Balt., 1964-66; mem. Pierson and Pierson, 1966-69; mem. Clapp, Somerville, Black & Honemann, Balt., 1969-74; Law Offices H. Russell Smouse, 1974-81; mem. Melnicove, Kaufman, Weiner & Smouse, P.A., Balt., 1981-89, Whiteford, Taylor & Preston, Balt., 1989-93, chair, litigation dept., 1989-93; head gen. litigation Law Offices Peter G. Angelos, 1993—; v.p. Legal Aid Bur. Balt. City, 1972-73; bd. dirs. Md. Legal Svcs. Corp., 1987—. Fellow Am. Coll. Trial Lawyers; mem. ABA, Md. State Bar Assn. (gov. 1981-83), Bar Assn. Balt. City (chmn. grievance com. 1969-70, chmn. judiciary com. and nominating com. 1980, mem. exec. com. 1969-70, 80, chmn. exec. com. lawyers' com. for ind. judiciary 1989—), Nat. Assn. R.R. Trial Counsel (exec. com., v.p. ea. region 1986-92). Republican. Presbyterian. Office: 210 W Pennsylvania Ave Ste 515 Baltimore MD 21204-5325

SMUCKER, BARBARA CLAASSEN, former librarian, writer; b. Newton, Kans., Sept. 1, 1915; dual citizen U.S. and Can.; d. Cornelius Walter and Addie (Lander) Claassen; m. Donovan Ebersole Smucker, Jan. 21, 1939; children: Timothy, Thomas, Rebecca. BS, Kans. State U., 1936; postgrad., Rosary Coll., 1963-65; LittD (hon.), U. Waterloo, 1986; DHL (hon.), Bluffton Coll., 1989. English tchr. Harper (Kans.) High Sch., 1937-38; reporter Evening Kansan Republican, Newton, 1939-41; tchr. Ferry Hall Sch., Lake Forest, Ill., 1960-63; children's librarian Kitchener (Ont.) Public Library, 1969-77; reference librarian, head librarian Renison Coll., U. Waterloo, Ont., 1977-82, sr. fellow Renison Coll., 1982—; writer Am. Educator Ency., Lake Bluff, Ill., 1960-63; convocation speaker U. Waterloo, Ont., 1986. Author: Henry's Red Sea, 1955, Cherokee Run, 1957, Wigwam in the City, Susan, 1970, Underground to Canada, 1977, Runaway to Freedom, 1977, Under Jorden Til Canada, 1977, Les Chemins Secrets de la Liberte, 1978, Folge dem Nordstern, 1979, Days of Terror, 1980, June Lilly, 1981, Amish Adventure, 1983, Huida al Canada, 1983, Nubes Negras, 1984, Dagen Van Angst, 1985, White Mist, 1985, Jacob's Little Giant, 1987 (selected as gift to Prince Harry by govt. Ont.), Incredible Jumbo, 1990, (I.O.D.E. award 1991), Race to Freedom, 1994, Selina and The Bear Paw Quilt, 1995, Selina and Shoo-Fly Pie, 1996; (oratorio, libretto) The Abiding Place, 1984, Garth and the Mermaid, 1992; (interpretation) Oxford Companion to Canadian Literature, 1985, Michelle Landsberg's Guide to Children's Books, 1986; illustrator (autobiography) Something About the Author, 1991. Recipient prizes Can. Council, 1980, Ruth Schwartz Found., 1980, Disting. Service award Kans. State U., 1980, Brotherhood award NCCJ, 1980; $2000 Vicki Metcalf prize for outstanding contbn. to Can. children's lit. Can. Authors Assn., 1988, Kitchener award, 1990. Mem. AAUW, Canadian Assn. Univ. Women, Canadian Soc. Children's Authors, Illustrators and Performers, Children's Reading Round Table, Chgo. Home: 20 Pinebrook Dr Bluffton OH 45817-1145

SMUCKLER, RALPH HERBERT, university dean, political science educator; b. Milw., Apr. 10, 1926; s. Robert H. and Celia (Berliand) S.; m. Lillian Zembrosky, July 6, 1946; children: Gary, Sandra, Harold. BA, U. Wis., 1948, MA, 1949, PhD, 1952. Mem. faculty Mich. State U., East Lansing, 1951-93, prof. polit. sci., 1963-93, dean internat. studies and programs, 1968-90, asst. to pres., 1987-91, emeritus prof., dean, 1993—; chief advisor tech. assistance team in Saigon, Mich. State U., 1955-56, 58-59; v.p. Edn. and World Affairs, N.Y.C., 1963-64; rep. Ford Found., Pakistan, 1967-69; dir. U.S. Internat. Sci. and Tech. Coop. Planning Office, Washington, 1978-79; mem. rsch. adv. com. AID, 1972-82, chmn., 1973-82, dep. asst. adminstr., 1991-92. Author: (with Leroy Ferguson) Politics in the Press, 1953, (with George Belknap) Leadership and Participation in Urban Political Affairs, 1956, (with R. Berg) New Challenges New Opportunities: U.S. Cooperation for International Growth and Development in the 1990s, 1988; contbr. articles to profl. jours. Bd. dirs. Midwest Univs. Consortium Internat. Activities, 1965-67, 69-90; trustee Inst. Internat. Edn., 1974-91; mem. adv. com. Kellogg Found. Nat. Fellowship Program, 1980-84; mem. bd. sci. and tech. for internat. devel. Nat. Acad. Sci., 1982-88, chmn., 1984-88; v.p. Mich. UN Assn., 1972-76; State of Mich. chmn. UN Day, 1960. With Inf. AUS, 1944-46. Recipient Disting. Citizen award Steuben Jr. High Sch., Milw., 1965, John Gilbert Winant Humanitarian award Marine City, Mich., 1976; Phi Beta Delta internat. scholar, Outstanding Faculty award, 1990. Mem. Am. Polit. Sci. Assn., Soc. Internat. Devel., Internat. Studies Assn., Assn. Internat. Edn. Adminstrs. (pres. 1986-87), Nat. Assn. State Univs. and Land-Grant Colls. (chmn. internat. acad. affairs com. 1986-90), Nat. Assn. Fgn. Student Affairs (governing bd. 1986, M. Houlihan award 1990), Mich. State Univ. Club, Phi Kappa Phi (named Disting. Mem. 1990). Jewish. Home: 4201 Cathedral Ave NW Apt 814W Washington DC 20016-4965

SMUIN, MICHAEL, choreographer, director, dancer; b. Missoula, Mont., Oct. 13, 1938; m. Paula Tracy; 1 child, Shane. Studied with Christensen Bros.; studied, San Francisco Ballet Sch.; DFA, U. Mont., 1984. Dancer U. Utah Ballet, Salt Lake City, 1955-57; dancer, choreographer, dir. San Francisco Ballet, 1957-62, 73-85; dancer Am. Ballet Theatre, N.Y. State Theatre, N.Y.C., 1967; prin. dancer, choreographer Am. Ballet Theatre, 1969-73; resident choreographer Am. Ballet Theatre, N.Y.C., 1992—; founder, dir. Smuin Ballets/SF, 1994—; worked as free-lance dancer with wife Paula Tracy, ind. choreographer; co-chmn. dance adv. panel Nat. Endowment for the Arts, Washington; mem. U.S. dance study team, People's Republic of China, 1983. Dir., musical stager, choreographer: (with Donald McKayle) Sophisticated Ladies, 1981 (Tony award nomination best direction of musical 1981, Outer Critics Circle award 1981); dir., choreographer: Chaplin, 1983, Shogun, 1990; choreographer: Anything Goes, 1987 (Tony award best choreography 1988, Drama Desk award best choreography 1988), Pulcinella Variations, Private Lives, 1991; staged dance works for Leslie Caron, Mikhail Baryshnikov, Rudolf Nureyev with Am. Ballet Theatre/Paris Opera Ballet, 1986; prodr. for San Francisco Ballet: Cinderella, Romeo and Juliet, The Tempest, A Song for Dead Warriors; dir.: Faustus in Hell, Peter and the Wolf; choreographer: (films) Rumble Fish, 1983, The Cotton Club, 1984, Fletch Lives, 1989, Bram Stoker's Dracula, 1992, So I Married an Axe Murderer, 1993, Angie, 1994, The Fantasticks, 1995; tech. adviser: (film) The Golden Child, 1986; choreographer: (TV) The Tempest, 1981 (Emmy award nomination outstanding achievement in choreography, 1981), A Song for Dead Warriors, 1984 (Emmy award outstanding achievement in choreography 1984), Cinderella, 1985, Romeo and Juliet; dir.: (TV spls.) Jinx, 1985, Voice/Dance: Bobby McFerrin and the Tandy Beal Dance Company, 1987; choreographer: (TV episode) Corridos! Tales of Passion and Revolution, 1987; creator: (TV show) The Omo, 1987; dir., choreographer: (TV spl.) Linda Ronstadt's Canciones de Mi Padre, 1989, Aid and Comfort. Recipient Dance Magazine award, 1983. Office: Smuin Ballets/SF 1314 34th Ave San Francisco CA 94122-1309

SMULYAN, JEFFREY, radio station executive, owner pro baseball team; children: Cari, Bradley. AB in History and Telecommunications, U. So. Calif., 1969, JD, 1972. Prin., owner, chmn. Seattle Mariners; chmn. bd. Emmis Broadcasting Corp., Indpls. Recipient Tree of Life award Jewish Nat. Fund; named Entrepreneur of Yr. Indpls. Bus. Jour., 1986. Mem. ABA, Ind. Bar Assn., Fed. Bar Assn., Communications Bar Assn. Office: Seattle Mariners PO Box 4100 Seattle WA 98104-0100 also: Emmis Broadcasting Corp. 200 S Capitol Ave Indianapolis IN 46225-1023

SMURFIT, MICHAEL WILLIAM JOSEPH, manufacturing company executive; b. 1936. With Jefferson Smurfit Group PLC, Dublin, Ireland, 1961—, pres., from 1966, now chmn., chief exec. officer; pres. Jefferson Smurfit Corp., Alton, Ill., 1979-82, now chief exec. officer, chmn. bd., 1982—. Office: Jefferson Smurfit Corp 8182 Maryland Ave Saint Louis MO 63105-3786*

SMUTNY, JOAN FRANKLIN, academic director, educator; b. Chgo.; d. Eugene and Mabel (Lind) Franklin; m. Herbert Paul Smutny; 1 child, Cheryl Anne. BS, Northwestern U., MA. Tchr., New Trier High Sch., Winnetka, Ill.; mem. faculty, founder, dir. Nat. High Sch. Inst., Northwestern U. Sch. Edn., Chgo.; mem. faculty, founder dir. high sch. workshop in critical thinking and edn., chmn. dept. communications Nat. Coll. Edn., Evanston, Ill., exec. dir. high sch. workshops, 1970-75, founder, dir. Woman Power Through Edn. Seminar, 1969-74, dir. Right to Read seminar in critical reading, 1973-74, seminar gifted high sch. students, 1973, dir. of Gifted Programs for 6, 7 and 8th graders pub. schs., Evanston, 1978-79, 1st-8th graders, Glenview (both Ill.) 1979—; dir. gifted programs Nat.-Louis U., Evanston, 1980-82, dir. Center for Gifted, 1982—; dir. Bright and Talented and Project 1986—, North Shore Country Day Sch., Winnetka, 1982—; dir. Job Creation Project, 1980-82; dir. New Dimensions for Women, 1973, dir. Thinking for Action in Career Edn. project, 1974-77 , dir. Individualized Career Edn. Program, 1976-79, dir. TACE, dir. Humanities Program for Verbally Precocious Youth, 1978-79; co-dir., instr. seminars in critical thinking Ill. Family Svc., 1972-75 . Writer ednl. filmstrips in Lang. arts and Lit. Soc. for Visual Edn., 1970-74 ; mem. speakers bur. Counc. Fgn. Rels., 1968-69 ; mem. adv. com. edn. professions devel. act U.S. Office Edn., 1969—; mem. state team for gifted, Ill. Office Edn., Office of Gifted, Springfield, Ill., 1977; writer, cons. Radiant Ednl. Corp., 1969-71 ; cons. ALA, 1969-71 , cons., workshop leader and speaker in area of gifted edn., 1971—; coord. of career edn. Nat. Coll. Edn., 1976-78, dir. Project 1987—, dir. Summer Wonders, 1986—, Creative Children's Acad., bd. dirs., Worlds of Wisdom and Wonder, 1978—; dir. Future Tchrs. Am. Seminar in Coll. and Career, 1970-72; cons. for research and devel. Ill. Dept. Vocat. Edn., 1973—; cons. in career edn. U.S. Office Edn., 1976—; evaluation cons. DAVTE, IOE, Springfield, Ill., 1977, mem. Leadership Tng. Inst. for Gifted, U.S. Office Edn., 1973-74; dir. workshops for high sch. students; cons., speaker in field; dir. Gifted Young Writer's and Young Writer's confs., 1978, 79; dir. Project '92 The White House Conf. on Children and Youth; mem. adv. bd. Educating Able Learners, 1991—; chmn. bd. dirs. Barbereux Sch., Evanston, 1992—; asst. editor, mem. editl. bd. Understanding Our Gifted, 1994—. Mem. AAUP, Nat. Assn. for Gifted Child (nat. membership chmn. 1991—, co-chmn. schs. and programs, co-editor newsletter early childhood divsn.), Nat. Soc. Arts and Letters (nat. bd., 1st and 3d v.p. Evanston chpt., dir. 1983-92, pres. Evanston chpt. 1990-92), Mortar Bd., Outstanding Educators of Am. 1974, Pi Lambda Theta, Phi Delta Kappa (v.p. Evanston chpt., rsch. chmn. 1990-92). Author: (with others) Job Creation: Creative Materials, Activities and Strategies for the classroom, 1982, A Thoughtful Overview of Gifted Education, 1990, Your Gifted Child - How to Recognize and Develop the Special Talents in Your Child from Birth to Age Seven, 1989, paperback, 1991, Education of the Gifted: The Young Gifted Child: An Anthology, 1990, Potential and Promise: The Young Gifted Child, 1996; contbg. editor Roepper Review, 1994—; asst. editor Understanding a Gift, 1995—; editor, contbr. Maturity in Teaching; writer ednl. filmstrips The Brother's Grimm, How the West Was Won, Mutiny on the Bounty, Dr. Zhivago, Space Odessey 2001, Christmas Around the World; editor Jour. for Gifted, Ill., 1984—, Ill. Coun. Gifted Jour., 1985-93; contbg. editor Roeper Review, 1994—; editor IAGC Jour. for Gifted, 1994—; contbg. editor numerous books in field; contbr. articles to profl. jours. including Chgo. Parent Mag. Reviewer of Programs for Gifted and Talented, U.S. Office of Edn., 1976-78. Home: 633 Forest Ave Wilmette IL 60091-1713 *Commitment to education is defined as contribution. We who are privileged to work in education know that the focus is the educant-the learner. Gifted education is particulalry vital in that it discerns the needs of bright, talented children who have an immense amount to contribute to our country and our world. Gifted children are our country's most neglected resource--and most needed. It is my privilege to work in this area, to work with children, parents and teachers. The community of mankind is neede to support the talent and growth of the gifted. Then we are really contributing to the educant.*

SMYER, MYRNA RUTH, drama educator; b. Albuquerque, June 10, 1946; d. Paul Anthony and Ruth Kelly (Klein) S.; m. Carlton Weaver Canaday, July 5, 1980. BFA, U. N.Mex., 1969; MA, Northwestern U., 1971. Pvt. practice drama instr. Albuquerque, 1974-78; dir. drama Sandia Preparatory Sch., Albuquerque, 1977—, chmn. dept. fine arts, 1980—; dialect coach, dir. Chgo. Acting Ensemble, 1969-71; lectr., performer Albuquerque Pub. Schs. and various civic orgns., Albuquerque, 1974—; writer, dir., performer Arts in the Pks., Albuquerque, 1977-80; performer, crew various indsl. videos, 1981-86; instr. workshops and continuing edn. U. N.Mex. 1977-80. Writer, dir., designer children's plays including May The Best Mammal (Or Whatever) Win, 1977, A Holiday Celebration, 1977, Puppets on Parade, 1978, A Witch's Historical Switches, 1979, Once Upon a Rhyme, 1987— (Outstanding Contbn. Arts in Edn. Bravo award Albuquerque Arts Alliance 1995), Little Red Riding Hood, 1987, Goldilocks and The Three Bears, 1988, Cinderella, 1989, Hansel and Gretel, 1990, Rumpelstiltskin, 1991, The Dancing Princesses, 1992, The Three Pigs, 1994, Sleeping Beauty, 1996; dir. numerous other children and adult plays. Instr., writer, dir. various community theatres including Albuquerque Little Theatre, Corrales Adobe Theatre, Kimo Theatre, Albuquerque Civic Light Opera, Now We Are Theatre; mem. Albuquerque Cable TV Adv. Bd.; mem. task force on the arts for children Albuquerque Little Theatre. Recipient 1st Pl. award for quality in edn. N.Mex. Rsch. and Study Coun., U. N.Mex., 1989-90, Albuquerque Acad. grant (children theatre), 1993, 95, Neighborhood Appreciation award Four Hills, 1993. Mem. Am. Alliance for Theatre and Edn., Theater N.Mex., Albuquerque Arts Alliance. Avocations: travel, reading, hiking, dancing. Office: Sandia Preparatory Sch 532 Osuna Rd NE Albuquerque NM 87113-1031

SMYNTEK, JOHN EUGENE, JR., newspaper editor; b. Buffalo, Aug. 24, 1950; s. John Eugene Sr. and Leona (Kluczynski) S.; m. Barbara Murphy, 1972 (div. Mar. 1980); m. Rebecca Anne Van Dine, 1982 (div. July 1988). BA, U. Detroit, 1972. Asst. instr. Mich. State U., East Lansing, 1981; features editor Free Press, 1985-92; dir. online svcs. and dir. libr. Free Press Plus, Detroit, 1992-95, spl. features & syndicate editor, 1995—; vis. fellow in journalism Duke U., 1988; profl. student publs. advisor U. Detroit Mercy, 1992-94. Recipient Fine Arts Reporting award Detroit Press Club, 1985. Roman Catholic. Office: Detroit Free Press 321 W Lafayette Blvd Detroit MI 48226-2705

SMYRL, WILLIAM HIRAM, chemistry educator; b. Brownfield, Tex., Dec. 12, 1938; s. Garvin H. and Opal Faye (Coor) S.; m. Donna Kay Clayton, Nov. 29, 1964; children: Eliot K., Clifford G. BS in Chemistry, Tex. Tech U., 1961; PhD in Chemistry, U. Calif., Berkeley, 1966. Asst. prof. U. Calif., San Francisco, 1966-68; mem. tech. staff Boeing Sci. Rsch. Lab., Seattle, 1968-72, Sandia Nat. Lab., Albuquerque, 1972-84; prof., dir. corrosion rsch. ctr. U. Minn, Mpls., 1984-96. Contbr. over 100 articles to refereed jours. Mem. AAAS, AIChE, Am. Chem. Soc., Electrochem. Soc. (chair corrosion divsn. 1990-92, H.H. Uhlig award 1995), Sigma Xi (Am. editor Corrosion Sci.). Democrat. Baptist. Office: U Minn Corrosion Rsch Ctr 221 Church St SE Minneapolis MN 55455-0152

SMYSER, ADAM ALBERT, newspaper editor; b. York, Pa., Dec. 18, 1920; s. Adam Milton and Miriam (Stein) S.; m. Elizabeth Harrison Avery, Dec. 25, 1943 (dec. 1983); children: Heidi, Avery; m. Doris H. Prather, Apr. 24, 1984. B.A., Pa. State U., 1941. Rewrite man Pitts. Press, 1941-42; with Honolulu Star-Bull., 1946—, city editor, 1953-60, mng. editor, 1960-65, editor, 1966-75, editor editorial page, 1975-83, contbg. editor, 1983—; mem. Pulitzer Journalism Awards Jury, 1970. Author: Hawaii's Future in the Pacific: Disaster, Backwater or Future State?, 1988, Hawaii as an East-West Bridge, 1990; past freelance writer McGraw-Hill mags. Chmn. temp. commn. on statewide environ. planning, 1973; bd. dirs. Corp. for Community TV; chmn. steering com. Gov.'s Congress on Hawaii's Internat. Role, 1988; mem. community adv. bd. Tokai U. Pacific Ctr.; Lt. USNR, 1942-46, PTO. Recipient Disting. Alumnus award Pa. State U., 1976, Hawaii's Outstanding Journalist award, 1989, Award for Disting. Contbn. to Hawaii Journalism Honolulu Cmty.-Medic Coun., 1994, award for promotion of U.S.-Asia/Pacific rels. Pacific and Asian Affairs Coun., 1994. Mem. Hawaii Econ. Assn., Honolulu Social Sci. Assn., Honolulu Acad. Arts, Am. Soc. Newspaper Editors, Japan-Am. Soc. Hawaii, Honolulu Cmty.-Media Coun., Honolulu Press Club (named to Hall of Fame 1987), Honolulu Rotary. Home: 1052 Iiwi St Honolulu HI 96816-5111 Office: Honolulu Star-Bull 605 Kapiolani Blvd Honolulu HI 96813-5129

SMYTH, ANNE, elementary school educator; b. Oceanside, N.Y., Sept. 28, 1943; d. David Anthony and Filomena Mary (Pascale) Caruso; m. Denis Charles Smyth, apr. 6, 1968; children: Michael David, Carolyn Anne. BS in Edn. and Social Studies, Cabrini Coll., 1965; MS in Spl. Edn., Adelphi U., 1980. Cert. tchr., (life), N.Y. Tchr. Belmnot Elem. Sch., North Babylon, N.Y., 1965-68, Forrest Sherman Elem. Sch., Naples, Italy, 1968-71, Centre Ave. Elem. Sch., E. Rockaway, N.Y., 1971—; supr. Great Books Club, E. Rockaway, 1988—; mem. Ctr. Ave Teacher Adv. Com., E. Rockaway, 1988—. Pub. rels. agt. (vol.) Boy Scouts Am., Troop 163, Rockville Ctr., N.Y., 1988—. Mem. Am. Fedn. Tchrs. Roman Catholic. Avocations: reading, skiing, aerobic dancing, hiking, family activities. Home: 92 Muirfield Rd Rockville Centre NY 11570-2701

SMYTH, BERNARD JOHN, retired newspaper editor; b. Renovo, Pa., Nov. 16, 1915; s. John Bernard and Alice C. (Russell) S.; m. Eva Mae Stone, Dec. 31, 1936; children: Constance, Joe, Pamela, Lisa. Grad., Dickinson Jr. Coll., 1935. Machinist helper Pa. R.R. Renovo Shops, 1936-39; mgr. Smyth Bros., Renovo, 1939-45; editor, pub., owner Renovo Daily Record, 1946-53; owner, editor, pub. Del. State News, Dover, 1953-70; chmn. bd. Independent Newspapers Inc., 1970-85; pres. Valley Newspapers Inc., Tempe, Ariz., 1971-85. Served with AUS, 1944-45. Mem. Soc. Profl. Journalists, Ariz. Newspaper Assn., Sigma Delta Chi. Home: 4200 N Miller Rd Apt 422 Scottsdale AZ 85251-3631

SMYTH, CRAIG HUGH, fine arts educator; b. N.Y.C., July 28, 1915; s. George Hugh and Lucy Salome (Humeston) S.; m. Barbara Linforth, June 24, 1941; children: Alexandra, Edward Linforth (Ned). BA, Princeton U., 1938, MFA, 1941, PhD, 1956; MA (hon.), Harvard U., 1975. Rsch. asst. Nat. Gallery Art, Washington, 1941-42; officer-in-charge, dir. Cen. Art Collecting Point, Munich, 1945-46; lectr. Frick Collection, N.Y.C., 1946-50; asst. prof. Inst. Fine Arts NYU, 1950-53, assoc. prof. Inst. Fine Arts, 1953-57, prof. Inst. Fine Arts, 1957-73, acting dir. Inst. Fine Arts, acting head dept. fine arts Grad. Sch. Arts and Scis., 1951-53, dir. inst., head dept. fine arts Grad. Sch., 1953-73; prof. fine arts Harvard U., 1973-85, prof. emeritus, 1985—; Samuel Kress prof. Ctr. for Advanced Study in Visual Arts Nat. Gallery Art, Washington, 1987-88; dir. Villa I Tatti Harvard U. Ctr. Italian Renaissance Studies, Florence, 1973-85; art historian in residence Am. Acad. in Rome, 1959-60; mem. U.S. Nat. Com. History Art, 1955-85; alt. U.S. mem. Comité Internat. d'Histoire de l'Art, 1970-83, U.S. mem., 1983-85; chmn. adv. com. J. Paul Getty Ctr. History of Art and Humanities, 1982—; mem. architect selection com. J. Paul Getty Trust, 1983-84; mem. organizing com., keynote speaker 400th Anniversary of Uffizi Gallery, 1981-82; vis. scholar Inst. Advanced Study, Princeton, N.J., 1971, mem., 1978, visitor, 1983, 85-86; vis. scholar Bibliotheca Hertziana, Max Planck Soc., Rome, 1972, 73; mem. vis. com. dept. art and archaeology Princeton U., 1956-73, 85-89; mem. adv. com. Villa I Tatti, 1985-92; trustee Hyde Collection, Glens Falls, N.Y., 1985-87, The Burlington mag., 1987—; mem. commn. Ednl. & Cultural Exch. between Italy and U.S., 1979-83. Author: Mannerism and Maniera, 1963, rev. edit. with introduction by E. Cropper, 1992, Bronzino as Draughtsman, 1971, Michelangelo Architetto (with H.M. Millon), 1988,

English edit., 1988, Repatriation of Art from the Collecting Point in Munich After World War II, 1988; editor: Michelangelo Drawings (Nat. Gallery of Art), 1992; editor (with Peter M. Lukehart), contbr.: The Early Years of Art History in the United States, 1994; contbr.: (with H.M. Millon) articles on Michelangelo and St. Peter's to profl. jours. Hon. trustee Met. Mus. Art, N.Y.C., 1968—; trustee Inst. Fine Arts, NYU, 1973—; mem. mayor's com. Piazza Della Signoria, Florence, 1975-78. Lt. USNR, 1942-46. Decorated Chevalier Legion of Honor France, U.S. Army Commendation medal; sr. Fulbright Rsch. fellow, 1949-50. Mem. Am. Acad. Arts and Scis., Am. Philos. Soc., Coll. Art Assn. Am. (bd. dirs. 1953-57, sec. 1956), Accademia Fiorentina delle Arti del Disegno (academician, assoc.), Accademia di San Luca, Harvard Club, Century Assn. (N.Y.C.). Address: PO Box 39 Cresskill NJ 07626-0039

SMYTH, DAVID SHANNON, real estate investor, commercial and retail builder and developer; b. Denver, May 13, 1943; s. William James and Constance Ruth (Sherman) S.; student Regis Coll., 1967-69, USAF Acad., 1961-65, U. No. Colo., 1965-67; m. Sharon Kaye Swiderski, Jan. 3, 1980; children: Julia Caitlin, Alexander Jeremiah, Matthew Davis; 1 son by previous marriage, Shannon David. Accountant, Colo. Nat. Bank, 1966-69; bus. analyst Dun & Bradstreet, 1969-70; pres., dir. Georgetown Valley Water & Sanitation Dist., 1973-74, Realists, Inc., 1973-74, Silver Queen Constrn. Co., 1973-74; v.p., sec., dir. Georgetown Assocs., Inc. (Colo.), 1970-74; pres., chief ops. officer Lincoln Cos., Denver, 1975-76; project mgr., sales mgr., prin. Brooks-Morris Homes, Fox Ridge, Colo., 1976-77; project mgr. U.S. West Homes, Denver, 1977-78; pres., dir. Denver Venture Capital, 1978-81; prin., dir., exec. v.p. Shelter Equities, Inc., 1982-87; prin., dir., exec. v.p. Comml. Constrn. Mgmt. Services, Inc., 1987-88, Shelter Equities, Inc., 1984-87; owner, dir., exec. v.p. Maple Leaf Realty Corp.; v.p., dir. Gibraltar Devel. Corp., Dominion Properties Ltd., 1978-82; investment dir. Van Schaack & Co., 1987-91; prin. investor, head devel. The Farkas Group, 1991-92; sr. residential loan officer, Freedom Mortgage Co., 1992-93; sr. loan officer, dir. builder mktg. NVR Mortgage Co., Englewood, Colo., 1994—; sr. loan officer Market St. Mortgage, 1996—. Served with USAF, 1961-65. Lic. real estate broker. Home: 8680 S Aberdeen Cir Highlnds Rnch CO 80126-3947 Office: Market St Mortgage 6025 S Quebec St #120 Englewood CO 80111

SMYTH, DONALD MORGAN, chemical educator, researcher; b. Bangor, Maine, Mar. 20, 1930; s. John Robert and Selma (Eubanks) S.; m. Elisabeth Luce, Aug. 1, 1951; children: Carolyn, Joanne. BS in Chemistry, U. Maine, 1951; PhD in Inorganic Chemistry, MIT, 1954. Sr. chemist Sprague Electric Co., North Adams, Mass., 1954-58, sect. head, 1958-61, dept. head, 1961-71; assoc. prof. Lehigh U., Bethlehem, Pa., 1971-73, prof., 1973-95, dir. Materials Rsch. Ctr., 1971-92, Paul B. Reinhold prof. materials sci., engring. and chemistry, 1988-95; emeritus, 1995—; mem. various coms. Lehigh U., 1973-95; mem. materials rsch. adv. com. NSF, 1984-88, chmn., 1985-86, co-chair ad-hoc com. to brief dir., 1986; mem. coun. materials sci. Dept. Energy, 1986-90; presenter in field. Contbr. articles to profl. jours. Recipient Libsch Rsch. award Lehigh U., 1990, Buessem award Dielectrics Rsch. Ctr., Pa. State U., 1991; grantee in field. Fellow Am. Inst. Chemists, Am. Ceramic Soc. (com. edn. electronics divsn. 1974-78, chmn. Lehigh Valley sect. 1978-79, counselor 1982—, assoc. editor jour. 1988-92, best paper award 1987, 95, Kraner award Lehigh Valley sect. 1990, Sosman lectr. 1996); mem. Am. Chem. Soc., Nat. Acad. Engring., Materials Rsch. Soc., Electrochem. Soc. (various coms., sec. dielectrics and insulation divsn. 1967-69, vice chmn. 1969-70, chmn. 1970-71, rsch. award battery divsn. 1960). Achievements include patents (with others) for Solid-State Battery Cell with Complex Organic Electrolyte Material, Capacitor with Dielectric Film Having Phosphorous-Containing Component Therein, Solid Barrier Electrolyte Incorporating Additive, others; research in defect chemistry and electrical properties of complex oxides. Home: 3429 Mountainview Cir Bethlehem PA 18017-1807 Office: Lehigh U Materials Rsch Ctr 5 E Packer Ave Bethlehem PA 18015-3102

SMYTH, GEORGE, electronics company executive, researcher. With Northern Telecom Ltd., Can.; now pres. BNR Inc., Research Triangle Park, N.C., 1987—. Office: BNR Inc 35 Davis Rd Research Triangle Park NC 27709*

SMYTH, GLEN MILLER, management consultant; b. Abingdon, Va., July 26, 1929; s. Glen Miller and Kathleen (Dunn) S.; m. Cynthia Olson, Aug. 25, 1954 (div. 1967); children: Catherine Ellen, Glen Miller, III, Cynthia Allison; m. Lilian Castel Edgar, Oct. 31, 1968; children: Stephanie Castel, Kimberley Forsyth, Lindsay Dunn. BA, Yale U., 1951; MS in Psychology, Rutgers U., 1958. Mktg. rep. Wheeling Stamping Co., N.Y.C., 1953-56; personnel dir. Celanese Internat., N.Y.C., 1958-71; mgr. orgn. and Manpower Internat. and Can. group Gen. Electric Co., N.Y.C., 1971-73; sr. v.p. human resources Northwest Bancorp., Mpls., 1973-82; sr. v.p. Calif. Fed. Savs., L.A., 1983-85; v.p. Career Transition Group, L.A., 1985-87; pres. Fuchs, Cuthrell & Co., Inc., L.A., 1987-93, Fuchs & Co., L.A., 1993-94; pres., CEO Smyth, Fuchs & Co., Inc., L.A., 1995—; leader seminars. Co-author: International Career Pathing, 1971; Contbr. articles to profl. jours. Served with AUS, 1951-53. Mem. Am. Psychol. Assn., Nat. Fgn. Trade Coun. (founder, past chmn. human resources, orgn. com. 1966—), Human Resources Planning Soc., Employment Mgmt. Assn., Jonathan Club, Yale Club of N.Y., North Ranch Country Club, Phi Gamma Delta. Home: 1115 Westcreek Ln Westlake Village CA 91362

SMYTH, JOEL DOUGLAS, newspaper executive; b. Renovo, Pa., Nov. 8, 1941; s. Bernard John and Eva Mae (Stone) S.; m. Madonna Robertson, Nov. 29, 1959; children: Deborah Sue, Susan Kelly, Michael Robertson, Patricia Ann, Rebecca Lee, Jennifer Neilia. Student, Lycoming Coll., 1959. Reporter Del. State News, Dover, 1960-62, news editor, 1962-65, mng. editor, 1965-70, editor, pres., 1970-78; editor Del. Sunday News, 1964-65; pres. Ind. Newspapers, Inc., Dover, 1970-89, chmn., CEO, 1989—. Founding pres. Valley Citizen's League, 1987-90. Recipient writing awards. Mem. AP Mng. Editors Assn. (dir.), Am. Soc. Newspaper Editors, Young Pres.'s Orgn., Sigma Delta Chi. Winter home: 33811 N 70th Way Scottsdale AZ 85262-7009 Summer home: 260 Forest Highlands Flagstaff AZ 86001-8422

SMYTH, JOSEPH PATRICK, retired naval officer, physician; b. Norwalk, Conn., Mar. 2, 1933; s. Patrick and Helen (Heffernan) S.; m. Ursula Marie (Kirwin), Dec. 28, 1960; children: Donna, Jennifer, Joseph. BA, Fairfield U., 1960; MD, Creighton U., 1964. Diplomate Am. Bd. Med. Examiners. Commd. ensign USN, 1963, advanced through grades to rear adm., 1988; intern Phila. Naval Hosp., 1964-65, internal medicine resident, 1965-68, staff physician, 1968-69; internist, chief of medicine U.S. Naval Hosp., DaNang, Vietnam, 1969-70, Orlando, Fla., 1970-76; chief of medicine, exec. officer U.S. Naval Hosp., Yokosuka, Japan, 1976-80; exec. officer U.S. Naval Hosp., Oakland, Calif., 1980-82, comdg. officer, 1984-86; comdg. officer U.S. Naval Hosp., Okinawa, Japan, 1982-84, Naval Med. Command European Region, London, 1986-90; dep. dir. for med. readiness The Joint Staff, Pentagon, Washington, 1990-92; retired US Navy, 1992; med. dir. Volusia County (Fla.) Dept. of Corrections, 1994—; instr. medicine Jefferson Med. Coll., 1966-69; preceptor USN Physician Asst. Program, Orlando, 1971-76; inst. mgmt. course Navy Med. Dept., Washington, 1986; Joint Staff coord. for entire mil. med. build-up for Operation Desert Shield/Storm, Saudi Arabia, 1990-91. Physician Orange County, Fla. Alcohol Ctr., Orlando, 1974-76. Decorated Def. Superior Svc. medal, Legion of Merit, Meritorious Svc. medals with 2 oak leaf clusters, Navy Commendation medal. Mem. AMA, Assn. Mil. Surgeons of U.S., Am. Acad. Med. Adminstrs. (Levandowski award 1991), Fla. Med. Assn., Am. Acad. Physician Execs., Orange County Med. Soc. Republican. Roman Catholic. Home: 400 Sweetwater Blvd S Longwood FL 32779-3422

SMYTH, JOSEPH PHILIP, travel industry executive; b. N.Y.C., Aug. 16, 1939; s. Joseph P. and Virginia S. (Gibbs) S.; m. Janet Hughes; 1 child, Philip. BA, Hamilton U., 1961; MBA, Harvard U., 1967; student, Naval Intelligence Sch., 1961-62. Dir. planning N.E. Airlines, Boston, 1967-70; acct. supr. Wells, Rich, Greene, N.Y.C., 1970-72; sr. v.p. mktg. Inter-Continental, N.Y.C., 1972-86, Hilton Hotels, Beverly Hills, Calif., 1986-88; head of ops. Cunard, N.Y.C., 1988-94; sr. v.p. fleet ops. Holland Am., Seattle, 1994; chmn Gibbs Bros., Huntsville, Tx., 1995—. Bd. mem. First Nat. Bank Huntsville, Tex. Lt. USN, 1961-65, ETO. Mem. Univ. Club, Harvard Club. Avocation: running. Home: 1088 Park Ave New York NY 10128-1132 Office: Gibbs Bros PO Box 711 Huntsville TX 77342-0711

SMYTH, JOSEPH VINCENT, manufacturing company executive; b. Belfast, Ireland, July 18, 1919; s. Joseph Leo and Margaret M. (Murray) S.; m. Marie E. Cripe, Mar. 22, 1941; children: Kevin W., Brian J., Ellen M., Vincent P. B.S. cum laude, U. Notre Dame, 1941. With Arnolt Corp., Warsaw, Ind., 1946-63; exec. v.p., gen. mgr. Arnolt Corp., until 1963; pres., gen. mgr. Hills-McCanna Co., Carpentersville, Ill., 1963-72; pres. Lunkenheimer Co., Cin., 1972-79; v.p. Condec Flow Control Group, Chgo., 1979-82; cons., 1982—. Club: Pinecrest Golf and Country (N.C.). Lodge: K.C. Home: 740 Saint Andrews Ln Apt 34 Crystal Lake IL 60014-7043 also: 299 Peppard Dr Fort Myers Beach FL 33931

SMYTH, PAUL BURTON, lawyer; b. Phila., Aug. 15, 1949; s. Benjamin Burton and Florence Elizabeth (Tomlinson) S.; m. Denise Elaine Freeland, May 31, 1975. BA, Trinity Coll, Hartford, Conn., 1971; JD, Boston Coll., 1974. Bar: Conn. 1974, D.C. 1975, U.S. Dist. Ct. D.C., 1980, U.S. Supreme Ct., 1985. With Dept. Interior, 1974—, atty. Office of Hearings and Appeals, Arlington, Va., 1974-76, atty. Office of Solicitor, Washington, 1976-82, asst. solicitor for land use and realty, Washington, 1982-87; deputy assoc. solicitor for energy and resources, Washington, 1987-93, acting dir. Office of Hearings and Appeals, Arlington, 1993-94, dep. assoc. solicitor. for energy and resources, Washington, 1994-95, for land and water resources, 1995—. Editor: Federal Reclamation and Related Laws Annotated, Reclamation Reform Act Compilation, 1982-88; contbr. articles to legal publs. Mem. ABA (coun. 1991-94, budget officer 1994—, sect. natural resources, energy and environ. law). Office: Office of Solicitor Dept Interior 18th and C Streets NW Washington DC 20240

SMYTH, PETER HAYES, radio executive; b. Apr. 25, 1952; s. Arthur and Irene (McNamara) S; m. Catherine Comerford Smyth, Aug. 8, 1976; children: Nancy, Colin, Kathleen. BA, Holy Cross Coll., Worcester, Mass., 1975; postgrad., Fordham U., 1975-76. Retail sales man Sta. WROR Radio, Boston, 1975-76, gen. sales mgr., 1976-83; gen. sales mgr. Sta. WOR Radio, N.Y.C., 1983-86; v.p. greater media sales Sta. WMEX-AM/WMJX-FM/WBCS-FM, Boston, 1986—; cons. Greater Media Cable, North Oxford, Mass., 1988-89. Bd. dirs. Holy Cross Coll., Worcester, Univ. Club, Boston, United Way of Mass., 1993, 94. Mem. New England Broadcast Assn. (bd. dirs. 1987, v.p., pres. 1992—). Republican. Roman Catholic. Avocations: golfing, swimming, skiing. Office: WMEX-AM/WMJX-FM/WBCS-FM 330 Stuart St Boston MA 02116-5229

SMYTH, REGINALD (REGGIE SMYTHE), cartoonist; b. Hartlepool, Eng., Oct. 7, 1917; s. Richard Oliver and Florence (Ritson) S.; m. Vera Toyne, Aug. 13, 1949. Student, Galleys Field Sch., 1922-31. With Brit. Civil Service, 1945-54; cartoonist, 1955—. Creator: Andy Capp daily comic strip, 1956. Served with Brit. Army, 1936-45. Recipient Best Brit. Cartoon award, 1961-65; Premio Cartoon award Lucca, 1969; Best Cartoonist award Genoa, 1973; Best Strip Cartoonist award Am. Cartoonists Soc., 1974. Mem. Nat. Cartoonists Soc. Mem. Ch. of Eng. Address: Whitegates 96 Caledonian Rd, Hartlepool England

SMYTH, RICHARD HENRY, foreign service officer; b. Oakland, Calif., June 12, 1951; s. Ronald Henry and Alyce Miriam (Swensson) S.; m. Janice Eileen Sullivan, Mar. 10, 1979; children: Caitlin, Alison. BA, U. Wash., 1973; grad. cert., U. Ala., Tuscaloosa, 1977. Cmty. planner Tuscaloosa, 1975-78; 3d sec. U.S. Embassy, Kabul, Afghanistan, 1979-80; 2d sec. U.S. Embassy, New Delhi, India, 1980-81, Jakarta, Indonesia, 1985-87; 1st sec. U.S. Embassy, Copenhagen, 1987-90; 2d sec. Belgian Embassy, Baghdad, Iraq, 1981-84; with U.S. Dept. of State, Washington, 1990-92; consul gen. U.S. Consulate, Peshawar, Pakistan, 1992—. Vol. U.S. Peace Corps, Kabul, Afghanistan, 1973-75. Mem. Assn. Am. Geographers, Am. Fgn. Svc. Assn. Avocations: Oriental studies, angling. Home and Office: 11 Hosp Rd, Peshawar Pakistan Office: AMCONS Pesh APO AE 09812-2217

SMYTHE, CHEVES MCCORD, dean, medical educator; b. May 25, 1924. Attended, Yale Coll., 1942-43; MD cum laude, Harvard, 1947. Diplomate Am. Bd. Internal Medicine, Am. Bd. Geriatrics. Intern, asst. resident Harvard Med. Svc., Boston City Hosp., 1947-49, chief resident, 1954-55; resident chest svc. Bellevue, 1949-50; rsch. fellow Presbyn. Hosp., N.Y.C., 1950-52; with Med. Coll. Hosp., Charleston, S.C., 1955-66; instr. medicine Med. Coll. S.C. Sch. Medicine, 1955-56, assoc. medicine, 1956-58, asst. prof. medicine, 1958-60, assoc. prof. medicine, 1960-66, dean, 1963-65; lectr. medicine Sch. Medicine Northwestern U., 1966-70; attending physician Wesley Meml., Cook County North Side VA Hosps., Chgo., 1967-70; with Hermann Hosp., Houston, 1970, Aga Khan U. Hosp., Karachi, Pakistan, 1990-91; dean faculty health scis., prof. medicine Aga Khan U., Karachi, Pakistan, 1982-85, prof., chmn. dept. medicine, 1990-91; with Meml. Southwest Hosp., Houston, 1991, LBJ Hosp., Houston, 1991; chief Med. Svcs. at LBJ Hosp., Houston, 1991-95; prof. divsn. gen. medicine dept. internal medicine U. Tex. Med. Sch., Houston, 1970—, dean, 1970-75, dean pro tem, 1995-96; vis. prof., lectr. U. Va., 1976, U. Guadalajara, 1976, U. So. Calif. Sch. Medicine, 1986-87; adj. prof. dept. family practice and cmty. medicine U. Tex. Med. Sch., Houston, 1991; cons. Regional Med. Libr. Adv. Com., Uniformed Svcs. Health Scis. U., U. S.D., U. Conn., Mercer U. Sch. Medicine, Oral Roberts U. Sch. Medicine, others. Contbr. articles to profl. jours., chpts. to books. Mem. AAAS, AMA, ACP, Am. Fedn. for Clin. Rsch. (chmn. southern sect.), Assn. Am. Med. Colls. (assoc. dir. 1966-70, dir. dept. acad. affairs 1969-70, chmn. med. sch. admissions assessment program 1973, mem. mgmt. advancement program steering com. 1973-75, mem. task force health manpower legislation 1974-75, chmn. deans of new and developing med. schs. group 1975, disting. svc. mem. 1979, others), Am. Heart Assn., Am. Clin. and Climatological Assn., Am. Soc. Nephrology, Am. Geriatrics Soc., Soc. for Exptl. Biology and Medicine, Tex. Geriatric Soc. (pres. 1991), Tex. Med. Assn. (cons. coun. on edn. and hosps.), Tex. Med. Found., Harris County Med. Soc. (mem. adv. com. on aging 1991, chmn. subcom. on continuing edn.), Houston Soc. Internal Medicine (v.p. 1976), Houston Geriatric Soc. (pres. 1989), Houston Acad. Medicine (vice-chmn., bd. dirs.), Southern Med. Assn., Southern Soc. for Clin. Rsch., Alpha Omega Alpha. Office: Univ Tex Med Sch 6431 Fannin Houston TX 77030

SMYTHE, SHEILA MARY, academic dean and administrator; b. N.Y.C., Nov. 1, 1932; d. Patrick John and Mary Catherine (Gonley) S. Student, Creighton U., 1952; BA, Manhattanville Coll., 1952; MS, Columbia U., N.Y.C., 1956; LHD (hon.), Manhattanville Coll., 1974. From rsch. assoc. to asst. dir. of rsch. and planning Blue Cross Assn., Chgo., 1957-63; exec. assoc. to pres. Empire Blue Cross & Blue Shield, N.Y.C., 1963-72, v.p., 1972-74, sr. v.p., 1974-78, exec. v.p., 1978-82, pres., chief oper. officer, 1982-85; health fin. and mgmt. cons. N.Y.C. and Washington, 1986-87; chief health policy advisor GAO, Washington, 1987-95, cons., exec. v.p., 1995—; dean grad. sch. health scis. N.Y. Med. Coll., N.Y.C., 1990—; adj. asst. prof. Grad. Sch. Pub. Health, Columbia U., 1980-86; bd. dirs. Mut. of Am., product & mktg. com. 1991-93, nominating com., 1992-94, audit com., 1993—, strategic planning com., 1994—; bd. dirs. Nat. Health Coun., Inc., mem. fin. com., 1987-94; bd. dirs. Hudson Valley Health Sys. Agy., sec., 1993-94, 1st v.p., 1994-95, pres., 1995—; active N.Y. State Hosp. and Rev. Planning Coun., 1994—. Chmn. bd. Manhattanville Coll., Purchase, N.Y., 1994—, trustee affairs, acad. affaris, exec. coms.; bd. dirs. Cath. Charities-U.S.A., 1989-95, mem. exec. pers. coms.; bd. dirs. March of Dimes Birth Defects Found., 1989—, vice chair, mem. fin. com., chair pub. affairs com., dir. Greater N.Y. March of Dimes, 1985-89. Recipient Elizabeth Cutter Morrow award YWCA, N.Y., 1977, Disting. Alumni award Manhattanville Coll., 1981, Excellence in Leadership award Greater N.Y. March of Dimes, 1989. Mem. Nat. Arts Club N.Y.C. Roman Catholic. Office: NY Med Coll Grad Sch Health Scis Valhalla NY 10595

SMYTHE, WILLIAM RODMAN, physicist, educator; b. Los Angeles, Jan. 6, 1930; s. William Ralph and Helen (Keith) S.; m. Carol Richardson, Nov. 27, 1954 (dec. Dec. 1987); children: Stephanie, Deborah, William Richardson, Reed Terry; m. Judith Brean Travers, Jan. 1, 1989. B.S., Calif. Inst. Tech., 1951, M.S., 1952, Ph.D., 1957. Engr. Gen. Electric Microwave Lab., Palo Alto, Calif., 1956-57; asst. prof. U. Colo., 1958-63, assoc. prof., 1963-67, prof., 1967—, chmn. nuclear physics lab., 1967-69, 81-83, 90-92. Group leader Rocky Mountain Rescue Group, 1967-68. Mem. Am. Phys. Soc. Club: Colorado Mountain (Boulder). Achievements include inventing negative ion cyclotron, fractional turn cyclotron. Home: 2106 Knollwood Dr Boulder CO 80302-4706

SMYTHE-HAITH, MABEL MURPHY, consultant on African economic development, speaker, writer; b. Montgomery, Ala., Apr. 3, 1918; m. Hugh H. Smythe, June 22, 1939 (dec. 1977); 1 child, Karen Pamela; m. Robert Haith, Jr., Oct. 18, 1985. Student, Spelman Coll., 1933-36, LLD (hon.), 1980; BA, Mt. Holyoke Coll., 1937, LHD (hon.), 1977; MA, Northwestern U., 1940; PhD, U. Wis., 1942, LLD (hon.), 1991; LHD (hon.), U. Mass., 1979. Asst. prof. Lincoln U., Mo., 1942-45; prof. Tenn. A. and I. U., 1945-46, Bklyn. Coll., 1946-47; vis. prof. Shiga U., Japan, 1951-53; dep. dir. rsch. for sch. segregation cases NAACP Legal Def. and Edn. Fund, 1953; tchr., prin. New Lincoln High Sch., N.Y.C., 1954-69; with Phelps-Stokes Fund, 1970-77, dir. research and publs., 1970-72, v.p., 1972-77; U.S. amb. to United Republic of Cameroon, Yaounde, 1977-80; U.S. amb. to Equatorial Guinea, 1979-80; dep. asst. sec. for African affairs Dept. State, 1980-81; Melville J. Herskovits prof. African studies Northwestern U., Evanston, Ill., 1981-83, disting. prof., 1983-85, prof. emeritus, 1985—, co-dir. internat. internship program, 1983-85; co-dir. African seminar Nat. Assn. Equal Opportunity in Higher Edn., 1985; mem. Adv. Com. on Edn. Exchange U.S. Dept. State, 1961-62, Adv. Commn. on Internat. Ednl. and Cultural Affairs, 1962-65; mem. Dept. State adv. coun. on African Affairs, 1962-65; U.S. del. 13th gen. conf. UNESCO, 1964; trustee Conn. Coll., 1964-65, 69-77, Mt. Holyoke Coll., 1971-76, vice chmn., 1975-76, trustee fellow, 1988—, Spelman Coll., 1980-89, life trustee, 1991—, Hampshire Coll., 1971-77, 85-88, vice chair, 1975-76; mem. U.S. Nat. Com. for UNESCO, 1965-70, Nat. Adv. rev. Bd., 1974-77; co-dir. African seminar for pres. black colls., 1971; bd. dirs. Nat. Corp. for Housing Partnerships, 1972-77; scholar-in-residence U.S. Commn. on Civil Rights, 1973-74; U.S. del. Internat. Conf. for Assistance to Refugees in Africa, 1981, So. African Devel. Coordination Conf. II, 1980; guest scholar Woodrow Wilson Internat. Ctr. for Scholars, Smithsonian Instn., Washington, 1982; mem. Aspen Inst. Humanistic Studies Exec. Seminar, 1983; mem. study mission to Japan with Assn. Black Am. Ambassadors, 1984, 85; mem. com. on policy for racial justice Joint Ctr. for Polit. and Econ. Studies, 1983-92; co-leader: Md. Consortium to Togo, Sierra Leone, Senegal, Liberia and Cameroon from 1970; co-dir. Mission to Malawi Women's Commn. on Refugee Women and Children, Malawi, 1989; adv. commn. Howard Univ. Patricia Roberts Harris Public Affairs Program, 1989—; adv. bd. Lincoln Univ. (Pa.) Ctr. for Public Policy and Diplomacy, 1991—; bd. dirs. Ralph Bunche Inst. on UN, CUNY, 1986-94; co-chair African-Am. Inst. Del. to observe presdl. elections, Madagascar, Feb., 1993. Author introduction: A Slaver's Log Book or 20 Years Residence in Africa, 1976; co-author: The New Nigerian Elite, 3d edit, 1971, Intensive English Conversation, Vol. I, 1953, Vol. II, 1954; editor: The Black American Reference Book, 1976; co-editor: Curriculum for Understanding, 1965; contbr. chpts. to coop. books, articles to profl. jours. Bd. dirs. Refugee Policy Group, 1983-89, adv. coun., 1989—; cons. African Devel. Found., 1986—; mem. Friends Inst. for Democracy in South Africa (formerly Inst. for a Democratic Alternative in South Africa), 1990—. Decorated grand officer Order of Valor (Cameroon); Grand Dama D'Inore, Order of Royal Crown of Crete (Malta); recipient Top Hat award Pitts. Courier, 1979, Mary McLeod Bethune award, 1981, Decade of Service award Phelps-Stokes Fund, 1982, Ella T. Grasso award Mt. Holyoke Coll., 1982, Northwestern U. Alumna of Year award, 1983, Disting. Service award Nat. Coalition of 100 Black Women, 1984, Disting. Service award USIA, 1986, Am. Bicentennial Presdl. Inaugural award, 1989, Black History Makers award Associated Black Charities, 1990. Mem. Coun. Fgn. Rels., Nat. Coun. Women U.S., Coun. Am. Ambassadors, Assn. Black Am. Ambassadors (exec. com.). Hugh H. and Mabel M. Smythe Internat. Service citatiod annually by InterFuture, Inc. Address: Watergate South Ste 317 700 New Hampshire Ave NW Washington DC 20037-2406 *Living in challenging times brings, along with its problems, opportunities for discovering new and better solutions to our difficulties, for making creative contributions to a world which so sorely needs positive input, for learning to enjoy the beauty and hope which are within our grasp.*

SNADER, JACK ROSS, publishing company executive; b. Athens, Ohio, Feb. 25, 1938; s. Daniel Webster and Mae Estella (Miller) S.; m. Sharon Perschnick, Apr. 4, 1959; children: Susan Mae, Brian Ross. BS, U. Ill., 1959. Cert. mgmt. cons. With mktg. Richardson-Merrell, Cin., 1959-65, Xerox Corp., N.Y.C., 1965-67, Sieber & McIntyre, Chgo., 1967-69; pres. Systema Corp., Northbrook, Ill., 1969—; bd. dirs. 1st Fed. Bank, Waukegan, Ill., Instrnl. Systems Assn. Author Systematic Selling, 1987, The Sales Relationship, 1981. Mem. ASTD, Inst. of Mgmt. Cons., Am. Mgmt. Assn. Office: Systema Corporation 60 Revere Dr Ste 600 Northbrook IL 60062-1578

SNAPP, ELIZABETH, librarian, educator; b. Lubbock, Tex., Mar. 31, 1937; d. William James and Louise (Lanham) Mitchell; BA magna cum laude, North Tex. State U., Denton, 1968, MLS, 1969, MA, 1977; m. Harry Franklin Snapp, June 1, 1956. Asst. to archivist Archive of New Orleans Jazz, Tulane U., 1960-63; catalog librarian Tex. Woman's U., Denton, 1969-71, head acquisitions dept., 1971-74, coord. readers svcs., 1974-77, asst. to dean Grad. Sch., 1977-79, instr. libr. sci., 1977-88, acting Univ. libr., 1979-82, dir. librs., 1982—, univ. historian, 1995—; chair-elect Tex. Coun. State U. Librs., 1988-90, chmn., 1990-92; mem. adv. com. on libr. formula Coordinating Bd. Tex. Coll. and Univ. System, 1981-92; del. OCLC Nat. Users Council, 1985-87, mem. by-laws com., 1985-86, com. on less-than-full-svcs. networks, 1986-87; trustee AMIGOS Bibliographic Coun., Inc., 1994—; project dir. NEH consultancy grant on devel. core curriculum for women's studies, 1981-82; chmn. Blue Ribbon com. 1986 Gov.'s Commn. for Women to select 150 outstanding women in Tex. history; project dir. math./sci. anthology project Tex. Found. Women's Resources. Co-sponsor Irish Lecture Series, Denton, 1968, 70, 73, 78. Sec. Denton County Dem. Caucus, 1970. Recipient Ann. Pioneer award Tex. Woman's U., 1986. Mem. AAUP, ALA (standards com. 1983-85), Tex. Libr. Assn. (program com. 1978, Dist. VII chmn. 1985-86, archives and oral history com. 1990-92, co-chair program com. Tex. Libr Assn. Ann. Conf. 1994, mem. Tall Texan selection com. 1995-96; treas. exec. com. 1996—, treas. exec. bd. 1996—), Tex. Hist. Commn. (judge for Farenbach History prize 1990-93), Women's Collecting Group (chmn. ad hoc com. 1984-86), AAUW (legis. br. chmn. 1973-74, br. v.p. 1975-76, br. pres. 1979-80, state historian 1986-88), AAUW Ednl. Found. (rsch. and awards panel 1990-94), So. Conf. Brit. Studies, Tex. Assn. Coll. Tchrs. (pres. Tex. Woman's U. chpt. 1976-77), Alliance Higher Edn. (chair coun. libr. dirs. 1993-95), Woman's Shakespeare Club (pres. 1967-69), Beta Phi Mu (pres. chpt. 1976-78; sec. nat. adv. assembly 1978-79, pres. 1979-80, nat. dir. 1981-83), Alpha Chi, Alpha Lambda Sigma (pres. 1970-71), Pi Delta Phi. Methodist. Club: Soroptimist Internat. (Denton) (pres. 1986-88). Asst. editor Tex. Academe, 1973-76; co-editor: Read All About Her! Texas Women's History: A Working Bibliography, 1995; contbg. author: Women in Special Collections, 1984, Special Collections, 1986; book reviewer Library Resources and Tech. Services, 1973—. Contbr. articles to profl. jours. Home: 1904 N Lake Trl Denton TX 76201-0602 Office: TWU Sta PO Box 424093 Denton TX 76204-2093 *The idealistic dreams of youth can be translated into making a difference in the work place and in your personal life if you develop a big picture that includes the ideas of individuals of diversity and if you give life your full attention, enthusiasm, and courage and give a few your steadfast friendship.*

SNAPP, HARRY FRANKLIN, historian; b. Bryan, Tex., Oct. 15, 1930; s. H.F. and Ethel (Manning) S.; BA, Baylor U., 1952, MA, 1953; PhD, Tulane U., 1963; m. Elizabeth Mitchell, June 1, 1956. Instr., U. Coll. Tulane U., 1960-62; asst. prof. history Wofford Coll., 1963-64; asst. prof. history U. North Tex. (formerly North Tex. State U.), Denton, 1964-69, assoc. prof., 1969-94; dir. Tex. Rsch. Ctr. Biog. Study of Women, Denton, 1995—; pres., dir. Read All About Her Tex. Women's Biographic Ctr., Inc., 1995—. Editor Brit. Studies Mercury, 1970—, Tex. Academy, 1973-76; co-editor: Read All About Her! Texas Women's History: A Working Bibliography, 1995; author: (with others) West Texas Historical Association Year Book, 1994; contbr. articles to profl. jours. Mem. Friends of Winchester Cathedral, Am. Com. Irish Studies; mem. adv. com. on acad. freedom and tenure policy, coordinating bd. Tex. Coll. and Univ. System. Recipient North Tex. State U. Faculty Rsch. award, 1966, 67. Mem. AAUP (pres. North Tex. chpt. 1968-69, pres. Southwestern regional conf. 1971-72, pres. Tex. conf. 1974-76, nat. coun. 1976-86), So. Conf. Brit. Studies (sec.-treas. 1969-84), Am. Hist. Assn., Tex. State Hist. Assn., Hist. Assn. (London), Libr. Rsch. Round Table, Libr. History Round Table,

Northamptonshire Record Soc., Butler Soc. (Ireland), Econ. History Soc., Ch. Hist. Soc., Tulane U. Alumni Assn., Alpha Chi, Lambda Chi Alpha. Methodist. Home: 1904 N Lake Trl Denton TX 76201-0602 Office: Read All About Her Tex Women's Biographic Ctr Inc PO Box 424053 TWU Sta Denton TX 76204-4053

SNAPP, ROY BAKER, lawyer; b. Strang, Okla., May 9, 1916; s. Harry Moore and Verda Mildred (Austin) S.; m. Dorothy Faye Loftis, Jan. 27, 1942; children: Deborah, Bryan Austin, Martha Lynn, Barbara, James. Lawyer. B.S. in Pub. Adminstrn, U. Mo., 1936; LL.B., Georgetown U., 1941, LL.M., 1942. With U.S. State Dept., 1941; spl. adviser comdg. gen. (Manhattan (Atomic Bomb) Project), 1946; dir. internat. affairs U.S. AEC, 1947, sec., 1948-54, asst. to chmn., 1954-55, sr. staff mem. nat. security coun., 1953-55; v.p. atomic div. (Am. Machine & Foundry), 1957; v.p. Am. Machine & Foundry Co., Washington office, 1961; bd. dirs. Electro-Nucleonics, Inc.; ptnr. Bechhoefer, Snapp and Trippe, 1966. Commd. ensign USNR 1942; assigned secretariat of U.S. Joint Chiefs of Staff and Combined (U.S.-Brit), Chiefs of Staff; naval mem. 1945; Intelligence Staff of Joint Chiefs Staff and Combined Chiefs Staff promoted to lt. comdr. 1945. Recipient D.S.M. AEC, 1955. Mem. SVC, Nat. Assn. Mgrs. (chmn. atomic energy com. 1963-64, dir. 1964-65), Phi Gamma Mu, Delta Theta Phi. Baptist. Clubs: Univ. (Washington), Columbia Country (Washington). Home: 11446 Savannah Dr Fredericksburg VA 22407-9108

SNAPPER, ERNST, mathematics educator; b. The Netherlands, Dec. 2, 1913; came to U.S., 1938, naturalized, 1942; s. Isidore and Henrietta (Van Buuren) S.; m. Ethel Lillian Klein, June 1941; children—John William, James Robert. MA, Princeton U., 1939, PhD, 1941; MA (hon.), Dartmouth Coll., 1964. Instr. Princeton, 1941-45, vis. asso. prof., 1949-50, vis. prof., 1954-55; asst. prof. U. So. Calif., 1945-48, asso. prof., 1948-53, prof., 1953-55; NSF post-doctoral fellow Harvard, 1953-54; Andrew Jackson Buckingham prof. math. Miami U., Oxford, Ohio, 1955-58; prof. math. Ind. U., 1958-63; prof. math. Dartmouth, 1963—, Benjamin Pierce Cheney prof. math., 1971—. Mem. Am. Math. Soc., Math. Assn. Am. (pres. Ind. sect. 1962-63, Carl B. Allendoerfer award 1980), Assn. Princeton Grad. Alumni (governing bd.), Soc. for Preservation Bridges of Konigsburg, Phi Beta Kappa (hon.), Pi Mu Epsilon (hon.). Home: PO Box 67 Norwich VT 05055-0067

SNAVELY, SHARON MARTIN, interior designer; b. Columbus, Ohio, July 31, 1946; d. John William and Patricia Mary (Mantel) Martin; m. Charles William Isaly, Nov. 5, 1966 (div. May, 1989); children: Jeffrey, Bradley. BA in Liberal Arts, No. Ariz. U., 1967. Interior designer John Martin Construction, Phoenix, 1967-73; v.p., owner Martin Constrn., Missoula, Mont., 1973-80; pres., owner SMI Interiors, Ariz., Mont., and Calif., 1980-92; constrn. adminstr. Trittipo & Assoc., Carlsbad, Calif., 1989-91; owner, ptnr. Design Group, Missoula, 1992-96; pres., owner Sharon Snavely, ASID, Missoula, 1996—. Mem. adv. bd. Florence Crittendon, Helena, Mont., 1994—, Missoula Symphony Bd., 1990—; pres. Symphony Guild; mem. action bd. Young Reps., Mont., 1994; bd. dirs. Extended Families, Missoula, 1994—. Mem. Am. Soc. Interior Designers, Am. Inst. Archs., Gen. Contractors Assn., Art Assocs. (pres.), Women in Art San Francisco, Missoula C. of C. Redcoats, Rotary. Avocations: skiing, golf, painting, horticulture. Home: 2020 W Greenough Dr Missoula MT 59802 Office: 201 N Higgins Missoula MT 59802

SNAVELY, WILLIAM PENNINGTON, economics educator; b. Charlottesville, Va., Jan. 25, 1920; s. Tipton Ray and Nell (Aldred) S.; m. Alice Watts Pritchett, June 4, 1942; children: Nell Lee, William Pennington, Elizabeth Tipton. Student, Hampden-Sydney Coll., 1936-37; BA with honors, U. Va., 1940, MA, 1941, PhD, 1950; postgrad. (Bennett Wood Green fellow), Harvard U., 1946-47. Mem. faculty U. Conn., 1947-73, prof. econs., 1961-73, chmn. dept., 1966-72, economist econ. edn. workshop, summers 1954, 55, 56; prof. econs. George Mason U., 1973-86, chmn. dept., 1973-81; acting dean CAS, summer 1981, 85-86, assoc. dean, 1982-85; prof. econs. Liberty U., 1986-93; cons. Ford Found., Jordan Devel. Bd., Amman, 1961-62, Ministry of Planning, Beirut, Lebanon, 1964-65, Saudi Arabian Cen. Planning Orgn., Riyadh, 1964-65, Am. U. Beirut, 1969-70, Bahrain Ministry Fin. and Nat. Economy, 1974, 75, 76, UN, Jordan Nat. Planning Coun., Amman, 1972; mem. Danforth Workshop, summer 1966; mem. adv. com. Willimantic Trust Co., Conn., 1968-73; v.p. Contemporary Econs. & Bus. Assn., 1988—. Author: (with W.H. Carter) Intermediate Economic Analysis, 1961, Theory of Economic Systems, 1969, (with M.T. Sadik) Bahrain, Qatar and the United Arab Emirates, 1972; contbr. articles to jours.; articles Ency. Americana. Bd. regents Liberty U. Capt. AUS, 1942-46. Fellow Fund Advancement Edn. Harvard, 1951-52; faculty-bus. exchange fellow Chase Nat. Bank, N.Y.C., summer 1952; fellow Merrill Center Econs., summer 1957; Fulbright research fellow Rome, 1958-59. Mem. Am. Econ. Assn., So. Econ. Assn., Assn. Christian Economists, Assn. Comparative Econs., Va. Assn. Economists (pres. 1979-80), Phi Beta Kappa, Phi Kappa Phi. Home: 1551 Dairy Rd Charlottesville VA 22903-1303

SNEAD, DAVID L., superintendent; b. Detroit, Oct. 15, 1943; s. Herman Jr. and Edythe (Burrell) S.; children by previous marriage: Deborah, David, Brandon; m. Sharon McPhail, May 1995. BS in Edn. and Kinesiology, Tuskegee Inst., 1968; MA in Urban Edn. and Kinesiology, U. Mich., 1970, PhD in Ednl. Adminstrn., 1984. Cert. tchr., Mich. Tchr., coach Detroit Pub. Schs., 1968-74; dept. chair health, athletics and phys. edn. Ctrl. H.S., Detroit, 1974-85, supr. health, tchr. phys. edn., 1985; asst. prin. Osborn H.S., Detroit, 1985-87; prin. Redford H.S., Detroit, 1987-89, Cass Tech. H.S., Detroit, 1989-93; asst. supt. for parent and adult edn. Detroit Bd. Edn., 1993, gen. supt., 1993—. Contbr. articles to profl. jours. Vol. ARC, 1970—; mem. youth adv. bd. St. Matthews-St. Joseph Episc. Ch. With AUS, 1961-64. Mem. U. Mich. Accreditation Adv. Com., Oreg. Sch. Adminstrs. and Suprs., Contract Negotiating Team. Office: 5057 Woodward Ave Detroit MI 48202-4000

SNEAD, GEORGE MURRELL, JR., army officer, scientist, consultant; b. San Diego, Nov. 6, 1922; s. George Murrell and Helen (Olsen) S.; m. Kathleen Hill Dawson, Apr. 26, 1947; children: George Murrell III, James M., William M., John P., Edward W. B.S., Va. Mil. Inst., 1943; M.S., U. Ill., 1948; Ph.D., U. Va., 1953. Commd. 2d lt. U.S. Army, 1943, advanced through grades to brig. gen., 1969; with Central Germany campaign 805th Signal Co., Europe, 1945-46; Aleutian sector comdr. Alaska Communication System, 1948-50; sta. at Electronic Warfare Center Ft. Monmouth, N.J. and Ft. Huachuca, Ariz., 1953-56; student U.S. Army Command and Gen. Staff Coll., 1956-57; signal adviser MAAG Vietnam, 1957-58; signal officer Dept. Army, 1958-60; acting dir. research ballistic missile def. Advanced Research Projects Agy., 1960; with U.S. Army Satellite Communications Agy. Ft. Monmouth, 1960-63; student Nat. War Coll., 1963-64, div. signal officer 24th Inf. Div., 1964-65, comdg. officer 7th Signal Group, 1965; dir. Communication /ADP Lab. Ft. Monmouth, 1966-68; exec. asst. chief of staff Communications Electronics, Dept. Army, 1968; dir. army research Dept. Army Washington, 1968-71; dep. comdr. Army Strategic Communications Command, 1971-73; prin. scientist Gen. Research Corp. McLean, Va., 1973-82; pres. Nat. Sci. Ctr. Found., Burke, Va., 1982-84; chmn. bd. Am. Fed. Savs. & Loan Assn., Lynchburg, Va., 1985-86; sci./bus. cons., 1986—. Active Boy Scouts Am., 1958-68; bd. dirs. Ctrl. Youth Summer Activities, Ft. Monmouth, 1960-63, Arthritis Found., Washington, 1981-84, Lynchburg Symphony, 1990-95; pres. Acad. Music Theatre, Lynchburg, 1985-95; trustee Sci. Mus. Va., 1995—; elder Presbyn. Ch., 1986—. Decorated D.S.M., Legion of Merit with oak leaf cluster, Bronze Star, Air medal, Army Commendation medal with 4 oak leaf clusters. Mem. Assn. U.S. Army, Armed Forces Communications and Electronics Assn. (sec. Washington chpt. 1968-69), Sigma Xi, Kappa Alpha. Home: 957 Rothowood Rd Lynchburg VA 24503-1113 Office: PO Box 3306 Lynchburg VA 24503-0306

SNEAD, JAMES ARRINGTON, architect; b. Richmond, Va., June 24, 1950; s. John Elwood and Anna Ruth (Reiche) S. BA, U. N.C., 1972; MArch, Va. Tech. U., 1978. Designer Hord Coplan & Macht, Balt., 1978-80; assoc. CS&D Architects, Balt., 1980-84; v.p., pres. Ziger Hoopes & Snead, Balt., 1984-93; pres. Ziger/Snead Architects, Balt., 1994—. Trustee Gilman Sch., Balt., 1990—; mem. adv. bd. Md. Inst. Sch. Continuing Studies, Balt., 1991—. Mem. AIA. Democrat. Presbyterian. Avocations: golf, travel, sailing. Office: Ziger &Snead Architects 1006 Morton St Baltimore MD 21201-5411

SNEAD, RICHARD THOMAS, retail company executive; b. Washington, Apr. 19, 1951; s. Walter Thomas and Ruth Claire (Reeves) S.; m. Marilyn Wolke; children: Richard Adam, Eric Thomas. BS in Engring., U. Tenn., 1973. Project mgr. First Fla. Bldg. Corp., Miami, 1974-78; constrn. mgr. Burger King Corp., San Francisco, 1978-79; nat. constrn. dir. Miami, 1979-81; dir. devel. Boston, 1981-84; regional v.p. Detroit, 1984-86; sr. v.p. devel. Miami, 1986-87, exec. v.p. devel., eastern div. mgr. (including responsibility for black minority affairs), 1987-88; pres. Burger King Internat. Div., 1988-89; mng. dir. Burger King U.K., 1989-92, Lenscrafters div. of U.S. Shoe, U.K., 1992-93; sr. v.p. Lenscrafters U.S.A., Cin., 1993-94, pres. Sight & Save div. and new bus. devel. Internat. div., 1994—. Republican. Avocations: running, golf, snow skiing, motorcycling. Office: 8650 Governors Hill Dr Cincinnati OH 45249-1386

SNEAD, SAMUEL JACKSON, former professional golfer; b. Hot Springs, Va., May 27, 1912; m. Audrey; children: Samuel Jackson, Terrance. Profl. golfer, from 1935. Author: How To Hit a Golf Ball, 1940, How To Play Golf, 1946, (with Al Stump) Education of a Golfer, 1962, The Driver, 1974, Golf Begins at Forty, 1978. Served with USNR, 1942-45. Recipient Vardon trophy Profl. Golfers' Assn., 1938, 49, 50, 55, Player of Year award, 1949, elected to Hall of Fame, 1963. Winner Profl. Golfers' Assn. Championship, 1942, 49, 51, Brit. Open, 1946, Masters Golf Tournament, 1949, 52, 54, Legends of Golf Championship, 1982. Office: care PGA of Am 100 Ave of the Champions Palm Beach Gardens FL 33410-9601

SNEDAKER, CATHERINE RAUPAGH (KIT SNEDAKER), editor; b. Fargo, N.D., Apr. 2; d. Paul and Charity (Primmer) Raupagh; B.A., Duke U.; m. William Brooks; children—Eleanor, Peter William; m. 2d, Weldon Snedaker. Pub. relations exec. United Seamen's Service, 1950-57; promotion mgr. sta. WINR-TV and WNBF-TV, Binghamton, N.Y., 1957-60; TV editor, feature writer Binghamton Sun, 1960-68; mem. staff Los Angeles Herald Examiner, 1968—, food editor, 1978—, restaurant critic, 1978-80, food and travel editor, 1980-86; editor The Food Package. Author: The Great Convertibles; contbr. numerous articles on food and travel to nat. mags. and newspapers; guest editor Mademoiselle mag., 1942. Recipient 3 awards Los Angeles Press Club, VISTA award, 1979. Mem. Soc. Am. Travel Writers, Travel Journalist's Guild. Democrat. Home: 140 San Vicente Blvd Apt A Santa Monica CA 90402-1533

SNEDDEN, JAMES DOUGLAS, health service management consultant; b. Toronto, Ont., Can., Mar. 4, 1925; s. David Morrison and Sarah Hayton (Monteith) S.; m. Elizabeth Ann McCauley, Dec. 20, 1953. B.Comm., U. Toronto, 1948; C.A., Inst. Chartered Accts. Ont., 1951. With Hosp. for Sick Children, Toronto, 1952-86, asst. dir., 1961-67, adminstr., 1967-70, chief exec. officer, 1970-86; nat. dir. health and social service cons. Peat, Marwick & Ptnrs., 1986-87; pres. J. Douglas Snedden and Assocs., 1987—; bd. dirs. Mallinckrodt Can., Cyberfluor Can. Hon. dir. Woodgreen Community Centre, Toronto, 1963-65, v.p., 1965-67, pres., 1967-69, hon. mem. bd. dirs., 1973—; past bd. dirs. Hosp. Coun. Met. Toronto; mem. Bd. Trade Met. Toronto, 1965—; bd. dirs. United Way Met. Toronto, 1986-89; bd. dirs. Wedgewood at Bonita Bay, Bonita Springs, 1990-94, pres., 1992-94. Served with RCAF, 1943-45. Decorated Can. Centennial medal. Fellow Can. Coll. Health Svc. Execs. (founding mem. 1970, bd. dirs. 1972-83, treas. 1978-81, chmn. 1981-82, past chmn. 1982-83), Inst. Chartered Accts. Ont. (life), Acad. of Medicine, Toronto; mem. Am. Coll. Healthcare Execs. Presbyterian. Clubs: University, Bd. of Trade. Office: #1005, 1 Aberfoyle Crescent, Etobicoke, ON Canada M8X 2X8

SNEDEKER, JOHN HAGGNER, university president; b. Plainfield, N.J., May 30, 1925; s. Alfred H. and Anna Marie (Ward) S.; m. Noreen I. Davey, Dec. 30, 1950; children—John D., Philip A., Patrick W. B.S. cum laude, N.Y. U., 1951, M.A., 1951; Ed.D., Ind. U., 1959. Dir. lab. human devel. U. Mont., 1952-56; cons. psychologist research Purdue U., 1955; asso. prof., dir. bur. research Ball State U., 1956-61; instr. higher edn., research asso. Ind. U., 1958; prof., chmn. div. edn. Western Wash. State U., Bellingham, 1961-62; pres. Western N.Mex. U., Silver City, 1962—; mem. exec. bd. Internat. Coun. Spl. Edn., 1952-56; Rocky Mountain regional rep. APA, 1953-56; mem. Gov. Wash. Com. Licensing Tchr. Edn., 1961, Wash. State Legislature Rsch. Tech. Com., 1961. Author or co-author rating scales, attitude and opinion measurement devices; contbr. jours. Bd. dirs. Nat. Sci. Fair; trustee N.Mex. Health Found. Served with AUS, 1943-48. Fellow AAAS; mem. Midwest Psychol. Assn., Inter-Am. Soc. Psychology, Am. Ednl. Research Assn., Holland Soc. N.Y. Address: 2117 Pinon St Silver City NM 88061-7734

SNEED, JOSEPH DONALD, philosophy educator, author; b. Durant, Okla., Sept. 23, 1938; s. Dabney Whitfield and Sallybelle (Atkinson) S. B.S., Rice U., 1960; M.S., U Ill., 1962; Ph.D., Stanford U., 1964. Prof. Stanford U., Palo Alto, Calif., 1966-73; policy analyst SRI Internat., Menlo Park, Calif., 1973-74; prof. U. Munich, 1974-75, U. Eindhoven, Holland, 1976-77, SUNY, Albany, 1977-79; prof. philosophy Colo. Sch. Mines, Golden, 1980—. Author: The Logical Structure of Mathematical Physics, 1971, (with W. Balzer and C. Moulines) An Architectonic for Science, 1987; editor: (with S. Waldhorn) Restructuring the Federal System, 1974. Mem. Am. Philos. Assn. Office: Colo Sch Mines Golden CO 80401

SNEED, JOSEPH TYREE, III, federal judge; b. Calvert, Tex., July 21, 1920; s. Harold Marvin and Cara (Weber) S.; m. Madelon Juergens, Mar. 15, 1944; children—Clara Hall, Cara Carleton, Joseph Tyree IV. B.B.A., Southwestern U., 1941; LL.B., U. Tex., Austin, 1947; S.J.D., Harvard, 1958. Bar: Tex. bar 1948. Instr. bus. law U. Tex., Austin, 1947; asst. prof. law U. Tex., 1947-51, asso. prof., 1951-54, prof., 1954-57, asst. dean, 1949-50; counsel Graves, Dougherty & Greenhill, Austin, 1954-56; prof. law Cornell U., 1957-62, Stanford Law Sch., 1962-71; dean Duke Law Sch., 1971-73; dep. atty. gen. U.S. justice dept., 1973; judge U.S. Ct. Appeals (9th cir.), San Francisco, 1973—, now sr. judge; Cons. estate and gift tax project Am. Law Inst., 1960-69. Author: The Configurations of Gross Income, 1967; Contbr. articles to profl. jours. Served with USAAF, 1942-46. Mem. ABA, State Bar Tex., Am. Law Inst., Order of Coif. Office: US Ct Appeals PO Box 193939 San Francisco CA 94119-3939

SNEED, MICHAEL (MICHELE), columnist; b. Mandan, N.D., Nov. 16, 1943; d. Richard Edward and June Marie (Ritchey) S.; m. William J. Griffin, Sept. 16, 1978; 1 child, Patrick. B.S., Wayne State U., 1965. Tchr. Barrington High Sch., Ill., 1965-66; legis. asst. Congressman Ray Clevenger, 1966-67; reporter City News Bur., Chgo., 1967-69; reporter Chgo. Tribune, 1969-86, columnist, 1981-86; pres. sec. Mayor Jane Byrne, Chgo., 1979; gossip columnist Chgo. Sun-Times, 1986—. Co-editor Chgo. Journalism Rev., 1971-72. Vice pres. No. Mich. U. chpt. Young Democrats, 1962. Roman Catholic. Club: Women's Athletic. Avocation: gardening. Office: Chgo Sun-Times Inc 401 N Wabash Ave Rm 110 Chicago IL 60611-3532

SNEED, RONALD ERNEST, engineering educator emeritus; b. Oxford, N.C., Nov. 23, 1936; s. Henry Ernest and Jewel Leigh (Hughes) S.; m. Shelba Jean Walters, June 8, 1958; children: Kathy Geneva Grosvenor, Jennie Leigh Berrier. BS in Agrl. Engring., N.C. State U., 1959, PhD in Biol. and Agrl. Engring., 1971. Registered profl. engr., N.C.; cert. irrigation designer. Sales trainee John Deere Co., 1959-60; ext. specialist N.C. State U., 1960-62, ext. instr., 1962-69, 70, ext. asst. prof., 1971-75, ext. assoc. prof., 1971-80, prof., 1980-92, prof. emeritus, 1993—; project engr. Agri-Waste Tech., Inc., 1993—, Irrigation Consulting and Engring., Inc., 1995; cons. Lexington (N.C.) Swine Breeders, 1973, 1st Colongy Farms, Creswell, N.C., 1977-78, Greek Tobacco Co. Uruguay, 1973-84, Internat. Potato Ctr., Lima, Peru, 1981-85, Philip Morris Tobacco Co., Richmond, Va., 1992-94, Stowe's Nursery, Inc., Belmont, N.C., 1993-94, Floyd Harrell Farms, Inc., Conetoe, N.C., 1994, Gilliam & Mason, Inc., Harrellsville, N.C., 1994, Craven County Com. of 100, Ltd., 1995. Active Civitan, Raleigh, 1994—. Maj. Gen. retired, U.S. Army, 1960-95. Recipient Outstanding Paper award So. region Am. Soc. Horticultural Sci., 1986, 91; Ronald E. Sneed Irrigation Soc., Inc. scholarship established in his honor, 1991. Fellow Am. Soc. Agrl. Engrs. (ednl. aids competition Blue Ribbon 1963-64, 68, 78-79, 85, 89, 91-92, Gunlogson Countryside Engring. award 1992, Outstanding Paper award 1984), The Irrigation Assn. (life tech. mem., Man of Yr. 1981), N.C. Irrigation Soc., Inc. (Oustanding Contbn. to Irrigation award 1973, former tech. advisor), Soil and Water Conservation Soc., N.C. Land Improvement Contractors Assn. (former tech. advisor), Carolinas Irrigation Assn. (hon.), Res. Officers Assn. (life). Democrat. Baptist. Office: 3405 Malibu Dr Raleigh NC 27607-6505

SNEIRSON, MARILYN, lawyer; b. Yonkers, N.Y., July 23, 1946. BA, Brandeis U., 1968; JD, Rutgers U., 1981. Bar: N.J. 1981, N.Y. 1989, U.S. Ct. Appeals (3d cir.) 1988, U.S. Supreme Ct. 1989. Law clerk Hon. Sylvia Pressler Superior Ct. N.J. Appellate, Hackensack, N.J., 1981-82; assoc. Pitney, Hardin, Kipp & Szuch, Morristown, N.J., 1982-84, Cole, Schotz et als, Hackensack, 1984-89; ptnr. Beattie, Padovano, Montvale, N.J., 1989-94; ptnr., prin. Price, Sneirson, Shulman & Meese, Woodcliff Lake, N.J., 1994—; commentator Court TV. contbr. articles to profl. jours. Committeewoman Dem. County Com., Ridgewood, N.J., 1980—. Mem. N.J. Bar Assn., Justice Pashman Am. Inns Court (master), Bergen County Bar Assn. Avocation: art. Office: Price Sneirson Shulman & Meese 50 Tice Blvd Woodcliff Lake NJ 07675

SNELL, BRUCE M., JR., state supreme court justice; b. Ida Grove, Iowa, Aug. 18, 1929; s. Bruce M. and Donna (Potter) S.; m. Anne Snell, Feb. 4, 1956; children: Rebecca, Brad. AB, Grinnell Coll., 1951; JD, U. Iowa, 1956. Bar: Iowa 1956, N.Y. 1958. Law clk. to presiding judge U.S. Dist. Ct. (no. dist.) Iowa, 1956-57; asst. atty. gen., 1961-65; judge Iowa Ct. Appeals, 1976-87; justice Iowa Supreme Ct., 1987—. Comments editor Iowa Law Rev. Mem. ABA, Iowa State Bar Assn., Am. Judicature Soc., Order of Coif. Methodist. Home: PO Box 192 Ida Grove IA 51445-0192 Office: Iowa Supreme Ct St Capitol Bldg Des Moines IA 50319

SNELL, DAVID D., retail executive; b. 1949. CEO United Supermarkets, Lubbock, Tex., 1970—. Office: PO Box 6840 Lubbock TX 79493

SNELL, ESMOND EMERSON, biochemist; b. Salt Lake City, Sept. 22, 1914; s. Heber Cyrus and Hedwig Emma (Ludwig) S.; m. Mary Caroline Terrill, Mar. 15, 1941; children: Esmond Emerson (dec.), Richard T., Allan G., Margaret Ann. B.A., Brigham Young U., 1935; M.A., U. Wis., 1936, Ph.D., 1938, D.Sc. (hon.), 1982. Rsch. assoc. chemistry U. Tex., 1939-41, asst. prof. chemistry, 1941-43, assoc. prof., 1943-45, prof. chemistry, 1951-56; assoc. prof. biochemistry U. Wis., 1945-47, prof., 1947-53, on leave 1951-53; prof. biochemistry U. Calif., 1956-76, chmn. dept., 1956-62; prof. microbiology and chemistry U. Tex., Austin, 1976-90, Ashbel Smith prof., 1981-90, prof. emeritus, 1990—, chmn. dept. microbiology, 1976-80; Guggenheim Meml. Found. fellow U. Cambridge, 1954-55, Max-Planck Institut für Zellchemie, München, 1962-63, U. Wash., Seattle, Rockefeller U., N.Y.C., Hebrew U., Jerusalem, 1969; Walker-Ames prof. biochemistry U. Wash., Seattle, spring 1953. Author numerous research articles in sci. jours.; Editor: Volume III Biochemical Preparations, 1963-64, Chemical and Biological Aspects of Pyridoxal Catalysis, 1963, Pyridoxal Catalysis, Enzymes and Model Systems, 1968; Mem. editorial bd. Jour. Am. Chem. Soc. 1948-58, Jour. Biol. Chemistry, 1949-59, Biochemistry, 1961-70, Biochem. and Biophys. Research Communication, 1970-85, Biofactors, 1988-91; editor: Ann. Rev. Biochemistry, 1969-83. Recipient U.S. Sr. Scientist award Alexander von Humboldt Found., 1977. Fellow AAAS, Am. Inst. Nutrition (Meade-Johnson B-Complex award 1946, Osborne-Mendel award 1951); mem. Nat. Acad. Scis., Am. Acad. Arts and Scis., Japanese Biochem. Soc. (hon.), Am. Chem. Soc. (chmn. div. biol. chemistry 1954, Kenneth A. Spencer award 1974, Nebr. Lectureship award 1983), Am. Soc. Biol. Chemists (pres. 1961-62, William Rose award 1985), Soc. Am. Bacteriologists (Eli Lilly award in bacteriology and immunology 1945), Am. Acad. Microbiology. Home: 5001 Greystone Dr Austin TX 78731-1118

SNELL, JACK EASTLAKE, federal agency administrator; b. Evanston, Ill., Nov. 29, 1935; s. Clarence Eastlake and Ruth (Meloy) S.; m. Elizabeth Kercher, Oct. 15, 1966; children: Jeffrey Eastlake, Julie Elizabeth. B.S.E. with honors in Aero. Engring, Princeton U., 1957; M.S. in Indsl. Engring, Northwestern U., 1965, Ph.D. in Civil Engring; Ph.D. (Walter P. Murphy scholar, Transp. Center fellow), 1966; grad., Fed. Exec. Inst., 1979. Aircraft maintenance engr. Pan Am. World Airways, N.Y.C., 1960; asst. prof. transp. engring., and dir. Transp. and Urban Systems Lab., Princeton U., 1966-71; chief bldg. service systems sect. Nat. Bur. Standards, Washington, 1971-73; asst. chief bldg. environ. div. Nat. Bur. Standards, 1973-74; chief Office Energy Conservation, 1974-76; dir. Office Energy Programs, 1976-81; dir. Ctr. Fire Research Nat. Engring. Lab., 1981-91, deputy dir. bldg. and fire rsch. lab., 1991—; mem. various fed. interagy. energy task forces, 1973-79; steering com. Intersoc. Energy Conversion Engring. Conf.; mem. Md. Gov.'s Sci. Adv. Council, 1976—; chmn. U.S.-Japan Panel on Fire Research and Safety. Contbr. articles to profl. jours. Served to 1st lt. USAF, 1953-60. Recipient Silver medal Dept. Commerce, 1975, Gold medal Dept. Commerce, 1987. Fellow ASME (chmn. advanced energy systems divsn. 1981), Nat. Fire Protection Assn. (bd. dirs., chmn. toxicity adv. com.). Presbyterian. Office: Natl Inst Standards & Technology Gaithersburg MD 20899

SNELL, JAMES LAURIE, mathematician, educator; b. Wheaton, Ill., Jan. 15, 1925; s. Roy Judson and Lucille (Ziegler) S.; m. Joan Perry, Dec. 30, 1952; children: John, Mary Paige. BA, U. Ill., 1947, MA, 1948, PhD, 1951. Instr. math. Princeton U., 1951-54; mem. faculty Dartmouth Coll., Hanover, N.H., 1954—, prof. math., 1962-95, prof. emeritus, 1995—. Author: (with J.G. Kemeny and G.L. Thompson) Introduction to Finite Mathematics, 1959, (with J.G. Kemeny) Finite Markov Chains, 1960, (with J.G. Kemeny and A.W. Knapp) Denumerable Markov Chains, 1966; Introduction to Probability, 1988. With USNR, 1944-46. Mem. Am. Math. Soc., Math. Soc. Am. Home: 34 E Wheelock St Hanover NH 03755-1514 Office: Dartmouth Coll Dept of Math Hanover NH 03755

SNELL, JOHN RAYMOND, civil engineer; b. Soochow, China, Dec. 9, 1912; (parents Am. citizens); s. John A. and Grace (Birkett) S.; m. Florence Moffett, Dec. 8, 1939; children: Dorothea Snell Fenska, Karen Snell Dailey, Martha E. Snell Rood, John Raymond, David Moffett. BE, Vanderbilt U., 1934; MS, U. Ill., 1936; DSc, Harvard U., 1939. Registered profl. engr., Mass., Mich., Ohio, Ill., Ind., La. Wis., N.Y., Tex. Fla., Idaho, Oreg., Ont., Can.; cert. san. engr.; diplomate Am. Acad. Environ. Engrs. Instr. civil engring. Hangchow U., 1934-35; with Water Supply Fed. Pub. Works Dept., Venezuela, 1939-40; design engr. Metcalf & Eddy, also Fay Spofford and Thorndyke, Stone & Webster, Boston, 1941-42; san. engr., head water and sewage sect. 1st Svc. Command, Boston, 1946; assigned UNRA restoration water, sewage, solid wastes 5 no. provinces China San. Engring. Services Inc., 1945-46; project engr. Burns & Kenerson, Boston, 1947; pres., chief engr. Engring. Svcs. Inc., Boston, 1948-51; lectr. MIT, 1949-51; prof., head dept. civil and san. engring. Mich. State U., 1951-55; owner John R. Snell & Assocs., 1956; sr. prin. Mich. Assocs., cons. engrs., 1956-60; pres. John R. Snell Engrs. Inc., 1960-75; pres. Snell Environ. Group, 1975-80, hon. chmn. bd., spl. cons., 1980-88; joint venturer Snell-Republic Assocs. Ltd., Lahore, West Pakistan, 1961-80; with Assoc. Architects & Engrs., Dacca, Bangladesh, 1965-80; pres. Caribbean Devel. Corp. and subs. Gen. Shrimp Ltd., Belize, 1984-92; sr. adj. scientist Mich. Biotech. Inst., 1990—; 1994 guest of China-Suzhou Hosp. 110 Aniv.; solid waste cons. Xiaogan Recycling Treatment Utilization of Organics, Peoples Republic of China, 1995; founder Trans Mich. Waterway Inc., S.W. Waterway (Ont.) Ltd., N.Y.; spl. cons. on ast high rate compost plant to Govt. of Japan, 1955-56; cons. in Orient, WHO, 1956; chmn. bd. Bootstrap Internat. Inc., 1972; expert witness on over 50 ct. cases. Author 12 sects. Environment Engineering Handbook; coauthor: Municipal Solid Waste Disposal; contbr. articles to profl. jours.; patentee in composting field. Maj. USPHS, 1945-47. Recipient Prescott Eddy award, 1944. Mem. Nat., Mich. (life) socs. profl. engrs., Am. Water Works Assn., Hwy. Rsch. Bd., ASTM, ASCE, Am. Pub. Works Assn., Water Pollution Control Fedn. (life), Mich. Engring. Soc. (life), Cons. Engrs. Coun. (past dir.), Cons. Engrs. Assn. Mich. (past pres.), Inter-Am. Assn. San. Engrs., World Aquaculture Soc., Composters Inc. (pres. Worldwide Techs. Inc. East Lansing 1980—), Rotary, Tau Beta Pi, Chi Epsilon. Home and Office: 918 Rosewood Ave East Lansing MI 48823-3127

SNELL, LORI B., corporate, transactional paralegal; b. L.A., Apr. 30, 1958; d. Melvil N. and Freda B. Snell. BA, UCLA, 1982, Paralegal Cert., 1983, JD, 1986. Corp. paralegal Cooper, Epstein & Hurewitz, Beverly Hills, Calif., 1989-93, Silverberg, Katz, Thompson & Braun, L.A., 1993-94, Unihealth, Burbank, Calif., 1994—; pres. Corp. Paralegal Svcs., Encino, Calif., 1989—.

SNELL, NED COLWELL, financial planner; b. Cowley, Wyo., May 16, 1944; s. Jay Hatton and Freda Hope (Colwell) S.; m. Barbara Anne Frandsen, Apr. 24, 1969; children: Taylor Anthony, Trevor Cameron. BA, U. Utah, 1969; CLU, Am. Coll., 1983, ChFC, 1985. English tchr. Granite Sch. Dist., Salt Lake City, 1969-71; ins. agt. Prudential Ins. Co., Salt Lake City, 1971-76; pres. Snell Fin. Corp., Salt Lake City, 1976—. Bd. dirs. Utah chpt. Arthritis Found., Salt Lake City, 1980-82, pres. 1982-83; missionary Mormon Ch. 1963-66; chmn. voting dist. 2604 Rep. Nominating Convs., 1986, 90. Recipient Golden Key Soc. Devel. award, 1990. Mem. NALU (Nat. Sales Achievement award 1971-89, Nat. Quality award), Am. Soc. CLU and ChFC (bd. dirs. Utah chpt. 1990-93, treas. 1993-94, v.p. 1994-96, pres. 1996—), Million Dollar Round Table (knight 1988-94), Salt Lake Assn. Life Underwriters (bd. dirs. 1974-76, 80-82). Republican. Avocations: creative writing, fly tying, fishing, basketball, tennis. Home: 1101 S 2000 E Salt Lake City UT 84108-1971 Office: 1800 S West Temple Ste 416 Salt Lake City UT 84115-1874

SNELL, PATRICIA POLDERVAART, librarian, consultant; b. Santa Fe, Apr. 11, 1943; d. Arie and Edna Beryl (Kerchmar) Poldervaart; m. Charles Eliot Snell, June 7, 1966. BA in Edn., U. N.M., 1965; MSLS, U. So. Calif., 1966. Asst. edn. libr. U. So. Calif., L.A., 1966-68; med. libr. Bedford (Mass.) VA Hosp., 1968-69; asst. law libr. U. Miami, Coral Gables, Fla., 1970-71; acquistions libr. U. N.Mex. Law Sch. Libr., Albuquerque, 1971-72; order libr. Los Angeles County Law Libr., 1972-76, cataloger, 1976-90; libr. Parks Coll., Albuquerque, 1990-92; records technician Technadyne Engring. Cons. to Sandia Nat. Labs., 1992-93; instr. libr. sci. program Coll. Edn. U. N.Mex., Albuquerque, 1991—, libr. Tireman Learning Materials Ctr., 1993—. Ch. libr., Beverly Hills Presbyn. Ch., 1974-90, ch. choir libr., 1976-90. Southwestern Library Assn. scholar 1965. Mem. ALA, N.Mex. Libr. Assn., Pi Lambda Theta. Avocations: travel, reading, gospel singing. Office: U N Mex Coll Edn EM/LS Program Tireman Libr Albuquerque NM 87131

SNELL, RICHARD, holding company executive; b. Phoenix, Nov. 26, 1930; s. Frank L. and Elizabeth (Berlin) S.; m. Alice Cosette Wiley, Aug. 1, 1954. BA, Stanford U., 1952, JD, 1954. Bar: Ariz. Ptnr. firm Snell & Wilmer, Phoenix, 1956-81; pres., chmn., chief exec. officer Ramada Inc., Phoenix, 1981-89; chmn., chief exec. officer Aztar Corp., 1989-90, chmn., bd. dirs., 1990-92; chmn., chief exec. officer, pres. Pinnacle West Capital Corp., Phoenix, 1990—, bd. dirs.; bd. dirs. Bank One Ariz. Corp., Bank One Ariz. NA, Aztar Corp.; bd. dirs., chmn. Ariz. Pub. Svc. Co. Trustee Am. Grad. Sch. Internat. Mgmt., Phoenix; past pres. YMCA Met. Phoenix and Valley of Sun. With U.S. Army, 1954-56. Mem. ABA, Ariz. Bar Assn., Paradise Valley Country Club, Phoenix Country Club. Republican. Lutheran. Office: Pinnacle West Capital Corp 400 E Van Buren St Phoenix AZ 85004 also: Arizona Public Service Co PO Box 53999 # 9960 Phoenix AZ 85072-3999

SNELL, RICHARD SAXON, anatomist; b. Richmond, Surrey, Eng., May 3, 1925; came to U.S., 1963; s. Claude Saxon and Daisy Lilian S.; m. Maureen Cashin, June 4, 1949; children: Georgina Sara, Nicola Ann, Melanie Jane, Richard Robin, Charles Edward. M.B., B.S., Kings Coll., U. London, 1949, Ph.D., 1955, M.D., 1961. House surgeon Sir Cecil P.G. Wakeley, Kings Coll. Hosp. and Belgrave Hosp. for Children, London, 1948-49; lectr. anatomy Kings Coll., U. London, 1949-59, U. Durham, Eng., 1959-63; asst. prof. anatomy and medicine Yale U., 1963-65, assoc. prof., 1965-67, vis. prof. anatomy, 1969; prof., chmn. dept. anatomy N.J. Coll. Medicine and Dentistry, Jersey City, 1967-69; vis. prof. anatomy Harvard U., 1970, 71, 80, 86; prof. anatomy Coll. Medicine, U. Ariz., Tucson, 1970; prof., chmn. dept. anatomy George Washington U. Med. Ctr., Washington, 1972-88, prof. emeritus, 1988—. Author: Clinical Embryology for Medical Students, 1972, 3d edit., 1983, Clinical Anatomy for Medical Students, 1973, 5th edit., 1995, Atlas of Normal Radiographic Anatomy, 1976, Atlas of Clinical Anatomy, 1978, Gross Anatomy Dissector, 1978, Clinical Neuroanatomy for Medical Students, 1980, 3d edit., 1992, Student's Aid to Gross Anatomy, 1986, Clinical Anatomy for Anesthesiologists, 1988, Clinical Anatomy of the Eye, 1989, Gross Anatomy: A Review with Questions and Explanations, 1990, Neuroanatomy: A Review with questions and Explanations, 1992, Clinical Anatomy for Emergency Medicine, 1993, Clinical Anatomy: An Illustrated Review with Questions and Explanations, 2d edit., 1996; contbr. articles to med. jours. Med. Research Council grantee, 1959; NIH grantee, 1963-65. Mem. Anat. Soc. Gt. Britain, Am. Soc. Anatomists, Alpha Omega Alpha. Home: 518 Boston Post Rd Madison CT 06443-2930

SNELLING, BARBARA W., state official; b. Fall River, Mass., Mar. 22, 1928; d. Frank Taylor and Hazel (Mitchell) Weil; m. Richard Arkwright Snelling, June 14, 1947 (dec. Aug. 1991); children: Jacqueline, Mark, Diane, Andrew. AB magna cum laude, Radcliffe Coll., 1950; D of Pub. Svc. (hon.), Norwich U., 1981. V.p. U. Vt., 1974-82; pres. Snelling and Kolb, Inc., 1982-95; lieut. gov. State of Vt., 1993—; chmn. bd. dirs. Chittenden Bank Corp., 1990—. Trustee Radcliffe Coll., 1990-95; bd. dirs. Vt. Community Found., 1986-94, Shelburne Mus., 1988—; mem. Vt. Ednl. Partnerships, 1992—; v.p. for devel. and external affairs U. Vt., 1974-82; mem. Vt. State Bd. Edn., 1971-77; trustee Champlain Coll., 1971-74; mem. Vt. Alcohol and Drug Rehab. Commn., 1970-73, Shelburne Sch. Bd., 1958-73, chmn. 1965-73; mem. Vt. Edn. Adv. Coun., 1968-71, Vt. Tchr. Edn. Adv. Com., 1966-70, Bd. of Sch. Dirs., Champlain Valley Union High Sch., 1962-69, chmn. 1962-68, others. Recipient Fanny G. Shaw award for Disting. Community Svc., Burlington Community Coun., 1972, Laymen's award Vt. Edn. Assn., 1965. Office: Office of Lieutenant Governor State House Montpelier VT 05633*

SNELLING, GEORGE ARTHUR, banker; b. St. Petersburg, Fla., June 27, 1929; s. William Henry and Eula Hall S.; m. Carolyn Shiver, Mar. 3, 1963; children—George, John S. B.S.B.A., U. Fla., 1951. Partner Smoak, Davis, Nixon & Snelling, C.P.A.s, Jacksonville, Orlando, Fla., 1956-66; v.p. planning Barnett Banks of Fla., Jacksonville, 1966-76; exec. v.p. 1st Bancshares of Fla., Boca Raton, 1976-78; exec. v.p. Fla. Nat. Banks of Fla., Jacksonville, 1978-80; exec. v.p. corp. devel., chief fin. officer Sun Banks of Fla., Orlando, 1981-85; exec. v.p. corp. devel. SunTrust Banks, Inc., Atlanta, 1986-90; pres. Unicoy, Inc., Atlanta, 1991—. Trustee Fla. So. U. Served with USAF, 1951-55. Mem. AICPA. Democrat. Methodist. Home: 2682 Varner Dr NE Atlanta GA 30345-1559 Office: Unicoy Inc 2682 Varner Dr NE Atlanta GA 30345-1559

SNELLING, NORMA JUNE, retired music educator, English educator; b. Brooten, Minn., June 1, 1928; d. Harold Melvin and Mabel Olga (Markuson) Hellickson; m. Douglas Howard Snelling, June 27, 1953; children: Julie Marie, Mary Merced, Steven Douglas. BA, Concordia Coll., Moorhead, Minn., 1949. Cert. tchr., Minn. Tchr. Wolverton (Minn.) Sch. Dist., 1949-51, Kimball (Minn.) Sch. Dist., 1951-52, Benson (Minn.) Sch. Dist., 1952-53, Belgrade (Minn.) Sch. Dist., 1953-57, Hutchinson (Minn.) Sch. Dist., 1964-66, Litchfield (Minn.) Sch. Dist., 1966-92; mem. staff edn. liaison 2d Congl. Dist. Minn., Litchfield, 1992—. Assoc. chairperson county level, del. Dem. Farmer Labor Party, Minn., 1992—, chair 1994; del. to Dem. Nat. Conv., 1984; co-chairperson Concert Series, Litchfield, 1962, Cancer Dr., Litchfield, 1960; dir. Choralaires, Eden Valley, Minn., 1976—; dir. music Zion Luth. Ch., Litchfield, 1962-85, poet ch. pubs., dedications, etc., also Big Grove Luth. Ch.; speech coach Litchfield Jr. H.S., 1972-77; mem. VFW Aux., Am. Legion Aux. 94m. NEA (life, congl. contact person 1985-90), Minn. Edn. Assn. (govtl. rels. uniserve chairperson, Leadership award medal 1986), Ret. Educators Minn. (legis. chairperson 1993—), Internat. Platform, Sons of Norway (musician, pres. Vannland Lodge 1993-94, Bronze medal 1993-94), Gen. Fedn. Women's Study Clubs, Halling Laget, Delta Kappa Gamma. Avocations: reading, bowling, flower arranging, painting, golf. Home: 621 W Crescent Ln Litchfield MN 55355-1830

SNELLING, ROBERT ORREN, SR., franchising and employment executive; b. Phila., Aug. 16, 1932; s. Louis Raymond and Gwendolyn Anne (Preble) S.; m. Joan E., 1951 (dec. 1979); children—Robert, Krista; m. Anne Morris, June 30, 1979; children—Rick Spragins, Leigh Crews, Linda Paulk. Student, Pa. State U., 1951-52; Dr. Lit. (hon.), Albright Coll., 1968. Profl. employment counsellor, Snelling & Snelling, Phila., 1952-53, gen. mgr., 1954-67, pres., 1962-68, chmn. bd., 1969—; speaker, lectr. in field. Author: The Opportunity Explosion, 1969, Jobs-What They Are-Where They Are-What They Pay, 1985, rev. edit., 1992, The Right Job, 1987, rev. edit., 1992; contbr. articles to profl. jours. Mem. long-range planning Sarasota 2000, 1976; mem. pvt. sector employment svcs. com. Dept. Labor, 1982; mem. Com. on Skilled Employment Brokering Svcs., 1984; mem. White Ho. Com. on Small Bus., 1986; mem. adv. com to U.S. Sec. William Brock, 1986; mem. Gov.'s Select Com. on Workforce 2000, 1988-89, chmn. govtl. regulations and benefits subcom., 1989; apptd. to Nat. Commn. for Employment Policy, 1994—. With U.S. Army, 1953-54. Recipient Golden Plate award, 1964; W.O. Blanchet award Pa. Assn. Personnel Service, 1976; Outstanding Citizen award Assn. Personnel N.Y., 1977; award for excellence Am. Acad. Achievement, 1964; Harold B. Nelson award, 1985. Mem. Internat. Franchise Assn., Nat. Assn. Personnel Cons., Nat. Assn. Temp. Svcs., U.S. C. of C. Republican. Avocations: reading, photography.

SNELSON, KENNETH DUANE, sculptor; b. Pendleton, Oreg., June 29, 1927; s. John Tavner and Mildred F. (Unger) S.; m. Katherine Eve Kaufmann, May 2, 1972; 1 child, Andrea Nicole. Numerous. Student, U. Oreg., 1946-47, Black Mountain Coll., 1948-49, Chgo. Inst. Design, 1950-51, Academie Montmartre, Paris, 1951-52; D of Arts and Humane Letters (honoris causa), Rensselaer Poly. Inst., 1985. Subject of articles in art publs.; one-man shows U.S. and Germany, Holland, including Portrait of an Atom, Balt., 1979-80, De Cordova and Dana Mus. and Park, Lincoln, Mass., 1984, Zabriskie Gallery, 1984, Yoh Art Gallery, Osaka, Japan, 1991, Contemporary Sculpture Ctr., Tokyo, 1995, Maxwell Davidson Gallery, N.Y.C., 1994; major retrospective, Hirshhorn Mus. and Sculpture Garden of Smithsonian Instn., 1981, Albright-Knox Art Gallery, Buffalo, 1981, N.Y. Acad. Scis., 1989; group shows include Mus. Modern Art, N.Y.C., 1967, Whitney Mus., N.Y.C., 1966, 69, 70, Albright Knox Gallery, 1968, Prospect '68, Dusseldorf, Germany, 1968, Salon International de Galeries Pilotes, Lausanne, Switzerland, 1970, Sammlun Etzold, Kolnischer Kunstverein, Cologne, Germany, 1970, Expo '70, Osaka, Japan, 1970, Fondation Maeght, St. Paul de Vence, France, 1970, Art Inst. Chgo., 1972; represented in permanent collections including, Mus. Modern Art, Whitney Mus. Am. Art, cities of Hannover and Hamburg, Germany, Rijksmuseum Kroller Muller, Otterlo, Holland, Rijksmuseum, Amsterdam, Holland, Japan Iron, Steel Fedn., Osaka, City of Balt., Hirshhorn Mus., Milw. Art Center, City of Buffalo, Mus. Modern Art, Shiga, Japan; author: Full Circle: Panoramas of Paris, Venice, Rome, Siena and Kyoto, 1990. Served with USNR, 1945-46. DAAD fellow Berlin Kunstlerprogram, 1976; recipient AIA Artist's medal, 1981, Art award Am. Inst. Arts and Letters, 1987, Prix Ars Electronica Siemens AG for Computer Graphics, Linz, Austria, 1989. Mem. Am. Acad. Arts and Letters. Patentee discontinuous compression structures, model for atomic forms. *My art is concerned with nature in its most fundamental aspect, the patterns of physical forces in space.*

SNETSINGER, DAVID CLARENCE, retired animal feed company executive; b. Barrington, Ill., Apr. 22, 1930; s. Clarence J. and Helen (Mills) S.; m. Phoebe Burnett; children: Penny, Tom, Carol, Susan. BS, U. Ill., 1952, MS, 1957, PhD, 1959. Registered profl. animal scientist. Asst. prof. U. Minn., 1959-62, assoc. prof., 1962-67; poultry area mgr. Purina Mills Inc., St. Louis, 1967-69, dir. poultry group, 1970-87, v.p. rsch., 1987-91; ret., 1991. Patentee in field of poultry feeding programs and equipment; author 116 sci. and popular trade articles on poultry nutrition. 1st lt. U.S. Army, 1952-54. Fellow Poultry Sci. Assn. (pres. 1988-89); mem. World's Poultry Sci. (v.p. 1989-92), Fedn. Food Animal Scis. (sec.-treas. 1989-92), Animal Sci. Assn., Am. Inst. Nutrition, Dairy Sci. Assn., Internat. Brotherhood Magicians (pres. 1982-83, 93-94), Soc. Am. Magicians (v.p. St. Louis chpt. 1980-81), Sigma Xi.

SNIBBE, PATRICIA MISCALL, advertising agency executive; b. Hackensack, N.J., June 1, 1932; d. Jack and Margaret Lois (Drake) Miscall; m. Richard Wilson Snibbe, Sept. 8, 1962; stepchildren: John Robinson, Paul Clor. BFA, R.I. Sch. Design, 1954; postgrad., New Sch. for Social Rsch., 1975-80, U. London, 1989. Art dir., film producer Peckham Prodns., N.Y.C., 1960-64; dir. art, ptnr. Stallman and Snibbe, N.Y.C., 1964-66; dir. art Shevlo Advt., N.Y.C., 1966-72, Bernard Hodes Advt., N.Y.C., 1972-77; owner, creative dir. Designstuff, N.Y.C., 1978-88; creative dir. Archtl. Film Libr., N.Y.C., 1980—; pres. Crommelin and Bliss, Parfumier, 1988—. Author and artist: Feminist Funnies, 1981—. Recipient Golden Cir. award Affiliated Advt. Agys. Internat., 1975-77, Creativity award of Distinction, 1978. Mem. NOW (bd. dirs. N.Y.C. 1983-84), Graphic Artists Guild (steering com. Cartoonists Guild div. 1984-85), NATAS, Archael. Inst. Am. Home: 139 E 18th St New York NY 10003-2470

SNIBBE, RICHARD W., architect; b. Balt., Oct. 31, 1916; s. George W. and Mildred (Robinson) S.; m. Miriam Bergman, Jan. 3, 1942 (dec.); children: John Robinson, Paul Clor; m. Patricia Lois Miscall, Sept. 8, 1962. B.A., St. Johns Coll., 1939; postgrad., Harvard Grad. Sch. Design, 1939-41. Registered profl. architect, lic. architect N.Y. Asso. Edward D. Stone (architect), N.Y.C., 1951-56; partner Ballard, Todd & Snibbe, N.Y.C., 1957-61; individual practice architecture N.Y.C., 1962; partner Myller, Snibbe, Tafel, N.Y.C., 1962-67, Snibbe, Tafel, Lindholm, 1967-73, Wilson & Snibbe (architects, planners, engrs.), N.Y.C., from 1970; formed Snibbes Inc. (producers archtl. films), 1981; instr. Cooper Union, N.Y.C., 1949; vis. critic Columbia, N.Y.C., 1956, Pratt Inst., N.Y.C., 1962; founder Archtl. Film Library, 1982. Author: Small Commercial Buildings, 1956, Snibbe, Selected Works and Essays, 1983; important works include U.S. embassy, New Delhi, India (as assoc.), 1955, Tennis Pavilion, Princeton, 1960 (AIA honor award 1962), grad. dormitories Princeton U., 1961, comprehensive campus plan and bldgs. State U. Coll, Geneseo, N.Y., 1962-72, Handloser Project, Future Town, 1973, entry to Paris Opera Competition, 1983; pub. L'Arca, 1990; exhibited in Mus. Modern Art, N.Y.C., Transformations in Modern Architecture, 1979; producer: (film) Maison La Roche-Jeanneret by Le Corbusier, 1983, (TV film) Great Modern Architecture of the Last 25 Years, 1994. Chmn. aesthetics com., bd. dirs. Gramercy Neighborhood Assn. Inc. Brunner scholar N.Y. chpt. AIA, 1957. Fellow AIA (chmn. nat. com. on aesthetics 1963, mem. emeritus 1990—); mem. Nat. Com. on Aesthetics (founder, chmn. 1963, mem. emeritus 1990—), Harvard Grad. Sch. Design Assn., Am. Arbitration Assn., Players Club. Patentee for suspended structure, Landspan. Address: 139 E 18th St New York NY 10003-2470

SNIDER, EDWARD MALCOLM, professional hockey club executive; b. Washington, Jan. 6, 1933; s. Sol C. and Lillian (Bonas) S.; m. Martha McGeary, March 4, 1984; children: Craig Alan, Jay Thomas, Lindy Lou, Tina Suzanne, Sarena Lynn, Samuel Everett. B.S., U. Md., 1955. CPA, Md. Maj. stockholder, exec. v.p. Edge Ltd., Washington, 1957-63; v.p. Phila. Eagles Football Club, 1964-67; owner Phila. Flyers Hockey Club, 1967—; chmn. bd. Spectrum Arena, Phila., 1967—; bd. govs. NHL, 1967—; established spectator, sports, entertainment and comm. firm adv. bd. Sol C. Snider Entrepreneurial Ctr. U Pa.; bd. overseers Wharton Sch. U. Pa.; bd. dirs. Inst. for Cancer and Blood Diseases Hahnemann U., Simon Weisenthal Ctr.; bd. trustees Inst. for Objectivist Studies. Office: Phila Flyers Pattison Pl Philadelphia PA 19148

SNIDER, ELIOT I., lumber company executive; b. Cambridge, Mass., Apr. 10, 1921; s. Harry and Lena (Korelitz) S.; m. Ruth Freund, 1945; children: Andrew, Paul, Nancy. BA, Harvard U., 1941, MBA, 1943. Pres. Mass. Lumber Co., Cambridge, 1953-95; chmn., dir. George McQuesten Co., Inc., Eastern Terminals, Inc.; dir. Kravis Ctr.; dir. corps. Chmn. Beth Israel Hosp., Boston, 1982-86, trustee 1976—; overseer Mus. Fine Arts; mem. dean's coun. Harvard U. Sch. Pub. Health. Pres. Snider Charitable Trust. Served to lt. USN, 1943-45. Mem. Chief Execs. Orgn., World Bus. Coun. Republican. Clubs: Longwood, Harvard, N.Y. Yacht, Rotary. Office: Mass Lumber Co 929 Massachusetts Ave Cambridge MA 02139-3143

SNIDER, ERIC ROSS, music critic; b. Cleve., Apr. 21, 1954; s. Donald ross and Erma Marie (Ceschini) S.; m. Barbara Ann Gartner, June 12, 1982; children: Karin Alison, Daniel Ryan. BA, SUNY, Cortland, 1976. Critic Jazziz Mag., Gainesville, Fla., 1982-88; editor, writer Music Mag., St. Petersburg, Fla., 1980-87; pop music critic St. Petersburg Times, 1987—. Recipient Gen. Excellence in Criticism award Fla. Press Club, 1987, 89. Avocations: basketball, softball, general sports. Office: St Petersburg Times 490 1st Ave S Saint Petersburg FL 33701-4204

SNIDER, GORDON LLOYD, physician; b. Toronto, Apr. 11, 1922; came to U.S., 1946, naturalized, 1956; s. Isadore Leonard and Rebecca (Freeman) S.; m. Ruth Charlotte Tobias, May 18, 1945; children: Barry Bernard, Martin David, Rebecca Eve. MD, U. Toronto, 1944. Intern Toronto Gen. Hosp., 1944-45; resident in medicine Bronx Hosp., N.Y.C., 1946-47; resident in pathology Mass. Meml. Hosps., Boston, 1947-48; fellow in medicine Lahey Clinic, Boston, 1948-49; fellow in pulmonary medicine Trudeau San., Trudeau, N.Y., 1949-50; asst. dir. chest dept. Michael Reese Hosp., Chgo., 1950-61; attending physician Winfield (Ill.) Hosp., 1950-61; cons. physician, dir. pulmonary function lab. Mcpl. Tb San., Chgo., 1954-68; chief div. thoracic medicine Mt. Sinai Hosp., Chgo., 1961-66; acting chmn. depts. medicine Chgo. Med. Sch. and Mt. Sinai Hosp., 1965-66; chief pulmonary disease sect. Wood VA Hosp.; attending physician Milwaukee County Gen. Hosp., Wood, Wis., 1966-68; asst. prof. Chgo. Med. Sch., 1958-61, assoc. prof., 1961-64, prof., 1964-66; prof. Marquette U. Sch. Medicine, 1966-68; prof. medicine, head pulmonary medicine sect. Boston U. Sch. Medicine, 1968-87; chief pulmonary medicine sect., Boston VA Med. Ctr., 1968-88, chief med. svc., 1986—; pulmonary sect. mem. Evans Dept. Clin. Rsch., Univ. Hosp., Boston, 1968—; Maurice B. Strauss prof. medicine, Boston U. and Tufts U. Schs. Medicine, 1986-93, Boston U. Sch. Medicine, 1993—; Presdl. lectr. Soc. European Pulmonologists, 4th Ann. Congress, Stressa-Milan, Italy, 1986, Blankenhorn lectr. Cin. Soc. Ind. Medicine, 1989; Parker B. Francis lectr. 6th Thomas L. Petty Aspen Lung Conf., 1991, Theodore Badger Meml. lectr. Mass. Thoracic Soc., 1995; vis. prof. U. Cin. Sch. Medicine, 1989; Frank T. Fulton vis. physician-in-chief pro tempore R.I. Hosp. and Brown U., Providence, 1988; med. adv. bd. Puritan-Bennett Corp.; chmn. sci. adv. com. Norman B. Salvesen Emphysema Trust, U. Edinburgh, 1981-93; Theodore Badger Meml. lecture Mass. Thoracic Soc., 1995, Irving Kass lectr. U. Nebr., 1992. Served to capt. M.C. Royal Can. Army, 1945-46. Co-recipient Alton Ochsner award relating smoking and health, 1990; NIH grantee, 1962-91; Francis S. North travel fellow, 1978; 6th Robert K. Match Disting. scholar L.I. Jewish Hosp., 1991. Fellow Am. Coll. Chest Physicians (Simon Rodbard lectr. 1985), ACP; mem. Am. Fedn. Clin. Research, Am. Thoracic Soc. (pres. 1986, Amberson lectr. 1992), Central Soc. Clin. Research, Sigma Xi, Alpha Omega Alpha. Jewish. Home: 24 Holly Rd Newton MA 02168-1449 Office: VA Med Center 150 S Huntington Ave Jamaica Plain MA 02130-4817

SNIDER, HARLAN TANNER, former manufacturing company executive; b. Owensboro, Ky., July 20, 1926; s. George William and Lydia (Tanner) S.; m. Helen Boswell, Mar. 7, 1953; children—William Jeffrey, Katherine Snider. B.A., Transylvania U., 1949. Territory salesman Sunray DX Corp., Owensboro, 1950-57; dist. sales mgr. Sunray DX Corp., Ind., 1958-63; div. mgr. Sunray DX Corp., Iowa, 1963-65; dir. mktg. services Sunray DX Corp., Tulsa, 1955-67; pres. Red Bar Chems., Tulsa, 1967-69; dir. petrochems. Sun Oil Co., Phila., 1969-71; v.p. mktg. Sun Oil Co., 1973-75; pres. Sunmark Industries, Phila., 1975-79; sr. v.p., external affairs Sun Co., Inc., Radnor, Pa., 1980-84; sr. v.p. planning pub. affairs Sun Co., Inc., 1984-88; ret., 1988. Served with USAF, 1944-46. Mem. Am. Petroleum Industry, 25 Yr. Club Petroleum Industry. Club: Union League (Phila.), Aronimink Golf (Newtown Square, Pa.), Mariner Sands Golf Club (Stuart, Fla.). Home (winter): 7013 Pacific Dr SE Stuart FL 34997

SNIDER, HAROLD WAYNE, risk and insurance educator; b. Puyallup, Wash., Apr. 16, 1923; s. P. Marion and Grace Stevenson (Short) S.; m. Isobel Milne Dice, Jan. 20, 1961. BA, U. Wash., 1946, MA, 1950; PhD, U. Pa., 1955. Instr. bus. U. Wash., 1952-54; assoc. prof. Ill. Wesleyan U., 1954-57; asst. prof. U. Pa., 1957-64; prof. risk mgmt. and ins. Temple U., Phila., 1964-91, prof. emeritus, 1991—; dir. Planned Protection Ins. Co. Author: Life Insurance Investment in Commercial Real Estate, 1956, Risk Management, 1963, (with Denenberg and others) Risk and Insurance, 1964, The Automobile Accident Problem: Saskatchewan Approach, 1973, Employee Benefit Administration, 1981; contbg. author: The Job of Risk Management, 1962. Bd. dirs. Planned Parenthood Fedn. Am., 1980-83. Served with AUS, 1943-46. S.S. Huebner Found. fellow, 1950-52. Mem. Risk and Ins. Mgmt. Soc., Am. Mgmt. Assn., Am. Risk and Ins. Soc., Phi Beta Kappa, Beta Gamma Sigma. Home: Unit 2A The Meadows 501 N Bethlehem Pike Apt 2A Ambler PA 19002-2516 Office: Sch Bus Adminstrn Temple U Philadelphia PA 19122 *If one has not failed, one's aspiration levels have been too low.*

SNIDER, JAMES RHODES, radiologist; b. Pawnee, Okla., May 16, 1931; s. John Henry and Gladys Opal (Rhodes) S.; B.S., U. Okla., 1953, M.D., 1956; m. Lynadell Vivion, Dec. 27, 1954; children—Jon, Jan. Intern, Edward Meyer Meml. Hosp., Buffalo, 1956-57; resident radiology U. Okla. Med. Center, 1959-62; radiologist Holt-Krock Clinic and Sparks Regional Med. Center, Ft. Smith, Ark., 1962—, dir. Fairfield Community Land Co., Little Rock, 1968-87, Fairfield Communities, Inc., 1968-87. Mem. Ark. Bd. Pub. Welfare, 1969-71. Bd. dirs. U. Okla. Assn., 1967-70, U. Okla. Alumni Devel. Fund, 1970-74; bd. visitors U. Okla. Served to lt. comdr. USNR, 1957-62. Mem. Am. Coll. Radiology, Radiol. Soc. N.Am., Am. Roentgen Ray Soc., AMA, Phi Beta Kappa, Beta Theta Pi, Alpha Epsilon Delta. Asso. editor Computerized Tomography, 1976-88. Home: 5814 S Cliff Dr Fort Smith AR 72903-3845 Office: 1500 Dodson Ave Fort Smith AR 72901-5128

SNIDER, JEROME GUY, lawyer; b. Lakewood, N.J., Mar. 14, 1950; s. Theodore Charles and Minnie Snider; m. Naomi S. Herman, Sept. 20, 1981; 1 child, Benjamin Herman. AB, Rutgers U., 1972; JD, U. Pa., 1975. Bar: N.Y. 1976, U.S. Dist. Ct. (so. and ea. dists.) N.Y. 1976, U.S. Dist. Ct. (no. dist.) Calif. 1979, U.S. Supreme Ct. 1980, U.S. Dist. Ct. D.C. 1983, U.S. Ct. Appeals (6th cir.) 1984, U.S. Ct. Appeals (D.C. cir.) 1986. Law clk. to chief judge U.S. Dist. Ct. (so. dist.) N.Y., N.Y.C., 1975-77; assoc. Davis Polk & Wardwell, N.Y.C., 1977-82, ptnr., Washington, 1983—. Mem. ABA, Fed. Bar Assn. Jewish. Home: 4821 43rd St NW Washington DC 20016-4064 also: Davis Polk & Wardwell 450 Lexington Ave New York NY 10017-3911*

SNIDER, JOHN JOSEPH, lawyer; b. Seminole, Okla., July 25, 1928; s. George Nathan and Katherine (Harris) S.; m. Harriet Jean Edmonds, June 14, 1952; children—John Joseph, Dorothy Susan (Mrs. Mark E. Blohm), William Arnold. A.B., U. Okla., 1950, LL.B., 1955. Bar: Okla. bar 1955. Since practiced in Oklahoma City; atty. Fellers, Snider, Blankenship, Bailey & Tippens, 1964-93, counsel to, 1993—; mem. Okla. adv. council Nat. Legal Services Corp., 1976-77. Pres. Okla. Soc. to Prevent Blindness, 1965-71; bd. dirs. Hosp. Hospitality House, Okla., 1978-86; bd. dirs. Nat. Soc. Prevention Blindness, 1971-75; vice chmn. Oklahoma City Crime Prevention Council, 1976-77. Served to 1st lt. USAF, 1950-53. Fellow Am. Bar Found. (Okla. chmn. 1986-88); mem. Oklahoma City C. of C., Okla. Bar Assn., Okla. County Bar Assn., Am. Judicature Soc., Phi Delta Phi, Phi Kappa Psi. Methodist. Home: 2018 Redbud Pl Edmond OK 73013-7733 Office: First Nat Bldg Oklahoma City OK 73102

SNIDER, L. BRITT, government executive; b. Rocky Mount, N.C., Jan. 12, 1945; s. Arnold Holmes and Kate Mills (Suiter) S.; m. Virginia Lansford, Aug. 24, 1974; 1 child, Britt Arnold. BA, Davidson (N.C.) Coll., 1966; JD, U. Va., 1969. Counsel judiciary subcom. on constl. rights U.S. Senate, Washington, 1971-75, counsel select com. on intelligence, 1975-76; ptnr. Ketner & Snider, Salisbury, N.C., 1976-77; counsel govt. ops. subcom. on govt. info. U.S. Ho. Reps., Washington, 1977; asst. dep. undersec. counterintelligence and security Dept. Def., Washington, 1977-87; minority counsel U.S. Senate Intelligence Com., Washington, 1987-89, gen. counsel, 1989-95, staff dir. commn. on roles and capabilities of U.S. Intelligence Cmty., 1995—; staff dir. Commn. to Rev. Security Practices and Procedures Dept. Def., Washington, 1985. Served to capt. U.S. Army, 1969-71, Vietnam. Mem. Va. Bar Assn., D.C. Bar Assn. Democrat. Episcopalian. Avocations: tennis, jogging, reading.

SNIDER, LAWRENCE K., lawyer; b. Detroit, Dec. 28, 1938; s. Ben and Ida (Hertz) S.; m. Maxine Bobman, Aug. 12, 1962; children: Stephanie, Suzanne. BA, U. Mich., 1960, JD, 1963. Bar: Mich. 1964, Ill. 1991. Ptnr. Jaffe, Snider, Raitt & Heuer, Detroit, 1968-91, Mayer, Brown & Platt, Chgo., 1991—; mem. Nat. Bankruptcy Conf., Am. Coll. Bankruptcy, 1991—. Contbr. articles to profl. jours. Mem. Mich. Coun. for the Arts, 1990-91. Avocations: photography, collections. Office: Mayer Brown & Platt 190 S La Salle St Chicago IL 60603-3410

SNIDER, ROBERT F., chemistry educator, researcher; b. Calgary, Alta., Can., Nov. 22, 1931; s. Edward C. and Agnes S. (Klaeson) S.; children: Wendy A., Timothy J., Terry E., Geoffrey Y, Eric A. M. Burrough. B.S., U. Alta., 1953; Ph.D., U. Wis., 1958. Postdoctoral fellow Nat. Research Council Can., Ottawa, 1958; instr. II U. B.C., Vancouver, 1958-60, asst.

prof., 1960-65, assoc. prof., 1965-69, prof., 1969—; vis. research prof. U. Leiden, Netherlands, 1973-74. Recipient gov. gen. gold medal U. Alta., 1953; U. Wis. WARF unassigned fellow, 1953-55; Izaac Walton Killam Meml. fellowship, 1985-86. Fellow Chem. Inst. Can., Royal Soc. Can.; mem. Am. Phys. Soc., Can. Assn. Physicists. Home: 3952 W 29th St. Vancouver, BC Canada V6S 1T9 Office: U BC, 2036 Main Mall, Vancouver, BC Canada V6T 1Z1

SNIDER, ROBERT LARRY, management consultant; b. Muskogee, Okla., Aug. 10, 1932; s. George Robert and Kathryn (Smiser) S.; m. Gerlene Rose Tipton, Nov. 26, 1953; children: Melody Kathryn Porter, Rebecca Lee. B.S. in Indsl. Engring., U. Houston, 1955, postgrad., 1956; postgrad., Pomona Coll., 1960. Cert. mgmt. cons. Instr. U. Houston Coll. Engring., 1955-56; sr. indsl. engr. Sheffield Steel Corp., Houston, 1955-59, Kaiser Steel Co., Fontana, Calif., 1959-60; cons. Arthur Young & Co., Los Angeles, 1960-61; mgmt. analyst Iranian Oil Exploration & Producing Co., Masjidi-Suliman, Iran, 1961-62; cons., 1962-65; v.p. operating methods div. Booz, Allen & Hamilton, Inc., Dallas, 1965-67; chmn., CEO RLS Profl. Svcs., Houston, Tex., 1995—; prin., gen. cons. practice Peat Marwick Mitchell, CPAs, Houston, 1969-71; exec. v.p. mfg. Sterling Electronics Corp., Houston, 1971-72, pres., chief operating officer, 1972-77; pres., chief exec. officer Rapoca Energy Corp., Cin., 1977-79; mng. partner, cons. Coopers & Lybrand, Southwest, Houston, 1979-81; mng. dir. Southwest region Korn Ferry Internat., Houston, 1981-86; ptnr.-in-charge Houston Mgmt. Cons. Practice, 1986-91; ptnr. cons. Southwest Enterprise Coopers & Lybrand, Houston, 1991-92; ptnr. S.W. Mfg. Consulting Process Improvement Group Coopers & Lybrand, Houston, Pakistan/Mid. Asia, 1992-93; internat. cons. ptnr. Coopers & Lybrand, Houston, 1993-95; chmn./CEO RLS Profl. Svcs., 1995—. Past mem. bd. dirs., exec. com. Houston Jr. Achievement; pastchmn. bd. mem. found. bd.and adminstrv. bd. Chapel Wood Meth. Ch.; ret. exec. com., bd. dirs. Houston Grand Opera. With C.E. AUS, 1956. Recipient Outstandng Mil. Engr. award Soc. Mil Engrs., 1955; named Disting. Alumni, Cullen Coll. Engring., U. Houston, 1991. Mem. Soc. Mining Engrs., U. Houston Alumni Assn. (past bd. dirs., exec. com., past pres., chmn.), Houston club, Houstonian Club, Phi Theta Kappa, Phi Kappa Phi. Home: 11643 Greenbay St Houston TX 77024-6430 Office: RLS Profl Svcs 681 Tealwood Rd Montgomery TX 77356

SNIDER, RUTH ATKINSON, retired counselor; b. Louisville, Jan. 7, 1930; d. Ellis Orrell and Fanola Blanche (Miller) Atkinson; m. Arnold Wills Snider, Feb. 17, 1950; children: Yvonne Marie, Ray Wills, Mark Alan. Student, Centre Coll., 1947-48; BS, Spalding U., 1965, MEd, 1970; rank I, Western Ky. U., 1981. Cert. sch. psychometrist, sch. prin., supr. of instrn. Tchr. Shelby County (Ky.) Bd. Edn., 1949-50, Louisville Pub. Schs., 1956-57; tchr. Jefferson County Pub. Schs., Louisville, 1965-67, counselor, 1967-92; vol. co-chairperson for mentor program Spalding U., Louisville, 1991. Vol. Ky. Ctr. for Arts, 1989, 90, 91, Actors Theatre of Louisville, 193-94, 95, 96, Klondike Elem. Sch. Libr., 1994-95; pub. chair World Day of Prayer, 1996; sec. adv. com. Beechwood Bapt. Ch. Mem. ACA (del.), Am. Sch. Counselors Assn. (del. nat. conf.), Ky. Assn. Counseling and Devel., Ky. Sch. Counselors Assn. (conf. chairperson), Spalding Soc. (pres. 1995-96), Spalding Alumni Assn. (sec. 1994-96, Caritas award), Jefferson County Ret. Tchrs. Assn., Christian Women's Club. Avocations: sewing, travel. Home: 2428 Chattesworth Ln Louisville KY 40242-2849

SNIDER, TIM, mining executive. Pres. Phelps Dodge Morenci Inc., Morenci, Ariz. Office: Phelps Dodge Morenci Inc 4521 US Hwy 191 Morenci AZ 85540*

SNIFFEN, MICHAEL JOSEPH, hospital administrator; b. Ossining, N.Y., June 16, 1949; s. John Francis and Mary Agnes (Madden) S.; m. Anne Marie Gillick; children: Kevin, Kristina. BS, Fordham U., 1971; MBA in Hosp. Adminstrn., Baruch Coll., 1977. Dir. of fin. planning Westchester div. N.Y. Hosp., White Plains, N.Y., 1971-74; assoc. dir. N.Y. Hosp., N.Y.C., 1974-80, sr. assoc. dir., assoc. dean Cornell Med. Ctr., 1980-87; pres., chief exec. officer Overlook Hosp., Summit, N.J., 1987—; exec. v.p., chief exec. officer Atlantic Health Corp., Florham Park, N.J., 1996—; exec. dir. Cornell Health Policy Program, N.Y.C., 1984-87; adminstr. program Commonwealth Fund, N.Y.C., 1978-81; adv. bd. Robert Wood Johnson Found.-Teaching Nursing Home Program, Princeton, N.J., 1980-86. Vol. March of Dimes, Tarrytown, N.Y., 1984-88; bd. dirs. St. Columbans Sch., Peekskill, N.Y., 1981-84; mem. various Father's Clubs, Westchester County, N.Y., 1976-91. Mem. Am. Coll. Healthcare Execs., Hosp. Fin. Mgmt. Assn. (advanced mem.), Echo Lake Country Club (Westfield, N.J.), Beacon Hill Country Club, Baltusrol Country Club (Springfield, N.J.)., Rotary. Roman Catholic. Avocations: golf, college basketball. Home: 49 Drum Hill Rd Summit NJ 07901-3141 Office: Atlantic Health Corp. 24 Hanover Rd Florham Park NJ 30071*

SNIFFIN, JOHN HARRISON, retail executive; b. N.Y.C., Feb. 25, 1942; s. Harrison Webb and Elizabeth (Wood) S.; m. Beverly Ann Bailey, Sept. 24, 1966; children: Christine, John, Ned, Ellen. BBA, Ga. State U., 1967, MBA, 1969. Internal audit mgr. Sears, Roebuck and Co., Atlanta, 1961-69; asst. controller Heilig-Meyers Co., Richmond, Va., 1969-72, asst. treas., 1972-84, treas., 1984-86, v.p., treas., sec., 1986, v.p. mdse., 1986-89, sr. v.p. merchandising, 1989-92; sr. v.p. govt. rels., 1992—. Mem. retail exec. adv. com. Ctr. for Retailing, James Madison U. Mem. Fin. Execs. Inst., So. Home Furnishings Assn. (pres., exec. com.), Va. Retail Mchts. Assn. (bd. dirs., exec. com., asst. treas.), N.C. Retail Mchts. Assn. , bd. dirs.), Ky. Retail Fedn. (bd. dirs.), Pa. Retailers Assn. (bd. dirs.), Fla. Retail Fedn. (bd. dirs.). Republican. Roman Catholic. Avocations: music, golf. Office: Heilig-Meyers Co 2235 Staples Mill Rd Richmond VA 23230-2942

SNIPES, WESLEY, actor. Grad., SUNY, Purchase, 1980. Appeared in Broadway plays Boys of Winter, Execution of Justice, Death and King's Horsemen; films include Streets of Gold, 1986, Vietnam War Story (ACE award for best actor 1989), Mo'Better Blues, 1989, Major League, 1989, New Jack City, 1991, Jungle Fever, 1991, The Waterdance, 1992, White Can't Jump, 1992, Passenger 57, 1992, Rising Sun, 1993, Demolition Man, 1993, Boiling Point, 1993, Sugar Hill, 1994, Drop Zone, 1994, To Wong Foo, Thanks for Everything, Julie Newmar, 1995, The Money Train, 1995.

SNITOW, CHARLES, lawyer; b. N.Y.C., Feb. 7, 1907; m. Virginia Levitt, Nov. 2, 1935; children: Ann Barr, Alan Mark. AB, Cornell U., 1928, JD, 1930. Ptnr. Pomerance & Snitow, N.Y.C., 1931—; pres. Nat. Hardward Show Inc., N.Y.C., 1945-70, World Hobby Exposition, Chgo., Phila., 1948-53, Charles Snitow Orgn., N.Y.C., 1950-79, Internat. Auto Show, N.Y.C., 1952-80, Nat. Fancy Food Conf. Show, N.Y.C., 1955-70, U.S. World Trade Fair Inc., N.Y.C., San Francisco, 1957-66, Internat. Photography & Travel Show Inc., N.Y.C., 1960-72, Consumer Electronics Show, N.Y.C., 1967-77, Snitow Show Consultants, Inc., N.Y.C., 1975—; cons. Soviet Expn. Sci. and Tech., N.Y.C., 1959, N.C. Internat. Fair, Charlotte, 1959, Brit. Expn., N.Y.C., 1960, Cahners Expn. Group divsn. Reed Exhbn. Cos., N.Y.C., 1970-87, Brazil Expo, N.Y., Chgo., L.A., Dallas, Atlanta, Miami, Fla., 1981, Greater N.Y. Internat. Auto Show, 1982—, East/Cen. Europe Trade Expo, N.Y., 1994. Contbr. articles to Cornell Law Quar. Bd. dirs. Bill of Rights Found., N.Y.C., 1980; mem. Met. Opera Chorus, Schola Cantorum, Collegiate Chorale. Recipient cert. of honor March of Dimes, Gold Key-Medal of Honor, City of N.Y., 1960-62, Gran Prix Am., France, 1965, Garcia Moreno medal Equador, 1966; named Knight, Order of Merit, Republic of Italy, 1963; named to Order Hon. Ky. Cols., La. Cols. Mem. Nat. Assn. Expn. Mgrs. (hon., Kings Glove award for excellence 1991), Latin Am. C. of C., Cornell Club, Savage Club, Phi Beta Kappa, Alpha Kappa Delta. Avocation: singing. Home: 81 Walworth Ave Scarsdale NY 10583-1140 Office: Snitow Show Cons Inc 4 Sniffen Ct New York NY 10016-3505

SNODDY, JAMES ERNEST, education educator; b. Perrysville, Ind., Oct. 6, 1932; s. James Elmer and Edna May (Hayworth) S.; m. Alice Joanne Crowder, Aug. 15, 1954; children—Ryan Anthony, Elise Suzanne. B.S., Ind. State U., 1954; M.Ed., U. Ill., 1961, Ed.D., 1967. Tchr. Danville (Ill.) Public Schs., 1954-57, prin., 1961-64; instr. U. Ill., Champaign, 1965-67; prof. edn. Mich. State U., East Lansing, 1967-72; chmn. dept. elem. and spl. edn. Mich. State U., 1972-78, prof. edn., 1978—; dir. Program CORK, 1978-82. Served with U.S. Army, 1955-57. Mem. Am. Assn. for Adult and Continuing Edn., Commn. of Profs. of Adult and Continuing Edn. Methodist. Home: 2194 Lagoon Dr Okemos MI 48864-2711 Office: Mich State U 419 Erickson Hall East Lansing MI 48824-1034

SNODGRASS, ROBERT EUGENE, psychiatrist; b. Indpls., Feb. 27, 1930; s. William Howard and Della Gladys (Satterly) S.; m. Constance Fusco, Mar. 1, 1958; 1 child, Robert Brent. AB in Anatomy and Physiology, Ind. U., 1952, MD, 1955. Diplomate Am. Bd. Psychiatry and Neurology. Intern Marion County Gen. Hosp., Indpls., 1955-56; resident in psychiatry Ind. U. Med. Ctr., Indpls., 1964-67; pvt. gen. practice Greenwood, Ind., 1958-64; pvt. practice Indpls., 1967-90; staff psychiatrist Madison (Ind.) State Hosp., 1991—. Author: Beloved Madison, 1990; contbr. articles to profl. jours. Mem. Hist. Dist. Bd. Rev., Madison, 1992—. Capt. U.S. Army, 1956-58. Decorated Meritorious Svc. Commendation medal. Fellow Am. Psychiatric Assn.; mem. AMA, Ind. Psychiatric Soc. (past pres.), Jefferson County Hist. Soc. (bd. dirs. 1989—), Elks. Avocation: foreign languages. Home: 707 E Main St Madison IN 47250-3650 Office: Madison State Hosp 711 Green Rd Madison IN 47250-2143

SNODGRASS, W. D., writer, educator; b. Wilkinsburg, Pa., Jan. 5, 1926; s. Bruce DeWitt and Jesse Helen (Murchie) S.; m. Lila Jean Hank, June 6, 1946 (div. 1953); 1 child, Cynthia Jean; m. Janice Marie Ferguson Wilson, Mar. 19, 1954 (div. Aug. 1966); children—Kathy Ann Wilson (stepdau.), Russell Bruce; m. Camille Rykowski, Sept. 13, 1967 (div. 1977); m. Kathleen Brown, June 20, 1985. Student, Geneva Coll., 1943-44, 46-47; B.A., State U. Iowa, 1949, M.A., 1951, M.F.A., 1953; hon. doctorate, Allegheny Coll., 1991. Faculty English dept. Cornell U., Ithaca, N.Y., 1955-57; faculty English dept. U. Rochester, N.Y., 1957-58; prof. English Wayne State U., Detroit, until 1968; prof. English and speech Syracuse U., N.Y., 1968-76; Disting. prof. of creative writing and contemp. poetry U. Del., Newark, 1979-94, retired, 1994; faculty Morehead Writers' Conf., Ky., summer 1955, Antioch Writers' Conf., Yellow Springs, Ohio, summer 1958, 59; disting. vis. prof. Old Dominion U., Norfolk, Va.; instr. Narrative Poetry Workshop SUNY, Binghamton, 1977, Cranbrook Writers' Conf., Birmingham, Mich., 1981. Author: (poems) Heart's Needle (Pultizer prize 1960), 1959, After Experience, 1968, Remains (under pseudonym S.S. Gardons) 1970, The Fuhrer Bunker, 1977, If Birds Build With Your Hair, 1979, The Boy Made of Meat, 1982, Magda Goebbels (poems from The Fuhrer Bunker, 1983), Heinrich Himmler (poems from The Fuhrer Bunker) 1983, D.D. Byrde Calling Jennie Wrenne, 1984, A Colored Poem, 1986, The House the Poet Built, 1986, 1987, Selected Poems, 1957-87, W.D.'s Midnight Carnival: Poems by W.D. Snodgrass and Paintings by DeLoss McGraw, 1988, The Death of Cock Robin: Poems by W.D. Snodgrass and Paintings by DeLoss McGraw, 1989, Autumn Variations, 1990; translator: (with Lore Segal) Gallows' Songs of Christian Morgenstern, Six Troubadour Songs, 1977, Traditional Hungarian Songs, 1978, Six Minnesinger Songs, 1983, The Four Seasons (translations of Vivaldi's Sonnets) 1984, (essays) In Radical Pursuit, 1975, Star and Other Poems, 1990, Five Romanian Ballads, 1991, Snow Songs, 1992, Each in His Season, 1993, The Fuhrer Bunker: The Complete Cycle, 1995; contbr. essays, poems, translations to lit. mags. Recipient Ingram-Merrill award, 1958, Longview lit. award, 1959, spl. citation Poetry Soc. Am., 1960, Pulitzer prize for poetry, 1960, Guinness Poetry award, 1961, Miles Modern Poetry award, 1966; Hudson Rev. fellow in poetry, 1958-59; fellow Guggenheim Found., 1972-73, Acad. Am. Poets, 1973, Bi-Centennial Medal William and Mary Coll., 1976, Centennial Medal Govt. Romania, 1977; Ingram-Merrill fellow 1979; sabbatical grantee Nat. Council on Arts, 1966-67, Ctr. for Advanced Study U. Del. grantee, 1983-84. Mem. PEN, Nat. Inst. Arts and Letters (grantee 1960), Poetry Soc. Am. Home: RD 1 Box 51 Erieville NY 13061-9801

SNORTLAND, HOWARD JEROME, educational financial consultant; b. Sharon, N.D., June 22, 1912; s. Thomas and Aline (Vig) S.; m. Anna Adeline Anderson, Sept. 1, 1940; children—Jan Signe, Kristi Jo, Howard Jay. B.A., U. N.D., 1937, M.S., 1958. Cashier N.D. Workmen's Compensation Bur., 1937-42, N.D. State Treas.'s Office, 1945-48; with N.D. Dept. Pub. Instrn., Bismarck, 1948-81; supt. pub. instrn. N.D. Dept. Pub. Instrn., 1977-81; ednl. fin. cons., 1981—; pres. State Econ. Council, 1978; nat. pres. Com. Ednl. Data Systems, 1965-67. Chmn. Burleigh ARC, 1963-67, bd. dirs., 1946—, vice chmn., 1964—; bd. dirs. Burleigh County Tb Assn., 1950—; stated clk. United Presbyterian Ch., 1942—; pres. N.D. United Christian Campus Fellowship, 1964-67, N.D. Westminster Found., 1963-70; mem. N.D. Synod Council, 1970—; chmn. United Way Fund, 1983. Served with USAAF, 1942-45. Recipient Summit Conf. award for outstanding pub. service, 1976. Mem. NEA, N.D. Edn. Assn., N.D. Sch. Bus. Ofcls., N.D. Assn. Adminstrs., Nat. Assn. Adminstrs., N.D. Assn. Ret. Employees (pres. 1987—), Am. Assn. Ret. Persons (vice chmn. N.D. legis. com. 1992-94, chmn. 1994—), Kiwanis, Phi Beta Kappa, Phi Delta Kappa.

SNOUFFER, NANCY KENDALL, English and reading educator; b. Long Branch, N.J., Aug. 22, 1941; d. Percival Wallace and Ruby Mae (Braswell) Kendall; m. Eugene Joseph Snouffer, Aug. 27, 1966; 1 child, Kendall Ann. BA in English, Gettysburg (Pa.) Coll., 1962; MA in English and Journalism, U. N.C., 1964; MS in Edn. and Reading, Western Ill. U., 1974; postgrad., U. Mo., 1976-78. Instr. English U. N.C., Wilmington, 1963-65, Shaw U., Raleigh, N.C., 1965-66; from instr. to asst. prof. English Wright Coll. and Chgo. City Colls., 1967-74; from instr. to asst. prof. reading Western Ill. U., Macomb, 1974-81; assoc. prof. ESL and reading Del Mar Coll., Corpus Christi, Tex., 1982—; mem. adv. bd. Tex. A&M U., Corpus Chrisit, 1993—; cons. in field. Author: College Reading Power, 4th edit., 1976-92; assoc. editor jour. Epistle, 1980-83, mem. editoral bd., 1983-85; contbr. articles to profl. jours. Master Tchr. Del Mar, 1986. Grantee Western Ill. U., 1974-81, Del Mar Coll., 1982—, NISSOD Teaching Excellence award, 1993. Mem. Tex. Assn. Developmental Educators, Tex. Coll. Reading Learning Assn. (chair So. membership 1994—), Nat. Assn. Developmental Educators, Internat. Reading Assn., Corpus Christi Literacy Coun. (bd. dirs., sec. 1988-93, vice-chair 1991-92), Harbor Playhouse (bd. dirs. 1988, 91-93), Alliance Francaise. Republican. Episcopalian. Avocations: tennis, travel, reading. Home: 4206 Acushnet Dr Corpus Christi TX 78413-2004 Office: Del Mar Coll 101 Baldwin Blvd Corpus Christi TX 78404-3805

SNOW, ALAN ALBERT, publisher; b. Van Nuys, Calif., July 20, 1946; s. Perry William and Virginia (Show) S. BA, Pepperdine U., L.A., 1969; MA, Sch. of Theology, Claremont, Calif., 1974; Magister Operae Onerosae (hon.), Inst. Antiquity-Christianity, Claremont, 1972; ThD, Andersonville Bapt. Sem., 1994. bd. dirs. Inst. for Study of Judeo-Christian Origins Calif. State U., Long Beach; mem. Jesus seminar Weststar Inst. Contbg. author to anthologies: The Book Your Church Does Not Want You to Read, 1993, 95, Sydney Omarr's Astrol. Guides for Your, 1994, 95, 96, 97. Mem. Nat. Notary Assn. (ethics com., Cert. Accomplishment), Am. Soc. Notaries, Dead Sea Scroll Rsch. Coun., Bibl. Archaeology Soc. Democrat. Home: 518 S Bay Front Balboa Island CA 92662

SNOW, CUBBEDGE, JR., lawyer; b. Macon, Ga., May 20, 1929. AB, Emory U., 1951; JD magna cum laude, Mercer U., 1952. Bar: Ga. 1952. Ptnr. Martin, Snow, Grant, Napier, Macon. Col. JAGC, USAFR, 1952-89. Fellow Am. Coll. Trial Lawyers, Am. Bar Found. (state chmn. 1988-92), Fedn. Ins. and Corp. Counsel, Ga. Def. Lawyers Assn., Am. Prepaid Legal Svcs. Inst. (bd. dirs. 1983-85); mem. ABA (ho. of dels. 1984—, chmn. prepaid legal svcs. com. 1986-88, bd. govs. 1993-96), Macon Bar Assn. (pres. 1967), State Bar Ga. (pres. 1974-75), Am. Judicature Soc. (bd. dirs. 1978-82, Herbert Harley award 1986), Phi Beta Kappa, Phi Alpha Delta, Omicron Delta Kappa. Office: Martin Snow 240 3rd St PO Box 1606 Macon GA 31202

SNOW, DAVID FORREST, judge; b. Boston, Mar. 15, 1932; s. Albert Grindle and Hope (Farrington) S.; m. Rosemary Allsman, Oct. 7, 1957 (div. Jan. 1982); children: Nicholas David, Sarah Alison, Catherine Ann; m. Joyce Neiditz, Mar. 15, 1985. BA, Dartmouth Coll., 1954; JD, Harvard U., 1960. Bar: Ohio 1961, U.S. Dist. Ct. Ohio 1965. Ptnr. Jones, Day, Reavis & Pogue, Cleve., 1960-88; asst. prof. law U. Iowa, Iowa City, 1967-68; bankruptcy judge U.S. Dist. Ct., Cleve., 1988—. Mem. ABA, Cleve. Bar Assn. Home: 2330 Ardleigh Dr Cleveland OH 44106-3128 Office: US Bankruptcy Ct 127 Public Sq 3101 Keycorp Tower Cleveland OH 44114-1309

SNOW, GEORGE ABRAHAM, physicist; b. N.Y.C., Aug. 24, 1926; s. Joseph and Anna (Snow) Ginsberg; m. Lila Alpert, June 20, 1948; children: Zachary, Andrew, Sara Ellen. B.S., CCNY, 1945; M.A., Princeton U., 1947, Ph.D., 1949. Jr. physicist Brookhaven Nat. Lab., Upton, N.Y., 1948-51; assoc. physicist Brookhaven Nat. Lab., 1951-55; physicist Naval Research Lab., Washington, 1955-58; vis. prof. dept. physics and astronomy U. Md., College Park, 1957-58, assoc. prof., 1958-61, prof., 1961-92, prof. emeritus, sr. rsch. scientist, 1992—; mem. Inst. for Advanced Study, Princeton, 1952-53; vis. lectr. U. Wis., Madison, 1955-56; vis. prof. U. Rome, 1965-66, U. Paris (France), Oxford, 1972-73, Tohoku U., Sendai, Japan, 1979; vis. scientist CERN, 1980, U. Bologna, 1986; mem. high energy physics adv. panel AEC, 1970-72; mem. high energy physics vis. com. Argonne Nat. Lab., 1969-71, Princeton-Pa. Accelerator, 1969-70, Lawrence Radiation Lab., Berkeley, Calif., 1980-83; mem. high energy physics adv. com. Brookhaven Nat. Lab., 1967-69; cons. to physics editor Prentice Hall, Inc., 1971-76. Cameraman, editor cable TV program: The Art Scene with Lila Snow, 1995—. Trustee URA, 1973-78, vice chmn., 1974, chmn. sci. com., 1975-77. Recipient Disting. Scholar-Tchr. award U. Md., 1988-89; NSF sr. postdoctoral fellow, 1961-62, John S. Guggenheim sr. fellow, Fulbright scholar, 1965-66; cited by Washington Acad. Scis., 1963. Fellow AAAS, Am. Phys. Soc. (mem. exec. coun. div. particles and fields 1968-70, vice chmn. div. particles and fields 1975, chmn. 1976, editor Phys. Rev. D 1981-83); mem. Fedn. Am. Scientists, European Phys. Soc., Phi Beta Kappa. Home: 4816 Essex Ave Bethesda MD 20815-5548 Office: U Md Dept Physics College Park MD 20742

SNOW, JAMES B., health science association administrator. MD cum laude, Harvard U., 1956. Intern surgery Johns Hopkins Hosp., Balt.; resident otolaryngology Mass. Eye and Ear Infirmary, Boston; prof., head dept. otorhinolaryngology U. Okla. Med. Ctr.; prof., chair dept. otorhinolaryngology and human comm. U. Pa. Sch. Medicine, 1972-90; dir. Nat. Inst. Deafness and Other Communication Disorders NIH, Bethesda, Md., 1990—; cons. prof. Shanghai Second U. Med. Scis., China. Author over 175 articles, abstracts and books. Recipient Regent's award U. Okla., 1970, Disting. Achievement award Deafness Rsch. Found., 1993, Presdl. Meritorious Exec. Rank award, 1994; named to Soc. Scholars Johns Hopkins U., 1991. Fellow Japan Broncho-Esophagological Soc.; mem. Am. Broncho-Esophagological Assn., Soc. Univ. Otolaryngologists-Head and Neck Surgeons, Assn. Acad. Depts. Otolaryngology-Head and Neck Surgery, Am. Laryngological Assn., Internat. Fedn. Oto-rhino-laryngological Socs. (Golden award 1989).

SNOW, JAMES BYRON, JR., physician, research administrator; b. Oklahoma City, Mar. 12, 1932; s. James B. and Charlotte Louise (Andersen) S.; m. Sallie Lee Ricker, July 16, 1954; children: James B., John Andrew, Sallie Lee Louise. BS, U. Okla., 1953; MD cum laude, Harvard U., 1956; MA (hon.), U. Pa., 1973. Diplomate: Am. Bd. Otolaryngology (dir. 1972-90). Intern Johns Hopkins Hosp., Balt., 1956-57; resident Mass. Eye and Ear Infirmary, Boston, 1957-60; prof., head dept. otorhinolaryngology Sch. Medicine U. Okla., Oklahoma City, 1962-72; prof., chmn. dept. otorhinolaryngology and human communication U. Pa. at Phila., 1972-90; dir. Nat. Inst. on Deafness and Other Comm. Disorders/NIH, Bethesda, Md., 1990—; mem. nat. adv. coun. neurol. and communicative disorders and stroke NIH, 1972-76, 82-86; chmn. Nat. Com. Rsch. Neurol. and Communicative Disorders, 1979-80. Editor: Am. Jour. Otolaryngology, 1979-83; Contbr. articles to sci. and profl. jours. Served with M.C. AUS, 1960-62. Recipient Regents award for superior tchg. U. Okla., 1970, Golden award Internat. Fedn. Otorhinolaryngological Socs., 1989, Disting. Achievement award Deafness Rsch. Found., 1993, Presdl. Meritorious Exec. Rank award, 1994; named to Soc. Scholars Johns Hopkins U., 1991. Fellow Japan Broncho-Esophagological Soc. (hon.), Am. Laryngological Assn. (hon.); mem. ACS (regent 1982-90), AMA (coun. on sci. affairs 1975-86), Soc. Univ. Otolaryngologists (pres. 1975), Am. Acad. Otolaryngology-Head and Neck Surgery, Assn. Acad. Depts. Otolaryngology (pres. 1981-82), Am. Laryngol., Rhinol. and Otol. Soc., Am. Otol. Soc., Am. Laryngol. Assn. (editor 1983-89, pres. 1990-91), Am. Broncho-Esophagol. Assn. (editor trans. 1973-77, pres. 1979), Collegium Otorhinolaryngologicum, Phi Beta Kappa, Alpha Omega Alpha. Home: 119 Driscoll Way Gaithersburg MD 20878-5210 Office: Nat Inst Deafness & Other Comm Disorders 9000 Rockville Pike Bldg 31 Bethesda MD 20892-0001

SNOW, JEFFREY SCOTT, fuels engineer; b. Princeton, Ind., Feb. 27, 1959; s. Wilford Lee and Lois Jean (Spaw) S.; m. Debra Rose Stout, Mar. 27, 1982; children: Bryan Robert, Scott Harrison. AS in Mining Engring. Tech., U. So. Ind., Evansville, 1980, BS in Mining Engring. Tech., 1981; BS in Mgmt. of Human Res., Oakland City (Ind.) Coll., 1990; MS in Mgmt., Oakland City U., 1996. Engring. coop. Old Ben Coal Co., Oakland City, 1978-80; engring. asst. PSI, Plainfield, 1982-83; sr. engring. asst. Pub. Svc. Ind. Energy, Plainfield, 1983, sta. engring. technologist, 1983-85, site and fueling engr., 1985-96, analyst power ops., 1996—. Mem. Soc. Mining Engrs. of AIME (assoc.), ASTM (mem. DO5 com. 1988—, E31 com. 1988—), Nat. Conf. on Weights and Measures, Omicron Psi. Lutheran. Achievements include coal handling system automation - Gibson Generating Station; avocations: golf, coin collecting. Office: PSI Energy Inc Gibson Generating Sta RR 1 Box 300 Owensville IN 47665

SNOW, JOEL ALAN, research director; b. Brockton, Mass., Apr. 1, 1937; s. George H. and Mary W. (Sproul) S.; m. Laetitia Harrer, June 29, 1957 (div. 1983); children: Jonathan, Nicholas; m. Barbara Kashian, Feb. 7, 1992; stepchildren: James, Alexander. BS in Physics, U. N.C., 1958; MA in Physics, Washington U., St. Louis, 1963, PhD in Physics, 1967. Program dir. for theoretical physics NSF, Washington, 1968-70, head office of interdisciplinary rsch., 1970-71, dep. asst. dir. for sci. and tech., rsch. applications, 1971-74, dir. office of planning and resources, 1974-76, dir. div. of policy rsch. and analysis, 1976; sr. policy analyst, office of sci. and tech. policy Exec. Office of the Pres., Washington, 1976-77; assoc. dir. for rsch. policy U.S. Dept. Energy, Washington, 1977-81, dir. sci. and tech. affairs, 1981-88; assoc. v.p. for rsch. and Argonne, U. Chgo., 1988-92; dir. Inst. for Phys. Rsch. and Tech. Iowa State U., Ames, 1993—, prof. elec. and computer engring., 1993—; rsch. assoc. dept. physics U. Ill., Urbana, 1967-68; instr. physics and electronics U.S. Navy Nulcear Power Shc., New London, Conn., 1958-61; sci. organizer Pres.'s Conf. on Superconductivity, 1987, NSF program rsch. applied to nat. needs, 1971, NSF program interdisciplinary rsch. relevant to problems of society, 1969. Contbr. over 130 articles to mags. and profl. jours. Lt. (j.g.) USN, 1958-61. Recipient Meritorious Svc. award NSF, 1972, Meritorious award William A. Jump Found., 1973, Arthur S. Fleming award Downtown Jaycees, 1974; NSF postdoctoral fellow Ctr. for Advanced Study U. Ill., 1967-68; NSF fellow, 1963-65. Fellow AAAS, Am. Phys. Soc.; mem. Am. Chem. Soc., Am. Nuc. Soc., World Future Soc., Sigma Xi, Phi Beta Kappa. Achievements include pioneering development of federal programs in solar and geothermal energy and energy conservation and federal programs in technology transfer. Office: IPRT/Iowa State U 112 Office Lab Bldg Ames IA 50011

SNOW, JOHN WILLIAM, railroad executive; b. Toledo, Aug. 2, 1939; s. William Dean and Catharine (Howard) S.; m. Fredrica Wheeler, June 11, 1964 (div. 1973); children: Bradley, Ian; m. Carolyn Kalk, Aug. 31, 1973; 1 child, Christopher. B.A., Kenyon Coll., 1962; Ph.D., U. Va., 1965; LL.B., George Washington U., 1967. Asst. prof. econs. U. Md., College Park, 1965-67; assoc. Wheeler & Wheeler, Washington, 1967-72; asst. gen. counsel Dept. Transp., Washington, 1972-73, dep. asst. sec. for policy, plans and internat. affairs, 1973-74, asst. sec. for govtl. affairs, 1974-75, dep. under sec., 1975-76; adminstr. Nat. Hwy. Traffic Safety Adminstrn., Washington, 1976-77; v.p. govt. affairs Chessie System Inc., Washington, 1977-80; sr. v.p. corp. services CSX Corp., Richmond, Va., 1980-84, exec. v.p., 1984-85; pres., chief exec. officer Chessie System R.R.s, Balt., 1985-86, CSX Rail Transport, Jacksonville, Fla., 1986-87, CSX Transp., Jacksonville, Va., 1987-88; pres., chief operating officer CSX Corp., Richmond, Va., 1988-89, pres., chief exec. officer, 1989-91, chmn., pres., chief exec. officer, 1991—, also bd. dirs.; adj. prof. law George Washington U., 1972-75; vis. prof. econs. U. Va., Charlottesville, spring 1977; vis. fellow Am. Enterprises Inst., Washington, spring 1977; bd. dirs. NationsBank Corp., Bassett Furniture Industries Inc., USX Corp., Textron Inc. Bd. trustees Johns Hopkins U., chmn. The Bus. Roundtable. Mem. Va. State Bar. Episcopalian. Clubs: Chevy Chase, Metropolitan (Washington); Commonwealth, Country of Va. (Richmond).

SNOW, KARL NELSON, JR., public management educator, university administrator, former state senator; b. St. George, Utah, July 1, 1930; s. Karl Nelson and Wanda (McGregor) S.; m. Donna Jean Dain, Jan. 29, 1960; children: Karl Nelson, III, Melissa, Daniel D., Jeanmarie, Elisabeth, Howard H. B.S., Brigham Young U., Provo, Utah, 1956; M.A. (State of Minn. Adminstrv. fellow 1956-57), U. Minn., 1958; M.P.A. (univ. fellow 1959-61),

U. So. Calif., 1965, D.P.A., 1972. Budget examiner Minn. Dept. Adminstrn., 1956-59; staff asst., instr. Sch. Pub. Adminstrn. U. So. Calif., 1959-62; mem. faculty Brigham Young U., Provo, Utah, 1962—, dir. Inst. Govt., 1969-79, prof. public mgmt., 1979—, asst. exec. v.p., 1987-91; state legis. fiscal analyst, 1966-70; mem. Utah Senate from 16th Dist., 1972-85, majority leader, 1981-85; chmn. Utah State House Fellowship Commn., 1973-79, Utah Constl. Revision Commn., 1977-89; bd. dirs. Legis. Leaders Found., 1981-85; chmn. bd. trustees Utah Tech. Fin. Corp., 1983-94; pres., trustee Utah Tech. Equity Found., 1994-96; chmn. Conf. of State Sponsored Seed and Venture Funds, 1993-96. Bd. editors Public Adminstrn. Rev, 1969-70, State and Local Govt. Rev, 1977-83; contbr. articles to profl. jours. Missionary Mormon Ch., 1950-52, mem. stake high council, 1975-85, 91—, bishop, 1985-90; mem. Warren Burger Prison Task Force, 1983-87; bd. dirs. Utah Innovation Found., 1984-88. Mem. Am. Soc. Pub. Adminstrn. (chpt. pres. 1968-69), dir. nat. council (1969-72), Sons Utah Pioneers. Home: 1847 Oak Ln Provo UT 84604-2140 Office: Brigham Young U 760 Tnrb Provo UT 84602-1133

SNOW, MARINA SEXTON, author; b. Boston, Apr. 9, 1937; d. Charles Ernest Snow and Katherine Alice Townsend; m. Richard DeVere Horton, Aug. 30, 1958 (div. 1968); children: Heather Kertchem, James Horton; m. Charles A. Washburn, Jan. 7, 1978 (div. 1979). BA, U. Iowa, 1958; MA in Speech Pathology, N.Mex. State U., 1967; MA in Librarianship, San Jose State U., 1976; MA in Theatre Arts, Calif. State U., Sacramento, 1979. Cert. clin. competence Am. Speech and Hearing Assn. Tchr. ESL Inst. Colombo-Americano, Cali, Colombia, 1958-59; tchr. Las Cruces (N.Mex.) Pub. Schs., 1964-66; speech therapist Sutter County Schs., Yuba City, Calif., 1967-72; reference libr. Calif. State U. Libr., Sacramento, 1976-95. Contbr. articles to profl. jours.; author 2 plays: Apricot Coffee, Alkali Flat. Pres. Alkali Flat Neighborhood Assn., Sacramento, 1987-94, Sacramento Old City Assn., 1979—. Mem. Sacramento Old City Assn. Avocations: theatre arts, historic preservation, gardening.

SNOW, MARLON O., trucking executive, state agency administrator; m. Ann; children. Gen. mgr. spl. commadities Milne Truck Lines, Phoenix, L.A., 1970-81; gen. mgr. spl. commodities, sales Motor Cargo, Salt Lake City, Utah, 1981-82; owner MST Trucking, Inc., Salt Lake City, Utah, 1982—. Mem. Utah Valley State Coll. Found. (bd. dirs. 1991—), Alpine Sch. Dist. Found. (bd. dirs. 1990—). Office: 1247 East 430 N Orem UT 84057

SNOW, ROBERT ANTHONY, journalist; b. Berea, Ky., June 1, 1955; s. James Allen and Betty Jo (Threlkeld) S.; m. Jill Ellen Walker, Sept. 26, 1987; children: Kendall Elizabeth, Robert Walker. BA, Davidson Coll., 1977; postgrad. in Philosophy and Econs., U. Chgo., 1978-79. Editorial writer The Greensboro (N.C.) Record, 1979-81, The Virginian Pilot, Norfolk, 1981-82; editorial page writer The Daily Press, Newport News, Va., 1982-84; dep. editorial page editor The Detroit News, 1984-87, columnist, 1993—; editorial page editor The Washington Times, 1987-91; dep. asst. to pres. comm., dir. speechwriting The White House, Washington, 1991-92, dep. asst. for media affairs to Pres., 1992-93; columnist USA Today, Arlington, 1993—; syndicated columnist Creators Syndicate, 1993—; substitute host Teh Rush Limbaugh Radio Program, 1994—; polit. analyst Good Morning America, 1995; host Fox News Sunday, 1996—. Active Leadership Washington. Mem. Coun. Fgn. Rels., Nat. Conf. Edtl. Writers. Avocations: sports, music, traveling, writing. Office: Gannett News Svc 1000 Wilson Blvd Arlington VA 22209-3901

SNOW, THEODORE PECK, astrophysics educator; b. Seattle, Jan. 30, 1947; s. Theodore P. and Louise (Wertz) S.; s. Constance M. Snow, Aug. 23, 1969; children: McGregor A., Tyler M., Reilly A. BA, Yale U., 1969; MS, U. Wash., 1970, PhD, 1973. Mem. rsch. staff Princeton (N.J.) U., 1973-77; prof. U. Colo., Boulder, 1977—, dir. Ctr. for Astrophysics and Space Astronomy, 1986—. Author: (textbook) The Dynamic Universe, 1983, 4th edit., 1991, Essentials of the Dynamic Universe 4th edit., 1993 (textbook excellence award Text and Academic Authors Assn. 1994), Physics, 1986; contbr. over 200 articles to profl. jours. Fellow Royal Astron. Soc.; mem. Am. Astron. Soc., Astron. Soc. Pacific, Sigma Xi. Achievements include discovery, through observations in ultraviolet visible, and infrared wavelengths, of several important processes involving interstellar gas and dust, and their roles in star formation and late stages of stellar evolution. Office: U Colo Ctr Astrophysics Space Astronomy Campus Box 389 Boulder CO 80309

SNOW, TOWER CHARLES, JR., lawyer; b. Boston, Oct. 28, 1947; s. Tower Charles and Margaret (Harper) S.; m. Belinda L. Snow. AB cum laude English, Dartmouth Coll., 1969; JD, U. Calif., Berkeley, 1973. Bar: Calif. 1973, U.S. Dist. Ct. (no. dist.) Calif. 1973, U.S. Ct. Appeals (9th cir.) 1973, U.S. Supreme Ct. 1976, U.S. Dist. Ct. (ea. dist.) Calif. 1979, U.S. Ct. Appeals (fed. cir.) 1980, U.S. Ct. Claims 1980, U.S. Ct. Appeals (2d cir.) 1987, N.Y. 1988, U.S. Dist. Ct. (ea. and so. dists.) N.Y. 1988, U.S. Dist. Ct. (ctrl. dist.) Calif. 1989, U.S. Dist. Ct. (no. dist.) Tex. 1995. Ptnr., chmn. litigation dept. Orrick, Herrington & Sutcliffe, San Francisco, 1973-89; ptnr. Shearman & Sterling, San Francisco, 1989-94; ptnr., chmn. securities litigation, intellectual property and antitrust groups Brobeck, Phleger & Harrison, San Francisco, 1995—; arbitrator Nat. Assn. Securities Dealers, Am. Stock Exch., N.Y. Stock Exch., Pacific Coast Stock Exch., Superior Ct. City and County San Francisco, Am. Arbitration Assn.; lectr. in field. Author numerous law handbooks and articles to profl. jours. Mem. San Francisco Mus. Soc., San Francisco Symphony, San Francisco Ballet, San Francisco Opera, Am. Conservatory Theatre. Mem. ABA (chmn. subcom. pub. offering litig. 1984-88, co-chair task force on securities arbitration 1988-89, vice chair securities litig. com. 1986-88), Continuing Edn. Bar (bus. law inst. planning com. 1986), Securities Industry Assn., Nat. Inst. Trial Advocacy, San Francisco Bar Assn. (pres. securities litig. sect.). Democrat. Avocations: internat. travel, skiing, running, scuba diving, photography. Home: 177 Ridge Dr Napa CA 94558-9777 Office: Brobeck Phleger & Harrison Spear St Tower One Market St San Francisco CA 94105

SNOW, VELMA JEAN, secondary education educator; b. Hardaway, Ala., Oct. 29, 1952; d. Oliver and Lucy Ann (Carter) Harris; m. Joe Lee Snow Jr., July 8, 1979; children: Joe Lee, Jeffrey Oliver. BS in Biology, Ala. State U., 1974, MS, 1976. Cert. secondary tchr., Mich. Tchr. Perry County Schs., Marion, Ala., 1974-76, Montgomery (Ala.) Pub. Schs., 1976-78, Detroit Pub. Schs., 1979—. Vol. NAACP, Southfield, Mich., 1993. Recipient educators Achievement award Booker T. Washington Bus. Assn., 1988; NIH fellow, 1992, Am. Physiol. Soc. fellow, 1994. Mem. Mich. Sci. Tchrs. Assn., Detroit Sci. Tchrs. Assn., Young Astronauts Pilots (chpt. leader, coord. 1990-94, cert. 1993). Democrat. Baptist. Avocations: reading, golfing, singing, computer graphics. Home: 20477 Willowick Dr Southfield MI 48076-1765 Office: Detroit Pub Schs 2200 W Grand Blvd Detroit MI 48208-1178

SNOW, W. STERLING, secondary education educator, sports coach; b. Devils Lake, N.D., Feb. 14, 1947; s. Morgan Williams and Josephine Elizabeth Ann (Erickstad) S.; m. Barbara Kay Jolley, Aug. 29, 1976; 1 child, Michelle Rene. AB, U. Calif., Santa Cruz, 1970; postgrad., U. Calif., Santa Barbara, 1970-71; MA, Chapman Coll., 1976. Cert. secondary sch. tchr., Calif., Alaska, Arizona; Arizona, cert. adminstrn., Calif. Tchr., coach Monterey (Calif.) Peninsula Unified Sch. Dist., 1972-76; tchr., coach Anchorage (Alaska) Sch. Dist., 1976—, athletic dir., 1987-92, tchr., 1992—; conf. asst. U. Calif., Santa Cruz, 1971-78. Bd. dirs. Dimond Alumni Found., Anchorage, 1987-92. Recipient Merit award for outstanding athletic program Alaska Dept. Edn., 1990. Mem. AAAS, ASCD, Am. Chem. Soc., Nat. Sci. Tchrs. Assn., Nat. Assn. Biology Tchrs. (life), Nat. Interscholastic Athletic Adminstrs. Assn. (life), Nat. Assn. Basketball Coaches, Alaska Sci. Tchrs. Assn., Alaska Athletic Adminstrs. Interscholastic Assn. (Athletic Dir. of Yr. 1990), N.Y. Acad. Scis., Kappa Delta Pi. Lutheran.

SNOWBARGER, VINCENT KEITH, lawyer, state representative; b. Kankakee, Ill., Sept. 16, 1949; s. Willis Edward and Wahnona Ruth (Horger) S.; m. Carolyn Ruth McMahon, Mar. 25, 1972; children: Jeffrey Edward, Matthew David. BA in History, So. Nazarene U., 1971; MA in Polit. Sci., U. Ill., 1974; JD, U. Kans., 1977. Bar: Kans. 1977, U.S. Dist. Ct. Kans. 1977, Mo. 1987. Instr. Mid-Am. Nazarene Coll., Olathe, Kans., 1973-76; ptnr. Haskin, Hinkle, Slater & Snowbarger, Olathe, 1977-84, Dietrich, Davis, Dicus et al, Olathe, 1984-88, Armstrong, Teasdale, Schafly & Davis, Overland Park, Kans., 1989-92; Holbrook, Heaven & Fay, P.C., Merriam, Kans., 1992-94; ptnr. Snowbarger & Veatch LLP, Olathe, Kans., 1994—. Mem. Kans. Legislature, Topeka, 1985—; majority leader Ho. of Reps., 1993—; mem. Olathe Planning Commn., 1982-84, Leadership Olalthe; bd. dirs. Johnson County Cert. Devel. Corp.; divsn. chmn. United Way, Olathe, 1985-88, chmn. citizen rev. com., 1991—. Mem. Kans. Bar Assn., Kans. Assn. Hosp. Attys., Johnson County Bar Assn., Olathe Area C. of C. (bd. dirs. 1984). Republican. Nazarene. Avocation: politics. Home: 1451 E Orleans Dr Olathe KS 66062-5728 Office: PO Box 10121 110 S Cherry Ste 103 Olathe KS 66051-1421

SNOWBERGER, JANE ARDETH, geriatrics nurse, educator; b. Coffeeville, Kans., Nov. 4, 1945; d. Carl Fredrick and Mary Jane Emaline (Wood) Sonenberg; m. David E. Snowberger, Apr. 13, 1973; children: Tammy, Deena, John. Cert., N.Mex. State U., Las Cruces, 1980; AA, N.Mex. State U., 1983, ADN, 1990; BA, Graceland Coll., 1995. Med.-surg. nurse Gerald Champion Hosp., Alamogordo, N.Mex., 1980-82; ob-gyn staff nurse Gerald Champion Hosp., Alamogordo, 1990-91; office nurse Dr. A. Austin, M.D., Alamogordo, 1982-83; supr. charge nurse Betsy Ross ICF Facility, Rome, N.Y., 1984-86; med. records clk. Rome murphy Hosp., 1987-88; supr. charge nurse Planned Parenthood, Alamogordo, 1988-89; coord. NA program N.Mex. U., Alamogordo, 1991—. Sewing instr. Sr. Citizens, Alamogordo, 1989—. Mem. Nat. League for Nursing, LOCO Credit Union (supr. bd.). Democrat. Baptist. Avocations: sewing, serging, reading, dancing, hand crafts. Home: 1306 Greenwood Ln Alamogordo NM 88310-5742 Office: NMex U Scenic Dr Alamogordo NM 88310

SNOWDEN, FRANK MARTIN, JR., classics educator; b. York County, Va., July 17, 1911; s. Frank Martin and Alice (Phillips) S.; m. Elaine Hill, June 8, 1935; children: Jane Alice, Frank Martin III. Grad., Boston Latin Sch., 1928; AB, Harvard U., 1932, AM, 1933, PhD, 1944; postgrad., Am. Acad. in Rome, summer 1938; Fulbright research scholar, Italy, 1949-50; LLD (hon.), Bard Coll., 1957; DLitt (hon.), Union Coll., 1979; LHD (hon.), Georgetown U., 1985, Howard U., 1985; LHD, U. Md., 1993. Instr. classics Va. State Coll., 1933-36, Spelman Coll., 1936-40; instr. classics Howard U., 1942-44, chmn. dept., 1942-77, asso. prof., 1944-45, prof., 1945-90, prof. emeritus, 1991—; dir. Howard U. (Summer Sch.), 1942-54, Howard U. (Evening Sch. and Adult Edn.), 1942-48; chmn. Howard U. (Humanities Program), 1950-51; dean Howard U. (Coll. Liberal Arts), 1956-68; specialist lectr. Internat. Information Adminstrn., Dept. State, French West Africa, Gold Coast, Nigeria, Libya, Italy, Greece, Austria, 1953; cultural attaché Am. Embassy, Rome, Italy, 1954-56; vis. lectr. Fgn. Service Inst., 1956-62, 66-68; U.S. specialist in, India, lectr., Bombay, New Delhi, Lucknow, Calcutta, Madras areas, 1957, lectr. as U.S. specialist, Brazil, summer 1960, studied higher edn., Soviet Union, 1958; participant internat. seminar University Today, Dubrovnik, Yugoslavia, 1958; mem. U.S. del. UNESCO, Paris, 1958, 60, U.S. nat. commn. for, 1958-61; mem. Nat. Humanities Faculty, 1969-70, mem. bd., 1970-73; ann. lectr. Archaeol. Inst. Am., 1970-71, 74-76; vis. scholar U. Center Va., 1971-72; mem. com. Internat. Exchange Persons, 1970-73; mem. jury to select fellows in classics Am. Acad. Rome, 1971-73; mem. com. Folger Fellowship Program, 1972-75; Am. Council Learned Socs. rep. Council on Internat. Exchange of Scholars, 1973-77; mem. D.C. com. on Fulbright scholarships, 1951-54, 68-74; fellow Woodrow Wilson Internat. Center for Scholars, 1977; scholar-in-residence Rockefeller Found., Bellagio, Italy, fall 1977; adj. prof. classics Georgetown U., 1991-92, Blegen vis. disting. rsch prof. Vassar Coll., 1992-93. Author: Blacks in Antiquity: Ethiopians in the Greco-Roman Experience, 1970; coauthor: The Image of the Black in Western Art I: From the Pharaohs to the Fall of the Roman Empire (also pub. in French), 1976, Before Color Prejudice: The Ancient View of Blacks, 1983; contbr. chpts. to books, articles to classical and ednl. jours. Mem. D.C. Mayor's Commn. Arts and Humanities, 1972-74; vis. com. bd. overseers dept. classics Harvard Coll., 1977-83. Decorated Medaglia d'Oro for outstanding work in Italian culture and edn. Italy, 1958; Am. Council Learned Socs. fellow, 1962-63; NEH grantee, summer 1970. Mem. Am. Conf. Acad. Deans (sec., editor 1959-62, chmn. 1963-64), Am. Council on Edn., Vergilian Soc. Am. (trustee 1956-60), Am. Philol. Assn. (Charles J. Goodwin award of merit 1973, bd. dirs. 1976-79, 2d v.p. 1983-84), Archeol. Inst. Am. (pres. Washington soc. 1971), Classical Soc. Am. Acad. in Rome, Washington Classical Soc. (v.p. 1949-50, pres. 1974-75), Washington Fedn. Chs. (v.p. 1951-53). Clubs: Cosmos, Harvard. Home: 4200 Massachusetts Ave NW Washington DC 20016-4744

SNOWDEN, GUY BERNHARD, manufacturing executive; b. Peekskill, N.Y., Sept. 11, 1945; s. Frederick and Grace (Martin) S.; divorced; children: Guy Jr., Sean, Heather, Aubrey; m. Diane Pailthorpe, 1987; 1 child, Stephanie. Student, Syracuse U., 1963-64, Pace U., 1966-67, Elizabethtown Coll., 1972. Syss. analyst IBM Corp., Yorktown, N.Y., 1966-70; mgr. syss. support Bunker Ramo Corp., N.Y.C., 1970-72; mgr. sys. design Mathematica/Syss. Opers., Inc., 1972-76; co-founder Gaming Dimensions, Inc., 1976-79; exec. v.p. Datatrol, Providence, 1979-80; co-chmn., ceo, pres. GTECH Corp., West Greenwich, R.I., 1980—. Office: GTECH Corp 55 Technology Way West Greenwich RI 02817-1711

SNOWDEN, LAWRENCE FONTAINE, retired aircraft company executive, retired marine corps general officer; b. Charlottesville, Va., Apr. 14, 1921; s. Lawrence Fontaine Snoddy and Beatrice M. (Huffman) S.; m. Martha Roselyn Ham, Nov. 17, 1942; children: John Stephen, Brian Fontaine. Student, Stetson U., 1938-39; BS, U. Va., 1942; MA, Northwestern U., 1950; advanced mgmt. program, Harvard U., 1968; grad., Indsl. Coll. Armed Forces, 1967. Commd. 2d lt. USMC, 1942, advanced through grades to lt. gen., 1975; comdr. 7th Marine Regt., Vietnam, 1966; ops. officer III Marine Amphibious Force, Vietnam, 1967; asst. dir. personnel Hdqrs. Marine Corps, Washington, 1968-69; dir. systems support group Hdqrs. Marine Corps, 1969-70; dir. Marine Corps Devel. Ctr., Quantico, Va., 1970-72; chief of staff U.S. Forces, Japan, 1972-75; U.S. chmn. UN Bd., Japan, 1973-75; chief of staff Hdqrs. U.S. Marine Corps, 1977-79; ret., 1979; v.p. Far East Internat. Service Co. Hughes Aircraft Co., 1979-86; group v.p. Internat. Ground Systems Group Hughes Aircraft Co., Fullerton, Calif., 1986-88; pres. Snowden Internat. Assocs., Tallahassee, Fla., 1988—. Recipient Disting. Eagle Scout award, Silver Beaver award Boy Scouts Am.; decorated Legion of Merit (5), Army Commendation medal, Navy Commendation medal, D.S.M. (2), Purple Heart (2), Cross of Gallantry (3) Vietnam, Second Order of Sacred Treasure Japan). Mem. Marine Corps League, U.S. Navy League, Am. C. of C. in Japan, Am.-Japan Soc., Marine Corps Assn., Sigma Nu. Clubs: Tokyo, Killearn Country.

SNOWE, OLYMPIA J., senator; b. Augusta, Maine, Feb. 21, 1947; d. George John and Georgia G. Bouchles; m. John McKernan. BA, U. Maine, 1969; LLD (hon.), U. Maine, Machias, 1982, Husson Coll., 1981, Bowdoin Coll., 1985, Suffold U., 1994. Businesswoman; mem. Maine Ho. of Reps., 1973-76, Maine Senate, 1976-78; mem. 96th-103d Congresses from 2d Maine Dist., 1979-94; mem. budget com., mem. commerce sci. and transp. com., chmn. fgn. rel.subcom. on internat. ops. US Sen. from Maine; co-chair Congl. Caucus for Women's Issues; dep. Republican whip, U.S. senator from Maine, 1995—; corporator Mechanics Savs. Bank. Republican. Greek Orthodox. Club: Philoptochos Soc. Office: US Senate 495 Russell Senate Bldg Washington DC 20510-1903

SNYDER, ALAN CARHART, insurance company executive; b. N.Y.C., May 25, 1946; s. John I. and Elfrida (Bendix) S.; m. Mary Burgoyne, Feb. 9, 1974. BS, BA, Georgetown U., 1968; MBA, Harvard U., 1973. Cons. Reynolds Securities, N.Y.C., 1972-73; exec. v.p. Dean Witter Reynolds, N.Y.C., 1975-85; sole proprietor Shinnecock Ptnrs., N.Y.C., 1985-89, mng. ptnr., 1989—; pres., chief oper. officer, bd. dirs. First Exec. Corp., L.A., 1990-91; chief oper. officer Exec. Life Ins. Co., L.A., 1991-93; CEO Aurora Nat. Life Assurance Co., L.A., 1993-94; cons. Aurora Nat. Life Assurance Co., L.A., 1994-95; mng. ptnr. Shinnecock Group, L.A., 1994—. Baker scholar Harvard Bus. Sch., 1973.

SNYDER, ALLEGRA FULLER, dance educator; b. Chgo., Aug. 28, 1927; d. R. Buckminster and Anne (Hewlett) Fuller; m. Robert Snyder, June 30, 1951 (div. Apr. 1975, remarried Sept. 1980); children: Alexandra, Jaime. BA in Dance, Bennington Coll., 1951; MA in Dance, UCLA, 1967. Asst. to curator, dance archives Mus. Modern Art, N.Y.C., 1945-47; dancer Ballet Soc. of N.Y.C. Ballet Co., 1945-47; mem. office and prodn. staff Internat. Film Found., N.Y.C., 1950-52; editor, dance films Film News mag., N.Y.C., 1966-72; lectr. dance and film adv., dept. dance UCLA, 1967-73, chmn. dept. dance, 1974-80, 90-91, acting chair, spring 1985, chair of faculty Sch. of the Arts, 1989-91, prof. dance and dance ethnology, 1973-91, prof. emeritus, 1991—; pres. Buckminster Fuller Inst., Santa Barbara, Calif.; vis. lectr. Calif. Inst. Arts, Valencia, 1972; co-dir. dance and TV workshop Am. Dance Festival, Conn. Coll., New London, 1973; dir. NEH summer seminar for coll. tchrs. Asian Performing Arts, 1978, 81; coord. Ethnic Arts Intercoll. Interdisciplinary Program, 1974-73, acting chmn., 1986; vis. prof. performance studies NYU, 1982-83; hon. vis. prof. U. Surrey, Guildford, Eng., 1983-84; cons. Thyodia Found., Salt Lake City, 1973-74; mem. dance adv. panel Nat. Endowment Arts, 1968-72, Calif. Arts Commn., 1974-91; mem. adv. screening com. Coun. Internat. Exch. of Scholars, 1979-82; mem. various panels NEH, 1979-85; core cons. for Dancing, Sta. WNET-TV, 1988—. Dir. film Baroque Dance 1625-1725, in 1977; co-dir. film Gods of Bali, 1952; dir. and wrote film Bayanihan, 1962 (named Best Folkloric Documentary at Bilboa Film Festival, winner Golden Eagle award); asst. dir. and asst. editor film The Bennington Story, 1952; created films Gestures of Sand, 1968, Reflections on Choreography, 1973, When the Fire Dances Between Two Poles, 1982; created film, video loop and text Celebration: A World of Art and Ritual, 1982-83; supr. post-prodn. film Erick Hawkins, 1964, in 1973. Also contbr. articles to profl. jours. and mags. Adv. com. Pacific Asia Mus., 1980-84, Festival of the Mask, Craft and Folk Art Mus., 1979-84; adv. panel Los Angeles Dance Currents II, Mus. Ctr. Dance Assn., 1974-75; bd. dirs. Council Grove Sch. III, Compton, Calif., 1976-81; apptd. mem. Adv. Dance Com., Pasadena (Calif.) Art Mus., 1970-71, Los Angeles Festival of Performing Arts com., Studio Watts, 1970; mem. Technology and Cultural Transformation com., UNESCO, 1977. Fulbright research fellow, 1983-84; grantee Nat. Endowment Arts, 1981, Nat. Endowment Humanities, 1977, 79, 81, UCLA, 1968, 77, 80, 82, 85; recipient Amer. Dance Guild Award for Outstanding Achievement in Dance, 1992. Mem. Am. Dance Therapy Assn., Congress on Rsch. in Dance (bd. dirs. 1970-76, chmn. 1975-77, nat. conf. chmn. 1972), Coun. Dance Adminstrs., Am. Dance Guild (chmn. com. awards 1972), Soc. for Ethnomusicology, Am. Anthrop. Assn., Am. Folklore Soc., Soc. Anthropology of Visual Comm., Soc. Humanistic Anthropology, Calif. Dance Educators Assn. (conf. chmn. 1972), L.A. Area Dance Alliance (adv. bd. 1978-84, selection com. Dance Kaleidoscope project 1979-81), Fulbright Alumni Assn. Home: 15313 Whitfield Ave Pacific Palisades CA 90272-2548 Office: Buckminster Fuller Inst Ste 224 2040 Alameda Padre Serra Santa Barbara CA 93103

SNYDER, ARTHUR, publishing company executive; b. Valley Stream, N.Y., Feb. 6, 1925; s. Arthur and Kathryn (Staubitzer) S.; m. Betty Lain Harper, July 8, 1950; children—Susan, Arthur, Betsy, Jack, Heidi, Bonnie. B in Metall. Engring., Cornell U., 1950, MBA, 1952. Mfg. engr. Norton Co., Worcester, Mass., 1952-56; chief accountant Norton Co., 1956-58, asst. controller, 1958-59, mgr. data processing, 1959-61, controller, 1961-65; exec. v.p. A.M. Best Co., Oldwick, N.J., 1965-67; pres. A.M. Best Co., 1968—, chmn., 1971—. Author: Principles of Inventory Control and Managing Capital Expenditures. 1st lt. 95th Inf. div. AUS, 1942-45. Decorated Bronze Star with oak leaf cluster, Purple Heart. Mem. Fin. Execs. Inst., Cornell Soc. Engrs., Roxiticus Golf Club (Mendham, N.J.), Baltusrol Golf Club (Springfield, N.J.), U.S. Srs. Golf Assn., Mendham Valley Gun Club (Green Village, N.J.), Pawling (N.Y.) Mountain Gun Club. Presbyterian. Home: Lloyd Rd Bernardsville NJ 07924-1710 Office: AM Best Company Inc Ambest Rd Oldwick NJ 08858

SNYDER, CAROLYN ANN, university dean, librarian; b. Elgin, Nebr., Nov. 5, 1942; d. Ralph and Florence Wagner; m. Barry Snyder, Apr. 24, 1969. Student, Nebr. Wesleyan U., 1960-61; BS cum laude, Kearney State Coll., 1964; MS in Librarianship, U. Denver, 1965. Asst. libr. sci. and tech. U. Nebr., Lincoln, 1965-67, asst. pub. svc. lit , 1967-68, 70-73; pers. libr. Ind. U. Librs., Bloomington, 1973-76, acting dean of univ. librs., 1980, 88-89, assoc. dean for pub. svcs., 1977-88, 89-91, interim devel. officer, 1989-91; adminstrv. army libr. Spl. Svcs. Agy., Europe, 1968-70; dean libr. affairs So. Ill. U., Carbondale, 1991—; team leader Midwest Univs. Consortium for Internat. Activities-World Bank IX project to develop libr. system and implement automation U. Indonesia, Jakarta, 1984-86; libr. devel. cons. Inst. Tech. MARA/Midwest Univs. Consortium for Internat. Activities Program in Malaysia, 1985. Contbr. chpt. to book and articles to profl. jours. Mem. Humane Assn. Jackson County, 1991—, Carbondale Pub. Libr. Friends, 1991—. Recipient Cooperative Rsch. grant Coun. on Libr. Resources, Washington, 1984. Mem. ALA (councilor 1985-89, Bogle Internat. Travel award 1988, H.W. Wilson Libr. Staff devel. grantee 1981), Libr. Adminstrn./Mgmt. Assn. (pres. 1981-82), Com. on Instnl. Coop./Resource Sharing (chair 1987-91), Coalition for Networked Info. (So. Ill. U. at Carbondale rep. 1991—), Coun. Dirs. State Univ. Librs. in Ill. (chair 1992-93), Ill. Asn. Coll. and Rsch. Librs. (chair Ill. Bd. Higher Edn. liaison com. 1993-94), Ill. Network (bd. dirs.), Ind. Libr. Assn. (chair coll./univ. divsn. 1982-83), U.S. Grant Assn. (bd. dirs. 1992—), Ill. Libr. Computer Sys. Orgn. (policy coun. 1992-95), Nat. Assn. State Univs. and Land-Grant Colls. (commn. on info. tech. and its distance learning bd. 1994—), NetIllinois (bd. dirs. 1994—), OCLC Users Coun. (elected rep. 1995—). Avocations: antiques, theater, movies. Office: So Ill U Morris Libr Carbondale IL 62901-6632

SNYDER, CHARLES AUBREY, lawyer; b. Bastrop, La., June 19, 1941; s. David and Shirley Blossom (Haas) S.; m. Sharon Rae Veta, Aug. 29, 1963; children: David Veta, Shelby Haas, Claire Frances. B.B.A., Tulane U., 1963; J.D., La. State U., 1966. Bar: La. 1966. Assoc. firm. Milling, Benson, Woodward, Hillyer, Pierson & Miller, and predecessors, New Orleans, 1966-69, ptnr., 1969—; bd. dirs. Delta Petroleum Co., La. Motel and Investment Corp. Trustee Kathryn O'Brien Found., 1970; bd. dirs. New Orleans Speech and Hearing Ctr., pres., 1978-80; bd. dirs. City Pk. Commn., 1991—, pres., 1995; fellow La. Coll. Securities Counsel. Mem. ABA, La. Bar Assn. (chmn. sect. on corp. and bus. law 1982-83), New Orleans Bar Assn., La. Law Inst. (coms. on mineral code and revision of partnership law and community property law), Beta Gamma Sigma. Clubs: Metairie Country, City Energy, Plimsoll. Home: 74724 River Rd Covington LA 70433 Office: Milling Benson Woodward Hillyer Pierson & Mill 909 Poydras St Ste 2300 New Orleans LA 70112-4000

SNYDER, CHARLES ROYCE, sociologist, educator; b. Haverford, Pa., Dec. 28, 1924; s. Edward D. and Edith (Royce) S.; m. Patricia Hanson, June 30, 1951; children—Stephen Hoyt, Christiana Marie, Constance Patricia, Daniel Edward. BA, Yale U., 1945, M.A., 1949, Ph.D., 1954. Mem. staff Ctr. Alcohol Studies Yale U., 1950-60, asst. prof. sociology, 1956-60; prof. sociology So. Ill. U., Carbondale, 1960-85; chmn. dept. So. Ill. U., 1964-75, 81-85, prof. emeritus, 1985—; vis. prof. human genetics Sackler Sch. Medicine, Tel Aviv U., 1980; cons. behavioral scis. tng. com. Nat. Inst. Gen. Med. Scis., NIH, 1962-64; mem. planning com., chmn. program 28th Internat. Congress Alcohol and Alcoholism, 1964. Author: Alcohol and the Jews, 1958; editor: (with D.J. Pittman) Society, Culture and Drinking Patterns, 1962; editorial bd. Quar. Jour. Studies on Alcohol, 1957-83; assoc. editor Sociol. Quar., 1960-63. Mem. theol. commn. United Ch. of Christ, 1964-71; bd. dirs. Ill. Stewardship Alliance, 1990-95. With USNR, WWII. Fellow Am. Sociol. Assn.; mem. Soc. Study Social Problems (v.p. 1963-64, rep. to council Am. Sociol. Assn. 1964-66), Midwest Sociol. Soc. (bd. dirs. 1970-71), AAUP. Home: 705 S Taylor Dr Carbondale IL 62901-2217

SNYDER, CHARLES THEODORE, geologist; b. Powell, Wyo., July 19, 1912; s. Lee G. and Eda Belle (Hansen) S.; m. Marion Ruth Harris, Dec. 22, 1945 (dec. 1973); children: Anita Maria, Kristin Eileen; m. Alberta Irene Dangel, Oct. 15, 1973. BS, U. Ariz., 1948. Registered profl. geologist, Calif. Hydrologist U.S. Geol. Survey, Menlo Park, Calif., 1948-75; dir. Scotts Valley (Calif.) Water Dist., 1980-84; vis. scientist Carter County Mus., Ekalaka, Mont., 1983-84; researcher Resurgent Lakes in Western U.S. Author: Effect of Off-Road Vehicles, 1976. Disaster chmn. ARC, 1982-83. Mem. AAAS, Arctic Inst. N.Am., Soc. Vertebrate Paleontologists. Democrat. Presbyterian. Home: 552-17 Bean Creek Rd Scotts Valley CA 95066

SNYDER, CLAIR ALLISON, banker; b. Reading, Pa., June 12, 1921; s. Augustus M. and Estella G. (Bright) S.; m. Jean Doris George, June 27, 1948; children: Joan Marie Snyder Ferguson, Jerry George. Student, W.Va. U., 1943-44, U. Mich., 1944-45. With Meridian Bancorp, Inc. and Meridian Bank, Reading, 1938-43, 46-88; exec. v.p., gen. banking Meridian Bancorp, Inc. and Meridian Bank, 1973-78, exec. v.p., chmn. credit policy com., 1978-

86; pvt. practice fin. cons. Snyder Svcs. Co., Reading, 1987—; sr. cons. Marston Group, Inc., Harrisburg, Pa.; bd. dirs. Magnus Corp t/a Progressive Info. Techs., York, Pa., Terre Hill (Pa.) Concrete Corp., Am. Beton Systems, Terre Hill; asst. sec. Bi-Products, Inc., Fairfax, Va. Bd. dirs. Pa. divsn. Am. Cancer Soc., 1965-87, chmn. bd. dirs., 1975-77; bd. dirs. Berks County (Pa.) unit Am. Cancer Soc., 1955—, pres., bd. dirs., 1964-66; chmn. Hope Lodge Com.; chmn. Property Mgmt. Com. With U.S. Army, 1943-46. Recipient Luther Halsey Gulick award Camp Fire Girls, 1966; div. Bronze medal Am. Cancer Soc., also Sword of Hope award. Mem. Internat. Soc. for Philosophic Inquiry, Am. Bankers Assn. (cert.), Pa. Bankers Assn. (group chmn. 1972-73), Robert Morris Assocs. (pres. 1972-73), Am. Legion (post comdr. 1948-49), Old Point Golf and Country Club, Moselem Springs Golf Club, Belvedere Plantation Golf and Country Club. Republican. Mem. United Chs. of Christ. Home: Flying Hills 92 Medinah Dr Reading PA 19607-3313 also: 616 Sawgrass Rd Olde Point Hampstead NC 28443 *My life has been dedicated to personal achievement, but always with the knowledge that mankind's progress can only occur if each of us is willing to commit some of our efforts and resources to the future.*

SNYDER, DAVID L., film production designer; b. Buffalo, Sept. 22, 1944; s. Albert R. and Louise M. (Passero) S.; m. Terry Finn, Aug. 1, 1990; children: David Michael, Amy Lynne. Grad. high sch., Niagara Falls, N.Y. Ind. film prodn. designer Hollywood, Calif.; pres. Snyder Bros. Prodns., Inc., Hollywood; guest speaker Tokyo Internat. Film Festival, 1985. Art dir.: (films) In God We Trust, 1980, The Idolmaker, 1980, Blade Runner, 1982 (Academy award nomination best art direction 1982), Brainstorm, 1983, Racing With the Moon, 1984, The Woman In Red, 1984, My Science Project, 1985, (TV movies) Sins of the Past, 1984; prodn. designer: (films) Strange Brew, 1983, Pee-Wee's Big Adventure, 1985, Armed and Dangerous, 1986, Back to School, 1986, Summer School, 1987, Moving, 1988, She's Out of Control, 1989, Bill & Ted's Bogus Journey, 1991, Class Act, 1992, Super Mario Brothers, 1993, Demolition Man, 1993; assoc. prodr.: (film) Cold Dog Soup, 1990, Terminal Velocity, 1994, Rainbow, 1995; exec. prodr. (film) Rainbow, 1995. Mem. Soc. Motion Picture and TV Art Dirs., Acad. Motion Picture Arts and Scis., Nat. Acad. TV Arts and Scis. Democrat. Avocation: researching history of the film industry in America. Office: care Mirisch Agy Ste 700 10100 Santa Monica Blvd Los Angeles CA 90067

SNYDER, DAVID RICHARD, lawyer; b. Kalamazoo, Mich., Oct. 9, 1949; s. Richard E. and Margaret L. (Vanderplough) S.; m. Phyllis Alford, Aug. 14, 1971; children: Jason Richard, Carrie Lynn. BA with high honors, Mich. State U., 1971; JD with distinction, Cornell U., 1974. Bar: Calif. 1974. Assoc. Jenkins & Perry, San Diego, 1974-77, ptnr., 1978-83; ptnr. Aylward, Kintz & Stiska, San Diego, 1983-86, Luce, Forward, Hamilton & Scripps, San Diego, 1986-93, Pillsbury Madison & Sutro LLP, San Diego, 1993—; v.p., dir. San Diego Venture Group, 1989-91; adj. prof. Calif. Western Sch. Law, San Diego, 1982-84; lectr. Calif. Continuing Edn. of Bar, 1983—. Co-author: Drafting Legal Instruments, 1982; editor Cornell Law Rev., 1973-74. Bd. dirs. Boys Club Chula Vista, Calif., 1979-83; pres. Corpus Christi Parish Coun., Bonita, Calif., 1988-90; mem. Children's Hosp. Found., San Diego, 1988—, chmn., 1990-92. Mem. ABA (fed. securities law com. 1987—), State Bar Calif., San Diego County Bar Assn., Am. Electronics Assn. (bd. dirs., mem. exec. com. San Diego chpt. 1991-93), Order of Coif, Phi Beta Kappa. Republican. Roman Catholic. Office: Pillsbury Madison & Sutro 101 W Broadway Ste 1800 San Diego CA 92101-8219

SNYDER, DON, retail automotive executive; b. 1939. With Bob Moore Leasing Co., Oklahoma City, 1967-70; gen. mgr. Bob Moore Cadillac, Oklahoma City, 1970-79; pres. Don Davis Auto Group Inc., Arlington, Tex., 1979—, Don Davis Nissan Inc., Arlington, 1979—; with Don Davis Auto Inc., Arlington, 1994—, now v.p.-contr. Office: Don Davis Auto Inc 1661 Wet N Wild Way Arlington TX 76011*

SNYDER, DONALD EDWARD, corporate executive; b. Rochester, N.Y., Nov. 10, 1928; s. Benjamin Orman and Arlien Henrietta (Wing) S.; m. Dorothy Edna Stanke, Oct. 16, 1954; children—Donald Edward, Anne Arlien Snyder Marone, Barbara Lynn Snyder Mitchell, Richard John Snyder. A.B., Cornell U., 1950, J.D., 1952; postgrad., Ind. U., 1962. Bar: N.Y. 1953. Pvt. practice law, 1953-56; with Eastman Savs. and Loan Assn., 1956-68, pres., 1970-75, chmn. bd., 1979-88; asst. to treas. Eastman Kodak Co., Rochester, 1968-70; gen. credit mgr. Eastman Kodak Co., 1975-77, with Comptroller's div., 1977-78, asst. treas., 1978-79, treas., 1979-88; chmn. Eastman Kodak Credit Corp., 1985-88; chief exec. officer, chmn. bd., pres. Corp. Officers and Dirs. Assurance Ltd., Hamilton, Bermuda, 1990-93. Bd. dirs. Greater Rochester chpt. Epilepsy Found. Am., 1979-85, Allendale Mut. Ins. Co., 1983-92; bd. dirs. Luth. Ch.-Mo. Synod, 1983-95; vice chmn. bd., chmn. fin. com., mem., chmn. audit com., 1989-95; bd. dirs., mem. exec. com. ACE Ltd., 1985-90, EXEL Ltd., 1985-90, CODA Ltd., 1986-93; mem. investment rev. com. United Way of Greater Rochester, 1979—; trustee Seneca Zool. Soc., 1983-90. With USNR, 1946-48. Mem. N.Y. State Bar Assn., Monroe County Bar Assn., Rochester C. of C. (trustee 1980-86), Cornell Club (Rochester), Phi Kappa Tau (nat. fin. advisor, mem. nat. coun. 1988-95, treas., mem. exec. com. Phi Kappa Tau Found. 1991—). Home and Office: 48 Church Hill Rd Henrietta NY 14467-9711

SNYDER, FRANKLIN FARISON, hydrologic engineering consultant; b. Holgate, Ohio, Nov. 11, 1910; s. Samuel Lewis and Nettie May (Farison) S.; m. Mary Elizabeth Bruton, Oct. 1, 1938; children: Marilyn Kay Snyder Lutz, Carol Lamb Snyder Garnett, Gregory Lewis. Student, U. Toledo, 1928-30; B.C.E., Ohio State U., 1932, C.E., 1942; postgrad., Dept. Agr. Grad. Sch., 1940-42, 62. Registered profl. engr., Ohio. Hydraulic engr. U.S. Geol. Survey, Washington, 1934-35; hydraulic engr. TVA, Knoxville, 1936-37, Pa. Dept. Forests and Waters, Harrisburg, 1938-39, U.S. Weather Bur., Pitts. and Washington, 1940-42, Office Chief Engrs., Washington, 1942-66; ptnr. Nunn, Snyder & Assocs., Fairfax, Va., 1972-78; hydrologic engring. cons., McLean, Va., Can., Mex., Sudan, Greece, Bangladesh, Pakistan, Colombia, Jamaica, 1954-90; mem. Internat. St. Lawrence River Bd. Control., 1961-74, U.S. Nat. Com. for Internat. Hydrol. Decade, 1964-67, mem. commn. for Hydrology, Wold Meteorol. Orgn., 1960-72. Contbr. articles to profl. publs. Supr. Citizens Assn. Security Patrol, Chesterbrook Woods, McLean, 1978-94. Recipient exceptional civilian service award War Dept., 1946, Outstanding Civil Engring. Alumnus award Ohio State U. Civil Engring. Alumni Assn., 1989, Disting. Alumnus award Ohio State U., 1990; named to Gallery of Disting. Civilian Employees, C.E., 1983. Fellow ASCE (Cross medal); mem. Am. Geophys. Union, Am. Meteorol. Soc., Nat. Acad. Engring., Cosmos Club Washington, Officers Club Ft. Myer, Va., Sigma Xi, Tau Beta Pi. Republican. Presbyterian. Avocations: genealogy; golf; travel. Address: 1516 Laburnum St Mc Lean VA 22101-2527

SNYDER, GARY SHERMAN, poet; b. San Francisco, May 8, 1930; s. Harold Alton and Lois (Wilkie) S.; m. Masa Uehara, Aug. 6, 1967 (div.); children: Kai, Gen; m. Carole Koda, Apr. 28, 1991. B.A., Reed Coll., 1951; postgrad., Ind. U., 1951-52, U. Calif.-Berkeley, 1953-56. Gen. Lookout Mount Baker Forest, 1952-53; research in Japan, 1956-57, 59-64; lectr. U. Calif., Berkeley, 1964-65; prof. U. Calif., Davis, 1985—. Author: poems Riprap, 1959, Myths and Texts, 1960, Six Sections from Mountains and Rivers Without End, 1965, The Back Country, 1968, Regarding Wave, 1970, Turtle Island, 1974, Axe Handles, 1983, Left Out in the Rain, 1986, No Nature, 1992; prose Earth House Hold, 1969, The Old Ways, 1977, He Who Hunted Birds in His Father's Village, 1979, The Real Work, 1980, Passage Through India, 1984, The Practice of the Wild, 1990, A Place in Space, 1995. Bollingen fellow, 1966-67, Guggenheim fellow, 1968-69; recipient Pulitzer prize for poetry, 1975. Mem. Am. Acad. Arts and Letters, Am. Acad. Arts and Scis. *My work as artist and citizen has been driven by the insight that all is connected and interdependent—nature, societies, rocks, stars. If I seem to set myself "against the times" it is in the name of a larger process; of clarity and of sanity.**

SNYDER, GEORGE EDWARD, lawyer; b. Battle Creek, Mich., Feb. 7, 1934; s. Leon R. and Edith (Dullabahn) S.; m. Mary Jane Belt, July 27, 1957 (div. Sept. 23, 1982); children: Sara Lynn, Elizabeth Jane; m. Claudia Gage Brooks, Feb. 25, 1984. B.S., Mich. State U., 1957; J.D., U. Mich., 1960. Bar: Mich. 1961, U.S. Dist. Ct. (we. and ea. dists.) Mich. 1961. With Gen. Electric Co., 1957-58; assoc. firm Miller, Johnson, Snell & Commisky, Grand Rapids, 1960-62, Goodenough & Buesser, Detroit, 1962-66; partner firm Buesser, Buesser, Snyder & Blank, Detroit and Bloomfield Hills, 1966-85, Meyer, Kirk, Snyder & Safford, Bloomfield Hills, 1985—; dir. Bill Knapps Mich., Inc. Chmn. E. Mich. Environ. Action Council, 1974-78; pub. mem. inland lakes and streams rev. com. Mich. Dept. Natural Resources, 1975-76. Served as 2d lt. AUS, 1957. Fellow Am. Acad. Matrimonial Lawyers (pres. Mich. chpt. 1991-92), Am. Coll. Family Trial Lawyers, Am. Bar Found., Internat. Acad. Matrimonial Lawyers, Mich. Bar Found; mem. ABA, Am. Judicature Soc., Am. Arbitration Assn. (panel arbitrators), State Bar Mich. (chmn. family law com. 1968-72, mem. rep. assembly 1972-78, chmn. rules and calendar com. 1977-78, mem. family law sect. coun. 1973-76, environ. law sect. coun. 1980-85, prepaid legal svcs. com. 1973-82, com. on judicial selection 1974, com. on specialization 1976-82), Detroit Bar Assn. (chmn. family law com. 1966-68), Oakland County Bar Assn., Delta Upsilon (chmn. trustees, alumni chpt. dep. 1965-70), Tau Beta Pi, Pi Tau Sigma, Phi Eta Sigma. Episcopalian. Clubs: Detroit Athletic, Thomas M. Cooley, Birmingham (Mich.) Athletic. Home: 32965 Outland Trl Bingham Farms MI 48025-2555 Office: Meyer Kirk Snyder & Safford Ste 100 100 W Long Lake Rd Bloomfield Hills MI 48304-2773

SNYDER, GILES D. H., lawyer; b. Charleston, W.Va., May 28, 1931; s. Harry L. and Cora Ella (Houston) S.; m. Dale S. Davis, May 23, 1975; children—Jesse D. H., Benjamin D. H.; children by previous marriage—Anne H., Giles G., Matthew D. A.B., W.Va.U., 1952, LL.B., 1954. Bar: W.Va. Ohio 19, D.C. 19, U.S. Ct. Appeals 19, U.S. Supreme Ct. Asst. atty. gen. State of W.Va., Charleston, 1956-60; atty. Columbia Gas System, N.Y.C., 1960-68; asst. sec. Columbus Group of Columbia System, Ohio, 1968-73; asst. sec. Columbia Gas Transmission Corp., Charleston, W.Va., 1973-83, sec., gen. counsel, 1983-94; spl. counsel Bowles Rice McDavid Graff and Love, Charleston, 1994—. Mem. ABA, W.Va. Bar Assn., Ohio State Bar Assn., Fed. Energy Bar Assn., Order of Coif, Phi Beta Kappa. Democrat. Episcopalian. Home: 1661 Woodvale Dr Charleston WV 25314-2547 Office: Bowles Rice McDavid PO Box 1386 Commerce Sq Charleston WV 25325-1386

SNYDER, HARRY COOPER, retired state senator; b. July 10, 1928. Student, Wilmington Coll., Ohio U. Mem. Ohio State Senate, Columbus, 1979-96; ret., 1996; chmn. edn. and retirement com. Ohio State Senate, Columbus. Former mem. exec. com. Ohio Sch. Bds. Assn.; commr. Ohio High Speed Rail Devel. Authority; mem. Edn. Commn. of the States; chmn. Ohio Retirement Study Commn.; chmn. Legis. Office on Edn. Oversight; ad hoc mem. State Bd. Edn., Ohio Bd. Regents; mem. Jobs for Ohio Grads.; founder Clinton County Family Y; mem. Clinton County Bd. Edn. Recipient Outstanding Legis. Svc. award Citizens United for Responsible Edn., Ohio Ret. Tchrs. Assn., Ohio Coalition for Edn. of Handicapped Children, Ohio Assn. Civil Trial Attys., Guardian of Small Bus. award Nat. Fedn. Ind. Bus., Outstanding Contbr. to Edn. in Ohio award Ohio Confedn. Tchr. Edn. Orgn., Disting. Govtl. Svc. award Ohio Coun. Pvt. Colls. and Schs., Legis. of Yr. Ohio Sch. and Transit Assn. Mem. Am. Legis. Exch. Coun. (edn. com., Outstanding State Legis.-Jefferson award), Nat. Conf. State Legislatures (state/fed. assembly, edn. and job tng. com., assembly of legislature, edn. com.), Rotary Club (pres.), Great Oaks Task Force. Republican. Methodist. Avocations: reading, gardening, sailing. Home: 6508 Spring Hill Dr Hillsboro OH 45133-9209

SNYDER, HENRY LEONARD, history educator, bibliographer; b. Hayward, Calif., Nov. 3, 1929; s. Henry Runyon and Mary (Rosenberg) S.; m. Janette Marie Hannus, July 21, 1961; children: Michael Jesse, Christopher Henry, David Lyle. BA, U. Calif., Berkeley, 1951, MA, 1960, PhD, 1963. Sr. buyer Dohrmann Comml. Co., San Francisco, 1951-59; instr. to prof. U. Kans., Lawrence, 1963-78; assoc. dean to dean research adminstrn. U. Kans., 1967-78; prof. history, dean arts and scis. La. State U., Baton Rouge, 1979-86; prof. history U. Calif., Riverside, 1986—; dir. Ctr. for Bibliog. Studies, 1989—; dean humanities and social scis. U. Calif., Riverside, 1986; vis. lectr. Bedford Coll., U. London, 1965-66; Fulbright lectr., research scholar U. Hamburg, Fed. Republic Germany, 1974; dir. English Short Title Catalogue for N.Am., 1978—. Editor: The Marlborough Godolphin Correspondence, 1975; co-editor: The Scottish Heritage, 1981. Pres. Baton Rouge Opera, 1981-83, Riverside Opera, 1987-90; pres. United Way, Lawrence, 1977; bd. dirs. Arts and Humanities Com., Baton Rouge, 1981-85; Sigmund, Martin, Heller Traveling fellow U. Calif.-Berkeley, 1962-63. Am. Council Learned Soc. sr. fellow, 1969-70. Fellow Royal Hist. Soc. Gt. Brit. Bibliog. Soc. London; mem. Am. Soc. 18th Century Studies (pres. 1980-81), Conf. Brit. Studies (exec. com. 1978-83), Am. Hist. Assn., Internat. Fed. Librs. (chair rarebooks and ms. sect. 1995—). Republican. Congregationalist. Home: 220 Trinity Ave Kensington CA 94708-1139 Office: U Calif- Riverside Ctr for Bibliog Studies Riverside CA 92521-0154

SNYDER, IRVIN STANLEY, microbiologist, educator; b. Nanticoke, Pa., May 29, 1931; s. Irvin William and Wanda Dolores S.; m. Marlene Ann Smetana, Sept. 3, 1955; children—Mary Ellen, Carole Jeanne, Irvin John. B.S., Wilkes Coll., 1953; M.A., U. Kans., 1958, Ph.D., 1960. Instr. microbiology U. Iowa Med. Sch., 1960-61, asst. prof., 1961-67, assoc. prof., 1967-72, prof., 1972-73; research prof. Bryn Mawr (Pa.) Coll., 1966; prof., chmn. dept. microbiology W.Va. U. Med. Center, Morgantown, 1973-91, prof., 1991—. Author: (with J.M. Slack) Bacteria and Human Disease, 1978; contbr.: (with R. Finch) chpts. to Modern Pharmacology; author several slide-tape teaching programs; contbr. articles to profl. jours. Served with AUS, 1953-55. Recipient Silver medal Kaw Valley Heart Assn., 1960, teaching awards U. Iowa, teaching awards W.Va. U., Alumni Faculty Appreciation award W.Va. U. Fellow Am. Acad. Microbiology; mem. Am. Soc. Microbiology, Am. Bd. Microbiology, Soc. Exptl. Biology and Medicine, Am. Inst. Biol. Scis., Sigma Xi, Phi Delta Kappa, Omicron Kappa Upsilon. Office: W Va U/Dept Microbiol & Imm Robt C Byrd Health Sci Ctr PO Box 9177 Morgantown WV 26506-9177

SNYDER, JACK L., social sciences administrator. Dir. Columbia U. Inst. War & Peace Studies. Office: Columbia Univ Inst War & Peace Studies 420 W 118th New York NY 10027*

SNYDER, JACK RALPH, lawyer; b. Gary, Ind., June 24, 1940; s. Jack T. and Margaret (Considine) S.; m. Barbara C. Goins, June 23, 1962 (div. Sept. 1985); children: John, Hilary, Alison, Alfred; m. Mary L. Brzezinski Forster, Oct. 1987. AB, Brown U., 1962; LLB, U. Mich., 1964. Bar: Ind. 1965, U.S. Dist. Ct. (so. dist.) 1965, U.S. Ct. Appeals (7th cir.) 1965, (D.C. cir.) 1980. Assoc. ICE Miller Donadio & Ryan, Indpls., 1965-71, ptnr., 1972—, mng. ptnr., 1990-93; bd. dirs. Indpls. Motor Speedway Corp. Counsel Midwestern Collegiate Conf.; trustee Marian Coll.; v.p. Ind. Sports Corp., 1989—. Recipient Louis A. Dawson Outstanding Vol. award Tabernacle Presbyn. Ch., 1980, Monsignor Albert Basalt Outstanding Vol. award Indsl. Cath. Youth Orgn., 1982, Knight of Svc. award Marian Coll., 1995. Fellow Ind. Bar Assn.; mem. ABA, Indpls. Bar Assn., Skyline Club (Indpls.), Ind. Conv. and Visitors Assn. (bd. dirs.), Phi Delta Phi, Delta Kappa Epsilon. Avocations: running, photography, sports, travel. Office: Ice Miller Donadio & Ryan 1 American Sq Indianapolis IN 46282-0001

SNYDER, JAMES R., wholesale distribution executive, textiles executive; b. 1948. Sec., treas. Shelter Components Indiana, Elkhart, Ind. Office: Shelter Components Indiana 27217 County Road 6 Elkhart IN 46514-5601*

SNYDER, JAN LOUISE, administrative aide; b. Warrington Twp., Pa., Sept. 15, 1935; d. Wilbert Adam and Alice (Myers) March; divorced; children: Steven Michael Krone, David Sylvan Snyder. Grad. high sch., Dover, Pa. With McCrory Stores Divsn. McCrory Corp., York, 1966, receptionist exec. buying divsn. Active Northwestern region York Hosp. Aux., 1979—, York Symphony Assn., 1990—, membership com., 1992—; active York chpt. Am. Cancer Soc. Am., 1990—, York Chorus, 1988-90; mem. Ch. of the Open Door of Shiloh, 1956—, Dover Twp. Fire Co. Aux. for Women, 1975—, Harrisburg Jr. League Lectr. Series, 1980-95, York Jr. League Lectr. series, 1989—. Mem. Am. Bus. Womens Assn. (pres. Colonial York charter chpt. 1980, mem. adv. bd. 1980-89), Nat. Trust for Historic Preservation. Democrat. Avocations: travel, music, lecturing, church activities, flower and vegetable gardening. Home: 2823 Grandview Ave York PA 17404-3905

SNYDER, JEAN MACLEAN, lawyer; b. Chgo., Jan. 26, 1942; d. Norman Fitzroy and Jessie (Burns) Maclean; m. Joel Martin Snyder, Sept. 4, 1964; children: Jacob Samuel, Noah Scot. BA, U. Chgo., 1963, JD, 1979. Bar: Ill. 1979, U.S. Dist. Ct. (no. dist.) Ill. 1979, U.S. Ct. Appeals (7th cir.) 1981. Ptnr. D'Ancona & Pflaum, Chgo., 1979-92; prin. Law Office of Jean Maclean Snyder, Chgo., 1993—. Contbr. articles to profl. publs. Mem. ABA (mem. coun. on litigation sect. 1989-92, editor-in-chief Litigation mag. 1987-88, co-chair First Amendment and media litigation com. 1995-96, co-chair the woman advicate com. 1996—). Office: Law Office Jean M Snyder 3 First Nat Plaza 70 W Madison St Ste 3600 Chicago IL 60602

SNYDER, JEANNE ANNE, interior designer, educator; b. Detroit, July 23, 1945; d. Paul G. and Mary T. Thoen; m. James C. Snyder, July 13, 1968; children: Jamie Moore, Jennifer Thoen. BS in Design, U. Mich., 1967. Interior designer Skidmore Owings, Chgo., 1967-68, Interior Design Svc., U. Mich., Ann Arbor, 1968-72, Associated Space Design, Atlanta, 1972-76, Kahler, Slater, Fitzhugh Scott, Milw., 1976-80; interior designer Hobbs & Black, Ann Arbor, 1984-91, dir. interior design, 1991—; asst. prof. interior design U. Mich., Ann Arbor, 1980-90. Prin. works include Waukesha Meml. Hosp., 1979, Hobbs & Black Corp. Ctr., 1986, Peachwood Nursing Faculty, 1988, Olds Plaza, 1990, Lansing Ctr., 1994. Mem. Ins. Bus. Designers (assoc.). Roman Catholic. Home: 2963 Warren Rd Ann Arbor MI 48105-9717

SNYDER, JO ANNA W., cartographer, computer graphics designer; b. Atlanta, July 10, 1961; d. Joseph Hans Werner and Ruby Lee (Patty) Horton; m. Edward H. Snyder, Feb. 4, 1992. Grad. high sch., Ooltewah, Tenn., 1979; cert. computer drafting and design specialist, Charter Coll., Anchorage, 1994. Freelance graphics designer; typesetter, artist Printer's Workshop, Anchorage, 1984-85, Pip Printing, Anchorage, 1985-87; computer graphics designer BP Exploration (Alaska) Inc., Anchorage, 1987-92, cartographer, 1990-92; owner desktop pub. firm Graphics Alaska; freelance graphics designer, Wasilla, Alaska, 1989-94; CAD technician, then mktg. specialist New Horizons Telecom., Inc., Palmer, Alaska, 1994-96. Checker Iditarod Trail Sled Dog Assn., Wasilla, 1990-91. Mem. NAFE, nat. Contract Mgmt. Assn., Nat. Computer Graphics Assn., Computer Graphics Network (founder, chmn. 1989-91). Avocations: fishing, hiking, gardening. Home: HC 89 Box 330 Willow AK 99688-9704

SNYDER, JOHN C., oil and gas industry executive; b. 1942. BA in Petroleum Engring., U. Okla., 1964; MBA, Harvard U., 1968. Petroleum engr. Humble Oil & Refining, Houston, 1964-66; with Devtek Inc., Ft. Worth, 1968-69; founder Can.-Am. Resource Fund Inc., Ft. Worth, 1969-71; exec. v.p. May Petroleum Inc., Dallas, 1971-73; ind. oil operator Midland, Tex., 1974-77; founder Tucker-Snyder Exploration Co. (name now Snyder Oil Co.), Ft. Worth, 1977—, now chmn. bd. dirs. Office: Snyder Oil Co 777 Main St Ste 2500 Fort Worth TX 76102-5329*

SNYDER, JOHN JOSEPH, bishop; b. N.Y.C., Oct. 25, 1925; s. John Joseph and Katherine Marie (Walsh) S. Ordained priest Roman Cath. Ch., 1951, consecrated bishop, 1973. Assoc. pastor St. Mel's Parish, Flushing, N.Y., 1951-57; sec. to bishops Diocese Bklyn., 1957-72; titular bishop Forlimpopoli, vicar gen., aux. bishop Diocese Bklyn., 1972-79; bishop Diocese of St. Augustine, Fla., 1979—. Office: Chancery Office 11625 Old St Augustine Rd Jacksonville FL 32258-2060*

SNYDER, JOHN MILLARD, recreation resources executive, educator; b. Chelsea, Mass., Apr. 3, 1946; s. John Henry and Grace (Eby) S.; m. Barbara Ripple, Nov. 8, 1969 (div. 1979); 1 child, Logan; m. Glenda Allene Snyder, Sept. 10, 1983; children: Erika, Kimberly. BA, Franklin & Marshall Coll., 1968; MS, Colo. State U., 1974, PhD, 1982; cert., Harvard Sch. Design, 1987. Econ. rsch. asso. Coll. Natural Resources, Ft. Collins, Colo., 1972-76; econ devel. City Devel. Dept., Kansas City, Mo., 1976-77; v.p. Oblinger Smith Corp., Denver, 1977-79; sr. resource analyst Abt Assocs., Denver, 1979-80; dir. devel. analysis URS Engrs., Denver, 1980-83; pres. Strategic Studies, Inc., Littleton, Colo., 1983—; pres. Glacier Bay Outfitters, 1990—; co-founder Ecotourism Internat., 1994—; faculty environ. policy and mgmt. U. Denver, 1990—; econ. faculty Regis U., 1984—. Author: (poems) A Far Off Place, 1995, Best Poems of 1995, 1995; contbr. articles to profl. jours. Econ. advisor Treas. and Gov. Colo., Denver, 1979-84; officer YMCA Guides Program, LIttleton, 1984-85; sr. advisor Spl. Family Recreation, Denver, 1985-90; benefactor Le Bal de Ballet, Denver, 1989—. 1st lt. U.S. Army military intelligence, 1968-72. Mem. Ctr. for Whale Studies, Stanford Libr. (assoc.), Denver Zoological Found., Nat. Parks and Conservation Assn., several environ. orgns., Phi Kappa Phi, Xi Sigma Pi. Office: Strategic Studies Inc 2275 E Arapahoe Rd Ste 303 Littleton CO 80122-1540

SNYDER, JOSEPH JOHN, editor, author, lecturer, historian, consultant; b. Washington, Aug. 27, 1946; s. Joseph John and Amy Josephine (Hamilton) S.; m. Sally Hale Walker, July 4, 1973; children: Lauren Elizabeth, Brian Joseph Seth. BA in Anthropology, George Washington U., 1968; MA in Anthropology, U. N.Mex., 1973. With U.S. CSC, Washington, 1974-77; editor, writer U.S. Nat. Park Svc., Harpers Ferry, W.Va., 1977-81; cons. editor Early Man mag., Evanston, Ill., 1978-83; cons. editor Sea Power Mag., 1987—; freelance writer, 1981—; pres. Sta. at Shepherdstown Inc., 1992—; pres., chmn. bd. dirs., Atlantic & Pacific High Speed Railway, Inc., 1993—; lectr. Maya archaeology Norwegian-Caribbean Lines, Miami, Fla., 1982; cons. mus. design. Chmn. parks com. Neighborhood Planning Adv. Group, Croydon Park, Rockville, Md., 1980-81; bd. dirs. Agrl. R & D Orgn, 1985—; v.p., bd. dirs., Hagerstown (Md.) Roundhouse Mus., 1989-91; sec. bd. dirs. Hagerstown-Washington County Conv. and Visitors. Bur., 1993—. With U.S. Army, 1970-71, Vietnam. Decorated Bronze Star. Mem. Coun. Md. Archaeology, Hakluyt Soc., Am. Com. to Advance Study of Petroglyphs and Pictographs, Nat. Geog. Soc. (cons. 1987—), Nat. Ry. Hist. Soc. Cons. editor jour. Archaeoastronomy, 1987—; contbr. articles to popular mags. Democrat. Home and Office: 2008 Ashley Dr Shepherdstown WV 25443

SNYDER, KENNETH F., lawyer; b. Cleve., Ohio, Sept. 10, 1941. BA, Western Reserve U., 1963; JD, U. Mich., 1966; LLM Taxation, NYU, 1967. Bar: Ohio 1966. Ptnr. Baker & Hostetler, Cleve. Office: Baker & Hostetler 3200 Nat City Ctr 1900 E 9th St Cleveland OH 44114-3401*

SNYDER, LEE H., lawyer; b. Oct. 9, 1931. BS, Albright Coll., 1955; JD, U. Mich., 1958. Bar: Pa. 1958, Fla. 1978. Ptnr. Morgan, Lewis & Bockius, Phila. Office: Morgan Lewis & Bockius 2000 One Logan Sq Philadelphia PA 19103*

SNYDER, LESLIE, newspaper editor. Education educator Dallas Morning News, Tex. Office: The Dallas Morning News Communications Ctr PO Box 655237 Dallas TX 75266-5237

SNYDER, LEWIS EMIL, astrophysicist; b. Ft. Wayne, Ind., Nov. 26, 1939; s. Herman Lewis and Bernice (McKee) S.; m. Doris Jean Selma Lautner, June 16, 1962; children: Herman Emil, Catherine Jean. BS, Ind. State U., 1961; MA, So. Ill. U., 1964; PhD, Mich. State U., 1967. Research assoc. Nat. Radio Astronomy Obs., Charlottesville, Va., 1967-69; prof. astronomy dept. U. Va., Charlottesville, 1969-73, 74-75; vis. fellow Joint Inst. for Lab. Astrophysics, U. Colo., Boulder, 1973-74; prof. astronomy dept. U. Ill., Urbana, 1975—. Co-editor: Molecules in the Galactic Environment, 1973; contbr. articles to sci. jours. NASA-Am. Soc. Engring. Edn. summer fellow, 1972, 73; Alexander von Humboldt Found. sr. U.S. scientist award, 1983-84. Mem. AAAS, Astron. Soc. Pacific, Am. Phys. Soc., Am. Astron. Soc., Internat. Astron. Union, Union Radio Scientifique Internationale, Sigma Xi. Lutheran. Office: U Ill 1002 W Green St Urbana IL 61801-3074

SNYDER, MARIAN H., nursing educator and administrator; b. Webster, S.D., June 10, 1942; d. Harry C. and Helen L. (Potter) Walker; 1 child, Susan Marin. BSN, U. Conn., 1964; MS in Nursing, U. Ky., 1977; PhD, Marquette U., 1987. Staff nurse USAF, San Antonio, 1965-67; instr. Norton-Children's Hosp., Louisville, 1967-77; faculty Columbia Coll., Milw., 1977-81; dean, chief exec. officer Carroll-Columbia Coll. Nursing, Milw., 1981—. 1st lt. Nurses Corps, USAF. Mem. ANA, NLN, Sigma Theta Tau. Office: Columbia College 2121 E Newport Ave Milwaukee WI 53211-2952

SNYDER, MARION GENE, lawyer, former congressman; b. Louisville, Jan. 26, 1928; s. M. G. and Lois (Berg) S.; 1 son, Mark; m. Patricia C. Robertson, Apr. 10, 1973; 3 step-children. LLB cum laude, Jefferson Sch. Law, Louisville, 1950; JD, U. Louisville, 1969. Bar: Ky. bar 1950, D.C. bar

1970. Practiced law Louisville, 1950-76; ret., farmer, 1957-80; city atty. Jeffersontown, 1953-57; magistrate 1st dist. Jefferson County, 1957-61; real estate broker, 1949—; mem. 88th Congress from 3d Ky. Dist., 1963-65; mem. 90th-99th congresses from 4th Ky. Dist., 1967-87, ret., 1987; sole practice, 1987-91; v.p. Ky. Magistrates and Commrs., 1958. Vice pres. Jeffersontown Civic Center, 1953-54; pres. Lincoln Republican Club Ky., 1960-61, 1st Magisterial Dist. Rep. Club, 1955-57. Mem. Ky. Bar Assn., Ky. Farm Bur., Ky. Real Estate Brokers, Lions, Optimists (prs. Jeffersontown club 1957-58), Jesters, Shriners, Masons. Home (winter): 383 Juli Fe Dr Naples FL 33942-1123

SNYDER, MARVIN, neuropsychologist; b. Bklyn., Oct. 14, 1940; s. Samuel and Sarah (Seidman) S.; m. Arlyne S. Naphtali, June 23, 1963; 1 dau., Sian Leslie. BA (N.Y. State Regents scholar 1958-62, Meml. award psychology 1962), Bklyn. Coll., 1962; PhD (NDEA fellow 1962-65, USPHS fellow 1965-66, trainee 1966-67), Duke U., 1967. Research psychologist NIMH, 1967-71; Nat. Eye Inst., 1971-72; program dir., neuroscis. Nat. Inst. Drug Abuse, 1974-79, dir. div. research, 1979-90, dir. Office of Sci. Policy, Edn. and Legislation, 1990-94; acting dep. dir. Nat. Inst. on Drug Abuse, 1992-93; pres. Snyder Assocs., 1995; dir. life scis. rsch. office Fedn. of Am. Socs. for Exptl. Biology, 1995—; mem. sr. exec. svc. USPHS exec. com. AIDS, 1983-85; mem. DDHS Orphan Products Bd., 1982-88; mem. The White House Task Force on Drug Abuse Health Issues; co-chmn. Interagy. Com. on Smoking and Health, Interagy. Com. on New Therapies for Pain and Discomfort; exec. sec. Interagy. com. on Pain and Analgesia, chmn. subcom. on edn. and tng., 1985—; cons. to WHO on drug abuse policy issues, 1985-87; testifier on drug abuse sci. and policy issues to U.S. Congress; mem. FCCSET Com. onBrain and Behavior, 1990-91, Devel. Guidelines for Protection Human Subjects in Drug Abuse Studies, 1991. Author papers on comparative neurology. Recipient Michael Morrison award for excellence in sci. adminstrn. Com. on Problems of Drug Dependence, 1988, Presdl. Meritorious Rank award 1990. Office: Fedn Am Socs Exptl Biology Life Scis Rsch Office 9650 Rockville Pike Bethesda MD 20814-3998

SNYDER, MIKE, newspaper editor. Day city editor Houston Chronicle. Office: Houston Chronicle Pub Co 801 Texas St Houston TX 77002-2906

SNYDER, NANCY MARGARET, translator, language services company executive; b. Detroit, Sept. 24, 1950; d. Estle M. and Noreen V. (Woodruff) S.; m. P. W. Denton, July 15, 1972 (div. Feb. 1980); 1 child, Virginia. BA in German, Mich. State U., 1972; cert. in programming and ops., Control Data Inst., 1984. Office mgr. Detroit Translation Bur., Southfield, Mich., 1980-82; bilingual sec. Volkswagen Am., Troy, Mich., 1984-85, translator, 1985-88; owner, operator Tech. Lang. Svcs., Birmingham, Mich., 1988—; guest speaker Kent State U. Inst. Applied Linguistics, 1992, Ferndale (Mich.) High Sch., 1992. Contbr. articles to profl. jours. Stadium usher Olympic Games, Munich, 1972; mem., worker Cass Corridor Food Coop., Detroit, 1986-90. Mem. S.E. Mich. Translators and Interpreters Network (newsletter editor 1993), Am. Translators Assn. (accredited German to English translator), Chgo. Area Translators Assn., Am. Mensa Ltd., Amherst Block Club. Avocations: exercise, socializing. Office: Tech Lang Svcs 600 S Adams Rd Ste 210 Birmingham MI 48009-6863

SNYDER, NATHAN, entrepreneur; b. Hartford, Conn., Oct. 7, 1934; s. Saul and Betsy (Wand) S.; m. Geraldine Wolff, Dec. 27, 1964; children: Hannah Abigail, Alexander Lowell Wolff. AB, Harvard U., 1956; LLB, Columbia U., 1963; postgrad. in bus., NYU, 1967-68. Bar: N.Y. 1963. Assoc. Paul, Weiss, Rifkind, Wharton & Garrison, N.Y.C., 1963-66; v.p., sec. Randolph Computer Corp., Greenwich, Conn., 1966-69, exec. v.p., gen. counsel, bd. dirs., 1969-73; exec. v.p., chief operating officer BanCal Tri-State Corp. (holding co. Bank of Calif.), San Francisco, 1974-76; v.p. acquisitions CBS Inc., N.Y.C., 1976-87; pres. VS & A Communications Ptnrs., N.Y.C., 1987-89, The Snyder Co., New Canaan, Conn., 1989—; lectr. of mgmt. Golden Gate U., San Francisco, 1974-76, Annenberg Sch. Comms., Phila., 1982-87; bd. dirs. Sogen Funds, N.Y.C. Editor: Columbia Law Rev., 1962-63. Vol. legal services Office Econ. Opportunity, 1963. Served to lt. USNR, 1956-60. Harlan Fiske Stone scholar, 1964-65. Mem. ABA, Columbia Law Sch. Alumni Assn. (bd. dirs. 1979), Harvard Club (N.Y.C.), Harvard Club (v.p. Fairfield County). Office: The Snyder Co 163 Parish Rd New Canaan CT 06840-4427

SNYDER, PATRICIA DI BENEDETTO, theater director and administrator. BA in English and Speech Edn., SUNY, Albany, 1967; MA in Theater Arts, Syracuse U., 1967; PhD in Arts and Humanities, NYU, 1991. Tchr. English, speech and drama West Genesee Sr. High Sch., Camillus, N.Y., 1962-64; tchr. English and drama, chair humanities teaching team Chestnut Hill Mid. Sch., Liverpool, N.Y., 1964-66; grad. asst. Syracuse (N.Y.) U., 1966-67; instr. dept. theatre SUNY, Albany, 1967-74, spl. asst. to chancellor, adj. assoc. prof. dept. theatre, 1974-75, founder, producing dir. Empire State Youth Theatre Inst., 1975-92; exec. dir. Gov. Nelson A. Rockefeller Empire State Plz. Performing Arts Ctr. Corp., 1982-89; producing dir., CEO N.Y. State Theatre Inst. Corp., 1992—; cons. Spanish and Portuguese Mins., Madrid and Lisbon, 1968, U.S. Office Edn. 1979, Spanish Min. Culture, 1982, Time Warner, Inc., 1991; mem. edn. bd. Saratoga Performing Arts Ctr., 1973; apptd. arts and humanities planning com. N.Y. State Edn. Dept., 1975; mem. arts task force on arts in edn. NEH, 1977; apptd. N.Y. State Edn. Commr.'s Adv. Coun., 1978; panelist U.S. Children;s Lit. Assn., 1978; del. UNESCO Conf., Sibenek, Yugoslavia, 1979; lectr. Syracuse U., 1988; mem. acad. coun. Richard Porter Leach Fund for Arts, 1989; adj. prof. theatre Russell Sage Coll., 1992.; lectr. and presenter in field. Prodr. (stage prodns.) The Wizard of Oz, 1977, Lancashire Lad, 1980, Sleeping Beauty, 1981, 83, 90, Handy Dandy, 1985, Rag Dolly, 1986, Aladdin, 1987, Hizzoner!, 1988, 89, Beauty and the Beast, 1991, Slow Dance on the Killing Ground, 1993 (Best dir. theatre N.E. Metroland for '94); exec. prodr. (CD) Atlantic Theatre, A Tale of Cinderella, 1995; stage and video dir. A Tale of Cinderella, 1995; contbr. articles to profl. jours. Guest fellow Hungairan Theatre Inst., 1970, USSR Min. Culture, 1970, 84; recipient Mayor's medal City of Milan, Italy, 1977, Spl. Recognition award John F. Kennedy Ctr. for Performing Arts, 1978, 81, Recognition award NATAS, 1986, Albany League Arts award, 1986, Spl. Recognition award N.Y. State Theatre Edn Assn., 1993. Mem. Am. Theatre Assn. (commn. on theatre devel. 1976, Spl. Recognition citation 1973, 74, Jennie Heiden award 1985), Children's Theatre Assn. Am. (Zeta Phi Eta award 1972), League Am. Theatres and Prodrs., Soc. State Dirs. and Choreographers, Assn. Internat. du Theatre pour l'Enfants et al Jeunesse (del. 1968, 70, 74, 78, 79 congresses, exec. com. 1969, fundraiser 1972 conf., editor ofcl. report 1973, chair U.S. ctr. 1977), N.Y. League Profl. Theatre Women, U. Albany Alumni Assn. (Disting. Alumni award 1987), Cosmopolitan Club, Phi Delta Kappa. Home: 722 N Broadway Saratoga Springs NY 12866-1621 Office: NY State Theatre Inst PO Box 28 Troy NY 12181-0028

SNYDER, PETER LARSEN, public relations executive; b. Phila., Apr. 28, 1952; s. Philip Lerch and Adrienne Louise (Larsen) S.; m. Karen Suzanne Stachiw, June 1, 1973; children: P. Evan, Erik D. BS, Cornell U., 1975. Account exec. Gibbs & Soell Pub. Rels., N.Y.C., 1975-78; account assoc. Ruder & Finn Pub. Rels., N.Y.C., 1978-80; exec. v.p., mng. ptnr. Dorf & Stanton Communications, St. Louis, 1980—, COO, 1992—, pres., 1995—; mng. dir. Shandwick U.S.A. (merger with Dorf & Stanton), 1996—. Cons. Harbor Festival '78, N.Y.C., 1978, St. Louis Pub. Sch. Partnership program, 1985-87, St. Louis area ARC, 1987-88, Muscular Dystrophy Assn. St. Louis, 1988; bd. dirs., capital chmn. Rohan-Woods Sch., Warson Woods, Mo., 1986-88; bd. dirs. Kirkwood/Webster YMCA, Webster Groves, Mo., 1984-87, The New Theater, St. Louis, 1994—, Riverway Sch., 1994—, Downtown St. Louis, 1995—, Emmanuel Ch. Found., 1989-92; co-founder, asst. scoutmaster Troop 39, Boy Scouts Am.; chmn. Downtown Parks Bus. Dist., 1990—; co-chair security com. Downtown St. Louis Inc., 1991—; comms. com. Diocese Mo. Episcopal Ch., 1993—; trustee world affairs coun. St. Louis, 1993, v.p. 1994—; commr. downtown pks. taxing dist., 1994—. Mem. Nat. Agri-Mktg. Assn. (named Best of 1983), Cornell Club St. Louis (bd. dirs. 1988—), Media Club, The Newcomen Soc. Episcopalian. Avocations: sailing, scuba diving, skiing. Office: Shandwick USA 1221 Locust St Ste 555 Saint Louis MO 63103-2364

SNYDER, RALPH SHELDON, lawyer; b. Harrisburg, Pa., May 15, 1922; s. Louis Sidney and Ann Margaret (Shulman) S.; m. Janet Gushner, Aug. 29, 1948; 1 child, Randy. BA, Pa. State U., 1942; JD, Dickinson Sch. Law, 1948. Bar: Pa. 1949, U.S. Dist. Ct. (ea. dist.) Pa., U.S. Ct. Appeals (3d cir.), U.S. Ct. Appeals (10th cir.), U.S. Supreme Ct. Dep. atty. gen. Commonwealth of Pa., Harrisburg, 1949-62; ptnr. Schnader, Harrison, Segal & Lewis, Phila., 1963—; lectr. law master's program Temple U., Phila., 1977, Villanova U., Phila., 1981-83—; lectr. Pa. Bar Inst., Harrisburg, 1979—. Trustee Fedn. of Jewish Agys., Phila., v.p., 1985-88, 94—, chmn. project renewal campaign, 1984-93; bd. dirs. Jewish Cmty. Ctrs., Phila., 1985—; vice chmn. Fedn. Com. on Jewish Edn., 1971-73; bd. govs. Dropsie U., Phila., 1975-80; pres. Har Zion Temple, Penn Valley, Pa., 1980-82; v.p. Phila. Geriatric Ctr., 1985-89; pres., cabinet Jewish Theol. Sem. Am., Phila., 1984-88. Served to sgt. USAAF, 1942-46. Mem. ABA, Pa. Tax Commn., Pa. Bar Assn. (past chmn. tax law sect., ho. of dels.), Pa. Bar Inst. (pres. 1992-93), Pa. Bar Found. (treas. 1984—), Phila. Bar Assn. (past chmn. state and local tax law), Green Valley Country Club, The Locust Club, Phila. Club. Republican. Avocations: golfing; acting; singing. Office: Schnader Harrison Segal & Lewis 1600 Market St Ste 3600 Philadelphia PA 19103-7240

SNYDER, RICHARD ELLIOTT, publishing company executive; b. N.Y.C., Apr. 6, 1933; s. Jack and Molly (Rothman) S.; children: Jacqueline, Matthew, Elliott; m. Laura Yorke, Jan.17, 1992. B.A., Tufts U., 1955. Asst. mktg. dir. Doubleday & Co., N.Y.C., 1958-60, sales mgr., 1960-64; dir. sales Simon & Schuster, N.Y.C., 1964-66, dir. mktg., 1967-68, pub., exec. v.p., 1969-75, pres., 1975—, chief exec. officer, 1979, chief exec. officer, chmn. bd., 1981-94; chmn., CEO Golden Press Inc., N.Y.C., 1995—; cons. N.Y.C., 1995—; bd. dirs. Reliance Group Holdings, Franklin Electric Pubs., Inc. Contbr. articles to profl. jours. Chmn. N.Y. area com. PEN, 1988; co-chmn. benefit com., 1992, chmn. pubs. com. for 48th Internat. PEN Congress; founding mem. Nat. Book Found., Nat. Book Awards, Inc.; mem. bus. com. N.Y. Zool. Soc., Coun. on Foreign Rels., Soc. Fellows, libr. com. Am. Mus. Natural History; mem. bd. overseers Univ. Librs., Tufts U.; vice chmn. benefit Literacy Vols., N.Y.C., 1991. Mem. Assn. Am. Pubs. (bd. dirs. 1976-79, 82-85), Econ. Club of N.Y.C. Office: Ste 2112-2110 237 Park Ave 21st Fl New York NY 10017

SNYDER, RICHARD G., transportation services executive; b. 1932. BS, Rutgers U. Various mgmt. and exec. positions Kearfott divsn. Gen. Precision, Little Falls, N.J., 1954-79, v.p. bus. devel.; v.p. internat. bus. devel. aerospace sys. group Singer Co., 1979-80; v.p. missile and space programs Kearfott divsn. Gen. Precision, 1980-84; pres. link tactical simulation divsn. CAE Industries Ltd., Silver Spring, Md., 1984-90; pres., CEO Reflectone Inc., Tampa, Fla., 1990—. Office: Reflectone Inc 4908 Tampa West Blvd Tampa FL 33634-2411*

SNYDER, RICHARD JOSEPH, lawyer; b. Boston, June 18, 1939; s. Harris H. and Ruth (Galner) S.; m. Joyce Marshall Aug. 19, 1962 (div.); children: Robert M., Lauren E., John K.; m. Susana Gohiman, Apr. 11, 1982; stepchildren: Joanna Maixner, Adriana Maixner. BSBA with honors, Babson Coll., 1960, LLD, 1994; JD with honors, Boston U., 1963; LLM, Georgetown U., 1966; LLD (hon.), Babson Coll., 1994. Bar: Mass. 1963, U.S. Claims Ct., 1964, U.S. Tx Ct. 1966, U.S. Dist. Ct., 1967, U.S. Ct. Appeals (1st Cir.) 1968, U.S. Supreme Ct. 1968, Vt. 1988. Sr. trial atty. Dept. Justice, Washington, 1963-66; assoc. Epstein & Salloway, Boston, 1966-67, Cohn, Reimer & Pollack (now Reimer & Braunstein), Boston, 1967-69; assoc. then ptnr. Widett & Widett (now Widett, Slater & Goldman), Boston, 1969-76; ptnr. Goldstein & Manello, Boston, 1976-88, chmn., 1988—; lectr. law Babson Coll., Wellesley, Mass., 1967-76; bd. advisors WBUR Pub. Radio, 1995—. Contbr. Boston U. Law Rev., 1962; contbg. editor Direct Sales Mag., 1976-78. Bd. dirs. Sundy Sch., Inc., 1974-85, pres., 1976-85; trustee Babson Coll., Wellesley, Mass., 1977-89, exec. com., 1979-89, chmn. bd., 1984-89, chmn. Corp., 1989—; mem. bus. and profl. leadership com. Boston Symphony Orch., 1989-91; hon. chmn. Presidents at Pops, 1980, ann. fund com., 1992; bd. dirs. Babson Recreation Ctr., 1987—, chmn. bd. dirs., 1987-89; bd. dirs. Mass. Corp. for Ednl. Telecom., 1985—, vice chmn. bd. dirs., 1986-88, chmn., 1989—; mem. corp. New Eng. Deaconess Hosp, 1992—. Fellow Mass. Bar Found.; mem. ABA, Mass. Bar Assn., Vt. Bar Assn., Boston Bar Assn., Am. Bus. Law Assn. (chmn. real property com. 1976-77, pres. North Atlantic region 1976-77), Nat. Assn. Coll. and Univ. Attys., Mass. Conveyancers Assn., New Eng. Land Title Assn., Babson Coll. Alumni Assn. (pres. 1977-79), Minuteman Yacht Club, Algonquin Club, Downtown Club, Greater Boston C. of C. (chmn. econ. devel. com.). Avocation: sailing. Home: 40 Pearl Rd Nahant MA 01908-1162 Office: Goldstein & Manello 265 Franklin St Fl 20 Boston MA 02110-3113

SNYDER, RICHARD LEE, consumer products company executive; b. Carlisle, Pa., June 24, 1940; s. Paul Bear and Mary (Fishburn) S.; m. Roberta Fitzgerald, Nov. 15, 1970 (div. July 1991). B.S. magna cum laude, Pa. State U., 1961. C.P.A., N.Y. With Coopers & Lybrand, N.Y.C., 1961-64; chief fin. officer Bell Equipment Corp., N.Y.C., 1964-71; treas. Wheelabrator-Frye, N.Y.C., 1971-73, v.p. fin. internat., 1973-75; v.p. fin. and adminstrn. Philip Morris USA, N.Y.C., 1975-79; corp. contr. Philip Morris, Inc., N.Y.C., 1979-81; sr. v.p. adminstrn. Philip Morris Internat., 1981-83, exec. v.p., 1983-87, 90-91; sr. v.p. human resources and adminstrn. Philip Morris Cos., N.Y.C., 1987-90; owner Snyder Quality Llamas. Treas. Sutton Area Comty. Assn., 1976-79; bd. dirs. Nat. Multiple Sclerosis Soc., 1981—, chmn. 1994—; bd. dirs. N.Y. Urban League, 1988-90. With U.S. Army, 1962. Recipient Alumni Achievement award Pa. State U., 1980. Mem. AICPA, Philippine Am. C. of C. (pres. 1986-87). Office: PO Box 927 Milford PA 18337

SNYDER, ROBERT MARTIN, agriculture consultant, retired government official; b. Lahmansville, W.Va., Sept. 6, 1912; s. Noah W. and Maggie M. (Varner) S.; m. Gail M. Hiser, Nov. 25, 1937; children: Rebecca J. Snyder Peters, Margaret A. Snyder Bensenhaver, Shirley L. Snyder Williams, Robert Martin Jr. B.S. in Agr, W.Va. U., 1937. Engaged in farming, 1929-90; agrl. extension agt. Nicholas County, W.Va., 1937-41; adminstrn. commodity loans crop ins. and program performance AAA, Morgantown, W.Va., 1941-42; adminstrn. grain and oilseed program E central region, AAA USDA, 1942-47, asst. coordinator, CCC, 1947-50, coordinator dairy, poultry, fruit and vegetable programs, CCC, 1950-52; chief agriculturist U.S. mission to Karachi, Pakistan FOA, 1952-54; dir. U.S. Mission and counselor U.S. Embassy Afghanistan, Kabul, 1954-59; rep. ICA to, Brit. East Africa, Kenya, Uganda, Tanganyika, Zanzibar, 1959-60; food and agr. officer West African countries of Ivory Coast, Upper Volta, Niger, Dahomey, 1961-62; acting dir. U.S. AID Mission, Ivory Coast, 1961-63; agr. adviser, area office rep. AID mission to, Rhodesia and Nyasaland, 1964; attache, AID affairs officer Malawi, Africa, 1964-68; cons. World Bank, IBRD, 1967; detail officer fgn. direct investments Dept. Commerce, 1968; AID affairs officers Washington, 1968-69; food and agr. officer U.S. AID, Amman, Jordan, 1969-70; planning adviser Ministry Natural Resources, Nigeria, 1970-72; cons., 1972—; Mem. del. Gen. Mem. Agreements Tariffs and Trade Conf., Torquay, Eng., 1951; mem. Mus. Commn., Library Commn. Served to lt. USNR, 1944-46, PTO. Recipient nat. 4-H alumni award Nat. 4-H Congress, Chgo., 1982, Disting. Alumnus award W.Va. Coll. Agriculture and Forestry, 1987; named to W.Va. Agrl. and Forestry Hall of Fame, 1991. Mem. Fgn. Service Assn., Am. Legion, W.Va. U. Alumni Assn., Am. Acad. Polit. and Social Sci., Soc. Internat. Devel., Internat. Platform Assn., U.S. Nat. Trust for Historic Preservation, Nature Conservancy, Commn. on Aging, Alpha Zeta. Clubs: Masons, Kiwanis, Explorers. Home: Noah Snyder Farm HC 84 Box 32 Lahmansville WV 26731-9702 *I feel that any success which I have achieved in life is in direct relationship to my interest in others and my ability to contribute to a better world situation in which each person can develop and achieve a better life for himself or herself and family.*

SNYDER, SCOTT WILLIAM, geology educator; b. Canton, Ohio, Apr. 8, 1946; s. Russell William and Merrie Elizabeth (Landis) S.; m. Lorna Jean Richmond, Sept. 3, 1966; 1 child, Kimberly Ann. BA in Geology, Coll. of Wooster, 1968; MS in Geology, Tulane U., 1970, PhD in Paleontology, 1974. Lic. geologist, N.C. Asst. prof. East Carolina U., Greenville, N.C., 1972-76, assoc. prof., 1976-83, prof., 1983—, chmn. geology dept., 1988—; acting assoc. dean Coll. Arts and Scis., 1990-91; scientist aboard R/V Glomar Challenger (sponsored by NSF), 1981, R/V Joides Resolution, 1993; mem. adv. com. N.C. State Geol. Map, Raleigh, 1983-85. Assoc. editor Jour. Foraminiferal Rsch., 1986-94, editor, 1995—, Spl. Pub. #25 Cushman Found., 1988; contbr. articles to profl. jours. Mem. Nat. Wildlife Fedn., 1988—; bd. dirs. Cushman Found., 1991—. Grantee NOAA, 1982, 84, 91, 93, NSF, 1982, 86, Petroleum Rsch. Fund, Am. Chem. Soc., 1988. Fellow Cushman Found. for Foraminiferal Rsch.; mem. Geol. Soc. Am., Paleontol. Soc., Paleontol. Rsch. Inst., Am. Geophys. Union, N.Am. Micropaleontol. Soc., Nat. Assn. Geology Tchrs., Sigma Xi. Democrat. Avocations: jogging, woodworking. Office: East Carolina U Dept Geology Greenville NC 27858

SNYDER, SOLOMON HALBERT, psychiatrist, pharmacologist; b. Washington, Dec. 26, 1938; s. Samuel Simon and Patricia (Yakerson) S.; m. Elaine Borko, June 10, 1962; children: Judith Rhea, Deborah Lynn. M.D. cum laude, Georgetown U., 1962, D.Sc. (hon.), 1986; D.Sc. (hon.), Northwestern U., 1981; PhD (hon.), Ben Gurion U., 1990. Intern Kaiser Found. Hosp., San Francisco, 1962-63; rsch. assoc. NIMH, Bethesda, Md., 1963-65; resident psychiatry Johns Hopkins Hosp., Balt., 1965-68; assoc. prof. psychiatry and pharmacology Johns Hopkins Med. Sch., 1968-70, prof., 1970-77, disting. svc. prof. psychiatry and pharmacology, 1977-80, disting. svc. prof. neurosci., psychiatry, and pharmacology, 1980—, dir. dept. neurosci., 1980—; NIH lectr., 1979. Author: Uses of Marijuana, 1971, Madness and the Brain, 1973, Opiate Receptor Mechanisms, 1975, The Troubled Mind, 1976, Biologic Aspects of Mental Disorder, 1980, Drugs and the Brain, 1986, Brainstorming, 1989; editor Perspectives in Neuropharmacology, 1971, Frontiers in Catecholamine Research, 1973, Handbook of Psychopharmacology, 1974; contbr. articles to profl. jours. Served with USPHS, 1963-65. Recipient Outstanding Scientist award Md. Acad. Scis., 1969, John Jacob Abel award Am. Pharmacology Soc., 1970, A.E. Bennett award Soc. Biol. Psychiatry, 1970; Gaddum award Brit. Pharm. Soc., 1974, F.O. Schmitt award in neuroscis. MIT, 1974, Nicholas Giarman lecture award Yale U., 1975, Rennebohm award U. Uis., 1976, Salmon award 1977, Stanley Dean award Am. Coll. Psychiatrists, 1978, Harvey Lecture. award, 1978, Lasker award, 1978, Wolf prize, 1983, Dickson prize, 1983, Sci. Achievement award AMA, 1985, Ciba-Giegy-Drew award, 1985, Strecker prize, 1986, Edward Sachar Meml. award Columbia U., 1986, Paul K. Smith Meml. lecture award George Washington U., 1986; Sense of Smell award Fragrance Rsch. Found., 1987, Julius Axelrod lecture award CUNY. 1988, John Flynn Meml. lecture award, Yale U., 1988, V. Erspamer lecture award Georgetown U., 1990, J. Allyn Taylor prize, 1990, Pasarow Found. award, 1991; Bower award Achievement Sci. Franklin Inst., 1991, Chauncey Leake Lecture award, 1992; William Veatch lecture award Harvard Med. Sch., 1992, Joseph Priestley prize Dickinson Coll., 1992, Konrad Bloch lecture award Harvard U., 1992, Basic Neurochem. lecture award Am. Soc. Neurochem., 1993, Nanine Duke lecture award Duke U., 1993, Salvador Luria lecture award MIT, 1993, Rudin lecture award Columbia U., 1995, Christian Herter lecture award NYU, 1995, Maclean lecture award, Baylor Med. Coll., 1995, Baxter award Am. Assn. Med. Colls., 1995, Bristol-Myers-Squibb Neurosci. prize, 1996. Fellow Am. Coll. Neuropsychopharmacology (Daniel Efron award 1974), Am. Psychiat. Assn. (Hofheimer award 1972, Disting. Svc. award 1989), Am. Acad. Arts and Scis., Am. Philosophical Soc.; mem. Nat. Acad. Scis., Soc. for Neuroscis. (pres. 1979-80), Am. Soc. Biol. Chemists, Am. Pharmacology Soc., Inst. Medicine. Home: 3801 Canterbury Rd Apt 1001 Baltimore MD 21218-2315 Office: Johns Hopkins U Med Sch Dept Neurosciences 725 N Wolfe St Baltimore MD 21205-2105

SNYDER, STEPHEN EDWARD, lawyer, mediator; b. Albuquerque, Sept. 14, 1942; s. John Royden and Elaine Stella (Draper) S.; m. Judith Anne Swall, Oct. 27, 1967; children: Sara, Katherine. BBA, U. N.Mex., 1965, MBA, 1967; JD, U. Tex., 1972. Bar: Colo. 1973, N.Mex. 1984. Ptnr. Holme Roberts & Owen, Denver, 1973—. Author: Commercial Bankruptcy Litigation, 1989. Chmn. bd. trustees Mile High Transplant Bank, Denver, 1995; trustee The Transplant Found., 1992-96, Allosource, 1994-96. Lt. (j.g.) USN, 1967-70. Office: Holme Roberts & Owen 1700 Lincoln St Ste 4100 Denver CO 80203-4541

SNYDER, SUSAN BROOKE, retired English literature educator; b. Yonkers, N.Y., July 12, 1934; d. John Warren and Virginia Grace (Hartung) S. BA, Hunter Coll., CUNY, 1955; MA, Columbia U., 1958, PhD, 1963. Lectr. Queens Coll., CUNY, N.Y.C., 1961-63; instr. Swarthmore Coll., Pa., 1963-66, asst. prof. English lit., 1966-70, assoc. prof., 1970-75, prof., 1975-93, Eugene M. Lang research prof., 1982-86, Gil and Frank Mustin prof., 1990-93; ret.; prof. emeritus Swarthmore Coll., 1993—; rschr. Folger Shakespeare Libr. Author: The Comic Matrix of Shakespeare's Tragedies, 1979; editor: Divine Weeks and Works of Guillaume de Saluste, Sieur du Bartas, 1979, Othello: Critical Essays, 1988, All's Well that Ends Well, 1993; mem. editl. bd. Shakespeare Quar., 1972—. Folger Library sr. fellow, 1972-73; Nat. Endowment for Humanities fellow, 1967-68; Guggenheim Found. fellow, 1980-81; Huntington Library summer grantee, 1966, 71; Folger Library grantee, 1969; Nat. Endowment for Humanities grantee, 1970; Nat. Endowment for Humanities summer grantee, 1976. Mem. Renaissance Soc. Am. (coun. 1979-81), Shakespeare Assn. Am. (trustee 1980-83).

SNYDER, THOM, lawyer; b. Glendale, Calif., Oct. 28, 1945; s. Walter and Jeanne (Mott) S.; m. Georgina Rae Totoian, Apr. 6, 1968; children: Chad Thomas, Seth Michael. BA, Calif. State U., Fresno, 1968; MA, Calif. State U., 1976; JD, San Joaquin Coll. of Law, 1982. Tchr. Riverdale (Calif.) Elem. Sch., 1968-70; tchr., adminstr. Am. Union Sch., Fresno, 1972-78; assoc. McInturff & Behrens, Hanford, Calif., 1983-85; ptnr. Behrens, Snyder & Romaine, Hanford, 1985—; adj. prof. Coll. of the Sequoias, Visalia, Calif., 1987-90. Pres., bd. dirs. Ctrl. Valley Regional Ctr., Fresno, 1987-93; pres. Assn. Regional Ctr. Agys., Sacramento, 1989-92; v.p., bd. dirs. Career Devel. Program, Escondido, Calif., 1994—; bd. dirs. Hanford YMCA, 1994—; sponsor, coach local youth sports, Hanford, 1986—. With U.S. Army, 1970-72. Named Tchr. of Yr. Coll. of Sequoias, 1989; recipient Svc. Appreciation award Ctrl. Valley Regional Ctr., 1992, 93. Mem. Kiwanis (v.p. Hanford club 1994—). Republican. Presbyterian. Home: 350 W Trinity Cir Hanford CA 93230 Office: Behrens Snyder & Romaine 522 N Redington St Hanford CA 93230

SNYDER, THOMAS DANIEL, retired electronics engineer, consultant; b. Phila., Aug. 30, 1925; s. Thomas Daniel and Edith May (Lees) S.; Asso. in Applied Sci. in Radio and TV Tech., Milw. Sch. Engring., 1951; m. Mary Ann Wilson, Aug. 28, 1954; children: Thomas Daniel, Ellen Mary, John W. Foreman Prime Mfg. Co., Milw., 1951; with engring. dept. No. Light Co., Milw., 1951-52; communications clk. fgn. service U.S. Dept. State, 1952-55; electronics engr. U.S. Dept. Def., Warrenton, Va., 1955-85; staff cons. Am. Elect. Labs. Cons. accoustics and magnetics govt. agys., 1964—; lectr. metric conversion; participant Solid States Application Conf., Fla. Atlanta U., 1971; participant profl. seminars Mass. Inst. Tech., 1962, 64, 66, Columbia, 1963, Pa. State U., 1967, U. Wis., 1969. Pres., PTA, Fairfax, Va., 1971, county rep., 1972. Served with USNR, 1943-46; PTO. Recipient Meritorious award for outstanding design in electronics equipment, U.S. Govt., 1969. Mem. AAAS, IEEE, Optical Soc. Am., Metric Assn., Am. Nat. Metric Coun., Am. Legion, Cath. War Vets. (adj. 1964-67). Roman Catholic. Contbr. articles to profl. jours. Patentee in field. Home: 4246 Worcester Dr Fairfax VA 22032-1140

SNYDER, WILLARD BREIDENTHAL, lawyer; b. Kansas City, Kans., Dec. 18, 1940; s. N.E. and Ruth (Breidenthal) S.; m. Lieselotte Dieringer, Nov. 10, 1970 (dec. Nov. 1975); 1 child, Rolf; m. T.J. Sewall, May 17, 1996. BA, U. Kans., 1962, JD, 1965; postgrad., Hague Acad. Internat. Law, The Netherlands, 1965-66, U. Dijon, France, 1966; grad., Command and Gen. Staff Coll., Ft. Leavenworth, Kans., 1977. Bar: Kans. 1965, Mo. 1986, U.S. Tax Ct. 1977, U.S. Ct. Mil. Appeals 1981, U.S. Dist. Ct. Kans. 1965, U.S. Supreme Ct. 1977. Atty. Kansas City, 1970-80, 85—; trust officer, corp. trust officer Security Nat. Bank., Kansas City, 1980-83, corp. sec., 1983-85; pres. Real Estate Corp. Inc., Leawood, Kans., 1984—; dir., mem. trust and investment com. Blue Ridge Bank; German Consul (H) for Kans., Western Mo., 1972—. Mem. Platte Woods (Mo.) City Coun., 1983-84; mem. exec. bd. dirs. regional coun. Boy Scouts Am.; bd. govs. Liberty Meml. Assn.; bd. dirs., v.p., treas. MacJannett Found., Talloires, France; pres. Breidenthal-Snyder Found.; bd. dirs., mem. exec. com. CORO Found.; Trustee Hoover Presdl. Libr. Col. Kans. Army N.G., ret.; col. USAR. Decorated Bundesverdienst Kreuz, 1982, BVK 1KL (Germany), 1992, Bundeswehr Kreuz (silver), 1987, Ge. Abn., Legion of Merit, Meritorious Svc. medal, Army commendation medal; named to Hon. Order Ky. Cols., 1988; recipient Golden Honour badge German Vet. Orgn., Bavaria, 1988, Mil. Order of WW award, OCS Hall of Fame. Mem. Mo. Bar Assn., Kansas City Bar Assn., Kansas City Hosp. Attys., Kansas City Bd. Trade, Mil. Order of World Wars (chpt. comdr. 1983-84, regional comdr. 1987-91, Patrick Henry award), Nat. Eagle Scout Assn. Avocations: scuba, hunting,

Notgeld collections, cartridge collection. Office: 8014 State Line Rd Ste 203 Leawood KS 66208-3712

SNYDER, WILLIAM BURTON, insurance executive; b. Clarksburg, W.Va., July 9, 1929; s. William Burton and Mary Catherine (Cornwell) S.; m. Georgie Gaye, Oct. 27, 1951; children: William Burton, Melissa Ann. B.B.A. in Acctg. cum laude, Tex. Tech. U., 1955. With Travelers Ins. Co., 1955-77, v.p., 1970-77; with Govt. Employees Ins. Co., Washington, 1977-93; chmn., pres., CEO GEICO Corp., 1985-93; chmn. and mem. bd. So. Heritage Ins. Co./Merastar Ins. Co., 1991—; chmn., pres., CEO So. Heritage Holdings, Inc., Merastar Corp., Washington, 1993—; adv. bd. mem. Riggs Nat. Bank, Washington Mut. Investors Fund. Past chmn., mem. econ. adv. coun. Montgomery County; bd. dirs. Capital Area coun. Boy Scouts Am.; past chmn., mem. Nat. Assn. Ind. Insurers. Capt. USAF, 1950-53. Decorated Air medal. Mem. Kenwood Country Club (Bethesda, Md.). Republican. Baptist.

SNYDER, WILLIAM HARRY, financial advisor; b. Newport, Pa., May 11, 1934; s. William Harry and Mary (Barner) S.; m. Irvil Kear, June, 1956 (div. 1961); 1 child, Geoffrey W.; m. Sandra Elizabeth Wolff, June 25, 1966; 1 child, Tara Elizabeth. BS in Indsl. Engring., Lehigh U., 1956; MS in Applied Stats., Rutgers U., 1961. Cert. fin. planner. Research engr. Johns-Manville Corp., Manville, N.J., 1956-61; indsl. engr., mgr. services and quality control Johns-Manville Corp., Nashua, N.H., 1961-69; mgr. phys. distbn. Johns-Manville Corp., N.Y.C., 1969-72; mgr. div. and corp. planning. Johns-Manville Corp., Denver, 1972-82; dir. corp. devel. Manville Corp. (formerly Johns-Manville Corp.), Denver, 1982-85; prin. Snyder Fin. Services, Littleton, Colo., 1985—; bd. dirs. Manville Employees Fed. Credit Union, Denver, 1985-88; rep. Fin. Network Investment Corp., 1988—; sec., founding mem. Manville Retirees Assn., 1992—; assoc. Fin. Network Adv. Corp., 1993—. Patentee process for making chalkboard; author: (with others) Standard Handbook of Plant Engineering, 1983. Vol. AARP Tax Coun. Program for the Elderly, 1987—. Served as 2d lt. U.S. Army, 1957-58. Mem. Colo. Soc. of Cert. Fin. Planners, Inst. of Cert. Fin. Planners, Pi Kappa Alpha (pres. 1954-55), Tau Beta Pi, Alpha Pi Mu. Republican. Methodist. Lodge: Mason. Avocations: backpacking, skiing, sailing, cycling. Home and Office: Snyder Fin Svcs 1952 W Ridge Rd Littleton CO 80120-3139

SNYDER, WILLIAM PENN, III, manufacturing company executive; b. Pitts., Mar. 11, 1918; s. William Penn and Marie Elise (Whitney) S.; m. Jean Evans Rose, Sept. 30, 1939; children: Marie Elise, J. Brandon. Student, U. Pitts. With The Wilpen Group Inc., now pres.; dir. H.J. Heinz Co., all Pitts., Whitney Nat. Bank, New Orleans. Bd. dirs. Pa. Economy League; chmn. bd. Allegheny Health, Edn. and Rsch. Found., Pitts.; v.p. bd. mgrs. Allegheny Cemetery; trustee Carnegie-Mellon U., Pitts., Carnegie Inst., Carnegie Hero Fund Commn., Western Res. Hist. Soc. Served as lt. (s.g.) USNR, 1942-45. Republican. Episcopalian. Clubs: Duquesne (Pitts.); Rolling Rock (Ligonier, Pa.); Allegheny Country (Sewickley, Pa.); Gulf Stream Golf (Delray Beach, Fla.). Home: Blackburn Rd Sewickley PA 15143-1416

SNYDERMAN, RALPH, medical educator, physician; b. Bklyn., Mar. 13, 1940; m. Judith Ann Krebs, Nov. 18, 1967; 1 child, Theodore Benjamin. B.S., Washington Coll., Chestertown, Md., 1961; M.D., SUNY-Bklyn., 1965. Diplomate Am. Bd. Internal Medicine, Am. Bd. Allergy and Immunology. Med. intern Duke U. Hosp., Durham, N.C., 1965-66, med. resident, 1966-67, asst. prof. medicine and immunology, 1972-74, assoc. prof., 1974-77, chief, div. rheumatology and immunology, 1975-87, prof. medicine and immunology, 1980-87, Frederic M. Hanes prof. medicine, prof. immunology, 1984-87, adj. prof. medicine, 1987-89; surgeon USPHS, NIH, Bethesda, Md., 1967-69; sr. staff fellow Nat. Inst. Dental Research, NIH, Bethesda, Md., 1969-70, sr. investigator immunology sect. lab. microbiology and immunology, 1970-72; chief, div. rheumatology Durham VA Hosp., Bethesda, Md., 1972-75; v.p. med. rsch. and devel. Genentech, Inc., South San Francisco, Calif., 1987-88, sr. v.p. med. rsch. and devel., 1988-89; chancellor for health affairs, dean Sch. Medicine Duke U., Durham, 1989—, James E. Duke prof. medicine, 1989—; CEO Duke U. Health System; adj. asst. prof. oral biology U. N.C. Sch. Dental Medicine, Chapel Hill, 1974-75; Howard Hughes med. investigator, Durham, 1972-77; dir. Lab Immune Effector Function, Howard Hughes Med. Inst., Durham, 1977-87; adj. prof. medicine U. Calif., San Francisco, 1987-89. Editor: Contemporary Topics in Immunobiology, 1979, Inflammation: Basic Concepts and Clinical Correlates, 1988, 2d edit., 1992; contbr. articles to profl. jours. Recipient McLaughlin award for inflammation rsch., 1978, Alexander von Humboldt award Fed. Republic Germany, 1985, award for lifetime achievements in inflammation rsch. Ciba-Geigy Morris Ziff, 1991, Bonnizinga award for excellence in leukocyte biology rsch., 1993, Disting. Alumni Achievement award SUNY Bklyn., 1995, Disting. Alumni citation Washington Coll., 1996, others. Mem. NAS, Inst. Medicine, Assn. Am. Physicians, Am. Assn. Immunologists, Am. Soc. Clin. Investigation, Am. Acad. Allergy, Am. Assn. Cancer Rsch., Soc. for Leukocyte Biology, Am. Fedn. Clin. Rsch., Am. Assn. Pathologists, Am. Soc. for Biochemistry and Molecular Biology, Assn. Acad. Health Ctrs., Am. Coll. Rheumatology, Am. Assn. for Med. Colls., Soc. for Med. Adminstrs., Sigma Xi. Office: Duke U Sch Medicine PO Box 3701 Durham NC 27710

SNYDERMAN, REUVEN KENNETH, plastic surgeon, educator; b. Phila., July 6, 1922; s. Harry S. and Anna (Koss) S.; m. Patricia Dawn Kennedy, June 29, 1955 (div. 1969); children: Peri Lynne, Lisa Mari, Scott R.; m. Adrienne E. Nordenschild, Dec. 6, 1970 (dec); m. Catherine Weisel Birkhahn, Jan. 16, 1993. AB, U. Pa., 1943, MD, 1946. Intern U.S. Naval Hosp., Phila., 1946-47; resident in gen. surgery Montefiore Hosp., NYU Med. Center, N.Y.C., 1949-51; resident in plastic and reconstructive surgery Columbia-Presbyn. Med. Center, N.Y.C., 1951-53; resident Meml. Sloan-Kettering Hosp., N.Y.C., 1953; pvt. practice medicine specializing in plastic, reconstructive surgery N.Y.C., 1954-73, Princeton, N.J., 1973-92; mem. staff plastic and reconstructive surgery, head of tissue transplantation sect Sloan-Kettering Inst. Cancer Research, N.Y.C., 1955-73; attending surgeon Princeton Hosp.; assoc. prof. surgery Med. Sch. Cornell U.; chief div. plastic and reconstructive surgery Robert Wood Johnson Univ. Hosp.; prof. emeritus div. plastic surgery U. Medicine and Dentistry of N.J.; chief div. Comprehensive Breast Svcs. Robert Wood Johnson Med. Sch., to 1991, prof. emeritus, 1992—; chmn. Plastic Surgery Research Council; cons. Nathan Littauer Hosp., Gloversville, N.Y.; spl. cons. Auerbach Corp., Phila. Author: New Parts for People, 1969, Symposium on Neoplastic and Reconstructive Problems of the Female Breast, 1973, The Breast, 1978; contbr. numerous articles to med. jours. With USNR, 1943-45; lt. (j.g.) USMC, 1947-49. Recipient Honor award N.Y. chpt. Hadassah, 1969. Fellow ACS; mem. AMA, N.Y. Regional Soc. Plastic and Reconstructive Surgery (historian), Am. Soc. Plastic and Reconstructive Surgery, N.J. Med. Soc., Mercer County Med. Soc., Webster Soc. (sec.-treas.), Am. Assn. Plastic Surgeons, N.Y. Cancer Soc. Home: 20 Constitution Hl W Princeton NJ 08540-6748 Office: U Medicine and Dentistry NJ Robert Wood Johnson Med Sch 1 Robert Wood Johnson Pl # 19 New Brunswick NJ 08901-1928

SOBCZAK, JUDY MARIE, clinical psychologist; b. Detroit, Dec. 28, 1949; d. Thaddeus Joseph and Bernice Agnes (Sowinski) Gorski; m. John Nicholas Sobczak, Aug. 17, 1974. BE cum laude, U. Toledo, 1971; postgrad., Ea. Mich. U., 1980-82; PhD, U. Toledo, 1987. Lic. psychologist. Tchr. Ottawa (Ohio)-Glandorf Schs., 1971-73; prin., tchr. St. Mary Sch., Assumption, Ohio, 1973-77; tchr. Our Lady of Perpetual Help Sch., Toledo, 1978-79; staff psychologist Outer Dr. Hosp., Lincoln Park, Mich., 1987-90; psychologist Adult/Youth Devel. Svcs., Farmington, Mich., 1991-95, Daivs Counseling Ctr., Farmington Hills, Mich., 1996—; with Northwestern Cmty. Svcs., Livonia, Mich., 1996—, Orchard Hills Psychiat. Ctr., Plymouth, Mich., 1996—; adj. asst. prof. Madonna U., Livonia, Mich., 1987-94. Eucharistic minister St. Anthony Cath. Ch., Belleville, Mich., 1991—, parish coun. 1993-96; Cath. Svc. Appeal co-chmn., 1993—; sec. bd. dirs. Children Are Precious Respite Care Ctr., 1995. Fellow Mich. Women Psychologists (charter; newsletter editor 1987-92, treas 1989-93, Plaque of Appreciation 1992-96, sec. 1993—); mem. Mich. Psychol. Assn., Phi Kappa Phi. Home: 41498 Mckinley St Belleville MI 48111-3439 Office: Davis Counseling Ctr 37923 W Twelve Mile Rd Farmington Hills MI 48331

SOBEL, ALAN, electrical engineer, physicist; b. N.Y.C., Feb. 23, 1928; s. Edward P. and Rose (Naftalison) S.; m. Marjorie Loebel, June 15, 1952; children: Leslie Ann, Edward Robert. BSEE, Columbia U., 1947, MSEE, 1949; PhD in Physics, Poly. Inst. Bklyn., 1964. Lic. Profl. Engr., N.Y. and Ill. Asst. chief engr. The Electronic Workshop, N.Y.C., 1950-51; head, functional engr. Fairchild Controls Corp., 1951-56; project engr. Skiatron Electronics and TV Corp., 1956-57; sr. rsch. engr. Zenith Radio Corp., Glenview, Ill., 1964-78; v.p. Lucitron inc., Northbrook, Ill., 1978-87, pres., 1987; pvt. practice cons. Evanston, Ill., 1988—; asst., instr. Poly. Inst. Bklyn.,1957-64; mem. program coms. SID Internat. Symposium, Internat. Display Rsch. Conf., 1970—. Inventor: 14 patents on various display and electron devices; author 50 papers on electronics, physics, electronic displays, etc.; editor Jour. Soc. Info. DIsplay, 1991—; contbg. editor Info. Display; assoc. editor: IEEE Trans. on Electron Devices, N.Y., 1970-77. Mem. Democratic Party of Evanston and Ward Orgn., various neighborhood orgns. NSF fellow, 1959, 60. Fellow Soc. Info. Display; mem. IEEE (sr., life), Am. Phys. Soc., Inst. Soc. for Optical Engring., Sigma Xi. Democrat. Home and Office: 633 Michigan Ave Evanston IL 60202-2552

SOBEL, ARNOLD I., mining executive; b. 1917. With Material Svc. Corp., Chgo., 1948—, now vice chmn. bd. dirs.; also bd. dirs. for other subs. and parent co. Office: Material Svc Corp 222 N La Salle St Chicago IL 60601-1003*

SOBEL, BURTON ELIAS, physician, educator; b. N.Y.C., Oct. 21, 1937; s. Lawrence J. and Ruth (Schoen) S.; m. Susan Konheim, June 19, 1958; children: Jonathan, Elizabeth. A.B., Cornell U., 1958; M.D. magna cum laude, Harvard U., 1962. Intern Peter Bent Brigham Hosp., Boston, 1962-63; resident Peter Bent Brigham Hosp., 1963-64, 66-67; clin. asso., cardiology br. NIH, Bethesda, Md., 1964-66, 67-68; asst. prof. medicine U. Calif. at San Diego, La Jolla, 1968-71; asso. prof. medicine, dir. myocardial infarction research unit, dir. coronary care, 1971-73; asso. prof. medicine Barnes Hosp.-Washington U., St. Louis, 1973-75; prof. Barnes Hosp.-Washington U., 1975—, dir. cardiovascular div., 1973—, program dir. specialied ctr. rsch. in ischemic heart disease, 1975-89, program dir. specialized ctr. rsch. in coronary and vascular diseases, 1990-94, program dir. principles in cardiovascular rsch., 1975-94; chmn., prof. medicine U. Vt., Burlington, 1994—; physician-in-chief Med. Ctr. Hosp. Vt., Burlington, 1994—; program dir. Collaborative Clin. Trial Therapy to Protect Ischemic Myocardium, Washington U., 1977; chmn. cardio renal drugs U.S. Pharmacopeial Conv., 1990—. Assoc. med. editor The Heart Bull, 1971-72; editor Clin. Cardiology, 1971-74; mem. circulation bd., 1971—; editor Circulation, 1983-88; mem. editorial bd. Circulation Research, 1974—, Annals of Internal Medicine, 1976—, Am. Jour. Cardiology, 1976—, Cardiology Digest, 1976-77, Jour. Continuing Edn. in Cardiology, 1978—, Cardiology in the Elderly, 1991—; mem. editorial bd., assoc. editor Jour. Clin. Investigation, 1977—; assoc. editor, Am. Jour. Physiology: Heart and Circulatory Physiology, 1978—; Churchill Livingstone editorial advisory bd. Internat. Seminars in Cardiovascular Medicine, 1978—, Cardiology in Review, 1992—; mem. editorial bd. Current Med. Lit., Current Opinion in Cardiology, editor, 1989—, Internat. Jour. Cardiology, Fibrinolysis, 1986, assoc. editor, 1990—; cons. editor Circulation, 1988—; editor Coronary Artery Disease, 1989—, Can. Jour. Cardiology, 1995—. Served to lt. comdr. USPHS, 1964-68. Recipient Career Rsch. Devel. award USPHS, 1972, internat. recognition award Heart Rsch. Found., 1981, Disting. Achievement award Am. Heart Assn. Sci. Couns., 1984, award Robert J. and Claire Posatow Found., 1988, award Va. Heart Ctr., 1991, Drake award Maine Heart Assn., 1992. Fellow ACP; mem. Royal Soc. Medicine, Am. Fedn. Clin. Rsch. (councilor), Am. Heart Assn. (James B. Herrick award 1992), Am. Coll. Cardiology (Disting. Scientist award 1987), Assn. Univ. Cardiologists, Am. Soc. Clin. Investigation (councilor), Assn. Am. Physicians, Am. Physiol. Soc., Cardiac Muscle Soc., Western Soc. Clin. Rsch., Internat. Soc. Fibrinolysis and Thrombolysic (councilor), Assn. Profs. Cardiology (pres.-elect 1992), Internat. Soc. Applied Cardiovasc. Biology, Alpha Omega Alpha. Home: 2 Lost Cove Rd Colchester VT 05446-1840 Office: Fletcher Allen-MCHV Campus Fletcher 311 Burlington VT 05401

SOBEL, HOWARD BERNARD, osteopath; b. N.Y.C., May 15, 1929; s. Martin and Ella (Sternberg) S.; m. Ann Louise Silverbush, June 16, 1957 (dec. May 1978); children—Nancy Sobel Schumer, Janet Sobel Medow, Robert; m. Irene S. Miller, June 8, 1980; stepchildren—Avner Saferstein, Daniel Saferstein, Naomi Saferstein. A.B., Syracuse U., 1951; D.O., Kansas City Coll. Osteopathy and Surgery, 1955. Intern Zieger Osteo. Hosp., Detroit, 1955-56; gen. practice osteo. medicine Redford Twp., Mich., 1956-74, Livonia, Mich., 1974—; chief of staff Botsford Gen. Hosp., Farmington, Mich., 1978; mem. faculty Mich. State U. Coll. Osteo. Medicine, 1969—, clin. assoc. prof. family practice, 1973—; mem. exec. and med. adv. coms. United Health Orgn. Mich.; mem. Venereal Disease Action Com., Mich.; apptd. to asst. impaired osteo. physicians Mich., 1983. Mem. Am. Osteo. Assn. (ho. of dels. 1981—), Mich. Assn. Osteo. Physicians and Surgeons (ho. of dels.), Am. Coll. Osteo. Rheumatologists, Coll. Am. Osteo. Gen. Practitioners, Osteo. Gen. Practice Mich., Wayne County Osteo. Assn. (pres.). Jewish. Home: 6222 Northfield Dr West Bloomfield MI 48322-2431 Office: 28275 5 Mile Rd Livonia MI 48154-3944

SOBEL, SHEPARD MICHAEL, artistic director; b. N.Y.C., Mar. 28, 1947; s. Daniel and Pearl (Schwartz) S.; m. Rhonda Plotkin, Aug. 4, 1968 (div. 1972); 1 child, Sabrina; m. Joanne Camp, Oct. 24, 1983. BA, Hobart Coll., 1968; MA, U. Fla., 1974. Tchr. Canandaigua (N.Y.) Acad., 1968-70, South Fla. State Hosp., Hollywood, 1970-71, Annandale (Va.) High Sch., 1974-78; freelance actor, dir. Washington, 1974-79, N.Y.C., 1979-84; artistic dir. Pearl Theatre Co., N.Y.C., 1982—. Jewish. Office: Pearl Theatre Co 80 Saint Marks Pl New York NY 10003-8129

SOBELLE, RICHARD E., lawyer; b. Cleve., Mar. 18, 1935. BA, Stanford U., 1956, JD, 1960; LLM, U. So. Calif., 1967. Bar: Calif. 1961, U.S. Supreme Ct. 1969. Exec. Tracinda Corp., Las Vegas. Mem. ABA (mem. corp., banking and bus. law sect. 1969—), State Bar Calif. (del. to conf. state bar dels. 1965-77, mem. exec. com. bus. law sect. 1977-78), L.A. County Bar Assn. (mem. exec. coun., jr. barristers 1965-68, mem. exec. com. bus. and corps. sect. 1973-75). Office: Tracinda Corp 4835 Koval Ln Las Vegas NV 89109

SOBERON, PRESENTACION ZABLAN, state bar administrator; b. Cabambangan, Bacolor, Pampanga, Philippines, Feb. 23, 1935; came to U.S., 1977, naturalized, 1984; d. Pioquinto Yalung and Lourdes (David) Zablan; m. Damaso Reyes Soberon, Apr. 2, 1961; children: Shirley,Sherman, Sidney, Sedwin. Office mgmt., stenography, typing cert. East Cen. Colls., Philippines, 1953; profl. sec. diploma, Internat. Corr. Schs., 1971; student Skyline Coll., 1979, LaSalle Ext. U., 1980-82; AA, cert. in Mgt. and Supervision, Diablo Valley Coll. With U.S. Fed. Svc. Naval Base, Subic Bay, Philippines, clerical, stenography and secretarial positions, 1955-73, adminstrv. asst., 1973-77; secretarial positions Mt. Zion Hosp. and Med. Center, San Francisco, 1977, City Hall, Oakland, Calif., 1978; secretarial positions gen. counsel div. and state bar court divsn., State Bar of Calif., San Francisco, 1978-79, adminstrv. asst. fin. and ops. div., 1979-81, office mgr. sects. and coms. dept., profl. and pub. svcs. div., 1981-83, appointment adminstr. office of bar rels., 1983-86; adminstr. state bar sects. bus. law sect., estate planning, trust and probate law sect., labor and employment law section, office of bar rels., 1986-89, adminstr. antitrust and trade regulation law sect., labor and employment law sect., workers' compensation sect., edn. and meeting svcs., 1989-96, adminstrn. estate planning, trust and probate law sect., 1996—, family law sect., 1996—, internat. law sect., 1996—, workers' compensation sect., 1996—, edn. and meeting svcs., 1996—; disc jockey/announcer Philippine radio stas. DZYZ, DZOR and DWHL, 1966-77. Organizer Neighborhood Alert Program, South Catamaran Circle, Pittsburg, Calif., 1979-80. Recipient 13 commendation certs. and outstanding pers. monetary awards U.S. Fed. Svc., 1964-77, 20 Yr. U.S. Fed. Svc. pin and cert., 1975; Nat. 1st prize award for community svc. and achievements Nat. Inner Wheel Clubs Philippines, 1975; several plaques and award certs. for community and sch. activities and contbrns. Olongapo City, Philippines. Mem. NAFE, Am. Soc. Assn. Execs., N.Y.C. Olongapo-Subic Bay Assn. No. Calif. (Pittsburg rep. 1982-87, bus. mgr. 1988—, pub. rels. officer 1993-94), Castillejos Assn. of No. Calif. Roman Catholic. Home: 207 S Catamaran Cir Pittsburg CA 94565-3613 Office: State Bar of Calif 555 Franklin St San Francisco CA 94102-4456

SOBEY, DAVID FRANK, food company executive; b. Stellarton, N.S., Can., Mar. 22, 1931; s. Frank Hoyse and Irene (MacDonald) S.; m. Faye B. Naugle, June 2, 1953; children: Paul David, Janis Irene Hames. D of Commerce (hon.), St. Mary's U., 1991. With Sobeys Inc., Stellarton, 1949—, store mgr., dir. merchandising and advt., v.p., exec. v.p., pres., dep. chmn., chief exec. officer, dir., 1981-85, chmn., dir., 1985—; bd. dirs. Empire Co. Ltd., Sobey Leased Properties Ltd., Atlantic Shopping Ctrs. Ltd., Sobeys Land Holdings Ltd., Clover Group, Ea. Sign Print Ltd., Lumsden Bros. Ltd., Dominion Textile Inc., Evangeline Fin. Svcs. Corp., T.R.A. Foods Ltd., Hannaford Bros. Co., CHC Helicopter Corp.; chmn. The Sobey Found., Frank H. Sobey Fund for Excellence in Bus. Studies. Bd. dirs. Retail Coun. Can., Internat. Assn. Chain Stores, C.I.E.S., Food Mktg. Inst., Tim Horton Children's Found., The Sobey Art Found., Boy Scouts Can., Atlantic Salmon Fedn.; bd. govs. St. Mary's U., chmn. fin. campaign; mem. Halifax Bd. Trade. Mem. Order of Can., 1996. Clubs: Royal N.S. Yacht Squadron; Halifax; City (New Glasgow), Abercrombie Country. Office: Sobeys Inc, 115 King St, Stellarton, NS Canada B0K 1S0

SOBEY, DONALD CREIGHTON RAE, real estate developer; b. New Glasgow, N.S., Can.; s. Frank Hoyse and Irene (MacDonald) S.; m. Elizabeth H. Purvis; children: Robert George Creighton, Irene Elizabeth, Kent Richard. B of Commerce, Queen's U.; LLD (hon.), Dalhousie U., 1989. Vice chmn. Halifax Devels. Ltd., 1989—; pres. Empire Cos. Ltd., 1969; chmn. Empire Co. Ltd., 1985—; also bd. dirs.; bd. dirs. Paribas Participations Limitee PPL, Merchant Pvt. Ltd., Atlantic Shopping Ctrs. Ltd., Jannock Ltd., Lawton's Drug Stores Ltd., Tibbetts Paints Ltd., Toronto-Dominion Bank, Wajax Ltd., Sobeys Inc., Maritime Telegraph and Telephone Co. Ltd. Gov. Olympic Trust Can.; patron 1986 World Congress on Edn. and Tech.; bd. govs. Dalhousie U.; mem. task force Future of Port Halifax; mem. Conf. Bd. Can.; founding chmn. Camp Hill Med. Ctr.; mem. Club de Rels. d'Affaires Can.-France; chmn. Friends of the Nova Scotia Mus. Industry Soc.; co-chair fin. com. Gov. Gen.'s Can. Study Conf.; bd. dirs. Nat. Gallery Can. Mem. Internat. Assn. for Students Econs. and Commerce, Lloyd's of London (underwriting). Avocations: skiing, tennis, music, art, travel. Office: Empire Co Ltd, 115 King ST, Stellarton, NS Canada B0K 1S0

SOBEY, EDWIN J. C., museum director, oceanographer, consultant; b. Phila., Apr. 7, 1948; s. Edwin J. and Helen (Chapin) S.; m. Barbara Lee, May 9, 1970; children: Ted Woodall, Andrew Chapin. BS, U. Richmond (Va.), 1969; MS, Oreg. State U., 1974, PhD, 1977. Rsch. scientist Sci. Applications, Inc., Boulder, Colo., 1977-79, div. mgr., 1979-81; exec. dir. Sci. Mus., West Palm Beach, Fla., 1981-88, Mus. Sci. and History, Jacksonville, Fla., 1988, Nat. Invention Ctr., Akron, Ohio, 1989-92, Fresno (Calif.) Met. Mus., 1993—, devel. dir. Sch. Natural Scis., Calif. State U., Fresno; exec. prodr. (t.v. show) Idea Factory, KFSN-30, Fresno, 1995—. Alumni v.p. Leadership Palm Beach County; expdn. leader Expdn. Tng. Inst., S.E. Alaska, 1980; mem. U.S. Antarctic Research Program, 1974. Author: Complete Circuit Training Guide, 1980; Strength Training Book, 1981; (with others) Aerobic Weight Training Book, 1982, Increasing Your Audience, 1989, Inventing Stuff, 1995; mem. editorial adv. bd. Invent Mag., 1989-92. Founder, bd. dirs. Visually Impaired Sports Program, Boulder, 1978-81; fitness instr. YMCA Boulder, 1977-81; convener 1st Nat. Conf. Sports for the Blind, 1979; bd. dirs. Leadership Palm Beach; vice chmn. County Com. on Artificial Reefs; treas. Leaderdeship Akron Alumni Assn., 1990-91, class pres. Leadership Akron; v.p. Ohio Mus. Assn., 1991-92, pres., 1992-93; co-host Blow the Roof Off Ednl TV show, 1992; bd. dirs. Fla. Mus. Assn., 1988-89; mem. adv. bd. Marine Sci. Inst., 1990—. Lt. USN, 1970-73. Fellow Explorers Club; mem. Marine Tech. Soc. (sect. chmn. 1982-84), Coral Reef Soc. (chpt. pres. 1982-87), Nat. Inventive Thinking Assn. (bd. dirs. 1989—). Home: 8806 N 5th St Fresno CA 93720-1724

SOBIESKI, JAROSLAW, aerospace engineer; b. Wilno, Poland, Mar. 11, 1934; came to U.S., 1966; naturalized, 1971.; s. Stanislaw and Sabina Sobieszczanski; m. Wanda Dlugosz, Dec. 31, 1958; children: Margaret Ann, Ian Patrick. BS aeros., Tech. U. Warsaw, 1955, MS aeros., 1957, DEng, 1964. Cons. Polish Aircraft Industries, Warsaw, Poland, 1957-64; asst. and adj. prof. Tech. U. Warsaw, Warsaw, Poland, 1955-64; rsch. assoc. Tech. U. Norway, Trondheim, 1964-66; assoc. prof. St. Louis U., 1966-71; aerospace engr. NASA Langley Rsch. Ctr., Hampton, Va., 1971-89, head rsch. office, 1979-93, chief scientist, 1993-94, multidisciplinary rsch. coord., 1994—, mgr. computational AeroScis. team, 1996—; mem. faculty George Washington U., 1972-92, U. Va., 1982—; pres. and cons. engr. Tech. Analysis Optimization, Inc. Hampton, Va., 1983—. Contbr. articles to profl. jours. Recipient medal for exceptional achievement in engring. NASA, 1988. Fellow AIAA (mem. tech. com.). Home: 518 Elizabeth Lake Dr Hampton VA 23669-1724 Office: NASA Langley Rsch Ctr Hampton VA 23681-0001

SOBIN, JULIAN MELVIN, international consultant; b. Boston, July 14, 1920; s. Irving Maxwell and Selma Helen (Brodie) S.; m. Leila Feinburg, May 3, 1942; children: Patricia, Jonathan. A.B., Harvard U., 1941; LL.D. (hon.), William Penn Coll., 1979. Trainee to chmn. Sobin Chems. Inc., Boston, 1946-75; sr. v.p. Internat. Minerals & Chem. Corp., 1975-77, dir. internat. bus. devel., 1976-77, exec. cons., 1977-78; exec. v.p. IMC Chem. Group, 1975-76; chmn. trustees Internat. Mktg. Inst., Cambridge, Mass., 1975-84; v.p. Assoc. Metals & Minerals Corp., 1978-82; dir. Comml. Solvents Corp.; exec. cons. China trade Laporte Industries U.K. and U.S.A.; lectr. in field; corporator South Boston Savs. Bank; advisor, cons. to Spl. Rep. of Pres. for Trade Negotiations, Kennedy Round of Tariff Reductions, 1962-63; mem. Pres.'s Adv. Com. Nat. Trade Policy, 1968-69; mem. adv. com. on East/West trade Dept. Commerce, 1976—; internat. trade cons. Internat. Exec. Svc. Corps to San Miguel Corp., Manila, 1984-85; mem. exec. com. Mass. Gov.'s Fgn. Bus. Coun., 1977—; cons. dir. NYBO Internat. Inc., 1987—; sr. advisor C.P. Group, Bangkokk, 1992—, Harcros Chemicals, London, 1992—. Author: (audio album) The China Trader; co-author: Ency. of China Today, The China Guide, 12th edit., 1992; mem. adv. bd. Partisan Review; contbr. numerous articles to profl. jours. Gen. chmn. New Eng. Trade Week, 1959; trustee Nat. Jewish Hosp. and Research Center, Denver, Emerson Coll.; bd. advisors Stonehill Coll., 1975-78; mem. overseers com. to visit dept. fine arts Harvard U., 1968-74; mem. Boston Com. on Fgn. Relations; bd. dirs. Nat. Council U.S.-China Trade, 1976-77; bd. dirs., mem. exec. com. Internat. Trade Ctr. New Eng. Inc.; trustee Lesley Coll., Boston U., Am. Grad. Sch. Internat. Mgmt. (Thunderbird); mem. overseers com. to visit Ctr. Internat. Affairs Harvard U., 1981—. Served to maj. F.A. AUS, 1941-46, CBI. Decorated Legion of Merit; recipient Annual Honor medal Nat. Jewish Hosp. and Rsch. Ctr., 1975; fellow Harvard U. Ctr. for Internat. Affairs, 1987-88; hon. royal consul of Nepal in Boston, 1993—. Mem. Mfg. Chemists Assn., Chemists Club of N.Y., Hong Kong-Am. C. of C., Fgn. Correspondents Club Hong Kong, Internat. Mgmt. Devel. Inst. (corp. strategic planning coun.), Soc. Am. Chem. Industry, Am. Radio Relay League, Harvard Club (Boston, N.Y.C.), Univ. Club (Boston). First Am. businessman invited to Peking, China, spring 1972. Home: 790 Boylston St Boston MA 02199-7928

SOBKOWICZ, HANNA MARIA, neurology researcher; b. Warsaw, Poland, Jan. 1, 1931; came to U.S., 1963; d. Stanislaw and Jadwiga (Ignaczak) S.; m. Jerzy E. Rose, Mar. 12, 1972. B.A., Girls State Lyceum, Gilwice, Poland, 1949; M.D, Med. Acad., Warsaw, 1954, Ph.D., 1962. Intern. 1st Internal Med. Clinic Med. Acad., Warsaw, 1954-55; resident 1st Internal Med. Clinic, Med. Acad., Warsaw, 1955-59; resident Neurol. Clinic, Med. Acad., 1959, jr. asst., 1959-61, sr. asst., 1961-63; research fellow neurology Mt. Sinai Hosp., N.Y.C., 1963-65; Nat. Multiple Sclerosis Soc. fellow Columbia U., N.Y.C., 1965-66; asst. prof. neurology U. Wis., Madison, 1966-72, assoc. prof., 1972-79, prof., 1979—. Contbr. articles to profl. jours. NIH research grantee, 1968—. Mem. Internat. Brain Rsch. Orgn., Assn. Rsch. in Otolaryngology, Soc. Neurosci., Internat. Soc. Devel. Neurosci. (editorial bd. 1984—), Electron Microscopy Soc. Am. Office: U Wis Dept Neurology 1300 University Ave Madison WI 53706-1510

SOBLE, JAMES BARRY, lawyer; b. Chgo., Apr. 14, 1942; s. Julius R. Soble and Bernyce (Morris) Rossuck; children—Debra, Jeffrey, Tony, Leslie; m. Ann S. Valenstein, June 29, 1980. B.A., Grinnell Coll., 1963; J.D., Northwestern U., 1966. Bar: Ill. 1966, Fla. 1974. Assoc. Deutsch & Peskin, Chgo., 1966-68; ptnr. Siegel & Soble, 1969-71 Peskin & Soble, 1972-73; exec. v.p., corp. counsel Millstream Corp., Sunrise, Fla., 1973-79; pvt. developer, Ft. Lauderdale, Fla., 1979-81; ptnr., shareholder Jacobs, Robbins, Gaynor,

Hampp, Burns, Cole & Shasteen, P.A., St. Petersburg, Fla., 1981-83; ptnr. Taub & Williams, Tampa, Fla., 1984-88; ptnr. Honigman Miller Schwartz and Cohn, 1988—; lectr. Law Forum, Inc., 1982-84. Pres., bd. dirs. Gulf Coast Jewish Family Services of Pinellas County, 1984—; bd. dirs. Better Bus. Bur. West Florida, Inc.; pres. Jewish Fedn. Pinellas County, 1989-91, 93-95. Mem. ABA, Ill. Bar Assn., Hillsborough County Bar Assn. Jewish. Home: 2996 Sandpiper Pl Clearwater FL 34622-3058 Office: Honigman Miller Scharwtz & Cohn 2700 SunTrust Fin Ctr 401 E Jackson St Tampa FL 33602

SOBOL, HAROLD, retired dean, manufacturing executive, consultant; b. Bklyn., June 21, 1930; s. Stanley and Minnie S.; m. Marion Gross, Dec. 29, 1957; children—Diane, Neil, Jessica, Martin. B.S.E.E., CUNY, 1952; M.S.E.E., U. Mich., 1956, Ph.D., 1960. Research asst. Willow Run Labs. U. Mich., 1952-55, research assoc., 1956-59; staff mem. IBM Research, Yorktown Heights, N.Y., 1960-62; with RCA Labs., Princeton, N.J., 1962-73; staff engr. RCA Labs., 1970-72, head communication tech., 1972-73; sr. mem. tech. staff Collins Radio Rockwell-Internat., Dallas, 1973-74; dir. product devel. Collins Transmission Systems div., 1974-85; dir. engring. Rockwell Telecommunications, 1985-86, v.p. engring., 1986-88, ret., 1988; prof. elec. engring., assoc. dean U. Tex., Arlington, 1988-93. Author: Advances in Microwaves Volume 8, 1974; contbr. in field. Cubmaster Tex.-Okla. council Boy Scouts Am., Dallas, 1978-80. Sperry fellow, 1955-56. Fellow IEEE (pres. microwave theory and techniques soc. 1979); mem. Am. Phys. Soc., Nat. Mgmt. Assn., Sigma Xi, Tau Beta Pi, Eta Kappa Nu. Office: U Tex PO Box 19019 Arlington TX 76019

SOBOL, LAWRENCE RAYMOND, lawyer; b. Kansas City, Mo., May 8, 1950; s. Haskell and Mary (Press) S.; m. Maureen Patricia O'Connell, May 29, 1976; children: David, Kevin. BBA, U. Tex., 1972; JD, U. Mo., 1975. Bar: Mo. 1975, U.S. Dist. Ct. (ea. dist.) Mo. 1975. Gen. counsel, gen. ptnr. Edward D. Jones & Co., Maryland Heights, Mo., 1975—; allied mem. N.Y.C. Stock Exchange, 1977—; sec. Lake Communications Corp., Conroe, Tex., 1984-86, LHC Inc., EDJ Holding Co. Inc.; sec., bd. dirs. Cornerstone Mortgage Inc., St. Louis, 1986; v.p., bd. dirs. Tempus Corp., St. Louis, 1984—. Omar Robinson Meml. scholar U. Mo., 1974-75. Mem. ABA (securities law com. 1982—), Met. St. Louis Bar Assn. (securities law sect.), Nat. Assn. Securities Dealers (dist. bus. com., registered prin. officer, nat. arbitration com. 1991—), Securities Industry Assn. (fed. rebulation securities com. 1987-88), Forest Hills Country Club, Phi Eta Sigma. Republican. Jewish. Avocations: tennis, golf. Office: Edward D Jones & Co 201 Progress Pky Maryland Heights MO 63043

SOBOL, THOMAS, state education commissioner; b. Jan. 11, 1932; m. Harriet Sobol; three children. BA in English, Harvard U., 1953, grad., 1954; PhD, Columbia U., 1969. Head dept. English pub. sch. system Bedford, N.Y., 1961-65; dir. instrn., 1965-69; asst. supt. instrn. pub. sch. system Great Neck, N.Y., 1969-71; supt. sch. systems Scarsdale, N.Y., 1971-87; commr. N.Y. State edn. Albany, 1987—; Christian A. Johnson Prof. Columbia Univ. Teacher's College, N.Y.C. also: Columbia Univ. Teachers College 525 W 120th St New York NY 10027

SOBOLEWSKI, JOHN STEPHEN, computer information scientist, director computer services, consultant; b. Krakow, Poland, July 14, 1939; came to U.S., 1966; s. Jan Zygmund and Stefania (Zwolinska) S.; m. Helen Skipper, Dec. 17, 1965 (div. July 1969); m. Carole Straith, Apr. 6, 1974; children: Anne-Marie, Elisa, Martin. BE, U. Adelaide, Adelaide, South Australia, 1962, ME, 1966; PhD in Computer Sci., Wash. State U., 1971. Sci. officer Weapons Research Establishment, Salisbury, South Australia, 1964-66; asst. prof. computer sci. Wash. State U., Pullman, 1966-73; dir. research, assoc. prof. U. Wash., Seattle, 1973-80, dir. computer svcs., 1980-88; assoc. v.p. computing U. N.Mex., Albuquerque, 1988—; cons. govt. and industry, Seattle, 1973—; mem. bd. trustees Fisher Found., Seattle, 1984—. Author: Computers for the Dental Office, 1986; contbr. articles to profl. jours. Served as engr. with Royal Australian Army, 1957-60. Australian govt. scholar, 1954-60, Elec. Res. Bd. scholar CSIRO, Melbourne, Australia, 1961-64. Mem. IEEE, Computer Soc. Roman Catholic. Avocation: mineral collecting. Home: 8501 Northridge Ave NE Albuquerque NM 87111-2107 Office: U NMex CIRT 2701 Campus Ave NE Albuquerque NM 87131

SOCARIDES, CHARLES WILLIAM, psychiatrist, educator; b. Brockton, Mass., Jan. 24, 1922; s. James and Theodora (Cokas) S.; m. Veronica Rak (div.); children: Richard, Daphne; m. Barbara Bonner, Jan. 28, 1973 (div. Apr. 1987); children: Alexandra, Charles Jr.; m. Claire Alford, Oct. 19, 1988; 1 child, Jacqueline Nichole. Cert., Harvard Coll., Cambridge, Mass., 1945; MD, N.Y. Med. Coll., 1947; cert., Columbia U., N.Y.C., 1952. Diplomate Am. Bd. Psychiatry and Neurology. Instr. in psychiatry Columbia U., N.Y.C., 1956-60, assoc. in psychiatry, 1960-62; clin. asst. prof. psychiatry SUNY, N.Y.C., 1955-58, clin. prof. psychiatry, 1976-78; assoc. attending psychiatrist Vanderbilt Clinic Coll. U., N.Y.C., 1960-62; assoc. clin. prof. psychiatry Albert Einstein Coll. Medicine, N.Y.C., 1969-76, clin. prof., 1976—; clin. prof. psychiatry Montefiore Med. Ctr., N.Y.C., 1978—; med. cons. Armed Svcs. Dept. Def., Washington, 1978—; tng. psychiat. residents Albert Einstein Coll. Medicine, 1968—. Author: The Overt Homosexual, 1968, Homosexuality, 1978, The Preoedipol Origin and Psychoanalytic Treatment of Sexual Perversion, 1988, Beyond Sexual Freedom, On Sexuality: Psychoanalytic Observations, 1979, The Homosexualities and the Therapeutic Process; contbr. articles to profl. jours.; numerous book reviews. Lt. USNR, 1952-54. Recipient Sigmund Freud award Am. Soc. Psychoanalytic Physicians, 1987, N.Y. Soc. for Psychoanalytic Tng., 1975. Fellow Am. Psychoanalytic Assn., Am. Psychiat. Assn., Am. Coll. Psychoanalysts, Am. Soc. Psychoanalytic Physicians (hon. fellow); mem. AMA, N.Y. County Med. Soc., Internat. Psychoanalytic Assn., Royal Soc. of Medicine London (affiliate), Coral Beach Club. Democrat. Greek Orthodox. Avocations: tennis, writing, professional books. Home and Office: 242 E 94th St New York NY 10128-3706

SOCHACKI, TINA MARIE, secondary education educator; b. Evergreen Park, Ill., July 10, 1967; d. Alex Wayne and Judith Anne (Zicha) Spirakes; m. Matthew Zygmunt Sochacki, June 18, 1993. BA in French and Spanish Edn., U. Ill., 1989; postgrad., Gov.'s State U., University Park, Ill., 1994-96. Cert. 6-12 tchr., Ill.; Ill. type 75 cert. Tchr. fgn. lang. Bremen H.S., Midlothian, Ill., 1989-90, Acad. of Our Lady H.S., Chgo., 1990-91, Evergreen Park H.S., 1991—. Mem. ASCD, Am. Assn. Tchrs. French, Ill. Coun. on Tchg. Fgn. Langs., U. Ill. Alumni Assn., Golden Key. Avocations: billiards, reading, spending time with family and pet pug. Office: Evergreen Park HS 9901 S Kedzie Ave Evergreen Park IL 60805

SOCHEN, JUNE, history educator; b. Chgo., Nov. 26, 1937; d. Sam and Ruth (Finkelstein) S. B.A., U. Chgo., 1958; M.A., Northwestern U., 1960, Ph.D., 1967. Project editor Chgo. Superior and Talented Student Project, 1959-60; high sch. tchr. English and history North Shore Country Day Sch., Winnetka, Ill., 1961-64; instr. history Northeastern Ill. U., 1964-67, asst. prof., 1967-69, assoc. prof., 1969-72, prof., 1972—. Author: The New Woman, 1971, Movers and Shakers, 1973, Herstory: A Woman's View of American History, 1975, 2d edit., 1981, Consecrate Every Day: The Public Lives of Jewish American Women, 1981, Enduring Values: Women in Popular Culture, 1987, Cafeteria America: New Identities in Contemporary Life, 1988, Mae West: She Who Laughs Lasts, 1992; editor: Women's Comic Visions, 1991; contbr. articles to profl. jours. Nat. Endowment for Humanities grantee, 1971-72. Office: Northeastern Ill U 5500 N Saint Louis Ave Chicago IL 60625-4625

SOCIE, DARRELL FREDERICK, mechanical engineering educator; b. Toledo, Oct. 28, 1948; s. Frederick James and Emerence (Lupinski) S.; m. Pamela Sue Doll, 1977; children: Benjamin, Bethany, Michael. BS in Metall. Engring., U. Cin., 1971, MS, 1973; PhD, U. Ill., 1977. Registered profl. engr., Ill., Ohio. Research asst. dept. theoretical and applied mechanics U. Ill., Urbana, 1974-77, vis. asst. prof. dept. theoretical and applied mechanics, 1977-78; asst. prof. Dept. Mech. and Indsl. Engring. U. Ill., Urbana, 1978-81, assoc. prof., 1981-85, prof., 1986—; panelist Coopers & Lybrand Trendsetter Barometer, 1993—; cons. Structural Dynamics, 1974-80, Owens-Corning Fiberglass, 1974-82; pres. SOMAT Corp., 1982—. Recipient Ralph R. Teetor award Soc. Automotive Engrs., 1980, Comdr.'s award for disting. pub. svc. U.S. Army, 1990, Disting. Alumni award U. Cin., 1991. Mem. ASTM (Fatigue Achievement award 1992), SAE (Arch T. Colwell award 1994), ASM, Sigma Xi, Alpha Sigma Mu. Office: U Ill 144 Mech Engring Bldg 1206 W Green St Urbana IL 61801-2906

SOCOL, HOWARD, department store executive. Chmn. Burdine's, Miami, Fla. Office: Burdines 22 E Slagler St Miami FL 33130*

SOCOL, JERRY M., retail executive; b. 1942. Grad., Ind. U. With Federated Dept. Stores, Cin., 1963-64, Marshall Field, Louisville, 1964-84, The Limited, Columbus, Rich's Dept. Stores, Cin.; pres. Filene's, Boston, chmn., CEO, pres., CEO; pres. J. Baker Inc., Canton, Mass., 1988-90, CEO, 1990—; CEO WGS Corp.; pres., CEO Morse Shoe Inc., JBI Inc.; bd. dirs. Casual Male Inc. Office: J Baker Inc 555 Turnpike St Canton MA 02021-2724*

SOCOL, MICHAEL LEE, obstetrician/gynecologist, educator; b. Chgo., Oct. 3, 1949; s. Joseph and Bernice (Bofman) S.; m. Donna Kaner, Dec. 17, 1972. BS, U. Ill., 1970; MD, U. Ill., Chgo., 1974. Diplomate Am. Bd. Ob-Gyn., Am. Bd. Maternal-Fetal Medicine. Resident obstetrics and gynecology U. Ill. Hosp., Chgo., 1974-77; clin. rsch. fellow dept. obstetrics and gynecology L.A. County-U. So. Calif. Med. Ctr., 1977-79; assoc. attending physician Northwestern Meml. Hosp., Chgo., 1980-86, attending physician dept. ob-gyn., 1986—; co-dir. Northwestern Perinatal Ctr., Chgo., 1987—; head maternal-fetal medicine, chief obstetrics Northwestern U. Med. Sch., Chgo., 1987—, dir. maternal-fetal medicine fellowship program, 1987—, asst. prof. obstetrics and gynecology, 1979-84, assoc. prof., 1984-92, prof., 1992—; mem. appointment and promotions and departmental com. on clin. privileges Northwestern Meml. Hosp., Chgo., 1987—, vice-chmn. dept. ob-gyn., 1992—; mem. residencey edn. com., 1987—; mem. appointments, promotions and tenure com., 1991—. Author: (with others) Clinical Obstetrics and Gynecology, 1982, 1984, Diagnostic Ultrasound Applied to Obstetrics and Gynecology, 1987, Principles and Practice of Medical Therapy in Pregnancy, 1992; peer reviewer Am. Jour. Obstetrics and Gynecology, 1980—, Obstetrics and Gynecology, 1984—; contbr. numerous articles to profl. jours. Fellow Am. Coll. Ob-Gyn., Soc., Perinatal Obstetricians, Ctrl. Assn. Ob-Gyn., Chgo. Gynecol. Soc., Soc. for Gynecol. Investigation, Am. Gynecol. and Obstetrical Soc.; mem. AMA, Assn. Profs. of Gynecology and Obstetrics, Ill. State Med. Assn., Chgo. Med. Soc. Avocation: marathon running. Office: 333 E Superior St # 410 Chicago IL 60611-3015

SOCOL, SHELDON ELEAZER, university official; b. N.Y.C., July 10, 1936; s. Irving and Helen (Tuchman) S.; m. Genia Ruth Prager, Dec. 26, 1959; children: Jeffrey, Steven, Sharon, Robyn, Leslie, Steven Warren. BA, Yeshiva U., 1958; JD, NYU, 1963. Asst. bursar Yeshiva U., N.Y.C., 1958-60, assoc. bursar, 1960-62, dir. student fins., 1962-70, sec., 1970—, chief fiscal officer, 1971-72, v.p. bus. affairs, 1972—; mem. N.Y. State Adv. Coun. on Fin. Assistance to Coll. Students, 1969-76; asst. dir. Tng. Inst. for Fin. Aid Officers, Hunter, Coll., CUNY, 1970-71; mem. presdl. adv. com. Temple U., 1986; mem. regents adv. task force N.Y.C. Regional Plan for Higher Edn., 1971-73; speaker Prentice Hall Law and Bus. Series, 1989, KPMG Peat Marwick Conf., 1990, Inst. for Endowment Mgmt., 1992. Pres. Minyon Park Estates, Inc. Mem. NEA, Nat. Assn. Coll. and Univ. Attys., Met. N.Y.C. Fin. Aid Adminstrs. Assn., Ea. Assn. Student Fin. Aid Officers, Am. Mgmt. Assn., Am. Assn. for Higher Edn., Nat. Assn. Coll. and Univ. Bus. Officers, Soc. Coll. and Univ. Planning, Mid. States Assn. Colls. (evaluation team Commn. on Higher Edn., U. Medicine and Dentistry N.J., 1985, Upstate Health Sci. Ctr. 1986, Carnegie-Mellon U. 1988, Albany Med. Ctr. 1989).

SOCOLOFSKY, JON EDWARD, banker; b. Chgo., Mar. 27, 1946; s. E. E. and Jane C. (Ward) S.; married; 1 child, Brian Edward. BA, DePauw U., 1968; MBA, Ind. U., 1970. Auditor No. Trust Co., Chgo., 1970-79, v.p., 1979-86, sr. v.p., 1986—. Pres. Cass Sch. Dist. # 63, Darien, Ill., 1987-93. Mem. Internat. Ops. Assn., Internat. Soc. Securities Adminstrs. Republican. Congregationalist. Avocations: water skiing, volleyball, motorcycles. Office: The Northern Trust Co 50 S La Salle St Chicago IL 60603-1003

SOCOLOW, ARTHUR ABRAHAM, geologist; b. Bronx, N.Y., Mar. 23, 1921; s. Samuel and Yetta (Solomon) S.; m. Edith S. Blumenthal, Apr. 10, 1949; children: Carl, Roy. Jeff. BS, Rutgers U., 1942; MA, Columbia U., 1947, PhD, 1955. Photogrammetrist, U.S. Geol. Survey, 1942, 46; with Eagle Picher de Mexico, 1947; instr. geology So. Methodist U., 1948-50; dir. geology field camp Colo., 1948-50; asst. prof. Boston U., 1950-55; geologist Def. Minerals Exploration Authority, Alaska, 1952; assoc. prof. U. Mass., 1955-57; econ. geologist Pa. Geol. Survey, 1957-61, dir., state geologist, 1961-86; cons. geologist Gloucester, Mass., 1986—; prof. environ. geology Salem (Mass.) State Coll., 1993-95; dir. New Eng. Govs. Conf. Project on Aggregate Resources New Eng., 1990-95; cons. geologist Gloucester; mem. Outer Continental Shelf Policy Com., 1974-88, Pa. rep., 1978-88; lectr. mineral conservation Pa. State U., 1959-75; mem. conf. earth sci. source materials NSF, 1959; chmn. ann. field conf. Pa. Geologists, 1961-86; past mem. U.S. Nat. Com. on Tunnelling Tech.; mem. com. on N.Y. State low level waste program Nat. Acad. Sci.; past mem. gov.'s adv. com. Nat. Coun. on Environ. Quality; past chmn. Pa. Water Resources Coordinating Com.; geol. advisor Boston Mus. Sci., 1955-57. Former editor Pa. Geol. Bull.; mem. editorial bd. Northeastern Geol. Jour.; contbr. over 100 publs. and papers on environ. and econ. geology to profl. jours. Served with USAAF, 1942-46. Fellow Geol. Soc. Am. (sec.-treas. N.E. sect., past nat. councilor), Mineral Soc. Am., AAAS (past pres. geography-geology sect.); mem. AAUP, Soc. Econ. Geologists, Phila. Geol. Soc. (past pres.), Am. Geol. Inst. (com. on manpower), Nat. Assn. Geology Tchrs. (past regional pres., Ralph Digman award for contbns. to geologic edn. 1980), Pa. Acad. Sci., Am. Meteoritical Soc., Am. Assn. State Geologists (past pres., editor, compiler State Geological Surveys-A History 1988), Am. Geophys. Union, Am. Commn. Stratigraphic Nomenclature (past chmn.), Harrisburg Geol. Soc., Interstate Oil Compact Commn. (rsch. com., environ. com.), Gloucester Conservation Commn. (chmn.), Fgn. Policy Assn. (past chpt. pres.), Sigma Xi. Club: Internat. Torch (past pres. chpt.). Home and Office: 26 Salt Island Rd Gloucester MA 01930-1945 *I have great respect for the individualism of man in the midst of a society and a world where there is an unavoidable interrelationship and interdependence of man upon man, and of man upon his environment. While we strive to maintain our individualism, we must share our common resources and our common aspirations. This is the challenge that makes our lives worth living.*

SOCOLOW, ROBERT HARRY, engineering educator, scientist; b. N.Y.C., Dec. 27, 1937; s. A. Walter and Edith (Gutman) S.; m. Elizabeth Anne Sussman, June 10, 1962 (div. Apr. 27, 1982); children: David, Seth; m. Jane Ries Pitt, May 25, 1986; stepchildren—Jennifer, Eric. B.A., Harvard U., 1959, M.A., 1961, Ph.D., 1964. Asst. prof. physics Yale U., New Haven, 1966-71; assoc. prof. mech. and aerospace engring. Princeton U. (N.J.), 1971-77, prof. mech. and aerospace engring., 1977—; mem. Inst. Advanced Study, Princeton, 1971; dir. Center for Energy and Environmental Studies, Princeton, 1978—. Author: (with John Harte) Patient Earth, 1971, (with K. Ford, G. Rochlin, M. Ross) Efficient Use of Energy, 1975, (with H.A. Feiveson, F.W. Sinden) Boundaries of Analysis: An Inquiry into the Tocks Island Dam Controversy, 1976, Saving Energy in the Home: Princeton's Experiments at Twin Rivers, 1979, (with C. Andrews, F. Berkhout, V. Thomas) Industrial Ecology and Global Change, 1994; editor Ann. Rev. of Energy and Environment, 1992—. Chmn. bd. Am. Coun. for Energy Efficient Econ., 1989-93; bd. dirs. Nat. Audubon Soc., 1992—. John Simon Guggenheim fellow, 1976-77; German Marshall Fund fellow, 1976-77; NSF Postdoctoral fellow, 1964-66; NSF Predoctoral fellow, 1960-64. Fellow AAAS, Am. Phys. Soc. Jewish. Home: 34 Westcott Rd Princeton NJ 08540-3060 Office: Princeton U H102 Engineering Quad Princeton NJ 08544

SOCWELL, MARGARET GERTRUDE OSBORN HARRIS, reading and language arts educator, consultant; b. Avoca, Iowa, Oct. 7, 1946; d. Fay and Mary Gertrude (Grote) Osborn; m. Richard John Socwell, Mar. 11, 1971 (div. May 1979); 1 child, Benjamin Adam. BS, Ohio State U., Columbus, 1968; MS, U. Wis., 1979. Cert. reading specialist, libr. media specialist, Spanish and French tchr., Ariz. Tchr. French Mason (Ohio) Pub. Schs., 1969-70; tchr. Spanish and French St. Matthias Cath. Girls High Sch., L.A., 1970-71; tchr. French Whitewater (Wis.) Pub. Schs., 1971-72, tchr. Spanish, 1972-78; reading specialist Chilton (Wis.) Pub. Schs., 1978-79, Tolleson (Ariz.) Elem. Schs., 1979-80; tchr. reading and Spanish Deer Valley Unified Schs., Phoenix, 1980-88; tchr. reading Rio Salado C.C., Phoenix, 1987-91, tchr. lang. arts, 1989-93, tchr. social studies, 1993—; state forensics judge Whitewater Pub. Schs., 1974—; test designer Deer Valley Reading Curriculum Com., Phoenix, 1986-87, participant lang. arts pilot program Deer Valley Unified Sch. Dist., 1989. Recipient grant Deer Valley Edn. Found., Inc., 1992. Mem. Internat. Assn. Near-Death Studies. Democrat. Avocations: reading, embroidery, cross-stitch, knitting, travel. Office: Deer Valley Pub Schs #97 20402 N 15th Ave Phoenix AZ 85027-3636

SODAL, INGVAR EDMUND, electrical engineer, scientist; b. Hemne, Norway, Feb. 12, 1934; came to U.S., 1962; s. Ingebrigt L. and Johanna (A.) Sodal; m. Sally Rollins; 1 child, Silje M. Degree in elec. engring., Trondheim Tech. Coll., Norway, 1959; BSEE, U. Colo., 1964. Engr. Fjeldseth Engring., Trondheim, 1959-61; rsch. engr. U. Norway, Trondheim, 1961-62; rsch. engr. U. Colo. Med. Ctr., Denver, 1964-66, rsch. assoc., 1966-75, instr., lectr., 1975-79; vis. rsch. assoc. dept. engring. U. Colo., Boulder, 1974-75, lectr., 1975-76; asst. prof., div. head. Ohio State U., Columbus, 1979-82, mem. grad. faculty, 1982; pres., chief exec. officer Masstron, Inc., Boulder, Colo., 1983-87; chief scientist Paradygm, Boulder, 1987-89; pres. Pacemark, Inc., Boulder, 1989-90, Med. Physics Colo., Inc., 1991—. Contbr. articles to profl. jours., chpts. to books; holder 6 patents in field. Instr. and/or program coord. in Scandinavian folklore and folk dancing for numerous groups and instns. throughout U.S., Can., and Norway, 1959—. Grantee NIH and various pvt. orgns. Mem. Assn. for Advancement Med. Instrumentation, Instrument Soc. Am., Soc. for Technology in Anesthesia, Biomed. Engring. Soc., Sons of Norway. Office: 1550 Moss Rock Pl Boulder CO 80304-1543

SODD, VINCENT JOSEPH, nuclear medicine researcher, educator; b. Toledo, Ohio, Nov. 20, 1934; s. Abraham and Sarah (Hamway) S.; m. Dorothy P. Langenderfer, Oct. 20, 1956; children: Vincent Joseph, Anthony Newman, Joseph William, Anne Marie. B.S., Xavier U., Cin., 1956, M.S., 1958; Ph.D., U. Pitts., 1964. Dep. chief nuclear medicine lab. FDA, Cin., 1974-77, acting chief, 1971-72, dir., 1974-84; assoc. prof. radiology U. Cin., 1974-77; prof. U. Cinn., 1977—; mem. radiation safety com. U. Con., 1975-86, mem. radioactive drug research com., 1979-86, mem. com. on human research, 1982-86. Author: Radiopharmaceuticals and Radiopharmaceuticals II, 1975,79, Radiation Safety in Nuclear Medicine-A Practical Guide, 1981; contbr. more than 150 articles to profl. jours.; patantee in field. Served to capt. USPHS, 1957-84. Recipient Dorst Chemistry Key Xavier U., 1956; recipient Silver award Ohio State Med. Assn., 1968. Mem. Soc. Nuclear Medicine (pres. S.E. chpt. 1979, 80, exec. dir. 1984—, exec. dir. Ctrl. chpt. 1991—, coun. 1981—, trustee 1980-81, bd. govs. Instrumentation Coun. 1982—), Internat. Commn. Radiol. Protection. Roman Catholic. Office: U Cin Coll Applied Sci ML 103 Cincinnati OH 45267

SODEN, PAUL ANTHONY, lawyer; b. N.Y.C., Feb. 3, 1944; s. Leo J. and Mildred E. (Callahan) S.; m. Irene M. Davis, Aug. 3, 1968; children—Christina M., Paul A. A.B., Fordham U., 1965, J.D., 1968. Bar: N.Y. 1968. Assoc. Cahill, Gordon & Reindel, N.Y.C., 1968-74; corp. counsel Technicon Corp., Tarrytown, N.Y., 1974-76, asst. gen. counsel, asst. sec., 1976-78, sr. v.p., gen. counsel, sec., 1978-87; v.p., dir. internat. law Sterling Winthrop Inc., 1987-88; v.p., gen. counsel, sec. Sterling Drug Inc., 1988-95; sr. v.p., gen. counsel The Reader's Digest Assn., Inc., 1995—. Mem. Am. Bar Assn., N.Y. State Bar Assn. Club: Scarsdale (N.Y.) Golf. Office: Reader's Digest Rd Pleasantville NY 10570-7000

SODEN, RICHARD ALLAN, lawyer; b. Bklyn., Feb. 16, 1945; s. Hamilton David and Clara Elaine (Seale) S.; m. Marcia LaMonte Mitchell, June 7, 1969; children: Matthew Hamilton, Mark Mitchell. AB, Hamilton Coll., 1967; JD, Boston U., 1970. Bar: Mass. 1970. Law clk. to judge U.S. Ct. Appeals (6th cir.), 1970-71; assoc. firm Goodwin, Procter & Hoar, Boston, 1971-79, ptnr., 1979—; instr. Law Sch. Boston Coll., Chestnut Hill, Mass., 1973-74. Mem. South End Project Area Com.; past pres., bd. dirs. United South End Settlements; mem. adv. council Suffolk U. Sch. Mgmt.; chmn. Boston Mcpl. Rsch. Bur.; bd. dirs. Greater Boston council Boy Scouts Am.; chmn., trustee Judge Baker Guidance Ctr.; bd. govs. New England Aquarium; trustee Boston U., Harvard Med. Ctr.; bd. visitors Boston U. Goldman Sch. Grad. Dentistry; mem. bd. overseers WGBH; mem. Mass. Minority Bus. Devel. Commn.; mem. Adv. Task Force on Securities Regulation; mem. Adv. Com. on Legal Edn.; past chmn. Lawyers Com. for Civil Rights Under Law. Mem. ABA, Nat. Bar Assn., Mass. Bar Assn. (past vice chmn. bus. law coun., 1990-91), Boston Bar Assn. (immediate past pres. 1994-95), Mass. Black Lawyers Assn. (pres. 1980-81). Home: 42 Gray St Boston MA 02116-6210 Office: Goodwin Procter & Hoar Exchange Pl Boston MA 02109

SODER-ALDERFER, KAY CHRISTIE, counseling administrator; b. Evanston, Ill., Oct. 25, 1949; d. Earl Eugene and Alice Kathryn (Lien) Soder; m. David Luther Alderfer, May 15, 1976. BSE, No. Ill. U., 1972; postgrad., Luth. Sch. Theology, Phila., 1973; MA, Gov.'s State U., University Park, Ill., 1978; PhD, Walden U., 1985. Consecrated deaconess Luth. Ch., 1974. News reporter Suburban Life Newspaper, La Grange Park, Ill., 1972; counselor various orgns. Ill. & Pa., 1973—; parish worker Luth. Ch., De Kalb, Ill., 1973-74; pub. rels. asst. Luth. Ch. Women, Phila., 1974-76; editor Luth. Ch., Chgo., 1979—; spiritual dir. Gentle Pathways, Downers Grove, Ill., 1988—, counseling psychologist, 1990—, also bd. dirs.; cons. Evang. Luth. Ch. in Am., Chgo., 1988—, Lehigh Valley Hosp. Assn., Allentown, Pa., 1986. Author: Gentle Journeys, 1993, With Those Who Grieve, 1995, Help! There's a Monster in My Head, 1996; editor Entree, 1988-93, Multicultural Jour., 1992—; graphic designs exhbn. Franklin Mus., Phila., 1981. Spokeswoman Progressive Epilepsy Network, Phila., 1980-85; chair spiritual life com. Luth. Deaconess Cmty., Gladwyne, Pa., 1990-92; founder Teens with Epilepsy and Motivation, 1995; vol. March of Dimes, Ill., 1991-93; amb. of goodwill Good Bears of the World, 1993-94; spiritual dir. Evang. Luth. Ch. in Am. Recipient Silver award Delaware Valley Neographics Soc., 1981; 50th anniversary scholar Luth. Deaconess Community, 1983. Mem. AAUW, APA (div. women and psychology, div. psychology and the arts, div. psychology and religion). Avocations: painting, mixed media, story telling, traveling, Native American studies, culture and art. Office: Gentle Pathways 1207 55th St Downers Grove IL 60515-4810

SODERBERG, DAVID LAWRENCE, chemist; b. Evergreen Park, Ill., Jan. 28, 1944; s. Arthur Lawrence and Jean Van Norden (Freeman) S. AB in Chemistry, Ripon (Wis.) Coll., 1969. Rsch. asst. Ripon Coll., 1968-69, Pomona Coll., Claremont, Calif., 1969-70; chemist animal and plant health inspection svc. USDA, N.Y.C., 1972-73; chemist food safety and quality svc. USDA, Athens, Ga., 1974-83; supervisory chemist food safety and inspection svc. USDA, St. Louis, 1983-87; chemist, program devel. and tech. mgmt. USDA, Washington, 1987—. Contbr. articles to profl. jours. With U.S. Army, 1965-67, Vietnam. Recipient awards USDA, 1976, 87, cert. of merit, 1980. Mem. AAAS, ASTM, Am. Chem. Soc., Assn. Official Analytical Chemists (gen. referee meat and poultry products). Office: USDA FSIS DTMB 300 12th St SW Rm 524 Washington DC 20024

SODERBERG, NANCY, federal agency administrator; b. San Turce, P.R., Mar. 13, 1958; d. Lars Olof and Nancy (MacGilvrey) S. BA in French and Econs., Vanderbilt U., 1980; MS in Fgn. Svc., Georgetown U., 1984. Budget and reports analyst Bank of New England, Boston, 1980-82; rsch. asst. Brookings Inst., Washington, 1982-83; summer intern UN Devel. Program, Brazzaville, Congo, 1983; rsch. asst. Agy. Internat. Devel., Washington, 1983; del. selection asst. Mondale-Ferraro Com., Washington, 1983, fgn. policy advisor, 1984; dep. issues dir. fgn. policy Dukakis for Pres. Com., Boston, 1988; fgn. policy advisor Senator Edward M. Kennedy, Washington, 1985-88, 89-92; fgn. policy dir. Clinton/ Gore Campaign, Little Rock, 1992; dep. asst. dir. transition nat. security Clinton/ Gore Transition, Little Rock, 1992-93; dep. asst. to Pres. for nat. security affairs Nat. Security Coun., Washington, 1993—; mem. Coun. Fgn. Rels. *

SODERBERGH, STEVEN ANDREW, filmmaker; b. Atlanta, Jan. 14, 1963; s. Peter Andrew and Mary Ann (Bernard) S.; m. Elizabeth Jeanne Brantley, Dec. 1, 1989 (div. Oct. 1994). Writer, dir., editor: (film) sex, lies, and videotape, 1989 (Palme d'Or award Cannes Film Festival 1989), King of the Hill, 1993; dir., editor: (film) Kafka, 1991; exec. prodr.: (film) Suture, 1994, The Daytrippers, 1996; dir.: (film) The Underneath, 1995. Mem.

AMPAS, Dirs. Guild Am. Democrat. Office: PO Box 2000 Orange VA 22960

SODERLIND, STERLING EUGENE, newspaper industry consultant; b. Rapelje, Mont., Sept. 6, 1926; s. William John and Florence (Longbotham) S.; m. Helen Boyce, Apr. 9, 1955; children: Steven (dec.), Sarah, Lori. B.A., U. Mont., 1950; B.A. Rhodes Scholar, Oxford U., Eng., 1950-52. Reporter Mpls. Tribune, 1952-55; reporter Wall St. Jour., Chgo., 1955-56; Southeastern bur. chief Wall St. Jour., Jacksonville, Fla., 1956-57; mem. page one editing staff Wall St. Jour., N.Y.C., 1957-65, asst. mng. editor, 1966-70, mng. editor, 1970; econs. editor Dow Jones & Co., Inc., N.Y.C., 1970-77, asst. to pres., 1975-77, v.p., 1977-91; newspaper industry cons., 1992—. Served with USNR, 1944-46. Congregationalist. Home: 58 Wellington Ave Short Hills NJ 07078-3308

SODERQUIST, LARRY DEAN, lawyer, educator, consultant; b. Ypsilanti, Mich., July 20, 1944; s. Hugo E. and Emma A. (Johanson) S.; m. Ann Mangelsdorf, June 15, 1968; children: Hans, Lars. BS, Ea. Mich. U., 1966; JD, Harvard U., 1969. Bar: N.Y. 1971, Tenn. 1981. Assoc. Milbank, Tweed, Hadley & McCloy, N.Y.C., 1971-76; assoc. prof. law U. Notre Dame, South Bend, Ind., 1976-80, prof. 1980-81; vis. prof. law Vanderbilt U. Law Sch., Nashville, 1980-81, prof. 1981—, dir. corp. and securities law inst. 1993—; of counsel Tuke Yopp & Sweeney; spl. master U.S. Dist. Ct. (no. dist.) Ohio, 1977. Capt. U.S. Army 1969-71. Decorated Army Commendation medal. Mem. ABA, Am. Law Inst. Presbyterian. Author: Corporations, 1979, 3d edit., 1991, Understanding Corporation Law, 1990, Understanding the Securities Laws, 3d edit., 1993, Securities Regulation, 3d edit., 1994, Law of Federal Estate and Gift Taxation: Code Commentary, 1978, Analysis, 1980, Investor's Rights Handbook, 1993; contbr. numerous articles to legal jours. Home: 421 Sunnyside Dr Nashville TN 37205-3413 Office: Vanderbilt U Sch Law 21st Ave S Nashville TN 37240

SODERQUIST, RONALD BRUCE, minister, ministry director; b. Pine City, Minn., Mar. 16, 1943; s. Russell Eugene and Abigail Mae (Berger) S.; m. Carol Lynn Peterson, Aug. 20, 1966; children: Peter Gustav, Ingrid Ann-Marie, Anna Kristine.; BA, Northwestern Coll., 1965; MA, U. Wis., 1967; D in Ministry, Bethel Theol. Sem., 1993. Ordained min. So. Bapt. Conv., 1988. Acad. dean Kings Inst. Coll., Koronodal, Cotabato, The Philippines, 1967-69; asst. prof. English Trinity Coll., Deerfield, Ill., 1969-70; student ministry staff Campus Crusade for Christ, L.A., Mpls., Madison, 1970-77; regional dir. midwest Campus Crusade for Christ, 1977-80; internat. rep. Campus Crusade for Christ, Gothenburg, Sweden, 1980-84; spl. rep. Christian Embassy, Washington, 1984-87, dir. mil. ministry, 1987—. Avocations: travel, photography, reading. Office: Christian Embassy Ste 730 2000 14th St N Arlington VA 22201

SODOLSKI, JOHN, retired association administrator; b. Menasha, Wis., Apr. 11, 1931; s. L.V. and L.W. (Pinkowski) S.; m. C.J. Eppard. BS, U. Wis., 1953. Vice pres. Electronic Industries Assn., Washington, 1961-83; pres. U.S. Telephone Assn., Washington, 1983-93; ret., 1993. Served to 1st lt. USMC, 1955.

SOECHTIG, JACQUELINE ELIZABETH, telecommunications executive; b. Manhasset, N.Y., Aug. 12, 1949; d. Alvin Hermann and Regina Mary (Murphy) Venzke; m. James Decatur Miller, July 4, 1976 (div. Oct. 1982); M. Clifford Jon Soechtig, Oct. 19, 1983. B.A. cum laude, Coll. of New Rochelle (N.Y.), 1974; M.A. summa cum laude, U. So. Calif., 1979. Computer operator IBM, White Plains, N.Y., 1970-72, ops. job scheduler, 1972-74, various spl. assignments, 1974-75, mktg. rep., Bethesda, Md., 1975-76, Charleston, W. Va., 1979-81, adv. regional mktg. rep. Dallas, 1981-82; dist. mgr. Am. Speedy Printing Co., Dallas, 1982-83, nat. sales devel. mgr., Detroit, 1984; regional mgr. major and nat. accounts MCI Telecommunications, Southfield, Mich., 1984-85, dir. nat. accounts, 1985-86, v.p. nat. accounts, 1987-88, v.p. mktg. and customer svc., 1988-89, v.p. consumer segment, 1989-90; v.p. integrated telecommunications solutions Sprint United, Atlanta, 1990-92; pres., chief exec. officer Precision Systems, 1992-94; interviewer, Sergio Segre, Bolonga, Italy, 1977, Radio Free Europe, Brussels, 1978, World Health Program, Rome, 1978, ITT, Brussels, 1977, Franz Josef Strauss, 1978. Recipient Golden Circle Achievement award IBM, 1980, Quar. Recognition award, 1980, 81; named New Bus. Pacesetter, 1980, 81. Republican. Club: German Am. Women's (v.p. Stuttgart, W.Ger. 1977-78). Office: Lasergate Syss Inc 28050 US 19 N Ste 502 Clearwater FL 34621

SOEDERSTROM, ELISABETH ANNA, opera singer; b. Stockholm, May 7, 1927; d. Emanuel Albert and Anna (Palasova) S.; student Opera Sch., Stockholm, also pupil of Andrejewa Skilondz; m. Sverker Olow, Mar. 29, 1950; children: Malcolm, Peter, Jens. Appearances include Stockholm Opera, 1950, Salzburg Festival, 1955, Glyndebourne Opera, 1957, 59, 61, 63, 64, Met. Opera, 1959, 60, 62, 63, 83, 86-87; sang three leading roles in Rosencavalier within one year, 1959; toured USSR, 1966; others roles include Fiordiligi in Cosi Fan Tutte, Susanna and Countess in Figaro, Countess in Capriccio; radio, TV and concert appearances in U.S. and Europe; artistic leader Drottingholm Ct. Theatre; author: I Min Tonart, 1978, Sjung ut, Elisabeth!, 1986. Decorated Order of Vasa (Sweden); Stelle Della Solidarieta Dell'Italia; King Olav's reward (Norway); comdr. Most Disting. Order Brit. Empire, CBE; comdr. des Arts et des Lettres; named Singer of the Court (Sweden); recipient prize for best acting Royal Swedish Acad., 1965, Literis et Artibus award, 1969. Mem. Royal Acad. Music Gt. Britain (hon.). Office: Drottningholms Theatre Mus, Box 27050, S-10251 Stockholm Sweden also: care Columbia Artists Mgmt 165 W 57th St New York NY 10019-2201

SOENS, LAWRENCE D., bishop; b. Iowa City, Aug. 26, 1926. Student, Loras Coll., Dubuque, Iowa, St. Ambrose Coll., Davenport, Iowa, Kenrick Sem., St. Louis, U. Iowa. Ordained priest Roman Catholic Ch., 1950, consecrated bishop, 1983. Bishop of Sioux City Iowa, 1983—. Office: Chancery Office PO Box 3379 1821 Jackson St Sioux City IA 51105-1055*

SOERGEL, KONRAD HERMANN, physician; b. Coburg, Germany, July 27, 1929; came to U.S., 1954, naturalized, 1962; s. Konrad Daniel and Erna Henrietta (Schilling) S.; m. Rosina Klara Rudin, June 24, 1955; children: Elizabeth Ann, Karen Theresa, Marilyn Virginia, Kenneth Thomas. M.D., U. Erlangen, Germany, 1954, Dr. med., 1958. Intern Bergen Pines County Hosp., Paramus, N.J., 1954-55; resident in pathology West Pa. Hosp., Pitts., 1955-56; resident in medicine Mass. Meml. Hosp., Boston, 1957-58; fellow in gastroenterology Boston U. Med. Sch., 1958-60, instr., 1960-61; mem. faculty Med. Coll. Wis., Milw., 1961—, prof. medicine, 1969—, prof. physiology, 1993—; chief sect. gastroenterology Med. Coll. Wis., 1961-93, dir. fellowship program, dept. medicine, 1993—; chmn. gastroenterology and clin. nutrition study sect. NIH, 1979-80. Contbr. articles to profl. jours., chpts. to books. Recipient Research Career Devel. award USPHS, 1963-72; Alexander von Humboldt Found. sr. fellow, 1973-74. Mem. Am. Gastroenterol. Assn., Am. Soc. Clin. Investigation, Am. Assn. Physicians, German Soc. for Digestive and Metabolic Disorders (hon.), Ger. Soc. Internal Medicine (hon.). Home: 14245 Hillside Rd Elm Grove WI 53122-1677 Office: Med Coll Wis 9200 W Wisconsin Ave Milwaukee WI 53226-3522

SOETEBER, ELLEN, journalist, newspaper editor; b. East St. Louis, Ill., June 14, 1950; d. Lyle Potter and Norma Elizabeth (Osborn) S.; m. Richard M. Martins, Mar. 16, 1974. BJ, Northwestern U., 1972. Edn. writer, copy editor Chgo. Today, 1972-74; reporter Chgo. Tribune, 1974-76, asst. met. editor, 1976-84, assoc. met. editor, 1984-86, TV and media editor, 1986, met. editor, 1987-89, assoc. mng. editor for met. news, 1989-91, dep. editor editorial page, 1991-94; mng. editor Ft. Lauderdale (Fla.) Sun-Sentinel, 1994—; fellow journalism U. Mich., Ann Arbor, 1986-87. Office: The Sun-Sentinel 200 E Las Olas Blvd Fort Lauderdale FL 33301-2248

SOETH, SARAH LAVERNE REEDY MCMILLAN, psychiatric nurse; b. Amory, Miss., Feb. 20, 1925; d. Samuel Thomas and Bessie Lee (Franklin) Reedy; m. Urshel E. McMillan, Jan. 16, 1944 (dec. 1964); children: David Thomas McMillan, Joy Laverne McMillan Keys; m. Glenn Eugene Soeth, Nov. 27, 1976 (dec. 1995). Student, Miss. State Coll. Women, 1943-44; LPN, Tupelo Sch. Nursing, 1968; MSN, U. Miss., Jackson, 1972. RN, Miss. Pvt. duty nurse Evart, Mich., 1960-64; staff nurse Aberdeen (Miss.) Monroe County Hosp., 1965-72; lic. psychiat. nurse Hinds Gen. Hosp., Jackson, Miss., 1972-78; charge nurse Tigard (Oreg.) Psychiat. Convalescent Hosp., 1978-79; staff nurse VA Med. Ctr., Reno, 1979-80, Glenn County Hosp., Willows, Calif., 1980-81; staff nurse VA Med. Ctr., Martinez, Calif., 1981-91, Fresno, Calif., 1991-93; ret., 1993; vol. Mental Health Treatment Ctr. Active Diabetes Assn.; dir. sr. branch Faith Assembly God Presbyn. Ch., Tupelo, Miss., 1996, pres. women's ministry. Mem. Nat. Assn. Ret. Fed. Employees. Presbyterian. Avocations: music, reading, genealogy, hand crafts, travel.

SOFAER, ABRAHAM DAVID, lawyer, legal advisor, federal judge, legal educator; b. Bombay, India, May 6, 1938; came to U.S., 1948, naturalized, 1959; m. Marian Bea Scheuer, Oct. 23, 1977; children: Daniel E., Michael J., Helen R., Joseph S., Aaron R., Raphael J. BA in History magna cum laude, Yeshiva Coll., 1962; LLB cum laude, NYU, 1965. Bar: N.Y. 1965. Law clk. to Hon. J. Skelly Wright, U.S. Ct. Appeals, Washington, 1965-66; to Hon. William J. Brennan, Jr., U.S. Supreme Ct., Washington, 1966-67; asst. U.S. atty. So. Dist. N.Y., N.Y.C., 1967-69; prof. law Columbia U., N.Y.C., 1969-79; judge U.S. Dist. Ct. for So. Dist. N.Y., 1979-85; legal advisor Dept. State, Washington, 1985-90; ptnr. Hughes Hubbard & Reed, Washington, 1991-94; George P. Shultz disting. scholar, sr. fellow Hoover Instn., Stanford U., 1994—; hearing officer N.Y. Dept. Environ. Conservation, 1975-76. Author: War, Foreign Affairs and Constitutional Power: The Origins, 1976; contbr. articles to legal, polit., fgn. jours.; editor-in-chief: NYU Law Rev, 1964-65. Served with USAF, 1956-59. Root-Tilden scholar NYU, 1965. Mem. Fed. Bar Assn., Am. Bar Assn., N.Y. Bar Assn., Am. Law Inst. Jewish. Office: Stanford Univ The Hoover Instn Stanford CA 94305-6010

SOFFAR, WILLIAM DOUGLAS, lawyer; b. Houston, Sept. 8, 1944; s. Benjamin and Esther Goldy (Garfinkel) S.; m. Nancy Elise Axelrod, Mar. 29, 1969 (div. Sept. 1989); children: Pamela Beth, Stephanie Michelle, Jill Denise. BA, U. Houston, 1966, JD, 1969. Bar: Tex. 1969, U.S. Dist. Ct. (so. dist.) Tex. 1970, U.S. Ct. Appeals (5th cir.) 1974, U.S. Supreme Ct. 1974; cert. mediator in civil law and family law. Atty. examiner U.S. Interstate Commerce Commn., Washington, 1969-70; atty. Law Office of Adolph Uzick, Houston, 1970-72, Walsh & Soffar, Houston, 1972-73; lawyer, sole practice Law Offices of William D. Soffar, Houston, 1973-74; ptnr. Soffar & Levit, Houston, 1974—; family law and civil mediator, basic mediation and family mediation trainer Atty.-Mediator's Inst. Bd. dirs. Miller Theater Adv. Coun., Houston, 1985-90, Zina Garrison Found., Houston, 1989-91. Mem. Houston Bar Assn. (bd. dirs., family law sect. mem. 1989-90), Jewish Cmty. Ctr. (health club com. 1971—), Jewish Family Svc. (bd. dirs. 1970-71), Phi Delta Phi. Jewish. Avocations: travel, reading, raquetball. Office: Soffar & Levit 6575 W Loop South Ste 630 Bellaire TX 77601

SOFFER, ROSEMARY S., community health nurse, consultant, educator; b. N.Y.C., June 29, 1953; d. E.F. Harvey and Paula L. Show. Diploma, Hosp. U. Pa. Sch. Nursing, 1975; BSN, Neumann Coll., 1980; postgrad., Temple U./Beh Sci, 1983—, Neumann Coll., 1994—. RN, Pa., Del.; cert. CPR instr. Educator nursing sch., consulting nurse practitioner, educator Ambilikkai Village Health Clinic, India; program devel., nurse cons. Anglican Ch. India, 1995; charge nurse Hosp. of U. Pa., Phila., adult ventricular tachycardia, 1980; community nurse Community Nursing Svc., Chester, Pa.; program devel. nurse cons. Anglican Ch. India, Phila./Delaware County, Pa., 1995; ind. nurse contractor, 1994, 95; spkr. in field at Neumann Coll., chs. and orgns.; presenter numerous seminars on internat. nursing issues; exec. dir. Christian Ministry Internat. Author: The Real Rambo, 1989, Coping Mechanism of the Chronically Ill During Separation, 1983, Opened Eyes, 1990. Exec. com. Rambo Co., Inc. Sight for Curable Blind; bd. dirs. Ecumenical Caring Coalition-Chester Food Cupboard; elder Yeadon Presbyn. Ch., 1990-93; pres., dir. Ministry Internat., 1995—. Named one of Outstanding Young Women of Am., nominated by Dept. Atty. Gen. Harrisburg, 1991-92, Professionalism award Yeaden High Sch., 1971. Mem. Internat. Nursing Soc., Pa. Med. Missionary Soc. (bd. dirs. 1990-95), Sigma Theta Tau.

SOFIA, SABATINO, astronomy educator; b. Episcopia, Italy, May 14, 1939; married, 1963; 2 children. BS, Yale U., 1963, MS, 1965, PhD in Astrophysics, 1966. Rsch. assoc. astrophysics Goddard Inst. Space Studies NASA, 1966-67; from assoc. prof. to prof. astronomy U. South Fla., 1967-73; vis. fellow Joint Inst. Lab. Astrophysics, 1973-74; sr. rsch. assoc. U. Rochester, 1974-75; adj. prof. astronomy U. Fla., 1975—; staff scientist NASA, 1975-77; sr. rsch. assoc. solar physics Nat. Acad. Sci., Nat. Rsch. Coun., 1977-79; space scientist Goddard Space Flight Ctr., 1979-85; mem. space and earth sci. adv. com. NASA, 1985-88. Mem. Am. Astron. Soc., Internat. Astron. Union, Am. Geophys. Union. Office: Yale U Astronomy Dept 260 Whitney Ave PO Box 6666 New Haven CT 06511*

SOFRANKO, JOEL E., pension fund administrator. Audit supr. Coopers & Lybrand, Columbus, Ohio, 1978-82; gen. manager Muirfield Ltd., Columbus, Ohio, 1982-87; cfo Health Power Management Corp., Columbus, Ohio, 1987-89, School Employees Retirement System, Columbus, Ohio, 1989—. Office: School Empl Retrmnt Sys 45 N 4th St Columbus OH 43215-3602*

SOFRO, BARNEY, retail executive; b. 1942. BS, San Jose State Coll., 1964. With House of Fabrics Inc., 1964—, exec. v.p., sec., 1978-81, pres., COO, 1981-85, also bd. dirs., co-chmn. bd. dirs., now chmn. bd. dirs. Office: House of Fabrics Inc 13400 Riverside Dr Van Nuys CA 91423-2511*

SOFTNESS, DONALD GABRIEL, marketing and manufacturing executive; b. Bklyn.; s. Burt H. and Ida (Kaiser) S.; m. Sydell Meyerson; children: Michael, Anita May, Beth. A.B., NYU, 1949, M.B.A., 1959; L.H.D., St. John's U., 1979. Chmn. Softness Group, Inc., N.Y.C., 1960-79; pres. Softness Enterprise, N.Y.C., 1979—, SecureVue, Inc., N.Y.C., 1984—; v.p., maj. prin. Radio Stas. WVNJ-AM-FM, Newark and N.Y.C.; mem. faculty Advt. Week seminars Advt. Age; prodr., sponsor Bklyn. Rollathon (skating marathon). Co-author: Cardiologists' Guide to Health and Fitness Through Exercise, 1979; contbr. articles to bus. and trade jours. Patentee in field. Served with USN. Mem. Public Relations Soc. Am., Internat. Radio TV Soc., Am. Coll. Sports Medicine. Club: N.Y. Yacht. Home and Office: 28 Trues Dr West Islip NY 11795-5139 Office: SecureVue Inc 251 E 51st St New York NY 10022-6534

SOFTNESS, JOHN, public relations executive; b. Bklyn., Nov. 7, 1930; s. Burt H. and Ida (Kaiser) S.; m. Leona Ruth Golden; children: Barney, David, Daniel. B.A., U. Miami, 1955. Reporter Miami Herald, 1953; reporter Sta. WTVJ, Miami, Fla., 1954; asso. pub. relations dir. aviation dept. Shell Oil Co., N.Y.C., 1958-60; pres., chief exec. officer The Softness Group, Inc., N.Y.C., 1960-91, chmn., 1992—; spl. counselor to Bklyn. Borough pres., 1966-76; adj. prof. communications arts St. John's U., 1981—; counselor communications com. N.Y. Heart Assn. Served to capt. USAF, 1955-58. Mem. Pub. Rels. Soc. Am., Pride and Alarm (chmn.), Counselors' Acad. Home: 245 E 54th St Apt 14F New York NY 10022-4719 Office: The Softness Group Inc 381 Park Ave S New York NY 10016-8806

SOGABE, AKIKO, artist; b. Mishima, Japan, June 1, 1945; came to the U.S., 1987; d. Kaoru and Miki (Takahashi) Hirata; m. William Sogabe, Jan. 29, 1971; children: Steve, Sandy. Student, Tokyo Flower Acad., 1970; diploma, Japan Art Inst., 1972. Illustrator: Cinnamon, Mint & Mthballs, 1993, Washington Water Weeks, 1994, The Loyal Cat, 1995, Oregon Trout, 1995. Mem. Guild Am. Paper Cutters, Northcoast Collage Soc., Soc. Children's Book Writers and Illustrators. Home: 3319 170th Ave NE Bellevue WA 98008-2038

SOGARD, HAROLD ROSHER, advertising executive; b. Red Wing, Minn., Aug. 2, 1952; m. Susan Bolle; 1 child, Lucy. BA, Wesleyan U., 1974; MBA, U. Chgo., 1978. Ptnr., dir. account mgmt. Ogilvy & Mather, N.Y.C., 1984-90, Hal Riney & Ptnrs., San Francisco, 1990-91, Goodby, Silverstein & Ptnrs., San Francisco, 1991—. Office: Goodby Silverstein & Ptnrs 921 Front St San Francisco CA 94111

SOGG, WILTON SHERMAN, lawyer; b. Cleve., May 28, 1935; s. Paul P. and Julia (Cahn) S.; m. Saralee Frances Krow, Aug. 12, 1962 (div. July 1975); 1 child, Stephanie; m. Linda Rocker Lehman, Dec. 22, 1979 (div. Dec. 1990). A.B., Dartmouth Coll., 1956; J.D., Harvard U., 1959; Fulbright fellow, U. London, 1959-60. Bar: Ohio 1960, D.C. 1970, Fla. 1970, U.S. Supreme Ct., N.Y. 1985, U.S. Tax Ct. Assoc. Gottfried, Ginsberg, Guren & Merritt, 1960-63, ptnr., 1963-70; ptnr. Guren, Merritt, Feibel, Sogg & Cohen, Cleve., 1970-84; of counsel Hahn, Loeser, Freedheim, Dean and Wellman, Cleve., 1984-85; ptnr. Hahn Loeser & Parks, 1986—; trustee, pres. Cleve. Jewish News; adj. prof. Cleve. State Law Sch., 1960—; lectr. Harvard U. Law Sch., 1978-80. Author (with Howard M. Rossen); new and rev. vols. of Smith's Review Legal Gems series, 1969—; editor: Harvard Law Rev.; contbr. articles to profl. jours. Trustee Jewish Cmty. Fedn. of Cleve., 1966-72; bd. overseers Cleveland Marshall Coll. Law, Cleve. State U., 1969—; dir. Project for Improving Delivery of Legal Svcs., Case Western Res. U. Law Sch., 1991—; mem. U.S. and State of Ohio Holocaust commns. Mem. Ohio Bar Assn., Cleve. Bar Assn., Cuyahoga County Bar Assn., Fla. bar Assn., D.C. Bar Assn., N.Y. State Bar Assn., German Philatelic Soc., Oakwood Club, Union Club, Chagrin Valley Hunt Club, Phi Beta Kappa. Home: 22176 Parnell Rd Cleveland OH 44122-2727 Office: Hahn Loeser & Parks 3300 BP America Bldg 200 Public Sq Cleveland OH 44114-2301

SOH, CHUNGHEE SARAH, anthropology educator; b. Taegu, Korea, May 1, 1947; came to U.S., 1970; d. Sang Yung and Ock Yun (Choi) S.; m. Jerry Dee Boucher. BA summa cum laude, Sogang U., 1971; postgrad., U. Calif., Berkeley, 1971; MA in Anthropology, U. Hawaii, 1983, PhD in Anthropology, 1987. Staff instr. English Korean Air Lines, Edn. & Tng. Ctr., Seoul, 1978-79; instr. anthropology Ewha Women's U., Seoul, 1985; asst. prof. U. Hawaii, 1990; asst. prof. anthropology Southwest Tex. State U., San Marcos, 1991-94; asst. prof. anthropology San Francisco State U., 1994-96, assoc. prof. anthropology, 1996—; guest lectr. Chaminade U. Honolulu, 1988; vis. asst. prof. anthropology U. Ariz., 1990-91; cons. in field. Author: Women in Korean Politics; contbr. articles to profl. jours. Recipient East-West Ctr. grantee, 1981-87. Fellow Am. Anthrop. Assn.; mem. Am. Ethnological Soc., Soc. Psychol. Anthropology, Assn. Asian Studies (exec. bd. Com. Women Asian Studies), Western Social Sci. Assn., Korean Assn. Women's Studies, Royal Asiatic Soc. Korean Br. Office: San Francisco State U Dept Anthropology 1600 Holloway Ave San Francisco CA 94132-1722

SOHMER, BERNARD, mathematics educator, administrator; b. N.Y.C., July 16, 1929; s. Sol and Florence (Schonfeld) S.; m. Margot Rosette, July 27, 1952; children—Emily, Olivia. B.A., N.Y. U., 1949, M.S., 1951, Ph.D., 1958. Lectr. CCNY, 1952-57, faculty, 1958—, prof. math., 1969—, dean students, 1969-72, v.p. student affairs, 1972-75, chmn. faculty senate, 1977-79, 85-91, ombudsman, 1991—, chmn. liberal arts and sci. faculty council, 1979-85, pres. Hillel, 1988—; asst. prof. N.Y. U., 1957-58; trustee PSC-CUNY Welfare Fund, 1982—. Sec. Univ. Faculty Senate, 1992-94, vice chair, 1994—. Mem. AAAS, AAUP (pres. CCNY chpt. 1966-67, sec. 1977-78), Am. Math. Soc., Math. Assn. Am. (pres. elect N.Y. Met. sect. 1989-90, pres. 1992-93, past pres. 1993-94, councillor 1996-99), Profl. Staff Congress (pres. CCNY chpt. 1993—). Home: 3345 92nd St Jackson Hts NY 11372-1851 Office: CCNY 139th and Convent Ave New York NY 10031

SOHN, CHANG WOOK, energy systems researcher, educator; b. Seoul, Korea, Jan. 10, 1947; parents Kye Taek and Young Bo (Koh) S.; m. Chung Hae Han Sohn, Aug. 24, 1974; children: Douglas Jemin, Sammy Sungmin. BS in Engring., Seoul Nat. U., 1969; MS in Mech. Engring., Tex. Tech. U., 1975; PhD in Mech. Engring., U. Ill., Urbana, 1980. Registered profl. engr., Ill. 1st lt. Korean Army, 1969-71; tchr. KyungGi H.S., Seoul, 1971-72; rsch. asst. Tex. Tech. U., Lubbock, 1973-74; rsch. asst. U. Ill., Urbana, 1974-79, rsch. assoc., 1979-80; rsch. engr. U.S. Army Constrn. Engring. Rsch. Lab., Champaign, Ill., 1980-84, acting. team leader, 1992, prin. investigator, 1984—; adj. assoc. prof. U. Ill., Urbana, 1992—. Contbr. articles on fluid mechanics, heat transfer to profl. jours, ASHRAE transactions. Recipient Tech. Transfer award U.S. Army Corps of Engrs., Washington, 1991, Spl. Act award U.S. Army Yuma (Ariz.) Proving Ground, 1988. Mem. ASME (K-19 com. 1993—), ASHRAE (com. chair Cool Storage Design Guide 1992, air conditioning rsch. ctr. industry adv. bd. mem. 1991—). Avocations: golf, reading, classical. Home: 2910 Robeson Park Dr Champaign IL 61821-7609 Office: U S Army CERL PO Box 9005 Champaign IL 61826

SOHN, HONG YONG, chemical and metallurgical engineering educator, consultant; b. Kaesung, Kyunggi-Do, Korea, Aug. 21, 1941; arrived U.S., 1966; s. Chong Ku and Soon Deuk (Woo) S.; m. Victoria Bee Tuan Ngo, Jan. 8, 1972; children: Berkeley Jihoon, Edward Jihyun. BS in Chem. Engring., Seoul (Korea) Nat. U., 1962; MS in Chem. Engring., U. N.B., Can., 1966; PhD in Chem. Engring., U. Calif., Berkeley, 1970. Engr., Cheil Sugar Co., Busan, Korea, 1962-64; rsch. assoc. SUNY-Buffalo, 1971-73; research engr. DuPont Co., Wilmington, Del., 1973-74; prof. metall. engring., adj. prof. chem. engring. U. Utah, Salt Lake City, 1974—; cons. Lawrence Livermore Nat. Lab., 1976—, Kennecott Co., Salt Lake City, 1976—, Cabot Corp., 1984—, DuPont Co., 1987—, Utah Power and Light Co., 1987—. Co-author: Gas-Solid Reactions, 1976; co-editor: Rate Processes of Extractive Metallurgy, 1979, Extractive Metallurgy of Refractory Metals, 1980, Advances in Sulfide Smelting, 2 vols., 1983; Recycle and Secondary Recovery of Metals, 1985, Gas-solid Reactions in Pyrometallurgy, 1986, Flash Rection Processes, 1988, Metallurgical Processes for the Year 2000 and Beyond, 1988, Metallurgical Processes for the Early Twenty-First Century, 2 vols., 1994; patentee process for treating sulfide-bearing ores; contbr. numerous articles to sci., tech. jours. Camille and Henry Dreyfus Found. Tchr. Scholar awardee, 1977; Fulbright Disting. lectr., 1983; Japan Soc. for the Promotion of Sci. fellow, 1990. Mem. The Minerals, Metals and Materials Soc. (past dir., Extractive Metallurgy Lectr. award, 1990, Champion H. Mathewson Gold Medal award, 1993, Extractive metallurgical sci. award 1990, 94), Am. Inst. Chem. Engrs., Korean Inst. Chem. Engrs. Office: U Utah 412 Browning Building Salt Lake City UT 84112-1118 *Fortunate are those who earn a living by doing what they would rather be doing even if they do not have to do it to earn a living. Material wealth accumulated by doing what one does not enjoy doing is not worth the effort.*

SOHN, JEANNE, librarian; b. Milton, Pa.; d. Robert Wilson and Juliette Lightner (Hedenberg) Gift; m. Steven Neil Sohn, Nov. 23, 1962. BA, Temple U., 1966; MSLS, Drexel U., 1971. Lit. bibliographer Temple U., Phila., 1971-75, chief of collection devel., 1975-81; asst. dean for collection devel. U. N.Mex., Albuquerque, 1981-86, assoc. dean for libr. svcs., 1986-89; dir. libr. svcs. Cen. Conn. State U., New Britain, 1989—; cons. New Eng. Assn. Schs. and Colls., Winchester, Mass., 1991—. Mem. editorial bd. Collection Mgmt., 1984—; contbr. articles to profl. jours. Mem. Gov.'s Blue Ribbon Commn. on the Future of Libraries, 1994—. Mem. ALA, New Eng. Libr. Assn., Conn. Libr. Assn., Assn. Coll. and Rsch. Librs., Beta Phi Mu. Home: 1820 Boulevard West Hartford CT 06107-2815 Office: Cen Conn State Univ Elihu Burritt Libr New Britain CT 06050

SOHN, LOUIS BRUNO, lawyer, educator; b. Lwów, Poland, Mar. 1, 1914; came to U.S., 1939, naturalized, 1943; s. Joseph and Fryderyka (Hescheles) S.; m. Elizabeth Mayo. LLM, Diplomatic ScM, John Casimir U., 1935; LLM, Harvard U., 1940, SJD, 1958; LLD (hon.), Free U. Brussels (Flemish sect.), 1990. Asst. to Judge M. O. Hudson, 1941-48; John Harvey Gregory teaching fellow Harvard Law Sch., 1946-47, lectr. law, 1947-51, asst. prof. law, 1951-53, John Harvey Gregory lectr. in world orgn., 1951-81, prof. law, 1953-61, Bemis prof. internat. law, 1961-81; Woodruff prof. internat. law U. Ga., 1981-91; disting. rsch. prof. and dir. rsch. and studies Internat. Rule of Law Inst., 1992—; vis. Congl. prof. George Washington U., 1991-92; Disting. fellow Jennings Randolph Program, U.S. Inst. Peace, 1991-92; cons. U.S. ACDA, 1960-70, Office Internat. Security Affairs, Dept. Def., 1963-70; asst. to del. Permanent Ct. Internat. Justice, San Francisco Conf. UN, 1945; exec. sec. legal subcom. on atomic energy Carnegie Endowment for Internat. Peace, 1946; asst. reporter on progressive devel. internat. law Am. and Canadian bar assns., 1947-48; cons. UN secretariat, 1948, 69, legal officer, 1950-51; counselor internat. law Dept. State, 1970-71; U.S. del. to UN Law of Sea Conf., 1974-82; U.S. del. head Athens Conf. on Settlement Internat. Disputes, 1984. Author: Cases on World Law, 1950, Cases on United Nations Law, 1956, 2d edit., 1967, (with G. Clark) World Peace Through World Law, 1958, 3d edit., 1966, Basic Documents of African Regional Organizations, 4 vols, 1971-72, (with T. Buergenthal) International Protection of Human Rights, 1973, (with K. Gustafson) The Law of the Sea, 1984, International Organization and Integration: student edit. 1986; also articles on legal subjects; editor devel. internat. law: Am. Bar Assn. Jour, 1947-50; editorial bd.: Am. Jour. Internat. Law, 1958—. Recipient World Peace Hero award World Federalists of Can., 1974, Grenville Clark award, 1984, William A. Owens award for creative rsch. in social and behavioral scis. U. Ga., 1985, Harry Leroy Jones award Washington Fgn. Law Soc., 1993. Mem. ABA (hon., co-rapporteur joint working group with Can. Bar Assn. on peaceful settlement of disputes 1976—, vice chmn. internat. law and practice sect. 1983-91, chmn. 1992-93, Leonard J. Theberge award 1992), Am. Soc. Internat. Law (mem. exec. coun. 1954-57, v.p. 1965-66, hon. v.p. 1980-87, 90—, pres. 1988-90, Manley O. Hudson medal 1996), World Parliament Assn. (legal advisor 1954-64), Internat. Law Assn. (v.p. Am. br.), Am. Law Inst. (assoc. reporter Fgn. Rels. Law 1978-87), Inst. Internat. Law (Geneva), Fedn. Am. Scientists (vice chmn. 1963, mem. coun. 1964-65, 68-69), Commn. Study Orgn. Peace (chmn. 1986—). Home: 801 15th St S Apt 1504 Arlington VA 22202-5023 Office: George Washington U Law Sch 720 20th St NW Washington DC 20052

SOIKA, HELMUT EMIL, retirement plan executive; b. N.Y.C., May 22, 1941; s. Hubert E. and Berta Antonia (Metzger) S. BS, Fordham U., 1963, JD, 1968. Asst. trust officer Nat. Bank of N.Am., N.Y.C., 1968-71; trust officer Bank of N.Y., Westchester, 1971-72; atty. O'Neill, DiManno & Kelly, N.Y.C., 1972-76; atty. & div. mgr. Mut. of Am., N.Y.C., 1976-82; v.p., mgr. retirement plans Prudential-Bache Securities, N.Y.C., 1982-86; sr. v.p., dir. retirement plans Gruntal & Co. Inc., N.Y.C., 1986—. Office: Gruntal & Co Inc 14 Wall St New York NY 10005-2101

SOILEAU, MARION JOSEPH, engineering and physics educator; b. Simmesport, La., June 27, 1944; s. Marion and Mary Ann (Rabalais) S.; m. Cheryl A. Meche; children: Bruce, Aimee. BS in Astronomy/Physics, La. State U., 1967; MS in Physics/Optics, U. Utah, 1968; PhD in Quantum Electronics, U. So. Calif., 1979. Prof. Elec. Engring., Physics. Various positions in field to physicist Naval Weapons Ctr., China Lake, Calif., 1973-80; assoc. prof. physics North Tex. State U., 1980-84, prof. physics, 1984-87; prof. elec. engring. and physics, dir. Ctr. Rsch. and Edn. in Optics and Lasers, U. Ctrl. Fla., Orlando, 1987—. Contbr. over 100 sci. papers on nonlinear optics; contbr. articles to profl. jours. Trustee Orlando Sci. Ctr., 1991—. Capt. USAF, 1967-72. Co-recipient North Tex. State U. Pres.'s award, 1983. Fellow Optical Soc. Am., Soc. Photo-Optical and Instrumentation Engrs. (bd. govs. 1990-92), SPIE-The Internat. Optical Engring. Soc. (bd. govs. 1990-92, 94, sec. 1995, v.p. 1996); mem. AAAS, IEEE (sr.), Laser Inst. Am., K.C., others. Democrat. Roman Catholic. Avocation: fishing. Home: 100 Tuskawilla Rd Winter Spgs FL 32708-2830 Office: U Cen Fla PO Box 162700 Orlando FL 32816-2700

SOIN, RAJESH K., business executive; b. New Delhi, India, July 27, 1947; came to U.S., 1969; m. Indu Soin; children: Vishal, Amol. BSME, Delhi U.; MSIE, Bradley U.; postgrad., Harvard U., U. Pa. Indsl. engr. Firestone Tire & Rubber Co., 1971-78; corp. system mgr. Williams Internat., Walled Lake, Mich., 1978-84; pres., CEO Modern Techs. Corp., Dayton, Ohio, 1984—; pres. JMD Devel. Corp., Dayton, Emerald Constrn. Corp., Dayton; pres. Asian Indian Am. Bus. Group, Dayton. Bd. dirs. Dayton Coun. on World Affairs, Needy Children's Found., Dayton; trustee Ohio/India Project, Dayton Art Inst.; mem. bd. advisors Wright State U. Coll. Bus. and Adminstrn., Dayton. Mem. Dayton Area C. of C. (bd. dirs.), Dayton Rotary Club. Avocation: golf. Home: 2624 Lantz Rd Beavercreek OH 45434-6627 Office: Modern Techs Corp 4032 Linden Ave Dayton OH 45432-3015*

SOJKA, GARY ALLAN, biologist, educator, university official; b. Cedar Rapids, Iowa, July 15, 1940; s. Marvin F. and Ruth Ann (Waddington) Sojka Green; m. Sandra Kay Smith, Aug 5, 1962; children: Lisa Kay, Dirk Allan. BS, Coe Coll., 1962; MS, Purdue U., 1965, PhD, 1967; LLD (hon.), Lycoming Coll., 1995. Rsch. assoc. Ind. U., Bloomington, 1967-69, asst. prof., 1969-73, assoc. prof., 1973-79, prof., 1979-84, assoc. chmn. biology, 1977-79, chmn. biology, 1979-81, dean arts and scis., 1981-84; pres. Bucknell U., Lewisburg, Pa., 1984-95; prof. biology, 1995—; mem. higher edn. commn. Mid. States Assn. Colls. and Schs., 1992—; chmn. tax policy subcom. Nat. Assn. Ind. Colls. and Univs., 1991-93; mem. study group on internat. edn. Am. Coun. Edn., 1992-94. Chmn. bd. dirs. Stone Belt Coun. Ret. Citizens, Bloomington, 1977-78; mem. nominating com. Ind. Assn. Ret. Citizens, Indpls., 1979; mem. So. Ind. Health Sys. Agy., Bedford; bd. dirs. Geisinger Med. Found., Danville, Pa., Inst. European Studies; trustee St. Mary-of-the-Woods Coll., Ind., 1988-94; chmn. Pa. Commn. Ind. Colls. and Univs., 1989-90; dir. Suncom Industries, Northcumberland, Pa., 1991-93; mem. Pres.'s Commn. NCAA, 1993-95; bd. dirs. Bethesda Found., Lewisburg, 1996—. Recipient Ind. U. Sr. Class Tchg. award, 1975, Frederick B. Lieber award, 1977, Coe Coll. Alumni award of merit, 1982, Gary A. Sojka award Bucknell U., 1992, Cmty. Leadership award Susquahanna Valley Boy Scouts, 1994; named to Coe Coll. Athletic Hall of Fame, 1988. Mem. Am. Assn. Microbiology, Am. Acad. Microbiology, Am. Soc. Biol. Chemists, Soc. Gen. Microbiology, Nat. Assn. Independent Colls. and Univs. (subcom. chmn. 1991-93), Am. Coun. Edn. (mem. study group on internat. edn. 1992—), Sigma Xi, Sigma Nu, Omicron Delta Kappa. Baptist. Home: Bend-in-the-Creek Farm 141 Creek Rd Middleburg PA 17842 Office: Bucknell U Dept Biology Lewisburg PA 17842

SOKAL, ROBERT REUVEN, biology educator, author; b. Vienna, Austria, Jan. 13, 1926; came to U.S., 1947, naturalized 1958; s. Siegfried and Klara (Rattner) S.; m. Julie Chen-Chu Yang, Aug. 12, 1948; children: David Jonathan, Hannah Judith. BS in Biology, St. John's U., Shanghai, Republic of China, 1947; PhD in Zoology, U. Chgo., 1952; DSc (hon.), U. Crete (Greece), 1990. From instr. to prof. U. Kans., Lawrence, 1951-69; prof., then leading prof., Disting. prof. SUNY, Stony Brook, 1969-95, dept. chmn., 1980-83, vice provost for rsch. and grad. studies, 1981-82, disting. prof. emeritus, 1995; Fulbright vis. prof. Hebrew/Tel Aviv U., Israel, 1963-64, U. Vienna, Austria, 1977, 78, 84; vis. prof. Inst. Adv. Studies, Oeiras, Portugal, 1971-80; vis. disting. prof. U. Mich., 1975-76; vis. prof. Coll. de France, Paris, 1989. Author: Principles of Numerical Taxonomy, 1963, Biometry, 1969, 3d rev. edit., 1994, Statistical Tables, 1969, 3rd rev. edit. 1994, Introduction to Biostatistics, 1973, 2d rev. edit., 1987, Numerical Taxonomy, 1973; editor Am. Naturalist Jour., 1969-84. Career investigator NIH, 1964-69; sr. fellow NSF, 1959-60, NATO fellow, 1974, Guggenheim fellow, 1975-76, 84; Ctr. Advanced Study in Behavioral Sci. fellow, 1992-93. Fellow AAAS, Am. Acad. Arts and Scis.; mem. Soc. Study Evolution (pres. 1977), Am. Soc. Naturalists (pres. 1984), The Classification Soc. (pres. 1969-71), Internat. Fedn. Classification Socs. (pres. 1988-89), Nat. Acad. Scis., Linnean Soc. London (fgn.), Soc. Systematic Zoology (hon.), Natural History Mus. (Paris, corr. mem.), B'nai Brith (pres. 1966). Democrat. Jewish.

SOKMENSUER, ADIL, physician, educator; b. Izmir, Turkey, Jan. 24, 1928; came to U.S., 1956; s. Cevat and Rukiye (Sun) S.; m. Ulku Sakizlioglu, June 22, 1956; children: G. Hakan, Cem Yanki, Kent Halit. BA with honors, Inönü Lisesi, Izmir, 1945; MD, U. Istanbul, Turkey, 1951; student, U. Pa., 1970-71. Intern Loretto Hosp., Chgo., 1956-57; resident Phila. Gen. Hosp., 1957-59; staff physician Cen. Fla. Tb Hosp., Orlando, Fla., 1959; mem. staff A.G. Holley State Hosp., Lantana, Fla., 1959—, dir. clin. svcs., 1963-66, med. dir., supt., 1966-73, cons., 1973-75; pvt. practice internal medicine West Palm Beach, Fla., 1973-89; med. dir. Palm Beach County Home & Gen. Care Facility; cons. chest svc. VA Hosp., Miami (Fla.), 1969-76; clin. instr. Sch. Medicine, U. Miami, 1969-71, asst. prof., 1971-80, assoc. prof. chest medicine, 1980-84; med. dir., cons. internist Palm Beach County GCF, 1973—. With Turkish Army, 1951-52. Mem. Am. Coll. Chest Physicians, Fla. Med. Assn., Palm Beach County Med. Soc., S.E. Fla. Chest Physicians Soc., Am. Thoracic Soc., Fla. Thoracic Soc. (pres. 1972-73), Gerontology Soc. Rsch. in chemotherapy of Tb and Atypical Tb. Home: 320 Dunbar Rd Palm Beach FL 33480-3763 Office: Palm Beach County Home & Gen Care Facility 1200 45th St West Palm Beach FL 33407-2342

SOKOL, MARC JEFFREY, arts administrator; b. Phila., Apr. 18, 1961; s. Arnold and Phyllis (Goldman) S. BA in Architecture and Art History, U. Pa., 1984; MFA in Arts Adminstrn., Columbia U., 1992. Instr. Am. architecture and art history Rio de Janeiro, 1984-85; exec. dir. Paris Edits., Cherry Hill, N.J., 1985-87, L'Imagerie Gallery, L.A., 1987-88; pvt. art dealer, Phila., 1988-89; exec. program dir. Sculpture in Environ., Inc (SITE), N.Y.C., 1990-94; program officer for arts and humanities Ventures in Edn. Inc., N.Y.C, 1994—; mem. edn. adv. com. High Sch. Art and Design, N.Y.C. Contbr. articles to profl. publs. Co-founding mem. night without light com. Visual AIDS for Arts, N.Y.C.; mem. bus. coalition steering com. Walks of Life. Grantee Van Nostrand Reinhold Co., N.Y. Times Co. Found., Nat. Endowment for Arts, Dreyfus Corp. N.Y. State Coun. on the Arts, Ark. Arts Coun., Recipient of the Am. Inst. of Arch. N.Y. State, 1993 Pres. Citation. Mem. AIA (learning by design com. N.Y.C. chpt.). Avocations: travel, scuba diving, architectural walking tours. Office: Ventures in Edn 245 Fifht Ave Ste 802 New York NY 10016

SOKOL, ROBERT JAMES, obstetrician/gynecologist, educator; b. Rochester, N.Y., Nov. 18, 1941; s. Eli and Mildred (Levine) S.; m. Roberta Sue Kahn, July 26, 1964; children: Melissa Anne, Eric Russell, Andrew Ian. BA with highest distinction in Philosophy, U. Rochester, 1963, MD with honors, 1966. Diplomate Am. Bd. Ob-Gyn (assoc. examiner 1984-86), Sub-Bd. Maternal-Fetal Medicine. Intern Barnes Hosp., Washington U., St. Louis, 1966-67, resident in ob-gyn., 1967-70, asst. in ob-gyn., 1966-70, rsch. asst., 1967-68, instr. clin. ob-gyn., 1970; Buswell fellow in maternal fetal medicine Strong Meml. Hosp.-U. Rochester, 1972-73; fellow in maternal-fetal medicine Cleve. Met. Gen. Hosp.-Case Western Res. U., Cleve., 1974-75, assoc. obstetrician and gynecologist, 1973-83, asst. prof. ob-gyn., 1973-77; asst. program dir. Perinatal Clin. Rsch. Ctr., 1973-78, co-program dir., 1978-82, program dir., 1982-83, acting dir. obstetrics, 1974-75, co-dir., 1977-83, assoc. prof., 1977-81, prof., 1981-83, assoc. dir. dept. ob-gyn., 1981-83; prof. ob-gyn. Wayne State U., Detroit, 1983—, chmn. dept. ob-gyn., 1983-89, mem. grad. faculty dept. physiology, 1984—, interim dean Med. Sch., 1988-89, dean, 1989—, pres. Fund for Med. Rsch. and Edn., 1988—; chief ob-gyn. Hutzel Hosp. Detroit, 1983-89; dir. C.S. Mott Ctr. for Human Growth and Devel., 1983-89; interim chmn. med. bd. Detroit Med. Ctr., 1988-89, chmn. med. bd., 1989—, sr. v.p. med. affairs, 1992—, trustee, 1990—; past pres. med. staff Cuyahoga County Hosps.; mem. profl. adv. bd. Educated Childbirth Inc., 1976-80; sr. Ob cons. Symposia Medicus; cons. Nat. Inst. Child Health and Human Devel., Nat. Inst. Alcohol Abuse and Alcoholism, Ctr. for Disease Control, NIH, Health Resources and Services Adminstrn., Nat. Clearinghouse for Alcohol Info., Am. Psychol. Assn.; mem. alcohol psychosocial research rev. com. Nat. Inst. Alcohol Abuse and Alcoholism, 1982-86; mem. ob/gyn adv. panel U.S. Pharmacopeial Conv., 1985-90. Mem. internat. editorial bd. Israel Jour. Obstetrics and Gynecology; reviewer med. jours.; mem. editorial bd. Jour. Perinatal Medicine; editor-in-chief Interactions: Programs in Clinical Decision-Making, 1987-90; researcher computer applications in perinatal medicine, alcohol-related birth defects, perinatal risk and neurobehavioral devel.; contbr. articles to profl. jours. Mem. Pres.'s leadership council U. Rochester, 1976-80; mem. exec. com. bd. trustees Oakland Health Edn. Program, 1987—; mem. voluntary alumni admissions com. U. Rochester, 1986—. Served to maj. M.C. USAF, 1970-72. Mem. AMA, NAS (Inst. of Medicine), ACOG (chmn. steering com. drug and alcohol abuse contract 1986-87), Am. Med. Informatics Assn., Soc. Gynecologic Investigation, Perinatal Rsch. Soc., Assn. Profs. Gyn.-Ob, Royal Soc. Medicine, Mich. Med. Soc., Wayne County Med. Soc., Detroit Acad. Medicine, Cen. Assn. Obstetricians-Gynecologists, Rsch. Soc. Alcoholism, Soc. Perinatal Obstetricians (v.p., pres.-elect 1987-88, pres. 1988-89, achievement award 1995), Liaison Com. for Ob-Gyn., Am. Gynecol. and Obstetrical Soc., Neurobehavioral Teratology Soc., APHA, Am. Med. Soc. on Alcoholism and Other Drug Dependencies, Soc. for Neuroscis. (Mich. chpt.), Internat. Soc. Computers in Obstetrics, Neonatology, Gynecology (v.p. 1987-89, pres. 1989-92, immediate past pres. 1992—), World Assn. Perinatal Medicine, Soc. Physicians Reproductive Choice and Health, Am. Assn. Med. Colls. (coun. of deans), Detroit Physiol. Soc. (hon.), Polish Gynecologists World Club, Phi Beta Kappa, Sigma Xi, Alpha Omega Alpha. Republican. Jewish. Home: 5200 Rector Ct Bloomfield Hills MI 48302-2654 Office: Wayne State U Sch Medicine 540 E Canfield St Detroit MI 48201-1928 *The drive for academic accomplishment was instilled early in childhood in a home environment which placed value on a multiplicity of interests in science and the arts-my parents taught me what to do. In retrospect, exposure to strong role models-professors of philosophy, pathology, psychiatry and obstetrics-gynecology-takes on increased importance-these individuals showed me how to do it. My family continues to support me in seeking and meeting new challenges. The opportunity to develop and transmit new knowledge sustains a high level of activity. I enjoy what I do.*

SOKOL, SAUL, insurance agency executive; b. Columbus, Ohio, Mar. 27, 1920; s. Nathan and Rose (Klyst) S.; m. Phyllis Davis, Jan. 15, 1950; children: Jay Bradford, Samara Sokol Fields. Student, Ohio State U., 1939-40. CLU, CPCU. Propr. Sokol Ins. Agy., Columbus, 1946—; bd. dirs. Ohio Indemnity Co., Columbus, Bancinsurance Corp., Columbus. Author: Your Insurance Adviser, 1977; writer ins. articles The Columbus Dispatch. Mem. adv. bd. Salvation Army, Columbus, 1972—; trustee Alzheimer's Assn., Columbus, 1987-94, Wexner Heritage Village, Columbus, 1991—; trustee Syntaxis Youth Homes, Columbus, 1973. S/Sgt. Signal Corps, U.S. Army, 1942-46, ETO. Recipient Vol. Svcs. award Salvation Army, 1990. Mem. Am. Soc. CLU (Hall of Fame award 1992), Am. Soc. CPCU (pres. Columbus chpt. 1984-85), Columbus Life Underwriters Assn. (disting. hon.; pres. 1976-77), Ind. Ins. Agts. Assn., Profl. Ins. Agts. Assn., Press Club of Ohio, Univ. Club (Columbus), B'nai B'rith (pres. 1953-54). Home: 360 S Roosevelt Ave Columbus OH 43209-1832 Office: Sokol Ins Agy 3242 E Main St Columbus OH 43213-3807

SOKOLOF, PHIL, industrialist, consumer advocate; b. Omaha, Dec. 14, 1922; s. Louis and Rose (Jacobson) S.; m. Ruth Rosinsky, June 1, 1947 (dec. Feb. 1982); children: Steven, Karen Sokolof Javitch. Grad. high sch., Omaha, 1939. Founder and chief exec. officer Phillips Mfg. Co., Omaha, 1955-92; founder, pres. Nat. Heart Savers Assn., Omaha, 1985—. Author: Bridge Philosophy, 1971; contbg. editor N.Y. Times, 1991; featured in Time mag., Mar. 1990, in Journal of American Medicine, Dec. 1990 as catalyst of American public's cholesterol consciousness; contbg. ed. Sunday New York Times, 1991. Designated by Congress hon. co-sponsor 1990 Nutrition Labeling and Edn. Act; conducted Poisoning of Am. nat. media campaigns against major food processors for high colesterol, high fat content in foods, 1988-93 (citation FDA 1993); activist in lowering fat content Nat. Sch. Lunch Program; conducted, funded $1 million Nutrition Facts sweepstakes quiz to educated pub. regarding nutrition food labels, 1994; ran nat. advt. campaign promoting skim milk and alerting Ams. that 2% milk is not low fat, 1995; pioneered mass cholesterol testing, Grand Island, Nebr., 1985; tested cholesterol levels 200,000 people in 16 cities, 1985-87; created, won congl. appropral designating March as Nat. Know Your Cholesterol Month, 1987, Cholesterol Kills pub. svc. announcements featured on over 100 TV stas., 1987—; nat. spokesperson to creatd pub. awarness of danger of cholesterol and saturated fats in food products which promote heart disease. Named Person of Week, ABC News, Mar. 15, 1991; recipient Food & Drug Admin. Commr's. Spl. Achievement citation, 1993, C. Everett Koop Health Advocate award Am. Hosp. Assn., 1994. Mem. Am. Contract Bridge League (life master), King Solomon's Cir. philanthropy,1990 (charter). Office: Nat Heart Savers Assn 9140 W Dodge Rd Omaha NE 68114-3306

SOKOLOFF, LOUIS, physiologist, neurochemist; b. Phila., Oct. 14, 1921; married; 2 children. BA, U. Pa., 1943, MD, 1946. Intern Phila. Gen. Hosp., 1946-47; rsch. fellow in physiology U. Pa. Grad. Sch. Medicine, 1949-51, instr., then assoc., 1951-56; assoc. chief, then chief sect. cerebral metabolism NIMH, Bethesda, Md., 1953-68; chief lab. cerebral metabolism NIMH, 1968—. Chief editor Jour. Neurochemistry, 1974-78. Served to capt. M.C. U.S. Army, 1947-49. Recipient F.O. Schmitt medal in neurosci., 1980, Albert Lasker clin. med. research award, 1981, Karl Spencer Lashley award Am. Philos. Soc., 1987, Disting. Grad. award U. Pa., 1987, Nat. Acad. Scis. award in Neurosci., 1988, Georg Charles de Hevesy Nuclear Medicine Pioneer award Soc. Nuclear Medicine, 1988, Mihara Cerebrovascular Disorder Rsch. Promotion award, 1988. Mem. Am. Physiol. Soc., Assn. Rsch. Nervous and Mental Diseases, Am. Biophys. Soc., Am. Acad. Neurology, Am. Neurol. Assn., Am. Soc. Biol. Chemists, Am. Soc. Neurochemistry, U.S. Nat. Acad. Scis. Achievements include development of methods for measurement of cerebral blood flow and metabolism in animals and man.

SOKOLOV, JACQUE JENNING, health care executive, nuclear cardiologist; b. L.A., Sept. 13, 1954; s. Albert I. and Frances (Burgess) S. BA in Medicine magna cum laude, U. So. Calif., 1974, MD with hons., 1978; postgrad., Mayo Clinic, Rochester, Minn., 1978-81, U. Tex., Dallas, 1981-83. Med. diplomate. Cardiologist, nuclear cardiologist Health Sci. Ctr. U. Tex., 1981-84; chief med. officer Baylor Ctr. for Health Promotion Wellness & Lifestyle Corp., Dallas, 1985-87; v.p., dir. health care dept., corp. med. dir. So. Calif. Edison Co., Rosemead, Calif., 1987-92; CEO Advanced Health Plans, Inc./Sokolov Strategic Alliance, L.A., 1992—; chmn. bd. Coastal Physician Group, Inc., 1994—; cons. Health Care Strategic Planning Southwestern Bell, AT&T, Wang, Rosewood Corp., Dallas, 1985-87; bd. dirs. Calif. Health Decisions. Contbr. articles to profl. jours. Tech. advisor Coun. Social Security; bd. dirs. Washington Bus. Group Health. Grantee NIH, Bethesda, Md., 1983. Office: Ste 800 9000 Sunset Blvd Los Angeles CA 90069

SOKOLOV, RICHARD SAUL, real estate company executive; b. Phila., Dec. 7, 1949; s. Morris and Estelle Rita (Steinberg) S.; m. Susan Barbara Saltzman, Aug. 13, 1972; children: Lisa, Anne, Kate. BA, Pa. State U., 1971; JD, Georgetown U., 1974. Assoc. Weinberg & Green, Balt., 1974-80, ptnr., 1980-82; v.p., gen. counsel The Edward J. DeBartolo Corp., Youngstown, Ohio, 1982-86, sr. v.p. devel., gen. coun., 1986-94; pres., CEO DeBartolo Realty Corp., Youngstown, Ohio, 1994—. Mem. investment com. Jewish Fedn., Youngstown, 1992—; bd. dirs. Heritage Manor, Youngstown, United Way 1995—. Mem. Internat. Coun. Shopping Ctrs. (trustee 1994—), Urban Land Inst. (assoc.). Office: DeBartolo Realty Corp 7655 Market St Youngstown OH 44513

SOKOLOW, MAURICE, physician, educator; b. N.Y.C., May 19, 1911; s. Alexander and Anna (Spiegelman) S.; m. Ethel Schwabacher, June 30, 1941 (dec. 1970); children: Gail Anne, Jane Carol (dec.), Anne May. A.B. cum laude, U. Calif., Berkeley, 1932; M.D., U. Calif., San Francisco, 1936. Intern San Francisco Gen. Hosp., 1935-36; resident U. Calif., San Francisco, 1936-37, research fellow, 1939-40; resident New Eng. Med. Ctr., Boston, 1937-38; research fellow Michael Reese Hosp., Chgo., 1938-39; gen. practice medicine San Francisco, 1946-62; mem. faculty cardiovascular div. Sch. Medicine, U. Calif., San Francisco, 1946—, assoc. prof. medicine, 1952-58, prof., 1958-78, prof. emeritus, 1978—, chief electrocardiograph dept., chief hypertension clinic, 1946-78, chief cardiovascular div., 1954-73; program and founding dir. cardiology tng. grant USPHS, San Francisco, 1960-73; sr. mem. Cardiovascular Rsch. Inst., 1957—; cons. in field. Author: Clinical Cardiology; Contbr. articles to med. jours., texts.; mem. editorial bd.: Jour. Cardiovascular Medicine, 1975—, Western Jour. Medicine, 1946-68. Bd. dirs. Fromm Inst Life Long Learning, U. San Francisco. Served to lt. comdr. M.C. USN, 1942-46. Nat. Heart Inst. grantee, 1950-78; named U Calif. San Francisco Alumnus of Yr., 1986. Fellow Am. Coll. Cardiology (hon.); mem. Am. Fedn. Clin. Research (v.p. 1948-49), Assn. Univ. Cardiologists, Am. Soc. Clin. Investigation, Brit. Cardiac Soc. (corr.), Am. Heart Assn., San Francisco Heart Assn. (pres. 1950-51). Club: Menlo Circus. Home: 3452 Jackson St San Francisco CA 94118-2021 Office: U Calif Sch of Medicine San Francisco CA 94143

SOKOLSKY, ROBERT LAWRENCE, journalist, entertainment writer; b. Boston, May 18, 1928; s. Henry and Lillian (Gorodetzky) S.; m. Sally-Ann Moss, Aug. 11, 1955; 1 son, Andrew E. A.B., Syracuse (N.Y.) U., 1950. Reporter Springfield (Mass.) Union, 1950; asst. dir. pub. info. ARC, Syracuse, 1952-54; entertainment editor Syracuse Herald-Jour., 1954-61, Buffalo Courier Express, 1961-72, Phila. Bull., 1972-82; entertainment writer Riverside (Calif.) Press-Enterprise, 1983—; syndicated TV columnist Ottaway News Svc., 1988—; radio show host; freelance writer; guest lectr. Contbr. articles to profl. jours. Bd. dirs. Brush Hollow Civic Assn., Evesham Twp., N.J. Served with U.S. Army, 1950-52. Recipient Sigma Delta Chi award for feature writing, 1950, award for entertainment coverage Twin Counties Press Club, 1984, 87. Mem. Am. Newspaper Guild (Page One award for opinion writing), Syracuse Press Club, Greater Buffalo Press Assn., TV Critics Assn., Soc. Profl. Journalists (Excellence in Journalism award 1989, 93), Pen and Pencil Club of Phila., Variety Club. Republican. Jewish. Home: 3080 Saratoga St Riverside CA 92503-5435 Office: Riverside Press-Enterprise 3512 14th St Riverside CA 92501-3814

SOLA, JURE, electronics executive. BSEE, San Jose State U., 1972. Various mgmt. positions Lika Corp., Stockton, Calif., 1972-80; with Sanmina Corp. and predecessor, 1980—, now pres., chmn. bd. dirs. Office: Sanmina Corp 355 E Trimble Rd San Jose CA 95131-1314*

SOLAN, LAWRENCE MICHAEL, lawyer; b. N.Y.C., May 7, 1952; s. Harold Allen and Shirley (Smith) S.; m. Anita Lois Rush, Mar. 27, 1982; children: Renata, David. BA, Brandeis U., 1974; PhD, U. Mass., 1978; JD, Harvard U., 1982. Bar: N.J. 1982, N.Y. 1984. Clk. to Justice Pollock Supreme Ct. N.J., Morristown, 1982-83; assoc. Orans, Elsen & Lupert, N.Y.C., 1983-89, ptnr., 1989—; mem. panel of arbitrators Am. Arbitration Assn., N.Y.C. Author: The Language of Judges, 1993, Pronominal Reference, 1983. Mem. Phi Beta Kappa. Home: 163 Ralston Ave South Orange NJ 07079-2344 Office: Orans Elsen & Lupert One Rockefeller Plz New York NY 10020

SOLAND, NORMAN R., corporate lawyer; b. Duluth, Minn., Oct. 17, 1940; m. Carol A. Isaacson, Aug. 29, 1964; children: Kirk, Lisa, Kari, Chad. BA, U. Minn., 1963; JD, Am. Univ., 1972. Bar: Minn. 1973. Analyst CIA, 1963-73; assoc. Thompson, Hessian, Fletcher, McKasy & Soderberg, Thompson, Fletcher, Stone & Morse, 1973-79; corp. counsel Nash-Finch Co., Mpls., 1979-84, asst. sec., counsel, 1984-86, sec., gen counsel, 1986-88, v.p., sec. & gen. counsel, 1988—. Mem. ABA, Minn. State Bar Assn., Hennepin County Bar Assn., Am. Corp. Counsel Assn. Office: Nash Finch Co 7600 France Ave S PO Box 355 Minneapolis MN 55440-0355

SOLANO, CARL ANTHONY, lawyer; b. Pittston, Pa., Mar. 26, 1951; s. Nick D. and Catherine A. (Occhiato) S; m. Nancy M. Solano, 1989; 1 child, Melanie A. BS magna cum laude, U. Scranton, 1973; JD cum laude, Vilanova U., 1976. Bar: Pa. 1976, U.S. Dist. Ct. (ea. dist.) Pa. 1978, U.S. Ct. Appeals (3rd cir.) 1980, U.S. Ct. Appeals (5th cir.) 1981, U.S. Supreme Ct. 1982, U.S. Ct. Appeals (9th cir.) 1986, U.S. Dist. Ct. (mid. dist.) Pa. 1988, U.S. Ct. Appeals (6th cir.) 1988, U.S. Ct. Appeals (Fed. cir.) 1989. Law clerk Hon. Alfred L. Luongo U.S. Dist. Ct., Ea. Dist. Pa., Phila., 1976-78; assoc. Schnader, Harrison, Segal & Lewis, Phila., 1978-84, ptnr., 1985—. Mem. ABA, Am. Law Inst., Pa. Bar Assn. (statutory law com. 1980—), Phila. Bar Assn., St. Thomas More Soc., Justinian Soc., Order of Coif, Pi Gamma Mu. Roman Catholic. Home: 5 Barrister Ct Haverford PA 19041-1137 Office: Schnader Harrison Segal & Lewis 1600 Market St Ste 3600 Philadelphia PA 19103-7240

SOLAR, RICHARD LEON, banker; b. Boston, Aug. 15, 1939; s. Hervey L. and Mildred (Beckerman) S.; m. Stephanie Bennett; children: Andrew, Lisa. BA, Harvard U., 1961; MBA, Columbia U., 1963. Asst. v.p. Bankers Trust Co., N.Y.C., 1963-71; treas. Val D'Or Inds., N.Y.C., 1971-74, Diamondhead Corp., Mountainside, N.J., 1974-75, mng. dir., 1984—; sr. v.p. Bankers Trust Co., N.Y.C., 1975-84 ; chmn., dir. Bankers Trust Comml. Corp., 1983-90; sr. v.p. Gerber Childrens Wear Inc., N.Y.C., 1996—. Mem. Nat. Comml. Fin. Assn. (chmn., dir.). Club: Wyantenuck Country (Great Barrington, Mass.). Office: Gerber Childrens Wear Inc 1333 Broadway New York NY 10018

SOLARI, R. C., heavy construction company executive; b. 1925; married. With Granite Construction Co., 1946—, formerly pres.; now pres., chief exec. officer, dir. Granite Construction Co., Watsonville, Calif., chmn. bd. dirs. Office: Granite Constrn Co PO Box 50085 Watsonville CA 95077-5085*

SOLARO, ROSS JOHN, physiologist, biophysicist; b. Wadsworth, Ohio, Jan. 9, 1942; s. Ross and Lena (Chuppa) S.; m. Kathleen Marie Cole, Sept. 18, 1965; children: Christopher, Elizabeth. BS, U. Cin., 1965; PhD, U. Pitts., 1971. Asst. prof. Med. Coll. Va., Richmond, 1973-77; assoc. prof. pharmacology and physiology U. Cin., 1977-81, prof. pharmacology and cell biophysics, 1981-85, prof. physiology, 1981-88; prof. physiology, head U. Ill., Chgo., 1988—; sec. gen. Internat. Soc. Heart Rsch., 1989-93; chmn. exptl. cardiovascular study sect. NIH, 1990-92; vice-chmn. physiology U. Cin., 1995—. Editor: Protein Phosphorylation in Heart Muscle, 1986; contbr. articles to profl. jours. including Nature, Jour. Biol. Chemistry, Circulation Rsch. Chmn. rsch. coun. Am. Heart Assn., Met. Chgo., 1990—. Grantee NIH, 1977—, 77-82, 89—, Fogarty fellow, 1986; Brit. Am. Heart fellow Am. Heart Assn., 1974-75; Sr. Internat. fellow U. Coll. London, 1987. Mem. Am. Physiol. Soc. (chmn. subgroup), Am. Soc. Pharm. Exptl. Therapeutics, Biophys. Soc. (chmn. subgroup 1983-84). Office: U Ill at Chgo Dept MC901 Physiology & Biophysics 901 S Wolcott Ave Chicago IL 60612-7340

SOLBERG, ELIZABETH TRANSOU, public relations executive; b. Dallas, Aug. 10, 1939; d. Ross W. and Josephine V. (Perkins) Transou; m. Frederick M. Solberg, Jr., Mar. 8, 1969; 1 son, Frederick W. BJ, U. Mo., 1961. Reporter, Kansas City (Mo.) Star, 1963-70, asst. city editor, 1970-73; reporter spl. events, documentaries Sta. WDAF-TV, Kansas City, Mo., 1973-74; prof. dept. journalism Park Coll., Kansas City, Mo., 1975-76, advisor, 1976-79; mng. ptnr. Fleishman-Hillard, Inc., Kansas City, Mo., from 1979, now exec. v.p., sr. ptnr., gen. mgr. Kansas City br.; pres. Fleishman-Hillard/Can. Mem. Kansas City Commn. Planned Indsl. Expansion Authority, 1974-91; mem. long-range planning com. Heart of Am. council Boy Scouts Am., 1980-82, bd. dirs., 1986-89; mem. Clay County (Mo.) Devel. Commn., 1979-88; bd. govs. Citizens Assn., 1975—; mem. exec. com. bd. Kansas City Area Devel. Coun., 1989-96, co-chair, 1991-93; trustee Pembroke Hill Sch., 1987-93, U. Kansas City, 1990—, exec. com., 1992—, Midwest Rsch. Inst., 1995—; bd. dirs. Greater Kansas City Cmty. Found. and Affiliated Trusts, 1996—, Starlight Theatre, 1996—; regent Rockhurst Coll., 1984-96; active Bus. Coun., Nelson Gallery Found., Nelson-Atkins Mus. Art, 1990—; bd. dirs. Civic Coun. Greater Kansas City, 1992—. Recipient award for contbn. to mental health Mo. Psychiat. Assn., 1973, Arthur E. Lowell award for excellence in orgn. comm. Kansas City/IABC, 1985, Kansas City Spirit award Gillis Ctr., 1994. Mem. Pub. Relations Soc. Am. (nat. honors and awards com., co-chmn. Silver Anvil com. 1983, Silver Anvil award 1979-82, chair nat. membership com. 1989-91, assembly del.-at-large 1995-96), Counselor's Acad. (exec. com. 1991-92), Mo. C. of C. Pub. Relations Council, Greater Kans. City C. of C. (chair 1994-95, bd. exec. com.), Pi Beta Phi. Clubs: Jr. League, River Kansas City, Carriage, Central Exchange. Office: Fleishman Hillard Inc 2405 Grand Blvd Ste 700 Kansas City MO 64108-2519

SOLBERG, LOREN ALBIN, state legislator, secondary education educator; b. Blackduck, Minn., Nov. 3, 1941; s. Albin Andy and Mabel Ethel (Bergen) S.; m. Joan Maxine Olsen, Aug. 9, 1969; children: Sean, John, Previn, Kjirstin. BS, Bemidji (Minn.) State U., 1965, MS, 1974; MPA, Harvard U., 1990. Tchr. math. Ind. Sch. Dist. 316, Coleraine, Minn., 1965—; mem. Minn. Ho. of Reps., St. Paul, 1983—; instr. math. Itasca C.C., Grand Rapids, Minn., 1981-83; instr. computer sci. Harvard U., Cambridge, Mass., 1988. Mayor City of Bovey, Minn., 1970-82. Democrat. Lutheran. Home: PO Box 61 Bovey MN 55709-0061 Office: Minn Ho of Reps State Office Bldg Saint Paul MN 55155-1201

SOLBERG, MYRON, food scientist, educator; b. Boston, June 11, 1931; s. Alexander and Ruth (Graff) S.; m. Rona Mae Bernstein, Aug. 26, 1956; children: Sara Lynn, Julie Sue, Laurence Michael. BS in Food Tech, U. Mass., 1952; PhD, MIT, 1960. Commd. 2d lt. USAF, 1952, advanced through grades to lt. col., 1973, ret., 1991; cons. to food industry, 1956-60, 64—; mem. rsch. staff food tech. MIT, 1954-60; quality control mgr. Colonial Provision Co., Inc., Boston, 1960-64; sci. editor Meat Processing mag., Chgo., 1968-69; mem. faculty Rutgers U., 1964—, prof. food sci., 1970—, dir. Ctr. for Advanced Food Tech., 1984—; UN expert on food product quality control, 1973-74; vis. prof. Technion, Israel Inst. Tech., Haifa, 1973-74. Co-editor Jour. Food Safety, 1977-88; contbr. articles to profl. jours. Pres. Highland Park (N.J.) Bd. Health, 1971-72. Recipient numerous research grants. Fellow AAAS, Am. Chem. Soc., Inst. Food Technologists (pres. N.Y. sect. 1971-72, Food Scientist of Yr. N.Y. sect. award 1981, Nicholas Appert award 1990); mem. Am. Soc. Microbiology, Am. Soc. Quality Control, Am. Meat Sci. Assn., N.Y. Acad. Scis., N.J. Acad. Sci. Home: 415 Grant Ave Highland Park NJ 08904-2705 Office: Rutgers U Cook Coll Food Tech Inst Ctr for Advanced Food Tech New Brunswick NJ 08903

SOLBERG, NELLIE FLORENCE COAD, artist; b. Sault Ste. Marie, Mich.; d. Sanford and Mary (McDonald) Coad; m. Ingvald Solberg, Aug. 24, 1930; children: Jeanne Elaine Solberg Unruh, Walter Eugene, Kay Louise Solberg Link. BA, Minot State U., 1930; MA, N.D. State U., 1963; postgrad. Wash. State U., 1960, U. Wyo., 1964, St. Cloud Coll., 1971. Tchr. Bismarck Elem. Schs., N.D., 1954-63, art dir. high sch., 1963-72; instr. art Bismarck Jr. Coll., 1964-67; cons. Bismarck Art Assn. Galleries, 1973-79, State Capitol Galleries, 1973-78; dir. arts festivals including Statewide Religious Arts Festival, Bismarck, 1969-85, State Treas.'s Gallery, 1977, N.D. State Capitol, Bismarck, 1973-78; co-dir. Indian Art Show, Nat. Congress Am. Indians, Bismarck, 1963. Artist: (print) Prairie Rose for N.D. centennial, 1989; one-woman shows include Minot State Coll., 1963, Dickinson State Coll., 1964, Jamestown Coll., 1964, U. N.D., Valley City State Coll., Bismarck Jr. Coll., 1963, 65, 68, 69, N.D. State U., 1970, 74, Linha Gallery, Minot N.D., 1972, 74-77, Bank of N.D., 1972-74, 76-77, Elan Gallery, 1982; exhibited in group shows at Gov. John Davis Mansion, 1960, Concordia Coll., Moorhead, Minn., 1965, N.D. Capitol, 1968, 69, Internat. Peace Gardens, 1969, Gov. William Guy Mansion, 1971, Gov. George Sinner Mansion, 1991. Mem. Indian Culture Found., 1964—, Civic Music Assn., 1942-89; works included in numerous pvt. collections U.S., Can., Europe; religious arts com. Conf. Chs., 1973; bd. dirs. Citizens for Arts, 1978-81; mem. The Statue of Liberty/Ellis Island Found., 1984-89. Recipient numerous awards including Gov.'s award for arts, 1977, Gov. Allen Olson award, 1982, Gov.'s award Bismarck Art Show, 1982, Dakota Northwestern Bank award, 1983, Dr. Shari Orser Purchase award Religious Arts Festival, 1984, William Murray award Religious Arts Festival, 1984, Mandan Art Assn. award, 1986, 18th ann. 3d prize weaving Festival of Arts, 1987, Dr. Cy Rinkel watercolor purchase award, 1987, Heritage Centennial Art award Heritage Arts, Inc., 1988; named N.D. Woman Artist of Yr., 1974, Heritage Centennial award, 1989; the New Visual Arts Gallery named the Children's Gallery in name of Nellie Solberg; Mem. Bismarck Arts and Galleries Assn. (membership com., mem. Gallery 522, mem. Visual Arts Ctr.), Bismarck Art Assn. (charter, Honor award 1960, pres. 1963-64, 71-72), Jamestown Art Assn., Linha Gallery (Minot), Nat. League Am. Pen Women (pres. N.D. 1964-66, pres. Medora br. 1972-74, treas. 1975-86), Mpls. Soc. Fine Arts, P.E.O. (pres. chpts. 1967-69), Bismarck Vets., Meml. Library (life), Soc. Preservation Gov.'s Mansion (charter, bd. dirs.), Women in the Arts Nat. Mus. (charter), Zonta, Order of Ea. Star, Sigma Sigma Sigma. Republican. Home: 925 N 6th St Bismarck ND 58501-3922

SOLBERG, RONALD LOUIS, investment manager, international economist; b. Madison, Wis., May 15, 1953; s. Carl Louis and Gladys Irene Evelyn (Oen) S.; m. Anna Maria Teresa Gorgol, May 16, 1983 (div. Aug. 1992). BA in Econs. with honors, U. Wis., 1975; MA, U. Calif., Berkeley, 1977, PhD, 1984. Country risk analyst Wells Fargo Bank, San Francisco, 1978-79; asst. v.p., economist Wells Fargo Ltd., London, 1979-81; cons. RAND Corp., Santa Monica, Calif., 1982-84; acting instr. econs. U. Calif., Berkeley, 1983; 1st v.p., portfolio risk policy mgr. Security Pacific Corp., L.A., 1984-92; internat. fin. cons., 1992-94; v.p., fixed-income credit rschr. Pacific Investment Mgmt. Co., 1994-95; v.p., head Asian econ. rsch. Chase Manhattan Bank, Hong Kong, 1995—; adj. asst. prof. U. So. Calif., L.A., 1985-92. Author: (monograph with G. Grossman) The Soviet Union's Hard-Currency Balance of Payments and Creditworthiness in 1985, 1983; (book) Sovereign Rescheduling: Risk and Portfolio Management, 1988, Country Risk Analysis, 1992; contbr. articles to profl. jours. Research fellow Inst. Internat. Studies, Berkeley, 1982-84. Mem. Am. Econ. Assn., Asia Soc., Nat. Assn. for Bus. Economists, Soc. for Internat. Devel. Avocations: fly fishing, cross-country skiing, squash, billiards. Home: Borrett Mansions Apt 6B, 9 Bowen Rd, Mid-levels, Hong Kong Hong Kong Office: Chase Manhattan Bank, One Exch Sq, 39/F Central, Hong Kong Hong Kong

SOLBERG, WINTON UDELL, history educator; b. Aberdeen, S.D., Jan. 11, 1922; s. Ole Alexander and Bertha Georgia (Tschappat) S.; m. Ruth Constance Walton, Nov. 8, 1952; children—Gail Elizabeth, Andrew Walton, Kristin Ruth. A.B. magna cum laude, U. S.D., 1943, LHD (hon.), 1987; student, Biarritz (France) Am. U., 1946; A.M., Harvard, 1947, Ph.D., 1954. Instr., then asst. prof. social scis. U.S. Mil. Acad., 1951-54; instr., then asst. prof. history Yale U., 1954-58; fellow Pierson Coll., 1955-58, Morse fellow, 1958; James Wallace prof. history Macalester Coll., 1958-62; vis. prof. U. Ill., 1961-62, assoc. prof. history, 1962, prof., 1967—, chmn. dept. history, 1970-72; research fellow Ctr. Study History of Liberty in Am., Harvard U., 1962-63; summer research scholar Henry E. Huntington Library, San Marino, Calif., 1959; dir. Coe Found. Am. Studies Inst., summers 1960-62; lectr., cons. Army War Coll., 1959-62; lectr. U.S. Command and Gen. Staff Sch., 1963-64; Fulbright lectr. Johns Hopkins U. Bologna, 1967-68, Moscow (USSR) State U., 1978, U. Calcutta India, 1993; vis. prof. Konan U., Kobe, Japan, 1981; USIA Lectr., Korea and Malaysia, 1985, Korea, 1992. Author: The Federal Convention and the Formation of the Union of the American States, 1958, The Constitutional Convention and the Formation of the Union, 1990, The University of Illinois, 1867-1894, 1968, Redeem the Time: The Puritan Sabbath in Early America, 1977, History of American Thought and Culture, 1983, Cotton Mather, The Christian Philosopher, 1994; also articles. Mem. Ill. Humanities Council, 1973-75; sec. Council on Study of Religion, 1981-85. Served to maj. inf. AUS, 1943-46, 51-54; lt. col. U.S. Army Res. Recipient Faculty Achievement award Burlington No. Found., 1986, Disting. Teaching award U. Ill. Coll. Liberal Arts and Scis., 1988; NEH sr. fellow, 1974-75; NSF research grantee, 1981-82. Mem. Am. Hist. Assn., So. Hist. Assn., Orgn. Am. Historians, Am. Studies Assn. (pres. Mid-Am. 1985-86), Am. Soc. Ch. History (pres. 1985-86), AAUP (chpt. pres. 1965-66, mem. council 1969-72, 1st v.p. 1974-76), Phi Beta Kappa. Episcopalian. Home: 8 Lake Park Rd Champaign IL 61821-7101 Office: U Ill History Dept Urbana IL 61801

SOLBRIG, INGEBORG HILDEGARD, German literature educator, author; b. Weissenfels, Germany, July 31, 1923; came to U.S., 1961, naturalized, 1966; d. Reinhold J. and Hildegard M.A. (Ferchland) S. Grad. in chemistry, U. Halle, Germany, 1948; BA summa cum laude, San Francisco State U., 1964; postgrad., U. Calif., Berkeley, 1964-65; MA, Stanford U., 1966, PhD in Humanities and German, 1969. Asst. prof. U. R.I., 1969-70, U. Tenn., Chattanooga, 1970-72, U. Ky., Lexington, 1972-75; assoc. prof. German U. Iowa, 1975-81, prof., 1981-93, prof. emerita, 1993—. Author: Hammer-Purgstall und Goethe, 1973; main editor Rilke Heute, Beziehungen und Wirkungen, 1975; translator, editor: (bilingual edit.) Reinhard Goering: Seeschlacht/Seabattle, 1977, Orient-Rezeption, 1995; contbr. numerous articles, revs. and transls. to profl. jours., chpts. to books. Mem. Iowa Gov.'s Com. on 300th Anniversary German-Am. Rels. 1683-1983, 1983. Recipient Hammer-Purgstall Gold medal Austria, 1974; named Ky. col., 1975; fellow Austrian Ministry Edn., 1968-69, Stanford U., 1965-66, 68-69; Old Gold fellow Iowa, 1977; Am. Coun. Learned Socs. grantee; German Acad. Exch. Svc. grantee, 1980; sr. faculty rsch. fellow in the humanities, 1983; NEH grantee, 1985; May Brodbeck fellow in the humanities, 1989; numerous summer faculty rsch. grants. Mem. MLA (life), Internat. Verein fur Germanishce Sprach und Lit. Wiss., Goethe Gesellschaft, Deutsche Schiller Gesellschaft, Am. Soc. for 18th Century Studies, Can. Soc. for 18th Century Studies, Goethe Soc. N.Am., Inc. (founding mem.), Internat. Herder Soc. Prin. Rsch. Interest: contact of eastern and western cultures. Avocations: English and western styles horseback riding, photography. Home: 1126 Pine St Iowa City IA 52240 *The circumstances of my life took me to many places and cultures. Despite the discord and problems plaguing many parts of this planet, let us not forget that it's the home of the human family, our home. Always remember: Life is, by definition, change.*

SOLDATOS, PAUL W., holding company executive; b. 1950. BA, U. Wis.; MBA, U. Pa. With Chase Manhattan Bank, N.Y.C., 1974-81, Mfrs. Hanover Bank, N.Y.C., 1981-88, Investcorp Internat. Inc., 1988—; with Saks Holding Inc., N.Y.C., now pres.; CEO Saks Holding Inc., London, Eng. Office: Saks Holdings Inc 280 Park Ave Fl 37W New York NY 10017-1216*

SOLDNER, PAUL EDMUND, artist, ceramist, educator; b. Summerfield, Ill.; s. Grover and Beulah (Geiger) S.; m. Virginia I. Geiger, June 15, 1947; 1 child, Stephanie. BA, Bluffton Coll., 1946; MA, U. Colo., 1954; MFA, L.A. County Art Inst., 1956; DFA (hon.), Westminster Coll., 1992. Tchr. art Medina (Ohio) County Schs., 1946-47; supr. art, asst. county supr. Wayne County Schs., Wooster, Ohio, 1951-54; tchr. adult edn. Wooster Coll., 1952-54; vis. asst. prof. ceramics Scripps Coll., 1957-66, prof., 1970-91, prof. emeritus, 1991—; prof. Claremont (Calif.) Grad. Sch., 1957-66, prof., 1970-92; prof. U. Colo., Boulder, 1966-67, U. Iowa, Iowa City, 1967-68; pres. Soldner Pottery Equipment, Inc., Aspen, Colo., 1956-77; mem. steering com. Internat. Sch. Ceramics, Rome, 1965-77; advisor Vols. for Internat. Assistance, Balt., 1966-75; craftsman, trustee Am. Craft Coun., N.Y.C., 1970-74, trustee emeritus, 1976-77; dir. U.S. sect. World Craft Coun., 1970-74; dir. Anderson Ranch Ctr. for Hand Art Sch., 1974-76; speaker 6th Internat. Ceramics Symposium Syracuse, 1989; participant Internat. Russian Artists Exchange Program, Riga, Latvia, 1989; cons. in field. Author: Kilns and Their Construction, 1965, Raku, 1964, Paul Soldner, A Retrospective View, 1991; contbr. articles to profl. jours.; subject of 5 films; 156 one-man shows including Cantini Mus. Modern Art, Marseille, France, 1981, Thomas Segal Gallery, Boston, 1982, Elements Gallery, N.Y., 1983, Louis Newman Gallery, L.A., 1985, Susan Cummins Gallery, Mill Valley, Calif., 1989, Great Am. Gallery, Atlanta, 1986, Patricia Moore Gallery, Aspen Colo., 1987, Coleg Prifysgol Cymru, Aberystwyth, Wales, 1987, Joan Hodgell Gallery, Sarasota, Fla., 1988, Esther Saks Gallery, Chgo., 1986, 88, El Camino Gallery Art, Toraance, Calif., 1987, San Antonio Art Ctr., San Angelo, Tex., 1988, traveling exhibit, 12 U.S. mus., 1992—; 335 group shows including Nelson-Atkins Mus., Kansas City, Mo., 1983, Los Angeles Mcpl. Art Gallery, 1984, 27th Ceramic Nat. Exhibition, Everson Mus. Art, Syracuse, N.Y., 1986, Victoria & Albert Mus., London, 1986, Chicago Internat. New Art Forms Exposition, 1986, Hanover Gallery, Syracuse, N.Y., 1987, L.A. County Mus. of Art, 1987, Crain/Wolov Gallery, Tulsa, 1987, Contem Crafts Gallery, Portland, Oreg., 1988, Oakland (Calif.) Art Mus., 1988, Munson Gallery, Santa Fe, 1988, Japanese Influence on Am. Ceramics, Everson Mus., Syracuse, N.Y., 1989, traveling retrospective, 1991-93; hon. vis. artist Shigaraki Ceramic Cultural Park, Japan, 1994; works in permanent collections, Nat. Mus. Modern Art, Kyoto, Japan, Victoria and Albert Mus., London, Smithsonian Instn., Washington, Los Angeles County Mus. Art, Oakland Art Mus., Everson Mus. Art, Syracuse Australian Nat. Gallery, Taipei Fine Arts Mus.; curator Mirror Images Exhibit, Craft Alliance Gallery, St. Louis, 1989. Served with U.S. Army, 1941-46. Decorated Purple Heart; grantee NEA, 1991, Louis Comfort Tiffany Found., 1966, 72, Nat. Endowment for Arts, 1976, Colo. Gov.'s award for the Arts & Humanities, 1975; voted one of Top Twelve Potters World-Wide, Ceramics Monthly mag., 1981; Scripps Coll. Faculty Recognition award, 1985; named Hon. Mem. Coun., Nat. Coun. on Edn. for Ceramic Arts, 1989. Fellow Collequim of Craftsmen of the U.S.; mem. Internat. Acad. Ceramics, Nat. Coun. on Edn. for Ceramic Arts. Originator Am. Raku philosophy and techniques in ceramics. Home: PO Box 90 Aspen CO 81612-0090 also: 743 W Baseline Rd Claremont CA 91711

SOLDO, BETH JEAN, demography educator, researcher; b. Binghamton, N.Y., Sept. 30, 1948; d. Frank E. and Ruth E. (Dayton) S.; m. T. Peter Bridge, Sept. 20, 1975. BA, Fordham U., 1970; MA, Duke U., 1973, PhD, 1977. Asst. dir. Ctr. Demographic Studies Duke U., Durham, N.C., 1974-77; sr. rsch. scholar Ctr. Population Rsch. Georgetown U., Washington, 1977, sr. rsch. fellow Kennedy Inst. Ethics, 1978—, assoc. prof. demography, 1985-92, prof., 1992—, dept. chair, 1986-95; cons. White House Conf. on Aging, Washington, co-investigator 1990—, U. Mich. Health and Retirement Survey, Survey Asset and Health Dynamics of Oldest-Old; mem. com. on population NRC/NAS, 1992—. Co-author: (with R.J. Struyk) Improving the Elderly's Housing: A Key to Preserving the Nation's Housing Stock and Neighborhoods, 1980; contbr. articles to profl. jours. and chpts. in books. Grantee Atlantic Richfield Found., 1984, Commonwealth Fund, 1984-85, Retirement Rsch. Found., 1986-88, competitive grantee Nat. Inst. on Aging, 1986—. Fellow Gerontol. Soc. Am.; mem. Am. Sociol. Assn., Population Assn. Am. (bd. dirs. 1990-92, chair pub. affairs com. 1995—). Office: Georgetown U Dept Demography 233 Poulton Washington DC 20057

SOLE, MICHAEL JOSEPH, cardiologist; b. Timmins, Ont., Can., Mar. 5, 1940; s. Fred and Lillian Sole; m. Susan Karen Samuels, May 26, 1964; children: David Frederick, Leslie Meredith. BSc, U. Toronto, Ont., Can., 1962, MD, 1966. Cert. Coll. Physicians and Surgeons Ont.; diplomate Am. Bd. Internal Medicine. Rotating intern, jr. asst. resident, sr. asst. resident in internal medicine Toronto Gen. Hosp., 1966-69; cardiology fellow cardiovascular rsch. inst. U. Calif., San Francisco, 1969-71; cardiology fellow Peter Bent Brigham Hosp., Boston, 1971-73, jr. assoc. medicine, 1973-74; rsch. assoc. MIT, Cambridge, 1973-74; instr. medicine Harvard Med. Sch., 1973-74; from asst. to assoc. prof. medicine U. Toronto, 1974-83, prof. medicine and physiology, 1983, mem. staff inst. med. sci., 1978—, dir. cardiology rsch., 1987-89, dir. centre cardiovascular rsch., 1989—; staff cardiologist Toronto Hosp., 1974-89, dir. non-invasive cardiology, 1974-79, dir. cardiology rsch., 1979-89, dir. divsn. cardiology, 1989—, dir. cardiovascular program, 1992-93, dir. cardiac centre, 1993—; vis. prof. Harvard U., 1975, NIH, Bethesda, Md., 1981, U. B.C., 1982, 91, 92, Capital Med. Sch. and Beijing Hosp., 1985, U. Tokyo, 1992, others; mem. Can. Govt. Task Force Diagnostic Ultrasound, 1976-78; vice-chmn. econs. com. dept. medicine Toronto Gen. Hosp., 1977, chmn., 1978, 79, chmn. emeritus, 1980, mem. various coms., 1981—, chmn. cardiology rsch. com., 1988-89, mem. cardiovascular collaborative practice group, 1989-92; rsch. assoc. Ont. Heart Found., 1979-89; assoc. rsch. inst. pediatrics Hosp. Sick Children, Toronto, 1979—; mem. med. staff Mt. Sinai Hosp., Toronto, 1979—; mem. adv. bd. Merck Pharms., 1983—, Boots Pharms., 1992-93; mem. Health Rsch. and Devel. Coun., Province of Ont., 1983-86, mem. exec. com., 1984-86; Levesque lectr. Montreal Heart Inst., 1984; mem. cardiovascular panel Med. Rsch. Coun. Can., 1985-87; mem. heart and blood vessel rsch. adv. com. Toronto Hosp., 1986-89; chmn. cardiovascular rsch. adv. com. faculty medicine U. Toronto, 1986-87, mem. various coms., 1987—, chmn. rsch. com. dept. medicine, 1987-88, mem. rsch. adv. bd., 1989—, chair life scis. com., 1990-92, chair decanal promotions com. faculty medicine, 1992-94; mem. exec. com. Centre Cardiovascular Rsch., 1988—, chmn. sci. com., 1989—, mem. exec. com. cardiovascular clin. rsch. lab., 1992—, chmn. rsch. com., 1992—; Pfizer vis. fellow Clin. Rsch. Inst., Montreal, 1988; mem. sr. adv. com. Toronto Western Hosp., 1989-90; Katz vis. prof. U. Chgo., 1989; mem. provincial working group cardiovascular svcs. Ministry of Health, 1990-91, mem. ctrl. east region cardiovascular patient care mgmt. group, 1990-91; mem. trial devel. com. diabetes atherosclerosis intervention study WHO and Fournier Pharms., 1991-93, mem. trial exec. com., 1993—; mem. Joint Med. Rsch. Coun. Can./Pharm. Mfrs. Assn. Can. Adv. Com. Sci., 1993; mem. organizing coms. various sci. meetings; presenter in field. Mem. editl. bd. Can. Jour. Cardiology, 1988-94, Index and Revs. Congestive Heart Failure, 1988-90, Hypertension Can., 1988-90, European Jour. Pharmacology, 1992—, Cardiosci., 1993, Jour. Heart Failure, 1994—, Circulation, 1996—, Jour. Molecular Medicine, 1996—; mem. internat. editl. bd. Cardiology Digest, 1992—; reviewer Can. Jour. Cardiology, New Eng. Jour. Medicine, European Jour. Pharmacology, others; contbr. chpts. to books and articles to profl. jours.; patentee Bis Adducts of Tertiary Alcohols and Discyanates. Grantee Heart & Stroke Found. Ont., 1969—, Med. Rsch. Coun. Can., 1982-92; Ivan Smith Rsch. fellow U. Toronto, 1964, Hunter fellow Ont. Heart Found., 1973; Walter Watkins scholar U. Toronto, 1962. Fellow Am. Coll. Cardiology (abstract reviewer 1989, 91), Royal Coll. Physicians and Surgeons; mem. Am. Soc. Clin. Investigation, Assn. Am. Physicians, Am. Heart Assn. (fellow couns. clin. cardiology, hypertension, circulation and basic sci., mem. exec., basic sci. coun. 1986-89, mem. Katz prize selectionSoc. Clin. Investigation, Can. Cardiovascular Soc. (mem. young investigators award panel 1982-84, mem. student presentation award com. 1988-90, mem. nat. task force cardiovascular sci. 1992-93, Ann. Rsch. award 1975, Rsch. Achievement award 1989), Heart and Stroke Found. Can. (mem. sci. rev. bd. 1976-79, vice-chmn. 1980-83, chmn. hypertension and cardiovascular pharmacology panel 1982-83, chmn. molecular biology, biochemistry, pathology panel 1989-90), Can. Med. Assn. (mem. coun. 1982-87), Am. Fedn. Clin. Rsch., Ont. Med. Assn. (alt. del. Toronto Gen. Hosp. bd. 1988-90), Heart and Stroke Found. Ont. (mem. med. rsch. com. 1978-81, bd. dirs. 1986-92, mem. fin. com. 1986-90, mem. corp. rels. com. 1990-92, mem. rsch. policy com. 1991-93, Disting. Rsch. prof. 1989-96, Murray Robertson Meml. lectr. 1989), Internat. Soc. Heart Rsch. (exec. Am. sect. 1979-88), Banting Rsch. Found. (hon. sec.-treas. 1979-81), Gairdner Found. (mem. rev. panel 1979-94), Alpha Omega Alpha. Office: Toronto Hosp Eaton North 13-208, 200 Elizabeth St, Toronto, ON Canada M5G 2C4

SOLECKI, R. STEFAN, anthropologist, educator; b. Bklyn., Oct. 15, 1917; s. Kazimierz John and Mary (Tarnawski) S.; m. Rose Muriel Lilien, June 24, 1955; children—John Irwin, William Duncan. B.Sc., City Coll. N.Y., 1941; M.A., Columbia, 1950, Ph.D. in Anthropology, 1958. Archaeologist Smithsonian Instn., 1948-54; archaeol. asst. anthropology Columbia U., N.Y.C., 1954-55, mem. faculty, 1959-88, prof. anthropology, 1965-88, prof. emeritus, 1988—, chmn. dept., 1975-78; adj. prof. dept. anthropology Tex. A&M Univ., College Station, 1989—; assoc. curator old world U.S. Nat. Mus., 1957-59; archael. expdns. to Alaska, 1949, 61, Iraq, 1950-51, 53, 56-57 (field dir.), 60, 78, Sudanese Nubia, 1961, Turkey, 1963, Syria, 1963, 64, 65, 88, 89, Iran, 1968, Lebanon, 1969-73, France, 1975, Ea., Midwestern and Western U.S.; collaborator in archaeology Smithsonian Instn., 1953; cons. UNESCO, 1959. Served with AUS, 1943-45. Fulbright scholar, Iraq, 1952-53; William Bayard Cutting travelling fellow Columbia, 1956-57; Fulbright-Hays faculty research awardee Syria, 1980-81; Fulbright fellow, Iraq, 1988-89. Fellow Am. Anthrop. Assn., Arctic Inst. Am., N.Y. Acad. Scis. (chmn. anthropology sect. 1977-79); mem. N.Y. Archaeol. Assn. (pres. 1960-62), N.Y. Oriental Club (pres. 1965), Profl. Archeologists of N.Y.C. (pres. 1980-81), Soc. Archaeology, Am. Schs. Oriental Research (assoc. trustee 1969-71), Prehistoric Soc., Deutsches Archaeologisches Inst., Soc. Préhistorique Français, Archaeol. Inst. Am. (exec. com. 1968-70), Assn. Field Archaeology (pres. 1972-74). Home: 500 Crescent Dr Bryan TX 77801-3713 Office: Tex A&M Univ Dept Anthropology College Station TX 77843

SOLENDER, ROBERT LAWRENCE, financial, newsprint manufacturing executive; b. Rochester, N.Y., Sept. 1, 1923; s. Samuel S. and Catherine (Goldsmith) S.; m. Ellen Van Raalte Karelsen, Nov. 25, 1948; children: Elizabeth, Jefferson, Katherine. BA, Oberlin Coll., 1943. Asst. to pres. Craven & Hedrick, Inc., N.Y.C., 1946-49; with Dallas Times Herald, 1949-75, v.p., advt. dir., 1964-69, v.p., gen. mgr., 1969-75; prin. Robert L. Solender & Assocs., Dallas, 1975—; mng. ptnr. The Devonshire Co., Dallas, 1978-95; vice chmn. Southland (Tex.) Newsprint LLC, 1996—; interim chmn., CEO, AccuBanc Mortgage Corp., 1992. Pres. Dallas Child Guidance Clinic, 1956, Dallas Assn. Mental Health, 1958, Hope Cottage Children's Bur., 1973—; bd. dirs. Dallas Theatre Center, Child Care Assn. Met. Dallas; trustee Southwestern Med. Found.; mem. adv. council Communities Found. of Tex.; assoc. Dallas Mus. Art; bd. dirs., mem. exec. com. Dallas County United Way, 1973. Served to lt. USNR, 1944-46, PTO. Mem. Dallas C. of C., Park City Club, Masons. Home: 9131 Devonshire Dr Dallas TX 75209-2411 Office: 5600 W Lovers Ln Ste 300 Dallas TX 75209-4319

SOLENDER, SANFORD, social worker; b. Pleasantville, N.Y., Aug. 23, 1914; s. Samuel and Catharine (Goldsmith) S.; m. Ethel Klonick, June 19, 1935; children: Stephen, Peter, Ellen, Susan. BS, NYU, 1935; MS, Columbia U., 1937. Dir. activities Neighborhood House, Bklyn., 1935-36; asst. headworker Bronx House, N.Y., 1936-39; headworker Madison House, N.Y.C., 1939-42; exec. dir. Coun. Ednl. Alliance, Cleve., 1942-48; dir. bur. pers. and tng., also dir. Jewish community ctr. divsn. Nat. Jewish Welfare Bd., N.Y.C., 1948-60, exec. v.p. bd., 1960-70; exec. v.p. Fedn. Jewish Philanthropies N.Y., 1970-81, exec. cons., 1982-86; exec. v.p. United Jewish Appeal Fedn. Campaign, 1975-81; past pres. Nat. Conf. Jewish Communal Svc.; past chmn. planning com. Internat. Conf. Jewish Communal Svc.; chmn. Task Force on N.Y.C. Crisis, 1976-81. Contbr. articles to profl. jours., chpts. in books. Mem. Mt. Vernon Bd. Edn., 1953-58, pres., 1957-58, chmn. sec. HEW's ad hoc. com. to study fed. govt. social welfare programs, 1961; adv. coun. pub. welfare HEW, 1963-65; mem. Gov. Hugh Carey's Task Force on Human Svcs., N.Y. State, 1975; bd. dirs. Lavanburg Corner House, Herman Muehlstein Found.; adv. bd. Brandeis U., Hornstein Program in Jewish Communal Svc.; mem. Md. East Watch, Am.'s Watch coms. bds., Nat. Found. for Jewish Culture, 1985—, Jewish Mus., 1982—, Nat. Jewish Ctr. for Learning and Leadership, 1984—. Named Most Disting. Citizen of Mt. Vernon, 1960; recipient Joseph E. Kappel award Nat. Conf. Jewish Communal Svc., 1968, Florence G. Heller award Nat. Jewish Welfare Bd., 1972. Mem. Nat. Assn. Jewish Ctr. Workers (past pres.), Nat. Conf. Social Welfare (past pres.). Home: 1935 Gulf of Mexico Dr Seaplace G7-107 Longboat Key FL 34228 Office: 130 E 59th St New York NY 10022-1302

SOLENDER, STEPHEN DAVID, philanthropic organization executive; b. N.Y.C., Feb. 25, 1938; s. Sanford L. and Ethel (Klonick) S.; m. Elsa Adelman, June 5, 1960; children: Michael, Daniel. BA, Columbia U., 1960, MS, 1962. Dir. community ctrs., community orgn. and fundraising Am. Jewish Joint Distbn. Com., Geneva, 1969-75, dir. svcs. Muslim and Arab countries, 1969-75; dir. social planning and budgeting Assoc. Jewish Charities and Welfare Fund, Balt., 1975-79, pres., 1979-86; exec. v.p. United Jewish Appeal-Fedn. Jewish Philanthropies N.Y. Inc., N.Y.C., 1986—; mem. profl. adv. com. Brandeis U. Hornstein Ctr., Boston, 1982—; mem. health policy forum United Hosp. Fund, N.Y.C., 1987—; mem. presdl. coun., founding chmn. Human Svcs. Coun. N.Y.C., 1990-93; pres. World Coun. Jewish Communal Svc., 1994—; co-chair Human Svcs. Action Group. Bd. dirs. Jill Fox Meml. Fund, Balt., 1979-86, JCC Assn. N.A., 1984-92; bd. govs. Wurzweiler Sch. Social Work, N.Y.C., 1987—; mem. City of N.Y. Man. Boro Com., United Negro Coll. Fund, 1991—; pres. Internat. Conf. of Jewish Communal Svc., 1994—; mem. nat. adv. bd. Balt. Inst. for Jewish

Communal Svc., 1995—. Office: UJA-Fedn NY 130 E 59th St New York NY 10022-1302

SOLERI, PAOLO, architect, urban planner; b. Turin, Italy, June 21, 1919; came to U.S., 1947; m. Corolyn Woods, 1949 (dec. 1982); children: Kristine, Daniela. D.Arch., Turin Poly., 1946; hon. doctorates, Dickinson Coll., Moore Coll. Art, Ariz. State U. Fellowship with Frank Lloyd Wright, Taliesin West, Ariz., 1947-49; pvt. practice Turin and So., Italy, 1950-55; founder Cosanti Found., Scottsdale, Ariz. Major works include Dome House, Cave Creek, Ariz., 1956, Mesa City project, 1958-61, Outdoor Theatre, Inst. Am. Indian Arts, Santa Fe, 1966, Arcosanti (cmty. for 5,000 people), nr. Cordes Junction, ARiz., 1970—, Paolo Soleri Amphitheatre, Glendale Cmty. Coll., 1995, Minds for History Inst., 1986, Via Deliziosa (NEA grantee), 1987; exhbns., Mus. Modern Art, N.Y.C., 1961, Brandeis U., Waltham, Mass., 1964, Corcoran Gallery, Washington, 1970, Space for Peace, 1985, also on tour, Xerox Ctr., Rochester, N.Y., 1976, Space for Peace Exhgn. at NAD and Pacific Design Ctr., San Diego, 1989, Architecture for the Plant Earth and Beyond, Scottsdale Ctr. for the Arts, 1993; collection Howe Architecture Libr., Ariz. State U., Tempe; author 7 books. Recipient Craftsmanship medal AIA, 1963, Silver medal Academie d'Architecture in Paris, 1984, Gold medal World Biennale of Architecture, Sofia, Bulgaria, Utopis award Univ. di Bologna, 1989; Graham Found. fellow, 1962; Guggenheim Found. grantee, 1964-67. Address: Cosanti Found 6433 Doubletree Rd Scottsdale AZ 85253

SOLES, ADA LEIGH, former state legislator, government advisor; b. Jacksonville, Fla., May 19, 1937; d. Albert Thomas and Dorothy (Winter) Wall; B.A., Fla. State U., 1959; m. James Ralph Soles, 1959; children—Nancy Beth, Catherine. Mem. New Castle County Library Adv. Bd., 1975-80, 95—, chmn., 1975-77; chmn. Del. State Library Adv. Bd., 1975-78; mem. Del. State Ho. Reps., 1980-92; sr. advisor Gov. of Del., 1993-94; mem. U. Del. Libr. Assocs. Bd., 1995—. Adminstrv. asst. U. Del. Commn. on Status of Women, 1976-77; acad. advisor U. Del. Coll. Arts and Scis., 1977-92. Mem. LWV (state pres. 1978-80), Phi Beta Kappa, Phi Kappa Phi, Mortar Bd., Alpha Chi Omega. Episcopalian.

SOLES, WILLIAM ROGER, insurance company executive; b. Whiteville, N.C., Sept. 16, 1920; s. John William and Margaret (Watts) S.; m. Majelle Marrene Morris, Sept. 22, 1956 (dec. 1993); children: William Roger, Majelle Janette. B.S. in Commerce, U. N.C., 1947, postgrad., 1956; LLD, Campbell U., 1981. With Jefferson Standard Life Ins. Co., Greensboro, N.C., 1947—, v.p., mgr. securities dept., 1962-64, asst. to pres., 1964-66, exec. v.p., mgr. securities dept., 1966, pres., also dir., 1967-86; chmn., pres., chief exec. officer Jefferson-Pilot Life Ins. Co.; retired, 1993; chmn., pres. Jefferson-Pilot Corp., retired, 1993. Trustee, past chmn. High Point U.; past chmn. Wesley Long Community Hosp.; trustee, past chmn. Ind. Coll. Fund N.C.; past pres. Bus. Found. of N.C.; bd. dirs. N.C. Ins. Edn. Found. Served with USAAF, 1941-45. Mem. N.C. Citizens for Bus. and Industry (past chmn.), Am. Council Life Ins. (past chmn., dir.), Beta Gamma Sigma. Club: Greensboro Country. Home: 604 Kimberly Dr Greensboro NC 27408-4914 Office: Jefferson-Pilot Corp PO Box 21008 Greensboro NC 27420-1008

SOLET, MAXWELL DAVID, lawyer; b. Washington, May 15, 1948; s. Leo and Pearl (Rose) S.; m. Joanne Marie Tolksdorf, Sept. 27, 1970; children: David Marc, Paul Jacob. AB, Harvard U., 1970, JD, 1974. Bar: Mass. 1974, U.S. Tax Ct. 1976, U.S. Ct. Claims 1976, U.S. Supreme Ct. 1976. Assoc. Gaston Snow & Ely Bartlett, Boston, 1974-79, Mintz, Levin, Cohn, Ferris, Glovsky & Popeo, P.C., Boston, 1979-82; ptnr. Mintz, Levin, Cohn, Ferris, Glovsky & Popeo, P.C., 1982—. Mem. ABA, Mass. Bar Assn., Boston Bar Assn. (chmn. tax sect. 1987-89), Nat. Assn. Bond Lawyers (mem. steering com. bond atty.'s workshop 1992-95). Home: 15 Berkeley St Cambridge MA 02138-3409 Office: Mintz Levin Cohn Ferris Glovsky & Popeo PC One Financial Ctr Boston MA 02111

SOLGANIK, MARVIN, real estate executive; b. Chgo., Nov. 7, 1930; s. Harry and Dora (Fastoff) S.; m. Judith Rosenberg, Sept. 11, 1960; children: Randall, Janet, Robert. B.B.A., Western Res. U., 1952. Real estate broker Cleve., 1950-65, Herbert Laronge Inc., Cleve., 1965-68; sr. v.p. real estate Revco D.S., Inc., Twinsburgh, Ohio, 1968—, corp. dir., 1974—; guest lectr. Cleve. State U., Case Western Res. U., Cuyahoga Community Coll., Ohio No. U., Cleve. Real Estate Bd. Vol. jewish Welfare Fund, Shaker heights, Ohio; chmn. capital and budget coms. Jewish Fedn.; chmn. Agnon Sch. Bdlg. Com.; bd. dirs. Bellfair-J.C.B.-Home for Emotionally Disturbed Children. Recipient Appreciation award Am. Soc. Real Estate Appraisers, Akron-Cleve. chpt., 1971. Mem. Nat. Assn. Corp. Real Estate Officers, Internat. Council Shopping Ctrs. Office: D S Revco 1925 Enterprise Pky Twinsburg OH 44087-2207

SOLHEIM, JAMES EDWARD, church executive, journalist; b. Thief River Falls, Minn., May 16, 1939; s. Edward and Verna (Sagmoen) S. BA, St. Olaf Coll., 1961; MDiv, Luther Sem., 1968; MS in Journalism, Columbia U., 1975. Admissions counselor St. Olaf Coll., 1962-67; editor Am. Luth. Ch., Mpls., 1968-74; dir. communications St. Peter's Ch., N.Y.C., 1975-77; editor A.D. mag., N.Y.C., 1977-83, Luth. Ch. in Am., Phila., 1984-88; dir. communications Episcopal Diocese Mass., Boston, 1988-89; news dir. Episcopal Ch. in U.S.A., N.Y.C., 1989—. Bush Found. fellow, 1974. Mem. Assn. Ch. Press (v.p. 1987-89, Merit award 1969-89, Writing fellow 1969), Religious Pub. Rels. Coun. (v.p.), St. Olaf Alumni Assn. (pres.), Sigma Delta Chi. Democrat. Lutheran. Avocation: photography. Home: 168 W 100th St New York NY 10025-5145 Office: Episcopal Ch in USA 815 2nd Ave New York NY 10017-4503

SOLHEIM, WILHELM GERHARD, II, anthropologist, educator; b. Champaign, Ill., Nov. 19, 1924; s. Wilhelm Gerhard and Ragnhild Risty S.; m. Ludy Montenegro, Sept. 10, 1973; children: Gary, Kristina, Valerie, Lisa, Mei Li, Siri, Edwin. Student, U. Wis., 1943, U. Chgo., 1943-44; BS, U. Wyo., 1947; MA, U. Calif., 1949; PhD, U. Ariz., 1959. Mus. preparator Mus. Anthropology, U. Calif., Berkeley, 1947-49; research assoc. Mus. Archaeology and Ethnology, U. Philippines, 1950-54; lectr. U. East, Manila, 1950-52; provincial public affairs officer USIA, Manila, 1953-54; asst. prof. anthropology Fla. State U., Talahassee, 1960-61; mem. faculty dept. anthropology U. Hawaii, Honolulu, 1961—; prof. U. Hawaii, 1967-91, prof. emeritus, 1992—; asso. archaeologist Social Sci. Research Inst., 1963-67, archaeologist, 1967-70, editor, 1976-87; vis. prof. Inst. Advanced Studies, U. Malaya, Kuala Lumpur, Malaysia, 1979-80; v.p. R&D Transpacific Assocs., Guam, 1992; rsch. in Sarawak, The Philippines, 1983, Ea. Indonesia, 1990; dir. Ctr. for S.E. Asian Studies, U. Hawaii, 1986-89; bd. dirs. Austro-Tai Studies Inst., Guam, 1992—. Author: The Archaeology of Central Philippines, 1964, (with Avelino M. Legaspi and Jaime S. Neri), Archaeological Survey in Southeastern Mindanao, 1979; editor Asian Perspectives, 1957-91, Asian and Pacific Archaeology Series, 1967-91, History of Humanity Vol. I Prehistory and the Beginnings of Civilization, 1994; contbr. articles to profl. jours. Trustee Hawaii Found. for History and Humanities, 1969-74, 1st v.p., 1972, 2d v.p., 1974; bd. dirs. Balik Bahay, Inc., Honolulu, 1976-93, pres., 1977-93; mem. Hawaii Com. Humanities, 1978-79. With USAF, 1943-46. Fulbright grantee, 1958-59, 83, 90; NSF grantee, 1963-66, 69-72; NEH fellow, 1967-68; Ford Found. grantee, 1972, 75-76; Vis. Scholar Exchange Program fellow Com. on Scholarly Communication with Peoples Republic of China, 1986. Fellow Philippine Assn. Advancement Sci. (founding); mem. Siam Soc., Société des Etudes Indochinoises, Royal Asiatic Soc. (Malaysian br.), Burma Research Soc., Assam Sci. Soc., Indian Archaeol. soc., Far-Eastern Prehistory Assn. (pres. 1971-76), Indo-Pacific Prehistory Assn. (pres. 1976-80), Sigma Xi, Phi Kappa Phi, Phi Delta Theta. Office: U Hawaii Dept Anthropology 2424 Maile Way Honolulu HI 96822-2223

SOLIDUM, JAMES, finance and insurance counselor; b. Honolulu, Mar. 12, 1925; s. Narciso and Sergia (Yabo) S.; student U. Hawaii, 1949-50; m. Vickie Mayo, Aug. 14, 1954; children: Arlin James, Nathan Francis, Tobi John, Kamomi Teresa. BA, U. Oreg., 1953. Promotional salesman Tongg Pub. Co., 1953-54; editor Fil-Am. Tribune, 1954-55; master planning technician Fed. Civil Svc., 1955-57; publs. editor Hawaii Sugar Planters Assn., 1957; field agt. Grand Pacific Life Ins. Co., 1957-59, home office asst., 1959-60, supr., 1960-62, asst. v.p., 1962-64; propr. J. Solidum & Assos., Honolulu, 1964—; pres. Fin. Devel. Inst., 1967—; contbg. writer Paradise of Pacific Mag., 1957-58, Hawaii Agrl. Mag., 1957-58; gen. ptnr. R.Z. Limited Partnership, 1981—; v.p. Grand Pacific Life Ins. Co., 1983-90; bd. dirs. Hawaii Econ. Devel. Corp., 1982-89. Mem. adv. com. Honolulu dist. SBA, 1971-77; bd. advisors Philippine Consulate of Hawaii, 1959. Pres., Keolu Elem. P.T.A., 1960-62; mem. satisfaction com. Hawaii Visitors Bur., 1963-66; chmn. budget and rev. panel IV, Aloha United Fund, 1966-72, bd. dirs., 1971-77, 82-88, chmn. bd., 1984; mem. mgmt. svcs. com., 1977, mem. cen. com., 1977-82, chmn. budget and allocations com., 1982-84; chmn. Kamehameha Dist. fin. com. Aloha coun. Boy Scouts Am., 1966; vice chmn. Businessmen's Cancer Crusade, 1965; chmn. Operation Bayanihan, Hawaii Immigration Task Force, 1970; participant Oahu Housing Workshop, State of Hawaii, Hawaii chpt. HUD, 1970; mem. task force on housing and transp. Alternative Econ. Futures for Hawaii, 1973; chmn. Bicentennial Filipiniana, 1976; chmn. SBA Bicentennial Com., 1976; campaign chmn. State Rep. Rudolph Pacarro, 1964-68; mem. exec. com. Campaign for Reelection U.S. Senator Hiram L. Fong, 1970, Gov. William Quinn for U.S. Senate, 1976; Rep. candidate for Hawaii Ho. of Reps., 1972; mem. Rep. Citizens Task Force on Housing, 1973; trustee St. Louis Alumni Found., 1970—, Kuakini Med. Ctr., 1984-86, Palama Settlement, 1975-82, v.p., 1976, treas., 1980-82; bd. mgrs. Windward YMCA, 1964-67; bd. advisers St. Louis H.S., 1963-64; bd. govs. Goodwill Industries, 1964; bd. dirs. Children's Ctr., Inc., 1975-77, Hawaii Multi-Cultural Arts Ctr., 1977-81, treas., 1979; fin. fin. chmn. St. Stephen's Parish Coun., 1974—; bd. dirs. St. Louis Fine Arts Ctr., 1985-88. With U.S. Army, 1945-47. C.L.U. Recipient Man of Year award Filipino C. of C., 1965; cert. of merit Aloha United Fund, 1971; Wisdom mag. honor award, 1974; Outstanding Alumnus honor medal St. Louis High Sch., 1976. Mem. Hawaii State C. of C. (bd. dirs. 1964-67, chmn. legis. com. 1966-67, v.p. 1970, chmn. election judges 1971, mem. ad hoc com. bus.-youth rels. 1970), Filipino C. of C. (past pres. 1965, com. chmn.), Am. Soc. CLU, Honolulu Assn. Life Underwriters (bd. dirs. 1963-66, del. nat. conv. 1967, chmn. life underwriters tng. coun. 1962-67), Hawaii Estate Planning Coun., Hawaii Plantation Indsl. Editors Assn. (sec.-treas. 1957), St. Louis Alumni Assn. (bd. dirs. 1964—, chmn. fin. 1969-75, pres. 1976, treas. 1977—), Phi Kappa Sigma. Republican. Roman Catholic. Home: 2622 Waolani Ave Honolulu HI 96817-1362 Office: 225 Queen St Apt 12-a Honolulu HI 96813-4608

SOLIS, HILDA LUCIA, educational administrator, state legislator; b. Los Angeles, Oct. 20, 1957; d. Raul and Juana (Sequiera) S.; m. Sam H. Sayyad, June 26, 1982. BA in Polit. Sci., Calif. State Poly U., 179; MA in Pub. Adminstrn., U. So. Calif., 1981. Interpreter Immigration and Naturalization Service, Los Angeles, 1977-79; editor in chief Office Hispanic Affairs, The White House, Washington, 1980-81; mgmt. analyst Office Mgmt. and Budget, Washington, 1981-82; field rep. Office Assemblyman Art Torres, L.A., 1982; dir. Calif. Student Opportunity and Access, Whittier, 1982—; rep. 57th assembly dist. Calif. State Assembly, Sacramento, 1992—; elected state sen. 24th Dist., 1994-98; cons. South Coast Consortium, L.A., 1986—; mem. South Coast Ednl. Opportunity Pers. Consortium. Bd. dirs. Calif. Commn. on Status of Women, 1993—; corr. pres. Friendly El Monte (Calif.) Dem. Club, 1986—; mem. credentials com. Calif. Dem. Com., 1987-88; trustee Rio Hondo C.C., 1985—. Recipient Meritorious Svc. award Dept. Def., 1981, Young Careerist award El Monte Bus. and Profl. Women, 1987; fellow Nat. Edn. Inst., Kellogg Found., 1984-85. Mem. Western Assn. Ednl. Opportunity Pers. (sec. bd. dirs. 1986—), Comision Feminil de Los Angeles (bd. dirs. 1983-84, edn. chmn.), Women of Moose. Roman Catholic. Home: 11724 E Roseglen St El Monte CA 91732-1446 Office: Calif Student Opportunity and Access 9401 Painter Ave Whittier CA 90605-2729

SOLIS, JIM, state legislator, lawyer; b. Weslaco, Tex., July 7, 1963; s. Santiago Sr. and Maria (Cobarrubias) S. BBA, U. Tex.-Pan Am., Edinburg, 1985; JD cum laude, Thurgood Marshall Sch. Law, Houston, 1989. Ptnr. Law Office of Bello & Solis, Houston, 1989-90; assoc. Law Office of Albert Villegas, Brownsville, Tex., 1990-94; mem. Tex. Ho. of Reps., 1993—; pvt. practice law Harlingen, Tex., 1994—; mem. Tex. Pro Bono Legal Project, Brownsville, 1991—. Recipient Cert. of Appreciation, Tex. Assn. Pub. Employees, 1993, Meritorious awrd Tex. Assn. Chicanos in Higher Edn., 1993, others. Mem. State Bar Tex., Cameron County Bar Assn., Nat. Bar Assn., Mexican-Am. Bar Assn., Mexican-Am. Dems. of Tex. (cert. of honor 1993), Dem. Party Club, Tex. Young Dems., AFL-CIO, Phi Kappa Theta. Roman Catholic. Avocations: tennis, golf, hunting, fishing, music (playing the drums). Home: Rt 3 Box 207 Harlingen TX 78552 Office: 501 E Tyler Harlingen TX 78550

SOLIS, JORGE ANTONIO, federal judge; b. 1951. BA, McMurray Coll., 1973; JD, U. Tex., 1976. Clk. Indsl. Accident Bd., 1975-76; asst. criminal dist. atty. U.S. Attys. Office, 1976-81; with Moore & Holloway, 1981-82; criminal dist. atty. U.S. Attys. Office, 1983-87, spl. prosecutor narcotics task force, 1988; judge 350th Dist. Ct., 1989-91; fed. judge U.S. Dist. Ct. (no. dist.) Tex., 1991—. Bd. dirs. HRC Drug Abuse Treatment Ctr., Abilene, Tex., 1979—, pres. bd. dirs., 1982-83, Meals on Wheels, 1984—, Abilene (Tex.) Girls Home, 1985—; active Gov. Task Force on Drug Abuse, 1987—. Mem. State Bar Tex., Abilene Bar Assn. (past bd. dirs.), Abilene Young Lawyers Assn. (sec.-treas. 1977-78), Tex. Dist. and County Attys. Assn. Office: US Dist Ct 1100 Commerce St # 13F31 Dallas TX 75242-1027*

SOLIZ, JOSEPH GUY, lawyer; b. Corpus Christi, Tex., June 25, 1954; s. Oscar and Ola Mae (Trammell) S.; m. Juanita Solis, June 3, 1978; children: Lauren Michelle, Michael. BA with highest honors, S.W. Tex. State U., 1976; JD, Harvard U., 1979. Bar: Tex. 1979, U.S. Dist. Ct. (no. dist.) Tex. 1980, U.S. Ct. Appeals (5th cir.) 1980, U.S. Dist. Ct. (so. dist.) 1987. Atty. Gulf Oil Corp., Houston, 1979-81; assoc. Chamberlain, Hrdlicka, White, Johnson & Williams, Houston, 1981-85, ptnr., 1985-91; of counsel Brill, Sinex & Stephenson, 1991-92, Sinex & Stephenson, 1993—; v.p., gen. counsel, Golden Engring., Inc., 1992-93; pres. ECO Solutions, Inc., Houston, 1993—; adj. prof. South Tex. Coll. of Law, 1990-91; bd. dirs. Costal Water Authority, 1994-95. Bd. dirs. Wilde-West Recreation Club, Inc., 1988-89, Harris County Pvt. Industry Coun., 1989-93, Big Bros., Big Sisters of Houston, 1989-95, treas., 1992-93, High-Tech Carpets, Inc., 1993—; mem. exec. com. Harris County Dem. Party, 1988-92, 94—; dir. Houston Hispanic Forum, 1989-96, treas. 1992-95. Mem. ABA (natural resources sect.), Tex. Bar Assn., Hispanic Bar Assn. (dir. 1988-89, sec. 1989-90, treas. 1990-93), Houston Bar Assn., Houston Young Lawyers Assn. (Outstanding Com. Leader 1986-87, 87-88, 88-89, dir. 1988-89), Tex. Bd. Legal Specialization (cert. in oil, gas and mineral law), Jobs for Progress of Tex. Gulf Coast Inc. (dir. 1990-96, vice chmn. 1991-92, chmn. 1992-96), Houston Hispanic C. of C. (dir. 1989-90), Delta Tau Kappa, Alpha Chi, Pi Gamma Mu. Democrat. Roman Catholic. Home: 9406 Beverly Hill St Houston TX 77063-3908 Office: 9800 Richmond Ave Ste 320 Houston TX 77042-4519

SOLLENBERGER, HOWARD EDWIN, retired government official; b. N. Manchester, Ind., Apr. 28, 1917; s. Oliver Clark and Hazel (Coppock) S.; m. Agnes Hafner, Dec. 31, 1944; children—David Olaf, Roger Hafner (dec.), Zoe Karin. B.A., Manchester Coll., 1941, LL.D. (hon.), 1963. Relief adminstr. Brethern Services Com., also Am. Friends Service Com., N. China, 1938-40; engaged in civilian pub. service, 1941-44; orientation officer UNRRA, 1945-46; liaison officer UNRRA, Shanghai, China, 1946-47; with Fgn. Svc. Inst., State Dept., 1947-76; dir. Chinese lang. and area sch. Fng. Service Inst., State Dept., Peiping, China, 1947-50; asso. prof. Chinese Studies Fng. Service Inst., State Dept., Washington, 1950, 55; dean Fng. Service Inst., State Dept. (Sch. Lang. and Area Studies), 1956-65; acting dir. Fng. Service Inst., State Dept. (Inst.), 1965-66, 69-71, asso. dir., 1966-69, dir., 1971-76; cons. internat. edn., 1976—; mem. adv. com. lang. and area programs NDEA, 1962-64; adv. com. Center Applied Linguistics, 1959-62; adviser Georgetown U. Sch. Langs. and Linguistics, 1964-84; Unitarian-Universalist rep. Interfaith Action for Econ. Justice, 1977-88. Author: Read Chinese Script, 1949, Chinese Newspaper Syllabus, 1949, Documentary Chinese, 1949. Pres. McLean (Va.) PTA, 1960; v.p. Fairfax Unitarian Ch., 1961-62, 66-67; pres. Fairfax Meml.Soc., 1969-74; bd. dirs. No. Va. Meml. Soc., 1989-95. Recipient Superior Honor award Dept. State, 1964, John Jacob Rogers award, Dept. State, 1976, Svc. citation Brethren Health and Welfare Assn. Mem. MLA, Linguistics Soc. Am., Assn. Asian Studies, Tau Kappa Alpha. Home: 1287 Berry Pl Mc Lean VA 22102-1503

SOLLENDER, JOEL DAVID, management consultant, financial executive; b. N.Y.C., Nov. 11, 1924; s. Samuel and Flora (Blumenthal) S.; m. Dorothy Leaf, Aug. 6, 1958; children: Jeffrey D., Jonathan L. B.S., N.Y. U., 1946. C.P.A., N.Y. Staff auditor Ernst & Young, N.Y.C., 1946-50; with United Mchts. & Mfrs., Inc., N.Y.C., 1950-86; corp. contr. United Mchts. & Mfrs., Inc., 1977—, sr. v.p., 1980—, chief acctg. officer, 1976—, also bd. dirs., officer various subs., mem. mgmt. com. parent co., 1986-88; assoc. dir. N.Y. Hist. Soc., N.Y.C.; mem. adv. coun. to Office of Charities Registration Dept. State, N.Y. State, 1986-89; v.p. fin. Piedmont Industries, N.Y.C., 1989-90; exec. v.p., CFO Earthworm Inc., 1990-92; fin. mgmt. cons., 1992—. Served with U.S. Army, World War II. Decorated Combat Infantry Badge, Purple Heart with cluster, Prisoner of War medal. Mem. AICPA, N.Y. State Soc. CPAs (chief fin. officer com.), Am. Inst. Corp. Controllers. Clubs: Bailiwick (Greenwich, Conn.); Greenhaven Yacht (Rye).

SOLLID, FAYE EISING, volunteer; b. Milw., Aug. 31, 1913; d. George Walter and Jessie Belle (Davey) Eising; m. Erik Sollid, Aug. 1, 1936 (dec. Mar. 1977); 1 child, Jon Erik. BA in Journalism, U. Wis., 1936; postgrad., U. Denver, 1947. Asst. in basic communications U. Denver, 1947. Editor Am. Hindi cookbook for Am. Woman's Club New Delhi, 1956; mem. Clearwater (Fla.) Libr. Bd., 1981-89, liaison between Libr. Bd. and Friends of Libr. Bd., 1984-89; mem. Clearwater Beautification Com., 1989-92. Recipient Citation of Sincere Appreciation for pub. svc. as mem. libr. bd. 1981-89 Mayor City of Clearwater, 1989. Mem. AAUW, Internat. Graphoanalysis Soc., Nat. Mus. Women in Arts, Upper Pinellas African Violet Soc. (v.p. 1973-74, pres. 1974-75), Sovereign Colonial Soc. Ams. Royal Descent, Plantagenet Soc., Soc. Descs. Most Noble Order Garter, Order of Crown Charlemagne in U.S.A., Colonial Order of the Crown, Suncoast Magna Charta Dames (rec. sec. 1980-83), Nat. Soc. Colonial Dames XVII Century (v.p. 1983-85, 89-93). Avocations: genealogy, handwriting analysis.

SOLLIE, DIANN THORNTON, education educator, counselor; b. Jackson, Miss., Sept. 29, 1960; d. Jerry L. Thornton and Helen (Chambers) Taylor; m. William D. Sollie, Apr. 15, 1983; children: Steven, Caitlin. BS, U. So. Miss., 1981; MEd, Miss. State U., 1986; PhD Candidate, U. Ala., 1990—. Lic. profl. counselor, Miss. Field rep. Sigma Sigma Sigma Sorority, Woodstock, Va., 1981-82; police officer Meridian (Miss.) Police Dept., 1982-83; counselor Lauderdale County Juvenile Ctr., Meridian, 1983-86; program coord. Naval Air Sta. Family Svc. Ctr., Meridian, 1987-88; family counselor Laurelwood Ctr., Meridian, 1988-89; assoc. prof. U. So. Miss., Hattiesburg, 1988-92; program dir. Laurelwood Ctr., Meridian, 1992; prof. Meridian C.C., 1992—; cons. Laurelwood Ctr., Meridian, 1989-93; expert witness, Jackson, Miss., 1990-92; cons. Ala. Power, Tuscaloosa, 1991, City of Meridian, 1991. Contbr. articles to profl. jours. Exec. bd. mem. Boy Scouts Am., Meridian, 1992—; bd. dirs. Miss. Juvenile Justice Adv. Bd. State of Miss., 1984-88; faculty advisor Criminal Justice Assn., Meridian C.C., 1990—, faculty sponsor Internat. Studies Program, 1993—, faculty senate vice chair, 1993-94, chair, 1995—. Named Outstanding Young Educator of Yr. Jaycees, 1995. Mem. Soc. Police and Criminal Psychology (pres. 1992-93, v.p. 1991-92), Am. Counseling Assn., Miss. Criminal Justice Assn., Mid-South Sociol. Assn., Miss. Sociol. Assn., Ala. Sociol. Assn. Office: Meridian Community Coll 910 Highway 19 S Meridian MS 39301-8204

SOLLMAN, GEORGE HENRY, telecommunications company executive; b. Michigan City, Ind., Nov. 2, 1941; s. Henry Charles and Margaret Elisabeth (Gockel) S.; m. Maureen Tosh, July 12, 1968; children: Jennifer, Erich. Spl. student, MIT, 1965-66; BSEE, Northwestern U., 1964; MSEE, Northeastern U., 1967. Engring. dir. Honeywell Info. systems, Waltham, Mass., 1964-73; product line mgr. Control Data, Hawthorne, Calif., 1973-76; v.p., gen. mgr. Shugart/Xerox, Sunnyvale, Calif., 1976-84; spl. ptnr. Sand Hill Venture Group, Menlo Park, Calif., 1984; pres., chief exec. officer Centigram Corp., San Jose, Calif., 1985—; chmn. nat. bd. dirs. Am. Elec. Assn.; presdl. nomination Semicondr. Tech. Coun.; co-chmn. Alexis d'Toqueville Soc.; adv. coun. Joint Venture Silicon Valley. Patentee in field. Co-chmn. United Way of Santa Clara County. Mem. steering com. George Lucas Ednl. Found., Marin County. Home: 242 Polhemus Ave Atherton CA 94027-5439 Office: Centigram Corp 91 E Tasman Dr San Jose CA 95134-1618

SOLLORS, WERNER, English language, literature and American studies educator. Dr. phil., Freie Universität, Berlin, 1975. Wissenschaftlicher asst. and assistenzprofessor John F. Kennedy Inst. Freie Universität, Berlin; from asst. to assoc. prof. English and Comparative Lit. Columbia U.; Henry B. and Anne M. Cabot Prof. English Lit., prof. Afro-Am. studies Harvard U., Cambridge, Mass. Author: Amiri Baraka/LeRoi Jones: The Quest for a Populist Modernism, 1978, Beyond Ethnicity: Consent and Descent in American Culture, 1986; contbr.: Das amerikanische Drama der Gegenwart, 1976, The Harvard Encyclopedia of American Ethnic Groups, 1980, Reconstructing American Literary History, 1986, Columbia Literary History of the United States, 1988, Critical Terms for Literary Study, 1990, Looking Inward, Looking Outward: From the 1920s through the 1940s, 1990, Nationale und kulturelle Identität: Studien zur Entwicklung des kollektiven Bewusstseins in der Neuzeit, 1991, Immigrants in Two Democracies: French and American Experience, 1992, Intersecting Boundaries: The Theatre of Adrienne Kennedy, 1992, Il razzismo e le sue storie, 1992, Swedes in America: Intercultural and Interethnic Perspectives on Contemporary Research, 1993, Multiculturalism and the Canon of American Culture, 1993, Configurations de l'ethnicité aux États-Unis, 1993, History & Memory in African-American Culture, 1994, Thematics: New Approaches, 1995, Neither Black Nor White Yet Both: Thematic Approaches to Interracial Literature, 1996, New Essays on Henry Roth's Call It Sleep, 1996; editor: A Bibliographic Guide to Afro-American Studies, 1972, A Bibliographic Guide to Afro-American Studies Supplement I, 1974; co-editor: Bibliographie amerikanistischer Veröffentlichungen in der DDR bis 1968, 1976, Varieties of Black Experience at Harvard, 1986, The Invention of Ethnicity, 1989, The Life Stories of Undistinguished Americans As Told by Themselves, 1990, The Return of Thematic Criticism, 1993, Cane, 1993, Blacks at Harvard: A Documentary History of African-American Experience at Harvard and Radcliffe, 1993, The Black Columbiad: Defining Moments in African-American Literature and Culture, 1994, Ethnic Theory: A Classical Reader, 1996, The Promised Land, 1996; contbr. articles to profl. jours. John Simon Guggenheim Meml. fellow, Andrew W. Mellon faculty fellow Harvard U.; recipient Constance Rourke prize Am. Studies Assn., 1990. Office: Harvard U 11 Prescott St Cambridge MA 02138-3902

SOLLOWAY, C. ROBERT, forest products company executive; b. Vancouver, B.C., Can., May 19, 1935; s. Harold Eugene and Elva Merle (McAllister) S.; m. Ila Noreen Kelly. B in Commerce, U. B.C., 1959, LLB, 1960. Bar: Can., 1961. Asst. to exec v.p., asst. to pres. West Coast Transmission Co. Ltd., Vancouver, 1962-68; corp. counsel, asst. sec. Weldwood of Can. Ltd., Vancouver, 1968-73, gen. counsel, sec., 1973-75, v.p., gen. counsel, sec., 1975—. Mem. Law Soc. B.C., Can. Bar Assn., Vancouver Bar Assn. Anglican. Clubs: Vancouver; Vancouver Lawn Tennis and Badminton. Office: Weldwood of Can Ltd, 1055 W Hastings PO Box 2179, Vancouver, BC Canada V6B 3V8

SOLMAN, JOSEPH, artist; b. Vitebsk, Russia, Jan. 25, 1909; came to U.S. 1912; s. Narciso and Rose (Peskin) S.; m. Ruth Romanofsky, Nov. 19, 1908; children: Paul, Ronni. Nat. Acad. of Design, 1927-30. Nat. Academician 1967. Easel painter WPA, N.Y.C., 1935-41; pvt. art instr. N.Y.C., 1951-66; art instr. CUNY, N.Y.C., 1967-75; artist N.Y.C., 1935—. Exhibitions: Retrospective at Phillips Mem. Mus., Washington, 1949, Retrospective at Wichita (Kansas) Mus. of Art, 1984; author: books, Joseph Solman, Crown Publishers, 1966, Monotypes of Joseph Solman, Da Capo Press, 1977; artist: several paintings. Recipient of several awards for paintings and portraits including the Nat. Inst. of Arts & Letters, 1961, and 8 prizes from the Nat. Acad. of Design Annuals, 1967-89. Mem. Nat. Acad. of Design (treas. 1979-85), Fedn. of Modern Painters & Sculptors (exec. bd. 1968-89); fellow (life) Art Student League. Home: 156 2nd Ave New York NY 10003-5716

SOLMSSEN, PETER, academic administrator; b. Berlin, Nov. 1, 1931. A.B., Harvard U., 1952; J.D., U. Pa., 1959. Atty. Ballard, Spahr, Andrews & Ingersoll, Phila., 1959-60; with U.S. Fgn. Service, 1961; vice consul Singapore, 1962-63; asst. to under sec. of state, 1963-65; 2d sec. Rio de Janeiro, 1965-67; Cultural attache U.S. Dept. State, Sao Paulo, Brazil, 1967-70; adviser on arts Washington, 1974-80, dep. ambassador at large for cultural affairs, 1981-83; pres. Phila. Coll. Art, 1983-87, U. of the Arts, Phila., 1987—. One-man photography exhbns. include: Mus. Art, Sao Paulo. Author and illustrator. Clubs: Philadelphia; Century Assn. Office: Univ Arts Office of Pres Broad And Pine St Philadelphia PA 19104

SOLNIT, ALBERT JAY, physician, commissioner, educator; b. Los Angeles, Aug. 26, 1919; s. Benjamin and Bertha (Pavin) S.; m. Martha Benedict, 1949; children—David, Ruth, Benjamin, Aaron. B.A. in Med. Scis., U. Calif., 1940, M.A. in Anatomy, 1942, M.D., 1943; M.A. (hon.), Yale U., 1964. Rotating intern L.I. Coll. Hosp., 1944, asst. resident in pediatrics, 1944-45; resident in pediatrics and communicable diseases U. Calif. div. San Francisco Hosp., 1947-48; asst. resident dept. psychiatry and mental hygiene Yale U., 1948-49, sr. resident, 1949-50, fellow in child psychiatry, 1950-52, instr. pediatrics and psychiatry, 1952-53, asst. prof., 1953-60, assoc. prof., 1960-64, prof., 1964-70, Sterling prof., 1970—, dir. Child Study Ctr., 1966-83; commr. dept. mental health and addiction svcs. State of Conn., Hartford, 1991—; tng. and supervising analyst Western New Eng. Inst. Psychoanalysis, 1962—, N.Y. Psychoanalytic Inst., 1962—; cons. Childrens Bur., HEW; mem. adv. coun. Erikson Inst. for early Childhood Edn., 1966—; nat. adviser Children, publ. of Children's Bur., 1965—; mem. com. on publs. Yale U. Press, 1971—; adv. bd. Action for Children's TV, Newtonville, Mass., 1973—; mem. div. med. scis. Assembly Life Scis., NRC, 1974—; cons. div. mental health svc. program NIMH, 1974—; Sigmund Freud Meml. prof. U. Coll. London, 1983-84; Sigmund Freud prof., dir. Freud Ctr. Psychoanalytic Studies Hebrew U., Jerusalem, 1985-87. Author: (with M.J.E. Senn) Problems in Child Behavior and Develpment, 1968), (with A. Freud, J. Goldstein) Beyond the Best Interests of the Child, 19732, (with Goldstein) Divorce and Your Child, 1983, (with R. Lord, B. Nordhaus) When Home Is No Haven, 1992; The Many Meanings of Play, 1993; editor: (with S. Provence) Modern Perspectives in Child Development, 1963; mng. editor Psychoanalytic Study of the Child, 1971—; mem. editorial bd. Israel Annals Psychiatry and Related Disciplines, 1969—. WHO prof. psychiatry and human devel. U. Negev, Beer-Sheva, Israel, 1973-74. With USAAF, 1945-47. Recipient Disting. Svc. award Am. Psychiatric Assn., 1992. Mem. AAAS, Inst. Medicine of NAS, Am. Orthopsychiatric. Assn. (editorial bd. jour. 1974-82), Am. Psychoanalytic Assn. (past pres., editorial bd. jour. 1972-74), Am. Acad. Child and Adolescent Psychiatry (past pres., editorial bd. jour. 1975, Simon Wile Award, 1991), Internat. Pediatric Soc., Am. Assn. Child Psychoanalysis (past pres.), Am. Acad. Pediatrics (editorial bd. jour. 1968-76, task force pediatric edn.), Internat. Psychoanalytic Assn., Internat. Assn. Child and Adolescent Psychiatry (pres. 1974-78, hon. pres. 1990—), N.Y. Psychoanalytic Soc., Soc. Profs. Child Psychiatry. Home: 107 Cottage St New Haven CT 06511-2465 Office: 333 Cedar St New Haven CT 06510-3206 also: 410 Capitol Ave Hartford CT 06106

SOLO, ALAN JERE, medicinal chemistry educator, consultant; b. Phila., Nov. 7, 1933; s. David H. and Marion J. (Gottschall) S.; m. Elma Mardirosian, Oct. 5, 1963; children: David Matthew, Julia Ann. SB, MIT, 1955; MA, Columbia U., 1956, PhD, 1959. Rsch. assoc. Rockefeller U., N.Y.C., 1958-62; asst. prof. med. chemistry SUNY, Buffalo, 1962-65, assoc. prof., 1965-70, dir. grad. studies med. chemistry, 1967-69, chmn. med. chemistry, 1969—, prof., chmn., 1970—; cons. Westwood Pharms. Inc., Buffalo, 1971-92. Predoctoral fellow NSF, 1955-56, NIH, 1957-58. Mem. Am. Chem. Soc., N.Y. Acad. Scis., Sigma Xi. Achievements include synthesis and structure-activity correlation of steroid hormone analogs and of calcium channel antagonists of the Dihydropyridine type. Office: SUNY Sch Pharmacy 439 Cooke Hall Buffalo NY 14260

SOLO, JOYCE R., volunteer; b. Buffalo, N.Y., Feb. 14, 1924; d. Jay Harry and Rose (Maisel) Rubenstein; m. Richard D. Solo, Jan. 6, 1946; children: Harry Jay Solo, Eleanor Solo, Sally Solo. BA, Wellesley Coll., 1945. Pres. LWV, Sarasota County, Fla., 1990-92; healthcare com. chair, 1988-90, 92—; sec. Sarasota County Health Care Coord. Adv. Coun., 1993-95; active Planned Approach to Cmty. Health/Healthy Sarasota 2000; chair sr. adv. com. Sarasota Meml. Hosp.; vol. Reach to Recovery Breast Cancer Task Force, Manatee County Am. Cancer Soc.; pres. Beth Israel Women Bd., Temple Beth Israel, numerous others health and civic orgn. activities.

SOLO, ROBERT ALEXANDER, economist, educator; b. Phila., Aug. 2, 1916; s. Louis C. and Rebecca (Muchnick) S.; m. Roselyn Starr; 1 dau., Tova Maria. B.S., Harvard U., 1938; M.A., Am. U., 1941; Ph.D., Cornell U., 1953. Economist fed. and war agys., 1939-41; author, script chief Sta. WCAU-TV, Phila., 1949-50; mem. faculty Rutgers U., New Brunswick, N.J., 1953-55, McGill U., Montreal, Que., Can., 1955-56, CCNY, 1956-58; sr. research economist Princeton U., 1965-66; prof. dept. econs. Mich. State U., East Lansing, 1966-87, prof. emeritus, 1987—; dir. Inst. Internat. Bus. and Devel. Studies, 1966-68; mem. faculty Johns Hopkins U., Balt., summer 1953, U. Mich., Ann Arbor, summer 1957; lectr. L'Ecole Practique des Hautes Etudes, Sorbonne, Paris, 1964-65; research Institut Recherch Economique et Planification, lectr. U. Grenoble, France, 1972-73; prof. associe U. Paris IV, Dauphine, 1971, 73; cons. NASA, 1965-67, OECD, 1963-64, Commonwealth of P.R., 1959-61; project chmn. Study on Info. Tech., Nat. Conf. Bd., 1969-72; project dir. Nat. Planning Assn., Washington, 1961-63; U.S. del. Yugoslavian Conf. on Transfer of Tech., Belgrade, 1974; mem. Alan T. Waterman award Com., 1976-77. Author: Economics and the Public Interest, 1955, Synthetic Rubber: A Case Study in Technological Development under Public Direction, 1959 (reprinted as Across the High Technology Threshold 1980), Economic Organizations and Social Systems, 1967, (with Everett Rogers) Inducing Technological Change for Economic Growth and Development, 1973, The Political Authority and the Market System, 1974, Organizing Science for Technology Transfer in Economic Development, 1975, The Positive State, 1981, (with Charles Anderson) Value Judgement and Income Distribution, 1981, Opportunity Knocks: American Economic Policy after Gorbachev, 1991, The Philosophy of Science and Economics, 1991, also other books in field; contbr. chpts. to books, articles to profl. jours. Fulbright fellow, 1972-73. Mem. Council European Studies (steering com., exec. com., chmn. research com. 1974-77). Home: 4609 Chippewa Dr Okemos MI 48864-2009

SOLOFF, LOUIS ALEXANDER, physician, educator; b. Paris, Oct. 4, 1904; came to U.S., 1905, naturalized, 1930; s. Abraham and Rebecca (Wagenfeld) S.; m. Mathilde Robin, 1933 (dec.); 1 child, Joann Soloff Green. B.A, U. Pa., 1926; M.D., U. Chgo., 1930. Dir. pathology St. Joseph's and St. Vincent's hosps., Phila., 1933-45; dir. pathology Eagleville Sanitorium, Norristown, Pa., 1933-45; with Temple U. and Hosp., Phila., 1930—; chief div. cardiology Temple U. and Hosp., 1956-70, prof. medicine, 1966—, Blanche P. Levy disting. svc. prof., Florence P. Bernheimer prof. cardiology emeritus, 1970—; now chief cardiology emeritus Temple U. Hosp.; chief div. cardiology Episcopal Hosp., 1950-56. Mem. A.C.P., AMA, Am. Heart Assn., Am. Fedn. Clin. Research, Pa. Med. Soc., Am. Heart Assn., Council on Clin. Cardiology, AAUP, Assn. Univ. Cardiologists, Sigma Xi, Alpha Omega Alpha. Research, publs. on cardiovascular disease. Home: 1901 Walnut St Philadelphia PA 19103-4605 Office: Temple U Health Scis Center Philadelphia PA 19140

SOLOMAN, WILLIAM T., industrial services executive; b. Dallas, Aug. 11, 1942; m. Gay Ferguson; 2 children. BSCE, So. Meth. U., 1965; MBA, Harvard U., 1967. With Austin Indsl. Inc., 1967—; now chmn. bd. dirs. Austin Industries, Inc.; bd. dirs. A.H. Belo Corp. Past bd. dirs. Dallas Mus. Art, Dallas Symphony Assn., Inc.; bd. dirs. Baylor U. Med. Ctr. Found.; trustee So. Meth. U., exec. bd. chmn. Sch. Engring. & Applied Sci.; trustee Southwestern Med. Found.; chmn. bd. dirs. Dallas Citizens Coun., 1989-90; founding co-chmn. Dallas Together Forum, 1991-94; mem. Dallas Assembly; past bd. chmn. Northaven United Meth. Ch.; mem. Dallas County adv. bd. The Salvation Army. Recipient Humanitarian award NCCJ, 1982, Champion Free Enterprise award Associated Builders & Contractors, 1985, citation of honor Dallas chpt. AIA, 1985, Disting. Alumnus award So. Meth. U., 1988, Skill, Integrity, Responsibility award Assoc. Gen. Contractors, 1990, Dreamers, Doers and Unsung Heroes award The Real Estate Coun., 1994; named for Excellence in Cmty. Svc., Dallas Hist. Soc., 1993, Tex. Minority Bus. Adv. of Yr., U.S. Small Bus. Adminstrn., 1995. Mem. ASCE, Dallas C. of C. (chmn. bd. dirs. 1982-84), Young Press.' Orgn. (internat. bd. dirs., past chmn. Dallas chpt.), Salesmanship Club of Dallas. Office: Austin Industries Inc PO Box 1590 Dallas TX 75221

SOLOMON, ALAN, physician, medical oncologist and clinical investigator; b. N.Y.C., May 16, 1933; s. Joseph and Rita (Schwartz) S.; m. Frances N. Jacobs, June 14, 1959 (div. Jan. 1972); children: David A., Joseph A.; m. Doris A Creekmore Waters, Nov. 27, 1977. BS, Bucknell U., 1953; BS in Medicine, Duke U., 1956, MD, 1957. Diplomate Nat. Bd. Med. Examiners, Am. Bd. Internal Medicine. Intern Mt. Sinai Hosp., N.Y.C., 1957-58; asst. resident medicine Montefiore Hosp., N.Y.C., 1958-59, Mt. Sinai Hosp., N.Y.C., 1959-60; clin. assoc. Nat. Cancer Inst., NIH, Bethesda, Maryland, 1960-62; chief resident medicine Mt. Sinai Hosp., N.Y.C., 1962-63; guest investigator, asst. physician Rockefeller U., N.Y.C., 1963-65; assoc. rsch. prof. U. Tenn., Meml. Rsch. Ctr. Hosp., Knoxville, Tenn., 1966-69, rsch. and clin. prof., 1970-80, prof. medicine, 1981—; Am. Cancer Soc. clin. rsch. prof. U. Tenn. Med. Ctr., Knoxville, Tenn., 1992—; chmn. Clin. Cancer Project Review Com. Nat. Cancer Inst./NIH, Bethesda, 1978-83, mem. sci. counselors divsn. cancer biology, 1993-95; head human immunology cancer program U. Tenn. Med. Ctr., Knoxville, 1990—. Contbr. to over 140 profl jours. Bd. trustees Knoxville Mus. Art, Tenn., 1982—. Sr. Surgeon USPHS 1960-62, (inactive) 1962-63. Named Special Fellow NIH/Rockefeller Inst., N.Y.C., 1963-65, Laszlo Meml. Lecturer Montefiore Hosp., N.Y.C., 1984; recipient Rsch. Career Devel. award NIH/U. Tenn. Med. Ctr., 1968-72. Fellow Am. Coll. Physicians; mem. Am. Assn. Cancer Rsch., Am. Soc. Hematology, Am. Assn. Immunologist, Am. Soc. Clin. Investigators, Am. Soc. Clin. Oncology. Jewish. Avocations: gardening, hiking, sculpture. Office: U Tenn Med Ctr 1924 Alcoa Hwy Knoxville TN 37920-1511

SOLOMON, ARTHUR CHARLES, pharmacist; b. Gary, Ind., May 30, 1947; s. Laurence A. and Dorothy B. (Klippel) S.; m. Janet Evelyn Irak, Aug. 23, 1969; children: Thomas, Michael, Mark, Jill. BS in Pharmacy, Purdue U., 1970, MS in Clin. Pharmacy, 1972; PharmD. Registered pharmacist; cert. nuclear pharmacist. Clin. prof. pharmacy U. Tex., Austin, 1972-75; v.p. Nuclear Pharmacy, Inc., Atlanta, 1975-83; exec. v.p., managed care officer Diagnostek, Inc., Albuquerque, 1983-95; pres. Health Care Svcs., Inc., 1990-95; exec. v.p., COO Value Rx, Albuquerque, 1995—; adj. prof. U. N.Mex., 1992—. Contbr. articles to profl. jours. Mem. Am. Pharm. Assn., Am. Soc. Hosp. Pharmacy, Nat. Assn. Retail Druggists, Nat. Coun. Prescription Drug Programs, Am. Managed Care Pharmacy Assn. (pres., dir.), Am. Soc. Cons. Pharmacists, Rho Chi, Pi Kappa Phi. Republican. Roman Catholic. Avocations: golf, fishing, gardening, tennis. Home: 1504 Catron Ave SE Albuquerque NM 87123-4218 Office: Value Rx 4500 Alexander Blvd NE Albuquerque NM 87107-6805

SOLOMON, ARTHUR KASKEL, biophysics educator; b. Pitts., Nov. 26, 1912; (married); 2 children. A.B., Princeton U., 1934; M.A., Harvard U., 1935, Ph.D. in Phys. Chemistry, 1937; Ph.D. in Physics, Cambridge U., Eng., 1947, Sc.D., 1964. Research assoc. in physics and chemistry Harvard, 1939-41; officer Brit. Ministry Supply, 1941-43; mem. staff Radiation Lab., Mass. Inst. Tech., 1945; asst. prof. phys. chemistry Med. Sch., Harvard, 1946-57, asso. prof. biophysics, 1957-68, prof., 1968-82, prof. emeritus, 1982—; assoc. in biophysics Peter Bent Brigham Hosp., Boston, 1950-72; dir. Read's Inc., Balt., 1946-77; pres. Read's Inc., 1961-77; Mem. U.S. Nat. Com. for Pure and Applied Biophysics, 1965-72, U.S. Nat. Com. for Biology, 1966-71; mem. U.S. Nat. Com. for UNESCO, 1969-74, mem. U.S. del. to gen. assembly, Nairobi, 1976; mem. vis. com. biology dept. Brookhaven Nat. Lab., 1961-65; mem. NRC com. on radiology, 1957-59, com. on growth, 1954-57; sec. Gen. Internat. Union for Pure and Applied Biophysics, 1961-72; mem. NIH radiation study sect., 1960-63, biophys. sci. tng. com., 1963-68, chmn., 1966-68; mem. U.S. del. Gen. Assembly of UNESCO, Paris, 1978; mem. adv. panel on sci., tech. and society UNESCO, 1981-84; mem. bd. internat. orgns. and programs Nat. Acad. Scis., 1973-80, chmn., 1977-79; mem. Commn. on Internat. Relations, 1977-79; mem. exec. com. Internat. Council Sci. Unions, 1966-72; U.S. del. 17th, 18th Gen. Assemblies of Internat. Council Sci. Unions, Athens, 1978, Amsterdam, 1980; chmn. disting. fellowship com. Internat. Council Sci. Unions-UNESCO, 1980-85; chmn. Harvard com. on higher degrees in biophysics, 1959-80; chmn. Harvard Med. Sch. Oral History Com.; chmn. Harvard Council on the Arts, 1973-76. Mem. editorial bds.: Quarterly Revs. of Biophysics, 1972-74, Journal Gen. Physiology, 1958—. Trustee Inst. Contemporary Art, Boston, 1946-76, pres., 1965-71; bd. overseers Boston Mus. Fine Arts, 1978-84; mem. collectors com. Nat. Gallery Art, Washington, 1985-88. Decorated Order Andres Bello Venezuela). Fellow AAAS, Am. Acad. Arts and Scis.; mem. Am. Chem. Soc., Am. Physiol. Soc., Biophysics Soc., Soc. Gen. Physiology. Clubs: Cosmos (Washington); St. Botolph (Boston); Harvard (N.Y.C. and Boston). Home: 27 Craigie St Cambridge MA 02138-3457 Office: Harvard Med Sch Biophysics Lab 221 Longwood Ave Boston MA 02115-5817

SOLOMON, BARRY JASON, healthcare administrator, consultant; b. Boston, May 16, 1934; s. Samuel and Ethel (Fleishman) S.; m. C. Priscilla Fugate, June 29, 1958; children: R. Stephen, Jon, Julie Ellen. BS in Biology and Chemistry, Tufts U., 1955; MBA in Health Care Adminstrn., Xavier U., Cin., 1960; MPH in Health Care Adminstrn., U. N.C., 1989. Chief med. record adminstr. USPHS Hosp., Lexington, Ky., 1956-59; asst. dir. Union Meml. Hosp., Balt., 1960-61; asst. adminstr. James Lawrence Kernan Hosp., Balt., 1961-67; asst. to dean, lectr. health edn. and med. care sects. Yale U. Sch. Medicine, New Haven, 1967-70; dir. health svcs., clin. asst. prof. pharmacy adminstrn. U. R.I., Kingston, 1970-76; assoc. dir. for adminstrn. USPHS Hosp., Norfolk, Va., 1976-81; dir., COO, sr. fellow in social medicine Montefiore Hosp., Bronx, N.Y., 1981-84; assoc. v.p. for med. affairs, mem. exec. coun. of Med. Sch. U. South Fla., Tampa, 1984-89; assoc. prof., acting chmn. dept. comprehensive medicine U. So. Fla., Tampa, 1984-89, assoc. prof. Coll. Pub. Health, 1984-89; cons. in health adminstrn., Columbia, Md., 1989-93; v.p. for acad. affairs North Broward Hosp. Dist., Ft. Lauderdale, Fla., 1993—; bd. dirs. Vis. Nurse Corp., 1987-90; bd. dirs., mem. exec. and nominating coms. Vis. Nurse Assn. Tampa Bay, 1987-90; mem. planning com. of bd. trustees Hillsborough County Hosp. Authority, 1986-88; mem. profl. affairs com. of bd. trustees H. Lee Moffitt Cancer Ctr. and Rsch. Inst., 1986-88; mem. affiliation com. S.W. Fla. Blood Bank, 1988-89; instr. hosp. adminstrn. Xavier U., 1960; course asst., instr. Am. Med. Record Assn., 1962-72; instr. Howard U. Coll. Continuing Edn., Washington, 1993; cons. St. Elizabeth Hosp., Covington, Ky., 1959, City Hosp. Ctr. at Elmhurst, 1965, Hall-Brooke Hosp., Westport, Conn., 1968-69, Conn. Mental Health Ctr., New Haven, 1969-70, South County Hosp., Wakefield, R.I., 1970-76, Centurion Hosp., Tampa, 1989, Primary Care Svcs., Tampa, 1991, Holland & Knight, Tampa, 1991, NCC Internat., Colchester, Eng., 1991, F.W. Assocs., Tampa, 1989-92, Decking Design, Norfolk, 1986-93, SMSinc., Columbia, 1993, Internat. Flooring & Protective Coatings, Inc., Norfolk, 1993—; sr. cons. Meisel Assocs., Inc., N.Y.C., 1983—. Contbr. articles to profl. jours. Trustee Montefiore-Moshulu Cmty. Ctr., 1981-84; mem. Nat. Com. on Religion and Health, 1982-84; mem., vice chmn. Chariho Sch. Bd., Richmond, R.I., 1974-76; mem. Broward Econ. Devel. Coun., Inc. Lt. USPHS, 1956-59, capt., 1976-81. Recipient citation Suncoast chpt. Am. Heart Assn., 1988. Fellow Am. Coll. Healthcare Execs.; mem. APHA. Avocation: tennis. Home: 2863 Via Venezia Deerfield Beach FL 33442 Office: North Broward Hosp Dist 303 SE 17th St Fort Lauderdale FL 33316

SOLOMON, CAREN G., internist; b. N.Y.C., Feb. 20, 1963. MD, Harvard U., 1988. Resident Brigham Womens Hosp., Boston, 1988-90, fellow in endocrinology, 1990-93, assoc. physician, 1993—; instr. medicine Harvard Med. Sch., 1993—. Recipient Clinican Scientist award Am. Heart Assn., 1995-96. Mem .ACP. Office: Brigham Womens Hosp 75 Francis St Boston MA 02215

SOLOMON, DAN EUGENE, bishop; b. Matador, Tex., Dec. 15, 1936; s. Henry Monroe and Mabel Amy (Jenkins) S.; m. Joy Causseaux, May 30, 1957; children: Stuart, Paul, Julie Beth. BA summa cum laude, McMurry Coll., 1958; M Div with honors, Perkins Sch. Theology, 1961; D Ministry, United Theol. Sem., Dayton, 1973; DD (hon.), Oklahoma City U., 1989. Assoc. pastor First Meth. Ch., Plainview, Tex., 1961-62; sr. pastor St. Stephen United Meth. Ch., Amarillo, Tex., 1962-69, St. John's United Meth. Ch., Corpus Christi, Tex., 1969-76; supt. Kerrville (Tex.) Dist., 1976-77; sr. pastor Travis Park United Meth. Ch., San Antonio, 1977-83, First United Meth. Ch., Corpus Christi, 1983-88; bishop Okla. area, Okla. Ann. Conf., Okla. Indian Missionary Conf. United Meth. Ch., Oklahoma City, 1988—; mem. Gen. Conf. and Jurisdictional Conf., Gen. Bd. Ch. and Soc., Gen. Bd. Status and Role of Women. Author/creator simulation game Cabinet; contbr. articles to profl. pubs. Trustee Oklahoma City U.; bd. dirs. Suicide Prevention Group, Crimestoppers. Recipient Homiletics award Perkins Sch. Theology. Avocation: golf. Office: United Meth Ch 2420 N Blackwelder Ave Oklahoma City OK 73106-1410

SOLOMON, DAVID, investment banker. Pres. Mortgage Acquisition Corp., Boston. Office: Mortgage Acquisition Corp 18 Newbury St 3rd Fl Boston MA 02116-3201*

SOLOMON, DAVID EUGENE, engineering company executive; b. Milton, Pa., June 22, 1931; s. Oren Benjamin and Bernardine Claire Solomon; m. Joyce Marie Hoffman, June 24, 1950; children: Timothy, Melissa, Daniel. AB, Susquehanna U., 1958; MS, Bucknell U., 1960; MBA, Ea. Mich. U., 1974. Sr. engr. Westinghouse Electric Corp., Balt., 1959-65; rsch. engr. U. Mich., 1965-67; chief engr. Electro-Optics divsn. Bendix Corp., 1967-72; v.p. ops. KMS Fusion, Inc., Ann Arbor, Mich., 1972-85; pres., CEO Solohill Engring. Inc., 1985—; bd. dirs. Ann Arbor Engring. Inc., SoloHill Labs. Inc. With USN, 1950-55. Fellow IEEE. Patentee in field. Office: 1919 Green Rd Ann Arbor MI 48105-2554

SOLOMON, DAVID HARRIS, physician, educator; b. Cambridge, Mass., Mar. 7, 1923; s. Frank and Rose (Roud) S.; m. Ronda L. Markson, June 23, 1946; children: Patti Jean (Mrs. Richard E. Sinaiko), Nancy Ellen (Mrs. Marvin Evans.). A.B., Brown U., 1944; M.D., Harvard U., 1946. Intern Peter Bent Brigham Hosp., Boston, 1946-47, resident, 1947-48, 50-51; fellow endocrinology New Eng. Center Hosp., Boston, 1951-52; faculty UCLA Sch. Medicine, 1952—, prof. medicine, 1966-93, vice chmn. dept. medicine, 1968-71, chmn. dept., 1971-81, assoc. dir. geriatrics, 1982-89; dir. UCLA Ctr. on Aging, 1991—; prof. emeritus UCLA, 1993—; chief med. svc. Harbor Gen. Hosp., Torrance, Calif., 1966-71; cons. Wadsworth VA Hosp., L.A., 1952—, Sepulveda VA Hosp., 1971—; cons. metabolism tng. com. USPHS, 1960-64, endocrinology study sect., 1970-73. Editor: Jour. Am. Geriatric Soc., 1988-93; contbr. numerous articles to profl. jours. Recipient Mayo Soley award, 1986. Master ACP; mem. Assn. Am. Physicians, Am. Soc. Clin. Investigation, Western Soc. Clin. Research (councillor 1963-65), Endocrine Soc. (Robert H. Williams award 1989), Am. Thyroid Assn. (pres. 1973-74, Disting. Service award 1986), Inst. Medicine Nat. Acad. Scis., AAAS, Assn. Profs. Medicine (pres. 1980-81), Western Assn. Physicians (councillor 1972-75, pres. 1983-84), Am. Fedn. Aging Rsch. (Irving S. Wright award), Am. Geriatrics Soc. (bd. dirs. 1985-93, Milo Leavitt award 1992, Disting. Svc. award 1993), Phi Beta Kappa, Sigma Xi, Alpha Omega Alpha. Home: 863 Woodacres Rd Santa Monica CA 90402-2107 Office: UCLA Sch Medicine Dept Medicine Los Angeles CA 90024-1687

SOLOMON, EDWARD IRA, chemistry educator and researcher; b. N.Y.C., Oct. 20, 1946; s. Mordecai L. and Sally S. Solomon; m. Darlene Joy Spira, Sept. 15, 1984; children: Mitchell Landau, Paige Elana. BS, Rensselaer Poly. Inst., 1968; PhD, Princeton U., 1972. Rsch. assoc. Princeton (N.J.) U., 1972-73; postdoctoral fellow H.C. Ørsted Inst., Copenhagen, 1973-74, Calif. Inst. Tech., Pasadena, 1974-75; asst. prof. MIT, Cambridge, Mass., 1975-79, assoc. prof., 1979-81, prof., 1981-82; prof. Stanford (Calif.) U., 1982-91, Monroe E. Spaght prof. humanities and sci., 1991—; cons. prof., World Bank lectr. Xiamen U., People's Republic of China, 1984: O.K. Rice lectr. U. N.C., 1984, Reilly lectr. U. Notre Dame, 1985; invited prof. U. Paris, 1987; 1st Glen Seaborg lectr. U. Calif., 1990; Frontiers in Chem. Rsch. lectr. Tex. A&M U., 1990; ACS lectr., Argentina, 1992; invited prof. Tokyo Inst. Tech., 1992; Xerox lectr. U. Alta., 1993; lectr. NSC Republic of China, 1993; Leermakers lectr. Wesleyan U., 1994; Amoco lectr. Ind. U., 1995. Assoc. editor Inorganic Chemistry, 1985—; mem. editl. adv. bd. Chem. Revs., 1990—, Jour. Inorganic Biochemistry, Chemtracts, Chemistry and Biology, Jour. Biol. Inorganic Chemistry; contbr. 225 articles to profl. publs., including Jour. Am. Chem. Soc., Inorganic Chemistry, Procs. of NAS, Phys. Rev. Mem. panels NIH, NSF, Washington; mem. vis. coms. Exxon, U. Calif., Santa Cruz. Sloan fellow; recipient Ramsen award Md. ACS and Johns Hopkins U., 1994, NIH Merit award, 1995, Dean award for disting. tchg., 1990. Fellow AAAS, Japan Soc. for Promotion of Sci.; mem. Am. Chem. Soc. (chmn. bioinorganic divsn.), Am. Phys. Soc., Sigma Xi. Achievements include research in structure/function correlations in copper cluster proteins, in electronic structure of the blue copper active site, in spectroscopic definition of the active site in the Cu/ZnO methanol synthesis catalyst, in new spectroscopic probes of non-heme iron enzymes, in excited state potential energy surfaces of inorganic complexes and their contribution to reactivity, on new methods of inorganic spectroscopy; covalency in transition metal complexes. Office: Stanford U Dept Chemistry Roth Way Stanford CA 94305

SOLOMON, ELDRA PEARL BROD, psychologist, educator, biologist, author; b. Phila., Apr. 9, 1940; d. Theodore and Freda Miriam (Warhaftig) Brod; m. Edwin Marshall Solomon, June 28, 1959 (div. Jan. 1985); children: Mical Kenneth, Amy Lynn, Belicia Efros. BS, U. Tampa, 1961; MS, U. Fla., 1963; MA, U. South Fla., 1987, PhD, 1989. Lic. psychologist. Adj. biology prof. Hillsborough Community Coll., Tampa, Fla., 1968-86; biopsychologist Ctr. for Rsch. in Behavioral Medicine, U. South Fla., Tampa, 1985-89; dir. rsch. Advanced Devel. Systems, Tampa, 1989-92; pvt. practice clin. psychologist Tampa, 1990—; clin. dir. Ctr. for Mental Health Edn., Assessment and Therapy, Tampa, Fla., 1992—; adj. prof., mem. grad. faculty U. South Fla., 1992—; expert witness, psychol. expert county and cir. cts., 1989—; health edn. cons. Advanced Devel. Sys., Tampa, 1985-92. Author: Human Anatomy and Physiology, 1990, The World of Biology, 5th edit., 1995, Biology, 4th edit., 1996; author: (with others) Health Psychology: Individual Differences and Stress, 1988; contbr. chpt. to book. Mem. APA, Am. Soc. Criminology, Fla. Psychol. Assn., Internat. Soc. for the Study of Dissociation (chairperson Tampa chpt.). Democrat. Jewish. Avocations: boating, swimming, reading. Office: Ctr Mental Health Edn Assessment & Therapy Tampa Medical Tower Ste 770 2727 W Martin Luther King Blvd Tampa FL 33607-6383

SOLOMON, ELINOR HARRIS, economics educator; b. Boston, Feb. 26, 1923; d. Ralph and Linna Harris; m. Richard A. Solomon, Mar. 30, 1957; children: Joan S. Griffin, Robert H., Thomas H. AB, Mt. Holyoke Coll., 1944; MA, Radcliffe U., 1945; PhD, Harvard U., 1948. Jr. economist Fed. Res. Bank Boston, 1945-48; economist Fed. Res. Bd. Govs., Washington, 1949-56; internat. economist U.S. State Dept., Washington, 1957-58; professorial lectr. Am. U., Washington, 1964-66; sr. economist antitrust div. U.S. Dept. Justice, Washington, 1966-82; prof. econs. George Washington U., Washington, 1982—; econ. cons., Washington, 1982—; expert witness antitrust, electronic funds transfer cases, Washington, 1988—. Author, editor: Electronic Funds Transfers and Payments, 1987, Electronic Money Flows, 1991; contbr. articles on econs., banking and law to profl. jours. Mem. Am. Econs. Assn., Nat. Economist Club. Home: 6805 Delaware St Bethesda MD 20815-4164 Office: George Washington U Dept Econs Washington DC 20052

SOLOMON, EZRA, economist, educator; b. Rangoon, Burma, Mar. 20, 1920; came to U.S., 1947, naturalized, 1951; s. Ezra and Emily (Rose) S.; m. Janet Lorraine Cameron, May 7, 1949; children—Catherine Shan, Janet Ming, Lorna Cameron. A.B. (hons.), U. Rangoon, 1940; Ph.D., U. Chgo., 1950. Instr. U. Chgo., 1948-51, asst. prof. fin., 1951-55, assoc. prof., 1955-57, prof., 1957-61; Dean Witter prof. fin. Stanford U., 1961-71, 73-90; dir. Internat. Ctr. Mgmt. Edn.; mem. Coun. Econ. Advisers, 1971-73; Bd. dirs. Benham Capital Funds. Author: The Theory of Financial Management, 1963, Money and Banking, 5th edit, 1968, The Management of Corporate Capital, 1959, Metropolitan Chicago: An Economic Analysis, 1958, The Anxious Economy, 1975, An Introduction to Financial Management, 2d edit, 1980, Beyond the Turning Point, 1981; editor: International Patterns of Inflation— A Study in Contrasts, 1984, Jour. Bus, 1953-57; bd. editors Jour. of Finance, 1965-66, Jour. Bus. Finance, 1969-73, Jour. Quantitative and Financial Analysis, 1969-71. Served as lt., Burma div. Royal Naval Vol. Res., 1942-47. Mem. Am. Econ. Assn., Am. Finance Assn. Home: 775 Santa Ynez St Stanford CA 94305-8478 Office: Stanford Univ Grad School of Busines Stanford CA 94305

SOLOMON, GEORGE FREEMAN, academic psychiatrist; b. Freeport, N.Y., Nov. 25, 1931; s. Joseph C. and Ruth (Freeman) S.; children: Joshua Ben, Jared Freeman. A.B., Stanford U., 1952, M.D., 1955. Intern, Barnes Hosp., St. Louis, 1955-56; resident in psychiatry Langley Porter Neuropsychiat. Inst., U. Calif. Med. Sch., San Francisco, 1956-59; asst. to asso. prof. psychiatry Stanford U. Med. Sch., 1962-73; dir. med. edn. Fresno County (Calif.) Dept. Health, 1973-83; clin. prof. UCLA Med. Sch., 1974-78; clin. prof. psychiatry U. Calif. Med. Sch., San Francisco, 1976-79, prof., 1980-84, vice-chmn. dept., 1978-83; adj. prof. U. Calif., San Francisco, 1984-90; prof.

psychiatry and biobehavioral sci. UCLA, 1984-95, prof. emeritus, 1995—; chief chem. dependency treatment ctr. VA Med. Ctr., Sepulveda, Calif., 1984-89; chief psychoneuroimmunology, 1989-94; chief psychiatry Valley Med. Center, Fresno, 1974-83. Co-author: The Psychology of Strength, 1975; contbr. over 150 papers and articles on psychoneuroimmunology, violence, Vietnam and other topics to profl. jours. and various publs. Capt. USAR, 1959-61. Fellow Internat. Coll. Psychosomatic Medicine, Am. Psychiat. Assn., Acad. of Behavioral Med. Research., Royal Coll. Psychiatrists. Home: 19054 Pacific Coast Hwy Malibu CA 90265-5406 Office: UCLA Sch Med Dean's Office N Cousins Prog Psychoneuro 12-138CHS Los Angeles CA 90025

SOLOMON, GEORGE M., newspaper editor; b. N.Y.C., July 19, 1940; s. Sidney and Fannie (Seidel) S.; m. Hazel Stephanie Bakst, July 23, 1967; children—Aaron, Mark, Gregory. B.S. in Journalism, U. Fla., 1963. Sports editor Sun-Sentinel, Fort Lauderdale, Fla., 1965-70; reporter, columnist Washington Daily News, 1970-72; reporter sports Washington Post, 1972-74, asst. sports editor, 1974-75, asst. mng. editor sports, 1975—. Author: Team Nobody Wanted: the Washington Redskins, 1973. Democrat. Jewish. Avocations: running; tennis. Office: Washington Post 1150 15th St NW Washington DC 20071-0001

SOLOMON, GERALD BROOKS HUNT, congressman; b. Okeechobee, Fla., Aug. 14, 1930; s. Seymour and Rlee Eugenia (Hunt) S.; m. Freda Frances Parker, Feb. 5, 1955; children: Susan, Daniel, Robert, Linda, Jeffrey. Student, Siena Coll., Albany, N.Y., 1948-49, St. Lawrence U., Canton, N.Y., 1953-54. Town supr., chief exec. Queensbury, N.Y., 1967-72; legislator Warren County, N.Y., 1968-73; mem. N.Y. State Assembly, 1972-78, 96th-97th Congresses from 29th N.Y. dist., 1979-83; 98th-104th Congresses from 24th (now 22d) N.Y. dist. 98th-103rd Congresses from 24th (now 22nd) N.Y. dist., Washington, D.C., 1983—; chmn. Rules com., mem. joint com. orgn. congress; ambassador del. UN, 1985; house com. mem. Vets. Affairs Com., 1979-89, Pub. Wks. Com., 1979-83, Fgn. Affairs Com., 1983-89, 2d ranking rep. 1989—, 1st ranking rep. 1991—; founding ptnr. Assoc. of Glens Falls (N.Y.) Inc. ins. and stockbrokerage firm, 1964—. Chmn. Warren County Social Svc. Com., 1968-72; active Ea. Adirondack Heart Assn., Adirondack Muscular Dystrophy Assn.; mem. Queensbury Ctrl. Vol. Fire Co., from 1967; bd. dirs. Adirondack Park Assn., Glens Falls Area Youth Ctr.; coun. Boy Scouts Am.; mem. house rules com. U.S. Congress, 1989—, Task Force, Prisoner and Missing in S.E. Asia; former mem. Ho. Fgn. Affairs Com.; former sr. ranking rep. Vets. Affairs Com.; amb. UN, N.Y., 1985, also congl. advisor to UN session on disarmament; former congl. del. North Atlantic Assembly, vice chmn., active, 1982—; chmn. polit. fgn. affairs com. Assembly. With USMC, 1951-58, Korean War. Mem. Queensbury C. of C. (pres. 1972), Queensbury Jaycees (pres. 1964-65). Presbyterian. Lodges: Masons, Shriners, K.T, Elks, Kiwanis (bd. dir. Queensbury club 1965-69), Grange. Office: US Ho of Reps 2206 Rayburn House Office Bldg Washington DC 20515-3222

SOLOMON, HENRY, university dean; b. Bronx, N.Y., Nov. 28, 1926; s. Max and Tillie (Gilerowitz) S.; m. Jacqueline Mona Cohen, May 31, 1953; 1 son, Michael Robert. B.A., Bklyn. Coll., 1949; M.A., NYU, 1950, Ph.D., 1960. Research assoc., then sr. staff investigator and dep. prin. investigator, logistics research project George Washington U., 1950-66, prof. econs., chmn. dept., 1962-74, 91—; dean George Washington U. (Grad. Sch. Arts and Scis.), 1974-90; dep. asst. adminstr. econs., acting asst. adminstr. planning, research and analysis SBA, 1966-67; cons. in field. Assoc. editor: Naval Research Logistics Quar, 1957-90 . Served with U.S. Army, 1945-46. Recipient Founder's Day award N.Y. U., 1960. Mem. Am. Econ. Assn., Am. Statis. Assn. Home: 6311 Stratford Rd Chevy Chase MD 20815-5355 Office: 801 22nd St NW Washington DC 20037-2515

SOLOMON, IRVIN D., history educator, author; b. Alexandria, La., July 20, 1946; s. Mary Katherine (Rohaly) Solomon Beer. BS in Edn., Edinboro U. of Pa., 1971, MA in History, 1973; PhD in History, U. Akron, 1983. Teaching fellow, teaching asst. U. Akron, 1973-78; tchr. Fairfax County Sch. Dist., Falls Church, Va., 1978-83; instr. Afro-Am. history Prince George's C.C., Largo, Md., 1979-83; grad. instr. human relations George Mason U., Fairfax, Va., 1980-82; prof. history and African-Am. studies Edison C.C., Ft. Myers, Fla., 1988-94; asst. prof. History U. South Fla., Ft. Myers, Fla., 1994—; adj. prof. history and African-Am. studies U. Cen. Fla., 1983-88, U. South Fla., Ft. Myers, Fla., 1990-94; instr. evening sch. Columbia Coll., Orlando, 1983-88; cons. in human rels., Washington, 1978-83. Author: Make It Happen: A Comprehensive Guide and Directory for Americans Wishing to Teach Overseas, 1985, Feminism and Black Activism in Contemporary America: An Ideological Assessment, 1989; editor: Readings in American History: Key Social Issues, 1994; contbr. articles to profl. jours. and newspapers. Co-sponsor Black History Month, Ft. Myers, 1988-90, Women's History Month, Ft. Myers, 1990. Recipient citations for excellence in writing Orlando Sentinel, 1985, 86, 87, tchg. student svc. award U. South Fla., 1995; Univ. fellow, 1977-78. Mem. Phi Alpha Theta, Phi Delta Kappa. Avocation: travel. Office: U South Fla at Ft Myers Coll Arts and Scis 8111 College Pky Fort Myers FL 33919-5162

SOLOMON, JACK AVRUM, lawyer, automotive distributor, art dealer; b. Omaha, Oct. 25, 1928; s. John A. and Matilda (Bienstok) S.; m. Josephine J. Kleiman, June 1948 (div. Mar. 1971); children: Debra, Alisa, Michael, Rena; m. Carolyn Summers, Dec. 1973. B.S., U. Nebr., 1950, LL.B. cum laude, 1952; LL.M. (Cook fellow), U. Mich., 1953. Bar: Nebr. 1950, Ill. 1951. Practice law Chgo., 1950—; with firm Stiefel, Greenberg, Burns, Baldridge & Solomon, 1953-66, ptnr., 1958-66; ptnr. Solomon, Rosenfeld, Elliot & Stiefel, and predecessor, 1966—, sr. ptnr., 1966—; dir. Amco Industries, Inc., Chgo., 1968—, chmn. bd., 1968-69, sec., gen. counsel, 1969—; sec., dir. Mogen David Wine Corp., Chgo., 1964-71; chmn. bd., dir. Arts and Leisure Corp., 1969-76; pres., chmn. bd., dir. Circle Fine Art Corp., 1968-95; chmn. bd. Solomon and Solomon Fine Art, Ltd., 1996—. Mem. Ill., Nebr. bar assns.; mem. Fine Art Pubs. Assn. (pres. 1982—); Mem. Order of Coif. Jewish (pres. temple 1959-61). Club: Nat. Arts (N.Y.C.). Home: 950 N Michigan Ave Chicago IL 60611-4503 Office: 303 E Wacker Dr Ste 207 Chicago IL 60601-5212

SOLOMON, JOHN DAVIS, aviation executive; b. Kingfisher, Okla., Oct. 22, 1936; s. Edward Dempsey and Mary Blanche (Smith) S.; m. Mildred Oraline Brammer, July 16, 1968 (div. Mar. 1984); children: Jennifer Leigh, Jason Lewis; m. Sheila Mary McLeod, Nov. 23, 1985. BA, Okla. State U., 1958. Asst. mgr. airport City of Oklahoma City Dept. Aviation, 1963-66, City of Tulsa Airport Authority, 1966-70; dir. aviation City of Oklahoma City, 1970-77, Clark County Dept. Aviation, Las Vegas, Nev., 1977-86; dir. environ. planning Landrum & Brown, Aviation Planners, Cin., 1986-88; dep. dir. aviation City of Houston Airport System, 1988-90; dir. aviation City of Kansas City, Mo., 1990—. Editor Airport Mgmt. Jour., 1975; contbr. articles to aviation jours. Mem. Am. Assn. Airport Execs. (bd. dirs., ex-officio, accredited 1965, pres. 1979, Pres.'s award 1975, Disting. Svc. award 1991), Airports Coun. Internat. (bd. dirs. 1985-86), Kappa Sigma. Avocations: art, music, collecting military miniatures. Office: Dept Aviation Kansas City Internat. Airport PO Box 20047 Kansas City MO 64195-0047

SOLOMON, JOSEPH, lawyer; b. N.Y.C., Mar. 11, 1904; s. Abraham and Rebecca (Rubin) S.; m. Rita Schwartz, Aug. 31, 1929; children: Alan, Diane Solomon Kempler. LL.B., N.Y. Law Sch., 1927, LL.D. with honors, 1976; L.H.D. (hon.), Bar-Ilan U., 1986. Bar: N.Y. 1928. With Leventritt, Cook, Nathan & Lehman, N.Y.C., 1919-22; asst. to mng. clk. Leventritt, Cook, Nathan & Lehman, 1922-28, mem. legal staff, 1928-45; partner firm Lehman, Rohrlich & Solomon (and predecessor firms), 1945-63, sr. partner, 1963-79; sr. ptnr. firm Pincus, Ohrenstein, Bizar, De Alessandro and Solomon, 1980-83; counsel Ohrenstein & Brown, 1983-87, Milman, Stone, Poltarak, Finell & Solomon, N.Y.C., 1987-90, Gallet, Dreyer & Berkey, N.Y.C., 1990—; mem. com. on character and fitness of applicants for admission to bar appellate div. 1st Jud. Dept., 1977—. Author: Jewish Rights in a Jewish Land, 1987; bd. editors N.Y. Law Jour. Mem. Dr. Alfred Meyer Found. Mt. Sinai Hosp., 1951—; trustee Milton Helpern Libr. Legal Medicine Award, 1980; hon. trustee N.Y. Law Sch., 1985; bd. visitors Columbia U. Sch. Law, 1993—. Decorated cavaliere dell' Ordine al Merito (Italy); recipient Horatio Alger Nat. award, 1978, Disting. Alumnus award N.Y. Law Sch., 1986; Joseph Solomon chair in wills, trusts and estates named in his honor Columbia U. Sch. Law, 1974, Joseph Solomon Fund for arts law internship, Joseph Solomon Presdl. Scholars and Fellows Fund; Joseph Solomon chair in law N.Y. Law Sch., 1975, Rita and Joseph Solomon prof. wills, trusts and estates, 1983, Joseph Solomon Pub. Svc. Scholarship and Endowment Fund N.Y. Law Sch., 1990; Joseph Solomon chair in medicine Mt. Sinai Sch. Medicine, 1976. Mem. ABA, New York County Lawyers Assn. (bd. dirs. 1974-78, certification of appreciation), New York County Lawyers Assn. Found., Assn. Bar City N.Y., Lawyers Club (bd. govs. 1975-79), Am. Soc. Italian Legions of Merit, Phi Delta Phi (hon.). Home: 1025 Fifth Ave New York NY 10028-0134 Office: 845 3rd Ave New York NY 10022-6601 *Mindful of my debt to various institutions and individuals in my formative years, I have constantly sought to make repayment in some small measure by my acts for the betterment of society in general and people in particular.*

SOLOMON, JULIUS OSCAR LEE, pharmacist, hypnotherapist; b. N.Y.C., Aug. 14, 1917; s. John and Jeannette (Krieger) S.; student Bklyn. Coll., 1935-36, CCNY, 1936-37; BS in Pharmacy, U. So. Calif., 1949; postgrad. Long Beach State U., 1971-72, Southwestern Colls., 1979, 81-82, San Diego State U., 1994—; PhD, Am. Inst. Hypnotherapy, 1988; postgrad. San Diego State U., 1994—. m. Sylvia Smith, June 26, 1941 (div. Jan. 1975); children: Marc Irwin, Evan Scott, Jeri Lee. Cert. hypnotherapist; cert. hypnoanaesthesia therapist. Dye maker Fred Fear & Co., Bklyn., 1935; apprentice interior decorator Dorothy Draper, 1936; various jobs, N.Y. State Police, 1940-45; rsch. asst. Union Oil Co., 1945; lighting cons. Joe Rosenberg & Co., 1946-49; owner Banner Drug, Lomita, 1949-53, Redondo Beach, Calif., 1953-72, El Prado Pharmacy, Redondo Beach, 1961-65; pres. Banner Drug, Inc., Redondo Beach, 1953-72, Thrifty Drugs, 1972-74, also Guild Drug, Longs Drug, Drug King, 1976-83; pres. Socoma, Inc. doing bus. as Lee & Ana Pharmacy, 1983-86, now Two Hearts Help Clinic, 1986—. Charter commr., founder Redondo Beach Youth Baseball Council; sponsor Little League Baseball, basketball, football, bowling; pres. Redondo Beach Boys Club; v.p. South Bay Children's Health Ctr., 1974, Redondo Beach Coordinating Coun., 1975; bd. dirs. So. Bay Assn. Little Theatres, 1972-75; actor in 8 shows; founder Redondo Beach Community Theater, 1975; actor Man of La Mancha Vangard Theatre, San Diego, 1995; active maj. gift drive YMCA, 1975; mem. SCAG Com. on Criminal Justice, 1974, League Calif. Environ. Quality Com., 1975; mem. Dem. State Cen. Com., Los Angeles County Dem. Cen. Com.; del. Dem. Nat. Conv., 1972; chmn. Redondo Beach Recreation and Parks Commn.; mem. San Diego County Parks Adv. Commn., 1982; mem. San Diego Juvenile Justice Commn., 1986-92; mem. San Diego County Adv. Com. Adult Detention, 1987-92; mem. human resource devel. com., pub. improvement com. Nat. League of Cities; v.p. Redondo Beach Coordinating Coun.; councilman, Redondo Beach, 1961-69, 73-77; treas. 46th Assembly Dist. Coun.; candidate 46 Assembly dist. 1966; nat. chmn. Pharmacists for Humphrey, 1968, 72; pres. bd. dirs. South Bay Exceptional Childrens Soc., Chapel Theatre; bd. dirs. so. div. League Calif. Cities, U.S.-Mex. Sister Cities Assn., Boy's Club Found. San Diego County, Autumn Hills Condominium Assn. (pres.), Calif. Employee Pharmacists Assn. (pres. 1985), Our House, Chula Vista, Calif., 1984-86; mem. South Bay Inter-City Hwy. Com., Redondo Beach Round Table, 1973-77; mem. State Calif. Commn. of Californias (U.S.-Mexico), 1975-78; mem. Chula Vista Safety Commn., 1978, chmn., 1980-81; chmn. San Diego County Juvenile Camp Contract Com., 1982-83; mem. San Diego County Juvenile Delinquency Prevention Commn., 1983-85, 89-91, San Diego County Juvenile Justice Commn., 1986-91, San Diego County Adv. Com. for Adult Detention, 1987-91; spl. participant Calif. Crime and Violence Workshop; mem. Montgomery Planning Commn., 1983-86; mem. Constnl. Observance Com., 1990-93, Troubled Teenagers Hypnosis Treatment Program, 1989—. With USCGR, 1942-45. Recipient Pop Warner Youth award, 1960, 1962, award of merit Calif. Pharm. Assn., 1962, award Am. Assn. Blood Banks, 1982. Diplomate Am. Bd. Diplomates Pharmacy Internat., 1977-81; Fellow Am. Coll. Pharmacists (pres. 1949-57); mem. South Bay Pharm. Assn. (pres.), South Bay Councilman Assn. (founder, pres.), Palos Verdes Peninsula Navy League (charter), Am. Legion, U. So. Calif. Alumni Assn. (life), Assn. Former N.Y. State Troopers (life), AFTRA, Am. Pharm. Assn., Nat. Assn. Retail Druggists, Calif. Pharmacists Assn., Calif. Employee Pharmacist Assn. (bd. dirs. 1980-81), Hon. Dep. Sheriff's Assn., San Ysidro C. of C. (bd. dirs. 1985-87), Fraternal Order of Police, San Diego County Fish and Game Assn., Rho Pi Phi (pres. alumni). Club: Trojan (life). Lodges: Elks (life), Masons (32 deg.; life), Lions (charter mem. North Redondo). Established Lee and Ana Solomon award for varsity athlete witghest scholastic average at 10 L.A. South Bay High Schs. in Los Angeles County and 3 San Diego area South Bay High Schs.

SOLOMON, MARILYN KAY, educator, consultant; b. Marshall, Mo., Oct. 16, 1947; d. John W. and Della M. (Dille) S. BS, Ctrl. Mo. State U., 1969; MS, Ind. U., 1974. Cert. in early childhood and nursery sch. edn., Mo., Ind. Tchr. Indpls. Pub. Schs., 1969-74; dir. Singer Learning Ctrs., Indpls., 1974-78; v.p. ECLC Learning Ctrs., Inc.; Early Learning Ctrs., Inc., Indpls., 1995—; pres., CEO, owner Solomon Antique Restoration, Inc., Indpls., 1996—; owner, pres., CEO, Early Learning Ctrs., Inc., Indpls., 1995—, Solomon Antique Restoration, Inc., Indpls., 1996—; mem. OJT tng. task force Dept. Labor, Washington; mem. nat. task force for parenting edn. HEW, Washington; cons. to numerous corps. on corp. child care. Co-author curricula. Founding bd. dirs. Mid City Pioneer, Indpls., 1977, Enterprise Zone Small Bus. Incubator, Indpls., 1995—, Family Support Ctr., Indpls., 1983, pres. bd. dirs., 1985-87. Recipient Outstanding Leadership award Ind. Conf. on Social Concerns, 1975, 76, 77, Children's Mus. Edn. award, 1974; named to Outstanding Young Women of Am., 1984. Mem. Indpls. Mus. Art, Ind. Lic. Child Care Assn. (v.p. 1992, pres. 1974, 75), State of Ind. Quality and Tng. Coun. (chair 1992), Step Ahead-Marion County (rep. for child care 1992—), Ind. Alliance for Better Child Care (bd. dirs. 1992), Order Eastern Star, Indpls. Zool. Soc. (charter). Office: Early Learning Ctrs Inc 1315 S Sherman Dr Indianapolis IN 46203-2210

SOLOMON, MARK RAYMOND, lawyer, educator; b. Pitts., Aug. 23, 1945; s. Louis Isadore and Fern Rhea (Josselson) S. BA, Ohio State U., 1967; MEd, Cleve. State U., 1971; JD with honors, George Washington U., 1973; LLM in Taxation, Georgetown U., 1976. Bar: Ohio, Mich. Tax law specialist corp. tax br. Nat. Office of IRS, 1973-75; assoc. Butzel, Long, Gust, Klein & Van Zile, Detroit, 1976-78; dir., v.p. Shatzman & Solomon, P.C., Southfield, Mich., 1978-81; prof., chmn. tax and bus. law dept., dir. MS in Taxation Program, Walsh Coll., Troy, Mich., 1981—; of counsel in tax matters Meyer, Kirk, Snyder and Safford PLLC, Bloomfield Hills, Mich., 1981—; adj. prof. law U. Detroit, 1977-81. Editor: Cases and Materials on Consolidated Tax Returns, 1978, Cases and Materials on the Application of Legal Principles and Authorities to Federal Tax Law, 1990. Mem. ABA, Mich. Bar Assn., Phi Eta Sigma. Lodge: Kiwanis (bd. dirs). Avocation: bridge (life master). Home: 2109 Golfview Dr Apt 102 Troy MI 48084-3926 Office: Meyer Kirk Snyder & Safford PLLC 100 W Long Lake Rd Ste 100 Bloomfield Hills MI 48304-2773

SOLOMON, MARSHA HARRIS, draftsman, artist; b. Tulsa, Oct. 21, 1940; d. Ruel Sutton and Anna May (Fellows) Harris; m. Robert E. Collier, Aug. 13, 1960 (div. Dec. 1968); 1 child, Craig Robert Collier; m. Louis G. Solomon, Sept. 5, 1984. Student, U. Tex., 1958-61; BFA, U. Houston, 1966. Chief draftsman Internat. Paper, Petroleum & Minerals Divsn., Houston, 1985—; artist, ptnr. Archway Gallery, Houston, 1994. Mem. Nat. Mus. Women in Art (charter). Mem. Watercolor Art Soc. Houston (bd. dirs. 1984-91, treas. 1987-89, pres. 1990-91), N.Mex. Watercolor Soc. (signature mem.). Home: 5832 Valley Forge Dr Houston TX 77057-2248

SOLOMON, MARTIN M., judge; b. Jan. 24, 1950; BA magna cum laude, SUNY, Albany; LLB, N.Y. Law Sch. admitted to N.Y. bar, 1976; judge N.Y.C. Civil Ct., Brooklyn; mem. N.Y. State Senate, 1978-95, mem. exec. com. Nat. Conf. Ins. Legislators, ranking mem. sen. ins. com., mem. health, bank, judiciary coms. Mem. Oddfellows, KP. Office: NYC Civil Ct 141 Livingston St Brooklyn NY 11201

SOLOMON, MARVIN H., computer science educator, researcher, consultant; b. Chgo., Mar. 11, 1949; s. Jerome R. and Harriet A. (Arenberg) S.; m. Betsy Cromey, Aug. 12, 1984; children: Carlin L. Daley, Rebecca C. BS in Math., U. Chgo., 1970; MS in Computer Sci., Cornell U., 1974, PhD in Computer Sci., 1977. Tchg. asst., rsch. asst. Cornell U., Ithaca, N.Y., 1970-75; vis. lectr. Aarhus (Denmark) U., 1975-76; lectr. U. Wis., Madison, 1976-77, from asst. prof. to assoc. prof., 1977-88, prof., 1988—, chair computer scis., 1993—; vis. scientist IBM, San Jose, Calif., 1984-85; cons. IBM, Digital Equipment, Cross & Trecker; tech. adv. bd. Legato Network Sys., Palo Alto, Calif.; presenter papers at refereed confs. Contbr. articles to profl. jours. Recipient numerous rsch. grants. Mem. IEEE Computer Soc., Assn. for Computing Machinery (mem. program com. 11th symposium on principles of programming langs.). Achievements include research in object-oriented systems, software development support environments, distributed operating systems, computer networks, design and implementation of programming languages, programming language theory. Home: 1106 Mohican Pass Madison WI 53711 Office: U Wis Computer Scis Dept 1210 W Dayton St Madison WI 53706

SOLOMON, MAYNARD ELLIOTT, music historian, former recording company executive; b. N.Y.C., Jan. 5, 1930; s. Benjamin and Dora (Levine) S.; m. Eva Georgiana Tevan, Jan. 22, 1951; children: Mark Jonathan, Nina Stephanie, Maury David. BA, Bklyn. Coll., 1950; postgrad., Columbia U., 1950-51. Co-founder, co-owner Vanguard Rec. Soc., Inc., N.Y.C., 1950-86; faculty grad. div. CUNY, 1979-81; vis. prof. SUNY Stony Brook, 1988, Columbia U., N.Y.C., 1990, Harvard U., Cambridge, Mass., 1992, Yale U., New Haven, 1994-95. Author: Marxism and Art, 1973, Beethoven, 1977 (translated into German, French, Spanish, Portuguese, Japanese, Italian, Bulgarian), Myth, Creativity and Psychoanalysis, 1978, Beethoven's Tagebuch, 1982, Beethoven's Tagebuch, German translation, 1990, Italian translation, 1992, Beethoven Essays, 1988; Mozart: A Life, 1995; contbg. editor: Am. Imago; mem. editorial bd. Beethovenhaus edit. Beethoven's Letters; editor: Memories of Beethoven, 1992; contbr. articles to profl. jours. Recipient Deems Taylor award ASCAP, 1978, 89. Mem. PEN, Am. Musicol. Soc. (bd. dirs. 1984-86, Otto Kinkeldey award 1989), Authors Guild, N.Y. Inst. for Humanities, Phi Beta Kappa. Home: 1 W 72nd St New York NY 10023-3486

SOLOMON, MICHAEL BRUCE, lawyer; b. Chgo., Nov. 8, 1945; s. Arthur J. and Ruth H. (Halpert) S.; m. Tunny Jamri, Dec. 17, 1983. BA, U. Miami, Coral Gables, Fla., 1967, JD, 1970. Bar: Fla. 1970; U.S. Dist. Ct. (so. dist.) Fla. 1972; U.S. Ct. Appeals (5th cir.) 1989, U.S. Ct. Appeals (11th cir.). Assoc. Theodore M. Trushin P.A., Miami Beach, Fla., 1970-77; ptnr. Klein, Oshinsky & Solomon, Hallandale, Fla., 1978-87; pvt. practice Hallandale, Fla., 1988—; spl. asst., pub. defender, Dade County, Fla., 1972-78; ombudsman Dade County pub. defender's office, Miami, 1972. Contbr. article to profl. jour. Mem. ATLA, So. Dist. Fla. Trial Bar, Broward County Bar Assn. Office: 1150 E Hallandale Beach Blvd Ste A Hallandale FL 33009

SOLOMON, MICHAEL ROBERT, marketing educator; b. Washington, Apr. 18, 1956. BA magna cum laude, Brandeis U., 1977; MA, U.N.C., 1979, PhD, 1981. Assoc. dir. Inst. Retail Mgmt. NYU, 1983-85, asst. prof. mktg., 1981-86, assoc. prof. mktg., 1986-87; assoc. prof., chmn. dept. mktg. Rutgers U., New Brunswick, N.J., 1987-95; human scis. prof. of consumer behavior Sch. of Human Scis. Auburn (Ala.) U., 1995—; lectr., presenter in field. Editor: The Psychology of Fashion, 1985, others; contbr. articles to profl. jours.; reviewer jours./books in field. Recipient numerous grants including Burlington Industries, 1985, Mktg. Sci. Inst., 1986, others; faculty fellow Am. Mktg. Assn. Doctoral Consortium, 1987, fellow Nat. Rsch. Svc., 1980, Fulbright fellow, 1996, others. Mem. APA, Assn. Consumer Rsch. Conf. (co-chmn. 1990), Am. Mktg. Assn. (co-chmn. mktg. educator's conf., Toronto 1987), Soc. Consumer Psychology, Ea. Psychol. Assn., Retail Rsch. Soc., Assn. Coll. Profs. Textiles and Clothing, Soc. Study Symbolic Interaction, Popular Culture Assn., others. Office: Dept Consumer Affairs Sch Bus Dept Mktg Auburn U Sch Human Scis Auburn AL 36849

SOLOMON, PAUL ROBERT, neuropsychologist, educator; b. Bklyn., Aug. 27, 1948; s. Maynard and Norma Harris (Ruben) S.; m. Suellen Zablow, Aug. 16, 1970; children: Todd, Jessica. BA in Psychology, SUNY, New Paltz, 1970, MA in Psychology, 1972; PhD in Psychology, U. Mass., 1972. lic. Psychologist, Mass. Prof. psychology and neuroscience Williams Coll, Williamstown, Mass., 1976—, neuroscience program chmn., 1990—; dir. memory disorders clinic S.W. Vt. Med. Ctr., Bennington, 1990—; bd. dirs. No. Berkshire Mental Health Assn., North Adams, Mass. Author: Scientific Writings, 1985, Memory, 1989, Psychology 4th edit., 1993; contbr. articles to profl. jours. Bd. dirs. W. Mass. Alzheimers Assn., 1992—. Recipient Distinguished Teaching award U. Mass., Amherst, 1975; Rsch. grantee EPA, NIH, NSF, 1978—; Rsch. fellowships NIH, 1979, NSF, 1980. Fellow APA, AAAS, Am. Psychol. Soc.; mem. Soc. for Neuroscience. Home: 130 Forest Rd Williamstown MA 01267-2029 Office: Williams Coll Dept Psychology Williamstown MA 01262

SOLOMON, PETER R., physicist, physical chemist, engineering executive; b. N.Y.C., Feb. 19, 1939; married 1975; 3 children. BS, CCNY, 1960; MA, Columbia U., 1963, PhD in Physics, 1965. Rsch. asst. physics Watson Lab. IBM Corp., 1963-65; exptl. physicist United Technol. Rsch. Ctr., 1965-68, prin. scientist, 1968-71, asst. to dir. rsch. progs., technol, 1971-73, prin. physicist, 1973-80; pres. Advanced Fuel Rsch. Inc., Hartford, Conn., 1980—. Mem. Am. Phys. Soc., Am. Chem. Soc. (Henry H. Storch award 1991), Combustion Inst. Achievements include research in low-temperature physics, electrical instabilities in semiconductors, coal science, superconductivity, instabilities in solids. Office: Advanced Fuel Rsch Inc PO Box 18343 Hartford CT 06118-0343

SOLOMON, PHILIP MYRON, astronomer, atmospheric scientist; b. N.Y.C., Mar. 19, 1939; s. Nathan and Betty (Safer) S.; m. Sheila Movit; 1 child, Nina Beth. BS in Physics, U. Wis., 1959, MS in Astronomy, 1961, PhD, 1964. Postdoctoral fellow Princeton U., 1964-66; rsch. assoc., lectr. Columbia U., N.Y.C., 1966-71; assoc. prof. Sch. Physics and Astronomy U. Minn., 1971-73; prof. astronomy dept. earth and space scis. SUNY, Stony Brook, 1974—; vis. scientist Inst. Astronomy, Cambridge (Eng.) U., 1967-69, 72, sr. vis. scientist, 1981-82; mem. in Sch. Natural Scis., Inst. for Advanced Study, Princeton, N.J., 1973-74, 86; overseas fellow Churchill Coll., Cambridge, U., 1981-82; vis. prof. Ecole Normale Superieure, Paris, 1989, Max Planck Inst. for Radioastronomie, Bonn, 1989, Inst. d'Astrophysique, Paris, 1993. Editor: Giant Molecular Clouds in the Galaxy, 1980; contbr. numerous articles to profl. jours. Recipient Sr. Humboldt award Alexander von Humboldt Found., 1989. Mem. Am. Astron. Soc., Internat. Astron. Union. Home: 440 Riverside Dr New York NY 10027-6828 Office: SUNY Stony Book Astronomy Program Dept Earth And Scis Stony Brook NY 11794

SOLOMON, RANDALL L., lawyer; b. Dayton, Ohio, June 8, 1948. BA summa cum laude, Wright State U., 1970; JD, Case Western Res. U., 1973. Bar: Ohio 1973, U.S. Dist. Ct. (no. dist.) Ohio 1973, U.S. Ct. Appeals (6th cir.) 1973, U.S. Ct. Appeals (fed. cir.) 1988. Ptnr. Baker & Hostetler, Cleve.; speaker in field. Fellow Am. Coll. Trial Lawyers; mem. ABA (mem. litigation, tort and ins. practice sects., mem. toxic and hazardous substances and environ. law coms.), Ohio State Bar Assn., Cleve. Bar Assn. (chair litigation sect. 1991-92), Nat. Inst. Trial Advocacy (mem. nat. session 1978), Def. Rsch. Inst. (mem. industrywide litigation com.), Master of Bench, Am. Inn of Ct. Office: Baker & Hostetler 3200 Nat City Ctr 1900 E 9th St Cleveland OH 44114-3401

SOLOMON, RICHARD HARVEY, political scientist; b. Phila., June 19, 1937; s. Bertram Harvey and Ellen (Harris) S.; m. Anne G. Keatley, Dec. 16, 1991. Part-time student, Harvard U., 1959-63, Yale U., 1961, 63-64; SB, MIT, 1960, PhD, 1966. Tech. photographer, lab. worker Photon, Inc., Cambridge, Mass., 1957; researcher Polaroid Corp., 1959-61; research assoc. Ctr. for Chinese Studies U. Mich., Ann Arbor, Mich., 1966-71, from asst prof. to prof. polit. sci., 1966-71; staff mem. NSC, Washington, 1971-76; head. polit. sci dept. The Rand Corp., Santa Monica, Calif., 1976-86, program dir. Internat. Security Policy Research, 1977-83; mem. Pres.' Commn. on Fgn. Lang. and Internat. Studies Washington, 1978-80, mem. Chief of Naval Ops. exec. panel, 1983—; dir. policy planning staff Dept. of State, Washington, 1986-89, asst. sec. of state for East Asian and Pacific affairs, 1989-92; U.S. ambassador to Philippines, 1992-93; pres. U.S. Inst. of Peace, Washington, 1993—. Author: Mao's Revolution and the Chinese Political Culture, 1971, Chinese Political Negotiating Behavior, 1986; contbr. articles to profl. jours. Office: US Inst of Peace 1550 M St NW Ste 700 Washington DC 20005-1708

SOLOMON, RISA GREENBERG, video software industry executive; b. N.Y.C., June 22, 1948; d. Nathan and Frances (Guttman) Greenberg; m. Philip Howard Solomon, June 21, 1970; children: Elycia Beth, Cynthia Gayle. BA, NYU, 1969, MA, 1970. Asst. editor Redbook Mag., N.Y.C., 1969-70; assoc. editor Greenwood Press, Westport, Conn., 1970-71; mng. editor Dushkin Pub., Guilford, Conn., 1971-72; freelance editor Yale U. Press, New Haven, Conn., 1972-75; v.p. ops. Videoland, Inc., Dallas, 1980-82; v.p. Video Software Dealers Assn., Cherry Hill, N.J. and Dallas, 1981-83; pres. Videodome Enterprises, Dallas, 1983—; cons. Home Recording Rights Coalition, Washington, 1983-84. Contbr. articles to video mags. Bd. dirs. Congregation Anshai Emet, Dallas, 1985-86. Mem. Video Software Dealers Assn. (founder, dir. 1981-82). Democrat. Jewish. Avocations: world travel, tennis, water and snow skiing. Office: Videodome Enterprises 11420 St Michaels Dr Dallas TX 75230-2436

SOLOMON, ROBERT, economist; b. N.Y.C., May 2, 1921; s. Sol and Betty (Brownstone) S.; m. Fern Rice, Sept. 11, 1946; children: Carol Ann, Barbara Betty, Anne Eleanor. B.A., U. Mich., 1942; M.A., Harvard U., 1947, Ph.D., 1952. With Fed. Res. Bd., 1947-76, assoc. adviser research div., 1963-65, adviser research div., 1965, adviser to bd. govs., 1965-76, dir. div. internat. fin., 1966-72; sr. fellow Brookings Instn., Washington, 1976-80; guest scholar Brookings Instn., 1980—; pres. RS Assos., pub. Internat. Econ. Letter, 1981—; vice chmn. deps. of com. of 20 IMF, 1972-74; adj. prof. Am. U., 1962-67; sr. staff economist Council Econ. Advisers, 1963-64. Author: The International Monetary System, 1945-81, 1982, Partners in Prosperity, 1991, The Transformation of the World Economy, 1980-93, 1994; contbr. articles to profl. jours. Served to 1st lt. USAAF, 1942-45. Decorated D.F.C., Air medal, officier Legion of Honor France; recipient Rockefeller Pub. Service award, 1971. Mem. Am. Econ. Assn., Council on Fgn. Relations. Club: Cosmos (Washington). Home and Office: 8502 W Howell Rd Bethesda MD 20817-6827

SOLOMON, ROBERT CHARLES, philosopher, educator; b. Detroit, Sept. 14, 1942; s. Charles M. and Vita (Petrosky) S. BA, U. Pa., 1963; MA, U. Mich., 1965, PhD, 1967. Teaching fellow U. Mich., Ann Arbor, 1965-66; lectr. Princeton (N.J.) U., 1966-67, 67-68; asst. prof. U. Pitts., 1969-71, CUNY, 1971-72; assoc. prof. philosophy U. Tex., Austin, 1972-77, prof., 1977—, Quincy Lee Centennial prof., 1986—; vis. prof. U. Pa., UCLA, U. Auckland, N.Z., La Trobe U., Melbourne, Australia, U. B.C.; chmn. Phi Beta Kappa Emerson Award Com.; cons. in field. Author: From Rationalism to Existentialism, 1972, The Passions, 1976, Introducing Philosophy: Problems and Perspectives, 1977, History and Human Nature: A Philosophical Review of European History and Culture, 1750-1850, 1979, Love: Emotion, Myth and Metaphor, 1981, In the Spirit of Hegel, 1983, (with C. Calhoun) What Is an Emotion?, 1984, It's a Good Business, 1985, (with Kristine Hanson) Above the Bottom Line, 1983, From Hegel to Existentialism, 1987, Continental Philosophy After 1750, 1988, About Love, 1988, A Passion for Justice, 1990, Ethics: A Briefer Introduction, 1991, Ethics and Excellence, 1992, Entertaining Ideas, 1992, (with J. Solomon) Up the University, 1993, (with Kathleen Higgins) A Short History of Philosophy, 1996; editor: Phenomenology and Existentialism, 1972, Nietzsche, 1973, Existentialism, 1974, (with Kathleen Higins) Reading Nietzsche, 1988, From Africa to Zen, 1993, The Age of German Idealism, 1993, (with Mark A. Murphy) What Is Justice?, 1990; contbr. articles to profl. jours. Recipient Outstanding Tchr. award Standard Oil Co., 1973, Pres.' Teaching Excellence award, 1985. Mem. Am. Philos. Assn., N.Am. Nietzsche Soc. (exec. bd.), Internat. Soc. Research on Emotions (bd. dirs.), Soc. for Bus. Ethics.

SOLOMON, ROBERT DOUGLAS, pathology educator; b. Delavan, Wis., Aug. 28, 1917; s. Lewis Jacob and Sara (Ludgin) S.; m. Helen Fisher, Apr. 4, 1943; children: Susan, Wendy, James, William. Student, MIT, 1934-36; BS in Biochemistry, U. Chgo., 1938; MD, Johns Hopkins U., 1942. Intern John's Hopkins Hosp., 1942-43; resident in pathology Michael Reese Hosp., 1947-49; lectr. U. Ill., Chgo., 1947-50; fellow NIH pathology U. Ill., 1949-50; asst. prof. U. Md., Balt., 1955-60; assoc. prof. U. So. Calif., L.A., 1960-70; chief of staff City of Hope Nat. Med. Ctr., 1966-67; prof. U. Mo., Kansas City, 1977-78, SUNY, Syracuse, 1968-78; chief of staff The Hosp., Sidney, N.Y., 1985-86; adj. prof. U. N.C., Wilmington, 1988—; cons. VA Hosp., Balt., 1955-60, Med. Svc. Lab., Wilmington, 1989-93. Co-author: Progress in Gerontological Research, 1967; contbr. papers and profl. jours. and rsch. in biochemistry, revascular of heart, carcinogenesis, cancer chemotherapy, atherogenesis, discovery of reversibility of atherosclerosis. V.p. Rotary, Duarte, Calif., 1967; v.p. and pres. Force for an Informed Electorate. Capt. Med. Corps, AUS, 1943-46, PTO. Grantee NIH, Fleischmann Found., Am. Heart Assn., Nat. Cancer Inst., 1958-70. Fellow ACP (pres. Md. chpt.); mem. Coll. Am. Pathologists (past pres. Md. chpt.), Am. Soc. Clin. Pathologists, Assn. Clin. Scientists, Am. Chem. Soc., Royal Soc. Medicine (London). Avocations: cruising, astronomy, mathematics, fishing, stamps. Home: 113 S Belvedere Dr Hampstead NC 28443-2504

SOLOMON, RUSSELL, retail products executive; b. 1925. CEO MTS. Office: MTS PO Box 919001 Diamond Springs CA 95619*

SOLOMON, SAMUEL, biochemistry educator, administrator; b. Brest Litovsk, Poland, Dec. 5, 1925; s. Nathan and Rachel (Greenberg) S.; m. Sheila R. Horn, Aug. 11, 1953 (div. 1974); children—David Horn, Peter Horn, Jonathan Simon; m. Augusta M. Vineberg, July 12, 1974. B.S. with honors, McGill U., 1947, M.S., 1951, Ph.D. in Biochemistry, 1953. Research asst. Columbia, 1953-55, asso. in biochemistry, 1958-59, asst. prof., 1959-60; asso. prof. biochemistry and exptl. medicine McGill U., 1960-66, prof., 1967-95; prof. emeritus, 1995—; prof. ob-gyn. McGill U., 1976-95; dir. endocrine lab. Royal Victoria Hosp., Montreal, Que., 1965-95, dir. research inst., 1982-85; mem. endocrinology and metabolism grants com. Med. Rsch. Coun. Can., 1967-71, regional dir. for Que., 1993-95; vis. prof. endocrinology U. Vt., 1964; cons. in field; Joseph Price orator, 1982, Am. OB-GYN Soc.; mem. steering com. Pharm. Mfg. Assn. Med. Rsch. Coun. Can. Partnership, 1993—; Med. Rsch. Coun. Can. dir. for McGill U., 1993-95. Co-editor: Chemical and Biological Aspects of Steroid Conugation, 1970; Editorial bd.: Endocrinology, 1962; asso. editor: Can. Jour. Biochemistry, 1967-71, Jour. Med. Primatology, 1971; Contbr. articles profl. jours. Mem. bd. govs. McGill U., 1975-78; mem. steering com. European Study Group on Steroid Hormones, 1974—, chmn. steering com., 1983-95, chmn. program com., 1990-91; mem. Dubin Commn. on Inquiry Drugs in Athletes, 1988-90. Recipient McLaughlin medal Royal Soc. Can., 1989. Fellow Chem. Inst. Can., Am. Ob-Gyn. Soc. (hon.), Perinatal Rsch. Soc. Am. (pres. 1976), Soc. Gynecol. Investigation (program chmn. 1980), Endocrine Soc. (publ. com. 1986-89). Home: 239 Kensington Ave 804, Montreal, PQ Canada H3Z 2H1 Office: Royal Victoria Hosp Dept Endocrinology, 687 Pine Ave W, Montreal, PQ Canada H3A 1A1

SOLOMON, SEAN CARL, geophysicist, lab administrator; b. L.A., Oct. 24, 1945. BS geophysics, Calif. Inst. Tech., 1966; PhD geophysics, MIT, 1971. From asst. prof. to prof. geophysics Mass. Inst. Tech., Cambridge, 1972-92; dir. dept. terrestrial magnetism Carnegie Instn., Washington, 1992—; vis. scientist Lunar Sci. Inst., 1975, Jet Propulsion Lab., 1978; guest investigator Woods Hole Oceanographic Inst., 1979-92; vis. faculty Inst. Geophysics and Planetary physics, dept. earth and space scis., UCLA, 1982-83; Roland and Jane Blumberg vis. prof. planetary scis. U. Tex., Austin, 1988; vis. assoc. divsn. geol. and planetary scis. Calif. Inst. Tech., 1990-91; mem. various groups, teams, coms. NASA, 1974—, earthquake hazards reduction program peer review panel U.S. Geol. Survey, 1975, 85; lunar and planetary sci. coun. Univs. Space Rsch. Assn., 1978-80, 91-93; tech. review panel, geophysics review panel Dept. Def., 1981-86; chmn. steering com. space sci. working group Assn. Am. Univs., 1984-91; review panelist NSF, 1986, 88, 95, 96; chmn. standing com. global seismic network Inc. Rsch. Instns. Seismology, 1987-90; participant numerous oceanographic expeditions, 1967-88. Assoc. editor Proceedings of the Lunar and Planetary Sci. Conf., 1976, 78, Jour. Geophys. Rsch., 1976-78, Physics Earth and Planetary Interiors, 1977, Eos Transactions of Am. Geophys. Union, 1979-81, Geophys. Rsch. Letters, 1986-88; editor Tectonophysics, 1981; edit. bd. Physics and Chemistry of Earth, 1981-85; edit. com. Ann. Review Earth and Planetary Scis., 1993—; contbr. over 150 articles to profl. jours. Grad. fellow NSF, 1966-68, postdoctoral fellow, 1971-72; Fannie and John Hertz Found. fellow, 1968-71; Alfred P. Sloan rsch. fellow, 1977-81; John Simon Guggenheim meml. fellow, 1982-83. Fellow AAAS, Am. Acad. Arts and Scis., Am. Geophys. Union (pres. elect and pres. 1994—, pres. planetology sect. 1984-88, chmn. geophys. monograph bd. 1983-84, numerous coms.); mem. Seismological Soc. Am., Geol. Soc. Am., Am. Astron. Soc. (divsn. planetary scis.), Tau Beta Pi. Office: Carnegie Instn Dept Terrestrial Magnetism 5241 Broad Branch Rd NW Washington DC 20015-1305

SOLOMON, SOLOMON SIDNEY, endocrinologist, pharmacologist, scientist; b. N.Y.C., Dec. 2, 1936; s. Nathan and Irene (Oransky) S.; m. Linda M. Shaw, June 17, 1962 (div. 1980); children: Joan Geller, Rebecca Karen. AB in Chemistry, Harvard U., 1958; MD, U. Rochester, 1962. Intern in internal medicine New Eng. Med. Ctr., Tufts U., Boston, 1963; resident in internal medicine Boston City Hosp., 1964, 65; fellow in endocrinology and metabolism U. Wash. Sch. Medicine, Seattle, 1965-67; teaching fellow Tufts U. and Boston City Hosp., Boston, 1964-65; asst. prof., assoc. prof. then prof. medicine U. Tenn. Sch. Medicine, Memphis, 1969—, assoc. dean for rsch., 1983—, prof. pharmacology, 1986—; chief endocrinology and metabolism VA Med. Ctr., Memphis, 1971—; cons. in field; mem. merit rev. bd. VA Rsch. Svc., Washington, 1978-81. Coeditor: The Lab in Clinical Diagnosis, 1981; contbr. numerous articles and abstracts to profl. jours. Capt. MC, USAF, 1967-69. Harvard Coll. scholar, 1954-58; Whipple scholar, 1959-62; VA and NIH grantee, 1965—. recipient career and devel. award VA Ctrl. Office Rsch. Svc., 1969-71, 1st place for excellence in clin. rsch. Memphis Area Health Industry Couns., 1994. Fellow Am. Coll. Endocrinology; mem. Am. Diabetes Assn. (pres. Tenn. chpt. 1975-76, rsch. com., chmn. metabolism sect. 1982), So. Soc. Clin. Investigation (chmn. metabolism sect. 1975, 88, nominating com. 1989), Endocrine Soc., Am. Fedn. for Clin. Rsch. (counselor south sect. 1976-79), Am. Soc. Clin. Investigation, Cen. Soc. for Clin. Rsch., Am. Soc. Pharmacology and Exptl. Therapy, Fedn. Am. Soc. Exptl. Biology. Jewish. Avocations: antique furniture, history, music, tennis, running. Home: 5196 Longmeadow Dr Memphis TN 38134-4316 Office: VA Med Ctr 1030 Jefferson Ave Memphis TN 38104-2127 *At the risk of being mundane, my philosophy in life has always been to get involved...my motto is "I came to play, not to watch."*

SOLOMON, VITA PETROSKY, artist; b. Phila., Dec. 16, 1916; d. Harry and Rose (Bobrow) Petrosky; m. Charles M. Solomon, Apr. 8, 1941; children: Robert Charles, Henry Andrew, Jon David. Diploma, Moore Inst. Art, 1937; B.F.A., Tyler Sch. Fine Arts, Temple U., 1958, B.S. in Edn, 1958, M.F.A., 1960. tchr. art and art history Cheltenham High Sch.; tchr. art and English Elkins Park Jr. High Sch. Exhibited in group shows at United Soc. Artists, London, Pa. Acad. Fine Art, Phila. Art Mus., Detroit Inst. Art, Butler Inst. Art, Silvermine Guild, Conn., N.A.D., Am. Water Color Soc., Audubon Soc., Royal Acad. Arts, London, Paris Salon, Woodmere Art Gallery, Phila. Art Alliance, Royal Inst. London, Nat. Arts Club, N.Y., Met. Mus. Art , others; represented in permanent collections Nat. Portrait Gallery, Phila. Mus. Art, Fed. Res. Bank, Temple U., U. Pa., Phila. City Hall, Free Library Phila., Phila. Psychiat. Inst., Cheltenham Twp. Adminstrn. Bldg., others, including portraits on commn.; one-artist shows include Phila. Art Alliance, 1953, 54, 58, Red Door Gallery, 1959, 60, 61, Newman Gallery, 1964, Moore Coll. Art, 1974, Suzanne Gross Gallery, 1979. J.F. Lewis traveling fellow Europe, by Moore Inst., 1937; recipient Gross Meml. award Silvermine Guild, 1958, Chandler prize Allied Artists Am., 1960, Nat. Arts Club award, 1974, prizes Moore Inst., 1957, 60, 61, purchase prize Temple U., 1959 (2), 1960, painting prize, 1966, Burdine meml. prize Woodmere Gallery, 1964, painting prize Wharton Art Ctr., 1964, Lowell Painting prize C.L. Wolfe Club, Nat. Arts Club, 1966, Painting prize Silver medal Paris Salon, 1966, award Phila. Watercolor Club, 1973, Benedictine Art award, 1972, Blumenthal prize Cheltenham Art Center, 1973, Jane Peterson medal Audubon Artists, 1975, Eugenia Atwood purchase prize Phila. Print Club, 1975, Eyre medal Phila. Watercolor Club, 1977, Best Figure Painting prize Woodmere Gallery, 1977, Best in Show award Moore Coll. Art, 1980, award of excellence Ariz. Aqueous VII, 1992, 2nd prize Phila. Plastic Show, 1993, Best in Show award Tubac Ctr. Arts, Ariz., 1995, Spl. Recognition & Best of Show So. Ariz. Watercolor Guild, 1996. Mem. Am. Watercolor Soc., Cheltenham Twp. Art Centre (award for best profl. painting 1980, 83, 85), Am. Watercolor Soc., Artists Equity, Phila. Water Color Club (Pennell Meml. prize 1987, 88), Allied Artists Am., Am. Color Print Soc. (prize 1987), Western Fedn. Watercolor Socs. (award of excellence 1991), So. Ariz. Watercolor Guild (Excellence award U. Ariz. 1991, Signature mem. 1992, Past Pres.'s award 1994), So. Ariz. Tubac Ctr. Arts (award of excellence 1991, hon. mention 1993), Phila. Sketch Club (Best in Show award ann. pastel show, hon. mention 1990, 3d prize ann. print show 1993). Home: 200 Locust St Apt 24G Philadelphia PA 19106-3920 also: 6298 N Campbell Ave Tucson AZ 85718-3150

SOLOMON, WILLIAM TARVER, general construction company executive; b. Dallas, Aug. 11, 1942; s. Marion Bryant and Margaret (Moore) S.; m. Gay Ferguson, Feb. 15, 1964; children—William Tarver Jr., Meredith M. BSCE, So. Meth. U., 1965; MBA, Harvard U., 1967. With Austin Industries, Inc., Dallas, 1967—, chmn., pres., CEO, 1970—; chmn. Austin Comml., Inc., Dallas, Brit. Am. Ins. Co., Dallas; bd. dirs. A.H. Belo Corp., Chilton Corp., Fidelity Union Life, Nat. Bank Tex. Immediate past chmn. Dallas Citizens Coun.; bd. dirs. Baylor U. Med. Ctr. Found., Dallas Mus. Art; trustee Southwestern Med. Found., So. Meth. U. Recipient citation of honor Dallas chpt. AIA, 1985, Humanitarian award NCCJ, Dallas, 1982, Champion of Free Enterprise award Associated Builders and Contractors, 1985, Outstanding Alumni award Southern Meth. U., 1988. Mem. ASCE, Young Pres.'s Orgn. (past chmn. Dallas chpt.), Dallas Assembly, Salesmanship Club Dallas, Dallas C. of C. (bd. dirs.). Republican. United Methodist. Home: 3830 Windsor Ln Dallas TX 75205-1743 Office: Austin Industries Inc PO Box 1590 Dallas TX 75221*

SOLOMON, ZACHARY LEON, apparel manufacturing company executive; b. N.Y.C., July 22, 1934; s. Nathan and Rose Solomon; children: Lisa, Michael, Andrew, Romy; m. Susan Phillips. BA, Bklyn. Coll., 1957; MBA, NYU, 1962. Div. mdse. mgr. Abraham & Strauss, Bklyn., 1957-72; v.p., gen. mdse. mgr. Apparel Buying Svcs., Secaucus, N.Y., 1972-73; sr. v.p., gen. mdse. mgr. May Co., L.A., 1974-75, exec. v.p., 1980-82; exec. v.p. The Emporium, San Francisco, 1976-77, pres., 1978-80; exec. v.p. Manhattan Industries, N.Y.C., pres., CEO Perry Ellis, 1983-87; pres. Ellen Tracy Co., N.Y.C., 1987-90; pres., chief exec. officer Associated Merchandising Corp., N.Y.C., 1991—. Trustee Bklyn. Coll. Jewish. Office: Associated Merchandising 1440 Broadway New York NY 10018

SOLOMONS, GUS, JR. (GUSTAVE MARTINEZ), choreographer, dancer, writer; b. Boston; s. Gustave Martinez and Olivia Mae. Student, Boston Conservatory of Music, 1956-59; BArch, MIT, 1961; postgrad., Martha Graham Sch., N.Y.C., 1961-66. Dance soloist Martha Graham Co., N.Y.C., 1964-65, Donald McKayle Co., 1961-64, Merce Cunningham Co., N.Y.C., 1965-68; artistic dir. The Solomons Dance Co., N.Y.C., 1972—; dean, artistic dir. Calif. Inst. of the Arts, Valencia, 1976-78; vis. artist-in-residence U. Calif., Santa Cruz, Calif. State U., Long Beach, others; dance panelist Nat. Endowment Arts; various other other state art couns., 1983—; assoc. prof. dance numerous colls., univs., including UCLA, Un. Nev.-Las Vegas, Tex. Christian U., York, Simon Fraser, NYU; mem. faculty Tisch Sch. of Arts, 1994—; USIA cons. to Nat. Dance Co., Tanzania, East Africa, 1988, Argentina, 1994. Appearances maj. TV networks, Sta. WGBH-TV, Boston; choreographr for various univs. and dance cos.; writer dance criticism for Village Voice, Dance Mag., others. Recipient numerous grants Nat. Endowment for Arts, 1983—, N.Y. State Coun. on the Arts, 1972—; fellow Nat. Endowment for Arts, 1978-80. Studio: 889 Broadway New York NY 10003-1212 *The content of a good dance is the truth about its maker. Performing it is a confession to the audience. The dancer places himself in the position of ultimate vulnerability each time he performs; it is at once cleansing, fulfilling, and courageous.*

SOLOMONS, MARK ELLIOTT, lawyer; b. Buffalo, Mar. 4, 1946; s. Alvin and Trude (Salant) S.; m. Jill E. Kent, Aug. 20, 1978. BA, U. Rochester, 1967; JD, U. Pa., 1970; LLM, George Washington U., 1973. Bar: N.Y. 1971, D.C. 1981. Staff atty. U.S. Dept. Labor, Washington, 1970-73, counsel coal miners benefits, 1973-77, legis. counsel, 1977-80; prin. Kilcullen Wilson & Kilcullen, Washington, 1980-86; ptnr. Arter and Hadden, Washington, 1986—, mem. exec. com., 1989—; guest lectr. law and history SUNY-Stony Brook, 1970-76, U. Mich., 1977-78, Hobart Coll., 1972-76; prin. Coun. for Excellence in Govt., 1991—. Contr. articles to profl. jours. Vice chair Appellate Advocacy Com., 1994—. Mem. ABA (chair workers compensation and employers liability com. 1987-88, sr. vice chair 1988-94), Fed. Bar Assn. (chair regulatory com. 1988—), D.C. Bar Assn., N.Y. Bar Assn., Am. Inn of Ct. (master 1991, counselor 1996—). Republican. Office: Arter & Hadden 1801 K St NW Washington DC 20006-1301

SOLOMONSON, CHARLES D., corporate executive; b. 1930; m. Sarah B. Auer, 1952; children: Katherine M., Charles W. B.S., Columbia U., 1954; M.B.A., Harvard U., 1956. With Denver Union Stock Yard Co., 1956-60; sec., asst. treas. G. D. Searle & Co., 1960-68; with Jos. Schlitz Brewing Co., 1968-69, treas., 1968-69; v.p. fin. Fairmont Food Co., Omaha, 1969-73, pres., 1973-74, dir., 1972-75; v.p. fin., treas. Hobart Corp., Troy, Ohio, 1975-77, v.p. fin. and Adminstrn., dir., 1977-79; sr. v.p., chief fin. officer Holiday Corp., Memphis, 1979, dir., 1980-86, exec. v.p., chief fin. and adminstrv. officer, 1981-87; ret. Trustee Nebr. Meth. Hosp., 1973-75, Miami Valley Hosp., Dayton, Ohio, 1977-79, Sta. WKNO-TV-FM, Memphis, 1983-88, Dixon Gallery and Gardens, 1985-88. Episcopalian. Home: 1030 N State St Apt 42H Chicago IL 60610-2837

SOLON, MELVA JUNE, mental health nurse; b. Streator, Ill., Mar. 12, 1943; d. Melvin L. and Vincentina J. (Verdiramo) Chalfant; m. Thomas P. Solon, July 25, 1964; children: Thomas P. (dec.), Susan Denise. Diploma, St. Charles Hosp. Sch. Nursing, 1964; BSN, Gov.'s State U., University Park, 1981; MSN, Ind. U.-Purdue U., Indpls., 1996. RN, Ill., Ind.; cert. mental health nurse. Night supr. Chastain's Nursing Home & Convalescent Ctr., Highland, Ill.; staff charge nurse night shift Norman (Okla.) Mcpl. Hosp., Wesley Meml. Hosp., Chgo.; staff nurse, night charge nurse Danville (Ill.) VA Med. Ctr. Mem. AAUW (charter), Am. Psychiat. Nurses Assn. (charter), Ill. Psychiat. Nurses Assn. (charter), Sigma Theta Tau (charter). Home: 1644 N Franklin St Danville IL 61832-2364

SOLOTOROVSKY, JULIAN, lawyer; b. Plainfield, N.J., Oct. 12, 1951; s. Morris and Mary Louise (Whitty) S.; m. Stacee Levy, Sept. 13, 1980; children: Alec, Scott, Laura. BA, U. Va., 1973; JD, John Marshall Law Sch., Chgo., 1978. Bar: Ill. 1978, U.S. Dist. Ct. (no. dist.) Ill. 1978, U.S. Ct. Appeals (7th cir.) 1978. Asst. U.S. atty., dep. chief spl. prosecutions U.S. Dept. Justice, Chgo., 1978-87; mem. Kelley Drye & Warren, Chgo., 1987—; mem. 7th Cir. Jury Instrn. Com., Chgo., 1979-82. Avocations: running, gardening, carpentry. Office: Kelley Drye & Warren 303 W Madison St Chicago IL 60606*

SOLOV, ZACHARY, choreographer, ballet artist; b. Phila., Feb. 15, 1923; s. Carl Nathan and Sima (Silnutzer) S. Student, Littlefield Ballet Sch., 1937-40, U. of the Dance, 1947. Appeared with, Am. Jubilee, N.Y. World's Fair, 1940, tour with, Littlefield Ballet, 1941, Am. Ballet, S.A., 1941; with, Dance Players, summer quarters, New Hope, Pa., 1942, The Lady Comes Across, N.Y. City, 1942, Ballet Theatre, London, 1946; choreographer ballet master, Met. Opera, N.Y. City. Served as staff sgt. A.A.C., 1943-46. Recipient Capezio Dance award, 1952. Office: 200 W 58th St New York NY 10019-1401

SOLOVY, JEROLD SHERWIN, lawyer; b. Chgo., Apr. 10, 1930; s. David and Ida (Wilensky) S.; m. Kathleen Hart; children: Stephen, Jonathan. B.A., U. Mich., 1952; LL.B., Harvard U., 1955. Bar: Ill. 1955. Assoc. Jenner & Block, Chgo., 1955-63, ptnr., 1963—, chmn., 1991—. Active Cook County Jud. Adv. Council, Chgo., 1975-77, 82-89, chmn., 1989-91. Fellow Am. Coll. Trial Lawyers; mem. ABA, Chgo. Bar Assn., Ill. State Bar. Assn. Clubs: Standard; Lake Shore Country (Chgo.). Office: Jenner & Block Bldg 4400 1 IBM Plaza Chicago IL 60611-3586

SOLOW, HERBERT FRANKLIN, film producer, writer; b. N.Y.C., Dec. 14, 1930; s. Morris David and Frances Louise (birnbaum) S.; m. Maxine Debra Turner, Aug. 6, 1954 (div. 1974); children: Jody, Bonnie, Jamie; m. Yvonne Fern, 1996. AB, Dartmouth Coll., 1953. Agt. William Morris Agy., N.Y.C., 1954-58; dir., exec. NBC, N.Y.C., 1958-59, Los Angeles, 1958-60, CBS, Los Angeles, 1961-63; v.p. Desilu Studios, Los Angeles, 1964-69; v.p. prodn. Paramount TV, Los Angeles, 1969; v.p. worldwide prodn. Metro-Goldwyn-Mayer, Los Angeles, 1969-73; pres. Solow Prodn. Co., Los Angeles, 1976-79; v.p. Sherwood Prodns., Los Angeles, 1980-83; ind. producer, writer Los Angeles, 1984—. Mem. Writers Guild Am., Dirs. Guild Am., Acad. Motion Picture Arts and Scis., Acad. TV Arts and Scis.

SOLOW, ROBERT MERTON, economist, educator; b. Brooklyn, N.Y., Aug. 23, 1924; s. Milton Henry and Hannah Gertrude (Sarney) S.; m. Barbara Lewis, Aug. 19, 1945; children: John Lewis, Andrew Robert, Katherine. BA, Harvard U., 1947, MA, 1949, PhD, 1951, DLitt (hon.), 1992; LLD (hon.), U. Chgo., 1967, Brown U., 1972, U. Warwick, 1976, Tulane U., 1983, Dartmouth Coll., 1990; DLitt (hon.), Williams Coll., 1974, Lehigh U., 1977, Wesleyan U., 1982, Boston Coll., 1986, Harvard U., 1992, Colgate U., 1990; DSc (hon.), U. Paris, 1975, U. Geneva, 1982, Bryant Coll., 1988; D of Social Sci. (hon.), Yale U., 1976, U. Mass., Boston, 1989; D Social Sci. (hon.), U. Helsinki, 1990, SUNY, Albany, 1991, U. Glasgow, 1992, Rutgers U., 1994; D honoris causa, U. Chile, 1992; Conservatoire, Nat. des Arts et Métiers, Paris, 1994; D in Engring., Colo. Sch. Mines, 1996. Mem. faculty MIT, 1949-95, prof. econs., 1958-95, inst. prof., 1973-95, prof. emeritus, 1995—; W. Edwards Deming prof. NYU, 1996; sr. economist Coun. Econ. Advisers, 1961-62, cons., 1962-68; cons. RAND Corp., 1952-64; Marshall lectr., fellow commoner Peterhouse, Cambridge (Eng.) U., 1963-64; Eastman vis. prof. Oxford U., 1968-69; overseas fellow Churchhill Coll., Cambridge; sr. fellow Soc. Fellows, Harvard U., 1975-89; bd. dirs. Boston Fed. Res. Bank, 1975-80, chmn., 1979-80; active President's Commn. on Income Maintenance, 1968-70, President's Com. on Tech., Automation and Econ. Progress, 1964-65, Carnegie Commn. Sci., Tech. and Govts., 1988-93, Nat. Sci. Bd., 1994—. Author: Linear Programming and Economic Analysis, 1958, (with R. Dortman, P. Samuelson) Capital Theory and the Rate of Return, 1963, The Sources of Unemployment in the United States, 1964, Growth Theory, 1970, Price Expectations and the Behavior of the Price Level, 1970, (with M. Dertouzos, R. Lester) Made in America, 1989, The Labor Market as a Social Institution, 1990, (with F. Hahn) A Critical Essay on Modern Macroeconomic Theory, 1995. Bd. dirs., mem. exec. com. Nat. Bur. Econ. Rsch.; trustee Inst. for Advanced Study, Princeton U., 1972-78, Woods Hole Oceanographic Inst., 1988—, Alfred P. Sloan Found., 1992—, Resources for the Future, 1994—, Urban Inst., 1994—, German Marshall Fund of U.S., 1994—. With AUS, 1942-45. Recipient David A. Wells prize Harvard U., 1951, Seidman award in polit. economy, 1983, Nobel prize in Econs., 1987; fellow Ctr. Advanced Study Behavioral Scis., 1957-58, trustee, 1982-95, chmn., 1987-95. Fellow Am. Acad. Arts and Scis., Brit. Acad. (corr.); mem. AAAS (v.p. 1970), Am. Philos. Soc., Nat. Acad. Scis. (coun. 1977-80, 95), Acad. dei Lincei, Order Pour le merite (Germany), Am. Econ. Soc. (exec. com. 1964-66, John Bates Clark medal 1961, v.p. 1968, pres. 1979), Econometric Soc. (pres. 1964, mem. exec. com.). Home: 528 Lewis Wharf Boston MA 02110-3920 Office: MIT Dept Econs Cambridge MA 02139

SOLOWAY, ALBERT HERMAN, medicinal chemist; b. Worcester, Mass., May 29, 1925; s. Bernard and Mollie (Raphaelson) S.; m. Barbara Berkowicz, Nov. 29, 1953; children: Madeleine Rae, Paul Daniel, Renee Ellen. Student, U.S. Naval Acad., 1945-46; BS, Worcester Poly. Inst., 1948; PhD, U. Rochester, 1951. Postdoctoral fellow Nat. Cancer Inst. at Sloan-Kettering Inst., N.Y.C., 1951-53; research chemist Eastman Kodak Co., Rochester, N.Y., 1953-56; asst. chemist Mass. Gen. Hosp., Boston, 1956-61, asso. chemist, 1961-73; asso. prof. med. chemistry Northeastern U., Boston, 1966-68, prof. medicinal chemistry, chmn. dept., 1968-71, prof. medicinal chemistry and chemistry, chmn. dept. medicinal chemistry and pharmacology, 1971-74; dean Coll. Pharmacy and Allied Health Professions, 1975-77; dean Coll. Pharmacy Ohio State U., Columbus, 1977-88, prof. medicinal chemistry, 1977—. Author rsch. in medicinal chemistry, boron neutron caputre therapy of cancer. Recipient Disting. Achievements in Boron Sci. award Boron USA, 1994. Fellow AAAS, Acad. Pharm. Soc.; mem. Am. Chem. Soc., Am. Assn. Coll. Pharmacy, Am. Assn. Cancer Research, Am. Assn. Pharm. Sci., Am. Nuclear Soc. Office: Ohio State U 500 W 12th Ave Columbus OH 43210-1214

SOLTANOFF, JACK, nutritionist, chiropractor; b. Newark, Apr. 24, 1915; s. Louis and Rose (Yomteff) S.; m. Esther Katcher, Sept. 29, 1939; children: Howard, Ruth C. Soltanoff Jacobs, Hillory Soltanoff Seaton. N.M.D. Mecca Coll. Chiropractic Medicine, 1938, U.S. Sch. Naturopathy and Allied Scis.,

1951; D.Chiropractic, Chiropractic Inst. N.Y., 1956; postgrad. Atlantic States Chiropractic Inst., 1962-63, Nat. Coll. Chiropractic, 1964-65; PhD, diplomate in nutrition Fla. Natural Health Coll., 1982. Gen. practice chiropractic medicine, cons. in nutrition, N.Y.C., 1956-75, West Hurley, N.Y. and Singer Island, Fla., 1975—; lectr., cons. in field. Author: Natural Healing; pub. Warner Books; contbr. articles to profl. jours. Syndicated newspaper columnist. Fellow Internat. Coll. Naturopathic Physicians; mem. Am. Chiropractic Assn., Internat. Chiropractic Assn., Brit. Chiropractic Assn., N.Y. Acad. Scis., Am. Council on Diagnosis and Internal Disorders, Council on Nutrition, Ethical Culture Soc. Unitarian. Instrumental in instituting chiropractic care in union contracts for mems. of Teamsters Union. Home: 25 Holiday Dr West Hurley NY 12491 also: Martinique II 4100 N Ocean Dr West Palm Beach FL 33404-2855 Office: RR 28 Kingston NY 12401

SOLTERO, MARY ANN, elementary education educator; b. Bellingham, Wash., Feb. 25, 1949; d. Thomas Redmond and Berniece Olive (Walker) Maloney; m. Gregory Alan Soltero, Aug. 18, 1978; children: Ann Marie, Elizabeth Elaine. BS, Eastern Mont. Coll., 1971, MS, 1979. Third grade tchr. Cody (Wyo.) Pub. Schs., 1971-72; second grade tchr. Sunset Elem. Sch., Cody, Wyo., 1972-81, remedial reading tchr., 1981-89, third grade tchr., 1989—; writer lang. art curriculum com., Cody Pub. Schs., 1992-94. Recipient grant State of Wyo., 1994. Mem. NEA, Wyo. Edn. Assn., Cody Edn. Assn. (treas. 1987-88), Internat. Reading Assn., Nat. Coun. Tchrs. Eng., Delta Kappa Gamma (1st v.p. 1994). Democrat. Roman Catholic. Avocations: quilting, counted cross stitch, sewing. Home: 1013 Aspen Dr Cody WY 82414-4513 Office: Sunset Sch 1520 21st St Cody WY 82414-4412

SOLTI, SIR GEORG, conductor; b. Budapest, Hungary, Oct. 21, 1912; naturalized Brit. citizen, 1972; s. Mor Stern and Theres (Rosenbaum) S.; m. Hedi Oechsli, Oct. 29, 1946; m. Anne Valerie Pitts, Nov. 11, 1967; 2 daus. Ed., Budapest Music High Sch.; MusD (hon.), Leeds U., 1971, Oxford U., 1972, DePaul U., Yale U., 1974, Harvard U., 1979, Furman U., 1983, Sussex U., 1983, London U., 1986, Rochester U., 1987, Bologna (Italy) U., 1988, Roosevelt U., Chgo., 1990. Music dir. Chgo. Symphony Orch., 1969-91, music dir. laureate, 1991—; MusD (hon.) U. Durham, 1995. Mus. asst. Budapest Opera House, 1930-39, pianist, Switzerland, 1939-45; gen. music dir. Munich (Germany) State Opera, 1946-52, Frankfurt (Germany) City Opera, 1952-60; mus. dir. Royal Opera House Covent Garden, London, 1961-71, Orchestre de Paris, 1972-75; prin. condr. and artistic dir. London Philharm., 1979-83; condr. emeritus London Philharm., 1983-90, music dir. laureate Royal Opera House Covent Garden, London, 1992—; pianist Concours Internat., Geneva, 1942; guest condr. various orchs. including N.Y. Philharm., Vienna Philharm., Berlin Philharm., London Symphony, Bayerischer Rundfunk, Norddeutscher Rundfunk, Salzburg, Edinburgh, Glyndebourne, Ravinia and Bayreuth Festivals, Vienna State, Met. Opera; condr. concert tours with Chgo. Symphony to Europe, 1971, 74, 78, 81, 85, 89, 90, Chgo. Symphony to Japan, 1977, 86, 90, Chgo. Symphony to Australia, 1988; artistic dir. Salzburg Easter Festival and Whitsun Concerts, 1992-93; prin. guest condr. Paris Opera Bicentennial Tour, 1976, rec. artist for London Records. Recipient 31 Grammys, Lifetime Achievement Grammy award, 1996, Gold medal Royal Philharm. Soc., Gt. Britain, 1992, honored by John F. Kennedy Ctr. for Performing Arts, Washington, for lifetime achievement in music. Hon. fellow Royal Coll. Music (London). Office: care Chgo Symphony Orch 220 S Michigan Ave Chicago IL 60604-2508

SOLTMAN, NEIL M., lawyer; b. Phila., July 20, 1949. BA magna cum laude, Temple U., 1971; JD, Cath. U. Am., 1975. Bar: Calif. 1975. Ptnr. Mayer, Brown & Platt, L.A. Editor articles, book reviews Cath. U. Am. Law Review, 1974-75. Mem. ABA (litigation sect.). Office: Mayer Brown & Platt 350 S Grand Ave 25th Fl Los Angeles CA 90071-3406*

SOLTYS, JOHN JOSEPH, JR., lawyer; b. Portsmouth, Va., Feb. 4, 1942; s. John J. Sr. and Antoinette N. Soltys; children: John J. III, Amy Elaine. BS, USCG Acad., 1963; JD, Willamette U., 1970. Bar: Wash. 1970, U.S. Dist. Ct. (we. and ea. dists.) Wash. 1970. From assoc. to sr. ptnr. Karr, Tuttle, Seattle, 1970-89; sr. ptnr. Cozen & O'Connor, Seattle, 1989—. Lt. (j.g.) USCG, 1963-67. Mem. Wash. Def. Trial Lawyers (pres. 1986-87), Fedn. Ins. & Corp. Counsel. Avocations: fishing, hunting, soccer, gardening. Office: Cozen & O'Connor 1201 3d Ave Ste 5200 Seattle WA 98101-3033

SOLURSH, LIONEL PAUL, psychiatrist; b. Toronto, Jan. 14, 1936; came to U.S., 1986, naturalized, 1994; s. Coleman Bernard and Zelma Dorothy (Singer) S.; m. Marcia Persin (div.); children: Fern, Susan, Marc; m. Diane Sue Mullenax; children: Lia, Janine. MD, U. Toronto, 1959; Diploma in Psychiatry, U. Toronto, Can., 1962; CRCPC, Royal Coll. Physicians, 1964, FRCPC, 1965. Diplomate Am. Bd. Sexology; bd. cert. sex educator and clin. supr. Asst. prof. U. Toronto, 1965-73; staff psychiatrist Toronto Western Hosp., 1966-80, assoc. head psychiatry, 1973-79; outpatient psychiatrist Toronto East Gen. and Orthopaedic Hosp., 1980-86; assoc. prof. psychiatry U. Toronto, 1974-86; cons. psychiatrist Augusta (Ga.) Correctional Med. Inst., 1990—, chief psychiat. cons., 1992—; dir. PTSD out-patient psychiatry VA Med. Ctr., Augusta, 1986-95, med. dir. SIPU/PTSD rehab. unit, 1991-95; med. dir. trauma team SIPU/PTSD rehab. unit, 1995—; med. dir. PTSD treatment team VA Med. Ctr., Augusta, 1995—; prof. psychiatry and health behavior Med. Coll. of Ga., Augusta, 1986—; assoc. fellow Am. Coll. Sexology, 1995—; cons. Ga. Regional Hosp. and Richmond County Cmty. Mental Health Ctr., 1995—; spkr. in field. Author: (audiotape) Human Sexuality, 1967, 71, 95, (videotape) Art, Symbolism & Mental Health, 1991; contbr. chpts. to books and book revs. and more than 148 papers to profl. jours. Named R.S. McLaughlin Traveling fellow, 1966, Outstanding Young Canadian, 1974, Minister of Health Gold medalist U. Toronto, 1962. Fellow Am. Orthopsychiat. Assn., Am. Psychiat. Assn., Am. Acad. Clinical Sexologists; mem. Am. Acad. Psychiatrists in Alcoholism & Addictions, AMA, Can. Psychiat. Assn., Internat. Soc. for Traumatic Stress Studies, Am. Assn. Sex Educators, Counselors and Therapists. Jewish. Avocations: photography, scuba diving, travel, performing arts, cyberspace touring. Office: VA Med Ctr 1 Freedom Way Augusta GA 30904-6258

SOLURSH, MICHAEL, biology educator, researcher; b. L.A., Dec. 22, 1942; s. Louis and Helen (Schwartz) S.; m. Victoria R. Raskin, Mar. 21, 1964; 1 child, Elizabeth. BA, UCLA, 1964; PhD, U. Wash., 1969. Asst. prof. U. Iowa, Iowa City, 1969-73, assoc. prof., 1973-79, prof., 1979—. Mem. Am. Soc. Zoologists (program officer 1990-93), Soc. for Developmental Biologists, Am. Assn. Anatomists (program chairperson 1992-93), Tissue Culture Assn., Am. Soc. for Cell Biology. Achievements include research in morphogenetic mechanisms in mesenchyme.

SOLYMOSY, EDMOND SIGMOND ALBERT, international marketing executive, retired army officer; b. Budapest, Pest, Hungary, Sept. 3, 1937; came to U.S., 1949; s. Sigmond Ladislas and Gabrielle (Lindelof) S.; m. Mary Ellen Via, Sept. 9, 1961; children: Edmond S.A. Jr., Stephan G., Philip A. BSME, Tex. A&M U., 1960, BBA, 1961, MBA, 1970; postgrad., Mich. U., 1985, Harvard U., 1991. Commd. 2d lt. U.S. Army, 1961, advanced through grades to gen., 1985; student Nat. Def. U., Washington, 1980-81; comdr. 1st Air Def. Arty. Brigade, Ft. Bliss, Tex., 1981-83; chief of staff U.S. Army Air Def. Ctr., Ft. Bliss, 1983; dir. Human Resources Directorate, Hdqrs. Dept. Army, Washington, 1983-85; dep. comdr. U.S. Army Community and Family Support Ctr., Alexandria, Va., 1985-86; chief of staff U.S. Army I Corps, Ft. Lewis, Wash., 1986-88; chief exec. U.S. Office of Def. Coop., Athens, Greece, 1988-91; ret., 1991; pres. Global Project Mgmt., Houston, 1991—; advisor Sec. of Army Panel, Washington, 1983-86, Hellenic-Am. C. of C., Athens, 1988-91; bd. dirs. Am. Ikarus, Inc. Author: Continental Economic Alliances, 1981. Sponsor Spl. Olympics, Ft. Lewis, 1986; advisor Mil. Mus., Ft. Lewis, 1986-88; regional v.p. Mediterranean coun. Boy Scouts Am., Athens, 1988-91; mem. devel. com. Tex. A&M U., College Station, 1991, advisor Ctr. for Internat. Bus.; mem. bd. advisors Mosher Inst. for Internat. Policy Studies; mem. Mil. Com., Houston. Decorated D.S.M., Def. D.S.M., Combat Infantryman's Badge, Airborne Parachutist's Badge, Army Ranger, Legion of Merit (3); recipient U.S. and Vietnamese awards for heroism, Greek Disting. Svc. award, 1991. Mem. Assn. U.S. Army (Svc. to Soldiers award 1985), VFW, Armed Forces YMCA (chmn. com. 1982, Nat. Vol. of Yr. award 1983), Internat. Propeller Club (Greece advisor 1989). Republican. Lutheran. Avocations: sports, jogging, sailing, fishing, hunting. Home: 2438 Stanmore Dr Houston TX 77019-3424 Office: Global Project Mgmt PO Box 27253 Houston TX 77227-7253

SOLYMOSY, HATTIE MAY, writer, publisher, storyteller, educator; b. Kew Gardens, N.Y., Apr. 1, 1945; d. Julius and Sylvia Becky (Glantz) Fuld; m. Richard Milk, June 30, 1966 (div. Feb. 1974); 1 child, Jared Marc Milk.; m. Abraham Edward Solymosy, Apr. 21, 1974. BA, Queens Coll., 1966, MS in Edn., 1973. Cert. tchr., N.Y.C. and N.Y. Actress, model, 1950-60; elem. tchr. N.Y.C. Bd. of Edn., 1966—; owner Ultimate Jewelry, N.Y.C., 1976-80; tutor N.Y.C., 1983-91; children's writer N.Y., 1991—, romance writer, 1993—; owner Hatties' Tales, Cedarhurst, N.Y., 1993; storyteller Mo. flood victims, Okla. Fed. Bldg. bombing victims, various children's hosps.; exec. Hamajama Gifts. Author: (sound recs.) Delancy Dolphin, 1993, Thaddius Thoroughbred, 1993, Willie's War, 1993, Noodles-An Autobiography, 1993, (with Jared Marc Milk) Trapped With The Past, 1993, Thick Slick Tangled Webs, 1993, Cinderella Cockroach, 1993, A Christmas Tale, 1993, Chanukah Tale, 1993, Doc Simon, 1995, Mr. Music, 1996, Women on Film, 1996, Buying a Dream, 1996, Rock and Roll, 1996; owner Cigar Box Factory. Social sec., fundraiser Children's Med. Ctr., N.Y.C., 1969-79; aux. mem. St. John's Hosp., N.Y., 1987—; contbr. children's stories Okla. Bombing, Mo. Flood Victims, Children's Hosps. Mem. Romance Writers of Am., Soc. of Children's Writers and Illustrators, Simon Wiesenthal Ctr., World Jewish Congress. Democrat. Jewish. Avocations: music, tennis, movies, gardening, dance. Home: 470 W Broadway Cedarhurst NY 11516-1531 Office: Hatties' Tales PO Box 24 Cedarhurst NY 11516-0024

SOLZHENITSYN, ALEKSANDR ISAYEVICH, author; b. Kislovodsk, Russia, Dec. 11, 1918; imprisoned under Joseph Stalin for critical comments, 1945-53; exiled to Soviet Cen. Asia, 1953; freed from exile, 1956; expelled from USSR, 1974; now living in U.S.; m. Natalya Reshetovskaya, 1940 (div.), remarried, 1956 (div.); m. Natalia Svetlova, 1973; children: Yermoli, Ignat, Stepan. Corr. student in philology, Moscow Inst. History, Philosophy and Lit., 1939-41; degree in math. and physics, U. Rostov, 1941; Litt.D., Harvard U., 1978. Author: Odin den' Ivana Denisovicha, 1962 (pub. as One Day in the Life of Ivan Denisovich, 1963), Dlia pol'zy dela, 1963 (pub. as For the Good of the Cause, 1964), Sluchai na stantsii Krechetovka/Matrenin dvor, 1963 (pub. as We Never Make Mistakes, 1963), Etudy i krokhotnye rasskazy, 1964 (pub. as Stories and Prose Poems, 1971, as Prose Poems, 1971, as Matryona's House and Other Stories, 1975), V kruge pervom, 1968 (pub. as The First Circle, 1968; Prix du Meilleur Livre Etranger France 1969), Rakovyi korpus, 1968 (pub. as Cancer Ward, 1968; Prix du Meilleur Livre Etranger France 1969), Le Droits de l'écrivain, 1969, Sobranie sochinenii (6 vols.), 1969-70, Six Etudes, 1971, Avgust chetyrnadtsatogo, 1971 (pub. as August 1914, 1972), Nobelevskaia lektsiia po literature, 1972 (pub. as Nobel Lecture, 1972, as One Word of Truth, 1972), Arkhipelag Gulag (3 vols.), 1973-76 (pub. as The Gulag Archipelago, 1974-78), Prusskie nochi: poema napisannaia v lagere v 1950, 1974 (pub. as Prussian Nights, 1977), Iz-pod glyb, 1974 (pub. as From Under the Rubble, 1975), Mir i nasilie, 1974, Pis'mo vozhdiam Sovetskogo soiuza, 1974 (pub. as Letter to the Soviet Leaders, 1974), A Pictorial Autobiography, 1974, Solzhenitsyn, the Voice of Freedom, 1975, Bodalsia telenok s dubom, 1975 (pub. as The Oak and the Calf, 1980), Lenin v Tsiurikhe, 1975 (pub. as Lenin in Zurich, 1976), Detente: Prospects for democracy and Dictatorship, 1975, America, We Beg You to Interfere, 1975, Amerikanskie rechi, 1975, Warning to the Western World, 1976, A World Split Apart, 1978, Alexander Solzhenitsyn Speaks to the West, 1978, Sobranie sochinenii, 1978, The Mortal Danger, 1980, East and West, 1980, Issledovaniia noveishei russkoi istorii, 1980, Publitsistika: stat'i i rechi, 1981, Krasnoe koleso: povestvovan'e v otmerennykh srokakh Uzel I: Avgust chetyrnadtsatogo, 1983 (pub. as The Red Wheel: A Narrative in Discrete Periods of Time, 1989), Krasnoe koleso: povestvovan'e v otmerennykh srokakh Uzel II: Oktiabr'shestnadtsatogo, 1984, Krasnoe koleso: povestvovan'e v otmerennykh srokakh Uzel III: Mart semnadtsatogo, 1986, Rasskazy, 1990, Kak nam obustroit' Rossiiu, 1990, Krasnoe koleso: povestvovan'e v otmerennykh srokakh Uzel IV: Aprel'semnadtsatogo, 1991, Rebuilding Russia: Toward Some Formulations, 1991, Les Invisibles, 1992, Nashi pliuralisty: otryvok iz vtorogo toma "Ocherkov literaturnoi zhizni", 1992, The Russian Question Toward the End of the Twentieth Century, 1995; (plays) Olen' i shalashovka, 1968 (pub. The Love-Girl and the Innocent, 1969), Svecha na vetru, 1968 (pub. Candle in the Wind, 1973), Pir podebitelei, 1981 (pub. as Victory Celebrations, 1983), Plenniki, 1981 (pub. as Prisoners, 1983), P'esy i kinostsenarii, 1981; editor: Russkii slovar' iazykovogo rasshireniia, 1990. Arty. officer Russian Army, World War II. Recipient Lenin prize nomination, 1964, Nobel prize for lit., 1970, Freedoms Found. award Stanford U., 1976, Templeton Found. prize, 1983. Mem. Am. Acad. Arts and Scis., Hoover Inst. War, Revolution and Peace (hon.). *

SOMASUNDARAN, PONISSERIL, surface and colloid engineer, applied science educator; b. Pazhookara, Kerala, India, June 28, 1939; came to U.S., 1961; s. Kumara Moolayil and Lakshmikutty (Amma) Pillai; m. Usha N., May 25, 1966; 1 child, Tamara. BS, Kerala U., Trivandrum, India, 1958; BE, Indian Inst. Sci., Bangalore, 1961; MS, U. Calif., Berkeley, 1962, PhD, 1964. Rsch. engr. U. Calif., 1964, Internat. Minerals & Chem. Corp., Skokie, Ill., 1965-67; rsch. chemist R.J. Reynolds Industries, Inc., Winston-Salem, N.C., 1967-70; assoc. prof. Columbia U., N.Y.C., 1970-78, prof. mineral engring., 1978-83, La Von Duddleson Krumb prof., 1983—; chmn. Henry Krumb Sch. Chem. Engring., Materials Sci. and Mining Engring., Columbia, U., 1988—, dir. Langmuir Ctr. for Colloids and Interfaces, 1987—; cons. numerous agys., cos., including NIH, 1974, B.F. Goodrich, 1974, NSF, 1974, Alcan, 1981, UNESCO, 1982, Sohio, 1984-85, IBM, 1984, Am. Cyanamd, 1988-89, Duracell, 1988-89, DuPont, 1989, Canmet, 1990-93, Unilever, 1991—, Engelhard, 1991-94, UoP, 1991-92, Alcoa, 1991-92; mem. panel NRC; chmn. numerous internat. symposia and NSF workshops; mem. adv. panel Bur. Mines Generic Ctr., 1983-91; keynote and plenary lectr. internat. meetings; hon. prof. Ctrl. South U. Tech., China, Brahm Prakash chair in metallurgy and material sci. Indian Inst. Sci., Bangalore, 1990; hon. rsch. advisor Bejing Gen. Rsch. Inst., 1991—. Editor books, including Fine Particles Processing, 1980 (Publ. Bd. award 1980); editor-in-chief Colloids and Surfaces, 1980—; Henry Krumb lectr. AIME, 1988; contbr. numerous articles to profl. publs., patentee in field. Pres. Keralasamajam of Greater N.Y., N.Y.C., 1974-75; bd. dirs. Fedn. Indian Assocs., N.Y.C., 1974—, Vols. in Svc. to Edn. in India, Hartford, Conn., 1974—; mem. planning bd. Village of Piermont, N.Y., 1995—. Recipient Disting. Achievement in Engring. award, AINA, 1980, Antoine M. Gaudin award Soc. Mining Engrs.-AIME, 1983, Achievements in Applied Sci. award 2d World Malayalam Conf., 1985, Robert H. Richards award, AIME, 1986, Arthur F. Taggart award Soc. Mining Engrs.-AIME, 1987, honor award Assn. Indian in Am., 1988, VHP award of Excellence, Ellis Island medal of Honor, 1990, Commendations citation State of N.J. Senate, 1991; named Mill Man of Distinction, Soc. Mining Engrs.-AIME, 1983, Disting. Alumnus award Indian Inst. Sci., Bangalore, 1989, Outstanding Contbns. and Achievement award Cultural Festival India, 1991, Recognition award SIAA, 1992, Asian-Am. Heritage award Asian Am. Higher Edn. Coun., 1994. Fellow Instn. Mining and Metallurgy (U.K.); mem. AICE, NAE, Soc. Mining Engrs. (bd. dirs. 1982-85, Disting. mem. award, also others), Engring. Found. (chmn. bd. 1994—, chmn. conf. com. 1985-88, bd. exec. com. 1985-88, bd. dirs. 1991—, Frank Aplan award 1992), Am. Chem. Soc., N.Y. Acad. Scis., Internat. Assn. Colloid and Surface Scientists (councillor 1989-92), Indian Material Rsch. Soc. (hon.), Sigma Xi.

SOMBROTTO, VINCENT R., postal union executive; b. N.Y.C., June 15, 1923; s. Raymond and Agnes (McCormick) S.; Feb. 23, 1957; children: Gloria, Vincent, Lisa, Leslie, Jacqueline, Stephen, Mara. Grad. high sch. Letter carrier N.Y.C., 1947-71; br. pres. Nat. Assn. Letter Carriers, N.Y.C., 1971-79; pres. Nat. Assn. Letter Carriers, Washington, 1979—; dir. Fund For Assuring An Ind. Retirement; v.p., mem. exec. council AFL-CIO; bd. dirs. Ctr. Nat. Policy; chmn. Employee Thrift Adv. Council of Fed. Retirement Thrift Investment Bd. Bd. adv. Sidney Harmon Program on Tech. Pub. Policy and Human Devel., Harvard U.; adv. com. Nat. Assembly Vol. Health and Social Welfare Orgns.; nat. v.p. Muscular Dystrophy Assn.; mem. adv. council Am. Diabetes Assn.; mem. President's Commn. Employment of Handicapped. Served with AUS, 1943-45. Mem. Fed. Adv. Council Occupational Safety and Health, Postal Telephone and Telegraphy Internat. (mem. exec. council). Office: Nat Assn Letter Carriers 100 Indiana Ave NW Washington DC 20001-2144

SOMERS, ANNE RAMSAY, medical educator; b. Memphis, Sept. 9, 1913; d. Henry Ashton and Amanda Vick (Woolfolk) Ramsey; m. Herman Miles Somers, Aug. 31, 1946; children: Sara Ramsay, Margaret Ramsay. BA, Vassar Coll., 1935; postgrad., U. N.C., 1939-40; DSc (hon.), Med. Coll. Wis., 1975. Ednl. dir. Internat. Ladies Garment Workers Union, 1937-42; labor economist U.S. Dept. Labor, 1943-46; rsch. assoc. Haverford Coll., 1957-63; rsch. assoc. indsl. rels. sect. Princeton U., 1964-84; prof. U. Medicine and Dentistry of N.J.-R. Wood Johnson Med. Sch. (formerly Rutgers Med. Sch.), 1971-84, adj. prof., 1984—; adj. prof. geriat. medicine U. Pa. Sch. Medicine, 1990—; mem. Nat. Bd. Med. Examiners, 1983-86; cons. in health econs., health edn., geriats., gerontology, realted areas. Author: Hospital Regulation: The Dilemma of Public Policy, 1969, Health Care in Transition: Directions for the Future, 1971, (with H.M. Somers) Workmen's Compensation: The Prevention, Rehabilitation and Financing of Occupational Disability, 1954, Medicare and the Hospitals, 1967, Doctors, Patients and Health Insurance, 1961, Health and Health Care: Policies in Perspective, 1977, (with N.L. Spears) The Continuing Care Retirement Community: A Significant Option for Long Care?, 1992; editor: (with D.R. Fabian) The Geriatric Imperative: An Introduction to Gerontology and Clinical Geriatrics, 1981. Mem. bd. visitors. Duke U. Med. Ctr., 1972-77, U. Tex. Health Scis. Ctr., Houston, 1980-86. Recipient Elizur Wright award Am. Risk and Ins. Assn., 1962; named to Health Care Hall of Fame, 1993. Fellow Am. Coll. Hosp. Adminstrs. (hon.), Coll. Physicians Phila. (hon.); mem. Inst. Medicine of NAS, Soc. Tchrs. of Family Medicine (hon.). Home: Pennswood Vlg # G-205 Newtown PA 18940

SOMERS, GEORGE FREDRICK, biology educator; b. Garland, Utah, July 9, 1914; s. George Fredrick and Elizbuth (Sorenson) S.; m. Beulah Rich Morgan, June 24, 1939; children: Ralph M., Steven J., Gary F. B.S., Utah State U., 1935; B.A., Oxford U., 1938, B.Sc., 1939; Ph.D., Cornell U., 1942. Faculty Cornell U., 1941-51, asso. prof. biochemistry, 1949-51; plant physiologist U.S. Dept. Agr., 1944-51; faculty U. Del., Newark, 1951—; assoc. dir. Del. Agrl. Expt. Sta., 1951-59; assoc. dean Coll. Agr., 1954-59; chmn. dept. biol. scis. U. Del., 1959-71, H. Fletcher Brown prof. biology, 1962-81, emeritus prof., 1981—; vis. prof. U. Philippines, 1958-59. Author: (with J.B. Sumner) Chemistry and Methods of Enzymes, 3d edit, 1953, Laboratory Experiments in Biological Chemistry, 2d edit, 1949; also articles.; Editor: biochem. sect. Chem. Abstracts, 1968-75. Union Pacific scholar, 1930; Rhodes scholar, 1936; Henry Strong Denison fellow, 1939. H.C. fellow AAAS; mem. Am. Assn. Plant Physiology, Bot. Soc. Am., Sigma Xi, Phi Kappa Phi. Research on influence of environ. factors on vitamin C content of vegetables; viscoelasticity in plant tissues as related to cell wall properties; chem. properties of algal cell walls; salt-tolerant plants as food crops. Home: 22 Minquil Dr Newark DE 19713-1312

SOMERS, HANS PETER, lawyer; b. Berlin, Germany, Nov. 11, 1922; came to U.S., 1938; s. Fritz A. and Karoline E. (Neuert) S.; m. Claudia C. Schuette, May 3, 1947; children: Daniel E., Stephen A., Deborah J., Conrad S. B.A., Cornell Coll., 1944; M.A., U. Iowa, 1948; LL.B. magna cum laude, Harvard U., 1951. Bar: Mass. 1951, Pa. 1957. Assoc. Hill & Barlow, Boston, 1951-56; assoc. Morgan, Lewis & Bockius, Phila., 1956-60, ptnr., 1960-88, counsel, 1988—; lectr. law Northeastern U., Boston, 1951-53, Boston U. Law Sch., 1953-55; lectr. Villanova U. Law Sch., Phila., 1959-63; research assoc. Am. Law Inst., Cambridge, Mass., 1955-56. Editor: Harvard Law Rev., 1949-51; contbr. articles to legal jours. Served to 2d lt. AUS, 1943-46, ETO. Mem. ABA (chmn. com. tax sect. 1967-69, real property, probate and trust law 1974-77), Nat. Conf. Lawyers and Corp. Fiduciaries (chmn. 1978-81), Am. Coll. Probate Counsel (mem. editorial bd. dirs. 1976-77), Internat. Acad. of Estate and Trust Law (exec. council 1974-78, 81—). Clubs: Radnor Hunt (Malvern, Pa.) (bd. govs.); Union League (Phila.). Home: 8024 Goshen Rd Newtown Square PA 19073-1122 Office: Morgan Lewis & Bockius 2000 One Logan Sq Philadelphia PA 19103

SOMERS, HAROLD MILTON, economist, educator; b. Toronto, Ont., Can., Sept. 30, 1915; came to U.S., 1937, naturalized, 1947; s. Joseph and Elizabeth (Behr) S.; m. Claire Rosen, June 12, 1939; children: Joan, Margery, Warren. B.Com., U. Toronto, 1937; Ph.D., U. Calif., 1942; student, U. Chgo., 1940; LL.B., U. Buffalo, 1956. Teaching asst. in econs. U. Calif., 1937-39; research asst. govt. fin. U. Chgo., 1940; fellow Social Sci. Research Council, 1940-41; mem. research staff Brookings Instn., summer 1941; teaching fellow in econs. U. Mich., 1941-42, instr. in econs., summer 1942; asst. prof. econs. U. Buffalo, 1942-45, assoc. prof., 1945-46, prof., 1946-61, dean. sch. bus. adminstrn., 1947-61; lectr. U. Buffalo Sch. Law, 1957-59; prof. econs. UCLA, 1961-86, prof. emeritus, 1986—, chmn. dept. econs., 1961-66, dean div. social scis., 1967-70; vis. prof. econs. U. Calif. at Berkeley, summer 1947, Columbia, summer 1954, U. B.C., summer 1953; vis. prof. law Yale Law Sch., 1968; econ. affairs officer in fiscal div. UN, summer 1950, cons., 1950-53; cons. to research div. O.P.A., 1943; arbitrator Fed. Conciliation and Mediation Service, 1950-86, Am. Arbitration Assn., 1955-86, N.Y. State Bd. Mediation, 1952-61, Los Angeles County Employee Relations Commn. Arbitration, 1970-73; cons. U.S. Office Edn., Bur. Higher Edn., 1965-69; mem. Personnel Security bd. AEC, 1957-59; cons. N.Y. State Legis. Com. on Constn., 1957- 58; economist N.Y. State Dept. Commerce, summer 1944, cons., 1944-45; tech. adviser to mayor's full employment com., City of Buffalo, 1945-46, cons. to budget div., 1946-47; chmn. exec. com., fin. subcom. Capital Expenditures Com., 1956-57; chmn. N.Y. State Minimum Wage Bd. for Restaurant Industry, 1956-58; mem seminar adv. com. Fed. Res. Bank, N.Y., 1952; editorial cons. Blakiston Co., Phila., 1947-52; cons. Employment and Youth Opportunities Agy., Los Angeles, 1966, Calif. Adv. Commn. on Tax Reform, 1968. Author: American Policies of Postwar Readjustment (monograph), 1944, Public Finance and National Income, 1949; co-author: Industrial Conflict, 1939, Growth of the American Economy, 1944, rev. edit., 1951, Readings in Business Cycle Theory, 1944, Readings in the Theory of Income Distribution, 1946, Taxation and Business Concentration, 1952, Corporate Tax Problems, 1952, Taxation of Corporate Income in California, 1964, Taxation of Property in California, 1964, Public Finance and Welfare, 1966, A Search for City Revenue, 1968; author monographs The Sales Tax, 1964, Capital Gains, Death and Gift Taxation, 1965; editor: Estate Taxes and Business Management, 1957; editor Western Econ. Jour., 1966-69; editorial bd.: Am. Econ. Rev., 1952-54; contbr.: articles to Ency. Brit. and econ. and law jours. Mem. Am., N.Y. State bar assns., Am. Econ. Assn. (nominating com. 1969, 70), Econometric Soc. (session chmn. 1947, 51, program chmn. 1949), Am. Fin. Assn. (dir. pub. fin. 1969-71), Nat. Tax Assn. (mem. sales tax com. 1975-77, fed. taxation and fin. com. 1981-84), Phi Beta Kappa, Alpha Kappa Psi, Beta Gamma Sigma. Home: 152 N Kenter Ave Los Angeles CA 90049-2730 Office: Dept Econs U Calif Los Angeles CA 90024

SOMERS, JAMES WILFORD, information management company executive; b. Akron, Ohio, Apr. 19, 1951; s. Gilbert N. and Yvonne E. (Thuma) S.; m. Judith Field Smith, Nov. 20, 1986; children: James A., Elizabeth A. BS in Aerospace Engring., U.S. Naval Acad., 1973; MS in Aero. Engring., U.S. Naval Postgrad. Sch., 1974. Commd. ens. USN, 1973, advanced through grades to lt. comdr. select, 1981, resigned, 1981; program mgr. ASD Def. Nuclear Agy., Alexandria, Va., 1978-84, divsn. dir. lethality and target hardening, 1984-86; dir. staff GRCI/ATD, Vienna, Va., 1986-87, group dir. engring., 1993-94, ops. dir. senser and comml. ops., 1993-94, ops. dir. mission support ops., 1994-95; pres. Info. Mgmt. Group, Great Falls, Va., 1995—. Active various Rep. Campaigns, 1988—. Capt. USNR. Mem. AIAA, Am. Def. Preparedness Assn. Lutheran. Avocations: sailing, skiing. Home: 9123 Maria Ave Great Falls VA 22066 Office: Info Mgmt Group Inc Ste 710 9893 Georgetown Pike Great Falls VA 22066

SOMERS, JOHN ARTHUR, insurance company executive; b. Cin., Feb. 24, 1944; s. Arthur Edward and Margaret Mary (Netschke) S.; m. Ann-Christin Ahlander, Dec. 28, 1968; children—Monica Ann, Christina Elizabeth, Mark Edward. B.S. in Econs., Villanova U., 1966; postgrad., Sch. Law, U. Conn., 1966-67; M.B.A. in Fin., U. Conn., 1972. Asst. town mgr. Town of Newington, Conn., 1970-72; v.p. Prudential Ins. Co. Am., Newark, 1972-81; sr. v.p. Tchrs. Ins. & Annuity Assn., N.Y.C., 1981—; bd. dirs., vice chmn. Nat. Realty Com.; bd. dirs. Cmty. Preservation Corp., Emigrant Bank; chmn., adv. bd. N.Y.U. Real Estate Inst. Mem. Urban Land Inst., Nat. Assn. Indsl. and Office Parks, Mortgage Bankers Assn. Am., Internat. Council Shopping Ctrs., N.Y. Real Estate Bd. Roman Catholic. Office: Tchrs Ins & Annuity Assn Am 730 3rd Ave New York NY 10017-3206*

SOMERS, LOUIS ROBERT, retired food company executive; b. Pontiac, Mich., Aug. 8, 1926; s. Jay G. and Maggie (Gee) S.; m. Rynda Horinga, July 28, 1950; children: Linda, Laurie. B.S., Mich. State U., 1950. With Kellogg Co., Battle Creek, Mich., 1955-88; controller Kellogg Internat., 1967-70, 72-75; fin. dir. Kellogg Gt. Brit. Ltd., 1970-72; v.p. fin., treas. Kellogg Co., 1975-85, sr. v.p. fin., 1985-88; bd. dirs. Purity Foods, Inc. Trustee Alma Coll., 1982—; bd. dirs. Mich. State U. Devel. Fund, 1983-88; bd. govs. ARC, 1985-92, chmn. audit com.

SOMERSET, HAROLD RICHARD, retired business executive; b. Woodbury, Conn., Sept. 25, 1935; s. Harold Kitchener and Margaret Mary (Roche) S.; m. Marjory Deborah Ghiselin, June 22, 1957 (dec. Jan. 1984); children: Timothy Craig, Paul Alexander; m. Jean MacAlpine DesMarais, Jan. 2, 1985; stepchildren: Cheryl Lyn DesMarais, James Fenelon DesMarais. B.S., U.S. Naval Acad., 1957; B.C.E., Rensselaer Poly. Inst., Troy, N.Y., 1959; LL.B., Harvard U., 1967. Bar: Mass. 1967, Hawaii 1973. Commd. ensign U.S. Navy, 1957, advanced through grades to lt., 1961; service in U.S. and Hawaii; resigned, 1964; with firm Goodwin, Procter & Hoar, Boston, 1967-72; corp. counsel Alexander & Baldwin, Inc., Honolulu, 1972-74, v.p., gen. counsel, 1974-78, group v.p.-sugar, 1978-79, exec. v.p.-agr., 1979-84; with Calif. & Hawaiian Sugar Co., San Francisco, 1984-93, exec. v.p., chief operating officer, 1984-88, pres., chief exec. officer, 1988-93, bus. cons., 1994—; bd. dirs. Longs Drug Stores Corp., Brown and Caldwell, PLM Internat., Inc., Calif. and Hawaiian Sugar Co. Trustee San Francisco Nat. Maritime Mus., Carquinez Strait Preservation Trust (mgmt. com., pres.). Mem. St. Mary's Coll. Sch. Edn. (adv. coun.). Home: 19 Donald Dr Orinda CA 94563-3646 Office: Calif & Hawaiian Sugar Co 830 Loring Ave Crockett CA 94525-1104

SOMERSON, ROSANNE, artist; b. Phila., June 21, 1954; d. Herbert M. and Ileana V. (Reiver) S.; m. Alphonse Mattia, Nov. 9, 1947; 1 child, Isabel Giani. BFA, R.I. Sch. Design, 1976. Mem. staff Fine Woodworking mag., 1976-81; furniture designer and builder, 1978—; mem. faculty grad. furniture design program RISD, Providence, 1985—, head program, 1992—, head furniture design dept., 1995—; instr. Boston Archtl. Ctr., 1981; teaching fellow continuing edn. sculpture and design in wood Harvard U., 1977-79; lectr. in field. Exhibited works at Brockton (Mass.) Art Mus., 1981, 84, 86, Workbench Gallery, N.Y.C., 1982, 83, Hudson River Mus., 1983, Pitts. Ctr. for Arts, 1984-85, Susan Carr Gallery, Houston, 1985, Ester Saks Gallery, Chgo., 1985, Soc. Arts and Crafts, Boston, 1986, 89, Mus. Art of RISD, 1987, Sothebys, N.Y.C., 1987, Am. Craft Mus., N.Y.C., 1986-89, Mus. Fine Arts, Boston, 1989, Oakland (Calif.) Mus., 1990, Musee des Arts Decoratifs, Paris, Oslo Mus. Applied Art, Slovak Nat. Gallery, Peter Joseph Gallery, N.Y.C., 1991-95, Pritain and Eames Gallery, N.Y.C., 1984-94, also others. Address: 771 Division Rd Westport MA 02790-1350

SOMERVILLE, CAROLYN JOHNSON, principal; b. Parkersburg, W.Va., Mar. 11, 1942; d. George Hughes and Nellie Maude (Cather) Johnson; m. Ron D. Somerville, Aug. 22, 1965 (div. 1981); children: Jennifer Nicole Somerville Moon, Ron Dean. BS, Asbury Coll., 1963; MEd, Ohio U., 1966. Cert. elem. prin., Okla. Tchr. jr. high Prince George County Schs., Md., 1963-64; grad. asst. Ohio U., Athens, 1964-65; social worker W.Va. Dept. of Welfare, Huntington, 1965-67; counselor jr. high Wood County Schs., Parkersburg, W.Va., 1972-78, tchr. jr. high, 1979-81; substitute tchr. Yukon (Okla.) Schs., 1982-83; asst. prin. elem. Western Heights Schs., Oklahoma City, 1983-85, Skyview Elem. Sch., 1985—; presenter workshops; cons. in field. Mem. adv. bd. Planned Parenthood, Parkersburg, W.Va., 1974-77; counselor, speaker Gov. Com. on Crime and Delinquency, Parkersburg, 1974-77; tchr. Sunday sch. Trinity Bapt. Ch., Yukon, 1982-83; sponsor Alateen, 1988-93. Named Adminstr. of Yr. Dist. 11A, 1995. Fellow Nat. Prins. Assn., State of Okla. Prins. Assn.; mem. ASCD, Okla. Assn. Elem. Sch. Prins. (com.), Coop. Coun. Okla. Sch. Adminstrn., Yukon Curriculum Coun. Avocations: reading, writing, sewing, boating. Home: 113 W Vail Dr Yukon OK 73099-5829 Office: Skyview Elem Sch 2800 Mustang Rd Yukon OK 73099

SOMERVILLE, MARGARET ANNE GANLEY, law educator; b. Adelaide, Australia, Apr. 13, 1942; d. George Patrick and Gertrude Honora (Rowe) Ganley; divorced. A.u.A. (pharm.), U. Adelaide, 1963; LLB (hon. I), U. Sydney, 1973; D.C.L., McGill U., 1978; LLD (hon.), U. Windsor, Ont., 1992, Macquarie, NSW, 1993, St. Francis Xavier, Antigonish, Nova Scotia, 1996. Registered pharmacist; Bar: Supreme Ct. New South Wales 1975, Quebec 1982. New South Wales; Pharmacist NSW, Australia; atty. Mallesons, Sydney, Australia, 1974-75; cons. Law Reform Com. Can., 1976-85; asst. prof. faculty of law Inst. of Comparative Law, 1978, assoc. prof. faculty of law, 1979; prof., faculty law, faculty medicine McGill U., 1984—; founding dir. McGill Ctr. Medicine Ethics & Law, 1986—; Gale prof. law McGill U., 1989—; vis. prof. Sydney U., 1984, 86, 90, Ctr. for Human Bioethics, Monash U., 1985-86; cons. to numerous orgns. Editl. bd. Bioethics, 1986—, Kennedy Inst. Ethics Jour., 1990—, Health and Human Rights, 1993—, Ecosystem Health and Medicine, 1993—; Adv. editor Social Sci. and Medicine, 1988—; reviewer Cmty. Health Studies, Jour. Clin. Epidemiology, Can. Jour. Family Law, Jour. Pharmacy Practice, Jour. AIDS, New Eng. Jour. Medicine, Can. Jour. Law and Soc., Dalhousie Law Jour., Am. Jour. Law, Medicine and Ethics, others; contbr. articles to profl. jours. Clin. ethics com. Royal Victoria Hosp., 1980-95; prin. investigator Nat. Health R&D Program, 1986-89; assoc. mem. McGill AIDS Ctr., 1990—, Nat. Adv. Com. on AIDS in Can., 1986-92; chmn. Nat. Rsch. Coun. Can., Ethics Com., 1991-95; bd. dirs. Can. Ctr. for Ethics in Sport. Australian Commonwealth scholar, McGill U., 1975; recipient U. Sydney medal, 1976, Joseph Dainow prize McGill U., 1976, Disting. Svc. award Am. Soc. Law & Medicine, 1985; named to Order of Australia. Fellow Royal Soc. Can.; mem. Am. soc. Pharm. Law, Inst. Soc., Ethics & Life Sci., Hastings Ctr., Am. Soc. Law, Medicine, and Ethics, Assn. des Prof. de Droit du Que., Can. Law Tchrs. Assn. Office: McGill Ctr Medicine Ethics & Law, 3690 Peel St, Montreal, PQ Canada H3A 1W9

SOMERVILLE, MARY ROBINSON, library director; b. Fairfield, Ala., Aug. 16, 1941; d. E. Bryce Robinson, Jr. and Margaret Allen m. Ormond Somerville, July 10, 1964 (d. 1976). BA in English with honors in Writing, U. N.C., 1963; MA in English, U. Colo., 1965; MLS, U. Okla., 1971. Youth svcs. adminstr. Lincoln City (Nebr.) Librs., 1973-78; youth svcs. mgr. Louisville (Ky.) Free Pub. Libr., 1978-88, proj. dir. automation, 1985-86, grants adminstr., 1986-87, mgr. employee rels., 1987-88; youth svcs. adminstr. Broward County Libr., Ft. Lauderdale, Fla., 1988-90; youth svcs. adminstr. Miami-Dade Pub. Libr., 1990-91, asst. dir. branches and spl. svcs., 1991-93, interim dir., 1993-94, dir., 1994—. Named Outstanding Alumnus Sch. Libr. and Info. Studies U. Okla., 1995. Mem. ALA (spkr., lectr. 22 states, pres. Assn. for Libr. Svc. to children 1987-88, mem. 5 person del. to former Soviet Union 1989, cons. U.S. Dept. Edn. 1988, chair nominating com. 1992, planning and budget assembly 1992, coun. 1992, mem. exec. bd. 1993-95, pres. 1996-97, initiator projects that won H.W. Wilson Staff Devel. award and 4 John Cotton Dana awards), Phi Beta Kappa. Home: 800 West Ave # 735 Miami Beach FL 33139 Office: Miami Dade Pub Libr System 101 W Flagler St Miami FL 33130-1523

SOMERVILLE, MASON HAROLD, mechanical engineering educator, university dean; b. Worcester, Mass., Dec. 21, 1941; s. Harold Mervin and Eleanor Ruth (Archibald) S.; children: Mark, Matthew, Meredith, Michael, Michelle. B.S.M.E., Worcester Polytech. Inst., 1964; M.S.M.E., Northeastern U., 1966; Ph.D. in Mech. Engring., Pa. State U., 1971. Profl. engr., N.D., Ark., Tex. Grad. teaching asst Northeastern U., Boston, 1964-66; engr. Norton Co., Worcester, Mass., 1965; instr. mech. engring. dept. Pa. State U., State College, 1966-71; sr. engr. Bettis Atomic Power Lab., West Mifflin, Pa., 1971-73; prof., dir. Engring. Expt. Sta., U. N.D., Grand Forks, 1973-80; prof., head mech. engring dept. U. Ark., Fayetteville, 1980-84; prof., dean engring. Tex. Tech U., Lubbock, TX, 1984-94; dean engring. No. Ariz. U., Flagstaff, 1994—; cons. Natural Gas Pipeline, Chgo., 1974-79, Archtl. Alliance, Mpls., 1978-80; bd. dirs. Mid-Am. Solar Energy Corp., Mpls., 1978-80, Ctr. for Advanced Engring and Rsch., TTU/HSC Rsch. Found.; chmn. bd. dirs. N.D. Energy Assn., 1979-80; energy advisor State of N.D., 1978-80; mem. ABET/EAC Commn., 1987-92; speaker to pub. service groups. Author: Coal Gasification Environmental Impact, Analysis of U.S. Weather, 1980; numerous tech. papers. Mem. Lubbock Bd. City Devel., 1985-87. Recipient Ralph R. Teetor award Soc. Automotive Engrs., 1974, Haliburton award; rsch. grantee. Mem. ASME, ASHRAE, Am. Soc. Engring. Edn., Sigma Xi, Pi Tau Sigma. Republican. Episcopalian. Home: 3260 S Gillerwater Dr Flagstaff AZ 86001-8970 Office: Northern Arizona Univ Coll of Engring/Tech PO Box 15600 Flagstaff AZ 86011

SOMERVILLE, RICHARD CHAPIN JAMES, atmospheric scientist, educator; b. Washington, May 30, 1941; s. James William and Mollie (Dorf) S.; m. Sylvia Francisca Bal, Sept. 17, 1965; children: Anatol Leon, Alexander Chapin. BS in Meteorology, Pa. State U., 1961; PhD in Meteorology, NYU, 1966. Postdoctoral fellow Nat. Ctr. Atmospheric Rsch., Boulder, Colo., 1966-67; rsch. assoc. geophysical fluid dynamics lab. NOAA, Princeton, N.J., 1967-69; rsch. scientist Courant Inst. Math. Scis., N.Y.C., 1969-71; meteorologist Goddard inst. space studies NASA, N.Y.C., 1971-74; adj. prof. Columbia U., NYU, 1971-74; head numerical weather prediction sect. Nat. Ctr. Atmospheric Rsch., Boulder, 1974-79; prof. meteorology, dir. climate rsch. divsn. Scripps Inst. Oceanography, U. Calif.-San Diego, La Jolla, 1979—; chmn. bd. dirs. Aspen Global Change Inst.; mem. adv. com. on geoscis. NSF; mem. panel on climate and global change NOAA. Author: The Forgiving Air: Understanding Environmental Change, 1996. Fellow AAAS, Am. Meterol. Soc.; mem. Am. Geophysical Union, Oceanography Soc. Office: U Calif San Diego Scripps Inst Oceanography 9500 Gilman Dr Dept 0224 La Jolla CA 92093-0224

SOMERVILLE, ROMAINE STEC, arts administrator; b. Scranton, Pa., May 24, 1930; d. Michael John and Julia (Skweir) Stec; m. Frank P.L. Somerville, Sept. 29, 1962; 1 child, Julia Hooper. B.A., Marymount Coll., 1951; M.A., Columbia U., 1953; postgrad., Yale U., 1958-60. Instr. art history Marywood Coll., 1954-58; curator art Everhart Mus., Scranton, 1954-58; curator decorative arts Balt. Mus. Art, 1960-63; exec. dir. Commn. for Hist. and Archtl. Preservation, Balt., 1966-72; chief curator, asst. dir. Md. Hist. Soc., Balt., 1972-78, dir., 1978-84; field cons. Nat. Endowment for Arts, Washington, 1984-86; exec. dir. The Preservation Soc., Balt., 1993—; mem. faculty Goucher Ctr. Ednl. Resources, Johns Hopkins U. Evening Sch., 1978-80; regional advisor Am. Friends of Attingham. contbg. author, editor: exhibit catalogues Md. Hist. Soc., 1975-90. Bd. dirs. Balt. Heritage, Inc., 1975—, Corpus Christi Hist. Trust, Balt., 1976—, Hampton Hist. Site, Towson, Md., 1989—; mem. adv. bd. Soc. Colonial Dames Am. Md., 1984-88, Gov.'s House, Annapolis, 1978-86; guest curator Roman Cath. Ch. bicentennial exhibit Archdiocese of Balt., 1986-91; cons. Mother Seton House, Balt., 1980-89; pres. Balt. Coalition of Hist. Neighborhoods, 1992—; mem. gov.'s adv. com. Save Outdoor Sculpture, 1992-95. Mem. Victorian Soc. Am., Md. Hist. Soc. (gallery com. 1988—), Preservation Md., Balt. Found. for Architecture, Nat. Trust for Hist. Preservation. Office: 201 W Monument St Baltimore MD 21201-4601

SOMERVILLE, WALTER RALEIGH, JR., government official; b. Macon, N.C., Feb. 17, 1930; s. Walter Raleigh and Bettie Lou (Hunt) S.; student Morgan State Coll., 1957-60; BA in Bus. Adminstrn., U. Md., 1970; diploma program sr. mgrs. in govt. John F. Kennedy Sch. Govt. Harvard U., 1992; m. Jean Renwick (Nava), Sept. 12, 1975; 1 child, Thomasine A. Walker Adams; 1 stepchild, Pamela Nava-Whitter. Personnel staffing specialist FAA, Washington, 1962-65; personnel mgmt. specialist OEO, 1965-67; personnel mgmt. specialist Office Sec. Transp., 1967-70; chief civilian equal opportunity div. U.S. Coast Guard, Transp. Dept., 1970-83, dir. civil rights, 1983—, trainee Fed. Exec. Devel. Program, 1975-76. Chmn. fin. com. Christ United Meth. Ch., Washington, 1976-85, chmn. adminstrv. coun., 1985-86; mem. human relations edn. bd. Dept. Def., 1983-85; mem. Dept. of Def. Equal Opportunity Coun.; chmn. placement and counseling com. for industry cluster Paul Quinn Coll.; bd. trustees USCG Acad., 1994—. With USAF, 1951-60. Recipient Outstanding Performance award, 1981, 82, 83, Proclamation award City Coun. of New Orleans, 1987, Key to City of Franklin, Ky., 1992, Sr. Exec. Svc. Cash Perf. award, 1993, Outstanding Contbns. to Higher Edn. Spl. award Nat. Assn. Equal Opportunity in Higher Edn., 1995; named to Nat. Assn. Equal Opportunity in Higher Edn. Registry of Disting. Individuals, 1995. Mem. Am. Mgmt. Assn., NAACP (golden heritage life mem., Roy Wilkins Meritorious Svc. award, 1987, Benjamin L. Hooks Disting. Svc. award 1993), Sr. Execs. Assn., Washington Urban League (life), U. Md. Alumni Assn. (century club), Nat. Urban League (charter mem. Pres.'s Club, mem. black exec. exch. program, vis. prof. historically black colls. and univs.). Home: 1228 4th St SW Washington DC 20024-2302 Office: 2100 2nd St SW Washington DC 20593-0001

SOMIT, ALBERT, political educator; b. Chgo., Oct. 25, 1919; s. Samuel and Mary (Rosenblum) S.; m. Leyla D. Shapiro, Aug. 31, 1947; children: Scott H., Jed L. A.B., U. Chgo., 1941, Ph.D., 1947. Prof. polit. philosophy N.Y. U., 1945-65; chmn. dept. polit. sci. State U. N.Y. at Buffalo, 1966-69, exec. v.p., 1970-80; acting pres. SUNY, Buffalo, 1976-77; pres. So. Ill. U., Carbondale, 1980-87, disting. service prof., 1987—; fellow Netherlands Inst. Advanced Study, 1978-79; Nimitz prof. polit. philosophy U.S. Naval War Coll., 1961-62. Author: (with Joseph Tanenhaus) The Development of American Political Science: From Burgess to Behavioralism, 1967, expanded edit., 1982, (with Tanenhaus) American Political Science: A Profile of A Discipline, 1964, Political Science and the Study of the Future, 1974, Biology and Politics: Recent Explorations, 1976, (with others) The Literature of Biopolitics 1963-1977, 1978, 1980, 1983, 1986, Biopolitics and Mainstream Political Science A Master Bibliography, 1990, (with Wildenmann) Hierarchy and Democracy, 1991, (with Peterson) The Dynamics of Evolution, 1992, (with Wildenmann) The Victorious Incumbent: A Threat to Democracy?, 1994, (with Peterson) The Political Behavior of Older Americans, 1994, Research in Biopolitics: Human Nature and Politics, 1995, Birth Order and Political Behavior, 1996. Served with AUS, 1950-52. Office: So Ill U Lesar Law Bldg Carbondale IL 62901

SOMJEN, GEORGE GUSTAV, physiologist; b. Budapest, Hungary, May 2, 1929; came to U.S., 1962; s. Laszlo and Margit (Ranschburg) S.; m. Eva Herman, 1952 (dec. 1974); children: Monika, Maria, Georgette, Evelyn; m. Amalia Deutsch, 1976. Grad., U. Amsterdam Med. Faculty, 1956; M.D., U. N.Z., 1962. Research asst. Pharmaco-therapeutic Lab., U. Amsterdam, 1953-56; lectr., sr. lectr. dept. physiology U. Otago, Dunedin, N.Z., 1956-62; prof. physiology Duke U., Durham, N.C., 1963—; cons. Nat. Inst. Environ. Health Scis., 1971-75. Author: Sensory Coding in the Mammalian Nervous System, 1972, Neurophysiology: The Essentials, 1983; editor: Neurophysiology Studied in Man, 1972, Mechanisms of Cerebral Hypoxia and Stroke, 1988. Recipient research grants NIH, 1964—. Mem. Am. Physiol. Soc., Soc. Neurosci., Internat. Union Physiol. Sci. (mem. com. edn. 1986-93, chmn., 1993—), Internat. Pathophysiol. Soc. (mem. com. edn.), Am. Epilepsy Soc. Office: Duke U Dept Cell Biology Div Physiology PO Box 3709 Durham NC 27710

SOMLYO, ANDREW PAUL, physiology, biophysics and cardiology educator; b. Budapest, Hungary; s. Anton and Clara Maria (Kiss) S.; m. Avril V. Russell, May 25, 1961; 1 child, Andrew Paul. BS, U. Ill., 1954, MS, 1956, MD, 1956; MS, Drexel Inst. Tech., Phila., 1963; MA (hon.), U. Pa., Phila., 1981. Asst. physician Columbia-Presbyn. Med. Ctr., N.Y.C., 1960-61; rsch. assoc. Presbyn. Hosp., Phila., 1961-67; asst. prof. pathology U. Pa., Phila., 1964-67, assoc. prof., 1967-71, prof., 1971-88, prof. physiology and pathology, 1973-88, dir. Pa. Muscle Inst., 1973-88; Charles Slaughter prof. molecular physiology-biol. physics U. Va., Charlottesville, 1988—, chmn. dept., 1988—, prof. cardiology, 1988—; cons. NIH; Brit. Heart Found. vis. prof. Hammersmith Hosp., London, Shanghai (China) Med. U.. Author: (with others) Vascular Neuroeffector Systems, 1971, The Handbook of Physiology, Vascular Smooth Muscle, 1981, Microprobe Analysis of Biological Systems, 1981, Recent Advances in Light and Optical Imaging in Biology and Medicine, 1986; editor: Jour. Muscle Research and Cell Motility; contbr. numerous articles to jours. including Biol. Chemistry, Jour. Physiology, Am. Heart Jour., Jour. Pediatrics, Jour. Cell Biology, Cell Calcium, others; mem. editl. bd. Blood Vessels, Am. Jour. Physiology, 1979-83, Magnesium: Experimental and Clinical Rsch., Jour. Structural Biology. Recipient The Louis and Artur Lucian award for rsch. in circulatory diseases, 1995. Mem. AAAS, Soc. Gen. Physiologists, Am. Physiol. Soc. Biophys. Soc., Electron Microscopy Soc., Microbeam Analysis Soc. (Presdl. award 1996), Am. Soc. for Cell Biology, Hungarian Physiol. Soc. (hon.), Microscopy Soc. Am. (Disting. Scientist award for biol. scis. 1994), Alpha Omega Alpha Med. Soc. (CIBA-GEIGY award for Hypertension Rsch. 1991). Office: U Va Sch Medicine Dept Molec Physiol & Biol Phyics 449 Jordan Hall Charlottesville VA 22908

SOMMER, ALFRED, medical educator, researcher, ophthalmologist; b. N.Y.C., Oct. 2, 1942; s. Joseph and Natalie Sommer; m. Jill Abramson, Sept. 1, 1963; children: Charles Andrew, Marni Jane. BS summa cum laude, Union Coll., 1963; MD, Harvard U., 1967; MHS in Epidemiology, Johns Hopkins U., 1973. Diplomate Am. Bd. Ophthalmology, Nat. Bd. Med. Examiners. Teaching fellow in medicine Harvard U. Med. Sch., Boston, 1968-69; dir. Nutritional Blindness Prevention Rsch. Program, Bandung, Indonesia, 1976-79; vis. fellow Inst. Ophthalmology U. London, Eng., 1979-80; founding dir., Dana Ctr. for Preventive Ophthalmology Johns Hopkins Med. Insts., Balt., 1980-90; assoc. prof. Johns Hopkins U., Balt., 1981-85, prof. ophthalmology, epidemiology and internat. health, 1985—, dean Johns Hopkins Sch. Hygiene and Pub. Health, 1990—; vis. prof. ophthalmology U. Padjadjaran, Indonesia, 1976-79; cons., advisor Helen Keller Internat., N.Y.C., 1973—; cons., chmn. com. NIH, Bethesda, Md., 1981—; bd. dirs. Internat. Agy. for the Prevention of Blindness, Geneva, Switzerland, 1978—; cons., com. mem. Nat. Acad. Scis., Washington, 1989; chmn. program adv. group on blindness prevention WHO, Geneva, 1989-90, com. mem., 1978-90, expert com., 1990—; chmn. steering com. Internat. Vitamin A Cons. Group, Washington, 1975—; pres. Internat. Fedn. of Tissue Banks; chmn. sci. adv. bd. Edna McConnell Clark Found.; mem. adv. com. Internat. Coun. Ophthalmology. Author: Epidemiology and Statistics for the Ophthalmologist, 1980, Nutritional Blindness: Xerophthalmia and Keratomalacia, 1982, Vitamin A Deficiency: Health, Survival and Vision, 1995, Detection and Control of Vitamin A Deficiency and Xerophthalmia, 1978, 82, 95; chmn. bd. overseers Am. Jours. Epidemiology and Epidemiologic Revs., 1990—. Charles A. Dana Found. award for Pioneering Achievement in Health, 1988, Disting. Svc. award for Contbn. to Vision Care AOHA, 1988, E.V. McCollum Internat. Lectureship in Nutrition Am. Inst. Nutrition, 1988, Second Ann. Am. Coll. Advancement in Medicine Achievement award in Preventive Medicine, 1990, Disting. Contbn. to World Ophthalmology award Internat. Fedn. Ophthalmol. Socs., 1990, Smadel award Infectious Diseases Soc. Am., 1990, Doyne Meml. award Oxford. Mem. Inst. Medicine of NAS (Food and Nutrition bd.), Am. Acad. Opthalmology (chmn. pub. health com. 1982-88, chmn. Quality of Care/Clin. Guidelines 1986-90, Hon. award 1986), Nat. Soc. to Prevent Blindness (bd. dirs. 1989) Internat. Assn. to Prevent Blindness (bd. dirs. 1978—). Achievements include first to detail and publish epidemiologic approach to disaster assessment; nutritional indices predict subsequent mortality in free-living children, surveillance and containment is effective intervention strategy for controlling and eradicating smallpox, vitamin A deficiency increases childhood mortality and vitamin A supplementation decreases childhood mortality, nerve fiber layer is valuable diagnostic and prognostic sign of early glaucoma; routine preventive services cost-effective in eye disease; clinical guideline development and importance of outcome assessment; research in epidemiologic and public health approaches to ophthalmology, blindness prevention, and improved health and survival. Office: Johns Hopkins Sch Hygiene and Pub Health 615 N Wolfe St Rm 1041 Baltimore MD 21205-2103

SOMMER, ALPHONSE ADAM, JR., lawyer; b. Portsmouth, Ohio, Apr. 7, 1924; s. A.A. and Adelaide (Orlett) S.; m. Storrow Cassin, June 13, 1951; children: Susan, Edward, Nancy. A.B., U. Notre Dame, 1948; LL.B., Harvard U., 1950; LL.D., Cleve. State U., 1976. Bar: Ohio 1951, D.C. 1976. Assoc. Calfee, Halter, Calfee, Griswold & Sommer, Cleve., 1950-60; ptnr. Calfee, Halter, Calfee, Griswold & Sommer, 1960-73; commr. SEC, 1973-76; ptnr. Morgan, Lewis & Bockius, Washington, 1979-94, counsel, 1994—; chmn. pub. oversight bd., AICPA. Contbr. articles to profl. jours. Chmn. pub. oversight bd. AICPA. Served with AUS, 1943-46. Mem. Nat. Assn. Securities Dealers (bd. dirs.). Home: 7105 Heathwood Ct Bethesda MD 20817-2915 Office: Morgan Lewis & Bockius 1800 M St NW Ste 925 Washington DC 20036-5802

SOMMER, HOWARD ELLSWORTH, textile executive; b. Kansas City, Mo., May 1, 1918; s. Frederick H. and Edna O. (Olsen) S.; m. Sarah Scott McElevey, June 20, 1942; children: Scott E., Paul F. BA magna cum laude, Dartmouth Coll., 1940; MBA, Harvard U., 1942. With Wolf & Co. CPAs, Chgo., 1946-76, chmn. mng. group, 1960-76; dir. Jockey Internat., Kenosha, Wis., 1959—, sr. v.p., chmn. audit com., 1979-89. Author: Procedural Routine for a Business Audit, 1947; also articles. Counsellor, Chgo. chpt. Boy Scouts Am. Lt. col. AUS, 1942-46. Decorated Bronze Star; Croix de Guerre with palms; Medaille de la Reconnaissance (France). Mem. ASME, Assn. Cons. Mgmt. Engrs. (cert. of Award 1956, v.p. 1970-72), Inst. Mgmt. Cons. (cert. mgmt. cons., past dir.), Univ. Club (pres., dir. Chgo. chpt. 1959-61), Indian Hill Club, Harvard Bus. Sch. Club (dir. Chgo. chpt. 1958-59), North Shore Cotillion Club, Dartmouth Club, Halter Wildlife Club, Masons (32 deg.), Shriners, Phi Beta Kappa, Chi Phi. Episcopalian (vestryman, warden).

SOMMER, JEFF, journalist. BA in History with distinction, Cornell U., 1974; MS in Journalism, Columbia U., 1977; MS in Regional Studies-East Asia, Harvard U., 1978. Local reporter The Albany (N.Y.) Knickerbocker News, 1977-79, The Record, Bergen County, N.J., 1979-81, Newsday, N.Y.C., 1981-82; Asia bur. chief Newsday, Beijing, 1983-86; chief corr. Soviet & East European affairs Newsday, Moscow, 1986-89; fgn. editor Newsday, N.Y.C., 1989—. Recipient Hal Boyle award Overseas Press Club, 1985; edited Pulitzer prize-winning coverage in internat. news, 1992, 93. Office: Newsday 235 Pinelawn Rd Melville NY 11747-4226

SOMMER, WILLIAM P., think tank executive. Pres. SRI Internat., Arlington, Va. Office: SRI Internat 1611 N Kent St Arlington VA 22209*

SOMMERER, JOHN, accountant; b. Mt. Holly, N.J., Oct. 30, 1947; s. John Price and Barbara Elizabeth (Davis) S.; m. Diane Catherine Kuszaj, Aug. 5, 1967; children: James Peter, John Joseph, Paul Andrew, Matthew Thomas. BS, U. Hartford, 1969; MBA, U. Toronto, 1972; postgrad., Columbia U., 1972-74. CPA, Fla., N.J., N.Y. Sr. cons. Deloitte and Touche, N.Y.C., 1974-78; dir. mgmt. info. systems Pantry Pride Enterprises, Ft. Lauderdale, Fla., 1978-82; mng. ptnr. John Sommerer and Co., P.A., Coral Springs, Fla., 1982—; mayor City of Coral Springs, 1994—. Treas. Coral Springs Cmty. Chest, 1988-94. Mem. Coral Springs Kiwanis (bd. dirs. 1990, 92), Coral Springs C. of C. (pres. 1987, treas. 1986, bd. dirs. 1986-88). Roman Catholic. Home: 9501 NW 44th Pl Coral Springs FL 33065-6602 Office: John Sommerer and Co PA 1881 N University Dr Coral Springs FL 33071-8915

SOMMERFELD, NICHOLAS ULRICH, lawyer; b. Frankfurt, Fed. Republic Germany, Sept. 3, 1926; came to U.S., 1933; s. Martin and Helene (Schott) S.; m. Charlotte Ann Abrams, Sept. 11, 1954; children: Gretchen, Amy Fiore. AB, Princeton U., 1948; JD, Harvard U., 1952. Assoc. Gaston Snow & Ely Bartlett, Boston, 1954-61, ptnr., 1961-91; of counsel Hutchins Wheeler & Dittmar, Boston, 1991—. Trustee Perkins Sch. for the Blind, Watertown, Mass., 1982—, Boston Bar Found., 1994—. Lt. USN, 1952-54. Fellow Am. Coll. Trust Estate Counsel; mem. Boston Bar Assn. (chmn. probate com. 1986-87, chmn. steering com., lawyers com. for civil rights 1980-84, mem. coun. 1993—), Boston Bar Found. (trustee 1994—). Office: Hutchins Wheeler & Dittmar 101 Federal St Boston MA 02110-1800

SOMMERFELDT, JOHN ROBERT, historian; b. Detroit, Feb. 4, 1933; s. Melvin John and Virginia Zita (Gruenheck) S.; m. Patricia Natalie Levinske, Aug. 25, 1956; children: Ann, James, John, Elizabeth. AB, U. Mich., 1954, AM, 1956, PhD, 1960. Instr. history Stanford U., 1958-59; from instr. to prof. Western Mich. U., 1959-78; prof. history U. Dallas, 1978—, chmn. dept. history, 1984-87, univ. pres., 1978-80; dir. Medieval Inst., Western Mich. U., 1961-76; exec. dir. Inst. Cistercian Studies, 1973-78; dir. Center Contemplative Studies, 1976-78; pres. Cistercian Publs., 1973-79, chmn. bd., 1976-79. Author: The Spiritual Teachings of Bernard of Clairvaux, 1991; editor: Studies in Medieval Culture, 12 vols., 1964-78, Studies in Medieval Cistercian History, II, 1977, Cistercian Ideals and Reality, 1978, Simplicity and Ordinariness, 1980, The Chimaera of His Age: Studies in Bernard of Clairvaux, 1980, Abba: Guides to Wholeness and Holiness, East and West, 1981, Erudition at God's Service, 1987, Bernardus Magister, 1992, Studiosorum Speculum, 1993. Fulbright scholar, 1954-55; Univ. fellow U. Mich., 1960. Mem. Mediaeval Acad. Am., Am. Hist. Assn., Am. Catholic Hist. Assn., Am. Soc. Ch. History, Phi Beta Kappa, Phi Eta Sigma, Phi Kappa Phi. Republican. Roman Catholic. Home: 2809 Warren Cir Irving TX 75062-8938 Office: U Dallas Dept History Irving TX 75062-4799

SOMMERFELT, SOREN CHRISTIAN, foreign affairs, international trade consultant, former Norwegian diplomat, lawyer; b. Oslo, May 9, 1916; s. Soren Christian and Sigrid (Nicolaysen) S.; m. Frances Bull, June 27, 1947; 1 child, Cathrine. LLD, Oslo U., 1940. Joined Norwegian Fgn. Svc., 1941; pvt. sec. to fgn. minister, UN sec. gen. Trygve Lie, 1941-44; assigned to UN Secretariat, 1946, Div. Refugees' and Displaced Persons, 1st sec. Norwegian Embassy, Copenhagen, 1948-50; counselor Norwegian del. to NATO, 1950-52; dep. head. econ. dept. Norwegian Ministry Fgn. Affairs, 1953-56, head, 1956-60; amb., head Norwegian del. to European Free Trade Assn., Gen. Agreement on Tariffs and Trade (GATT), and UN European Office, 1960-68; chmn. GATT Contracting Parties, 1968; amb. to Fed. Republic Germany, 1968-73, U.S.A., 1973-79, Italy, 1979-81; head Norwegian del. negotiating entry into European Communities, 1970-72; counsel Arent, Fox, Kintner, Plotkin & Kahn, Washington, 1982-84; ptnr. cons. firm Washington Resources, Inc., 1984-91; sr. ptnr. Sommerfelt Assocs., Washington, 1992—; bd. dirs. Nordic Enterprises, Inc. Decorated comdr. Order St. Olav, Norway, grand cross Order of Merit, Fed. Republic Germany, grand cross Order of Merit, Italy, comdr. with star Order of North Star, Sweden, comdr. Order of Leopold II, Belgium, knight Order of Falcon, Iceland, knight Order of Dannebrog, Denmark. Mem. Metropolitan Club (Washington), Chevy Chase Club (Md.), Norske Selskab Club (Oslo). Home: 2700 Calvert St NW Washington DC 20008-2621 Office: Sommerfelt Assocs 1250 24th St NW Washington DC 20037-1124

SOMMERLAD, ROBERT EDWARD, environmental research engineer; b. Jersey City, Aug. 27, 1937; s. Herman Francis and Helen Rita (Joyce) S.; m. Margaret Doreen Breen, Sept. 9, 1961; children: Sharon K., Michael E., Ellen J. BSME, N.J. Inst. Tech., 1960, MSME, 1963, postgrad., 1965. Devel. engr., rsch. assoc. Foster Wheeler Energy Corp., Livingston, N.J., 1960-71, head air pollution control sect., 1971-74; v.p. contract ops. Foster Wheeler Devel. Corp., Livingston, 1974-84; pres. Envirespone Inc., Livingston, 1985-86; dir. bus. devel. Energy and Environ. Rsch. Corp., Edison, N.J., 1987-88; cons., 1988-89; dir. environ. bus. devel. Midwest Rsch. Inst., Falls Church, Va., 1989-90; mgr. combustion tech. Rsch.-Cottrell Cos ., 1990-92, cons., 1992-93; mktg. dir. PSI Powerserve, Andover, Mass., 1993-94, cons., 1994-95; cons. Gas Rsch. Inst., Chgo., 1995—; mem. coal combustion and applications working group U.S. Dept. Energy U. San Diego, 1981-84. Patentee in field. V.p. Cranford (N.J.) Cmty. Pools Parents Assn., 1975-77, 86-87, pres., 1977-79, 84-86, 87-89; chmn. N.J. Swimming and Diving Conf., Cranford, 1986-89. Recipient Outstanding Achievement award Westfield YMCA, 1975. Fellow ASME (mem. rsch. com. indsl. and mcpl. waste 1971—, vice chmn. 1972-74, sec. 1987-91, mem. environ. affairs com. 1982-92, mem. dioxin com. 1985-92, mem. bd. performance test codes 1986—, chmn. boiler-calorimeter com. 1986-89, numerous com. and conf. chairmanships); mem. Air and Waste Mgmt. Assn. (vice chmn. 1994—, sec. 1991-94, vice-chair 1994, mem. AE-1 com. on particulate and associated acid gases), Watchung Amateur Ski Club (mem. exec. bd. 1986-87) (Mountainside, N.J.). Roman Catholic. Home: 1368 Knottingham Dr Gurnee IL 60031

SOMMERS, GEORGE R., lawyer; b. N.Y.C., Jan. 27, 1955. BA, U. So. Fla., 1975; JD, NYU, 1987. Bar: N.J. 1987, U.S. Dist. Ct. N.J. 1987, N.Y. 1988, U.S. Dist. Ct. (all dists.) N.Y. 1988, U.S. Ct. Appeals (3d cir.) 1988, U.S. Ct. Appeals (2d cir.) 1989, U.S. Supreme Ct. 1992. Assoc. Sullivan & Cromwell, N.Y.C., 1987-90; pvt. practice lawyer N.Y.C., 1990—; pres. Bill of Rights Found., N.Y.C., 1994—. Seidler scholar NYU Sch. Law, N.Y.C., 1985. Mem. Hoboken Bar Assn. (pres. 1994). Jewish. Avocations: sailing, chess. Office: Ste 2411 67 Wall St New York NY 10005

SOMMERS, GORDON L., religious organization administrator. Pres. Moravian Ch. in Am., Bethlehem, Pa. Office: Moravian Ch in Am PO Box 1245 1021 Center St Bethlehem PA 18016-1245

SOMMERS, LAWRENCE MELVIN, geographer, educator; b. Clinton, Wis., Apr. 17, 1919; s. Emil L. and Inga (Anderson) S.; m. Marjorie Smith, Apr. 26, 1948; 1 dau., Laurie Kay. B.S., U. Wis., 1942, Ph.M., 1946; Ph.D., Northwestern U., 1950. Prof. geography Mich. State U., East Lansing, 1949—, successively instr., asst. prof. dept. geography, assoc. prof., 1949-55, prof., 1955-89, prof. emeritus, asst. provost emeritus, 1989—; chmn. dept. geography Mich. State U., East Lansing, 1955-79, mem. Environ. Quality Ctr., 1979-81, asst. provost, 1987-89; Mem. adv. com. geography Office Naval Research and NRC, 1958-61; Fellow Am. Scandinavian Found. Co-author: Outside Readings in Geography, 1955, Introduction to Geography-Selected Readings, 1967, Cultural Geography-Selected Readings, 1967, Physical Geography-Selected Readings, 1967, Economic Geography-Selected Readings, 1970, World Regional Geography, 1976, Energy and the Adaptation of Human Settlements, 1980, Planning Issues in Marginal Areas, 1991; author: Michigan: A Geography, 1984; editor: Atlas of Michigan, 1977, Fish in Lake Michigan, 1981, Land Use: A Spatial Approach, 1981; contbr. articles on Norwegian, European, Mich., marginal areas, and econ. geography to profl. jours. Served with adj. gen. dept. AUS, 1942-45. Office Naval Rsch. grant for rsch. in Denmark, 1953, Travel grant to Europe, 1960, 82, 86, Social Sci. Rsch. Coun. and Am. Scandinavian Found. grantee for rsch. in Norway, 1948. Mem. AAAS, Am. Geog. Soc., Assn. Am. Geographers (exec. com. 1967-70, chmn. cons. svc. 1970-77, publ. com. 1968-70), Mich. State U. Acad. Coun. and Grad. Coun. (chmn. steering com. 1981-84), Am. Scandinavian Found., Scandinavian Studies Assn., Explorers Club, Sigma Xi (pres. Mich. State U. chpt. 1959-60), Phi Kappa Phi (pres. Mich. State U. chpt. 1980-82, v.p. North Ctrl. region 1986-89, nat. pres.-elect 1989-92, exec. com. 1992—, nat. pres. 1992-95, past pres. 1995—), Phi Delta Beta. Home: 4292 Tacoma Blvd Okemos MI 48864-2734 Office: Mich State Univ Geography Dept East Lansing MI 48824

SOMMERS, MAXINE MARIE BRIDGET, writer, educator, publisher; b. Crystal Falls, Mich., May 7, 1932; d. Francis Ernest and Irene Catherine (Raher) Munns; m. Clemens Struve, June 10, 1952 (div. 1975); children: Stephen, Joseph; m. Norval Isom Sommers (dec. 1989). Student, Milw. Downer Coll. for Women, 1948-49, U. Tex. Med. Br., Galveston, 1949-50, St. Mary's Hosp., 1950-51. Owner, operator Pound Sterling Publ., 1982—, Pound Sterling Media Svc., 1983—. Author: A Texan on the Road Again to the Far East, 1992; author 28 books and mini-books on cuisine, and travel, also children's books. Pres. Corpus Christi Symphony Guild, 1967-69, Tex. Assn. Symphony Orchestras, 1969; bd. dirs. Corpus Christi Symphony Soc., 1975—, South Tex. Health Syss. Agy., 1982-85; bd. dirs., pvt. svc. trainer Tex. divsn. Am. Cancer Soc., 1974-94; pres. Tex. Coastal Bend Mental Health Assn., 1976-78. Recipient cert. of award Byliners Tex. Wide Writers, 1992, Bus. Assoc. Night award Am. Bus. Women's Assn., 1992, cert. merit Corpus Christi Symphony Guild, 1969, cert. recognition Tex. Women's Assn. Symphony Orchestras, 1969, various awards Am. Cancer Soc. Mem. Byliners, Austin Writers League, Internat. Platform Assn. Avocations: gardening, cooking, traveling. Home: 4270 Ocean Dr Corpus Christi TX 78411-1283

SOMMERS, ROBERT THOMAS, editor, publisher, author; b. Balt., Aug. 6, 1926; s. Thomas Michael and Pearl Florence (Glendenning) S.; m. Helen Louise Ray, Oct. 19, 1952; children—Thomas Michael II, Patricia Ray. B.S., U. Md., College Park, 1950. Reporter Evening Sun, Balt., 1950-62; reporter Evening Star, Washington, 1962-66; editor U.S. Golf Assn. Jour., N.Y.C., 1966-72, Far Hills, N.J., 1972-92. Author: The Oxford Book of Golf Anecdotes, 1995, The U.S. Open: Golf's Ultimate Challenge, 1987, 2nd edit., 1996, Bobby Jones in Chapman's Library of Golf, 1992; co-author: Great Shots, 1989; contbr. articles to profl. jours. Served with U.S. Coast Guard, 1944-46, PTO. Mem. Golf Writers Assn. Am., Assn. Golf Writers Gt. Britain, Authors Guild, Plainfield (N.J.) Country Club, Ballybunion Golf Club (Ireland), Kingston Heath Golf Club (Australia), Royal and Ancient Golf Club of St. Andrews (Scotland), The Reserve Golf and Tennis Club (Fla.). Republican. Episcopalian. Avocations: reading, golf, music. Home and Office: 8083 Spendthrift Ln Port Saint Lucie FL 34986-3122

SOMMERS, WILLIAM PAUL, management consultant, think tank executive; b. Detroit, July 22, 1933; s. William August and Mary Elizabeth (Baietto) S.; m. Josephine A. Sommers; children: William F., Clare M., John C. Hughes, Joanna M. Weems, Russell L. Hughes. B.S.E. (scholar), U. Mich., 1955, M.S.E., 1956, Ph.D. (Riggs fellow, Texaco fellow, Univ. fellow), 1961. Research asso. U. Mich. Inst. Sci. and Tech., Ann Arbor, 1958-61; chief chem. propulsion space and missile systems Martin Marietta Corp., Balt., 1956-58, 61-63; v.p. Booz, Allen & Hamilton, Inc., Bethesda, Md., 1963-70; pres. Tech. Mgmt. Group Booz, Allen & Hamilton, Inc., 1973-79, sr. v.p., 1979-92; exec. v.p. Iameter, Inc., San Mateo, Calif., 1992-94; pres., CEO SRI Internat., Menlo Park, Calif., 1994—; bd. dirs. Kember Fin. Svcs., Rohr Inc., Therapeutic Discovery Corp., Litton Inc. Contbr. articles to profl. jours., also chpt. in book. Pres. Washington chpt. U. Mich. Alumni Club, 1970-71; v.p. Wildwood manor Citizens Assn., 1968-70; chief Adventure Guide program YMCA, 1971-72; bd. visitors Coll. Engring. U. Calif., Davis; mem. nat. adv. bd. Coll. Engring. U. Mich.; mem. conf. bd. Internat. Coun. on Innovation and Tech. Mem. Columbia Country Club, Willow Bend Country Club, Sigma Xi, Tau Beta Pi, Pi Tau Sigma. Republican. Roman Catholic. Home: 2181 Parkside Ave Hillsborough CA 94010-6452 Office: SRI Internat 333 Ravenswood Ave Menlo Park CA 94025-3453

SOMMESE, ANDREW JOHN, mathematics educator; b. N.Y.C., May 3, 1948; s. Joseph Anthony and Frances (Lia) S.; m. Rebecca Rooze DeBoer, June 7, 1971; children: Rachel, Ruth. BA in Math., Fordham U., 1969; PhD in Math., Princeton U., 1973. Gibbs instr. Yale U., New Haven, 1973-75; asst. prof. Cornell U., Ithaca, N.Y., 1975-79; assoc. prof. U. Notre Dame, Ind., 1979-83, prof. of math., 1983—, chair dept. math., 1988-92, Vincent J. Duncan and Annamarie Micus Duncan chair math., 1994—; mem. Inst. for Advanced Study, Princeton, N.J., 1975-76; guest prof. U. Bonn, Germany, 1978-79; guest rschr. Max Planck Inst. for Math., Bonn, 1992-93; cons. GM Rsch., Warren, Mich., 1986—. Editor: Manuscripta Mathematica jour., 1986-93; contbr. articles to profl. publs. Recipient Rsch. award for Sr. U.S. Scientists Alexander Von Humboldt found., 1993; A.P. Sloan Found. rsch. fellow, 1979. Mem. Am. Math. Soc., Soc. for Indsl. and Applied Math., Phi Beta Kappa. Office: U Notre Dame Dept Math Notre Dame IN 46556

SOMORJAI, GABOR ARPAD, chemist, educator; b. Budapest, Hungary, May 4, 1935; came to U.S., 1957, naturalized, 1962; s. Charles and Livia (Ormos) S.; m. Judith Kaldor, Sept. 2, 1957; children: Nicole, John. BS, U. Tech. Scis., Budapest, 1956; PhD, U. Calif., Berkeley, 1960; D (hon.), Tech. U. Budapest, 1989, U. Paris, 1990, Free Univ Brussels, Belgium, 1992. Mem. research staff IBM, Yorktown Heights, N.Y., 1960-64; dir. Surface Sci. and Catalysis Program Lawrence Berkeley Lab., Calif., 1964—; mem. faculty dept. chemistry U. Calif.-Berkeley, 1964—, assoc. prof., 1967-72, prof., 1972—, Miller prof., 1978; Unilever prof. dept. chemistry U. Bristol, Eng., 1972; vis. fellow Emmanuel Coll., Cambridge, Eng., 1989; Baker lectr. Cornell U., Ithaca, N.Y., 1977; mem. editorial bds. Progress in Solid State Chemistry, 1973—, Jour. Solid State Chemistry, 1976-92, Nouveau Jour. de Chemie, 1977—, Colloid and Interface Sci., 1979—, Catalysis Revs., 1981, Jour. Phys. Chemistry, 1981-91, Langmuir, 1985—, Jour. Applied Catalysis, Molecular Physics, 1992—. Author: Principles of Surface Chemistry, 1972, Chemistry in Two Dimensions, 1981, Introduction to Surface Chemistry and Catalysis, 1994; editor-in-chief Catalysis Letters, 1988—; contbr. articles to profl. jours. Recipient Emmett award Am. Catalysis Soc., 1977, Kokes award Johns Hopkins U., 1976, Albert award Precious Metal Inst., 1986, Sr. Disting. Scientist award Alexander von Humboldt Found., 1989, E.W. Mueller award U. Wis., Chemical Pioneer award Am. Inst. of Chemists, 1995; Guggenheim fellow, 1969. Fellow AAAS, Am. Phys. Soc.; mem. NAS, Am. Acad. Arts and Scis., Am. Chem. Soc. (chmn. colloid and surface chemistry 1981, Surface and Colloid Chemistry award 1981, Peter Debye award 1989, Arthur W. Adamson award 1994), Catalysis Soc. N.Am., Hungarian Acad. Scis. (hon. 1990). Home: 665 San Luis Rd Berkeley CA 94707-1725 Office: U Calif Dept Chemistry D 58 Hildebrand Hall Berkeley CA 94720

SONDE, THEODORE IRWIN, lawyer; b. N.Y.C., Jan. 7, 1940; s. Martin and Anne (Greenbaum) S.; m. Susan Kolisch, Sept. 10, 1964; children: Andrea Martine, David Ian. BA, CCNY, 1961; LLB, NYU, 1964; LLM, Georgetown U., 1967. Bar: N.Y. 1964, D.C. 1978, U.S. Supreme Ct. With SEC, Washington, 1964-80, asst. gen. counsel, office of Gen. Counsel, 1970-74, assoc. dir. div. of enforcement, 1974-80; dir. Office of Enforcement, Fed. Energy Regulatory Commn., 1980-81; mem. Cole, Corette & Abrutyn, Washington, 1982-90, Dechert, Price & Rhodes, 1990—; adj. prof. Georgetown U. Law Sch. 1977-95, George Washington U. Nat. Law Ctr., 1976-82. Contbr. articles to legal jours. Office: Dechert Price & Rhoads 1500 K St NW Washington DC 20005-1209

SONDEL, PAUL MARK, pediatric oncologist, educator; b. Milw., Aug. 14, 1950; s. Robert F. and Audrey J. (Dworkus) S.; m. Sherie Ann Katz, Jan. 1, 1973; children: Jesse Adam, Beth Leah, Elana Rose, Jodi Zipporah. BS with honors, U. Wis., 1971, PhD in Genetics, 1975; MD magna cum laude, Harvard Med. Sch., Boston, 1977. Diplomate Nat. Bd. Med. Examiners, Am. Bd. Pediatrics; lic. physician, Wis. Postdoctoral rsch. fellow Harvard Med. Sch., Boston, 1975-77; intern in pediatrics U. Minn. Hosp., Mpls., 1977-78; resident in pediatris U. Wis. Hosp. and Clinics, Madison, 1978-80; asst. prof. pediatrics, human oncology and genetics U. Wis., Madison, 1980-84, assoc. prof., 1984-86, prof. pediatrics, human oncology and genetics, 1987—, head divsn. pediatric hematology/oncology, program leader, 1990—; sub-fellow pediatric oncology; Midwest Children's Cancer Ctr., Milw., 1980; vis. scientist dept. cell biology Weizmann Inst. Sci., Rehovot, Israel, 1987. Mem. editorial bd. Jour. Immunology, 1985-87, Jour. Nat. Cancer Inst., 1987—, Jour. Biol. Response Modifiers, 1990—, BLOOD, 1992—, Natural Immunity, 1992—; contbr. articles to Jour. Exptl. Medicine, Jour. Immunology, Cellular Immunology, Immunol. Revs., Med. Pediatric Oncology, Wis. State Med. Jour., Jour. Biol. Response Modifiers, Jour. Pediatrics, Jour. Clin. Oncology, Jour. Clin. Investigation, and others. State of Wis. Regents scholar, 1968; J.A. and G.L. Hartford Found. fellow, 1981-84. Mem. Am. Assn. Immunologists, Am. Assn. Clin. Histocompatibility Typing, Am. Fedn. Clin. Rsch., Am. Soc. Pediatric Hematology/Oncology, Am. Assn. Cancer Rsch., Am. Soc. Transplant Physicians, Am. Soc. Clin. Oncology, Am. Acad. Pediatrics, Leukeima Soc. Am. (bd. dirs. Wis. chpt. 1987—), Disting. Physicians Am., Am. Cancer Soc. (sci. adv. com. immunology 1992—), Midwest Soc. Pediatric Rsch., Soc. Biol. Therapy (bd. dirs. 1989—, sci. adv. bd. 1989—), Transplantation Soc., Phi Beta Kappa, others. Achievements include patent for Typing Leukocyte Antigens; research in breast cancer cells enhances resistance to doxorubicin but not lymphocyte mediated killing, clinical and immunological effects of human recombinant Interleukin-2. Home: 1114 Winston Dr Madison WI 53711-3161 Office: U Wis K4/448 Clin Sci Ctr 600 Highland Ave Madison WI 53792-0001

SONDERBY, SUSAN PIERSON, federal bankruptcy judge; b. Chgo., May 15, 1947; d. George W. and Shirley L. (Eckstrom) Pierson; m. James A. De Witt, June 14, 1975 (dec. 1978); m. Peter R. Sonderby, Apr. 7, 1990. AA, Joliet (Ill.) Jr. Coll., 1967; BA, U. Ill., 1969; JD, John Marshall Law Sch., 1973. Bar: Ill. 1973, U.S. Dist. Ct. (cen. and so. dists.) Ill. 1978, U.S. Dist. Ct. (no. dist.) Ill. 1984, U.S. Ct. Appeals (7th Cir.) 1984. Assoc. O'Brien, Garrison, Berard, Kusta and De Witt, Joliet, 1973-75, ptnr., 1975-77; asst. atty. gen. consumer protection div., litigation sect. Office of the Atty. Gen., Chgo., 1977-78; asst. atty. gen., chief consumer protection div. Office of the Atty. Gen., Springfield, Ill., 1978-83; U.S. trustee for no. dist. Ill. Chgo., 1983-86; judge U.S. Bankruptcy Ct. (no. dist.) Ill., Chgo., 1986—; adj. faculty De Paul U. Coll. Law, Chgo., 1986; spl. asst. atty. gen., 1972-78; past mem. U.S. Trustee adv. com., consumer adv. coun. Fed. Res. Bd.; past sec. of State Fraudulent I.D. com., Dept. of Ins. Task Force on Improper Claims Practices. Mem. Fourth Presbyn. Ch., Art Inst. Chgo.; past mem. Westminster Presbyn. Ch., Chgo. Coun. of Fgn. Rels.; past bd. dirs. Land of Lincoln Coun. Girl Scouts U.S.; past mem. individual guarantors com. Goodman Theatre, Chgo.; past chmn. clubs and orgns. Sangamon County United Way Capital campaign; past bd. dirs., chmn. house rules com. and legal subcom. Lake Point Tower; past mem. Family Svc. Ctr., Aid to Retarded Citizens, Henson Robinson Zoo. Master Abraham Lincoln Marovitz Inn of Ct.; fellow Am. Coll. Bankruptcy; mem. Nat. Conf. Bankruptcy Judges (legis. outreach com.), Am. Bankruptcy Inst., Comml. Law League Am. (exec. coun. bankruptcy and insolvency sect., bankruptcy com., past vice chmn. U.S. Trustee Rev. com., edn. com.), Law Club of Chgo., Legal Club of Chgo. (hon.), Nordic Law Club. Avocations: travel, flying, interior decorating. Office: US Bankruptcy Ct 219 S Dearborn St Ste 638 Chicago IL 60604-1704

SONDEREGGER, THEO BROWN, psychology educator; b. Birmingham, Ala., May 31, 1925; d. Ernest T. and Vera M. (Sillox) Brown; children: Richard Paul, Diane Carol, Douglas Robert. BS, Fla. State U., 1946; MA in Chemistry, U. Nebr., 1948, MA in Exptl. Psychology, 1960; PhD in Clin. Psychology, U. Nebr., 1965. Lic. psychologist, Calif; clin. lic., cert. Nebr. Asst. prof. U. Nebr. Med. Ctr., Omaha, 1965-71, Nebr. Wesleyan U., Lincoln, 1965-68; asst. prof. U. Nebr., Lincoln, 1968-71, assoc. prof., 1971-76, prof., 1976-94; ret., 1994, prof. emeritus, 1995—; vol. assoc. prof. U. Nebr. Med. Ctr., 1972-77, courtesy prof. med. psychology, 1977-95. Editor: Nebr. Symposium on Motivation, 1974, 84, 91, Problems of Perinatal Drug Dependence: Research and Clinical Implications, 1986, Neurobehavioral Toxicology and Teratology vol. 8, 1988-89, Problems of Perinatal Drug Dependence, 1979, 82, 84, Feminist Therapy Interchange, 1988-89, 91, Perinatal Substance Abuse: Research and Clinical Implications, 1992, Agendas for Aging, 1994—. Mem. grant rev. coms. Nat. Inst. Drug Abuse, 1983-84, 85, 91-94. Tribute to Women award Lincoln YMCA, 1985, named Outstanding Rsch. Scientist Nebr. Chpt. Sigma Xi, 1991, Outstanding Contbn. to Status of Women, N N-L Chancellors Commn. on Status of Women, 1994, Pound Howard Disting. Career Achievement award, 1996. Fellow AAAS, Am. Psychol. Assn., Am. Psychol. Soc.; mem. Midwestern Psychol. Assn., Internat. Soc. Devel. Psychobiology, Internat. Soc. Psychoneuroendocrinolty, Nebr. Psychol. Assn. (pres. 1972), Soc. Neuroscis., Advanced Feminist Therapy Inst., Region V Adv. Coun. on Drugs, Fetal Alcohol Adv. Coun., Phi Beta Kappa (sec. Nebr. chpt. 1974), Sigma Xi (pres. 1986). Club: Altrusa YWCA. Avocations: painting, photography.

SONDHEIM, STEPHEN JOSHUA, composer, lyricist; b. N.Y.C., Mar. 22, 1930; s. Herbert and Janet (Fox) S. B.A., Williams Coll., 1950. vis. prof. contemporary theater Oxford U., England, 1990. Composer incidental music Girls of Summer, 1956, Invitation to a March, 1961, Twigs, 1971; lyrics West Side Story, 1957, Gypsy, 1959, Do I Hear A Waltz?, 1965; music and lyrics A Funny Thing Happened on the Way to The Forum, 1962, Anyone Can Whistle, 1964, Evening Primrose, 1966, Company, 1970 (Tony award 1971), Follies, 1971 (Tony award 1972), A Little Night Music, 1973 (Tony award 1973), The Frogs, 1974, Pacific Overtures, 1976, Sweeney Todd, 1979 (Tony award 1979), Merrily We Roll Along, 1981, Sunday in the Park with George, 1984 (Pulitzer prize 1985), Into the Woods, 1987 (Tony award 1988), Assassins, 1991, Passion, 1994 (Tony award 1994); additional lyrics Candide, 1973; anthologies Side by Side by Sondheim, 1976, Marry Me a Little, 1981, You're Gonna Love Tomorrow, 1983, Putting It Together, 1993; film scores Stavisky, 1974, Reds, 1981; composer songs for film Dick Tracy, 1990 (Acad. award); co-author film The Last of Sheila, 1973. Recipient Creative Arts medal Brandeis U., 1982, Grammy award, 1970, 73, 75, 79, 84, 88, Kennedy Ctr. Honor for Lifetime Achievement, 1993. Mem. Am. Acad. and Inst. Arts and Letters.

SONDHEIMER, JUDITH MCCONNELL, pediatrician, educator; b. Englewood, N.J., Apr. 20, 1944; d. John W. and Harriet H. (Barlow) McConnell; m. Henry M. Sondheimer, June 30, 1969; 2 children. BA, Swarthmore Coll., 1966; MD, Columbia U., 1970. Diplomate Am. Bd. Pediatrics, Am. Bd. Pediatric Gastroenterology. Intern then resident U. Colo., Denver, 1970-72; pediatric GI fellow Hosp. for Sick Children, Toronto, Ont., Can., 1974-76; asst. prof. pediatrics SUNY, Syracuse, 1976-80, assoc. prof. pediatrics, 1980-85; assoc. prof. pediatrics U. Colo., Denver, 1985-89, prof. pediatrics, 1989—; chief GI/Nutrition, Children's Hosp., Denver, 1985—. Fellow Am. Acad. Pediatrics; mem. Am. Gastroenterol. Soc., N.Am. Soc. Pediatric Gastroenterology and Nutrition. Office: Childrens Hosp-GI/Nutrition 1056 E 19th Ave Denver CO 80218-1007

SONEGO, IAN G., lawyer; b. Louisville, May 27, 1954; s. Angelo and Zella Mae (Causey) S. BA in Polit. Sci. with high honors, U. Louisville, 1976, JD, 1979. Bar: Ky. 1979, U.S. Dist Ct. (ea. dist.) Ky. 1980, U.S. Dist. Ct. (we. dist.) Ky. 1989, U.S. Ct. Appeals (6th cir.) 1989, U.S. Supreme Ct. 1990. Asst. atty. Office Commonwealth's Atty. Pike County, Pikeville, Ky., 1980, sr. asst. atty., 1988-89; assoc. John Paul Runyon Law Firm, Pikeville, 1981-87; asst. atty. gen. Office Atty. Gen., Frankfort, Ky., 1989—; lectr. criminal law Ky. Bar Assn., Jenny Wiley Park, 1981, Ky. Prosecutors Confs., 1989, 93; mem. Atty. Gen.'s task force child sexual abuse, 1992-94. Contbg. editor Ky. Prosecuter Newsletter, 1991—. Recipient Kessleman award U. Louisville, 1975, Bd. Trustee award 1979. Outstanding Prosecutor award Ky. Atty. Mem. Ky. Commonwealth's Attys. Assn. (hon., lectr. 1987, 90, chmn. com. ethics 1984-86, bd. dirs. 1983-85, Outstanding Svc. award 1985, Spl. award 1987). Office: Office Atty Gen PO Box 2000 1024 Capital Ctr Dr Frankfort KY 40602-2000

SONENBERG, JACK, artist; b. Toronto, Ont., Can., Dec. 28, 1925; s. Solomon and Leah (Saltzman) S.; m. Phoebe Helman, June 7, 1949; 1 dau., Maya. Student, N.Y. U., 1949; B.F.A., Washington U., 1951. Mem. faculty dept. art Queens Coll., 1970-72, Bklyn. Coll., 1972, Bklyn. Coll. (Sch. of Visual Arts), 1962-73; mem. faculty Pratt Inst., Bklyn., 1968—; chmn. painting and drawing dept. Pratt Inst. Bklyn., 1973—. One-man shows, Byron Gallery, N.Y.C., 1965, 68, Hampton Inst., 1968, U. No. Iowa, 1969, Grand Rapids (Mich.) Art Mus., 1968, Flint Inst. Arts, 1972, Fischbach Gallery, N.Y.C., 1973, 55 Mercer Gallery, N.Y.C., 1980, group shows include, Whitney Mus., 1967, 73, Mus. Modern Art, 1974, Art Inst. Chgo., 1975, Pratt Inst., Bklyn., 1980, Rutgers U., N.J., 1980, Nat. Gallery, Washington, 1980, Moscow Artists Union, 1989; group shows include Painting Self-Evident, Piccolo Spolete, 1992; represented in permanent collections, Guggenheim Mus., Whitney Mus., Washington U., Met. Mus., Bradley U., Nat. Gallery Can., W.Va. U. Ford Found. grantee, 1966; Guggenheim Found. grantee, 1973, N.Y. State CAPS, 1973-76, Nat. Endowment Arts grantee (sculpture), 1984-85, N.Y. Found. for the Arts grantee (painting) 1989. Office: Pratt Inst Sch Art and Design Brooklyn NY 11205

SONENBERG, MARTIN, biochemistry educator, physician; b. N.Y.C., Dec. 1, 1920; s. Berl and Nellie (Gordon) S.; m. Dellie Madeleine Ellis, Jan. 17, 1956; children: Santha, Andrea. B.A., U. Pa., 1941; M.D., NYU, 1944, PhD in Chemistry, 1952. Mem. Sloan-Kettering Cancer Center, N.Y.C., 1950, chief endocrinology, 1972-94; faculty Cornell U., 1950—, prof. biochemistry, 1967-83, prof. medicine, 1972—, prof. cell biology and genetics, 1983—. Mem. editorial bd.: Endocrinology, 1967-75; contbr. articles to profl. jours. Mem. biomed. adv. com. Population Coun., 1960; mem. adv. com. Am. Cancer Soc., 1971; chmn. endocrinology study sect. NIH, mem. adv. com. divsn. rsch. grants, 1989-91. Recipient Van Meter award Am. Thyroid Assn., 1952; Am. Cancer Soc. scholar, 1952-55; Guggenheim fellow, 1957-58; recipient Sloan award for cancer research, 1968. Mem. Am. Thyroid Assn., Am. Soc. Clin. Investigation, Am. Soc. Biol. Chemists, Endocrine Soc. Research on role of pituitary gland in normal and abnormal growth. Office: 1275 York Ave New York NY 10021-6007

SONENSHEIN, ABRAHAM LINCOLN, microbiology educator; b. Paterson, N.J., Jan. 13, 1944; s. Israel Louis and Celia (Rabinowitz) S.; m. Gail Entner, Jan. 28, 1967; children: Dina Miriam, Adam Israel. AB, Princeton U., 1965; PhD, MIT, 1970. Postdoctoral fellow U. Paris, Orsay, France, 1970-72; asst. prof. Tufts U., Boston, 1972-78, assoc. prof., 1978-82, prof., 1982—. Rsch. grantee NIH, 1972—; fellow Am. Cancer Soc., 1970-72. Mem. AAAS, Am. Soc. for Microbiology, Am. Acad. Microbiology, Fedn. Am. Scientists, Sigma Xi. Office: Tufts U 136 Harrison Ave Boston MA 02111-1800

SONENSHEIN, NATHAN, marine consulting company executive, retired naval officer; b. Lodi, N.J., Aug. 2, 1915; s. H. W. and Sarah S.; m. Ila Nina Maria Baker, May 11, 1941; children: Carol Dale Manashil, William Baker. B.S., U.S. Naval Acad., 1938; M.S., MIT, 1944; grad. Advanced Mgmt. Program, Harvard U., 1964. Commd. ensign U.S. Navy, 1938, advanced through grades to rear adm., 1965; various assignments U.S. and Japan, 1938-49; dir. navy facilities div. Bur. Ships, 1949-51; engring. officer U.S.S. Philippine Sea, 1951-53; planning and estimating supt. N.Y. Naval Shipyard, 1953-56; head hull design br. Bur. Ships, 1956-60; fleet and force maintenance officer on staffs comdr.-in-chief and comdr. service force U.S. Pacific Fleet, 1960-62; dir. ship design div. Bur. Ships, 1962-64, asst. chief for design, shipbldg. and fleet maintenance, 1965; project mgr. Fast Deployment Logistics Ship Project, 1965-66; dep. chief naval material for logistic support, 1967-69; comdr. Naval Ship Systems Command, 1969-72; chmn. NMC Shipbldg. Council, 1972-73; dir. for energy Dept. Def., 1973-74, ret., 1974; asst. to pres. Global Marine Devel., Inc., Newport Beach, Calif., 1974-84; pres. Sonenshein and Assocs., marine cons. co., Moraga, Calif., 1985—; mem. nat. adv. com. Oceans and Atmosphere, 1984-86. Decorated Legion of Merit with 2 Gold stars. Mem. Am. Soc. Naval Architects and Marine

Engrs. (v.p.), Am. Soc. Naval Engrs. (past pres., H.E. Saunders medal 1982), Sigma Xi. Home and Office: 1884 Joseph Dr Moraga CA 94556-2711

SONES, SHARI CAROLYN, counselor, educator; b. Warner Robins, Ga., May 3, 1966; d. Jon Chalmers and Eleanor Jean (Spaulding) Niemeyer. BS, Brenau Coll., 1988; MS, Ga. State U., 1991. Cert. Nat. Bd. for Cert. Counselors, Inc.; lic. profl. counselor. Asst. tchr. Hi Hope, Lawrenceville, Ga., 1988; counselor Anxiety Disorder Inst. Atlanta, 1991-94; pvt. practice Atlanta, Ga., 1994—; tchr. Oglethorpe U., Atlanta, 1993; clin. dir. Trauma and Abuse Resource Program, 1994—. Vol. group leader Ga. Counsel on Child Abuse, Atlanta, 1991-92. Mem. ACA, Nat. Assn. Alcoholism and Drug Abuse Counselors. Avocations: riding horses, running, reading, learning sign language. Office: Anxiety Disorders Inst 1 Dunwoody Pk Ste 112 Atlanta GA 30338

SONFIELD, ROBERT LEON, JR., lawyer; b. Houston, Oct. 28, 1931; s. Robert Leon and Dorothy Harriett (Huber) S.; 1 dau., Sheree. B.A., U. Houston, 1956, LL.B., J.D., 1959; Ph.D. (hon.), U. Eastern Fla., 1962; LL.D. (hon.), London Inst. Applied Research, 1973; certificate fed. taxation, NYU, 1973; certificate securities regulation, Harvard U., 1983. Bar: Tex. 1959, U.S. Supreme Ct. 1959, U.S. Dist. Ct. Tex. 1960, U.S. Tax Ct. 1960, U.S. Ct. Appeals 1960, U.S. Ct. Claims 1974. Mng. dir. Sonfield & Sonfield, Houston, 1959—; Mem. nat. adv. council Nat. Fedn. Ind. Bus. Author: Corporate Financing by Sale of Securities to the Public, 1969, Mergers and Acquisitions, 1970, Student Rights, 1971, The Limited Partnership as a Vehicle for Real Estate Investment, 1971, Integration of Partnership Offerings, 1974, The Grantor Trust Rules After The Tax Reform Act of 1986, Incentive Equity Program, Corporate Name Protection Along With Name Registration, A Guide to SEC Corporate Filing, Organizational Professionals' Residual Litigation and Investment Strategy, Comparing California, Delaware and Nevada: Corporate Laws in Light of California Corporations Code Section 2115 and Offering of Unregistered Securities Only to Accredited Investors, Disclosure Policies, Practices and Procedures For Public Companies, Regulation of Franchises, How to Become a Publicly Held Company Via the Registered Ditribution of a Percentage of Your Company's Stock to Shareholders, numerous others. Recipient St. John Garwood award, 1957, Frio-Finnegan Outstanding Alumnus award, 1970-71, citation for outstanding contbn. to legal profession, 1971. Mem. Am. Tax Lawyers Assn. (pres.), Lawyers Soc. Houson, Am. Judicature Soc., ABA, Tex. Bar Assn. (dist. com. on admission to state bar, chmn. clients security fund com.), Houston Bar Assn. (com. chmn. council, tax sect.), Tex. Equal Access to Justice Found., Houston Bar Found., Real Estate Securities and Syndication Inst., Huguenot Soc. of London, Order Stars and Bars, SAR, Sons Confederate Vets., Mil. Order World Wars, Mil. and Hospitaller Order St. Lazarus of Jerusalem, Knightly Assn. St. George the Martyr, Smithsonian Assocs., Houston Heritage Soc., Houston Mus. Fine Arts, Newcomen Soc. N.Am., Phi Delta Phi, Delta Sigma Phi. Clubs: Metropolitan (N.Y.C.); Argyle (San Antonio); Houston, Houstonian. Office: Sonfield & Sonfield 770 S Post Oak Ln Houston TX 77056-1913

SONG, XIAOTONG, physicist, educator; b. Taizhou, Jiangsu, People's Republic of China, Oct. 18, 1934; came to U.S., 1989; s. Hoshu Song and Jingying Wang; m. Chuchu Zhu, 1966; 1 child, Jianyang. BS in Physics, Fudan U., Shanghai, China, 1955, PhD in Physics, 1963. Rsch. fellow Dept Def., China, 1955-58; asst. prof. Hangzhou U., China, 1958-63; lectr., 1963-66, 77-83, assoc. prof., 1983-86, prof., 1986—; rsch. cons. dept. physics Inst. Nuclear and Particle Physics, U. Va., Charlottesville, 1989-90, rsch. prof., cons., 1990—; adv. com. for professorship exam., Zhejiang, China; dir. theory divsn. dept. physics Hangzhou U., China, 1984-89; referee Phys. Rev., High Energy Physics and Nuclear Physics, Nat. Natural Sci. Found., China; vis. scientist Tech. U. Munich, 1986, 88-89, European Lab. for Particle Physics, Geneva, 1986-87, Inst. Nat. Fisica Nuclear Turin Sect., Italy, 1986-88, Internat. Ctr. Theoretical Physics, Italy, 1986-88, Los Alamos Nat. Lab., 1987, Utah State U., 1987, Kans. State U., 1989, Brookhaven Nat. Lab. Contbr. articles to profl. jours. Recipient Prize of Natural Sci., Com. Sci. and Tech., Zhejiang Province, China, 1983, 84; grantee Nat. Natural Sci. Found., 1984-87. Mem. AAAS, Internat. Ctr. Theoretical Physics (sr. assoc.), Am. Phys. Soc., Chinese High Energy Physics Soc., Chinese Phys. Soc., N.Y. Acad. Sci., Sigma Xi. Achievements include research in theoretical nuclear and particle physics. Office: U Va Physics Dept Mccormick Rd Charlottesville VA 22901

SONGSTER, JOHN HUGH, legal administrator; b. Springfield, Pa., Mar. 20, 1934; s. James Thomas and Sarah Boyce (McMichael) S. BA, LaSalle Coll., Phila., 1956. Commd. ensign USN, 1956, advanced through grades to comdr., 1971, ret., 1976; asst. treas. Bradford Trust Co., N.Y.C., 1976-80; staff acct. Harcourt Brace Jovanovich, N.Y.C., 1980-83, Software Design Assocs., N.Y.C., 1983-87; legal adminstr. Gold Farrell & Marks, N.Y.C., 1988—. Mem. Assn. Legal Adminstrs. Republican. Roman Catholic. Avocations: reading biographies and mysteries, opera. Office: Gold Farrell & Marks 41 Madison Ave New York NY 10010-2202

SONIN, AIN A., mechanical engineering educator, consultant; b. Tallinn, Estonia, Dec. 24, 1937; came to U.S., 1965; s. Elmar and Ina (Herman) S.; m. Epp Jurima, July 24, 1971; children: Juhan, Aldo. BA Sc., U. Toronto, Ont., Can., 1960, MA Sc., 1961, PhD, 1965. Rsch. fellow, teaching asst. U. Toronto, 1960-65; asst. prof. MIT, Cambridge, 1965-68, assoc. prof., 1968-74, prof. mech. engring., 1974—; sr. scientist Thermo Electron Corp., Waltham, Mass., 1981-82; cons. in field. Contbr. over 60 articles to profl. jours. in fluid and thermal sciences. Mem. ASME, AAAS, Am. Phys. Soc., Am. Nuclear Soc. Achievements include 3 patents in field. Office: MIT Rm 3-256 Cambridge MA 02139

SONJU, NORM ARNOLD, professional sports team manager, executive; b. Chgo., Sept. 30, 1938; s. Marinius Anton and Anna (Nesse) S.; m. Carole Lynne Thiesen, June 10, 1967; children: Lynne, Scott, David. B.A., Grinnell Coll., 1960; M.B.A., U. Chgo., 1967. Vice pres., gen. mgr. Service-Master Contract Services, Downers Grove, Ill., 1967-77; pres., gen. mgr. Buffalo Braves, N.Y., 1977-78; v.p. Dallas Mavericks, 1979-87, gen. mgr., 1979—, chief operating officer, 1987—; dir., founder Camp of Woods Basketball Clinic, Speculator, N.Y., 1963—; dir. Correct Craft Boat Co., Orlando, Fla. Bd. dirs. Gospel Vols., Speculator, 1976—; trustee Taylor U., Upland, Ind., 1981—; mem. Dallas Assembly, 1983—. Mem. Nat. Basketball Assn. (bd. govs. 1977—, chmn. mktg. com. 1982—). Republican. Clubs: Cress Creek Country (Naperville, Ill.); Brookhaven Country (Dallas). Office: Dallas Mavericks Reunion Arena 777 Sports Pl Dallas TX 75207-4411*

SONKA, STEVEN T., agricultural economics educator, consultant; b. Cedar Rapids, Iowa, July 4, 1948; s. Jerome and Marcella (Pickert) S.; m. Karilyn Mae Stephen, June 5, 1970; children: Tracy, Melissa, Julie, Teresa. BS in Agrl. Bus., Iowa State U., 1970, PhD in Econs., 1974. Resident assoc./staff economist Iowa State U., 1971-75; asst. prof. U. Ill., Urbana, 1975-79, assoc. prof., 1979-83, prof. agr. econ., 1983—; ptnr. Agrl. Edn. and Cons., Champaign, Ill., 1983—; vis. faculty in residence Arthur Andersen & Co., summer 1982, Monstanto Co., summer 1993; resident assoc. Ctr. for Advanced Study, Champaign, fall 1986; vis. prof. Inst. Agrl. Bus., Santa Clara, Calif., 1986-87; cons. Orgn. Econ. Coop. and Devel., Paris, 1989, office tech. assessment U.S. Congress, Washington, 1989-90. Author: (books) American Farm Size, 1975, Hail Suppression, 1977, Computers in Farming, 1983. Task force mem. U.S. Senate, Washington, 1982-83. Recipient Van Nostrand Reinhold/A V I Press Teacher awd., Nat. Assn. of Colleges and Teachers of Agriculture, 1992. Mem. Am. Agrl. Econ. Assn. (chair 1987-90). Office: U Ill 1301 W Gregory Dr Urbana IL 61801-3608

SONKOWSKY, ROBERT PAUL, classicist, educator, actor; b. Appleton, Wis., Sept. 16, 1931; s. Paul and Loretta Stella (Nooyen) S.; m. Barbara Lou Zierke, June 8, 1956; children—Paul Victor, Steven Robert, Michael Edward. B.A., Lawrence Coll., 1954; postgrad., U. Rome, 1956-57; Ph.D., U. N.C., 1958. Instr., asst. prof. U. Tex., 1958-61; fellow Inst. Research in Humanities, U. Wis., 1961-62; asso. prof. U. Mo., 1962-63, U. Minn., Mpls., 1963-64; chmn. dept. classics U. Minn., 1964-78, prof., 1964—; disting. Marbrook vis. prof. Macalester Coll., 1987-88; actor Attic Theatre, Appleton, Wis., 1950-54, Wilderness Rd. Theater Co., Berea, Ky., The Confederacy Co. Virginia Beach, Va., summers, 1955-58, Pillsbury House and Lyric Theaters, Mpls., 1991, Looking Glass Theater, St. Paul, 1993, Theater on the Park, Mpls., 1994-96. Author books; contbr. articles to profl. jours.; also recitations and recordings of classical Latin lit. in restored pronunciation; lit. recs., ednl. feature and indsl. films, TV commls. Lay reader Episc. Cathedral Ch. of St. Mark; lector Gregorian Singers, 1980-89; mem. St. Paul Sch. Com., 1971-76. Mem. AFTRA, Am. Philol. Assn., Soc. for Oral Reading of Greek and Latin Lit., Classical Assn. Mid West and South Internat. Soc. Chronobiology (nomenclature com.), Fulbright Assn. (pres. Minn. chpt. 1991-92), Phi Beta Kappa (pres. U. Minn. chpt. 1973-74, nat. senator 1976-82, pres. Minn. Assn. 1991-95, books reviewer for Key Reporter). Office: U Minn Classical & Near Ea Studies 330 Folwell Hall 9 Pleasant St SE Minneapolis MN 55455-0194

SONNABEND, ROGER PHILIP, hotel company executive; b. Boston, Sept. 17, 1925; s. Abraham M. and Esther (Lewitt) S.; m. Elsa Golub, July 17, 1949 (div.); children: Andrea, Stephanie, Jacqueline, Alan; m. Joan Snider, Feb. 18, 1971; stepchildren: Heidi Norton, Andrea Stoneman. B.A., MIT, 1946; M.B.A., Harvard U., 1949; LL.D. (hon.), U. N.H., 1969. Chief exec. officer Sonesta Internat. Hotel Corp., Boston, 1954—, chmn., 1970—. Contbr. chpts. to books and articles to profl. jours. Mem. exec. com. Nat. Alliance of Businessmen, 1968-69; bd. dirs. Bus. Execs. for Nat. Security, Inc., Washington, 1983-86; exec. com. Northeast NCCJ, 1957, regional co-chmn., nat. v.p., 1960-68; trustee Inst. Contemporary Art. Mem. World Bus. Coun., Chief Execs. Orgn., Harvard Club (Boston). Home: 170 Rushton Ln Tavernier FL 33070-3015 Office: Sonesta Internat Hotels Corp 200 Clarendon St Boston MA 02116-5021

SONNE, MAGGIE LEE, sales executive; b. Pasadena, Calif., July 14, 1958; d. Roscoe Newbold Jr. and Ann Miriam (Vierhus) S.; m. Donald Alan Blackburn, Sept. 8, 1979 (div. 1983). AS, Oreg. Inst. Tech., 1981, BS, 1983. Sales trainee NCR Corp., Dayton, Ohio, 1983-84; sales rep. NCR Corp., Portland, Oreg., 1984-86; account mgr. NCR Corp., Seattle, 1986-87; sr. account mgr. NCR Corp., Portland, 1987-88; sr. account rep. Wang Labs., Portland, 1988-91; account exec. Tandem Computers, Portland, 1991-94; sr. acct. exec. Fin. Svcs., L.A., 1994—. Active Emily's List, Project Vote Smart, Spl. Olympics, Ams. for Change, Presdl. Task Force, Pres. Coun., Tandem Computers, Inc. Mem. Soc. Advancement Mgmt., Costeau Soc., Alpha Chi. Avocations: sailing, diving, skiing, biking, golf. Home: PO Box 323 Surfside CA 90743-0323

SONNEBORN, HENRY, III, former chemical company executive, business consultant; b. Balt., Mar. 11, 1918; s. Henry, Jr. and Lillian B. (Hamburger) S.; m. Clara Louise Lauer, Nov. 12, 1942; 1 child, Peter. A.B., Johns Hopkins U., 1938, Ph.D., 1941; doctorate (hon.), Hebrew U., Jerusalem, 1976. V.p., bd. dirs. Sonneborn Chem. and Refining, N.Y.C., 1950-60; bus. cons., Larchmont, N.Y.; bus. cons. Contbr. articles to profl. jours. Mem. PMI-Strang Clinic, 1969-72; trustee Hosp. for Joint Diseases, 1961—, chmn. bd., 1985-88; pres. Am. Friends Hebrew U., 1974-77; trustee Johns Hopkins U., 1978—. Served to lt. USNR, 1942-46. Jewish. Home: 110 N Chatsworth Ave Larchmont NY 10538-1638 Office: 2 Madison Ave Larchmont NY 10538-1947*

SONNECKEN, EDWIN HERBERT, management consultant; b. New Haven, July 22, 1916; s. Ewald and Pauline (Halfmann) S.; m. Elizabeth Gregory, June 3, 1939; children: William H., Richard G., Paul D. B.S., Northwestern U., 1938, M.B.A., 1940. With Montgomery Ward & Co., Chgo., 1940-42; price adminstr. OPA, Chgo., 1943; mgr. sales B.F. Goodrich Co., Akron, Ohio, 1943-53; dir. planning Ford Motor Co., Dearborn, Mich., 1953-57; pres. Market Planning Corp., N.Y.C., 1957-61; from dir. corp. planning and research to v.p. corp. bus. planning Goodyear Tire & Rubber Co., 1961-80; chmn. Mktg. Sci. Inst., Cambridge, Mass., 1980-84; also trustee, chmn. research policy com. Mktg. Sci. Inst.; mgmt. cons., Akron, 1985—; Pres. Akron (Ohio) chpt. Am. Mktg. Assn., 1950, v.p. Detroit chpt., 1955, nat. v.p., dir., 1957, nat. pres., 1964-65, mem. global mktg. coun., 1986—. Pres. YMCA, Akron, 1978; chmn. trustees First Congl. Ch., Akron, 1985, chmn. endowment trust, 1987—. Served with AUS, 1945-46. Mem. Am. Statis. Assn., Am. Assn. Pub. Opinion Research, Nat. Assn. Bus. Economists, Am. Mktg. Assn., Internat. Mktg. Fedn. (pres.), European Soc. for Opinion and Market Research, Beta Gamma Sigma, Portage Country (Akron). Avocation: golf. Home: 736 Hampton Ridge Dr Akron OH 44313-5024

SONNEDECKER, GLENN ALLEN, historian of pharmacy; b. Creston, Ohio, Dec. 11, 1917; s. Ira Elmer and Letia (Linter) S.; m. Cleo Bell, Apr. 3, 1943; 1 child, Stuart Bruce. BS, Ohio State U., 1942; MS, U Wis., 1950, PhD, 1952; Dr. Sci. honoris causa, Ohio State U., 1964, Phila. Coll. Pharmacy and Sci., 1989; PharmD honoris causa, Mass. Coll. Pharmacy, 1974. Lic. pharmacist. Mem. editorial staff Sci. Service, Washington, 1942-43; editor Jour. Am. Pharm. Assn. (practical pharmacy edit.), Washington, 1943-48; asst. prof. U. Wis., 1952-56, asso. prof., 1956-60, prof., 1960-81, Edward Kremers prof., 1981-86; sec. Am. Inst. History of Pharmacy, 1949-57, dir., 1957-73, 81-85, hon. dir. life, chmn. bd., 1988-89; editor-in-chief RPh, 1978-80; sec., bd. dirs. Friends of Hist. Pharmacy, 1945-49; chmn. Joint Com. on Pharmacy Coll. Librs., 1960-61; U.S. del. Internat. Pharm. Fedn., 1953, 55, 62; U.S. rep. to Mid. East Pharm. Congress, Beirut, 1956; sec. sect. history of pharmacy and biochemistry Pan-Am. Congress Pharmacy and Biochemistry, 1957. Co-author books; contbr. to pharm. and hist. publs. Recipient Edward Kremers award (for writings), 1964, Nat. award Rho Chi, 1967, Schelenz plaquette Internat. Soc. for History of Pharmacy, 1971, Remington honor medal Am. Pharm. Assn., 1972, Urdang medal, 1976, Folch Andreu prize, Spain, 1985, Profile award Am. Found. Pharm. Edn., 1994; Am. Found. fellow, 1948-52, Guggenheim fellow, 1955, Fulbright Rsch. scholar, Germany, 1955-56. Mem. Am. Pharm. Assn. (life mem.; sec. sect. history of pharmacy 1949-50, vice chmn. 1950-51, chmn. 1951-52, rsch. assoc. 1964-65, chmn. joint task force with Acad. Pharm Scis. 1985, hon. chmn. bd. trustees 1985), Internat. Acad. History Pharmacy (1st v.p. 1970-81, pres. 1983-91, hon. pres. 1991—), Am. Assn. History of Medicine (exec. coun. 1966-69), Internat. Gesellschaft fur Geschichte der Pharmazie (exec. bd. 1965-89), hon. mem. socs. for history of pharmacy of Italy, Benelux, pan-Arab, Spain; mem. Sigma Xi, Rho Chi (mem. nat. exec. coun. 1957-59), Phi Delta Chi. Unitarian. Home: 2030 Chadbourne Ave Madison WI 53705-4047 Office: Univ Wis Pharmacy Bldg Madison WI 53706

SONNEMAN, EVE, artist; b. Chgo., 1946; d. Eric O. and Edith S. BFA, U. Ill., 1967; MFA, U. N.Mex., 1969. One-woman shows include Castelli Gallery, N.Y.C., 1976, 78, 80, 82, 84-86, Tex. Gallery, Houston, 1976, 78, 80, 82, 85, Galerie Farideh Cadot, Paris, 1978, 80, 83, François Lambert Gallery, Milan,Italy, 1980, 87, Mpls. Inst. Arts, 1980, La Noveau Musèe, Lyon, France, 1980, Musèe de Toulon (France), 1983, Centre Georges Pompidou, Paris, 1984, Circus Gallery, L.A., 1989, Jones Troyer Fitzpatrick, Washington, 1989, Zabriskie Gallery, N.Y., 1990, Gloria Luria Gallery, Miami, 1990, Grand Central Terminal, N.Y.C., 1991, Charles Cowles Gallery, 1992, Sidney Janis Gallery, N.Y.C., 1996, La Geode Mus., Paris, 1996; author: America's Cottage Gardens, 1990, Where Birds Live, 1992; photographs subject of book Real Time, 1976. Grantee Nat. Endowment Arts, 1971, 78, Polaroid Corp., 1978; Cartier fellowship, France, 1989. Address: 684 Avenue Of The Americas New York NY 10010-5110

SONNEMANN, HARRY, electrical engineer, consultant; b. Munich, Germany, Sept. 3, 1924; came to U.S., 1938, naturalized, 1944; s. Leopold and Emmy (Markus) S.; m. Shirley E. Battles, Nov. 25, 1949; children: Carol Jean, Joyce Elaine, Patricia Ann. B.S., Poly. Inst. Bklyn., 1954. Research electroence-phalography, 1944-47; asst. to dir. electronics dept. AEC contract, Columbia U., 1947-50; supr. electronics shop Columbia Hudson Labs., 1951-53, head electronics dept., 1954-59; asst. dir. Project Artemis, 1959-64, Project Artemis (Hudson labs.), 1961-64; asst. dir. field engring. Advanced Research Projects Agy., Nuclear Test Detection Office, 1964-67; acting dep. dir. Nuclear Test Detection Office, 1967-68; spl. asst. in electronics to asst. sec. navy for research and devel. Navy Dept., 1968-76, spl. asst. to asst. sec. navy for research and devel., 1976-77; asst. to chief engr. NASA, 1977-78, dep. chief engr., 1978-84, asst. chief engr., 1984-86, cons., 1986—; pres. SBC Assocs. Inc., McLean, Va., 1988—; chmn. Dept. Def. Tactical Satellite Exec. Steering Group, 1968-69, chmn. Dept. Def. nav. satellite exec. steering group, 1969-70, 72-73. Treas. Art League. No. Va., 1967-68; pres. Rotonda Condominium Unit Owners Assn., 1982-84. Clubs: Washington Figure Skating (dir. 1968-73, treas. 1969-72), Ice of Washington (pres. 1974-76). Home and Office: 8360 Greensboro Dr Apt 907 Mc Lean VA 22102-3514

SONNENBERG, BEN, playwright, poet, editor; b. N.Y.C., Dec. 30, 1936; s. Benjamin and Hilda (Caplan) S.; m. Dorothy Gallagher, Mar. 10, 1981; children by previous marriages: Susanna, Emma, Saidee. Literary advisor Oxford (Eng.) Playhouse, 1963-65; lit. mgr. Repertory Theatre of Lincoln Ctr., N.Y.C., 1971-72; lectr. drama ctr. Juilliard Sch., N.Y.C., 1977-78; editor Grand Street, N.Y.C., 1981-90; pub. Grand Street Books, N.Y.C., 1990—. Author: Poems of Anna Comnena and More Poems, 1990, Lost Property, Memoirs and Confessions of a Bad Boy, 1991; editor: Grand Street Reader, 1986, Performance and Reality: Essays from Grand Street, The Courtship of Rita Hayworth, Mole Wedding; contbr. articles to The Nation, London mag., Yale Rev., Raritan, Harper's/Queen (Eng.). Fellow Royal Soc. of Lit.; mem. PEN. Office: Grand Street Pubs Inc 50 Riverside Dr New York NY 10024-6555

SONNENBERG, HARDY, data processing company research and development executive, engineer; b. Schoenese, Fed. Republic Germany, Apr. 12, 1939; s. Gustav and Wanda (Neumann) S.; m. Doris Linda Adam, June 20, 1964; children: Kevin, Denise. BS, U. Alta., 1962; MS, Stanford U., 1964, PhD, 1967. Registered profl. engr., Ont. Advanced devel. engr. GTE Sylvania, Mountain View, Calif., 1966-68, engring. specialist, 1968-70, sect. mgr., 1970-73; dir. rsch. Optical Diodes Inc., Palo Alto, Calif., 1973-74; mem. rsch. staff Xerox Rsch. Centre Can., Mississauga, Ont., 1975-78, area mgr., 1978-80, lab. mgr., 1980-86, mgr. rsch. ops., 1986-87, mgr. tech. and engring. systems, 1987-94, v.p. rsch. and tech., 1994—; chmn. indsl. adv. coun. McMaster U., Hamilton, Ont., 1990-93, active, 1987-94. Contbr. articles to profl. jours. Patentee in field. Chmn. bd. dirs. local ch., Hamilton, Ont., 1983-85, 89-93; pres. Sheridan Park Assn., Mississauga, 1988-89; chmn. Conf. Bd. Can. Rsch. Mgrs. Forum, 1991-93. Recipient cert. of recognition for invention NASA, 1973, 74, Achievement award Xerox Corp., 1981, Charles E. Ives Engring. award, 1983. Mem. IEEE, Am. Phys. Soc., Assn. Profl. Engrs. Ont., Soc. for Imaging Sci. and Tech., Soc. Photographic Scientists and Engrs., Sigma Xi. Avocations: outdoor activities, singing, church participation. Home: 900 Hwy 97 Box 126, Freelton, ON Canada L0R 1K0 Office: Xerox Graphic Systems, 2660 Speakman Dr, Mississauga, ON Canada L5K 2L1

SONNENFELD, BARRY, cinematographer, film director. Cinematographer: (films) Blood Simple, 1984, Compromising Positions, 1985, Three O'Clock High, 1987, Raising Arizona, 1987, Throw Momma from the Train, 1987, Big, 1988, When Harry Met Sally..., 1989, Miller's Crossing, 1990, Misery, 1990, (TV movies) Out of Step, 1984 (Emmy award best cinematography 1984); dir.: (films) The Addams Family, 1991, Addams Family Values, 1993; dir., co-prodr.: For Love or Money, 1993. Office: Gersh Agency 232 North Canon Dr Beverly Hills CA 90210 also: United Talent Agency 9560 Wilshire Blvd Beverly Hills CA 90212

SONNENFELD, MARION, linguist, educator; b. Berlin, Feb. 13, 1928; d. Kurt and Sibylla (Lemke) S. BA with high honors, Swarthmore Coll., 1950; MA, Yale U., 1951, PhD, 1956. Instr., asst. prof. Smith Coll., Northampton, Mass., 1954-62; assoc. prof. Wells Coll., Aurora, N.Y., 1962-67, German chmn., dir. German sch., 1965-67; assoc. prof., prof. SUNY Coll., Fredonia, 1967-77, SUNY disting. teaching prof., 1977-93, emerita, 1993, acting dean arts and humanities, 1980-81; mem. com. on learning assessment Fund for the Improvement of Post Secondary Edn., 1988-90, nat. screening com. for Fulbright grants, 1989-91. English translator of German books and plays. Active Literacy Vols. Am., 1994—. Yale U. Jr. Sterling fellow, 1951-53, NEH postdoctoral fellow Ind. U., 1977; SUNY faculty exch. scholar, 1984—. Mem. MLA, AAUP. Office: SUNY Dept Fgn Langs Lit Fredonia NY 14063

SONNENFELDT, HELMUT, former government official, educator, consultant, author; b. Berlin, Germany, Sept. 13, 1926; came to U.S., 1944, naturalized, 1945; s. Walter H. and Gertrud (Liebenthal) S.; m. Marjorie Hecht, Oct. 4, 1953; children—Babette Sonnenfeldt Lubben, Walter H., Stewart H. A.B., Johns Hopkins, 1950, M.A., 1951. With Dept. State, Washington, 1952-77; formerly dir. Office Rsch. and Analysis for USSR and Eastern Europe, 1965-69; lectr. Sch. Advanced Internat. Studies, Johns Hopkins U., 1958-69, vis. scholar, 1977-78; guest scholar Brookings Instn., Washington, 1978—; sr. mem. Nat. Security Coun., 1969-74; counselor Dept. State, 1974-77. Former gov. UN Assn. of U.S.; dir. Atlantic Coun. of U.S., World Affairs Coun. Washington; trustee Johns Hopkins U. With AUS, 1945-46. Mem. Inst. Strategic Studies (London) (mem. exec. com.), Coun. on Fgn. Rels. N.Y., Pi Delta Epsilon. Home: 4105 Thornapple St Chevy Chase MD 20815-5129 Office: Brookings Instn 1775 Massachusetts Ave NW Washington DC 20036-2188

SONNENFELDT, RICHARD WOLFGANG, management consultant; b. Berlin, July 3, 1923; s. Walter H. and Gertrude (Liebenthal) S.; m. Shirley C. Aronoff, Dec. 23, 1949; m. Barbara A. Hausman, Mar. 8, 1981; children: Ann Elizabeth, Lawrence Alan, Michael William. BSEE, Johns Hopkins U., 1949; postgrad., U. Pa., 1953-56. Mgr. engring. and prodn. RCA, 1949-62; gen. mgr. digital systems div. Foxboro Co., 1962-65; chief exec. officer, pres., dir. Digitronics Corp., 1965-70; v.p. RCA Corp., 1970-79; chmn. bd. dirs., CEO Electronic Indsl. Engring. Corp., 1972-75; exec. v.p. ops. NBC, N.Y.C., 1979-82; dean Sch. Mgmt. Poly Inst. N.Y., Bklyn., 1982-84, prof. mgmt., 1982—; chmn. bd. dirs., CEO NAPP Systems, Inc., 1987-90; lectr. Harvard U. Bus. Sch., Sloan Sch., MIT; cons. in field; bd. dirs. Tetktronix, Inc., Foxboro Co., Lee Enterprises, Decision Industries Corp., Compuflight Corp., Biospherics Inc., Deerpark Baking Co., Tridex Corp., Internat. Harvest Group, Comm. Satellite Network Corp., Medlife Software Inc., Solar Outdoor Lighting Inc. Contbr. articles to profl. jours.; patentee in field. Fellow IEEE; mem. Am. Coun. Germany, Coun. Fgn. Rels., Tau Beta Pi, Omicron Delta Kappa. Home and Office: 4 Secor Dr Port Washington NY 11050-3418

SONNENSCHEIN, ADAM, lawyer; b. N.Y.C., Oct. 15, 1938; s. Harry D. and Sybil (Reinus) S.; m. Phyllis Cokin, Oct. 25, 1968; children: Andrew, Michael. BA, Amherst Coll., 1960; LLB, Columbia U., 1965. Bar: N.Y. 1965, Mass. 1970. Assoc. Berlack, Israels & Liberman, N.Y.C., 1965-70; ptnr. Sprague Assocs., Boston, 1970-72, Walter & Sonnenschein, Boston, 1972-78, Hausserman, Davison & Shattuck, Boston, 1978-83, Foley, Hoag & Eliot, Boston, 1983—. Mem. ABA, Mass. Bar Assn., Boston Bar Assn., Assn. of Bar of City of N.Y. Office: Foley Hoag & Eliot 1 Post Office Sq Boston MA 02109-2103

SONNENSCHEIN, HUGO FREUND, academic administrator, economics educator; b. N.Y.C., Nov. 14, 1940; s. Leo William and Lillian Silver S.; m. Elizabeth Gunn, Aug. 26, 1962; children: Leah, Amy, Rachel. AB, U. Rochester, 1961; MS, Purdue U., 1963, PhD, 1964; PhD (hon.), Tel Aviv U., 1993; D (honoris causa), U. Autonoma Barcelona, Spain, 1994; hon. degree, Purdue U., 1996. Mem. faculty dept. econs. U. Minn., 1964-70, prof., 1968-70; prof. econs. U. Mass., Amherst, 1970-73, Northwestern U., 1973-76; prof. econs. Princeton U., 1976-87, Class of 1926 prof., 1987-88; dean and Thomas S. Gates prof. Sch. Arts and Scis. Sch. Arts & Scis., U. Pa., Phila., 1988-91; provost Princeton (N.J.) U., 1991-93; pres., prof. dept. econs. and Coll., U. Chgo., 1993—; vis. prof. U. Andes, Colombia, 1965, Tel-Aviv U., 1972, Hebrew U., 1973, U. Paris, 1978, U. Aix-en-Provence, France, 1978, Stanford U., 1984-85. Editor: Econometrica, 1977-84; asso. editor: Jour. Econ. Theory, 1972-75; bd. editors: Jour. Math. Econs, 1974—, SIAM Jour, 1976-80; Contbr. articles to profl. jours. Trustee U. Rochester, 1992, U. Chgo., 1993—. Social Sci. Research Council fellow, 1967-68; NSF fellow, 1970—; Ford Found. fellow, 1970-71; Guggenheim Found. fellow, 1976-77. Fellow Am. Acad. Arts and Scis., Econometric Soc. (pres. 1988-89); mem. NAS.

SONNENSCHEIN, RALPH ROBERT, physiologist; b. Chgo., Aug. 14, 1923; s. Robert and Flora (Kieferstein) S.; m. Patricia W. Niddrie, June 21, 1952; children—David, Lisa, Ann. Student, Swarthmore Coll., 1940-42, U. Chgo., 1942-43; B.S., Northwestern U., 1943, B.M., 1946, M.S., 1946, M.D., 1947; Ph.D., U. Ill., 1950. Research asst. in physiology Northwestern U. Med. Sch., 1944-46; intern Michael Reese Hosp., Chgo., 1946-47; successively research fellow clin. sci., research asst. psychiatry, research asso. psychiatry U. Ill. Med. Sch., Chgo., 1947-51; mem. faculty U. Calif. Med. Sch., Los Angeles, 1951-88, prof. physiology, 1962-88, prof. emeritus, 1988—; liaison scientist Office Naval Research, London, 1971-72. Author papers on pain, innervation of skin, peripheral circulation. Served with AUS,

1943-46. Spl. research fellow USPHS, 1957-58; fellow Swedish Med. Research Council, 1964-65; grantee USAF; grantee Office Naval Research; grantee NIH; grantee NSF. Mem. Am. Physiol. Soc., Microcirculatory Soc., Soc. Exptl. Biology and Medicine, AAAS, Hungarian Physiol. Soc. (hon.). Home: 18212 Kingsport Dr Malibu CA 90265-5636 Office: U Calif Sch Medicine Dept Physiology Los Angeles CA 90095-1751

SONNINO, CARLO BENVENUTO, electrical manufacturing company executive; b. Torino, Italy, May 12, 1904; came to U.S., 1952, naturalized, 1959; s. Moise and Amelia S.; m. Mathilde Girodat, Jan. 21, 1949; children—Patricia, Frederic, Bruno. Ph.D., U. Milano, Italy, 1927, LL.B., 1928. Dir. research Italian Aluminum Co., Milano, 1928-34; pres. Laesa Cons. Firm, Milano, 1934-43; tech. adviser Boxal, Fribourg, Switzerland, 1944-52, Thompson Brand, Rouen, France, 1972-76; materials engring. mgr. Emerson Electric Co., St. Louis, 1956-72; staff scientist Emerson Electric Co., 1973—; prof. metall. engring. Washington U., St. Louis, 1960-68, U. Mo., Rolla, 1968—; cons. Monsanto Chem. Co., Wagner Co., other maj. firms, U.S., Europe. Decorated knight comdr. Italian Republic. Fellow Am. Soc. Metals, ASTM (hon.), Alpha Sigma Mu. Patentee process for synthetic cryolite; patentee in field of metallurgy, corrosion; mfr. 1st aluminum cans in world, 1940. Home: 7206 Kingsbury Blvd Saint Louis MO 63130-4140 Office: Emerson E and S Div Emerson Electric Co 8100 W Florissant Ave Saint Louis MO 63136-1417 *I have always been guided by the highest ethical standards in professional, business, and civic life, even in the most difficult moments, and by strong dislike for hypocrisy and greed.*

SONNTAG, BERNARD H., agrologist, research executive; b. Goodsoil, Sask., Can., June 27, 1940; s. Henry R. and Annie (Heesing) S.; m. Mary L. Ortman, Aug. 10, 1963; children: Calvin, Galen, Courtney Anne. BSA, Sask. U., Saskatoon, 1962, MSc, 1965; PhD, Purdue U., 1971. Economist Agriculture Can., Saskatoon, 1962-66; cons. D.W. Carr & Assoc., Ottawa, Ont., Can., 1966-68; economist Agriculture Can., Lethbridge, Alta., 1968-79, Saskatoon, 1979-80; dir. rsch. sta. Agriculture Can., Brandon, Man., 1980-86, Swiftcurrent, Sask., 1986-89, Lethbridge, 1989-95; dir. gen. Prairie Farm Rehab. Adminstrn., Regina, Sask., Can., 1996—; pres. Man. Inst. Agrologists, Brandon, 1984. Recipient Leadership award Bell Can., 1993. Mem. Rotary. Roman Catholic. Home: 3123 Winchester Rd, Regina, SK Canada S4V 2T4 Office: Agriculture Can PFRA, 1800 Hamilton St, Regina, SK Canada S4P 4L2

SONS, RAYMOND WILLIAM, journalist; b. Harvey, Ill., Aug. 25, 1926; s. William Henry and Gladys Lydia (Steinko) S.; m. Bettina Dieckmann; children: David, Pamela Sons Clarke, Ronald. B.A., U. Mich., 1950. Reporter, mng. editor Murphysboro (Ill.) Daily Ind. edit. So. Illinoisan newspaper, 1950-52; assoc. news editor Middletown (Ohio) Jour., 1952-53; reporter, asst. city editor, sportswriter, sports editor Chgo. Daily News, 1953-78; sports editor, columnist Chgo. Sun-Times, 1978-92. Served with USAAF, 1945-46. Recipient Best Sports Story in Ill. award U.P.I., 1970, Marshall Field award for outstanding editorial contbn. to Chgo. Daily News, 1972; Best Sports Column award AP Sports Editor, 1979, Best Sports Column award Ill. AP, 1987, Chgo. Journalism Hall of Fame, 1996. Roman Catholic. Home: 4100 Torrington Ct Fort Collins CO 80525-3419

SONSINI, LARRY W., lawyer; b. Rome, N.Y., Feb. 5, 1941. AB, U. Calif., Berkeley, 1963; LLB, U. Calif., 1966. Bar: Calif. 1966. Ptnr. Wilson, Sonsini, Goodrich & Rosati, Palo Alto; prof. securities regulation Boalt Hall Sch. law U. Calif., Berkeley, 1984—; mem. exec. com. Securities Re. Mem. ABA (com. on fed. regulation securities, subcom. on registration statements), Am. Law Inst. Office: Wilson Sonsini Goodrich & Rosati 650 Page Mill Rd Palo Alto CA 94304-1001*

SONSKY, STEVE, newspaper editor. Features executive editor Miami Herald, Fla. Office: The Miami Herald Pub Co One Herald Plz Miami FL 33132-1693

SONTAG, FREDERICK EARL, philosophy educator; b. Long Beach, Calif., Oct. 2, 1924; s. M. Burnett and Cornelia (Nicholson) S.; m. Carol Furth, June 10, 1950; children: Grant Furth, Anne Burnett Karch. BA with great distinction, Stanford U., 1949; MA, Yale U., 1951, PhD, 1952; LLD (hon.), Coll. Idaho, 1971. Instr. Yale U., 1951-52; asst. prof. philosophy Pomona Coll., Claremont, Calif., 1952-55, assoc. prof., 1955-60, prof., 1970—, Robert C. Denison prof. philosophy, 1972—, chmn. dept. philosophy, 1960-67, 76-77, 80-84; chmn. coordinating com. in philosophy Claremont Grad. Sch. and Univ. Ctr., 1962-65; vis. prof. Union Theol. Sem., N.Y.C., 1959-60, Collegio di Sant' Anselmo, Rome, 1966-67, U. Copenhagen, fall 1972; theologian-in-residence Am. Ch. in Paris, fall 1973; Fulbright regional vis. prof., India, East Asia, Pacific areas, 1977-78; mem. nat. adv. council Kent Fellowship Program of Danforth Found., 1963-66. Author numerous books, the most recent being: Love Beyond Pain: Mysticism Within Christianity, 1977; Sun Myung Moon and the Unification Church, 1977, also German, Japanese and Korean transl.; (with John K. Roth) God and America's Future, 1977; What Can God Do?, 1979; A Kierkegaard Handbook, 1979; The Elements of Philosophy, 1984, (with John K. Roth) The Questions of Philosophy, 1988, Emotion, 1989, The Return of the Gods, 1989, Willgenstein and the Mystical, 1995, Uncertain Truth, 1995, The Descent of Women, 1995, The Acts of the Trinity. Pres. bd. dirs. Claremont Family Svc., 1960-64; trustee The Coro Found., Los Angeles and San Francisco, 1967-71; bd. dirs., chmn. ways and means com. Pilgrim Place, Claremont, 1970-77. Served with AUS, 1943-46. Vis. scholar Ctr. for Study Japanese Religions, Kyoto, Japan, spring 1974; vis. fellow East-West Ctr., Honolulu, summer 1974. Wig Disting. Prof. award, 1970, 76; Fulbright regional vis. prof. India, East Asia, Pacific Areas, 1977-78. Mem. Am. Philos. Assn., Metaphys. Soc. Am., Soc. on Religion in Higher Edn. (Kent fellow 1950-52), Am. Acad. Religion, Phi Beta Kappa. Congregationalist. Office: Pomona Coll 551 N College Ave Claremont CA 91711-6355

SONTAG, FREDERICK H., public affairs and research consultant; b. Breslau, Germany, Apr. 29, 1924; came to U.S., 1937, naturalized, 1943; s. Hugo and Lotte (Lab) S.; m. Edith Virginia Sweeney, Feb. 8, 1958. Grad., Phillips Acad., 1942; A.B., Colby Coll., 1946; grad. student, Columbia, 1947-48. Asso. Earl Newsom & Co. (pub. relations counsel), N.Y.C., 1947-48; asst. dir. Citizens Found., Syracuse, N.Y., 1948-50; pub. relations and advt. cons. Merchants Nat. Bank, Syracuse, 1948-51; central N.Y. corr. Business Week, other McGraw-Hill publs., 1950-51; dir. pub. relations Bus. Week mag., 1951-55; manuscript cons. McGraw-Hill Book Co., 1951-60; spl. cons. to U.S. Sec. Labor, 1954-61, congressman Thomas B. Curtis, 1957-69, Civic Service, Inc., St. Louis and Washington, 1957-83; spl. cons. to 1960 Winter Olympics, Sec. HEW, 1969, 72, U.S. Internat. Trade Commn. chmn., 1975-77; assoc. Anna M. Rosenberg Assos., 1957-60; spl. cons. Monsanto Co., 1962-77; spl. cons. to Edwin J. Putzell, Coburn, Croft & Putzell, St. Louis and Naples, Fla., 1977-83, 1st Caribbean Mainland Capital Co., Inc., N.Y.C., San Juan, P.R., 1962; pub. affairs cons. Office of Sec. HUD, 1981-83, spl. asst. to regional adminstr., 1983-85, regional program liaison officer, 1985-90; spl. cons. bishop Episcopal Diocese of Springfield, Ill., 1947-72; program and planning assoc. to dir. broadcasting Nat. Council Episcopal Ch., 1956-61; exec. dir. com. increased minority staffing U.S. Ho. of Reps., Washington, 1961-69; co-dir. Study of Am. Polit. Parties, Cambridge, Mass., also South Orange, N.J., 1969-73, dir., 1973—; vis. lectr. Colby Coll., Waterville, Maine, 1975; lectr., discussion leader John F. Kennedy Sch. Govt., Inst. Politics, Harvard, Brookings Inst., Washington, Woodrow Wilson Internat. Center Scholars, Washington, Am. Assembly, Arden House, Columbia.; Analyst-commentator Maine Pub. Broadcasting Network, 1973-75, Suburban Cablevision TV3, East Orange, N.J., 1977-79; spl. cons. Pres.'s Com. on Govt. Employment Policy, 1955-60; bd. advisers Husson Coll., Bangor, Maine, 1965-79, trustee, 1979-89; mem. Com. on Party Renewal, 1982—; cons. Bd. Christian Social Concerns, United Meth. Ch., 1965-71; legis. cons. to N.J. State Senator James H. Wallwork, 1968-79, N.J. Assemblyman C. L. Hardwick, 1979-83, N.J. Assemblyman Harry McEnroe, 1983; free-holder-at-large Lincoln Turner, 1979-82, Senator Carmen Orechio, 1984. Co-author: Parties: The Real Opportunity for Effective Citizen Politics, 1972, softcover, 1973; Editorial adv. bd.: Electoral Studies Yearbook; Contbr.: Op-ed page Los Angeles Times, N.Y. Times; nat. corr.: Scroll; contbg. writer, reviewer: Worrall Newspapers, No. N.J. Trustee Pres. James Monroe Found., Fredericksburg, Va., 1992—. Recipient certificates achievement Am. Pub. Relations Assn., 1952, 54, Silver Anvil award, 1953; Spl. Achievement award U.S. Internat. Trade Commn., 1976; HUD award for superior service on fair housing, 1984; Studer award Montclair Coll., 1984; Outstanding Performance awards HUD 1985-88; special recognition award Martin Luther King, Jr. fed. holiday commn., 1989; named Alumnus of Yr., Harvey Sch., Katohah, N.Y., 1983. Mem. Pub. Relations Soc. Am., Am. Polit. Sci. Assn., Am. Assn. Polit Cons. (charter), N.J. Conf. Promotion Better Govt., Phi Delta Theta, Phi Gamma Mu. Anglo-Catholic. Club: Overseas Press (N.Y.C.). Home: Ste 45 764 Scotland Rd Apt 45 South Orange NJ 07079-3023 also: General Delivery Seal Harbor ME 04675-0207

SONTAG, JAMES MITCHELL, cancer researcher; b. Denver, Dec. 8, 1939; s. Samuel Henry and Rose Hazel (Silverman) S.; m. Elizabeth Crockett Tunis; children: Ariella, Eythan. BS, Lamar State Coll. Tech., Beaumont, Tex.; MS, U. Ill., 1967; PhD, Weizmann Inst. Sci., Rehovot, Israel, 1971; MPH, Harvard U., 1982. Damon Runyon Meml. Fund Cancer Research postdoctoral fellow, 1971-72; guest worker Nat. Cancer Inst., NIH, Bethesda, Md., 1972-73; staff fellow Nat. Cancer Inst., NIH, 1973-74, exptl. oncologist, 1973-76, mgr. carcinogen bioassay program, 1973-76, asst. to divsn. dir. cancer cause and prevention, 1976-80; exec. sec. Clearinghouse on Environ. Carcinogens, 1976-80, asst. dir. for interagy. affairs Office of Dir., 1980-82, spl. asst. epidemiology and biostatistics program, 1982-96; chief office of program planning, coord. divsn. cancer epidemiology and genetics Nat. Cancer Inst., 1996—. Author, editor in field. Served with AUS, 1956-59. Beaumont LWV scholar, 1963-65. Mem. Beta Beta Beta. Home: 10500 Rockville Pike Apt 610 Rockville MD 20852-3341 Office: Nat Cancer Inst Exec Plaza North Room 543 Bethesda MD 20892

SONTAG, PETER MICHAEL, travel management company executive; b. Vienna, Austria, Apr. 25, 1943; came to U.S., 1960; s. Otto Schiedeck and Maria Katharina (Schmidt) Cigalle; m. Eleanor Ann Alexander, Jan. 24, 1971; children: Alicia Alexandra, Julie Katherine. Diploma in hotel mgmt., Schule fuer Gastgewerbe, Vienna, 1960; BS magna cum laude, West Liberty State Coll., 1969, LLD, 1991; MBA, Columbia U., 1971. Steel worker Weirton (W.Va.) Steel Co., 1965-69; fin. analyst Citicorp, N.Y.C., 1970-71; ops. staff exec. ITT, N.Y.C., 1971-73; asst. v.p. Sun Life Ins. Co. Am., Balt., 1974-75; exec. v.p. Travel Guide, Inc., Balt., 1975-76; pres. Travelwhirl, Inc., Balt., 1976-78; founder Gelco Travel Services, Mpls., 1978-83; chmn., chief exec. officer Sontag, Annis & Assocs., Washington, 1983-86, US Travel Systems, Inc., Washington, 1986—; prin. CORVES Cons., Inc., Rockville, Md., 1983-86; pub. Travel Bus. Mgr., 1983-86; speaker in field, 1983—. With Austrian Air Force, 1963-64. Named one of Twenty Five Most Influential Execs. in Travel Industry Travel Bus. News, 1985, 87, 88, 89; named Delta Sigma Pi scholar. Mem. Alpha Phi Sigma, Delta Mu Delta (charter), Lakewood Country Club. Republican. Avocations: skiing, sailing, photography, collecting antique cars. Office: Travelogue Inc Ste 280 1201 New York Ave NW Washington DC 20005

SONTAG, SUSAN, writer; b. N.Y.C., Jan. 16, 1933; m. Philip Rieff, 1950 (div. 1958); 1 son, David. BA, U. Chgo., 1951; MA in English, Harvard U., 1954, MA in Philosophy, 1955. Instr. English U. Conn., Storrs, 1953-54; editor Commentary, N.Y.C., 1959; lectr. philosophy City Coll., N.Y.C., 1959-60, Sarah Lawrence Coll., Bronxville, 1959-60; instr. dept. religion Columbia U., N.Y.C., 1960-64; writer in residence Rutgers U., 1964-65. Author: (novels) The Benefactor, 1963, Death Kit, 1967, The Volcano Lover: A Romance, 1992; (plays) Alice in Bed: A Play in Eight Scenes, 1993; (stories) I, etcetera, 1978, The Way We Live Now, 1991; (essays) Against Interpretation, 1966 (Mat. Book award nomination 1966), Styles of Radical Will, 1969, Trip to Hanoi, 1969, On Photography, 1977 (Nat. Book Critics Circle award for criticism 1978), Illness as Metaphor, 1978, Under the Sign of Saturn, 1980, AIDS and Its Metaphors, 1989; (anthology) A Susan Sontag Reader, 1982; screenwriter, dir.: (films) Duet for Cannibals, 1969, Brother Carl, 1971; dir.: (films) Promised Lands, 1974, Unguided Tour, 1983; editor, author of introduction: Antonin Artaud: Selected Writings, 1976, A Roland Barthes Reader, 1982, Danilo Kis's Homo Poeticus: Essays & Interviews, 1995. Guggenheim fellow, 1966, 75, Rockefeller Found. fellow, 1965, 74, MacArthur fellow, 1990-95; recipient George Polk Meml. award, 1966, Ingram Merrill Found. award in lit. in field of Am. Letters, 1976, Creative Arts award Brandeis U., 1976, Malaparte prize, 1992; named Officier de l'Ordre des Arts et des Lettres, France, 1984. Mem. Am. Acad. Arts and Scis. (elected 1993), Am. Acad. Arts and Letters (Arts and Letters award 1976), PEN (pres. Am. Ctr. 1987-89). Address: 470 W 24th St New York NY 10011

SOO, SHAO LEE, mechanical engineer, educator; b. Peking, China, Mar. 1, 1922; came to U.S., 1947, naturalized, 1962; s. Hsi Yi and Yun Chuan (Chin) S.; m. Hermia G. Dan, June 7, 1952; children: Shirley A. Soo Gorman, Lydia M., David D. BS, Nat. Chiaotung U., 1945; MS, Ga. Inst. Tech., 1948; ScD, Harvard U., 1951. Engr. China Nat. Aviation, Calcutta and Shanghai, 1945-47; lectr. Princeton (N.J.) U., 1951-54, asst. prof., 1954-57, assoc. prof. mech. engring., 1957-59; prof. mech. engring. U. Ill., Urbana, 1959-93, prof. emeritus, 1993—; cons. NASA, NIH, ANL, Dept. Energy, EPA, NATO, Nat. Inst. Standards and Tech.; mem. sci. adv. bd. EPA, 1976-78; adv. energy transp. World Bank, 1979; China, UNDP, 1985, 92, NATO AGARD lectr.; Fulbright-Hays Disting. lectr., 1974—, lectr. Chinese Acad. Sci., 1980; guest lectr. China-Japan Conf. Fluidized Beds, 1985, 88, 91, bd. dirs. S.L. Soo Assocs., Ltd., Urbana; vis. prof. Delft Tech. U., The Netherlands, 1993. Author 7 books on thermodynamics, energy conservation and multiphase flow; mem. editorial bd. Internat. Jour. Multiphase Flow, 1972—, Jour. Pipelines, 1980—, Internat. Jour. Sci. and Engring., 1983, Jour. Engring. Chem. and Metallurgy China, 1990—; contbr. numerous articles to profl. jours. Recipient Applied Mechanics Rev. award, 1972, Disting. Lecture award Internat. Pipeline Assn., 1981, Alcoa Found. award, 1985, NASA award for creative devel., 1992. Fellow ASME; mem. ASEE, AIChE (Particle Tech. Forum), Combustion Inst., Fine Particle Soc. (chmn. fluidized beds com.), Chinese Acad. Sci. (hon. prof.), Internat. Freight Pipeline Soc. (Plaque of Appreciation 1995), Sigma Xi, Pi Tau Sigma (hon.), Phi Kappa Phi. Methodist. Patentee in field (6). Home: 2020 Cureton Dr Urbana IL 61801-6226 Office: 1206 W Green St Urbana IL 61801-2906

SOOCHER, STAN, editor, lawyer; b. Bangor, Maine, Jan. 10, 1951. BA in English, U. Fla., 1973, MA in English, 1974; JD, N.Y. Law Sch., 1983. Bar. N.Y. 1984. Dir. Ind. Prodn. Workshop, Miami, 1974-76; freelance entertainment journalist Musician Mag., Rolling Stone, N.Y.C., 1976—; staff writer Nat. Law Jour., N.Y.C., 1981—; founding editor Entertainment Law & Finance, N.Y.C., 1985—. Recipient Deems Taylor Journalism award ASCAP, 1986. Avocation: song writing.

SOONG, TSU-TEH, engineering science educator; b. Honan, China, Feb. 10, 1934; s. Tung and Yu-Hsieh (Lee) S.; m. Dorothy Yen-Ling Tsai, June 5, 1959; children—Karen, Stephen, Susan. B.S., U. Dayton, 1955; postgrad., U. Ill., 1955-56; M.S., Purdue U., 1958, Ph.D., 1962. Instr. engring. sci. Purdue U., 1958-62; sr. research engr. Jet Propulsion Lab., Pasadena, Calif., 1962-63; asst. prof. engring. sci. State U. N.Y. at Buffalo, 1963-66, asso. prof., 1966-68, prof., 1968-89; Samuel P. Capen prof., 1989—; part-time lectr. engring. U. Calif. at Los Angeles, 1962-63; part-time research mathematician Cornell Aero. Lab., Buffalo, 1964-67, prin. research mathematician, 1967-70. NSF Sci. Faculty fellow Tech. U. Delft, Netherlands, 1966-67; Humboldt Sr. Scientist, U. Hanover, Fed. Republic of Germany, 1987-88. Mem. ASCE, NSPE, Earthquake Engring. Rsch. Inst., Sigma Xi, Tau Beta Pi. Research in stochastic processes and structural control in engring. Home: 249 Wellingwood Dr East Amherst NY 14051-1750

SOPER, D. E., physical science research administrator; b. Milw., Mar. 21, 1943; married, 1971; 2 children. AB, Amherst Coll., 1965; PhD in Physics, Stanford U., 1971. From instr. to asst. prof. physics Princeton (N.J.) U., 1971-77; from asst. prof. to assoc. prof. physics U. Oreg., Eugene, 1977-82, prof. physics, dir. inst. theoretical sci., 1982—. Mem. Am Physics Soc. Office: Univ Oregon Inst Theoretical Sci Eugene OR 97403*

SOPER, JAMES HERBERT, botanist, curator; b. Hamilton, Ont., Can., Apr. 9, 1916; s. Herbert Armitage and Anna Eliza Gertrude (Cooper) S.; m. Jean Elizabeth Morgan, Aug. 17, 1946; children: Nancy Elizabeth, Mary Florence, Daphne Evans, Ian Morgan. B.A., McMaster U., 1938, M.A., 1939; Ph.D. (Harris fellow, Austin fellow), Harvard U., 1943. Mem. faculty U. Toronto, 1946-67, curator, 1946-67, prof. botany, 1966-67; chief botanist Can. Mus. Nature, Ottawa, Ont., 1967-81, curator emeritus, 1981—, rsch. assoc., 1993-95. Author: Mt. Revelstoke National Park Wildflowers, 1976, Shrubs of Ontario, 1982; contbr. articles to profl. jours. Served with RCAF, 1943-45. Recipient Royal Jubilee medal, 1978. Mem. Royal Canadian Inst. (life) (pres. 1962-63), Canadian Bot. Assn. (pres. 1982-83), Ottawa Field Naturalists Club, Fedn. Ont. Naturalists (hon.).

SOPER, QUENTIN FRANCIS, chemist; b. Buhl, Minn., Dec. 3, 1919; s. Claude E. and Dessie E. (Zern) S.; m. Genevieve Landreth, Oct. 5, 1946; children—John, Julia, Dan, Jean. B.Chem., U. Minn., 1940; Ph.D. in Organic Chemistry, U. Ill., 1943. Sr. organic chemist Eli Lilly & Co., Indpls., 1944-62; research scientist Eli Lilly & Co., 1962-66; head agrl. organic chemistry research Eli Lilly & Co., Greenfield, Ind., 1965-72, sr. agrl. assoc., 1972-76, research adviser, 1976-84; ret., 1984. Co-inventor Penicillin V; inventor herbicides Treflan, Balan, Paarlan, Surflan, Sonalan, Dipan. Recipient Outstanding Achievement award U. Minn., 1977, John Scott award City of Phila., 1980, Pioneer award Am. Inst. Chemists, 1981. Mem. Am. Chem. Soc., Weed Sci. Soc., N.Y. Acad. Scis. Presbyterian. Home: 2120 W 38th St Indianapolis IN 46208-3202

SOPHER, VICKI ELAINE, museum director; b. Streator, Ill., May 22, 1943; d. Donald Bird and Thelma Elsie (Saxton) Watson; m. Terry Ray Sr., Jan. 20, 1962 (div. Aug. 1982); 1 child, Terry Ray Jr. AA, No. Va. Community Coll., 1973; BA, Am. U., 1976; MS, Bank State Coll. Edn., 1986. Adminstrv. asst. Decatur & Wilson House, Washington, 1977-81; asst. dir. Decatur House/Nat. Trust for Hist. Preservation, Washington, 1981-84, dir., 1984-95; cons. curator Monmouth Mus., Freehold, N.J., 1978-80; founder, pres. Historic House Mus. Metropolitan Wash. Mem. Am. Assn. Museums, Mid-Atlantic Assn. Museums, Am. Assn. for State and Local History, Victorian Soc. Am. (bd. dirs.). Home: 2621 12th St S Arlington VA 22204-4819

SOPINKA, JOHN, Canadian supreme court justice; b. Broderick, Sask., Can., Mar. 19, 1933; s. Metro and Nancy (Kikcio) S.; m. Marie Wilson, 1956; children: Randall, Melanie. BA, U. Toronto, 1955, LLB, 1958; JD (hon.), Ukrainian Free U., Munich. Bar: Nfld. 1973, N.B. 1975, Sask. 1984, Alta. 1987, Y.T. 1987, N.W.T.1987. Assoc. Fasken & Calvin, Barristers and Solicitors, Toronto, 1960-66, ptnr., 1966-77; ptnr., head litigation dept. Stikeman, Elliott, Barristers & Solicitors, Toronto, 1977-88; puisine judge Supreme Ct. of Can., Ottawa, Ont., 1988—; apptd. Queen's Counsel, 1975; lectr. civil procedure Osgoode Hall Law Sch., 1974-82, U. Toronto Law Sch., 1976-84; mem. Commns. of Inquiry into Royal Can. Mounted Police relationship with Dept. Nat. Revenue, into Certain Deaths Hosp. for Sick Children and Related Matters, into Facts of Allegations of Conflict of Interest Concerning Hon. Sinclair M. Stevens; chief counsel Commn. on Aviation Safety; counsel Commn. of Inquiry into Cessation of Ops. Can. Comml. Bank and Northland Bank; mem. Task Force on Equality of Opportuniy in Athletics; former bencher Law Soc. Upper Can., frequent lectr. continuing edn. series. Author: (with Lederman and Bryant) The Law of Evidence in Canada, 1992, The Trial of an Action, 1981, (with Gelowitz) The Conduct of an Appeal, 1993; contbr. articles to profl. jours. Bd. dirs. Hockey Can., 1960—; mem. Bd. Edn. Town of Oakville, 1967-69; co-chmn. Acad. Tribunal U. Toronto, 1975-80; mem. Police Complaints Bd. Met. Toronto; mem. bd. fgn. advisors Ukranian Legal Found. Fellow Am. Coll. Trial Lawyers (jud.); mem. Advocate's Soc. (bd. dirs., chmn. subcom. adminstrn. Ont. cts., lectr.), Can. Bar Assn. (chmn. Ont. subsect. comparative law sect. 1967-68, nat. chmn. of sect. 1970, lectr.), County of York Law Assn., Univ. Club, Blvd. Club, Lawyer's Club. Avocations: squash, skiing, tennis, music. Home: 161 Carleton St, Rockcliffe Pk, Ottawa, ON Canada K1M OG6 Office: Supreme Ct Can, Wellington St, Ottawa, ON Canada K1A 0J1*

SOPKIN, GEORGE, cellist, music educator; b. Chgo., Apr. 3, 1914; s. Isador and Esther (Sopkin) S.; m. Thelma Friedman, July 5, 1936; children—Monica, Paula; m. Carol Borchard Durham, Aug. 30, 1956; children—Edwin, Anthony. Student with, Daniel Saidenberg, Am. Conservatory Music, 1930-32; with, Emmanuel Feurermann, Chgo., Mus. Coll., 1932-34; D.Mus. (hon.), Northland Coll., 1977. Assoc. prof. music U. Wis., 1940-42, artist-in-residence, 1963-79, prof., 1967-77, Disting. prof., 1977-85; prof. Carnegie Mellon U., 1985—, formed trio concert tour of Europe, 1985; staff ABC, Chgo., 1946-52; artist-in-residence Northwestern U., 1952-55, U. Wisconsin-Milw., Cleve. Inst.; founder New Eng. Piano Quartette, 1980. Mem., Kansas City (Mo.) Philharmonic Orch., 1933-34, Chgo. Symphony Orch., 1934-40, Pro Arte String Quartet, 1940-42, founder, 1946, since mem., Fine Arts Quartet, Chgo., soloist, Kansas City (Mo.) Philharmonic Orch., Chgo. Symphony Orch., Ill. Symphony Orch., Milw. Chamber Orch., Saidenberg Symphonette, frequent TV appearances; artist of film for, Ency. Brit. films, Nat. Ednl. TV films; recording artist for, Mercury, Decca, Concert-disc, Everest, numerous tours, Europe. Bd. dirs. Contemporary Concerts, Inc., Chgo. Served with USAAF, 1943-45. Mem. Lincoln Acad. Address: Newbury Neck Rd Surry ME 04684

SOPKO, MICHAEL D., mining company executive; b. Montreal, Que., Can., Jan. 22, 1939; s. John and Mary Sopko; m. Mary Raatikainen, Dec. 28, 1979; children: David, Stuart, Andrew. B Metall. Engring., McGill U., Mont., Que., 1960, M Metall. Engring., 1961, PhD, 1964. Jr. engr., mgr. Inco Ltd. Ont. Div., Copper Cliff, Ont., 1964-73; mgr. Iron Ore Recovery Plant, Inco, Copper Cliff, Ont., 1973; ops. mgr. Exmibal (Inco), Guatemala, 1973-78; mgr. copper refinery Inco Ltd.-Ont. Div., Copper Cliff, 1978-79, v.p., 1980-84, pres., 1984-80; v.p. human resources Inco Ltd., Toronto, Ont., 1989-91; pres. Inco Ltd., Toronto, 1991-92, chmn., chief exec. officer, 1992—, also bd. dirs.; bd. dirs. Inco Ltd., The Toronto Dominion Bank; bd. dirs. Conf. Bd. Can., 1994—; mem. Toronto Bd. Trade. Mem. Mining Assn. Can. (bd. dirs. 1991-95, chmn. 1995—), Nickel Devel. Inst. (bd. dirs. 1991-95), Credit Valley Golf and Country Club. Office: Inco Ltd, Ste 1500, 145 King St W, Toronto, ON Canada M5H 4B7

SOPKO, THOMAS CLEMENT, lawyer; b. Warren, Ohio, Mar. 21, 1945; s. Clement and Mary (Sroka) S.; m. Joyce Ann Deffenbaugh, Aug. 5, 1967; children: Amy L., Kathleen A. BS in History, Xavier U., 1967; JD, U. Notre Dame, 1970. Bar: Ind. 1970, U.S. Dist. Ct. (no. dist.) Ind. 1970, U.S. Dist. Ct. (so. dist.) Ind. Assoc. Edward Kalamaros and Assocs., South Bend, Ind., 1970-75; ptnr. Hardig & Sopko, South Bend, 1976-85; pvt. practice South Bend, 1986-91; ptnr. Sopko & Firth, South Bend, 1991—; dep. prosecutor County of St. Joseph, South Bend, 1976-79; town atty. Town of Osceola, Ind., 1975-82; gen. counsel Notre Dame Fed. Credit Union, 1986—, Holy Cross Coll., Notre Dame, 1989—, speaker for continuing legal edn. seminars on civil litigation, trial practice and procedure, family law and mediation matters. Chmn. profl. divsn. United Way St. Joseph County; bd. dirs. St. Joseph County Alcoholism Coun., South Bend; active Jud. Nominating Com., St. Joseph County, 1985-88; chmn. St. Anthony's Parish Coun., South Bend, 1991-93. Scholar U. Notre Dame Law Sch., 1967-70. Fellow Ind. Bar Assn. Found.; mem. St. Joseph County Bar Assn. (pres. 1994-95, bd. govs. 1990—, pres.-elect 1993-94, v.p. 1992-93, chmn. continuing legal edn. 1992-94), Ind. Trial Lawyers Assn. (dist. chmn. 1979-80), Assn. Trial Lawyers Am., ABA. Republican. Roman Catholic. Avocations: downhill skiing, tennis, golf, jogging. Home: 1418 E Washington St South Bend IN 46617-3343 Office: Sopko & Firth 5th Fl Plaza Bldg 210 S Michigan St South Bend IN 46601-2017

SOPPELSA, GEORGE NICHOLAS ANGELO, artist; b. Youngstown, Ohio, July 16, 1939; s. Joseph and Rose (Gaiarsa) S. BFA, Ohio State U., 1961. vis. artist Weir Farm Nat. Hist. Site, Wilton, Conn., 1994-95. One-man shows include Mulvane Art Ctr., Washburn U., Topeka, 1985, John Szoke Gallery, N.Y.C., 1989, Homer Babbidge Libr., U. Conn., Storrs, 1990, Inter Art Galerie Reich, Cologne, Germany, 1994, The Gallery, St. Mary's Coll. of Md., St. Mary's City, 1991; exhibited in group shows at John Szoke Gallery, N.Y.C., 1989, Art at 100 Pearl, Hartford, Conn., 1989, Butler Inst. Am. Art, Youngstown, Ohio, 1990, Hurlbutt Gallery, Greenwich, Conn., 1993, Mattatuck Mus., Waterbury, Conn., 1995, Aldrich Mus., Ridgefield, Conn., 1995; represented in permanent collections at Mulvane Art Ctr., Topeka, Conn. Collection, Hartford. Fellow Nat. Endowment for Arts, 1987, Vt. Studio Colony, 1988; grantee Conn. Commn. on Arts, 1991, vis. artist Weir Farm Nat. Hist. Site, Wilton, Conn., 1994-95. Office: Brairton & Tubbs Art Agts 135 Central Ave East Hartford CT 06108-3103

SOPRANOS, ORPHEUS JAVARAS, manufacturing company executive; b. Evanston, Ill., Oct. 4, 1935; s. James Javaras and Marigoula (Papalexatou)

S.; m. Angeline Buches, Dec. 31, 1959; children—Andrew, Katherine. A.B., U. Chgo., 1957, M.B.A., 1957. Mgmt. trainee Ford Motor Co., Chgo., 1958-59; with Amsted Industries, Chgo., 1959—; dir. bus. research Amsted Industries, 1966-70, treas., 1970-80, v.p., 1980—; pres. Amsted Internat., 1991-93, corp. v.p., 1993—. Served with U.S. Army, 1958, 61-62. Mem. Am. Inst. C.P.A.s, Ill. Soc. C.P.A.s. Clubs: Univ. (Chgo.), Skokie Country, Mid-Am. Office: 205 N Michigan Ave Chicago IL 60601-5925

SORA, SEBASTIAN ANTONY, business machines manufacturing executive, educator; b. N.Y.C., June 29, 1943; s. Joseph Louis and Angelina Maria (Maletta) S.; m. Janet Lee Dietz, Apr. 11, 1970 (dec. July 1972); 1 child, Joseph Walter; m. Mary Frances Elizabeth Boscketti, Oct. 12, 1974; children: Joseph Walter, Sebastian Nicholas, Frances Ann, Jenny Concetta. BS, Bklyn. Coll., 1964; MBA, Iona Coll., 1974, PMC, 1976; DPS, Pace U., 1989. Math. modeller Assoc. Univs. Inc., 1964-66; with U.S. Coast and Geodetic Survey, Washington, 1967-70; mgr. programming IBM, Yorktown, N.Y., 1966-67, 70-75, programmer, modeller, 1970-72; mgr. program system and design IBM, Fishkill, N.Y., 1971-77; analyst on market models IBM, Harrison, N.Y., 1977-81; sr. programmer IBM, Boeblingen, Fed. Republic Germany, 1981-82; mgr. rsch. staff 1st Josephson system IBM, Yorktown, 1982-84; program dir. Systems Rsch. Inst. IBM, N.Y.C., 1984-87; mgr. edn. program World Trade Corp. IBM, North Tarrytown, N.Y., 1989-90; mgr. promotional-artificial intelligence systems IBM, White Plains, N.Y., 1990—; assoc. prof. MIS Montclair State Coll., Upper Montclair, N.J., 1992-95; pres. Bus. Edn. Systems Tech., 1992—; assoc. prof. info. sci. Pace U., White Plains, N.Y., 1977—; asst. prof. telecommunications Iona Coll., New Rochelle, N.Y., 1986; asst. prof. mgmt. Manhattan Coll., Bronx, N.Y., 1988; cons. AID, Washington, 1989. Editor Jour. Value Based Mgmt., 1987—, Jour. Cross Cultural Mgmt., Jour. of Am. Mgmt., 1994-95; contbr. articles to profl. jours.; patentee fluxless solder, also others. Mem. IEEE (technol. leadership com. 1986—, info. policy com. 1986-95), Data Processing Mgmt. Assn. Roman Catholic. Home: Christie Ct Somers NY 10589 Office: IBM Mktg & Svcs Hdqrs 1133 Westchester Ave White Plains NY 10604-3505

SORAN, ROBERT L., manufacturing executive; b. 1944. With Beatrice Cos., Inc., 1973-85; pres. Tropicana Products, Inc., 1985-91; pvt. practice cons. Sarasota, Fla., 1991-92; pres. Uniroyal Tech. Corp., Sarasota, 1992—, now CEO. Office: Uniroyal Tech Corp 2 N Tamiami Trl Ste 900 Sarasota FL 34236-5568*

SORBER, CHARLES ARTHUR, academic administrator; b. Kingston, Pa., Sept. 12, 1939; s. Merritt Walter and Marjory (Roachford) S.; m. Linda Ellen Babcock, Feb. 20, 1972; children: Kimberly Ann, Kingsley Charles. BS in Sanitary Engring., Pa. State U., 1961, MS in Sanitary Engring., 1966; PhD, U. Tex., 1971. Sanitary engr. U.S. Army, France and Fed. Republic Germany, 1961-65; chief gen. engring. br. U.S. Army Environ Hygiene Agy., Edgewood Arsenal, Md., 1966-69; comdr. U.S. Army Med. Environ. Research Unit, Edgewood Arsenal, 1971-73; dir. environ. quality div. U.S. Army Med. Bioengring. R&D Lab., Frederick, Md., 1973-75; asst. dean coll. scis. and math. U. Tex., San Antonio, 1976-77, acting dir. div. earth & phys. scis., 1977-80, dir. Ctr. Applied Research & Tech., 1976-80; assoc. dean coll. engring. U. Tex., Austin, 1980-86, L.B. (Preach) Meaders prof., 1985; dean sch. engring. U. Pitts., 1986-93; pres. U. Tex.-Permian Basin, Odessa, 1993—; bd. dirs. Pitts. Applied Rsch. Corp., chmn., 1992-93; bd. dirs. Tex. Commerce Bank-Odessa, Wilkes U. Coun.; cons. various cos. and agys. Author, co-author more than 140 papers, book chpts., reports on land application of wastewater and sludges, water and wastewater reuse, water and wastewater disinfection, and higher edn. Recipient Disting. Alumnus award Wilkes Coll., 1987, Disting. Grad. award Coll. of Engring., U. Tex., Austin, 1994, Outstanding Engring. Alumnus award Pa. State U., 1994; John A. Focht teach fellow U. Tex.-Austin, 1982. Fellow ASCE; mem. NSPE, Am. Acad. Environ. Engrs. (trustee 1994—, diplomate, Gordon Maskew Fair award 1993), Water Environ. Fedn. (com. chmn. 1983-85, 86-89, 93—, bd. control 1988-94, Svc. award 1985, 89, 90, v.p. 1990-91, pres.-elect 1991-92, pres. 1992-93), Am. Soc. Engring. Edn., Am. Water Works Assn., Coun. Pub. Univ. Pres. and Chancellors (exec. com. Tex. 1994-95), Odessa Country Club, Club at Mission Dorado, Petroleum Club (Midland), Horseshoe Bay Resort and Conf. Club. Office: U Tex Permian Basin 4901 E University Blvd Odessa TX 79762-8122

SORBY, DONALD LLOYD, university dean; b. Fremont, Nebr., Aug. 12, 1933; s. Lloyd A. and Orpha M. (Simmons) S.; m. Jacquelyn J. Burchard, Nov. 7, 1959; children: Thomas, Sharon. B.S. in Pharmacy, U. Nebr., 1955; M.S., U. Wash., 1958, Ph.D., 1960. Dir. pharm. services U. Calif., San Francisco, 1970-72; chmn. dept. pharmacy practice Sch. Pharmacy, U. Wash., Seattle, 1972-74; dean Sch. of Pharmacy, U. Mo., Kansas City, 1974-84; dean Sch. of Pharmacy, U. Pacific, Stockton, Calif., 1984-95, dean emeritus, 1995—; bd. dirs. Lougs Drugstores Inc. Contbr. articles in field to profl. jours. Mem. Am. Pharm. Assn. (Linwood F. Tice award 1995), Am. Assn. Colls. of Pharmacy (pres. 1980-81), Calif. Pharm. Assn., Acad. Pharm. Rsch. and Scis., Calif. Soc. Health-sys. Pharmacists, Assn. Pharm. Scis., Sigma Xi, Phi Kappa Phi, Rho Chi. Home: 4362 Yacht Harbor Dr Stockton CA 95204-1126 Office: U Pacific Sch Pharmacy Stockton CA 95211

SORBY, J(OSEPH) RICHARD, artist, educator; b. Duluth, Minn., Dec. 21, 1911; s. Joseph Austin and Lydia A. (Esterly) S.; m. P. Elizabeth Ferguson, Dec. 9, 1950. B.A., U. Northern Colo., 1937, M.A., 1952; post-grad., UCLA, 1953, U. of Americas, 1952, U. Colo., 1954. Instr. art Greeley High Sch., Colo., 1937-41; asst. prof. art U. Nebr., Lincoln, 1941-43; assoc. prof. art U. Denver, 1946-59; prof. design and painting Calif. State U., San Jose, 1959-72, prof. emeritus, 1972—; guest prof. Southern Utah U., Cedar City, June, July 1964; rep. by Spectrum Gallery, Estes Park, Colo.; artist in residence Casa de las Campanas, Rancho Bernardo, Calif., 1988—. Exhibited in numerous nat. competitive exhbns. including Rocky Mountain Nat. Watermedia Exhbn. and various publ. collections. Served with USN, 1943-46, lt. comdr. USNR, ret. Recipient Purchase award Joslyn Art Mus., Omaha, Mid-Am. Annual, William Rockhill Nelson Gallery, Kansas City, Nat. Watercolor Competition, Washington, Denver Art Mus., Mus. N.Mex., Southwestern Artist's Annual; selected for U.S. nat. traveling exhbn. Mem. Fifteen Colo. Artists (pres. 1957-58), Retired officers Assn., Mil. Order World Wars, East Bay Art Assn. (v.p. 1966-68), Group 21 (pres. Los Gatos, Calif. 1970-71). Home and Office: 18655 W Bernardo Dr San Diego CA 92127-3020 Studio (summer): Morningsun Studio 15 N Fork Rd Glen Haven CO 80532-3020

SORCE, DAVID SAMUEL, lawyer; b. Rochester, N.Y., Feb. 20, 1954; s. James Salvatore and Domenica (Gligora) S. BA, St. Bonaventure, Olean, N.Y., 1976; JD, Syracuse U., 1980. Bar: N.Y. 1981, U.S. Dist. Ct. (we dist.) N.Y., 1984, U.S. Bankruptcy Ct. 1984, U.S. Supreme Ct. 1991. Assoc. Harter, Secrest & Emery, Rochester, 1984-92; assoc. gen. counsel Canandaigua Wine Co., 1992—. Cmty. svc. Meml. Art Gallery, Rochester, Rochester Mus. Sci. Ctr., Rochester Philharmonic Orch. Mem. Monroe County Bar Assn. (bus. coun. 1994—). Avocations: reading, racquetball. Office: Canandaigua Wine Co Inc 116 Buffalo St Canandaigua NY 14424

SOREFF, STEPHEN MAYER, artist; b. N.Y.C., Feb. 2, 1931; s. Joseph and Jeanne (Goldring) S.; m. Almeda Helen Soreff; children: Alexander, Zachary. BA, Bklyn. Coll., 1954; AA, Pratt Inst., Bklyn., 1960. Engring. designer Slocum & Fuller, N.Y.C., 1954-58; indsl. designer George Kress Assocs., Newark, 1958-62, Walter Darwin Teague Assocs., N.Y.C., 1962-68; prof. art U. Wash., Seattle, 1968-70, C.W. Post Ctr. L.I. U., Greenvale, N.Y., 1970-95; pvt. practice artist N.Y.C., 1965—. exhibited works include Crystall Art, Mus. Hudson Highlands, 1988, Star Lake, Emporia Coll., 1988, The Infinite Painting, U. Md., 1988, The Artists Tomb, W&J Coll., 198, The Information Shower, 1992, Richard Humphrey Gallery, N.Y.C., 1995, Reading (Pa.) Mus., 1996, Eighth Flr. Gallery, N.Y.C., 1996; works in collections of Mus. of Modern Art, N.Y.C., Whitney Mus., Guild Hall Mus. Recipient award Art Quest, Inc., Los Angeles, 1987, Metro Art, Inc., Scarsdale, N.Y., 1987, N.Y. chpt. Nat. Drawing Assn., 1987; fellow Macdowell, Va. Ctr., Altosde Chavon, Cite des Arts Internat. Home: 79 Mercer St New York NY 10012-4430

SOREL, CLAUDETTE MARGUERITE, pianist; b. Paris; d. Michel M. and Elizabeth S. Grad. with top honors, Juilliard Sch. Music, 1947, post-grad., 1948; student of, Sigismund Stojowski, Sari Biro, Olga Samaroff Stokowski, Mieczyslaw Horszowski, Rudolf Serkin; ensemble with, Felix Salmond; musicology with, Dr. Robert Tangeman; music history with, Marian Bauer; grad., Curtis Inst. Music, 1953; B.S. cum laude in Math., Columbia U., 1954. music faculty, vis. prof. Kans. U., 1961-62; assoc. prof. music Ohio State U., 1962-64; prof. music, head piano dept. SUNY Fredonia, 1964—. Disting. Univ. prof., 1969—, univ. artist, 1969—, faculty exchange scholar, 1976—; mem. internat. jury Van Cliburn Internat. Piano Competition, Tex., 1966, Que. and Ont. Music Festivals, 1967, 75; chmn. music panel Presdl. Scholars in Arts Program, 1979—; juror numerous nat. and internat. music competitions; cons. Ednl. Testing Service, Princeton. Author: Compendium of Piano Technique, 1970, 2d edit., 1987, Japanese edit., 1987, Mind Your Musical Manners - Off and On Stage, 1972, 3d revised edit., 1995, The 24 Magic Keys, 3 vols., 1974, The Three Nocturnes of Rachmaninoff, 1974, 2d edit., 1975, 3d edit. with cassette in compact disc, 1988, Fifteen Smorgasbord Studies for the Piano, 1975, 2d edit., 1995, 17 Little Piano Studies, 1995, Arensky Piano Etudes, 1976; spl. editor: Music Insider; painter of oil portraits; contbr. articles to profl. mags.; compiler: The Modern Music of Today, 1974, Serge Prokofieff - His Life and Works, 1947, The Ornamentations in Mozart's Music, 1984; debut at Town Hall, N.Y.C., 1943; since appeared in leading cities of U.S.; performed with N.Y. Philharm., London Philharm., Zurich, Boston, San Antonio, Milw., NBC, Phila., New Orleans and Cin. symphony orchs., Youth Orch. of Am., 200 others; appeared at Aspen, Berkshire, Chautauqua, other festivals, European concert tours, 1956, 57, 58, to Eng., Sweden, Holland, Germany, Switzerland, France; appeared on various radio, TV programs; made recs. for RCA Victor Rec. Co., Monitor Records, Mus. Heritage; compact disc MacDowell Piano Concerto #2 with N.Y. Philharm. Orch., 1993; 2000 solo appearances, U.S. and Europe. Bd. dirs. Olga Samaroff Found.; Jr. com. aux. bd. N.Y. Philharmonic Symphony Orch., N.Y. State Nat. Fedn. Music Clubs; mem. adv. bd. Univ. Library Soc.; pres. Shelton Apartments, Inc. Fulbright fellow, 1951; Ford Found. Concert grantee, 1962; winner Phila. Orch. Youth Auditions, 1950, to appear with orch. under direction of Eugene Ormandy; U.S. Senatorial Bus. Adv. Com. Fulbright scholar, 1951; recipient Harry Rosenberg Meml., Frank Damrosch prizes, 1947, Nat. Fedn. Music Clubs Young Artist award, 1951; citation svc. to Am. music Nat. Fedn. Music Clubs, 1966, citations Nat. Assn. Composers & Condrs., 1967, Mu Phi Epsilon, 1968, Freedom medal U.S. Senatorial Com., 1994; nominated Kyoto Japan Humanitarian award, 1989, 92; Claudette Sorel Scholarship for Women Ctr. in Music created by NYU. Mem. Nat. Music Coun. (dir. 1973—, chmn. performance com.), Nat. Arts Club, Music Critics Assn., Broadcast Music Incorp., Columbia Univ. Club (N.Y.C.), Nat. Arts Club, Pi Kappa Lambda, Mu Phi Epsilon (dir. Meml. Found., nat. chmn. Sterling Staff Concert Series, citation 1968). Home: 333 W End Ave New York NY 10023-8131 *The most difficult achievement in life is to try to reach one's goals while keeping one's highest idealism and integrity. If these aims can also be maintained in an atmosphere of freedom and respect for quality in all aspects of life, then the individual is most fortunate.*

SOREL, EDWARD, artist; b. N.Y.C., Mar. 26, 1929; s. Morris and Rebecca (Kleinberg) Schwartz; m. Nancy Caldwell, May 29, 1965; children: Jenny, Katherine; children by previous marriage: Madeline, Leo. Diploma, Cooper Union, 1951. Co-founder Pushpin Studio, 1953; free-lance artist, 1956—; syndicated Sorel's News Service, 1969-70, King Features. Author, illustrator: Making the World Safe for Hypocrisy, 1972; exhibited in, Pushpin Studio retrospective at the Louvre, 1970, other European galleries, 1970-71; exhibited one-man show, Graham Galleries, N.Y.C., 1973, 78, Galerie Bartsch & Chariau, Munich, 1986, Retrospective Exhibition Cooper Union, 1987, Susan Conway Galleries, Washington, 1992, Soc. Illustrators Am. Mus. Illustration, N.Y.C., 1993, Davis and Langdale Galleries, N.Y.C., 1994; illustrator: Pablo Paints a Picture, 1961, Gwendolyn the Miracle Hen, 1963 (N.Y. Herald Tribune Book award for illustration 1962), What's Good for a Five-Year-Old, 1969, The Duck in the Gun, 1969, Word People, 1970, Magical Storybook, 1972, Superpen, 1978, The Zillionaire's Daughter, 1990, First Encounters, 1994; contbr. to The Nation, The New Yorker, American Heritage and The Atlantic mags. Recipient awards Soc. Illustrators, Art Dirs. Club N.Y.; Augustus St. Gauden's medal Cooper Union; George Polk award for satiric drawing, 1981; Page One award Newspaper Guild of N.Y. for best editorial cartoon (magazines), 1988, Hamilton King award Soc. Illustrators, 1990.

SORELLE, RUTH DOYLE, medical writer, journalist; b. Port Arthur, Tex., Oct. 9, 1948; d. Richard Thomas and Ruth Elaine (Droddy) D.; m. Paul Charles SoRelle, Apr. 10, 1970; children: Danielle Amanda, Richard Paul. BJ, U. Tex., 1971; MPH, U. Tex., Houston, 1988. Reporter Port Arthur News, summer 1968, 69, Univ. and Info. Svc., Austin, Tex., 1970-71; med. editor U. Tex. MD Anderson Hosp., Houston, 1973-74; editor Resources Devel. Corp., Houston, 1974-76; med. editor Baylor Coll. Medicine, Houston, 1977-78; copy editor Houston Chronicle, Houston, 1978-79; med. writer Houston Chronicle, 1979—; instr. U. Houston, 1986, 87, 89. Leader Presbyn. Youth Fellowship, Houston, 1989. Recipient John P. McGovern award Am. Med. Writers Assn., Community Svc. award Tex. Assoc. Press, 1993, Katie award Dallas Press Club, 1992, 93, Anson Jones award Tex. Med. Assn., 1981, 83, 85, 86, 88, 90, 92, Francis C. Moore award Harris County Med. Assn., 1984-94, Silver Star Tex. award Tex. Hosp. Assn., 1984, 86, 89, 92, Tex. Pub. Health Assn. award, 1981, 89, 90, 91, 94, Houston Area Health Care Coalition's Health Policy Leadership award, 1990, Paul Ellis award Am. Heart Assn., 1988, 95, others. Mem. Am. Med. Writer's Assn. (bd. dirs. southwest chpt. 1994-95), Press Club of Houston (Deadline Coverage award 1984, Investigative Series award 1990, Mag. Feature award 1994). Home: 5814 Warm Springs Rd Houston TX 77035-2428

SOREN, DAVID, archaeology educator, administrator; b. Phila., Oct. 7, 1946; s. Harry Friedman and Erma Elizabeth (Salamon) Soren; m. Noelle Louise Schattyn, Dec. 22, 1967. B.A., Dartmouth Coll., 1968; M.A., Harvard U., 1972, Ph.D., 1973. Cert. Rome Classics Ctr. Curator of coins Fogg Art Mus., Cambridge, Mass., 1972; asst. prof. U. Mo., Columbia, 1972-76, assoc. prof., dept. head, 1976-81; prof. archaeology U. Ariz., Tucson, 1982-83, dept. head, 1984-89; guest curator Am. Mus. Natural History, N.Y.C., 1983-90, lectr., 1993—; creator/dir. Kourion Excavations, Cyprus, 1982-89, Portugal, 1983-84, Am. Excavations at Lugnano, Italy, 1988-93; pot cons., field dir. Tunisia Excavations, Chgo. Oriental Inst./Smithsonian Instn., 1973-78; bbd. dirs. humanities program U. Ariz., 1992-94; dir. excavations Chianciano Terme, Italy, 1995; subject of The Learning Channel TV program: series "Archaeology", 1995. Author: (books) Unreal Reality, 1978, Rise and Fall of Fantasy Film, 1980, Carthage, 1990, French edit., 1994; co-author: Kourion: Search for a Lost Roman City, 1988, Corpus des Mosaiques de Tunisie, 1972, 3rd rev. edit., 1986, Carthage: A Mosaic of Ancient Tunisia, 1987; editor: Excavations at Kourion I, 1987; producer: (film) Carthage: A Mirage of Antiquity, 1987; creator and guest curator: (internat. traveling exhbn.) Carthage: A Mosaic of Ancient Tunisia, 1987-92; editor, founder Roscius, 1993—; creative cons. TV miniseries Lost Civilizations, 1994; contbr. articles to profl. jours. Subject of National Geographic spl. Archeological Detectives, 1985; work subject of feature articles in Newsweek, Conoisseur, National Geographic and others; recipient Cine Golden Eagle, 1980, Angenieux Film award Industrial Photography mag., 1980, Outstanding American Under 40 award C. Johns Hopkins-Britain's Royal Inst. Internat. Affairs, 1985; named Outstanding American Under 40 Esquire mag., 1985, hon. Italian citizen Lugnano, Italy, 1989; grantee NEH, 1979, 87, Fulbright, Lisbon, 1983. Mem. Nat. Geog. Soc. (project dir. 1983-84), Am. Sch. Oriental Rsch. (dept. rep. 1981-85), Archaeol. Inst. Tucson (pres. 1983-86), Luso-Am. Commn. (citation 1983-84), Explorer's Club. Office: U Ariz Dept Classics 371 MLB Tucson AZ 85721

SOREN, TABITHA L., television newscaster, writer; b. San Antonio, Aug. 19, 1967; d. John Thomas and Mary Jane (Quinn) Sornberger. BA cum laude in Journalism, NYU, 1989. Intern Cable News Network, N.Y.C., Sta. WNBC TV, N.Y.C.; desk asst. ABC TV, N.Y.C.; news anchor, statehouse correspondent ABC Sta. WVNY-TV, Vt.; news reporter, anchor MTV News Dept., N.Y.C., 1991—; contbg. corr. NBC News, N.Y.C., 1992—; columnist N.Y. Times Syndication Sales Corp., N.Y.C.; cons. editor Elle, N.Y.C. Contbr. articles to various periodicals. Recipient Peabody Journalism award U. Ga., 1993, Leadership award Nat. League Women Voters, 1993. Office: MTV News 1515 Broadway New York NY 10036

SORENSEN, ALLAN CHRESTEN, service company executive; b. Edson, Alta., Can., Apr. 27, 1938; came to U.S., 1962, naturalized, 1965; s. Henry and Vivien A. (Howie) S.; children: Scott, Jody. B.S. in Pharmacy, Drake U., 1961. Salesman Hoffman LaRoche Pharm. Co., Kitchener, Ont., Can., 1961-62; salesman Personnel Pool of Am., Inc., Chgo., 1962-63; sales mgr. Personnel Pool of Am., Inc., 1963-67, dir., pres., 1967-89, chief exec. officer, 1978-91; chmn. interim svcs. Personnel Pool of Am., Inc. (name changed to Interim Svcs. Inc. 1992), 1993—; dir., vice chmn. Let's Talk Cellular & Wireless, 1994—; dir. The Apple Tree Cos., Inc. Bd. dirs. Broward Workshop. Mem. Nat. Assn. Temp. Svcs. (past pres., bd. dirs.), Exec. Assn. Ft. Lauderdale, Home Health Svcs. and Staffing Assn. (past chmn., bd. dirs.). Republican. Club: Rotary. Home: 1500 S Ocean Dr Fort Lauderdale FL 33316-3242 Office: Interim Svcs Inc 2050 Spectrum Blvd Fort Lauderdale FL 33309-3008

SORENSEN, ANDREW AARON, academic administrator; b. Pitts., July 20, 1938; s. Albert Aaron and Margaret (Lindquist) S.; m. Donna Ingemie, Aug. 4, 1968; children: Aaron Ashley, Benjamin Samuel. BA, U. Ill., 1959; BDiv, Yale U., 1962, MPh, 1970, PhD, 1971; MPH, U. Mich., 1966. Asst. prof. Cornell U., Ithaca, N.Y., 1971-73; asst. prof. U. Rochester, N.Y., 1973-76, assoc. prof., 1976-83; prof., dean U. Mass., Amherst, 1983-86; prof. Johns Hopkins U., Balt., 1986-90; provost, v.p. acad. affairs U. Fla., Gainesville, 1990-96; pres. U. Ala., Tuscaloosa, 1996—; chmn. adminstrv. bd. Whitney Marine Biol. Lab., 1990-96; chmn. editl. bd. Univ. Press Fla., 1990-96. Author 5 books; contbr. over 100 articles to profl. jours. Exec. dir. Johns Hopkins AIDS Inst., Balt., 1987-90. U.S. Dept. Edn. fellow Lincoln U., 1966-67, NSF fellow Harvard U., 1975-76. Democrat. Presbyterian. Office: Office of Pres U Ala 205 Rose Adminstrn Bldg Box 870100 Tuscaloosa AL 25487-0100

SORENSEN, BURTON ERHARD, investment banker; b. Chgo., Oct. 28, 1929; s. Soren Kirsten and Christine (Petersen) S.; m. Linda Graf, Aug. 28, 1954 (div. 1970); children: Debra, Jack, Peter, Janice; m. France Elizabeth Pepinger, Dec. 28, 1972. Student, Northwestern U., 1949; B.A., Wheaton Coll., 1955. Vice pres. Kidder, Peabody & Co., N.Y.C., 1956-71; v.p. Goldman, Sachs & Co., N.Y.C., 1972-76, ptnr., 1977-84; chief exec. officer, chmn. Lord Securities Corp., N.Y.C., 1984—; dir. Provident Companies, Inc., Chattanooga, Tenn., Servicemaster Industries Inc. Served to cpl. USMC, 1951-53, Korea. Mem. N.Y. Soc. Security Analysts, City Midday Club (N.Y.C.), Morris County Golf Club (Covent, N.J.), Baltusrol Golf Club, Grandfather Golf and Country Club (Linville, N.C.), The Sanctuary Golf Club (Sanibel Island, Fla.). Republican. Office: Lord Securities Corp 2 Wall St New York NY 10005-2001

SØRENSEN, ERIK, international company executive; b. Randers, Denmark, July 19, 1944; s. Christen and Erna Sørensen; m. Brigitte Berg; children: Anne Marie, Thomas, Anne Louise, Anne Mette, Anne Sophie. MS in Chemistry, Tech. U. Denmark, 1968; MBA in Internat. Fin., Cph Sch. Econs., 1971. Sr. economist Novo Industri A/S, Bagsvaerd, Denmark, 1970-71, mgr. econs. and planning, 1972-74, v.p. sales and mktg., 1974-80; pres. bioindsl. group Novo Industri A/S, Denmark, 1980-88; pres. Health Care Grp Novo Nordisk A/S, Denmark, 1988-1995; pres., CEO Christian Hansen Group, Denmark, 1995—. Lt. Danish Army, 1968-70. Office: Chr. Hansen Group, Bøge Allé 10, 2970 Hoersholm Denmark

SORENSEN, GILLIAN MARTIN, United Nations official; b. Columbus, Ohio, Mar. 4, 1941; d. John Butlin and Helen (Hickam) Martin; m. Theodore C. Sorensen, June 28, 1969; 1 child, Juliet. BA, Smith Coll., 1963. Commr. N.Y.C. Commn. for UN and Consular Corps, 1978-90; pres. Nat. Conf., 1990-93; undersec gen., spl. advisor for pub. policy UN, N.Y.C., 1993—. Del. Dem. Nat. Conv., 1976, 84, 88. Mem. Coun. on Fgn. Rels., Bus. Coun. for UN (bd. dirs. 1990—), Women's Forum. Avocations: skiing, tennis, jogging. Office: Rm S-3161 Rm S-3194A UN New York NY 10017

SORENSEN, HAROLD W., engineering executive; b. Omaha. BS in Aeronautical Engring., Iowa State U., 1957; MS in Engring., UCLA, 1963, PhD in Engring., 1966. With Gen. Dynamics/Aeronautics, San Diego, 1957-62, GM, AC Electronics Divsn., El Segundo, Calif., 1963-66; prof. engring. U. Calif., San Diego, 1968-69; group v.p., gen. mgr. MITRE Corp., Bedford, Mass., 1969—; co-founder, pres. Orincon Corp., LaJolla, Calif., 1973-81; guest scientist Inst. Guidance and Control, Oberpfaffenhofen, Germany; chief scientist USAF, Washington, 1985, mem. scientific adv. bd., 1981-85, 88—, vice chmn., 1990-93; mem. adv. bd. Defense Intelligence Agy., 1993—. Contbr. tech. papers to profl. publs. Fellow IEEE (past pres. control systems soc., bd. dirs. 1984-86, dir. systems and control divsn. X); mem. AAAS. Avocations: tennis, golf, scuba diving, classic automobiles. Office: Mitre Corp Burlington Rd Bedford MA 01730

SORENSEN, HENRIK VITTRUP, electrical engineering educator; b. Skanderborg, Denmark, Jan. 17, 1959; came to U.S. 1983; s. Evan Anton and Anne Marie (Vittrup) S.; m. Karen Ann Taylor, Mar. 5, 1988; 1 child, Amanda Elisabeth. MS, Aalborg U. Ctr., 1983; PhD, Rice U., 1988. Asst. prof. Dept. Electrical Engring. U. Pa., Phila., 1988-95; dir. Ariel Corp., Cranbury, N.J., 1995—; cons. AT&T Bell Labs., Murray Hill, N.J., 1990-95. Author: Handbook for Digital Signal Processing, 1992, The FRT Bibliography, 1995; contbr. articles to profl. jours. Fellow Rotary; mem. IEEE (editor 1990-94, vice chmn. Phila. sect. 1991-94), Sigma Xi, Eta Kappa Nu. Lutheran. Achievements include development of fast algorithms for the split radix fast Fourier transform and for the fast Hartley transform. Home: 75 Franklin Dr Plainsboro NJ 08536 Office: Ariel Corp 2540 Rt 130 Cranbury NJ 08512

SORENSEN, JACKI FAYE, choreographer, aerobic dance company executive; b. Oakland, Calif., Dec. 10, 1942; d. Roy C. and Juanita F. (Bullon) Mills; m. Neil A. Sorensen, Jan. 3, 1965. BA, U. Calif., 1964. Cert. tchr., Calif. Ptnr., Big Spring Sch. Dance, 1965; tchr. Pasadena Ave. Sch., Sacramento, 1968; founder, pres., choreographer Jacki's Inc., DeLand, Fla., 1990—; cons., lectr. on phys. fitness. Author: Aerobic Dancing, 1979, Jacki Sorensen's Aerobic Lifestyle Book, 1983; choreographer numerous dance exercises for records and videocassettes. Trustee Women's Sports Found. Recipient Diamond Pin award Am. Heart Assn., 1979, Individual Contbn. award Am. Assn. Fitness Dirs. in Bus. and Industry, 1981, Spl. Olympics Contbn. award, 1982, Contbn. to Women's Fitness award Pres.'s Coun. Phys. Fitness and Sports, 1982, Healthy Am. Fitness Leader award U.S. Jaycees, 1984, Lifetime Achievement award Internat. Dance Exercise Assn., 1985, New Horizons award Caldwell (N.J.) Coll., 1985, Legend of Aerobics award City Sports mag., 1985; Pres. Coun. award Calif. Womens' Leadership Conf., 1986, Hall of Fame award Club Industry mag., 1986, IDEA, 1992. Mem. AAHPERD, AFTRA, Am. Coll. Sports Medicine, Nat. Intramural and Recreation Assn. Office: Jacki's Inc PO Box 289 Deland FL 32721-0289

SORENSEN, JOHN FREDERICK, retired minister; b. Cadillac, Mich., Apr. 4, 1923; s. Neil Thomas and Helga S. (Anderson) S.; m. D. Marieta Moore, Mar. 16, 1944; children: Jack, Keith, Robert. BA, Mich. State U., 1957; MDiv, Garrett Theol. Sem., 1962; DD (hon.), Holy Trinity Coll., 1996. Ordained to ministry United Meth. Ch. as deacon, 1960, as elder, 1962. Pastor Mulliken (Mich.) United Meth. Ch., 1951-55, Upton Ave. United Meth. Ch., Battle Creek, Mich., 1955-64, Haven United Meth. Ch., Jackson, Mich., 1964-67, Ithaca (Mich.) United Meth. Ch., 1967-72, 1st United Meth. Ch., Lansing, Mich., 1972-78; assoc. pastor Community United Meth. Ch., Holiday, Fla., 1985-93; mem. various coms. for Conf. Dist., United Meth. Ch., 1962-85; summer exch. pastor to Loughton, Eng., 1975. Contbr. columns to newspapers, 1967-72. Founder Free Health Clinic. With USN, 1942-46. Recipient Spl. Tribute Gov. Mich., 1985, Ionia Hospice award, 1986; named Rural Pastor of Yr. United Meth. Ch., Mich., 1955, Amb., Ionia C. of C., 1983-85; commd. Ky. Col., 1995. Fellow Designate Acad. Parish Clergy (edn. coom. 1982-84, state sec. 1994-96), West Pasco Ministerial Assn. Shriners (past master 1972), Masons, commd. a Ky. Col. (1995). Home: 4427 Pelorus Dr New Port Richey FL 34652-5810

SORENSEN, JOHN NOBLE, mechanical and nuclear engineer; b. Mpls., Jan. 2, 1934; s. Alfred Noble and Helen Viola (Baker) S.; m. Joan Elizabeth Reiche, Sept. 15, 1954; children: Laura Elizabeth, Nancy Helen, Karen Lynn. BSME, U. N.D., 1955; MSME, U. Pitts., 1958. Cert. engr. Sr. engr. Westinghouse Electric, Pitts., 1955-67; v.p., gen. mgr. NUS Corp., Rockville, Md., 1967-86; v.p., dir. Grove Engring., Inc., Rockville, 1986-93; tech. asst. to commr. U.S. NRC, Washington, 1993—. Mem. ASME, NSPE, Am. Nuclear Soc., Sigma Xi. Home: 629 Crocus Dr Rockville MD 20850-2046 Office: US NRC Washington DC 20555

SORENSEN, LEIF BOGE, physician, educator; b. Odense, Denmark, Mar. 25, 1928; came to U.S., 1955, naturalized, 1963; s. Henry V. and Mary (Nielsen) S.; m. Janice D. Nolan; 1 child, Heidi. BS, Odense Katedralskole, 1946; MD, U. Copenhagen, Denmark, 1953, PhD in Biochemistry, 1960. Intern Copenhagen County Hosp., Hellerup, Denmark, 1954; resident Copenhagen Municipal Hosp., 1955, U. Chgo. Hosp., 1957-60; mem. faculty, scientist U. Chgo. and Franklin McLean Meml. Research Inst., 1956—; prof. medicine U. Chgo., 1970—; attending physician dept. medicine, assoc. chmn. dept. Pritzker Sch. Medicine, U. Chgo., 1976—; cons. FDA, 1972—. Mem. editorial bd.: Jour. Lab. and Clin. Medicine, 1964-70, Arthritis and Rheumatism, 1965-72; Contbr. articles to profl. jours. With M.C. Danish Army, 1951. Fulbright scholar, 1955; Ill. Arthritis Found. grantee, 1970-72; NIH Fogarty Internat. Center sr. fellow, 1980. Mem. AAAS, Am. Rheumatism Soc., Am. Soc. Clin. Investigation, Central Soc. Clin. Research, N.Y. Acad. Scis., Danish Med. Assn., Ill. Acad. Gen. Practice., Am. Geriatrics Soc., Gerontologic Soc. Am., Am. Fedn. Aging Research. Home: 1700 E 56th St Apt 2801 Chicago IL 60637-1935

SORENSEN, ROBERT HOLM, diversified technology company executive, retired; b. Racine, Wis., Mar. 14, 1921; s. Viggo Marius and Lydia Marie (Holm) S.; m. Harriet Norma Kruse, Feb. 27, 1944; children: Anitra A., Scott E., Lyle R. B.S.E.E., Northwestern U., 1947; grad. advanced mgmt. program, Harvard U., 1957; DSc (hon.), Grand View Coll., 1991. Sr. engr. Engrng. Research Assocs., Inc., St. Paul, 1947-51; ops. mgr. Sperry Rand Corp. (formerly Remington Rand Inc.), Norwalk, Conn., 1952-59; with Perkin-Elmer Corp., 1959-86; v.p. optical group Perkin-Elmer Corp., Norwalk, 1965-66; sr. v.p. Perkin-Elmer Corp., 1966-73, pres., chief operating officer, 1973-77, chief exec. officer, 1977-84, chmn. bd., 1980-85; retired, 1986. With USN, 1943-46. Recipient Award of Merit, Northwestern U., 1987. Mem. Tau Beta Pi, Eta Kappa Nu. Club: Silver Spring Country (Ridgefield, Conn.).

SORENSEN, SHEILA, state senator; b. Chgo., Sept. 20, 1947; d. Martin Thomas Moloney and Elizabeth (Koehr) Paulus; m. Wayne B. Slaughter, May, 1969 (div. 1976); 1 child, Wayne Benjamin III; m. Dean E. Sorensen, Feb. 14, 1977; (stepchildren) Michael, Debbie, Kevin, Dean C. BS, Loretto Heights Coll., Denver, 1965; postgrad. pediatric nurse practicioner, U. Colo., Denver, 1969-70. Pediatric nurse practicioner Pub. Health Dept., Denver, 1970-71, Boise, Idaho, 1971-72; pediatric nurse practicioner Boise (Idaho) Pediatric Group, 1972-74, Pediatric Assocs., Boise, 1974-77; mem. Idaho State Ho. Reps., 1987-92; mem. Idaho Senate, 1992—, chair senate health and welfare com., 1992-94, chair senate majority caucus, vice chair state affairs com., 1994—. Precinct committeeman Ada County Rep. Ctrl. Com., Boise, 1982-86, dist. vice chair, 1985-88; polit. chair Idaho Med. Assn. Aux., 1984-87, Ada County Med. Assocs., 1986-87; bd. dirs. Family Practice Residency Program, 1992—, Univ./Cmty. Health Sci. Assn., Bishop Kelly Found., 1993—; chair Senate Majority Caucus, 1995, vice chair state affairs com. Recipient AMA Nathan Davis award for Outstanding State Legislator, 1994. Mem. Nat. Conf. State Legislators, Nat. Orgn. Women Legislators (state chair), Am. Legis. Exch. Coun. Roman Catholic.

SORENSEN, THEODORE CHAIKIN, lawyer, former special counsel to President of United States; b. Lincoln, Nebr., May 8, 1928; s. Christian Abraham and Annis (Chaikin) S.; m. Gillian Martin, June 28, 1969; 1 child, Juliet Suzanne; children from previous marriage: Eric Kristen, Stephen Edgar, Philip Jon. B.S. in Law, U. Nebr., 1949, LL.B., 1951, LL.D. (hon.), 1969; LL.D. (hon.), U. Canterbury, 1966, Alfred U., 1969, Temple U., 1969, Fairfield U., 1969. Bar: Nebr. 1951, N.Y. 1966, U.S. Supreme Ct. 1966, D.C. 1971. Atty. Fed. Security Agy., 1951-52; mem. staff joint com. r.r. retirement U.S. Senate, 1952; asst. to Sen. John F. Kennedy, 1953-61; sec. New Eng. Senators' Conf., 1953-59; spl. counsel to pres. U.S., 1961-64; mem. firm Paul, Weiss, Rifkind, Wharton & Garrison, N.Y.C., 1966—; mem. Pres.'s Adv. Com. Trade Negotiations, 1978; chmn. Gov.'s panel on N.Y. State Export Credit Agy., 1982. Editor: Nebr. Law Rev, 1950-51; author: Decision Making in the White House, 1963, Kennedy, 1965, The Kennedy Legacy, 1969, Watchmen in the Night: Presidential Accountability After Watergate, 1975, A Different Kind of Presidency, 1984, (with Ralf Dahrendorf) A Widening Atlantic? Domestic Change and Foreign Policy, 1986; editor: Let the Word Go Forth: The Speeches, Statements and Writings of John F. Kennedy, 1988. Dem. candidate for U.S. Senate, 1970; chmn. Dem. Nat. Com. task force on polit. action, 1981-82, mem. task force on fgn. policy, 1986; mem. Internat. Trade Roundtable, 1985; dir. Twentieth Century Fund, 1984—, Coun. on Fgn. Rels., 1993—, Nat. Dem. Inst. for Internat. Affairs, 1993—; trustee N.Y. Acad. Medicine, 1991—; advisor Russian-Am. Press and Info. Ctr., 1993—. Named by Jr. C. of C. as one of ten Outstanding Young Men of Year, 1961. Mem. Order of Coif, Phi Beta Kappa. Office: Paul Weiss Rifkind Wharton & Garrison 1285 Avenue Of The Americas New York NY 10019-6028*

SORENSEN, THOMAS CHAIKIN, retired financial executive; b. Lincoln, Nebr., Mar. 31, 1926; s. Christian and Annis (Chaikin) S.; m. Mary Barstler (div.); children: Ann Christine Sorensen Ketter, Alan Thomas, Jens Christian.; m. Pamela A. Berse; children—Matthew Thomas, Adam Lincoln. B.A., U. Nebr., 1947, LHD (hon.), 1996. Radio announcer, 1943-44, newspaper reporter, 1945-46; asst. night editor Nebr. State Jour., 1946-49; dir. news and pub. affairs radio sta. KLMS, Lincoln, 1949-51; instr. U. Nebr. Sch. Journalism, 1948-50; info. officer, press attaché Am. Embassy, Beirut, Lebanon, 1952-56, Baghdad, Iraq, 1956, Cairo, Egypt, 1957-59; program officer for Near East USIA, Washington, 1959-61; dep. dir. for policy USIA, 1961-65; v.p. U. Calif., 1966-68; sr. fellow Adlai Stevenson Inst., 1968-69; v.p. Leasco Corp., 1969-70; ptnr. Sartorius & Co., N.Y.C., 1971-74; sr. v.p., dir. Advest Inc., 1974-80; v.p. Capital Rsch. Internat., 1980-90; cons. Capital Group Inc., 1990-96; lectr. govt. and fgn. affairs U. Va., 1995-96. Author: The Word War, 1968. Named one of 10 Outstanding Young Men in Fed. Service, 1961. Mem. Washington Inst. of Fgn. Affairs, Va. Inst. Polit. Leadership, Phi Beta Kappa, Sigma Delta Chi, Delta Sigma Rho. Home: Matfield 2725 Hunt Country Ln Charlottesville VA 22901-8989

SORENSEN, W. ROBERT, clergy member, church administrator. Exec. dir. Division for Higher Education and Schools, Evangelical Lutheran Churchin America, Chgo. Office: Evangelical Lutheran Church Am 8765 W Higgins Rd Chicago IL 60631-4101

SORENSON, JAMES ROGER, public health educator; b. Yakima, Wash., Feb. 9, 1943; s. Paul Olaf and Helen Leona (Anderson) S.; m. Nancy Ellen O'Neal, May 24, 1968;1 child, Peter Matthew. BA in Sociology, U. Wash., 1965, MA in Sociology, 1966; PhD in Sociology, Cornell U., 1970. Asst. prof. Princeton (N.J.) U., 1969-74; assoc. prof. Boston U. Sch. of Medicine, 1974-84, Boston U. Sch. of Pub. Health, 1979-84; prof. Boston Univ. Schs. of Medicine and Pub. Health, 1984-85; prof. Sch. Pub. Health U. N.C., Chapel Hill, 1985—; cons. NIMH (Changing Role of Women Com.), 1971, Rutgers U. Ednl. Decision Making Project, 1970-74, Nat. Inst. Child Health and Human Devel., 1977-79, Nat. Heart , Lung and Blood Inst., Sickle Cell Br., 1977-80, 1991-92, Boston Comprehensive Sickle Cell Ctr., 1979-85, Nat. Ctr. for Human Genome Rsch., 1990-91; com. mem. Ea. Sociol. Soc. Papers Com., 1970-73, Genetics Core Group, Inst. for Soc., Ethics and the Life Scis., 1971-76, NYU com. on Med. and Ethical Issues in Treating Spina Bifida, 1973-74, Nat. Found. March of Dimes Clin. Rsch. (Human) adv. com. 1974-75; sci. assoc. Boston City Hosp., 1975-85, N.E. Group on Med. Edn., 1976-77; also many coms. at U. N.C. including Dean's Cabinet Sch. of Pub. Health, 1985—; dir. and chair steering com. Sch. of Pub. Health Promotion/Disease Prevention Program, 1986-89; adv. bd. Injury Prevention Rsch. Ctr., many others. Author: (with others) In Sickness and in Health: Social Dimensions of Medical Care, 1981, Reproductive Pasts, Reproductive Futures: Genetic Counseling and Its Effectiveness, 1981; also numerous articles to profl. jours. and chpts. to books; reviewer Am. Jour. Med. Genetics, Am. Jour. Preventive Medicine, Am. Jour. Pub. Health, Archives of Pathology and Laboratory Medicine, Human Relations, Jour. of Health and Social Behavior, Jour. Am. Geriatrics Soc., Milbank Meml. Fund Quarterly, New Eng. Jour. of Medicine, Patient Edn. and Counseling, Prenatal Diagnosis, Sci., Tech. and Human Values, Social Sci. and Medicine. Mem. adv. coun. Com. to Combat Huntington's Disease, Mass. chpt., 1979-85, edn. and comty. adv. bd. Am. Heart Assn., N.C. affiliate, 1986-89. Named fellow NIMH, Cornell U., 1967-69, Inst. of Soc., Ethics and Life Scis; named Falk lectr. Ea. Sociol. Soc., 1975-76; recipient Disting. Alumnus award Yakima Valley Coll., 1985; grantee; Mass. Dept. Pub. Health, Nat. Found., March of Dimes, NIDA, Nat. Cancer Inst. and others (18 grants in all). Mem. Am. Pub. Health Assn., Soc. Profl. Health Educators, N.C. Soc. Profl. Health Educators, Coun. on Health Edn. in Higher Edn., N.C. Pub. Health Assn., Phi Beta Kappa, Delta Omega. Avocations: music, theatre. Home: 21 Wysteria Way Chapel Hill NC 27514 Office: U NC Sch Pub Health 318 Rosenau CB 7400 Chapel Hill NC 27599

SORENSON, JEANNE, nursing consultant; b. Longmont, Colo., July 11, 1941; d. Dell Edwin and Verna Elizabeth (Nelson) Waggener; m. Roy Everett Sorenson, Sept. 15, 1962; children: JoDee Sorenson Wells, Roy E. III. Student, Sacramento State U., 1959, Contra Costa C.C., 1959-61; diploma, Kaiser Found. Sch. Nursing, 1962; postgrad., Am. River C.C., 1982. RN, Calif.; cert. rehab. RN, case mgr. Charge nurse Roseville (Calif.) Hosp., 1962-64; float nurse Mercy Gen. Hosp., Sacramento, 1964-66; float nurse Am. River Hosp., Carmichael, Calif., 1966-67, admissions nurse, 1967-73; sr. coord. Greater Sacramento Profl. Stds. and Rev. Orgn., 1973-80; med. rev. specialist ComputerSci Corp., Sacramento, 1980-86; sr. case mgr. Blue Shield of Calif., Folsom, 1986-91; ind. RN cons. SorensonEtal, Inc., Carmichael, 1991—; presenter seminars in field; mem. adv. bd. Casa Colina Rehab. Ctr., Pomona, Calif., 1989—, No. Valley Rehab. Ctr., Chico, Calif., 1989—, Kangaroo Kids, Sacramento, 1987—. Bd. dirs. No. Calif. Girls Softball Assn., Carmichael, 1975-80, Del Campo Little League, Carmichael, 1982-84, Childrens' Respit Ctr., Sacramento, 1990—. Mem. Nat. Head Injury Found. (mem. pediatric task force 1991—), Assn. Rehab. Nurses, Am. Assn. Spinal Cord Injury Nurses, Case Mgmt. Soc. Am., Nat. Assn. Rehab. Profls. Avocations: collecting kachina dolls and baseball cards, backpacking, family activities. Home: 5119 Mckinney Way Carmichael CA 95608-0762 Office: SorensonEtal Inc PO Box 1147 Carmichael CA 95609-1147

SORENSON, LIANE BETH MCDOWELL, women's affairs director, state legislator; b. Chgo., Aug. 13, 1947; d. Harold Davidson McDowell and Frances Elanor (Williams) Daisey; m. Boyd Wayne Sorenson, June 30, 1973; children: Nathan, Matthew, Dana. BS in Edn., U. Del., 1969, M in Counseling with honors, 1986. Tchr. Avon Grove Sch. Dist., West Grove, Pa., 1969-70, Alexis I. duPont Sch. Dist., Wilmington, Del., 1970-73, Barrington (Ill.) Sch. Dist., 1973-75; counseling intern Medill Intensive Learning Ctr.-Christina Sch. Dist., Newark, Del., 1985; counselor Family Violence Shelter CHILD, Inc., Wilmington, 1985, 86-87, dir. parent edn. programs, 1987-88; dir. Office Women's Affairs, exec. dir. Commn. on Status of Women U. Del., Newark, 1988—; mem. Del. Legislature, Dover, 1992—; chair Del. Ho. Edn. Com., 1992—; commr. Edn. Commn. State Del.; mem. tng. com. Nat. Conf. State Legislatures; mem. joint sunset com. Del. Legislature, Del. House of Reps., 1992-94, Del. Senate, 1994—, Del. Legis. Joint Fin. Com. Del. Legis., 1994—. Presenter papers various meetings & confs. Pres. bd. dirs. Nursing Mothers, Inc., 1980-81; trustee Hockessin Montessori Sch., 1982-84, enrollment chair, 1982-83; trustee Hockessin Pub. Libr., 1982-84, pres. bd., 1982-84; bd. dirs. Del. Coalition for Children, 1986-88; bd. dirs. Children's Bur. Del., 1984-87, sec., 1985-87; pres. Jr. League Wilmington, 1986-87, rsch. coun. v.p., 1985-86; bd. dirs. YWCA New Castle County, 1989-91; pres. Del. Women's Agenda, 1986-88; vice-chair Women's Leadership Ctr., 1992—; mem. Del. Work Family Coalition. Grantee Del. Dept. Svcs. to Children, Youth and Their Families, 1987-88, 1988, State of Del. Gen. Assembly, 1992. Mem. Am. Assn. for Higher Edn. (chair women's caucus 1991-92, program chair women's caucus 1990-91, pre-conf. workshop coord. women's caucus 1990 Ann. Conf.), Del. Greenway and Trails Coun., Rotary (charter mem. Hackessin Pike Creek club 1994—), Del. Alliance for Arts in Edn., Del. Family Law Commn. Republican. Methodist. Avocations: camping, hiking. Office: State of Delaware Legislative Hall Dover DE 19901

SORESE, DENISE POWERS, reading consultant, educator; b. N.Y.C., Sept. 11, 1945; d. Daniel Dennis and Frances Louise (Kruft) Powers; m. Vincent James Sorese, Aug. 12, 1967; children: Jaclyn, Lauren. BS in Edn., SUNY, Cortland, 1967; M of Reading, U. Bridgeport, 1970; cert. advanced study in adminstrn., Fairfield U., 1993. Tchr. early childhood N.Y.C. Bd. Edn., 1965-67; tchr. elem. sch. Greenwich (Conn.) Bd. Edn., 1967-72, reading specialist, 1972-77, 91—, learning facilitator, 1995—, mainstreaming assoc., 1986-91, adminstr. summer sch., 1993—; dir. summer acad. Convent of Sacred Heart Sch., 1994—; learning facilitator Hamilton Ave. Sch., Greenwich, Conn., 1995—; afterschool. adminstr. Hamilton Ave. Sch., Greenwich, 1993—; state assessor Conn. State Dept. Edn., Hartford, 1993—, tech. advisor, 1993—; presenter in field. Mem., project Charlie chmn. Jr. League Greenwich, 1989-92; bd. dirs. St. Pauls Day Sch., Riverside, Conn., 1981-92, PTA, Greenwich, 1984-93, St. Catherines Players, Riverside, 1993-94. Reading grantee State of Conn., 1973, 74. Mem. NEA, ASCD, Conn. Edn. Assn., Conn. Reading Assn. (bd. dirs., exemplary reading award, chairperson 1994—), Conn. Coun. Tchrs. English, Internat. Reading Assn., Delta Kappa Gamma. Roman Catholic. Avocations: tennis, reading, theatre,. Office: Hamilton Ave Sch 184 Hamilton Ave Greenwich CT 06830-6113

SORGEN, RENÉE BERKMAN, health facility administrator; b. Princeton, N.J., Apr. 15, 1945; d. Leon and Edna (Erhlichman) Berkman; m. Fred N. Sorgen, June 13, 1971; 1 child, Leigh Jason. RN, Helen Fuld Sch. of RN Hosp. for Joint Diseases, N.Y.C., 1967; postgrad., Fla. Internat. U. Asst. DON Sunrise (Fla.) Health Ctr., 1983-89, John Knox Village, Pompano Beach, Fla., 1989-90, Broward Convalescent, Ft. Lauderdale, Fla., 1990-91; DON Tamarac (Fla.) Convalescent Ctr., 1991—. Author: (manuals) Pressure Ulcer Management Manual and Program, 1994, Corporate Nursing Policy and Procedure Manual, Disaster and Safety Manual, 1991, Infectious Control Manual, 1991. Active South Fla. Assn. for Quality Assurance, Ft. Lauderdale, 1983-89; mem. adv. bd. Broward County Allied Health Professions, Ft. Lauderdale, 1983-91. Mem. Infection Control Practitioners, Phi Kappa Phi Honor Soc. Democrat. Avocations: reading, swimming, traveling. Home: 9330 NW 8th Cir Plantation FL 33324-4929

SORGENTI, HAROLD ANDREW, petroleum and chemical company executive; b. Bklyn., May 28, 1934; s. Louis J. and Lucille (Sisti) S.; m. Ann Rusnack, June 30, 1962; children: Elizabeth, Lucille. B.S.Ch.E., CCNY, 1956; M.S., Ohio State U., 1959. Research engr. Battelle Meml. Inst., Columbus, Ohio, 1956-59; with Atlantic Richfield Co., 1959-91, v.p. research and engrng., products div., 1975-76; sr. v.p. chem. devel. Arco Chem. Co. subs. Atlantic Richfield Co., Phila., 1977-79, pres., 1979-87, pres., CEO, 1987-90, vice chmn. bd., 1991; ptnr. Freedom Group Partnership, Phila., 1991-92; chmn. Freedom Chem. Co., 1992—; bd. dirs. Provident Mut. Life Ins. Co., Core States Fin. Corp., Crown Cork & Seal. Bd. dirs. Phila. Orch. Assn., Pa. Acad. Fine Arts. Mem. Am. Chem. Soc., Am. Inst. Chem. Engrs., Soc. Chem. Industry, Ohio State U. Alumni Assn., CCNY Alumni Assn., Union League. Office: Freedom Chem Co 1735 Market St Ste 3500 Philadelphia PA 19103-7501*

SORKIN, ALAN LOWELL, economist, educator; b. Decatur, Ill., Nov. 2, 1941; s. Martin and Sally Eileen (Steinberg) S.; m. Sylvia Jean Smardo, Sept. 9, 1967; children: David, Suzanne. BA, Johns Hopkins U., 1963, MA, 1964, PhD, 1966. Rsch. assoc. Brookings Instn., Washington, 1967-69; asst. prof. internat. health and econs. Johns Hopkins U., Balt., 1969-72, assoc. prof. internat. health and econs., 1972-74, adj. prof. dept. internat. health Sch. Hygiene and Pub. Health, 1986—; prof., chmn. dept. econs., 1974—; also adj. prof. preventive and social medicine Med. Sch., U. Md., 1974—. Author: Education, Unemployment and Economic Growth, 1974, Health Economics: An Introduction, 1975, 2d edit., 1983, 3d edit., 1992. The Urban American Indian, 1978, Economic Aspects of Natural Hazards, 1982, Health Care and the Changing Economic Environment, 1986, Monetary and Fiscal Policy and Business Cycles in The Modern Era, 1988, Public Health and Development, 1988, (with others) Female Labor Force and Development, 1990, Nutrition, Food Policy and Development, 1995, others; contbr. articles to profl. jours. Mem. Am. Econs. Assn., Phi Beta Kappa, Delta Omega. Republican. Lutheran. Home: 1694 Campbell Rd Forest Hill MD 21050-2342 Office: U Md Dept Econ 5401 Wilkens Ave Baltimore MD 21228-5329 *Personal relationships are more important than material possessions. Persons with many friends have a sense of well-being that can never be embodied in materialism.*

SORKIN, LAURENCE TRUMAN, lawyer; b. Bklyn., Oct. 20, 1942; s. Sidney and Lilly (Kowensky) S.; m. Joan Carol Ross, June 25, 1972; children: Andrew Ross, Suzanne Ross. AB summa cum laude, Brown U., 1964; LLB, Yale U., 1967; LLM, London Sch. Econs. and Polit. Sci., 1968. Bar: N.Y. 1968, D.C. 1972, U.S. Supreme Ct. 1973. Law clk. to judge U.S. Ct. Appeals (2d cir.), Hartford, Conn., 1968-69; assoc. Cahill Gordon & Reindel, N.Y.C., 1969-75, ptnr., 1975—; vis. lectr. Yale U., 1972, 73; lectr. Practicing Law Inst., 1977—, and various other profl. orgns.; rsch. asst. to Lester and Bindman for book Race and Law in Great Britain, 1972. Contbr. to State Antitrust Law (Lifland), 1984; author (with Lifland, Sorkin and Van Cise): Understanding the Antitrust Laws, 1986. Fulbright scholar, 1967-68. Bd. dirs. The Legal Aid Soc., N.Y.C., 1988-94, N.Y. Lawyers for Pub. Interest, 1990-93. Mem. ABA (antitrust law sect. 1978—), N.Y. State Bar Assn. (mem. antitrust sect. 1978—, chmn. com. on legis. 1978-79, sec. 1979-80, chmn. com. on mergers 1987-89, chmn. Clayton Act com.1989-94, exec. com. 1989-94), Assn. of Bar of City of N.Y. (mem. com. trade regulation 1974-77, 95—, com. on electronic funds transfer 1979-80), Phi Beta Kappa. Office: Cahill Gordon & Reindel 80 Pine St New York NY 10005-1702

SORO, MAR BAWAI, bishop; b. Kirkuk, Iraq, Mar. 3, 1954; s. Andrew Athniel and Souria (Sada) S. MA in Theology, Cath. U. Am., 1994. Ordained priest Holy Apostolic Cath. Assyrian Ch. of the East. Parish priest Assyrian Ch., Toronto, Ont., Can., 1982-85; diocesian bishop Diocese of Western U.S. Assyrian Ch., San Jose, Calif., 1985-95; gen. sec. Assyrian Ch. of East Commn. on Inter-ch. Rels. and Edn. Devel., Seattle, 1995—; mem. Ctrl. Com., W.C.C., Geneva, 1982-91; mem. official dialogue with Roman Cath. Ch., Vatican City, 1984—, with Middle East Coun. Chs., Limassol, Cypress, 1991—. Pub. The Messenger, 1993—. Avocations: reading, computer applications.

SOROKA, CYNTHIA ANNE, writer, photographer; b. N.Y.C., Sept. 28, 1967; d. George E. and Diane (Feldman) S. AS in Broadcasting, Bergen C.C., Paramus, N.J., 1987; BA in Comm., SUNY, New Paltz, 1989. Payroll clk., audit clk., receptionist Howard Johnson Hotel, Saddle Brook, N.J., 1987-88; intern WPDH, Poughkeepsie, N.Y., 1989; disc jockey WALL-AM/WKOJ-FM, 1989; weekend anchor and newscaster WGNY-FM Radio, Newburgh, N.Y., 1989-90; disc jockey WCZX-FM, Poughkeepsie, N.Y., 1990; disc jockey, traffic dir., producer WRKL-AM 91, Pomona, N.Y., 1990-91; disc jockey, accts. payable, traffic dir. WVIP-AM&FM, Mt. Kisco, N.Y., 1991; from photo asst. to v.p. Expressions Photography, Closter, N.J., 1982—; pres. Ariel Starr Prodns., Closter, 1991—; v.p. Flash Blasters Inc., Closter, 1992-95. Author: The Dark Chronicles, vol. 1, 1993, vol. 2, 1994, vol. 3, 1995, The Dark Chronicles Years of Light Part 1, 1996; poems included: Distinguished Poets of Am., 1991-93, Outstanding Poets of 1994. Vol. Englewood (N.J.) Hosp., 1982-83. Mem. Nat. Assn. Broadcast Employees, Authors Guild Am., Bergen County Sci. Fiction Assn., Horror Writers Assn. Home: 32A Hawthorne Ter Closter NJ 07624-2435 Office: Expressions Photography 253 Closter Dock Rd Closter NJ 07624-2619

SOROKIN, PETER PITIRIMOVICH, physicist; b. Boston, July 10, 1931; s. Pitirim Alexandrovich and Elena Petrovna (Baratynskaya) S.; m. Anita J. Schell, Oct. 1, 1977; children: Elena P., Paul P. A.B., Harvard U., 1952, M.S., 1953, Ph.D., 1958. Staff physicist IBM Watson Rsch. Ctr., Yorktown Heights, N.Y., 1957-68, fellow, 1968—. Contbr. articles in quantum electronics to profl. jours. Recipient Michelson medal Franklin Soc., 1974; R.W. Wood award Optical Soc. Am., 1978; Harvey prize, 1984; IBM fellow, 1968—; APS Schawlow prize, 1991. Mem. Nat. Acad. Sci. (Comstock award 1983), Am. Acad. Sci., N.Y. Acad. Sci. Patentee laser devices. Home: 5 Ashwood Rd South Salem NY 10590 Office: IBM T J Watson Rsch Ctr PO Box 218 Yorktown Heights NY 10598-0218

SOROS, GEORGE, fund management executive; b. Budapest, Hungary, Aug. 12, 1930; came to U.S., 1956; s. Tivadar and Elisabeth (Szucs) S.; m. Annaliese Witschak, Sept. 17, 1960 (div. June 1983); children: Robert, Andrea, Jonathan; m. Susan Weber, June 19, 1983; children: Alexander, Gregory. BS, London Sch. Econs., 1952; LLD (hon.), New Sch. for Social Rsch., 1990; D. Civil Law, U. Oxford, Eng., 1990; LHD (hon.), Yale U., 1991. Arbitrage trader F.M. Mayer, N.Y.C., 1956-59; analyst Wertheim & Co., N.Y.C., 1959-63; v.p. Arnhold and S. Bleichroeder, N.Y.C., 1963-73; pres. Soros Fund Mgmt., N.Y.C., 1973—. Author: The Alchemy of Finance, 1987, 2nd edit., 1994, Opening the Soviet System, 1990, Underwriting Democracy, 1991. Mem. Coun. on Fgn. Rels., N.Y.C., 1988—, Royal Inst. Internat. Affairs, London, 1990—, Bretton Woods Com., Washington, 1989; mem. exec. com. Helsinki Watch, N.Y.C., 1982—; mem. com. Americas Watch, N.Y.C., 1982—; chmn., founding pres. Ctrl. European U., Prague, Budapest, 1991; chmn. Open Soc. Fund, 1981, Open Soc. Inst., 1993, founds. in Albania, Belarus, Bosnia and Herzegovina, Bulgaria, Croatia, Czech Republic, Estonia, Georgia, Hungary, Kazakhstan, Kyrgyzstan, Latvia, Lithuania, Macedonia, Moldova, Poland, Romania, Russia, Slovakia, Slovenia, South Africa, Rroma, Ukraine, Yugoslavia. Recipient honor Lawyers Co. for Human Rights, N.Y.C., 1990. Mem. Brooks' London, Queens Club (London), N.Y. Athletic Club, Town Tennis, Meadow Club (Southampton, N.Y.). Avocations: tennis, skiing, chess, backgammon. Office: Soros Fund Mgmt 888 7th Ave Ste 3300 New York NY 10106*

SORREL, WILLIAM EDWIN, psychiatrist, educator, psychoanalyst; b. N.Y.C., May 27, 1913; s. Simon and Lee (Lesenger) S.; m. Rita Marcus, July 1, 1950; children: Ellyn Gail, Joy Shelley, Beth Mara. BS, NYU, 1932; MA, Columbia U., 1934, MD, 1939; PhD, NYU, 1963. Diplomate Am. Bd. Med. Psychotherapists (profl. adv. coun. 1992—); qualified psychiatrist, also cert.examiner N.Y. State Dept. Mental Hygiene. Intern Madison (Tenn.) Sanitarium and Hosp., 1939; resident physician Alexian Bros. Hosp., St. Louis, 1940; officer instrn. St. Louis U. Sch. Medicine, 1940-41; asst. psychiatrist Central State Hosp., Nashville, 1941; assoc. psychiatrist Eastern State Hosp., Knoxville, 1942-44; assoc. attending neuropsychiatrist, chief clin. psychiatry Jewish Meml. Hosp., N.Y.C., 1946-59; assoc. attending neuropsychiatrist, chief clin. child psychiatry Lebanon Hosp., Bronx, N.Y., 1947-65; psychiatrist-in-chief Psychiatry Clinic, Yeshiva U., 1950-66, asst. prof. psychiatry, 1952-54, assoc. prof., 1954-58, prof., 1959-62, psychiatrist-in-chief, assoc. dir. Psychol. Center,, 1957-67; prof. human behavior Touro Coll., 1974—; attending psychiatrist St. Clare's Hosp., N.Y.C., 1983—; asst. prof. clin. psychiatry Albert Einstein Coll. Medicine, 1986—; psychiat. cons. SSS, 1951, N.Y. State Workmens Compensation Bd., 1951—, Bronx-Lebanon Med. Ctr., 1985—; vis. psychiatrist Fordham Hosp., N.Y.C., 1951; attending neuropsychiatrist, chief mental hygiene svc. Beth-David Hosp., 1950-60; attending neuropsychiatrist Grand Central Hosp., 1958-66, Morrisania Hosp., 1959-72; psychiatrist-in-chief Beth Abraham Hosp., 1954-60; psychiat. cons. L.I. U. Guidance Ctr., 1955-60, Daytop Village, 1970-71; assoc. psychiatrist Seton City Hosp., 1955; guest lectr. U. London, 1947; vis. prof. Jerusalem, Israel Acad. Med., 1960, Hebrew U., 1960; mem. psychiat. staff Gracie Sq. Hosp., 1960—; chief psychiatry Trafalgar Hosp., 1962-72; vis. prof. psychiatry Tokyo U. Sch. Medicine, 1964; adj. prof. N.Y. Inst. Tech., 1968; vis. lectr. in psychiatry N.Y. U., 1971-73; Am. del. Internat. Conf. Mental Health, London, 1948; mem. Am. Psychiat. Commn. to USSR, Poland and Finland, 1963, Empire State Med., Sci. and Ednl. Found. Author: (booklets) Neurosis in a Child, 1949, A Psychiatric Viewpoint on Child Adoption, 1954, Shock Therapy in Psychiatric Practice, 1957, The Genesis of Neurosis, 1958, The Prejudiced Personality, 1962, The Schizophrenic Process, 1962, The Prognosis of Electroshock Therapy Success, 1963, Psychodynamic Effects of Abortion, 1967, Violence Towards Self, 1971, Basic Concepts of Transference in Psychoanalysis, 1973, A Study in Suicide, 1972, Masochism, 1973, Emotional Factors Involved in Skeletal Deformities, 1977, Cults & Cult Suicide, 1979; assoc. editor: Jour. Pan Am. Med. Assn., 1992—; contbr. articles on the psychoses. Vice pres. Golden Years Found.; N.Y.C. chmn. Com. Med. Standards in Psychiatry, 1952-54. Recipient Sir William Osler Internat. Honor Med. Soc. Gold Key; 3d prize oil paintings N.Y. State Med. Art Exhibit, 1954; NYU Founders Day award, 1963; Presdl. Achievement award, 1984; others. Fellow Am. Psychiat. Assn. (life, pres. Bronx dist. 1960-61, other offices, Gold medal 1974, 94), Am. Assn. Psychoanalytic Physicians (pres. 1971-72, bd. govs. 1972—); mem. AMA, Ea. Psychiat. Assn., N.Y. State Soc. Med. Rsch., Am. Med. Writers Assn., N.Y. Med. Soc., N.Y. County Med. Soc., N.Y. Soc. for Clin. Psychiatry, Pan Am. Med. Assn. (various offices including pres. 1989—, assoc. editor jour. 1992—), Assn. for Advancement Psychotherapy, Bronx Soc. Neurology and Psychotherapy (pres. 1960-61, Silver medal 1970), Mensa. Home: 23 Meadow Rd Scarsdale NY 10583-7642 Office: 263 W End Ave New York NY 10023-2612 *Very meaningful to me is the matter of professionalism in the practice of my discipline. A helping service to individuals is to add and enhance their contentment of living; especially in a world of* *turmoil. Medical science has added greatly to the art of my training: and I apply it daily.*

SORRELL, FURMAN YATES, mechanical engineering educator; b. Wadesboro, N.C., July 14, 1938; s. Furman Yates and Julia Lee (Little) S.; 1 dau., Shannon Lea. B.S., N.C. State U., Raleigh, 1960; M.S., Calif. Inst. Tech., 1961, Ph.D., 1966. Research engr. Pratt & Whitney Aircraft Corp., West Palm Beach, Fla., 1961-62; asst. prof. U. Colo., Boulder, 1966-68; mem. faculty N.C. State U., Raleigh, 1968—; asso. prof. mech. engring. N.C. State U., 1970-76, prof., 1976—; with Perry Assos. (Cons. Engrs.), 1974-75; tech. dir. N.C. Alt. Energy Corp., 1981-82 (on leave); cons. NASA, Langley Research Center, Babcox & Wilcox, Fram Corp., IBM, U.S. Army Chem. Systems Labs.; chmn. marine waste disposal panel NOAA Conf. Ocean Pollution and Monitoring, 1979-80. Contbr. articles to profl. jours. Grantee NSF, NOAA, NASA. Mem. Am. Geophys. Union, Am. Acad. Mechanics, Am. Phys. Soc., N.Y. Acad. Scis., ASME. Home: 930 Ralph Dr Cary NC 27511-4623 Office: Box 7910 NC State U Raleigh NC 27695

SORRELL, MARTIN STUART, advertising and marketing executive; b. London, Feb. 14, 1945; s. Jack and Sally (Goldberg) S.; m. Sandra Carol Ann Finestone, Apr. 25, 1971; children: Mark, Robert, Jonathan. BA, Cambridge (Eng.) U., 1966, MA, 1970; MBA, Harvard U., 1968. Cons. Glendinning Assoc., Conn., 1968-70; v.p. Mark McCormack Orgn., London, 1970-74; dir. James Gulliver Assoc., London, 1975-77; group fin. dir. Saatchi & Saatchi, London, 1977-86; group chief exec. WPP Group PLC, London, 1986—; non-exec. dir. Storehouse, London, 1994—. Trustee U. Cambridge Found., Princess Royal Trust for Carers; mem. governing body London Bus Sch.; mem. adv. bd. Instituto de Estudios Superiores de la Empresa, Judge Inst. Mgmt. Studies. Avocation: cricket, skiing. Office: WPP Group PLC, 27 Farm St, London W1X 6RD, England

SORRELLS, FRANK DOUGLAS, mechanical engineer, consultant; b. Toccoa, Ga., May 14, 1931; s. Ralph Price and Ila B. (Freeman) S.; m. Alma M. West, June 19, 1954; 1 child, Desiree G. BSME, U. Tenn., 1957, MS, 1968. Registered profl. engr., Tenn. Chief engr. Formex Co., Greeneville, Tenn., 1960-67; exec. v.p. Charles Lee Assoc., Knoxville, Tenn., 1967-76; pvt. practice consulting engr. Knoxville, Tenn., 1976-78, 83-88; dir. engring. Cole Nat. Corp., Knoxville, Tenn., 1978-83; mgr. tech. transfer Valmet Paper Machinery div. Valmet-Enerdry, Knoxville, Tenn., 1988-93; pres. PEPE Software LLC, Knoxville, Tenn., 1996—; cons., Knoxville, 1976—; mem. Advanced Toroidal Facility Design Team, cons. Oak Ridge (Tenn.) Nat. Lab., 1984-85. Inventor, patentee of 8 patents and co-inventor, patentee of 14 patents in fields of filtration, web processing, plastic forming and lens processing. Staff sgt. USAF, 1950-54. Mem. NSPE, ASME (Energy Resources Rech. award 1987), Tenn. Soc. Profl. Engrs. Avocations: fishing, boating. Home and Office: 5516 Timbercrest Trl Knoxville TN 37909-1837

SORRELS, RANDALL OWEN, lawyer; b. Va., Dec. 11, 1962; s. Charles Vernon and Marjorie Elaine (Jones) S.; m. Cheryl Ann Casas, June 29, 1985; children: Ashley Michelle, Stephanie Leigh. BA in Polit. Sci.and Speech Comm. magna cum laude, Houston Bapt. U., 1984; JD magna cum laude, South Tex. Coll. Law, 1987. Bar: Tex. 1987, U.S. Dist. Ct. (so. dist.) Tex.; bd. cert. in civil trial law and personal injury trial law tex. Bd. Legal Specialization. Assoc. Fulbright & Jaworski, Houston, 1987-90; ptnr. Abraham, Watkins, Nichols, Ballard & Friend, Houston, 1990—. Mem. ABA, ATLA, State Bar Tex. (bd. dirs. 1994—, bd. advisor pattern jury charge commt. Vol. 1 1994—, Vol. 4, 1995—, chmn. profl. devel. com. 1996—, vice chair legis. com. 1996—), Tex. Trial Lawyers Assn. (sustaining life mem., bd. dirs.), Houston Trial Lawyers Assn. (bd. dirs., chmn. CLE com. 1993—), Houston Young Lawyers Assn., Tex. Young Lawyers Assn., Coll. of the State Bar of Tex., Assn. of Civil Trial and Appellate Specialists. Home: 4524 Palmetto St Bellaire TX 77401-3710 Office: Abraham Watkins Nichols Ballard & Friend 800 Commerce St Houston TX 77002-1707

SORRENTINO, GILBERT, English language educator, novelist, poet; b. Bklyn., Apr. 27, 1929; s. August E. and Ann Marie (Davis) S.; m. Victoria Ortiz; children: Jesse, Delia, Christopher. Student, Bklyn. Coll., 1949-51, 54-56. In various positions, 1947-70; including reins. clk. Fidelity and Casualty Co., N.Y.C., 1947-48; freight checker Ace Assembly Agy., N.Y.C., 1954-56; packer Bennett Bros. Inc., N.Y.C., 1956-57; messenger Am. Houses, Inc., N.Y.C., 1948-49; shipping-room supr. Thermo-fax Sales, Inc., Queens, N.Y., 1957-60; editor Grove Press, N.Y., 1965-70; tchr. Columbia U., 1966, Aspen Writers Workshop, 1967, Sarah Lawrence Coll., 1972, The New Sch. for Social Rsch., 1976—; NEH chairperson in lit. U. Scranton, 1979; prof. English Stanford (Calif.) U., 1982—; editorial cons. Contemporary Lit., 1989—. Author: The Darkness Surrounds Us, 1960, Black and White, 1964, The Sky Changes, 1966, The Perfect Fiction, 1968, Steelwork, 1970, Imaginative Qualities of Actual Things, 1971, Corrosive Sublimate, 1971, Splendide-Hotel, 1972, Flawless Play Restored, 1974, A Dozen Oranges, 1976, White Sail, 1977, Sulpiciae Elegidia/Elegiacs of Sulpicia, 1977, The Orangery, 1978, Mulligan Stew, 1979, Aberration of Starlight, 1980, Selected Poems, 1958-80, 1981, Crystal Vision, 1981, Blue Pastoral, 1983, Something Said: Essays, 1984, Odd Number, 1985, Rose Theatre, 1987, Misterioso, 1989, Under the Shadow, 1991, Red the Fiend, 1995. With U.S. Army, 1951-53. Recipient Samuel Fels award in fiction Coord. Coun. Lit. Mags., 1974, John Dos Passos prize, 1981, Am. Acad. and Inst. Arts and Letters award in lit., 1985, Lannan Lit. award for fiction, 1992; John Simon Guggenheim Meml. fellow, 1973-74, 87-88; grantee Creative Artists Pub. Svc. Program, 1974-75, Nat. Endowment for Arts, 1974-75, 78-79, 83-84. Mem. PEN Am. Ctr. Office: Stanford U Dept English Stanford CA 94305

SORRENTINO, RALPH JOSEPH, communications executive; b. Bklyn., June 28, 1952; s. Vincent Sorrentino and Carmela (Visciano) La Rosa; m. Jean Marie McAuliffe, Sept. 8, 1984. BS in Acctg., Bklyn. Coll., 1979. CPA, N.Y. Controller Lowe Marschalk, N.Y.C.; pres., COO Bohbot Comm. Inc., N.Y.C. Mem. Am. Inst. CPA's. Avocation: stock and bond markets. Home: 407 Blauvelt Rd Pearl River NY 10965-2845 Office: Bohbot Communications Inc 41 Madison Ave New York NY 10010

SORRENTINO, RENATE MARIA, illustrator; b. Mallnitz, Carinthia, Austria, June 21, 1942; came to the U.S., 1962; d. Johann and Theresia (Kritzer) Weinberger; m. Philip Rosenberg, Nov. 22, 1968 (dec. 1982); m. Francis J. Sorrentino, Sept. 4, 1988. Grad. gold and silversmith artist, Höhere Technische Lehranstalt, Austria, 1961. Draftswoman Elecon Inc., N.Y.C., 1962-65; jr. designer Automatics Metal Prod. Corp., N.Y.C., 1965-70; designer, art dir. Autosplice, Inc., Woodside, N.Y., 1970-90; freelance artist Jupiter, Fla., 1990—. Patentee Quick Disconnect from Continuous Wire, 1977. Home: 2301 Marina Isle Way Apt 404 Jupiter FL 33477-9423 Office: Autosplice Inc 10121 Barnes Canyon Rd San Diego CA 92121-2725

SORTE, JOHN FOLLETT, investment firm executive; b. Boston, June 30, 1947; s. Martin Eugene and Elizabeth Foster (Bradley) S.; m. Colleen Sarah Costello, July 28, 1979; children: Bradley Follett, Laura Elizabeth, Kathryn Clare. BA in Chem. Engring., Rice U., 1969, M in Chem. Engring., 1970; MBA, Harvard U., 1972. Assoc. Shearson Hammill & Co., Inc., N.Y.C., 1972-74; v.p. Shearson Hayden Stone, Inc., N.Y.C., 1974-79; 1st v.p. Shearson Loeb Rhoades, Inc., N.Y.C., 1979-80; 1st v.p. Drexel Burnham Lambert, Inc., N.Y.C., 1980-82, mng. dir., 1982-88, exec. v.p., 1989-90, pres., chief exec. officer, dir., 1990-92; pres., chief exec. officer New Street Capital Corp., N.Y.C., 1992-94; pres. New Street Advisors L.P., N.Y.C., 1994—; chmn. N.Y. Media Group, Inc., 1995—; bd. dirs. Gillett Holdings, Inc., WestPoint Stevens, Inc. V.p., bd. dirs. DBL Found., Inc., N.Y.C., 1991-95; bd. trustees Rippowam Cisqua Sch. Office: New Street Advisors LP 17th Fl 99 Park Ave New York NY 10016-1503

SORTER, BRUCE WILBUR, federal program administrator, educator, consultant; b. Willoughby, Ohio, Sept. 1, 1931; s. Wilbur David and Margaret Louise (Palmer) S.; m. Martha Ann Weirich, Sept. 2, 1960 (div. 1967); 1 child, David Robert. BA, U. Md., 1967; MCP, Howard U., 1969; PhD, U. Md., 1972. Cert. community developer. Commd. USAFR, 1967, advanced through grades to lt. col., 1964; sr. planner, cons. Md. Nat. Capital Park and Planning Com., 1968-71; instr. psychology, sociology Howard and P.G. C.C., Columbia and Largo, Md., 1971-72; cmty. resource devel. dept. Md. Coop. Extension Svc., U. Md., College Park, Md., 1972-92; coord. rural info. ctr. Md. Coop. Ext. Svc., U. Md., College Park, 1989-92; affiliate prof. U. Md., 1985-92, ret., 1996; ext. advisor USDA Internat. Programs, Washington, 1991-96; co-author, co-dir. Dept. Edn. Coun. Effectiveness Tng. Program, 1979-81; author First County Energy Conservation Plan, Prince George's County, 1978-85. Author, co-author 12 books; contbr. articles to profl. publs., chpts. to books. Developer, dir. teamwork tng. programs U.S. Dept. Edn., U.S. Dept. Agriculture, Brazil, Poland, Nat. Grange, 1972-92; cons. Fed. Power Commn. U.S., 1973-75, State Dept. Natural Resources, Md., 1978-79, Dept. Edn., Brazil, 1981-82, Nat. Grange, 1987, Edn. Ext. Svcs., Poland, 1991-92. Urban Planning fellow Howard U., 1968, Human Devel. fellow U. Md., 1970; recipient Meritorious Svc. award Dept. Def., 1983, Disting. Community Svc. award Md. Community Resource Devel. Assn., 1983, Citation for Outstanding Svc., Ptnrs. of Am., 1983, Excellence in Ednl. Programs award Am. Express, 1984, Project of Yr. award Am. Psychol. Assn., 1976, Award of Yr. Am. Vol. Assn., 1976, Achievement award Nat. Assn. of Counties, 1980. Mem. Internat. Cmty. Devel. Soc. (bd. dirs., Achievement award for outstanding contbn. to cmty. devel. 1985, Disting. Svc. award 1990), Md. Cmty. Resource Devel. Assn. (sec.-treas. 1979, pres. 1980, 88-89). Republican. Methodist. Avocations: volunteer work, tennis, sailing, skiing. *Decide where you want to go. Ask yourself, is it worth the cost? If the answer is yes, then go with determination for time is in short supply.*

SORTER, GEORGE HANS, accounting and law educator, consultant; b. Vienna, Austria, Dec. 2, 1927; came to U.S., 1938; s. Alfred and Hertha (Kohn) S.; m. Dorienne Lachman, Aug. 18, 1966; children: David, Ivan, Adrienne. Ph.B., U. Chgo., 1953, M.B.A., 1955, Ph.D., 1963. C.P.A., N.Y. Instr. U. Chgo., 1955-58, asst. prof., 1959-63, assoc. prof., 1963-65, prof., 1966-74; Vincent C. Ross prof. acctg., prof. of law NYU, N.Y.C., 1974—; Arthur Young prof. U. Kans., 1969; Coopers & Lybrand prof. Tuck Sch. Dartmouth Coll., 1982; bd. dirs. NYU Credit Union, 1982-85; dir. Greater N.Y. Savs. Bank, N.Y.C., 1983—; audit com. City of N.Y., 1985—. Author: Accounting Theory, 1963, Accounting Thoughts of W.W. Werntz, Boundaries of Accounting Universe, 1978, Relevant Financial Statements, 1978, Financial Accounting: An Events and Cash Flow Approach, 1990, The Mix-Max Co., 1990. Mem. Ill. Sch. Bd. Dist. 233, Flossmoor, 1970-74; bd. dirs. Sch. Emotionally Disturbed Children, Chgo., 1960-74, Renaissance Soc., 1956-74, Found. Acctg. Edn., N.Y.C., 1975-79. Erskine fellow U. Canterbury, 1979. Mem. Am. Acctg. Assn. (v.p 1980-81 Outstanding Acctg. Educator), N.Y. State Soc. C.P.A.s (dir. 1980-82), Am. Inst. C.P.A.s, Fin. Acctg. Standard Adv. Com. Home: 37 Washington Sq W New York NY 10011-9181 Office: NYU Tisch Hall 40 W 4th St New York NY 10012-1118

SORTOR, HAROLD EDWARD, financial executive; b. Craig, Nebr., Jan. 18, 1925; s. Harold E. and Ruth (Oldham) S.; m. Dorothy M. Johnson, Oct. 9, 1954; 1 child, Georgia Lynn. B.S., U. Ill., 1949, J.D., 1950. Bar: Ill. bar 1950; C.P.A., Ill. Tax supr. Ernst & Ernst, Chgo., 1950-56; mem. firm McDermott, Will & Emery, Chgo., 1956-59; tax mgr. Amphenol-Borg Electronics Corp. (name changed to Amphenol Corp. 1965), Oak Brook, Ill., 1959-62; asst. controller Amphenol-Borg Electronics Corp. (name changed to Amphenol Corp. 1965), 1962-63, treas., 1963-68; treas. Bunker Ramo Corp., 1968, Montgomery Ward & Co., Chgo., 1968-73; sr. v.p. corporate finance CNA Financial Corp., 1973-75; group v.p. finance Pennzoil Co., 1975-85; lectr. Northwestern U., 1954-59. Mem. Sch. Bd. Dist. 25, Cook County, Ill., 1962-67, pres., 1965-67; bd. dirs. United Charities Chgo., 1971-75, Ill. sect. Am. Cancer Soc., 1972-75. Served with AUS, 1943-46. Mem. AICPA. Home: 11 Little Comfort Rd Savannah GA 31411-1446

SORVINO, MIRA, actress; b. 1968; d. Paul S. AB, Harvard U., 1990. Appeared in films including Amongst Friends, 1993, The Second Greatest Story Ever Told, 1993, Quiz Show, 1994, Parallel Lives, 1994, Barcelona, 1994, Tarantella, 1995, Sweet Nothing, 1995, Mighty Aphrodite, 1995 (Oscar for Best Supporting Actress), The Dutch Master, 1995, Blue in the Face, 1995, Beautiful Girls, 1996, (TV) The Buccaneers, 1995, Norma Jean and Marilyn, 1996, Jake's Women, 1996; assoc. prodr. Amongst Friends, 1993. Office: The William Morris Agy 151 El Camino Dr Beverly Hills CA 90212*

SORVINO, PAUL, actor; b. N.Y.C., 1939. Attended, Am. Musical and Dramatic Acad. N.Y.C. stage debut in Bajour, 1964; actor in (plays) including The Baker's Wife, Mating Dance, Skyscraper, That Championship Season, King Lear, An American Millionaire, For My Last Number, We'll Get By, Philemon, (films) including The Gambler, 1970, Where's Poppa, 1970, Panic in Needle Park, 1971, Cry Uncle, Made for Each Other, 1971, The Day of the Dolphin, 1973, A Touch of Class, 1973, I Will, I Will ... For Now, 1976, Oh God!, 1977, The Brink's Job, 1978, Shoot It, Black, Shoot It, Blue, Slow Dancing in the Big City, 1978, The Bloodbrothers, 1979, Lost and Found, 1979, Cruising, 1980, Reds, 1981, That Championship Season, 1982, I, The Jury, 1982, Off the Wall, Turk 182, A Fine Mess, 1985, The Stuff, 1986, Vasectomy, 1986, Dick Tracy, 1990, Goodfellas, 1990, The Rocketeer, 1991, The Firm, 1993, Nixon, 1995; (TV miniseries) Seventh Avenue, 1977, (TV films) including Tell Me Where it Hurts, 1974, It Couldn't Happen to a Nicer Guy, 1974, Dummy, 1979, A Question of Honor, 1982, Chiefs, 1983, My Mother's Secret Life, 1984, With Intent to Kill, 1984, Surviving, 1985, Betrayed by Innocence, 1986, Don't Touch My Daughter, 1991, Perry Mason: The Case of the Wicked Wives, 1993, Parallel Lives, 1994; star (TV series) We'll Get By, 1975, Bert D'Angelo/Superstar, 1976, The Oldest Rookie, 1987, Law and Order, 1991-92, Star Trek: The Next Generation (guest appearance), 1994; artistic dir. Am. Stage Co., Teaneck, N.J.; dir., star: All the Kings Men; dir. Two for the Seesaw, The Rainmaker, 1986. Office: C/O William Morris Agency care Michele Stern 151 El Camino Beverly Hills CA 90212*

SOSA, ERNEST, philosopher, educator; b. Cardenas, Cuba, June 17, 1940; s. Ernesto and Maria (Garriga) S.; m. Sara Mercedes, Dec. 21, 1961; children: E. David, Adrian J. BA, U. Miami, 1961; MA, U. Pitts., 1962, PhD, 1964. Instr. U. Western Ontario, London, Ontario, Can., 1963-64, U. Pitts., 1964; postdoctoral fellow Brown U., Providence, 1964-66; asst. prof. U. Western Ontario, London, Ontario, 1966-67; asst. prof. to full prof. Brown U., Providence, 1967-74, chmn. of philosophy, 1970-76, full prof., 1974—, Romeo Elton prof., 1981—; vis. prof. U. Miami, 1970, Nat. U. Mexico, 1979, 80, 81, Harvard U., Cambridge, Mass., 1982. Author: Knowledge in Perspective, 1991; gen. editor book series, Cambridge Univ. Pres., 1990—, Blackwell Publishers, 1991—; contbr. numerous articles to profl. jours. Grantee NSF, 1970-72, Exxon Ednl. Found., 1980-82; recipient Sr. fellowship NEH, 1988-89. Mem. Am. Philos. Assn. (sec.-treas. 1974-82, chair internat. coop. com. 1984-89), Am. Coun. Learned Socs./Soviet Acad. Commn., Internat. Fedn. Philos. Soc. (steering com. mem. 188-89, v.p. 1988-93), Institut Internat. de Philosophie (exec. com. 1993—). Avocations: running, travel. Office: Brown U Providence RI 02912

SOSA, SAMUEL (SAMMY SOSA), professional baseball player; b. San Pedro de Macoris, Dominican Republic. With Tex. Rangers, 1989; outfield Chgo. Cubs, 1989—. Selected to N.L All-Star Team, 1995. Office: Chgo Cubs 1060 W Addison St Chicago IL 60613-4397*

SOSHNIK, JOSEPH, investment banking consultant; b. Omaha, Feb. 14, 1920; s. Ben Nathan and Clara (Lehman) S.; m. Miriam Saks, June 29, 1941; children—David, Allan (dec.), Robert. B.S.C. summa cum laude, Creighton U., 1941; M.S. (Alfred P. Sloan fellow), U. Denver, 1943; student, U. Colo., 1943-44; Ph.D., U. Nebr., 1952, LHD (hon.), 1988. Instr., asst. prof., asso. prof. Creighton U., 1946-57, auditor, budget cons., 1952-57; with U. Nebr., 1957-71, prof. bus. adminstrn., 1966-71, comptroller, 1957-62, vice chancellor, 1962-68, pres. Lincoln campuses and outstate activities, 1968-71; v.p. Kirkpatrick, Pettis, Smith, Polian, Inc., 1971-73, exec. v.p., 1973-90, chmn. exec. com., 1973-85, also bd. dirs.; investment banking cons. Omaha, 1990—. Contbr. articles to profl. jours. Chmn. Nebr. Commn. Higher Edn. Facilities Act, 1964-71; chmn. Omaha Tomorrow, 1981-82; trustee Nebr. Council Econ. Edn., 1969—, chmn., 1974-75, 83; trustee Nebr. Ednl. TV Council Higher Edn., 1969-71, Omaha Indsl. Found., 1979-91, v.p., 1986-91; trustee U. Nebr. Found., 1978—; mem. higher edn. adv. com. Midwest Regional Conf. Council State Govts., 1963-71; mem. Citizens Adv. Com. Omaha Pub. schs., 1954-57; trustee Lincoln Gen. Hosp. and Lincoln Gen. Hosp. Assn., 1962-71, treas., 1963-67; nat. trustee NCCJ, 1978-83, co-chmn. Midlands exec. bd., 1973-80, bd. govs., 1989—; bd. dirs. Lincoln Hosp. and Health Council, 1962-69, sec. treas., 1962-64; bd. dirs. Lincoln Community Chest, 1963-69, Child Guidance Center, 1960-63, Nebraskans for Pub. TV, 1972-76, Jewish Fedn. Omaha, 1975-78, Father Flanagan's Boys Home, 1978-88, Jr. Achievement Omaha, 1981-83, Met. Arts Council Omaha, 1987—, treas., 1989-93, Nebr. Found. for the Humanities, 1993—; mem. Boys Town Nat. Coun. Friends, 1989—; bd. govs. Omaha Boys' Clubs, 1972-76; mem. Lincoln Found., 1968-71; mem. council bus. execs. Creighton U. Coll. Bus. Adminstrn., 1972-77, chmn., 1973-77; mem. pres.'s council Creighton U., 1973—; trustee Temple Israel, 1973-75, 91-93; mem. citizens assembly United Way Midlands, 1975—; bd. visitors Creighton Inst. Bus., Law and Social Research, 1976-78; mem. pres.'s adv. council U. Nebr., 1977-87; mem. Nebr. Com. for Higher Edn., 1986—; treas., mem. exec. com. St. Joseph Health Care Found., 1982-84; chmn. Leadership Omaha, 1986-88. Served with USNR, 1943-46. Recipient Bus. Leadership award Alumni Assn. U. Nebr., Spl. Charter award Nebr. Council Econ. Edn., Disting. Svc. award; John P. Begley award Creighton U., Alumni Achievement citation Creighton U., Alumni Merit award Creighton U. Mem. Nebr. Assn. Commerce and Industry (dir. 1982-88), Am. Council Edn., Nat. Assn. State Univs. and Land-Grant Colls. (senate joint com. bus. officers 1959-66), Nat. Assn. Coll. and Univ. Bus. Officers, Nebr. Securities Industry Assn. (pres. 1986-87), Greater Omaha C. of C. (bd. dirs. 1980-90, dir. emeritus 1991—, v.p. 1986-88, dir. found. 1985—), Innocents Soc., Highland Country Club, Order of Artus, Beta Gamma Sigma, Alpha Sigma Nu, Pi Lambda Phi, Delta Sigma Pi, Delta Sigma Rho. Home: 834 S 112th Plz Omaha NE 68154-3310

SOSNIK, DOUG, federal government official. Asst. to pres., dir. polit. affairs Office of Dir of Polit Affairs, Washington, 1995—. Office: Office of Dir Polit Affairs 1600 Pennsylvania Ave NW Washington DC 20500

SOSNOW, LAWRENCE IRA, health care company executive; b. Newark, Mar. 7, 1935; s. Emanuel and Edith (Grunt) S.; m. Ellen N. Rosenthal, May 30, 1965; children: Peter, Meg. BBA, Upsala Coll., East Orange, N.J., 1957; postgrad., NYU Grad. Sch. Bus., 1958. Pres. Sosnow & Co., Inc., Newark, 1960-66; chmn., pres. Spade & Archer, N.Y.C., 1966-69; chmn. Gilbert Youth Research, N.Y.C., 1968-69; pres. MIND, Inc., N.Y.C., 1969-74; vice chmn. MIND, Inc., 1974-75; chmn. Patient Care Inc., West Orange, N.J., 1975-95, vice-chmn., 1995—; dir. Home Health Agy. Assembly of N.J., 1985-88; chmn. I.V. Therapy Products, Inc., 1989-92; mem. N.Y. State Dept. Health Adv. Com. on Licensure, 1985-86, Home Care Assn. N.Y. Legis. Commn., 1992—. Bd. govs. Boy's Athletic League, N.Y.C., 1969-85, United Cerebral Palsy No. N.J., 1983-86, McBurney Sch., 1985-86. Served with AUS, 1957, 61-62. Mem. Nat. Assn. Home Care (dir. 1979-82). Home: 850 Park Ave New York NY 10021-1845 Office: 100 Executive Dr West Orange NJ 07052-3309

SOSOKA, JOHN RICHARD, mechanical engineer; b. L.A., Nov. 30, 1929; s. John and Mary (Kovach) S.; m. Audrey T. Trezona, Apr. 26, 1952; children: John Richard Jr., Cathie Ann, Karen Elizabeth. BS in Gen. Engring., UCLA, 1952; MBA, Calif. State U., 1975. Registered profl. engr., Calif. Project engr. Stathem Instrument, L.A., 1954-55; staff engr. Aerojet Gen., Azusa, Calif., 1955-60; tech. dir. Unitek Corp., Monrovia, Calif., 1960-65; staff engr. TRW Systems, Redondo Beach, Calif., 1965-69; engr. mgr. Allen-Jones Electronics, Gardena, Calif., 1969-70; sect. head City of Long Beach, Calif., 1970-79; pres. Sosoka & Assoc.s, Los Alamitos, Calif., 1979-90; exec. v.p. Sparvan, Inc., Long Beach, Calif., 1990-91; pres. PSI Engrs., Inc., Long Beach, Calif., 1991—. Fellow ASHRAE (dir. and regional chair 1990-93, Disting. Svc. award 1988); mem. Assn. Energy Engrs. (v.p. 1980-81, Energy Engr. of Yr. award 1985), Optimists. Republican. Episcopalian. Achievements include patent in Welding. Home: 848 Roxanne Ave Long Beach CA 90815 Office: PSI Engrs Inc 5000 E Spring St #800 Long Beach CA 90815

SOSSAMAN, JAMES J., state legislator; b. Phoenix, July 17, 1932; s. Jasper H. and Faith Carolyn (Mather) S.; m. Carolyn Sue Peters, Dec. 12, 1953; children—Kimberlee, Stephen, Scott. Student, Ariz. State U., 1950-52. Mem. Ariz. Ho. of Reps., 1969-87, majority whip, 1976-84, speaker, 1985-87, senator, 1987-93. Precinct committeeman, 1958—; mem. Queen Creek Sch. Bd., 1965-80. Lt. USN, 1952-56, Korea. Recipient Outstanding Young Farmer award Flying Farmers, 1966, Legislator of Yr. award Ariz. Students' Assn., 1977, 78, Disting. Citizen award U. Ariz., 1979, hon. state farmer degree Future Farmers Am., 1980. Mem. Am. Legis. Exchange Council, Western Conf. Council State Govts., Maricopa County Farm Bur. (pres.), Ariz. Cotton Growers Bd. (agriculturalist for 1986). Republican. Methodist. Home: 19105 E Ocotillo Rd Queen Creek AZ 85242-4077

SOTER, GEORGE NICHOLAS, advertising executive; b. Chgo., May 16, 1924; s. Nicholas A. and Emily (Damascus) S.; m. Effie Hartocollis, Feb. 7, 1949; children: Nicholas, Thomas, Peter. Student, U. Chgo., 1947-51. Writer McCann-Erickson, Chgo., 1951-53; with Needham, Louis & Brorby, Chgo., 1954-62; v.p., creative dir. Needham, Louis & Brorby, N.Y.C., 1958-62; v.p., assoc. creative dir. Lennen & Newell Inc., N.Y.C., 1962-67; v.p., co-dir. creative svcs., mgmt. supr. Kenyon & Eckhardt Inc., N.Y.C., 1968-73; exec. v.p., creative dir. Pampuzac-Soter Assocs. Inc., N.Y.C., 1974-76; sr. writer Marsteller Inc., N.Y.C., 1980-82; v.p., creative Lord, Geller, Federico, Einstein, Inc., N.Y.C., 1982-87; sr. v.p., creative dir. Great Scott Advt. Co. Inc., N.Y.C., 1987-93; dir. Soter Advt. & Mktg. Consulting Svcs., N.Y.C., 1993—; founder, pres. Greek Island Ltd., N.Y.C., 1963—; dir. Interpub. Product Devel. Workshop, N.Y.C., 1967. With U.S. Army, 1943-47, ETO. Home: 404 Riverside Dr New York NY 10025-1861

SOTIR, THOMAS ALFRED, healthcare executive, retired shipbuilder; b. Marlboro, Mass., July 8, 1936; s. Nisi and Pauline Violet (Theodore) S.; m. Sandra Losano, Oct. 2, 1960; children: Laura Jean, Mark Joseph, Christine Marie. BS in Indsl. Engring., Northeastern U., 1959; MBA, Xavier U., Cin., 1966. Employee rels. generalist GE, Cin., 1959-66, mgr. incoming materials, 1966-67, mgr. adminstrn., 1967-68, mgr. employee rels., Arkansas City, Kans., 1968-71, mgr. grievance negotiations, Lynn, Mass., 1971-77; with Electric Boat div. Gen. Dynamics Corp., Groton, Conn., 1977-91, dir. labor rels., 1977-79, v.p. human resources, 1979-89, dir. total quality mgmt., 1989-91; cons. human resources R.A. Flath Assocs., New London, Conn., 1991-92; v.p. human resources Kennebec Health System, Augusta, Maine, 1992—; mem. faculty U. New Haven Bus. Sch., 1979-91; adv. panel job evaluation State of Conn., 1985-91. Trustee, exec. com. Thames Sci. Ctr., New London, Conn., 1987-89; bd. dirs. United Way, Groton, 1979-87. Capt. USAR, 1959-69. Mem. Shipbuilders Coun. Am. (chmn. indsl. rels. com. Washington chpt. 1987-88), Kennebec Valley C. of C. (bd. dirs.), Rotary. Republican. Roman Catholic. Avocations: hunting, fishing, cooking. Home: 21 Sewall St Augusta ME 04330-5531

SOTIRHOS, MICHAEL, ambassador; b. N.Y.C., Nov. 12, 1928; m. Estelle Manos; 2 children. B.B.A., CCNY, 1950. Ptnr. Ariston Sales Co., Ltd., 1948, founder, chmn., 1958—; chmn. bd. Ariston Interior Designers, Inc., 1973-85; U.S. amb. to Jamaica, 1985-89; U.S. amb. to Greece Athens, 1989-93; bd. dirs. Atlantic Bank of N.Y., Alexander S. Onassis Found.; cons. various internat. shipping & pharm. firms. Former mem. Nat. Vol. Service Adv. Council; former chmn. Internat. Ops. Com., Peace Corps; mem. nat. adv. council SBA, 1976; former chmn. Nat. Republican Heritage Groups Council. Decorated comdr. Order of Distinction (Jamaica); recipient Man of Yr. award Nat. Rep. Heritage Groups Coun.

SOTIRIOS OF TORONTO See ATHANASSOULAS, SOTIRIOS

SOTO, JOCK, dancer; b. Gallup, N.M., 1965. Student, Phoenix Sch. Nallet, Sch. Am. Ballet. Mem. corps de ballet N.Y.C. Ballet, 1981-84, soloist, 1984-85, prin. dancer, 1985—. Appeared in The Magic Flute, 1981, Bagaku, The Nutcracker, Mozartiana, Rubies, Symphony in C, The Four Temperaments, Western Symphony, Stravinsky Violin Concerto, Symphony in Three Movements, Cortege Hongrois, Liebeslieder Walzer, A Midsummer Night's Dream, Brahms/Handel, Glass Pieces, Moves, The Four Seasons, In The Night, Opus 19/The Dreamer, I'm Old Fashioned, Delibes Divertissement, A Schubertiad, Concerto for Two Solo Pianos, Celebration, Allegro Brillante, A Schubert Sonata, X-Ray; N.Y.C. Ballet's Balanchine Celebration, 1993. Office: NYC Ballet NY State Theater Lincoln Ctr Plz New York NY 10023

SOTO, RAMONA, training specialist; b. East Chicago, Ind., Apr. 14, 1963; d. Robert Rudy and Antonia (Perez) S. Student, Purdue U., 1982-86, U. Ill., Chgo., 1990, DePaul U., 1992-95. Salesperson The Gap, Inc., Ind.,

1979-84; asst. mgr. The Gap, Inc., Ind. and Ill., 1984-88; tng. mgr. The Gap, Inc., Ill., 1988-90; tng. specialist Montgomery Ward & Co., Ill., 1990-93; temp. worker The Richard Michael Group, Chgo., 1993, Resort Travel Corp, Oakbrook Terrace, Ill., 1993; ind. tng. cons. Chgo., 1994—; tutor tng. mgr. The Cabrini Green Tutoring Program, Chgo., 1991-94, jr. asst. coord., 1995—, tutor Preparing An Attitude for Learning, Leadership and Success, 1991-94, jr. asst. advisor, 1995—. Mem. ASTD. Avocations: fitness, reading, volunteering, cooking, biking. Home: 3550 N Lake Shore Dr Chicago IL 60657-1916

SOTOMAYOR, SONIA, federal judge; b. N.Y.C., June 25, 1954; d. Juan Luis and Celina (Baez) S.; m. Kevin Edward Noonan, Aug. 14, 1976 (div. 1983). AB, Princeton (N.J.) U., 1976; JD, Yale U., 1979. Bar: N.Y. 1980, U.S. Dist. Ct. (ea. and so. dists.) N.Y. 1984. Asst. dist. atty. Office of Dist. Atty. County of N.Y., N.Y.C., 1979-84; assoc., ptnr. Pavia & Harcourt, N.Y.C., 1984-92; fed. judge U.S. Dist. Ct. (so. dist.) N.Y., N.Y.C., 1992—. Editor Yale U. Law Rev., 1979. Bd. dirs. P.R. Legal Def. and Edn. Fund, N.Y.C., 1980-92, State of N.Y. Mortgage Agy., N.Y.C., 1987-92, N.Y.C. Campaign Fin. Bd., 1988-92; mem. State Adv. Panel on Inter-Group Rels., N.Y.C., 1990-91. Mem. Phi Beta Kappa. Office: US Courthouse 500 Pearl St New York NY 10007

SOTOMORA-VON AHN, RICARDO FEDERICO, pediatrician, educator; b. Guatemala City, Guatemala, Oct. 22, 1947; s. Ricardo and Evelyn (Von Ahn) S.; m. Eileen Marie Holcomb, May 9, 1990. M.D., San Carlos U., 1972; M.S. in Physiology, U. Minn., 1978; m. Victoria Monzon, Nov. 26, 1971; children—Marisol, Clarisa, Ricardo, III, Charlotte Marie. Rotating intern Gen. Hosp. Guatemala, 1971-72; pediatric intern U. Ark., 1972-73, resident, 1973-75; fellow in pediatric cardiology U. Minn., 1975-78; research assoc. in cardiovascular pathology United Hosps., St. Paul, 1976; fellow in neonatal-perinatal medicine St. Paul's Children's Hosp., 1977-78, U. Ark., 1981-82; instr. pediatrics U. Minn., 1978-79; pediatric cardiologist, unit cardiovascular surgery Roosevelt Hosp., Guatemala City, 1979-81; asst. prof. pediatrics (cardiology and neonatology), U. Ark., Little Rock, 1981-83; practice medicine specializing in pediatric cardiology-neonatology, 1983—. Diplomate Am. Bd. Pediatrics, Sub-Bd. Pediatric Cardiology, Neonatal-Perinatal Medicine. Fellow Am. Acad. Pediatrics, Am. Coll. Cardiology, Am. Coll. Chest Physicians, Am. Coll. Angiology; mem. AMA, AAAS, Ark. Med. Soc., N.Y. Acad. Scis., Am. Heart Assn., Soc. Pediatric Echocardiography, Guatemala Coll. Physicians and Surgeons, Central Ark. Pediatric Soc., So. Soc. Pediatric Research, Soc. Critical Care Medicine. Clubs: Pleasant Valley Country (Little Rock). Home: 25 River Ridge Cir Little Rock AR 72227 Office: # 5 Office Park Dr Ste 105 Little Rock AR 72211

SOTT, HERBERT, lawyer; b. Detroit, Jan. 26, 1920; s. Harry and E. Helen (Nalven) S.; m. Elaine D. Davidson, Oct. 14, 1987; children by previous marriage; Lesley Sott Geary, Lynne Sott Jackson. A.B., U. Mich., 1940, M.B.A., 1942, J.D. with distinction, 1943. Bar: Mich. 1946. Since practiced in Detroit; ptnr. Friedman, Meyers & Keys, 1951-68; partner Barris, Sott, Denn & Driker, 1968—. Active Founders Soc. Detroit Inst. Arts, Detroit Grand Opera Assn., Detroit Symphony Assn., Detroit Zool. Assn.; bd. dirs. Detroit Symphony Orch., Mich. Heart Assn., Mich. Cancer Found., Jewish Home for Aged, Jewish Family and Children's Service, Jewish Vocat. Service. Served as lt. (j.g.) USNR, 1943-46. Mem. Detroit, Mich., Am. bar assns. Clubs: Detroit, Franklin Hills. Office: Barris Sott Denn & Driker 15th Flr 211 W Fort St Ste 15 Detroit MI 48226-3211

SOTTILE, BENJAMIN JOSEPH, greeting card company executive; b. Bklyn., 1937; s. John and Nicoletta Sottile; m. Ileana Nardone; children: John, Robert. BSEE, U.S. Naval Acad., 1961. With Colgate Palmolive, 1965-68, Vick Chem. co., 1968-69, Warner Lambert, 1969-80, Warner Communications, Inc., 1980-83; sr. v.p. Revlon, Inc., 1983-86; pres., chief operating officer Gibson Greetings, Inc., Cin., 1986, pres. chief exec. officer, 1987, chief exec. officer, pres., chmn. bd., 1989—; also bd. dirs.; bd. dirs. Decker Communications, San Francisco. Bd. govs. USO, Washington, 1989—. Lt. USN, 1961-65. Mem. Nat. Assn. Chain Drug Stores (adv. bd.). Office: Gibson Greetings Inc 2100 Section Rd Cincinnati OH 45237-3510

SOUDER, MARK EDWARD, government official; b. Ft. Wayne, Ind., July 18, 1950; s. Edward Getz and Irma (Fahling) S.; B.S., Ind. U., Ft. Wayne, 1972; M.B.A., U. Notre Dame, 1974; m. Diane Kay Zimmer, July 28; children—Brooke Diane, Nathan Elias. Mgmt. trainee Crossroads Furniture Co., Houston, 1974; mktg. mgr. Gabberts Furniture & Studio, Mpls., 1974-76; mktg. mgr., exec. v.p. Souder's Furniture & Studio, Grabill, Ind., 1976-80, pres., 1981-84; econ. devel. liaison for U.S. Rep. Dan Coats, 1983—; U.S. congressman, Ind. 4th Dist., 1995— . Publicity chmn. Grabill County Fair, 1977—; advisor Dan Coats for Congress Com., 1980-81; mem. Ind. Area Devel. Council; mem. bus. alumni adv. com. Ind. U.-Ft. Wayne. Mem. Midwest Home Furnishings Assn. (dir. 1976-84, past treas., exec. v.p.), Ft. Wayne, Grabill chambers commerce, Allen County Hist. Soc., Alumni Assn. Ind. U. at Ft. Wayne (dir., past pres.), Alumni Assn. U. Notre Dame. Republican. Mem. Apostolic Christian Ch. Home: 13733 Ridgeview Ct Grabill IN 46741 Office: US House Reps 508 Cannon House Office Bldg Washington DC 20515-1404*

SOUDERS, JAMES P., professional association executive; b. Kansas City, Mo., Mar. 17, 1938; s. Harley Hugh and Mabel V. (Duffels) S.; m. Marianne Geier, June 25, 1959 (div. 1984); children: Suzanne Baldwin, Andrew, Matthew, Christopher. BSBA, Rockhurst Coll., 1959. Commd. officer U.S. Marine Corps., 1959-79; asst. exec. dir. Assn. Records, Mgrs., Adminstrs., Prairie Village, Kans., 1979-87; exec. dir. Assn. Records, Mgrs., Adminstrs., Prarie Village, Kans., 1987—. Lt. col. USMC, 1955-79. Republican. Roman Catholic. Avocations: hunting, fishing. Office: Assoc of Records Managers & Adminstrn 4200 Somerset Dr Ste 215 Prairie Village KS 66208

SOUHAM, GÉRARD, communications executive; b. Paris, May 30, 1928; s. Lucien and Mary-Françoise (Husson) S.; m. Eliane Meyrat, June 23, 1951; children: Glenn (dec.), Yan, Philip. Diploma, Am. Community Sch., Paris, 1948; cert., Ecole Commerciale de Paris. Chargé de mission State Dept., Europe, 1950-52; pub. info. officer Allied Air Forces NATO, Fontainebleau, 1953-55; chmn. bd., chief exec. officer J. Walter Thompson, Paris, 1955-75; v.p. J. Walter Thompson, N.Y.C., 1970-75; prin. SC3 Gerard Souham Group Communication Cos., Paris and Lausanne, Switzerland, 1975—, N.Y.C., 1979—; bd. dirs. Am. Overseas Meml., I.T. Fin., AVON, France; bd. dirs. Turner Prodn. S.A., chmn., 1994—; chmn. bd. Turner Prodn. Europe, 1994. Author: Général Souham Comte de l'Empire, 1964, Impressions sur..., 1970, Souham, 1989, Sur les Champs de Bataille de la Révolution et de l'Empire, 1990. Mem. pvt. sector internat. and pub. rels. coms. USIA, 1985; mem. world bd. govs. USO, Washington, 1984, chmn. fundraising com., 1989—, pres., Paris, 1995. Decorated Knight of Legion of Honor (France); Officer Order of Leopold (Belgium), Knight of Belgian Crown. Mem. Internat. Advt. Assn. (v.p. pub. svc., bd. dirs.), Internat. Inst. Strategic Studies London, France, USA (bd. dirs.), Am. Overseas Meml. Assn. (bd. dirs. 1988—). Roman Catholic. Clubs: HM Guards Polo (Windsor, Eng.) (life); Polo de Bagatelle (Paris); N.Y. Athletic; Yacht of Monaco. Avocation: collecting fine bindings. Office: Souham Group Comm 500 5th Ave New York NY 10110

SOUJAH, JAKE, investment company executive; b. Beirut, Lebanon, Mar. 11, 1954; came to U.S., 1984; s. Atif M. and Mona Aida (Ashkar) S. BS, Am. U. Beirut, 1976; MBA, George Washington U., 1986. V.p. sales Arapco Internat., Inc., Beirut, 1976-81, Arapco Ltd., Inc., Riyadh, Saudi Arabia, 1981-84; exec. v.p, coo Aramnet Internat., Inc., Washington, 1986-91; chmn., ceo Orca Holdings Inc., San Francisco, 1990—; ceo Ivan Holdings Co., San Francisco, 1992—; bd. dirs. Personal Image Inc., San Rafael, Calif., Centauri Comms., Inc., San Francisco, K. Lee Internat. Corp., San Francisco. Avocations: birdwatching, skiing, sailing. Office: Ivan Holdings Co 350 Townsend St Ste 250 San Francisco CA 94107

SOULE, CHARLES EVERETT, insurance executive; b. Middleboro, Mass., June 7, 1934; s. Albert Foster and Alberta Nancy (Soule) S.; m. Elna Louise Eayrs, Sept. 4, 1955; children: Kimberly, Charles, Jonathan, Peter. BA, Dartmouth Coll., 1956. Underwriter Paul Revere, Worcester, Mass., 1956-68; 2d v.p. Paul Revere, Worcester, 1968-72, v.p., 1972-78, sr. v.p., 1978-84, exec. v.p., 1984-91; pres., CEO Paul Revere Corp., Worcester, Paul Revere Life Ins. Co., Worcester, Paul Revere Protective Life Ins. Co., Worcester, Paul Revere Variable Annuity Ins. Co., Worcester, 1991—; bd. dirs. New Eng. Electric System, Westboro, Mass. Author: Disability Income Insurance-The Unique Risk, 1984, 2d edit., 1989, 3d edit., 1994. Bd. dirs. Worcester Bus. Devel. Corp., 1988—, Worcester Found. for Exptl. Biology, Shrewsbury, Mass., 1992—; chmn. Worcester C. of C., 1987-88. Fellow Life Office Mgmt. Assn. Republican. Avocations: reading, running. Home: 50 Oneil Dr Westboro MA 01581-3008 Office: Paul Revere Corp 18 Chestnut St Worcester MA 01608-1528

SOULE, GARDNER BOSWORTH, writer; b. Paris, Tex., Dec. 16, 1913; s. Edgar Huckabee and Floy DeVore (Perfect) S.; m. Janie Lee McDowell, Sept. 20, 1940 (dec.); m. Mary Muir Downing, Apr. 23, 1994. B.A., Rice Inst., 1933; B.S., Columbia U., 1935, M.S., 1936. With A.P., N.Y.C., 1936-41, Newspaper PM, 1942; mng. editor Better Homes and Gardens, Des Moines, 1946-50. Free-lance writer articles, books, N.Y.C., 1950—; Author: The Maybe Monsters, 1963, Tomorrow's World of Science, 1963, Gemini and Apollo, 1964, The Mystery Monsters, 1965, Trail of the Abominable Snowman, 1966, The Ocean Adventure: Science Explores the Depths of the Sea, 1966, Sea Rescue, 1966, UFO's and IFO's, 1967, Undersea Frontiers, 1968, Under the Sea, 1969, Strange Things Animals Do, 1970, Wide Ocean, 1970, The Greatest Depths, 1970, Surprising Facts, 1971, New Discoveries in Oceanography, 1974, Wide Ocean, Brit. edit, 1974, Remarkable Creatures of the Seas, 1975, Men Who Dared The Sea: The Ocean Adventures of the Ancient Mariners, 1976, German edit., 1978, The Long Trail: How Cowboys and Longhorns Opened The West, 1976, Mystery Monsters of the Deep, 1981, Mystery Creatures of the Jungle, 1982, Antarctica, 1985, Christopher Columbus, 1988; Contbr.: articles to mags. including Boys' Life. Served to lt. USNR, 1943-46. Mem. Authors League, Columbia University Club (N.Y.C.), Sigma Delta Chi, Sigma Nu. Address: 85 River Rd Apt I3 Essex CT 06426-1343

SOULE, GEORGE ALAN, literature educator; b. Fargo, N.D., Mar. 3, 1930; s. George Alan and Ruth Georgia (Knudsen) S.; m. Carolyn Richards, Nov. 24, 1961; 1 child, Katherine. BA, Carleton Coll., 1947; postgrad., Corpus Christi Coll., Cambridge (Eng.) U., 1952-53; MA, Yale U., 1956, PhD, 1960. Instr. English lit. Oberlin (Ohio) Coll., 1958-60; asst. prof. U. Wis., Madison, 1960-62; from asst. prof. to prof. Carleton Coll., Northfield, Minn., 1962-95, prof. emeritus, 1995—, dir. Centennial, 1965-67; chair English dept. Carleton Coll., Northfield, 1980-83; dir. summer writing program Carleton Coll., Northfield, Minn., 1980-86; cons. Ednl. Testing Svc., Princeton, N.J., 1967-84, 94—. Editor (book) Theatre of the Mind, 1974; contbr. articles, revs. to profl. jours. With U.S. Army, 1954-55. Internat. fellow Rotary, 1952-53, Sterling pre-doctoral fellow Yale U., 1957-58. Mem. Johnson Soc. of Lichfield, Boswell Soc. of Auchinleck, Friends of Dove Cottage, The Charles Lamb Soc., Rotary. Episcopalian. Avocations: cooking, traveling, Jeopardy (Champion Sr. Tournament 1990). Home: 313 Nevada St Northfield MN 55057-2346 Office: Carleton Coll 1 N College St Northfield MN 55057-4001

SOULE, ROBERT D., safety and health educator, administrator; b. DeTour Village, Mich., July 8, 1941; s. Harold M. and Mildred M. (Abear) S.; m. Mary Ann Kretzschmar, June 13, 1964; children: Dawn Marie, Robert John, Rebecca Leigh. BS, Mich. State U., 1963; MS in Chem. Engring., Purdue U., 1965; EdD in Higher Edn. Adminstrn., U. Pitts., 1993. Cert. safety profl. cert in indsl. hygiene; registered profl. engr., Mich., Ind., Tex. Calif. Environ. health engr. Dow Chem. Co., Midland, Mich., 1965-69; sr. indsl. hygienist Dow Chem. Co., Freeport, Tex., 1969-70; v.p. Clayton Environ. Cons., Southfield, Mich., 1970-77; prof. safety and health Indiana U. of Pa., 1977—; cons. in pvt. practice, Indiana, Pa., 1977—. Contbr. chpts. to books; mem. editorial bd. Am. Indsl. Hygiene Assn. Jour., 1979-85, Occupational Hazards, 1992—. Fellow Am. Indsl. Hygiene Assn.; mem. Am. Conf. Govtl. Indsl. Hygienists, Am. Soc. Safety Engrs. (profl.), Am. Acad. Indsl. Hygiene (sec.-treas.). Office: Indiana U Pa Dept Safety Scis 117 Johnson Hall Indiana PA 15705

SOULE, SALLIE THOMPSON, retired state official; b. Detroit, May 13, 1928; d. Hayward Stone and Elizabeth Robinson Thompson; A.B., Smith Coll., 1950; M.A., U. Vt., Burlington, 1952; m. Gardner Northup Soule, July 26, 1958; stepchildren: Gardner Northup, Nancy Soule Brown; children: Sarah Goodwin, Trumbull Dickson. Sec. trade sales dept. Macmillan Pub. Co., N.Y.C., 1952-57; tech. writer sales svc. div. Eastman Kodak Co., Rochester, N.Y., 1957-58; feature writer Brighton-Pittsford Post, Pittsford, N.Y., 1958-68; v.p., gen. mgr. F. H. Horsford Nursery, Inc., Charlotte, Vt., 1968-76; ptnr., pres. Bygone Books, Inc., Burlington, Vt., 1978—; mem. Vt. Ho. of Reps., 1976-80, mem. ways and means com., 1976-80; mem. Vt. Senate, 1980-84, mem. appropriation com., energy and natural resources com. 1980-84; commr. Vt. Dept. Employment and Tng., Montpelier, 1985-88; chmn. Vt. Employment Security Bd., 1985-88.

SOURKES, THEODORE LIONEL, biochemistry educator; b. Montreal, Que., Can., Feb. 21, 1919; s. Irving and Fannie (Golt) S.; m. Shena Rosenblatt, Jan. 17, 1943; children: Barbara, Myra. B.Sc., McGill U., 1939, M.Sc. magna cum laude, 1946; Ph.D., Cornell U., 1948; D.U. honoris causa, U. Ottawa, Can., 1990. Asst. prof. pharmacology Georgetown U. Med. Sch., 1948-50; research asso. dept. enzyme chemistry Merck Inst. Therapeutic Research, Rahway, N.J., 1950-53; sr. research biochemist Allan Meml. Inst., Montreal, 1953-65; dir. lab. neurochemistry Allan Meml. Inst. Psychiatry, 1965—; mem. faculty McGill U., Montreal, 1954—; prof. biochemistry McGill U., 1965—, prof. psychiatry, assoc. dean of medicine for research Faculty Medicine, 1972-75; prof. pharmacology, 1990—, emeritus, 1991; Mem. Que. Med. Research Council, 1971-77; sr. fellow Parkinson's Disease Found., N.Y.C., 1963-66; assoc. mem. McGill Ctr. for Medicine, Ethics and Law, 1991. Author: Biochemistry of Mental Disease, 1962, Nobel Prize Winners in Medicine and Physiology, 1901-1965, 1967. Decorated Officer Order of Canada. Fellow Royal Soc. Can.; mem. Canadian Biochem. Soc., Pharmacol. Soc. Can., Canadian Coll. Neuropsychopharmacology (Heinz Lehmann award 1982, medal 1990), Am. Soc. Biol. Chemists, Am. Soc. Pharmacology and Exptl. Therapeutics, Am. Soc. Neurochemistry, Internat. Soc. Neurochemistry, Internat. Brain Research Orgn., Venezuelan Order Andrés Bello, Sigma Xi. Research and publs. on drugs for treatment high blood pressure; 1st basic research on methyldopa; elucidation of role of dopamine and other monamines in nervous system; first trials of L-dopa in Parkinson's disease, biochemistry of mental depression, pathways of stress in the nervous system, imaging serotonin in brain, history of biochemistry. Home: 3033 Sherbrooke St W # 303, Montreal, PQ Canada H3Z 1A3

SOURS, JAMES KINGSLEY, association executive, former college president; b. Corydon, Iowa, Sept. 16, 1925; s. James N. and Virginia (Kantor) S.; m. Alice Hyde, July 11, 1947; children—James W., Mary Jan. David Bryan. Student, Phillips U., 1943; B.A., U. Wichita, 1949; M.P.A. (Administration fellow 1949-51), Harvard, 1951, Ph.D., 1954. Adminstrv. aid City Mgr.'s Office, Wichita, 1947-49; mem. faculty Wichita State U., 1951-65; prof. polit. sci., head dept., 1958-62; dean Fairmount Coll. Arts and Scis., 1962-65; chmn. Fairmount Coll. Arts and Scis. (Center Urban Studies), 1957-63; pres. So. Oreg. State Coll., Ashland, 1969-79; ednl. cons. Dankook U., Seoul, 1979-80, dir. Inst. Asian Studies and Cultures, 1990—; ednl. cons. Korean Ministry Edn., 1979-80; exec. v.p. Am. Coll. Testing Program, Iowa City, 1965-68; vis. prof. polit. sci. U. Istanbul, Turkey, 1968-69; vis. prof. Dankook U., Seoul, Korea, 1976, 79-80; dir. devel. Oreg. Shakespearean Festival Assn., 1980-85; v.p., bd. dirs. Dankook U. Am., 1990—; bd. dirs. Oreg. Partnership for Internat. Edn., Internat. Wildlife Recovery Ctr., Eagle Point, Oreg., Rogue Valley Manor Found.; chmn. bd. dirs. Aletheia Psycho-Phys. Found., 1988—. Author: series Some Observations on the Management of Large Cities, 1957; also numerous articles. V.p. NCAA, 1959-64; founding pres. Urban League Wichita, 1953-56, Wichita City Commn. Human Rels., 1962; trustee Carpenter Found., 1983-87, v.p., 1984-87; chmn. Sedgwick County chpt. ARC, 1964, Jackson County chpt., 1973-75; bd. dirs. So. Oreg. Hist. Soc., 1987-89; mem. Oreg. Am. Revolution Bicentennial Commn., 1972-76; chmn. com. nursing edn. Wesley Med. Ctr., Wichita, 1962-64. Served with USNR, 1943-46. Democrat. Unitarian. Home: 3100 Payne Rd Medford OR 97504-9407

SOUSA, JOSEPH PHILIP, secondary education educator; b. Azores, Portugal, May 26, 1943; s. Agostinho and Emilia Augusta (Freitas) S.; m. Filomena Alice Castro, Apr. 1, 1967 (div. Aug. 1983); children: Yvette Marie, John Philip. BA in Math., San Jose State U., 1981. Cert. tchr., Calif., Ga.; ordained priest Cath. and Apostolic Ch. of Antioch, 1989, bishop, 1991. Tchr. math. Milpitas (Calif.) Unified Sch. Dist., 1981-93, mentor tchr., 1989-91; tchr. Cobb County Sch. Dist., 1993, South San Francisco Unified Sch. Dist., 1994—; advisor math. engring. and sci. achievement San Jose (Calif.) State U., 1982—; cons. math. Coll. Bd., 1986-88. With USAR, 1965-83. Mem. NEA, Nat. Coun. Tchrs. Math., Calif. Tchrs. Assn., Calif. Union Portuguese (pres. 1984), Irmandade Divino Espirito Santo (sec. 1982-85). Avocations: collecting stamps, soccer, meditation, Tai-Chi, Regenesis. Home: 4349 La Cosa Ave Fremont CA 94536-4721

SOUTAR, CHARLES FREDERICK, utilities executive; b. N.Y.C., 1936. BCE, Poly. Inst. Bklyn., 1958, MCE, 1965. Engr. Consol. Edison N.Y., N.Y.C., 1958-75, asst. pres., 1975-77, v.p. cen. services, 1977-80, sr. v.p. constrn. engring. environ. affairs, 1980-85, exec. v.p. cen. services, 1985—. Office: Consol Edison Co NY Inc 4 Irving Pl New York NY 10003-3502*

SOUTAS-LITTLE, ROBERT WILLIAM, mechanical engineer, educator; b. Oklahoma City, Feb. 25, 1933; s. Harry Glenn and Mary Evelyn (Miller) Little; m. Patricia Soutas, Sept. 3, 1982; children: Deborah, Catherine, Colleen, Jennifer, Karen. B.S. in Mech. Engring, Duke U., 1955; M.S., U. Wis., 1959, Ph.D., 1962. Design engr. Allis Chalmers Mfg. Co., Milw., 1955-57; instr. mech. engring. Marquette U., 1957-59; instr. U. Wis., Madison, 1959-62; asst. prof. U. Wis., 1962-63, Okla. State U., 1963-65; prof. Mich. State U., 1965—, chmn. dept. mech. engring., 1972-77, chmn. dept. biomechanics, 1977-90; dir. biomechanics evaluation lab., 1989—; Cons. A. C. Electronics Co., Ford Motor Co., CBS Research Lab., B. F. Goodrich Co.; lectr. AID, India, 1965. Author: Elasticity, 1973; Contbr. articles to profl. jours. Vice pres. Okemos (Mich.) Sch. Bd., 1967-72; mem. Meridian Twp. (Mich.) Charter Commn., 1969-70, Meridian Twp. Zoning Bd. Appeals, 1969-71. Recipient award for excellence in instrn. engring. students Western Electric Co., 1970-71, Disting. Faculty award, 1996; NSF grantee, 1964-69, 79, NIH grantee, 1973-75, 79—. Mem. ASME, Soc. Engring. Sci., Am. Soc. Biomechanics, Internat. Soc. Biomechanics, N.Am. Soc. Clin. Gait and Movement Analysis, Sigma Xi, Pi Tau Sigma, Ta Beta Pi. Home: 2402 Hulett Rd Okemos MI 48864-2512 Office: Mich State U Dept Matls Sci Mechani East Lansing MI 48824

SOUTER, DAVID HACKETT, United States supreme court justice; b. Melrose, Mass., Sept. 17, 1939; s. Joseph Alexander and Helen Adams (Hackett) S. BA, Harvard U., 1961, LLB, 1966; Rhodes scholar, Oxford U., 1961-63, MA, 1989. Bar: N.H. Assoc. firm Orr & Reno, Concord, 1966-68; asst. atty. gen. N.H., 1968-71, dep. atty. gen., 1971-76, atty. gen., 1976-78; assoc. justice Superior Ct. N.H., 1978-83, N.H. Supreme Ct., 1983-90; judge U.S. Ct. Appeals (1st cir.) N.H., 1990; assoc. justice U.S. Supreme Ct., Washington, 1990—. Trustee Concord Hosp., 1973-85, pres. bd. trustees, 1978-84; bd. overseers Dartmouth Med. Sch., 1981-87. Mem. N.H. Bar Assn., N.H. Hist. Soc. (v.p. 1980-85, trustee 1976-85), Phi Beta Kappa. Republican. Episcopalian.

SOUTER, ROBERT TAYLOR, retired banker; b. Melrose, Mass., Feb. 17, 1909; s. Walter Wilson and Mary (Taylor) S.; m. Barbara P. Claybourne, Sept. 7, 1935; children—Scott C., Pamela (Mrs. Darroll Hanssen). Student, Harvard, 1934. Treas. Braintree Coop. Bank, Mass., 1937-42; v.p. U.S. Savs. and Loan League, 1942-47; v.p., dir. Coast Fed. Savs. & Loan Assn., Los Angeles, 1947-55; pres., dir. World Savs. and Loan Assn., Oakland, Calif., 1955-86. Republican. Methodist. Home: 4 Windsor Dr Burlingame CA 94010-6359

SOUTH, FRANK EDWIN, physiologist, educator; b. Norfolk, Nebr., Sept. 20, 1924; s. Frank Edwin and Gladys (Brinkman) S.; m. Berna Deane Phyllis Casebolt, June 23, 1946; children: Frank Edwin, Robert Christopher. AB, U. Calif., Berkeley, 1949, PhD, 1952. Asst. prof. physiology U. P.R. Sch. Medicine, 1953-54, U. Ill. Coll. Medicine, 1954-61; asso. prof. Colo. State U., 1961-62, prof., 1962-65; prof. U. Mo., 1965-76; prof., dir. Sch. Life and Health Scis., U. Del., Newark, 1976-82; prof. emeritus U. Del., Newark, 1989, Sch. Life and Health Scis., U. Del., Newark, 1989—; mem. governing bd., dir. Hibernation Info. Exchange, 1959—. Mem. editorial bd. Cryobiology, 1989; contbr. numerous articles on physiology of hibernation, temperature regulation, renal function, marine mammals, artificial atmospheres, and sleep to profl. jours. Bd. dirs. Del. Lung Assn., 1976-82, Del. Cancer Network, 1977-82; mem. research com. Del. Heart Assn., 1977-82; mem. N.E. regional research com. Am. Heart Assn.; mem. med. adv. bd. A.I. DuPont Inst., Wilmington, Del., 1978-83. Served with AUS, 1943-45. Decorated Purple Heart with oak leaf cluster, Bronze Star with oak leaf cluster, Pres. unit citation, Croix de Guerre (unit); NIH career devel. awardee, 1961-65; recipient European African Mid East campaign medal with bronze spear head and silver star, World War II victory medal, Army of Occupation medal with Germany clasp, combat med. badge. Fellow AAAS, Sigma Xi; mem. Am. Physiol. Soc., Soc. Hist. Preservation. Episcopalian. Clubs: Ranger Battalions Assn. World War II, Marathon Yacht Club.

SOUTHALL, IVAN FRANCIS, author; b. Melbourne, Victoria BNA, Australia, June 8, 1921; s. Francis Gordon and Rachel Elizabeth (Voutier) S.; m. Joy Blackburn, Sept. 8, 1945; children—Andrew John, Roberta Joy, Elizabeth Rose, Melissa Frances; m. Susan Helen Westerlund, Nov. 11, 1976. Ed., pub. schs., Victoria. Free-lance writer, 1947—. Author over 60 books in 22 langs., including: Ash Road, 1965 (Book of Yr. 1966), To the Wild Sky, 1967 (Book of Yr. 1968), Bread and Honey, 1970 (Book of Yr. 1971), Josh, 1971 (Carnegie medal 1971), Fly West, 1975 (Book of Yr. 1976), The Long Night Watch, 1983 (Nat. Children's Book award 1986). Found. pres. Knoxbrooke Day Tng. Centre for Intellectually Handicapped, Victoria, 1967-69. Served as flight lt. Royal Australian Air Force, 1942-47, Europe. Decorated D.F.C., RAF, Order Australia; recipient emeritus fellowship award Australia Coun., 1993. Methodist. Home: PO Box 25, Healesville, 3777 Victoria Australia Office: Farrar Straus & Giroux Inc 19 Union Sq W New York NY 10003-3307

SOUTHAN, ARTHUR, insurance company executive. Pres. Care Am. So. Calif., Chatsworth, Calif., 1988—. Office: Care Am So Calif 6300 Canoga Ave Woodland Hills CA 91367*

SOUTHARD, BILL, public relations executive; b. Passaic, N.J., May 8, 1957. BA in Comms. and Journalism, Seton Hall U., 1979. Asst. A/E Ardrey, 1980-81; A/E Ardrey, Inc., 1981-82; mgr. pub. rels. ApolloTechs., 1982; A/E Dorf., 1982-83; sr. A/E Dorf/MJH, 1983-84; A/S D & S, 1984-86; sr. v.p. Dorf & Stanton, 1986-88; exec. v.p. and gen. mgr. Dorf & Stanton Comms., 1988-92; pres. N.Y. Earle Palmer Brown Pub. Rels., 1992-94., Southard Communications, N.Y.C., 1995—. Mem. Am. Agricultural Editors Assn., Nat. Agricultural Mktg. Assn., Pub. Rels. Soc. Am. Office: Southard Communications 24 E 23rd St 6th Fl New York NY 10010*

SOUTHARD, WILLIAM G., lawyer; b. Toledo, Ohio, May 6, 1953; s. James Theodore and Dorothy (Fergusson) S.; m. Martha Donelan, Aug. 14, 1976; children: Abigail, Margaret, Michael. BA, Williams Coll., 1975; JD, Columbia U., 1978. Bar: Ill. 1978, U.S. Dist. Ct. Ill. 1979, Mass. 1981, U.S. Dist. Ct. Mass. 1981, U.S. Ct. Appeals (1st cir.) 1985. Assoc. Schiff Hardin & Waite, Chgo., 1978-81; assoc. Bingham, Dana & Gould, Boston, 1981-85, ptnr., 1985—; dep. chmn. litigation, 1994—. Assoc. editor Columbia Jour. Transnat. Law, 1978; contbr. articles to profl. jours. Mem. ABA, ASTM, Boston Bar Assn. Office: Bingham Dana & Gould 150 Federal St Boston MA 02110-1745

SOUTHARD-RITTER, MARCIA, nursing administrator; b. Cape Girardeau, Mo., Dec. 12, 1942; d. Leebert Melton and Katherine Louise (Goslin) Loyd; m. C. John Ritter, Dec. 20, 1986; children: Robin Hacket, Emilie Clardy, Stephen Southard, Benjamin Ritter, Daniel Southard. Diploma, Jewish Hosp. Sch. Nursing, St. Louis, 1963; BS in Health Care Adminstrn., St. Joseph Coll., North Windham, Maine, 1984; MS in Health Sci. Adminstrn., Cen. Mich. U., 1986. RN, Mo.; cert. nursing adminstr., healthcare exec.; lic. nursing home adminstr. Head nurse, staff nurse S.E. Mo. Hosp., Cape Girardeau, 1963-69; cardiovascular nurse Internal Medicine Group, Cape Girardeau, 1969-72; staff nurse, head nurse St. Francis Hosp., Cape Girardeau, 1972-76, dir. critical care, 1976-82, dir.

patient care adminstrv. svcs., 1982, v.p. patient care, 1982—. Contbr. articles to profl. jours. Mem. NAFE, AACN, ANA, Mo. Nurses Assn., Am. Coll. Health Care Execs., Am. Orgn. Nurse Execs. Office: St Francis Med Ctr 211 Saint Francis Dr Cape Girardeau MO 63703-5049

SOUTHERLAND, S. DUANE, manufacturing company executive; b. Durham, N.C., Apr. 24, 1949; s. Sydney Duane and Beatrice Marie (Carver) S.; m. Linda F. Lewis, Jan. 5, 1974, 1 child, S. Duane III. BSE, Duke U., 1971, MS in Engring., 1973, MBA, 1974. Ops. analyst Cooper Group Div. Cooper Industries, Apex, N.C., 1974-78; planning analyst Cooper Industries, Houston, 1978-81; dir. fin. Cooper Electronics Div. Cooper Industries, Nashua, N.H., 1981-83; gen. mgr. Conn. ops. Kirsch Div. Cooper Industries, Beacon Falls, Conn., 1983-87; pres. Kirsch Div. Cooper Industries, Sturgis, Mich., 1987-94; pres., CEO Conso Products Co., Union, S.C., 1995—. Republican. Baptist.

SOUTHERLIN, KENNETH GOWAN, principal; b. Greenville, S.C., May 29, 1950; s. William Bates and Nancy Ellen (Hightower) S.; m. Donna Elizabeth Sloan, Aug. 8, 1971; children: Kenneth Gowan Jr., Krystal Danielle. AA, North Greenville Coll., 1969; BS, Clemson U., 1971, MA, 1973. Tchr. James F. Byrnes H.S., Duncan, S.C., 1971-72; tchr. Blue Ridge H.S., Greer, S.C., 1972-74, asst. prin., 1974-77, prin., 1977—; budget com. The Sch. of Greenville, 1993, sch. to work com., 1994. Mem. Tigerville Vol. Fire Dept., 1978-79, commr., 1979-84; mem. Blue Ridge Ruritan, Greer, 1974—; mem. Locust Hill Bapt. Ch., 1985—; chmn. Locust Hill Bapt. Ch., 1994, deacons, 1994, fin. com., 1994. Named Outstanding Educator First Union Corp., 1994. Mem. ASCD, Assn. of Secondary Prins., Phi Delta Kappa. Home: 441 N Southerlin Rd Taylors SC 29687-7036 Office: Blue Ridge HS 2151 Fews Chapel Rd Greer SC 29651

SOUTHERN, HUGH, performing arts consultant; b. Newcastle-on-Tyne, Eng., Mar. 20, 1932; came to U.S., 1955; s. Norman and Phyllis Margaret (Hiller) S.; m. Jane Rosemary Llewellyn, Dec. 18, 1954 (div.); children: Hilary, William Norman; m. Kathy Ayers Dwyer, Dec. 10, 1989; 1 child, Jaime Andres. B.A., King's Coll., Cambridge, Eng., 1956. Assoc. account exec. Fuller & Smith & Ross, N.Y.C., 1956-58; treas. Westport Country Playhouse Conn., 1958; adminstrv. mgr. Theatre Guild-Am. Theatre Soc., N.Y.C., 1959-62; asst. dir. Repertory Theatre, Lincoln Ctr., N.Y.C., 1962-65; gen. mgr. Nat. Repertory Theatre, N.Y.C., 1965-67; mgmt. assoc. San Francisco Opera, 1967-68; exec. dir. Theatre Devel. Fund, N.Y.C., 1968-82; dep. chmn. programs Nat. Endowment for Arts, Washington, 1982-89, acting chmn., 1989; gen. mgr. Met. Opera Assn. Inc., N.Y.C., 1989-90; dir. Va. Festival of Am. Film, Charlottesville, Va., 1995-96; acting dir. performing arts program N.Y. State Council on Arts, N.Y.C., 1974-75, acting exec. dir., 1976; dir. New Dramatists, N.Y.C., 1978-82, Film Forum, N.Y.C., 1978-82; trustee Actor's Fund Am., N.Y.C., 1978-85. Trustee Manhattan Country Sch., N.Y.C., 1970-82, chmn., 1971-74; mem. Mayor's Com. on Cultural Policy, N.Y.C., 1974-75; dir. Vol. Cons. Group, Inc., N.Y.C., 1976-82, 92—. Home: PO Box 68 Montpelier Station VA 22957-0068

SOUTHERN, ROBERT ALLEN, lawyer; b. Independence, Mo., July 17, 1930; s. James Allen and Josephine (Ragland) S.; m. Cynthia Agnes Drews, May 17, 1952; children: David D., William A., James M., Kathryn S. O'Brien. B.S. in Polit. Sci., Northwestern U., 1952, LL.B., 1954. Bar: Ill. 1955. Assoc. Mayer, Brown & Platt, Chgo., 1954-64, ptnr., 1965—, mng. ptnr., 1978-91; mng. ptnr. Mayer, Brown & Platt, L.A., 1991—. Editor in chief Northwestern U. Law Rev., 1953-54. Trustee, v.p., gen. counsel LaRabida Children's Hosp. and Rsch. Ctr., Chgo., 1974-89; trustee Kenilworth (Ill.) Union Ch., 1980-88; pres. Joseph Sears Sch. Bd., 1977-79; trustee Rush-Presbyn.-St. Luke's Med. Ctr., 1983-91, life trustee, 1991—; bd. dirs. Boys and Girls Clubs Chgo., 1986-91; governing mem. Orchestral Assn. Chgo., 1988-93. With U.S. Army, 1955-57. Mem. ABA, Chgo. Bar Assn., Law Club Chgo., Legal Club Chgo., Econ. Club Chgo., Order of Coif, Indian Hill Club, Chgo. Club, City Club on Bunker Hill (L.A.). Office: Mayer Brown & Platt 350 S Grand Ave Ste 25 Los Angeles CA 90071-1503

SOUTHERN, RONALD D., diversified corporation executive; b. Calgary, Alta., Can., July 25, 1930; s. Samuel Donald and Alexandra (Cuthill) S.; m. Margaret Visser, July 30, 1954; children: Nancy, Linda. BSc, U. Alta., Edmonton, 1953; LLD (hon.), U. Calgary, 1976, U. Alberta, 1991. Pres., CEO ATCO Ltd., Calgary, 1954-85, dep. chmn., CEO, 1985-91, chmn., pres., CEO, 1985-93; chmn., CEO ATCO Ltd. and Can. Utilities Ltd., Calgary, 1994—, ATCO Ltd., Calgary, 1994—, Can. Utilities Ltd., Calgary, 1994—; chmn. Akita Drilling Ltd.; bd. dirs. Fletcher Challenge Can. Ltd., Can. Airlines Corp., Can. Pacific Ltd., Chrysler Can. Ltd., IMASCO Ltd., LaFarge, Royal Ins. Ltd., Xerox of Can. Inc., Fletcher Challenge Ltd., New Zealand; co-chmn. Spruce Meadows Tournaments. Recipient Holland Trade award Gov. of The Netherlands, 1985, (with wife) Sportsmen of Yr. award Calgary Booster Club, Internat., Disting. Entrepreneur award U. Man. Faculty Mgmt., 1990; inducted into Can. Bus. Hall, 1995; named Businessman of Yr. U. Alta., 1986, to Order of Can. Brit. Empire, 1986, Comdr. Brit. Empire, 1995. Mem. Ranchmen's Club. Calgary Golf and Country Club. Home: 67 Massey Pl SW, Calgary, AB Canada T2V 2G7 Office: ATCO Ltd & Can Utilities Ltd, 1600 909-11 Ave SW, Calgary, AB Canada T2R 1N6

SOUTHWARD, GLEN MORRIS, statistician, educator; b. Boise, Idaho, Oct. 8, 1927; s. Glen P. and Emma M. (Martin) S.; m. M. Louise Kissack, Oct. 3, 1974; children from previous marriage: Judith Ann, Richard Todd. BS, U. Wash., 1949, MS, 1956, PhD, 1966. Asst. prof. Stats. Wash. State U., Pullman, 1967-71; biometrician Internat. Pacific Halibut Commn., Seattle, 1971-75; assoc. prof. stats. N.Mex. State U., Las Cruces, 1975-80, prof., 1980-93, prof. emeritus, 1993—. Contbr. articles to profl. jours. Fellow Am. Inst. Fishery Research Biologists; mem. Am. Statis. Assn., Biometric Soc. (sec., treas. Western N.Am. region 1984-91), Sigma Xi. Avocations: photography, cooking. Office: NMex State U Dept Exptl Stats PO Box 30003 Las Cruces NM 88003-8003

SOUTHWAY, PETER, bank holding company executive; b. 1935. Pres., COO Valley Nat. Bancorp, Wayne, N.J., 1952—. Office: Valley Nat Bancorp 1445 Valley Rd Wayne NJ 07470-2088 also: 505 Allwood Rd Clifton NJ 07012-2160

SOUTHWELL, LEONARD J., dairy corporation executive; b. Sioux City, Iowa, Nov. 9, 1924; s. George P. and Nellie (Van Houten) S.; m. Rosemary Kathern Kirsch, June 9, 1951; children: George, Christine, John. BS in Dairy Ind., Iowa State U., 1951. Mgr. Equity Creamery, Pana, Ill., 1951-64; sales mgr. Prairie Farms Dairy, Carlinville, Ill., 1964-72, asst. gen. mgr., 1972-80, chief oper. officer, 1980-88, chief exec. officer, 1988—; bd. dirs. Milk Industry Found. With USN, 1943-46. Mem. Elks, Masons, Shrine, Consistory. Home: 1000 S Hickory St Pana IL 62557-1928 Office: Prairie Farms Dairy Inc PO Box 560 Carlinville IL 62626-0499*

SOUTHWICK, ARTHUR FREDERICK, legal educator; b. Pitts., Nov. 22, 1924. BA, Coll. of Wooster, 1947; MBA, U. Mich., 1950, JD, 1951. Bar: Ohio 1951. Atty. trust dept. Nat. City Bank, Cleve., 1951-56; asst. prof. law U. Mich., Ann Arbor, 1956-61, assoc. prof., 1961-66, prof. bus. law, health svcs. mgmt. and policy, 1966-90, prof. emeritus, 1990—. Author: The Law of Hospital and Health Care Administration, 1988; contbr. articles to legal publs. and med. jours. Elder 1st Presbyterian Ch., Ann Arbor, 1963—. Mem. Am. Acad. Health Care Attys., Acad. of Legal Studies in Bus., Nat. Health Lawyers Assn., Am. Soc. Law, Medicine and Ethics. Home: 26 Southwick Ct Ann Arbor MI 48105-1410 Office: U Mich Sch Bus Adminstrn Ann Arbor MI 48109

SOUTHWICK, CHARLES HENRY, zoologist, educator; b. Wooster, Ohio, Aug. 28, 1928; s. Arthur F. and Faye (Motz) S.; m. Heather Milne Beck, July 12, 1952; children: Steven, Karen. B.A., Coll. Wooster, 1949; M.S., U. Wis., 1951, Ph.D., 1953. NIH fellow, 1951-53; asst. prof. biology Hamilton Coll., 1953-54; NSF fellow Oxford (Eng.) U., 1954-55; faculty Ohio U., 1955-61; assoc. prof. pathobiology Johns Hopkins Sch. Hygiene and Pub. Health, Balt., 1961-68; prof. Johns Hopkins Sch. Hygiene and Pub. Health, 1968-79; assoc. dir. Johns Hopkins Internat. Ctr. for Med. Rsch. and Tng., Calcutta, India, 1964-65; chmn. dept. environ., population and organismic biology U. Colo., Boulder, 1979-82, prof. biology, 1979—, prof. emeritus, 1993—; researcher and author publs. on animal social behavior and population dynamics, influences animal social behavior on demographic characteristic mammal populations, primate ecology and behavior, estuarine ecology and environmental quality; mem. primate adv. com. Nat. Acad. Sci.-NRC, 1963-75, com. primate conservation, 1974-75; mem. Gov.'s Sci. Adv. Com. State of Md., 1975-78; mem. com. on rsch. and exploration Nat. Geog. Soc., 1979—; mem. adv. bd. Caribbean Primate Rsch. Ctr., 1987—, Wis. Primate Rsch. Ctr., 1990—; mem. Integrated Conservation Rsch., 1989—. Editor, author: Primate Social Behavior, 1963, Animal Agression, 1970, Nonhuman Primates in Biomedical Research, 1975, Ecology and the Quality of Our Environment, 1976, Global Ecology, 1985; Ecology and Behavior of Food-Enhanced Primate Groups, 1988; author: Global Ecology in Human Perspective, 1996. Recipient Fulbright Rsch. award India, 1959-60. Fellow AAAS, Acad. Zoology, Animal Behavior Soc.; mem. Am. Soc. Zoologists, Ecol. Soc. Am., Am. Soc. Mammalogists, Am. Soc. Primatology (Disting. Primatologist award 1994), Internat. Primatology Soc., Am. Inst. Biol. Scis., Primatology Soc. Gt. Britain, Internat. Soc. Study Aggression.

SOUTHWICK, DAVID LEROY, geology researcher; b. Rochester, Minn., Aug. 30, 1936; m. 1959; 3 children. BA, Carleton Coll., 1958; PhD in Geology, Johns Hopkins U., 1962. Geologist U.S. Geol. Survey, 1962-68; asst. prof. to prof. geology Macalester Coll., 1968-77; sr. geologist Minn. Geol. Survey, St. Paul, 1977-89, asst. dir., rsch. assoc., 1989-93, acting dir., 1993-94, dir., 1994—; adj. assoc. prof. U. Minn., 1983-94, prof., 1994—. Fellow Geol. Assn. Can., Geol. Soc. Am.; mem. Am. Geophys. Union. Office: Minnesota Geological Survey 2642 University Ave W Saint Paul MN 55114-1057

SOUTHWICK, E. MICHAEL, diplomat; b. Willits, Calif., 1945; m. Susan Obee; children: Edward, Andrew, Katherine. Grad., Stanford U., 1966. Consular officer, staff asst. to amb. Carol Laise U.S. Dept. State; adminstr., consular officer Kigali, Rwanda; dep. chief of mission Bujumbura, Burundi & Niamey, Niger; assignments officer for Africa Bu. Pers.; exec. dir. Bur. Intel & Rsch.; dep. chief of mission Nairobi, Kenya, 1990-94; U.S. amb. to Uganda, 1994—. Recipient Meritorious Honor award, Order of Merit Govt. of Niger. Office: US Ambassador Kampala Uganda US Dept of Washington Washington DC 20521-2190*

SOUTHWICK, HARRY WEBB, surgeon; b. Grand Rapids, Mich., Nov. 21, 1918; s. G. Howard and Jessie (Webb) S.; m. Lorraine Hinsdale, June 27, 1942; children: Harry Webb Jr., Sandra, Charles Howard, Gay. B.S., Harvard U., 1940, M.D., 1943. Intern Presbyn. Hosp., Chgo., 1944-45, resident in surgery, 1945-46; surg. resident U. Ill. Research and Ednl. Hosps., 1948-50; chmn. dept. gen. surgery Rush-Presbyn.-St. Luke's Med. Center, Chgo., 1970-84; pvt. practice surgery Chgo., 1950-84; clin. assoc. prof. surgery U. Ill. Med. Sch., 1957-63, clin. prof., 1963-71; Helen Shedd Keith prof. surgery Rush Med. Coll., 1971-84; bd. dirs. Howard Young Med. Ctr., sec., 1987-89, vice-chmn., 1989-90, chmn., 1990—; bd. dris. Howard Young Health Care, Eagle River Meml. Hosp. Contbr. articles to med. jours. Pres. Chgo. unit Am. Cancer Soc., 1964-66, pres. Ill. div. 1972-73; bd. dirs. Eagle River Meml. Hosp., 1989—. Lt. (j.g.) M.C., USNR, 1946-48. Fellow ACS; mem. Am. Surg. Assn., Pan Am. Surg. Soc., Minn. Surg. Soc. (hon.), Western Surg. Soc., Cen. Surg. Soc., Chgo. Surg. Soc. (pres. 1979-80), Soc. Head and Neck Surgeons (sec.-treas. 1956-63, pres. 1964-65), Soc. Surgery Alimentary Tract, Soc. Surg. Oncology, Plum Lake Golf Club. Home and Office: 8155 N Lost Lake Dr Sayner WI 54560

SOUTHWICK, LAWRENCE, JR., management educator; b. Northampton, Mass., Sept. 5, 1938; s. Lawrence Sr. and Caroline (Ingram) S.; m. Patricia A. Matthews, Oct. 21, 1961; children: Lawrence III, Rebecca A., Catherine A. BS in Math., Case Western Res. U., Cleve., 1960; MBA, Western Mich. U., 1963; MS in Indsl. Adminstrn., Carnegie-Mellon U., 1965, PhD in Econs., 1967. Cert. mgmt. acct. Asst. prof. mgmt. SUNY, Buffalo, 1966-70, assoc. prof., 1970—; chmn. dept. mgmt. SUNU, Buffalo, 1976-81, 91-94; cons. in field. Author: Managerial Economics, 1985. Councilman Town of Amherst, 1972-91. Mem. NAFE, Am. Law and Econ. Assn., Am. Econ. Assn., Seneca Nation of Indians Econ. Devel. Corp. (bd. dirs.), Restoration Soc. (bd. dirs., pres.), Friendship Found. (bd. dirs.). Republican. Unitarian. Home: 100 Oakland Rd Williamsville NY 14221-6816 Office: SUNY Sch Mgmt Buffalo NY 14260

SOUTHWICK, PAUL, retired public relations executive; b. West Newton, Mass., Mar. 27, 1920; s. Alfred and Pauline (Winkler) S.; m. Susan Barbara Heider, Feb. 24, 1947; children: Thomas Paul, Peter Alfred, Linda Susan. AB in Econs. cum laude, Harvard Coll., 1943. Coor. AP, Concord, N.H., 1947-49; UP UPI, Washington, 1949-57; mem. profl. staff govt. info. subcom. U.S. Ho. Reps., 1957-59; legis. asst., adminstrv. asst. U.S. Senator Long of Hawaii, 1959-62; dep. adminstr. charge accelerated pub. works program Area Redevel. Adminstrn., 1962-63; spl. asst. The White House, 1963-65; spl. asst. for congl. rels. Office of U.S. Sec. Commerce, 1965-67; v.p. Newmyer Assocs., Inc., Washington, 1967-87; ind. cons., 1987-93, ret., 1993. With USNR, 1941-45, PTO. Mem. Nat. Press Club (Washington), Bethesda (Md.) Country Club. Democrat. Presbyterian. Home: 4012 Underwood St Bethesda MD 20815-5028

SOUTHWORTH, HORTON COE, educational educator, education scholar; b. Monroe, Mich., Apr. 2, 1926; s. Frederick Osgood and Bertha Southworth; m. Jannene MacIntyre, Apr. 1971; children: Sueann, Nancy, Jim, Janet, Jaye, Bradford, Alexandra. BS, Mich. State U., East Lansing, 1950, MA, 1953, EdD, 1962. Cert. K-8 tchr., elem. prin., Mich. Mid. sch. tchr. Bellevue (Mich.) Pub. Schs., 1950-51, elem. prin., 1951-53, supervising prin., 1953-55; elem. prin. Pontiac (Mich.) Pub. Schs., 1955-59; coord. Macomb Tchr. Ctr. Mich. State U., Warren, 1959-67, asst. prof., 1962-64, assoc. prof., 1964-67; prof. edn., chmn. elem. edn. dept. U. Pitts., 1967-91; scholar-in-residence Duquesne U., Pitts., 1990—, cons., 1991-92; cons. Pa. Dept. Edn., Harrisburg, 1968-91; treas. Learning Tree Assocs. Pitts., 1974—. Chmn. Three Rivers dist. Boy Scouts Am., Pitts., 1980-90; pres. Univ. Childrens Sch., California, Pa., 1988—, mem. adv. com. grad. program in Pa., Nova Southeastern U., Harrisburg, 1989—; invited participant Leadership Conf., Oxford U., 1995. With USNR, 1944-46, PTO. Recipient Chancellor's Disting. Tchr. award U. Pitts., 1988, Prof. Emeritus award, 1991. Mem. Assn. Tchr. Educators (33 Yr. Mem. award 1991), Pa. Assn. Colls. and Tchr. Educators (exec. bd. 1985-91), Masons (life), Kappa Delta Pi (5 Yr. Chpt. Counselor award 1989), Phi Delta Kappa (25 Yr. Mem. award 1985, 40 Yr. Mem. award 1996), Theta Chi. Democrat. Presbyterian. Avocations: skiing, reading, gardening. Home: 619 S Linden Ave Pittsburgh PA 15208-2812 Office: Learning Tree Schs Corp Penn West Bldg Pittsburgh PA 15221

SOUTHWORTH, JAMIE MACINTYRE, education educator; b. Ironton, Ohio, Oct. 16, 1931; d. Gaylord and Lydia Marcum (Adkins) MacIntyre; m. Horton C. Southworth; children: Jaye, Brad, Alexandra, Sueann, Janet, Jim. BS, Ball State U., 1952, MA, 1961; EdD, U. Pitts., 1981. Cert. adminstr. and tchr., reading specialist, Pa. Instr. Mich. State U., East Lansing, 1964-67; instr., coord. U. Minn., Mpls., 1967-71; rsch. assoc. Pitts. Pub. Schs., 1971-80; assoc. prof. California U. Pa., 1988; prof. edn. California U., Pa., 1993—; state grants educator, 1990-95; univ. faculty devel. com. mem., 1992—; chair the dept. promotion and tenure com., 1993—; mem. the evaluation com., 1994—; chancellor State Adv. Com., Calif. Univ. rep., 1994—; invited participant Oxford (Eng.) U. Leadership Studies, 1995; dir. leadership tng. proposal, 1996—. Contbr. articles to profl. jours. U.S. Office of Edn. title III & IVC grantee; grantee Pa. Vocat. Tech. State, 1990-91, 93, Bibliotherapy Project California Univ. Pa., 1992, Pa. State, 1993, Pa. Campus Compac, 1993. Mem. Am. Assn. Colls. Tchr. Edn., NEA Young Children, Kappa Delta Pi (counselor), Phi Delta Kappa.

SOUTHWORTH, LINDA JEAN, artist, critic, educator; b. Milw., May 11, 1951; d. William Dixon and Violet Elsie (Kuehn) S.; m. David Joseph Roger, Nov. 16, 1985 (div. July 1989). BFA, St. John's U., Queens, N.Y., 1974; MFA, Pratt Inst., Bklyn., 1978. Printmaker, still life and portrait painter, collage artist, photographer self-employed, N.Y.C., 1974—; art critic Resident Publs., N.Y.C., 1993—; adj. prof. art history St. Francis Coll., Bklyn., 1985-94; artist-in-residence Our Saviour's Atonement Luth. Ch., N.Y.C., 1993-95. Exhibited in solo shows at Galimaufry, Croton-on-Hudson, N.Y., 1977, Kristen Richards Gallery, N.Y.C., 1982, Gallery 84, N.Y.C., 1990, The Bernhardt Collection, Washington, 1991, The Netherland Club, N.Y.C., 1992; group shows include Union St. Graphics, San Francisco, 1974, Nuance Gallery, Tampa, 1987, 88, Soc. Illustrators Ann. Drawing Show, N.Y.C., 1989, 90, Salmagundi Club, N.Y.C., 1991, 92, Henry Howells Gallery, N.Y.C., 1992, 93, Mus. Gallery, N.Y.C., 1994, Cavalier Gallery, Greenwich, Conn., 1995, Carib Gallery, N.Y.C., 1995, Chuck Levitan Gallery, N.Y.C., 1996; artist Christmas card/UNICEF, 1992. Avocations: ballroom dancing, old inns and architecture, cycling. Home: 106 Cabrini Blvd Apt 5D New York NY 10033-3422

SOUTHWORTH, ROD BRAND, computer science educator; b. Binghampton, N.Y., Aug. 24, 1941; s. William Tanner Southworth and Ruth Evelyn (Brabham) Woods; m. Patrice Marie Gapen, Jan. 10, 1978; children: Suzi Lynn, Judi Leigh, Megan Marie, Robin Ashley. BS in Bus., U. Ariz., 1965; MS in Mgmt. Sci. and Info Systems, Colo. State U., 1978. Mktg. rep. IBM, Denver, 1966-69; system analyst Colo. State U., Fort Collins, 1969-73, grad. teaching asst., 1978-79; project mgr. Systems and Computer Tech., Portland, Oreg., 1973-75; asst. dir. Systems and Computer Tech., Fairbanks, Alaska, 1975-77; instr. in computer info. systems Laramie County C.C., Cheyenne, Wyo., 1979—. Author: (software) PC-DOS/MS-DOS Simplified, 1st edit. 1988, 3rd edit. 1992, DOS Complete and Simplified, 1990, DOS Essentials, 1991, DOS 5 Simplified, 1992, DOS 6.2 Simplified, 1994. Mem. Civil Air Patrol, Cheyenne, 1991. Mem. Data Processing Mgmt. Assn. (mem. assoc. level model curriculum 1984-85), Assn. Computing Machinery (mem. assoc. level computer info. processing model curriculum 1991-92). Avocations: boating, water skiing, fishing, stamp collecting, tennis. Home: PO Box 5457 Cheyenne WY 82003-5457 Office: Laramie County Comm Coll 1400 E College Dr Cheyenne WY 82007-3204

SOUTHWORTH, WILLIAM DIXON, retired education educator; b. Union City, Tenn., Dec. 28, 1918; s. Thomas and Gertrude (Dyer) S.; m. Violet Kuehn, July 22, 1944; children: Geoffrey Scott, Linda Jean. PhB, Marquette U., 1948, MEd, 1950; PhD, NYU, 1961. Tchr., coach La Follette Sch., Milwaukee County, Wis., 1948-51; teaching dist. prin. Grand View Sch., Milwaukee County, 1951-56; supervising dist. prin. Maple Dale Sch., Milwaukee County, 1956-58; bldg. prin. Main St. Sch., Port Washington, N.Y., 1958-65; asst. supt. for elem. edn. Huntington (N.Y.) pub. schs., 1965-67; assoc. prof., acting head dept. adminstrn. and supervision St. John's U., Jamaica, N.Y., 1967, chmn. dept., 1968-73, prof., 1968-84; adj. prof. Berne U. (as dissertation adviser); parliamentarian for 35 internat., nat. regional orgns., expert witness, pub. moderator, and workshop leader. Author: (pamphlet) Care and Nurture of the Doctoral Candidate, 1968, 74, (unpublished books) Murder on the Flagship, The Art of the Meeting--How to Run Successful Meetings, The Sensual Sailor--Seven Years of Lusty Living, contbg. editor Condominium Times; contbr. 220 articles to ednl. jours., condiminium and parliamentary publs. Served with USN, 1938-44. Lutheran. Home: Apt 608 7100 Sunshine Skyway Ln S Saint Petersburg FL 33711-4926 *In the conflicting demands of self and society, one must strike a balance by retaining the uniqueness of one's individuality while serving the society that nurtured that uniqueness. It is in the balance thus struck that the complete person evolves—self-esteeming, and socially able.*

SOUTTER, THOMAS DOUGLAS, retired lawyer; b. N.Y.C., Nov. 1, 1934; s. Thomas G. and Hildreth H. (Callanan) S.; m. Virginia Hovenden; children: Alexander D., C. Anson, Hadley H. BA, U. Va., 1955, LL.B., 1962; postgrad., Advanced Mgmt. Program, Harvard U., 1980. Bar: N.Y. 1962, R.I. 1969. Atty. Breed, Abbott & Morgan, N.Y.C., 1962-68; with Textron Inc., Providence, 1968-95; gen. counsel Textron Inc., 1968-95, v.p., 1973-80, sr. v.p., 1980-85, exec. v.p., gen. counsel, 1985-95; cons., 1995—; mem. adv. bd. Internat. and Comparative Law Ctr., 1975-95; mem. Assn. Gen. Counsel; bd. dirs. Avco Fin. Svcs., Inc., 1985-95, Paul Revere Corp. 1993-95; trustee New England Legal Found. Nat. chmn. ann. giving campaign U. Va. Law Sch., 1992-94; former trustee Providence Preservation Soc., Providence Performing Arts Ctr.; mem. U. Va. Arts and Scis. Alumni Coun.; mem. Narragansett coun. Boy Scouts Am. Lt. USNR, 1955-59. Mem. ABA, N.Y. State Bar Assn., R.I. Bar Assn., Internat. Bar Assn. Office: P O Box 878 40 Westminster St 17th Fl Providence RI 02903-2525

SOUVEROFF, VERNON WILLIAM, JR., corporate executive, investor, author; b. L.A., Aug. 12, 1934; s. Vernon William Sr. and Aileen (Young) S.; m. Aileen Patricia Robinson; children—Gail Kathleen, Michael William. B.S. in E.E., Stanford U., 1957; postgrad., Ohio State U., 1958-59. With Litton Industries, Beverly Hills, Calif., 1960-75; with ITT Corp., N.Y.C., 1975-87, corp. v.p., 1983-84, sr. v.p., 1984-87; pres. ITT Gilfillan, 1979-83; group exec. ITT Def. Space Group, 1983-84; dir. ITT Telecom and Electronics N.Am., 1984-86; pres., chief exec. officer ITT Def. Tech. Corp., 1986-87; exec. dir. Nat. Ctr. for Career Change, 1990—; mem. U.S. Def. Policy Adv. Com. on Trade, Washington, 1984-88; bd. advisors, investor Venture Resources, Venture Capital, 1988—; prin. Bus. Acquisitions and Investments, 1988—; bd. dirs. Elanix, Inc. Author books on career changes. Served as officer USAF, 1957-60. Recipient Exec. Salute award Los Angeles C. of C., 1981; Ring of Quality ITT Corp., 1983. Mem. IEEE, Nat. Contracts Mgmt. Assn., Electronics Industries Assn., Am. Def. Preparedness Assn. (former dir.), Nat. Security Indsl. Assn., Air Force Assn., Navy League, Assn. U.S. Army, Rancho Mirage Racquet Club (Calif.). Presbyterian.

SOUW, BERNARD ENG-KIE, physicist, consultant; b. Pekalongan, Java, Indonesia, Jan. 7, 1942; came to U.S., 1984, naturalized citizen, 1990; s. Tjwan-Ling and Pek-Liang (Kwee) S.; m. Martha Tjoei-Lioe Lim, July 17, 1967; children: Victor, Verena. Diploma in Physics, Tech. U. of Clausthal, Zellerfeld, Fed. Republic of Germany, 1972; D in Natural Scis., U. Duesseldorf, Fed. Republic of Germany, 1981. Rsch. assoc. U. Duesseldorf, 1973-83; rsch. scientist Isotope Rsch. Inst., Haan, Fed. Republic of Germany, 1983; univ. asst. Free U. of Berlin, 1984; vis. scientist A. F. Wright Aero. Labs., Dayton, Ohio, 1984-85; rsch. scientist Brookhaven Nat. Lab., Upton, N.Y., 1985—; cons. cvd-diamond, plasma and laser applications; adj. prof. N.J. Inst. Tech., 1994—. Contbr. articles to Jour. Applied Physics, Jour. Quantitative Spectroscopy, Jour. Plasma Physics, Plasma Physics and Controlled Fusion, Physica. Mem. Am. Phys. Soc., L.I. Optical Soc., Materials Rsch. Soc. Office: Brookhaven Nat Lab Bldg 820M Upton NY 11973

SOUZA, MARCO ANTONIO, civil engineer, educator; b. Valença, Rio de Janeiro, Sept. 26, 1951; s. Oldemar and Elza Souza; m. Silvia Marina Pinto Souza, May 6, 1982. Degree in structural engring., Pontificia U. Cath., Rio de Janeiro, 1975, MS, 1978; PhD, Univ. Coll. London, 1982. Design engr. Montreal Engenharia S.A., Rio de Janeiro, 1975-76; assoc. prof. civil engring. dept. Pontificia U. Cath. Rio de Janeiro, 1982-89, assoc. prof., 1991-93; v.p. tech. divsn. COREV Am. Inc., 1993—; vis. prof. Va. Poly. Inst. and State U., Blacksburg, 1989-91, U. Alberta, Edmonton, Can., 1987; cons. Ecopetrol, Bogota, Colombia, 1988; chmn. local arrangements com. 1st Pan Am. Congress Applied Mechanics, 1989; mem. organizing and editorial com. 2d and 3d Pan Am. Congresses Applied Mechanics, 1991, 93, program com. 2d Biennial European Joint Conf. on Engring. Systems Design and Analysis, London, 1994; reviewer jours.; leader presentations and seminars in field. Assoc. editor Ocean Engring., 1990—; contbr. numerous articles to profl. jours. Coun. Nat. Desenvolvimento Tech. and Sci. scholar, 1976-78, 79-82, grantee, 1983—. Mem. AIAA, ASCE, ASME (reviewer Jour. Applied Mechanics), Am. Soc. Engring. Edn., Am. Acad. Mechanics (steering com. Pan Am. Congresses), Brazilian Soc. Mech. Sci. (reviewer jour.), Soc. Engring. Sci., Structural Stability Rsch. Coun., Sigma Xi. Home: 10131 Briar Dr Houston TX 77042-1208 Office: Corev Am Inc 11620 Brittmoore Park Dr Houston TX 77041-6917

SOVERN, MICHAEL IRA, law educator; b. N.Y.C., Dec. 1, 1931; s. Julius and Lillian (Arnstein) S.; m. Lenore Goodman, Feb. 21, 1952 (div. Apr. 1963); children: Jeffrey Austin, Elizabeth Ann, Douglas Todd; m. Eleanor Leen, Aug. 25, 1963 (div. Feb. 1974); 1 child, Julie Danielle; m. Joan Wit, Mar. 9, 1974 (dec. Sept. 1993); m. Patricia Walsh, Nov. 12, 1995. AB summa cum laude, Columbia U., 1953, LLB (James Ordronaux prize), 1955, LLD (hon.), 1980; PhD (hon.), Tel Aviv U., 1982; LLD (hon.), U. So. Calif., 1989. Bar: N.Y. 1956, U.S. Supreme Ct. 1976. Asst. prof., then assoc. prof. law U. Minn. Law Sch., 1955-58; mem. faculty Columbia Law Sch., 1957—, prof. law, 1960—, Chancellor Kent prof., 1977—, dean Law Sch., 1970-79; chmn. exec. com. faculty Columbia U., 1968-69, provost, exec. v.p., 1979-80, univ. pres., 1980-93, pres. emeritus, 1993; rsch. dir. Legal Restraints on

Racial Discrimination in Employment, Twentieth Century Fund, 1962-66; spl. counsel to gov. N.J., 1974-77; cons. Time Mag., 1965-80; dir. Chem. Bank, AT&T, GNY Ins. Group, Warner Lambert; mem. panel of arbitrators N.J. Bd. Mediation, Fed. Mediation and Conciliation Svc.; bd. dirs. Asian Cultural Coun., Shubert Orgn., Shubert Found., Sta. WNET-TV, NAACP Legal Def. Fund; chmn. N.Y.C. Charter Revision Commn., 1982-83; co-chmn. 2d Cir. Commn. on Reducation of Burdens and Costs in Civil Litigation, 1977-80; chmn. Commn. on Integrity in Govt., 1986; pres. Italian Acad. Advanced Studies in Am., 1991-93; chmn. Japan Soc., 1993—, Am. Acad. Rome, 1993—; chmn. nat. adv. coun. Freedom Forum Media Studies Ctr., 1993—. Author: Legal Restraints on Racial Discrimination in Employment, 1966, Law and Poverty, 1969, Of Boundless Domains, 1994; host Sta. WNET-TV series Leading Questions. Mem. Pulitzer Prize Bd., 1980-93, chmn. pro tem, 1986-87; trustee Kaiser Family Found., Presidential Legal Expense Trust. Commendatore in the Order of Merit of the Republic of Italy, 1991; recipient Alexander Hamilton medal, 1993, Citizens Union Civic Leadership award, 1993. Fellow Am. Acad. Arts and Scis.; mem. ABA, Coun. Fgn. Rels., Assn. Bar City N.Y., Am. Arbitration Assn. (panel arbitrators), Am. Law Inst., Econ. Club, Nat. Acad. Arbitrators. Office: Columbia U Sch Law 435 W 116th St New York NY 10027-7201

SOVEY, WILLIAM PIERRE, manufacturing company executive; b. Helen, Ga., Aug. 26, 1933; s. Louis Terrell and Kathryn Bell (White) S.; m. Kathryne Owen Doyle, Dec. 28, 1958; children: Margaret Elizabeth, John Todd. B.S.I.E., Ga. Inst. Tech., 1955; grad., Advanced Mgmt. Program, Harvard U., 1976. Gen. mgr. automotive div. Atwood Vacuum Machine Co., Rockford, Ill., 1963-68; v.p. internat. A.G. Spalding & Bros., Inc., Chicopee, Mass., 1968-71; pres. Ben Hogan Co. div. AMF Inc., Ft. Worth, 1971-77; corp. v.p., group exec. indsl. products group AMF Inc., Stamford, Conn., 1977-79; pres., chief operating officer, dir. AMF Inc., White Plains, N.Y., 1982-85; pres., chief operating officer Newell Co., Freeport, Ill., 1986-92, vice chmn. CEO, 1993, also bd. dirs. Served with USN, 1955-58. Home: 5349 Winding Creek Dr Rockford IL 61114-5483 Office: Newell Co PO Box 117 Beloit WI 53512-0117*

SOVIE, MARGARET DOE, nursing administrator, college dean, educator; b. Ogdensburg, N.Y., July 7, 1934; d. William Gordon and Mary Rose (Bruyere) Doe; m. Alfred L. Sovie, May 8, 1954; 1 child, Scot Marc. Student, U. Rochester, 1950-51; diploma in nursing, St. Lawrence State Hosp. Sch. Nursing, Ogdensburg, 1954; postgrad., St. Lawrence U., 1956-60; BS in Nursing summa cum laude, Syracuse U., 1964, MS in Edn., 1968, PhD in Edn., 1972; DSc (hon.), Health Sci. Ctr. SUNY, Syracuse, 1989; MSN, U. Pa., 1995. Cert. adult health nurse practitioner. Staff nurse, clin. instr. St. Lawrence State Hosp., Ogdensburg, 1954-55, instr. nursing, 1955-62; staff nurse Good Shepherd Hosp., Syracuse, 1962; nursing supr. SUNY Upstate Med. Ctr., Syracuse, 1963-65, insvc. instr., 1965-66, edn. dir. and coord. nursing svc., 1966-71, asst. dean Coll. Health Related Professions, 1972-84, assoc. prof. nursing, 1973-76, dir. continuing edn. in nursing, 1974-76, assoc. dean and dir. div. continuing edn. Coll. Health Related Professions, 1974-76; spl. assignment in pres.'s office SUNY Upstate Med. Ctr. and Syracuse U., 1972-73; assoc. dean for nursing U. Rochester, N.Y., 1976-88, assoc. prof. nursing, 1976-85, prof., 1985-88; assoc. dir. for nursing Strong Meml. Hosp., U. Rochester Med. Ctr., 1976-88; chief nursing officer Hosp. U. Pa., Phila., 1988-96, assoc. exec. dir., 1988-94, assoc. dean for nursing practice Sch. Nursing, 1988-96, Jane Delano prof. nursing adminstrn. Sch. Nursing, 1988—, chief nursing officer, 1988-96; sr. fellow Leonard Davis Inst. Health Econs. U. Pa., Phila., 1992—; trustee bd. U. Pa. Health Sys., Phila., 1993-96; nursing coord. and project dir. Cen. N.Y. Regional Med. Program, Syracuse, 1968-71; mem. edn. dept. State Bd. Nursing, Albany, N.Y., 1974-84, chmn., 1981-83, chmn. practice com., 1975-80, mem. joint practice com., 1975-80, vice chmn., 1980-81; mem. adv. com. to clin. nurse scholars program Robert Wood Johnson found., Princeton, N.J., 1982-88; adj. assoc. prof. Syracuse U. Sch. Nursing, 1973-76; mem. Gov.'s Health Adv. Panel N.Y. State Health Planning Commn., 1976-82, task force on health manpower policy, 1978, informal support networks sect. steering com., 1980; mem. health manpower tng. and utilization task force State N.Y. Commn. on Health Edn.and Illness Prevention, 1979; mem. task force on nursing personnel N.Y. State Health Adv. Coun., 1980; mem. adv. panel on nursing svcs. U.S. Pharm. Conv. Inc., Washington, 1985-90; cons. Nat. Ctr. for Svcs. Rsch. and Health Care Tech. Assessment, Rockville, Md., 1987; mem. nursing stds. task force Joint Commn. Accreditation Health Care Orgns., 1988-90; mem. various other adv. coms.; lectr. in field. Mem. editl. bd. Health Care Supr., 1982-87, Nursing Econs., 1983—, Best Practices and Benchmarking in Health Care, 1995—; manuscript rev. panel Nursing Outlook, 1987-91; mem. editorial bd. Seminars for Nurse Mgrs., 1994—; contbr. articles to profl. jours., chpts. to books. Mem. bd. visitors Sch. Nursing U. Md., Balt., 1984-89; mem. bd. mgrs. Strong Meml. Hosp., Rochester, 1983-88; bd. dirs. Monroe County Assn. for Hearing, Rochester, 1979-82, Vis. Nurse Svc., Rochester and Monroe County, 1978, Southeastern Pa. chpt. ARC, 1991—. Ann. Margaret D. Sovie lectureship inaugurated Strong Meml. Hosp. U. Rochester, 1989; spl. nurse rsch. fellow NIH, 1971-72; grantee various orgns.; recipient Dean's Outstanding Alumni award Coll. of Nursing, Syracuse U., 1994. Fellow Am. Acad. Nursing (program com. 1980-81, task force on hosp. nursing 1981-83, chair expert panel on quality health 1994—); mem. ANA (nat. rev. com. for expanded role programs 1975-78, site visitor to programs requesting accreditation 1976-78, cabinet on nursing svcs. 1986-90, cert. bd. nursing adminstrn. 1983-86, Ad Hoc com. on advanced practice 1992-95), Am. Orgn. Nurse Execs. (stds. task force 1987), N.Y. State Nurses Assn. (med. surg. nursing group, chmn. edn. com. dist. 4 1974-76, chmn. cmty. planning group for nursing dist. 4 1974-75, couegional planning in nursing 1974-76, del. to conv. 1978, Nursing Svc. Adminstrn. award 1985), Inst. Medicine (com. design strategy for quality rev. and assurance in Medicare 1988-90), Sigma Theta Tau, Pi Lambda Theta. Republican. Roman Catholic. Avocations: golf, cross-country skiing, swimming, dancing. Office: U Pa Sch Nursing 420 Guardian Dr Philadelphia PA 19104-6096

SOVIERO, DIANA BARBARA, soprano; b. Jersey City, Mar. 19, 1946; d. Amerigo and Angelina Catani; student Juilliard Sch. Music, Hunter Coll. Opera Workshop. Appearances with opera cos. including Tulsa Opera, Houston Grand Opera, San Diego Opera, Ottawa (Ont., Can.) Opera, Zurich Opera, Goldovsky Opera Theatre, Lake George Opera, New Orleans Opera, Hamburg (W.Ger.) Opera, Dallas Opera, Chgo. Opera, Rome Opera, Paris Opera, Nice Opera, Avignon Opera, San Francisco Opera, Montreal (Que., Can.) Opera, Toulouse, France, Caracas, Venezuela, Vienna Opera, Parma Opera, Italy, Munich Opera, W.Ger., Edmonton (Alta., Can.) Opera, Winnipeg (Man., Can.) Opera, Calgary (Alta.) Opera, Madrid Opera, Greater Miami Opera, Bastille Opera, Montreal Opera, Covent Garden, Florence Opera, Opera Pacific at Costa Mesa; with Met. Opera, 1986—, now leading soprano; instr. master classes The Faculty, sch. for actors, Los Angeles. Recipient Richard Tucker award. Mem. AFTRA, Am. Guild Musical Artists, SAG. Office: care Royal Opera House-Contracts, Convent Gardens, London WC2, England

SOVIERO, JOSEPH C., chemical company executive; b. 1938. BS, Polytech. Inst. Bklyn., 1960; MS, NYU, 1965. With Union Carbide Corp., Danbury, Conn., 1960—, corporate v.p. Office: Union Carbide Corp 39 Old Ridgebury Rd Danbury CT 06810*

SOVIK, EDWARD ANDERS, architect, consultant; b. Honan, China, June 9, 1918; s. Edward Anderson and Anna (Tenwick) S.; m. Genevieve Elaine Hendrickson, June 29, 1946; children: Rolf, Martin, Peter. BA, St. Olaf Coll., 1939; student, Art Students League N.Y., 1939-40, Luther Theol. Sem., 1940-42; MArch, Yale U., 1949; DFA (hon.), Concordia Coll., 1981. Ret. chmn. SMSQ, Architects and predecessors, Northfield, Minn.; prof. art emeritus St. Olaf Coll., Northfield; lectr. on ch. design at various confs., schs., univs.; participant, planner, del. numerous domestic and fgn. confs. on religion and architecture; mem., officer various profl., religious and pub. bds. and commns. Author: Architecture for Worship; Contbr. numerous articles to mags., anthologies.; works include chs., coll. and univ. bldgs., instns. With USMC, 1942-45; maj. Res. Decorated D.F.C., Purple Heart, Air medal. Fellow AIA; mem. AIA Minn. (pres. 1977, Gold medal 1981), Phi Beta Kappa. Republican. Lutheran. Home: 711 Summit Ave Northfield MN 55057-1568

SOWADA, ALPHONSE AUGUSTUS, bishop; b. Avon, Minn., June 23, 1933; s. Alphonse B. and Monica (Pierskalla) S. Student, Onamia (Minn.) Sem., 1947-53; grad., Crosier House of Studies, Ft. Wayne, Ind., 1959; M.A., Cath. U. Am., 1961. Ordained priest Roman Cath. Ch., 1958; arrived in Irian Jaya to work among Asmat, 1961, selected as mission superior, 1966; ordained bishop Diocese Agats-Asmat, 1969—; mem. exec. com. Indonesian Conf. of Bishops, 1991—. Contbr. to: Nat. Geog. Yearbook, 1968, other publs. Mem. Order of Alhambra, Crosier Order, Kappa Delta Gamma. Office: Kantor Keuskupan Agats, Asmat Agats 99677, Irian Jaya Indonesia

SOWDER, FRED ALLEN, foundation administrator, alphabet specialist; b. Cin., July 17, 1940; s. William Franklin and Lucille (Estes) S.; m. Sandra Ann Siegman, July 15, 1961 (div. Sept. 1963); 1 child, William. Student, Cin. Sch. Ct. Reporting, 1975; diploma Self-Health Insts., Sch. of Med. Masso-Therapy, 1985; diploma, Cin. Sch. Hypnosis, 1989. Founder World Union Universal Alphabet, Cin., 1981—, Internat. Assn. Sch. Massage, Cin., 1988—. Inventor of hundreds of published and unpublished alphabets and writing systems, including light wave, color and musical tone systems and tactile systems for the blind; author: Sowder Shorthand, 1980, Universal Alphabet: What and Why, 1981, Your Intimacy Quotient: The Symptoms, Causes & Consequences of Intimacy Deprivation, 1996; contbr. numerous articles to mags. State dir. Soc. Separationists, Cin., 1967-70; bd. dirs. ACLU of Ohio, ACLU Found., 1984-89, sec., Cin. chpt., 1984-89. Mem. AAAS, Amnesty Internat., Ohio Com. to Abolish Capital Punishment, Assn. for Humanistic Psychology, Internat. Soc. for Gen. Semantics, Am. Sunbathing Assn., The Naturist Soc., Am. Massage Therapy Assn., Urban Appalachian Coun. Democrat. Home: PO Box 252 Cincinnati OH 45201-0252 Office: World Union Universal Alphabet PO Box 252 Cincinnati OH 45201-0252

SOWDER, KATHLEEN ADAMS, marketing executive; b. Person County, N.C., Feb. 9, 1951; d. George W. and Mary W. (Woody) A.; BS, Radford Coll., 1976; MBA, Va. Poly. Inst., 1978; m. Angelo R. LoMascolo, Apr. 11, 1980 (div.); 1 child, Mary Jennifer; m. Terry Tetirick, Dec. 27, 1995. Asst. product mgr. GTE Sylvania, Waltham, Mass., 1978-79, product mgr. video products, 1979-80; comml. mktg. mgr. Am. Dist. Telegraph, N.Y.C., 1980-87; v.p. mktg. ESL, Hingham, Mass., 1987-91; pres. Q.B. Air dba Falcon Holdings, Summit, N.J., 1991—; exec. v.p. Falcon Detection Techs., Inc., Plymouth, Mass., 1991-94; v.p. mktg. Westec Security, Irvine, Calif., 1995—. Mem. Am. Mktg. Assn., Am. Soc. Indsl. Security (past chair standing com. on phys. security). Republican. Home: 2521 E Gelid Ave Anaheim CA 92506 Office: Westec 5 Mason Irvine CA 92718

SOWDER, ROBERT ROBERTSON, architect; b. Kansas City, Kans., Dec. 29, 1928; s. James Robert and Agnes (Robertson) S.; m. Joan Goddard, July 26, 1954; 1 dau., Lisa Robertson Lee. B.A., U. Wash., 1953; B.Arch., U. Va., 1958; grad. diploma in Architecture, Ecole Des Beaux Arts, Fontainebleau, France, 1952. Designer Architects Collaborative, Boston, 1958-59, Peirce & Pierce (architects), Boston, 1959-63; asso. Fred. Bassetti & Co. (architects), Seattle, 1963-67; partner Naramore, Bain, Brady & Johanson (architects), Seattle, 1967-81; pres. NBBJ Internat., 1976-81; architect TRA, Seattle, 1981-83; v.p. Daniel, Mann, Johnson & Mendenhall, San Francisco, 1983-93; prin. RRS Consulting, 1993—; archtl. design critic Boston Archtl. Ctr., 1961-62. Important works include Ridgeway III Dormitories, Bellingham, Wash. (Dept. Housing and Urban Devel. Honor award), Seattle Rapid Transit (HUD Excellence award), Safeco Ins. Co. Home Office Complex, Seattle, King County Stadium, Balt. Conv. Ctr., Oreg. Conv. Ctr., San Francisco (Moscone) Conv. Ctr. Expansion, Honolulu Conv. Ctr., Wilmington (Del.) Conv. Ctr. Served with CIC U.S. Army, 1954-56. Recipient Premier Prix D'Architecture Ecole Des Beaux Arts, Fontainebleau, 1951, 52, Prix D'Remondet Fontainebleau, 1952. Mem. AIA, Internat. Assn. Auditorium Mgrs., Scarab, Seattle Tennis Club, Sigma Chi. Episcopalian. Home and Office: 17032 NE 135th Ct Redmond WA 98052-1715

SOWELL, THOMAS, economist; b. Gastonia, N.C., June 30, 1930. A.B., Harvard U., 1958; A.M., Columbia U., 1959; Ph.D., U. Chgo., 1968. Economist Dept. Labor, 1961-62; instr. econs. Douglass Coll., Rutgers U., 1962-63; lectr. econs. Howard U., 1963-64; econ. analyst AT&T, 1964-65; asst. prof. Cornell U., 1965-69; asso. prof. Brandeis U., 1969-70; asso. prof. econs. UCLA, 1970-74, prof., 1974-80; project dir. Urban Inst., Washington, 1972-74; fellow Center Advanced Study Behavioral Scis., Stanford, Calif., 1976-77; sr. fellow Hoover Instn., 1977, 80—; vis. prof. Amherst Coll., 1977. Author: Ethnic America, 1981, A Conflict of Visions, 1987, Inside American Education, 1993, Race and Culture, 1994, The Vision of the Anointed, 1995; contbr. articles to profl. publs. Served with USMC, 1951-53. Mem. Am. Econ. Assn., Nat. Acad. Edn. Office: Stanford Univ Hoover Instn Stanford CA 94305

SOWERS, WESLEY HOYT, lawyer, management consultant; b. Whiting, Ind., Aug. 26, 1905; s. Samuel Walter and Bertha E. (Spurrier) S.; m. Gladys Krueger, Jan. 21, 1929; children: Penny (Mrs. David Buxton), Wesley Hoyt. BS, Purdue U., 1926, MS, 1927; JD, DePaul U., 1941; grad., Advanced Mgmt. Program, Harvard, 1960. Bar: Ill. 1940; registered patent atty. and practitioner ICC. Chemist Shell Oil Co., East Chicago, Ind., 1927-29; sales engr. Nat. Lead Co., St. Louis, 1929-31; lab. supr. patent atty. Pure Oil Co., Chgo., 1932-42; v.p. Bay Chem. Co., New Orleans, 1942-50, Frontier Chem. Co., Wichita, Kans., 1950-57; pres. Frontier Chem. div. Vulcan Materials Co., 1957-65; exec. v.p., dir. Vulcan Materials Co., Birmingham, 1958-65; mgmt. counsel, 1965—; former bd. dirs. Gt. Lakes Chem. Co., West Lafayette, Ind., Huntsman Chem. Corp., Salt Lake City; health professions vis. com. Wichita State U. Patentee in field. Past chmn. Met. Planning Commn., Wichita and Sedgwick County, 1958; commr. Kans. Econ. Devel. Bd.; chmn. Kansas Com. for Constitutional Revision, Sedgwick County U.S. Savs. Bonds Sales; past chmn. Kans. Radio Free Europe; past mem. adv. com. Kans. Geol. Survey; mem. Kans. Senate, 1970-81; former mem. engring. adv. council Sch. Engring. and Architecture, Kans. State U.; regent, trustee Wichita State U., HCA/Wesley Med. Ctr., Wichita; bd. dirs. Health Systems Agy. of Southeast Kans., Bd. of Health Sedgwick County, Inst. Logopedics, Quivira council Boy Scouts Am., YMCA, Health Systems Agy. S.E. Kans.; past trustee Midwest Research Inst.; mem. adv. bd. Kans. U. Bus. Sch.; vis. com. Coll. Health Profession, Wichita State U.; chmn. Kans. Health Care Providers Malpractice Commn.; mem. Kans. Health Care Costs Commn., Kans. Health Coordinating Council, Wichita/Sedgwick County Bd. Health; mem. gov.'s adv. commn. Kans. Dept. Health and Environment. Mem. AAAS, Kans. C. of C. (past pres., past dir.), Wichita C. of C. (past pres. 1959, past dir., Uncommon Citizen award 1988), Kans. Assn. Commerce and Industry (past pres., dir.), Am. Chem. Soc., AAAS, Smithsonian Assocs., Soc. Chem. Industry, Ill. Bar Assn., Wichita Bar Assn., Phi Delta Theta. Lodge: Rotary. Home and Office: 2414 N Woodlawn St Ste 170 Wichita KS 67220-3900

SOWERS, WILLIAM ARMAND, civil engineer; b. Willis, Va., Apr. 23, 1923; s. Harry Cline and Effie Vivian (Slusher) S.; m. Gale Johnson, May 20, 1978; children: Jane Dixon, Jean Marie. Student, Roanoke Coll., 1940-42; BCE, Va. Poly. Inst., 1947, BS in Archtl. Engring., 1948. Registered profl. engr., Va. Assoc. Brown, Wells & Meagher, Roanoke, Va., 1948-50; ptnr. R.L. Brown and Assocs., Roanoke, 1950-53, Sowers, Knowles & Rodes, Roanoke, 1953-59, Sowers, Rodes & Whitescarver, Roanoke, 1959-84, Sowers & Assocs., Roanoke, 1984-94; DJG Sowers, Mann Sowers, Mann, Inc., Roanoke, 1994—. Trustee ACEC Health Life Ins., St. Louis, 1975-83; commr. city planning City of Roanoke, 1976-92. Mem. Am. Cons. Engrs. (nat. pres. 1970-72), Cons. Engrs. Coun. Va. (svc. award 1972), Va. Soc. Profl. Engrs. (Svc. to Profession award 1972), Illuminating Engring. Soc., Hunting Hills Country Club, Masons. Office: PO Box 4038 Roanoke VA 24015-0038

SOWLE, DONALD EDGAR, management consultant; b. Mt. Pleasant, Mich., May 27, 1915; s. Sidney Edgar and Mary Agnes (West) S.; m. Gretchen Elizabeth MacRae, July 4, 1942 (dec. Feb. 1993); children: Lisa Sowle Cahill, Mary Ann Sowle Messing; m. Catherine Taggart Lewis, Nov. 25, 1995. B.S., Central Mich. U., 1940; postgrad., Harvard U., 1942, M.I.T., 1942; M.B.A., U. Chgo., 1950. Sales rep. Armour & Co., Grand Rapids, Mich., 1940-41; commd. 2d lt. USAF, advanced through grades to col., 1958; asst. dir. Jet Propulsion Lab., Calif. Inst. Tech., Pasadena, 1965-68; group v.p. Gulf & Western Industries, Los Angeles, 1968-69; dir. studies Congl. Commn. on Govt. Procurement, Washington, 1970-73; pres., chmn. bd. dirs. Don Sowle Assocs., Inc., Arlington, Va., 1973-81; adminstr. Fed. Procurement Policy, Exec. Office of The Pres. of The U.S., Washington, 1981-85; mgmt. cons., 1985—; dir. Procurement Round Table, 1985; mem. adv. bd. Fed. Contracts Report, Bur. Nat. Affairs, 1965-91; nat. regent Inst. Cost Analysis, 1981; instr. Georgetown U., 1961-65; adj. prof. and mem. adv. council procurement mgmt. program Kogod Coll. Am. U., Washington. Mem. adv. coun. Sch. Bus. Marymount U., 1985-94. Recipient Dept. Def. Joint Svc. Commendation medal, 1963, Legion of Merit award Sec. Def., 1964, Pub. Svc. award Los Angeles County, 1969, award Cen. Mich. U., 1968, 92. Fellow Nat. Contract Mgmt. Assn. (cert. profl. contract mgr., bd. advisers, Herbert Roback Meml. award 1990); mem. U.S. C. of C. (procurement coun. 1985), Nat. Security Indsl. Assn. (hon. life), Nat. Assn. Uniforms Svcs. (life mem., bd. dirs. 1984-88), Ret. Officers Assn. (life), Ronald Regan Alumni Assn., Am. Legion, Capitol Hill Club, Officers Club, NASA Alumni League, Beta Gamma Sigma. Republican. Roman Catholic. Home: 2795 N Quebec St Arlington VA 22207

SOWMAN, HAROLD GENE, ceramic engineer, researcher; b. Murphysboro, Ill., July 21, 1923; s. Harold Thomas and Thelma (Crombar) S.; m. Gladys May Wright, Dec. 8, 1945; children—Letitia Ann, Daniel Patrick. B.S. in Ceramic Engring., U. Ill., 1948, M.S. in Ceramic Engring., 1949, Ph.D. in Ceramic Engring., 1951. Assoc. ceramist Titanium Alloy, Niagara Falls, N.Y., 1951-52; research assoc. Knolls Atomic Power Lab., Gen. Electric Co., Schenectady, 1952-57; various supervisory and mgmt. positions in nuclear materials research and devel. 3M Co., St. Paul, 1957-65; research specialist 3M Co., 1965-67, sr. research specialist, 1967-70, corp. scientist, 1970-87; Friedberg Meml. lectr. Nat. Inst. Ceramic Engrs., 1988. Author articles, govt. reports on research and devel. of ceramic and nuclear materials; patentee in field. Served to 2d lt. AUS, 1943-46. Recipient Hon. Alumni award for disting. service in engring. U. Ill. Coll. Engring., 1983. Fellow Am. Ceramic Soc. (John Jeppson medal 1985, Samuel Geijsbeek award 1989); mem. Nat. Acad. Engring., Acad. of Ceramics, 3M Carlton Soc., Sigma Xi, Tau Beta Pi (chpt. Eminent Engr. award 1983). Home: 855 Towne Cir Stillwater MN 55082-4131

SOX, HAROLD CARLETON, JR., physician, educator; b. Palo Alto, Calif., Aug. 18, 1939; s. Harold Carleton and Mary (Griffiths) S.; m. Carol Helen Hill, Aug. 26, 1962; children: Colin Montgomery, Lara Katherine. BS, Stanford U., 1961; MD cum laude, Harvard U., 1966. Diplomate Am. Bd. Internal Medicine (pretest writing com. 1992-94). Intern and resident Mass. Gen. Hosp., Boston, 1966-68; clin. assoc. Nat. Cancer Inst., Bethesda, Md., 1968-70; instr. Dartmouth Med. Sch., Hanover, N.H., 1970-73; asst. prof. medicine to prof. Stanford U. Sch. Medicine, Calif., 1973-88; Joseph Huber prof., chmn. dept. medicine Dartmouth Med. Sch., 1988—; panel mem. Nat. Bd. Med. Examiners, Physicians Assts. Nat. Certifying Exam., 1973-76, chair com. on priority-setting for health tech. assessment Inst. Medicine, 1990-91, chair U.S. preventive svcs. task force, 1990-95, chair Inst. Medicine com. on HIV and U.S. blood supply, 1994-95; chair task force to revise internal medicine residency curriculum Federated Coun. Internal Medicine, 1993—. Author: Medical Decision Making, 1988; editor: Common Diagnostic Tests, 1987, 2d edit., 1990; mem. editorial bd. Med. Decision Making, 1980-87, Jour. Gen. Internal Medicine, 1985-87, New Eng. Jour. Medicine, 1990—; cons. assoc. editor Am. Jour. Medicine, 1988-95; assoc. editor Sci. Am. Medicine, 1995—; contbr. chpts. to books and articles to profl. jours. Fellow ACP (clin. efficacy assessment subcom. 1985-92, bd. regents, 1991—, chmn. ednl. policy com. 1994—); mem. Soc. for Gen. Internal Medicine (coun. 1980-83), Soc. for Med. Decision Making (trustee 1980-83, pres. 1983-84), Am. Fedn. Clin. Rsch., Assn. Am. Physicians, Assn. Profs. Medicine, Inst. Medicine of NAS, Alpha Omega Alpha. Home: Faraway Ln Hanover NH 03755-2312 Office: Darthmouth-Hitchcock Med Ctr Dept Lebanon NH 03756

SOYER, DAVID, cellist, music educator; b. Phila., Feb. 24, 1923; s. Samson and Esther (Faggin) S.; m. Janet Putnam, June 23, 1957; children: Daniel, Jeffrey. Student pub. schs., N.Y.C.; D.F.A. (hon.), U. South Fla., 1976, SUNY, 1983. Prof. cello Curtis Inst. Music, 1967; prof. music U. Md. Cellist with, Bach Aria Group, 1948-49, Guilet Quartet, 1949-51, New Music Quartet, 1954-55, Guarneri String Quartet, N.Y.C., 1964—, (Recipient 5 Grammy awards for Guarneri Quartet recs. 1965-74). Served with USNR, 1942-46. Mem. Century Assn. Jewish. Home: 6 W 77th St New York NY 10024-5125 also: Box 903 RFD 4 West Brattleboro VT 05301 Office: Herbert Barrett Mgmt care H Beall Mgmt 1776 Broadway New York NY 10019-2002

SOYFER, VALERY NIKOLAYEVICH, molecular geneticist and biophysicist; b. Gorky, RSFSR, USSR, Oct. 16, 1936; came to U.S., 1988; s. Nikolay Ilya Soyfer and Anna A. Kuznetsova; m. Nina I. Yakovleva, Aug. 12, 1961; children: Marina, Vladimir. BA in Agronomy, Timiryazev Agrl. Acad., Moscow, 1957; MA in Biophysics, Lomonosov State U., Moscow, 1961; PhD in Molecular Genetics, Kurchatov Inst. Atomic Energy, Moscow, 1964; D Phys. and Math. Scis., Moscow, 1994. Head Group Inst. Gen. Genetics, Moscow, 1966-70; dir. Lab. Molecular Genetics, Moscow, 1970-79; sci. dir. USSR Inst. Applied Molecular Biology and Genetics, Moscow, 1974-76; pres. Moscow Ind. U., 1985-88; disting. prof. Ohio State U., Columbus, 1988-90; Robinson prof. George Mason U., Fairfax, Va., 1990-93, disting. prof. molecular genetics, 1993—; sci. sec. Coun. on Molecular Biology and Genetics, Moscow, 1972-80; mem. USSR Govtl. Coun. on Molecular Biology and Molecular Genetics, 1974-80; invited lectr. Halle-Wittenburg U., German Democratic Republic, 1975; prin. investigator USSR State Com. on Sci., 1972, 74, 78, NIH, 1990. Author: Molecular Mechanisms of Mutagenesis, 1969, History of Molecular Genetics, 1970, Molekulare Mechanismen der Mutagenese und Reparatur, 1976, Power and Science, History of the Crushing of Soviet Genetics, 1989, Lysenko and the Tragedy of Soviet Science, 1994, Triple Helical Nucleic Acids, 1995; contbr. more than 200 articles on molecular genetics, biophysics and history of sci. to Nature, Mutation Rsch., Nucleic Acids Rsch., others. Chmn. bd. Friends of St. Petersburg Ind. U., N.Y., 1990—; pres. USSR Amnesty Internat. Group, Moscow, 1983-88. Mem. USSR Soc. Geneticists and Breeders (founding), Gt. Britain Genetical Soc., USSR Biochem. and Microbiol. Soc., Internat. Soc. for History, Philosophy and Social Studies of Biology (charter), European Culture Club (charter), Internat. Sci. Fedn. (bd. dirs. 1992—, chmn. bd. Internat. Soros Sci. Edn. program), Nat. Acad. Scis. Ukraine (fgn. mem.), Russian Acad. Natural Sci. (fgn. mem.), others. Achievements include discovery of DNA Repair in higher plants; establishment of correlation between structural damages in DNA and mitagenesis rate in higher plants; co-development of the method of photofootprinting of DNA triplexes. Office: George Mason U 200 E Bldg Fairfax VA 22030

SOYSTER, MARGARET BLAIR, lawyer; b. Washington, Aug. 5, 1951; d. Peter and Eliza (Shumaker) S. AB magna cum laude, Smith Coll., 1973; JD, U. Va., 1976. Bar: N.Y. 1977, U.S. Dist. Ct. (so. and ea. dists.) N.Y. 1977, U.S. Ct. Appeals (2nd cir.) 1979, U.S. Supreme Ct. 1981, U.S. Ct. Appeals (4th cir.) 1982, U.S. ct. Appeals (11th cir.) 1987, U.S. Ct. Appeals (7th cir.) 1991, U.S. Ct. Appeals (3d cir.) 1992. Assoc. Rogers & Wells, N.Y.C., 1976-84, ptnr., 1984—. Mem. ABA, Assn. of Bar of City of N.Y., Nat. Assn. Coll. and Univ. Attys., Phi Beta Kappa. Office: Rogers & Wells 200 Park Ave Ste 5200 New York NY 10166-0005

SOZEN, METE AVNI, civil engineering educator; b. Turkey, May 22, 1930; m. Joan Bates; children: Timothy, Adria, Ayshe. BCE, Roberts Coll., Turkey, 1951; MCE, U. Ill., 1952, PhD in Civil Engring., 1957; hon. doctorate, Bogazici U., Istanbul, Turkey, 1988. Registered structural engr., Ill. Jr. engr. Kaiser Engrs., Oakland, Calif., 1952; structural engr. Hardesty and Hanover, N.Y.C., 1953; research asst. civil engring. U. Ill., Urbana, 1953-55, research assoc., 1955-57, asst. prof. civil engring., 1957-59, assoc. prof., 1959-63, prof., 1963-94; prof. Purdue U., 1994—; cons. problems related to earthquake-resistant constrn. VA, various firms Europe, S.Am., U.S., UNESCO, UN Devel. Programs; cons. criteria for mass housing projects P.R.; adv. com. structural safety VA, rsch. project NSF, Applied Tech. Coun., Los Alamos and Sandia Nat. Labs.; chief investigator various NSF contracts and grants. Contbr. over 125 tech. papers, monographs, procs., reports to profl. jours.; presenter numerous papers to profl. meetings U.S.A, Japan, Italy, India, Turkey, Mexico. Recipient Drucker award U. Ill., 1986, Howard award, 1987, Boase award, 1988, Parlar Sci. and Tech. prize Mid. East Tech. U., Ankara, Turkey, 1995. Mem. NAE, ASCE (hon.,

Rsch. prize 1963, Raymond C. Reese award 1971, 94, Moiseiff award 1972, Howard award 1987, Raymond C. Reese Rsch. award 1994), Am. Concrete Inst. (Kelly award 1975, Bloem award 1985, Lindau award 1993), Am. Arbitration Assn. (nat. panel) Seismological Soc. Am., Swedish Royal Acad. Engring. Office: Purdue Univ Sch of Civil Engring 4149 Civil Engring Bldg West Lafayette IN 47907-1284

SPACE, THEODORE MAXWELL, lawyer; b. Binghamton, N.Y., Apr. 3, 1938; s. Maxwell Evans and Dorothy Marie (Boone) S.; m. Susan Shultz, Aug. 18, 1962 (div. Apr. 1979); children: William Schuyler, Susanna; m. Martha Collins, Apr. 6, 1991. AB, Harvard U., 1960; LLB, Yale U., 1966. Bar: Conn., 1966. Assoc. Shipman & Goodwin, Hartford, Conn., 1966-71, ptnr., 1971—, mng. ptnr., 1984-87, adminstv. ptnr., 1988-91. Mem. Bloomfield (Conn.) Bd. Edn., 1973-85, chmn., 1975-85; treas. Citizens Scholarship Found., Bloomfield, 1971-73, bd. dirs., 1973-91; mem. Bloomfield Human Rels. Commn., 1973-75; mem. Bloomfield Town Dem. Com., 1976-83; corporator Hartford Pub. Libr., 1976—; libr. com. Conn. Hist. Soc., 1990—, chair, 1993—; chair fin. com., coun. mem. Unitarian Soc. Hartford, 1988-91. Lt. (j.g.) USN, 1960-63. Mem. ABA, Conn. Bar Assn. (exec. com. adminstrv. law sect. 1980—), Hartford County Bar Assn., Am. Law Inst., Nat. Health Lawyers Assn., Conn. Health Lawyers Assn., Swift's Inn, Hartford Club. Democrat. Unitarian Universalist. Avocations: reading, classical music. Home: 59 Prospect St Bloomfield CT 06002-3038 Office: Shipman & Goodwin One American Row Hartford CT 06103-2833

SPACEK, SISSY (MARY ELIZABETH SPACEK), actress; b. Quitman, Tex., Dec. 25, 1949; d. Edwin S. and Virginia S.; m. Jack Fisk, 1974; children: Schuyler Elizabeth, Virginia Madison. Student, Lee Strasberg Theatrical Inst. Motion picture appearances include Prime Cut, 1972, Ginger in the Morning, 1972, Badlands, 1974, Carrie, 1976 (Acad. award nomination for best actress 1976), Three Women, 1977, Welcome to L.A., 1977, Heartbeat, 1980, Coal Miner's Daughter, 1980 (Acad. award for best actress 1980), Raggedy Man, 1981, Missing, 1982 (Acad. award nomination for best actress), The River, 1984 (Acad. award nomination for best actress), Marie, 1985, 'Night Mother, 1986, Crimes of the Heart, 1986 (Acad. award nomination for best actress), Violets Are Blue, 1986, JFK, 1991, The Long Walk Home, 1990, Hard Promises, 1992, Trading Mom, 1994, The Grass Harp, 1995, Streets of Laredo, 1995; TV movie appearances include The Girls of Huntington House, 1973, The Migrants, 1973, Katherine, 1975, Verna: USO Girl, 1978, A Private Matter, 1992, A Place for Annie, 1994, The Good Old Boys, 1995; guest host TV show Saturday Night Live, 1977; appeared in episode TV show The Waltons. Named Best Actress for Carrie, Nat. Soc. Film Critics, 1976, Best Supporting Actress, N.Y. Film Critics, 1977. Office: care Creative Artists 9830 Wilshire Blvd Beverly Hills CA 90212-1804*

SPACEY, KEVIN, actor; b. South Orange, N.J., July 26, 1959. Student, Juilliard Sch., 1979-81. Stage appearances include Henry IV, part I, 1981, Barbarians, 1982, Hurlyburly, 1985, Long Days Journey into Night, 1986, National Anthems, 1988, Lost in Yonkers, 1991 (Tony award for Best Featured Actor, 1991, Drama Desk award, 1991), Playland, 1993; TV appearances include (series) Wiseguy, 1987-88, (films) The Murder of Mary Phagan, 1988, Will You Remember Me, 1990, Fall From Grace, 1990, Darrow, 1991; films include Heartburn, 1986, Working Girl, 1988, Rocket Gibraltar, 1988, Dad, 1989, See No Evil, Hear No Evil, 1989, A Show of Force, 1990, Henry and June, 1990, Glengarry Glen Ross, 1991, Consenting Adults, 1992, The Ref, 1994, Outbreak, 1995, Swimming With Sharks, 1995, The Usual Suspects, 1995 (Acad. award for best supporting actor 1996), Seven, 1995. Office: Altman Greenfield & Salvaje 36th Fl 120 W 45th St New York NY 10036

SPACH, JULE CHRISTIAN, church executive; b. Winston-Salem, N.C., Dec. 21, 1923; s. Jule Christian and Margaret Stockton (Coyner) S.; m. Nancy Clendenin, Sept. 18, 1948; children: Nancy Lynn Lane, Margaret Cunningham, Ann Thomerson, Cecelia Welborn, Robert. Student, Va. Mil. Inst., 1942-43; B.S. in Chem. Engring, Ga. Inst. Tech., 1949; postgrad., Union Theol. Sem., Richmond, Va., 1951-52, Duke U., 1955-56; M.A. in Ednl. Adminstrn, U. N.C. at Greensboro, 1976; L.H.D. (hon.), Stillman Coll., Tuscaloosa, Ala., 1977; Litt.D. (hon.), Belhaven Coll., Jackson, Miss., 1977; LL.D., King Coll., Bristol, Tenn., 1977. Salesman Mengle Corp. subs. Internat. Container Corp., Winston-Salem, 1950-52; prof. scis., athletic dir. Quinze de Novembro Coll., Garanhuns, Pernambuco, Brazil, 1952-56; pres. Quinze de Novembro Coll., 1956-64; edn. dir. Cruzada ABC-Recife, Pernambuco, 1965-70; pres. Cruzada ABC-Recife, 1969-70; exec. sec. Parliamentary Christian Leadership, Brasilia, Fed. Dist., Brazil, 1970-73; exec. dir. Presbyn. Mission in Brazil, Campinas, Sao Paulo, 1973-75; moderator Gen. Assembly of Presbyn. Ch. in U.S., Atlanta, 1976-77; exec. dir. Triad United Meth. Home, Inc., Winston-Salem, 1977—; dir. First Home Fed. Savs. and Loan. Bd. dirs. Instituto Gammon, Presbyn. Ch. U.S., Forsyth County Coun. on Aging Forsyth County Sr. Svcs. Forsyth County, Covenent Fellowship of Presbyns., William Black Lodge, Synod of N.C., Presbyn. Ch. U.S.A.; bd. visitors Lee's McRae Coll., Montreat Anderson Coll.; mem. cabinet United Way, 1987; chmn. Winston-Salem Forsyth County Coun. on Svcs. to Homeless; chmn. bd. dirs. Sr. Svcs., Inc., Winston-Salem. With USAAF, 1943-45, prisoner of war, Poland. Decorated Purple Heart; recipient Jefferson award, 1991. Mem. Sertoma Club (recipient 3 svc. awards). Republican. Clubs: Lions (Brazil); Rotary (Winston Salem). Home: Arbor Acres 1244 Arbor Rd Apt 197 Winston Salem NC 27104-1136 Office: 1240 Arbor Rd Winston Salem NC 27104-1106 *The Christian faith teaches us that the greatest of all gifts is love. This gift comes from God, and it is ours through the presence of His spirit dwelling in us. This love gives man peace within and with his fellow man.*

SPACH, MADISON STOCKTON, cardiologist; b. Winston-Salem, N.C., Nov. 10, 1926; s. Jule Christian and Margaret (Stockton) S.; m. Cecilia Goodson, June 25, 1949; children: Madison Jr., Joyce, Susan, David. AB, Duke U., 1950, MD, 1954. Diplomate Am. Bd. Pediatrics, Am. Bd. Pediatric Cardiology. Intern and resident dept. pediatrics Duke U., Durham, N.C., 1954-57, resident, 1955-56, fellow cardiology, 1956-57; prof. pediatrics Duke U. Sch. Medicine, Durham, N.C., 1968—, James B. Duke prof. pediatrics, 1977, prof. physiology, 1978-88, chief pediatric cardiology, 1986-91, prof. cell biology, 1988—; pres. Soc. for Pediatric Rsch., 1974; chmn. Sub-Board of Pediatric Cardiology, 1975-77, Nat. Heart, Lung, Blood Inst. Manpower Com., 1982-85. Author 167 published papers on cardiovascular rsch.; mem. editorial bd. Circulation, 1981-91. With USN, 1944-46, PTO. Fellow Am. Coll. Cardiology, Am. Inst. for Med. and Biomed. Engring.; mem. N.Y. Acad. Scis., Internat. Soc. for Heart Rsch. (Am. sect.), Am. Physiol. Soc., Phi Beta Kappa, Alpha Omega Alpha. Democrat. Presbyterian. Office: Duke U Sch Medicine PO Box 3475 Durham NC 27702-3475

SPACKMAN, DAVID GLENDINNING, lawyer; b. Wilkes Barre, Pa., Aug. 15, 1948; s. John Worth and Ethel Coates (Farley) S.; m. Judy Ellen Selednik, June 29, 1980; children: Jenna Reiss, Britt Farley. BA, Beloit Coll., 1970; JD, Suffolk U., 1976. Bar: Mass. 1977, U.S. Dist. Ct. Mass. 1977. Gen. counsel Dept. Health and Hosps., Boston, 1976-84; assoc. Gaston & Snow, Boston, 1984-87, ptnr., 1988-90; ptnr. Mintz, Levin, Cohn, Ferris, Glovsky & Popeo, P.C., Boston, 1990—. Office: Mintz Levin Cohn Ferris Glovsky & Popeo PC One Financial Ctr Boston MA 02111

SPACKMAN, THOMAS JAMES, radiologist; b. Oak Park, Ill., Apr. 24, 1937; s. Thomas Frederick and Louise Mary (Kaiser) S.; m. Donna S. Stewart, June 25, 1960; children—Kirsten, Thomas James, Victoria. BA, DePauw U., 1959; MD, Western Res. U., 1964; Diploma in Bus. Studies, London Sch. Econs., 1987. Intern, then resident in internal medicine Yale-New Haven Med. Center, 1964-66, resident in diagnostic radiology, 1966-68, fellow clin. research tng. unit, 1968-69; instr., then asst. prof. radiology Yale U. Med. Sch., 1969-74; asso. prof. U. Pa. Med. Sch., 1974-78; prof. radiology U. Conn. Med. Sch., Farmington, 1978—; head dept. U. Conn. Med. Sch., 1978-90; dir. radiology St. Francis Hosp. and Med. Ctr., Hartford, Conn., 1992-93; pres. Elscint, Inc., Hackensack, N.J., 1993—; sr. v.p. Elscint, Ltd., Haifa, Israel, 1993—; mem. Conn. Med. Exam. Bd., 1980-86; bd. dirs. Elscint, Inc. Mem. editorial adv. bd. Diagnostic Imaging, 1989-92; author articles in field, chpts. in books. Fellow Am. Coll. Radiology; mem. AMA, Assn. Univ. Radiologists, Soc. Pediatric Radiology, Radiol. Soc. N.J. Office: Elscint Inc 505 Main St Hackensack NJ 07601-5900

SPACKS, PATRICIA MEYER, English educator; b. San Francisco, Nov. 17, 1929; d. Norman B. and Lillian (Talcott) Meyer; 1 child, Judith Elizabeth Spacks. BA, Rollins Coll., Winter Park, Fla., 1949, DHL, 1976; MA, Yale U., 1950; PhD, U. Calif., Berkeley, 1955. Instr. English Ind. U., Bloomington, 1954-56; instr. humanities U. Fla., Gainesville, 1958-59; from instr. to prof. Wellesley Coll., Mass., 1959-79; prof. English Yale U., New Haven, 1979-89, chmn. dept., 1985-88; Edgar F. Shannon prof. English U. Va., 1989—, chmn. dept., 1991—. Author: The Poetry of Vision, 1967, The Female Imagination, 1975, Imagining a Self, 1976, The Adolescent Idea, 1982, Gossip, 1985, Desire and Truth, 1990, Boredom: The Literary History of a State of Mind, 1995. Fellow Guggenheim Found., 1969-70, NEH, 1974, Am. Council Learned Socs., 1978-79, Nat. Humanities Ctr., 1982-83, 89. Mem. MLA (2nd v.p. 1992, 1st v.p. 1993, pres. 1994, mem. adv. com. 1976-80, mem. exec. coun. 1986-89), Am. Acad. Arts and Scis., Am. Coun. Learned Socs. (mem. bd. trustees 1992—, v.p. 1994—). Home: 1830 Fendall Ave Charlottesville VA 22903-1614 Office: U Va Dept English Bryan Hall Charlottesville VA 22903

SPADA, JAMES, author, publisher; b. S.I., N.Y., Jan. 23, 1950; s. Joseph Vincent and Mary (Ruberto) S. Student, Wagner Coll., 1968-71, Calif. State U., 1979-80. Pres., Spada Pubs, Los Angeles, pub. Barbra Quar., Los Angeles, 1980-83. Mem. Authors Guild, ACLU. Democrat. Author: Barbra: The First Decade-The Films and Career of Barbra Streisand, 1974, The Films of Robert Redford, 1977, The Spada Report, 1979, Streisand-the Woman and the Legend, 1981, Monroe-Her Life in Pictures, 1982, Judy and Liza, 1983, Hepburn: Her Life in Pictures, 1984, The Divine Bette Midler, 1984, Fonda: Her Life in Pictures, 1985, Shirley and Warren, 1985, Grace: The Secret Lives of a Princess, 1987, Peter Lawford: The Man Who Kept the Secrets, 1991, More Than a Woman: An Intimate Biography of Bette Davis, 1993, Streisand: Her Life, 1995; book packager The 1984 Marilyn Monroe Pin-Up Calendar, 1983, The Telephone Book, 1984, Elizabeth Taylor: A Biography in Photographs, 1984, Bette Davis: A Biography in Photographs, 1985, Natalie Wood: A Biography in Photographs, 1986.

SPADER, JAMES, actor; b. Mass., Feb. 7, 1960. Student, Phillips Acad., Michael Chekhov Studio. Appeared in pictures Endless Love (debut 1981), The New Kids, 1985, Tuff Turf, 1985, Pretty in Pink, 1986, Mannequin, 1987, Wall Street, 1987, Less Than Zero, 1987, Baby Boom, 1987, Jack's Back, 1988, The Rachel Papers, 1989, sex, lies and videotape (Best actor award Cannes Festival 1989), 1989, Bad Influence, 1990, White Palace, 1990, True Colors, 1991, Storyville, 1992, Bob Roberts, 1992, The Music of Chance, 1993, Dream Lover, 1994, Wolf, 1994, Stargate, 1994; TV movies Cocaine: One Man's Seduction, 1983, A Killer in the Family, 1983, Family Secrets, 1984, Starcrossed, 1985; TV series The Family Tree, 1983. Office: care Tony Howard/ICM 8942 Wilshire Blvd Beverly Hills CA 90211-1934*

SPAEDER, ROGER CAMPBELL, lawyer; b. Cleve., Dec. 20, 1943; s. Ferd N. and Luceil (Campbell) S.; m. Frances DeSales Sutherland, Sept. 7, 1968; children: Michael, Matthew. BS, Bowling Green U., 1965; JD with honors, George Washington U., 1970. Bar: D.C. 1971, U.S. Dist. Ct. D.C. 1971, U.S. Ct. Appeals (D.C. cir.) 1971, U.S. Supreme Ct. 1976, U.S. Ct. Claims 1979, U.S. Dist. Ct. Md. 1984, U.S. Ct. Appeals (2d and 4th cirs.) 1985. Asst. U.S. atty. D.C., Washington, 1971-76; ptnr. Zuckerman, Spaeder, Goldstein, Taylor & Kolker, Washington, 1976—; faculty Atty. Gen. Advocacy Inst., 1974-76, Nat. Inst. Trial Adv., 1978-79; adj. faculty Georgetown U. Law Ctr., 1979-80, Am. U. Ctr. Adminstrn. Justice, 1976-79; lectr. D.C. Bar Continuing Legal Edn. Programs, 1980—. Recipient Spl. Achievement award Dept. Justice, 1971. Mem. ABA (co-chair com. on complex crimes litigation 1989-92, divsn. co-dir. sect. litigation 1992—), Bar Assn. D.C. (lectr. Criminal Practice Inst. 1977-80), D.C. Bar (com. criminal jury instrns. 1972, div. courts, lawyers, adminstrn. of justice, 1976-78; adv. com. continuing legal edn. 1986), Def. Rsch. Inst., Assn. Trial Lawyers Am., Assn. Plaintiffs' Trial Attys., Nat. Assn. Criminal Def. Lawyers, Omicron Delta Kappa. Contbr. articles to profl. jours. and chpts. to books. Home: 7624 Georgetown Pike Mc Lean VA 22102-1412 Office: Zuckerman Spaeder Goldstein Taylor & Kolker 1201 Connecticut Ave NW Fl 12 Washington DC 20036-2605

SPAEH, WINFRIED HEINRICH, retired banker; b. Essen, Fed. Republic of Germany, Dec. 23, 1930; came to U.S., 1961; s. Josef and Anna (Belker) S.; m. Waltraut Schab, Aug. 15, 1964; children: Andrea, Olivier. Abitur, Gymnasium Essen-Werden, 1951; postgrad. Columbia U., 1961-62; With Dresdner Bank, Essen and Düsseldorf, 1951-60; with internat. banking div. Morgan Guaranty Trust Co. of N.Y., N.Y.C., 1961-66, v.p. German offices, Frankfurt, 1969, gen. mgr., 1972; exec. mgr. Dresdner Bank AG, Frankfurt/Main., 1975, dep. of mng. dirs., 1979-82, sr. officer, N.Y.C., 1982-95; ret. 1995; dir. Dresdner (SE Asia) Ltd., Singapore, 1978-80, Aseambankers Malaysia Berhad, Kuala Lumpur, 1977-80, P.T. Asian and Euro-Am. Capital Corp. Ltd., Jakarta, 1977-80; chmn. Conf. State Bank Suprs./Fgn. Bankers Adv. Coun., Washington, 1993—. Mem. Am. Inst. Contemporary German Studies (bd. dirs. 1983—), Bankers Assn. Fgn. Trade (chmn. 1982-90, internat. adv. coun. 1982-95), Inst. Internat. Bankers (bd. dirs. 1989-92), German-Am. C. of C. (bd. dirs. 1985-93), N.Y. C. of C. (bd. dirs.), N.Y.C. Partnership (bd. dirs., internat. bus. coun.), Muenchener Herren Club, Union Internat. Club (Frankfurt), Belle Haven Club (Greenwich, Conn.). Home: 25 Turner Dr Greenwich CT 06831-4415

SPAEPEN, FRANS AUGUST, applied physics researcher, educator; b. Mechelen, Belgium, Oct. 29, 1948; came to U.S., 1971; s. Jozef F.M. and Ursula (Roppe) S.; m. Moniek Steemans, Aug. 21, 1973; children: Geertrui M., Elizabet U., Hendrik J.L. Burgerlijk Metaalkundig Ingenieur, U. Leuven, Belgium, 1971; PhD, Harvard U., 1975. IBM postdoctoral fellow Harvard U., Cambridge, Mass., 1975-77; asst. prof. applied physics Harvard U., 1977-81, assoc. prof., 1981-83, Gordon McKay prof. applied physics, 1983—; vis. prof. U. Leuven, 1984; chmn. Gordon Conf. on Phys. Metallurgy, 1988; dir. Harvard Materials Rsch. Lab., 1990—; solid state scis. com. NRC, 1990-93; Krengel lectr. Technion, Israel, 1994. Co-editor: Solid State Physics; mem. editl. bd. Jour. Applied Physics, Applied Physics Letters, 1990-93, Applied Physics Revs., 1991—, Phys. Rev., 1994—, Jour. Non-Crystalline Solids, 1990-94; contbr. numerous articles to profl. publs., chpts. to books. Recipient Best Paper award Acta Metallurgica, 1994. Fellow Am. Phys. Soc. (chmn. divsn. materials physics 1992), AIME-The Metall. Soc.; mem. Am. Soc. Metals (lectr.), Materials Rsch. Soc. (councillor 1986-88, 90-92, co-chmn. fall meeting Boston 1990, chmn. program com. 1993—), Koninklijke Vlaamse Ingenieurs Vereniging, Böhimische Physikalische Gesellschaft, Order van den Prince. Office: Harvard U Div Applied Scis 29 Oxford St Cambridge MA 02138-2901

SPAETH, C. EDMOND, library media specialist; b. Yonkers, N.Y., May 3, 1945; s. Camille and Ida Mae (Therrien) S.; m. Merrill Hunting, Sept., 1973; 1 child, Erin Elise. BA, Mich. State U., 1974; MS, L.I. U., 1981. Cert. sch. libr. specialist, N.Y. Libr. media specialist West Park (N.Y.) Union Free Sch., Valley Central Schs., Kingston (N.Y.) City Schs.; reference libr. Newburgh (N.Y.) Free Libr.; freelance storyteller. Reviewer ABC/CLIO Video Rating Guide for Librs.; contbr. entries premier edit. Hudson River Almanac; contbr. articles to JeMe Souviens. Chairperson Town of Fishkill Parks Bd.; trustee Mt. Gulian Historic Site. With USN, 1967-71. Recipient Storybook Garden grant. Mem. SLMSSENY (pres., v.p., editor newsletter), Ulster County Sch. Libr. System Bd., Kingston City Schs. Libr. Bd., Beta Phi Mu.

SPAETH, EDMUND BENJAMIN, JR., lawyer, law educator, former judge; b. Washington, June 10, 1920; s. Edmund B. and Lena (Link) S. AB magna cum laude, Harvard U., 1942, LLB, 1948. Bar: Pa. 1949. Judge Ct. of Common Pleas, Phila., 1964-73; judge Superior Ct of Pa., 1973-86, pres. judge, 1983-86; of counsel Pepper, Hamilton & Scheetz, Phila., 1986—; adj. prof. U. Pa. Law Sch., 1986—, cons. Ctr. on Professionalism, 1993—. Bd. dirs. Pub. Interest Law Ctr. of Phila., 1987—. Fellow Am. Bar Found. (life); mem. ABA, Am. Law Inst. (life), Pa. Bar Assn., Phila. Bar Assn., Am. Judicature soc., Order of Coif, Phi Beta Kappa. Home: Cathedral Village Apt L-206 600 E Cathedral Rd Philadelphia PA 19128-1933 Office: 3000 Two Logan Sq Philadelphia PA 19103

SPAETH, GEORGE LINK, physician, ophthalmology educator; b. Phila., Mar. 3, 1932; s. Edmund Benjamin and Lena Marie (Link) S.; m. Ann Ward, May 17, 1955; children: Kristin Lea Crowley, George Link Jr., Eric Edmund. BA magna cum laude, Yale U., 1954; MD cum laude, Harvard U., 1959; postgrad., U. Mich., 1960, U. Pa., 1971. Diplomate Am. Bd. Ophthalmology. Resident surgeon Wills Eye Hosp., Phila., 1960-63, attending surgeon, 1970—, dir. glaucoma svc., 1968—; clin. fellow NIH, Bethesda, Md., 1963-65; instr. U. Pa., Phila., 1965-68; pvt. practice Phila., 1965-68; prof. ophthalmology Temple U. Med. Sch., Phila., 1968-75, Jefferson Med. Coll., Phila., 1975—; ophthalmologist Chestnut Hill Hosp., Phila., 1975—; pres. Am. Glaucoma Soc., Boston, 1983-85; attending surgeon, Graduate Hosp.; cons., Bryn Mawr Hosp. Author: 14 books in ophthalmology and surgery, 1970—; contbr. over 500 articles to profl. jours.; editor: Ophthalmic Surgery jour., 1985; patentee differometer, tonometer tip cover. Pres. Chestnut Hill Cmty. Assn., Phila., 1970-72; trustee, treas. Thomas Harrison Found., 1975—; founder, pres. E.B. Spaeth and The Eye Disease Found., 1978—, Profls. for Nuclear Army Control, 1985-88; interviewer Yale Alumni Schs. Com., Phila., 1965—; Yale Class coun., 1968—; curriculum com. Jefferson Med. Coll. 1987-90; institutional review bd. Jefferson Med. Coll., 1990—. Lt. comdr. USPHS, 1963-68. Recipient Sir Stuart Duke Elder Glaucoma award Internat. Glaucoma Soc., 1986, Newberg award Lawyers Alliance for World Security, 1995; NIH grantee, 1968—. Fellow Am. Acad. Ophthalmology (chmn. ethics com. San Francisco 1987-95, coun. 1980-93, vice chmn. residency rev. com. Chgo. 1982-88, Sr. honor award 1988), Ind. Assn. Rsch. in Vision and Ophthalmology, Royal Coll. Ophthalmologist, United Kingdom, Danish Ophthalmological Soc.; mem. Coll. Physicians Phila. (sec. 1976-84), Phila. County Med. Soc., Pa. Acad. Ophthalmology (pres. coun.), Physicians for Social Responsibility (pres. Phila. chpt.), Assn. Computing Machinery (bd. govs., chmn. adv. coun., chmn. subcom. monitoring), Phila. Club, Phila. Cricket Club, Franklin Inn Club (Phila.), Moral Values Book Club, Phi Beta Kappa, Alpha Omega Alpha. Democrat. Episcopalian. Avocations: playing piano, sports, photography, gardening, poetry writing. Office: Wills Eye Hosp 900 Walnut St Philadelphia PA 19107-5509

SPAETH, KARL HENRY, retired chemical company executive, lawyer; b. Phila., Mar. 12, 1929; s. Edmund Benjamin and Lena Marie (Link) S.; m. Ann Dashiell Wieland, Sept. 14, 1963; children—Karl Henry, Edmund Alexander, Christopher Philip. AB, Haverford Coll., 1951; postgrad. Oxford U., 1955; JD, Harvard U., 1958. Bar: Pa. 1959, U.S. Ct. (ea. dist.) Pa. 1959, U.S. Ct. Appeals (3d cir.) 1959. Assoc. MacCoy, Evans & Lewis, Phila., 1959-62; counsel for fgn. ops. Scott Paper Co., Phila., 1962-69; v.p., corp. sec. Quaker Chem. Corp., Conshohocken, Pa., 1969-95, ret., 1995; bd. dirs. Greater Phila. Internat. Network, 1991-94, Cen. Phila. Devel. Corp., 1991—; bd. dirs., sec.-treas. Edmund B. Spaeth Clin. Rsch. Found., 1982—; chmn. bd. dirs. Pa. Chem. Industry Coun., 1984-86. Chmn. bd. trustees Quaker Chem. Found., 1982—; bd. overseers Univ. Mus., U. Pa., Phila., 1983-89, 90—; bd. dir. Opera Co. Phila., 1988—; vestry Ch. St. James the Less, Phila., 1992—; bd. dirs. Chestnut Hill Acad., Phila., 1976-83, pres., 1979-83; mem. Whitemarsh Twp. Bd. Suprs., Pa., 1969-75, chmn., 1972-74; mem. Com. of Seventy, Phila., 1984—; internat. adv. com. Phila. First Partnership Econ. Devel., 1994—. Comdr. USNR, 1952-55. Mem. Am. Soc. Corp. Secs., Pa. Bar Assn. (chmn. sect. on internat. and comparative law 1980-92), Montgomery Bar Assn., Phila. Com. on Fgn. Rels. (exec. com., sec. 1984-94), Phila. Club, Phila. Athenaeum, Libr. Co. of Phila., Phila. Cricket Club. Republican. Anglican. Oxford Union, Univ. Barge (sec. 1988-94), Mil. Order Fgn. Wars (registrar 1989-91, vice commdr. 1991-93). Home: 2129 Harts Ln Conshohocken PA 19428

SPAETH, NICHOLAS JOHN, lawyer, former state attorney general; b. Mahnomen, Minn., Jan. 27, 1950. A.B., Stanford U., 1972, J.D., 1977; B.A., Oxford U., Eng., 1974. Bar: Minn. 1979, U.S. Dist. Ct. (Minn.) 1979, U.S. Ct. Appeals (8th cir.) 1979, N.D. 1980, U.S. Dist. Ct. (N.D.) 1980, U.S. Supreme Ct. 1984. Law clk. U.S. Ct. Appeals (8th cir.), Fargo, N.D., 1977-78; law clk. to Justice Byron White U.S. Supreme Ct., Washington, 1978-79; pvt. practice, 1979-84; atty. gen. State of N.D., Bismarck, 1984-93; ptnr. Dorsey & Whitney, Fargo, 1993—; adj. prof. law U. Minn., 1980-83. Rhodes scholar, 1972-74. Democrat. Roman Catholic. Office: Dorsey & Whitney PO Box 1344 Fargo ND 58107-1344

SPAFFORD, MICHAEL CHARLES, artist; b. Palm Springs, Calif., Nov. 6, 1935. BA, Pomona Coll., 1959; MA, Harvard U., 1960. One man shows include Seattle Art Mus., 1982, 86, Reed Coll., 1984, Whtcom county Mus., 1987, U. Puget Sound, Tacoma, Wash., 1973, Tacoma Art Mus., 1975, 86, Utah Mus. Fine Arts, Salt Lake City, 1975, Francine Seders Gallery, Seattle, 1965—, Bellevue Art Mus., 1991, Cheney-Cowles Mus., Spokane, Wash., 1994; exhibited in group shows at Wilcox Gallery, Swarthmore Coll., Pa., 1977, Seattle Art Mus., 1977, 80, 84, Am. Acad. and Inst. Arts and Letters, N.Y.C., 1980, 83, 89, Kobe, Japan, 1981, Eastern Wash. U., 1982, Henry Art Gallery, 1982, 86, Bellevue Art Mus., 1987, Cheney Cowles Mus., 1988. Recipient Prix de Rome, 1967-69, award Am. Acad. and Inst. Arts and Letters, 1983; Louis Comfort Tiffany Found. grantee, 1965-66. Home: 2418 E Interlaken Blvd Seattle WA 98112-3029

SPAFFORD, MICHELLE, special education educator; b. New Kensington, Pa., June 7, 1964; d. Del John and Joan Elizabeth (Dunlap) S. BA in Therapeutic Recreation, Alderson-Broaddus Coll., Philippi, W.Va., 1986; M in Spl.Edn., Clarion (Pa.) U., 1991. Cert. tchr. mentally and physically handicapped, Pa. Resident care specialist Verland Found., Sewickley, Pa., 1986; child care specialist Luth. Youth and Family Svc., Pa., 1986-87; mental health therapist DuBois (Pa.) Regional Med. Ctr., 1987-90, recreational therapist, 1990-91; supr. Clearfield County Child & Youth Svcs., Clearfield, Pa., 1990-91; grad. asst. Clarion U., 1990-91; spl. edn. tchr. DuBois Area Sch. Dist., 1992—; recreational therapist The Golden Age, DuBois, 1994-95; mem. Perkins participatory planning com. Jefferson Tech., DuBois, 1994—; mem. Sandy Twp. Recreation Bd., 1995—. Tchr. pioneer club Christian Missionary Alliance, DuBois, 1993; tchr., coach Spl. Olympics, DuBois, 1991; advisor Environ. Club, DuBois Area H.S., 1994—. Mem. Council for Exceptional Children, Pa. Therapeutic Recreation Assn., The Wilderness Soc. Republican. Baptist. Avocations: swimming, water skiing, volleyball, cooking. Home: 1229 Treasure Lk Du Bois PA 15801-9029 Office: Du Bois Area Sch Dist Liberty Blvd Du Bois PA 15801

SPAGNOLO, SAMUEL VINCENT, internist, pulmonary specialist, educator; b. Pitts., Sept. 3, 1939; s. Vincent Anthony and Mary Grace (Culotta) S.; m. Lucy Aleta Weyandt, June 20, 1961 (div. Feb., 1992); children: Samuel, Brad, Gregg. BA, Washington & Jefferson Coll., 1961; MD, Temple U., 1965. Diplomate Am. Bd. Internal Medicine, Bd. of Pulmonary Disease; active lic. physician in Fla., Calif., Md., D.C.; inactive Pa., Mass. Sr. resident in medicine VA Med. Ctr., Boston, 1969-70, chief resident in medicine, 1970-71; Harvard Clin. and Rsch. fellow in pulmonary diseases Mass. Gen. Hosp., Boston, 1971-72; asst. chief med. svc. VA Med. Ctr., Washington, 1972-75, acting chief med. svc., 1975-76, chief pulmonary disease sect., 1976-94; instr. in medicine Boston U. Sch. of Medicine, Tufts u. Sch. Medicine, Boston, 1970-71; clin. and rsch. fellow in pulmonary diseases Harvard U. Sch. of Medicine, Mass. Gen. Hosp., Boston, 1971-72; clin. asst. prof. medicine Georgetown U., Washington, 1975-77; asst. prof. medicine George Washington U. Sch. of Medicine and Health Scis., Washington, 1972-75, assoc. prof., 1975-81, prof. medicine, 1981—, dir. divsn. pulmonary diseases and allergy, 1978-93; assoc. chmn. dept. medicine George Washington U. Med. Ctr., Washington, 1986-89; cons. in pulmonary diseases The Washington Hosp. Ctr., Washington, D.C., 1977—, Will Rogers Inst., White Plains, N.Y., 1980—, U.S. Dept. Labor, Washington, 1980—, Walter Reed Army Med. Ctr., Washington, 1987; rep. Am. Coll. Chest Physicians to Am. Registry Pathology, Washington, 1981-92; numerous radio tv appearances on Health Oriented Programs; invited lectr. in U.S., Russia, Jordan; chmn., mem. many coms. George Washington U. Sch. of Medicine, George Washington Med. Ctr., VA Med. Ctr., Washington; med. chest cons. in attempted assasination of former Pres. Regan. Author: (books): Clinical Assessment of Patients with Pulmonary Disease, 1986; co-author: (with A.E. Medinger) Handbook of Pulmonary Emergencies, 1986, (with others) Handbook of Pulmonary Drug Therapy, 1993, (with Witorsch, P.) Air Pollution and Lung Disease in Adults, 1994; contbr. numerous articles to profl jours. including Med. Clin. N. Am., Chest, So. Med. Jour., Am. Jour. Cardiology, Jour. Am. Med. Assn., Clin. Rsch., Am. Rev. Respiratory Disease, Am. Lung Assn. Bull., Clin. Notes on Respiratory Diseases, Jour. Nuclear Medicine, Drug Therapy; presented abstracts at over 13 profl. meetings; reviewer for Chest, Am. Review Respiratory Diseases. Lt. cmmdr. U.S. Pub. Health Svc., 1966-68. Decorated Cavaliere in Order of Merit, Republic of Italy, 1983; nominated for Golden Apple award by med. students Geo. Washington Sch.

of Medicine, Phila., 1977; recipient cert. appreciation D.C. Lung Assn., 1983. Fellow Am. Coll. Physicians (coun. critical care 1983-85), Am. Coll. Chest Physicians (gov. D.C., coun. of govs. 1989-96); mem. Am. Thoracic Soc. (exec. com. D.C. chpt. 1978, 85, 89, mem. adv. com. tuberculosis control, 1978-84, pres. D.C. chpt. 1981-83), Nat. Assn. VA Physicians (sec. 1987-89, v.p. 1989-91, pres. 1992—), Internat. Lung Found. (pres. 1991—). Achievements include first major review of patient outcome during early history of intensive care units; an analysis of mechanisms of hypoxemia in patients with chronic liver disease; first report of Pneumocystis Carinii Pneumonitis in patients with lung cancer; first prospective evaluation of short course therapy reported in U.S. using Isoniazid and Rifampin; first American report using laser through fiberoptic bronchoscope to treat lung cancer; first report to evaluate continuous intravenous morphine to control pain in cancer patients; description of a simple technique to measure the total lung volume non-invasively using the routing chest x-ray. Avocations: reading, swimming, stamp collecting, gardening, chess. Office: Geo Washington U 2150 Pennsylvania Ave NW Washington DC 20037

SPAGNUOLO, PASQUALINA MARIE, rehabilitation nurse; b. Phila., Jan. 21, 1942; d. Charles and Lena (Damiano) Caruolo; children: Louis, Charles, Jason. Lic. practical nurse diploma, Salem (N.J.) Community Coll., 1985; BSN, Widener U., Chester, Pa., 1989. Lic. practical nurse, Del., N.J., Pa.; RN, Del., N.J., Pa. Practical nurse A.I. Dupont Rehab. Hosp., Wilmington, Del.; med. sec. Underwood Meml. Hosp., Woodbury, N.J., nurse's aide; pvt. duty nurse, Mt. Ephraim, N.J. Merit scholar Widener U., 1985-86, Charlotte Newcomb scholar, 1986-87; recipient Eleanore O. Dower award, 1988.

SPAHN, GARY JOSEPH, lawyer; b. N.Y.C., July 23, 1949; s. Harry G. and Mary (Hopkins) S.; m. Lois Luttinger, Aug. 9, 1975; children: Gary J. Jr., Lori J. BA, L.I. U., 1971, MA, 1976; JD, U. Richmond, 1975. Bar: Va. 1975, U.S. Ct. Appeals (4th cir.) 1975, U.S. Supreme Ct. 1980. Law clk. to Hon. Judge Dortch U.S. Dist. Ct. (ea. dist.) Va., Richmond, 1975-77; from assoc. to ptnr. Mays & Valentine, Richmond, 1977—, now ptnr., chmn. products liability and ins. sect.; lectr. in field, 1980—; mem. judicial conf. U.S. Ct. Appeals (4th cir.). Co-author: Virginia Law of Products Liability, 1990. Pres. Southhampton Citizens Assn., Richmond, 1982-85; dir. Southhampton Recreation Assn., Richmond. 1983; mem. coun. Southside Montessori Sch., Richmond, 1983-85. With USAF, 1967-73. Mem. ABA (litigation and tort and ins. sects.), Am. Assn. Ins. Attys., Assoc. Def. Trial Attys., Def. Rsch. Inst., Va. Assn. Def. Attys., Va. Mfrs. Assn., Products Liability Adv. Counsel, Va. Power Boat (commodore). Avocations: boating, basketball, racquetball. Office: Mays & Valentine PO Box 1122 1111 E Main St Richmond VA 23208-1122

SPAHN, MARY ATTEA, retired educator; b. Buffalo, July 16, 1929; d. George H. and Madeline Barbara (Bitar) Attea. A.B., Nazareth Coll., Rochester, N.Y., 1950; Ed.M., SUNY, Buffalo, 1952, Ed.D., 1966. Tchr. Clarence (N.Y.) Cen. Schs., 1951-65; tchr. reading Sweet Home Cen. Schs., Amherst, N.Y., 1965-68; assoc. prof. elem. edn. D'Youville Coll., Buffalo, 1970-75; prof. curriculum and supervision SUNY Coll., Buffalo, 1975-85, prof. emeritus, 1985—; part time tchr. creativity East Aurora Schs., N.Y., 1988; coordinator Sweet Home secondary sch. summer reading program, 1968-70; cons. to Niagara Wheatfield, Clarence Central, Sweet Home schs. Author: Turning Students on Through Creative Writing, 2d edit., 1979; (poetry) Weep Willow Weep, 1974; Fragments, 1979, Busy Bodies, 1975, Flutterbyes, A Collection of Easy Readings, 1985, (with others) Flutterbyes II, 1992; contbr. articles to profl. jours. Vol. Creative Edn. Found., Creative Problem Solving Inst., Ministry of Care, McCaulley House, 1988—; leader Bishop's Com., 1987. Mem. NEA, Internat. Reading Assn. (pres. 1968 Niagara Frontier coun.), N.Y. State Reading Assn. (sec. 1970), Am. Ednl. Rsch. Assn., United Univ. Profs., Nat. Coun. Tchrs. English, East Aurora Writers Guild, Southtown's Quilters Club, Bernina Club, Penwomen, Grief Counselling, Phi Delta Kappa. Home: 58 Buffalo Rd East Aurora NY 14052-1628 *Persistence, determination, sensitivity, sharing, willingness to take risks and give of myself, plus a faith in God...these are the qualities which have helped me on the road to success.*

SPAIN, JACK HOLLAND, JR., lawyer; b. Greenville, N.C., Jan. 24, 1939; s. Jack Holland and Lucy Marie (Hardee) S.; m. Mary Elizabeth Rhamstine, May 9, 1964; children: John Hardee, Sidney Holland. AB, U. N.C., 1960; JD, Harvard U., 1963. Bar: Va. 1964, U.S. Dist. Ct. (ea. dist.) Va. 1964. Assoc. Hunton & Williams, Richmond, Va., 1964-71; ptnr. Hunton & Williams, Richmond, 1971—. Bd. dirs. Maymount Found., Richmond, 1975—, pres., 1980-82; mem. bd. elders 2d Presbyn. Ch., Richmond, City Dem. Com., Richmond; spl. counsel Local Govt. Com., Va. Constl. Revision Com. Lt. comdr. USN. Mem. ABA (chmn. taxation com., local govt. sect.), Va. Bar Assn., Richmond Bar Assn., Harvard U. Law Sch. Assn. Va. (pres.), Phi Beta Kappa, Phi Eta Sigma, Phi Alpha Theta. Club: Bull & Bear (Richmond). Avocations: spectator sports, antiques, Chinese art, farming. Office: Hunton & Williams River Front Pla E Twr 951 E Byrd St Richmond VA 23219-4040

SPAIN, JAMES DORRIS, JR., biochemist, educator; b. Washington, Feb. 3, 1929; s. James Dorris and Frances (Pitkin) S.; m. Patricia Mann, Oct. 3, 1952; children: James Williamson, Caryn Ann, Mary Alisa. Student, Tulane U., 1947-48; B.S., Mich. Technol. U., 1951; M.S., Med. Coll. Va., 1953; Ph.D., Stanford, 1956. Research fellow biochemistry U. Tex.-M.D. Anderson Hosp. and Tumor Inst., 1955-56; assoc. prof. dept. chemistry Mich. Technol. U., Houghton, 1956-62; head dept. biol. scis. Mich. Technol. U., 1962-68, prof. biochemistry, 1962-84, prof. emeritus, 1985—; dir. Ctr. for Instrnl. Computing, Ea. Mich. U., Ypsilanti, 1984-85; vis. prof. Clemson U., S.C., 1985-94; pres. Electronic Homework Sys., Inc., 1994—; cons. Computer Applications in Biology and Chemistry; dir. SUMIT Courseware Devel. Project, 1979-82. Author: Some Computer Programs for Biology, 1970, Biological Simulation Techniques, 1972, Lake Superior Basin Bibliography, 1976, BASIC Computer Models in Biology, 1978, BASIC Microcomputer Models in Biology, 1982, Developing Chemical Skills with Computerized Instruction, 1990, Computer Simulation in Biology: A BASIC Introduction, 1992, CHEMI-SKILL-BILDR Electronic Homework System, 1994; contbr. articles to profl. jours. Chmn. adv. council St. Josephs Hosp. Sch. Nursing, 1967; Trustee, pres. Portage Twp. Sch. Bd., 1968-76; trustee Copper Country Intermediate Sch. Dist., 1975-78. Recipient Faculty Research award Mich. Technol. U., 1965. Mem. Am. Chem. Soc. (past sect. v.p., chmn.), Sigma Xi, Phi Lambda Upsilon. Episcopalian. Clubs: Miscowaubik (gov. 1971-74, 79-82), Boscobel Country; Lodge: Rotary. Home: 129 Leslie Ln Pendleton SC 29670-9697

SPAIN, JAMES WILLIAM, political scientist, writer, investor; b. Chgo., July 22, 1926; s. Patrick Joseph and Mary Ellen (Forristal) S.; m. Edith Burke James, Feb. 21, 1951; children: Patrick, Sikandra, Stephen, William. M.A., U. Chgo., 1949; Ph.D., Columbia U., 1959. Cons. sec. army, 1949-50; with U.S. Fgn. Service, 1951-53; researcher, lectr. Columbia, 1955-62; mem. policy planning council State Dept., 1963-64; dir. Office Research and Analysis for Near East and South Asia, 1964-66; country dir. for Pakistan and Afghanistan, 1966-69; charge d'affaires Am. embassy, Rawapindi, 1969; consul gen. Istanbul, Turkey, 1970-72; minister Am. embassy, Ankara, 1972-74; diplomat-in-residence, vis. prof. history and govt. Fla. State U., Tallahassee, 1974-75; amb. to Tanzania Dar es Salaam, 1975-79; amb., dep. permanent rep. UN, N.Y.C., 1979; amb. to Turkey, Ankara, 1980-81; amb. to Sri Lanka, Colombo, 1985-89; fgn. affairs fellow Carnegie Endowment for Internat. Peace and Rand Corp., Washington, 1982-84; chmn. CML Spain Perry Fin. Svcs. Ltd., Colombo; chmn. Lanka Infrastructure Ltd.; bd. dirs. Hawk Mountain Fed. Express, Ltd.; adj. prof. polit. sci. Am. U., Washington, 1965-67. Author: The Way of the Pathans, 1962, The Pathan Borderland, 1963, American Diplomacy in Turkey, 1984, Pathans of the Latter Day, 1995. Pres. bd. trustees Joseph Frazer Meml. Hosp.; bd. dirs. Inst. Technol. Studies, Philharm. Soc., Rainbow Found. With U.S. Army, 1946-47. Fellow Ford Found., 1953-55; recipient Presdl. Exec. award, 1983, Wilbur I. Carr award for Disting. Diplomacy, 1989. Mem. Coun. Fgn. Rels., Washington Inst. Fgn. Affairs, Am. Fgn. Svc. Assn., Assn. Diplomatic Studies and Tng., Cosmos Club. Home: Galle Face Ct II # 42, Colombo 3, Sri Lanka

SPAIN, JAYNE BAKER, corporate executive, educator; b. San Francisco; d. Lawrence Ian and Marguerite (Buchanan) Baker; student U. Calif. at Berkeley, 1944-47, Music U. Cin., 1947-50; LL.D., Edgecliff Coll., Cin., 1969; Dr. Pub. Service, George Washington U., 1970; LL.D., U. Cin., 1971, Dumbarton Coll., 1972, Springfield (Mass.) Coll., 1973, Gallaudet Coll., Washington, 1973; L.H.D. Bryant Coll., 1972, Russell Sage Coll., Troy, N.Y., 1973, Loyola Coll., Balt., 1975; m. John A. Spain, July 14, 1952; children—Jeffry Alan, Jon Kimberly. Pres., Alvey-Ferguson Co., Cin., 1952-66, pres. Alvey-Ferguson Operations div. Litton Industries, Inc., 1966-70, also dir. parent co., 1970—; vice chmn. CSC, 1971—; sr. v.p. Gulf Oil Corp., Pitts., from 1975; Disting. vis. prof. and exec.-in-residence George Washington U., Washington, 1979—; dir. Beatrice Foods, Chgo., Ohio Nat. Life Ins., Cin. Vice chmn. Pres.'s Com. on Employment Handicapped, 1966—; participant internat. trade fairs U.S. Depts. State, Commerce, Europe, North Africa, 1961-66, mem. trade and investment mission, India, 1965; mem. U.S. com. Internat. Council Social Welfare; mem. Pres.'s Adv. Com. on Productivity; dir. Pvt. Sector Council, Washington, Dean's Adv. com. Coll. of Bus. U. Cin.; mem. Internat. Soc. Rehab. Disabled; mem. adv. com. sheltered workshops U.S. sec. labor; mem. Ohio Gov.'s Commn. on Status of Women; mem. bldg. com. Children's Med. Center, Cin. Bd. dirs., past pres. Convalescent Hosp. Children, Cin., Greater Cin. Hosp. Council, Children's Neuromuscular Diagnostic Center, Cin., Cin. Sci. Center; bd. dirs. President's Commn. on Personnel Interchange; chmn. bd. trustees Fed. Women's Award; mem. dean's adv. council Coll. Bus. Adminstrn. U. Cin.; chmn. Found. of Ams. for the Handicapped; bd. dirs. Recs. for the Blind. Recipient Distinguished Service award for work overseas blind People Com., Washington, 1965; Migel medal Am. Found. Blind, N.Y., 1966; Golden Plate award industry Acad. Achievement, Dallas, 1967; Top Hat award Bus. and Profl. Women's Clubs. Am., N.Y., 1967; named to Cin. Bus. Hall Fame, 1994. Mem. Conveyor Equipment Mfrs. Assn. (sec., treas., dir. 1960-63), Machinery and Allied Products Inst., Am. Mgmt. Assn., Internat. Platform Assn. Episcopalian. Contbr. articles to profl. jours.

SPAIN, NETTIE EDWARDS (MRS. FRANK E. SPAIN), civic worker; b. Alexandria, La., Oct. 9, 1918; d. John Henry and Sallie Tamson (Donald) Edwards; student Alexandria Bus. Coll., 1936-37, Birmingham-So. Coll., 1958-59, Nat. Tng. Inst., United Community Funds and Councils Am., 1965-66; m. Frank E. Spain, May 18, 1974. Reporter, Alexandria Daily Town Talk, 1942-45; staff writer Birmingham (Ala.) Post, 1945-49; pub. rels. dir. Community Chest, Birmingham, 1949-53; dir. info. services Pa. United Fund, Phila., 1953-55; asst. exec. dir. Ala. Assn. Mental Health, Birmingham, 1956-57; pub. rels. dir. United Appeal, Birmingham, 1958-68, asst. exec. dir., 1968-71; asst. to pres. for devel. U. Ala., Birmingham, 1971-74, acting dir., 1975. Mem. pub. rels. com. Ala. Heart Assn., Birmingham, 1972-75; bd. dirs. Kate Duncan Smith DAR Sch., Grant, Ala., 1981-82; bd. dirs. Children's Aid Soc., 1971-77, 79, v.p., 1976-77; bd. dirs. Jefferson-Shelby Lung Assn., 1972-75, Vol. Bur. Greater Birmingham, 1973-77, Hale County chpt. ARC, Hale County Library; advisor fin. Hale County Library Bd., 1988; adv. com. Jr. League, 1974-75; exec. com. Historic Hale County Preservation Soc.; hon. mem. president's council U. Ala., Birmingham; bd. dirs. Norton Center Continuing Edn., Birmingham-So. Coll., mem. Edward Lee Norton Bd. Advisers for Mgmt. and Profl. Edn., internat. progam com.; charter mem. bd. Birmingham Children's Theater. Recipient 1st Place awards Nat. Photos for Fedn., 1966-67; citation Pa. United Fund, 1955, citation for service Jefferson-Shelby Lung Assn., 1975, citation Ala. Heart Assn., 1974, Vol. Bur. Greater Birmingham, 1977; award of Merit, Ala. Hist. Commn., 1977, Disting. Svc. award, 1987; Rotary Found. Paul Harris fellow; Benjamin Franklin fellow Royal Soc. Arts, London, U.S.A.; citation Veritas Club, Gt. Am. Citizen of Greensboro, Ala., 1987. Mem. Nat. Pub. Rels. Council of Health and Welfare Services (bd. dir. 1967-69), Birmingham Women's Com. of 100, Pub. Rels. Council Ala. (hon. life), Order of Crown in Am., Ala. Hist. Soc., Nat. Soc. Colonial Dames Am., English Speaking Union, Nat. Trust for Historic Preservation, Met. Opera Guild, Guy E. Snavely Soc. (Birmingham-So. Coll.), Colonial Dames Am., DAR, First Families of Va., Burgess for Ala., Birmingham Astron. Soc. (hon.), Children's Aid Foundation (charter mem). Episcopalian. Clubs: Lakeview Country (Greensboro, Ala.), Mountain Brook Country, The Summit (Birmingham), The Club (Birmingham), Northriver Yacht (Tuscaloosa), Mountain Brook Club (Birmingham). Home: Medley PO Box 400 Greensboro AL 36744-0400

SPAIN, RICHARD COLBY, lawyer; b. Evanston, Ill., Nov. 17, 1950; s. Richard Francis and Anne Louise (Brinckerhoff) S.; m. Nancy Lynn Mavec, Aug. 3, 1974; children: Catherine Day, Sarah Colby. BA cum laude, Lawrence U., 1972; JD, Case Western Reserve U., 1975; LLM in taxation, John Marshall Law Sch., 1985. Bar: Ohio 1975, Ill. 1982, U.S. Dist. Ct. (no. dist.) Ohio 1977, U.S. Dist. Ct. (no. dist.) Ill. 1982, Mass. 1996. Ptnr. Spain & Spain, Cleve., 1975-82, Whitted & Spain, P.C., Chgo., 1985-89, Spain, Spain & Varnet P.C., Chgo., Northborough, Mass., 1989—; assoc. Canel Whitted & Aronson, Chgo., 1982-85; dir., sec. Stone Perforating Co., Chgo., 1988—, Chgo. EDM, Inc., Chgo., Highland Park, Ill., 1994—. Contbr. articles to profl. jours. Dir., co-chair devel. com. ARC Ill., 1993—; dir., pres. Hanover Condominium Assn., Chgo., 1992—; dir. Chgo. Youth Symphony Orch., 1983—. Mem. Chikaming Country Club (dir.), The Winter Club Lake Forest. Home: 1780 Bowling Green Dr Lake Forest IL 60045 Office: Spain Spain & Varnet PC 33 N Dearborn St Ste 2220 Chicago IL 60602

SPAINHOWER, JAMES IVAN, retired college president; b. Stanberry, Mo., Aug. 3, 1928; s. Elmer Enoch and Stella Irene (Cox) S.; m. Joanne Steanson, June 10, 1950; children: Janet Dovell, James Jeffrey. BA, Phillips U., Enid, Okla., 1950, LLD (hon.), 1967; BD, Lexington (Ky.) Theol. Sem., 1953; MA in Polit. Sci., U. Mo., Columbia, 1967, PhD, 1971; U. Ark., 1954; diploma, U. Pacific Sch. Religion, Berkeley, Calif., 1958; DPA (hon.), Culver-Stockton Coll., 1973; LL.D. (hon.), Maryville Coll., St. Louis, 1976; Litt.D. (hon.), Kirksville (Mo.) Coll. Osteo. Medicine, 1977; D.H.L. (hon.), Mo. Valley Coll., 1984; LLD (hon.), Eureka Coll., 1989, Lynchburg Coll., 1993. Ordained to ministry Christian Ch. (Disciples of Christ), 1950; pastor chs. in Ark. and Mo., 1953-70; mem. Mo. Ho. of Reps. from, Saline County, 1963-70; pres. Asso. Med. Schs. Mo., Jefferson City, 1970-72; part-time prof. polit. sci. Lincoln U., Jefferson City, 1970-72; treas. State of Mo., 1973-80; pres. Sch. of Ozarks, Point Lookout, Mo., 1981-82, Lindenwood Coll., St. Charles, Mo., 1983-89; pres. divsn. higher edn. Christian Ch. (Disciples of Christ), 1989-93. Author: Pulpit, Pew and Politics, 1979. Chmn. Mo. del. Dem. Nat. Conv., 1976; elected mem. Acad. Squires, 1981; 1st chmn. Mo. Children's Trust Fund, 1984-86. Recipient Mental Health award Mo. Mental Health Assn., 1967, Meritorious Service award St. Louis Globe Dem., 1968, Harry S. Truman award Saline County Young Democrats, 1970, citation of merit Alumni Assn. U. Mo., 1975; named Mo. Lay Educator of Year Mo. chpt. Phi Delta Kappa, 1968. Home and Office: 8067 Old White River Rd Rogers AR 72756-7662

SPAKE, NED BERNARR, energy company executive; b. Montpelier, Ohio, Sept. 18, 1933; s. Lewis W. and Gertrude E. (Foley) S.; m. Marilyn Rae Faulk, July 14, 1956; children: Julie Ann Spake Scott, Cynthia Ann Spake Lovern. B. Indsl. Engring., U. Fla., Gainesville, 1957; MBA, Rollins Coll., Winter Park, Fla., 1967. Mgr. Fla. Power Corp., Winter Park, Fla., 1962-72; dir. Fla. Power Corp., St. Petersburg, Fla., 1972-76, asst. v.p., 1976-78, v.p., 1978-83; v.p. Fla. Progress Corp., St. Petersburg, 1983-86; pres., chief exec. officer, dir. Progress Technologies Corp., St. Petersburg, Fla., 1985-89; pres., chief exec. officer, chmn. bd. Advanced Separation Technologies, Inc., St. Petersburg, Fla., 1985-89, Rein Energy Corp., Alachua, Fla., 1989-92; pres., CEO The Nouveau Group Inc., Winter Park, Fla., 1992—, also bd. dirs. Patentee in field. Mem. adv. coun. Engring. Sch. U. Fla., Gainesville, 1978—; bd. dirs. U. Fla. Rsch. Found., Inc., 1986-94; dir. GelTech, Inc., 1986-87. Lutheran. Home: 2711 Summerfield Rd Winter Park FL 32792-5111 Office: The Nouveau Group Inc 2711 Summerfield Rd Winter Park FL 32792-5111

SPALDING, ANDREW FREEMAN, lawyer; b. Toledo, June 24, 1951; s. Dean and Shirley Louise (Maitland) S.; m. Adele Taylor, May 17, 1980; children: Amy Louise, Adam Freeman, Audrey Wade, Abigail Maitland. BA, U. Calif.-Berkeley, 1973; JD, So. Meth. U., 1977. Bar: Tex. 1977, U.S. Dist. Ct. (so., ea., and we. dists.) Tex. 1978, U.S. Ct. Appeals (5th cir.) 1978; bd. cert. Civil Trial Law Tex., Personal Injury Trial Law, Tex.. Bd. Legal Specialization. Assoc. Bracewell & Patterson, Houston, 1977-84, ptnr., 1984—. Notes and comments editor Southwestern Law Jour., Dallas, 1976-77. Fellow Tex. Bar Found., Houston Bar Found.; mem. State Bar Tex., Tex. Assn. Def. Counsel, Houston Bar Assn., Def. Rsch. Inst., Knights Momus, Krewe Maximilian. Clubs: Houston. Office: Bracewell & Patterson 2900 S Tower Pennzoil Pla 711 Louisiana St Houston TX 77002-2716

SPALDING, JAMES STUART, retired telecommunications company executive; b. Edinburgh, Scotland, Nov. 23, 1934; arrived in Can., 1957, permanent resident, 1962; Student, Edinburgh U., 1951-52, Glasgow U., 1953. Gen. mgr., dir. United Corps. Ltd., Montreal, Que., Can., 1970-72; pension fund mgr. BCE, Inc., Montreal, 1972-74, sr. asst. treas., 1974-76, treas., 1976-79, v.p., 1979-83, v.p. fin., 1983-84, exec. v.p. fin., 1984-90; ret., 1990; pub. gov. Can. Investor Protection Fund. Mem. Inst. Chartered Accts. Scotland, Order Chartered Accounts Que., Fin. Execs. Inst. Can. (past chmn.). Home: 54 Aberdeen Ave, Westmount, PQ Canada H3Y 3A4

SPALTY, EDWARD ROBERT, lawyer; b. New Haven, Oct. 1, 1946; s. Kermit and Elinor (Phelan) Turgeon; m. Suzy Clune; children: Thomas John, Kathleen Tess. AB, Emory U., 1968; JD, Columbia U., 1973. Bar: Mo. 1975, U.S. Dist. Ct. (we. dist.) Mo. 1975, U.S. Ct. Claims 1977, U.S. Ct. Appeals (8th cir.) 1984, U.S. Supreme Ct. 1994. Assoc. Webster & Sheffield, N.Y.C., 1973-74; mng. atty. Armstrong, Teasdale, Schlafly & Davis, Kansas City, Mo., 1974—. Contbr. articles to profl. jours. Chmn. bd. dirs. Mo. Easter Seals Soc., 1990-92; bd. dirs. Nat. Easter Seal Soc., former chmn. rules, agenda and resolutions com., former chmn. membership and orgnl. structure com. ho. of dels.; founding mem. Heartland Franchise Assn. With U.S. Army, 1968-70. Mem. ABA (litigation sect., franchising forum com.), Mo. Bar Assn. (civil rules and procedures com.), Kansas City Met. Bar Assn. (chmn. antitrust and franchise law com., co-chair 14th and 16th ann. Nat. Franchise Law Inst.), Lawyers Assn. Kansas City, Mo. Orgn. Def. Attys., Def. Rsch. Inst., Am. Judicature Soc., Internat. Rels. Coun. Kansas City, Am. Arbitration Assn. (nat. panel arbitrators 1987, arbitrator U.S. Dist. Ct. we. dist. Mo. 1986—), Kansas City (Mo.) Club, Columbia Club (v.p.), Sigma Nu, Pi Sigma Alpha, Phi Delta. Home: 13703 NW 73rd St Parkville MO 64152-1120 Office: Armstrong Teasdale et al Ste 2000 2345 Grand Blvd Kansas City MO 64108

SPAN, ROBERT STEVEN, lawyer; b. N.Y.C., June 30, 1947; s. A. Noel and Dorothy (Heinze) S.; m. Crystal Elizabeth Wampler, May 2, 1971; 1 child, Evan Noel. AB, Dartmouth Coll., 1967; JD, Yale U., 1971. Bar: N.H. 1971, Calif. 1976, U.S. Ct. Appeals (9th cir.), 1976, U.S. Dist. Ct. (cen. dist.) Calif., 1976, U.S. Supreme Ct. 1987. Assoc. Normandin, Cheney & O/Neill, Laconia, N.H., 1971-73; legis. dir. to U.S. Senator Thomas J. McIntyre Washington, 1973-76; assoc. Paul, Hastings, Janofsky & Walker, L.A., 1976-81, ptnr., 1981—. Pres. Westside Legal Svcs., Santa Monica, Calif., 1983-84. Fellow Am. Bar Found.; mem. ABA, L.A. County Bar Assn. (trustee 1989-91), Santa Monica Bar Assn. (trustee 1985-90, pres. 1988-89), Phi Beta Kappa. Office: Paul Hastings Janofsky & Walker 555 S Flower St Fl 23 Los Angeles CA 90071-2300

SPANBAUER, JAMES, chemicals executive; b. 1939. BS in Math., U. Wis., Oshkosh, 1962, MBA, 1979. EDP-operator Soo Line R.R., Janesville, Wis., 1957-63; sys. traffic mgr. Am. Can Co., Elm Grove, Wis., 1963-70; with Reynolds Consumer Products, Appleton, Wis., 1970—, now v.p. adminstrn. Office: Reynolds Consumer Products PO Box 2399 670 N Perkins St Appleton WI 54914-3133*

SPANDER, ART, sportswriter; b. L.A., Aug. 30, 1938; m. Elizabeth Newman, June 17, 1962; children: Debbie, Wendy. BA in Polit. Sci., UCLA, 1960. With UPI, 1960; joined Santa Monica (Calif.) Evening Outlook, 1963-65, San Francisco Chronicle, 1965-79; columnist San Francisco Examiner, 1979—. Author: Golf: The Passion and the Challenge, 1978, The Art Spander Collection, 1989. Recipient AP Sports Editors awards, Profl. Football Writers Am. awards, 1st place awards San Francisco Press Club, 1st Place Golf Writers Assn. Am. awards, Hayward-Newland Lifetime Achievement award Calif. Golf Writers. Office: San Francisco Examiner 110 5th Ave San Francisco CA 94103-1310

SPANDORFER, MERLE SUE, artist, educator, author; b. Balt., Sept. 4, 1934; d. Simon Louis and Bernice P. (Jacobson) S.; m. Lester M. Spandorfer, June 17, 1956; children: Cathy, John. Student, Syracuse U., 1952-54; BS, U. Md., 1956. Mem. faculty Cheltenham (Pa.) Sch. Fine Arts, 1969—; instr. printmaking Tyler Sch. Art Temple U., Phila., 1980-84; faculty Pratt Graphics Ctr., N.Y.C., 1985-86. One woman shows include Richard Feigen Gallery, N.Y.C., 1970, U. Pa., 1974, Phila. Coll. Textiles and Sci., 1977, Ericson Gallery, N.Y.C., 1978, 79, R.I. Sch. Design, 1980, Syracuse U., 1981, Marian Locks Gallery, Phila., 1973, 78, 82, Temple U., 1984, Tyler Sch. Art, 1985, University City Sci. Ctr., 1987, Gov.'s Residence, 1988, Wenniger Graphics Gallery, Provincetown, Mass., 1989, Mangel Gallery, Phila., 1992, Widener U. Art Mus., 1995; group shows Bklyn. Mus. Art, 1973, San Francisco Mus. Art, 1973, Balt. Mus. Art, 1970, 71, 74, Phila. Mus. Art, 1972, 77, Fundacio Joan Miro, Barcelona, Spain, 1977, Del. Mus. Art, Wilmington, 1978, Carlsberg Glyptotek Mus., Copenhagen, 1980, Moore Coll. Art, Phila., 1982, Tyler Sch. Art, 1983, William Penn Meml. Mus., Harrisburg, Pa., 1984 Ariz. State U., 1985, Tiajin Fine Arts Coll., China, 1986, Beaver Coll., Phila., 1988, The Port of History Mus., Phila., 1987, Sichuan Fine Arts Inst., Chong Qing, People's Republic China, 1988, Glynn Vivian Mus., Swansea, Wales, 1989, Phila. Mus. Art, 1990, Fgn. Mus., Riga, Latvia, 1995; represented in permanent collections Met. Mus. Art, N.Y.C., Whitney Mus. Am. Art, N.Y.C., Mus. Modern Art, N.Y.C., The Israel Mus., Balt. Mus. (gov's prize and purchase award 1970), Phila. Mus. Art (purchase award 1977), Toyoh Bijutsu Gakko, Tokyo, Library of Congress, Temple U.; commd. works represented in U. Pa. Inst. Contemporary Art, 1991; co- author: Making Art Safely, 1993. Recipient award Balt. Mus. Art/Md. Inst. Art, 1971, Govs. prize and Purchase award Balt. Mus. Art, 1970, Outstanding Art Educators award Pa. Art Edn. Assn., 1982, Purchase award Berman Mus., 1995; grantee Pa. Coun. Arts, 1989. Mem. Am. Color Print Soc., Pa. Art Edn. Assn. Jewish. Studio: 307 E Gowen Ave Philadelphia PA 19119-1023

SPANEL, HARRIET ROSA ALBERTSEN, state senator; b. Audubon, Iowa, Jan. 15, 1939; m. Leslie E. Spanel, June 3, 1961; 3 children. BS in Math., Iowa State U., 1961. Rep. Wash. State, 1987-93, senator, 1993—. Home: 901 Liberty St Bellingham WA 98225-5632 Office: PO Box 40482 Olympia WA 98504-0482

SPANGLER, ARNOLD EUGENE, investment banker; b. Ft. Dodge, Iowa, Aug. 1, 1948; s. Kermit Charles and Cora (Buroos) S.; m. Penelope Angell, Nov. 8, 1980; children: Christopher Paul, Allison Elizabeth. BS, Iowa State U., 1970; MBA, Harvard U., 1972. Assoc. Hornblower & Weeks-Hemphill, Noyes, N.Y.C., 1972-74; product officer Citibank, N.Y.C., 1974-76; with Lazard Freres & Co., N.Y.C., 1976-89, gen. ptnr., 1983-89; mng. dir. mergers and acquisitions Paine Webber Inc., N.Y.C., 1989-91; sr. advisor Bentley Assocs., L.P., N.Y.C., 1992-93; mng. dir. Mancuso & Co., N.Y.C., 1993—; bd. dirs. Syncor Internat. Corp., L.A. Home: 1165 Park Ave New York NY 10128-1210

SPANGLER, CLEMMIE DIXON, JR., academic administrator; b. Charlotte, N.C., Apr. 5, 1932; s. Clemmie Dixon and Veva C. (Yelton) S.; m. Meredith Jane Riggs, June 25, 1960; children: Anna Wildy, Abigail Riggs. BS, U. N.C., 1954; MBA, Harvard U., 1956; LHD (hon.), Queens Coll., 1985; LLD (hon.), Davidson Coll., 1986, Furman U., 1993. Pres. C.D. Spangler Constrn. Co., Charlotte, 1958-86, Golden Eagle Industries, Inc., 1968-86; chmn. bd. Bank of N.C., Raleigh, 1973-82; dir. NCNB Corp., 1983-86; chmn. N.C. Bd. Edn., 1982-86; pres. U. N.C., Chapel Hill, 1986—; bd. dirs. BellSouth Corp., Atlanta, Nat. Gypsum Co., Charlotte. Past deacon Myers Park Bapt. Ch., vice-chmn. Charlotte-Mecklenburg Bd. Edn., Charlotte, 1972-76, So. Regional Edn. Bd., 1987—; past trustee Charlotte Nature Mus., Charlotte Symphony Orch., Crozer Theol. Sem.; past chmn. Charlotte adv. bd. Salvation Army; past bd. dirs. YMCA, Equitable Life Assurance Soc., Jefferson-Pilot Corp.; pres. bd. trustees Mint Mus. Art; bd. dirs. Union Theol. Sem., 1985-90, Assocs. Harvard Bus. Sch. With U.S. Army, 1956-58. Recipient Liberty Bell award Mecklenburg County Bar Assn., 1985, Alumni Achievement award Harvard Bus. Sch., 1988. Mem. Assn. Am. Univs., Bus. Higher Edn. Forum, Harvard Club (N.Y.C.), Univ. Club (N.Y.C.), Quail Hollow Country Club (Charlotte). Office: U NC Gen Adminstrn Office of President PO Box 2688 Chapel Hill NC 27515-2688

SPANGLER, DAISY KIRCHOFF, educator, educational consultant; b. Lancaster, Pa., Jan. 27, 1913; d. Frank Augustus and Lida Flaharty (Forewood) Kirchoff; BS, Millersville State Coll., 1963; MEd, Pa. State U., 1966, EdD, 1972; PhD, Stanton U., 1974; m. Francis R. Cosgrove Spangler, June 3, 1939 (dec.); children: Stephen Russell, Michael Denis. Tchr. rural sch., Providence, Pa., 1933-35, Rapho Twp., Pa., 1935-42, Mastersonville, Pa., 1942-51; elem. sch. prin. Manheim Cen., Pa., 1952-66; tchr., Manheim, Pa., 1967-68; assoc. prof. elem. edn. Millersville U., Pa., 1968-78, prof. emeritus, 1978—, advisor Kappa Delta Phi, 1968-88; tchr. Buckview Parachiol Sch., 1989-93; ednl. cons., 1978—. Author: Teacher Daisy, 1994, Good Morning Teacher Daisy, 1994. Dist. chmn. ARC, 1965-66; mem. Hempfield PTA, 1966-67. Mem. Pa. Edn. Assn., Pa. Elem. Prins. Assn., Assn. Pa. State Coll. and Univ. Profs., Nat. Prin. Assn., Lancaster Prin. Assn. (pres. 1963-64), Pa. Assn. Ret. State Employees, Pa. Assn. State Retirees, Lancaster Area Ret. Pub. Sch. Employees Assn., Am. Ednl. Rsch. Assn., Manheim Tchrs. Assn. (pres. 1964-65), Hempfield Profl. Women, Am. Assn. Ret. Persons (chpt. pres. 1983-85, 89-90), Pi Lambda Theta (nat. com. 1980—, advisor Millersville U. 1968-78, named outstanding advisor 1988, 89), Delta Kappa Gamma (pres. 1976-78), Order Eastern Star. Lutheran (pres. Luth. Women 1966-67, 79-81). Home and Office: 2906 Spooky Nook Rd Manheim PA 17545-9127

SPANGLER, DAVID ROBERT, college administrator, engineer; b. Flint, Mich., Aug. 17, 1940; s. John Solomon and Margaret Inger (McKinley) S.; m. Sally Jeanne Henry, Aug. 28, 1965; children: Timothy David, Megan Marie. BS, U.S. Mil. Acad., 1962; MS in Engring., U. Ill., 1966, PhD in Structural Dynamics, 1977. Registered profl. engr. Commd. 2d lt. U.S. Army, 1962, advanced through grades to lt. col., 1979; prof. math. U.S. Mil. Acad. U.S. Army, West Point, N.Y., 1968-71; engr. Korea Support Command U.S. Army, 1972-73; dep. dist. engr. C.E. U.S. Army, Walla Walla, Wash., 1973-74; research coordinator Def. Nuclear Agy. U.S. Army, Washington, 1976-79; bn. comdr. U.S. Army, Hawaii, 1979-81; inspector C.E. U.S. Army, San Francisco, 1981-82; ret. U.S. Army, 1982; prof. engring. St. Martin's Coll., Lacey, Wash., 1982-84, pres., 1984—; mem. Nat. Com. for Tunnelling Tech., Washington, 1977-79; cons. Thurston County, Olympia, Wash., 1982-84. Contbr. articles to profl. jours. Bd. dirs. Econ. Devel. Coun., Thurston County, 1985-88, Wash. State Capitol Mus., 1988-91. Decorated Bronze Star with 2 oak leaf clusters, Meritorious Service medal, Def. Nuclear Agy. Joint Service medal. Mem. Soc. Mil. Engrs. (v.p. 1980-81, pres. 1973-74), Nat. Assn. Ind. Colls. and Univs. (bd. dirs. 1992-95, treas. 1994), Ind. Colls. Wash. (bd. dirs.), Assn. Benedictine Colls. and Univs. (pres. 1994-95), Rotary (mem. gov.'s oversight com. on tech. 1996), Sigma Xi. Roman Catholic. Avocation: running. Office: St Martin's Coll Office of Pres Lacey WA 98503

SPANGLER, MILLER BRANT, science and technology analyst, planner, consultant; b. Stoyestown, Pa., Sept. 1, 1923; s. Elbert Bruce and Raye Isabel (Brant) S.; m. Claire Labin Kussart, Sept. 20, 1947; children: Daryl Claire, Philip Miller, Coreen Sue. BS with honors, Carnegie-Mellon U., 1950; MA, U. Chgo., 1953, PhD, 1956. Chem. engr. Gulf Rsch. Corp., Harmarville, Pa., 1950-51; assoc. engr. rsch. corp. IBM, Yorktown Heights, N.Y., 1956-60; mgr., market rsch. fed. systems div. IBM, Rockville, Md., 1960-63; program economist U.S. Agy. for Internat. Devel., Turkey, India, 1963-66; dir. ctr. for techno-econ. studies Nat. Planning Assn., Washington, 1966-72; chief, cost benefit analysis br. U.S. Atomic Energy Commn., Washington, 1972-75; spl. asst. policy devel. U.S. Nuclear Regulatory Commn., Washington, 1975-89; pres. Techno-Planning, Inc., Bethesda, Md., 1989-94; freelance author Bethesda, 1994—; mem. adv. bd. NSF Sea Grant Program, Washington, 1969, Environ. Profl. Jour., L.A., 1981-88. Author: New Technology and the Supply of Petroleum, 1956, New Technology and Marine Resource Development, 1970, The Role of Research and Development in Water Resources Planning, 1972, U.S. Experience in Environmental Cost-Benefit Analysis, 1980; contbr. numerous articles and papers to profl. jours. Recipient Planning Rsch. award Program Edn. and Rsch. in Planning U. Chgo., 1953. Mem. N.Y. Acad. Scis., Am. Assn. for the Advancement Sci., Nat. Assn. Environ. Profls., Soc. for Risk Analysis, Internat. Assn. for Impact Assessment., Tau Beta Pi. Republican. Methodist. Avocations: oriental gardening, traveling, photography, fishing. Home: 9115 Mcdonald Dr Bethesda MD 20817-1941

SPANGLER, RONALD LEROY, television executive, aircraft distributor; b. York, Pa., Mar. 5, 1937; s. Ivan L. and Sevilla (Senft) S.; children: Kathleen, Ronald, Beth Anne. Student U. Miami (Fla.), 1955-59. Radio announcer Sta. WSBA, York, 1955-57; TV producer-dir. Sta. WBAL-TV, Balt., 1959-65; pres., chmn. bd. LewRon Television, N.Y.C., Hollywood, Calif., 1965-74; now pres., chmn. bd. Spanair Inc., distbr. Rockwell Comdr. aircraft; owner Prancing Horse Farm. Mem. Video Tape Producers Assn. N.Y., Rolls Royce Owners Club, Ferrari Clubs Am. Avocation: racing Ferrari automobiles, collecting and dealing in vintage Ferrari automobiles. Home: Prancing Horse Farm 3710 Ady Rd Street MD 21154

SPANGLER, SCOTT MICHAEL, private investor; b. Toledo, Aug. 4, 1938; s. Walter James and Martha Zoe (Hirscher) S.; m. Jean Galt Schmonsees, June 10, 1963; children—Karen Elizabeth, Scott Michael, Andrew Galt. B.M.E., U. Cin., 1961; M.B.A., Harvard U., 1963. Research asso. M.I.T., 1963-65; fin. exec. Cooper Industries, Inc., Mt. Vernon, Ohio, 1965-68; v.p. indsl. group White Motor Corp., Cleve., 1968-70; pres. Spangler and Co., Houston, 1970-73; dir., pres., chief exec. officer AZL Resources, Inc. (and affiliates), Phoenix, 1973-84; pres., chief exec. officer First Phoenix Capital, Inc., Scottsdale, Ariz., 1984-90; assoc. adminstr. AID, Washington, 1990-93; pres. First Phoenix Capital Inc., Phoenix and Washington, 1993—; bd. dirs. First So. Capital Corp., Alamosa Nat. Bank, Cen. Ariz. Bank, New London Oil Inc. Mem. World Pres.' Orgn., Chief Execs. Orgn., Harvard Club, Paradise Valley Country Club, Met. Club. Republican. Presbyterian. Office: 700 New Hampshire Washington DC 20037-2406

SPANGLER, VERA MAE, mental health nurse; b. Montebello, Va., Jan. 21, 1939; d. Roy Hall and Flora May (Smiley) Allen; m. Jerry Cleveland Utt, Jan. 20, 1956 (div. June 1981); 1 child, Sherry Lynn; m. Danny Eugene Spangler, Apr. 16, 1994. AAS, Piedmond Va. C.C., 1984. RN, Va. Staff nurse, RN Kings' Daughter's Hosp., Staunton, Va., 1984-87; nurse supr., unit mgr. Liberty House Nursing Home, Waynesboro, Va., 1987-90; quality assurance nurse supr. Walnut Hills Convalescent Ctr., Petersburg, Va., 1990-92; RN, clinician A Ctrl. State Hosp., Petersburg, 1992—. Republican. Presbyterian. Avocation: doll collecting. Home: 4607 Woodstream Ct Petersburg VA 23803-8856 Office: Ctrl State Hosp PO Box 4030 Petersburg VA 23803-0030

SPANIER, GRAHAM BASIL, academic administrator, family sociologist, demographer, marriage and family therapist; b. Capetown, South Africa, July 18, 1948; s. Fred and Rosadele (Lurie) S.; m. Sandra Kay Whipple, Sept. 11, 1971; children: Brian Lockwood, Hadley Alison. BS, Iowa State U., 1969, MS, 1971; PhD, Northwestern U., 1973. Assoc. dean, prof. in charge Pa. State U., University Park, 1973-82, pres., 1995—; vice provost, prof. SUNY, Stony Brook, 1982-86; provost, v.p. for acad. affairs Oreg. State U., Corvallis, 1986-91; chancellor U. Nebr., Lincoln, 1991-95; pres. Pa. State U., 1995—. Author 10 books and 100 articles to profl. jours. Pres., chmn. bd. dirs. Christian Children's Fund, Richmond, Va., 1985-94; del. White House Conf. on Families, Washington, 1980; host Pub. Broadcast TV programs, 1973-76. Recipient Moran award Am. Assn. Family and Consumer Scis., 1987; named Outstanding Young Alumnus Iowa State U., 1982; Am. Assn. Marriage and Family Therapy fellow, 1983—, Woodrow Wilson fellow, 1972. Mem. Nat. Coun. Family Rels. (pres. 1987-88, Outstanding Grad. Student award 1972), Population Assn. Am., Am. Sociol. Assn. (family sect. chmn. 1983-84), Internat. Sociol. Assn., Am. Assn. Higher Edn., Am. Assn. Family and Consumer Scis., Nat. Assn. State Univs. and Land Grant Colls. (exec. com. coun. on acad. affairs 1990-91, bd. pres. commn. on info. technologies 1993-96), Am. Coun. on Edn. (commn. on women 1992-95), Nat. Collegiate Athletic Assn. (pres. commn. 1995), Am. Assn. State Colls. (joint commn. on accountability report 1993-95). Democrat. Avocations: aviation, magic, athletics. Office: Pa State U Office of Pres 201 Old Main University Park PA 16802

SPANN, GEORGE WILLIAM, management consultant; b. Cuthbert, Ga., July 21, 1946; s. Glinn Linwood and Mary Grace (Hiller) S.; B.S. in Physics with honors, Ga. Inst. Tech., 1968, M.S., 1970, M.S. in Indsl. Mgmt., 1973; m. Laura Jeanne Nason, June 10, 1967; children: Tanya Lynne, Stephen William. Engr., Martin Marietta Corp., Orlando, Fla., 1968-70; research scientist Engring. Expt. Sta., Ga. Inst. Tech., 1970-75; v.p., dir. Metrics, Inc., mgmt. and engring. cons., Atlanta, 1973-78, pres., dir., 1978—; v.p., dir. Exec. Data Systems, Inc., 1981—; mem. Ga. Energy Policy Council, Ga. Metrication Council, NASA applications survey group for Landsat follow-on; mem. com. on practical applications of remote sensing from space Space Applications Bd. Nat. Research Council; market research cons. NOAA, NASA, pvt. cos. Regents scholar, 1964. Mem. Am. Soc. Photogrammetry, Urban and Regional Info. Systems Assn., Atlanta Jaycees, Tau Beta Pi, Phi Kappa Phi, Sigma Pi Sigma. Author papers, reports. Home: 3475 Clubland Dr Marietta GA 30068-2509 Office: 1640 Powers Ferry Rd Bldg 27 Marietta GA 30067-5485

SPANN, JAMES J., JR., lawyer; b. Westfield, N.Y., July 8, 1955; s. James J., Sr. and Jean (Killmeyer) S.; m. June M. Miller, May 27, 1995. BA, SUNY, Fredonia, 1974; JD, Thomas M. Cooley Law Sch., 1984. Bar: N.Y. 1985, D.C. 1986. Assoc. Anthony J. Spann, P.C., Dunkirk, N.Y., 1985—; magistrate N.Y. State Magistrate, Westfield, 1987—; bd. dirs. Westfield (N.Y.) Counseling Svcs. Mem. N.Y. State Bar Assn., N.Y. State Trial Lawyers Assn., Chautauqua Bar Assn. Office: Anthony J Spann PC 427 Ctrl Ave Dunkirk NY 14048

SPANN, KATHARINE DOYLE, marketing and communications executive; b. Holton, Kans.; d. Edward James and Josephine (Hurla) Doyle; m. Hugh J. Spann; 1 dau., Susan Katharine. BS, Emporia State Coll. V.p. Bozell & Jacobs Advt. (formerly L.C. Cole Co.), San Francisco, 1951-76; pres. Katharine Doyle Spann Assos., 1977—; propr. Kate's Vineyard, Napa Valley, Calif. Bd. dirs. No. Calif. Am. Inst. Wine and Food, Napa Valley Opera House. Named Advt. Woman of Yr., 1962; recipient El Capitan award Peninsula chpt. Pub. Relations Soc. Am., 1962, 66, Am. Silver Anvil award, Pub. Relations Soc. Am., 1962, 66, Excellence award Publicity Club of Bay Area, 1966. Trustee, bd. dirs., mem. exhbn. com., audience devel. com. Fine Arts Mus. San Francisco. Mem. Am. Soc. Enology, Am. Inst. Wine and Food, Napa Valley Women in Wine, Calif. Vintage Wine Soc. (wine com.), Officier Commandeur, Conferie des Chevaliers du Tastevin (events com.), Delta Sigma Epsilon. Club: Metropolitan (San Francisco). Home: 1447 Whitehall Ln Saint Helena CA 94574-9684

SPANN, WILMA NADENE, educational administrator; b. Austin, Tex., Apr. 24, 1938; d. Frank Jamison and Nadene (Burns) Jamison Plummer; m. James W. Spann II, Aug. 2, 1958; children: James III, Timothy, Terrance, Kemberly, Kelby, Elverta, Peter, Margo. BA, Marquette U., 1974; MS, U. Wis., 1985. Sec. Spandagle Coop., Milw., 1969-89; tchr. adult basic edn. Milw. area Tech. Coll., Milw., 1975-80; tchr. Milw. Pub. Sch. System, 1975-90, adminstrv. intern, 1990-91; asst. prin. Clara Barton Elem. Sch., Milw., 1992-93; asst. prin. in charge Greenfield Montessori Sch., Milw., 1993-94, 1993-94, prin., 1993—; prin. Greenfield Montessori Sch., 1993—; del. Inter Group Coun. Contbr. articles to profl. jours. Dir. Vacation Bible Sch., Tabernacle Cmty. Bapt. Ch., Milw., 1977-80, bd. dirs. Christian edn., 1981-90; v.p. women's aux. Wis. Gen. Bapt. State Conv., 1985-95, pres. women's aux., 1995—; instr. Wis. Congress Christian Edn., 1982—; asst. dean Wis. Gen. Bapt. State Congress Christian Edn., 1985; mem. sr. retreat com. Nat. Bapt. Youth Camp; fin. sec. Interdenominational Min.'s Wives Wis. Recipient cert. of Recognition, women's auxiliary Wis. Gen. Bapt. State Conv., 1986, Bd. Edn. Tabernacle Bapt. Ch., 1990. Mem. NAACP, Internat. Assn. Childhood Edn. (sec. 1990-92), Met. Milw. Alliance Black Sch. Educators, Nat. Bapt. Conv. (life, del. intergroup coun., Myra Taylor shcolar com.), Marquette U. Alumni Assn., Assn. Childhood Edn. Internat. (sec. 1990-92), Interdenominational Alliance Minister's Wives & Widows of Wis. (fin. sec.), Assn. Women in Adminstrn., N.Am. Baptist Women's Union, Ch. Women United (life, del. to intergroup), Phi Delta Kappa, Eta Phi Beta. Democrat. Avocations: writing, public speaking, traveling, reading. Home: 1906 W Cherry St Milwaukee WI 53205-2046 Office: Greenfield Montessori Sch 1711 S 35th St Milwaukee WI 53215-2004

SPANNAGEL, ALAN WAYNE, physiologist; b. Harlingen, Tex., May 9, 1958; s. Billy Wayne and Ersel Lou (Jones) S.; m. Kathy Lynn Lang, Aug. 16, 1980 (div. 1982); m. Maristella Partin, 1987 (div. 1988). BS in Marine Biology, Tex. A&M U., 1980; MS in Biology, U. Houston, Clear Lake City, 1985; postgrad., U. Tex. Health Sci. Ctr., San Antonio. Rsch. technician U. Tex. Med. Br., Galveston, 1981-85, rsch. assoc., 1985-87; grad. rsch. asst. dept. physiology U. Tex. Health Sci. Ctr., San Antonio, 1987—; instr., lectr. Physiology for Occupl. Therapy Students, 1990-93; reviewer and cons. on Physiol. Studies. Contbr. articles to profl. sci. jours. Mem. Am. Pancreatic Assn. Achievements include isolation, purification and physiological studies on a novel gastrointestinal peptide, the luminal CCK-releasing factor; demonstration that adapted changes in pancreatic juice composition have physiological effects on gastrointestinal hormone secretion and gastrointestinal function; showed that dietary peptides, not intact protein, stimulated pancreatic secretion during a meal. Home: 154 Barbara Bend Universal City TX 78148 Office: Univ Tex Health Sci Ctr Dept of Physiology 7703 Floyd Curl Dr San Antonio TX 78284

SPANNUTH, JOHN ROY, aquatics association executive; b. Reading, Pa., Oct. 7, 1933; s. John R. and Virginia Spannuth; children: John III, Virginia. BA in Health and Phys. Edn., West Chester U., 1961. Aquatics dir. YMCA, Reading, 1956-59; swimming coach West Chester (Pa.) U., 1959-61; aquatics dir. Phillips Petroleum Co., Bartlesville, Okla., 1961-68; exec. dir. Amarillo (Tex.) Aquatic Club, 1968-69; nat. aquatics adminstr. Nat. AAU, Indpls., 1970-74; exec. dir. Spl. Olympics Kennedy Found., Washington, 1974-75; nat. swimming coach Country of Bahrain, 1980-83; dir. recreation Saudi Arabian Air Force, Riyadh, 1984-86; sr. aquatics dir. Cleve. County Family YMCA, Norman, Okla., 1986-89; pres., CEO U.S. Water Fitness Assn., Boynton Beach, Fla., 1989—; spkr. in field. Recipient C. Carson award Health & Fitness Leaders, Ranson Arthur award U.S. Masters Swimming Assn. Mem. Am. Swimming Coaches Assn. (past pres.). Office: US Water Fitness Assn PO Box 3279 Boynton Beach FL 33424-3279

SPANOGLE, ROBERT WILLIAM, marketing and advertising company executive, association administrator; b. Lansing, Mich., Nov. 13, 1942; s. William P. and Mary A. (Lenneman) S.; m. Ruth Ann Long, Jan. 14, 1967; children: John Paul Stephen Donald, Amy Lynn. AA, Lansing C.C., 1969; BA, Mich. State U., 1971; postgrad., U. Pa., 1985. Cons. Nat. League Cities, Washington, 1971-72; cons. Am. Legion, Indpls., 1972-75, dir. membership, 1975-79; exec. dir. Am. Legion, Washington, 1975-81, nat. adjutant, 1981—; chmn. HP Direct, Inc., Indpls., 1985—; chmn. exec. com. HP Direct, Inc., Washington, 1989—; mem. individual investors adv. com. N.Y. Stock Exch., N.Y.C., 1989-92. Bd. govs. USO, Washington, 1986-92; trustee St. Mary of the Woods Coll., Terre Haute, Ind., 1991—; treas. Civil War Battle Flags Commn. State of Ind., Indpls., 1994—; sec. 500 Festival Assocs., Indpls., 1985-91; mem. Vet.'s Day Coun., Indpls., 1989; bd. dirs. Indpls. Athletic Club, Crossroads Coun. Boy Scouts Am., 1985-92. With U.S. Army, 1962-65. Mem. Am. Legion of Mich. (Hon. Comdr. 1985), Kiwanis (exec. com. 1989-92). Roman Catholic. Avocations: golf, hunting, reading. Home: 672 Yosemite Dr Indianapolis IN 46217-3962 Office: Am Legion 700 N Pennsylvania Indianapolis IN 46204

SPANOS, ALEXANDER GUS, professional football team executive; b. Stockton, Calif., Sept. 28, 1923; m. Faye Spanos; children: Dean, Dea Spanos Berberian, Alexis Spanos Ruhl, Michael. LLD (hon.), U. Pacific, 1984. Chmn. bd. dirs. A.G. Spanos Constrn. Inc., Stockton, Calif., 1960—; chmn. bd. dirs. A.G. Spanos Properties Inc., Stockton, Calif., 1960—, A.G. Spanos Mgmt. Inc., Stockton, Calif., 1967—, A.G. Spanos Enterprises Inc., Stockton, Calif., 1971—, A.G. Spanos Devel. Inc., Stockton, Calif., 1973—, A.G. Spanos Realty Inc., Stockton, Calif., 1978—, A.G. Spanos Jet Ctr. Inc., Stockton, Calif., 1980—, A.G.S. Fin. Corp., Stockton, Calif., 1980—; pres., chmn. bd. dirs. San Diego Chargers, 1984—; Chmn. bd. dirs. A.G.S. Spanos Land Co., Stockton, Calif., 1982—. Former trustee Children's Hosp., San Francisco, San Francisco Fine Arts Mus.; trustee Eisenhower Med. Ctr., Rancho Mirage, Calif.; hon. regent U. Pacific, Stockton, 1972-82; gov. USO, Washington, 1982—. Served with USAF, 1942-46. Recipient Albert Gallatin award Zurich-Am. Ins. Co., 1973, Horatio Alger award Horatio Alger Found., 1982, medal of Honor Statue of Liberty-Ellis Islan Found., 1982. Mem. Am. Hellenic Ednl. Progressive Assn., Calif. C. of C. (bd. dirs. 1980-85). Republican. Greek Orthodox. Avocation: golfing. Office: San Diego Chargers Jack Murphy Stadium PO Box 609609 San Diego CA 92160-9609 also: A G Spanos Constrn Co 1341 W Robinhood Dr Stockton CA 95207-5511*

SPANOS, DEAN A., business executive; b. Stockton, Calif., May 26, 1950; s. Alex G. Spanos; m. Susan Spanos; children: Alexander Gus, John Dean. BBA, U. Pacific, 1972. Pres., vice chmn. San Diego Chargers, from 1984; pres. Spanos corp. entities; vice chmn. AGS Fin. Corp. Former mem. bd. regents U. Pacific. Co-winner Bing Crosby Nat. Pro-Am. Golf Tournament, 1985; winner Bob Hope Chrysler Classic, 1990, 91, AT&T Nat. Pro-Am. Golf Tournament, 1990; recipient Most Valuable Amateur trophy; mem. winning team in Sr.'s Reunion Tournament, Dallas, 1985. Avocation: golf. Office: San Diego Chargers San Diego Jack Murphy Stad PO Box 609609 San Diego CA 92160-9609

SPANOS, POL DIMITRIOS, engineering educator; b. Messini, Peloponnesus, Greece, Feb. 27, 1950; came to U.S., 1973; s. Dimitrios Constandin Spanos and Aicaterine Polychronis Bonaros; m. Olympia Constandin Critikou, Mar. 22, 1976; children: Demetri, Eudokia. Diploma in mech. engring., Nat. Tech. U., Athens, 1973; MS in Civil Engring., Calif. Inst. Tech., 1974, PhD in Applied Mechanics, 1976. Registered profl. engr., Tex., Greece. Rsch. asst. Calif. Inst. Tech., Pasadena, 1973-76, rsch. fellow, 1976-77; from asst. prof. to assoc. prof. U. Tex.-Austin, 1981-84, P.D. Henderson assoc. prof. engring., 1983-84; prof. mech. engring. and civil engring. Rice U., Houston, 1984-88, L.B. Ryon endowed chair in engring., 1988—; cons. on analytical and numerical applications of theory of dynamics and vibrations, worldwide. Author: Random Vibrations, Probabilistic Offshore Mechanics, Probabilistic Methods in Civil Engineering, Random Vibration and Statistical Linearization, Dynamic Analysis of Non-Linear Structures by the Method of Statistical Quadratization, Stochastic Finite Elements: A Spectral Approach, Computational Stochastic Mechanics, Probabilistic Structural Mechanics: Advances in Structural Reliability Methods, Random Vibrations: A Broad Perspective; contbr. to profl. jour. issues devoted to dynamics and vibrations; mem. editorial bd. 8 jours.; editor or co-editor 2 primary jours. on mechanics. Recipient European award of sci. N.V. Phillips Co., Eindhoven, Netherlands, 1969, Presdl. Young Investigator award in earthquake engring. NSF, 1984-89, Cert. merit McDonnell Douglas Astronautics Co., Houston, 1987, Humboldt Rsch. award for Sr. Scientists, Alexander von Humboldt Found., Germany, 1995; scholar Greek Scholarships Instn., 1968-72. Fellow ASME (participant tech. confs. and coms., Pi Tau Sigma Gold medal 1982, G.L. Larson Meml. award 1991), ASCE (participant tech. confs. and coms., W.L. Huber Civil Engring. Rsch. prize 1989, Alfred M. Freudenthal medal 1992, Humboldt Rsch. award for sr. scientists, from Alexander von Humboldt Found., Germany, 1995), Am. Acad. Mechanics; mem. Earthquake Engring. Rsch. Inst., Internat. Assn. for Structural Safety and Reliability, Hellenic Profl. soc. (sponsor scholarship com.). Office: Rice U Dept Mech Engring MS 321 6100 Main St Houston TX 77005-1892

SPANOVICH, MILAN, civil engineer; b. Steubenville, Ohio, Feb. 19, 1929; s. Stanley and Katherine (Komazec) S.; m. Sylvia J. Tomko, Apr. 16, 1971. B.S. Civil Engring, Carnegie-Mellon U., 1956, M.S. Civil Engring., 1957. Registered profl. engr., Pa., N.Y., Ohio, Va., W.Va., Mich., N.Mex., Ky., Md., Colo., N.J., Del., N.C., Fla. Instr. Carnegie-Mellon U., 1957-60; charter assoc., v.p. E. D'Appolonia Assocs., 1957-61; mem. civil engring. staff U. N.Mex., 1961-63; founder, sr. cons. Engring. Mechs., Inc., Pitts., 1963—. Contbr. articles on soil mechs. to tech. jours.; mem. editorial bd. Carnegie-Mellon Mag. Bd. dirs. Carnegie Mellon U. Andrew Carnegie Soc. Recipient Pitts. Young Civil Engr. of Yr. award, 1969. Fellow ASCE (Pitts. Civl Engr. of the Yr. 1987, chmn. numerous coms.), Am. Cons. Engrs. Council (mem. numerous coms.); mem. Cons. Engrs. Council Greater Pitts. (pres. 1972-74), Engring. Soc. Western Pa. (dir. 1972, 77-83), Nat. Soc. Profl. Engrs., Pa. Soc. Profl. Engrs. (pres. Pitts. chpt. 1971, Hornfeck award Pitts. chpt. 1979, state dir. 1976-79, Disting. Service award Pitts. chpt. 1985, Pa. Engr. of the Yr. 1988, Profl. Devel. award 1989, Outstanding Svc. award Pitts. chpt. 1993), ASTM (chmn. task com. on relative density of granular soils 1959-63), Am. Concrete Inst., Hwy. Research Bd., Internat. Soc. Soil Mechs. and Found. Engring., Pitts. Geol. Soc., Am. Arbitration Assn., Profl. Engrs. in Pvt. Practice (chmn. 1970-71), Pitts. Builders Exchange, Soc. Explosives Engrs., Am. Soc. Hwy. Engrs., Carnegie-Mellon U. Alumni Assn. (mem. planning com.), Chi Epsilon Nat. Civil Engring. Honor Soc. Patentee found. systems. Home: 216 Eton Rd Pittsburgh PA 15205-1733 Office: 4636 Campbells Run Rd Pittsburgh PA 15205-1316

SPAR, EDWARD JOEL, demographer; b. N.Y.C., Jan. 2, 1939; s. Max and Dora (Miller) S.; m. Rosalind Getzoff, June 10, 1962; 1 dau., Zoe; m. 2d Elizabeth A. Harrington, Sept. 10, 1977; children: Melissa, Daniel, Matthew. B.B.A., CCNY, 1961. Statistician Alfred Politz Research, N.Y.C., 1962-65; sr. statistician Computer Users Co., N.Y.C., 1965-68; v.p. Daniel Starch, Mamaroneck, N.Y., 1968-71; pres. Market Statistics, N.Y.C., 1971—; demographic cons. N.Y. Times, 1982—; exec. dir. Coun. Profl. Assns. on Fed. Stats.; dir. Bill Comms., Strategy Rsch., Miami, Fla., Dualabs, Arlington, Va. Mem. Assn. Pub. Data Users, Am. Statis. Assn., Coun. Profl. Assocs. Fed. Statistics, (exec. dir.), Am. Mktg. Assn. Democrat. Jewish. Home: 5400 Bradley Blvd Bethesda MD 20814-1002 Office: 633 3d Ave 1429 Duke St Alexandria VA 22314

SPARANO, VINCENT THOMAS, editor; b. Newark, Apr. 7, 1934; s. Gaetano and Agnes (Martucci) S.; m. Elizabeth Frances Rooney, Nov. 21, 1959; children: Donna Marie, Michael Thomas, Matthew John, Ellen Elizabeth. Student, Newark Coll. Engring., 1952-53; BS, NYU, 1959. Assoc. editor Sports Afield Mag., N.Y.C., 1959-60; editor Outdoor Life Mag., N.Y.C., 1960-95; outdoor life, editor emeritus, sr. field editor Gannett News Svc., 1996—. Author: Complete Outdoors Encyclopedia, 1972 (Library Assn. Outstanding Reference Work award 1973), The Outdoor Sportsman's Illustrated Dictionary, 1980, The American Fisherman's Fresh and Salt Water Guide, 1976; editor: Shooting-Why We Miss, 1977, Greatest Hunting Stories Ever Told, 1983, Classic Hunting Tales, 1986, Tales of Woods and Waters, 1989, Hunting Dangerous Game, 1992, Game Birds and Gun Dogs, 1992. editor-in-chief, pub. Northeast Guides to Saltwater Fishing and Boating, Southeast Guides to Saltwater Fishing and Boating. Committeeman Boy Scouts Am., 1970; chmn. Fairfield Fishing Derby, 1971—; trustee Camp Wyanokie Commn., Fairfield, 1976; bd. dirs. Catch and Release Found. Served to cpl. U.S. Army, 1954-56. Mem. Outdoor Writers Assn. Am. (bd. dirs.), Rod and Gun Editors Assn. Met. N.Y. (pres. 1977-78), Nat. Rifle Assn. (cert. firearms instr.), Fairfield Conservation and Sportsman's Assn. (pres. 1983-85), Sigma Delta Chi, Theta Chi. Roman Catholic. Lodges: Elks, K.C. Avocations: hunting; fishing; boating. Home: 17 Henning Dr Fairfield NJ 07004-1744 also: PO Box 821 190 Arnold Blvd, Barnegat Light Long Beach Island NJ 08008

SPARBERG, ESTHER B., chemist, educator; b. N.Y.C., June 17, 1922; d. Abraham and Sarah (Kurnick) Braun; m. Lester S. Sparberg, Dec. 31, 1944; children—Andrew, Alice. B.S. in Chemistry, U. N.C., 1943; M.A., Columbia U., Tchrs. Coll., 1945, Ed.D., 1958. Chemist Interchem. Corp., 1943; technician Rockefeller Inst. Med. Research, 1943-44; tchr. chemistry Julia Richman High Sch., N.Y.C., 1946-47; mem. faculty Hofstra U., 1959-95, prof. chemistry, 1977-89, prof. emerita, 1989; also dir. NSF projects for tchrs. Sci. Co-author: A Laboratory Manual of Concepts in Chemistry, 1968, Chemical Quantitative Analysis: A New Approach, 1972, Ideas, Investigation and Thought, A General Chemistry Laboratory Manual, 1978, The Physical Sciences: the Search for Order and Harmony, 1996; contbr. articles to profl. jours. Sci. manpower fellow Columbia U., 1956-57. Mem. Am. Chem. Soc., Am. Assn. Physics Tchrs., History Sci. Soc., Am. Sci. Tchrs. Assn., Kappa Delta Pi. Democrat. Jewish. Office: Hofstra U Hempstead NY 11550

SPARBERG, MARSHALL STUART, gastroenterologist, educator; b. Chgo., May 20, 1936; s. Max Shane and Mildred Rose (Haffron) S.; m. Eve Gaymont Enda, Mar. 15, 1987. B.A., Northwestern U., 1957, M.D., 1960. Intern Evanston Hosp., Ill., 1960-61; resident in internal medicine Barnes Hosp., St. Louis, 1961-63; fellow U. Chgo., 1963-65; practice medicine specializing in gastroenterolgy Chgo., 1967—; asst. prof. medicine Northwestern U., 1967-72, assoc. prof., 1972-80, prof. clin. medicine, 1980—; instr. Washington U., St. Louis, 1961-63, U. Chgo., 1963-65. Author: Ileostomy Care, 1969, Primer of Clinical Diagnosis, 1972, Ulcerative Colitis,

1978, Inflammatory Bowel Disease, 1982; contbr. numerous articles to profl. jours. Pres. Fine Arts Music Found., 1974-76, Crohn's Disease and Colitis Found. of Am., pres. Ill. chpt., 1994-97; bd. dirs. Lyric Opera Guild, 1974—, Chamber Music Soc. North Shore Chgo., 1984—; physician to Chgo. Symphony Orch., 1981—. With USAF, 1965-67. Named Outstanding Tchr. Northwestern U. Med. Sch., 1972. Mem. AMA, ACP, Am. Gastroent. Assn., Am. Coll. Gastroent. (bd. govs.), Chgo. Med. Soc., Chgo. Soc. Internal Medicine, Chgo. Soc. Gastroenterology (pres.), Chgo. Soc. Gastrointestinal Endoscopy (pres.). Democrat. Jewish. Office: 676 N Saint Clair St Ste 1525 Chicago IL 60611

SPARER, MALCOLM MARTIN, rabbi; b. N.Y.C.; m. Erna Reichl (dec. Sept. 1990); children: Ruth, Arthur (dec.), Jennifer, Shoshana. AB, M in Hebrew Lit., Yeshiva U.; MA in Sociology, CCNY; cert. in pastoral counselling, Des Moines Coll. Osteopathic Medicine; PhD in Sociology, NYU. Ordained rabbi, 1953. Rabbi Jewish Home for the Aged, San Francisco; exec. dir. Rabbinical Coun. Calif., L.A., 1957-66; chaplain VA; adminstr. Tchr's. Coll. of West Coast, Torah U. (later Yeshiva U.), 1957-66; rabbi Beth El Jacob, Des Moines, 1966-69, Chevra Thilim, San Francisco, 1969-72; pres. No. Calif. Bd. Rabbis, 1977-95, pres. emeritus, 1995—; sr. lectr. San Francisco C.C.; liason for Union of Orthodox Jewish Congregations Am., 1957-66, moderator radio series Lest We Forget, 1962, moderator TV spls. on Jewish religion and holiday observances Sta. KNXT, L.A., 1964-65, Des Moines, 1967-69; instr. dept. philosophy Drake U., 1966-69; pres. San Francisco dist. Zionist Orgn. Am., 1969-82, also bd. dirs.; chmn., mem. nat. bd. San Francisco Bay Area Zionist Fedn., 1971-84; co-chmn. Jerusalem Fair, 25th Anniversary of State of Israel, 1973; chmn. Commn. on Soviet Jewry, Jewish Cmty. Rels. Coun., 1974-81; bd. dirs. Jewish Cmty. Fedn., 1982-84; cons. internat. leaders, founder Menorah Inst.; cons. Commn. on Christian-Jewish and Moslem Rels. to European Parliament Nations; cons. various govt. and non-govt. orgns.; writer, frequent lectr. colls., ch. groups on Judaica and world affairs; chmn. dept. world affairs/internat. politics C.C. San Francisco; former chaplain Letterman Army VA Hosp., San Francisco Presidio; co-founder Black and Jewish Clergy; mem. San Francisco Coun. Chs. (bd. dirs. food bank program), United Jewish Appeal (chmn. rabbinic cabinet of western region); invited mem. del. bishops and ch. leaders various denominations conducting meml. svc. at Dachau, Fed. Republic Germany, 1988. Hon. chmn. Mayor's Commn. on Holocaust Meml., San Francisco; mem. Mayor's Task Force for Homeless; co-chmn. Gov.'s Family Task Force, San Francisco. With USN, World War II, Korean War, chaplain USAF. Address: PO Box 15055 San Francisco CA 94115-0055

SPARK, DAME MURIEL SARAH, writer; b. Edinburgh, Scotland, Feb. 1, 1918; d. Bernard and Sarah Elizabeth Maud (Uezzell) Camberg; m. S.O. Spark, (marriage dissolved); 1 son. Student, Heriot Watt Coll., Edinburgh; DLitt (hon.), Strathclyde U., 1971, U. Edinburgh, 1989, Aberdeen U., 1995; DUniv. (hon.), Heriot-Watt U., 1995. Gen. sec. Poetry Soc., 1947-49; editor Poetry Rev., 1949. Author: (non-fiction) Child of Light: A Reassessment of Mary Wollstonecraft Shelley, 1951 (rev. as Mary Shelley, 1987), Emily Brontë: Her Life and Work, 1953, John Masefield, 1953, revised, 1992, The Essence of the Brontës, 1993; (poetry) The Fanfarlo and Other Verse, 1952, Collected Poems I, 1967, Going Up to Sotheby's and Other Poems, 1982; (autobiography) Curriculum Vitae, 1992; (fiction) The Comforters, 1957, Robinson, 1958, The Go-Away Bird and Other Stories, 1958, Memento Mori, 1959, The Ballad of Peckham Rye, 1960, The Bachelors, 1960, Voices at Play, 1961, The Prime of Miss Jean Brodie, 1961, The Girls of Slender Means, 1963, The Mandelbaum Gate, 1965 (James Tait Black Meml. prize 1966, Yorkshire Post Book of Yr. award 1965), Collected Stories I, 1968, The Public Image, 1968, (juvenile) The Very Fine Clock, 1968, The Driver's Seat, 1970, Not to Disturb, 1971, The Hothouse by the East River, 1973, The Abbess of Crewe, 1974, The Takeover, 1976, Territorial Rights, 1979, Loitering with Intent, 1981, Bang-Bang You're Dead and Other Stories, 1982, The Only Problem, 1984, The Stories of Muriel Spark, 1985, A Far Cry from Kensington, 1988, Symposium, 1990, (juvenile) The French Window and the Small Telephone, 1993; (play) The Doctors of Philosophy, 1962; (radio plays) The Party Through the Wall, 1957, The Interview, 1958, The Dry River Bed, 1959, The Ballad of Peckham Rye, 1960 (Prix Italia 1962), The Danger Zone, 1961; editor: A Selection of Poems by Emily Brontë, 1952, My Best Mary: The Letters of Mary Shelley, 1953, The Letters of the Brontës: A Selection, 1954, Letters of John Henry Newman, 1957. Decorated Officier de l'Ordre das Arts et de Lettres (France), dame Order Brit. Empire; recipient Observer short story prize, 1951, Ingersoll T.S. Eliot award, 1992. Fellow Royal Soc. Edinburgh; mem. AAAL (hon. 1978). Address: care David Higham Assocs Ltd, 5-8 Lower John St, London W1R 4HA, England

SPARKES, CHERYL FLOWERS, accountant; b. Texarkana, Ark., July 31, 1956; d. Charles Glendon and Mary Carolyn (Caldwell) Flowers; m. Jay Bedford Sparkes, July 14, 1984. BSBA, U. Ark., 1978. CPA, Tex., CMA. Staff acct. Ernst & Ernst, Dallas, 1978-80; sr. acct. Ernst & Whinney, Dallas, 1980-82, mgr., 1983-84, sr. mgr., 1984-89; sr. mgr. Ernst & Young, Dallas, 1989-94, fin. adv. svcs. regional dir. human resources, 1993-95, ptnr., cons. dispute resolution & litigation svcs., 1994-95; dispute resultion & litigation cons., chmn. nat. FAS edn. Ernst & Young, N.Y.C., 1995—. Chmn. Nat. Edn. Com., 1996—; neighborhood capt. Am. Cancer Soc., Dallas, 1990-92; active Dallas Mus. Art, 1985-95, Jr. League Dallas, 1990-95. Mem. AICPA, Inst. Mgmt. Accts., Tex. Soc. CPAs, Delta Delta Delta. Avocations: weight training, traveling. Home: 250 E 54th St Apt 9C New York NY 10022 Office: Ernst & Young LLP 787 7th Ave New York NY 10019

SPARKMAN, BRANDON BUSTER, educator, writer, consultant; b. Hartselle, Ala., Aug. 2, 1929; s. George Olen and Mary Louise (Jones) S.; m. Wanda Phillips, Sept. 13, 1952; children—Ricky Brandon, Rita Sharon, Robert Lee. B.S., Florence (Ala.) State U., 1952; M.A., U. Ala., 1958, Ednl. Specialist, 1961; Ed.D., Auburn (Ala.) U., 1970. Tchr., asst. prin. Phllips High Sch., Bear Creek, Ala., 1954-57; prin. Tuscumbia, Ala., 1957-65; asst. supt., 1965-69; ednl. cons. Auburn Center, 1969-70; mem. faculty dept. sch. adminstrn. Auburn U., 1970; asst. supt. for staff personnel devel. Jackson (Miss.) Pub. Schs., 1970-71, supt., 1971-73; sch. supt. Richland County Sch. Dist. 1, Columbia, S.C., 1973-75; asst. supt. instruction Hartselle (Ala.) City Schs., 1975-80; supt. Guntersville (Ala.) City Schs., 1980-88; adj. prof. Auburn U., 1988—; pres., chief exec. officer The Right Combination Pub. & Ednl. Svcs. Corp., Guntersville, Ala., 1984-93; writer, cons. in field. Sr. author: Blueprint for a Brighter Child, 1973, STEPS (System for Teacher Evaluation of Pre-reading Skills), 1974; co-author: Preparing Your Preschooler for Reading, 1977, Competency Tests for Basic Reading Skills, 1978, Soaring High with Science, 1985, Soaring High with Social Studies, 1985; author: How Well Does Your Child Read, 1979; editor: The In-Between Years, 1979; creator: CORE (Program Management Through Computer Systems), 1975; editor, contbg. author: The Advantaged, A Preschool Program for the Disadvantaged, 1969, Writing Composition Made Easy, 1991, Expository Writing, 1993; contbr. articles to profl. jours. Bd. dirs. Morgan County chpt. ARC, United Givers Fund, Colbert-Lauderdale Child Study Center, Sheffield-Tuscumbia Credit Union; bd. govs. Jackson Symphony Orch.; adv. bd. Jackson Mental Health Center. Served with AUS, 1952-54. Recipient Human Relations award Jackson. Mem. Am., Ala assns. sch. adminstrs. (past pres.), Ala. Council Sch. Adminstrn. and Supervision (past pres.), Assn. Supervision and Curriculum Devel., Ala. Assn. Supervision and Curriculum Devel. (past pres.), Florence State U. Alumni Assn. (past pres.). Methodist (ch. sch. tchr., supt., vice chmn. ofcl. bd., chmn. commn. edn.). Lodge: Kiwanis. Home and Office: PO Box 961 Guntersville AL 35976-0961

SPARKMAN, CATHRYN, lawyer, health facility administrator; b. June 4, 1947; d. Henry and Miriam Gerhauser; m. Allen Sparkman; children: David, Miriam. BA cum laude, U. Colo., 1969; JD, U. Tex., 1973. Bar: Colo. Atty. Passman, Jones, Dallas, 1973-75, Burford & Ryburn, Dallas, 1976-84, Hall & Evans, Denver, 1986-91; pvt. practice Denver, 1991-92; asst. gen. counsel Rocky Mountain Health Care Corp., Denver, 1992-93, v.p., gen. counsel, 1993—. Home: 2185 Stony Hill Rd Boulder CO 80330 Office: Rocky Mountain Health Care Corp 700 Broadway Denver CO 80273

SPARKMAN, LILA GILLIS, health care facility administrator; b. Cumby, Tex., Feb. 24, 1930; d. William Paul and Cora (Caviness) Gillis; m. Alton C. Sparkman, July 26, 1947; children: Claudia, Vivian, Alan. BS summa cum laude in Social Work, East Tex. State U., 1978, MA, 1980; postgrad. U. Tex., Tyler, 1982; PhD in Clin. Sociology, U. N. Tex. Cert. social worker, mental retardation diagnostic and evaluation specialist, mental retardational profl. Prof. sociology Paris (Tex.) Jr. Coll., 1980; coordinator geriatric services Sabine Valley Regional Mental Health-Mental Retardation Ctr., Marshall, Tex., 1980-82, adminstr. Mental Retardation Residential Homes, Longview, Tex., 1983—; clin. dir. Hunt County Family Svcs. Ctr., Greenville, Tex., 1987; pvt. clin. practice, Winnsboro, Tex., 1989—; sec.-treas. KAM Well Service, New London, Tex., 1981—; social work cons. Forest Acres, Longview, 1983. Author: Comparison of Traditional and Non-traditional Female Students and Their Perceived Reasons for University Attendance, 1980 co-author: Day Care Centers for the Elderly: An Alternative, 1983. Mem. Am. Sociol. Assn., Nat. Assn. Social Workers, Mid South Sociol. Assn., Pub. Health Assn., Alpha Kappa Delta, Alpha Chi, Cap and Gown. Democrat. Methodist. Lodge: Rebekah. Home: PO Box 529 Winnsboro TX 75494-0529

SPARKMAN, ROBERT SATTERFIELD, retired surgeon, educator; b. Brownwood, Tex., Feb. 18, 1912; s. Ellis Hugh and Ola (Stanley) S.; m. Willie Ford Bassett, Feb. 21, 1942. B.A., Baylor U., 1935, M.D., 1935, LL.D., 1974. Diplomate Am. Bd. Surgery. Intern Cin. Gen. Hosp., 1935-36, resident in surgery, 1938-40; intern Good Samaritan Hosp., Lexington, Ky., 1936-37; resident in pathology Baylor Hosp., Dallas, 1937-38; practice medicine specializing in surgery Dallas, 1946—; chief dept. surgery Baylor U. Med. Center, Dallas, 1969-81; emeritus chief Baylor U. Med. Center, 1982—; mem. staff Parkland Meml. Hosp., Dallas; clin. prof. surgery U. Tex. Southwestern Med. Sch., Dallas, 1963—; chief civilian surg. cons. 5th U.S. Army Area, 1950-73; cons. to surgeon gen. U.S. Army, 1950—. Editor, also prin. author: The Texas Surgical Society—The First Fifty Years, 1965; editor: Essays of a Louisiana Surgeon, 1977, Minutes of the American Surgical Association, 1880-68, 1972, The Southern .Surgical Association; The First 100 Years, 1887-1987, 1989—; mem. editorial bd.: Am. Jour. Surgery; Contbr. articles to profl. jours. Bd. dirs. Friends of Dallas Pub. Libr., 1968—. Served to col. M.C. AUS, 1940-46, PTO. Decorated Bronze Star medal; recipient Disting. Alumnus award Baylor U., 1976, Disting. Alumnus award Coll. Medicine, 1976, Disting. Alumnus award Tex. Beta chpt. Alpha Epsilon Delta, A.C. Greene award Friends of Dallas Pub. Libr., 1993; commd. hon. Ky. col., 1980. Fellow ACS (bd. govs. 1962-70); mem. AMA, Am. Surg. Assn. (2d v.p. 1977-78), So. Surg. Assn. (pres. 1978, hon. mem. 1983), Okla. Surg. Assn. (hon.), Tex. Surg. Soc. (pres. 1965), Dallas Gen. Surgeons Soc. (pres. 1961), Internat. Soc. Surgery, Tex. Med. Assn., Soc. Med. Cons. to Armed Forces, James D. Rives Surg. Soc., Soc. Surgery Alimentary Tract, Internat. Biliary Assn., Philos. Soc. Tex., Alpha Omega Alpha, Parkland Surg. Soc. (hon. mem.), Petroleum Club, Dallas Country Club. Home: 5351 Wenonah Dr Dallas TX 75209-5517

SPARKMAN, STEVEN LEONARD, lawyer; b. Sarasota, Fla., May 30, 1947; s. Simeon Clarence and Ursula (Wahlstrom) S.; m. Terry Jeanne Gibbs, Aug. 23, 1969; children: Joanna Jeanne, Kevin Leonard. BA, Fla. State U., 1969, JD, 1972. Bar: Fla. 1972, U.S. Dist. Ct. (mid. dist.) Fla. 1974, U.S. Ct. Appeals (5th cir.) 1975. Legal rsch. asst. Office Gen. Counsel, Fla. Dept. Revenue, Tallahassee, 1971; legis. intern com. on community affairs Fla. Ho. of Reps., Tallahassee, 1971-72; jud. rsch. aide Fla. 2d Dist. Ct. Appeals, Lakeland, 1972-73; asst. county atty. Hillsborough County, Tampa, Fla., 1973-75; assoc. Carlton, Fields, Ward, Emmanuel, Smith & Cutler, P.A., Tampa, 1975-80, sr. atty., 1980—; mem. Fla. State U. Coll. Law Bd. Visitors, 1994—. Sec., bd. dirs. Bapt. Towers Plant City, Inc., 1981-84; deacon 1st Bapt. Ch., Plant City, 1980—. 1st lt. USAFR, 1973. Mem. ABA, Fla. Bar Assn. (exec. coun. local govt. law sect. 1978-79), Hillsborough County Bar Assn., Tampa Kiwanis (bd. dirs. 1980-82, Layman of Yr. 1984, 89). Democrat. Office: Carlton Fields Ward Emmanuel Smith & Cutler PA 777 S Harbour Island Blvd Tampa FL 33602

SPARKS, DAVID EMERSON, bank holding company executive; b. L.I., N.Y., May 7, 1944; m. Anne M. McLaughlin; children—Christopher Drew, Deborah Lee. B.A., Furman U., 1966; A.M.P., Harvard U., 1980. C.P.A. Coopers & Lybrand, 1969-73; chief fin. officer Provident Nat., 1973-81; exec. v.p. and chief fin. officer Provident Nat. Corp. Bank, 1981-83; treas. PNC Fin. Corp., 1983—; exec. v.p. Midlantic Corp., Edison, N.J., 1983-89, ret., 1989; vice chmn., CFO Meridian Bancorp, Reading, Pa., 1990—. Mem. Am. Inst. C.P.A.s, Pa. Inst. C.P.A.s, Fin. Execs. Inst. Office: Meridian Bancorp Inc 35 N 6th St Reading PA 19601-3539*

SPARKS, DAVID STANLEY, university administrator; b. Phila., Dec. 8, 1922; s. Richard Frederick and Grace Dorothy (Tuttle) S.; m. Phyllis Ann Bate, June 12, 1949; children: Robert F., E. Anne. A.B., Grinnell (Iowa) Coll., 1944; M.A., U. Chgo., 1945, Ph.D., 1951. Instr., asst. prof., asso. prof. U. Md., College Park, 1947-65; prof. history U. Md., 1965—, assoc. dean grad. studies and research, 1967-70, dean, 1970-77, acting vice chancellor for acad. affairs, 1976-77, acting v.p. grad. studies and research, 1978-79, v.p. grad. studies and research, 1979-87, acting v.p. for acad. affairs, 1982-83, v.p. acad. affairs, grad. studies and research, 1987-88, vice chancellor for acad. affairs, 1988-91, vice chancellor emeritus, 1991; vis. professorial lectr. dept. history Johns Hopkins, 1965. Co-editor, author: American Civilization: A History of the United States, 1960, The Making of American Democracy, Readings and Documents, 2 vols, 1962; Editor: Inside Lincoln's Army: The Diary of General Marsena Rudolph Patrick, 1964. Recipient research awards Am. Philos. Soc., 1958, Social Sci. Research Council, 1957. Mem. Am., So. hist. assns., Orgn. Am. Historians, Am. Assn. U. Profs. (pres. U. Md. chpt.), Nat. Acad. Univ. Research Adminstrs., Phi Kappa Phi. Club: Cosmos (Washington). Home: 10500 Rockville Pike Apt 1309 Rockville MD 20852-3350

SPARKS, DONALD EUGENE, interscholastic activities association executive; b. St. Louis, May 26, 1933; s. Lloyd Garland and Elsie Wilma (Finn) S.; m. Gloria Mae Helle, Sept. 22, 1951; children: Robert, Michael, Donna Lyn. BS in Edn., N.E. Mo. Univ., 1956, MA, 1959, postgrad., 1962-63. Cert. tchr. and principal, Mo. High sch. coach, athletic dir. The Parkway Sch. Dist., Chesterfield, Mo., 1959-77; assoc. dir. Mo. High Sch. Activity Assn., Columbia, 1977-81; asst. dir. Nat. Fedn. State High Sch. Assns., Kansas City, Mo., 1981—. Recipient spl. Nat. Athletic Dir.'s citation Nat. Fedn. State High Sch. Assns., 1972. Mem. Nat. Interscholastic Adminstrs. Assn. (Disting. Service award 1979). Home: 5204 NW 84th Ter Kansas City MO 64154-1420 Office: Nat Fedn State High Sch Assns 11724 NW Plaza Cir Kansas City MO 64153-1158

SPARKS, HARVEY VISE, JR., physiologist; b. Flint, Mich., June 22, 1938; s. Harvey Vise and Ellen Louise (Paschall) S.; m. Barbara M. Taylor, Jan. 17, 1969; children—Matthew Taylor, Catherine Elliott, Wendy Sue, Harvey Vise. Student, U. Mich., 1956-59, M.D., 1963. Postdoctoral fellow dept. physiology Harvard Med. Sch., Boston and; U. Goteborg, Sweden; instr. U. Mich., 1966-67, asst. prof. physiology, 1967-70, assoc. prof., 1970-74, prof., 1974-78; asst. to dean U. Mich. (Med. Sch.), 1970-71, asst. dean, 1971-72; prof. physiology Mich. State U., East Lansing, 1978—, chmn. dept., 1979-89, vice provost human health programs, 1989-93; Fulbright lectr. U. Zimbabwe, 1986-87; vis. prof. U. Zimbabwe, 1995; mem. survey team, liaison com. on med. edn. AMA Am. Assn. Med. Colls.; mem. rev. teams NIH. Author: Casebook of Physiology, 1973, Essentials of Cardiovascular Physiology, 1987; contbr. numerous articles to profl. jours.; editor: (with others) Handbook of Physiology, 1979. Recipient Meritorious Service award Mich. Heart Assn., 1962, Borden award for med. student research, 1963, Merit award NIH, 1988; Mich. Heart Assn. student fellow, 1962-63; John and Mary Markle scholar, 1967-72; USPHS postdoctoral fellow, 1963-66; U. Mich. student research fellow, 1960-61; USPHS grantee, 1963—. Fellow Royal Soc. Medicine; mem. AAAS, Am. Physiol. Soc. (pres. 1987-88, editl. bd. Am. Jour. Physiology 1974-88), Microcirculatory Soc., Am. Heart Assn. (coun. on circulation, editl. bd. Circulation Rsch.), Mich. Pub. Health Inst. (bd. dirs. 1989-94), Internat. Union Physiol. Scis. (treas. 1990—), Coun. Internat. Exch. Scholars (Africa area com. 1988-91), Russian Acad. Sci. (fgn.), Victor Vaughn Soc., Alpha Omega Alpha, Phi Kappa Phi, Phi Zeta. Home: 8122 W Lovejoy Rd Perry MI 48872-8902 Office: Mich State U Dept Physiology East Lansing MI 48824

SPARKS, IRVING ALAN, biblical scholar, educator; b. Ft. Wayne, Ind., June 15, 1933; s. James Edwin and Isabelle Mildred S.; A.B., Davidson (N.C.) Coll., 1954; B.D., Union Theol. Sem., Richmond, Va., 1959; S.T.M., Lancaster (Pa.) Theol. Sem., 1970; Ph.D., Claremont (Calif.) Grad. Sch., 1970; m. Helen Daniels, Sept. 3, 1954; children—Lydia Isabelle Sparksworthy, Leslie Bishop, Robin Bond. Lectr. philosophy and religion LaVerne (Calif.) Coll., 1965-69; asst. prof. religion Claremont Grad. Sch., 1970-74, assoc. dir. Inst. Antiquity and Christianity, 1970-74; mem. faculty San Diego State U., 1974—, prof. religious studies, 1980—, chmn. dept. religious studies, 1983-90, 92—, assoc. dean grad. div. and research, 1974-83; adj. faculty Sch. Theol. Claremont, Calif., 1970-74, 89—; founder/pres. Inst. Bibl. Studies, 1983-85; cons. photog. archival conservation of Dead Sea Scrolls in Jerusalem, 1980; mem adv. bd. Inst. Antiquity and Christianity, 1974—. Trustee, Claremont Collegiate Sch., 1970-75, pres., 1972-74; trustee, mem. exec. com. Ancient Bibl. Manuscript Ctr., 1981—. Fellow Lilly Found., 1964-65, Layne Found., 1965-66; disting. vis. scholar James Madison U., 1982. Mem. Am. Soc. Papyrologists, Soc. Bibl. Lit., Phi Beta Delta. Author: The Pastoral Epistles: Introduction and Commentary, 1981, Exploring World Religions: A Reading and Writing Workbook, 1986, 4th edit., 1991; editor Studies and Documents, 1971-92; contbr. articles on papyrology and bibl. studies to scholarly jours. Office: San Diego State U Dept Religious Studies San Diego CA 92182-0304

SPARKS, JOHN EDWARD, lawyer; b. Rochester, Ind., July 3, 1930; s. Russell Leo and Pauline Anna (Whittenberger) S.; m. Margaret Joan Snyder, Sept. 4, 1954; children: Thomas Edward, William Russell, Kathryn Chapman. A.B., Ind. U., 1952; LL.B., U. Calif., Berkeley, 1957; postgrad., London Sch. Econs., 1957-58. Bar: Calif. 1958. Assoc. Brobeck, Phleger & Harrison, San Francisco, 1958-66, ptnr., 1967—; adj. prof. law U. San Francisco, 1967-69; pres. Legal Aid Soc. San Francisco, 1978-79, dir., 1971-81; trustee Pacific Legal Found., Sacramento, 1975-80. Editor U. Calif. Law Rev., 1956-57. Served to 1st lt. Q.M.C. U.S. Army, 1952-54, Korea. Recipient Wheeler Oak Meritorious award U. Calif., Berkeley, 1986. Fellow Am. Bar Found., Am. Coll. Trial Lawyers; mem. State Bar Calif., Bar Assn. San Francisco (bd. dirs. 1974-75), ABA, Am. Judicature Soc., Boalt Hall Alumni Assn. (pres. 1983-84), Bankers Club, Pacific Union Club (San Francisco), World Trade Club. Democrat. Office: Brobeck Phleger & Harrison Spear St Tower 1 Market Plz San Francisco CA 94105*

SPARKS, LARRY EDWARD, elementary school educator; b. Berea, Ky., Feb. 23, 1954; s. Clifton Eugene and Delores Jean (Robinson) S. BA in Elem. Edn., Berea Coll., 1976; exch. student, Newberry Coll., 1976; MA in Ednl. Adminstrn., George Peabody Coll. Tchrs., 1979; Rank I Ednl. Adminstrn., Ea. Ky. U., 1988. Cert. tchr. elem. k-8, prin. k-8, supr. instrn. k-12, Ky. Tchr. Sand Gap (Ky.) Elem. Sch., Jackson County Bd. Edn., 1976-78; substitute tchr. Garrard and Madison Counties, Ky., 1979-80; adminstrv. dir. Ky. Jr. Coll. Bus., Richmond, Ky., 1980-84; tchr. math. and social scis. grades 5 and 6 Paint Lick (Ky.) Elem. Sch., Garrard County Bd. Edn., 1984—; sch. dist. tech. grant writer, 1986-87, mem. dist. tech. com., 1987-88, coord. sch. computer lab., 1984-87, basketball coach, 1986-87, yearbook sponsor, 1986-89, newspaper sponsor, 1990-91, mem. sch. handbook com., 1988—, mem. sch. guidance com., 1990-92, mem. sch. dedication com., mem. sch. primary action plan com., 1992, mem. sch. tech. com., 1990-94; sponsor Nat. Jr. Beta Club, 1991—; coach Elem. Acad. Team, 1991-95; chmn. Elem. Social Studies, 1994—. V.p. PTO, Paint Lick, 1984-86; mem. Nat. Trust for Hist. Preservation, 1992—, Ky. Farm Bur., Lancaster, 1980—. Coach dist. champions Elem. Acad. Team, 1994, Quick Recall champions, 1994, 95, Future Problem Solving champions, 1995; grantee Garrard County Sch. Dist., 1986-87. Mem. ASCD, Nat. Coun. Tchrs. of Math., Ky. Edn. Assn. (state del. 1984-85), Future Tchrs. of Am., Future Farmers of Am., Berea C. of C., Kappa Delta Pi. Democrat. Avocation: Antique collector and dealer. Home: 212 Boone St Berea KY 40403-1605

SPARKS, MORGAN, physicist; b. Pagosa Springs, Colo., July 6, 1916; s. Harry Lysinger and Pearl (Morgan) S.; m. Elizabeth MacEvoy, Apr. 30, 1949; children: Margaret Ellen, Patricia Rae, Morgan MacEvoy, Gordon K. B.A., Rice U., 1938, M.A., 1940; Ph.D., U. Ill., 1943. With Bell Telephone Labs., Murray Hill, N.J., 1943-72; exec. dir. semicondr. components Bell Telephone Labs., 1968-69, v.p. tech. info. and personnel, 1969-71, v.p. electronic tech., 1971-72; pres. Sandia Nat. Labs., Albuquerque, 1972-81; dean Anderson Sch. Mgmt., U. N.Mex., Albuquerque, 1981-84. Contbr. articles on transistors, pn junctions and properties of semicondrs. to profl. jours. Rockefeller Found. fellow U. Ill., 1940-43. Fellow Am. Phys. Soc., IEEE (Jack A. Morton award 1977), Am. Inst. Chemists; mem. Am. Chem. Soc., Nat. Acad. Engring., Phi Beta Kappa, Sigma Xi, Phi Lambda Upsilon. Patentee semicondr. electronics. Home: 904 Lamp Post Cir SE Albuquerque NM 87123-4119

SPARKS, ROBERT DEAN, medical administrator, physician; b. Newton, Iowa, May 6, 1932; s. Albert John and Josephine Emma (Kleinendorst) S.; children: Steven, Robert, Ann Louise, John James. BA, U. Iowa, 1955, MD, 1957; D of Humanitarian Service, Creighton U., 1978. Diplomate Am. Bd. Internal Medicine. Intern Charity Hosp. of La., New Orleans, 1957-58, resident in internal medicine, 1958-59; asst. in medicine Charity Hosp. of La., 1958-59; fellow in gen. medicine and gastroenterology Tulane U. Sch. Medicine, 1959-62, instr. medicine, 1959-63, asst. prof., 1963-64, assoc. prof., 1964-68, prof., 1968-72, asst. dean, 1964-67, assoc. dean, acting dean, 1967-68, vice dean, 1968-69, dean, 1969-72, chief sect. gastroenterology, 1968-72; chancellor Med. Ctr. U. Nebr., 1972-76, prof. medicine, 1972-76; v.p. U. Nebr. System, 1972-76; health program dir. W.K. Kellogg Found., Battle Creek, Mich., 1976-81, v.p. programming, 1981-82, sr. v.p., 1982, pres., chief programming officer, 1982-86, pres., 1982-87, trustee, 1982-87, pres. emeritus, cons., 1988-92; exec. dir., CEO, Calif. Med. Assn. Found., San Francisco, 1995—; cons. U. Tenn. Health Sci. Ctr., 1988-90, Boston U. Health Policy Inst., 1989-90; bd. dirs., mem. sci., compensation and trust rev. coms. Syntex Corp., Palo Alto, Calif., 1987-91, v.p. product safety and compliance, 1991-93; mem. overseers com. to visit Harvard U. Med. and Dental Schs., 1984-90; mem. vis. com. U. Miami Sch. Medicine, 1982-86; assoc. med. dir. for addiction treatment svcs., dir. for edn. and rsch., Battle Creek Adventist Hosp., 1990-91; v.p. Howe-Lewis Internat Inc., Menlo Park, N.Y., 1993-94, cons., 1994-95. Contbr. articles to profl. jours. Bd. dirs. Nat. Coun. on Alcoholism and Drug Dependence, N.Y.C., 1982-93, treas., 1986-88, chmn., 1989-90, past chmn., 1991-92; bd. dirs. Battle Creek Symphony Orch., 1981-88, Lakeview Sch. Dist., Battle Creek, 1979-83, 88-91; trustee Monsour Med. Found., Jeannette, Pa., 1976-90, interim pres., 1989, chmn. bd., pres., 1989-90; mem. Pres. Reagan's Adv. Bd. Pvt. Sector Initiatives, Washington, 1986-89; chmn. bd. dirs. Bard Coll. Health Policy and Practice Inst., 1988—, Consumer Health Info. Rsch. Inst., 1990—, Chelsea-Arbor Treatment Ctr., 1990-91, Calhoun County Bd. Health, 1988-91, chmn., 1989-91; mem., bd. dirs. Mental Health and Addictions Found. of Mich., Battle Creek, 1991-93. Recipient Harvard Dental award Harvard U. Sch. Dental Medicien, 1992. Fellow ACP; mem. AMA, Nat. Acad. Scis. Inst. Medicine (com. study of treatment and rehab. svcs. for alcoholism and alcohol abuse, bd. mental health and behavioral medicine), Coun. Mich. Founds. (trustee 1986-88), Assn. Am. Med. Colls. (disting. svc. mem. award 1975), Phi Eta Sigma, Alpha Omega Alpha. Republican. Presbyterian. Avocations: tennis, bridge, reading, travel. Home: 7 Robert S Dr Menlo Park CA 94025-5543 Office: Calif Med Assn Found PO Box 7690 221 Main St San Francisco CA 94120-7690

SPARKS, ROBERT RONOLD, JR., lawyer; b. Bklyn., Dec. 4, 1946; s. Robert Ronold Sr. and Marjorie Anne (Boehm) S. BA, Va. Mil. Inst., 1969; JD, U. Va., 1972. Bar: U.S. Dist. Ct. (D.C. cir.) 1979, U.S. Dist. Ct. (ea. dist.) Va. 1979, U.S. Ct. Appeals (2d cir.) 1986, U.S. Ct. Appeals (D.C. cir.) 1975, Va. 1972, U.S. Ct. Appeals (4th cir.) 1982, U.S. Ct. Mil. Appeals 1976, U.S. Tax Ct. 1978, U.S. Supreme Ct. 1981, U.S. Dist. Ct. Md. 1993. From assoc. to ptnr. Sedam & Herge, McLean, Va., 1978-85; ptnr. Herge, Sparks & Christopher, McLean, 1985-90; mem. bd. regents James Monroe Law Office Mus. and Meml. Library, Fredericksburg, Va., 1983-86. Mem. Fairfax County Redevel. and Housing, Fairfax, 1981-82; commr. Fairfax County Indsl. Devel. Authority, 1980-81, Fairfax County Planning Comm., 1983-89. Lt. USNR, 1972-77, Philippines. Mem. Va. Bar Assn., D.C. Bar Assn., Rotary (treas., bd. dirs. 1978-80). Roman Catholic. Home: 6448 Spring Ter Falls Church VA 22042-3141 Office: Herge Sparks Christopher 8201 Greensboro Dr Ste 200 Mc Lean VA 22102-3810

SPARKS, ROBERT WILLIAM, publishing executive; b. Seattle, Dec. 30, 1925; s. James Donald and Gladys (Simmons) S. Student, U. Wash., 1947-50; B.A., U. Hawaii, 1954, M.A., 1965. Editor, various publs., 1947-64; mng. editor U. Hawaii Press, 1964-66, dir., 1967-87; cons. East-West Ctr.,

Jour. Hawaiian History, Japanese and Chinese book pubs., 1987-92; mem. adv. bd. to pres. Kamehameha Schs. Served with AUS, 1944-46, PTO. Recipient McInerny editorship, 1953; Pacific House citation Pacific and Asian Affairs Council, 1974. Mem. Assn. Am. Univ. Presses, Assn. Am. Publishers, Internat. Assn. Scholarly Publishers, Soc. for Scholarly Pub., Hawaiian Hist. Soc., Hawaii Found. History and Humanities, Honolulu Acad. Arts, Bishop Mus. Assn. Home: 3634 Nihipali Pl Honolulu HI 96816-3307

SPARKS, SAM, federal judge; b. 1939. BA, U. Tex., 1961, LLB, 1963. Aide Rep. Homer Thornberry, 1963; law clk. to Hon. Homer Thornberry U.S. Dist. Ct. (we. dist.) Tex., 1963-65; assoc. to ptnr., shareholder Hardie, Grambling, Sims & Galatzan (and successor firms), El Paso, Tex., 1965-91; dist. judge U.S. Dist. Ct. (we. dist.) Tex., 1991—. Fellow Am. Coll. Trial Lawyers, Tex. Bar Found. (life); mem. Am. Bd. Trial Advocates (advocate), State Bar Tex. Office: US Dist Ct Judge 200 W Eighth St Ste 100 Austin TX 78701-2333

SPARKS, SHERMAN PAUL, osteopathic physician; b. Toledo, Jan. 23, 1909; s. Earnest Melvin and Nancy Jane (Keller) S.; m. Helen Mildred Barnes, Aug. 1, 1930 (div. July 1945); 1 child, James Earl; m. Billie June Wester, Feb. 20, 1946 (dec. Apr. 1959); children: Randal Paul, Robert Dale; m. Joyce Marie Sparks, Jan. 23, 1965 (dec.); 1 child, David Paul. BS, U. Ill., 1932, MS, 1938; DO, Kirksville Coll. Osteopathy and Surgery, 1945. Diplomate Am. Bd. Osteo. Medicine. Tchr. high schs., Kincaid, Pesotum, Mt. Olive, Ill., 1930-42; intern Sparks Hosp. and Clinic, Dallas, 1945-46; pvt. practice, Rockwall, Tex., 1946-95; part-time cons., sci. rschr., ret.; team physician Rockwall High Sch., 1946-78; med. examiner Am. Cancer Soc., Rockwall, 1946-76. Coord. CD, Rockwall, 1946-80; chmn. Rockwall Centennial Assn., 1954, Rockwall County Rep. Com., 1964-78; pres. Rockwall PTA, 1961. Recipient Spirit of Tex. award, TV sta., Dallas, 1985; named Hon. State Farmer, Future Farmer's Am., 1980. Mem. Am. Coll. Gen. Practitioners, Tex. Osteo. Med. Assn. (chmn. chmn. 1946-54, numerous offices), Rockwall C. of C. (pres. 1961), SAR (pres. Plano chpt. 1989), Masons, Psi Sigma Alpha, Alpha Phi Omega. Avocations: travel, inventing. Home: 1405 Ave L Galveston TX 77550

SPARKS, THOMAS E., JR., lawyer; b. Little Rock, Jan. 11, 1942; s. Thomas E. and Marie Christine Lundgren, Sept. 11, 1976; children: Thomas Gunnar, Erik Richard, Andrew Pal. BS, Washington and Lee U., 1963; JD, U. Ark., 1968; LLM, Harvard U., 1970. Bar: Ark. 1968, Calif. 1970. Assoc. Pillsbury Madison & Sutro, San Francisco, 1970-76; ptnr. Pillsbury, Madison & Sutro, San Francisco, 1977-84, Baker & McKenzie, San Francisco, 1984-87, Pillsbury Madison & Sutro, San Francisco, 1987—. Trustee Grace Cathedral, San Francisco. 1st lt. U.S. Army, 1965. Mem. ABA, Calif. Bar Assn., Olympic Club (San Francisco). Office: Pillsbury Madison Sutro LLP 235 Montgomery St San Francisco CA 94104-2902

SPARKS, WALTER CHAPPEL, horticulturist, educator; b. New Castle, Colo., Aug. 22, 1918; s. Lester Elroy and Jean Ivene (Murray) S.; m. Barbara Ferne Gardner, May 31, 1942; children: Robert, Richard, Eugene. Student, Western State Coll., 1936-37; BS, Colo. State U., 1941, MS, 1943; postgrad., U. Minn., 1945, Wash. State U., 1949, 56-57; DSc (hon.), U. Idaho, 1984. Instr., head dept. agr. Pueblo Jr. Coll., 1941; grad. asst. Colo. State U., 1941-43, instr. horticulture, 1943-44, asst. prof., 1944-47, assoc. prof., 1947; assoc. horticulturist U. Idaho, Aberdeen, 1947-57; acting supt. Aberdeen br. Agrl. Expt. Sta., 1951, 57, 65, horticulturist, 1957—, research prof. horticulture, 1968—, prin. liaison coordinator for potato program, 1976—; exchange prof. Research Inst., Kolding, Denmark, 1972-73; adviser and lectr. on potato problems to various fgn. govts.; cons., adv., Israel, 1980, Philippines, 1981, Jamaica, 1988; dir. Postharvest Inst. Perishables, 1980—. Contbr. articles to profl. jours. Recipient 50th Anniversary medal Fed. Land Banks, 1967, Disting. Svc. in Potato Industry award Gov. of Idaho, 1967, Alimni Svc. award 1980, Disting. Faci;tu award Phi Kappa Phi, 1980, Disting. Svc. award for rsch. in potato postharvest storage tech., 1987, Cert. of Appreciation Nat. Potato Rsch. Edn. Found., 1986, Agriculture Svc. award N.W. Food Processor Field Reps., 1987; named to Hall of Fame Potato Mus. Brussels, 1977, Idaho Agrl. Hall of Fame, 1983, Idaho Potato Hall of Fame for outstanding contbn. to Idaho Potato Industry, 1996; Eldred Jenne Rsch. fellow, 1957; named 1 of 100 "People Make the Difference" in Idaho, 1990. Mem. AAAS, Am. Inst. Biol. Scis., Am. Soc. Hort. Sci. (life), European Assn. Potato Research, N.W. Assn. Horticulturists, Entomologists and Plant Pathologists, Idaho Acad. Sci., Nat. Potato Research and Edn. Found. (cert. appraciation seed potato storage tech. 1986), N.W. Food Processors Assn. (Disting. Service award, 1987), N.W. Fieldman's Assn. (Disting. Agrl. Service award, 1987), Potato Assn. Am. (life mem., past pres., dir.), Western Regional Potato Improvement Group (past pres.), C. of C., Scabbard and Blade, Sigma Xi (Outstanding Research Paper award 1974), Gamma Sigma Delta (Outstanding Research Worker award 1977, award of merit 1978), Alpha Zeta, Beta Beta Beta, Epsilon Rho Epsilon. Club: Rotary. Home: 1100 Burnett Dr Apt 513 Nampa ID 83651-7578 Office: U Idaho Reseach & Extension Center Aberdeen ID 83210 *If the food losses occurring from the farmer to the consumer (including storage) could be minimized or completely eliminated, the food supply could be significantly increased without bringing one more acre of land into production, or using one more pound of fertilizer, or using one additional gallon of fuel. Proper handling and storage can accomplish this goal.*

SPARLING, MARY CHRISTINE, foundation executive; b. Collingwood, Ont., Can., July 8, 1928; d. Alexander and Catherine Henrietta (MacDonald) Malcolm; m. Wintfield Henry Sparling, June 17, 1950; children: Margaret, John. BA, Queen's U., Kingston, Ont., 1949; BEd (Gold medal 1970), St. Mary's U., Halifax, N.S., 1970; MA in Edn., Dalhousie U., 1978; DFA (hon), Nova Scotia Coll. Art & Design, 1994. Curator edn. N.S. Mus., Halifax, 1968-73; dir. art gallery Mt. St. Vincent U., Halifax, 1973-94; v.p. Neptune Theatre Found., Halifax, 1994—; cons. in field; bd. mem. Pier 21 Soc. Recipient Ohio State award for film script The Artist in Nova Scotia, 1977, Queen's Silver Jubilee medal, 1977, Outstanding Cultural Exec. award N.S. Cultural Fedns., 1991; Warner-Lambert award for disting. arts adminstrn. in Can., 1993. Fellow Can. Mus. Assn. (pres. 1974-76, coun. 1972-78); mem. N.S. Coalition on Arts and Culture. Unitarian. Home: 6030 Jubilee Rd, Halifax, NS Canada B3H 2E4

SPARLING, MARY LEE, biology educator; b. Ft. Wayne, Ind., May 20, 1934; d. George Hewson and Velmah Evelyn (McClain) S.; m. Albert Alcide Barber, Sept. 1, 1956 (div. Jan. 1975); children: Bonnie Lee Barber, Bradley Paul Barber. BS, U. Miami, Coral Gables, Fla., 1955; MA, Duke U., 1958; PhD, UCLA, 1962. Lectr. UCLA, 1962-63; asst. prof. Calif. State U., Northridge, 1966-72, assoc. prof., 1972-76, prof., 1976—. Contbr. articles to profl. jours. NSF grantee Calif. State U., Northridge, 1971-72, 81-83, 89, NIH grantee Calif. State U., Northridge, 1987-89. Mem. AAUP (pres. 1981-82), Am. Soc. Cell Biology, Soc. for Devel. Biology, Am. Soc. Zoologists, Sigma Xi (bd. dirs. Research Triangle, N.C. 1974-91). Avocations: tennis, gardening, backpacking, travel. Home: 8518 White Oak Ave Northridge CA 91325-3940 Office: Calif State U Biology Dept Northridge CA 91330

SPARLING, PETER DAVID, dancer, dance educator; b. Detroit, June 4, 1951; s. Robert Daniel and Emily Louise (Matthews) S. BFA, Juilliard Sch., N.Y.C., 1973. Dancer José Limón Co., N.Y.C., 1971-73; co. instr. London (Eng.) Contemporary Dance Theatre, 1983-84; prin. dancer Martha Graham Dance Co., N.Y.C., 1973-87; asst. prof. dance U. Mich., Ann Arbor, 1984-87, chmn. dance dept., assoc. prof., 1987—; artistic dir. Peter Sparling Presents Solo Flight, N.Y.C., 1977-82, Peter Sparling Dance Co., N.Y.C., 1980-84; co-dir. Ann Arbor Dance Works, 1984—; guest choreographer Victorian Coll. Arts, 1981, 84, Dance Uptown, Am. Ballet Theatre II, Cloud Dance Theatre, Taiwan, Ballet Gulbenkian, Lisbon, Utah Repertory Dance Theatre, Joseph Holmes Dance Theatre, Corning Dances, Fla. State U. Choreographer Divining Rod, 1973, Little Incantations, 1974, Three Farewells, 1977, Suite to Sleep, 1978, A Thief's Progress or The Lantern Night, 1979, Excursions of Chung Kuei, 1978, Nocturnes for Eurydice, 1978, Once in a Blue Moon, 1978, Harald's Round, 1979, Hard Rock, 1979, What She Forgot He Remembered, 1979, Sitting Harlequin, 1979, In Stride, 1979, Elegy, 1979, The Tempest, 1980, Orion, 1980, Landscape with Bridge, 1980, Nocturnes, Modern Life, Bright Bowed River, A Fearful Symmetry, Alibi, Rounding the Square, De Profundis, Rondo, Wings, Witness, The Boy Who Played With Dolls. Louis Horst Meml. scholar Juilliard Sch., 1973; Nat. Endowment for the Arts fellow 1971, 79, 83; grantee U. Mich., 1985-86, 89, Mich. Coun. for the Arts, 1986; recipient Choreographer's award Mich. Dance Assn., 1988, Artist's award Arts Found. Mich., 1989. Office: Univ of Michigan Dept of Dance Dance Bldg Ann Arbor MI 48109

SPARR, DANIEL BEATTIE, federal judge; b. Denver, June 8, 1931; s. Daniel John and Mary Isabel (Beattie) S.; m. Virginia Sue Long Sparr, June 28, 1952; children: Stephen Glenwood, Douglas Lloyd, Michael Christopher. BSBA, U. Denver, 1952, JD, 1966. Bar: Colo. U.S. Dist. Ct. Assoc. White & Steele, Denver, 1966-70; atty. Mountain States Telephone & Telegraph Co., Denver, 1970-71; ptnr. White & Steele, Denver, 1971-74; atty. Wesley H. Doan, Lakewood, Colo., 1974-75; prin. Law Offices of Daniel B. Sparr, Denver, 1975-77; judge 2d dist. Colo. Dist. Ct., Denver, 1977-90; judge U.S. Dist. Ct. Colo., Denver, 1990—. Mem. Denver Bar Assn. (trustee 1975-78), Denver Paralegal Inst. (bd. advs. 1976-88), William E. Doyle's/Am. Inns of Ct., Am. Bd. Trial Advs., ABA, Colo. Bar Assn. Office: US Dist Ct US Courthouse Rm 334 1929 Stout St Denver CO 80294-2900*

SPARROW, EPHRAIM MAURICE, mechanical engineering scientist, educator; b. Hartford, Conn., May 27, 1928; s. Charles and Frieda (Gottlieb) S.; m. Ruth May Saltman, Nov. 2, 1952; 1 child, Rachel Bernarr. BS, MIT, 1948, MS, 1949; MA, Harvard Coll., 1950, PhD, 1956; Doutor Honoris Causa, U. Brazil, 1967. Heat transfer specialist Raytheon Mfg. Co., 1952-53; rsch. specialist Lewis Rsch. Ctr., NASA, Cleve., 1953-59; prof. mech. engring. U. Minn., 1959—, chmn. fluid dynamics program, 1968-80; program dir. NSF, 1986-87, dir. chem., biochem. and thermal engring. divsn., 1986-88; vis. prof., chief AID mission U. Brazil, 1966-67; adv. prof. Xi'an Jiaotong U., 1984—; cons. in field, 1960—; pres. 1st Brazilian Symposium on Heat Transfer and Fluid Mechanics, 1966; mem. solar energy panel Fed. Coun. on Sci. and Tech., 1972; U.S. sci. committeeman 5th Internat. Heat Transfer Conf., 1973-74. Author: (with R.D. Cess) Radiation Heat Transfer, 1966, 2nd edit., 1978; editor: Handbook of Numerical Heat Transfer; hon. mem. editorial bd. Internat. Jour. Heat Mass Transfer, 1964—, Internat. Comm. in Heat Mass Transfer, 1975—; sr. editor Jour. Heat Transfer, 1972-80; editor Series in Computational and Phys. Processes in Mechanics and Thermal Scis., 1980—; chmn. editorial adv. bd. Numerical Heat Transfer, 1978—; contbr. over 560 tech. articles to profl. jours. Recipient Ralph Coates Roe award Am. Soc. Engring. Edn., 1978, Outstanding Teaching award U. Minn., 1985, Fed. Engr. of Yr. award NSF, 1988, Sr. Rsch. award Am. Soc. Engring. Edn., 1989, Horace T. Morse award for outstanding contbns. to undergraduate teaching, 1993; named George Hawkins Disting. lectr. Purdue U., 1985. Fellow ASME (Meml. award for outstanding contbn. to sci. heat transfer 1962, Max Jakob award for eminent contbn. 1976, Centennial medal 1980, Disting. Svc. award heat transfer div. 1982, Charles Russ Richards Meml. award 1985, Worcester Reed Warner medal 1986, 50th Anniversary award heat transfer div. 1988, Disting. lectr. 1986-91, 93-94); mem. NAE, Biomed. Engring. Soc. (faculty advisor 1994—), Sigma Xi (Monie A. Ferst medal for contbn. to rsch. through edn. 1993), Pi Tau Sigma. Home: 2105 Hoyt Ave W Saint Paul MN 55108-1314 Office: U Minn Minneapolis MN 55455-0111

SPARROW, HERBERT GEORGE, III, lawyer; b. Ft. Bragg, N.C., May 26, 1936; s. Herbert George and Virginia (Monroe) S.; m. Nancy Woodruff, Mar. 4, 1962; children: Amy Winslow, Edward Harrison, Herbert G. IV, Alison Kidder. AB cum laude, Princeton U., 1958; JD, U. Mich., 1961. Bar: Mich. 1961, Calif. 1964, D.C. 1979, U.S. Ct. Claims 1982, U.S. Tax Ct. 1983, U.S. Ct. Mil. Appeals 1962, U.S. Supreme Ct. 1976. Assoc. Dickinson, Wright, Moon, Van Dusen & Freeman, Detroit, 1965-70, ptnr., 1970—; adj. prof. Detroit Coll. Law, 1977—. Author numerous articles environ. law.; speaker in field. Bd. dirs. Family Life Edn. Coun., Grosse Pointe, Mich., 1982-88, Adult Well-Being Svcs., Inc., Detroit, 1995—. Capt. JAGC, U.S. Army, 1962-65. Mem. ABA, Mich. Bar Assn. (rep. assembly 1979-85, environ. law sect. coun. 1985-91), Calif. Bar Assn., D.C. Bar Assn., Detroit Bar Assn., Am. Arbitration Assn. (panel arbitrators 1975—), Mich. State Bar Found. (fellow 1989—), Environment Law Inst. (assoc.), Phi Delta Phi (pres. Kent Inn Assn., Ann Arbor 1985—). Office: Dickinson Wright Moon 500 Woodward Ave Ste 4000 Detroit MI 48226-3425

SPARROW, LARRY J., telecommunications executive. With GTE Corp., Thousand Oaks, Calif., 1967—; pres. GTE Northwest Inc., Thousand Oaks, Calif., 1992—; also prin. GTE Calif., Inc., Thousand Oaks, Calif., 1992—; pres. GTE, Irving, Tex, 1993—. Office: GTE PO Box 152092 Irving TX 75015-2092*

SPARSHOTT, FRANCIS EDWARD, poet, educator; b. Chatham, Eng., May 19, 1926; emigrated to Can., 1950, naturalized, 1970; s. Frank Brownley and Gladwys Winifred (Head) S.; m. Kathleen Elizabeth Vaughan, Feb. 7, 1953; 1 dau., Pumpkin Margaret Elizabeth. B.A., M.A., Corpus Christi Coll., Oxford, Eng., 1950. Lectr. dept. philosophy U. Toronto, Ont., Can., 1950-55, Univ. Prof., 1982-91; asst. prof. Victoria Coll., 1955-62, assoc. prof., 1962-64, prof., 1964-91, dept. chmn., 1965-70; vis. assoc. prof. Northwestern U., Evanston, Ill., 1958-59; vis. prof. U. Ill., Urbana, 1966. Author: An Enquiry into Goodness and Related Concepts, 1958, The Structure of Aesthetics, 1963, A Divided Voice, 1965, The Concept of Criticism, 1967, A Cardboard Garage, 1969, Looking for Philosophy, 1972, The Naming of the Beasts, 1979, The Rainy Hills, 1979, The Theory of the Arts, 1982, The Cave of Trophonius, 1983, The Hanging Gardens of Etobicoke, 1983, Storms and Screens, 1986, Off the Ground, 1988, Sculling to Byzantium, 1989, Taking Life Seriously, 1994, Views from the Zucchini Gazebo, 1994, A Measured Pace, 1995. Served with Brit. Army, 1944-47. Am. Council Learned Socs. fellow, 1961-62; Killam sr. research fellow, 1977-78. Fellow Royal Soc. Can.; mem. Can. Philos. Assn. (pres. 1975-76), League Canadian Poets (pres. 1977-79), Am. Soc. for Aesthetics (pres. 1981-82), Aristotelian Soc., Classical Assn. Can. Home: 50 Crescentwood Rd, Scarborough, ON Canada M1N 1E4

SPARTZ, ALICE ANNE LENORE, retired retail executive; b. N.Y.C., May 14, 1925; d. John Francis and Alice Philomena (Murray) Rattenbury; m. George Eugene Spartz, Oct. 29, 1949; children: Mary Elizabeth, James, Barbara, Anne, Thomas, William, Michael, John, Matthew, Clare, Robert, Richard. Student, Wright Coll., 1945-47, No. Ill. U., 1950; AA, Triton Coll., 1987. Svc. rep. Ill. Bell Tel., Chgo., 1945-46; stewardess United Airlines, Denver, 1947-49; mgr. Family Life League Resale Shop, Oak Park, Ill., 1987-95; retired, 1995. Mem. Cicero (Ill.) Cmty. Coun., 1967-69; mem. Park Dist. Oak Park Com., 1973-74; active Ill. Right to Life Com., Chgo., 1971—, Com. Pro-Life Caths., Chgo., 1992—; former bd. dirs. Ill. Pro-Life Coalition, Family Life League; vol. canteen workers ARC, Chgo., 1942-45. Mem. St. Edmunds Womens Club. Democrat. Roman Catholic. Avocations: travel, sewing, reading, swimming, pro-life activist. Office: 226 N Ridgeland Oak Park IL 60302

SPATOLA, JOANNE POLLARA, special education educator; b. Hoboken, N.J., Apr. 18, 1954; d. Ralph Frank and Katharine Stark (Cunningham) Pollara; m., Anthony Francis Spatola, Dec. 28, 1975; children: Angela, Joshua. BA, St. Joseph Coll., 1976; MA, Montclair State U., 1994. Cert. tchr. elem., spl. edn., L.D.T.C., N.J. 4th grade tchr. Holy Trinity Sch., Hackensack, N.J., 1976-77; tchr. of handicapped Kessler Inst., West Orange, N.J., 1978-86; bedside instructor West Orange Bd. of Edn., 1976-86, spl. edn. inst. aide, 1986-88; tchr. of handicapped Redwood Sch., West Orange, N.J., 1988—; mem. spl. edn. curriculum com., W. Orange, N.J., 1989, bldg. mgmt. com., 1991-92; spl. edn. rep. reading curriculum com., W. Orange, 1990; PTA faculty rep. Redwood Sch., W. Orange, 1994-95. Religious educator Our Lady of Lourdes Ch., West Orange, N.J., 1984-85, Notre Dame Ch., North Caldwell, N.J., 1991-92; girl scout leader Girl Scouts of U.S., W. Orange, N.J., 1983-84, 86-87. Mem. Coun. for Exceptional Children (learning disabilities divsn.), Coun. for Ednl. Diagnostic Svcs., Phi Kappa Phi. Avocations: reading, music (piano, guitar), swimming. Home: 50 Beverly Rd West Caldwell NJ 07006-6531 Office: Pleaseantdale Sch Pleasant Valley Way West Orange NJ 07052-3623

SPATT, ARTHUR DONALD, federal judge; b. 1925. Student, Ohio State U., 1943-44, 46-47; LLB, Bklyn. Law Sch., 1949. Assoc. Davidson & Davidson, N.Y.C., 1949, Lane, Winard, Robinson & Schorr, N.Y.C., 1950, Alfred S. Julien, N.Y.C., 1950-52, Florea & Florea, N.Y.C., 1953; pvt. practice N.Y.C., 1953-67, Spatt & Bauman, N.Y.C., 1967-78; justice 10th judicial cir. N.Y. State Supreme Ct., 1979-82; adminstrv. judge Nassau County, 1982-86; assoc. justice appellate div. Second Judicial Dept., 1986-89; dist. judge U.S. Dist. Ct. (ea. dist.) N.Y., Bklyn., 1989-90, Uniondale, N.Y., 1990—. Active South Nassau Communities Hosp., Jewish War Vets. Mem. ABA, Assn. Supreme Ct. Justices State of N.Y., Bar Assn. Nassau County, Assn. of Bar of City of N.Y., Jewish Lawyers Assn. Nassau County, Bklyn. Law Rev. Assn., Long Beach Lawyers Assn., Bklyn. Law Sch. Alumni Assn., Theodore Roosevelt Am. Inn of Ct., Master of the Bench. Office: US Dist Ct 2 Uniondale Ave Uniondale NY 11553-1259

SPATT, ROBERT EDWARD, lawyer; b. Bklyn., Mar. 26, 1956; s. Milton E. and Blanche S. (Bakstansky) S.; m. Lisa B. Malkin, Aug. 11, 1979; 1 child, Mark Eric. AB, Brown U., 1977; JD magna cum laude, U. Mich., 1980. Bar: N.Y. 1981. Assoc. Simpson Thacher & Bartlett, N.Y.C., 1980-87, ptnr., 1987—. Mem. ABA, N.Y. State Bar Assn., City of N.Y. Bar Assn., Order of Coif, ACLU. Avocations: photography, boating, reading. Home: 286 West Trl Stamford CT 06903-2402 Office: Simpson Thacher & Bartlett 425 Lexington Ave New York NY 10017-3903

SPATTA, CAROLYN DAVIS, education consultant; b. Gauhati, Assam, India, Jan. 20, 1935; d. Alfred Charles and Lola Mildred (Anderson) Davis; m. John Robert Spatta, June 2, 1957 (div. Feb. 1964); children: Robert Alan, Jennifer Lynn Spatta-Harris; m. S. Peter Karlow, July 25, 1981. AB, U. Calif., Berkeley, 1964; MA, U. Mich., 1968, PhD, 1974. Rsch. asst. U. Calif., Berkeley, 1963-65; instr. Schoolcraft Coll., Livonia, Mich., 1968-74; corp. sec. Oberlin (Ohio) Coll., 1974-78; pres. Damavand Coll., Tehran, Iran, 1978-79; cons. pvt. practice, Washington, 1979-80; v.p., adminstr. E. Mich. U., Ypsilanti, Mich., 1980-81; Dir. Inst. grants programs, and adv. svc. Assn. Am. Colls., Washington, 1982-84; v.p., adminstrn. and bus. affairs Calif. State U., Hayward, 1984-92, prof. geography and environ. studies, 1992-94; ind. mediator, cons. higher edn., 1995—; vis. lectr. E. Mich. U., Ypsilanti, 1969, 1970; mem. accreditation team Western Assn. Schs. Colls.; Fulbright scholar, Malaysia, 1994. Contbr. articles to profl. jours. Bd. dirs. Wellness, Inc.; mem. Trinity Parish, Menlo Pk., Calif. (pers., bldg. coms.), U. Mich. Alumni Assn., St. John's Episc. Ch. (pastoral care commn.), Chevy Chase, Md., Oberlin Open Space Com., Tenaya Guild, John Muir Hosp., Walnut Creek, Calif. (pres.), steering com. Ann Arbor Citizens for Good Schs.; trustee Pacific Sch. of Religion, 1992—. Recipient fellowship Nat. Defense Foreign Lang., 1966-68; Fulbright scholar, Malaysia, 1994—. Mem. Am. Assn. Higher Edn., Asian Studies on Pacific Coast, Assn. Asian Studies, Assn. Am. Geographers, Assn. Pacific Coast Geographers. Avocations: travel, reading, walking, cooking and entertaining, golf, art, music.

SPATZ, HUGO DAVID, film producer; b. Zanesville, Ohio, Nov. 29, 1913; s. Charles Edwin and Mary Jane (Elias) S.; m. Ruth D. Wallie, Nov. 26, 1945. BA, Ohio State U., 1933, MA, 1935; PhD, Columbia Pacific U., San Pedro, Calif., 1986. Buyer Schiff Shoe Corp., Columbus, Ohio, 1936-39; gen. mgr. Zenith Precision Optics Corp., Wheeling, W.Va., 1940-42; v.p. Fredrick Optical Co., Cleve., 1945-56; pres. The House of Hugo Opticians, Cleve., 1957-73, Away to Adventure Travelogues, Port Charlotte, Fla., 1974—. Columnist weekly column "Profiles". Pres. Charlotte County (Fla.) Civic Coalition, 1985-86; v.p. The Alliance of th e Arts; adv. bd. Cultural Ctr., Charlotte County; pres. Home Owners, N.Y. Area, Port Charlotte, 1984-85; chmn. Water & Sewer Bd., Charlotte County, 1988; mem. Comprehensive Land Plan Com., Charlotte County, 1987; pub. mem. Polit. Sign Com., 1988. With U.S. Army, 1942-45. Named Citizen of Yr., Citizens of University Heights, 1975; commd. Ky. col., 1987. Mem. Masons (master 1968-69). Republican. Home: 22525 Nyack Ave Port Charlotte FL 33952-7116

SPAULDING, FRANK HENRY, librarian; b. Danielson, Conn., July 12, 1932; s. Jacob Lindhurst and Frances (Upham) S.; m. Eugenia Jenewicz, May 25, 1963; children—Geoffrey Michael, Jennifer Anne. A.B., Brown U., 1957; M.S.L.S., Case Western Res. U., 1961. Supr. info. ctr. Colgate-Palmolive Co., Piscataway, N.J., 1961-65; group supr. library tech. processes Bell Labs., Holmdel, N.J., 1965-70, head library ops., 1970-84; mgr. library services AT&T Bell Labs., Holmdel, 1985-87, mgr. mktg. library network, 1984-86; library/info. cons., 1987—; pres. Sp. Libraries. Assn. 1986-87; treas. Am. Soc. for Info. Sci., 1983-86; pres. Documentation Abstracts, N.Y.C., 1983-85; dir. Universal Serials and Book Exchange, Washington, 1983-85, Palinet, Phila., 1979-81. Compiler: Managing the Electronic Library, 1983; author: Today's Information Specialist Tomorrow's Knowledge Technician, Knowledge Counselor in 2006, International Information: International Librarianship; creator: Task Force on the Value of the Informational Professional. Mem. Buten Mus. Wedgwood. Served to lt. USN, 1957-60. Mem. ALA (com. on accreditation 1989-93), Spl. Librs. Assn. (del. to Internat. Fedn. Libr. Assn. and Inst. 1987-89).

SPAULDING, JOHN PIERSON, public relations executive, marine consultant; b. N.Y.C., June 25, 1917; s. Forrest Brisbine and Genevieve Anderson (Pierson) S.; m. Eleanor Rita Bonner, Aug. 18, 1947; children: Anne Spaulding Balzhiser, John F., Mary T. Spaulding Calvert; m. 2d, Donna Alene Abrescia, May 15, 1966. Student Iowa State Coll., 1935-36, Grinnell Coll., 1936-38, U. Chgo., 1938-39. Reporter, Chgo. City News Bur., UPI, 1939-40; editor Cedar Falls (Iowa) Daily Record, 1940-41; picture editor Des Moines Register & Tribune, 1941-42, 47-50; pub. relations dir. Motor Club Iowa, Davenport, 1950-51; commd. 2d. lt. USAF, 1942, advanced through grades to maj., 1947, recalled, 1951, advanced through grades to lt. col.; ret., 1968; v.p. Vacations Hawaii, Honolulu, 1969-70; dir. pub. relations, mgr. pub. relations services Alexander & Baldwin, Inc., Honolulu, 1970-76; mgr. community relations Matson Navigation Co., Honolulu, 1976-81. Pres., Econ. Devel. Assn., Skagit County, Wash., 1983-85, Fidalgo Island Ednl. Youth Found.; mem. Anacortes (Wash.) Sch. Bd., 1982-88; mem. Gov.'s Tourism Devel. Council, 1983-85; mem. adv. com. State Ferry System, 1982—, productivity coun., 1990—; chmn. Everett chpt. S.C.O.R.E., 1984-86, Bellingham chpt., 1991—; mem. citizens adv. com. SKAGIT Trans., 1995—. Decorated Air medal. Mem. Pub. Relations Soc. Am. (pres. Hawaii chpt. 1974), Hawaii Communicators (pres. 1973), Nat. Def. Transp. Assn. (pres. Aloha chpt. 1980-81, Disting. Service award 1978-79), Air Force Assn., Can. Inst. Internat. Affairs, Anacortes C. of C., Sigma Delta Chi (life). Clubs: Propeller (pres. Port of Honolulu 1979-80), Honolulu Press, Fidelgo Yacht, Hawaii Yacht, Royal Hawaiian 400 Yacht (comdr. 1977-81), Rotary (sec.-elect 1996—), Elks. Home: 6002 Sands Way Anacortes WA 98221-4015

SPAULDING, ROBERT MARK, lawyer; b. Buffalo, June 2, 1929; s. Mark Spaulding and Alice (Dee) Sparks; m. Mary Jean Tillett, Aug. 22, 1953; children: Joseph, M. Celia, Robert Mark Jr., William, Alyson. BA, St. Bonaventure U., Allegany, N.Y., 1951; JD, Harvard U., 1954. Bar: N.Y. 1954, U.S. Dist. Ct. (we. dist.) N.Y. 1955, U.S. Dist. Ct. (no. dist.) N.Y. 1972, U.S. Ct. Appeals (2d cir.) 1980. Mem. firm Phillips, Lytle, Hitchcock, Blaine & Huber, Buffalo, 1954—; lectr. in field. Author: Commentaries on Commercial Law. Mem. ABA, N.Y. State Bar Assn., Erie County Bar Assn. Office: Phillips Lytle Hitchcock Blaine & Huber 3400 Marine Midland Ctr Buffalo NY 14203-2834

SPEAKES, LARRY MELVIN, public relations executive; b. Cleveland, Miss., Sept. 13, 1939; s. Harry Earl and Ethlyn Frances (Fincher) S.; m. Laura Christine Crawford, Nov. 3, 1968; children: Sondra LaNell, Barry Scott, Jeremy Stephen. Student, U. Miss., 1957-61; Litt. D. (hon.), Ind. Central U., 1982. News editor Oxford (Miss.) Eagle, 1961-62; news editor Bolivar Comml., Cleveland, 1962-63; mng. editor Bolivar Comml., 1965-66; dep. dir. Bolivar County Civil Def., 1963-65; gen. mgr. Progress Pubs., Leland, Miss., 1966-68; editor Leland Progress, Hollandale Herald, Bolivar County Democrat, Sunflower County News; press sec. U.S. Senator J.O. Eastland of Miss., 1968-74; staff asst. Exec. Office of Pres., Mar.-May 1974; press asst. to spl. counsel to Pres., May-Aug. 1974; asst. White House press sec., 1974-76, asst. press sec. to Pres., 1976-77; press sec. to Gerald R. Ford, 1977; v.p. Hill & Knowlton, Inc., internat. pub. relations and pub. affairs counsel, Washington, 1977-81; prin. dep. press sec. and asst. to Pres. of U.S., Washington, 1981-87; sr. v.p. Merrill Lynch & Co., Inc., N.Y.C., 1987-88; v.p. comm. No. Telecom Ltd., Washington and Toronto, Ont., Can., 1991-93; sr. v.p. corp. and legis. affairs U.S. Postal Svc., Washington, 1994—; corp. comm. cons., lectr. on press and politics, 1988-91; mem. pub. rels. seminar. Author: Speaking Out: The Reagan Presidency From Inside the White House; contbr. Crisis Repsponse: Inside Stories on Managing Image Under Siege. Recipient Presdl. Citizens medal, 1987, Gen. Excellence award

Miss. Press Assn., 1988, Disting. Journalism Alumni award U. Miss., 1981, Hall of Fame, 1985, Silver Em. Miss. Scholastic Press Assn., 1988, Spl. Achievement award Nat. Assn. Govt. Communications, 1983, Silver Anvil award Pub. Rels. Soc. Am., 1988. Mem. Arthur Page Soc. (trustee), Sigma Delta Chi, Kappa Sigma (Man of Yr. 1982), Lambda Sigma, Omicron Delta Kappa. Methodist. Home: 4800 Thiban Ter Annandale VA 22003-4250

SPEAKS, RUBEN LEE, bishop; b. Lake Providence, La., Jan. 8, 1920; s. Benjamin and Jessie Bell (Nichols) S.; m. Janie Angeline Griffin, Aug. 31, 1947; children: Robert Bernard, Joan Cordelia, Faith Elizabeth. A.B., Drake U., 1946; M.Div., Drew Theol. Sem., 1949; S.T.M., Temple U., 1952; postgrad., Div. Sch., Duke U., 1961; D.D., Hood Theol. Sem., 1972. Ordained deacon Christian Ch., 1942; elder A.M.E. Zion Ch., 1947; minister St. Thomas A.M.E. Zion Ch., Somerville, N.J., 1947, Wallace Chapel A.M.E. Zion Ch., Summit, N.J., 1948-50, Varick A.M.E. Zion Ch., Phila., 1950-56, St. Mark A.M.E. Zion Ch., Durham, N.C., 1956-64, 1st A.M.E. Zion Ch., Bklyn., 1964-72; bishop 10th Episcopal Area, Roosevelt, N.Y., 1972-84, 8th Episcopal Area, Wilmington, N.C., 1984-88, 6th Episcopal Area, Salisbury, N.C., 1988—; ch. world service chmn. Overseas Mission Bd., A.M.E. Zion Ch. Author: Higher Catechism for Ministers and Laymen, 1966, The Minister and His Task, 1968, The Church and Black Liberation, 1972, God, In An Age of Scarcity, 1981, Prelude to Pentecost, A Theology of the Holy Spirit, 1985. Bd. dirs. Durham Com. on Negro Affairs, 1958-63, N.Y. Urban League, 1967-72; trustee Lincoln Hosp., Durham, Livingstone Coll., 1972—, U. N.C., Wilmington, 1984-88; chmn. exec. com. NAACP, 1958-63. Recipient Citizens award City of Durham, 1964, Meritorious Service award N.Y. Urban League, 1968, Chancellor's award for meritorious services as trustee U. N.C. at Wilmington, 1988. Mem. Nat. Acad. Sci. and Religion, World Methodist Coun. (exec. com.), Nat. Coun. Chs. U.S.A., World Coun. Chs. Home: PO Box 986 Salisbury NC 28145-0986

SPEAR, ALLAN HENRY, state senator, historian, educator; b. Michigan City, Ind., June 24, 1937; s. Irving S. and Esther (Lieber) S. BA, Oberlin Coll., 1958; MA, Yale U., 1960, PhD, 1965. Lectr. history U. Minn., Mpls., 1964-65, asst. prof., 1965-67, assoc. prof., 1967—; mem. Minn. State Senate, St. Paul, 1973—, chmn. jud. com., 1983-93; chmn. crime prevention com., 1993—; pres. Minn. State Senate, 1993—; vis. prof. Carleton Coll., Northfield, Minn., 1970, Stanford U., Palo Alto, Calif., 1970. Author: Black Chicago, 1967. Mem. Internat. Network Gay and Lesbian Elected Offcls., Com. on Suggested State Legislation of Coun. of State Govts.; bd. dirs. Family and Children's Svc. of Mpls. Mem. Dem. Farm Labor Party. Avocations: cooking, travel, reading, classical music. Home: 2429 Colfax Ave S Minneapolis MN 55405-2942 Office: Minn State Senate 27 State St Saint Paul MN 55107-1408

SPEAR, HARVEY M., lawyer; b. Providence, May 24, 1922; s. Alfred and Esther (Marcus) S.; m. Ruth Abramson, June 27, 1965; children: Jessica Tjernberg, Elizabeth Anne. A.B., Brown U., 1942; LL.B., Harvard, 1948; M.A., George Washington U., 1949, LL.M., 1952, S.J.D., 1955. Bar: Mass. 1948, D.C. 1948, N.Y. 1954, U.S. Supreme Ct. 1954; CPA, Md. Asst. U.S. atty. D.C., 1948; legal asst. to chmn., asst. to vice chmn. SEC, 1948-50; spl. asst. to atty. gen. Dept. Justice, 1951-54; pvt. practice law N.Y.C. and Washington, 1956—; counsel Cadwalader Wickersham & Taft, N.Y.C., 1996—. Contbr. articles to legal jours. Founding trustee Harlem Prep. Sch., 1967; mem. Met. Opera Assn., 1961—. Served to maj. USMCR, 1942-45. Mem. ABA, Assn. of Bar of City of N.Y. Home: 765 Park Ave New York NY 10021-4254 also: 78 Hither Ln East Hampton NY 11937-2635 Office: 77 Water St Fl 17 New York NY 10005-4401

SPEAR, H(ENRY) DYKE N(EWCOME), JR., lawyer; b. New London, Conn., Feb. 26, 1935; s. Henry D. N. and Helene (Vining) S.; m. Karla A. Dalley, Sept. 9, 1995. BA, Trinity Coll., Hartford, Conn., 1958; JD, U. Conn., 1960. Bar: Conn. 1960. Pvt. practice matrimonial law Hartford, 1961—. Mem. Conn. Bar Assn., Hartford County Bar Assn. Republican. Methodist. Office: 10 Trumbull St Hartford CT 06103-2404

SPEAR, LAURINDA HOPE, architect. BFA, Brown U., 1972; MArch, Columbia U., 1975. Registered architect, Fla., N.Y., Colo.; cert. Nat. Coun. Archtl. Registration. Founding prin. Arquitectonica, Coral Gables, Fla.; mem. faculty U. Miami; lectr. in field. Prin. works include Pink Ho., Miami, Fla., 1978, The Palace, Miami, 1982 (Honor award Miami chpt. AIA 1982), Overseas Tower (Honor award Fla. chpt. AIA 1982, Honor award Miami chpt. 1982), The Atlantis, Miami, 1982 (Miami chpt. AIA award 1983), The Sq. at Key Biscayne (Honor award Miami chpt. AIA 1982), The Imperial, Miami, 1983, Casa los Andes (Record Hos. award Archtl. Record 1986), North Dade Justice Ctr., Miami, 1987 (Honor award Miami chpt. AIA 1989), Rio, Atlanta, 1988 (Honor award Miami chpt. AIA 1989), Banco de Credito del Peru, Lima, 1988 (Honor award Miami chpt. AIA 1989), The Ctr. Innovative Tech., Herndon, Va., 1988 (Honor award Va. chpt. AIA 1989, Honor award Miami chpt. 1990, Merit award Fairfax, Va., County Exceptional Design Awards Program 1990), Sawgrass Mills (Merit award Miami chpt. AIA 1990, Honor award Fla. chpt. 1991), Miracle Ctr. (Honor award Miami chpt. AIA 1989), Internat. Swimming Hall of Fame, Ft. Lauderdale, Fla., 1991, Banque de Luxembourg, 1993, Disney All-Star Resorts, Orlando, Fla., 1994, Foster City (Calif.) Libr., 1994, U.S. Embassy, Lima, 1994, USCG Family Housing, Bayamon, P.R., 1994, Altamira Ctr., Caracas, Venezuela, 1994. Mem. beaux arts support group Lowe Art Mus., Miami; bd. dirs. Miami Youth Mus. Recipient Design Awards citation Progressive Architecture, 1975, 80, Rome Prize in Architecture, 1978, Award of Excellence, Atlanta Urban Design Commn., 1989. Fellow AIA. Office: Arquitectonica 426 Jefferson Ave Miami FL 33139

SPEAR, RAYMOND E., school system administrator. Supt. Coventry (R.I.) Pub. Schs. State finalist Nat. Supt. Yr., 1993. Office: Coventry Pub Schs 60 Wood St Coventry RI 02816-5825

SPEAR, RICHARD EDMUND, art history educator; b. Michigan City, Ind., Feb. 3, 1940; s. Irving S. and Esther Marion (Lieber) S.; m. Athena Tacha, June 11, 1965. B.A., U. Chgo., 1961; M.F.A., Princeton U., 1963; Ph.D., 1965. Mem. faculty Oberlin (Ohio) Coll., 1964—, prof. art history, 1975-83, Mildred Jay prof. art history, 1983—; dir. Allen Meml. Art Mus., 1972-83; disting. vis. prof. George Washington U., Washington, 1983-84; trustee Intermuseum Conservation Assn., 1972-83, pres., 1975-77. Author: Caravaggio and His Followers, 1971, 75, Renaissance and Baroque Paintings from the Sciarra and Fiano Collections, 1972, Domenichino, 1982; editor-in-chief Art Bull., 1985-88; contbr. articles to profl. jours. Regional exec. bd. ACLU, 1974-76. Recipient Premio Daria Borghese Gold medal, 1972; Fulbright scholar Italy, 1966-67; Am. Coun. Learned Socs. fellow, 1971-72; NEH fellow, 1980-81, sr. fellow Ctr. Advanced Study in Visual Arts Nat. Gallery Art, 1983-84, Guggenheim fellow, 1987-88; Nat. Humanities Ctr. fellow, 1992-93. Mem. Coll. Art Assn. Am. Democrat. Home: 291 Forest St Oberlin OH 44074-1509 Office: Oberlin Coll Dept Art Oberlin OH 44074

SPEAR, ROBERT CLINTON, environmental health educator, consultant; b. Los Banos, Calif., June 26, 1939; s. Clinton Wentworth Spear and Maytie Izetta (Patten) Gill; m. Patricia Warner, Dec. 15, 1962; children—Andrew Warner, Jennifer Ellen. B.S., U. Calif.-Berkeley, 1961, M.S., 1962; Ph.D., Cambridge U., 1968. Registered profl. engr., Calif. Systems engr. U.S. Naval Weapons Ctr., China Lake, Calif., 1962-65, 68-69; asst. prof. environ. health Sch. Pub. Health, U. Calif.-Berkeley, 1970-76, assoc. prof., 1976-81, prof., 1981—, dir. No. Calif. Occupational Health Ctr., 1980-89, assoc. dean, 1988-91, dir. Environ. Engring. and Health Scis. Lab., 1991-96; assoc. dean Coll. of Engring. U. Calif.-Berkeley, 1994-96. Contbr. articles on engring. aspects of environ. health to profl. jours. Mem. Nat. Adv. Com. on Occupational Safety and Health, U.S. Dept. Labor, 1986-88. NSF grad. fellow Cambridge U., 1965-68, sr. internat. fellow Fogarty Ctr., NIH, Australian Nat. U., 1977-78, research grantee Nat. Inst. Occupational Safety and Health NIH, State of Calif., 1971—. Mem. ASME, AAAS, Am. Indsl. Hygiene Assn., Assn. Univ. Programs in Occupational Health and Safety (pres. 1984-85). Democrat. Avocation: sailing. Home: 1963 Yosemite Rd Berkeley CA 94707-1631 Office: U Calif Sch Pub Health Berkeley CA 94720

SPEAR, THOMAS TURNER, history educator; b. Coral Gables, Fla., Dec. 23, 1940. BA, Williams Coll., 1962; MA, U. Wis., 1970, PhD, 1974; postgrad., Sch. Oriental and African Studies, 1976-77. Sr. lectr. La Trobe U., Melbourne, Australia, 1973-80; Charles R. Keller prof. Williams Coll., Williamstown, Mass., 1981-92; prof. U. Wis., Madison, 1993—; reviewer NEH. Author: The Kaya Complex: A History of the Mijikenda Peoples of the Kenya Coast to 1900, 1978, Kenya's Past: An Introduction to Historical Method in Africa, 1981, (with Derek Nurse) The Swahili: Reconstructing the History and Language of and African Soc., 800-1500, 1985; editor: (with Richard Waller) Being Maasai: Ethnicity and Identity in East Africa, 1993; contbr. articles to profl. jours. Grantee Williams Coll., 1984, 87-89, 91-92, NEH, 1984, Am. Coun. Learned Socs., 1982, La Trobe U., 1976-77; recipient A.C. Jordan prize U. Wis., 1972, Fgn. Area fellowship Social Sci. Rsch. Coun./Am. Coun. Learned Socs., 1970-72, Coll. Tchrs. fellowship NEH, 1987-88, Guggenheim fellowship, 1995-96, U. Wis., 1995—. Mem. Am. Hist. Soc. (contbr. Guide to Hist. Lit.), African Studies Assn., African Studies Assn. Australia (founder, exec. sec. 1978-80), Internat. African Inst. Office: U Wis Dept History 3211 Humanities 455 N Park St Madison WI 53706-1405

SPEARING, ANTHONY COLIN, English literature educator; b. London, Jan. 31, 1936; came to U.S., 1987; s. Frederick and Gertrude (Calnin) S. MA, Cambridge U., Eng., 1960. W.M. Tapp rsch. fellow Gonville-Caius Coll. Cambridge U., 1959-60, asst. lectr. in English, 1960-64, official fellow Queens' Coll., 1960-87, life fellow, 1987—, dir. studies in English, 1967-85, lectr. in English, 1964-85, reader in medieval English lit., 1985-87; vis. prof. English U. Va., Charlottesville, 1979-80, 84, prof. English, 1987-89, Kenan prof. English, 1989—; William Matthews lectr. Birkbeck Coll., London, 1983-84; invited lectr. numerous colls. and univs. in U.K., Europe, Can. and U.S.; Lansdowne vis. fellow U. Victoria, 1993. Author: Criticism and Medieval Poetry, 1964, rev. edit., 1972; (with Maurice Hussey and James Winny) An Introduction to Chaucer, 1965; The Gawain-Poet: A Critical Study, 1970, Chaucer: Troilus and Criseyde, 1976, Medieval Dream-Poetry, 1976, Medieval to Renaissance in English Poetry, 1985, Readings in Medieval Poetry, 1987, The Medieval Poet as Voyeur, 1993; editor: The Pardoner's Prologue and Tale (Chaucer), 1965, rev. edit., 1994, The Knight's Tale (Chaucer), 1966, rev. edit., 1995, The Franklin's Prologue and Tale (Chaucer), 1966, rev. edit., 1994; co-editor: (with J.E. Spearing) Shakespeare: The Tempest, 1971, Poetry of the Age of Chaucer, 1974, The Reeve's Prologue and Tale (Chaucer), 1979; contbr. numerous articles to profl. jours. Mem. Medieval Acad. Am., Internat. Assn. U. Profs. English, New Chaucer Soc. (trustee 1986-90). Office: Univ Va Dept English Bryan Hall Charlottesville VA 22903

SPEARING, KAREN MARIE, physical education educator, coach; b. Chgo., Apr. 17, 1949; d. John Richard and Naomi (Allen) Miller; m. Edward B. Spearing III, Apr. 28, 1973. BS in Phys. Edn., U. Wis., Whitewater, 1972; MS in Outdoor Edn., No. Ill. U., 1978. Cert. phys. edn. tchr., Ill. Tchr., coach Glenside Mid. Sch., Glendale Heights, Ill., 1973—, athletic dir., 1981-92, 95—, dept. chairperson, 1992-93. Awards chairperson U.S. Power Squadron, Chgo., 1987-93, mem. exec. com. DuPage br., 1993-96, edn. officer, 1996—; mem. com. Ill. Hunting and Fishing Days, Silver Springs State Pk., 1993—; amb. People to People Citizen Amb. Program, Russia and Belarus, 1993. Mem. AAHPERD, Ill. Assn. Health, Phys. Edn., Recreation and Dance, Ill. H.S. Assn. (volleyball referee). Avocations: clock collecting, hunting, fishing, boating. Office: Glenside Mid Sch 1560 Bloomingdale Rd Glendale Heights IL 60139

SPEARMAN, DAVID HAGOOD, veterinarian; b. Greenville, S.C., Nov. 16, 1932; s. David Ralph and Elizabeth (Hagood) S.; student Clemson Coll., 1950-52, BS, 1975; DVM, U. Ga., 1956; m. Patsy Lee Cordle, Dec. 18, 1954; children: Kathleen Elizabeth, David Hagood. With Cleveland Park Animal Hosp., Greenville, 1956-57; individual practice vet. medicine, Easley and Powdersville, S.C., 1957—. Mem. S.C. State Bd. Vet. Examiners, 1981-87, chmn. 1987, Pickens County Planning and Devel. Bd., 1972—; pres. Northside Parent-Tchr. Orgn., 1965-67; mem. adv. bd. vet. technicians program Tri-County Tech., 1975-76; mem. admissions com. Vet. Coll., U. Ga., 1975; mem. adv. com. Pre-Vet Club, Clemson U.; chmn. Easley Zoning Bd., 1980-83; mem. S.C. Bd. Vet. Examiners, 1982-89, chmn., 1987. Mem. AVMA (alt. del. 1992-95, S.C. del. 1996—), Blue Ridge Veterinary Med. Assn., (founder, pres., sec.), S.C. Assn. Veterinarians (pres. 1974-75, publicity chmn. 1975—, chmn. animal health technician com., Veterinarian of Yr. 1985), Am. Animal Hosp. Assn. (assoc.), S.C. Wildlife, Pickens County Horse, Cattle, and Fair Assn. (pres.), Jr. C. of C. (past officer, Key Man award 1959), Trout Unltd. (state dir.), Pickens County Foxhunters Assn., Clemson U. Tiger Lettermen Assn., Easley Boosters Club, Easley C. of C., World Wildlife Fund, Nat. Wildlife Fedn., Audubon Soc., Nature Conservancy, Internat. latform Assn., Pickens County Hist. Soc., Lions (pres., internat. del. 1971, 73) Pendelton Farmers Soc., Alpha Psi, Alpha Zeta. Presbyterian (deacon, elder, youth leader 1972-74, chmn. orgn. com. 1973-75, 83-85, pulpit com.). Avocation: photography, fly fishing. Home: Burdine Springs 505 Asbury Cir PO Box 327 Easley SC 29640-1343 Office: 6714 Calhoun Memorial Hwy Easley SC 29640

SPEARS, ALEXANDER WHITE, III, tobacco company executive; b. Grindstone, Pa., Sept. 29, 1932; s. Alexander White and Eva Marie (Elliott) S.; m. Shirley Pierce; 1 child, Craig Stewart. BS, Allegheny Coll., Meadville, Pa., 1953; PhD, SUNY, 1960. Research asso., then research fellow SUNY, Buffalo, 1956-58; instr. Millard Fillmore Coll., Buffalo, 1958-59; with Lorillard Corp., Greensboro, N.C., 1959—, v.p. R & D, 1971-74, sr. v.p. ops. and rsch., 1975-79, exec. v.p. ops. and rsch., 1979-91, vice chmn., COO, 1991-95; also bd. dirs., 1991—, chmn., CEO, 1995—; asst. prof. Guilford Coll., 1961-65, mem. bd. assocs., 1990, 91, trustee, 1995—; chmn. bd. visitors Greensboro Coll., 1990-94. Patentee in field; past editor: Tobacco Sci. Jour. Chmn. Coun. on Edn., 1974, mem. exec. com., 1987; chmn. model sch. task force Greensboro Bd. Edn. and Greensboro C. of C., 1975; mem. N.C. Humanities Coun., 1978-81, Piedmont Triad Airport Authority, 1993—; bd. dirs. United Way of Greensboro, 1980-85, N.C. Bus. Com. on Edn., 1983-84, Greensboro Devel. Corp., 1985—, pres., 1992-94; chmn. Greensboro Area United Negro Coll. Fund, 1982, N.C. AT&T St. U., Focus on Excellence campaign, 1984-86, Greensboro Pub. Sch. Fund, 1987; capital campaign chmn. Greensboro Area Girl Scouts U.S., 1987; bd. dirs. N.C. A&T U. Found., 1985-93, trustee, 1990—; bd. dirs. Greensboro NCCJ, 1990-92, chmn. ann. dinner, 1991, N.C. Citizens for Bus. and Industry, 1984-88, YMCA, 1989—, chmn., 1993-95; chmn. Hayes-Taylor Capital Campaign, 1990; bd. dirs. Ctr. Indoor Air Rsch., 1988—, chmn., 1991-95, Coun. for Tobacco Rsch., 1990—; mem. U.S. Tech. Study Group Cigarette Safety Act of 1984, U.S. Study CPSC Tech. Adv. Group Cigarette Safety Act. of 1990; adv. bd. U. N.C., Greensboro, 1988-94; chmn. fundraiser campaign Greensboro Hist. Mus., 1988-89, trustee, 1989—. Recipient Disting. Achievement award in tobacco sci. Philip Morris, 1970; named to Jr. Achievement Bus. Leaders Hall of Fame, 1994, and YMCA Hall of Fame, 1994. Mem. AAAS, Am. Chem. Soc., Soc. Applied Spectroscopy, Am. Mgmt. Assn., N.Y. Acad. Scis., Internat. Coop. Ctr. Sci. Rsch. Relative to Tobacco (sci. com. 1972), Greensboro C. of C. (bd. dirs. 1974-75, 86-87, 96—, Nathaniel Greene award 1975, hon. chmn. 1994 Kmart Greater Greensboro Open). Presbyterian. Office: Lorillard Tobacco Co 2525 E Market St Greensboro NC 27401-4815 also: One Park Ave New York NY 10016-5895

SPEARS, GREGORY LUTTRELL, journalist; b. N.Y.C., Mar. 14, 1956; s. Robert Rae and Charlotte Lee (Luttrell) S.; m. Laurie Beth Chamlin, June 26, 1983; children: Michael Chamlin, Genevieve Rachel. Diploma, Kent Sch., 1974; MA, U. Rochester, 1979; MS in Journalism with honors, Northwestern U., 1981. Reporter Brandenton (Fla.) Herald, 1981-82; bus. reporter St. Petersburg (Fla.) Times, 1983-85; Washington corr. Knight-Ridder Newspapers, 1985-94; assoc. editor Kiplinger's Personal Fin. Mag., Washington, 1994—. Chmn. Nat. Press Bldg. Bd., 1993. Mem. Nat. Press Club (pres. 1992). Episcopalian. Home: 6508 40th Ave University Park MD 20782 Office: Kiplinger's 1729 H St NW Washington DC 20006-3904

SPEARS, JAE, state legislator; b. Latonia, Ky.; d. James and Sylvia (Fox) Marshall; m. Lawrence E. Spears; children: Katherine Spears Cooper, Marsha Spears-Duncan, Lawrence M., James W. Student, U. Ky. Reporter Cin. Post, Cin. Enquirer newspapers; rschr. Stas. WLW-WSAI, Cin.; tchr. Jiya Gakuen Sch., Japan; lectr. U.S. Mil. installations East Anglia, Eng.; del. State of W.Va., Charleston, 1974-80; mem. W.Va. Senate, Charleston, 1980-1993; mem. state visitors com. W.Va. Extension and Continuing Edn., Morgantown, 1977-91, W.Va. U. Sch. Medicine, 1992—. Chmn. adv bd. Sta. WNPB, 1992-94; congl. liaison Am. Pub. TV Stas. and Sta. WNPB-TV, 1992—; mem. coun. W.Va. Autism Task Force, Huntington, 1981-90; mem. W.Va. exec. bd. Literacy Vols. Am., 1986-90, 94—, pres., 1990-92; mem. Gov.'s State Literacy Coun., 1991—; bd. dirs. Found. Ind. Colls. W.Va., 1986—; mem. regional adv. com. W.Va. Gov.'s Task Force for Children, Youth and Family, 1989; mem. USS W.Va. Commn., 1989; mem. exec. com. W.Va. Employer Support Group for Guard and Res., 1989, mem. steering com., 1990—. Recipient Susan B. Anthony award NOW, 1982, nat. award Mil. Order Purple Heart, 1984, Edn. award Profl. Educators Assn. W.Va., 1986, Ann. award W.Va. Assn. Ret. Sch. Employees, 1985, Meritorious Service award W.Va. State Vets. Commn., 1984, Vets. Employment and Tng. Service award U.S. Dept. Labor, 1984, award W.Va. Vets. Council, 1984; named Admiral in N.C. Navy, Gov. of N.C., 1982, Hon. Brigadier Gen. W.Va. N.G., 1984. Mem. Bus. and Profl. Women (Woman of Yr. award 1978), Nat. League Am. Pen Women (Pen Woman of Yr. 1984), Nat. Order Women Legislators, DAR, VFW (aux.), Am. Legion (aux.), Delta Kappa Gamma, Alpha Xi Delta. Democrat. Home and Office: PO Box 2088 Elkins WV 26241-2088

SPEARS, JAMES GRADY, small business owner; b. Port Arthur, Tex., July 20, 1941; s. John Grady and Dorothy Nell (Haney) S. Grad. high sch., Port Arthur. Adminstr. Child Health & Devel. Studies, Oakland, Calif., 1962-69; sales mgr. Sunshine Biscuits Inc., Houston, 1969-75; owner, pres. S.W. Tookie Inc./Tookie's Restaurant, Seabrook, Tex., 1975—. Mem. Greater Houston Convention & Visitors Bur., Clear Lake Convention & Visitors Bur. With USN, 1959-62. Mem. Tex. Restaurant Assn., Houston Restaurant Assn., Seabrook Assn., Old Seabrook Assn. Republican. Roman Catholic. Avocations: collectibles, fine art, antiques, listening to records, self improvement. Home: 16310 Hickory Knoll Dr Houston TX 77059-5311 Office: SW Tookie Inc/Tookie's Restaurant 1202 Bayport Blvd Seabrook TX 77586-3406

SPEARS, KENNETH GEORGE, chemistry educator; b. Erie, Pa., Oct. 23, 1943. BS, Bowling Green State U., 1966; MS, PhD in Phys. Chemistry, U. Chgo., 1970. NIH predoctoral fellow U. Chgo., 1968-70; NRC-NOAA postdoctoral fellow NOAA, Boulder, Colo., 1970-72; prof. dept. chemistry Northwestern U., 1972—, mem. biomedical engring. dept., 1987—. Bd. editors The Rev. Scientific Instruments, 1980-83; conbtr. articles to profl.jours. Alfred P. Sloan Found. fellow, 1974-76. Fellow AAAS; mem. Am. Phys. Soc., Am. Chem. Soc., Midwest Bio-Laser Inst. (adv. bd. 1985—). Office: Northwestern U Dept Chemistry Evanston IL 60208-3113

SPEARS, MARIAN CADDY, dietetics and institutional management educator; b. East Liverpool, Ohio, Jan. 12, 1921; d. Frederick Louis and Marie (Jerman) Caddy; m. Sholto M. Spears, May 29, 1959. BS, Case Western Res. U., 1942, MS, 1947; PhD, U. Mo., 1971. Chief dietitian Bellefaire Children's Home, Cleve., 1942-53; head dietitian Drs. Hosp., Cleve., 1953-57; assoc. dir. dietetics Barnes Hosp., St. Louis, 1957-59; asst. prof. U. Ark., Fayetteville, 1959-68; assoc. prof. U. Mo., Columbia, 1971-75; prof., head dept. hotel, restaurant, instn. mgmt. and dietetics Kans. State U., Manhattan, 1975-89; cons. dietitian small hosps. and nursing homes; cons. dietetic edn. Author: Foodservice Organizations Textbook, 3d edit., 1995; contbr. articles to profl. jours. Mem. Am. Dietetic Assn. (Copher award 1989), Am. Sch. Foodsvc. Assn., Food Systems Mgmt. Edn. Coun., Soc. Advancement of Foodsvc. Rsch., Nat. Restaurant Assn., Coun. Hotel, Restaurant, Inst. Mgmt. Edn., Manhattan C. of C., Sigma Xi, Gamma Sigma Delta, Omicron Nu, Phi Kappa Phi. Home: 1522 Williamsburg Dr Manhattan KS 66502-0408 Office: Kans State U 105 Justin Hall Manhattan KS 66506-1400

SPEARS, MONROE KIRK, English educator, author; b. Darlington, S.C., Apr. 28, 1916; s. James Monroe and Lillian (Fair) S.; m. Betty Greene, Sept. 3, 1941; 1 dau., Julia Herndon. A.B., A.M., U. S.C., 1937; Ph.D., Princeton U., 1940; D. Letters (hon.), U. of South, 1983. Instr. English U. Wis., 1940-42; asst. prof., then assoc. prof. English Vanderbilt U., 1946-52; prof. English U. South, 1952-64; Libbie Shearn Moody prof. English Rice U., 1964-86, prof. emeritus, 1986—; vis. prof. U. Wash., summer 1960, U. Mich., summer 1961, Swarthmore Coll., 1961-62; mem. adv. council dept. English Princeton U., 1960-66, Christian Gauss lectr., 1975; dir. NEH Seminars for Coll. Tchrs. Rice U., 1975, 78. Author: The Poetry of W.H. Auden: The Disenchanted Island, 1963, Hart Crane, 1965, Dionysus and the City: Modernism in Twentieth Century Poetry, 1970, Space Against Time in Modern American Poetry, 1972, The Levitator and Other Poems, 1975, American Ambitions: Selected Essays on Literary and Cultural Themes, 1987, Countries of the Mind: Literary Explorations, 1992, One Writer's Reality, 1996; editor: (with H.B. Wright) The Literary Works of Matthew Prior, 2 vols., 1959, W.H. Auden: A Collection of Critical Essays, 1964, The Narrative Poetry of Shakespeare, 1968, Sewanee Rev., 1952-61, adv. editor., 1961-73. Served to capt. AUS and USAAF, 1942-46, ETO. Am. Philos. Soc. and Carnegie Found. grantee, 1949; Rockefeller fellow, 1956, Guggenheim fellow, 1965-66, 72-73, Brown Found. fellow, U. South, 1988. Fellowship So. Writers, S.C. Acad. Authors. Democrat. Episcopalian. Home: 117 Carruthers Rd Sewanee TN 37375-2007

SPEARS, RICHARD W., oil company executive; b. 1936; married. BA, Georgetown Coll., 1957; LLB, U. Ky., 1961. Atty. Texaco Inc., 1961-64; staff atty. Ashland Oil Inc., Russell, Ky., 1964-75; gen. counsel Ashland Oil Inc., Russell, 1975-76, v.p. law, 1976-79, adminstrv. v.p., 1979-80, sr. v.p. human resources, 1980-81, sr. v.p. group operating officer human resources and law; now sr. v.p. human resources and law Ashland Oil Inc. With USAR, 1954-61. Office: Ashland Oil Inc 1401 Winchester Ave Ashland KY 41114*

SPEARS, SALLY, lawyer; b. San Antonio, Aug. 29, 1938; d. Adrian Anthony and Elizabeth (Wylie) S.; m. Tor Hultgreen, July 15, 1961 (div. Jan. 1983); children: Dagny Elizabeth, Sara Kirsten, Kara Spears. BA, U. Tex., 1960, LLB, 1965. Bar: Tex. 1961, Ill. 1971. Practice law Stamford, Conn., 1966-67, Chgo., 1970-71, Northbrook, Ill., 1972-73, Toronto, Ont., Can., 1973-81; assoc. firm Cummings & Lockwood, Stamford, 1966-67, Kirkland & Ellis, Chgo., 1970-71; sr. atty. Allstate Ins. Co., Northbrook, Ill., 1971-73; gen. counsel, sec. Reed Paper Ltd., Reed Ltd., Toronto, 1973-78, Denison Mines Ltd., Toronto, 1978-81; pvt. practice law San Antonio, 1981—. Mem. Tex. Bar Assn., San Antonio Bar Assn., Bankruptcy Bar Assn., Bexar County Women's Bar Assn., San Antonio Country Club, The Club at Sonterra. Home: 433 Evans Ave San Antonio TX 78209-3725 Office: Ste 211 4600 Broadway San Antonio TX 78209-6262

SPEAS, CHARLES STUART, personnel director; b. Phila., Jan. 1, 1944; s. Austin LeRoy and Peggy Elaine (Drake) S.; m. Julie Ellen Royce, Apr. 10, 1965; children: Eric S. Speas, Robert Austin Speas. Student, Tri-State Coll., U. Notre Dame, Purdue U. Lic. agt. in life, accident and health ins., Ind. Sr. scheduling coord. Excel Industries, Elkhart, Ind., 1966-73; corp. dir. pers. EFP Corp., Elkhart, 1973—; cons. various Elkhart, Goshen area bus., 1980—. Contbr. articles profl. jours. Participant Soviet/Am. Conf. on Trade and Econ. Cooperation, Kremlin, 1991. With USAF, 1962-66. Mem. Ind. Pers. Assn., Goshen Indsl. Club (recipient cert. of appreciation 1990), Soc. for Human Resources Mgmt., Elkhart C. of C. (task force on healthcare availability/cost). Republican. Avocations: woodworking, fishing, gardening. Home: 23683 River Dr Goshen IN 46526-9000 Office: EFP Corp 223 Middleton Run Rd Elkhart IN 46516-5429

SPEAS, RAYMOND AARON, retired insurance company executive; b. Lynneville, Iowa, Feb. 10, 1925; s. Harold H. and Susie B. Speas; m. Betty Jane Welshhons, Apr. 27, 1945; children: Raymond D., Gaylynn J. BS in Bus. Adminstrn., Drake U., 1951. CLU. With Equitable Life Ins. Co. of Iowa, Des Moines, 1951—, v.p., contr., 1967-76; sr. v.p., adminstrn. Equitable of Iowa Cos., Des Moines, 1976-77, sr. v.p., treas., 1977-82, exec. v.p., treas., 1982-92, also bd. dirs.; bd. dirs. E.I. Sales Inc.; exec. v.p., treas. Equitable Am. Life Ins. Co. Mem. Internat. Youth Coun. YMCA, 1966-74, bd. dirs. Des Moines, 1960-63; exec. bd. Iowa Soc. Christian Chs., 1977; past pres., bd. dirs. Des Moines Jr. Achievement. With U.S. Army, 1943-46. Fellow Life Office Mgmt. Assn.; mem. Life Ins. Agy. Mgmt. Assn., Des Moines Golf and County Club. Home: 3524 Grand Des Moines IA 50312 Office: Equitable of Iowa Cos 604 Locust St Des Moines IA 50309-3705 also: Equitable of Iowa Cos 699 Walnut Hub Tower PO Box 9107 Des Moines IA 50306

SPEAS, ROBERT DIXON, aeronautical engineer, aviation company executive; b. Davis County, N.C., Apr. 14, 1916; s. William Paul and Nora Estelle (Dixon) S.; m. Manette Lansing Hollingsworth, Mar. 4, 1944; children: Robert Dixon, Jay Hollingsworth. BS, MIT, 1940; Air Transport Pilot rating, Boeing Sch. Aero., United Air Lines, 1938; DBA in Aviation (hon.), Embry Riddle Aero. U., 1995. Aviation reporter Winston Salem Jour., 1934; sales rep. Trans World Airlines, 1937-38; engr. Am. Airlines, 1940-44, asst. to v.p., 1944-46, dir. maintenance and engring., cargo div., 1946-47, spl. asst. to pres., 1947-50; U.S. rep. A.V. Roe Can., Ltd., 1950-51; pres., chmn. bd. R. Dixon Speas Assocs., Inc. (aviation cons.), 1951-76; chmn., chief exec. officer Speas-Harris Airport Devel., Inc., 1974-76; chmn. bd., pres. Aviation Consulting, Inc., 1976-82, chmn. bd., 1982-84; pres. PRC Aviation, 1984—; mem. aeros. and space engring. bd. Nat. Rsch. Coun., 1980-84. Author: Airplane Performance and Operations, 1945, Pilots' Technical Manual, 1946, Airline Operation, 1949, Technical Aspects of Air Transport Management, 1955, Financial Benefits and Intangible Advantages of Business Aircraft Operations, 1989. Recipient 1st award Ann. Nat. Boeing Thesis Competition, 1937, rsch. award Am. Transport Assn., 1942, William A. Downes Airport Operators Coun. Internat. award, 1992; inductee Ariz. Aviation Hall of Fame, 1995, William Littlewood Memorial lecture Am. Inst. of Aeronautics and Astronautics, 1994. Fellow AIAA (treas. and coun. 1963-64, chmn. ethics com. 1989-92, AIAA-SAE Williams Littenwool lectr. 1994), Royal Aero. Soc., Soc. Automotive Engrs. (v.p. 1955, coun. 1964-66); mem. ASME, Flight Safety Found. (bd. govs. 1958-71, 79-90, exec. com. 1979-90), Inst. Aero Scis. (past treas., coun. 1959-62, exec. com. 1962), Coll. Aeronautics (trustee 1967—), Soc. Aircraft Investigators, Manhasset C. of C. (pres. 1962), Wings Club (pres. 1968-69, coun. 1966-71, 73-90, 92-95, chmn. devel. com. 1989—, Sight lectr. 1992), Skyline Country Club. Home: 4771 E Country Villa Dr Tucson AZ 85718-2640 Office: 6262 N Swan Rd Tucson AZ 85718-3600

SPECCHIO, LISA ANNA, lawyer; b. Reno, May 31, 1963; d. Michael Ronald Specchio and Kathleen Christina (Baldwin) Duncan. BA, U. Nev., 1985; JD, U. Pacific, 1988. Bar: Calif. 1988, U.S. Ct. Appeals (9th cir.) 1989, U.S. Dist. Ct. (ctrl. dist.) Calif. 1989. Assoc. Barton Klugman & Oetting, L.A., 1988-89, Harry Scolinos Law Firm, Pasadena, Calif., 1989-90, Hampton & Wilson, North Hollywood, Calif., 1991-92, Bower & Weiner, Van Nuys, Calif., 1992—. Roman Catholic. Avocations: drawing, art, racquetball. Home: 514 Hill Dr Glendale CA 91206-2839 Office: Bower & Weiner 16600 Sherman Way Ste 200 Van Nuys CA 91406-3733

SPECHT, ALICE WILSON, library director; b. Caracus, Venezuela, Apr. 3, 1948; (parents Am. citizens); d. Ned and Helen (Lockwood) Wilson; m. Joe W. Specht, Dec. 30, 1972; 1 child, Mary Helen. BA, U. Pacific, 1969; MLS, Emory U., 1970; MBA, Hardin-Simmons U., 1983. Libr. social scis. North Tex. State U., Denton, 1971-73; reference libr. Lubbock (Tex.) City and County Libr., 1974-75; system coord. Big Country Libr. System, Abilene, Tex., 1975-79; assoc. dir. Hardin-Simmons U., Abilene, 1981-88, dir. univ. librs., 1988—; apptd. Mayor's Task Force Libr. Svcs., 1995-96. Author bibliog. instrn. aids, 1981-90; editor; The College Man, For Pilots Eyes Only. Mem. mayor's task force Abilene Pub. Libr., 1995-96. Recipient Boss of Yr., Am. Bus. Women's Assn., 1994. Mem. ALA, Tex. Libr. Assn. (chair com. 1978-84, sec.-treas. coll. and univ. librs. divsn. 1993-94, legis. com. 1994—), Abilene Libr. Consortium (chair adminstrv. coun. 1990, 93, coord. nat. conf. 1991, 93), Rotary (chair com. 1989-90). Home: 918 Grand Ave Abilene TX 79605-3233 Office: Hardin-Simmons U PO Box 16195 2200 Hickory Abilene TX 79698-0001

SPECHT, CHARLES SHERMAN, pathologist; b. Pitts., Apr. 7, 1957; s. Charles Kenneth and Audrey Marie (Sherman) S.; m. Jo Anne Lavelle, Dec. 18, 1982; 1 child, Kurt Ehrlich. La Roche Coll., Allison Park, Pa., U. Pitts.; MD, U. Md. at Balt., 1980. Diplomate Am. Bd. Pathology; lic. MD, Md., Pa., Mass. Resident in anatomic pathology Shadyside Hosp., Pitts., 1981-83; resident in neuropathology U. Mass. Med. Ctr., Worcester, 1983-85, chief resident, 1984-85; rsch. fellow in ophthalmic pathology Harvard Med. Sch., Mass. Eye and Ear Infirmary, Boston, 1985-86; staff Dept. Ophthalmic Pathology Armed Forces Inst. Pathology, Washington, 1986-91; staff Dept. Pathology, dir. autopsy svc. Shadyside Hosp., Pitts., 1991—. Contbr. chpt. to book, numerous articles and abstracts to profl. jours. Recipient Commendation for Exceptional Performance, Dept. of Army, 1990, 91, Cert. of Appreciation, Armed Forces Inst. Pathology, 1991. Fellow Coll. Am. Pathologists; mem. Boston Soc. Psychiatry and Neurology, New Eng. Soc. Pathologists, Assn. for Rsch. in Vision and Ophthalmology, Am. Assn. Neuropathologists, Georgiana Dvorak Theobald Soc., Assn. for Rsch. in Nervous and Mental Disease, Am. Assn. Ophthalmic Pathologists, Internat. Soc. for Neuropathology, Pitts. Pathology Soc., Pa. Assn. Pathologists, Pitts. Ophthalmology Soc., Med. Alumni Assn. U. Md., Assn. Ophthalmic Alumni, Friends and Alumni Soc. of the AFIP. Avocations: fishing, hunting, reading, travel. Home: 802 Cottingham Ct Allison Park PA 15101-2069 Office: Shadyside Hosp Dept of Pathology 5230 Centre Ave Pittsburgh PA 15232-1304

SPECHT, GORDON DEAN, retired petroleum executive; b. Garner, Iowa, June 3, 1927; s. Reuben William and Gladys (Leonard) S.; m. Cora Alice Emmert, May 24, 1952; children: Mary Ellen, Grant. BS in Chem. Engring., Iowa State U., 1950, MS in Chem. Engring., 1951; SM in Chem. Engring., MIT, 1954. Engr. Exxon Corp. Bayway Refinery, Linden, N.J., 1951-59, systemn services div. mgr., 1960-61, engring. services div. mgr., 1962-63, chem. coordination div. mgr., 1964; mgr. systems dept. Exxon Corp.-Exxon Chem. Co., N.Y.C., 1965-70; sr. advisor communications and computer scis. dept. Exxon Corp., Florham Park, N.J., 1971-76, assoc. cons., 1977-85; retired, 1986. Patentee in field. Asst. scoutmaster Boy Scouts Am., Westfield, N.J., 1986—; sr. qualified observer Sperry Obs., Cranford, N.J., 1986—; celestial navigation instr. U.S. Power Squadrons, 1990—. With U.S. Army, 1945-46, 1st lt. C.E., 1952-53, Korea. Decorated Bronze Star. Mem. Am. Inst. Chem. Engrs., Amateur Astronomers, Inc., No. N.J. Power Squadron, MIT Club of N.J., Nat. Eagle Scout Assn., MIT Club Princeton, Tau Beta Pi, Phi Lambda Upsilon, Phi Kappa Phi, Tau Kappa Epsilon. Republican. Methodist. Avocations: astronomy, sailing, canoeing, swimming, bicycling. Home: 15 Normandy Dr Westfield NJ 07090-3431

SPECIALE, RICHARD, bank executive; b. N.Y.C., Aug. 16, 1945. B.S.B.A., Georgetown U., 1967; M.B.A., NYU, 1976. Sr. acct. Price Waterhouse & Co., N.Y.C., 1969-74; sr. v.p. J.P. Morgan and Co. Inc., N.Y.C., 1974—; bd. dirs. instnl. owners divsn. Real Estate Bd. N.Y., 1984—, chmn., 1991—, mem. bd. govs., 1988-90, 92—; bd. dirs. Downtown-Lower Manhattan Assn., Inc., N.Y.C., Grand Ctrl. Partnership Inc.; mem. adv. bd. Real Estate Inst., NYU, 1984—; dir. Realty Found. of N.Y., 1994—. Bd. dirs. Children's Arts and Scis. Workshops, N.Y.C., 1978-84; trustee Dance Theatre Found., N.Y.C., 1984—, Alvin Ailey Am. Dance Theatre, N.Y.C., 1984—; mem. real estate and constrn. coun. Lincoln Ctr., 1985—. Mem. AICPA, N.Y. State Soc. CPAs, Industrial Devel. Rsch. Coun. Office: JP Morgan & Co Inc 60 Wall St New York NY 10005-2807

SPECK, EUGENE LEWIS, internist; b. Boston, Dec. 17, 1936; s. Robert A. and Anne (Rosenberg) S.; m. Rachel Shoshana; children: Michael Robert, Keren Sara. AB, Brandeis U., Waltham, Mass., 1958; MS, U. Mass., 1961; PhD, George Washington U., 1966, MD, 1969. Diplomate Am. Bd. Internal Medicine with subspecialty in infectious diseases. Intern N.Y. Hosp.-Cornell, 1969-70; rsch. assoc. NIH, Bethesda, Md., 1970-72; resident Barnes Hosp.-Washington U., 1972-73; instr. medicine Washington U., St. Louis, 1972-73; fellow Strong Meml. Hosp.-U. Rochester, 1973-75; instr. medicine U. Rochester, N.Y., 1973-75, asst. prof. medicine, 1975-80; asst. prof. medicine U. Nev., Las Vegas, 1980-85, assoc. prof., 1985-95, prof. medicine, 1995—; dir./co-dir. infectious disease unit U. Med. Ctr. of So. Nev., Las Vegas, 1980—; ptnr. Infectious Diseases Consultants, 1983—; cons. Clark County Health Dept., Las Vegas, 1980—, U. Med. Ctr. So. Nev., Las Vegas, 1980—, Sunrise Hosp., Las Vegas, 1980—, Valley Hosp., Las Vegas, 1980—. Contbr. articles to profl. jours., chpts. to books. Fellow ACP; mem. Am. Soc. Microbiology, Infectious Disease Soc. Am., Alpha Omega Alpha. Avocations: tennis, skiing, racquetball. Home: 2228 Chatsworth Ct Henderson NV 89014-5309 Office: Infectious Diseases Cons 3006 S Maryland Pky # 780 Las Vegas NV 89109

SPECK, LAWRENCE W., architect; b. Houston, Apr. 22, 1949; s. H.K. and Esther (Elliot) S.; m. Cynthia Alexander, Jan. 2, 1971; children: Sloan Garret, Harrison Alexander. BS in Mgmt., MIT, 1971, BS in Art and Design, 1971, MArch, 1972. Registered architect, Mass., Tex. Instr. MIT, Boston, 1972-75; asst. prof. U. Tex., Austin, 1975-79, assoc. prof., 1979-84, prof., 1984—; prin. Lawrence W. Speck Assocs., Austin, 1975—; dir. Ctr. Study Am. Architecture U. Tex. at Austin; adj. curator architecture Dallas Mus. Art, 1985-87. Editor: Architecture for the Emerging American City, 1985; author: Landmarks of Texas Architecture, 1986; co-editor: New Regionalism, 1987. Bd. dirs. Buell Ctr. Columbia U., N.Y.C., 1985-87. Fulbright sr. scholar Council for Internat. Exchange Scholars, 1978. Mem. AIA (5 design awards Austin chpt. 1984-87), Tex. Soc. of Architects (3 design awards 1986), Soc. Arch. Historians, Sigma Chi. Avocations: athletics, children's literature. Home: 1708 Cromwell Hl Austin TX 78703-3307 Address: 3209 Tarryhollow Dr Austin TX 78703-1638

SPECK, MARVIN LUTHER, microbiologist, educator; b. Middletown, Md., Oct. 6, 1913; s. John Luther and Pearl Lighter (Wilhide) S.; m. Jean Moler Critchlow, Sept. 11, 1940; children: Linda Jean, Martha Loraine, Susan Carol. B.S., U. Md., 1935, M.S., 1937; Ph.D., Cornell U., 1940. Instr. microbiology U. Md., 1940-41; asst. chief bacteriologist Nat. Dairy Research Labs., Balt., 1941-47; mem. faculty N.C. State U. at Raleigh, 1947—, prof. food microbiology, 1951-79, William Neal Reynolds prof. food sci., 1957-79, prof. emeritus, 1979—; lectr. Am. Inst. Chem. Engrs., 1978-79; spl. con. USPHS, 1950-62, HEW, 1967-70. Author: (with others) Dairy Microbiology, 1957; editor: Methods for the Microbiological Examination of Foods, 1976, 84; mem. editorial bd. Jour. Dairy Sci, 1953-68. Recipient J.M. Jarrett award N.C. Pub. Health Assn.; Nordica Internat. Research award Am. Cultured Dairy Products Inst., 1981; Nat. Award for Agrl. Excellence Nat. Agri-Mktg. Assn., 1984. Fellow Am. Acad. Microbiology (bd. govs. 1976), Inst. Food Technologists (nat. lectr. 1968); mem. Am. Soc. Microbiology (vice chmn. 1976-77, chmn. sect. 1977-79), Am. Dairy Sci. Assn. (Borden award dairy mfg. 1959, Pfizer-Lewis award for rsch. on cheese 1967), N.C. Dairy Products Assn. (Disting. Svc. award 1976), Sigma Xi, Phi Kappa Phi, Gamma Sigma Delta, Alpha Zeta. Presbyterian (elder). Home: 3204 Churchill Rd Raleigh NC 27607-6806

SPECK, SAMUEL WALLACE, JR., academic administrator; b. Canton, Ohio, Jan. 31, 1937; s. Samuel Wallace Sr. and Lois Ione (Schneider) S.; m. Sharon Jane Anderson, Jan. 20, 1962; children: Samuel Wallace III, Derek Charles. BA, Muskingum Coll., 1959; postgrad., U. Zimbabwe, Harare, 1961; MA, Harvard U., 1963, PhD, 1968. Prof. polit. sci. Muskingum Coll., New Concord, Ohio, 1964—, asst. to pres., 1986-87, exec. v.p., 1987, acting pres., 1987-88, pres., 1988—; mem. Ohio Ho. of Reps., 1971-76; state senator from Ohio 20th Dist., 1977-83; assoc. dir. Fed. Emergency Mgmt. Agy., 1983-86; bd. dirs. Camco Fin. Corp., Cambridge, Ohio, Cambridge (Ohio) Savs. Bank; pres. Eastern Ohio Devel. Alliance, 1990-92; Fund for Improvement of Postsecondary Edn., 1990-91, chmn. 1991. Contbr.: Southern Africa in Perspective, 1972; also numerous articles on African and Am. govt. and pub. policy. Bd. dirs. Ohio Tuition Trust Authority, 1991-93, Internat. Ctr. for Preservation Wild Animals. Recipient Outstanding Legislator award VFW/DAV/Am. Legion, Conservation Achievement award State of Ohio. Mem. Assn. Ind. Colls. and Univs. of Ohio (chmn. 1992-94). Republican. Presbyterian. Home: 57 College Pl New Concord OH 43762-1101 Office: Muskingum Coll Office of Pres New Concord OH 43762

SPECK, WILLIAM T., physician, health facility administrator. MD. Pres., CEO Presbyn. Hosp. in City of N.Y./Columbia-Presbyn. Med. Ctr., N.Y.C. Office: Presbyn Hosp the City NY Columbia-Presbyn Med Ctr New York NY 10032-3784

SPECTER, ARLEN, senator; b. Wichita, Kans., Feb. 12, 1930; s. Harry and Lillie (Shanin) S.; m. Joan L. Levy, June 14, 1953; children: Shanin, Stephen. Student, U. Okla., 1947-48; BA Internat. Rels., U. Pa., 1951; LL.B., Yale U., 1956. Asst. counsel Warren Commn., Washington, 1964; magisterial investigator Commn. of Pa., 1965; asst. dist. atty. City of Phila., 1959-63, dist. atty., 1966-74; ptnr. Dechert Price & Rhoads, Phila., 1956-66, 74-80; U.S. senator from Pa., 1981—; lectr. law Temple U., 1972-75, U. Pa., 1968-72; chmn. Appropriations Subcom. on Labor, Health and Human Svcs., sel. com. in intelligence, judiciary subcom. on terrorism, tech. and gov. info., spec. com. on aging, vet. affaors, sen. rep. policy com. Bd. editors Law Jour.; contbr. articls to profl. jours. Served to 1st U.S. Army, 1951-53. Recipient Youth Svcs. award B'nai B'rith, 1966; recipient Sons of Italy award, 1968, Community Humanitarian award Bapt. Ch., 1969, man of Yr. award, Temple Beth Ami, 1971, N.E. Cath. High Sch. Outstanding Achievement award, 1973. Mem. Phi Beta Kappa. Republican. Jewish. Office: US Senate 530 Senate Hart Bldg Washington DC 20510-3802*

SPECTOR, ABRAHAM, ophthalmic biochemist, educator, laboratory administrator; b. Nyack, N.Y., Jan. 14, 1926; s. Benjamin and Eva (Kaplovitz) S.; m. Joan Gruden, June 25, 1950 (dec. Jan. 1981); children: David Julian, Paul Joseph; m. Marguerite B. Filson, May 27, 1983. AB, Bard Coll, 1947, DS (hon.), 1985; PhD, NYU, 1957; MD (hon.), U. of the Republic, Uruguay, 1981. Rsch. chemist Lederle Lab., Pearl River, N.Y., 1948-52; instr. ophthalmic rsch. Harvard U., Boston, 1958-64, assoc. ophthalmic rsch., 1964-65; lectr. biol. chemistry Northeastern U., Boston, 1959-62; asst. prof. ophthalmic biochemistry Columbia U., N.Y.C., 1965-67, assoc. prof., 1967-73, prof., 1973—, dir. lab. biochemistry and molecular biology, 1976—, dir. rsch., dept. ophthalmology, 1989-90; mem. Vision Research and Tng. Com., Nat. Eye Inst., 1970-71, chmn. cataract workshop, 1973, mem. visual scis. study sect., 1976-80, chmn., 1978-80, bd. sci. advisors, 1982-85, chmn., 1983-85. mem. sci. adv. com. Fight for Sight, Inc., 1980-84; bd. sci. advisors Inst. Biol. Scis. Oakland U., 1982—; vis. prof. ophthalmology U. P.R., 1982—; vis. prof. biochemistry Med. U. Shanghai, 1986—. Assoc. editor Archives of Ophthalmology, 1968-70; sect. editor Experimental Eye Rsch., 1985-92; mem. editorial bd. Investigative Ophthalmology and Visual Sci., 1968-82, 87-92, Experimental Eye Rsch., 1974-85; contbr. numerous articles to profl. jours. Recipient Bausch & Lomb Sci. medal, 1944, Merit award NIH, 1987, Japanese Coop. Cataract Rsch. Group Internat. award, 1987, Sr. Scientific Investigators award Rsch. to Prevent Blindness, 1987, 94, Alcon Rsch. Inst. award, 1994; Guggenheim fellow, 1971-72, Fulbright fellow, 1981. Mem. AAAS, Assn. for Rsch. in Vision and Ophthalmology (pres. 1976, trustee 1970-75, Proctor medal 1983), Am. Soc. Biol. Chemistry, Am. Chem. Soc., Am. Soc. for Cell Biology, Harvey Soc., Marine Biol. Lab., Oxygen Soc. Home: 808 Broadway Apt 612 New York NY 10003-4806 Office: Columbia U Dept Ophthalmology Eye Research Addition 5th Fl 630 W 168th St New York NY 10032-3702

SPECTOR, DAVID M., lawyer; b. Rock Island, Ill., Dec. 20, 1946; s. Louis and Ruth (Vinikour) S.; m. Laraine Fingold, Jan. 15, 1972; children: Rachel, Laurence. BA, Northwestern U., 1968; JD magna cum laude, U. Mich., 1971. Bar: Ill. 1971, U.S. Dist. Ct. (no. dist.) Ill. 1971, U.S. Ct. Appeals (7th cir.) 1977, U.S. Ct. Appeals (4th cir.) 1984, U.S. Dist. Ct. (cen. dist.) Ill. 1984. Clk. Ill. Supreme Ct., Chgo., 1971-72; ptnr., assoc. Isham, Lincoln & Beale, Chgo., 1972-87; ptnr. Mayer, Brown & Platt, Chgo., 1987—; chair ABA Nat. Inst. on Ins. Co. Insolvency, Boston, 1986; co-chair ABA Nat. Inst. on Internat. Reins.: Collections and Insolvency, New York, 1988; chair ABA Nat. Inst. on Life Ins. Co. Insolvency, Chgo., 1993. Editor (book): Law and Practice of Insurance Company Insolvency, 1986, Law and Practice of Life Insurer Insolvency, 1993; co-editor (book) Law and Practice of International Reinsurance Collections and Insolvency, 1988; contbr. articles to profl. jours.; speaker in field. Mem. ABA (chair Nat. Inst. on Life Insurer Insolvency 1993), Chgo. Bar Assn., Legal Club of Chgo. Home: 2100 N Lincoln Park W Chicago IL 60614-4648 Office: Mayer Brown & Platt 190 S La Salle St Chicago IL 60603-3410

SPECTOR, ELEANOR RUTH, government executive; b. N.Y.C., Dec. 2, 1943; d. Sidney and Helen (Kirschenbaum) Lebost; m. Mel Alan Spector, Dec. 10, 1966; children: Nancy, Kenneth. BA, Barnard Coll., 1964; postgrad. sch. pub. adminstrn., George Washington U., 1965-67; postgrad sch. edn., Nazareth Coll., 1974. Indsl. investigator N.Y. State Dept. Labor, White Plains, 1964-65; mgmt. intern Navy Dept., Washington, 1965, contract negotiator, 1965-68, contract specialist, 1975-78, contracting officer/br. head, 1978-82, dir. div. cost estimating, 1982-84; dep. asst. sec. def. for procurement Washington, 1984-91; dir. Def. Procurement, Washington, 1991—; advisor Nat. Contract Mgmt. Assn., 1984—. Recipient Def. Meritorious Civilian Svc. medal, 1986, 93, Meritorious Svc. Presdl. award, 1989, 94, Disting. Civilian Svc. medal, 1991, 94, Presd. award 1990, Def. Disting. Civilan Svc. Office: Office Under Sec Defense Acquisition & Technology 3060 Def Pentagon Rm 3E144 Washington DC 30301-3060

SPECTOR, GERSHON JERRY, physician, educator, researcher; b. Rovno, Poland, Oct. 20, 1937; came to U.S., 1949; naturalized, 1956; m. Patsy Carol Tanenbaum, Aug. 28, 1966. BA, Johns Hopkins U., 1960; MD cum laude, U. Md., 1964. Intern Beth Israel Hosp., Boston, 1964-65; resident in surgery Sinai Hosp., Balt., 1965-66; resident in otolaryngology Mass. Eye and Ear Infirmary, Boston, 1966-69, Peter Bent Brigham Hosp., Boston, 1968-69; teaching fellow in otolaryngology Harvard U. Med. Sch., Boston, 1968-69; assoc. physician Ill. Crippled Children's Svc., Carbondale, 1971; mem. faculty Washington U. Med. Sch., St. Louis, 1971—, assoc. prof. otolaryngology, 1974-76, prof., 1976—; chief dept. otolaryngology St. Louis County Hosp., 1971-77; mem. staff Washington U. Med. Ctr., Barnes Hosp.; dir. temporal bone bank, 1971-81; guest examiner Am. Bd. Otolaryngology, 1975-77; rsch. cons. neurosci. group, G.D. Searle Pharm. Corp. Mem. editl. bd. Laryngoscope, 1978, editor-in-chief, 1984-94; contbr. articles to med. jours. With U.S. Army, 1969-71. Hancock scholar, 1962. Fellow ACS; mem. AAAS, AMA, Am. Acad. Ophthalmology and Otolaryngology (Honor award 1979), St. Louis Med. Soc., St. Louis County Med. Soc., Am. Coun. Otolarygology, St. Louis Ear, Nose and Throat Club (pres. 1986), So. Med. Assn., Deafness Rsch. Found., Pan. Am. Assn. Otorhinolaryngology and Broncho Esophagology, Am. Soc. Head and Neck Surgery, Soc. Univ. Otolaryngologists, Am. Laryngological, Rhinological and Otological Soc. (Edmund Prince Fowler award 1974), Am. Soc. Cell Biology, Electron Microscopy Soc., N.Y. Acad. Scis., Am. Assn. Anatomists, Am. Acad. Facial Plastic and Reconstructive Surgery, Am. Neuro-Otology Soc., Gesellschaft fur Neurootologie und Aequilibrimoetrie A.V., Barany Soc., Am. Radium Soc., Assn. Acad. Surgery, Am. Fedn. Clin. Oncologic Socs., Am Otological Soc., Acoustical Soc. Am., Soc. for Neurosci., Internat. Skull Base Soc. (founding), Brazilian Skull Base Soc. (hon.), Centurion Club, Alpha Omega Alpha, Psi Chi. Home: 7365 Westmoreland Dr Saint Louis MO 63130-4241 Office: Washington U Med Sch Saint Louis MO 63110

SPECTOR, HARVEY M., osteopathic physician; b. Phila., July 10, 1938; s. Philip and Sylvia (Rischall) S.; m. Rochelle Fleishman, June 16, 1963; children: Jill, Larry. DO, Phila. Coll. Osteo. Medicine, 1963. Osteopathic physician Phila., 1964—; preceptor Hershey (Pa.) Med. Sch., 1987—, Phila. Coll. Osteopathic Medicine, 1989—; assoc. prof. medicine Med. Coll. Pa., 1991—. Recipient Humanitarian award, Chapel of Four Chaplains, Phila., 1984. Mem. Am. Osteo. Assn. (del.), Pa. Osteo. Med. Assn. (del.), Am. Acad. Osteo. Gen. Practitioners, Phila. County Osteo Med. Soc., Med. Club Phila., Abington Dolphins Aquatic Club (pres. 1984-86), B'nai B'rith. Jewish. Avocations: golf, swimming. Office: 1220 Cottman Ave Philadelphia PA 19111-3650

SPECTOR, JOHANNA LICHTENBERG, ethnomusicologist, former educator; b. Libau, Latvia; came to U.S., 1947, naturalized, 1954; d. Jacob C. and Anna (Meyer) Lichtenberg; m. Robert Spector, Nov. 20, 1939 (dec. Dec. 1941). DHS, Hebrew Union Coll., 1950; MA, Columbia U., 1960. Rsch. fellow Hebrew U., Jerusalem, 1951-53; faculty Jewish Theol. Sem. Am., N.Y.C., 1954—, dir., founder dept. ethnomusicology, 1962-85, assoc. prof. musicology, 1966-70, Sem. prof., 1970-85, prof. emeritus, 1985—. Author: Ghetto-und Kzlieder, 1947, Samaritan Chant, 1965, Musical Tradition and Innovation in Central Asia, 1966, Bridal Songs from Sana Yemen, 1960; documentary film The Samaritans, 1971, Chicago International, 1973, Middle Eastern Music, 1973, About the Jews of India: Cochin, 1976 (Cine Golden Eagle 1979), The Shanwar Telis or Bene Israel of India, 1978 (Cine Golden Eagle 1979), About the Jews of Yemen, A Vanishing Culture, 1986 (Cine Golden Eagle 1986, Blue Ribbon, Am. Film Festival 1986), 2000 Years of Freedom and Honor: The Cochin Jews of India, 1992, Margaret Mead, 1992, Columbus International, 1993; religious and folk recs. number over 10, 000; contbr. articles to encys., various jours.; editorial bd. Asian Music. Fellow Am. Anthrop. Assn.; mem. Am. Ethnol. Soc., Am. Musicol. Soc., Internat. Folks Music Coun., World Assn. Jewish Studies, Yivo, Asian Mus. Soc. (v.p. 1964—, pres. 1974-78), Soc. Ethnomusicology (sec.-treas. N.Y.C. chpt. 1960-64). Home: 400 W 119th St New York NY 10027-7125

SPECTOR, JOSEPH ROBERT, retired diversified manufacturing executive; b. N.Y.C., Apr. 16, 1923; s. Benjamin and Julia (Wagner) S. A.B., Dartmouth Coll., 1946; LL.B., Cornell U., 1952. Bar: N.Y. bar 1952, Fla. bar 1953. Asst. counsel Equitable Life Assurance Soc., N.Y.C., 1956-64; asst. gen. counsel Gen. Precision Co., Tarrytown, N.Y., 1964-68; corp. counsel Singer Co., N.Y.C., 1968-70; v.p., gen. counsel, sec. UMC Industries, Inc., Stamford, Conn., 1970-81, ret., 1981. Trustee Morocco-Am. Cultural Assn. Charitable Trust, No. Dispemsar, 1974-90; pres. 20 East 11 Owners Corp. With USNR, 1942-46. Mem. ABA, Am. Soc. Corp. Secs., Fla. Bar Assn., Assn. of Bar of City of N.Y., Yale Club. Home: 236 Loch Rd Columbia SC 29210-4406 also: 1 Blvd Mohammed V, Tangier Morocco

SPECTOR, LOUIS, retired federal judge, lawyer, arbitrator, consultant; b. Niagara Falls, N.Y., Apr. 4, 1918; s. Jacob and Gussie (Yochelson) S.; children: Gale Anne Spector Pasternack, Arthur George, James Aland. Student (N.Y. State scholar), Niagara U., 1936-37; LL.B. with honors, U. Buffalo (later State U. N.Y.), 1940. Bar: N.Y. bar 1940, D.C. bar 1972, U.S. Supreme Ct. bar 1971, U.S. Ct. Claims bar 1968. Asso. firm Saperston, McNaughton & Saperston, Buffalo, 1941-42; asst. chief legal div. U.S. Army C.E., Buffalo Dist., 1942-43; chief sect. claims appeals and litigation U.S. Army C.E. (Great Lakes Div.), Chgo., 1946; chief legal br. and real estate div. U.S. Army C.E. (Great Lakes Div.), Buffalo Dist., 1946-53; exec. dir. Buffalo Port Authority, 1953-54; mem. Bd. Contract Appeals, Washington, 1954-59; chmn. Army panel Armed Services Bd. Contract Appeals, Washington, 1959-62, Unified Armed Services Bd. Contract Appeals, 1962-68; trial judge U.S. Ct. Claims, Washington, 1968-82, judge, 1982-85; cons., arbitrator, mediator Falls Church, Va., 1985—; lectr., speaker, writer public contracts; Congressional appearances, 1953, 66, 69, 77. Contbr. articles to profl. publs. Served with C.E. U.S. Army, 1943-46. Recipient Freshman medal Niagara U., 1936, Sophomore medal, 1937. Fellow Am. Bar Found.; mem. ABA (chmn. sect. pub. contract law 1967-68); Fellow Nat. Contract Mgmt. Assn. (nat. bd. advisers 1967—); mem. ABA (ho. of dels. 1968-70), Fed. Bar Assn. (gen. editor jour. 1960-74, nat. chmn. com. govt. contracts and procurement law 1961-63, Distinguished Service award D.C. chpt. 1974), Lincoln Law Soc. (alumni pres. 1951). Club: Cosmos. Home: 6219 Beachway Dr Falls Church VA 22041-1425 *The concept of justice has been a central concern of my life. It is not a unique concern. Daniel Webster described it as "the great interest of man on earth . . . the ligament which holds civilized beings and nations together." And Reinhold Neibuhr reflected that: "Man's capacity for justice makes democracy possible; but man's inclination to injustice makes democracy necessary.".*

SPECTOR, MARSHALL, philosophy educator; b. Chgo., Feb. 11, 1936; s. Israel Hayyim Spector and Pauline (Futorian) Axelrood; m. Nan Shipman, Dec. 26, 1959; children: Anthony, Jessica. BS in Physics, Ill. Inst. Tech., 1957; MS in Physics, U. Chgo., 1959; PhD in Philosophy, Johns Hopkins U., 1963. Asst. prof. philosophy Duke U., Durham, N.C., 1963-68; assoc. prof. SUNY, Stony Brook, 1968-74, prof., 1974—. Author: Methodological Foundations of Relativistic Mechanics, 1972, Concepts of Reduction in Physical Science, 1978. NSF grantee. Office: SUNY Stony Brook Dept Philosophy Stony Brook NY 11794-3750

SPECTOR, MARTIN WOLF, lawyer, business executive; b. Phila., 1938. BA, Pa. State U., 1959; JD, U. Pa., 1962. Bar: Pa. 1962. Judge U.S. Dist. Ct., until 1967; asst. gen. counsel ARA Services, Phila., assoc. gen. counsel, 1969-76, v.p., 1976-83, gen. counsel, 1983—, formerly sr. v.p., exec. v.p., 1985—. Served to lt. USN, 1953-56. Office: ARA Svcs Inc 1101 Market St Philadelphia PA 19107-2934*

SPECTOR, MELBOURNE LOUIS, management consultant; b. Pueblo, Colo., May 7, 1918; s. Joseph E. and Dora (Bernstein) S.; m. Louise Vincent, Nov. 23, 1948; 1 son, Stephen David. B.A. with honors, U. N.Mex., 1941. Intern U.S. Bur. Indian Affairs, 1941, Nat. Inst. Pub. Affairs, 1941; personnel asst. Office Emergency Mgmt., 1941-42; chief classification div. War Relocation Authority, 1942-43, Hdqrs. USAAF, 1943-45; employment officer UNRRA, 1945-46; pvt. employment, 1946-47; personnel officer Dept. State, 1947-49; dep. dir. personnel ECA, Marshall Plan, Paris, 1949-51; dep. dir., acting dir. personnel Econ. Adminstrn., Mut. Security Adminstrn.,

FOA, 1951-54; asst., dep. dir. Mission to Mexico, ICA, 1954-57, acting dir., 1957-59; chief C. Am., Mex. and Caribbean div. ICA, 1959-61; dir. Office Personnel Mgmt., AID, 1961-62; exec. dir. Bur. Inter-Am. Affairs, Dept. State, 1962-64; commd. fgn. service officer, 1964; counselor for adminstrv. affairs Am. embassy, New Delhi, India, 1964-66; seminar Sr. Seminar Fgn. Policy, Dept. State, 1966-67; exec. dir. U.S.-Mex. Commn. for Border Devel. and Friendship, 1967-69, Am. Revolution Bicentennial Commn., 1969-71; mem. mgmt., policy and coordination staffs Dept. State, 1971-73; ret., 1973, cons., 1973—; mem. Fgn. Svc. Grievance Bd., 1976-77; exec. dir. Am. Consortium for Internat. Pub. Adminstrn., 1980-84, 93-94, dir. Marshall Plan Oral History Project, 1987—. Mem. Cosmos Club, Am. Soc. Pub. Adminstrn., Pi Kappa Alpha, Phi Kappa Phi. Home: 6414 Bannockburn Dr Bethesda MD 20817-5430

SPECTOR, MICHAEL JOSEPH, agribusiness executive; b. N.Y.C., Feb. 13, 1947; s. Martin Wilson and Dorothy (Miller) S.; BS in Chemistry, Washington and Lee U., 1968; m. Margaret Dickson, Sept. 14, 1977. Research chemist Am. Viscose, Phila., 1968-69; pres. MJS Entertainment Corp., Miami, Fla., 1970-84, also MJS Internat., Inc.; ptnr. Old Town Key West Devel. Ltd. (Fla.), 1977—; founder, dir. Plz. Bank of Miami, Fla., 1980-83; pres. MJS Entertainment of Can. Inc., Toronto, Ont., Margo Farms, MJS Prodns., Inc., N.Y.C.; chmn., pres., CEO Margo Nursery Farms, Inc., Dorado, P.R., 1981—, also bd. dirs.; bd. dirs. Goodwill Industries So. Fla., v.p. fin., 1980, bd. dirs. Plz. Bank of Miami. Served with AUS, 1969-70. Recipient Robert E. Lee rsch. grant Washington and Lee U., 1967-68. Mem. Nat. Assn. Record Merchandisers (dir. Nova div., chmn. one-stop distbn. com. 1982-83), Country Music Assn., Dorado Beach, Golf and Tennis Club. Patentee synthetic stretching process. Home: Hyatt Dorado Beach PO Box 8 Dorado PR 00646-0008

SPECTOR, MORTON, wholesale distribution executive; b. 1929. Attended, Cornell U. With D&H Dist. Co., Harrisburg, Pa., 1950—, now CHB, treas. With U.S. Army (2 years). Office: D & H Dist Co PO Box 5967 252535 N 7th St Harrisburg PA 17110*

SPECTOR, PHIL, record company executive; b. Bronx, N.Y., Dec. 25, 1940; m. Veronica Bennett, 1968 (div. 1974); children: Gary Phillip and Louis Phillip (twins), Donte Phillip, Nicole and Phillip (twins). Student, UCLA. Producer with Atlantic Records, 1960-61; founder Philles Records, 1962; now pres. Warner-Spector Records, Inc.; also Mother Bertha Music. Mem. mus. group: Teddy Bears, 1958-59; producer records for Gene Pitney, Ike and Tina Turner, Ben E. King, the Beatles, Righteous Bros., Checkmates, Crystals, Ronettes, John Lennon, George Harrison, The Ramones, Yoko Ono, others; producer album A Concert for Bangladesh (Grammy award); composer songs including You've Lost That Lovin' Feelin', others; appeared in films Tami, Easy Rider; prod., TV documentary film A Giant Stands 5 Ft. 7 In.; prod. film That Was Rock. Named to Rock and Roll Hall of Fame, 1989; named Country Music Song of Yr. Songwriter and Pub. for To Know Him Is To Love Him, 1989; recipient lifetime achievement award U. Calif., Berkeley, 1994, Phila. award Phila. Music Alliance, 1994 (includes star on Phila.'s Walk of Fame). Office: Care Warner-Spector Records Inc 686 S Arroyo Pky Pasadena CA 91105-3233

SPECTOR, ROBERT DONALD, language professional, educator; b. N.Y.C., Sept. 21, 1922; s. Morris and Helen (Spiegel) S.; m. Eleanor Helen Luskin, Aug. 19, 1945; children: Stephen Brett, Eric Charles. BA, L.I. U., 1948, DHL, 1994; MA, NYU, 1949; PhD, Columbia U., 1962. Instr. L.I. U., Bklyn., 1948-59; asst. prof. L.I. U., 1959-62, assoc. prof., 1962-65, prof. English, 1965-94, chmn. senate, 1966-67, 69-70, chmn. dept., 1970-75, dir. humanities and comm. arts, 1975-84, coord. div. of humanities and div. of comms. and performing arts, 1990—, dir. humanities, 1984-90; prof. emeritus L.I. U., 1994—, 1993—; editor, cons. Johnson Reprint Corp., 1967-84. Author: English Literary Periodicals, 1966, Tobias George Smollett, 1968, updated edit., 1989, Pär Lagerkvist, 1973, Arthur Murphy, 1979, Tobias Smollett: A Reference Guide, 1980, The English Gothic, 1983, Backgrounds to Restoration and Eighteenth-Century English Literature, 1989, Political Controversy, 1992, Smollett's Women, 1994; editor: Essays on the Eighteenth Century Novel, 1965, Great British Short Novels, 1970, 9 other vols. English and Am. lit., revs. and articles, poetry. Trustee L.I. U., 1969-70; chmn. George Polk Award Com., 1977—. Served with USCGR, 1942-46. Recipient L.I. U. Trustee award for scholarly achievement, 1978, Tristram Walker Metcalfe Alumnus of Year, 1981; Swedish Govt. travel and research grantee, 1966; fellow Huntington Library, 1974; fellow Folger Library, 1975; fellow Newberry Library, 1976. Mem. MLA, Am.-Scandinavian Found. (publs. com. 1962-84), P.E.N. Home: 1761 E 26th St Brooklyn NY 11229-2405

SPECTOR, STANLEY, historian, foreign language educator; b. N.Y.C., June 10, 1924; s. Irving and Sophie (Braun) S.; m. Betty Peishan Yue, Mar. 8, 1963; children—Pat Lee, Stephanie Spector Van Denberg, Lee Paul, Jon Marc. B.S., Coll. City N.Y., 1945; Ph.D., U. Wash., 1953; postgrad., London Sch. Oriental and African Studies, 1950-51. Instr. history CCNY, 1946; instr. Far Eastern history U. Wash., Seattle, 1951-52, asst. prof., 1955; lectr. history UCLA, 1953; lectr. in history, post-certificate class Chung Cheng Chung Hsueh Singapore, 1954; asst. prof. Far Eastern history Washington U., St. Louis, 1955-58, assoc. prof., 1959-64, assoc. prof. Chinese history, 1964-65, prof. emeritus Asian studies, 1965-89, prof. emeritus, 1989—; chmn. dept. Chinese and Japanee studies, 1964-72, dir. East Asian Lang. and AreaCtr., 1964, Office Internat. studies, 1969; vis. prof. Chinese and Japanese history Columbia U., 1962; vis. prof. U. Singapore, summers 1967-69, 71-73, Waseda U., Tokyo, 1966-67, Ikip U., Bandung, Indonesia, summer 1969. Author: Li Hung-chang and the Huai Army, 1964; co-editor: Guide to the Memorials of Seven Leading Officials of the 19th Century China, 1955. Chmn. Seattle chpt. Am. Vets. Com., 1948-49; co-chmn. Citizens for Stevenson, Seattle, 1952; chmn. St. Louis-Nanjing (Peoples Republic China) Sister City Com. Served with USNR, 1942-43. Social Sci. Research Council fellow, 1950-51, 58-59; Ford Found. fellow, 1953-55; Social Sci. Research Council, Toyo Bunko, 1966-67; Fulbright research scholar Japan, People's Republic of China, Hong Kong, Singapore, Malaysia, 1966-67; Fulbright research scholar USSR, 1975-76. Mem. AAUP, Midwest Conf. on Asian Studies (pres. 1967-68), Chinese Lang. Tchrs. Assn. (pres. 1971—), Am. Polit Sci. Assn., Assn. Asian Studies, Am. Hist. Assn., Internat. Studies Assn. Home: 50 Arundel Pl Saint Louis MO 63105-2278 Office: Washington U PO Box 1088 Saint Louis MO 63130

SPEDALE, VINCENT JOHN, manufacturing executive; b. Chgo., Dec. 2, 1929; s. Joseph and Mildred (Satarino) S.; m. Joan Deeny, Apr. 11, 1953; children: Kathleen, Joseph, Barbara, Judith, Robert, Anthony. BSME, Ill. Inst. Tech., 1952; MS in Indsl. Engring., Wayne State U., 1959; postgrad. in mgmt., MIT, 1977. With Chrysler Corp., 1952-70; v.p. mfg. solar gas turbine div. Internat. Harvester Co., San Diego, 1971-73; v.p. mfg. truck div. Internat. Harvester Co., Chgo., 1973-78, v.p., gen. mgr. engine div., 1978-81; pres. machine tool div. ACME Precision Products, Inc., Detroit, 1982-87; v.p. ops. ICM Industries, Inc., Chgo., 1987-91; CEO, K-Whit Inc, air conditioning equipment mfrs., Fishers, Ind., 1993-94; pres. Hwy. Recycling Sys. Corp., Wasau, Wis., Vinco Mgmt. Cons., Wheaton, Ill.; bd. dirs. Spartan Diesel Co., Harbor Beach, Mich.; CEO Forum Group, Inc., Indpls., 1991-92, Union City (Ind.) Body Co., 1992-93; mfg. cons. Kamaz Truck and Diesel Engine Mfr., Naberezhniye-Chelny, Tartarstan, Russia, 1995—. Mem. Soc. Automotive Engrs. Roman Catholic. Home: 1260 Shady Ln Wheaton IL 60187-3722

SPEECE, RICHARD EUGENE, civil engineer, educator; b. Marion, Ohio, Aug. 23, 1933; s. Irvin Ward S. and Desta May (Speece); m. Jean Margaret Edscorn, Nov. 15, 1969; children: Eric Jordan, Lincoln Dana. BCE, Fenn. Coll., 1956; M of Engring., Yale U., 1958; PhD, MIT, 1961. Assoc. prof. civil engring. U. Ill., Urbana, 1961-65; prof. N.Mex. State U., 1965-70, U. Tex., Austin, 1970-74; Betz chair prof. environ. engring. Drexel U., Phila., 1974-88; Centennial prof. Vanderbilt U., Nashville, 1988—; vis. scholar Cambridge (Eng.) U., 1994; cons. to govt., industry. Contbr. articles to profl. jours.; patentee in field. Recipient hon. mention for best paper Trans. Am. Fisheries Soc., 1973. Mem. Assn. Environ. Engring. Profs. (Disting. Faculty award 1970, disting. lectr. 1978, trustee 1981-83, Engring. Sci. award 1982), ASCE (J. James Cross medal 1983), Am. Soc. Microbiologists, Water Environ. Fedn. (Harrison Prescott Eddy medal 1966), U.S. ANC (Founder's award 1991), Internat. Assn. on Water Pollution Rsch. and Control. Office: Vanderbilt U Civil Engring Dept Nashville TN 37203

SPEED, BILLIE CHENEY (MRS. THOMAS S. SPEED), retired editor, journalist; b. Birmingham, Ala., Feb. 21, 1927; d. John J. and Ruby (Petty) Cheney; m. Thomas S. Speed, July 7, 1968; children: Kathy Lovell Windham Williams, Donna Lovell Adams, Melanie Lovell Wright. Grad., W.Ga. Coll. Reporter, sports writer Birmingham News, 1945; sports writer, gen. assignment reporter, ch. editor Atlanta Jour., 1947-53, with promotion dept., 1955-57, religion editor, 1965-89; feature editor Coach and Athlete Mag., 1958, So. Outdoors, 1958. Recipient Sharp Tack award Cumberland dist. Seventh Day Adventists; Spl. Service award Christian Council of Metro Atlanta, 1974, award for outstanding personal ministry, 1986, personal service award, 1986; Arthur West award for religious feature writing United Meth. Ch., 1977; Alumni Achievement award West Ga. Coll., 1985; Trustee award Protestant Radio & TV Ctr., 1986; Faith & Freedom award Religious Heritage of Am., 1986. Fellow Religious Pub. Relations Council; mem. Nat. Religion Newswriters Assn., Nat. Fedn. Press Women, Theta Sigma Chi. Methodist. Home: 559 Rays Rd Stone Mountain GA 30083-3142

SPEED, JOHN SACKETT, insurance company executive; b. Dubuque, Iowa, Aug. 29, 1927; s. Lloyd Jeter and Marion (Whitbread) S.; m. Anne Carter Stewart, Apr. 28, 1951; children: Virginia Lyons, Lloyd Rogers (Mrs. William C. Ciccariello), Anne Carter (Mrs. John B. Meyers). A.B., Princeton U., 1950; M.B.A., Harvard Bus. Sch., 1955. V.p. Commonwealth Life Ins. Co., Louisville, 1955-72; v.p., sec., treas. Capital Holding Corp., Louisville, 1972-88; cons. Johnson & Higgins of Ky., Inc., Louisville, 1988—. Bd. dirs. Hist. Homes Found., Greater Louisville Fund for Arts, 1989—; chmn. J.B. Speed Art Mus., 1992-94; v.p. Filson Club Hist. Soc. Served with USN, 1945-46. Republican. Episcopalian. Clubs: Louisville Country (treas. 1963-70), Pendennis, River Valley, Wynn Stay, Little Harbor. Home: 5913 Brittany Valley Rd Louisville KY 40222-5905 also: 760 Sextant Dr Sanibel FL 33957-3825 also: 3320 Forrest Dr Harbor Springs MI 49740 Office: Starks Bldg Ste 370 Louisville KY 40202

SPEED, TERENCE PAUL, statistician, educator; b. Victor Harbor, Australia, Mar. 14, 1943; came to the U.S., 1987; s. Harold Hector and Jeanette Elisabeth (Hacklin) S.; m. Freda Elizabeth Pollard, Dec. 22, 1964. BS, Melbourne U., Victoria, Australia, 1965; PhD, Monash U., Victoria, 1969. Tutor Monash U., 1965-67, lectr., 1967-69; lectr. U. Sheffield, United Kingdom, 1969-73; prof. U. Western Australia, 1974-82; chief CSIRO Div. Math. and Statistics, Canberra, Australia, 1983-87; prof. U. Calif., Berkeley, 1987—. Home: 1830 Arch St Berkeley CA 94709-1310 Office: U Calif Dept Statistics Berkeley CA 94720

SPEEDY, ERIC DAWSON, laboratory technician; b. York, Pa., July 11, 1969; s. Harry Wilson and Janet Patricia (Roney) S. BS, Allegheny Coll., 1991. Biology technician Allegheny Coll., Meadville, Pa., 1991-93; lab. technician Hilltop Lab. Animals, Inc., Scottdale, Pa., 1994—. Bd. dirs. Greater Latrobe Recreation Soccer Assn, Latrobe, Pa., 1995. Mem. Am. Assn. Lab. Animal Sci., Nat. Ski Patrol Systems. Avocations: skiing, golf, outdoor activities, reading. Home: 5614 Pocusset St Pittsburgh PA 15217-2217

SPEER, C. A., veterinary science rsch. administrator, biologist; b. Lamar, Colo., Feb. 14, 1945; married, 1977; 2 children. BS, Colo. State U., 1967; MS, Utah State U., 1970, PhD in Zoology, 1972. Asst. prof. U. Tex., Houston, 1972-73; rsch. assoc. U. N.Mex., 1973-75; from asst. prof. to assoc. prof. microbiology U. Mont., Bozeman, 1975-83; assoc. prof. vet. sci. Mont. State U., Bozeman, 1983-86, prof., head dept. vet. sci., 1986—. Mem. Am. Assn. Immunologists, Am. Soc. Parasitologists, Can. Soc. Zoologists, Soc. Protozoologists. Office: Vet Molecular Lab Mont State U Bozeman MT 69717*

SPEER, DAVID BLAKENEY, industrial executive; b. Sault Ste. Marie, Ont., Apr. 6, 1951; s. Richard Norwood and Mary (Davis) S.; m. Barbara Ann Brugenhemre, June 22, 1974; children: Blake, Sarah. BS in Indsl. Engring., Iowa State U., 1973; MBA, Northwestern U., 1977. Sales engr. Precision Paper, Wheeling, Ind., 1976-78; sales mgr. Precision Paper, Wheeling, 1976-78; regional sales mgr. ITW Buildex, Itasca, Ill., 1978-81; nat. sales mktg. mgr. ITW Buildex, Itasca, 1981-84, v.p., gen. mgr., 1984-92; v.p., gen. mgr. ITW Paslode, Lincolnshire, Ill., 1992—; group v.p., constrn. products, 1994—. Mem. Am. Mgmt. Assn., Am. Mktg. Assn., Am. Soc. Indsl. Engrs., Midwest Indsl. Mfg. Assn. Office: Ill Tool Works Inc 3600 W Lake Ave Glenview IL 60025

SPEER, DAVID JAMES, public relations executive; b. Mpls., Apr. 30, 1927; s. Ray Patterson and Grace Elizabeth (Kane) S.; m. Nancy How Girouard; children: Robert J. Girouard, Mark J. Girouard. B.A. in Polit. Sci., U. Minn., 1950. Sports reporter Mpls. Tribune, 1945-50; night radio editor AP, Mpls., 1950-51; ptnr. Speer's Publicity Service, Mpls., 1950-59; pres. Sullivan & Speer Inc., Mpls., 1959-61; sr. v.p. Padilla, Sarjeant, Sullivan & Speer, Inc., Mpls., 1961-71, pres., sec., 1971-77; pres., chief operating officer Padilla and Speer, Inc., Mpls., 1977-86; Minn. commr. Trade and Econ. Devel., 1987-91; cons. Padilla Speer Beardsley Inc., Mpls., 1991-93; exec. dir. Friends of the Communication Ctr., St. Paul, Minn., 1993—; cons. pub. relations, Mpls., N.Y.C., 1961-86; dir. pub. relations Minn. State Fair, 1961-68, St. Paul Winter Carnival Assn., 1952-68. Past chmn. Minn. Multiple Sclerosis Soc.; bd. dirs. St. Paul Chamber Orch.; consul of Finland in Minn. Served with USN, 1945-46. Mem. Pub. Rels. Soc. Am. (pres. chpt. 1967), U. Minn. Alumni Assn. (pres. 1975-76), Mpls. Club. Home: 23235 Saint Croix Trl N Scandia MN 55073-9725 Office: Padilla Speer Beardsley Inc 224 W Franklin Ave Minneapolis MN 55404-2331

SPEER, GLENDA O'BRYANT, middle school educator; b. Uvalde, Tex., Mar. 30, 1956; d. Harvey Glen and Mary (Miller) O'Bryant; m. Weldon Michael Speer, July 12, 1975; children: Janena Lea, Jon Michael. BS, Sul Ross State U., Alpine, Tex., 1978; MA, U. Tex., San Antonio, 1984. Tchr. math. Jackson Middle Sch., San Antonio, 1978-82; tchr. math., computers Bradley Middle Sch., San Antonio, 1982-86, chmn. dept. math., 1986—; computer edn. tchr. trainer N.E. Ind. Sch. Dist., San Antonio, 1984—; acad. pentathlon coach Bradley Middle Sch., 1988-92; software reviewer Nat. Coun. Tchrs. Math., Reston, Va., 1994. Editor Math Matters newsletter, 1989—; writer curriculum guide: Computer Literacy Guide for Teachers, 1992. Black belt Karate and self-defense instr. Tang So Do Karate Assn., San Antonio, 1994—. Recipient Supt.'s award N.E. Ind. Sch. Dist., 1990, 92, 93, Red Apple Tchrs. award St. Mary's U., San Antonio, 1992. Mem. Nat. Coun. Tchrs. Math., Tex. Coun. Tchrs. Math., Bradley Middle Sch. PTA. Avocations: geneology, Southwest history. Office: Bradley Middle Sch 14819 Heimer Rd San Antonio TX 78232-4528

SPEER, JACK ATKESON, publisher; b. Wichita, Kans., July 3, 1941; s. Jack Shelley and Shannon Speer; m. Judith Ann Fuller, Aug. 5,1967; children: Martin Fuller, Elizabeth Fuller. BS in Bus. Adminstrn., Kansas. State U., 1966, ML, 1967; postgrad., U. Mo., 1967, U. So. Calif., 1969; IBM Pres.'s Class, Harvard U., 1980. Mem. advt., editorial, mech. staffs Wichita Eagle-Beacon, 1954-64; editorial asst. Emporia (Kans.) Gazette, 1964-65; supr. libr. data processing Kans. State U., Emporia, 1965-67; mgr. data processing ctr. Kans. State U., Manhattan, 1967-69; mgr. systems and programming John Wiley Inc.-Becker & Hayes Inc., Bethesda, Md., 1969-72; dir. libr. info. systems Informatics Inc. Info. Systems Group, Rockville, Md., 1972-77; v.p. ops. Arcata Real Estate Data Inc., Miami, Fla., 1977-79; mgr. electronic info. systems Arcata Publs. Group, Norwalk, Conn., 1979-83; v.p. mktg./sales, data imaging group The William Byrd Press, Richmond, Va., 1983-84; sr. v.p. ops. NewsBank Inc., New Canaan, Conn., 1984-85; pres., pub. Buckmaster Pub., Mineral, Va., 1986—; mem. faculty Cath. U. Am. Libr. Sch., Kans. State U. Libr. Sch. Author: Amateur Radio Call Directory, 1982—, Buckmaster's Ann. Stockholder Reports, 1986—, Front-Page-News (CD-ROM), 1989, HamCall (CD-ROM), 1988—; compiler Libraries and Automation: A Bibliography, 1967, The Living Bible Concordance, 1972. Trustee Jefferson-Madison Regional Libr., 1990-91; commr. Louisa County Planning Commn., 1992—; mem. adv. coun. Louisa County High Sch., 1992. Mem. ALA, NRA, Am. Radio Relay League, Nat. Info. Standards Orgn. (CD-ROM com), D.C. Libr. Assn. (pres.), Sigma Tau Gamma. Office: Buckmaster Pub 6196 Jefferson Hwy Mineral VA 23117-0010

SPEER, JAMES, religious organization administrator. Dir. Daniel Springs Encampment, Gary, Tex. Office: Daniel Springs Encampment PO Box 310 Gary TX 75643-0310

SPEER, JOHN E., freelance legal assistant, reporter; b. Conrad, Mont., Mar. 19, 1956; s. Elmer Constant and Mildred Saphronia (LaBelle) S.; m. Sharron D. Knotts, May 23, 1982 (div. Mar. 1986); 1 child: Jeremy Keith; 1 foster child: Casey. Paralegal assoc., Coll. of Great Falls, Mont., 1994. Farmer Valier, Mont., 1956-73; janitor Shelby (Mont.) pub. schs., 1974-75; freelance news reporter KSEW Radio, Shelby, 1980—, various TV stas., newspapers, Great Falls, 1980—; office cleaner Parkdale Housing Authority, Great Falls, 1990—; freelance paralegal Great Falls, 1993—; rschr. line-up identification appeal binder to U.S. Supreme Ct., 1993. Contbr. victim-witness assistance program operating manual, 1992. Counselor and adv. Victim-Witness Assistance Svcs., Great Falls, 1991-93. Mem. Mont. Big Sky Paralegal Assn., Am. Counseling Assn. Jehovah's Witness. Avocations: hiking, fishing, cooking, travel, swimming. Home: 3308 Lower River Rd Apt 19 Great Falls MT 59405-7215

SPEER, PHILLIP BRADFORD, commercial business executive; b. Deering, Mo., Jan. 31, 1927; s. Aiser Jacob and Bertha Mary (Black) S.; m. Sylvia June Petersen, Nov. 5, 1948; children: Mark Stephen, Philip Craig, Kim Gregory, Todd Jeffrey, Dana Paige. Grad., Logistics Devel. Sch., Ft. Lee, Va., 1977; BA, U. Ariz., 1954, Command & Gen. Staff Coll., Ft. Leavenworth, Kans., 1969, Nat. Def. U., 1972; MA, George Washington U., 1982. Cert. logistician. Pres., CEO Lollesgard Splty. Co., Inc., Tucson, 1954-84, TLC Med. Alert, Inc., Tucson, 1984-87, Treasured Family Ties, Inc., Tucson, 1990—; cons. Kwik Change Tables, Inc., Tucson, 1990—. V.p., charter mem. Srs. Achievement and Growth through Edn., Tucson, 1989-90. Col. U.S. Army, 1977-82. Decorated Legion of Merit. Mem. Res. Officers Assn., Ret. Officers Assn. Avocations: travel, reading, tennis. Home: 1316 S Camino Seco Tucson AZ 85710-6527

SPEER, ROY M., broadcasting executive; b. 1932. BA, So. Meth. U., 1956; JD, Stetson U., 1959. Pres. Aloha Utilities, Inc., Tarpon Springs, Fla., 1966—; ptnr. Speer & Olson, Clearwater, Fla., 1979-86; chmn., chief exec. officer Home Shopping Network, 1982—, also bd. dirs. Office: Home Shopping Network Inc PO Box 9090 12000 25th Ct N Saint Petersburg FL 33716-1923

SPEER, WILLIAM THOMAS, JR., banker, investor, consultant, rancher; b. Boston, Feb. 17, 1936; s. William Thomas and Marie Dorothy (DeWolfe) S.; m. Glenda Jane Farris, Nov. 15, 1972; children: Jason Farris, Tyson DeWolfe, Courtland Conley, William Thomas III. AA, Marin Jr. Coll., Kentfield, Calif., 1955; BA in Bus., Calif. State U.-Fullerton, 1962; postgrad. U. Calif.-San Francisco, 1955-56. Bank examiner Fed. Res. Bank, 1962-67, 68-70; exec. v.p. First Nat. Bank, Cañon City, Colo., 1967-68; v.p., then sr. v.p. Bank of Idaho, Boise, 1970-74; sr. v.p. Bank of N.Mex., Albuquerque, 1975; prin. organizer, founder, pres., CEO, chmn. bd. Am. Bank of Commerce, Boise, 1975-94; exec. cons. First Security Bank, N.A., 1994-95, cons., 1995—; developer Willowgrove Estates, Meridian, Idaho, Rivers Bend Condominiums, McCall, Idaho, Snake Riverview Ranches, Inc. (pres.), King Hill, Idaho; guest lectr. Boise State U.; cons. in field. Contbr. articles to profl. jours. Bd. dirs. Idaho chpt. Am. Heart Assn., 1983, chmn. bd., 1985; bd. dirs. Boise Philharm., 1984, Boise Better Bus. Bur., 1994, Boise Sr. Sitizens, 1994; active Pub. TV Sta., 1981-83. With U.S. Army, 1957-61. Recipient gov.'s appreciation award Idaho-Oreg. Lions Club, 1982. Mem. Am. Bankers Assn., Idaho Bankers Assn. (exec. coun.), BBB, Western Ind. Bankers Assn., Idaho Ind. Bankers Assn. (pres. 1986), Robert Morris Assocs., Nat. Assn. Home Builders, U.S. Indsl. Council, Greater Boise C. of C., Nat. Fedn. Ind. Bus., Idaho Water Users Assn., Boise State U. Club, Ducks Unltd., Pheasants Forever, Hillcrest Country Club, Centurion Club, Bronco Boosters Club, Elks. Home: PO Box 7566 Boise ID 83707-1566

SPEERING, ROBIN, educator, computer specialist; b. Athens, Ga., Apr. 23, 1937; s. Harry and Effie (Adams) S. BS, U. Ga., 1962, MEd, 1970, EdS, 1974; MRE, Southwestern Bapt. Sem., 1964. Cert. tchr., Ga. Ind. audio-visual equipment specialist Athens, 1957-69; mgr. Speering Printing Co., Athens, 1965-67, asst. mgr., computer specialist, 1986—; tchr. Oconee County High Sch., Watkinsville, Ga., 1968-69, Barrow County Schs., Winder, Ga., 1970-73, Comer (Ga.) Elem. Sch., 1974-76, Tadmore Elem. Sch., Hall County, Ga., 1976-77, Richmond County Schs., Augusta, Ga., 1977-85, Truett-McConnell Coll., Watkinsville, Ga., 1995—; freelance writer, Athens, 1986—. Contbr. articles to newsletters, area newspapers. Organist, tchr. Christian Fellowship Ch., Athens, 1990—. Mem. ASCD, NEA, Ga. Assn. Educators, Printing Industry Assn. Ga., Kappa Delta Pi. Avocations: music, photography, electronics. Home: PO Box 6943 Athens GA 30604-6943 Office: Speering Printing Co 278 Hodgson Dr Athens GA 30606-2962

SPEERS, ROLAND ROOT, II, lawyer; b. Jacksonville, Fla., Oct. 8, 1933; s. Roland Root and Alice (Calkins) S.; m. Florence Briscoe, Dec. 18, 1954; children: Kirsten, Guy, Gina Marie. B.A. cum laude, UCLA, 1955, J.D., 1958. Bar: Calif. 1958, D.C. 1978. Dep. commr. corps. Calif. Dept. Corps., Los Angeles, 1958-59; sec., gen. counsel Suburban Cos., Pomona, Calif., 1959-64, Amcord, Inc., Los Angeles, 1964-67; asst. to pres. Amcord, Inc., 1967, v.p. corp. devel., 1968; v.p., gen. counsel Amcord, Inc., Newport Beach, Calif., 1970; sr. v.p. Amcord, Inc., 1971, exec. v.p., 1972-75, pres., 1975-94; ptnr. Speers, Dana, Teal Balfour & MacDonald, Costa Mesa, Calif., 1977-94; dir. Logicon, Inc., Torrance, Calif. Trustee Pitzer Coll., Pomona, 1975-80; bd. councillors Center Pub. Affairs U. So. Calif., 1976-81; bd. dirs. Newport Harbor Art Mus., 1977-82. Mem. D.C. Bar Assn., State Bar Assn. Calif., UCLA Alumni Assn., UCLA Law Sch. Alumni Assn., Phi Alpha Delta. Clubs: Big Canyon Country (Newport Beach). Office: 611 Anton Blvd PO Box 3936 Costa Mesa CA 92628

SPEERT, ARNOLD, college president, chemistry educator; b. Bronx, N.Y., June 19, 1945; s. David Jack and Dorothy Bernice (Feldman) S.; m. Myrna Goldstein, June 11, 1967; children: Alan Michael, Debra Beth. BS, CCNY, 1966; PhD, Princeton U., 1971. Asst. to dean grad. and rsch. program William Paterson Coll., Wayne, N.J., 1970-71, from asst. to assoc. prof. chemistry, 1970-80, prof., 1980—, asst. to v.p. acad. affairs, 1971-78, assoc. dean acad. affairs, 1978-79, v.p. acad. affairs, 1979-85, pres., 1985—; bd. dirs. State Farm Indemnity Co., Better Bus. Bur. Trustee Barnert Hosp., Paterson, 1986—, Jewish Fedn. North Jersey, Wayne, 1986—, YM & YWHA No. N.J., Wayne, 1988—, Respiratory Health Assn., 1990-93; bd. dirs. William Paterson Coll. Found., 1985—. Mem. Am. Assn. State Colls. and Univs. (bd. dirs. 1993-95), Tri-County C. of C. (bd. dirs. 1986-94), N.J. State Bd. Examiners. Home: 48 Brandon Ave Wayne NJ 07470-6032 Office: William Paterson Coll 300 Pompton Rd Wayne NJ 07470-2103

SPEICE, CHARLES BOARDMAN, retired geological engineer, and geology educator; b. North Platte, Nebr., May 21, 1935; s. Boardman Elias and Margerat (Schipke) S.; m. Jane Davis, Oct. 17, 1959 (dec. Apr. 23, 1990); children: Charles B., David E., John R.; m. Mary Bell, June 25, 1994. BS in Geol. Engring., S.D. Sch. Mines and Tech., 1957. Sr. staff geol. engr. Shell Offshore Inc., New Orleans, 1957-91; ret., 1991; part-time prof. geology North Ark. Cmty. and Tech. Coll., Harrison, 1994—; speaker in field. Author, instr. co. sch.. Capt. Shell team Christmas in Oct., New Orleans, 1990, 91. Served to capt. U.S. Artillery, 1957. Mem. Am. Assn. Petroleum Geologists, New Orleans Geol. Soc. (Boy Scout com. 1980—). Republican Episcopalian. Achievements include research in field of seismic and 3D in oil field development; in house work in shallow hazards offshore Gulf Mex. Avocations: fishing, woodworking, gardening. Home: Rt 7 Box 238B Harrison AR 72601

SPEICHER, OPAL, church administrator. Pres. Missionary Women Intern. of the Missionary Church, Fort Wayne, Ind.

SPEIDEL, DAVID HAROLD, geology educator; b. Pottsville, Pa., Aug. 10, 1938; s. Harold O. and Edith M. (Rosser) S.; m. Margaret Helen Liebrecht, Sept. 8, 1962. B.S., Franklin and Marshall Coll., Lancaster, Pa., 1960; Ph.D., Pa. State U., 1964. Research asso. Pa. State U., 1964-66; asst. prof. to prof. dept. geology Queens Coll., CUNY, Flushing, 1966—; chmn. dept. Queens Coll., CUNY, 1980-88, dean faculty sci., 1970-79, chmn. faculty senate, 1992-96; maj. projects sect. head, earth scis. NSF, 1988-89; vis.

scholar Sr. Specialists div. Congl. Research Service, Washington, 1977-78. Author: (with A.F. Agnew) Natural Geochemistry of Our Environment; editor (with L. Ruedisili and A.F. Agnew) Perspectives on Water: Uses and Abuses; contbr. articles to profl. jours. Mem. AAAS, Geol. Soc. Am., Am. Ceramic Soc., Mineral. Soc. Am., Am. Geophys. Union, Am. Inst. Profl. Geologists, Nat. Hazards Soc., N.Y. Acad. Scis., Soc. Environ. Geochemistry and Health, Sigma Xi. Office: Queens Coll Dept Geology Flushing NY 11367

SPEIDEL, JOHN JOSEPH, physician, foundation officer; b. Iowa City, Iowa, Sept. 17, 1937; s. Thomas Dennis and Edna (Warweg) S.; divorced; 1 child, Sabrina Brett. A.B. cum laude, Harvard U., 1959, M.D., 1963, M.P.H., 1965. Diplomate: Nat. Bd. Med. Examiners, Am. Bd. Preventive Medicine. Intern St. Luke's Hosp., N.Y.C., 1963-64; resident N.Y.C. Dept. Health, 1965-67, dep. dir. maternal and infant care project, 1966-67; chief research div. Office of Population, AID, Dept. State, Washington, 1969-76; assoc. dir. Office of Population, 1977, dep. dir., acting dir. office, 1978-83; v.p. Population Action Internat. (formerly Population Crisis Com.), 1983-87, pres., 1987-95; program officer for population Hewlett Found., 1995—; lectr. population and family planning Georgetown U., 1973-75. Contbr. articles to profl. jours.; Editor: (with others) Female Sterilization, 1971, Hysteroscopic Sterilization, 1974, Intrauterine Devices, 1974, Control of Male Fertility, 1975, Advances in Female Sterilization Technology, 1976, Risks, Benefits and Controversies in Fertility Control, 1978, Reversal of Sterilization, 1978, Pregnancy Termination, 1979, Vaginal Contraception, 1979. Served to maj. U.S. Army, 1967-69. Recipient Meritorious Unit citation Office of Population, 1969-71, Arthur S. Flemming award Washington Downtown Jaycees, 1972. Mem. Am. Pub. Health Assn. (Carl S. Shultz award 1982), Population Assn. Am. Office: William & Flora Hewlett Found 525 Middlefield Rd Ste 200 Menlo Park CA 94025-3447

SPEIER, JOHN LEO, JR., retired chemist; b. Chgo., Sept. 29, 1918; s. John L. and Mary Jane (Dickman) S.; m. A. Louise Kimmel, Oct. 21, 1944; children—Susan, Genevieve, Dorothy, Margaret, John L. III, Thomas J. B.Sc., St. Benedict's Coll., 1941; M.Sc., U. Fla., 1943; Ph.D., U. Pitts., 1947. Naval Stores research fellow U. Fla., 1941-43; research fellow Mellon Inst., Pitts., 1943; sr. fellow Mellon Inst., 1947-56; mgr. organic research Dow Corning Corp., Midland, Mich., 1956-69; scientist in corp. research Dow Corning Corp., 1969-75, sr. scientist in corp. research, 1975-93; retired, 1994. Contbr. numerous articles to profl. jours., 1950—; holder 100 patents prodn. organosilicon compounds and allied products. Named Indsl. Research and Devel. Scientist of Yr. Indsl. Research/Devel. mag., 1978. Mem. AAAS, Am. Chem. Soc. (Frederick Stanley Kipping award 1990), Sigma Xi. Office: Dow Corning Corp Dept Research Midland MI 48640

SPEIGHT, JAMES GLASSFORD, research company executive; b. Murton, Eng., June 24, 1940; came to U.S., 1980; s. George Madison and Elizabeth (Glassford) S.; m. Sheila Elizabeth Stout, Dec. 28, 1963; 1 child, James. BSc in Chemistry with honors, Manchester U., Eng., 1961, PhD in Organic Chemistry, 1965. Research fellow Manchester U., 1965-67; research officer Research Council, Edmonton, Alta., Can., 1967-80; research assoc. Exxon Corp., Linden, N.J., 1980-84; chief sci. officer Western Rsch. Inst., Laramie, Wyo., 1984-89, chief exec. officer, 1990—; adv. com. Grant McEwan Community Coll., Edmonton, 1975-80; chmn. petroleum-natural gas research task force, Alta. Research Council, 1978-79; search com. V.P. for Research and Grad. Studies, U. Wyo., 1985; external mem. promotions com. U. Mosul, Iraq, 1985; thesis examiner, Indian Inst. Techn., Bombay, 1974, U. Mosul, 1976, 77, 78; vis. lect. petroleum sci., U. Mosul, Iraq, 1978; lectr. petroleum sci., U. Alberta, Edmonton, Can., 1976-80, U. Calgary, Alta., 1979-80. Editor Fuel Sci. and Tech. Internat., 1983—, Energy Sources, 1983—; referee numerous jours., manuscripts; contbr. more than 200 sci. articles to profl. jours. Fellow Am. Inst. Chemists, Royal Soc. Chemistry (chartered chemist), Chem. Inst. Can. (treas. Edmonton sect. 1971-78, editor newsletter 1975-77); mem. Am. Chem. Soc. (program com. petroleum divsn. 1981-91, 94—, bus. mgr. petroleum divsn. 1982-85), Sigma Xi. Office: Western Rsch Inst 365 N 9th St Laramie WY 82070-3380

SPEIGHT, VELMA RUTH, alumni affairs director; b. Snow Hill, N.C., Nov. 18, 1932; d. John Thomas and Mable Lee (Edwards) S.; m. Howard H. Kennedy, 1953 (div. 1961); 1 child, Chineta. BS, N.C. A&T U., 1953; MEd, U. Md., 1965, PhD, 1976. Cert. counselor, tchr., Md. Tchr. math., French Kennard High Sch., Centreville, Md., 1954-60; counselor Kennard High Sch., Centreville, 1960-66; coord. guidance dept. Queene Anne's County High Sch., Centreville, 1966-69; adv. specialist in civil rights Md. State Dept. Edn., Balt., 1969-72, supr. guidance, 1972-76, dep. asst. state supt., 1976-82, asst. state supt., 1982-86; dir. EEO recruitment U. Md., College Park, 1972; coord. guidance and counseling U. Md. Ea. Shore, Princess Anne, 1986-87; assoc. prof. counselor edn. East Carolina U., Greenville, 1989; chmn. dept. edn., coord. grad. prog. guidance and counseling U. Md., Eastern Shore, Greenville, 1989-93, chmn. dept. edn., 1990-94; dir. alumni affairs N.C. A&T U., Greensboro, 1993—; adj. prof. Loyola U., Balt., 1976-80, Johns Hopkins U., Balt., 1980; cons., 1987—; speaker numerous seminars. Mem. Nat. Coalition for Chpt. I Parents, Washington, 1980-87, Human Rights Commn., Howard County, Md., 1987—; chmn. Gov.'s com. Studying Sentencing Alternatives for Women, Annapolis, Md., 1987; founder, chmn. Mothers to Prevent Dropouts, Centreville. Recipient Early Childhood Edn. award Japanese Govt., 1984, Md. State Tchrs'. Assn. Minority award Black Chs. for Excellence in Edn.; Fulbright Hayes scholar, 1991. Mem. Am. Counseling Assn., Nat. Alliance Black Educators, Assn. for Supervision and Curriculum Devel., Assn. Tchr. Edn., Md. Assn. Coll. Tchr. Edn., Md. Counseling Assn., N.C. A&T U. Alumni Assn. (nat. pres. 197983, Excellence award 1983), Tchr. Edn. and Profl. Standards Bd. Democrat. Presbyterian. Club: Community Action (Centreville). Avocations: reading, cooking, sewing, bicycling. Home: 11 Carissa Ct Greensboro NC 27407-6366 Office: NC A&T State U Off of Dir Alumni Affairs Greensboro NC 27411

SPEILLER-MORRIS, JOYCE, English composition educator; b. Utica, N.Y., Nov. 11, 1945; d. Arnold Leonard Speiller and Sybil (Sall) McAdam; m. Joseph Raymond Morris, Mar. 17, 1984. BS, Syracuse U., 1968; MA, Columbia U., 1969. Cert. tchr., N.Y., Fla. Chmn. upper sch. social studies dept., tchr. grade 6 social studies and English Cathedral Heights Elem. Sch., N.Y.C., 1969-74; adj. prof. Broward Community Coll., Hollywood, Davie and Pompano, Fla., 1982-90, Biscayne Coll., Miami, Fla., 1983, Miami-Dade Community Coll., 1983, Nova U., Miami and Davie, 1983-84; adj. prof., semester lectr. U. Miami, Coral Gables, 1985—; master tchr. U. Miami, 1990, 92, 94, faculty fellow, 1990-94, mem. curriculum devel., 1991-94; contbr. presentation to Fla. Coll. English Assn., 1991-92, Wyo. Conf. English, 1991; guest spkr. in field of svc.-learning, 1992-94; cons. svc.-learning curriculum design, 1994; acad. advisor U. Miami, 1994, 95, 96. Reviewer textbook McGraw Hill, 1993; contbr. instr.'s manual of textbook, 1994; contbr. poetry to revs., articles to profl. jours. Founder, dir. Meet the Author program, Coral Gables, 1989—. Recipient V.P. award U. Miami, 1992, cert. recognition West Palm Beach, Fla., TV sta., 1992; grantee Fla. Office for Campus Vols., 1992, Dade Community Found., 1992. Mem. MLA, Nat. Soc. Experiential Edn., Fla. Coll. English Assn., Coll. English Assn., Nat. Coun. Tchrs. English, Fla. Chpt. of Tchrs. of English to Spkrs. of Other Langs. (spkr. conf. 1992), Am. Correctional Assn., Phi Delta Kappa, Phi Lambda Theta. Avocations: reading, community svc. Home: Tower 200 Apt 806 19101 Mystic Pointe Dr North Miami Beach FL 33180 Office: U Miami Office English Composition PO Box 248145 Coral Gables FL 33124-8145

SPEIRS, DEREK JAMES, diversified corporation financial executive; b. Montreal, Que., Can., Dec. 21, 1933; s. James B. and Marie C. (Hunt) S.; m. Carol Alice Cumming, Dec. 8, 1967 (div. Feb. 1989); children: Lara Marie, Gregory Ross, Scott Lawrence Gordon. B. Commerce with honors in Econs., McGill U., 1954, M.B.A., 1959. Chartered acct., Can., chartered corp. sec. Devel. dir. fine papers, corp. acctg. dir. Domtar, Inc., Montreal, 1970-72, dir. corp. devel., 1976-78, v.p. fin., corp. devel., 1978-89, sr. v.p. fin. and corp. devel., 1989-91; v.p., sec. fin. Consoltex, Montreal, 1972-76, bus. cons., 1991—; pres. Speirs Cons. Inc. Mem. Can. Inst. Chartered Accts., Fin. Execs. Inst., C.D. Howe Inst., Lac Marois Country Club, St. James Club, Montreal Amateur Athletic Assn. Avocations: travel, skiing. Home: 365 Stanstead Ave, Ville Mont-Royal, Montreal, PQ Canada H3R 1X5 Office: Ste 1100, 2 Pl Alexis Nihon, Montreal, PQ Canada H3Z 3C1

SPEISER, THEODORE WESLEY, astrophysics, planetary and atmospheric sciences educator; b. Del Norte, Colo., Nov. 23, 1934; s. Alfred Theodore and Virginia Melva (Pickens) S.; m. Patricia Jane McCrummen, June 10, 1956; children: Tanya Lee, Kelly Ann, Tertia Ava. BS, Colo. State U., 1956; MS, Calif. Inst. Tech., 1959; PhD, Pa. State U., 1964. Asst. prof. U. Colo., Boulder, 1969-74, assoc. prof., 1974-85, prof. astrophysics, planetary and atmospheric scis., 1985—; cons. NOAA, Boulder, 1970—. Contbr. articles to profl. jours. Served to capt. U.S. Army, 1960-61. Recipient U.S. Sr. Scientist award A.V. Humboldt Found., 1977; Fulbright fellow, 1956. Mem. Am. Geophys. Union (local br. v.p. 1986-87, pres. 1987). Avocations: photography, hiking, cross-country skiing, tennis. Home: 2335 Dartmouth Ave Boulder CO 80303-5209 Office: U Colo Dept of Astrophysics Planetary & Atmospheric Scis C Box 391 Boulder CO 80309

SPEITEL, GERALD EUGENE, consulting environmental engineer; b. Phila., Feb. 4, 1930; s. Edmond Joseph and Lillian M. (Kohlschreiber) S.; m. Rosemarie Noller, Aug. 22, 1953; children: Gerald Eugene, Edmond C. BS, Drexel Evening Coll., 1963; M.S. in Engring. Mgmt, Drexel U., 1967. With Dept. Water, City of Phila., 1948-51, Day & Zimmerman, Phila., 1953-54; with John G. Reutter Assos., Camden, N.J., 1954-72, v.p., 1970-72; pres. Speitel Assos., Marlton, N.J., 1972-88; dir. Environ. Measurements and Analysis, Hammonton, N.J., 1979-86; sr. v.p. BCM Engrs., Inc., 1986-90; prin. Gerald E. Speitel, Forensic Engr., 1991—. Served with C.E. U.S. Army, 1951-53. Named Honor Man of Yr. Drexel Evening Coll., 1983, 90; recipient Del. Valley Engr. of Yr. award, 1989, Disting. N.J. Civil Engr. award ASCE, 1989, Penjerdel award, 1989, Mary S. Irick Drexel medal, 1991. Fellow ASCE (life, pres. South Jersey br. 1978-79, N.J. sect. 1979-80, nat. dir. dist. 1 1981-84, v.p. 1987-89, N.J. Engr. of Yr. 1984), Am. Cons. Engrs. Coun.; mem. NSPE (life), N.J. Soc. Profl. Engrs. (Disting. Svc. award 1993), Nat. Acad. Forensic Engrs. (diplomate), Am. Acad. Environ. Engrs. (diplomate), Cons. Engrs. Coun. N.J. (pres. 1967-68, Engring. Excellence award 1979, 80, Grand award 1980), KC, Atlantic City Country Club. Roman Catholic. Home and Office: 921 Third St Ocean City NJ 08226-4019

SPEJEWSKI, EUGENE HENRY, physicist, educator; b. East Chicago, Ind., Sept. 15, 1938; s. Henry Louis and Carrie Jane (Fuss) S.; m. Norma Beverly Seekins, June 8, 1963; children: Maria Suzanne, Beverly Anne, Andrew John, Jeannette Michelle. B.S., U. Notre Dame, 1960; Ph.D., Ind. U., 1966. Research assoc. Ind. U., Bloomington, 1965-67; research assoc. Princeton U., 1967-69, instr., 1969-71; asst. prof. Oberlin Coll., Ohio, 1971-72; dir. UNISOR, Oak Ridge Assoc. Univs., 1972-85, mgr. SDS program, 1985-86, chmn. spl. projects div., 1986-89; v.p., dir. tng. and mgmt. systems div. Oak Ridge Inst. for Sci. and Edn., 1989-95, assoc. dir. for edn. and tng. group, 1995—; vis. prof. physics U. Tenn., Knoxville, 1981-84; mem., chmn. HHIRF Users Exec. Com., Oak Ridge Nat. Lab., 1982-84; referee U.S. Dept. Energy, various profl. jours. Co-editor: Future Directions in Studies of Nuclei Far from Stability, 1980; contbr. articles to profl. jours. Referee U.S. Soccer Fedn.; bd. dirs. Oak Ridge Community Playhouse, 1985-88. Mem. AAAS, Am. Phys. Soc., Am. Mgmt. Assn., Oak Ridge Sertoma Club (sec., treas., pres., chair bd. dirs.), Sigma Xi.

SPELLACY, WILLIAM NELSON, obstetrician, gynecologist, educator; b. St. Paul, May 10, 1934; s. Jack F. and Elmyra L. (Nelson) S.; m. Lynn Larsen; children: Kathleen Ann, Kimberly Joan, William Nelson. B.A., U. Minn., 1955, B.S., 1956, M.D., 1959. Diplomate: Am. Bd. Ob-Gyn, subsplty. cert. in maternal and fetal medicine. Intern Hennepin County Gen. Hosp., Mpls., 1959-60; resident U. Minn., Mpls., 1960-63; practice medicine specializing in ob-gyn. Mpls., 1963-67, Miami, Fla., 1967-73, Gainesville, Fla., 1973-79, Chgo., 1979-88; prof., head dept. U. Ill. Coll. Medicine, Chgo., 1979-88; prof., chmn. dept. U. So. Fla. Coll. Medicine, Tampa, 1988—; prof. dept. obstetrics and gynecology U. Miami, 1967-73; prof., chmn. dept. U. Fla., 1974-79. Contbr. articles to med. jours. Mem. AMA, Am. Gynecol. Soc., Am. Assn. Obstetricians and Gynecologists, Am. Gynecol. and Obstet. Soc., Soc. Gynecol. Investigation, Am. Coll. Obstetricians and Gynecologists, Endocrine Soc., Am. Fertility Soc., Assn. Profs. Gynecology and Obstetrics, Am. Diabetes Assn., Perinatal Research Soc., South Atlantic Soc. Obstetrics and Gynecology, Central Assn. Obstetrics and Gynecology, Soc. Perinatal Obstetricians, Ill. Med. Soc., Inst. of Medicine. Episcopalian. Club: Rotary. Home: 845 Seddon Cove Way Tampa FL 33602-5704 Office: U South Fla Coll Medicine Dept OBGYN 4 Columbia Dr Ste 514 Tampa FL 33606-3589

SPELLING, AARON, film and television producer, writer; b. Dallas, Apr. 22, 1923; s. David and Pearl (Wall) S.; m. Carole Gene Marer, Nov. 23, 1968; children: Victoria Davey, Randall Gene. Student, Sorbonne, U. Paris, France, 1945-46; B.A., So. Meth. U., 1950. Co-owner with Danny Thomas Thomas-Spelling Prodns., 1969-72; co-pres. Spelling-Goldberg Prodns., 1972-76; pres. Aaron Spelling Prodns., Inc., Los Angeles, 1977-86, chmn., chief exec. officer, 1986—. Writer numerous TV plays and movies; producer over 58 TV series including Dynasty, The Colbys, Love Boat, Hotel, Beverly Hills 90210, Melrose Place, 1992; also 130 TV movies for ABC, CBS, NBC; producer 10 theatrical films including Mr. Mom, Knight, Mother, Surrender, Cross My Heart, Soapdish. Bd. dirs. Am. Film Inst. Served with USAAF, 1942-45. Decorated Bronze Star medal, Purple Heart with oak leaf cluster; recipient Eugene O'Neill awards, 1947, 48, NAACP Image awards 1970, 71, 73, 75; named Man of Yr., Publicists Guild Am., 1971, Man of Yr. B'nai B'rith, Beverly Hills chpt., 1972, 85, Humanitarian of Yr., 1983, Man of Yr. Scopus Orgn., 1993. Mem. Writers Guild Am. (award 1962), Producers Guild Am., The Caucus of Producers, Writers and Directors, Hollywood Radio and TV Soc., Hollywood TV Acad. Arts and Scis., Acad. Motion Picture Arts and Scis. Democrat. Jewish. Clubs: Friars, Big Brothers of Am. Office: Spelling Television Inc 5700 Wilshire Blvd Ste 575 Los Angeles CA 90036*

SPELLMAN, GEORGE GENESER, SR., internist; b. Woodward, Iowa, Sept. 11, 1920; s. Martin Edward and Corinne (Geneser) S.; m. Mary Carolyn Dwight, Aug. 26, 1942; children: Carolyn Anne Spellman Rambow, George G. Jr., Mary Alice, Elizabeth Spellman-Chrisinger, John Martin Pile-Spellman, Loretta Suzanne Spellman Hoffman. B.S., St. Ambrose Coll., 1940; M.D., State U. Iowa, 1943. Diplomate Am. Bd. Internal Medicine. Intern Providence Hosp., Detroit, 1944; resident in internal medicine State U. Iowa, Iowa City, 1944-46; practice medicine specializing in internal medicine Mitchell, S.D., 1948-50, Sioux City, Iowa, 1950-91; instr. Coll. Medicine U. Iowa, 1975-77, clin. assoc. Coll. Medicine, 1977-95, ret., 1995; mem. Iowa Bd. Med. Examiners, 1989-95; instr. schs. nursing St. Vincent Hosp. and Luth. Hosp.; bd. dirs. St. Joseph Mercy Hosp. (merged with St. Vincent's Hosp. into Marian Health Ctr. 1977), 1977-80, 87-90, mem. staff, 1950-91, chief of staff, 1963; bd. dirs. St. Vincent's Hosp., 1965-77, also bd. dirs.; clin. assoc. prof. medicine State U. Iowa; bd. dirs. Mid-Step Svcs. Mentally Handicapped, Hospice of Siouxland, Marian Health Ctr., 1974-80, 89-91, also co-founder, 1st pres., chmn. dependency unit, founder renal dialysis unit, 1964, St. Joseph Mercy-St. Vincent's Hosps., 1977-89. Contbr. articles to med. jours. Ordained deacon Cath. Ch., 1988; vol. cons. Siouxland Community Health Ctr., 1993—. Capt. M.C., U.S. Army, 1946-48. Decorated Knight of St. Gregory (Vatican); named Internist of Yr., Iowa Soc. Internal Medicine, 1987; recipient Laureate award Iowa Chpt. ACP, 1991, Humanitarian award Siouxland Community, 1991. Fellow ACP; mem. AMA, Am. Acad. Scis., Iowa State Med. Soc., Woodbury Med. Soc., Am. Soc. Internal Medicine, Iowa Soc. Internal Medicine, Am. Thoracic Soc., Iowa Thoracic Soc., Am. Heart Assn., Iowa Heart Assn., Am. Geriatric Soc., Alpha Omega Alpha. Home: 3849 Jones St Sioux City IA 51104-1447 *I've loved the practice of medicine. The challenge presented by a difficult patient's illness, to diagnosing then witnessing the patient's response to your treatment are rewards experienced in no other profession. In medicine also, one is always thankful for the help of the divine healer.*

SPELLMAN, J. R., book publishing executive. Treas., office manager Steckley Hybrid Corn Co., Lincoln, Nebr., 1954-1964; pres. Cliffs Notes Inc., Lincoln, Nebr., 1964-94; pres. emeritus Clifs Notes Inc., Lincoln, Nebr., 1995—. Office: Cliffs Notes Inc PO Box 80728 Lincoln NE 68501-0728

SPELLMAN, JOHN DAVID, retired electrical engineer; b. Beaver Dam, Wis., July 27, 1935; s. John Joseph and Elsie Marguerite (Schultz) S.; B.S. in Elec. Engring., U. Wis., 1959; m. Kathleen Burns King, May 26, 1972; stepchildren: Kathleen Biegel, Karen Zarling, Kimberly Lyon. Jr. engr., part time, Malleable Iron Range Co., Beaver Dam, 1952-59; mem. tech. staff Rockwell Internat., Anaheim, Calif., 1961-85, lead engr., 1969-78, 81-85; mgr. ground instrumentation ops. unit Rockwell Internat., Vandenberg AFB, 1985-88, mgr. data ops., 1988-91; cons. Data Processing, Santa Maria, Calif., 1965. Served to 1st lt. Signal Corps, AUS, 1959-61. Recipient U.S. Army Accomodation award, 1961, USAF Outstanding Achievement award for Civilian Personnel. Mem. Assn. Computing Machinery, Air Force Assn., Res. Officers Assn. Clubs: Birnam Wood Golf (Montecito, Calif.); Santa Maria Country. Contbr. publs. on minutemen data systems, PCM Telemetry systems. Home: 642 Meadowbrook Dr Santa Maria CA 93455-3604 Office: PO Box 2669 Santa Maria CA 93457-2669

SPELLMAN, MITCHELL WRIGHT, surgeon, academic administrator; b. Alexandria, La., Dec. 1, 1919; s. Frank Jackson and Altonette Beulah (Mitchell) S.; m. Billie Rita Rhodes, June 27, 1947; children: Frank A., Michael A., Mitchell A., Maria A., Melva A., Mark A., Manly A., Rita A. A.B. magna cum laude, Dillard U., 1940, LL.D. (hon.), 1983; M.D., Howard U., 1944; Ph.D. in Surgery (Commonwealth Fund fellow), U. Minn., Mpls., 1955; D.Sc. (hon.), Georgetown U., 1974, U. Fla., 1977. Intern Cleve. Met. Gen. Hosp., 1944-45, asst. resident in surgery, 1945-46; asst. resident in surgery Howard U. and Freedmen's Hosp., Washington, 1946-47; chief resident in thoracic surgery Howard U. and Freedmen's Hosp., 1947-48, teaching asst. in physiology, 1948-49, chief resident in surgery, 1949-50, teaching asst. in surgery, 1950-51; asst. prof. surgery Howard U., 1954-56, assoc. prof., 1956-60, prof., 1960-68; dir. Howard surgery service at D.C. Gen. Hosp., 1961-68; fellow in surgery U. Minn., 1951-54; sr. resident in surgery U. Minn. Med. Sch. and Hosp., 1953-54; dean Charles R. Drew Postgrad. Med. Sch., Los Angeles, 1969-77; prof. surgery Charles R. Drew Postgrad. Med. Sch., 1969-78; asst. dean, prof. surgery Sch. Medicine, U. Calif. at Los Angeles, 1969-78; clin. prof. surgery Sch. Med., U. So. Calif., 1969-78; dean for med. svcs., prof. surgery Harvard Med. Sch., Boston, 1978-90, dean emeritus for med. svcs., 1990—, dean emeritus for internat. projects, 1990—, prof. surgery emeritus, 1990—; dir. internat. exch. programs Harvard Med. Internat., 1995—; exec. v.p. Harvard Med. Ctr., 1978-90; fellow Ctr. for Advanced Study in Behavioral Scis.; vis. prof. Stanford, 1975-76; bd. dirs. Kaiser Found. Hosps., Kaiser Found. Health Plan, 1971-89; mem. D.C. Bd. Examiners in Medicine and Osteopathy, 1955-68; mem. Nat. Rev. Com. for Regional Med. Programs, 1968-70; mem. spl. med. adv. group, nat. surg. cons. VA, 1969-73; mem. Commn. for Study Accreditation of Selected Health Ednl. Programs, 1970-72; chmn. adv. com. br. med. devices Nat. Heart and Lung Inst., 1972; Am. health del. to visit People's Republic of China, 1973; hon. dir. State Mut. Cos., 1990—; mem. com. mandatory retirement in higher edn. NAS/NRC, 1989-91. Mem. editorial bd.: Jour. Medicine and Philosophy, 1977-90; Contbr. articles on cardiovascular physiology and surgery, measurement of blood volume, and radiation biology to profl. jours. Past bd. dirs. Sun Valley Forum on Nat. Health; mem. ethics adv. bd. HEW, 1977-81; bd. dirs. Harvard Comty. Health Plan, 1979-84; former trustee Occidental Coll.; former bd. overseers com. to visit univ. health svc. Harvard, bd. overseers Harvard Comty. Health Plan, 1984-95; former regent Georgetown U.; former vis. com. U. Mass. Med. Ctr.; mem. bd. visitors UCLA Sch. Medicine; mem. corp. MIT; adv. bd. PEW Scholars Program in Biomed. Scis., 1984-86; bd. dirs. Med. Edn. for South African Blacks, 1985—. Markle scholar in med. scis., 1954-59; recipient Distinguished Alumnus award Dillard U., 1963; Distinguished Postgrad. Achievement award Howard U., 1974; Outstanding Achievement award U. Minn., 1979. Mem. AMA, AAAS, AAUP, ACS, Nat. Med. Assn. (William A. Sinkler Surgery award 1968), Soc. Univ. Surgeons, Am. Coll. Cardiology, Am. Surg. Assn., Inst. of Medicine of Nat. Acad. Scis. (chmn. program com. 1977-79, governing coun. 1978-80), Nat. Acad. Practice in Medicine, Am. Assn. Sovereign Mil. Order of Malta (Knights and Dames of Malta), MIT Corp. (life mem. emeritus), Cosmos Club. Roman Catholic. Office: 138 Harvard St Ste 300 Brookline MA 02146-6418

SPELLMAN, THOMAS JOSEPH, JR., lawyer; b. Glen Cove, N.Y., Nov. 11, 1938; s. Thomas J. and Martha H. (Erwin) S.; m. Margaret Mary Barth, June 23, 1962; children: Thomas Joseph, Kevin M., Maura N. BS, Fordham U., 1960, JD, 1965. Bar: N.Y. 1966, U.S. Dist. Ct. (so. and ea. dist.) N.Y. 1968, U.S. Ct. Appeals (2nd cir.) 1980, U.S. Supreme Ct. 1981. Staff atty. Allstate Ins. Co., N.Y.C., 1966-69; trial atty. Hartford Ins. Co., Hauppauge, N.Y., 1969-71; ptnr. Wheller & Spellman, Farmingville, N.Y., 1971-76, Devitt Spellman Barrett Callahan Leyden & Kenney LLP and predecessors, Smithtown, N.Y., 1976—; mem. grievance com. 10th Jud. Dist., Westbury, N.Y., 1984-92. Capt. USAR, 1960-68. Fellow Am. Bar Found., N.Y. Bar Found; mem. Suffolk County Bar Assn. (bd. dirs., sec.-treas., v.p. 1982, pres. 1992-93), N.Y. State Bar Assn. (Ho. of Dels. 1989—, nominating com. 1992-93, v.p. 1996—). Home: 8 Highwoods Ct Saint James NY 11780-9610 Office: Devitt Spellman et al 50 Route 111 Smithtown NY 11787-3700

SPELLMIRE, GEORGE W., lawyer; b. Oak Park, Ill., June 10, 1948. Attended, Brown U.; BA, Ohio State U., 1970; JD, De Paul U., 1974. Bar: Ill. 1974, U.S. Dist. Ct. (no. dist.) Ill. 1974, U.S. Tax Ct. 1984, U.S. Ct. Appeals (7th cir.) 1984, U.S. Supreme Ct. 1994. Ptnr. Hinshaw & Culbertson, Chgo. Author: Attorney Malpractice: Prevention and Defense, 1988; co-author: Accountants' Legal Liability Guide, 1990, Illinois Handbook on Legal Malpractice, 1982, Associates Primer for the Prevention of Malpractice, 1987. Mem. ABA, Am. Coll. Trial Lawyers, Soc. Trial Lawyers, Fed. Trial Bar, Internat. Assn. Def. Counsel (legal malpractice com., def. counsel practice mgmt. com.), Ill. State Bar Assn., Chgo. Bar Assn., Trial Lawyers Club Chgo. Office: Hinshaw & Culbertson 222 N La Salle St Ste 300 Chicago IL 60601-1005

SPELTS, RICHARD JOHN, lawyer; b. Yuma, Colo., July 29, 1939; s. Richard Clark and Barbara Eve (Pletcher) S.; children: Melinda, Meghan, Richard John Jr.; m. Gayle Merves, Nov. 14, 1992. BS cum laude, U. Colo., 1961, JD, 1964. Bar: Colo. 1964, U.S. Dist. Ct. Colo. 1964, U.S. Supreme Ct. 1968, U.S. Ct. Appeals (10th cir.) 1970, U.S. Dist. Ct. (ea. dist.) Mich. 1986. With Ford Motor Internat., Cologne, Germany, 1964-65; legis. counsel to U.S. Senator, 89th and 90th Congresses, 1967-68; minority counsel U.S. Senate Subcom., 90th and 91st Congresses, 1968-70; asst. U.S. atty., 1st asst. U.S. atty. Fed. Dist. of Colo., 1970-77; pvt. practice Denver, 1977-89; risk mgr. sheriff's dept. Jefferson County, Golden, Colo., 1990-91; owner Video Prodn. for Lawyers, 1991—. Selected for Leadership Denver, 1977; recipient cert. for outstanding contbns. in drug law enforcement U.S. Drug Enforcement Adminstrn., 1977, spl. commendation for criminal prosecution U.S. Dept. Justice, 1973, spl. commendation for civil prosecution U.S. Dept. Justice, 1976. Mem. Fed. Bar Assn. (chmn. govt. torts seminar 1980), Colo. Bar Assn. (bd. govs. 1976-78), Denver Bar Assn., Colo. Trial Lawyers Assn., Denver Law Club, Order of Coif. Republican. Methodist. Home and Office: 6697 W Hinsdale Ave Littleton CO 80123-4511

SPENCE, A. MICHAEL, economics educator, academic administrator; b. Montclair, N.J., 1943; m. Ann Spence. BA summa cum laude, Princeton U., 1966; MA, Oxford U., 1968; PhD in Econs., Harvard U., 1972. Instr. Harvard U., Cambridge, Mass., 1971-72, prof. econs., 1976-90, prof. bus. adminstrn., 1979-90, chmn. econ. dept., George Gund prof. of econ. and bus. adminstrn., 1983-90, dean faculty arts and scis., 1984-90; assoc. prof. econs. Stanford (Calif.) U., 1973-75, Philip H. Knight prof. econs. and mgmt., 1990—, dean Grad. Sch. Bus., 1990—; bd. dirs. BankAm. Corp., Sun Microsystems, Gen. Mills Inc., VeriFone, Inc., Bay Area Coun.; chmn. Nat. Rsch. Coun. on Sci., Tech. and Econ. Policy; mem. econs. adv. panel, NSF, 1977-79. Author: Market Signaling: Information Transfer in Hiring and Related Screening Processes, 1974; (with R.E. Caves and M.E. Porter) Competition in the Open Economy, 1980; mem. editorial bd. various jours. including Bell Jour. Econs., Jour. Econ. Theory, Pub. Policy. Rhodes scholar, 1966-68; recipient Galbraith Prize for Teaching Excellence, 1978, John Bates Clark Medal, Am. Econ. Assn., 1981. Office: Stanford U Grad Sch Bus Stanford CA 94305

SPENCE, ANDREW, artist, painter; b. Bryn Mawr, Pa., Oct. 4, 1947; s. Thomas and Elizabeth Spence; m. Mary Stewart Stoll, June 24, 1977. BFA, Temple U., 1969; MFA, U. Calif., Santa Barbara, 1971. One-man shows include TransAvant Garde Gallery, Austin, Tex., 1989, Barbara Krakow Gallery, Boston, 1989, Barbara Toll Fine Arts, N.Y.C., 1982-83, 85, 87-88, 90, Compass Rose Gallery, Chgo., 1990, James Corcoran Gallery, L.A., 1990, Max. Protetch Gallery, N.Y.C., 1992-93, Barbara Scott Gallery, Miami, 1993, 96, Worcester (Mass.) Art Mus., 1991; exhibited in group shows including Corcoran Gallery of Art, Washington, 1987, Hirshhorn

Mus. and Sculpture Garden, Smithsonian Instn., Washington, 1989, Whitney Mus. Am. Art, N.Y., 1989, 91-92, Met. Mus. Art, N.Y.C., 1993; represented in permanent collections including Balt. Mus. Art, Cleve. Mus. Art, Cin. Art Mus., Hirshhorn Mus. and Sculpture Garden, Laguna Gloria Art Mus., Met. Mus. Art, N.Y.C., San Diego Mus. Contemporary Art, Walker Art Ctr., Whitney Mus. Am. Art, N.Y.C. Painting grantee Nat. Endowment for Arts, 1987; Guggenheim fellow, 1994.

SPENCE, BARBARA E., publishing company executive; b. Bryn Mawr, Pa., July 8, 1921; d. Geoffrey Strange and Mary (Harrington) Earnshaw; m. Kenneth M. Spence Jr., June 29, 1944; children: Kenneth M. III, Christopher E., Hilary B. Grad. high sch. Movie, radio editor Parade Mag., N.Y.C., 1941-45; with Merchandising Group, N.Y.C., 1946-47; exec. dir. Greenfield Hill Congl. Ch., Fairfield, Conn., 1958-74, dir. religious edn., 1968-74; assoc. Ten Eyck-Emerich Antiques, 1974-76; personnel dir. William Morrow & Co., Inc., N.Y.C., 1976-91; ret., 1991. Chmn. pub. relations, bd. dirs. ARC, 1951-56, Family Service Soc., Fairfield, 1956-57, 61-63; chmn. pub. relations Citizens for Eisenhower, 1952, Fairfield Teens Players, 1968-71; bd. dirs. Fairfield Teens, Inc., 1965-70, Planned Parenthood of Greater Bridgeport, 1969-75, chmn. pub. affairs, 1971-72, chmn. personnel, 1972-73, chpt. vice chmn., 1973-75; pres. steering com. Am. Playwrights Festival Theatre, Inc., Fairfield, 1969-70, v.p., bd. dirs., 1971—; bd. govs. Unquowa Sch., Fairfield, 1963-69; bd. dirs. Fairfield U. Playhouse, 1971-73, Downtown Cabaret Theatre, Bridgeport, 1975-76. Mem. AAP (compensation survey com.), Fairfield Women's Exch. (bd. dirs. 1993). Home: 101 Twin Brook Ln Fairfield CT 06430-2834

SPENCE, CLARK CHRISTIAN, history educator; b. Great Falls, Mont., May 25, 1923; s. Christian Edward and Lela (Killian) S.; m. Mary Lee Nance, Sept. 12, 1953; children: Thomas Christian, Ann Leslie. B.A., U. Colo., 1948, M.A., 1951; Ph.D, U. Minn., 1955. Instr. Carleton Coll., Northfield, Minn., 1954-55; instr., then assoc. prof. Pa. State U., 1955-60; vis. lectr. U. Calif.-Berkeley, 1960-61; mem. faculty U. Ill., Champaign, 1961—; prof. history U. Ill., 1964-90, prof. emeritus, 1990—, chmn. dept., 1967-70, assoc. mem. Ctr. for Advanced Study, 1975; vis. lectr. Yale, summer 1964; vis. prof. U. Colo., summer 1967; disting. vis. prof. Ariz. State U., spring 1988. Author: British Investment and the American Mining Frontier, 1958, God Speed the Plow: The Coming of Steam Cultivation to Great Britain, 1960, Sinews of American Capitalism: An Economic History, 1964, The American West, 1966, Mining Engineers in the American West, 1970, Territorial Politics and Government in Montana, 1864-89, 1975, Montana: A Bicentennial History, 1978, The Rainmakers: American Pluviculture to World War II, 1980, The Salvation Army Farm Colonies, 1985, The Conrey Placer Mining Company, 1989. Served with USAAF, 1943-46. Fulbright fellow Eng., 1953-54; Ford Found. fellow, 1963-64; Guggenheim fellow, 1970-71; recipient ann. book award Agrl. History Soc., 1959. Mem. Western History Assn. (pres. 1969-70), Mining Hist. Assn. (pres. 1990-91), Phi Beta Kappa, Phi Alpha Theta. Home: 1107 Foley St Champaign IL 61820-6326

SPENCE, DONALD POND, psychologist, psychoanalyst; b. N.Y.C., Feb. 8, 1926; s. Ralph Beckett and Rita (Pond) S.; m. Mary Newbold Cross, June 2, 1951; children: Keith, Sarah, Laura, Katherine. AB, Harvard U., 1949; PhD, Columbia U., 1955. Lic. psychologist, N.Y., N.J. From rsch. asst. to prof. psychology NYU, 1954-74; prof. psychiatry Robert Wood Johnson Med. Sch., Piscataway, N.J., 1974-95; ret., 1995; vis. prof. psychology Stanford (Calif.) U., 1971-72, Princeton (N.J.) U., 1975—, Louvain-la-Neuve, Belgium, 1980, William Alanson White Inst., N.Y.C., 1992; mem. personality and cognition rsch. rev. com. NIMH, 1969-73. Author: Narrative Truth and Historical Truth, 1982, The Freudian Metaphor, 1987, The Rhetorical Voice of Psychoanalysis, 1994; mem. editl. bd. Psychoanalysis and Contemporary Thought, Psychol. Inquiry, Theory and Psychology; contbr. articles to profl. jours. With U.S. Army, 1944-46, ETO. Recipient rsch. scientist award NIMH, 1968-74. Mem. APA (pres. theoretical and philos. divsn. 1992-93), Am. Psychoanalytic Assn., N.Y. Acad. Sci., Sigma Xi. Democrat. Home: 9 Haslet Ave Princeton NJ 08540-4913

SPENCE, EDWARD LEE, publisher, marine archeologist; b. Munich, Germany, Nov. 6, 1947; s. Judson Cauthen and Mary Virginia (Truett) S.; m. Mary Tabb Gildea, Sept. 11, 1979 (div. Feb. 1981); 1 child, Matthew Lee. BA in Marine Archeology, U. S.C., 1967, postgrad., 1977; D of Marine Histories, Coll. of Marine Arts, 1972; PhD (hon.), Sea Rsch. Soc., 1976, Colombian Rsch. Inst., 1993. Pres. Shipwreck Cons., Sullivan's Islands, S.C., 1976-94; marine archeology cons. Coll. Charleston, S.C., 1983-84; underwater archeologist Shipwrecks Inc., Munhall, Pa., 1985-87; archeol. dir. Ocean Enterprises, Ltd., Nassau, The Bahamas, 1986-87; underwater archeologist Freedom Marine Ltd., Vancouver, B.C., Can., 1988-89; pub., sr. editor Shipwreck Press Inc., Sullivan's Island, 1988-91; chief underwater archeology Old Providence Island, Colombia, 1992-94; contbg. editor America's Treasure Search, Yucaipa, Calif., 1994; pub., sr. editor Narwhal Press Inc., Miami, Fla., 1994—; curator Mus. Sunken Treasure, Cape Canaveral, Fla., 1980; mem. adv. bd. Contemporary U., U. S.C., Columbia, 1971; cons. Seahawk Deep Ocean Tech., Tampa, Fla., 1991—. Author: Shipwrecks of South Carolina and Georgia 1521-1865, 1985, Shipwrecks of the Civil War, 1994, Romance on the Confederate Coast, 1994, Treasures of the Confederate Coast: The Real Rhett Butler and Other Revelations, 1995, Shipwrecks, Pirates & Privateers, 1995. Co-founder Hot Line, Charleston, 1971; mem. maritime subcom. S.C. Bi-Centennial Commn., Charleston, 1975-76; co-founder S.C. Underwater Archeol. Rsch. Coun., 1971. Grantee S.C. Com. for Humanities, 1983-84, NEH, 1983-84; Nat. Honors scholar U. Miami, 1966. Mem. Sea Rsch. Soc. (pres., pres. emeritus 1970—), Intertel, French Honor Soc. (alumnus), Mensa, Order of De Molay (alumnus, chaplain, historian), Tau Kappa Epsilon (alumnus), Mu Alpha Theta (alumnus). Republican. Avocations: sailing, photography, fishing, hunting, numismatics. Home: 1750 I'on Ave Sullivan's Island SC 29482 Office: Narwhal Press Inc 1629 Meeting St Charleston SC 29405-9408

SPENCE, FLOYD DAVIDSON, congressman; b. Columbia, S.C., Apr. 9, 1928; s. James Wilson and Addie (Lucas) S.; m. Deborah Williams, July 3, 1988; children from previous marriage: David, Zack, Benjamin, Caldwell. A.B., U. S.C., 1952, J.D., 1956. Bar: S.C. 1956. Former partner firm Callison and Spence, West Columbia, S.C.; mem. S.C. Ho. Reps., 1956-62; mem. S.C. Senate, 1966-70, minority leader, 1966-70, chmn. joint com. internal security, 1967-70; mem. 92nd-103rd Congresses from 2nd S.C. dist., Washington, D.C., 1971—; chmn. nat. security com. 104th Congress, mem. subcom. mil. procurement; ranking minority mem. Armed Svcs. com., 1992-94; mem. Ho. of Reps. com. on coms. 103d Congress; mem. Rep. policy com. 104th Congress; mem. Vietnam Era Vets in Congress. Editor S.C. Law Quarterly. Past chmn. Indian Waters Coun. S.C. Boy Scouts Am., 1965-66, exec. bd., 1963—; chmn. Lexington County Mental Health Assn., 1959; former mem. bd. visitors U.S. Naval Acad. Served as capt. USNR, ret. Recipient Watchdog of the Treasury award, Order of the Palmetto award. Mem. ABA, U.S. Supreme Ct. Bar Assn., Lexington County Bar Assn., Am. Legion, VFW, Res. Officers Assn., Navy League, Kappa Alpha Order, Phi Alpha Delta (former chief justice), Kappa Sigma Kappa, Omicron Delta Kappa. Lutheran. Office: US Ho Reps 2405 Rayburn House Office Bldg Washington DC 20515-4002*

SPENCE, FRANCIS JOHN, archbishop; b. Perth, Ont., Can., June 3, 1926; s. William John and Rose Anna (Jordan) S. BA, St. Michael's Coll., Toronto, 1946; postgrad., St. Augustine's Sem., Toronto, 1946-50; JCD, St. Thomas U., Rome, 1955. Ordained to priest Roman Cath. Ch., 1950. Consecrated bishop, 1967; diocesan sec. Kingston, Ont., 1950-52; parish asst., 1955-61; mem. Marriage Tribunal, 1961-66; diocesan dir. hosp. and charities, 1961-66; pastor Sacred Heart Ch., Marmora, Ont., 1966-67; aux. bishop Mil. Vicar Canadian Forces, 1967-70; bishop of Charlottetown P.E.I., 1970-82; archbishop of Kingston Ont., 1982—; mil. vicar of Can., 1982-88. Office: Catholic Diocesan Centre, 390 Palace Rd, Kingston, ON Canada K7L 4T3

SPENCE, GERALD LEONARD, lawyer, writer; b. Laramie, Wyo., Jan. 8, 1929; s. Gerald M. and Esther Sophie (Pfleeger) S.; m. Anna Wilson, June 20, 1947; children: Kip, Kerry, Kent, Katy; m. LaNelle Hampton Peterson, Nov. 18, 1969. BSL, U. Wyo., 1949, LLB, 1952, LLD (hon.), 1990. Bar: Wyo. 1952, U.S. Ct. Claims 1952, U.S. Supreme Ct. 1982. Sole practice Riverton, Wyo., 1952-54; county and pros. atty. Fremont County, Wyo., 1954-62; ptnr. various law firms, Riverton and Casper, Wyo., 1962-78; sr. ptnr. Spence, Moriarity & Schuster, Jackson, Wyo., 1978—; lectr. legal orgns. and law schs. Author: (with others) Gunning for Justice, 1982, Of Murder and Madness, 1983, Trial by Fire, 1986, With Justice for None, 1989, From Freedom to Slavery, 1993, How To Argue and Win Every Time, 1995. Mem. ABA, Wyo. Bar Assn., Wyo. Trial Lawyers Assn., Assn. Trial Lawyers Am., Nat. Assn. Criminal Def. Lawyers. Office: Spence Moriarity & Schuster PO Box 548 Jackson WY 83001-0548

SPENCE, GLEN OSCAR, clergyman; b. Willow Springs, Mo., Jan. 20, 1927; s. John Oscar and Emma Adelia (Kentch) S.; m. Margaret Carolyn Hunter, Sept. 10, 1948; children: Rodney Glen, Randall Eugene. B.S. in Agr, U. Mo., 1950; B.A. in Bible, Oakland City (Ind.) Coll., 1957, D.Div. (hon.), 1982. Tchr. agr. Mountain View, Mo., 1950-55; instr. biology Oakland City Coll., 1955-57; ordained to ministry Gen. Bapt. Ch., 1954; pastor chs. in Evansville, Ind., 1958-65, 73-76; dir. denominational affairs Oakland City Coll., 1965-72; exec. dir. Gen. Assn. Gen. Bapts., Poplar Bluff, Mo., 1977-92; moderator Gen. Assn. Gen. Bapts., 1961, pres. gen. bd., 1963-64. Served with USNR, 1945-46. Mem. Kiwanis (lt. gov. Mo.-Ark. dist. divsn. 15 1992-93, chmn. human and spiritual values com. Mo.-Ark. dist. 1993-94).

SPENCE, JAMES ROBERT, JR., television sports executive; b. Bronxville, N.Y., Dec. 20, 1936; s. James Robert and Mary Jeffery (Grant) S.; m. Betsy Jo Viener, June 16, 1992. B.A., Dartmouth Coll., 1958. Prodn. asst. ABC Sports, Inc. (known as Sports Programs, Inc. through 1966), N.Y.C., 1960-63; asst. to exec. producer ABC's Wide World of Sports, 1963-66, coordinating producer, 1966-70; v.p. program planning ABC Sports, Inc., 1970-78, sr. v.p., 1978-86; pres. Sports Television Internat. Inc., N.Y.C., 1986—. Author: Up Close and Personal - The Inside Story of Network Television Sports, 1988. Served with U.S. Army, 1958-60. Club: Westchester Country (Rye, N.Y.). Office: Sports TV Internat Inc 545 Madison Ave New York NY 10022-4219

SPENCE, JANET BLAKE CONLEY (MRS. ALEXANDER PYOTT SPENCE), civic worker; b. Upper Montclair, N.J., Aug. 17, 1915; d. Walter Abbott and Ethel Maud (Blake) Conley; m. Alexander Pyott Spence, June 10, 1939; children: Janet Blake Spence Kerr, Robert Moray, Richard Taylor. Student, Vassar Coll., 1933-35; cert., Katharine Gibbs Sch., 1936. formerly active Jr. League, Neighborhood House, ARC, Girl Scouts U.S.A.; active various community drives; chmn. Darien (Conn.) Assembly, 1955-56; sec., chmn. Wilton Jr. Assembly, 1961-63; subscription chmn. Candlelight Concerts Wilton, Conn., 1963-65; rec. sec. Pub. Health Nursing Assn. Wilton Bd., 1964-67; corr., rec. sec. Royle Sch. Bd., Darien, 1952-55; fund raiser Vassar Class of 1937; mem. Washington Valley Community Assn.; mem. N.J. Symphony Orch. League, treas. Morris County br. 1978-83, corr. sec. 1982-83, pres. 1985-89, acting pres. 1989—, state coun. mem. 1985-89, acting pres. Morris br. 1989-90; docent Macculloch Hall Historica Mus., Morristown, N.J., 1992—. Mem. Vassar Alumni Assn., Dobbs Alumni Assn., Jersey Hills Vassar Club (ann. fund raiser), Wilton Garden Club (life), Washington Valley Cmty. Assn. (life corr. sec. 1977-82, pres. 1982-84, v.p. 1984-85, co-pres. 1985-86, chmn. membership com. 1987-89, mem. archives com. 1988—, treas. 1990—), Washington Valley Home Econs. Club. Congregationalist. Home: 168 Washington Valley Rd Morristown NJ 07960-3333

SPENCE, JONATHAN DERMOT, historian, educator; b. Surrey, Eng., Aug. 11, 1936; came to U.S., 1959; s. Dermot Gordon Chesson and Muriel (Crailsham); m. Helen Alexander, Sept. 15, 1962 (div. 1993); children: Colin Chesson, Ian Alexander; m. Chin Annping, Aug. 12, 1993. B.A., Cambridge (Eng.) U., 1959; Ph.D., Yale U., 1965; L.H.D. (hon.), Knox Coll., 1984, U. New Haven, 1989; DLitt. (hon.), Wheeling Coll., 1985, Chinese U. Hong Kong, 1996, Gettysburg Coll., 1996. Asst. prof. history Yale U., New Haven, 1966-71; prof. Yale U., 1971—, chmn. dept. history, dir. div. humanities.; Wiles lectr. Queens's U., Belfast, 1985; Gauss lectr. Princeton U., 1987; vis. prof. Peking U., 1987; chmn. Council on East Asian Studies; bd. govs. Yale U. Press, 1988—; hon. prof. Nanjing U., 1993. Author: Ts'Ao Yin and the K'Ang-Hsi Emperor, 1966, To Change China, 1969, Emperor of China, 1974, The Death of Woman Wang, 1978, The Gate of Heavenly Peace, 1981, The Memory Palace of Matteo Ricci, 1984, The Question of Hu, 1988, The Search for Modern China, 1990, Chinese Roundabout, 1992, God's Chinese Son, 1996; editor: Ch'ing-Shih We'T'I, 1965-73, (with others) From Ming to Ch'ing, 1979; mem. editorial bd. Am. Hist. Rev., 1990-93, Yale Jour. Criticism, 1989, Yale Rev., 1991, China Quar., 1992. Served with Brit. Army, 1954-56. Recipient John Adison Porter prize, 1965, Christopher award, 1975, Devane teaching medal, 1978, L.A. Times book award, 1982, Vursell prize Am. Acad. and Inst. Arts and Letters, 1983, Comisso prize (Italy), 1987, Gelber prize (Can.), 1990; named to Coun. of Scholars, Libr. of Congress, 1988—; Yale fellow in East Asian Studies, 1962-65, 68-70, Guggenheim fellow, 1979-80, John D. and Catherine T. MacArthur Found. fellow, 1988-93. Mem. Am. Acad. Arts and Scis., Am. Philos. Soc., Assn. Asian Studies. Home: 691 Forest Rd New Haven CT 06515-2520 Office: Yale U History Dept PO Box 208324 New Haven CT 06520

SPENCE, PAUL HERBERT, librarian; b. Geraldine, Ala., Dec. 25, 1923; s. John Clardy and Leila (Carrell) S.; m. Ruth Schmidt, May 9, 1954; children—John Carrell, Peter Schmidt, Robert McCollough. A.B., Emory U., 1948, M.A., 1956; Ph.D., U. Ill., 1969. Asst. reference librarian Emory U., Atlanta, 1950-53; periodical reference librarian Air U., Maxwell AFB, 1953-56; dir. library Air Force Inst. of Tech., Wright-Patterson AFB, Ohio, 1957-58; asst. dir. social studies U. Notre Dame, South Bend, Ind., 1959-60, U. Nebr., Lincoln, 1960-63; history and polit. sci. librarian U. Ill., Urbana, 1963-66; assoc. dir. libraries U. Ga., Athens, 1966-70; dir. libraries U. Ala., Birmingham, 1970-84, collection devel. librarian, 1985-89, prof. emeritus, 1989—, libr. cons., 1990—. Bd. dirs. Southeastern Library Network, Atlanta, 1973-75. Served with U.S. Army, 1943-46, ETO. Mem. ALA (council mem. 1976-78), Ala. Library Assn. (treas. 1975-76), Southeastern Library Assn. (pres. 1980-82). Democrat. Presbyterian. Home: 614 Warwick Rd Birmingham AL 35209-4426 Office: U Ala at Birmingham 172 Sterne Libr Birmingham AL 35294

SPENCE, RICHARD DEE, paper products company executive, former railroad executive; b. Tucumcari, N.Mex., Apr. 7, 1925; s. Andrew Doke and Myrtle Hannah (Roach) S.; m. Mary Ames Kellogg, July 24, 1976; children: Mary B., Ames T., Richard T.; children from previous marriage: Diana, Richard N. BS, UCLA, 1949; grad., Transp. Mgmt. Program, Stanford U., 1956, Sr. Execs. Program, MIT, 1962. With So. Pacific Transp. Co., San Francisco, 1946-75, asst. v.p. ops., 1967-69, v.p. ops., 1969-75; pres., chief oper. officer Consol. Rail Corp., Phila., 1975-78; pres. L&N R.R. Co., Louisville, 1978-80; exec. v.p. ops. Family Lines Rail System, 1980-84; ptnr. Skippingdale Paper Products, Eng., 1985—. With USN, 1943-46. Mem. Ponte Vedra Club, Tournament Players Club, Sawgrass Club, Bohemian Club, Golf House Club of Elie (Scotland), Plantation Club at Ponte Vedra, Phi Kappa Sigma. Republican. Episcopalian. Home and Office: 339 Ponte Vedra Blvd Ponte Vedra Beach FL 32082-1813

SPENCE, ROBERT DEAN, physics educator; b. Bergen, N.Y., Sept. 12, 1917; s. La Vergne Robert and Jennie (Waterman) S.; m. Helen Holbrook, June 14, 1942; children—John, Elizabeth, Janet, Barbara. B.S., Cornell U., 1939; M.S., Mich. State U., 1942; Ph.D., Yale, 1948. Asst. prof. physics Mich. State U., East Lansing, 1947-49, assoc. prof., 1949-52, prof., 1952-86, emeritus, 1986—; vis. prof. U. Bristol, Eng., 1955-56, Technische Hogesch., Eindhoven, Netherlands, 1964, Rijks universiteit, Leiden, Netherlands, 1970-71. Recipient Distinguished Faculty award Mich. State U., 1963; Guggenheim fellow, 1955-56. Mem. Nat. Soc. Profl. Engrs., Sigma Xi, Phi Kappa Phi. Research and publs. on math. physics, chem. physics, magnetism. Home: 1849 Ann St East Lansing MI 48823-3707

SPENCE, ROBERT LEROY, publishing executive; b. Carlisle, Pa., Sept. 13, 1931; s. Leroy Oliver and Esther Helen (Lau) S.; m. Barbara Amelia Hunter, Sept. 1, 1954 (div. Sept. 1978); children—Robert Roy, Bonnie Leigh; m. 2d, Maryanne Elizabeth Yacono, Jan. 10, 1979. B.A., Dickinson Coll., 1953; postgrad, Temple U., 1955-57, Rutgers U., 1956, 59-60, U. Pa., 1960. Cert. tchr., N.J. Chmn. dept. math. Haddon Heights High Sch., N.J., 1954-62; sr. editor Silver Burdett Co., Morristown, N.J., 1962-64; editor-in-chief Harcourt Brace Jovanovich, Inc., N.Y.C., 1964-81; v.p., pub. Harper & Row Publishers, Inc., N.Y.C., 1981-85, Scribner Ednl. Pubs. div. Macmillan, Inc., N.Y.C., 1985; pres. R&M Spence, Inc., Sparta, N.J., 1985—. Author textbook series: Growth in Mathematics, 1978, Excel in Mathematics, 1989-90, Mathematics Plus: Multicultural Projects, 1993. Mem. Assn. Am. Pubs. (mem. exec. com. 1981-84), Nat. Council Tchrs. Math., Internat. Reading Assn., Am. Numismatic Assn. Avocations: rare coin collecting; coin newsletter author and publisher; artist; writer. Home and Office: 37 Heather Ln Sparta NJ 07871-3538

SPENCE, SANDRA, professional administrator; b. McKeesport, Pa., Mar. 25, 1941; d. Cedric Leroy and Suzanne (Haudenshield) S. BA, Allegheny Coll., 1963; MA, Rutgers U., 1964. With Pa. State Govt., Harrisburg, 1964-68, Appalachian Regional Commn., Washington, 1968-75; legis. rep. Nat. Assn. Counties, Washington, 1975-77; fed. rep. Calif. Dept. Transp., Washington, 1977-78; dir. congl. affairs Amtrak, Washington, 1978-81, corp. sec., 1981-83; dir. computer svcs. Nat. R.R. Passenger Corp., Washington, 1983-84; co-owner Parkhurst-Spence Inc., 1985; owner The Spence Group, 1986-90; v.p. Bostrom Corp., Washington, 1990-92; exec. dir. Soc. Glass and Ceramic Decorators, 1992—; chmn. legis. com. Womens Transp. Seminar, 1977-79, dir., 1982-83, v.p., 1983-84, chmn. edn. com., 1982-83; com. on edn. and tng. Transp. Rsch. Bd., 1982-85. Contbr. articles to profl. jours. Commr., sec. D.C. Commn. for Women, 1983-88; del. Ward III Dem. Com., 1982-90, 1st vice chmn., 1987-88. Fellow Eagleton Inst. Politics, 1963-64; recipient Achievement award Transp. Seminar, 1982, 83. Mem. Greater Washington Soc. Assn. Execs. (vice-chair law and legis. com. 1989-90, chmn. 1990-91, chmn. scholarship com. 1992-93, bd. dirs. 1993-96, Rising Star award 1989, Chmn.'s award for Govt. Rels. 1991), Am. Soc. Assn. Execs. (mgmt. cert. 1987), Phi Beta Kappa. Home: 3701 Appleton St NW Washington DC 20016-1807 Office: Soc Glass and Ceramic Decorators 1627 K St NW Ste 800 Washington DC 20006-1702

SPENCER, ALBERT FRANKLIN, physical education and education educator; b. Pitts., Dec. 31, 1943; s. Albert Clair and Ann Mary (Kielbas) S. BS in Edn., Slippery Rock (Pa.) State, Coll., 1966; MS, Clarion (Pa.) State Coll., 1981; PhD in LS, Fla. State U., Tallahassee, 1985, PhD in Phys. Edn., 1992. Phys. edn. tchr., libr., coach St. John's Indian Sch., Komatke, Ariz., 1976-79, Duncan (Ariz.) H.S., 1977-79; tchr. math. and sci. Army and Navy Acad., Carlsbad, Calif., 1979-80; phys. edn. tchr., libr., coach Baboquivari H.S., Sells, Ariz., 1980-81; asst. men's intercoll. basketball coach Fla. State U., Tallahassee, 1981-83; asst. prof. phys. edn., dir. audiovisual svcs. St. Leo (Fla.) Coll., 1983-86; asst. prof. Atlanta U., Emory U., Atlanta, 1986-87; assoc. prof. phys. edn./athletics, libr. dir., coach Ga. Mil. Coll., Milledgeville, 1987-90; asst. prof. edn. U. Nev., Las Vegas, 1991-94; asst. prof. phys. edn., dept. human performance/health scis. Rice U., Houston, 1994—; cons. ednl. tech. Atlanta Pub. Schs., 1986-87; profl. basketball scout Bertka Agy. and L.A. Lakers, 1985-91; deptl. dir. KMart, New Kensington, Pa., 1972-74; dir. athletics YMCA, Kittanning, Pa., 1969. Contbg. author: Twentieth-Century Young Adult Writers, 1994; contbr. articles and revs. to profl. jours. Fundraiser KC, Las Vegas; vol. coach for youth league St. Anthony Elem. Sch., San Antonio, Fla.; scoutmaster Boy Scouts Am., New Kensington. Mem. AAHPERD, ALA, Am. Libr. and Info. Sci. Educators, Fla. Assn. for Health, Phys. Edn., Recreation and Dance, Tex. Assn. for Health, Phys. Edn., Recreation and Dance, U.S. Phys. Edn. Assn., Tex. Faculty Assn., Beta Phi Mu, Omicron Delta Kappa. Roman Catholic. Avocations: writing, golf, basketball, hiking. Office: Rice U Dept Human Perf/Hlth Svcs PO Box 1892 Houston TX 77251

SPENCER, BRUCE DAVID, statistics educator. BS in Biometry, Cornell U., 1973; MS in Stats., Fla. State U., 1974; PhD in Stats., Yale U., 1979. Sr. staff officer, study dir. Com. on Nat. Stats., NAS, 1978-80; sampling statistician Nat. Opinion Rsch. Ctr., U. Chgo., 1982-85, dir. Methodology Rsch. Ctr., 1985-92, sr. rsch. statistician, 1992-94; asst. prof. stats. and edn. and social policy Northwestern U., Evanston, Ill., 1980-86, assoc. prof., 1986-92, prof., 1992—, chmn. dept. stats., 1988—; mem. NAS math. scis. assessment panel, 1991-93; mem. U.S. Steering Com., Third Internat. Math. and Sci. Study, 1991—. Author: Benefit-Cost Analysis of Data Used to Allocate Funds, 1980, Estimating Population and Income of Small Areas, 1980; contbr. articles to profl. jours. Recipient Palmer O. Johnson Meml. award Am. Ednl. Rsch. Assn., 1985; AT&T rsch. fellow, 1992-93. Fellow Am. Statis. Assn. (com. on energy stats. 1990-93, JES mgmt. com. 1989—); mem. Inst. Math. Stats., Royal Statis. Soc. Home: 1404 Asbury Ave Evanston IL 60201 Office: Northwestern U Dept Stats 2006 Sheridan Rd Evanston IL 60208

SPENCER, CAROL BROWN, association executive; b. Normal, Ill., Aug. 26, 1936; d. Fred William and Sorado (Gross) B.; m. James Calvin Spencer, Dec. 18, 1965 (div. July 1978); children: James Calvin Jr., Anne Elizabeth. BA in English, Calif. State U., Los Angeles, 1964, MA in Pub. Adminstrn., 1986. Cert. secondary edn. tchr., Calif. Tchr. English Seneca Vocat. High Sch., Buffalo, 1966-70; pub. info. officer City of Pasadena, Calif., 1979-90, City of Mountain View, Calif., 1990-93; exec. dir. Calif. Assn. for the Gifted, 1993—; owner PR to Go, 1994—. Sec., bd. dirs. Calif. Music Theatre, 1987-90; bd. dirs. Pasadena Beautiful Found., 1984-90, Pasadena Cultural Festival Found., 1983-86, Palo Alto-Stanford Heritage, 1990-93; mayoral appointee Strategic Planning Adv. Com., Pasadena, 1985-86. Mem. NOW, Pub. Rels. Soc. Am., Calif. Assn. Pub. Info. Ofcls. (exec. bd., Paul Clark Achievment award 1986, award for mktg. 1990), City/County Comms. and Mktg. Assn. (bd. dirs. 1988-90, Savvy award for mktg. 1990), Nat. Assn. for Gifted Children. Democrat. Episcopalian. Home: 426 Escuela Ave Apt 19 Mountain View CA 94040-2022

SPENCER, CAROL DIANE, consulting company executive; b. Pitts., Mar. 12, 1952; d. Louis John and Elinor Edwinna (Clark) Kacinko; m. Dirk Victor Spencer, May 12, 1993; children: Erick Jon Powell, Tiffani Dawn Showalter. AS in Computer Sci., C.C. Allegheny County, 1974; BSBA, U. Pitts., 1979. Data base adminstr. Beckwith Machinery, Murrysville, Pa., 1974-78; systems analyst Mode Inc., Irwin, Pa., 1978-80; supr. data base Tex. Instruments, Dallas, 1980-83, E-Systems Melpar, Falls Church, Va., 1983; dep. dir. Vanguard Techs., Fairfax, Va., 1983-85; mgr, data base Siecor, Hickory, N.C., 1985-86; sr. cons. Computer Task Group, Raleigh, N.C., 1986-88; prin. cons., mgr. Tex. Instruments, 1988-94; pres. Kacinko Consulting, Reston, Va., 1994—; speaker Computer Assocs., Atlanta, 1994. Mem. Digital Users Group, DB2 Users Group. Home and Office: 12608 Bridoon Ln Herndon VA 22071-2827

SPENCER, CONSTANCE MARILYN, secondary education educator; b. New York, Jan. 2, 1942; d. Edward Bennett and Blanche Lloyd (Miller) Asbury; m. Robert William Spencer, Dec. 30, 1966; children: Keane Thomas, Keith Lyle. BA, U. Calif., Santa Barbara, 1964; MA in English, U. West Fla., 1974. Cert. lang. devel. specialist, preliminary adminstr. Tchr. Valley Stream (N.Y.) N. H.S., Workman Jr. H.S., Pensacola, Fla., Imperial Beach (Calif.) Elem. Sch.; substitute tchr. South Bay Union Sch., Imperial Beach; mgr. Geni, Inc., Pasadena, Calif., Avon Products, Inc., Pasadena; tchr. Walnut (Calif.) H.S., 1985—; pres. Am. Computer Instrn. Inc., Upland, Calif.; grant writer Walnut Valley Unified Sch. Dist., 1986-94, mentor tchr., 1988-94; accreditation co-chair Walnut H.S., 1993-94. Mem., sec. Toastmistress, Ontario, Calif., 1977-86. Grantee Calif. Dept. Edn., 1987, Walnut Valley Unified Sch. Dist., 1988, Diamond Bar (Calif.) Rotary, 1994. Republican. Roman Catholic. Avocation: writing. Home: 2238 Coolcrest Way Upland CA 91784-1233 Office: Walnut HS 400 Pierre Rd Walnut CA 91789-2535

SPENCER, DALE A., medical products executive; b. 1945. BS in Engring., U. Maine, 1968; MBA, So. Ill. U., 1973. With Kuken Steel Co., Cin., 1973-75; sales and mktg. mgr. Baxter Travenol Labs., Mpls., 1975-80; with Scimed Life Systems Inc., Osseo, Minn., 1980—, pres., CEO, 1982, now chmn. and CEO, 1994; also, pres. (subsidiary) Scimed, Inc., Osseo, Minn. With USAF, 1968-73. Office: Scimed Life Systems Inc 1 Scimed Pl Osseo MN 55311-1565

SPENCER, DAVID JAMES, lawyer; b. Altadena, Calif., June 23, 1943; s. Dorcy James and Dorothy Estelle (Pingry) S.; m. Donna Rae Blair, Aug. 22, 1965; children: Daniel, Matthew. BA, Rocky Mountain Coll., 1965; JD, Yale U., 1968. Bar: Minn. 1968, U.S. Dist. Ct. Minn. 1968, U.S. Ct. Appeals (8th cir.) 1970. Mem. firm Briggs and Morgan, P.A., Mpls. and St. Paul, 1968—. Contbg. author 10 William Mitchell Law Rev., 1984; contbr.

articles to profl. jours. Trustee Rocky Mountain Coll., Billings, Mont., 1980—; bd. dirs. Reentry, Inc., 1993—, River Valley Arts Coun., 1996—; pres., bd. dirs. St. Croix Friends of Arts, Stillwater, Minn., 1981-84; bd. dirs. Valley Chamber Chorale, Stillwater, 1989-92; v.p. Minn. Jaycees, St. Paul, 1974; elder Presbyn. Ch. Recipient Silver Key St. Paul Jaycees, 1974; Disting. Svc. award Rocky Mountain Coll., 1981, Outstanding Svc. award, 1988, Disting. Achievement award, 1992. Fellow Am. Coll. Real Estate Lawyers; mem. ABA, Minn. Bar Assn., Hennepin County Bar Assn., Stillwater Country Club, Mpls. Athletic Club. Presbyterian. Avocations: trout fishing, golf, singing. Home: 9987 Arcola Ct N Stillwater MN 55082-9523 Office: Briggs & Morgan 2400 IDS Ctr 80 S 8th St Minneapolis MN 55402-2100

SPENCER, DAVID MILLS, library administrator; b. Eugene, Oreg., Dec. 7, 1950; s. Richard J. and Adelaide (Marsh) S. BA in English Lit., Lewis & Clark Coll., 1973; M in Urban and Regional Planning, U. Oreg., 1978; MLS, Cath. U. Am., 1988. Asst. planner Linn County Planning Dept., Albany, Oreg., 1979-80; from asst. planner to dir. Benton County Devel. Dept., Corvallis, Oreg., 1980-87; from reference libr. to br. libr. Nat. Air & Space Mus. Br. Libr. Smithsonian Instn. Librs., Washington, 1989—. Vestryman St. Thomas Episcopal Ch., Washington, 1993-95, jr. warden, 1995—. Mem. Spl. Libr. Assn., Nat. Trust for Hist. Preservation. Democrat.

SPENCER, DONALD CLAYTON, mathematician; b. Boulder, Colo., Apr. 25, 1912; s. Frank Robert and Edith (Clayton) S.; m. Mary Jo Halley (div.); children: Maredith (dec.), Marianne; m. Natalie Robertson (dec.); 1 child, Donald Clayton Jr. BA, U. Colo., 1934; BS, MIT, 1936; PhD, Cambridge (Eng.) U., 1939, ScD, 1963; ScD (hon.), Purdue U., 1971. Instr. MIT, Cambridge, 1939-42; assoc. prof. Stanford (Calif.) U., 1942-46, prof., 1946-50, 63-68; assoc. prof. Princeton (N.J.) U., 1950-53, prof., 1953-63, 68-78, Henry Burchard Fine prof. emeritus, 1978—. Co-author: (with A.C. Schaeffer, monograph) Coefficient Regions for Schlicht Functions, 1950, (with M. Schiffer) Functionals of Finite Riemann Surfaces, 1954, (with A. Kumpera) Lie Equations, vol. I: General Theory, 1972, (with H.K. Nickerson and N.E. Steenrod, textbook) Advanced Calculus, 1959. Recipient Bocher prize Am. Math. Soc., 1948, Nat. medal of sci. Pres. of U.S., 1989, George Norlin award U. Colo., 1990. Fellow Am. Acad. Arts and Scis.; mem. NAS. Home: 943 County Rd 204 Durango CO 81301-8547

SPENCER, DONALD SPURGEON, historian, academic administrator; b. Anderson, Ind., Jan. 29, 1945; s. Thomas E. and Josephine (Litz) S.; m. Pamela Sue Roberts, June 19, 1965; 1 child, Jennifer Wynne. BA, Ill. Coll., 1967; PhD, U. Va., 1973. Asst. prof. history Westminster Coll., Fulton, Mo., 1973-76, Ohio U., Athens, 1976-77; from asst., assoc. to full prof., assoc. dean, asst. provost U. Mont., Missoula, 1977-90; provost SUNY, Geneseo, 1990-93; pres. Western Ill. U., Macomb, 1994—. Author: Louis Kossuth and Young America, 1978, The Carter Implosion: Jimmy Carter and the Amateur Style of Diplomacy,1989; contbr. articles to jours. in field. With U.S. Army, 1968-71, Korea. Woodrow Wilson Found. fellow, 1968; Danforth Found. univ. teaching fellow, 1971. Mem. Phi Beta Kappa. Congregationalist. Home: 2001 Wigwam Hollow Rd Macomb IL 61455-9336 Office: W Ill Univ Office of the President Sherman Hall Macomb IL 61455

SPENCER, EDGAR WINSTON, geology educator; b. Monticello, Ark., May 27, 1931; s. Terrel Ford and Allie Belle (Shelton) S.; m. Elizabeth Penn Humphries, Nov. 26, 1958; children: Elizabeth Shawn, Kristen Shannon. Student, Vanderbilt U., 1949-50; B.S., Washington and Lee U., 1953; Ph.D., Columbia U., 1957. Lectr. Hunter Coll., 1954-57; mem. faculty Washington and Lee U., 1957—, prof. geology, head dept., 1962-95, Ruth Parmly prof.; pres. Rockbridge Area Conservation Coun., 1978-79, 95-96; NSF sci. faculty fellow, New Zealand and Australia; dir. grant for humanities and pub. policy on land use planning Va. Found., 1975; dir. grant Petroleum Rsch. Fund, 1981-82; leader field trip Ctrl. Appalachian Mts. Internat. Geol. Congress, 1989. Author: Basic Concepts of Physical Geology, 1962, Basic Concepts of Historical Geology, 1962, Geology: A Survey of Earth Science, 1965, Introduction to the Structure of the Earth, 1969, 3d edit., 1988, The Dynamics of the Earth, 1972, Physical Geology, 1983, Geologic Maps, 1993. Recipient Va. Outstanding Faculty award Va. Coun. of Higher Edn., 1990. Fellow Geol. Soc. Am., AAAS; mem. Am. Assn. Petroleum Geologists (dir. field seminar on fold and thrust belts 1987, 88-91), Am. Inst. Profl. Geologists, Am. Geophys. Union, Nat. Assn. Geology Tchrs., Yellowstone-Bighorn Rsch. Assn., Phi Beta Kappa (hon.), Sigma Xi. Home: PO Box 1055 Lexington VA 24450-1055

SPENCER, ELIZABETH, author; b. Carrollton, Miss., 1921; d. James Luther and Mary James (McCain) S.; m. John Arthur Blackwood Rusher, Sept. 29, 1956. BA, Belhaven Coll., 1942; MA, Vanderbilt U., 1943; LittD (hon.), Southwestern U. at Memphis, 1968; LLD (hon.), Concordia U. at Montreal, 1988; LittD (hon.), U. of the South, 1992. Instr. N.W. Miss. Jr. Coll., 1943-44, Ward-Belmont, Nashville, 1944-45; reporter The Nashville Tennessean, 1945-46; instr. U. Miss., Oxford, 1948-51, 52-53; vis. prof. Concordia U., Montreal, Que., Can., 1976-81, adj. prof., 1981-86; vis. prof. U. N.C., Chapel Hill, 1986-92. Author: Fire in the Morning, 1948, This Crooked Way, 1952, The Voice at the Back Door, 1956, The Light in the Piazza, 1960, Knights and Dragons, 1965, No Place for an Angel, 1967, Ship Island and Other Stories, 1968, The Snare, 1972, The Stories of Elizabeth Spencer, 1981, Marilee, 1981, The Salt Line, 1984, Jack of Diamonds and Other Stories, 1988, (play) For Lease or Sale, 1989, On the Gulf, 1991, The Night Travellers, 1991; contbr. short stories to mags. and anthologies. Recipient Women's Democratic Com. award, 1949, recognition award Nat. Inst. Arts and letters, 1952, Richard and Hinda Rosenthal Found. award Am. Acad. Arts and Letters, 1957; Guggenheim Found. fellow, 1953, 1st McGraw-Hill Fiction award, 1960, Henry Bellamann award for creative writing, 1968; Award of Merit medal for the short story Am. Acad. Arts and Letters, 1983, Salem award for lit., 1992, Dos Passos award for fiction, 1992; Kenyon Rev. fellow in fiction, 1957; Bryn Mawr Col. Donnelly fellow, 1962; Nat. Endowment for Arts grantee in lit., 1983, Sr. Arts Award grantee Nat. Endowment for Arts, 1988, N.C. Gov.'s award for lit., 1994. Mem. Am. Acad. Arts and Letters, Fellowship of So. Writers (charter; vice chancellor 1993—). Home: 402 Longleaf Dr Chapel Hill NC 27514-3042

SPENCER, FOSTER LEWIS, newspaper editor; b. Putnam, Conn., Dec. 18, 1932; s. Ralph Washburn and Helen (Thompson) S.; m. Dorothy Virginia Purda, Aug. 18, 1956; children: Faith Elizabeth, Beth Mary. B.A., U. Mass., 1960. News editor Palmer (Mass.) Jour.-Register, 1956-60; Sunday feature editor Springfield (Mass.) Republican, 1960-65; mng. editor Buffalo News, 1966—; chmn. N.Y. State adv. bd./UPI, 1980-86. Served with USAF, 1952-56, Korea. Recipient Spl. award AP, 1979. Mem. N.Y. AP Assn. (pres. Albany 1976-77), N.Y. State Soc. Newspaper Editors (pres. 1983). Democrat. Congregationalist. Home: 292 Summer St Buffalo NY 14222-2114 Office: Buffalo News 1 News Plaza Buffalo NY 14203-2994

SPENCER, FRANK COLE, medical educator; b. Haskell, Tex., 1925. MD, Vanderbilt U., 1947. Intern Johns Hopkins U., Balt., 1947-48, fellow in surgery, 1947-48, asst. resident in surgery, 1953-54; resident in surgery Johns Hopkins Sch. Medicine, Balt., 1954-55; surgeon, outpatient dept. Johns Hopkins Hosp., 1955; resident in surgery Wadsworth VA Ctr. Hosp., 1949-50; fellow cardiovascular surgery USPHS, Los Angeles, 1951; asst. prof. surgery Johns Hopkins U., 1955-59, assoc. prof., 1959-61; prof. surgery U. Ky.; now chmn. dept. surgery, George David Steward prof. surgery NYU. Served to lt. M.C., USN, 1951-53. John and Mary R. Markle scholar in med. sci. Johns Hopkins U., 1956. Office: NYU Sch of Medicine Dept of Surgery 550 1st Ave New York NY 10016-6481

SPENCER, FREDERICK GILMAN, newspaper editor in chief; b. Phila., Dec. 8, 1925; s. F. Gilman and Elizabeth (Hetherington) S.; m. Isabel Brannon, July 3, 1965; 1 child, Isabel; children by previous marriage: Amy, Elizabeth Blair, F. Gilman, Jonathan. Student pub. and pvt. schs. Copyboy Phila. Inquirer, 1947-49; photographer-reporter Chester (Pa.) Times, 1949, 1952-59; photographer, sports editor Mt. Holly (N.J.) Herald, 1949-52; mng. editor Main Line Times, Ardmore, Pa., 1959-63; asst. city editor Phila. Bull., 1963-64; editorial spokesman Sta. WCAU-TV, Phila., 1964-67; editor The Trentonian, Trenton, N.J., 1967-75, Phila. Daily News, 1975-84, N.Y. Daily News, N.Y.C., 1984-89; editor-in-chief Denver Post, 1989-93, columnist, 1993—. With USNR, 1943-46. Recipient Pulitzer prize for editorials, 1974. Mem. Am. Soc. Newspaper Editors, Sigma Delta Chi. Office: Denver Post 1560 Broadway Denver CO 80202-5133

SPENCER, GAYLE, middle school education educator; b. Charlotte, N.C., Aug. 14, 1947. BA in Health and Phys. Edn., U. S.C., 1969, MA in Health and Phys. Edn., 1973; postgrad., U. N.C., Charlotte, 1983, Coastal Carolina Coll. Tchr. Keenan Jr. High, Columbia, S.C., 1969, Saluda (S.C.) High, 1969-70, Hyatt Pk. Elem., Columbia, 1970-72; tchr. high sch. Providence Day Sch., Charlotte, 1973-84, tchr. elem. and mid. sch., 1975-84; tchr. Waccamaw Elem., Conway, S.C., 1984-85, Conway Elem., 1984-85, Homewood Elem., Conway, 1986-93, Horry Elem., Aynor, S.C., 1986-91, St. James Mid. Sch., Surfside, S.C., 1994—; instr. Francis Marion Coll., Florence, S.C., 1973-74, Coastal Carolina Coll., Conway, 1974-75; dir. Tchrs. Understand Fun and Fitness (TUFF); mem. S.C. Tchr. Forum Leadership Coun., 1992—; mem. Horry County Tchr. of Yr. Selection Com., 1992, 93, Horry County Tchr. Forum Steering Com., 1994—; coach various jr. high, high sch. and coll. athletic teams; presenter in field. Contbr. articles to profl. publs. Mem. Horry County Target 2000 Com., 1990, S.C. Health Frameworks Com., 1992-93; vol. ARC, Am. Heart Assn., Conway C. of C. Named Tchr. of Yr., Homewood Elem. Sch., 1991, 92, Horry County, 1992; scholar Sun News, 1990-91. Mem. NEA, S.C. Edn. Assn. (mem. delegate assembly 1993—), Horry County Edn. Assn. (sec. 1992-94, v.p. 1994-95, pres. 1995—), S.C Assn. Health, Phys. Edn., Recreation and Dance. Home: 36 Retreat Rd # D3 Pawleys Island SC 29585-6418

SPENCER, GEOFFREY F., church administrator; b. Teralba, NSW, Australia; came to U.S., 1966; m. Jill Marcia Godwin; children: Paul, Mark, Shelly. Grad., Newington Coll., NSW, Australia; BA, Sydney (Australia) U.; MA in Am. History, U. Mo., Kansas City; MDiv, St. Paul Sch. Theology. Ordained to ministry, 1954, ordained high priest, 1958, ordained apostle, 1984. With dept. Christian edn. Reorganized Ch. of Jesus Christ of Latter Day Saints, 1966, commr. pastoral svcs., dir. program svcs. divsn., pres. Temple Sch., asst. to 1st pres., commr. religious edn., acting dir. program svcs. divsn., mem. Coun. Twelve Apostles; mem. ch. history commn., theology com.; pres. Quorum of High Priests, 1974-84; mem. Standing High Coun., 1976-84. Author: The Burning Bush, Strangers and Pilgrims, The Promise of Healing; contbr. articles to profl. jours. Avocations: literature, psychology, music. Office: Reorganized Ch of Jesus Christ of Latter Day Saints PO Box 1059 Independence MO 64051

SPENCER, HARRY CHADWICK, minister; b. Chgo., Apr. 10, 1905; s. John Carroll and Jessie Grace (Chadwick) S.; m. Mary Louise Wakefield, May 26, 1935; children: Mary Grace Spencer Lyman, Ralph Wakefield. B.A., Willamette U., 1925, D.D. (hon.), 1953; M.Div., Garrett Bibl. Inst., 1929; M.A., Harvard U., 1932. Ordained to ministry Meth. Ch., 1931; pastor Washington Heights Ch., Chgo., 1931-33, Portage Park Ch., Chgo., 1933-35; rec. sec. bd. missions Meth. Ch., 1935-40, asst. exec. sec., 1940-45, sec. dept. visual edn., 1945-52, exec. sec. radio and film commn., 1952-56, gen. sec. TV, radio and film commn., 1956-68, asso. gen. sec. program council div. TV, radio and film communication, 1968-72; asso. exec. sec. joint commn. on communications United Meth. Ch., 1972, ret., 1973; mem. exec. com. Nat. Council Chs. Broadcasting and Film Commn., 1952-73, chmn., 1960-63; mem. exec. com. Nat. Council Chs., 1960-63, mem. gen. bd., 1967-72, v.p. Cen. div. communications, 1969-72; chmn. constituting assembly World Assn. for Christian Broadcasting, 1963; mem. constituting assembly World Assn. Christian Communication, 1968, dir. assembly, 1975; mem. adminstrv. com. Ravemco, 1950-70, Intermedia, 1970-72; vis. prof. Garrett Evang. Theol. Sem., 1975; lectr. in field. Exec. producer: TV series Learning to Live; radio series Night Call; motion pictures John Wesley, etc.; Contbr. articles on films to ch. publs. Trustee Scarritt Coll., 1967-74, emeritus, 1974-88; bd. dirs. Outlook Nashville, 1977-83, sec., 1980; bd. dirs. Nashville chpt. UN Assn., 1976-83. Recipient award excellence art communications Claremont Sch. Theology, 1973, The Pioneer in Religious Communications award World assn. for Christian Communication, 1989; inducted into United Meth. Communicators Hall of Fame, 1983. Mem. United Meth. Assn. Communicators, World Assn. Christian Communications (award). Clubs: Kiwanis (Woodmont); Harvard (Nashville). Home: PO Box 150063 Nashville TN 37215-0063 *The most precious quality we know is human personality. Unfortunately, innumerable hazards constantly beset each individual even from the time of conception. Nevertheless, every person has inherited many priceless advantages. The ability to store up knowledge and the imagination to foresee future events, which make possible human communication, have enhanced the value of human personality and brightened our hope for the future—if human beings can now learn the secret of self-discipline and will use it to achieve long-range benefits for a world community.*

SPENCER, HARRY IRVING, JR., retired banker; b. Worcester, Mass., Feb. 3, 1925; s. Harry Irving and Bertha (Johnson) S.; m. Violet Virginia Bergquist, Sept. 16, 1950; children—Nancy Elaine, Harry Irving III, Carol Helen. B.A., Clark U., 1950. With Worcester County Nat. Bank, 1950-82, asst. treas., 1954-58, cashier, 1958-82, v.p., 1966-69, sr. v.p., 1969-77, exec. v.p., cashier, 1977-82, clk., dir., 1980-82; exec. v.p., cashier, sec. Shawmut Worcester County Bank, N.A., 1982-88, also bd. dirs.; sec., treas., dir. Nobility Hill Realty Corp.; dir. Worcester Capital Corp., Wornat Leasing Corp. Bd. dirs. Worcester Taxpayers Assn. Methodist (trustee). Clubs: Kiwanis; Economic (Worcester, Mass.), Plaza (Worcester, Mass.). Home: 79 Birchwood Dr Holden MA 01520-1939 Office: 446 Main St Worcester MA 01608-2302

SPENCER, IVAN CARLTON, clergyman; b. nr. West Burlington, Pa., July 8, 1914; s. Ivan Quay and Annie Minnie (Back) S.; m. Elizabeth Garate, Apr. 14, 1935; children: David Carlton, Esther Elizabeth (Mrs. Saied Adour), John Wesley. Grad., Elim Bible Inst., 1933; D.D., Am. Bible Coll., 1966. Ordained to ministry Elim Missionary Assemblies. Pastor various chs., 1935-38; instr. Elim Bible Inst., 1938, campus pastor, 1938-44, pres., 1949-82; gen. sec. Elim Missionary Assemblies (now Elim Fellowship), 1940-54, gen. chmn., 1954-85; bd. dirs. Nat. Assn. Evangs., 1958-85, Pentecostal Fellowship of N. Am., 1961-86, treas., 1963-65, 73-81. Address: 7245 College St Lima NY 14485

SPENCER, JAMES CALVIN, SR., humanities educator; b. Detroit, Oct. 21, 1941; s. Donald and Beulah S.; m. Linda J. Voloshen, Nov. 21, 1987; children: James, Anne. BA, Calif. State U., 1966; MA, SUNY, 1970, PhD in Philosophy, 1973. NDEA fellow SUNY, Buffalo, 1968-70, SUNY fellow, 1970-71; instr. Cuyahoga C.C., Parma, Ohio, 1971-73, asst. prof., 1973-77, assoc. prof., 1977-81, prof. philosophy and art, 1981—; cons. continuing edn. divsn. Kans. State U., 1986, Case Western U., Cleve., 1973, Ford Motor Co., Brookport, Ohio, 1990, Campus Planning Ins., Cleve., 1991-94; pres. Spencer Enterprises, Brecksville, Ohio, 1991—; reviewer manuscripts for Wadsworth Pub. Author: The Nightmare Never Ends, 1992; co-author: Instructor's Manual for the Voyage of Discovery: A History of Western Philosophy, 1996; contbr. articles to profl. jours. Ward com. Democratic Party, Ashland, Brecksville, Ohio, Libertarian Party, Buffalo, N.Y.; Chevalier de la Chaine des Rotisseurs, Chevalier Ordre Mondial, 1996—. Grantee Nat. Sci. Found., 1979. Mem. French Food Soc., French Wine Soc. Office: Cuyahoga Community College 11000 W Pleasant Valley Rd Cleveland OH 44130-5114 *My life has demonstrated the correctness of what the wise have known since Mesopotamia as the formula for success: Hard work, much luck and enough intelligence to know when to take advantage of them both.*

SPENCER, JAMES H., art director, production designer. Prodn. designer: (TV movies) Friendly Persuasion, 1975, Red Alert, 1977, King, 1978, Some Kind of Miracle, 1979, Son Rise: A Miracle of Love, 1979, Not in Front of the Children, 1982, Journey to the Center of the Earth, 1993, (films) Fire Sale, 1977, Die Laughing, 1980, King of the Mountain, 1981, Stripes, 1981, Poltergeist, 1982, The Sender, 1982, Gremlins, 1984, Innerspace, 1987, The 'Burbs, 1989, Gremlins 2: The New Batch, 1990, Lethal Weapon 3, 1992; art dir.: (films) Bound for Glory, 1976, Rocky, 1976, Twilight Zone-The Movie ("Nightmare at 20,000 Feet"), 1983. Office: care Lawrence Mirisch The Mirisch Agency 10100 Santa Monica Blvd Ste 700 Los Angeles CA 90067-4011

SPENCER, JAMES JEFFREY, executive director; b. Oil City, Pa., Nov. 19, 1958; s. Donald Ralph and Betty Jane (Coughlan) S. BS in Music Edn., Clarion U., 1981; MusB in Mktg., 1981. Chpt. cons. Alpha Chi Rho, Neptune, N.J., 1981-83; dir. Chpt. Svcs., 1983-86, exec. dir., nat. sec., 1986—; trustee Alpha Chi Rho Edl. Found., Neptune, N.J., 1986—. Contbr. articles to profl. jours. Republican. Methodist. Avocations: music, reading, skiing. Home: Tree Haven III Apt 346B Matawan NJ 07747 Office: Alpha Chi Rho 109 Oxford Way Neptune NJ 07753

SPENCER, JAMES R., federal judge; b. 1949. BA magna cum laude, Clark Coll., 1971; JD, Harvard U., 1974, MDiv, 1985. Staff atty. Atlanta Legal Aid Soc., 1974-75; asst. U.S. atty. Washington, 1978, U.S. Dist. Ct. (ea. dist.) Va., 1983; judge U.S. Dist. Ct. (ea. dist.) Va., Richmond, 1986—; adj. prof. law U. Va., 1987—. Capt. JAGC, U.S.Army, 1975-78, res. 1981-86. Mem. ABA, Nat. Bar Assn., State Bar Ga., D.C. Bar, Va. State Bar, Richmond Bar Assn., Washington Bar Assn., Old Dominion Bar Assn., Omega Psi Phi, Sigma Pi Phi. Office: US Courthouse 1000 East Main St Richmond VA 23219-3525

SPENCER, JEFFREY PAUL, art educator; b. Omaha, Oct. 31, 1962; s. James Stanley and Darlene (Rahe) S. BFA, U. Nebr., 1987; MFA, U. Tenn., 1990. Instr. Met. C.C., Omaha, 1990—. Mem. Young Dems., Omaha, 1993—. NEA grantee, 1991. Mem. Coll. Art Assn. Home: 815 S 46th Ave Omaha NE 68106

SPENCER, JOHN HEDLEY, biochemistry educator; b. Stapleford, Eng., Apr. 10, 1933; emigrated to Can., 1956; s. Thomas and Eva (Johnson) S.; m. Magdeliene Vera Kulin, Sept. 16, 1958; children—Robin Anne, David Thomas, Mark Stewart. BSc, U. St. Andrews, Scotland, 1955, BSc with honors, 1956; student, Montreal Cancer Rsch. Soc., 1956-59; PhD, McGill U., 1960. Damon Runyon Meml. Fund postdoctoral fellow Columbia U., N.Y.C., 1959-61; mem. faculty McGill U., Montreal, 1961-78, assoc. prof. biochemistry, 1966-71, prof., 1971-78; prof. biochemistry Queen's U., Kingston, Ont., 1978—, head biochemistry, 1978-90; vis. prof. U. Montreal, 1992-93. Author: The Physics and Chemistry of DNA and RNA, 1972; co-editor: Planet Earth: Problems and Prospects, 1995. Recipient Ayerst award Can. Biochem. Soc., 1972. Fellow Royal Soc. Can.; mem. AAAS, Can. Biochem. Soc. (treas. 1966-69, pres. 1979-80), Can. Fedn. Biol. Socs. (pres. 1981-82), Biochem. Soc., Am. Soc. Biochemistry and Molecular Biology, Royal Soc. Can., Sigma Xi. Home: 36 Kenwoods Cir, Kingston, ON Canada K7K 6Y1

SPENCER, KENDALL L., banking executive; b. Linton, Ind., Aug. 8, 1952; s. Emil M. and Patricia A. (Elliot) S.; m. Sylvia Morgan, Aug. 24, 1973; children: Rachel, Rebecca. BS in Fin. and Acctg., U. Fla., 1974; MDiv, Trinity Evang., Chgo., 1978; banking cert., Stonier Grad. Sch. Banking, 1995. Bank mgmt. staff Am. Fletcher Nat. Bank, Indpls., 1978-81; CFO Concord, Inc., Fargo, Ill., 1981-83; dir. corp. banking Barnett Bank of Alachua County, N.A., Gainesville, Fla., 1984-88; CEO, pres. Barnett Bank of Lake Co. N.A., Eustis, Fla., 1988-93, Barnett Bank of Pasco County, Port Richey, Fla., 1993—; mem. bank credit and ops. coun. Fla. Bankers Assn., Fla. Dept. Edns. State Tech. Com. for Bus. Tech. Edn. Chmn. bd. trustees Lake-Sumter C.C.; capital campaign chmn. Salvation Army Pasco County, 1993-94; bd. dirs. Pasco County Com. of 100, pres., 1995; bd. Sertoma Speech and Hearing Found. Fla., Inc.; bd. mgrs. West Pasco County Family YMCA; bd. dirs., exec. com. Pasco County United Way, campaign chmn., 1995; mem. Pasco County Bd., Bd. of Trustees for Jr. Achievement of the Suncoast, Inc.; campaign chmn. Jr. Achievement in Pasco County, 1995; trustee All Children's Hosp. Found., Inc., St. Petersburg, Fla.; bd. dirs. Tampa Bay Capital Initiative; mem. math. dept. external adv. coun. U. Fla.; bd. dirs. Leadership Tampa Bay; charter mem. Jobs and Edn. Partnership Com.; others. Mem. New Port Richey Rotary Club, Pasco County Gator Club. Office: Barnett Bank Pasco County 10220 US Hwy 19 Port Richey FL 34668

SPENCER, LEWIS DOUGLAS, lawyer; b. Frankfort, Ind., Feb. 6, 1917; s. Clarence D. and Hazel (Ghormley) S.; m. Marcia Jane Maish, Jan. 29, 1947; children: Karen Jane Spencer Redman, Margo Linn Spencer Estruth. AB, DePauw U., 1939; LLB, Columbia, 1942; student, Motorola Exec. Inst., 1969. Bar: N.Y. 1942, Ind. 1943, Ill. 1947. Assoc. firm Carter, Ledyard and Milburn, N.Y.C., 1942-43, Barnes, Hickam, Pantzer & Boyd, Indpls., 1943-44, O'Connor & Farber, N.Y.C., 1944-47, Peterson, Rall, Barber, Ross & Seidel, Chgo., 1947-51; atty. Motorola, Inc. (and subsidiaries), 1951-77, asst. sec., 1956-74, sec., 1974-77, gen. atty., 1959-73, gen. counsel, 1973-77, v.p., 1965-77; lectr. sch. law Loyola U., Chgo., 1978-79, prof. sch. law, 1979-86. Contbr. articles to profl. jours. Mem. Park Ridge (Ill.) Bd. Fire and Police Commrs., 1964-67; mem. Park Ridge Zoning Bd. Appeals and Zoning Commn., 1967-75, chmn., 1968-75; bd. dirs. Park Ridge United Fund, 1966-69, pres., 1968. Mem. Chgo. Tax Club (bd. dirs. 1965-71, pres. 1969), The Nat. Soc., SAR. Mem. Park Ridge Community Ch. (bd. dirs. 1964-72, chmn. congregation 1970-71). Home: 5555 N Sheridan Rd Apt 1602 Chicago IL 60640-1628

SPENCER, MARGARET GILLIAM, lawyer; b. Spokane, Wash., Aug. 30, 1951; d. Jackson Earl and Margaret Kathleen (Hindley) Gilliam; m. John Bernard Spencer, Feb. 21, 1993. BA in Sociology, U. Mont., 1974, MA in Sociology, 1978, JD, 1982. Bar: Mont. 1982, Colo. 1982. Assoc. Holland & Hart, Denver, 1982-84; assoc. Roath & Brega, P.C., Denver, 1984-88, shareholder, dir., 1988-89; spl. counsel Brega & Winters, P.C., Denver, 1989; corp. counsel CH2M Hill, Inc., Denver, 1989—. Democrat. Episcopalian. Avocations: skiing, scuba diving. Office: CH2M Hill Inc PO Box 22508 Denver CO 80222-0508

SPENCER, MARY EILEEN, biochemist, educator; b. Regina, Sask., Can., Oct. 4, 1923; d. John J. and Etta Christina (Hamren) Stapleton; m. Henry Anderson Spencer, July 3, 1946; 1 child, Susan Mary. AA, Regina Coll., 1942; BA with high honors in Chemistry, U. Sask., 1945; MA in Chemistry, Bryn Mawr Coll., 1946; PhD in Agrl. Chemistry, U. Calif.-Berkeley, 1951. Chemist, Ayerst, McKenna and Harrison Ltd., Montreal, Que., Can., summer 1945, full time, 1946-47, Nat. Canners Assn., San Francisco, 1948; teaching fellow U. Calif.-Berkeley, 1949-51, faculty food chemistry, 1951-53; faculty U. Alta., Edmonton, Can., 1953-61, instr., asst. prof., assoc. prof., acting head biochem. dept., 1960-61, assoc. prof. plant sci. dept., 1962, prof. plant sci., 1964-83, McCalla rsch. prof., 1983-84, univ. prof., 1984—; pres. Rootrainers Corp.; mem. NRC Can., 1970-73, 73-76, Task Force on Post-Secondary Edn., Alta. Govt. Com. on Ednl. Planning, 1970-72; chmn. nat. adv. com. on biology NRC, mem. adv. bd. NRC Prairie Regional Lab.; mem. adv. bd. NRC Atlantic Regional Lab.; mem. adv. bd. NRC Biol. Sci. Divsn.; chmn. ad hoc vis. com. in forestry rsch. NRC, 1975-76; bd. govs. U. Alta. 1976-79; mem. Agr. Can. Cons. Com. IBT Pesticides, 1981-82; mem. coun. Natural Scis. and Engring. Rsch. Coun. Can., 1986-92, mem. mins. adv. com. Networks Ctrs. Excellence, 1989-92; mem. Premier's Coun. on Sci. and Tech., 1990-94. Recipient Queen Elizabeth II Silver Jubilee medal, 125th Ann. Can. Confedn. Commemorative medal. Fellow Royal Soc. Can., Chem. Inst. Can.; mem. Can. Soc. Plant Physiologists (pres. 1971-72, Gold medal 1990), Plant Growth Regulator Soc. Am., Am. Soc. Plant Physiologists, Can. Assn. Univ. Tchrs., Internat. Plant Growth Regulator Soc. Office: U Alta Dept Agrl Food and Nutritional Sci, Faculty Agr & Forestry, Edmonton, AB Canada T6G 2E3

SPENCER, MARY MILLER, civic worker; b. Comanche, Tex., May 25, 1924; d. Aaron Gaynor and Alma (Grissom) Miller; 1 child, Mara Lynn. BS, U. North Tex., 1943. Cafeteria dir. Mercedes (Tex.) Pub. Schs., 1943-46; home economist coordinator All-Orange Dessert Contest, Fla. Citrus Commn., Lakeland, 1959-62, 64; tchr. purchasing sch. lunch dept. Fla. Dept. Edn., 1960. Clothing judge Polk County (Fla.) Youth Fair, 1951-68, Polk County Federated Women's Clubs, 1964-66; pres. Dixieland Elem. Sch. PTA, 1955-57, Polk County Council PTA's, 1958-60; chmn. public edn. com. Polk County Unit Am. Cancer Soc., 1959-60, bd. dirs., 1962-70; charter mem., bd. dirs. Lakeland YMCA, 1962-72; sec. Greater Lakeland Community Nursing Council, 1965-72; trustee, vice chmn. Polk County Eye Clinic, Inc., 1962-64, pres., 1964-82; bd. dirs. Polk County Scholarship and Loan Fund, 1962-70; mem. exec. com. West Polk County (Fla.) Community Welfare Council, 1960-62, 65-68; mem. budget and audit com. Greater Lakeland United Fund, 1960-62, bd. dirs., 1967-70, residential chmn. fund drive, 1968; mem. adv. bd. Polk County Juvenile and Domestic Relations Ct., 1960-69; worker children's services div. family services Dept. Health and Rehab. Services, State of Fla., 1969-70, social worker, 1970-72, 74-82, social worker OFR unit, 1977-81, with other pers. svcs., 1981-82; supr. OFR unit 1982-83, pub. assistance specialist IV, 1984-89; with other pers. svcs. Emergency Fin. Assistance Housing Program, 1990-95. Mem. exec. com. Suncoast Health Council, 1968-71; mem. Polk County Home Econs. Adv. Com., 1965-71; sec. bd. dirs. Fla. West Coast Ednl. TV, 1960-81; bd. dirs.

Lake Region United Way, Winter Haven, 1976-81; mem. Polk County Community Services Council, 1978-88. Mem. Nat. Welfare Fraud Assn., Fla. Congress Parents and Tchrs. (hon. life; pres. dist. 7 1961-63, chmn. pub. relations 1962-66), AAUW (pres. Lakeland br. 1960-61), Polk County Mental Health Assn., Fla. Health and Welfare Council, Fla. Health and Social Service Council, U. North Tex. Alumni Assn. Democrat. Methodist. Lodge: Order of Eastern Star. Home and Office: PO Box 2161 Lakeland FL 33806-2161

SPENCER, MELVIN JOE, hospital administrator, lawyer; b. Buffalo Center, Iowa, Jan. 2, 1923; s. Kenos W. and Jennie (Michaelson) S.; m. Dena Joyce Butterfield, Mar. 1, 1952; children: Dennis Norman, Gregory Melvin, Shelly Lynn Spencer Goodnight. AB, U. Mich., 1948, JD, 1950. Bar: Iowa 1950, Mo. 1950, Okla. 1961. Practiced in Kansas City, Mo., 1950-61, Oklahoma City, 1961—; assoc., then ptnr. Watson, Ess, Marshall & Enggas, 1950-61; ptnr. Miller & Spencer (and predecessor firm), 1961-75, of counsel, 1975-80; adminstr. Deaconess Hosp., 1975-92, cons., 1992-93; dir. Union Bank & Trust Co., Oklahoma City, 1977-88, 89-96, adv. dir., 1996—; dir., sec. Hosp. Casualty Co., 1977-92; dir., treas. VHA of Okla., Inc., 1986-92. Assoc. editor Mich. Law Rev., 1949-50. Mcpl. judge City of Roeland Park, Kans., 1952, mem. city coun., 1954; area Rep. precinct chmn., 1968-69; del. Rep. State Conv., 1968, 96; bd. dirs. Deaconess Hosp., Oklahoma City, Christian Counseling Ctr., 1973-75; trustee Okla. Hosp. Assn., 1978-84, chmn. bd. trustees, 1983; trustee, vice chmn. bd. dirs. Ctrl. Coll., McPherson, Kans., 1972-86; trustee Okla. Ambulance Trust, 1984-87; mem. adv. bd. Okla. State U. Tech. Inst., 1980-92; mem. Okla. Hist. Soc.; bd. dirs. Emergency Med. Svcs. Ctrl. Okla., 1975-78, FMC Ministries, Inc.; mem. const. coun. Free Meth. Ch. World Fellowship; chmn. Free Meth. Found.; gen. counsel Free Meth. Ch. N.Am., 1969-95, sec., mem. bd. adminstrn., chmn. investment com., 1986-88. Capt. USAAF, 1943-46. Named Layman of Yr., Free Meth. Ch. N.Am., 1984; recipient W. Cleveland Rodgers Disting. Svc. award Okla. Hosp. Assn., 1985; fellow Cen. Coll. Acad. of Achievers, 1990. Mem. Okla. Bar Assn., Oklahoma County Bar Assn., Men's Dinner Club, Order of Coif, Phi Beta Kappa, Phi Kappa Phi. Home: 5910 N Shawnee Ave Oklahoma City OK 73112-1627

SPENCER, MILTON HARRY, economics and finance educator; b. N.Y.C., Mar. 25, 1926; m. Roslyn Pernick; children: Darcy, Robin, Cathy. BS, NYU, 1949, MA, 1950; PhD, Cornell U., 1954. Instr. econs., fin. Queens Coll., N.Y.C., 1949-52; research asst. Cornell U., Ithaca, N.Y., 1952-54; economist Armour & Co., Chgo., 1954-55; assoc. prof. Wayne State U., Detroit, 1955-62, prof., 1962-91, prof. emeritus, 1991—; vis. prof. U. Hawaii, Honolulu, 1965-66; lectr., U.S., Australia, Europe, Asia, Africa, South Am.; cons. U.S. Dept. State, Washington, 1959—, govts. of Chile, Israel, Eng., France, Italy, Australia, Hong Kong, Japan, Rep. of China and various domestic and fgn. corps. Author: Basic Economics, 1951, Economic Thought, 1954, Business and Economic Forecasting, 1958, Managerial Economics, 3 edits., 1959-68, Contemporary Economics, 8 edits., 1971-93; various monographs: contbr. numerous articles to profl. jours. Served as cpl. U.S. Army, 1943-45. Recipient Disting. Service awards from U.S. Dept. State, Govts. of Chile, Israel, France, Spain, England, Italy, Belgium. Mem. Am. Econ. Assn., Am. Fin. Assn., Nat. Assn. Bus. Economists. Avocations: piloting vintage planes, hang gliding.

SPENCER, PETER LEVALLEY, clergyman; b. Providence, Nov. 18, 1938; s. Lee Valley and Mary Josephine (Henry) S.; m. Eugenia Louise DiCostonzo-Bruno, May 4, 1961; children: Peter LeValley, David Louis, Mary Lee, Sarah Eugenia. BA, Brown U., 1960; ThM, Gen. Sem., 1965. Ordained to ministry Episcopal Ch. as priest, 1966. Curate St. Paul's Episcopal Ch., Pawtucket, R.I., 1965-67; curate St. Paul's Episcopal Ch., North Kingstown, R.I., 1967-71, rector, 1971—; canon Diocese of R.I., Providence, 1972—, spiritual dir., 1984—. Pres. Am. Cancer Soc., South County Div., Washington County, R.I., 1980. Lt. USN, 1960-62. Home: 14 Gold St North Kingstown RI 02852-5014 Office: St Pauls Church 5 S Main St North Kingstown RI 02852-5111

SPENCER, RICHARD HENRY, lawyer; b. Kansas City, Mo., Nov. 29, 1926; s. Byron Spencer and Helen Elizabeth (McCune) Hockaday; m. Barbara G. Rau, Aug. 2, 1952 (div. 1955); 1 chlid, Christina G. Cuevas; m. Katherine Graham, Dec. 28, 1957; children: Elisabeth M., Katherine S. Rivard. BS in Engring., Princeton U., 1949; LLB, U. Mo., 1952. Bar: Mo. 1952, U.S. Dist. Ct (we. dist.) Mo. 1955. Assoc. Spencer, Fane, Britt & Browne, Kansas City, 1952-59, ptnr., 1959-94; ret. ptnr., 1995—; bd. dirs., sec. Daniels-McCray Lumber Co., Kansas City, 1975—, First Am. Fin. Corp., Kansas City, 1971—, First Am. Ins. Co., Kansas City, 1971—. Co-author: Fiduciary Duties, Rights and Responsibilities of Directors, 1985. Sec. Kansas City Symphony, 1983—; sec., bd. dirs. Met. Performing Arts Fund, Kansas City, 1984—. Mem. ABA, Mo. Bar Assn., Lawyers Assn. Kansas City, Kansas City Club (pres. 1974), Kansas City Country Club (pres. 1986), Rotary. Republican. Episcopalian. Avocations: hunting, golf, traveling. Home: 77 Le Mans Ct Shawnee Mission KS 66208-5230 Office: Spencer Fane Britt & Browne 1400 Commerce Bank Bldg 1000 Walnut St Kansas City MO 64106-2107

SPENCER, RICHARD PAUL, biochemist, educator, physician; b. N.Y.C., June 7, 1929; s. David E. and Frances (Fried) S.; m. Gwendolyn Enid Williams, Apr. 7, 1956; children: Carolyn Roberts, Jennifer Holt, Priscilla James. AB, Dartmouth Coll., 1951; MD, U. So. Calif., 1954; MA (NSF fellow, Helen Hay Whitney fellow), Harvard U., 1958, PhD, 1961. Intern Beth Israel Hosp., Boston, 1954-55; practice medicine specializing in nuclear medicine; mem. faculty biophysics U. Buffalo, 1961-63; chief radioisotope service VA Hosp., Buffalo, 1961-63; asso. prof. nuclear medicine Yale Sch. Medicine, 1963-68, prof., 1968-74; prof., chmn. dept. nuclear medicine U. Conn. Health Center, 1974—. Author: The Intestinal Tract, 1960, (with others) Biophysical Principles, 1965, Radionuclide Studies of the Spleen, 1975, Clinical Focus on Nuclear Medicine, 1977, Handbook of Nuclear Medicine, 1977, Therapy in Nuclear Medicine, 1978, Radiopharmaceuticals: Structure-Activity Relationships, 1981, Interventional Nuclear Medicine, 1984, New Procedures In Nuclear Medicine, 1988; contbr. (with others) articles to profl. jours. Mem. Am. Physiol. Soc., AAAS, Soc. Nuclear Medicine, Biophys. Soc. Achievements include discovery of functional asplenia; developed first complete description of relationship of food intake to reproductive success and to longevity in a species. Office: U Conn Health Ctr Farmington CT 06030

SPENCER, RICHARD PRAIL, property management educator, job placement counselor; b. Mar. 1, 1948; s. Richard Victor and Doris Louise (Byington) S.; m. Carol J. Vassar, Apr. 16, 1981; children: Chris, Matthew, Nicholas. Lic. postsecondary tchr., Calif. Real estate assoc. Spencer Realty & Investments, Ukiah, Calif., 1975-81; resort owner Headwater's Inn, Lake Wenatchee, Wash., 1981-83; property mgr. Spencer Property Mgmt., Santa Rosa, Calif., 1983-86; property mgmt. instr., founder Agapé Sch. Property Mgmt., Forestville, Calif., 1986—; spkr., Santa Rosa. Author: Professional Development, 1987; co-author: The Complete Reference Manual for Property Owners and Managers, 1988, The Complete Maintenance Manual for Property Owners and Managers, 1988. Founder Agapé Project for the Homeless, Forestville, Calif., 1989. Recipient SBA award Nat. Bank Score, 1993. Democrat. Avocations: fly fishing, jazz music, drums, harmonica, singing.

SPENCER, RICHARD THOMAS, III, healthcare industry executive; b. Oak Park, Ill., Mar. 18, 1936; s. Richard Thomas Jr. and Lois Anne (Pollock) S.; m. Andrea B. Schlickeiser, June 29, 1962; 1 child, Richard Thomas IV. BA, U. Mich., 1959; postgrad., U. Pa., 1976, Stanford U., 1984, Clemson U., 1985. Mktg. group Mobil Oil Co., Detroit, 1962; internat. trade specialist U.S. Dept. Commerce, Detroit, 1963-64; account exec. J. Walter Thompson Co., Detroit, 1965-66; sales mgr. Sarns Inc., Ann Arbor, Mich., 1967-69; v.p. mktg. Cordis Dow Corp., Miami, Fla., 1970-81; pres. mktg. div. Cordis Corp., Miami, Fla., 1982-87; pres., CEO Uni-Med Internat. Corp., Miami, Fla., 1988—; sr. advisor, bd. dirs. World Med. Mfg. Corp., Sunrise, Fla., 1993—; cons. in field. Contbr. articles to profl. jours. With U.S. Army, 1959-61. Republican. Avocations: skiing, scuba diving, running, stereo equipment, geopolits. Office: Uni-Med Internat Corp PO Box 331120 Miami FL 33233-1120

SPENCER, ROBERT C., political science educator; b. Chgo., Mar. 28, 1920; m. Edith Maxham McCarthy, Sept. 13, 1941; children: Margaret, Catherine, Anne, Thomas More, David. AB, U. Chgo., 1943, MA, 1952, PhD in Polit. Sci. (Univ. fellow 1952-53), 1955. Instr. polit. sci. and sociology St. Michaels Coll., 1949-51, asst., then assoc. prof. polit. sci., 1953-60, prof. govt., 1960-63, dir. summer sessions, 1960-61, asst. to pres., 1963-65; prof. polit. sci., chmn. dept., dean summer sessions U. R.I., 1965-67; grad. dean U. R.I. (Grad. Sch.), 1967-69; founding pres. Sangamon State U., Springfield, Ill., 1969-78; prof. govt. and public affairs Sangamon State U., 1978-88, prof. emeritus, 1988—; research assoc. Indsl. Relations Center, U. Chgo., 1952-53; extension lectr. N.Y. State Sch. Indsl. and Labor Relations, Cornell U., 1956-57; vice chmn. West Central Ill. Ednl. Telecommunications Consortium, 1975-77, chmn., 1977-78; chmn. task force personnel Vt. Little Hoover Commn., 1957-58; mem. Ill. adv. com. U.S. Commn. on Civil Rights, 1979-87; bd. mgrs. Franklin Life Variable Annuity Funds, 1974—; vis. prof. polit. sci., sr. rsch. assoc. local govt. ctr. Mont. State U., Bozeman, 1985, 89, 90—. Author: (with Robert J. Huckshorn) The Politics of Defeat, 1971. Bd. dirs. City Day Sch., Springfield, 1979-83, Gt. Am. People Show Repertory Co., 1980-90; vice chmn. Petersburg Libr. Bd., 1982-88; chmn. Petersburg Zoning Bd. Appeals, 1984-90; mem. Vt. Senate, 1959-63; faculty fellow Ford Found.'s Nat. Ctr. for Edn. in Politics, rsch. dir. Dem. Nat. Com., 1962-63; mem. adv. bd. Landmark Preservation Coun. Ill., 1986-89; mem., treas. Gallatin County Coun. on Aging, 1993—. Roman Catholic. Home: 2303 S 3rd Ave Bozeman MT 59715-6009

SPENCER, ROGER FELIX, psychiatrist, psychoanalyst, medical educator; b. Vienna, Austria, Apr. 19, 1934; s. Eugene S. Spitzer and Santa (Kurz) Spencer; m. Barbara Ann Houser, Aug. 18, 1958; children—Geoffrey, Jennifer, Rebecca. B.S., Yale Coll., 1956; M.D., Harvard Med. Sch., 1959. Diplomate Am. Bd. Psychiatry. Intern, N.C. Meml. Hosp., Chapel Hill, 1959-60, resident in psychiatry, 1960-63; instr. U. N.C. Sch. Medicine, 1963-66, asst. prof., 1966-69, assoc. prof., 1969-76, prof., 1976—, dir. of liaison and cons., 1967-77, dir. out patient psychiatry, 1977—. Recipient Career Tchr. award NIMH, 1965-67. Fellow Am. Psychiat. Assn., Am. Psychoanalytic Assn.; mem. N.C. Psychoanalytic Soc., N.C. Neuropsychiat. Assn. Club: Chapel Hill Tennis. Contbr. articles to profl. jours. Office: UNC Hosps Psychiatry Dept CB 7160 Chapel Hill NC 27599

SPENCER, SAMUEL, lawyer; b. Washington, Dec. 8, 1910; s. Henry Benning and Katharine (Price) S.; children from previous marriage: Henry B., Janet Spencer Dougherty, Richard A.; m. June Byrne, May 29, 1982. Student, Milton (Mass.) Acad., 1924-29; A.B. magna cum laude, Harvard U., 1932, LL.B., 1935. Bar: N.Y. 1937, D.C 1938, U.S. Supreme Ct 1950. Assoc. Shearman & Sterling, N.Y.C., 1935-37, Covington, Burling, Rublee, Acheson & Shorb, Washington, 1937- 40, 45-47; ptnr. Spencer, Graham & Holderman, 1947—; pres. bd. commrs., D.C., 1953-56; pres., chmn. bd. Tenn. R.R. Co., 1956-73. Bd. dirs. Nat. Symphony Orch., 1949-51, Garfield Hosp., 1947-53, 56-62; bd. dirs. Children's Hosp., 1948-53, sec., 1951-53; trustee Potomac Sch., 1947-53; pres. Washington Hosp. Ctr., 1958-60, bd. dirs., 1958-65; mem. Washington Nat. Monument Soc., 1958-91. Served to comdr. USNR, 1940-45. Decorated Bronze Star with combat V. Mem. ABA, Bar Assn. D.C., Am. Cancer Soc. (trustee D.C. chpt. 1951-53), AIA (hon.), Washington Inst. Fgn. Affairs (bd. dirs. 1961-89, sec. 1961-81), Jud. Council D.C. Circuit (com. on adminstrn. of justice 1966-70), Soc. of Cincinnati, Phi Beta Kappa. Episcopalian (sr. warden). Clubs: Metropolitan of Washington (bd. govs. 1949-53, 56-61, pres. 1959-60); Chevy Chase (Md.). Home: 5904 Cedar Pky Bethesda MD 20815-4251 Office: 2000 Massachusetts Ave NW Washington DC 20036-1022

SPENCER, SAMUEL REID, JR., educational consultant, former university president; b. Rock Hill, S.C., 1919; m. Ava Clark; 1948; children: Samuel Reid, Ellen Spencer Henschen, Clayton, Frank. AB summa cum laude, Davidson Coll., 1940, LLD (hon.), 1964; MA, Harvard U., 1947, PhD, 1951; LHD (hon.), Oglethorpe U., 1977, Queens Coll., 1983, Bridgewater Coll., 1986, Marymount U., 1988, Hollins Coll., 1991, Mary Baldwin Coll., 1992; LittD (hon.), Washington and Lee U., 1991. With Vick Chem. Co., N.Y.C., 1940; research asst. to Grenville Clark, Dublin, N.H., 1947-48; asst. to pres. Davidson Coll., 1951-54, dean of students, asso. prof. history, 1954, dean of students, prof. history, 1955-57; pres. Mary Baldwin Coll., 1957-68; pres. Davidson (N.C.) Coll., 1968-83, pres. emeritus, 1983—; pres. Va. Found. for Ind. Colls., Richmond, 1983-88; sr. cons. Acad. Search Consultation Svc., 1989—; interim pres. Hollins Coll., 1990-91; dir. Piedmont Bank & Trust Co.; Fulbright lectr. U. Munich, 1965-66; mem. Bd. Fgn. Scholarships, 1980-83, chmn., 1982-83; bd. dirs. Assn. Am. Colls., 1976-83, chmn. assn., 1981-82; pres. So. Univ. Conf., 1979-80; mem. commn. govtl. relations Am. Council Edn., 1973-76. Author: Decision for War, 1917, 1953, Booker T. Washington and the Negro's Place in American Life, 1955, (with J. Garry Clifford) The First Peacetime Draft, 1986. Bd. dirs. Grenville Clark Fund, Dartmouth Coll., 1973—, Charlotte-Mecklenburg chpt. Urban League, 1979-83; trustee Agnes Scott Coll., 1975-91; trustee Union Theol. Sem., Richmond, Va., 1985-94, chmn., 1988-94. Maj. AUS, 1940-45. Austin fellow Harvard, 1947-48; Rosenwald fellow, 1948-49; Kent fellow Nat. Council on Religion in Higher Edn., 1949-51. Mem. Fulbright Assn. (bd. dirs. 1989-92), Phi Beta Kappa, Omicron Delta Kappa. Presbyterian (bd. Christian edn.). Address: PO Box 1117 Davidson NC 28036-1117

SPENCER, STEVEN D., lawyer; b. Mar. 22, 1953. BS, Cornell U., 1975; JD, Columbia U., 1979. Bar: Pa. 1978, N.Y. 1979. Ptnr. Morgan, Lewis & Bockius, Phila.; adj. prof. Villanova U. law sch. 1991-92. Office: Morgan Lewis & Bockius 2000 One Logan Sq Philadelphia PA 19103*

SPENCER, STEVEN SEARS, medical consultant; b. Phila., Aug. 27, 1929; s. Steven Murray and Mary Emma (Sears) S.; m. Joan Esther Price, June 11, 1955; children: Mary Elizabeth, Margaret Ruth, Sarah Price, Rebecca Louise. BA, Swarthmore Coll., 1951; MD, U. Pa., 1955. Diplomate Am. Bd. Internal Medicine; lic. physician Republic of Tanzania, N.Mex., Ariz.; cert. correctional health profl. Intern U. Mich., 1955-56; fellow in internal medicine Mayo Found. and Mayo Clinic, 1959-62; pvt. practice Flagstaff, Ariz., 1963-70; assoc. prof. U. Dar es Salaam, Tanzania, 1970-74; assoc. prof. U. Ariz., 1974-79, clin. lectr., 1979-94; clin. assoc. prof. U. N.Mex., 1986-94; pvt. cons. Santa Fe, 1994—; mem. cons. staff Albert Schweitzer Hosp., 1960; mem. med. staff Flagstaff Cmty. Hosp., 1963-70, chief of staff, 1966-67, chief of medicine, 1964-67, 69-70; mem. staff Muhimbili Hosp., Dar es Salaam, 1970-74, U. Hosp., Tucson, 1974-79, Tucson VA Hosp., 1974-79, Sage Meml. Hosp., 1979-85; med. dir. Navajo Nation Health Found., Sage Meml. Hosp., Ganado, Ariz., 1979-85, N.Mex. Corrections Dept., 1985-93; cons. in field of prison and jail health care. Contbr. numerous articles to profl. jours. Mem. Ariz. Bd. Med. Examiners, 1979-85, chmn., 1984-85, Gov.'s Task Force on HIV/AIDS, 1986-93; bd. dirs. St. Elizabeth Shelter for the Homeless, 1991—; mem. N.Mex. Com. to Stop Executions, 1993—, Cert. Correctional Health Profl. Bd. Trustees, 1995—. Sr. asst. surgeon USPHS, 1956-59. Fellow Nat. Heart Inst., 1960, NEH, 1975. Fellow SCP; mem. APHA (mem. jail and prison health com.), Am. Correctional Health Svcs. Assn. (bd. dirs. 1991-95, chairperson policy and stds. com.), Am. Correctional Assn., Internat. Physicians for Prevention of Nuclear War, Soc. Correctional Physicians, Physicians for Human Rights (mem. internat. adv. com.). Democrat. Mem. Soc. of Friends. Avocations: choral singing, fly fishing, skiing.

SPENCER, WILLIAM A., physician, educational administrator; b. Oklahoma City, Feb. 16, 1922. B.S. cum laude, Georgetown U., 1942; M.D., Johns Hopkins U., 1946. Diplomate Am. Bd. Pediatrics. Intern Johns Hopkins Hosp Harriet Lane Home, Balt., 1946-47, resident, 1947-48; med. dir. Southwestern Poliomyelitis Respiratory Ctr., Houston, 1950-59; dir. Tex. Inst. Rehab. and Research, Houston, 1959-77; pres. Inst. for Rehab. and Research, Houston, 1977—; instr. dept. pediatrics Baylor Coll. Medicine, Houston, 1950-55, asst. prof. dept. pediatrics, 1955-57, asst. prof. dept. physiology, 1954-57, prof., chmn. dept. rehab. medicine, 1957—; vis. mem. grad. faculty Tex. A&M U., College Station; cons. staff VA Hosp., Houston; cons. spinal injury service and phys. medicine and rehab. VA Hosp., Houston; cons. dept. biomath. and phys. medicine and rehab. M.D. Anderson Hosp. and Tumor Inst., Houston; asst. attending physician Ben Taub Gen. Hosp., Houston; mem. active staff Tex. Children's Hosp., Houston, Inst. for Rehab. and Research, Houston; mem. courtesy staff St. Anthony's Ctr., Houston; Horowitz vis. prof. Inst. Phys. Medicine and Rehab., NYU Med. Ctr., 1964; mem. U. Houston Ctr. for Pub. Policy Adv. Council, 1981—; mem. VA Rehab., Research and Devel., Sci. Merit Rev. Bd., 1981—; mem. sci. adv. bd. Paralyzed Vets. Am. Tech. and Research Found., 1981—; mem. com. on health care of racial/ethnic minorities and handicapped persons Nat. Acad. Sci., 1980-81; mem. panel on testing of handicapped Nat. Acad. Sci., 1980-81; intermittent cons. Nat. Inst. Handicapped Research, Washington, 1979—; mem. Inst. Medicine, Nat. Acad. Scis., 1971—; mem. phys. medicine services adv. com. Joint Commn. on Accreditation of Hosps., 1972—; mem. med. commn. Rehab. Internat., 1977—; ad hoc mem. VA Sci. Rev. and Evaluation Bd. for Rehab. Engring. Research and Devel., 1981—. Cons. editor Jour. Am. Phys. Therapy Assn., 1965-71; mem. editorial bd. Med. Informatics Jour., Health Services Hosp. Research and Ednl. Trust, 1967-73, Computer Programs in Biomedicine, 1968—, Stroke-A Jour. of the Cerebral Circulation, 1969-70, Computers and Human Concern, 1973—, Am. Jour. Phys. Medicine, 1975—, Informatique Medicine, 1975—, Bull. Prosthetics Research, 1982—. Served to capt., M.C., U.S. Army, 1948-50. Recipient Physician's award Pres. Commn. on Employment of Handicapped, 1964, Gold medal 6th Internat. Congress Phys. Medicine, 1972, Disting. Citizens award Goodwill Industries, 1976. Mem. AMA, Am. Physiol. Soc., Am. Congress Rehab. Medicine (Gold Key 1972, Culter award 1978), AAAS, Tex. Med. Assn., Harris County Med. Soc., Houston Pediatric Soc., Nat. Rehab. Assn., N.Y. Acad. Scis., So. Med. Assn., So. Soc. Pediatric Research, Soc. Advanced Med. Systems, Assn. Computing Machinery, Am. Assn. Med. Systems and Informatics, Am. Documentation Inst., Internat. Rehab. Medicine Assn., Am. Acad. Orthopedics (assoc.), Am. Acad. Phys. Medicine (hon.), Am. Coll. Physicians in Computation, Tex. Soc. Profl. Engrs. (hon.), Nat. Assn. Rehab. and Research Ctrs. (exec. com. of bd. 1982—), Houston C. of C., Sigma Xi, Phi Beta Kappa, Alpha Omega Alpha. Office: Baylor Coll of Medicine Dept Of Rehabilitation Houston TX 77025

SPENCER, WILLIAM COURTNEY, foundation executive, international business executive; b. Uniontown, Pa., Sept. 15, 1919; s. Clarence Ashley and Hazel (Stark) S.; m. Evelyn Van Cleve Bailey, Aug. 6, 1942; children: Courtney Lloyd, Henry Bailey, Edward Ashley. AB, Drew U., 1941; AM, Columbia U., 1946, EdD, 1952. Tchr. Scarsdale (N.Y.) Pub. Schs., 1946-49; dir. Univ. Sch. Columbia, 1949-52; prof. edn. and adminstrn. U. Del., 1952-55; prof., dir. grad. program tchr. edn. NYU, 1955-59, prof. higher edn. and internat. affairs, 1960-61; prof. adminstrn. U. Chile, Santiago, 1959-60; dir. Interam. affairs Inst. Internat. Edn. and asst. sec. gen. Coun. Higher Edn. in Am. Republics, 1961-65; assoc. dean Grad. Sch. Bus. Columbia U., 1965-67, spl. asst. to pres., 1967-69; pres. Western Coll., Oxford, Ohio, 1969-74, The Lindenwood Colls., 1974-79, Fund for Peace, 1979-80; v.p. Trans Internat. Mgmt. Corp., 1979-88; spl. adviser Fund for Higher Edn., 1979-82, pres., 1982-86; spl. asst. to pres. Internat. Exec. Svc. Corps, Stamford, Conn., 1988; dir. internat. devel. svcs. Nippon Manpower Ltd, Tokyo, 1988-91; pres. Trans Internat Exec. Svcs., 1988—; cons. UNESCO Latin Am. major project in edn., Chile, 1959-60, project edn. and econ. planning, India, 1962; cons. Am. Coun. Edn., 1960-61; del. Pan-Am Assembly on Population, 1965; mem. standing com. on internat. edn. Coll. Entrance Exam. Bd., 1972-74; cons. Am. Med. Internat. Inc., 1980, McGraw Hill Internat. Book Co., 1981, AID, Indonesia, 1982, Thermo-Electron Corp., China, 1984, Internat. Exec. Svc. Corps, Jamaica, 1989, Costa Rica, 1991, 93, Hungary, 1991. Author: Education and World Responsibility, 1965, also articles; editor: Art and the University, 1964, University and National Development, 1965, Agriculture and the University, 1965. Bd. dirs. Internat. Sch. Svc., 1963-69, chmn., 1967-69; mem. Mo. master planning com. Coordinating Bd. Higher Edn., 1975-79; pres. Ind. Colls. and Univs. of Mo., 1977-79; bd. dirs. St. Louis Coun. on World Affairs, 1977-79; mem. scholarship bd. Timken Co. Ednl. Fund, 1971-76; bd. dirs. Internat. Inst. Energy Conservation, 1984-89, Conn. River Mus., 1988—. Lt. comdr. USNR, 1942-46. Decorated Purple Heart; commendation medals from Royal Navy, U.S. Navy. Mem. Coun. Fgn. Relations, N.Y. Yacht Club, Essex (Conn.) Yacht Club, North Cove Yacht Club. Home: 100 Dudley Ave Apt C-11 Old Saybrook CT 06475-2339

SPENCER, WILLIAM FRANKLIN, SR., soil scientist, researcher; b. Carlinville, Ill., Mar. 4, 1923; s. Jesse H. and Mayme (Wohlert) S.; m. Marjorie Ann Hall, June 2, 1946; children: Barbara Annette, William Franklin Jr., Gary Alan. BS in Agr., U. Ill., 1947, MS in Chemistry, 1950, PhD in Agronomy, 1952. Asst. chemist U. Fla., Lake Alfred, 1951-54; soil scientist USDA Agrl. Rsch. Svc., Laramie, Wyo., 1954-55, Brawley, Calif., 1955-57; assoc. soil chemist U. Fla., Lake Alfred, 1957-62; rsch. leader USDA Agrl. Rsch. Svc., Riverside, Calif., 1962-95; mem. Western Soil & Water Rsch. Com., Riverside, 1965-75; cons. Cen. U., Maracay, Venezuela, 1959. Contbr. over 105 articles to profl. jours. With U.S. Army, 1943-46, PTO. Fellow AAAS, Am. Soc. Agronomy, Soil Sci. Soc. Am.; mem. Soc. Environ. Toxicology and Chemistry, Internat. Soil Sci. Soc., Gamma Sigma Delta, Sigma Xi. Methodist. Achievements include research on behavior and fate of pesticides. Home: 2935 Arlington Ave Riverside CA 92506-4450 Office: U Calif USDA Agrl Rsch Svc Riverside CA 92521

SPENCER, WILLIAM H., ophthalmologist; b. N.Y.C., 1925. MD, U. Calif., San Francisco, 1954. Diplomate Am. Bd. Ophthalmology (exec. dir.). Intern Phila. Gen. Hosp., 1954-55; resident in ophthalmology U. Calif., San Francisco, 1955-58. Office: Calif-Pacific Med Ctr 2340 Clay St 5th Fl San Francisco CA 94115-1932

SPENCER, WINIFRED MAY, art educator; b. Tulsa, Oct. 7, 1938; d. Len and Madge (Scofield) S. BA in Comml. Art, U. Tulsa, 1961, Cert. in Tchg., 1962. Cert. comml. art, K-12 art, English/journalism tchr. Freelance comml. artist Tulsa, 1962-63; art/sci. educator Pleasant Porter Elem. Tulsa Pub. Schs., 1963-65, art educator, supervising tchr. Kendall Elem., 1965-70, art educator, team leader pilot program Bunche Elem., 1970-75, art educator Carnegie Elem., 1975-81, art educator, fine arts dept. chair Foster Jr. High, 1982-83, art educator, fine arts dept. chair Foster Mid. Sch., 1983—; judge Okla. Wildlife Arts Festival, Okla. Wildlife Arts Assn., Tulsa, 1988; supervising tchr., tchr. tng. U. Tulsa, 1965-70, Northeastern State U., Tahlequah, Okla, 1965-70; pres. Tulsa Elem. Art Tchrs., Tulsa Pub. Schs., 1967-68, curriculum writing/curriculum cons., 1970-75, 91—; coord. summer arts/artists in the schs. program Tchr. Adv. Bd., Summer Arts Tulsa Arts and Humanities Coun., 1986-94. Exhibited in group shows at Tulsa City-County Ctrl. Libr., 1989, Philbrook Art Mus., 1993, 94. Mem. Rep. Nat. Com., 1994-96; art adv. PTA, Tulsa, 1970—; ch. leader Christian Sci. Ch., Tulsa, 1960—; mem. city of Tulsa goals for tomorrow task force on cultural affairs, 1995—. Invited U.S. China Joint Conf. on Edn., Citizen Amb. Program People to People Internat., 1992, U.S. Spain Joint Conf. on Edn., Citizen Amb. Program People to People Internat., 1995. Mem. AAUW, NEA, ASCD, Okla. Edn. Assn., Tulsa Classroom Tchrs. Assn., Okla. Mid. Level Edn. Assn. (del. 1994), Nat. Art Edn. Assn. (del. 1992, 94, 96), Okla. Art Edn. Assn. Avocation: travel. Home: 439 S Memorial Dr Tulsa OK 74112-2203 Office: Foster Mid Sch 12121 E 21st St Tulsa OK 74129-1801

SPENCER-DAHLEM, ANITA JOYCE, medical, surgical and critical care nurse; b. Weirton, W.Va., Aug. 26, 1961; d. Carlas A. and Evelyn Faye (Miller) Spencer; m. Terry Dahlem. BS, Alderson-Broaddus Coll., Philippi, W.Va., 1984. Staff nurse, orthopedic unit Charleston (W.Va.) Area Med. Ctr., 1984-86; ICU staff nurse Ohio Valley Hosp., Steubenville, Ohio, 1986—; nurse on cardiac catheterization unit Ohio Valley Hosp., Steubenville, 1994—. Mem. Ohio Nurses Assn.

SPENGLER, DAN MICHAEL, orthopedic surgery educator, researcher, surgeon; b. Defiance, Ohio, Feb. 25, 1941; s. Harold A. and Wilhelmina Spengler; m. Cynthia Niswonger; children: Christina, Craig. BS, Baldwin-Wallace Coll., 1962; MD, U. Mich., 1966. Diplomate Am. Bd. Orthopaedic Surgery (bd. dirs. 1988—). Intern in gen. surgery King County Hosp., Seattle, 1967-68; resident in orthopedics U. Mich., Ann Arbor, 1970-73; asst. prof. U. Wash., Seattle, 1974-78, assoc. prof., 1978-83; bd. dirs. Am. Bd. Orthopaedic Surgery. Author: Low Back Pain, 1982. Fellow Am. Acad. Orthopaedic Surgeons; mem. Am. Orthopaedic Assn., ACS, Am. Bd. Orthopaedic Surgeons (pres. 1993-94), Assn. Bone and Joint Surgeons, Internat. Soc. for Study of Lumbar Pain, U. Nashville Club. Avocations: flying, golf, running, skiing. Office: Vanderbilt U Dept Orthopedic Rehab 1211 21st Ave S # D-4208 Nashville TN 37212-2717

SPENGLER, KENNETH C., meteorologist, professional society administrator; b. Harrisburg, Pa.. BA, Dickinson Coll., 1936; MS, MIT, 1941; DSc (hon.), U. Nev., 1966. Sec. Weather Rsch. Ctr. Hdqs., Air Weather Svc., organizer Army Weather Ctrl., chief climatological and statistical divsn. and Army Weather Ctrl., spl. asst. for interdepartmental and internat. affairsto comdr.; exec. dir. Am. Meteorol. Soc., Boston, 1946-88, sec.-treas., 1986—, emeritus exec. dir., 1988—; adv. com weather svc. U.S. Dept. Commerce, 1950-51; appointed by Pres. Eisenhower to com. on weather control, 1953-58; panel on edn. and scientific manpower and com. atmospheric sci. NAS, 1962-64; adv. bd. earth sci. curriculum project Am. Geol. Inst., 1964-70; nat. adv. com. oceans and atmosphere, 1976-77; U.S. Nat. com. Internat. Union Geodesy and Geophysics, 1987—; chair Nat. com. Internat. Assn. Meteorology and Atmospheric Physics, 1991—; founder, pres. Nat. Fedn. Abstracting and Indexing Svcs., Coun. Scientific Soc. Execs. With USAF 1940-45, USAFR 1946-75. Decorated Legion of Merit, 1975; recipient Disting. Alumni award Dickinson Coll., Leadership award Coun. Scientific Soc. Execs; The Spengler award named in his honor Air Weather Svc. 1975. Fellow AAAS, Royal Meteorol. Soc., Am. Meteorol. Soc. (recipient Charles Franklin Brooks award 1968, 89, Cleveland Abbe Disting. Svc. award 1993, hon. mem. 1996; mem. AIAA, Chinese Meteorol. Soc. (hon. mem. 1994), Am. Geophys. Union, Coun. Engring. & Sci. Soc. Home: 189 Jason St Arlington MA 02174

SPENSER, IAN DANIEL, chemist educator; b. Vienna, Austria, June 17, 1924; m. Anita Fuchs, Sept. 5, 1951; children: Helen Ruth, Paul Andrew. B.Sc. with honors, U. Birmingham (Eng.), 1948; Ph.D. in Biochemistry, U. London, 1952, D.Sc. in Organic and Biochemistry, 1969. Demonstrator in biochemistry King's Coll., U. London, 1948-52, asst. lectr. in biochemistry Med. Coll. St. Bartholomew's Hosp., 1952-54, lectr., 1954-57; postdoctoral fellow div. pure chemistry NRC Can., Ottawa, Ont., 1953-54; asst. prof. biochemistry McMaster U., Hamilton, Ont., Can., 1957-59; assoc.prof. McMaster U., 1959-64, prof., 1964-68, prof. chemistry, 1968-89, prof. emeritus, 1989—; Akademischer Gast Laboratorium für Organische Chemie/Eidgenössische Technische Hochschule, Zürich, Switzerland, 1971, 89; vis. prof. Inst. Organic Chemistry, Tech. U. Denmark, Lyngby, 1977, Inst. Organische Chemie/Univ. Karlsruhe, Fed. Republic Germany, 1981, Institut für Pharmazeutische Biologie, Universität Bonn, Federal Republic of Germany, 1989. Research in biosynthesis of alkaloids, biosynthesis of vitamin Bl and vitamin B6. Recipient Sr. Scientist award NATO, 1980; recipient Can.-Japan Exchange award, 1982-83, Univ. Club of Hamilton award, 1990. Fellow Royal Soc. Can., Chem. Inst. Can. (John Labatt Ltd. award 1982-83), Royal Soc. Chemistry (U.K.); mem. Biochem. Soc., Am. Soc. Biochemistry Molecular Biol., Am. Soc. Pharmacognosy, Phytochem. Soc. N. Am. Office: McMaster U, Dept Chemistry, Hamilton, ON Canada L8S 4M1

SPERAKIS, NICHOLAS GEORGE, artist; b. N.Y.C., June 8, 1943; s. George and Cathren (Cokatas) S.; m. Yolanda de Carmen Mesa, Feb. 1, 1983. Student, Pratt Inst., 1960, NAD, 1960-61, Art Students League N.Y., Pratt Graphic Art Center, 1961-63. Instr. Summit (N.J.) Art Center, 1971, New Sch. Social Research, N.Y.C., 1972—, Fashion Inst. Tech., N.Y.C., 1977—. Exhibited one-man shows at Paul Kessler Gallery, 1963, 64, Provincetown, Mass., Hinckley and Brohel Art Gallery, Washington, 1964, N.Y.C., 1965, Mari Galleries, Woodstock, N.Y., 1966, 67, 68, Larchmont, N.Y., 1967, Eric Schindler Galleries, 1965, Richmond (Va.) Art Gallery, N.Y. U. Student Loeb Center, 1969, L.I. U., 1971, Pratt Inst., 1971, Bienville Gallery, New Orleans, 1972, 74, Pace U., N.Y.C., 1972, Lerner-Heller Gallery, N.Y.C., 1975, 76, Daedal Gallery, Balt., 1976, Reading Mus. Art, (Pa.), 1977, Bklyn. Mus., 1977, Washington Irving Gallery, N.Y.C., 1982, Museo Universitario Del Chopo, Mexico City, 1984, Forum Gallery, N.Y.C., Mus. Contemporary Art, Bogota, The Atler Gallery, Munich, 1989, Galeriever Blankenese, Hamburg, Fed. Republic Germany, 1988, Galeria Sextante, Bogota, 1989, La Francia, Centro de Arte, Medellin, Colombia, 1989, various woodcut exhbns., , Alexander S. Onassis Ctr. N.Y.U., 1995, others; exhibited group shows, Mercy Hurst Coll., Erie, Pa., 1963, 64, Bklyn. Mus., 1964, 77, Jewish Mus., 1964, Chrysler Mus., 1964, 65, Assoc. Am. Artists Galleries, N.Y.C., 1965, Norfolk (Va.) Mus. Arts Scis., 1965, Long Beach (Calif.) Coll., 1969, Am. Acad. and Nat. Inst. Arts and Letters, 1969, 75, Mid West Mus-Am-Art, 1981, numerous others, print exhbns., France, Italy, Spain, other European Countries, Far East, 1970-71, Lerner-Heller Gallery, 1973, 76, Amherst Coll., 1974, Worcester (Mass.) Mus. Fine Art, 1977, Reading (Pa.) Mus. Art, 1977, Galeria El Museo Santate de Bogota, Colombia, 1992, Mus. Modern Art, Rio de Janeiro, Brazil, 1992, travel Ams., Europe, 1992, Rhino Horn, N.Y.C., 1994, WhiteHall, N.Y.C., 1993, 94, Barnard/Biderman Fine Art, N.Y.C., 1994; represented in permanent collections Bklyn. Mus., Walter P. Chrysler Mus., Norfolk, Va., Norfolk Mus. Arts and Scis., N.Y.C. Public Library, Phila. Mus. Fine Arts, Worcester Mus. Fine Art, Flint (Mich.) Art Inst., Mus. Modern Art, N.Y.C., U. Conn., Storrs, Amherst Coll., Okla. Fine Arts Center Mus., Am. Acad. and Nat. Inst. Arts and Letters, Detroit Inst. Fine Art, Corcoran Gallery of Art, Midwest Mus. Am. Art, Exeter Acad., Conn., Mus. Modern Art, N.Y.C., print collections Nat. Mus. Am. Art Smithsonian Instn., DeHunter Mus. Art, Chattanooga, Libr. of Congress, Washington, High Mus. Art, Atlanta, Free Libr., Phila., Kunst Mus., Fine Arts Mus. Bern Switzerland, Australian Nat. Gallery, Canberra, Snite Mus. Art, U. Notre Dame, Ind., Bibliotheque Royale Albert/ER, Bruxelles, Belgium, Museo Rayo, Roldanillo, Colombia, Stedelijk Mus., Amsterdam, The Netherlands, Hirshhorn Mus., Washington, Mus. Modern Art Santa Fe de Bogota, Nordjyllands Kunstmus., Aalborg, Denmark, Banco Bozano Simonsen, Rio de Janeiro, Mus. Modern Art, Bogota, Rose Art Mus. Brandeis U., Conn.; organized (with others), Rhino Horn artist group, N.Y.C., 1970. Recipient First Prize Purchase award Mercy Hurst Coll., 1964; Lawrence and Hinda Rosenthal award Am. Acad. and Nat. Inst. Arts and Letters, 1969; Guggenheim graphics fellow, 1970; McDowell Colony summer residency, 1976. Mem. Soc. Am. Graphic Artists. Address: 245 W 29th St Floor 12A New York NY 10001 *Art doesn't bring out the voters for candidates X or Z. Art brings forth an experience and enters the knowledge of the viewer, so it helps the individual consider new channels and modes of behavior. One of the reasons there is so much censorship of art is due to the power art has to transform people at the roots not into some action but in a more generalized manner in terms of understanding institutions and traditions for what they really are. I think art changes emotions more than it changes specific ideas.*

SPERANDIO, GLEN JOSEPH, pharmacy educator; b. Glen Carbon, Ill., May 8, 1918; s. Henry A. and Marjorie (Dunstedter) A.; m. Dorys Bell, June 21, 1946; 1 child, James Glen. B.S., St. Louis Coll. Pharmacy, 1940; M.S., Purdue U., 1947, Ph.D., 1950. Pharmacist, 1936-41; analytical chemist Grove Labs., St. Louis, 1941-43, 45; mfg. pharmacist William R. Warner Co., St. Louis, 1944; instr. Purdue U., 1946-50, asst. prof. pharmacy, 1950-53, assoc. prof., 1953-62, prof., 1962—, head dept., 1966-78, assoc. dean, 1978-83, assoc. dean emeritus, 1984—; exec. dir. Ind. Soc. Hosp. Pharmacists, 1984—; indsl. cons., 1955-81; pharm. cons. VA Hosp., Indpls., 1963-69; mem. blue ribbon com. on standardized bd. exams. Nat. Assn. Bds. Pharmacy, 1969; cons. on clin. pharmacy Surgeon Gen., U.S. Army, 1973-80. Author: Laboratory Manual of Cosmetics, 1956, (with others) Scoville's Art of Compounding, 1959, (with others) Clinical Pharmacy, 1966; author, editor: (with others) Hosp. Pharmacy Notes, 1959-74. Served with USCGR, 1944. Named 1st prof. clin. pharmacy in U.S., Distinguished Alumnus St. Louis Coll. Pharmacy, 1969. Mem. AMA, Am. Soc. Hosp. Pharmacists, Parenteral Drug Assn. (regional v.p. 1965-67), Nat. Formulary, Ind. Soc. Hosp. Pharmacists (pres. 1955-57, hon. mem., disting. educator 1980), Am. Pharm. Assn. (sec.-treas. sect. practical pharmacy 1956), Ind. Pharm. Assn., Tipp County Pharm. Assn., Internat. Fedn. Pharmacists, Soc. Cosmetic Shemists, Am. Legion, Masons (32 deg.), Golden Key, Sigma Xi, Kappa Psi (nat. svc. award 1967, nat. pres. 1963-67), Rho Chi, Phi Lambda Upsilon. Research in drug, cosmetic formulation. Home: PO Box 2509 West Lafayette IN 47906-0509 Office: Purdue U Sch Pharmacy Lafayette IN 47907 *A great help in solving problems is to look at the situation from the other person's point of view.*

SPERBER, DANIEL, physicist; b. Vienna, Austria, May 8, 1930; came to U.S., 1955, naturalized, 1967; s. Emanuel and Nelly (Liberman) S.; m. Ora Yuval, Nov. 29, 1963; 1 son, Ron Emanuel. M.Sc., Hebrew U., 1954; Ph.D., Princeton U., 1960. Tng. and rsch. asst. Israel Inst. Tech., Haifa, 1954-55, Princeton U., 1955-60; sr. scientist, rsch. adviser Ill. Inst. Tech. Rsch. Inst., Chgo., 1960-67; assoc. prof. physics Ill. Inst. Tech., 1964-67, Rensselaer Poly. Inst., Troy, N.Y., 1967-72; prof. Rensselaer Poly. Inst., 1972—; Nordita prof. Niels Bohr Inst., Copenhagen, 1973-74, NATO research fellow, vis., prof., 1974-77; vis. prof. G.S.I., Darmstadt, Fed. Republic Germany, 1983; sr. Fulbright research scholar, Saha Inst. Nuclear Physics, Calcutta, India, 1987-88. Contbr. over 100 sci. papers to profl. jours. Served to capt. Israeli Army, 1948-51. Fellow Am. Phys. Soc.; mem. Israel Phys. Soc., N.Y. Acad. Scis., Sigma Xi. Jewish. Home: 1 Taylor Ln Troy NY 12180-7162 Office: Rensselaer Poly Inst Dept Physics Troy NY 12180-3590 *My goals are to further an understanding of nature by basic research in nuclear theory and to introduce a new generation to this research.*

SPERBER, MARTIN, pharmaceutical company executive, pharmacist; b. N.Y.C., Aug. 6, 1931; s. David and Gertrude (Besen) S.; m. Ellen Claire Marx, June 7, 1953; children—Steven Jay, Susan Barbara Parnes. B.S., Columbia U., N.Y.C., 1952. Registered pharmacist. Pharmacist, dir. sales and mktg. Henry Schein, Inc., N.Y.C., 1953-65, v.p., 1965-80; pres., chief oper. officer Henry Schein, Inc., Port Washington, N.Y., 1980-89, vice chmn., 1989—, also bd. dirs.; pres., chief oper. officer Schein Pharm., Inc., Port Washington, 1985-89, chmn., chief exec. officer, 1989—, also bd. dirs.; chmn., chief exec. officer Danbury Pharm. Inc., Carmel, N.Y., 1989—, also bd. dirs.; chmn., chief exec. officer Steris Labs., Inc., Phoenix, 1989—, also bd. dirs. Mem. coun. of overseers Arnold and Marie Schwartz Coll. Pharmacy, L.I. U. Mem. Am. Pharm. Assn. Office: Schein Pharm Inc 100 Campus Dr # 375 Florham Park NJ 07932-1006*

SPERDUTO, LEONARD ANTHONY, mathematics eductor; b. Philadelphia, Jan. 19, 1958; s. Anthony and Lena (Maio) S. AAS, Camden County Coll., Blackwood, N.J., 1982, 87; BA, Rutgers U., 1989. Cert. tchr. math., N.J. Math. tutor Rutgers U., Camden, N.J., 1987-89; substitute tchr. Maple Shade (N.J.) Bd. Edn., 1989-90; math. tutor Camden County Coll., Blackwood, 1992-94, adj. instr. basic skills math., 1992—. Mem. Math. Assn. Am., Nat. Coun. Tchrs. Math. Home: 6849 Clark Ave Camden NJ 08105-3101 Office: Camden County Coll PO Box 200 Blackwood NJ 08012

SPERELAKIS, NICHOLAS, SR., physiology and biophysics educator, researcher; b. Joliet, Ill., Mar. 3, 1930; s. James and Arestia (Kayadakis) S.; m. Dolores Martinis, Jan. 28, 1960; children: Nicholas Jr., Mark, Christine, Sophia, Thomas, Anthony. BS in Chemistry, U. Ill., 1951; diploma, U.S Navy & Marine Corps Electronics Sch., 1952; MS in Physiology, U. Ill., 1955, PhD in Physiology, 1957. Teaching asst. U. Ill., Urbana, 1954-57; instr. Case Western Res. U., Cleve., 1957-59, asst. prof., 1959-66, assoc. prof., 1966; prof. U. Va., Charlottesville, 1966-83; Joseph Eichberg prof. physiology Coll. Medicine U. Cin., 1983—, chmn. dept., 1983-93; cons. NPS Pharm., Inc., Salt Lake City, 1988-95, Carter Wallace, Inc. Cranbury, N.J., 1988-91; vis. prof. U. St. Andrews, Scotland, 1972-73, U. San Luis Potosi, Mex., 1986, U. Athens, Greece, 1994; Rosenblueth prof. Centro de Investigacion y Avanzades, Mex., 1972; mem. sci. adv. com. several internat. meetings, editorial bd. numerous sci. jours. Co-editor: Handbook of Physiology and Pathophysiology of the Heart, 1984, 2d edit., 1988, 3d edit., 1995, Calcium Antagonists: Mechanisms of Action on Cardiac Muscle and Vascular Smooth Muscle, 1984, Cell Interactions and Gap Junctions, vols. I and II, 1989, Frontiers in Smooth Muscle Research, 1990, Ion Channels in Vascular Smooth Muscle and Endothelial Cells, 1991, Essentials of Physiology, 1992, 2d edit., 1996, Cell Physiology Source Book, 1995, Electrogenesis of Biopotentials, 1995; assoc. editor Circulation Rsch., 1970-75, Molecular Cellular Cardiology; contbr. articles to profl. jours.; author/co-author over 490 rsch. publs. and book chpts. Lectr. Project Hope, Peru, 1962. Sgt. USMC, 1951-53, Res., 1953-59. Recipient Disting. Alumnus award Rockdale (Ill.) Pub. Schs., 1958; U. Cin. Grad. fellow, 1989; NIH grantee, 1959—. Mem. Am. Physiol. Soc. (chair steering com. sect. 1981-82), Biophys. Soc. (coun. 1990-93), Am. Soc. Pharmacology and Exptl. Therapeutics, Internat. Soc. Heart Rsch. (coun. 1980-89, 92—), Am. Heart Assn. (established investigator 1961-66, Rsch. Merit award 1995, Sam Kaplan Rsch. award, 1996), Am. Hellenic Ednl. Progressive Assn. (pres. Charlottesville chpt. 1980-82), Ohio Physiol. Soc. (pres. 1990-91), Phi Kappa Phi. Democrat. Greek Orthodox. Avocations: ancient coins, stamp collecting. Office: U Cin Coll Medicine 231 Bethesda Ave Cincinnati OH 45229-2827 *One of the most important contributions to society and civilization that we can make is to express our serious and urgent concern for the well-being of planet Earth, the environment, plants, animals, and humans, and to educate the public worldwide accordingly.*

SPERGER, COURTLAND, food products executive; b. 1922. Chmn. Alto Dairy Coop, Waupun, Wis., 1944—. Office: Alto Dairy Coop N 3545 County EE Waupun WI 53963*

SPERLING, ALLAN GEORGE, lawyer; b. N.Y.C., Dec. 10, 1942; s. Saul and Gertrude (Lober) S.; m. Susan Kelz, June 27, 1965; children: Matthew Laurence, Stuart Kelz, Jane Kendra. Bar: N.Y. 1969, U.S. Ct. Appeals (2d cir.) 1975. Law clk. to presiding justice U.S. Dist Ct., New Haven, 1967-68; assoc. Cleary, Gottlieb, Steen & Hamilton, N.Y.C., 1968-75, ptnr., 1976—. Editor Yale Law Jour. Chmn. bd. Merce Cunningham Dance Found., N.Y.C., 1992—, vice-chmn., 1985-92; chmn. bd. Rye (N.Y.) Arts Ctr. Inc., 1985-88, bd. dirs., 1990-94; bd. dirs. Friends of the Neuberger Mus., Purchase, N.Y., 1989—. Mem. ABA, N.Y. State Bar Assn., Order of Coif, Phi Beta Kappa. Home: Kirby Ln Rye NY 10580 Office: Cleary Gottlieb Steen & Hamilton 1 Liberty Plz New York NY 10006-1404

SPERLING, ELLIOT HARRIS, history educator; b. N.Y.C., Jan. 4, 1951; s. Solomon and Edith (Kantor) S.; m. Annie Joly, Apr. 10, 1982; 1 child, Coline Joly. BA, Queens Coll., CUNY, 1973; MA, Ind. U., 1980, PhD, 1983. Vis. asst. prof. of history U. So. Miss., Hattiesburg, 1984-85; asst. prof. of Tibetan studies dept. of Uralic and Altaic studies Ind. U., Bloomington, 1986-93; vis. asst. prof. of Tibetan and Himalayan studies, dept. Sanskrit and Indian studies Harvard U., Cambridge, Mass., 1992-93; assoc. prof. of Tibetan studies, dept. ctrl. Eurasian studies Ind. U., 1993—; vis. lecturer U. Delhi, India, 1994—. Contbr. articles to profl. jours. John D. & Catherine T. MacArthur Found. fellow, 1984-89, Fulbright scholar, 1994. Mem. The Tibet Soc., The Mongolia Soc., The Am. Oriental Soc., The Assn. for Asian Studies. Democrat. Jewish. Office: Ind U Dept Uralic and Altaic Studies Goodbody Hall Bloomington IN 47405

SPERLING, GEORGE, cognitive scientist, educator; s. Otto and Melitta Sperling. BS in Math., U. Mich., 1955; MA in Psychology, Columbia U., 1956; PhD in Psychology, Harvard U., 1959. Rsch. asst. in biophysics Brookhaven Nat. Labs., Upton, N.Y., summer 1955; rsch. asst. in psychology Harvard U., Cambridge, Mass., 1957-59; mem. tech. rsch. staff Acoustical and Behavioral Rsch. Ctr., AT&T Bell Labs., Murray Hill, N.J., 1958-86; prof. psychology and neural sci. NYU, N.Y.C., 1970-92; disting. prof. cognitive scis. U. Calif., Irvine, 1992—; instr. psychology Washington Sq. Coll., NYU, 1962-63; vis. assoc. prof. psychology Duke U., spring 1964; adj. assoc. prof. psychology Columbia U., 1964-65; acting assoc. prof. psychology UCLA, 1967-68; hon. rsch. assoc. Univ. Coll., U. London, 1969-70; vis. prof. psychology U. Western Australia, Perth, 1972, U. Wash., Seattle, 1977; vis. scholar Stanford (Calif.) U., 1984; mem. sci. adv. bd. USAF, 1988-92. Recipient Meritorious Civilian Svc. medal USAF, 1993; Gomberg scholar U. Mich., 1953-54; Guggenheim fellow, 1969-70. Fellow AAAS, APA (Disting. Sci. Contbn. award 1988), Am. Acad. Arts and Sci., Optical Soc. Am.; mem. NAS, Assn. for Rsch. in Vision and Ophthalmology, Ann. Interdisciplinary Conf. (founder, organizer 1975—), Eastern Psychol. Assn. (bd. dirs. 1982-85), Soc. for Computers in Psychology (steering com. 1974-78), Psychonomic Soc., Soc. Exptl. Psychologists (Warren medal 1996), Soc. for Math. Psychology (chmn. 1983-84, exec. bd. 1979-85), Phi Beta Kappa, Sigma Xi. Office: U Calif Dept Cognitive Scis SS Tower Irvine CA 92717

SPERLING, GEORGE ELMER, JR., lawyer; b. Phila., Feb. 5, 1915; s. George E. and Margaret Ethel (Fulton) S.; m. Elizabeth Ruth Smollett, Feb. 3, 1945; children: Mary Elizabeth, Doris Fulton, Patricia Anne. A.B., Pa. State Coll., 1936, M.A., 1937; J.D., U. Mich., 1940. Bar: Mich. 1940. Practice in Ann Arbor, 1940-42; counsel Standard Oil Co., Cleve., 1943-45, Carnation Co., Los Angeles, 1946-82; asst. sec. Carnation Co., 1951-63, sec., 1963-82, mem. jr. bd. dirs., 1952-62; v.p. Buckley & Sperling, Monterey, Calif., 1982-85; ptnr. Buckley, Sperling & Frey, Monterey, 1985-87; ptnr. Buckley & Sperling, Santa Monica, 1987—, pres., 1992—. Chmn. Wilshire YMCA, 1952—; pres. Brentwood Protective Assn., 1958-60; trustee Bel Air Town and Country Sch.; mem. pres.' coun. San Francisco Theol. Sem., San Anselmo, Calif., 1993—; pres. Clara Schmidt Found., 1992—. Mem. Navy League, Pa. State Coll. Alumni Assn. of So. Calif. (v.p.), Mich., Ohio, Calif., Wis. bar assns., Brentwood Youth Council (pres. 1959). Presbyn. Clubs: Toastmasters, Riviera Country, President's (U. Mich.). Lodge: Miracle Mile Kiwanis (pres. dir.). Home: 347 25th St Santa Monica CA 90402-2521 Home: 347 25th St Santa Monica CA 90402-2521 *The most important thing for a person to do is to keep your mind alert at all times. You will never get old if you keep thinking of ways to help your country, your neighbors, your friends, and yourself.*

SPERLING, GODFREY, JR., journalist; b. Long Beach, Calif., Sept. 25, 1915; s. Godfrey and Ida (Bailey) S.; m. Betty Louise Feldmann, June 22, 1942; children—Mary (Mrs. John H. McAuliffe), John Godfrey. B.S., U. Ill., 1937; J.D., U. Okla., 1940. Bar: Ill. bar 1940. Practice in Urbana, Ill.; also reporter Champaign-Urbana News-Gazette, 1940-41; mem. staff Christian Sci. Monitor, 1946—, Midwest bur. chief, 1957-62, N.Y. bur. chief, 1962-65, news mgr., asst. chief Washington bur., 1965-73, nat. polit. corr., 1970-83, chief Washington Bur., 1973-83, sr. Washington columnist, 1984—; lectr. nat. affairs, 1955—, Woodrow Wilson vis. fellow, 1976—. Served to maj. USAAF, 1941-46; col. Res. Recipient Alumnus Achievement award U. Ill., 1987, Spl. Citation, Nat. Press Found. for unique contbns. to Am. journalism, 1994. Mem. Okla. Bar Assn., Ill. Bar Assn., Mass. Bar Assn., Congl. Press Corr. Assn., White House Press Corr. Assn., Nat. Press Club (Washington), Overseas Writers Club (Washington), Gridiron of Washington (pres. 1991), Sperling Breakfast Group (host 1966—), Kenwood Country Club (Bethesda, Md.), Navy Officers Club (Bethesda), Sigma Delta Chi. Christian Scientist. Office: Christian Science Monitor 910 16th St NW Washington DC 20006-2903

SPERLING, ROBERT Y., lawyer; b. Chgo., July 14, 1947. AB, U. Ill., 1969; JD, De Paul U., 1972. Bar: Ill. 1972, U.S. Dist. Ct. (no. dist.) Ill. 1972, U.S. Ct. Appeals (7th cir.) 1975, U.S. Supreme Ct. 1978. Ptnr. Katte Muchin & Zavis, Chgo. Mem. ABA (local govt. law sect., litigation sect., antitrust law legis. com. 1977-79), Ill. State Bar Assn., Chgo. Bar Assn. (jud. com. 1972, local govt. com. 1972, young lawyers divsn.). Address: Katten Muchin & Zavis 525 W Monroe St Ste 1600 Chicago IL 60661-3629*

SPERLING-ORSECK, IRENE, publishing company executive. V.p., pub. Tradeshow Week, L.A. Office: Tradeshow Week 5700 Wilshire Blvd Los Angeles CA 90036*

SPERO, BARRY MELVIN, medical center executive; b. Richmond, Va., July 13, 1937; s. Stanley Leo and Jean (Marmorstein) S.; m. Merle Burns, May 29, 1960; children: Amy, Robin, Melissa. BA, U. Richmond, 1959; MHA, Med. Coll. Va., 1961. Asst. adminstr. Bapt. Hosp., Nashville, 1963-66, adminstrv. dir., 1966-68; v.p., dir. hosp. adminstrn. Hosp. Affiliates, Inc., Nashville, 1968-71; exec. dir. Bon Secours Hosp., Grosse Pointe, Mich., 1971-77; pres. The Mt. Sinai Med. Ctr., Cleve., 1977-85; pres., pres. NeWell Health Care System Newton-Wellesley Hosp., 1985-90; pres. Maimonides Med. Ctr., Bklyn., 1990-95, Masonicare, Wallingford, Conn., 1995—; bd. dirs. Premier Health Alliance, chmn., 1981-84, Premier Preferred Care, Healthfirst; bd. trustees Villa Maria Nursing Ctr./Bon Secours Hosp., 1974-94, chmn., bd., 1988-94; bd. dirs. Conn. Assn. Not-for-Profit Providers for the Aging, bd. dirs. League Vol. Hosps. and Homes, 1991-95, chmn.-elect, 1992-95; coun. overseers Arnold & Marie Schwartz, Coll. Pharmacy and Health Scis., 1992-95; mem. State of Ohio Gov.'s Commn. on Health Care Cost, 1984-85; mem. various coms. Coun. Tchg. Hosps., 1992-95; treas. Vol. Hosps. Am., Mass., 1986-90; chmn. hosp. adv. com. Blue Cross N.E. Ohio, 1983-85; bd. trustees Med. Instrumentation Systems, 1978-84. Mem. personnel practice com. Combined Jewish Philanthropies; chmn. United Way, West Suburban Hosp. Div.; regional bd. Bay Bank Middlesex; mem. Perpetual Benevolent Fund Com., Blue Print 2000, Commonwealth Mass. Fellow Am. Coll. Healthcare Execs.; mem. Greater N.Y. Hosp. Assn. (bd. govs. 1992-94), Am. Hosp. Assn. (com. on Medicare payment for outpatient svcs. 1989-90), Mass. Hosp. Assn. (bd. trustees 1987-90, com. on Medicare payment for outpatient svcs. 1989-90), Mass. Hosp. Assn. (bd. trustees 1987-90, com. on health systems 1986-90, Met. Boston Hosp. Coun. (chmn. 1988-90), New Eng. Healthcare Assembly (Blue Ribbon com. 1985-90), Ohio Hosp. Assn. (exec. coun., bd. trustees 1981-85), Greater Cleve. Hosp. Assn. (exec. coun., bd. trustees 1978-85), Coun. Tchg. Hosps. (various coms. 1992-94). Jewish. Avocations: golf, tennis, scuba diving. Office: Masonicare PO Box 70 Wallingford CT 06492

SPERO, DIANE FRANCES, school director; b. Glen Ridge, N.J., Sept. 4, 1949; d. Gerard Anthony and Frances Dolores (Duffy) Racioppi; m. John David Spero, Feb. 21, 1971; children: John, Lisa. BA in Elem. Edn., Trenton (N.J.) State Coll., 1971; postgrad., Ariz. State U. Tchr. Mount Laurel (N.J.) Twp. Schs., 1971-75, Chandler (Ariz.) Unified Schs., 1975-77, Madison Sch. Dist., Phoenix, 1977-78; dir., tchr. Creative Art Sch. for Youth, Scottsdale, Ariz., 1985—. Choir dir., youth choir dir. St. Patricks Ch., Scottsdale, 1986-92; vol. Am. Diebetes Assn., 1990—, Am. Cancer Soc., 1990-93. Mem. ASCD, Nat. Assn. for the Edn. of Young Children, Ariz. assn. for the Edn. of Young Children, Assn. for Childhood Edn. Internat. Roman Catholic. Avocations: writing musical shows, reading. Home: 9208 N 83rd Pl Scottsdale AZ 85258-1884 Office: CASY Country Day Sch 7214 E Jenan Dr Scottsdale AZ 85260-5416

SPERO, JOAN EDELMAN, federal agency administrator; b. Davenport, Iowa, Oct. 2, 1944; d. Samuel and Sylvia (Halpern) Edelman; m. C. Michael Spero, Nov. 9, 1969; children: Jason, Benjamin. Student, L'Inst. d'Etudes Politiques, Paris, 1964-65; BA, U. Wis., 1966; MA, Columbia U., 1968, PhD, 1973. Asst. prof. Columbia U., N.Y.C., 1973-79; ambassador of U.S. to UN Econ. and Social Council, N.Y.C., 1980-81; v.p. Am. Express Co., N.Y.C., 1981-83, sr. v.p. internat. corp. affairs, 1983-89; treas., sr. v.p., 1989-91; exec. v.p. corp. affairs and communications Am. Express Co., 1991-93; under sec. for econ., bus. and agrl. affairs Dept. of State, Washington, 1993—; vis. scholar Fed. Res. Bank N.Y., 1976-77; mem. U.S.-Japan Bus. Coun., Washington, 1983—. Author: The Politics of International Economic Relations, 4th edit., 1990, The Failure of the Franklin National Bank, 1980; contbr. articles to profl. jours. Trustee Amherst Coll.; bd. dirs. French-Am. Found.; mem. Coun. Am. Ambassadors. Named to Acad. Women Achievers, YWCA, 1983; named Fin. Woman of Yr., Fin. Women's Assn., 1990; recipient George Washington Disting. Statesperson award, 1994; Woodrow Wilson fellow. Mem. Coun. on Fgn. Rels. (Internat. Affairs fellow), The Trilateral Commn., Svcs. Policy Adv. Com., Phi Beta Kappa. Democrat. Jewish. Avocations: writing; swimming. Office: US Dept State Econ Bus and Ag Affairs 2201 C St NW Washington DC 20520-7512

SPERO, NANCY, artist; b. Cleve., 1926. BFA, Sch. Art Inst. Chgo., 1949; student, Ecole des Beaux-Arts, Paris, 1950, Atelier Andre l'Hote, Paris, 1950. One-woman shows include Burnett Miller Gallery, L.A., 1985, 89, Rhona Hoffman Gallery, Chgo., 1986, Inst. Contemporary Art, London, 1987, Everson Mus. Art, Syracuse, N.Y., 1987, Mus. Contemporary Art, L.A., 1988, Smith Coll. Mus. Art, Northampton, Mass., 1990, Haus am Walsee, Berlin, Germany, 1990, Barbara Gross Galerie, Munich, Salzburger Kunstverein, Austria, 1991, Christine König Gallery, Vienna, Austria, 1992, Ulmer Mus., Ulm, Germany, 1992, Josh Baer Gallery, N.Y.C., 1993, Nat. Gallery Can., Ottowa, 1993, Greenville (S.C.) County Mus. Art, 1993, Rhona Hoffman Gallery, Chgo., 1994, Printworks, Chgo., 1994, Kunststichting Kanaal Art Found., Kortrijk, Belgium, 1994, Malmö (Sweden) Konshal, 1994, Am. Ctr., Paris, MIT List Visual Arts Ctr., Cambridge, 1994, Arthur M. Sackler Mus., Harvard U., 1995, Fine Arts Gallery, U. Md. Baltimore County, 1995, Barbara Gross Gallerie, Munich, 1995, N.Y. Kunsthalle, 1996, Vancouver Art Gallery, 1996, Hiroshima City Mus. Contemporary Art, 1996, Jüdisches Mus. der Stad Wier, 1996, Heeresspital, Innsbruck, Tyrol, 1996, Jack Tilton Gallery, N.Y.C., 1996, others; exhibited in group shows at The Biennial of Sydney, Australia, 1986, Mus. Modern Art, N.Y.C., 1988, The Bertha and Karl Leubsdorf Art Gallery, Hunter Coll., N.Y.C., 1988, Le Grande Halle de La Villette, Paris, 1989, Bullet Space, N.Y.C., 1989, Ctr. Internat. d'Art Contemporain, Montreal, 1990, dum Umeni Mesta Brna, Brünn, Czechoslowakia, 1991, Boston (Mass.) U. Art Gallery, 1991, Mus. der Stadtentwässerung, Zurich, 1994, Stichting Artimo, Beurs van Berlage, Amsterdam, 1994, Sch. Art Inst. Chgo., Betty Rymer Gallery, Chgo., 1994, MIT List Visual Arts Ctr., Cambridge, 1995, Southeastern Ctr. for Contemporary Art, Winston-Salem, N.C., 1995, Ctr. Georges Pompidou, Paris, 1995, Uffizi Gallery, Florence, Italy, 1995, Mus. Modern Art, N.Y.C., 1996, numerous others.

SPEROS, RICHARD LEE, state official, resort executive; b. Oil City, Pa., Oct. 16, 1936; s. Louie T. and Leona (Regal) S.; m. Millie Evelyn O'Camb, June 11, 1955; children: Penny, Jason, Jeff. BA in History, Alliance Coll., Cambridge Springs, Pa., 1961; MA in Edn., Troy (Ala.) State U., 197. Commd. 2d lt. USAF, 1961, advanced through grades to maj., fighter pilot,, 1961-78; ret., 1978; owner, mgr. Tiger Musky Resort, Coudenay, Wis., 1976—; sec. Wis. Dept. Tourism, Madison, 1991—; bd. dirs. Heritage Bank, Hayward, Wis. Bd. dirs. Fishing Hall of Fame, Hayward, 1990—. Decorated DFC with two oak leaf clusters, Air medal with nine oak leaf clusters. Mem. Rotary. Office: Wis Dept Tourism 123 W Washington Madison WI 53707

SPERTUS, PHILIP, investment company executive; b. Chgo., 1934; grad. MIT, 1956. With Intercraft Industries Corp., Chgo., pres., 1969-79, chmn. bd., 1979-92, also chief exec. officer and dir. Office: 3321 Bee Caves Rd Ste 333 Austin TX 78746-6769

SPERZEL, GEORGE E., JR., personal care industry executive; b. 1951. BS in Bus. Adminstrn./Mgmt., U. Louisville, 1977. With General Electric Co., 1977-93; with Andrew Jergens Co., Cin., 1993—, now v.p., CFO; v.p., CFO Kao Corp. of Am., Wilmington, Del., 1995—. Office: Andrew Jergens Co 2535 Spring Grove Ave Cincinnati OH 45214-1729 also: Kao Corp Am Ste 404 902 Market St Wilmington DE 19801

SPETH, JAMES GUSTAVE, United Nations executive, lawyer; b. Orangeburg, S.C., Mar. 4, 1942; s. James Gustave and Amelia St. Clair (Albergotti) S.; m. Caroline Cameron Council, July 3, 1964; children: Catherine Council, James Gustave, Charles Council. BA summa cum laude, Yale U., 1964, LLB, 1969; MLitt, Oxford U., 1966; LLD (hon.), Clark U., 1995. Bar: D.C. 1969. Law clk. to Justice Hugo L. Black U.S. Supreme Ct., 1969-70; sr. staff atty. Natural Resources Def. Council, Washington, 1970-77; mem. Council Environ. Quality, Washington, 1977-79, chmn., 1979-81; prof. law Georgetown U. Law Ctr., Washington, 1981-82; pres. World Resources Inst., Washington, 1982-93; adminstr. UN Devel. Program, N.Y.C., 1993—; founded World Resources Inst.; organized Western Hemisphere Dialogue environ. and devel., 1990; chaired U.S. Task Force internat. devel. and environ. security. Contbr. articles to profl. jours.; speaker in field. Bd. dirs. World Resources Inst., Nat. Resources Def. Coun., Woods Hole Rsch. Ctr., Keystone Ctr., Leadership award 1994. Recipient Resources Def. award Nat. Wildlife Fedn., 1976, Barbara Swain award of honor Nat. Resources Coun. Am., 1992; named to Global 500 Honor Role United Nations Environ. Program, 1988; Rhodes scholar, 1964-66. Mem. Coun. on Fgn. Rels. (N.Y.C.), China Coun. for Internat. Coop. on Environment and Devel. Episcopalian. Home: 350 E 57th St Apt 10A New York NY 10022-2953 Office: UNDP 1 United Nations Plz New York NY 10017-3515

SPETRINO, RUSSELL JOHN, retired utility company executive, lawyer; b. Cleve., Apr. 22, 1926; s. John Anthony and Madeline Spetrino; m. Marilyn Folk, July 17, 1954 (dec.); children: Michael J., Ellen A. Spetrino Raines; m. Mildred Pilkton, June 26, 1993. B.S., Ohio State U., 1950; LL.B., Western Res. U., 1954. Bar: Ohio 1954. Asst. atty. gen. Ohio, 1954-57; atty.-examiner Public Utilities Commn. of Ohio, Columbus, 1957-59; atty. Ohio Edison Co., Akron, 1959-69, sr. atty., 1970-73, gen. counsel, 1973-78, v.p., gen. counsel, 1978-87, exec. v.p., gen. counsel, 1987-89, ret., 1989. Served with inf. U.S. Army, 1944-46. Mem. Portage Country Club. Republican. Home: 333 N Portage Path Unit 34 Akron OH 44303-1252 *The importance of—and the strength that can be derived from—simple intellectual honesty never ceases to amaze me. It is so much easier to deal successfully with others when every effort is made to understand their views, and your own views are based upon thoughtful, honest conviction.*

SPEVACK, MARVIN, English educator; b. N.Y.C., Dec. 17, 1927; s. Nathan and Miriam (Propper) S.; m. Helga Husmann, May 28, 1962; 1 child, Edmund Daniel. B.A., CCNY, 1948; M.A., Harvard U., 1950, Ph.D., 1953. Instr. English CCNY, 1955-61; asst. prof. City Coll. N.Y., 1961-63; prof. English, U. Muenster, Germany, 1963-89, dir. English seminar, 1964-89, dir. Inst. Erasmianum, 1974-89; Fulbright lectr. U. Münster, Germany, 1961-62; vis. prof. U. Munich, 1962-63, NYU, summer 1966, Harvard U., summer 1973, U. N.Mex., 1985-86, Bowling Green State U., fall 1989; fellow Folger Shakespeare Libr., 1970; hon. rsch. fellow Univ. Coll., London, 1980-81, 95—; vis. fellow Wolfson Coll., Cambridge (Eng.) U., 1984; scholar-in-residence Ctr. for Renaissance and Baroque Studies, U. Md., spring 1989; vis. rsch. fellow Inst. for Advanced Studies in Humanities, U. Edinburgh, Scotland, 1991. Author: Harvard Concordance to Shakespeare, 1973, A Complete and Systematic Concordance to the Works of Shakespeare, 9 vols., 1968-80, Robert Burton, Philosophaster, 1984, Shakespeare: The second, Third, and Fourth Folios, 1985, New Cambridge Julius Caesar, 1988, Shakespeare-Text, Language and Criticism: Essays in Honor of Marvin Spevack, 1988, New Variorum Antony and Cleopatra, 1990, A Shakespeare Thesaurus, 1993; also articles and editions. Served with AUS, 1953-55. Guggenheim fellow, 1973-74, Andrew W. Mellon Found. fellow Huntington Libr., 1992, Ctr. for Book fellow Brit. Libr., London, 1994-95. mem. MLA, Internat. Assn. Univ. Profs. English, Internat. Shakespeare Assn., The Bibliog. Soc., Deutsche Shakespeare Gesellschaft W., Shakespeare Assn., Soc. Textual Scholarship, Harvard Club (N.Y.C.), Harvard of Rhein-Ruhr Club (Germany, Phi Beta Kappa. Home: 14 Potstiege, 48161 Münster Germany Office: 12-20 Johannisstrasse, 48143 Münster Germany

SPEWOCK, THEODOSIA GEORGE, reading specialist, educator; b. Canton, Ohio, Sept. 11, 1951; d. George Eleftherios and Despina George (Ilvanakis) Sideropoulos; m. Michael Andrew Spewock, Aug. 23, 1974. BS, Kent State U., 1974; MEd in reading, Pa. State U., 1978; cert. in early childhood edn., Ind. U. of Pa., 1989, cert. elem. prin., 1994. Tchr. Winnisquam Regional Sch. Dist., Tilton, N.H., 1974-77; reading specialist Tyrone (Pa.) Area Sch. Dist., 1978-80, home-sch. liaison, 1980—, title 1 coord., 1994—; chair adv. bd. Family Ctr., Tyrone, 1994; steering com. Altoona Reading Inst., Altoona, Pa., 1991—; chair state reading conf. Keystone Reading Assn., 1994-96. Creator and host (weekly radio story hour): Mrs. Spewock & Friends, 1990—; author: Just for Five's, 1995, Just for Four's, 1995, Just for Three's, 1995, Just for Two's, 1995, Just for One's, 1995, Just for Babies, 1995, Getting Ready to Read, 1996; contbr. articles to profl. jours. Assoc. contbr. Altoona Symphony Orch., 1994; mem. adv. bd. strategic planning Tyrone Area Sch. Dist., 1994; rep. Pa. in Washington D.C., 1992. Recipient Dist. Svc. award Tyrone Area Cmty. Orgn., 1992, Outstanding Employee award, 1989. Mem. Keystone State Reading Assn. (pres. 1995), Internat. Reading Assn., Blair County Reading Coun. (pres. 1986-88), Assn. Supervision and Curriculum Devel., Nat. Assn. Edn. Young Children, Pa. Assn. Elem. Sch. Prins., Phi Delta Kappa. Avocations: piano, reading, folk dancing, cross-country skiing, walking for fitness. Office: Tyrone Area Sch Dist 1317 Lincoln Ave Tyrone PA 16686-1415

SPEYER, JASON LEE, aeronautical engineer, educator; b. Boston, Apr. 30, 1938; s. Joseph Louis and Ruth Sylvia (Steinmetz) S.; m. Barbara Joan Sachs, Sept. 11, 1966; children—Gil, Gavriel, Rakhel, Joseph. B.S., MIT, 1960; M.S., Harvard U., 1964, Ph.D., 1968. Registered profl. engr., Tex. Engr. Boeing Co., Seattle, 1960-61; sr. engr. Raytheon Co.,, Bedford, Mass., 1961-68; sr. analyst Analytical Mechanics Assocs., Inc., Cambridge, Mass., 1968-70; mem. research staff Charles Stark Draper Lab., Cambridge, Mass., 1970-76; Harry H. Power prof. engring. U. Tex., Austin, 1976-90; lectr. MIT, 1971-76; vis. scientist Weizmann Inst. Sci., 1972-73; Lady Davis prof. Technion, Haifa, Israel, 1983; Hunsaker vis. prof. aeros. and astronautics MIT, 1989-90. Recipient Hocott Disting. Engring. Rsch. award Coll. Engring., U. Tex., 1985, Exceptional Civil Svc. award USAF, 1991; Raytheon fellow, 1963-67; Hugh L. Dryden lectureship Am. Inst. of Aeronautics and Astronautics, 1995. Fellow IEEE (bd. govs. Control Sys. Soc. 1982—, assoc. editor Transaction on Automatic Control), AIAA (Mechanics and Control of Flight award 1985, Dryden lectureship in rsch. 1995, assoc. editor Jour. Spacecraft and Rockets, Jour. Guidance and Control). Home: 11358 Chalon Rd Los Angeles CA 90049-1721 Office: UCLA Dept Mech Aerospace & Nuclear Engring Los Angeles CA 90024

SPEYRER, JUDE, bishop; b. Leonville, La., Apr. 14, 1929. Ed., St. Joseph Sem., Covington, La., Notre Dame Sem., New Orleans, Gregorian U., Rome. Ordained priest Roman Cath. Ch., 1953. Consecrated bishop Lake Charles, La., 1980—. Office: PO Box 3223 414 Iris St Lake Charles LA 70602*

SPEZIALE, A. JOHN, organic chemist, consultant; b. Rocky Hill, Conn., Nov. 3, 1916; s. Antonio and Giovina (DiMarco) S.; m. Dorothy Baumeister, May 2, 1942; children: Dona Speziale Luedde, Karen Speziale Hutcheson, Wendy Speziale Tarson. B.S. in Pharmacy, U. Okla., 1942, M.S., 1943; Ph.D., U. Ill., 1948. With Monsanto Co., St. Louis, 1948-79; sr. scientist agrl. div. Monsanto Co., 1960-63; dir. research Monsanto Agrl. Products Co., 1963-79; chem., agrl. and indsl. cons., 1979—; vis. lectr. Washington U., St. Louis, 1950-53; bd. dirs. Mycogen Corp., EOSystem, Inc. Author publs. Served with U.S. Army, 1944-46. Recipient Kenneth A. Spencer award, 1981. Mem. AAAS, Am. Chem. Soc. (exec. com. organic div. 1974-76, mem. editorial bd. Jour. Organic Chemistry 1964-69, lectr. 1970-74, St. Louis sect. award 1973), Weed Sci. Soc. Am. (hon.), Sigma Xi. Patentee synthesis and mechanism action pesticides, phosphorus chemistry, enamines, epoxides, heterocyclics, haloamides. Home: 2635 Saklan Indian Dr # 2 Walnut Creek CA 94595

SPEZIALE, JOHN ALBERT, lawyer; b. Winsted, Conn., Nov. 21, 1922; s. Louis and Mary (Avampato) S.; m. Mary Kocsis, Aug. 12, 1944; children: John Albert, Marcia Jean. BA in Econs., Duke U., 1943, JD, 1947. Bar: Conn. 1948. Clk. Judiciary Com. of Conn. Gen. Assembly, 1949; judge Mcpl. Ct., Torrington, Conn., 1949-51; dir. CD, 1951-52; fed. atty. OPS, 1951-52; mem. Conn. State Jud. Council, 1955-59; sr. partner firm Speziale, Mettling, Lefebre & Burns, Torrington, 1958-61; city atty. Torrington, 1957-59; treas. State of Conn., 1959-61; judge Conn. Ct. Common Pleas, 1961-65, Conn. Superior Ct., 1965-77; presiding judge Conn. Superior Ct. (Appellate div.), 1975-77, chief judge, 1975-77, mem. exec. com., 1975-84, chmn. exec. com., 1977-81; justice Conn. Supreme Ct., 1977-81, chief ct. adminstr., 1978-81, chief justice, 1981-84; sr. ptnr. Cummings & Lockwood, Hartford, 1984-92; of counsel, 1992—; state trial referee Conn., 1986—; mem. exec. com. Nat. Conf. State Trial Judges, 1970-74; faculty advisor grad. session Nat. Coll. State Judiciary, U. Nev., 1973; mem. Conn. Jud. Rev. Coun., 1975-77; co-chmn. planning commn. criminal adminstrn. Conn. Justice Commn., 1975-78; mem. Conn. Commn. on Adult Probation, 1976-77, Adv. Coun. on Ct. Unification, 1976-78, Conn. Bd. Pardons, 1977-78; mem. exec. com. Nat. Bd. Trial Advocacy, 1983-88, dir. 1988—; mem. mediation com. Ctr. Pub. Resources, 1985—. chmn. State-Fed. Relations Com. Conf. of Chief Justices, 1983-84; chmn. adv. bd. Use of Vol. Lawyers to Supplement Jud. Resources, Nat. Inst. Justice and Nat. Ctr. for State Ctrs., 1983-87; mem. lawyers com. Nat. Ctr. for State Cts., 1985-88; chmn. subcom. jud. decisions Nat. Assn. Ins. Commrs. adv. Com. Environ. Liability Ins., 1985-87; mem. Panel of Trial and Appellate Judges, Asbestos Claims Facility, 1986—;l arbitrator Ins. Arbitration Forums, Inc., 1986—; others. Trustee Conn. Jr. Republic, 1975-83; bd. dirs. Newington Children's Hosp. 1983-86, corporator 1983—; chmn. awards com. Freedoms Found. at Valley Forge, 1982, trustee Nat. Council, 1986—; fellow Pvt. Adjudication Found. Duke U. Sch. Law, 1986—. Lt. (j.g.) USNR, 1942-46, PTO. Recipient Conn. Trial Lawyers Jud. award, 1977; 1st Unico Nat. Disting. Key award, 1977; Citizen of Yr. award Elks, 1982; Alva P. Loiselle lifetime achievement award, 1984; Disting. Service award Nat. Ctr. for State Cts., 1985; Significant Practical Achievement award Ctr. for Pub. Resources Legal Program, 1985; Conn. Law Rev. award, 1985. Fellow Am. Bar Found. (life), Conn. Bar Found. (charter life fellow, chmn. James W. Cooper fellows 1994—); mem. ABA (vice chmn. 1984-86, com. on stds. jud. adminstrn. jud. adminstrn. divsn.), Inst. Jud. Adminstrn., Am. Judicature Soc. (dir. 1978-82), Conn. Bar Assn. (com. on alternative dispute resolution 1985-87, com. on liaison with state cts. 1986-92), Hartford Bar Assn., Litchfield County Bar Assn., Supreme Ct. Hist. Soc., Am. Arbitration Assn. (comml. panel arbitrators 1987—, panelist large complex case program 1993—), Am. Fedn. Musicians (life), Sons of Italy of Am., Conn. State Srs. Golf Assn., Inc., Litchfield County Univ. Club, Torrington Country Club, Unico Club (life), Bear Lakes Country Club (Fla.), K.C., Phi Beta Kappa. Roman Catholic. Home: 278 Windtree St Torrington CT 06790-7904 Office: Cummings & Lockwood City Place 1 Hartford CT 06103

SPEZZANO, VINCENT EDWARD, newspaper publisher; b. Retsof, N.Y., Apr. 3, 1926; s. Frank and Lucy S.; m. Marjorie Elliott, Dec. 18, 1948; children: Steve, Judy, Mark, Christine (dec.). BA in Journalism, Syracuse (N.Y.) U., 1950. Reporter Livingston Republican, Geneseo, N.Y., 1950-51, Lynchburg (Va.) News, 1951-54, St. Louis Globe-Democrat, 1954-55; polit. writer, then dir. public service and research Rochester (N.Y.) Times Union, 1955-68; dir. public service, then dir. promotion and public service Gannett Co., Inc., 1968-75; pres., publisher Cape Publs., Inc., Cocoa, Fla., 1975-84; chmn. Cape Publs., Inc., 1984-91; asst., then v.p. Gannett/South, Gannett Co., Inc., 1977-79; pres. Gannett Southeast Newspaper Group, Gannett Co., Inc., 1979-82; exec. v.p. USA Today, 1982-83, pres., 1983; sr. v.p. communications Gannett Co., 1983-84, bd. dirs.; pres., pub. Gannett Rochester Newspapers, 1984-90, chmn., 1990-91; pres. Gannett N.E. Div., 1984-86; past mem. journalism endowment adv. com. U. Fla.; bd. dirs. Marine Midland Bank. Editor handbook. Past trustee St. John Fisher Coll., Rochester; trustee Brevard Art Ctr. and Mus., Melbourne, Fla.; bd. dirs. Cape Canaveral Hosp., 1991—, Fla. Inst. Tech., 1991—, Astronauts Meml. Found., 1991—, vice-chmn., space camp adv. bd.; bd. vice-chmn. Rochester Conv. Bur., 1986-91; mem. Founder's Com. The Rochesterians, 1986—; mem. adv. bd. Space Pioneers, Inc. With A.C., USNR, 1944-46. Recipient News Ariting award Va. Press Assn., 1953, Citizen of Yr. award Citizens Club Rochester, 1960, Disting. Svc. award for non-members Kiwanis Club, 1960, Pub. Svc. Reporting award Am. Polit. Sci. Assn., 1963; named NE Kiwanis Citizen of Yr., 1987, Boss of Yr. Coca Beach chpt. Nat. Secretaries Assn., 1977, Rochester Communicator of Yr., 1987, Rochester Citizen of Yr., 1987, Cavaliere (Knight) in Order of Merit Republic of Italy, 1994. Mem. Internat. Newspaper Promotion Assn. (pres. 1970-71, Silver Shovel award 1975), Am. Newspapers Pubs. Assn., So. Newspaper Pubs. Assn. Found. (chmn.), Fla. Press Assn. (bd. dir., pres. 1984), N.Y. Newspaper Pubs. Assn. (bd. dirs.), Cocoa Beach Area C. of C., Rochester Area C. of C. (bd. dir. 1985—, chmn. bd. 1989-90). Roman Catholic. Home: 855 S Atlantic Ave Cocoa Beach FL 32931-2424 Office: 1 Gannett Plz Melbourne FL 32940 also: Cape Pubs Inc PO Box 363000 Melbourne FL 32936

SPHAR, RAYMOND LESLIE, JR., physician, research administator; b. Charleroi, Pa., July 27, 1934; s. Raymond Leslie and Alma Josephine (Massey) S.; m. Jean Frances Cusick, June 24, 1961 (div. 1976); 1 child, Christina Leslie. BS, Westminster Coll., 1956; MD, Jefferson Med. Coll., 1961; MPH, Yale U., 1972. Commd. lt. USN, 1961, advanced through grades to capt., 1975; resident in preventive medicine Yale U., New Haven, 1969-72; rsch. med. officer Naval Submarine Med. Rsch. Lab., Groton, Conn., 1972-73, comdg. officer, 1973-78; program mgr. med. rsch. Office of Naval Tech., 1978; dir. undersea and radiation medicine Bur. of Medicine and Surgery, Navy Dept., 1978-81; exec. officer Naval Med. Rsch. and Devel. Command, Bethesda, Md., 1981-83; comdg. officer Naval Med. Rsch. Inst., Bethesda, Md., 1983-86; asst. for med., life scis. rsch. Office of Sec. of Def., 1986-89; dir. R&D Bur. Medicine & Surgery, Washington, 1989-90; dir. med. rsch. svc. Dept. Vets. Affairs, Washington, 1991-92, dep. assoc. chief med. dir., 1992-95, chief rsch. and devel., 1995—; U.S. rep. to NATO panel, Brussels, 1986-89; DOD rep. Nat. Adv. Rsch. Resources Coun., NIH, 1986-89; VA rep. Nat Cancer Adv. Bd., NIH, 1991—. Fellow Coll. of Physicians of Phila.; mem. Am. Coll. Preventive Medicine, Am. Coll. Occupational and Environ. Medicine (master), Army and Navy Club, English-Speaking Union, Yale Club. Presbyterian. Home: 2475 Virginia Ave NW Washington DC 20037-2639 Office: Dept Vets Affairs 810 Vermont Ave NW Washington DC 20420-0001

SPHEERIS, PENELOPE, film director; b. New Orleans, 1945. MFA, UCLA Film Sch. Producer: TV series of shorts for Saturday Night Live; films include: The Decline of Western Civilization II: The Metal Years, 1988, Real Life, 1979; dir. (documentary) the Decline of Western Civilization, 1981, (films) Suburbia, 1984, (also screenwriter) The Boys Next Door, 1985, Hollywood Vice Squad, 1986, Dudes, 1987, Wayne's World, 1992, The Beverly Hillbillies, 1993, The Little Rascals, 1994; screenwriter: Summer Camp Nightmare, 1987; actress: Wedding Band, 1990; tv films directed include: Prison Stories: Women on the Inside, 1990. Office: The Gersh Agency Inc 232 N Canon Dr Beverly Hills CA 90210-5302

SPHIRE, RAYMOND DANIEL, anesthesiologist; b. Detroit, Feb. 12, 1927; s. Samuel Raymond and Nora Mae (Allen) S.; m. Joan Lois Baker, Sept. 5, 1953; children—Suzanne M., Raymond Daniel, Catherine J. BS, U. Detroit, 1948; MD, Loyola U., Chgo., 1952. Diplomate Am. Bd. Anesthesiology. Intern Grace Hosp., Detroit, 1952-53; resident Harvard Anesthesia Lab.-Mass. Gen. Hosp., 1953-55; attending anesthesiologist Grace Hosp., Detroit, 1955-72, dir. dept. inhalation therapy, 1968-70; sr. attending anesthesiologist, dir. dept., dir. dept. respiratory therapy Detroit-Macomb Hosps. Assn., 1970—, trustee, 1978—, chief of staff, 1980—; clin. asst. prof. Wayne State U. Sch. Medicine, 1967—; clin. prof. respiratory therapy Macomb Community Coll., Mount Clemens, Mich., 1971—; examiner Am. Registry Respiratory Therapists, 1972—; insp. Joint Rev. Com. Respiratory Therapy Edn., 1972—. Co-author: Operative Neurosurgery, 1970, First Aid Guide for the Small Business or Industry, 1978. With AUS, 1944-45; 1st lt. M.C., USAF, 1952. Fellow Am. Coll. Anesthesiologists, Am. Coll. Chest Physicians; mem. AMA, Am. Soc. Anesthesiologists, Wayne County Soc. Anesthesiologists (pres. 1967-69), Am. Assn. Respiratory Therapists, Soc. Critical Care Medicine, Detroit Athletic Club, Country Club of Detroit, Cumberland Club (Portland, Maine), Severance Lodge. Roman Catholic. Home: 19874 Westchester Dr Clinton Township MI 48038 Office: 119 Kercheval Ave Grosse Pointe MI 48236-3618

SPICER, HAROLD GLENN, chemical engineer; b. Cin., Aug. 4, 1960. BS in Chemistry, U. Dayton, 1983, BSChemE, 1983, MS, 1987. Rsch. assoc. U. Dayton, Ohio, 1982-84; dir. R&D Isotec Inc., Dayton, 1983—. Office: Isotec Corp 3858 Benner Rd Miamisburg OH 45342-4304

SPICER, HOLT VANDERCOOK, speech and theater educator; b. Pasadena, Calif., Feb. 1, 1928; s. John Lovely and Dorothy Eleanor (Clause) S.; m. Marion Arel Gibson, Aug. 16, 1952; children: Mary Ellen, Susan Leah, Laura Alice, John Millard. BA, U. Redlands, 1952, MA, 1957; Ph.D., U. Okla.-Norman, 1964. Instr. speech and theatre Southwest Mo. State Coll., 1952-59, assoc. prof., 1959-64, prof., 1964-93, emeritus prof., 1993—, head dept. speech and theatre, 1967-71, dean Sch. Arts and Humanities, 1971-85; chmn. Dist. 4 Nat. Debate Tournament Com., 1955, 58, 64, 68. Bd. dirs. Springfield Community Ctr., Mo., 1981—. Named Debate Coach of Decade U.S. Air Force Acad., 1965, Holt V. Spicer Debate Forum, 1988; recipient Alumni Achievement award in Speech and Debate U. Redlands, 1991; team won CEDA Nat. Debate championship, 1992. Mem. Speech Communication Assn., Am. Forensic Assn., AAUP. Episcopalian (vestryman 1981-85). Home: 2232 E Langston St Springfield MO 65804-2646 Office: SW Mo State U 901 S National Ave Springfield MO 65804-0027

SPICER, KEITH, federal official, journalist, educator; b. Toronto, Can., Mar. 6, 1934. BA Modern Langs. and Lit., U. Toronto, PhD Polit. Scis.; diploma French civilization, La Sorbonne, Paris; MA Internat. Rels. Inst. d'Etudes Politiques, U. Paris; PhD (hon.), York U., Ottawa U., Laurentian U. TV, radio host, interviewer, commentator Radio Can., Radio Quebec, Can. Broadcasting Corp., TVOnt., TVA, CKVU, Radio-Can. Internat.; pres. Spicer Comm. Group Inc., Can., U.S., 1984-89; spl. asst. to Minister Justice, Can., 1970-77; 1st commr. Ofcl. Langs., Can.; chmn. Can. Radio-TV Comm. Commn., Can., 1989-90, 91-96, Citizen's Forum on Can.'s Future, 1990-91; prof. U. Ottawa, U. Toronto, Dartmouth Coll., N.H., York U., U. B.C., Simon Fraser U. Author: A Samaritan Stae, Cher péquiste...et nèanmoins ami, The Winging It Logic System, Think on Your Feet; editor The Ottawa Citizen, 1985-89; editorial writer The Globe and Mail, Toronto; mag. columnist L'Actualité; contbr. articles to profl. jours. Mem. Order Can. (officer), Union des Parlementaires of French Lang. (officer). Office: CRTC, Ottawa, ON Canada K1A 0N2

SPICER, WILLIAM EDWARD, III, physicist, educator; b. Baton Rouge, Sept. 7, 1929; s. William Edward II and Kate Crystal (Watkins) S.; m. Cynthia Stanley, June 12, 1951 (div. 1969); children: William Edward IV, Sally Ann; m. Diane Lubarsky, Apr. 24, 1969; 1 dau., Jacqueline Kate. B.S., Coll. William and Mary, 1949, MIT, 1951; M.A., U. Mo., 1953, Ph.D., 1955; D.Tech. (hon.), U. Linköping, Sweden, 1975. Scientist RCA Labs, 1955-61, Lawrence Radiation Lab., U. Calif.-Livermore, 1961-62; mem. faculty Stanford U., 1962—, prof. elec. engring. and materials sci. engring., 1965—, prof. by courtesy applied physics, 1976—, Stanford Ascherman prof. engring., 1978—, prof. Stanford Synchrotron Radiation Lab, 1992—; dir. Acad. Skills, Inc., Los Altos, Calif., 1971-73; dep. dir. Stanford Synchrotron Radiation Lab., 1973-75, cons. dir., 1975—, prof., 1992—; cons. to govt. and industry, 1962—; mem. solid state scis. panel Nat. Acad. Sci.-NRC, 1965-73; cons., lectr. Chinese Univ. devel. project World Bank-Fudan U., 1983; mem. panel atomic and molecular physics div. Nat. Bur. Standards, 1966-73, chmn., 1971-73; mem. adv. group election devices Dept. Def., 1975-82; fellow Churchill Coll., Cambridge U., Eng., 1979; mem. panel Japanese tech. evaluation program U.S. Dept. Commerce and NSF, 1983-84; acting dir. Stanford Photon. Lab., 1987-99; chmn. affiliated faculty Stanford Syncrotron Radiation Lab., 1988-92. Mem. editorial bd. Jour. Crystal Growth, 1981-85; author publs. theory and experiment solid state and surface physics and chemistry, photoemission, optical properties solids, electronic structure metals, semiconductors, insulators, high temperature superconductors. Bd. dirs. Princeton (N.J.) YMCA, 1960-62. Recipient Achievement award RCA, 1957, 60, mentor award Nat. Conf. Black Phys. Students, 1992; named Scientist of Yr., Indsl. Research and Devel. mag., 1981; Guggenheim fellow, 1978-79. Fellow IEEE, Am. Phys. Soc. (Oliver Buckley Solid State Physics prize 1980), Am. Vacuum Soc. (chmn. electronics material div. 1978-79, dir. 1979-80, trustee 1981-82, Medard W. Welch award 1984); mem. Phi Beta Kappa. Home: 785 Mayfield Ave Palo Alto CA 94305-1043 Office: Stanford U Mccullough Bldg Stanford CA 94305

SPICKLER, JOSEPH WILLIAM, researcher, physician; b. Leaksville, N.C., Nov. 5, 1940; s. Joseph Creath and Helen (Williams) S.; m. Sarah Schneider, June 23, 1962 (div.); 1 child, Scott William Spickler Chesney; m. Delores Papp, Nov. 28, 1969 (div.); 1 child, Nicole Dianna; m. Marilyn Marie Holmes, Jan. 22, 1981. BSEE, Northwestern U., 1962, MSEE, 1964, PhD in Physiology, 1968; MD, Med. Coll. Ohio, 1975. Cert. Nat. Bd. Med. Examiners, 1976, cert. Am. Bd. Internal Medicine, 1978. Head physiology and bio-engring. dept. Cox Heart Inst., Dayton, Ohio, 1968-72; intern internal medicine Presbyn. Med. Ctr., Denver, 1975-76, resident internal medicine, 1976-78; pvt. practice internal medicine Denver, 1978-86; med. dir. Astra Pharm. Products, Westborough, Mass., 1986-89; dir. clin. investigation Syntex Labs., Palo Alto, Calif., 1989-92; v.p., dir. Syntex Rsch., Palo Alto, 1992—; adj. asst. prof. dept. biol. scis. Wright State U., Dayton, 1970-72; presenter in field. Patentee in field; contbr. articles to profl. jours. Mem. ACP. Home: 1501 Dominion Ave Sunnyvale CA 94087-4025

SPIEGEL, ARTHUR HENRY, III, managing director, president; b. Chgo., June 25, 1939; s. Arthur Henry II and Eleanor F. Spiegel; children: Julia M., Adam H.; m. L. Pollock; 1 child, Samuel. BA, Stanford U., 1965; MBA, Harvard U., 1967. Assoc. dir. ACCION, Venezuela, 1959-61; assoc. adminstr. N.Y.C. Housing and Devel. Adminstrn., 1967-70; dep. adminstr. N.Y.C. HRA, 1970-74; chief oper. officer for Medicaid Dept. Social Svcs. and Child Welfare, N.Y.C., 1970-74; exec. dir. Dept. Social Svcs., N.Y.C., 1970-74; pres., founder APM, Inc., N.Y.C., 1974—; bd. dirs., treas. Nat. Ctr. for Health Edn., N.Y.C., 1988—. Bd. dirs., past pres. Greater N.Y. chpt. March of Dimes, 1985—. Mem. Harvard Club, N.Y. Athletic Club. Office: APM Inc 1675 Broadway Fl 18 New York NY 10019-5820*

SPIEGEL, DANIEL LEONARD, diplomat; b. Balt., Sept. 5, 1945; s. William and Anna (Stiffman) S.; m. Marianne Albertson; 1 child, Anna. AB, Washington U., St. Louis, 1967; MPA, Harvard U., 1969; JD, Georgetown U., Washington, 1979. Legis. asst. U.S. Senate, Washington, 1969-76; spl. asst. to Sec. of State Dept. of State, Washington, 1977-78, mem. policy planning staff, 1978-79; ptnr. Akin, Gump, Strauss, Hauer, LLP, Washington, 1983-90, dir. internat. practice, 1991-93; sr. advisor Clinton-Gore transition Dept. of State, Washington, 1992-93; amb., permanent rep. U.s. Mission to UN, Geneva, 1993—. Office: US Mission to UN, Rt de Pregny 11, 1292 Chambesy Switzerland

SPIEGEL, FRANCIS HERMAN, JR., pharmaceutical company executive; b. Bethlehem, Pa., Apr. 25, 1935; s. Francis H. and Elizabeth (Redding) S.; m. Nancy Starner; children: Todd, Tadd, Thomas. B.A. in Acctg., Lehigh U., 1957. C.P.A., Pa. Account analyst Merck & Co., Inc., Rahway, N.J., 1966, mgr. internal auditing, 1967-70, dir. acctg., 1970-72, asst. controller, 1972-76, controller, 1976-79, treas., 1979-81, v.p. corp. planning, 1981-82; v.p. planning and devel. Merck & Co., Inc., 1983-84, v.p. fin., 1985-87, sr. v.p., 1987—, exec. v.p., 1992—; bd. dirs. Arkwright Ins. Co. Chmn. vis. com. Lehigh U., Bethlehem, Pa., 1980-83, now trustee; trustee Fin. Execs. Rsch. Found. Served to capt. USMC, 1958-61. Mem. AICPA, Fin. Execs.

Inst., Conf. Bd. Coun. Fin. Execs. Office: Merck & Co Inc 1 Merck Dr PO Box 100 Whitehouse Station NJ 08889*

SPIEGEL, HART HUNTER, retired lawyer; b. Safford, Ariz, Aug. 30, 1918; s. Jacob B. and Margaret (Hunter) S.; m. Genevieve Willson, Feb. 12, 1946; children: John Willson, Claire Margaret Spiegel Brian, Jennifer Emily Spiegel Grellman. BA, Yale U., 1940, LLB, 1946. Bar: Calif. 1946, D.C. 1960. Assoc. Brobeck, Phleger & Harrison, San Francisco, 1947-55, ptnr., 1955-90; chief counsel IRS, Washington, 1959-61, mem. adv. group to commr., 1975. Served to lt. USMC, 1942-46, PTO. Mem. ABA (coun. mem. tax sect. 1966-68), Am. Law Inst., Bar Assn. San Francisco (pres. 1983), Pacific Union Club, Berkeley Tennis Club (pres. 1964-65). Home: 3647 Washington St San Francisco CA 94118-1832 Office: Brobeck Phleger & Harrison 1 Market Pla Spear St Tower San Francisco CA 94105

SPIEGEL, HERBERT, psychiatrist, educator; b. McKeesport, Pa., June 29, 1914; s. Samuel and Lena (Mendlowitz) S.; m. Natalie Shainess, Apr. 24, 1944 (div. Apr. 1965); children: David, Ann; m. Marcia Greenleaf, Jan. 29, 1989. B.S., U. Md., 1936, M.D., 1939. Diplomate: Am. Bd. Psychiatry. Intern St. Francis Hosp., Pitts., 1939-40; resident in psychiatry St. Elizabeth's Hosp., Washington, 1940-42; practice medicine specializing in psychiatry N.Y.C., 1946—; attending psychiatrist Columbia-Presbyn. Hosp., N.Y.C., 1960—; faculty psychiatry Columbia U. Coll. Physicians and Surgeons, 1960—; adj. prof. psychology John Jay Coll. Criminal Justice, CUNY, 1983—; mem. faculty Sch. Mil. Neuropsychiatry, Mason Gen. Hosp., Brentwood, N.Y., 1944-46. Author: (with A. Kardiner) War Stress and Neurotic Illness, 1947, (with D. Spiegel) Trance and Treatment: Clinical Uses of Hypnosis, 1978; subject of book: (by Donald S. Connery) The Inner Source: Exploring Hypnosis with Herbert Spiegel, M.D.; Mem. editorial bd.: Preventive Medicine, 1972; Contbr. articles to profl. jours. Mem. profl. advisory com. Am. Health Found.; mem. pub. edn. com., smoking and health com. N.Y.C. div. Am. Cancer Soc.; mem. adv. com. Nat. Aid to Visually Handicapped. Served with M.C. AUS, 1942-46. Decorated Purple Heart. Fellow Am. Psychiat. Assn., Am. Coll. Psychiatrists, Am. Soc. Clin. Hypnosis, Am. Acad. Psychoanalysis, Internat. Soc. Clin. and Exptl. Hypnosis, William A. White Psychoanalytic Soc., N.Y. Acad. Medicine, N.Y. Acad. Scis.; mem. Am. Orthopsychiat. Assn., Am. Psychosomatic Soc., AAAS, AMA, N.Y. County Med. Soc. Office: 19 E 88th St New York NY 10128-0557

SPIEGEL, JERROLD BRUCE, lawyer; b. N.Y.C., Apr. 11, 1949; s. Seymour S. and Estelle (Minsky) S.; m. Helene Susan Cohen, Mar. 3, 1972; children: Dana Sean, Amy Barrett, Evan Tyler. BS, Queens Coll., 1970; JD cum laude, NYU, 1973. Bar: N.Y. 1974. Assoc. Austrian, Lance & Stewart, N.Y.C., 1973-75, Gordon Hurwitz Butowsky Baker Weitzen & Shalov, N.Y.C., 1975-79; ptnr. Shapiro Spiegel Garfunkel & Driggin, N.Y.C., 1979-86, Frankfurt, Garbus, Klein & Selz P.C., N.Y.C., 1986—. Editor Ann. Survey Am. Law, 1972-73,. Mem. ABA (corp. law sect.), Order of the Coif, Omicron Delta Epsilon. Office: Frankfurt Garbus Klein & Selz PC 488 Madison Ave New York NY 10022-5702

SPIEGEL, JOHN WILLIAM, banker; b. Indpls., Mar. 14, 1941; s. William Sordon and Elizabeth (Hall) S.; children: W. Robert, John F., Bradley H.; m. Elizabeth Devereux Morgan, Aug. 16, 1986; stepchildren: David P. Adams III, Morgan G. Adams, Devereux Socas. BA, Wabash Coll., 1963; MBA, Emory U., 1965; postgrad., Nova U., 1993-95. Rsch. assoc. IMEDE (Mgmt. Inst.), Lausanne, Switzerland, 1965-66; mgmt. trainee Trust Co. Bank, Atlanta, 1966-67, bond portfolio mgr., 1967-72; data processing mgr. Trust Co. Ga., Atlanta, 1972-78, treas., 1978-85; exec. v.p., chief fin. officer SunTrust Banks Inc., Atlanta, 1985—; mem. Emory U. Bd. Visitors, 1991—; bd. dirs. Rock Tenn. Co., Sallie Mae; former mem. taxation and payment systems com. ABA; former instr. Morehouse Coll. and Banking Schs.; mem. exec. com. CFO divsn. ABA, 1987-90, chair, 1989-90. Mem. exec. com., bd. dirs. Alliance Theatre, Atlanta, 1985-92, pres., 1989-91; bd. dirs. High Mus. Art, Atlanta, 1985—; pres. Young Audiences Atlanta Inc., 1981-84, bd. dirs., 1985, mem. adv. bd., 1986—; pres. bd. visitors Grady Meml. Hosp., Atlanta, 1983-90; v.p. exec. bd. Atlanta Area coun. Boy Scouts Am., 1983-92, treas., 1989-91, mem. adv. bd., 1992; mem. adv. coun. Ga. State U. Sch. Accountancy, 1981-85, chmn. curriculum subcom., 1983-84; mem. exec. com., trustee Morehouse Sch. Medicine, 1984-93, chmn. fin. com., 1987-90, chmn., 1990-92; mem. Leadership Atlanta, 1976—, trustee, 1990-94; trustee, mem. exe. com. Robert W. Woodruff Arts Ctr. Inc., 1976—, treas., 1976-83, chmn. fin. com., 1984-89, 93—; chmn. fin. com., bd. dirs. Schenck Sch., Atlanta, 1986-88; exec. vice chmn. bd. trustees Holy Innocents Episcopal Sch., Atlanta, 1976-79, bd. dirs., treas., 1987-90; bd. dirs. Atlanta Opera, 1986—, United Way Met. Atlanta, Inc., 1994—. mem. Emory U. Bd. Visitors, 1991-95; bd. dirs. Rock Tenn. Co., Sallie Mae, Conti Fin. Corp.; former mem. taxation and payment syss. com. ABA, mem. exec. com. divsn., 1987, 90, chair, 1989-90; former isntr. Morehouse Coll. and Banking Schs. Episcopalian. Home: 3043 Nancy Creek Rd NW Atlanta GA 30327-1901 Office: SunTrust Banks Inc PO Box 4418 Atlanta GA 30302-4418

SPIEGEL, LAWRENCE HOWARD, advertising executive; b. N.Y.C., Oct. 9, 1942; s. Melvin Arthur and Rose (Black) S.; m. Christy Mansfield; children from previous marriage: Robert, David. BA, NYU, 1963. Print buyer William Esty Co., N.Y.C., 1964-65, broadcast buyer, 1965-66; media planner Batten, Barton, Durstine & Osborn, Inc., N.Y.C., 1966-67, media supr., 1967-68, assoc. media dir., 1969-72, v.p., 1972-74; media group head Jack Tinker & Ptnrs., N.Y.C., 1968-69; v.p. Tracy-Locke, Dallas, 1974-80, sr. v.p., 1980-84, exec. v.p., 1984-89; prin. The Richards Group, Dallas, 1989—; Richards/Spiegel Value Added, Dallas, 1994—; pres. Tex. Coun. Advt., 1991—. Guest editor Mktg. and Media Decision mag., June 1982. Mem. Dallas Cable Bd., 1983-86; chmn. mktg. com. U. Tex., Dallas, 1984-89; pres. Cable Access Dallas, Inc., 1985-86; trustee Dallas Symphony Assn., 1978—; bd. dirs. Equest Inc., 1991-92; bd. dirs. I Have a Dream Found., 1994—. Mem. Assn. Broadcasting Execs. Tex. (pres. 1975-76), Am. Women in Radio and TV, Inc. (bd. dirs. 1992-93). Republican. Avocations: skiing, sailing. Office: The Richards Group Ste 1200 8750 N Central Expy Dallas TX 75231-2318

SPIEGEL, MARILYN HARRIET, real estate executive; b. Bklyn., Apr. 3, 1935; d. Harry and Sadie (Oscher) Unger; m. Murray Spiegel, June 12, 1954; children: Eric Lawrence, Dana Cheryl, Jay Barry. Grad. high sch., Bklyn. Exec. sec. S & W Paper Co., N.Y.C., 1953-54, Japan Paper Co., N.Y.C., 1954-58; salesperson Red Carpet Realtors, Los Alamitos, Calif., 1974-75, Coll. Park Realtors, Garden Grove, Calif., 1975-79; owner, broker S & S Properties, Los Alamitos, Calif., 1979—. Named Realtor of Yr., 1989. Mem. Calif. Assn. Realtors (bd. dirs. 1984—), West Orange County Bd. Realtors (bd. dirs. 1984—, 1st v.p. 1987, pres. 1988), Million Dollar Sales Club, Long Beach C. of C., Seal Beach C. of C., Orange County C. of C., Summit Orgn., Toastmasters (pres. founders group Garden Grove, Calif. 1990). Home: 1371 Oakmont Rd 150-D Seal Beach CA 90740-3035 Office: S & S Properties 3502 Katella Ave Ste 208 Los Alamitos CA 90720-3115

SPIEGEL, MELVIN, retired biology educator; b. N.Y.C., Dec. 10, 1925; s. Philip Edward and Sadie (Friedman) S.; m. Evelyn Sclufer, Apr. 16, 1955; children: Judith Ellen, Rebecca Ann. B.S., U. Ill., 1948; Ph.D., U. Rochester, 1952; M.A. (hon.), Dartmouth Coll., 1967. Research fellow U. Rochester, 1952-53, Calif. Inst. Tech., 1953-55, 64-65; asst. prof. Colby Coll., 1955-59; mem. faculty Dartmouth Coll., Hanover, N.H., 1959—, prof. biology, 1966-93; prof. emeritus Dartmouth Coll, Hanover, N.H.; chmn. dept. biol. scis. Dartmouth Coll., Hanover, N.H., 1972-74; summer investigator Marine Biol. Lab., Woods Hole, Mass., 1954—; sr. research biologist U. Calif.-San Diego, 1970-71; vis. prof. biochemistry Nat. Inst. Med. Research, Mill Hill, London, 1971; vis. prof. Biocenter, U. Basel, 1979-82, 85; Wilson Meml. lectr. U. N.C., 1975; program dir. developmental biology NSF, 1975-76; mem. cell biology study sect. NIH, 1966-70. Editorial bd.: Biol. Bull., 1966-70, 71-75, Cell Differentiation, 1979-88 ; contbr. articles to profl. jours. Trustee Marine Biol. Lab. Corp.; mem. exec. com., trustee Marine Biol. Lab., 1976-80. Served with AUS, 1943-46, ETO. Decorated Purple Heart with 2 oak leaf clusters, Combat Inf. badge. Fellow AAAS; mem. Am. Soc. Cell Biology, Am. Soc. Devel. Biology, Internat. Soc. Devel. Biologists (sec.-treas. 1977-81, bd. dirs. 1981-85). Home: 15 Barrymore Rd Hanover NH 03755-2401

SPIEGEL, S. ARTHUR, federal judge; b. Cin., Oct. 24, 1920; s. Arthur Major and Hazel (Wise) S.; m. Louise Wachman, Oct. 31, 1945; children: Thomas, Arthur Major II, Andrew, Roger Daniel. BA, U. Cin., 1942, postgrad., 1949; LLB, Harvard U., 1948. Assoc. Kasfir & Chalfie, Cin., 1948-52; assoc. Benedict, Bartlett & Shepard, Cin., 1952-53, Gould & Gould, Cin., 1953-54; ptnr. Gould & Spiegel, Cin., 1954-59; assoc. Cohen, Baron, Druffel & Hogan, Cin., 1960; ptnr. Cohen, Todd, Kite & Spiegel, Cin., 1961-80; judge U.S. Dist Ct. Ohio, Cin., 1980—; sr. status, 1995—. Served to capt. USMC, 1942-46. Mem. ABA, FBA, Ohio Bar Assn., Cin. Bar Assn., Cin. Lawyers Club. Democrat. Jewish. Office: US Dist Ct 838 US Courthouse 5th Walnut St Cincinnati OH 45202

SPIEGEL, SIEGMUND, architect; b. Gera, Germany, Nov. 13, 1919; s. Jakob and Sara (Precker) S.; ed. Coll. City N.Y., 1939-40, Columbia, 1945-50; m. Ruth Josias, Apr. 13, 1945; children: Sandra Renee, Deborah Joan. Came to U.S., 1938, naturalized, 1941. DHL (hon.) Hofstra U., 1993. Draftsman, Mayer & Whittlesey, architects, N.Y.C., 1941-47, office mgr., 1947-55; pvt. practice architecture, East Meadow, N.Y., 1956—. Served with AUS, 1941-45; ETO. Decorated Purple Heart, Bronze Star, Croix de Guerre with palme (Belgium); recipient grand prize for instnl. bldgs. (for Syosset Hosp.), L.I. Assn., 1963; grand prize Human Resources Sch., 1966; grand prize Stony Brook Profl. Bldg., 1966; Beautification award, Town Hempstead, N.Y., 1969; Archi award for Harbour Club Apts., L.I. Assn., 1970, for Birchwood Blue Ridge Condominiums, 1974; Dr. Martin Luther King Jr. award Nassau County, 1986; Louis E. Yavner award N.Y. State Bd. Regents, 1992. Fellow Acad. Marketing Sci., L.I.U., 1971. Registered architect, N.Y., N.J., Mass., Md., Va., Pa., Conn., Ga., Vt., Tenn., N.H., Fla.; lic. profl. planner, N.J. Mem. AIA, N.Y. State Assn. Archs., East Meadow C. of C. (pres. 1966). Club: Kiwanis. Author: The Spiegel Plan. Contbr. articles to Progressive Architecture. Prin. works include: Syosset (N.Y.) Hosp., 1962; Reliance Fed. Savs. and Loan Assn. Bank, Queens, N.Y., 1961; Louden Hall Psychiat. Hosp., 1963; Human Resources Sch., Albertson, N.Y., 1964; Nassau Center for Emotionally Disturbed Children, 1968; Harbor Club Apt., Babylon, N.Y., 1968; Reliance Fed. Bank, Albertson, 1967; North Isle Club and Apt. Cmty., Coram, N.Y., 1972; County Fed. Savs. & Loan Assn., Commack, N.Y., 1972; Birchwood Glen Apt. Cmty., Holtsville, N.Y., 1972; Bayside Fed. Savs. & Loan Bank Plaza, Patchogue, N.Y., 1973; L.E. Woodward Sch. for Emotionally Disturbed Children, Freeport, N.Y., 1974, Birchwood Sagamore Hills, Blue Ridge and Bretton Woods Condominium Cmtys., Coram, N.Y., 1975, Maple Arms Condos, Westbury, N.Y., 1982, Dept. Pub. Works, Freeport, N.Y., Nuc. Molecular Resonance Bldg., 1983. Home: 1508 Hayes Ct East Meadow NY 11554-4418

SPIEGELBERG, EMMA JO, business education educator; b. Mt. View, Wyo., Nov. 22, 1936; d. Joseph Clyde and Dorcas (Reese) Hatch; BA with honors, U. Wyo., 1958, MEd, 1985; EdD Boston U., 1990; m. James Walter Spiegelberg, June 22, 1957; children: William L., Emory Walter, Joseph John. Tchr. bus. edn. Laramie (Wyo.) High Sch., 1960-61, 65-93, adminstr., 1993—. Bd. dirs. Cathedral Home for Children, Laramie, 1967-70, 72—, pres., 1985-88, Laramie Plains Mus., 1970-79. Author: Branigan's Accounting Simulation, 1986, London & Co. II, 1993; co-author: Glencoe Computerized Accounting, 1993, 2nd edit., 1995, Microcomputer Accounting: Daceasy, 1994, Microcomputer Accounting: Peachtree, 1994, Microcomputer Accounting: Accpac, 1994, Computerized Accounting with Peachtree, 1995, Glencoe Computerized Accounting: Peachtree, 1995. Named Wyo. Bus. Tchr. of Yr., 1982. Mem. Am. Vocat. Assn. (policy com. region V 1984-87, region V Tchr. of Yr. 1986), Wyo. Vocat. Assn. (exec. bd. 1978-80, pres. 1981-82, Outstanding Contbns. to Vocat. Edn. award 1983, Tchr. of Yr. 1985, exec. sec. 1986-89), Nat. Bus. Edn. Assn.(bd. dirs. 1987-88, 1991—, Sec. Tchr. of the Yr. 1991), Mt. Plains Bus. Edn. Assn. (Wyo. rep. to bd. dirs. 1982-85, pres. 1987-88, Sec. Tchr. of the Yr. 1991, Leadership award 1992), Internat. Soc. Bus. Edn., Wyo. Bus. Edn. Assn. (pres. 1979-80), NEA, Wyo. Edn. Assn., Albany County Edn. Assn. (sec. 1970-71), Laramie C. of C. (bd. dirs. 1985-88), U. Wyo. Alumni Assn. (bd. dirs. 1985-90pres. 1988-89), Kappa Delta Pi, Phi Delta Kappa, Alpha Delta Kappa (state pres. 1978-82), Chi Omega, Pi Lambda Theta, Delta Pi Epsilon. Mem. United Ch. of Christ. Club: Zonta. Home: 3301 Grays Gable Rd Laramie WY 82070-5031 Office: Laramie High Sch 1275 N 11th St Laramie WY 82070-2206

SPIEGELBERG, HANS LEONHARD, medical educator; b. Basel, Switzerland, Jan. 8, 1933; came to U.S., 1961; s. Hans G. S.; m. Elizabeth von der Crone, May 19, 1962; children: Franzi, Daniel, Markus. MD, U. Basel, Basel, 1958. Med. diplomate, Switzerland. Intern and resident in pediatric allergy and immunology Dept. of Medicine, U. of Basel, Switzerland; intern and resident in allergy and immunology NYU, N.Y.C., 1961-63; with Scripps Rsch. Inst., La Jolla, Calif., 1963-90; prof. U. Calif., San Diego, 1990—; cons. VA Med. Ctr., L.A., 1966-90. Editor (jour.) Seminars in Immunopathology, 1988—. Home: 2234 Paseo Dorado La Jolla CA 92037 Office: U Calif San Diego 9500 Gilman Dr La Jolla CA 92093-0609

SPIEGELBERG, HARRY LESTER, retired paper products company executive; b. New London, Wis., Apr. 24, 1936; s. Harry Henry and Gladys Louise (Kalt) S.; m. Bonnie Faye Ludden, Jan. 23, 1960; children: Susan Faye Spiegelberg Schuldes, Sharon Louise Spiegelberg Kozlowski, Stephen Harry, Scott Charles. BSChemE, U. Wis., 1959; MS, Inst. Paper Chemistry, Appleton, Wis., 1963, PhD, 1966; MBA, U. Chgo., 1980. Teaching asst. U. Wis. Coll. Engring., Madison, 1957-59; engr. Kimberly-Clark Corp., Neenah, Wis., 1959-61, rsch. scientist, 1965-68, mgr. new concepts, 1968-73, dir. R & D, 1973-84, v.p. consumer tissue rsch., 1985-92; v.p. tech. and patent strategy Kimberly-Clark Corp., 1992-93, v.p. tech. transfer, 1993-96, ret., 1996; mem., past chmn. vis. com. dept. chem. engring. U. Wis., 1985—, mem., past chmn. indsl. liaison coun. Coll. Engring., 1987-93; founder, vice chmn. Paper Industry Hall of Fame; pres. Ctr. Project Inc. Contbr. chpt. to book; patentee in nonwovens and tissue fields. Pres. Ctr. Project, Inc. Capt. C.E. USAR, 1959-67. Recipient Disting. Svc. citation U. Wis., 1986. Congregationalist. Avocations: bicycling, backpacking. Home: 3624 S Barker Ln Appleton WI 54915-7038

SPIEGELMAN, ART, author, cartoonist; b. Stockholm, Feb. 15, 1948; s. Wladek and Andzia (Zylberberg) S.; m. Francoise Mouly, July 12, 1977; children: Nadja, Dashiell. Student, Harpur Coll. (now SUNY), Binghamton, N.Y. Creative cons., artist, designer, editor, writer Topps Chewing Gum, Inc., Bklyn., 1966-88; editor Douglas Comix, 1972; contbg. editor Arcade, the Comics Revue, 1975-76; founding editor Raw, 1980—; artist, contbg. editor New Yorker, 1992—; instr. San Francisco Acad. Art, 1974-75, N.Y. Sch. Visual Arts, 1979-87. Author, illustrator: The Complete Mr. Infinity, 1970, The Viper Vicar of Vice, Villainy, and Vickedness, 1972, Ace Hole, Midge Detective, 1974, The Language of Comics, 1974, Breakdowns: From Maus to Now: An Anthology of Strips, 1977, Work and Turn, 1979, Every Day Has Its Dog, 1979, Two-Fisted Painters Action Adventure, 1980, Maus: A Survivor's Tale, 1986 (Joel M. Cavior award for Jewish Writing 1986, Nat. Book Critics Cir. nomination 1986, Pulitzer prize 1992), Maus, Part Two, 1992 (Nat. Book Critics Cir. nomination 1992, Pulitzer prize 1992), The Wild Party, 1994, (with F. Mouly) Read Yourself Raw, 1987; contbr. The Apex Treasury of Underground Comics, 1974; compiling editor (with B. Schneider) Whole Grains: A Book of Quotations, 1972; exhbns. include N.Y. Cultural Ctr., Inst. Contemporary Art, London, Seibu Gallery, Tokyo, Mus. Modern Art, N.Y.C., 1991, Galerie St. Etienne, N.Y.C., 1992, Ft. Lauderdale Mus. Art, 1993; creator Wacky Packages, Garbage Pail Kids and other novelties; contbr. to numerous underground comics. Recipient Playboy Editorial award for best comic strip, 1982, Yellow Kid award for best comic strip author, 1982, Regional Design award Print mag., 1983, 84, 85, Inkpot award San Diego Comics Conv., 1987, Stripschappening award for best fgn. comics album, 1987, Alpha Art award Angoulerne, France, 1993. Office: Raw Books & Graphics 27 Greene St New York NY 10013-2537

SPIELBERG, STEVEN, motion picture director, producer; b. Cin., Dec. 18, 1947; m. Amy Irving, Nov. 27, 1985 (div.); 2 children: Max Samuel, Sasha; m. Kate Capshaw; 1 dau. BA, Calif. State Coll., Long Beach; Hon. Doctorate in Creative Arts, Brandeis U., 1986. Founder Amblin Entertainment (Universal Studios), Dreamworks SKG (with Jeffrey Katzenberg and David Geffen); directed segments of TV series Columbo; dir. TV movies Night Gallery, 1969, Duel, 1971, Savage, 1972, Something Evil, 1972; exec prodr. series: Steven Spielberg's Amazing Stories, Tiny Toon Adventures, Family Dog, seaQuest DSV; films include (dir.): The Sugarland Express, 1974 (also story), Jaws, 1975, Close Encounters of the Third Kind, 1977 (also co-writer), 1941, 1979, Raiders of the Lost Ark, 1981, Indiana Jones and the Temple of Doom, 1984, Indiana Jones and the Last Crusade, 1989, Hook, 1991, Jurassic Park, 1993, Men in Black, 1996; (dir., prodr.): E.T. The Extra-Terrestrial, 1982, The Color Purple, 1985, Empire of the Sun, 1987, Always, 1989, Schindler's List, 1993 (Best Drama & Best Dir. Golden Globe awards, Best Picture & Best Dir. Acad. awards); (dir., exec. prodr.): Twilight Zone: The Movie, 1983; (prodr.): Poltergeist, 1982 (also co-writer), An American Tail: Fievel Goes West, 1991, Casper, 1995; (exec. prodr.): I Wanna Hold Your Hand, 1978, Used Cars, 1980, Continental Divide, 1981, Gremlins, 1984, The Goonies, 1985, Back to the Future, 1985, Young Sherlock Holmes, 1985, The Money Pit, 1986, An American Tail, 1986, Innerspace, 1987, *batteries not included, 1987, Who Framed Roger Rabbit?, 1988, The Land Before Time, 1988, Dad, 1989, Back to the Future Part II, 1989, Joe Verses the Volcano, 1990, Back to the Future Part III, 1990, Gremlins 2: The New Batch, 1990, Arachnophobia, 1990, Cape Fear, 1991, We're Back!: A Dinosaur's Story, 1993, The Flintstones, 1994, The Little Rascals, 1994, Balto, 1995, Twister, 1996; (actor): The Blues Brothers, 1980. Recipient Man of Yr. award Hasty Pudding Theater, Harvard U., 1983, Outstanding Directorial Achievement award for feature films Dirs. Guild Am., 1985, Film award Brit. Acad. Film and TV Arts, 1986, Irving Thalberg Mem. award Acad. Motion Picture Arts and Scis., 1987, Golden Lion award for career achievement Venice Film Festival, 1993, Life Achievement award Am. Film Inst., 1995. Fellow Brit. Acad. Film and TV Arts. Won film contest with 40-minute war movie, Escape to Nowhere, at age 13; made film Firelight at age 16, and made 5 films while in coll.; became TV dir. at Universal Pictures at age 20. Office: CAA 9830 Wilshire Blvd Beverly Hills CA 90212-1804*

SPIELMAN, BARBARA HELEN NEW, editor, consultant; b. Canton, Ohio, June 28, 1929; d. Arthur Daniel and Helen Barbara (Rickenmann) New; m. David Vernon Spielman, Nov. 24, 1956; children: Daniel Bruce, Linda Barbara. BS in English and History Edn. cum laude, Miami U., Oxford, Ohio, 1951. Cert. tchr., Ohio, Tex. Tchr. Canton Pub. Schs., 1951-53; vets. aide U. Tex., Austin, 1954-57; copy editor, mng. editor U. Tex. Press, Austin, 1964-91; ret., 1991; editorial cons. Chicago Manual of Style, 13th edit., 1975, Amon Carter Mus., Ft. Worth, 1970—, Ctr. for Mex. Am. Studies, Austin, 1980, Archer M. Huntington Art Gallery, Austin, 1975—, 64 Beds Project for Homeless and Hungry, Austin, 1989—; mem. search com. for dir., U. Tex. Press, 1991. Troop leader Girl Scouts Am., Austin, 1970-73; officer PTA, Austin, 1964-73. Mem. Am. Assn. Univ. Presses, Smithsonian Instn., Nat. Geog. Soc., Althenoi, Seton Med. Ctr. Aux., Phi Beta Kappa, Kappa Delta Pi, Sigma Sigma Sigma. Democrat. Presbyterian. Avocations: reading, gardening, piano, painting, drawing. Home: 3301 Perry Ln Austin TX 78731-5330

SPIELMAN, CHRIS, professional football player; b. Canton, Ohio, Oct. 11, 1965. Student, Ohio State U. With Detroit Lions, 1988—. Recipient Lombardi award, 1987; named to Sporting News Coll. All-Am. team, 1986, 87, Pro Bowl team, 1989-91. Office: Detroit Lions 1200 Featherstone Rd Pontiac MI 48342-1938

SPIELMAN, JOHN PHILIP, JR., historian, educator; b. Anaconda, Mont., June 16, 1930; s. John Philip and Lewanna (Coleman) S.; BA, U. Mont., 1951; MA, U. Wis., 1953, PhD, 1957; m. Danila B. Cole, Sept. 14, 1955. Instr., U. Mich., Ann Arbor, 1957-59; asst. prof. history Haverford (Pa.) Coll., 1959-65, assoc. prof., 1965-70, prof., 1970-85, Audrey Dusseau meml. prof. humanities, 1985—, dean, 1966-68. Served with U.S. Army, 1953-55. Mem. Am. Hist. Assn., Soc. French Hist. Studies, Soc. Austrian and Habsburg Historians. Author: Leopold I of Austria, 1977, The City and the Crown, 1993; co-author 2 textbooks; translator: Simplicissimus (Grimmelshausen), 1981. Home: 749 Millbrook Ln Haverford PA 19041-1210 Office: Haverford Coll 370 Lancaster Ave Haverford PA 19041-1309

SPIELVOGEL, CARL, international business and marketing executive; b. N.Y.C., Dec. 27, 1928; s. Joseph and Sadie (Tellerman) S.; m. Barbaralee Diamonstein, Oct. 27, 1981; children: David Joseph, Rachel Fay, Paul Abram. BBA, CUNY, 1956, LLD (hon.), 1984. Reporter, columnist N.Y. Times, 1950-60; with McCann-Erickson, Inc., Interpublic Group of Cos., Inc., N.Y.C., 1960-74; vice chmn., chmn. exec. com., dir. Interpublic Group of Cos., Inc., 1974-80; chmn., chief exec. officer Backer & Spielvogel, Inc., 1980-87; chief exec. officer, chmn. bd. dirs. Backer Spielvogel Bates Worldwide, Inc., N.Y.C., 1987-94; chmn., CEO, United Auto Group, Inc., 1994—; dir. Manhattan Industries, Franklin Corp.; bd. dirs. Hasbro, Inc. Chmn. Com. in Pub, Interest, 1975-79, Tri-State United Way, 1984; pres. bd. trustees Baruch Coll. Fund, 1979; mem. Bus. Com. Arts; bd. dirs., mem. exec. com. Mt. Sinai Hosp., N.Y.C.; bd. dirs. N.Y. Coun. Humanities, N.Y. Philharm., 1987—, Asia Soc., 1989—; trustee Lincoln Ctr. for Performing Arts, 1987—; chmn. Mayor's Com. for Pub.-Pvt. Partnerships; mem. exec. com. Bus. Mktg. Corp., N.Y.C.; chmn. com. div. WNET-Pub. Broadcasting; trustee, mem. exec. com., chmn. bus. com. Met. Mus. Art; mem. internat. adv. bd. bus. coun. UN; bd. govs. U.S. Govt. Broadcasting, 1995—. Recipient Human Relations award Anti-Defamation League, 1972, Achievement award Sch. Bus. Alumni, CCNY, 1972, Citizens Union award, 1980, Disting. Alumni award for Outstanding Career Accomplishment Baruch Coll., 1990; named Marketer of Yr. N.Y. chpt. Am. Mktg. Assn., 1982, Outstanding Exec. Crain's N.Y. Bus., 1987. Mem. Mcpl. Art Soc. Clubs: Princeton (N.Y.C.), Yale. Office: United Auto Group Inc 375 Park Ave Ste 2201 New York NY 10152

SPIELVOGEL, SIDNEY MEYER, investment banker; b. N.Y.C., July 14, 1925; s. Hyman and Rae (Mandel) S.; m. Beverly Anne Gold, Dec. 18, 1960; 1 son, Peter James. B.S.S., CCNY, 1944; A.M., Harvard U., 1946, M.B.A., 1949. Economist Treasury Dept., Washington, 1946-47; assoc. dept. mgr. Alexander's Dept. Stores, 1949-53; asst. to mdse. mgr., dept. mgr. Bloomingdale's Dept. Store, 1953-56; with Prudential-Bache Securities Inc., 1956-88, 1st v.p., 1971-75, sr. v.p., 1975-85, mng. dir., 1986-88; dir. MoneyMart Assets Inc., pres., 1981-87; lectr. Hunter Coll., N.Y.C., 1963-68. Bd. dirs. Emanu-el Midtown YM-YWHA, N.Y.C., 1975-91; mem. Harvard Grad. Soc. Coun., 1983-88, 89-92, 94—, chmn., 1985-87. Mem. Phi Beta Kappa. Clubs: Harvard (N.Y.C.), Harvard Bus. Sch. (N.Y.C.), World Trade Center (N.Y.C.). Home: 245 E 19th St New York NY 10003-2639 Office: Corp Capital Cons Inc 1185 Avenue Of The Americas New York NY 10036-2601

SPIER, PETER EDWARD, artist, author; b. Amsterdam, Netherlands, June 6, 1927; came to U.S., 1952, naturalized, 1958; s. Joseph Eduard and Albertine Sophie (Van Raalte) S.; m. Kathryn M. Pallister, July 12, 1958; children: Thomas P., Kathryn E. Student, Ryks Academie Voor Beeldende Kunsten, Amsterdam, 1945-47. Jr. editor Elsevier's Weekly, Amsterdam, 1950-51, Elsevier Pub. Co., Houston, 1952. Free-lance author, illustrator, N.Y.C., 1952—, speaker, lectr. schs. and libraries.; author, illustrator: 38 books, including: The Star-Spangled Banner, 1973, Fast-Slow, High-Low, 1972, Crash! Bang! Boom!, 1972, Tin Lizzie, 1975, Noah's Ark, 1977, Oh, Were They Ever Happy!, 1978, Bored—Nothing to Do, 1978, The Legend of New Amsterdam, 1979, People, 1980, Peter Spier's Village Books, 1981, Rain, 1982, Christmas!, 1983, The Book of Jonah, 1985, Dreams, 1986, We The People, 1987, Peter Spier's Circus, 1992, Father, May I Come?, 1993; illustrator over 150 books; contbr., illustrator many nat. mags. Lt. Royal Netherlands Navy, 1947-58. Runner-up for Caldecott medal, 1960; recipient Christopher award, 1970, Boston Globe award, 1967, Caldecott medal, 1978, Christopher award, 1978, Nat. Religious Book award, 1978, Lewis Carroll Shelf award, 1978, Media award NCCJ, 1980, David McCord award, 1989. Clubs: Shoreham (N.Y.); Country; Netherlands (N.Y.C.). Address: PO Box 566 5 Warden Cliff Rd Shoreham NY 11786-0566

SPIERKEL, GREG, electronics executive; b. 1957. BA, Carleton U. With Mitel Corp., Reston, Va., 1986—, now pres., CEO. Office: Mitel Inc 205 Van Buren St Ste 400 Herndon VA 22070*

SPIERS, RONALD IAN, diplomat; b. Orange, N.J., July 9, 1925; s. Thomas Hoskins and Blanca (De Ponthier) S.; m. Patience Baker, June 11, 1949; children: Deborah Wood, Peter, Martha, Sarah. BA, Dartmouth Coll., 1948; M in Pub. Affairs, Princeton U., 1950. With U.S. Atomic Energy Commn., 1950-54; officer-in-charge disarmament and arms control Dept. State, 1955-61; dir. NATO Affairs, 1962-66; polit. counselor London,

1966-69; asst. sec. for Bur. Politico-Mil. Affairs U.S. Dept. State, Washington, 1969-73; U.S. ambassador Nassau, Bahamas, 1973-74; dep. chief-of-mission Am. Embassy, London, 1974-77; U.S. permanent rep. to Cento Coun., 1977-79; U.S. ambassador Ankara, Turkey, 1977-80; asst. sec. for intelligence and rsch., mem. U.S. Intelligence Bd. U.S. Dept. State, Washington, 1980-81; U.S. ambassador Islamabad, Pakistan, 1981-83; under-sec. for mgmt. U.S. Dept. State, Washington, 1983-89; under-sec. gen. for polit. affairs UN, N.Y.C., 1989-92; internat. affairs cons. U. S. Dept. State, Washington, 1992—; career ambassador U.S. Fgn. Svc., 1984. Served to lt. (j.g.) USN, 1943-46, PTO. Woodrow Wilson fellow Princeton U., 1948. Fellow Nat. Acad. of Pub. Adminstrn.; mem. Am. Fgn. Svc. Assn., Internat. Inst. Strategic Studies, Coun. on Fgn. Rels., Am. Acad. of Diplomacy, Washington Inst. Fgn. Affairs. Home: RR 1 Box 54A South Londonderry VT 05155-9706

SPIERS, TOMAS HOSKINS, JR., architect; b. Paris, Jan. 26, 1929; s. Tomas Hoskins and Blanca Genevive (DePonthier) S. (parents Am. citizens); m. Nancy M. Fenold, Aug. 10, 1952; children: Merrick David, Jordan Henry, Corey Albert. Student Mohawk Coll., 1946-48; BA, Hobart Coll., 1951; MArch, Yale U., 1960. Registered architect, Pa., N.J., N.Y., Mass., Md., Ohio, Conn., S.C., R.I., Ind., Va., W.Va., Fla., Ga., Vt. Archtl. designer Pederson & Tilney, New Haven, 1955-60; mng. dir. Pederson & Tilney Italia SpA, Milan, Italy, 1960-66; v.p. European ops. Pederson/Tilney/Spiers, Milan, 1963-66; v.p. S.E. Asia, Louis Berger, Inc., Bangkok, Thailand, 1966-68; v.p. architecture Benatec Assos., Harrisburg, Pa., 1968-75, v.p. design, 1975-78, sr. v.p., 1979-87; pres., 1987-91, chief exec. officer, 1991-94, pres. Spiers, McDonald, Bharueha & Royal, Inc., 1994—; lectr. archtl. restoration Pa. State U., 1975-80; cons. Pa. Hist. & Mus. Commn., Bur. Historic Sites; mem. Pa. State Hist. Preservation Bd., 1980-84, chmn. 1986-88. Prin. works include restoration of Gen. Knox quarters, Valley Forge, Pa., Eagle Hotel, Waterford, Pa., The Highlands, Whitemarsh, Pa., Washington Monument, Balt. Bd. dirs. Urban League of Harrisburg, Inc., 1977-84. Served with USN, 1951-55. Mem. AIA (com. on hist. resources 1977-94, exec. com. 1980-82, chmn. 1983), ASCE, Am. Arbitration Assn. (arbitrator 1974—), Assn. Preservation Tech. (bd. dirs., editor bull. 1979-82, v.p. 1984-87, pres. 1988-92), Soc. Am. Mil. Engrs. Home: 357 N 27th St Camp Hill PA 17011-3629 Office: Spiers McDonald Bharucha & Royal Inc 150 Corporate Center Dr Ste 101 Camp Hill PA 17011-1759

SPIES, CLAUDIO, composer, educator; b. Santiago, Chile, Mar. 26, 1925; came to U.S., 1942, naturalized, 1966; s. Mauricio and Gertrudis (Heilbronn) S.; m. Emmi Vera Tobias, June 10, 1953 (div. 1986); children: Caterina, Michael, Tatiana, Leah, Susanna. AB, Harvard, 1950, MA, 1954. Instr. music Harvard U., 1953-57; lectr. music Vassar Coll., 1957-58; asst. prof. music, condr. orch. Swarthmore Coll., 1958-63, assoc. prof., 1964-69, prof., 1969-70; prof. music Princeton U., 1970-95, prof. music emeritus, 1995—. Conducted 1st performances of new works, Stravinsky, Boston, 1954, Santiago, 1954, Swarthmore Coll., 1963-68, Harvard, 1968, cond. own works, Composer's Forum, N.Y.C., 1961, Los Angeles County Museum, 1965, Columbia U. Group for Contemporary Music, 1966 (recipient prize for composition U. de Chile 1948, 54, 56); (Brandeis U. Creative Arts citation 1967); composer: orch. Music for a Ballet, 1955, Descanso en jardín; woodwind quartet, tenor and baritone; text by Jorge Guillén, 1957, Il Cantico di Frate Sole; bass. and orch., 1958, Five Psalms; soprano, tenor and 6 instruments; commd. by Harvard Mus. Assn., 1959, Verses from the Book of Ruth; women's voices and piano; commd. by Phila. Art Alliance, 1959, Tempi; music 14 instruments; commd. by Fromm Music Found., 1962, Proverbs on Wisdom; male voices, piano and organ; commd. by Colgate U., 1964, Animula Vagula, Blandula; 4 parts, a cappella, 1964, Viopiacem; duo for viola and keyboard instruments, 1965, LXXXV, Eights and Fives; strings and clarinets, 1967, Times Two; horns, 1968, Three Songs on Poems by May Swenson, 1969, Bagatelle for piano, 1970, 7 Enzensberger-Lieder; baritone, 4 instrumentalists, 1972, Shirim le Hathunatham; soprano, 5 instruments, 1975, Five Sonnet-Settings; Shakespeare; vocal quartet and piano, 1976-77; 5 Dádivas, occasional pieces for piano, 1977-81, Half-Time; for clarinet and trumpet, 1981, Rilke: Rühmen; soprano, clarinet, trumpet, piano, 1981, Tagyr for baritone, flute, clarinet, bassoon, horn and viola, 1983, Seven Sonnets; Shakespeare/Celan; soprano, bass, clarinet, bass clarinet, string trio, 1989; Lament and a Complementary Envoi, Dylan Thomas, baritone, piano, 1990, Dreimal Sieben, oboe and piano, 1991, Insieme, flute and violin, 1994, Beisammen, 2 oboes, also English horns, 1995, Bis, Oboe and Piano, 1996; contbr. numerous articles and revs. to Perspectives of New Music, Mus. Quarterly, Notes, Tempo, Coll. Music Symposium, Jour. of Arnold Schoenberg Inst., vols. essays Berg, Brahms, Mendelssohn, Stravinsky; mem. editorial bd. Perspectives of New Music. Recipient Bohemian Club prize Harvard, 1950; John K. Paine Traveling fellow, 1950-51; Lili Boulanger Meml. Fund award, 1956; grantee The Ingram Merrill Found., 1966; sr. fellow Council Humanities, Princeton, spring 1966, fall 1966-67; award Nat. Inst. Arts and Letters, 1969; fellow Nat. Endowment Arts, 1975. Mem. Am. Soc. U. Composers (mem. founding bd.), Internat. Alban Berg/Soc. Ltd. (mem. founding bd.), Phila. Composers' Forum (exec. com. 1966-67), League-ISCM (mem. bd. 1970-73), Am. Brahms Soc., Phi Beta Kappa. Office: Princeton U Music Dept Woolworth Ctr Mus Stud Princeton NJ 08544-1007

SPIES, DENNIS J., editor; b. Hays, Kans., Dec. 20, 1941; s. Joseph A. and Germaine A. (Giebler) S.; (widowed Apr. 1985); children: Quentin, Tracy, Angie; m. Linda Yarbrough, Feb., 1990. BA, West Tex. State U., 1970. Draftsman Jeppesen and Co., Denver, 1963-65; tech. illustrator Emerson Electric, St. Louis, 1965-66; reporter Amarillo (Tex.) Globe-News, 1966-68, copy editor, 1968-80, news editor, 1980-84, night city editor, 1984-86, mng. editor, 1986—. Author: (poetry) Sharing, 1984, Kansas Moon, 1989, Road Kill, 1995. Bd. dirs. Adult Literacy Coun., Amarillo, 1987-91, Goodwill Industries, 1987-93, United Way, 1989-90; mem. steering com. Leadership Amarillo, 1989-90. With USAF, 1960-63. Mem. AP Mng. Editors, Lions. Avocations: poetry, cooking, music, cars, motorcycles. Office: Amarillo Globe-News 907 S Van Buren St Amarillo TX 79101-3329

SPIESS, FRED NOEL, oceanographer, educator; b. Oakland, Calif., Dec. 25, 1919; s. Fred Henry and Elva Josephine (Monck) S.; m. Sarah Scott Whitton, July 25, 1942; children: Katherine Spiess Dallaire, Mary Elizabeth Spiess DeJong, John Morgen Frederick, Helen Spiess Shamble, Margaret Josephine Deligio-Spiess. A.B., U. Calif., Berkeley, 1941, Ph.D., 1951; M.S., Harvard U., 1946. With Marine Phys. Lab., U. Calif., San Diego, 1952—; dir. Marine Phys. Lab., U. Calif., 1958-80, U. Calif. Inst. Marine Resources, 1980-88; dir. Scripps Inst. Oceanography, La Jolla, 1964-65, prof. oceanography, 1961—; chair U. Calif. Acad. Coun. and Assembly U. Calif. Bd. Regents, 1988-90; Mem. Naval Research Adv. Commn., 1978-81; mem. com. on geodesy Nat. Acad. Scis., 1980-84; mem. Def. Sci. Bd., 1976-79. Capt. USNR, 1941-79. Decorated Silver Star medal, Bronze Star medal; recipient John Price Wetherill medal Franklin Inst., 1965; Compass Disting. Scientist award Marine Technol. Soc., 1971; Robert Dexter Conrad award U.S. Sec. of Navy, 1974, Navy Disting. Pub. Svc. award, 1990; Newcomb Cleveland prize AAAS, 1981. Fellow Acoustical Soc. Am. (Pioneers of Underwater Acoustics medal 1985), Am. Geophys. Union (Maurice Ewing award 1983), Marine Tech. Soc. (Lockheed award 1985); mem. Nat. Acad. Engring., Phi Beta Kappa, Sigma Xi. Home: 9450 La Jolla Shores Dr La Jolla CA 92037-1137 Office: U Calif San Diego Scripps Inst Oceanogra La Jolla CA 92093

SPIKER, BECKY JO, elementary school educator; b. Charleroi, Pa., July 22, 1969; d. James Edward McClain Jr. and Penelope Ann Leasure Sparrow; m. Elmer Clayton Spiker Jr. BSEd, Slippery Rock U., 1991. Tchr. 4th grade Charleroi Elem. Sch., 1991—; family devel. specialist East Allegheny Sch. Dist. Family Ctr. Vol. Spl. Olympics, Slippery Rock, Pa., 1987—, Slippery Rock U. Primary Lab. Sch., 1988-89, Slippery Rock U. Child Care Ctr., 1988-89, Pitts. Blind Assn., 1994-95. Deno Castelli scholar, 1987. Methodist. Avocations: reading, music, swimming, walking. Home: 214 Clark St Belle Vernon PA 15012

SPIKINGS, BARRY PETER, film company executive; b. Boston, Eng., Nov. 23, 1939; came to U.S., 1986; children from previous marriage: Nicolas, Rebecca. Student, Boston (Eng.) Grammar Sch. Dir. Great Western, 1969-72; ptnr. Brit. Lion Films Holdings Ltd., Eng., 1972-75; chmn. Shepperton Studios, Eng., 1972-75; joint mng. dir., chmn., chief exec. officer E.M.I. Film & Theater Corp., 1975-82, chm., chief exec., 1982-85; ind. producer, 1982-85; dir. Galactic Films, 1985-86; pres., chief oper. officer Nelson Entertainment Group Inc., Beverly Hills, Calif., 1986-91; ptnr. Pleskow Spikings Partnership, Beverly Hills, 1991—; creator contractual arrangements with Orion, Columbia, Showtime, Viacom. Producer The Deer Hunter, 1978 (Oscar award for best picture). Office: Spikings Entertainment Ste 135 335 North Maple Dr Beverly Hills CA 90210

SPIKOL, ART, editor, writer, illustrator; b. Phila., Mar. 22, 1936; s. Emanuel and Yetta (Levy) S.; m. Rosalind Noshay, Jan. 12, 1958 (div.); 1 child, Victoria; m. Linda Parent, May 28, 1967; 1 child, Elizabeth. Student, Phila. Coll. Art, 1959-62. Art dir. Phila. mag., 1969-74, exec. editor, 1975-78, editor, 1980-82; art dir. Boston mag.; v.p. communications Einstein Med. Ctr., Phila., 1982-85; pres. Art Spikol, Inc., Phila., 1985—. Author: Magazine Writing: The Inside Angle, 1979, The Physalia Incident, 1988; columnist Writer's Digest, 1976-94, contbg. editor, 1994—. Recipient Best Feature Writing award Sigma Delta Chi, 1972, Penney-Mo. Mag. award U. Mo., 1974, Nat. Mag. Editor award Columbia Sch. Journalism, 1982. Jewish. Avocations: sketching, painting, pocket billiards. Office: Art Spikol Inc 751 S 5th St Philadelphia PA 19147-3042

SPILHAUS, ATHELSTAN, meteorologist, oceanographer; b. Cape Town, Union of South Africa, Nov. 25, 1911; came to U.S., 1931, naturalized, 1946; s. Karl Antonio and Nellie (Muir) S.; m. Kathleen Fitzgerald, 1978; children by previous marriage: Athelstan F., Mary Muir, Eleanor (dec.), Margaret Ann, Karl Henry. B.Sc., U. Cape Town, 1931, D.Sc., 1948; M.S., Mass. Inst. Tech., 1933; D.Sc., Coe Coll., 1961, Hahnemann Med. Coll., 1968, U. R.I., 1968, Phila. Coll. Pharmacy and Sci., 1969, Hamilton Coll., 1970, U. S.E. Mass., 1970, U. Durham, Eng., 1970, U. S.C., 1971, Southwestern U. at Memphis, 1972; LL.D., Nova U., 1970, U. Md., 1978. Research asst. Mass. Inst. Tech., 1934-35; asst. dir. tech. services Union of South Africa Def. Forces, Pretoria, 1935-36; research asst. Woods Hole (Mass.) Oceanographic Instn., and Cambridge, Mass., 1936-37; investigator in phys. oceanography Woods Hole (Mass.) Oceanographic Instn., and Cambridge, 1938, phys. oceanographer, 1940—; asst. prof. meteorology N.Y. U., 1937, asso. prof., 1937-42, prof., 1942, dir. research, 1946; meteorol. adviser to Union S. Africa Govt., 1947; dean Inst. Tech. U. Minn., 1949-66, prof. physics, 1966-67; pres. Franklin Inst., Phila., 1967-69, Aqua Internat. Inc., 1969-70; fellow Woodrow Wilson Internat. Center for Scholars, 1971-74; with NOAA, Dept Commerce, Washington, 1974-80; disting. scholar Annenberg Center, U. So. Calif., 1981; vis. scholar Inst. Marine and Coastal Studies, U. So. Calif., 1982-83; pres. Pan Geo, Inc., 1984—; Dir. Sci. Service, Inc., Am. Dynamics Corp., Donaldson Co., Minn.; trustee Aerospace Corp., Los Angeles; U.S. commr. Seattle World's Fair, 1961-62; chmn. nat. fisheries center and aquariam adv. bd. U.S. Dept. Interior; mem. adv. coms. for armed forces; mem. nat. com. IGY; mem com. on oceanography, com. on polar research Nat. Acad. Scis.; mem. exec. bd. UNESCO, 1955-58; mem. sci. adv. com. Am. Newspapers and Pubs. Assn.; sr. summer fellow Woods Hole Oceonographic Instn., 1990. Contbr.: numerous articles to profl. jours. including Jour. of Meterology; author: numerous articles to profl. jours. including The Ocean Laboratory. Trustee Woods Hole Oceanographic Instn., St. Paul Inst.; mem. Nat. Sci. Bd., 1966-72; vice chmn. Invest-in-America. Served from capt. to lt. col. USAAF, 1943-46. Decorated Legion of Merit, Exception Civilian Service medal USAF; recipient Patriotic Civilian Service award Dept. Army. Fellow AAAS (pres. 1970, chmn. 1971), Am. Geog. Soc., Geog. Soc., Royal Meteorol. Soc., Am. Geophys. Union; mem. AIAA, NAS (mem. com. pollution), Am. Philos. Soc. Episcopalian. Clubs: Cosmos (Washington); Bohemian (San Francisco). Inventor of Bathythermograph, 1938. Home: PO Box 1063 Middleburg VA 22117-1063 Office: Pan Geo Inc PO Box 2000 Middleburg VA 22117-2000

SPILHAUS, KARL HENRY, textiles executive, lawyer; b. N.Y.C., July 19, 1946; s. Athelstan Frederick and Mary (Atkins) S.; m. Constance DeLaMater, Dec. 30, 1989; stepchildren: Mary Alexis Welch, Antonia Morrow Welch. BA, U. Pa., 1971; JD, New Eng. Sch. Law, 1975. Bar: Mass. 1975. Staff atty. Legal Svcs., Cape Cod and the Islands, 1975-76; with No. Textile Assn., 1976—, pres., 1982—; pres. No. Textile Export Trading Co., Boston, 1992—; pres. Cashmere and Camel Hair Mfrs. Inst., 1984—; U.S. del. Internat. Labor Orgn. Textiles Com.; mem. adv. coun. U. Mass., Dartmouth, 1979—; arbitrator Am. Arbitration Assn., Boston. Trustee Mus. Am. Textile History, Bacon Free Libr., South Natick, Mass.; mem. Eliot Ch. of South Natick. With USMC, 1966-69, Vietnam. Mem. Textile Club Boston (pres.), Soc. King's Chapel, Phi Psi (hon.). Office: No Textile Assn 230 Congress St Boston MA 02110-2409

SPILKA, MARK, retired English language educator; b. Cleve., Aug. 6, 1925; s. Harvey Joseph and Zella (Fenberg) S.; m. Ellen Potter, May 6, 1950 (div. Dec. 1965); children: Jane, Rachel, Aaron; m. Ruth Dane Farnum, Jan. 18, 1975 (div. May 1993); stepchildren: Betsy, Polly; m. Shelly Regenbaum, July 4, 1993; stepchildren: Shir, Livi. BA magna cum laude, Brown U., 1949; MA, Ind. U., 1953, PhD, 1956. Editl. asst. Am. Mercury, 1949-51; instr. U. Mich., 1954-58, asst. prof., 1958-63; assoc. prof. Brown U., Providence, 1963-67, prof., 1967-95, prof. emeritus, 1995—, Israel J. Kapstein prof. English, 1990, chmn. English dept., 1968-73; Summer seminar dir. Nat. Endowment for Humanities, 1974; pres. Conf. Editors of Learned Jours., Modern Lang. Assn., 1974-75; vis. prof. Grad. Inst. Modern Letters U. Tulsa, summer 1975, Hebrew U., Jerusalem, 1972, Ind. U., summer 1976. Author: The Love Ethic of D.H. Lawrence, 1955, Dickens and Kafka: A Mutual Interpretation, 1963, Virginia Woolf's Quarrel with Grieving, 1980, Hemingway's Quarrel with Androgyny, 1990, Renewing the Normative D.H. Lawrence: A Personal Progress, 1992; editor: D.H. Lawrence: A Collection of Critical Essays, 1963, Towards a Poetics of Fiction: Essays from Novel: A Forum on Fiction, 1967-76, 1977, (with Caroline McCracken-Flesher) Why the Novel Matters: A Postmodern Perplex, 1990; mng. editor: Novel: A Forum on Fiction, 1967-77; editor, 1978—. Served with USAAF, 1944-46. Named Harry T. Moore Disting. D.H. Lawrence scholar MLA and D.H. Lawrence Soc., 1988; Ind. Sch. Letters fellow, 1961, 63; Guggenheim fellow, 1967-68; Nat. Endowment for Humanities fellow, 1978-79, 87. Mem. MLA (pres. Dickens Soc. 1986), AAUP, Phi Beta Kappa. Home: 294 Doyle Ave Providence RI 02906-3355

SPILKER, JAMES J., JR., electronics executive; b. 1933. PhD, Stanford U. Mgr. Lockheed Corp., 1958-63; mgr. WDL divsn. Philco Ford, 1963-73; co-founder Stanford Telecommunications, Sunnyvale, Calif., 1973—, now chmn., pres., CEO. Office: Stanford Telecommunications 1221 Crossman Ave Sunnyvale CA 94089-1103*

SPILLANE, MICKEY (FRANK MORRISON SPILLANE), author; b. Bklyn., Mar. 9, 1918; s. John Joseph and Catherine Anne S.; m. Mary Ann Pearce, 1945 (div.); children: Kathy, Ward, Mike, Carolyn; m. Sherri Malinou, Nov. 1964 (div.); m. Jane Rodgers Johnson, Oct. 1983. Attended, Kans. State Coll. Scripter, asst. editor Funnies, Inc., in 1940's; co-founder Spillane-Fellows Prodns., Nashville, 1969. Author: (mystery-suspense novels) I, the Jury, 1947, Vengeance is Mine!, 1950, My Gun Is Quick, 1950, The Big Kill, 1951, One Lonely Night, 1951, The Long Wait, 1951, Kiss Me, Deadly, 1952, Tough Guys, 1960, The Deep, 1961, The Girl Hunters, 1962, Day of the Guns, 1964, The Snake, 1964, Bloody Sunrise, 1965, The Death Dealers, 1965, The Twisted Thing, 1966, The By-Pass Control, 1967, The Delta Factor, 1967, Body Lovers, 1967, Killer Mine, 1968, Me. Hood!, 1969, Survival: Zero, 1970, Tough Guys, 1970, The Erection Set, 1972, The Last Cop Out, 1973, The Flier, 1973, Tomorrow I Die, 1984, The Killing Man, 1989, (children's books) The Day the Sea Rolled Back, 1979 (Junior Literary Guild award 1979), The Ship That Never Was, 1982; screenwriter, actor: (films) The Girl Hunters, 1963; creator: (TV series) Mike Hammer, 1984-87; editor: Murder Is My Business, 1994; appeared in Miller Lite Beer commls. Served to capt. USAAF, World War II. *

SPILLANE, ROBERT RICHARD, school system administrator; b. Lowell, Mass., Oct. 29, 1934; s. John Joseph and Catherine (Barrett) S.; children: Patricia, Robert Jr., Kathleen, Maura. BS, Ea. Conn. State Coll., 1956; MA, U. Conn., 1959, PhD, 1967. Elem. and secondary tchr. Storrs, Conn., 1956-60, Chaplin, Conn., 1960-62; elem. prin. Trumbull, Conn., 1962-63; secondary prin. Trumbull, 1963-65; asst. supt. Glassboro (N.J.) Pub. Schs., 1966-68, Roosevelt (L.I., N.Y.) Schs., 1968-70, New Rochelle (N.Y.) Pub. Schs., 1970-78; dep. commr. N.Y. State Dept Edn., Albany, N.Y., 1978-81; supt. Boston Pub. Schs., 1981-85, Fairfax (Va.) County Pub. Schs., 1985—; bd. dirs. Council Great City Schs.; mem. adv. bd. Met. Ctr. Ednl. Research, Devel. and Tng. NYU, Instr. Mag.; chmn. pres.' adv. bd. Tchrs. Coll. Columbia U.; co-chmn. adminstrs. com. study on edn. and edn. of tchrs. U.S. Office Edn., Washington; mem. N.Y. State Sch. Officers Resolutions Com. on Legislation, Westchester County Chief Sch. Officers Legis. Com.; bd. dirs. Curriculum Devel. Council So. N.J., Impact II, N.Y.C.; adj. prof. sch. edn. Fordham U., N.Y.C., Iona Coll., New Rochelle, Bank St. Coll. Edn., N.Y.C., Glassboro State Coll.; instr. NYU; vis. lectr. U. Bridgeport, Conn. Author: You and Smoking, 1970, Management by Objectives in the Schools, 1978; contbr. articles to profl. jours. Trustee Mus. Fine Arts, Boston; bd. dirs. Jr. Achievement Ea. Mass., Inc.; mem. adv. com. Boston Pub. Library, The Statue of Liberty-Ellis Island Found., Inc., commn. on Bicentennial U.S. Constitution. Recipient Disting. Alumni award Ea. Conn. State Coll., 1969, Disting. Alumni award U. Conn., 1986; named one of Outstanding Young Men of Am. Mem. Am. Assn. Sch. Adminstrs. (Nat. Supt. of the Year award 1995), Mass., Conn., N.J., N.Y. Assns. Sch. Adminstrs., Sch. Mgmt. Study Group (pres. 1971-73, Hall of Fame award 1974), Assn. Supervision and Curriculum Devel., Nat. Sch. Pub. Relations Assn., Phi Delta Kappa. Avocations: swimming, sailing, skiing, theater and the arts, entertaining. Office: Fairfax Cty Public Schools 10700 Page Ave Fairfax VA 22030-4006

SPILLARD, ERNEST JOHN, oil company executive; b. London, June 14, 1939; came to U.S., 1981; s. Richard John and Iris Ethel (Turpy) S.; divorced; children: Dinah Susan, Mark John; m. Marray Candice Miller, July 21, 1989. MBA, U. Tex., 1989. Various exec. positions FG Minter Group, London, 1964-75; mng. dir. Ferry Works Plant Hire Ltd., London, 1975-77; v.p. Beck Arabia Ltd., Alkhobar, Saudi Arabia, 1977-79; contr. Pool Arabia Ltd., AlKhobar, 1979-81; various positions Pool Co., Houston, 1981-86, sr. v.p., 1986—. Fellow Assn. Chartered Cert. Accts. Home: 540 Wilcrest Dr Houston TX 77042-1076 Office: Pool Energy Svcs Co 10375 Richmond Ave Houston TX 77042-4124*

SPILLENKOTHEN, MELISSA J., federal agency administrator. Asst. sec. for adminstrn. U.S. Dept. Transp., Washington, 1995—. Office: US Dept Transp Office of Adminstrn 400 7th St SW Washington DC 20590

SPILLER, EBERHARD ADOLF, physicist; b. Halbendorf, Ger., Apr. 16, 1933; came to U.S., 1968; s. Walter Richard and Ruth Elfriede (Radzey) S.; m. Marga Dietz, Dec. 18, 1964; children—Michael, Bettina. Diploma, U. Frankfurt, Ger., 1960, Ph.D., 1964. Asst. U. Frankfurt, 1960-68, mem. faculty, 1966-68; physicist IBM Research Center, Yorktown Heights, N.Y., 1968-93; emeritus physicist IBM, 1993—; guest prof. Tech. U. Denmark, 1994-95, U. Ctrl. Fla., 1996. Author: Soft X-Ray Optics, 1994. Fellow AAAS, Am. Optical Soc.; mem. German Phys. Soc., Photo-Optic Instrumentation Soc. Research in solid state physics, laser and coherence optics, nonlinear optics, thin films, soft x-rays, x-ray microscopy, lithography; inventor multilayer x-ray optics, x-ray astronomy, x-ray lithography. Home: 60 Lakeside Rd Mount Kisco NY 10549 Office: IBM Corp TJ Watson Research Ctr Yorktown Heights NY 10598

SPILLER, PAT, critical care nurse, educator; b. Wichita Falls, Tex., Nov. 12, 1953; d. William Herman and Frances Euleane (Kimbrell) Webb; m. Tommy Spiller, Sept. 3, 1971; children: Patrick Todd, Tara Dyann. ADN, Northwest Community Coll., Phil Campbell, Ala., 1979; BSN, U. Ala., Tuscaloosa, 1985. Asst. coord. spl. care unit Walker Regional Med. Ctr., Jasper, Ala., 1986-87, coor. spl. care unit, 1987-88, coor. spl. care unit/spl. ICU, 1988-89, nursing insvc. coord., 1990—. Author book on Messianic Jewish Festivals; contbg. author profl. reference book. Mem. AACCN, Am. Heart Assn. (nurse edn. com., pres.-elect), Ala. Soc. for Healthcare Edn. and Tng. (speakers bur.), Nat. Nursing Staff Devel. Orgn. Office: Walker Regional Med Ctr Edn and Tng Dept PO Box 3547 Jasper AL 35502-3547

SPILLERS, WILLIAM RUSSELL, civil engineering educator; b. Fresno, Calif., Aug. 4, 1934; s. William Horton and Marguerite Ester (Johnson) S.; m. Priscilla Watson, Sept. 10, 1960 (div. 1981); children: Sarah, William, Lars; m. Sandra Lynn Newsome, July 15, 1983. Student, Fresno State Coll., 1951-53; BS, U. Calif., Berkeley, 1955, MS, 1956; PhD, Columbia U., 1961. Registered profl. engr., N.Y., N.J. Structural engr. John Blume Assocs., San Francisco, 1956-57; teaching asst. Columbia U., N.Y.C., 1957-61, prof. civil engring. and engring. mechanics, 1961-76; prof. civil engring. Rensellaer Poly. Inst., Troy, N.Y., 1976-90; prof., chmn. civil and environ. engring. N.J. Inst. Tech., Newark, 1990—; disting. prof. civil and environ. engring. N.J. Inst. Tech., 1995—; cons. Weidlinger Assoc., N.Y.C., 1957-76, Geiger Berger Assoc., N.Y.C., 1957-76, DeLeuw Oh Eocha, Manchester, Eng., 1974, Parsons Hawaii, Los Angeles, 1983, Horst Berger Ptnrs., N.Y.C., 1980; organizer NSF workshop on design theory, Troy, N.Y., 1988. Author: Automated Structural Analysis, 1972, Iterative Structural Design, 1975, Intro Structures, 1985, (with R. Levy) Analysis of Geometrically Nonlinear Structures, 1995; editor 4 books including Design Theory, 1988; contbr. more than 130 articles to profl. jours. NSF fellow, 1976, Guggenheim fellow, 1968. Mem. ASCE (numerous coms., chmn. exec. com. TCCP, 1987), Internat. Assn. Bridge & Structural Engrs. Democrat. Achievements include contribution to the development of fabric structures; initiated the science of design theory; participated in development of applications of digital computers to large structural systems. Home: 571 Parker St Newark NJ 07104-1523 Office: NJ Inst Tech Dept Civil & Environ Engring Newark NJ 07102

SPILLIAS, KENNETH GEORGE, lawyer; b. Steubenville, Ohio, Nov. 8, 1949; s. George and Angeline (Bouyoucas) S.; m. Monica Mary Saumweber, May 10, 1975; children: Geoffrey David, Alicia Anne, Stephanie Marie. BA, Pa. State U., 1971; JD magna cum laude, U. Pitts., 1974. Bar: Pa. 1974, Fla. 1978, U.S. Supreme Ct. 1978, U.S. Ct. Appeals (2d, 3d, 4th, 5th, 6th cirs.) 1975, (11th cir.) 1981, U.S. Dist. Ct. (mid. dist.) Fla. 1979, U.S. Dist. Ct. (so. dist.) Fla. 1978. Trial atty. U.S. Dept. Justice, Washington, 1974-76; asst. dist. atty. Dist. Atty. of Allegheny County, Pitts., 1976-78; asst. atty. gen. Fla. Dept. Legal Affairs, West Palm Beach, Fla., 1978-79; ptnr. Spillias & Mitchell, West Palm Beach, 1979-82, Considine & Spillias, West Palm Beach, 1982-83, Schneider, Maxwell, Spillias et al, West Palm Beach, 1984-86, Wolf, Block, Schorr et al, West Palm Beach, 1986-88, Shapiro & Bregman, West Palm Beach, 1988-91; of counsel Greenberg, Traurig et al, West Palm Beach, 1991; pvt. practice West Palm Beach, 1991—; instr. bus. law Coll. of the Palm Beaches, West Palm Beach, 1980-81; CLE lectr. Palm Beach County Bar Assn., 1983—. County commr. Bd. County Commrs., Palm Beach County, 1982-86; co-founder, mem. Children's Svcs. Coun., Palm Beach County, 1986-91; steering com. Fla. Atlantic U. Inst. of Govt., Boca Raton, 1983-94; bd. dirs. The Literacy Coalition of P.B.C., West Palm Beach, 1990—, health and human svcs. Fla. Dist. IX, 1995—, Ctr. for Family Svc., West Palm Beach, 1992-96, Palm Beach County Coun. of Arts, 1985-86; mem. policy coun. Fla. Inst. Govt., Tallahassee, 1985-86; fund raising chmn. United Cerebral Palsey Telethon, West Palm Beach, 1984-85; judge Palm Beach Post Pathfinders Awards, 1992-96. Recipient Cmty. Svc. award Downtown Civitan Club, West Palm Beach, 1983, Man of the Day award United Cerebral Palsey, 1986, Spl. Honoree award Palm Beach County Child Advocacy Bd., 1986, Children's Trust award Exch. Club/Dick Webber Ctr. for Prevention Child Abuse, 1991, Up and Comers Award in Law, South Fla. Bus. Jour./Price Waterhouse, 1988, Achievement award Nat. Assn. Counties, 1986; named to Outstanding Young Men of Am., U.S. Jaycees, 1975, 84. Mem. ABA, Acad. Fla. Trial Laywers, Assn. Trial Lawyers Am. (judge student trial competition 1995-96), Allegheny County Bar Assn., Palm Beach County Bar Assn. (appellate practice com. 1990—), Order of the Coif. Avocations: sports, scuba diving, theater, reading, music. Home: 147 Gregory Rd West Palm Beach FL 33405 Office: 250 S Australian Ave #1504 West Palm Beach FL 33401

SPILLMAN, JANE SHADEL, curator, researcher, writer; b. Huntsville, Ala., Apr. 30, 1942; d. Marvin and Elizabeth (Russell) Shadel; m. Don Lewis Spillman, Feb. 18, 1973; children: K. Elizabeth, Samuel Shadel. AB, Vassar Coll., 1964; MA, SUNY, 1965. Rsch. asst. Corning (N.Y.) Mus. Glass, 1965-70, asst. curator, 1971-73, assoc. curator Am. glass, 1974-77, curator, 1978—, head of curatorial dept., 1994—; cons. New Bedford (Mass.) Glass Mus., 1986, The White House Curator's Office, Washington, 1987-90. Author: Complete Cut and Engraved Glass of Corning, 1979, Knopf Collectors Guide to Glass, Vol. 1, 1982, Vol. 2, 1983, White House Glassware, 1989, Masterpieces of American Glass, 1990, The American Cut Glass Industry: T.G. Hawkes and His Competitors, 1996, also 6 other books, numerous articles. Mem. Am. Assn. Mus. (chairperson curators com. 1989-

93), Nat. Early Am. Glass Club (bd. dirs. 1989-95), Glass Circle of London. Office: Corning Mus Glass 1 Museum Way Corning NY 14830-2253

SPILLMAN, ROBERT ARNOLD, architect; b. Bethlehem, Pa., May 21, 1931; s. Otto Henry and Ruth Meredith (Miller) S.; m. Cidney Jane Brandon, July 7, 1956; children—Catherine, Sarah, Peter. B.Arch., Cornell U., 1954. Registered profl. architect Pa., N.J., Va., Del., Ga., N.Y. Archl. designer office Douglass Orr, New Haven, 1956-58; ptnr. Lovelace & Spillman, Architects, Bethlehem, 1959-70; sr. ptnr. Spillman Farmer Architects, Bethlehem, 1971-82; pres. Spillman Farmer Shoemaker Pell Whildin, P.C, Bethlehem, 1983-96. Trustee, Laros Found., Bethlehem, 1970—; pres. Bethlehem Library Bd., 1970-74, United Way Northampton and Warren Counties, 1979-81, Lehigh River Found., 1992-95; v.p. Lehigh Valley Indsl. Parks, 1985-96, pres. 1996—; chmn. City of Bethlehem Bd. Historic Archl. Rev., 1961-82. Recipient New Constrn. award Historic Easton, Inc. (Pa.), 1981. Mem. Pa. Soc. Architects (disting. bldg. awards 1971, 76, 78, 94), AIA, Soc. Coll. and Univ. Planners, Eastern Pa. chpt. AIA (pres. 1969-70). Democrat. Episcopalian. Served as 1st lt. USAF, 1954-56. Clubs: Bethlehem; Bay Head Yacht (N.J., rear commodore 1985-87). Office: Spillman Farmer Shoemaker Pell 1 Bethlehem Plz Ste 1000 Bethlehem PA 18018-5716

SPILMAN, RAYMOND, industrial designer; b. Wichita, Kans., Jan. 12, 1911; s. Robert Bruce and Willa (Wood) S.; m. Mary Jordan, May 15, 1937; children: Susan, Alden. Student, Kans. State U., 1933. Stylist Gen. Motors Corp., 1935-39; staff designer Walter Dorwin Teague, N.Y.C., 1940-42; chief designer Johnson Cushing & Nevell, N.Y.C., 1942-46; propr. Raymond Spilman Indsl. Design, N.Y.C., 1946, Stamford, Conn., 1963, Darien, Conn., 1983—; ednl. adviser, lectr. design and design curriculums, color applications in design. Mem. edit. bd., Color Rsch. and Applications Quar., 1976-80; producer films on color and design; collections included in Archives of Domestic Life Smithsonian Inst., 1950—. Recipient Elec. Mfg. Design award Gates Pub. Co., 1950, award U.S. Trade Fair Exhbns., Yugoslavia, 1955, Italy, 1957, Peru, 1959 and 63, Poland, 1964, Graphis award, Graphis mag. Italy, 1957, Internat. Triennale award Undicesima Triennale di Milano, Milan, Italy, 1957, Wescon award of merit West Cost Elec. Prodn. Mfg. Assn., 1959, Design USA award Indsl. Design Soc. Am., 1965, Product Engring. Master Design awards, 1959, 66, Housewares Design award, 1967, 68, citation for design in steel Am. Iron and Steel Inst., 1974, John Vassos award Indsl. Design Soc. Am., 1985, Personal Recognition award Indsl. Designers Soc. Am., 1993; Endowment Arts design project fellow Nat. Endowment Arts, 1977; Design Advancement grantee Nat. Endowment Arts, 1989-90. Fellow Indsl. Design Soc. Am. (Personal Achievement award 1993, Personal Recognition award 1993); mem. Am. Soc. Indsl. Designers (pres. 1960-62, chmn. bd. dirs. 1963-64), Am. Inter-Soc. Color Coun. (bd. dirs. 1970-72, 76-77), Phi Delta Theta. Home and Office: Raymond Spilman Indsl Design 1 Althea Ln Darien CT 06820-2501

SPILMAN, ROBERT HENKEL, furniture company executive; b. Knoxville, Tenn., Sept. 27, 1927; s. Robert Redd and Lila (Henkel) S.; m. Martha Jane Bassett, Apr. 2, 1955; children: Robert Henkel Jr., Virginia Perrin, Vance Henkel. BS, N.C. State U., 1950. With Cannon Mills, 1950-57; with Bassett Table Co., Va., 1957-60; dir. Bassett Furniture Industries Inc., 1960—, exec. v.p., 1966, pres., 1966-89, CEO, 1979—, chmn., 1982—; bd. dirs. Pittston Co., Greenwich, Conn., Nations Bank Corp., Charlotte, Trinova Corp., Maumee, Ohio, Dominion Resources, Inc., Richmond, Va., Dominion Energy, Richmond, Va. Elec. & Power Co.; chmn. bd. dirs. Jefferson-Pilot Corp., Greensboro, N.C., Internat. Home Furnishing Ctr., High Point, N.C.; mem. adv. bd. Liberty Mut. Ins. Co. Trustee Va. Found. Ind. Colls., Darden Sch. Found., N.C. State U.; bd. dirs. Blue Ridge Airport Authority. Lt. U.S. Army, WWII and Korea. Recipient Best Chief Exec. Officer in Home Furnishing Industry award Wall Street Transcript, 1981, 82; named Humanitarian of Yr., City of Hope, 1982. Mem. Am. Furniture Mfrs. Assn. (James T. Ryan award 1984), Nat. Furniture Mfrs. Assn. (bd. dirs., past pres.), Furniture Factories Mktg. Assn. (past chmn., bd. dirs.), Va. Mfrs. Assn. (past dir. exec. com.), Bassett Country Club, Chatmoss Country Club, Hunting Hills Country Club, Brook Club, Commonwealth Club, Linville Golf Club, Waterfront Golf Club (Moneta, Va.), Grandfather Golf and Country Club (Linville, N.C.). Episcopalian. Avocation: fishing. Office: Bassett Furniture Industries Inc PO Box 626 Bassett VA 24055-0626 Home: PO Box 874 Bassett VA 24055*

SPINA, ANTHONY FERDINAND, lawyer; b. Chgo., Aug. 15, 1937; s. John Dominic and Nancy Maria (Ponzio) S.; m. Anita Phyllis, Jan. 28, 1961; children—Nancy M. Spina Okal, John D., Catherine M. Spina Samatas, Maria J. Spina Samatas, Felicia M. B.S. in Social Sci., Loyola U., Chgo., 1959; J.D., DePaul U., 1962. Bar: Ill. 1962. Assoc. Epton, Scott, McCarthy, & Bohling, Chgo., 1962-64; sole practice, Elmwood Park, Ill., 1964-71; pres. Anthony & Spina, P.C., 1971-84, Spina, McGuire & Okal, P.C., 1985—; atty. Leyden Twp., Ill., 1969-89, Village of Rosemont, Ill., 1971; counsel for Pres. and dir. Cook County Twp. Ofcls. of Ill., 1975—; counsel for exec. dir. Ill. State Assn. Twp. Ofcls.; counsel Elmwood Park Village Bd., 1967-89, Norwood Park St. Lighting Dist., 1988—, various Cook County Twps. (including DuPage, 1980-82, Maine, 1981—, Norwood Park, 1982—, Wayne, 1982-84), all Cook County Hwy. Commrs. Traffic Fine Litigation, Hanover Twp. Mental Health Bd., 1991—, Glen Edens Assn., 1994—; mem. Elmwood Park Bldg. Code Planning Commn. Bd. Appeals. Recipient Lacodaire medal, Dean's Key Loyola U.; Loyola U. Housing awards, 1965, 71, 76; award of appreciation Cook County Twp. Ofcls., av rating Martindale-Hubbel. Mem. Ill. Bar Assn., ABA, Chgo. Bar Assn., West Suburban Bar Assn. of Cook County (past chmn. unauthorized practice of law sect.), Am. Judicature Soc., Justinian Soc. Lawyers, Ill. State Twp. Attys. Assn. (past v.p., pres. 1982-86, dir. 1986—), Nat. Inst. Town and Twp. Attys. (past v.p., pres. 1993-95, Ill. del.), Montclare/Leyden C. of C., Edgebrook C. of C. (past bd. dirs.), Nat. Assn. Italian Am. Lawyers, World Bocce Assn. (dir.), Blue Key, Delta Theta Phi, Tau Kappa Epsilon, Pi Gamma Mu. Roman Catholic. St. Rocco Soc. of Simbario (auditor-trustee Chgo.), KC (scribe, trustee, past grand knight, bldg. corp. dir. 1967—, Calabresi in Am. Orgn. (bd. dirs. 1990—). Author Rosemont Village Ordinances, 1971; Elmwood Park Bldg Code, 1975, Leyden Twp. Codified Ordinances, 1987. Office: 7610 W North Ave Elmwood Park IL 60635-4142

SPINA, HORACIO ANSELMO, physician; b. Buenos Aires, Mar. 19, 1939; came to U.S., 1970; s. Antonio and Rosa Palma S.; m. Patricia Anne Duffy, Apr. 4, 1985; children: Alicia V., Cristina V., Mario A. Nat. U. Cordoba, Universidad Nacional Cordoba, Argentina, 1968; MD in Psychiatry, U. Pitts., 1974. Diplomate Am. Bd. Psychiatry and Neurology. Resident U. Pitts., 1971-74; rotating intern Shadyside Hosp., Pitts., 1970-71; med. dirs. psychiat. svcs. and chem. dependence program St. Clair Mem. Hosp., Pitts., 1980—; clin. asst. prof. psychiatry U. Pitts. Mem. APA, InterAm. Coll. Physicians and Surgeons, Psychiat. Physicians Pa., Cordoba Soc. Pharmacology and Therapeutics, N.Y. Acad. Scis., Am. Soc. Clin. Psychopharmacology, Acad. Psychosomatic Medicine, Nat. Alliance for the Mentally Ill. Avocations: cooking, gardening, music, computers. Office: 1050 Bower Hill Rd Ste 303 Pittsburgh PA 15243-1869

SPINALE, FRANCIS G., medical educator, research cardiologist; b. Beverly, Mass., July 14, 1956; m. Molly R. Thomas, Sept. 11, 1982. BS in Biology, Northeastern U., 1979; MS in Biometry, Med. U. S.C., 1984, PhD in Pathology, 1988, MD, 1993. Diplomate Nat. Bd. Med. Examiners. Rsch. assoc., divsn. cardiothoracic surgery Med. U. S.C., Charleston, 1985-88, asst. prof., divsn. cardiothoracic surgery, 1988-92, assoc. prof. cardiothoracic surgery and physiology, 1992—, assc. prof. pediat., 1994—; adj. prof. dept. bioengring. Clemson U., 1988—. Contbr. over 100 articles to profl. jours.; editl. rev. bd. Am. Jour. Physiology, Jour. Molecular and Cellular Cardiology, Circulation Rsch., Annals of Thoracic Surgery, Cardiovascular Rsch., Basic Rsch. in Cardiology, PACE, Circulation; abstract reviewer Am. Heart Assn. 66th Scientific Sessions, 1993, 94, 95; editor: (book) The Pathophysiology of Tachycardia Induced Heart Failure,, 1995. Recipient Sec.'s Cmty. Health Promotion award for excellence, U.S. Dept. Health and Human Svcs., 1984, grad. rsch. scholarship award Am. Lung Assn. S.C., 1986, Young Investigators award Am. Heart Assn., 1989, 1st prize Young Investigator Award Heart Inst. for Children, Chgo., 1990, 1st Investigator award R29 NIH, Heart Lung and Blood Inst., 1991, Est. Investigator award Am. Heart Assn., 1994-99; invited spkr. various confs. Mem. AMA, Acad. Surg. Rsch., Soc. Exptl. Biology and Medicine, Internat. Soc. Heart Rsch., Am. Physiol. Soc. (fellow cardiovasc. sect. 1994), S.C. Med. Assn. Home: 1528 Newberry St Charleston SC 29412 Office: Med Univ SC Divsn Cardiothoracic Surg 171 Ashley Ave Charleston SC 29425

SPINDEL, ROBERT CHARLES, electrical engineering educator; b. N.Y.C., Sept. 5, 1944; s. Morris Tayson and Isabel (Glazer) S.; m. Barbara June Sullivan, June 12, 1966; children—Jennifer Susan, Miranda Ellen. B.S.E.E., Cooper Union, 1965; M.S., Yale U., 1966, M.Phil., 1968, Ph.D., 1971. Postdoctoral fellow Woods Hole Oceanographic Instn, Mass., 1971-72, asst. scientist, 1972-76; assoc. scientist Woods Hole Oceanographic Instn., Mass., 1976-82; sr. scientist Woods Hole Oceanographic Instn, Mass., 1982-87, chmn. dept. ocean engring., 1982-87; dir. applied physics lab. U. Wash., 1987—. Contbr. articles to profl. jours.; patentee on underwater nav. Recipient A.B. Wood medal Brit. Inst. Acoustics, 1981, Gano Dunn medal The Cooper Union, 1989. Fellow IEEE (assoc. editor jour. 1982—), Acoustical Soc. Am. (exec. coun. 1985-86), Marine Tech. Soc. (pres. elect 1991-93, pres. 1993-95). Independent. Jewish. Avocations: automobile restoration, hiking. Home: 14859 SE 51st St Bellevue WA 98006-3515 Office: U Wash Applied Physics Lab 1013 NE 40th St Seattle WA 98105-6606

SPINDEL, WILLIAM, chemist, consultant; b. N.Y.C., Sept. 9, 1922; s. Joseph and Esther (Goldstein) S.; m. Sara Lew, 1942 (div. 1966); children: Robert Andrew, Lawrence Marshall; m. Louise Phyllis Hoodenpyl, July 30, 1967. B.A., Bklyn. Coll., 1944; M.A., Columbia U., 1947, Ph.D., 1950. Jr. scientist Los Alamos Lab, Manhattan Dist., 1944-45; instr. Poly. Inst., Bklyn., 1949-50; assoc. prof. State U. N.Y., 1950-54; rsch. assoc., vis. prof. Columbia, 1954-57, vis. prof., sr. lectr., 1962-74; assoc. prof., then prof. Rutgers U., 1957-64; prof., chmn. dept. chemistry Belfer Grad. Sch. Sci., Yeshiva U., 1964-74; exec. sec., office chemistry and chem. tech. NAS-NRC, 1974-81, also staff dir. bd. on chem. scis. and tech., prin. staff officer commn. phys. scis., math. and resources, 1982-90, sr. cons., 1990—; vis. Am. scientist, Yugoslavia, 1971-72. Contbr. articles to profl. jours. Served with AUS, 1943-46. Recipient prof. staff award NRC, 1985; Guggenheim fellow, 1961-62; Fulbright Research scholar, 1961-62. Fellow AAAS; mem. Am. Chem. Soc. Club: Cosmos. Achievements include research on separation of stable isotopes, isotope effects on chemical and biological processes; developed chemical exchange process for concentrating nitrogen-15. Home: 6503 Dearborn Dr Falls Church VA 22044-1116 *Working at and for the sciences has yielded a most fulfilling professional life.*

SPINDLER, G. R., mining company executive. Chief oper. officer Pyxis Resources Co., Abingdon, Va.; pres. coal div Cyprus Minerals Inc, Englewood, CO. Office: Cyprus Minerals Inc 9904 E Mineral Circle Englewood CO 80112*

SPINDLER, GEORGE DEARBORN, anthropologist, educator, author, editor; b. Stevens Point, Wis., Feb. 28, 1920; s. Frank Nicholas and Winifred (Hatch) S.; m. Louise Schaubel, May 29, 1942; 1 dau., Sue Carol Spindler Coleman. B.S., Central State Tchrs. Coll., Wis., 1940; M.A., U. Wis., 1947; Ph.D., U. Calif. at Los Angeles, 1952. Tchr. sch. in Wis., 1940-42; research asso. Stanford, 1950-51, mem. faculty, 1951—, prof. anthropology and edn., 1960-78, exec. head dept., 1963-67, 84; vis. prof. U. Wis., Madison, 1979, 80, 81, 82, 83, 84, 85; editor Am. Anthropologist, 1962-66; cons. editor Holt, Rinehart & Winston, 1965-91, Harcourt, Brce, 1991—; vis. prof. U. Calif., Santa Barbara, 1986-91. Author: Menomini Acculturation, 1955, (with A. Beals and L. Spindler) Culture in Process, 1967, rev. edit., 1973, Transmission of American Culture, 1959, (with L. Spindler) Dreamers Without Power, 1971, rev. edit., 1984, Burgbach: Urbanization and Identity in a German Village, 1973, (with Louise Spindler) The American Cultural Dialogue and its Transmission, 1990; editor: Education and Anthropology, 1955, (with Louise Spindler) Case Studies in Cultural Anthropology, 1960—, Methods in Cultural Anthropology, 1965—, Case Studies in Education and Culture, 1966—, Basic Units in Anthropology, 1970; editor, contbr.: Education and Culture, 1963, Being An Anthropologist, 1970, Education and Cultural Process, 1974, rev. edit., 1987, The Making of Psychological Anthropology, 1978, 2nd edit., 1994, Doing the Ethnography of Schooling, 1982, Interpretive Ethnography of Schooling at Home and Abroad, 1987, Pathways to Cultural Awareness: Cultural Therapy with Students and Teachers, 1994. Pres. Peninsula Sch. Bd., Menlo Park, Calif., 1954-56. Served with AUS, 1942-45. Recipient Lloyd W. Dinkelspell award Stanford U., 1978, Disting. Svc. award Soc. Internat. Diplomacy and Third World Anthropologists, 1984, Disting. Career Contbn. award Com. on Role and Status of Minorities, Am. Edn. Rsch. Assn., Nat. Acad. Edn., 1994; fellow Ctr. Advanced Study of Behavioral Scis., 1956-57; subject of Vol. 17 Psychoanalytic Study of Soc. essays, 1992. Fellow Am. Anthrop. Assn.; mem. Southwestern Anthrop. Assn. (pres. 1962-63), Coun. for Anthropology and Edn. (pres. 1982, George and Louise Spindler award for outstanding contbns. to ednl. anthropology 1987), Nat. Acad. Edn. Home: 489 Kortum Canyon Rd Calistoga CA 94515-9703 Office: Ethnographics PO Box 38 Calistoga CA 94515-0038 *My major aims as a professional observer and interpreter of human behavior are to acquire knowledge by research and disseminate understanding to others by teaching, writing, and editing. As a person I try to keep love, work, play in balanced relationship to each other, and strive for tolerance at least, and hopefully appreciation for others who are different than myself.*

SPINDLER, GEORGE S., lawyer, oil industry executive. BCE, Ga. Inst. Tech., 1961; JD, DePaul U., 1966. Bar: Ill. 1966. Asst. gen. counsel, patents and licensing Amoco Corp., Chgo., 1979-81, gen. mgr. info. svcs., 1981-85, v.p. planning and adminstrn., 1985-87, assoc. gen. counsel, 1987-88, dep. gen. counsel, 1988-89, v.p., gen. counsel, 1989-92, sr. v.p., gen. counsel, 1992-95, sr. v.p. law and corporate affairs, 1995—. Office: Amoco Corp 200 E Randolph Dr Chicago IL 60601

SPINDLER, JOHN FREDERICK, lawyer; b. Milw., Aug. 23, 1929; s. Howard L. and Margaret (Knauf) S.; m. Martha Murdoch, June 26, 1952; children: Susan Spindler Nelson, Elizabeth Spindler, John F. Jr., Robert P. BA, U. Mich., 1951, JD, 1953. Bar: Mich. 1953, Pa. 1954, U.S. Ct. Claims 1955, U.S. Ct. Mil. Appeals 1955, Conn. 1956, U.S. Supreme Ct. 1956, U.S. Dist. Ct. Conn. 1960, U.S. Tax Ct. 1967, Fla. 1977. Assoc. Cummings & Lockwood, Stamford, Conn., 1956-63, ptnr., 1963—. Bd. dirs. Stamford YMCA, 1987-93, Stamford Hist. Soc., 1984-90. 1st lt. JAGC, U.S. Army, 1953-56. Home: 175 Saddle Hill Rd Stamford CT 06903-2306 Office: Cummings & Lockwood Four Stamford Plz PO Box 120 Stamford CT 06904-0120

SPINDLER, MICHAEL H., computer company executive; b. 1942. MBA, Rheinische Fachochschule. European mktg. mgr. Apple Computer Inc., 1980-88, pres. Apple Europe divsn., 1988-90, exec. v.p., COO, 1990-91, pres., COO, 1991-93, now pres., CEO, 1993—; also chmn. Claris Corp., Santa Clara, Calif. Office: Apple Computer Inc 1 Infinite Loop Cupertino CA 95014-6201*

SPINDLER, PAUL, public relations executive; b. Chgo., May 2, 1931; s. Isaac Edward and Sophia (Stein) S.; m. Gail Klynn; children from previous marriage: Kevin, Makayla, Sydney, Jeffrey. BA in Journalism, Temple U., 1952. Reporter Akron Beacon Jour., Akron, Ohio, 1955-58, San Francisco Examiner, 1958-59; editor Santa Clara (Calif.) Daily Jour., 1959-63; dir. pub. affairs Litton Industries, Inc., Beverly Hills, Calif., 1963-68; dir. pub. relations Internat. Industries, Beverly Hills, 1968-70; pres. Paul Spindler & Co., L.A., 1970-75; exec. v.p. Manning Selvage & Lee, Inc., N.Y.C., 1975-85; pres. The Spindler Co., L.A., 1985-87; pres. Western div. GCI Group, L.A., 1987-91; pres. GCI Spindler, L.A., 1991—; bd. dirs. Phoenix House Calif., Inc.; vis. com. mem. Sch. Bus. Adminstrn. U. So. Calif. Cpl. U.S. Army, 1952-54. Mem. Pub. Relations Soc. Am., Fin. Analysts Fedn., Mountain Gate Country Club (L.A.). Democrat. Jewish. Office: GCI Spindler 6100 Wilshire Blvd Los Angeles CA 90048-5115

SPINELLA, DENNIS MICHAEL, education educator; b. Mt. Pleasant, Pa., Feb. 21, 1945; s. Michael Louis and Veronica Joan Spinella; m. Bernadette Marie Beitle, July 17, 1976; children: Melissa, Jennifer, Lauren. BS in Elem. Edn., Calif. U. Pa., 1966; MEd in Elem. Edn., U. Pitts., 1967, PhD in Sch. Adminstrn., 1986. Tchr. Allegheny Valley Sch. Dist., Springdale, Pa., 1966-71; lectr. in edn. U. Pitts., Pitts., 1971-74; asst. elem. sch. prin. Keystone Oaks Sch. Dist., Pitts., 1974-76; prin. elem. sch. North Hills Sch. Dist., Pitts., 1976-88, dir. edn., 1988-92; lectr. in edn. Carlow Coll., Duquesne U., Pitts., 1992—, U. Pitts., Pitts., 1995—; bd. govs. Pa. Congress of Sch. Adminstrn., Pa., 1978-82; v.p. dean's alumni coun. U. Pitts., 1986—; pres. U. Pitts. Alumni Assn., 1995. Vol. sch. bd. election, Penn Hills, Pa., 1988; v.p. Northaven Civic Assn., Glenshaw, Pa., 1990-91. PEELS leadership sci. scholar Clarion U. Pitts., 1985. Mem. ASCD, Pa. Staff Devel. Coun. (charter mem.), U. Pitts. Assn. Doctoral Educators (v.p. 1994-95), Phi Delta Kappa (pres. 1992-94, Western Pa. Consortium of Educators rep. 1990—, Leadership award), Pitts. Oldies Music Assn. Democrat. Avocations: professional radio disk jockey, professional research reading, travel, dancing. Home: 316 Sunnyfield Dr Glenshaw PA 15116-1936 Office: Carlow Coll DuQuesne U Pittsburgh PA 15116

SPINELLA, JUDY LYNN, healthcare administrator; b. Ft. Worth, Apr. 8, 1948; d. Gettis Breon and Velrea Inez (Webb) Prothro; children: Scott Slater, Jennifer. BS, U. Tex., 1971; MS, Tex. Woman's U., 1973; MBA, Vanderbilt U., 1993. RN, Tex., Calif., Tenn. Asst. prof. U. Tex., Arlington, 1976-81; dir. emergency svcs. San Francisco Gen. Hosp., 1981-84, assoc. adminstr. for clin. svcs., 1984-88; exec. dir. for nursing svcs. Vanderbilt U. Med. Ctr., Nashville, 1988-93, dir. patient care svcs., 1993-94; dir., COO Vanderbilt U. Hosp., Nashville, 1994-96; healthcare cons. APM, Inc., N.Y.C., 1996—. Wharton fellow Johnson & Johnson, 1987. Mem. Am. Orgn. Nurse Execs., Emergency Nurses Assn. (bd. dirs., treas. 1979-86), Tenn. Orgn. Nurse Execs. (bd. dirs. 1989-91), Sigma Theta Tau. Avocations: hiking, skiing, travel. Home: 784 Harpeth Trace Dr Nashville TN 37221-3144

SPINELLA, STEPHEN, actor. Student, NYU Grad. Acting program. Stage appearances include The Age of Assassins, La Fin de la Baleine, Heavenly Theatre, A Bright Room Called Day, Hydriota, The Illusion, Burrhead, Tartuffe, 7 By Beckett, Serious Money, Major Barbara, The Virgin Molly, King Lear, Angels in America: Millenium Approaches, 1993 (Tony award 1993), Angels in America: Peristroika, 1993 (Tony award 1994); film appearances include: Virtuosity, 1995; TV movies include: And The Band Played On, 1994. Recipient Marion Scott Actor Achievement award. Office: William Morris Agy 1325 Ave Americas New York NY 10019*

SPINELLI, ANNE CATHERINE, elementary education educator; b. Chgo., Dec. 19, 1943; d. Stanley J. and Lucy A. (Schmidt) Malaski; m. Joseph P. Spinelli Jr., May 28, 1966. BS in Edn., Ohio U., 1965; postgrad., Ashland U., 1989—. Lic. tchr. kindergarten - 8th grade. Tchr. K-3 North Olmsted (Ohio) City Schs., 1965-70, master tchr., 1970-71, kindergarten tchr., 1971-74; kindergarten tchr. Cloverleaf Schs., Lodi, Ohio, 1974—; seminar presenter sci. dept. Ednl. Rsch. Coun. Am., Cleve., 1969-74, State of Ohio Supr. Assn., Columbus, 1986, Great Lakes Interant. Reading Assn., Chgo., 1993; panelist Ohio Coun. Elem. Sch. Sci. Conv., Akron, 1969; speaker Nat. Sci. Tchrs. Assn. Great Lakes Conf., Cleve., 1971. Co-author: North Olmsted Schools Motor Perception Book for Kindergarten, 1970, Kingergarten Home Activities Book, 1991. Mem. Zoning Commn., Westfield Twp., Medina County, Ohio, 1978-90; area coord. Cancer Soc., Medina County, 1983, 85, 89. Jennings scholar Jennings Found., N.E. Ohio, 1987-88; named Outstanding Educator/Acad. Subjects Mid East Ohio/Spl. Edn. Regional Resouce Ctr., 1994, Medina County (Ohio) Tchr. of the Year, 1995. Mem. ASCD, NEA, Ohio Edn. Assn., No. Ohio Edn. Assn., N.E. Ohio Edn. Assn., Cloverleaf Edn. Assn. (bldg. reps. 1985-94), Internat. Reading Assn., Lizotte Reading Coun., Elem., Kindergarten, Nursery Sch. Educators. Avocations: travel, gardening. Office: Westfield Elem Sch 9055 S LeRoy Rd Westfield Center OH 44251

SPINELLI, JERRY, writer; b. Norristown, Pa., Feb. 1, 1941; s. Louis Anthony and Lorna Mae (Bigler) S.; m. Eileen Mesi, May 24, 1977; children: Kevin, Barbara, Lana, Jeffrey, Molly, Sean, Benjamin. BA, Gettysburg (Pa.) Coll., 1963; MA, Johns Hopkins U., 1964. Editor Chilton Co., Radnor, Pa., 1966-89. Author: Space Station Seventh Grade, 1982, Who Put That Hair in My Toothbrush?, 1984, Night of the Whale, 1985, Jason and Marceline, 1986, Dump Days, 1988, Maniac Magee, 1990 (Newbery medal 1991, Boston Globe/Horn Book award 1991), Bathwater Gang, 1990, There's a Girl in My Hammerlock, 1991, Dump Days, 1991, Fourth Grade Rats, 1991, Bathwater Gang Get Down to Business, 1992, Do the Funky Pickle, 1992, Report to the Principal's Office!, 1992, Who Ran My Underwear Up the Flagpole?, 1992, Picklemania, 1993, Tooter Pepperday, 1995, Crash, 1996. Avocations: tennis, reading, country music, travel.

SPINK, FRANK HENRY, JR., association manager, publisher, urban planner,; b. Chgo., Sept. 23, 1935; s. Frank Henry and Madeline Imogene (Ryan) S.; m. Barbara Jean Westbrook, June 30, 1962; children: Christina Jean, Suzan Josette. BArch, U. Ill., 1958; M of Urban Planning, U. Wash., 1963. Planner City of Bellevue, Wash., 1961-62, City of Fremont, Calif., 1963-66; planning dir. City of Pleasanton, Calif., 1966-67; community builders coun. dir. ULI-The Urban Land Inst., Washington, 1967-72; program div. dir. ULI-The Urban Land Inst., 1972-74, tech. publs. div. dir., 1974-75, publs. dir., 1976-80, publs. v.p., pub., 1981—; founding mem. and trustee emeritus Partners for Liveable Places, Washington. Creator/pub.: (subscription svc.) Project Reference File, 1971—; creator (reference book series) Community Builders Handbook Series, 1975—; contbr. numerous books by ULI, 1975—. Lt. USNR, 1958-61. Mem. Am. Inst. of Cert. Planners, Va. Watercolor Soc. (founder artist), Sumi'e Soc. of Am. (gold medal 1990, Best of Show 1991), Potomac Valley Watercolorists (pres.), Fremont Artist Assn. (pres.), Soc. of Western Artists, Lambda Alpha Internat. (pres. George Washington chpt. 1990-91, v.p. East 1992-95, 1st v.p. 1996—). Republican. Episcopal. Avocations: watercolorist, oriental watercolorist. Home and Studio: 5158 Piedmont Pl Annandale VA 22003-5527 Office: ULI-The Urban Land Inst 1025 Thomas Jefferson St NW Washington DC 20007

SPINKS, JOHN LEE, retired engineering executive; b. Central City, Ky., June 19, 1924; s. William Lee and Lucy Susan (Greenwood) S.; m. Marion Louisa Mutz, Dec. 24, 1951; children—Susan Marie, Douglas John. B.S.M.E., U. Ky., 1951; postgrad., U. So. Calif., 1951-52, UCLA, 1957-58; grad., Res. Police Acad., 1977; Ph.D. (hon.), World U., 1984. Registered profl. engr., Calif., La., Tex., Del., Wis., N.H., Okla., Ky., Miss.; diplomate Am. Acad. Environ. Engrs. Aerodynamicist Rockwell Internat., Los Angeles, 1951-52, Downey, Calif., 1954-55; engr. Bell Telephone Labs., Burlington, N.C., 1952-54, Mobil Oil Corp., Torrance, Calif., 1955-56; supervising engr. II S. Coast Air Quality Mgmt. Dist., El Monte, Calif., 1956-83; pres. Environ. Emissions Engring. Co., Palos Verdes Peninsula, Calif., 1983-95; ret., 1995; dep. dir. civil engring. divsn., space divsn. USAFR, L.A. AFB, 1961-73; past cons. nat. and internat. govt. air quality agys. Co-author: Air Pollution Engineering Manual, 1967, 2d edit., 1973. Former res. police officer Hermosa Beach Police Dept.; mgr. Little League Baseball, 1966-70; instr. rock and ice mountaineering dir. AQMD Golf League, 1968-81; formre lectr. marathon running; usher St. Francis Episcopal Ch., Palos Verdes Estates, 1968-81. Lt. col. USAAF, 1943-46. Decorated Air Force Commendation medal; recipient U.S. Presdl. Sports award in running, 1977, Sierra Peaks emblem; named to Hon. Order Ky. Cols. Fellow Inst. for Advancement Engring.; mem. Am. Assn. Engring. Socs., Sierra Club, Triangle. Clubs: Srs. Track, Pacific Crest. Home: 26856 Eastvale Rd Palos Verdes Peninsula CA 90274-4007 *The achievement of one's personal goals in itself has little meaning. Complete fulfillment comes with guiding youngsters in their formative years, helping them reach higher levels of motivation and social behavior to insure saneness for tomorrow.*

SPINKS, MICHAEL, retired professional boxer; b. 1956; s. Leon and Kay S.; m. Sandy (dec.); 1 child, Michelle. Profl. boxer, 1976—. World Boxing Assn. Light-Heavyweight champion, 1981-86; World Boxing Council Light-Heavyweight champion, 1983-85; Internat. Boxing Fedn. Heavyweight champion, 1985-87; Gold medalist 1976 Olympics, Montreal, Can. Office: care Butch Lewis 250 W 57th St New York NY 10102-0158*

SPINKS, PAUL, retired library director; b. London, Mar. 7, 1922; came to U.S., 1952; m. Clarice Ada Goode, Jan. 27, 1946; 1 child, Philip Andrew. B.A., U. Okla., Norman, 1958; M.L.S., U. Okla., 1959. Catalog asst. Brit. Mus. Library, London, 1939-52; research reports librarian Naval Postgrad. Sch., Monterey, Calif., 1959-61; assoc. librarian Naval Postgrad. Sch., 1961-74, dir. libraries, 1975-93; prof. emeritus, 1993—. Author studies in field. Recipient Civilian Svc. Meritorious award USN, 1993. Mem. ALA, Spl. Libraries Assn., Am. Soc. Info. Sci. Episcopalian. Club: Brit.-Am. (sec. Monterey 1982-85). Home: 855 Capistrano Dr Salinas CA 93901-2420

SPINNATO, JOSEPH ANTHONY, II, obstetrician; b. Ketchikan, Alaska, May 10, 1949; s. Joseph Anthony and Anne Spinatto; m. Diane Dusak, Apr. 26, 1969; children: Joseph Anthony III, Mark Andrew, Julie Anne. BS, U. Dayton, 1970; MD, U. Louisville, 1974. Diplomate Am. Bd. Obstetricians and Gynecologists. Resident on ob/gyn U. Louisville, 1974-77; asst. prof. ob/gyn Sch. Medicine Tex. Tech U., Lubbock, 1979-82; nutrition intern Montreal (Can.) Diet Dispensary, 1980; fellow in maternal-fetal medicine U. Tenn. Ctr. for Health Scis., Memphis, 1982-84, clin. instr. dept. ob/gyn, 1982-84; assoc. prof. divsn. maternal-fetal medicine dept. ob/gyn Coll. Medicine U. South Ala., 1984-88; dir. and prof. divsn. maternal-fetal medicine dept. ob/gyn. Sch. Medicine/U. Louisville, 1988—; mem. ob/gyn staff Lubbock Gen. Hosp., 1979-82, City of Memphis Hosps., 1982-84, U. South Ala. Med. Ctr., Mobile, 1984-88, Norton Hosp., Louisville, 1988—, U. Louisville Hosp., 1988—; mem. birth defects adv. com., human resources dept. Commonwealth of Ky., 1992; dir. maternal transport North Hosp., 199-92, dir. women's reproductive testing cir., 1988—; dir. improved pregnancy outcome project U. Louisville, 1988-92; dir. Fetal Rev. Bd., 1990-92; presenter, lectr., rschr. in field. Spl. reviewer jours. in field; contbr. articles, abstracts to profl. publs. Dir. teenage parent program Emerson Sch., Louisville, 1988-92. Lt. comdr. Med. Corps USN, 1977-79. Nutrition intern March of Dimes, 1980; grantee Smith Kline French Labs., 1986, NIH, 1986, NKC Cmty. Trust Fund, 1988, WHAS Crusade for Children, 1989, 90, 92, Ky. Human Resources Dept., 1990, 93, 94, Outstanding Tchr. award, 1991, 93. Mem. Am. Coll. Obstetricians and Gynecologists, Assn. Profs. of Gynecology and Obstetrics (Excellence in Tchg. award 1994), Soc. Perinatal Obstetricians, So. Perinatal Assn., Nat. Perinatal Assn., Jefferson County Med. Soc., Louisville Obgyn Soc., Am. Inst. Ultrasound in Medicine. Avocations: tennis, golf, music, basketball. Office: U Louisville Dept Ob/Gyn Louisville KY 40292

SPINNER, ROBERT JAY, orthopedic surgeon; b. N.Y.C., Dec. 8, 1961; s. Morton and Paula (Lerner) S. SB, MIT, 1984; M of Studies, Oxford (Eng.) U., 1985; MD, Mayo Clinic, 1989. Rsch. fellow, Luce scholar Prince of Wales Hosp., Hong Kong, 1989-90; intern in surgery Duke Univ., Durham, N.C., 1990-91, jr. resident in surgery, 1991-92, resident in orthopaedic surgery, 1992-96; resident in neurosurgery Mayo Clinic, Rochester, Minn., 1996—. Recipient Davison Teaching award Duke U. Med. Sch., 1993, Schilling scholar Mayo Found., 1984-86. Mem. Phi Beta Kappa, Sigma Xi, Alpha Chi Sigma. Avocations: travel, reading. Office: Mayo Clinic Dept Neurosurgery Rochester MN 55905

SPINNER, ROBERT KEITH, hospital administrator; b. Mpls., Nov. 2, 1942; married. B, St. John's U., 1964; M, U. Minn., 1969. Adminstrv. resident Fairview Hosps., Mpls., 1968-69; administrv. trainee Abbott-Northwestern Hosp., Mpls., 1966-67, asst. adminstr., 1969-72, assoc. administr., 1972-76, administr., 1976-81, v.p. ops., 1981-82, exec. v.p., 1982-88, pres., 1988—. Home: 7722 Lochmere Ter Edina MN 55439-2618 Office: Abbott-Northwestern Hosp 800 E 28th St Minneapolis MN 55407-3723*

SPINOTTI, DANTE, cinematographer. Cinematographer: (films) Sotto, Sotto, 1984, The Berlin Affair, 1985, Manhunter, 1986, Choke Canyon, 1986, Crimes of the Heart, 1986, From the Hip, 1987, Illegally Yours, 1987, Beaches, 1988, Mamba, 1988, The Legend of the Holy Drinker, The Comfort of Strangers, 1989, Torrents of Spring, 1989, Hudson Hawk, 1990, True Colors, 1991, Frankie and Johnny, 1992, (with Doug Milsome) The Last of the Mohicans, 1992, Blink, 1993, The Quick and the Dead, 1994, Nell, 1994, The Man of the Stars, 1994, Heat, 1995. Office: Smith/Gosnell/Nicholson & Assoc PO Box 1166 1515 Palisades Dr Pacific Palisades CA 90272

SPINRAD, BERNARD ISRAEL, physicist, educator; b. N.Y.C., Apr. 16, 1924; s. Abraham and Rose (Sorrin) S.; m. Marion Eisen, June 29, 1951; children: Alexander Abraham, Mark David, Jeremy Paul, Diana Esther; m. Lois Ringston Helton, Jan. 28, 1983. BS with honors, Yale, 1942, MS, 1944, PhD in Phys. Chemistry, 1945, Sterling fellow postdoctoral research, 1945-46. Physicist Oak Ridge Nat. Lab., 1946-48; mem. staff Argonne Nat. Lab., 1949-67, 70-72, dir. reactor engring. div., 1957-63, sr. physicist applied physics div., 1963-67, 70-72; dir. div. nuclear power and reactors IAEA, Vienna, Austria, 1967-70; prof. nuclear engring. Oreg. State U., Corvallis, 1972-82, prof. emeritus, 1983—; prof., chmn. dept. nuclear engring. Iowa State U., Ames, 1983-90, prof. emeritus, 1990—; adviser U.S. delegation Internat. Conf. Peaceful Uses Atomic Energy, Geneva, 1955, 58; cons. IAEA, 1961, 63, 72, 74; chmn. European-Am. Com. Reactor Physics, 1962-64; mem. com. nuclear and alternative energy systems NRC, 1974-79, com. innovative concepts and approaches to energy conservation, 1984-85, com. univ. research reactors, 1986-88; vis. researcher Internat. Inst. Applied Systems Analysis, Vienna, 1978-79, chmn. nuclear engring. dept. head orgn., 1986-87. Author books, papers and reports in field; mem. editorial bd. Annals of Nuclear Energy. Named Man of Year Chgo., 1956, Man of Year Hinsdale, Ill., 1958. Fellow Am. Phys. Soc., Am. Nuclear Soc. (past dir.); mem. AAAS, Am. Chem. Soc., UN Assn. Am., Sigma Xi. Address: 18803 37th Ave NE Seattle WA 98155-2713 *I have lived by trying to understand the rich fabric of the world and our lives, and I love the richness. All the elements should be in it, and this means that apparent contradictions are to be harmonized and resolved, rather than set against each other. I find that I have to be selectively moderate, aggressively opposing the nonsense which is bound up with the valid points in polarized ideologies. It is an attitude which is a bit lonely, for it rejects blind loyalty and blind faith, but I value the dignity of it.*

SPINRAD, HYRON, astronomer; b. N.Y.C., Feb. 17, 1934; s. Emanuel B. and Ida (Silverman) S.; m. Bette L. Abrams, Aug. 17, 1958; children—Michael, Robert, Tracy. A.B., U. Calif. at Berkeley, 1955, M.A., 1959, Ph.D. (Lick Obs. fellow), 1961. Studied galaxies U. Calif. at Berkeley, 1960-61; planetary atmospheres work Jet Propulsion Lab., Pasadena, Calif., 1961-63; investigation atmospheres of coolest stars U. Calif. at Berkeley, 1964-70. Mem. Am. Astron. Soc., Astron. Soc. Pacific. Spl. research water vapor on Mars, molecular hydrogen on Jupiter, Saturn, Uranus and Neptune, temperature measurements on Venus atmosphere, spectra of galaxies and near-infrared observations, 71-72, location of faint radio galaxies, redshifts of galaxies, galaxy evolution and cosmology, 1973, spectroscopic observations of volatile gases in comets. Home: 7 Ketelsen Ct Moraga CA 94556-1814 Office: Univ California Dept Astronomy Berkeley CA 94720

SPINRAD, ROBERT JOSEPH, computer scientist; b. N.Y.C., Mar. 20, 1932; s. Sidney and Isabel (Reiff) S.; m. Verna Winderman, June 27, 1954; children: Susan Irene, Paul Reiff. B.S., Columbia U., 1953, M.S. (Bridgham fellow), 1954; Ph.D. (Whitney fellow), MIT, 1963. Registered profl. engr., N.Y. Project engr. Bulova Research & Devel. Lab., N.Y.C., 1953-55; sr. scientist Brookhaven Nat. Lab., Upton, N.Y., 1955-68; v.p. Sci. Data Systems, Santa Monica, Calif., 1968-69; v.p. programming Xerox Corp., El Segundo, Calif., 1969-71; dir. info. scis. Xerox Corp., 1971-76, v.p. systems devel., 1976-78; v.p. research Xerox Corp., Palo Alto, 1978-83; dir. systems tech. Xerox Corp., 1983-87, dir. corp. tech., 1987-92, v.p. tech. analysis and devel., 1992-94; v.p. technology strategy, 1994—; cons. Contbr. articles to profl. jours. Mem. IEEE, Assn. for Computing Machinery, Nat. Acad. Engring., Calif. Coun. on Sci. and Tech., Sigma Xi, Tau Beta Pi. Achievements include patents in field. Office: Xerox Corp 3333 Coyote Hill Rd Palo Alto CA 94304-1314

SPINWEBER, CHERYL LYNN, research psychologist; b. Jersey City, July 26, 1950; d. Stanley A. And Evelyn M. (Pfleger) S.; m. Michael E. Bruich, June 18, 1977; children: Sean Michael Bruich, Gregory Alan Bruich. AB with distinction, Cornell U., 1972; PhD in Exptl. Psychology, Harvard U., 1977. Lic. psychologist, Calif. Asst. prof. psychiatry Tufts U. Sch. Medicine, Medford, Mass., 1977-79; asst. dir. sleep lab. Boston State Hosp., 1973-79; dep. head dept. behavioral psychopharmacology Naval Health Research Ctr., San Diego, 1978-86, head dept. behavioral psychopharmacology, 1986-89; research asst. prof. dept. psychiatry Uniformed Svcs. U. of the Health Scis., Bethesda, Md., 1985—; lectr. workshop instr. U. Calif. San Diego, La Jolla, 1979-81, vis. lectr. 1979-86; assoc. adj. prof. Dept. Psychology, 1989-94, adj. prof., 1994—; courtesy clin. staff appointee dept. psychiatry Naval Hosp., San Diego, 1984-89, clin. dir. Sleep Disorders Ctr. Mercy Hosp., San Diego, 1991—; pediatric sleep specialist Children's Hosp., San Diego, 1992-95. Contbr. articles to profl. jours. Scholar Cornell U., Ithaca, N.Y., 1968-72, West Essex Tuition, 1968-72, Cornell U. Fedn. Women, 1917-72, Harvard U., 1972-73, 74-76, NDEA Title IV, 1973-74; postdoctoral associateship Nat. Research Council, 1978-80, Outstanding Tchg. award U. Calif. San Diego, 1994. Fellow Am. Sleep Disorders Assn., Clin. Sleep Soc., We. Psychol. Assn. (sec.-treas. 1986—); mem. Am. Men and Women of Sci., Sleep Rsch. Soc. (exec. com. 1986-89), Calif. Sleep Soc., Sigma Xi. Office: U Calif San Diego Dept Psychology 0109 La Jolla CA 92093

SPIOTTA, RAYMOND HERMAN, consulting editor; b. Bklyn., Feb. 24, 1927; s. Michael Joseph and Olga Elizabeth (Schmidt) S.; m. Maria Theresa Attanasio, Apr. 17, 1949; children: Robert, Michael, Ronald, Mark, Sandra. B.M.E., Pratt Inst., 1953. Mfg. engr. Arma div. Am. Bosch Arma Corp., Garden City, N.Y., 1948-53; mng. editor Machinery mag., N.Y.C., 1953-65; editor Machine and Tool Blue Book, Wheaton, Ill., 1965-89; editorial dir. Machine and Tool Blue Book & Mfg. Systems, Carol Stream, Ill., 1989-90; cons. editor Cutting Tool Engring., Northbrook, Ill., 1992-95; acquisitions editor Hanser Gardner Publs., Cin., 1995—. Contbr. to Am. Peoples Ency. Yearbook; contbr. articles to profl. jours. Mem. DuPage County (Ill.) area council Boy Scouts Am., 1966-73. Served with AC USNR, 1944-48. Mem. Numerical Control Soc. of AIM-Tech., Soc. Am. Value Engrs., Soc. Mfg. Engrs., Am. Inst. Indsl. Engrs., Robotics Internat. Roman Catholic. Home and Office: 1484 Aberdeen Ct Naperville IL 60564-9796

SPIOTTO, JAMES ERNEST, lawyer; b. Chgo., Nov. 25, 1946; s. Michael Angelo and Vinnetta Catherine (Henninger) S.; m. Ann Elizabeth Humphreys, Dec. 23, 1972; children: Michael Thomas, Mary Catherine, Joan Elizabeth, Kathryn Ann. AB, St. Mary's of the Lake, 1968; JD, U. Chgo., 1972. Bar: Ill. 1972, U.S. Dist. Ct. (no. dist.) Ill. 1973, U.S. Ct. Appeals (3rd and 7th cir.) 1974, U.S. Supreme Ct. 1978, U.S. Ct. Appeals (9th cir.) 1984, U.S. Dist. Ct. (so. dist.) Calif. 1984. Exclusionary rule study-project dir. Law Enforcement Assistance Agy. Grant, Chgo., 1972; law clk. to presiding justice U.S. Dist. Ct., Chgo., 1972-74; assoc. Chapman and Cutler, Chgo., 1974-80, ptnr., 1980—; chmn. program on defaulted bonds and bankruptcy Practising Law Inst., 1982—, chmn program on troubled debt financing, 1987—. Author: Defaulted Securities, 1990; contbr. numerous articles to profl. jours. With USAR, 1969-75. Mem. Assn. Bond Lawyers, Law Club of City of Chgo., Union League, Econs. Club Chgo. Roman Catholic. Office: Chapman and Cutler 111 W Monroe St Chicago IL 60603

SPIRA, MELVIN, plastic surgeon; b. Chgo., July 3, 1925; s. Samuel and Jessie (Tivin) S.; m. Rita Silver, Nov. 27, 1952; children—Mary Ann, Joel Bennett, Pamela Beth. Student, Wright Jr. Coll, Chgo., 1942-43, Franklin and Marshall Coll., Lancaster, Pa., 1943-44; DDS, Northwestern U., 1947, MSD, 1951; MD, Med. Coll. of Ga., 1956. Diplomate Am. Bd. Plastic Surgery. Intern Duke U. Hosp., Durham, N.C., 1956-57, jr. asst. resident, 1958-59, asst. resident, 1959-60; resident Jefferson Davis Hosp, Houston, 1960-61, asst. in surgery and plastic surgery; sr. attending physician Ben Taub Gen. Hosp, Houston, chief of plastic surgery; attending physician Tex. Children's Hosp., Houston; chief plastic surgery Meth. Hosp., Houston, St. Lukes Episc. Hosp., Houston, VA Hosp., Houston; prof. Baylor Coll. Medicine, Houston, head div. plastic surgery; chmn. Am. Bd. Plastic Surgery, 1984-85. Served with USN, 1943-45, 48-50. Fellow ACS; mem. Houston Surg. Soc., Am. Soc. Maxillofacial Surgeons (pres. 1974-75), Am. Soc. Plastic and Reconstructive Surgeons, Harris County Med. Soc., Plastic Surgery Research Council, So. Med. Assn., Tex. Med. Assn., Am. Trauma Soc., G.V. Black Soc., Internat. Soc. for Burn Injuries, Am. Burn Assn., Am. Cleft Palate Assn., Am. Assn. Plastic Surgeons (pres. 1992-93), Acad. Plastic Surgery Forum, Internat. Soc. Reconstructive Microsurgery, Tex. Surg. Soc., Michael E. DeBakey Internat. Cardiovascular Soc., Baron Hardy Soc., Am. Soc. for Aesthetic Plastic Surgery, Alpha Omega Alpha, Sigma Xi. Avocations: snow skiing; photography; painting; tennis. Office: Baylor Coll Medicine Div Plastic Surgery 6560 Fannin St Ste 800 Houston TX 77030-2725

SPIRA, PATRICIA GOODSITT, performing arts association executive; b. Milw.; d. Lawrence Manfred and Ruth Pauline (Miller) Goodsitt; m. Marvin Alfred Spira, July 12, 1952; children: David, James, Ann, Ellen. BA in History, U. Wis., Milw., 1967. Dir. group sales Swan Theatre and Supper Club, Milw., 1962-63; mgr. box office Performing Arts Ctr., Milw., 1969-80; dir. devel. St. Louis Conservatory and Schs., 1980-81; pres. Box Office Mgmt. Internat., N.Y.C., 1981—; tchr. Creative Dramatics, Milw., 1962-66; adv. coun. Town Hall, N.Y.C., 1989—; bd. dirs. Theatre and Dance Co., N.Y.C., 1986-89. bd. dirs. Milw. Chamber Music Soc., 1974-80. Mem. Am. Soc. Assn. Execs. (cert.), N.Y. Soc. Assn. Execs. Avocations: reading, travel, theater. Office: Box Office Mgmt Internat 250 W 57th St # 722 New York NY 10107

SPIRE, NANCY WOODSON (MRS. LYMAN SPIRE), civic worker; b. Wausau, Wis., May 6, 1917; d. Aytchmonde Perrin and Leigh (Yawkey) Woodson; B.S., Radcliffe Coll., 1939; postgrad. Syracuse U., 1957; m. Lyman J. Spire, June 29, 1940; children: Stephen Crittenden Woodson, Abigail Lyman. Vice pres. Woodson Fiduciary Corp., Wilmington, Del. Trustee Aytchmonde Woodson Found., pres., 1963—; trustee Corinthian Found., 1958-63, 68—, Syracuse Child and Family Service, 1957-62; trustee, sec. Crouse-Irving Meml. Hosp., Syracuse; trustee Syracuse Symphony Orch.; mem. exec. com. Syracuse U. Library Assos., 1958-63, trustee, 1958—. Bd. visitors N.Y. State Tng. Sch. for Girls; v.p. bd. dirs. Leigh Yawkey Woodson Art Mus. Mem. Syracuse Symphony Guild (treas. 1958-59), U.S. Trotting Assn. Republican. Universalist (trustee). Club: Virgin Islands Game Fishing. Office: Yawkey Lumber Co PO Box 65 Wausau WI 54402-0065 also: 707 Kimry Moor Fayetteville NY 13066-1834 also: Cowpet Bay W 24 Windward Way Saint Thomas VI 00802

SPIRER, JUNE DALE, marketing executive, clinical psychologist; b. N.Y.C., May 14, 1943; d. Leon and Gloria (Wagner) Spirer; BA, Adelphi U., 1965; MS, Yeshiva U., 1980, PhD in Psychology, 1984, postgrad. NYU, 1988. TV/radio buyer BBD&O, 1965-66, SSC&B, 1966-68; sr. media planner Norman, Craig & Kummel, N.Y.C., 1968-71; assoc. media dir. Ted Bates Co., 1971-72; v.p., account supt. C.T. Clyne Co., N.Y.C., 1972-74; dir. advt. Am. Express, 1974-75; corp. dir. advt. Del Labs., Farmingdale, N.Y., 1975-79; pres. J. Spirer & Assocs., Inc., N.Y.C., 1978-96; pres., CEO Media Placement Svcs., Inc., 1985-95, Tactics, Inc., 1988-95; CEO 75 Main St. Restaurant, Southampton, N.Y., 1990—; Mem. Am. Psychol. Assn. Home: PO Box 490 Southampton NY 11969-0490 Office: 2 Horatio St New York NY 10014-1608

SPIRES, ROBERT CECIL, foreign language educator; b. Missouri Valley, Iowa, Dec. 1, 1936; s. Roy C. and Ellen M. (Epperson) S.; m. Roberta A. Hyde, Feb. 2, 1963; children: Jeffrey R., Leslie Ann. BA, U. Iowa, 1959, MA, 1963, PhD, 1968. Asst. prof. Ohio U., Athens, 1967-69; asst. prof. dept. Spanish and Portuguese U. Kans., Lawrence, 1969-72, assoc. prof., 1972-78, prof., 1978—, chmn. dept., 1983-92. Author: La novela española, 1978, Beyond the Metafictional Mode, 1984, Transparent Simulacra, 1988, Post-Totalitarian Spanish Fiction, 1996; contbg. editor SigloXX/20th Century; editl. bd. Jour. of Interdisciplinary Literary Studies, 1993—, Ind. Jour. of Hispanic Lit., 1992—. Served with U.S. Army, 1959-61. NEH fellow, 1981-82, U.S.-Spain Joint Com. fellow, 1985-86, Hall Ctr. for Humanities fellow, 1992, Program Cultural Coop. fellow, 1993. Mem. Revista de Estudios Hispánicos (editorial bd. 1985—), Anales de Literatura Contemporánea (editorial bd. 1981—), Letras Peninsulares (editorial bd. 1987—), MLA (del. assembly 1989-91), MLA 20th Century Spain (exec. com. 1983-89), 20th Century Spanish Assn. Am. (v.p. 1989-92). Home: 2420 Orchard Ln Lawrence KS 66049-2710 Office: U Kans Dept Spanish & Portuguese Lawrence KS 66045-0239

SPIRN, MICHELE SOBEL, communications professional, writer; b. Newark, Jan. 26, 1943; d. Jack and Sylvia (Cohen) Sobel; m. Steven Frederick Spirn, Jan. 27, 1968; 1 child, Joshua. BA, Syracuse U., 1965. Creative dir. Planned Communications Svcs., N.Y.C., 1966-72, EDL Prodns., N.Y.C., 1972-73; free-lance writer Bklyn., 1973-83; dir. pub. rels. Nat. Coun. Jewish Women, N.Y.C., 1983-90, dir. communications, 1990-95; freelance writer Bklyn., 1995—; adj. lectr. CUNY, Bklyn., 1977-81. Author: The Fast Shoes, 1985, The Boy Who Liked Green, 1985, The Know-Nothings, 1995; co-author: A Man Can Be..., 1981; editor, columnist Children's Entertainment Rev. mag., N.Y.C., 1982; columnist The Phoenix newspaper, Bklyn., 1983. Pres. Tenth St. Block Assn., Bklyn., 1989-91; vol. Model Media Program, Bklyn., 1985—. Recipient Silver medal for pub. svc. film N.Y. Internat. Film and TV Festival, 1972. Mem. Editl. Freelancers Assn., Soc. Children's Book Writers and Illustrators. Avocations: reading, gardening.

SPIRO, BENJAMIN PAUL, economist, consultant; b. Concise, Switzerland, June 6, 1917; came to U.S., 1941, naturalized, 1948; s. Louis and Jeanne (Secretan) S.; m. Nelly Riveros, Oct. 2, 1963; 1 son, Cyril Sven. Lic.Sc.Pol., U. Lausanne, 1939, Lic.Sc.Ec., 1940, Dr.Sc.Pol., 1941; postgrad., Columbia U., 1941-42. Sec. to Swiss Legation, Washington, 1943-45; with Irving Trust Co., N.Y.C., 1945-46; mem. faculty Duke U., 1946-47; with World Bank, 1947-59; pres. Bank-Fund (credit union), 1959-60; with Stanford Research Inst., 1959; fgn. econ. and financial cons. to internat. orgns., govts., pvt. cos. San Francisco, 1961—; pres. Benjamin Spiro Assos., Inc., San Francisco, 1962—; Adviser Central Bank and Nat. Bank Econ. Devel., Brazil, 1965-67, Indonesian Devel. Bank, 1968; integrated regional devel. projects in, Morocco, 1969-71, Iran, 1972-75, East Africa, 1975-76, Yemen, 1977; promoted small-scale industry devel. in, Latin Am., Africa, 1978—. Contbr. articles to profl. lit. Active Boy Scouts Am., 1941-60. Served with Swiss Army, 1937-41. Recipient Silver Beaver award, 1953. Mem. Nat. Democratic Club. Home: Le Mazot, 1884 Huemoz Switzerland Office: 3309 Stephenson Pl NW Washington DC 20015-2451

SPIRO, HERBERT JOHN, political scientist, politician, educator, ambassador; b. Hamburg, Germany, Sept. 7, 1924; came to U.S., 1938, naturalized, 1944; s. Albert John and Marianne (Stiefel) S.; m. Elizabeth Anna Petersen, June 7, 1958 (div.); children: Peter John, Alexander Charles Stiefel; m. Marion Ballin, July 22, 1985. Student, San Antonio Jr. Coll., 1942-43; AB summa cum laude, Harvard U., 1949, MA, 1950, PhD, 1953; MA (hon.), U. Pa., 1971. Adminstrv. asst. U.S. War Dept., Vienna, Austria, 1945-46; mem. faculty Harvard U., Cambridge, Mass., 1950-61, asst. prof., 1957-61; assoc. prof. polit. sci. Amherst (Mass.) Coll., 1961-65; prof. polit. sci. U. Pa., Phila., 1965-73; mem. policy planning staff Dept. State, Washington, 1970-75; ambassador to Cameroon, 1975-77; amb. to Equatorial Guinea, 1975-76; fellow Woodrow Wilson Internat. Ctr. for Scholars, Smithsonian Instn., Washington, 1978; vis. prof. polit. sci. Def. Intelligence Sch., Washington, 1979-80; univ. prof. polit. sci. John F. Kennedy Inst. for N.Am. Studies, Free U. Berlin, 1980-89; Fulbright sr. research prof. U. Coll. Rhodesia and Nyasaland, 1959-60; cons. Brit. Commn. to Rev. Constn., Fedn. Rhodesia and Nyasaland, 1960, Japanese Commn. on Revision Constn., 1962; vis. assoc. prof. U. Chgo., 1961, Stanford (Calif.) U., 1963; chmn. Asian and African Studies program, Amherst-Smith-Mt. Holyoke Colls., U. Mass., 1964-65; vis. prof. internat. affairs Woodrow Wilson Sch., Princeton (N.J.) U., 1966; mem. adv. council polit. sci. Haverford Coll., 1966-71; affiliated with Nuffield Coll., Oxford (Eng.) U., 1967-68; resident scholar Rockefeller Found. Study Ctr., Bellagio, Italy, 1968, 78; vis. prof. govt., guest scholar Ctr. for Internat. Affairs, Harvard U., 1983; vis. scholar U. Tex., Austin, 1984-89; life mem. Brit. studies faculty seminar U. Tex., Austin, 1983—; researcher Lyndon Baines Johnson Presdl. Library, 1985-86; fellow Aspen (Colo.) Inst. Humanistic Studies, 1986; adj. prof. govt. U. Tex., Austin, 1989-91; participant internat scholarly and diplomatic confs.; lectr. various univs. Author: Politics of German Codetermination, 1958, (with others) Patterns of Government, 1958, 2d edit., 1962, Government by Constitution, 1959, Politics in Africa, 1962, 2d edit., 1975, Five African States, 1963, World Politics: The Global System, 1966, (with others) Authority, Nomos I, 1958, Responsibility, Nomos III, 1960, Privacy Nomos XIII, 1971, Why Federations Fail, 1968, Responsibility in Government, 1969, The Dialectic of Representation 1619-1969, 1969, Politics as the Master Science: From Plato to Mao, 1970, Theory and Politics, 1971, Between Sovereignty and Integration, 1974, A New Foreign Policy Consensus?, 1979, (with others) The Legacy of the Constitution, 1987, (with others) Anti-Americanism, 1988; editor, contbr.: (with others) Africa: The Primacy of Politics, 1966, Patterns of African Development, 1967, 'Privatization' of U.S. Foreign Relations, 1995; contbr. to: World Book Ency., Ency. Britannica, Intern. Ency. of the Social Scis.; host Spiro's Conversations, Austin Community TV, 1992—; contbr. articles to profl. jours. Del. Tex. State Rep. Conv., 1990-92; precinct chmn. Travis County; Rep. cand. for Tex. Ho. of Reps., 1991, U.S. House of Reps., 1992, 94, U.S. Senate, 1993, cand. U.S. Senate, 1993; vol. interviewer Survivors Shoah Visual History Found. Decorated Bronze Star with oak leaf cluster, Purple Heart; grand officer Legion of Valor Cameroon, 1977; recipient Detur prize Harvard Coll., 1948, Bowdoin prize, 1952; John Harvard scholar, 1949-51, Holzer scholar, 1949-51; Guggenheim fellow, 1959-60, Social Sci. Research Council faculty fellow, 1962, 67-68, Rockefeller Found. fellow, 1958, Sheldon travelling fellow Harvard U., also Fulbright fellow, 1953-54; Moody grantee Lyndon Baines Johnson Found., 1985. Fellow Assn. for Diplomatic Studies; mem. African Studies Assn., Am. Polit. Sci. Assn. (coun. 1968-70, chmn. election com. 1969), Internat. Polit. Sci. Assn., Am. Soc. Polit. and gal Philosophy, Ambs. Forum Reps. Abroad, Coun. Fgn. Rels., Internat. Rep. Inst., Am. Coun. on Germany, Coun. Am. Ambs., Am. Fgn. Svc. Assn., Mil. Order Purple Heart, Austin Com. Fgn. Affairs (dir.), Harvard Alumni Assn. (appointed regional dir. Tex. 1994—), Wissenschaftliche Gesellschaft Berlin, Signet Soc., Harvard U. Faculty Club, Harvard Club (N.Y.C.), Harvard Club Berlin (pres. 1985-89), Harvard Club Austin (pres. 1990-92), Phi Beta Kappa. Republican. Address: Towers of Town Lake 40 N I H 35 Apt 4b3 Austin TX 78701-4329

SPIRO, HOWARD MARGET, physician, educator; b. Cambridge, Mass., Mar. 23, 1924; s. Thomas and Martha (Marget); m. Marian Freelove Wagner, Mar 11, 1951; children—Pamela Marget, Carolyn Standish, Philip Marget, Martha Standish. B.A., Harvard, 1944, M.D., 1947; M.A., Yale, 1967. Intern Peter Bent Brigham Hosp., Boston, 1947-48; resident Peter Bent Brigham Hosp., 1948-51, Mass. Gen. Hosp., 1953-55; practice medicine, specializing in gastroenterology New Haven, 1955—; chief gastrointestinal unit Yale Sch. Medicine, 1955-82, prof. medicine, 1967—, dir. program for humanities in medicine, 1983—. Author: Clinical Gastroenterology, 1970, 4th edit., 1993, Doctors, Patients and Placebos, 1986; editor: Jour. Clin. Gastroenterology, 1979—, (with others) When Doctors Get Sick, 1987, Empathy and the Practice of Medicine, 1993, Facing Death--Where Culture, Religion and Medicine Meet, 1996. Served with USNR, 1943-45; Served with AUS, 1951-53. Mem. ACP (master). Club: Madison Beach. Home: 89 Middle Beach Rd Madison CT 06443-3006 Office: Box 208019 333 Cedar St New Haven CT 06520-8019

SPIRO, MELFORD ELLIOT, anthropology educator; b. Cleve., Apr. 26, 1920; s. Wilbert I. and Sophie (Goodman) S.; m. Audrey Goldman, May 27, 1950; children: Michael, Jonathan. B.A., U. Minn., 1941; Ph.D., Northwestern U., 1950. Mem. faculty Washington U., St. Louis, 1948-52, U. Conn., 1952-57, U. Wash., 1957-64; prof. anthropology U. Chgo., 1964-68; prof., chmn. dept. anthropology U. Calif., San Diego, 1968—; Bd. dirs. Social Sci. Research Council, 1960-62. Author: (with E.G. Burrows) An Atoll Culture, 1953, Kibbutz: Venture in Utopia, 1955, Children of Kibbutz, 1958, Burmese Supernaturalism, 1967, Buddhism and Society: A Great Tradition and Its Burmese Vicissitudes, 1971, Kinship and Marriage in Burma, 1977, Gender and Culture: Kibbutz Women Revisited, 1979, Human Nature and Culture, 1993; editor: Context and Meaning in Culture Anthropology, 1965, Oedipus in the Trobriands, 1982, Burmese Brother or Anthropological Other?, 1992. Fellow Am. Acad. Arts and Scis., Nat. Acad. Scis.; mem. Am. Anthrop. Assn., Am. Ethnol. Soc. (pres. 1967-68), AAAS, Soc. for Psychol. Anthropology (pres. 1979-80). Home: 2500 Torrey Pines Rd La Jolla CA 92037

SPIRO, ROBERT HARRY, JR., foundation and business executive, educator; b. Asheville, N.C., Dec. 5, 1920; s. Robert Harry and Eoline Peterson (Shaw) S.; m. Terrie C. Gay, May 17, 1980; children by previous marriage: Robert Timothy, Elizabeth Susan, James Monroe. BS, Wheaton (Ill.) Coll., 1941; postgrad. Navy Supply Sch., Harvard U., 1943; postgrad., U. N.C., 1945-46; PhD, U. Edinburgh, Scotland, 1950; student, Union Theol. Sem., summers 1951-53; postdoctoral, Duke U., summer 1956; ScD (hon.), Fla. Inst. Tech. Assoc. prof. King Coll., Bristol, Tenn., 1946-50; prof. history Miss. Coll., 1950-57; pres. Blue Ridge Assembly, Black Mountain, N.C., 1957-60; dean Coll. Liberal Arts Mercer U., prof. history, 1960-64; pres. Jacksonville U., Fla., 1964-79; under sec. of Army, 1980-81; cons. to bus., 1981-84, 86—; nat. exec. dir. Res. Officers Assn. U.S., 1984-86; chmn. RHS Imprinted Products Inc.; v.p. Crescent Fin. Corp.; bd. mgrs. Voyager Variable Annuity of Fla., 1972-79; v.p. Am. Sec. Coun. Found.; past pres. Fla. Assn. Colls. and Univs.; mem., past chmn. Ind. Colls. and Univs., 1964-79, chmn., 1967; sec.-treas. Assn. Urban Univs., 1968-76; mem. Fla.-Columbia Ptnrs.; gen. chmn. Jacksonville Sesquicentennial Commn., 1970-72; mem.

N.C. Tricentennial Commn., 1962—; past mem. adv. coun. Robert A. Taft Inst. Govt., Inst. Internat. Edn. Contbr. articles to profl. publs. and encys. Trustee Southwestern Bapt. Theol. Sem., 1968-78; mem. Fla.-Colombia Ptnrs.; gen. chmn. Jacksonville Sesquicentennial Commn., 1970-72; mem. N.C. Tricentennial Commn., 1962—; chmn. bd. Bapt. Coll. and Sem., Washington. Lt. USNR, 1941-45; ret. rear adm. USNR, 1978. Decorated Palmes Academique (France); recipient Disting. Civilian Svc. award Dept. of Army, 1981. Mem. Navy League U.S. (former pres. Jacksonville coun.), Naval Res. Assn. (nat. adv. coun.), Res. Officers Assn., Ret. Officers Assn., Am. Legion, Kiwanis (pres. Georgetown, D.C. club 1991-92), Army-Navy Country Club (Arlington, Va.), Army and Navy Club (Washington), Phi Delta Kappa, Alpha Kappa Psi, Phi Alpha Theta, Phi Kappa Phi. Home: 105 Follin Ln SE Vienna VA 22180-4957 *Esse Quam Videre—"To Be Rather than to Seem" —is an eloquent apothegm I learned in high school Latin classes. For me it has been a demanding goal for daily living, a worthy aspiration for each task in life and a challenging vision of what I wish and ought to be.*

SPIRO, THOMAS GEORGE, chemistry educator; b. Aruba, Netherlands Antilles, Nov. 7, 1935; s. Andor and Ilona S.; m. Helen Handin, Aug. 21, 1959; children—Peter, Michael. BS, UCLA, 1956; PhD, MIT, 1960. Fulbright rschr. U. Copenhagen, Denmark, 1960-61; NIH fellow Royal Inst. Tech., Stockholm, 1962-63; research chemist Calif. Research Corp., LaHabra, 1961-62; mem. faculty Princeton U., 1963—, prof. chemistry, 1974—, head dept., 1979-88, Eugene Higgins prof., 1981—. Author: (with William M. Stigliani) Environmental Issues in Chemical Perspective, 1980, Chemistry of the Environment, 1995; contbr. articles to profl. jours. Recipient Bomem-Michelson award Bomem Corp., 1986; NATO sr. fellow, 1972, Guggenheim fellow, 1990. Fellow AAAS; mem. Am. Chem. Soc., Phi Beta Kappa, Sigma Xi. Office: Princeton U Dept Chemistry Princeton NJ 08544

SPIRO, WALTER ANSELM, advertising and public relations agency executive; b. Berlin, Germany, Aug. 10, 1923; came to U.S., 1940, naturalized, 1945; s. Harry L. and Kate (Loewenstein) S.; children: Karen Leslie, Pamela Anne, Paul David, Amy Eloise. Student, Athelton Coll., affiliate Cambridge U., Folkestone, Eng., 1938-40. Display dir. Allied Stores, N.Y.C., 1947-51; advt. dir. Gimbel Bros., Phila., 1951-58; exec. v.p. Lavenson Bur. Advt., Phila., 1958-64; chmn. Spiro & Assocs. (now Earle Palmer Brown & Spiro), Phila., 1964—; now CEO Earle Palmer Brown & Spiro, Philadelphia, PA. Bd. dirs. Pa. Ballet, 1982—; bd. dirs. Pa. Hosp., 1984—; trustee Phila. United Fund, 1973—, Phila. Orch. Assn., 1981—, Phila. Mus. Art, 1981—; bd. dirs., mem. exec. com. Urban Affairs Partnership; mem. founding group Global InterDependence Center, 1978—; mem. leadership com. Bus. Leaders Organized for Catholic Schs., 1981—; founding mem. Bus. Execs. for Nuclear Arms Control, 1983—; bd. dirs. Greater Phila. First Corp., 1983—, WHYY-TV & FM radio broadcasting stas. Mem. World Affairs Council Phila. (dir. 1971—, vice-chmn. 1974-78), Am. Assn. Advt. Agys. (com. of bd. agy. mgmt.). Clubs: Downtown, Urban, Vesper, Peale, Sunday Breakfast. Home: 1900 Rittenhouse Sq Philadelphia PA 19103-5735 Office: Earle Palmer Brown & Spiro 1 Liberty Pl 1650 Market St Philadelphia PA 19103-7301*

SPISAK, JOHN FRANCIS, environmental company executive; b. Cleve., Mar. 27, 1950; s. Ernest Lawrence and Adele Marie (Chipko) S.; m. Barbara Ann Heisman, June 10, 1972; children: John Stefan, Theresa Rose. BS in Chemistry, Purdue U., 1972, BS in Biology with honors, 1972. Rsch. engr. Anaconda Minerals, Tucson, 1972-79; chief metallurgist Fed. Am. Uranium, Riverton, Wyo., 1979-80; v.p. ops. Anschutz Mining Corp., Denver, 1980-87; chmn. bd. dirs. Warrenton Refining (subs. of Anschutz Corp.), Denver, 1987-89; CEO Terranext, Inc., Denver, 1989—; mem. Western States-U.S. Senate Coalition for Superfund Reform. Contbr. articles to profl. publs.; patentee sequential flotation of sulfide ores. Named One of Fifty Colo. Top Bus. Leaders, Colo. Assn. Commerce and Industry. Mem. AIME, Soc. Mining, Metallurgy and Exploration, Nat. Assn. Environ. Mgrs. (co-founder, bd. dirs. Washington chpt., co-chmn. govt. liaison and advocacy com.), Denver Petroleum Club, Elks. Republican. Roman Catholic. Avocations: classical piano, cycling, model railroads. Home: 9570 Lacosta Ln Littleton CO 80124-8909 Office: Terranext Union Tower 165 S Union Blvd Ste 1000 Lakewood CO 80228-2214

SPITALERI, VERNON ROSARIO, newspaper publisher, manufacturing company executive; b. Pelham, N.Y., Aug. 2, 1922; s. Rosario S. and Martha (Landerer) S.; m. Marjorie A. Ferrar, Oct. 14, 1952; children: Marc, Eric, Kris, Lynn. B.S., Carnegie Mellon U., 1942. Mgr. mech. dept. Am. Newspaper Pubs. Assn., N.Y.C., 1946-53; research dir., gen. adminstr. Miami Herald and Knight Newspapers (Fla.), 1953-57; chmn. bd., pres. Sta-Hi Corp., Newport Beach, Calif., 1957-74; v.p. Republic Corp., 1974-76, Sun Chem. Corp., 1976-79; chmn. bd. Sta-Hi Color Service, Sta-Hi Europe, Brussels, Concrete Floats-Huntington Engring. Corp., Huntington Beach, Calif.; editor, pub. Laguna Beach (Calif.) News-Post, 1967-81; pres. Laguna Pub. Co., Nat. Newspaper Found.; dir. Suburban Newspapers Am.; chmn. bd. Victory Profl. Products, Mango Surfware. Pres., Boys Club, Laguna Beach; mem. citizens adv. com. Laguna Beach; pres. Laguna Beach Library Bd., Laguna Playhouse, Laguna Coordinating Council; bd. dirs. Sta-Hi Found.; dir. Opera Pacific. Served to lt. comdr. USNR, 1942-46. Decorated Purple Heart. Mem. Am. Mgmt. Assn., Nat. Newspaper Assn. (dir.), Calif. Newspaper Pubs. Assn. (dir.), Laguna Beach C. of C. (bd. dir.), Alpha Tau Omega. Republican. Roman Catholic. Club: Dana Point Yacht.

SPITLER, KENNETH F., wholesale distribution executive; b. 1949. With Miesel/Sysco Food Svc. Co., Canton, Mich., 1986—, pres. Office: Miesel/Sysco Food Svc Co 535 Portwall St Houston TX 77029*

SPITLER, LEE WILLIAM, banker; b. Racine, Wis., Feb. 14, 1919; s. Marion Albert and Agnes Elizabeth (Lowe) S.; m. Helen Deloris Krejci, Mar. 19, 1949; children—Susan D., Lee William, Anne M., James E. B.S., U. Md., 1956; M.B.A., George Washington U., 1962; postgrad. advanced mgmt. program, Harvard U., 1963; grad., U.S. Air Force War Coll., 1959, U.S. Air Force Command and Staff Coll., 1955. Commd. 2d lt. U.S. Air Force, 1943, advanced through grades to col., 1954; chief personnel stats. div. Hdqrs. U.S. Air Force, Washington, 1950-54; asst. dir. statis. services U.S. Air Force, 1958-63; asst. comptroller Hdqrs. U.S. European Command U.S. Air Force, Paris, 1955-58; asst. comptroller Hdqrs. Air Tng. Command U.S. Air Force, Randolph AFB, Tex., 1963-64; ret. U.S. Air Force, 1964; v.p. Computax Corp., El Segundo, Calif., 1965-69; exec. v.p. Irving Bank Corp., N.Y.C., 1969-84; sr. exec. v.p. Irving Trust Co., N.Y.C., 1969-84; ret., 1984; pres. Spitler Fin. Svcs., Monterey, Calif., 1985—; dir. Turkiye Tutunculer Bankasi AS, Izmir, Turkey, 1984-87. mem. nat. adv. bd. Am. Security Council. Decorated Legion of Merit. Mem. Internat. Assn. Fin. Planning, Am. Bankers Assn., Am. Mgmt. Assn., Soc. for Mgmt. Info. Systems, Ret. Officers Assn., Nat. Assn. Uniformed Services, Mil. Order World Wars, Am. Assn. Mil. Comptrollers, Am. Legion, Veterans of Fgn. Wars, Am. Assn. Ret. Personnel, Inst. Cert. Planners, Air War Coll. Alumni Assn., First Fighter Group Assn. Clubs: Harvard, West Point Officers. Home: 200 Glenwood Cir Apt 525 Monterey CA 93940-6747 Office: 200 Glenwood Circle Monterey CA 93940

SPITZ, ARNOLDT JOHN, corporate professional, consultant; b. Koenigsberg, East Prussia, Germany, Nov. 20, 1929; s. Josef and Edith (Simon) S; m. Eleanor Marie; children: Allyson, Neil, Nicholas, Francesa. PhD, Ruprecht Karls U., Heidelberg, Fed. Republic Germany, 1952; MS, NYU, 1954; Hon. Doctorate in Internat. Econs., London Inst. Applied Rsch., 1992. Internat. economist Elektro Watt, Sindelfingen, Fed. Republic Germany, 1954-57, Arlen Industries, N.Y.C., 1957-66; sr. cons. and prof. Econ. Adv. Group Freiburg U., Fed. Republic Germany, 1966-70; exec. v.p. VAS Industries, Inc., NYC, 1970-74; exec. v.p., treas. Internat. Seaway Trading Corp., Boynton Beach, Fla., 1974—; exec. v.p. Unitech Steel, Inc., Chardon, Ohio and Frankfurt, Germany, 1991—; pres. emeritus bd. Geauga Campus Kent State U., 1974—; sr. cons. Yonsei U., Seoul, Republic of Korea, 1982—; sr. cons. Beijing U., People's Republic of China, 1986—. Adv. Chardon (Ohio) Bd. Edn., 1987; dir. German-Am. Nat. Congress, Chgo., 1970-74. Recipient Spl. Recognition, George Washington U., 1979; named Hon. Prof., Inst. of Documentation and Study of Europe, Brussels, 1992; established Josef Spitz Meml. Scholarship Fund for Study of Humanities, Kent State U., 1985, Arnoldt J. Spitz Study of Humanities Fund, Ruprecht Karls U, 1988. Mem. Nat. Assn. Accts., Nat. Assn. Bus. Economists, Am. Econ. Assn., Soc. Govt. Econs., Rep. Nat. Com., Schurman Soc. at Heidelberg Univ. Roman Catholic. Avocations: farming, horses, scouting. Home: 7580 Kimberly Ln Chesterland OH 44026 Office: Internat Seaway Trading Corp 7100 W Camino Real Ste 110 Boca Raton FL 33433 also: Unitech Steel Inc 12573 Chillicothe Rd Ste 4 Chesterland OH 44026

SPITZ, BARBARA SALOMON, artist; b. Chgo., Jan. 8, 1926; d. Fred B. and Sadie (Lorch) Salomon; m. Lawrence S. Spitz, Mar. 19, 1949; children—Thomas R., Linda J., Joanne L. A.B., Brown U., 1947; student, Art Inst. Chgo., 1942-43, R.I. Sch. Design, 1945. One-woman exhbns. include Benjamin Galleries, Chgo., 1971, 73, Kunsthaus Buhler, Stuttgart, Germany, 1973, Van Straaten Gallery, Chgo., 1976, 80, Elca London Studio, Montreal, Que., Can., 1977, Loyola U. Chgo., 1988, Schneider, Bluhm, Loeb gallery, Chgo., 1993, The Ctr. Gallery, 1994; group exhibitions include Am. Acad. Arts and Letters, Library of Congress traveling print exhbn., Tokyo Cen. Mus. Arts, Nat. Acad. Design, N.Y.C., Pratt Graphic Ctr., Honolulu Acad. Arts, Wadsworth Atheneum, Nat. Aperture, 1986—, others; represented in permanent collections, Phila. Mus. Art, DeCordova Mus., Okla. Art Ctr., Milw. Art Ctr., Los Angeles County Mus. Art, Art Inst. Chgo., Portland Mus. Art. Vice-chmn. Chgo. area Brown U. Bicentennial Drive; treas. Hearing and Speech Rehab. Ctr., Michael Reese Hosp., 1960; fine arts patron bd. Newport Harbor Art Mus. Mem. Print Club Phila., Boston Printmakers, Arts Club of Chgo., Soc. Am. Graphic Artists. Address: 1106 Somerset Ln Newport Beach CA 92660-5629

SPITZ, CHARLES THOMAS, JR., clergyman; b. Hazard, Nebr., May 26, 1921; s. Charles Thomas and Magdalene (Schneemann) S.; m. Dorothy O. Gross, June 11, 1944 (dec. 1982); children: Charles Thomas III, Gretchen Ann.; m. Karen Ankener Lucas, Aug. 25, 1983; 1 child, Garrett Richard. Grad., St. Paul's Coll., Concordia, Mo., 1939; AB, Concordia Sem., St. Louis, 1944, DD, 1965; DD, Capital U., Columbus, Ohio, 1967, Muhlenberg Coll., 1967, Gettysburg Coll., 1970; LHD, Luther Coll., Decorah, Iowa, 1967. Ordained to ministry Lutheran Ch., 1944; pastor in Waterloo, Iowa, 1944-46, Marengo, Iowa, 1947-53; dir. broadcasting Luth. Laymen's League, St. Louis, 1953-66; gen. sec. Luth. Council U.S., 1966-73; pastor in Manhasset, L.I., N.Y., 1974-84; exec. assoc. Fuchs, Cuthrell & Co., 1984-85; sr. ptnr. Corp. Exec. Outplacement, 1986-91; pres. Creative Energetics, 1985—; exec. asso. Evang. Lutheran in Mission, 1974-76; pres. Luth. Ch. in Mission, 1975-78; dir. Assn. Evang. Luth. Chs., 1976-83; mem. Commn. Luth. Unity, 1978-83; mem. commn. on faith and order Nat. Council Chs., 1977-83, vice chmn., 1979-82. Trustee Eger Luth. Home, 1987-92; bd. dirs., treas. Licensing Link, 1995—. Home: 21 Deepdale Dr Manhasset NY 11030-3303

SPITZ, LEWIS WILLIAM, historian, educator; b. Bertrand, Nebr., Dec. 14, 1922; s. Lewis William and Pauline Mary (Griebel) S.; m. Edna Marie Huttenmaier, Aug. 14, 1948; children: Stephen Andrew, Philip Mathew. AB, Concordia Coll., 1944; MDiv, Concordia Sem., 1946; MA, U. Mo., 1947; PhD, Harvard U., 1954; DD (hon.), Concordia Theol. Sem., 1977; LLD (hon.), Valparaiso (Ind.) U., 1978; LittD (hon.), Wittenberg U., 1983; DLitt (hon.), Concordia Coll., 1988. With U. Mo., Columbia, 1953-60, assoc. prof. history, 1958-60; Fulbright prof. U. Mainz, Fed. Republic of Germany, 1960-61; prof. history Stanford (Calif.) U., 1960—, William R. Kenan Jr. prof., 1974—, assoc. dean humanities and scis., 1973-77; vis. prof. Harvard U., Cambridge, Mass., 1964-65; dir. rsch. Ctr. for Reformation Rsch., Clayton, Mo., summer 1964, mem. bd. control, 1973—; sr. fellow Southeastern Medieval and Renaissance Inst., Duke U., summer 1968; vis. prof. Barnard Coll., 1980-81; sr. fellow Inst. Advance Study Princeton U., 1979-80; vis. prof. Institut für Europäische Geschichte, Mainz, Ger., 1992. Author: Conrad Celtis: The German Arch-Humanist, 1957, The Religious Renaissance of the German Humanists, 1963, Life in Two Worlds: A Biography of William Sihler, 1968, The Renaissance and Reformation Movements, 2 vols., 1987, Humanismus und Reformation in der Deutschen Geschichte, 1980, The Protestand Reformation, 1517-1559, 1985; contbr. The Harvest of Humanism in Central Europe: Essays in Honor of Lewis W. Spitz, 1992; co-author (with Barbara Sher Tinsley): Johann Sturm on Education, 1995, Luther and German Humanism, 1996; mem. editl. bd. Soundings, 1973-79; mng. editor: Archive for Reformation History, 1968-76. Recipient Harbison award for teaching Danforth Found., 1964; Guggenheim fellow, 1956; Nat. Endowment for Humanities sr. fellow, 1965; Am. Council Learned Socs. fellow, 1971; Huntington Library fellow, 1959; Inst. Advanced Study Princeton fellow, 1979-80; Pew Found. fellow, 1983. Fellow Am. Acad. Arts and Scis.; mem. Am. Soc. Reformation Rsch. (pres. 1963-64), Am. Hist. Assn., No. Calif. Renaissance Soc. (pres. 1964-65), Am. Soc. Ch. History (pres. 1976-77). Home: 827 Lathrop Dr Stanford CA 94305-1054 Office: Stanford U Dept History Stanford CA 94305 *College teaching has enabled me to develop a career which coincides perfectly with my inner needs and goals in life, which have more to do with service than with ambition, more with love of people than wish to dominate, more with mind and spirit than with material things.*

SPITZ, SEYMOUR JAMES, JR., retired fragrance company executive; b. Milw., Nov. 17, 1921; s. Seymour James and Marie (Spinette) S.; m. Elizabeth Taylor Parks, Feb. 7, 1948 (div. Aug. 1967); children: William Taylor, Elizabeth Seymour, Anne Bellin; m. Ellen C. Flynn, July 25, 1969; 1 dau., Ellen Christina. SB, MIT, 1943. With Newport Industries div. Heyden Newport Chem. Corp., Pensacola, Fla., 1946-65; asst. chief engr., 1955-57, asst. v.p., 1957-58; v.p. Newport Industries div. Heyden Newport Chem. Corp., 1959-60, exec. v.p., 1960-61, pres., 1961-65; v.p. parent co. Heyden Newport Chem. Corp., 1962-65, became group v.p., 1965; exec. v.p. Heyden Newport Chem. Corp. (name now Tenneco Chems., Inc.), 1966; pres. Tenneco Chems., Inc., 1967-69; sr. v.p. parent co. Tenneco Inc.; pres. and dir. Internat. Flavors & Fragrances Inc., N.Y.C., 1970-85. Mem. MIT Corp. Devel. Com., 1977-86; trustee Spence Sch., 1982-88, Savannah Symphony, 1990-95, Telfair Mus. Art, Savannah, 1993-96. With USN, WWII, 1943-46. Mem. Univ. Club (N.Y.C.), Larchmont Yacht Club (N.Y., trustee 1986-89), Landings Club, Oglethorpe Club (sav., bd. dirs. 1995—), Chatham Club. Home: 6 Brandenberry Rd Savannah GA 31411-2201

SPITZBERG, IRVING JOSEPH, JR., lawyer, corporate executive; b. Little Rock, Feb. 9, 1942; s. Irving Joseph and Marie Bettye (Seeman) S.; m. Roberta Frances Alprin, Aug. 21, 1966 (div. 1988); children—Edward Storm, David Adam; m. Virginia V. Thorndike, Dec. 24, 1988. B.A., Columbia U., 1964; B.Phil., Oxford U., 1966; J.D., Yale U., 1969. Bar: Calif. 1969, D.C. 1985, Va. 1995. Asst. prof. Pitzer Coll., Claremont, Calif., 1969-71; fellow Inst. Current World Affairs, N.Y.C., 1971-74; vis. lectr. Brown U., Providence, 1973; prof. SUNY, Buffalo, 1974-78; dean of coll. SUNY, 1974-78; gen. sec. AAUP, Washington, 1980-84; exec. dir. Coun. for Liberal Learning of Assn. Am. Colls., Washington, 1985-89; pres. The Knowledge Co., Fairfax, Va., 1985—; ptnr. Spitzberg & Drew, Washington, 1990-92; of counsel Spirer & Goldberg, Washington, 1993—; coord. Alvan Ikoku Coll., Nigeria, 1979-80; cons. Bd. Adult Edn., Kenya, 1973-74, Philander Smith Coll., Little Rock, 1978-80; co-dir. nat. study on campus life for Carnegie Found. for Advancement Teaching, 1989-90. Author and editor: Exchange of Expertise, 1978, Universities and the New International Order, 1979, Universities and the International Exchange of Knowledge, 1980; author: Campus Programs on Leadership, 1986, Racial Politics in Little Rock, 1987; co-author: (with Berdahl and Moodie), Quality and Access in Higher Education, 1991, (with Virginia Thorndike) Creating Community on College Campuses, 1992. Founder Coalition for Ednl. Excellence, Western N.Y., 1978-80; founding mem. Alliance for Leadership Devel., Washington, 1985; counsel GASP, Pomona, Calif., 1969-71; Dem. Committeeman, Erie County, N.Y., 1978-80; founding pres. Internat. Found. for St. Catherine's Coll., Oxford, 1986—; founder Coun. for Liberal Learning. Nat. winner Westinghouse Sci. Talent Search, 1960; Kellett scholar Trustees of Columbia U., 1964-66. Mem. AAAS, Internat. Soc. Ednl., Cultural, and Sci. Exchs., Washington Ethical Soc. Jewish. Clubs: Columbia, Yale (Washington). Avocations: kids, the InterNet. Office: The Knowledge Co 10301 Democracy Ln Ste 403 Fairfax VA 22030

SPITZE, ROBERT GEORGE FREDERICK, agricultural economics educator; b. Berryville, Ark., Oct. 12, 1922; s. Wesley Henry and Nora Catherine (Stullken) S.; m. Hazel Cleo Taylor, Mar. 4, 1944; children—Glenna Dean Spitze Franklin, Ken Rollin. Student, Columbia U., 1944; BS (Sears Roebuck nat. fellow), U. Ark., 1947; PhD (Knapp research fellow), U. Wis., 1954. Instr. U. Wis., Madison, 1950; asst. prof. to prof. U. Tenn., Knoxville, 1951-60; prof. agrl. econs. U. Ill., Urbana, 1960-93; vis. prof. Wye Coll., U. London, 1967-68; vis. research prof. policy U.S. Dept. Agr., Washington, 1975; vis. lectr. various univs., U.S. and Eng.; cons. Fed. Intermediate Credit Bank, 1958-59, Ill. Gen. Assembly Commn. on Revenue, 1963, Tex. A&M U., 1970, Am. Farm Bur. Fedn., Chgo., 1971, Ill. Gov.'s Commn. on Farm Income, 1972, Nat. Agrl. Research Policy Adv. Com., 1975, U.S. Dept. Agr. Econs. Research Service, 1976, Wharton Econometric Forecasting Inc., 1977, Nat. Rural Center, Washington, 1979-80, Nat. Public Policy Com., 1980, Okla. State U., 1986; mem. Ill. Gov.'s Council Econ. Advisers, 1974-76. Co-author: Food and Agricultural Policy, Economics and Politics, 1994; co-editor Policy Rsch. Notes, 1975—, Food, Agriculture, and Rural Policy into the Twenty-first Century, 1994; editor: Agricultural and Food Policy: Issues and Alternatives for the 1990s, 1990; contbr. articles to profl. jours., chpts. to books. Lt. USNR, 1943-47. Recipient Funk recognition award, 1973, Excellence in Teaching award U. Ill., 1977, Outstanding Agr. Coll. Alumni award U. Ark., 1994. Mem. AAAS, Am. Econ. Assn., Am. Agrl. Econs. Assn. (Disting. Policy award 1981, Disting. Teaching award 1972, travel study grantee to France 1964), Internat. Assn. Agrl. Econs., Agrl. Econs. Soc. (U.K.), AAUP, Blue Key, Sigma Xi, Omicron Delta Kappa, Gamma Sigma Delta, Phi Eta Sigma, Alpha Zeta, Phi Sigma. Office: U Ill Dept Agr Econ 1301 W Gregory Dr Urbana IL 61801-3608

SPITZER, ADRIAN, pediatrician, medical educator; b. Bucharest, Rumania, Dec. 21, 1927; came to U.S., 1963, naturalized, 1968; s. Osias and Sophia S. S.; m. Carole Zelter, Oct. 31, 1951; 1 son, Vlad. B.S., Matei Basarab Lyceum, Bucharest, 1946; M.D., Med. Sch. Bucharest, 1952. Diplomate: Am. Bd. Pediatrics. Intern White Plains (N.Y.) Hosp., 1964; resident Hosp. Med. Coll. Pa., 1965-66; postdoctoral fellow pediatric nephrology Albert Einstein Coll. Medicine, 1966-67; postdoctoral fellow in renal physiology Cornell U. Med. Sch., 1967-68; practice medicine specializing in pediatric nephrology Bronx, N.Y., 1968—; asst. prof. pediatrics Albert Einstein Coll. Medicine, 1968-72, assoc. prof., 1972-76, prof., 1976—, dir. div. nephrology, 1973—; mem. staff Bronx Mcpl. Hosp. Ctr., Hosp. Albert Einstein Coll. Medicine/Montefore Med. Ctr.; mem. Medicine B Study sect.-NIH, 1976-80; Prof. C. Dunders rotating chmn. U. Utrecht, The Netherlands, 1990—; vis. fellow St. Catherine's Coll.; vis. fellow dept. biochemistry Oxford U., 1981-82; coord. Internat. Study Kidney Disease in Children; chmn. organizing com. 1st-6th Internat. Workshop on Devel. Renal Physiology, 1980-95; mem. renal adv. com. N.Y.C. Dept. Health; sci. adv. bd. rsch. and grant com. Nat. Kidney Found., 1982; chmn. pediatric nephrology bd. Am. Bd. Pediat., 1982-83. Mem. editorial bd.: Pediatric Nephrology, Seminars in Nephrology; assoc. editor: Pediatric Renal Disease, 1979, 2d edit., 1992; editor: The Kidney Development, 1982. NIH spl fellow, 1967; John E. Fogarty Sr. Internat. fellow, 1981-82; grantee NIH, N.Y. State Health Research Council, Nat. Kidney Found.; recipient Bela Schick medal for extraordinary achievements in acad. and clin. pediatrics. Mem. Am. Soc. Nephrology, Am. Soc. Pediatric Nephrology (council 1977-80, pres. 1981-82), Am. Fedn. Clin. Research, Am. Physiol. Soc., Soc. Pediatric Research, Salt and Water Club, Am. Acad. Pediatrics, Am. Pediatrics Soc., Intersoc. Council for Kidney and Urinary Tract Research (sec.-treas. 1984-89). Office: Albert Einstein Coll Medicine 1410 Pelham Pky S Bronx NY 10461-1101

SPITZER, CARY REDFORD, avionics consultant, electrical engineer; b. New Hope, Va., July 31, 1937; s. Clyde Burke and Marion Jeanette (Redford) S.; m. Carrie Laura Ruth Logan, June 18, 1960; 1 child, Stiegel Logan. BSEE, Va. Poly. Inst. & State U., 1959; MS in Engring. Mgmt., George Washington U., 1970. Rsch. engr., engring. mgr. Langley Rsch Ctr., NASA, Hampton, Va., 1962-94; founder, pres. AvioniCon, Inc., 1993—; lectr. UCLA, 1989—, George Washington U., 1994. Author: Viking Orbiter Views of Mars, 1981, Digital Avionics Systems, 1987, 2d edit., 1993, Avionics Handbook, 1996; contbr. articles to sci. publs. 1st lt. USAF, 1959-62. Recipient Volare award Airline Avionics Inst., 1988; named Va. Peninsula Engr. of Yr., 1993; recipient Digital Avionics award Am. Inst. of Aeronautics and Astronautics, 1994. Fellow AIAA (assoc., Digital Avionics award 1994), IEEE (Centennial medal 1984), Aerospace and Electronic Systems Soc. of IEEE (pres. 1973-74), Exch. Club (pres. Williamsburg 1985). Methodist. Avocations: kite flying, car mechanics. Home and Office: 3409 Foxridge Rd Williamsburg VA 23188-2499

SPITZER, HUGH D., lawyer; b. Seattle, Feb. 14, 1949; s. George Frederick and Dorothy Lea (Davidson) S.; m. Ann Scales, Oct. 14, 1983; children: Johanna Spitzer, Claudia Spitzer, Jenny Spitzer. BA, Yale U., 1970; JD, U. Wash., 1974; LLM, U. Calif., 1982. Bar: Wash. 1974, U.S. Dist/ Ct. (ea. and we. dists.) Wash. 1975, U.S. Ct. Appeals (9th and D.C. cirs.) 1975, U.S. Supreme Ct. 1980. Program analyst N.Y.C. Health and Hosp. Corp., 1970-71; labor lawyer Hafer, Cassidy & Price, Seattle, 1974-76; legis. asst. Seattle City Coun., 1976-77; legal counsel to mayor City of Seattle, 1977-81; mcpl. bond lawyer Foster Pepper & Shefelman, Seattle, 1982—. Contbr. articles to profl. jours. bd. dirs. King County Housing Ptnrship, Seattle; vice chair Puget Sound Water Quality Authority Wash. State, 1989—; chair Seattle Law Income Housing Levy Oversight com., 1988—. Mem. Nat. Assn. Bond Lawyers. Democrat. Avocations: hiking, skiing. Office: Foster Pepper & Shefelman 1111 3rd Ave Bldg Ste 3400 Seattle WA 98101

SPITZER, JACK J., banker; b. N.Y.C., Sept. 11, 1917; s. Ira I. and Jennie (Brody) S.; m. Charlotte May Braunstein, Dec. 21, 1941; children: Jil Spitzer-Fox, Robert Braunstein. BA, UCLA, 1938; LLD (hon.), Adelphi U., 1980, Ben-Gurion U.of the Negev, 1991. Pres., CEO Spitzer Co., L.A., 1951-59; pres., chief exec. officer Brentwood Savs. & Loan, L.A., 1959-66, Sterling Savs. & Loan, Riverside, Calif., 1966-72, Security Savs. & Loan, Seattle, 1972-78; chmn. bd. dirs. Cert. Reports, Kinderhook, N.Y., 1967—; chmn. bd. dirs., chief exec. officer Covenant Mortgage, Mercer Island, Wash., 1982—, Pacific Linen, Bothell, Wash., 1984—; chmn. Vitritek Environ., Inc., Columbia, Md., 1993—. Pres. United Way, Riverside, 1970; nat. chmn. David Ben-Gurion Centennial Com. of the U.S., Inc., 1985-87; mem. U.S. Del. to Inauguration of Pope John Paul II, apptd. by Pres. Carter, 1978; 1st v.p. Dem. County Cen. Com., Los Angeles, 1953-62; Vice chmn., bd. govs. Ben-Gurion Univ. of Negev, 1984—, pres. Am. Assocs., 1985; founder, chmn. Seattle-Beer Sheva (Israel) Sister City Com., 1977; exec. committeeman Am. Jewish Joint Distbn. Com., v.p., Conf. on Jewish Material Claims, 1978—; vice chmn. bd. trustees Med. Edn. for South African Blacks, 1984—. Served to 2d lt. U.S. Army, 1943-46. Spitzer dept. of Social Work at Ben-Gurion Univ. named in his honor, 1986; recipient Outstanding Communal Svc. award Wurtzweiler Sch. Social Work, 1987, Gold medal for Humanitarian Svc., B'nai B'rith, 1994. Mem. Meml. Found. for Jewish Culture (treas. 1978—, chmn. exec. com. 1990—, pres. 1994—), Alexis de Tocqueville Soc., United Way, Rainier Club (Seattle), A.Z.A. of B'nai Brith (internat. pres. 1938-39, Harry Lapidus Communal Svc. award 1936, Sam Beber Outstanding Alumnus award 1970), B'nai Brith (west coast pres. 1968-69, internat. pres. 1978-82, hon. pres. 1982—, internat. chmn. susquicentennial celebration 1992-94), Rotary (World Cmty. Svc. award 1994). Avocation: ping pong. Home: PO Box 2008 Kirkland WA 98083-2008 Office: Covenant Mortgage Corp 9725 SE 36th St Ste 304 Mercer Island WA 98040-3840

SPITZER, JOHN BRUMBACK, lawyer; b. Toledo, Mar. 6, 1918; s. Lyman and Blanche (Brumback) S.; m. Lucy Ohlinger, May 10, 1941 (dec. Oct. 13, 1971); children: John B., Molly (Mrs. Edmund Frost), Lyman, Adelbert L.; m. Vondah D. Thornbury, July 3, 1972; stepchildren: Vondah, Barbara, James R. Thornbury. Grad., Phillips Andover Acad., 1935; B.A., Yale, 1939, LL.B., 1947. Bar: Ohio 1947. Since practiced in Toledo; law clk. to U.S. Supreme Ct. Justice Stanley Reed, 1947-48; ptnr. Marshall, Melhorn, Cole, Hummer & Spitzer, Toledo, 1955-86, Hummer & Spitzer, Toledo, 1986-89; with Hummer Legal Svcs. Corp., Perrysburg, Ohio, 1990—; pres. Spitzer Box Co., 1955-63; v.p. Spitzer Bldg. Co., 1960-91, pres. 1992—. Pres. Toledo Symphony Orch., 1956-58, v.p., sec., 1958-86. Maj. AUS, World War II. Mem. Belmont Country Club. Congregationalist. Home: 29620 Gleneagles Rd Perrysburg OH 43551-3515 Office: Hummer Legal Svcs Corp 353 Elm St Perrysburg OH 43551-2167

SPITZER, LEO, historian, educator; b. La Paz, Bolivia, Sept. 11, 1939; came to U.S., 1950; s. Eugene and Rose (Wolfinger) S.; m. Manon S. Spitzer,

Aug. 23, 1961 (div. 1980); 1 child, Alexander; m. Marianne Hirsch, May 9, 1981; children: Oliver, Gabriel. BA in Spanish magna cum laude, Brandeis U., 1961; MA in History, U. Wis., 1963, PhD, 1969; MA (hon.), Dartmouth Coll., 1982. Instr. dept. history Dartmouth Coll., Hanover, N.H., 1967-69, asst. prof. history, 1969-75, assoc. prof., 1975-81, prof., 1981—, chair dept., 1989-92; rsch. assoc. Inst. African Studies U. Coll. Sierra Leone, 1965-66, 70, 76; rsch. assoc. Centro de Estudos Afro-Asiaticos-CEAA, Rio de Janeiro, Brazil, 1980-82, Boston U., 1986-92; rsch. affiliate Ctr. European Studies Harvard U., Cambridge, Mass., 1984-85. Author: The Sierra Leone Creoles: Responses to Colonialism 1870-1945, 1974, Lives In Between: Assimilation and Marginality in Austria, Brazil, West Africa 1780-1945, 1990; author chpts. to books; contbr. articles to profl. jours. Recipient Ford Found. award, 1974; Am. Philos. Soc. grantee, 1970, Hewitt Presdl. Devel. grantee, 1987, Sloan Found. grantee, 1985; Social Sci. Rsch. Coun. fellow, 1972, Marion and Jasper Whiting Found. fellow, 1991, Littauer Found. fellow, 1992, Nat. Humanities Ctr. fellow, 1992-93, John Simon Guggenheim fellow, 1995. Home: RFD Box 75 East Thetford VT 05043 Office: Dartmouth Coll Dept History Hanover NH 03755

SPITZER, LYMAN, JR., astronomer; b. Toledo, June 26, 1914; s. Lyman and Blanche C. (Brumback) S.; m. Doreen D. Canaday, June 29, 1940; children: Nicholas, Dionis, Lutetia, Lydia. AB, Yale U., 1935, DSc, 1958; Henry Fellow, Cambridge (Eng.) U., 1935-36; PhD, Princeton U., 1938; Nat. Rsch. fellow, Harvard U., 1938-39; DSc, Case Inst. Tech., 1961, Harvard U., 1975, Princeton U., 1984; LLD, Toledo U., 1963. Instr. physics and astronomy Yale U., 1939-42; scientist Spl. Studies Group, Columbia U. Div. War Research, 1942-44; dir. Sonar Analysis Group, 1944-46; assoc. prof. astrophysics Yale U., 1946-47; prof. astronomy, chmn. dept. and dir. obs. Princeton U., 1947-79, Charles A. Young prof. astronomy, 1952-82, chmn. rsch. bd., 1967-72, dir. project Matterhorn, 1953-61, chmn. exec. com. Plasma Physics Lab., 1961-66, sr. rsch. astronomer, 1982—; trustee Woods Hole Oceanographic Inst., 1946-51; mem. Com. on Undersea Warfare, NRC, 1948-51; mem. Yale U. Council, 1948-51; chmn. Scientists Com. on Loyalty Problems, 1948-51; chmn. Space Telescope Inst. Council, Assoc. Univs. Rsch. Astronomy, 1981-90. Author: monograph Physics of Fully Ionized Gases, 1956, rev., 1962; Diffuse Matter in Space, 1968, Physical Processes in the Interstellar Medium, 1978, Searching Between The Stars, 1982, Dynamical Evolution of Globular Clusters, 1987; editor: Physics of Sound in the Sea, 1946; contbr. articles to Astrophysical Jour., Physics of Fluids, Phys. Rev., others. Recipient Rittenhouse medal, 1957, Exceptional Sci. Achievement medal NASA, 1972, Bruce Gold medal, 1973, Henry Draper Gold medal, 1974, James C. Maxwell prize, 1975, Karl Schwarzschild medal, 1975, Disting. Pub. Svc. medal NASA, 1976, Gold medal Royal Astron. Soc., 1978, Nat. medal sci., 1980, Janssen medal, 1980, Franklin medal Franklin Inst., 1980, Crafoord prize Royal Swedish Acad. Scis., 1985, Madison medal Princeton U., 1989, Franklin medal Am. Philos. Soc., 1991. Mem. NAS, Am. Acad. Arts and Scis., Am. Philos. Soc., Am. Astron. Soc. (past pres.), Royal Soc. (London, fgn.), Royal Astron. Soc. (assoc.), Royal Soc. Scis. Liège (fgn. corr.), Am. Phys. Soc., Astron. Soc. Pacific, Am. Alpine Club, Alpine Club (London). Unitarian. Research on interstellar matter, space astronomy, stellar dynamics, broadening of spectral lines, conductivity of ionized gases, controlled release of thermonuclear energy.

SPITZER, ROBERT RALPH, academic administrator emeritus; b. Waukesha, Wis., May 4, 1922; s. John and Ruth S.; m. Marie L. Woerfel, 1946; children: John, Jeffrey, Susan. B.S. in Agr, U. Wis., 1943, M.S. in Animal Nutrition and Biochemistry, 1945, Ph.D. in Animal Nutrition and Med. Physiology, 1947. With Murphy Products Co., Burlington, Wis., 1947-75; pres. Murphy Products Co., 1958-74, chmn. bd., 1974-75; coordinator Food for Peace, U.S. Dept. State, Washington, 1975-76; pres. Milw. Sch. Engring., 1977-91, pres. emeritus, 1991—; chmn. Norman Vincent Peale Nat. Cabinet, Pawling, N.Y.; bd. dirs. State Fin. Svcs., Hales Corners, Kikkoman Foods, Inc., Maple Leaf Farms, Milford, Ind., Roundy's Inc., Pewaukee, Wis.; past citizen mem. Wis. State Bar, bd. govs., 1992-94. Author: Family Organizer, 1977, The American Challenge, 1980, No Need for Hunger, 1981, The Enterprise Collection, 1991, Help the Hungry Feed Themselves, 1994. Chmn. adv. com. Milw. Billy Graham Crusade, 1979; mem. adv. com. on edn. Rickover Found., past mem. com.; pres. Nat. 4-H Coun., 1975; past trustee Farm Found., Nutrition Found., N.Y.C.; active Gov.'s Coun. on Sci. and Tech.; bd. dirs., mem. edn. com. Wis. Mfrs. and Commerce Found. Recipient Freedom's Found. award, 1964, 82, 83, Freedoms Found. award, 1987; Coll. Agr. award U. Wis., 1971; Disting. Service award, 1972; Disting. Lectr. award Mich. State U., 1976; SBA Wis. Agribus. Advocate of Yr., 1985; Disting. Service award Wis. Farm Bur. Fedn., 1984; Wis. Agri-Bus. Adv. of Yr. award U.S. Small Bus. Adminstrn., 1985; Hon. Legion of Honor award Internat. Supreme Order DeMolay, 1987; Disting. Svc. award Pub. Expenditure Survey Wis., 1987; Educator of Yr. award Sales and Mktg. Execs. Milw., 1988; Wis. Leadership Network award, 1993; Patrick Henry citation Mil. Order of World Wars, 1993. Mem. Lake Geneva Country Club, Milw. Athletic Club, Navy League, Milw. Rotary Club, (pres. 1954-55, 89-90, Vocat. Recoognition award 1989, hon. mem. 1993), Sigma Xi, Phi Lamda Upsilon, Alpha Zeta, Phi Eta Sigma, Phi Sigma, Delta Phi Zeta, Phi Kappa Phi, Delta Theta Sigma, Gamma Sigma Delta. Republican. Episcopalian. Home and OFfice: 1134 North Rd Burlington WI 53105-9056 *Peace and freedom from hunger will be a reality in our time with enlightened moral leadership in government and if economic and technical literacy are achieved. Service to our fellow human beings is a privilege.*

SPITZER, WALTER OSWALD, epidemiologist, educator; b. Asuncion, Paraguay, Feb. 19, 1937; children—Paul, Pamela, Carl, Brenda. M.D., U. Toronto, 1962; M.H.A., U. Mich., 1966; M.P.H., Yale U., 1970. Gen. dir. Internat. Christian Med. Soc., 1966-69; asst. prof. clin. epidemiology McMaster U., Hamilton, Ont., Can., 1969-73; assoc. prof. McMaster U., 1973-75; prof. epidemiology McGill U., Montreal, Que., Can., 1975—; prof. medicine McGill U., 1983—, Strathcona prof. and chmn. dept. epidemiology and biostats., 1984—; cons. PanAm. Health Orgn., Washington, 1975, 77, Aga Khan Found., Geneva, 1983-84, Can. Ministry of Transport, 1977—. Editor Jour. Clin. Epidemiology, 1981—; contbr. articles to biomed. jours. Named Nat. Health Scientist of Can., 1981. Fellow Am. Coll. Epidemiology; mem. Can. Oncology Soc. (bd. dirs. 1983-85, pres. 1987—), Inst. Medicine of Nat. Acad. Scis. (U.S.). Mem. Liberal party. Anglican. Avocations: skiing; photography; flying. Office: McGill U Purvis Hall, 1020 Pine Ave W, Montreal, PQ Canada H3A 1A2

SPITZER, WILLIAM GEORGE, university dean, physicist, educator, researcher; b. L.A., Apr. 24, 1927; s. Max and May Lea (Axleband) S.; m. Jeanette Dorothy Navsky, June 23, 1949; children—Matthew Laurence, Margaret Ilene. B.A., UCLA, 1949; M.S., U. So. Calif., 1952; Ph.D., Purdue U., 1957. Mem. tech. staff Bell Telephone Lab., Murray Hill, N.J., 1957-62; mem. tech. staff Bell & Howell Research Ctr., Pasadena, Calif., 1962-63; prof. material sci. and physics U. So. Calif., Los Angeles, 1963—, chmn. dept. material sci., 1967-69, chmn. dept. physics, 1969-72, 78-81, vice provost, dean Grad. studies, 1983-85; dean Letters, Arts and Scis. U. So. Calif., 1985-89; retired, 1992; acting provost U. So. Calif., 1993. Contbr. chpts. to books, articles to profl. jours. Served with U.S. Army, 1945-46. Hon. DHL awarded by Hebrew Union Coll., Jewish Inst. of Religion, 1992. Fellow Am. Phys. Soc.; mem. IEEE (sr.). Home: 4995 Lamia Way Oceanside CA 92056-7431 Office: U So Calif Material Sci Dept Vivian Hall Engring University Park Los Angeles CA 90089

SPITZNAGEL, JOHN KEITH, microbiologist, immunologist; b. Peoria, Ill., Apr. 11, 1923; s. Elmer Florian and Anna S. (Kolb) S.; m. Anne Moulton Sirch, Feb. 2, 1947; children: John, Jean, Margaret, Elizabeth, Paul. B.A., Columbia U., 1943, M.D., 1946. Diplomate Nat. Bd. Med. Examiners, Am. Bd. Internal Medicine. Intern Johns Hopkins Hosp., Balt., 1946-47; resident in internal medicine Barnes Hosp., St. Louis, 1949-51; vis. investigator Rockefeller Inst., N.Y.C., 1952-53, Nat. Inst. Med. Research, London, 1967-68; mem. faculty U. N.C., Chapel Hill, 1957-79; prof. microbiology and infectious diseases U. N.C., 1957-79; cons. N.C. Meml. Hosp., Chapel Hill, 1974-79; ad hoc adviser NIH, 1971—; prof. microbiology and immunology, chmn. dept. Emory U., Atlanta, 1979-93, prof. emeritus microbiology and immunology, 1993—; mem. study sect. bacteriology and mycology NIH, 1975-79, 85-89, chmn., 1977-79. Editor: Infection and Immunity, 1970-80, Jour. Immunology, 1973-80, Jour. Reticuloendothelial Soc, 1973-80. Served with M.C. AUS, 1947-57. Recipient Research Career Devel. award USPHS, 1957-67, Disting. Service award Sch. Medicine U. N.C., Chapel Hill, 1987; USPHS postdoctoral fellow, 1968; USPHS and AEC grantee. Fellow ACP, Infectious Disease Soc.; mem. AAAS, AAUP, Am. Soc. Microbiology (div. group councilor 1977-79), Am. Assn. Immunologists, Reticuloendothelial Soc. (pres. 1982), Infectious Disease Soc., So. Soc. Clin. Rsch., Assn. Am. Med. Sch. Microbiology and Immunology Chmn. (pres. 1990-91), Sigma Xi. Research on cell biology of human neutrophil polymorphonuclear leukocytes, and oxygen ind. mechanisms of antimicrobial phagocytoses; first to demonstrate cationic antimicrobial proteins of polymorphonuclear leukocytes granules; co-discoverer of a cationic protein of polymorph granules with antimicrobial action and a powerful attractant for mononuclear phagocytes. Home: 2251 Brianwood Ct Decatur GA 30033-1715 Office: 1440 Clifton Rd NE Atlanta GA 30307-1053

SPIVACK, GORDON BERNARD, lawyer, lecturer; b. New Haven, June 15, 1929; s. Jacob and Sophie (Ocheretianski) S.; m. Dolores Olivia Traversano, Jan. 16, 1956; children—Michael David, Paul Stephen. B.S. with philosophic orations and honors with exceptional distinction, Yale U., 1950, LL.B. magna cum laude, 1955. Bar: Conn. 1955, U.S. Supreme Ct. 1962, N.Y. 1970. Trial atty. antitrust div. Dept. Justice, Washington, 1955-60; asst. chief field ops. antitrust div. Dept. Justice, 1961-64, chief field ops. antitrust div., 1964-65, dir. ops. antitrust div., 1965-67; assoc. prof. law Yale U., New Haven, 1967-70; vis. lectr. Yale U., 1970-78; ptnr. Lord, Day & Lord, N.Y.C., 1970-86, Coudert Bros., N.Y.C., 1986—; speaker on antitrust law; mem. Pres.'s Nat. Commn. for Rev. Antitrust Law and Procedures, Washington, 1978-79. Contbr. numerous articles on antitrust law to profl. jours. Served with U.S. Army, 1950-52. Recipient Sustained Superior Performance award Dept. Justice, 1955-60. Fellow Am. Coll. Trial Lawyers; mem. ABA, N.Y. State Bar Assn., Bar Assn. City N.Y., Yale Club (N.Y.C.), Pine Orchard Yacht and Country Club (Conn.). Jewish. Avocation: detective stories. Home: 118 Townsend Ter East Haven CT 06512-3129 Office: Coudert Bros 1114 Avenue Of The Americas New York NY 10036-7703

SPIVACK, HENRY ARCHER, life insurance company executive; b. Bklyn., Apr. 15, 1919; s. Jacob and Pauline (Schwartz) S.; m. Sadie Babe Meiseles, Jan. 1, 1941; children: Ian Jeffrey, Paula Janis. Student CCNY, 1936-42; BBA, Am. Coll., Bryn Mawr, Pa., 1965. CLU. Comptroller Daniel Jones, Inc., N.Y.C., 1947-59; field underwriter Union Cen. Life Ins. Co., N.Y.C., 1959-79, mgr. programming dept., 1966-69, assoc. agy. mgr., 1977-79; pension dir. Bleichroeder, Bing & Co., N.Y.C., 1975-77, sr. v.p. NCA Agy., Inc. (formerly New Confidence Agy.), 1979-90, Bentley Agy., Inc., 1990-92; Luxco & Assocs., 1990—; pension dir., employee benefit plan cons., estate and fin. planning, pres. Profl. Benefit Planners Inc. N.J.; instr. N.Y. State Ins. Dept., C.W. Post Coll., L.I. U., N.Y. Ctr. for Fin. Studies; coord. Ins. Dept. Yeshiva U., N.Y.; ins. courses instr.; also lectr., moderator. Contbr. articles to publs. Served with USN, 1943-46. Mem. Life Underwriters Assn. N.Y. (past chmn. blood bank), Am. Soc. CLU's (past chmn. N.Y. chpt. pension sect., past chmn. profl. liaison com.), Am. Soc. Pension Actuaries, Pensioneers at C.W. Post Coll., C.W. Post Coll. Tax Inst. and Fin. Planning Inst., Practising Law Inst., Internat. Assn. Fin. Planners, Internat. Assn. Registered Fin. Cons. (registered fin. cons.), Internat. Platform Assn., Greater N.Y. Brokers Assn. Lodge: K.P. (life; past dep. grand chancellor N.Y. state). Office: 500 N Broadway Jericho NY 11753-2111

SPIVAK, ALVIN A., retired public relations executive; b. Phila., Nov. 30, 1927; s. Herman and Bella (Haimovitz) S.; m. Martha Barry, Nov. 26, 1965; 1 dau., Denise. B.S., Temple U., 1949. With I.N.S., 1949-58; Senate reporter, also mem. gen. staff I.N.S., Washington, 1951-58; with U.P.I., 1958-67, White House reporter, 1960-67; pub. affairs dir. Nat. Adv. Commn. on Civil Disorders, 1967-68, Democratic Nat. Com., 1968-70; corp. pub. affairs dir. Gen. Dynamics Corp., 1970-94, ret., 1994. Served with USAAF, 1946-47. Mem. Nat. Press Club, Sigma Delta Chi, Beta Gamma Sigma. Home: 9201 Fernwood Rd Bethesda MD 20817-3315

SPIVAK, JOAN CAROL, medical public relations specialist; b. Phila., May 12, 1950; d. Jack and Evelyn Lee (Copelman) S.; m. John D. Goldman, May 17, 1980; children: Jesse, Marcus. AB, Barnard Coll., 1972; M of Health Scis., Johns Hopkins U., 1980. Freelance writer N.Y.C., 1980-84; project dir. Impact Med. Communication, N.Y.C., 1984-87; exec. v.p. Daniel J. Edelman Inc., N.Y.C., 1987—. Co-author: (pamphlet) Lead: New Perspectives on an Old Problem, 1978; contbr. The Book of Health, 1981. Bd. dirs. May O'Donnell Dance Co., N.Y.C., 1983-85, Chamber Ballet U.S.A., N.Y.C., 1985-87, Nat. Child Labor Commn., 1991—, Cases, 1995—. Mem. N.Y. Acad. Sci. Democrat. Jewish. Avocations: pottery, sailing. Office: Daniel J Edelman Inc 1500 Broadway New York NY 10036-4015

SPIVAK, JONATHAN M., journalist; b. Boston, Sept. 2, 1928; s. Lawrence E. and Charlotte (Ring) S.; m. Dorothy A. Amendt, Jan. 10, 1953 (div.); children: Jennifer Lee, Timothy L.A.; m. 2d Micheline Aler, Dec. 18, 1980. B.A. magna cum laude, Harvard U., 1950. Reporter Hollister Evening Free Lance, Calif., 1954-55, UP, San Francisco, 1955, San Francisco Call Bull., 1956-57; staff corr. Wall St. Jour., San Francisco, 1957-58, Washington, 1959-78, London, 1978-83, N.Y.C., 1984; writer Paris. Served to 2d lt. U.S. Army, 1951-53. Recipient several writing awards. Mem. Inst. Medicine, Acad. Scis., Phi Beta Kappa, Athenaeum Club (London), Harvard Club (N.Y.C.). Jewish. Home: Ferme le Gres, Lauris France 84360

SPIVAK, ROBERT ELLIOT, financial consultant; b. Phila., Dec. 30, 1936; s. Philip and Helen (Kramer) S.; m. Willa Cohen, June 21, 1958 (div. 1973); children: Michael, Merri, Gregory; m. Ann Taylor Hogge, Sept. 11, 1976. BSBA, Muhlenburg Coll., 1958; postgrad., U. Pa., 1960-61; degree in fin. cons., Am. Coll., 1987. Fin. cons. CMS Cos., Phila., 1968—; lectr. in field. Contbr. articles to profl. jours. Pres. U.S. Com. Sports for Israel, 1981—; chmn. So. N.J. Cystic Fibrosis, 1975; mem. Drug Edn. Info. Clinic, Cherry Hill, N.J., 1972; bd. dirs. Internat. Jewish Sports Hall of Fame, Israel, 1981—, Wingate Inst. for Phys. Fitness, 1981—, Phila. JCC Coun., 1980-88; bd. dirs. Phila. chpt. ADC, 1995, Boys' Town Jerusalem, 1995-96; del. U.S. Olympic Com., 1989; bd. dirs. Einstein Med. Ctr., 1992. Honoree Phila. Office Israel Bonds, 1988; named Man of Yr., U.S. Com. Sports for Israel, 1995. Mem. Nat. Assn. Security Dealers, Million Dollar Round Table, Assn. Advanced Life Underwriting, Am. Soc. CLUs, Woodcrest Country Club (pres. 1975), B'rith Shalom (v.p. 1970-72), B'nai B'rith. Democrat. Jewish. Home: 2330 Pine St Philadelphia PA 19103-6415 Office: CMS Cos 1926 Arch St Philadelphia PA 19103-1444

SPIVEY, BRUCE E., integrated delivery systems management executive; b. Cedar Rapids, Iowa, Aug. 29, 1934; s. William Loranzy and Grace Loretta (Barber) S.; children: Lisa, Eric; m. Patti Amanda Birge, Dec. 20, 1987. B.A., Coe Coll., 1956; M.D., U. Iowa, 1959, M.S., 1964; M.Ed., U. Ill., 1969; hon. doctorate Sci., Coe Coll., 1978. Diplomate Am. Bd. Ophthalmology (fellow, bd. dirs. 1975-83). Asst. prof. U. Iowa Coll. Medicine, Iowa City, 1966, assoc. prof., 1966-71; dean Sch. Med. Scis. U. Pacific, San Francisco, 1971-76; prof., chmn. dept. ophthalmology Pacific Med. Ctr. (now Calif. Pacific Med. Ctr.), San Francisco, 1971-87, pres., chief exec. officer, dir., 1976-91; exec. v.p., chief exec. officer Am. Acad. Ophthalmology, San Francisco, 1978-93; pres., chief exec. officer Calif. Healthcare System, Bay area, 1986-92, Northwestern Healthcare Network, Chgo., 1992—; bd. dirs. Ophthalmic Pub. Co., Chgo., 1977—, pres., 1993—; v.p. Am. Bd. Med. Specialties, 1978-82, pres., 1980-82; chmn. bd. dirs. Vol. Hosps. of Am.-No. Calif., 1985-87, nat. bd. dirs., 1991—; mem. nat. adv. eye coun. NEI, NIH, 1987-92; mem. spl. med. advisors group Dept. Vets. Affairs, 1987-93; trustee, bd. dirs., sec. bd. Ophthal. Mut. Ins. Co., 1988—, Phoenix Alliance, Inc., 1993—. Contbr. over 110 articles to profl. jours.; inventor instruments for eye surgery. Bd. dirs. Pacific Vision Found., San Francisco, 1978—, U.S.-China Ednl. Inst., 1979—; trustee Coe Coll., 1985—, Found. AAO, 1981—. Served to capt. U.S. Army, 1964-66. Decorated Bronze Star; recipient Emile Javal Gold medal Internat. Contact Lens Council, San Francisco, 1982, Gradle medal Pan-Am. Assn. Ophthalmol., others. Fellow ACS, Am. Acad. Ophthalmology (Disting. Svc. award 1972, Sr. Honor award 1986); mem. AMA, Am. Ophthal. Soc. (Howe medal 1993, bd. dirs. 1986-91, pres. 1994-95), Academia Ophthal. Internat., Soc. Med. Adminstrs., Internat. Congress Ophthalmology (sec.-gen. 1978-82), Internat. Coun. Ophthalmology (sec.-gren. 1994—, trustee 1986—), Pacific-Union Club. (San Francisco), Chgo. Club, Chevy Chase Club, Racquet Club Chgo., Glen View Club. Republican. Presbyterian. Office: Northwestern Healthcare Network 980 N Michigan Ave Chicago IL 60611-4501

SPIVEY, JOSEPH M., III, lawyer; b. Richmond, Va., Aug. 10, 1935; s. Joseph M. and Ethel Clarke (Dorsey) S.; m. Ann Dare Davis, Feb. 1, 1958; children—Joseph M., IV, Timothy Andrew Woodland, Thomas Nelson Carpenter. B.S. in Civil Engring., Va. Mil. Inst., 1957; LL.B., Washington and Lee U., 1962. Bar: Va. 1962, D.C. 1979, U.S. Supreme Ct. 1972, U.S. Ct. Appeals (4th cir.) 1965, U.S. Ct. Appeals (10th cir.) 1981, U.S. Ct. Appeals (D.C. cir.) 1978, U.S. Ct. Appeals (2d cir.) 1983, U.S. Dist. Ct. (ea. and we. dists.) Va. 1963, U.S. Dist. Ct. D.C. 1978. Assoc. Hunton & Williams, Richmond, 1962-69, ptnr., 1969—; now of counsel; gen. counsel Va. Mil. Inst. Found., Inc. Bd. visitors Va. Mil. Inst. Served to capt., arty. U.S. Army, 1957-59. Mem. ABA, Richmond Bar Assn. (pres. 1982-83), Va. Bar Assn., Am. Coll. Trial Lawyers. Clubs: Country of Va., Commonwealth (Richmond). Office: Hunton & Williams Riverfront Plaza East Tower 951 E Byrd St Richmond VA 23219-4040*

SPIVEY, TED RAY, English educator; b. Fort Pierce, Fla., July 1, 1927; s. Theodore Roosevelt and Etty Pearl (Sumner) S.; m. Julia Brannon Douglass, June 30, 1962; children—Mary Leta, John Andrew. A.B., Emory U., 1949; M.A., U. Minn., 1951, Ph.D., 1954. Reporter Greenville Reporter, S.C., 1949-50; instr. Emory U., Atlanta, 1954-56; mem. faculty Ga. State U., Atlanta, 1956-89, assoc. prof. English, 1960-64; prof. Ga. State U., 1964-89, Regents' prof., 1984-89, emeritus, 1989—. Author: (with Kenneth M. England) A Manual of Style, 1960, The Renewed Quest, 1969, The Coming of the New Man, 1971, The Journey Beyond Tragedy, 1980, Revival: Southern Writers in the Modern City, 1986, The Writer as Shaman: The Pilgrimages of Conrad Aiken and Walker Percy, 1986, To Die in Atlanta; Poems of the Civil War and After, 1987, Beyond Modernism: Toward a New Myth Criticism, 1988, A City Observed: Poems of the New Age, 1988, (with Arthur Waterman) Conrad Aiken: A Priest of Consciousness, 1989, Flannery O'Connor: The Woman, The Thinker, The Visionary, 1995, Airport: America Rediscovered, 1996. Served with USN, 1945-46. Urban Life Center grantee, 1977-80. Mem. So. Atlantic Modern Lang. Assn. Democrat. Episcopalian. Club: Brittany. Home: 3181 Frontenac Ct NE Atlanta GA 30319-2414

SPLANE, RICHARD BEVERLEY, social work educator; b. Calgary, Alta., Can., Sept. 25, 1916; s. Alfred William and Clara Jane (Allyn) S.; m. Verna Marie Huffman, Feb. 22, 1971. BA, McMaster U., 1940, LLD (hon.), 1990; cert. social sci. and adminstrn., London Sch. Econs., 1947; MA, U. Toronto, 1948, MSW, 1951, PhD, 1961; LLD (hon.), Wilfrid Laurier U., 1988, U. B.C., Can., 1996. Exec. dir. Children's Aid Soc., Cornwall, Ont., Can., 1948-50; with Health and Welfare Can., Ottawa, 1952-72; exec. asst. to dep. minister nat. welfare Health and Welfare Can., 1959-60, dir. unemployment assistance, 1960-62, dir. gen. welfare assistance and services, 1960-70, asst. dep. minister social allowances and services, 1970-72; vis. prof. U. Alta., Edmonton, 1972-73; prof. social policy Sch. Social Work, U. B.C., Vancouver, 1973—; cons. Govt. Can., Govt. Alta., UNICEF. Author: The Development of Social Welfare in Ontario, 1965; (with Verna Huffman Splane) Chief Nursing Officers in National Ministries of Health, 1994. Served with RCAF, 1942-45. Recipient Centennial medal Govt. Can., 1967, Charles E. Hendry award U. Toronto, 1981, Commemorative medal for 125th anniversary of Confederation of Canada, 1992. Mem. Can. Assn. Social Workers (Outstanding Nat. Svc. award 1985), Can. Inst. Pub. Adminstrn., Can. Hist. Assn., Can. Coun. on Social Devel. (Lifetime Achievement award 1995), Internat. Assn. Schs. Social Work, Internat. Confs. Social Devel. (pres.), World Federalists of Can. (pres. Vancouver br.), Vancouver Club, Order of Can. Mem. United Ch. Can. Office: U BC Sch Social Work, 208 West Mall, Vancouver, BC Canada V6T 1Z2

SPLETE, ALLEN PETERJOHN, association executive, educator; b. Carthage, N.Y., June 24, 1938; s. Howard Henry and Minnie Bertha (Peterjohn) S.; m. Marilyn Lois Detweiler, June 18, 1966; children—Heidi, Michael. BA, St. Lawrence U., 1960; MA with distinction, Colgate U., 1962; PhD, Syracuse U., 1968; LHD, Campbellsville Coll., 1990; LLD, Davis and Elkins Coll., 1990; LHD, Mt. Union Coll., 1992, St. Thomas Aquinas Coll., 1992, U. Indpls., 1994, Juniata Coll., 1994, Hastings Coll., 1994; EdD, Marywood Coll., 1995; LHD, Holy Family Coll., 1996. Adminstrv. asst. to v.p. acad. affairs Syracuse U., N.Y., 1965-68, assoc. dean, exec. asst. to provost, 1968-70; v.p. for acad. planning St. Lawrence U., Canton, N.Y., 1970-82; pres. Westminster Coll., New Wilmington, Pa., 1982-85; exec. v.p. Coun. Ind. Colls., Washington, 1985-86, pres., 1986—; dir. Nat. Prepaid Tuition Plan, 1988-91; cons. York Coll., Pa., 1974; mem. planning and research com. N.Y. State Com. on Ind. Colls. and Univs., 1975-82; mem. statewide higher edn. adv. com. N.Y. State Senate Com. on Higher Edn., 1979-82; mem. nat. adv. bd. Flaming Rainbow U., 1989—; mem. adv. bd. Assn. Gov. Bds. Presdl. Search Consultation Svc., 1987-94, Academic Search Consultation Svc., 1989—, mem. Harvard Sem. for new pres. adv. bd., 1990—; bd. dirs. Am. Coun. on Edn., 1991-92; mem. oversight and review com. leadership and orgnl. devel. program United Negro Coll. Fund, 1991—. Co-author: Frederic Remington-Selected Letters, 1988, A Good Place To Work: Sourcebook for the Academic Workplace, 1991; editor: (with others) Confs. on Adirondack Park, 1972-82, Can.-Am. Relations, 1974-75; contbr. articles to profl. jours. Chmn. planning bd. Village of Canton, 1974-81; elder Neelsville Presbyn. Ch., 1986-89; trustee Adirondack Conservancy, Wilsboro, N.Y., 1980-82. Served to 1st lt. U.S. Army, 1960-62. Recipient Alumni citation St. Lawrence U., 1987; John Ben Snow Found. grantee, 1981. Mem. Pa. Assn. Colls and Univs. (govt. relations com. 1983-85), Middle States Assn. (team chmn. com. on higher edn. 1976-78, 81), Assn. Am. Colls. (project rev. cons. 1981-82), Soc. Educators and Scholars (bd. editors), Assn. Am. Colls. (pres. adv. com. 1977-78, reviewer Quill project 1978-79), St. Lawrence County Hist. Assn. (pres. 1977-82), Frederic Remington Mus. Assn., Beta Theta Pi (v.p. 1980-83). Republican. Home: 10821 Longmeadow Dr Damascus MD 20872-2240 Office: Coun Ind Colls 1 Dupont Cir NW Ste 320 Washington DC 20036-1110

SPLIETHOFF, WILLIAM LUDWIG, chemical company executive; b. Matamoras, Pa., Apr. 8, 1926; s. Oscar and Louisa (Rummel) S.; m. Dorothy Coffman, June 11, 1949; children: Christina Spliethoff Hansen, Karen Spliethoff Walker, William Mark; m. Marjorie Ann Johnson, Nov. 15, 1971. BS in Chemistry, Pa. State U., 1946, MS, 1948; PhD in Organic Chemistry, Mich. State U., 1953. Rsch. chemist E.I. duPont de Nemours & Co., Wilmington, Del., 1952-60; dir. market rsch. chem. divsn. Gen. Mills, Inc., Kankakee, Ill., 1960-62, mgr. comml. devel., 1962-67; asst. mng. dir. Polymer Corp., Sydney, Australia, 1967-69; v.p. Gen. Mills Chems., Inc., Mpls., 1969-77; exec. v.p. Henkel Corp., Mpls., 1977-86; mgmt. cons. Chanhassen, Minn., 1986—; bd. dirs. Princess Soft Toys, Inc.; sr. v.p. Henkel of Am., N.Y.C., 1981-86; chmn. Habib-Gen., Ltd., Karachi, Pakistan, 1970-79, Nutralgum, S.P.A., Milan, 1972-85, Henkel Ireland Ltd., Cork, 1975-86; v.p. Chem-Plast, S.P.A., Milan, 1977-86, Poliamidas de Venezuela, S.A., Caracas, 1975-86, Gemisa, S.A. de C.V., Mexico City, 1979-86. Mem. bd. edn., Kankakee, 1964-67. Mem. Am. Chem. Soc., Chem. Market Rsch. Assn., Comml. Devel. Assn. (honor award 1982), Sigma Xi, Phi Lambda Upsilon.

SPLINTER, WILLIAM ELDON, agricultural engineering educator; b. North Platte, Nebr., Nov. 24, 1925; s. William John and Minnie (Calhoun) S.; m. Eleanor Love Peterson, Jan. 10, 1953; children: Kathryn Love, William John, Karen Ann, Robert Marvin. BS in Agrl. Engring., U. Nebr., 1950; MS in Agrl. Engring., Mich. State U., 1951, PhD in Agrl. Engring., 1955. Instr. agrl. engring. Mich. State U., East Lansing, 1953-54; assoc. prof. biology and agrl. engring. N.C. State U., Raleigh, 1954-60, prof. biology and agrl. engring., 1960-68; prof., chmn. dept. agrl. engring. U. Nebr., Lincoln, 1968-84, George Holmes Disting. prof., 1984—, head dept. agrl. engring., 1984-88, assoc. vice chancellor for rsch., 1988-90, intermim vice chancellor for rsch., dean grad. studies, 1990-92, vice chancellor for rsch., 1992-93, George Holmes Disting. prof. emeritus, 1993-94; interim dean Coll. of Engring. and Tech., 1995—; cons. engr. Mem. exec. bd. Am. Assn. Engring. Socs.; hon. prof. Shengyang (People's Republic of China) Agrl. U. Contbr. articles to tech. jours.; patentee in field. Served with USNR, 1946-51. Recipient Massey Ferguson gold medal, 1978, John Deere gold medal, 1995, Kiwanis award for disting. svc., 1994; named to Nebr. Hall of Agrl. Achievement. Fellow AAAS, Am. Soc. Agrl. Engrs. (pres., adminstrv. council, found. pres.); mem. Nat. Acad. Engring., Soc. Automotive Engrs., Am. Soc. Engring. Edn., Nat. Soc. Profl. Engrs., Sigma Xi, Sigma Tau, Sigma Pi Sigma, Pi Mu Epsilon, Gamma Sigma Delta, Phi Kappa Phi, Beta Sigma Psi. Home: 4801 Bridle Ln Lincoln NE 68516-3436 Office: U Nebr 202 Biol Systems Engring Labs Lincoln NE 68583-0832

SPLITSTONE, GEORGE DALE, retired hospital administrator; b. Sharon, Pa., Oct. 10, 1925; s. Paul R. and Rose (Kelly) S.; divorced; children by previous marriage: David, Scott. B.A., Westminster Coll., 1951; M.S., Columbia U., 1953. Asst. adminstr. Denver Gen. Hosp., 1953-56, Reid Meml. Hosp., Richmond, Ind., 1956-59; adminstr. Reid Meml. Hosp., 1959-68; pres. Univer. Community Hosp., Tampa, Fla., 1968-87. Dist. dir. Boy Scouts Am., 1983. Served with U.S. Army, 1943-46. Kellogg Found. grantee, 1977. Mem. Am. Coll. Hosp. Adminstrs., Fla. Hosp. Assn. (dir. 1973), Tampa Area Hosp. Council (v.p. 1980-83). Democrat.

SPLITTSTOESSER, WALTER EMIL, plant physiologist; b. Claremont, Minn., Aug. 27, 1937; s. Waldemar Theodore and Opal Mae (Young) S.; m. Shirley Anne O'Connor, July 2, 1960; children: Pamela, Sheryl, Riley. B.S. with distinction (univ. fellow), U. Minn., 1958; M.S., S.D. State U., 1960; Ph.D., Purdue U., 1963. Plant breeder U. Minn., 1956-58; weed scientist S.D. State U., 1958-60; plant physiologist Purdue U., 1960-63, Shell Oil Co., Modesto, Calif., 1963-64; biochemist U. Calif., Davis, 1964-65; mem. faculty U. Ill., Urbana, 1965—; prof. plant physiology U. Ill., 1974—, head vegetable crops div., 1972-82; vis. prof. Unov. Coll., Dublin, Ireland, 1987, Univ. Coll., London, 1972, La Trobe U., Melbourne, Australia, 1995; biologist Parkland Coll., Champaign, Ill., 1974; vis. rsch. assoc. Rothamsted Exptl. Sta., Herpenden, England, 1980; disting. vis. prof. Nagoya (Japan) U., 1982; biotechnologist U. Coll., Dublin, 1987. Author: Vegetable Growing Handbook, 1979, 2d edit., 1984, 3d edit., 1990; contbr. over 200 articles to sci. jours.; rev. editor: Analytical Biochemistry, 1969-78, NSF, 1978-79; numerous others. Recipient J.H. Gourley award Am. Fruit Grower-Am. Soc. Hort. Sci., 1974, Outstanding Grad. Educator award, 1990; NIH fellow, 1964-65. Fellow Am. Soc. Hort. Sci. (rev. editor jour. 1969—), Japanese Soc. Promotion of Sci.; mem. Am. Soc. Plant Physiologists, Japanese Soc. Plant Physiologists, Sigma Xi (pres. 1990-91), Alpha Zeta, Gamma Sigma Delta, Delta Theta Sigma, Phi Kappa Phi. Home: 2006 Cureton Dr Urbana IL 61801-6226 Office: U Ill 1102 S Goodwin Ave Urbana IL 61801-4730

SPOCK, BENJAMIN MCLANE, physician, educator; b. New Haven, Conn., May 2, 1903; s. Benjamin Ives and Mildred Louise (Stoughton) S.; m. Jane Davenport Cheney, June 25, 1927 (div. 1976); children: Michael, John Cheney; m. Mary Morgan Councille, Oct. 24, 1976. B.A., Yale U., 1925, student Med. Sch., 1925-27; M.D., Columbia U., 1929. Intern in medicine Presbyn. Hosp., N.Y.C., 1929-31; in pediatrics N.Y. Nursery and Child's Hosp., 1931-32; in psychiatry N.Y. Hosp., 1932-33; practice pediatrics N.Y.C., 1933-44, 46-47; instr. pediatrics Cornell Med. Coll., 1933-47; asst. attending pediatrician N.Y. Hosp., 1933-47; cons. in pediatric psychiatry N.Y. City Health Dept., 1942-47; cons. psychiatry Mayo Clinic and Rochester Child Health Project, Rochester, Minn.; asso. prof. psychiatry Mayo Found., U. Minn., 1947-51; prof. child devel. U. Pitts., 1951-55, Western Res. U., 1955-67. Author: Baby and Child Care, 1946, (with J. Reinhart and W. Miller) A Baby's First Year, 1954, (with M. Lowenberg) Feeding Your Baby and Child, 1955, Dr. Spock Talks with Mothers, 1961, Problems of Parents, 1962, (with M. Lerrigo) Caring for Your Disabled Child, 1965, (with Mitchell Zimmerman) Dr. Spock on Vietnam, 1968, Decent and Indecent, 1970, A Teenagers Guide to Life and Love, 1970, Raising Children in a Difficult Time, 1974, Spock on Parenting, 1988, (with Mary Morgan) Spock on Spock: A Memoir of Growing Up With the Century, 1989, A Better World for Our Children, 1994. Presdl. candidate Peoples Party, 1972, advocator Nat. Com. for a Sane Nuclear Policy (SANE), co-chmn., 1962 . Served to lt. comdr. M.C., USNR, 1944-46. Home: PO Box 1268 Camden ME 04843-1268 *In pediatric practice I was trying, with difficulty, to reconcile concepts gained in psychoanalytic training with what mothers told me about their children. After ten years of that, I was able to write Baby & Child Care, which, in turn, brought invitations to research and teaching jobs. To save children from radiation I became a public supporter of a test ban treaty and co-chairman of SANE in 1962, which led, eventually to full-time opposition to the Vietnam war, conviction for conspiracy, conversion to socialism.*

SPODAK, MICHAEL KENNETH, forensic psychiatrist; b. Bklyn., Nov. 5, 1944; s. Harry and Betty (Rahn) S.; children: Lisa Beth, Brett David. B.S., Union Coll., 1966; M.D., SUNY-Syracuse, 1970. Diplomate: Nat. Bd. Med. Examiners, Am. Bd. Neurology and Psychiatry. Intern Mary Imogene Bassett Hosp., Cooperstown, N.Y., 1970-71; resident John Hopkins Hosp., Balt., 1974-77; practice medicine specializing in civil and criminal forensic psychiatry Towson, Md., 1977—; chief dept. psychiatry Balt. County Gen. Hosp., Randallstown, 1978-85; mem. staff Clifton T. Perkins Hosp. Ctr., Jessup, Md., 1977-92; clin. asst. prof. psychiatry U. Md. Hosp., Balt., 1983—; psychiat. cons. Bur. Disability Ins., Social Security Adminstrn., Workmen's compensation Commn., Balt., 1981—; dir. community forensic services Mental Hygiene Adminstrn., Md., 1982-92; faculty Nat. Jud. Coll., 1988—; mem. Md. Task Force on Somatic Therapies. Contbr. numerous articles on forensic psychiatry to profl. jours., chpt. to book. Served with M.C. USN, 1972-74. Mem. Am. Acad. Psychiatry and Law, Am. Psychiat. Assn., Md. Psychiat. Soc., Md. Med. Soc. (chmn. occupational health com. 1983-90), Baltimore County Med. Soc. Office: 26 W Pennsylvania Ave Towson MD 21204-5001

SPODEK, BERNARD, curriculum educator; b. Bklyn., Sept. 17, 1931; s. David and Esther (Lebenbaum) S.; m. Prudence Debb, June 21, 1957; children: Esther Yin-ling, Jonathan Chou. BA, Bklyn. Coll., 1952; MA, Columbia U., 1955, EdD, 1962. Cert. early childhood edn. tchr., N.Y. Tchr. Beth Hayeled Sch., N.Y.C., 1952-56, N.Y. City Pub. Schs., Bklyn., 1956-57, Early Childhood Ctr., Bklyn. Coll., 1957-60; asst. prof. elem. edn. U. Wis.-Milw., 1961-65; assoc. prof. early childhood edn. U. Ill., Champaign, 1965-68, prof. dept. curriculum and instrn., 1968—, dir. dept. grad. programs, 1986-87, chair dept., 1987-89, dir. hons. program, Coll. Edn., 1984-86, mem. faculty Bur. Ednl. Rsch., 1981-85; dir. insts. Nat. Def. Edn. Act, 1965-67, dir. experienced tchr. fellowship program, 1967-69, co-dir. program for tchr. trainers in early childhood edn., 1969-74; vis. prof. Western Wash. State U., 1974, U. Wis., Madison, 1980; vis. scholar Sch. Early Childhood Studies, Brisbane (Australia) Coll. Advanced Edn., Delissa Inst. Early Childhood Studies, S. Australia Coll. Advanced Edn., 1985, Beijing Normal U., Nanjing Normal U., E. China Normal U., Shangai, People's Republic China, 1986; rsch. fellow Kobe U., Japan, 1996. Author or co-author 28 books including: (with others) A Black Studies Curriculum for Early Childhood Eduication, 1972, 2d edit., 1976, Teaching in the Early Years, 1972, 3d edit., 1985, Early Childhood Education, 1973, Studies in Open Education, 1975 (Japanese trans.), Early Childhood Education: Issues and Perspectives, 1977, (with Nir-Janiv and Steg) International Perspectives on Early Childhood Education, 1982 (Hebrew trans.), with Saracho and Lee (Mainstreaming Young Children, 1984, (with Saracho and Davis) Foundations of Early Childhood Education, 1987, 2d edit. (Japanese trans.), 1991, (with Saracho) Right from the Start, 1994, Dealing with Individual Differences in the Early Childhood Classroom, 1994; editor: Handbook of Research in Early Childhood Education, 1982, Today's Kindergarten, 1986, (with Saracho and Peters) Professionalism and the Early Childhood Practitioner, 1988, (with Saracho) Early Childhood Teacher Education, 1990, Issues in Early Childhood Curriculum, 1991, Educationally Appropriate Kindergarten Practices, 1991, Issues in Childcare, 1992, Handbook of Research on the Education of Young Children, 1993, (with Saracho) Language and Literacy in Early Childhood Education, 1993; (with Sufford and Saracho) Early Childhood Special Education, 1994; (with Garcia, McLaughlin & Saracho) Meeting the Challenge of Cultural and Linguistic Diversity, 1995; series editor Yearbook in Early Childhood Education, early childhood edn. publs., 1971-79; guest editor Studies in Ednl. Evaluation, 1982; also contbr. chpts to books, articles to profl. jours. Mem. Assn. for Childhood Edn. Internat. (nursery sch. com. 1964-66), Am. Ednl. Rsch. Assn. (chair early childhood and child devel. spl. interest group 1983-84, publs. com. 1984-86), AAUP, Nat. Assn. Edn. Young Children (sec. 1965-68, bd. govs. 1968-72, pres. 1976-78, editorial adv. bd. 1972-76, book rev. editor, 1972-74, cons. editor, 1985-87 Young Children jour., mem. tchr. edn. commn. 1981-88, chair commn. on appropriate edn. 4-5 yr. old children, 1984-85, cons. editor Early Childhood Rsch. Quar. 1987-90), Nat. Soc. for Study of Edn. (1972 yearbook com.), Soc. Rsch. Child Devel., Early Education and Development. Office: U Ill Dept Curriculum & Instrn 1310 S 6th St Champaign IL 61820-6925

SPOELHOF, JOHN, consumer products company executive. CEO Prince Corp. Office: Prince Corp 1 Prince Ctr Holland MI 49423-5407 Office: One Prince Ctr Holland MI 49423

SPOFFORD, ROBERT HOUSTON, advertising agency executive; b. N.Y.C., Apr. 3, 1941; s. Robert Knowlton and Linda Prieber (Houston) S.; m. Susan Proctor Allerton; children—Margaret, Robert Christopher. B.E.E., Cornell U., 1964. Account exec. Batten, Barton, Durstine & Osborn, Inc., N.Y.C., 1964-71, v.p., 1971-84, sr. v.p., 1984-88, exec. v.p., dir. strategic planning, 1988—. Contbr. articles to advt. and data processing jours. Mem. Westchester County Democratic Com. N.Y. 1974-78; ch. organist. First recipient Founder's medal Batten, Barton, Durstine & Osborn, Inc., 1985. Unitarian. Home: 449 35th St Manhattan Beach CA 90266-3320 Office: BBDO LA 10960 Wilshire Blvd Los Angeles CA 90024-3702

SPOFFORD, SALLY HYSLOP, artist; b. N.Y.C., Aug. 20, 1929; d. George Hall and Esther (McNaull) Hyslop; m. Gavin Spofford, Mar. 11, 1950 (dec. Jan. 1976); children: Lizabeth Spofford Smith, Leslie Spofford Russell. Student, The China Inst., N.Y.C., 1949, The Art Students League, N.Y.C., 1950; BA with high honors, Swarthmore Coll., 1952. Instr. Somerset Art Assn., Peapack, N.J., 1978-95, Hunterdon Art Ctr., Clinton, N.J., 1985—; adv. bd., lectr. Apollo Muses, Inc., Gladstone, N.J.; bd. trustees Artshowcase, Inc. One-man show Riverside Studio, Pottersville, N.J., 1985, Morris Mus., Morristown, N.J. 1989, Schering-Plough Gallery, Madison, N.J., 1989, Phoenix Gallery, N.Y.C., 1990, Robin Hutchins Gallery, Maplewood, N.J., 1992, Berlex Labs. Corp. Office, Wayne, N.J., 1992, Hunterdon Art Ctr., Clinton, N.J., 1993; exhibited in group shows at Hickory (N.C.) Mus., 1983, Purdue U., 1983, Monmouth (N.J.), 1984, Nabisco Brands Gallery, E. Hanover, N.J., 1985, 89, Hunterdon Art Ctr., Clinton, N.J., 1988, 93, Schering-Plough Gallery, Madison, 1988, Morris Mus., Morristown, 1989, Montclair (N.J. State U., 1995; represented in permanent collections N.J. State Mus., Trenton, Newark Mus. Painting residency fellow Vt. Studio Ctr., 1992. Mem. Assoc. Artists N.J. (pres. 1985-87), N.J. Watercolor Soc., Federated Art Assns. of N.J. (panel mem. 1985, demonstrator 1991). Home: PO Box 443 Bernardsville NJ 07924-0443

SPOHN, HERBERT EMIL, psychologist; b. Berlin, Germany, June 10, 1923; s. Herbert F. and Bertha S.; m. Billie M. Powell, July 28, 1973; children—Jessica, Madeleine. B.S.S., CCNY, 1949; Ph.D., Columbia U., 1955. Research psychologist VA Hosp., Montrose, N.Y., 1955-60; chief research sect. VA Hosp., 1960-64; sr. research psychologist Menninger Found., Topeka, 1965-80; dir. hosp. research Menninger Found., 1979-94, dir. research dept., 1981-94; ret., prof. emeritus for rsch., 1994—; mem. mental health small grant com. NIMH, 1972-76, mem. treatment assessment rev. com., 1983-86, chmn. 1986-87. Author: (with Gardner Murphy) Encounter with Reality, 1968; assoc. editor: Schizophrenia Bull, 1970-87, 91—; contbr. articles to profl. jours. Served with AUS, World War II. USPHS grantee, 1964—. Fellow Am. Psychopath. Assn.; mem. AAAS, N.Y. Acad. Sci., Soc. Psychopath. Research, Phi Beta Kappa, Sigma Xi. Office: Menninger Found PO Box 829 Topeka KS 66601-0829

SPOHN, JANICE, elementary education educator, consultant; b. Pitts., Jan. 12, 1952; d. James Arthur and Jean Edna (Smithyman) Rowan; m. Chester Michael Spohn II, Oct. 23, 1972; children: Chester M. III, Lisa Marie. BE, Clarion U., 1973; ME, Slippery Rock U., 1989; supervisory cert., Duquesne U., 1992. Cert. reading specialist, gifted edn., supervisor reading, Pa. Group supr. Butler County (Pa.) Children Ctr., 1974-87; temp. instr. Slippery Rock U., Slippery Rock, Pa., 1989; reading specialist North Allegheny Schs., Pitts., 1990—; coord. Pa. Framework Network, North Allegheny Schs., 1991—; inservice com. Allegheny Intermediate Unit, 1993—; Pa. Framework steering com. Allegheny Intermediate Unit, 1993—. Co-author/editor: (book) Pennsylvania Framework-Portfolio Implementation Guide, 1993. Mem. ASCD, Nat. Coun. Tchrs. of English, Internat. Reading Assn., Keystone State Reading Assn., Three Rivers Reading Coun., Butler County Reading Coun. Avocations: reading, crafts, camping. Home: 520 Herman Rd Butler PA 16001-9517 Office: Peebles Elem N Allegheny Schs 8526 Peebles Rd Pittsburgh PA 15237

SPOHR, ARNOLD THEODORE, artistic director, choreographer; b. Rhein, Sask., Can., Dec. 26, 1927. Student, Winnipeg (Can.) Tchrs. Coll., 1942-43; Assocs., Royal Conservatory Music, Toronto, Can.; cert., Royal Acad. Dance; LLD (hon.), U. Man., Can., 1970, U. Winnipeg, 1984; DFA (hon.), U. Victoria, Can., 1987. Cert. tchr. pub. schs. Tchr. piano, 1946-51; prin. dancer Winnipeg Ballet (now Royal Winnipeg Ballet), 1945-58, artistic dir., tchr. dance, 1958-88, artistic dir. emeritus, 1988—; choreographer, performer Rainbow Stage Sta. CBC-TV, 1957-60; dir. dept. dance Nelson Sch. Fine Arts, 1964-67; artistic dir. dept. dance Banff Sch. Fine Arts, 1967-81; bd. dirs. Can. Theatre Centre; vice chmn. Bd. Dance Can.; adjudicator Can. Council, Can. Dance Tchrs. Assn., N.Y. Internat. Ballet Competitions. Choreographer Ballet Premier, 1950, Intermede, 1951, E Minor, 1959, Hansel and Gretal, 1960, also 18 musicals for Rainbow Stage. Decorated Order of Can., 1970; recipient Centennial medal Govt. of Can., 1967, Manitoba's Order of Buffalo, 1969, Molson prize, 1970, Can. Actor's Equity Assn. Champagne award, 1979, Dance mag. Ann. award, 1981, Diplome D'honneur Can. Conf. of Arts, 1983, Can. Tourism medal, 1985, Royal Bank award, 1987. Mem. Dance in Can. Assn. (bd. dirs., Can. Dance award 1986). Office: Canada's Royal Winnipeg Ballet, 380 Graham Ave, Winnipeg, MB Canada R3C 4K2

SPOLAN, HARMON SAMUEL, banker; b. Phila., Dec. 12, 1935; s. Jay and Edythe (Greenberg) S.; m. Betty Jane Evnitz, Mar. 30, 1958; children: Michael, Suzanne. AB, Temple U., 1957, LLB, 1959; postgrad. Oxford U., 1966. Bar: Pa. 1960. Ptnr. Ravetz & Shuchman, Phila., 1960-68, Blair & Co., N.Y.C., 1968-72; v.p. Butcher & Singer, Phila., 1972-74; pres. Capital First Corp., Phila., 1974-75, State Nat. Bank, Rockville, Md., 1975-78, Jefferson Bank, Phila., 1978—; pres., bd. dirs. JeffBanks, Inc., Phila., Bryn Mawr Resources, Phila.; lectr. law U. Pa., Phila., 1964-68. Author: Federal Aids to Financing, 1970; contbr. articles to profl. jours. Former chmn. bd. Huntingdon Hosp., Willow Grove, Pa., 1982-89; bd. dirs. YMHA, Phila., 1978—; dir. Anti-Defamation League, 1982. Named Man of the Yr., Nat. Assn. Women Bus. Owners, 1978; Disting. Alumnus, Central High Sch., 1975. Mem. ABA, Phila. Bar Assn., Locust Club, Oxford and Cambridge Club (London). Republican. Jewish. Office: Jefferson Bank 250 S 18th St Philadelphia PA 19103-6140

SPOLLEN, JOHN WILLIAM, lawyer; b. Bklyn., Aug. 26, 1944. AB, Fordham U., 1966, JD, 1973. Bar: N.Y. 1974, U.S. Dist. Ct. (so. dist.) N.Y. 1975. Ptnr. Simpson, Thacher & Bartlett, N.Y.C., 1973—. 1st lt. U.S. Army, 1967-69. Mem. ABA, N.Y. State Bar Assn., N.Y. County Lawyers Assn. Club: Larchmont Shore.

SPONG, JOHN SHELBY, bishop; b. Charlotte, N.C., June 16, 1931; s. John Shelby and Doolie Boyce (Griffith) S.; m. Joan Lydia Ketner, Sept. 5, 1952 (dec. 1988); children: Ellen Elizabeth, Mary Katharine, Jaquelin Ketner; m. Christine Mary Bridger, Jan. 1, 1990. A.B., U. N.C., 1952; M.Div., Va. Theol. Sem., 1955; D.D., St. Paul's Coll., 1976, Va. Theol. Sem., 1977. Ordained to ministry Episcopal Ch., 1955, bishop, 1976; rector St. Joseph's Ch., Durham, N.C., 1955-57, Calvary Ch., Tarboro, N.C., 1957-65, St. John's Ch., Lynchburg, Va., 1965-69, St. Paul's Ch., Richmond, Va., 1969-76; bishop Diocese of Newark, 1976—; mem. governing body Nat. Episc. Ch., 1973-76. Author: Honest Player, 1973, This Hebrew Lord, 1974, Dialogue--In Search of Jewish-Christian Understanding, 1975, Christpower, 1976, The Living Commandments, 1977, The Easter Moment, 1980, Into the Whirlwind: The Future of the Church, 1983, Beyond Moralism, 1986, Survival and Consciousness, 1987, Living in Sin? A Bishop Rethinks Human Sexuality, 1988, Rescuing the Bible from Fundamentalism--A Bishop Rethinks the Meaning of Scripture, 1991, Born of a Woman, 1992, Resurrection: Myth or Reality?, 1994, Liberating the Gospels, Reading the Bible with Jewish Eyes, 1996. Mem. Richmond Human Relations Commn. Club: Rotary. Home: 43 Ogden Pl Morristown NJ 07960-5248 Office: 24 Rector St Newark NJ 07102-4512

SPONG, WILLIAM BELSER, JR., lawyer, educator; b. Portsmouth, Va., Sept. 29, 1920; s. William Belser and Emily (Nichols) S.; m. Virginia Wise Galliford, June 3, 1950 (dec. May 1993); children: Martha Kingman, Thomas Nichols. Student, Hampden-Sydney Coll., 1937-40, LLD (hon.), 1968; LLB, U. Va., 1947; postgrad., U. Edinburgh, Scotland, 1947-48; LLD (hon.), Roanoke Coll., Washington and Lee U. and Coll. William and Mary. Bar: Va. 1947. Lectr. law Coll. William and Mary, 1948-49, 75-76; practice law Portsmouth, 1949-76; mem. Va. Ho. Dels., 1954-55, Va. Senate, 1956-66, U.S. Senate, 1966-73; gen. counsel Comm. for Conduct Fgn. Policy, 1973-75; dean Marshall-Wythe Sch. Law Coll. William and Mary, 1976-85, Woodbridge prof. emeritus, 1985—; pres. Old Dominion U., 1989-90; spl. master Va. Electric & Power Co., et al vs. Westinghouse Corp., 1977-80, re Dalkon Shield litigation, 1983-85, Smith vs. Morton-Thiokol, 1988; ptnr. Cooper, Spong & Davis, Portsmouth, 1990—; guest scholar Woodrow Wilson Center Smithsonian Instn.; vis. scholar U. Va. Sch. Law, 1973; adj. prof. law U. Richmond, 1974-75, Salzburg Seminar, 1979; sr. visitor Inst. Advanced Legal Studies, U. London, 1985; vis. prof. Washington and Lee U., 1986; Ewald Disting. vis. prof. U. Va. Sch. Law, 1987; Menzies lectr. Australian Nat. U., 1990. Chmn. Va. Commn. Pub. Edn., 1958-62, Gov.'s Commn. on Va.'s Future, 1982-84; mem. Va. Coun. Higher Edn., 1985-89; trustee Hampden-Sydney Coll., 1951-72, Va. Hist. Soc., 1990—; mem. bd. visitors Air Force Acad., 1970, Naval Acad., 1971, Coll. William and Mary, 1992—. With USAAF, 1942-45. Mem. Va. Bar Assn. (pres. 1976), Portsmouth Bar Assn. (past pres.), Order of Coif, Phi Beta Kappa, Phi Alpha Delta, Omicron Delta Kappa, Pi Kappa Alpha. Home: 351 Middle St Portsmouth VA 23704-2826 Office: Cooper Spong & Davis PO Box 1475 Portsmouth VA 23705-1475

SPONSLER, GEORGE CURTIS, III, research administrator, lawyer; b. Collingswood, N.J., Dec. 2, 1927; s. George Curtis and Mary Grace (Hollinberger) S.; m. Bridget Ruth Butcher, Sept. 3, 1955; children: Freda Grace, Naomi Margaret Bride, Curtis Alexander. B.S. in Engring., Princeton U., 1949, M.A., 1951, Ph.D., 1952; J.D., George Washington U., 1981. Bar: Md. 1981, D.C. 1982, U.S. Ct. Appeals (4th cir.) 1982, U.S. Ct. Appeals (fed. cir.) 1984. U.S. Supreme Ct. 1986. With Lincoln Lab., MIT, 1952-56; liaison officer Office Naval Research, London, 1956-58; head spl. projects br. Office Naval Research, Washington, 1958-59; sr. scientist Hoffman Sci. Center, Santa Barbara, Calif., 1959-60; chief sci., dir. tech. analysis and ops. research U.S. Navy Bur. Ships, 1960-63; dir. advanced planning, fed. systems div. IBM, 1963-66, dir. center exploratory studies, 1966-68; exec. sec. div. engring. Nat. Acad. Sci.-NRC, 1968-70; pres. Law Math. and Tech. Inc., 1970—; on leave, Congl. fellow U.S. Senate, Washington, 1987-88; mem. adv. com. to Office Emergency Planning, Nat. Acad. Sci., 1967-72, chmn. subcom. automation, 1966-68, mem. joint adv. com. on electromagnetic pulse, 1970-74; cons. Exec. Office of Pres., 1971-73. Contbr.: Tech. Innovation, Harper Ency. of Sci.; author articles in field. Fellow AAAS (electorate nominating com. 1980-83, chmn.-elect sect. X, 1983-84, chmn. 1984-85, mem. coun. 1985-86), Am. Physics Soc.; mem. IEEE (sr., chmn. subcom. on privacy of communications and info. policy com. 1982-85, aerospace R&D policy com. 1990-92), Phi Beta Kappa, Sigma Xi. Democrat. Episcopalian. Club: Cosmos (Washington). Home: 7804 Old Chester Rd Bethesda MD 20817-6280

SPOOLSTRA, LINDA CAROL, minister, educator, religious organization administrator; b. Hillsdale, Mich., July 11, 1947; d. Jay Carroll and Carol Elsa (Linstrom) Lehmann; m. Gerald William Spoolstra, Feb. 17, 1973. BA, Bethel Coll., 1969; MA, Fla. State U., 1970; M of Div., McCormick Theol. Sem., Chgo., 1978; DD (hon.), Cen Bapt. Theol. Sem., Kansas City, Kans., 1988. Ordained Am. Bapt. Clergywoman. Tchr. Dade County Pub. Schs., Miami, Fla., 1970-71; ins. claims adjustor Safeco Ins. Co., Chgo., 1971-72; dir. of community outreach and edn. N. Shore Bapt. Ch., Chgo., 1972-78, assoc. pastor, 1978; pastor First Bapt. Ch., Swansea, Mass., 1978-84; exec. dir. commn. on the ministry Am. Bapt. Chs. U.S.A., Valley Forge, Pa., 1984-90; exec. minister Am. Bapt. Chs. Mass., Dedham, 1990—; mem. Nat. Coun. Chs. Profl. Ch. Leadership, N.Y.C., 1984-90; mem. commn. on pastoral leadership Bapt. World Alliance, McLean, Va., 1986-90; mem. gen. bd. Nat. Coun. Chs. of Christ, 1990-96. Trustee Andover-Newton Theol. Sch., 1990—. Avocations: sailing, tennis, travel, classical music. Office: Am Bapt Chs Mass 20 Milton St Dedham MA 02026-2954

SPOON, ALAN GARY, communications and publishing executive; b. Detroit, June 4, 1951; s. Harry and Mildred (Rudman) S.; m. Terri Alper, June 3, 1975; children: Ryan, Leigh, Randi. B.S., MIT, 1973, M.S., 1973; J.D., Harvard U., 1976. Cons. The Boston Cons. Group, 1976-79, mgr., 1979-81, v.p., 1981; v.p. The Washington Post Co., 1984-85; v.p., contr. Washington Post, 1985-86, v.p. mktg., 1986-87; v.p. fin., CFO The Washington Post Co., 1987-89; pres. Newsweek mag., 1989-91; COO The Washington Post Co., 1991—, pres., 1993—; dir. Info. Industry Assn., Washington, 1982-83, 88-89; bd. dirs., trustee WETA-Pub. Broadcasting, 1987; bd. dirs. The Riggs Nat. Bank of Washington, 1991-93. Dir. Norwood Sch., 1989-93, chmn., 1993-95; dir. Internat. Herald Tribune, 1991—, Smithsonian Nat. Mus. Natural History, 1994—. Recipient award for scholarship and athletics Eastern Coll. Athletic Conf. and MIT, 1973. Mem. New Eng. Intercollegiate Sailing Assn. (pres. 1972). Home: 7300 Loch Edin Ct Rockville MD 20854-4835 Office: The Washington Post Co 1150 15th St NW Washington DC 20071-0001

SPOONER, ED THORNTON CASSWELL, geology educator and researcher; b. Blandford, Dorset, Eng., June 16, 1950; m. 1972; two children. BA, U. Cambridge, 1971, MA, 1975; MA, Oxford U., 1975; PhD in Geology, U. Manchester, 1976. Demonstrator mineral Oxford U., 1973-77; lecr. geology Oriel & Pembroke Colls., Oxford U., 1974-77; asst./assoc. prof. geology U. Toronto, 1977-90, prof., 1990—. Natural Sci. and Engring. Rsch. Coun. Can. grantee, 1978—. Mem. Soc. Econ. Geology. Office: University of Toronto, Dept Geology/22 Russell St, Toronto, ON Canada M5S 3B1

SPOOR, WILLIAM HOWARD, food company executive; b. Pueblo, Colo., Jan. 16, 1923; s. Charles Hinchman and Doris Field (Slaughter) S.; m. Janet Spain, Sept. 23, 1950; children: Melanie G., Cynthia F., William Lincoln. BA, Dartmouth Coll., 1949; postgrad., Denver U., 1949, Stanford U., 1965. Asst. sales mgr. N.Y. Export divsn. Pillsbury Co., 1949-53; mgr. N.Y. office Pillsbury Co., 1953-62; v.p. export divsn. Pillsbury Co., Mpls., 1962-68, v.p., gen. mgr. internat. ops., 1968-73, CEO, 1973-85, also bd. dirs., chmn. exec. com., 1987, pres., CEO, 1988, past chmn. bd. dirs.; bd. dirs. Coleman Co. Mem. regional export expansion coun. Dept. Commerce, 1966-74; bd. dirs. exec. coun. Fgn. Diplomats, 1976-78; mem. bd. visitors Nelson A. Rockefeller Ctr., Dartmouth Coll., 1992-95; Minn. Orchestral Assn., United Negro Coll. Fund, 1973-75; chmn. Capitol City Renaissance Task Force, 1985; trustee Mpls. Found., 1985-92; mem. sr. campaign cabinet Carlson Com. U. Minn., 1985; mem. corps. rels. com. Nature Conservancy, 1985; mem. Nat. Cambodia Crisis Com., pres. pvt. sector Dept. Transp. task force, 1982, pres. pvt. sector survey on cost control, 1983; chmn. YWCA Tribute to Womwn in Internat. Industry. 2d lt. inf. U.S. Army, 1943-46. Recipient Golden Plate award, Am. Acad. Achievement, Disting. Bus. Leadership award, St. Cloud State U., Miss. Valley World Trade award, Outstanding Achievement award, Dartmouth Coll., Horatio Alger award, 1986, Medal of Merit, U.S. Savs. Bond Program; honored with William H. Spoor Dialogues on Leadership, Dartmouth Coll., honored Fair Player Minn. Women's Polit. Caucus, 1989. Mem. Grocery Mfrs. Am. (treas. 1973-84), Nat. Fgn. Trade Coun., Minn. Hist. Soc. (mem. exec. com. 1983, bd. dirs.), Minn. Bus. Partnership, River Club N.Y.C., Woodhill Country Club, Lafayette Club (Wayzata, Minn.), Mpls. Club (bd. govs. 1985, pres. 1986), Little Club, Gulf Stream Bath and Tennis Club, Delray Beach Yacht Club, Gulf Stream Golf Club, Old Baldy Club (Saratoga, N.Y.). Home: 622 Ferndale Rd W Wayzata MN 55391-9628 Office: 4900 IDS Ctr Minneapolis MN 55402

SPORE, KEITH KENT, newspaper executive; b. Milw., May 29, 1942; s. G. Keith and Evelyn A. (Morgan) S.; divorced; children: Bradley, Julie; m. Kathy Stokebrand. BS in Journalism, U. Wis., Milw., 1967. City editor Milw. Jour. Sentinel, 1977-81, asst. mng. editor/news, 1981-89, mng. editor, 1989-91, editor, 1991-95, editl. page editor, 1995, pres., 1995—. Author: (novels) The Hell Masters, 1977, Death of a Scavenger, 1980. With U.S. Army, 1961-64. Recipient Freedom of Info. award Soc. Profl. Journalists, 1995; named Mass Comms. Alumnus of Yr., U. Wis.-Milw., 1994. Mem. Milw. Press Club. Office: Milw Jour Sentinel 333 W State St PO Box 661 Milwaukee WI 53203-1500

SPORE, RICHARD ROLAND, III, lawyer, educator; b. Memphis, May 28, 1962; s. Richard R. Jr. and Melba (Cullum) S.; m. Patricia Ann Witherspoon, Aug. 15, 1987; 1 child, Caroline Dare. BA, U. of the South, 1984; JD, U. Va., 1987; MBA, Christian Bros. U., 1992. Bar: Tenn. 1987. Assoc. Burch, Porter & Johnson, Memphis, 1987-94, ptnr., 1995—; adj. prof. bus. law Christian Bros. U., Memphis, 1992—; chmn. Tenn. Bus. Law Forum. Author: The Partnering Paradigm: An Entrepreneur's Guide to Strategic

Alliances, 1994, Business Organizations in Tennessee, 1995. Mem. Pro Bono Panel for Sr. Citizens, Memphis, 1987—; chmn. small bus. coun. Memphis Area C. of C., 1993; pres. Sewanee Club of Memphis, 1989. Recipient Disting. Svc. award Pro Bono Panel for Sr. Citizens, 1992. Mem. ABA, Tenn. Bar Assn., Memphis Bar Assn. Republican. Methodist. Office: Burch Porter & Johnson 130 N Court Memphis TN 38103

SPORES, RONALD MARVIN, anthropology educator, ethnohistorian; b. Eugene, Oreg., Jan. 25, 1931; s. Marvin C. and Marie (Norwood) S.; children: Lisa France, Ronald Jonathan. B.S., U. Oreg., 1953; M.A., Mexico City Coll., 1960; Ph.D., Harvard U., 1964. Asst. prof. anthropology U. Mass., Amherst, 1964-65; prof. anthropology Vanderbilt U., Nashville, 1965—, dir. anthropology program, 1967-77. Author: The Mixtec Kings and Their People, 1967, The Mixtecs, 1984; co-author: The Cloud People, 1983; series editor: Vanderbilt Publications in Anthropology, 1971—. Served with U.S. Army, 1953-55, Korea. Mem. Am. Soc. for Ethnohistory (pres. 1978-79). Republican. Methodist. Home: 3415 W End Ave Nashville TN 37203-1077 Office: Vanderbilt U Anthropology Dept Nashville TN 37235

SPORKIN, STANLEY, federal judge; b. Phila., 1932; m. Judith Sally Imber, Sept. 30, 1955; children: Elizabeth Michael, Daniel Paul, Thomas Abraham. AB, Pa. State U., 1953; LLB, Yale U., 1957. Bar: Del. 1958, Pa. 1958, U.S. Dist. Ct. D.C. 1963, U.S. Supreme Ct. 1964, U.S. Ct. Appeals (2d cir.) 1975, U.S. Ct. Appeals (4th cir.) 1978. Law clk. to presiding justice U.S. Dist. Ct. Del., 1957-60; assoc. Haley Woolenberg & Bader, Washington, 1960-61; staff atty. spl. study securities markets U.S. SEC, Washington, 1961-63, atty., 1963, chief atty. enforcement br., 1963-66, chief enforcement atty., 1966, asst. dir., 1967, assoc. dir., 1968-72, dep. dir. div. trading and markets, 1972-73, dir. div. enforcement, 1973-81; gen. counsel CIA, Washington, 1981-86; judge U.S. Dist. Ct. D.C., Washington, 1985—; adj. prof. Antioch Law Sch., 1974-81, Howard U., 1981—; mem. exec. com. U. Calif. Securities Regulation Inst., 1977—. Contbr. articles to profl. jours. Recipient Nat. Civil Svc. League's Spl. Achievement award, 1976, Rockefeller Pub. Svc. award, 1978, Pres.' Disting. Fed. Civilian Svc. award, 1979, Pa. State U. Almunus of Yr. award, 1979, William O. Douglas award for lifetime achievement Assn. Securities and Exch. Commn. Alumni, 1994; honored by B'nai B'rith Hall of Fame; named Alumni Fellow Coll. Bus. Administrn. Pa. State U., 1990. Fellow Am. Bar Found.; mem. ABA, Fed. Bar Assn. (exec. council securities law sect. 1978—), Del. Bar Assn., Bar Assn. of D.C., Am. Law Inst., Am. Inst. CPA's, Fed. Legal Council, Adminstrv. Conf. of U.S., Phi Beta Kappa, Phi Kappa Phi. Office: US Dist Ct US Courthouse 3rd & Constitution Ave NW Washington DC 20001

SPORN, STANLEY ROBERT, retired electronic company executive; b. N.Y.C., Dec. 10, 1928; s. Max and Mollie (Thau) S.; m. Audrey Brandfield, June 29, 1952; children: Lawrence (dec.), David, Howard. BEE, CCNY, 1950; MSEE, U. Tenn., 1951. Devel. engr. Arma div. AMBAC Industries, N.Y.C., 1951-55, sr. engr., 1958-60, supr., then sect. head, 1960-76, dir. engring., 1976-78; sr. devel. engr. Norden Labs., White Plains, N.Y., 1955-58; dir. engring. Gull Airborne Equipment, Smithtown, N.Y., 1978-81, v.p. engring., 1981-86; v.p. advanced tech. Gull Electronic Systems Divsn. Parker Hannifin Corp., Smithtown, 1986-95; ret., 1995. Author: (with others) Mechanical Design and Systems Handbook, 1964; patentee accelerometers, servos, electronics. Mem. Tau Beta Pi, Eta Kappa Nu. Office: Gull Inc Electronic Systems Divsn 300 Marcus Blvd Smithtown NY 11788-2044

SPOSITO, JAMES A., lawyer, consultant; b. Carbondale, Pa., Jan. 11, 1943; s. Anthony James and Hortense (Talarico) S.; m. Karen Mascelli, Nov. 25, 1966 (div. Nov. 1976); children: James A. Jr., Angela; m. Patricia A. Dee, June 25, 1994. BS in History, U. Scranton, 1964; MS, Marywood Coll., Scranton, 1969; JD, George Mason U., 1980; D Law, Strasburg (France) U., 1980. Bar: Pa. 1980, U.S. Dist. Ct. (mid. dist.) Pa. 1980, U.S. Ct. Appeals (3d cir.) 1983; cert. tchr., Pa. Tchr. elem. and secondary schs., Pa., 1966-76; aide to Congressman Phil Sharp, U.S. Ho. of Reps., Washington, 1977-78; pres. James A. Sposito & Assocs., Scranton, 1980—; pres. Spo-Jac Enterprises, Carbondale, 1964—; pres., owner Sposito Realty Co., Carbondale, 1965—. Advisor 114th legis. dist. State Rep.'s Office, Pa., 1978—. Acting 2d lt. U.S. Army N.G., 1964-71. Mem. ATLA, Pa. Bar Assn., Pa. Trial Assn., Susquehanna County Bar Assn., Lackawanna Bar Assn., Thunderbird Investment Club (pres. 1966-70), Elkview Country Club. (sr. golf mem.). Roman Catholic. Avocations: golf, hunting, fishing. Home: RR 1 Box 1155 Carbondale PA 18407-9016 Office: 547 Hickory St Scranton PA 18505-1322

SPOTO, DONALD, writer, educator; b. New Rochelle, N.Y., June 28, 1941; s. Michael George and Anne Hortense (Werden) S. BA summa cum laude, Iona Coll., New Rochelle, 1963; MA, Fordham U., 1966, PhD, 1970. Instr. Fairfield U., Conn., 1966-68; asst. prof. Coll. New Rochelle, 1968-74; mem. faculty CUNY, N.Y.C., 1974-75, New Sch. for Social Rsch., N.Y.C., 1975-86; adj. prof. U. So. Calif., L.A., 1987-89; vis. lectr. Brit. Film Inst., Nat. Film Theatre, London, 1980-86; nat. lectr. Am. Film Inst., Washington, 1979-82. Author: The Art of Alfred Hitchcock, 1976, 2d edit., rev., 1992, Camerado, 1978, Stanley Kramer: Film Maker, 1978, The Dark Side of Genius: The Life of Alfred Hitchcock, 1983 (Edgar award Mystery Writers Guild 1984), The Kindness of Strangers: The Life of Tennessee Williams, 1985, Falling In Love Again, 1985, Lenya: A Life, 1989, Madcap: The Life of Preston Sturges, 1990, Laurence Olivier: A Biography, 1991, Blue Angel: The Life of Marlene Dietrich, 1992, Marilyn Monroe: The Biography, 1993; author numerous revs., essays; contbr. articles to mags. and newspapers. Mem. Authors Guild Am., Writers Guild Am. Roman Catholic. Office: care Elaine Markson Literary Agy 44 Greenwich Ave New York NY 10011-8347

SPOTSWOOD, ROBERT KEELING, lawyer; b. Balt., July 11, 1952; s. William Syson and Helen Marie (Fairchild) S.; m. Ashley Hayward Wiltshire, Aug. 19, 1978; children: Robert Keeling, Mary Hayward. BS with highest distinction in Applied Math., U. Va., 1974, JD, 1977. Bar: Ala. 1977, U.S. Dist. Ct. (no. dist.) Ala. 1979, U.S. Dist. Ct. (so. dist.) Ala. 1980, U.S. Ct. Appeals (5th cir.) 1979, U.S. Ct. Appeals (11th cir.) 1981, U.S. Dist. Ct. (mid. dist.) Ala. 1986, U.S. Supreme Ct. 1987. Ptnr. Bradley, Arant, Rose & White, Birmingham, Ala., 1977—. Mem. Birmingham Bar Assn., ABA. Club: Mountain Brook. Home: 3865 Cove Dr Birmingham AL 35213-3801 Office: Bradley Arant Rose & White PO Box 830709 Birmingham AL 35283-0709

SPRABERY, CAROL ANN, health facility administrator; b. North Island, Calif., July 6, 1945; d. Thomas Eugene and Dorothy Frances (Grimes) Forister; div.; children: Scott Ellis, Cynthia Anne. BS, U. Miss., 1967; MEd, Miss. State U., 1986, PhD, 1990. Lic. profl. counselor; cert. psychometrist, nat. counselor. Adolescent counselor Laurelwood Psychiat., Meridian, Miss.; counselor Lamar Sch., Meridian; tchr. counselor edn. Weems Cmty. Mental Health Ctr., Meridian, 1990-95; pvt. practice Glen Burnie, Md., 1995—; mem. adj. faculty Miss. State U., 1990—. Mem. ACA, Miss. Counselors Assn., Assn. Mental Health Counselors, Assn. Sch. Counselors, Lauderdale County Mental Health Bd. Office: Ste 409 1600 S Crain Hwy Glen Burnie MD 21061 Office: 1600 Crain Hwy S Ste 409 Glen Burnie MD 21061

SPRADLEY, DEBBY HAY, advertising executive; b. Dallas, Dec. 8, 1952; d. Jess Thomas and Betty Jo (Peacock) Hay; children: Jessica Kathryn, Rachel Hay. BFA, So. Meth. U., 1975. Vice pres. Dallas Market Ctr., 1975-83; pres. The Hay Agy., Inc., Dallas, 1983—; bd. dirs. Turtle Creek Nat. Bank, New Bus. Devel. Bd. dirs. Dallas Democratic Forum, 1983, TACA, Inc., 1983—, The Family Place, 1985, The Hockaday Sch., 1992—, Dallas Summer Musicals, 1993—; active Jr. League Dallas, 1981—, Dallas Symphony Orch. League, Mental Health Assn.. Mem. Dallas Ad League, Fashion Group, Dallas Mus. Art, Dallas Comm. Coun. Democrat. Methodist. Home: 7226 Desco Dr Dallas TX 75225-2003 Office: Hay Agency 2200 Ross Ave Ste 4300E Dallas TX 75201-2764

SPRAGENS, THOMAS ARTHUR, educational consultant; b. Lebanon, Ky., Apr. 25, 1917; s. William Henry and Lillian (Brewer) S.; m. Catharine Smallwood, May 24, 1941; children: Thomas Arthur, Barbara Allen, David William. A.B., U. Ky., 1938, LL.D., 1964; Maxwell fellow pub. adminstrn., Syracuse U., 1939-40; LL.D., Westminster Coll., Fulton, Mo., 1958, Berea Coll., 1982, Centre Coll., 1982; Litt. D., U. Ala., 1967; H.H.D., Ky. State U., 1984. Research asst. Ky. Dept. Revenue, 1938-39, adminstrv. asst. to commr., 1941-42; adminstv. analyst U.S. Bur. Budget, 1940-41, sr. analyst, 1942-45; asst. chief food allocations Fgn. Econ. Adminstrn., 1945; asst. to pres. Stanford U., 1945-51; sec., treas. Fund for Advancement Edn., 1951-52; pres. Stephens Coll., 1952-57; pres. Centre Coll. of Ky., Danville, 1957-81, pres. emeritus, 1981—; pres. Spragens Assocs., Inc.; cons. in institutional devel. Mem. Ohio Valley Regional Coun., 1973-75; pres. So. Coll. Univ. Union, 1970-74, So. Univ. Conf., 1975; trustee Pikeville Coll., 1985-91; bd. dirs. Shakertown at Pleasant Hill, Ky., 1973-91, Leadership Ky., Inc., 1985—; city commr. Danville, Ky., 1990-94; del. Nat. Dem. Conv., 1968. Mem. Am. Council Edn. (dir. 1966-69), Ky. Hist. Soc. (bd. dirs.), Pendennis Club, Filson Club, Rotary, Phi Beta Kappa, Omicron Delta Kappa. Presbyterian (mem. bd. Christian edn. 1968-73). Home: 3 Charleston Greene Danville KY 40422-1800 Office: Centre Coll Library Danville KY 40422

SPRAGENS, WILLIAM CLARK, public policy educator, consultant; b. Lebanon, Ky., Oct. 1, 1925; s. Thomas Eugene and Edna Grace (Clark) S.; m. Elaine Jean Dunham, June 14, 1964. AB in Journalism, U. Ky., 1947, MA, 1953; PhD, Mich. State U., 1966. Instr. U. Tenn., Knoxville, 1962-64; part-time instr. Mich. State U., East Lansing, 1964-65; asst. prof. Millikin U., Decatur, Ill., 1965-67, Wis. State U., Oshkosh, 1967-69; assoc. prof. Bowling Green (Ohio) State U., 1969-82, prof., 1982-86, prof. emeritus, 1986—; owner Spragens Rsch./Analysis, Reston, Va., 1989—. Author: Electronic Magazines, 1995; editor-in-chief: Popular Images of American Presidents, 1988. Del. candidate McGovern for pres. campaign, Bowling Green, 1972; co-dir. Nat. Convs. Program, 1972, 76, 80, 84. Lyndon Baines Johnson Found. grantee, 1977, 78. Mem. World Affairs Coun. Washington, Am. Polit. Sci. Assn., Internat. Soc. for Polit. Sociology, Am. Soc. for Pub. Adminstrn. Democrat. Presbyterian. Avocations: coin collecting, first day cover collecting, psychology. Home and Office: PO Box 410 Herndon VA 22070-0410

SPRAGUE, CHARLES CAMERON, medical foundation president; b. Dallas, Nov. 14, 1916; s. George Able and Minna (Schwartz) S.; m. Margaret Frederica Dickson, Sept. 7, 1943; 1 dau., Cynthia Cameron. BBA, BS, DSc, So. Meth. U.; MD, U. Tex. Med. Branch, Galveston, 1943; DSc (hon.), U. Dallas, 1983, Tulane U., 1991. Diplomate Am. Bd. Internal Medicine. Intern U.S. Naval Med. Center, Bethesda, Md., 1943-44; resident Charity Hosp., New Orleans, 1947-48, Tulane U. Med. Sch., 1948-50; Commonwealth research fellow in hematology Washington U. Sch. Medicine, St. Louis, also Oxford (Eng.) U., 1950-52; mem. faculty Med. Sch. Tulane U., 1952-67, prof. medicine, 1959-67; dean Med. Sch. Tulane U. (Sch. Medicine), 1963-67; prof., dean U. Tex. Southwestern Med. Sch., Dallas, 1967-72; pres. U. Tex. Health Sci. Center, Dallas, 1972-86; pres. SW Med. Found., 1987-88, chmn. bd., chief exec. officer, 1988—; pres. emeritus U. Tex. SW Med. Ctr., 1988-95; chmn. emeritus SW Med. Found., 1995—. Mem. Nat. Adv. Council, 1966-70; mem. adv. com. to dir. NIH, 1973—; chmn. Gov.'s Task Force Health Manpower, 1981, Gov.'s Med. Edn. Mgmt. Effectiveness Com.; chmn. allied health edn. adv. com., coordinating bd. Tex. Coll. and Univ. System.; mem. coordinating bd., Tex. Higher Edn., 1989—, vice chmn., 1990—. Adv. com. Ctr. Sci. and Soc., U. Tex., Dallas, 1991—. With USNR, 1943-47. Recipient Ashbel Smith Disting. Alumnus award U. Tex. Med. Br., 1967; Disting. Alumnus award So. Meth. U., 1965; recipient Sports Illustrated Silver Anniversary award, 1963. Mem. Assn. Am. Med. Colls. (chmn. council deans 1970, chmn. exec. council and assembly 1972-73), Am. Soc. Hematology (pres. 1966), Assn. Acad. Health Ctrs. (bd. dirs. 1982—, chmn. bd. 1985-86). Office: Southwestern Medical Found PO Box 45708 5323 Harry Hines Blvd Dallas TX 75245-0708

SPRAGUE, EDWARD AUCHINCLOSS, retired association executive, economist; b. N.Y.C., Oct. 9, 1932; s. Irvin Auchincloss and Maude Browning (Fisher) S.; m. Patricia Ivy Cannon, Apr. 27, 1957; children: James Edward, Elizabeth Mary, Jennifer Ann. BA, Princeton U., 1954; MA, NYU, 1961. Rsch. analyst N.J. State C. of C., Newark, 1957-59; assoc. economist F.W. Dodge Corp., N.Y.C., 1959-62; economist Lehman Bros., N.Y.C., 1962-67; v.p. Nat. Assn. Mfrs., N.Y.C. and Washington, 1967-77; dir. tax policy The Tax Found., Washington, 1977-82; sr. v.p. The Tax Found., 1985-89; exec. dir. Tax Exec. Inst., 1982-85; v.p., exec. dir. The Tax Coun., 1979-82, 86-91, cons., 1991-92; cons. Employers Coun. on Flexible Compensation, Washington, 1992-93; ret., 1993. Editor: Building Business, 1961-62; jour. The Tax Executive, 1983-85. With U.S. Army, 1955-57. Mem. Nat. Tax Assn. Republican. Home: 623 Running Fox Rd Lusby MD 20657-3141

SPRAGUE, GEORGE FREDERICK, geneticist; b. Crete, Nebr., Sept. 3, 1902; s. Elmer Ellsworth and Lucy Kent (Manville) S. B.S., U. Nebr., 1924, M.S., 1926, D.Sc., 1958; Ph.D., Cornell U., 1930. With Dept. Agr., 1924-72, leader corn and sorghum investigations, 1958-72; mem. faculty U. Ill., Urbana, 1973-86; prof. emeritus U. Ill., 1986-93. Editor: Corn and Corn Improvement, 3d edit, 1989; contbr. articles to profl. jours. Recipient Superior Svc. award USDA, 1960, Disting. Svc. award, 1970, Wolf Found. award, Nat. Coun. Plant Breeders award, DeKalb Career award; inducted into USDA-Agrl. Rsch. Svc. Sci. Hall of Fame. Fellow AAAS, Washington Acad. Scis., Am. Soc. Agronomy (pres. 1960, Crops Rsch. award 1957); mem. NAS, Crops Sci. Soc. (pres. 1951), Am. Genetics Assn., Genetics Soc. Am., Am. Soc. Plant Physiologists, Am. Naturalists, Biometrics Soc. Home: 494 W 10th Ave Apt 208 Eugene OR 97401-2880

SPRAGUE, JAMES MATHER, medical scientist, educator; b. Kansas City, Mo., Aug. 31, 1916; s. James P. and Lelia (Mather) S.; m. Dolores Marie Eberhart, Nov. 25, 1959; 1 son, James B. B.S., U. Kans., 1938, M.A., 1940; Ph.D., Harvard U., 1942; A.M. (hon.), U. Pa., 1971. From asst. to asst. prof. anatomy Hopkins Med. Sch., 1942-50; asst. prof. to prof. anatomy U. Pa. Med. Sch., Phila., 1950-83; chmn. dept. U. Pa. Med. Sch., 1967-76, Joseph Leidy prof. anatomy, 1973-83, emeritus Joseph Leidy prof., 1983—, dir. Inst. Neurol. Sci., 1973-80, chmn. univ. faculty senate, 1963; vis. prof. Northwestern U., 1948, U. Oxford, 1949, Rockefeller U., 1955, Cambridge U., 1956, U. Pisa, 1966, 74-75, U. Leuven, 1984—, Kyushu U., 1988; sci. cons. NIH, 1957-60. Co-editor: Progress in Psychobiology and Physiological Psychology, 1966-84; asso. editor: Acta Neurobiol. Exper., 1976; contbr. articles to profl. jours. Recipient Macy faculty award, 1974-75; Guggenheim fellow, 1948-49. Mem. NAS, Am. Assn. Anatomists (v.p. 1976-78), Japanese Assn. Anatomists (hon.), Soc. Neurosci. (founding coun.). Democrat. Home: 410 Lantern Ln Berwyn PA 19312-2011 Office: Dept Cell & Devel Biology Dept Neurosci Sch Medicine U Pa Philadelphia PA 19104-6058

SPRAGUE, JOHN LOUIS, management consultant; b. Boston, 1930; s. Robert Chapman and Florence Antoinette (van Zelm) S.; m. Mary-Jane Whitney, June 19, 1952; children—John Louis, William Whitney, Catherine van Zelm, David Hyatt. A.B., Princeton, 1952; Ph.D., Stanford, 1959. With Sprague Electric Co., North Adams, Mass., 1959-87; co-dir. engring. labs., sr. v.p. engring. Sprague Electric Co., 1964-65, v.p. research and devel., 1965-66, sr. v.p. semi-condr. div., 1967-76, pres., 1976-87, chief exec. officer, 1981-87; pres. John L. Sprague Assocs. Inc., 1988—; bd. dirs. Sipex Corp., Allmerica Fin., Aerovox, Inc., MRA Labs., Inc., Calif. Micro Devices, Aerospace Coating Sys., Inc., Boyd Converting Co. Chmn. Williamstown United Fund-ARC Campaign, 1961; trustee Pine Cobble Sch., 1978, Middlesex Sch., 1994—. Served to lt. (j.g.) USNR, 1952-55. Mem. IEEE, Electrochem. Soc., Am. Chem. Soc., Sci. Research Soc. Am., Confrerie des Chevaliers du Tastevin, Confrerie de la Chaine des Rotisseurs, Mayflower Hist. Soc., Sigma Xi, Phi Lambda Upsilon. Club: Princeton (N.Y.C.). Home: 175 Bee Hill Rd Williamstown MA 01267

SPRAGUE, NORMAN FREDERICK, JR., surgeon, educator; b. L.A., June 12, 1914; s. Norman F. and Frances E. (Ludeman) S.; m. Caryll E. Mudd, Dec. 27, 1941 (dec. Apr. 1978); children: Caryll (Mrs. Mingst), Norman Frederick III, Cynthia Sprague Connolly, Elizabeth (Mrs. Day); m. Erlenne Estes, Dec. 31, 1981. AB, U. Calif., 1933; MD, Harvard U., 1937. Intern Bellevue Hosp., N.Y.C., 1937, house surgeon, 1938-39; pvt. med. practice L. A., 1946—; mem. hon. staff Hosp. of Good Samaritan, L. A.; mem. staff St. Vincent Med. Ctr., L. A.; asst. clin. prof. surgery UCLA, 1951—; dir. emeritus Western Fed. Savs. & Loan Assn.; chmn. bd. dirs. Western Pioneer Co., 1961-63, Pioneer Savs. & Loan Assn., 1959-63; dir. Arden-Mayfair, Inc., 1966-69; also chmn. exec. com.; dir., mem. exec. com. Cyprus Mines Corp., 1959-79; trustee Mesabi Trust, 1964-76. Chmn. exec. com., v.p. Harvard Sch., 1954-65; mem. Cmty. Redevel. Agy. City of L.A., 1966-69, vice-chmn., 1967-69; mem. Calif. Regional Med. Programs Area IV Coun., 1970-75; bd. dirs., v.p. Calif. Inst. Cancer Rsch., 1974-80, pres., 1980-82; bd. dirs. Cancer Assoc., 1975-80; trustee UCLA Found., Marlborough Sch., 1981-90, Mildred E. and Harvey S. Mudd Found., Hollywood Bowl Assn., 1962-66; hon. trustee Calif. Mus. Found.; mem. exec. com., trustee Youth Tennis Found., 1960-70; trustee, pres., mem. exec. com. S.W. Mus.; founding trustee Harvey Mudd Coll.; chmn. bd. trustees Caryll and Norman Sprague Found., 1957—, Harvard Sch.; mem. bd. visitors UCLA Med. Sch.; nat. bd. dirs. Retonitis Pigmentosa Internat.; mem. adv. com. Univs. Space Rsch. Assn., Divsn. Space Biomedicine, 1982-94. Maj. M.C. AUS, 1941-46. Decorated Bronze Star; recipient Bishop's award of Merit Episc. Diocese L.A., 1966, Highest Merit award So. Calif. Pub. Health Assn., 1968. Mem. AMA, SAR, Calif. Med. Assn., L.A. County Med. Assn., Univ. Space Rsch. Assn. (mem. adv. com. divsn. space biomedicine 1982-94), Am. Cattlemen's Assn., Symposium Soc., Tennis Patrons Assn. (dir. 1960-70), Calif. Club, Harvard Club, L.A. Country Club, Delta Kappa Epsilon. Home: 550 S Mapleton Dr Los Angeles CA 90024-1811 Office: 2049 Century Park E Ste 2760 Los Angeles CA 90067-3202

SPRAGUE, PETER JULIAN, semiconductor company executive, lecturer; b. Detroit, Apr. 29, 1939; s. Julian K. and Helene (Coughlin) S.; m. Tjasa Krofta, Dec. 19, 1959; children: Carl, Steven, Kevin, Michael. Student, Yale U., 1961, MIT, 1961, Columbia U., 1962-66. chmn. Wave Sys., Inc.; bd. dirs. Software Profls., Inc. Trustee Strang Clinic. Club: Yale. Home: 399 Under Mountain Rd Lenox MA 01240-2036 Office: Wave Sys Corp 540 Madison Ave New York NY 10022-3213

SPRAGUE, WILLIAM, insurance company executive, farmer; b. 1938. Pres. Ky Farm Bur Mutual Inc., Louisville; farmer Sturgis, Ky. Office: Ky Farm Bur Ins Co 9201 Bunsen Pky Louisville KY 40220-3792*

SPRAGUE, WILLIAM DOUGLAS, lawyer, company executive; b. Houston, Dec. 23, 1941; s. William Douglas and Helen (Mims) S.; m. Marilyn Wells, Aug. 7, 1965; children: William Douglas III, Anne W., Robert L. BS, U. Wis., 1964; JD, Harvard U., 1967. Bar: Mich. 1972, Ind. 1978, Pa. 1991. Assoc. Reinhart, Boerner, Van Deuren, Norris & Rieselbach, Milw., 1967-71; lawyer Ford Motor Credit Co., Dearborn, Mich., 1971-77; various legal positions to sr. v.p. adminstrn. AMAX Coal Co., Indpls., 1977-87; assoc. gen. counsel Alumax Inc., San Mateo, Calif., 1987-88; v.p., gen. counsel Lukens Inc., Coatesville, Pa., 1988—. Gen. campaign chmn. United Way Chester County, Exton, Pa., 1990. Mem. ABA, Wis. Bar Assn., Mich. Bar Assn., Ind. Bar Assn., Pa. Bar Assn., Phi Kappa Phi, Phi Eta Sigma. Avocations: golf, bridge. Office: Lukens Inc 50 S 1st Ave Coatesville PA 19320-3418

SPRAGUE, WILLIAM WALLACE, JR., retired food company executive; b. Savannah, Ga., Nov. 11, 1926; s. William Wallace and Mary (Crowther) S.; m. Elizabeth Louise Carr, Oct. 3, 1953; children: Courtney, Lauren Duane, William Wallace III, Elizabeth Louise. BSME, Yale U., 1950. With Savannah Foods & Industries, Inc., 1952-94, ret., 1994, sec., 1961-62, v.p., 1962-72, pres., chief exec. officer, 1972-92, chmn. bd. dirs., CEO, 1993-94, also bd. dirs., mem. asset quality rev. com. NationsBank Corp., Charlotte, N.C.; mem. adv. bd. NationsBank Ga., N.A., Savannah; bd. dirs. Everglades Sugar Refinery, Clewiston, Fla.; chmn. bd. dirs. Mich. Sugar Co., Saginaw, Colonial Sugars, Gramercy, La., Food Carrier, Inc., Savannah, Raceland (La.) Sugars, Inc., Savannah Foodsvc., Inc.; bd. dirs., pres. Adeline Sugar Factory Co., Ltd., Savannah, Coastal Mgmt. Corp., Savannah. Trustee Savannah Bus. Group, Savannah Benevolent Assn.; chmn., mem. steering com. United Way Savannah; vice chmn. Savannah CEO Coun.; chmn. emeritus Youth Futures Authority, Savannah. With USN, 1945-46. Named Sugar Man of Yr. and recipient Dyer Meml. award B.W. Dyer & Co., 1985; named Industrialist of Yr. Internat. Mgmt. Coun., 1988. Mem. World Sugar Rsch. Orgn. (chmn. 1982-85), Grocery Mfrs. Assn. (bd. dirs.), The Sugar Assn. (bd. dirs.), NAM, Carolina Plantation Soc., St. Andrews Soc., Oglethorpe Club, Century Club (Savannah). Office: Savannah Foods & Industries PO Box 339 Savannah GA 31402-0339*

SPRALEY, JUDITH ANN, nursing educator, administrator; b. Gross Point, Mich., Jan. 11, 1936; d. Leonard Joseph and Margaret (McCloskey) S. BSN, Mount St. Joseph Coll., 1958; MEd, U. Cin., 1986. RN, Ohio; CNOR. Dir. nursing svc. Otto C. Epp Meml. Hosp., Cin.; nursing instr. Deaconess Hosp. Sch. Nursing, Cin.; nursing administr. U. Hosp., Cin.; chair surg. tech. program Cin. State Tech. Coll. and C.C.; p.r.n. charge/treatment nurse Twin Towers Retirement Cmty., Cin.; author, instr. operating rm. courses for nurses & surg. technologists; acute and long term patient advocate; cons. in field. Mem. AAUP, Assn. Oper. Rm. Nurses, Assn. Surg. Technologists (liaison com. on cert for surg. technologist), Nat. C.C. Chair Acad. Home: 8034 Mildmay Ct Cincinnati OH 45239-4012 Office: Twin Towers Retirement Cmty 5343 Hamilton Ave Cincinnati OH 45224

SPRANG, MILTON LEROY, obstetrician, gynecologist, educator; b. Chgo., Jan. 15, 1944; s. Eugene and Carmella (Bruno) S.; m. Sandra Lee Karabelas, July 16, 1966; children: David, Christina, Michael. Student, St. Mary's Coll., 1962-65; MD, Loyola U., 1969. Diplomate Am. Bd. Ob-gyn; Nat. Bd. Med. Examiners; CME accreditation. Intern St. Francis Hosp., Evanston, Ill., 1969-70, resident, 1972-75, sr. attending physician, 1985—; assoc. attending physcian Evanston Hosp., 1975-79, attending physician, 1980-84, sr. attending physician, 1985—, v.p. med. staff, 1990-91, pres.-elect, 1991-92, pres., 1992-93; also bd. dirs., 1991-94; sec. exec. com. Evanston Hosp., 1993-94; chmn. ob-gyn Cook County Grad. Sch. Medicine,, Chgo., 1983-91; instr. Northwestern U. Med. Sch., Chgo., 1975-78, asst. prof., 1984-85, assoc. prof., 1995—; pres. Northwestern Healthcare Network Physician Leadership, 1994; lectr. acad. and civic groups OB-Gyn. Nat. Ctr. Advanced Med. Edn., 1991—; bd. dirs. Ill. Found. Med. Rev.; bd. trustees Ill. State Ins. Svcs., 1992-96; bd. govs. Ill. State Med. Inter-Inst. Exch., 1987-92. Editor: Profl. Staff News, 1992-93; chmn. editorial bd. Jour. Chgo. Medicine, 1986-91; contbr. articles to profl. jours. Bd. dirs. Am. Cancer Soc., chmn. profl. edn. com. North Shoore unit, 1982-85; bd. dirs. Chgo. Community Info. Network, 1994-95; mem. Nat. Rep. Congrl. Com., 1981—, Ill. Med. Polit. Action Com. With USN, 1970-72. Fellow ACS, Am. Coll.Ob-Gyn. (chmn. Ill. sect. 1975-76), Am. Soc. Colposcopy and Cervical Pathology; mem. AMA (Physician Recognition award 1977, 80, 83), Ill. Med. Soc. (del. to AMA 1987, 91—, ho. dels., govt. affairs com. 1988-96, chmn. reference com. 1989, chmn. bd. trustees 1996—, chmn. fin. com. 1992-94, sec.-treas. 1994-96), Chgo. Med. Soc. (v.p. 1984-85, adv. com. advt. stds. 1978-84, counselor, physician's rev. com. 1980-85, chmn. 1985, , sec. 1989—, exec. coun. north suburban br. 1981-82, 86, chmn. 1985, trustee ins. bd. 1982—, nominating com. 1985-96, trustee 1986-92, treas. 1986-89, sec. 1989-90, pres.-elect 1990-91, pres. 1991-92, chmn. fin. com. 1986-89, pres. 1991-93, chmn. ethical rels. com. 1994-96, chmn. bd. trustees 1990-91), Chgo. Found. Med. Care (nominating com. 1980-84, med. care evaluation and edn. com. 1980-83, practice guidelines com. 1984), Physician Benefit Trust (chmn. fin. com. 1993-96). Roman Catholic. Avocations: reading, raising fish, swimming. Home: 4442 Concord Ln Skokie IL 60076-2606 Office: AGSO 1000 Central St Evanston IL 60201-1777

SPRATT, JOHN MCKEE, JR., congressman, lawyer; b. Charlotte, N.C., Nov. 1, 1942; s. John McKee and Jane Love (Bratton) S.; m. Jane Stacy, May 31, 1968; children: Susan Elizabeth, Sarah Stacy, Catherine Bratton. A.B., Davidson Coll., 1964; M.A., Corpus Christi Coll., Oxford U., 1966; LL.B., Yale U., 1969. Ops. analyst Office of Asst. Sec. of Def., 1969-71; ptnr. Spratt, McKeown & Spratt, Mork, S.C., 1971-83; pres. Spratt Ins. Agy., Ft. Mill, 1973-82, Bank of Ft. Mill, S.C., 1973-82; mem. 98th-104th Congresses from 5th S.C. dist., Washington, D.C., 1983—; mem. Armed Svcs. com., subcoms. oversight and investigations, military acquisitions, govt. opns. com., subcom. commerce, consumer, monetary affairs, joint com. orgn. congress; former dir. Bank of York. Chmn. bd. trustees Divine Saviour Hosp., York, 1980-82; bd. dirs. Piedmont Legal Services, Inc., 1978-82; bd. visitors Davidson Coll., 1978-80; chmn. bd. visitors Winthrop Coll., 1976. Served to capt. JAGC, U.S. Army, 1969-71. Mem. S.C. Bar Assn. (ho. of dels.), ABA. Democrat. Presbyterian. Office: US Ho of Reps 1536 Longworth House Office Bldg Washington DC 20515-4005*

SPRAUER, CYNTHIA CAROL, optometrist; b. Bridgeton, N.J., Apr. 11, 1962; d. Frederick Henry and Edna Catherine (Hepner) S. BS in Biology, Va. Tech., 1984; BS in Visual Sci., Pa. Coll. Optometry, 1988, OD, 1991.

Tech. rep. Vineland (N.J.) Chem., 1984-87; optometrist Office of Drs. Klein & Schwab, Mays Landing, N.J., 1991-93, Nu Vision, Northfield, N.J., 1993—. Mem. Am. Optometric Assn., N.J. Optometric Assn., South Jersey Optometric Soc., Beta Sigma Kappa. Avocations: roller skating, dance, photography. Home: 3627 Whitehall Ct Mays Landing NJ 08330-3244

SPRAY, PAUL, surgeon; b. Wilkinsburg, Pa., Apr. 9, 1921; s. Lester E. and Phoebe Gertrude (Hull) S.; m. Mary Louise Conover, Nov. 28, 1943; children: David C., Thomas L., Mary Lynn (Mrs. Thomas Branham). BS, U. Pitts., 1942; MD, George Washington U., 1944; MS, U. Minn., 1950. Diplomate Am. Bd. Orthopedic Surgery. Intern U.S. Marine Hosp., S.I., 1944-45; resident Mayo Found., Rochester, Minn., 1945-46, 48-50; practice medicine specializing in orthopedic surgery Oak Ridge, Tenn., 1950—; mem. staff Oak Ridge Hosp., Park West Hosp., Knoxville, Harriman Hosp., Tenn.; vol. vis. cons. CARE Medico, Jordan, 1959, Nigeria, 1962, 65, Algeria, 1963, Afghanistan, 1970, Bangladesh, 1975, 77, 79, Peru, 1980, U. Ghana, 1982; AMA vol. physician, Vietnam, 1967, 72; vis. assoc. prof. U. Nairobi, 1973; mem. tchg. team Internat. Coll. Surgeons to Khartoum; vis. prof. orthop. surgery U. Khartoum, 1976; hon. prof. San Luis Gonzaga U., Ica, Peru; AmDoc vol. cons. U. Biafra Tchg. Hosp., 1969; vis. prof. Mayo Clinic, 1988; sec. orthops. overseas divsn. CARE Medico, 1971-76, sec. Medico adv. bd., 1974-76, vice chmn., 1976, chmn., 1977-79, v.p. CARE, Inc., 1977-79, pub. mem. CARE bd. dirs., 1980-90, mem. bd. overseers, 1991—; chmn. Orthops. Overseas, Inc., 1982-86, treas., 1986-88, emeritus mem., 1994; mem. U.S. organizing com. 1st Internat. Acad. Symposium on Orthops., Tianjin, China, 1983; mem. CUPP Internat. Adv. Coun., 1986—; invited guest spkr. Japan Orthop. Assn., 1994. Mem. editorial bd. Contemporary Orthopedics, 1984—. V.p. Anderson County Health Coun., 1975, pres., 1976-77, hon. bd. dirs., 1991; pres. health commn. Coun. So. Mountains, 1958-65, sec., bd. dirs., 1965-66; Tenn. pres. UN Assn., 1966-67; vice-chmn. bd. Camelot Care Ctr., Tenn., 1979-82, chmn., 1982-86; chmn. bd. dirs. Camelot Found., 1986-87; hon. mem. World Orthopedic Concern, 1990; with del. to Vietnam People to People, 1993, citizen amb. to Vietnam, 1993; del. to Oak Ridge's Sister City, Obinsk, Russia, 1993; bd. dirs. Vietnam Am. Student found.; trustee Vietnam Am. Scholarship Fund, 1992-95. Recipient Svc. to Mankind award Sertoma, 1967, Humanitarian award Lions Club, 1968, Freedom Citation, 1978, Amb. Goodwill award 1979, Medico Disting. Svc. award, 1990, 1st Ann. Vocat. Svc. award Oak Ridge Rotary, 1979, Tech. Communication award East Tenn. chpt. Soc. for Tech. Communication, 1983, Individual Achievement award Meth. Med. Ctr. of Oak Ridge, 1991, Humanitarian award Orthopaedics Overseas, 1992; Melvin Jones fellow Lions Club, 1993. Fellow ACS, Internat. Coll. Surgeons (Tenn. regent 1976-80, bd. councillors 1980-84, hon. chmn. bd. turstees 1981-83, trustee 1983-84, v.p. U.S. sect. 1982-83, mem. surg. teams com. 1983-90, Humanitarian award 1992); mem. AMA (Humanitarian Svc. award 1967, 72), Sociètè International Chirugie Orthopèdique et de Traumuatologie, So. Orthopedic Assn., Western Pacific Orthopedic Assn., Am. Fracture Assn., Am. Acad. Orthopedic Surgeons (mem. com. on injuries 1980-86), Tenn. Med. Assn. (com. on emergency med. svcs. 1978-88), Peru Acad. Surgery (corr.), Peruvian Soc. Orthopedic Surgery and Traumatology (corr.), Clin. Orthopedic Soc., Mid-Am. Orthopaedic Soc., Rotary Club (Oak Ridge chpt.). Home: 507 Delaware Ave Oak Ridge TN 37830-3902 Office: Ste C 160 W Tennessee Ave Oak Ridge TN 37830

SPRAYBERRY, SHERYL MCARTHUR, rehabilitation nurse; b. Pitts., Dec. 5, 1947; d. Edwin Ross Jr. and Virginia Wilma (Herchenroether) McA.; m. Bert Powell Craft, May 24, 1968 (div. June 1984); children: David Preston Craft, Kim Alissa Craft; m. Spencer Lesley Sprayberry, Apr. 21, 1990. BSN, U. Miss., Jackson, 1971, postgrad., 1974-75; MSN, U. Ala., 1978; cert. in exec. mgmt., So. Meth. U., 1987. RN, Tex. Staff nurse CCU, head nurse med.-surg. unit U. Miss. Med. Ctr., Jackson, 1971-74; clin. specialist, asst. DON, liaison nurse Miss. Meth. Rehab. Ctr., Jackson, 1974-85; clin. coord., rehab. clin. inpatient units Dallas Rehab. Inst., 1985-86, 86-88, asst. adminstr. nursing svcs., 1985-88; DON Houston Rehab. Inst., 1989-91; program cons. Rehab. Care Corp., St. Louis, 1991-95; dir. rehab. svcs. St. Joseph's Hosp. and Health Ctr., Paris, Tex., 1995—; adj. instr. Alcorn State U., Natchez, Miss., 1981-82; adj. clin. instr. Sch. Nursing, U. Miss., 1978-85; clin. preceptor, guest instr. U. Tex., Arlington, 1985-88; clin. preceptor U. Tex., Houston, 1989-91; co-author, developer CEU courses, seminars, various nursing splty. presentations; lectr. in field. Mem. adv. bd. Crippled Children's Agy., Jackson, 1977; vol. med. asst. Tenneco Marathon, Houston, 1991. Mem. Nat. Assn. Rehab. Nurses (cert.), S.E. Tex. Assn. Rehab., Sigma Theta Tau. Methodist. Avocations: painting, needle work, exercise, reading, ch. choir. Home: 2526 Lamar Ave 135 Paris TX 75460

SPRECHER, DAVID A., university administrator, mathematician; b. Saarbrucken, Fed. Republic Germany, Jan. 12, 1930; s. Wolfgang and Karolina (Jung) S.; children: Lorrie, Jeannie. Student, Hebrew U., 1952-54; A.B., U. Bridgeport, 1958; Ph.D., U. Md., 1963. Instr. math. U. Md., 1961-63; asst. prof. Syracuse U., 1963-66; asso. prof. math. U. Calif.-Santa Barbara, 1966-71, prof., 1971-92, prof. emeritus, 1993—, chmn. dept., 1972-75, assoc. dean Coll. of Letters and Sci., 1975-78, dean Coll. of Letters and Sci., 1978-81, provost/dean, 1981-91. Author: Elements of Real Analysis, 1970, 2nd edit., 1987, Precalculus Mathematics, 1974, Finite Mathematics, 1976; (with P. Frank and A. Yaqub) A Brief Course in Calculus With Applications, 1971, 2nd edit., 1976; (with P. Frank) Calculus, 1975; contbr. articles to profl. jours. Served with Israeli Army, 1948-50. Mem. Am. Math. Soc., Math. Assn. Am. Office: U Calif 6607 South Hall Santa Barbara CA 93106

SPRECHER, BARON WILLIAM GUNTHER, pianist, composer, conductor, diplomat; b. Saarbrucken, Germany, Jan. 20, 1924; came to U.S., 1952.; s. Wolf and Karoline (Jung) Sprecher; m. Blossom Tag, Aug. 6, 1952. Studied piano with Prof. Wittels, Tel Aviv; studied piano with Madame Vengerova, N.Y.C.; studied composition with Paul Ben-Haim, Tel Aviv, studied conducting with Georg Singer; hon. degree, Inst. of Vocal Arts, 1957; Dr. honoris causa in Philosophy of Music, World Univ. Roundtable, 1988; MusD (hon.), London Inst. Applied Rsch., 1991, DFA (hon.), 1993, HHD, 1993; MusD (hon.), Australian Inst. Coord. Rsch., 1991; diploma, Gran Premio Am., 1990, Paladino del Tricolore, 1990; D Musicology, Somerset U.; D Music (hon.), Atlantic Southeastern U.; Diploma, Acad. Argentina de Diplomacia; Assoc. (hon.), Inst. Affairs Internat., Paris, 1993; DD (hon.), The Christian Congregation; D rerum politicarum (hon.), LittD, U. Aeterna Lucina Vitama, 1991; DD (hon.), LittD, Eng., 1994; PhD (hon.), Germany, 1994. Korrepetitor Israel Folk Opera, Tel-Aviv, 1940-43; piano soloist Israel Philharm. Orch., Tel-Aviv, 1946-48; pres., music dir. Bronx Philharm., N.Y.C., 1971-83; music dir. Sta. WEVD, N.Y.C., 1969-85; asst. pianist accompanying Lotte Lenya, Richard Tucker, Jan Peerce, Itzhak Perlman, Jan Kiepura, Ilona Massey; prof. Inst. Hautes Etudes Economiques et Sociales; rsch. prof. Alliance Universelle Paix Connaissance, Paris, 1991; prof. Haute Ecole de Recherche, Inst. des Hautes Etudes Economiques et Sociales; mem. coun. Inst. de Documentation et D'Etudes Europeennes; dep. mem., diplomat Internat. State Parliament. Composer: (Song Book) Yinglish, piano soloist 1st performance of Gershwin's Concerto in F in Israel; composer Piano Sonata, 1945, Jerusalem Concerto for Piano and Orch., 1967, (TV spl.) Great is Thy Faith, 1970; pianist-condr. 24 record albums; mem. The First Piano Quartet (Acad. award nomination, Peabody award). Consul Sovereign State Aeterna Lucina for State and City of N.Y.; comdr. fgn. rels. Island Du Caricom, 1995; diplomat World Jewish Congress; senator Coun. of States for Protection of Life and Human Rights, Palermo, Italy. Decorated noble knight Noble House of Amena, knight order Knight Templars of Jerusalem, knight comdr. Lofsensis Ursinius Order, baron Order of Bohemian Crown, comdr. Order of Golden Lance (Austrlia), Capt. Légion de L'Aigle Mer, Baron of Montsalvat, knight Holy Grail, count San Ciriaco, comdr. fgn. rels. Island du Caricom, 1995, Sen Maison Internationale Des Intellectuels, Sen European Parliament, Internat. Parliament for Safety and Peace, diplomat World Jewish Congress, Laird-Lord of Camster, Caithness, Scotland, 1995; recipient Diplomatic medal Internat. Parliament for Safety and Peace, 1995, Gold Cross of Honour, Albert Schweitzer Soc. Austria, Albert Einstein medal, Circulo Nobiliario Caballeros Universales, 1992, Swan Knight (Chevalier du Cygne), Order of the Swan, Knight of Yr. award Internat. Writers and Artists Assn., 1995, Noble Conquistador, Internat. Chivalric Order of the Knights of Justice, and other.s. Fellow United Writers' Assn. India; mem. ASCAP, Maison Internat. des Intellectuels, Internat. Parliament for Safety and Peace, World Parliament Confedn. of Chivalry (Grand Coun.), World Acad. Assn. of the Universe (life), Bronx Philharm. Symphony Soc., Inc. (founder, pres.), Internat. Platform Assn., Am. Fedn. Musicians, Robert Stolz Soc. Gt. Britain, World Univ. Roundtable (trustee, founder), Internat. Cultural Corr. Inst., Circulo Nobiliario de los Caballeros Universales (grandmaster U.S.), Royal Order Bohemian Crown (baron), Lègion de L'Aigle de Mer (capt.). Avocations: walking, chivalry and heraldry, cats, collecting rare musical books and recordings, collecting rare medieval coins and antique Coptic Ethiopian Crosses. Home and Office: Res Montsalvat 1D 2235 Cruger Ave Bronx NY 10467-9411

SPREITER, JOHN ROBERT, engineering educator, space physics scientist; b. Oak Park, Minn., Oct. 23, 1921; s. Walter F. and Agda E. (Hokanson) S.; m. Brenda Owens, Aug. 7, 1953; children: Terry A., Janet L., Christine P., Hilary M. B Aero. Engring., U. Minn., 1943; MS, Stanford U., 1947, PhD, 1954. Research scientist Ames Research Ctr. NASA, Moffett Field, Calif., 1943-69, chief theoretical studies br., 1962-69; prof. applied mechanics, mechanical engring. and aeros. and astronautics Stanford (Calif.) U., 1968-92, prof. emritus, 1992—; lectr. Stanford U., 1951-68; cons. Nielsen Engring. and Research Inc., Mountain View, Calif., 1968-85, RMA Aerospace, Mountain View, 1985—. Contbr. numerous articles to profl. jours. and books. Served with USN, 1944-46. Fellow AIAA, Royal Astron. Soc., Am. Geophys. Union; mem. AAAS, Am. Phys. Soc., The Planetary Soc., Saratoga Tennis Club (treas. 1955-65), Fremont Hills Country Club (Los Altos Hills, Calif.), Stanford Faculty Club, Sigma Xi, Tau Beta Pi, Tau Omega. Democrat. Achievements include pioneering studies in transonic aerodynamics; numerous contributions to studies of solar terrestrial relations, solar wind interaction with the earth, moon, other planets, and the local interstellar medium. Home: 1250 Sandalwood Ln Los Altos CA 94024-6739 Office: Stanford U Div Applied Mechanics Stanford CA 94305

SPRENGER, GORDON M., hospital administrator; b. Albert Lea, Minn., Apr. 30, 1937. Bachelors degree, St. Olaf Coll., 1959; masters degree, U. Minn., 1961. Registrar USAF Hosp., Hamilton AFB, Calif., 1961-64; with St. Luke's Hosp., Milw., 1964-67, Northwestern Hosp., Mpls., 1967-71; exec. v.p. Abbott-Northwestern Hosp., Mpls., 1971-75, pres., 1975—; exec officer Allina Health System, Mpls., MN; prof. U. Minn., 1976—; acad. lectureship; preceptor. Mem. Am. Hosp. Assn., Minn. Hosp. Assn. (bd. dirs. 1978-81, chmn. 1983-84, community svc., treas., 1981. Office: Allina Health System PO Box 9310 Minneapolis MN 55440-9310*

SPRENKLE, CASE MIDDLETON, economics educator; b. Cleve., Aug. 18, 1934; s. Raymond E. and Helen K. (Middleton) S.; m. Elaine Elizabeth Jensen, June 22, 1957; children: David, Peter, Amy. B.S., U. Colo., 1956; M.A., Yale U., 1957, Ph.D., 1960. Instr. econs. Yale U., New Haven, 1959-60; mem. faculty U. Ill., Urbana, 1960—, prof. econs., 1970—, chmn. dept. econs., 1976-80, acting head dept. econs., 1995-96, asst. dean Coll. Commerce, 1962-65; dir. U. Ill.-U. Warsaw MBA program, 1991—; faculty Econs. Inst., Boulder, Colo., 1965, 72, 81; vis. scholar London Sch. Econs., 1967, 74, 81, 88; vis. lectr. City of London U., 1981; cons. Ill. Revenue Commn., 1962—; bd. dirs. Aggregate Equipment co. Contbr. articles to profl. jours. Bd. dirs. Champaign-Urbana Symphony, treas., 1972-74, pres., 1975-77; bd. dirs. Champaign County Arts and Humanities Coun., 1977-79; bd. dirs. Champaign-Urbana Mass Transit Dist., 1983—, vice chmn., 1985, 93-94. Am. Bankers Assn. grantee, 1970-71. Mem. Am. Econs. Assn., Am. Fin. Assn., Omicron Delta Epsilon. Presbyterian. Home: 3403 S Persimmon Cir Urbana IL 61801-7128 Office: U Ill Dept Econs 1201 S 6th St Champaign IL 61820

SPREWELL, LATRELL FONTAINE, professional basketball player; b. Milw., Sept. 8, 1970; s. Latoska Fields and Pamela Sprewell; children: Aquilla, Page, Latrell II. Student, Three Rivers C.C., Poplar Bluff, Mo., 1988-90, Ala. U., 1990-92. Profl. basketball player Golden State Warriors, Oakland, Calif., 1992—. Avocations: music, repairing stereo equipment. Office: Oakland Coliseum Arena 700 Coliseum Way Oakland CA 94612-1918

SPRICK, DENNIS MICHAEL, critic, copy editor; b. Passaic, N.J., Sept. 2, 1956; s. Frederick Vincent and Jeannette Mary (Claudepierre) S. BA, Lehigh U., 1978. Copy editor Daily Advance, Roxbury, N.J., 1978-80; film and Broadway critic, copy editor Times Herald-Record, Middletown, N.Y., 1980—. Mem. Phi Beta Kappa. Roman Catholic. Avocations: yoga, singing, vegetarian cooking, massage. Office: Times Herald-Record 40 Mulberry St Middletown NY 10940-6302

SPRIESTERSBACH, DUANE CARYL, university administrator, speech pathology educator; b. Pine Island, Minn., Sept. 5, 1916; s. Merle Lee and Esther Lucille (Stucky) S.; m. Bette Rae Bartell, Aug. 31, 1946; children: Michael Lee, Ann. B.Ed., Winona State Tchrs. Coll., 1939; M.A., U. Iowa, 1940, Ph.D., 1948. Asst. dir. pers. rels. Pacific Portland Cement Co., San Francisco, 1946-47; prof. speech pathology U. Iowa, Iowa City, 1948-89, prof. emeritus, 1989—, dean. Grad. Coll., v.p. ednl. devel. and rsch., 1965-89, v. pres. and dean emeritus, 1989—, acting pres., 1981-82; v.p. ops. Breakthrough, Inc., Oakdale, Iowa, 1993-94; cons., 1994—; com. mem. Nat. Inst. Neurol. Disease and Blindness; chmn. dental tng. com. Nat. Inst. Dental Research, 1967-72, chmn. spl. grants rev., 1978-82; chmn. bd. Midwest Univs. Cons. Internat. Activities, Columbus, 1978-87. Author: Psychosocial Aspects of Cleft Palate, 1973, (with others) Diagnostic Methods in Speech Pathology, 1978; co-editor: Cleft Palate and Communication, 1968, Diagnosis in Speech Language Pathology, 1994. Pres. Iowa City Community Theater, 1964, 77, 83. Served to lt. col. U.S. Army, 1941-46, ETO. Decorated Bronze Star; Nat. Inst. Dental Rsch. fellow, 1971. Fellow AAAS; mem. Assn. Grad. Schs. (pres. 1979-80), Am. Speech and Hearing Assn. (pres. 1965, honor award), Am. Cleft Palate Assn. (pres. 1961-62, disting. service award), Midwestern Assn. Grad. Schs. (chmn. 1979-80), Mortar Board, Sigma Xi. Episcopalian. Club: Cosmos (Washington). Home: 2 Longview Knl N E Iowa City IA 52240-9148 Office: Univ Iowa M212 Oakdale Hall Oakdale IA 52319

SPRIGGS, RICHARD MOORE, ceramic engineer, research center administrator; b. Washington, Pa., May 8, 1931; s. Lucian Alexander and Kathryn (Aber) S.; m. Patricia Anne Blaney, Aug. 1, 1953; children—Carolyn Elizabeth Spriggs Muchna, Richard Moore, Alan David. BS in Ceramics, Pa. State U., 1952; MS in Ceramic Engring., U. Ill., 1956, PhD, 1958. Sr. research engr. Ferro Corp., Cleve., 1958-59; sr. staff scientist, group leader, ceramics rsch. AVCO Corp., Wilmington, Mass., 1959-64; assoc. prof. metall. engring. Lehigh U., Bethlehem, Pa., 1964-67, prof. metallurgy and materials sci. and engring., 1967-80, adminstrv. asst. to pres., 1970-71, asst. v.p. for adminstrn., 1971-72, v.p. for adminstrn., 1972-78, dir. phys. ceramics lab., 1964-70, assoc. dir. Materials Research Ctr., 1964-70; vis. sr. staff assoc. Nat. Materials Adv. Bd. NRC, Washington, 1979-80, sr. staff officer, staff scientist, 1980-87, staff dir. bd. on assessment of NBS programs, 1984-87; J.F. McMahon prof. ceramic engring., dir. NYS Ctr. Advanced Ceramic Tech. N.Y. State Coll. Ceramics, Alfred (N.Y.) U., 1987—, dir. office of sponsored programs, 1988—; affiliate staff scientist Pacific Northwest Lab., 1994—. Contbr. articles to profl. publs. Co-patentee in field. Pres., bd. dirs. YMCA, Bethlehem, Pa., 1978-79. Served to lt. USNR, 1952-56. Fellow Armco Steel Corp., 1956-58, Am. Council on Edn., 1970-71. Fellow Am. Ceramic Soc. (disting. life, pres. 1984-85, Ross Coffin Purdy award 1965, Hobard M. Kraner award Lehigh Valley sect. 1980, trustee pension trust fund 1979-84, Orton lectr. 1988, McMahon lectr. 1988, Mueller lectr. 1996, coord. programs and meetings 1991-92), Ceramic Soc. Japan (Centennial medal 1991), Brit. Inst. Ceramics; mem. AAAS, N.Y. Acad. Scis., Internat. Inst. for Sci. of Sintering, Nat. Inst. Ceramic Engrs., Materials Rsch. Soc. Japan (hon.), Ceramic Ednl. Coun., Brit. Ceramic Soc., Internat. Acad. Ceramics (trustee 1988—), Am. Soc. Engring. Edn., Materials Rsch. Soc., Fed. Materials Socs. (trustee 1978-84), Ceramic Assn. N.Y. (sec.-treas. 1988—), Serbian Acad. Scis. and Arts (fgn.), Rotary (dir. 1982-87, pres. 1985-86). Office: Alfred U Ctr Advanced Ceramic Tech NY State College of Ceramics Alfred NY 14802

SPRING, MICHAEL, editor, writer; b. N.Y.C., Oct. 14, 1941; s. Sol and Muriel (Roth) S.; m. Marjorie Hornblower Bauer, Mar. 1965 (div. 1980); children: Declan, Evan; m. Janis Abrahms, 1993. B.A., Haverford Coll., Pa., 1964; M.A., Columbia U., N.Y.C., 1970. Reporter Bergen Record, Hackensack, N.J., 1969-71; editor Scholastic Inc., N.Y.C., 1971-87; editorial dir. Fodor's Travel Publs., 1987-94, v.p., 1989-94; pub. Macmillan Travel, N.Y.C., 1994—; broadcaster, writer WNCN-FM, N.Y.C., 1983-84. Author: Great Weekend Escape Book, 1982, 4th rev. edit. 1990, Student's Guide to Julius Ceasar, 1984; editor: American Way of Working, 1980, 50 vol. Barron's Book Notes series, 1984, Scholastic Literature Anthologies, 4 vols., 1985, 87, Great European Itineraries, 1987, Touring Europe, 1990, 3d edit. 1994; contbg. editor Conde Nast's Traveler, 1987—; travel expert CNN Travel Show, 1991-94. Democrat. Jewish. Home: 20 Country Rd Westport CT 06880-2525 Office: Macmillan Travel 1633 Broadway New York NY 10019-6785

SPRING, PAULL E., bishop. Bishop Northwestern Pa. Evang. Luth. Ch. in Am., Oil City. Office: Evang Luth Ch in Am PO Box 338 Rte 257 Salina Rd Seneca PA 16346-0338

SPRING, RAYMOND LEWIS, legal educator; b. Warsaw, N.Y., Aug. 5, 1932. AB, Washburn U., 1957, JD, 1959. Bar: Kans. 1960, U.S. Ct. Appeals (10th cir.) 1960. Assoc. Crane, Martin, Claussen & Ashworth, Topeka, 1959-65; examiner Workmen's Compensation program State of Kans., 1961-62; asst. prof. law Washburn U., Topeka, 1965-68, assoc. prof., 1968-71, acting dean Sch. of Law, 1970-71, prof., dean Sch. of Law, 1971-78, Disting. prof., 1978—, interim v.p. for acad. affairs, 1988-91; faculty Karl Menninger Sch. Psychiatry and Mental Health Scis., 1987—; mem. cts. subcom. Kans. Gov.'s Com. on Criminal Adminstrn., 1970-79; dir. Century Savs. Assn., Shawnee Mission, Kans., 1978-84, chmn., 1980-82. Author: (with Ryan) Vernon's Kansas Criminal Code Annotated, 1971, Vernon's Kansas Code of Criminal Procedure, 1973; The End of Insanity, 1983, (with Lacoursiere and Weissenberger) Patients, Psychiatrists and Lawyers: Law and the Mental Health System, 1989. Bd. dirs. Topeka Welfare Planning Coun., 1964-66, Kans. Adv. and Protective Svcs., Inc., 1987—, Shawnee Coun. Campfire Girls, 1965-68; chmn. Shawnee County Young Reps., 1962-64; leader edn. divsn. Topeka United Fund, 1972; deacon Ctrl. Congrl. Ch., 1972-74, 79-80, 85-87, trustee, 1980-81, moderator, 1988; mem. Kans. Bd. Admissions of Attys., 1979-86, Kans. Gov.'s adv. com. mental Health and Retardation Svcs., 1983-90; mem. human studies commn. Colmery-O'Neil VA Med. Ctr., 1982-89. Recipient Disting. Svc. award Washburn Law Sch. Assn., 1987, William O. Douglas Outstanding Prof. award, 1980. Mem. ABA, Kans. Bar Assn. Topeka Bar Assn., Barristers, Kans. Hist. soc. (bd. dirs. 1980-93), Phi Kappa Phi, Delta Theta Phi, Phi Sigma Kappa. Home: 1616 SW Jewell Ave Topeka KS 66604-2737 Office: 1700 SW College Ave Topeka KS 66621-0001

SPRINGEL, BARRY L., lawyer; b. Detroit, Sept. 5, 1942. BS, Drexel Inst. Tech., 1964; JD, U. Mich., 1967; LLM, George Washington U., 1968. Bar: Mich. 1968, Ohio 1969. Ptnr. Jones, Day, Reavis & Pogue, Cleve. Office: Jones Day Reavis & Pogue North Point 901 Lakeside Ave E Cleveland OH 44114-1116*

SPRINGER, CHARLES EDWARD, state supreme court justice; b. Reno, Feb. 20, 1928; s. Edwin and Rose Mary Cecelia (Kelly) S.; m. Jacqueline Sirkegian, Mar. 17, 1951; 1 dau., Kelli Ann. BA, U. Nev., Reno, 1950; LLB, Georgetown U., 1953; LLM, U. Va., 1984; student Grad. Program for Am. Judges, Oriel Coll., Oxford (Eng.), 1984. Bar: Nev. 1953, U.S. Dist. Ct. Nev. 1953, D.C. 1954, U.S. Supreme Ct. 1962. Pvt. practice law Reno, 1953-80; atty. gen. State of Nev., 1962, legis. legal adv. to gov., 1958-62; legis. bill drafter Nev. Legislature, 1955-57; mem. faculty Nat. Coll. Juvenile Justice, Reno, 1978—; juvenile master 2d Jud. Dist. Nev., 1973-80; justice Nev. Suprem Ct., Carson City, 1981—; mem. Jud. Selection Commn., 1981, Nev. Supreme Ct. Gender Bias Task Force, 1981—; trustee Nat. Coun. Juvenile and Family Ct. Judges, 1983—; mem. faculty McGeorge Sch. Law, U. Nev., Reno, 1982—; mem. Nev. Commn. for Women, 1991-95. With AUS, 1945-47. Recipient Outstanding Contbn. to Juvenile Justice award Nat. Coun. Juvenile and Family Ct. Judges, 1989, Midby-Byron Disting. Leadership award U. Nev., 1988. Mem. ABA, Am. Judicature Soc., Am. Trial Lawyers Assn., Phi Kappa Phi. Office: Nev Supreme Ct Capitol Complex 201 S Carson St Carson City NV 89710

SPRINGER, DAVID EDWARD, lawyer; b. Chgo., Jan. 20, 1952; s. Edward W. and Mildred (Bergmark) S. AB summa cum laude, Yale U., 1974, JD, 1977. Bar: Ill. 1977, U.S. Ct. Appeals (5th cir.) 1978, U.S. Dist. Ct. (no. dist.) Ill. 1978, U.S. Ct. Appeals (7th cir.) 1981, U.S. Supreme Ct. 1981, U.S. Ct. Appeals (4th cir.) 1982, U.S. Ct. Appeals (fed. cir.) 1983, Wis. 1990, U.S. Dist. Ct. (D.C. cir.) 1991, U.S. Ct. Appeals (8th cir.) 1992. Atty., ptnr. Kirkland & Ellis, Chgo., 1977-86, Skadden, Arps, Slate, Meagher & Flom, Chgo., 1986—. Mem. Chgo. Club, City Club Chgo., Phi Beta Kappa. Republican. Protestant. Office: Skadden Arps Slate 333 W Wacker Dr Ste 2100 Chicago IL 60606-1288

SPRINGER, DOUGLAS HYDE, retired food company executive, lawyer; b. Englewood, N.J., Jan. 31, 1927; s. Arthur Hyde and Melicent Katherine (Messenger) S.; m. Virginia Helen Chouinard, Nov. 23, 1949; children: Susan Compton, Debora Lee. Student, Wesleyan U., 1944-45; AB, Yale U., 1947; LLB, Columbia U., 1950. Bar: N.Y. 1950. Atty. Port of N.Y. Authority, 1950-52; legal counsel Worthington Corp., Harrison, N.J., 1953-61, asst. sec., 1956-61; asst. counsel Campbell Soup Co., Camden, N.J., 1961-65, asst. sec., 1965, spl. assignments, 1966, dir. spl. studies, corp. planning, 1966-69, dir. corp. planning frozen foods, 1969-70, asst. treas., 1970-71, treas., 1971-73, v.p. fin. planning, 1973-75, v.p., controller, 1975-78, v.p., treas., 1978-88, v.p. investment mgmt., 1988-90; trustee Meml. Health Allience; mem. adv. bd. Pa. Liberty Mut. Ins. Co., 1971-88; mem. Eastern regional adv. bd. Arkwright-Boston Mfrs. Mut. Ins. Co., 1985-90; exec. sec. Gov.'s Interstate Adv. Com., 1966; asst. to mem. Pres.'s Commn. on Postal Orgn., 1967-68; spl. asst. to chmn South Jersey Port Corp., 1969-71; mem. N.J. Econ. Devel. Council, 1972-76; mem. adv. coun. Tax Found., 1980-89. Trustee Nat. Food Processors Assn. Retirement Plan and Trust Indenture Fund, 1976-89, Perkins Ctr. for Arts, 1979-88, Ind. Coll. Fund, N.J., 1982-88; mem. exec. bd., v.p. fin. Camden County coun. Boy Scouts Am., 1978-90; mem. Y's Men's Club, Moorestown, N.J., 1990—, v.p., 1992-94, pres., 1994-95; mem. found. bd. Family "Y" of Burlington County, 1995—. With USNR, 1944-46. Mem. Nat. Assn. Corp. Treas. (bd. dirs. 1982-88), Phila. Treas. Club, Internat. Bus. Forum (bd. dirs. 1980-88), Phi Nu Theta, Phi Delta Phi, N.J. Soc. Pa. (pres. 1992-93). Clubs: Yale (Phila., N.Y.C.); Nassau (Princeton, N.J.). Home: 735 Mill St Moorestown NJ 08057-1803

SPRINGER, FLOYD LADEAN, architect; b. Goodrich, N.D., Feb. 1, 1922; s. George Roy Springer and Louise Baumbach; m. Dorothy Mae Shepard (dec. Sept. 1995); children: Debra Louise, Tami June. Student, U. Denver, 1948-51; BS in Archtl. Engring., U. Colo., 1952; postgrad., U. Wash., 1953-54, U. Utah, Portland, Oreg., 1980. With Seattle Delta Investment Group, 1984—. Cpl. inf. U.S. Army, 1941-44, PTO. Decorated Silver Star. Presbyterian. Avocations: photography, landscaping, leaded art glass, oil painting, writing. Home and Office: 18548 60th Ave NE Seattle WA 98155-4453

SPRINGER, FRED EVERETT, federal agency administrator; b. Washington, June 30, 1945; s. Sidney and Janet L. (Bushlow) Kurland; m. Lola Weinberg Springer, Aug. 3, 1946; children: Eileen Gerri Frazier, Michelle Sherrie, Paul Louis. BSCE, U. Md., 1967; postgrad., George Washington U. Civil engr. Naval Facilities Engring. Command, Bur. of Stds., 1967-70, FPC, Washington, 1970-76; chief project mgmt. br. Divsn. of Lic. Projects, Office of Elec. PowerRegulation FPC/FERC, Washington, 1976-83; dep. dir. project mgmt. divsn. hydropower lic. Office of Elec. Power Regulation FERC, Washington, 1983-84; dir. divsn. project mgmt. FERC, Washington, 1984-87, dir. Office Hydropower Licensing, 1987—; tchr. specialty courses to numerous fed. and state agys.; mem. steering com. Hydrovision 94, 96; mem. exec., steering coms. Waterpower 97. Pres., v.p. Highland of Olney (Md.) Civic Assn.; v.p., treas. B'nai Shalom of Olney; coach Olney Boys and Girls Club. Mem. ASCE, Tau Beta Pi, Chi Epsilon. Democrat. Jewish. Office: OHL-FERC 888 First St NE Rm SA-01 Washington DC 20426

SPRINGER, GEORGE STEPHEN, mechanical engineering educator; b. Budapest, Hungary, Dec. 12, 1933; came to U.S., 1959; s. Joseph and Susan (Grausz) S.; m. Susan Martha Flory, Sept. 15, 1963; children: Elizabeth Anne, Mary Katherine. B in Engring., U. Sydney, Australia, 1959; M in Engring., Yale U., 1960, MSc in Engring., 1961, PhD, 1962. Registered profl. engr., Mass. Asst. prof. mech. engring. MIT, Cambridge, Mass., 1962-67; prof. mech. engring. U. Mich., Ann Arbor, 1967-83; Paul Pigott prof., chmn. dept. aeronautics and astronautics Stanford (Calif.) U., 1983—. Author: Erosion by Liquid Impact, 1975; co-author, co-editor 12 books; contbr. over 150 articles to scholarly and profl. jours. Recipient Pub. Svc.

Group Achievement award, NASA, 1988. Fellow AIAA (Engr. of Yr. 1995), ASME (Worcester Reed Warner medal 1994), Soc. Advancement Materials and Process Engring. (Delmonte award 1991); mem. Am. Phys. Soc., Soc. Automotive Engrs. (Ralph Teetor award 1978), Nat. Acad. Engring., Hungarian Nat. Acad. Sci. (fgn. mem.). Achievements include patent in field. Office: Stanford U Dept Aeronautics and Astronautics Stanford CA 94305

SPRINGER, JAMES VAN RODEN, lawyer; b. N.Y.C., July 9, 1934; s. Charles Meredith and Jeanne (Nehrbas) S.; m. Carol Murphy, Mar. 31, 1962; children: Stephen, Catherine. AB, Harvard U., 1955, LLB, 1961. Bar: N.Y. 1962, D.C. 1962, U.S. Ct. Appeals (D.C. cir.) 1963, U.S. Ct. Appeals (10th cir.) 1972, U.S. Ct. Appeals (2d cir.) 1973, U.S. Ct. Appeals (5th cir.) 1976, U.S. Ct. Appeals (6th and 7th cirs.) 1977, U.S. Ct. Appeals (11th cir.) 1981, U.S. Ct. Appeals (1st cir.) 1984, U.S. Ct. Appeals (4th cir.) 1986, U.S. Ct. Appeals (9th cir.) 1990, U.S. Ct. Appeals (fed. cir.) 1991, U.S. Supreme Ct. 1968. Law clk. to chief judge U.S. Ct. Appeals for 2d Cir., N.Y.C., 1961-62; assoc. Covington and Burling, Washington, 1962-67; asst. legal advisor U.S. Dept. State, Washington, 1967-68; dep. solicitor gen. U.S. Dept. Justice, Washington, 1968-71; ptnr. Dickstein, Shapiro and Morin, Washington, 1972-. Pres. Harvard Law Rev., 1960-61; contbr. articles to profl. jours. With U.S. Army, 1955-58, Korea. Mem. ABA, D.C. Bar. Democrat. Home: 3017 44th Pl NW Washington DC 20016 Office: Dickstein Shapiro & Morin LLP 2101 L St NW Washington DC 20037-1526

SPRINGER, JEFFREY R., bank officer; b. 1944. With Chemical Bank, N.Y., 1968-74, Md. Nat. Bank, 1974-85, Diversified Investments Assn., Balt., 1985-87; with Citizens Bancorp, Laurel, Md., 1987, now pres. Office: Citizens Bancorp 14401 Sweitzer Ln Laurel MD 20707-2922

SPRINGER, JOHN SHIPMAN, public relations executive; b. Rochester, N.Y., Apr. 25, 1916; s. Wilfred A. and Alice Jane (Grosjean) S.; m. June Alicia Reimer, June 3, 1953; children: Gary John, Alicia Ann, Cynthia Lynn. Student, U. Toronto, Ont., Can., 1935-37; Ph.B., Marquette U., 1939. Feature writer Rochester Democrat and Chronicle, 1940-41; head mag. publicity RKO Radio Pictures, N.Y.C., 1946-57, 20th Century-Fox Films, N.Y.C., 1957-59; v.p. Arthur Jacobs, Pub. Relations, 1959-60; ptnr. Jacobs & Springer (pub. relations), 1960-62; pres. John Springer Assos., Inc., N.Y.C., Los Angeles, London, Paris and Rome, 1964—. Author: All Talking! All Singing! All Dancing!, 1966, The Fondas, 1970, They Had Faces Then, 1975, Forgotten Films to Remember, 1980, They Sang, They Danced, They Romanced, 1991; contbr. to: Close Ups, Conversations with Joan Crawford; author mag. articles and newspaper features.; creator/producer "Film Segments" Night of 100 Stars; producer/host stage-screen shows starring Bette Davis, Myrna Loy, Sylvia Sidney, Joan Crawford, Rosalind Russell, Debbie Reynolds, Joanne Woodward, Lana Turner, Henry Fonda, others in, N.Y.C., U.S. tour, Australia, Gt. Britain; writer/producer Ann. Am. Mus. Moving Image ann. tributes to Sidney Lumet, Elia Kazan, James Stewart, Sidney Poitier, Mike Nichols, Robert DeNiro, Al Pacino; producer, dir. three films/live events at 92d St. Y, New York, with in person guest stars including Ginger Rogers, Liv Ullmann, Tony Randall, Sylvia Sidney, Van Johnson, Geraldine Fitzgerald, Farley Granger, Betty Comden, Adolph Green, etc., 1991. Bd. dirs. Actors Studio, Nat. Theatre of Deaf. With USAAF, 1942-45. Recipient Byline award Coll. Journalism, 1970, By-line award Marquette U., 1970. Mem. Players Club (honored with Pipe Night 1995). Democrat. Roman Catholic. Home and Office: 130 E 67th St New York NY 10021-6136

SPRINGER, MARLENE, university administrator, educator; b. Murfreesboro, Tenn., Nov. 16, 1937; d. Foster V. and Josephine Jones; children: Ann Springer, Rebecca Springer. BA in English & Bus. Adminstrn., Centre Coll., 1959; MA in Am. Lit., Ind. U., 1963, PhD in English Lit., 1969. Chair English dept. U. Mo., Kansas City, 1980-81, acting assoc. dean grad. sch., 1982; Am. Coun. of Edn. Adminstrn. fellow U. Kans., Laurence, 1982-83; dean of grad. sch. U. Mo., Kansas City, 1983-84, assoc. vice chancellor for acad. affairs & grad. studies, 1985-89; vice chancellor for acad. affairs East Carolina U., Greenville, N.C., 1989-94; pres. CUNY Coll. S.I., 1994—. Author: What Manner of Woman: Essays, 1977, Thomas Hardy's Use of Allusion, 1983, Plains Woman: The Diary of Martha Farnsworth, 1986 (Choice award 1986), Ethan Frome: A Nightmare of Need, 1993. Huntington Libr. fellow, 1988. Mem. Am. Coun. on Edn. (profl. devel. com. 1991—, invited participant Nat. Forum 1984), Am. Assn. State Colls. & Univs. (exec. com. 1992-94), Acad. Leadership Acad. (exec. com. 1992-94), Assn. Tchr. Educators (chair 1992), Coun. Grad. Schs. (chair 1986-88). Office: Coll Staten Island 2800 Victory Blvd Staten Island NY 10314-6600

SPRINGER, MICHAEL LOUIS, federal agency administrator; b. Sarasota, Fla., Jan. 28, 1938; s. Stewart and Vergie (Fayard) S.; m. Afife Camila Chamas, Aug. 31, 1963; children: Elizabeth Karime, Michele Renee, John David. BA, George Washington U., 1964; MPA, The Am. U., 1978. With fin. mgmt. office Nat. Libr. Medicine, Bethesda, Md., 1969-71; dep. dir. mgmt. and orgn. div. U.S. EPA, Washington, 1971-73, dir. mgmt. info. and data systems div., 1973-75; sr. mgmt. assoc. mgmt. improvement and evaluation U.S. Office Mgmt. and Budget, Washington, 1977-82; dep. dir. Office Adminstrn. U.S. NRC, Washington, 1982-86; staff dir. Office Consolidation, Washington, 1987-88; dir. Office Consolidation U.S. Nuclear Regulatory Commn., Washington, 1988-94, dir. divsn. facilities and property mgmt., 1994—; bd. dirs. Transp. Action Partnership North Bethesda and Rockville, Md., 1988—. Mem. Citizens Adv. Com. for North Bethesda Master Plan, Montgomery County, 1990-91. Roman Catholic. Office: Nuclear Regulatory Commn Mail Stop T-7D59 Washington DC 20555

SPRINGER, PAUL DAVID, lawyer, motion picture company executive; b. N.Y.C., Apr. 27, 1942; s. William W. and Alma (Markowitz) S.; m. Mariann Frankfurt, Aug. 16, 1964; children: Robert, William. BA, U. Bridgeport, 1963; JD, Bklyn. Law Sch., 1967. Bar: N.Y. 1968, U.S. Dist. Ct. (so. and ea. dists.) N.Y. 1968, U.S. Ct. Appeals (2d cir.) 1970, U.S. Supreme Ct. 1973, Calif. 1989. Assoc. Johnson & Tannenbaum, N.Y.C., 1968-70; assoc. counsel Columbia Pictures, N.Y.C., 1970; assoc. counsel Paramount Pictures, N.Y.C., 1970-79, v.p., theatrical distbn. counsel, 1979-85, sr. v.p., chief resident counsel East Coast, 1985-87; sr. v.p., asst. gen. counsel Paramount Pictures, L.A., 1987—; Bar: N.Y. 1968, U.S. Dist. Ct. (so. and ea. dists.) N.Y. 1968, U.S. Ct. Appeals (2d cir.) 1970, U.S. Supreme Ct. 1973, Calif. 1989. Trustee West Cunningham Park Civic Assn., Fresh Meadows, N.Y., 1978—. Mem. ABA, Assn. of Bar of City of N.Y., L.A. Copyright Soc., Acad. Motion Picture Arts and Scis., Motion Picture Pioneers.

SPRINGER, ROBERT DALE, retired air force officer, consultant, lecturer; b. Millheim, Pa., Jan. 17, 1933; s. Simon Peter and Ruth Olive (McCool) S.; m. Bonnie Joan Brubaker, Aug. 30, 1953; children: Robert Dale Jr., Debra K. Springer Miller, Curtis A., Michele L. Demmy, Tania. BA in Social Sci., George Washington U., 1964, MS in Internat. Affairs, 1969. Cert. command pilot. Commd. 2d lt. U.S. Air Force; advanced through grades to lt. gen.; comdr. 435th Tactical Airlift Wing, Rhein-Main Air Base, Federal Republic Germany, 1978-80, 322d Airlift Div, Ramstein Air Base, Federal Republic Germany, 1980-81, Air Force Manpower and Personnel Ctr., Randolph AFB, Tex., 1982-84, 21 A.F., McGuire AFB, N.J., 1984-85; insp. gen. USAF, Washington, 1985-87; with DCS-personnel Mil. Airlift Command, Scott AFB, Ill., 1981-82, vice comdr.-in-chief, 1987-88; ret., 1988; media cons., lectr., 1989—; dir. Air Force Commissary Svc., San Antonio, 1982-84, Army-Air Force Exch. Svc., Dallas, 1982-84; chmn. bd. dirs. Air Force Welfare Bd., San Antonio, 1982-84. Exec. dir Air Force Meml. Found., 1992—; trustee Aerospace Edn. Found., 1992-94. Mem. Air Force Assn. (Presdl. Citation 1984), Airlift-Tanker Assn. (life mem., sr. v.p. 1989-94), Arnold Air Soc. (exec. dir. 1990-93, trustee 1993—), Ret. Officers Assn. (life), Daedalians (life). Lutheran. Lodge: Masons. Avocations: tennis; golf; reading.

SPRINGER, STANLEY G., lawyer; b. Newburgh, N.Y., Sept. 27, 1927; s. Allen Paul and Mabel (Thorn) S.; m. Roberta Gietz, Sept. 14, 1947 (div. 1975); children—Valerie, Beverly, Jeffrey, Gregory, Kimberly, Lindsay; m. Vallie Strong, July 2, 1979 (dec. 1987). B.A., Union Coll., 1949; LL.D. with distinction (1st Fraser scholar), Cornell U., 1953. Bar: Wis. 1953, Ill. 1958, Tex. 1970, Calif. 1988. Mem. firm Whyte, Hirschboeck, Minahan, Harding & Harland, Milw., 1953-58; atty. Libby, McNeill & Libby, Chgo., 1958-63; gen. counsel, v.p. J.I. Case Co., Racine, Wis., 1963-69; v.p., gen. counsel, dir. Mich. Gen. Corp., Dallas, 1969-83; pvt. practice Dallas, 1983-88; gen. counsel George Realty Co., Inc. and affiliated cos., San Gabriel, Calif., 1988-90; dir. J.I. Case Credit Corp., 1963-69, Colt Mfg. Co., Inc., 1967-69. Chmn. Racine Heart Fund campaign, 1964; commr. Racine Redevel. Authority, 1965-69; bd. dirs., sec., pres. Prestonwood Country Club Condominium Assn., 1981-84; dir. and legal advisor Friends of the Point Vicente Interpretive Ctr., Inc., Rancho Palos Verdes, Calif., 1988-90, also docent at ctr. Served with AC, USNR, 1945-47. Recipient 1st prize WPB Carey Exbn., Cornell U., 1953. Mem. ABA, Wis. Bar Assn., Tex. Bar Assn., Dallas Bar Assn., Calif. Bar Assn., Lawyer-Pilots Bar Assn., Order of Coif, Phi Delta Phi, Phi Kappa Phi. Home: 3721 Spring Valley Rd Apt 202 Dallas TX 75244-3311

SPRINGFIELD, JAMES FRANCIS, retired lawyer, banker; b. Memphis, Nov. 5, 1929; s. C.L. and Mildred (White) S.; m. Shirley Burdick, June 1, 1951 (div.); children: Sidney, Susan, James Francis; m. Nancy Hardwick Ragan, Feb. 8, 1987 (dec. Jan. 1988); m. Donna Thomas Moore, Feb. 22, 1989. BA with distinction in econs., Southwestern at Memphis (now Rhodes Coll.), 1951; LLB, U. Memphis, 1960. Bar: Tenn. 1960. With Union Planters Nat. Bank, Memphis, 1951-94; exec. v.p., sr. trust officer, head trust dept. Union Planters Nat. Bank, 1968-85, gen. counsel, sec. bd., 1985-94; sec. bd., exec. v.p., gen. counsel Union Planters Corp., 1985-94; ret., 1994. Mem. president's coun. Rhodes Coll., Memphis, chmn., 1991-92, internat. chmn. ann. fund, 1995-96; chmn. bd. trustees So. Coll. Optometry, 1978-80; trustee Plough Found., Memphis Conf. United Meth. Ch. Found., 1978-85, U. Tenn. Med. Units Found., 1975-82, MidSouth Pub. Comm. Found., 1985-87; chmn. fin. com. Hutchinson Sch.; sec. bd. trustees Vision Edn. Found., 1977-78; bd. regents Tenn. Trust Sch., chmn., 1977; mem. president's adv. coun. Lambuth Coll., 1982-85; mem. exec. bd. Chickasaw coun. Boy Scouts Am., 1983-87; bd. visitors Memphis State U. Cecil C. Humphreys Sch. Law, treas. Balmoral Civic Club, 1967-68. Lt. (j.g.) USNR, 1951-54. Mem. Tenn. Bar Assn. (chmn. interprofl. rels. com. 1976), Memphis and Shelby County Bar assn. (chmn. moral fitness com. 1972), Tenn. Bankers Assn. (chmn. legis.com. trust div. 1976-77, treas. 1972-73, pres. 1976-77, bd. dirs. 1976-77), Bank Adminstrn. Inst. (chmn. trust commn. 1981-82), Estate Planning Coun. Memphis (pres. 1973-74), Sigma Nu (div. comdr. 1967-68, treas., bd. dirs. House Corp. 1966-81), Omicron Delta Kappa (Rhodes Coll. chpt.). Republican. Home: 8334 Heatherglen Dr Memphis TN 38138-6209

SPRINGGATE, CLARK FRANKLIN, physician, researcher; b. Champaign, Ill., Nov. 14, 1946; s. William F. and Marjorie E. (Fitch) S.; children from a previous marriage: Elizabeth, Benjamin; m. Diane Louise Rotnem, Oct. 19, 1991. AB in Biology, Boston U., 1967; PhD in Biochemistry, Boston Coll., 1972; MD, U. Miami, 1983. Diplomate Nat. Bd. Med. Examiners, Am. Bd. Pathology. Med. dir. Richardson Vicks Pharm., Shelton, Conn., 1989-91; v.p., med. dir. TSI Biomed. Rsch. Group, Medford, Mass., 1992-94; v.p. Scicor, Indpls., 1988-89; pres. Springgate Biotech, Guilford, Conn., 1991—, Biotech Regular Cons., Guilford, 1994—. Contbr. articles to jours. Heart Transplant, Am. Soc. Hist. Immunogey. Bd. dirs. AIDS Protect New Haven, 1994-95; funding bd. Leap Youth Program, New Haven, 1991-92. Leukemia Soc. Am. fellow, 1972-74. Mem. AAAS, ACP Execs., Conn. State Med. Soc. Achievements include research in immune monitoring of heart transplant patients to prevent rejection and infection, diagnostic flow cytometry-oncology. Home: 1320 Little Meadow Guilford CT 06437

SPRINGSTEEN, BRUCE, singer, songwriter, guitarist; b. Freehold, N.J., Sept. 23, 1949; s. Douglas and Adele S.; m. Julianne Phillips, May 13, 1985 (div. 1988); m. Patti Scialfa; children: Evan James, Jessica Rae. Attended community coll. Performed in N.Y. and N.J. nightclubs; signed with Columbia Records in 1972; first album Greetings from Asbury Park, New Jersey, 1973; nationwide concert tours with The E-Street Band, 1974-92; albums include The Wild, The Innocent and the E-Street Shuffle, 1974, Born to Run, 1975 (Gold Record award), Darkness on the Edge of Town, 1978, The River, 1980, Nebraska, 1982, Born in the U.S.A., 1984 (Best Pop/Rock Album of Yr., Downbeat Readers Poll 1984), Bruce Springsteen and the E-Street Band Live/1975-1985, 1986, Tunnel of Love, 1987, Chimes of Freedom, 1988, Human Touch, 1992, Lucky Town, 1992, Bruce Springsteen Greatest Hits, 1995. The Ghost of Tom Joad, 1995; songs composed include Thunder Road, Glory Days, Rosalita, Pink Cadillac, Jersey Girl, Hungry Heart, Streets of Philadelphia (Golden Globe award for Best Original Song in a Film, 1994, Acad. award for best original song in a film 1994, MTV Best Video from a Film award 1994), Dead Man Walking (Acad. award nominee for best original song in a film 1996); appears on Patti Scialfa's album, Rumble Doll, 1993. Recipient Grammy award for best male rock vocalist, 1984, 87, 94. Office: care Premier Talent Agy 3 E 54th St New York NY 10022-3108*

SPRINGSTEEN, DAVID FOLGER, financial consultant; b. N.Y.C., Mar. 29, 1932; s. Nelson J. and Gwendolyn (Folger) S.; BS, MIT, 1954; MBA, Harvard U., 1958; m. Nancy Neller, Oct. 22, 1955; children: Susan S. Jamieson, Page S. Vanatta. Aero. rsch. scientist Lewis Flight Propulsion Lab. NASA, Cleve., 1955-57; with Chase Manhattan Bank, N.Y.C., 1958-71, asst. treas., 1961-64, 2d v.p., 1964-68, v.p. Energy div., 1969-71; v.p. corp. fin. Stone & Webster Securities Corp., 1971-74; v.p. corp. fin. E.F. Huttons & Co., Inc., N.Y.C., 1974-78; fin. cons., corp. fin. David F. Springsteen Co., Greenwich, Conn., 1978—; Dir. Eastman Community Assn., Delta Cooling Towers, Inc. Served to lt. USAF, 1955-57. Mem. Holland Soc. Home: PO Box 248 Lakeview Pl Grantham NH 03753 Office: PO Box 248 Grantham NH 03753-0248

SPRINKEL, BERYL WAYNE, economist, consultant; b. Richmond, Mo., Nov. 20, 1923; s. Clarence and Emma (Schooley) S.; m. Lory Kiefer, Aug. 29, 1993; children: Gary L., Kevin G. Student, N.W. Mo. State U., 1941-43, U. Oreg., 1943-44; BS, U. Mo., 1947; MBA, U. Chgo., 1948, PhD, 1952; LHD (hon.), DePaul U., 1975; LLD (hon.), St. Michael's Coll., 1981, U. Mo., 1985, U. Rochester, 1985, Govs. State U., 1988, U. Nebr., 1988; Doctor of Pub. Adminstrn., Marion Coll., 1988. Instr. econs. and fin. U. Mo., Columbia, 1948-49, U. Chgo., 1950-52; with Harris Trust & Savs. Bank, Chgo., 1952-81, v.p., economist, 1960-68, dir. rsch., 1963-69, sr. v.p., 1968-74, economist, 1968-81, exec. v.p., 1974-81; undersec. monetary affairs Dept. Treasury, Washington, 1981-85; chmn. Coun. Econ. Advisers, The White House, Washington, 1985-89, mem. Pres.'s Cabinet, 1987-89; pvt. cons. economist, 1989—; cons. Fed. Res. Bd., 1955-59, Bur. of Census, 1962-70, Joint Econ. Com. U.S. Congress, 1958, 62, 67, 71, Ho. of Reps. Banking and Currency Com., 1963, Senate Banking Com., 1975; econ. adv. bd. to sec. commerce, 1967-69; bd. economists Time mag., 1968-80; bd. dirs. US Life Corp., Duff and Phelps Utilities Income Fund, Inc. Author: Money and Stock Prices, 1964, Money and Markets-A Monetarist View, 1971; co-author: Winning with Money, 1977;. Pres. Homewood-Flossmoor (Ill.) Community High Sch., 1959-60. With AUS, 1943-45. Recipient Hamilton Bolton award Fin. Analysts Assn., 1968, Alexander Hamilton award U.S. Treasury, 1985. Fellow Nat. Assn. Bus. Economists; mem. Am. Econ. Assn., Nat. Assn. Bus. Economists, Beta Gamma Sigma. Home: 20140 Saint Andrews Dr Olympia Fields IL 60461-1169

SPRINSON, DAVID BENJAMIN, biochemistry educator; b. Raigorod, Ukraine, Apr. 5, 1910; came to U.S., 1921; s. Moses and Rebecca (Skolnick) S.; m. Helen Evans Yeargain, Oct. 8, 1943; children: Joan, Mary, John. BS, CCNY, 1931; MS, NYU, 1936; PhD, Columbia U., 1946, DSc (honoris causa), 1991. Rsch. assoc. Columbia U., N.Y.C., 1946-51, asst. prof. biochemistry, 1951-54, assoc. prof., 1954-58, prof., 1958-78, prof. biochemistry and molecular biology emeritus, 1978—; prof. biochemistry and molecular biology emeritus St. Luke's/Roosevelt Hosp. Ctr., N.Y.C., 1979—; career investigator Am. Heart Assn., 1958-75. Contbr. articles to sci. jours. Grantee NIH, NSF, Am. Heart Assn., Am. Cancer Soc., 1950-91; recipient Disting. Svc. award Coll. Physicians and Surgeons, 1995. Mem. NAS, AAAS, Am. Soc. for Biochemistry and Molecular Biology. Office: St Luke's/Roosevelt Hosp Ctr 1000 10th Ave New York NY 10019-1056

SPRINTHALL, NORMAN ARTHUR, psychology educator; b. Attleboro, Mass., Aug. 19, 1931; s. William Archie and Edith Jarvis (Clark) S.; m. Lois May Thies; children: Douglas, Jane, Carolyn. AB magna cum laude, Brown U., 1954, MA, 1959; EdD, Harvard U., 1963. Dir. fin. aid Brown U., 1955-60; asst. prof., then asso. prof. psychology, program chmn. counseling Harvard U., 1963-72; mem. faculty U. Minn., Mpls., 1972-82; prof. ednl. psychology U. Minn., 1973-82, program chmn. counseling, 1972-74; prof., head counselor edn. program N.C. State U., Raleigh, 1982-87, prof., counselor, educator, 1987-95, prof. emeritus; cons. Bur. Educational Handicapped; co-dir. Ethical Reasoning Project in Pub. Adminstrn., U.S. and Poland, 1993—. Author: Educational Psychology: Readings, 1969, Guidance for Human Growth, 1971, Educational Psychology: A Developmental Approach, 6th edit., 1994, Value Development as the Aim of Education, 2d edit., 1981, Adolescent Psychology: A Developmental View, 1984, 2d rev. edit., 1988, 3d edit., 1995; co-author: Stewart-Sprinthall Management Survey (SSMS) Ethics and Public Administration; mem. editorial bd. profl. jours. Bd. dirs. Josephson Inst. Advancement of Ethics, 1986-90, mem. bd. advisors Character Counts Coalition, 1994—. Fellow APA; mem. ACA, Am. Edn. Rsch. Assn., Phi Beta Kappa.

SPRIZZO, JOHN EMILIO, federal judge; b. Bklyn., Dec. 23, 1934; s. Vincent James and Esther Nancy (Filosa) S.; children—Ann Esther, Johna Emily Sprizzo Bolka, Matthew John. BA summa cum laude, St. John's U., Jamaica, N.Y., 1956; LLB summa cum laude, St. John's U., 1959. Bar: N.Y. 1960. Atty. U.S. Dept. Justice, 1959-63; asst. U.S. atty. so. dist. N.Y. Dept. Justice, N.Y.C., 1963-68, chief appellate atty., 1965-66, asst. chief criminal div., 1966-68; assoc. prof. Fordham U. Law Sch., N.Y.C., 1968-72; ptnr. Curtis, Mallet-Prevost, N.Y.C., 1972-81; dist. judge U.S. Dist. Ct. (so. dist.) N.Y., N.Y.C., 1981—; cons. Nat. Com. for Reform of Criminal Laws, N.Y.C., 1971-72; mem. Knapp Commn., 1971-72; assoc. atty. Com. of Ct. on Judiciary, N.Y.C., 1971-72. Co-contbr. articles to profl. law revs. Mem. ABA, D.C. Bar Assn., Assn. of Bar of City of N.Y. Office: US Dist Ct US Courthouse Foley Sq New York NY 10007-1501

SPROAT, JOHN GERALD, historian; b. L.A., Apr. 1, 1921; s. John Gerald and Grace (Elwell) Drummond S.; m. Ruth Christensen, Mar. 18, 1967; 1 child by previous marriage, Barbara. B.A., San Jose State Coll., 1950; M.A., U. Calif.-Berkeley, 1952, Ph.D., 1959. Instr. Mich. State U., 1956-57; asst. prof. Williams Coll., 1957-63; prof. Lake Forest Coll., Ill., 1963-74; prof. history U. S.C., Columbia, 1974-92, chmn. dept., 1974-83; dist. prof. emeritus, 1992—; sr. fellow Inst. for So. Studies, 1992—; Fulbright prof. Hamburg U., Fed. Republic Germany, 1961-62; vis. fellow Cambridge U., Eng., 1970; vis. prof. U. Calif.-Berkeley, 1972; Fulbright prof. U. Munich, Fed. Republic Germany, 1982, Indonesia, 1993-94; Am. participant lectr. USIA, India, Pakistan, 1987; mem. S.C. Commn. Archives and History, 1974-83, chmn., 1979-83; mem. S.C. Bd. Rev. Hist. Places, 1974-86, chmn., 1978-83; del. Am. Council Learned Socs. Author: The Best Men: Liberal Reformers in the Gilded Age, 1988; (with others) The Shaping of America, 1972, Making Change: South Carolina Banking in the 20th Century, 1990; contbr. chpts. to books; exec. producer A Bond of Iron, S.C. ETV, 1979; gen. editor So. Classics Series. Past pres., trustee Columbia Mus. Art; v.p. Historic Columbia Found., 1995—. Served with USAAF, 1941-45. NEH grantee, 1976, 77, 79, 85; Shell Found. grantee, 1967, 70, 73; Lilly Endowment grantee, 1966-67. Mem. Am. Hist. Assn., Orgn. Am. Historians, So. Hist. Assn. Episcopalian. Clubs: Capital City (Columbia). Home: 1686 Woodlake Dr Columbia SC 29206-4647 Office: U SC Inst For So Studies Columbia SC 29208

SPROGER, CHARLES EDMUND, lawyer; b. Chgo., Feb. 18, 1933; s. William and Minnette (Weiss) S. BA (David Himmelblau scholar), Northwestern U., 1954, JD, 1957. Bar: Ill. 1957. Practiced in Chgo., 1958—; assoc. Ehrlich & Cohn, 1958-63, Ehrlich, Bundesen, Friedman & Ross, 1963-72; partner Ehrlich, Bundesen, Broecker & Sproger, 1972-77; pvt. practice, 1977—; mem. adv. com. curriculum Ill. Inst. Continuing Legal Edn., Chgo., 1976—; v.p. Mediation Coun. of Ill., 1986-87; arbitration panelist for Cir. Ct. Cook County, 1990—. Editor: Family Lawyer, 1962-63; contbr. articles to legal publs. Mediator Pastoral Psychotherapy Inst., 1982-86. Fellow Am. Acad. Matrimonial Lawyers (bd. examiners 1972-86, chmn. Law Day U.S.A. 1975); mem. ABA, Ill. Bar Assn. (chmn. coun. family law 1970-71), Chgo. Bar Assn. (matrimonial law com. 1958—), Am. Arbitration Assn. (divorce mediation com. 1983—), Decalogue Soc., U. Mich. Club Chgo. (pres. 1988-89), Phi Alpha Delta. Office: 155 N Michigan Ave Chicago IL 60601-7511

SPROLE, FRANK ARNOTT, retired pharmaceutical company executive, lawyer; b. Bklyn., Sept. 13, 1918; s. Frank Newland and Eleanor Arnott (Greenberg) S.; m. Sarah Louise Knapp, Sept. 23, 1944; children—Wendy Sprole Bangs, Frank J., Anne Sprole Mauk, Jonathan K., Sarah Sprole Obregon. B.A., Yale U., 1942; LL.B., Columbia U., 1949. Bar: N.Y. 1949. Assoc. firm Winthrop Stimson, Putnam & Roberts, N.Y.C., 1949-50; atty. Bristol-Myers Co., N.Y.C., 1950-52, asst. sec., 1952-55, sec., 1955-67, v.p., 1965-73, sr. v.p., 1973-77, vice chmn. bd., 1977-84; bd. dirs., officer Proprietary Assn., Washington, 1978-84; dir., officer Knapp Fund, N.Y.C., 1960-93. Pres. bd. trustees Hotchkiss Sch., Lakeville, Conn., 1980-85; trustee Internat. Inst. Rural Reconstrn., N.Y.C., and Manila, 1983-87. Served to lt. comdr. USNR, 1942-45, PTO. Mem. Assn. of Bar of City of N.Y., Yale Club of N.Y.C., Wee Burn Country Club, Bohemian Club, Mid Ocean Club, John's Island Club, Riomar Country Club. Republican. Episcopalian. Avocation: golf. Home: 394 Mansfield Ave Darien CT 06820-2112

SPROTT, DAVID ARTHUR, statistics and psychology educator; b. Toronto, Ont., Can., May 31, 1930; s. Arthur Frederick and Dorothy (Barry) S.; m. Muriel Doris Vogel; children: Anne, Jane. BA, U. Toronto, 1952, MA, 1953, PhD, 1955. Rsch. asst. Galton Lab., London, 1955-56; biogeneticist, clin. tchr. dept. psychiatry U. Toronto, 1956-58; assoc. prof. stats. U. Waterloo, Ont., 1958-61, prof., 1961—, prof. psychology, 1964—, dean math., 1966-72, chmn. dept. stats., 1966-75; prof. Centro de Investigacion en Matematicas, Guanajuato, Mex., 1993—; vis. prof. various univs. and colls. Contbr. numerous articles to profl. jours. Recipient Gold medal Statis. Soc. Can., 1988. Fellow Am. Statis. Assn., Inst. Math. Stats., Royal Soc. Can., Royal Photog. Soc.; mem. Internat. Statis. Inst., Statis. Soc. Can. (hon.). Avocations: photography, wine making. Office: U Waterloo Math Faculty, Waterloo, ON Canada N2L 3G1

SPROTT, JOHN T., ambassador; b. Phoenix, Apr. 6, 1933; m. Jeanne S.; 5 children. B.A., Northern Ariz. Univ.; Ph.D., Univ. of Colorado. Econ. instructor Univ. of Colorado, 1960-61; asst. econ. prof. Duquesne Univ., Penn., 1962-65; chmn., Econ. & Comml. Study Prog. Frn. Svc. Inst., 1966-67; sr. econ. adviser U.S. Econ. Mission to Chile, 1968-71; dep. coord., then coord. Econ. & Comml. Studies div. Fgn. Svc. Inst., 1971-75, dean, Sch. of Profl.Studies, 1975-81, dep. dir., 1981-93; U.S. amb. to Swaziland Mbabane, 1993—; lect. Johns Hopkins Univ., 1967-68. with U.S. Navy 1951-55. Mem. Sr. Exec. Svc. Assn., Aircraft Owners and Pilots Assn. Office: Am Embassy Mbabane Dept State Washington DC 20521

SPROTT, RICHARD LAWRENCE, government official, researcher; b. Tampa, Fla., Aug. 9, 1940; s. Joseph Albert and Marie Marguerite (Goaper) S.; m. Margaret Ann Weidel, June 19, 1965; children—Lynn Marie, Deborah Ann. Student, Franklin and Marshall Coll., 1958-60; B.A., U. N.C., 1962, M.A. in Psychology, 1964, Ph.D. in Psychology, 1965. Asst. prof. Oakland U., Rochester, Mich., 1967-69; assoc. staff scientist Jackson Lab., Bar Barbor, Maine, 1969-71, staff scientist, 1971-80; health scientist adminstr. Div. Research Resources, NIH, Bethesda, Md., 1980-81; br. chief Nat. Inst. on Aging, Bethesda, 1981-84, assoc. dir., 1984—. Editor: Hormonal Correlates of Behavior, 1975, Age, Learning Ability and Intelligence, 1980; mem. editorial bd. Exptl. Aging Research jour., 1978—; contbr. articles to profl. jours. Mem. Bar Harbor Town Council, 1975-79, chmn., 1978-79; mem. bd. appeals Town of Bar Harbor, 1972-75, mem. warrant com., 1972-75. NIH fellow, 1965-67; NIH grantee, 1969-79. Fellow Am. Psychol. Assn.; mem. Behavior Genetics Assn. (membership chmn. 1979). Home: 11514 Regency Dr Potomac MD 20854-3733 Office: Nat Inst on Aging 7201 Wisconsin Ave Rm 2c231 Bethesda MD 20814-4810

SPROUL, JOAN HEENEY, elementary school educator; b. Johnstown, Pa., July 17, 1932; d. James L. and Grace M. (Dunn) Heeney; m. Robert Sproul, July 31, 1957; 1 child, Mary Claire. BS, Clarion U., 1954; MA, George Wash. U., 1963; postgrad., U. Va., 1966-88. Cert. tchr., Va. Kindergarten tchr. Jefferson Sch., Warren, Pa., 1954-55; primary grades tchr. Alexandria (Va.) Pub. Schs., 1955-64; elem. tchr. Fairfax County Schs., Springfield, Va., 1965—; math. lead tchr. West Springfield (Va.) Sch., 1987—. Contbr. (with others) Virginia History, 1988. Advisor Springfield Young Organists Assn., 1971-83; mem. Fairfax County Dem. Com., 1988-94,

West Springfield Civic Assn., 1965—. Grantee Impact II, 1985-86. Mem. NEA, Nat. Fedn. Bus. and Profl. Women (pres., dir., dist. VIII 1984—, Woman of Yr. 1985, 88), Delta Kappa Gamma (2d v.p. Va. chpt. 1963—), Phi Delta Kappa. Episcopalian. Avocations: reading, music, gardening, fashion design. Home: 8005 Greeley Blvd West Springfield VA 22152-3036 Office: West Springfield Elem Sch 6802 Deland Dr Springfield VA 22152-3009

SPROUL, JOHN ALLAN, retired public utility executive; b. Oakland, Calif., Mar. 28, 1924; s. Robert Gordon and Ida Amelia (Wittschen) S.; m. Marjorie Ann Hauck, June 20, 1945; children: John Allan, Malcolm J., Richard O., Catherine E. A.B., U. Calif., Berkeley, 1947, LL.B., 1949. Bar: Calif. 1950. Atty. Pacific Gas & Electric Co., San Francisco, 1949-52, 56-62, sr. atty., 1962-70, asst. gen. counsel, 1970-71, v.p. gas supply, 1971-76, sr. v.p., 1976-77, exec. v.p., 1977-89; gen. counsel Pacific Gas Transmission Co., 1970-73, v.p., 1973-79, chmn. bd., 1979-89, also bd. dirs.; atty. Johnson & Stanton, San Francisco, 1952-56; bd. dirs. Oreg. Steel Mills, Inc. Bd. dirs. Hastings Coll. of Law. Served to 1st lt. USAAF, 1943-46. Mem. Calif. Bar Assn. (inactive), Pacific Coast Gas Assn., World Trade Club, Pacific-Union Club, Orinda Country Club. Home: 8413 Buckingham Dr El Cerrito CA 94530-2531 Office: Pacific Gas and Electric Co Mail Code H17F PO Box 770000 San Francisco CA 94177

SPROULE, BETTY ANN, computer industry strategic planning manager; b. Evanston, Ill., Dec. 30, 1948; d. Harold Fletcher and Lois (Reno) Mathis; m. J. Michael Sproule, Mar. 3, 1973; children: John Harold, Kevin William. BS, Ohio State U., 1969, MS, 1970, PhD, 1972. Mem. tech. staff Bell Telephone Labs., Columbus, Ohio, 1973-74; asst. prof. U. Tex., Odessa, 1974-77; analyst bus. systems Maj. Appliance Bus. div. GE, Louisville, 1977-78; dir. forecasting and analysis Brown and Williamson Tobacco, Louisville, 1978-86; strategic planning mgr. Hewlett-Packard Co., Santa Clara, Calif., 1986—. Contbr. articles to profl. jours.; patentee in field. Sr. mem. IEEE, Soc. Women Engrs. Home: 4135 Briarwood Way Palo Alto CA 94306-4610 Office: Hewlett-Packard Co 5301 Stevens Creek Blvd Santa Clara CA 95052

SPROULL, ROBERT LAMB, retired university president, physicist; b. Lacon, Ill., Aug. 16, 1918; s. John Steele and Chloe Velma (Lamb) S.; m. Mary Louise Knickerbocker, June 27, 1942; children: Robert F., Nancy M. AB, Cornell U., 1940, PhD, 1943; LLD (hon.), Nazareth Coll., 1983. Research physicist RCA labs., 1943-46; faculty Cornell U., 1946-63, 65-68, prof. physics, 1956-63, dir. lab. atomic and solid state physics, 1959-60, dir. materials sci. center, 1960-63, v.p. for acad. affairs, 1965-68; dir. Advanced Research Projects Agy., Dept. Def., Washington, 1963-65; v.p., provost U. Rochester, N.Y., 1968-70; pres. U. Rochester, 1970-84, pres. emeritus, 1984—; prin. physicist Oak Ridge Nat. Lab., 1952; physicist European Rsch. Assoc., Brussels, 1958-59; lectr. NATO, 1958-59; past bd. dirs., John Wiley & Sons, Charles River Labs., United Technols. Corp., Xerox Corp., Bausch & Lomb; mem. sci. adv. com. GM Corp., 1971-80, chmn., 1973-80; mem. Def. Sci. Bd., 1966-70, chmn., 1968-70; mem. Naval Rsch. Adv. Com., 1974-76, Sloan Commn. Higher Edn., 1977-79, N.Y. Regents Commn. Higher Edn., 1992-93. Author: Modern Physics, 1956; Editor: Jour. Applied Physics, 1954-57. Trustee Deep Springs Coll., 1967-75, 83-87, Cornell U., 1972-77. Ctr. for Advanced Study in Behavioral Scis. fellow, 1973; Meritorious Civilian Svc. medal Sec. of Def., 1970. Fellow Am. Acad. Arts and Scis.; mem. Telluride Assn. (pres. 1945-47), Inst. of Def. Analysis (trustee 1984-92). Home: 16910 Bay St Jupiter FL 33477-1206 Office: U Rochester Off of Pres Rochester NY 14627

SPROUSE, CHERYL LYNNE, principal; b. Lynchburg, Va., May 29, 1951; d. Elwood Gleason and Essie Ellen (Campbell) S. AS in pre-teaching, Ctrl. Va. C.C., 1971; BS, Radford Coll., 1973; MS, Radford U., 1978. Cert. tchr. Va. 5th and 7th grade tchr. Amherst (Va.) County Pub. Schs., 1973-78; asst. prin., 4th and 5th grade tchr. Amherst Elem. Sch., 1978-79, asst. prin., 1979-80, prin., 1989—; asst. prin. Amelon Elem. Sch., Madison Heights, Va., 1979-80, Monelison Jr. High Sch., Madison Heights, 1980-89; prin. Amherst (Va.) Elem. Sch., 1989-93, Check (Va.) Elem. Sch., 1993—; family life facilitator Amherst County Pub. Schs., 1985-87, family life curriculum Va. Dept. Edn., 1986-87, chpt. 1 adv. bd., 1989-91. Dir. Young Musicians Choir, Grades 1 to 6, Rivermont Ave. Bapt. Ch., Lynchburg, 1990—, pres. adult choir, 1991-93; mem. adult choir 1st Bapt. Ch., Roanoke, 1994—, dir. young musicians grade 4 choir. Mem. ASCD, Va. Assn. Elem. Sch. Prins., Piedmont Assn. Elem. Prins., Radford U. Alumni (pres. 1983-85), Order Eastern Star (electa 1994-95, soloist 1991-93), Phi Delta Kappa. Republican. Avocations: singing, swimming, tennis, reading, crafts. Home: 3108K Honeywood Ln Roanoke VA 24014-2101 Office: Check Elem Sch Rte 221 PO Box 8 Check VA 24072

SPROUSE, EARLENE PENTECOST, educational diagnostician; b. Hopewell, Va., Apr. 23, 1939; d. Earl Paige and Sophia Marlene (Chairky) Pentecost; m. David Andrew Koren, July 3, 1957 (div. Jan. 1963); children: David Andrew Jr., Elysia Marlene, Merri Paige; m. Wayne Alexender Sprouse, Sept. 2, 1964; 1 child, Michael Wayne. AS, Paul D. Camp C.C., Franklin, Va., 1973; BS in Comm. Disorders, Old Dominion U., 1975, MEd in Spl. Edn., 1977. Tchg. cert. with endorsement in speech lang. pathology, learning disabilities and emotional disturbance, Va. Speech lang. pathologist Southampton County Schs., Va., 1975-76; learning disabled tchr. itinerant Franklin (Va.) City Pub. Schs., 1976-78, emotionally disturbed/learning disabled tchr., 1978-85, speech lang. pathologist, 1986-91, ednl. diagnostician, 1992—; com. mem. The Childrens Ctr., Franklin, 1986—, Early Childhood Coun., Franklin, 1992—; needs assessment com. Juvenile Domestic Rels. Ct., Franklin, 1993—; project leader curriculum guide Listening and Lang. Processing Skills, 1990-91. Com. mem. Dem. Com., Suffolk, Va., 1985-92, Family Fair, Franklin, 1993—. Recipient Excellence in Edn. award C. of C., Hampton Roads, Va., 1988-89; grantee Va. Edn. Assn., Richmond, 1994—, Project UNITE Dept. Edn., Richmond, 1994—. Mem. ASCD, Coun. for Exceptional Children (com. mem.), Speech and Hearing Assn. Va., Franklin City Edn. Assn. (pub. rels. com., pres. 1980, 91), Orton Dyslexia Soc. Presbyterian. Avocations: fishing, music. Home: 319 Gray's Creek Ln Surry VA 23883 Office: Franklin City Pub Schs 800 W 2nd Ave Franklin VA 23851-2162

SPROUSE, JAMES MARSHALL, retired federal judge; b. Williamson, W.Va., Dec. 3, 1923; s. James and Garnet (Lawson) S.; m. June Dolores Burt, Sept. 25, 1952; children: Tracy Sprouse Ferguson, Jeffrey Marshall, Andrew Michael, Sherry Lee Sprouse Shinholser, Shelly Lynn Sprouse Schneider. A.B., St. Bonaventure (N.Y.) U., 1947; LL.B., Columbia U., 1949; postgrad. in internat. law, U. Bordeaux, France, 1950. Bar: W.Va. Asst. atty. gen. State of Va., 1949; with W.Va. CIA, 1952-57; pvt. practice W.Va., 1957-72, 75-79; justice W.Va. Supreme Ct. Appeals, 1972-75; judge U.S. Ct. Appeals (4th cir.), Lewisburg, W.Va., 1979-92, sr. cir. judge, 1992-95; retired, 1995, pvt. practice, 1995—. Served with AUS, 1942-45. Fulbright scholar. Mem. Am. Bar Assn., W.Va. State Bar, W.Va. Bar Assn., W.Va. Trial Lawyers Assn., Kanawha County Bar Assn., VFW, Am. Legion. Democrat. Presbyterian. Clubs: Shriners, Aheppa. Office: PO Box 159 Union WV 24983

SPROUSE, ROBERT ALLEN, II, retail chain executive; b. Portland, Oreg., Dec. 25, 1935; s. John Alwyn and Mary.Louise (Burpee) S.; m. Frances Carolyn Russell, June 22, 1957. Student, Williams Coll., 1953-57. With Sprouse-Reitz Stores Inc., Portland, 1957—; buyer, sec. Sprouse-Reitz Stores Inc., 1963-69, v.p., 1969-73, pres., 1973—, chief exec. officer, 1986-91, also bd. dirs., chmn., 1991-94. Active Good Samaritan Hosp. Found. Mem. Chief Execs. Orgn., Theta Delta Chi. Republican. Episcopalian. Clubs: Multnomah Athletic (Portland); Arlington. Lodge: Rotary.

SPROUSE, SUSAN RAE MOORE, human resources specialist; b. Amsterdam, N.Y., Feb. 23, 1948; d. Charles Franklin and Alice Rae (Lawson) Moore; m. Richard D. Sprouse, May 5, 1973; children: Jennifer Lynn, Melinda Rae. BS, U. So. Miss., 1970, MBA, 1971. Spl. non-exempt employee rels. GE Co., Owensboro, Ky., 1972-74; from instr. entry level tng. to spl. profl. rels. and EEO GE Co., Chgo., 1974-78; from employee rels. clk. to material control specialist GE Co., Ft. Smith, Ark., 1978-82; employee rels. rep. Mason Chamberlain Inc., Stennis Space Ctr., Miss., 1982-90; human resource specialist Inst. for Naval Oceanography, Stennis Space Ctr., Miss., 1990-92; program coord. Ctr. for Ocean and Atmospheric Modeling, Stennis Space Ctr., Miss., 1992-95; human resources specialist Computer Scis. Corp., Stennis Space Ctr., Miss., 1995—; co. rep. Jr. Achievement, Owensboro, 1972-74. Libr., Am. flag chair DAR, Picayune, Miss., 1967-92; bd. dirs. Picayune On Stage, v.p., sec., 1982—. Named Outstanding Jr. Mem. DAR, Picayune, 1970; profiled in Picayune Item, 1988. Mem. Nat. Soc. Magna Charta Dames, Sigma Sigma Sigma, Phi Delta Rho. Republican. Church of Christ. Avocations: community theater, reading. Office: CSC Bldg 3205 Stennis Space Ctr Bay Bay Saint Louis MS 39529

SPROW, HOWARD THOMAS, lawyer, educator; b. Atlantic City, Dec. 4, 1919; s. Howard Franklin and Elizabeth B. (Riley) S.; m. Mildred J. Fiske, July 22, 1945; children—Howard Hamilton, Mildred Elizabeth (Mrs. Wilson), Matthew Thomas. A.B. cum laude, Colgate U., 1942; J.D., Columbia, 1945; LLD (hon.), St. Lawrence U., 1987. Bar: N.Y. 1946. Assoc. Brown, Wood, Fuller, Caldwell & Ivey, N.Y.C., 1945-53; ptnr. Brown, Wood, Fuller, Caldwell & Ivey, 1954-70; gen. counsel, v.p. corporate and pub. affairs, sec. Merrill Lynch, Pierce, Fenner & Smith Inc., N.Y.C., 1970-77, Merrill Lynch & Co., Inc., 1973-77; ptnr. Rogers & Wells, N.Y.C., 1977-80; of counsel Rogers & Wells, 1980-87; prof. law Albany Law Sch., Union U., 1980-90, prof. emeritus, 1990—; of counsel Crane & Mackrell, Albany, 1990-92; sr. counsel Whiteman Osterman & Hanna, Albany, 1992—; adj. prof. law Fordham U., 1974-80; mem. adv. panel to Law Revision Commn. on Recodification N.Y. State Ins. Law, 1973-84, chmn., 1976-80; bd. dirs. Farm Family Holdings, Inc., Glenmont, N.Y. Mem. editorial bd. Columbia Law Rev, 1944-45; editor: Financing in the International Capital Markets, 1982. Mem. ABA, N.Y. State Bar Assn., Assn. of Bar of City of N.Y. Home: 55 Marion Ave Albany NY 12203-1820 Office: Whiteman Osterman & Hanna One Commerce Plz Albany NY 12260

SPROWL, CHARLES RIGGS, lawyer; b. Lansing, Mich., Aug. 22, 1910; s. Charles Orr and Hazel (Allen) S.; m. Virginia Lee Graham, Jan. 15, 1938; children: Charles R., Robert A., Susan G., Sandra D. A.B., U. Mich., 1932, J.D., 1934. Bar: Ill. 1935. Pvt. practice, 1934—; of counsel Taylor, Miller, Sprowl, Hoffnagle & Merletti, 1986—; dir. Simmons Engring. Corp., Petersen Aluminum Corp. Mem. Bd. Edn., New Trier Twp. High Sch., 1959-65, pres. 1962-65; mem. Glencoe Zoning Bd. Appeals, 1956-76, chmn., 1966-76; mem Glencoe Plan Commn., 1962-65; bd. dirs. Glencoe Pub. Libr., 1953-65, pres. 1955-56; trustee Highland Park Hosp., 1959-69; bd. dirs. Cradle Soc., 1968-92. Fellow Am. Coll. Trial Lawyers; mem. Chgo. Bar Assn. (bd. mgrs. 1949-51), Ill. Bar Assn., ABA, Juvenile Protective Assn. (dir. 1943-53), Northwestern U. Settlement (pres. 1963-70, dir.), Soc. Trial Lawyers, Delta Theta Phi, Alpha Chi Rho. Presbyn. Clubs: Law (pres. 1969-70), Legal (pres. 1953-54), Univ, Monroe, Skokie Country. Home: 558 Washington Ave Glencoe IL 60022-1837 Office: 33 N La Salle St Chicago IL 60602-2600

SPROWLS, ROBERT WAYNE, veterinarian, laboratory administrator; b. Phillips, Tex., Mar. 19, 1946; s. Charlie and Nettie Elizabeth (Green) S.; m. Linda Sue Rhoades, Aug. 11, 1966; children—Kimberly, Kari. B.S. in Vet. Sci., Tex. A&M U., 1968, D.V.M., 1969, Ph.D., 1973. NIH fellow pathology Tex. A&M U., College Station, 1969-73; asst. prof. Med. Ctr., U. Ark., Little Rock, 1973-75; pathologist Nat. Ctr. Toxicological Research, Jefferson, Ark., 1973-75; head pathologists Tex. Vet. Med. Diagnostic Lab., Amarillo, 1975-81; dir. Tex. Vet. Med. Diagnostic Lab., 1981—. Contbr. articles to profl. jours. Chmn. Valley View Nazarene Ch., Amarillo, 1984—. Mem. AVMA, Am. Assn. Vet. Lab. Diagnosticians (mem. exec. bd. 1992—, mem. accreditation com. 1990—), Acad. Vet. Cons. (corr. sec. 1992—), Tex. Vet. Medicine Assn., High Plains Vet. Medicine Assn. (sec.-treas. 1980-81, 90—), Am. Assn. Bovine Practitioners, Amarillo A&M Club (v.p. 1977-78). Office: Tex A&M Vet Med Diagnostic Lab PO Box 3200 Amarillo TX 79116-3200

SPRUGEL, GEORGE, JR., ecologist; b. Boston, Sept. 26, 1919; s. George and Frances Emily (Strong) S.; m. Catharine Bertha Cornwell, Oct. 27, 1945; 1 son, Douglas George. B.S., Iowa State U., 1946, M.S., 1947, Ph.D., 1950. Instr., then asst. prof. zoology and entomology Iowa State U., 1946-54; asst. head biology br. Office Naval Research, 1951-53; spl. asst. to asst. dir., div. biology and medicine NSF, 1953-54, program dir. environ. biology, 1954-64; chief scientist Nat. Park Service, 1964-66; chief Ill. Natural History Survey, 1966-80, chief emeritus, 1980—; Cons. in field; mem. adv. com. environ. biology NSF, 1965; dir. program conservation of ecosystems U.S. Internat. Biol. Program, 1969-72; mem. study group on role lunar receiving lab. NASA, 1969-70, mem. life scis. com., 1972-78; mem. ecology adv. com. Bur. Reclamation, 1972-74; mem. Gov. of Ill. Sci. Adv. Com., 1967-80, Ill. Environ. Quality Council, 1970-73; mem. environ. studies bd. com. to devel. protocol for toxic substances Nat. Acad. Scis.-Nat. Acad. Engring., 1972-73; mem. NRC, 1968-72. Served as officer USNR, 1940-45, 51-53. Fellow AAAS (council 1961-73, v.p., chmn. sect. biol. scis. 1971); mem. Am. Inst. Biol. Scis. (mem.-at-large gov. bd. 1969-72, exec. com. 1972-75, pres. 1974), Ecol. Soc. Am. (council 1961-78, v.p. 1968), Am. Soc. Zoologists (sec. 1970-72, chmn. div. ecology 1971), Sci. Research Soc. Am., Sigma Xi. Home: 2710 S 1st St Champaign IL 61821-7114

SPRUIELL, VANN, psychoanalyst, educator, editor, researcher; b. Leeds, Ala., Oct. 16, 1926; s. Vann Lindley and Zada (Morton) S.; m. Iris Taylor, Sept. 20, 1951 (div. Oct. 1966); children: Graham, Fain, Garth; m. Joyce Ellis, Feb. 11, 1967; stepchildren: Sidney Reavey, Catherine Ellis, Matson Ellis. BS, U. Ala., Tuscaloosa, 1948; MD, Harvard U., 1952. Resident Bellevue Hosp., N.Y.C., 1952-53, N.Y. Hosp., N.Y.C., 1953-55; fellow Tulane Sch. Medicine, New Orleans, 1955-57; pvt. practice New Orleans, 1957—; vis. rschr. Anna Freud Ctr., London, 1972-73; co-pub. JOURLIT and BOOKREV; pres. and founding mem. Psychoanalytic Archives CD-ROM Texts, New Orleans, 1993—; clin. prof. psychiatry La. State U. Sch. Medicine, Tulane U. Sch. Medicine; sec. Ctr. for Advanced Studies in Psychoanalysis, 1989—. Editl. bd. Psychoanalytic Quarterly, 1973—; N.Am. editor Internat. Jour. Psychoanalysis, London; mem. various other editl. bds.; contbr. articles to profl. jours. and books. Sgt. U.S. Army, 1944-46. Mem. Am. Psychoanalytic Assn. (sec. bd. on profl. stds. 1979-92), Wyvern Club. Avocations: interdisciplinary studies, sailing. Home: 215 Iona St Metairie LA 70005-4137

SPRUNG, DONALD WHITFIELD LOYAL, physics educator; b. Kitchener, Ont., Can., June 6, 1934; s. Lyall MacAulay and Doreen Bishop (Price) S.; m. Hannah Sueko Nagai, Dec. 12, 1958; children: Anne Elizabeth, Carol Hanako. BA, U. Toronto, Ont., 1957; PhD, U. Birmingham, Eng., 1961, DSc, 1977. Asst lectr. U. Birmingham, Eng., 1960-61; instr. Cornell U., Ithaca, N.Y., 1961-62; rsch. staff lab. nuclear sci. MIT, Boston, 1964-65; asst. prof. McMaster U., Hamilton, Ont., 1962-66, assoc. prof., 1966-71, physics prof., 1971—, dean faculty sci., 1975-84, mem. bd. govs., 1986-90, chair dept. physics and astronomy, 1991—; vis. prof. U. Barcelona, Spain, 1991-92, 95. Contbr. articles to profl. jours. C.D. Howe fellow, 1969-70. Fellow Royal Soc. Can.; mem. Can. Assn. Physicists (Herzberg medal 1972), Am. Phys. Soc.; mem. Inst. Physics. Avocations: bicycling, cabinet making. Office: McMaster Univ Dept Physics and Astronomy, 1280 Main St W, Hamilton, ON Canada L8S 4M1

SPUDICH, JAMES A., biology educator; b. Collinsville, Ill., Jan. 7, 1942; married, 1964; 2 children. BS, U. Ill., 1963; PhD in Biochemistry, Stanford U., 1968. USPHS trainee Stanford (Calif.) U., 1968; asst. prof. biochemistry U. Calif., San Francisco, 1971-74, assoc. prof., 1974-76; prof., 1976; prof. biochemistry and devel. biology Beckman Ctr., Stanford U. Sch. Medicine, 1977—. Editor: Annual Rev. Cell Biology, 1994. Mem. Am. Soc. Cell Biologists (pres. 1989). Research in molecular basis of cytokine amoeboid movement and other forms of cell motility. Office: Stanford U Dept Biochemistry Stanford Med Ctr Stanford CA 94305

SPULBER, NICOLAS, economics educator emeritus; b. Brasov, Romania, Jan. 1, 1915; m. Pauline, Aug. 5, 1950; 1 son, Daniel Francis. MA, New Sch. Social Rsch., 1950, PhD magna cum laude, 1952. Rsch. assoc. Ctr. Internat. Studies, Mass. Inst. Tech., 1952-54; mem. faculty Ind. U., Bloomington, 1954—; prof. econs. Ind. U., from 1961, acting chmn. Inst. East European Studies, 1956-59, Disting. prof. econs., 1974-80, Disting. prof. emeritus, 1980—; vis. prof. City Coll., City U. N.Y., 1963-64. Author: The Economics of Communist Eastern Europe, 1957, reissued 1976, The Soviet Economy: Structure, Principles, Problems, 2d edit, 1969, Soviet Strategy for Economic Growth, 1964, The State and Economic Development, 1966, Socialist Management and Planning, 1971, Organizational Alternatives in Soviet-Type Economies, 1979, Managing the American Economy from Roosevelt to Reagan, 1989, Restructuring The Soviet Economy: In Search of the Market, 1991, The American Economy: The Struggle for Supremacy in the 21st Century, 1995; co-author: Quantitative Economic Policy and Planning, 1976, Economics of Water Resources: From Regulation to Privatization, 1994; editor, co-editor 5 books; contbr. numerous articles to profl. jours. in, U.S. and fgn. countries. Halle fellow, 1951-52; grantee Am. Philos. Soc., 1956; grantee Ford Found., 1962-63; rsch. fellow Ford Faculty Found., 1960-61; sr. fellow Internat. Devel. Rsch. Ctr., Ind. U., 1969-71. Mem. Am. Econ. Assn. Office: Ind U Dept Econs Bloomington IN 47405

SPUNT, SHEPARD ARMIN, realty executive, management and financial consultant; b. Cambridge, Mass., Feb. 3, 1931; s. Harry and Naomi (Drooker) S.; B.S., U. Pa., 1952, M.B.A., 1956; m. Joan Murray Fooshee, Aug. 6, 1961 (dec. June 1969); children—Erica Frieda and Andrew Murray (twins). Owner, Colonial Realty Co., Brookline, Mass., 1953—, Cambridge, 1960—; sr. assoc. Gen. Solids Assocs., 1956—; chmn. bd. Gen. Solids Systems Corp., 1971-74; trustee Union Capital Trust, Boston; incorporator Liberty Bank & Trust Co., Boston; dir., clerk The Computer Co., Somerville, Mass., 1986—. Chmn., Com. for Fair Urban Renewal Laws, Mass., 1965—; Boston Area assoc. trustee U. Pa.; treas. Ten Men of Mass., 1980. Pres., New Eng. Council of Young Republicans, 1964-67, 69-71; vice chmn. Young Rep. Nat. Fedn., 1967-69, dir. region I, 1964-67, 69-71; mem. Brookline Rep. Town Com., 1960—, treas., 1996; del. Atlantic Conf. Young Polit. Leaders, Brussels, 1973; bd. dirs. Brookline Taxpayers Assn., 1964—, v.p., 1971-72, pres., 1972—. Registered profl. engr., Mass. Mem. Nat. Soc. Profl. Engrs., Rental Housing Assn., Greater Boston Real Estate Bd., Navy League, Boston Athenaeum, Copley Soc. Boston. Lodges: Masons, Shriners. Author: (with others) A Business Data Processing Service for Small Business Practitioners, 1956; A Business Data Processing Service for Medical Practitioners, 1956, rev. edit., 1959. Author, sponsor consumer protection and election law legislation Mass. Gen. Ct., 1969—. Patentee in field of automation, lasers, dielectric bonding. Home: 177 Reservoir Rd Chestnut Hill MA 02167-1426 Office: 21 Elmer St Cambridge MA 02138-6107

SPURGEON, EDWARD DUTCHER, law educator; b. Newton, N.J., June 2, 1939; s. Dorsett Larew and Mary (Dutcher) S.; m. Carol Jean Forbes, June 17, 1963; children: Michael Larew, Stephen Edward. AB, Princeton U., 1961; LLB, Stanford U., 1964; LLM in Taxation, NYU, 1968. Bar: Calif. 1965. Assoc. atty. Stammer McKnight et al, Fresno, Calif., 1964-67; assoc. atty. Paul Hastings Janofsky and Walker, L.A., 1968-70, ptnr., 1971-80; prof. law U. Utah, Salt Lake City, 1980-90, Wm. H. Leary prof. law and policy, 1990-93, assoc. dean acad. affairs Coll. Law, 1982-83, dean Coll. Law, 1983-90; dean, prof. Sch. of Law U. Ga., Athens, 1993—; pres., dir. Albert and Elaine Borchard Found., L.A., 1983—; vis. prof. law Univ. Coll. London, fall 1990, Stanford U. Law Sch., spring 1991; ex-officio mem. Utah State Bar Commn., 1984-90; cons. devel. office U. Utah, 1991-93. Co-author: Federal Taxation of Trusts, Grantors and Beneficiaries, 1st edit., 1978, 2d edit., 1989. Mem. Utah Gov.'s Task Force Officers and Dirs. Liability Ins., 1985-87, Utah Dist. Ct. Reorgn. Commn., 1986-87, Justice in 21st Century Commn., Utah, 1989-91; bd. visitors, exec. com. Stanford U. Law Sch., 1988-93. Mem. ABA (Commn. on Legal Problems of the Elderly 1991-95, spl. advisor 1995—), Am. Bar Found. Office: U of Ga Law School Athens GA 30602

SPURLING, EVERETT GORDON, JR., architect, construction specifications consultant; b. Fallston, N.C., Sept. 5, 1923; s. Everett Gordon and Vera Mae (Lattimore) S.; m. Margaret Ball Duckworth, Sept. 9, 1944; children: David Steven, Diana Lynn, Norman Kent. AS, Mars Hill Coll., 1940-42; B in Archtl. Engring. with high honors, N.C. State U., 1947, postgrad., 1948. Registered architect, N.C., Va., Md. Inspector aircraft Glenn Martin Co., Balt., 1942; draftsman, architect F. Carter Williams, Architect, Raleigh, N.C., 1947-52; staff architect C.E. Silling and Assocs., Charleston, W.Va., 1952-53, Greife and Daley, Architects, Charleston, 1953-55; ptnr. Hunter and Spurling, Architects, Charleston, 1955-57; project architect, assoc. McLeod and Ferrara, Architects, Washington, 1957-64; owner, cons. E.G. Spurling Jr., Architect, Washington and Bethesda, Md., 1964—; guest lectr. Montgomery Coll., Cath. U., U. Mo.-Rolla, George Washington U.; guest speaker, panelist numerous constrn. orgns. Contbr. articles to profl. jours. Served as sgt. C.E., U.S. Army, 1944-46, ETO. Recipient Design award GSA, 1990. Fellow AIA, Constrn. Specifications Inst. (hon. mem. 1995, cert. of appreciation 1971, 93, Ben John Small Meml. award 1979, edn. commendation 1979, Master Format spl. award 1983, Mid-Atlantic Region cert. of appreciation 1990, 92); mem. ASTM, Am. Arbitration Assn. (panelist 1979-96), Specifications Cons. in Ind. Practice (pres. 1977-80), Tau Beta Pi, Phi Kappa Phi. Democrat. Baptist. Avocations: fishing, woodworking, art, fgn. travel. Home and Office: 6312 Marjory Ln Bethesda MD 20817-5804

SPURR, HARVEY W., plant pathology research administrator; b. Oak Park, Ill., June 8, 1934; m. Idamarie Thome, 1956; 3 children. BS, Mich. State U., 1956; PhD in Plant Pathology, U. Wis., 1961. Fellow plant pathology NIH U. Wis., Madison, 1961-63; plant pathologist agrl. rsch. sta. Union Carbide Corp., N.C., 1963-69; assoc. prof. plant pathology N.C. State U., Oxford, 1969-74, prof. plant pathology, 1974—; rsch. plant pathologist Oxford (N.C.) Tobacco Lab. USDA, 1969—, rsch. leader, lab. dir., 1988—. Mem. Am. Phytopath Soc., Am. Soc. Microbiology. Home: USDA Crops Rsch Lab 4185 Tommie Sneed Rd Oxford NC 27565 Office: USDA Crops Rsch Lab PO Box 1168 Oxford NC 27565*

SPURRIER, STEVE, university athletic coach, former professional football player. Quarterback San Francisco 49'ers, 1967-75, Tampa Bay Buccaneers, 1976; head football coach Duke U., 1987-89, U. Fla. Gators, 1990—. Winner Heisman Trophy, U. Fla., 1966. Office: Univ Fla PO Box 14485 Gainesville FL 32604-2485*

SPYERS-DURAN, PETER, librarian, educator; b. Budapest, Hungary, Jan. 26, 1932; came to U.S., 1956, naturalized, 1964; s. Alfred and Maria (Almasi-Balogh) S-D; m. Jane F. Cumber, Mar. 21, 1964; children: Kimberly, Hilary, Peter. Certificate, U. Budapest, 1955; M.A. in L.S, U. Chgo., 1960; Ed.D., Nova U., 1975. Profl. asst. libr. adminstrn. div. ALA, Chgo., 1961-62; assoc. dir. librs., assoc. prof. U. Wis., 1962-67; dir. librs., prof. Western Mich. U., 1967-70; dir. librs., prof. libr. sci. Fla. Atlantic U., 1970-76; dir. libr. Calif. State U., Long Beach, 1976-83; prof. libr. and info. sci., dir. libr. Wayne State U., Detroit, 1983-86, dean, prof. libr. and info. sci. program, 1986-95, dean and prof. emeritus, 1995—; cons. Spyers-Duran Assocs., 1995—; vis. prof. State U. N.Y. at Geneseo, summers 1969-70; cons. publs., libr. and info. scis.-related enterprises; chmn. bd. internat. confs., 1970—. Author: Moving Library Materials, 1965, Public Libraries - A Comparative Survey of Basic Fringe Benefits, 1967; editor: Approval and Gathering Plans in Academic Libraries, 1969, Advances in Understanding Approval Plans in Academic Libraries, 1970, Economics of Approval Plans in Research Libraries, 1972, Management Problems in Serials Work, 1973, Prediction of Resource Needs, 1975, Requiem for the Card Catalog: Management Issues in Automated Cataloging, 1979, Shaping Library Collections for the 1980's, 1981, Austerity Management in Academic Libraries, 1984, Financing Information Systems, 1985, Issues in Academic Libraries, 1985; mem. editorial bd. Jour. of Library Adminstration, 1989-95. Mem. Kalamazoo County Library Bd., 1969-70; Bd. dirs. United Fund. Mem. ALA, Mich. Libr. Assn., Internat. Fed. Libr. Assns., Assn. Info. Sci., Fla. Libr. Assn., Calif. Libr. Assn., Fla. Assn. Community Colls., Boca Raton C. of C., U. Chgo. Grad. Libr. Sch. Alumni Club (pres. 1973-75), Mich. Libr. Consortium (bd. dirs. 1983-87), Detroit Area Libr. Network (pres. bd. dirs. 1985-95), Mich. Ctr. for Book (pres. 1988-89), Am. Soc. Info. Sci., Assn. Libr. and Info. Sci. Edn. Republican. Methodist. Home: 8000 Sailboat Key Blvd S Saint Petersburg FL 33707-6340 Office: Wayne State Univ Librs Detroit MI 48202

SQUARCIA, PAUL ANDREW, school superintendent; b. Yukon, Pa., Nov. 17, 1939; s. Paul and Lucy (Nardonne) S.; m. Gena Maria Porreca, Aug. 18, 1962; children: Paul, Stephanie, Suzanne. BS, Boston U., 1961, cert. advanced studies, 1974; EdD, Boston Coll., 1987; MEd, U. N.H., 1967. Sci. tchr. Berlin (N.H.) Sch. Dept., 1961-63, asst. prin., 1963-66; prin. Oxford Hills High Sch., South Paris, Maine, 1967-70; prin. Silver Lake Regional Dist., Kingston, Mass., 1970-72, asst. supt. schs., 1972-78, supt. schs., 1978—; adj. prof. Bridgewater (Mass.) State Coll., 1980—, Lesley Coll.,

Cambridge, Mass., 1980—. Recipient Nat. Superintendent of the Yr. awd., Massachusetts, Am. Assn. of School Administrators, 1993. Mem. ASCD, Am. Assn. Sch. Adminstrs., Mass. Assn. Sch. Supts. (pres. 1992-93). Roman Catholic. Avocations: reading, traveling, spectator sports. Home: 28 Holmes Ter Plymouth MA 02360-4013 Office: Silver Lake Regional Dist 130 Pembroke St Kingston MA 02364-1066

SQUIBB, SAMUEL DEXTER, chemistry educator; b. Limestone, Tenn., June 20, 1931; s. Benjamin Bowman and Lou Pearl S.; m. JoAnn Kyker, Dec. 15, 1951; children—Sandra Lavanne, Kevin Dexter. B.S., E. Tenn. State U., 1952; Ph.D., U. Fla., 1956. Assoc. prof., dir. chemistry Western Carolina U., Cullowhee, N.C., 1956-60; asst. prof., dir. chemistry Eckerd Coll., St. Petersburg, Fla., 1960-63; asso. prof. Eckerd Coll., 1963-64; prof. chemistry U. N.C., Asheville, 1964-94, prof. emeritus, 1994—, chmn. dept., 1964-94; vis. prof. U. N.C., Chapel Hill, 1976-81, 83-87, 92-95, Clemson U., S.C., 1982; cons. So. Assn. Colls. and Schs., State of W.Va. Author: Experimental Organic Chemistry, 1972, Understanding Chemistry One, 1979, rev. 1990, Two, 1981, rev. 1991, Three, 1981, rev. 1992, Four, 1981, rev. 1992, Five, 1981, rev. 1989, Six, 1984, Chemistry One, 1976, rev. 1987, Two, 1980, rev. 1990, Experimental Chemistry One, 1976, rev. 1988, Two, 1981, rev. 1991; contbr. articles to profl. jours. Mem. Grose United Meth. Ch. Disting. Tchr. award U. N.C.-Asheville, 1983. Fellow Am. Inst. Chemists (life, nat. publs. bd. 1988-92); mem. Am. Chem. Soc. (Charles H. Stone award Carolina Piedmont sect. 1979, Disting. Chemist award Western Carolinas sect. 1993, chmn. Tampa Bay subsect. 1963, Western Carolina sect. 1981, editor Periodic News Western Carolina sect. 1980—, Disting. Chemist award 1993), N.C. Inst. Chemists (pres. 1977-79, sec. 1975-77, 85-91, Disting. Chemist award 1986), Skyland Twirlers Square Dance Club, Silver Spurs Advanced Square Dance Club, Skylark Round Dance Club, Phi Beta Kap.

SQUIER, JACK LESLIE, sculptor, educator; b. Dixon, Ill., Feb. 27, 1927; s. Leslie Lee and Ruth (Barnes) S.; m. Jane Bugg, June 9, 1950. Student, Oberlin Coll., 1945-46; B.S., Ind. U., 1950; M).F.A., Cornell U., 1952. Instr. Cornell U., 1952, asst. prof. art, 1958-61, asso. prof., 1961-65, prof., 1965—; designer Howatt Pottery Co., N.Y.C., 1953; account exec. Jamian Advt. Co., N.Y.C., 1954-58; asst. prof. U. Calif., Berkeley, 1960; mem. Internat. Assn. Art, UNESCO, 1964-72, mem. exec. com., 1966-69, v.p., 1969-72. One-man shows include Alan Gallery, N.Y.C., 1956, 59, 62, 64, White Mus., Cornell U., 1959, 68, Instituto de Arte Contemporaneo, Lima, Peru, 1963, Landau-Alan Gallery, N.Y.C., 1966, 69, Herbert F. Johnson Mus., Corwell Univ. (retospective of work , 1953-93); exhibited in group shows at Mus. Modern Art, N.Y.C., 1957, Whitney Mus., N.Y.C., 1952, 54, 56, 58, 62, 67, 78, Hirshhorn Mus., Washington, 1978, Mus. Fine Arts, Boston, 1958, Chgo. Art Inst., 1960, Brussel's Worlds Fair, 1956, competition, Auschwitz, Poland, 1957, Albright-Knox Mus., Buffalo, 1968, Claude Bernard Gallery, Paris, 1957, Hanover Gallery, London, 1958; represented in permanent collections Mus. Modern Art, N.Y.C., Whitney Mus. Art, Hirshhorn Mus., Instituto de Arte Contemporaneo, Everson Mus., Syracuse, N.Y., Stanford U. Mus., St. Lawrence U. Mus., SUNY at Potsdam, Ithaca Coll., Johnson Mus. at Cornell U., Houston Mus., Hood Mus.-Dartmouth (N.H.) U.; retrospective exhbn. Herbert F. Johnson Mus. Cornell U., 1993; work pub. in various, books, mags., newspapers, slide collections, catalogs. Served with AC USN, 1945-47. Office: Cornell U Dept Art 100 Tjaden Hall Ithaca NY 14853-7301

SQUIER, LESLIE HAMILTON, psychology educator; b. San Francisco, Nov. 17, 1917; s. Leslie Hamilton and Alma Ida (Bergmann) S.; m. Anne Frances Wood, Dec. 12, 1959; children—Renata, Leslie III, Stafford, Kurt. B.A., U. Calif.-Berkeley, 1950, Ph.D., 1953. From instr. to prof. psychology Reed Coll., Portland, Oreg, 1953-88, dean of students, 1955-61, prof. emeritus, 1988—; vis. scientist Oceanic Inst., Makapuu, Oahu, Hawaii, 1969-70, 71; vis. prof. Paine Coll., Augusta, Ga., 1984; NSF fellow U. Oreg. Med. Sch., Portland, 1976, U. Hawaii Med. Sch., Honolulu, 1977. Trustee Portland Zool. Soc., 1962-68. Served with USAF, 1942-46. Mem. AAAS, APA, Am. Psychol. Soc., Oreg. Psychol. Assn. (pres. 1965), Western Psychol. Assn., Assn. for the Study of Dreaming, Phi Beta Kappa, Sigma Xi. Home: 5647 SE 38th Ave Portland OR 97202-7501 Office: Reed Coll Portland OR 97202

SQUIRE, ALEXANDER, management consultant; b. Dumfrieshire, Scotland, Sept. 29, 1917; s. Frederick John and Lillian (Ferguson) S.; m. Isabelle L. Kerr, June 23, 1945; children: Jonathan, David, Deborah, Stephen, Philip, Martha, Timothy, Rebecca, Elizabeth. B.S., MIT, 1939. Research metallurgist Handy and Harman, Fairfield, Conn., 1939-41; devel. metallurgist Sullivan Machinery Co., Michigan City, Ind., 1941-42; head powder metallurgy br. Watertown Arsenal Lab., Mass., 1942-45; mgr. metall. devel. Westinghouse Electric Corp., Pitts., 1945-50; project mgr. Bettis Atomic Power Lab., Pitts., 1950-62; gen. mgr. plant apparatus div. Westinghouse, 1962-69; dir. purchases and traffic Westinghouse Electric Corp., 1969-71; pres. Westinghouse Hanford Co., Richland, Wash., 1971-79; bus. cons. Richland, 1979-80; dep. mng. dir. Wash. Public Power Supply System, 1980-85, cons., 1985—. Mem. Nat. Acad. Engring., Am. Nuclear Soc., Am. Soc. Metals, AIME, Am. Def. Preparedness Assn. Address: 2415 Winburn Ave Durham NC 27704-5145

SQUIRE, ANNE MARGUERITE, religious leader; b. Amherstburg, Ont., Can., Oct. 17, 1920; d. Alexander Samuel and Coral Marguerite Park; m. William Robert Squire, June 24, 1943; children: Frances, Laura, Margaret. BA, Carleton U., Ottawa, 1972, BA with honors, 1974, MA, 1975; LLD (hon.), Carleton U., 1988; DD (hon.), United Theol. Coll., 1979, Queen's U., 1985. Cert. tchr., Ont. Adj. prof. Carleton U., 1975-82; sec. div. ministry personnel and edn. United Ch. Can., Toronto, 1982-85, moderator, 1986-88. Author curriculum materials, 1959—; contbr. articles to profl. jours. Mem. bd. mgmt. St. Andrew's Coll., Saskatoon, Sask., 1982, Queens Theol. Coll., Kingston, Ont., 1980-82. Recipient Senate medal Carleton U., 1972. Mem. Can. Research Inst. for Advancement Women, Delta Kappa Gamma (pres. 1978-79). Office: 731 Weston Dr, Ottawa, ON Canada K1G 1W1

SQUIRE, JAMES ROBERT, retired publisher, consultant; b. Oakland, Calif., Oct. 14, 1922; s. Harry Edwin and Ruby (Fulton) S.; m. Barbara Lyman, Jan. 20, 1946; children: Kathryn Elizabeth, Kevin Richard, David Whitford. BA, Pomona Coll., 1947, DLitt, 1966; MA, U. Calif., Berkeley, 1949, PhD, 1956. Tchr. secondary sch. Oakland, Calif., 1949-54; supr., lectr. English edn. U. Calif. at Berkeley, 1951-59; prof. English U. Ill., Urbana, 1959-67; exec. sec. Nat. Council Tchrs. English, 1960-67; editor-in-chief, sr. v.p. Ginn & Co., Lexington, Mass., 1968-74; sr. v.p., pub. Ginn & Co., 1975-80, sr. v.p., dir. research and devel., 1980-82, sr. v.p., sr. cons., 1983-84; cons., 1984-94; lectr. grad. sch. edn. Harvard U., 1990-95; pres. Nat. Conf. Rsch. in English, 1982-83; pres. Hall of Fame in Reading, 1995-96; sr. rsch. assoc. Boston U., 1996—. Author: (with W. Loban, M. Ryan) Teaching Language and Literature, 1961, 69, (with R.K. Applebee) High School English Instruction Today, 1968, (with B.L. Squire) Greek Myths and Legends, 1967, Teaching English in the United Kingdom, 1969, A New Look at Progressive Education, 1972; editor: Teaching of English, 76th Yearbook Nat. Soc. Study Edn., 1977, Dynamics of Language Learning, 1987, Writing K-12 Exemplary Programs, 1987, (with J. Jensen, D. Lapp, J. Flood) Handbook of Research on Teaching the English Language Arts, 1991, (with E.J.. Farrell) Transactions in Literature: A Fifty Year Perspective; section editor: Ency. of English Studies and Language Arts, 1994. Bd. dirs. Am. Edn. Publ. Inst., 1968-70. With AUS, 1943-45. Recipient Creative Scholarship award Coll. Lang. Assn., 1961, Lifetime Rsch. award Nat. Conf. Rsch. in English, 1992; named Ky. col., 1966; named to Hall of Fame in reading, 1987. Mem. MLA (pres. 1995), Assn. Am. Pubs. (vice chmn. sch. divsn. 1971-73, chmn. 1974-76, 81-82, Mary McNulty award 1983), Nat. Coun. Tchrs. English (Exec. Com. award 1967,l Disting. Svc. award 1991), Internat. Reading Assn., Coll. Conf. on Composition and Communication, Phi Delta Kappa. Home: 1 Nubanusit Rd Marlborough NH 03455 Office: Harvard Grad Sch Edn 205 Larsen Hall Cambridge MA 02138

SQUIRE, RUSSEL NELSON, musician, emeritus educator; b. Cleve., Sept. 21, 1908. B.Mus. Edn., Oberlin Coll., 1929; A.M., Case Western Res. U., 1939; Ph.D., NYU, 1942; postgrad. U. So. Calif. Dir. Oberlin Summer Music Sch., Ohio, 1929; dir. instrumental music instrn. Chillicothe Pub. Schs., Ohio, 1929-37; faculty Pepperdine U., Malibu, Calif., 1937-56, prof. music, 1937-56, now prof. emeritus, also chmn. fine arts div., 1940-56; faculty Calif. State U.-Long Beach, 1956-72, prof. music, 1964-72, now prof. emeritus; vis. prof. Pacific Christian Coll., 1970-74; prof. philosophy Sch. Edn., Pepperdine U., 1972-78; profl. theater orch. pianist, 1926-28; founder/propr./dir. Ednl. Travel Service involving study residencies in Europe, the Near East, China, India, Australia, Africa; Service: Agoura, Calif., 1958-84. Author: Studies in Sight Singing, 1950; Introduction to Music Education, 1952; Church Music, 1962; Class Piano for Adult Beginners, 1964, 4th edit., 1990; also contbr. articles to profl. jours. Founder/pres. Council for Scholarship Aid to Fgn. Students, Inc.; mem. Los Angeles County Music Commn., 1948-60; bd. dirs. Opera Guild So. Calif., 1948-60; pres. Long Beach Symphony Assn., 1963-64 (bd. dirs 1961-64). Mem. Music Tchrs. Assn. Calif. (br. pres. 1948-51), AAUP (chpt. founding pres. 1948-49), Rotary, Phi Mu Alpha Sinfonia (life). Club: Twenty (Los Angeles), Bohemians (Los Angeles). Home: 350 Robin Rd Waverly OH 45690-1521

SQUIRE, WALTER CHARLES, lawyer; b. N.Y.C., Aug. 5, 1945; s. Sidney and Helen (Friedman) S.; m. Sara Jane Abramson; children: Harrison, Russell, Zachary, Andrew. BA, Yale U., 1967; JD, Columbia U., 1971. Bar: N.Y. 1971, U.S. Dist. Ct. (so. and ea. dists.) N.Y. 1975, U.S. Ct. Appeals (2d cir.) 1974, U.S. Supreme Ct. 1977. Ptnr. Jones Hirsch Connors & Bull, N.Y.C., 1986—. Bd. govs. Arthritis Found. N.Y., Inc., 1993—; bd. dirs. MedicAlert Found., N.Y., 1990—. Mem. ABA, N.Y. State Bar Assn., Assn. of Bar of City of N.Y., Internat. Bar Assn., Licensing Execs. Soc., Am. Arbitration Assn. (arbitrator 1975—, mediator 1993—), Am. Acad. Hosp. Attys., Risk Ins. Mgmt. Soc. (lectr. 1983, 84). Office: Jones Hirsch Connors & Bull 101 E 52nd St New York NY 10022-6018

SQUIRES, ARTHUR MORTON, chemical engineer, educator; b. Neodesha, Kans., Mar. 21, 1916; s. Charles Loren and Vera Amber (Moore) S. A.B. with distinction in Chemistry, U. Mo., 1938; Ph.D, Cornell U., 1947. Design engr. M.W. Kellogg Co., N.Y.C., 1942-46; asst. dir. process devel. Hydrocarbon Research, Inc., N.Y.C., 1946-51, dir. process devel., 1951-59; cons. chem. process industries N.Y.C., 1959-67; prof. chem. engring. CUNY, 1967-74, disting. prof., 1974-76, chmn. dept. chem. engring., 1970-73; Vilbrandt prof. chem. engring. Va. Poly. Inst. and State U., Blacksburg, 1976-82, disting. prof., 1978-86, disting. prof. emeritus, 1986—. Author: The Tender Ship, 1986; editor: (with D.A. Berkowitz) Power Generation and Environmental Change, 1971; contbr. articles to profl. jours.; patentee in field. Mem. N.Y. Pro Musica, 1953-60. Fellow Am. Acad. Arts and Scis., AAAS; mem. Nat. Acad. Engring., Am. Inst. Chem. Engrs. (inst. lectr.), Am. Chem. Soc. (Henry H. Storch award 1973), ASME, Sigma Xi, Tau Beta Pi. Avocation: performing medieval and Renaissance music. Home: 2710 Quincy Ct Blacksburg VA 24060-4124 Office: Va Poly Inst and State U Dept Chem Engring Blacksburg VA 24061

SQUIRES, BONNIE STEIN, fundraising consultant; b. Phila., May 12, 1940; d. Joseph and Lillian (Ponnock) Stein; children: Deborah Rose, David Abram; m. Sami Ouahada. BE, U. Pa., MA. Various positions Temple U., Phila., 1983-89, exec. dir. capital campaign, 1992-94; asst. exec. dir. Pa. Edn. Assn., Harrisburg, 1989-92; v.p. for devel. Phila. Geriatric Ctr., 1994-95; pres. Squires Consulting, Wynnewood, Pa., 1995—. Author: (poetry) New Eden, 1977; editor: (poetry) This Land of Fire, 1988, (student essays, poems and photos) A New Nation, 1976. Mem. Fedn. Jewish Agys., Citizens' Crime Commn., Ctr. UN Reform Edn.; bd. dirs. Phila. com. Am. Jewish Congress, Phila. Mus. Art, Am. Friends Hebrew U., Harrisburg Jewish Community Rels. Coun.; del. Israel's Prime Minister's Solidarity Conf., 1989, Pres. Bush's regional Edn. Summit, 1989; pres. Pa. region Am. Jewish Congress; v.p. Pa. Breast Cancer Coalition. Recipient Torch award and Lillian Alpers award Am. Friends Hebrew U., Louise Waterman award Am. Jewish Congress. Mem. AAUW (del. Beijing UN Conf. Women), LWV. Home: 11 Arthurs Round Table Wynnewood PA 19096-1202

SQUIRES, JOHN HENRY, judge; b. Urbana, Ill., Oct. 21, 1946; s. Henry Warrick and Nell Catherine (McDonough) S.; m. Mary Kathleen Damhorst, June 7, 1969; children: Jacqueline Marie, Mary Elizabeth, Katherine Judith, Emily Jean, Grace Dorothy. AB cum laude, U. Ill., 1968, JD, 1971. Bar: Ill. 1971, U.S. Dist. Ct. (cen. dist.) Ill. 1972, U.S. Tax Ct. 1978. Assoc. Brown, Hay & Stephens, Springfield, Ill., 1971-76, ptnr., 1977-87; judge U.S. Bankruptcy Ct. No. Dist. of Ill., ea. div., 1988—; trustee in bankruptcy, 1984-87; adj. prof. law The John Marshall Law Sch., Chgo., 1994, DePaul U., Chgo., 1996; lectr. Chgo. Bar Assn., Ill. Inst. Continuing Legal Edn. , Comml. Law League Am., Ill. Credit Union League; mem. lay adv. bd. St. Joseph's Home, Springfield, 1980-84, sec., 1982-83, v.p., 1983-84. With USAF, 1969. Mem. Chgo.-Lincoln Am. Inn of Ct., Am. Bus. Club, Union League of Chgo., Nat. Conf. of Bankruptcy Judges. Office: US Bankruptcy Ct No Dist Ill Ea Div Rm 656 219 S Dearborn St Chicago IL 60604-1702

SQUIRES, RICHARD FELT, research scientist; b. Sparta, Mich., Jan. 15, 1933; s. Monas Nathan and Dorothy Lois (Felt) S.; m. Else Saederup, 1 child, Iben. BS, Mich. State U., 1958; postgrad., Calif. Inst. Tech., 1961. Rsch. biochemist Pasadena Found. for Med. Rsch., 1961-62; chief biochemistry sect. rsch. dept. A/S Ferrosan, Soeborg, Denmark, 1963-78; neurochemistry group leader CNS Biology sect. Lederle Labs. div. Am. Cyanamid Co., Pearl River, N.Y., 1978-79; prin. rsch. scientist The Nathan S. Kline Inst. for Psychiat. Rsch., Orangeburg, N.Y., 1979—. Contbr. articles to profl. jours.; patentee in field. Nat. Inst. Neurol. and Communication Disorders and Stroke grantee, 1981-84. Mem. Soc. Neurosci., Collegium Internat. Neuro-Psychopharmacologicum, Internat. Soc. Neurochemistry, European Neurosci. Assn., Am. Soc. Neurochemistry, Am. Soc. Biochemistry and Molecular Biology, Am. Soc. Pharmacology and Exptl. Therapeutics. Home: 10 Termakay Dr New City NY 10956-6434 Office: Nathan S Kline Inst Psychiat Rsch Orangeburg NY 10962

SQUIRES, SCOTT WILLIAM, special effects expert, executive. With Indsl. Light & Magic, San Rafael, Calif., 1975-79, visual effects supr., 1985—; co-founder, pres. Dreamquest Visual Effects, 1979-85. Asst. cameraman (film) Close Encounters of the Third Kind, 1977; cameraman (film) Buck Rogers and the Battleship Galactica, 1977; rsch. designer (film) Star Trek I, 1979; spl. effects supr. films including Blue Thunder, Buckeroo Bonzai, Deal of the Century, One From the Heart, Blade Runner, Dentsu, 1988, Micronauts, 1988; tech. dir. Witches of Eastwick, 1986, Willow, 1987, Who Framed Roger Rabbit, 1988; visual effects supr. (film) The Hunt for Red October, 1990; dir. visual effects (film) Showscan, 1991; effects supr. (comml.) Disney Coke. Recipient Acad. Tech. award pioneering work on input scanners, 1995, several effects awards as effects supr. Brit. Petroleum Elevator comml. Office: Indsl Light & Magic PO Box 2459 San Rafael CA 94912-2459

SQUIRES, WILLIAM RANDOLPH, III, lawyer; b. Providence, Sept. 6, 1947; s. William Randolph and Mary Louise (Gress) S.; m. Elisabeth Dale McAnulty, June 23, 1984; children: Shannon, William R. IV, Mayre Elisabeth, James Robert. BA in Econs., Stanford U., 1969; JD, U. Tex., 1972. Bar: Wash. 1973, U.S. Dist. Ct. (we. dist.) Wash. 1973, U.S. Dist. Ct. (ea. dist.) Wash. 1976, U.S. Ct. Appeals (9th cir.) 1976, U.S. Supreme Ct. 1976, U.S. Claims Ct. 1982. Assoc. Oles, Morrison, Rinker, Stanislaw, & Ashbaugh, Seattle, 1973-78; ptnr., chmn. litigation group Davis Wright Tremaine (formerly Davis, Wright, Todd, Riese & Jones), Seattle, 1978—. Mem. ABA, Wash. State Bar Assn., Seattle-King County Bar Assn. Episcopalian. Clubs: Wash. Athletic, Rainier (Seattle). Home: 5554 NE Penrith Rd Seattle WA 98105 Office: Davis Wright Tremaine 2600 Century Sq Seattle WA 98101

SQUYRES, STEVEN WELDON, astronomy educator, planetary geology researcher; b. Woodbury, N.J., Jan. 9, 1956. BA, Cornell U., 1978, PhD in Geology, 1981. Assoc. NRC, Ames Rsch. Ctr., NASA, 1981—; assoc. prof. dept. astronomy Cornell U., 1985—; mem. Planetary Geol. Working Group, NASA, 1982—. Mem. AAAS, Am. Geophys. Union. Office: Cornell University Center for Radiophysics & Space Research Ithaca NY 14853*

SRACIC, KAREN K., librarian; b. Sharon, Pa., Sept. 16, 1955. BFA, Pa. State U., 1977; postgrad., Ill. State U., 1978-80; MLS, Clarion U., 1991, postgrad., 1991—. Grad. teaching asst. art Ill. State U., Normal, 1978-80; libr. tech. asst. III, cataloging, Milner Libr., 1980-88; work-study libr. tech. svcs. dept. Pub. Libr. of Youngstown (Ohio) and Mahoning County, 1988-91; catalog and ref. libr., instr. McGill Libr. Westminster Coll., New Wilmington, Pa., 1991-93; union catalog liaison INFOHio Project, Youngstown, 1996—. Contbr., reviewer: Plays for Children and Young Adults: An Evaluative Index and Guide, 1991. Mem. ALA, Assn. for Libr. Collections and Tech. Svcs., Pa. State U. Alumni Assn., Beta Phi Mu.

SRAGOW, ELLEN, gallery owner; b. N.Y.C., 1943. BA, Hofstra U., 1964; MA, NYU, 1966. Registrar art collection NYU, N.Y.C., 1967-71; dir. Sragow Gallery, N.Y.C., 1974—. Mem. Internat. Fine Print Dealers Assn. Office: Sragow Gallery 73 Spring St New York NY 10012

SREENIVASAN, KATEPALLI RAJU, mechanical engineering educator; b. Kolar, India, Sept. 30, 1947; married 1980; 2 children. BE, Bangalore U., 1968; ME, Indian Inst. Sci., 1970, PhD in Aeronautical Engring., 1975. JRD Tata fellow Indian Inst. Sci., 1972-74, project asst., 1974-75; fellow U. Sydney, Australia, 1975, U. Newcastle, 1976-77; rsch. assoc. Johns Hopkins U., Balt., 1977-79; from asst. prof. to assoc. prof. Yale U., New Haven, 1982-85, prof. mech. engring., 1985—, Harold W. Cheel prof. mech. engring., 1988—, prof. physics, 1990—, prof. applied physics, 1993—; vis. scientist Indian Inst. Sci., 1979, vis. prof., 1982, Calif. Inst. Tech., Pasadena, 1986, Rockefeller U., 1989, Jawaharlala Nehru Ctr. Advancement Sci. Studies, 1992, chmn. mech. engring. dept., 1987-92; vis. sci. DFVLR, Gottingen, Germany, 1983; mem. Inst. for Advanced Study, Princeton, N.J., 1995. Recipient Narayana Gold medal Indian Inst. Sci., 1975, Disting. Alumnus award, 1992; Humboldt Found. fellow, 1983, Guggenheim fellow, 1989. Fellow ASME, Am. Phys. Soc. (Otto Laporte award 1995), AIAA (assoc.); mem. Am. Math. Soc., Conn. Acad. Sci. and Engring., Sigma Xi. Achievements include research in origin and dynamics of turbulence; control of turbulent flows; chaotic dynamics; fractals.

SRERE, BENSON M., communications company executive, consultant; b. Rock Island, Ill, Aug. 13, 1928; s. Jacob H. and Margaret (Weinstein) S.; m. Betty Ann Cerruti, June 20, 1957; children: David Benson, Anne Michele, Peter John. BA magna cum laude, U. So. Calif., 1949. Newsman U.P., Los Angeles, 1948-56; assoc. editor Good Housekeeping mag., N.Y.C., 1956-59; sr. editor Good Housekeeping mag., 1959-67, asst. mng. editor, dir. spl. publs. div., 1967-68, mng. editor, 1968-72, exec. editor, v.p., 1972-75, v.p., editorial dir., 1975-76; v.p., gen. mgr. King Features Syndicate, 1976-81; v.p. Hearst Metrotone News, 1976-81; exec. asst. to pres. Hearst Corp., 1981—, v.p., 1983-94; dir. Hearst/ABC Video Svcs., Hearst/ABC Viacom Entertainment Svcs., A&E Cable Network, Lifetime Cable Network. Trustee Optometric Center of N.Y. Found., 1978-79. Served with U.S. Army, 1950-52. Mem. Soc. Profl. Journalists, Phi Beta Kappa, Phi Kappa Phi, Phi Eta Sigma. Home: 11 Lafayette Ct Greenwich CT 06830-5324

SRINIVASA, VENKATARAMANIAH, engineer; b. Mysore, India, Aug. 30, 1941; came to U.S., 1968; s. Venkataramaniah and Gowramma S.; m. Janakimala Muthiah, June 1972; children: Supreeth, Suman. BSc, Mysore U., 1962, MSc, 1964; MS, Rutgers U., 1972, PhD, 1975. Rsch. fellow CFTRI, Mysore, 1964-67; tech. officer Indian Inst. Packaging, Bombay, 1967; rsch. intern, rsch. and tching. asst. Rutgers U., New Brunswick, N.J., 1972-75, rsch. intern, tching. asst., rsch. fellow Bur. Engring. Rsch., 1970-75; sr. packaging engr. Abbott Labs., Abbott Park, Ill., 1975-78, sr. project engr., 1978-83, mgr., 1983—. Mem. Inst. Packaging Profls., Soc. Plastics Engrs., Am. Chem. Soc., Sigma Xi. Home: 2729 Sallmon Ave Waukegan IL 60087-3514

SRINIVASACHARI, SAMAVEDAM, chemical engineer; b. Visakhapatnam, India, Oct. 5, 1926; came to U.S., 1958; s. Appalachari Srinivasa and Chudamani Samavedam; m. Vasanta S. Chari, Feb. 11, 1955; children: Sarita, Roger. M of Chem. Engring., NYU, 1959; PhD in Chem. Engring., Poly. Inst. Bklyn., 1967. Registered profl. engr., Pa. Teaching fellow Poly. Inst. Bklyn., 1960-63; sr. process devel. engr. Internat. Latex & Chemical, Dover, Del., 1966-73; prin. process engr. Catalytic, Inc., Phila., 1973-75; sr. process engr. Coalcon/Union Carbide, N.Y.C., 1976-77, Foster Wheeler Energy Corp., Livingston, N.J., 1977-82; chemical and environ. engr. Duro-Test Corp., Clifton, N.J., 1987-92, mgr. environ. engring., 1992—. Mem. AICE, Am. Chem. Soc. Democrat. Hindu. Achievements include design of chem. and petroleum plants, design of synthetic fuels plants; rsch. in environ. and regulatory problems of indsl. plants, environ. clean up of indsl. plant sites. Home: 12 The Ter Rutherford NJ 07070-2028 Office: Duro-Test Corp 185 Scoles Ave Clifton NJ 07012-1125

SRINIVASAN, MANDAYAM PARAMEKANTHI, software services executive; b. Mysore City, India, July 1, 1940; s. Appalacharya Paramekanthi and Singamma Budugan; came to U.S., 1970, naturalized 1991; B.S., U. Mysore, 1959, B.E. in Mech. Engring., 1963; M.S. in Ops. Research, Poly. Inst. N.Y., 1974, M.S. in Computer Sci., 1983; m. Ranganayaki Srirangapatnam, June 18, 1967; children: Srikala, Srilatha, Sriharsha. Costing engr. Heavy Engring. Corp., Ranchi, Bihar, India, 1963-70; inventory analyst Ideal Corp., Bklyn., 1970-75; systems analyst Electronic Calculus, Inc., N.Y.C., 1975-76; cons. in software, project leader Computer Horizons Corp., N.Y.C., 1976-85; pres. Compmusic, Bellerose, N.Y., 1985—; tchr., cons. in-house tng. Founding mem. governing council Vishwa Hindu Parishad of U.S.A., 1973—, pres. N.Y. State chpt., 1977-86. Mem. IEEE, Inst. Engrs. (India). Republican. Hindu. Office: Compmusic Inc 8229 251st St Jamaica NY 11426-2527

SRINIVASAN, VENKATARAMAN, marketing and management educator; b. Pudukkottai, Tamil Nadu, India, June 5, 1944; came to U.S., 1968; s. Annaswamy and Jambagalakshmi Venkataraman; m. Sitalakshmi Subrahmanyam, June 30, 1972; children: Ramesh, Mahesh. B Tech., Indian Inst. Tech., Madras, India, 1966; MS, Carnegie-Mellon U., 1970, PhD, 1971. Asst. engr. Larsen & Toubro, Bombay, 1966-68; asst. prof. mgmt. and mktg. U. Rochester, N.Y., 1971-73, assoc. prof., 1973-74; assoc. prof. Stanford (Calif.) U., 1974-76, prof., 1976-82, dir. PhD program in bus., 1982-85, Ernest C. Arbuckle prof. mktg. and mgmt. sci., 1982—; mktg. area coord., 1976-78, 88-93; cons. in field. Mem. editorial bd. Jour. Mktg. Rsch., 1988—, Mktg. Sci., 1980—, Mgmt. Sci., 1974-91; contbr. articles to profl. jours. Mem. Am. Mktg. Assn., Inst. Ops. Rsch./Mgmt. Scis. Hindu. Avocation: classical music.

SRIRANGANATHAN, NAMMALWAR, veterinary microbiology educator; b. Kunigal, Karnataka, India, Dec. 12, 1944; came to U.S. 1970; s. Rangaiah and Shallamma (Shallamma) Nammalwar; m.Rukmini Pankajam, Oct. 3, 1980; children: Chakravarthy, Selvi. BVSc, Mysore Vet. Coll., India, 1966; MVSc, U. Agrl. Sci., Bangalore, India, 1968; PhD, Oreg. State U., 1974; DVM, Am. Vet. Coll., Chgo., 1975. Lic. veterinarian, Wash., Oreg.; diplomate Am. Coll. Vet. Microbiologists. Vet. surgeon Civil Vet. Hosp., Bangalore, India, 1968-69; instr. Mysore Vet. Coll., Bangalore, 1969-70; research asst. Oreg. State U., Corvallis, 1970-74; clin. intern Duby, Macomber & Wasselius Vet. Clinic, Centralia, Wash., 1974-75; postdoctoral fellow Nat. Inst. Allergy & Infectious Diseases, Pullman, Wash., 1976-77; research assoc. USDA, Pullman, 1977-78; asst. prof. Wash. State U., Pullman, 1979-84; asst. prof. vet. microbiology Va. Tech, Blacksburg, 1984-90; assoc., prof. vet. microbiology Va. Tech., Blacksburg, 1990—; dir. diagnostic vet. bacteriology and mycology Coll. Vet. Medicine, Wash. State U., Pullman, 1979-82, dir. clin. bacteriology and mycology Va. Med. Reg. Coll. Vet. Medicine, Blacksburg, 1984-87, cons., 1987—. Contbr. articles to profl. jours. Active various charitable orgns. Mem. AVMA, Am. Soc. Microbiology, Conf. Rsch. Workers in Animal Diseases, Microbiologists of India, Am. Assn. Vet. Lab. Diagnosticians, Phi Zeta. Avocations: soccer, tennis, racquetball, hiking. Home: 507 Cedar Orchard Dr W Blacksburg VA 24060-9151

SROGE, MAXWELL HAROLD, marketing consultant, publishing executive; b. N.Y.C., Oct. 9, 1927; s. Albert N. and Goldie (Feldman) S.; children: Roberta, David, Marc, Sarah. Student, CCNY, 1946-48, NYU, 1948, New Sch. Social Research, 1948. Dir. sales Bell & Howell Co., Chgo., 1950-60; dir. prodn. planning Bell & Howell Co., 1961-62, pres. Robert Maxwell div., 1962-63; pres. Maxwell Sroge Co., Inc., Chgo., 1965—, Telespond, Inc., Chgo., 1971—, Maxwell Sroge Pub., Inc., Chgo., 1976—; chmn. JUF Comm. Industry, 1974-75, Transatlantic Catalogue Corp.; chmn. Direct Mktg. Svcs., Inc.; pub. Non-Store Mktg. Report, Inside Leading Mail Order Houses, Mail Order Industry Ann. Report, Best in Catalogs, How to Create Successful Catalogs, The Catalog Marketer, 101 Ideas for More Profitable Catalogs; bd. dirs. Tools Direct; chmn. Telespond Inc. Mem. New Ill. Com., 1965; speakers bur. Percy for Gov., 1964, Citizens for Percy, 1972; co-chmn. Percy for Pres. Exploratory Com., 1974; mem. regional adv. bd. Nat. Jewish Hosp.,

1974-75; mem. devel. com. WTTW-Channel 11, 1975-76, NCCJ; founder Save the Tarryall, Inc., 1982. Served with USNR, World War II. Mem. Direct Mail Mktg. Assn. (Gold Mail Box award 1978, Internat. Gold Carrier Pigeon award 1979), Nat. Retail Merchants Assn., Retail Advt. Conf., World Futures Soc. *To succeed man must stretch himself, his mind, his heart, his grasp. Our capabilities far exceed our accomplishments. Within each of us there is the potential for greatness if we will dig deep enough to find it. Those of us who have been blessed to have discovered success owe a special responsibility to the world around us to make it a better place for all men to live.*

SROKA, JOHN WALTER, trade association executive; b. Perth Amboy, N.J., July 24, 1946; s. John and Mary (Teliszewski) S.; m. Paula J. Devitt, Aug. 17, 1968; children: Amanda, Alexandra. BA in Psychology, Fairleigh Dickinson U., 1968, postgrad., 1968-69; postgrad. in law, Am. U., 1972-73. Asst. exec. dir. Associated Gen. Contractors of Am., Washington, 1973-87; exec. v.p. Nat. Assn. Sheet Metal and Air Conditioning Contractors, Chantilly, Va., 1987—. Sgt. U.S. Army, 1969-71. Mem. Am. Soc. Assn. Execs. Roman Catholic. Office: SMACNA 4201 Lafayette Center Dr Chantilly VA 22021-1209

SROKA, PETER STANLEY, secondary school educator; b. Fall River, Mass., Oct. 16, 1944. BA, Southeastern Mass. U., 1970; MA, Am. U., 1976; postgrad., Antioch Sch. Law, 1978-79; cert. in secondary social sci. edn., U. Ga., 1995. Cert. secondary tchr., Ga. Asst. to dir. Project Upward Bound, Dartmouth, Mass., 1967-70; staff writer Daily and Sunday Standard-Times, New Bedford, Mass., 1970-74; legis. asst. in edn. U.S. Ho. of Reps., Washington, 1977-82; vis. lectr. English composition Southeastern Mass. U., Dartmouth, 1982-85; instr. Learning Skills, Inc., Amherst, Mass., 1985-86; equal opportunity specialist U.S. EEOC, Boston, 1987-91, FCC, Washington, 1991-92; student tchr. Clarke County Sch. Dist., Athens, Ga., 1995—; adj. instr. journalism Bristol C.C., Fall River, 1972-74; cons. Bonner & Assocs., Washington, 1992; debate cons. New Bedford (Mass.) Pub. Schs., 1970-74; grad. asst. to dean Am. U., Washington, 1975. Contbr. articles to profl. publs. Contbg. mem. Dem. Nat. Com., Washington, 1982—; founding mem. First Amendment Assn., New Bedford, 1972; v.p. local specialists union Nat. Equal Employment, Washington, 1990-91. Sgt. U.S. Army, 1963-66. Mem. ASCD, NEA, ACLU, Ga. Assn. Educators, Nat. Forensic League (coach 1970—, Superior Achievement award 1993), Am. Legion, Kappa Delta Epsilon. Roman Catholic. Avocations: baseball, jogging, research and study of origin and development of English language. Home: 685 Whit Davis Rd Athens GA 30605-4031

STAAB, THOMAS EUGENE, chemist; b. Peoria, Ill., Jan. 26, 1941; s. Leo Reuben and Mary Blanche (Griffin) S.; BS in Chemistry, St. Louis U., 1963; m. Donna Marie Murnighan, May 30, 1967; children: Lynn Anne, Thomas Patrick. Rsch. and devel. chemist for elastomers Victor Products div. Dana Corp., Chgo., 1963-65, application engr. for oil seals, 1965-68, application engrng. supr. for oil seals, 1968-70, chief product engr. for oil seals, 1970-72, mgr. sales and engrng., Ft. Wayne, Ind., 1972-73, chief product engr. for oil seals, Chgo., 1973-75, prodn. supr., 1975-77, materials engr. for gaskets, 1977-79, mgr. oil seal engrng., Lisle, Ill., 1979-82, chief devel. engr. materials, 1982-83, prodn. area mgr. 1983-84, mgr. materials devel., 1984-86, mgr. tech. svcs., 1986-90, environ. mgr., 1990-92, sen. tech. svc. engr. 1992—. Alliance chief Y Indian Guides, 1975-76; mgr./coach Little League, 1978-81. Mem. Rubber Mfrs. Assn. (past chmn. oil seal tech. com.), Soc. Automotive Engrs. (past mem. adv. bd. of sealing com.), Am. Chem. Soc. Roman Catholic. Patentee hydrodynamic shaft seal, rotary shaft seals, antistick, nonliquid absorbing gasket. Home: 512 S Lincoln St Hinsdale IL 60521-4012 Office: 1945 Ohio St Lisle IL 60532-2169

STAAB, THOMAS ROBERT, textile company financial executive; b. Beaver Falls, Pa., Apr. 23, 1942; s. Henry Louis and Margaret Constance (Clarke) S.; m. Angela Maria Simon, Aug. 5, 1965; children: Thomas II, Jennifer, Thea. BBA, U. Pitts., 1964, MBA, 1965. CPA, Pa. Sr. audit mgr. Price Waterhouse & Co., Pitts., 1970-77; practice fellow Fin. Acctg. Standards Bd., Stamford, Conn., 1978-80; dir. corp. acctg. and taxes Fieldcrest Cannon Inc., Eden, N.C., 1981-85, asst. contr., 1985-86, contr., 1986-92, v.p. fin., 1992-93; CFO, 1994—; mem. adv. bd. Arkwright Mut. Ins. Co. Served to lt. USN, 1966-70. Mem. Am. Inst. CPA's, Pa. Inst. CPA's, N.C. Textile Mfrs. Assn., Am. Textile Mfrs. Inst. Republican. Roman Catholic. Avocation: farming. Home: 3726 Nc # 65 Reidsville NC 27320 Office: Fieldcrest Cannon Inc 326 E Stadium Dr Eden NC 27288-3523

STAADT, THOMAS ARTHUR, financial company executive; b. Chgo., July 29, 1947; s. Peter and Wilma (Thompson) S.; m. Katherine Franzwa, Dec. 2, 1967; children: Michael W., Jeffery P., Matthew P. BA, De Paul U., 1989; grad., Command and Gen. Staff Coll., Ft. Leavenworth, Kans., 1989. Lic. comml. pilot. Commd. officer U.S. Army, 1966, helicopter pilot, 1966-76; resigned, 1976; sales rep. Pat Rogers Assocs., Chgo., 1976-79; regional mgr. Pat Rogers Assocs., Kansas City, Mo., 1979-82, Chgo., 1982-90; v.p., regional mgr. Rogers Benefit Group, Wellesley, Mass., 1990—. Bd. dirs. Northbook (Ill.) United Way, 1985; prin. emergency preparedness liaison officer Fed. Emergency Mgmt. Agy., Boston, 1992—. Col. USAR, 1976—. Decorated Bronze Star, Air medal. Fellow Nat. Assn. for Search and Rescue (life mem., treas., bd. dirs. 1971—). Republican. Avocations: flying, scuba diving, basketball. Office: Rogers Benefit Group 40 Washington St Wellesley Hills MA 92181

STAAR, RICHARD FELIX, political scientist; b. Warsaw, Poland, Jan. 10, 1923; s. Alfred and Agnes (Gradalska) S.; m. Jadwiga Maria Ochota, Mar. 28, 1950; children: Monica, Christina. B.A., Dickinson Coll., 1948; M.A. (Univ. fellow), Yale, 1949; Ph.D., U. Mich., 1954. Research analyst U.S. Dept. State, Washington, 1951-54; prof. polit. sci. Ark. State Coll., Jonesboro, 1957-58; lectr. overseas program U. Md., Munich, Germany, 1958-59; assoc. prof. to prof., chmn. dept. polit. sci. Emory U., 1959-69; sr. fellow Hoover Instn. on War, Revolution and Peace at Stanford, 1969—, prin. assoc. dir., 1969-81, dir. internat. studies program, 1975-81, 85-91; U.S. ambassador to Mut. and Balanced Force Reductions Negotiations, Vienna, 1981-83; Nimitz chair Naval War Coll., 1963-64; prof. polit. affairs Nat. War Coll., 1967-69; cons. Office Sec. Def., 1969-73; adj. prof. USMC Command and Staff Coll., 1971-81; sr. advisor to Comdg. Officer Politico-Mil. Affairs USNR, Treasure Island, Calif., 1975-81; disting. vis. prof. nat. security affairs Naval Postgrad. Sch., 1979; cons. U.S. ACDA, 1983-86, Sandia Nat. Labs., 1991—; mem. bd. visitors Def. Language Inst., 1988—. Author: Poland, 1944-62, The Sovietization of a Captive People, 1962, reprinted, 1975, Communist Regimes in Eastern Europe, 5th edit., 1988, USSR Foreign Policies After Detente, 1985, rev. edit., 1987, Foreign Policies of the Soviet Union, 1991, The New Military in Russia, 1996; co-author: Soviet Military Policies Since World War II, 1986; contbg. author and editor: Aspects of Modern Communism, 1968; editor: Yearbook on International Communist Affairs, 1969-91, Arms Control: Myth Versus Reality, 1984, Public Diplomacy: USA Versus USSR, 1986, Future Information Revolution in the USSR, 1988, United States - East European Relations in the 1990's, 1989, East-Central Europe and the USSR, 1991, Transition to Democracy in Poland, 1993; mem. editl. bd. Current History, Orbis, Strategic Rev., Mediterranean Quar.; contbr. articles to profl. jours. Asst. dist. commr. Quapaw Area council Boy Scouts Am., 1954-57; active Profs. for Goldwater, 1964; mem. Reagan for Pres. Com., 1980; dir. for nat. security affairs Office of Pres.-Elect, 1980-81; mem. Academicians for Reagan, 1984. Served to col. USMCR, 1960-83. Decorated Legion of Merit. Mem. Am. Polit. Sci. Assn., Internat. Studies Assn., Am. Assn. Advancement Slavic Studies, Phi Beta Kappa, Kappa Sigma. Republican. Methodist. Home: 36 Peter Coutts Cir Stanford CA 94305-2503 Office: Hoover Instn Stanford CA 94305-6010

STAAS, WILLIAM E., JR., physiatrist; b. Phila., 1936. MD, Jefferson Med. Coll., 1962. Intern Mercy Hosp., Darby, Pa., 1962-63; resident in phys. medicine and rehab. U. Pa. Hosp., 1965-68; attending physiatrist Magee Rehab. Hosp., Phila.; prof. rehab. medicine Jefferson Med. Coll. Office: Magee Rehab Hosp 6 Franklin Plz Philadelphia PA 19102-1177

STAATS, DEAN ROY, retired reinsurance executive; b. Somerville, N.J., Sept. 18, 1924; s. Roy Theodore and Mabel Ellen (Rhodes) S.; m. Marilyn Ann Hockenbury, 1947 (div. 1956; 1 child, Barry Clinton; m. Marilyn Lee Truitt, Dec. 16, 1961. B.Sc., Brown U., 1946, M.A., 1948. Asst. actuary N.Am. Reassurance Co., N.Y.C., 1959-67, data processing officer, 1967-69, v.p., actuary, 1969-71, sr. v.p., 1971-84, exec. v.p., 1984-86; pres., dir. NARe Life Mgmt. Co., N.Y.C., 1985-86; rep. Life Ins. Guaranty Corp, 1977-86; U.S. mgr. Can. Reassurance Co., 1984-86; cons. actuary, 1986-89. Served to lt. (j.g.), USN, 1943-46, PTO. Fellow Soc. Actuaries; mem. Am. Acad. Actuaries N.Y. Jr. Actuaries Club (pres. 1960-61), Soc. Actuaries (reins. adminstrn. com. 1984-85). Republican. Clubs: Anchor and Saber (pres. 1959-60). Avocations: art collectibles; tennis; gardening; travel. Home and Office: 234 Hansell Rd Newtown Square PA 19073-2509

STAATS, ELMER BOYD, foundation executive, former government official; b. Richfield, Kans., June 6, 1914; s. Wesley F. and Maude (Goodall) S.; m. Margaret S. Rich, Sept. 14, 1940; children: David Rich, Deborah Rich Staats Sanders, Catharine Rich Staats Taubman. AB, McPherson (Kans.) Coll., 1935, LLD (hon.), 1966; MA, U. Kans., 1936; PhD, U. Minn., 1939; D. in Pub. Service (hon.), George Washington U., 1971; D. in Adminstrn. (hon.), U. S.D., 1973; LLD (hon.), Duke U., 1975, Nova U., 1976, U. Pa., 1981, Lycoming Coll., 1982; LHD (hon.), Ohio State U., 1982. Research asst. Kans. Legis. Council, 1936; teaching asst. U. Minn., 1936-38; staff Pub. Adminstrn. Service, Chgo., 1937-38; staff mem. U.S. Bur. Budget, Exec. Office Pres., 1939-47, asst. to dir., 1947, asst. dir. charge legis. reference, 1947-49, exec. asst. dir., 1949-50, dep. dir., 1950-53, 58-66; comptroller gen. U.S. Washington, 1966-81; pres. Harry S. Truman Scholarship Found., 1981-84, chmn., 1984—; bd. dirs. rsch. dir. Marshall Field & Co., Chgo., 1953; exec. dir. ops. coord. bd., Nat. Security Coun., 1953-58; professorial lectr. pub. adminstrn. George Washington U., 1944-49; mem. bd. visitors Nat. Def. U., 1981-90; mem. vis. com. John F. Kennedy Sch. Govt., Harvard U., 1974-80, Grad. Sch. Mgmt., UCLA, 1976—; mem. Com. on Pub. Policy Studies U. Chgo., 1976—; trustee Nat. Inst. Pub. Affairs, 1969-77; mem. Conf. Bd., 1966; mem. dir.'s adv. coun. Met. Life Ins. Co., 1985-94, emeritus mem., 1994—; dir. Computer Data Systems, Inc., 1981—; bd. advisors Alexander Proudfoot & Co., 1981-85; mem. pub. rev. bd. Arthur Andersen & Co., 1981-91; bd. dirs. Air Products and Chems., 1981-85, Met. Life Ins. Co., 1981-85, Nat. Intergroup Inc. (formerly Nat. Steel Corp.), 1981-86; chmn. congl. panel on social security orgn., 1983-84; mem. nat. commn. on pub. svc., 1987-90; mem. commn. to rev. honor code of West Point U.S. Mil. Acad., 1988-89; mem. Govt. Acctg. Standards Bd., 1984-90; chmn. Fed. Acctg. Standards Adv. Bd., 1991—. Author: Personnel Standards in the Social Security Program, 1939; contbr. to: Am. Polit. Sci. Rev. Trustee Am. U., 1969-80; trustee McPherson Coll., 1969-79, mem. bd. trustees and research and policy com., com. for econ. devel., 1981—; bd. govs. Internat. Orgn. of Supreme Audit Instns., 1969-80; trustee Kerr Found., 1981—; bd. dirs. George C. Marshall Found., 1984—. Recipient Rockefeller Pub. Service award, 1961, Alumni achievement award U. Minn., 1964, Disting. Service citation U. Kans., 1966, Warner D. Stockberger Achievement award, 1973, Abraham O. Smoot Pub. Service award Brigham Young U., 1975, Person of Yr. award Washington chpt. Inst. Internal Auditors, 1975, Thurston award Inst. Internal Auditors, 1988, medal of honor Am. Inst. CPAs, 1980, Engr. of Yr. award San Fernando Valley Engrs. Council, 1980, Presdl. Citizens medal, 1981, Hubert Humphrey medal, 1981, Pub. Service Achievement award Common Cause, 1981; fed. exec. award Evaluation Research Soc., 1980; named to Acctg. Hall of Fame, 1981; fellow Brookings Instn., 1938-39. Mem. Nat. Acad. Pub. Adminstrn., Assn. Govt. Accountants, Am. Acad. Polit. and Social Sci. (dir. 1966—), Am. Soc. Public Adminstrn. (pres. Washington 1948-49, nat. coun. 1958-65, nat. pres. 1961-62), Am. Mgmt. Assns. (gen. mgmt. coun. 1966-85, trustee 1981-85), Cosmos Club (Washington), Chevy Chase (Md.), Phi Beta Kappa, Pi Sigma Alpha, Beta Gamma Sigma, Alpha Kappa Psi. Methodist. Office: Harry S Truman Scholarship Found 712 Jackson Pl NW Washington DC 20006-4901

STABA, EMIL JOHN, pharmacognosy and medicinal chemistry educator; b. N.Y.C., May 16, 1928; s. Frank and Marianna T. (Mack) P.; m. Joyce Elizabeth Ellert, June 19, 1954; children—Marianna, Joanna, Sarah Jane, John, Mark. B.S. cum laude, St. John's U., 1952; M.S., Duquesne U., 1954; Ph.D., U. Conn., 1957. Asst. prof. U. Nebr., 1957-60, prof., chmn. dept., 1968; prof. dept. pharmacognosy U. Minn., 1968—; cons. econs. plants and plant tissue culture U.S. Army Q.M.C.; cons. on drug plants and plant tissue culture NASA; cons. N.C.I. at NIH on anti-cancer natural product prodn., 1991-92; cons. Govt. of Korea, food and pharm. industry cons. NSF-Egyptian Acad. Sci. Rsch. Tech., 1984—; internat. vis. prof. Dalhousie U., 1983; cons. on Indonesia biotech. devel. World Bank-Midwestern Univs. Consortium for Internat. Activities, 1985-90, Thailand, 1989; mem. natural products revision com. U.S. Pharmacopeia, 1980—, chair subcom. natural products, 1995-2000; mem. adv. coun. on life scis. NASA, 1984-87. Mem. editorial bd.: Jour. Plant Cell, Tissue and Organ Culture, 1980-86, plant cellular and developmental biology sect. of In Vitro, 1988—. Served with USNR, 1945-46, PTO. Sr. fgn. fellow NSF, Poland, 1969; Fulbright fellow, Germany, 1970; Coun. Sci. and Indsl. Rsch.-NSF fellow, India, 1973, Pakistani Coun. Sci. and Indsl. Rsch.-NSF fellow, Pakistan, 1978; fellow U.K. Sci. Engring. Rsch. Coun., 1989. Fellow AAAS; mem. Am. Soc. Pharmacognosy (pres. 1971-72), Am. Assn. Colls. Pharmacy (chmn. tchrs. sect. 1972-73, dir. 1976-77), Tissue Culture Assn. (pres. plant sect. 1972-74), Am. Pharm. Assn. and Acad. (chmn. pharmacognosy and nat. products 1977), Soc. Econ. Botany, Am. Soc. Pharmacognosy. Home: 2840 Stinson Blvd Minneapolis MN 55418-3127 Office: U Minn Coll Pharmacy Unit F-9106 Minneapolis MN 55455

STABENAU, JAMES RAYMOND, research psychiatrist, educator; b. Milw., May 24, 1930; s. Walter Frederick and Ruth Emile (Jung) S.; m. Barbara Louise Burris, Oct. 3, 1981; children: Victoria Ruth, Erik Fowler. BS magna cum laude, Marquette U., 1952, MD cum laude, 1955; grad., Washington Psychoanalytic Inst. Diplomate: Am. Bd. Neurology and Psychiatry. Intern Johns Hopkins Hosp., 1955-56; clin. assoc. lab. chem. pharmacology Nat. Cancer Inst., NIH, 1956-58; asst., asso. and chief resident psychiatry U. Rochester Sch. Medicine and Dentistry, Strong Meml. Hosp., 1958-61; research psychiatrist sect. twin and sibling studies adult psychiatry br., clin. investigations NIMH, NIH, 1961-69; research cons. Washington Sch. Psychiatry, 1964-69; prof., chmn. dept. psychiatry U. Conn., Hartford, 1969-73; dir. research U. Conn., 1973-91, prof. emeritus sch. medicine; med. dir. behavioral health Med. Clinic, Sacramento, 1991; prof. sch. medicine U. Calif., Davis; vis. scientist Genetics Unit, Inst. Psychiatry, U. London, 1980-81. Contbr. articles to med. jours. Recipient Eben J. Carey Anatomy award Marquette U. Sch. Medicine, 1952, Lakeside prize, 1955, Lt. William Milman award, 1955; scholar in residence Rockefeller Found., Bellagio, Italy, 1978. Fellow Am. Psychiat. Assn.; mem. Conn. Psychiat. Soc., Washington Artists, Alpha Omega Alpha (v.p. Marquette U. chpt. 1955), Epsilon Phi Chi. Home: 14609 Guadalupe Dr Rncho Murieta CA 95683-9465 Office: 1792 Tribute Rd Ste 400 Sacramento CA 95815

STABILE, BENEDICT LOUIS, retired academic administrator, retired coast guard officer; b. Bklyn., Dec. 13, 1927; s. Domenic and Vita (Grillo) S.; m. Barbara Adele Thompson, June 10, 1951; children: Janet T., Bennett R., Gale V., Roderick T. BS, USCG Acad., 1950; naval engring. degree, MIT, 1956. Commd. USCG, 1950, advanced through grades to vice admiral; served aboard USCG cutters Eastwind, Unimak, Castle Rock, Reliance & Mellon; comdg. officer USCG Yard, Curtis Bay, Md., 1975-77; chief engr. USCG, Washington, 1977-79; dist. comdr. USCG (7th Dist.), Miami, Fla., 1979-82; vice comdt. USCG, Washington, 1982-86; ret. USCG, 1986; coll. pres. Webb Inst. Naval Architecture, Glen Cove, N.Y., 1986-90, ret., 1990. Decorated Meritorious Service medal (3), D.S.M. (2), Legion of Merit, Order of Merit of Italian Republic. Mem. Am. Soc. Naval Engrs., Soc. Naval Architects and Marine Engrs.

STABILE, ROSE K. TOWNE (MRS. FRED STABILE), building and management executive, public relations consultant; b. Sunderland, Eng.; d. Stephen and Amelia Bergman; student English schs., Tchrs. Coll., Columbia; m. Wilfred Kermode (dec. Feb. 1934); m. 2d, Arthur Whittlesey Towne, May 29, 1936 (dec. 1954); m. 3d, Norbert Le Veillie, June 10, 1961 (div. Feb. 1969); m. 4th, Fred Stabile, May 30, 1970. Formerly auditor Brit. Govt., Whitehall, London; activities and membership dir. N.Y. League of Girls Clubs, N.Y.C.; real estate exec., now semi-ret. bldg. mgr. State Tower Bldg., Syracuse, N.Y.; cons. public relations, office designer and decorator; lectr. real estate dept. Syracuse U. An initiator Syracuse Peace Council; mem. area sponsoring com. Assn. for Crippled Children and Adults; mem. Met. Mus., N.Y.C., The Met. Opera, N.Y.C. Mem. English Speaking Union (membership com.), Nat. N.Y. Assn. Real Estate Bd., Nat. Assn. Bldg. Owners and Mgrs., Syracuse C. of C., LWV, Assn. UN, Women of Rotary, Bus. and Profl. Women's Clubs, Everson Mus. Art Friends of Reading, Mus. Modern Art (N.Y.C.), Internat. Center of Syracuse, Hist. Soc. Syracuse, Opera Club of Syracuse, Corinthian Club. Unitarian (chmn. service com. 1956-57.). Home: 304 Malverne Dr Syracuse NY 13208-1843

STABLER, DONALD BILLMAN, business executive; b. Williamsport, Pa., Dec. 23, 1908; s. George William and Etta Mae (Billman) S.; m. Dorothy Louise Witwer, Aug. 10, 1952; 1 dau., Beverly Anne. B.S., Lehigh U., 1930, M.S., 1932, LL.D., 1974; LL.D., Dickinson Law Sch., 1981; LHD, Susquehanna Univ., 1995. Owner Donald B. Stabler (Contractor), Harrisburg, Pa., 1940-55; chmn. bd., chief exec. officer Stabler Cos. Inc., 1955-91, Stabler Constrn. Co., 1955-91, Protection Services Inc., 1955—, State Aggregates Inc., DBS Transit, Inc., 1964—, Stabler Devel. Co., Harrisburg, Pa., 1983—, Stabler Land Co., Harrisburg, Pa., 1984—, Ea. Industries, Inc., Elco-Hausman Constrn. Corp., 1976—, The Center Valley (Pa.) Club Inc., 1992—, Work Area Protection Corp., St. Charles, Ill., 1986—, Precision Solar Controls Inc., Garland, Tex., 1990—; bd. dirs. Millers Mut. Ins. Co., Harrisburg., Road Info. Program, Washington, pres., 1970-74, chmn. bd., 1975-78, chmn. emeritus, 1979—. Bd. dirs. Harrisburg Polyclinic Med. Center, Miami Heart Rsch. Inst.; trustee Lehigh U. Recipient silver hard hat award Constrn. Writers Assn., 1973, Humanitarian award Lions, 1973, Nat. Automobiler Dealers award, 1978, Man & Boy award Boys' Club, 1984, Man of Yr. March of Dimes, 1994, real estate award, 1994, rebuilding Am. award CIT, 1985, master entrepreneur of yr. award Cen. Pa. 1994; named man of yr. Pa. Hwy. Info. Assn., 1992. Mem. Am. Rd. and Transp. Builders Assn. (dir., ARBA award 1974, Nello L. Teer, Jr. award 1994), Associated Pa. Constructors (dir., adv. bd., pres. 1949-50), Nat. Asphalt Pavement Assn., Pa. Asphalt Pavement Assn., U.S. C. of C., Pa. C. of C., Harrisburg C. of C. (adm. 1960), Am. Soc. Hwy. Engrs. (Industry Man of Year 1975), Harrisburg Builders Exchange, Nat. Soc. Profl. Engrs., Pa. Soc. Profl. Engrs. (Engr. of Yr. Harrisburg chpt. 1981), Com. of 100 Miami Beach (dir.), Pa. Soc. N.Y., Lehigh U. Alumni Assn. (pres. 1965-66, L-in-Life award 1972), Navy League, Chi Epsilon, Pi Delta Epsilon. Presbyterian. Clubs: Tall Cedars; Surf (Miami Beach) (pres. 1974-76, chmn. bd. of govs. 1976-78, bd. govs. 1974—); Bal Harbour (Miami); Harrisburg Country (Harrisburg); Saucon Valley Country (Bethlehem, Pa.). Lodges: Masons, Shriners, Jesters, Elks, Rotary. Home: Stray Winds Farm 4001 Mcintosh Rd Harrisburg PA 17112-1927 also: 4001 Mcintosh Rd Harrisburg PA 17112-1927 Office: 635 Lucknow Rd Harrisburg PA 17110-1635

STABLER, LEWIS VASTINE, JR., lawyer; b. Greenville, Ala., Nov. 5, 1936; s. Lewis Vastine and Dorothy Daisy Stabler; m. Monteray Scott, Sept. 5, 1958; children: Dorothy Monteray Scott, Andrew Vastine, Monteray Scott Smith, Margaret Langston. BA, Vanderbilt U., 1958; JD with distinction, U. Mich., 1961. Bar: Ala. 1961. Assoc. firm Cabaniss & Johnston, Birmingham, Ala., 1961-67; assoc. prof. law U. Ala., 1967-70; ptnr. Cabaniss, Johnston, Gardner, Dumas & O'Neal (and predecessor firms), Birmingham, 1970-91, Walston, Stabler, Wells, Anderson and Bains, Birmingham, 1991—; Mem. com. of 100 Candler Sch. Theology, Emory U. Bd. editors: Mich. Law Rev, 1960-61. Fellow Am. Bar Found.; mem. Am. Law Inst., Ala. Law Inst. (mem. council, dir. 1968-70), ABA, Ala. Bar Assn., Birmingham Bar Assn., Am. Judicature Soc., Am. Assn. Railroad Trial Counsel, Order of Coif. Methodist (cert. lay speaker). Clubs: Country of Birmingham, Rotary. Home: 3538 Victoria Rd Birmingham AL 35223-1404 Office: Walston Stabler Wells Anderson & Bains PO Box 83064 Birmingham AL 35283-0642

STACEY, WESTON MONROE, JR., nuclear engineer, educator; b. Birmingham, Ala., July 23, 1937; s. Weston Monroe and Dorothy (Toole) S.; m. Penny Smith; children: Helen Lee, Weston Monroe III, Lucia Katherine. BS in Physics, Ga. Inst. Tech., 1959, MS in Nuclear Sci., 1963; PhD in Nuclear Engring., MIT, 1966. Nuclear engr. Knolls Atomic Power Lab., Schenectady, N.Y., 1962-64, 66-69, Argonne Nat. Lab., Chgo., 1969-77; Callaway Regents prof. Ga. Inst. Tech., Atlanta, 1977—. Author 5 books; contbr. more than 170 articles to profl. jours. 1st lt. USMC, 1959-61. Recipient Cert. Appreciation Dept. Energy, Disting. Assoc. award Dept. Energy, 1990. Fellow Am. Phys. Soc., Am. Nuclear Soc. (bd. dirs. 1974-77, Outstanding Achievement award); mem. AAAS, Soc. Engr. Educators. Office: Ga Inst Tech Nuclear Engring Dept 0225 Atlanta GA 30332

STACHO, ZOLTAN ALADAR, construction and engineering company executive; b. Budapest, Hungary, Mar. 16, 1930; came to U.S., 1957; s. Aladar and Elizabeth (Balazs) S.; m. Maria E. Belatini, July 4, 1951; children: Dorika, Carla. MSCE, U. Tech. and Ec. Sci., Budapest, 1952. Registered profl. engr. Colo., Calif., Mass., Mich., Ga., N.Y., Pa. Chief engr. U.S. Army, Air Force Exchange, 1963-65; project mgr. PBQ&D, San Francisco, Boston, 1965-70; projects mgr. Kaiser Engrs., Inc., Oakland, Calif., 1970-78, v.p., 1978-84, group v.p., 1984-86, exec. v.p., 1986-89, also bd. dirs.; sr. v.p., mgr. corp. ops. svcs. Holmes and Narver, Orange, Calif., 1989-90; with Bechtel Nat., Inc., San Francisco, 1990-91; pres. Holmes and Narver, Inc., Orange, Calif., 1991—. Contbr. articles to profl. jours. Fellow ASCE; mem. Project Mgmt. Inst. Roman Catholic. Home: 210 Lille Ln Apt 214 Newport Beach CA 92663-2694 Office: Holmes & Narver Inc 999 Town Country Rd Orange CA 92668

STACHOWSKI, MICHAEL JOSEPH, lawyer, consultant; b. Buffalo, Feb. 27, 1947; s. Stanley Joseph and Pearl (Wojcik) S.; children: Lisa Ann, Evan Michael, Crystal Lee; m. Deborah Ann Jakubczak, Oct. 19, 1979. BA, Canisius Coll., 1970; JD, SUNY-Buffalo, 1973; cert. Hague Acad. Internat. Law, Netherlands, 1976. Bar: N.Y. 1974, U.S. Dist. Ct. (we. dist.) N.Y. 1974, U.S. Ct. Appeals (2d cir.) 1974. Atty. Sportservice, Inc., Buffalo, 1973-74; assoc. Siegel & McGee, Buffalo, 1974-75; confidential clk. 8th dist. N.Y. Supreme Ct., Buffalo, 1975-77; rsch. counsel N.Y. State Assembly, Albany, 1977-80; sole practice, Buffalo, 1976-86, dep. atty. Town of Cheektowaga, N.Y., 1986—, spl. prosecutor; Michael J. Stachowski P.C., 1987—. Campaign mgr. various jud. candidates, Buffalo, 1977—; fund raiser Erie County Democrats, Buffalo, 1979—, vice chmn. 1988—, com.; bd. dirs. Buffalo Columbus Hosp., 1988—, sec., 1991-92, treas., 1993-95, chmn. merger com. with Buffalo Gen.; mem. N.Y. State Dem. Com., 1988—. Fellow Am. Acad. Matrimonial Lawyers; mem. Erie County Bar Assn., East Clinton Profl. Businessmen's Assn. (v.p. 1976—, pres. 1985). Roman Catholic. Home: 12 Beaverbrook Ct Depew NY 14043-4242 Office: 2025 Clinton St Buffalo NY 14206-3311

STACHOWSKI, WILLIAM T., state senator; b. Buffalo, Feb. 14, 1949; s. Stanley J. and Pearl (Wojcik) S. BA in Polit. Sci., Coll. Holy Cross, 1972. Legislator Erie County Legislature, Buffalo, 1974-81; senator N.Y. State Legislature, Albany, 1981—; mem. U.S. Rte. 19 Assn., Western N.Y., 1982—, U.S. Rte. 62 Assn., Western N.Y., 1985—, City of Buffalo Auditorium Task Force. Recipient Friend of Law Enforcement award N.Y. State Sheriffs, 1990, Fellow Medal Hilbert Coll., 1993. Mem. Erie County Dem. Party, 1967—. Roman Catholic. Avocations: sports. Home: 2030 Clinton St Buffalo NY 14206-3312 Office: NY State Senate State Capital Albany NY 12247

STACK, EDWARD WILLIAM, business management and foundation executive; b. Rockville Centre, N.Y., Feb. 1, 1935; s. Edward Henry and Helen Margaret (Leitner) S.; m. Christina Carol Hunt, Aug. 19, 1967; children: Amy Alison, Kimberly Anne, Suzanne Gail. BBA, Pace U., 1956; LLD (hon.), Hartwick Coll., 1982; LHD (hon.), Pace U., 1991, L.I. U., 1994. Sec., dir. Clark Estates, Inc., fin. and bus. mgmt., N.Y.C., 1956-90, pres., bd. dirs., 1990—; v.p., dir. Leatherstocking Corp., hotels and real estate, Cooperstown, N.Y., 1961-92, pres., bd. dirs., 1992—; sec.-treas., dir. The New Republic, Inc., mag., Washington, 1974—; regional adv. bd. Chase Manhattan Corp., N.Y.C., 1993—. Sec., trustee N.Y. State Hist. Assn., Cooperstown, 1961—; vice chmn., trustee Mary Imogene Bassett Hosp., 1961—; sec. Nat. Baseball Hall of Fame and Mus., Inc., Cooperstown, 1961-77, pres., chmn., 1977-93, chmn., 1993—; v.p., bd. dirs. Farmers' Mus., Inc., Cooperstown, 1964—; sec. Clark Found., N.Y.C., 1963-90, v.p., bd. dirs. 1990—; v.p., bd. dirs. Scriven Found., N.Y.C., 1976—; v.p., trustee Glimmerglass Opera, Cooperstown, N.Y.; trustee Hartwick Coll., Oneonta, N.Y.; trustee, treas. Bethany Deaconess Soc., Bklyn.; bd. dirs. United Meth. City Soc. of Meth. Ch., N.Y.C.; adv. coun. Salvation Army Nassau County. Mem. Downtown Assn. (N.Y.C.), Mohican Club (Cooperstown, N.Y.). Republican. Home: 25 Waverly St Glen Head NY 11545-1004 Office: 30 Wall St New York NY 10005-2201

STACK, GEOFFREY LAWRENCE, real estate developer; b. Trinidad, British West Indies, Sept. 16, 1943; s. Gerald Francis and V. Louise (Bell) S.; m. Victoria Hammack, 1970 (div. 1986); 1 child, Kathryn; m. Nancy J. Haarer, Apr. 19, 1987; children: Alexandra, Natalie. BA, Georgetown U., 1965; MBA, U. Pa., 1972. Dir. acquisitions J.H. Snyder Co., L.A., 1972-75; from project mgr. to exec. v.p. Richards West, Newport Beach, Calif., 1975-77; pres. Regis Homes Corp., Newport Beach, 1977-93; mng. dir. Sares-Regis Group, Irvine, Calif., 1993—; bd. dirs. WJS, Inc., Newport Beach, 1988—, Arral & Ptnrs., Hong Kong, 1981—, Calif. Housing Coun., Sacramento, 1986—. Mem. adv. bd. Coro So. Calif., Santa Ana, 1991—; bd. regents Franciscan Sch. of Theology, Berkeley, Calif., 1991—; bd. advisors Grad. Sch. Bus., U. Calif., Irvine, 1992. Capt. USMC, 1967-70. Decorated 2 Bronze Stars, 21 Air medals, Navy Commendation medal, Purple Heart. Mem. Young Pres. Orgn., Big Canyon Country Club, Pacific Club, Ctr. Club. Democrat. Roman Catholic. Office: Sares Regis Group 18802 Bardeen Ave Irvine CA 92715-1521

STACK, GEORGE JOSEPH, philosophy educator; b. N.Y.C.; s. George Francis and Elizabeth (Sullivan) S.; m. Claire Avena (dec.); children: Diane Joan, Christopher George. B.A., Pace U., 1960; M.A., Pa. State U., 1962, Ph.D., 1964. Instr. humanities Pa. State U., 1962-63; instr. philosophy L.I. U., 1963-64, asst. prof., 1964-67; asst. prof. SUNY, Brockport, 1967-68, assoc. prof., 1968-70, prof., chmn., 1970-77, prof., 1977-95, prof. emeritus, 1995—, also advisor Center for Philosophic Exchange, 1970-82; cons. to Choice. Author: Berkeley's Analysis of Perception, 1970, 2d edit., 1992, On Kierkegaard: Philosophical Fragments, 1976, Kierkegaard's Existential Ethics, 1977, 2d edit., 1992, Japanese transl., 1985, Sartre's Philosophy of Social Existence, 1978, reprinted 1992, Lange and Nietzsche, 1983; contbg. author: Nietzsche and Modern German Thought, 1991, Nietzsche and Emerson, 1992, Nietzsche: Man, Knowledge, Will to Power, 1994; editorial advisor: Folia Humanistica, Filosofia Oggi; contbr. over 180 philos. articles to profl. jours. Mem. United Univ. Profls. Home: PO Box 92 Grapevine TX 76099

STACK, J. WILLIAM, JR., management consultant; b. Lansing, Mich., July 13, 1918; s. Joseph William and Helen (Dodge) S.; m. Wolcott Rorick, Sept. 25, 1948; children: Christopher D., Nathan S., Joseph W., David R., Peter S. B.A., Yale U., 1940. With Gen. Motors Corp, 1945-57; dir. mktg. Gen. Motors Corp (AC Electronics div.), 1955-57; v.p. Kurth Malting Co., Milw., 1957-59; gen. sales mgr. Massey Ferguson, Inc., Toronto, Can., 1960-62; pres., founder Stancor Ltd., Toronto, 1963-68; pres. William Stack Assocs. Inc., N.Y.C., 1968—; mem. Navy and Marine Corps Acquisition Rev. Com., 1974-75. Active Rep. Town Com. Lt. comdr. USNR, 1940-45. Mem. Yale Club of N.Y.C., New Canaan Country Club. Episcopalian. Home: 31 Lakeview Ave New Canaan CT 06840-5947 Office: Stack Assocs 31 Lakeview Ave New Canaan CT 06840-5947 *Success is measured by what you give back; not what you take. To help one person, to advance one worthy cause is the mark of total achievement.*

STACK, JOHN WALLACE, lawyer; b. Chgo., May 30, 1937; s. Wallace and Irma Evelyn (Anderson) S.; m. Della Rae Melin, Feb. 1, 1975; children: James Randolph, Linnea Claire, Theodore. BBA, U. Wis., 1960; JD, U. Calif., Berkeley, 1963. Bar: Ill. 1963, D.C. 1963, U.S. Ct. Appeals (7th cir.) 1963, U.S. Supreme Ct. 1972. Assoc. Pattishall, McAuliffe & Hofstetter, Chgo., 1963-64; assoc. Winston & Strawn, Chgo., 1964-70, ptnr., 1970—. Contbg. editor U. Calif. Law Rev., 1963. Mem. ABA (antitrust and corp., banking and bus. law sects.), W Club of U. Wis. (Madison), Order of Coif, Phi Delta Phi, Beta Gamma Sigma. Republican. Lutheran. Avocations: sports, gardening, reading. Home: 2906 Lincoln St Evanston IL 60201-2047 Office: Winston & Strawn 35 W Wacker Dr Chicago IL 60601-1614

STACK, MAURICE DANIEL, retired insurance company executive; b. N.Y.C., Dec. 15, 1917; s. Maurice E. and Margaret (Brooks) S.; m. Catherine T. O'Connor, Nov. 25, 1943; children: Mary Jane, Eileen, Peter, Clare. Student, U. Notre Dame, 1935-36; BBA, Manhattan Coll., 1939; MBA, Harvard, 1941. Investment analyst Carnegie Corp., N.Y.C., 1946-48; adminstrv. asst. Tchrs. Ins. & Annuity Assn., 1948-49; investment analyst First Nat. Bank N.Y., 1949-54; fin. sec. Atlantic Mut. Ins. Co., N.Y.C., 1954-56; v.p. Atlantic Mut. Ins. Co., 1957-60, fin. v.p., trustee, 1961-66, chmn. fin. com., 1966-83; trustee emeritus Atlantic Mutual Ins. Co. Trustee emeritus, adviser St. Vincent's Hosp.; trustee emeritus YWCA. Served to maj. C.E., AUS, 1941-46. Mem. Soc. for Propagation of the Faith (dir.), K.M. Club (N.Y.C.), Harvard Club (N.Y.C.). Home: 85 Lynbrook Ave Point Lookout NY 11569-0095

STACK, MAY ELIZABETH, library director; b. Jackson, Miss., Nov. 10, 1940; d. James William and Irene Thelma (Baldwin) Garrett; m. Richard Gardiner, Apr. 15, 1962; children: Elinor, Harley David. BS, Miss. State Coll. for Women, 1962; MBA, Western New Eng. Coll., 1981; MLS, So. Conn. State U., 1989. Clk. Western New Eng. Coll., Springfield, Mass., 1965-66; acquisitions staff Western New Eng. Coll., Springfield, 1966-72, cataloger, 1972-84, asst. dir., 1984-89, acting dir., 1989-90, dir., 1990—; chair Ctrl./Western Mass. Automated Resource Sharing Collection Devel. Com., Paxton, Mass., 1993-95, exec. bd., 1993-96. mem. East Longmeadow (Mass.) Hist. Soc., 1989-92. Mem. ALA, Mass. Libr. Assn., Assn. Coll. and Rsch. Librs., Libr. and Mgmt. Assn., Libr. Info. and Technology Assn. Methodist. Avocations: horseback riding, show dogs. Office: Western New Eng Coll D'Amour Libr 1215 Wilbraham Rd Springfield MA 01119-2654

STACK, PAUL FRANCIS, lawyer; b. Chgo., July 21, 1946; s. Frank Louis and Dorothy Louise Stack; m. Nea Waterman, July 8, 1972; children: Nea Elizabeth, Sera Waterman. BS, U. Ariz., 1968; JD, Georgetown U., 1971. Bar: Ill. 1971, U.S. Ct. Claims 1975, U.S. Tax Ct. 1974, U.S. Ct. Internat. Trade 1977, U.S. Supreme Ct. 1975. Law clk., U.S. Dist. Ct., Chgo., 1971-72; Asst. U.S. Atty. No. Dist. Ill., Chgo., 1972-75; mng. dir. Stack & Filpi, Chgo., 1976—. Bd. dirs. Riverside (Ill.) Pub. Libr., 1977-83, Suburban Libr. Sys., Burr Ridge, Ill., 1979-82; mem. Mayor's ad hoc adv. com. on Ctrl. Libr., Chgo., Ill., 1987-88; mem. bd. edn. Twp. H.S. Dist. 208, Riverside, Ill., 1989—. Mem. Chgo. Zoological Soc. (governing mem.), Brookfield, Ill., 1982—, Chgo. Bar Assn., Union League Club of Chgo. (bd. dirs. 1986-89). Presbyterian. Home: 238 N Delaplaine Rd Riverside IL 60546-2035 Office: 140 S Dearborn St Ste 411 Chicago IL 60603-5892

STACK, R. TIMOTHY, health facility administrator; b. 1952. BA, Bethany (W.Va.) Coll., 1952; MA, Med. Coll. Va., 1977. Asst. adminstr. Southside Hosp., Pitts., 1977-79; sr. v.p., COO Cen. Med. Ctr., Pitts., 1980-81; pres. Southside Hosp., 1981-87; pres., adminstr. Borgess Health Alliance Inc., Kalamazoo, Mich., 1987—. Office: Borgess Health Alliance Inc 1521 Gull Rd Kalamazoo MI 49001-1640*

STACK, ROBERT LANGFORD, actor; b. Los Angeles, Jan. 13, 1919; s. James Langford and Elizabeth (Wood) S.; m. Rosemarie Bowe, Jan. 23, 1956; children: Elizabeth Langford, Charles Robert. Student, U. So. Calif., 1937-38. Pres. St. Pierre Prodns., Los Angeles, 1959—. Actor, co-producer: (TV series) The Untouchables, 1959-63 (2 nominations, 1 Emmy award); actor: The Name of the Game, 1968-71, Most Wanted, 1976-77, Strike Force, 1982-83, Unsolved Mysteries, 1986—; actor: (TV movies) The Strange and Deadly Occurence, 1974, The Adventure of the Queen, 1975, Murder on Flight 502, 1975, Undercover with the KKK, 1979 (narrator), Perry Mason: The Curse of the Sinister Spirit, 1987, The Return of Elliot Ness, 1991; (TV miniseries) George Washington, 1984, Hollywood Wives; (films) including First Love, 1940, When the Daltons Rode, 1940, Mortal Storm, 1940, Nice Girl, 1941, Badlands of Dakota, 1941, To Be or Not To Be, 1942, Eagle Squadron, 1942, Men of Texas Fighter Squadron, 1948, Date with Judy, 1948, Miss Tatlock's Millions, 1948, Mr. Music, 1950, The Bullfighter and the Lady, 1950, My Outlaw Brother, 1951, Bwana Devil, 1952, War Paint, 1953, The High and the Mighty, 1953, Iron Glove, 1954, Written on the Wind, 1956 (Acad. Award nomination for best supporting actor), The Last Voyage, 1959, John Paul Jones, 1959, The Caretakers, 1963, The Corrupt Ones, 1967, Story of a Woman, 1970, '1941', 1979, Airplane!, 1980, Uncommon Valor, 1983, Big Trouble, 1984, Glory Days, 1987, Caddyshack II, 1988, Joe Verses the Volcano, 1990. Served with USN, WWII. Recipient Emmy award Acad. TV Arts and Scis. Office: care Camden Artists 409 N Camden Dr Beverly Hills CA 90210-4417

STACK, STEPHEN S., manufacturing company executive; b. DuPont, Pa., Apr. 25, 1934; s. Steve and Sophie (Baranowski) Stasenko. BSME, Case Western Res. U., 1956; postgrad. Syracuse U. Registered profl. engr., Ill. Mech. engr. Kaiser Aluminum, Erie, Pa., 1956-58; instr. Gannon U., Erie, 1958-60, Syracuse (N.Y.) U., 1960-61; engring. supr. A. O. Smith Corp., Erie and Los Angeles, 1961-66; gen. mgr. Am. Elec. Fusion, Chgo., 1966-67; mgr. new products Maremont Corp., Chgo., 1967-69; dir. market planning Gulf and Western Ind., Bellwood, Ill., 1969-71; mgmt. and fin. cons. Stack & Assos., Chgo., 1971-76; pres. Seamcraft, Inc., Chgo., 1976—; mem. Ill. Legis. Small Bus. Conf., 1980, Gov.'s Small Bus. Adv. Commn., 1984-94, Ill. State House Conf. on Small Bus., 1984, 86; chmn. West Cell, 1988—, Bridge Pers. Svcs. Corp., 1989—; v.p. Ind. Bus. Assn. Ill., 1993-94; mem. small bus. adv. coun. Fed. Res. Bank of Chgo., 1989-91; del. White House Conf. on Small Bus., 1986. Patentee in liquid control and metering fields. Treas. Sem. Townhouse Assn., 1993-94; active Lincoln Park Conservation Assn., Sheffield Neighbors Assn. Recipient Am. Legion award, 1948, Case Western Res. U. Honor key, 1956, Eagle Scout award, 1949. Mem. Ill. Mfrs. Assn. (bd. dirs. 1986—, vice chmn. 1996), Small Mfrs. Action Council (vice chmn. 1986-87, chmn. 1988-89), Mfrs. Polit. Action Com. (exec. com. 1987—, vice chmn. 1993-95, chmn. 1996—), Am. Mgmt. Assn., Ind. Bus. Assn. Ill. (v.p. 1993), Pres.' Assn., Blue Key, Beta Theta Pi, Theta Tau, Pi Delta Epsilon. Clubs: Chgo. Yacht, Chgo. Execs., East Bank, Singapore (Mich.) Yacht, Capitol Hill (Washington), Fullerton Tennis (pres. 1971-79, treas. 1979-83, bd. dirs. 1983-86), Lake Shore Ski (v.p. 1982, 91), Lincoln Park Tennis Assn., Oak Park Tennis Club. Office: 932 W Dakin St Chicago IL 60613-2922

STACKABLE, FREDERICK LAWRENCE, lawyer; b. Howell, Mich., Dec. 4, 1935; s. Lawrence Peter and Dorothea R. (Kiney) S. BA, Mich. State U., 1959; JD, Wayne State U., 1962. Bar: Mich. 1962, U.S. Dist. Ct. (ea. and we. dists.) Mich. 1964; U.S. Supreme Ct. 1968. Lawyer Ingham County Cir. Ct. Commnr.; v.p. Mich. Assn. Cir. Ct. Commrs., 1963, pres., 1967-70; 18th dist. rep. Ingham County Bd. Suprs.; mem. Com. on Mich. Law Revision Commn.; state rep. 58th House Dist., 1971, 72, 73, 74. County del. Rep. Party, Ingham County, Mich., 1969-70, state del., Mich., 1971-74. Recipient Disting. Alumni award Wayne State U. Sch. Law, Detroit, 1987. Mem. Mich. Bar Assn., Ingham County Bar Assn., Ingraham Hounty Bar, Mich. Trail Rider's Assn. (dir., past pres.), Nat. Conf. Commrs. Uniform State Laws, Mich. Trail Rider's Assn. (dir.), Mich. Internat. Snowmobile Assn., Sportsman's Alliance Mich., Cycle Conservation Club, Am. Judicature Soc. Avocations: horseback riding, snowmobiling, skiing, traveling. Office: 300 N Grand Ave Lansing MI 48933

STACKELBERG, JOHN RODERICK, history educator; b. Munich, May 8, 1935; came to U.S., 1946; s. Curt Freiherr and Ellen (Biddle) von Stackelberg; m. Steffi Heuss, Oct. 10, 1965 (div. Apr. 1983); m. Sally Winkle, Mar. 30, 1991; children: Katherine Ellen, Nicholas Olaf, Emmet Winkle. AB, Harvard U., 1956; MA, U. Vt., 1972; PhD, U. Mass., 1974. Reading instr. Baldridge Reading Svcs., Greenwich, Conn., 1957-62; lang. tchr. Hartnackschule, Berlin, 1963-67; English and social studies tchr. Lake Region Union High Sch., Orleans, Vt., 1967-70; lectr. history San Diego State U., 1974-76; asst. prof. history U. Oreg., Eugene, 1976-77, U. S.D., Vermillion, 1977-78; asst. prof. history Gonzaga U., Spokane, Wash., 1978-81, assoc. prof. history, 1981-88, prof. history, 1988—. Author: Idealism Debased, 1981; contbr. articles to profl. jours. Pres. Spokane chpt. UN Assn., 1986-90. With U.S. Army, 1958-60. Leadership Devel. fellow Ford Found., 1969-70. Avocations: chess, tennis. Home: 9708 E Maringo Dr Spokane WA 99206-4429 Office: Gonzaga U Spokane WA 99258

STACKHOUSE, RICHARD GILBERT, retired financial company executive; b. Ottawa, Ont., Can., Nov. 26, 1929; s. A. Gilbert and Leone (Turner) S.; m. Edna Betty Fitzsimmons, July 9, 1955 (dec. July 1988); children: Brent Richard, Kerry Jane, Nancy Edna; m. Jean Elinor Stark, Nov. 3, 1990. B of Commerce, Queen's U., Kingston, Ont., 1953. Chartered acct., FCA, Ont. Contr. Goddard Enterprises Ltd., Barbados, W.I., 1964-65; staff acct. to mgr. Price Waterhouse, Toronto, Ont., 1953-64, mgr., 1965-67, ptnr., 1967-92; chmn. bd. Queen's U., 1990-95. Gov. Exhbn. Place, Toronto, 1988-94, The Shaw Festival Niagara-on-the-Lake, 1991-95. Lt. Royal Can. Navy Res., 1949-53. Mem. Can. Nat. Exhbn. Assn. (pres. 1990-92), Donwood Inst. (chmn. 1982-86), Ont. Safety League (chmn. 1984-86), Nat. Club (pres. 1986-87), Mississauga Golf and Country Club (pres. 1983-84), Masons (treas. 1983—). Office: Price Waterhouse, 1st Canadian Pl Box 190, Toronto, ON Canada M5X 1H7

STACKHOUSE, ROBERT, sculptor; b. Bronxville, N.Y., 1942. BA, U. South Fla., 1965; postgrad., U. Md., 1967. Vis. artist and lectr., U. Hawaii, Manoa, 1990, U. South Fla., Tampa, 1991, U. Denver, 1992. One-man shows Corcoran Gallery Art, Washington, 1973, 88, Honolulu Acad. Arts, 1990, Va. Mus. Fine Arts, Richmond, 1990, U. Denver Art Gallery, 1993, Struve Gallery, Chgo., 1993, Morgan Gallery, Kansas City, Mo., 1993, Baumgartner Galleries, Washington, 1993; exhibited in group shows Corcoran Gallery Art, 1970, Balt. Mus. Art, 1970, Walker Art Ctr., Mpls., 1977, Art Inst. Chgo., 1977, Hunter Mus. Art, Chattanooga, 1981, Bklyn. Mus., 1986, 89, Nat. Mus. Am. Art, Smithsonian Inst, Washington, 1989, William A. Farnsworth Libr. and Art Mus., Rockland, Maine, 1990, Am. Acad. and Inst. Arts and Letters, N.Y.C., 1991, U. Wyo. Art Mus., 1993, numerous others; travelling exhbns. Corcoran Gallery Art, 1975, 87, Ft. Worth Art Mus., 1975, Huntsville (Ala.) Mus. Art, Hunter Mus. Art, Chattanooga, 1984, Okla. Mus. Art, Oklahoma City; represented in permanent collections Mus. Modern Art, N.Y.C., Art Inst. Chgo., Mus. Contemporary Art, Chgo., Walker Art Ctr., Balt. Mus. Art, Hirshhorn Mus. and Sculpture Garden, Corcoran Gallery Art, also corp. collections; commns. include bronze On the Beach Again, Australia Nat. Gallery, Canberra; painted wood St. Louie Bones, Laumeier Sculpture Park, St. Louis, Oliver Ranch Project/Russian River Bones, Geyserville, Calif., 1989; extruded red brass Delaware Passage, Del. Art Mus., Wilmington, 1991, Divers, Marine Sci. Bldg., U. Hawaii, 1991.

STACKPOLE, LAURIE EVELETH, library director; b. Schenectady, N.Y., June 27, 1934; d. Lawrence Nelson and Genevieve (McCafferty) E.; m. John D. Stackpole, June 11, 1960; children: Mark L., Paul L., Jean S. Brown. AB, Trinity Coll., Washington, 1956; MA, Smith Coll., 1957; MSLS, Cath. U., 1977. Reference libr. NOAA, Rockville, Md., 1977-81, head libr. svcs., 1981-84, sys. libr., 1984-85, head libr. divsn., 1985-86; chief libr. Naval Rsch. Lab., Washington, 1986—; rep. Fed. Libr. and Info. Ctr. Com., Washington, 1992-94; mem. adv. coun. FEDLINK, Washington, 1992-94, chair, 1993. Contbr. articles to profl. jours. Mem. ALA (sec.-treas. Fed. Librs. Round Table 1992-94, bd. dirs. 1994-96), Spl. Libr. Assn. (chair-elect, chair mil. libr. divsn., 1990). Office: USN Naval Rsch Lab Ruth H Hooker Rsch Libr & Tech Info Ctr Code 5220 Washington DC 20375-5334

STACY, ALAN, gas industry executive; b. 1941. Degree, Lamar U., 1965. With Phillips Petroleum Co., Odessa, Tex., 1965-69; with Enogex Inc., Okla. City, 1969—, v.p., coo, now v.p. of pipeline & processing, 1986—; pres. Enogex Products Corp., Okla. City. Office: Enogex Inc 515 Central Park Dr PO Box 24300 Oklahoma City OK 73124-0300*

STACY, BILL WAYNE, academic administrator; b. Bristol, Va., July 26, 1938; s. Charles Frank and Louise Nelson (Altwater) S.; m. Sue Varnon; children: Mark, Sara, James. B.S.Ed., S.E. Mo. State U., 1960; M.S., So. Ill. U., 1965, Ph.D., 1968. Tchr. Malden High Sch., Mo., 1960-64; faculty Southeast Mo. State U., Cape Girardeau, 1967-89, dean Grad. Sch., 1976-79, interim pres., 1979, pres., 1980-89; pres. Calif. State U., San Marcos, 1989—; dir. Boatmen's Nat. Bank. Bd. dirs. San Diego United Way. Mem. Am. Assn. state Colls. and Univs. (dir.), Am. Assn. Higher edn., PIC Policy Bd., San Diego Rotary, Pvt. Industry Coun. Presbyterian.

STACY, CHARLES BRECKNOCK, lawyer; b. Charleston, W.Va., Sept. 2, 1924; s. George Palmer and Patti (Hubbard) S.; m. Judith Cook Willner, June 14, 1947 (dec. Jan. 1996); 1 child, Charles Brecknock. B.S., Yale U., 1948, LL.B., 1951. Bar: W.Va. 1951. Assoc. firm Spilman, Thomas & Battle, 1951-58; v.p. Lewis-Hubbard Corp., 1957; ptnr. Spilman, Thomas & Battle, Charleston, 1958—; mem. U.S. Circuit Ct. Judge Nominating Commn., 4th Circuit, 1977-79. Contbr. articles to law and tax publs. Pres. Kanawha-Charleston Vis. Nursing Assn., 1966-67; bd. dirs. Charleston Symphony Orch., 1960-70, pres., 1962-63; bd. trustees Woodberry Forest (Va.) Sch., 1970-76; pres. Woodberry Forest Alumni Assn., 1972-74; bd. dirs. Community Council of Kanawha Valley, Inc., 1971-79, pres., 1975-77; bd. dirs. United Way of Kanawha Valley, Inc., 1973-77, exec. com., 1975-77; trustee Greater Kanawha Valley Found., 1968-72, adv. bd., 1972—, chmn. bd., 1970-72; bd. dirs. W.Va. Tax Inst., 1958-67, pres., 1959-60. Served with USAAF, 1943-46. Fellow Am. Bar Found., Am. Coll. Trust and Estate Counsel, Am. Coll. Tax Counsel; mem. ABA (coun. 1977-83, vice chmn. adminstrn. sect. taxation 1980-83), Kanawha County Bar Assn., W.Va. State Bar (chmn. standing com. on state and fed. taxation 1959-70), W.Va. Bar Assn., Am. Law Inst., Am. Judicature Soc., Edgewood Country Club Charleston (gov. 1973-75, 83-86), Sea Pines Country Club (Hilton Head, S.C.), Yale Club N.Y.C., Rotary (bd. dirs. Charleston club 1979-80, 83-91, pres. 1989-90). Democrat. Presbyterian. Home: 1560 Thomas Cir Charleston WV 25314-1623 Office: Spilman Ctr 300 Kanawha Blvd E Charleston WV 25301-2531

STACY, DENNIS WILLIAM, architect; b. Council Bluffs, Iowa, Sept. 22, 1945; s. William L. and Mildred Glee (Carlsen) S.; BArch., Iowa State U., 1969; postgrad. U. Nebr., 1972. Registered architect, Iowa, Tex., Colo., Mo.; m. Judy Annette Long, Dec. 28, 1968; 1 child, Stephanie. Designer Troy & Stalder Architects, Omaha, 1967, Architects Assocs., Des Moines, 1968-69, Logsdon & Voelter Architects, Temple, Tex., 1970; project architect Roger Schutte & Assocs., Omaha, 1972-73; architect, assoc. Robert H. Burgin & Assocs., Coun. Bluffs, 1973-75, Neil Astle & Assocs., Omaha, 1975-78; owner, prin. Dennis W. Stacy, AIA, Architect, Glenwood, Iowa, 1978-81, Dallas, 1981—. Mem. City of Dallas Urban Design Adv. Com., 1992-96, chmn., 1995-96; chmn., Glenwood Zoning Bd. Adjustment, 1979-81; chmn. Mills County Plant Iowa Program, 1979-81; mem. S.W. Iowa Citizen's Adv. Com., Iowa State Dept. Transp., 1977-81; regional screening chmn. Am. Field Svc. Internat./Intercultural Programs, 1974-79, Iowa-Nebr. rep., 1978-80. With U.S. Army, 1969-71. Decorated Nat. Def. Svc. medal, Vietnam Svc. medal, Vietnam Campaign medal, Army Commendation medal. Mem. AIA (recipient Iowa Design Honor award 1981, Dallas AIA commendation awards (2) 1990, citation of honor award 1991, 92, Dallas Design awards (2) 1991, Texas Design Honor award 1992, Dallas AIA Firm of Yr. award 1992, Dallas commr. design, 1991, chmn. Dallas design awards 1992, pres Dallas AIA 1996), Nat. Coun. Archtl. Registration Bds., Tex. Soc. Archs. (environ. resource com. 1994-95, chmn., Tex. arch. pub. com., 1992-95), The 500 Inc. (outstanding mem. 1985), Glenwood Optimist (Disting. Svc. award 1982, pres. 1980-81), Masons. Archtl. Works include: Davies Amphitheater, 1980, Addison Nat. Bank Bldg., 1985, Fairview Recreation Complex, 1984, Computer Lang. Rsch. Corp. Learning Ctr., 1987., Villa Roma, 1988, C.U. Performing Arts Ctr., 1989, Mercedes-Benz Distbn. Ctr., 1987, Dallas Chpt. AIA Offices, 1990, Janadria Festival Arena, 1994, Surg. Ctr. Pain Mgmt. Inst., 1995, Physicians Consultants Clinic, 1994, rheumatology assoc. clinic Horizon Pain Mgmt. Ctr., 1995. Home: 4148 Cobblers Ln Dallas TX 75287-6725 Office: 2136 N Harwood St Ste 100 Dallas TX 75201-2253

STACY, RICHARD A., administrative law judge; b. Eldorado, Ark., Mar. 7, 1942; s. Jack Leonard S. and Estelle (Mabry) Carrier; m. Karen Kay King, Aug. 20, 1961; children: Mark L., Andrea L. BA, U. Wyo., 1965, JD, 1967. Bar: Wyo. 1967, Colo. 1967, U.S. Supreme Ct. 1972. Revisor Wyo. Statute Revision Com., Cheyenne, 1967-69; asst. atty. gen. State of Wyo., 1969-72; asst. U.S. atty. Dept. Justice, Cheyenne, 1972-75; U.S. atty. Dis. Wyo., Cheyenne, 1981-94; adminstrv. law judge Office of Hearing & Appeals, San Jose, Calif., 1994—; mem. atty. gen's adv. com. of U.S. attys. Dept. Justice, 1981-84. Mem. Gov.'s Statewide Drug Alcohol Adv. Bd., 1988-94. Mem. ABA, Wyo. Bar Assn., Colo. State Bar, Santa Clara County Bar Assn. (hon., com. on bench, bar, media, police relationships 1995—). Republican. Episcopalian. Club: Kiwanis (charter pres. Wheatland 1977). Office: Hearings & Appeals 280 S 1st St San Jose CA 95113-3002

STADDON, JOHN ERIC RAYNER, psychology, zoology, neurobiology educator; b. Grayshott, Hampshire, Eng.; came to U.S., 1960; s. Leonard John and Dulce Norine (Rayner) S.; m. Lucinda Paris. BSc, Univ. Coll., London, 1960; PhD, Harvard U., 1964. Asst. prof. psychology U. Toronto, Ont., Can., 1964-67; from asst. prof. to prof. Duke U., Durham, N.C., 1967-72, prof., 1972-83, J.B. Duke prof. psychology, prof. neurobiology and zoology, 1983—. Author: Adaptive Behavior and Learning, 1983, Behaviorism, 1993; editor: Behavioral Processes, 1979; cons. editor Behavior and Philosophy, 1993; assoc. editor Jour. Exptl. Analysis of behavior, 1979-82. Recipient von Humboldt prize, 1985. Fellow AAAS, N.Y. Acad. Scis., Soc. Exptl. Psychologists; mem. Phi Beta Kappa (hon.), Sigma Xi. Avocations: history, philosophy of science, public policy. Office: Duke U Dept Exptl Psychology PO Box 90086 Durham NC 27708-0086

STADE, GEORGE GUSTAV, humanities educator; b. N.Y.C., Nov. 25, 1933; s. Kurt Herman and Eva Bergit (Aronson) S.; m. Dorothy Louise Fletcher, Dec. 16, 1957; children: Bjorn, Eric, Nancy, Kirsten. B.A., St. Lawrence U., 1955; M.A., Columbia U., 1958, Ph.D., 1965. Tchr. Collegiate Sch., N.Y.C., 1957-58; instr. Bernard Baruch Sch. Bus., N.Y.C., 1958-59, Bklyn. Poly. Inst., 1959-60, Rutgers U.-Newark, 1960-62; instr. Columbia U., N.Y.C., 1962, asst. prof., 1965, assoc. prof., 1968, prof. English, 1971—; cons. various law firms, N.Y.C., 1960—. Author: Robert Graves, 1967, Confessions of a Lady-Killer, 1979; editor: European Writers, 13 vols., Selected Letters of E.E. Cummings, 1968, Six Modern British Writers, 1974, Six Contemporary British Writers, 1976, European Writers: Selected Authors, 3 Vols., 1992, British Writers Supplement II, 1992, British Writers Supplement III, 1995; contbr. over 100 articles to profl. jours. Mem. PEN, N.Y. Book Critics Circle, Popular Culture Assn., MLA. Home: 430 W 116th St New York NY 10027-7239 Office: Columbia U 604 Philosophy Hall New York NY 10027

STADELMAN, WILLIAM RALPH, chemical institution executive; b. Ont., Can., July 18, 1919; s. John Joseph and Lillian (Trachsell) S.; m. Jean MacLaren, Nov. 2, 1951; 1 child, Mary Laren. B.A.Sc., U. Toronto, 1941; M.B.A., U. Pa., 1949. Chief process engr. Can. Synthetic Rubber, Ltd., 1943-47; lectr. mktg. U. Pa., 1948-49; asst. to mgr. Pa. Salt Mfg. Co., 1950; sec.-treas. Ont. Research Found., Mississauga, 1950-64, pres., 1964-84; pres. WRS Assocs., 1984—; dir., sr. exec. Inst. Chem. Sci. and Tech., 1985-89; dir. Med. Tech. Investment Corp. Fellow World Acad. Art and Sci.; mem. Assn. Profl. Engrs. Ont., Can. Rsch. Mgmt. Assn., Bd. Trade Met. Toronto, Club of Rome, Caledon Ski Club. Home and Office: WRS Assocs, 31 Rykert Crescent, Toronto, ON Canada M4G 2T1

STADLER, CRAIG ROBERT, professional golfer; b. San Diego, June 2, 1953; s. Donald Edwin and Betty M. (Adams) S.; m. Susan Barrett, Jan. 6, 1979; children: Kevin Craig, Christopher Barrett. Student, U. So. Calif. Profl. golfer Palm Beach Gardens, Fla.; winner Hope Classic, 1980, Greater Greensboro Open, 1980, Kemper Open, 1981-82, Tucson Open, 1982, Masters, 1982, World Series of Golf, 1982, 92, Tour Championship, 1991. U.S. amateur champion, 1973; mem. U.S. Walker Cup team, 1975; leading money winner PGA Tour, 1982. Mem. Golf Mag. (Player of Yr. 1982). *

STADLER, GERALD P., transportation executive; b. 1937; married. Student, Loyola U. Sec. United Van Lines, Fenton, Mo., 1981-84, vice chmn., 1984—, also bd. dirs. Office: United Van Lines Inc 1 United Dr Fenton MO 63026-2535*

STADLEY, PAT ANNA MAY GOUGH (MRS. JAMES M. STADLEY), author; b. El Paso, Tex., Aug. 31, 1918; d. Thomas and Leona (Plitt) Gough; A.A., Chaffey Jr. Coll., 1936; m. James M. Stadley, Aug. 15, 1936; children—William T., Jerry M. Author books, anthologies, short stories published in over 15 fgn. langs., works include: The Black Leather Barbarians, 1960; Autumn of a Hunter (Edgar Allen Poe spl. award 1970, produced as The Deadly Hunt TV Friday Night Movie Week 1971), 1970; The Deadly Hunt; 1977; The Murder Hunt, 1977; also numerous short stories including The Doe and The Gantlet, 1957, The Waiting Game, 1961, Kurdistan Payload, 1962, Something for the Club, 1963, The Big Measure, 1976, The Tender Trap, 1977, The Stranger, 1980. Democrat. Mem. Christian Ch. Clubs: Calif. Writers (v.p. 1967) (Citrus Heights), Calif. Writers (v.p. 1967—), Mystery Writers Am. Home: 15079 Pinon Rd Magalia CA 95954-9124

STADTER, PHILIP AUSTIN, classicist, educator; b. Cleve., Nov. 29, 1936; s. John M. and Mary Louise (Jones) S.; m. Lucia Angela Ciapponi, July 6, 1963; children: Paul, Maria, Mark. B.A., Princeton U., 1958; M.A., Harvard U., 1959, Ph.D., 1963. Instr. U. N.C., Chapel Hill, 1962-64, asst.

prof., 1964-67, assoc. prof., 1967-71, prof., 1971—, chmn. dept. classics, 1976-86, prof. comparative lit., 1991—, Falk prof. humanities, 1991—. Author: Plutarch's Historical Methods, 1965, The Public Library of Renaissance Florence, 1972, Arrian of Nicomedia, 1980, A Commentary on Plutarch's Pericles, 1989; editor: The Speeches of Thucydides, 1973, Plutarch and the Historical Tradition, 1992. Fulbright fellow Rome, 1960-61; Guggenheim fellow Florence, Italy, 1967-68; NEH fellow, 1974-75; fellow Am. Council Learned Socs., Oxford, Eng., 1982-83. Fellow Nat. Humanities Ctr.; mem. Am. Philol. Assn. (dir. 1977-80), Am. Assn. Ancient Historians, Soc. Promotion of Hellenic Studies, Classical Assn. Middle West and South. Democrat. Roman Catholic. Office: U NC Dept Classics Chapel Hill NC 27599-3145

STADTLER, BEATRICE HORWITZ, author; b. Cleve., June 26, 1921; d. David and Minnie (Gorelick) Horwitz; m. Oscar Stadtler, Jan. 31, 1945; children—Dona Stadtler Rosenblatt, Sander, Miriam Stadtler Rosenbaum. MS in Religious Edn., John Carroll U., 1983, M Judaic Studies, 1988. Sec. Cleve. Dept. Pub. Health and Welfare, 1940; sec., dept. mgr. Fed. Pub. Housing Authority, Cleve., 1943; primary supr. Temple Beth Shalom Religious Sch., Cleve., 1953; registrar Cleve. Coll. Jewish Studies, 1958-83; asst. editor Israel Philatelist, 1975—; speaker on holocaust, lectr. at writer's confs. and classes; scholar-in-residence various cities; tchr. Cleve. Hebrew Schs., 1992—. Author: Once Upon a Jewish Holiday, 1963, The Story of Dona Gracia, 1969, The Adventures of Gluckel of Hamlen, 1967, Rescue From the Sky (in Hebrew), 1972, Personalities of the Jewish Labor Movement, 1972, The Holocaust: A History of Courage and Resistance, 1975 (prize outstanding juvenile book, Jewish Book Coun. Nat. Jewish Welfare Bd. 1975), The History of Israel Through Her Postage Stamps, 1993 (Silver medals Can. Nat. Philatelic Lit. Competition and Nat. Philatelic Lit. Competition); also stories and articles for children in Chattanooga Shofar newspaper; poems in book Women Speak to God; film strip The Adventures of Mirkee Pirkee and Danny Dollar, 1963 (prize Nat. Coun. Jewish Audio Visual Materials 1963); libertto rock opera Solomon the King; contbr. articles to Shofar mag., Uoung Judean; contbr. articles on Holocaust to New Book of Knowledge; author weekly column Cleve. Jewish News, 1964-70, Boston Jewish Advocate, 1970-92; contbr. articles to publs. Adviser youth group United Synagogue, 1967-70; mem. Holocaust task force Jewish Community Fedn. Cleve.; mem. Educator's Assembly, Pioneer Women., Edn. Council N. Am.; mem. U.S. Holocaust Meml. Council, chmn. adv. panel Holocaust edn., judge writing contest for students 9th-12th grades.; mem. Gov.'s commn. of the State of Ohio on Holocaust Edn.; mem. State of Ohio Holocaust Commn., Cleve. Holocaust Ctr. (chmn. edn.), Bd. Cleve. Hebrew Schs. (chmn. edn.); bd. dirs. Women's Div. Jewish Nat. Fund. Recipient Leslie Reggel award for outstanding contbns. to Israel Philately, 1994, prizes Fedn. and Welfare Funds Audio Visual Coun. of Am. Assn. Jewish Edn., prize by Judah Magnes Mus., Berkeley, Calif. Democrat. Home: 24355 Tunbridge Ln Cleveland OH 44122-1631

STADTMAN, EARL REECE, biochemist; b. Carrizozo, N.Mex., Nov. 15, 1919; s. Walter William and Minnie Ethyl (Reece) S.; m. Thressa Campbell, Oct. 19, 1943. B.S., U. Calif., Berkeley, 1942, Ph.D, 1949. With Alcan Hwy. survey Pub. Rds. Adminstrn., 1942-43; rsch. asst. U. Calif., Berkeley, 1938-49, sr. lab. technican, 1949; AEC fellow Mass. Gen. Hosp., Boston, 1949-50; chemist lab. cellular physiology Nat. Heart Inst., 1950-58, chief enzyme sect., 1958-62, chief lab. biochemistry, 1962—; biochemist Max Planck Inst., Munich, Germany, Pasteur Inst., Paris, 1959-60; faculty dept. microbiology U. Md.; prof. biochemistry grad. program dept. biology Johns Hopkins U.; adv. com. Life Scis. Rsch. Office, Am. Fedn. Biol. Sci., 1974-77; bd. dirs. Found. Advanced Edn. Scis., 1966-70, chmn. dept. biochemistry, 1966-68; biochem. study sect. rsch. grants NIH, 1959-63. Editor Jour. Biol. Chemistry, 1960-65, Current Topics in Cellular Regulation, 1968—, Circulation Rsch., 1968-70; exec. editor Archives Biochemistry and Biophysics, 1960—, Life Scis., 1973-75, Procs. NAS, 1975-81, Trends in Biochem. Rsch., 1975-78; mem. editorial adv. bd. Biochemistry, 1969-76, 81—. Recipient medallion Soc. de Chemie Biologique, 1955, medallion U. Pisa, 1966, Presdl. Rank award as Disting. Sr. Exec., 1981, Welch Found. Award in Chemistry, 1991, Rsch. award Am. Aging Assn., 1992, Paul Glen award Am. Gerontology Soc., 1993. Mem. Am. Chem. Soc. (Paul Lewis Lab. award in enzyme chemistry 1952, exec. com. biol. div. 1959-64, chmn. div. 1963-64, Hillebrand award 1969), Am. Soc. Biol. Chemists (publs. com. 1966-70, coun. 1974-77, 82-84, pres. 1983—, Merckaward 1983), Nat. Acad. Sci. (award in microbiology 1970), Am. Acad. Arts and Scis., Am. Soc. Microbiology, Washington Acad. Scis. (award biol. chemistry 1957, Nat. medal sci. 1979, meritorious exec. award 1980, Robert A. Welch award in chemistry 1991, Paul Glenn award in aging, 1993). Office: Nat Heart and Lung Inst 9000 Rockville Pike Bethesda MD 20892-0001

STADTMAN, VERNE AUGUST, former foundation executive, editor; b. Carrizoso, N.Mex., Dec. 5, 1926; s. Walter William and Minnie Ethel (Reece) S.; m. Jackolyn Carol Byl, Aug. 26, 1949; children: Kristen Karen, Rand Theodore, Judith Dayna, Todd Alan. A.B., Calif.-Berkeley, 1950. AUS, 1945-47; mng. editor Calif. Monthly, Calif. Alumni Assn., Berkeley, 1950-64; centennial editor U. Calif., Berkeley, 1964-69; assoc. dir., editor Carnegie Commn. on Higher Edn., Berkeley, 1969-73, Carnegie Council on Policy Studies in Higher Edn. Berkeley, 1973-80; v.p. gen. services Carnegie Found. for Advancement Teaching, Princeton, N.J., 1980-89; trustee Editorial Projects Edn., Inc., 1957-91, pres., 1962-63, chmn. bd., 1980-86; guest scholar Hiroshima U., Japan, 1978. Author: California Campus, 1960, University of California, 1868-1968, 1970, Academic Adaptations, 1980; editor: (with David Riesman) Academic Transformation: Seventeen Institutions Under Pressure, 1973 (Book of Yr. award Am. Council Edn.); compiler-editor: Centennial Record of the University of California, 1967. Served with AUS, 1945-47. Recipient Alumnus Service award Calif. Alumni Assn., 1970. Mem. Am. Alumni Council (pres. 1963-64). Home: 182 St James Dr Sonoma CA 95476-8336

STADTMUELLER, JOSEPH PETER, federal judge; b. Oshkosh, Wis., Jan. 28, 1942; s. Joseph Francis and Irene Mary (Kilp) S.; m. Mary Ellen Brady, Sept. 5, 1970; children: Jeremy, Sarah. B.S. in Bus. Adminstrn., Marquette U., 1964, J.D., 1967. Bar: Wis. 1967, U.S. Supreme Ct. 1980. with Kluwin, Dunphy, Hankin and McNulty, 1968-69; asst. U.S. atty. Dept. Justice, Milw., 1969-74; 1st. asst. U.S. atty. Dept. Justice, 1974-75; with Stepke, Kossow, Trebon and Stadtmueller, Milw., 1975-76; asst. U.S. atty. Dept. Justice, 1977-78, dep. U.S. atty., 1978-81, U.S. atty., 1981-87; judge U.S. Dist. Ct. (ea. dist.) Wis., Milw., 1987—, chief judge, 1995—. Recipient Spl. Commendation award Atty. Gen. U.S., 1974, 80. Mem. ABA, State Bar Wis. (bd. govs. 1979-83, exec. com. 1982-83), Am. Law Inst., Fed. Judges Assn. (bd. dirs. 1995—), Univ. Club (Milw.). Republican. Roman Catholic. Club: University (Milw.). Office: 471 US Courthouse 517 E Wisconsin Ave Milwaukee WI 53202

STAEHELIN, LUCAS ANDREW, cell biology educator; b. Sydney, Australia, Feb. 10, 1939; came to U.S., 1969; s. Lucas Eduard and Isobel (Malloch) S.; m. Margrit Weibel, Sept. 17, 1965; children: Daniel Thomas, Philip Roland, Marcel Felix. Dipl. Natw., Swiss Fed. Inst. Tech., Zurich, 1963, Ph.D. in Biology, 1966. Research scientist N.Z. Dept. Sci. and Indsl. Research, 1966-69; research fellow in cell biology Harvard U., Cambridge, Mass., 1969-70; asst. prof. cell biology U. Colo., Boulder, 1970-73, assoc. prof., 1973-79, prof., 1979—; vis. prof. U. Freiburg, 1978, Swiss Fed. Inst. Tech., 1984, 92; mem. cellular biology and physiology study sect. NIH, Bethesda, Md., 1980-84; mem. DOE panel on rsch. directions for the energy bioscis., 1988, 92; mem. NSF adv. panel for cellular orgn., 1994—. Editor Jour. Cell Biology, 1977-81, European Jour. Cell Biology, 1981-90, Plant Physiology, 1986-92, Plant Jour., 1991—; editor: (with C.J. Antzen) Encyclopedia of Plant Physiology, Vol. 19, Photosynthesis III, 1986; contbr. numerous articles to sci. jours. Recipient Humboldt award Humboldt Found., 1978, Sci. Tchr. award U. Colo., 1984, NIH research grants, 1971—. Mem. AAAS, Am. Soc. Cell Biology, Am. Soc. Plant Physiology, German Acad. Natural Scis. Leopoldina. Home: 2855 Dover Dr Boulder CO 80303-5305 Office: U Colo Dept Molecular Cell/Devel Biology Campus Box 347 Boulder CO 80309-0347

STAEHLE, ROBERT L., foundation executive; b. Rochester, N.Y., Apr. 22, 1955; s. Henry Carl and Isabel Montgomery S. BS in Aero. and Astronautic Engring., Purdue U., 1977. Prin. investigator Skylab Expt. ED-31 (bacteria aboard Skylab), NASA/Marshall Space Flight Center, Huntsville, Ala., 1972-74; student trainee engring. Skylab Expt. ED-31 (bacteria aboard Skylab), NASA/Marshall Space Flight Center, 1974-77; sci. observation analyst Caltech/Jet Propulsion Lab., Pasadena, Calif., 1977-78; engr. advanced projects group, 1978-83, mem. tech. staff system integration sect. of Space Sta., 1983-87, mem. tech. staff and space sta., user ops. team leader, 1987-88; tech. mgr. Jet Propulsion Lab., Pasadena, Calif., 1988—, mgr. space sta. Freedom support office Pasadena ops., 1990-92, Pluto team leader, 1992-93, mgr. Pluto Express preproject, 1993—; prin. founder, pres. World Space Found., South Pasadena, Calif., 1979—; founding dir. So. Calif. Space Bus. Roundtable, 1987-95. Co-author: Project Solar Sail, New Am. Libr., 1990; contbr. articles to profl. jours. Mem. Cmty. Leaders Adv. Bd. for Irvine Scholars, Occidental Coll., L.A., 1996—; bd. dirs. Caltech Y, 1987-93. Nat. Space Club Goddard scholar, 1977; Charles A. Lindbergh Fund grantee, 1986. Fellow Brit. Interplanetary Soc.; mem. AIAA, Tau Beta Pi, Sigma Gamma Tau. Avocations: photography, hiking. Office: Jet Propulsion Lab Pasadena CA 91109

STAELIN, DAVID HUDSON, electrical engineering educator, consultant; b. Toledo, May 25, 1938; s. Carl Gustav and Margaret E. (Hudson) S.; m. Ellen Mahoney, June 16, 1962; children: Carl H., Katherine E., Paul H. SB, MIT, 1960, SM, 1961, ScD in Elec. Engring., 1965. Instr. elec. engring. MIT, Cambridge, 1965, asst. prof., 1965-69, assoc. prof., 1969-76, prof., 1976—; asst. dir. Lincoln Lab. MIT, Lexington, 1990—; vis. asst. scientist Nat. Radio Astronomy Obs., Charlottesville, Va., 1968-69; cons. Jet Propulsion Lab., Pasadena, Calif., 1969, Wellesley, Mass., 1965—; dir. Environ. Rsch. and Tech., Inc., Concord, Mass., 1969-78; co-founder, chmn. PictureTel Corp., Peabody, Mass., 1984-87; mem. com. on radio frequency requirements for rsch., NAS, Washington, 1980-86, chmn. 1983-86; chmn. advanced microwave sounder working group NASA, Washington, 1981-82, mem. space applications adv. com.,NASA, 1983-86. Co-author: Made in America, 1989, Electromagnetic Waves, 1994; also articles; patentee grinding and polishing sheet glass, display of dynamic images, ribbon-beam cathode ray tube. Fellow IEEE, AAAS; mem. Am. Geophys. Union, Am. Meteorl. Soc., Internat. Union for Radio Sci. Office: MIT Rm 26-341 Cambridge MA 02139

STAELIN, RICHARD, business administration educator; b. Larchmont, N.Y., Aug. 3, 1939; s. Richard Carl and Dorothy (Potts) S.; m. Julie Ann Fischer, Aug. 24, 1963; children: Adam, Kate. BSME, U. Mich., 1961, BS in Math., 1962, M.B.A., 1963, Ph.D., 1969. Market planner IBM, Harrison, N.Y., 1963-66; prof. Carnegie-Mellon U., Pitts., 1969-82; Edward and Rose Donnell prof. Duke U., Durham, N.C., 1982—, assoc. dean faculty affairs, 1982-91, mng. dir., 1995—; exec. dir. Mktg. Sci. Inst., Cambridge, Mass., 1991-93; vis. prof. Australian Grad. Sch., Kensington, Australia, 1980-81. Author: Consumer Protection Legislation and the U.S. Food Industry, 1980; mem. editorial bd. Jour. Mktg. Rsch., 1974-82, Jour. Consumer Rsch., 1976-87; area editor Mktg. Sci., 1983-88; editor-in-chief Mktg. Sci., 1995—. Mem. Pitts. Exec. Bd.; treas. Pitts. Arts and Crafts Ctr., 1976-79; bd. dirs. Dispute Settlement Ctr., Chapel Hill, N.C.; bd. vis. drama dept. Duke U., 1990—. Recipient Best Mktg. Paper award Inst. Mgmt. Sci., 1985, hon. mention, 1986; HEW grantee, 1972-74; NSF grantee, 1973-79. Mem. Am. Mktg. Assn., Assn. Consumer Research, Inst. Mgmt. Sci. Office: Fuqua School of Business Science Dr Rm 339 Durham NC 27706-2597

STAFF, CHARLES BANCROFT, JR., music and theater critic; b. Franklin, Ind., July 2, 1929; s. Charles Bancroft and Clara Margaret (Jennings) S. AB, Franklin Coll., 1951; BM, Ind. U., 1955. Copy editor Indpls. News, 1955-58, movie, TV critic, 1958-65, music, drama critic, 1965—; pianist dance band, Franklin, 1943-46. Composer numerous musical pieces string quartet, 1954, wind quintet, 1954, violin sonata, 1955, Deat Under A Tree, Wicked Tales for Evil Children, 1980. Organist Presbyn. Ch., Franklin, 1945-48, Bapt. Ch. Franklin, 1948-51. Recipient Best Critical Writing award Indpls. Press Club, 1977, 78. Democrat. Office: Indpls News 307 N Pennsylvania St Indianapolis IN 46204-1811

STAFFIER, PAMELA MOORMAN, psychologist; b. Passaic, N.J., Dec. 7, 1942; d. Wynant Clair and Jeannette Frances (Rentzsch) Moorman; B.A., Bucknell U., 1964; M.A. in Psychology, Assumption Coll., Worcester, Mass., 1970, C.A.G.S., 1977; Ph.D., Union Inst., 1978; m. John Staffier, Jr., Apr. 5, 1975; children—M. Anthony, C. Matthew. Psychologist, Westboro (Mass.) State Hosp., 1965, prin. psychologist, also asst. to supt., 1973-76; psychologist Moriarty Mental Health Clinic; psychiat. cons. local gen. hosp.; research psychologist Wrentham (Mass.) State Sch., 1966, Cushing Hosp., Framingham, Mass., 1967; prin. psychologist, also asst. to supt. Grafton (Mass.) State Hosp., 1967-72; dir. Staffier Psychol. Assocs., Inc., 1978—. Mem. Am. Psychol. Assn. (assoc.), Am. Psychol. Practitioners Assn. (founding mem.), Mass. Psychol. Assn., Nat. Register Health Service Providers in Psychology. Research, publs. on state hosp. closings, biochem. basis of Schizophrenia. Home: 68 Adams St PO Box 1103 Westborough MA 01581 Office: 57 E Main St Westborough MA 01581-1464

STAFFORD, DONALD GENE, chemistry educator; b. Valliant, Okla., Oct. 9, 1930; s. Otto Lewis and Rose Lavelle (Osterdock) S.; m. Jane Wright, July 5, 1951; children—Michael Royce, Robert Gene, Joel Dan. B.S., U. Okla., 1957, Ph.D., 1969; M.S., Okla. State U., 1961. Prof. sci. edn. East Cen. U., Ada, Okla., 1961-73, prof. chemistry, 1973—; adj. prof. U. Okla., Norman, 1970—. Author: The Improvement of Science in Oklahoma (7-12), 1970, Guidelines and Successful Practices in Elementary Edn, 1970, Wings for a Dinosaur, 1972, Early Childhood Resource Book, 1972, Teaching Science in the Elementary School, 1973, 3d edit., 1979, Teaching Science in the Secondary School, 1973, Research, Teaching, and Learning with the Piaget Model, 1976, Investigations in Physical Science, 1976, The Learning Science Program K-6 (7 children's books and 7 tchr.'s guides), 1976, TOP, The Oklahoma Project, Chemistry, 1987, The Learning Cycle, 1988. Served with AUS, 1948-53. Mem. Am. Chem. Soc., Nat. Sci. Tchrs. Assn., Okla. Sci. Tchrs. (pres. 1973-74, 78-79), Sigma Xi. Home: 2202 Fullview Dr Ada OK 74820-4436

STAFFORD, EARL, conductor. Began piano studies at age 8; profl. and solo debut with Thunder Bay Symphony at age 10; studied at Faculty of Music, U. Toronto, with Milton Kaye in N.Y.C., at Paris Conservatory with Franco Ferrara and Aldo Ciccolini; joined Royal Winnipeg Ballet as prin. pianist, 1975, appointed assoc. music dir., 1982, now music dir. and condr.; also music dir. dance div. Banff Ctr. Fine Arts. Orchestrator numerous ballets for Royal Winnipeg Ballet, including Five Tangos, Bluebird Pas De Deux, Giselle Pas De Deux, Tchaikovsky Pas De Deux, Nuages; guest condr. various Can. orchs. including Vancouver Symphony, Calgary Philharmonic, Regina Symphony, Winnipeg Symphony, Saskatoon Symphony Orch., Nat. Arts Ctr. Orch., Thunder Bay Symphony. Recipient Gold medal for accompanying, Internat. Ballet Competition, Varna, Bulgaria, 1980. Office: EML Internat Artist Mgmt Inc, 219 Baseline Rd East, London, ON Canada N6C 2N6

STAFFORD, FRANK PETER, JR., economics educator, consultant; b. Chgo., Sept. 17, 1940; s. Frank Peter and Ida Gustava (Tormala) S.; m. Lilian Elisabeth Lundin, Aug. 8, 1964; children: Craig Peter, Jennifer Elisabeth, Christine Anna. BA, Northwestern U., 1962; MBA, U. Chgo., 1964, PhD, 1968. Asst. prof. econs. U. Mich., 1966-71, assoc. prof., 1971-73, 74-75, prof., 1976—, chmn. dept. econs., 1980—, rsch. scientist Inst. Social Rsch., 1995—, chair budget study com., 1995—; vis. assoc. prof. Grad. Sch. Bus.-Stanford U., 1973-74; spl. asst. for econ. affairs U.S. Dept. Labor, Washington, 1975-76; vis. prof. dept. econs. U. Saarlandes, Fed. Republic Germany, 1986; faculty rsch. assoc. Inst. Social Rsch., Ann Arbor, 1979—; vis. scholar Indsl. Inst. for Econs. and Social Rsch., Stockholm, 1979, 83, 90, Worklife Study Ctr., Stockholm, 1988, 90; Tinbergen Found. prof. U. Amsterdam, 1992, 94; panel mem. Social Sci. Rsch. Coun., N.Y.C., 1979—; rsch. assoc. Nat. Bur. Econ. Rsch., Cambridge, Mass., 1983—; prof. econs. Tinbsrgne Found. U. Amsterdam, 1992; vis. scholar U. Stockholm, 1994. Author, editor: Time Use Goods and Well Being, 1986, Studies in Labor Market Behavior: Sweden and the United States, 1981; mem. editorial bd.: Am. Econ. Rev., 1976-78; contbr. articles to profl. jours. Co-dir. Panel Study of Income Dynamics, 1995—. Grantee NSF, 1973, 80, 95—, NICHD, 1995—. Mem. Am. Econs. Assn. Home: 3535 Daleview Dr Ann Arbor MI 48105-9686 Office: U Mich Dept Econs Lorch Hall Rm 312 Ann Arbor MI 48105

STAFFORD, J. FRANCIS, archbishop; b. Balt., July 26, 1932; s. F. Emmett and Mary Dorothy S. Student, Loyola Coll., Balt., 1950-52; B.A., St. Mary's Sem., Balt., 1954; S.T.B., S.T.L., Gregorian U., Rome, 1958; M.S.W., Catholic U., 1964; postgrad., Rutgers U., 1963, U. Wis.-Madison, 1969, St. Mary's Sem. and Univ., Balt., 1973-75. Spiritual moderator Ladies of Charity Ch., Balt., 1966-76; spiritual moderator Soc. St. Vincent de Paul, Balt., 1965-76; urban vicar Archdiocese of Balt., 1966-76, monsignor, 1970, vicar gen., auxiliary bishop, 1976-83; bishop Diocese of Memphis, 1983-86; archbishop Archdiocese of Denver, 1986—; dir. Assn. Cath. Charities, Balt., 1966-76; archdiocesan liaison to Md. Cath. Conf., Balt, 1975-78; Oriental Orthodox/Roman Cath. consultation Nat. Cath. Conf. Bishops, 1977-85, com. on doctrine, 1978-82, chmn. ecumenical and interreligious affairs com., 1987-90; co-chmn. bilateral dialogue Roman Cath./World Meth. Council, 1977-86; co-chmn. U.S. Roman Cath.-Luth. Dialogue, 1986—; chmn. Bishops' com. marriage and family life U.S. Cath. Conf., 1978-84; mem. gen. Synod Bishops, Vatican City, 1980. Contbr. articles to profl. jours. Trustee Good Samaritan Hosp., Balt., 1973-77, Cath. U. Am., 1990—, Blue Cross of Md., Inc., 1973-76, Balt. Urban Coalition, 1970-75; trustee, chmn., St. Thomas Theol. Sem., 1987—; bd. dirs. Sch. Social Work and Planning, U. Md., 1973-76. Recipient Father Kelly Alumni award Loyola High Sch., 1978; Alumni Laureate, Loyola Coll., 1979. Mem. World Meth. Conf. Roman Cath. Dialogue (co-chmn. 1977-86), Oriental Orthodox Roman Cath. Consultation (co-chmn. 1977-85), Nat. Conf. Cath. Bishops, Luth. Roman Cath. Dialogue, Congregation for Doctrine of Faith. Office: 200 Josephine St Denver CO 80206-4710*

STAFFORD, JAMES F., electronics executive; b. 1944. With Honeywell Inc., 1965-73, Bendix, 1973-76, Fairfield Camera & Instrument Corp., 1976-79, Synertek, 1979-81; dir. materials Seeq Technology, Inc., San Jose, Calif., 1981-84; pres., CEO Chips & Tech. Inc., San Jose, 1985—. Office: Chips & Tech Inc 2950 Zanker Rd San Jose CA 95134-2113*

STAFFORD, JOHN ROGERS, pharmaceutical and household products company executive; b. Harrisburg, Pa., Oct. 24, 1937; s. Paul Henry and Gladys Lee (Sharp) S.; m. Inge Paul, Aug. 22, 1959; children—Carolyn, Jennifer, Christina, Charlotte. AB, Dickinson Coll., 1959; LLB with distinction, George Washington U., 1962, Degree (hon.), 1994. Bar: D.C. 1962. Assoc. Steptoe & Johnson, Washington, 1962-66; gen. atty. Hoffman-LaRoche, Nutley, N.J., 1966-67, group atty., 1967-70; gen. counsel Am. Home Products Corp., N.Y.C., 1970-74, v.p., 1972-77, sr. v.p., 1977-80, exec. v.p., 1980-81, pres., 1981—, chmn., chief exec. officer, 1986—; bd. dirs. The Chase Manhattan Corp., Allied Signal Inc., Grocery Mfrs. Am., Inc., Met. Life Ins. Co., Nynex Corp., Pharm. Rsch. and Mfrs. Am., chmn., 1991-92. Bd. dirs. Ctrl. Park Conservancy, Project Hope, Am.-China Soc., Am. Paralysis Assn. Recipient John Bell Larner 1st Scholar award George Washington U. Law Sch., 1962, Outstanding Achievement Alumnus award, 1981. Mem. ABA, D.C. Bar ASsn., Nat. Assn. Mfrs. (bd. dirs.), Sky Club (N.Y.C.), Essex Fells (N.J.) Country, Links Club (N.Y.C.), Baltusrol (N.J.), Robert Trent Jones (Va.). Office: American Home Products Corp 5 Giralda Farms Madison NJ 07940-1027

STAFFORD, JOSEPHINE HOWARD, lawyer; b. San Antonio, July 27, 1921; d. Joseph and Olive Maeblume (Goodson) Howard; m. Harry B. Stafford (div. 1958); 1 child, Julie. BA, U. N.C., 1942, LLB, 1952. Bar: N.C. 1952, Fla. 1953, U.S. Dist. Ct. (mid. dist.) Fla. 1954, U.S. Ct. Appeals (11th cir.), U.S. Ct. Appeals (5th cir.); lic. real estate broker; cert. arbitrator, Hillsborough County Cir. Ct. Assoc. Fowler, White, Gillen, Yancey and Humkey, Tampa, Fla., 1952-54; pvt. practice Tampa, 1954-57, 69-72; exec. dir., atty. Legal Aid Bur., Tampa, 1957-69; atty. City of Tampa, 1972—; instr. U. South Fla., Tampa, 1971-72; adj. prof. Hillsborough Community Coll., Tampa, 1980-86; lectr. U. South Fla., Tampa, 1973, U. Tampa, U. Fla., Gainesville, 1959; atty. Housing Authority City of Tampa, 1970-72; substitute judge mcpl. ct., 1958-71, interim mcpl. ct. judge, 1971-72; mem. Grievance Com. "13C". Author: Amendments to Search Warrant Law; Tax Laws, Agencies and Divorce, 1979; author Mayor's Proclamation Commemorating D-Day, 1994. Precinct committeewoman Hillsborough County Dem. Exec. Coun., Tampa, 1991, co-chmn., 1970; bd. mem., past pres., chmn. com. Travelers Aid Soc., Tampa, 1971-93, life mem., 1994; bd. mem., fin. com. Girl Scouts Am., Tampa, 1991-95; bd. mem., exec. com., past pres. Police Athletic League, Tampa, 1984-88, 90—; mem. Fla. Commn. on Status of Women; co-chmn. Selective Svc. System, 1971-76; bd. dirs. ARC, Tampa chpt., 1964-79, Am. Cancer Soc., Hillsborough County unit, 1982-84. Recipient Svc. to Mankind award Sertoma Internat., Tampa, 1969, Outstanding Bus. and Profl. Woman of Yr. award Bus. and Profl. Women, Tampa, 1959, 69, Women Helping Women award Soroptimist Club, Tampa, 1979, Excellence award Hillsborough County Dem. Women's Club, 1991. Mem. ABA (Nat. Conf. Lawyers and Social Workers, Nat. Conf. Lawyers and Realtors, Standing Com. on Nat. Conf. Groups), Fla. Bar assn. (chmn., legal aid com.), Tampa and Hillsborough County Bar Assn. (dir. 1958-63, chmn. elder law com. 1991-93, mem Liberty Bell award com. 1996), Nat. Legal Aid and Defender Assn. (nat. bd. dirs.), Fla. Assn. Women Lawyers (pres.), Tampa Assn. Women Lawyers (pres., named Outstanding Women Lawyers of Achievement 1993), Fla. Fedn. Social Workers (pres. Hillsborough County chpt. 1964, pres. state bd. 1969), Tampa Legal Sec. Assn., U.S. Navy League. Democrat. Methodist. Avocations: poetry, art, theatre, pottery, gardening, swimming. Home: 3402 S Gardenia Dr Tampa FL 33629-8208 Office: City of Tampa Legal Dept 315 E Kennedy Blvd Tampa FL 33602-5211

STAFFORD, PATRICK MORGAN, biophysicist; b. Roanoke, Va., June 3, 1950; s. Jess Woodrum and Georgine Elna (Morgan) S.; m. Kristina Lee Troyer, July 10, 1976; children: Kathryn Lee, Jess Walter. BS in Physics, Va. Poly. Inst., 1972; M Med. Sci. in Medical Physics, Emory U., 1979; PhD in Biophysics, U. Tex., Houston, 1987. Diplomate Am. Bd. Radiology. Assoc. engr. Duke Power Co., Charlotte, N.C., 1973-78; rsch. scientist U. N.Mex., Los Alamos, 1979-81; asst. physicist U. Tex., Houston, 1981-87; asst. prof. U. Pa., Phila., 1987-91; v.p. Radiation Care, Inc., Atlanta, 1991-95, Oncology Therapies, Inc., 1995—; adj. prof. Ga. Inst. Tech., 1993—; lectr. in field. Author: Dynamic Treatment with Pions at Lampf, 1980, Critical Angle Dependance of CR-39, 1986, Real-Time Portal Imaging; jour. reviewer Medical Physics, Internat. Jour. Radiation Oncology, Biology and Physics. Active Atlanta Emory Symphony, 1978; deacon Crabapple Bapt. Ch., Alpharetta, Ga., 1992. Rosalie B. Hite fellow U. Tex., 1983. Mem. Am. Assn. Physicists in Medicine (radiation therapy com. 1989-92, liaison from ASTRO 1995—, continuing edn. com. 1995—), Am. Coll. Med. Physics (commn. on comm. 1991-94), Am. Coll. Radiology, Am. Soc. for Therapeutic Radiology and Oncology. Home: 430 Kensington Farms Dr Alpharetta GA 30201-3740 Office: Oncology Therapies Inc 1155 Hammond Dr NE Ste A Atlanta GA 30328-5332

STAFFORD, REBECCA, academic administrator, sociologist; b. Topeka, July 9, 1936; d. Frank C. and Anne Elizabeth (Larrick) S. AB magna cum laude, Radcliffe Coll., 1958, MA, 1961; PhD, Harvard U., 1964. Lectr. dept. sociology Sch. Edn., Harvard U., Cambridge, Mass., 1964-70, mem. vis. com. bd. overseers, 1973-79; assoc. prof. sociology U. Nev., Reno, 1970-73, prof., 1973-80, chmn. dept. sociology, 1974-77, dean Coll. Arts and Scis., 1977-80; pres. Bemidji (Minn.) State U., 1980-82; exec. v.p. Colo. State U., Ft. Collins, 1982-83; pres. Chatham Coll., Pitts., 1983-91, Monmouth U., West Long Branch, N.J., 1993—; bd. dirs. First Fidelity Bancorp, N.J. Contbr. articles to profl. jours. Trustee Monmouth Med. Ctr.; bd. dirs. Univ. Presbyn. Hosp., 1985-93, Pitts. Symphyony, 1984-93, Winchester-Thurston Sch.; chmn. Harvard U. Grad. Soc. Coun., 1987-93. Recipient McCurdy-Rinkle prize for rsch. Eastern Psychiat. Assn., 1970; named Man of Yr. in Edn., City of Pitts., 1986, Woman of Yr. in Edn., YWCA Tribute to Women, 1989; grantee Am. Coun. Edn. Inst. Acad. Deans, 1979, Inst. Ednl. Mgmt., Harvard U., 1984. Mem. Harvard U. Alumni Assn. (bd. dirs. 1985-87), Phi Beta Kappa, Phi Kappa Phi. Office: Monmouth University West Long Branch NJ 07764

STAFFORD, ROBERT THEODORE, lawyer, former senator; b. Rutland, Vt., Aug. 8, 1913; s. Bert L. and Mable R. (Stratton) S.; m. Helen C. Kelley, Oct. 15, 1938; children—Madelyn, Susan, Barbara, Dianne. B.S., Middlebury Coll., 1935, LL.D., 1960; postgrad., U. Mich., 1936; LL.B., Boston U., 1938, LL.D., 1959; LL.D., Norwich U., 1960, St. Michaels Coll., 1967, U. Vt., 1970. Bar: Vt. bar 1938. City prosecutor Rutland, 1939-42; state's atty. Rutland County, 1947-51; dep. atty. gen. Vt., 1953-54, atty. gen., 1954-

56, lt. gov., 1957-58, gov., 1959-60; mem. 87th to 92d Congresses, Vt.-at-large; apptd. U.S. Senate, 1971, mem., 1972-89, chmn. com. on environment and public works, 1981-87, chmn. edn. subcom., 1981-87, ranking mem., 1987-89; ptnr. Stafford, Abiatell & Stafford, 1938-46; sr. ptnr. Stafford & LaBrake, 1946-51. Chmn. UN-U.S.A. Assn. Panel UNESCO, 1989—. Lt. comdr. USNR, 1942-46, 51-52; capt. Res. Named Disting. Scholar U. Vt., 1989, Disting. Prof. Pub. Affairs Castleton State Coll., 1989. Mem. V.F.W., Am. Legion. Club: Elk. Home and Office: 1 Sugarwood Hill Rd RR 1 Box 3954 Rutland VT 05701 Office: Castleton Coll Coolidge Libr Bldg Castleton VT 05735

STAFFORD, SHANE LUDWIG, lawyer; b. Camden, N.J., Mar. 10, 1955; s. Joseph and Victoria Stafford; m. Connie, Jan. 19, 1980; children: Courtney, Ashley and Shaun (twins). BS, Calif. State U., 1977; JD, Southwestern U., L.A., 1980; LLD, U. Miami, 1980. Bar: Fla. 1980, U.S. Dist. Ct. (so. dist.) Fla. 1981. Intern Ins. Co. North Am., Miami, Fla., 1980-81; assoc. Miami, Fla., 1981-83; ptnr. Varner & Stafford, Lake Worth, Fla., 1983-85, Varner, Stafford & Seaman, Lake Worth, 1985—. Mem. Assn. Trial Lawyers Am., Acad. Trial Lawyers Fla., Palm Beach County Bar Assn., Phi Delta Phi. Avocations: golf, family. Office: Varner Stafford & Seaman 2328 10th Ave N Ste 2B Lake Worth FL 33461-6606

STAFFORD, THOMAS PATTEN, retired military officer, former astronaut; b. Weatherford, Okla., Sept. 17, 1930; m. Linda A. Dishman; children: Dionne, Karin. BS, U.S. Naval Acad., 1952; student, USAF Exptl. Flight Test Sch., 1958-59; DSc (hon.), Oklahoma City U., 1967; LLD (hon.), Western State U. Coll. Law, 1969, U. Cordoba, Argentina; D Communications (hon.), Emerson Coll., 1969; D Aero. Engring. (hon.), Embry-Riddle Aero. Inst., 1970; LHD (hon.), U. Okla., 1994; M of Humane Letters (hon.), Southwestern U., 1994; HHD (hon.), Oklahoma Christian U. Commd. 2d lt. USAF, 1952; advanced through grades to lt. gen.; chief performance br. Aerospace Research Pilot Sch., Edwards AFB, Calif.; with NASA, Houston, 1962-75; assigned Project Gemini, pilot Gemini VI, 1965, command pilot Gemini IX, 1966, comdr. Apollo X, 1969, chief astronaut office, 1969-71; dep. dir. flight crew operations, comdr. Apollo-Soyuz flight, 1975; comdr. Air Force Flight Test Ctr., Edwards AFB, 1975; lt. gen., dep. chief staff Research, Devel. and Aquisition, 1979; ret., 1979; chair The White House/NASA Com. to Independently Advise NASA How to Return to Moon and Explore Mars, 1990-91; chmn. bd. Omega Watch Co. Am.; dir. start F-117A Stealth Fighter, B-2 Stealth Bomber program, 1978; co-founder tech. cons. firm, Stafford, Burke, Hecker, Inc., Alexandria, Va.; adv. numerous govtl. agys. including NASA, Air Force Systems Command; defense advisor to Ronald Reagan during presdl. campaign; bd. dirs. numerous cos. Co-author: Pilot's Handbook for Performance Flight Testing, Aerodynamics Handbook for Performance Flight Testing. Decorated DFC with oak leaf cluster, D.S.M. (3), Disting. Flying Cross (2); recipient NASA Disting. Svc. medal (2), NASA Exceptional Svc. medal (2), Air Force Command Pilot Astronaut Wings; Chanute Flight award AIAA, 1976, VFW Nat. Space award, 1976; Gen. Thomas D. White USAF Space trophy Nat. Geog. Soc., 1976; Gold Space medal Fedn. Aeronautique Internationale, 1976, Laurel Award, Space/Missiles, Aviation Week & Space Tech., 1991, Congl. Space medal honor V.P. Dan Quayle, 1993, Rotary Nat. award Space Achievement, 1993, Goddard award Astronaut Hall of Fame, 1993, Pub. Svc. award NASA, 1994; co-recipient AIAA, 1966, Harmon Internat. Aviation trophy, 1966, Spl. Trustees award NATAS, 1969. Fellow Am. Astronautical Soc., Soc. Exptl. Test Pilots; mem. AIAA, AFTRA (hon. life). Holder all-time world speed record for space flight, 24,791.4 miles per hour. Address: 1006 Cameron St Alexandria VA 22314-2427 *As we move through life, each of us has an opportunity to make a contribution to humanity. In this respect, I have been extremely fortunate as I have been privileged to help explore new frontiers in space and aviation technology. But, it is clear to me that the most important element in a successful program is people. Their willingness to discipline their efforts and to work together to achieve important objectives remains the most important factor in a successful operation.*

STAFFORD, WILLIAM HENRY, JR., federal judge; b. Masury, Ohio, May 11, 1931; s. William Henry and Frieda Gertrude (Nau) S.; m. Nancy Marie Helman, July 11, 1959; children: William Henry, Donald Helman, David Harrold. B.S., Temple U., 1953, LL.B., 1956; J.D., 1968. Bar: Fla. 1961, U.S. Ct. Appeals (5th cir.) 1969, U.S. Supreme Ct. 1970. Assoc. firm Robinson & Roark, Pensacola, 1961-64; individual practice law Pensacola, 1964-67, state atty., 1967-69, U.S. atty., 1969-75; U.S. dist. judge U.S. Dist. Ct. for No. Dist. Fla., Tallahassee, 1975—, U.S. dist. judge, chief judge, 1981-93, sr. judge, 1996—; instr. Pensacola Jr. Coll., 1964, 68; mem. judicial council U.S. Ct. Appeals (11th cir.), 1986-89; apptd. com. on intercircuit assignments, 1987-92, subcom. on fed. jurisdiction, 1983-87. Lt. (j.g.) USN, 1957-60. Mem. Fla. Bar (mem. numerous comns., bench/bar commn. 1991-92, bench/bar implementation commn. 1993), Dist. Judges Assn. 11th Cir. (pres. 1984-85), State Fed. Judicial Council Fla., Am. Inns of Ct., Tallahassee Bar Assn., Tallahassee Inn (pres. 1989-91), Masons, Shriners, Rotary, Sigma Phi Epsilon, Phi Delta Phi. Republican. Episcopalian. Office: US Dist Ct 110 E Park Ave Tallahassee FL 32301

STAGE, THOMAS BENTON, psychiatrist; b. Marietta, Ohio, July 23, 1926; s. John Douglas and Grace (Shawhan) S.; m. Doris Jeane Weinstock, Dec. 22, 1951; children: Samuel Ray, Amy Elizabeth, James Robert; m. Alicia Anderson Marsh, June 7, 1993. B.A. cum laude, Marietta Coll., 1949; M.D., Ohio State U., 1952. Diplomate: Am. Bd. Psychiatry and Neurology. Intern Detroit Receiving Hosp., 1952-53; psychiat. resident, fellow Menninger Sch. Psychiatry, Topeka, 1953-56; sect. chief, chief psychiatry VA Hosp., Topeka, 1956-62; adminstr. VA Hosp., Sheridan, Wyo., 1962-66; dir. VA Hosp., Salem, Va., 1967-72; dep. asst. chief med. dir. for ambulatory care VA Central Office, Washington, 1972-74; dir. No. Va. Mental Health Inst., Falls Church, 1974-78; asst. commr. for mental health State of Va., Richmond, 1978-79; dir. clin. services Fairfax-Falls Church Community Services Bd., Vienna, Va., 1979-82, psychiat. cons. for med. affairs, 1982—; instr. Menninger Sch. Psychiatry, 1958-62, U. Wyo. Sch. Nursing, 1963-66; assoc. prof. U. Va. Med. Sch., 1972-74; cons. surveyor Joint Commn. on Accreditation of Hosps., 1976—; cons. Crow-No. Cheyenne USPHS Hosp., 1963-66, Ala. Dept. Mental Health (Wyatt Com.), 1986-91; psychiatric cons. on accreditation Commonwealth of Va. Dept. Mental Health, Mental Retardation and Substance Abuse, 1982—; mem. Comprehensive Mental Health Ctr. Com., 1968-73, Gov.'s Adv. Commn. on Mental Health, 1971-74; chmn. Drug Abuse Rehab. Com., 1970-73; cons. adminstrv. psychiatry NIMH, 1975-78; chmn. steering com. Asso. Faculties Program Community Psychiatry, Washington, 1975-77; mem. State Health Coordinating Coun., 1976-89. Contbr. articles to profl. jours. Served wtih USNR, 1944-46, PTO. Fellow Am. Psychiat. Assn. (life); mem. Am. Assn. Psychiat. Adminstrs., Washington Psychiat. Soc., Psychiat. Soc. Va., Am. Assn. Community Psychiatrists. Home: 11410 Hollow Timber Way Reston VA 22094-1906 Office: Fairfax-Falls Ch Comty Svcs Ste 800 12011 Government Center Pky Fairfax VA 22035-1105

STAGER, DONALD K., construction company executive. Chmn. Dillingham Constrn. Corp., Pleasanton, Calif. Recipient, Roebling award Am. Soc. of Civil Engineers, 1995. Office: Dillingham Constrn Corp 5960 Inglewood Dr Pleasanton CA 94588-8535

STAGER, LAWRENCE E., archaeologist, educator; b. Kenton, Ohio, Jan. 5, 1943; married; 2 children. BA, Harvard U., 1965, MA, 1972, PhD in Syro-Palestinian Archeology and History, 1975. Instr. Oriental Inst., U. Chgo., 1973-74, asst. prof., 1974-75, assoc. prof. Syro-Palestinian archaeology, 1976-87; Dorot prof. archeology of Israel, Dept. Near Eastern Langs. and Civilizations and Anthropology Harvard U., Cambridge, Mass., 1986—; co-dir. Am. Expdn., Idalion, Cyprus, 1972-74; dir. UNESCO Save Carthage Project, Am. Punic Archaeol. Expdn., 1975-80, Harvard Semitic Mus., 1987—, Leon Levy Expdn. to Ashkelon, Israel, 1985—. Author: Ashkelon Discovered, 1991, A Heap of Broken Images: Essays in Biblical Archaeology, 1997; co-author: Idalion I, Idalion II; contbr. articles to profl. jours. Mem. Am. Schs. Oriental Rsch. (editor newsletter 1975-76, assoc. trustee 1977-80, trustee 1987-90, assoc. editor bull. 1978—), Archaeol. Inst. Am. (v.p. 1986-88, trustee 1989-91), Am. Orient Soc., Soc. Bibl. Lit. Rsch. in economy, society and religion of ancient Israel; archaeology of Philistines, Canaanites and Phoenicians. Office: Harvard U Semitic Mus Dept Near Ea Langs/Civil Cambridge MA 02138-2091

STAGG, EVELYN WHEELER, educator, state legislator; b. Waterbury, Vt., Sept. 30, 1916; d. Aiton Grover and Edythe (Boyce) Wheeler; m. David Stagg, May 15, 1942; children: Christie Stagg Austin, Bonnie, Carol Stagg Kevan. BA, Middlebury Coll., 1939; MA, U. Vt., 1971. Assoc. prof. Castleton State Coll., Vt., 1966-82; mem. Vt. Ho. of Reps., 1982-90, chmn. house edn. com., 1982-90, vice chmn. health and welfare com., 1985-86, mem. ways and means com., 1989-90; Commn. of the States, 1987-88; cons. communications projects, Bomoseen, Vt., 1982—. Contbr. articles to profl. jours. Chmn. Women's Legis. Caucus, 1984-88; pres., bd. dirs. Rutland Area Vis. Nurse Assn., 1969-75, 89-92; bd. dirs. Rutland Mental Health Assn., 1986-88; adv. bd. nursing Castleton State Coll.; vol. LUVS for abused children; trustee pub. funds, 1990—, Castle Libr., 1992—; bd. civil authority, 1984-93; justice of peace Town of Castleton, 1984-93; mem. customer adv. coun. U.S. Postal Svc., Naples. Mem. Women's Caucus, Vt. Women's Polit. Caucus of Collier County, Nat. Women's Polit. Caucus, Inst. for Gen. Semantics, Internat. Soc. for Gen. Semantics, Am. Philatelic Soc., Democratic Women's Club of Collier County, Castleton Hist. Soc. Clubs: Women's, Rutland County Stamp. Avocations: stamp and coin collecting, sailing, skiing, traveling. Home: 222 Harbour Dr Naples FL 33940-4022 also: Mason Point Bomoseen VT 05732 Office: Evelyn Stagg Literary Agy Naples FL 33940

STAGG, LOUIS CHARLES, English language and literature educator; b. New Orleans, Jan. 3, 1933; s. Louis Anatol and Gladys (Andrews) S.; BA in English, La. Coll., 1955; MA in English U. Ark., 1957, PhD in English, 1963; m. Mary Casner, June 5, 1959; children: Robert Charles, Helen Marie. Teaching asst. English U. Ark., 1955-59; asst. prof. William Jewell Coll., 1959-60; instr. Stephen F. Austin State U., 1960-62; asst. prof. Memphis State U. (name changed to U. Memphis), 1962-69, assoc. prof., 1969-77, prof., English language and literature 1977—, dir. grad. studies in English, 1985-88, dir. English Drama Players, 1968—, dir undergrad. advising for English, 1970-80, 88-91, chair policies and procedures com. for English, 1983-95, tenure and promotion com. for English, 1978-80, 82-86, 89—; chmn. acad. policies com. Memphis State U. Senate, 1981-82, 88-90, 93-94, 95—, mem. exec. com. senate, 1987-91, 93—, parliamentarian of senate, 1987-88, 90-91, 94-95, humanities rep. budget adv. com. dean coll. arts and scis., 1992-93, mem. steering com., chair of schedules, originator Alliance Creative Theatre, Edn. and Rsch. series, 1989, 90, 92, 94, 96; cons. NEH, 1975, 76, 78, Ohio State U. Press, summer 1985, 86, U. Jordan, Aman, 1985; chair policies and procedures subdivsn. Eng. Dept. so. assn. colls., schs. self study, mem. steering com., 1992-93; cons. Memphis State U. Learning Media-Ctrs. catalogue Shakespeare holdings, 1992-93, rev., 1993-94, 94-95. Mem. Memphis Oratorio Soc. Chorus, 1969-92, diction coach, 1987, Memphis Symphony Chorus, 1993—, Memphis in May Tattoo Chorus, 1993, Memphis in May Sunset Symphony Choir, 1996, Martin Luther King Tribute Concert Choir, 1995, 96. Recipient summer stipend NEH, 1967; Memphis State U. grantee, 1965—; travel grantee to U.S. Library of Congress, summer 1971. Mem. MLA, So. Humanities Coun. (sec.-treas. 1974-76, exec. com. 1976-83, 94—, chmn. coun. 1993-94, chmn. sect. humanities in pluralistic society 1984, ad hoc com. on crisis in teaching humanities 1977—, chmn. local arrangements for convs. 1975, 94), Tenn. Philol. Assn. (pres. 1976-77, exec. com. 1977, local arrangements chmn. 1987), Marlowe Soc. Am. (book reviewer 1984, 86, 87, 88, 93), Am. Soc. for Theatre Rsch., Samuel Beckett Soc., Conf. on Christianity and Lit., South Cen. Conf. on Christianity and Lit. Soc. for Study of Works of Harold Pinter (asst. constitution revision 1988, asst. with planning 1992, treas. 1994—, mem. exec. com. 1994—), Ark. Philol. Assn., Shakespeare Assn. Am. (local arrangements host com. 1985), Stratford-Upon-Avon Shakespeare Festival, Eng.; Eugene O'Neill Soc., Alliance for Creative Theatre, Edn. and Rsch. (chmn. schedules com., rep. for English, mem. steering com., originator of proposal 1986, 89, 90, 92, 94, 96), Internat. Shakespeare Assn., Am. Soc. Theatre Rsch., Internat. Soc. Theatre Rsch., Medieval and Renaissance Drama Soc., Renaissance Soc. Am., South Cen. Renaissance Conf. (chmn. nominations 1976, exec. com. 1978-80, program com. 1981-83, chmn. sect. Shakespeare 1981, 85, 95, 16th Century lit. 1982, chmn. local arrangements 1983, symposium on humanism 1984, chmn. Shakespeare on film and the teaching of Brit. Drama 1986, chmn. music in Shakespeare's plays 1987, chmn. sect. Thematic Approaches to Tudor/Stuart Drama 1988, chmn. sect. Medieval influences on Renaissance drama 1993, chmn. Shakespeare's Villains: Stage and Page 1995, chmn. local arrangements for convention 1990, chmn. spl. session 1989, 95), South Cen. MLA (assoc. editor for English, South Cen. Bull. 1982-84, nominations com. 1985-86, 95—, book reviewer South Cen. Rev. 1983, 85, 86, sec. English I.B. Renaissance, 1986, chair, 1987, sec. spl. sect. Renaissance Drama, 1988, chair Shakespeare's Tragi-comedies and tragi-comic romances, 1989, co-chair local arrangements 1980, 92, chair panel on renaissance drama criticism 1995), South Atlantic MLA, South Cen. Coll. English Assn. (sec.-treas. 1980-81, v.p. 1981-82, pres. 1982-83, exec. com. 1983-90, co-host 19stitution revision 1989), Coll. English Assn., Internat. Patristic Medieval and Renaissance Conf. (sect. chmn. Medieval drama 1977, chair Shakespeare session 1994, chair renaissance drama section 1995), Am. Theatre Assn. (chmn. sect. combining Brit. lit. and theatre in teaching of drama 1983, chmn. Shakespeare sect. 1994), The Stratford Can. Shakespeare Festival, AAUP (sec. treas. Memphis State U. chap. 1982-86, v.p. 1986-88, pres. 1988-90), Phi Beta Kappa (pres. Memphis alumni assn. 1985-88, mem. spl. panel The Soc. and the New Scholarship at 37th triennial coun. 1994), Alpha Chi. Democrat. Episcopalian (lay reader 1969-86). Author: (with J. Lasley Dameron) Poe's Critical Vocabulary, 1966; author series: Index To The Figurative Language of John Webster's Tragedies, 1967, of Ben Jonson's Tragedies, 1967, of Thomas Heywood's Tragedies, 1967, of George Chapman's Tragedies, 1970, of John Marston's Tragedies, 1970, of Thomas Middleton's Tragedies, 1970, of Cyril Tourneur's Tragedies, 2d edit. all 7 under title Index to the Figurative Language of the Tragedies of Shakespeare's Chief 17th Century Contemporaries 1977), 3d edit., 1982; Index to the Figurative Language of the Tragedies of Shakespeare's Chief 16th Century Contemporaries, 1984; contbr. to Great Writers of the English Language: Dramatists, 1979, 87; circulation editor Interpretations, 1976-80; contbr. articles on English and American drama to profl. jours., publs. on Shakespeare, other lit. publs. Home: 5219 Mason Rd Memphis TN 38117-2104 Office: U Memphis Dept English Memphis TN 38152 *It's time—past time— we realized we all belong to one race, human, and that we have only one world, this one, only one ecological system, this one, if we want humanity to survive beyond our own life times.*

STAGG, TOM, federal judge; b. Shreveport, La., Jan. 19, 1923; s. Thomas Eaton and Beulah (Meyer) S.; m. Margaret Mary O'Brien, Aug. 21, 1946; children: Julie, Margaret Mary. B.A., La. State U., 1943, J.D., 1949. Bar: La. 1949. With firm Hargrove, Guyton, Van Hook & Hargrove, Shreveport, 1949-53; pvt. practice law Shreveport, 1953-58; sr. ptnr. firm Stagg, Cady & Beard, Shreveport, 1958-74; judge U.S. Dist. Ct. (we. dist.) La., 1974-84, 91-92, chief judge, 1984-90, sr. judge, 1992—; Pres. Abe Meyer Corp., 1960-74, Stagg Investments, Inc., 1964-74; mng. partner Pierremont Mall Shopping Center, 1963-74; v.p. King Hardware Co., 1955-74; Mem. Shreveport Airport Authority, 1967-73, chmn., 1970-73; chmn. Gov.'s Tidelands Adv. Council, 1969-70; del. La. Constl. Conv., 1973-74; chmn. rules com., com. on exec. dept.; mem. Gov.'s Adv. Com on Offshore Revenues, 1972-74. Active Republican party, 1950-74, del. convs., 1956, 60, 64, 68, 72; mem. Nat. Com. for La., 1964-72, mem. exec. com., 1964-68; Pres. Shreveport Jr. C. of C., 1955-56; v.p. La. Jr. C. of C., 1956-57. Served to capt., inf. AUS, 1943-46, ETO. Decorated Bronze Star, Purple Heart with oak leaf cluster. Mem. Am., La., Shreveport bar assns., Photog. Soc. Am. Office: US Dist Ct 300 Fannin St Ste 4100 Shreveport LA 71101-3121

STAGLIN, GAREN KENT, finance and computer service company executive; b. Lincoln, Nebr., Dec. 22, 1944; s. Ramon and Darlene (Guilliams) S.; m. Sharalyn King, June 8, 1968; children: Brandon Kent, Shannon King. BS in Engring. with honors, UCLA, 1966; MBA, Stanford U., 1968. Treas. Stanco, Inc., 1968—; assoc. Carr Mgmt. Co., N.Y.C., 1971-75; v.p. Crocker Nat. Bank, San Francisco, 1975-76; dir. fin. Itel Corp., San Francisco, 1976-77, pres. ins. services div., 1977-79; corp. v.p., gen. mgr. ADP Automotive Svcs. Group, San Ramon, Calif., 1978-91; chmn., chief exec. officer Safelite Glass Corp., Columbus, Ohio, 1991—; owner Staglin Family Vineyard, 1985—; bd. dirs. Grimes Aerospace Corp. Bd. dirs. Peralta Hosp. Cancer Inst., 1977-78, Berkeley Reportory Theatre, 1979-85, Summa Care, Inc., 1988-90, Quick Response Svcs., Inc., 1991—, First Data Corp., 1992—; bd. trustees Justin Sienna H.S., 1995—; chmn. major gifts program Ea. Bay region, Stanford (Calif.) U., 1989-92. Lt. USN, 1968-71. Mem. Stanford Assocs. (bd. govs. 1985-92), World Pres. Orgn., Internat. Inst. Soc. (bd. govs. 1985-92), Stanford Bus. Sch. (adv. bd. 1995—). Democrat. Lutheran. Home: PO Box 680 1570 Bella Oaks Ln Rutherford CA 94573

STAHELI, DONALD L., grain company executive; b. 1931. BS, Utah State U., 1953; MS, U. Ill., 1954, PhD, 1956. With Swift & Co., 1958-69, Allied Mills (now World Meat and World Milling Groups of Continental Grain Co., 1969—; dir. Continental Grain Co., N.Y.C., 1977—, exec. v.p., 1977-84, pres., COO, 1984-88, CEO, chmn., 1988—. With USAF, 1956-58. Office: Continental Grain Co 277 Park Ave New York NY 10172-0099*

STAHELI, LYNN TAYLOR, pediatric orthopedist, educator; b. Provo, Utah, Nov. 13, 1933; s. Harvey Roulin and Letha (Taylor) S.; m. Ann Lee Smith, June 4, 1957 (div. 1976); children: Linda Ann, Diane Kay, Todd Kent; m. Lana Ribble, June 11, 1977. BS, Brigham Young U., 1956; MD, U. Utah, 1959. Intern U. Utah, Salt Lake City, 1960; resident in orthopedic surgery U. Wash., 1964-68; dir. rsch. and edn. Children's Hosp., Seattle, 1968-77, dir. dept. orthopedics, 1977-92; prof. dept. orthopedics U. Wash., Seattle, 1968—; mem. med. exec. com. Children's Hosp. and Med. Ctr., Seattle, 1977-92; cons. Fircrest Sch., Seattle, 1968-80, Boyer Children's clinic, Seattle, 1968-80, Seattle Pub. Schs. Spl. Edn. Program, 1968-80; invited speaker for more than 1000 individual presentations in 30 countries, 1960—; founder Duncan Seminar for Cerebral Palsy, 1980. Editor: Jour. Pediatric Orthopedics, 1981—; author: Med. Writing and Speaking, 1986, Fundamentals of Pediatric Orthopedics, 1992; contbr. articles to numerous profl. jours. Founding mem. bd. N.W. Inst. Ethics and Life Scis., Seattle, 1974—; bd. dirs. Rainier Found., Seattle, 1988—; founder Internat. Scholarship for Pediatric Orthopedics, Seattle, 1988-93. Capt. USAF, 1960-63. Mem. Pediatric Orthopedic Soc. N.Am., Am. Acad. Orthopedic Surgeons (pediatric orthopedics com. 1980-86), Am. Acad. Pediatrics (chmn. com. on shoewear 1985—, Disting. Svc. award 1995), Am. Acad. Cerebral Palsy and Devel. Medicine (chmn. instrnl. course com. 1982—), Alpha Omega Alpha. Avocations: flying, sailing, boating, canoeing, photography. Home: 4116 48th Ave NE Seattle WA 98105 Office: Childrens Hosp Dept Orthopedics 4800 Sand Point Way NE Seattle WA 98105

STAHL, ALAN MICHAEL, curator; b. Providence, Aug. 7, 1947; s. Benjamin and Evelyn (Miller) S.; m. Pamela McAbee Dec. 28, 1968 (div. 1976). BA, U. Calif., Berkeley, 1968; MA, U. Pa., 1973, PhD, 1977. Asst. curator Am. Numismatic Soc., N.Y.C., 1980-82, assoc. curator, 1982-86, curator, 1986—; visiting prof. Universita di Venezia, Venice, Italy, 1987-88. Author: Merovingian Coinage/Metz, 1982, Venetian Tornesello, 1985, Medal in America, 1988. Recipient Research Grant G.K. Delmas Found., 1981, 83, 85. Mem. Fed. Internat. de la Medaille (USA del.), Am. Medallic Sculpture Assn., Nat. Sculpture Soc. (councillor), Medieval Acad. Am., N.Y. Numismatic Club. Home: 565 Ft Washington Ave New York NY 10033-1935 Office: Am Numismatic Soc Broadway at 155th St New York NY 10032

STAHL, ALICE SLATER, psychiatrist; b. Vienna, Austria, Jan. 28, 1913; came to U.S., 1938; d. Sam and Helen (Bluman) Slater; widowed; chidlren: Kenneth Lee, June Audrey. Baccalaureate, Gymnasium, Vienna, 1932; Med. Dr., U. Vienna Med. Sch., 1938. Intern Williamsport (Pa.) Gen. Hosp., 1939-40; resident in psychiatry Gallinger Mcpl. Hosp., Washington, 1940-41, Independence State Hosp., 1941-42; resident in psychiatry Bellevue Hosp., N.Y.C., 1942-43, attending psychiatry, 1945-48; staff psychiatrist Jewish Bd. of Guardians, N.Y.C., 1943-45; attending psychiatrist Jamaica Hosp., Queens, N.Y., 1948-52; dir. adolescent psychiatry Hillside Hosp., Glen Oaks, N.Y., 1954-62, attending staff psychiatrist, 1962—; supervising psychiatrist Bergen Pines County Hosp., Paramus, N.J., cons. psychiatrist, 1988—; asst. prof. clin. psychiatry Yeshiva U. Med. Sch., 1978—. Fellow AMA (life), Am. Psychiat. Assn. (life); mem. Am. Psychoanalytic Assn. (life), Am. Soc. for Adolescent Psychiatry (life). Avocations: swimming, hiking, gardening, grandmotherhood. Home and Office: 305 Joan Pl Wyckoff NJ 07481-2818

STAHL, CHARLES EUGENE, lawyer; b. Washington, Sept. 23, 1944; s. George P. Sr. and Dorothy G. (McCaffrey) S. BA, U. Notre Dame, 1967; JD, Northwestern U., 1971. Bar: Ill. 1972, Calif. 1980. Assoc. Newman & Hess, Chgo., 1971-73; ptnr. Newman & Stahl, Chgo., 1973-83, Arvey, Hodes, Costello & Berman, Chgo., 1984, Friedman & Koven, Chgo., 1985, Winston & Strawn, Chgo., 1986—; lectr. Ill. Inst. For Continuing Edn., Chgo., 1975—; speaker Infocast Banking Semminars, Santa Monica, Calif., 1987—. Bd. dirs. Chgo. Symphony Orch., 1987—, William Ferris Chorale, Chgo., 1988—. Mem. Univ. Club. Democrat. Roman Catholic. Avocations: classical music, sports collectibles, history. Office: Winston & Strawn 35 W Wacker Dr Chicago IL 60601-1614

STAHL, DAVID EDWARD, trade association administrator; b. Chgo., Apr. 10, 1934; s. Archie Edward and Dorothy (Berning) S.; m. Carolyn Downs Stahl, June 23, 1956; children: Stephen, Michael, Kurt, Thomas. B.S., Miami U., 1956. Exec. v.p. Republic Realty Mortgage Corp., Chgo., 1963-66; dep. mayor City of Chgo., 1966-70, city comptroller, 1971-73; exec. v.p. Urban Land Inst., Washington, 1973-76, Nat. Assn. Home Builders, Washington, 1977-84; pres. Nat. Forest Products Assn., Washington, 1984-87; exec. v.p. Urban Land Inst., Washington, 1987-92; exec. dir. Young Pres.'s Orgn., Irving, Tex., 1992-96; del. 6th Ill. Constl. Conv., Springfield, 1970. Served to lt. USAF, 1956-59. Mem. Am. Soc. Assn. Execs., Econ. Club (Chgo.), Wayfarers Club, Annapolis Yacht Club, Ocean Reef Club, Lambda Alpha. Roman Catholic. Home: 529 Rock Bluff Austin TX 78734

STAHL, DAVID M., lawyer; b. Chgo., Sept. 22, 1946. BA, U. Ill., 1968; JD magna cum laude, U. Mich., 1971, MA, 1971. Bar: Ill. 1972, U.S. Dist. Ct. (no. dist.) Ill. 1973, U.S. Ct. Appeals (D.C. and 5th cirs.) 1979, U.S. Ct. Appeals (9th cir.) 1984, U.S. Ct. Appeals (7th cir.) 1986, U.S. Dist. Ct. (ea. dist.) Mich. 1989. Ptnr. Sidley & Austin, Chgo. Office: Sidley & Austin 1 First Nat Plz Chicago IL 60603*

STAHL, FRANK LUDWIG, civil engineer; b. Fuerth, Germany, 1920; came to U.S., 1946, naturalized, 1949; s. Leo E. and Anna (Regensburger) S.; m. Edith Cosmann, Aug. 31, 1947; children—David, Robert. BSCE, Tech. Inst. Zurich, Switzerland, 1945. With Ammann & Whitney, Cons. Engrs., N.Y.C., 1946-93, project engr., 1955-67, assoc., 1968-76, sr. assoc., 1977-81, chief engr. Transp. div., 1982-93; author and lectr. in field. Prin. works include: Verrazano-Narrows Bridge, Throgs Neck Bridge, Walt Whitman Bridge, Improvements to Golden Gate Bridge, rehab. of Williamsburg Bridge, N.Y.C. Royal Gorge Bridge, Colo., Interstate-10 Deck Tunnel, Phoenix, Ariz.; contbr. articles to profl. jours. on bridge design and construction. Recipient Gold award The James F. Lincoln Arc Welding Found., 1986, John A. Roebling medal Internat. Bridge Conf., 1992. Fellow ASCE (Thomas Fitch Rowland prize 1967, Innovation in Civil Engring. award of mert 1983, Metro. Civil Engr. of Yr. award 1987, Roebling award 1990), ASTM (vice chmn. com. A-1 on steel, stainless steel and related alloys 1978-83, chmn. steel reinforce-subcom. 1971-82, award of merit 1982); mem. Am. Inst. Steel Constrn. (Prize Bridge award 1986), Engring. Found. (rsch. coun. on structural connections), Internat. Assn. Bridge and Structural Engring., Internat. Bridge Tunnel and Turnpike Assn. Home: 20911 28th Rd Flushing NY 11360-2412

STAHL, JACK LELAND, real estate company executive; b. Lincoln, Ill., June 28, 1934; s. Edwin R. and Edna M. (Burns) S.; m. Carol Anne Townsend, June 23, 1956; children: Cheryl, Nancy, Kellea. BS in Edn., U. N.Mex., 1957. Tchr. Albuquerque Public Schs., 1956-59; pres. House Finders, Inc., Albuquerque, 1959-65; v.p. N.Mex. Savs. & Loan Assn., Albuquerque, 1965-67; chmn. bd. Hooten-Stahl, Inc., Albuquerque, 1967-77; mem. N.Mex. Ho. of Reps., 1969-70; pres. The Jack Stahl Co., Albuquerque, 1977—; mem. N.Mex. Senate, 1981-86; lt. gov. State of N.Mex., 1987-90. Mem. N. Mex. Ho. of Reps., 1969-70, exec. bd. Gr. S.W. Coun. Boy Scouts Am, 1982-89; bd. dirs. BBB N. Mex., 1968-82, pres. 1975-76; trustee Univ Heights. Hosp.,1980-85; vice chmn. N. Mex. Bd. Fin., 1987-90, N. Mex. Cmty. Devel. Coun., 1987-90; bd. dirs. Ctr. for Entrepreneurship and Econ. Devel., 1994—; mem. Gov.'s Bus. Adv. Coun., 1995—. Named Realtor of Yr., Albuquerque Bd. Realtors, 1972. Mem. Nat. Assn. Realtors, Nat. Homebuilders Assn., N.Mex. Amigos, 20-30 Club (pres. 1963-64), Rotary. Republican. Methodist. Office: 1911 Wyoming Blvd NE Albuquerque NM 87112-2865

STAHL, LADDIE L., electrical engineer, manufacturing company executive; b. Terre Haute, Ind., Dec. 23, 1921; s. Edgar Allen and Martha (Llewellyn) S.; m. Thelma Mae Beasley, Dec. 11, 1942; children: Stephanie, Laddie L., Craig. B.S. in Civil Engring., Purdue U., 1942; M.S. in Engring., Johns Hopkins U., 1950. With GE, 1954-90; mgr. planning and resources, electronics sci. and engring., corp. research and devel. GE, Schenectady, N.Y., 1974-76, mgr. electronics systems programs ops., elec. sci. and engring., 1976-84, mgr. spl. programs and project devel. operation, 1984-90; dir. tech. transfer program Data Storage Systems Ctr. Carnegie Mellon U., Pitts., 1990—; chmn. adv. group U.S. Army Electronics Command, 1971-74; mem. U.S. Army Sci. Bd., 1978-87; cons. in field. Contbr. articles to profl. publs. Mem. alumni bd. dirs. Purdue U., 1979-82. Served with U.S. Army, 1942-54, ETO; maj. gen. Res. (ret.), 1954-77. Decorated D.S.M., Legion of Merit. Mem. AIAA (sr.), IEEE (life), Am. Def. Preparedness Assn., Tau Beta Pi, Chi Epsilon. Clubs: Mohawk (Schenectady); Army and Navy (Washington). Home: 29 Fairway Ln Rexford NY 12148-1213 Office: Carnegie Mellon U Hamerschlag Hall A206 ECE Dept Hamburg Hall 2505 Pittsburgh PA 15213-3890

STAHL, LESLEY R., journalist; b. Lynn, Mass., Dec. 16, 1941; d. Louis and Dorothy J. (Tishler) S.; m. Aaron Latham; 1 dau. B.A. cum laude, Wheaton Coll., Norton, Mass., 1963. Asst. to speechwriter Mayor Lindsay's Office, N.Y.C., 1966-67; researcher N.Y. Election unit London-Huntley Brinkley Report, NBC News, 1967-69; producer, reporter WHDH-TV, Boston, 1970-72; news corr. CBS News, Washington, from 1972; moderator Face the Nation, 1983-91; co-editor, corr. CBS News, 60 Minutes, 1991—. Trustee Wheaton Coll. Recipient Tex. Headliners award, 1973, Dennis Kauff award for lifetime achievement in journalism; named Best White House Corr., Washington Journalism Rev., 1991. Office: CBS News 60 Minutes 555 W 57th St New York NY 10019-2925

STAHL, MARGO SCHNEEBALG, marine biologist; b. Coral Gables, Fla., June 24, 1947; d. Martin and Rose (Osman) Schneebalg; m. Glenn Stahl, Aug. 17, 1969 (div. June 1988); 1 child, Shaina Flori Georgina. BS in Biology, U. Miami, 1969, MS in Marine Biology, 1973. Fish and wildlife aide Calif. Dept. Fish and Game, Long Beach, 1973; assoc. rsch. engr. So. Calif. Edison Co., Rosemead, 1973-75; rsch. assoc. in urban and regional planning U. Hawaii, Honolulu, 1975-76, Hawaii Inst. Marine Biology, Kaneohe, 1975-77, Anuenue Fisheries Rsch. Ctr., Honolulu, 1977-79; aquatic biology Hawaii Dept. Land and Natural Resources, Honolulu, 1979-83; instr. sci. U. Hawaii Windward C.C., Kaneohe, 1985-88; ecologist U.S. Army C.E., Honolulu, 1988-93; supervisory fish and wildlife biologist U.S. Fish and Wildlife Svc., Honolulu, 1993—; pres. Mermaid Aquatic Cons., Honolulu, 1979-81, 84-88; mem. Hawaii Water Quality Tng. Interagy. Com., Honolulu, 1991-93. Contbg. author: Taste of Aloha, 1983 (Jr. League award 1985); contbr. articles to profl. jours. Project mgr. Kokokahi Aquaculture Model, Kaneohe, 1978-80; mem. adv. bd. Windward C.C., 1982-83; hon. coord. RESULTS Hunger Lobby, Honolulu, 1989. Recipient Stoye award in icythyology Am. Soc. Ichtyologists and Herpetologists, 1972, Career Woman award Sierra Mar dist. Calif. Bus. and Profl. Womens Club, 1975, Comdr's award for exceptional performance U.S. Army C.E., Ft. Shafter, Hawaii, 1990. Mem. Nat. Assn. Environ. Profls. (cert. environ. profl., chmn. cert. com. 1992-93, C.E.P. award 1991), Assn. for Women in Sci. (bd. dirs. 1985), Hawaii Assn. Environ. Profls. (bd. dirs. 1991-93, pres.-elect 1993-94), World Mariculture Soc. (bd. dirs. 1981), Am. Fisheries Soc., Western Soc. Naturalists. Avocations: scuba diving, gardening, classical music, animals. Home: 46-436 Holopeki St Kaneohe HI 96744-4227 Office: US Fish and Wildlife Svc Honolulu HI 96850

STAHL, NORMAN H., federal judge; b. Manchester, N.H., 1931. BA, Tufts U., 1952; LLB, Harvard U., 1955. Law clk. to Hon. John V. Spalding Mass. Supreme Ct., 1955-56; assoc. Devine, Millimet, Stahl & Branch, Manchester, N.H., 1956-59, ptnr., 1959-90; dist. judge U.S. Dist. Ct. (N.H. dist.), 1990-92; cir. judge U.S. Ct. Appeals (1st cir.), Concord, N.H., 1992—. Del. to Rep. Nat. Conv., 1988. Mem. N.H. Bar Assn. Office: US Ct Appeals 55 Pleasant St Rm 220 Concord NH 03301-3938

STAHL, O(SCAR) GLENN, writer, lecturer, former government official; b. Evansville, Ind., Apr. 30, 1910; s. Oscar and Mayme (Wittmer) S.; m. Marie Jane Rueter, June 26, 1934; children: Elaine Marie, Alan G. A.B., U. Evansville, 1931, LL.D., 1984; M.A., U. Wis., 1933; Ph.D., N.Y. U., 1936. Instr. govt. NYU, 1933-35; personnel officer TVA, 1935-41; with Fed. Security Agy. (later HEW), 1941-51; dir. personnel, 1948-51; with U.S. CSC (now OPM), 1951-69, dir. bur. policies and standards, 1955-69; adj. prof. public adminstrn. Am. U., 1949-69; part time prof. U. Tenn., 1939, Dept. Agr. Grad. Sch., 1941-49; vis. lectr. various univs., U.S. and abroad; lectr. Salzburg Seminar in Am. Studies, 1965; tech. assistance adviser to Venezuela UN, 1958-59, 72; U.S. rep. UN Conf., Ethiopia, 1964; Ford Found. cons. to, India, 1968-69, 71, Nepal, 1969, Pakistan, 1974; AID adviser, Pakistan, 1969, 71; U.S. rapporteur Internat. Congress Adminstrv. Scis., Dublin, 1968; U.S. rep. UN Seminar, Tashkent, Uzbekistan, 1969; spl. advisor to W. Ger., 1971; spl. cons. Public Adminstrn. Service-Govtl. Affairs Inst. and Internat. Personnel Mgmt. Assn., 1973-76; dir. Internat. Symposium on Public Personnel Adminstrn., Salzburg, 1973, 75; speaker Latin Am. Conf. on Civil Service Tng., Venezuela, 1982. Author: Training Career Public Servants for the City of New York, 1936, Public Personnel Administration, 8th edit, 1983, The Personnel Job of Government Managers, 1971, Frontier Mother, 1979, The Need for a Public Philosophy, 1987, Standing Up for Government, 1990; editor: Personnel Adminstrn, 1945-55, Improving Public Services, 1979, (with others) Police Personnel Administration, 1974; contbr. numerous articles to jours. Mem. Arlington County (Va.) Sch. Bd., 1948-50; pres. Arlington Com. to Preserve Public Schs., 1958-61. Recipient Disting. Service award CSC, 1960; Stockberger award Soc. Personnel Adminstrn., 1962; Career Service award Nat. Civil Service League, 1967; medal of Honor U. Evansville, 1981; hon. fellow Nat. Acad. Pub. Adminstrn., 1988. Mem. Am. Polit. Sci. Assn., Am. Soc. Public Adminstrn. (editorial bd. 1955-58), Internat. Inst. Adminstrv. Sci., Internat. Personnel Mgmt. Assn. (hon. life mem., exec. com. Public Personnel Assn. 1951-54, pres. 1965-66, Washington rep. 1971-73). Presbyterian. Home: 3600 N Piedmont St Arlington VA 22207-5333

STAHL, RICHARD G. C., journalist, editor; b. Chgo., Feb. 22, 1934; m. Gladys C. Weisbecker; 1 child, Laura Ann. Student, Northwestern U., U. Ill., Chgo. Editor Railway Purchases and Stores Mag., Chgo., 1960-63; editor pub. rels. dept. Sears Roebuck & Co., Chgo., 1963-68; dir pub. rels. dept. St. Joseph's Hosp. Med. Ctr., Phoenix, 1968-72; v.p. pub. rels. Consultation Svcs., Inc., Phoenix, 1972-73; creative dir. Don Jackson and Assoc., Phoenix, 1973; editor, pub. rels. mgr. Maricopa County Med. Soc., Phoenix, 1974-76; mng. editor Ariz. Hwys. mag., Phoenix, 1977—. Regional editor: (travel guides) Budget Travel, 1985, USA, 1986, Arizona, 1986; free-lance writer and editor. Mem. Soc. Profl. Journalists. Avocation: woodworking. Office: Ariz Hwys Mag 2039 W Lewis Ave Phoenix AZ 85009-2819 *Personal philosophy: Follow your dream and fulfill your potentialities.*

STAHLMAN, MILDRED THORNTON, pediatrics and pathology educator, researcher; b. Nashville, July 31, 1922; d. James Geddes and Mildred (Thornton) S. AB, Vanderbilt U., 1943, MD, 1946; MD (hon.), U. Goteborg, Sweden, 1973, U. Nancy, France, 1982. Diplomate Am. Bd. Pediatrics, Am. Bd. Neonatology. Cardiac resident La Rabida Sanitarium, Chgo., 1951; instr. pediatrics Vanderbilt U., Nashville, 1951-58, instr. physiology, 1954-60, asst. prof. pediatrics, 1959-64, asst. prof. physiology, 1960-62, assoc. prof. pediatrics, 1964-70, prof., 1970—, prof. pathology, 1982—, Harvie Branscomb Disting. prof., 1984, dir. div. neonatology, 1961-89. Editor: Respiratory Distress Syndromes, 1989; contbr. over 140 articles to profl. publs. Recipient Thomas Jefferson award Vanderbilt U., 1980, Apgar award Am. Acad. Pediatrics, 1987; NIH grantee, 1954—. Mem. AAAS, Am. Pediatric Soc. (pres. 1984), Soc. Pediatric Rsch., Am. Physiology Soc., So. Soc. Pediatric Rsch. (pres. 1961-62), Royal Swedish Acad. Scis., Inst. of Medicine of the Nat Acad. of Scis. Episcopalian. Home: 538 Beech Creek Rd S Brentwood TN 37027-3421 Office: Vanderbilt U Med Ctr 21st Ave Nashville TN 37232*

STAHMANN, ROBERT F., education educator; b. Peoria, Ill., Nov. 26, 1939; s. Fred Soeffner and Mary Emma (Thompson) S.; m. Kathleen Cook, Dec. 21, 1965; children: Benjamin C., John C., Paul C., Mark C., Anne. BA, Macalester Coll., 1963; MS, U. Utah, 1965, PhD, 1967. Research fellow U. Utah, 1966-67; sr. counselor U. Iowa, Iowa City, 1967-71; coordinator counseling service U. Iowa, 1971-72, dir. counseling service, 1972-75, asst. prof. edn., 1967-71, asso. prof., 1971-75; prof. family scis. Brigham Young U., Provo, Utah, 1975—, chmn. dept. family scis., 1983-89, dir. Marriage and Family Counseling Clinic, 1976-83, coordinator program in marriage and family therapy, 1977-83; vis. prof. sex and marital therapy clinic Coll. Medicine, U. Utah, 1980-81; mem. Utah State Marriage and Family Therapy Licensing Bd., 1982-92; mem. Commn. Accreditation for Marriage and Family Therapy Edn., 1989-94, chair, 1990-94. Co-author: Premarital Counseling, 1980, 2d edit., 1987, Dynamic Assessment in Couples Therapy, 1993; co-editor: Ethical and Professional Issues for Marital and Family Therapists, 1980; co-editor, contbr.; Counseling in Marital and Sexual Problems: A Clinician's Handbook, 1977, 3d edit., 1984; assoc. editor: Jour. Coll. Student Pers., 1971-77; editor: Jour. Assoc. Mormon Counselors and Psychotherapists, 1977-78; contbr. chpts. to books., articles to profl. jours. Scoutmaster Boy Scouts Am., 1969-72, 83-87, cubmaster, 1976-79; mem. Orem City Beautification Commn., 1986-87; mem. adv. bd. Ret. Sr. Vol. Program for Utah County, 1987-89. Fellow Am. Assn. Marriage and Family Therapy (bd. dirs. 1977-79); mem. ACA, Am. Assn. Sex Educators, Counselors and Therapists (cert.), Utah Assn. Marriage and Family Counselors (pres. 1978-80), Nat. Coun. on Family Rels., Utah Coun. on Family Rels. (pres. 1987-88), Sigma Xi, Phi Kappa Phi. Mem. LDS Ch. Office: Brigham Young Dept Edu Dept Provo UT 84602

STAHR, CURTIS BRENT, photographer, art association administrator, educator; b. West Union, Iowa; s. Freman H. and Lucile M. (Schreiner) S. AA, Ellsworth Coll., 1966; BFA, Peru (Nebr.) State U., 1968. Cert. tchr., Iowa, Colo., Ariz. Art dir. Iowa Falls (Iowa) High Sch., 1968-70, Wiley (Colo.) Schs., 1971-72, Judson Sch., Scottsdale, Ariz., 1973-79; freelance graphic artist, photographer and mktg. dir., 1979-88; prof. photography Des Moines Area Community Coll., 1988—; art dir. Homestead Assn., Des Moines, 1993—; bd. dirs. Homestead Corp.; art dir. Starland Design Band Group, 1979-86, graphic effects dept. Bischoff's, 1987-88; photographic dir. ednl. exchange trip to China. Exhibited in 14 one-man art shows, in 27 invited/juried art shows; represented in numerous pvt. collections; photographer numerous field trips including migration of Am. eagle from Alaska to Fla., all 99 Iowa County Courthouses, Yellowstone Nat. Park, Grand Teton Nat. Park, Waterton-Glacier Internat. Peace Park (U.S. and Can.), Isle Royale Nat. Park, Grand Canyon Nat. Park, Denali Nat. Park, Arctic Nat. Park & Preserve, Canyon de Chelly Nat. Monument, Rainbow Bridge Nat. Monument, Devils Tower Nat. Monument, Effigy Mounts Nat. Monument, Yosemite Nat. Park, Sequoia Nat. Park, Kings Canyon Nat. Park, Japser Nat. Park (Can.), Glacier Nat. Park (Can.), Banff (Can.) Nat. Park, numerous cross coutnry trips to U.S., Can., Mex., Cen. Am., S.Am., Yukon Territory and Arctic Cir. Speaker Ariz.-Calif. Lecture Series, 1982-84; chairperson art evaluation com. State of Iowa, 1970; bd. dirs. Ariz. Arts Festival, 1974-79, Muscular Dystrophy Assn. Fund Drive, Ariz., 1982-85. Recipient 8 purchase awards. Democrat. Office: Des Moines Area CC 2006 S Ankeny Blvd Ankeny IA 50021-8995

STAHR, ELVIS J(ACOB), JR., lawyer, conservationist, educator; b. Hickman, Ky., Mar. 9, 1916; s. Elvis and Mary Anne (McDaniel) S.; m. Dorothy Howland Berkfield, June 28, 1946; children: Stephanie Ann, Stuart Edward Winston, Bradford Lanier. AB, U. Ky., 1936; BA (Rhodes scholar), U. Oxford, Eng., 1938; BCL, 1939, MA, 1943; diploma in Chinese Lang., Yale U., 1943; LL.D., W.Va. Wesleyan Coll., Waynesburg Coll., 1959, Concord Coll., 1960, U. Md., U. Pitts., 1961, La. State U., Tex. Christian U., U. Ky., 1962, U. Notre Dame, 1964, Ind. State U., 1966, Brown U., 1967, Northwestern U., U. Fla., 1968, U. Tampa, 1972, Ind. U., 1976, Cumberland Coll., 1990; D.Environ. Sci., Rollins Coll., 1973; Dr.Mil. Sci., Northeastern U., 1962; D.Pub. Adminstrn., Bethany Coll., 1962; D.H.L., DePauw U., 1963, Rose Hulman Inst., 1965, Transylvania U., 1973; Litt.D., U. Cin., 1966, U. Maine, 1976; Pd.D., Culver-Stockton Coll., 1966; D.Sc., Norwich U., 1968, Hanover Coll., 1975. Bar: N.Y. State 1940, Ky. 1948, D.C. 1983, U.S. Supreme Ct. 1950, U.S. Ct. Mil. Appeals 1952. Practiced as assoc. Mudge, Stern, Williams & Tucker, N.Y.C., 1939-41; sr. assoc. Mudge, Stern, Williams & Tucker, 1946-47; assoc. prof. law U. Ky., 1947-48, prof. law, 1948-56; dean U. Ky. (Coll. Law), 1948-56, provost, 1954-56; exec. dir. Pres. Eisenhower's Com. on Edn. Beyond High Sch., 1956-57; vice chancellor professions U. Pitts., 1957-58; pres. W.Va. U., Morgantown, 1958-61; spl. asst. Sec. Army, Washington, 1951-52, cons., 1953; Sec. of the Army Dept. Def., Washington, 1961-62; pres. Ind. U., 1962-68, Nat. Audubon Soc., N.Y.C., 1968-79; sr. counselor Nat. Audubon Soc., 1979-81, pres. emeritus, 1981—; ptnr. Chickering & Gregory, San Francisco, 1982-85; of counsel Chickering & Gregory P.C., San Francisco, 1986—; dir. Acacia Mut. Life Ins. Co., 1968-85; pres. Univ. Assocs., Inc., 1981-90; exec. v.p. Pub. Resource Found., 1982—; sr. cons. Cassidy & Assocs., Inc., 1984—; chmn. Washington Conservation Roundtable, 1986-87; dir. Chase Manhattan Corp. and Bank, 1976-79, Fed. Res. Bank Chgo., 1966-68, dep. chmn., 1967, 68; Mem. Constn. Rev. Commn. Ky., 1949-56, Ind., 1967-68; mem. U.S. del. UN Conf. on Human Environment, Stockholm, 1972, Joint U.S.-USSR Com. on Cooperation for Protection of Environment, 1973, Internat. Whaling Commn., London, 1975, 78; mem. U.S. Aviation Adv. Commn., 1970-73, Nat. Commn. for World Population Yr., 1974; nat. chmn. U.S.O., 1973-76; pub. mem. Nat. Petroleum Council, 1974-79; mem. Summit Conf. on Inflation, 1974. Author: (with others) Economics of Pollution, 1971. Mem. Nat. Commn. on Accrediting, 1963-68; trustee Transylvania U., 1969-76, mem. founders bd. 1978-80; pres. Midwestern Univs. Rsch. Assn., 1963-66; incorporator Argonne Univs. Assn., 1965, trustee, 1965-67; trustee Univs. Rsch. Assn., 1965, mem. coun. pres' 1965-68, chmn. 1968; bd. dirs. Alliance to Save Energy, 1977-88, Resolve, 1977-81, Coun. Fin. Aid to Edn., 1966-69; chmn. higher edn. adv. com. Edn. Commn. States, 1966-68; mem. bd. Govtl. Affairs Inst., 1968-72, Inst. Svcs. to Edn., 1965-67; chmn. Commn. on Fed. Rels., Am. Coun. on Edn., 1966-68; mem. exec. com. Nat. Assn. State Univs. and Land Grant Colls., 1965-68; mem. at-large bd. dirs. Am. Cancer Soc., 1970-76; trustee Com. Econ. Devel., 1964-82, hon.trustee, 1982—; mem. exec. bd. Nat. Assn. Ednl. Broadcasters, 1969-72; adv. coun. Elec. Power Rsch. Inst., 1971-77, Gas Rsch. Inst., 1977-83, Population Inst., 1981—, FAIR, 1982—; mem. Govtl. Affairs Com. of Ind. Sector, 1980-91; bd. dirs. Regional Plan Assn. Greater N.Y., 1970-75; evaluation panel Nat. Bur. Standards, 1975-77; adv. coun. Nat. Energy Project, Am. Enterprise Inst. Pub. Policy Rsch.1974-76; chmn. Coalit. Concerned Charities, 1972-78; mem. exec. bd. Am. Com. for Internat. Conservation, 1978-80; bd. dirs. World Environ. Ctr., 1978-85, Environ. and Energy Study Inst., 1983-90, mem. chmn.'s coun. 1990—; Green Fire Cnserv. Assn., 1988-91, bd. dirs. com. Constnl. System, 1985—, Nat. Water Alliance, 3-86, Land Betwen the Lakes Assn., 1986-89, Pvt. Trust for Pub. Edn., 1990-92, Pub. Mems. Assn. of Fgn. Svc., 1991-94. Lt. col. AUS, 1941-46, N. Africa, China. Decorated Spl. Breast Order of Yun Hui (2) Army Navy and Air Force medal 1st class (China); Bronze Star medal with oak leaf cluster (U.S.); Order of Grand Cross (Peru); recipient Algernon Sydney Sullivan medallion of N.Y. So. Soc., 1936, Meritorious Civiliam Svc. medal Dept. Army, 1953, Disting. Civilian Svc. medal, 1971, Disting. Svc. award U. Ky. Alumni Assn., 1961, Disting. Svc. award Res. Officers Assn. U.S., 1962, Kentuckian of Yr. award Ky. Press Assn., 1961, WHAS (Louisville), 1968, Conservation Svc. award Dept. Interior, 1979, Conservation Achievement award Nat. Wildlife Fedn., 1978, Barbara Swain Award of Honor Natural Resources Coun. of Am., 1988, Sequicentennial medal U. Mich., 1967, Centennial medal U. Ky., 1965 ; named One of Am.'s Ten Outstanding Young Med U.S. Jr. C. of C., 1948, named Ky. Col. and Gen., U. Ky. Hall of Disting. Alumni, named to Tennis Hall of Fame, ROTC Hall of Fame, named hon. citizen of Tex., Ind. and Sagamore; awarded keys to cities of San Francisco, San Juan, New Orleans, Orlando, others. Mem. Assn. U.S. Army (life, pres. 1965-68, chmn. coun. trustees 1969-74), Ind. Soc. of Chgo. (hon. life), Jr. C. of C. Internat. (hon. life senator), Assn. Am. Rhodes Scholars, ABA, Fed. Bar Assn., Kentuckians (pres. N.Y.C. 1976-79, life trustee), S.R., SAR, Ky. Bar Assn., D.C. Bar Assn., Ind. Bar Assn. (hon.), Disciples of Christ Hist. Soc. (life mem.), Army-Navy (Washington), Field (Greenwich), Pilgrims of U.S., Boone and Crockett, Order of Coif, Phi Beta Kappa, Sigma Chi (Balfour Nat. award 1936, Significant Sig 1961, found bd. 1974-91, Order of Constantine 1981), Omicron Delta Kappa (dir. found. 1984-90, Laurel Crowned Circle award), Phi Delta Phi, Tau Kappa Alpha (Dist. Alumni award 1966), Merton Soc. (Oxford, Eng.), Oxford Soc.: hon. mem. Blue Key, Beta Gamma Sigma, Alpha Kappa Psi, Kappa Kappa Psi. Presbyterian. Home: 16 Martin Dl N Greenwich CT 06830-4719 Office: Chickering & Gregory PC 1815 H St NW # 650 Washington DC 20006-3604 *Focus on getting good results rather than on getting credit for them.*

STAILEY, JANIE RUTH, occupational health nurse; b. DeRidder, La., Nov. 23, 1946; d. James Raynie and Betty Lou (Bolding) Whiteley; m. Claude Perry Spicer (div. 1992); 1 child, Cherie Suzanne; m. Ronald Ira Stailey, 1993; stepchildren: Melissa Elliott, Ron, Bobby. Diploma in Nursing, Confederate Meml. Med. Ctr., Shreveport, La., 1968; BS, St. Joseph's Coll., Windham, Maine, 1991. RN, La.; cert. occupl. health nurse specialist. Head nurse Merryville (La.) Gen. Hosp., 1970-79; employee health coord., indsl. hygiene technician, hazard comm. coord. Westvaco Corp., DeRidder, La., 1980—; health care cons. So. Insulation, DeRidder, 1989—, JM&M Constrn., DeRidder, 1988—, Ron Williams Constrn., 1995—. Sec. Beauregard Parish chpt. Am. Cancer Soc., DeRidder, 1988-91, Beauregard Cmty. Concerns, DeRidder, 1988-91. Named La. Occupl. Health Nurse of Yr., Schering Pharm./La. Assn. Occupl. Health Nurses, 1989, Beauregard Parish Woman of the Yr., 1994. Mem. ANA, S.W. La. Dist. Nurses Assn. (Occupl. Health Nurse of Yr. 1989), La. State Nurses Assn., VFW Ladies Aux. (v.p. 1994-95), Am. Assn. Occupl. Health Nurses (bd. dirs. 1989-94, rep. nurse in Washington intership 1993), La. Assn. Occupl. Health Nurses (treas., bd. dirs. 1986—), S.W. La. Assn. Occupl. Health Nurses (pres., v.p.), Beta Sigma Phi. Home: 1124 Elm Rd DeRidder LA 70634 Office: Westvaco Corp 400 Crosby Rd DeRidder LA 70634

STAINE, ROSS, lawyer; b. El Paso, Tex., July 13, 1924; s. Adelbert Claire and Dennie Joe (Stowe) S.; m. Mary Louise Sibert, Aug. 15, 1947; children: Martha Louise, Julie Ann, Ross. B.A., Tex. A&M U., 1947; LL.B., U. Tex., 1950. Bar: Tex. Assoc. Baker & Botts, Houston, 1947, ptnr., 1962—. Served with AUS, 1943-46; served to 1st lt. U.S. Army, 1950-52, PTO. Mem. State Bar Tex., Houston Bar Assn., Tex. Law Rev. Assn., Order of Coif, Phi Delta Phi. Baptist. Clubs: Forest (Houston), Coronado (Houston), Univ. (Houston). Home: 5555 Del Monte Dr Apt 807 Houston TX 77056-4117 Office: Baker & Botts 3000 One Shell Plaza Houston TX 77002

STAINES, DAVID MCKENZIE, English educator; b. Toronto, Aug. 8, 1946; s. Ralph McKenzie and Mary Rita (Hayes) S. BA, U. Toronto, 1967; AM, Harvard U., 1968, PhD, 1973. Asst. prof. English Harvard U., Cambridge, Mass., 1973-78, vis. assoc. prof., summers 1980, 82; assoc. prof. English U. Ottawa, Ont., 1978-85, prof., 1985—; vice-dean faculty of Arts U. Ottawa, Ont., 1994—. Author: Tennyson's Camelot, 1982, Beyond the Provinces: Literary Canada at Century's End, 1995; contbr. articles and revs. Arthurian lit., medieval drama and romance to profl. jours.; editor: The Canadian Imagination, 1977, The Forty-ninth and Other Parallels, 1986; editor Jour. Can. Poetry, 1984—; gen. editor New Can. Libr., 1988—; translator The Complete Romances of Chrétien de Troyes, 1990; co-editor Elements of Literature, 1990, The Short Story in English, 1991. Ind. study fellow NEH, London, 1977-78, fellow Huntington Libr., San Marino, Calif., 1979. Mem. Medieval Acad. Am. (chmn. com. on ctrs. and regional assn. 1981-87), MLA, Internat. Arthurian Soc., Assn. Can. Univ. Tchrs. English. Roman Catholic. Avocations: theater, bridge. Home: 12 Galt St, Ottawa, ON Canada K1S 4R4 Office: Univ Ottawa, Dept English, Ottawa, ON Canada K1N 6N5

STAINES, MAVIS AVRIL, artistic director, ballet principal; b. Cownsville, Que., Can., Apr. 9, 1954; d. David Russell and Betty (Knott) S.; m. Jyrki Virsunen, Feb. 4, 1988. Student, Nat. Ballet Sch., 1968-73, 81-83. Dancer Nat. Ballet of Can., 1973-78, 1st soloist, 1975-78; dancer Dutch Nat. Ballet, 1978-81; artistic dir. Nat. Ballet Sch., Toronto, Ont., Can., 1989—; mem. artistic staff Nat. Ballet Sch., 1982, assoc. artistic dir., 1984; juror Prix de Lausanne, Switzerland, 1993, 94, 95; mem. task force on classicl ballet tng. DANCE/USA, Phila., 1994; mem. dance adv. com. The Can. Coun.; mem. Dance 20/20 Com., mem. DAN/CE--The Dance Comty. of Educators; bd. dirs. Kala Nidhi Fine Arts of Can. Office: The Nat Ballet Sch, 105 Maitland St, Toronto, ON Canada M4Y 1E4

STAINROOK, HARRY RICHARD, banker; b. Phila., Jan. 11, 1937; s. Millward M. and Janet (Cruickshank-Smith) S.; m. Judith Ann Swann, May 21, 1966; children: Jennifer, Eric. B.A., Rutgers U., 1970. Mgr. bank ops. First Pa. Bank, Phila., 1956-61, asst. v.p. br. dept., 1964-73, v.p., mgr. London office, 1973-75, v.p. internat. dept., 1975-78; sr. v.p. comml. group First Pa. Bank, 1978-81, exec. v.p., trust and investments, 1981-85; exec. v.p. trust and investments Mfrs. and Traders Trust Co., Buffalo, 1985—. Chmn., bd. dirs. Greater Buffalo Opera Co.; bd. dirs. Buffalo Philharm. Orch., U. Buffalo Found.; adv. bd. Buffalo Coun. on World Affairs. With U.S. Army, 1961-64. Mem. N.Y. State Bankers Assn., Buffalo C. of C., English Speaking Union, Saturn Club. Lutheran. Office: Mfrs and Traders Trust Co One M and T Pla Buffalo NY 14240

STAIR, FREDERICK ROGERS, retired foundation executive, former seminary president; b. Knoxville, Tenn., Mar. 7, 1918; s. Fred Rogers and Cristyne (Miller) S.; m. Martha Osborne, Dec. 19, 1942; children: Mary Miller, Thomas Osborne. B.S., Davidson Coll., 1939, D.D., 1960; postgrad., U. Edinburgh, 1945-46; B.D., Union Theol. Sem., Va., 1947, Th.M., 1948; LL.D., Davis and Elkins Coll., 1969; postgrad., Advanced Mgmt. Program, Harvard, 1972-73. Ordained to ministry Presbyn. Ch., 1943; asst. to pres. Union Theol. Sem., Va., 1948-53; pastor Central Presbyterian Ch., Hickory, N.C., 1953-59; pastor in Atlanta, 1959-67; pres. Union Theol. Sem., Va., 1967-81; exec. dir. Presbyn. Ch. (U.S.A.) Found., Charlotte, N.C., 1981-88. Trustee Davidson Coll., 1954-59, 74-85, chmn. bd., 1980-85; program coord. Inst. for Theol. Edn. Mgmt. Served with inf. AUS, 1942-46. Moses D. Hoge fellow, 1948, rsch. fellow Yale Divinity Sch., 1973, Ecumenical Inst., U. Salamanca, Spain, 1979. Mem. Phi Beta Kappa, Phi Gamma Delta, Omicron Delta Kappa, Sigma Upsilon. Home: 5150 Sharon Rd Charlotte NC 28210-4720

STAIR, GOBIN, publishing executive, painter, graphic designer; b. S.I., N.Y., July 30, 1912; s. Gobin and Elsie (Wilson) S.; m. Julia Sitterly, Oct. 5, 1933; children—Adrian, Charlotte. A.B., Dartmouth, 1933; L.H.D., Starr King Sch. for Ministry, 1975. With Beacon Press, Boston, 1956-75, dir., 1962-75. Illustrator: Gulliver's Travels (Swift), 1967, Middle Passage (Coxe), 1960, Old Quotes at Home (Darling), 1965, The King Lear Experience, 1976, Old Tales for a new Day (Fahs and Cobb), 1980, True to Form, 1988; creator: Alphabet Mural, Kingston Mass. Pub. Libr., 1994; creator: Evolution of Spirituality Mural, Unitarian Universalist Ch., Kingston, 1996. Mem Bookbuilders of Boston (pres. 1961-62, William A. Dwiggins award 1965), Boston Soc. Printers. Home: 9 Wapping Rd PO Box 123 Kingston MA 02364

STAIR, THOMAS OSBORNE, physician, educator; b. Richmond, Va., Jan. 10, 1950; s. Frederick Rogers Jr. and Martha (Osborne) S.; m. Lucy Caldwell, Dec. 28, 1973; children: Rebecca Caldwell, Peter Caldwell. AB, U. N.C., 1971; MD, Harvard U., 1975. Diplomate Am. Bd. Emergency Medicine (examiner 1982-88). Residency dir. emergency dept. Georgetown U. Hosp., Washington, 1979-85, asst. dir. emergency dept., 1979-89; asst. dean for continuing med. edn. Georgetown U. Sch. Medicine, Washington, 1985-89; chair dept. emergency medicine, 1989-95; prof. U. Md., Balt., 1995—. Co-author: Common Simple Emergencies, 1985. Recipient Excellence in Teaching award Emergency Medicine Residents Assn., 1986. Fellow Am. Coll. Emergency Physicians; mem. Soc. Acad. Emergency Medicine, Am. Med. Informatics Assn. Home: 4822 Quebec St NW Washington DC 20016-3229 Office: Univ Maryland Baltimore MD

STAIRS, DENIS WINFIELD, political science educator; b. Halifax, N.S., Can., Sept. 6, 1939; s. Henry Gerald and Freda (Winfield) S.; m. Valerie Downing Street, Aug. 10, 1963 (div. Dec. 1986); children: Robert Woodliffe, Christopher Winfield; m. Jennifer Smith, July 18, 1987. BA, Dalhousie U., 1961, Oxford U., 1964; MA, Oxford U., 1968; PhD, U. Toronto, 1969. Asst. prof. dept. polit. sci. Dalhousie U., 1966-70, assoc. prof., 1970-75, dir. Centre Fgn. Policy Studies, 1971-75, prof. polit. sci., 1975—, McCulloch prof., 1995—, chmn. dept., 1980-85, mem. adv. com. acad. relations, dept. external affairs, 1978—, v.p., acad. and research, 1988-93; bd. dirs. Atlantic Coun. Can., 1979—; mem. coun. Social Sci. and Humanities Rsch. Coun. Can., 1981-87; mem. rsch. coun. Can. Inst. Advanced Rsch., 1986—; bd. dirs. Inst. for Rsch. on Pub. Policy, 1989—. Author: The Diplomacy of Constraint: Canada, the Korean War, and the United States, 1974. Rhodes scholar, 1961; J.W. Dafoe postgrad. fellow internat. studies, 1965-66; Can. Council leave fellow, 1972-73; Social Scis. and Humanities Research Council Can. leave fellow, 1979-80. Fellow Royal Soc. Can.; mem. Can. Polit. Sci. Assn. (pres.), Can. Inst. Internat. Affairs, Internat. Studies Assn., Internat. Polit.

Sci. Assn. Club: Royal N.S. Yacht Squadron. Office: Dalhousie U, Dept Polit Sci, Halifax, NS Canada B3H 4H6

STAKER, ROBERT JACKSON, senior federal judge; b. Kermit, W.Va., Feb. 14, 1925; s. Frederick George and Nada (Frazier) S.; m. Sue Blankenship Poore, July 16, 1955; 1 child, Donald Seth; 1 stepson, John Timothy Poore. Student, Marshall U., Huntington, W.Va., W.Va. U., Morgantown, U. Ky., Lexington; LL.B, W.Va. U., 1952. Bar: W.Va. 1952. Practiced in Williamson, 1952-68; judge Mingo County Circuit Ct., Williamson, 1969-79; U.S. dist. judge So. Dist. W.Va., Huntington, 1979-95, sr. U.S. dist. judge, 1995—. Served with USN, 1943-46. Democrat. Presbyterian.

STAKGOLD, IVAR, mathematics educator; b. Oslo, Dec. 13, 1925; came to U.S., 1941, naturalized, 1947; s. Henri and Rose (Wishengrad) S.; m. Alice Calvert O'Keefe, Nov. 27, 1964 (dec. Jan. 1994); 1 dau., Alissa Dent. BME, Cornell U., 1945, MME, 1946; PhD, Harvard U., 1949. Instr., then asst. prof. Harvard, 1949-56; head math. and logistics brs. Office Naval Research, 1956-59; faculty Northwestern U., 1960-75, prof. math. and engring. scis., 1964-75, chmn. engring. scis., 1969-75; prof. math. U. Del., 1975—, chmn., 1975-91; dir. Washington office Am. Math. Soc., 1994-95; mem. U.S. Army basic rsch. com. NRC, 1977-80, MS 2000 oversight com., 1989-91; mem. com. on applications of math. NAS-NRC, 1982-86; mem. adv. panel on computational and applied math. Nat. Inst. Standards and Tech., 1990-95; vis. faculty Math. Inst., Oxford (Eng.) U., 1973, 92, Univ. Coll., London, 1978, Victoria U., Wellington, N.Z., 1981, Ecole Polytechnique Federale de Lausanne, Switzerland, 1981, Bari U., 1987, U. Complutense, Madrid, 1987, 92, U. Milan, 1992. Author: Boundary Value Problems of Mathematical Physics, Vols. I and II, 1967, Green's Functions and Boundary Value Problems, 1978; mem. editl. bd. Am. Math. Monthly, 1975-80, Jour. Applicable Analysis, 1977-90, Internat. Jour. Engring. Sci., 1977—, Jour. Integral Equations, 1978—, Jour. Math. Analysis and Applications, 1988-94, SIAM Rev., 1989-94. Mem. Soc. Indsl. and Applied Math. (trustee 1976-85, chmn. 1979-85, pres. 1989-90, past pres. 1991), Conf. Bd. Math. Sci. (chmn. 1990-92), Coun. Sci. Soc. Pres. (exec. bd. 1990), Am. Math. Soc. (dir. Washington office). U.S. rep. World Bridge Championships, 1959, 60; holder 7 nat. bridge championships. Home: 19 Wood Rd Wilmington DE 19806

STAKIAS, G. MICHAEL, lawyer; b. Norfolk, Va., Feb. 2, 1950; s. George and Gloria May (Hoggard) S. BA, William & Mary, 1972; JD, Thomas M. Cooley Law Sch, 1976; LLM, NYU, 1977. Bar: Mich., 1976, D.C. 1980, Pa. 1980, N.Y. 1994. Atty. U.S. SEC, Washington, 1977-80; ptnr. Blank, Rome, Comisky & McCauley, Phila., 1980—. Bd. dirs. Thomas M. Cooley Law Sch., Lansing, Mich., 1988—. Mem. ABA (bus. law sect., chmn. small bus. capital formation subcom. 1988), Patrons Found. Office: Blank Rome Comisky & McCauley 1200 Four Penn Ctr Plz Philadelphia PA 19103

STALBERG, ZACHARY, newspaper editor; b. Phila., Apr. 6, 1947; m. Deborah Lock, Sept. 2, 1990. Student polit. sci., Temple U., 1968. Reporter Bucks County Courier Times, Levittown, Pa., 1970-71; reporter Phila. Daily News, 1971-75, city editor, 1975-77, mng. editor, 1977-79, exec. editor, 1979-84, editor, 1984—. Served with U.S. Army, 1968-70. Mem. Am. Soc. Newspaper Editors. Home: 413 S 49th St Philadelphia PA 19143-1709 Office: Philadelphia Daily News 400 N Broad St Philadelphia PA 19130-4015

STALCUP, JOE ALAN, lawyer, clergyman; b. Hooker, Okla., Feb. 13, 1931; s. Herbert I. and Ruby (Gantt) S.; m. Nancy Jo Vaughn, Sept. 3, 1950; children: Melinda, Sondra Jo, Cheri Ann. B.B.A. cum laude, So. Methodist U., 1951, J.D. magna cum laude, 1959, M.Th. magna cum laude, 1978. Bar: Tex. 1959. Tchr. Dallas Ind. Sch. Dist., 1951-57; assoc. mem. firm Locke, Purnell, Boren, Laney & Neely, Dallas, 1959-66; assoc. atty., partner firm Geary, Brice & Lewis, Dallas, 1966-67; founder, sr. partner firm Stalcup, Johnson, Meyers & Miller (and predecessor firm), Dallas, 1968-75; dean Sch. Theology for the Laity, 1978-80, 92-96. Pres. Dallas County Young Democrats, 1952-54; Bd. dirs., mem. exec. com. N. Tex. Christian Communications Commn., 1972-78; bd. dirs., v.p. Greater Dallas Council Chs., 1972-75; bd. dirs., chmn. Christian Ch. Found., 1976-84, 86-91, Christian Bd. Publ., 1991—. Mem. ABA, Tex. Bar Assn., Dallas Bar Assn., Am. Judicature Soc., Phi Alpha Delta. Mem. Christian Ch. (minister). Home: 7594 Benedict Dr Dallas TX 75214-1903 Office: 6510 Abrams Rd Dallas TX 75231-7217

STALCUP, RANDY STEPHEN, lawyer; b. Great Bend, Kans., Feb. 3, 1947; s. Lawrence Clark and Wanda Lee (Pundsack) S.; m. Clara Belle Coltrane, July 30, 1976; children: William, Stephen, Laurie, Bradley. BA in Polit. Sci., Wichita State U., Kans., 1969; JD, Washburn U. Sch. Law, Topeka, Kans., 1975. Bar: U.S. Dist. Ct. 1976, U.S. Ct. Appeals (10th cir.) 1978, Kans. County and juvenile ct. probate judge Stafford County, Kans., 1971-72; ptnr. Williamson & Stalcup, Wichita, Kans., 1975-83; pvt. practice Wellington, Kans., 1983-89; assoc. atty. Brian Tamara Pistotnik P.A., Wichita, Kans., 1989—. Mem. Am. Trial Lwyers Assn., Kans. Trial Lawyers Assn., Sedgwick County Bar Assn. Home: 1728 Tamarisk Dr Wichita KS 67230 Office: 2831 E Central Ave Wichita KS 67214-4706

STALDER, FLORENCE LUCILLE, secondary education educator; b. Fairmont, W.Va., Jan. 3, 1920; d. Brooks Fleming and Sally May (Odewalt) Clayton; m. Bernard Nicholas Stalder, Sept. 14, 1946; children: Kathryn Lynn Stalder Mirto, Susan May Stalder Woodard. BA in Edn. with honors, Fairmont State Coll., 1966; MA, W.Va. U., 1973; postgrad., Kent State U., 1973, U. Va., Charlottesville, 1981. Cert. elem. tchr., W.Va. Sec. to mgr. Hall Agy., Inc., Fairmont, W.Va., 1941-43; sec. to supt. Westinghouse Electric Corp., Fairmont, 1943-47; sec. to purchasing agt. Fairmont Supply Co., 1947-48; sec. to dist. mgtr. Ea. Gas & Fuel Assoc., Gen. Stores Div., Grant Town, W.Va., 1948-50; sec. to pres., v.p. Hutchinson Coal Co., Fairmont, 1950-52; sec. to personnel mgr. Consolidation Coal Co., Fairmont, 1957-61; sec. and asst. to adminstr. Fairmont Clinic (Monongahela Valley Assoc. Health Ctrs.), 1965-70; instr. Fairmont Jr. High, Miller Jr. High Schs., 1968-85; instr., dir. W.Va. Univ. Younger Youth Sci. Camps, Fairmont, 1966-72; workshop instr. W.Va. State Bd. Edn. Energy Workshops, Fairmont, 1973-74; adult edn. instr., Fairmont, 1985—. Pres. PTA, 1958-61; troop leader Girl Scouts USA, 1961-64; sec., mem. League of Women Voters, Fairmont, 1968—. Mem. AAUW (pres. 1972-74), NEA, DAR (1st v.p. regent 1986-92, regent 1992-95, state good citizen chmn.), Svc. Corps Of Ret. Execs., Marion County Edn. Assn., W.Va. Edn. Assn., W.Va. Adult Edn. Assn., Daus. of Founders and Patriots of Am. (pres. 1979-85, nat. officers club 1985—), Daus. of Am. Colonists (vice regent 1988-91, regent 1991-94), Daus. Am. Pioneers, Alpha Delta Kappa (pres. 1979-81). Republican. Methodist. Avocations: ecology and conservation issues, humane education, food preservation, gardening. Home: 1208 Bell Run Rd Fairmont WV 26554-1400

STALEY, DELBERT C., telecommunications executive; b. Hammond, Ind., Sept. 16, 1924; s. Eugene and Nellie (Downer) s.; m. Ingrid Andersen, Mar. 16, 1946; children—Crista Staley Ellis, Cynthia Staley-Ianoale, Clifford, Corinn. Student, Rose Poly. Inst., Hammond, 1943-44; grad. advanced mgmt. program, Harvard U., 1962; D. Engring. (hon.), Rose Hulman Inst. Tech., 1981; LL.D. (hon.), Skidmore Coll., 1983. With Ill. Bell Telephone, 1946-76, v.p. ops., 1972-76; pres. Ind. Bell, 1976-78; v.p. residence mktg. AT&T, 1978-79; pres. N.Y. Telephone, 1979-83, chmn. bd., chief exec. officer, 1983; chmn. bd., chief exec. officer NYNEX Corp., White Plains, N.Y., 1983-89, chmn., dir. internat. mgmt. com., 1989-91; chmn. bd. dirs. Alcatel Network Systems, Inc.; prin. East Haven Investments Ltd.; bd. dirs. John Hancock Mut. Life Ins. Co., Polaroid Corp., Digital Equipment Corp., Maynard, Mass. With U.S. Army, 1943-46; ETO. Recipient Puerto Rican Legal Def. and Edn. Fund award, 1981, Cleveland Dodge award YMCA Greater N.Y., 1983, New Yorker for N.Y. award Citizens Com. for N.Y., 1984, Leadership in Mgmt. award Pace U., 1988, Albert Schweitzer Leadership award Hugh O'Brian Youth Found., 1988, Hammond Achievement award The Hammond Hist. Soc., 1988, Gold Medal award USO, 1988, Am. Vocation Success award Pres. George Busch, 1989. Mem. Ind. Acad. (hon.), Telephone Pioneers Am. (pres. 1983-84), Westchester Country Club, Blind Brook Club, Royal Poinciana Club. Presbyterian. Home: 32 Polly Park Rd Rye NY 10580-1927 Office: NYNEX Corp 1095 Avenue of the Americas New York NY 10036

STALEY, FRANK MARCELLUS, JR., mathematics educator; b. Columbia, S.C., July 21, 1930; s. Frank Marcellus and Sarah (Ryan) S.; m. Valeria Howard, June 9, 1956; children: Frank Howard, Elisa Claire. Student, Morehouse Coll., Atlanta, 1946-48; BS, S.C. State U., 1951; MA, Columbia U., 1958; postgrad., various colls. Tchr. math. Ft. Valley (Ga.) State Coll., 1955-57, Va. State Coll., Petersburg, 1957-58; assoc. prof. math. S.C. State Coll., Orangeburg, 1958-90. Active Boy Scouts Am., Den Leader award, Silver Beaver award, Vigil award, mem. exec. bd. 1971-74, Dist. Award of Merit; chmn. bd. Orangeburg County Dept. Social Svcs., ARC; vol. Orangeburg Regional Hosp., Dist. 5 Sch. Sys., Orangeburg Recreation Department. Decorated Army Commendation medal, Purple Heart, Army Res. medal, Korean Svc. medal, others; life mem. Basketball Hall of Fame; names to ROTC Hall of Fame, S.C. State U. Mem. AAUP, Math. Assn. Am., Nat. Coun. Tchrs. Math., Am. Legion (past vice comdr.), VFW (past post comdr.), Res. Officers Assn. (life), Ret. Officers Assn., Assn. U.S. Army, Scabbard and Blade, Omega Psi Phi (life, Man of the Yr. 1975), Alpha Kappa Mu, Kappa Delta Pi, Phi Delta Kappa, Kappa Mu Epsilon, Masons, Shriner. Democrat. Home: 1756 Belleville Rd NE Orangeburg SC 29115-3809 Office: SC State Coll Box 1947 300 College St NE Orangeburg SC 29117-0001

STALEY, HENRY MUELLER, manufacturing company executive; b. Decatur, Ill., June 3, 1932; s. Augustus Eugene, Jr. and Lenore (Mueller) S.; m. Violet Lucas, Feb. 4, 1955; children—Mark Eugene, Grant Spencer. Grad., Governor Dummer Acad., 1950; B.S. in Psychology, Northwestern U., 1954, M.B.A. in Finance, 1956. Salesman Field Enterprises, Chgo., 1953; salesman A.E. Staley Mfg. Co., 1951, mgmt. trainee, 1956-57, ins. mgr., 1957-59, asst. treas., 1959-65, treas., asst. sec., 1965-73, v.p., treas., asst. sec., 1973-77, v.p. bus. and econ. analysis, 1977-87, also dir., 1969-85; pvt. investor Decatur, 1987—; dir. Staley Continental, Inc., 1985-88. Crusade chmn. Macon County unit Am. Cancer Soc., 1964-65, mem. bd. dirs., 1965-71, vice chmn. bd., 1965-66, chmn. bd., 1966-69; bd. dirs. United Way Decatur and Macon County, 1972-74; mem. adv. council Millikin U., 1968—, chmn. adv. council, 1970-71; mem. Decatur Meml. Hosp. Devel. Council, 1969-71, mem. finan. com., bd. dirs., 1970-79, mem. long-range planning com., 1976-77, mem. devel. and community relations com., 1977-78. Mem. Decatur C. of C. (dir. 1967-72), Sigma Nu. Clubs: Decatur, Decatur Country. Home and Office: 276 N Park Pl Decatur IL 62522-1952 also: 74 Ironwood Ln Lahaina HI 96761-9062

STALEY, LYNN, English educator; b. Madisonville, Ky., Dec. 24, 1947; d. James Mulford and Florine (Hurt) Staley. AB, U. Ky., 1969; MA, PhD, Princeton U., 1973. Grad. asst. Princeton (N.J.) U., 1971-73; instr. English Colgate U., Hamilton, N.Y., 1974-75, from asst. to assoc. prof., 1975-86, prof., 1986—. Author: The Voice of the Gawain-Poet, 1984, The Shepheardes Calendar: An Introduction, 1990, Margery Kempe's Dissenting Fictions, 1994; contbr. articles to profl. jours. Mem. MLA, Medieval Acad. Am., Renaissance Soc. Am., New Chaucer Soc., Spenser Soc. Office: Colgate U Dept English 13 Oak Dr Hamilton NY 13346-1338

STALEY, THOMAS FABIAN, language professional, academic administrator; b. Pitts., Aug. 13, 1935; s. Fabian Richard and Mary (McNulty) S.; m. Carolyn O'Brien, Sept. 3, 1960; children: Thomas Fabian, Caroline Ann, Mary Elizabeth, Timothy X. A.B., Regis Coll., 1957, B.S., 1957, M.A., U. Tulsa, 1958; Ph.D., U. Pitts., 1962; D.H.L., Regis Coll., 1979. Asst. prof. English Rollins Coll., 1961-62; mem. faculty U. Tulsa, 1962-88, prof. English, 1969-88, dean Grad. Sch., 1969-77; dir. Grad. Inst. Modern Letters, Trustees prof. modern lit. U. Tulsa (Grad. Sch.), 1977—; dean Coll. Arts and Scis. U. Tulsa, 1981-83, provost, v.p. acad. affairs, 1983-88, McFarlin prof. modern lit., 1988—; prof. English, dir. Ransom Humanities Rsch. Ctr. U. Tex., Austin, 1988—, Chancellor's Centennial prof. of the Book, 1989-92, Harry Huntt Ransom chair liberal arts, 1992—; Fulbright prof., Italy, 1966-67; Fulbright lectr., 1971; Danforth assoc., 1962-67; chmn. Internat. James Joyce Symposium; dir. Grad. Inst. Modern Letters, 1970-81. Author: James Joyce Today, 1966, James Joyce's Portrait of the Artist, 1968, Italo Svevo: Essays on His Work, 1969, (with H.J. Mooney) The Shapeless God: Essays on the Modern Novel, 1968, (with B. Benstock) Approaches to Ulysses: Ten Essays, 1970, Approaches to Joyce's Portrait: Ten Essays, 1977, Jean Rhys: A Critical Study, 1979; editor: Il Punto Su Joyce, 1973, Dorothy Richardson, 1975, Ulysses: Fifty Years, 1974, Twentieth-Century Women Novelists, 1982, British Novelists, 1890-1929, Traditionalists, Dictionary of Lit. Biography, Vols. 34, 36, 70, 77, An Annotated Critical Bibliography of James Joyce, 1989, Joyce Studies: An Annual edit., 1990, Studies in Modern Literature Series, 1990, Reflections on James Joyce: Stuart Gilbert's Paris Journal, 1993, James Joyce Quar., 1963-89; adv. editor Twentieth-Century Lit., 1966—; bd. dirs. Eighteenth-Century Short Title Catalogue/North America, 1990; contbr. articles to profl. jours. Bd. dirs. Tulsa Arts Coun., 1969-76, NCCJ, 1979—; pres. James Joyce Found., 1968-72; chmn. bd. Undercroft Montessori Sch., 1968-70, Marquette Sch., 1969-70; bd. dirs. Cascia Hall Prep. Sch.; chmn. disting. authors com. Tulsa Libr. Trust, 1984; mem. bd. commrs. Tulsa City-County Libr., chmn., 1980-82; mem. adv. coun. Tex. Inst. for Humanities; trustee Regis U., 1992—; bd. dirs. Libr. Am., 1994—, Harlick Trust, 1994—. Recipient Am. Council Learned Socs. award, 1969, 80. Mem. MLA, Internat. Assn. Univ. Profs. English, Anglo-Irish Studies Assn., Am. Com. for Irish Studies, Assn. Internat. de Bibliophilie, James Joyce Soc., Hopkins Soc., Tex. Philos. Soc. (bd. dirs. 1991—), U.S. Tennis Assn., Tulsa Tennis Club, Westwood Country Club, The Athenaeum Club (London), Grolier Club (N.Y.), Edgecomb Tennis Club (Kennebunk, Maine), Tarry House, Phi Beta Kappa. Home: 2528 Tanglewood Trl Austin TX 78703-1540

STALFORT, JOHN ARTHUR, lawyer; b. Balt., June 9, 1951; s. John Irving and Libby Jean (Adams) S.; m. Rebecca Higgins, Aug. 21, 1976 (div. 1984); m. Anne Cheesman, July 19, 1985. BA, U. Va., 1973, MBA, JD, 1977. Bar: Md. 1977. Assoc. Miles & Stockbridge, Balt., 1977-84, ptnr., 1984—. Author: Commercial Financing Forms-Maryland, 1986. Sec. Roland Pk. Rds. and Maintenance Corp., Balt., 1978-83. Mem. ABA, Md. State Bar Assn. Bond Lawyers (chmn. sect. bus. law 1995-96), Roland Pk. Civic League, Balt. Country Club, Ctr. Club, Md. Club, Talbot Country Club, Phi Beta Kappa. Republican. Presbyterian. Avocations: skiing, tennis, golf, lacrosse, running. Office: Miles & Stockbridge 10 Light St Baltimore MD 21202-1435

STALKER, JACQUELINE D'AOUST, academic administrator, educator; b. Penetang, Ont., Can., Oct. 16, 1933; d. Phillip and Rose (Eaton) D'Aoust; m. Robert Stalker; children: Patricia, Lynn, Roberta. Teaching cert., U. Ottawa, 1952; tchr. music, Royal Toronto Conservatory Music, 1952; teaching cert., Lakeshore Tchrs. Coll., 1958; BEd with honors, U. Manitoba, 1977, MEd, 1979; EdD, Nova U., 1985. Cert. tchr. Ont., Man., Can. Adminstr., tchr., prin. various schs., Ont. and Que., 1952-65; area commr. Girl Guides of Can., throughout Europe, 1965-69; administr., tchr. Algonquin Community Coll., Ottawa, Ont., 1970-74; tchr., program devel. Frontenac County Bd. Edn., Kingston, Ont., 1974-75; lectr., faculty advisor dept. curriculum, edn. U. Man., Can., 1977-79; lectr. U. Winnipeg, Man., Can., 1977-79; cons. colls. div. Man. Dept. Edn., 1980-81, sr. cons. programming br., 1981-84, sr. cons. post secondary, adult and continuing edn. div., 1985-88, dir. post secondary career devel. br. and adult and continuing edn. br., 1989; asst. prof. higher edn., coord. grad. program in higher edn. U. Man., 1989-92, assoc. prof., coord. grad. program in higher edn., 1992-95; cons. lectures, seminars, workshops throughout Can. Contbr. articles to profl. jours.; mng. editor Can. Jour. of Higher Edn., 1989-93. Mem. U. Man. Senate, 1976-81, 86-89, bd. govs., 1979-82; Can. rep. Internat. Youth Conf., Garmisch, Fed. Republic of Germany, 1968; vol. Can. Cancer Soc.; mem. Assn. RN Accreditation Coun., 1980-85; chair Child Care Accreditation Com., Man., 1983-90; chair Task Force Post-Secondary Accessibility, Man., 1983; vol. United Way Planning and Allocations; provincial dir., mem. nat. bd. Can. Congress for Learning Opportunities for Women. Recipient award for enhancing the Outreach activities of the univ. U. Man., 1994. Mem. Can. Soc. Study Higher Edn., Man. Tchrs. Soc., U. Man. Alumni Assn., Women's Legal Edn. and Action Fund, Am. Assn. Study Higher Edn. Home: 261 Baltimore Rd, Winnipeg, MB Canada R3L 1H7 also: 3844 N W 94 Way Sunrise FL 33351

STALLARD, HUBERT R., telecommunications industry executive; b. 1937. Degree, Hampden-Sydney (Va.) Coll. Engr. staff asst. Bell Atlantic Va. Inc., Richmond, 1959-85, pres., CEO, 1985—; mem. bd. dirs. Universal Corp., Richmond. Office: Bell Atlantic Va Inc 600 E Main St Richmond VA 23219*

STALLARD, HUGH R., telephone company executive; b. Norton, Va., Jan. 31, 1937; s. Nathaniel Winfield and Evelyn (Stewart) S.; m. Alice Cheatwood, Aug. 1, 1959; children: Craig Winston, Brian Kendrick, Mark Brian. BS, Hampden-Sydney Coll., 1959. Successively staff asst. engr., foreman svc., plant supr., foreman supr., dist. plant supr., dist. plant mgr. Chesapeake and Potomac Telephone Co. of Va., Richmond, Roanoke, Newport News, Norfolk, 1960-68; from staff supr. to div. plant mgr. Chesapeake and Potomac Telephone Co. of Va., Northern and Culpeper, 1969-73; from gen. engring. mgr. to gen. mgr. network engring. and provisioning, Richmond Chesapeake and Potomac Telephone Co. of Va., Richmond, 1977-80, asst. v.p. revenue requirements, 1980-82, asst. v.p. external affairs, 1982-85, v.p., 1985-88, pres., 1988-90, pres., chief exec. officer, 1990—; staff supr. Chesapeake and Potomac Telephone Cos., Washington, 1968-69; gen. plant mgr. Chesapeake and Potomac Telephone Co. of Washington, 1973-77; pres., ceo Bell Atlantic Va., Richmond. Exec. adv. bd. Jr. Achievement of Richmond, 1981; adv. bd. U. Richmond, 1982; bd. dirs. Richmond Renaissance, 1985, Va. Literacy Found., 1989; mem. Va. Bus. Coun., Richmond, 1985, corp. bd. YMCA of Greater Richmond, 1986, capital funds bd. United Way Greater Richmond, 1988—; trustee Va. Found. for Ind. Colls., 1986, Hampden-Sydney (Va.) Coll., 1987. Lt. comdr. Va. C.G., 1960—. Named Chief Exec. Officer of Yr. Minority Devel. Coun., 1989, Bus. Man of Yr. Va. Literacy Found., 1989. Mem. Va. Mfrs. Assn., Va. Telephone Assn. (bd. dirs. 1984-85). Presbyterian. Office: Bell Atlantic Va. 600 E Main St Richmond VA 23219-2441*

STALLINGS, CHARLES HENRY, physicist; b. Durham, N.C., Dec. 28, 1941; s. Henry Harroll and Dorothy (Powers) S.; m. Elizabeth Bright, Sept. 4, 1965; children: Deborah, Sharon. BS, N.C. State U., 1963, MS, 1964; PhD, U. Wis., 1970. Sr. physicist Physics Internat. Co., San Leandro, Calif., 1970-73, dep. dept. mgr., 1974-76, dept. mgr., 1976-79, dir. satellite X-ray test facility office, 1979-81, dir. bus. devel., 1981-83, v.p., dir. rrsch. devel., 1983—. Contbr. articles to tech. jours. Patentee in field. Mem. Gen. Plan Rev. Com., Pleasanton, Calif., 1983. Mem. Am. Phys. Soc., IEEE (assoc.). Home: 1717 Courtney Ave Pleasanton CA 94588-2692 Office: Olin Corp Physics Internat 2700 Merced St San Leandro CA 94577-5633

STALLINGS, GENE CLIFTON, university athletic coach, former professional coach; b. Paris, Tex., Mar. 2, 1935; s. Eugene C. and Neil (Moye) S.; m. Ruth Ann Jack, Dec. 1, 1956; children: Anna Lee, Laura Nell, John Mark, Jacklyn Ruth, Martha Kate. B.S., Tex. A&M U., 1958. Asst. football coach U. Ala., 1958-64; head football coach, dir. athletics Tex. A&M U., 1964-72; asst. coach Dallas Cowboys, 1972-85; head football coach St. Louis Cardinals (now known as Phoenix Cardinals), 1986-89, U. Ala. Crimson Tide, 1990—; dir. Bank of A&M, College Station, Tex., Rolling Internat., Inc., Dallas; Spalding sports cons. Mem. Sam Houston council Boy Scouts Am.; trustee Abilene (Tex.) Christian U. Named 1983 Dallas Father of the Yr.; elected to Tex. A&M U. Hall of Fame, 1982. Mem. Nat. Assn. Collegiate Dirs. Athletics, Am. Football Coaches Assn., Fellowship Christian Athletes. Mem. Ch. of Christ. Coached NCAA divisional IA U. Ala. Nat. Champions, ranked # 1 by UPI and AP, 1992. *

STALLINGS, JAWANNIA HERMENE, surgical nurse; b. Chgo., Jan. 1, 1952; d. John and Elizebeth Miles; m. Roosevelt J. Stallings, Dec. 27, 1973; children: Howard, Jarmaur, Sincerai, Hassan. BSN cum laude, Med. Coll. Ga., 1987. RN, Ga. Staff nurse CCU St. Joseph Hosp., Augusta, Ga., 1987-88; surg.-clin. asst. West Augusta Surg. Assocs., Augusta, 1988—, office bus. mgr., 1988—; developer surg. patient edn. program. With U.S. Army, 1976-79. Mem. NAFE, Richmond County Med. Aux., Stoney Med. Aux., Columbia County C. of C., Richmond County C. of C., Sigma Theta Tau, Chi Eta Phi. Roman Catholic. Avocations: bowling. Office: West Augusta Surg Assocs 1242 Augusta West Pky Augusta GA 30909-1854

STALLINGS, (CHARLES) NORMAN, lawyer; b. Tampa, Fla., Apr. 3, 1914; s. Otto Pyromus and Minnie Henderson (Mitchell) S.; m. Mary Phillips Powell, Feb. 6, 1943; children: Charles Norman, Jean Katherine, Mary Anne. A.B., U. Fla., 1935; J.D., Harvard U., 1938, LL.M., 1940. Bar: Mo. 1939, Fla. 1940, D.C. 1941, Ga. 1946. Asso. firm Ryland, Stinson, Mag & Thomson, Kansas City, Mo., 1938-39, Sutherland, Tuttle & Brennan, Washington, 1940-41, Atlanta, 1946-49; mem. firm Shackleford, Farrior, Stallings & Evans, Tampa, Fla., 1949-84, of counsel, 1984—. Vice chmn. Hillsborough County (Fla.) Aviation Authority, 1955-61. Served to lt. col. U.S. Army, 1941-46, ETO. Decorated Bronze Star; Croix de Guerre avec Palma, Belgium). Fellow Am. Coll. Trial Lawyers; mem. ABA, Hillsborough County Bar Assn. (past pres.), Fla. Bar Assn. (past gov.), Univ. Club (past pres.), Tampa Yacht and Country Club (past gov.), Ye Mystic Krewe of Gasparilla (past capt. and king), Phi Delta Phi, Kappa Alpha. Republican. Episcopalian. Home: 1901 S Ardsley St Tampa FL 33629-5930 Office: PO Box 3324 Tampa FL 33601-3324

STALLINGS, VIOLA PATRICIA ELIZABETH, systems engineer, educational systems specialist; b. Norfolk, Va., Nov. 6, 1946; d. Harold Albert and Marie Blanche (Welch) S.; m. (div. Oct. 1984); 1 child, Patricia N.P. Stallings. BS in Psychology, Va. State U., 1968; MBA with distinction, U. Pa., 1975; postgrad., Temple U., 1972-74, Calif. State U., San Francisco, 1973; EdD with specialization in tech., Nova Southeastern U., Ft. Lauderdale, Fla., 1996. Tchr., supr. Peace Corps, Liberia, West Africa, 1968-71; tchr. Day Care Ctr., disruptive h.s. students Tioga Comm. Youth Ctr., 1972-73; tchr. Phila. Sch. Dist., 1972-76; bus. cons. Phila., 1976; sr. sys. engr./sr. industry svcs. specialist IBM/K-12 Edn., Mt. Laurel, N.J., 1976—; bd. dirs. Woodrock, Inc., Phila., 1974-84, 87-95; mem. nat. edn. rsch. fund com.; task force leader IBM Corp., 1990-91. Bd. dirs., v.p. Unity Ch. of Christ, 1993-95. Recipient Outstanding Svc. award IBM Black Workers Alliance, Washington, 1984. Mem. AAUW, Assn. for Ednl. Comm. and Tech., Beta Gamma Sigma. Baptist. Avocations: reading, writing, drawing, gardening, cooking, dancing, sewing. Home: 105 Burnamwood Ct Mount Laurel NJ 08054-3106 Office: IBM/EduQuest IBM 1000 Atrium Way Mount Laurel NJ 08054

STALLMEYER, JAMES EDWARD, engineer, educator; b. Covington, Ky., Aug. 11, 1926; s. Joseph Julius and Anna Catherine (Scheper) S.; m. Mary Katherine Davenport, Apr. 11, 1953; children: Cynthia Marie, James Duncan, Michael John, Catherine Ann, John Charles, Gregory Edward. BS, U. Ill., 1947, MS, 1949, PhD, 1953. Jr. engr. So. Ry. System, 1947; research asst. U. Ill., Urbana, 1947-49; research asso. U. Ill., 1951-52, asst. prof. civil engring, 1952-57, assoc. prof., 1957-60, prof., 1960—; cons. on structural problems various indsl. and govt. agys. Author: (with E.H. Gaylord Jr.), Design of Steel Structures. Served with USN, 1944-46. Standard Oil fellow, 1949-51; recipient Adams meml. award, 1964, Everitt award for teaching excellence, 1981. Mem. ASCE, Am. Concrete Inst., Am. Ry. Engring. Assn., ASTM, Am. Welding Soc., Am. Soc. Metals, Soc. Exptl. Stress Analysis, Scabbard and Blade, Sigma Xi, Chi Epsilon, Sigma Tau, Tau Beta Pi, Phi Kappa Phi. Republican. Roman Catholic. Club: KC. Office: Newmark Civil Engring 205 N Mathews Ave Urbana IL 61801-2350

STALLONE, SYLVESTER ENZIO, actor, writer, director; b. N.Y.C., July 6, 1946; s. Frank and Jacquline (Labofish) S.; m. Sasha Czack, Dec. 28, 1974 (div.); children: Sage, Seth; m. Brigitte Nielsen, Dec. 15, 1985 (div. 1987). Student, Am. Coll. of Switzerland, 1965-67, U. Miami, 1967-69. Formerly, usher, fish salesman, horse trainer, delicatessen worker, truck driver, bouncer, zoo attendant, short order cook, pizza demonstrator, phys. edn. tchr., motel supt., bookstore detective. Appeared in motion pictures Lords of Flatbush, 1973, Capone, 1974, Rocky, 1976, (Oscar for Best Picture 1976, Golden Globe award for best picture 1976, Donatello award for best actor in Europe 1976, Christopher Religious award 1976, Bell Ringer award Scholastic Mag. 1976, Nat. Theatre Owners award 1976) F.I.S.T, 1978, Paradise Alley, 1978, Rocky II, 1979, Nighthawks, 1981, Victory, 1981, Rocky III, 1982, First Blood, 1982, Rhinestone, 1984, Rambo: First Blood Part II, 1985, Rocky IV, 1985, Cobra, 1986, Over the Top, 1987, Rambo III, 1988, Lock Up, 1989, Tango and Cash, 1989, Rocky V, 1990, Cliffhanger, 1993, Demolition Man, 1993, The Specialist, 1994, Judge Dredd, 1995, Assassins, 1995, Firestorm, 1996, Daylight; producer, dir. film Staying Alive, 1983; author: Paradise Alley, 1977, The Rocky Scrapbook, 1977; novel Rocky II. Recipient Star of the Year award 1977, named Show West actor of the year 1979, Artistic Achievement award Nat. Italian Am. Found., 1991, Order of Arts and Letters, French Ministry, 1992, Caesar award for Career Achievement, 1992. Mem. Screen Actors Guild, Writers Guild, Stuntmans Assn. (hon.), Dirs. Guild. Nomination for two Oscars (acting and writing) in same year (1976) occurred for only 3d time in history. Office: Creative Artists Agy 9830 Wilshire Blvd Beverly Hills CA 90212-1804 *Once in one's life, for one mortal moment, one must make a grab for immortality; if not, one has not lived.**

STALLWORTH-BARRON, DORIS A. CARTER, librarian, educator; b. Ala., June 12, 1932; d. Henry Lee Carter and Hattie Belle Stallworth; m. George Stallworth, 1950 (dec.); children: Annette LaVerne, Vanzette Yvonne; m. Walter L. Barron, 1989. BS, Ala. State U., 1955; MLS, CUNY, 1968; postgrad., Columbia U., St. John's U., NYU. Cert. supr. and tchr. sch. libr. media, N.Y. Libr. media specialist N.Y.C. Bd. Edn.; head libr. Calhoun County High Sch., Hobson City, Ala.; cons. Libr. Unit, N.Y.C. Bd. Edn.; cons. evaluator So. Assn. Secondary Schs., Ala.; supr., adminstr., liason rep. Community Sch. Dist. #24 N.Y.C. Sch. System; previewer libr. media Preview Mag., 1971-73; mem. ednl. svcs. adv. coun. Sta. WNET, 1987-89; mem. coun. N.Y.C. Schs. Libr. System, 1987-90; turn-key tchr. trainer N.Y. State Dept. Edn., 1988; spl. guest speaker and lectr. Queens Coll., City U., Community Sch. Dist. #24, PTA, N.Y. City Sch. System, Libr. unit, 1980-90; curriculum writer libr. unit N.Y.C. Bd. Edn., 1985-86. Contbr. articles to ednl. publs. Mem. State of Ala. Dem. Exec. Com., 1994—; active A+ for Kids. Mem. NAFE, ALA, Am. Assn. Sch. Librs. (spl. guest speaker and lectr. for conv. 1987), Am. Sch. Libr.'s Assn., Nat. Assn. Black Pub. Adminstrs., N.Y. State Libr. Assn., N.Y.C. Sch. Librs. Assn., Nat. Forum for Black Pub. Adminstrs., N.Y. Coalition 100 Black Women, Lambda Kappa Mu Sorority, Inc., Alpha Kappa Alpha Sorority.

STALNAKER, JOHN HULBERT, physician; b. Portland, Oreg., Aug. 29, 1918; s. William Park II and Helen Caryl (Hulbert) S.; m. Louise Isabel Lucas, Sept. 8, 1946; children: Carol Ann, Janet Lee, Mary Louise, John Park, Laurie Jean, James Mark. Student, Reed Coll., Portland, 1936-38; AB, Willamette U., Salem, Oreg., 1941; MD, Oreg. Health Scis. U., 1945. Diplomate Am. Bd. Internal Medicine. Intern Emanuel Hosp., Portland, 1945-46; resident in internal medicine St. Vincent Hosp., Portland, 1948-51; clin. instr. U. Oreg. Med. Sch., 1951-54, 60-62; staff physician VA Hosp., Vancouver, Wash., 1970-79; cons. in internal medicine, 1951-79. Contbr. articles to profl. jours. Pianist various civic and club meetings, Portland; leader Johnny Stalnaker's Dance Orch., 1936-39. Lt. (j.g.) USNR, 1946-48. Fellow ACP; mem. AMA, Multnomah County Med. Soc., Oreg. State Med. Assn., N.Am. Lily Soc., Am. Rose Soc. Avocations: music, photography, horticulture. Home: 2204 SW Sunset Dr Portland OR 97201-2068

STALOFF, ARNOLD FRED, financial executive; b. Dover, N.J., Dec. 12, 1944; s. William and Ida (Greenberg) S.; m. Sharon Marcia Teplitsky, June 10, 1967; children: Kimberly, Lindsay. BBA, U. Miami, 1967. Statistician U.S. Census Bur., Washington, 1967-68; fin. analyst SEC, Washington, 1968-71; sr. v.p. Phila. Stock Exch., 1971-78; v.p. Securities Industry Automation Corp., N.Y.C., 1978-80; pres. Fin. Automation Corp., Phila., 1980-83, Phila. Bd. Trade, 1983-89; pres., CEO Commodity Exch., Inc. (COMEX), N.Y.C., 1989-90; CEO Bloom Staloff Corp., Phila., 1990—; bd. dirs. Phila. Stock Exch., Lehman Bros. Fin. Products, Inc. Bd. dirs. Variety Club for Handicapped Children, Phila., 1987-92; mem. adv. bd. Phila. Internat. Airport, 1988—. Mem. Nat. Futures Assn. (bd. dirs. 1987-90). Avocations: fly fishing, golf, skiing. Office: Bloom Staloff Corp 2000 Market St Philadelphia PA 19103-3231

STALON, CHARLES GARY, retired economics educator, institute administrator; b. Cape Girardeau, Mo., Oct. 26, 1929; s. Charles Douglas and Lucy Idell (Row) S.; m. Marie Allene Hitt, Mar. 15, 1952; children: Connie Lucille Stalon Babbitt, Donna Jean Stalon Williams. Student, Ohio State U., 1955-56; BA, Butler U., 1959; MS, Purdue U., 1963, PhD, 1966. Econs. instr. Purdue U., Lafayette, Ind., 1962-63; econs. prof. So. Ill. U., Carbondale, 1963-77; rsch. economist Fed. Power Commn., Washington, 1969-70; commr. Ill. Commerce Commn., Springfield, 1977-84, Fed. Energy Regulatory Commn., Washington, 1984-89; dir. Putnam, Hayes & Bartlett, Inc., Washington, 1989-91; dir. Inst. Pub. Utilities, prof. econs. Mich. State U., East Lansing, 1991-93; pres. Mid-Am. Regulatory Commn., Chgo., 1983-84; mem. adv. coun. Gas Rsch. Inst., 1982-84, 91—; bd. dirs. N.J. Resources Corp. Author: (book chpt.) Papers in Quantitative Economics, 1968, The Future of Electrial Energy, 1986; contbr. articles to profl. jours. With USN, 1948-49, 52-54. Mem. Am. Econ. Assn., Transp. and Pub. Utility Group, Nat. Soc. Rate of Return Analysts (bd. dirs. 1982-90), Coun. on Econ. Regulation (bd. dirs. 1986—), Nat. Assn. Regulatory Utilities Commns., Nat. Regulatory Rsch. Inst. (bd. dirs. 1983-84, 91-94), Inst. for Study of Regulation (bd. dirs. 1984-87).

STAM, DAVID HARRY, librarian; b. Paterson, N.J., July 11, 1935; s. Jacob and Deana B. (Bowman) S.; m. Deirdre Corcoran, May 15, 1963; children—Julian, Wendell, Kathryn. AB, Wheaton Coll., 1955; postgrad., New Coll., U. Edinburgh, 1955-56; MLS, Rutgers U., 1962; postgrad., CUNY, 1963-64; PhD, Northwestern U., 1978. Asst. editor library publs., reference librarian, manuscript cataloguer New York Pub. Library, 1959-64; librarian Marlboro (Vt.) Coll., 1964-67; head tech. services dept. Newberry Library, Chgo., 1967-71; assoc. librarian Newberry Library, 1969-73; librarian Milton S. Eisenhower Library, Johns Hopkins U., Balt., 1973-78; Andrew W. Mellon dir. rsch. libraries N.Y. Pub. Library, N.Y.C., 1978-86; Univ. librarian Syracuse U., 1986—; trustee Gladys K. Delmas Found. Author: Wordsworthian Criticism 1964-1973: An Annotated Bibliography, 1974, (with Rissa Yachnin) Turgenev in English: A Checklist of Works by and about Him, 1960; Contbr. articles to profl. jours. Served with USNR, 1956-58. Brit. Acad. Overseas fellow, 1975, Brit. Libr. fellow, 1995-96. Mem. Am. Hist. Assn., Am. Antiquarian Soc., Caxton Club (Chgo.), Princeton Club N.Y., Grolier Club (N.Y.C.). Home: 2400 Euclid Ave Syracuse NY 13224-1811 Office: Syracuse U E S Bird Libr 222 Waverly Ave Syracuse NY 13244-2010

STAMAS, STEPHEN, investment executive; b. Salem, Mass., Apr. 26, 1931; s. Theodore and Georgia (Fotopulos) S.; m. Elaine Heidi Zervas, Apr. 24, 1955; children: Heidi, Theodore. A.B., Harvard, 1953, Ph.D., 1957; B.Phil. (Rhodes scholar), Oxford U., 1955. Budget examiner Bur. Budget, Washington, 1957-59; loan officer Devel. Loan Fund, Washington, 1959-60; mgr. internat. div. treasurer's dept. Standard Oil Co. (N.J.), N.Y.C., 1960-63; dep. European financial rep. Standard Oil Co. (N.J.), London, Eng., 1963-64; govt. relations mgr. Esso Europe, 1964-67; petroleum planning mgr. Esso Internat., 1967-68; dep. asst. sec. for financial policy Dept. Commerce, Washington, 1968-69; chief economist Standard Oil Co. (N.J.), N.Y.C., 1969-70; dep. mgr. pub. affairs dept. Standard Oil Co. (N.J.), 1971; v.p., pub. affairs Exxon Corp., N.Y.C., 1973-86; pres. Wallace Funds, N.Y.C., 1986-87; pres. N.Y. Philharm., 1984-89, chmn., 1989—; pvt. investment exec. Windcrest Ptnrs., N.Y.C., 1992—. Trustee, pres. Am. Ditchley Found.; trustee, vice chmn. Rockefeller U.; chmn. Am. Assembly, Columbia U., Marlboro Sch. Music; mem. bd. overseers Harvard Coll., 1979-85; chmn. N.Y. Philharm.-Symphony Soc.; vice chmn. Lincoln Ctr. for the Performing Arts; bd. dirs. The Greenwall Found., BNY Hamilton Funds, Inc., Seacor Holdings Inc. Mem. Coun. Fgn. Rels., Acad. Polit. Sci., Am. Coun. on Germany, Phi Beta Kappa. Clubs: Harvard (N.Y.C.), Century Assn. (N.Y.C.), Manursing Island (Rye, N.Y.). Home: 325 Evandale Rd Scarsdale NY 10583-1505 Office: New York Philharm Avery Fisher Hall 10 Lincoln Center Plz New York NY 10023-6912 also: Windcrest Ptnrs 122 E 42nd St New York NY 10168-0002

STAMATAKIS, CAROL MARIE, state legislator, lawyer; b. Canton, Ohio, Apr. 27, 1960; d. Emmanuel Nicholas and Catherine Lucille (Zam) S.; m. Michael Charles Shklar, Mar. 23, 1985. BA in Criminology and Criminal Justice, Ohio State U., 1982; JD, Case Western Res., 1985. Bar: N.H. 1985, U.S. Dist. Ct. N.H. 1985. Atty. Law Office Laurence F. Gardner, Hanover, N.H., 1985-87, Law Office William Howard Dunn, Claremont, N.H., 1987-90, Elliott, Jasper & Stamatakis, Newport, N.H., 1990-93; state rep. N.H. State Legislature, 1988-94; of counsel Law office of Michael C. Shklar, Newport, 1994—; staff atty. N.H. Dept. Health and Human Svcs., Keene, 1994—; instr. Am. Inst. Banking, Claremont, 1987-88, 91-92, 95. Asst. editor: (jours.) Health Matrix: The Jour. of Health Services Mangement, 1983-85. Treas., mem. Town of Lempster N.H. Conservation Commn., 1987—; bd. dirs. Orion House, Inc., Newport, N.H., 1987-91; town chair N.H. Dem. Party, 1987—; mem. Town of Lempster Recycling Com., 1988—, Community Task Force on Drug and alcohol Abuse, 1988. Mem. N.H. Bar Assn., Sierra Club, Upper Valley Group (former vice chair and solid waste chair). Avocations: drawing, painting. Home: PO Box 807 Newport NH 03773-0807

STAMATY, MARK ALAN, cartoonist, author, artist; b. Bklyn., Aug. 1, 1947; s. Stanley and Clara Gee (Kastner) S. B.F.A., The Cooper Union, 1969. Mem. faculty Parson's Sch. Design, N.Y.C., 1977-81. Author-illustrator: (children's books) Who Needs Donuts, 1973 (Bklyn. Art Books For Children award 1974), Small in the Saddle, 1975, Minnie Maloney & Macaroni, 1976, Where's My Hippopotamus?, 1977, (comic strip collections) Macdoodle St., 1981, Washingtoon, 1983; cartoonist: Macdoodle St., Village Voice newspaper, 1978-79, Carrrttooooonn, Village Voice newspaper, 1980-81, (Washington Post and syndication) Washingtoon, 1981—; polit. cartoonist TIME mag., 1994—; illustrator various publs., including: (children's book) Yellow Yellow, 1971, (Bklyn. Art Books for Children award). Recipient Purchase award N.J. State Mus., about 1969, Gold medal Soc. Illustrators, 1974. Mem. PEN Am. Ctr. Avocations: impersonating Elvis Presley; watching the world; softball; swimming. Office: care Village Voice 842 Broadway New York NY 10003-4801

STAMBAUGH, ARMSTRONG A., JR., restaurant and hotel executive; b. Cleve., Nov. 1, 1920; s. Armstrong Alexander and Beatrice (Snyder) S.; m. Janet Turley Marting, July 26, 1943 (div. 1958); children—Susan Reed (Mrs. Roy H. Beaton, Jr.), Sally Russell (Mrs. Michael H. Huber), Elizabeth Renshaw (Mrs. James W. Ewing); m. Aagot Hinrichsen Cain, June 10, 1972. B.A., Dartmouth, 1942; Indsl. Adminstr., Harvard, 1943, M.B.A., 1946. Research asst., then instr. bus. adminstrn. Harvard Grad. Sch. Bus. Adminstrn., 1946-48; with Gulf Oil Corp., 1948-66; coord. sales devel. mktg. hdqrs. Gulf Oil Corp., Houston, 1962-63; v.p. Eastern marketing region Gulf Oil Corp., Phila., 1963-66; exec. v.p. adminstrn. Howard Johnson Co., Inc., 1966-70, exec. v.p. ops. and adminstrn., 1970-79, exec. v.p., asst. to pres., 1979-81, dir., 1969-81; operator, developer food and lodging facilities, 1981—. Pres. trustees Fox Chapel Country Day Sch., Pitts., 1955-57; div. vice chmn. Boston United Fund, 1961; bd. dirs. Houston Internat. Trade and Travel Fair, 1962-63, World Affairs Coun. Phila., 1964-65; dir. Phila. C. of C., 1964, 65, 66; bd. overseers Hanover Inn, Dartmouth Coll., 1979-85, chmn., 1984-85; trustee Old Sturbridge Village, Mass., 1979—. Served to lt. (j.g.) USNR, 1943-46. Mem. Pine Valley Golf Club (N.J.), Weston (Mass.) Golf Club, Kittansett Golf Club (Mass.), Boston Skating Club, Harvard Club (Boston), Vineyard Haven Yacht Club (Mass.), Paradise Valley Country Club (Ariz.), Delta Tau Delta. Home: 474 Concord Rd Weston MA 02193-1313 Office: 301 W Wyoming Ave Stoneham MA 02180-9999

STAMBAUGH, RONALD DENNIS, physicist; b. Milw., May 15, 1947; s. Wilbert Foster and Joyce Elaine (Miller) S.; m. Mildred Alice Considine, June 22, 1968; children: James, Emily, Claire, Margaret. BS, U. Wis., 1969; MPhil, Yale U., 1971, PhD, 1974. Computer programmer U. Wis., Madison, 1967-69; rsch. asst. Yale U., New Haven, Conn., 1970-74; sr. scientist Gen. Atomics, San Diego, 1975-77, br. mgr., 1978-79, plasma control coord., 1979-84, mgr. physics dept., 1984-91, divsn. dir., 1991—; chmn. divertor expert group ITER, 1994—; BPX dep. physics head Princeton (N.J.) Plasma Lab., 1990-91; exec. com. APS-DPP, 1987-89, 91-92. Mem. editl. bd. Nuclear Fusion, 1991—. Recipient award for Excellence in Plasma Physics Research Am. Physical Society, 1994. Fellow Am. Phys. Soc. (Excellence in Plasma Physics 1994). Achievements include experimental verification of plasma stability theory for Tokamaks. Office: Gen Atomics PO Box 85608 San Diego CA 92186-9784

STAMBERG, SUSAN LEVITT, radio broadcaster; b. Newark, Sept. 7, 1938; d. Robert I. and Anne (Rosenberg) Levitt; m. Louis Collins Stamberg, Apr. 14, 1962; 1 child, Joshua Collins. BA, Barnard Coll, 1959; DHL (hon.), Gettysburg Coll., 1982, Dartmouth Coll., 1984, Knox Coll., U. N.H., SUNY, Brockport. Editorial asst. Daedalus, Cambridge, Mass., 1960-62; editorial asst. The New Republic, Washington, 1962-63; host, producer, mgr., program dir. Sta. WAMU-FM, Washington, 1963-69; host All Things Considered Washington, 1971-86; host Weekend Edition Nat Pub. Radio, Washington, 1987-89; spl. corr. Nat. Pub. Radio, 1990—; bd. dirs. AIA, Washington, 1983-85, PEN/Faulkner Fiction Award Found., 1985—. Author: Every Night at Five, 1982, The Wedding Cake in the Middle of the Road, 1992, Talk: NPR's Susan Stamberg Considers All Things, 1993. Recipient Honor award Ohio U., 1977, Edward R. Murrow award Corp. for Pub. Broadcasting, 1980; named Woman of Yr., Barnard Coll., 1984; fellow Silliman Coll. Yale U., 1984—; inducted Broadcasting Hall of Fame, 1994. Avocations: sketching; piano; knitting. Office: Nat Pub Radio 635 Massachusetts Ave NW Washington DC 20001-3752

STAMELMAN, RICHARD HOWARD, French and humanities educator; b. Newark, Mar. 7, 1942; s. Louis Robert and Gilda (Senzer) S.; m. Rebecca White, June 5, 1965; children—Emily Gibson, Jeremy White. B.A., Hamilton Coll.; Ph.D., Duke U. Asst. prof. French and humanities Wesleyan U., Middletown, Conn., 1967-74, assoc. prof., 1974-79, prof., 1979-93, William R. Kenan Jr. prof. humanities, 1983-92, dean humanities, 1986-89, dir. Ctr. for the Humanities, 1976-82, dir. humanities devel., 1982-85; dir. Weston Ctr. for Fgn. Langs., Lits. and Cultures Williams Coll., Williamstown, Mass., 1992—, prof. Romance langs., 1992—; chair dept. French and Italian U. Colo., Boulder, 1991-92; organizer (study group) Écrire le Livre: Autour d'Edmond Jabès, Cerisy-la-Salle, France, 1987; co-dir. Edouard Morot-Sir Summer Inst. for French Cultural Studies, Hanover, N.H., 1994. Author: The Drama of Self in Guillaume Apollinaire's Alcools, 1976, Claude Garache: Prints, 1965-85, 1985, Lost Beyond Telling: Representations of Death and Absence in Modern French Poetry, 1990; editor: Contemporary French Poetry, Studies in 20th Century Literature, 1989, Ecrire le Livre: Autour d'Edmond Jabès, 1989, Italian transl., 1991, French Poetry since the War, L'Esprit Créateur, 1992; editor, prin. translator: The Lure and the Truth of Painting, Selected Essays by Yves Bonnefoy, 1995; translator: The Grapes of Zeuxis and Other Fables by Yves Bonnefoy, 1987, Once More the Grapes of Zeuxis by Yves Bonnefoy, 1989, The Last Grapes of Zeuxis by Yves Bonnefoy, 1993; mem. editorial bd. French Forum; contbr. articles to profl. jours. Recipient Chevalier dans l'ordre des Palmes Académiques award French Govt., 1993; NEH fellow, 1973; Am. Council Learned Socs. grantee, 1983. Mem. MLA (regional del. 1987-90, mem. program com. 1996—), Am. Assn. Tchrs. French, Acad. Lit. Studies. Home: 21 Southworth St Williamstown MA 01267 Office: Williams Coll Weston Ctr Fgn Langs Lits Culture Williamstown MA 01267

STAMES, WILLIAM ALEXANDER, realtor, cost management executive; b. Douglas, Ariz., Mar. 26, 1917; s. Alex Basil and Teresa (Ruis) S.; AA, Long Beach Coll., 1941; postgrad. U. Calif., Berkeley, 1962-64; cert. mgmt. practices Naval Officers CIC Sch., Glenview, Ill., 1955; grad. Real Estate Inst., Calif.; m. Marguerite Winifred Nelson, June 11, 1943; 1 child, Wynn Lorain. Owner, Stames Beverage Co., Brawley, Calif., 1945-50; liaison engr. Lockheed Missiles & Space Co., Sunnyvale, Calif., 1958-60, liaison engr. sr., 1960, adminstr., 1960-62, staff adminstr., 1962-63, liaison engr., sr., design engr. sr., 1965-76; owner, mgr. Cost Reduction Equipment Sales & Tech., Sunnyvale, 1967-76; realtor Cornish & Carey, 1988—. Comdr. USNR, 1941-69, ret., World War II, Korea, Vietnam. Decorated D.F.C., Air medal with two gold stars, Presdl. citation. Mem. Am. Mgmt. Assn., Mountain View Real Estate Bd. (pres.), Calif. Assn. Realtors (bd. dirs.), Tailhook Assn. Clubs: Commonwealth San Francisco, Ret. Officers (past pres. Peninsula chpt.), Lions. Author: Polaris Electrical Subsystems Design History, 1964; Poseidon Subsystem Invention, 1971. Home: 1060 Coronado Ave Coronado CA 92118-2439

STAMEY, THOMAS ALEXANDER, physician, urology educator; b. Rutherfordton, N.C., Apr. 26, 1928; s. Owen and Virginia (Link) S.; m. Kathryn Simmons Dec. 1, 1973; children: Fred M., Charline, Thomas A. III, Allison, Theron. BA, Vanderbilt U., 1948; MD, Johns Hopkins U., 1952. Diplomate Am. Bd. Urology. Intern, then resident Johns Hopkins Hosp., 1952-56; asst. prof. urology Johns Hopkins U. Sch. Medicine, Balt., 1958-60, assoc. prof., 1960-61; assoc. prof. Stanford (Calif.) U., 1961-64, 1964-90, prof., chmn. dept., 1991—, chmn. div. urology, 1961-90. Author: Renovascular Hypertension, 1967, Pathogenesis and Treatment of Urinary Tract Infections, 1980, Urinalysis and Urinary Sediment: A Practical Guide for the Health Science Professional, 1985; editor: Campbell's Urology, Monographs in Urology, 1980—. Capt. M.C., USAF, 1956-58. Recipient Sheen award ACS, 1990, Ferdinand C. Valentine award N.Y. Acad. Medicine, 1991. Mem. Am. Urol. Assn., Am. Surg. Assn. (sr.), Inst. Medicine of NAS. Avocation: fishing. Office: Stanford U Med Ctr 300 Pasteur Dr Palo Alto CA 94304-2203*

STAMM, ALAN, lawyer; b. Galesburg, Ill., Nov. 22, 1931; s. Gustave Frederick and Miriam (Simon) S.; m. Shelley Lynn Ramage, Mar. 19, 1978; 1 child, Lucinda Anne. Student, Universidad Nacional de Mex., summer 1950; AB, Yale U., 1952; JD, Harvard U., 1957. Bar: Calif. 1957, U.S. Supreme Ct. 1963. Assoc. Thelen, Marrin, Johnson & Bridges, San Francisco, 1957-60; staff atty. Litton Industries Inc., Beverly Hills, Calif., 1960-66; asst. sec. Litton Industries Inc., Beverly Hills, 1963-66; sec., gen. counsel Internat. Rectifier Corp., L.A., 1966-69, v.p., 1968-69; v.p., gen. counsel Republic Corp., L.A., 1969-71, also bd. dirs., 1970-71; v.p., gen. counsel Sat. Rev. Industries, N.Y.C., 1971-72; v.p., gen. counsel Mattel Inc., Hawthorne, Calif., 1972-74, staff cons., 1974-75; of counsel Long & Levit, L.A., 1975-82, O'Donnell & Gordon, L.A., 1983-87, Hedges, Powe & Caldwell, L.A., 1988-90; pvt. practice L.A., 1990—; judge pro tem Mcpl. Ct. L.A. Jud. Dist., 1977—; arbitrator L.A. Superior Ct. 1979—, judge pro tem L.A. Superior Ct. 1989—, arbitrator Nat. Assn. Securities Dealers, 1981—. Founding trustee Ctr. for Law in the Pub. Interest; adv. trustee L.A. Ctr. for Photog. Studies; Eagle Scout. Served from ensign to lt. (J.G.) USNR, 1952-54; now lt. comdr. Res.; ret. Mem. ABA, Calif. Bar Assn., L.A. Bar Assn., Am. Jewish Com., Harvard Law Sch. Assn., L.A. County Art Mus., Am. Arbitration Assn. (nat. panel arbitrators), NAACP, Sierra Club, Nat. Assn. Yale Alumni (former bd. govs.), Yale Club of So. Calif. (former dir.), Harvard Club of So. Calif., Phi Beta Kappa. Home: 422 Denslow Ave Los Angeles CA 90049-3507 Office: 1840 Century Park E Fl 8 Los Angeles CA 90067-2101

STAMM, GEOFFREY EATON, arts administrator; b. Washington, July 30, 1943; s. George Edward Stamm and Dorothy Bourne (Baden) Elliott; m. Florence Theresa Ryan, Nov. 19, 1983. AB, Hamilton Coll., 1965; diploma in arts adminstrn., Harvard U., 1974. Mus. tech. Indian Arts and Crafts Bd., Washington, 1965-67, rsch. asst., 1967-69, coord. spl. projects, 1969-74, asst. to gen. mgr., 1974-78, asst. gen. mgr., 1978-93, gen. mgr., 1993-94, dir., 1994—. Chmn. Foggy Bottom and West End Adv. Neighborhood Commn., Washington, 1983-86; pres. St. Mary's Ct. Housing Devel. Corp., Washington, 1988-93. Mem. Am. Assn. Mus., Am. Craft Coun., Native Am. Art Studies Assn. Office: Indian Arts and Crafts Bd 1849 C St NW MS 4004-MIB Washington DC 20240

STAMM, ROBERT JENNE, building contractor, construction company executive; b. Albuquerque, Nov. 17, 1921; s. Roy Allen and Elizabeth C. (Baldridge) S.; m. Florence I. Bradbury, May 14, 1943; children—R. Brad, Susan Stamm Evans. BSCE, U. N.Mex., 1942; postgrad. in Naval Architecture, U.S. Naval Acad., 1943. Registered profl. engr. and surveyor, N.Mex. With Bradbury & Stamm Constrn. Co., Albuquerque, 1946—; chmn., chief exec. officer Bradbury & Stamm Constrn. Co., 1975—, former pres. Mem. U. N.Mex. Found., 1982-94, N.Mex. Commn. on Higher Edn., 1986-95; mem. centennial exec. com. U. N.Mex., chmn. devel. fund, 1984-85, 89-94; trustee Albuquerque Cmty. Found., 1983—; trustee Albuquerque Mus., 1993—, chmn. 1995—; bd. dirs. N.Mex. Mus. Natural History, 1995—; bd. dirs., pres. Albuquerque Bus.-Edn. Compact, 1987-88, Albuquerque Mus. Found., 1986-91, Indsl. Found. Albuquerque; past bd. dirs., officer United Way, Girl Scouts U.S.A., Boy Scouts Am., Presbyn. Hosp. Ctr. Found., Presbyn. Heart Inst., Greater Albuquerque Cmty. Ednl. Alliance, N.Mex. First, Albuquerque Econ. Forum, Albuquerque YMCA, Anderson-Abruzzo Internat. Balloon Mus. Comdr. USNR, 1943-69, ret. Recipient Regents Recognition medal U. N.Mex., 1986, Zimmerman award, 1988, U. N.Mex. Centennial Alumnus awrad Nat. Assn. State Univ. and Land Grant Colls., 1987, Disting. Pub. Svc. award State N.Mex., 1990, Award of Excellence, Presbyn. Helath Fedn., 1991, Disting. Citizen award Boy Scouts-Great S.W. Coun., 1994; named Most Admired Co., N.Mex. Pvt. 100, 1990, 92, 94, 95; named to Albuquerque Sr. Citizen Hall of Fame, 1994; named for N.Mex. Outstanding Philanthropic Leadership, 1994. Mem. NSPE (Albuquerque Engr. of Yr. 1987, N.Mex. Lifetime Svc. award 1995), Assoc. Gen. Contractors N.Mex. (pres. bldg. br. 1962), Econ. Forum Albuquerque, Exec. Assn. Greater Albuquerque, Exec. Assn. Greater Albuquerque, Albuquerque country Club (bd. dirs. 1972-76, 87-89), Albuquerque Tennis Club (bd. dirs. 1978-80). Episcopalian. Clubs: Albuquerque Country (bd. dirs. 1972-76, 87-89), Albuquerque Tennis (bd. dirs. 1978-80). Lodge: Elks. Avocations: tennis; skiing; golf. Home: 1524 Las Lomas Rd NE Albuquerque NM 87106-4532 Office: Bradbury & Stamm Constrn Co PO Box 25027 Albuquerque NM 87125-0027

STAMOS, JOHN, actor; b. Orange County, Calif., Aug. 19, 1963; s. Bill and Loretta Stamos. Drummer with various bands. Actor: (TV series) General Hospital (Emmy award, 2 Soapy awards), Dreams, 1984, You Again?, 1986-87, Full House, 1988-95, (TV movies) Daughter of the Streets, 1990, Captive, 1991, (feature film) Never Too Young to Die, 1986, Born to Ride, 1991. Recipient Youth in Film award. Mem. AFTRA, Child Help U.S.A. (nat. spokesperson). Office: William Morris Agy 151 S El Camino Dr Beverly Hills CA 90212-2704*

STAMOS, JOHN JAMES, judge; b. Chgo., Jan. 30, 1924; s. James S. and Katherine (Manolopoulos) S.; m. Helen Voutiritsas, Sept. 3, 1955 (dec. 1981); children—James, Theo, Colleen, Jana; m. Mary Sotter, March 21, 1986. LL.B., DePaul U., 1948. Bar: Ill. 1949. Since practiced in Chgo.; asst. corp. counsel City Chgo., 1951-54; asst. states atty. Cook County, 1954-61; chief criminal div. States Attys. Office, 1961-64, 1st asst. states atty., 1964-66, states atty., 1966-68; judge Appellate Ct. of State of Ill., 1968-88; Judge Ill. Supreme Ct., Springfield, 1988-90; ret., 1990; of counsel Stamos and Trucco, Chgo., 1991—. Served with AUS, 1943-45.

STAMP, FREDERICK PFARR, JR., federal judge; b. Wheeling, W.Va., July 24, 1934; s. Frederick P. Sr. and Louise (Aul) S.; m. Joan A. Corson, Sept. 20, 1975; children: Frederick Andrew, Joan Elizabeth. BA, Washington and Lee U., 1956; LLB, U. Richmond, 1959. Bar: W.Va. 1959, Va. 1959, Pa. 1986, U.S. Supreme Ct. 1973, U.S. Ct. Appeals (4th cir.) 1962, U.S. Dist. Ct. (no. dist.) W.Va. 1959, U.S. Dist. Ct. (so. dist.) W.Va. 1975, U.S. Dist. Ct. (we. dist.) Pa., U.S. Tax Ct. 1973, W.Va. Supreme Ct. Appeals 1966, Va. Supreme Ct. Appeals 1959. Assoc., then ptnr. Schrader, Stamp, Byrd, Byrum & Companion and predecessor firms, Wheeling, 1960-90; judge U.S. Dist. Ct. (no. dist.) W.Va., Wheeling, 1990-94, apptd. chief judge, 1994—; mem. ho. of dels. W.Va. Legislature, Charleston, 1966-70. Mem. W.Va. Bd. Regents, Charleston, 1970-77; trustee Linsly Sch., Wheeling, 1977—. Fellow Am. Bar Found., Am. Coll. Trial Lawyers; mem. W.Va. Bar Assn. (pres. 1981-82), W.Va. Commn. on Uniform State Laws, Nat. Conf. Commrs. on Uniform State Laws.

STAMP, NEAL ROGER, lawyer; b. Watkins Glen, N.Y., Sept. 19, 1918; s. Nelson Mathews and Mae Emma (Broderick) S.; m. Maja Stina Cavetz, Apr. 24, 1946; children: Thomas G., Gayle E. A.B., Cornell, 1940, J.D., 1942. Bar: N.Y. 1943. Pvt. practice Rochester, 1946-47; asst. sec. corp., asso. legal counsel Cornell U., Ithaca, N.Y., 1947-59; sec. corp., asso. legal counsel Cornell U., 1959-62, sec. corp., 1959-79, univ. counsel, 1962-79, sr. counsel, 1979-84, univ. counsel emeritus, 1979—, dir. aero. lab., research found.; higher edn. cons., 1979—; lectr. Practicing Law Inst.; dir. First Bank & Trust Co., Ithaca, 1971-84, chmn., 1978-84. Trustee Tompkins County Meml. Hosp., 1959-66, pres., 1961-62; dir. Visiting Nurse Svc. of Tompkins County, 1996—. 1st lt. inf. AUS, 1942-46, MTO. Mem. ABA (ho. of dels. 1977-79), N.Y. State Bar Assn., Tompkins County Bar Assn., Assn. of Bar of City of N.Y., Nat. Assn. Coll. and U. Attys. (exec. bd. 1964-68, 72-79, life mem., pres. 1976-77). Home: Apt 14-2-F PO Box 4508 700 Warren Rd Ithaca NY 14852-4508

STAMPER, JOE ALLEN, lawyer; b. Okemah, Okla., Jan. 30, 1914; s. Horace Allen and Ann (Stephens) S.; m. Johnnie Lee Bell, June 4, 1936; 1 child, Jane Allen (Mrs. Ernest F. Godlove). B.A., U. Okla., 1933, LL.B., 1935, J.D., 1970. Bar: Okla. bar 1935. Practice in Antlers, 1935-36, 46—; mem. firm Stamper, Burrage & Hadley, 1974—; atty. Pushmataha County, 1936-39; spl. justice Okla. Supreme Ct., 1948. Mem. Okla. Indsl. Commn., 1939-40; pres. Antlers Sch. Bd., 1956-67, Pushmataha Found., 1957—; mem.

Okla. Bicentennial Com., 1971—; vice chmn. bd. U. Okla. Law Center, 1975-78; mgr. Okla. Democratic party, 1946, dist. chmn., 1946-50; alt. del. Dem. Nat. Conv., 1952. Served to col. AUS, 1935-46, E O. Decorated Bronze Star. Fellow Am. Bar Found., Am. Coll. Trial Lawyers, Am. Bd. Trial Advocates (advocate); mem. ABA (del. 1974-91, state del. 1975-86, mem. com. on law book pub. practices 1974-76, bd. govs. 1986-89, standing com. on fed. jud. improvement 1989-92), SAR, Okla. Bar Assn. (bd. govs. 1969-73, Pres.'s award 1977, 80, 93), Okla. Bar Found. (pres. 1977), Mil. Order World Wars, Pi Kappa Alpha. Baptist (deacon). Clubs: Petroleum (Oklahoma City). Lodges: Masons, Shriners, Lions. Home: 1000 NE 2nd St Antlers OK 74523-2822 Office: PO Box 100 112 N High St Antlers OK 74523-2250

STAMPER, MALCOLM THEODORE, aerospace company executive; b. Detroit, Apr. 4, 1925; s. Fred Theodore and Lucille (Cayce) S.; m. Marion Philbin Guinan, Feb. 25, 1946; children: Geoffrey, Kevin, Jamie, David, Mary, Anne. Student, U. Richmond, Va., 1943-44; BEE, Ga. Inst. Tech., 1946; postgrad., U. Mich., 1946-49; DHumanities, Seattle U., 1994. With Gen. Motors Corp., 1949-62; with Boeing Co., Seattle, 1962-90; mgr. electronics ops., v.p., gen. mgr. turbine div. Boeing Co., 1964-66; v.p., gen. mgr. Boeing Co. (747 Airplane program), 1966-69, v.p., gen. mgr. comml. airplane group, 1969-71, corp. sr. v.p. ops., 1971-72; pres. Boeing Co., 1972-85, vice chmn., 1985-90; chief exec. officer Storytellers Ink Pub., Seattle, 1990—, also chmn. bd. dirs.; bd. dirs. Esterline Co., Chrysler Co., Whittaker Corp.; trustee The Conf. Bd., 1988—. Candidate for U.S. Ho. of Reps., Detroit, 1952; trustee, chmn. Seattle Art Mus.; nat. bd. dirs. Smithsonian Assocs. With USNR, 1943-46. Named Industrialist of Year, 1967; recipient Educator's Golden Key award, 1970, Elmer A. Sperry award, 1982, AIEE award, Ga. Inst. Tech. award, Sec. Dept. Health and Human Services award, Silver Beaver award Boy Scouts Am., 1989, Literary Lions award, 1995. Mem. Nat. Alliance Businessmen, Phi Gamma Delta.

STAMPER, ROBERT LEWIS, ophthalmologist, educator; b. N.Y.C., July 27, 1939; m. Naomi T. Belson, June 23, 1963; children: Juliet, Marjorie, Alison. BA, Cornell U., 1957-61; MD, SUNY-Downstate, 1965. Diplomate Am. Bd. Ophthalmology (assoc. examiner 1976-92, bd. dirs. 1992—, mem. glaucoma panel 1993—); lic. physician, Calif. Intern Mt. Sinai Hosp., N.Y.C., 1965-66; resident in ophthalmology Washington U.-Barnes Hosp., St. Louis, 1968-71; Nat. Eye Inst.-NIH fellow dept. ophthalmology Washington U., St. Louis, 1971-72, from instr. ophthalmology to asst. prof. dept. ophthalmology, 1971-72; asst. prof. dept. ophthalmology Pacific Presbyn. Med. Ctr., San Francisco, 1972-76, assoc. prof. ophthalmology, 1976-87; chmn. dept. ophthalmology Calif. Pacific Med. Ctr. (formerly Pacific Presbyn. Med. Ctr.), San Francisco, 1987—; asst. opthalmologist Barnes Hosp., St. Louis, 1971-72, Harkness Hosp., San Francisco, 1973-74; dir. ophthalmic photography and fluorescin angiography, dept. ophthalmology Washington U., St. Louis, 1969-72; dir. resident tng. Pacific Presbyn. Med. Ctr., 1972-89, dir. glaucoma svc., vice-chmn. dept. ophthalmology, 1974-87; chief ophthalmology svc. Highland Hosp., Oakland, Calif., 1974-76; clin. instr. dept. ophthalmology U. Calif., San Francisco, 1974-77; clin. asst. prof. opthalmology U. Calif., Berkeley, 1974-78, asst. clin. prof. ophthalmology, 1978-85; sr. rsch. assoc. Smith-Kettlewell Inst. Visual Scis., San Francisco, 1972-89; project co-dir. ophthalmic curriculum for med. students Nat. Libr. Medicine, 1973-75; commr. Joint Commn. on Allied Health Pers. in Ophthalmology, 1975-87, bd. dirs., 1978-88, sec., 1980, v.p., 1982-83, pres., 1984-85; provisional asst. chief dept. ophthalmology Mt. Zion Hosp., San Francisco, 1976-87, assoc. chief dept. ophthalmology, 1982-86; ophthalmic cons. Ft. Ord, Calif., 1976—, Oakland (Calif.) Naval Hosp., 1978-83; instr. Stanford (Calif.) U., 1977—; glaucoma cons. U. Calif., Davis, 1978-84; vis. lectr. dept. ophthalmology Hadassah Hebrew U. Med. Ctr., Jerusalem, 1978, Oxford (Eng.) U. Eye Hosp., 1986; ind. med. examiner State of Calif., 1979—; mem. appeals hearing panel Accreditation Coun. for Grad. Med. Edn., 1986-93, mem. residency rev. com. for ophthalmology, 1993—; mem. provisional courtesy staff Peralta Hosp., Oakland, 1988-92; mem. ophthalmic devices adv. panel USFDA, 1989-92; presenter, lectr. in field. Editor Ophthalmology Clinics of North Am., 1988—; mem. editl. adv. com. Ophthalmology, 1982-89, mem. editl. bd., 1983-94; contbr. articles to profl. jours. Chmn. bd. Agy. for Jewish Edn., Oakland, 1986-89; bd. dirs. Jewish Fedn. Greater East Bay, Oakland, 1992-94; bd. dirs. Found. for Glaucoma Rsch.; mem. glaucoma adv. com. Nat. Soc. to Prevent Blindness, 1981—; mem. Am. Diabetes Assn. Surgeon USPHS, 1966-68. Recipient Nat. Soc. for Performance and Instrn. award for self-instrnl. material in ophthalmology, 1975, Honor award Am. Acad. Ophthalmology, 1982, Statesmanship award Joint Commn. on Allied Health Pers. in Ophthalmology, 1989; N.Y. State Regents scholar, 1961, N.Y. State scholar in medicine, 1965; Blalock student fellow UCLA Sch. Medicine, 1961, Fight for Sight student fellow dept. ophthalmology N.Y. Hosp. and Cornell Med. Ctr., 1962, 63, 64. Fellow Am. Acad. Ophthalmology and Otolaryngology (rep. to joint commn. on allied health pers., faculty home study course sect. X, chmn. sect. VIII 1983-85, bd. councilors, editl. adv. com. Opthalmology jour. 1982-89, editl. bd. Ophthalmology jour. 1983-94, and many others), ACS; mem. AMA (Physician's Recognition award 1989), Am. Ophthalmologic Soc., Assn. for Rsch. in Vision and Ophthalmology, Calif. Med. Assn. (asst. sec. sect. ophthalmology, chmn., sci. bd. rep. adv. panel on ophthalmology 1985-91), Nat. Soc. Prevent Blindness (mem. glaucoma adv. com. 1981—, bd. dirs. 1986—), No. Calif. Soc. Prevent Blindness, Calif. Assn. Ophthalmology, Pan Am. Ophthalmological Soc., N.Y. Acad. Scis., Las Vegas Ophthalmological Soc. (hon.). Office: ic Med Ctr 2340 Clay St San Francisco CA 94115-1932

STAMPFLI, JOHN FRANCIS, international business consultant; b. Dhahran, Saudi Arabia, Oct. 27, 1957. BA in History, Calif. State U., Fullerton, 1980; profl. designation in internat. trade, UCLA, 1983, profl. designation internat. bus. mgmt., 1985. Substitute tchr. East Whittier City Sch. Dist., Whittier, Calif., 1980-81; various positions for customshouse broker, Long Beach, Calif., 1981-87; mgr. logistics ops. peripherals group UNYSIS, Santa Clara, Calif., 1987-90; mgr. logistics Orange County Ops.-Peripheral Products divsn. UNYSIS, Mission Viejo, Calif., 1990-93; internat. bus. cons. Irvine, Calif., 1993—. Contbr. commentaries and editls. to various publs. Mem. Armed Forces Comm. and Electronics Assn., Assn. Old Crows, U.S. Naval Inst., Phi Alpha Theta. Home: 26191 La Real E Mission Viejo CA 92691

STAMPLEY, NORRIS LOCHLEN, former electric utility executive; b. Bentonia, Miss., Dec. 21, 1920; s. Orville K. and Norma Eloise S.; m. Mary Virginia Russum, May 28, 1942; children: Mary Lynn, Virginia Kaye. Registered profl. engr., Miss. Engr. U.S. Navy Dept., Washington, 1942-45; with Miss. Power & Light Co., Jackson, 1947-84, chief engr., 1968-72, v.p., 1972-80, sr. v.p., 1980-84; now ret. Miss. Power & Light Co. Pres. Met. YMCA, Jackson, 1980, 85; trustee Mcpl. Separate Sch. Dist., 1980-90, Miss. Baptist Found., 1981-85, 87-92; chmn. So. Baptist Conv. Brotherhood Commn., 1985-86. Served with Signal Corps, U.S. Army, 1945-47. Named Alumnus of Yr. Hinds Jr. Coll., 1980. Mem. Nat. Soc. Profl. Engrs., Miss. Engring. Soc. (Engr. of Yr. 1974), IEEE, Am. Nuclear Soc., Jackson C. of C. (dir.), Phi Theta Kappa (Alumnus of Yr. 1977). Clubs: Exchange (pres. 1975). Home: 343 Elms Court Cir Jackson MS 39204-4333

STAMPS, THOMAS PATY, lawyer, consultant; b. Mineola, N.Y., May 10, 1952; s. George Moreland and Helen Leone (Paty) S.; children: Katherine Camilla, George Belk, Elizabeth Margaret; m. Diana Lynn Whittaker, Dec. 11, 1993. BA, U. Ill., 1973; postgrad., Emory U., 1975-76; JD, Wake Forest U., 1979. Bar: Ga. 1979, N.C. 1979. Pers. dir. Norman Jaspan, N.Y.C., 1973-74; assoc. Macey & Zusmann, Atlanta, 1979-81; prin. Zusmann, Small, Stamps & White PC, Atlanta, 1981-85; cons. GMS Cons., Oxford, Ga., 1975—; ptnr. Destin Enterprises, Atlanta, 1983-85. Author: Study of a Student, 1973, History of Coca-Cola, 1976; asst. editor Ga. Jour. So. Legal History, 1991-94. Chmn. Summer Law Inst., Atlanta, 1981-85; mem. Dem. Party Ga., Atlanta, 1983—; atty. Vol. Lawyers for Arts, Atlanta, 1981-94, Atlanta Vol. Lawyers Found.; panel mem. U.S. Bankruptcy Trustees No. Dist. Ga., 1982-89; active High Mus. Art, 1986—, Atlanta Hist. Soc., Atlanta Bot. Gardens, Atlanta Symphony Orch., Ga. Trust Hist. Preservation, Ind.; sec. Friends of Woodrow Wilson, 1988—, chmn. dinner, 1990—; trustee Ga. Legal History Found., 1989—. Named to Honorable Order of Ky. Colonels; recipient Svc. award Inst. Continuing Legal Edn., Athens, Ga., 1981, 86. Mem. ABA, Atlanta Bar Assn. (com. chmn. 1981-85), N.C. Bar Assn., Lawyers Club, Phi Alpha Delta (justice, Atlanta 1982-83, emeritus 1983). Office: 314 Buckhead Ave NE Atlanta GA 30305-2306

STAMSTA, JEAN F., artist; b. Sheboygan, Wis., Nov. 2, 1936; d. Herbert R. and Lucile Caroline (Malwitz) Nagel; m. Duane R. Stamsta, Aug. 18, 1956; children: Marc, David. BS, BA, U. Wis., 1958. guest curator Milw. Art Mus., 1986; resident artist Leighton Artist Colony, Banff, Alta., Can., 1987. One-woman shows Am. Craft Mus., N.Y.C., 1971, Winona (Minn.) State U., 1986, Lawrence U., Appleton, Wis., 1990, Walkers Point Ctr. Arts, Milw., 1990, U. Wis. Ctr., Waukesha, 1995; exhibited in group shows, incuding Cleve. Mus. Art, 1977, Milw. Art Mus., 1986, 88, Nat. Air and Stace Mus., Smithsonian Instn., Washington, 1986, Madison (Wis.) Art Ctr., 1987, 90, Paper Press Gallery, Chgo., 1988, North Arts Ctr., Atlanta, 1990, Dairy Barn Cultural Arts Ctr., Athens, Ohio, 1991, Paper Arts Festival, Appleton, 1992, Fine Arts Mus., Budapest, Hungary, 1992, Tilburg Textile Mus., The Netherlands, 1993, U. Wis. Union Gallery, 1994, Holland Area Arts Coun. Gallery, U. Mich., Ann Arbor, 1996. NEA craftsman fellow, 1974. Avocations: swimming, travel. Home and Studio: 9313 Center Oak Rd Hartland WI 53029

STANAITIS, SANDRA LEE, nurse; b. Chester, Pa., Dec. 27, 1958; d. Leon David and Margaret (Sharpless) S. BA in Psychology, Widener U., 1980; BS in Biology, SUNY, Albany, 1983; postgrad., East Carolina U., 1984; BSN, West Chester U., 1993; student perioperative program, Delaware County C.C., Media, Pa., 1994. RN, Del., N.J., Pa.; cert. in venipuncture, perioperative nursing, intravenous therapy/ctrl. lines scis. Instr. biology lab. East Carolina U., Greenville, N.C., 1987-88, tutor math. and sci., 1986-88, technician biol. lab. Sea Grant Program, 1987, adj. lectr. biology, 1987-88; tutor math. and sci. Vocat. Rehab., Greenville, 1987-88; technician environ. lab. Weyerhauser Pulp Mill, New Bern, N.C., 1987-88; insp. pharm. quality control Burroughs-Wellcome, Greenville, 1988; clin. data asst. Wyeth Labs., Radnor, Pa., 1988-89; rep. customer svc. Met. Pers., Wayne, Pa., 1989-92, Bayada Nurses Home Health Care Specialist, 1993—; charge nurse subacute care ctr. Genesis Health Ventures, Suburban Woods, Norristown, Pa., 1994—; instr. med.-surg. clin. nursing Delaware County C.C., 1995. James McDaniel Meml. scholar East Carolina U., 1986-88, Army Nurse Corps scholar, 1991-93, U. N.C. Inst. Nutrition scholar, 1985-87. Mem. Nat. League for Nursing, Assn. Oper. Rm. Nurses, U.S. Figure Skating Assn., Recreation Skating Inst. Am., Skating Club of WEilmington, Competitor U.S. Adult Nat. Figure Skating Championships, West Chester U. Nursing Honor Soc., Sigma Xi, Sigma Theta Tau. Home: Suburban Woods 2751 DeKalb Pike Norristown PA 19403

STANALJCZO, GREGG, computer services executive; b. 1959. Degree, Oakland U. With CDI Computer Svcs., Inc., Troy, Mich., 1982—, now pres., 1994—; exec. v.p. Tech. Teammates Inc., 1996. Office: Technology Teammates Inc 1111 Rosedale Ct Detroit MI 48211*

STANBERRY, DOSI ELAINE, English literature educator, writer; b. Elk Park, N.C.; m. Earl Stanberry; 1 child, Anita St. Lawrence. Student in Bus. Edn., Steed Coll. Tech., 1956; BS in Bus. and English, East Tenn. State U., 1961, MA in Shakespearean Lit., 1962; EdD, East Tex. State U., 1975; postgrad., North Tex. State U., U. South Fla., NYU, Duke U., U. N.C. Prof. Manatee Jr. Coll., Bradenton, Fla., 1964-67, Dickinson State U., N.D., 1967-81; retired, 1981. Author: Poetic Heartstrings, Mountain Echoes, Love's Perplexing Obsession Experienced by Heinrich Heine and Percy Bysshe Shelley, Poetry from the Ancients to Moderns: A Critical Anthology, Finley Forest, Chapel Hill's Tree-lined Tuck, (plays) The Big Toe, The Funeral Factory; contbr. articles, poetry to jours., mags. Recipient Editor's Choice award Nat. Libr. Poetry, 1988, 95, Distinguished Professorof English Award, Dickinson State U., 1981; included in Best Poems of 1995. Mem. Acad. Am. Poets, N.C. Writers Network, N.C. Poetry Soc. (Carl Sandburg Poetry award 1988), Poetic Page, Writers Jour., Poets and Writers, Friday-Noon Poets, Delta Kappa Gamma. Home: Finley Forest 193 Summerwalk Cir Chapel Hill NC 27514-8642

STANBURY, JOHN BRUTON, physician, educator; b. Clinton, N.C., May 15, 1915; s. Walter A. and Zula (Bruton) S.; m. Jean F. Cook, Jan. 6, 1945; children: John Bruton, Martha Jean, Sarah Katherine, David McNeill, Pamela Cook. A.B., Duke U., 1935; M.D., Harvard U., 1939; M.D. (hon.), U. Leiden (Netherlands), 1975; postgrad., U. Pisa, Italy, 1994. House officer Mass. Gen. Hosp., 1940-41, asst. resident, 1946, chief med. resident, 1948, mem. med. staff, 1949—; research fellow pharmacology Harvard Med. Sch., 1947; vis. prof. medicine U. Leiden, 1955; prof. exptl. medicine MIT, Cambridge, 1966-80; emeritus MIT, 1980—; cons. Pan Am. Health Orgn., WHO, UNICEF, U.S. AEC. Author: Endemic Goiter: The adaptation of man to iodine deficiency, 1954, Metabolic Basis of Inherited Disease, 5th edit., 1984, The Thyroid and Its Diseases, 5th edit., 1984, Endemic Goiter, 1969, Human Development and the Thyroid, 1972, Endemic Goiter and Endemic Cretinism, 1980, Prevention and Control of Iodine Deficiency Disorders, 1987, A Constant Ferment, 1991, The Damaged Brain of Iodine Deficiency, 1994, The Inborn Errors of the Thyroid System, 1994. Served from lt. (j.g.) to comdr. USNR, 1941-45. Recipient Delmar S. Fahrney medal Franklin Inst., 1993, Prince Mahidol award, Thailand, 1994. Mem. Am. Assn. Physicians, Soc. Clin. Investigation, Am. Thyroid Assn. (pres. 1969), Am. Acad. Arts and Scis., Endocrine Soc., Endocrine Socs. Finland, Colombia, Peru, Ecuador and Argentina, Internat. Coun. for Control of Iodine Deficiency Disorders. Democrat. Episcopalian. Home: 43 Circuit Rd Chestnut Hill MA 02167-1802

STANBURY, ROBERT DOUGLAS GEORGE, lawyer, executive; b. Exeter, Ont., Can., Oct. 26, 1929; s. James George Stuart and Elizabeth Jean (Hardy) S.; m. Miriam R. Voelker, June 21, 1952; children: Susan, Carol, Ian, Duncan. B.A. in Journalism, U. Western Ont., 1950; grad., Osgoode Hall Law Sch., 1955; LLB, York U., 1991. Bar: Ont. 1955, Queen's counsel 1974. Account exec. Public and Indsl. Relations Ltd., Toronto, 1950-51; ptnr. Hollingworth & Stanbury, Toronto, 1955-65; mem. Can. Parliament, 1965-77; minister of citizenship and info., 1969-71, of communications, 1971-72, of nat. revenue, 1972-73; del. to UN Gen. Assembly, 1974-76; v.p., gen. counsel, sec. Firestone Can. Inc., Hamilton, Ont., 1977-83; chmn., chief exec. officer Firestone Can. Inc., 1983-85; sec., dir. Dayton Tire Can. Ltd., 1977-83; dir. Workers Compensation Bd. (Ont.), 1985-88; counsel Inch Easterbrook & Shaker Barristers & Solicitors, Hamilton, Ont., 1986—; pres., CEO Can. Coun. for Native Bus., 1988-91; vice chmn. bd. dirs. Workers Compensaton Bd., Ont., 1991-94. Mem. N.Y. Bd. Edn., 1961-64, chmn., 1963-64; mem. Met. Toronto Sch. Td., 1963-64, Met. Toronto Planning Bd., 1963; bd. dirs. Hamilton and Dist. C. of C., 1979-85, pres., 1983-84; bd. dirs. Hamilton Found., 1980-84, pres., 1982-83; bd. dirs. Art Gallery Hamilton, 1980-88, v.p., 1984-86, pres., 1986-87, bd. govs., 1988—; bd. dirs. Art Gallery Hamilton Found., 1996—; bd. dirs. Can. C. of C., 1982-86, mem. exec. com., 1983-86; mem. bus. adv. coun. McMaster U., 1983-89, chmn., 1987-88; bd. dirs., v.p. Inst. Corp. Dirs. in Can., 1986-87, pres., 1987-88, vice chmn., 1988-91; bd. govs. Jr. Achievement Hamilton-Wentworth, 1988-91; mem. Can. Broadcast Stds. Coun., Ont., 1990—, vice chmn., 1996—; mem. adv. coun. U. Western Ont. Grad. Sch. Journalism, 1994—; mem. Nunavut Arbitration Bd., 1994—; chmn. Employers Coun. on Workers Compensation, 1996—. Recipient Can. Centennial medal, 1967, Queen's Jubilee medal, 1977, Confedn. medal, 1993; apptd. mem. for life Queen's Privy Coun. for Can., 1969; hon. mem. InterParliamentary Union. Fellow Inst. Dirs. (U.K.); mem. Law Soc. Upper Can., Internat. Commn. Jurists, Can. Coun. Adminstrv. Tribunals, Soc. Ont. Adjudicators and Regulators, Can. Club of Hamilton (bd. dirs. 1986-89), Kappa Alpha, Phi Delta Phi. Liberal. Presbyterian. Home: 607 Edgewater Cres, Burlington, ON Canada L7T 3L8 Office: 1 King St W, Hamilton, ON Canada L8P 4X8

STANCIL, IRENE MACK., family counselor; b. St. Helena Island, Sept. 29, 1938; d. Rufus and Irene (Wilson) Mack; m. Nesby Stancil, Dec. 29, 1968; 1 child, Steve Lamar. BA, Benedict Coll., 1960, CUNY, 1983; MA, New World Bible Coll., 1984; SSD, United Christian Coll., 1985. Supr. City of New York; tchr. local bd. edn., S.C. Mem. Am. Ctr. for Law & Justice.

STANCILL, JAMES MCNEILL, finance educator, consultant; b. Orange, N.J., July 30, 1932; s. James Sr. and Anne Jeanne (Sauter) S.; m. Catherine Jackson, Sept. 25, 1954; children: Martha A., Mary C., Christine E. AB, George Washington U., 1954, MBA, 1957; PhD in Fin. and Econs., U. Pa., 1965. Buyer Melpar Inc., Falls Church, Va., 1954-59; instr., adminstrv. officer U. Pa., Phila., 1959-64; prof. fin. U. So. Calif., Los Angeles, 1964—; prin. Stancill & Assocs., Pasadena, Calif., 1964—. Author: Management of Working Capital, 1970; contbr. numerous articles to Harvard Bus. Rev., 1977—. Avocations: genealogy, sailing. Office: Grad Sch Bus Univ Of So Calif Los Angeles CA 90089

STANCZAK, JULIAN, artist, educator; b. Borownica, Poland, Nov. 5, 1928; came to U.S., 1950, naturalized, 1957; s. Victor and Elizabeth (Cwynar) S.; m. Barbara M. Meerpohl, June 10, 1963; children: Danuta M., Christopher. B.F.A., Cleve. Inst. Art., 1954; M.F.A., Yale U., 1956. Tchr. Art Acad. Cin., 1957-64, Cleve. Inst. Art, 1965—. One-man shows include Dayton Art Inst., 1964, Martha Jackson Gallery, N.Y.C., 1964, 65, 68, 71, 72, 75, 77, 79, Miami U., Oxford, Ohio, 1965, Feingarten Galleries, Los Angeles, 1966, Kent State U., 1968, Dartmouth, 1968, Akron (Ohio) Art Inst., 1969, Cleve. Inst. Art, 1971, London Arts Gallery, 1971, Cin. Art Mus., 1972, 80, Corcoran Gallery Art, Washington, 1972, Canton (Ohio) Art Inst., 1974, Pollack Gallery, Toronto, 1975, Ohio State U., 1976, IMF and CARE, Washington, 1978, Butler Inst. Am. Art, Youngstown, Ohio, 1980, Nat. Mus., Warsaw, Poland, 1981, Alice Simsar Gallery, Ann Arbor, Mich., 1982, 88, New Gallery, Cleve., 1983, Charles Foley Gallery, Columbus, Ohio, 1984, 88, Walker Gallery, Chgo., 1986, Carl Solway Gallery, Cin., Jane Haslem Gallery, Washington, 1986, Standard Oil Co. Hdqrs., Cleve., 1987, Alice Simsar Gallery, Ann Arbor, Mich., Boca Raton Mus. Art, Fla., 1989, Carl Solway Gallery, Cin., Charles Foley Gallery, Columbus, Ohio, Ctr. for Contemporary Art, Cleve., 1990; one man retrospective David Anderson Gallery, Buffalo, N.Y., Dennos Mus.,Traverse City, Mich.; exhibited in group shows: Mus. Modern Art, N.Y.C., 1965, Albright Knox Art Gallery, Buffalo, 1965, 68, Detroit Art Inst., 1965, Larry Alrich Mus., 1965, U. Ill., 1965, Gallery Moos, Toronto, 1965, Kranert Art Mus., Urbana, Ill., 1965, San Francisco Mus. Art, 1965, Flint (Mich.) Inst. Art, 1966, Carnegie Inst., Pitts., 1967, Japan Cultural Forum, 1967, Smithsonian Instn., Washington, 1967, 69, 85, Dept. State, Washington, 1968, Cin. Art Mus., 1968, 83, Del. Art Ctr., 1970, Seibu, Tokyo, 1971, Mansfield (Ohio) Art Ctr., 1973, Butler Art Inst., Youngstown, Ohio, 1973, Minn. Art Mus., Mpls., 1973, Akron Art Inst., 1975, Indpls. Mus. Art, 1976, Bklyn. Mus. Art, 1976, 80, Cleve. Mus. Art, 1976, 77, 83, Memphis Acad. Art, 1981, Nat. Gallery Art, 1981, 85, Hirshhorn Mus. Art, 1981, Montclair Art Mus., N.J., 1982, Art Acad. Cin., 1986, Embassies Travelling Exhbn., Madrid, 1987, Warsaw, Poland, 1991; represented in permanent collections: Nat. Mus. Am. Art, Albright Knox Art Gallery, Larry Aldrich Mus., Mus. Modern Art, Dayton Art Inst., Hirshhorn Mus., Washington, Butler Inst. Am. Art, Youngstown, Ohio, Rufino Tomajo Mus., Mex., Cleve. Art Assn., Milw. Art Inst., Canton (Ohio) Art Inst., USIA, N.Y.C., Balt. Mus. Art, San Francisco Mus. Art, Herron Mus. Art, Indpls., Okla. Art Ctr., Oklahoma City, Pa. Acad. Fine Arts, Phila., Carnegie Inst., Pitts., Cleve. Mus. Art, Cin. Art Mus., Tulsa Mus. Fine Arts, Columbus (Ohio) Art Mus., Akron Art Inst., Corcoran Art Mus., Nat. Gallery, Washington, Lowe Art Mus., Coral Gables, Fla., Contemporary Art Mus., Houston, Winnipeg Fine Arts Ctr., Man., Can., Dracket Fine Art Collection, Cin., Kalamazoo Inst. Arts, Worcester Art Mus., Phoenix Art Mus., Indpls. Mus. Art, Wasserman Devel. Corp., Cambridge, Dartmouth Coll., Hanover, N.H., Etzold Sammlung, Cologne, Fed. Republic Germany, Johnson & Johnson Fine Art Collection, Conn., Nelson Rockefeller Collection, N.Y., Chase Manhattan Bank, N.Y., Mus. Fine Arts, Los Angeles, Newport Harbor Mus., Newport Beach, Calif., N.Y. State U. at Buffalo. Recipient 1st prize Dayton Art Inst., 1964; recipient Butler Inst. Am. Art award, 1966, Cleve. Fine Arts prize, 1970, Ohio Arts Council award, 1972, Best of Show award Internat. Platform Assn., 1973-76. Mem. Abstract Artists Am., Internat. Platform Assn. Pioneer optical art. Address: 6229 Cabrini Ln Seven Hills OH 44131-2848

STANDAERT, FRANK GEORGE, medical research administrator, physician; b. Paterson, N.J., Nov. 12, 1929; s. George Joseph and Ethel Mirene (Miller) S.; m. Joan Frances Cairns, Feb. 7, 1959; children: David, Robert, Christopher. AB, Harvard Coll., 1951; MD, Cornell U., 1955. Lic. physician Ohio, Md., D.C., N.Y. Intern in medicine Johns Hopkins Hosp., Balt., 1955-56; rsch. fellow Cornell U. Med. Coll., N.Y.C., 1956-57, instr. pharmacology, 1959-60, from asst. to assoc. prof. pharmacology, 1960-67; Schering Found. Prof., chmn. dept. pharmacology Georgetown U. Schs. Medicine and Dentistry, Washington, 1967-86, acting chmn. dept. biochemistry, 1985-86; v.p. acad. affairs, dean Coll. Medicine Med. Coll. Ohio, Toledo, 1986-89, prof. pharmacology and anesthesiology, 1986-91; assoc. v.p. for rsch. Med. Coll. Ohio, 1990-91; dir. rsch. Toledo Hosp., 1990—; adj. prof. anesthesiology U. Mich. Sch. Medicine, 1993—; active various coms. NIH, 1968-86; mem. merit rev. bd. neurobiology VA, 1974-77, chmn., 1976-77, cons., 1977; mem. Commn. Fed. Drug Approval Process U.S. Congress, 1981-82; discussion leader toxicology and safety evaluation Gordon Rsch. Conf., 1983; cons. FTC, 1971-74, 78, Occupational Safety and Health Adminstrn., 1974, FDA, initial rev. group orphan products devel., 1984—; del. U.S. Pharmacopeial Conv., 1970-86; adj. prof. anesthesiology Med. Sch. U. Mich., 1992—. Contbr. over 75 articles to profl. jours. Served to lt. USN, 1957-59. Recipient Career Devel. award USPHS, 1961-65, 66-67, Golden Apple award Georgetown Med. Sch., 1968. Fellow AAAS; mem. AMA, Am. Soc. Clin. Pharmacology and Therapeutics, Drug Info. Assn., Soc. Neurosci., The Peripatetic Soc., Am. Soc. Pharmacology and Exptl. Therapeutics (active various coms., 1966—, pres. 1990—), Fedn. Am. Socs. for Exptl. Biology (treas. 1982-84, bd. dirs. 1991—, various coms.), Assn. Med. Sch. Pharmacology (councilor 1974-75, sec. 1975-76, pres. 1982-84), Am. Assn. Med. Colls. (audit com. 1984), Soc. Toxicology (sect. mechanisms, founding mem. Nat. Capital Area chpt., 1982), Georgetown Inst. Neurosci. (bd. dirs. 1985-90, bd. scientific advisors 1985-90), Pharm. Mfr.'s Assn. Found., Nat. Bd. Med. Examiners (pharmacology com. 1983-86, comprehensive part II com. 1986-89), Nat. Research Council (div. biology and agr., various coms.), Am. Heart Assn. (nat. capital affiliate, bd. dirs. 1972-78, Exceptional Service award 1983), Sigma Xi, Alpha Omega Alpha. Clubs: Cosmos (Washington), Toledo Country. Office: The Toledo Hosp PO Box 691 Toledo OH 43697-0691*

STANDBERRY, HERMAN LEE, school system administrator, consultant; b. Oran, Mo., Feb. 22, 1945; s. Willie Standberry and Bettie Mae (Thompson) Standberry-Taylor; m. Barbara Irene Palmer, July 1, 1942; children: Donna, Debra, Nina, Miriam, Miranda, Gretchen, Charles, Mary, Dwayne, Helena, Regina, Lakesha. BS, So. Ill. U., 1968; MA, Newport U., 1981, LHD (hon.), 1990; EdD, Walden U., 1992; D Ministry, U. Bibl. Studies and Sem., 1996. Cert. supt., gen. adminstr., curriculum, tchr. Tchr. Community H.S. Dist. 428, Blue Island, Ill., 1968-70; exec. dir. Kane County Coun. for Econ. Opportunity, Batavia, Ill., 1970-75; dep. dir./program planner, Head-Start dir., casemgr., youth supr., educator State of Ill., Dept. Pub. Aid., Dept. Corrections, Chgo., Joliet and St. Charles, Ill., 1975-85; adminstrv. asst. to prin. Bloom High Sch. Dist. 206, Chicago Heights, Ill., 1992-93; asst. prin. Rogers High Sch., Michigan City, Ind., 1994-95; prin. Mich. City (Ind.) Area Alternative H.S., 1995—; chmn. bd. dirs. Greater Chgo. Coun. of Religious Orgns., 1985-89; mem. George Bush's Rep. Presdl. Task Force, Washington, 1989; nominated mem. U.S. Rep. Senatorial Inner Cir., Washington, 1989. Author (curriculum) Business Law I & II, 1968, Career Counseling and Survival, 1978. Bd. dirs. United Way, Elgin, Ill, 1972, City of Elgin-Fremont Youth Orgn., 1971-72; host agy. rep. Dept. Human Svcs., Chgo., 1985-90; sustaining mem. Ill. Rep. Party, Springfield, 1989; host agy. Percy Julian High Sch., Chgo., 1989-90, Ill. Dept. Pub. Aid, Chgo., 1987. Recipient grant Ill. Dept. Pub. Aid, 1984-87, hon. award Christian World Affairs Conf., 1985-86. Mem. Internat. Assn. Police and Community Rel. Officers, United Evangelistic Consulting Assn. (chmn. bd. dirs., pres. 1985—). Home: 803 E 193rd St Glenwood IL 60425-2011 Office: United Evangelistic Assn 1236-42 W 103d St Chicago IL 60643

STANDBRIDGE, PETER THOMAS, retired insurance company executive; b. Norristown, Pa., Mar. 30, 1934; s. Henry Kay and Helen Margaret (Ballard) S.; m. Jean Ann Sire, Sept. 29, 1956; children: Kevin Scot, Keith Alan, Kathryn Ann, Steven Todd. A.B., Lafayette Coll., Easton, Pa., 1955. Regional mgr. Kemper Group, Richmond, Va., 1961-63; div. sales mgr. Kemper Group, Syracuse, Summit, N.Y., N.J., 1963-73; spl. planning officer Kemper Group, Long Grove, Ill., 1973; v.p. mktg. Kemper Group, 1973-86, sr. v.p., 1986-87, exec. v.p., 1988-96; dir. Kemper County Mut. Ins., Garland, Tex., 1978-85, Am. Protection Ins. Co., Long Grove, 1976-96, Acord Corp., Oradell, N.J., 1978-82. Mem. Henrico County (Va.) Rep. Com., 1960-64; trustee Village of Manlius, N.Y., 1966-68; bd. govs. Good Shepherd Hosp., Barrington, Ill., 1983-92; chmn. Marquis Soc. Lafayette Coll., 1984-86; bd. dirs. Buehler YMCA, Palatine, Ill., 1989-92; trustee Lafayette Coll., 1991-93. Mem. Lake Zurich (Ill.) Golf Club, The Landing Club (Ga.). Republican. Episcopalian. Home: 5 Moonrise Circle Savannah GA 31411

STANDEN, MICHAEL, metal products company executive. Pres., chmn., ceo Metallurg Inc., N.Y.C. Office: Metallurg Inc 27 E 39th St New York NY 10016-0903*

STANDER, JOSEPH WILLIAM, mathematics educator, former university official; b. Covington, Ky., Dec. 2, 1928; s. Charles G. and Rosa (Kerner) S. B.S., U. Dayton, Ohio, 1949; M.S., Cath. U. Am., 1957, Ph.D. in Math, 1959. Joined Soc. of Mary Roman Cath. Ch., 1946; tchr. Hamilton (Ohio) Cath. High Sch., 1949-50, Colegio Ponceno, Ponce, P.R., 1950-55; mem. faculty U. Dayton, 1960—, prof. math., 1970—; dean U. Dayton (Grad. Sch.), 1968-74, v.p. acad. affairs, 1974-89, prof. math. dept., 1990—. Mem. Math. Assn. Am. Office: U Dayton Math Dept 300 College Park Ave Dayton OH 45469-0001

STANDIFER, SABRINA, state legislator; m. Brad Barkley. Mem. Kans. Ho. of Reps., 1993—; self-employed computer cons. Democrat. Home: 317 W 41st St N Wichita KS 67204-3203 Office: Kans Ho of Reps State Capitol Topeka KS 66612*

STANDIFORD, SALLY NEWMAN, technology educator; b. Berkeley, Calif., Dec. 25, 1941; d. Richard Lancaster and Eleanor June (Wagstaff) Newman; m. Jay Cary Standiford, Nov. 21, 1964; children: Barbara, Susan. AB, Georgian Ct. Coll., Lakewood, N.J., 1963; MA in Teaching, The Citadel, 1972; PhD, U. Ill., 1980. Tchr. Goose Creek High Sch., Hanahan, S.C., 1969-73; rsch. and teaching asst. U. Ill., Urbana, 1974-78, rsch. asst. Inst. Aviation, 1979-80, vis. asst. prof., 1980-84; adminstr. City Colls. Chgo., 1978; mgr. Control Data Corp., Champaign, Ill., 1978-79; instrnl. design specialist Control Data Corp., Savoy, Ill., 1979-80; asst. prof. U. St. Thomas, St. Paul, 1984-88; assoc. prof. tech. U. Wis., River Falls, 1988-92, prof., 1992—; dir. Ednl. Tech. U. Wis., 1988—; tech. coord. telecomms. curriculum project, U. Wis., 1993—; advisor N.W. Instrnl. Broadcast Svc., 1989—; evaluator Wis. Dept. Pub. Instrn., Madison, 1990—; rschr. Saturn Sch. Tomorrow, St. Paul, 1991—; cons. Met. State U., Mpls., 1992—, Hamline U., St. Paul, 1994—; mem. U. Wis. Sys. Distance Edn. Policy Task Force, 1993—. Author: Computers in English Classroom, 1983; contbg. author: Language Arts Methods, 1987; also numerous articles; designer instrnl. software. Del. Minn. Dem.-Farmer-Labor Conv., Rochester, 1988; computer cons. Women Against Mil. Madness, Mpls., 1988-91; marcher Honeywell Project, Mpls., 1988-91; pres. faculty senate U. Wis., 1992-94. Grantee NSF, 1970-71, fellow, 1973-74; ssummer faculty rsch. fellow USAF, 1987; U. Wis. Lighthouse Tech. Innovation, 1994—. Mem. Am. Assn. Colls. of Tchr. Edn. (co-chair spl. study group on tech. in edn.), Nat. Coun. Tchrs. English (instrnl. tech. com. 1983-88, commn. on media 1985-88, cons. 1992—), Assn. Women in Computing, Western Wis. Alliance in Tech. (advisor 1990—), Computer Profls. for Social Responsibility (charter). Office: U Wis A12 Ames River Falls WI 54022

STANDING, KIMBERLY ANNA, educational researcher; b. Hagerstown, Md., Mar. 24, 1965; d. Thomas Townsend and Ruth Annadeane (Powell) Stone; m. Christopher G. Standing, May 20, 1989; 1 child, Iain Christopher. BA in Math., St. Mary's Coll., 1988; MA in Higher Edn. Adminstrn., George Washington U., 1996. Rsch. analyst Westat, Inc., Rockville, Md., 1988—. Mem. Am. Ednl. Rsch. Assn., Assn. Study Higher Edn. Home: 11545 Brundidge Ter Germantown MD 20876-5500 Office: Westat Inc 1650 Research Blvd # TB243 Rockville MD 20850-3129

STANDING BEAR, ZUGGUELGERES GALAFACH, criminologist, forensic scientist, educator; b. Boston, Jan. 10, 1941; m. Nancy Lee Karlovic, July 13, 1978 (div. Aug. 1985); m. Virginia Anne Red Hawk, Mar. 22, 1988. BS, U. Nebr., 1971; MS in Forensic Sci., George Washington U., 1974; postgrad. cert. in forensic medicine, Armed Forces Inst. Pathology, 1974; MSEd, U. So. Calif., 1976; MPA, Jacksonville State U., 1981; PhD in Criminology, Fla. State U., 1986. Diplomate Am. Bd. Forensic Examiners, Am. Bd. Forensic Medicine; cert. coroner, Ga., 1988-92; cert. criminal justice instr., Calif., Ga. Criminal investigator U.S. Army, 1965; dist. comdr. 7th region U.S. Army Criminal Investigation Command, Seoul, 1974-77; course mgr. U.S. Army Mil. Police Sch., Ft. McClellan, Ala., 1978-81; ret. U.S. Army, 1981; instr. Fla. State U., Tallahassee, 1981-85; asst. prof. No. Ariz. U., Flagstaff, 1985-86; program coord., prof. Valdosta (Ga.) State U., 1986-95; assoc. prof. Colo. State U., Ft. Collins, 1995—; v.p. Bearhawk Cons. Group, Ft. Collins, 1986—. Editor Jour. Contemporary Criminal Justice, 1992. Mem., task group coord. Com. for Sexual Assault Evidence Stds., ASTM, 1993—; mem. leadership coun. Cmty. Policing Project, Valdosta, Ga., 1993-95; v.p. edn. and rsch. No. Colo. WOLF rescue, edn., and rsch. project, LaPorte, Colo., 1995—. Decorated Bronze Star medal. Fellow Am. Acad. Forensic Scis. (gen. sec. 1987-88, gen. chmn. 1988-90, gen. program co-chair 1995-96), Am. Coll. Forensic Examiners, Internat. Assn. Forensic Nurses (disting. fellow, mem. exec. bd. dirs., cons. and permissions exec., chmn. ethics com.),; mem. ASTM (co-coord. sexual assault evidence stds. task group), Am. Sociol. Assn., Acad. Polit. Sci., Am. Soc. Criminology, Acad. Criminal Justice Scis. (program com. 1996—). Democrat. Haudenosaunee (Native Am.). Avocations: wolf behavior, traditional Native American religious counseling. Office: Colo State U Dept Sociology Fort Collins CO 80523

STANDISH, JOHN SPENCER, textile manufacturing company executive; b. Albany, N.Y., Apr. 17, 1925; s. John Carver and Florence (Spencer) S.; m. Elaine Joan Ritchie, Oct. 20, 1962 (div. 1984); children: John Carver, Christine Louise; m. Patricia Hunter, Nov. 9, 1985. BS, MIT, 1945. Asst. to prodn. mgr. Forstmann Woolen Co., Passaic, N.J., 1945-52; various positions Albany Internat. Corp., 1952-72, v.p., 1972-74, exec. v.p., 1974-76, vice chmn., 1976-84, chmn., 1984—; bd. dirs. Berkshire Life Ins. Co., Pittsfield, Mass. Bd. dirs. Albany chpt. ARC, 1966-92, chpt. chmn., 1971-74, bd. govs., Washington, 1980-86; bd. dirs. United Way Northeastern N.Y., Albany, 1980—, pres., 1984-85; trustee Albany Med. Coll. and Ctr., 1984-93, Sienna Coll., Loudonville, N.Y., 1987—; chmn. U. Albany Fund, 1982-87, 89-92; pres. U. Albany Found., 1992—. Sgt. U.S. Army, 1945-46. Mem. Am. Mgmt. Assn., World Econ. Forum, Ft. Orange Club, Wolferts Roost Country Club, Schuyler Meadows Country Club, John's Island Club (Fla.). Republican. Episcopalian. Avocations: bridge, tennis, golf. Home: 1 Schuyler Meadow Club Rd Loudonville NY 12211-1423 Office: Albany Internat Corp PO Box 1907 Albany NY 12201-1907

STANDISH, SAMUEL MILES, oral pathologist, college dean; b. Campbellsburg, Ind., July 6, 1923; s. Irvin Arthur and Etta May (Smedley) S.; m. Gertrude Elizabeth Eberle, Aug. 6, 1949; children—Nancy Jo, Linda Sue. D.D.S., Ind. U., 1945, M.S., 1956. Diplomate: Am. Bd. Oral Pathology (dir. 1973-80), Am. Bd. Forensic Odontology. Practice dentistry, specializing in oral pathology Indpls., 1948-58; mem. faculty Sch. Dentistry Ind. U., 1958-88, emeritus prof. oral pathology, 1967-88, chmn. div. clin. oral pathology, 1967-77, asst. dean sch., 1969-74, asso. dean, 1974-88; cons. Nat. Cancer Inst., 1969-73, Nat. Bd. Dental Examiners, 1966-74, ADA, 1971-77. Author: (with others) Oral Diagnosis/Oral Medicine, 1978, Maxillofacial Prosthetics: Multidisciplinary Practice, 1972, Outline of Forensic Dentistry, 1982. Served with USNR, 1945-47. Fellow Am. Acad. Oral Pathology (pres. 1972-73); mem. ADA, Internat. Assn. Dental Research, Am. Acad. Forensic Sci., Sigma Xi, Omicron Kappa Upsilon, Xi Psi Phi. Home: 4548 Manning Rd Indianapolis IN 46208-2768 Office: Ind U Sch Dentistry Indianapolis IN 46202

STANDISH, WILLIAM LLOYD, judge; b. Pitts., Feb. 16, 1930; s. William Lloyd and Eleanor (McCargo) S.; m. Marguerite Oliver, June 12, 1963; children: Baird M., N. Graham, James H., Constance S. Bar: Pa. 1957, U.S. Supreme Ct. 1967. Assoc. Reed, Smith, Shaw & McClay, Pitts., 1957-63, ptnr., 1963-80; judge Ct. Common Pleas of Allegheny County (Pa.), 1980-87; judge U.S. Dist. Ct., Pa. we. dist., 1987—; solicitor Edgeworth Borough Sch. Dist., 1963-66. Bd. dirs. Sewickley (Pa.) Community Ctr., 1981-83, Staunton Farm Found., mem, 1984—, trustee, 1984-92; corporator Sewickley Cemetery, 1971-87; trustee Mary and Alexander Laughlin Children's Ctr., 1972-90; trustee Leukemia Soc. Am., 1978-80, trustee western Pa. chpt., 1972-80, Western Pa. Sch. for the Deaf. Recipient Pres. award Leukemia Soc. Am., 1980. Mem. ABA, Pa. Bar Assn., Allegheny County Bar Assn., Am. Judicature Soc., Acad. Trial Lawyers Allegheny County (treas. 1977-78, bd. dirs. 1979-80), Am. Inn of Ct. (Pitts. chpt. 1993—). Office: US Dist Ct 605 US Courthouse Pittsburgh PA 15219

STANDLEY, MARK, school program administrator, consultant; b. Waco, Tex., Feb. 12, 1954; s. Troy and Julia (Crockett) S.; m. Christine Selin Standley, Dec. 31, 1986; children: Aron, Robin Joanne. BA, S.W. Tex. State U., 1976; MS, U. Oreg., 1993. Cert. tchr., adminstr. Vol. U.S. Peace Corps, South Korea, 1976-79; tchr. Northway (Ala.) Sch., 1985-90; prin. Mentasta (Ala.) Lake Sch., 1990-92; program mgr. Ala. Gateway Sch. Dist., Tok, 1993-95; account exec. Apple Computer, TOK, Alaska, 1995—; co-founder Nat. Acad. for Ednl. Tech., Eugene, Oreg., 1993; ednl. advisor Dynamix Software, Eugene, 1993—; team leader Tech. Leadership Retreats, Ala., 1992—. Co-author: Technology Advisory Councils, 1993, Teacher's Guide to the Incredible Machine, 1994. Bd. dirs. No. Ala. Environ. Ctr., Fairbanks, 1983-84; v.p. Upper Tanana Natural History Assn., Tok, 1988-89; mem. Tom Snyder Prodns. Presenters Club, 1994—. Recipient Tchr. Fellowship grant Am. Indian Soc. for Engring. and Sci., 1987, Tech. Incentive grant Apple Computer, Inc., 1989. Mem. ASCD, Internat. Soc. for Tech. in Edn., Ala. Soc. for Tech. in Edn. (bd. dirs. 1992—, pres.-elect 1994—, Pres.'s award 1994). Avocations: kayaking, snow shoe racing. Home: PO Box 714 Tok AK 99780-0714 Office: Apple Computer Inc PO Box 714 Tok AK 99780

STANEK, ALAN EDWARD, music educator, performer, music administrator; b. Longmont, Colo., July 3, 1939; s. Edward Thomas Stanek and Mary Rose (Hicks) Stanek MacDougall; m. Janette Elizabeth Swanson, Aug. 23, 1963; children: Michael Alan, Karen Leigh. B in Mus. Edn., U. Colo., 1961; MusM, Eastman Sch. Music, 1965; MusD, U. Mich., 1974. Dir. instrumental music Ainsworth Pub. Sch., Nebr., 1961-64, Cozad Pub. Sch., Nebr., 1965-67; asst. prof. music Hastings Coll., Nebr., 1967-76; prof., chmn. dept. music Idaho State U., Pocatello, 1976—. . Contbr., editor, reviewer for profl. jours. including Clarinet, Idaho Music Notes, Nebr. Music Educator. Mem. Music Educators Nat. Conf., Idaho Music Educators Assn. (chmn. higher edn. 1978-86, pres. 1988-90, chair state solo contest 1990-92), Internat. Clarinet Assn. (sec. 1978-84, v.p. 1986-88, pres.-elect 1994-96, pres. 1996—), Coll. Music Soc., Nat. Assn. Coll. Wind and Percussion Instrs. (chmn. Idaho 1978-88), Nat. Assn. Schs. Music (sec. N.W. region 1979-82, vis. evaluator 1990—, chair N.W. region 1991-94), Rotary (pres. Gate City chpt. 1994-95). Office: Idaho State U Dept Music PO Box 8099 Pocatello ID 83209

STANFILL, DENNIS CAROTHERS, business executive; b. Centerville, Tenn., Apr. 1, 1927; s. Sam Broome and Hattie (Carothers) S.; m. Therese Olivieri, June 29, 1951; children: Francesca (Mrs. Peter Tufo), Sara, Dennis Carothers. BS, U.S. Naval Acad., 1949; M.A. (Rhodes scholar), Oxford U., 1953; LHD (hon.), U. S.C. Corporate finance specialist Lehman Bros., N.Y.C., 1959-65; v.p. finance Times Mirror Co., Los Angeles, 1965-69; exec. v.p. 20th Century-Fox Film Corp., 1969-71, pres., 1971, chmn. bd., chief exec. officer, 1971-81; pres. Stanfill, Bowen & Co., 1981-90; chmn. bd. dirs., chief exec. officer AME, Inc., 1990-91; co-chmn., co-CEO Metro-Goldwyn-Mayer, Inc., 1992-93; sr. advisor Credit Lyonnais, 1993-95; pres. Dennis Stanfill Co., 1995—; bd. dirs. Dial Corp., Weingart Found. Trustee Calif. Inst. Tech. Served to lt. USN, 1949-59; politico-mil. policy div. Office Chief Naval Ops., 1956-59.

STANFILL, SHELTON G., performing arts administrator; m. Brigitte. BA in History and Social Scis., Colo. State U., postgrad. Exec. dir. Hopkins Ctr. Dartmouth Coll.; dir. cultural programs Colo. State U.; dir. Nat. Arts Festival 12th Winter Olympic Games; ptnr. Brown, Stanfill & Brown; pres., CEO Wolf Trap Found. for Performing Arts, Vienna, Va.; pres. Music Ctr. L.A. County, 1994—; chair panels, cons. Nat. Endowment for Arts, Lincoln Ctr., Bklyn. Acad. Music, UCLA; advisor Telluride Film Festival. Avocations: reading, wine, dancing, film, medieval history. Office: Music Ctr LA County 135 N Grand Ave Los Angeles CA 90012-3013

STANFORD, DENNIS JOE, archaeologist, museum curator; b. Cherokee, Iowa, May 13, 1943; s. William Erle and Mary L. (Fredenburg) S.; m. Margaret Brierty, June 4, 1988; 1 dau., Brandy L. BA, U. Wyo., 1965; MA, U. N.Mex., 1967, PhD, 1972. Archeologist, curator Smithsonian Instn., Washington, 1972—, head div. archeology, 1990-92, chmn. dept anthropology, 1992—; v.p., dir. Taraxacum Press, 1981—; mem. adv. bd. Ctr. for the Study of the First Americans, 1985—; rsch. assoc. Denver Mus. Natural History, 1989—. Author: The Walakpa Site, Alaska, 1975; editor: (with Robert L. Humphrey) Pre-Llano Cultures of the Americas, 1979, (with George C. Frison) The Agate Basin Site, 1982, (with Jane Day) Ice Age Hunters of the Rockies, 1992. Mem. Anthrop. Soc. Washington (gov. 1974-77), Soc. Am. Archeology, Am. Quaternary Assn. Research, publs. on Paleo-Indian Studies, N.Am., S.Am., N.E. Asia, especially Western U.S., Arctic. Home: 1350 Massachusetts Ave SE Washington DC 20003-1556 Office: Smithsonian Instn Washington DC 20560

STANFORD, DONALD ELWIN, English educator, editor, poet, critic; b. Amherst, Mass., Feb. 7, 1913; s. Ernest Elwood and Alice (Carroll) S.; m. Edna Goodwin, July, 1937 (div. 1946); 1 child, Don David; m. Maryanna Peterson, Aug. 14, 1953 (dec. Mar. 1992). B.A., Stanford U., 1933, Ph.D., 1953; M.A., Harvard U., 1934. Instr. La. State U., Baton Rouge, 1949-50, asst. prof. English, 1953-54, assoc. prof., 1954-62, prof., 1962-79, Alumni prof. English, 1979-83, Alumni prof. emeritus, 1983—; vis. prof. Duke U., Durham, N.C., 1961-62, Tex. A&M U., College Station, 1984. Author: New England Earth, 1941, The Traveler, 1955, In the Classic Mode: The Achievement of Robert Bridges, 1978, Revolution and Convention in Modern Poetry, 1983; editor: The Poems of Edward Taylor, 1960, Dictionary of Literary Biography, vol. 19, 1981, Dictionary of Literary Biography, vol. 20, 1983, Selected Letters of Robert Bridges, 2 vols., 1983, Humanities Series, 1963-66, The So. Rev., 1963-83, cons. editor The So. Rev., 1987—; mem. adv. bd.: Hopkins Quar., 1981—. Recipient Disting. Research Master award La. State U., 1982; Guggenheim Found. fellow, 1959-60; La. State U. Disting. Faculty fellow, 1973-74; NEH research scholar, summers 1972, 78. Mem. PEN, MLA, South Atlantic MLA, Phi Beta Kappa, Phi Kappa Phi. Democrat. Club: Athenaeum (London). Home: 776 Delgado Dr Baton Rouge LA 70808-4730

STANFORD, HENRY KING, college president; b. Atlanta, Apr. 22, 1916; s. Henry King and Annie Belle (Callaway) S.; m. Laurie Ruth King, Sept. 19, 1936; children: Henry, Lowry, Rhoda, Peyton. AB, Emory U., 1936, MA, 1940, LLD, 1961; postgrad., U. Heidelberg, Germany, 1936-37; MS in Govt. Mgmt. (Alfred P. Sloan Found. fellow 1941-43), U. Denver, 1943, LLD, 1962; PhD (Tax Found. fellow 1943-44), NYU, 1949; DCL Jacksonville (Fla.) U, 1963; LLD, Loyola U., New Orleans, 1968, U. Akron, Kyung Hee U., Seoul, Korea, 1968, Rollins Coll., 1977, Barry Coll., 1979; DHL, U. Tampa, 1969; DLitt, U. R.I., 1970; D in Higher Edn., U. Miami, 1981; DHL, Birmingham-So. Coll., 1987. Instr., Emory U., 1937-40; asst. prof. Ga. Inst. Tech., 1940-41; instr. NYU, 1943-46; prof. pub. administrn., also dir. sch. pub. administrn. U. Denver, 1946-48; pres. Ga. Southwestern Coll., Americus, 1948-50; dir. U. Center in Ga., 1950-52; asst. chancellor U. System of Ga., 1952-53; pres. Ga. State Coll. for Women, Milledgeville, 1953-56; chief of party NYU-Internat. Cooperation Adminstrn. Contract, Ankara, Turkey, 1956-57; pres. Birmingham-So. Coll., 1957-62, U. Miami, Fla., 1962-81; pres. emeritus U. Miami, 1981—; interim pres. U. Ga., 1986-87, pres. emeritus, 1987—; bd. dirs. Avatar Holdings, 1980—, DWG, Southeastern Pub. Service, Wilson Bros., 1982-86, Fischbach Corp., 1985-86, NVF, 1985-86, So. Bell, 1969-85; research asst. Tax Found., N.Y.C., 1943-44; staff N.A.M. com. exec., 1944-46; mem. bd. dirs. Birmingham br. Fed. Res. Bank Atlanta, 1960-62, Jacksonville br., Atlanta, 1967-72, chmn., 1969, 72. Trustee Knight Found., 1982—; vice chmn. Invest-in-Am., 1984-86, chmn. 1986-87; chmn. Dade County Community Relations Bd., 1969-71; bd. visitors Air U., Maxwell AFB, Ala., 1963-66; trustee Caribbean Resources Devel. Found., 1978—, pres., 1978-83, chmn., 1983-84; chmn. Jimmy Carter Hist. Site Adv. Commn., 1990—. Decorated Star of Africa medal Liberia; officer Order of Merit Fed. Republic of Germany; recipient Eleanor Roosevelt-Israel Humanitarian award, 1965, Outstanding Civilian Svc. award U.S. Army, 1966, Silver Medallion Fla. Region NCCJ, 1968, Ga. Region, 1987, Disting. Svc. award Ga. Coll., 1979, hon. alumnus, 1996, C.H.I.E.F. award Ind. Colls. and Univs. Fla., 1983, Sibley award Ga. Mil. Coll., 1991, Emory medal, 1991, Adrian Dominican Ednl. Leadership award Barry U., 1991, Atlanta Boys' High Alumnus award, 1992, James Blair Humanitarian award Americus, Ga., 1993, Westmeyer award pub. svc. NYU, 1993. Mem. So. Assn. Colls. and Schs. (chmn. commn. colls. 1960-62, pres. 1972-73), Nat. Assn. Ind. Colls. and Univs. (dir. 1976-80), Assn. Caribbean Univs. and Rsch. Insts. (v.p. 1965-79), Golden Key Honor Soc. (bd. dirs. 1982-91), Internat. Assn. Univ. Pres. (exec. com. 1977-81), Delta Phi Alpha, Phi Beta Kappa, Omicron Delta Kappa, Phi Sigma Iota, Alpha Kappa Psi, Phi Mu Alpha, Phi Kappa Phi, Rotary. Methodist. Lodge: Rotary (Americus, Ga.) (pres. 1984-85). Office: PO Box 1065 510 W Lamar St Americus GA 31709-3443 *The greatest literary influence on my life has been Goethe's Faust, Part I. Reading it in the original German as a college student, I was struck immediately with the demands Faust made of himself in concluding the contract with Mephistopheles: he would lose his soul if he ever chose a "bed of ease," succumbed to flattery, opted for pleasure alone, or said to any one moment, "Linger awhile: you are so nice!" In other words, whenever he ceased striving, he was lost.*

STANFORD, JOSEPH STEPHEN, diplomat, lawyer, educator; b. Montreal, Que., Can., May 7, 1934; s. Walter Albert and Geraldine (O'Loghlin) S.; m. Agnes Mabelle Walker, Nov. 16, 1957; children: Kevin, Karen, Michael. BA, U. Montreal, 1953; LLB, U. Alta., Edmonton, Can., 1956. Bar: Alta. 1957; called to Queen's Counsel 1984. Mem. Greenan, Cooney & Stanford, Calgary, Alta., 1957-60; joined Fgn. Svc., Dept. External Affairs, Govt. of Can., 1960; amb. to Israel Tel Aviv, 1979-82; also Can. high commr. to Cyprus; asst. dep. min. for Africa and Mid. East Dept. External Affairs, Ottawa, Ont., 1983-85, asst. dep. min. for Europe, 1985-87, assoc. undersec. of state for external affairs, 1987-88; dep. solicitor gen. Govt. of Can., Ottawa, 1988-93; sr fellow, conflict mgr. Canadian Center Mgmt. Devel., Ottawa, 1993—; assoc. Conflict Mgmt. Group, Cambridge, Mass. Contbr. articles on internat. law, fgn. investment and conflict resolution to profl. jours. Roman Catholic. Avocations: wilderness canoeing, tennis, skiing. Home: 58 Amberwood Cres, Nepean, ON Canada K2E 7C3 Office: Canadian Center Mgnt Devel, 373 Sussex Dr, Ottawa, ON Canada K1N 8V4

STANFORD, MELVIN JOSEPH, retired dean, educator; b. Logan, Utah, June 13, 1932; s. Joseph Sedley and Ida Pearl (Ivie) S.; m. Yvonne Watson, Feb. 8, 1951 (div. 1956); children: Connie Stanford Tendick, Cheryl Stanford Bohn; m. Linda Barney, Sept. 2, 1960; children: Joseph Barney Stanford, Theodore Barney Stanford, Emily Stanford, Charlotte Stanford Vaughan, Charles Barney Stanford, Sarah Stanford. B.S. (First Security Found. scholar), Utah State U., 1957; M.B.A. (Donald Kirk David fellow), Harvard U., 1963; Ph.D., U. Ill., 1968. CPA, Utah. Asst. audit supr. Utah Tax Commn., 1959-61, auditor, 1958-59; acct. Haskins & Sells, C.P.A.s, Boston, 1961-62; acctg. staff analyst Arabian Am. Oil Co., Dhahran, Saudi Arabia, 1963-66; teaching and rsch. asst. U. Ill., Urbana, 1966-68; mem. faculty Brigham Young U., Provo, Utah, 1968-82; dir. mgmt. devel. programs Brigham Young U., 1970-73, prof. bus. mgmt., 1974-82; dean Coll. Bus., Mankato (Minn.) State U., 1982-89, prof. mgmt., 1989-94, prof. emeritus, 1994—; mem. adv. bd. M.L. Bigelow & Co., Inc., Organ Builders; cons. Strategic Planning, Decision Case Mgmt., New Enterprise Mgmt.; vis. prof. mgmt. Boston U., Europe, 1975-76; vis. prof. agrl. mgmt. U. Minn., 1991-92. Author: New Enterprise Management, 1975, 82, Management Policy, 1979, 83; co-author: Cases in Business Policy and Strategy, 1990, Decision Cases for Agriculture, 1992, Business Plan Guidebook, 1995; also articles, mgmt. cases; founder Midwestern Jour. Bus. and Econs., 1985. Bishop, Mankato ward LDS Ch., 1987-91. With USAF, 1951-55, USAR, 1956-80. Named Amb. of City of Mankato, 1988. Fellow N.Am. Case Rsch. Assn. (v.p. for rsch. 1985-86, pres. 1987-88, Curtis E. Tate Jr. Outstanding Case Writer award 1992); mem. SAR (pres. Utah 1978-79, nat. trustee 1979-81, Meritorious Svc. medal 1981, Patriot medal 1991), Kiwanis, Sons of Utah Pioneers, Alpha Kappa Psi, Phi Kappa Phi. Home: 1754 Cobblestone Dr Provo UT 84604-1155

STANG, PETER JOHN, organic chemist; b. Nürnberg, Germany, Nov. 17, 1941; came to U.S., 1956; s. John Stang and Margaret Stang Pollman; m. Christine Schirmer, 1969; children: Antonia, Alexandra. BS, DePaul U., Chicago, 1963; Ph. D., U. California, Berkeley, 1966; hon. degr., Moscow State Lomonossov U., 1992, Russian Academy of Sciences, 1992. Instr. Princeton (N.J.) U., 1967-68; from asst. to assoc. prof. U. Utah, Salt Lake City, 1969-79, prof., 1979-92, Disting. prof. chemistry, 1992—. Co-author: Organic Spectroscopy, 1971; author: (with others) Vincy Cations, 1979; contbr. 300 articles to sci. publs. Humboldt-Forschungspreis, 1977; JSPS Fellowship, 1985; Fulbright-Hays Sr. Scholarship, 1988. Fellow AAAS; mem. Am. Chem. Soc. (assoc. editor Jour. Am. Chem. Soc. 1982—). Office: Univ Utah Dept Chemistry Salt Lake City UT 84112

STANGE, JAMES HENRY, architect; b. Davenport, Iowa, May 25, 1930; s. Henry Claus and Norma (Ballhorn) S.; m. Mary Suanne Peterson, Dec. 12, 1954; children: Wade Weston, Drew Dayton, Grant Owen. BArch, Iowa State U., 1954. Registered architect, Iowa, Nebr., Kans., Mo., Okla. Designer Davis & Wilson, Lincoln, Nebr., 1954-62, v.p., 1962-68; v.p., sec. Davis, Fenton, Stange, Darling, Lincoln, Nebr., 1968-76, pres., 1976-92, chmn., 1978-94; mem. State Bd. Examiners for Engrs. and Architects, 1989-92, chmn. region V NCARB, 1991. Prin. works include Lincoln Airport Terminal, Sq. D Mfg. Plant, Lincoln, Bryan Meml. Hosp. (masterplans and additions), 1970, 80, 90, Bryan Ambulatory Care Ctr. Med. Office Bldg., Same Day Surgery Conf. Ctr., Parking Garage, 1993-95, Nebr. Wesleyan Theatre, Lincoln, Hasting (Nebr.) YMCA, various structures U. Nebr., Lincoln, ctr. and br. offices Am. Charter Fed. Savs & Loan, Southeast High Sch. (addition), 1984, U. Nebr. Animal Sci. Bldg., 1987, Beadle Ctr., UNL, 1991. Pres. Lincoln Ctr. Assn., 1979, Capitol Assn. Retarded Citizens, 1972-96; chmn. United Way Campaign, 1986, chmn. bd., 1988; chmn. Bryan Hosp. Found. Endowment Com., 1988-90; bd. dirs. Delta Dental, 1987-92, Downtown Lincoln Assn., 1985-94, steering com. 1989, v.p. Nebr. Jazz Orch., 1995, pres. 1996—, Nebr. Art Assn., 1996—; mem. mayor's com. Study Downtown Redevel., 1989, pub. bldg. commn., masterplan rev. com., 1994; deacon Presbyn. Ch., 1960, chmn. bd. trustees, 1968-90, elder, 1972-87. Recipient Honor award Conf. on Religious Architecture-1st Plymouth Ch. Addition, 1969, also numerous state and nat. awards from archtl. orgns. Mem. AIA (Nebr. bd. dirs. 1964-65, treas. 1965, sec. 1966, v.p. 1967, pres. Nebr. 1968, mem. com. on architecture for health, 1980-94, Regional Design award 1976, 88), Am. Assn. Health Planners, Interfaith Forum on Religion, Art, Architecture, Lincoln C. of C. (bd. dirs. 1982). Republican. Clubs: Exec. (pres. 1972), Crucible, 12, Hillcrest Country (pres. 1977), Lincoln Univ. (sec. 1992—, bd. dirs. 1991—, pres. 1995, 96). Avocations: travel, photography, golf. Home: 3545 Calvert St Lincoln NE 68506-5744 Office: Davis/Fenton/Stange/Darling Inc 211 N 14th St Lincoln NE 68508-1616

STANGELAND, ROGER EARL, retail chain store executive; b. Chgo., Oct. 4, 1929; s. Earl and Mae E. (Shaw) S.; m. Lilah Fisher, Dec. 27, 1951; children: Brett, Cyndi Stangeland Meili, Brad. Student, St. Johns Mil. Acad., 1943-47, Carleton Coll., 1947-48; B.S., U. Ill., 1949-51. With Coast to Coast Stores, Mpls., 1960-78, pres., 1972-77; sr. v.p., exec. v.p. Household Merchandising, Chgo., 1978-84; chief exec. officer, chmn. bd. Vons Grocery Co., Los Angeles, 1984-85; past CEO The Vons Cos., Inc., Arcadia, Calif., chmn., 1986—, now chmn. emeritus. Chmn. Wauconda (Ill.) Bd. Edn., 1957-60, Hopkins (Minn.) Bd. Edn., 1968-74; bd. fellows Claremont (Calif.) U. Ctr. and Grad. Sch., 1986; bd. dirs. L.A. area Boy Scouts Am.; trustee Hugh O'Brian Youth Found.; mem. CEO bd. advisors U. So. Calif. Sch. Bus. Adminstrn.; trustee St. John's Mil. Acad; bd. visitors Peter F. Drucker Grad. Mgmt. Ctr. Mem. Am. Inst. Wine and Food (bd. dirs.), Food Mktg. Inst. (chmn. bd. dirs.), Food Employers Coun. (exec. com., bd. dirs.), Mchts. & Mfrs. Assn. (bd. dirs.), L.A. Area C. of C. (bd. dirs.), Jonathan Club (L.A.), Calif. Club. Home: 842 Oxford Rd San Marino CA 91108-1214 Office: Vons Cos Inc PO Box 3338 618 Michillinda Ave Arcadia CA 91007-6300*

STANGER, ABRAHAM M., lawyer; b. N.Y.C., Sept. 25, 1921; s. Joseph I. and Tillie (Rothfield) S.; m. Claire Y. Schwebel, Sept. 18, 1948; children: Richard, Jordan, Hope. BA cum laude, CCNY, 1941; LLB, NYU, 1948, LLM, 1952, Dr. Jud. Sci., 1958. Bar: N.Y. 1949, U.S. Tax Ct. 1951, U.S. Dist. Ct. (so. dist.) N.Y. 1951, U.S. Dist. Ct. (ea. dist.) N.Y. 1953, U.S. Supreme Ct. 1958, U.S. Ct. Appeals (2d cir.) 1960, U.S. Ct. Claims 1984; CPA, N.Y. Sr. ptnr. corp. fin. reporting, disclosure issues and tax matters Stanger, Robson & Rothstein, N.Y.C., 1960-72; sr. ptnr. corp. div. fin. reporting, disclosure issues and tax matters Trubin Sillcocks Edelman & Knapp, N.Y.C., 1972-83; sr. ptnr. corp. fin. reporting, disclosure issues and tax matters Seyfarth, Shaw, Fairweather & Geraldson, N.Y.C., 1983—; adj. prof. law NYU, 1958—; mem. Fin. Acctg. Standards Adv. Council, 1979-83. Contbr. numerous articles on fin. reporting and disclosure to profl. jours;

edit. staff NYU Law Rev., 1947-48; columnist Corp. Law Rev., 1978-86. Recipient Scroll Appreciation award, NYU. Fellow Am. Bar Found.; mem. AICPA (futures issues com. 1985-88), ABA (chmn. com. law and acctg. sect. bus. law 1980-85, chmn. subcom. lawyers replies to auditors 1985—, chmn. subcom. acctg. methods of com. tax acctg. problems sect. of taxation 1982-86, vice chmn. com. tax acctg. problems 1986-90, mem. nat. conf. of lawyers and CPA's 1988-91), N.Y. State Bar Assn., Assn. of Bar of City of N.Y., N.Y. County Lawyers Assn., Internat. Bar Assn. (rep. on consultative group internat. acctg. stds. com. 1987—, rep. on consultative group internat. auditing practices com. 1995—), Am. Judicature Soc. Home: 605 Park Ave New York NY 10021-7016 Office: Seyfarth Shaw Fairweather & Geraldson 900 3rd Ave New York NY 10022-4728

STANGER, ILA, writer, editor; b. N.Y.C.; d. Jack Simon and Shirley Ruth (Nadelson) S. B.A., Bklyn. Coll., 1961. Feature and travel editor Harpers Bazaar, N.Y.C., 1969-75; exec. editor Travel and Leisure mag., N.Y.C., 1975-85; editor in chief Food and Wine Mag., N.Y.C., 1985-89, Travel and Leisure mag., N.Y.C., 1990-93; contbg. editor Town and Country and Quest mag., 1993—; writer on arts, features and travel; consulting editor Internat. Masters Pubs., London. Mem. N.Y. Travel Writers., Am. Soc. Mag. Editors. Home and Office: 115 W 71st St New York NY 10023-3838

STANGER, JOHN WILLIAM, finance company executive; b. Boston, Jan. 24, 1923; s. John Sawyer and Lenora (Leo) S.; m. Valerie Gudel, Apr. 14, 1951; 1 dau., Pamela Beth. Student, Boston U., 1941-43; A.B., Harvard U., 1947. With G.E. Capital Corp., N.Y.C., 1947-85; v.p., gen. mgr. comml. and indsl. fin. G.E. Capital Corp., 1962-75; pres., gen. mgr. G.E. Capital Corp. subs. G.E. Co., 1975-79, chief exec. officer, 1979-84, vice chmn., 1984-85, also bd. dirs.; chmn., dir. Signal Capital Corp., 1985-93, Stanger, Miller Inc., 1985-91; dir. Monetary Mgmt. Corp. Served to capt. USAAF, 1943-45, 51-53. Decorated D.F.C. Mem. Harvard Lower Fairfield Club, Greenwich Country Club, City Club, Jupiter Golf Club. Republican. Home and Office: 18305 SE Village Cir Tequesta FL 33469-1790

STANHOPE, WILLIAM HENRY, lawyer; b. Chillicothe, Ohio, Aug. 17, 1951; s. William Wallace and Elizabeth C. Stanhope; m. Kristen A. Keirsey, July 26, 1976; children: Liesel, Sally, Kaitlyn. BA, Duke U., 1973; JD, Northwestern U. Law Sch., 1976. Bar: Minn. Supreme Ct. 1976, U.S. Dist. Ct. Minn. 1976, U.S. Dist. Ct. Ga. 1979, Ga. Supreme Ct. 1979, Ga. Ct. Appeals 1979. Assoc. Robins, Kaplan, Miller & Ciresi, Mpls., Atlanta, 1976-82; ptnr. Robins, Kaplan, Miller & Ciresi, Atlanta, 1982-91, mng. ptnr. SE Regional Office., 1991—; instr. NITA, Raleigh, N.C., 1988, Emory U., Atlanta, 1990—. Contbr. articles to profl. jours. Mem. ABA, Assn. Trial Lawyers Am., Ga. State Bar Assn., Ga. Trial Lawyers Assn. Office: Robins Kaplan Miller & Ciresi 2600 One Atlantic Plz 950 E Paces Ferry Rd NE Atlanta GA 30326-1119

STANIAR, BURTON B., television company executive; b. Summit, N.J., Jan. 30, 1942; s. George Andrew and Marion (Dreher) S.; m. Vicki Campbell, Apr. 13, 1968; children—Judson Campbell, Guy Shepard. B.A., Washington and Lee U., 1964; M.B.A., Columbia U., 1966. New products mgr. Colgate Palmolive Co., N.Y.C., 1966-70; v.p., prin. Artcraft Concepts, N.Y.C., 1970-74; dir. mktg. Church & Dwight Co., Piscataway, N.J., 1974-80; sr. v.p. mktg. Group W Cable, Inc., N.Y.C., 1980-81, sr. v.p. mktg., programming, 1981-82, pres., 1982-86, sr. exec. v.p. Westinghouse Broadcasting Co., Inc., N.Y.C., 1986-87, chmn., chief exec. officer, 1987—; bd. dirs. Gibson Greetings, Inc. Trustee Mus. Broadcasting; chmn. Ctr. for Communication, Inc. Mem. Internat. TV and Radio Soc. (bd. govs.), TV Operator's Caucus (chmn.), Adv. Bd. for Rsch. Program in Telecommunications and Info. Policy at Columbia U., Met. Mus. Bus. Com. (vice chmn.), Columbia U. Bus. Sch. Alumni Assn. (bd. dirs.), Nat. Urban League (trustee). Office: Westinghouse Broadcasting Co 888 7th Ave New York NY 10106

STANISLAO, JOSEPH, consulting engineer, educator; b. Manchester, Conn., Nov. 21, 1928; s. Eduardo and Rose (Zaccaro) S.; m. Bettie Chloe Carter, Sept. 6, 1960. BS, Tex. Tech. U., 1957; MS, Pa. State U., 1959; Eng.ScD, Columbia U., 1970. Registered profl. engr., Mass., Mont. Asst. engr. Naval Ordnance Research, University Park, Pa., 1958-59; asst. prof. N.C. State U., Raleigh, 1959-61; dir. research Darlington Fabrics Corp., Pawtucket, R.I., 1961-62; from asst. prof. to prof. U. R.I., Kingston, 1962-71; prof., chmn. dept. Cleve. State U., 1971-75; prof., dean N.D. State U., Fargo, 1975-94, acting v.p. agrl. affairs, 1983-85, asst. to pres., 1983—; dir. Engring. Computer Ctr. N.D. State U., 1984—; prof. emeritus indsl. engring. and mgmt. N.D. State U., Fargo, 1994—; pres. XOX Corp., 1984-90; chmn. bd., chief exec. officer ATSCO, 1989-94, chief engr., 1993—; prof. emeritus N.D. State U., 1994; adj. prof. Mont. State U., 1994—. Contbr. chpts. to books, articles to profl. jours.; patentee pump apparatus, pump fluid housing. Served to sgt. USMC, 1948-51. Recipient Sigma Xi award, 1968; Order of the Iron Ring award N.D. State U., 1972, Econ. Devel. award, 1991; USAF recognition award, 1979, ROTC appreciation award, 1982. Mem. Am. Inst. Indsl. Engrs. (sr.; v.p. 1964-65), ASME, Am. Soc. Engring. Edn. (campus coord. 1979-81), Acad. Indsl. Engrs. Tex. Tech U., Lions, Elks, Am. Legion, Phi Kappa Phi, Tau Beta Pi (advisor 1978-79). Roman Catholic. Home: 8 Park Plaza Dr Bozeman MT 59715-9343

STANKEY, SUZANNE M., editor; b. Grand Rapids, Mich., Apr. 4, 1951; d. Robert Michael and Elizabeth (Rogers) Stankey; m. Homer Brickey, Jr. B.A., Ohio U., Athens, 1973; B.J., U. Mo., Columbia, 1977. Editor Living Today, The Blade, Toledo, 1980-82, Toledo Mag., The Blade, 1982-92, Living Today, Toledo, 1992—. Mem. Toledo Press Club, Toledo Sailing Club, Toledo Rowing Club. Home: 2510 Kenwood Blvd Toledo OH 43606-3601 Office: The Blade 541 N Superior St Toledo OH 43660-1000

STANKIEWICZ, WLADYSLAW JOZEF, political philosopher, educator; b. Warsaw, Poland, May 6, 1922; s. Jozef Edmund and Helena Kamilla (Pawlowicz) S. M.A., U. St. Andrews, Scotland, 1944; Ph.D., London Sch. Econs. and Polit. Sci., 1952. Lectr. Polish U. Coll., London, 1947-52; research asso. Mid-European Studies Center, N.Y.C., 1952-54; vis. postdoctoral fellow Princeton U., 1954-55; economist Govt. of Ont., Can., 1956-57; mem. faculty U. B.C., Vancouver, 1957-87; prof. polit. sci. U. B.C., 1965-87, prof. emeritus, 1987—; lectr. in over 60 univs. in, Europe, N.Z., Australia, Africa, and Asia. Author numerous books, 1955—, latest being Canada-U.S. Relations and Canadian Foreign Policy, 1973, Aspects of Political Theory: Classical Concepts in an Age of Relativism, 1976, Approaches to Democracy, 1980, Am. edit., 1981, In Search of a Political Philosophy: Ideologies at the Close of the Twentieth Century, 1993, Jottings: Thoughts & Aphorisms, 1995; editor books, 1964—, latest being In Defense of Sovereignty, 1969, British Government in an Era of Reform, 1976, The Tradition of Polish Ideals, 1981. Served with Polish Army, 1940-46. Fellow Can. Council, 1968-69, 74-75; Social Scis. and Humanities Research Council Can., 1979-80; I.W. Killam Sr. fellow, 1969-70, 71-72, 77-78. Mem. Am. Soc. Polit. and Legal Philosophy, Am. Polit. Sci. Assn. Office: Univ BC, Dept Polit Sci, Vancouver, BC Canada V6T 1Z1 *I think it is important to believe in a hierarchy of values; to eschew what is merely practical or popular; to shape one's thoughts into a coherent system of ideas reflecting a Weltanschauung; to pursue long-range goals; not to commit oneself to secondary objectives; to see a project through all its stages; to avoid the distinction between working and living; to preserve a sense of the joy of life.*

STANLEY, ARTHUR JEHU, JR., federal judge; b. nr. Lincoln, Kans., Mar. 21, 1901; s. Arthur and Bessie (Anderson) S.; m. Ruth Willis, July 16, 1927; children: Mary Louise Stanley Andrews, Carolyn Stanley Lane, Constance Stanley Yunghans, Susan Stanley Hoffman. LL.B., Kansas City Sch. Law (U. Mo.), Kansas City, 1928. Bar: Kans. bar 1928. County atty. Wyandotte County, Kans., 1935-41; U.S. dist. judge Dist. of Kans., Leavenworth, 1958-71; chief judge Dist. of Kans., 1961-71, sr. U.S. dist. judge, 1971—; mem. Jud. Conf. U.S., 1967-70, chmn. com. on operation jury system, 1973-78, mem. bicentennial com., 1975-78. Mem. Kans. Senate, 1941. Served with 7th U.S. Cav. Can. Army, World War I; with USN, 1921-25; Yangtze Patrol Force 1923-25; 9th Air Force USAAF, 1941-45; disch. to Inf. Res. as lt. col. Fellow Am. Bar Found.; mem. ABA, Kans. Bar Assn., Wyandotte County Bar Assn. (past pres.), Leavenworth County Bar Assn., Am. Judicature Soc., Kans. Hist. Soc. (pres. 1974-75), Am. Legion. Anglican. Home: 501 N Esplanade St Leavenworth KS 66048-2027 Office: US Dist Ct 235 Fed Bldg Leavenworth KS 66048 *My goal in life has been to have and deserve the affection of my family and the respect of my professional colleagues.*

STANLEY, BOB, artist; b. Yonkers, N.Y., Jan. 3, 1932; s. Robert and Margaret (Druitz) S.; m. Marylin Herzka, 1970. B.A., Oglethorpe U., 1953; postgrad., Columbia U., 1953, Bklyn. Mus. Art Sch., 1954-56. faculty Sch. Visual Arts, N.Y.C., 1970-72, 84—; vis. artist La. State U., 1976, Syracuse U., 1978, Princeton U., 1979-80, St. Lawrence U., Canton, N.Y., 1978, New Arts Program, Kutztown, Pa., 1984. One man exhbns. include Bianchini Gallery, N.Y.C., 1965, 66, Internat. Gallery Orez, The Hague, Holland, 1966, Contemporary Art Center, Cin., 1966, Galerie Ricke, Kassel, Germany, 1966, 67, Gegenverkehr, Aachen, Germany, 1969, On 1st, N.Y.C., 1969, Warren Benedek Gallery, 1972, N.Y. Cultural Center, 1974, La. State U. Union Gallery, Baton Rouge, 1976, Hal Bromm Gallery, N.Y.C. & Elizabeth Weiner Gallery, 1978, 80, Bucklew Goehring Gallery, Tampa, Fla., 1983, Centre d'Art Contemporain, Dijon, France, 1986, John Davis Gallery, N.Y.C., 1986, 87, Galerie G. Lavrov, Paris, 1987, 88, Gallerie Bébert, Rotterdam, The Netherlands, 1989, The Painted Bride Gallery, Phila., 1990, The Greenville County (S.C.) Art Mus., 1991, Barbierato Arte Contemporanea, Asiago, Italy, 1992, Moderne Künst Dietmar Werle, Köln, Germany, 1992, Conde Gallery, N.Y.C., 1996; retrospective exhibit at Holly Keenberg-Contemporary Art, Winnipeg, Man., Can., 1980; group exhbns. include 2 man show, P.S.I. Long Island City, 1977, Antisensitivity Show, Ohio U., 1964, Pop and Circumstance, Four Seasons, N.Y.C., 1965, Contemporary Americans, Art Inst. Chgo., 1965, John G. Powers Collection, Larry Aldrich Mus., Ridgefield, Conn., 1966, Hanford Yang Collection, Larry Aldrich Mus., Ridgefield, 1968, 29th Ann., Art Inst. Chgo., 1969, Aspects of a New Realism, Milw. Art Center, 1969, Ann. Exhbn, Whitney Mus. Am. Art, N.Y.C., 1967, 69, 72, 73, 17th, Nat. Print Exhbn, Bklyn. Mus., 1970, Monumental Art, Contemporary Arts Center, Cin., 1970, Recent Aquisitions, Washington U. Mus., St. Louis, 1967, Obsessive Image, Inst. Contemporary Art, London, Eng., 1968, Documenta 68, Kassel, Germany, Another Aspect of Pop, P.S.I. Long Island City, 1978, Milw. Art Center, 1969, Corcoran Gallery Art, 1980, Parrish Art Mus., Southampton, N.Y., 1980, Des Moines Art Center, 1980, Krannert Art Mus., Champaign-Urbana, Ill., 1980, William Paterson Coll., Wayne, N.J., 1980, Worcester Art Mus., Mass., 1981, Orozco Gallery, Mexico City, 1981, Am. Acad. and Inst. Arts and Letters, 1982, Daniel Wolf Gallery, N.Y.C., 1982, Ft. Worth Art Mus., 1984, Harcus Gallery, Boston, 1984, Fuji I, Tokyo, 1985, U. R.I. Fine Arts Ctr., 1985, Art Mus. Princeton, N.J., 1985, White Columns, N.Y.C., 1987, Lyman Allyn Mus., New London, Conn., 1987, High Mus. Art, Atlanta, 1988, Lehigh U., Bethlehem, 1988, Nelson-Atkins Mus. Art, Kansas City, 1989, Contemporay Arts Ctr., Cin., 1990, Centro Cultural La Gerneral Granada, Spain, 1990, Greenville Coounty Mus. Art., 1995, Shardin Art Gallery, Kutztown (Pa.) U., 1996, numerous others. Recipient Casandra Found. award, 1969, Igor Found. award, 1987. Address: 95 Van Dam St 2R New York NY 10013

STANLEY, CAROL JONES, academic administrator, educator; b. Durham, N.C.; m. Donald A. Stanley. BS, N.C. Ctrl. U., Durham, 1969; MS, N.C. Ctrl. U., 1975; spl. student, U. N.C., Greensboro, 1987-90. Master's G teaching cert. Instr. Fayetteville (N.C.) State U., 1975-76, adj. instr., 1986-89; instr. Durham Tech. C.C., 1977; adminstrv. sec., adj. instr., rsch. asst. N.C. Ctrl. U., Durham, 1989. Mem. ASCD, Nat. Bus. Edn. Assn., Delta Sigma Theta (scholarship 1989). Home: 1611 N Duke St # 8F Durham NC 27701-1240

STANLEY, DANIEL JEAN, geological oceanographer, senior scientist; b. Metz, France, Apr. 14, 1934; came to U.S., 1941, naturalized, 1946; s. Paul Emile and Madeleine (Simon) Streisguth; m. Adrienne N. Ellis, Mar. 5, 1988; children: Marc Michel, Eric Paul, Brian, Natalie Anne, Susan. B.Sc., Cornell U., 1956; M.Sc., Brown U., 1958; D.Sc., U. Grenoble, France, 1961. Research geologist French Petroleum Inst., Paris, 1958-61; asst. to dir. U.S. Waterways Expt. Sta., Vicksburg, Miss., 1961-63; asst. prof. geology Ottawa U., Ont., Can., 1963-64; research assoc. prof. Dalhousie U., Halifax, N.S., Can., 1964-66; sr. scientist, oceanographer, dir. Deltas-Global Change Program div. sedimentology Smithsonian Instn., Washington, 1966—; adj. prof. U. Québec, 1992—; cons. to govts. Mediterranean countries; sci. expert Internat. Ct. Justice, 1981—; curator Smithsonian Instn., Washington. Editor: New Concepts of Continental Margin Sedimentation, 1969, Mediterranean Sea: A Natural Sedimentation Laboratory, 1972, Marine Sediment Transport and Environmental Management, 1976, Sedimentation in Submarine Canyons, Fans and Trenches, 1978, The Shelfbreak: A Critical Interface on Continental Margins, 1983, Geological Evolution of the Mediterranean Basin, 1985; contbr. chpts to books, articles to profl. jours. Bd. dirs. Mediterranean Basin and Deltas Programs. Served to capt. C.E., U.S. Army, 1961-63. Recipient médaille Alpes Maritimes, France, 1976, F.P. Shepard medal Soc. for Sedimentary Geology, 1990; named Hon. Prof., East China U., 1995; grantee in field. Fellow Geol. Soc. Am., AAAS, Geol. Soc. Belgium; mem. Internat. Assn. Sedimentologists, Am. Assn. Petroleum Geologists, Soc. Econ. Paleontologists and Mineralogists, Geol. Soc. Washington, Sigma Xi. Republican. Club: Cosmos (Washington). Office: Smithsonian Instn Sedimentology Dv Washington DC 20560

STANLEY, DAVID, retail company executive; b. Kansas City, Mo., 1935; married. Grad., U. Wis., 1955; LLB, Columbia U., 1957. Assoc. Paul, Weiss, Rifkind, Wharton & Garrison, N.Y.C., 1957-60; ptnr. Faegre & Benson, Mpls., 1960-71; exec. v.p. Piper, Jaffray & Hopwood, Mpls., 1971-80; pres. Payless Cashways, Inc., Kansas City, 1980-86, chief exec. officer, 1982—, chmn., 1985—, also bd. dirs.; bd. dirs. Local Initiaves, Support Corp., Nat. Equity Fund, Inc., Piper Jaffray Inc. Bd. dirs. Dole Found. Office: Payless Cashways Inc PO Box 419466 2300 Main St Kansas City MO 64108-2415*

STANLEY, EDWARD ALEXANDER, geologist, forensic scientist, technical and academic administrator; b. N.Y.C., Apr. 7, 1929; s. Frank and Elizabeth (Wolf) S.; m. Elizabeth Ann Allison, June 7, 1958; children: Karen (dec.), Scott. B.S., Rutgers U., 1954; M.S., Pa. State U., 1956, Ph.D., 1960. Geologist, Amoco Petroleum Co., Tulsa, 1960-62; prof. U. Del., 1962-64, U. Ga., 1964-77; assoc. dean rsch., chmn. geology dept. Indiana (Pa.) U. , 1977-81; supr. Phillips Petroleum Co., Bartlesville, Okla., 1981-86, dir., comdg. officer N.Y.C. Police Dept. Crime Lab., 1986-94, cons. geology, forensic sci., microscopy 1994—; cons. geology, Athens, Ga., 1963-77, Indiana, Pa., 1977-81. Contbr. articles to profl. jours. Served to sgt. USAF, 1947-50. NSF grantee 1965-68, 74, Office Water Resources Rsch. grantee, 1965-68; NAS exch. prof. Soviet Union, 1968-69, 73; invited guest Moscow Forensic Labs., 1990; invited speaker FBI Internat. Symposium on Forensic Trace Evidence, 1991. Fellow AAAS, Geol. Soc. Am., Royal Microscopical Soc.; mem. Am. Assn. Petroleum Geologists, Am. Acad. of Forensic Sci., Am. Assn. Crime Lab Dirs., Internat. Assn. for Identification, , Am. Assn. Stratigraphic Palyologists, N.Y. Microscopical Soc., Sigma Xi. Presbyterian. Avocations: photography, music, firearms. Home: 2004 Haverford Rd Ardmore PA 19003-3010

STANLEY, ELLEN MAY, historian, consultant; b. Dighton, Kans., Feb. 3, 1921; d. Delmar Orange and Lena May (Bobb) Durr; m. Max Neal Stanley, Nov. 5, 1939; children: Ann Y. Stanley Epps, Janet M. Stanley Horsky, Gail L. Stanley Peck, Kenneth D., Neal M., Mary E. Stanley McEniry. BA in English and Journalism, Ft. Hays (Kans.) State U., 1972, MA in History, 1984. Pvt. practice local/state historian, cons., writer local history Dighton, 1973—, cons. genealogy, 1980—; vice chmn. State Preservation Bd. Rev., Kans., 1980-87; area rep. Kans. State Mus. Assn., 1978-84. Author: Early Lane County History: 12,000 B.C.—A.D. 1884, 1993 (cert. of commendation Am. Assn. State and Local History), Cowboy Josh: Adventures of a Real Cowboy, 1996; contbr. articles to profl. jours. Precinct woman com. Alamota Township, Kans., 1962-86; mem. Dem. State Affirmative Action Com., 1975. Recipient hon. mention for photography Ann. Christian Arts Festival, 1974, Artist of Month award Dane G. Hansen Mus., 1975. Mem. Kans. State Hist. Soc. (pres. 1990-91), Lane County Hist. Soc. (pres. 1970-78). Methodist. Avocations: fossil hunting, walking, photography, antiques. Home: 100 N 4th Dighton KS 67839 Office: 116 E Long St Dighton KS 67839

STANLEY, H(ARRY) EUGENE, physicist, educator; b. Norman, Okla., Mar. 28, 1941; s. Harry Eugene and Ruth S.; m. Idahlia Dessauer, June 2, 1967; children: Jannah, Michael, Rachel. BA in Physics (Nat. Merit scholar), Wesleyan U., 1962; postgrad. (Fulbright scholar), U. Cologne, W. Ger., 1962-63; PhD in Physics, Harvard U., 1967; PhD (hon.), Bar-Ilan U., Ramat-Gan, Israel, 1994. NSF predoctoral rsch. fellow Harvard U., 1963-67; mem. staff Lincoln Lab MIT, 1967-68, asst. prof. physics, 1969-71, assoc. prof., 1971-73; Miller rsch. fellow U. Calif., Berkeley, 1968-69; Hermann von Helmholtz assoc. prof. health scis. and tech. Harvard U.-MIT Program in Health Scis. and Tech., 1973-76; vis. prof. Osaka (Japan) U., 1975; univ. prof., prof. physics, prof. physiology Sch. Medicine, dir. Ctr. Polymer Studies Boston U., 1976—; Joliot-Curie vis. prof. Ecole Superieure de Physique et Chimie, Paris, 1979; vis. prof. Peking U., 1981, Seoul Nat. U., 1982, 30th Ann. Saha Meml. Lecture, 1992; dir. NATO Advanced Study Inst., Cargese, Corisca, 1985, 88, 90; dir. IUPAP Internat. Conf. on Thermodynamics and Statis. Mechanics, 1986; dir. Enrico Fermi Sch., Varenna, Italy, 1996; cons. Sandia Nat. Lab., 1983—, Dowell Schlumberger Co., 1982—, Elscint Co., 1983-85; nat. co-chmn. Com. of Concerned Scientists, 1974-76. Author: Introduction to Phase Transitions and Critical Phenomena, 1971, From Newton to Mandelbrot: A Primer in Theoretical Physics, 1990, Fractal Forms, 1991, Fractal Concepts in Surface Growth, 1995; editor: Biomedical Physics and Biomaterials Science, 1972, Cooperative Phenomena Near Phase Transitions, 1973, On Growth and Form: Fractal and Non-Fractal Patterns in Physics, 1985, Statistical Physics, 1986, Random Fluctuation and Pattern Growth, 1988, Correlations and Connectivity: Geometric Aspects of Physics, Chemistry and Biology, 1990, Fractals in Science, 1994, Disordered Materials and Interfaces, 1996; assoc. editor Phys. A., 1988-91, editor, 1991—. Recipient Choice award Am. Assn. Book Pubs., 1972, Macdonald award, 1986, Venture Rsch. award British Petroleum, 1989, Mass. Prof. of Yr. award Coun. Advancement and Support of Edn., 1992; John Simon Guggenheim Meml. fellow, 1979-80. Fellow AAAS, Am. Phys. Soc. (chmn. New Eng. sect. 1982-83); mem. Non-Linear Sci. Panel of Nat. Acad. Sci. Home: 50 Metacomet Rd Newton MA 02168-1465 Office: Boston U Ctr for Polymer Studies Boston MA 02215 *The greatest joy of my professional life is to share in the excitement of learning something new—however minor—about the workings of Nature. The greatest joy of my personal life is to be able to imagine that I've done my very best to meet the needs of my family and my co-workers. The greatest obstacle to happiness is the persistent feeling that it is impossible to find that tortuous path whereby both joys may occasionally be experienced.*

STANLEY, HUGH MONROE, JR., lawyer; b. Ft. Lewis, Wash., Oct. 25, 1944; s. Hugh Monroe Sr. and Rita (McHugh) S.; m. Patricia Page, Aug. 17, 1968; children: Allison Michelle, Matthew Monroe, Trevor Marshall. BA magna cum laude, U. Dayton, 1966; JD, Georgetown U., 1969. Bar: Ohio 1969, U.S. Ct. Appeals (6th cir.) 1983, U.S. Supreme Ct. 1979. Assoc. Arter & Hadden, Cleve., 1969-76, ptnr., 1976—, chmn. litigation dept., 1983-96. Staff editor Georgetown Law Jour., bd. editors. Fellow Am. Bar Found., Bar Assn. Greater Cleve., Am. Coll. Trial Lawyers, Internat. Acad. Trial Lawyers, Internat. Soc. Barristers, Nat. Assn. R.R. Trial Counsel; mem. ABA, Fed. Bar Assn., Def. Rsch. Inst., Cleve. Assn. Civil Trial Attys., Ohio Assn. Civil Trial Attys. Republican. Roman Catholic. Avocation: reading. Office: Arter & Hadden 1100 Huntington Bldg 925 Euclid Ave Cleveland OH 44115

STANLEY, JACK H., newspaper publishing executive. V.p.- operations The Houston Chronicle, Tex. Office: Houston Chronicle Pub Co 801 Texas St Houston TX 77002-2906

STANLEY, JAMES PAUL, printing company executive; b. Montreal, Que., Can., Aug. 15, 1915; s. Paul Garton and Florence May (Tooke) S.; m. Anne Seymour Raynsford ; children—Marie, Susan, James, Sarah. B.Engring., McGill U., Montreal, 1938. Staff engr. Stevenson, Kellogg Ltd., 1938-41; plant mgr. Dow Brewery Ltd., 1947-53; v.p., then pres. Ronalds-Federated Ltd., Montreal, 1954-77; chmn. bd., chief exec. officer Ronalds-Federated Ltd., 1977-80. Gov. Montreal Gen. Hosp. Served with RCAF, 1941-46. Fellow Graphic Arts Tech. Found. Mem. Ch. of Eng. Clubs: St. James's. Home: 799 Wartman Ave, Kingston, ON Canada K7M 4M3

STANLEY, JAMES RICHARD, lawyer; b. Williamsport, Pa., Oct. 23, 1931; s. Leslie Wright and Hazel (Stryker) S.; m. Darlene Foster, Nov. 18, 1961; children: Susan A., Sandra R., James F., Jeffrey W. BA, Pa. State U., 1953; JD, Dickinson Sch. Law, 1958. Bar: Pa. 1959, N.Y. 1963, U.S. Supreme Ct. 1967, Ill. 1983. Atty. Duquesne Light Co., Pitts., 1958-62, Hazeltine Corp., Little Neck, N.Y., 1962-64; div. counsel Sealtest Foods, Phila. and Schenectady, N.Y., 1964-71; dir. legal dept. Thiokol Corp., Newtown, Pa., 1971-82; assoc. gen. counsel specialty chems. group Morton Thiokol, Inc., Chgo., 1982-86, gen. counsel, 1986-87; v.p. legal affairs, gen. counsel Morton Internat., Inc., Chgo., 1987—; mem. adv. bd. Northwestern U. Corp. Counsel Ctr., Chgo., 1986—. Served to 1st lt. U.S. Army, 1953-55. Mem. ABA (com. on corp. law depts. 1986—), Phila. Bar Assn., Ill. Bar Assn., Chgo. Bar Assn. Republican. Presbyterian. Clubs: Met., Tower (Chgo.). Office: Morton Internat Inc 100 N Riverside Plz Chicago IL 60606-1518

STANLEY, JANICE FAYE, special education educator; b. Montgomery, Ala., Nov. 21, 1953; d. Holley Moring and Miriam Elizabeth (Long) S. BS in Edn., Auburn U., 1977, EdS, 1992; M of Spl. Edn., Troy State U., 1982. Spl. edn. tchr. Fews Elem. Sch., Montgomery, 1977-79, Vaughn Rd. Elem. Sch., Montgomery, 1979-81, Dunbar Elem. Sch., Montgomery, 1981-91, Catoma Elem. Sch., Montgomery, 1991-95, Chisholm Elem. Sch., 1995—. Edn. mgr. Civitan Club, Montgomery, 1992-93, bd. dirs., 1992—, sec. edn. meeting, 1996—. Mem. Kappa Delta Pi. Methodist. Avocations: reading, swimming, attending plays. Home: 8500 English Oak Loop Montgomery AL 36117-6822 Office: Catoma Elem Sch 1780 Mitchell Young Rd Montgomery AL 36108

STANLEY, JULIAN CECIL, JR., psychology educator; b. Macon, Ga., July 9, 1918; s. Julian Cecil and Ethel (Cheney) S.; m. Rose Roberta Sanders, Aug. 18, 1946 (dec. Nov. 1978); 1 child, Susan Roberta Willhoft; m. Barbara Sprague Kerr, Jan. 1, 1980. B.S., Ga. So. U., 1937; Ed.M., Harvard U., 1946, Ed.D., 1950; D of Ednl. Excellence (hon.), U. North Tex., 1990. Tchr. Fulton and West Fulton high schs., Atlanta, 1937-42; instr. psychology Newton (Mass.) Jr. Coll., 1946-48; instr. edn. Harvard U., 1948-49; asso. prof. ednl. psychology George Peabody Coll. Tchrs., 1949-53; assoc. prof. edn., 1953-57, prof. edn., 1957-62, prof. ednl. psychology, 1962-67, chmn. dept., 1962-63; dir. lab. exptl. design U. Wis., Madison, 1961-67; prof. edn. and psychology Johns Hopkins U., 1967-71, prof. psychology, 1971—, dir. study mathematically precocious youth, 1971—; mem. rsch. adv. coun. Coop. Rsch. Br., U.S. Office Edn., 1962-64; mem. com. examiners for aptitude tests Coll. Entrance Exam. Bd., 1961-65, chmn., 1965-68; mem. rsch. com. Ednl. Testing Svc., 1962-67; fellow Social Sci. Rsch. Coun. Inst. Math. for Social Scientists, U. Mich., summer 1955; postdoctoral fellow statistics U. Chgo., 1955-56; Fulbright rsch. scholar U. Louvain, Belgium, 1958-59; Fulbright lectr. New Zealand and Australia, 1974; cons. U. Western Australia, 1980; fellow Ctr. for Advanced Study in Behavioral Sci., 1965-67, vis. scholar, 1983; hon. prof. Shanghai (People's Republic of China) Tchrs. U.; disting. tchr. Commn. on Presdl. Scholars, 1987, 92; disting. vis. prof. U. Ga., 1947, U. Hawaii, 1960, Harvard U., 1963, U. North Tex., 1990, U. NSW, Australia, 1992; mem. adv. bd. Tex. Acad. Maths. and Sci., 1988—; trustee Ctr. for Excellence in Edn., 1989-93. Author: Measurement in Today's Schools, 4th edit., 1964, (with D.T. Campbell) Experimental and Quasi-Experimental Designs for Research, 1963, 66, (with Gene V. Glass) Statistical Methods in Education and Psychology, 1970, (with K.D. and B. Hopkins) Educational and Psychological Measurement and Evaluation, 3d edit., 1990, (with K.D. Hopkins, G.H. Bracht) Perspectives in Educational and Psychological Measurement, 1972; editor: Improving Experimental Design and Statistical Analysis, 1967, Preschool Programs for the Disadvantaged, 1972, Compensatory Education for Children, Ages 2-8, 1973, (with D.P. Keating, L.H. Fox) Mathematical Talent: Discovery, Description, and Development, 1974, (with W.C. George, C.H. Solano) The Gifted and the Creative: A Fifty-Year Perspective, 1977, Educational Programs and Intellectual Prodigies, 1978, (with W.C. George, S.J. Cohn) Educating the Gifted: Acceleration and Enrichment, 1979, (with C.P. Benbow) Academic Precocity: Aspects of Its Development, 1983; adv. editor jours. Served with USAAC, 1942-45. Julian C. Stanley chair in ednl. psychology created U. Wis., Madison, 1995. Fellow APA (pres. div. ednl. psychology 1965-66, div. evaluation and measurement 1972-73, Thorndike award for disting. psychol. contbns. to edn. 1978), AAAS, Am. Statis. Assn., Am. Psychol. Soc. (J.

McKeen Cattell award 1994); mem. Nat. Council Measurement Edn. (pres. 1963-64), Am. Ednl. Research Assn. (pres. 1966-67, award for disting. contbns. to research in edn. 1980), Nat. Assn. for Gifted Children (2d v.p. 1977-79, Disting. Scholar award 1982), AAUP (past pres. chpt.), Psychometric Soc. (past dir.), AAUP (past chpt. pres.), Tenn. Psychol. Assn. (past pres.), Nat. Acad. Edn., Phi Beta Kappa (past chpt. pres.), Phi Beta Kappa Assocs., Sigma Xi, Phi Delta Kappa. Office: Johns Hopkins U 351 Bloomberg Ctr Baltimore MD 21218-2695 *I am deeply indebted for my graduate education to the G.I. Bill following World War II.*

STANLEY, JUSTIN ARMSTRONG, lawyer; b. Leesburg, Ind., Jan. 2, 1911; s. Walter H. and Janet (Armstrong) S.; m. Helen Leigh Fletcher, Jan. 3, 1938; children: Janet Van Wie Hoffmann, Melinda Fletcher Douglas, Justin Armstrong, Harlan Fletcher. AB, Dartmouth Coll., 1933, AM (hon.), 1952, LLD (hon.), 1983; LLB, Columbia U., 1937; LLD (hon.), John Marshall Law Sch., 1976, Suffolk U., 1976, Vt. Law Sch., 1977, Norwich U., 1977, Ind. U., 1981, Oklahoma City U., 1981, IIT-Chgo.-Kent Coll. Law, 1988, William Mitchell Coll. Law, 1989. Bar: Ill. 1937. Since practiced in Chgo.; assoc. Isham, Lincoln & Beale, 1937-48, ptnr., 1948-66; ptnr. Mayer, Brown & Platt, 1967-91; of counsel, 1991—; v.p. Dartmouth Coll., 1952-54; asst. prof. law Chgo.-Kent Coll. Law, 1938-43, prof., 1943-46; pub. mem. disputes sect. Nat. War Labor Bd., 1943-44. Trustee Presbyn.-St. Luke's Hosp., Wells Coll., 1960-69, Rockford Coll., 1962-70; trustee Ill. Childrens Home and Aid Soc., pres., 1963-64. Served as lt. USNR, 1944-46. Recipient medal for excellence Columbia U. Law Sch., 1984, Disting. Svc. award, 1994. Fellow Am. Bar Found., Am. Coll. Trial Lawyers; mem. ABA (chmn. pub. utility sect. 1970-71, ho. of dels. 1973—, pres. 1976-77, chmn. commn. on professionalism 1985-86, ABA medal 1986), Fed. Energy Bar Assn., Chgo. Bar Assn. (pres. 1967-68), Ill. Bar Assn. (Disting. Svc. award 1986), Alumni Coun. Dartmouth (pres. 1952), Am. Law Inst., Am. Judicature Soc., Supreme Ct. Hist. Soc. (pres. 1987-91, chmn. 1995—), Alpha Delta Phi. Episcopalian. Office: Mayer Brown & Platt 190 S La Salle St Chicago IL 60603-3410

STANLEY, KAREN FRANCINE MARY LESNIEWSKI, human resources professional; b. Amsterdam, N.Y., Oct. 10, 1948; d. Francis Raymond and Genievive Mary (Klementowski) Lesniewski; m. Mark Anthony Stanley, Nov. 11, 1972. BA, Alliance Coll., 1970; MA, The Coll. St. Rose, 1976, CAS, 1987. English tchr. Middle Country Sch., Centereach, N.Y., 1970-71; English and social studies tchr. Mt. Carmel, Gloversville, N.Y., 1971-72; English tchr. Bishop Scully H.S., Amsterdam, 1972-80, Shenendehowa Ctrl., Clifton Park, N.Y., 1980-82; English tchr., head dept. Broadalbin (N.Y.) Ctrl. Sch., 1982-86; adminstrv. intern Saratoga Springs (N.Y.) City Sch. Dist., 1986-87, dir. for human resource svcs., 1987—; bd. dirs. N.Y. State Staff Devel. Coun., 1990-92. Mem. Am. Soc. for Human Resource Mgrs., N.Y. State Assn. Women Adminstrs., Nat. Assn. Schs., Colls. and Univs., Nat. Assn. Ednl. Negotiators, Soroptimist Internat. (sec. Saratoga County chpt. 1991-92, del. Dist. I 1992-93, 96-97, asst. treas. 1994-95, treas. 1995-96), Ednl. Adminstrn. Assn./Coll. St. Rose (bd. dirs., sec. 1986-89, pres. 1989-92). Republican. Roman Catholic. Avocations: gardening, reading, sailing, golf. Office: Saratoga Springs City Schs 5 Wells St Saratoga Springs NY 12866-1205

STANLEY, MARGARET KING, performing arts administrator; b. San Antonio, Tex., Dec. 11, 1929; d. Creston Alexander and Margaret (Haymore) King; children: Torrey Margaret, Jean Cullen. Student, Mary Baldwin Coll., 1948-50; BA, U. Tex., Austin, 1952; MA, Incarnate Word Coll., 1959. Tchg. cert. 1953. Elem. tchr. San Antonio Ind. Sch. Dist., 1953-54, 55-56, Arlington County Schs., Va., 1954-55, Ft. Sam Houston Schs., San Antonio, 1955-57; art, art history tchr. St. Pius X Sch., San Antonio, 1959-60; tchr. Trinity U., 1963-65; designer-mfr., owner CrisStan Clothes, Inc., San Antonio, 1967-73; founder, exec. dir. San Antonio Performing Arts Assn., 1976-92, founder Arts Council of San Antonio, 1962; founding chmn. Joffrey Workshop, San Antonio, 1979; originator, founding chairwoman Student Music Fair, San Antonio, 1963; radio program host On Stage, San Antonio, 1983—. Originator of the idea for a new ballet created for the City of San Antonio, "Jamboree," commd. from the Joffrey Ballet, world premiere in San Antonio, 1984. Pres. San Antonio Symphony League, 1971-74; v.p. Arts Council of San Antonio, 1975; bd. govs. Artists Alliance of San Antonio, 1982; v.p. San Antonio Opera Guild, 1974-76, founder Early Music Festival, San Antonio, 1990; mem. adv. bd. Hertzberg Circus Mus. Recipient Outstanding Tchr. award Arlington County Sch. Dist., 1954, Today's Woman award San Antonio Light Newspaper, 1980, Woman of Yr. in Arts award San Antonio Express News, 1983, Emily Smith award for outstanding alumni Mary Baldwin Coll., 1973, Erasmus medal The Dutch Consulate, 1992, Mary Baldwin Sesquicentennial medallion, 1992; named to Women's Hall of Fame, San Antonio, 1984, Disting. Alumnae, St. Mary's Hall, 1995; teaching fellow Trinity U., San Antonio, 1964-66. Mem. Internat. Soc. for the Performing Arts (regional rep. 1982-85, bd. dirs. 1991—), Met. Opera Nat. Coun., Assn. Performing Arts Presenters, Women in Comm. (Headliner award 1982, San Antonio chpt.), Jr. League of San Antonio, Battle of Flowers Assn., S.W. Performing Arts Presenters (chmn. 1988-92). Avocations: traveling, reading.

STANLEY, MARLYSE REED, horse breeder; b. Fairmont, Minn., Sept. 19, 1934; d. Glenn Orson and Lura Mabel (Ross) Reed; m. James Arthur Stapleton, 1956 (div. 1976); 1 child, Elisabeth Katharene; m. John David Stanley, Oct. 22, 1982. BA, U. Minn., 1957. Registered breeder Arabian horses in Spain, 1976-94. Chmn. bd. dirs. Sitting Rock Spanish Arabians, Inc., Greensboro, N.C., 1978-81; pres. Sitting Rock Spanish Arabians, Inc., Hollister, Calif., 1981-91, Stanley Ranch, Yerington, Nev., 1991—; bd. dirs. Glenn Reed Tire Co., Fairmont, Minn. Author Arabian hunter/jumper rules Am. Horse Shows Assn.; contbr. articles to horse jours. Named Palomino Queen of Minn., 1951, Miss Fairmont, 1954, Miss Minn., 1955. Mem. AAUW, Arabian Horse Registry Am., Internat. Arabian Assn. (bd. dirs. region 10, Minn. and Wis. 1973-76, nat. chmn. hunter-jumper com. 1976-81), Minn. Arabian Assn. (bd. dirs. 1972-75), Am. Paint Horse Assn. (nat. bd. dirs. 1967-70), Assn. Española de Criadores de Caballos Arabes (Spain), World Arabian Horse Assn., Alpha Xi Delta. Republican. Episcopalian. Avocations: fox hunting, fishing, breeding and importing Arabian horses.

STANLEY, PETER WILLIAM, academic administrator; b. Bronxville, N.Y., Feb. 17, 1940; s. Arnold and Mildred Jeanette (Pattison) S.; m. Joan Olivia Hersey, Sept. 14, 1963 (div. 1978); m. Mary-Jane Cullen Cosgrove, Sept. 2, 1978; 1 dau., Laura. B.A. magna cum laude, Harvard U., 1962, M.A., 1964, Ph.D., 1970; LHD (hon.), Occidental Coll., 1994. Asst. prof. history U. Ill., Chgo., 1970-72; asst. prof. history Harvard U., 1972-78, lectr. history, 1978-79; dean of coll. Carleton Coll., Northfield, Minn., 1979-84; program officer in charge edn. and culture program Ford Found., 1984-87, dir. edn. and culture program, 1987-91; pres. Pomona Coll., Claremont, Calif., 1991—; lectr. Fgn. Service Inst., Arlington, Va., 1977-89. Author: A Nation in the Making: The Philippines and the United States, 1974; co-author: Sentimental Imperialists: The American Experience in East Asia, 1981; editor, contbr.: Reappraising an Empire: New Perspectives on Philippine-American History, 1984; contbr. numerous articles to scholastic jours., 1966—. Trustee The Coll. Bd., 1991—, vice chair, 1993-94, chair, 1994—; dir. The Hitachi Found., 1993—, Assn. Am. Colls. and Univs., 1995—; bd. fellows Claremont U. Ctr., 1991—; active humanities and scis. coun. Stanford U., 1986—; nat. adv. bd. Ctr. for Rsch. on Effective Schooling for Disadvantaged Students, Johns Hopkins U., 1989-92; nat. adv. coun. Nat. Fgn. Lang. Ctr., 1992—; mem. exec. com. Consortium Financing Higher Edn., 1992—; bd. dirs. Nat. Assn. Latino Elected Ofcls. Edn. Fund, Commn. on Internat. Edn., Am. Coun. Edn., 1992-95. Fellow Charles Warren Ctr. for Studies in Am. History-Harvard U., 1975-76; Frank Knox Meml. fellow Harvard U., 1962-63. Mem. AAUP, Am. Hist. Assn., Assn. Asian Studies, Coun. on Fgn. Rels., Phi Beta Kappa. Home: 345 N College Ave Claremont CA 91711-4408 Office: Pomona Coll Pres Office Claremont CA 91711-6301

STANLEY, RALPH, bluegrass musician; b. Stratton, Va., Feb. 25, 1927. Founder (with Carter Stanley) band, Stanley Bros. and Clinch Mountain Boys, 1946; albums include: Old Country Church, Hills of Home, Old Home Place, The Stanley Sound Around The World, Plays Requests, A Man and His Music, I Want to Preach the Gospel, Cry From the Cross, Let Me Rest on Peaceful Mountain, Banjo in the Hills, Best of Bluegrass, Folk Song Festival, In Person, 1983, Collector's Edition Vols. 1-6, Long Journey Home, Rank Strangers, Together for the Last Time; appeared at Royal Albert Hall, London, 1966. Grammy nomination, Best Country Vocal Collaboration for Miner's Prayer" (with Dwight Yoakam), 1994. Office: Rebel Records PO Box 3057 Roanoke VA 24015-1057

STANLEY, RICHARD HOLT, consulting engineer; b. Muscatine, Iowa, Oct. 20, 1932; s. Claude Maxwell and Elizabeth Mabel (Holthues) S.; m. Mary Jo Kennedy, Dec. 20, 1953; children: Lynne Elizabeth, Sarah Catherine, Joseph Holt. BSEE and BSME, Iowa State U., 1955; MS in Sanitary Engring., U. Iowa, 1963. Lic. profl. engr., Iowa, other states. With Stanley Cons. Inc., Muscatine, Iowa, 1955—, pres., 1971-87, chmn., 1984—; also bd. dirs. Stanley Cons. Inc.; bd. dirs. HON Industries, Inc., vice-chmn., 1979—; chmn. Nat. Constrn. Industry Coun., 1978, Com. Fedn. Procurement Archtl.-Engring. Svcs., 1979; pres. Eastern Iowa C.C., Bettendorf, 1966-68; mem. indsl. adv. coun. Iowa State U. Coll. Engring., Ames, 1969—, chmn., 1979-81. Contbr. articles to profl. jours. Bd. dirs. Northeast-Midwest Inst., 1989-95, treas., 1991-93, chmn., 1993-95; bd. dirs. Stanley Found., 1956—, pres., 1984—; bd. dirs. Muscatine Health Support Found., pres., 1984—; bd. dirs. Muscatine United Way, 1969-75, Iowa State U. Meml. Union, 1968-83, U. Dubuque, Iowa, 1977-93, Inst. Social and Econ. Devel., 1992—; bd. govs. Iowa State U. Achievement Found., 1982-96. With C.E., U.S. Army, 1955-57. Recipient Young Alumnus award Iowa State U. Alumni Assn., 1966, Disting. Svc. award Muscatine Jaycees, 1967, Profl. Achievement citation Coll. Engring., Iowa State U., 1977, Anson Marston medal Iowa State U., 1991; named Sr. Engr. of Yr., Joint Engring. Com. Quint Cities, 1973. Fellow ASCE, Am. Cons. Engrs. Coun. (pres. 1976-77), Iowa Acad. Sci.; mem. IEEE (sr.), ASME, Am. Soc. Engring. Edn., Nat. Soc. Profl. Engrs., Cons. Engrs. Coun. Iowa (pres. 1967), Iowa Engring. Soc. (pres. 1973-74, John Dunlap-Sherman Woodward award 1967, Disting. Svc. award 1980, Voice of Engr. award 1987, Herbert Hoover Centennial award 1989), Muscatine C. of C. (pres. 1972-73), C. of C. of U.S. (constrn. action coun. 1976-91), Tau Beta Pi, Phi Kappa Phi, Pi Tau Sigma, Eta Kappa Nu. Presbyterian (elder). Club: Rotary. Home: 601 W 3rd St Muscatine IA 52761-3119 Office: Stanley Cons Inc Stanley Bldg Muscatine IA 52761

STANLEY, ROBERT ANTHONY, artist, educator; b. Defuniac Springs, Fla., Mar. 10, 1942. BA cum laude, U. Dayton, 1964; MS, Pratt Inst., N.Y.C., 1969. Dir. art program Upward Bound project Earlham Coll., Richmond, Ind., 1967-68; lectr. art dept. U. Dayton, Ohio, 1967-68; asst. prof. art and humanities Harrisburg (Pa.) C.C., 1969-71; prof. art Oakton Coll., Des Plaines, Ill., 1971—; mem. com. League for Humanities Study Grant, Des Plaines, 1988-89; assoc. dir. Inst. for Environ. Response, N.Y.C., 1968-70; presenter League for Innovation Conf., 1994. Author: Exploring the Film, 1968 (Maxi award 1969), (interactive multimedia) VisLang, 1994; contbr. articles to profl. jours.; shows include William Penn Mus., Harrisburg, Pa., New Horizons in Art Chgo., 1974, Internat. All on Paper, Buffalo, 1979, Zaner Gallery, Rochester, N.Y., 1983, Germanow Art Gallery, Rochester, 1985, Joy Horwich Gallery, Chgo., 1988, 95, U. Oreg., Portland, 1991, Atrium Gallery, N.Y.C., 1991, Shelter Gallery, Chgo., 1992, Matrix Gallery, Chgo., 1994, Ctr. for Visual and Performing Arts, Munster, Ind., 1994, Galerie d'Art Contemporain, Chamalieres, France, 1994, Horwich Gallery, Chgo., 1995. Vol. Ctr. of Concern, Park Ridge, Ill., 1993—; bd. dirs. Kloempken Prairie Restoration, Des Plaines, 1987-89. Grantee OCC Ednl. Found., 1989; recipient 2d Place Paragon award for video Nat. Coun. Cmty. Rels., 1985, 1st place Gold award for graphics Art Ctr. Show, Dayton Art Inst., 1969, award of merit Internat. Works on Paper, 1979. Mem. NEA, Ill. Higher Art Edn. Assn. (founding mem., bd. dirs. 1975-76, 83-84). Office: Joy Horwich Gallery 226 E Ontario Chicago IL

STANLEY, ROBERT MICHAEL, professional baseball player; b. Fort Lauderdale, Fla., June 25, 1963. Degree, U. Fla. With Tex. Rangers, 1987-91; catcher N.Y. Yankees, 1992—. Named to The Sporting News Am. League All-Star Team, 1993, The Sporting News Am. League Silver Slugger Team. Office: Yankee Stadium E 161 St and River Ave Bronx NY 10451*

STANLEY, RONALD ALWIN, environmental scientist, poet; b. Edinburg, Tex., June 18, 1939; s. Hamlet Alwin and Gloria Goldie (Rinkel) S.; m. Dorothy Thibault, Aug. 29, 1963 (div. July 1982); children: Ronald Alwin Jr., David A., Catherine A. Stanley Brookes; m. Susan Absher, Sept. 25, 1982 (div. Dec. 1986); 1 child, Angela M.; m. Mary M. Aldridge, Dec. 26, 1992. AS, Coll. of the Ozarks, 1959; BS, U. Ark., 1961, MS, 1963; PhD, Duke U., 1970; MPA, U. So. Calif., 1982. Intern Oak Ridge (Tenn.) Nat. Lab., summer 1963; scientist Tenn. Valley Authority, Muscle Shoals, 1964-75; asst. prof. biology Memphis State U., 1975, U. S.D., Springfield, 1975; scientist, mgr. EPA, Washington, 1976-96, dir. contracts mng. group, 1992-94, coord. trade and environment policy, 1994-95, program mgr. for multimedia assessment, 1995-96; program mgr. Agy. for Internat. Devel., Washington, 1989-90; tchr. Frostburg State U., 1996—; co-mgr. Blackberry Hills Farm, Clearville, Pa., 1992—. Author: Dark Vision, 1990; co-author: Environmental Management of Water Projects, 1987; author, pub.: My Mother, The Earth, 1990, With All My Heart, 1990, Fragments of the Journey, 1991; pub.: Holding to the Light, 1991; contbr. articles to profl. jours. Overseer Potomac Appalachian Trail Club, Washington, 1990-92, One-Plus-One Social Svc. Soc., Washington, 1992—; usher Arena Stage, 1985—; mentor Environmentors, 1994-95; Duke Club of Washington Internat. Interest Group, 1995. Mem. Ecol. Soc. Am., Am. Chestnut Found., Nature Conservancy, Soc. Wetland Scientists, Sierra Club, Phi Beta Kappa, Sigma Xi. Office: US EPA 401 M St SW Washington DC 20460-0001

STANLEY, SCOTT, JR., editor; b. Kansas City, Kans., July 11, 1938; s. Winfield Scott and Irene Mae (Flint) S.; m. Janice Johns, Aug. 30, 1959 (dec. July 1992); children: Leslie, Scott, Margaret; m. Cynthia Ward, Dec. 30, 1995. BA, Earlham Coll., 1960. Mng. editor Am. Opinion mag., Boston, 1961-85; editor Rev. of The News mag., Boston, 1965-85; editor-in-chief Conservative Digest, Washington, 1985-88, Am. Press Internat., Washington, 1987—; pres. USA Tech., 1991-92; mng. editor Nutrition and Healing, 1994—; dep. editor Insight on the News, Washington, 1995—; mem. nat. bd. dirs. Young Ams. for Freedom, 1960-62; public speaker and univ. lectr., 1962—. Keynote speaker Am. Party Nat. Conv., 1976; pres. Ams. Legal Def. Fund, 1977—; bd. govs. Council for Nat. Policy, 1981—; bd. dirs. Free Congress Polit. Action Com. Recipient award of merit Young Ams. for Freedom, 1970, Freedom award Nat. Congress for Freedom, 1969-79. Congregationalist. Clubs: Nat. Press, Meganset Yacht. Home: 1211 S Eads Arlington VA 22202

STANLEY, SHIRLEY DAVIS, artist; b. Mt. Vernon, N.Y., Dec. 5, 1929; d. Walter Thompson and Elsie Viola (Lumpp) Davis; m. Charles B. Coble Jr., June 11, 1951 (div. 1968); children: Jennifer Susan Farmer, Charles B. Coble III; m. Marvin M. Stanley, Dec. 18, 1983 (dec.). BA in Home Econs. and Gen. Sci., Greensboro Coll., 1951; grad., Real Estate Inst., 1962. Tchr. Dryher H.S., Columbia, S.C., 1951-52, Haw River (N.C.) Sch., 1954-56, Alexander Wilson Sch., Graham, N.C., 1957-58; guest essayist for news Mebane (N.C.) Enterprise, 1955-56; pres. Shirley, Inc., Burlington, N.C., 1962-94; artist, 1956—. One woman show Art Gallery Originals, Winston-Salem, 1976, Olive Garden Gallery, 21st Century Gallery, Williamsburg, Va., numerous galleries in Fla., N.C. Bd. dirs. Girl Scouts Am., Burlington, 1961; mem. disaster bd. ARC, 1990—; life mem. Rep. Inner Cir., Washington, 1990—; active Salvation Army; vol. fundraiser Physicians for Peace; com. mem. York County Rep. Party, 1995; vol., mem. Jeff Jays Take Charge Am. Program. Recipient Rep. Medal of Freedom, 1994. Mem. AAUW, Am. Watercolor Soc. (assoc.), Va. Watercolor Soc., Nat. Soc. Amateur Dancers, Sierra Club, Williamsburg Bibliophiles. Episcopalian. Avocations: travel, gardening, writing, dancing, reading. Home and Studio: 103 Little John Rd Williamsburg VA 23185-4907

STANLEY, STEVEN MITCHELL, paleobiologist, educator; b. Detroit, Nov. 2, 1941; s. William Thomas and Mildred Elizabeth (Baker) S.; m. Nell Williams Gilmore, Oct. 11, 1969. A.B. with highest honors, Princeton U., 1963; Ph.D., Yale U., 1968. Asst. prof. U. Rochester, 1967-69; asst. prof. paleobiology Johns Hopkins U., 1969-71, assoc. prof., 1971-74, prof., 1974, chmn. Dept. Earth and Planetary Scis., 1987-88; assoc. in research Smithsonian Instn., 1972—; mem. bd. earth scis. NRC, 1985—, vice chmn., 1988, mem. bd. earth scis. resources, 1988-88, com. on solid earth scis., exec. and steering com., 1988, com. on geosciences, environ. and resources, 1990—. Author: Relation of Shell Form to Life Habits in the Bivalvia, 1970, (with D.M. Raup) Principles of Paleontology, 1971, Macroevolution: Pattern and Process, 1979, The New Evolutionary Timetable: Fossils, Genes, and the Origin of species, 1981, Earth and Life Through Time, 1986, Extinction, 1987, Exploring Earth and Life Through Time, 1992, Children of the Ice Age: How a Global Catastrophe Allowed Humans to Evolve, 1996; mem. editl. bd. Am. Jour. Sci., 1975—, Paleobiology, 1975-82, 88—, Evolutionary Theory, 1973—. Recipient Outstanding Paper award Jour. Paleontology, 1968, Allan C. Davis medal Md. Acad. Scis., 1973, Outstanding Tech. Paper award Washington Geol. Soc., 1986; Guggenheim fellow, 1981. Fellow Am. Acad. Arts and Scis., Nat. Acad. Scis., Geol. Soc. Am. (chmn. Penrose com. 1978); mem. Paleontol. Soc. (councilor 1976-77, sr. councilor 1991-93, pres. 1993-94, Charles Schuchert award 1977), Soc. for Study Evolution (councilor 1982-84), Am. Geophys. Union, Paleontol. Rsch. Inst. Office: Johns Hopkins U Dept Earth Planetary Sciences Baltimore MD 21218

STANLEY, THOMAS BAHNSON, JR., investor; b. Martinsville, Va., Jan. 9, 1927; s. Thomas B. and Anne (Bassett) S.; m. Ruth Barnes, Sept. 10, 1949; children: Thomas Bahnson III, Susan Walker, Andrew. B.S. in C.E., Va. Mil. Inst., 1946; B.S.C., U. Va., 1948; grad., Advanced Mgmt. Program, Harvard U., 1970. With Stanley Furniture Co., Stanleytown, Va., 1948-79, dir., 1950-79, exec. v.p., 1952-62, pres., 1962-71, chmn., 1971-79; pres. Mead Interiors, Stanleytown, 1969-74; group v.p. Mead Corp., Dayton, Ohio, 1969-74; also dir. Mead Corp.; bd. dirs. Main Street Bank Group, Martinsville, Va., Stanley Land & Lumber Co., Drakes Branch, Va.; treas., bd. dirs. Hobe Sound (Fla.) Co. Inc., 1989—. Mem. Henry County Sch. Bd., 1957-80; chmn. bd. trustees Ferrum Coll., 1977-79. Mem. So. Furniture Mfrs. Assn. (dir., pres. 1966, chmn. 1967). Methodist. Lodge: Masons (32 deg.). Home: Land's End 100 Hunter's Green Dr Stanleytown VA 24168 Office: PO Box 26 Stanleytown VA 24168-0026

STANLEY, THOMAS EDWARD, publishing company executive; b. Springfield, Ill., June 10, 1948; m. Christine Lloreda, 1989; children: Robert, Laurel, Evan. BS in Econs., MacMurray Coll., 1971. Mgr. ops. Hertzberg New Method, Jacksonville, Ill., 1971-78; dir. sales Bantam Books, N.Y.C., 1978-82, 1978-82; v.p., dir. mktg. Avon Books, Hearst Corp., N.Y.C., 1982-84; exec. v.p. Simon & Schuster, N.Y.C., 1984-89; pres. Stanley & Assocs., N.Y.C., 1989-92; sr. v.p., pub. Merriam-Webster Inc., Springfield, Mass., 1991—. Avocations: coach youth sports, running, reading. Office: Merriam-Webster Inc PO Box 281 47 Federal St Springfield MA 01102

STANLEY, TIMOTHY WADSWORTH, economist; b. Hartford, Conn., Sept. 28, 1927; s. Maurice and Margaret Stowell (Sammond) S.; m. Nadia Leon, June 7, 1952; children: Timothy Wadsworth III, Alessandra Maria, Christopher Maurice, Flavia Margaret. Student, Choate Sch., 1943-45; B.A., Yale, 1950; LL.B., Harvard, 1955, Ph.D., 1957. Bar: Conn. 1956, U.S. Supreme Ct. 1971. Mem. staff Office Sec. Def., 1955; teaching fellow Harvard U., 1955-56; spl. asst. White House staff, 1957-59, spl. asst. to asst. sec. def. for internat. security affairs, 1959-62; vis. research fellow Council on Fgn. Relations, N.Y.C., 1962-63; div. dir. policy planning staff Office Sec. Def., 1963-64; asst. to sec. def. for NATO force planning, Paris, 1965-67; def. adviser (minister) U.S. Mission to NATO, Paris and Brussels, 1967-69; vis. prof. internat. relations Johns Hopkins Sch. Advanced Internat. Studies, 1969-70; exec. v.p. Internat. Econ. Policy Assn., Washington, 1970-74; pres. Internat. Econ. Policy Assn., 1974-84, chmn., 1984-87; pres. Internat. Econ. Studies Inst., 1974—; prof. lectr. George Washington U., 1957-60; cons. to various govt. agys., univs., bus. orgns., 1969-70; spl. rep. ACDA in negotiations for East-West Mut. Balanced Force Reductions, 1973-74, cons., 1974-80; mem. U.S. Govt. Adv. Com. on Investment, Tech. and Devel., 1974—; mem. Nat. Strategic Materials and Minerals Program Adv. Com., 1984-88. Author: American Defense and National Security, 1955, NATO in Transition, 1965, Detente Diplomacy, 1970; co-author: U.S. Troops in Europe, 1971, The United States Balance of Payments, 1972, Raw Materials and Foreign Policy, 1977, Technology and Economic Development, 1979, U.S. Foreign Economic Strategy for the Eighties, 1982, Mobilizing U.S. Industry: A Vanishing Option for National Security?, 1987, To Unite our Strength: Enhancing the United Nations Peace and Security System, 1992; contbr. articles to profl. jours. Bd. dirs. Atlantic Coun. U.S., UN Assn. U.S., Nat. Capital Area, v.p., 1992-96; mem. transition team Pres.-elect George Bush, 1988-89. Served to 1st lt. AUS, 1946-48, 51-52. Recipient Distinguished Civilian Service medal Dept. Def., 1969. Mem. Coun. on Fgn. Rels. N.Y., Inst. for Strategic Studies London, Met. Club. Congregationalist. Home: 3028 O St NW Washington DC 20007-3107 Office: Internat Econ Studies Inst 1064 Paper Mill Ct NW Washington DC 20007-3619

STANNERS, CLIFFORD PAUL, molecular and cell biologist, biochemistry educator; b. Sutton, Surrey, Eng., Oct. 19, 1937; married; 3 children. BSc, McMaster U., 1958; MSc, U. Toronto, 1960, PhD, 1963. Fellow molecular biology MIT, Cambridge, Mass., 1962-64; from asst. prof. to prof. med. biophysics U. Toronto, Can., 1964-82; sr. sci. biol. rsch. Ont. (Can.) Cancer Inst., 1964-82; prof. biochemistry McGill U., Montreal, 1982—, dir. McGill Cancer Ctr., 1988—; mem. grants Med. Rsch. Coun. & Nat. Cancer Inst. Can., 1965—, U.S. Nat. Cancer Inst., 1973-79. Assoc. editor Jour. Cell Physiology, 1973-92, Cell, 1975-84. Mem. AAAS, Can. Biochem. Soc., Can. Soc. Cell Biology, Am. Assn. Cancer Rsch. Achievements include rsch. in growth control of animal cells; protein synthesis somatic cell genetics; cell virus interactions; intercellular adhesion molecules; human cancer; human carcinoembryonic antigen cloning and function. Office: McGill U, 3655 Drummond St, Montreal, PQ Canada H3G 1Y6

STANO, CARL RANDOLPH (RANDY STANO), newspaper editor, art director, educator; b. Russellville, Ark., Apr. 1, 1948; s. Carl J. Stano and Martha Lee (Linton) Partain. AA, San Jacinto Coll., 1968; BS in Edn., U. Tex., Austin, 1971; MA, Syracuse U., 1979. Cert. tchr., Tex. Dir. student publs., tchr. A.N. McCallum High Sch., Austin, Tex., 1971-78; grad. asst. S.I. Newhouse Sch. Pub. Communications Syracuse (N.Y.) U., 1978-79; asst. editor, art dir. Kansas City (Mo.) Star Times, 1980-81; dir. graphic arts Democrat and Chronicle, Rochester, N.Y., 1981-85; dir. editorial art and design The Miami (Fla.) Herald, 1985-95; Knight prof. commn. U. Miami, Coral Gables, Fla., 1995—; bd. dirs. PBC Internat. Publ.; instr. summer workshops U. Tex., Austin, U. Iowa, Ball State U., Columbia U., Tex. Tech U., U. Okla., U. Houston, N.Mex. State U., Syracuse U., Kans. State U., Ctrl. Mich. State U., Ouachita State Bapt. U., 1970—; instr., lectr. Syracuse U., 1980, 1982-83, St. John Fisher Coll., Rochester, 1983-85, U. Miami, 1985-95; instr. profl. seminars Poynter Inst. for Media Studies, So. Newspapers Pubs. Assn. Newpaper redesigns Democrat and Chronicle, 1982, Olympian, Olympia, Wash., 1985, Sentinel Newspapers, East Brunswick, N.J., 1986, Jacksonville, N.C. Daily News,1988, El Nuevo Herald, 1987, Miami Herald, 1991. Recipient numerous Tex. State H.S. awards, 1971-78, Edith Fox King Tchg. award Tex. Interscholastic League Press Conf., Austin, 1972, Tex. H.S. Jour. Tchr. of Yr. award, 1974, Lifetime Achievement award Am. Student Press Assn., 1989, Nat. Jour. Tchr. of Yr. award Newspaper Fund and Wall St. Jour., Princeton, N.J., 1974, Pub. Svc. award Miami Herald, 1993; mem. Pulitzer Prize reporting team Kansas City Times/Star, 1981; named to Nat. Scholastic Journalism Hall of Fame U. Okla., 1987, Gallery of Profls. S.I. Newhouse Sch. Pub. Commns. Syracuse U., 1994. Mem. Sco. Newspaper Design (contest chmn. 6th edit. 1985e, southeast chmn. 1985-89, competition chmn. 1987-90, sec. 1989, exec. bd. dirs. 1989-93, 2d v.p. 1990, 1st v.p. 1991, pres.s 1992, immediate past pres. 1993, excellence awards 3d-16th edits., bronze award 1991, 92, 93, silver award 1983, 85, 89-95, gold award 1986, 89, 92, Best of Show, 1992), Fla. Soc. News Editors (illustration graphic award 1987, 88, 90-95, page design award 1988, 90-95, pring mag. award 1989-92), Columbia Scholastic Press Advisors Assn. (Gold Key award 1980, five Trendsetter awards 1975-77), Nat. Scholastic Press Assn. (3 five-star/Pacemaker awards). Home: 4718 SW 67th Ave Apt 8B Miami FL 33155-6849 Office: The Miami Herald One Herald Plaza Miami FL 33132 also: U Miami Sch Comm Merrick Bldg 314E Miami FL 33124-2030

STANS, MAURICE HUBERT, retired business consultant, former government official; b. Shakopee, Minn., Mar. 22, 1908; s. J. Hubert and Mathilda (Nyssen) S.; m. Kathleen Carmody, Sept. 7, 1933 (dec. Oct. 1984); children: Steven, Maureen (dec.), Theodore, Terrell. Student, Northwestern U., 1925-28, Columbia U., 1929-30; LL.D., Ill. Wesleyan U., 1954, Northwestern U., 1960, DePaul U., 1960; D.P.A., Parsons Coll., 1960; LL.D., Grove City Coll., St. Anselm's Coll., 1969, U. San Diego, Gustavus Adolphus Coll., 1970, Pomona Coll., 1971, Maryville Coll., 1971, Rio

Grande Coll., 1972, Nat. U., 1979, Pepperdine U., 1984. C.P.A. With Alexander Grant & Co. (C.P.A.'s), Chgo., 1928, exec. ptnr., 1940-55; pres., dir. Moore Corp. (stove mfrs.), Joliet, Ill., 1938-45; dir., mem. exec. com. James Talcott, Inc., N.Y.C., 1941-55; fin. cons. to postmaster gen. U.S., 1953-55, dep. postmaster gen. U.S., 1955-57; dep. dir. U.S. Bur. Budget, 1957-58, dir., 1958-61; pres. Western Bancorp., Los Angeles, 1961-62; also vice chmn. United Calif. Bank; sr. ptnr. William R. Staats & Co., 1963-64; pres. William R. Staats Co., Inc., 1964-65, Glore Forgan, William R. Staats, Inc., N.Y.C., 1965-69; syndicated columnist, 1961-62; sec. of Commerce Washington, 1969-72; Bd. dirs. Uniglobe Travel (Internat.), Vancouver; pres., bd. dirs. Farmont Corp., L.A.; bd. dirs., treas. Electronic Town Hall Meetings, Inc., 1992-93; bd. dirs., chmn. AT&D Inc., 1993—; bus. cons., L.A., 1975-92; chmn., bd. dirs. Weatherby, Inc., 1986-91. Author: The Terrors of Justice, 1978, One of the Presidents' Men, Twenty Years With Eisenhower and Nixon, 1995; contbr. numerous articles on govt. fin., fgn. trade and bus. to profl. publs. Founder, past pres., now chmn., dir. Stans Found., Chgo.; chmn. Nixon Finance Com., 1968, Republican Nat. Finance Com., 1968-69, 72-73, Finance Com. to Re-Elect Pres., 1972-73; fin. chmn., bd. dirs. Nixon Presdl. Library, 1985—; trustee Pomona Coll., 1962-69; bd. dirs. Huntington Med. Rsch. Inst.; bd. dirs. Arnold and Mabel Beckman Found., Irvine, Calif., 1988-92, Eisenhower World Affairs Inst., Washington, 1987—, chmn. 1991-93; chmn. Minority Enterprise Devel. Adv. Coun., Washington, 1989-91; founding dir. African Wildlife Found., Washington, 1958. Recipient Great Living Am. award U.S. C. of C., 1961, Tax Found. award, 1960, Free Enterprise award Internat. Franchise Assn., 1988; named to Acctg. Hall of Fame, 1968; creator Stans African Halls sect. Mus. York County, Rock Hill, S.C., 1980; financed and constructed Stans Hist. Ctr. Shakopee, Minn., 1995, deeded to Scott County Hist. Soc. Mem. NAM (dir. 1968-69), AICPA (pres. 1954-55, Pub. Service award 1954), Ill. Soc. CPAs (dir. 1944-46), D.C. Soc. CPAs (hon.), Hawaii Soc. CPAs (hon.), Am. Acctg. Assn. (nat. Alpha Kappa Psi award 1952), Fed. Govt. Accountants Assn., Nat. Assn. Postmasters (hon.), Iron Molders and Foundry Workers Union (hon.). Clubs: Union League, Adventurers (Chgo.), California (Los Angeles), Athenaeum (Pasadena), Shikar-Safari Club Internat. (founding 1952, trustee internat. found.), Safari Club Internat., East African Profl. Hunters (hon.), Explorers (N.Y.C.), African Safari (Washington, founding bd. dirs. 1957), Jamhuri of Garissa (Kenya) (hon.), Valley Hunt (Pasadena).

STANSBERRY, JAMES WESLEY, air force officer; b. Grafton, W.Va., Dec. 29, 1927; s. William Adrian and Phyllis Gay (Robinson) S.; m. Audrey Mildred Heinz, May 7, 1950; children: Nora G. Fitzpatrick, Amy G. Stansberry Goodhand, Lisa Stansberry De Regis. BS, U.S. Mil. Acad., 1949; MBA, Air Force Inst. Tech., 1956. Advanced through grades from pvt. to lt. gen. USAF; chief prodn. (Kawasaki Gifu Contract Facility), Gifu, Japan, 1956-57; dep. asst. to Sec. of Def. for atomic energy Washington, 1970-71; dep. dir. procurement policy U.S. Air Force, 1972-73; dep. chief staff contracting and mfg. (Hdqrs. Air Force Systems Command), Andrews AFB, Md., 1977-81; comdr. Electronic Systems Div. Hanscom AFB, Mass., 1981-84; pres. Stansberry Assocs. Inc., 1984—. Decorated DSM with oak leaf cluster, Legion of Merit with oak leaf cluster; named Disting. grad. Lancaster (N.Y.) H.S. Methodist. Home: 43 Monadnock Dr Westford MA 01886-3021 *The real secrets are enthusiasm, competence and good luck; and it helps immensely to marry a good woman. Work and persistence define us, accomodating various levels of talent, intelligence and luck. Work and persistence prevail, witnessed by discipline and determination, and perhaps supported by a sense of humor.*

STANSBURY, PHILIP ROGER, lawyer; b. Milw., May 7, 1931; s. Carroll and Margaret (Manning) S.; m. Daviette Clagett Hill, Dec. 5, 1959; children: Henry Tayloe, Catherine Contee. AB, Haverford (Pa.) Coll., 1953; JD, Harvard U., 1956. Bar: D.C. 1956, U.S. Ct. Appeals (D.C. crct.) 1956. Assoc. Covington & Burling, Washington, 1958-66, ptnr., 1966—. Contbr. articles to profl. jours. Mem. Southwestern Legal Found. (adv. bd.). Republican. Roman Catholic. Office: Covington & Burling 1201 Pennsylvania Ave NW PO Box 7566 Washington DC 20044

STANSEL, JAMES W., agricultural research administrator; b. Angleton, Tex., Apr. 8, 1934; married, 1954; 2 children. BS, Tex. A&M U., 1956, MS, 1959; PhD in Plant Breeding and Genetics, Purdue U., 1965. Asst. geneticist Tex. A&M U., Beaumont, 1960-66, asst. prof. genetics, 1966-70, asst. prof. agronomy Agrl. Rsch. and Ext. Ctr., 1970-77, assoc. prof. genetics/environ., scientist in charge we. div., 1972-77, assoc. prof. agronomy, 1978-82, resident dir., prof. agr. Tex. Agrl. Exptl. Sta., 1982—. Mem. Am. Soc. Agronomy, Soil Sci. Soc. Am., Am. Assn. Cereal Chemists, Am. Genetics Assn. Office: Tex A&M U Agrl Rsch & Extension Ctr Rte 7 Box 999 Beaumont TX 77713-8530*

STANSFIELD, CHARLES W., educational administrator; m. Charlene Rivera, Sept. 6, 1989. BA in Spanish, Fla. State U., 1968, MA in Fgn. Lang. Edn., 1969, MS in Teaching English as Second Lang., 1970, PhD in Fgn. and Second Lang. Edn., 1973. Tchr. English, Centro Colombo-Americano, Bogota, Colombia, 1966; 2jr. high sch. tchr. Spanish Fla. State U. Demonstration Sch., 1968-69; instr. Spanish, U. Colo., Boulder, 1970-73, asst. prof., 1973-80, assoc. prof., 1980-81; assoc. program dir. lang. programs Ednl. Testing Svc., Princeton, N.J., 1981-86; dir. fgn. lang. edn. and testing div. Ctr. for Applied Linguistics, Washington, 1986-94, dir. ERIC Clearinghouse Lang. and Linguistics, 1986-94; pres. Second Lang. Testing, Inc., Bethesda, Md., 1994—; dir. Peace Corps Tng. Ctr., Managua, Nicaragua, 1978; mem. exec. com. Joint Nat. Com. on Langs., 1988-93; conf. coord. Interagy. Lang. Roundtable Invitational Symposium on Lang. Aptitude Testing, Rosslyn, Va., 1988; mem. adv. bd. Nat. Fgn. Lang. Resources Ctr., U. Hawaii, 1991-93; numerous presentations at profl. meetings, 1970—. Author: Cuaderno de ejercicios, 1976, rev. edit., 1981; co-author: Manual de laboratorio, 2d rev. edit., 1981, The Test of Spoken English as a Measure of Communicative Ability in the Health Professions,: Validation and Standard Setting, 1983, (with others) Multiple-Choice Cloze Items and the Test of English as a Foreign Language, 1988; co-editor: Second Language Proficincy Assessment: Current Issues, 1988, Language Aptitude Reconsidered, 1990; also numerous articles. Named Outstanding Alumnus Fla. State U., 1994; Colo. Congress Fgn. Lang. Tchrs. scholar, 1981. Mem. Am. Assn. Tchrs. Spanish and Portuguese (life), Am. Coun. on Teaching Fgn. Langs. (Paul Pinsleur award 1984), Am. Ednl. Rsch. Assn., Internat. Assn. Applied Linguistics, Nat. Assn. for Bilingual Edn., Nat. Coun. on Measurement in Edn., Internat. Lang. Testing Assn. (pres. 1992-93), Tchrs. English to Speakers Other Langs., Washington Area Tchrs. English to Speakers Other Langs., Colo. Tchrs. English to Speakers Other Langs. (Gladys Doty award 1987). Home and Office: 10704 Mist Haven Ter Rockville MD 20852

STANSKY, PETER DAVID LYMAN, historian; b. N.Y.C., Jan. 18, 1932; s. Lyman and Ruth (Macow) S. B.A., Yale U., 1953, King's Coll., Cambridge (Eng.) U., 1955; M.A., King's Coll., Cambridge (Eng.) U., 1959; Ph.D., Harvard U., 1961; D.L. (hon.), Wittenburg U., 1984. Teaching fellow history and lit. Harvard U., 1957-61, instr., then asst. prof. history, 1961-68; assoc. prof. history Stanford U., 1968-73, prof., 1973-74, Frances and Charles Field prof., 1974—, chmn. dept. history, 1975-78, 79-82, 89-90, assoc. dean humanities and scis., 1985-88; chmn. publs. com. Conf. Brit. Studies, 1970-78; pres. Pacific Coast Conf. Brit. Studies, 1974-76, N. Am. Conf. Brit. Studies, 1983-85; vis. fellow Wesleyan Center Humanities, Middletown, Conn., 1972, All Soul's Coll., Oxford (Eng.) U., 1979, St. Catherine's Coll., Oxford (Eng.) U., 1983. Author: Ambitions and Strategies, 1964, England Since 1867, 1973, Gladstone, 1979, William Morris, 1983, Redesigning the World, 1985, On or About December 1910, 1996; co-author: Journey to the Frontier, 1966, The Unknown Orwell, 1972, Orwell: The Transformation, 1979, London's Burning, 1994. Guggenheim fellow, 1966-67, 73-74; Am. Council Learned Socs. fellow, 1978-79; NEH fellow, 1983, Royal Hist. Soc. fellow Ctr. for Advanced Study Behavioral Scis., 1988-89. Fellow Am. Acad. Arts and Scis. (coun. 1994—); mem. Am. Hist. Assn. (pres. Pacific Coast br. 1988-89), Conf. on Brit. Studies, Victorian Soc., William Morris Soc., AAUP, Century Assn. Home: 375 Pinehill Rd Hillsborough CA 94010-6612 Office: Stanford U Dept History Stanford CA 94305

STANTON, DONALD SHELDON, academic administrator; b. Balt., June 8, 1932; s. Kenneth Gladstone and Dorothy Erma (Hettrick) S.; m. Barbara Mae Hoot, June 25, 1955; children: Dale Richard, Debra Carol, Diane Karen. AB, Western Md. Coll., 1953, LLD, 1981; MDiv magna cum laude, Wesley Theol. Sem., 1956; MA, Am. U., 1960; Ed.D., U. Va., 1965; L.H.D., Columbia Coll., 1979; Litt.D., Albion Coll., 1983. Ordained to ministry United Methodist Ch., 1956; pastor Balt. and Va. confs. United Meth. Ch., 1953-59; dir. Richmond (Va.) Area Wesley Found., 1959-63; chaplain, dean of students Greensboro Coll., 1963-65; chaplain Wofford Coll., 1965-69; dir. office coll. services United Meth. Div. Higher Edn., Nashville, 1969-75; v.p. for devel. Wesleyan Coll., 1975-78; pres. Adrian Coll., 1978-88, Oglethorpe U., Atlanta, 1988—; adminstr., prof. European internat. ednl. programs, summers 1960, 69-71, 73; chmn. pres.'s assn. Mich. Intercollegiate Athletic Assn., 1986-87; mem. exec. com. Mich. Colls. Found., 1985-88. Contbr. articles, revs. to profl. publs. in U.S., Japan, Argentina, chpts. to books; editor: Faculty Forum, 1972-74; bass-baritone soloist. Bd. dirs. Toledo (Ohio) Symphony, 1980-83, Lewanee County Jr. Achievement, 1980-83; chair bd. trustees U. Ctr. Ga., 1994-96; mem. exec. com. So. Collegiate Athletic Conf., 1995—; bd. dirs. Found. Ind. Higher Edn., 1996—. Adminstrn. bldg. at Adrian Coll. named in honor of Stanton and his wife, 1988. Mem. Am. Assn. Univ. Adminstrs. (bd. dirs. 1990-93), Ga. Assn. Colls. (pres. 1992), Soc. Wesley (Disting. Alumni Recognition award 1988), Ga. Found. for Ind. Colls. (vice chair 1992), Nat. Assn. Ind. Colls. and Univs. (past mem. pub. rels. com.), Commerce Club, Rotary, Omicron Delta Kappa, Order of Omega, Tau Kappa Epsilon, Psi Chi, Phi Eta Sigma. Home: 1571 Windsor Pky NE Atlanta GA 30319-2740 Office: Oglethorpe U Office of Pres 4484 Peachtree Rd NE Atlanta GA 30319-2737

STANTON, ERIC, wholesale distribution executive. Co-chmn., sec., CFO, treas. Simon Mktg. Inc., L.A., 1974—. Office: Simon Mktg Inc 1900 Avenue Of The Stars ste 400 Los Angeles CA 90067-4301*

STANTON, FRANK, communications executive; b. Muskegon, Mich., Mar. 20, 1908; s. Frank Cooper and Helen Josephine (Schmidt) S.; m. Ruth Stephenson, 1931 (dec. 1992). BA, Ohio Wesleyan U., 1930; PhD, Ohio State U., 1935. Diplomate Am. Bd. Profl. Psychology. Audience researcher CBS, N.Y.C., 1935-45; pres. CBS Inc., N.Y.C., 1946-71, vice chmn., 1971-73; chmn. The Rand Corp., 1961-67, Capital Income Builder, Inc., Sony Music Entertainment Inc., Internat. Herald Tribune (Paris), Interpub. Group of Cos., 1976-95; dir. Capital World Growth & Income Fund, London Observer, 1977-85; chmn. U.S. Adv. Commn. Info., Washington, 1964-73. Coauthor: The Study of Psychology, 1935, Radio Research, 1941, 42-43; author: International Information, Education and Cultural Relations: Recommendations for the Future, 1975; co-editor Communications Rsch., 1943-49. Bd. overseers Harvard Coll., 1978-84, chmn. vis. com. Kennedy Sch. Govt., 1979-85, chmn. vis. com. Harvard Grad. Sch. Design, 1990-91; founding mem., chmn. Ctr. for Advanced Study in Behavioral Scis., Stanford, Calif., 1953-60, trustee, 1953-71; chmn. ARC, Washington, 1973-79, vice chmn. League of Red Cross Socs., Geneva, Switzerland, 1973-80; mem. Pres.'s Com. Arts and Humanities, Washington, 1983-90, Nat. Portrait Gallery Commn., Washington, 1973-92, Bus. Coun., Washington, 1956— (hon.); dir., trustee Bryant Park Restorarion Corp., Ednl. Broadcasting Corp. (hon.), Internat. Design Conf. in Aspen, Colo., Lincoln Ctr. Inst., Mus. of TV and Radio, Recorded Anthology Am. Music; emeritus trustee, dir. Lincoln Ctr. for Performing Arts, Rockefeller Found., Carnegie Instn. Washington. Recipient Peabody awards, 1959, 60, 61, 64, 72, Trustees award Nat. Acad. TV Arts and Scis., 1959, 72, Paul White Meml. award Radio and TV News Dirs. Assn., 1957, 71, Spl. Honor award AIA, 1967, Internat. Directorate award Nat. Acad. TV Arts and Scis., 1980, Trustees award Calif. Inst. Arts, 1994; named to TV Acad. Hall of Fame, 1986, Market Rsch. Coun. of N.Y., 1988. Fellow AAAS, Am. Psychol. Assn., Am. Acad. Arts and Scis., N.Y. Acad. Scis., Century Assn., Harvard Club, Cosmos Club. Office: 25 W 52nd St New York NY 10019-6101

STANTON, GEORGE BASIL, JR., engineering executive, chemical engineer, consultant; b. Bklyn., Nov. 3, 1926; s. George B. and Despina Stanton. B in Chem. Engring., Poly. Inst., Bklyn., 1945, M in Chem. Engring., 1948; MBA, NYU, 1971, MA in Safety and Health, 1975. Cert. safety profl., indsl. hyfienist; registered profl. engr., N.J. Chief occupl. health Dept. Labor State of N.J., 1971-74; cons. engr. N.J., 1974-79; pres. Am. Hazard Control Cons., Inc., Caldwell, N.J., 1979—; adj. prof. N.J. Inst. Tech., 1974-92, Ctr. for Safety NYU, 1977-84; organizer, pres. Essex Fells Found. for Ednl. Excellence, Inc., 1994-95; ASME rep. Joint Coun. for Health, Safety and Environ. Edn. of Profls., 1995—. Fellow Royal Soc. Health; mem. ASME (joint coun. health, safety and environ. edn. of profls. 1995—, Centennial medal 1980), Am. Soc. Safety Engrs. (award 1989). Office: Am Hazard Control Cons Inc PO Box 231 Caldwell NJ 07006-0231

STANTON, HARRY DEAN, actor; b. Ky., July 14, 1926. Actor: (feature films) Tomahawk Trail, 1957, The Proud Rebel, 1958, Pork Chop Hill, 1959, A Dog's Best Friend, 1959, Cool Hand Luke, 1967, Kelly's Heroes, 1970, Two-Lane Blacktop, 1971, Pat Garrett and Billy the Kid, 1971, Dillinger, 1973, Zandy's Bride, 1974, The Godfather, Part II, 1974, Rancho Deluxe, 1974, Farewell, My Lovely, 1975, The Missouri Breaks, 1976, 92 in the Shade, 1976, Renaldo and Clara, 1977, Straight Time, 1977, The Rose, 1979, Wise Blood, 1979, Alien, 1979, Deathwatch, 1979, The Black Marble, 1980, UFOria, 1980, Private Benjamin, 1980, Escape from New York, 1981, Young Doctors in Love, 1982, One From the Heart, 1982, Tough Enough, 1983, Christine, 1983, Repo Man, 1984, The Bear, 1984, Red Dawn, 1984, Paris, Texas, 1984, One Magic Christmas, 1985, Pretty in Pink, 1986, Fool for Love, 1986, The Last Temptation of Christ, 1988, Dream A Little Dream, 1989, Twister, 1989, The Fourth War, 1990, Wild at Heart, 1990, Man Trouble, 1992, Twin Peaks: Fire Walk With Me, 1992; (TV spl.) Faerie Tale Theatre, Showtime, 1987; (TV film) Flatbed Annie and Sweetie Pie: Lady Truckers, 1979, I Want to Live, 1983, Payoff, 1992, Hostages, 1993, Hotel Room, 1993. Mem. Screen Actors Guild. Office: Bresler Kelly Kipperman 15760 Ventura Blvd Ste 1730 Encino CA 91436-3002*

STANTON, JAMES ADKINS, high technology integration company executive; b. Tallahassee, Jan. 24, 1941; s. Charles Newton and Louise (Harris) S.; m. Diane Rae Stovall, June 2, 1962; children: Nancy Rae Stanton Stamm, James Adkins Jr., Suzanne Louise. BS in Math., U. Ala., Tuscaloosa, 1963. Systems analyst Boeing Co., Huntsville, Ala., 1963-68; pres. VEE, Inc., Rosslyn, Va., 1968-70, Psi Tran Corp., Rosslyn, 1973-75, Sci. Mgmt. Systems Co., Landover, Md., 1975-80, Stanton Group, Inc., Herndon, Va., 1984-88; v.p. Computer Data Systems, Bethesda, Md., 1970-73; v.p. cons. Morino Assocs., Inc., Vienna, Va., 1980-84; sr. v.p. adminstrn. Comdisco, Inc., Rosemont, Ill., 1988-95; pres. Wireless Tech. Group, Barrington, Ill., 1995—; mem. adv. bd. So. Ill. U. Coll. Bus. Adminstrn., Carbondale, 1988—, Pontikes Ctr. for Mgmt. Info., Carbondale, 1988—. Author: Bull Moose School of Modern Management, 1987; also over 30 articles. Mem. Am. Mgmt. Assn., Data Processing Mgmt. Assn., Computer Measurement Group (best mgmt. devel. paper award 1987). Avocations: Ferrari automobiles, vintage racing. Office: Comdisco Inc 6111 N River Rd Rosemont IL 60018-5158

STANTON, JEANNE FRANCES, retired lawyer; b. Vicksburg, Miss., Jan. 22, 1920; d. John Francis and Hazel (Mitchell) S.; student George Washington U., 1938-39; BA, U. Cin., 1940; JD, Salmon P. Chase Coll. Law, 1954. Admitted to Ohio bar, 1954; chief clk. Selective Svc. Bd., Cin., 1940-43; instr. USAAF Tech. Schs., Biloxi, Miss., 1943-44; with Procter & Gamble, Cin., 1945-84, legal asst., 1952-54, head advt. svcs. sect. legal div., trade practices dept., 1954-73, mgr. advt. svcs., legal div., 1973-84, ret., 1984. Team capt. Community Chest Cin., 1953; mem. ann. meeting com. Archaeol. Inst. Am., 1983; trustee, asst. corr. sec., statutory agt. Friends of Bronze Age Archaeology in the Aegean area, 1987—. Mem. ABA (chmn. subcom. D of com. 307 copyright sect. 1987-88, 89, 90), Ohio Bar Assn. (chmn. uniform state laws com. 1968-70), Cin. Bar Assn. (sec. law day com. 1965-66, chmn. com. on preservation hist. documents 1968-71), Vicksburg and Warren County Hist. Soc., Cin. Hist. Soc., Intercontinental Biog. Assn., Lawyers Club Cin. (exec. com. 1979—, pres. 1983), Cin. Women Lawyers (treas. 1958-59, nominating com. 1976), Terrace Park Country Club. Personal philosophy: Most people are good and honest. If a person does the honorable thing, that is its own reward. Home: 2302 Easthill Ave Cincinnati OH 45208-2608

STANTON, JOHN JEFFREY, editor, broadcast journalist, government programs director, analyst; b. Wichita Falls, Tex., July 19, 1956; s. John Joseph Jr. and Joan (Marley) S.; m. Scylla Maria Silva, Jan. 6, 1981; 1 child, Damien Kristian. BS in Pub. Adminstrn. and Bus. Adminstrn., Nichols Coll., 1978; M in Pub. Adminstrn., U. Detroit, 1980. Rsch. asst. Am. Enterprise Inst., Washington, 1977; rep. aide R.I. Ho. of Reps., Providence, 1977-78; mng. editor Am. Politics, Washington, 1982, assoc. editor, 1983, corp. advisor, 1984, sr. editor, 1985-87; editor, govt. programs mgr. ENTEK, Alexandria, Va., 1988-90; govt. programs dir., cons. Tuckerman Group, Springfield, Va., 1991; comm. industry writer Arlington, Va., 1991—; program dir. TeleStrategies, McLean, Va., 1991-93; Washington corr., editorial bd. mem. Tech. Transfer Jour., 1994—; editor Tech. Transfer Newsletter; asst. to pres., info. transfer specialist Am. Def. Preparedness Assn., Arlington, 1994—; creator, co-host (radio programs) Power Breakfast, Sta. WNTR, Washington, 1987, Am. Politics Radio, 1987; frequent guest broadcast journalist Stas. WNTR, WAMU-NPR, Washington, WBAL, Balt. and Washington areas. Polit. campaign cons. to Glenn Tenney, 1992—; commr. Arlington Little League Baseball, 1993; mem. Arlington Edn. Adv. Com. Recipient Doers Honoree The Washington Times, 1988. Roman Catholic. Avocations: coaching youth league sports programs.

STANTON, LEA KAYE, elementary school educator, counselor; b. Denver, Nov. 13, 1930; d. Edgar Malcolm and Eunice Lois (Chamberlain) Wahlberg; m. Charles M. Stanton, June 15, 1952; children: Gary Charles, Thomas Edgar, Brian Paul, Craig John, William Mayne. BS, Ea. Mich. U., 1954, MA, 1977, postgrad., 1984. 1st grade tchr. Taylor (Mich.) Pub. Schs., 1952-53; 1st-8th grade tchr., 7th-9th grade counselor Dearborn (Mich.) Pub. Schs., 1972-75; tutor YWCA, Dearborn and Inkster, Mich., 1956-59; mem. sch. adv. com. Salina Elem. Sch., Dearborn, 1972-80. V.p. Dearborn Ink Human Rels. Coun., 1960-75; bd. dirs. Dearborn Interfaith Action Coun., 1960-75; union rep. McDonald Pub. Sch., Dearborn, 1985-90; mem. Vanguard Voices Cmty. Chorale, Dearborn, 1993-94; den mother Boy Scouts Am., Dearborn. Mem. AAUW (new mem. chmn.), Women's Internat. League for Peace and Freedom, Mich. Group Psychotherapy Soc., Nat. Bd. Cert. Counselors. Avocations: hiking, reading, singing. Home: Box 2383 Estes Park CO 80517

STANTON, LOUIS LEE, federal judge; b. N.Y.C., Oct. 1, 1927; s. Louis Lee and Helen Parsons (La Fétra) S.; m. Berit Eleonora Rask; children: L. Lee, Susan Helen Benedict, Gordon R., Fredrik S. BA, Yale U., 1950; JD, U. Va., 1955. Assoc. Davis Polk Wardwell Sunderland & Kiendl, N.Y.C., 1955-66; assoc. Carter, Ledyard & Milburn, N.Y.C., 1966-67, ptnr., 1967-85; judge U.S. Dist. Ct. (so. dist.) N.Y., N.Y.C., 1985—. Served to 1st lt. USMCR, 1950-52. Fellow Am. Coll. Trial Lawyers, N.Y. Bar Found.

STANTON, MARSHALL P., academic administrator, minister; b. Satanta, Kans., Oct. 15, 1935; s. Vernon and Julia (Beatrice) S.; m. Janice Marie Duryee, Dec. 20, 1956; children: Eric, Kirsten, Nathan. BA, Friends U., 1957, DD, 1986; BD, Asbury Theol. Sem., 1960; ThM, Princeton Theol. Sem., 1961. Ordained minister United Meth. Ch. Pastor United Meth. Ch., Laurel, Ohio, 1958-60, Jewell, Kans., 1961-66, Salina, Kans., 1966-67, Colby, Kans., 1971-78; dist. supt. United Meth. Ch., Hutchinson, Kans., 1978-84; pres. Kans. Wesleyan U., Salina, 1984—, also bd. dirs. Bd. dirs. Southwestern Coll., Winfield, Kans., 1978-84. Mem. Kans. Ind. Coll. Assn. (chmn. bd. dirs. 1989-90), Assoc. Colls. Ctrl. Kans. (chmn. bd. dirs. 1988-89, 95-96), Ministerial Assn. (pres. Salina chpt. 1969-70, pres. Colby chpt. 1973-74), Salina C. of C. (bd. dirs. 1986-99), vice chmn. 1996). Avocations: jogging, bicycling, radio-control model aircraft. Home: 151 Aspen Rd Salina KS 67401-3609 Office: Kans Wesleyan U Office of Pres 100 E Claflin Ave Salina KS 67401-6146

STANTON, MICHAEL JOHN, newspaper editor; b. New Britain, Conn., Mar. 30, 1944; s. John Martin and Helen (McNally) S.; m. Barbara Ann Mucha, Aug. 27, 1966; 1 child, Sean. A.B. in English, Holy Cross Coll., 1966. Reporter, editor Providence (R.I.) Jour., 1968-72; press sec. Gov. R.I., Providence, 1972-77; asst. news editor St. Louis Globe-Dem., 1977-81; news copy desk chief Detroit Free Press, 1981-83, exec. news editor, 1983-85, asst. to exec. editor, 1985-86; exec. news editor Seattle Times, 1986—. Office: The Seattle Times PO Box 70 Fairview Ave N & John St Seattle WA 98111

STANTON, PATRICK MICHAEL, lawyer; b. Phila., Sept. 8, 1947; s. Edward Joseph and Helen Marie (Coghlan) S.; m. Kathleen Ann Fama, Aug. 22, 1970; children: Cheryl Marie, Susan Elizabeth. BS in History, St. Joseph's U., 1969; JD, U. Va., 1972; MBA, Fairleigh Dickinson, 1984. Bar: Ohio 1972, U.S. Dist. Ct. (so. dist.) Ohio 1972, N.J. 1982, U.S. Dist. Ct. N.J. 1982, N.Y. 1984. Assoc. Taft, Stettinius & Hollister, Cin., 1972-80; labor counsel Union Camp Corp., Wayne, N.J., 1980-83; dir. labor relations, equal employment oppurtunity programs W.R. Grace & Co., N.Y.C., 1983-86; of counsel Shanley & Fisher, P.C., Morristown, N.J., 1986-89, ptnr., chmn. labor and employment group, 1989-95; Stanton, Hughes, Diana & Zucker, P.C., Florham Park, N.J., 1995—; adj. prof. bus. law Fairleigh Dickinson Univ.; exec. dir. Sidney Reitman employment law Am. Inn. Ct., 1993—. Pres., bd. dirs. N.Y. State Adv. Coun. on Employment Law, Inc., N.Y.C., 1985-86. DuPont scholar U. Va., 1970. Mem. ABA, N.J. State Bar Assn. (exec. com. labor employment law sect. 1989—, rec. sec. 1995—), Phi Alpha Theta, Delta Mu Delta. Roman Catholic. Home: 292 Forest Ave Glen Ridge NJ 07028-1808 Office: Stanton Hughes Diana & Zucker PC 30A Vreeland Rd Ste 340 Florham Park NJ 07932

STANTON, ROBERT JAMES, JR., geologist, educator; b. L.A., June 17, 1931; s. Robert James and Audrey (Franke) S.; m. Patricia Ann Burns, Sept. 13, 1953; children—John, Carol. B.S., Calif. Inst. Tech., 1953; Ph.D., 1960; M.A., Harvard U., 1956. Research geologist Shell Devel. Co., Houston, 1959-67; mem. faculty Tex. A&M U., 1967—, prof. geology, 1972-86, Ray C. Fish prof. geology, 1986—, head dept., 1979-83; vis. prof. U. Nuremburg-Erlangen, Germany, 1984. Co-author: Paleoecology: Principles and Applications, 1981, 2d edit., 1990. Served with AUS, 1953-55. Fellow Geol. Soc. Am.; mem. Internat. Paleontol. Union, Paleontol. Soc., Paleontol. Research Inst., Soc. Econ. Paleontologists and Mineralogists (Outstanding Paper award 1970), Sigma Xi, Tau Beta Pi. Home: 3609 Sunnybrook Ln Bryan TX 77802-3922 Office: Tex A&M U Dept Geology College Station TX 77843

STANTON, ROGER D., lawyer; b. Waterville, Kans., Oct. 4, 1938; s. George W. and Helen V. (Peterson) S.; m. Judith L. Duncan, Jan. 27, 1962; children: Jeffrey B., Brady D., Todd A. AB, U. Kans., 1960, JD, 1963. Bar: Kans. 1963, U.S. Dist. Ct. Kans. 1963, U.S. Ct. Appeals (10th cir.) 1972, U.S. Supreme Ct. 1973. Assoc. Stanley, Schroeder, Weeks, Thomas & Lysaught, Kansas City, Kans., 1963-68; ptnr. Weeks, Thomas, Lysaught, Bingham & Johnston, Kansas City, 1968-72, Weeks, Thomas & Lysaught, 1969-80, also bd. dirs., chmn. exec. com., 1981-82, Stinson, Mag & Fizzell, 1983—; chmn. products practice group, also bd. dirs., 1993-95. Active Boy Scouts Am., 1973-79; pres. YMCA Youth Football Club, 1980-82; co-chmn. Civil Justice Reform Act com. Dist. of Kans., 1991-95. Fellow Am. Coll. Trial Lawyers (state chmn. 1984-86); mem. Internat. Assn. Def. Counsel, Am. Bd. Trial Adv., Def. Rsch. Inst. (state co-chmn. 1979-90, Exceptional Performance award 1979), Kans. Bar Assn. (Pres.'s award 1982), Johnson County Bar Found. (v.p., trustee), Kans. Assn. Def. Counsel (pres. 1977-78), Kans. Inn. Ct., U. Kans. Sch. Law Alumni Assn. (bd. dirs. 1972-75). Chmn. bd. editors Jour. Kans. Bar Assn., 1975-83; contbr. articles to legal jours. Office: Stinson Mag & Fizzell 7500 W 110th St Overland Park KS 66210-2328

STANTON, RONALD P., export company executive. Chmn. Transammonia, Inc., N.Y.C., 1965—. Office: Transammonia Inc 350 Park Ave New York NY 10022-6022*

STANTON, THOMAS MITCHELL, lawyer, educator; b. Vicksburg, Miss., Sept. 30, 1922; s. John Francis and Hazel Florence (Mitchell) S.; m. Jean Aldrich Herron, Oct. 31, 1953; children: Lucinda S. Duddy, Amy S. Conklin, Thomas Herron. BS, Harvard U., 1943, JD, 1948. Bar: Ohio 1949, Wis. 1962. Pvt. practice law Cin., 1949-56; corp. atty. Kroger Co., Cin., 1957-61; with Kimberly-Clark Corp., Neenah, Wis., 1962-86; v.p., gen. counsel Kimberly-Clark Corp., Neenah, 1971-84, v.p., internat. counsel, 1985-86; ret. Kimberly-Clark Corp., 1986; lectr. litigation decision analysis Boston U., Northwestern U., U. Wis., also others, 1986—; pvt. practice law Neenah, 1987—; v.p., sec., bd. dirs. Tango, Inc.; pres., dir. Dataphon Co. of S.C. Trustee Friends of Bronze Age Archeology in the Aegean Area. Capt. AUS, 1943-46. Mem. ABA, Wis. Bar Assn., Am. Corp. Counsel Assn. (internat. legal affairs com.), North Shore Golf Club, Univ. Club. Home: 390 Park St Menasha WI 54952-3428 Office: 101 W Canal St Ste 25 Neenah WI 54956-3000

STANTON, VIVIAN BRENNAN (MRS. ERNEST STANTON), retired educator; b. Waterbury, Conn.; d. Francis P. and Josephine (Ryan) Brennan; B.A., Albertus Magnus Coll.; M.S., So. Conn. State Coll., 1962, 6th yr. degree, 1965; postgrad. Columbia U.; m. Ernest Stanton, May 31, 1947; children—Pamela L., Bonita F., Kim Ernest. Tchr. English, history, govt. Milford (Conn.) High Sch., 1940-48; tchr. English, history, fgn. Born Night Sch., New Haven, 1954-58, Simon Lake Sch., Milford, 1960-62; guidance counselor, psychol. examiner Jonathan Law High Sch., Milford, 1962-73, Nat. Honor Soc. adv., 1966-73, mem. Curriculum Councils, Graduation Requirement Council, Gifted Child Com., others, 1940-48, 60-73; guidance dir. Foran High Sch., Milford, 1973-79, career center coordinator, 1976-79, ret., 1979. Active various community drives; mem. exec. bd. Ridge Rd PTA, 1956-59; mem. Parent-Tchr. council Hopkins Grammer Sch., New Haven; mem. Human Relations Council, North Haven, 1967-69; vol., patient rep. surg. waiting rm. Fawcett Meml. Hosp., P.C., Sun City Ctr. Emergency Squad, Good Samaritans. Mem. Nat. Assn. Secondary Schs. and Colls. (evaluation com.; chmn. testing com.), AAUW, LWV, Conn. Personnel and Guidance Assn., Conn. Sch. Counselors Assn., Conn. Assn. Sch. Psychol. Personnel, Conn., Milford (pres. 1945-47) edn. assns. Clubs: Univ., Charlotte Harbor Yacht, Sun City Ctr. Golf and Racquet. Home: 237 Courtyard Blvd Apt 202 Sun City Center FL 33573-5779

STANTON, WILLIAM JOHN, JR., marketing educator, author; b. Chgo., Dec. 15, 1919; s. William John and Winifred (McGann) S.; m. Imma Mair, Sept. 14, 1978; children by previous marriage: Kathleen Louise, William John III. BS, Ill. Inst. Tech., 1940; MBA, Northwestern U., 1941, PhD, 1948. Mgmt. trainee Sears Roebuck & Co., 1940-41; instr. U. Ala., 1941-44; auditor Olan Mills Portrait Studios, Chattanooga, 1944-46; asst. prof., asso. prof. U. Wash., 1948-55; prof. U. Colo., Boulder, 1955-90; prof. emeritus, 1990—; head mktg. dept. U. Colo., 1955-71, acting dean, 1963-64; assoc. dean U. Colo. (Sch. Bus.), 1964-67; Author: Economic Aspects of Recreation in Alaska, 1953, (with Richard H. Buskirk and Rosann Spiro) Management of a Sales Force, 9th edit., 1995 (also Spanish transl.), (with others) Challenge of Business, 1975, (with M. Etzel and B. Walker) Fundamentals of Marketing, 11th edit., 1996 (also Spanish, Portuguese and Indonesian transls.), (with M.S. Sommers and J.G. Barnes) Can. edit. Fundamentals of Marketing, 7th edit., 1995, (with K. Miller and R. Layton) Australian edit., 3d edit., 1994, (with R. Varaldso) Italian edit., 2d edit., 1990, (with others) South African edit., 1992; monographs on Alaska Tourist Industry, 1953-54; contbr. articles to profl. jours. Author: Economic Aspects of Recreation in Alaska, 1953; (with Richard H. Buskirk and Rosann Spiro) Management of a Sales Force, 9th edit., 1995 (also Spanish transl.), (with others) Challenge of Business, 1975, (With M. Etzel and B. Walker) Fundamentals of Marketing, 11th edit., 1997 (also Spanish, Portuguese and Indonesian transls.), (with M.S. Sommers and J.G. Barnes) Can. edit. Fundamentals of Marketing, 7th edit., 1995, (with K. Miller and R. Layton) Australian edit., 3d edit., 1994, (with R. Varaldo) Italian edit., 2d edit., 1990, (with others) South African edit., 1992; monographs on Alaska Tourist Industry, 1953-54; contbr. articles to profl. jours. Mem. Am. Mktg. Assn., Western Mktg. Assn., Beta Gamma Sigma. Roman Catholic. Home: 1445 Sierra Dr Boulder CO 80302-7846

STANWAY, PAUL WILLIAM, newspaper editor; b. Manchester, Eng., Apr. 22, 1950; arrived in Canada, 1976; s. William and Gladys (Wright) S.; m. Erina Danyluk, May 5, 1976; children: Scott, Nicole. Reporter Nottingham (Eng.) Post, 1969-72, Express and Star, Wolverhampton, Eng., 1972-76, Free Press, Winnipeg, Can., 1976-77; city editor Edmonton (Can.) Sun, 1978-80, news editor, 1980-81, mng. editor, 1981-84, assoc. editor, columnist, 1988-90; editor Calgary (Can.) Sun, 1988-90; European bur. chief Toronto Sun Pub., London, 1990-96; editor-in-chief Edmonton Sun, 1992—. Avocations: skiing, golf, fishing, travel. Office: The Edmonton Sun, 4990 92d Ave Ste 250, Edmonton, AB Canada T6B 3A1

STANWICK, TAD, retired systems engineer; b. Severn, Md., May 4, 1916; s. Walter L. and Mary Ann (Pfeiffer); m. Wickliffe Shackleford, Dec. 16, 1941; children: Covington Philip, Wickliffe Mary, Wells Thomas. Student, St. John's Coll., Annapolis, Md., 1935, U.S. Naval Acad., 1936. Asst. to pres. and chmn. bd. Am. Machine & Foundry Co., N.Y.C., 1952-55, v.p., 1955-57; v.p., dir. Cleve. Pneumatic Industries, Inc., 1957-62; pres. Pneumo Dynamics Corp., 1959-62; pres., chmn. bd. Stanwick Corp., 1962-92. Author: Lacrosse, 1939. Bd. dirs. U.S. Bus. and Indsl. Council. Served as comdr. USNR, 1940-53. Mem. Philos. Soc. Washington, Soc. Naval Architects and Marine Engrs., Internat. Oceanographic Found., Def. Orientation Conf. Assn., Internat. Christian Union Bus. Execs., Metaphys. Soc. Am., IEEE, Philos. Soc. Am., Holy Name Soc., Phi Sigma Kappa. Clubs: U.S. Yacht Racing Union, Chesapeake Bay Yacht Racing Assn, Annapolis Yacht, CIMAV Yacht, Army and Navy. Home: 4715 Upton St NW Washington DC 20016-2369 : 1800 K St NW Washington DC 20006-2202

STANZLER, JORDAN, lawyer. AB, Harvard U., 1967; JD, U. Chgo., 1972; LLM in Taxation, NYU, 1987. Bar: Calif. 1972, R.I. 1975, N.Y. 1981. Asst. U.S. atty. So. Dist. N.Y., 1982-88, chief tax unit, 1987-88; ptnr. Anderson Kill Olick & Oshinsky, San Francisco, 1988—; lectr. ins. coverage matters. Contbr. articles to profl. jours. Office: Anderson Kill Olick & Oshinsky CT 1 Sansome St San Francisco CA 94104

STAPELL, RAYMOND JAMES, lawyer, partner; b. Buffalo, N.Y., Dec. 24, 1947; s. Howard J. and Gertrude P. (Balke) S.; m. Janice M. Rosa, Aug. 2, 1980; children: Hamilton M., Elizabeth C., Paul M. BA Polit. Sci., Le Moyne Coll., 1969; JD, SUNY, 1975. Bar: N.Y. 1976, PA. 1987, U.S. Dist. Ct. (ea. dist.) 1976. Assoc. atty. Gross, Schuman, Laub & David, Buffalo, N.Y., 1975-77; ptnr. Pusatier, Sherman & Stapell, Buffalo, N.Y., 1977-83; gen. counsel Universal Resources Holdings, Dunkirk, N.Y., 1983-85; ptnr. Birzon, Zakia & Stapell, Buffalo, N.Y., 1985-90, Stapell, Townsend, Clifford & Mussenden, Buffalo, N.Y., 1990-92, Harris, Beach & Wilcox, Buffalo, N.Y., 1992—; estate tax atty. N.Y. State Dept. Taxation, 1977-83; participating atty. Aircraft Owners and Pilots Assn., 1989—; adv. bd. mem. Monroe Title Ins. Corp., Buffalo, N.Y., 1992-93. Mem. Greater Buffalo Devel. Found., 1992-93; adv. bd. mem. Gateway Family Svcs., Buffalo, 1992-93. Capt. U.S. Army, Lt. USN, 1969-73, Vietnam. Mem. Am. Arbitration Assn. (arbitrator 1987—), Erie County Bar Assn., N.Y. State Bar Assn., Aerospace Edn. Assn. Roman Catholic. Avocations: commercial pilot, rock climbing, skiing.

STAPH, JACK A., corporate lawyer; b. 1945. BSBA, Youngstown State U., 1967; JD, Cleve. State U., 1973. Bar: Ohio 1973. Ins. mgr. Revco D.S. Inc., Twinsburg, Ohio, 1972-73, asst. sec., corr. counsel, 1974-86, v.p., gen. counsel, sec., 1986-87, sr. v.p., sec., gen. counsel, 1987—; sec. Hook-Superx Inc., Twinsburg, Hook's Drug Stores, Twinsburg, Revco Discount Drug Ctrs., Twinsburg, Superx Drug Stores, Twinsburg. Office: Revco D S Inc 1925 Enterprise Pky Twinsburg OH 44087*

STAPLE, BRUCE WILLIAM, acoustical engineer; b. Bklyn., Aug. 31, 1935; s. Carl and Sylvia (Shapiro) S. Grad., RCA Inst., N.Y.C., 1957. Lab. technician Hazeltine Elec., Bayside, N.Y., 1953-55; group leader quality RCA Victor Studios, N.Y.C., 1956-61; pres., chief engr. Allegro Sound Studios, N.Y.C., 1961-71; engring. cons. N.Y.C., 1972-74; exec. dir. Elec. Lady Studios, N.Y.C., 1974-76; v.p., gen. mgr. Soundmixer/Sound One, N.Y.C., 1976-81; sr. staff acoustical engr. Motorola, Plantation, Fla., 1983—; acoustical cons., Ft. Lauderdale, Fla., 1982—. Author: Determining Speech Intelligibility of a Transceiver in a Customers Environment, 1993. With U.S. Army, 1958-60. Mem. IEEE, Audio Engring. Soc., Acoustical Soc. Am., Am. Loudspeaker Mfrs. Assn. Achievements include patents for microphone, noise cancelling microphone, wind noise and vibration noise reducing microphone; avocations: tennis, bicycle, fishing. Office: Motorola 8000 W Sunrise Blvd Plantation FL 33322

STAPLES, JOHN NORMAN, III, lawyer; b. Durham, N.C., Aug. 1, 1946; s. Norman Appleton Staples and Elizabeth (Stewart-Richardson) Smith; m. Lila Banks James, May 18, 1968; children: Susan Banks, John William, James Nicholas. BA in English, Trinity Coll., 1968; JD, Pepperdine U., 1976. Bar: Calif. 1976. Former ptnr. Millard, Morris & Staples, Carmel; v.p. Bank of America, Monterey, Calif.; bd. dirs. Household Credit Svcs., Salinas, Calif. Bd. dirs. Monterey Peninsula United Way, 1980-83, Planned Parenthood Monterey County, 1986-90; chmn. bd. dirs. All Sts. Episcopal Day Sch., Carmel Valley, Calif., 1986-89; trustee Monterey Peninsula Mus. Art; trustee Calif. Assn. Ind. Schs., 1986-89. Capt. USMC, 1968-73, lt. col. USAFR, Ret. Mem. ABA, Monterey County Bar Assn., Calif. Bar Assn., Old Capital Club (Monterey), Pacheco Club (Monterey), Cypress Point Club. Office: Bank of Am 6th and Dolores Sts 200 E Franklin St Monterey CA 93940

STAPLES, O. SHERWIN, orthopedic surgeon; b. Boston, May 19, 1908; s. Oscar S. and Nellie E. (Barnes) S.; m. Mable Hughes, Dec. 11, 1945; children—Katherine E., Thomas H. A.B., Harvard, 1930, M.D., 1935. Diplomate: Am. Bd. Orthopaedic Surgery (examiner 1964-69). Intern Boston City Hosp., 1935-37; resident Mass. Gen., Children's hosps., Boston, 1937-39; asst. orthopaedic surgery (Mass. Gen. Hosp.), 1939-46; asst. orthopaedic surgeon New Eng. Peabody Home Crippled Children, 1939-46; chmn. orthopaedic surgery sect. Hitchcock Clinic and Mary Hitchcock Meml. Hosp., 1946-73; cons. VA Hosp., White River Junction, Vt., 1947-73, chief, orthopedic sect., 1973-81, cons. orthopedics, 1981-92; asst. orthopaedic surgery Harvard Med. Sch., 1939-46; mem. faculty, chmn. orthopaedic sect. Dartmouth Med. Sch., 1946-73, clin. prof. surgery, 1967-73, emeritus, 1973—. Asso. editor: Jour. Bone and Joint Surgery, 1961-67; Contbr. articles to med. jours. Served from capt. to lt. col. M.C. AUS, 1942-45, MTO. Mem. Aesculapian Club, N.H. Med. Soc., Grafton County Med. Soc. (pres. 1963), Boylston Med. Soc., Boston Orthopaedic Club (pres. 1960-61), Am. Acad. Orthopaedic Surgeons, A.C.S., Am. Orthopaedic Assn., New Eng. Surg. Soc., Soc. Internat. de Chirurgie Orthopedique et de Traumatologie, Am. Orthopaedic Foot Soc. (founding), Assn. Orthopaedic Chmn. (founding). Home: Hemlock Rd Hanover NH 03755

STAPLES, RICHARD CROMWELL, microbiologist, researcher; b. Hinsdale, Ill., Jan. 29, 1926; s. George Allen and Ruth Larken (Maxted) S.; children: Cynthia, Laura, Robert. BS, Colo. State U., 1950; AM, Columbia U., 1954, PhD, 1957. Asst. plant biochemist Boyce Thompson Inst., Yonkers, N.Y., 1957-61, plant biochemist, 1962-66, program dir. plant stress, 1966-76; program dir. plant stress Boyce Thompson Inst. Cornell U., Ithaca, N.Y., 1977-88, G.L. McNew scientist, 1988-92, G.L. McNew scientist emeritus, 1993—; adj. prof. plant pathology Cornell U., Ithaca, 1988—. Editor: Stress Physiology of Crop Plants, 1979, Linking Research to Crop Production, 1980, Plant Disease Control, 1981; editor FEMS Microbiology Letters, 1994—; contbr. more than 140 articles to profl. jours. Alexander von Humboldt Stiftung Sr. Scientist award, Bonn, 1981, Ruth Allen award, 1994. Fellow Am. Phytopathology Soc.; mem. Phi Kappa Phi, Beta Beta Beta, Gamma Sigma Delta. Avocations: birding, hunting. Office: Cornell Univ Boyce Thompson Inst of Plant Res 207 Klinewoods Rd Ithaca NY 14850-2230

STAPLES, RICHARD FARNSWORTH, lawyer; b. Providence, Nov. 24, 1919; s. Harold E. and Margaret (Smith) S.; m. Mary Kingsbury, June 20, 1942; children: Richard Farnsworth, Jr., Benjamin T., Edward K. A.B., Harvard U., 1941, LL.B., 1949. Bar: R.I. 1949. Ptnr. Tillinghast, Collins & Graham, Providence, 1949-81; ptnr. Hinckley, Allen & Snyder, Providence, 1981-87, of counsel, 1987—; mem. commn. on jud. tenure and discipline, 1987-93; mem. ethics adv. panel R.I. Supreme Ct., 1995—. Chmn. sch. com. Town of Barrington (R.I.), 1956-62, mem., 1957-62; mem. State Bd. Edn., Providence, 1964-69, chmn., 1968-69; pres. R.I. Hist. Soc., 1981-83. Served to 1st lt. U.S. Army, 1943-46. Decorated Bronze Star. Mem. ABA, R.I. Bar Assn., Soc. Colonial Wars, Providence Art Club, Harvard Club. Home: 180 Slater Ave Providence RI 02906-5723 also: Loon Lake Rd Freedom NH 03836-0298

STAPLETON, CAROLYN LOUISE, lawyer, clergywoman; b. West Point, N.Y., July 19, 1947; d. Carl William and Louise Maxine (Starrett) S. BA, Mich. State U., 1969; MTh, So. Meth. U., 1972, D Ministry, 1983; JD, U. Hawaii, 1987. Bar: Hawaii 1987, U.S. Dist. Ct. Hawaii; ordained deacon United Meth. Ch., 1971, ordained elder, 1973. Assoc. min. St. John's United Meth. Ch., Corpus Christi, Tex., 1972-74; Methodist campus min. Emory U., Atlanta, 1974-78; chaplain Punahou Sch., Honolulu, 1978-80; civilian contract chaplain Aliamanu Mil. Housing, Honolulu, 1981; dir. family ministries Naval Sta. Chapel, Pearl Harbor, Hawaii, 1983-84; law clerk Family Ct. (1st cir.) Hawaii, 1985, Supreme Ct. Federated States of Micronesia, 1986, Office Disciplinary Counsel, Hawaii Supreme Ct., 1986-87; dep. atty. gen. State of Hawaii, Honolulu, 1987-88, staff atty. labor appeals bd., 1988-89; exec. dir., legal counsel Ethics Commn. City and County of Honolulu, 1989—; staff assoc. for social justice and spiritual concerns Hawaii Coun. Churchs., 1990—; bd. dirs., sec. Spiritual Life Ctr., Honolulu, 1990-95; trustee 1st United Meth. Ch., Honolulu, 1986-95; mem. Hawaii dist. div. ch. and society United Meth. Ch., 1979-95; mem. nominating com. Coun. on Govtl. Ethics Laws, 1995. Contbg. author: Called from Within: Early Women Lawyers of Hawaii, 1992; prodr. slide and tape show Womanriver Flowing On: Glimpses of Some Foremothers in the United Methodist Tradition, 1981; contbr. articles to religious jours. Bd. dirs., v.p. Hawaii Lawyers Care, Honolulu, 1990—; bd. dirs. Advs. for Pub. Interest Law, Honolulu, 1986-89; del., com. mem. Hawaii Dem. Conv., 1984, 86, 88, 90, 92, 94; precinct treas. Honolulu Dem. Party, 1986—; mem. Neighborhood Bd. 5, Honolulu, 1983-89; cofounder, bd. dirs. Hawaii Women's Polit. Action League, Honolulu, 1982-85; bd. dirs. Friends Judiciary History Ctr., sec., 1991—; bd. dirs. Interfaith Network Against Domestic Violence, 1990-95. Named One of 10 Outstanding Young Women Am., Pres. of U.S., 1974; Laskey scholar women's div. bd. missions United Meth. Ch., 1971; rsch. grantee Women's Studies Coun., So. Meth. U., 1981. Mem. AAUW (bd. dirs., various state and br. offices 1979—), Phi Delta Phi (parliamentarian, historian 1985—), Alpha Delta Pi (chaplain, historian 1966—). Avocations: photography, needlework. Office: Ethics Commn City & County Honolulu 715 S King St Ste 211 Honolulu HI 96813-3091

STAPLETON, HARVEY JAMES, physics educator; b. Kalamazoo, Dec. 22, 1934; s. Herbert James and Viola Delia (Early) S.; m. Joan Eilleen Sylvander, June 22, 1957; children: Patricia Lynne, Susan Joan, Jeffrey Denis. B.S., U. Mich., 1957; Ph.D., U. Calif., Berkeley, 1961. Faculty physics U. Ill., Urbana, 1961—, prof., 1969-95, prof. emeritus, 1995—, assoc. dean Grad. Coll., 1980-95, assoc. vice chancellor for rsch., 1987-95; interim dean Grad. Coll., 1992; interim vice chancellor for rsch. U. Ill., 1992; Alfred P. Sloan fellow, 1962-64. Contbr. articles to profl. jours. Fellow Am. Phys. Soc.; mem. Phi Beta Kappa, Sigma Xi, Phi Sigma Kappa, Phi Kappa Phi, Phi Eta Sigma. Roman Catholic. Home: 3806 Gulf Of Mexico Dr #310 Longboat Key FL 34228-2706

STAPLETON, JAMES FRANCIS, lawyer; b. Bridgeport, Conn., June 30, 1932; s. James M. and Lucy V. (Moran) S.; m. Margaret M. Daly, July 13, 1957; children: James F., Mark T., Paul and Kathleen. BSS, Fairfield U., 1954; LLB, Boston U., 1957; LLM, Georgetown U., 1958. Bar: Conn. 1957, U.S. Dist. Ct. (ea. and so. dists.) N.Y. 1979, U.S. Ct. Appeals (2d cir.) 1966, U.S. Dist. Ct. Conn. 1961, Mass. 1957, U.S. Supreme Ct. 1965, U.S. Ct. Appeals, (D.C. cir.) 1958. Atty., Appellate Sect., Antitrust Div., U.S. Dept. Justice, 1957-58; assoc., ptnr. Marsh, Day & Calhoun, Bridgeport, Conn., 1958-73; city atty. City of Bridgeport, 1971-73; legis. counsel Conn. Bankers Assn., 1971-73; judge Conn. Superior Ct., 1973-78; chmn. Criminal Justice Commn., State of Conn., 1991-95; ptnr. Day, Berry & Howard, Stamford, Conn., 1978—. Mem. Bridgeport Bd. Edn., 1960-69. Fellow Am. Bar Found., Am. Coll. Trial Lawyers (chmn. state com. 1994—); mem. Am. Bd. Trial Advocates, Conn. Bar Assn. (bd. govs., ho. of dels., v.p., pres.), Fed. Bar Coun. Found. for 2d Circuit (chmn.), ABA, Bridgeport Bar Assn., Stamford-Darien Bar Assn. Home: 225 Winton Rd Fairfield CT 06430-3858 Office: Day Berry & Howard One Canterbury Green Stamford CT 06901

STAPLETON, JAMES HALL, statistician, educator; b. Royal Oak, Mich., Feb. 8, 1931; s. James Leo and Dorothy May (Hall) S.; m. Alicia M. Brown, Apr. 3, 1963; children: James, Lara, Sara. B.A., Eastern Mich. U., 1952; M.S., Purdue U., 1954, Ph.D., 1957. Statistician Gen. Electric Co., 1957-58; asst. prof. stats. and probability Mich. State U., East Lansing, 1958-63; assoc. prof. Mich. State U., 1963-72, prof., 1972—, chmn. dept., 1968-75, grad. dir., 1985-96; cons. Gen. Telephone Co. of Ind., 1961; vis. prof. U. Philippines, 1978-79. Mem. USS-Mich. Swim Com., AAU, 1976-84, chmn., 1976-78; mem. Mich. AAU Exec. Bd., 1976-81. NSF fellow, 1966-67. Mem. Inst. Math. Stats., Am. Statis. Assn. Office: Mich State U Dept Statistics East Lansing MI 48823

STAPLETON, JEAN, think-tank executive, actress. Chairwoman bd. dirs., pres. bd. dirs. Woman's Rsch. and Edn. Inst., Wash., D.C. Office: Women's Rsch and Edn Inst 1750 New York Ave NW Ste 350 Washington DC 20006*

STAPLETON, JEAN (JEANNE MURRAY), actress; b. N.Y.C.; d. Joseph E. and Marie (Stapleton) Murray; m. William H. Putch (dec.); 2 children. Student, Hunter Coll., N.Y.C., Am. Apprentice Theatre, Am. Actors Co., Am. Theatre Wing; student with, Harold Clurman; LHD (hon.), Emerson Coll.; hon. degree, Hood Coll., Monmouth Coll. Opera debut in Candide with Balt. Opera Co.; appeared in The Italian Lesson with Balt. Opera; first N.Y. stage role in The Corn is Green, Equity Library Theatre; starred as mother in Am. Gothic, Circle-in-the-Sq.; Broadway debut with Judith Anderson In The Summer House; also appeared on Broadway in Damn Yankees, Bells Are Ringing, Juno, Rhinoceros and Funny Girl; first major break in comic ingenue role as Myrtle Mae with Frank Fay in Harvey on-tour; played with nat. tour of Come Back, Little Sheba starring Shirley Booth; starred in tour of Morning's at Seven, The Show-Off, Daisy Mayme; appeared in motion pictures including Damn Yankees, 1958, Bells Are Ringin, 1960, Up the Down Staircase, 1967, Cold Turkey, 1971, The Buddy System, 1984, Klute; appeared in numerous TV shows including Studio One, Naked City, Armstrong Circle Theatre, The Defenders, Jackie Gleason show, PBS-TV appearances Grown-ups, Trying Shakespeare Co. D.C., 1994, Night Seasons, Signature Theatre N.Y., 1994, Blithe Spirit, Costa Mesa, Calif.; guest star Grace Underfire (Emmy nomination); stepmother in N.Y.C. Opera's Cinderella, 1995. U.S. commr. to Internat. Woman's Yr. Commn. and Nat. Conf. Women, Houston, 1977; bd. dirs. Women's Rsch. and Edn. Inst.; trustee Actors' Fund Am. Recipient Emmy award for best performance in comedy series 1970-71, 71-72, 78, Golden Globe awards Hollywood Fgn. Press Assn. 1972, 73, Obie award, 1990. Mem. AFTRA, SAG, Actors Equity Assn. Office: care Bauman & Hiller 5757 Wilshire Blvd Los Angeles CA 90036*

STAPLETON, JEAN, journalism educator; b. Albuquerque, June 24, 1942; d. James L. and Mary (Behrman) S.; m. John Clegg, Apr. 15, 1965 (dec. Sept. 1972); m. Richard Bright, Jan. 13, 1973 (div. 1985); children: Lynn, Paul. BA, U. N.Mex., 1964; MS in Journalism, Northwestern U., 1968. Reporter Glenview (Ill.) Announcements, 1967-68, Angeles Mesa News Advertiser, L.A., 1968-69, City News Svc., Radio News West, L.A., 1969-71; press sec. polit. campaign, 1972; instr. journalism East L.A. Coll., 1973-75, prof., dept. chair, 1975—. Author: Equal Marriage, 1975, Equal Dating, 1979; co-editor Star, Am. Yankee Assn., 1987-88. Mem. NOW (pres. L.A. chpt. 1973-74), Women in Comm., Soc. Profl. Journalists, Ninety Nines. Democrat. Methodist. Home: 3232 Philo St Los Angeles CA 90064-4719 Office: East LA Coll 1301 Avenida Cesar Chavez Monterey Park CA 91754-6001

STAPLETON, KATHARINE HALL (KATIE STAPLETON), food broadcaster, author; b. Kansas City, Mo., Oct. 29, 1919; d. William Mabin and Katharine (Hall) Foster; m. Benjamin Franklin Stapleton, June 20, 1942; children: Benjamin Franklin, III, Craig Roberts, Katharine Hall. BA, Vassar Coll., 1941. Cookbook reviewer Denver Post, 1974-84; producer, writer, host On the Front Burner, daily radio program Sta. KOA-CBS, Denver, 1976-79, Sta. WGN, Portland, Maine, 1979-81, Cooking with Katie, live one-hour weekly, Sta. KOA, 1979-88; guest broadcaster Geneva Radio, 1974, London Broadcasting Corp., 1981, 82; tour leader culinaries to Britain, France and Switzerland, 1978-85. Eng., 1978. Chmn. women's div. United Fund, 1955-56; founder, chmn. Denver Debutante Ball, 1956, 57; hon. chmn. Nat. Travelers Aid Assn., 1952-56, 93-96; commr. Denver Centennial Authority, 1958-60; trustee Washington Cathedral, regional v.p., 1967-73; mem. world service council YWCA, 1961-87; trustee, Colo. Women's Coll., 1975-80; sole trustee Harmes C. Fishback Found. Decorated Chevalier de L'Etoile Noire (France); recipient People-to-People citation, 1960, 66, Beautiful Activist award Altrusa Club, 1972, Gran Skillet award Colo./Wyo. Restaurant Assn., 1981, Humanitarian of Yr. award Arthritis Found., 1995; named Chevalier du Tastevin, 1989, Outstanding Vol. Fundraiser Nat. Philanthropy Day, 1995. Republican. Episcopalian. Clubs: Denver Country, Denver. Author: Denver Delicious: 150 Past and Present Recipes from the Queen City, 1980, 3d. edit., 1983; High Notes: Favorite Recipes of KOA, 1984. Home: 8 Village Rd Cherry Hills Village CO 80110

STAPLETON, KATHARINE LAURENCE, English literature educator, writer; b. Holyoke, Mass., Nov. 20, 1911; d. Richard Prout and Frances (Purtill) S. A.B., Smith Coll., 1932; postgrad., U. London, Eng., 1932-33. Registrar Mass. Pub. Employment Service, 1933-34; mem. faculty Bryn Mawr Coll., 1934—, prof. English and polit. theory, 1948-64, chmn. dept. English, 1954-65, Mary E. Garrett prof. English, 1964-80, prof. emeritus, 1980—. Author: Justice and World Society, 1944, The Design of Democracy, 1949, H.D. Thoreau: A Writer's Journal, 1960, Yushin's Log and Other Poems, 1969, The Elected Circle: Studies in the Art of Prose, 1973, Marianne Moore: The Poet's Advance, 1978, Some Poets and Their Resources: The Future Agenda, 1995. Mem. bd. sponsors Nat. Com. for an Effective Congress. Recipient Lindback Found. award, 1980; Smith Coll. Alumnae fellow, 1932-33; Guggenheim fellow, 1947-48; Nat. Endowment for Arts fellow, 1972-73. Mem. MLA, Renaissance Soc., Thoreau Soc., Assn. Lit. Scholars and Critics, Four Chaplains Legion of Honor, Phi Beta Kappa. Home: 229 N Roberts Rd Bryn Mawr PA 19010-2817

STAPLETON, MARLIN GLENN, lawyer; b. Walla Walla, Wash., July 19, 1932; s. Glenn Douglas and Pearl (Hatch) S.; m. Janet Louise, Oct. 29, 1955; children: Wendy Assn, Marlin G., Jr., Robin L. AA, Police Sci., 1960; BS, Western State U., Anaheim, Calif., 1969; JD, 1970. Bar: Calif., 1971. With USN, 1951-55; police officer City of Hawthorne, Calif., 1955-63; hwy. patrol, motorcycle riding instr. State of Calif., 1964-71; atty. Calif. State Bar, 1971—; arbitrator, 1984-94, judge pro tem, 1980-94, Orange County Bar, Calif.; expert witness on numerous subjects, Calif. Contbr. articles to profl. jours.; many speaking engagements in field. State bar mem. Calif., 1995—; Orange County Bar mem., 1995—; homicide panel Orange County, Calif., 1981-93. Named Class Pres. Western State U., 1970; recipient Martindale-Hubbell Highest Profl. Rating, 1988. Mem. Calif. State Bar, Orange County Bar, Pilot's Assn., Safari Club Internat. (pres. Orange County, Calif. chpt.). Avocations: bush flying, guiding people on fishing adventures. Office: 17621 Irvine Blvd Ste 114 Tustin CA 92680-3130

STAPLETON, MAUREEN, actress; b. Troy, N.Y., June 21, 1925; d. John P. and Irene (Walsh) S.; m. Max Allentuck, July 1949 (div. Feb. 1959); children: Daniel, Katharine; m. David Rayfiel, July, 1963 (div.). Student, Siena Coll, 1943. Debut in Playboy of the Western World, 1946; toured with Barretts of Wimpole Street, 1947; plays include Anthony and Cleopatra, 1947, Detective Story, The Bird Cage, Rose Tattoo, 1950-51, The Sea Gull, Orpheus Descending, The Cold Wind and the Warm, 1959, Toys in the Attic, 1960-61, Plaza Suite, 1969, The Gingerbread Lady, 1970 (Tony award 1970), 27 Wagons Full of Cotton, Country Girl, 1972, Secret Affairs of Mildred Wild, 1972, The Gin Game, 1977-78, The Little Foxes, 1981; motion pictures include Lonely Hearts, 1959, The Fugitive Kind, 1960, A View from the Bridge, 1962, Bye Bye Birdie, 1963, Trilogy, 1969, Airport, 1970, Plaza Suite, 1971, Interiors, 1978, The Runner Stumbles, 1979, Reds, 1981 (Oscar award as best supporting actress), The Fan, 1981, On the Right Track, 1981, The Electric Grandmother, 1982, Mother's Day, 1984, Johnny Dangerously, 1984, Cocoon, 1985, The Money Pit, 1986, Nuts, 1987, Made in Heaven, 1987, Cocoon: The Return, 1990, Passed Away, 1992, Trading Mom, 1994, The Last Good Time, 1995; TV films include Tell Me Where It Hurts, 1974, Cat On a Hot Tin Roof, 1976, All the King's Men, 1958, For Whom the Bell Tolls, 1959, Save Me a Place at Forest Lawn, 1966, Mirror, Mirror, Off the Wall, 1969, Queen of the Stardust Ballroom, 1975, The Gathering, 1977, Part II, 1979, Letters From Frank, 1979, Little Gloria ... Happy at Last, 1982, Sentimental Journey, 1984, Private Sessions, 1985, Liberace: Behind the Music, 1988, Last Wish, 1992, Miss Rose White, 1992. Recipient Nat. Inst. Arts and Letters award, 1969. *

STAPLETON, NIGEL JOHN, multinational information publishing executive; b. London, Nov. 1, 1946; s. Frederick Ernest John and Katie Margaret (Tyson) S.; m. Johanna Augusta Molhoek, Dec. 20, 1982; children: Henry James, Elizabeth Jane. BA with honors, Cambridge U., Eng., 1968; MA, Cambridge U., 1971. Internal auditor Unilever, Ltd., London, 1968-70; group mgr. internal audit Unilever, Ltd., 1970-73, sr. auditor, 1973-75; corp. planning mgr. Bocm Silcock, Hampshire, Eng., 1975-77; devel. dir. Bocm Silcock, 1977-80; comml. mem. N.Am. office Unilever PLC, London, 1980-

83; v.p. fin. Unilever U.S., Inc., N.Y.C., 1983-86; fin. dir. Reed Internat. P.L.C., London, from 1986; dep. chmn. Reed Internat., 1994—; CFO Reed Elsevier PLC, 1994—; chmn. exec. bd. Lexis-Nexis, 1995—. Fellow Chartered Inst. Mgmt. Accts.; mem. United Oxford and Cambridge Club. Avocations: tennis, opera, classical music, gardening. Office: Reed Internat PLC, 6 Chesterfield Gardens, London W1A 1EJ, England*

STAPLETON, RICHARD D., construction company executive; b. 1936. Grad., Lehigh U., 1958; JD, U. Conn., 1961; LLM, Boston U., 1962. Bar: Conn. 1961; CPA, Conn. Tax mgr. Peat, Marwick, Mitchell & Co., Waterby, Conn., 1961-66; from various positions to exec. v.p., sec., gen. counsel Lane Constrn. Co., Meriden, Conn., 1966—. Office: Lane Constrn Corp 965 E Main St Meriden CT 06450-6006

STAPLETON, WALTER KING, federal judge; b. Cuthbert, Ga., June 2, 1934; s. Theodore Newton and Elizabeth Grantland (King) S.; m. Georgianna Duross Stapleton; children: Russell K., Theodore N., Teryl J. B.A., Princeton, 1956; LL.B., Harvard, 1959; LL.M., U. Va., 1984. Bar: Del. Assoc. mem. firm Morris, Nichols, Arsht & Tunnell, Wilmington, Del., 1959-65; dep. atty. gen. State of Del., 1963; partner Morris, Nichols, Arsht & Tunnell, 1966-70; judge U.S. Dist. Ct. Del., Wilmington, 1970-85; chief judge U.S. Dist. Ct. Del., 1983-85; judge U.S. Ct. Appeals (3d cir.), 1985—; Dep. atty. gen., Del., 1964; mem. Jud. Conf. U.S., 1984-85. Bd. dirs. Am. Bapt. Chs., U.S.A., 1978. Baptist. Office: US Ct Appeals 844 N King St Wilmington DE 19801-3519

STAPP, DAN ERNEST, retired lawyer, utility executive; b. New Orleans, July 1, 1934; s. James Frank, Jr. and Marguerite Edna (Joubert) S.; m. Barbara Allan Wilmot, June 10, 1961; children: Marguerite Wilmot (dec.), Mary Darby, Paul Wilmot, James Andrew. B.B.A., Loyola U., New Orleans, 1955, LL.B., 1957. Bar: La. 1957. With New Orleans Pub. Service Inc., 1958-68, asst. to v.p., 1965-68; with Entergy Svcs. (formerly MSU System Svcs. Inc.), New Orleans, 1968-92; v.p., sec., asst. treas. Entergy Svcs., 1968-80; sr. v.p., 1980-92; sec. System Fuels, Inc., New Orleans, 1972-92, Entergy Corp. (formerly Middle South Utilities, Inc.), New Orleans, 1974-92, Systems Energy Resources, Inc., Jackson, Miss., 1974-91, Electec, Inc., 1984-91, Entergy Ops., Inc., 1990-91, Enterg Power, Inc., 1990-92. Trustee Mercy Hosp., New Orleans, 1973-80, pres., 1975, chmn. bd. devel., 1971-72; mem. pres.'s coun. Loyola U., 1975-85, chmn., 1980-82; adv. coun. Coll. Bus. Adminstrn., 1969-70; mem. adv. bd. Asso. Cath. Charities, 1979-82; gen. chmn. United Way Greater New Orleans, 1978, trustee, 1978-84; mem. exec. bd. New Orleans Area coun. Boy Scouts Am., 1980-85, pres., 1984-85. 2d lt. AUS, 1957. Mem. ABA, La. Bar Assn., New Orleans Country Club, Pickwick Club, Blue Key (past chpt. pres.), Alpha Sigma Nu, Delta Theta Phi. Republican. Roman Catholic. Home: 401 Bellaire Dr New Orleans LA 70124-1014

STAPP, JOHN PAUL, surgeon, former air force officer; b. Bahia, Brazil, July 11, 1910; s. Charles Franklin and Mary Louise (Shannon) S.; m. Lillian Lanese, Dec. 23, 1957. B.A., Baylor U., 1931, M.A. cum laude, 1932, D.Sc., 1956; Ph.D., U. Tex., 1939; M.D., U. Minn., 1943; grad., Army Field Service Sch., 1944, Sch. Aviation Medicine, 1945, Indsl. Med. Course, 1946; D.Sc., N.Mex. State U., 1979. Diplomate Am. Bd. Preventive Medicine, Am. Bd. Aerospace Medicine. Intern St. Mary's Hosp., Duluth, Minn., 1944; commd. 1st lt. U.S. Army, 1944; advanced through grades to col. M.C. USAF, 1957; resident Lincoln Army AC Regional, 1944-45; research project officer (Aero Med. Lab.), Wright Field, Ohio, 1946; chief lab. (Aero Med. Lab.), 1958-60; chief scientist aerospace med. div. Brooks AFB, Tex., 1960-65; chief impact injury br. (Armed Forces Inst. Pathology), Washington, 1965-67; chief med. scientist Nat. Hwy. Safety Bur., 1967-70; now mem. staff N.Mex. Rsch. Inst., La Cruces; cons. Dept. Transp., Washington, 1970-72; adj. prof. Safety and Sys. Mgmt. Ctr., U. So. Calif., 1972-76, Sys. Mgmt. Ctr., L.A., 1973-76; cons. accident epidemiology and pathology Armed Forces, Bur. Stds., NIH, Nat. Acad. Scis., Gen. Svcs. Adminstrn.; chief Aero Med. Field Lab., Holloman AFB, Alamogordo, N.Mex., 1953-58; cons. N.Mex. State U. Phys. Scis. Lab., Las Cruces, 1972—; mem. subcom. on flight safety NACA; permanent chmn. Ann Stapp Car Crash Conf.; chmn. Gov.'s Commn. Internat. Space Ctr., 1986; pres. N.Mex. Rsch. Inst., 1987. Mem. N.Mex. Gov.'s Commn. Internat. Space Hall of Fame, 1974—; mem. N.Mex. Planning Bd., 1975—; Bd. dirs. Kettering Found.; v.p. Internat. Astronautical Fedn., 1959-60. Decorated DSM with bronze oak leaf, Legion of Merit (for crash rsch.) with bronze oak leaf; recipient award for outstanding rsch. by Air Force officer Nat. Air Coun., 1951, John Jeffries award for med. rsch. Inst. Aero. Sci., 1953, Air Power award for sci. Air Force Assn., 1954, Flight Safety Found. award for contbns. Air Transp. Safety, 1954, Air Force Cheney award, 1955, Gorgas award Assn.. Mil. Surgeons, 1956, Med. Tribune award for automotive safety, 1965, award for contbns. to automotive safety Am. Assn. for Automotive Medicine, 1972, Cresson medal Franklin Inst., 1973, Excalibur award safety rsch., 1975, Cert. of Achievement, Nat. Space Club, 1976, Lovelace award NASA Assn. Flight Surgeons, 1982, Outstanding Svc. award Aviation/Space Writers Assn., 1984, Honda medal ASME, 1984, Disting. Alumnus award Baylor U., 1986, Nat. medal for tech. Pres. Bush, 1991, Nat. Medal Tech., 1991; elected to Internat. Space Hall of Fame, 1979, Nat. Aviation Hall of Fame, 1985, Safety and Health Hall of Fame, Internat., 1991, Disting. Pub. Svc. award Nat. Aviation and Space Writers Assn., 1994; ann. John Paul Stapp medal biomechanics Aerospace Med. Assn., 1993—; dedicated Stapp Found., Soc. Automotive Engrs., 1995. Fellow Aero. Med. Assn. (Liliencrantz award for deceleration research 1957), Am. Astronautical Soc., Am. Rocket Soc. (pres. 1959, Wyld award 1955, Leo Stevens medal 1956), Soc. Automotive Engrs.; mem. U.S. Mil. Surgeons Assn., Internat. Acad. Astronautics, Internat. Acad. Aviation Medicine, Civil Aviation Medicine Assn. (pres. 1968), Am. Soc. Safety Engrs. (hon.), Order Daedalians (hon.), Sigma Xi. Achievements include research rocket sled experiments reproducing aircraft crash forces to determine human tolerance limits, 1947-51. Home: PO Box 553 Alamogordo NM 88311-0553 Office: NMex Rsch Inst PO Box 454 Alamogordo NM 88311-0454 *Life is consciousness involved in thinking and doing; it is valued in terms of the quality of resulting contributions to the stream of human advancement. I live in hopes of always doing better and producing more.*

STAPP, OLIVIA BREWER, opera singer; b. N.Y.C., May 31, 1940; d. Henry and Jean Brewer; m. Henry Stapp III; 1 child, Henry. BA, Wagner Coll; studied with, Marjorie Mayer Steen, Ettore Campogalliani, Rodolfo Ricci and Oren Brown; Dr. honoris causa, Wagner Coll., 1988. Appeared as leading soprano in Truandot, Idomeno at La Scala, Milano; Tosca, Elektra, Macbeth, Tabarro at Met. Opera, N.Y.C.; Erani, Macbeth, Il Tabarro at Liceo Barcelona; Macbeth, Madame Butterfly, Tosca, Aida, Fanciulla del West, Lohengrin at Deutche Oper Berlin; Vespre Sciciliani at Grand Theater, Geneva; Nabucco, Attila, Macbeth at Zurich Oper; Salome at The Colon Theater, Buenos Aires; Cavalleria Rusticana, Anna Bolena, Tosca, Nabucco at San Francisco; Elektra Cavalleria Rusticana at Vienna Staatsoper; Idameneo at Munich Staatsoper; Carmen, The Consul, Ariadne auf Naxos, Anna Bolena, Roberto Deveraux, Cavalleria Rusticana at City Opera, N.Y.C.; Lady Macbeth, Nabucco, Turandot at Hamburg Staatsoper; Fanciulla el West, Aida, Nabucco, Turandot at the Arena de Verona; Turandot at Seoul, Korea; Turandot in N.H.K. Tokyo; Norma in Winnipeg, Edmonto, Montreal and Vancouver, Can.; Lady Macbeth in Chatelet Theater, Paris, others. Recipient Puccini award Vissi d'Arde, 1991; Fulbright scholar. Address: Columbia Artist Mgmt Inc Zemsky Green Div 165 W 57th St New York NY 10019-2201

STAPP, WILLIAM FRANCIS, museum curator, photographic historian; b. McKinney, Tex., Mar. 2, 1945; s. Richard Michael and Barbara Louise (McTee) S.; m. Carol Buchalter, Aug. 27, 1967; 1 child, Rose Anna. BA in Polit. Sci., Tulane U., 1967; MA, U. Pa., 1970, Goddard Coll., 1976. Curator photographs Nat. Portrait Gallery, Smithsonian Instn., Washington, 1976-91; sr. curator 19-20th century photography Internat. Mus. Photography, George Eastman House, Rochester, N.Y., 1991-94; head of interpretation Nat. Mus. Photography, Film & TV, Bradford, Eng., 1995—; guest scholar J. Paul Getty Mus., Malibu, Calif., 1989. Co-author: Picture It!, Robert Cornelius, Irving Penn: Master Images, 1990. Model fellow Nat. Gallery Can., 1994. Office: Nat Mus Photography Film TV, Pictureville, Bradford West Yorkshire BD1 1NQ, England

STAPRANS, ARMAND, electronics executive; b. Riga, Latvia, Feb. 28, 1931; s. Theodore and Elvira (Ulmanis) S.; m. Vija Spalvins, Sept. 25, 1955; children: Silvija, Armin, Erik. Student, Willamette U., 1949-52; BSEE, U. Calif., Berkeley, 1954, MSEE, 1955, PhDEE, 1959. Rsch. asst. dept. elec. engring. U. Calif., 1955-57; engr. microwave tube div. Varian Assocs., Palo Alto, Calif., 1957-60, engring. mgr., 1960-68, ops. mgr., 1978-78, 86-89, chief engr., 1978-86, gen. mgr. coupled cavity tube divsn., 1989-92, v.p., 1990-95; gen. mgr. microwave power tube products, 1992-95; pres. microwave power tube products divsn. Comms. and Power Inds., Palo Alto, Calif., 1995—. Contbr. articles to profl. jours., chpt. to book; patentee microwave tubes field. Fellow IEEE (electron device adminstrv. com. 1983-88). Home: 445 Knoll Dr Los Altos CA 94024-4732 Office: Comm and Power Inds M/S B-100 Microwave Power Tube Prod Divsn 811 Hansen Wax Box 50750 Palo Alto CA 94303-0750

STARBIRD, LONNIE DARRYL, producer of custom car shows, designer and builder of custom automobiles; b. Topeka, Aug. 7, 1933; s. Austin Tyler and Lucy Marie (Campbell) S.; m. Donna Mae Gray, July 5, 1953; children: Debra Marie, Clifford Dean, Cristy Mae, Rick Alan. Student, Wichita State U., 1951-54. Owner Starbird Custom Autos, Wichita, Kans., 1955-86, Starbird Prodns., Wichita, 1957-83; pres. Nat. Rod & Custom Assn., Mulvane, Kans., 1970-84, Dickens Christmas Exposition, Mulvane, 1982-83, Nat. Show Prodn., Inc., Mulvane, 1983—, Nat. Ad Agy. Inc., Mulvane, 1983—; design cons. Monogram Models, Morton Grove, Ill., 1963-67; freelance photographer leading auto mags., 1957-86; builder, curator Nat. Rod and Custom Care Hall of Fame Mus., 1996—. Starbird creations featured in Stern Mag. in Germany, 1986, Custom Car mags. in England and Australia, 1979, 83; L & M Custom Car tour of Europe - 6 Starbird creations over 20 major cities, 1986. Named Custom Car Builder of Yr., Nat. Hot Rod Assn., 1960, Constructer of Yr., Internat. Show Car Assn., 1986; recipient Master Builder award Grand Nat. Roadster Show, 1963; winner of 500 trophies in leading auto shows throughout US. Mem. Internat. Auto Show Producers Assn. (v.p. 1986). Roman Catholic. Home: RR 3 Box 180 Afton OK 74331-9003 Office: Nat Show Producers Inc RR 3 Box 180 Afton OK 74331-9003

STARCHMAN, DALE EDWARD, medical radiation biophysics educator; b. Wallace, Idaho, Apr. 16, 1941; s. Hubert V. and Lottie M. (Alford) S.; m. Erlinda Socrates, Dec. 13, 1969; children: Ann, Cindy, Julie, Mark. Student, Rockhurst Coll., 1959-61; BS in Physics, Pitts. (Kans.) State U., 1963; MS in Radiation Biophysics, U. Kans., 1965, PhD in Radiation Biophysics, 1968. Cert. Radiol. Physicist, Health Physicist, Med. Physicist. Chief health physicist ITT Rsch. Inst., Chgo., 1968-71; radiol. physicist Mercy Hosp. Inst. of Radiation Therapy, Chgo., 1968-71; prof., head radiation biophysics Northeast Ohio U. Coll. of Medicine, Rootstown, Ohio, 1971—; pres. Med. Physics Svcs., Inc., Canton, Ohio, 1971—. Author: (with Wayne R. Hedrick and David L. Hykes) Ultrasound Physics and Instrumentation, 3rd edit., 1994; contbr. numerous articles in profl. jours., chpts. in books, monographs. Fellow Am. Coll. Radiology; mem. Am. Assn. Physicists in Medicine (bd. mem. at large 1984-86, pres. Penn-Ohio chpt. 1975-76, rec. sec. midwest chpt. 1970, mem. edn. coun. 1980-83, chmn. Am. assn. med. dosimetrists task group 1976-78, mem. diagnostic radiology task group on quality control 1975—, mem. numerous other coms. 1975-83), Health Physics Soc. (chmn. summer sch. sub. com. 1977-78), Radiol. Soc. N.Am. (assoc. scis. com. 1976-86, task force chmn. 1983-86, mem. 1975-86), Sigma Xi, Kappa Mu Epsilon. Achievements include research areas including selection, quality assurance and acceptance testing of diagnostic x-ray units, design of radiology facilities; effects of tissue inhomogeneities on electron therapy, radiation atrophy in bone, large field therapy swing technique, polymer dosimetry, photon spectra through thick shields, fetal effects, ultrasound. Home and Office: 5942 Easy Pace Cir NW Canton OH 44718-2216

STARE, FREDRICK JOHN, nutritionist, biochemist, physician; b. Columbus, Wis., Apr. 11, 1910; s. Fredrick Arthur and Susan (Seidell) S.; m. Joyce Allen, Sept. 14, 1935 (dec. May 1957); children: Fredrick Allen, David, Mary; m. Helen Haxton Foreman, June 9, 1959 (dec. Feb. 1974); m. Mary Bartlett Engle, Dec. 30, 1976 (div. 1983); m. Irene Mackey Kinsey, Sept. 15, 1984. B.S., U. Wis., 1931, M.S., 1932, Ph.D., 1934; M.D., U. Chgo., 1941; MA (hon.), Harvard U., 1945; D.Sc., Suffolk, 1963, Trinity Coll., Dublin, 1964, Muskingum Coll., 1977. Asst. biochemist U. Wis., 1931-34; Nat. Research fellow Washington U. Sch. Medicine, St. Louis, 1934-35; Gen. Edn. Bd. fellow Cambridge (Eng.) U., 1935-36, Szeged, Hungary, 1936, Zurich, 1937; research assoc. Bowman Cancer Found., Wis., 1937-39; intern Barnes Hosp., St. Louis, 1941-42; asst. prof. nutrition Harvard Med. Sch. and Sch. Pub. Health; prof. nutrition, chmn. dept. nutrition, 1942-76; prof. nutrition emeritus Harvard Sch. Pub. Health, 1976—; jr. asso. medicine Peter Bent Brigham Hosp., 1942-44, asso. in medicine, 1944-50, sr. asso. medicine, 1950-60, cons. medicine, 1960-70; co-founder syndicated radio program Healthline; dir. Continental Group; former mem. food and nutrition bd. NRC; cons. nutrition Sec. War, USPHS; mem. health adv. com. Fgn. Operations Administrn.; com. health Commn. on Inter-govtl. Relations; mem. Nat. Health Edn. Com. Author: Living Nutrition, Scope Manual on Nutrition, Eat OK-Feel OK, Food for Today's Teens, Food for Fitness After Fifty; The Executive Diet, Panic in the Pantry, Your Basic Guide to Nutrition, Dear Dr. Stare: What Shall I Eat?, The Harvard Square Diet; Nutrition for Good Health, The 100% Natural, Purely Organic, Cholesterol-Free, Megavitamin, Low-carbohydrate Nutrition Hoax, Balanced Nutrition Beyond The Cholesterol Scare, Adventures in Nutrition, Your Guide to Good Nutrition; nat. syndicated columnist: Food and Your Health; former editor: Nutrition Revs. Overseer emeritus New Eng. Conservatory Music; bd. dir. Lown Cardiovascular Found., Pathfinder Internat.; co-founder, bd. dirs. Am. Coun. Sci. and Health. Recipient Pub. Svc. award U. Chgo., 1982, medal of honor Internat. Found. for Nutrition Rsch. and Edn., 1989, Disting. Svc. award U. Chgo. Med. and Biol. Scis. Alumni Assn., 1992, Excellence in Med. Nutrition Edn. award Am. Soc. Clin. Nutrition, 1993, Disting. Emeritus Prof. award Harvard Sch. Pub. Health, 1993, citation for 50 yrs. of svc. Harvard U., 1993, Am. Coun. Sci. and Health award, 1994; Fredrick John Stare professorship of nutrition established by Harvard U., 1991; John Harvard fellow, 1996. Fellow APHA, Royal Irish Coll. Physicians (hon.); mem. AMA (Goldberger award 1961), Am. Acad. Arts and Scis., Mass. Med. Soc., Am. Chem. Soc., Am. Soc. Biol. Chemists, Am. Inst. Nutrition (Elvehjem award 1969), Biochem. Soc. (Eng.), Am. Soc. Clin. Investigation, Am. Soc. Arteriosclerosis, Am. Dietetic Assn. (hon.), Group of European Nutritionists (hon.), Soc. Nutrition Edn., Harvard Club (Boston, N.Y.C.), Cosmos Club, Sigma Xi. Home: 267 Cartwright Rd Box 812085 Wellesley MA 02181-0013 Office: Harvard U Sch Pub Health 665 Huntington Ave Boston MA 02115-6021 *I never expect anyone to work any harder than I do. Be overly generous in giving credit to others. Never ask anyone to do anything you are not willing to do yourself.*

STARER, ROBERT, composer; b. Vienna, Austria, Jan. 8, 1924; came to U.S., 1947, naturalized, 1957; s. Nison and Erna (Gottlieb) S.; m. Johanna Herz, Mar. 27, 1942; 1 child, Daniel. Student, State Acad., Vienna, 1938-39, Jerusalem Conservatory, 1939-42; postgrad. diploma, Juilliard Sch. Music, 1949. mem. faculty Juilliard Sch. Music, 1949-74; assoc. prof. Bklyn. Coll., 1963-66, prof., 1966-91, Disting. prof., 1986-91, ret., 1991. Composer: Symphony 1, 1950, Symphony 2, 1951, Piano Concerto 1, 1947, Piano Concerto 2, 1952, Concerto a Tre, 1954, Viola Concerto, 1958, Ariel, 1959, Joseph and His Brothers, 1966; opera The Intruder, 1956, Concerto for Violin Cello and Orch, 1967, Six Variations with Twelve Notes, 1967, On The Nature of Things (chorus), 1968, Symphony 3, 1969; ballets The Dybbuk, 1960, Samson Agonistes, 1961, Phaedra, 1963, Mutabili, 1965, Third St. Overture, 1970, (opera), Pantagleize, 1971, Concerto Piano 3, 1972, Images of Man, 1973, Stone Ridge Set, Mandala, Profiles in Brass, 1974, The Last Lover (opera), 1975, Journals of a Songmaker; text by Gail Godwin, 1975, The People, Yes; text by Carl Sandburg, 1976, Piano Quartet, 1977; song cycle Transformations, 1978; operas Apollonia, 1978, Anna Margarita's Will, 1979; chorus Voices of Brooklyn, 1980, Evanescence, 1981; Violin Concerto, 1982, Hudson Valley Suite, 1983, Concerto a Quattro, 1984, Piano Trio, 1985, Remembering Felix, 1986, Kaaterskill Quartet, 1987, Cello Concerto, 1987, Duo for violin and piano, 1988, Angel Voices for brass and organ, 1989, Night Thoughts for chorus and synthesizer, 1990, Yizkor and Anima Eterna for flute and harpsichord, 1991, Clarinet Quintet, 1992, Episodes for Viola, Cello and Piano, 1993, Concerto for Two Pianos, 1994, String Quartet No. 2, 1995; also chamber music, choral, piano music, songs.; author: Rhythmic Training, 1969, Continuo: A Life in Music, 1987; Symphonic works premiered by N.Y. Philharmonic condrs., other leading condrs. in, U.S., abroad, ballets commd. by Martha Graham, 1961-63, CBS TV for Anna Sokolow, 1964, Lincoln Center for John Butler, 1967. With Royal Air Force, 1943-46. Recipient award Am. Acad. and Inst. Arts and Letters, 1979; Guggenheim fellow, 1957, 63; Fulbright postdoctoral research grantee, 1964; Nat. Endowment for Arts grantee, 1974, 77. Mem. ASCAP, Am. Music Ctr. (dir. 1962-64), Am. Acad. Arts and Letters.

STARFIELD, BARBARA HELEN, physician, educator; b. Bklyn., Dec. 18, 1932; d. Martin and Eva (Illions) S.; m. Neil A. Holtzman, June 12, 1955; children—Robert, Jon, Steven, Deborah. A.B., Swarthmore Coll., 1954; M.D., SUNY, 1959; M.P.H., Johns Hopkins U., 1963. Teaching asst. in anatomy Downstate Med. Ctr., N.Y.C., 1955-57; intern in pediatrics Johns Hopkins U., 1959-60, resident, 1960-62, dir. pediatric med. care clinic, 1963-66, dir. community staff comprehensive child care project, 1966-67, dir. pediatric clin. scholars program, 1971-76, prof. health policy, head health policy div., joint appointment in pediatrics, 1975—; disting. univ. prof., 1994—; mem. Nat. Com. Vital Stats., 1994—; cons. DHHS; mem. nat. adv. coun. Agy. for Health Care Policy and Rsch., 1990-94; adv. subcom. on Health Systems and Svcs. Rsch. Pan Am. Health Orgn., 1988-92, 1995—; cons. Health Care Fin. Adminstrn., 1980—. Editorial bd. Med. Care, 1977-79, Pediatrics, 1977-82, Internat. Jour. Health Svcs.,1 978—, Med. Care Rev., 1980-84; contbr. articles to profl. jours. Recipient Dave Luckman Meml. award, 1958; HEW Career Devel. award, 1970-75, Am. Pub. Health Assn. Martha May Eliot award, 1995, Disting. Investigator award, Assn. for Health Svcs. Rsch., 1995, 1st Primary Care Achievement award, Pew Charitable Trust Fund, 1994, 1st Annual Rsch. award of Ambulatory Pediatric Assn., 1990. Fellow Am. Acad. Pediat.; mem. APHA (Martha May Eliot award 1995), NAS Inst. Medicine (governing coun. 1981-83), Am. Pediat. Soc., Soc. Pediat. Rsch., Internat. Epidemiologic Assn., Ambulatory Pediat. Assn. (pres. 1980), Sigma Xi, Alpha Omega Alpha. Office: Johns Hopkins Sch Hygiene 624 N Broadway Baltimore MD 21205-1901

STARGELL, WILLIE (WILVER DORNEL STARGELL), professional sports team coach, former baseball player; b. Earlsboro, Okla., Mar. 6, 1941. Student, Santa Rosa Jr. Coll. Player Pitts. Pirates, 1962-82, coach, 1982-85; coach Atlanta Braves, 1985-88, now special assistant; player All-Star Game, 1964-66, 71-73, 78. Named Sportsman of Yr. Sports Illus. mag., 1979, co-Most Valuable Player Nat. League, 1979, Major League Player of Yr. Sporting News, 1979; inducted into Baseball Hall of Fame, 1988. Office: Atlanta Braves PO Box 4064 Atlanta GA 30302*

STARING, GRAYDON SHAW, lawyer; b. Deansboro, N.Y., Apr. 9, 1923; s. William Luther and Eleanor Mary (Shaw) S.; m. Joyce Lydia Allum-Poon, Sept. 1, 1949; children: Diana Hilary Agnes, Christopher Paul Norman. Student, Colgate U., 1943-44; A.B., Hamilton Coll., 1947; J.D., U. Calif.-Berkeley, 1951. Bar: Calif. 1952, U.S. Supreme Ct. 1958. Atty. Office Gen. Counsel, Navy Dept., San Francisco, 1952-53; atty. admiralty and shipping sect. U.S. Dept. Justice, San Francisco, 1953-60; assoc. Lillick & Charles, San Francisco, 1960-64, ptnr., 1965—; titulary mem. Internat. Maritime Com.; bd. dirs. Marine Exchange at San Francisco, 1984-88, pres. 1986-88; instr. pub. speaking Hamilton Coll., 1947-48. Author: Law of Reinsurance, 1993; assoc. editor Am. Maritime Cases, 1966-92, editor, 1992—; contbr. articles to legal jours. Mem. San Francisco Lawyers Com. for Urban Affairs, 1972-90; bd. dirs. Legal Aid Soc., San Francisco, 1974-90, v.p., 1975-80, pres., 1980-82. With USN, 1943-46, comdr. USNR. Fellow Am. Bar Found., Am. Coll. Trial Lawyers; mem. ABA (chmn. maritime ins. com. 1975-76, mem. standing com. admiralty law 1976-82, 86-90, chmn. 1990, ho. dels. 1986-90), Fed. Bar Assn. (pres. San Francisco chpt. 1968), Bar Assn. San Francisco (sec. 1972, treas. 1973), Calif. Acad. Appellate Lawyers, Maritime Law Assn. U.S. (exec. com. 1977-88, v.p. 1980-84, pres. 1984-86), Brit. Ins. Law Assn., Brit.-Am. C. of C. (bd. dirs. 1987—), World Trade Club San Francisco, Tulane Admiralty Inst. (permanent adv. bd.), Assocs. Maritime Mus. Libr. (dir. 1990-92, pres. 1992-94). Home: 195 San Anselmo Ave San Francisco CA 94127-1513 Office: 2 Embarcadero Ctr Ste 2600 San Francisco CA 94111-3823 *"How small, of all that human hearts endure,/That part which laws or kings can cause or cure!".*

STARK, BRUCE GUNSTEN, artist; b. Queens, N.Y., Feb. 17, 1933; s. Richard M. and Karen (Gunsten) S.; m. Joan Patricia Lauer, Nov. 19, 1960; children: Robert, Ronald. Student, Sch. Visual Arts, N.Y.C., 1955-58. Artist, cartoonist N.Y. Daily News, N.Y.C., 1961—. Exhibited one-man shows Art Inst., Pitts., 1968, U. Kutztown, Pa., 1970, N.Y. Bank for Savs., N.Y.C., 1971; group shows Nat. Art Mus. Sport, N.Y.C., 1971; represented in permanent collections Everett Dirksen Library, L.D. Johnson Library, Baseball Hall Fame, Cooperstown, N.Y., Basketball Hall Fame, Mass. Served with USN, 1952-54. Recipient Nat. Cartoonist Soc.'s Rueben Catagory awards for sports, 1966, 75, spl. features, 1968; Page One award for best sports cartoon, 1970, 73 N.Y.C., 71; 3d, 4th, 6th prizes Internat. Salon de Caricatures Montreal, 1966, 68, 69; Most Outstanding Achievement award Sch. Visual Arts, 1982. Original cartoons requested by Pres. Nixon, Johnson; 1st color cartoon appearing on front page of N.Y. Daily News. Home: 212 Elm Ave Melbourne FL 32951-2420 *My goals, ideas, principles and standards of conduct are all helpfully outlined for me by God in His holy word—the Bible. I really need no other source. Whatever success has come to me, I think, is because of this, and what God has done for me, through His Son, Jesus Christ.*

STARK, CHARLES HENRY, III, architectural firm executive. BS in Architecture, U. Cin., 1959; student, Toledo Mus. Art. Registered arch., Ohio, Fla., Ind., Mich., Tenn., Conn., Ill., N.C., Okla.; cert. Nat. Coun. Archtl. Registration Bds. With Richards, Bauer & Moorhead, 1959-63; assoc. Bauer Stark & Laskbrook (formerly Richards, Bauer and Moorhead), Toledo, 1963-67, sr. assoc., 1967-70, dir. design, 1970-71, ptnr., 1971-80, pres., 1980—; nat. authority on the design of schs. of music. Pres. Maumee Valley Hist. Soc., chmn. long range planning com., bd. trustees; founder Landmark Com., mem. exec. com.; bd. trustees Toledo Repertoire Theatre, mem. new bldg. com.; mem. adv. com. Owens Tech. Coll.; mem. cmty. tech. adv. com. U. Toledo; active Ohio Hist. Soc., Maumee Heritage Corridor Planning Com. Recipient 1st Pl. award Nat. Ceramic Tile Competition, Cin. Illumniating Engrings. Soc. Competition. Mem. AIA (mem. urban design com., Toledo chpt. bd. trustees, pres., v.p., treas.), Archs. Soc. Ohio (mem. legis. rev. com., bd. trustees, past chmn. design awards com.), Nat. Trust Hist. Preservation, Vistula Soc. (founder), Toledo Met. Area Coun. Govts. (mem. energy guidance com., chmn. new constrn. task force), Toledo Area Small Bus. Assn., Toledo Area C. of C., U. Cin. Alumni Assn. (pres.), Lucas County Port Authority (mem. econ. devel. focus group), Com. of One Hundred (mem. downtown planning adv. com.), The Uptown Assn. (bd. trustees, mem. devel. com.). Office: Bauer Stark & Lashbrook 1600 Madison Ave Toledo OH 43624-1451

STARK, DENNIS EDWIN, banker; b. Springfield, Ill., Dec. 24, 1937; s. Edwin C. and Ida (Fentem) S. B.S., Ill. Wesleyan U., 1959; Sanxay fellow practical ethics, Princeton U., 1959-60; M.B.A., Harvard U., 1962. Adminstrv. asst. to chmn. bd. Industrial Valley Bank, Phila., 1962-64; fin. analyst E.I. DuPont de Nemours, Wilmington, Del., 1964-65; asst. treas. Old Stone Bank, Providence, 1965-68, treas., 1968-71; sr. v.p., treas., sec. Old Stone Bank and Old Stone Corp., Providence, 1971-76; exec. v.p., chief fin. officer Old Stone Corp., Old Stone Bank, 1976-86, Dime Savs. Bank, N.Y.C., 1986-88; ptnr. Bank Mgmt. Ptnrs., N.Y.C., 1988-90; sr. v.p., CFO, corp. sec. Cen Fed Bank, Pasadena, Calif., 1990-92; exec. v.p., CFO, Corp. sec. Ea. Bank, Lynn, Mass., 1992—. Mem. bd. overseers Peabody Essex mus., Salem, Mass.; mem. vestry, treas. St. Stephen's Ch., Providence; mem. bd. visitors Ill. Wesleyan U., Bloomington; trustee Gilbert Stuart Meml., Saunderstown, R.I. Mem. Fin. Execs. Inst., Fin. Mgrs. Soc., Am. Soc. Corp. Secs., Harvard Bus. Sch. Assn. of Boston, Acacia (co-founder Ill. Wesleyan U. chpt.), Providence Art Club, Hope Club, Harvard Club (N.Y.C., Boston), Agawam Hunt, Dunes Club. Republican. Episcopalian. Avocations: philately, numismatics. Home (summer): 41 Courtway St Narragansett RI 02882-3610 Office: 21 Hersey Rd Cranston RI 02910

STARK, EDWARD JOSEPH, banker; b. Exeter, N.H., Mar. 14, 1938; s. Joseph V. and Eleanor W. (Wood) S.; m. Rebecca McKenzie (div. Aug. 1984); children: Michael T., Amy C., Elizabeth C.; m. Fran Durbin, Jan. 26, 1985. BS in Bus., U. Md., 1980. Asst. v.p., asst. sec. Am. Security Bank, Washington, 1973-81, dept. head, v.p., asst. sec., 1981-83, corp. sec., v.p., 1983—; corp. sec., v.p. MNC Fin. Inc., Balt., 1987-89, corp. sec., sr. v.p., 1989—; bd. dirs. Va. Fed. Savs. Bank. Bd. dirs. Mary Washington Found., Fredericksburg, Va., 1987—. With U.S. Army, 1960-62. Mem. Am. Soc.

Corp. Secs., Greater Washington Bd. Trade. Republican. Episcopalian. Home: 10791 Crest St Fairfax VA 22030-5171 Office: MNC Fin Inc A-9 730 15th St NW # A-9 Washington DC 20005-1012

STARK, FORTNEY HILLMAN (PETE STARK), congressman; b. Milw., Nov. 11, 1931; s. Fortney Hillman Sr. and Dorothy M. (Mueller) S.; children: Jeffrey Peter, Beatrice Ann, Thekla Brumder, Sarah Gallun, Fortney Hillman Stark III; m. Deborah Roderick. BS, MIT; MBA, U. Calif. Teaching asst. MIT, Cambridge, 1953-54; prin. Skaife & Co., Berkeley, Calif., 1957-61; founder Beacon Savs. & Loan Assn., Antioch, Calif., 1961; pres., founder Security Nat. Bank, Walnut Creek, Calif., 1963-72; mem. 93d-102nd Congresses from 9th Calif. dist., 1973—; chmn. ways and means subcom. on health 93d-103d Congresses from 13th dist. Calif., 1973—; mem., chmn. D.C. com., Ways and Means com., subcom. Health, Select Revenue Measures, joint econ. com. Bd. dirs. ACLU, 1971, Common Cause, 1971, Starr King Sch.; del. Dem. State Cen. Com.; trustee Calif. Dem. Coun. Capt. USAF, 1955-57. Mem. Delta Kappa Epsilon. Office: House of Representatives 239 Cannon Bldg Washington DC 20515-0003*

STARK, FRANCIS C., JR., horticulturist, educator; b. Drumright, Okla., Mar. 19, 1919; s. Francis C. and Maude Salena (Crowder) S.; m. Dorothy Lucille Moore, Sept. 14, 1941; children: Carolyn P. Stark Reich, Francis C. III. B.S., Okla. A&M Coll., 1940; M.S., U. Md., 1941, Ph.D., 1948. Asst. prof. horticulture U. Md., College Park, 1945-49; asso. prof. U. Md., 1949-51, prof., 1951-80, prof. emeritus, 1980—, head dept. horticulture, 1964-74, chmn. food sci. program, 1966-73, provost agr. and life scis., 1974-80, acting vice chancellor acad. affairs, 1981-82, spl. asst. to v.p., 1982—. Contbr. articles to profl. jours. Mem. Md. Gov.'s Commn. on Migratory Labor, 1959-79, chmn., 1963-76; bd. dirs. Capital Area Christian Ch., 1961-66, 89-94, pres., 1963-66; bd. dirs. Christian Ch. Facilities for aging, 1965-96, pres., 1975-80; trustee Lynchburg (Va.) Coll., 1970-79. With USAAF, 1942-45. Recipient Hon. State Farmer award Md. Future Farmers Assn., 1966. Fellow Am. Soc. Hort. Sci., AAAS. Club: Rotary. Office: U Md Dept Horticulture College Park MD 20742

STARK, JACK LEE, academic administrator; b. Urbana, Ind., Sept. 26, 1934; s. Lynn C. and Helen (Haley) S.; m. Jil Carolyn Harris, June 14, 1958; children: Janet, Jeffrey, Jennifer, Jonathan. BA, Claremont McKenna Coll., 1957; hon. degree, Redlands U., LDH, 1973. Asst. to pres. Claremont (Calif.) McKenna Coll., 1961-70, pres., 1970—. Active Pomona Valley Cmty. Hosp.; bd. dirs. Thacher Sch., Ojai, Calif. Capt. USMCR, 1957-60. Mem. Assn. Ind. Calif. Colls. and Univs. (chmn.), Ind. Colls. So. Calif. (bd. dirs.), Western Coll. Assn. (bd. dirs.). Club: California (Los Angeles). Home: 1679 Tulane Rd Claremont CA 91711-3426 Office: Claremont McKenna Coll Office of Pres 500 E 9th St Claremont CA 91711-6400

STARK, JEFFREY ROZELLE, lawyer; b. Orange, Calif., Apr. 2, 1951; s. Harwood Milton and Jean Gladys (Rozelle) S.; m. Margaret Pagano, Feb. 23, 1991; children: Tyler Chase, Jennifer Rozelle. BA, UCLA, 1972; JD, Loyola U. Bar: Calif. 1976, U.S. Dist. Ct. Calif. 1976. Atty. Cadoo, Tretheway, McGinn & Morgan, Marina del Rey, Calif., 1976-80; pvt. practice Marina del Rey, 1980-89; atty. Stark & Rasak, Torrance, Calif., 1989-92, Stark, Rasak & Clarke, Torrance, 1992—; chmn. bd. dirs. Bay Harbor Hosp. and Harbor Health Sys., Harbor City, Calif. 1989-95. Bd. dirs. Billy Barty Found., Burbank, Calif., 1990-95; founding mem. Wellness, Redondo Beach, Calif., 1990-95. Mem. Phi Beta Kappa. Home: 52 Village Cir Manhattan Beach CA 90266-7222 Office: Stark Rasak & Clarke 20355 Hawthorne Blvd Torrance CA 90503-2401

STARK, JOAN SCISM, education educator; b. Hudson, N.Y., Jan. 6, 1937; d. Ormonde F. and Myrtle Margaret (Kirkey) S.; m. William L. Stark, June 28, 1958 (dec.); children: Eugene William, Susan Elizabeth, Linda Anne, Ellen Scism; m. Malcolm A. Lowther, Jan. 31, 1981. B.S., Syracuse U., 1957; M.A. (Hoadly fellow), Columbia U., 1960; Ed.D., SUNY, Albany, 1971. Tchr. Ossining (N.Y.) High Sch., 1957-59; free-lance editor Holt, Rinehart & Winston, Harcourt, Brace & World, 1960-70; lectr. Ulster County Community Coll., Stone Ridge, N.Y., 1968-70; asst. dean Goucher Coll., Balt., 1970-73; asso. dean Goucher Coll., 1973-74; assoc. prof., chmn. dept. higher postsecondary edn. Syracuse (N.Y.) U., 1974-78; dean Sch. Edn. U. Mich., Ann Arbor, 1978-83, prof., 1983—; dir. Nat. Ctr. for Improving Postsecondary Teaching and Learning, 1991-96. Editor: Rev. of Higher Edn., 1991-96; contbr. articles to various publs. Leader Girl Scouts U.S.A., Cub Scouts Am.; coach girls Little League; dist. officer PTA, intermittently, 1968-80; mem. adv. com. Gerald R. Ford Library, U. Mich., 1980-83; trustee Kalamazoo Coll., 1979-85; mem. exec. com. Inst. Social Research, U. Mich., 1979-81; bd. dirs. Mich. Assn. Colls. Tchr. Edn., 1979-81. Mem. Am. Assn. for Higher Edn., Am. Ednl. Rsch. Assn., Assn. Study Higher Edn. (dir. 1977-79, v.p. 1983, pres. 1984, Rsch. Achievement award 1992), Assn. Innovation Higher Edn. (nat. chmn. 1974-75), Assn. Instl. Rsch. (disting. mem.), Assn. Colls. and Schs. Edn. State Univs. and Land Grant Colls. (dir. 1981-83), Acctg. Edn. Change Commn., Phi Beta Kappa, Phi Kappa Phi, Sigma Pi Sigma, Eta Pi Upsilon, Lambda Sigma Sigma, Phi Delta Kappa, Pi Lambda Theta. Office: Univ Mich 2002 Sch of Edn Ann Arbor MI 48109-1259

STARK, MATTHEW, higher education and civil rights administrator; b. N.Y.C., Jan. 27, 1930; s. Edward and Frieda S.; m. Terri L. BA, Ohio U., 1951, BS in Edn., 1951; MA in Ednl. Psychology, U. Minn., 1959; PhD in Ednl. Adminstrn. & Counseling, Western Reserve U., 1963. Counselor jr. coll. counseling office U. Minn., 1953-54, coord. residence counseling program, 1954-60; dean of students Moorhead State U., 1962-63; asst. prof., coord. human rels. programs U. Minn., 1963-70, asst. prof., coord. edn. programs, 1970-73; exec. dir. Minn. Civil Liberties Union, 1973-87; ret., 1987; cmty. legal edn. bd. dirs. U. Minn.; v.p. Friends of Pub. Edn.; mem. bd. dirs. ACLU. Pres., bd. dirs. Minn. affiliate ACLU; mem. Minn. Farm. and Migratory Labor Com.; chmn. Minn. state adv. com. U.S. Commn. Civil Rights; mem. Bicentennial of U.S. Constitution Com., State of Minn.; mem. curriculum devel. task force Minn. State Bd. Edn.; mem. Gov.'s Blue Ribbon Task Force on Human Rights Dept.; founder, mem. ERA Coalition Minn., Minn. Coalition Against Censorship, Minn. Coalition Orgns. on Sex Equity in Edn., Minn. Gay and Lesbian Legal Assistance. Mem. Am. Personnel & Guidance Assn., Freedom to Read Found. (bd. dirs.). Home: 444 Penn Ave S Minneapolis MN 55405-2059

STARK, MEREDITH ANNE, television executive; b. N.Y.C., Sept. 12, 1955; d. Edward Emmett and Florence Audrey (Howard) Stark. B.F.A., U. Ariz., 1977. Prodn. assoc. ABC Sports, N.Y.C., 1977; with press info. staff CBS News, N.Y.C., 1978-79, coordinator affiliate services, 1979-81, mgr. affiliate services, 1981-83, dir. affiliate services, 1983-85, dir. news services, 1985-86, assoc. producer CBS Morning News, 1986-87; dir. Spl. Projects, CBS TV Stas., 1987-88; exec. producer WBBM-TV, Chgo., 1988—. Mem. Am. Women in Radio and Tev, Radio TV News Dirs. Assn., Women in Communications. Home: 70 E Scott St Chicago IL 60610-2344 Office: Sta WBBM-TV 630 N Mcclurg Ct Chicago IL 60611-3007

STARK, NATHAN J., lawyer; b. Mpls., Nov. 9, 1920; s. Harold and Anna (Berlow) S.; m. Lucile D. Seidler, Nov. 28, 1943; children: Paul S., David H., Robert, Margaret J. AA, Woodrow Wilson Jr. Coll., Chgo., 1940; BS, U.S. Mcht. Marine Acad., 1943; JD, Ill. Inst. Tech., 1948; LLD (hon.), Park Coll., 1969, U. Mo., 1980; DHL, Scholl Coll., Hahnemann U., 1987. Bar: Ill. 1947, Mo. 1952. Plant mgr. Englander Co., Inc., Chgo., 1949-51; partner law firm Downey, Abrams, Stark & Sullivan, Kansas City, Mo., 1952-53; v.p. Rival Mfg. Co., Kansas City, 1954-59; sr. v.p. ops. Hallmark Cards, Inc., Kansas City, 1959-74; dir. Hallmark Cards, Inc., 1960-74; pres., chmn. Crown Center Redevel. Corp., 1971-74; sr. vice chancellor health scis. Schs. Health Professions, U. Pitts., until 1984, sr. vice chancellor emeritus, 1984—, also pres. Univ. Health Center, 1974-79, 81—, also prof. Grad. Sch. Public Health; undersec. HEW, Washington, 1979-81; of counsel Fort & Schlefor, Washington; lawyer, treas., pres., CEO Nat. Acad. of Social Ins., 1992-95; dir. ERC Corp., 1970-79, Hallmark Continental Ltd., Ireland, 1971-73; mem. exec. bd. Nat. Bd. Med. Contbr. articles to prof. and bus. jours. Legal counsel Lyric Opera Theatre, Kansas City, Mo., 1958-72; mem. com. undergrad. med. edn. AMA, 1966-73; vice chmn. health ins. benefits adv. com. NEW, 1965-70; sec. task force on Medicaid, 1960-70, chmn. adv. commn. incentive reimbursement experimentation, 1968-70; chmn. capital investment conf. HEW-HRA, 1976; mem. liaison com. Am. Assn. Med. Colls.-AMA, 1970-74; chmn. task force life-long learning opportunities Kellogg Found., 1975-77; chmn. cmty. hosp.-med. staff group practice program Robert Wood Johnson Found., 1974-79; mem.-at-large Nat. Bd. Med. Examiners; mem. bd. Blue Cross Western Pa., 1975-79, Am. Nurses Found., 1975-77, Health Sys. Agy. SW Pa., 1976—; v.p. Kansas City Philharm. Assn., 1954; sec. Eddie Jacobson Meml. Found., 1960—; mem. tech. bd. Milbank Meml. Fund, 1976-78; pres., chmn. Kansas City Gen. Hosp. and Med. Ctr., 1962-74; trustee Allegheny Found., 1975—, Pitts. Ballet Theater, 1977-79, Pitts. Chamber Opera Theater, 1978—; mem. VA Scholars Bd. Governance, 1979—; hon. fellow, trustee Hastings Ctr., 1981; v.p. Pitts. Opera; adv. bd. of trustees St. Joseph Coll., trustee, 1994. Recipient Chancellor's medal U. Mo. at Kansas City, 1969; Pro-Meritus award Rockhurst Coll., 1967; Layman award; AMA, 1974. Fellow Am. Acad. Pediatrics (hon.); mem. Inst. Medicine of NAS (coun. 1973-76), Am. Hosp. Assn. (hon. mem., Trustee award 1968), Am. Coll. Hosp. Adminstrs., Nat. Acad. Social Ins. (bd. trustees, pres. 1992-94). Home: 4343 Westover Pl NW Washington DC 20016-5554

STARK, NELLIE MAY, forest ecology educator; b. Norwich, Conn., Nov. 20, 1933; d. Theodore Banjamin and Dorothy Josephine (Pendleton) Beetham; m. Oscar Elder Stark, Oct. 1962 (dec.). BA, Conn. Coll., 1956; AM, Duke U., 1958, PhD, 1962. Botanist Exptl. Sta., U.S. Forest Svc., Old Strawberry, Calif., 1958-66; botanist, ecologist Desert Rsch. Inst., Reno, Nev., 1966-72; prof. forest ecology Sch. Forestry, U. Mont., Missoula, 1972-92; pvt. cons. Philomath, Oreg.; pres. Camas Analytical Lab., Inc., Missoula, 1987-92. Contbr. articles to profl. jours. Named Disting. Dau. Norwich, Conn., 1985; recipient Conn. award Conn. Coll., 1986, 54 grants. Mem. Ecol. Soc. Am. (chair ethics com. 1974, 76), Soc. Am. Foresters (taskforce 1987-88).

STARK, NORMAN, secondary school educator; b. Bronx, N.Y., Sept. 15, 1940; s. Martin and Margaret (Neuman) S.; m. Betty Joanne Kelton, Sept. 4, 1994; 1 child, Michelle Allison. Student, Newark State Coll., Union, 1963-69. Creative writing tchr., acting tchr., singles forum tchr., film tchr. Plantation (Fla.) High Sch., 1988; Hoover Mid. Sch. and Palm Bay H.S., Melbourne, Fla., 1995. Editor West Palm Beach News, 1979; screenplay writer, actor. With U.S. Army, 1963-69. Avocations: reading, puzzles, movies. Home: 2732 Locksley Rd Melbourne FL 32935

STARK, RAY, motion picture producer. Student, Rutgers U. Publicity agt., lit. agt.; talent agt. Famous Artist Agy., to 1957; co-founder Seven Arts Prodn. Co., 1957; ind. film producer, 1966—. Producer : (films) The World of Suzie Wong, 1960, The Night of the Iguana, 1964, Reflections in a Golden Eye, 1967, Funny Girl, 1968, The Owl and the Pussycat, 1970, Fat City, 1972, The Way We Were, 1973, Funny Lady, 1975, The SUnshine Boys, 1975, Murder By Death, 1976, Smokey and the Bandit, 1977, The Goodbye Girl, 1977, The Cheap Detective, 1978, California Suite, 1978, Chapter Two, 1979, The Electric Horseman, 1979, Seems Like Old Times, 1980, Annie, 1982, Blue Thunder, 1983, Nothing in Common, 1986, Peggy Sue Got Married, 1986, The Secret of My Success, 1987, Biloxi Blues, 1988. Steel Magnolias, 1989, Revenge, 1990, Lost in Yonkers, 1993, Barbarians at the Gate, 1993 (Emmy award Outstanding Made to Television Movie 1993), Mr. Jones, 1993, Dr. Jekyll and Ms. Hyde, 1995, Mariette in Ecstacy, 1995, The Gillian on Her 37th Birthday, 1996, Harriet the Spy, 1996. Recipient Thalberg award Acad. Motion Picture Arts and Scis., 1980. Office: Hepburn Bldg W 10202 W Washington Blvd Culver City CA 90232-3119

STARK, RICHARD BOIES, surgeon, artist; b. Conrad, Iowa, Mar. 31, 1915; s. Eugene and Hazel (Carson) S.; m. Judy Thornton, Oct. 31, 1967. A.B., Stanford U., 1936; postgrad., U. Heidelberg, 1936-37; M.D., Cornell U., 1941. Diplomate Am. Bd. Plastic Surgery (pres. 1967-68). Intern Peter Bent Brigham Hosp., Boston, 1941-42; asst. resident surgery Childrens Hosp., Boston, 1942; plastic surgeon Northington Gen. Hosp., Ala., 1945-46, Percy Jones Gen. Hosp., Mich., 1946; postwar fellow anatomy and embryology Stanford U., 1946-47; from asst. resident to resident in head and neck surgery VA Hosp., Bronx, N.Y., 1947-50; asst. resident, resident surgery, plastic, head and neck and gen. surgery N.Y. Hosp., 1947-50; instr. surgery Cornell U., 1950-52, asst. prof., 1952-55, assoc. prof., 1955; asst. attending surgeon N.Y. Hosp., 1950-55; asst. prof. surgery Columbia U., 1955-58, assoc. prof., 1958-73, prof. clin. surgery, 1973—; assoc. attending surgeon St. Luke's Hosp., N.Y.C., 1955-58, founding attending surgeon dept. plastic surgery, 1958—; founder dept. plastic surgery, 1955; cons. Walter Reed Med. Ctr., 1970-77. Author: Plastic Surgery, 1962, Cleft Palate, 1968, Plastic Surgery at the New York Hospital 100 Years Ago, 1952, Aesthetic Plastic Surgery, 1980, Total Facial Reconstruction, 1985, Plastic Surgery of the Head and Neck, 1986; contbr. numerous chpts. to books, articles to profl. jours.; assoc. editor: Plastic Reconstructive Surgery, 1977-82; founding editor: Annals Plastic Surgery, 1978-81; 20 one-person art shows, 1946—. Chmn. Medico Adv. Bd., 1976-77; mem., v.p. CARE Bd.; v.p. Wellborn Found., N.Y.C. Served with AUS, 1943-46. Decorated Bronze Star (U.S.); Medal of Honor (2) (Vietnam); cavallero Order of San Carlos (Colombia), Dieffenbach medal (Berlin), Gold medal Nat. Inst. Social Scis. Fellow ACS; mem. Am. Assn. Plastic Surgeons, Am. Soc. Plastic and Reconstructive Surgery (pres. 1966, Spl. Achievement award), Found. Am. Soc. Plastic and Reconstructive Surgery (pres. 1961-65), Am. Surg. Assn., Soc. Univ. Surgeons, French Soc. Plastic Surgeons, Brasilian Soc. Plastic Surgeons, Colombian Soc. Plastic Surgeons, Argentina Soc. Plastic Surgeons, Brit. Assn. Plastic Surgery, Peruvian Acad. Surgeons, N.Y. Surg. Soc., N.Y. Acad. Medicine (pres. Friends Rare Book Room), Plastic and Reconstructive Surgery (sec., pres. 1966), N.Y. State Med. Soc. (pres., sec., med. history), N.Y. Regional Soc. Plastic and Reconstructive Surgery (pres. 1064-65), Halsted Soc. (pres. 1973-74), James IV Assn. Surgeons, Am. Soc. Aesthetic Plastic Surgery (pres. 1974-75), Nat. Arts Club (exhibiting mem.), Century Club (profl. artist), Artist Fellowship. Home: 35 E 75th St New York NY 10021-2761

STARK, ROBERT MARTIN, mathematician, civil engineer, educator; b. N.Y.C., Feb. 6, 1930; s. Alexander and Julia (Gross) S.; m. Carol LaSage, Jan. 13, 1955 (dec. Mar. 1988); children: Bradley R., Timothy D., Steven M., Candice B. AB, Johns Hopkins U., 1951; MA, U. Mich., 1952; PhD, U. Del., 1965. Rsch. scientist Bausch and Lomb, Rochester, N.Y., 1955; instr. Rochester Inst. Tech., 1956-57; asst. dean engring., asst. prof. math. Cleve. State U., 1957-62; instr. U. Del., 1962-64, asst. prof. civil engring. and ops. rsch., 1964-68, assoc. prof., 1968-76, prof., 1976—; pres., cons. applied sci. R.M. Stark & Co., Inc.; vis. assoc. prof. MIT, 1972-73; chmn. grad. program in ops. rsch.; cons. in field. Author: (with R.L. Nicholls) Mathematical Foundations for Design: Civil Engineering Systems, 1972; (with R.H. Mayer, Jr.) Quantitative Construction Management: Uses of Linear Optimization, 1983; (with R. Engelbrecht-Wiggans and M. Shubik) Auctioning, Bidding and Contracting, 1983; (with C. Sloyer, et al) Contemporary Applied Mathematics Series, 1987, Mathagrams, 1996. Bd. dirs. Geriatrics Svcs. Del., Inc., 1989—, Wilmington Sr. Ctr., 1994—, Meals on Wheels Found.; bd. dirs. Del. Acad. Sci., 1990—, pres., 1994-96; bd. dirs., v.p. White Clay Watershed Assn., 1992—; commr. Del. Heritage Commn., 1990—. Grantee Office Naval Rsch., 1974-81, NSF, 1969-70, U.S. Army Rsch. Office, 1966-68. Mem. AAAS, ASCE, Nat. Coun. Tchrs. Math., Inst. Mgmt. Sci., Ops. Rsch. Soc. Am., Phila. Ops. Rsch. Soc. (pres. 1970). Avocations: research, publs. ops. rsch., applied probability. Home: One Fox Ln Newark DE 19711 Office: U Del Dept Math Sci Newark DE 19716

STARK, ROHN TAYLOR, professional football player; b. Mpls., May 4, 1959; m. Ann Stark; 1 child, Rohn Jr. BS in Finance, Fla. State U., 1982. With Indpls. Colts, 1982-84; punter Indpls. Colts (formerly Balt. Colts), 1984—. Punter on the Sporting News Coll. All-Am. Team, 1981, NFL All-Pro team, 1992; played in Pro Bowl 1985, 86, 90, 92.

STARK, S. DANIEL, JR., convention and visitors bureau executive; b. Port Hueneme, Calif., Mar. 26, 1953; s. S. Daniel and Eloise Marie (Fisher) S.;1 child, Kaitlyn Elizabeth. BS, Calif. Poly. U., Pomona, 1981; cert. in exec. mgmt., Claremont Grad. Sch., 1989, MA in Mgmt., 1992. Driver-guide San Diego Wild Animal Pk./Zool. Soc. San Diego, Escondido, Calif., 1974-76; attractions host Disneyland div. The Walt Disney Co., Anaheim, Calif., 1976-80; mgmt. intern Disneyland div. The Walt Disney Co., Anaheim, 1981; supr. ops. Disneyland div. The Walt Disney Co., Anaheim, Calif., 1981-82, area supr. ops., dept. mgr., 1982-87; mgmt. cons. S.D. Stark, Jr., Redlands, Calif., 1987—; dir. mktg. Ramada Express Hotel & Casino, Laughlin, Nev., 1988-89; exec. dir. San Bernardino (Calif.) Conv. and Visitors Bur., 1989—; cons. Hemmeter Devel. Corp., Honolulu, 1985, Calif. Authority Racing Fairs, Sacramento, 1987-88, USIA for Latvian Ministry Transp., tourism div., 1992, U.S. Bur. Land Mgmt., tourism mgmt. project U. Alaska Sch. Mgmt.; adj. prof. Sch. Bus. and Pub. Adminstrn., Calif. State U., San Bernardino, 1992-93. Bd. dirs. Leadership So. Calif., 1993—, grad. pub. affairs tng., 1993; congl. appointee del. White House Conf. on Travel & Tourism, 1995; mem. regional econ. strategies consortium So. Calif. Assn. Govts. Recipient resolution Calif. Assembly, 1989, San Bernardino County Bd. Suprs., 1989, City of San Bernardino Mayor and Coun., 1989, Calif. Senate, 1989; selected as one of 1991 Up and Coming Young Bus. Leaders in San Bernardino County; named one of Inland Empire Bus. All Stars, 1991; recipient World Champion Trail Horse award Am. Jr. Quarter Horse Assn., 1972. Mem. Am. Horse Shows Assn. (life), Am. Quarter Horse Assn (life), Assn. Travel Mktg. Execs., Internat. Assn. Conv. and Visitors Burs. (cert. comm., conv. mktg., tourism mktg.), Pub. Rels. Soc. Am. (bd. dirs. Calif. Inland Empire chpt. 1990-95), Travel Industry Assn. Am., Calif. Festivals & Events Assn. (bd. dirs. 1994—), Inland Empire Tourism Coun. (bd. dirs. 1996—, exec. com. 1996—, chair tourism authority com. 1996—), Hospitality Sales and Mktg. Assn. Internat., Calif. Travel Industry Assn., Tourism Assn. So. Calif. (bd. dirs. 1990-95, vice chair 1992-95), Western Assn. Convs. and Vis. Bur. (chmn. Calif. coun. 1992-94), FarmHouse Fraternity (internat. bd. dirs. 1986-94, v.p. 1990-92, Snyder Alumni award 1984). Avocations: boating, fishing, films, equestrian competition. Office: San Barnardino Conv and Visitors Bur 201 N E St Ste 103 San Bernardino CA 92401-1520

STARK, SUSAN R., film critic; b. N.Y.C., July 9, 1940; d. Albert A. and Lillian H. (Landau) Rothenberg; m. Allan F. Stark, June 26, 1968 (div. 1983); children: Allana Fredericka, Paula-Rose. B.A., Smith Coll., 1962; M.A.T., Harvard U., 1963. Film critic Detroit Free Press, 1968-79, Detroit News, 1979—. Mem. Phi Beta Kappa. Office: Detroit News 615 W Lafayette Blvd Detroit MI 48226-3124

STARK, THOMAS MICHAEL, state supreme court justice; b. Riverhead, N.Y., Feb. 13, 1925; s. John Charles and Mary Ellen (Gaynor) S.; m. Jane Claire Crabtree, Dec. 30, 1954; children: Elizabeth Mary, Ellen Gaynor. BS cum laude, Holy Cross Coll., 1945; LLB, Harvard U., 1949. Bar: N.Y., 1950. Assoc. Zaleski & Jablonka, Riverhead, 1949-51; sole practice Riverhead, 1951-63, town atty., 1953, justice of peace, mem. town bd., 1956-57; mem. Riverhead Bd. Edn., Riverhead, 1960-63; judge county ct. County of Suffolk, Riverhead, 1963-68; justice 10th Jud. Dist. Supreme Ct. N.Y., Riverhead, 1969—, assoc. justice appellate term, 1985—; supervising judge Suffolk County Superior Criminal Cts., Riverhead, 1978-92; panel discussion leader Ann. Conf. N.Y. State Trial Judges, 1970-81; chmn. criminal law subcom. N.Y. State Trial Judges Benchbook, 1970-75; vice chmn. com. on criminal jury instrns. N.Y. State Office Ct. Adminstrn., 1975—; lectr. N.Y. State Office Ct. Adminstrn., 1977-87; mem. N.Y. State Ct. Facilities Task Force, 1980-84. Mem. exec. bd., v.p. Suffolk County council Boy Scouts Am., 1955-58; mem. exec. com., co-leader Riverhead, Suffolk County Republican Com., 1961-62. Served as ensign USNR, World War II. Recipient Silver Beaver award Boy Scouts Am., 1957, Disting. Eagle Scout, 1974; named Judge of Yr., Suffolk County Criminal Bar Assn., 1984. Mem. ABA (jud. adminstrn. sect.), N.Y. State Bar Assn. (presiding officer jud. sect. 1988-89, ho. dels. 1989-90), Suffolk County Bar Assn. (sec. 1959-62, 3d v.p. 1962-63). Home: Bay Woods Aquebogue NY 11931 Office: Suffolk County Criminal Bldg Riverhead NY 11901

STARKE, EDGAR ARLIN, JR., metallurgist, educator; b. Richmond, Va., May 10, 1936; s. Edgar Arlin and Mary Louise (Stein) S.; m. Donna Lee Frazier, June 10, 1961; children—John Arlin, Karen Lee. B.S. in Metall. Engring., Va. Poly. Inst., 1960; M.S., U. Ill., 1961; Ph.D. in Metall. Engring., U. Fla., 1964. Metallurgist Savannah River Lab., Aiken, S.C., 1961-62; asst. prof. Ga. Inst. Tech., Atlanta, 1964-68, assoc. prof. metallurgy, 1968-72, prof., 1972-82, dir. Fracture and Fatigue Research Lab., 1978-82; Earnest Oblesby prof. materials sci. U. Va., Charlottesville, 1983—, mem. staff Ctr. Advanced Studies, 1983-84, dean Sch. Engring. and Applied Sci., 1984-94; univ. prof., Oglesby prof. materials sci. and engring., 1994—; vis. scientist Oak Ridge Nat. Lab., 1967, Max-Planck Institut for Metallforschung, Stuttgart, Fed. Republic Germany, 1971; cons. Bell Tel. Labs., 1973-75, Lockheed Ga. Rsch. Lab., 1965-82, Southwire Co., 1967-82, Reynolds Metals Co., 1983-88, Northrop Corp., 1983—, Lockheed Missiles Space Co., 1983—, Kaiser Aluminum, 1984-86, GE, 1989—; mem. aeronautic adv. com. NASA, 1990-94, AGARD Structures and Materials panel, 1992—. Contbr. articles to profl. jours. Served with U.S. Army, 1954-56. Fellow ASM Internat.; mem. Am. Soc. Metals (sec. Atlanta chpt. 1974-75), AIME (sec.-treas. Ga. chpt. 1965-66, v.p. 1967, pres. chpt. 1968, sect. non-ferrous metallurgy com. 1973-74, vice chmn. 1974-75, chmn. 1976-78, vice chmn. program metals sci. bd. dirs. 1978-79), NRC (natural materials adv. bd.), Sigma Xi (sec. Ga. Inst. Tech. chpt. 1974-75), Tau Beta Pi, Alpha Sigma Mu, Omicron Delta Kappa, Phi Delta Epsilon. Home: RR 5 Box 331A Charlottesville VA 22901-8950

STARKEY, LUCILLE A., music educator; b. East Liverpool, Ohio; d. William Oscar and Goldie May (Cline) Mansfield; m. James Richard, Apr. 6, 1968; 1 child, Karen Michelle. BA, Northland Coll., 1966. Tchr. 1st grade Monroe Local Sch., Graysville, Ohio, 1967-68; tchr. music Caldwell (Ohio) Ex Village, 1969-71, Switzerland of Ohio, Woodsfield, 1971—. Avocations: archery - tournament and 3D. Home: 45518 Henthorn Rd Woodsfield OH 43793-9705 Office: Woodsfield Elem 118 N Paul St Woodsfield OH 43793-1151

STARKMAN, GARY LEE, lawyer; b. Chgo., Sept. 2, 1946; s. Oscar and Sara (Ordman) S. AB, U. Ill., 1968; JD cum laude, Northwestern U., 1971. Bar: Ill. 1971, U.S. Dist. Ct. (no. dist.) Ill. 1972, U.S. Ct. Appeals (7th cir.) 1972, U.S. Supreme Ct. 1974, Trial Bar U.S. Dist. Ct. (no. dist.) Ill. 1982, U.S. Ct. Appeals (3d cir.) 1984, U.S. Ct. Appeals (D.C. cir.) 1984. Asst. U.S. Atty. No. Dist. Ill., 1971-75; gen. counsel, dir. research Citizens for Thompson Campaign Com., 1975-77; counsel to Gov. of Ill., 1977-81; ptnr. Ross & Hardies, Chgo.; mem. admissions com. U.S. Dist. Ct. (no. dist.) Ill. Chmn. state agys. divsn. Jewish United Fund Met. Chgo., 1978-81; chmn. Ill. Racing Bd., 1991—; bd. dirs. Internat. Assn. Racing Commn., 1992-94; mem. community adv. bd. Jr. League of Chgo., 1979-83. Recipient John Marshall award for appellate litigation, Atty. Gen. U.S., 1974, Nat. Svc. award Tau Epsilon Phi, 1968; named to Ten Outstanding Young Citizens, Chgo. Jr. C. of C., 1978. Mem. ABA (litigation sect.), Chgo. Bar Assn. (constl. law com.), Decalogue Soc., Northwestern U. Law Alumni Assn. Co-author textbook: Cases and Comments on Criminal Procedure, 1974, 2d edit., 1980, 4th edit., 1992; contbr. writings to profl. publs., book revs. to periodicals. Office: Ross & Hardies 150 N Michigan Ave Ste 2500 Chicago IL 60601-7525

STARKS, ELIZABETH VIAL, gifted, talented education educator; b. Chgo., Feb. 2, 1943; d. George McNaughton and Mary Margaret (Beatty) Vial; m. Edward Arnold Kearns, June 6, 1964 (div. 1978); m. Kevin James Starks, Aug. 4, 1979; children: Lauren Elizabeth Kearns, Jason Edward Kearns. BA, U. Ariz., 1964; MA, Denver U., 1994. Tchr. grade 6 Tucson Pub. Schs., 1965-66; gifted/talented tchr. grades 4-6 Sch. Dist Re-3(J), Keenesburg, Colo., 1988—; gifted/talented coord. RE-3(J) Sch. Dist., 1992—, social studies curriculum com., 1993—, technology com., 1993-94. Bd. dirs. A Woman's Place (safe house), Greeley, Colo., 1994—; chmn. adv. bd. South County A Woman's Place, Ft. Lupton, Colo., 1994—; bd. dirs. Weld Mental Health Ctr., Greeley, 1984-87; County Dem. chairperson, Greeley, 1976-79. Mem. ASCD, ACLU, Nat. Assn. Gifted and Talented, Colo. Assn. Gifted and Talented, Phi Delta Kappa, Kappa Kappa Gamma. Avocations: reading, golf, swimming, gourmet cooking, theatre. Office: Hudson Elem Sch PO Box 278 Hudson CO 80642-0278

STARKS, FLORENCE ELIZABETH, retired special education educator; b. Summit, N.J., Dec. 6, 1932; d. Edward and Winnie (Morris) S. BA, Morgan State U., 1956; MS in Edn., CUNY, 1962; postgrad., Fairleigh Dickinson U., 1962-63, Seton Hall U., 1963, Newark State Coll. Cert. blind and visually handicapped and social studies tchr., N.J. Tchr. adult edn. Newark Bd. of Edn.; ret., 1995; tchr. N.Y. Inst. for Edn. of the Blind, Bronx; developer first class for multiple handicapped blind children in pub. sch. system, Newark, 1960; ptnr. World Vision Internat. Mem. ASCD, AFL-CIO, AAUW, Coun.

Exceptional Children, Nat. Assn. Negro Bus. and Profl. Women's Club Inc., N.J. Edn. Assn., Newark Tchrs. Assn., Newark Tchrs. Union-Am. Fedn. Tchrs., World Vision Internat. (ptnr.). Home: 4 Park Ave Summit NJ 07901-3942

STARKS, FRED WILLIAM, chemical company executive; b. Millford, Ill., Aug. 16, 1921; s. Otis Earl and Evelyn Viola S.; m. Minnie Jane Reynolds, Sept. 4, 1946; children: David F., Steven J., Daniel J. B.S., U. Ill., 1943, M.S., 1947; Ph.D., U. Nebr., 1950. Supr., U.S. Rubber Co., Torrance, Calif., 1943-44; supr. DuPont, Niagara Falls, N.Y., 1950-57; pres. Starks Assocs., Inc., Buffalo, N.Y., 1957-89, chmn., 1989—; spl. lectr. U. Buffalo, 1959-63. Lt. (j.g.) USNR, 1944-46. Avery fellow, 1948-49; USPHS fellow, 1949-50. Mem. Am. Chem. Soc., N.Y. Acad. Sci., Am. Inst. Chemists, Sigma Xi. Clubs: Buffalo, Cosmos, Chemists. Patentee in field. Home: 742 Highland Ave Buffalo NY 14223-1645 Office: Starks Assocs Inc 1280 Niagara St Buffalo NY 14213-1503

STARKS, RICHARD, newspaper publishing executive. V.p. advertising The Dallas Morning News, Tex. Office: The Dallas Morning News Communication Ctr Young & Houston Sts Dallas TX 75202

STARKS, SCOTT ALLEN, electrical and computer engineering educator; b. Houston, Dec. 5, 1951; s. Bernie Woodwell and Jewell Dean (Jones) S. BSEE, U. Houston, 1973; PhD in Elec. Engring., Rice U., 1978. Asst. prof. elec. engring. Auburn (Ala.) U., 1977-81; assoc. prof. computer sci. and engring. U. Tex., Arlington, 1981-86; prof. computer sci. East Tex. State U., Commerce, 1987-89; prof. elec. engring. U. Tex., El Paso, 1989—, assoc. dean, 1994-95, interim dean, 1995; dir. U. Tex. System AMP, 1992-95, NASA CTr. for Excellence, 1995—; sr. rsch. scientist NASA Ames Rsch. Ctr., Moffett Field, Calif., 1985-86; subpanel chmn. NASA Automation Robotics Panel, San Diego, 1984-89; cons. Univs. Space Rsch. Assn., Washington, 1987-89. Contbr. more than 100 articles to profl. jours. Grantee Electronics Sys. Command/USN, 1978-81, Johnson Space Ctr./NASA, 1990—, Ames Rsch. Ctr./NASA, 1983-86, 90—, NSF, 1992—. Mem. IEEE (sr.; program chmn. El Paso sect. 1990-92, treas. 1989-90), Am. Soc. Engring. Edn. (div. chmn. 1990-92, program chmn. 1988-89, Disting. Teaching and Svc. award 1995), Upsilon Pi Epsilon (Tchr. of Yr. 1986). Achievements include research in digital signal processing, pattern recognition, remote sensing, and automation and robotics. Home: 842 Espada Dr El Paso TX 79912-1900 Office: U Tex at El Paso Coll Engring El Paso TX 79968

STARKWEATHER, GARY KEITH, optical engineer, computer company executive; b. Lansing, Mich., Jan. 9, 1938; married; 2 children. BS, Mich. State U., 1960; MS, U. Rochester, 1966. Engr. Bausch & Lomb, Inc., 1962-64; area mgr. optical systems Xerox Palo Alto (Calif.) Rsch. Ctr., 1964-80, sr. rsch. fellow, 1980-88; Apple fellow advanced tech. group Apple Computer, Inc., Saratoga, Calif., 1988—; dir. Apple Computer, Inc., Cupertino, Calif.; instr. optics Monroe C.C., 1968-69. Recipient Johann Gutenberg prize Soc. Info. Display, 1987, Sci. and Tech. Acad. award for input scanning of film images, 1995. Mem. Optical Soc. Am. (David Richardson medal 1991), Soc. Photog. Inst. Engrs. Achievements include research in optics and electronics and their specific system interaction, involving display and hard copy image systems. Home: 10274 Parkwood Dr Apt 7 Cupertino CA 95014-1441

STARLEAF, DENNIS ROY, economics educator; b. Moline, Ill., Mar. 27, 1938; s. Carl Gustof and Helen Marie (Van Cleemput) S.; m. Elizabeth Ann Compton, June 3, 1961; children: Monica I., Katrina E., Christopher C. BA, U. Calif., Berkeley, 1959; MA, U. Calif., L.A., 1960; PhD, Vanderbilt U., 1967. Asst. prof. econs. Iowa State U., Ames, 1964-68, assoc. prof., 1968-71, prof., 1971—, chair of econs., 1984—; economist Fed. Res. Bd. of Govs., Washington, 1973-74; bd. dirs. Iowa State U. Press, Ames, 1987—; cons. Midwest Rsch. Inst., Kansas City, Mo., 1988—. Assoc. editor: Jour. of Fin., 1971-73; contbr. articles to profl. jours. Trustee Iowa State U. Found., Ames, 1984—. Doctoral dissertation fellow Ford Found., 1962-63; recipient Faculty Svc. award Nat. Univ. Continuing Edn. Assn., 1983, Gold Quil award Am. Soc. Farm Mgrs. and Rural Appraisers, 1989. Mem. Am. Econs. Assn., Am. Agrl. Econ. Assn., Phi Beta Kappa. Avocations: skeet, trap, scuba diving, swimming. Home: 2218 Northwestern Ave Ames IA 50010-4527 Office: Iowa State U Dept Econs Heady Hall Ames IA 50011

STARLING, JAMES LYNE, university administrator; b. Ridgeway, Va., Aug. 16, 1930; s. Leonard Anderson and Florine (Anderson) S.; m. Martha Elizabeth Lewis, Mar. 17, 1968; 1 child, Elizabeth Anne. B.S., Va. Polytech. Inst. & State U., Blacksburg, 1951; M.S., Pa. State U., 1955, Ph.D., 1958. Instr. agronomy Pa. State U., University Park, 1957-58, asst. prof. agronomy, 1958-63, assoc. prof. agronomy, 1963-69, prof., head dept. agronomy, 1969-85, assoc. dean for adminstrn., Coll. Agr., 1985-93, sr. assoc. dean, 1993-95; interm dean Pa. State U., 1996—. Served to 1st lt. U.S. Army, 1951-53, Korea. Fellow AAAS; mem. Am. Soc. Agronomy (pres. N.E. br. 1980-81), Crop Sci. Soc. Am., Am. Forage and Grassland Council, Pa. Grassland Council (pres. 1968), Pa. Plant Food and Protectant Edn. Soc. (pres. 1974-75), Phi Kappa Phi, Gamma Sigma Delta, Phi Epsilon Phi, Phi Sigma. Democrat. Methodist. Club: Kiwanis (State College, pres. 1982-83). Home: 1736 Princeton Dr State College PA 16803-3261 Office: Pa State U 201 Agr Adminstrn Bldg University Park PA 16802

STARNES, EARL MAXWELL, urban and regional planner, architect; b. Winter Haven, Fla., Sept. 14, 1926; s. Thomas Lowe and Kathryn Maxwell (Gates) S.; m. Dorothy Jean Prather, Aug. 21, 1949; children: Tom, Will, Janet, Patricia. Student, Fla. So. Coll., 1946-48; BArch cum laude, U. Fla., 1951; MS in Urban and Regional Planning, Fla. State U., 1973, PhD, 1977. Registered architect, Fla. Assoc. Courtney Stewart (Architect), Ft. Lauderdale, Fla., 1951-52, William Bigoney, Architect, Ft. Lauderdale, 1952-53, William T. Vaughn, Architect, Ft. Lauderdale, 1953, Alfred B. Parker, Architect, Miami, Fla., 1953-55, Rufus Nims, Architect, Miami, 1955-57; ptnr. Starnes & Rentscher, Architects, Miami, 1957-63, Starnes, Rentscher & Assocs., Architects, Miami, 1963-71; dir. div. mass transp. Fla. Dept. Transp., Tallahassee, 1971-72; dir. div. state planning Fla. Dept. Adminstrn., 1972-75; engaged in research and cons. service Tallahassee, 1975; prof., chmn. urban and regional planning Coll. Architecture U. Fla., Gainesville, 1976-88; prof. urban and regional plan coordination, doctorial studies Coll. of Architecture U. Fla., 1989-93, prof. emeritus, 1993—; instr. architecture U. Miami, 1953; adj. asst. prof. dept. urban and regional planning Coll. Social Scis., Fla. State U., 1971-74; mem. adv. panel B8-15, Nat. Coop. Hwy. Research Program, Transp. Research Bd., NRC-Nat. Acad. Scis., 1974—; mem. adv. bd. Pub. Tech., Inc., 1974—; mem. North Central Fla. Regional Planning Com., 1980-85, Fla. Substate Dist. Com., 1985-87; co-chmn. Joint Liaison Com. on Div. Responsibility for Urban Services, Dade County, Fla., 1965-71; chmn. joint policy com. U. Miami-Dade County Jackson Med. Center, 1966-71; chmn. Cape Fla. State Park Adv. Council, 1966-69, Dade County Landscape Ordinance Study Com., 1967-70, South Fla. Everglades Area Planning Council, 1969-71; vis. lectr. Calif. Poly. State U., San Luis Obispo, 1988-89; cons. Urban Planning Fla. and Caribbean. Prin. works include 1st Unitarian Ch., Miami; contbr. article on archtl. planning relationship Ency. Architecture Planning, 1987, chpt. to Growth Management, 1992; contbr. chpts. to books, articles on land use and urban devel. policies, wetland protection and state planning to profl. jours. Active South Dade Mental Health Soc., 1967-68, Cape Fla. Acquisition Com., 1966, Dade County Downtown Govtl. Center Com., 1967-71, Miami Downtown Devel. Authority, 1970, Gov.'s Task Force on Resource Mgmt., 1971-72, Nat. Task Force on Natural Resources and Land Use Info. and Tech., 1973-74, Fla. Gov.'s Commn. on Property Rights, 1993-94; county commr. Dist. 7, Dade County, 1964-71; vice mayor, 1964, 68; mem. adv. com. Legis. Council Subcom. on Constrn. Industry Study, 1966-68; bd. dirs., chmn. retirement and compensation com. State Assn. County Commrs., 1968-71; mem. Alachua County Budget Study Com., 1978, Fla. Land Use Adv. Com. for Phosphate Lands, 1978-80, Suwanee River Water Mgmt. Bd., 1982-87, 91—, chmn. 1987-88; chmn. Fla. Inst. Phosphate Research, 1984-87; bd. dirs. 1000 Friends of Fla, 1986—. With USCG, 1944-46. Fellow AIA (urban design com. 1976-80); mem. Am. Inst. Cert. Planners, Nat. Inst. Bldg. Scis. (steering com. for rsch. 1979-80), Assn. Collegiate Schs. of Planning (bd. dirs. 1986-88), Gargoyle Soc., Phi Kappa Phi. Democrat. Unitarian. Office: PO Box 234 Cedar Key FL 32625-0234

STARNES, JAMES WRIGHT, lawyer; b. East St. Louis, Ill., Apr. 3, 1933; s. James Adron and Nell (Short) S.; m. Helen Woods Mitchell, Mar. 29, 1958 (div. 1978); children: James Wright, Mitchell A., William B. II; m. Kathleen Israel, Jan. 26, 1985. Student St. Louis U., 1951-53; LLB, Washington U., St. Louis, 1957. Bar: Mo. 1957, Ill. 1957, Fla. 1992. Assoc. Stinson, Mag & Fizzell, Kansas City, Mo., 1957-60, ptnr., 1960-90; ptnr. Mid-Continent Properties Co., 1959-90, Fairview Investment Co., Kansas City, 1971-76, Monticello Land Co., 1973—, of counsel Yates, Mauck, Bohrer, Elliff, Croessmann & Wieland, P.C., Springfield, Mo., 1995—; sec. Packaging Products Corp., Mission, Kans., 1972-89; chmn., treas. Galerie of Naples (Fla.), Inc., 1990-92. Bd. dirs. Mo. Assn. Mental Health, 1968-69, Kansas City Assn. Mental Health, 1966-78, pres., 1969-70; bd. dirs. Heed, 1965-73, 78-82, pres., 1966-67, fin. chmn. 1967-68; bd. dirs. Kansas City Halfway House Found., exec. com., 1966-69, pres., 1966; bd. dirs. Joan Davis Sch. for Spl. Edn., 1972-88, v.p., 1972-73, 79-80, pres., 1980-82; bd. dirs. Sherwood Ctr. for Exceptional Child, 1977-79, v.p., 1978-79. Served with AUS, 1957. Mem. ABA, Mo. Bar, Fla. Bar, Springfield Bar Assn., Kansas City Bar Assn., Washington U. Law Alumni Assn. (bd. govs. 1990-92). Presbyterian (deacon). Mem. adv. bd. Washington U. Law Quar., 1957-90. Home: 2657 E Wildwood Rd Springfield MO 65804-5271 Office: Yates Mauck Bohrer Elliff Croessmann & Wieland 3333 E Battlefield Rd Ste 1000 Springfield MO 65804-4048

STARNES, MICHAEL S., trucking executive; b. 1945. BBA, U. Miss., 1968. Terminal mgr. Western Gillette Trucking, Fresno, Calif. and El Paso, Tex., 1968-73; gen. mgr. Rebel Motor Freight Lines, 1973-78; chmn. bd. dirs., pres., CEO M.S. Carriers, Inc., Memphis, 1977—; pres. TCX, Inc. Office: M S Carriers Inc 3150 Starnes Cv Memphis TN 38130*

STARNES, SUSAN SMITH, elementary education educator; b. Grinnell, Iowa, Oct. 8, 1942; d. Edwin Fay Smith Jr. and Miriam Jane (Spaulding) Smith Simms; m. Wayman J. Starnes, Apr. 25, 1964; children: Michele Ann Starnes Hoffman, Mary Shannon Starnes. BS in Edn. summa cum laude, Mo. Bapt. Coll., 1991. Cert. early childhood tchr., elem. tchr. 1-8. Adminstr. Presbyn. Ch. in Am. Hist. Ctr., St. Louis, 1985-90; tchr. 3rd grade Ctrl. Christian Sch., St. Louis, 1991—; chapel com. Ctrl. Christian Sch., St. Louis, 1991—. Children's dir. Canaan Bapt. Ch., St. Louis, 1991—, mission trip vol., 1992, 93; camp counselor Youth for Christ, Kansas City, 1992, 93. Avocations: recreational vehicling, swimming, scuba diving.

STARNES, WILLIAM HERBERT, JR., chemist, educator; b. Knoxville, Tenn., Dec. 2, 1934; s. William Herbert and Edna Margaret (Osborne) S.; m. Maria Sofia Molina, Mar. 4, 1986. BS with honors, Va. Poly Inst., 1955; PhD, Ga. Inst. Tech., 1960. Rsch. chemist Esso Rsch. & Engring. Co., Baytown, Tex., 1960-62, sr. rsch. chemist, 1962-64, polymer additives sect. head, 1964-65, rsch. specialist, 1965-67, rsch. assoc., 1967-71; instr. and rsch. assoc. dept. chemistry U. Tex., Austin, 1971-73; mem. tech. staff AT&T Bell Labs., Murray Hill, N.J., 1973-85; prof. chemistry Poly. U., Bklyn., 1985-89, head dept. chemistry and life scis., 1985-88, assoc. dir. polymer durability ctr. 1987-89, Floyd Dewey Gottwald Sr. prof. chemistry Coll. William and Mary, Williamsburg, Va., 1989—; invited lectr. several fgn. countries and U.S.; ofcl. guest U.S.S.R. Acad. Scis., 1990, Russian Acad. Scis., 1992; vis. scientist Tex. Acad. Scis., 1964-67; mem. bd. doctoral thesis examiners Indian Inst. Tech., New Delhi, 1988, McGill U., Montreal, 1989, MacQuarie U., Sydney, 1991, McMaster U., Hamilton, Can., 1994; panelist, reviewer NSF Acad. Rsch. Facilities Modernization Program, 1990; channel program mentor U. Cairo, 1994-95; mem. opinion leader panel Wall St. Jour., 1995—; mem. sci. adv. bd. European Vinyl Mfrs. Project on PVC in Landfills, 1996; cons. numerous indsl. cos.; course dir. continuing edn. Mem. adv. bd. and bd. reviewers Jour. Vinyl Tech., 1981-83; mem. editl. bd. Jour. of Chemical and Biochemical Kinetics, 1992—; contbr. articles to profl. jours., chpts. to books; patentee in field. NSF fellow 1958-60; recipient Profl. Progress award Soc. Profl. Chemists and Engrs. 1968, Disting. Tech. Staff award AT&T Bell Labs. 1982, Polymer Sci. Pioneer award Polymer News, 1988, Honor Scroll award N.J. Inst. Chemists, 1989; NSF grantee, Nat. Bur. Standards Ctr. for Fire Rsch. grantee, Internat. Copper Rsch. Assn. grantee, Va. Ctr. Innovative Tech. grantee, GenCorp Found. grantee. Fellow AAAS (Project 2061 1985-86, chmn. chemistry subpanel 1985-86, mem. panel on phys. scis. and engring., 1985-86), Am. Inst. Chemists (life); mem. Am. Chem. Soc. (bd. dirs. southeastern Tex. sect. 1970, speakers bur. div. polymer chemistry 1976—, mem.-at-large exec. com. Va. sect. 1995), Soc. Plastics Engrs. (Sponsoring Prof. award Vinyl Plastics divsn. 1996), N.Y. Acad. Scis. (life), Va. Acad. Sci., Sigma Xi (M.A. Ferst award Ga. Inst. Tech. chpt. 1960), Phi Kappa Phi, Phi Lambda Upsilon (pres. Va. Poly. Inst. chpt. 1954-55). Current work: Degradation, stabilization, flammability, microstructures, and polymerization mechanisms of synthetic polymers, especially poly (vinyl chloride); free radical chemistry; carbon-13 nuclear magnetic resonance and organic synthesis. Subspecialties: Organic chemistry; Polymer chemistry. Office: Coll William and Mary Dept Chemistry PO Box 8795 Williamsburg VA 23187-8795

STARPATTERN, RITA, arts administrator, sculptor; b. Dallas, Dec. 25, 1946; d. Wesley T. and Lillian (Gillespie) Murphey. BSA cum laude, U. Tex., Austin, 1967, postgrad., 1968-70, Spanish Lang. Competency Cert., 1992. Graphic designer Red River Womens Press, Austin, 1975-78; visual arts coord. Women & Their Work, Austin, 1978-81, exec. dir., 1981-86; program adminstr. spl. projects Tex. Commn. on Arts, Austin, 1986-89, program adminstr. visual arts and comm., 1990—; program mgr. Art in Pub. Places City of Austin, 1989-90; pubs. rep. Artweek, 1978; peer review panelist Nat. Endowment for Arts, Nat. Endowment for Arts/Rockefeller, Corp. for Pub. Broadcasting, State of Ohio, State of Ky., Arts MidWest, 1982—; presenter various confs.; mem. planning adv. task force Creative Support for the Individual Artist nat. conf., Orcas Island, 1989; program adv. cons. curriculum and media devel. program State of Tex. Region XIII Ednl. Svc. Ctr., 1982. One-woman shows at St. Edwards U., U. Tex. at Permian Basin; represented in permanent collections at Laguna Gloria Art Mus., Austin, Elisabet Ney Mus., Austin, Connemera Conservancy, Dallas, San Marcos Pub. Park Sys.; project coord. Project BRIDGE; prin. works include Outdoor Studio Plaza, City of Austin Cable Access TV Facility, 1988-90. bd. dirs., v.p. goals and planning Nat. Coalition Women's Arts Orgns., 1982-84; commr. City of Austin Cable Commn., 1984-86. NDEA Portuguese fellow U. Tex. summer 1967, HEW Art Edn. grad. study fellow U. TEx., 1969-70; recipient Amicus award Friends of the Dougherty Arts Ctr., Austin, 1983, Phoenix awardto women and minorities in the arts Black Arts Alliance, Austin, 1986. Mem. Nat. Assn. Artists Orgns., Assn. Am. Cultures. Home: 6408 Haney Austin TX 78723

STARR, CHAUNCEY, research institute executive; b. Newark, Apr. 14, 1912; s. Rubin and Rose (Dropkin) S.; m. Doris Evelyn Debel, Mar. 20, 1938; children: Ross M., Ariel E. E.E., Rensselaer Poly. Inst., 1932, Ph.D., 1935, D.Engring. (hon.), 1964; D.Engring. (hon.), Swiss ETH, 1980; D. Sci. (hon.), Tulane U., 1986—. Research fellow physics Harvard, 1935-37; research asso. Mass. Inst. Tech., 1938-41; research physicist D.W. Taylor Model Basin, Bur. Ships, 1941-42; staff radiation lab. U. Calif., 1942-43, Tenn. Eastman Corp., Oak Ridge, 1943-46, Tenn. Eastman Corp. (Clinton Labs.), 1946; chief spl. research N. Am. Aviation, Inc., Downey, Calif., 1946-49; dir. atomic energy research dept. N. Am. Aviation, Inc., 1949-55, v.p., 1955-66; gen. mgr. N. Am. Aviation, Inc. (Atomics Internat. div.), 1955-60, pres. div., 1960-66; dean engring. U. Calif. at Los Angeles, 1966-73; cons. prof. Stanford, 1974—; pres. Electric Power Research Inst., 1973-78, vice chmn., 1978-87, pres. emeritus, 1987—; Dir. Atomic Indsl. Forum. Contbr. sci. articles to profl. jours. Decorated Legion of Honor (France); recipient Henry D. Smyth award Atomic Indsl. Forum, 1983. Fellow Am. Nuclear Soc. (past pres.), Am. Phys. Soc., AAAS (dir.); mem. AIAA (sr.), Am. Power Conf., Nat. Acad. Engring., Am. Soc. Engring. Edn., Royal Swedish Acad. for Engring. Scis., Eta Kappa Nu, Sigma Xi. Home: 95 Stern Ln Atherton CA 94027-5422

STARR, CHESTER G., history educator; b. Centralia, Mo., Oct. 5, 1914; s. Chester Gibbs and Nettie (Glore) S.; m. Gretchen Daub, July 15, 1940; children: Jennifer (Mrs. Michael Johnson), Richard G., Thomas J.J. A.B. with distinction, U. Mo., 1934, LL.D., 1981; M.A., 1935; Ph.D., Cornell U., 1938; LLD (hon.), U. Ill., 1987, St. Michaels Coll., 1992. Faculty U. Ill. at Urbana, 1940-70, prof. history, 1953-70, chmn. div. humanities, 1953-55, chmn. dept. history, 1960-61; prof. U. Mich., Ann Arbor, 1970-85; Bentley prof. U. Mich., 1973-85, Hudson prof., 1981-82; Cons. World Book, 1963-67, Ency. Americana, 1966—. Author: Roman Imperial Navy, 1941, From Salerno to the Alps, 1948, Emergence of Rome, 1950, Civilization and the Caesars, 1954, Origins of Greek Civilization, 1961, History of Ancient World, 1965, Rise and Fall of Ancient World, 1965, Awakening of the Greek Historical Spirit, 1968, Athenian Coinage, 480-449 B.C, 1970, Ancient Greeks, 1971, Ancient Romans, 1971, Early Man, 1973, Political Intelligence in Classical Greece, 1974, 94, Economic and Social Growth of Early Greece, 1977, Essays on Ancient History, 1979, Beginnings of Imperial Rome, 1980, The Roman Empire: A Study in Survival, 1982, Individual and the Community: The Rise of the Polis, 1986, Past and Future in Ancient History, 1987, Influence of Sea Power on Ancient History, 1988, The Birth of Athenian Democracy, 1990, 93, The Aristocratic Temper of Greek Civilization, 1991. Served from 1st lt. to lt. col. AUS, 1942-46, MTO. Decorated Bronze Star; Croce di Guerra Italy).; Recipient certificate as distinguished grad. U. Mo., 1963; Am. Acad. in Rome fellow, 1938-40; Guggenheim fellow, 1950-51, 58-59. Fellow Am. Acad. Arts and Scis.; mem. Am. Hist. Assn. (chmn. com. on ancient history 1961-67, Disting. scholar 1991), AAUP (chpt. pres. 1956-57), Socs. for Promotion Roman and Hellenic Studies, Royal Numis. Soc., Assn. Ancient Historians (pres. 1974-78), Phi Beta Kappa, Phi Mu Alpha. Home: 2301 Blueberry Ln Ann Arbor MI 48103-2212

STARR, DARLENE R., special education educator, education educator; b. Bucyrus, Ohio, Aug. 25, 1943; d. Dale H. and Helen J. (Rettig) Laipply; m. Douglas K. Rudy, Sept. 12, 1987; children: Kris, Kim, Kirk, Shane, Aubry. BS in Elem. Edn., St. Cloud State U., 1976; reading specialist, Avila Coll., 1981; MS in Spl. Edn., Kans. U., 1987. Cert. grades K-9 elem. reading/learning disabilities. Tchr. Wright Devel. Ctr., Monticello, Minn., 1977-78; tchr., dir. chpt. 1 Maple Lake (Minn.) Dist. Schs., 1978-80; chpt. 1 tchr. Olate (Kans.) Dist. Schs., 1980-82; first grade tchr. Spring Hill (Kans.) Dist. Schs., 1982-85; kindergarten tchr. Marietta (Ga.) City Schs., 1985-86; learning disabilites tchr. Louisburg (Kans.) Dist. Schs., 1987-90, tchr. grade 2, 1990-91; learning disabilities tchr. Olathe (Kans.) Dist. Schs., 1991—; adj. prof. Ottawa U., Overland Park, Kans., 1993—; learning disabilities cons., Olathe, 1992—. Mem. Nat. Coun. for Tchrs. Math., Coun. for Learning Disabilities, Internat. Reading Assn., Kans. Reading Assn. (chair parents and reading com.), Delta Kappa Gamma. Lutheran. Avocations: golf, tennis, antiquing, reading. Home: 1929 E Frontier Ln Olathe KS 66062-2344

STARR, DAVID, newspaper editor, publisher; b. N.Y.C., Aug. 1, 1922; s. Aaron and Helen (Simon) S.; m. Marjorie Giffen, Aug. 3, 1943; children: Pamela, Peter. B.A., Queens Coll., 1942. Reporter, rewriteman L.I. Daily Press, 1942-50; exec. editor Nassau Daily Rev. Star, 1950-53; asst. editor Newark Star-Ledger, 1954-56; assoc. editor L.I. Press, 1953-54, 56-62, mng. editor, 1962-69, editor, 1969-77; sr. editor Newhouse Newspapers, 1971—; pub. Springfield Union-News, Sunday Republican, 1977—, now pres. and pub.; pres. Springfield Ctrl., Inc., 1978-88, chmn., 1989-95. Trustee Nassau Community Coll., SUNY, 1959-66; bd. dirs. Springfield Libr. and Mus. Assn., chmn., 1988-90; mem. Mass. Cultural Coun., 1980—; bd. dirs. Am. Arts Alliance, 1988-92, chmn., 1989-92. Mem. Am. Soc. Newspaper Editors, Am. Newspaper Pubs. Assn.

STARR, DAVID EVAN, corporate executive; b. Muscatine, Iowa, May 4, 1962; s. Walter C. and Ruth E. (Hayes) S. Grad. high sch., Marion, Iowa. Telemktg. dir. East-West Theatrical Prodns., West Port, Conn., 1983-85, WRG Enterprises, Sarasota, Fla., 1985-86; CEO Wolf Entr., 1982-84, Nat. Labyrinth Cos., Cedar Rapids, Iowa, 1989—, Megaplex Industries, Marion, Iowa, 1992—. Author: Girls of the Deep, 1989. Charter mem. Repub. Presdl. Task Force, Washington, 1982—; sustaining mem. Repub. Nat. Com., Washington, 1984—. Mem. Assn. MBA Execs., U.S. Jaycees. Methodist. Avocations: model building, reading, business. Office: Megaplex Industries PO Box 604 Marion IA 52302-0604

STARR, FREDERICK BROWN, furniture manufacturing executive; b. Wethersfield, Mass., Dec. 11, 1932; s. Frederick Rickaby and Virginia (Brown) S.; m. Sue Zook, June 1958; children: Jonathan, Curtis, Anne. BA in English, Trinity Coll., Hartford, Conn., 1955. Archtl. ceilings salesman Armstrong World Industries, Inc., Indpls., 1958-63, mktg. mgmt., Lancaster, Pa., 1963-73, v.p., gen. sales mgr. subs. co. Thomasville Furniture Industries, Inc., (N.C.), 1973-77, sr. v.p., gen. sales mgr., 1977-82, pres., CEO, 1982—, also dir.; bd. dirs. Furniture Libr., High Point, N.C. vice-chair U. N.C., Greensboro, 1985—. Reynolds House Mus., 1988—; pres. N.C. Shakespeare Theatre, 1987—; bd. dirs. Community Hosp., Thomasville, 1984—; chmn. TFI Found., Thomasville, 1984—. Served with U.S. Army, 1955-57. Mem. Internat. Home Furnishings Market Assn. (chmn. 1995—). Republican. Episcopalian. Home: 5506 E Rockingham Rd Greensboro NC 27407-7242 Office: Thomasville Furniture 401 E Main St Thomasville NC 27360-4152

STARR, HARVEY, political scientist; b. N.Y.C., Nov. 11, 1946; s. Nathan and Betty (Brand) S.; m. Madonna Kissel, June 1, 1969 (div. Dec. 1979); m. Dianne C. Luce, July 2, 1994. BA, SUNY, Buffalo, 1967; M of Philosophy, Yale U., 1970, PhD, 1971. Acting instr. Dept. Polit. Sci., Yale U., New Haven, Conn., 1970-71; visiting fellow in politics Dept. Politics, U. Aberdeen, Scotland, 1971-72, 78-79; asst. prof. Dept. Polit. Sci., Ind. U., Bloomington, 1972-77, assoc. prof., 1977-83, prof., 1983-89; prof. in internat. affairs Dept. Govt. & Internat. Studies, U. S.C., Columbia, 1989—; editl. bd. Am. Polit. Sci. Rev., 1985-89, 91-95, Internat. Studies Quar., 1985-90, Jour. of Politics, 1988—, Comparative Polit. Studies, 1979-82, Internat. Interactions, 1985-91, editor, 1991—; assoc. editor Teaching Polit. Sci., 1978-81. Author: Henry Kissinger: Perceptions of International Politics, 1984; co-author: Inquiry, Logic and International Politics, 1989, World Politics: Menu for Choice, 1981, 85, 89, 92, 96, The Diffusion of War: A Study of Opportunity and Willingness, 1991; contbr. articles to profl. jours. Grantee NSF, 1982-84. Mem. Peace Sci. Soc. Midwest (pres. 1978-80), Ind. Consortium for Security Studies (dep. dir. 1980-89), Data Devel. in Internat. Rsch. (exec. coun. 1986-87, 89-92), Conflict Processes Sect., Am. Polit. Sci. Assn. (exec. coun. 1989-91, pres. 1992-95, v.p. 1995—), So. Polit. Sci. Assn. (exec. coun. 1991-94). Office: U SC Dept Govt Internat Studies Columbia SC 29208

STARR, IRA M., lawyer; b. Jersey City, N.J., May 22, 1936; s. Hyman S. and Frances (Bauer) S.; m. Diane Steinberg, Dec. 24, 1961; children: Shari, Steven. AB, Rutgers U., 1957; LLB, U. Va., 1961. Bar: D.C. 1961, N.J. 1974. Tax law specialist IRS, Washington, 1961-62; sr. atty. advisor U.S. Securities and Exch. Com., Washington, 1962-66; dir. ops., gen. counsel H. Hentz and Co., Inc., N.Y.C., 1966-68, R. Gilder and Co., Inc., N.Y.C., 1968-70, Merkin and Co., Inc., N.Y.C., 1970-73; ptnr. Meltzer and Starr, Jersey City, N.J., 1974-81, Ruskin Meltzer Starr and Hoberman, Jersey City, 1981-83, Ruskin Kors Meltzer Rubin and Starr, Jersey City, 1983-93, Starr, Gern, Davison and Rubin, Roseland, N.J., 1993—; mem. adv. bd. First Jersey Nat. Bank, Jersey City, 1982-88; mem. Dist. Ethics Com., Jersey City, 1989-93; arbitrator NASD; mediator Am. Arbitration Assn. Trustee, pres. Temple B'nai Abraham, Livingston, N.J., 1974; trustee Vis. Homemakers Svc. Hudson County, Jersey City, 1977—; fin. sec., trustee Jewish Hosp. and Rehab. Ctr., Jersey City, 1981-87. Recipient U.S. Civil Svc. Sustained Performance award U.S., S.E.C., Washington, 1963. Mem. ABA, N.J. Bar Assn. Avocations: tennis, bridge, music. Office: Starr Gern Davison Rubin PC 103 Eisenhower Pkwy Roseland NJ 07068

STARR, ISIDORE, law educator; b. Bklyn., Nov. 24, 1911. BA, CCNY, 1932; MA, Columbia U., 1939; LLB, St. John's U., Jamaica, N.Y., 1936; JSD, Bklyn. Law Sch., 1942; PhD, New Sch. Social Rsch., 1957. Bar: N.Y. 1937. Tchr. N.Y.C. high schs., 1934-61; assoc. prof., prof. edn. Queens Coll., 1961-75, emeritus, 1975—; dir. Inst. on Law-Related Edn., Lincoln-Filene Ctr., Tufts U., 1963; dir. Law Studies Inst., N.Y.C., 1974; adv. on Our Living Bill of Rights Film Series (6 films) Encyclopedia Britannica Ednl. Corp.; mem. Ariz. Ctr. for Law-Related Edn.; cons. in field. Bd. dirs. Phi Alpha Delta Juvenile Justice Program, 1981—. 1st lt. U.S. Army, 1943-46. John Hay fellow, 1952-53. Recipient Outstanding Citizen award Philip Morris Cos., 1992. Mem. ABA (hon. chair adv. commn. on Youth Edn. for Citizenship, Isidore Starr award for Spl. Achievement in Law Studies, Leon Jaworski award 1989), Am. Judicature Soc., Am. Soc. for Legal History, Am. Legal Studies Assn., Nat. Coun. Social Studies (past pres.), Phi Beta Kappa, Phi Alpha Delta (cert. of appreciation 1981). Author: The Lost Generation of Prince Edward County, 1968, The Gideon Case, 1968, The Feiner Case, 1968, The Mapp Case, 1968, The Supreme Court and Contemporary Issues, 1968, Human Rights in the United States, 1969, The American Judicial System, 1972, The Idea of Libery, 1978, Justice: Due Process of Law, 1981; co-editor Living American Documents, 1971.. Address: 6043 E Harvard St Scottsdale AZ 85257

STARR, KENNETH WINSTON, lawyer; b. Vernon, Tex., July 21, 1946; s. W. D. and Vannie Maude (Trimble) S.; m. Alice Jean Mendell, Aug. 23, 1970; children: Randall Postley, Carolyn Marie, Cynthia Anne. B.A., George Washington U., 1968; M.A., Brown U., 1969; J.D., Duke U., 1973; LLD (hon.), Hampden Sydney Coll., Shenandoah U., Mitchell Coll. Law. Bar: Calif. 1973, D.C. 1979, Va. 1979. Law clk. to Judge David Dyer U.S. Ct. Appeals (5th cir.), Miami, Fla., 1973-74; assoc. Gibson, Dunn & Crutcher, Los Angeles, 1974-75; law clk. to Chief Justice Warren E. Burger, U.S. Supreme Ct., Washington, 1975-77; assoc., ptnr. Gibson, Dunn & Crutcher, Washington, 1977-81; counselor to atty gen. of U.S. Dept. Justice, Washington, 1981-83; judge U.S. Ct. Appeals (D.C. circuit), Washington, 1983-89; solicitor gen. Dept. Justice, Washington, 1989-93; ptnr. Kirkland & Ellis, Washington, 1993—; ind. counsel for Whitewater, 1994—. Contbr. articles to legal jours. Legal advisor CAB transition team office of pres.-elect, 1980-81, legal advisor SEC transition team, 1980-81; bd. adv. Duke Law Jour. Recipient Disting. Alumni awards George Washington U., Duke U.; recipient Atty. Gen.'s Award for Disting. Svc., 1993, Am. Values award U.S. Indsl. Coun. Ednl. Found., 1993. Fellow Am. Bar Found. (judicial fellows com., judicial conf. com. on bicentennial of U.S. constitution); mem. ABA, Am. Law Inst., Am. Judicature Soc., Inst. Jud. Adminstrn. (pres.), Supreme Ct. Hist. Soc., Calif. Bar Assn., D.C. Bar Assn., Va. Bar Assn., Order of Coif, Phi Delta Phi (Hughes chpt. Man of Yr. 1973).

STARR, LEON, retired chemical research company executive; b. Bronx, N.Y., May 2, 1937; s. Michael and Bella (Foux) S.; m. Joan Gail Linett, June 19, 1960; children—Michael Jason, Jennifer Nicole. B.S., Poly. Inst., Brooklyn, 1958; Ph.D., U. Mo., 1962. Teaching asst. U. Mo., Columbia, 1958-62; chem. researcher Mobil Chem. Co., Edison, N.J., 1962-67; various mgmt. positions then dir. tech. Celanese Corp., N.Y.C., 1967-83, corp. v.p. tech., 1983-86; pres. Celanese Research Co., N.Y.C., 1983-90; pres., corp. v.p. tech. Hoechst Celanese Corp., Chatham, N.J., 1986-90, ret., 1990; pres. Lee Starr Assocs., 1991—; adv. bd. U. Pa. 1988-90; adv. coun. Hampton U., 1988—; nat. adv. coun. Synthesis Coalition on Engring. Edn. 1991—. Contbr. chpt. to book; patentee in field. Fellow Phillips Corp., U. Mo., 1961-62, Poly. Inst. N.Y., 1985. Mem. AAAS, Assn. Rsch. Dirs., Am. Chem. Soc. (corp. assoc. 1983-90, bd. govs.), Natural Sci. Assn., N.Y. Acad. Scis., Soc. Chem. Industry, Chem. Mfrs. Assn. (chmn. chem. regulations and adv. com. 1977-82), Am. Inst. Chemists, Sales and Mktd. Execs. Internat. (v.p. 1972-73), Sigma Xi. Avocations: tennis; sailing; collecting antique scientific instruments.

STARR, MARTIN KENNETH, management educator; b. N.Y.C., May 21, 1927; s. Harry and Melanie (Krauss) S.; m. Polly Exner, Apr. 3, 1955; children: Christopher Herschel, Loren Michael. BS, MIT, 1948; MS, Columbia U., 1951, PhD, 1953. Ptnr., dir. M.K. Starr Assocs., 1956-61; prof. mgmt. sci. Columbia U., N.Y.C., 1961-96; dir. Ctr. for the Study of Ops. Columbia U., 1980-95, dir. Ctr. for Enterprise Mgmt., 1995-96, vice dean Grad. Sch. Bus., 1974-75; prof. ops. mgmt. Crummer Grad. Sch. Bus. Rollins Coll., Winter Park, Fla., 1996—, dir. Ctr. for Enterprise Mgmt., 1996—; guest lectr. Am. U., Beirut, 1964, MIT, 1964-67, U. Cape Town, S. Africa, 1976, 80, 82, 84, 86, 88; cons. GE, E.I. duPont de Nemours & Co., Eastman Kodak Co., Lever Brothers, TRW, R.J. Reynolds, Young & Rubicam, IBM. Author: The Structure of Human Decisions, Inventory Control-Theory and Practice, 1972, Product Design and Decision Theory, 1963, (with David W. Miller) Executive Decisions and Operations Research, 2d edit., 1969, Systems Management of Operations, 1971, Management: A Modern Approach, 1971, Production Management: Systems and Synthesis, 2d edit., 1972, (with Irving Stein) The Practice of Management Science, 1976, Operations Management, 1978, (with G. Dannebring) Management Science: An Introduction, 1981, (with Earl K. Bowen) Statistics for Business and Economics, 1982, (with Marion Sobol) Statistics for Business and Economics: An Action Learning Approach, 1983, Managing Production and Operations, 1989, Global Corporate Alliances and the Competitive Edge, 1991, (with Marion Sobol) Introduction to Statistics for Executives, 1993, Operations Management: A Systems Approach, 1996; editor: Executive Readings in Management Science, 1965, (with Milan Zeleny) Multiple Criteria Decision Making, 1977, Global Competitiveness: Getting the U.S. Back on Track, 1988; editor-in-chief Mgmt. Sci., 1967-82; mem. editl. bd. Behavioral Sci., 1970—; editl. adviser Operational Rsch. Quar., 1970-85; cons. editor: Columbia Jour. World Business: Focus: Decision Making, fall, 1977, Quantitative Methods in Mgmt., McGraw-Hill Book Co., N.Y.C.; contbr. articles to profl. jours. Mem. Inst. Mgmt. Scis. (pres. 1974-75), Prodn. and Ops. Mgmt. Soc. (pres.-elect 1994—, pres. 1995, past pres., bd. dirs. 1996—), Beta Gamma Sigma. Home: 100 S Interlachen Ave # 304 Winter Park FL 32789 Office: Rollins Coll 313 Crummer Grad Sch Bus Winter Park FL 32789 *The ability to manage complex systems has become the most pressing requirement as we move to and through the year 2000. Remarkable growth of strong systems interdependencies has occurred since 1990. Energy, ecology, international trade, quality, remanufacturing and productivity are some examples of critical issues for resolution. Management science using the systems approach combines art and logic with advancing computer-linked technology to achieve social benefit. Perhaps a new name is needed to describe this effort. By whatever name it is called, the impact of systems-oriented management science will determine the character of the 21st century and will, in turn, be changed by it.*

STARR, MARVIN BLAKE, lawyer; b. N.Y.C., May 11, 1928; s. Harry and Roslyn (Lapidos) S.; m. Anita Reizen, Sept. 15, 1951 (div.); children: Karen, Eric, Valerie; m. K. Jill Best, Aug. 3, 1980. BA, UCLA, 1952; JD, U. Calif., Berkeley, 1955. Bar: Calif. 1959. Shareholder Miller, Starr & Regalia, Oakland and Walnut Creek, Calif., 1964—; mem. faculty Sch. Bus. U. Calif., Berkeley, 1968-90; adj. prof. John F. Kennedy Sch. Law, 1992; speaker profl. and civic meetings, confs. and convs. throughout the U.S. Co-author: (with Harry D. Miller) The Current Law of California Real Estate, 3 vols., 1965-67, 5 vols., 1975-77, 9 vols., 1990; founder Real Estate Tax Digest, 1980, editor, prin. author, 1980-88. Office: Miller Starr & Regalia 1331 N California Blvd Ste 700 Walnut Creek CA 94596-4537

STARR, MELVIN LEE, counseling organization executive; b. N.Y.C., Mar. 17, 1922; s. Herman and Martha (Aberman) S.; m. Eileen Ferne Kagan, Sept. 7, 1947; children: Marianne, Lisa Caren. BBA, U. Miami, 1947; postgrad. Columbia U., 1949-53, U. Denver, 1955-56, Ariz. State U., 1956-57; MA, U. Ariz., 1950; EdD, Western Colo. U., 1974. Faculty, adminstrn. Tucson Pub. Schs., 1950—; tchr. Doolen Jr. High Sch., 1951-53, counselor high sch., 1953-62, asst. prin. Alice Vail Jr. High Sch., 1962-64, Catalina High Sch., 1964-68; prin. Rincon High Sch., 1968-71, Tucson High Sch., 1971-74; asst. supt. Tucson Pub. Schs., 1974-78, assoc. supt., 1978-82; pvt. practice family counseling; pres., CEO Psychol. Engring. for Bus. and Industry, Tucson, 1984—. Mem. Tucson Mayor's Com. on Human Relations, 1969—; mem. Ariz. state com. Anti Defamation League, 1971; Ariz. state adv. bd. Good Shepherd Sch. for Girls, 1971; mem. Dem. Cen. Com., Pima City, Ariz., 1968—; bd. dirs., Mobile Meals of Tucson, Pima County Bd. Health, So. Arix. Girl Scouts U.S. Council; chmn. Tucson Community Ctr. Commn.; bd. dirs. Amigos de los Americanos, AnyTown, Ariz., Lighthouse YMCA, Beacon Found., Big Bros., NCCJ, Jr. Achievement, Tucson Community Center, Pacific Western region Anti-Defamation League, Handmaker Nursing Home Pima County, United Way, CODAC, Planned Parenthood, Girl Scouts Am., Ariz. Mobile Meals, Epilepsy Soc. So. Ariz., Drug Abuse and Alcohol Consortium; adv. bd. Tucson Free Med. Clinic; bd. dirs. Los Ninos Crisis Ctr., 1995—. Mem. Ariz. Assn. Student Teaching (state treas.), NEA, Ariz. Interscholastic Assn. (pres. conf. 1971, legis. council), Ariz. Personnel and Guidance Assn., Nat. Assn. Secondary Sch. Prins., Am. Assn. Sch. Adminstrs., Assn. Supervision and Curriculum Devel., Ariz. Sch. Adminstrs., Phi Epsilon Pi, Phi Delta Kappa. Home: 7101 E River Canyon Rd Tucson AZ 85750-2111 Office: PO Box 30163 Tucson AZ 85751-0163 also: 482 Elm Dr Ste E Las Vegas NV 89109

STARR, MICHAEL SETH, critic; b. Hackensack, N.J., Nov. 18, 1961; s. Ivan Lee and Zelda Libby (Ladenheim) S.; m. Gail Ellen Fleisher, June 11, 1989; 1 child, Rachel Lara. BA in Am. Lit., George Washington U., 1983. Copy and rsch. editor Broadband Comms., N.Y.C., 1984-87; reporter, film citic Daily Register, Red Bank, N.J., 1987, Daily Local News, West Chester, Pa., 1987-90; entertainment editor North Jersey Herald-News, Passaic, N.J., 1990-93; TV critic North Jersey hearld-News, Passaic, N.J., 1993—. Author: Peter Sellers: A Film History, 1991, Works of Art: The Art Carney Story, 1995. Recipient 1st Pl. award Jersey Press assn., 1992, 3d Pl. award, 1993. Mem. TV Critics Assn. Jewish. Home: 840 Summit Ave Hackensack NJ 07601 Office: North Jersey Herald & News 988 Main Ave Passaic NJ 07055

STARR, PAUL ELLIOT, sociologist, writer, editor, educator; b. N.Y.C., May 12, 1949; s. Saul and Sarah Marion (Buzen) S.; m. Sandra Lurie Stein, Apr. 12, 1981. BA, Columbia U., 1970; PhD, Harvard U., 1978. Jr. fellow Harvard Soc. Fellows, 1975-78; asst. prof. Harvard U., Cambridge, Mass., 1978-82, assoc. prof., 1982-85; prof. sociology Princeton (N.J.) U., 1985—; founder, co-editor The Am. Prospect; founder The Electronic Policy Network, 1995. Author: The Discarded Army: Veterans After Vietnam, 1974, The Social Transformation of American Medicine, 1983 (C. Wright Mills award 1983, Pulitzer prize 1984, Bancroft award 1984), The Logic of Health-Care Reform, 1992. Guggenheim Found. fellow, 1981-82. Democrat. Office: Princeton U Dept of Sociology Green Hall Princeton NJ 08544-1010

STARR, RICHARD CAWTHON, botany educator; b. Greensboro, Ga., Aug. 24, 1924; s. Richard Neal and Ida Wynn (Cawthon) S. BS in Secondary Edn., Ga. So. Coll., 1944; MA, George Peabody Coll., 1947; postgrad. (Fulbright scholar), Cambridge (Eng.) U., 1950-51; PhD, Vanderbilt U., 1952. Faculty Ind. U., 1952-75, prof. botany, 1960-76; founder, head culture collection algae U. Tex., Austin, prof. botany, 1976—; Head course marine botany Marine Biol. Lab., Woods Hole, Mass., 1959-63. Algae sect. editor: Biol. Abstracts, 1959—; editorial bd.: Jour. Phycology, 1965-68, 76-78; assoc. editor: Phycologia, 1963-69; Contbr. articles to profl. jours. Trustee Am. Type Culture Collection, 1962-68, 80-85. Guggenheim fellow, 1959; sr. fellow Alexander von Humboldt-Stiftung, 1972-73; recipient Disting. Tex. Scientist award Tex. Acad. Sci., 1987. Fellow AAAS, Ind. Acad. Sci.; mem. NAS (Gilbert Morgan Smith Award 1985), Am. Inst. Biol. Scis. (governing bd. 1976-77, exec. com. 1980), Bot. Soc. Am. (sec. 1965-69, v.p. 1970, pres. 1971, Darbaker prize 1955), Phycological Soc. Am. (past pres., v.p., treas.), Soc. Protozoologists, Internat. Phycological Soc. (sec. 1964-68), Brit. Phycological Soc., Akademie Wissenschaft zu Göttingen (corr.), Sigma Xi. Office: U Tex Dept Botany Austin TX 78713

STARR, RICHARD WILLIAM, retired banker; b. Phila., Oct. 7, 1920; s. Edwin Bell and Bertha (Aurand) S.; student U. Buffalo, 1946-50; BS, U. So. Calif., evenings 1952-58; grad. Am. Inst. Banking, 1942, Pacific Coast Sch. Banking, U. Wash., 1968, Stanford Grad. Sch. Credit and Fin. Mgmt., 1958; Harvard U. Grad. Sch. Advanced Mgmt. Program, 1975; m. Evelyn Irene Johnson, Aug. 3, 1943; children—David Richard, Daniel Robert. With Marine Trust Co. of Buffalo, 1939-50, mgr. credit dept., 1947-50; with Calif. Bank, Los Angeles, 1952-61, with United Calif. Bank (formerley Calif. Bank), 1961-79, with First Interstate Bank (formerley United Calif. Bank), 1979-83; installment credit officer, 1952-53, mgr. credit dept., 1953-58, comml. lending officer, loan adminstr., 1958-61, br. mgr., 1961, asst. cashier, 1955, asst. v.p., 1956-63, v.p., 1963-71, sr. v.p., 1971-83, area adminstr. nat. div., 1969-70, br. adminstr., 1970-73, mgr. state div. corp. banking dept., 1973-74, mgr. so. div. Calif. Banking Group, Los Angeles 1974-76, adminstr. spl. credits div., 1976-79, with First Interstate Bank , exec. v.p., adminstr. Calif. div., 1979-80, sr. credit adminstr. bank credit policy and supervision div., 1980-83, also chmn. credit policy worldwide, pvt. practice cons., Orange, Calif., 1983-94; dir. I.C.N. Pharms., Inc., Costa Mesa, Calif. Served with USCGR, 1942-45, USNR, 1947-52. Mem. Mortgage Banking Assn. (chmn. Orange County 1962—), Robert Morris Assocs., Calif. Bankers Assn. (exec. com. 1972), Beta Gamma Sigma. Republican. Clubs: Santa Ana (Calif.) Country; Jonathan (Los Angeles), Masons. Home: 2849 N Rustic Gate Way Orange CA 92667-1709

STARR, RINGO (RICHARD STARKEY), musician, actor; b. Liverpool, Eng., July 7, 1940; s. Richard and Elsie (Gleave) Starkey; m. Maureen Cox, Feb. 11, 1965 (div. 1975); children: Zak, Jason, Lee; m. Barbara Bach, Apr. 27, 1981. Drummer, vocalist mus. group, The Beatles, 1962-69; musician with Rory Storme's Hurricanes, 1959-62; solo performer, 1970-77; toured with All-Starr Band, 1992; recs. include Ringo the 4th, Sentimental Journey, 1970, Beaucoups of Blues, 1970, Ringo, 1973, Goodnight Vienna, 1974, Blast From Your Past, 1975, Starrstruck: Ringo's Best, 1989, Ringo's Rotogravure, 1976, Ringo the Fourth, 1977, Bad Boy, 1978, Stop and Smell the Roses, 1981, Time takes Time, 1992; solo albumn It Don't Come East, 1971, Only You, 1975, No No Song, 1975, (with the Beatles) A Hard Day's Night, 1964, Rubber Seol, 1965, Sgt. Pepper's Lonely Hearts Club Band, 1967, Yellow Submarine, 1969, Let It Be, 1969, Hey Jude, 1970, Love Songs, 1977, Reel Music, 1982, numerous others; film appearances with the Beatles include A Hard Day's Night, 1964, Help!, 1965, Yellow Submarine, 1968, Let It Be, 1970, TV film Magical Mystery Tour, 1967; individual film appearances include Candy, 1968, The Magic Christian, 1969, 200 Motels, 1971, Blindman, 1971, Tommy, 1972, That'll Be the Day, 1973, Born to Boogie, also dir., producer, 1974, Son of Dracula, also producer, 1975, Lisztomania, 1975, Ringo Stars, 1976, Caveman, 1981, The Cooler, 1982, Give My Regards to Broad Street, 1984; appeared in TV miniseries Princess Daisy, 1983; star TV series Shining Time Station, PBS, 1989—. Decorated Order Brit. Empire; recipient numerous Grammy awards with The Beatles; inducted with The Beatles into Rock and Roll Hall of Fame, 1988. Office: 2 Glynde Mews, London SW3 1SB, England

STARR, ROSS MARC, economist, educator; b. Oak Ridge, Nov. 14, 1945; s. Chauncey and Doris E. S.; m. Susan S. Strauss, July 2, 1967; children: Daniel, Diana. B.S., Stanford U., 1966, Ph.D., 1972. Cons. Rand Corp., summers 1966, 67, Western Mgmt. Sci. Inst., Grad. Sch. Mgmt., UCLA, summers 1967, 71; Cowles Found. staff research economist Yale U., New Haven, 1970; faculty Yale U., 1970-74, assoc. prof. econs., 1974; assoc. prof. econs. U. Calif.-Davis, 1975-76, prof. econs., 1976-80; prof. econs. U. Calif.-San Diego, 1980—, chmn. dept., 1987-90; vis. lectr. London Sch. Econs., 1973-74; vis. scholar U. Calif.-Berkeley, 1978-80; vis. lectr. Peoples U. of China, Beijing, 1987. Co-editor: Essays in Honor of Kenneth J. Arrow, 1986: v.1, Social Choice and Public Decision Making, v.2, Equilibrium Analysis, v.3, Uncertainty, Information and Communication; editor: Gen. Equilibrium Models of Monetary Economies, 1989; contbr. articles to profl. jours. NDEA fellow, 1966-69; Yale jr. faculty fellow, 1973-74; Guggenheim fellow, 1978-79; NSF grantee, 1979-81, 83-85. Office: U Calif San Diego Dept Econs 0508 9500 Gilman Dr La Jolla CA 92093-5003

STARR, STEVEN DAWSON, photographer; b. Albuquerque, Sept. 6, 1944; s. Richard Vernon and Carol (Harley) S.; m. Marilynne Sue Anderson, Aug. 6, 1965; 1 child, Stephen Richard. Student, Antioch Coll., 1962-63, Bethel Coll., 1963-64; B.A., San Jose State Coll., 1967. Photographer San Jose Mercury-News, Calif., 1966-67; photographer, picture editor A.P., 1968-73; audiovisual producer Starr Productions, Inc., Coral Gables, Fla., 1974-85; photographer Picture Group Agy., 1986-88, Saba Press, N.Y.C., 1988—. Recipient Pulitzer prize for spot news photography, 1970, Nat. Headliners award, 1970, George Polk Meml. award, 1970, Pictures of Year hon. mention, 1970. Office: Saba Press 116 E 16th St 8th Fl New York NY 10003

STARR, V. HALE, communications executive; b. Winner, S.D., July 31, 1936; d. Achibald William and Alvena Lucille (Williams) Hale. BA in Drama, English, Dakota Wesleyan U., 1967, LLD (hon.), 1994; MEd in Speech, Black Hills State Coll., 1971; MA Communications Rsch., U. Iowa, 1976, PhD Communications Rsch., 1979; LLD (hon.), Dakota Wesleyan U., 1994. Personnel dir. Starr Enterprises, Mitchell, S.D., 1965-69, v.p., 1967-69; tchr. Mt. Vernon (Iowa) High Sch., 1967-68; asst. prof. English, speech, drama S.D. Sch. Mines & Tech., Rapid City, 1968-70, asst. prof. sociology, 1970-74; unwed pregnancy counselor Munson Clinic, Rapid City, 1972-74; marriage counselor N&S Assocs., Rapid City, 1973-74; div. counselor Women's Resource and Action Ctr. U. Iowa, Iowa City, 1974-76, curriculum and student teaching, supr. student tchrs., 1975-77; owner, CEO Starr & Assocs., West Des Moines, Iowa, 1978—; fin. dir./owner KEYNOTE, Inc., West Des Moines, 1985—; owner Starr-Terry, West Des Moines, 1983—; non-legal cons. grant writing, Iowa, Nebr., 1974—. Author: Voir Dire, 1993; co-author: Jury Selection, 1985, 2d edit., 1993; mem. editorial bd. Forensics Reports Critical Reviewer, 1987-90; contbr. articles to profl. jours. Pres. Common Cause Iowa, 1980-81; mem. regional bd. Common Cause, Washington, 1980-82; bd. dirs. Nat. Women's Polit. Caucus, Iowa, 1972-76. Named Greater Des Moines Woman of Achievement YWCA, 1986, Iowa Leader in Bus. Drake U. Leadership Inst., 1985, 86; recipient Communication and Leadership award Dist. 19 Toastmasters, Des Moines, 1986. Mem. Law and Soc. Assn. (bd. dirs. 1987—), Internat. Assn. Ethicists, Am. Soc. Trial Cons. (founding mem., bd. dirs. 1983-85, chair com. to develop profl. standards 1983-85), Speech Communication Assn. (conv. presenter 1983, 86, 91), Am. Sociol. Assn., Internat. Communication Assn., Cen. State Speech Assn., Iowa Communication Assn. (conv. presenter 1979), Polk County Assn. Women Attys., Consortium Club (founding mem.). Office: Starr & Assocs Inc 1201 Grand Ave West Des Moines IA 50265-3523 also: 3218 E Bell Rd # 304 Phoenix AZ 85032-2727

STARRETT, FREDERICK KENT, lawyer; b. Lincoln, Nebr., May 23, 1947; s. Clyde Frederick and Helen Virginia (Meyers) S.; m. Linda Lee Jensen, Jan. 19, 1969; children: Courtney, Kathryn, Scott. BA, U. Nebr., 1969; JD, Creighton U., 1976. Bar: Nebr. 1976, Kans. 1977, U.S. Dist. Ct. Nebr. 1976, Mo. 1987, U.S. Dist. Ct. Kans. 1977, U.S. Ct. Appeals (8th and 10th cirs.) 1983, U.S. Supreme Ct. 1993. Pvt. practice law Great Bend, Kans., 1976-77, Topeka, 1977-86; ptnr. Miller, Bash & Starrett, P.C., Kansas City, Mo., 1986-90, Lathrop Norquist & Miller, 1990-91, Lathrop and Norquist, Overland Park, Kans., 1991-95, Lathrop & Gage L.C., Overland Park, Kans., 1996—. Lt (j.g.) USNR, 1969-72. Mem. ABA, Kans. Bar Assn. (pres. litigation sect. 1985-86), Am. Bd. Trial Advs., Mo. Orgn. Def. Lawyers, Civitan Club (pres. 1985-86, Disting. Pres. award 1985-86). Democrat. Presbyterian. Avocations: aviation, scuba diving. Office: Lathrop and Gage LC 1050/40 Corporate Woods 9401 Indian Creek Pky Overland Park KS 66210-2005

STARRETT, PAMELA ELIZABETH, symphony executive director, violinist, conductor; b. Concord, N.H., July 15, 1962; d. John Frederick and Nancy Elizabeth (Garland) S.; m. John Peter Ingalls, May 14, 1988; children: Hugh Starrett Ingalls, Edmund Starrett Ingalls. B of Mus. Arts, U. Mich., 1984, MusM, MBA, 1988. Orch. mgr. Ann Arbor (Mich.) Symphony Orch., 1987-88, asst. condr., 1988; mktg. dir. Kalamazoo Symphony Orch., 1988-90; music dir. Battle Creek (Mich.) Youth Orch., 1989-91; exec. dir. Battle Creek Symphony Orch., 1990—. Chair young artists competition Kalamazoo Bach Festival, 1989-90; co-founder Cmty. Music Sch. Battle Creek Symphony Orch. Mem. Mich. Orch. Assn. (trustee 1990-91, 93—). Home: 153 Laurel Dr Battle Creek MI 49017-4666 Office: Battle Creek Symphony Orch 25 Michigan Ave W Ste 1206 Battle Creek MI 49017-7012

STARRS, JAMES EDWARD, law and forensics educator, consultant; b. Bklyn., July 30, 1930; s. George Thomas and Mildred Agatha (Dobbins) S.; m. Barbara Alice Smyth, Sept. 6, 1954; children: Mary Alice, Monica, James, Charles, Liam, Barbara, Siobhan, Gregory. BA and LLB, St. John's U., Bklyn., 1958; LLM, NYU, 1959. Bar: N.Y. 1958, D.C. 1966, U.S. Ct. Mil. Appeals 1959, U.S. Dist. Ct. (so. and ea. dists.) N.Y. 1960. Assoc. Lawless & Lynch, N.Y.C., 1958; teaching fellow Rutgers U., Newark, 1959-60; asst. prof. law DePaul U., Chgo., 1960-64; assoc. prof. law George Washington U., Washington, 1964-67, prof. law, 1967—, prof. forensic scis., 1975—; cons. Nat. Commn. Reform Fed. Criminal Laws, Washington, 1968, Cellmark Diagnostics, Germantown, Md., 1987—, Time-Life Books, 1993; participant re-evaluation sci. evidence and trial of Bruno Richard Hauptmann for Lindbergh murder, 1983; participant reporting sci. re-analysis of firearmes evidence in Sacco and Vanzetti trial, 1986; project dir. Alfred G. Packer Victims Exhumation Project, 1989, A Blace of Bullets: A Sci. Investigation into the Deaths of Senator Huey Long and Dr. Carl Austin Weiss, 1991, Meriwether Lewis Exhumation Project, 1992, Frank R. Olson Exhumation Project, 1994, Jesse W. James Exhumation Project, 1995. Author: (with Moenssens and Inbau) Scientific Evidence in Criminal Cases, 1986, (with Moenssens, Inbau and Henderson) Scientific Evidence in Civil and Criminal Cases, 1995; editor: The Noiseless Tenor, 1982; co-editor: (review) Scientific Sleuthing, 1976—; mem. editl. bd. Jour. Forensic Sci., 1980—; contbr. articles to profl. jours. Served to sgt. U.S. Army, 1950-53, Korea. Recipient Vidocq Soc. award, 1993; Ford Found. fellow, 1963; vis. scholar in residence USMC, 1984. Fellow Am. Acad. Forensic Sci. (chmn. jurisprudence sect. 1984, 94, 95, bd. dirs. 1986-89, Jurisprudence Sect. award 1988); mem. ABA, Mid-Atlantic Assn. Forensic Sci., Assn. Trial Lawyers Am., Internat. Soc. Forensic Sci. (chmn. jurisprudence sect. 1988—). Roman Catholic. Home: 8602 Clydesdale Rd Springfield VA 22151-1301 Office: George Washington U Nat Law Ctr 720 20th St NW Washington DC 20006-4306

STARRY, DONN ALBERT, former aerospace company executive, former army officer; b. N.Y.C., May 31, 1925; s. Donn Albert and Edith (Sortor) S.; m. Leatrice Hope Gibbs, June 15, 1948; children: Michael, Paul, Melissa, Melanie. B.S., U.S. Mil. Acad., 1948; M.S. in Internat. Affairs, George Washington U., 1966. Commd. 2d lt. U.S. Army, 1948, advanced through grades to gen., 1977; svc. in Europe, Korea and Vietnam; comdr. 11th armored cavalry rgt. Vietnam, Cambodia, 1969-70; assigned Dept. Army Staff, 1970-72; comdr. Armor Center and Ft. Knox, Ky., 1973-76, V Corps, Europe, 1976-77; comdr. Tng. and Doctrine Command Ft. Monroe, Va., 1977-81; comdr. in chief U.S. Readiness Command, 1981-83, ret., 1983; v.p. mission analysis and tech. affairs Ford Aerospace and Communications Corp., Detroit, 1983-84, v.p., gen. mgr. space missions div., 1984-86; exec. v.p. Ford Aerospace Corp., Arlington, Va., 1987-90; spl. asst. to pres. BDM Internat., McLean, Va., 1988-90; chmn. bd. Maxwell Labs. Inc., San Diego, 1995—; author, lectr., counselor to govt. and industry. Mem. Def. Sci. Bd., 1985-93, Order of Aaron and Hur, Friends of Fifth of May; trustee Eisenhower Found., 1995—; chmn. bd. U.S. Cavalry Meml. Found., 1995—. Decorated Def. D.S.M., Army D.S.M. with oak leaf cluster, Silver Star, Bronze Star with V, Soldier's medal, Purple Heart, Legion of Merit with 2 oak leaf clusters, French Ordre Nationale du Merite, German Knight Commdr.'s Cross of Order of Merit with Badge and Star, Disting. Flying Cross, Air Medal with 9 oak leaf clusters; named to U.S. Army Ft. Leavenworth Command and Gen. Staff Coll. Hall of Fame, 1993. Mem. U.S. Armor Assn., Assn. U.S. Army. Episcopalian. Office: 11401 Lilting Ln Fairfax Station VA 22039-1717

STARTUP, CHARLES HARRY, airline executive; b. Middletown, N.Y., Feb. 24, 1914; s. Charles H. and Laura Beatrice (Langan) S.; m. Jane Butler Williams, June 26, 1942; children—Charles Alan, Ann Elizabeth, Thomas Andrew. A.B., Middlebury Coll., 1936; postgrad., U. Cin., 1937-39. With Am. Airlines, N.Y.C., 1939-63, asst. v.p. customer service, 1957-59; v.p. passenger sales and service Am. Airlines, 1959-61, v.p. passenger sales, 1961-63, dir. admiralty bd., 1973-79; v.p. mktg. Nat. Car Rental System, 1963-64. Adminstr. Light Opera of Manhattan, 1981-84. Mem. Cin. Sales Execs. Council (pres. 1955), Soc. Consumer Affairs Profls. (dir.), Chi Psi. Club: Skal (N.Y.C.). Home: 221 W College St Oberlin OH 44074-1533

STARTUP, WILLIAM HARRY, chemist; b. Port Jervis, N.Y., Oct. 24, 1945; s. William George and Robina Victoria (Sutherland) S.; m. Frances Williams, Nov. 6, 1976; 1 child, Elizabeth. BS in Chemistry, SUNY, Cortland, 1974. Sr. flavor analyst PFW-Hercules, Middletown, N.Y., 1975-91; analytical supr. Tastemaker, Cin., 1991—. Bd. dirs. Humane Soc. Middletown N.Y., 1985-91. Sgt. USAF, 1967-71. Mem. Am. Chem. Soc., Assn. of Ofcl. Analytical Chemists. Home: 892 Sabino Ct Cincinnati OH 45231 Office: Tastemaker 100 E 69th St Cincinnati OH 45216

STARTZELL, DAVID N., sports association executive; b. Washington, June 16, 1949; s. James Startzell; m. Judith L. Jenner. BA in Sociology, Miami U., Oxford, Ohio, 1971; MS in Planning, U. Tenn., 1976. Planning com. Tech. Assistance Ctr., U. Tenn., Knoxville; asst. planning dept. City of Oxnard, Calif.; dir. trail mgmt. svcs. Appalachian Trail Conf., Harpers Ferry, W.Va., 1978-79, dir. resource protection, 1979-81, assoc. dir., 1981-86, exec. dir., CEO, 1986—; active various trails and conservation group coalitions; chmn. task force producing Trails for All Americans; former planning cons. Office of Mayor, Knoxville. Recipient Conservation Svc. award U.S. Dept. Interior, 1995. Office: Appalachian Trail Conf PO Box 807 Corner Washington-Jackson Harpers Ferry WV 25425-0807

STARYK, STEVEN S., violinist, concertmaster, educator; b. Toronto, Ont., Can., Apr. 28, 1932; s. Peter and Mary Staryk; m. Ida Elisabeth Busch, May 17, 1963; 1 child, Natalie. Student, Royal Conservatory of Music, Toronto, 1942-48, Harbord Collegiate Inst., Toronto, 1945-48; LittD (hon.), York U.,

Toronto, 1980. Soloist, concertmaster CBC-Radio Can., Toronto, 1951-55, Royal Philharmonic Orch., London, 1956-59; 1st concertmaster, tchr. Concertgebouw Orch. and Amsterdam Conservatory, 1960-63; concertmaster Chgo. Symphony Orch., 1963-67; prof. of violin Oberlin (Ohio) Coll. Conservatory, 1968-72, Acad. of Music, Vancouver, B.C., Can., 1972-75, Royal Conservatory of Music, Toronto, 1975-87; concertmaster Toronto Symphony, 1982-87; prof. of violin, chair string div. U. Wash. Sch. Music, Seattle, 1987—; faculty music U. Toronto, 1980-87; vis. prof. U. Victoria, 1972, U. Ottawa, 1975, Northwestern U., 1965-66; founding mem. Quartet Can., 1975-80. Soloist, recitalist, N.Am., Europe and the Far East; recording artist on EMI-HMV, CBC, Everest, Orion, other labels. Recipient 2 Arts awards Can. Council, Ottawa, 1968, 75, Queen's Silver Jubilee medal Govt. of Can., Toronto, Shevchenko medal, Winnipeg, Man., Can. Home: 5244 17th Ave NE Seattle WA 98105-3408 Office: U Wash Sch Music Mail Stop DN-10 Seattle WA 98195

STARZINGER, VINCENT EVANS, political science educator; b. Des Moines, Jan. 12, 1929; s. Vincent and Genevieve (Evans) S.; m. Mildred Hippee Hill, June 16, 1953; children: Page Hill, Evans. AB summa cum laude, Harvard U., 1950, LLB, 1954, PhD, 1959; AM (hon.), Dartmouth Coll., 1968. Bar: Iowa 1954. Practice with firm Bannister, Carpenter, Ahlers & Cooney, Des Moines, 1954; teaching fellow, then instr. govt. Harvard, 1957-60; mem. faculty dept. govt. Dartmouth, 1960-94, chmn. dept. govt., 1972-77, 83-85, Joel Parker prof. law and polit. sci., 1976-94, prof. emeritus, 1994—. Author: Middlingness: Juste Milieu Political Theory in England and France, 1815-48, 1965, repub. as The Politics of the Center, 1991; also articles. Served with AUS, 1955-56. Sheldon traveling fellow, 1950-51; Social Sci. Research Council fellow, 1958-59; Dartmouth faculty fellow, 1963-64; Am. Philos. Soc. award and Earhart Found. fellow, 1970-71. Mem. ABA, Am. Polit. Sci. Assn., Iowa Bar Assn., Am. Can. Alpine Club, Cambridge (Mass.) Boat Club, Phi Beta Kappa. Home: Elm St Norwich VT 05055 Office: PO Box 981 Hanover NH 03755-0981

STARZL, THOMAS EARL, physician, educator; b. Le Mars, Iowa, Mar. 11, 1926; s. Roman F. and Anna Laura (Fitzgerald) S.; m. Barbara Brothers, Nov. 27, 1954 (div.); children: Timothy, Rebecca, Thomas; m. Joy D. Conger, Aug. 1, 1981. BA, Westminster Coll., 1947, DSc (hon.), 1965; MA, Northwestern U., 1950, MD, PhD, 1952; DSc (hon.), N.Y. Med. Coll., 1970, Westmar Coll., 1974, Med. Coll. Wis., 1981, Northwestern U., 1982, Bucknell U., 1985, Muhlenberg Coll., 1985, Mt. Sinai Sch. Medicine, 1988; MD (hon.), U. Louvain, Belgium, 1985, U. Genova, 1988, U. Rennes, 1988; LLD (hon.), U. Wyo., 1971; LHD (hon.), LaRoche Coll., 1988. Intern Johns Hopkins U. Hosp., Balt., 1952-53, fellow, surg., 1953-54, resident, 1955-56; mem. faculty Northwestern U. Med. Sch., Evanston, Ill., 1958-61; mem. faculty U. Colo. Med. Sch., Denver, 1962-80, prof. surgery, 1964-80, chmn. dept. surgery, 1972-80; prof. surgery, dir. of Transplantation Inst. U. Pitts., 1981—; mem. staff Presbyn. Hosp., Univ. Hosp., Children's Hosp. of Pitts., Pitts. VA Hosp. Author: Experience in Renal Transplantation, 1964, Experience in Hepatic Transplantation, 1969; contbr. articles to profl. jours. Recipient award Westminster Coll., 1965, Achievement award Lund U., 1965, Eppinger award Soc. Internat. de Chirurgie, 1965, Eppinger prize, Freiburg, 1970, William S. Middleton award for outstanding research in VA system, 1968, Merit award Northwestern U., 1969, Disting. Achievement award Modern Medicine, 1969, Creative Council award U. Colo., 1971, Colo. Man of Yr. award, 1967, Brookdale award AMA, 1974, David Hume Meml. award Nat. Kidney Found., 1978, Pitts. Man of Yr. award, 1981; Markle scholar, 1958. Fellow ACS (Sheen award 1982), Am. Acad. Arts and Scis.; mem. Soc. Univ. Surgeons, Soc. Vascular Surgery, Am. Surg. Assn., Transplantation Soc., Deutsche Gesellschaft für Chirurgie, numerous others. Office: U Pitts Sch Med 3601 5th Ave 4th Fl Falk Clinic Pittsburgh PA 15213*

STARZYK, MARVIN J., plant biology research administrator; b. Chgo., Feb. 3, 1935; married, 1958; 4 children. BS, Loyola U., Chgo., 1957; PhD in Microbiology, U. Wis., 1962. Asst. prof. natural scis. No. Ill. U., De Kalb, 1961-64, asst. sect. leader, 1965-66; group leader microbiology rsch. dept. Brown & Williamson Tobacco Corp., Ky., 1964-65; asst. prof. No. Ill. U., De Kalb, 1966-71, assoc. prof., 1971-85, chmn. dept. biol. scis., 1984, prof. microbiology, 1985—; cons. Brown & Williamson Tobacco Corp., 1966-67. Mem. AAAS, Am. Soc. Microbiology, Sigma Xi. Office: Northern Illinois Univ Plant Molecular Biology Ctr Montgomery Hall De Kalb IL 60115-2861*

STASACK, EDWARD ARMEN, artist; b. Chgo., Oct. 1, 1929; s. Clifford Clement and Elizabeth Frances (Mallek) S.; m. Mary Louise Walters, June 20, 1953 (div. 1972); children: Caren Marie, Jennifer Elizabeth, John Armen, Michael Clifford; m. Diane Miura Hirsch, June 26, 1993. BFA with high honors, U. Ill., Urbana, 1955, MFA, 1956. Instr. in art U. Hawaii, 1956-61, prof. art, chmn. dept. art, 1969-72, program chmn. in printmaking, 1975-83, prof. emeritus, 1988; affiliate Downtown Gallery, N.Y.C., 1960-70; adj. prof. Prescott Coll. Author: (with J. Halley Cox) Hawaiian Petroglyphs, 1970, (with Georgia Lee) Petroglyphs of Kaho'olawe, 1993, Ka'upulehu Petroglyphs, 1994; one-man shows include Honolulu Acad. Arts, 1961, 66, 69, 76, 87, U.S. embassies Istanbul and Izmir, Turkey, 1976, Am. Cultural Ctr., Bucharest, Romania, 1976, Cleve. Inst. Art, 1976, Hilo (Hawaii) Coll. Gallery, 1976, Amfac Plaza Gallery, 1978, Ryan Gallery, 1981, Art Loft, Honolulu, 1983, Commons Gallery, U. Hawaii, 1996, Hawaii Volcano Nat. Park Art Ctr., 1996; group shows include Carnegie Inst., Pitts., 1964, Krakow (Poland) Biennial, 1966, 68, Smithsonian Instn., Washington, 1967, Mexico City Mus. Modern Art, 1968, Leicester Gallery, London, 1965, Art Mus. Manila, The Philippines, 1982, 2d Internat. Biennial Print Exhibit Republic of China, 1986, Yuma Art Ctr., 1990; represented in permanent collections Mus. Modern Art, N.Y.C., Met. Mus. Art, N.Y.C., Chgo. Art Inst., Bklyn. Mus., Honolulu Acad. Arts, Hawaii State Found. Culture and the Arts, Libr. of Congress, Phila. Mus. Art, Boston Pub. Libr. Served with U.S. Army, 1952-54. Recipient numerous prizes, including: Boston Printmakers Mems. prize, 1967; Juror's awards Honolulu Printmakers, 1957, 58, 59, 62, 63, 66, 67, 68, 74, 77, 87; Soc. Am. Graphic Artists prizes, 1956, 57, 61, 62, 63, 68, 73, 78, 79, 80, 91; Tiffany Found. fellow, 1958, 62; Rockefeller Found. grantee, 1959; MacDowell Colony fellow, 1971, 75; Hawaii State and U.S. Bicentennial Commns. fellow, 1975. Mem. Soc. Am. Graphic Artists, Australian Rock Art Rsch. Assn., Rock Art Assn. Hawaii (emeritus pres.), Am. Rock Art Rsch. Assn., Prescott Fine Arts Assn. Office: 1878 Paradise Ln Prescott AZ 86301

STASHEFF, JAMES DILLON, mathematics educator; b. N.Y.C., Jan. 15, 1936; s. Edward and Evelyn Columbia (Maher) S.; m. Ann Helen Pekarik; children: Steven, Kim. BA, U. Mich., 1956; MA, Princeton (N.J.) U., 1958, PhD, 1961; DPhil, Oxford (Eng.) U., 1961. Moore instr. MIT, Cambridge, Mass., 1960-62; asst. prof. Notre Dame U., South Bend, Ind., 1962-64, assoc. prof., 1964-68, prof., 1968-70; prof. Temple U., Phila., 1970-78, U. N.C., Chapel Hill, 1976—; vis. prof. Princeton U., 1968-69, U. Pa., Phila., fall 1983 and fall 1992, Rutgers U., New Brunswick, N.J., spring 1987, Lehigh U., spring 1993. Author: H-Spaces from a Homotopy Point of View, 1970, (with others) Characteristic Classes, 1974. Danforth fellow, 1956-60, Sloan fellow, 1967-69; Marshall scholar, 1958-60; NSF grantee 1964-84, 85-88, 89—. Mem. Am. Math. Soc., London Math. Soc., Math. Assn. Am., Phi Beta Kappa. Roman Catholic. Avocations: dancing. Office: U NC Math CB # 3250 Chapel Hill NC 27599

STASHOWER, SARA ELLEN, advertising executive; b. Cleve., Sept. 6, 1954; d. David Lippmann and Sally Carol (Weiss) S. BA cum laude, Macalester Coll., 1976; MEd, Harvard U., 1982. Lower sch. instr., curriculum supr. St. Paul Acad., 1976-81; cons. 3M Co., St. Paul, 1979-81; promotions dir. Robinson Broadcasting, Cleve., 1982-83; account exec. Liggett-Stashower Advt., Cleve., 1984-89, v.p., account supr., 1989-94, sr. v.p., 1994—; sr. v.p., gen. mgr. Liggett Stashower Consulting, Cleve., 1994; cons. Ctr. for Contemporary Art, Cleve., 1993-94. Trustee Playhouse Square Found., Cleve., 1993—, Cleve. Film Soc., 1990-96, Cleve. Children's Mus., 1996—; trustee, com. chair Montefiore Home, Cleve., 1991—; co-founder, co-chair exec. com. Playhouse Square Ptnrs., 1990-93; trustee New Orgn. for Visual Arts, 1991-96; Ohio co-chair, alumni rep. Macalester Coll. Alumni Admissions, 1981—. Recipient Achievement award No. Ohio Live Mag., 1992, 93; named one of Outstanding Young Women in Am., 1986. Mem. Cleve. Advt. Club (instr. 1990—), Jr. League Cleve. (community advisor 1990-94). Jewish. Home: 16300 Van Aken Blvd Shaker Hts OH 44120 Office: Liggett-Stashower Advt 1228 Euclid Ave Cleveland OH 44115-1831

STASIK, RANDY, health facility administrator. Treas., v.p. finance Borgess Health Alliance Inc., Kalamazoo, Mich. Office: Borgess Health Alliance Inc 1521 Gull Rd Kalamazoo MI 49001-1640*

STASIOR, WILLIAM F., engineering company executive; b. 1941. BSEE, Northwestern U., MSEE. With Booz Allen & Hamilton Inc., N.Y.C., 1967—, pres., COO, 1990—; CEO, chmn. bd. dirs. Booz Allen & Hamilton Inc., McLean, Va., 1991—. Office: Booz Allen & Hamilton Inc 8283 Greensboro Dr Mc Lean VA 22102*

STASSEN, JOHN HENRY, lawyer; b. Joliet, Ill., Mar. 22, 1943; s. John H. and Florence C. (McCarthy) S.; m. Sara A. Gaw, July 6, 1968; children: John C., David A. BS, Northwestern U., 1965, JD, Harvard U., 1968. Bar: Ill. 1968. Assoc. Kirkland & Ellis, Chgo., 1968, 73-76, ptnr. 1977—. Contbr. articles to legal jours. Lt. comdr., JAGC, USNR, 1969-72. Mem. ABA (past chmn. com. on futures regulation), Ill. Bar Assn., Chgo. Bar Assn., Phila. Soc., Mid America Club. Home: 1310 N Astor St Chicago IL 60610-2114 Office: Kirkland & Ellis 200 E Randolph St Ste 5900 Chicago IL 60601-6436

STASSI, RONALD V., electric power industry executive. Pres. So. Calif. Pub. Power Authority, Pasadena, 1990—; gen. mgr. Burbank (Calif.) Pub. Svc. Dept. Office: Burbank Public Services Dept 164 W Magnolia Blvd Burbank CA 91503*

STASSINOS, GAIL, lawyer; b. N.Y.C., July 6, 1949; d. John and Harriet (Katzen) S. BA in Psychology with honors, San Francisco State U., 1974; MA in Psychology with honors, Calif. State U., Sacramento, 1976; JD, U. Calif., Davis, 1987. Bar: Calif. 1987; Calif. C.C. counseling credential. Counselor Sacramento, 1976; head resident U. Wash., Pullman, 1976-78; pers. dir. Ctrl. Valley Opportunity Ctr., Merced, Calif., 1978-80; field rep. Calif. Sch. Employees Assn., Bakersfield, 1980; pers. analyst III Santa Barbara County, Calif., 1980-84; law clk. Beeson, Tayer, Badine, 1985; assoc. Canelo, Hansen & Wilson, Merced, Calif., 1987-89, Lea, Balavage & Arruti, Sacramento, 1989-90; pvt. practice Carmichael, Calif., 1990—; coord. ann. labor rels. conf. U. Calif., Davis, 1986; instr. U. Calif. Ext., Santa Cruz, 1978; pro tem judge small claims ct., Sacramento County. Author: (orgn. pers. manual) Central Valley Opportunity Center, 1979. Mem. ABA (litigation sect.), Sacramento Social Security Reps. Orgn., NOW (founding mem. Golden Gate chpt. 1968-69), Nat. Orgn. Social Security Reps., Calif. Trial Lawyers Assn., Calif. Women Lawyers, Capitol City Trial Lawyers, Women Lawyers of Sacramento, Bus. and Profl. Women (treas. 1984). Democrat. Jewish. Avocations: tri-lingual (English, Spanish, French), Karate greenbelt, agility dog shows, wine collecting, blues. Office: 5740 Windmill Way Carmichael CA 95608-1379

STASZESKY, FRANCIS MYRON, electric company consultant; b. Wilmington, Del., Apr. 16, 1918; s. Frank J. and Ruth (Jones) S.; m. Barbara F. Kearney, May 30, 1943; children—Francis Myron, John B., Barbara J., Faith A., Paul D. BSME, MIT, 1943; MSME, Mass. Inst. Tech., 1943. Mech. engr. Union Oil Co. Calif., L.A., 1943-45; with E.I. duPont de Nemours Co., Wilmington, Del., 1946-48; joined Boston Edison Co., 1948, supervising engr. design and constrn., 1948-57, supt. engring. and constrn. dept., 1957-64, v.p., asst. to pres., 1964-67, exec. v.p., 1967-79, pres., chief operating officer, 1979-83; cons., 1983—; dir. Boston Edison Co., 1968-83. Fellow ASME (life); mem. IEEE (sr., life), Nat. Acad. Engring., Engring., Soc. New Eng. (pres. 1961-62), Palm Valley Country Club (Palm Desert, Calif.), Brae Burn Country Club (West Newton, Mass.). Address: 166 Bank St Harwich Port MA 02646-1321

STATEN, DONNA KAY, elementary art educator; b. Temple, Tex., Apr. 17, 1958; d. Paul James and Doris Mary (Kleypas) Hoelscher; 1 child, Ryan. BS in Edn., U. Mary Hardin-Baylor, Belton, Tex., 1980. Cert. tchr. in art, elem. edn., health, phys. edn. and recreation, Tex. Art tchr. Meridith Magnet Sch., Temple, 1980-84; bank officer mktg. Tex. Am. Bank, Houston, 1985-88; self employed art tchr. and designer, Houston, 1989; tchr. ESL Aldine Ind. Sch. Dist., Houston, 1990; art tchr. Meridith Magnet Sch., 1991—; exec. dir. Visual Arts Friends of the Cultural Activities Ctr., Temple, 1993-95, Temple Sister Cities Corp., 1994—; chmn. fine arts team Meridith Campus, 1993—. Curator art exhibit From Russia with Love, 1993—, Internat. Children's Art Exhbn., 1996. Mem. The Contemporaries, Temple, 1994—; singer St. Luke's Ch. Choir, Temple, 1991—, mem. St. Luke's Women's Soc., 1993—; treas. Oaks Homeowners Assn., Temple, 1994—. Recipient Honorable Mention in Christmas Decorating Contest, Women's Day mag., 1989, Cert. of Recognition, Crayola/Binney & Smith, 1993-94, 95-96. Mem. AAUW, ASCD, Fine Arts Network, Internat. Soc. for Edn. Through Art, Nat. Art Edn. Assn., Tex. Art Edn. Assn., Tex. Classrm. Tchrs. Assn., Am. Craft Coun., Soc. Craft Designers, Tex. Computer Edn. Assn., Tex. Fine Arts Assn., Nat. Mus. Women in the Arts, Cultural Activities Ctr., Temple Assn. for the Gifted, Electronic Media Interest Group, Tex. Alliance Edn. and the Arts, Friends of the Temple Libr. Roman Catholic. Avocations: exercise, painting and drawing, singing. Home: 3927 River Oaks Cir Temple TX 76504-3566 Office: Meridith Magnet Sch 1717 E Avenue J Temple TX 76501-8414

STATKUS, JEROME FRANCIS, lawyer; b. Hammond, Ind., June 13, 1942; s. Albert William and Helen Ann (Vaicunas) S.; children: Wesley Albert, Nicholas Jerome. BA, So. Ill. U., 1964; JD, U. Louisville, 1968; MA, U. Wyo., 1974. Bar: Wyo. 1971, U.S. Dist. Ct. Wyo. 1971, Wis. 1989, D.C. 1977, U.S. Ct. Claims 1973, U.S. Supreme Ct. 1974, U.S. Ct. Appeals (10th and 7th cirs.) 1975. Law clk. U.S. Dist. Ct., So. Dist. Ill., Peoria, 1968-69; asst. atty. gen. State of Wyo., Cheyenne, 1971-75; legis. asst. to U.S. Senator Clifford Hansen, Washington, 1975-76; asst. U.S. atty. U.S. Dept. Justice, Cheyenne, 1976-77; sole practice, Cheyenne, 1978-79; assoc. Horisky, Bagley & Hickey, Cheyenne, 1979-81; ptnr. Rooney, Bagley, Hickey Evans & Statkus, Cheyenne, 1981-88; exec. dir. Wyo. State Bar, 1988-89; trustee Village of Germantown, Wis., 1991-93; pvt. practice, Douglas, Wyo., 1993-96, Germantown, 1996—; asst. pub. defender State of Wyo., Douglas, 1993-96. Pres. Ret. Sr. Vol. Program, Cheyenne, 1982-83; treas. Pathfinder (drug rehab.), Cheyenne, 1982-85; bar commr. 1st Jud. Dist., 1985-87; active Future Milw., 1991. Served with USNR, 1969-70. Mem. VFW, Wyo. Bar Assn., D.C. Bar Assn., Wis. State Bar Assn., Wyo. Trial Lawyers Assn. (bd. dirs.), Seventh Cir. Bar Assn., Wis. Vietnam Vets., KC. Republican. Roman Catholic. Home: PO Box 1523 Douglas WY 82633 Office: N93 W17744 White Oak Cir #29 Menomonee Falls WI 53051

STATLER, IRVING CARL, aerospace engineer; b. Buffalo, N.Y., Nov. 23, 1923; s. Samuel William and Sarah (Strauss) S.; m. Renee Roll, Aug. 23, 1953; children—William Scott, Thomas Stuart. B.S. in Aero. Engring., U. Mich., 1945, B.S. in Engring. Math., 1945; Ph.D., Calif. Inst. Tech., 1956. Research engr. flight research dept. Cornell Aero. Lab., Inc., Buffalo, 1946-53; prin. engr. flight research dept. Cornell Aero. Lab., Inc., 1956-57, asst. head aero-mechanics dept., 1957-63, head applied mechanics dept., 1963-70, sr. staff scientist aeroscis. div., 1970-71; research scientist U.S. Army Air Mobility Research and Devel. Lab., Moffett Field, Calif., 1971-73; dir. Aeromechanics Lab. U.S. Army Air Mobility Research and Devel. Lab., 1973-85, dir. AGARD, 1985-88; sr. staff scientist NASA Ames Rsch. Ctr., 1988-92, chief Human Factors Rsch. Divsn., 1992—; research scientist research analysis group Jet Propulsion Lab., Pasadena, Calif., 1953-55; chmn. flight mechanics panel adv. group aerospace research and devel. NATO, 1974-76; lectr. U. Buffalo, Millard-Fillmore Coll., Buffalo, 1957-58. Served with USAAF, 1945-46. Fellow AIAA (Internat. Cooperation in Space Sci. medal 1992), AAAS, German Aerospace Soc., Royal Aero Soc.; mem. Am. Helicopter Soc., Sigma Xi. Home: 1362 Cuernavaca Circulo Mountain View CA 94040-3571 Office: NASA Ames Rsch Ctr MS 262-7 Moffett Field CA 94035

STATLER, OLIVER HADLEY, writer; b. Chgo., May 21, 1915; s. Oliver Isaiah and Alice Mae (Hadley) S. BA, U. Chgo., 1936; LHD (hon.), Nat. Coll. Edn., Evanston, Ill., 1966. Administr. U.S. Civil Svc., Japan, 1947-54; writer, 1954—; tchr. U. Hawaii, Honolulu, 1977, adj. prof., 1977—. Sgt. U.S. Army, 1940-45, PTO. Guggenheim Found. fellow, 1973; Ctr. for Asian and Pacific Studies, U. Hawaii scholar-in-residence fellow, 1981; Japan Found. fellow, Tokyo, 1986. Mem. PEN, Authors Guild, Assn. for Asian Studies. Democrat. Home and Office: 1619 Kamamalu Ave Apt 302 Honolulu HI 96813-1720

STATMAN, JACKIE C., career consultant; b. Kingman, Kansas, June 15, 1936; d. Jack Carl and Dorothy E. (Kendall) Pulliam; m. Jerome Maurice Statman, Dec. 29, 1959; children: David Alan, Susan Gail. BA, U. Kans., 1958. Reg. music therapist Topeka State Hosp., Kans., 1958-59; caseworker Child Welfare, Pensacola, Fla., 1960-61; devel. rsch. tester The Children and Youth Project, Dallas, 1973-74; middle sch. counselor The Hockaday Sch., Dallas, 1981-84; career cons. Career Design Assocs., Inc., Garland, Tex., 1984-86; owner Career Focus Assocs., Plano, Tex., 1987—; pres. Assn. Women Entrepreneurs of Dallas, Inc., 1991-93; mem. career edn. adv. com. Plano Ind. Sch. Dist., 1993—. Author: (newspaper column) "Career Forum", 1991-92. With Cmty. Svcs. Commn., City of Plano, 1993—; mem. Leadership Plano Alumnae Assn., 1990—; mem. bd. dirs. Mental Health Assn. in Tex., 1989-93; founding pres. Mental Health Assn. Collin County, 1988-90. Recipient Child Advocacy award Mental Health Assn. of Greater Dallas, 1985, Golden Rule award JC Penney Comp., Inc., 1986, Humanitarian Vo. of the Yr. award Vol. Ctr. Collin County, 1990. Mem. Am. Counseling Assn., Nat. Assn. Women Bus. Owners (mem. Dallas/Ft. Worth bd. dirs. 1992-93), Nat. Career Devel. Assn., Plano C. of C. Avocations: community and civic volunteering. Office: Career Focus Assocs 1700 Coit Rd Ste 220 Plano TX 75075-6138

STAUB, AUGUST WILLIAM, drama educator, theatrical producer; b. New Orleans, Oct. 9, 1931; s. August Harry and Laurel (Elfer) S.; m. Patricia Gebhardt, Nov. 22, 1952; 1 child, Laurel Melicent. BA, La. State U., 1952, MA, 1956, PhD, 1960. Instr., tech. dir. La. State U., 1955; instr. Ea. Mich. U., 1956-58; assoc. dir. Dunes Summer Theatre, Michigan City, Ind., summers 1957-60; asst. prof., assoc. dir. univ. theatre U. Fla., 1960-64; assoc. prof. U. New Orleans, 1964-66, prof., chmn. dept. drama and communications, 1966-76; prof., head drama dept. U. Ga., 1976-95; exec. producer Jekyll Island Mus. Comedy Festival, 1984-88, Highlands (N.C.) Playhouse, 1989—, Ga. Repertory Theatre, 1991-95; exec. sec. Theatres of La.; v.p. New Orleans Internat. Jazz Festival, 1967-69; pres. S.W. Theatre Conf., 1973-74. Author: Lysistrata, 1968, The Social Climber, 1969, A Small Bare Space, 1970, Introduction to Theatrical Arts, 1971, Creating Theatre, 1973, Varieties of Theatrical Arts, 1980, 83, 94; gen. editor: Artists and Ideas in the Theatre (Peter Lang), 1989—; assoc. editor Speech Tchr., 1966-68, So. Speech Comm. Jour., 1974-77, Quar. Jour. Speech, 1977-79. Bd. dirs. Friends Ga. Mus., Ga. Symphony, Coun. Arts for Children, New Orleans, New Orleans Ctr. Creative Arts, Athens Arts. Commn., Ga. Alliance Arts Edn. Lt. AUS, 1952-54. Recipient Creativity in Rsch. medallion U. Ga., 1987, Disting. Svc. award S.W. Theater Conf., 1985; La. State U. Found. Disting. Faculty fellow, 1970-71. Fellow Coll. of Fellows of Am. Theatre; mem. Am. Theatre Assn. (pres. 1985-86, bd. dirs.), Univ. and Coll. Theatre Assn. (pres. 1974-75), Nat. Assn. Schs. Theatre (pres. 1981-83), Univ. Resident Theatre Assn. (bd. dirs.), Inst. European Theatre, Nat. Theatre Conf., Am. Soc. Theatre Rsch., Internat. Fedn. Theatre Rsch. Home: 400 Ponderosa Dr Athens GA 30605-3324 *How good it is to be able to earn a living doing what one loves to do.*

STAUB, W. ARTHUR, health care products executive; b. Detroit, Dec. 25, 1923; s. Edward Elmer and Emma Josephine (Fleury) S.; m. Alla Elizabeth Edwards, June 26, 1948; children: James Randall, Sally Ann, David Scott. BS, Dartmouth Coll., 1944; MD, Temple U., 1947. Intern Muhlberg Hosp., Plainfield, N.J., 1947-48; resident in pediatrics Abington (Pa.) Meml. Hosp., 1950-51; practice medicine specializing in pediatrics Westfield (N.J.) Med. Group, 1948-63; assoc. med. dir. Ciba Pharm. Co., Summit, N.J., 1963-66; med. dir., v.p. life sci. div. Becton-Dickinson and Co., Rutherford, N.J., 1966-70; v.p. med. affairs C. R. Bard Co., Murray Hill, N.J., 1970-88, also bd. dirs.; bd. dirs. Crestmont Fed. Savs. and Loan Assn., Edison, N.J., Colonial Trust Nat. Bank, North Palm Beach, Fla.; cons. Children's Specialized Hosp., Westfield, 1948-88, Overlook Hosp., Summit, 1948-88. Contbr. articles to profl. jours. Sec., treas. Westfield Med. Soc., 1961; deacon Presbyn. Ch., Westfield, 1959—. Served to capt. USAF, 1951-53. Fellow Am. Coll. Physician Execs.; mem. AAAS, Assn. Advancement Med. Instrumentation, Health Industry Mfrs. Assn. (chmn. med. and sci. steering com.). Republican. Presbyterian. Clubs: Echo Lake Country (Westfield) (bd. trustees 1984—); Lost Tree (North Palm Beach, Fla.); Skytop (Pa.). Avocations: golf, physical fitness, reading, sailing, travel. Home: 810 Village Rd North Palm Beach FL 33408-3334

STAUBER, DONNA BETH, education educator; b. Belton, Tex., Dec. 18, 1955; d. William R. and Pansy Joan (Bell) Parmer; 1 child, Chassati Thiele; m. George Russell Stauber, July 25, 1987; children: Blake, Michal. BS, Tex. A & M U., 1978; MS in Edn., Baylor U., 1983; PhD in Health Edn., Tex. Woman's U., 1993. Cert. health edn. specialist. Tchr., coach Sand Springs (Okla.) Ind. Sch. Dist., 1978-80, McGregor (Tex.) Ind. Sch. Dist., 1980-82, Leander (Tex.) Ind. Sch. Dist., 1983-87; grad. asst. Baylor U., Waco, Tex., 1982-83, lectr., 1987-94; lectr. Baylor U., 1994; product devel. coord. WRS Group, Inc., Waco; lectr. on stress mgmt. and self-esteem. Vol. Multiple Sclerosis Soc. Mem. AAHPERD, Tex. Assn. Health, Phys. Edn., Recreation and Dance, Soc. Pub. Health Edn., Nat. Wellness Assn., Assn. for Worksite Health Promotion, Am. Coll. Health Assn., Internat. Coun. Health, Phys. Edn., Recreation, Sport and Dance (health edn. commn. 1995). Home: 9601 Bryce Dr Waco TX 76712-3218

STAUBER, KARL NEILL, federal executive; b. Statesville, N.C., Jan. 4, 1951; s. Van G. and Dorthea (Mills) S.; m. Hollis Scott, Aug. 14, 1971. BA, U. N.C., 1973; Program for Mgmt. Devel., Harvard U., 1983; PhD, Union Inst., Cin., 1993. Asst. dir. Reynolds Babcock Found., Winston-Salem, N.C., 1974-79; exec. dir. Needmor Found., Toledo, Ohio, 1979-83; pres. Econ. Devel., Inc., Boulder, Colo., 1983-86; v.p. program N.W. Area Found., St. Paul, 1986-93; dep. under sec. reed USDA, Washington, 1993-94, under sec. ree, 1994—. Contbr. editorials to newspapers. Adv. bd. mem. Found. Mid South, Jackson, Miss., 1988-93, Mpls. Found., 1991-93. Avocations: furniture building, tractor restoration. Office: USDA 14th & Independence Ave Washington DC 20250

STAUBER, MARILYN JEAN, secondary and elementary school; b. Duluth, Minn., Feb. 5, 1938; d. Harold Milton and Dorothy Florence (Thompson) Froelich; children: Kenneth D. and James H. Atkinson; m. Lawrence B. Stauber Sr., Jan. 11, 1991. BS in K-6 Edn., U. Minn., Duluth, 1969, MEd in Math., 1977. Cert. elem. and secondary reading tchr., remedial reading specialist, devel. reading tchr., reading cons. Sec. div. vocat. rehab. State Minn., Duluth, 1956-59; sec. Travelers Ins. Co., Duluth, 1962-66; lead tchr. Title 1 reading and math. Proctor, Minn., 1969—. Mem. choir, comm. coord. Forbes Meth. Ch., Proctor. Mem. NEA, Internat. Reading Assn., Nat. Reading Assn., Minn. Arrowhead Reading Coun., Elem. Coun. (pres. 1983-84, 86-87), Proctor Fedn. Tchrs. (recert. com. 1980—, treas. 1981-86), Proctor Edn. Assn. Home: 6713 Grand Lake Rd Saginaw MN 55779-9782

STAUBITZ, ARTHUR FREDERICK, lawyer, healthcare products company executive; b. Omaha, Nebr., Mar. 14, 1939; s. Herbert Frederick Staubitz and Barbara Eileen (Dallas) Alderson; m. Linda Medora Miller, Aug. 18, 1962; children: Michael, Melissa, Peter. AB cum laude, Wesleyan U., Middletown, Conn., 1961; JD cum laude, U. Pa., 1964. Bar: Ill. 1964, U.S. Dist. Ct. (no. dist.) Ill. 1964, U.S. Ct. Appeals (7th cir.) 1964, Pa. 1972. Assoc. Sidley & Austin, Chgo., 1964-71; sr. internat. atty., asst. gen. counsel, dir. Japanese ops. Sperry Univac, Blue Bell, Pa., 1971-78; from asst. to assoc. to dep. gen. counsel Baxter Internat. Inc., Deerfield, Ill., 1978-85, v.p., dep. gen. counsel, 1985-90; v.p. Baxter Diagnostics, 1990-91; sr. v.p., sec., gen. counsel Amgen, Inc., Thousand Oaks, Calif., 1991-92; v.p., gen. mgr. Ventures Group Baxter World Trade Corp., Deerfield, Ill., 1992-93; v.p., sec., gen. counsel Baxter Internat. Inc., Deerfield, Ill., 1993, sr. v.p., gen. counsel, 1993—. Mem. Planning Commn., Springfield Twp., Montgomery County, Pa., 1973-74, mem. Zoning Hearing Bd., 1974-78; bd. dirs. Twp. H.S. Dist. 113, Deerfield and Highland Park, Ill., 1983-91, pres., 1989-91; trustee Food and Drug Law Inst., 1991-92, 93—; bd. dirs. Music of the Baroque, 1994—; vice-chmn. planning. Mem. ABA, Chgo. Bar Assn. Episcopalian. Home: 232 Deerfield Rd Deerfield IL 60015-4412 Office: Baxter Internat Inc 1 Baxter Pky Deerfield IL 60015-4625

STAUBS, JOYCE JARRETT, critical care nurse; b. Miami, Fla., May 15, 1947; d. Jones Eli and Maxine (Whitt) Jarrett; m. Ralph Arthur Staubs, Feb. 14, 1976; 1 child, Joel Eli. Diploma, Burge Sch. Nursing, Springfield, Mo., 1974; BA in Edn., Southwest Mo. State U., Springfield, 1971; teaching cert., Bapt. Bible Coll., Springfield, 1971. Staff nurse CCU Prince Georges Hosp. Ctr., Cheverly, Md., 1974-80, staff nurse clin. post anesthetic care unit, 1980-94; staff nurse level IV Dimensions Health Corp., Landover, Md., 1994—. Spl. editor The Recovery Rm. Home: 6908 Barton Rd Hyattsville MD 20784-2502

STAUBUS, GEORGE JOSEPH, accounting educator; b. Brunswick, Mo., Apr. 26, 1926; s. George Washington and Florence Lidwina (Pittman) S.; m. Sarah Mayer, Apr. 11, 1949; children: Lindsay, Martin, Paul, Janette. B.S., U. Mo., 1947; M.B.A., U. Chgo., 1949, Ph.D., 1954. C.P.A., Ill. Instr. U. Buffalo, 1947-49, U. Chgo., 1950-52; asst. prof. then assoc. prof. acctg. U. Calif.-Berkeley, from 1952, now Michael N. Chetkovich prof. emeritus; vis. prof. NYU, 1965, London Grad Sch. Bus. Studies, 1966-67, U. Kans., 1969-70; Erskine lectr. U. Canterbury, New Zealand, 1972, 91. Author: A Theory of Accounting to Investors, 1961, Activity Costing and Input-Output Accounting, 1971, Making Accounting Decisions, 1977, An Accounting Concept of Revenue, 1980, Activity Costing for Decisions, 1988, Economic Influences on the Development of Accounting in Firms, 1995—. Served with USN, 1944-46. Recipient Disting. prof. Calif. Soc. C.P.A.s, 1981. Fellow Acctg. Researchers Internat. Assn. (treas. 1981-83); mem. Am. Acctg. Assn. (disting. internat. lectr. 1982), Am. Inst. C.P.A.s, Fin. Execs. Inst. Office: UC Berkeley Acctg Dept Berkeley CA 94720

STAUDER, ALFRED MAX, wire products company executive; b. Mexico City, May 25, 1940; s. Hans and Charlotte (Mueller) S.; m. Deanna J. Woods, June 12, 1962; children—Carl, Monique. B.A., Principia Coll., 1962. Chief exec. officer Woods Wire Products, Inc., Carmel, Ind., 1965—. Served to 1st lt. U.S. Army, 1962-65. Mem. Young Pres. Orgn. Republican. Christian Scientist. Club: Palm Beach Polo and Country (Fla.). Home: PO Box 891 Carmel IN 46032-0891 Office: Woods Wire Products Inc 510 3rd Ave SW Carmel IN 46032-2032*

STAUDER, WILLIAM VINCENT, geophysics educator; b. New Rochelle, N.Y., Apr. 23, 1922; s. William P. and Margaret (Boll) S. A.B., St. Louis U., 1943, M.S. in Physics, 1948; S.T.L., St. Mary's (Kans.) Coll., 1953; Ph.D. in Geophysics, U. Calif. at Berkeley, 1959. Joined S.J., 1939, ordained priest Roman Catholic Ch., 1952. Faculty St. Louis U., 1959-92, prof. geophysics, 1966-92, prof. emeritus, 1992—, rector Jesuit community, 1967-73, 88-91, chmn. dept. earth and atmospheric scis., 1972-75, acting dean Grad. Sch., 1974-75, dean Grad. Sch., 1975-87, dir. univ. rsch., 1975-87, assoc. acad. v.p., 1989—; vis. research assoc. U. Calif.-Berkeley, 1984-85. Contbr. articles to profl. jours. Trustee Marquette U., 1978-90. Fellow Am. Geophys. Union; mem. Seismol. Soc. Am. (bd. dirs. 1962-68, pres. 1965, chmn. Eastern sect. 1964), Phi Beta Kappa, Sigma Xi. Home: 3601 Lindell Blvd Saint Louis MO 63108-3301

STAUDERMAN, BRUCE FORD, advertising executive, writer; b. Jersey City, Mar. 17, 1919; b. Herbert Henry and Helen Ann (Jacobus) S.; m. Claude Outhier, Mar. 23; 1946. Student, Syracuse U., 1936-38, TV Workshop, N.Y.C., 1949-50, Sch. TV Technique, 1950. V.p. TV, radio, films Meldrum & Fewsmith, Inc. (advt. agy.), Cleve., 1954-62; exec. v.p., chmn. plans bd., exec. creative dir. Meldrum & Fewsmith, Inc. (advt. agy.), 1973-79; v.p., creative dir. Ogilvy & Mather (advt. agy.), N.Y.C., 1962-69, Kenyon & Eckhardt, Inc. (advt. agy.), N.Y.C., 1979-83, Barnhart & Co. (advt. agy.), Denver, 1983-84; pres. Stauderman Advt., 1984—; v.p., creative dir. Mktg. Resources Group (advt. agy.), 1985-88; dir. TV, advt. cons. Intermarco-Elvinger (advt. co.), Paris, 1969-73; TV cons. gov., Ohio, 1958; council mem., judge C.L.I.O. Festival, 1960—; chmn. Paris jury, 1969-73; jury mem. Internat. Advt. Film Festival, Cannes, Venice, 1976—. Radio, TV program writer: House of Mystery, 1946-51; writer, producer, dir., WXEL-TV, Cleve., 1951-54. Mem. men's com. Cleve. Playhouse, 1958-62; chmn. TV com. Cleve. United Fund, 1958-59. Served from pvt. to 2d lt. AUS, 1941-46; to 1st lt. N.G. Essex Troop AUS, 1948-50. Mem. Am. Assn. Advt. Agys. (TV and radio adminstrs. com. 1958-62), Am. Fedn. TV and Radio Artists, Naval Club (London). Home: 30 Water St, Lavenham, Suffolk CO10 9RN, England

STAUFF, MICHAEL FREDERICK, financial manager; b. Frankfurt, Fed. Republic Germany, Feb. 22, 1950; came to U.S., 1950; s. Ralph Thomas and Leona Marie (McMahon) S.; m. Rosemary Chere Delaware, Aug. 2, 1975; children: Matthew, Adam. BS in Bus. Adminstrn., Northeastern U., 1972, MBA, 1983. Plant acct. Pandel Bradford, Lowell, Mass., 1972-73; fin. mgr. Modicon Corp., North Andover, Mass., 1973-75; asst. controller Simplex, Inc., Gardner, Mass., 1975-77, asst. to pres., 1977-80, materials mgr., 1980-83, mgr. corp. planning, 1983-85; v.p., chief fin. officer Internat. Marine Industries, Inc., Stamford, Conn., 1985-94; sr. v.p. TranSwitch Corp., Shelton, Conn., 1994—. Mem. Nat. Acctg. Assn., Fin. Execs. Inst. Roman Catholic. Avocations: skiing, boating, jogging. Home: 117 Settlers Farm Rd Monroe CT 06468-3334 Office: TranSwitch Corp 8 Progress Dr Shelton CT 06484-6219

STAUFF, WILLIAM JAMES, facility director; b. Providence, Mar. 2, 1949; s. William A. and Charlotte A. (Thorpe) S.; m. Bertha Nichols, Jan. 22, 1972; children: William J., Heidi A., Anneliese C. BS in Bus. Adminstrn., Northeastern U., Boston, 1977; MBA, Suffolk U., 1983; postgrad., U. Va., 1992—, Bethany Theol. Sem., Dothan, Ala. Process writer, indsl. engr. Rockwell Internat., Hopedale, Mass., 1972-77; bus. mgr., acct. Luth. Svc. Assn. New Eng., Framingham, Mass., 1977-80; mgr. acctg. and fin. Office Info. Tech. Harvard U., Cambridge, Mass., 1980-89; dir. bus. ops. facilities mgmt. U. Va., Charlottesville, Va., 1989—; pub. acctg. auditor Charles Murphy/Paul Haggerty, CPAs, Framingham, 1977-80. Mem. Assn. Higher Edn. Facilities Officers. Avocations: gardening, music, teaching. Home: RR 2 Box 286A Staunton VA 24401-9539 Office: U Va 575 Alderman Rd Charlottesville VA 22903-2405

STAUFFER, CHARLES HENRY, retired chemistry educator; b. Harrisburg, Pa., Apr. 17, 1913; s. Charles C. and Hannah (Henry) S.; m. Eleanor Ramsdell, July 8, 1939; children—Charles R., Anne Elizabeth, John E. A.B., Swarthmore Coll., 1934; M.A., Harvard U., 1936, Ph.D., 1937. Instr. Worcester (Mass.) Poly. Inst., 1937-43, asst. prof., 1943-52, assoc. prof., 1952-58; assoc. prof. affiliate Clark U., Worcester, 1941; prof., chmn. dept. chemistry St. Lawrence U., Canton, N.Y., 1958-65; prof. chemistry, chmn. div. natural scis. math. Bates Coll., Lewiston, Maine, 1965—, Charles A. Dana prof. chemistry, 1968-77, prof. emeritus, 1977—; dir. chem. kinetics data project Nat. Acad. Scis., 1954-64; mem. adv. com. Office Critical Constants, 1961-64. Fellow AAAS, Am. Chem. Soc. (sec., chmn. No. N.Y. sect., councilor Maine sect.); mem. Sigma Xi, Phi Beta Kappa (Swarthmore Coll. chpt.). Clubs: Mason, Searsport Yacht. Home: 10 Champlain Ave Lewiston ME 04240-5217

STAUFFER, DELMAR J., professional association executive; b. Saybrook, Ill., Nov. 22; s. Calvin Bishop and Lillian Ruth (Hammel) S.; m. Mary Barbara Gower, Oct. 22, 1939; children: Andrew Thomas, Matthew Eric. BS in Health Edn. and Biology, U. Ill., 1963, MS in Health Edn., 1967, postgrad., 1970. Sci. tchr. Glenwood (Ill.) Sch. for Boys, 1963-65, Edgewood Jr. High Sch., Highland Park, Ill., 1965-66; grad. instr. health and safety U. Ill., Champaign, 1966-70; health edn. adminstr. AMA, Chgo., 1970-71; dir. bur. health edn. and audio svcs. ADA, Chgo., 1971-77, sec. coun. on dental health and planning, 1976-78, asst. exec. dir., 1978-86; exec. dir. Chgo. Dental Soc., 1986-89, Radiol. Soc. N.Am., Oak Brook, Ill., 1989—; cons. Am. Fund for Dental Health, Chgo., 1978-85, advisor, trustee, 1988-89; cons. Fedn. Dentaire Internat., 1983-86. Co-author, editor strategic plan Future of Dentistry, 1983; contbr. articles to profl. jours. Mem. Lake Bluff (Ill.) Sch. Bd. Caucus, 1980-86. Recipient award of merit Am. Coll. Dentists, Washington, 1985. Fellow Am. Sch. Health Assn. (fin. com. 1985—); mem. Am. Soc. Assn. Execs., Chgo. Soc. Assn. Execs., Am. Pub. Health Assn., Ill. Soc. Pub. Health Edn., Town and Tennis Club (pres. 1984). Republican. Methodist. Office: Radiol Soc N Am 2021 Spring Rd Ste 600 Oak Brook IL 60521-1860

STAUFFER, ERIC P., lawyer; b. Tucson, Feb. 1, 1948; s. Robert D. and Jeanne E. (Catlin) S.; m. Jane F. Snyder, Aug. 2, 1969; children: Curtis Austen, Marcus Elias, Laura Afton. BA, U. South Fla., 1969; JD, Yale U., 1972. Bar: Ariz. 1972, Maine 1974, D.C. 1979. Spl. asst. to gov., fed. state coord. State of Maine, 1973-75; Maine alt. to New Eng. Regional Commn.; gen. counsel Maine State Housing Auth., 1976-77; adminstrv. asst. to chmn. Dem. Nat. Com., 1977-78; mem. Preti, Flaherty, Beliveau & Pachios, Portland, Maine, 1978—; Maine alt. to New England Regional Commn., 1973-75. Bd. dirs. Jr. Achievement Maine, Inc., 1995—; pres. Goodwill Industries, Maine, 1981-82, bd. dirs., 1979-93. Recipient Pub. Svc. award, 1992. Mem. Nat. Health Lawyers Assn., Maine State Bar Assn., Ariz. State Bar, D.C. Bar, Maine Real Estate Devel. Assn. (bd. dirs. 1990—), Maine Real Estate Devel. Assn. Office: Preti Flaherty Beliveau & Pachios PO Box 11410 443 Congress St Portland ME 04104-7410

STAUFFER, JOHN H., newspaper and broadcast executive; b. Arkansas City, Kans., Apr. 8, 1928; s. Oscar Stanley and Ethel Lucille (Stone) S.; m. Ruth Granger, June 3, 1950; children: John H. Jr., William H., Mary S. Brownback. BS Journalism, U. Kans., 1949. Reporter Topeka State Jour., 1949-54; editor The Kansan, Newton, 1954-57; pub. The Kansan, Kansas City, 1957-72, Topeka-Capital Jour., 1972-86; sr. v.p. Stauffer Comm. Inc., Topeka, 1969-86, pres., CEO, 1986-92; chmn. Topeka-Capital Jour., 1991—; also bd. dirs. Stauffer Comm. Inc., Topeka; dir. Mercantile Bank of Topeka. Pres. Kansas City Kans. United Way, 1968-69; chmn. bd. trustees Stormont-Vail Hosp., Topeka, 1984-86; mem. session 1st Presbyn. Ch., Topeka, 1986-89. Lt. U.S. Army, 1950-52. Mem. Kans. Press Assn. (pres. 1985-86), Inland Press Assn. (dir. 1980-88), Topeka Country Club (dir. 1978-83), Topeka C. of C. (pres. 1979), Kansas City C. of C. (pres. 1970-71), Top of the Tower, Phi Delta Theta. Republican. Presbyterian. Home: 2845 SW Jewell Ave Topeka KS 66611-1615 Office: Stauffer Comm Inc 616 SE Jefferson St Topeka KS 66607-1137

STAUFFER, ROBERT ALLEN, former research company executive; b. Dayton, Ohio, Jan. 26, 1920; s. John G. and Verna G. (Theobald) S.; m. Justine M. Wells, Mar. 20, 1943 (div. 1969); children—Susan, Nancy; m. Ruth Stanley Munro, Oct. 30, 1969. B.A. in Chemistry, Harvard, 1942. With Nat. Research Corp., Cambridge, 1942-67; gen. mgr. research div. Nat. Research Corp., 1949-63, dir., 1954-67, v.p., 1949-67; with Norton Co., Worcester, Mass., 1963-71; v.p. research Norton Co., 1963-71; v.p., gen. mgr. Norton Research Corp., Cambridge, 1968-71; v.p. NRC Metals Corp., 1955-56, Environ. Research and Tech., Concord, Mass., 1971-80. Patentee in field. Home: 3208 Heatherwood at Kings Way Yarmouth Port MA 02675

STAUFFER, RONALD EUGENE, lawyer; b. Hempstead, N.Y., Jan. 22, 1949; s. Hiram Eugene and Florence Marie (Hintz) S.; m. Vicki Lynn Hartman, June 12, 1973; children: Eric Alan, Craig Aaron, Darren Adam. SB, MIT, 1970; JD magna cum laude, Harvard U., 1973. Bar: D.C. 1973, U.S. Ct. Mil. Appeals 1976, U.S. Tax Ct. 1979. Ptnr. Hogan & Hartson, Washington, 1977-87, Sonnenschein Nath & Rosenthal, Washington, 1988—. Contbr. articles to profl. publs. Capt. U.S. Army, 1970-77. Mem. ABA (chair TIPS Employee Benefits Com. 1977—), D.C. Bar Assn., Tau Beta Pi, Sigma Gamma Tau. Avocations: running, water skiing. Home: 10207 Woodvale Pond Dr Fairfax Station VA 22039-1658 Office: Sonnenschein Nath & Rosenthal 1301 K St NW Ste 600 Washington DC 20005-3317

STAUFFER, STANLEY HOWARD, newspaper and broadcasting executive; b. Peabody, Kans., Sept. 11, 1920; s. Oscar S. and Ethel L. (Stone) S.; m. Suzanne R. Wallace, Feb. 16, 1945 (div. 1961); children: Peter, Clay, Charles; m. Elizabeth D. Priest, July 14, 1962 (div. 1991); children: Elizabeth, Grant; m. Madeline A. Sargent, Nov. 27, 1992. AB, U. Kans., 1942. Assoc. editor Topeka State Jour., 1946-47; editor, pub. Santa Maria (Calif.) Times, 1948-52; rewrite and copy editor Denver Post, 1953-54; staff mem. AP (Denver bur.), 1954-55; exec. v.p. Stauffer Publs., Inc., 1955-69; gen. mgr. Topeka Capital-Jour., 1957-69; pres. Stauffer Comm., Inc., 1969-86, chmn., 1986-92; bd. dirs. Topeka/Shawnee County Devel. Corp.; chmn. bd. dirs. Stauffer Comm. Found. Past pres. Topeka YMCA; past chmn. adv. bd. St. Francis Hosp.; past chmn. Met. Topeka Airport Authority; trustee William Allen White Found., Menninger Found., Midwest Rsch. Inst., Washburn U. Endowment Assn. With USAAF, 1942-45. Named Chpt. Boss of Yr. Am. Bus. Women's Assn., 1976, Outstanding Kans. Pub. Kappa Tau Alpha, 1980, Legion of Honor De Molay, Topeka Phi of Yr., 1971. Mem. Kans. Press Assn. (past pres.), Inland Daily Press Assn. (past dir.), Air Force Assn. (past pres. Topeka), Kans. U. Alumni Assn. (past dir.), Kans. C. of C. and Industry (past chmn.), Def. Orientation Conf. Assn., Topeka Country Club, Top of the Tower Club, Garden of the Gods Club, La Quinta (Calif.) Country Club, Masons (32d deg.), Shriners, Phi Delta Theta (past chpt. pres.), Sigma Delta chi (past chpt. pres.). Episcopalian (past sr. warden). Office: Stauffer Comm Inc 6th & Jefferson St Topeka KS 66607

STAUFFER, THOMAS GEORGE, hotel executive; b. Akron, Ohio, Mar. 4, 1932; s. Caldwell E. and Rose C. (Ortscheidt) S.; m. Lois Campsey, June 18, 1960. B.S., Case Western Res. U., 1954. Cert. hotel adminstr. Pres. Renaissance Hotels Internat. (Ams.), 1954—. Recipient Legion of Honor, Order of DeMolay. Mem. Am. Hotel and Motel Assn., Urban Land Inst., Nat. Restaurant Assn. (dir.), Rolling Rock Club, Clifton Club, Masons, Shriners, Sigma Chi (Significant Sigma Chi). Home: 1000 Estill Dr Cleveland OH 44107-1418 Office: Renaissance Hotels Internat 29800 Bainbridge Rd Solon OH 44139-2202

STAUFFER, THOMAS MICHAEL, university president; b. Harrisburg, Pa., Dec. 5, 1941; s. John Nisley and Louis Lee Stauffer; m. Marion Walker, Aug. 26, 1966 (div. Dec. 1989); children: Amity Juliet, Courtney Amanda, Winston Thomas; m. Deborah Whisnand, May 16, 1993; 1 stepchild, Elizabeth Stinson. Student, Juniata Coll., 1959-61; BA cum laude, Wittenberg U., Ohio, 1963; Cert. in E. European Politics, Freie U. Berlin, 1964; MA, PhD, U. Denver, 1973. Asst. dean coll., asst. prof. polit. sci. Keene State Coll., 1968-72; dir. fellows in acad. adminstrn., office leadership devel. Am. Coun. Edn., 1972-78; v.p., dir. div. external relations Am. Council on Edn., Washington, 1978-82; pres. Golden Gate Univ., San Francisco, present; exec. sec. Fedn. of Assn. of the Acad. Health Care Professions, 1975-80; chmn. task force on the future of Am. Coun. on Edn., 1978; exec. dir. Bus.-Higher Edn. Forum, 1978-81, Nat. Commn. on Higher Edn. Issues, 1980-81; pres., prof. pub. policy U. Houston, Clear Lake, 1982-91; pres., prof. pub. policy and internat. rels. Golden Gate U., 1992—; spl. asst. to adminstr. NASA, 1992; cons. NSF, Dept. State, Coun. for Internat. Exch. Scholars, Japan External Trade Orgn.; mem. commn. on credit and credentials, Am. Coun. Edn., Bay Area Internat. Forum; chair nat. bd. Challenger Ctr. for Space Sci. Edn., 1987-89, Ctr. for Advanced Space Studies, 1990-94; mem. dels. on higher edn. and econ. devel. to People's Republic of China, S.E. Asia, Japan, Rwanda, Sri Lanka, United Arab Emirates, 1978-94. Exec. editor Ednl. Record and Higher Edn. and Nat. Affairs, 1978-82; contbr. articles to profl. jours., newspapers, monographs, chpts. to books. Chmn. com. advanced tech. Tex. Econ. Devel., 1984, Houston Com. on Econ. Diversification Planning, 1984, Houston World Trade Ctr. Task Force, 1985, East Tex. 2000 Com. on Econ. Devel., S.E. Tex. Higher Edn. Coun., 1989, Clear Lake Area Econ. Devel. Found.; v.p. Inter-Am., U. Coun. for Econ. and Social Devel., Houston World Trade Assn.; vice chmn. Tex. Sci. and Tech. Coun., 1986; pres. St. John Hosp.; trustee San Francisco Consortium; bd. dirs. Houston Hosp. Coun. Found., Tex. Coun. on Econ. Edn., Tex. Senate Space Industry Tech. Commn., Tex. Innovation Info. Network Sys., San Francisco C. of C.; vice-chair San Francisco World Trade Assn.; mem. steering com. Houston Econ. Devel. Coun., Calif. Ind. Edn. Coun., blue ribbon com. City Coll., Bay Area Coun., Industry Edn. Coun. of Calif.; chair San Francisco Mayor's Blue Ribbon Com. on Econ. Devel.; cmty. bd. St. Mary's Hosp., San Francisco YMCA. Recipient Disting. Alumni award Grad. Sch. Internat. Studies U. Denver, 1989, Tex. Senate Resolution of Commendation, 1991; Am. Coun. on Edn. fellow in acad. adminstrn., 1972, Ford Found. and Social Sci. Found. fellow, 1963-68, sr. fellow Am. Leadership Forum. Mem. AAAS, Internat. Studies Assn. (co-chmn. ann. meeting 1978), Am. Hosp. Assn., Policy Studies Orgn., Internat. Assn. Univ. Pres., San Francisco Com. on Fgn. Rels., Oakland C. of C., San Francisco C. of C. (econ. devel. com., bd. dirs.), Commonwealth Club, San Francisco World Trade Club, Univ. Club San Francisco. Home: 1806 Green St San Francisco CA 94123-4922 Office: Golden Gate U Office of Pres 536 Mission St San Francisco CA 94105

STAUFFER, WILLIAM ALBERT, insurance company executive; b. Maryville, Mo., June 9, 1930; s. Marion W. and Louise (Mangelsdorf) S.; m. Jean VanSlyck Shanley, Apr. 11, 1953; children—Rebecca, John, Rachel. B.J., U. Mo., 1952. Gen. mgr. York (Nebr.) Daily News-Times, 1955-61, Grand Island (Nebr.) Daily Ind., 1961-63; with Northwestern Bell Telephone Co., 1963-83, sec.-treas., 1970-72; v.p., chief exec. officer Northwestern Bell Telephone Co., Fargo, N.D., 1972-74; v.p., chief exec. officer-Iowa Northwestern Bell Telephone Co., Des Moines, 1974-83; exec. v.p., chief operating officer Blue Cross-Blue Shield Iowa, Des Moines, 1984-87; bus. cons. Des Moines, 1987-95; bd. dirs. Hubbell Realty Co., Des Moines, Iowa-Des Moines Nat. Bank, Life Care Retirement Community, Inc., Nat. By-Products, Inc., Des Moines, POP Radio Corp., N.Y.C., Cable Com., Inc., Lithonia, Ga. Pres. Convalescent Home Children, Des Moines, 1969; v.p. Mid-Iowa council Boy Scouts Am.; pres. Hospice of Ctrl. Iowa Found., Regional Health Care Corp., Omaha, 1971, Mercy Hosp. Found., 1979-81; mem. adv. bd. Mercy Hosp., Des Moines.; Bd. dirs., sec. Omaha Symphony Orch. Assn., 1970, Iowa Coll. Found., Des Moines Symphony Orch. Assn., YMCA, Des Moines; bd. dirs. Blue Shield Iowa, Living History Farms; trustee Drake U., Des Moines; trustee devel. coun. U. Mo., pres. 1986-90. Served with USAF, 1952-54. Named to Mo. Basketball Hall of Fame, 1990, U. Mo. Intercollegiate Athletics Hall of Fame, 1991. Mem. C. of C. Des Moines (pres. 1981), Greater Des Moines Com., Phi Delta Theta. Clubs: Wakonda (pres. 1989), Des Moines. Home: 3920 Grand Ave Ste 301 Des Moines IA 50312-3525

STAUP, JOHN GARY, safety engineer; b. Cleve., May 10, 1931; m. Ellsworth Leroy and May Ann (Weisgerber) S.; m. Elizabeth Louise Friemoth, Jan. 10, 1953; children: Michael Steven, Valerie Elysa Staup Gerdemann, Timothy Karl. BA, Dayton U., 1949; student, U. Mich. Design engr. Gramm Trailer, Delphos, Ohio, 1955-57, F.C. Russell Co., Pandora, Ohio, 1957-59, Ins. Svc. Office, Lima, Ohio, 1959-65, Ctrl. Mut. Ins., Van Wert, Ohio, 1965-76, Mid. Am. Tech. Svcs., Delphos, 1980—; adminstr. safety programs and security programs for various firms. Sgt. USAF, 1951-55. Mem. Am. Single Shot Rifle Assn. (sec.-treas. 1991—), Maumee Valley Soc. Safety Engr., Optimist Club (v.p.). Avocations: gun collecting, civic involvement, public speaking, target shooting, travel. Home: 709 Carolyn Dr Delphos OH 45833

STAUTH, ROBERT E., food service executive; b. 1945. Grad., Kans. State U.; student, Stanford U. Exec. Program, 1989. Joined Fleming Cos., Inc., Oklahoma City, 1977, various mgmt. positions, 1977-93, pres., COO, bd. dirs., 1993, CEO, 1993—, chmn., 1994; bd. dirs. IGA, Inc. Adv. bd. Coll. Bus. Adminstrn., Okla. U., Kans. State U.; mem. Okla. State Fair Bd. Mem. Food Distbrs. Internat., Food Mktg. Inst. (exec. steering com. on efficient consumer response, industry rels. com.), Okla. State C. of C. (bd. dirs.), Okla. Bus. Roundtable (bd. dirs., state fair bd.). Office: Fleming Cos Inc PO Box 26647 6301 Waterford Blvd Oklahoma City OK 73118

STAVELY, KEITH WILLIAMS FITZGERALD, librarian; b. New Brunswick, N.J., May 13, 1942; s. Homer Eaton and Elizabeth (Williams) S.; m. Kathleen Fitzgerald, Aug. 19, 1978; 1 child, Jonathan Keith. BA, Yale U., 1964, PhD, 1969; MLS, Simmons Coll., 1980. Asst. prof. English Boston U., 1969-74, Ohio State U., 1990-91; lectr. in English Boston Coll., 1975-80; adult svcs. libr. Watertown (Mass.) Free Pub. Libr., 1979-89, br. libr., 1984-89, head adult svcs., 1989-90; reference libr. Somerville (Mass.) Pub. Libr., 1991-92; asst. adminstr. Fall River (Mass.) Pub. Libr., 1992—. Author: Puritan Legacies: Paradise Lost and the New England Tradition, 1630-1890, 1987, paperback edit., 1990, The Politics of Milton's Prose Style, 1975; co-author: Family Man: What Men Feel About Their Wives, Their Children, Their Parents, and Themselves, 1978; contbr. articles and revs. to profl. publs. Fellow Fulbright Found., India, 1964-65, Am. Coun. Learned Socs., 1988-89, John Simon Guggenheim Meml. Found., 1989. Mem. MLA (Prize for Ind. Scholars 1987), ALA, Mass. Libr. Assn., Phi Beta Kappa.

STAVER, LEROY BALDWIN, banker; b. Portland, Oreg., Oct. 1, 1908; s. Herbert LeRoy and Grace (Baldwin) S.; m. Helen M. Matschek, Oct. 16, 1937 (dec. Mar. 1995); 1 son, Roger. J.D., Northwestern Coll. Law, 1930; grad., Rutgers U. Grad. Sch. Banking, 1937-39. Bar: Oreg. bar 1929. With U.S. Nat. Bank of Oreg., 1925-74, asst. trust officer, 1936-42, trust officer, 1942-58, v.p., trust officer, 1958—, exec. trust officer, 1959-63, exec. v.p., exec. trust officer, 1963-66, pres., 1966-72, chmn., 1971-74, also dir.; chmn. Commerce Mortgage Co., 1967-74; chmn., chief exec. officer U.S. Bancorp., 1969-74, also dir. Hon. trustee Med. Rsch. Found. Oreg., pres., 1975-76; life trustee Willamette U., St. Vincent Med. Rsch. Found., Oreg. Grad. Inst. Sci. and Tech.; hon. bd. dirs. World Forestry Ctr. Named to Oreg. Bankers Assn. Hall of Fame, 1989. Mem. Am., Oreg. bar assns., C. of C. (pres. 1975), Oreg. Hist. Soc. (bd. dirs. 1978-91), Delta Theta Phi. Clubs: Arlington, Waverley Country. Home: 9908 SE Cambridge Ln Milwaukie OR 97222-7402 Office: US Nat Bank Oreg PO Box 4412 Portland OR 97208-4412

STAVERT, ALEXANDER BRUCE, bishop; b. Montreal, Que., Can., Apr. 1, 1940; s. R. Ewart and Kathleen H. (Rosamond) S.; m. Diana Greig, June 26, 1982; children: Kathleen, Rosamond, Timothy. Student, Lower Can. Coll., Montreal, 1957; BA, Bishop's U., 1961; STB, U. Toronto, Ont., Can., 1964, ThM, 1976, DD (hon.), 1986. Ordained to ministry Anglican Ch. as deacon, 1964, as priest, 1965. With Mission of Schefferville, Que., 1964-69; fellow, tutor in div. Trinity Coll., U. Toronto, 1969-70, chaplain, 1970-76; with St. Clement's Mission East, St. Paul's River, Que., 1976-81; chaplain Champlain Regional Coll., Bishop's U., 1981-84; dean, rector St. Alban's Cathedral, Prince Albert, Sask., Can., 1984-91; consecrated bishop Anglican Diocese of Que., Quebec, 1991—. Address: Diocese of Que, 31 rue des Jardins, Quebec, PQ Canada G1R 4L6

STAVES, SUSAN, English educator; b. N.Y.C., Oct. 5, 1942; d. Henry Tracy and Margaret (McClernon) S. AB, U. Chgo., 1963; MA, U. Va., 1964, PhD, 1967. Woodrow Wilson intern Bennett Coll., Greensboro, N.C., 1965-66; from asst. prof. to prof. Brandeis U., Waltham, Mass., 1967—, Paul Proswimmer prof. of Humanities, 1993—; dept. chair Brandeis U., Waltham, 1986-89, 95—; Clark prof. UCLA, 1989-90. Author: Players' Scepters: Fictions of Authority in the Restoration, 1979, Married Women's Separate Property in England, 1660-1833, 1990; co-author: (with John Brewer) Early Modern Conceptions of Property, 1994; also articles in Modern Philology, 18th-Century Studies, Studies in Eng. Lit., Studies in Eighteenth Century Culture, Law and History. Assoc. mem. Belmont (Mass.) Dem. Town Com.; mem. ACLU, 1967—. Woodrow Wilson fellow, 1963-64, Woodrow Wilson Dissertation fellow, 1966-67, Harward Liberal Arts fellow, 1980-81, John Simon Guggenheim fellow, 1981-82. Mem. MLA (exec. com. div. on late-18th century English lit. 1984-86), Am. Soc. for 18th-Century Studies (exec. bd. 1987-90), Am. Soc. for Legal History, AAUP, English Inst. Episcopalian. Avocations: tennis, squash. Office: Brandeis U Dept English Waltham MA 02254

STAVIG, MARK LUTHER, English language educator; b. Northfield, Minn., Jan. 20, 1935; s. Lawrence Melvin and Cora (Hjertaas) S.; m. Donna Mae Ring, July 3, 1957; children—Anne Ragnhild, Thomas Edward, Rolf Lawrence. B.A., Augustana Coll., 1956, Oxford U., 1958; M.A., Oxford U., 1962; Ph.D., Princeton U., 1961. Instr. to asst. prof. English U. Wis., Madison, 1961-68; from assoc. prof. to prof. English Colo. Coll., Colorado Springs, 1968—. Author: John Ford and the Traditional Moral Order, 1968, The Forms of Things Unknown: Renaissance Metaphor in Romeo and Juliet and A Midsummer Night's Dream, 1995; editor: Ford, 'Tis Pity She's a Whore, 1966. Fellow Danforth Found., 1956-61, Woodrow Wilson Found., 1956-57; Fulbright scholar Oxford U., 1956-58. Mem. MLA, Shakespeare Assn. Am. Democrat. Home: 1409 Wood Ave Colorado Springs CO 80907-7348 Office: Colo Coll Dept English Colorado Springs CO 80903

STAVIS, BARRIE, playwright, historian; b. N.Y.C., June 16, 1906; s. Abraham Max and Fanny Beatrice (Garfinkle) S.; m. Leona Heyert, 1925 (div. 1939); m. Bernice Sylvia Coe, May 17, 1950; children: Alexander Mark, Jane Devon. Student, Columbia U., 1924-27. Journalist, war corr. N.Y., Europe, 1937-47; guest spkr. seminars, colls., univs., insts., U.S. and abroad, 1938—; vis. fellow Inst. for the Arts and Humanistic Studies, Pa. State U., 1971; playwright, historian, lyricist; co-founder, mem. bd. New Stages, 1947, 48, U.S. Inst. for Theatre Tech., 1961-64, 69-72. Author: (novels) The Chain of Command, 1945, Home, Sweet Home!, 1949, (biography) John Brown:

The Sword and the Word, 1970, (plays) In These Times, 1932, The Sun and I, 1933, Refuge, 1938, Lamp at Midnight, 1948, one-hour abridgment, 1974, The Man Who Never Died, 1958, Harpers Ferry, 1967, Coat of Many Colors, 1968, The Raw Edge of Victory, 1976, The House of Shadows, 1992; contbr. articles to profl. jours.; librettist: opera Joe Hill (Alan Bush), 1970; oratorio Galileo Galilei (Lee Hoiby), 1975; author, co-editor: (with Frank Harmon) The Songs of Joe Hill, 1955. Served with AUS, 1942-45. Yaddo fellow, 1939; Am. Theatre Assn. fellow, 1982. Fellow Coll. Fellows Am. Theatre; mem. PEN, ASCAP, Dramatists Guild, Authors Guild, Nat. Theatre Conf. (award 1948, 49), U.S. Inst. for Theatre-Tech., Internat. Theatre Inst., ANTA. Office: care Coe Film Assn Inc 65 E 96th St New York NY 10128

STAVITSKY, ABRAM BENJAMIN, immunologist, educator; b. Newark, May 14, 1919; s. Nathan and Ida (Novak) S.; m. Ruth Bernice Okney, Dec. 6, 1942; children: Ellen Barbara, Gail Beth. AB, U. Mich., 1939, MS, 1940; PhD, U. Minn., 1943; VMD, U. Pa., 1946. Research fellow Calif. Inst. Tech., 1946-47; faculty Case Western Res. U., 1947—, prof. microbiology, 1962—, prof. molecular biology, 1983-89, emeritus, 1989; mem. expert com. immunochemistry WHO, 1963-83; mem. microbiology fellowship com. NIH, 1963-66; mem. microbiology test com. Nat. Bd. Med. Examiners, 1970-73; chmn. microbiology test com. Nat. Bd. Podiatry Examiners, 1978-82. Mem. editl. bd. Jour. Immunological Methods, 1979-88, Immunopharmacology, 1983-96. Vice pres. Ludlow Community Assn., 1964-66. Fellow AAAS; mem. Am. Assn. Immunologists, Am. Soc. Microbiology, Sigma Xi. Home: 14604 Onaway Rd Cleveland OH 44120-2845 Office: 2119 Abington Rd Cleveland OH 44106-2333

STAVITSKY, JEFFREY, wholesale distribution executive; b. 1949. With YKK Zipper Co., N.Y.C., 1970-77, D.B. Brown, Inc., Newark, 1977—; pres. D.B. Brown, Inc., Carteret. Office: D B Brown Inc 400 Port Carteret Dr Carteret NJ 07008*

STAVRO, STEVE A., professional hockey team executive. Chmn. bd., chief exec. officer Toronto Maple Leafs, Ont., Can. Office: Toronto Maple Leafs, 60 Carlton St, Toronto, ON Canada M5B 1L1*

STAVROPOULOS, WILLIAM S., chemical executive; b. Bridgehampton, N.Y., May 12, 1939; m. Linda Stavropoulos; children: S. William, Angela D. BA in Pharm. Chemistry, Fordham U.; PhD in Medicinal Chemistry, U. Washington. Research chemist in pharm. research Dow Chem. Co., Midland, Mich., 1967, research chemist for diagnostics product research, 1970, research mgr. diagnostics product research, 1973, bus. mgr. diagnostics product research, 1976, bus. mgr. polyolefins, 1977, dir. mktg. plastics dept., 1979; comml. v.p. Dow Chem. Co. Latin Am., Coral Gables, Fla., 1980; pres. Dow Latin Am., 1984; comml. v.p., basics and hydrocarbons Dow Chem. Co. U.S.A., Midland, 1985-87; group v.p. Dow Chem. Co. U.S.A., 1987-90; pres. Dow U.S.A., 1990—; v.p. The Dow Chemical Co., 1990; sr. v.p. The Dow Chem. Co., 1991, pres., 1992; pres., COO, bd. dirs. The Dow Chem. Co., Midland, 1993—; bd. dirs. Dow Corning Corp., The Dow Chem. Co., Marion Merrel Dow Inc.; CEO Essex Chem Corp, 1988-92. *

STAVROU, NIKOLAOS ATHANASIOS, political science educator; b. Griazdani-Delvino, Albania, May 5, 1935; came to U.S., 1956, naturalized, 1962; s. Athanasios Haritos and Aristoula F. (Laiou) S.; married. B.A., Hunter Coll., 1963; M.A. in Internat. Affairs, George Washington U., 1965, Ph.D. in Polit. Sci, 1970. Research fellow Inst. Sino-Soviet Studies, George Washington U., 1963-64; lectr. govt. Howard U., Washington, 1968-70; asst. prof. Howard U., 1970-72, assoc. prof. polit. sci., 1972-77, prof. polit. sci. and internat. affairs, 1978-79, assoc. chmn. dept. polit. sci., 1979-82; adj. professorial lectr. George Washington U., 1983; guest lectr. Fgn. Service Inst. State Dept.; coordinator Eastern Mediterranean Study Group; area specialist on Yugoslav, Albanian and Greek affairs. Author: Allied Politics and Military Interventions: The Political Role of the Greek Military, 1977, Albanian Communism and the Red Bishop, 1996; contbg. author: Political Parties of Europe; contbg. author: Yearbook on International Communism; editor: Edvard Kardelj: The Historical Roots of Non-Alignment, 1980, Greece under Socialism, 1988; author, editor Greece Under Socialism, 1988; editor Mediterranean Quar., 1991—; contbr. more than 200 articles to profl. jours., chpts. to books. Howard U. Research grantee, 1973-74, 77-78, 88-89. Mem. Internat. Studies Assn. (v.p. Mediterranean affairs). Eastern Orthodox. Club: Cosmos (Washington). Office: Howard Univ Dept Polit Sci Washington DC 20059

STAW, BARRY MARTIN, business and psychology educator; b. Los Angeles, Sept. 13, 1945; s. Harold Paul and Shirley C. (Posner) S.; m. Adrienne McDonnell; 1 child, Jonah Martin. BS, U. Oreg., 1967; MBA, U. Mich., 1968; PhD, Northwestern U., 1972. Asst. prof. bus. adminstrn. U. Ill., Urbana, 1972-75; assoc. prof. Northwestern U., Evanston, Ill., 1975-77, prof., 1977-80; prof. U. Calif., Berkeley, 1980—, Mitchell prof. Leadership and communication, 1986—; researcher in organizational psychology. Editor: Psychological Dimensions of Organizational Behavior; co-editor: New Directions in Organizational Behavior, (book series) Research in Organizational Behavior; mem. editl. bd. Adminstrv. Sci. Quar., Organizational Behavior and Human Decision Processes, 1974—, Basic and Applied Social Psychology; contbr. numerous articles to profl. jours. Fellow APA, Am. Psychol. Soc., Acad. Mgmt. Soc. for Organizational Behavior. Democrat. Jewish. Avocations: basketball, tennis, skiing. Office: Univ of Calif Haas Sch Bus Adminstrn Berkeley CA 94720

STAY, BARBARA, zoologist, educator; b. Cleve., Aug. 31, 1926; d. Theron David and Florence (Finley) S. A.B., Vassar Coll., 1947; M.A., Radcliffe Coll., 1949, Ph.D., 1953. Entomologist Army Research Center, Natick, Mass., 1954-60; vis. asst. prof. Pomona Coll., 1960; asst. prof. biology U. Pa., 1961-67; asso. prof. zoology U. Iowa, Iowa City, 1967-77; prof. U. Iowa, 1977—. Fulbright fellow to Australia, 1953; Lalor fellow Harvard U., 1960. Mem. Am. Soc. Zoologists, Am. Inst. Biol. Scis., Am. Soc. Cell Biology, Entomol. Soc. Am., Iowa Acad. Scis., Sigma Xi. Office: U Iowa Dept Biological Scis Iowa City IA 52242

STAYIN, RANDOLPH JOHN, lawyer; b. Cin., Oct. 30, 1942; s. Jack and Viola (Tomin) S.; children: Gregory S., Todd R., Elizabeth J. BA, Dartmouth Coll., 1964; JD, U. Cin., 1967. Bar: Ohio 1967, U.S. Dist. Ct. (so. dist.) Ohio 1968, U.S. Dist. Ct. D.C. 1977, U.S. Ct. Appeals (6th cir.) 1968, U.S. Ct. Appeals (fed. cir.) 1986, U.S. Supreme Ct. 1974, U.S. Ct. Appeals (D.C. cir.) 1976, U.S. Ct. Internat. Trade, 1985. Assoc. Frost & Jacobs, Cin., 1967-72; exec. asst., dir. of legislation U.S. Sen. Robert Taft, Jr., Washington, 1973-74, chief of staff, 1975-76; assoc. Taft, Stettinius & Hollister, Washington, 1977, ptnr., 1978-88; ptnr. Barnes & Thornburg, Washington, 1988—; bd. dirs. W.J.S. Holdings Ltd., W.J.S. Inc.; mem. adv. coun. U.S. and FGN. Comml. Svc., U.S. Dept. Commerce. Chmn., mem. numerous coms., chmn., worker campaigns for local politicians Rep. Party state and local orgns.; mem. Citizens to Save WCET-TV, 1967-72, Fine Arts Fund, 1970-72, Cancer Soc., 1970-72; chmn. agy. rels. com. Hamilton County Mental Health and Mental Retardation Bd., 1969-71, vice chmn., 1971, chmn., 1971-72; v.p. Recreation Commn., City of Cin., 1970-72; mem. funds mgmt. com. Westwood 1st Presbyn. Ch., 1968, v.p., 1969, pres., 1970, trustee, 1970, elder, 1971-72; bd. dirs. Evans Mill Pond Owners Assn., v.p., 1986, pres., 1987; active Washington Nat. Cathedral Fund Com. Mem. ABA (sect. on internat. law and practice, vice chmn. com. on nat. legislation 1977-79, internat. sect., anti-trust sect.), Am. Soc. Assn. Execs. (legal sect., internat. sect.), Internat. Bar Assn., D.C. Bar Assn. (com. on internat. law). Avocations: theater, tennis, skiing, travel, reading. Office: Barnes & Thornburg 1401 I St NW Ste 800 Washington DC 20005-2225

STAYTON, THOMAS GEORGE, lawyer; b. Rochester, Minn., May 1, 1948; m. Barbara Joan Feck, Aug. 8, 1970; children: Ryan, Megan. BS, Miami U., Oxford, Ohio, 1970; JD, U. Mich., 1973. Bar: Ind. 1973, U.S. Dist. Ct. (so. dist.) Ind. 1973, U.S. Ct. Appeals (7th cir.) 1977. Ptnr. Baker & Daniels, Indpls., 1973—. Recipient Sagamore of the Wabash Gov. of Ind., 1988. Mem. ABA, Ind. State Bar Assn., Indpls. Bar Assn. Club: Indpls. Athletic. Office: Baker & Daniels 300 N Meridian St Ste 2700 Indianapolis IN 46204-1755

STEAD, EUGENE ANSON, JR., physician; b. Atlanta, Oct. 6, 1908; s. Eugene Anson and Emily (White) S.; m. Evelyn Selby, June 15, 1940; children: Nancy White, Lucy Ellen, William Wallace. B.S., Emory U., 1928, M.D., 1932. Med. intern Peter Bent Brigham Hosp., Boston, 1932-33; surg. intern Peter Bent Brigham Hosp., 1934-35, assoc. medicine, 1939-42, acting physician-in-chief, 1942; research fellow medicine Harvard, 1933-34; asst. resident medicine Cin. Gen. Hosp., 1935-36, resident, 1936-37; instr. medicine U. Cin., 1935-37; resident phys. Thorndike Meml. Lab.; asst. medicine Harvard and Boston City Hosp., 1937-39; instr. medicine Harvard, 1938-41, assoc., 1941-42; prof. medicine Emory U.; physician-in-chief Grady Hosp., Atlanta, 1942-46; dean Emory U., 1945-46; physician in chief Duke Hosp., 1947-67; prof. medicine Duke U. Sch. Medicine, 1947-78; disting. physician VA, 1978-85. Editor: Circulation, 1973-78, N.C. Med. Jour., 1983-92; Contbr. numerous articles on various aspects of circulation to med. jours. Mem. N.C. Med. Soc., Am. Fedn. Clin. Research, Assn. Am. Physicians, Am. Soc. Clin. Investigation, Alpha Omega Alpha, Sigma Xi, Phi Beta Kappa. Methodist. Home: 5113 Townsville Rd Bullock NC 27507-9438 Office: Duke U Dept Medicine Durham NC 27710

STEAD, FRANCESCA MANUELA LEWENSTEIN, natural health care consultant, massage therapist; b. Bklyn., May 2, 1949; d. Robert Gottschalk Lewenstein and Shirley Winifred (Goodman) Lewenstein Ozgen; m. Thomas David Stead, May 28, 1975; children: Chandra Dharani, Thomas Robert. Student, Case Western Res. U., 1967-69; BA in Govt. cum laude, Ohio U., 1973; cert. in Massage Therapy, Cen. Ohio Sch. Massage, Columbus, 1978. Lic. massage therapist; cert. sports massage therapist. Youth service coordinator Adams-Brown Community Action Agy., Decatur, Ohio, 1973; child welfare worker Scioto Children's Services, Portsmouth, Ohio, 1975-77; project dir. youth services Scioto County Community Action Agy., Portsmouth, Ohio, 1978-79; co-owner Stead Enterprises, Otway, Ohio, 1978—; self employed massage therapist Portsmouth, Ohio, 1979—; owner Total Health Care Cons., Portsmouth, 1985—; drug and alcohol counselor Coun. on Alcoholism, West Union, Ohio, 1982; instr. Yoga, Cradtal, Shawnee State U., Portsmouth, 1985—; staff mem. Area Psychiatric and Psychotherapy Group, Health Ctr. One, Huntington, W.Va., 1986-90; instr. summer career edn. prog. Shawnee State U., 1986; reimbursement officer Ohio Dept. Mental Health, Columbus, 1982-85; cons. Portsmouth Dept., 1977; cons. drug abuse Aberdeen Sch., Ohio, 1982; Yoga instr. YMCA, Portsmouth, 1979-80, 85-87. Dem. campaign worker Ohio, 1968—; organizer So. Ohio Task Force on Domestic Violence, 1976; organizer campus ministry Shawnee State U., Portsmouth, 1976-77; organizer Portsmouth Food Coop., 1975. Flora Stone Mather scholar Case Western Res. U., 1967. Mem. Portsmouth Area Women's Network (adv. bd. 1988—), Am. Massage Therapy Assn. (govt. affairs com. Nat. Sports Massage Team Ohio chpt. 1990—, Ohio del. nat. conv. 1991, 93, sports massage team strategic planning com. 1995—), Women in Networking, Pi Gamma Mu. Democrat. Kagyupa Buddhist. Avocations: weaving, science fiction, painting, skiing, gardening, ethnology. Home: 4140 Mt Unger Rd Otway OH 45657-9515 Office: 11 Offnere St Portsmouth OH 45662

STEAD, JAMES JOSEPH, JR., securities company executive; b. Chgo., Sept. 13, 1930; s. James Joseph and Irene (Jennings) S.; m. Edith Pearson, Feb. 13, 1954; children: James, Diane, Robert, Caroline. BS, DePaul U., 1957, MBA, 1959. Asst. sec. C. F. Childs & Co., Chgo., 1957-62; exec. v.p., sec. Koenig, Keating & Stead, Inc., Chgo., 1962-66; 2d v.p., mgr. midwest mcpl. bond dept. Hayden, Stone Inc., Chgo., 1966-69; sr. v.p., nat. sales mgr. Ill. Co. Inc., 1969-70; mgr. instl. sales dept. Reynolds and Co., Chgo., 1970-72; partner Edwards & Hanly, 1972-74; v.p., instnl. sales mgr. Paine, Webber, Jackson & Curtis, 1974-76; v.p., regional instl. sales mgr. Reynolds Securities, Inc., 1976-78; sr. v.p., regional mgr. Oppenheimer & Co., Inc., 1978-88; sr. v.p., regional mgr. fixed income Tucker Anthony, 1988—; instr. Mcpl. Bond Sch., Chgo., 1967—. With AUS, 1951-53. Mem. Security Traders Assn. Chgo., Nat. Security Traders Assn., Am. Mgmt. Assn., Mcpl. Fin. Forum Washington. Clubs: Execs., Union League, Mcpl. Bond, Bond (Chgo.); Olympia Fields Country (Ill.); Wall Street (N.Y.C.). Home: 1005 Hickory Ridge Ct Frankfort IL 60423-2114 Office: 1 S Wacker Dr Chicago IL 60606-4614

STEAD, WILLIAM WHITE, physician, educator, public health administrator; b. Decatur, Ga., Jan. 4, 1919; s. Eugene Anson and Emily (White) S.; m. Ethel Barnett, June 14, 1947 (div.); 1 child, Richard Barnett; m. Joan Jordan DeVore, Apr. 22, 1975. A.B., Emory U., 1940, M.D., 1943. Intern Grady Meml. Hosp., Atlanta, 1944; resident in medicine Emory U., 1944-45, U. Cin., 1946-48; resident in medicine U. Minn., 1948-49, faculty med. schs., 1949-57; faculty med. schs. U. Fla., 1957-60; prof. medicine Med. Coll. Wis., Milw. County Gen. Hosp., Milw., 1960-72; med. dir. Muirdale Sanatorium, Milw., 1963-72; prof. medicine U. Ark. Med. Sch., 1972—; chief pulmonary diseases service VA Hosp., Little Rock, 1972-73; cons. VA Hosp., 1973—; dir. Tb control Ark. Health Dept., Little Rock, 1973—; Cons. VA Hosp., Wood, Wis., 1960-72. Author 3 books on Tb, also numerous articles. Served to lt. (j.g.) M.C. USNR, 1945-46; capt. M.C. AUS, 1953-54. Recipient Tom T. Ross award Ark. Public Health Assn., 1981; Robert S. Abernathy award for excellence in medicine Am. Coll. Physicians, 1984, James D. Bruce award Am. Coll. Physicians, 1988; research grantee in pulmonary emphysema, 1957-65. Master ACP; mem. AAAS, Am. Fedn. for Clin. Rsch. (nat. sec. 1955-58, v.p. 1958-59, pres. 1959-60), Ctrl. Soc. Clin. Rsch., Am. Soc. Clin. Investigation, Am. Thoracic Soc. (Trudeau medal 1988), Am. Coll. Chest Physicians. Research on unitary concept of Tb and epidemiology of Tb in prison and among elderly in nursing homes; chemotherapy of Tb; variation in susceptibility to Tb infection; history of Tb as a global epidemic; suggestion for genetic engineering of material to enhance resistance to initial infection with Tb. Office: Ark Dept of Health 4815 W Markham St Little Rock AR 72205-3866

STEADMAN, CHARLES WALTERS, lawyer, corporate executive, writer; b. Falls City, Nebr., July 25, 1914; s. William Sherman and Marie (Walters) S.; m. Dorothy Marie Fawick, Feb. 14, 1942 (dec. Sept. 1974); children: Suzanne Louise Steadman Hoerr (dec.), Carole Elaine Steadman Kinney, Charles T. W., Dorothy M. (Diana); m. Consuelo Matthews Artini, May 10, 1986. A.B., U. Nebr., 1935; J.D., Harvard U., 1938. Bar: Ohio 1939, D.C. 1956, U.S. Supreme Ct. 1950, U.S. Ct. Claims 1958. Partner Marshman, Hornbeck, Hollington, Steadman & McLaughlin, Cleve., 1946-65, Steadman, Jones & Baxter, 1956-70; chmn. bd. St. Regis Hotel Corp., 1960-63; vice chmn. Leaseway Intercontinental, 1961-65; prin. Charles W. Steadman Counselor-at-Law, 1970; chmn. com. to end govt. waste Nat. Taxpayers Union, 1979; chmn. bd., pres. Steadman Security Corp., Steadman Technology and Growth Fund, Steadman Investment Fund, Steadman Associated Fund, Steadman American Industry Fund; chief counsel Select U.S. Senate Com., 1956; spl. master commr. Matter of Dissolution of Cleve. Savs. Soc., 1959-62; spl. presdl. rep. to Oman, 1980. Author: Steadman's Revision of the Ohio Civil Practice Manual, 1950, The National Debt Conclusion: Establishing the Debt Repayment Plan, 1993; also legal and econ. articles.; editor: Charles W. Steadman Economic Review. Bd. govs. Investment Co. Inst., 1969-72; chmn. Washington met. area Rep. Nat. Fin. Com., 1980-81; mem. exec. com. Presdl. Inaugural Com., 1981; founder Presdl. Trust, 1981; trustee Tex. Wesleyan Coll., 1982-84; founder, chmn. Nat. Debt Repayment Found, 1982. Served as lt. col. AUS, World War II; chief counsel legal div. Cleve. Ordnance Dist. Recipient Disting. Service award U. Nebr., 1960. Mem. ABA (coun. corp., banking and bus. law 1958-60), Ohio Bar Assn., Cleve. Bar Assn., Ohio Bar, Bar Assn. D.C., Internat. Bar Assn., Am. Law Inst. (life), Am. Judicature Soc., 1925 F Street Club, Union Club (Cleve.), Beach Club (Palm Beach, Fla.), Everglades Club (Palm Beach, Fla.), Racquet and Tennis Club (N.Y.C.), Sky Club (N.Y.C.). Home: 425 Worth Ave Palm Beach FL 33480 also: 700 New Hampshire Ave NW Washington DC 20037 Office: 1730 K St NW Washington DC 20006-3868

STEADMAN, DAVID ROSSLYN AYTON, business executive, corporate director; b. Wembley, Eng., June 7, 1937; came to U.S., 1980; s. Eric and Iris Sina (Smith) S.; m. Beryl Ellen Giles, Jan. 5, 1963 (div.); children: Michael, Christopher, Timothy. B.Sc. in Engring. with honors, City U., London, 1960. Mng. dir. Cossor Electronics, Harlow, Eng., 1974-78; chmn. EMI med. Electronics, London, 1978-80; pres. Raytheon Data Systems, Norwood Mass., 1980-84, Raytheon Ventures, Lexington, 1985-87; chmn., chief exec. officer GCA Corp., Andover, Mass., 1987-88; pres. Atlantic Mgmt. Assocs., Inc., Wolfeboro, N.H., 1988—; chmn., CEO Integra-Hotel & Restaurant Co., 1990-94; chmn. Brookwood Cos., Inc., 1989—, Aavid Thermal Techs., Inc., 1993—, Tech. Svc. Group, Inc., 1994—; bd. dirs. Vitronics Corp., Telequip Corp., ElectroScan Corp., Wahlco Environ. Sys., Inc., Kurzweil Applied Intelligence, Inc. Fellow Instn. Elec. Engrs. (U.K.); mem. Inst. Mgmt. (U.K.; companion), Inst. Mech. Engrs. (U.K.). Avocations: music; sailing. Office: Atlantic Mgmt Assocs Inc PO Box 10670 Bedford NH 03110

STEADMAN, DAVID WILTON, museum official; b. Honolulu, Oct. 24, 1936; s. Alva Edgar and Martha (Cooke) S.; m. Kathleen Carroll Reilly, Aug. 1, 1964; children: Alexander Carroll, Kate Montague. B.A., Harvard U., 1960, M.A.T., 1961; M.A., U. Calif.-Berkeley, 1966; Ph.D., Princeton U., 1974. Lectr. Frick Collection, N.Y.C., 1970-71; asst. dir., acting dir., assoc. dir. Princeton U. Art Mus., 1971-73; dir. galleries Claremont Colls., (Calif.), 1974-80; art cons. Archtl. Digest, L.A., 1974-77; rsch. curator Norton Simon Mus., Pasadena, Calif., 1977-80; dir. Chrysler Mus., Norfolk, Va., 1980-89, Toledo Mus. Art, Ohio, 1989—. Author: Graphic Art of Francisco Goya, 1975, Works on Paper 1900-1960, 1977, Abraham van Diepenbeeck, 1982. Chester Dale fellow Nat. Gallery Art, Washington, 1969-70. Mem. Coll. Art Assn., Am. Assn. Mus. Dirs. Episcopalian. Office: Toledo Mus Art PO Box 1013 Toledo OH 43697-1013

STEADMAN, JACK W., professional football team executive; b. Warrenville, Ill., Sept. 14, 1928; s. Walter Angus and Vera Ruth (Burkholder) S.; m. Martha Cudworth Steinhoff, Nov. 24, 1949; children: Thomas Edward, Barbara Ann, Donald Wayne. B.B.A., So. Methodist U., 1950. Accountant Hunt Oil Co., Dallas, 1950-54; chief accountant W.H. Hunt, Dallas, 1954-58, Penrod Drilling Co., Dallas, 1958-60; gen. mgr. Dallas Texans Football Club, 1960-63; gen. mgr. Kansas City Chiefs Football Club, 1963-76, exec. v.p., 1966-76, pres., 1976-88; also chmn. bd., 1988—; chmn. benefit com. NFL; chmn. Hunt Midwest Enterprises, Inc., Kansas City; dir. Commerce Bank of Kansas City, Pvt. Industry Coun.; former chmn. Full Employment Coun. Former bd. dirs. Children's Mercy Hosp., bd. dirs. Civic Council, Starlight Theatre Assn., Kansas City, Am. Royal Assn.; pres. Heart of Am. United Way, 1981; adv. trustee Research Med. Ctr., Kansas City; trustee Midwest Research Inst.; mem. Village Presbyn. Ch.; past chmn. C. of C. of Greater Kansas City. Recipient Kans. Citian of Yr. award, 1988. Mem. Indian Hills Country Club, Kansas City Club (pres. 1988), 711 Inner, River, Carriage, Man-of-the-Month Fraternity. Home: 6436 Wenonga Ter Shawnee Mission KS 66208-1732 Office: Kansas City Chiefs 1000 Walnut St Ste 1528 Kansas City MO 64106-2123

STEADMAN, JOHN MARCELLUS, III, English educator; b. Spartanburg, S.C., Nov. 25, 1918; s. John Marcellus and Medora Rice (Rembert) S. AB, Emory U., 1940, MA, 1941, DHL (hon.), 1976; MA (T.W. Hunt scholar), Princeton U., 1948, PhD, 1949. Instr. English Ga. Inst. Tech., 1941-42; asst. prof. U. N.C., 1949-51; ind. study and rsch. in English lit., 1953-61; from rsch. assoc.to sr. rsch. assoc. Henry E. Huntington Libr., San Marino, Calif., 1962—; mem. faculty U. Calif., Riverside, 1966—; prof. English U. Calif., 1967—, faculty rsch. lectr., 1977, prof. emeritus, 1989—; vis. disting. prof. City U. N.Y., fall, 1974. Author numerous books including Disembodied Laughter: Troilus and the Apotheosis Tradition, 1972, The Lamb and The Elephant: Ideal Imitation and the Context of Renaissance Allegory, 1974, Epic and Tragic Structure in Paradise Lost, 1976, Nature into Myth: Medieval and Renaissance Moral Symbols, 1979, Milton's Biblical and Classical Imagery, 1984, The Hill and the Labyrinth: Discourse and Certitude in Milton and His Near-Contemporaries, 1984, The Wall of Paradise: Essays on Milton's Poetics, 1985, Milton and the Paradoxes of Renaissance Heroism, 1987, Redifining a Period Style: "Renaissance," "Mannerist," and "Baroque" in Literature, 1990, Ryoanji Temple and Other Poems, 1993, Moral Fiction in Milton and Spenser, 1995, Reconnaissances: Poems, 1996; co-editor latest being A Milton Ency., vols. I-IX, 1978-83; editor: latest being Huntington Libr. Quar., 1962-81. Capt. USAAF, 1942-46; capt. USAF, 1951-52. Grantee Huntington Libr., 1961-62; Procter fellow Princeton U., 1949, Guggenheim fellow, 1979. Mem. Milton Soc. Am. (pres. 1973, honored scholar 1976), So. Calif. Renaissance Conf., Phi Beta Kappa, Chi Phi, Fine Arts Club. Democrat. Home: 250 S Oak Knoll Ave Apt 109 Pasadena CA 91101-2923 Office: Henry E Huntington Libr San Marino CA 91108

STEADMAN, JOHN MONTAGUE, judge; b. Honolulu, Aug. 8, 1930; s. Alva Edgar and Martha (Cooke) S.; m. Alison Storer Lunt, Apr. 8, 1961; children—Catharine N., Juliette M., Eric C. Grad., Phillips Acad., Andover, Mass., 1948; BA summa cum laude, Yale U., 1952; LLB magna cum laude, Harvard U., 1955. Bar: D.C. 1955, Calif. 1956, U.S. Supreme Ct. 1964, Hawaii 1977. Assoc. Pillsbury, Madison & Sutro, San Francisco, 1956-63; atty. Dept. Justice, 1963-64; dep. under sec. army for internat. affairs, 1964-65; spl. asst. to sec. and dep. sec. def. Dept. Def., 1965-68; gen. counsel Dept. Air Force, 1968-70; vis. prof. law U. Pa. Law Sch., 1970-72; prof. law Georgetown U. Law Ctr., Washington, 1972-85, assoc. dean, 1979-84; assoc. judge D.C. Ct. Appeals, 1985—; instr. Lincoln Law Sch., San Francisco, 1961-62, San Francisco Law Sch., 1962-63; vis. prof. U. Mich. Sch. Law, 1976, U. Hawaii Sch. Law, 1977; of counsel firm Pillsbury, Madison & Sutro, Washington, 1979-85. Editor: Harvard Law Rev, 1953-55. Sinclair-Kennedy Traveling fellow, 1955-56. Mem. Am. Law Inst., Phi Beta Kappa, Delta Sigma Rho, Zeta Psi. Episcopalian. Home: 2960 Newark St NW Washington DC 20008-3338 Office: DC Ct Appeals 500 Indiana Ave NW Washington DC 20001-2131

STEAMER, ROBERT JULIUS, political science educator; b. Rochester, N.Y., Oct. 14, 1920; s. William August and Lotte (Becker) S.; m. Jean Worden, Apr. 12, 1947; children: Gregg Robert, James Worden. B.A. in Social Sci., Bucknell U., 1947; M.A. in Polit. Sci., U. Va., 1952; Ph.D., Cornell U., 1954; postgrad. law, Oxford (Eng.) U., 1968-69. Asst. prof. Oglethorpe U., 1952-55, U. Mass., 1955-56; assoc. prof. La. State U., 1956-62; prof. polit. sci., chmn. dept. Lake Forest (Ill.) Coll., 1962-72; prof. U. Mass., Boston, 1972-88, dean Coll. II, 1974-76, vice chancellor for acad. affairs, provost, 1976-79; vis. summer prof. Tulane U., 1958, Cornell U., 1960, UCLA, 1965; staff cons. La. sect. U.S. Commn. Civil Rights, 1961. Author: The Constitution: Cases and Comments, 1959, The Supreme Court in Crisis, 1971, The Supreme Court: Constitutional Revision and the New Strict Constructionism, 1973, Chief Justice: Leadership and the Supreme Court, 1986; sr. co-author: American Constitutional Law: Cases and Commentary, 1991; contbr. articles to profl. jours. Served with USAAF, 1942-46. Recipient Disting. Tchr. award Lake Forest Coll., 1965; Lilly Found. Research award, 1967; Major Research award Project 87, 1981; hon. research fellow U. Exeter, Eng., 1981. Mem. Am. Polit. Sci. Assn., Midwest Polit. Sci. Assn. (v.p. 1970-71), New Eng. Polit. Sci. Assn. (pres. 1979-80). Home: 439 Kilbourn Rd Rochester NY 14618-3635

STEANS, PHILLIP MICHAEL, lawyer; b. Oak Park, Ill., May 23, 1943; s. William B. and Evelyn A. (Leonetti) S.; m. Randi R. Solberg, Sept. 17, 1966; children: Erik, Joshua, Molly. BA summa cum laude, Ripon (Wis.) Coll., 1965; JD, U. Chgo., 1968. Bar: Wis. 1968, Ill. 1968, Minn. 1986, U.S. Dist. Ct. (we. dist.) Wis. 1968. Ptnr. Solberg & Steans, Menomonie, Wis., 1968-85; mng. ptnr. Steans, Skinner, Schefield & Higley, Menomonie, 1985-91; shareholder Bakke-Norman, S.C., Menomonie, 1991-94; pres. Phillip M. Steans, S.C., Menomonie, 1994—; dist. atty. Dunn County, Wis., Menomonie, 1969-75; asst. city atty. City of Menomonie, 1969-86; asst. family ct. commr. Dunn County, 1993. NCAA scholar, 1965. Mem. Nat. Bd. Trial Advocacy (mem. civil and criminal sects.). Avocations: racquetball, horseback riding, reading. Home: E 5745 708th Ave Menomonie WI 54751 Office: 393 Red Cedar St # 6 Menomonie WI 54751-2390

STEAR, EDWIN BYRON, corporate executive; b. Peoria, Ill., Dec. 8, 1932; s. Edwin Joseph and Juanita Blanche (Hoffman) S.; married; children—Brian Douglas, Linnea Susan. B.S. in Mech. Engring, Bradley U., 1954; M.S., U. So. Calif., 1956; Ph.D. (Hughes Staff fellow), UCLA, 1961. Mem. tech. staff Hughes Aircraft Co., Culver City, Calif., 1954-59; asst. research engr. U. Calif., Los Angeles, 1959-61; asst. prof. engring. U. Calif., 1964-68, assoc. prof., 1968-69; mgr. guidance and control research lab. Lear Siegler, Inc., Santa Monica, Calif., 1963-64; assoc. prof. elec. engring. U. Calif., Los Angeles and Santa Barbara, 1969-73; prof. U. Calif., 1973-79, chmn. dept., 1975-79; chief scientist USAF, 1979-82; dir. Wash. Technology Ctr., 1983-90; prof. elec. engring. U. Wash., Seattle, 1983-90, assoc. dean research Coll. Engring., 1983-85; corp. v.p. tech. assessment Boeing Co., Seattle, 1990—; mem. sci. adv. bd. USAF, 1971-79, 84-92, vice chmn., 1986-89, chmn., 1989-90; mem. aeros. adv. com. NASA, 1984-90; cons. to industry and govt., 1964-79, 82—; mem. SAE Tech. Stds. Bd., 1994—, chair, 1996—; mem.

Industry Adv. Coun. Accreditation Bd. Engring. and Tech., Inc., 1994—; mem. Ctr. for Strategic Internat. Studies, 1995—; trustee Analytical Svcs., Inc., 1984-90; mem. guidance and control panel NATO Adv. Group Aerospace R&D, 1981-92, dep. chmn. panel, 1988-90, chmn. 1990-92. Editor: (with A. Kadish) Hormonal Control Systems, 1969; mem. editorial bd. Aircraft jour. AIAA, 1974-77; contbr. articles to profl. lit. Served to 1st lt. USAF, 1961-63. Named Disting. Alumnus Bradley U., 1980; recipient civilian exceptional svc. medals USAF, 1982, 92; Arnold D. Beckman lectr. on rsch. and innovation U. Ill., Urbana, 1993; Mental Health Tng. Program fellow UCLA, 1972-74. Fellow IEEE, AIAA (assoc.); mem. AAAS, Internat. Fedn. Automation Control, Am. Electronics Assn. (sci. and tech. com. 1988-90), Sigma Xi, Eta Kappa Nu, Pi Mu Epsilon, Tau Beta Pi, Phi Eta Sigma, Tau Sigma. Home: 14010 SE 44th Pl Bellevue WA 98006-2331 Office: The Boeing Co PO Box 3707 MS 13-43 Seattle WA 98124-2207

STEARLEY, ROBERT JAY, retired packaging company executive; b. Brazil, Ind., Sept. 6, 1929; s. Melvin George and Hila Mona (Bolin) S.; m. Helen Louise Dellacca, Nov. 25, 1950; children: Rhonda Jo, Robert Thomas. B.S. in Mech. Engring., Rose Hulman Inst. Tech., 1957; postgrad., Harvard U., 1979. Gen. mgr. Poly Tech Corp., Mpls., 1961-63; gen. mgr. plastics Gt. Plains Bag Corp., Stamford, Conn., 1963-66, v.p., 1966-71, v.p. ops., 1971-75, pres., 1975-84, dir., 1966-84; v.p. Jefferson Smurfit Corp., Alton, Ill., 1984—. Mem. Paper Shipping Sack Mfg. Assn. (dir. 1980-82), Am. Legion. Republican. Methodist. Club: Norwood Hills Country (St. Louis). Lodge: Elks. Home: 2 Country Estate Pl Saint Louis MO 63131-3411

STEARN, TODD, federal government official. Asst. to pres., staff sec. Office of Staff Sec., Washington, 1995—. Office: Office of Staff Sec 1600 Pennsylvania Ave NW Washington DC 20508

STEARNS, CLIFFORD BUNDY, congressman, business executive; b. Washington, DC, Apr. 16, 1941; s. Clifford Robert and Emily Elizabeth (Newlin) S.; m. Joan Bette Moore; children: Douglas Moore, Clifford Bundy Jr., Scott Newlin. BSEE, George Washington U., 1963. Mgr. Control Data Systems, Inc., L.A., 1967-69; sr. contract adminstr. CBS, Inc., Stamford, Conn., 1969; account exec. Kutola Advt. Agy., Greenwich, Conn., 1970-71, Images 70/Wilson Haight Welch, Inc., Greenwich, 1971-72; motel owner Hatfield, Mass., 1972-77; pres., motel mgr. Stearns House, Inc., Silver Springs, Fla., 1977-88; mem. 101st-103rd Congresses from 6th Fla. dist., 1989—; mem. banking, fin. and urban affairs com., vets. affairs com. 101st Congress from 6th Fla. dist., mem. energy and commerce com., subcoms. energy and power, commerce, consumer protection and competetiveness; 104th Congress, mem. commerce and vets. coms., subcoms. telecom. and fin., healthcare, energy and power; broker Silver Springs (Fla.) Real Estate, 1981-88. Trustee, vice chmn. Monroe Regional Hosp., Ocala, Fla., 1984-89; bd. dirs. Boys Club of Ocala, 1980-84; pres. Toastmaster Club L.A., 1962. Capt. USAF, 1963-67. Mem. Am. Hotel/Motel Assn., Fla. Hotel/Motel Assn., Am. Assn. Realtors, Fla. Assn. Realtors, Marion County Motel Assn. (pres. 1979), Marion C. of C. (bd. dirs. 1987—), Kiwanis (pres. Ocala club 1984). Republican. Presbyterian. Avocations: basketball, swimming, computers. Home: 2071 SE 54th Ter Ocala FL 34471-8702 Office: US Ho of Reps 332 Channing St NE Bldg Washington DC 20002-1028 Office: Ho of Reps 2352 Rayburn Office Bldg Washington DC 20515 also: 115 SE 25th Ave Ocala FL 34471-9179

STEARNS, ELLIOTT EDMUND, JR., retired surgeon; b. Cleve., Jan. 11, 1923; s. Elliott Edmund and Sarah (Hoyt) S.; m. Martha Hudson Small, June 26, 1945; children: Michael Elliott, Philip Hoyt, Daniel Arthur. Student, Williams Coll., 1941-43; BS, U. Calif., Berkeley, 1945; MD, U. Calif., San Francisco, 1948. Diplomate Am. Bd. Urology. Intern U.S. Pub. Health Hosp., San Francisco, 1949-50; resident Sonoma Co. Hosp., Santa Rosa, Calif., 1950-51; fellow urology Cleve. Clinic, 1952-54; chief resident urology Cin. (Ohio) Gen. Hosp., U. Cin., 1954-56; med. staff St. Mary's Hosp., Tucson, 1956-87, St. Joseph's Hosp., Tucson, 1956-87, Tucson (Ariz.) Med. Ctr., 1956-87, Pima County Hosp., Tucson, 1956-87; ret., 1987; exec. com. mem. Pima County Med. Soc., Tucson, 1970s; chief of surgery St. Joseph's Hosp., Tucson, 1980s. Author: Catapult, 1994. Capt. USAF, 1954-56. Fellow ACS. Home: 2926 N Cascade Cir Tucson AZ 85715

STEARNS, JAMES GERRY, retired securities company executive; b. Lapine, Oreg., Jan. 29, 1922; s. Carey Summer and Betty (Hunt) S.; m. June Elizabeth Speer, Nov. 21, 1943; children: Robert Sumner, Katherine Inga, Gerry Marshall. Student, Oreg. State U. Flight instr. U.S. AAC, 1942-45; supr. Modoc County (Calif.), Alturas, 1951-67; dir. Calif. Dept. Conservation, Sacremento, 1967-72; sec. Calif. Agr. and Services Agy., Sacremento, 1972-75; dir. office alcohol fuels U.S. Dept. Energy, Washington, 1981-82; chmn., chief exec. officer Securities Investor Protection Corp., Washington, 1982-94; ret., 1994. With USAAC, 1942-45. Republican. Lodges: Masons; Shriners; Jesters. Office: Securities Investor Protection Corp 805 15th St NW Ste 800 Washington DC 20005-2207

STEARNS, LLOYD WORTHINGTON, investment adviser, oriental artifact consultant; b. Somerville, Mass., Feb. 16, 1910; s. Charles Victor and Flora D. (Liscom) S.; B.S. in Indsl. Engring., N.Y. U., 1934; m. Adelaide Church, Nov. 23, 1932; 1 child, Adelaide Liscom Stearns McRae. Indsl. security analyst Adminstrv. and Research Corp., 1934-38; asst. to treas., v.p. Northam Warren Corp., 1938-41; with Met. Life Ins. Co., 1941-75, sr. procedure analyst, mgmt. cons., exec. asst. to sr. v.p., to exec. v.p., 1941-60, to pres., 1960, sec., emergency com., 1950-75; coll. relations cons.; dir. Soundscriber, Inc.; pres., dir. Dispoz Sani Products, Ltd. Bd. dirs. Mil. Pub. Inst., Inc.; sec. N.Y. State Life Ins. Civil Def. Adv. Com., 1954-64; corp. mem. N.Y. World's Fair 1964-65 Corp.; mem. nat. def. com. U.S. C. of C. and NAM; mem. joint com. emergency operation Am. Life Conv.-Life Ins. Assn. Am.; mem. corps com. Lincoln Center for Performing Arts, 1959-62; v.p., treas., dir., vice chmn. N.Y. com. Nat. Strategy Seminars, Inc.; dir. Nat. Inst. Disaster Moblzn., Inc., Battery Park Colonnade Assocs., Inc.; sec. French-Polyclinic Fund, Inc. Trustee French Hosp., N.Y.C., N.Y. Polyclinic Med. Sch. and Hosp. Served to col. AUS, 1933-70; sec. gen. to chief commr. Allied Commn. Rome, Mediterranean Theater Opers., WWII, 1941-46, NATOUSA; with Res. 1946-70. Decorated Legion of Merit; recipient Outstanding Civilian Service medal U.S. Army; decorated comdr. Crown of Italy, comdr. Sts. Maurice and Lazarus (Italy); War Cross Commemorative Royal Yugoslav Army. Mem. Am. Ordnance Assn. (dir., chmn. programs), Am. Legion, Vet. Fgn. Wars, Soc. Colonial Wars (council), SAR (bd. mgrs.), N.Y. Soc. Mil. and Naval Officers World Wars (sec.), Mil. Order of World Wars, Assn. U.S. Army (pres. N.Y. chpt. 1961-62, regional pres. 1963-64), Def. Orientation Conf. Assn., N.Y. Chamber Commerce, Newcomen Soc., New Eng. Hist. and Geneal. Soc., U.S. Naval Inst., Statue of Liberty Found., Gateway Civic Assn (pres., sec., treas. 1983—), Phi Gamma Delta. Episcopalian. Clubs: University (N.Y.C.); Army and Navy (Washington); Masons. Home and Office: 410 Main St Keene NH 03431-4180

STEARNS, MILTON SPRAGUE, JR., financial executive; b. N.Y.C., June 3, 1923; s. Milton Sprague and Katherine (Stieglitz) S.; m. Virginia McCormick; children—Virginia Parker Stearns King, John Brackett, Barbara Ellison Stearns Terry, Kathryn Trowbridge Stearns Sergio, Elizabeth Sprague (dec.). Grad., Phillips Exeter Acad., 1942; BS cum laude, Harvard U., 1946, MBA, 1948. With The Fidelity Bank, Phila., 1948-72; group v.p. nat. lending div. The Fidelity Bank; pres. Charter Fin. Co., Radnor, Pa., 1972—; chmn., chief exec. officer Judson Infrared, Inc., 1976-87; bd. dirs. CFM Tech. Corp., Inc., West Chester, Pa., Infocore, King of Prussia, Pa.; ret. dir. The West Co., Phoenixville, Pa. Trustee Franklin Inst., Bryn Mawr Presbyn. Ch., pres. 1993-95. Served with USNR, WWII; lt. (j.g.) Res. ret. Mem. Robert Morris Assoc. (pres. Phila. chpt. 1961-62), Spee Club Cambridge, Mass., Merion Golf Club, Merion Cricket Club, Phila. Skating and Humane Soc., Union League Club of Phila., Delray Beach (Fla.) Club, Delray Beach Yacht Club, Country Club of Fla., Gulfstream Bath and Tennis Club, Pine Tree Golf Club. Home: 43 Righters Mill Rd Gladwyne PA 19035-1548 Office: Ste 300 290 King of Prussia Rd Radnor PA 19087-5111

STEARNS, NEELE EDWARD, JR., diversified holding company executive; b. Chgo., Apr. 2, 1936; s. Neele Edward Sr. and Grace (Kessler) S.; m. Bonnie Ann Evans; children: Katherine Grace, Kendra Ann. BA magna cum laude, Carleton Coll., 1958; MBA with distinction, Harvard U., 1960. Audit staff Arthur Andersen Co., 1962-66, audit mgr., 1966-67; asst. gen. mgr. internat. divsn. Imperial-Eastman Corp., 1967-68; asst. treas. Allied Products Corp., 1968-69, treas., 1969-72; v.p. Henry Crown (Ill.) and Co., 1972-75, v.p., controller, 1975-79; exec. v.p., chief oper. officer Henry Crown and Co., 1979-86; pres., chief exec. officer CC Industries, Inc., Chgo., 1986—. Trustee Ravinia Festival Assn., treas.; chmn. fin. com. Lakeland Health Svcs. (Highland Park Hosp.), trustee, treas. Mem. Commercial Club Chgo., Econ. Club Chgo., Univeristy Club Chgo., Chgo. Club, Skokie Country Club, Phi Beta Kappa. Office: CC Industries Inc 222 N La Salle St Chicago IL 60601-1003*

STEARNS, PETER NATHANIEL, history educator; b. London, Mar. 3, 1936; (parents Am. citizens); s. Raymond P. and Elizabeth (Scott) S.; m. Nancy Driessel (div. 1976); children: Duncan, Deborah; m. Carol Zisowitz, Mar. 26, 1978; children: Clio Elizabeth, Cordelia Raymond. AB, Harvard U., 1957, MA, 1959, PhD, 1963. Instr. to assoc. prof. U. Chgo., 1962-65; prof., chmn. history dept. Rutgers U., New Brunswick, N.J., 1965-74; Heinz prof. history Carnegie Mellon U., Pitts., 1974—, chmn. dept. history, 1986-92, dean Coll. Humanities and Social Scis., 1992—; co-dir. Pitts. Ctr. for Social History, 1986-92; chmn. acad. adv. coun. N.Y.C. Coll. Bd., 1982-85; chmn. Pacesetter World History commn., Coll. Bd., 1992-95. Author: European Society in Upheaval: Social History since 1800, 1967 (trans. Swedish), rev. edit., 1975, 3d edit., 1991, Priest and Revolutionary: Lamennais and the Dilemma of French Catholicism, 1967 (trans. Polish), Modern Europe, 1789-1914, 1969, Revolutionary Syndicalism and French Labor: a cause without rebels, 1971, (with Harvey Mitchell) Workers and Protest: The European Labor Movement, The Working Classes and the Rise of Socialism, 1890-1914, 1971, The European Experience since 1815, 1972, 1848: The Revolutionary Tide in Europe, 1974 (pub. in Eng. as The Revolutions of 1848), Lives of Labor: Work in Maturing Industrial Society, 1975 (trans. German), Old Age in European Society, 1977, Face of Europe, 1977, Paths to Authority: Toward the Formation of Middle Class Consciousness, 1978, Be A Man! Males in Modern Society, 1979, rev. edit., 1990, (with Linda Rosenzweig) Themes in Modern Social History, 1985, (with Carol Stearns) Anger: The Struggle for Emotional Control in America's History, 1986, World History: Patterns of Change and Continuity, 1987, (with others) Makers of Modern Europe, 1987, rev. edit., 1994, (with others) Readings in World History, Vol. 1: The Great Tradition and Vol. 2: The Modern Centuries, 1987, Expanding the Past: A Reader in Social History, 1988, Life and Society in the West, The Modern Centuries, 1988, World History: Traditions and New Directions, 1988, rev. edit., 1994, (with C. Stearns) Emotion and Social Change, Toward a New Psychohistory, 1988, (with Andrew Barnes) Social History and Issues in Consciousness and Cognition, 1989, Jealousy: Evolution of an Emotion in American History, 1989, Interpreting the Industrial Revolution, 1991, (with Michael Adas and Stuart Schwartz) World Civilizations, 1991, Meaning Over Memory: Issues in Humanities Education, 1993, The Industrial Revolution in World History, 1993, (translated into Swedish), American Cool: Developing a 20th Century Emotional Style, 1994, Turbulent Passage: A Global History of the 20th Century, 1994; editor: Century for Debate, 1969, The Impact of the Industrial Revolution, 1972, (with Walkowitz) Workers in the Industrial Revolution, 1974, The Other Side of Western Civilization, 1979, rev. edit., 1984, 4th edit., 1991, The Rise of Modern Women, 1977, (with Michael Weber) The Spencers of Amberson Avenue: A Turn-of-the-Century Memoir, 1983, (with Van Tassel) Old Age in a Bureaucratic Society, 1986; editor in chief Jour. Social History, 1967—; editor: Encyclopedia of Social History, 1993, Ency. World Hist., 1995, 5th edit. Encyclopedia World History rev.; contbg. editor history of emotions series NYU Press; contbr. over 150 articles to profl. and popular jours. Guggenheim Found. fellow, 1973-74; NEH grantee, 1981-84, 86, 90, Rockefeller Found. grantee, 1982-83. Fellow Internat. Soc. for Rsch. on Emotion; mem. Am. Hist. Soc., World History Assn., Am. Hist. Assn. (v.p., head teaching div. 1995—), Nat. Bd. Profl. Teaching Standards. Democrat. Avocations: racquet sports, travel. Home: 509 S Linden Ave Pittsburgh PA 15208-2846 Office: Carnegie Mellon U History Dept Pittsburgh PA 15213-3890

STEARNS, RICHARD GAYLORE, judge; b. L.A., June 27, 1944; s. Gaylore Rhodes and Jeannetta Viola (Hofheinz) S.; m. Patricia Ann McElligott, Dec. 21, 1975. BA, Stanford U., 1968; MLitt, Oxford U., Eng., 1971; JD, Harvard U., 1976. Bar: Mass. Dep. campaign mgr. McGovern for Pres., Washington, 1970-72; spl. asst. U.S. Senate, Washington, 1972-73; asst. dist. atty. Norfolk County, Dedham, 1976-79, 80-82; del. dir. Kennedy for Pres., Washington, 1979-80; asst. U.S. atty. U.S. Dept. Justice, Boston, 1982-90; assoc. justice Superior Ct. Mass., Boston, 1990-94; U.S. dist. judge U.S. Dist. Ct. Mass., Boston, 1994—. Author: Massachusetts Criminal Law: A Prosecutor's Guide, 15th edit., 1995. Rhodes scholar, 1968. Mem. ABA, Mass. Bar Assn., Phi Beta Kappa. Office: US Dist Ct 707 PO & Courthouse Bldg Boston MA 02109

STEARNS, ROBERT LELAND, curator; b. L.A., Aug. 28, 1947; s. Edward Van Buren and Harriett Ann (Hauck) S.; m. Sheri Roseanne Lucas, Oct. 2, 1982 (div. 1994); children: Marissa Hauck, Caroline Lucas. Student, U. Calif., San Diego, 1965-68, BFA, 1970; student, Calif. Poly. State U., San Luis Obispo, 1968. Asst. dir. Paula Cooper Gallery, N.Y.C., 1970-72; prodn. asst. Avalanche Mag., N.Y.C., 1972; dir. Kitchen Ctr. for Video/Music, N.Y.C., 1972-77, Contemporary Arts Ctr., Cin., 1977-82; dir. performing arts Walker Art Ctr., Mpls., 1982-88; dir. Wexner Ctr. for Arts, Columbus, Ohio, 1988-92; mem. Wexner Ctr. Found., Columbus, 1990-92; dir. Stearns & Assocs./Contemporary Exhbn. Svcs., Lancaster, Ohio, 1992—; adj. prof. dept. art, assoc. dean Coll. Art, Ohio State U., Columbus, 1988-92; cons. McKnight Found., St. Paul, 1978, Jerome Found., 1978-79; chmn. Artists TV Workshop, N.Y.C., 1976-77; bd. dirs., chmn. Minn. Dance Alliance, Mpls., 1983-88; bd. dirs. Haleakala, Inc., N.Y.C.; mem. various panels Nat. Endowment for Arts, Washington, 1977— ; mem. pub. arts policy Greater Columbus Arts Coun., 1988-90; adv. coun. Bklyn. Acad. Music, 1982-84, Houston Grand Opera, 1991-93. Author, editor: Robert Wilson: Theater of Images, 1980, Photography and Beyond in Japan, 1995; editor: Dimensions of Black, 1970; exec. editor: Breakthroughs, 1991; author and editor numerous catalogues. Decorated chevalier Order of Arts and Letters (France); Jerome Found. travel grantee, 1986, Japan Found. travel grantee, 1991.

STEARNS, SUSAN TRACEY, lighting design company executive, lawyer; b. Seattle, Oct. 28, 1957; d. Arthur Thomas and Roberta Jane (Arrowood) S.; m. Ross Alan De Alessi, Aug. 11, 1990; 1 child, Chase Arthur. AA, Stephens Coll., 1977, BA, 1979; JD, U. Wash., Seattle, 1990. Bar: Ct. Appeals (9th cir.) 1990, U.S. Dist. Ct. (no. dist.) Calif 1990, U.S. Dist. Ct. (we. dist.) Wash. 1991. TV news prodr. KOMO, Seattle, 1980-86; atty. Brobeck, Phleger & Harrison, San Francisco, 1990-92; pres. Ross De Alessi Lighting Design, Seattle, 1993—. Author periodicals in field. Alumnae Assn. Coun. Stephens Coll., Columbia, Mo., 1995—. Named Nat. Order of Barristers U. Washington, Seattle, 1990. Mem. ABA (mem. state labor and employment law subcom.), Wash. State Bar Assn. (mem. bench-bar-press com.), State Bar Calif., King County Bar Assn., Bar Assn.San Francisco, Wash. Athletic Club. Avocations: travel, dance. Office: Ross De Alessi Lighting Design 2815 2nd Ave Ste 280 Seattle WA 98121-1261

STEBBINS, GREGORY KELLOGG, foundation executive, chairman; b. Lafayette, Ind., Jan. 10, 1951; s. Albert Kellogg and Nancy Ruth (Osborn) S. BS in Data Processing, Calif. Poly., Pomona, 1974; MBA, U. So. Calif., 1976; EdD, Pepperdine U., 1985. Account exec. ADP, Long Beach, Calif., 1977-78; salesman Grubb & Ellis, L.A., 1978-81; v.p. Grubb & Ellis, Beverly Hills, Calif., 1981-83; regional mgr. Hanes Co., Beverly Hills, 1983-85; treas. U. Santa Monica, L.A., 1983—; pres. Stebbins Consulting Group, Santa Monica, 1989—; chair Santa Monica Inst., 1994—. Chair exec. com. Educare Found., 1994—. Mem. ASTD, Sigma Xi. Avocations: flying, scuba diving, photography. Home: 445 Washington Blvd Apt 15 Marina Dl Rey CA 90292-5271 Office: Santa Monica Inst 2101 Wilshire Blvd Santa Monica CA 90403-5735

STEBBINS, RICHARD HENDERSON, electronics engineer, peace officer, security consultant; b. Pittsburgh, Pa., Dec. 2, 1938; s. Earl Carlos and Esther Frances (Kusluch) S.; m. Rosemary Tanneberger, Aug. 12, 1984; children from previous marriage: Richard Earl, Susan Elizabeth. BSEE with high honors, U. Md., 1965; postgrad., Trinity U., 1973-74. cert. peace officer, Tex. Engring. tech. Nat. Security Agy., Ft. Meade, Md., 1960-65; design engr. Page Communications Engr., Washington, 1965-66, Electromechanical Rsch., Inc., College Park, Md., 1966-67, Honeywell, Inc., Annapolis, Md., 1967-68; electronics engr., intelligence rsch. specialist Fed. Civil Svc., San Antonio, 1968-91; pvt. cons. San Antonio, 1991—; comdr.'s advisor Air Force Cryptologic Support Ctr., San Antonio, 1988-91; deputy dir. countermeasures ops., intelligence rsch. specialist USAF HQ Electronic Security Command, San Antonio, 1981-88; mem. blue ribbon com. on ops. security & comm. security roles & relationships for command and svc. Author, lectr. in field; contbr. articles to profl. jours. With USN, 1956-59. Mem. NRA, Tau Beta Pi, Eta Kappa Nu, Phi Kappa Phi. Republican. Episcopalian. Avocations: hunting, fishing, target shooting, family history rsch. Home: 9602 Clear Falls San Antonio TX 78250-5067

STEBBINS, ROBERT ALAN, sociology educator; b. Rhinelander, Wis., June 22, 1938; s. William Nelson and Dorothy May (Guy) S.; m. Karin Yvonne Olson, Jan. 11, 1964; children: Paul, Lisa, Christi. B.A., Macalester Coll., 1961; M.A., U. Minn., 1962, Ph.D., 1964. Assoc. prof. Presbyterian Coll., Clinton, S.C., 1964-65; assoc. prof.to prof. Meml. U. Nfld., St. John's, Can., 1965-73; prof. U. Tex.-Arlington, 1973-76; prof. sociology U. Calgary, Alta., Can., 1976—, dept. head, 1976-82; head dept. sociology and anthropology Meml. U. Nfld., 1968-71. Author: Commitment to Deviance, 1971, The Disorderly Classroom: Its Physical and Temporal Conditions, 1974, Teachers and Meaning, 1975, Amateurs, 1979, The Magician, 1984, Sociology: The Study of Society, 2d edit., 1990, Canadian Football: The View from the Helmet, 1987, Deviance: Tolerable Differences, 1988, The Laugh-Makers: Stand-Up Comedy as Art, Business, and Life-Style, 1990, Amateurs, Professionals and Serious Leisure, 1992; co-editor: Fieldwork Experience, 1980, The Sociology of Deviance, 1982, Experiencing Fieldwork, 1991, Career, Culture, and Social Psychology in a Variety Art, 1993, Predicaments: Moral Difficulty in Everyday Life, 1993, The Franco-Calgarians: French Language, Leisure and Linguistic Lifestyle in an Anglophone City, 1994, The Connoisseur's New Orleans, 1995, The Barbershop Singer: Inside the Social World of a Musical Hobby, 1996, Tolerable Differences: Living with Deviance, 2d edit., 1996. Pres. St. John's Orch., 1967-68; mem. Dallas Civic Symphony, 1973-76, Orch. Soc. of Calgary, 1978—. Can. Coun. Sabbatical Leave fellow, 1972-72, Calgary Inst. for Humanities fellow, 1987-88, Killam resident fellow, 1990; NEH summer stipend, 1976. Mem. Leisure Studies Assn., Can. Sociology and Anthropology Assn. (pres. 1988-89), Internat. Sociol. Assn., Assn. for Can. Studies, World Leisure and Recreation Assn., Social Sci. Fedn. Can. (pres. 1991-92), Can. Assn. for Leisure Studies (v.p. 1993—), Internat. Soc. bassists Club (Ann Arbor, Mich., chmn. amateur divsn. 1974-84). Home: 144 Edgemont Estates Dr NW, Calgary, AB Canada T3A 2M3 Office: U Calgary Dept Sociology, 2500 University Dr NW, Calgary, AB Canada T2N 1N4

STEBBINS, THEODORE ELLIS, JR., museum curator; b. N.Y.C., Aug. 11, 1938; s. Theodore Ellis and Mary Emma Flood S.; children: Michael Morgan, Theodore Samuel, Susan Ellis. B.A., Yale U., 1960; J.D., Harvard U., 1964, Ph.D., 1971. Chester Dale fellow Nat. Gallery Art, Washington, 1967; instr. Smith Coll., 1968; assoc. prof. art history and Am. studies, curator Am. painting and sculpture Yale U., New Haven, 1969-77; John Moors Cabot curator Am. paintings Mus. Fine Arts, Boston, 1977—; lectr. fine arts Harvard U., 1979-81; prof. art history Boston U., 1982—; mem. governing bd. Yale U. Art Gallery; trustee Inst. Contemporary Art, Boston. Author: Life and Works of Martin Johnson Heade, 1975, American Master Drawings and Watercolors, 1976, The Hudson River School at the Wadsworth Atheneum, 1976, The Oil Sketches of Frederic Edwin Church, 1978, Drawings of Washington Allston, 1979, Luminism in Context, 1980, The Lane Collection, 1983, A New World: Masterpieces of American Painting, 1983, intro. to The Bostonians, 1986, Boston Collects Contemporary Painting and Sculpture, 1986, Charles Sheeler: The Photographs, 1987, Weston's Westons: Portraits and Nudes, 1989, The Lure of Italy: American Artists and the Italian Experience (Winner Minda de Gunzberg prize 1993), 1992, Weston's Westons: California and the West, 1994, Driftwood Winslow Homer's Final Painting, 1996. Trustee Howard Heinz Endowment; pres. Stebbins Fund. Recipient Joseph Coolidge Shaw medal Boston Coll., 1983. Club: Century Assn. Office: Mus Fine Arts 465 Huntington Ave Boston MA 02115-5523

STEBBINS, VRINA GRIMES, elementary school educator, counselor; b. Columbus, Ohio, Aug. 24, 1939; d. Marion Edward and Vrina Elizabeth (Davis) Grimes; m. Gary Frank Stebbins, Dec. 23, 1959; 1 child, Gregory Gary. Student, Ohio U., 1957-59; BS in Edn., Miami U., Oxford, Ohio, 1965; MS in Edn., St. Francis Coll., 1971; Counseling Endorsement, Ind.-Purdue U., Ft. Wayne, 1988. Cert. elem. classroom educator K-6, sch. counselor, social worker, Ind. 1st grade tchr. Greenville (Ohio) Pub. Schs., 1963-68; elem. educator East Allen County Schs., New Haven, Ind., 1969-84; elem. sch. counselor East Allen County Schs., New Haven, 1984—; presenter at Ind. profl. orgns., 1985-92, 1st Presbyn. Ch., Ft. Wayne, 1984—, Project 2000, Ft. Wayne, 1992—; participant Bus.-Edn. Exchange, Ft. Wayne C. of C., 1993. Mem. ACA, Ind. Counseling Assn. (com. mem. 1992-93, Ind. Elem. Counselor of Yr. 1991), East Allen Educators' Assn. (chair com. 1989—, East Allen County Schs. Elem. Educator of Yr. 1989), Arts United, Phi Delta Kappa, Delta Kappa Gamma (participant leadership mgmt. seminar 1993, 1st v.p. Ind. state 1993-95, Ind. state pres. 1995—). Democrat. Presbyterian. Avocations: travel, collecting antiques and angels. Home: 5712 Sandra Lee Ave Fort Wayne IN 46819-1118 Office: Village Elem Sch 4625 Werling Dr Fort Wayne IN 46806-3410

STEC, JOHN ZYGMUNT, real estate executive; b. Stalowawola, Poland, Jan. 21, 1925; Came to U.S.A. 1947.; s. Valenty and Maria (Madej) S. m. Wanda G. Baca, Oct. 13, 1956; children: David, Maria, Monica. Student, Poland, 1941-44, Kent St. U., Oh., 1965-66, Kent St. U., Oh., 1966-67. Cert. Master of Corporate Real Estate. With The Singer Co., Cleve., 1952-54, dis. mgr., 1954-60, sales supr., 1960-67; dir. real estate The Singer Co., Detroit and Chgo., 1967-73; v.p. Fabri Center of Am., Beachwood, Ohio, 1973—; sr. v.p. real estate Fabri-Centers of Am., Inc., Beachwood, Ohio, 1987—; With U.S. Army 1950-52. With U.S. Army, 1950-52. Mem. Nat. Assoc. of Corporate Real Estate (speaker, organizer 1974-77, audit Com. 1977-79, bd. dirs. 1970-82, Outstanding Achievement award 1982). Chagrin Valley Club. Repulican. Roman Catholic. Avocations: swimming, hiking, reading. Home: 9630 Stafford Rd Chagrin Falls OH 44023-5302 Office: Fabri-Ctrs Am Inc 5555 Darrow Rd Hudson OH 44236-4011 *Personal philosophy: Think success and you'll be successful. Perseverence of any goal leads to achievement. Learning is knowledge. Knowledge is the most powerful key that leads to greatness.*

STECK, THEODORE LYLE, biochemistry and molecular biology educator, physician; b. Chgo., May 3, 1939; s. Irving E. and Mary L. S.; children: David B., Oliver M. B.S. in Chemistry, Lawrence Coll., 1960; M.D., Harvard U., 1964. Intern Beth Israel Hosp., Boston, 1964-65; fellow Beth Israel Hosp., 1965-66; research assoc. Nat. Cancer Inst., NIH, Bethesda, Md., 1966-68, Harvard U. Med. Sch., Boston, 1968-70; asst. prof. medicine U. Chgo., 1970-74, asst. prof. biochemistry and medicine, 1973-74, assoc. prof., 1974-77, prof., 1977-84, chmn. dept. biochemistry, 1979-84, prof. biochemistry and molecular biology, 1984—, chair environ. studies program, 1993—. Office: 920 E 58th St Chicago IL 60637-1432

STECK, WARREN FRANKLIN, chemical company executive, former biochemistry researcher; b. Regina, Sask., Can., May 10, 1939; m. 1963; 2 children. B in Eng., McGill U., 1960; PhD in Organic Chemistry, U. Sask., 1964. Rsch. assoc. Rsch. Inst. Okla. U., 1963-64; asst. rsch. officer Nat. Rsch. Coun. Can., 1964-70, assoc. rsch. officer, 1970-76, sr. rsch. officer, 1976-80, asst. dir., 1980-81, assoc. dir., 1982-83, dir. Plant Biotech. Inst., 1983-90, dir. gen. Plant Biotech Inst., 1991-94; pres. Fytokem Inc., Saskatoon, Sask., 1995—. Mem. Phytochemical Soc. N.Am., Internat. Assn. Plant Tissue Culture, Internat. Soc. Chem. Ecology. Achievements include rsch. in insect sex attractants and pheromones, chem. ecology. Office: Fytokem Inc, 222-111 Research Dr, Saskatoon, SK Canada S7N3R2

STECKEL, BARBARA JEAN, city financial officer; b. L.A., Mar. 9, 1939; d. John Herschel and Bernice Evelyn (Selstad) Webb Banta; m. Jimmie Raeburn Lugenbeel, Feb. 16, 1957 (div. 1962); Leanna Virgina, Debra Lynn; m. Dale Robert Steckel, Mar. 16, 1962; 1 child, Richard Alan. AA in Bus., Anchorage Community Coll., 1975; BBA, U. Alaska, Anchorage, 1980. City clk., treas. City of Kotzebue, Alaska, 1973-74, city mgr., treas., 1974-76;

grants adminstr. Municipality of Anchorage, Alaska, 1976-79, contr., 1979-82, mcpl. mgr., 1982-84, chief fiscal officer, 1984-87; fin. dir., treas. City of Riverside, Calif., 1988—; bd. dirs. Riverside Cmty. Ventures, Corp., Cmty. Health Corp., chmn. fin. com. Mem. adv. coun. sch. bus. and pub. adminstrn. U. Alaska, Anchorage, 1982-85; bd. dirs. Anchorage Parking Authority, 1984-87, ICMA Retirement Corp., 1985-93, Police and Fire Retirement Sys. Mcpl. of Anchorage, 1982-87, chmn., 1986; devel. com. mem. Am. Heart Assn., Anchorage, 1987. Mem. Govt. Fin. Officers U.S. and Can. (bd. dirs. 1984-87), Mcpl. Fin. Officers Alaska (pres. 1981-82), Nat. Assn. Accts. (bd. dirs. 1986-87), Am. Soc. Women Accts., Calif. Soc. Mcpl. Fin. Officers (chmn. cash mgmt. com. 1989-91, bd. dirs. 1992-95, pres. elect 1995-96, pres. 1996-97), Mcpl. Treas. Assn. (R.E. Phillips award, Svc. award, debt com. chmn. 1992-95), Calif. Mcpl. Treas. Assn., Internat. City Mgrs. Assn., U. Alaska Alumni Assn., Rotary, Elks. Avocations: reading, sewing. Office: City of Riverside 3900 N Main St Riverside CA 92522-0001

STECKEL, RICHARD J., radiologist, academic administrator; b. Scranton, Pa., Apr. 17, 1936; s. Morris Leo and Lucille (Yellin) S.; m. Julie Raskin, June 16, 1960; children: Jan Marie, David Matthew. BS magna cum laude, Harvard U., 1957, MD cum laude, 1961. Diplomate: Am. Bd. Radiology. Intern UCLA Hosp., 1961-62; resident in radiology Mass. Gen. Hosp., Boston, 1962-65; clin./rsch. assoc. Nat. Cancer Inst., 1965-67; mem. faculty UCLA Med. Sch., 1967—, prof. radiol. scis. and radiation oncology, dir. Jonsson Comprehensive Cancer Ctr., 1974-94; chair dept. radiol. scis. UCLA Med. Ctr., 1994—; pres. Assn. Am. Cancer Insts., 1981. Author/editor 3 books; contbr. over 130 articles on radiology and cancer diagnosis-to profl. publs. Fellow Am. Coll. Radiology; mem. Radiol. Soc. N. Am., Am. Roentgen Ray Soc., Assn. Univ. Radiologists. Office: UCLA Med Ctr Dept Radiol Scis 10833 Le Conte Ave Los Angeles CA 90095-1721

STECKLER, LARRY, publisher, editor, author; b. Bklyn., Nov. 3, 1933; s. Morris and Ida (Beekman) S.; m. Catherine Coccozza, June 6, 1959; children: Gail Denise, Glenn Eric, Kerri Lynn, Adria Lauren. Student, CCNY, 1951. Assoc. editor Radio-Electronics mag., N.Y.C., 1957-62, editor, 1967-85; pub., editor in chief Radio Electronics mag., 1985-92; electronics editor Popular Mechanics mag., N.Y.C., 1962-65; assoc. editor Electronic Products mag., Garden City, N.Y., 1965-67; editorial dir. Merchandising 2-Way Radio mag., N.Y.C., 1975-77; v.p., dir. Gernsback Publs., N.Y.C., 1975-84, pres., dir., 1984—; pub., editorial dir. Spl. Projects mag., 1980-84, Radio-Electronics Ann., 1982-84; pub., editor in chief Hands-On Electronics, 1984-88; Popular Electronics Mag., 1988—, Hobbyists Handbook, 1989—; pub., editor in chief Experimenters Handbook, 1986—; Radio Craft, 1993; pub., editor in chief Computer Digest, 1985-90; pres. Claggk, Inc., 1986—; Silicon Chip, 1993-94; pub., editor in chief The Magic Course, Eating In/Dining Out on Long Island, Modern Short Stories, 1987-90, GIZMO, 1988—, Video/Stereo Digest, 1989-91; pres. Sci. Probe Inc., 1989-93; pub., editor in chief Sci. Probe! mag., 1989-93, StoryMasters, 1989—, Electronics Shopper, 1990—, Electronics Market Ctr., 1991—; mem. electronics adv. bd. Bd. Coop. Ednl. Services, Nassau County, N.Y., 1975-77; pres. Electronics Industry Hall of Fame, 1985—; bd. dirs. Pub. Hall of Fame, 1987-89. Author books, handbooks; pub.; contbr. articles to profl. jours. Bd. dirs. Nassau County council Camp Fire Girls, 1971-72. Served with U.S. Army, 1953-56. Recipient Coop. award Nat. Alliance TV and Electronic Services Assns., 1974, 75; inducted into Electronics Industry Hall of Fame, 1985. Mem. IEEE, Internat. Soc. Cert. Electronic Technicians (chmn. 1974-76, 79-81, 93-95, Chmn.'s award 1985, dir.-at-large 1991-93, rep. to NESDA bd. 1991-93, Region 9 dir. 1995—), Nat. Electronics Sales and Svc. Dealers Assn. (rec. sec. N.Y. state 1976-78, Man of Yr. award 1975, 85, treas. 1991-94, M.L. Finneyberg Excellence award 1994), Am. Mgmt. Assn., Radio Club Am., Internat. Underwater Explorers Soc., Am. Soc. Bus. Press Editors (sr.), Internat. Performing Magicians (exec. dir.), Soc. Profl. Journalists, L.A. Press. Home: 2601 Springridge Dr Las Vegas NV 89134-8848 Office: Gernsback Pub Inc 500 BiCounty Blvd Farmingdale NY 11735-3918 also: Claggk Inc 4820 Alpine Pl Ste A101 Las Vegas NV 89107-4065 *Do not be afraid to try the unaccepted. Do not be afraid to do the undesirable. Do what you enjoy. . .do it well. . .and after it is done. . .never regret having done it. . .only regret what you have not yet done.*

STECKLER, PHYLLIS BETTY, publishing company executive; b. N.Y.C.; d. Irwin H. and Bertha (Fellner) Schwartzbard; m. Stuart J. Steckler; children: Randall, Sharon Steckler-Slotky. BA, Hunter Coll.; MA, NYU. Editorial dir. R.R. Bowker Co., N.Y.C., Crowell Collier Macmillan Info. Pub. Co., N.Y.C., Holt Rinehart & Winston Info. Systems, N.Y.C.; pres., CEO Oryx Press, Scottsdale, Ariz., 1973-76, Phoenix, 1976—; adj. prof. mktg. scholarly publs. Ariz. State U., Tempe. Past chmn. Info. Industry Assn.; pres. Ariz. Ctr. for the Book; bd. dirs. Contemporary Forum of Phoenix Art Mus., Phoenix Pub. Libr. Friends; past pres. Friends of the Librs., U.S.A.; mem. edn. adv. coun. Senator John McCain; mem. Ariz. Women's Forum. Recipient Women Who Make a Difference award The Internat. Women's Forum, 1995; elected to Hunter Coll. Hall of Fame. Mem. ALA, Spl. Librs. Assn., Am. Soc. Info. Soc., Ariz. Libr. Assn., Univ. Club of Phoenix (bd. dirs.). Home: 6711 E Camelback Rd Unit 32 Scottsdale AZ 85251-2065 Office: Oryx Press 4041 N Central at Indian School Rd Phoenix AZ 85012

STECKLING, ADRIENNE See ADRI

STEDMAN, RICHARD RALPH, lawyer; b. Columbus, Ohio, July 18, 1936; s. Ralph Dale and Kathleen (Smith) S.; m. Elizabeth Ann Witschey, Dec. 18, 1965; children: Gretchen Kathleen, Richard Ralph II, Patrick Christopher Raymond. BBA, Ohio State U., 1958, JD, 1964. Bar: Ohio 1964; CPA, Ohio. Staff acct. Price Waterhouse & Co., Columbus, 1958-60; salesman Royal McBee Co., Columbus, 1960; ptnr. Vorys, Sater, Seymour & Pease, Columbus, 1964—. Contbr. articles to profl. jours. Trustee, counsel Found. Cath. Diocese of Columbus, 1985—; trustee, sec.-treas. Nat. Soc. Cath. Founds.; trustee Ohio Dominican Coll., 1990—, St. Charles Prep. Sch., 1990—, Edward Orton, Jr. Ceramic Found., 1994—. Merson fellow Ohio State U., 1963-64. Mem. Columbus Bar Assn., Fin. Execs. Inst., Athletic Club Columbus, Columbus Club, Brookside Golf and Country Club, Zanesfield Rod and Gun Club, Equestrian Order of Knights Holy Sepulchre of Jerusalem. Republican. Avocations: golfing, tennis, fishing. Office: Vorys Sater Seymour & Pease 52 E Gay St # 1008 Columbus OH 43215-3108

STEED, ROBERT LEE, lawyer, humor columnist; b. Augusta, Ga., Nov. 20, 1936; s. Robert Pentecost and Doris (Roop) S.; m. Linda (Lu) Ruth McElroy, Aug. 23, 1958; children: Joshua, Georgia, Nona Begonia. AB, Mercer U., 1958, LLB, 1961, LLD (hon.), 1979. Bar: Ga. 1959. Law clk. to presiding justice Supreme Ct. of Ga., Atlanta, 1961-62; assoc. King & Spalding, Atlanta, 1962-67, ptnr., 1967—. Author: Willard Lives, 1981, Lucid Intervals, 1983, Money Power and Sex (A Self-Help Guide for All Ages), 1985; editor: The First Hundred Years: A Centennial History of King and Spalding (Della Wager Wells), 1985, A Ship Without an Udder, 1995, The Sass Menagerie, 1988, Mail Fraud, The Laughable Letters of Robert L. Steed, 1991; columnist The Atlanta Jour. - Constn., 1978—. Mem., vice chmn. Met. Atlanta Crime Commn.; mem. bd. sponsors Atlanta Coll. Art; bd. dirs. 11 Alive Cmty. Svc. Awards, 1984—; chmn. bd. visitors Mercer Law Sch., 1970-71, 72-73, chmn. spl. gifts com. for renovation of Law Sch. Bldg., chmn. com. to select law sch. dean; trustee Mercer U., 1972-77, 79-84, 85-90, 91—, chmn. bd. trustees, 1985-90, mem. pres.'s coun., 1977-79, 84-85, mem. exec. com., 1974-77, chmn., 1982-84; bd. dirs. Walter F. George Found. for Mercer Law Sch., 1986—; trustee Walter F. George Sch. Law, George W. Woodruff Trust; bd. dirs. Clifton Corridor Coun., 1990-95. 1st lt. USAR, 1959. Recipient Journalistic Achievement award Dixie Coun. Authors, 1985, Humor award, 1985; Outstanding Alumnus award Mercer U., 1985, Disting. Alumnus award Mercer U. Coll. Liberal Arts, 1994. Mem. ABA, State Bar Ga. (bd. govs. 1967-68, pres. younger lawyers sect. 1967-68), Atlanta Bar Assn., Am. Coll. Investment Counsel, Ga. C. of C. (bd. dirs. 1982-85, chmn. Red Carpet Tour 1979-80, indsl. devel. commn. 1982-83), Bus. Coun. Ga. (bd. dirs. 1983-85), Mercer Alumni Assn. (exec. com. 1970-73), Mercer Law Alumni (pres.), U. Ga. Gridiron Secret Soc., Lawyers Club Atlanta, Old War Horse Lawyers Club, Capital City Club (bd. dirs. 1982-89, sec. 1985-87), Blue Key, Phi Delta Theta. Baptist. Home: 1058 Nawench Dr NW Atlanta GA 30327-1340 Office: King & Spalding 191 Peachtree St NE Atlanta GA 30303-1763

STEEDMAN, DORIA LYNNE SILBERBERG, advertising agency executive; b. L.A.; d. Mendel B. and Dorothy H. (Howell) Silberberg; m. Richard Cantey Steedman, Feb. 19, 1966; 1 child, Alexandra Loren. BA summa cum laude, UCLA. Producer EUE/Screen Gems, N.Y.C., 1963-66, Jack Tinker & Ptnrs., N.Y.C., 1966-68, Telpac Mgmt., N.Y.C., 1968-72; v.p. broadcast prodn. Geer DuBois Advt., N.Y.C., 1973-78, account mgr., dir. ops., 1979-92; exec. v.p., dir. creative devel. Partnership for a Drug-Free America, N.Y.C., 1992—. Recipient Andy award Art Dirs. Club, 1968, 71; named one of 100 Best and Brightest Women in Advt., Advt. Age mag., 1988. Mem. Advt. Women N.Y. (pres. 1993-95, Advt. Women N.Y. Found. (pres. 1994—), Phi Beta Kappa. Office: Partnership for a Drug-Free Am 405 Lexington Ave New York NY 10174

STEEG, MOISE S., JR., lawyer; b. New Orleans, July 25, 1916; s. Moise S. and Carrie (Gutmann) S.; m. Marion B., Sept. 14, 1943 (dec.); children: Barbara Steeg Midlo, Marion, Robert M.; m. Melba Law, Nov. 29, 1969. LLB, Tulane U., 1937. Bar: La. 1937, U.S. Dist. Ct. (ea. dist.) La. 1939, U.S. Ct. Appeals (5th cir.) 1946, U.S. Supreme Ct. 1950, U.S. Ct. Appeals (11th cir.) 1981. Practice, New Orleans, 1937—; assoc. Rittenberg & Rittenberg, 1937-38; sole practice, 1938-46; founder Gertler & Steeg, 1946-48, Steeg & Morrison, 1948-50, Marcus & Steeg, 1950-54, Steeg & Shushan, 1954-71; sr. ptnr. Steeg & O'Connor, 1972—. Bd. dirs. Loyola U., chmn., 1979—, mem. search com. for dean Coll. Law; chmn., founder New Orleans Hist. Dist. and Landmarks Com.; bd. dirs. chmn. bd. New Orleans Mus. Art, 1980; bd. overseers Hebrew Union Coll.; bd. dirs. Delgado Jr. Coll., New Orleans Symphony; founder, dir. New Orleans Ednl. and Rsch. Corp.; bd. dirs. Louise Davis Sch. for Retarded Children, Touro Infirmary, 1963-69; mem. Ochsner Found. Hosp. Bd., 1985—; bd. visitors Trinity Episcopal Sch., 1989—; organizer, sec. New Orleans Bus. Counsel, 1986; pres. Temple Sinai, 1966-67; chmn. Anti-Defamation League, Jewish Community Ctr., chmn. Acquarium Drive, Acquarium of Ams.; local counsel Nat. Dem. Party, 1966. Served to capt. USAF, 1942-46. Recipient Brotherhood Award, NCCJ, 1980, Disting. Alumnus award Tulane Law Sch., 1991. Mem. Paul Tulane Honor Soc. Home: One River Place 3 Poydras St New Orleans LA 70130-1665 Office: 201 Saint Charles Ave Ste 3201 New Orleans LA 70170-1000

STEEL, ADRIAN L., JR., lawyer; b. St. Louis, Jan. 2, 1950. AB, U. Mo., 1972; JD magna cum laude, U. Mich., 1975. Bar: Mo. 1975, Ill. 1976, U.S. Supreme Ct. 1979, D.C. 1981. Law clk. to Hon. William H. Webster U.S. Ct. Appeals (8th cir.), 1975-76; spl. asst. to dir. FBI, 1978-81; ptnr. Mayer, Brown & Platt, Washington. Mem. ABA, Ill. State Bar Assn., Mo. Bar, D.C. Bar Assn. Office: Mayer Brown & Platt 2000 Pennsylvania Ave NW St 6500 Washington DC 20006*

STEEL, DANIELLE FERNANDE, author; b. N.Y.C., Aug. 14, 1947; d. John and Norma (Stone) Schuelein-Steel. Student, Parsons Sch. Design, 1963, NYU, 1963-67. Vice pres. pub. relations and new bus. Supergirls Ltd., N.Y.C., 1968-71; copywriter Grey Advt., San Francisco, 1973-74. Author novels Going Home, 1973, Passion's Promise, 1977, Now and Forever, 1978, The Promise, 1978, Season of Passion, 1979, Summers End, 1979, To Love Again, 1980, The Ring, 1981, Loving, 1980, Love, 1981, Remembrance, 1981, Palomino, 1981, Once in a Lifetime, 1982, Crossings, 1982, A Perfect Stranger, 1982, Thurston House, 1983, Changes, 1983, Full Circle, 1984, (non-fiction) Having A Baby, 1984, Family Album, 1985, Secrets, 1985, Wanderlust, 1986, Fine Things, 1987, Kaleidoscope, 1987, Zoya, 1988, Star, 1988, Daddy, 1989, Message from Nam, 1990, Heartbeat, 1991, No Greater Love, 1991, Jewels, 1992, Mixed Blessings, 1992, Vanished, 1993, Accident, 1994, The Gift, 1994, Wings, 1994, Lightning, 1995; (children's) Martha's Best Friend, Martha's New School, Martha's New Daddy, Max's New Daddy, Max and The Babysitter, Max's Daddy Goes To The Hospital; contbr. poetry to mags., including Cosmopolitan, McCall's, Ladies Home Jour., Good Housekeeping. Home: PO Box 1637 New York NY 10156-1637 Office: 598 Madison Ave New York NY 10022-1614

STEEL, DAWN, motion picture producer; b. N.Y.C., Aug. 19; m. Charles Roven; 1 child, Rebecca. Student in mktg., Boston U., 1964-65, NYU, 1966-67. Sportswriter Major League Baseball Digest and NFL, N.Y.C., 1968-69; editor Penthouse Mag., N.Y.C., 1969-75; pres. Oh Dawn!, Inc., N.Y.C., 1975-78; v.p. merchandising, cons. Playboy mag., N.Y.C., 1978-79; v.p. merchandising Paramount Pictures, N.Y.C., 1979-80; v.p. prodn. Paramount Pictures, L.A., 1980-83, sr. v.p. prodn., 1983-85, pres. prodn., 1985-87; pres. Columbia Pictures, 1987-90; formed Steel Pictures (with Touchstone Pictures and Walt Disney Film & TV), 1990-94, Atlas Entertainment, 1994; mem. dean's adv. bd. UCLA Sch. Theater, Film, TV, 1993. First woman studio pres.; prodns. for Paramount include Flashdance, Footloose, Top Gun, Star Trek III, Beverly Hills Cop II, The Untouchables, The Accused, Fatal Attraction, 1985-87; prodns. for Columbia include Ghostbusters II, Karate Kid III, When Harry Met Sally, Look Who's Talking, Casualties of War, Postcards from the Edge, Flatliners, Awakenings; prodr. Steel Pictures for Disney: Honey, I Blew Up the Kid, 1992, Cool Runnings, 1993, Sister Act 2, 1993; prodr. (benefit concert) For Our Children, Pediatric AIDS Found., 1992; author: They Can Kill You, But They Can't Eat You, 1993. Appointeee Presdl. Commn. Scholars, 1993; mem. L.A. Mayor Richard Riordan's Transition Team, 1993, U.S. Del. to Winter Olympics, 1994; chair Mayor's Entertainment Industry Task Force, 1993; bd. dirs. Hollywood Supports, 1993. Recipient Women Film Crystal award Women in Film, 1989. Mem. Acad. Motion Picture Arts and Scis. Avocations: skiing, tennis. Office: Atlas Entertainment 9169 W Sunset Blvd Los Angeles CA 90069-3129

STEEL, DUNCAN GREGORY, physics educator; b. Cleve., Jan. 11, 1951; s. Robert John and Mildred (Graham) S.; m. Nancy Elizabeth Harknett, May 3, 1975; children: Adam, Benjamin. BA, U. N.C., 1972; MS, U. Mich., 1973, 75, PhD, 1976. Physicist Exxon Rsch. and Engring., Linden, N.J., 1977-78, Hughes Rsch. Labs., Malibu, Calif., 1975-85; prof. U. Mich., Ann Arbor, 1985—; scientist Inst. Gerontology Sch. Medicine, U. Mich., Ann Arbor, 1986—; topical editor Jour. Optical Soc., Washington, 1986-92. Contbr. articles to profl. jours. Fellow Optical Soc. Am., Am. Phys. Soc.; mem. IEEE (sr.). Achievements include first phase conjugate laser, first high resolution nonlinear laser spectroscopy of semiconductor heterostructures; demonstration of collision induced resonances in atoms; demonstration of low noise (below the standard quantum limit) room temperature semiconductor lasers; demonstration of in vitro trystophan phosphorescence for studies of protein structure in solution; discovery of structural annealing in proteins during protein folding. Office: U Mich Physics Dept 500 E University Ave Ann Arbor MI 48109-1120

STEEL, GORDON, electronics executive; b. 1944. BA, Pomona Coll., 1967; MBA, Stanford U., 1971. Divsn. mgr. Quantor, 1973-77; treas. Impell Corp., 1977-80; CFO Evotek, 1980-84, Pyramid Technology, 1984-87; with Xilinx Inc., San Jose, Calif., 1987—, v.p., CFO, sr. v.p. fin. Address: Xilinx Inc 2100 Logic Dr San Jose CA 95124*

STEEL, HOWARD HALDEMAN, pediatric orthopedic surgeon; b. Phila., Apr. 17, 1921; s. Howard Hinchman and Elizabeth (Haldeman) S.; m. Joan Elizabeth Clack, Aug. 16, 1964; children—Michael, Celia, Turner, Kathleen, Patrick, Townsend, Anna, Howard H. III. A.B., Colgate U., 1942; M.D., Temple U., 1945, M.S., 1951; Ph.D. in Anatomy, U. Wash., 1966. Enlisted U.S. Navy, 1941, advanced through grades to lt. comdr. M.C., 1955; ret., 1956; intern Temple U. Med. Center, Phila., 1945-46; resident in orthopaedic surgery Temple U. Med. Center, 1948-51; prof. orthopaedic surgery U. Wash., Seattle, 1965-66, Temple U., 1966—; endowed chair, prof. pediatric orthopaedics Temple U. Hosp., 1989—; clin. prof. orthopaedic surgery Med. Coll. Pa., 1985—; chief surgeon Shriners Hosp. for Crippled Children, Phila., 1966-86, emeritus chief of staff, 1986—; pres. Steel Fudge Shops, Inc., Atlantic City, 1958—; chmn. bd. Steels Fudge, Inc.; Hunterian lectr., London, 1958; med. cons. U.S. Army Med. Corps, USN, 1965-85; clin. prof. emeritus U. Pa., 1985—; prof. emeritus orthopaedic surgery Temple U., 1985—. Contbr. articles to profl. jours. Mem. Pine Barrens Conservation com. N.J. Legislature, Trenton, 1973-75; v.p. Colgate U. Alumni Corp., 1965-78; trustee Colgate U., 1972-78; hon. mem. Nat. Treasure of Japan, 1992. Recipient Apple Tchg. awards Sr. Class U. Wash., 1966, Temple U. Med. Sch., 1976, Disting. Alumnus award Colgate U., 1975, Humanitarian award City of Phila., 1978, Presdl. citation for rsch. in Berrylium, 1942, Humanitarian award Chapel of Four Chaplains, 1981. Fellow A.C.S.; mem. AMA (Billings Gold medal), Am. Orthopaedic Assn., Phila. Orthopaedic Soc. (pres. 1970), Am. Acad. Orthopaedic Surgeons, Pediatric Orthopaedic Soc., Orthopaedic Research Soc., Scoliosis Research Soc., Phila. Acad. Surgeons, Phila. Coll. Medicine, Eastern Orthopaedic Assn. (founder, 1st pres., Disting. Service award 1978), Jefferson Orthopaedic Soc., Phila. Roentgen Ray Soc., Am. Spinal Injury Assn., Hon. Nat. Treasure Japan, Phi Beta Kappa, Alpha Omega Alpha. Clubs: Phila. Country, Phila. Skating & Humane Soc., Merion Cricket, Merion Golf, The Courts Gladwyne, Wissahickon Skating, Wissahickon Ski, Confrerie des Chevalier du Tastevin, Union League Phila., Orpheus Club Phila., Ocean City Yacht, Corinthian Yacht, Masons (columbia 91 award 1981), Shriners. Researcher, developer orthopaedic procedures. Office: Shriners Hosp for Crippled Children 8400 Roosevelt Blvd Philadelphia PA 19152-1212

STEEL, JOHN M., electronics executive; b. 1944. Gen. mgr. OEM spares and tech. devices Control Data Corp., Mpls., 1968-83; with Zytec Corp., Eden Prairie, Minn., 1983—, v.p. sales & mktg. Office: Zytec Corp 7575 Market Place Dr Eden Prairie MN 55344-3637*

STEEL, KUNIKO JUNE, artist; b. San Francisco, June 3, 1929; d. Jirohei and Moriyo (Shiraishi) Nakamura; m. John Schulein-Steel, Jan. 26, 1963 (dec. May 1978). Student, U. Calif., 1948-49; diploma, Am. Acad. Art, Chgo., 1951; student, Academic Julian, Paris, 1952-53, Art Inst. Chgo., 1954-55, Art Students League, N.Y.C., 1959-62, 79-85. Exhibited in group shows at Rafilson Gallery, Chgo., 1954, Arts of N.E., Silvermine, Conn., 1966, 79, 90, 92, Modern Maturity Traveling Exhibit, 1990-92, Schoharie Exhibit, Cobleskill, N.Y., 1993-94, Mus. of Modern Art, Miami, Coral Gables, Fla., 1993, 37th Chautauqua Nat. Exhibit of Am. Art, 1994, Montclair State U., 1994, 95. Vol., crafts tchr. Hosp. for Spl. Surgery, N.Y.C., 1967-84; vol. Japanese Gallery Met. Mus., 1994; past vol. costume conservation Met. Mus., N.Y.C., 1979-94. Recipient scholarship Palo Alto Quota Club, 1948, Art Students League, 1960. Mem. N.Y. Artists Equity. Avocations: designing arts and crafts, painting.

STEEL, RONALD LEWIS, author, historian, educator; b. Morris, Ill., Mar. 25, 1931. BA magna cum laude, Northwestern U., 1953; MA, Harvard U., 1955. Vice consul U.S. Fgn. Service, 1957-58; editor Scholastic mag., N.Y.C., 1959-62; sr. assoc. Carnegie Endowment for Internat. Peace, 1982-83; fellow Woodrow Wilson Internat. Ctr. Scholars, 1984-85; prof. internat. relations U. So. Calif., Los Angeles, 1986—; fellow Wissenschaftskolleg zu Berlin, Federal Republic of Germany, 1988; vis. fellow Yale U., 1971-73; vis. prof. U. Tex., 1977, 79, 80, 85, Wellesley Coll., 1978, Rutgers U., 1980, UCLA, 1981, Dartmouth Coll., 1983, Princeton U., 1984; Shapiro prof. internat. rels. George Washington U., 1995-96. Author books including: The End of Alliance: America and the Future of Europe, 1964, (with G. Kimble) Tropical Africa Today, 1966, Pax Americana, 1967, Imperialists and Other Heroes, 1971, Walter Lippmann and the American Century, 1980, Temptations of a Superpower, 1995; editor various publs. for H.W. Wilson Co., 1961-67; contbr. to N.Y. Rev. Books; contbg. editor New Republic. Served with U.S. Army, 1954-56. Recipient Sidney Hillman award, 1968, Washington Monthly book award, 1980, Los Angeles Tims book award for nonfiction, 1980, Nat. Book Critics Circle award, 1981, Bancroft prize Columbia U., 1981, Am. History Bancroft prize, 1980, Am. Book award for biography, 1982; Guggenheim fellow, 1973-74. Mem. Council on Fgn. Relations. Office: U So Calif Sch Internat Rels Los Angeles CA 90089-0043

STEELE, ANA MERCEDES, government official; b. Niagara Falls, N.Y., Jan. 18, 1939; d. Sydney and Mercedes (Hernandez) S.; m. John Hunter Clark, June 2, 1979. AB magna cum laude, Marywood Coll., 1958. Actress, 1959-64; sec. Nat. Endowment for Arts, Washington, 1965-67, dir. budget and research, 1968-75, dir. planning, 1976-78, dir. program coordination, sr. exec. service, 1979-81, assoc. dep. chmn. for programs, dir. program coordination, sr. exec. service, 1982-93, acting chmn., acting sr. dep. chmn., 1993, sr. dep. chmn., sr. exec. svc., 1993-96; dep. chmn. for mgmt. and budget, sr. exec. svc., 1996—; guest lectr. George Washington U., 1987; trustee Marywood Coll., 1989—. Author, editor report: History of the National Council on the Arts and National Endowment for the Arts During the Johnson Administration, 1968; editor: Museums USA (Fed. Design Council award of Excellence 1975), 1974; National Endowment Arts 1965-1985; A Brief Chronology of Federal Involvement in the Arts, 1985. Former reader Rec. for the Blind, N.Y.C.; former tutor Future for Jimmy, Washington. Named Disting. Grad. in Field of Arts, Marywood Coll., 1976; recipient Sustained Superior Performance award Nat. Endowment for Arts, Washington, 1980, Disting. Service award, 1983, 84, 85, 89, 92. Mem. Actors' Equity Assn., Screen Actors Guild, Delta Epsilon Sigma, Kappa Gamma Pi. Office: Nat Endowment for Arts Nancy Hanks Ctr 1100 Pennsylvania Ave NW Washington DC 20004-2501

STEELE, ANITA MARTIN (MARGARET ANNE MARTIN), law librarian, legal educator; b. Haines City, Fla., Dec. 30, 1927; d. Emmett Edward and Esther Majulia (Phifer) Martin; m. Thomas Dinsmore Steele, June 10, 1947 (div. 1969); children: Linda Frances, Roger Dinsmore, Thomas Garrick, Carolyn Ann; m. James E. Beaver, Mar. 1980. BA, Radcliffe Coll., 1948; J.D., U. Va., 1971; M.Law Librarianship, U. Wash., 1972. Asst. prof. law U. Puget Sound, Tacoma, 1972-74, assoc. prof. law, 1974-79, prof. law, 1979—, dir. law library, 1972-94; prof. law, dir. law libr. Seattle U., Tacoma, 1994—. Author: (book) Martin and Carmichael Descendants in Georgia, 1811-1994, 1994; contbr. articles to profl. jours.; mem. editorial adv. bds. various law book pubs., 1980—. Treas., Congl. Campaign Orgn., Tacoma, 1978, 80; mem. adv. bd. Clover Park Vocat.-Tech. Sch., Tacoma, 1980-82. Mem. Am. Assn. Law Libraries, Internat. Assn. Law Libraries, Am. Soc. Internat. Law. Republican. Home: 1502 S Fernside Dr Tacoma WA 98465-1305 Office: Seattle U Sch Law 950 Broadway Tacoma WA 98402-4405

STEELE, ANTONIO L., principal, educator; b. Charlotte Amalie, St. Thomas, V.I., Oct. 4, 1947; s. Oliver O. and Viola A. (Smith) Steele; m. Floria R.; children: Monifa N., Renael E., Renan O., Rissah M. BA, Coll of V.I., 1970; MA, NYU, Washington Sq., 1977; postgrad., U. Ill., Taff Inst. Elem. tchr. George Washington Sch., St. Thomas, 1970; tchr. Eulalie Rivera Sch., St. Croix, V.I., 1971-73; tchr. Alfredo Andrews Sch., St. Croix, 1973, tchr. environ. edn., 1974, asst. prin., 1975-80; asst. prin. Juanita Gardina Elem. Sch., St. Croix, 1980; asst. prin. Evelyn M. Williams Elem. Sch., St. Croix, 1981, prin., 1982—; leader and presenter workshops, task force leader. Active ch. and community roles. Mem. LEAD (adv. bd.), Am. Fedn. Sch. Adminstrs., St. Croix Edn. Adminstrn. Assn. (pres. 1987—, adminstr. adult basic edn. 1989—).

STEELE, BETTY LOUISE, retired banker; b. Sigourney, Iowa, Nov. 20, 1920; d. Otto Orville and Freda Marie Christina (Strohman) Utterback; m. David L. Steele, Jan. 17, 1942; 1 child, David Leroy. Student pub. schs., Iowa. With N.W. Des Moines Nat. Bank, 1959-68, v.p., 1966-68; v.p., sec. Brenton Banks, Inc., Des Moines, 1968-86; mem. pension com. Brenton Banks, Inc., 1980-86, vice chmn. investment com., 1983-86, dir., 1976-83; sec. Brenton Found., 1970-83; mem. State Banking Bd., 1977-81. Author articles. Bd. dirs. Ctrl. Iowa chpt. ARC, 1984-90, mem. exec. com., asst. treas., 1984-90, mem. fin. audit com., 1985-93; mem. dean's com. Iowa State U. Coll. Home Econs., 1982-84; mem. Iowa Pub./Pvt. Sector Task Force, Gov.'s Com. for Volunteerism, 1984. Mem. Des Moines C. of C. (Nat. Leadership award 1976), Fin. Women Internat. (nat. pres. 1976-77, bd. dirs. 1970-78, trustee ednl. found. 1974-76, (Betty L. Steele award given in her honor Iowa chpt.), Am. Bankers Assn. (govt. relations council 1977-79), Iowa Bankers Assn. (legis. com. 1975-76). Republican. Mem. Ch. of Christ. Home: 6022 Terrace Dr Johnston IA 50131-1591

STEELE, CARL LAVERN, academic administrator; b. Patoka, Ill., Aug. 22, 1934; s. Boyd Alfa and Effie Jane (Corson) S.; m. Lula Irene Saliba, June 11, 1961; children: Jeffrey Van, Gregory Michael, Douglas Alan. BEd, So. Ill. U., 1956, MEd, 1960; MLS, No. Ill. U., 1971. Tchr. Shawneetown (Ill.) Community High. Sch., 1956-57; GED instr. U.S. Army, Ft. Hood, Tex. and Ulm, Fed. Republic of Germany, 1957-59; tchr. Forrest-Strawn-Wing Unit Dist., Forrest, Ill., 1959-61, Richwoods Community High Sch., Peoria, Ill., 1961-66; asst. dir. instructional materials Sauk Valley Coll., Dixon, Ill., 1966-68; dir. Ednl. Resources Ctr., Rock Valley Coll., Rockford, Ill., 1968-93; ret., 1993; part-time traffic safety instr. Rock Valley Coll., 1992—. Asst. World Record sec. Nat. Fresh Water Fishing Hall of Fame, Hayward, Wisc., 1977-79. Served with U.S. Army, 1957-59. Mem. ALA, Assn. Ednl. Communications and Technology, Ill. Assn. Ednl. Communications and Technology (conv. chmn. 1976), No. Ill. Media Assn. (conv. chmn.), Learning Resource Commn. ICCCA (chmn. 1981). Democrat. Presbyterian. Avocations: fishing, travel, reading, woodworking, gardening. Home: 5758 Weymouth Dr Rockford IL 61114-5569

STEELE, CHARLES GLEN, retired accountant; b. Faulkton, S.D., July 24, 1925; s. Clifford D. and Emily O. (Hanson) S.; m. Shirley June Ferguson, Nov. 9, 1947; children: Richard Alan (dec.), Deborah Ann Steele Most. B.B.A., Golden Gate U., San Francisco, 1951, M.B.A., 1962. With Deloitte Haskins & Sells, 1951-86, partner, 1963-86, partner charge Chgo. office, 1973-76; partner charge personnel and adminstrn. Deloitte Haskins & Sells, N.Y.C., 1976-78; chmn., chief exec. officer Deloitte Haskins & Sells, 1978-86; instr. evening program Golden Gate U., 1952-58. Served with USNR, 1943-48. Recipient Elijah Watts Sells Gold medal for highest grade in U.S. for C.P.A. exam., 1951. Mem. Am. Inst. C.P.A.s. Home and Office: 26349 Rio Ave Carmel CA 93923-9101

STEELE, CHARLES RICHARD, biomedical and mechanical engineering educator; b. Royal, Iowa, Aug. 15, 1933; married, 1969; 4 children. BS, Tex. A&M U., 1956; PhD in Applied Mechanics, Stanford U., 1960. Engring. specialist aircraft structure Chance-Vought Aircraft, Dallas, 1959-60; rsch. scientist shell theory Lockheed Rsch. Lab., Palo Alto, 1960-66; assoc. prof. Stanford (Calif.) U., 1966-71, prof. applied mechanics, 1971—; lectr. U. Calif., Berkeley, 1964-65; vis. prof. Swiss Fed. Inst. Technology, Zurich, 1971-72, U. Luleå, Sweden, 1982, Chung Kung U., Taiwan, 1985; tech. dir. Shelltech Assoc. Editor-in-chief: Internat. Jour. Solids Structures, 1985—. Fellow ASME (chmn. exec. com. applied mechanics divsn. 1983-84), Am. Acad. Mechanics (pres. 1989-90); mem. AIAA, NAE, Acoustical Soc. Am. Achievements include research in asymptotic analysis in mechanics; thin shell theory; mechanics of the inner ear; noninvasive determination of bone stiffness. Office: Stanford University Dept Applied Mechanics & Engin Stanford CA 94305

STEELE, DIANA ALEXANDER, lawyer; b. Phila., Oct. 3, 1946; d. Joseph Middleton and Martha Cynthia (Pound) S.; m. Eric John Heyer, June 8, 1980. BA, Wellesley Coll., 1968; JD, NYU, 1971, LLM in Taxation, 1982. Staff atty. Appeals Bur. Legal Aid Soc., N.Y.C., 1971-74, sr. supervising atty., 1974-78; staff counsel ACLU, N.Y.C., 1978-81; assoc. Reid & Priest, N.Y.C., 1982-86, ptnr., 1986—. Office: Reid & Priest 40 W 57th St New York NY 10019-4001

STEELE, EARL LARSEN, electrical engineering educator; b. Denver, Sept. 24, 1923; s. Earl Harold and Jennie (Larsen) S.; m. Martha C. Hennessey, June 27, 1953; children: Karl Thomas, Earl Robert, Karen Lynn, Kevin Douglas, Lisa Louise, Colleen Carol. B.S. with honors, U. Utah, 1945; Ph.D., Cornell U., 1952. Research physicist Gen. Electric Co., 1952-56; chief device devel. Motorola, Inc., 1956-58; mgr. devel. lab. Hughes Aircraft Co., 1958-64; research scientist N.Am. Rockwell Corp., 1964-69; prof. elec. engring. U. Ky., Lexington, 1969-90, prof. emeritus, 1991—; chmn. dept. U. Ky., 1971-80, 1988-89; Affiliate prof. Ariz. State U., 1956-58, U. Calif.-Irvine, 1966-69; adviser So. Calif. Coll., Costa Mesa, 1963-64; charter mem. Orange County Academic Decathlon (Calif.); bd. dirs. Southeastern Center for Elec. Engring. Edn., 1975—, treas., 1980-81, v.p., 1981-82, resident dir., 1981-82, 89-90, pres., 1982-83, mem. coun. of pres.', 1983—. Author: Optical Lasers in Electronics; contbr. articles to profl. jours. Fellow IEEE; mem. Am. Soc. Engring. Edn. (U. Ky. Coll. Engring. rep. to ASEE, 1988-90), Am. Phys. Soc., Internat. Soc. Hybrid Microelectronics, Sigma Xi, Tau Beta Pi, Eta Kappa Nu (dir. 1974-76, v.p. 1983-84, pres. 1984-85). Mem. LDS Ch. Home: 313 Blueberry Ln Lexington KY 40503-2004

STEELE, ELIZABETH MEYER, lawyer; b. San Mateo, Calif., Jan. 12, 1952; d. Bailey Robert and Kathryn Steele (Horrigan) Meyer; m. Gene Dee Fowler, Aug. 9, 1975 (div. Apr. 1985); 1 child, Steele Sternberg. BA, Kirkland Coll., 1974; JD, U. N.Mex., 1977. Counsel U.S. Dept. Energy, Los Alamos, N.Mex., 1977-78; law clk. to judge Howard C. Bratton U.S. Dist. Ct., Albuquerque, 1978-80; assoc. Davis, Graham & Stubbs, Denver, 1980-84, ptnr., 1985-87; v.p., gen. counsel Jones Intercable, Inc., Englewood, Colo., 1987—. Office: Jones Intercable Inc 9697 E Mineral Ave Englewood CO 80112-3408

STEELE, ERNEST CLYDE, retired insurance company executive; b. Corbin, Ky., May 11, 1925; s. J. Fred and Leona (McFarland) S.; m. Cora Jones, June 17, 1944 (dec. Nov. 1988); children: Gerald R., David. P.; m. Helen LeCoultre, July 7, 1990. BS with honors, U. Ky., 1948, MS, 1950. Asst. actuary Peninsular Life Ins. Co., Jacksonville, Fla., 1950-54; actuary Pioneer Life & Casualty Co., Gadsden, Ala., 1955; v.p., actuary Guaranty Savs. Life Ins. Co., Montgomery, Ala., 1956-57; exec. v.p., actuary Am. Investment Life Ins. Co., Nashville, 1958-59; pres., actuary Appalachian Nat. Life Ins. Co., Knoxville, Tenn., 1959-67; sr. v.p., chief investment officer, ops. analyst Coastal States Life Ins. Co., Atlanta, 1968-71; exec. v.p., dir. Coastal States Life Ins. Co., 1971-74, pres., dir., 1974-79; pres., dir. Occidental Life Ins. Co. of N.C., 1979-85, chmn., 1986-88; pres., dir. Peninsular Life Ins. Co., 1981-83, chmn., 1986-88; exec. v.p. investments MCM Corp., 1985-88; past pres. Ga. Assn. Life Inst. Cos., 1976-77. Mem. devel. coun. U. Ky. Served to 2d lt. U.S. Army, 1943-45. Fellow Life Mgmt. Inst.; mem. Life Office Mgmt. Assn. (past chmn. bd.), Am. Council Life Ins. (past dir.), U. Ky. Alumni Assn. (past bd. dirs.), Am. Acad. Actuaries, Pi Mu Epsilon. Republican. Baptist. Home: 103 Newell Village Dr Seymour TN 37865-5931 *My success in life is measured by the success of those with whom I have been associated.*

STEELE, GLENN DANIEL, JR., surgical oncologist; b. Balt., June 23, 1944; m. Diana; 1 child, Joshua; m. Lisa; children: Kirsten, Lara. AB magna cum laude, Harvard Coll., 1966; MD, NYU, 1970; PhD, Lund U., Sweden, 1975. Intern, then resident Med. Ctr. U. Colo., Denver, 1970-76; fellow NIH in immunology Univ. Lund, Sweden, 1973-75; asst. surgeon Sidney Farber Cancer Inst., Boston, 1976-78; clin. assoc. surgical oncology Sidney Farber Cancer Inst., 1978-79; jr. assoc. in surgery Peter Bent Brigham Hosp., Boston, 1976-82; instr. surgery Med. Sch. Harvard, Boston, 1976-78; asst. prof. surgery Med. Sch. Harvard Coll., 1978-81; asst. physician surgical oncology Sidney Farber Cancer Inst., 1979-82; assoc. prof. surgery Med. Sch. Harvard Coll., 1981-84; surgeon Brigham & Women's Hosp., 1982-84; assoc. physician surgical oncology Dana-Farber Cancer Inst., 1982-84, physician surg. oncology, 1984-95; chmn. dept. surgery, deaconess Harvard Surg. Svc. New England Deaconess Hosp., Boston, 1985-95; William V. McDermott prof. surgery Med. Sch. Harvard Coll., 1985-95; prof. Univ. Chgo.; dean biological scis. divsn. Pritzker Sch. Medicine, v.p. medical affairs; cons. surgeon Boston Hosp. for Women, 1977-80. assoc. editor Jour. of Clin. Oncology, 1986—, Jour. of Hepatobiliary-Pancreatic Surgery, 1993—; mem. editorial bd. Annals of Surgery, Annals of Surg. Oncology, British Jour. of Surgery, Surgery, Surgical Oncology; contbr. numerous articles to profl. jours. Recipient NIH fellow 1973-75, Am. Cancer Soc. fellow 1972-73, 76-79, various other rsch. grants. Fellow Am. Coll. Surgeons (chmn. patient care and rsch. com. commn. on cancer 1989-91, mem. bd. govs. 1991—, chmn. commn. on cancer 1991-93, exec. com. 1993—0); mem. Am. Assn. Immunologists, Am. Bd. Surgery (dir. 1993—), Ill. Surgical Soc., Am. Bd. Med. Specialists, Am. Soc. Clin. Oncology, Am. Surg. Assn., Assn. Program Dirs. in Surgery, Assn. for Surgical Edn., Internat. Fedn. Surg. Colls., Internat. Surg. Group, New England Cancer Soc., and numerous other mems. Office: Univ Chicago MC 1000 5841 S Maryland Ave MC1000 Chicago IL 60637-1470

STEELE, HILDA BERNEICE HODGSON, farm manager, retired home economics supervisor; b. Wilmington, Ohio, Mar. 24, 1911; d. George Sanders and Mary Jane (Rolston) Hodgson; m. John C. Steele, Aug. 10, 1963 (dec. Jan. 1973). BS, Wilmington Coll., 1935; MA, Ohio State U., 1941; postgrad., Ohio U., 1954, Miami U., Oxford, Ohio, 1959. Cert. elem. and high sch. gen. tchr. and vocat. supr., Ohio. Part-time tchr. Wilmington Pub. Schs., Midland Elem. Sch., 1931-32; tchr. Brookville (Ohio) Pub. Schs., 1932-37, Dayton (Ohio) Pub. Schs., Lincoln Jr. High Sch., 1937-40; tchr. practical arts, coord. home econs. Dayton Pub. Schs., 1940-45, supr. home econs., 1945-81; mgr. Steele's Farm, Xenia, Ohio, 1972—; mem. home econs. adv. com. Cen. State U., Wilburforce, Ohio, 1941-92, Miami Valley Hosp. Nursing Sch., Dayton, 1951-63; mem. adv. bd. Dayton Sch. Practical Nursing, 1951-92. Mem. adv. com. Montgomery County ARC, Dayton, 1940-80; mem. town and country career com. Miami Valley Br. YMCA, Dayton, 1948-59; mem. Ohio Electrification Com., Dayton, 1964-66; mem. corp. com. United Way, Dayton, 1970-96; bd. dirs. Ohio Future Homemakers of Am.-Home Econs. Related Occupations, Columbus, 1979-81; chmn. home econs. adv. com. Ohio Vets. Children Home, 1987-95. Recipient Outstanding Contbns. award Girls Scouts U.S., 1987, Appreciation award Dayton Practical Nursing Program, 1989; named Ohio Vocat. Educator of the Yr., 1981. Mem. NEA, Ohio Edn. Assn., Am. Home Econs. Assn. (Appreciation award 1990), Am. Vocat. Assn., Ohio Home Econs. Assn. (various coms., Friend of Family award 1994), Ohio Vocat. Assn. (life), Ohio Dist. C Home Econs. Assn., Ohio Ret. Tchrs. Assn. (life), Montgomery County Ret. Tchrs. Assn., Dayton Pub. Schs. Adminstrv. Assn., Met. Home Econs. Assn. (pres. 1949-50, 60-61), Greene County Landmark Assn., Electric Womens Roundtable Assn. (Dayton-Cin. chpt. 1951-72, mem.-at-large 1972—), U.S. C. of C., Phi Upsilon Omicron (hon.), Ea. Star, Zonta (pres. Dayton chpt. 1950-52). Mem. Ch. of Christ. Avocations: gardening, sewing, helping others. Home: 1443 State Route 380 Xenia OH 45385-9789

STEELE, JAMES HARLAN, former public health veterinarian, educator; b. Chgo., Apr. 3, 1913; s. James Hahn and Lydia (Nordquist) S.; m. Aina Oberg, 1941 (dec. 1969); children: James Harlan, David, Michael; m. Maria-Brigitte Meyer, 1969. DVM, Mich. State Coll., 1941; MPH, Harvard U., 1942. With Ohio Dept. Health, 1942-43; with USPHS, 1943-71; advancing through grades to asst. surgeon gen. for vet. affairs and chief vet. officer; chief vet. pub. health activities Communicable Disease Center, Atlanta, 1947-71; prof. environ. health U. Tex. Sch. Pub. Health, Houston, 1971-83, prof. emeritus, 1983—; cons. WHO, 1950—, Pan-Am. Health Orgn., 1945—, FAO, UN, 1960, German Health Svc., 1986-93; vis. prof. Tex. A&M U., 1976—, all univ. prof., 1981-82; trustee Nat. Found. Infectious Diseases. Author: Bovine Tuberculosis Control in Man and Animals, 1969, rev. (with Charles Thoen), 1995; editor-in-chief Zoonoses Handbooks, 1979-84, cons. editor, 1994; contbr. articles to profl. jours. and sects. to books on food hygiene and irradiation. Recipient Mich. State U. Alumni award, 1958, USPHS Order of Merit, 1963, Karl F. Meyer Gold Head Cane award, 1966, Disting. Svc. award USPHS, 1971, Mich. State U. Coll. Vet. Medicine award, 1972, hon. mem. Epidemic Intelligence Svc., 1975, Centennial award U. Pa., 1984, Am. Vet. Med. Assn. Internat. Vet. award, 1984, Pub. Svc. award, 1993; James H. Steele Vet. Pub. Health award World Vet. Epidemiology Soc., 1975, Disting. Svc. award Am. Vet. History Soc., 1995. Fellow Am. Pub. Health Assn. (emeritus, 1984; Bronfman award 1971, Centennial award 1972), Am. Coll. Epidemiology (founding fellow); mem. Conf. Pub. Health Vets. (founder), Am. Soc. Tropical Medicine (emeritus), Am. Coll. Vet. Preventive Medicine (founder, hon. diploma 1983, Pres.'s award 1994), Nat. Acad. Health Practitioners, World Vet. Epidemiology Soc. (founder, pres. 1971), Am. Vet. Epidemiology Soc. (pres. 1966-88), World Vet. Assn. (hon.), Philippines Vet. Med. Assn. (hon.), Peru Vet. Med. Assn. (hon.), Hellenic Vet. Soc. (Athens Greece, hon. diploma, 1977), U.S. Animal Health Assn. (life), U.S.-Mex. Pub. Health Assn. (hon., life), Mil. Surgeons Assn. (hon. life), Infectious Disease Soc. Am. (emeritus), Internat. Epidemiology Soc. (emeritus), XXI World Vet. Congress (Moscow, hon. diploma 1979), German Health Svc. (hon. diploma, 1988, Order of Merit 1993), Harvard U. Alumni Assn., Mich. State U. Alumni Assn., Alpha Psi. Episcopalian. Home: 10722 Riverview Way Houston TX 77042-1391 Office: School of Public Hlth University of Texas Houston TX 77225 *I have believed firmly throughout my career that I should share my knowledge and expertise with my fellow man, be he American or citizen of the world. Those of us who are more fortunate to be endowed with intellectual advantages have an even greater responsibility to share.*

STEELE, JOHN HYSLOP, marine scientist, oceanographic institute administrator; b. Edinburgh, U.K., Nov. 15, 1926; s. Adam and Annie H.; m. Margaret Evelyn Travis, Mar. 2, 1956; 1 son, Hugh. B.Sc., Univ. Coll., London U., 1946, D.Sc., 1964. Marine scientist Marine Lab., Aberdeen, Scotland, 1951-66; sr. prin. sci. officer Marine Lab., 1966-73, dep. dir., 1973-77; dir. Woods Hole Oceanographic Instn., Mass., 1977-89, pres., 1986-91; mem. NAS/NRC Ocean Sci. Bd., 1978-88, chmn., 1986-88; mem. rsch. and exploration com. Nat. Geog. Soc.; mem. Arctic Rsch. Commn., 1988-92; trustee U. Corp. Atmospheric Rsch., 1987-91, Bermuda Biol. Sta., R.W. Johnson Found.; del. Internat. Coun. Exploration Sea; bd. dirs. Exxon Corp.; hon. prof. U. Aberdeen. Author: The Structure of Marine Ecosystems, 1974; Contbr. articles to profl. jours. Served with Brit. Royal Air Force, 1947-49. Recipient Alexander Agassiz medal Nat. Acad. Sci., 1973. Fellow Royal Soc. London, AAAS, Royal Soc. Edinburgh, Am. Acad. Arts and Scis. Home: PO Box 25 Woods Hole MA 02543-0025 Office: Woods Hole Oceanographic Inst Woods Hole MA 02543

STEELE, JOHN LAWRENCE, journalist; b. Chgo., June 9, 1917; s. Leo M. and Helen (Schuhmann) S.; m. Louise V. Stein, June 27, 1940; children: Deborah, John Lawrence, Scott. Grad., Lake Forest Acad., 1935; A.B., Dartmouth Coll., 1939; Nieman fellow, Harvard U., 1951-52. With Chgo. City News Bur., 1939; staff Chgo. bur. U.P.I., 1939-41; bur. legislative corr. U.P., Washington, 1941-42, 45-53; legis. polit. corr. Time mag., 1953-55; White House corr., 1955-58; chief Washington bur.; Time-Life News Svc., 1958-69; sr. corr. Time-Life News Service, 1969-79; v.p. Time Inc., Washington, 1979-82, cons., 1982-84, pub. policy cons., 1985—. Collaborator: (with A.H. Vandenberg, Jr. and Joe A. Morris) The Private Papers of Senator Vandenberg, 1952; contbr. articles to mags. and jours., chpts. to books. Mem. Dartmouth Coll. Alumni Coun., 1971-74; mem. Native Am. Vis. Com., 1973-78, chmn., 1975-78; bd. dirs. Mag. Pubs. Assn., 1979-81; participant TV news interview programs NBC, CBS, BBC, 1950-79. Recipient The Dartmouth Alumni award for disting. svc. in journalism and pub. affairs. Mem. Burning Tree Club, Met. Club, Sigma Delta Chi (Hall of Fame 1979). Home and Office: 3100 Newark St NW Washington DC 20008-3343

STEELE, KAREN DORN, journalist; b. Portland, Oreg., Oct. 27, 1943; d. Ronald Gottche and Margaret Elizabeth (Cates) Moxness; m. Charles Stuart Dorn, Oct. 30, 1965 (div. Oct. 1982); children: Trilby Constance Elizabeth Dorn, Blythe Estella Dorn; m. Richard Donald Steele, July 4, 1983. BA, Stanford U., 1965; MA, U. Calif., Berkeley, 1967. Prodr. Sta. KSPS-TV, Spokane, Wash., 1970-72, dir. news and pub. affairs, 1972-82; reporter Spokesman-Rev., Spokane, 1982-87, environ./spl. projects reporter, 1987—. Contbr. articles to sci. publs. (Olive Br. award NYU Ctr. War, Peace & The Media 1989). Bd. dirs. Women Helping Women, Spokane, 1994; trustee St. George's Sch., Spokane, 1988-92. Mid-career fellow Stanford Knight Fellowship Program, 1986-87, Arms Control fellow Ctr. for Internat. Security and Arms Control, Stanford U., 1986-87; Japan Travel grantee Japan Press Found., Tokyo, 1987, rsch. grantee John D. and Catherine T. MacArthur Found., 1992; recipient Gerald Loeb award Anderson Sch. Mgmt. UCLA, 1995, George Polk award L.I. U., 1995, William Stokes award U. Mo., 1988; inductee State Hall of Journalistic Achievement, Wash. State U., Pullman, 1995. Unitarian. Avocations: literature, poetry, cooking, hiking, travel. Office: Spokesman-Rev PO Box 2160 W 999 Riverside Ave Spokane WA 99201

STEELE, KAREN KIARSIS, state legislator; b. Haverhill, Mass., Sept. 26, 1942; d. Victor and Barbara (McFee) Kiarsis; m. Edward E. Steele, Apr. 16, 1966; children: Shawn Robert, Gretchen Garvey. BA, U. Vt., 1964. Tchr. Waterbury Sch. System, 1964-65, Burlington (Vt.) Sch. System, 1965-67; legislator State of Vt., Montpelier, 1982—. Trustee Cen. Vt. Hosp., Berlin. Mem. Am. Legis. Exch. Coun. (nat. chmn. healthcare task force). Republican. Avocations: golf, swimming, reading, skiing. Home: RR 2 Box 796 Waterbury VT 05676-9713 Office: State House Montpelier VT 05602

STEELE, KATHLEEN FRANCES, federal official; b. Kansas City, Mo., Oct. 28, 1960; m. Steve Danner, Jan. 18, 1996. Admissions counselor N.E. Mo. State U., Kirksville, 1980-83, assoc. dir. admissions, 1983-86, programming coord. dept. pub. svcs., 1986-87; Iowa, N.H. dir. Gephardt for Pres., St. Louis, 1987-88; mem. Mo. Ho. of Reps., Jefferson City, 1988-94; state dir. Clinton for Pres., 1991-92; regional dir. U.S. Dept. Health and Human Svcs., Kansas City, Mo., 1994—; chair Freshman Dem. Caucus, 1989, chair sci., tech. and critical issues com. Bd. dirs. Adair County chpt. ARC, 1987. Recipient Young Careerist award Kirksville Bus. and Profl. Women, 1988. Mem. Nat. Order Women Legislators, Women Legislators of Mo. (pres. 1989-92). Roman Catholic. Avocations: sports enthusiast, dancing, reading, politics. Home: 6 Nantucket Ct Smithville MO 64089-9605 Office: US Dept Health and Human Svcs 601 E 12th St Ste 210 Kansas City MO 64106-2808

STEELE, KENNETH FRANKLIN, JR., hydrology educator, resource center director; b. Statesville, N.C., Jan. 16, 1944; s. Kenneth Franklin and Ruth Virginia (Wilhelm) S.; m. Sheila Kay Stumpf, Sept. 3, 1966; children: Krista Robin, Celisa Anne. BS in Chemistry, U. N.C., 1966, PhD in Geology, 1971. Registered profl. genealogist, Ark., registered hydrogeologist. From instr. to assoc. prof. geology U. Ark., Fayetteville, 1970-83, prof., 1983—, dir. Ark. Water Resources Ctr., 1988—; cons. in field. Contbr. numerous articles to profl. jours., chpts. to books; editor: Animal Waste and the Land-Water Interface. Summer faculty fellow Oak Ridge Associated Univs., 1981, 83, 85. Mem. Assn. Ground-Water Scientists and Engrs., Geol. Soc. Am. (regional bd. dirs. 1980-82, 84-86), Am. Water Resources Assn. (bd. dirs. 1991-94), Ark. Ground Water Assn. (bd. dirs. 1988-90, 93—, v.p. 1991, pres. 1992), Nat. Assn. Water Inst. Dirs. (counselor 1990-93). Achievements include research on the importance of rainstorms on spring water chemistry, nitrate and pesticide contamination of ground water. Home: 1115 Valley View Dr Fayetteville AR 72701-1603 Office: U Ark Water Resources Ctr 113 Ozark Hall Fayetteville AR 72701

STEELE, KURT D., publishing company executive; b. 1945; married. BA, Colgate U., 1967; JD, Columbia U., 1971. Assoc. Brown & Wood, 1971-74; atty. McGraw & Hill Inc., N.Y.C., 1974-85, v.p., assoc. gen. counsel, 1981-86; sr. v.p., gen. counsel, sec. Standard & Poor's Corp., N.Y.C., 1986-90; v.p., gen. counsel Rand McNally & Co., Skokie, Ill., 1990—. Office: Rand McNally Inc 8255 Central Park Ave Skokie IL 60076-2908

STEELE, LENDELL EUGENE, research scientist; b. Kannapolis, N.C., May 5, 1928; s. Robert Lee and Ina (Chapman) S.; m. Rowena Miller, Jan. 29, 1949; children—Joyce Lee Steele McCartney, Carol Ann Steele, Pamela Jane Steele Nelson, Linda Kay Steele Miller. B.S. in Chemistry, George Washington U., 1950; M.A. in Econs, Am. U., 1959. Registered profl. engr., Calif. Chemist U.S. Geol. Survey, Washington, 1949, U.S. Dept. Agr. Research Center, Beltsville, Md., 1949-50; chemist U.S. Naval Research Lab., Washington, 1950-51, chemist-research physicist, 1953-58, mgr. sci. research, 1958-86; metall. engr. AEC, Germantown, Md., 1966; cons. U.S. Metal Properties Council, 1968-70, 75-85; pvt. practice tech. cons. Springfield, Va., 1986—; U.S. rep. to IAEA, Vienna, Austria, 1967-93. Author: Analysis of Reactor Vessel Radiation Effects Surveillance Programs, 1970, Neutron Irradiation Embrittlement of Reactor Pressure Vessel Steels, 1975; Editor, contbg. author: Structural Integrity of Lightwater Reactor Components, 1983, Status of U.S.A. Nuclear Reactor Pressure Vessel Surveillance, 1983, Radiation Embrittlement and Surveillance of Nuclear Reactor Pressure Vessels: An International Study, Vol. I, 1983, Vol. II, 1986, Vol. III, 1989, Vol. IV, 1993; Light Water Reactor Structural Integrity, Vol. I, 1984, Vol. II, 1988, Component Repair, Replacement and Failure Prevention in Light Water Reactors, 1986; contbr. articles to profl. jours. Served with USAF, 1951-53. Recipient Superior Civilian Service medal U.S. Navy, 1976. Fellow Am. Soc. Metals, D.C. Acad. Sci. (Engring. Sci. award 1966), ASTM (life, Dudley award and medal 1972, bd. dirs. 1980-82, vice chmn. bd. 1983-84, chmn. bd. 1985, award of merit 1979); mem. Rsch. Soc. Am. (Applied Sci. award 1962), Am. Nuclear Soc. (Spl. award and prize 1972), Fedn. Materials Socs. (pres. 1984), Sigma Xi. Home and Office: 7624 Highland St Springfield VA 22150-3931

STEELE, MARY LINDA, nurse educator; b. Kansas City, Mo., Oct. 12, 1946; d. Dean Jenkins and Mary Margaret (Lichtenauer) Cloud; m. William Carl Steele III, Sept. 9, 1967; children: Paul Alan, Eric Brendan, Joshua Jon. Diploma, St. Margaret Hosp. Sch. Nursing, Kansas City, Kans., 1967; BSN, U. Ctrl. Okla., 1982; MSN, Okla. U., 1987. RN. From staff nurse to head nurse ICU St. Margaret Hosp., 1967-72; from head nurse CCU to respiratory nurse coord. Bethany Med. Ctr., Kansas City, Kans., 1972-76; from staff nurse CCU to dir. nursing edn. and devel. Presbyn. Hosp., Oklahoma City, 1976-88; edn. coord. Oklahoma City Clinic, 1988-90; instr. U. Ctrl. Okla., Edmond, 1990—; adv. bd. Rose State Coll. Nursing, 1990-94. Nursing cons. Am. Lung Assn., 1980-87; bd. dirs. Am. Diabetes Assn., 1994-95. Mem. Okla. Nurses Assn. (del. state conv. 1985-94, del. ANA conv. 1988, 90, 92), Sigma Theta Tau, Sigma Phi Omega, Kappa Omicron Nu. Office: U Ctrl Okla 100 N University Dr Edmond OK 73034

STEELE, OLIVER, English educator; b. Birmingham, Ala., May 13, 1928; s. Oliver L. and Mary Lucile (Abernethy) S.; m. Joy Cogdell, Dec. 23, 1950; children—Christopher, Mark, Eleanor, Andrew, Paul. B.S. in English, Auburn U., 1949, M.S. in English, 1951; Ph.D., U. Va., 1965. Instr. English U. Va., Charlottesville, 1959-65, asst. prof. English, 1965-67; assoc. prof. English U. Iowa, Iowa City, 1967-74, prof. English, 1974-92, prof. emeritus English, 1992—; Editor: Ellen Glasgow: a Bibliography, 1964, The Faerie Queene: Book I & II, 1965. Served with U.S. Army, 1953-55; Germany. Mem. Renaissance Soc. Am., Bibliographical Soc. U. Va., Raven Soc. Democrat. Avocation: music. Home: 1120 E Court St Iowa City IA 52240-3232 Office: Univ Iowa Dept English Iowa City IA 52240

STEELE, REBECCA ELIZABETH, insurance company administrator; b. Richlands, Va., May 17, 1949; d. Charlie Shade and Helen Elizabeth (Witt) S. BBA, East Tenn. State U., 1971. Cert. profl. ins. woman Nat. Assn. Ins. Women Internat. Uderwriting trainee State Farm Ins. Co., Charlottesville, Va., 1973-75, underwriter, 1975-77, sr. underwriter, 1977-87, underwriting specialist, 1987-91, personal lines supr., 1991—. Vol. Am. Cancer Soc., Charlottesville and Fredericksburg, Va., 1992, 93, 94, 95, Winter Spl. Olympics, Charlottesville, 1994, Am. Heart Assn., Charlottesville and Fredericksburg, 1992-95; vol. Multiple Sclerosis skiathon Charlottesville, 1991, 92, 93, Ronald McDonald House, 1994. Mem. Nat. Assn. Ins. Women (chairperson state pub. rels. 1993-95), Ins. Women Charlottesville/Albemerle (pres. pub. rels. 1991-93, Ins. Woman of Yr. award 1993), Ins. Inst. Am., East Tenn. State U. Alumni Club, Va. 4-H All Stars, Toastburners Toastmasters Club (sgt. at arms 1990, Competent Toastmaster award 1994). Republican. Methodist. Avocation: snow skiing. Office: State Farm Ins Co 1500 State Farm Blvd Charlottesville VA 22909-0001

STEELE, RICHARD J., management consultant; b. Elkhart, Ind., Sept. 27, 1925; s. Cornelius H. and Harriett (Poel) S.; m. Martha J. Micko, July 8, 1950; children: Barbara, Cheryl, Patricia, Thomas, Richard Jr., Marjorie, Gregory, Susan, Kathleen. SB, MIT, 1946; MBA, Ind. U., 1949. Cert. mgmt. cons. V.p. Fry Cons.'s, Inc., Chgo., 1950-70; pres. Richard Steele and Ptnrs., Inc., N.Y.C., 1970-72, Richard Steele Cons.'s, Inc., Columbia, Md., 1978—; group v.p. Macro Systems, Inc., Silver Spring, Md., 1972-78; sr. v.p. Birch & Davis Assocs., Inc., Silver Spring, 1979-94; counselor Nat. Health Coun., N.Y.C., 1971-94. Author: (with others) Determinants of HMO Success, 1988. Trustee Village of Riverwoods, Ill., 1967. Lt. USNR, 1943-75, WWII, Korea. Recipient Award of Merit Am. Heart Assn., 1974. Mem. World Future Soc., Inst. Mgmt. Cons. Republican. Unitarian. Home and Office: 5122 Durham Rd E Columbia MD 21044-1423

STEELE, ROBERT B., director vocational education; b. Pineville, W.Va., May 11, 1948; s. Hatler B. Steele and Pauline (Syck) Price; m. Sarah Lindbeck, Dec. 25, 1994; children: Jennifer, John. Assoc. degree, Cuyahoga C.C., 1972; BA, Cleve. State U., 1989; MEd in Spl. Edn. & Rehab., Kent State U., 1990, postgrad., 1992—. Cert. rehab. counselor. Psychiat. asst. State Dept. of Mental Health, Broadview, Ohio, 1972-74; instr. tech. English U. East Cen., Santo Domingo, San Pedro, Dominican Republic, 1974-77; behavior trainer Cuyahoga County Bd. Mental Retardation/Develop. Disabilities, Parma, Ohio, 1977-79; vocat. coord. Parma Adult Tng. Ctr., 1979-80; mobility and orientation specialist Cuyahoga County Bd. MR/DD, Cleve., 1980-85, employment and tng. specialist, 1985-91; supported employment coord. Kent (Ohio) State U., 1991-92; lectr., project coord. dept. teaching specialties U. N.C., Charlotte, 1992-94; coord. vocat. opportunities Collaborative Stark County Comty. Mental Health Bd., Canton, Ohio, 1994—; exec. bd. dirs. Supported Employment Tng. Inc., Charlotte; outcome based curriculum devel. com. Charlotte Mecklenburg Schs., Charlotte, 1992-94; cons. vocat. programming Hattie Larlham Found., Ravenna, Ohio, 1990-93; mem. Ohio interagy. employment tng. task force Ohio Interagy. Tng. Network, Akron, 1990-91; mem. N.C. State Vocat. Alternatives Task Force, 1992-94, Charlotte Mecklenburg Supported Employment Steering Com., Charlotte, 1992-94; mem. dirs. adv. com. Ohio State Dept. Mental Retardation and Devel. Disabilities, 1991-92; mem. vocational rehab. com. Ohio Coun. Cmty. Mental Health & Recovery Orgns., 1994—. Co-author: (book chpt.) Psychiatric Rehabilitation in Practice, 1993; author, editor: Job Placement Procedure Manual, 1991; co-author, editor: Cuyahoga Job Readiness Curriculum, 1990. Mem. human rights com. VOCA Residential Corp., 1993-94. Western Region Transition Svcs. tng. grantee N.C. Dept. Pub. Info., 1992, Undergrad. Specialization in Supported Employment grantee, Rehab. Svcs. Adminstrn., 1993, 94; doctoral leader fellow Kent State U., 1990-92. Mem. ASCD, Assn. for Persons in Supported Employment, Nat. Rehab. Assn., Am. Assn. on Mental Retardation, Assn. for Persons with Severe Handicaps, Vocat. Evaluation and Work Adjustment Assn., Internat. Assn. Psychosocial Rehab. Avocations: music, songwriting, camping, hiking. Home: 305 Roosevelt Ave Cuyahoga Falls OH 44221-2618 Office: Vocat Opportunities Collab 500 Cleveland Ave NW Canton OH 44702-1542

STEELE, ROBERT DOUGLAS, JR., nuclear engineer; b. Glens Falls, N.Y., May 20, 1949; s. Robert Doulgas and Josephine Westervelt (MacEwan) S.; m. Judith Lennore Wood, Dec. 21, 1968; children: Lisa Marie, Michael Douglas, Jennifer Leigh, Jessica May, Matthew Ryan, Adam Joshua. BE, SUNY, Cobleskill, 1969; BS in Engrng., Vanderbilt U., 1975; MS, Pa. State U., 1982. Cert. quality engr. Asst. to prin. rep. Naval Reactors Rep. Office Dept. Energy, Newport News, Va., 1982-84; sr. ship supt. and submarine type desk officer Portsmouth (N.H.) Naval Shipyard, 1985-89; dep. dir. submarine div. Bd. Inspection & Survey, Washington, 1989-92; asst. for engrng. Submarine Monitoring, Maintenance & Support, Arlington, Va., 1992-93; dep. dir. engrng. ADI Tech. Corp., Arlington, 1993—; adult ednl. adv. com. No. Va. C.C., Woodbridge, 1994—. Chmn. worship com. Ch. of Christ, Dale City, Va., 1993—. Cmdr. USN, 1970-93. Recipient outstanding profl. award USN League, 1972. Mem. Am. Soc. Quality Control, Am. Nuclear Soc. (sec.). Achievements include computer program simulation of dynamic performance for a nuclear reactor with various load and casualty conditions; engineering analysis of material condition data resulting in extending platform operating cycles leading to a cost avoidance of about $250M per hull; improved emergency diesel engine spare component reliability by more than half. Office: ADI Tech Corp 2231 Crystal Dr Arlington VA 22202

STEELE, ROBERT EDWIN, orthopedic surgeon; b. Kansas City, Mo., Jan. 8, 1937; s. Robert Edwin and Margaret Jane (Levens) S.; m. Emily Wells Stephens, May 9, 1964; children: Edward Stephen, Thomas McKewon, Linda Katherine. AB, U. Mo., 1959; MD cum laude, Harvard U., 1963. Diplomate Am. Bd. Orthopedic Surgery; cert. Am. Acad. Orthopedic Surgeons, Assn. Arthritic Hip and Knee Surgery. Intern Mass. Gen. Hosp., Boston, 1963-64; resident in orthopedics Harvard U., 1966-71; instr. in orthopedic surgery Harvard Med. Sch., Boston, 1971; mem. med. staff Good Samaritan Hosp., Corvallis, Oreg., 1971—; bd. dirs. Good Samaritan Hosp., 1984-88, pres. med. staff, 1985, chmn. peer rev. com., 1994. Author: Studies on Osteonecrusis, 1979. Lt. USNR, 1964-66, Vietnam. Recipient Kappa Delta award for Outstanding Orthopedic Rsch., Am. Acad. Orthopedic Surgeons, 1978. Mem. Corvallis Orthopedic Surgeons (pres. 1990). Achievements include performance of total knee replacement. Avocations: camping, cycling, hiking, skiing, white water boating. Office: Corvallis Orthopedic Surg 3640 NW Samaritan Dr Corvallis OR 97330

STEELE, RODNEY REDFEARN, judge; b. Selma, Ala., May 22, 1930; s. C. Parker and Miriam Lera (Redfearn) S.; m. Frances Marion Blair, Aug. 1, 1964; children: Marion Scott, Claudia Redfearn, Parker Blair. AB, U. Ala., 1950, MA, 1951; LLB, U. Mich., 1954. Bar: Ala. 1954, U.S. Dist. Ct. (mid. dist.) Ala. 1959, U.S. Ct. Appeals (5th cir., now 11th cir.) 1981. Law clk. Ala. Ct. Appeals, 1956-57; assoc. Knabe & Nachman, Montgomery, Ala., 1957-61; asst. U.S. atty. Dept. Justice, Montgomery, 1961-66; staff atty. So. Bell T&T Co., Atlanta, 1966-67; judge U.S. Bankruptcy Ct., Mid. dist. Ala., Montgomery, 1967—, chief judge, 1985—; adj. prof. Jones Law Sch. Served with U.S. Army, 1954-56, Korea. Mem. ABA, Ala. State Bar, Montgomery County Bar Assn. Democrat. Episcopalian. Office: US Bankruptcy Ct PO Box 1248 1 Court Sq Montgomery AL 36102-1248

STEELE, SHELBY, writer, educator; b. Chgo., 1946; s. Shelby Sr. and Ruth S. Grad., Coe Loll., 1968; M in Sociology, So. Ill. U., 1971; PhD in English, U. Utah, 1974. Prof. dept English Calif. State U., San Jose. Author: The Content of Our Character: A New Vision of Race in America, 1991 (Nat. Book Critics Circle award 1991); contbr. essays to profl. jours. Office: San Jose State U Dept English 1 Washington Sq San Jose CA 95112-3613

STEELE, THOMAS MCKNIGHT, law librarian, law educator; b. Bartlesville, Okla., June 4, 1948; s. James Robert and Erma Blanche (McKnight) S.; m. Barbara Van Curen, Mar. 23, 1973 (div. 1985); children: James Robert, Ryan Thomas, David Christopher Joyce, Justin Daniel Joyce; m. Martha Bolling Swann, Apr. 1985 (div. 1990); m. LeAnn P. Joyce, Jan. 1995. BA in History, Okla. State U., 1969; MLS, U. Oreg., 1974; JD, U. Tex., 1977. Adminstrv. asst. Tarlton Law Libr. U. Tex., Austin, 1975-77; acting law librarian Underwood Law Libr. So. Meth. U., Dallas, 1977-78, asst. law librarian, 1978-79; assoc. prof. law, dir. Franklin Pierce Law Ctr., Concord, N.H., 1979-82; asst. prof., dir. U. Miss. Law Libr., University, 1982-85; assoc. prof., dir. Wake Forest U. Sch. Law Libr., Winston-Salem, N.C., 1985-91; prof., dir. Profl. Ctr. Libr. Wake Forest U., Winston-Salem, N.C., 1991; cons. in field; exec. dir. SCRIBES--Am. Soc. Writers on Legal Subjects, 1988—. Editor (newsletter) Scrivener, 1986-88; mng. editor Scribes Jour. Legal Writing, 1989—; editor Pub. Librs. and Pub. Laws, 1986-88; compiler bibliography IDEA, 1981-83, Jour. Air Law and Commerce, 1977-81; co-author: A Law Library Move: Planning Preparation and Execution, 1994. With U.S. Army. Mem. Am. Assn. Law Librs. Democrat. Baptist. Office: Wake Forest U Sch Law Libr PO Box 7206 Winston Salem NC 27109-7206

STEELE, TODD BENNETT, lawyer; b. Brownwood, Tex., Mar. 31, 1967; s. Artie Ben and Cheri Suzanne (Bennett) S. BS in Criminal Justice, Tarleton State U., Stephenville, Tex., 1989; JD, Tex. Wesleyan U., Irving, 1994. Bar: Tex. 1994. Law clk. Jerry W. Hayes, Atty.-at-Law, Dallas, 1992-95; assoc. Bud Jones, Inc., Dallas, 1995 with Bryan Healer, Brownwood, Tex., 1995—. Mem. Assn. Trial Lawyers Am., Tex. Trial Lawyers Assn., State Bar of Tex. Avocation: hunting. Office: 208 E Anderson Brownwood TX 76801

STEELE, VICTORIA LEE, librarian; b. L.A., Feb. 24, 1952; d. John Wilms and Marjorie (Lee) Erpelding; m. Timothy Reid, Jan. 14, 1979. BA, UCLA, 1974, MLS, 1981; MA, U. So. Calif., 1993. Libr. Belt Libr. of Vinciana UCLA, 1981-82, head history and spl. collections Biomed. Libr., 1983-86, dir. devel. librs., 1986-88; head spl. collections U. So. Calif., L.A., 1988—; fundraising cons. Author: Becoming a Fundraiser, 1992; prodr. film: Every time I See a Patient..., 1994; contbr. articles to profl. publs. Mem. adv. bd. Fulbright Program for So. Calif., 1995—; mem. adv. coun. Annenberg Sch. for Communication U. So. Calif., 1994—; founder L.A. Preservation Network; vol. Save Outdoor Sculpture, 1995—. U. Calif. rsch. grantee, 1979, U. So. Calif. rsch. grantee, 1995; Fulbright fellow (U.K.), 1995. Mem. ALA (3M/JMRT award 1982, G.K. Hall award 1995). Office: U So Calif Doheny Libr University Park Los Angeles CA 90089-0182

STEEL-GOODWIN, LINDA, toxicologist; b. Belfast, U.K., Apr. 17, 1956; came to U.S., 1988; d. George William and Margaret (Corbett) Steel; m. Anthony E. Goodwin, Dec. 9, 1986; children: Anthony David Ezell William Goodwin, Barbara Mae Goodwin. BSc with honors, The Queen's U., Belfast, 1978, PhD, 1981. Registered toxicologist, U.K. Rsch. officer The Queen's U., Belfast, 1978-86; chemist toxcology divsn. U.S. Army Europe, Landstuhl, Germany, 1986-88; rsch. investigator U. Mo., Columbia, 1988-90; prin. investigator Armed Forces Radiobiology Rsch. Inst., Bethesda, Md., 1990-93; rsch. toxicologist Armstrong Lab., Dayton, Ohio, 1993—; sci. advisor NBC def. No. Ireland Office, Belfast, 1984-86. Co-author: Biology of Nitric Oxide, vol. 2, 1993, Radiation & The Gastrointestinal Tract, 1994; contbr. articles to profl. jours. Aux. nurse ambulance and surg. ward Belfast City Hosp./British Red Cross Assn., 1972-76. Maj. USAF, 1992-95. Rsch. grantee Air Force Office Sci. Rsch., 1995, Tri-Svc. Toxicology, 1995. Fellow Inst. Biomed. Scientists, Am. Clin. Scientists; mem. Inst. Biology (chartered mem.), British Toxicology Soc., Am. Chem. Soc. Achievements include rsch. in trace metal analysis and absorption in vasculary perfused digestive tract, effects of calcium blockers on gaba receptors in hippocampus brain slices, growth factor receptors in the digestive tract and liver, free radical analysis after radiation and chemical exposure.

STEELMAN, FRANK SITLEY, lawyer; b. Watsonville, Calif., June 6, 1936; s. Frank S. Sr. and Blossom J. (Daugherty) S.; m. Diane Elaine Duke, June 27, 1960; children: Susan Butler, Robin Thurmond, Joan Bentley, David, Carol. BA, Baylor U., 1958, LLB, 1962. Spl. agt. IRS, Houston, 1962-64, atty. for estate tax, 1964-68; trust officer First City Nat. Bank, Houston, 1968-71; sr. v.p., trust officer First Bank & Trust, Bryan, Tex., 1971-73; assoc. Goode, Skrivanek & Steelman, College Station, Tex., 1973-74; pvt. practice Bryan, 1974—; vis. lectr. Tex. A&M U., College Station, 1974-75; mcpl. judge City of Bryan, 1986-88. Bd. dirs. Bryan Devel. Found., 1994—; mem. Bryan Zoning Bd. Adjustments, 1992-94; pres. Brazos Valley Estate Planning Coun., 1973-74, Am. Heart Assn., 1975-76; deacon, mem. ch. choir, Sunday sch. tchr. So. Bapt. Ch. Mem. Rotary (bd. dirs. Bryan club 1973-74). Avocations: walking, golf. Office: 1810 Greenfield Plz Bryan TX 77802-3408

STEEN, CARLTON DUANE, private investor, former food company executive; b. Walnut Grove, Minn., June 12, 1932; s. Conrad Wendell and Hilda (Eng) S.; m. Dorothy Corinne Sorknes, Aug. 16, 1953; children: James, Craig, Jennifer. BA in Econs. cum laude, St. Olaf Coll., 1954; MA in Indsl. Relations, U. Minn., 1957. Job analyst Exxon Corp., Roselle, N.J., 1958-59; personnel adminstr. Kraft Inc., Chgo., 1959-65, compensation mgr., 1965-69; plant mgr. Kraft Inc., Decatur, Ga., 1969-70, Champaign, Ill., 1971-74; v.p. prodn. Kraft Inc., Chgo., 1974-76; pres. Indsl. Foods div., Memphis, 1976-82, Indsl. Foods Group, 1982-87. Served to capt. USAF, 1955-57. Republican. Lutheran.

STEEN, JOHN THOMAS, JR., lawyer; b. San Antonio, Dec. 27, 1949; s. John Thomas and Nell (Donnell) S.; m. Ida Louise Clement, May 12, 1979; children: John Thomas, Ida Louise Larkin, James Higbie Clement. AB, Princeton U., 1971; JD, U. Tex., 1974. Bar: Tex. 1974, U.S. Dist. Ct. (we. dist.) Tex. 1976, U.S. Ct. Appeals (5th cir.) 1989. Assoc. firm Matthews & Branscomb, San Antonio, 1977-82; ptnr. firm Soules, Cliffe & Reed, San Antonio, 1982-83; sr. v.p., gen. counsel, dir. Commerce Savs. Assn., San Antonio, 1983-88; pvt. practice, San Antonio, 1988—; bd. dirs. North Frost Bank, San Antonio, 1982-84. Trustee San Antonio Acad., 1976-81, 87-93, chmn. bd., 1989-91; adv. coun. San Antonio Acad., 1991—; v.p. Bexar County Easter Seal Soc., San Antonio, 1976-77; trustee, vice chmn. San Antonio C.C. Dist., 1977-82; bd. dirs. Tex. Easter Seal Soc., Dallas, 1977-80, San Antonio Rsch. and Planning Coun., 1978-81, Community Guidance Ctr., 1983-84; vice-chmn. Leadership San Antonio, 1978-79; dir. Fiesta San Antonio Commn., 1982-83, 93—; Bexar County commr., San Antonio, 1982, Tex. Commn. on Economy and Efficiency in State Govt., 1985-89; Coliseum Adv. Bd., 1985-91, chmn. bd., 1990-91; pres. San Antonio Performing Arts Assn., 1984-85; bd. trustees World Affairs Coun. San Antonio, 1982—, chmn. bd., 1984-86; trustee United Way San Antonio, 1985-92; bd. dirs. Accord Med. Found., 1987-92; mem. adv. bd. U. Tex., San Antonio, 1987—; trustee Tex. Cavaliers Charitable Found., 1994-95. 1st It. USAR, 1973-81. Fellow San Antonio Bar Found., Tex. Bar Found. (life); mem. Tex. Bar. Assn., San Antonio Acad. Alumni Assn. (pres. 1976-77), Ivy Club (Princeton, N.J.), San Antonio German Club (pres. 1982-83), Order of Alamo, Tex. Cavaliers (bd. dirs. 1989-92, 1994—, comdr. 1994-95, King Antonio LXXIV 1996—), San Antonio Country Club (bd. govs. 1990-93, v.p. 1992-93), Argyle Club, Conopus Club (bd. dirs. 1989-90), Princeton Club San Antonio and South Tex. (pres. 1980-81), Phi Delta Phi. Home: 207 Ridgemont Ave San Antonio TX 78209-5431 Office: 300 Convent St Ste 2440 San Antonio TX 78205-3725

STEEN, LOWELL HARRISON, physician; b. Kenosha, Wis., Nov. 27, 1923; s. Joseph Arthur and Camilla Marie (Henriksen) S.; m. Cheryl Ann Rectanus, Nov. 20, 1969; children—Linda C., Laura A., Lowell Harrison Jr., Heather J., Kirsten M. B.S., Ind. U., 1945, M.D., 1948. Intern Mercy Hosp.-Loyola U. Clinics, Chgo., 1948-49; resident in internal medicine VA Hosp., Hines, Ill., 1950-53; pvt. practice, Highland, Ind., 1953—; pres., chief exec. officer Whiting Clinic, 1960-85; mem. sr. staff St. Catherine Hosp., East Chicago, Ind.; staff Community Hosp., Munster, Ind.; bd. commrs. Joint Commn. Accreditation of Hosps. Served with M.C., AUS, 1949-50, 55-56. Recipient Disting. Alumni Service award Ind. U., 1983. Fellow ACP; mem. AMA (trustee 1975, chmn. bd. trustees 1979-81), Ind. Med. Assn. (pres. 1970, chmn. bd. 1968-70), World Med. Assn. (dir. 1978-82, chmn. 1981-82, del. world assembly), Ind. Soc. Internal Medicine (pres. 1963), Am. Soc. Internal Medicine (Disting. Internist award 1981), Lake County Med. Soc., Ind. U. Sch. Medicine Alumni Assn. (pres. 1989-90, Disting. Alumnus award 1981). Presbyterian. Home: 8800 Parkway Dr Hammond IN 46322-1520 also: Gateway 11481 Waterford Village Dr Fort Myers FL 33913-7917 Office: 3641 Ridge Rd Hammond IN 46322-2064

STEEN, LYNN ARTHUR, mathematician, educator; b. Chgo., Jan. 1, 1941; s. Sigvart J. and Margery (Mayer) S.; m. Mary Elizabeth Frost, July 7, 1940; children: Margaret, Catherine. BA, Luther Coll., 1961; PhD, MIT, 1965; DSc (hon.), Luther Coll., 1986, Wittenberg U., 1991. Prof. math. St. Olaf Coll., Northfield, Minn., 1965—; vis. scholar Inst. Mittag-Leffler, Djursholm, Sweden, 1970-71; writing fellow Conf. Bd. Math. Sci., Washington, 1974-75; exec. dir. Math. Sci. Edn. Bd., Washington, 1992-95. Author: Counterexamples in Topology, 1970, Everybody Counts, 1989; editor: Mathematics Today, 1978, On the Shoulders of Giants, 1990, Math. Mag., 1976-80; contbg. editor: Sci. News, 1976-82. NSF Sci. faculty fellow, 1970-71, Danforth Found. grad. fellow, 1961-65. Fellow AAAS (sec. math. sect. 1982-88); mem. Am. Math. Soc., Math. Assn. Am. (pres. 1985-86, Disting. Svc. award 1992), Coun. Sci. Soc. Pres. (chmn. 1989), Sigma Xi (Bd. Dirs. Spl. award 1989). Home: 716 Saint Olaf Ave Northfield MN 55057-1523 Office: St Olaf Coll Dept of Math Northfield MN 55057

STEEN, PAUL JOSEPH, retired broadcasting executive; b. Williston, N.D., July 4, 1932; s. Ernest B. and Inez (Ingebrigtson) S.; m. Judith Smith; children—Michael M., Melanie. BA, Pacific Luth. U., 1954; MS, Syracuse U., 1957. Producer, dir. Sta. KNTV, San Jose, Calif., 1957-58, Sta. KVIE, Sacramento, 1958-60; asst. prof. telecommunications Pacific Luth. U., Tacoma, 1960-67; dir. ops. Sta. KPBS San Diego State U., 1967-74; gen. mgr., 1974-93, prof. telecommunications and film, 1974-93, dir. univ. telecommunications; co-chmn. Office of New Tech. Initiatives. Dir. (tel. program) Troubled Waters (winner Nat. Ednl. TV award of excellence 1970). With AUS. Named Danforth Assoc. Mem. Pacific Mountain Network (bd. dirs., chmn., bd. of govs. award 1993), NATAS, Assn. Calif. Pub. TV Stas. (pres.), Pi Kappa Delta. Home: 4930 Campanile Dr San Diego CA 92115-2331

STEEN, WESLEY WILSON, former bankruptcy judge, lawyer; b. Abbeville, La., Feb. 15, 1946; s. John Wesley and Margaret (Chauvin) S.; m. Evelyn Finch, Aug. 29, 1970; children: Anna Frances, John Wesley, Lee Wilson. BA in English, U. Va., 1968; JD, La. State U., 1974. Bar: La. 1974, Tex. 1988. Assoc. Sanders, Downing, et al, Baton Rouge, 1974-77, ptnr., 1977-80; solo practice law, Baton Rouge, 1980-83; pres., atty. Steen, Rubin, et al, Baton Rouge, 1983-84; bankruptcy judge U.S. Bankruptcy Ct., Middle Dist. La., part time, 1983-84, full time, Baton Rouge, 1984-87; mem. Winstead, Sechrest & Minick, Houston, 1988—; mem. La. State Law Inst. Continuous Revision Com., La. Trust Code, 1980-87; mem. Baton Rouge Estate and Bus. Planning Council, 1980-87, State Bar Com. on Bar Admissions, Baton Rouge, 1981-85; adj. asst. prof. law La. State U., 1979-87, So. U. Law Sch., 1981; congl. page U.S. Ho. of Reps., 1963-64. Adv. editor Am. Bankruptcy Law Jour.; contbr. articles to profl. jours. Vestryman, St. James Episcopal Ch., 1980-83; bd. dirs., pres. Baton Rouge Symphony Assn., 1976-87, St. James Place, 1985-87, Cerebral Palsy Ctr., 1981, Baton Rouge Gallery, 1982. Fellow Am. Coll. Bankruptcy; mem. Baton Rouge Bar Assns., La. Bar Assn., Order of Coif, Omicron Delta Kappa. Republican. Episcopalian. Avocations: jogging, computers. Office: Winstead Sechrest & Minick 910 Travis St Ste 1700 Houston TX 77002-5807

STEENBURGEN, MARY, actress; b. Newport, Ariz., 1953; m. Malcolm McDowell, 1980 (div.); children: Lilly, Charlie. Student, Neighborhood Playhouse. Films: Goin' South, 1978, Time After Time, 1979, Melvin and Howard, 1980 (Academy Award, Best Supporting Actress), Ragtime, 1981, A Midsummer Night's Sex Comedy, 1982, Cross Creek, 1983, Romantic Comedy, 1983, One Magic Christmas, 1985, Dead of Winter, 1987, End of the Line, 1987 (also exec. prodr.), The Whales of August, 1987, Miss Firecracker, 1989, Parenthood, 1989, Back to the Future III, 1990, The Long Walk Home, 1990 (narrator), The Butcher's Wife, 1991, Philadelphia, 1993, What's Eating Gilbert Grape, 1993, Clifford, 1994, It Runs in the Family, 1994, Pontiac Moon, 1994; appeared in Showtime TV's Faerie Tale Theatre prodn. of Little Red Riding Hood and (miniseries) Tender Is the Night, 1985; TV films: The Attic: The Hiding of Anne Frank, 1988; theater appearances include: Holiday, Old Vic, London, 1987, Candida, Broadway, 1993. Office: William Morris Agy Inc 151 S El Camino Dr Beverly Hills CA 90212-2704*

STEENHAGEN, ROBERT LEWIS, landscape architect, consultant; b. Grand Rapids, Mich., July 11, 1922; s. Abraham and Rena (Vanden Broek) S.; m. Doris Brisentine, Aug. 2, 1952; children: Deborah, Cynthia, James. A.S., Grand Rapids Jr. Coll., 1942; B.S., Mich. State U., 1949. Chief landscape design Eastern design office Nat. Park Service, Phila., 1963-66; capt. planning team Nat. Park Service, Washington, 1966-70; asst. mgr. N.E. area Design Office Nat. Park Service, Denver, 1971-77, assoc. mgr., 1978-80; cons. landscape architecture Lakewood, Colo., 1980—. Served to sgt. U.S. Army, 1942-45, PTO. Recipient Meritorious Service award Nat. Park Service, 1971; recipient Performance award for Nat. Bicentennial Program, 1976. Fellow Am. Soc. Landscape Architects. Home: 2473 S Carr Ct Denver CO 80227-3104

STEENSLAND, RONALD PAUL, librarian; b. Dothan, Ala., Dec. 16, 1946; s. Maurice John and Claire Folkes S.; m. Nancy Hollister, Dec. 20, 1970; 1 child, Ronald Paul. B.A., Fla. State U., 1969, M.S., 1970; postgrad., Miami (Ohio) U., 1972, U. Md., 1980, U.S. Army War Coll., 1995. Dir. Davidson County Pub. Libr., Lexington, N.C., 1970-73, Hidalgo County Libr. System, McAllen, Tex., 1973-76, Los Alamos County Libr., 1976-77, Lexington (Ky.) Pub. Libr., 1977—; chmn. John Cotton Dana Library Public Relations Awards, 1977. Treas. Hildago County chpt. ARC, 1975. Served to col. USAR, 1969-70. Recipient Service award United Way. Mem. Res. Officers Assn. (sec.-treas. chpt. 100), Assn. U.S. Army (sec. Bluegrass chpt.), U.S. Chess Fedn., ALA, Southeastern Library Assn., Ky. Library Assn., Lexington C. of C., Alpha Tau Omega. Baptist. Clubs: Lafayette, Pres.'s, Lexington Chess, Rotary. Office: Lexington Pub Libr 140 E Main St Lexington KY 40507-1318

STEENSMA, ROBERT CHARLES, English language educator; b. Sioux Falls, S.D., Nov. 24, 1930; s. Anton Charles and Martha (Johnson) S.; m. Sharon Hogge, Sept. 5, 1964; children: Craig, Michael, Laura, Kathryn, Rebecca. BA, Augustana Coll., Sioux Falls, 1952; MA, U. S.D., 1955; PhD, U. Ky., 1961. Instr. English Augustana Coll., 1955-57; asst. prof. U. S.D., 1959-62; asst. prof., then asso. prof. Utah State U., Logan, 1962-66; mem. faculty U. Utah, 1966—, prof. English, 1971—; lectr. Utah Humanities Coun., 1992-94. Author: Sir William Temple, 1970, Dr. John Arbuthnot, 1979; Editor: On The Original and Nature of Government (Sir William Temple), 1965; Contbr. articles to profl. jours. Served to capt. USNR, 1948-83. Mem. Rocky Mountain MLA, U.S. Naval Inst., Am. Soc. 18th Century Studies, South Ctr. Soc. for 18th Century Studies (pres. 1994-95), Western Lit. Assn., S.D. Hist. Soc. Republican. Lutheran. Office: U Utah Dept English Salt Lake City UT 84112

STEEPLES, DOUGLAS WAYNE, university dean, consultant, researcher; b. Great Bend, Kans., Mar. 30, 1935; s. Marion Wayne and Dorothy Augusta (King) S.; children from previous marriage: Donald Bruce, John Douglas, Sheila Margaret; m. Christine Marie Webster, Dec. 8, 1990. B.A. summa cum laude, U. Redlands, 1957; M.A., U. N.C., 1958, Ph.D., 1961; cert., Inst. Ednl. Mgmt., Harvard U., 1981. Asst. prof. history Calif. State U.-Northridge, 1961-64; prof. history Earlham Coll., Richmond, Ind., 1963-80; acad. v.p. Wartburg Coll., Waverly, Iowa, 1979-80; exec. v.p. Westminster Coll., Salt Lake City, 1980-83; provost Ohio Wesleyan U., Delaware, Ohio, 1983-85, acting pres., winter 1984; dean Coll. Liberal and Fine Arts, U. So. Colo., Pueblo, 1985-89; v.p. for acad. affairs Aurora (Ill.) U., 1989-94; dean Coll. Liberal Arts, Mercer U., Macon, Ga., 1994—; cons. higher edn. mgmt.; cons., reader advanced placement program Ednl. Testing Service, Princeton, N.J., 1976—; cons., evaluator North Central Assn. Schs. and Colls., Chgo., 1985—; bd. dirs. Wesstern Ind. Colls. Fund, Salt Lake City, 1980-83; bd. dirs. Am. Con. of Acad. Deans, 1995; bd. trustees Econ. and Bus. Hist. Soc., 1995-98. Editor, contbg. author: Institutional Revival: Case Histories, 1986, Successful Strategic Planning Case Studies, 1989, Managing Change in Higher Education, 1990; assoc. editor Bus. Libr. Rev., 1996-98; contbr. articles to various publs. Pres. Luth. Inter-parish Coun., Richmond, 1975-78; bd. dirs. Soc. for Use and Preservation of Resources, Richmond, 1976-79; mem. adv. bd. Pueblo Symphony Orch., 1987-89; mem. allocations coms. United Way Richmond, 1976-79, Pueblo, 1988-89, Aurora, 1990-94. Scholar U. Redlands, Calif., 1953-57; Danforth fellow, 1957-61; Woodrow Wilson fellow, 1957-58; Found. for Econ. Edn. fellow in bus., 1963; Am. Philos. Soc. grantee, 1966. Mem. Am. Hist. Assn., Orgn. Am. Historians, So. Hist. Assn., Sierra Club, Phi Beta Kappa (senator united chpts. 1973-79), Omicron Delta Kappa. Republican. Lodges: Rotary (bd. dirs. 1983-84). Avocations: mountaineering, running, bagpiping. Office: Mercer U Coll Liberal Arts 1400 Coleman Ave Macon GA 31207-1000

STEER, ALFRED GILBERT, JR., foreign language educator; b. Lansdowne, Pa., May 30, 1913; s. Alfred Gilbert and Selma Elizabeth (Taber) S.; m. Elizabeth Jean Kell, Sept. 6, 1947; children: Susan Elizabeth, John Thomas. A.B., Haverford Coll., 1935; M.A., Duke U., 1938; Ph.D., U. Pa., 1954. Instr. Washington and Lee U., 1937-41, Haverford Coll., U. Pa., 1947-55; head lang. div Internat. Mil. Tribunal, Nurnberg, Germany, 1945-46; asst. prof., then assoc. prof. SUNY-Binghamton, 1955-59; assoc. prof. Columbia U., 1959-67; prof. Germanic and Slavic langs., head dept. Germanic and Slavic langs U. Ga., Athens, 1967-83, prof. emeritus, 1983—, chmn. linguistics com., 1969-83. Author: (with W.W. Pusey III and B.Q. Morgan) Readings in Military German, 1943, Goethe's Science in the Structure of the Wanderjahre, 1979, Goethe's Elective Affinities the Robe of Nessus, 1990, Interesting Times: A Memoir, 1992; contbg. author: Jahrbuch des Freien Deutschen Hochstifts, 1965, Approaches to Teaching Goethe's Faust, 1986, Science Skeleton of Goethe's Works, 1987; also articles. Bd. dirs. Univ. System of Ga. Studies Abroad Programs, 1969-70, Prospective Tchr. Fellowship Program, HEW. Served with USNR, World War II. Fellow Am. Philos. Soc., 1965-66; fellow Columbia Council for Research in Humanities, 1965-66. Mem. MLA, Am. Assn. Tchrs. German (v.p., pres. chpt. 1970-71). Home: 215 Bishop Dr Athens GA 30606-4013 Office: U Ga Dept Germanic Slavic L Athens GA 30602

STEER, REGINALD DAVID, lawyer; b. N.Y.C., July 16, 1945; s. Joseph D. and Rozica (Yusim) S.; m. Marianne Spizzy, July 22, 1984; children: Derek B., Trevor A. BA, U. Minn., 1966, JD, 1969. Bar: Minn. 1969, Calif. 1973, U.S. Dist. Ct. (no., ea. and cen. dists.) Calif., U.S. Ct. Mil. Appeals 1969, U.S. Ct. Appeals (9th cir.), U.S. Ct. Appeals (11th cir.), U.S. Supreme Ct. 1981, U.S. Ct. Internat. Trade, 1994. Assoc. Pillsbury, Madison & Sutro, San Francisco, 1973-79, ptnr., 1979—; lectr. Calif. Continuing Edn. of Bar, San Francisco, 1981, Petroleum Attys. Meeting, Washington, 1996. Capt. U.S. Army, 1969-73. Served to capt. U.S. Army, 1969-73. Mem. ABA (antitrust and litigation sects.). Club: Olympic (San Francisco). Avocations: piano, tennis, photography. Office: Pillsbury Madison & Sutro 235 Montgomery St San Francisco CA 94104-2902

STEERE, ALLEN CARUTHERS, JR., physician, educator; b. Apr. 11, 1943; m. Margaret Mercer, 1969; children: Allen Caruthers III, Margaret Hamilton, Samuel Mercer, John Summers. BA, Columbia U., 1965, MD, 1969; DSc. (hon.), Indiana U., 1992. Diplomate Am. Bd. Internal Medicine; lic. rheumatologist, N.Y., Ga., Ct., Mass. Intern St. Luke's Hosp., N.Y.C., 1969-70, asst., sr. resident, 1970-72, chief resident, instr. medicine, 1972-73; chief resident, instr. medicine Coll. Physicians and Surgeons Columbia U., N.Y.C., 1972-73; clin. instr. medicine Hosp. for Spl. Surgery Cornell U., N.Y.C., 1972-73; clin. instr. medicine Grady Meml. Hosp. Emory U., Atlanta, 1973-75; clin. fellow in rheumatology Yale U., New Haven, 1975-77, asst. prof. medicine, epidemiology and pub. health, 1977-81, assoc. prof. medicine, 1981-87; prof. medicine, chief rheumatology and immunology New Eng. Med. Ctr. Tufts U., Boston, 1987—. With USPHS, 1973-75. Recipient Citation for Elucidation of Lyme disease Infectious Diseases Soc. Am., 1984,

Ciba-Geigy Rheumatology prize Internat. League Against Rheumatism, 1985, award for discovery of Lyme disease Nat. Inst. Arthritis and Musculoskeletal Skin Diseases, 1988, Richard and Hinda Rosenthal award ACP, 1990, Joseph Mather Smith prize Coll. Physicians and Surgeons, Columbia U., 1990, Zucker Faculty prize Tufts U., 1990, award for studies Lyme disease Nat. Health Coun., 1990, Lee C. Howley Sr. prize Arthritis Found., 1993; Rsch. fellow Arthritis Found., 1977-80, Sr. fellow, 1981-86. Mem. Am. Soc. Clin. Investigation, Am. Fedn. Clin. Rsch., Am. Coll. Rheumatology. Office: Tufts U Sch Medicine New Eng Med Ctr # 406 750 Washington St Boston MA 02111-1533

STEERE, ANNE BULLIVANT, retired student advisor; b. Phila., July 27, 1921; d. Stuart Lodge and Elizabeth MacCuen (Smith) B.; m. Richard M. H. Harper Jr., Nov. 14, 1942 (div. Oct. 1967); children: Virginia Harper Kliever, Richard M. H. Harper III, Patricia Harper Flint, Stuart Lodge Harper, Lucy Steere, Grace Steere Johnson; m. Bruce Middleton Steere, July 5, 1968. BS in Sociology, So. Meth. U., 1978, M in Liberal Arts, 1985. Asst. to dir. Harvard Law Sch. Fund, Cambridge, Mass., 1958-68; advisor to older students So. Meth. U., Dallas, 1976-85. Contbr. articles to profl. jours. Trustee, Pine Manor Coll., Chestnut Hill, Mass., 1983—; bd. dirs. Planned Parenthood, Dallas, 1975-85. Mem. New Eng. Hist. and Geneal. Soc., Alpha Kappa Delta. Episcopalian. Clubs: Chilton (Boston); Jr. League. Avocations: reading, needlepoint, sailing. Home (winter): 1177 N Lake Way Palm Beach FL 33480-3245

STEERE, WILLIAM CAMPBELL, JR., pharmaceutical company executive; b. Ann Arbor, Mich., June 17, 1936; s. William Campbell and Dorothy (Osborne) S.; m. Lynda Gay Powers, Jan. 29, 1957; children: William, Mark, Christopher. BS, Stanford U., 1959. Sales rep. Pfizer & Co., Modesto, Calif., 1970-72; v.p., dir. ops. Pfizer Labs, N.Y.C., 1982-84; sr. v.p., dir. ops. Pfizer Pharms., N.Y.C., 1982-84, exec. v.p., 1984-86, pres., 1986-91; pres., CEO Pfizer Inc., 1991-92, chmn. bd., CEO, 1992—, also bd. dirs.; bd. dirs. Texaco Inc., NYU Med. Ctr., Minerals Techs. Inc., Fed. Res. Bank of N.Y., Sta. WNET-TV. Trustee N.Y. Bot. Garden; bd. overseers Meml. Sloan-Kettering Cancer Ctr. Mem. Pharm. Rsch. and Mfrs. Am. (bd. dirs.), Bus. Coun. (bd. dirs.), Bus. Roundtable, Univ. Club, N.Y. Yacht Club. Avocations: sailing, skiing. Office: Pfizer Inc 235 E 42nd St New York NY 10017-5703

STEFANE, CLARA JOAN, business education secondary educator; b. Trenton, N.J., Apr. 8; d. Joseph and Rose M. (Bonfanti) Raymond; m. John E. Stefane, July 19, 1975. BS in Bus. Adminstrn., Georgian Ct. Coll., Lakewood, N.J., 1968. Cert. tchr. gen. bus. and secretarial studies, N.J. Tchr. bus. Camden Cath. High Sch., Cherry Hill, N.J., 1960-68, Cathedral High Sch., Trenton, 1970-72; tchr., bus., chair dept. McCorristin Cath. High Sch., Trenton, 1972—; mem. Mercer County Task Force for Bus. Edn., Trenton, 1989-90. Sustaining mem. Rep. Nat. Com.; del. mem. 1992 Presdl. Trust; mem. Rosary Altar Soc., Incarnation Ch. Named Tchr. of Yr., The Cittone Inst., Princeton, N.J., 1991. Mem. ASCD, N.J. Bus. Edn. Assn., Nat. Cath. Edn. Assn., Sisters of Mercy of the Ams. (assoc.). Roman Catholic. Avocations: reading, creative writing, attending operas and Yankee baseball games. Home: 278 Weber Ave Trenton NJ 08638-3638 Office: McCorristin Cath High Sch 175 Leonard Ave Trenton NJ 08610-4807

STEFANIAK, NORBERT JOHN, business administration educator; b. Milw., Jan. 12, 1921; s. Peter Stephen and Mary Ann (Schlaikowski) S.; m. Elizabeth Jean Horning, Aug. 27, 1949; children—John, Mary, Jane, Beth, Joel, Peter, James, Thomas, Anne, Jean. B.B.A., U. Wis., 1948, M.B.A., 1950, Ph.D., 1960. C.P.A. Instr. U. Wis., Milw., 1950-53; treas., controller Wauwatosa (Wis.) Realty Co., 1953-56; prof. bus. adminstrn. U. Wis., Milw., 1957-75, prof. emeritus. Author: Real Estate Marketing, monograph and articles in field. Past commr. West Allis (Wis.) Planning Commn.; bd. dirs. Polish Festivals, Inc., Columbus KC, West Allis, Internat. Exch. Found.-Poland and Milw. County, Wis.; condemnation commr. Milw. County; bd. review City of West Allis, Wis. With USAAF, WWII. Named Polish-Am. Man of Yr., Polish Nat. Alliance (Milw. Soc.), 1990. Mem. Am. Real Estate and Urban Econs. Assn. (past pres.), Wis. Realtors Assn. (past dir.), Wis. Real Estate Exam. Bd. (past vice chmn.), Am. Soc. Real Estate Counselors (emeritus), Polish Nat. Alliance. Home: 865 S 76th St Milwaukee WI 53214-3026 Office: S63w13680 Janesville Rd Muskego WI 53150-2713

STEFANICS, ELIZABETH T. (LIZ STEFANICS), state legislator. BA, Eastern Ky. U.; MS, U. Wis.; PhD, U. Minn. Mem. N.Mex. Senate; mem. conservation com., judiciary com., chmn. health and human svcs. com., adminstr. health and human svcs. Democrat. Address: PO Box 10127 Santa Fe NM 87504-6127 Office: N Mex State Senate State Capitol Santa Fe NM 87503*

STEFANIDES, DEAN, advertising executive; b. New York, July 4, 1955; s. Stefanos and Mary (Karamicalos) S.; m. Maureen Stefanides. Student, Pratt Inst., 1972-76. Jr. art dir. BBDO, N.Y.C., 1976-77; art dir. Cavaliere, Klier, Pearlman, N.Y.C., 1977-78; v.p., art dir. Scali, McCabe, Sloves, N.Y.C., 1978-82, sr. v.p., assoc. creative dir., 1984—; v.p., art supr. Ammirati and Puris, N.Y.C., 1982-84.

STEFANIK, JEAN MARIANNE, educator, naturalist; b. Springfield, Mass., June 10, 1949; d. Edward Carl and Suzanne Florence (Chelkonas) S. BS in Elem. Edn.; MEd, Am. Internat. Coll.; postgrad. Norwich U., U. Vt., Merrimack Valley Coll., Franklin Pierce Coll., U. Mass., U. Hawaii. Reading specialist Easthampton (Mass.) Schs., 1973-74; dir. curriculum Barre Town (Vt.) Sch. Dist., 1974-80; extended edn. program dir., Amherst Sch. Dist., N.H., 1980—; part-time educator Computer Ctr., Tandy Corp., Manchester, N.H., 1981-82; part-time instr. Notre Dame Coll., Manchester, 1981-83, Merrimack Valley Coll., 1981-86, U. N.H. Coll. for Lifelong Learning, 1982-87, 92—, sabbitical including work for Smithsonian Inst. Marine Systems Lab. and New England Aquarium's Right Whale Rsch. Team, 1987-88; mem. Alaska Oil Spill and Ecology Info. Ctr., Juneau, 1989; mem. Earthwatch/Rsch. Teams Giant Clams of Tonga, 1988, Fijian Coral Reefs, 1993, field svc. rep., 1993-95. Mem. ASCD (internat., bd. dirs. 1979-80, 82—, mem. elem. global edn. pilot project 1992-94, issues com. 1995-96), Vt. Assn. Supervision and Curriculum Devel. (pres. 1979-80, treas. 1977-79), N.H. Assn. Supervision and Curriculum Devel. (pres. 1982-84, 86-87, bd. dirs. 1981—), New Eng. Aquarium Self Contained Underwater Breathing Apparatus Club (pres. 1990-93), Seamark (chmn. 1993), Mensa, Phi Delta Kappa, Alpha Chi. Home: 285 Beaver St Manchester NH 03104-5569

STEFANKO, ROBERT ALLEN, financial executive; b. Cleve., Jan. 20, 1943; s. John and Mary (Kovach) S.; m. Barbara Jane Gittner, Feb. 12, 1963; children—Sandra Marie, Robert Todd. B.S. in Acctg., Miami U., Oxford, Ohio, 1964. Mgr. Price Waterhouse, Cleve., 1964-72; chmn. bd., chief fin. officer A. Schulman Inc., Akron, Ohio, 1972—. Bd. dirs. Akron Gen. Devel. Found., Akron Community Found., Akron Gen. Med. Ctr. Mem. AICPA, Nat. Assn. Accts. Avocations: golf; reading. Office: A Schulman Inc 3550 W Market St Akron OH 44333-2658*

STEFANO, JOSEPH WILLIAM, film and television producer, author; b. Phila., May 5, 1922; s. Dominic and Josephine (Vottima) S.; m. Marilyn Epstein, Dec. 5, 1953; 1 son, Andrew Dominic. Ed. pub. schs. Pres. Villa di Stefano Prodns., 1962—. Toured as song and dance man in Student Prince, 1945, Merry Widow, 1946; composer music and lyrics popular songs, night club revues, indsl. shows, others, 1946-57; author screenplays The Black Orchid, 1958, The Naked Edge, 1960, Psycho, 1960, Anna di Brooklyn, 1962, Eye of the Cat, 1969, Futz, 1970, The Kindred, 1986, Blackout, 1989, Psycho IV: The Beginning, 1990, Two Bits, 1995; TV drama Made in Japan, 1959, movies for TV, 1970-78; prodr., author TV series The Outer Limits, 1963-64, Swamp Thing, 1990. Recipient Robert E. Sherwood award for Made in Japan, Fund for Republic, 1959, Edgar Allen Poe award for Psycho, Mystery Writers Am., 1960, Columbia award Federated Italo-Ams. Calif., 1964, Pres.'s award Acad. Sci.-Fiction Fantasy and Horror Films, 1987, Movieguide commendation for Two Bits, One of Ten Best Films of 1995; inducted into Cuiltural Hall Fame, South Phila. H.S. Mem. ASCAP, Writers Guild Am., Dirs. Guild Am., Producers Guild Am., Acad. Motion Pictures Arts and Scis., Mystery Writers Am. Home: 10216 Cielo Dr Beverly Hills CA 90210-2035 *For me it has always been important to succeed first in my own eyes. This personal sense of success seems warmer and surer and more likely to maintain the spirit during those moments when worldly success dances to tunes other than my own. Goals are golden. Guidelines are lines on a street map; they show how many different ways there are to go from where to when.*

STEFANO, ROSS WILLIAM, business executive; b. Cortland, N.Y., June 18, 1955; s. Nicola Sebastian and Gloria Maria (Saltarez) S.; m. Janet Stapleton, Apr. 2, 1977; children: Nicolas J.J., Christian A., Mari Elizabeth. BS, Cornell U., 1977, MBA, 1978. CPA, Calif. CPA Coopers & Lybrand, San Francisco, 1978-81; fin. mgr. Genstar Corp., San Francisco, 1981-83; v.p., treas., v.p. mktg. CIS Corp., Syracuse, N.Y., 1983-92; cons., 1992-94; pres. Pietrafesa Co., Liverpool, N.Y., 1994—. Bd. dirs., exec. dir. FM Soccer Club, 1984—; bd. dirs. Syracuse YMCA, 1986-89; fund raiser Boy Scouts Am., Syracuse, 1986-89, Cath. Charities, Syracuse, 1991. Mem. AICPA, Cavalry Club. Office: Peitrafesa Co 7400 Morgan Rd Liverpool NY 13090-3902

STEFANSCHI, SERGIU, dancer; b. Komralid, Romania, Mar. 2, 1941; emigrated to Can., 1971, naturalized, 1977; s. Alexander and Lidia S. Diploma, Acad. Dance, Leningrad, 1960. Tchr. Nat. Ballet Sch. and Nat. Ballet of Can., Toronto, 1978—. Prin. dancer, Bucharest (Romania) Opera, 1960-68, Jeunesse Musicale de France, 1969-70, Theatre Francaise de la Dance, Paris, 1970, Nat. Ballet of Can., Toronto, Ont., 1971-78, appeared with, Belgrade (Yugoslavia) Opera, 1966, 68, Coob Marieta (Ga.) Ballet, 1976 (Recipient Silver medal I, Internat. Ballet Concourse, Varna, Bulgaria 1964), Internat. Guest Theater. Mem. Actors Equity Can. Mem. Romania Orthodox Ch. Home: 319 Ave Keewatin, Toronto, ON Canada M4P 2A4 Office: 111 Maitland St, Toronto, ON Canada M4Y 1E4

STEFENSON, EVA, advertising agency executive; b. London, Eng.; d. Julius and Sofia Pietrzak von Habdank; m. Dana Stefenson, Oct. 27, 1985; 1 child, Audrey Caulfield Stefenson. BA in Advtg. & Graphic Design, Iowa State U.; postgrad. work in Painting, Acad. de Pitta, Florence, Italy. Assoc. art dir. Meredith Pub. Co., Des Moines, Iowa, 1976-81; sr. art dir. Conrans, N.Y.C., 1981-84; art dir. Clinque, N.Y.C., 1984-87; creative dir. Liz Claiborne, N.Y.C., 1987-90; ptnr., pres., creative dir. Calman & Stefenson, N.Y.C., 1990-94; v.p. creative dir. Arcade, Inc., N.Y.C., 1995—; cons. art direction Ann Taylor, N.Y.C., 1990-91; design cons. Coach Leatherware, N.Y.C., 1990-91. Editor Fine Arts Calendar, 1993 (Creativity award 1994). Co-chair benefit com. Cancer Rsch. Inst., N.Y.C., 1994-95. Recipient Daisy award Seventeen Magazine, 1969, 1st place Student Cosmetic Design, Clairol, N.Y.C., 1969. Fellow Mus. Modern Art; mem. Am. Inst. Graphic Artists (pkg. and corp. identity awards 1990. 91, 93), Internat. Ctr. of Photography.

STEFFAN, WALLACE ALLAN, entomologist, educator, museum director; b. St. Paul, Aug. 10, 1934; m. Sylvia Behler, July 16, 1966; 1 child, Sharon. B.S., U. Calif.-Berkeley, 1961, Ph.D., 1965. Entomologist dept. entomology Bishop Mus., Honolulu, 1964-85, head diptera sect., 1966-85, asst. chmn., 1979-85; dir. Idaho Mus. Natural History, Idaho State U., Pocatello, 1985-89, U. Alaska Mus., 1989-92; prof. biology U. Alaska Fairbanks, 1989-92; exec. dir. Great Valley Mus. Natural History, 1992-94; dir. Sun Cities Mus. Art, Sun City, Ariz., 1995—; mem. grad. affiliate faculty dept. entomology U. Hawaii, 1969-85; reviewer NSF, 1976—; mem. internat. editorial adv. com. World Diptera Catalog, Systematic Entomology Lab., U.S. Dept. Agr., 1983-85; mem. affiliate faculty biology, Idaho State U., 1986-89; bd. dirs. Idaho State U. Fed. Credit Union, 1986-89; mem. adv. coun. Modesto Conv. & Visitors Bureau, 1992-95; mem. Ft. Hall Replica Commn., 1986-89. Acting editor Jour. Med. Entomology, 1966; assoc. editor Pacific Insects, 1980-85. Judge Hawaii State Sci. and Engring. Fair, 1966-85, chief judge sr. display div., 1982, 83, 84; advisor to bd. Fairbanks Conv. and Visitors Bur., 1989-91; mem. vestry St. Christophers Episcopal Ch., 1974-76, St. Matthew's Episcopal Ch., Fairbanks, 1990-91; pres. Alaska Visitors Assn., Fairbanks, 1991; advisor Fairbanks Conv. Visitors Bur. Bd., 1989-91; bd. dirs. Kamehameha Fed. Credit Union, 1975-77, chmn., mem. supervisory com., 1980-84. Served with USAF, 1954-57. Grantee NIH, 1962, 63, 67-74, 76-81, 83-85. U.S. Army Med. Research and Devel. Command, 1964-67, 73-74, NSF, 1968-76, 83-89, City and County of Honolulu, 1977, U.S. Dept. Interior, 1980, 81. Mem. Entomol. Soc. Am. (mem. standing com. on systematics resources 1983-87), Am. Mosquito Control Assn., Pacific Coast Entomol. Soc., Soc. Systematic Zoology, Hawaiian Entomol. Soc. (pres. 1974, chmn. coms. 1966-85, editor procs. 1966), Hawaiian Acad. (councillor 1976-78), Entomol. Soc. Wash., Fairbanks C. of C. (adv. bd. Conv. Visitors Bur. 1989), Alaska Visitors Assn. (pres. Fairbanks chpt. 1991), Sigma Xi (pres. San Joaquin chpt. 1994-95, mem. bd. cultural connections 1994-95). Office: Sun Cities Art Mus 17425 N 115th St Sun City AZ 85373-2501

STEFFEL, SUSAN ELIZABETH, educator English; b. Muskegon, Mich., Feb. 9, 1951; d. Sherman Burgess and Geraldine (Westerman) Bos; m. Andrew John Steffel, July 12, 1975. BA, Hope Coll., 1973; MA in English, Mich. State U., 1978, PhD in English, 1993. Tchr. secondary English Maple Valley Schs., Vermontville, Mich., 1973-91; asst. prof. English Ctrl. Mich. U., Mt. Pleasant, 1991—; supr. secondary student tchrs. dept. English Ctrl. Mich. U., 1991—, vice-chair profl. educators, 1994-95, chair profl. educators coun., 1995—. Co-author: High School English: A Process for Curriculum Development, 1985, 20th Century Children's Authors, 1994. Recipient Excellence in End. award Lansing Regional C. of C., 1985, 86, 88, 89, 90, Excellence in Teaching award Ctrl. Mich. U., 1996. Mem. ASCD, AAUW, Am. Assn. Colls. for Tchr. Edn., Am. Ednl. Rsch. Assn., Nat. Coun. Tchrs. English (guest reviewer 1993—), Mich. Coun. Tchrs. English (mem. steering com. 1985—, asst. editor jour. 1993—), Assembly Lit. for Adolescents, Conf. English Edn., Golden Key Honor Soc. (hon.), Phi Kappa Phi, Phi Delta Kappa (sec. 1995—). Avocations: reading, gardening, pets, needlework. Office: Ctrl Mich U 242 Anspach Hall Mount Pleasant MI 48859

STEFFEN, CHRISTOPHER J., bank executive; b. 1942. BA, U. Mich., 1964; MBA, Wayne State U., 1967. With Ford Motor Co., 1967-74, Unarco, Price Waterhouse; cont. IC Indsl. Corp., 1974-80; v.p., contr. Chrysler Corp., 1981-88; CFO, exec. v.p., chief adminstrn. officer Honeywell, Inc., 1989-93; CFO Eastman Kodak, 1993; exec. v.p., CFO, vice Chmn. Citicorp, N.Y.C., 1993—. Office: Citicorp 153 E 53rd St 23rd Fl New York NY 10043*

STEFFEN, LLOYD HOWARD, minister, religion educator; b. Racine, Wis., Nov. 27, 1951; s. Howard C. and Ruth L. (Rode) S.; m. Emmajane S. Finney, Feb. 14, 1981; children: Nathan, Samuel, William. BA, New Coll., 1973; MA, Andover Newton Theol. Sch., 1978; MDiv, Yale U., 1978; PhD, Brown U., 1984. Ordained to ministry United Ch. of Christ, 1983. Chaplain Northland Coll., Ashland, Wis., 1983—, assoc. prof., 1982-90; assoc. prof. Lehigh U., Bethlehem, Pa., 1990—, chaplain, 1990—; mem. theol. com. Wis. Conf. United Ch. of Christ, Madison, 1985-87, mem. div. ch. and ministry NW assn. Wis. Conf., Eau Claire, 1987-90. Author: Self-Deception and the Common Life, 1986, Life/Choice: The Theory of Just Abortion, 1994, Abortion: A Reader, 1996; contbr. articles to profl. jours. Town supr. Town of La Pointe, Wis., 1984-87. Recipient NEH Inst. award Harvard U., 1988, East-West Ctr., 1995; Univ. fellow Brown U., 1982; faculty devel. grantee Northland Coll., 1986, 90, Lehigh U., 1994. Mem. Soc. Christian Ethics, Am. Acad. Religion, Assocs. for Religion and Intellectual Life, Assn. for Coordination of Univ. Religious Affairs. Home: 224 W Packer Ave Bethlehem PA 18015-1518 Office: Lehigh U Johnson Hall # 36 Bethlehem PA 18015

STEFFEN, PAMELA BRAY, secondary school educator; b. Bessemer, Ala., Mar. 9, 1944; d. James Ernest and Margaret Virginia (Parsons) Bray; m. Ted N. Steffen, June 17, 1972; children: Elizabeth, Thor. BA, U. Louisville, 1966; MA, Spalding U., 1975. Cert. tchr., gifted tchr., Ky. Tchr. English and German Louisville (Ky.) Pub. Schs., 1967-73; tchr. English to fgn. students Internat. Ctr., U. Louisville, 1970-78; bookkeeper T.N. Steffen PSC, Louisville, 1978-85; tchr. of adults Jefferson County Pub. Schs., Louisville, 1985-87, tchr. English and German, 1987—; network participant, bd. dirs. Foxfire, Louisville, 1990—; spokesperson Coalition Essential Schs., Providence, 1990—, Ctr. for LEadership in Sch. Reform, Louisville, 1990—; group leader AAUW, Louisville, 1983-88; presenter seminars; 94 AATG summer Austrian Inst. Graz; participant Austrian Landeskunde Internat., 1994. Bd. dirs. Jefferson County Med. Soc. Aux., Louisville, 1984-88, Highland Community Ministries, Louisville, 1980-87, Highland Ct. Apts. for Elderly, Louisville, 1984-87; nat. v.p. Deafness Rsch. Found. Aux., 1984-88; mem. vestry and rector search com. St. Andrew's Episcopal Ch., Louisville, 1985-88; active Louisville Fund for Arts campaign, 1980-93; Louisville Orch. Assn. fundraiser. Fulbright fellow Goethe Inst., Munich, 1969; grantee Ky. Arts Coun., 1991-92, artist-in-residence, 1992—; grantee Ky. Humanities Coun. CES, 1993, fall forum presenter; named to Ky.'s Commonwealth Inst. Tchrs. and Vis. Tchrs. Inst.; selected for Landeskunde in Österreich, 1994; sumer study scholar Freiberg, Germany. Mem. ASCD, Nat. Coun. Tchrs. English, Coalition Essential Sch., Nat. Coun. Tchrs. English, Greater Louisville Coun. Tchrs. English, Am. Assn. Tchrs. German. Avocations: swimming, travel, beagling, writing, reading. Home: 2404 Park Boundary Rd Louisville KY 40205-1620 Office: Fairdale High Sch 1001 Fairdale Rd Fairdale KY 40118-9731

STEFFENS, DONNA IRENE, gifted and talented education coordinator; b. Akron, Ohio, July 23, 1945; d. Harry Lee and Hazel Irene (Jay) Dye; m. Donald William Steffens, Dec. 18, 1971; children: Buddy Burgy, Jyl, Scott. BS in Edn., U. Akron, 1968, MS in Ednl. Adminstrn., 1972, postgrad., 1974. Cert. tchr., prin., supr./coord./dir. instrn., Wis. Tchr. elem. Copley (Ohio) Pub. Schs., 1966-74; inservice cons. Summit County Svcs., Akron, Ohio, 1973; tchr. Title 1 Cedarbur (Wis.) Pub. Schs., 1975, middle sch. tchr., 1988-90, dist. coord. gifted programming, 1990—; pvt. tutor Columbia, Md., 1978; day care operator Ellicott City, Md., 1978-79; instr. Cardinal Stritch Coll. of Edn., 1995 (curriculum coun. for dist., 1993-95, staff devel. com., 1993-95, assessment com., 1993-95); Christian edn. coord. Alliance Bible Ch., Cedarburg; adv. coun. chair Gifted Program, Cedarburg, 1988-92; enrichment program adv. com. U. Washington County. Mem. Libr. Bd., 1991, Cedarburg Cmty. Scholarship Bd., 1991, Jaycettes, 1979-81; bd. dirs. Workforce 2010, WATG; chair Parents Supporting Parents; mem. bldg. and scholarship coms. Alliance Bible Ch. Recipient Meritorious Svc. award Wis. Assn. Edn. Gifted and Talented, 1991, Jennings grant Copley Pub. Schs. Mem. ASCD, Wis. Coun. Gifted and Talented, Wis. Assn. Edn. Gifted and Talented. Avocations: singing, crafts, travel. Office: Cedarburg Sch Dist W68 N611 Evergreen Blvd Cedarburg WI 53012-1847

STEFFENS, DOROTHY RUTH, political economist; b. N.Y.C., May 5, 1921; d. Saul M. and Pearl Y. (Reiter) Cantor; m. Jerome Steffens, Nov. 19, 1940; children: Heidi Sue, Nina Ellen. BBA, CCNY, 1941; MEd, Temple U., 1961; PhD, Anthony U., 1981. Economist Nat. War Labor Bd., Washington, 1941-44, United Elec. Radio Machine Workers, Phila., 1944-46; instr. group dynamics Temple U., Phila., 1955-57; seminar program dir. Soc. Friends, Washington, 1958-61; tng. dir. Nat. Coun. Negro Women, Washington, 1967-68; edn. cons. Peace Corps, Nigeria, 1969-70; exec. dir. Women's Internat. League for Peace and Freedom, Phila., 1971-77, Fund for Open Info. and Accountability, Inc., 1978-80; conf. dir. Haverford Coll., 1980-84; exec. sec. Nigerian Women's Com., 1968-69; del. African Women's Seminar UN, Accra, Ghana, 1969; mem. Africa panel Am. Friends Svc. Com., 1976-88, mem. internat. divsn. exec. com., 1977-84; resource lectr. Internat. Women's Seminar, Lillehammer, Norway, 1991. Author: The Day after Summer, 1966; editorial bd. The Churchman, 1977—; mem. nat. bd. Gray Panthers, 1989-91; contbr. articles to profl. jours., newspapers, mags. N.Y. C. of C. scholar, N.Y. State Regents scholar CCNY, 1941. Quaker. *Women, minorities and the economically disadvantaged have the wisdom and the capacity to bring about a world of peace and social justice and to do it non-violently.*

STEFFENS, JOHN LAUNDON, brokerage house executive; b. Cleve., July 7, 1941; m. Louise Cullen, Nov. 25, 1967; children: Drew, Julie, Wesley. B in Econs., Dartmouth Coll., 1963. Various positions Merrill Lynch, 1963—, exec. v.p. Pvt. Client Group, 1990—. Office: Merrill Lynch & Co Inc World Fin Ctr N Tower 250 Vesey St New York NY 10281-1012*

STEFFER, ROBERT WESLEY, clergyman; b. Spokane, Wash., June 24, 1934; arrived in Can., 1987; s. Harold Wesley and Kathryne (Trumble) S.; m. Diane De'Moisey, Aug. 19, 1960; children: Erika Kirsten, Beauregard Gregory Robert. BA, Whitworth Coll., 1956; BD, Lexington Theol. Sem., 1959; MA, Ind. U., 1966, PhD, 1967. Ordained to ministry Christian Ch. (Disciples of Christ), 1959. Civilian dir. religious edn. U.S. Army Armor Ctr., Ft. Knox, Ky., 1960-64; assoc. min. Christian Ch. (Disciples of Christ), Oklahoma City, 1967-71; prof. Phillips U., Enid, Okla., 1971-76; fraternal worker div. overseas ministries Christian Ch. (Disciples of Christ), Barrow-in-Furness, Cumbria, Eng., 1976-79; Lilly vis. prof. religious edn. Christian Theol. Sem., Indpls., 1979-81; dir. edn. for mission div. homeland ministries Christian Ch. (Disciples of Christ), Indpls., 1981-87; exec. regional min. Christian Ch. (Disciples of Christ) in Can., Guelph, Ont., 1987—; sec. Coll. Chs. of Christ in Can., Guelph, 1987—. Contbr. articles to religious publs. and ency. Col. USAR, 1964—. Lilly Found. fellow in adult edn. Ind. U., 1964-66. Mem. Disciples of Christ Hist. Soc. (life, trustee 1990-94), Religious Edn. Assn. (bd. dirs. 1994—), Conf. Regional Mins. and Moderators (2nd v.p.), Ch. Fin. Coun. (bd. dirs. 1995—, exec. com. 1995). Democrat. Avocations: gardening, reading, travel, music. Home: RPO Park Mall, PO Box 30013 2 Quebec St, Guelph, ON Canada N1H 8J5 Office: All-Can Com Christian Ch, PO Box 64, Guelph, ON Canada N1H 6J6

STEFFES, DON CLARENCE, state senator; b. Olpe, Kans., Jan. 13, 1930; s. William A. and Marie M. (Dwyer) S.; m. Janie L. Steele, Oct. 10, 1953; children: Michael, Steve, David, Andrew, Nancy, Terrence, Jennifer. BS, Kans. State Tchrs. Coll., 1952, MS, 1958. Mgr. Abilene C. of C., Kans., 1955-57; mem. staff Topeka C. of C., 1957-60; mgr. McPherson C. of C., Kans., 1960-65; exec. v.p. Kans. Devel. Credit Corp., Topeka, 1965-68, McPherson Bank & Trust, 1968-73; pres., CEO BANK IV McPherson (formely McPherson Bank & Trust), 1973-91; mem. Kans. State Senate, Topeka, 1992—. Mem. Kans. Main St. Adv. Counsel, Topeka, 1978-82; pres., bd. dirs. Mingenback Found., McPherson, Kans., 1970—; vice chmn. Nat. Commn. Agrl. Fin., Washington, 1987-89; v.p. McPherson Indsl. Devel. Co., 1970-75. Named Man of Yr. McPherson Coll., 1989. Mem. Kans. Bankers Assn. (pres. 1985), KC. Roman Catholic. Home: 1008 Turkey Creek Dr Mc Pherson KS 67460-9763

STEFFES, KENT, volleyball player; b. Pacific Palisades, Calif., June 23, 1968. Student, Stanford U.; BA in Econ., UCLA, 1993. Profl. volleyball tour player. Named AVP Rookie of Yr., 1989, Up & Coming Player of Yr., 1988, AVP Most Valuable Player by Volleyball Monthly Mag., 1992. Mem. Assn. Volleyball Profls. (sec., bd. dirs.). First and only AVP mem. to win with 3 different ptnrs. in same yr., 1990; won 8 Miller Lite Opens, 1991; first and only AVP mem. to win 2 Joe Cuervo Gold Crown Series Events with different ptnrs. in same yr., 1991; won Miller Lite Tournament of Champions with Karch Kiraly, 1992, Miller Lite U.S. Championships, 1992, Miller Lite Grand Prix, 1992, with Karch Kiraly, 1993; compiled record 18 AVP Open wins, 1992; tied all-time consecutive open wins, 1992. Office: U S Volleyball Assn 15260 Ventura Blvd Sherman Oaks CA 91403-5307*

STEFFEY, EUGENE PAUL, veterinary medicine educator; b. Reading, Pa., Oct. 27, 1942; s. Paul E. and Mary M. (Balthaser) S.; children: Michele A., Bret E., Michael R., Brian T. Student, Muhlenberg Coll., 1960-63; D in Vet. Medicine, U. Pa., 1967; PhD, U. Calif., Davis, 1973. Diplomate Am. Coll. Vet. Anesthesiologists (pres. 1980). NIH spl. research fellow U. Calif., San Francisco, 1973; asst. prof. U. Calif., Davis, 1974-77, assoc. prof., 1977-80, prof. vet. medicine, 1980—, also chmn. dept. vet. surgery, 1980-93; mem. scientific reviewers Am. Jour. Vet. Research, Schaumburg, Ill., 1984-87. Contbr. numerous articles to profl. jours. Mem. AVMA, Am. Coll. Vet. Anesthesiologists, Am. Physiol. Soc., Am. Soc. Pharmocology Exptl. Therapeutics, Am. Soc. Anesthesiologists, Assn. Vet. Anaesthetists, Calif. Soc. Anesthesiologists, Comparative Respiratory Soc., Internat. Anesthesia Research Soc., Pa. Vet. Med. Assn., Sigma Xi, Phi Zeta. Office: U Calif Dept Surg/Radiol Scis School of Vet Medicine Davis CA 95616

STEFFY, JOHN RICHARD, nautical archaeologist, educator; b. Lancaster, Pa., May 1, 1924; s. Milton Grill and Zoe Minerva (Fry) S.; m. Esther Lucille Koch, Oct. 20, 1951; children: David Alan, Loren Craig. Student, Pa. Area Coll., Lancaster, 1946-47, Milw. Sch. Engring., 1947-49. Ptnr. M.G. Steffy & Sons, Denver, Pa., 1950-72; ship reconstructor Kyrenia Ship Project, Cyprus, 1972-73, Inst. Nautical Archaeology, College Station, Tex., 1973—; from lectr. to prof. anthropology Tex. A&M U., College Station, 1976-88, Sara W and George O. Yamani prof. nautical archaeology, 1989-90, prof. emeritus, 1990—; lectr. on ship constrn. Author: Wooden Shipbuilding and the Interpretation of Shipwrecks, 1994; co-editor: The Athlit Ram, 1991; contbr. chpts. to books and articles to profl. jours. Sec. Denver Borough Authority, Pa., 1962-72. Served with USN, 1942-45. MacArthur Found. fellow, 1985. Mem. Archaeol. Inst. Am., Soc. Nautical Research, N.Am. Soc. Oceanic History. Republican. Methodist. Office: Tex A&M U Inst Nautical Archaeology College Station TX 77843

STEG, LEO, research and development executive; b. Vienna, Austria, Mar. 30, 1922; came to U.S., 1941, naturalized, 1946; s. Jacob and Clara (Gellert) S.; m. Doreen Ethel Ray, June 12, 1947; children: Paula Jamie, Ellen Leslie, Audrey Leigh. B.S., City Coll. N.Y., 1947; M.S., U. Mo., 1948; Ph.D., Cornell U., 1951. Registered profl. engr., Pa. Chief engr. Fed. Design Co., N.Y.C., 1946-47; instr. mech. engring. U. Mo., Columbia, 1947-48; instr. applied mechanics and materials Cornell U., Ithaca, N.Y., 1948-51, asst. prof., 1951-55; systems engr., missile and space div. GE, Phila., 1955-56, mgr. space sci. lab., 1956-79, chief scientist, 1980-81; sr. v.p. University City Sci. Center, Phila., 1981-82; pres. Steg, Ray & Assocs., Villanova, Pa., 1980—; sci. and pub. policy fellow Brookings Inst., Washington, 1982-84; pres. Technical Applications Internat., Inc., McLean, Va., 1990—; adj. prof. Drexel U.; cons. to space scis. bd. Nat. Acad. Scis., other govt. agencies. Contbr. articles to profl. jours.; editor 2 books. Asso. trustee U. Pa. Named Engr. of Yr. Phila., 1965. Fellow AIAA (editor-in-chief jour. 1963-67), AAAS; mem. Phila. Acad. Scis. (founding), Franklin Inst. Phila. (past mem. bd. mgrs.), Long Beach Island Found. Arts and Scis. (past chmn. bd.), Sigma Xi, Phi Kappa Phi. Clubs: Cosmos, Cornell of N.Y. Home: 1616 Hepburn Dr Villanova PA 19085-2005

STEGEMAN, CHARLES, fine arts educator, lecturer, consultant; b. Ede, Netherlands, June 5, 1924; s. Leendert Gerrit and Christina Anna S.; m. Françoise André, Dec. 9, 1950 (div. July 1981); children: Charles François, Marc Alexandre, Daniel John; m. Marie-Thérèse Zenner, Nov. 9, 1984. Diploma in painting, Akademie van Beeldende Kunst, The Hague, Netherlands, 1945-46, Académie Royale des Beaux-Arts, Brussels, 1946-49, National Hoger Instituut van Schoone Kunsten, Antwerp, Belgium, 1949-50. Instr. U. B.C., Vancouver, 1953-62; tchr. summer sch. U. Calgary, Banff, Alberta, 1953-75; artist-in-residence Art Inst. Chgo., 1962-69; tchr. North Shore Art League, Winnetka, Ill., 1963-69; adj. faculty mem. Roosevelt U., Chgo., 1965-67; assoc. prof. Haverford Coll., Pa., 1969—; prof. Haverford Coll., 1972—; humanitites fellow Med. Coll. Pa., 1981-88, adj. faculty mem. New Sch. Music, 1982-85, Sch. Medicine U. Pa., 1986—. Author: (book) Les Cryptes de la Cathédrale de Chartres, 1993 (review) Bulletin de la Société archéologique d'Eure-et-loir, 1992; co-author: (article in collected work): The Humanities: From a Medical Point of View, 1987. Mem. Assn. Villard de Honnecourt for the Interdisciplinary Study of Medieval Tech., Sci. and Art (co-founder, pres. 1984-90, mem. bd. dirs. 1984-92, 94—), Socièté archèologique d'Eure-et-Loir, Coll. of Physicians (exec. com. sect. arts-medicine 1995—). Office: Haverford Coll 370 Lancaster Ave Haverford PA 19041-1309

STEGEMEIER, RICHARD JOSEPH, oil company executive; b. Alton, Ill., Apr. 1, 1928; s. George Henry and Rose Ann (Smola) S.; m. Marjorie Ann Spess, Feb. 9, 1952; children: Richard Michael, David Scott, Laura Ann, Martha Louise. BS in Petroleum Engring., U. Mo., Rolla, 1950, cert. petroleum engr. (hon.), 1981; MS in Petroleum Engring., Tex. A&M U., 1951; D of Engring. (hon.), U. Mo., Rolla, 1990. Registered profl. engr., Calif. Various nat. and internat. mgmt. positions with Unocal Corp. (formerly Union Oil Co.), L.A., 1951—, pres. sci. and tech. div., 1979-80, sr. v.p. corp. devel., 1980-85, pres., COO, 1985-88, CEO, also chmn. bd. dirs., 1988-94; bd. dirs. First Interstate Bancorp, Found. Health Corp., Halliburton Co., Northrop Corp., Outboard Marine Corp. Patentee in field. Bd. dirs. Calif. Econ. Devel. Corp.; bd. govs. Town Hall of Calif., The Music Ctr. of L.A. County; bd. overseers Exec. Coun. on Fgn. Diplomats, Huntington Libr.; chmn. L.A. World Affairs Coun., 1990-94; pres. World Affairs Coun. of Orange County, 1980-82; chmn. Brea (Calif.) Blue Ribbon Com., 1979-80 ; trustee Com. for Econ. Devel., U. So. Calif., Harvey Mudd Coll., Loyola Marymount U.; mem. adv. bds. Northwestern U. Kellogg Grad. Sch. of Mgmt.; bd. vis. UCLA Anderson Grad. Sch. of Mgmt., U. Mo., Rolla; mem. adv. bd. Calif. State U., Fullerton, adv. coun., Long Beach; bd. dirs. YMCA of L.A., L.A. Philharm. Assn., John Tracy Clinic; chmn. L.A. area coun. Boy Scouts of Am., Calif. C. of C. chmn., 1994; gen. campaign chmn. United Way of Greater L.A., 1990-91; trustee and immediate past pres. Hugh O'Brian Youth Found., 1993-94, L.A. Archidiocese Edn. Found. Recipient Merit award Orange County Engring. Coun., 1980, Outstanding Engr. Merit award Inst. Advancement Engring., 1981, Disting. Achievement medal Tex. A&M U., Hugh O'Brian Youth Found. Albert Schweitzer Leadership award, 1990, Human Rels. award Am. Jewish Com., 1990. Mem. AIChE (Disting. Career award So. Calif. sect. 1989), NAM (bd. dirs.), Nat. Acad. Engring., Am. Petroleum Inst. (bd. dirs.), Soc. Petroleum Engrs. (lectr. 1978), Nat. Petroleum Coun., 25 Yr. Club Petroleum Industry (past pres.), Calif. Bus. Roundtable, Calif. Coun. on Sci. and Tech., Calif. Club. Republican. Roman Catholic. Office: Unocal Corp 376 Valencia Ave Brea CA 92621*

STEGEMOELLER, HARVEY A., clergy member, church administrator. Exec. dir. Evangelical Lutheran Church of America Foundation, Chgo. Office: Evangelical Lutheran Church Am 8765 W Higgins Rd Chicago IL 60631-4101

STEGENGA, PRESTON JAY, international education consultant; b. Grand Rapids, Mich., July 9, 1924; s. Miner and Dureth (Bouma) S.; m. Marcia Jean DeYoung, July 28, 1950; children: James Jay, Susan Jayne. BA, Hope Coll., 1947; MA, Columbia U., 1948; PhD, U. Mich., 1952; LHD (hon.), Northwestern Coll., Iowa, 1989. Instr. history, polit. sci. Berea Coll., Ky., 1948-50; asoc. prof. Berea Coll., 1952-55; assistantship U. Mich., 1950-52; pres. Northwestern Coll., Orange City, Iowa, 1955-66; chief Cornell U. Project, U. Liberia-U.S. AID Program, Monrovia, W. Africa, 1966-68; coordinator internat. program Calif. State U., Sacramento, 1968-71; dir. Calif. State U. (Internat. Center), 1971-88; acting v.p. acad. affairs Calif. State U., 1974-75; spl. asst. to pres. Calif. State U., Sacramento, 1988-92; mem. Calif. State Liaison Com. for Internat. Edn.; ednl. cons. to Pres., Republic of Liberia, 1973-74; cons. internat. programs Am. Assn. State Colls. and Univs., 1975-89; cons. UN Devel. Programme, 1975-88; internat. edn. cons., 1992—; v.p. Sacramento chpt. UN Assn., U.S.A., 1969-71, pres., 1971-73, bd. dirs.; mem. Calif. UN Univ. Adv. Coun., 1976-80, internat. trade com. C. of C., 1984—, chair coll.-U. com., 1995—; pres. Tri-State Coll. Conf., 1963-64; dir. Fulbright project for Chinese scholars, 1985; cons. internat. projects Calif. State Fair, 1990—. Author: Anchor of Hope, 1954; asst. to editor History of Edn. Jour.; contbr. articles to profl. jours. Trustee Western Sem., Mich., Northwestern Coll., Iowa, 1955-66, 91—, New Brunswick Sem., N.J., 1955-66, Global Calif. Coun., 1991-93; trustee, v.p. World Affairs Coun., 1976-77, 85-90, pres., 1990-92, trustee, 1993-98; mem. Task Force for Improving Am. Competence in World Affairs, 1980-89; mem. internat. bd. Los Rios Coll. Found., 1980-85; mem. Am. Coun. for UN U., 1979-85, Interfaith Svc. Bd., 1985-90; bd. dirs. New Zealand-Sacramento Sister City, 1989—. With AUS, 1942-45. Decorated Purple Heart; named hon. chief Kpelle Tribe, West Africa, 1973, hon. commodore Port of Sacramento, 1983; recipient Disting. Svc. award UN Assn., 1971, Republic of Venezuela Edn. award, 1979, Outstanding Svc. award Fed. Republic of Germany, 1985, Disting. Svc. award Calif. State U. Chancellor, 1988, Citation of Achievement, Calif. Sec. of State, 1988, U.S. Congl. Register Recognition Citation, 1988, President's Award, World Affairs Coun., 1992, Gov.'s award Calif. State Fair, 1993, Internat. award Sacramento C. of C., 1993, Disting. Svc. award Assn. Citizens & Friends of Liberia, 1995; Ministry of Edn. scholar Republic of China, 1981; German Acad. Exch. Svc. fellow U. Bonn, 1981; Hon. Legis. Resolutions, Calif. State Senate and Assembly, 1988. Mem. Assn. Iowa Coll. and Univ. Pres. (v.p. 1965-66), NEA, Calif. State Univ. Student Personnel Assn., Am. Acad. Polit. and Social Sci., Assn. for Advancement of Dutch-Am. Studies, Phi Delta Kappa, Phi Kappa Phi, Phi Beta Delta. Mem. Reformed Ch. Am. Home: 545 Mills Rd Sacramento CA 95864-4911

STEGER, CHARLES WILLIAM, university administrator; b. Richmond, Va., June 16, 1947; s. Charles William and Virginia Belle (Garrett) S.; m. Janet Grey Baird, Sept. 13, 1969; children: Christopher B., David C. BArch, Va. Poly. Inst. & State U., 1970, MArch, 1971, PhD, 1978. Registered architect, Va. Project planner, architect Wiley & Wilson Inc., Lynchburg, Va., 1971-72, mgr. urban planning dept., 1973-74; dir. Environ. Design Consortium Inc., Blacksburg, Va., 1974-85; inst. grad. urban design program Coll. Architecture and Urban Studies , Va. Poly. Inst. and State U., Blacksburg, 1974-76, chmn. grad. urban design program, 1976-81; dean Coll. Architecture and Urban Studies, Va. Poly. Inst. and State U., Blacksburg, 1981-93; acting v.p. for pub. svc. Va. Poly. Inst. and State U., Blacksburg, 1990-93, v.p. for devel. and univ. rels., 1993—; bd. dirs. Va. Found. Architecture, Richmond. Contbr. articles to jours. in field. Bd. dirs. Va. Chamber Music Acad., Blacksburg, 1989—, Hollins Coll., Roanoke, Va., 1987—, Boswil (Switzerland) Found., 1986—, Ctr. in the Square, Roanoke, 1993—; v.p. Va. Tech. Found., Inc., 1993—; adv. coun. Va. Ctr. on Rural Devel., 1992—; commr. Govs. Commn. on Population Growth and Devel., Richmond, 1989-94. Fellow AIA (bd. dirs. ACSA Health Facilities Rsch. Program, Washington 1989—, ACSA Coun. on Arch. Rsch., 1987—); mem. Am. Planning Assn., Am. Inst. Cert. Planners, Commonwealth Club (Richmond, Va.), Shenandoah Club (Roanoke, Va.). Avocations: cattle farming, golf, canoeing. Office: Va Poly Inst and State U VP Devel Univ Rels 315 Burruss Hall Blacksburg VA 24061

STEGER, EVAN EVANS, III, lawyer; b. Indpls., Oct. 24, 1937; s. Charles Franklin and Alice (Hill) S.; m. Suzy Gillespie, July 18, 1964; children—Cynthia Anne, Emily McKee. A.B., Wabash Coll., 1959; J.D., Ind. U., 1962. Bar: Ind. 1962, U.S. Dist. Ct. (so. dist.) Ind. 1962, U.S. Ct. Appeals (7th cir.) 1972, U.S. Tax Ct. 1982, U.S. Supreme Ct. 1982. Assoc. Ice, Miller, Donadio and Ryan, and predecessor firm Ross, McCord, Ice and Miller, Indpls., 1962-69, ptnr., 1970-96, mng. ptnr., 1996— . Fellow Am. Coll. Trial Lawyers; mem. ABA, Ind. Bar Assn., Indpls. Bar Assn., Internat. Assn. Def. Counsel. Democrat. Presbyn. Office: Ice Miller Donadio & Ryan Box 82001 1 American Sq Indianapolis IN 46282

STEGER, JOSEPH A., university president. Formerly sr. v.p. and provost U. Cin., pres., 1984—. Office: U Cin PO Box 210063 Cincinnati OH 45221-0063

STEGER, WILLIAM MERRITT, federal judge; b. Dallas, Aug. 22, 1920; s. Merritt and Lottie (Reese) S.; m. Ann Hollandsworth, Feb. 14, 1948; 1 son, Merritt Reed (dec.). Student, Baylor U., 1938-41; LL.B., So. Meth. U., 1950. Bar: Tex. 1951. Pvt. practice Longview, 1951-53; apptd. U.S. dist. atty. Eastern Dist. Tex., 1953-59; mem. firm Wilson, Miller, Spivey & Steger, Tyler, Tex., 1959-70; U.S. dist. judge Ea. Dist. Tex. Tyler, 1970—. Republican candidate for gov. of Tex., 1960; for U.S. Ho. of Reps., 1962; mem. Tex. State Republican Exec. Com., 1966-69; chmn. Tex. State Republican Party, 1969-70. Pilot with ranks 2d lt. to capt. USAAF, 1942-47. Mem. ABA, State Bar Tex., Masons (32 degree, Shriner). Home: 801 Meadowcreek Dr Tyler TX 75703-3524 Office: US Courthouse PO Box 1109 Tyler TX 75710-1109

STEGMAN, MICHAEL ALLEN, city and regional planning educator; b. Bklyn., Oct. 12, 1940; s. Robert and Natalie (Ohrbach) S.; m. Nancy Weiss, Aug. 12, 1962; children—Laurie Michelle, Karen Jill. B.A. in Polit. Sci., Bklyn. Coll., 1962; M. City Planning, U. Pa., 1964, Ph.D. in City Planning, 1966. Asst. to assoc. prof. U. N.C., Chapel Hill, 1966-74; prof. city and regional planning U. N.C., 1974—, dept. chmn., 1983—; dep. asst. sec. research HUD, Washington, 1979-81. Author: Housing Investment in the Inner City, 1972, Dynamics of Rental Housing in New York City, 1982, Housing in New York: Study of a City, 1985, Cases in Housing Finance and Public Policy; editor: Housing and Economics: The American Dilemma, 1971. Chmn. Mayor's Task Force on Human Services, Chapel Hill, N.C., 1982; mem. Housing Policy Com. Legis. Task Force on Housing, 1981-83; mem. Govs. Commn. on Housing Options for Older Adults, N.C., 1981; chmn. Chapel Hill Housing Authority, 1973-75, Chapel Hill Redevelopment Authority, 1971-73. Mem. Am. Planning Assn., Nat. Housing and Redevel. Ofcls., Nat. Low Income Housing Coalition. Office: U N C Dept City & Regional Planning New East Bldg Chapel Hill NC 27514 Office: Dept Housing & Urban Devel Policy Devel & Rsch 451 7th St SW Washington DC 20410

STEGMAYER, JOSEPH HENRY, housing industry executive; b. Teaneck, N.J., Jan. 4, 1951; s. Arthur Harry and Alicia (Ward) S.; m. Delene Russell. BS in Fin., U. Louisville, 1973. Spl. projects Worthington Industries Inc., Columbus, Ohio, 1973-75, dir. investor rels., 1975-77, dir. corp. rels., 1977-80, v.p. corp. devel., 1980-82, v.p., CFO, 1982-93, treas., 1983-93, also bd. dirs.; pres. Clayton Homes, Inc., Knoxville, Tenn., 1993—, also bd. dirs.; bd. dirs. Cardinal Funds Inc., Columbus. Editor: We've Only Scratched the Surface, 1981. Chmn. YMCA, Columbus, 1981-83; pres. Columbus Zoo, 1987-90, chmn., 1990-93; bd. dirs. Muskingum Coll., 1984-93, Knoxville Zoo, Found. of Diocese of Columbus, United Way Knoxville; fin. chmn. Ronald McDonald House, Columbus. Named Citizen of Yr., Columbus Jaycees, 1984; recipient Outstanding Achievement in Fin. award Phi Beta Kappa, 1984. Mem. Fin. Execs. Inst., Knoxville C. of C. (bd. dirs.), Athletic Club, U. Tenn. Faculty Club. Roman Catholic. Avocations: scuba diving, travel, investing. Office: Clayton Homes Inc PO Box 15169 Knoxville TN 37901-5169

STEHLE, EDWARD RAYMOND, secondary education educator, school system administrator; b. Pitts., May 30, 1942; s. Edward August and Mary Josephine (Veverka) S.; m. Alberta McConnell; 1 child, Christian Dollison. BA, U. Pitts., 1964; MA, Columbia U., 1966, doctoral student, 1966-68. Instr. European history C.W. Post Coll., Long Island U., Greenville, N.Y., 1967-68, Middlebury (Vt.) Coll., 1968-69; history master The Lawrenceville Sch., Lawrenceville, N.J., 1969—, dir. day students, 1978-83, asst. dir. coll. counseling, 1983-88, chmn. history dept., 1988-94; asst. dir. The N.J. Scholars Program, Lawrenceville, 1981; vis. scholar Cambridge U., Lawrenceville, Eng., 1996, Cambridge (Eng.) U., 1996; cons. U. Del. Sea Grant Coll., Newark, 1981-82; cons. on history of migrations Statue of Liberty-Ellis Island Found., N.Y.C., 1985-88; mem. selection com. Morris County (N.J.) Summer Opportunities for Tchrs. Program, Morristown, 1985-86; bd. mem. N.J. Scholars Program, Lawrenceville, 1988—; bd. trustees Craftsbury Chamber Players, Greensboro, Vt., 1985-89; chmn. Bd. N.J. Scholar Program, 1988—. Co-author: A Guide to Programming in Basic Plus, 1975; contbr. Harper's Encyclopedia of the Modern World, 1972. Vice pres. Assoc. Mems., Ch. of Christ, Greensboro, 1974-76, pres., 1976-78. Mem. Am. Hist. Assn., Nassau Club (Princeton, N.J.), Mountainview Country Club (Greensboro, Vt.). Democrat. Episcopalian. Avocation: painting. Home: 2810 Main St Lawrenceville NJ 08648-1017 Office: The Lawrenceville Sch Main St Lawrenceville NJ 08620-2310

STEHLE, JOYCE MARIE, perinatal clinical nurse specialist; b. Islip, N.Y., Nov. 8, 1937; d. John Arthur and Mary Anna (Szuster) Engelbach; m. Joseph Michael Stehle, Sept. 27, 1958; children: Katherine Stehle Sarles, Elizabeth Stehle O'Neil, Paul, John. RN, Mt. Sinai Sch. Nursing, 1958; BSN, SUNY, Stony Brook, 1988; MSN, Wayne State U., 1992. Cert. ob/gyn. nurse practitioner. Staff nurse oper. rm. Mt. Sinai Hosp., N.Y.C., 1958-59; staff nurse labor and delivery Blvd. Hosp., L.I., N.Y., 1959-62; instr. practical nurse program Bd. of Coop. Ednl. Svcs. II Adult Edn., Bellport, N.Y., 1978-81; staff nurse L&D Southside Hosp., Bayshore, N.Y., 1963-79; tchg. and rsch. nurse II U. Hosp., Stony Brook, 1979-88; clin. nurse specialist Hurley Med. Ctr., Flint, Mich., 1988-94, Arnot Ogden Med. Ctr., Elmira, N.Y., 1995—; parent educator Perinatal Classes for Expectant Parents, Sayville, N.Y., 1985-88; presenter in field. Bd. dirs. H-PAC March of Dimes, Flint, 1993-94. Recipient Elizabeth Friedman award for patient care Mt. Sinai Sch. Nursing, 1958, Cert. of Achievement, Coun. Nursing, U. Hosp., Stony Brook, 1987. Fellow Nightingale Soc.; mem. Mich. Nurses Assn. (bd. dirs. 1988-94, legis. liaison 1992-94), Mich. Nurses Diagnosis Assn. (bd. dirs., secondary reviewer 1991-94), Assn. Women's Health, Obstetrics and Neonatal Nursing, ASPO/Lamase, Pre & Perinatal Psychology Assn. N.Am. Jacobs Inst. Women's Health, Sigma Theta Tau. Avocations: gardening-herbs, crafts-needlepoint, traveling-historic sites. Office: Arnot Ogden 600 Roe Ave Elmira NY 14890

STEHLI, FRANCIS GREENOUGH, geologist, educator; b. Upper Montclair, N.J., Oct. 16, 1924; s. Edgar and Emily (Greenough) S.; m. Irene Comfort, June 19, 1948; children: Anne, Robert, John, Edgar. B.S., St. Lawrence U., 1949, M.S., 1950; Ph.D., Columbia U., 1953. Asst. prof. invertebrate paleontology Calif. Inst. Tech., 1953-56; tech. group supr. research dept. Am. Petroleum Corp., 1956-60; prof. geology, chmn. dept. Case Western Res. U., 1960-73, Samuel St. John prof. earth scis., 1973-80, acting dean sci., 1975, acting dean sci. and engring., 1976, dean sci. and engring., 1977-80; dean grad. studies and research U. Fla., Gainesville, 1980-82; dean Coll. Geoscis. U. Okla., Norman, 1982-86; chmn. sci. adv. com. DOSECC, Inc., 1986—; rsch. assoc. Archeol. Rsch. Team, 1993—; geol. cons., 1960—. Author articles in field. Served with USNR, 1943-46. Fellow Geol. Soc. Am., AAAS; mem. Geochem. Soc., Paleontol. Soc. (pres.), Am. Soc. Engring. Edn., No. Ohio Geol. Soc. Home: 7711 SW 103rd Ave Gainesville FL 32608-6214 Office: DOSECC Sci Adv Com 7711 SW 103rd Ave Gainesville FL 32608-6214 also: Archeol Rsch Team 1519 NW 25 Terrace Gainesville FL 32605

STEHMAN, FREDERICK BATES, gynecologic oncologist, educator; b. Washington, July 20, 1946; s. Vernon Andrew and Elizabeth Coats (Bates) S.; m. Helen Sellinger, July 17, 1971; children—Christine Renee, Eileen Patricia, Andrea Kathleen, Lara Michelle. A.B., U. Mich., 1968, M.D., 1972. Diplomate Am. Bd. Ob-gyn. Resident in ob-gyn. U. Kans. Med. Ctr., Kansas City, 1972-75, resident in surgery, 1975-77; fellow in gynecol. oncology UCLA, 1977-79; asst. prof., attending staff Ind. U. Med. Ctr., Indpls., 1979-83, assoc. prof., 1983-87, prof., 1987—, chief gynecol. oncology, 1984-88, interim chmn., 1992-94, chair 1994—; chief ob-gyn service Wishard Meml. Hosp., Indpls., 1987-95. Author: (with B.J. Masterson and R.P. Carter) Gynecologic Oncology for Medical Students, 1975; also articles. Nat. Cancer Inst. grantee, 1981-89. Fellow Am. Coll. Obstetricians and Gynecologists, ACS (chpt. dir. 1984-92); mem. AMA, Am. Soc. Clin. Oncology, Am. Cancer Soc., Am. Gynecology and Obstetrics Soc., Ind. Med. Assn., Assn. Profs. Gynecology and Obstetrics, Central Assn. Obstetricians and Gynecologists, Gynecol. Oncology Group, K.E. Krantz Soc., Marion County Med. Soc., Soc. Gynecol. Oncologists, Western Assn. Gynecol. Oncologists, Phi Chi. Office: Ind U Med Ctr 550 N University Blvd 2440 UH Indianapolis IN 46202-5274

STEIB, JAMES TERRY, bishop; b. May 17, 1940. Ordained priest Roman Cath. Ch., 1967. Titular bishop Fallaba, 1983; aux. bishop St. Louis, 1983; consecrated bishop, 1984; bishop Diocese of Mempis, 1993—. Address: Diocese of Memphis PO Box 41679 Memphis TN 38174-1679

STEIG, WILLIAM, author, artist; b. N.Y.C., Nov. 14, 1907; s. Joseph and Laura (Ebel) S.; m. Elizabeth Mead, Jan. 2, 1936 (div.); children: Lucy, Jeremy; m. Kari Homestead, 1950 (div. 1963); 1 child, Margit Laura; m. Stephanie Healey, Dec. 12, 1964 (div. Dec. 1966); m. Jeanne Doron, 1969. Ed., Coll. City N.Y., 1923-25, NAD, 1925-29. Cartoonist New Yorker, N.Y.C., 1930—; author, illustrator for children's books, 1968—. Artist drawings in mags., water color collections, Bklyn. Mus.; one-man show wood sculpture Downtown Gallery, N.Y.C., 1939; exhibited drawsing and sculpture Smith Coll., 1940; author: Man About Town, 1932, About People: A Book of Symbolic Drawings, 1939, The Lonely Ones, a book of drawings, 1942, All Embarrassed, 1944, Small Fry, 1944, Persistent Faces, 1945, Till Death Do Us Part, 1947, The Agony in the Kindergarten, 1950, The Rejected Lovers, 1951, The Steig Album: Seven Complete Books, 1953, Dreams of Glory, 1953, Roland, the Minstrel Pig, 1968, CDB, 1968, Sylvester and the Magic Pebble, 1969 (Caldecott medal 1970), The Bad Island, 1969, An Eye for Elephants, 1970, The Bad Speller, 1970, Amos and Boris, 1971, Male/Female, 1971, Dominic, 1972 (Christopher award 1973, Priz de la Fondation de France 1983), The Real Thief, 1973 (Best Children's Book prize, Italy 1990), Farmer Palmer's Wagon Ride, 1974, Abel's Island, 1976 (Newbery Honor book), The Amazing Bone, 1976 (Caldecott Honor book), Caleb and Kate, 1977, Tiffky Doofky, 1978, Drawings, 1979, Gorky Rises, 1980, Doctor de Soto, 1982 (Am. Book award 1983), Yellow & Pink, 1984, Ruminations, 1984, Solomon and the Rusty Nail, 1984, Brave Irene, 1986, CDC?, 1986, Zabajaba Jungle, 1987, Spinky Sulks, 1988, Doctor De Soto Goes to Africa, 1992, (book of drawings) Strutters and Fretters, 1992; executed Wood sculpture R.I. Mus., Providence, Smith Coll. Mus., Northampton, Mass.; pub. Zabajaba Jungle, 1987, Shrek, 1990, Our Miserable Life, 1990. Recipient William Allen White award, 1975; Irma Simonton Black award, 1981. Home: 301 Berkeley St # 4 Boston MA 02116-2002

STEIGBIGEL, ROY THEODORE, infectious disease physician and scientist, educator; b. Bklyn., Nov. 23, 1941; s. Samuel and Lillian I. (Parker) S.; m. Julia Ann Enterline, June 10, 1967 (div. 1983); children: Keith D., Glenn N.; m. Sidonie Ann Morrison, Oct. 15, 1985; 1 child, Andrew M. BA, Carleton Coll., 1962; MD, U. Rochester, 1966. Diplomate Am. Bd. Internal Medicine, Am. Bd. Infectious Disease. Resident U. Rochester, N.Y., 1966-68; resident Stanford U., Palo Alto, Calif., 1970-71, fellow, 1971-73; from asst. to assoc. prof. U. Rochester, N.Y., 1973-83; prof. SUNY, Stony Brook, 1983—; mem. adv. bd. infectious disease U.S. Pharmacopea, Rockville, Md., 1980—; mem. adv. panels NIH, Bethesda, Md., 1985-87. Contbr. over 10 chpts. to books and over 95 articles to profl. jours. Served in USPHS, 1968-70. Fellow NIH, 1971-73, grantee, 1985—. Fellow ACP, Infectious Disease Soc. Am. Office: SUNY School of Medicine HSC-T-15-080 Stony Brook NY 11794-8153

STEIGER, GRETCHEN HELENE, marine mammalogist, research biologist; b. Williamsport, Pa., May 7, 1960; d. Robert Folk and Helene (Moltz) S.; m. John Calambokidis, July 29, 1989; 1 child, Alexei Steiger Calambokidis. BS in Zoology, U. N.C., 1982. Rsch. biologist Cascadia Rsch. Collective, Olympia, Wash., 1982—, also bd. dirs.; pres. Cascadia Rsch., 1988—; whale census technician, Barrow, Alaska, 1988; rsch. assoc. U. Alaska, Fairbanks, 1991; presenter in field. Author (with others) numerous govt. reports and pubs.; contbr. articles to profl. jours. Instr. Feminists Self-def. Tng., Olympia, 1984-92. Mem. Soc. Northwestern Vertebrate Biology, Soc. Marine Mammalogy (charter), Wildlife Soc. (Wash. chpt.). Office: Cascadia Research Collective 218 1/2 4th Ave W Olympia WA 98501-1004

STEIGER, JANET DEMPSEY, government official; b. Oshkosh, Wis., June 10, 1939; 1 child, William Raymond. BA, Lawrence Coll., 1961; postgrad., U. Reading, Eng., 1961-62, U. Wis., 1962-63; LLD (hon.), Lawrence U., 1992. Legis. aide Office of Gov., Wis., 1965; v.p. The Work Place, Inc., 1975-80; commr. Postal Rate Commn., Washington, 1980-89, acting chmn., 1981-82, chmn., 1982-89; commr. FTC, Washington, 1989—; U.S. del. OECD, Paris, 1989—. Author: Law Enforcement and Juvenile Justice in Wisconsin, 1965; co-author: To Light One Candle, a Handbook on Organizing, Funding and Maintaining Public Service Projects, 1978, 2d edit., 1980. Chmn. Commn. on Vets. Edn. Policy, 1987-90. Woodrow Wilson scholar; Fulbright scholar, 1961. Mem. Phi Beta Kappa. Office: FTC Office of Chmn 6th & Pennsylvania Ave NW Washington DC 20580-0002*

STEIGER, PAUL ERNEST, newspaper editor, journalist; b. N.Y.C., Aug. 15, 1942; s. Ernest and Mary Agnes (Walsh) S.; children: Erika Maren, Laura Arlene, Isabelle Amanda, William Ernest. B.A., Yale U., 1964. Staff reporter Wall Street Jour., San Francisco, 1966-68; asst. mng. editor Wall Street Jour., N.Y.C., 1983-85, dep. mng. editor, 1985-92, mng. editor, 1991—, also v.p.; bus. writer Los Angeles Times, 1968-71, econ. corr. Washington bur., 1971-78, bus. editor L.A., 1978-83. Co-author: The 70's Crash, 1970. Recipient G.M. Loeb award UCLA, 1971, 74, 78, John Hancock award, 1971. Office: Wall Street Journal Dow Jones & Co Inc 200 Liberty St New York NY 10281-1003*

STEIGER, ROD, actor; b. Westhampton, N.Y., Apr. 14, 1925; s. Fredrick and Lorraine (Driver) S.; m. Sally Gracie, 1952; m. Claire Bloom, Apr. 15, 1959 (div.); 1 daughter, Anna; m. Sherry Nelson, Apr. 1973 (div. 1979); m. Paula Ellis. Ed. pub. schs., Newark. Life mem. Met. Mus. Art, N.Y.C. Theatrical appearances include Night Music, 1951, Enemy of the People, 1953, Rashomon, 1959; motion picture appearances include On the Waterfront, 1953, Big Knife, 1955, Oklahoma, 1956, Jubal, 1957, Across the Bridge, 1958, Al Capone, 1959, Seven Thieves, 1959, The Mark, 1960, World in My Pocket, 1960, The Tiger Among Us, 1961, Convicts 4, 1961, The Longest Day, 1962, The Time of Indifference, 1962, Hands on the City, 1963, The Pawnbroker, 1964 (Berlin Film Festival award), The Loved One, 1964, Doctor Zhivago, 1966, In the Heat of the Night, 1967 (Golden Globe award, Acad. award for Best Actor), Waterloo, 1971, Happy Birthday, Wanda June, 1971, Duck You Sucker, 1972, Lolly-Madonna, 1973, Lucky Luciano, 1975, Hennessy, 1975, W.C. Fields and Me, 1976, F.I.S.T, 1978, Dirty Hands, 1978, Love and Bullets, 1979, The Amityville Horror, 1979, The Lucky Star, 1980, Lion of the Desert, 1981, Cattle Annie and Little

Britches, 1981, The Chosen, 1982, The Magic Mountain, 1982, Portrait of a Hitman, 1984, The Naked Face, 1985, The January Man, 1988, American Gothic, 1988, Tennessee Waltz, That Summer of White Roses, A Question of Life, Men of Respect, The Ballad of the Sad Cafe, 1991, Guilty As Charged, 1992, The Player, 1992, The Specialist, 1994; TV appearance as Marty, 1953 (Sylvania award), The Movie Maker, 1967, Jesus of Nazareth (miniseries), 1977, Cook and Peary: The Race to the Pole, 1983, Hollywood Wives (miniseries), 1985, Sword of Gideon, 1986, Desperado: Avalanche at Devil's Ridge, 1988, Passion and Paradise, 1989, In the Line of Duty: Manhunt in the Dakotas, 1991, Sinatra, 1992; appeared in play Moby Dick, 1962. Served with USNR, 1942-45. Office: c/o Gold/Marshak & Assoc 3500 W Olive Ave Burbank CA 91505-4628*

STEIGERWALDT, DONNA WOLF, clothing manufacturing company executive; b. Chgo., Apr. 2, 1929; d. Harry Hay and Donna (Currey) Wolf; m. William Steigerwaldt, Dec. 31, 1969; children: Debra, Linda. BA, U. Colo., Colo. Springs, 1950, LHD (hon.), 1987. Ins. broker Conn. Mut. Life Ins. Co., Chgo., 1950-53; vice chmn. Jockey Internat., Inc., Kenosha, Wis., 1978-80, chmn., chief exec. officer, 1980—. Pres. Donna Wolf Steigerwaldt Found., Inc.; mem. Infant Welfare Soc., Evanston Hosp.-Glenbrook Hosp. Corp., N.W. Cmty. Hosp. Aux., Aid to Animals No. Ill., Inc.; vice chmn. Carthage Coll., 1982-92, chmn., 1992—; bd. dirs. Century Club Sarasota Meml. Hosp. Paul Harris fellow, Rotary, 1984. Mem. Am. Apparel Mfrs. Assn., Navy League U.S., Glenview Hist. Soc., Exec. Women Internat. (hon.), Rotary (Paul Harris fellow 1984). Republican. Episcopalian. Clubs: North Shore Country, Plaza, Valley Lo Sports; Meadows Country (Sarasota, Fla.). Office: Jockey Internat Inc 2300 60th St Kenosha WI 53140-3822

STEIGMAN, CARMEN KAY, pathologist; b. Dallas, May 14, 1956; d. Walter Benjamin and Margaret Louise (Patton) S. BS, N.E. La. U., 1977; MD, La. State U., 1983; MPH, St. Louis U., 1994. Diplomate Am. Bd. Pathology; cert. anatomic, clin. and pediatric pathology. Pathology resident Fairfax Hosp., Falls Church, Va., 1983-87; pediatric pathology fellow Children's Hosp. of Phila., 1987-89; pathologist Sparrow Hosp., Lansing, Mich., 1989-90; asst. prof. pathology St. Louis U. Sch. Medicine, 1990—; pathologist Cardinal Glennon Childrens Hosp., 1990—. Fellow Coll. Am. Pathologists; mem. Soc. for Pediatric Pathology, Am. Assn. Clin. Chemistry, Am. Coll. Physician Execs., Am. Pathology Found. Office: Cardinal Glennon Childrens Hosp Dept Pathology 1465 S Grand Blvd Saint Louis MO 63104

STEIL, GEORGE KENNETH, SR., lawyer; b. Darlington, Wis., Dec. 16, 1924; s. George John and Laura (Donahoe) S.; m. Mavis Elaine Andrews, May 24, 1947; children: George Kenneth, John R., MIchelle Steil Bryski, Marcelaine Steil-Zimmermann. Student, Platteville State Tchrs. Coll., 1942-43; JD, U. Wis., Madison, 1950. Bar: Wis. 1950, U.S. Tax Ct. 1971, U.S. Dist. Ct. (western dist.) Wis. 1950. Assoc. J. G. McWilliams, Janesville, 1950-53; ptnr. McWilliams and Steil, Janesville, 1954-60, Brennan, Steil, Ryan, Basting & MacDougall (S.C., and predecessor), Janesville, 1960-72; pres. Brennan, Steil, Basting & MacDougall (S.C., and predecessor), 1972—; lectr. law U. Wis., 1974; bd. dirs. Heritage Mut. Ins. Co., Sheboygan, Wis., Blain Supply Inc., Blain's Farm & Fleet Stores; trustee, bd. dirs. Roman Cath. Diocese of Madison; mem. Wis. Supreme Ct. Bd. Atty. Profl. Responsibility, 1982-87, chmn., 1984-87; chmn. Gov.'s Adv. Coun. Jud. Selection, State of Wis., 1987-92; chmn. Wis. Lottery Bd., 1987-90. Bd. dirs. St. Coletta Sch. for Exceptional Children, Jefferson, Wis., 1972-76, 78-84, 86-89, chmn., 1982-83; bd. regents U. Wis., 1990—, pres., 1992-94; bd. dirs. U. Wis. Hosp. Authority, 1996—, U. Wis. Med. Found., 1996—. Recipient Disting. Svc. award U. Wis. Law Alumni, 1991. Fellow Am. Bar Found. (life), Am. Coll. Trust and Estate Counsel; mem. ABA, Jamesville Area C. of C. (pres. 1970-71), State Bar Wis. (pres. 1977-78), Wis. Bar Found. (bd. dirs. 1976—, Charles L. Goldberg Disting. Svc. award 1990). Roman Catholic. Home: 2818 Cambridge Ct Janesville WI 54545 Office: Brennan Steil Basting & MacDougall 1 E Milwaukee St Janesville WI 53545-3011

STEILEN, JAMES R., lawyer; b. Mitchell, S.D., Apr. 17, 1949; s. Ronald and Gladys M. (Aulner) S.; m. Carol Jane Scoonover, June 6, 1970; children: Matthew, Jennifer, Katherine, Daniel. BA, U. Iowa, 1971; JD, Harvard U., 1974. Bar: Minn. 1974. Shareholder Popham, Haik, Schnobrich & Kaufman Ltd., Mpls., 1974—. Capt. U.S. Army, 1971-76. Mem. Wayzata Country Club. Office: Popham Haik Schnobrich & Kaufman Ltd 3300 Piper Jaffray Tower 222 S 9th St Minneapolis MN 55402-3389

STEIN, A. C., clergy member, church administrator. Dir. of the dept of human resources Evangelical Lutheran Church in Am, Chgo. Office: Evang Luthern Ch Am 8765 W Higgins Rd Chicago IL 60631-4101

STEIN, ARLAND THOMAS, lawyer; b. Pitts., Nov. 19, 1938; s. Thomas Edward and Josephine Cecelia (Kiedaisch) S.; m. Helen Marie Horin, Aug. 14, 1965; children: Thomas Arland, John Andrew, Christian Michael. BS in Engring. Sci., Purdue U., 1961, postgrad., 1960-62; LLB, U. Va., 1965. Bar: Pa. 1965, Ohio 1966, U.S. Patent Office 1967, U.S. Supreme Ct. 1969. Assoc. Blenko, Leonard & Buell, Pitts., 1965-71; ptnr. Yeager, Stein & Wettach, Pitts., 1971-74; Reed Smith Shaw & McClay, Pitts., 1974—. Mem. ABA, Allegheny County Bar Assn., Am. Patent Law Assn., Pitts. Patent Law Assn., Lic. Execs. Soc., Tau Beta Pi, Omicron Delta Kappa (charter, life mem. Purdue chpt.), Rose Ade Found. Republican. Lutheran. Clubs: Masons, K.T., Duquesne Club. Home: 144 Riding Trail Ln Pittsburgh PA 15215 Office: Reed Smith Shaw & McClay Mellon Sq 435 6th Ave Pittsburgh PA 15219*

STEIN, ARNOLD, English educator; b. Brockton, Mass., Apr. 27, 1915; m. Bess Dworsky, June 20, 1942; children: Jonathan, Deborah. A.B., Yale U., 1936; A.M., Harvard U., 1938, Ph.D., 1942. Instr. U. Minn., Mpls., 1940-46; asst. prof. English Ohio State U., Columbus, 1946-48; assoc. prof. U. Wash., Seattle, 1948-53, prof., 1953-71; prof. English Johns Hopkins U., Balt., 1971-74, Sir William Osler prof., 1974-80; prof. U. Ill., Urbana, 1980-85, emeritus prof., 1985—; Fulbright lectr. Tel Aviv U., 1986-87. Author: Answerable Style, 1953, Heroic Knowledge, 1957, John Donne's Lyrics, 1962, George Herbert's Lyrics, 1968, The Art of Presence, 1977, The House of Death, 1987; mem. adv. bd. Poetry Northwest, 1960—; mem. editorial bd. Milton Studies, 1968—; editor: Theodore Roethke, 1965, On Milton's Poetry, 1970; editor: English Literary History, 1971—, sr. editor, 1974-80. Served as pvt. F.A. U.S. Army, 1943-45, ETO. Renaissance issue of ELH (English Lit. History) pub. in honor, 1982; Ford Found. fellow, 1953-54; Guggenheim Found. fellow, 1959-60. Mem. Renaissance Soc. Am., MLA, Milton Soc. Am. (Honored Scholar 1980), Folger Inst. Renaissance Studies (mem. central com. 1973-77).

STEIN, ARTHUR OSCAR, pediatrician; b. Bklyn., Apr. 3, 1932; s. Irving I. and Sadie (Brander) S.; AB, Harvard U., 1953; MD, Tufts U., 1957; postgrad. U. Chgo., 1963-66, San Jose State U., 1995—; m. Judith Lenore Hurwitz, Aug. 27, 1955; children: Susan, Jeffrey, Benjamin. Intern U. Chgo. Hosps., 1957-58, resident, 1958-59; resident N.Y. Hosp.-Cornell U. Med. Center, 1959-61; practice medicine specializing in pediatrics, 1963-95, ret., 1995; instr. pediatrics U. Chgo., 1963-66, asst. prof. pediatrics, 1966-70; mem. Healthguard Med. Group, San Jose, Calif., 1970-72; mem. Permanente Med. Group, San Jose, 1972-95; ret. 1995; asst. chief pediatrics Santa Teresa Med. Center, 1979-87; clin. instr. Santa Clara Valley Med. Center, Stanford U., 1970-72. Served to capt., M.C., AUS, 1961-63. USPHS Postdoctoral fellow, 1963-66. Fellow Am. Acad. Pediatrics. Jewish (v.p. congregation 1969-70, pres. 1972-73), Santa Clara County Med. Assn., Calif. Med. Assn. Clubs: Light and Shadow Camera (pres. 1978-80) (San Jose); Central Coast Counties Camera (v.p. 1980-81, pres. 1981-82), Santa Clara Camera. (pres. 1991). Co-discoverer (with Glyn Dawson) genetic disease Lactosylceramidosis, 1969. Home: 956 Redmond Ave San Jose CA 95120-1831

STEIN, BARRY EDWARD, medical educator. Prof. dept. physiology Med. Coll. Va.-Va. Commonwealth U., Richmond, 1982-94, affil. prof., 1994—; prof., chmn. dept. neurobiology and anatomy Bowman Gray Sch. Medicine-Wake Forest U., Winston-Salem, N.C., 1994—; bd. trustees The Gwendolyn Hardy Williams and Oliver Williams Found., Inc., 1992—; lectr. in field. Co-author: The Merging of the Senses, 1993; contbr. chpts. to books including The Cognotive Neurosciences, 1995, Electrophysiology of Vision, 1991, The Development of Intersensory Perception: Comparative Perspectives, 1994, others; contbr. numerous articles to profl. pubs. including Experimental Neurology, Jour. Experimental Psychology, Vision Rsch., others; mem. editl. bd. Somatosensory and Motor Rsch., Jour. Cognitive Neuroscience, The Behavioral and Brain Sciences. Home: 1825 Georgia Ave Winston Salem NC 27104 Office: Bowman Gray Sch Med Anatomy and Neurobiology Med Ctr Blvd Winston Salem NC 27157

STEIN, BENNETT MUELLER, neurosurgeon; b. N.Y.C., Feb. 2, 1931; s. Walter Charles and Marjorie Clare (Bennett) S.; m. Doreen Holmes, May 28, 1955 (dec. 1984); children: Susan, Marjorie; m. Bonita Soontit, Sept. 19, 1987; 1 child, Bennett Charles. A.B., Dartmouth Coll., 1952; M.D., C.M., McGill U., Montreal, Que., Can., 1955. Diplomate: Am. Bd. Neurol. Surgery, Nat. Bd. Med. Examiners. Rotating intern U.S. Naval Hosp., St. Albans, N.Y., 1955-56; Fulbright scholar Inst. Neurology, Nat. Hosp., London, 1958-59; asst. resident in surgery Presbyn. Hosp., N.Y.C., 1959-60; asst. resident in neurosurgery Presbyn. Hosp., 1960-63, chief resident, 1963-64; spl. fellow neuroanatomy Nat. Inst. Neurol. Diseases and Blindness, 1964-66; asso. in neurol. Surgery Columbia U. Coll. Phys. and Surgeons, 1964-68, mem. faculty, 1968—, Byron Stookey prof. neurol. surgery, 1980—; dir. service neurol. surgery Presbyn. Hosp., 1980—; prof. neurol. surgery, chmn. dept. Tufts-New Eng. Med. Center, Boston, 1971-80; dir. Am. Bd. Neurol. Surgeons, 1988—. Author articles in field; mem. editorial bds. profl. jours. Served as officer M.C. USNR, 1956-58. Fellow A.C.S.; mem. Am. Assn. Anatomists, AMA, Acad. Neurol. Surgeons, Congress Neurol. Surgeons, Am. Assn. Neurol. Surgeons, Am. Acad. Neurol. Surgeons, Soc. Neurol. Surgeons, Cajal Club, Brazilian Neurol. Soc. (corr.), N.Y. State Neurosurg. Soc., New Eng. Neurosurg. Soc., Mass. Med. Soc., Boston Surg. Soc., Boston Soc. Psychiatry and Neurology, Sigma Xi, Alpha Omega Alpha, Alpha Kappa Kappa. Lutheran. Office: Presbyn Hosp Columbia-Presbyn Med Ctr 710 W 168th St New York NY 10032-2603

STEIN, BERNARD, stockbroker; b. N.Y.C., Nov. 24, 1913; s. Abraham and Fannie (Zoob) S.; m. Marion Charlotte Holtsberg, Feb. 24, 1946; children: Robert Frederick, Ellen Frances (Mrs. Howard Lazarus). Student, Sch. Commerce, NYU, 1930-32. Ptnr. firm Ralph E. Samuel & Co., N.Y.C., 1947-70, Neuberger & Berman, Inc., 1970—; sr. v.p., treas., dir. Energy Fund, N.Y.C., 1962-80, pres., 1980-91, dir. emeritus; former vice chmn. Neuberger & Berman Mgmt. Co., N.Y.C. Served with USAAF, 1942-45. Clubs: Quaker Ridge Golf (Scarsdale); Beach Point (Mamaroneck, N.Y.). Home: 8 Split Tree Rd Scarsdale NY 10583-7900 Office: Neuberger & Berman 605 3rd Ave New York NY 10158

STEIN, BERNARD ALVIN, business consultant; b. Winnipeg, Can., June 4, 1923; s. Herman Louis and Rebecca (Harris) S.; m. Dorothy Lock, Jan. 1, 1942; 1 dau., Marilynn Stein Lakein. Vice-pres. food drug div. Giant Food, Inc., Washington, 1951-69; v.p., gen. mgr. Read Drug Stores, Balt., 1969-70; pres. Scotty Stores div. Sav-A-Stop, Jacksonville, Fla., 1970-71; pres., gen. mgr. Liberal Markets, Dayton, Ohio, 1971-72; pres. Pueblo Supermarkets, San Juan, P.R., 1972-74, Hills Supermarkets, Brentwood, N.Y., 1974-75, Allied Supermarkets, Detroit, 1976-78, Chatham Supermarkets, Detroit, 1978-81, Network Assocs., Chgo., 1981-92; bus. cons. Balt., 1992—. Mem. Presdl. Com. for Emergency Food Controls, 1969. Served with USAAF, 1943-45. Decorated Air medal. Home: 43 Stone Pine Ct Baltimore MD 21208 Office: 43 Stone Pine Ct Baltimore MD 21208-9999

STEIN, BOB, lawyer. Degree, U. Minn. Lawyer Minn. Timberwolves; former NFL player; former pres. Minn. Timberwolves; former pres. Target Ctr. Arena, Mpls., 1967-68. Home: Minn Timberwolves Wayzata Blvd Ste 700 Minneapolis MN 55416-1233

STEIN, CAREY M., lawyer; b. Chgo., July 15, 1947; s. Daniel and Shirley (Weinstein) S.; m. Seena R. Silverman, July 8, 1972; children: Allison, Amy. BS, So. Ill. U., 1970; JD, DePaul U., 1974. Bar: Ill. 1974, N.Y. 1988, Pa. 1990, Mo. 1992. Tax examiner IRS, Chgo., 1973-75; atty. Ill. Dept. Revenue, Chgo., 1975-77; asst. corp. counsel Hart, Schaffner & Marx, Chgo., 1977-83; Assoc. gen. counsel, asst. sec. Hartmarx Corp., Chgo., 1983-84, v.p., sec., gen. counsel, 1984—, exec. v.p., 1992, chief adminstrv. officer, 1993; ptnr. Ashman Stein, Chgo.; adv. bd. midwest region Arkwright Mutual Ins. Co., 1993. Mem. exec. com., bd. dirs. Ctr. for Enriched Living, Deerfield, Ill., 1984—, pres. 1990-91; mem. adv. bd. Northwestern U. Corp. Counsel Ctr., Chgo., 1984—; mem. exec. com., bd. dirs. Jewish Edn. Met. Chgo., 1987—, sec.-treas., 1988-89, v.p., 1989-91; mem. bd. dirs. Better Boys Found., 1993. Mem. ABA, Ill. Bar Assn., Chgo. Bar Assn., Am. Soc. Corp. Secs., Am. Apparel Mfrs. Assn. (legal com. 1985—). Am. Arbitration Assn. (adv. com., panel 1988—). Jewish. Office: Ashman & Stein 150 N Wacker Dr Chicago IL 60606*

STEIN, CARI WEISS, producer; b. Bklyn., July 4, 1957; d. Irwin and Beatrice (Siegel) Weiss; m. Irvin Stein, Mar. 25, 1986; children: Ivy Nicole, Blake Garrett. BA in Comm., SUNY, Buffalo, 1978; MA in Counseling Psychology, Loyola Coll., Balt., 1994. Prodr. WNYC-TV, N.Y.C., 1980; audio tape rschr. ABC Network News, N.Y.C., 1979-81; assignment editor Ind. TV News Assn., N.Y.C., 1981; news prodr. WVUE-TV, New Orleans, 1981-83; news prodr. WMAR-TV, Balt., 1983-86, exec. prodr., 1987-90; ind. prodr. Balt., 1990—; exec. prodr. To the Contrary, Md. Pub. TV. Mem. Washington Radio and TV Corr., Internat. Women's Media Found., Am. Women in Radio and TV.

STEIN, CARL, architect; b. N.Y.C., Jan. 27, 1943; s. Richard George and Ethel (Levy) S.; m. Nancy Ellen Jones, May 28, 1965; 1 child, Jesse Lee. BA, Middlebury (Vt.) Coll., 1964; BArch, Cooper Union Coll., N.Y.C., 1968; postgrad., Harvard U., 1966-67. With Marcel Breuer & Assocs., N.Y.C., 1968-71; assoc. Richard G. Stein & Assocs., N.Y.C., 1971—; ptnr. The Stein Partnership, N.Y.C., 1977—; pres., bd. dirs. Westbeth Housing Corp., N.Y.C., 1988—; co-founder Parents and Friends for Children's Survival, chair, 1982-89; prin. investigator Trenton Integrated Community Energy System. Prin. works include New Hdqrs. for Rescue Co. No. 1, N.Y.C., New 41st Precinct, Bronx, N.Y., Walt Whitman Birthplace Vis. Ctr., Huntington Sta., N.Y., Yantai (China) Kai Gang Houses, Ci Hou mixed use high rise, Shanghai, Crest Garden mixed use mid rise, Shanghai, Ctr. for Environ. Rsch. and Conservation Columbia U., Rockland County Courthouse Restoration, New City, N.Y., Cmty. Ch. of the Pelhams, N.Y., PS/IS 73, Bklyn., Bronx Biomed. Rsch. Park, 19th Precinct, N.Y.C., firehouse for Engine Co. 39 N.Y.C. Fire Dept. (Lucy G. Moses award 1992); reconstruction of Ctrl. Park Police Sta., N.Y.C., Shepard Hall, CCNY, (with R. Kinoshita and A. Marshall) Women's Rights Nat. Hist. Pk., Seneca Falls, N.Y., Energy Conscious Architecture (monograph), NW Corner master plan and Modular Units, World of Birds, Bronx Wildlife Conservation Park, Prototype Affordable Housing, Croton-on-Hudson, N.Y.; author Handbook of Energy Use for Building Construction; contbr. articles to profl. jours. Bd. dirs. Environ. Action Coalition, 1992—. Recipient N.Y. Soc. Architects Archtl. Achievement award, 1994, Presdl. award for Design Excellence Fed. Design Achievement award. Fellow AIA (chair energy profl. devel. program 1979, 81, chair N.Y.C. fellows com. 1994, 95). Office: The Stein Partnership Architect 20 W 20th St New York NY 10011-4213

STEIN, DALE FRANKLIN, retired academic administrator; b. Kingston, Minn., Dec. 24, 1935; s. David Frank and Zelda Jane S.; m. Audrey Dean Bloemke, June 7, 1958; children—Pam, Derek. B.S. in Metallurgy, U. Minn., 1958; Ph.D., Rensselaer Poly. Inst., Troy, N.Y., 1963. Metallurgist rsch. lab. GE, Schnectady, N.Y., 1958-67; assoc. prof. U. Minn., 1967-71; prof. metall. engring., head dept. Mich. Technol. U., Houghton, 1971-77; head mining engring. Mich. Technol. U., 1974-77, v.p. acad. affairs, 1977-79, pres., 1979-91; pres. emeritus, 1991—; cons. NSF, Dept. of Energy, 1972-90; trustee Rensselaer Poly. Inst., 1989-95; chmn. com. on decontamination and decommissioning uranium enrichment facilities Nat. Rsch. Coun., 1993—; active Nat. Materials Adv. Bd., 1987-93; chmn. adv. com. Ctr. for Nuclear Waste Regulatory Analyses. Contbr. articles to profl. jours. Paul Harris fellow. Fellow Metall. Soc. (pres. 1979, inst. Hardy Gold medal 1965), Am. Soc. Metals (Geisler award Eastern N.Y. chpt. 1967); mem. AIME, AAAS, NAE, Sigma Xi, Phi Kappa Phi, Tau Beta Pi, Alpha Sigma Nu.

STEIN, DAVID FRED, investment executive; b. N.Y.C., May 17, 1940; s. William Howard and Phoebe Louise (Hockstader) S.; m. Susan Vail Berresford, June 17, 1963 (div. 1970); 1 child, Jeremy Vail; m. Ellen Gail Cohen, Sept. 16, 1973; children: Katharine Ellen, Nicholas David. BA, Harvard U., 1962; MBA, Harvard Grad. Sch. Bus. Adminstrn., 1965. Assoc. Bache & Co., N.Y.C., 1965-68; assoc., then gen. ptnr. Kuhn Loeb & Co., N.Y.C., 1969-77; mng. dir. Lehman Brothers Kuhn Loeb, N.Y.C., 1977-83, Shearson Lehman Am. Express, N.Y.C., 1983-86; sr. exec. v.p., dir. Am. Express Bank, N.Y.C., 1986-87; mng. dir. Shearson Lehman Hutton, N.Y.C., 1987-89; mng. dir., mem. exec. com. The Stamford Co., N.Y.C., 1989-90, J & W Seligman & Co., N.Y.C., 1990—; co-chmn. Seligman, Henderson Co., N.Y.C., 1991—; mem. Internat. Com. of Nat. Assn. Security Dealers, 1970-85. Trustee P.R. Traveling Theatre, N.Y.C., 1970-72, Altro Health and Rebab. Ctr., Bronx, N.Y., 1975-82, Blythedale Children's Hosp., Valhalla, N.Y., 1977—, Montefiore Med. Ctr., Bronx, 1990—; trustee, chmn. fin. com. Riverdale Country Sch., Bronx, 1988—; mem. Coun. on Fgn. Rels. With U.S. Army, 1962-63. Mem. Century Country Club (Purchase, N.Y.), River Club (N.Y.C.), Harvard Club (N.Y.C.), Edgartown (Mass.) Yacht Club, Mill Reef Club (Antigua, B.V.I.), Chappaquiddick Beach Club (Edgartown). Democrat. Avocations: reading, sailing, fishing, skiing. Home: 875 Park Ave New York NY 10021-0341 Office: J & W Seligman 100 Park Ave New York NY 10017-5516

STEIN, ERIC, retired law educator; b. Holice, Czechoslovakia, July 8, 1913; came to U.S., 1940, naturalized, 1943; s. Zikmund and Hermina (Zalud) S.; m. Virginia Elizabeth Rhine, July 30, 1955. JUD, Charles U., Prague, Czechoslovakia, 1937; JD, U. Mich., 1942; Dr. honoris causa, Vrije U., Brussels, 1978, U. Libre, Brussels, 1979. Bar: Ill. 1946, D.C. 1953. Practiced law Prague, 1937; with State Dept., 1946-55; acting dep. dir. Office UN Polit. Affairs, 1955; mem. faculty U. Mich. Law Sch., Ann Arbor, 1956, prof. internat. law and orgn., 1958-76; Hessel E. Yntema prof. law U. Mich. Law Sch., 1976-83, emeritus prof., 1983—; co-dir. internat. legal studies, 1958-76, dir., 1976-81; vis. prof. Stanford Law Sch., 1956, 77, Law Faculties, Stockholm, Uppsala and Lund, Sweden, 1969, Inst. Advanced Legal Studies U. London, 1975, U. Ariz., 1991, 92; lectr. Hague Acad. Internat. Law, summer 1971; vis. lectr. European U. Inst., Florence, Italy, 1983, Beijing, Shanghai, Wuhan, 1986, U. Tokyo, Kyoto, 1986, Coll. of Europe, Bruges, Pontificia, Madrid, 1988; Jean Monnet prof. European U. Inst., Florence, Italy, 1991, Henry Morris lectr. Kent Coll. of Law, Chgo., 1992, Jeanne Kiewit Taylor design vis. lectr. U. Ariz., winter 1993; adviser U.S. delegation UN Gen. Assembly, 1947-55; mem. adv. panel, cons. Bur. European Affairs, State Dept., 1966-73; cons. U.S. rep. for trade negotiations, 1979; vice chmn. com. Atlantic studies Atlantic Inst., 1966-68; mem. adv. council Inst. European Studies, Free U., Brussels, Belgium, 1965-70; mem. U.S. Com. for Legal Edn. Exchange with China, 1983-91; lectr. Acad. of European Law, Florence, Italy 1990. Author: (with others) American Enterprise in the European Common Market-A Legal Profile, vols. I, II, 1960, (with H.K. Jacobson) Diplomats, Scientists and Politicians: The United States and the Nuclear Test Ban Negotiations, 1966, Harmonization of European Company Law: National Reform and Transnational Coordination, 1971, Impact of New Weapons Technology on International Law-Selected Aspects, 1971, Un Nuovo Diritto per l'Europa, 1991; editor: (with Peter Hay) Law and Institutions in the Atlantic Area Readings, Cases and Problems, 1967, (with Peter Hay and Michel Waelbroeck) European Community Law and Institutions in Perspective, 1976; co-author, co-editor: Courts and Free Markets-Perspectives From the United States and Europe, 1982; bd. editors: Am. Jour. Internat. Law, 1965—; mem. adv. bd. Common Market Law Rev., 1964—, Legal Issues of European Integration, 1974—, Rivista di Diritto Europeo, 1978—, Columbia Jour. East European Law, 1994—, Columbia Jour. European Law, 1994—; contbr. articles to profl. jours. Mem. Internat. Com. for Revision Czechoslovak Constn., 1990-92. With AUS, 1943-46. Decorated Bronze Star, Order Italian Crown, Italian Mil. Cross; Guggenheim fellow, 1962-63; Social Sci. Rsch. Coun. grantee; Rockefeller Found. scholar-in-residence, 1965, 73; Alexander von Humboldt Stiftung awardee, 1982; fellow Inst. Advanced Study, Berlin, 1984-85, IREX rsch. grant, 1995. Mem. ABA (co-chmn. European law com. 1982, mem. coun. sect. on internat. law and practice 1983-84), Internat. Law Assn., Coun. Fgn. Rels., Am. Soc. Internat. Law (exec. coun. 1954-57, bd. rev. and devel. 1965-67, 70-75, hon. v.p. 1982—), Brit. Inst. Internat. and Comparative Law, Internat. Acad. Comparative Law (assoc.). Home: 2649 Heatherway St Ann Arbor MI 48104-2850

STEIN, GEORGE HENRY, historian, educator, administrator; b. Vienna, Austria, May 18, 1934; came to U.S., 1939, naturalized, 1948; m. Dorothy Ann Lahm, Nov. 22, 1963; 1 child, Kenneth. B.A. with honors (N.Y. State Regents scholar), Bklyn. Coll., 1959; M.A. in History (Regents fellow), Columbia U., 1960, Ph.D. in History (Pres.'s fellow), 1964. Lectr. history City Coll., CUNY, 1962-63; instr. dept. history Columbia U., N.Y.C., 1963-65; asst. prof. Columbia U., 1965-66; assoc. prof. dept. history SUNY-Binghamton, 1966-70, prof., 1970—, disting. teaching prof., 1973—, vice chmn. grad. affairs, 1974-76, v.p. acad. affairs, 1976-87, provost, 1985-87, acting pres., 1986-87; manuscript evaluator and cons. to numerous publishers, 1964—. Author: The Waffen SS: Hitler's Elite Guard at War, 1939-45, 1966, paperback edit., 1984 (transl. into German, 1967, French, 1967, Spanish, 1973, Portuguese, 1970); contbr. articles on modern European history to scholarly pubs.; editor: Hitler, 1968; contbr. book revs. to hist. jours. Served with USAF, 1953-57. NEH fellow, 1970-71. Mem. Am. Hist. Assn. (mem. conf. group on cen. European history, conf. group for use of psychology in history), Acad. Polit. Sci., Assn. of Contemporary Historians, Am. Assn. Higher Edn., Nat. Assn. State Univs. and Land Grant Colls. (mem. council acad. affairs 1976-87), Am. Counc. Edn. (exec. com. nat. coun. chief acad. officers 1983-85), Com. Internat. d'Histoire de la Deuxieme Guerre Mondiale (mem. am. com. on history of WWII). Office: SUNY Dept History Binghamton NY 13901

STEIN, GILBERT, professional hockey executive; b. Phila., Jan. 11, 1928; m. Barbara Stein; children: Andrew, Holly Spinner, John. Grad., Temple U.; JD, Boston U. Exec. v.p., chief exec. officer Phila. Flyers Hockey Club; vice-chmn. NHL Enterprises, Inc., N.Y.; v.p., gen. counsel NHL, N.Y., pres., 1992—. Address: 1251 Avenue of the Americas #47 New York NY 10020-1104

STEIN, HERBERT, economist; b. Detroit, Aug. 27, 1916; s. David and Jessie (Segal) S.; m. Mildred Fishman, June 12, 1937; children: Rachel (Epstein), Benjamin. AB, Williams Coll., 1935, LLD (hon.), 1980; PhD, U. Chgo., 1958; LLD (hon.), Rider Coll., 1971, Hartford U., 1973, Roanoke Coll., 1984, New Haven U., 1987, Hofstra U., 1994. Economist FDIC, 1938-40, Nat. Def. Adv. Commn., 1940-41, WPB, 1941-44, Office War Moblzn. and Reconversion, 1945; economist Com. Econ. Devel., 1945-48, assoc. dir. research, 1948-56, dir. research, 1956-66, v.p., chief economist, 1966-67; sr. fellow Brookings Instn., 1967-69; mem. Pres.'s Council Econ. Advisers, Washington, 1969-72; chmn. Pres.'s Council Econ. Advisers, 1972-74; A. Willis Robertson prof. econs. U. Va., Charlottesville, 1974-84; weekly columnist The Economy Today, Scripps-Howard and other newpapers, 1974-80; bd. contbrs. Wall St. Jour., 1974—; cons. Congl. Budget Office, 1976-89; mem. Adv. Com. Nat. Growth Policy Processes, 1976-77, Pharm. Reimbursement Adv. Bd., 1976-77; adj. scholar Am. Enterprise Inst., 1975-77, sr. fellow, 1977—; cons. U.S. Dept. State, 1983-92; mem. Pres.'s Econ. Policy Adv. Bd., 1981-89; mem. Pres.'s Blue Ribbon Commn. on Def. Mgmt., 1985-86. Author: U.S. Government Price Policy during the World War, 1938, (with de Chazeau, Hart, Means, Myers, Yntema) Jobs and Markets, 1946, The Fiscal Revolution in America, 1969, rev. edit., 1990, Economic Planning and the Improvement of Public Policy, 1975, (with W. Leontief) The Economic System in an Age of Discontinuity, 1976, (with Benjamin Stein) On the Brink, 1977, (with Benjamin Stein) Money Power, 1980, Presidential Economics, 1984, rev. edit., 1994, Washington Bedtime Stories, 1986, Governing the $5 Trillion Economy, 1989, (with M. Foss) An Illustrated Guide to the American Economy, 1992, A New Illustrated Guide to the American Economy, 1995, On the Other Hand..., 1995; editor: Policies to Combat Depression, 1956, Tax Policy for the Twenty-First Century, 1988, AEI Economist, 1977-88; contbr. to: Agenda for the Nation, 1968, Contemporary Economic Problems, 1976, 77, 78, 79, 80. Co-chmn. Economists for Ford, 1976; founding mem. Ams. for An Effective Presidency, 1980; mem. vis. com. econs. dept. Harvard U., 1979-80; mem. Group of 30, 1978-81. Served as ensign USNR, 1944-45. Recipient 1st prize Pabst Post-War Employment awards, 1944, Frank Seidmann award polit. economy Rhodes Coll., Memphis, 1989; Center Advanced Study in Behavioral Scis. fellow, 1965-66. Mem. Am., Va. econ. assns., So. Econ. Assn. (pres. 1983-84), Nat. Economists Club (chmn., bd. govs. 1969-70), Am. Acad. Arts and Scis., Phi Beta Kappa. Club: Cosmos. Office: Am Enterprise Inst 1150 17th St NW Washington DC 20036-4603

STEIN, HERMAN DAVID, social sciences educator, past university provost; b. N.Y.C., Aug. 13, 1917; s. Charles and Emma (Rosenblum) S.; m. Charmion Kerr, Sept. 15, 1946; children: Karen Lou Gelender, Shoshi Stein Bennett, Naomi Elizabeth. B.S.S., CCNY, 1939; M.S., Columbia U., 1941, D. Social Welfare, 1958; L.H.D., Hebrew Union Coll.-Jewish Inst. Religion, Cin, 1969; LLD, Jewish Theol. Sem., 1995. Family case worker, dir. pub. relations Jewish Family Service, N.Y.C., 1941-45; mem. faculty Sch. Social Work, Columbia U., N.Y.C., 1945-47, 50-64, prof. social scis., 1958-64, dir. rsch. ctr., 1959-62; dean Sch. Applied Social Scis. Case Western Res. U., Cleve., 1964-68, provost for social and behavioral scis., 1967-71, John Reynolds Harkness prof., social adminstr., 1972-89, univ. provost, v.p., 1969-72, 86-88, univ. prof. and provost emeritus, 1990—, univ. prof., faculty Ctr. for Internat. Health, 1989—; founder, dir. Global Currents Lectures, 1983-88; vis. prof. Sch. Social Work, U. Hawaii, Honolulu, winter 1971-72; fellow ctr. for Advanced Study in Behavior Scis., 1974-75, 78-79; Dep. dir. budget and rsch. dir. welfare dept. Am. Joint Distbn. Com. (European Hdqrs.), Paris, 1947-50; sr. adviser to exec. dir. UNICEF, 1974-83; cons. UNICEF, UN Social Devel. Div., 1960-83; adv. com. NIMH, 1959-71; mem. Bd. Human Resources, Nat. Acad. Scis., 1972-74; lectr. Sch. Social Work, Smith Coll., 1951-62, Harvard U. Sch. Pub. Health, 1971-85; cons. indsl. and nonprofit orgns. Author: The Curriculum Study of the Columbia University School of Social Work, 1960; co-author: The Characteristics of American Jews, 1965; Editor: (with Richard A. Cloward) Social Perspectives on Behavior, 1958, Planning for the Needs of Children in Developing Countries, 1965, Social Theory and Social Invention, 1968, The Crisis in Welfare in Cleveland, 1969, Organization and the Human Services, 1981; mem. editorial bd.: Adminstr. in Social work, 1976—; contbr. to profl. jours. Chmn. Mayor's Commn. on Crisis in Welfare in Cleve., 1968. Recipient Disting. Svc. award Coun. on Social Work Edn., 1970, René Sand award Internat. Coun. on Social Welfre, 1984, Univ. medal Case Western Res. U., 1994. Mem. NASW (chmn. commn. internat. social welfare 1964-65, Lifetime Achievement award 1996), Am. Sociol. Assn., Soc. Applied Anthropology, Coun. Social Work Edn. (pres. 1966-69, Significant Lifetime Achievement award 1996), Internat. Assn. Schs. Social Work (pres. 1968-76), Internat. Conf. Social Welfare (exec. com. 1976-80, internat. adv. bd. 1986—, bd. dirs. coun. internat. programs 1965-92), Club of Rome (assoc. 1988—), Phi Beta Kappa. Office: Case Western Res U 436 Pardee Hall Cleveland OH 44106

STEIN, HOWARD, mutual fund executive; b. 1926. Student, Juilliard Sch. Music, 1944-46. With Seaporcel Metals Inc., 1950-53, Bache & Co., 1953-55; asst., dir. Dreyfus Investment Mgmt. of Dreyfus and Co., also gen. partner, 1965—; v.p. Dreyfus Fund Inc., 1961-65, pres., chmn. bd., 1965—; pres., dir. Dreyfus Corp., 1965-70, chmn. bd., chief exec. officer, 1970—. Office: Dreyfus Corp 200 Park Ave New York NY 10166-0005*

STEIN, HOWARD S., banker; b. N.Y.C., Dec. 27, 1939; s. J. Zachary and Adele (Epstein) S. B.A., U. Mich., 1961; M.B.A., Harvard U., 1963. Mem. treas.'s staff Gen. Motors Corp., N.Y.C., 1963-69; dep. dir., dir. fiscal ops. Human Resources Adminstrn., City of N.Y., 1969-71, dep. adminstr., 1972-74, 1st dep. adminstr., 1974-78; asst. commr. Manpower and Career Devel. Agy., N.Y.C., 1971-72; dep. commr. rent and housing maintenance Housing and Devel. Adminstrn., City of N.Y., 1972; v.p. Citicorp Credit Services Inc., N.Y.C., 1979-86; sr. v.p. Citicorp Retail Services Inc., N.Y.C., 1986-87; exec. dir. Landmark Mut. Funds Group of Citibank, N.A., N.Y.C., 1987-88; v.p. br. banking sect. devel. div. Citibank NA, 1989-91; sr. credit officer worldwide securities svcs. div. Fin. Instns. Group Citibank NA, N.Y.C., 1991-94; group risk mgr. Global Transaction Svcs., N.Y.C., 1995—; lectr. human resources policy Nova U., Ft. Lauderdale, Fla., 1973-74; field instr. adminstrn. specialization NYU Sch. Social Work, 1976-77. Past Bd. dirs., chmn. program com. Vol. Urban Cons. Group, Inc.; chmn. bd. dirs. Nova Inst; past treas., past pres., bd. dirs. Child Study Assn. Am./Wel-Met, Inc., 1963-85; past treas., bd. dirs. Career Center for Social Services Greater N.Y., Inc.; past treas., past pres. bd. dirs. Cavalier King Charles Spaniel Club U.S.A., Inc.; past bd. dirs., past sec. Child Welfare Info. Services; treas., bd. dirs., chmn. fin. com. WNYC Found.; bd. dirs. Senate Residence Owners Inc., New Goddard-Riverside Housing Devel. Fund Co., N.Y.C. Health and Hosps., Corp., 1976, Homes for the Homeless; mem. corp. Children's Mus., Boston; bd. dirs., treas., mem. fin. com. Goddard Riverside Neighborhood Houses; mem. Dept. Disciplinary com. Supreme Ct. State N.Y. Appellate Divsn. 1st Jud. Dept. Clubs: University, Harvard (N.Y.C.) (past mem. admissions com.). Home: 1158 5th Ave New York NY 10029-6917 Office: 339 Park Ave New York NY 10043-1000

STEIN, IRVIN, orthopedic surgeon, educator; b. Fayetteville, N.C., Oct. 17, 1906; s. Kalman and Fannie (Berman) S.; m. Dorothy Bluthenthal, Aug. 21, 1934 (dec. Sept. 1985); children: Jane (Mrs. Gerald Finerman), Margery (Mrs. Frederich Schab), Katherine (Mrs. Keith Sachs); m. Bernice Hutzler, July 1986. AB, U. N.C., 1926; MD, Thomas Jefferson U., Phila., 1930. Diplomate Am. Bd. Orthopedic Surgery. Intern Sinai Hosp., Balt., 1930-31; resident surg. pathology Johns Hopkins, 1931-32; resident Phila. Orthopaedic Hosp., 1932-33; resident orthopedic surgery Johns Hopkins Hosp. and Children's Hosp. Sch., 1933-34; chief orthopedic surgery Phila. Gen. Hosp., 1941—; dir. chmn. dept. orthopedic surgery Albert Einstein Med. Center, Phila., 1962-72; emeritus chmn. Albert Einstein Med. Center, 1972—; clin. prof. orthopedic surgery emeritus U. Pa. Sch. Medicine, Phila.; cons. dept. health svcs. Phila. Sch. System. Co-author: Living Bone in Health and Disease, 1955; contbr. numerous articles to profl. jours. Chmn. Phila. Chamber Orch. Soc., 1967-70; bd. dirs. emeritus Phila. Orch. Recipient Rehab. Physician of Year award Phila. Easter Seal Soc., 1971. Fellow ACS, Am. Assn. Study Neoplastic Diseases, N.Y. Acad. Scis., Coll. Physicians Phila., Am. Med. Writers Assn., Internat. Coll. Surgeons (pres. Pa. div. 1971, regent), Phila. Orthopedic Soc. (pres. 1970), Am. Acad. Orthopedic Surgery, Am. Geriatric Assn., Am. Acad. Surgery. Club: Broken Sound Golf. Home and Office: 2066 N Ocean Blvd Boca Raton FL 33431-7802

STEIN, JAY M., planning and design educator, consultant; b. N.Y.C., Dec. 21, 1946; s. Samuel and Helen (Hershkowitz) S.; m. Karen Lee Klenberg, Aug. 18, 1987; children: Danielle Eva, Melissa Ilana. BA, Harpur Coll., 1968; MA, York U., Toronto, Ont., Can., 1971; PhD, U. Mich., 1976. Cert. planner. Lectr. U. Mich., Ann Arbor, 1974-76; asst. prof. planning Ga. Inst. Tech., Atlanta, 1976-81, assoc. prof., 1981-86; prof., chmn. dept. SUNY, Buffalo, 1986-89, acting dean, 1988; prof., chmn. dept. urban and regional planning U. Fla., 1989—; vis. prof. Stanford (Calif.) U., 1984-85; prin. Jay M. Stein Assocs.; cons. Legal Svcs. Corp. Ga., Atlanta, 1980-84, Atlanta Regional Commn., 1982, Legal Svcs. Corp. Ala., Montgomery, 1983-84, New Orleans Legal Svcs., 1988-89. Editor: Public Infrastructure, 1988, Growth Management: The Planning Challenge of the 1990s, 1992, Classic Readings in Urban Planning, 1995, Classic Readings in Real Estate and Development, 1996; editl. bd. Jour. Arch. and Planning Rsch., Jour. Infrastructure Sys.; contbr. chpts. to books, articles to profl. jours. Mem. Am. Inst. Cert. Planners, Am. Planning Asasn. (mem. jour. editorial bd. 1984-88, 95—), Assn. Collegiate Schs. Planning (exec. com. 1980-82), Urban Land Inst. (affiliate). Avocations: tennis, photography. Office: Univ Fla Coll Architecture Dept Urban & Regional Planning Gainesville FL 32611

STEIN, JAY WOBITH, legal research and education consultant; b. Sauk Centre, Minn., June 19, 1920; s. Julius A. and Emaline (Wobith) S.; children: Holly Jayne, Navida Carol, April Jae, Andrew John, John Henry. BA cum laude, U. Minn., 1942; MA, Stanford U., 1949, Syracuse U., 1960; MS, Columbia U., 1950, PhD, 1952. Dir. CIA rsch. team, 1947-49; dir. library, asst. prof. social studies Southwestern U., Memphis, 1954-57; asst. dir. librs., adminstv. assoc. to v.p. Syracuse (N.Y.) U., 1958-61; faculty Maxwell Sch., Syracuse, 1959-61; asst. to pres. Drake U., Des Moines, Iowa, 1961-64; dir. State Higher Edn. Commn., Des Moines, 1964-67; dean Coll. Arts and Scis., prof. polit. sci. Western Ill. U., Macomb, 1967-69, prof. polit. sci. and edn., 1969-87; rsch. libr. John Marshall Law Sch. Libr., Chgo., 1989-94; ind. rsch. cons. law, libr., edn. Columbus, Ohio, 1995—; founder Rsch. & Resolution, Columbus, Ohio, 1996—; catalogue planner, econs. and govt., N.Y. Pub. Library, 1953; proposal reviewer U.S. Dept. Edn. Fund for the Improvement of Post-secondary Edn., 1982. Author: The Mind and the Sword, 1961, How Society Governs Education, 1975, Mass Media, Education and a Better Society, 1979, Society, Culture and Education, 1984, others; editor Scholar and Educator jour., 1977-85; contbr. articles to profl. jours. Mem. Coun. of Faculties of Bd. Govs. State Colls. and Univs., 1980-86, chmn., 1984-85; Family Cultural Ensemble, 1968-71; active with ch. and civic groups. With USN, 1942-46. Coolidge Found. fellow, 1984; grantee Univ. Rsch. Coun., others; recipient various overseas grants, 1970-80, including U. Bonn Acad. Exch., Germany, Internat. Recreation Assn., Switzerland, U.S. Dept. Edn., Europe and Egypt, also Iran, USSR. Mem. ABA (assoc.), ALA (life), ASPA, Am. Arbitration Assn. (panel of arbitrators), Am. Judicature Soc., Am. Polit. Sci. Assn., Soc. Advancement Edn., Soc. Educators and Scholars (founder 1976, exec. dir. 1976-82, chmn. bd. 1980-88), Rotary, Phi Beta Kappa, Phi Kappa Phi, Phi Delta Kappa, Alpha Mu Gamma, Pi Sigma Alpha, Lambda Alpha Psi. Avocations: books, swimming, running. Office: 518 E Town St Apt 510 Columbus OH 43215-4831

STEIN, JEROME LEON, economist, educator; b. Bklyn., Nov. 14, 1928; s. Meyer and Ida (Shapiro) S.; m. Hadassah Levow, Aug. 27, 1950; children: Seth, Gil, Ilana. B.A. summa cum laude, Bklyn. Coll., 1949; M.A., Yale U., 1950, Ph.D., 1955. Instr. Brown U., Providence, 1953-56; asst. prof. Brown U., 1956-60, assoc. prof., 1960-62, prof., 1962-70, Eastman prof. polit. economy, 1970-94; prof. emeritus Brown U., Providence, 1994—; vis. prof. Hebrew U., Jerusalem, 1965-66, 72-73, 78; Ford Found. rsch. prof. econs. U. Calif., Berkeley, 1979-80, Sorbonne, U. Paris, 1982, Tohoku U., Sendai, Japan, 1983, Haute Etudes Comml., France, 1987, Monash U., Melbourne U., Australia, 1989, U. Aix-en-Provence, Marseille, France, 1992, 95, U. Munich, 1994, La Sapienza, Rome, 1994. Author: Essays in International Finance, 1962, (with G.M. Borts) Economic Growth in a Free Market, 1964, Money and Capacity Growth, 1971, Monetarism, 1976, Monetarist, Keynesian and New Classical Economics, 1982, Economics of Futures Markets, 1986, International Finance Markets, 1991, Fundamental Determinants of Exchange Rates, 1995; bd. editors Am. Econ. Rev., 1974-80; assoc. editor Jour. Fin., 1964-70. Ford Found. faculty fellow, 1961-62; Social Sci. Research Council grantee, 1965-66; Guggenheim fellow, 1972-73. Mem. Am. Econ. Assn. Home: 77 Elton St Providence RI 02906-4505 Office: Brown U 79 Waterman St Providence RI 02912-9079

STEIN, JOSEPH, playwright; b. N.Y.C.; s. Charles and Emma S.; m. Elisa Loti, Feb. 7, 1975; children by previous marriage: Daniel, Harry, Joshua; children of present marriage: John, Jenny Lyn. BSS, CCNY, 1934; MSW, Columbia U., 1937. Psychiat. social worker N.Y.C., 1938-45. Writer: radio shows, including Raleigh's Room, 1948-49, Henry Morgan Show, 1949-52; TV shows, including Your Show of Shows, 1952-54; Sid Caesar Show, 1954-55; playwright Plain and Fancy, 1955; Mr. Wonderful, 1957, Juno, 1959, Take Me Along, 1959, Enter Laughing, 1963, Fiddler on the Roof, 1964 (Am. Theatre Wing Tony award for best musical, 1965, N.Y. Drama Critics Circle award Best Musical 1965), Zorba, 1968 (Tony nomination), Irene, 1975, King of Hearts, 1978, Carmelina, 1979, The Baker's Wife, 1983, (Olivier award nomination London 1989), Rags, 1986 (Tony nomination); screenplays Enter Laughing, 1970; Fiddler on the Roof, 1972 (Screen Actors Guild award). Mem. Authors League, Screen Writers Guild (award recipient), Dramatists Guild Coun. Home: 1130 Park Ave New York NY 10128-1255 Office: 250 W 57th St New York NY 10102-0158

STEIN, LAWRENCE A(LLEN), lawyer; b. Balt., Mar. 18, 1965; s. Hersh and Ellen (Hart) S.; m. Diane Wells, June 23, 1991; children: Joshua A., Julie E. AB, U. Chgo., 1988; JD, No. Ill. U., 1993. Bar: Ill. 1993, U.S. Dist. Ct. (no. dist.) Ill. 1993, U.S. Ct. Appeals (7th cir.) 1993, Md. 1994, U.S. Dist. Ct. Md. 1994. Assoc. Huck, Bouma, Martin, Charlton & Bradshaw, Wheaton, Ill., 1993—; advisor Prairie State Legal Svcs., Carol Stream, Ill., 1993—. Commr. Glen Ellyn (Ill.) Architecture Review Commn., 1994—. Recipient Am. jurisprudence award for excellence in appellate advocacy Lawyers Coop., 1991. Mem. ABA, Chgo. Bar Assn., DuPage County Bar Assn., Ill. State Bar Assn., Am. Inns Ct., Phi Delta Phi. Republican. Jewish. Home: 1255 Old Bond Ct Glen Ellyn IL 60137-7801 Office: Huck Bouma Martin Charlton & Bradshaw 1755 S Naperville Rd # 200 Wheaton IL 60187-8132

STEIN, MARVIN, psychiatrist, educator; b. St. Louis, Dec. 8, 1923; s. Samuel G. and Dora (Kline) S.; m. Ann Hackman, May 5, 1950; children: Leslie, David, Lisa. BS, MD, Washington U., St. Louis, 1949; grad., Phila. Psychoanalytic Inst., 1959. Intern St. Louis City Hosp., 1949-50; asst. resident in psychiatry Barnes Hosp., St. Louis, 1950-51; fellow in psychiatry Hosp. U. Pa., 1953-55; asst. prof., then assoc. prof. psychiatry U. Pa. Med. Sch., 1956-63; prof. psychiatry Cornell U. Med. Sch., N.Y.C., 1963-66; prof., chmn. dept. psychiatry SUNY Downstate Med. Ctr., Bklyn., 1966-71; chmn. dept. psychiatry Mt. Sinai Sch. Medicine, N.Y.C., 1971-87, Esther and Joseph Klingenstein prof., 1971-94, Esther and Joseph Klingenstein prof. emeritus, 1994—; mem. fellowships rev. panel NIMH, 1961-64, chmn. mental health extramural rsch. adv. com., 1968-71, chmn. rev. com. Mental Health Aspects of AIDS, 1988-90; mem. rsch. adv. com. VA, 1965-68, mem. rsch. svc. merit rev. bd. in behavioral sci., 1972-75; chmn. Mental Health Rsch. Career Award Com., 1963-67; chmn. bd. dirs. Founds. Fund for Rsch. in Psychiatry, 1967-70; mem. behavioral medicine study sect. NIH, 1981-83, geriatric rev. com., 1986-88. Contbr. articles on brain and behavior and immune function to med. jours. USPHS postdoctoral fellow, 1951-53; mental health career investigator, 1956-61; sr. fellow grantee, 1961-63. Mem. Am. Psychiat. Assn. (chmn. rsch. coun. 1981-84), N.Y. Acad. Medicine (Salmon com. 1984—). Home: 5700 Arlington Ave Bronx NY 10471-1503 Office: Mt Sinai Sch Medicine 1 Gustave L Levy Pl New York NY 10029-6504

STEIN, MICHAEL ALAN, cardiologist; b. Chgo., May 31, 1958; s. Harold Marc and Carlyne Mae (Skirow) S.; m. Ann Palmer Coe, June 9, 1984; 1 child, Sarah Elizabeth. BA, Lawrence U., 1980; MD, U. Ill., 1984. Diplomate in internal medicine and cardiovascular diseases Am. Bd. Internal Medicine. Intern, resident in medicine U. Ill., Chgo., 1984-87; fellow in cardiology, then interventional cardiology U. Iowa, Iowa City, 1987-91; asst. prof. Emory U., Atlanta, 1991-95; med. dir. CCU Atlanta VA Med. Ctr., Decatur, Ga., 1991-95; med. dir. cardiac catheterization lab., Dunwoody Med. Ctr., Atlanta, 1994-95; staff cardiologist Cardiology Cons., Pensacola, Fla., 1995—. Recipient clin. investigator award NIH, 1990-95. Fellow Am. Coll. Cardiology, Am. Heart Assn. (coun. clin. cardiology); mem. AAAS, Soc. for Cardiac Angiography & Interventions. Avocations: sailing, sailboat racing, hiking, scuba diving, fishing. Home: 2370 W Bayshore Rd Gulf Breeze FL 32561-2522 Office: 1717 N E St Ste 331 Pensacola FL 32501-6376

STEIN, MICHAEL HENRY, lawyer; b. New Haven, Conn., Aug. 28, 1942; s. Joseph and Sylvia (Susman) S.; m. Eileen McGinley, June 13, 1965. BA, Swarthmore Coll., 1964; LLB, Columbia U., 1968. Bar: D.C. 1971. Lectr. law U. Botswana, Lesotho, Swaziland, Roma, Lesotho, 1968-70; trial atty. U.S. Justice Dept., Washington, 1970-77; gen. counsel U.S. Internat. Trade Commn., Washington, 1977-84; ptnr. Verner, Liipfert, Bernhard, McPherson & Hand, Chartered, Washington, 1984-85, Dewey Ballantine, Washington, 1985—. Mem. Fed. Circ. Bar Assn. (bd. dirs. 1990—). Avocations: sailing, sheep dog trialing. Office: Dewey Ballantine 1775 Pennsylvania Ave NW Washington DC 20006-4605

STEIN, MILTON MICHAEL, lawyer; b. N.Y.C., Sept. 18, 1936; s. Isidore and Sadie (Lefkowitz) S.; m. Jacqueline Martin, June 17, 1962; children: April, Alicia. AB, Columbia U., 1958, LLB, 1961. Bar: N.Y. 1962, Pa. 1971, U.S. Supreme Ct. 1971. Asst. dist. atty. N.Y. County, 1962-67; sr. counsel Nat. Commn. for Reform of Fed. Criminal Law, Washington, 1967-70; asst. dist. atty., chief of appeals City of Phila., 1970-73; asst. dir. Nat. Wire Tapping Commn., Washington, 1973-75; dir. D.C. Law Revision, Washington, 1975-77; spl. asst. HUD, Washington, 1977-79; asst. gen. counsel U.S. Commodity Futures Trading Commn., Washington, 1979-83; v.p. N.Y. Futures Exch., N.Y.C., 1983-89, N.Y. Stock Exch., N.Y.C., 1989—. Mem. ABA, N.Y. State Bar Assn., Assn. of Bar of City of N.Y. Democrat. Jewish. Home: Hudson House PO Box 286 Ardsley On Hudson NY 10503-0286

STEIN, MYRON, internist, educator; b. Boston, May 27, 1925; s. Isador and Sara Esther (Zimble) S.; m. Pauline June Alpert, June 21, 1953 (dec. 1992); children: Lisa Jayne, Susan Jo Stein-Matthews, Amy Stein Weinberg, Laurie Jennifer. BA, Dartmouth Coll., 1948; MD, Tufts U., 1952. Diplomate Am. Bd. Internal Medicine. Assoc. medicine Med. Sch. Harvard U., Boston, 1957-65; assoc. prof. med. sci. Brown U., Providence, 1965-68, prof. med. sci., 1968-73; pvt. practice medicine Beverly Hills, Calif.; prof. medicine Sch. Medicine, UCLA, 1973-75, clin. prof., 1975—; cons. VA Hosp., Providence, 1965-73, L.A., 1975-89, Wadsworth VA Med. Ctr.; mem. pulmonary study sect. NIH, Bethesda, Md., 1971-95. Editor: Pulmonary Embolic Disease, 1965, Pulmonary Thromboembolism, 1973, New Directions in Asthma, 1975, Bronchial Asthma, 1985, 3d edit., 1993; contbr. 120 articles to med. jours. Mem. bd. corp. vis. com. Sch. Medicine Tufts U., Medford, Mass., 1986; bd. overseers, 1987. With AUS, 1943-46. Recipient Maimonides award Govt. of Israel, 1982. Fellow Am. Coll. Chest Physicians (sr. editor 1971-79); mem. Calif. Thoracic Soc. (sec.-treas. 1978, pres. 1981), L.A. Trudeau Soc., New Eng. Pulmonary Soc., Calif. Lung Assn. (chmn. edn. com. 1978-82, bd. dirs. 1981, Calif. medal 1989). Democrat. Jewish. Avocations: tennis, jogging, collecting lead soldiers. Office: 414 N Camden Dr Ste 1100 Beverly Hills CA 90210-4532

STEIN, OTTO LUDWIG, botany educator; b. Augsburg, Germany, Jan. 14, 1925; came to U.S., 1939, naturalized, 1944; s. Julius and Margaret (Haas) S.; m. Diana Borut, June 15, 1958; children: Deborah Lee, Judith Ann, Suzanne Beth, Jonathan Henri Richard. B.S. with distinction, U. Minn., 1949, M.S., 1952, Ph.D., 1954. Instr. botany U. Mo. at Columbia, 1955; USPHS research fellow Brookhaven Nat. Lab., 1955-57, research collaborator, 1958-68; asst. prof. botany U. Mont., Missoula, 1957-63; asso. prof. U. Mont., 1963-64; asso. prof. botany U. Mass., Amherst, 1964-70; prof. botany U. Mass., 1970-90, prof. emeritus, 1990—, head dept., 1969-74; dir. U. Mass./U. Freiburg (Germany) Exchange Program, 1979; vis. asst. prof. botany U. Calif., Berkeley, 1961-62. Served with AUS, 1944-46. NATO sr. research fellow Imperial Coll., London, Eng., 1971-72. Fellow Linnean Soc. (London), AAAS; mem. Bot. Soc. Am. (chmn. developmental sect. 1963-65), Soc. Developmental Biology, Soc. Exptl. Biology, Sigma Xi., Gamma Sigma Delta, Alpha Zeta, Gamma Alpha. Home: 140 Red Gate Ln Amherst MA 01002-1845 Office: U Mass Dept Biology Amherst MA 01003

STEIN, PAUL ARTHUR, financial services executive; b. St. Louis, Aug. 20, 1937; s. Harry Arthur and Julia (Vandivort) S.; m. Ann Garwood, Oct. 8, 1960 (dec. 1993); m. Marjorie Orr MacIver, 1996; children: Valerie Suzanne, Paul Garwood. AB, Dartmouth U., 1959. From trainee to dir. spl. market offices Merrill Lynch, N.Y.C. and Princeton, 1959—; chmn. bd. dirs. VPI, Inc. Mem. Beacon Hill Club (Summit, N.J.), N.J. Ctr. for Visual Arts (officer and trustee), Securities Industry Inst. (former trustee). Episcopalian.

STEIN, PAUL DAVID, cardiologist; b. Cin., Apr. 13, 1934; s. Simon and Sadie (Friedman) S.; m. Janet Louise Tucker, Aug. 14, 1966; children: Simon, Douglas, Rebecca. BS, U. Cin., 1955, MD, 1959. Intern Jewish Hosp., Cin., 1959-60, med. resident, 1961-62; med. resident Gorgas Hosp., C.Z., 1960-61; fellow in cardiology U. Cin., 1962-63, Mt. Sinai Hosp., N.Y.C., 1963-64; rsch. fellow Harvard Med. Sch., Boston, 1964-66; asst. dir. cardiac catheterization lab. Baylor U. Med. Ctr., Dallas, 1966-67; asst. prof. medicine Creighton U., Omaha, 1967-69; assoc. prof. medicine U. Okla., Oklahoma City, 1969-73; prof. rsch. medicine U. Okla. Coll. Medicine, Oklahoma City, 1973-76; dir. cardiovascular rsch. Henry Ford Hosp., Detroit, 1976-94, med. dir. cardiovascular rehab., 1994—; adj. prof. physics Oakland U., Rochester, Mich., 1985—; prof. medicine (Henry Ford) Case Western Res. U., Cleve., 1994—. Author: A Physical and Physiological Basis for the Interpretation of Cardiac Ausculation: Evaluations Based Primarily on Second Sound and Ejection Murmurs, 1981; contbr. articles to profl. jours. Coun. on Clin. Cardiology fellow Am. Heart Assn., 1971, Coun. on Circulation fellow, 1972. Fellow ACP, Am. Coll. Cardiology, Am. Coll. Chest Physicians (pres. 1993), Internat. Acad. Chest Physicians and Surgeons (pres. 1993); mem. ASME, Am. Physiol. Soc., Ctrl. Soc. Clin. Rsch. Office: Henry Ford Hosp New Center Pavillion 2921 W Grand Blvd Detroit MI 48202-2691

STEIN, PAUL E., superintendent; m. Carol Mannin; children: Christine, John, James. BS in polit. sci., U.S.A.F. Acad., Colo., 1966; MBA, Fla. State U., 1973; attended, Air War Coll., Maxwell Air Force Base, Ala., 1986. Commd. 2d lt. USAF, 1966, advanced through grades to lt. gen., 1994; asst. football coach USAF, Colo., 1966-67; chief personnel svcs. 7149th combat support group USAF, Spangdahlem Air Base, Germany, 1967-69; chief spl. svcs. divsn. 36th combat support group USAF, Bitburg Air Base, Germany, 1969-71; chief, spl. svcs. divsn. 2d comabt support group USAF, Barksdale Air Force Base, La., 1971-72; ops. analyst AWACS Test Ops. The Boeing Co., Washington, 1974-80; requirements program officer USAF, Washinton, 1980, tactical fighter requirements officer, 1980-82, 86-91; comdr. Keesler Tech. Training Ctr., Miss., 1991-92; dir., legislative liaison Office of the Sec., Washington, 1992-94; supr. USAF Acad., Colo., 1994—. Decorated Disting. Svc. medal, Legion of Merit with one bronze oak leaf cluster. Office: USAF Legislative Liason SAF/LL Washington DC 20330

STEIN, PAULA JEAN ANNE BARTON, hotel real estate consultant; b. Chgo., July 29, 1929; m. Marshall L. Stein; children: Guy G., George L. BA, Lake Forest (Ill.) U., 1951; postgrad., Roosevelt U., Chgo., 1955-77, UCLA, 1978-79. Lic. internat. hotel and mgmt. cons./broker, Ill. Adminstrv. asst. publicity Kefauver for Pres., Chgo., 1951; adminstrv. asst. Wells Orgns., Chgo., 1952; rschr., writer Employers Assn. Am., Chgo.; writer Woodworking Jobbers Assn., Chgo., 1953; cons. L.A., 1978-80; founder, pres., ptnr., cons. internat. hotel real estate Steinvest, Inc., Chgo., 1980—; cons., hotels Nat. Diversified Svcs., Inc., Chgo., 1990—, Chatmar, Inc., Bayview Hotels, Monterey, Calif. IBA fellow, 1990. Mem. World Future Soc. (profl.). Avocations: oil painting, grandparenting, social services causes, citizen-diplomacy. Home and Office: Steinvest Inc 641 W Willow St House 202 Chicago IL 60614-5176

STEIN, PAULA NANCY, psychologist, educator; b. N.Y.C., Aug. 23, 1963; d. Michael and Evelyn (Graber) S.; m. Andreas Howard Smoller, Sept. 2, 1991; 1 child, Rebecca Leigh Smoller. BA, Skidmore Coll., 1985; MA with distinction, Hofstra U., 1986, PhD, 1989. Lic. clin. psychologist, N.Y.; cert. in sch. psychology, N.Y. Intern NYU Med. Ctr.-Rusk Inst., N.Y.C., 1988-89; instr. Mt. Sinai Med. Ctr., N.Y.C., 1989-93, asst. prof. rehab. medicine, 1993—; chief psychologist Fishkill (N.Y.) Consultation Group, 1991—. Contbr. chpt. to book, articles to profl. jours. Kraewic scholar Skidmore Coll., 1985. Mem. APA, Am. Congress Rehab. Medicine (subcom. on tng.), Assn. for Advancement of Behavior Therapy, Hudson Valley Psychol. Assn., Phi Beta Kappa. Jewish. Avocations: skiing, swimming, tennis. Office: Fishkill Consultation Group Box 446 90 Main St Fishkill NY 12524

STEIN, RICHARD PAUL, lawyer; b. New Albany, Ind., Sept. 2, 1925; s. William P. and Lillian M. (Russell) S.; m. Mary Charlotte Key, June 22, 1959; children: Richard Paul, William, Patricia. Student, Miligan (Tenn.) Coll., 1943-44, Duke, 1944-45; J.D., U. Louisville, 1950. Bar: Ind., 1950. With labor relations Goodyear Engring. Co., Charlestown, Ind., 1952-54; ptnr. Naville & Stein, New Albany, 1954-61; pros. atty. 52d Jud. Circuit Ind., 1956-61; U.S. atty. So. Dist. Ind., 1961-67; chmn. Pub. Service Commn. of Ind., 1967-70; legis. counsel Eli Lilly Co., Indpls., 1970-74; v.p. pub. affairs Pub. Service Co. Ind., 1974-90; atty., pub. affairs cons., 1990—; dir. Indpls. Indians; Co-counsel New Albany-Floyd County Bldg. Authority, 1960-62; mem. State Bd. Tax Commrs. Adv. Bd., Jud. Study Commn. Sec. New Albany Dist. Dem. Com., 1956-61; chmn. New Albany United Way, 1957. Served to lt. USNR, 1943-46, 50-51; lt. Res. Named Floyd County Young Man of Yr. Floyd County Jr. C. of C., 1955, Outstanding Young Man of Yr. New ALbany Jaycees, 1958. Mem. Ind. Bar Assn., Marion County Bar Assn., Ind. Prosecutors Assn. (pres. 1960-61), Ind. Electric Assn. (dir.), Am. Legion, Pi Kappa Alpha, Phi Alpha Delta. Roman Catholic. Clubs: Highland Country, Skyline. Lodge: K.C. Avocations: tennis, golf, reading. Home: 9315 Spring Forest Dr Indianapolis IN 46260-1269

STEIN, RICHARD STEPHEN, chemistry educator; b. N.Y.C., Aug. 21, 1925; s. Isidor and Florence (Lewengood) S.; m. Judith Elma Balise, May 27, 1951; children: Linda Ann, Anne Marie, Carol Joan, Lisa Jean. BS, Poly. Inst. Bklyn., 1945; MA, Princeton U., 1948, PhD, 1949; DS (hon.), U. Ulm, Fed. Republic Germany, 1989; DSc (hon.), U. Mass., 1992. Postdoctoral fellow Cambridge U., 1948-49; research assoc. Princeton U., 1949-50; asst. prof. U. Mass., Amherst, 1950-57; asso. prof. U. Mass., 1957-59, prof., 1959-61, Commonwealth prof., 1961-80, Goessman prof. chemistry, 1980-92; Goessman prof. emeritus, 1992—; founder, dir. Polymer Research Inst. U. Mass., 1961—; cons. Monsanto Co., Procter and Gamble. Co-editor: Electromagnetic Scattering, 1967, Structure and Properties of Polymer Films, 1973; contbr. numerous articles to profl. jours. Recipient Internat. award Soc. Plastics Engrs., 1969, Bingham award Rheology Soc., 1972, Award for Disting. svc. for Advancement of Polymer Sci., Soc. Polymer Sci. Japan,

1988, Gordon Res. Conf. Huggins award, 1987. Mem. NAS, NAE, AAAS, AAUP, Am. Acad. Arts and Scis., Am. Chem. Soc. (Bordon award 1972, Polymer Chemistry award 1983), Am. Phys. Soc. (award in high polymer physics 1976), Rheology Soc., Sigma Xi. Founder sci. rheo-optics of polymers. Home: 5 Berkshire Ter Amherst MA 01002-1301

STEIN, ROBERT ALAN, electronics company executive; b. Chgo., Oct. 18, 1930; s. Manfred and Mildred (Rosenfield) S.; m. Frances Roslyn Berger, Dec. 25, 1960; 1 dau., Marcia Beth. B.A., U. Chgo., 1950, M.B.A., 1953. C.P.A., Ill. Sr. auditor Scovell, Wellington & Co., Chgo., 1955-63; supr. corp. acctg. Mack Trucks, Inc., Montvale, N.J., 1963-65; v.p. fin., treas. Lionel Corp., N.Y.C., 1965-82; pres. ITI Electronics, Inc., Fairfield, N.J., 1982—. Served with U.S. Army, 1953-55. Mem. Am. Inst. CPAs. Home: 32 Stonewall Dr Livingston NJ 07039-1822 Office: 12 Kulick Rd Fairfield NJ 07004-3308

STEIN, ROBERT BENJAMIN, biomedical researcher, physician; b. Buffalo, Oct. 28, 1950; s. Frank and Eleanor (Bankoff) S.; m. Marcia Joan Lieberman, Aug. 10, 1975 (div.); children: Rebecca Anne, Joshua David; m. Sophia Anne Rose, Dec. 29, 1989; children: Susan Claire, Stephanie Michelle. BS, Ind. U., 1972; MD, PhD, Duke U., 1979. Diplomate Am. Bd. Anatomic and Clin. Pathology. House staff Duke U. Med. Ctr., Durham, N.C., 1980-83; sr. research fellow Dept. Virus and Cell Biology Merck Sharp & Dohme Rsch. Labs., West Point, Pa., 1983-87, assoc. dir. molecular and cardiovascular pharmacology, 1987-89, sr. dir., head dept. pharmacology, 1989-90; v.p. rsch. Ligand Pharms., Inc., San Diego, 1990—. Contbr. articles to profl. jours., chpts. to books. Ins. Med. scholar, 1977-79; James B. Duke scholar, 1976-78; Lang Med. Pub. award, 1979; NIH grantee, 1974-75. Fellow Am. Soc. Clin. Pathologists, N.Y. Acad. Scis., Am. Physiol. Soc., AAAS, Sigma Xi, Phi Beta Kappa, Alpha Omega Alpha. Avocations: piano, history, literature, windsurfing. Office: Ligand Pharms Inc 9393 Towne Centre Dr San Diego CA 92121-3016

STEIN, ROBERT WILLIAM, actuary, accountant; b. Milw., Feb. 4, 1949; s. Herbert A. and Elizabeth (Greenman) S.; children: Paul, Jennifer, Margaret; m. Christine Marie Denham, May 14, 1988. BBA, Drake U., 1971. CPA, N.Y. Cons. actuary Milliman & Robertson, Inc., Milw., 1971-74, Denver, 1974-80; sr. mgr. Ernst & Whinney, Denver, 1976-80; ptnr. Ernst & Whinney, Chgo., 1980-87, N.Y.C., 1987—. Author: Universal Life, 1980; contbr. articles on fin. mgmt. Fellow Soc. Actuaries (bd. govs. 1990-93, exec. com. 1994—); mem. AICPA, Am. Acad. Actuaries. Avocations: raising and riding horses, skiing. Office: Ernst & Young 787 7th Ave New York NY 10019-6018

STEIN, RONALD JAY, artist, airline transport pilot; b. N.Y.C., Sept. 15, 1930; s. William and Ruth (Krasner) S. Diploma, The Cooper Union, 1953; BFA, Yale U., 1955; MFA, Rutgers U., 1960; grad., FAA Acad. Pilot Examiner Sch., 1980. Cons. Aviation Assocs., 1988—; mem. faculty Worcester Mus. Fine Arts, Rutgers U., 1960-63; aviation cons.; pilot examiner, accident prevention safety counselor FAA. One man shows sculpture and paintings include, Mirski Gallery, Boston, 1956, Inst. Contemporary Art, Boston, 1958, Irving Gallery, Milw., 1960, 71, Mayer Gallery, N.Y.C., 1960, 61, Rigelhaupt Gallery, Boston, 1966, Tibor Denagy Gallery, N.Y.C., 1964, N.Y. World's Fair, 1964, Marlborough Gallery, London, 1967, Kind Gallery, Chgo., 1969, Hokin Gallery, Palm Beach, Fla., 1974, Benson Gallery, L.I., N.Y., 1988, Benton Gallery, South Hampton, N.Y., 1988, 89, Odeon Gallery, Sag Harbor, N.Y., 1993; exhibited in group shows, Inst. Contemporary Art, Boston, Corcoran Gallery, Washington, Contemporary Arts Mus., Houston, U. N.C., Raleigh, Mus. Contemporary Art, Chgo., Benton Gallery, South Hampton, N.Y., Mus. Modern Art, N.Y.C., Cornell U., Ithaca, N.Y., Finch Coll. Mus. Fine Arts, N.Y.C.; represented in permanent collections, Am. Fedn. Art, N.Y.C., Guggenheim Mus., N.Y.C., Carnegie Inst., Chgo., Tenn. Fine Arts Ctr., Nashville, Mus. Contemporary Art, Chgo., Wadsworth Athenaeum, Hartford, Conn., Finch Coll. Mus. Art, N.Y.C., Guild Hall, East Hampton, N.Y., Mus. Modern Arts, N.Y.C., Smithsonian Instn., others. Commd. spl. min. of eucharist Most Holy Trinity Roman Cath. Ch., East Hampton, N.Y., 1992—. Capt. U.S. Mcht. Marine, 1976-81. Mem. NRA, Yale Club. Republican. Home: 836 Fireplace Rd East Hampton NY 11937-1512

STEIN, RUTH ELIZABETH KLEIN, physician; b. N.Y.C., Nov. 2, 1941; d. Theodore and Mimi (Foges) Klein; m. H. David Stein, June 9, 1963; children: Lynn Andrea Stein Melnick, Sharon Lisa, Deborah Michelle. AB, Barnard Coll., 1962; MD, Albert Einstein Coll. Medicine, 1966. Diplomate Am. Bd. Pediatrics. Intern, then resident Bronx Mcpl. Hosp. Ctr., 1966-68; sr. resident, fellow; instr. dept. pediatrics George Washington U., Washington, 1969-70; with Albert Einstein Coll. of Medicine, Bronx, 1970—, assoc. prof. pediatrics, 1977-83, prof., 1983—; vice chmn. dept. pediatrics Albert Einstein Coll., 1992—; pediatrician-in-chief, dir. pediatrics Bronx Mcpl. Hosp. Ctr., 1992—; vis. prof. pub. health dept. epidemiology Yale U. Sch. of Medicine, New Haven, 1986-87; scholar-in-residence United Hosp. Fund, N.Y., 1995—; dir., prin. investigator Preventive Intervention Rsch. Ctr. for Child Health, N.Y., Nat. Child Health Assessment Planning Project, N.Y., Behavioral Pediatric Tng. Program, N.Y.; dir. gen. pediatrics Pediatric Divsn., N.Y.; apptd. to Montefiore Med. Ctr., North Ctrl. Bronx Hosp. Editor: Caring for Children with Chronic Illness: Issues and Strategies, 1989; mem. editorial bd. Jour. Behavioral and Devel. Pediatrics; contbr. articles to profl. jours. Fellow Am. Acad. Pediatrics; mem. APHA, Am. Pediatric Soc., Soc. for Pediatric Rsch., Ambulatory Pediatric Assn. (bd. dirs. 1982-89, pres. 1987-88), Soc. for Behavioral Pediatrics, Alpha Omega Alpha. Jewish. Home: 91 Larchmont Ave Larchmont NY 10538-3748 Office: Albert Einstein Coll Medicine 1300 Morris Park Ave Bronx NY 10461-1926

STEIN, SEYMOUR, electronic scientist; b. Bklyn., Apr. 4, 1928; s. Louis Harry and Clara (Roth) S.; m. Corinne Leader, Sept. 14, 1954; children: Paul M., Emily L. BEE, CCNY, 1949; MS in Applied Physics, Harvard U., 1950, PhD in Applied Physics, 1955. Sr. engring. specialist Applied Rsch. Lab., GTE Sylvania, Waltham, Mass., 1954-56, sr. scientist, 1959-64, assoc. dir., 1964-66; dir. Communications Systems Lab., GTE Sylvania, Waltham, 1966-69; staff mem. Hermes Electronics, Cambridge, Mass., 1956-59; pres. Stein Assocs. div. Adams-Russell Co. Waltham, 1969-79; pres. SCPE, Inc., Newton Centre, Mass., 1979—. Co-author: Communications Systems and Techniques, 1966, 2nd edit., 1995, Modern Communication Principles, 1967. Fellow IEEE. Jewish. Office: SCPE Inc 56 Great Meadow Rd Newton MA 02159-2748

STEIN, SOL, publisher, writer, editor in chief; b. Chgo., Oct. 13, 1926; s. Louis and Zelda (Zam) S.; m. Patricia Day, Mar. 31, 1962; children: Kevin David, Jeffrey Lewelyn, Leland Dana, Robert Bruce, Andrew Charles, David Day, Elizabeth Day. BSS, CCNY, 1948; MA, Columbia U., 1949, postgrad., 1949-51. Lectr. social studies CCNY, 1948-51; sr. editor, ideological adv. staff Voice of Am., U.S. State Dept., 1951-53; gen. editor, originator Beacon Press Paperbacks, Boston, 1954—; cons. to pres. Harcourt, Brace, Jovanovich, N.Y.C., 1958-59; exec. v.p. The Mid-Century Book Soc., N.Y.C., 1959-62; pres., editor in chief Stein & Day Pubs., Briarcliff Manor, N.Y., 1962-89; pres. The Colophon Corp., Scarborough, N.Y., 1983—, The WritePro Corp., 1989—, The Stein Software Corp., 1993—; lectr., playwright Columbia U., 1958-60, Dialogue for Writers, Pub., U. Calif., Irvine, 1990-93; treas. The Forensic Found., N.Y.C., 1959-62; founding mem. Playwrights Group, The Actors Studio, 1957. Author: (plays) The Illegitimist, 1953 (1st prize Dramatists Alliance), A Shadow of My Enemy, 1957, (novels) The Husband, 1969, The Magician, 1971, Living Room, 1974, The Childkeeper, 1975, Other People, 1979, The Resort, 1980, The Touch of Treason, 1985, A Deniable Man, 1989, The Best Revenge, 1991 (computer software) WritePro, The Stein Creative Writing Program, 1989—, FirstAid for Writers, 1991, FictionMaster, 1993, WritePro for Business, 1996; (non-fiction) A Feast for Lawyers, 1989, Stein on Writing, 1995; also articles, revs. poetry. Exec. dir. Am. Com. for Cultural Freedom, 1953-56; mem. exec. com. Am. Friends of Captive Nations. Served to 1st lt. AUS, 1945-47. Fellow Yaddo Found., 1952, MacDowell Colony, 1952-56. Recipient Disting. Instr. award U. Calif. at Irvine, 1992. Mem. New Dramatists Com. (coun. mem.), Internat. Brotherhood Magicians (hon. life), Writers Guild Am. East. Avocations: tennis, inventing computer software programs. Home: 43 Linden Cir Scarborough NY 10510-2009 Office: The WritePro Corp 43 S Highland Ave Ossining NY 10562-5226

STEIN, STEPHEN WILLIAM, lawyer; b. N.Y.C., Apr. 12, 1937; s. Melvin S. and Cornelia (Jacobowitz) S.; m. Judith N., Jan. 22, 1966. AB, Princeton U., 1959; LLB, Columbia U., 1962; LLM, NYU, 1963. Bar: N.Y. 1962, Fla. 1962. Assoc. White & Case, N.Y.C., 1963-67; atty. advisor U.S. Agy. Internat. Devel., Washington, 1967-69; regional legal advisor Mission to India U.S. Agy. Internat. Devel., New Delhi, 1969-71; asst. gen. counsel U.S. Agy. Internat. Devel., Washington, 1971-73; assoc. ptnr. Delson & Gordon, N.Y.C., 1973-87; ptnr. Kelley Drye & Warren, N.Y.C., 1987—; mem. U.S. exec. com. Indonesian Trade, Tourism & Investment Promotion Program, 1990-92; mem. U.S.-Indonesia Trade & Investment Adv. Com., 1989-92; vis. instr. internat. Devel. Law Inst., 1993; lectr. Internat. Law Inst., Washington, 1984, 85; spkr. in field. Mem. ABA (mem. sect. internat. law, mem. various coms.), Internat. Bar Assn. (mem. sect. energy resources law, sect. bus. law, mem. various coms.), Assn. Bar of City of N.Y. (mem. com. internat. security affairs 1995—, former mem. others), Am. Indonesian C. of C. (bd. dirs. 1986—, pres. 1989-96). Home: 320 Central Park W New York NY 10025-7659 Office: Kelley Drye & Warren 101 Park Ave New York NY 10178

STEIN, THEODORE, state agency executive. Pres. City of L.A. Dept. Airports. Office: LA Internat Airport PO Box 92216 Los Angeles CA 90009-2216

STEIN, WILLIAM WARNER, anthropology educator; b. Buffalo, Oct. 9, 1921; s. Carl and Blanche (Gutman) S.; m. Rhoda Ruth Spector, June 12, 1949 (dec. 1993); children: Daniel Julian, Susan Isabel. AB, U. Buffalo, 1949; PhD, Cornell U., 1955. Asst. prof. U. Miami, Coral Gables, Fla., 1956-61, U. Alta., Calgary, Can., 1961-63; from asst. to assoc. prof. U. Kans., Lawrence, 1963-65; from assoc. prof. to prof. SUNY, Buffalo, 1965-94, prof. emeritus, 1994—. Author: Hualcan: Life in the Highlands of Peru, 1961, El levantamiento de Atusparia, 1988, Mariátegui y Norka Rouskaya, 1989, El caso de los becerros hambrientos y otros ensayos de antropologia económica peruana, 1991, A Peruvian Psychiatric Hospital, 1995; editor: Peruvian Contexts of change, 1985. Served with U.S. Army, 1941-45, ETO. Home: 131 Cadman Dr Buffalo NY 14221-6963 Office: SUNY at Buffalo Dept Of Anthropology Buffalo NY 14261

STEINBACH, ALICE, journalist; b. Balt.. Student, U. London. Feature writer Balt. Sun, 1981—; formerly dir. pub. info. Balt. Mus. Art. Recip. Pulitzer Prize for feature writing, 1985. Office: Balt Sun Calvert At Centre St Baltimore MD 21278

STEINBACH, TERRY LEE, professional baseball player; b. New Ulm, Minn., Mar. 2, 1962. Student, U. Minn. Catcher Oakland (Calif.) Athletics, 1986—. Named Southern League MVP, 1986. Office: Oakland Athletics Oakland Coliseum 7000 Coliseum Way Oakland CA 94621-1918*

STEINBACK, ROBERT LAMONT, newspaper columnist; b. N.Y.C., Nov. 20, 1955; s. Robert Lee Jr. and Trudy Marcella (Miller) S. BA in Econs., U. Rochester, 1977; MS in Journalism, Northwestern U., 1983. Comml. credit analyst Chem. Bank N.Y. N.Am., Rochester, N.Y., 1977-81; stockbroker Merrill Lynch Pierce Fenner & Smith, Rochester, 1981-82; intern reporter Green Bay (Wis.) Press Gazette, 1982; reporter, editor, columnist Miami (Fla.) Herald, 1983—. Recipient Explanatory Journalism award Fla. Soc. Newspaper Editors, 1990, Green Shade award for best serious commentary Soc. Profl. Journalists, 1991. Office: Miami Herald 1 Herald Plz Miami FL 33132-1609

STEINBAUM, ROBERT S., publisher, lawyer; b. Englewood, N.J., Oct. 13, 1951; s. Paul S. and Esther R. (Rosenberg) S.; m. Rosemary Konner, May 26, 1982; children: Marshall, Elliot. BA, Yale U., 1973; JD, Georgetown U., 1976. Bar: D.C. 1976, N.J. 1980, N.Y. 1982. Atty. Cole & Groner P.C., Washington, 1976-79; asst. U.S. atty. U.S. Atty.'s Office, Newark, 1979-84; atty. Scarpone & Edelson, Newark, 1984-87; publ. N.J. Law Jour., Newark, 1987—; trustee Met. West Jewish News, Whippany, N.J., 1990-95. Trustee North Jersey Blood Ctr., East Orange, N.J., 1987-93, Leadership N.J., 1990. Office: NJ Law Jour PO Box 20081 238 Mulberry St Newark NJ 07102-3528

STEINBERG, ALAN WOLFE, investment company executive; b. Bklyn., Oct. 26, 1927; s. Benjamin F. and Gertrude (Wolfe) S.; m. Suzanne Nichols, Oct. 12, 1958; children: Carol Albanese, Laura Frohman, Benjamin T. AB with honors and spl. distinction in math, Columbia U., 1947, MS, 1950. Indsl. engr. USDA, Washington, 1948-50; ops. rschr. Port of N.Y. Authority, 1950-55; prof. engring. NYU, 1956-63; pres. Am. Computing Ctrs., N.Y.C., 1962-66; v.p., dir. TBS Computer Ctrs., N.Y.C., 1967-76; mng. ptnr. Alan W. Steinberg Partnership, N.Y.C. and South Miami, Fla., 1974—. Contbr. articles to profl. jours. Nat. advisor automation United Jewish Appeal, N.Y.C., 1965-75; trustee Fla. Nature Conservancy, Winter Park, 1990—, treas., 1990—; bd. dirs., treas. Fla. Audubon Soc., Casselberry, 1984-95, Defenders of Wildlife, Washington, 1985-95, chmn. bd. dirs. 1995—; 1st v.p. Tropical Audubon Soc., South Miami, 1983-93. Recipient Chmn.'s award Fla. Audubon Soc., 1989, 93; funded named scholarship Columbia Coll. Fellow Fairchild Tropical Garden; mem. Columbia Coll. Alumni Assn. (bd. dirs. 1992-93, sustaining), Phi Beta Kappa (sustaining South Fla.). Home: 5522 Riviera Dr Coral Gables FL 33146-2747 Office: 7800 S Red Rd Ste 203 Miami FL 33143

STEINBERG, ARTHUR G(ERALD), geneticist; b. Port Chester, N.Y., Feb. 27, 1912; s. Bernard Aaron and Sarah (Kaplan) S.; m. Edith Wexler, Nov. 22, 1939; children: Arthur E., Jean E. Strimling. B.S., CCNY, 1933; M.A., Columbia U., 1934, Ph.D. (Univ. fellow), 1941. Mem. genetics dept. McGill U., Montreal, Que., Can., 1940-44; chmn. dept. genetics Fels Research Inst., asso. prof. genetics Antioch Coll., Yellow Springs, Ohio, 1946-48; cons. div. biometry and med. stats. Mayo Clinic, Rochester, Minn., 1948-52; geneticist Children's Cancer Research Found. and research asso. Children's Hosp., Boston, 1952-56; prof. biology Case Western Res. U., Cleve., 1956-72; asst. prof. human genetics, dept. preventive medicine Case Western Res. U., 1956-60, asso. prof., 1960-70, prof. human genetics, dept. reproductive biology, 1970—, Francis Hobart Herrick prof. biology, 1972-82, emeritus, 1982—, prof. human genetics, dept. medicine, 1975-82; lectr. genetics dept. orthodontics Harvard Sch. Dental Medicine, 1956-58; dir. heredity clinic Lakeside Hosp., Cleve., 1958-76; vis. prof. Albert Einstein Med. Coll., N.Y.C., 1962, 64, 66, Ind. U., Bloomington, 1972, N.Y. U. Sch. Medicine, 1977; XIIth Ann. Raymond Dart lectr. U. Witwatersrand, Johannesburg, S.Africa, 1975; mem. permanent com. to arrange Internat. Congresses Human Genetics; mem. med. adv. bd. Cystic Fibrosis Found. Cleve., 1957-69; mem. sci. adv. bd. Nat. Cystic Fibrosis Research Found., 1961-63; cons. to expert adv. panel on human genetics WHO, 1961, mem. expert adv. panel, 1965-85; mem. research adv. com. United Cerebral Palsy Found., 1962-65; mem. med. adv. bd. Nat. Genetics Found., 1966-68, chmn., 1968-80; dir. WHO Collaborating Centre for Reference and Research on Genetic Factors of Human Immunoglobulins, 1966-78; cons. study of diabetes in Pima Indians NIH, 1970—. Editor: Am. Jour. Human Genetics, 1956-61; sr. editor: Progress in Med. Genetics, 1960-83; mem. internat. bd. editors: Human Genetics Abstracts, 1962—; cons. editor: Transfusion, 1964—; contbg. editor: Vox Sanguinis, 1965-79; contbr. articles to sci. jours. Bd. dirs. Cleve. Zoo; mem. Cleve. Inst. Art, Cleve. Mus. Art, Cleve. Health Mus., Mus. Natural History. Fellow Australian Acad. Sci. (sr.), AAAS; mem. Am. Soc. Human Genetics (pres. 1964, dir. 1954-66), Genetics Soc. Am., Am. Assn. Immunologists, Japanese Soc. Human Genetics (hon.), Societe Francaise d'Anthropologie et d'Ecologie Humaine (fgn. mem. sci. counsel 1972), Sigma Xi. Home: 20300 N Park Blvd Apt 4B Cleveland OH 44118-5026 Office: 405Nc Millis Sci Center Case Western Res U Cleveland OH 44106 *The motivation for my life's work (research and teaching) has been to learn more about heredity and its application to humanity. I am fortunate in that my wife has always been supportive of my efforts, while pursuing a career of her own.*

STEINBERG, ARTHUR IRWIN, periodontist, educator; b. Pitts., Sept. 16, 1935; s. Ben and Sylvia (Jacobs) S.; B.S. in Microbiology, U. Pitts., 1957, D.M.D. cum laude, 1963, postgrad. in radiobiology, 1957-59; diploma in periodontology-immunology (USPHS fellow), Harvard U., 1966; m. Barbara Fay Ehrenkranz, May 23, 1959; children: Sharon Jill, Mindy Ruth, Michael Eli. Asst. prof. periodontology SUNY, Buffalo, 1966-67; assoc. prof. periodontology Temple U., Phila., 1967-68, assoc. prof. grad. periodontology, 1968-70; attending periodontist Phoenixville (Pa.) Hosp., 1971—, now mem. infections control com., by-laws com., religious affairs com., 1977—, credentials com., 1982—; mem. staff Suburban Gen. Hosp., Norristown, Pa., 1972—, Phoenixville Hosp., 1976—; asst. prof. periodontics U. Pa., 1973-82, clin. assoc. prof., 1982—; lectr. continuing edn., off-campus program U. Pitts., 1973—; Fulbright-Hays lectr. Nat. U. Ireland, Cork, 1970-71; vis. prof. Cork Dental Sch. and Hosp., 1971—; lectr. Periodontology Soc. Madrid, Spain, 1980, 5th region Soc. Periodontology Viña Del Mar, Chile, 1985; dentist in pediatrics Charlestown (Mass.) Boys Club, 1965-66; speaker Periodontists Conv., Chgo., 1966, N.J. Coll. Medicine and Dentistry, Conn. Dental Assn., 1967, U. Ind. Schs. Dentistry and Medicine, Phila. Ann. Dental Sci. Session, 1969, N.J. Dental Assn., 1970, Wilmington chpt. Sigma Epsilon Delta, 1974, Lehigh Valley Dental Soc., 1974, Inst. Medicine, Bucharest, Rumania, 1976, other confs. and convs.; participant Project Head Start, Childrens Hosp., Boston, 1966; mem. fund-raising subcom. Harvard U. Sch. Dental Medicine, 1980—; mem. faculty U. Pitts, 1988—; commencement speaker U. Pa. Sch. Dental Medicine, 1988, Harcum Coll. Dental Hygiene Program, 1994-95; presentor Phila. County Dental Soc. Ann. Meeting Liberty Dental Conf., 1988, 90, Acad. Gen. Dentistry Ann. Meeting, 1988. Contbg.-author The Fulbright Experience. Inducted into Phoenixville Hosps. Hall of Honor, 1996; mem. Legion Honor Chapel Four Chaplains, Valley Forge, Pa. Fellow Am. Coll. Dentists, Coll. Physicians Phila., Pierre Fauchard Acad., Acad. Dentistry Internat., Internat. Acad. Dental Studies; mem. AMA, Am. Dental Assn., AAUP, Harvard Dental, Fulbright (dir. 1977-79, mem. fin. resources com. 1983—) alumni assns., Pa. Soc. Periodontists (chmn. ins. com. 1967-69), Harvard Odontological Soc., Fulbright Assn., Nat. Fulbright-Alumni Assn. (a founder 1976, v.p. fin. affairs 1976-79), Am. Acad. Periodontology (ins. com. 1969, hosp. care com. 1973-74, continuing edn. speaker 1976 conv., 1983 conv.; nominating com. chmn. Pa. region to exec. council 1975, nat. clin. affairs com., 1984), Am. Coll. Clin. Pharmacology, Northeastern Soc. Periodontists, Acad. Stomatology Phila., Phila. Acad. Scis., Sigma Xi, Omicron Kappa Upsilon, Psi Omega (dep. councillor Zeta chpt. 1977-79). Clubs: Masons (32 deg., Shriner), Rotary (dir. 1973-76, chmn. found. com., chmn. internat. svc. 1974-76), B'nai B'rith, Harvard of Phila., Pottstown (Pa.) Area Study (pres. 1976-77). Contbg. author: Dentistry and the Allergic Patient, 1973; contbr. numerous articles to profl. jours. Home and Office: 1681 Pheasant Ln Norristown PA 19403-3331

STEINBERG, BURT, retail executive; b. N.Y.C., June 2, 1945; s. Harry and Etta (Lippman) S.; m. Francine Hershkowitz, Dec. 22, 1968; children: Michael, Jessica. BA, CCNY, 1968; MBA, Columbia U., 1970. Mdse. mgr. Abraham & Straus, Bklyn., 1972-77; sr. v.p. Brooks Fashion Stores, N.Y.C., 1977-82, Dress Barn Inc., Stamford, Conn., 1982—; Pres. Dress Barn Inc., Suffern, NY. Mem. Columbia Alumni Assn., Am. Mktg. Assn. Avocations: coaching youth soccer and baseball, travel, sports. Office: Dress Barn Inc 30 Dunningan Dr Suffern NY 10901*

STEINBERG, CHARLES ALLAN, electronics manufacturing company executive; b. Bklyn., June 7, 1934; s. Joseph and Rose (Graff) S.; m. Helen Greene, June 16, 1956; children—Ruth, Steven, Bruce. B.S.E.E., CCNY, 1955; M.S.E.E., M.I.T., 1958. Mem. tech. staff Bell Telephone Labs., Whippany, N.J., 1955; research and teaching asst. MIT, 1955-58; engring. sect. mgr. Airborne Instruments Lab. div. Eaton Corp., Deer Park, N.Y., 1958-63; exec. v.p. Ampex Corp., Redwood City, Calif., 1963-86, pres., chief exec. officer, 1986-88; pres. bus. and profl. group Sony Corp. Am., Montvale, N.J., 1988—. Contbr. numerous articles on med. electronics and diagnosis, info. systems to profl. jours.; patentee computer techniques in medicine. Bd. dirs. Santa Clara County (Calif.) United Fund, 1969-71. Mem. IEEE, CCNY Alumni Assn., M.I.T. Alumni Assn., Sigma Xi, Tau Beta Pi, Eta Kappa Nu. Office: Sony Electronics Inc 3 Paragon Dr Montvale NJ 07645-1725

STEINBERG, DANIEL, preventive medicine physician, educator; b. Windsor, Ont., Can., July 21, 1922; came to U.S., 1922; s. Maxwell Robert and Bess (Krupp) S.; m. Sara Murdock, Nov. 30, 1946 (dec. July 1986); children: Jonathan Henry, Ann Ballard, David Ethan; m. Mary Ellen Stratthaus, Aug. 11, 1991; 1 stepchild: Katrin Seifert. B.S. with highest distinction, Wayne State U., 1941, M.D. with highest distinction, 1944; Ph.D. with distinction (fellow Am. Cancer Soc. 1950-51), Harvard U., 1951; M.D. (hon.), U. Gothenburg, 1991. Intern Boston City Hosp., 1944-45; physician Detroit Receiving Hosp., 1945-46; instr. physiology Boston U. Sch. Medicine, 1947-48; joined USPHS, 1951, med. dir., 1959; research staff lab. cellular physiology and metabolism Nat. Heart Inst., 1951-53, chief sect. metabolism, 1956-61, chief of lab. metabolism, 1962-68; lectr. grad. program NIH, 1955, mem. sci. adv. com. ednl. activities, 1955-61, com. chmn., 1955-60; mem. metabolism study sect. USPHS, 1959-61; chmn. heart and lung research rev. com. B Nat. Heart, Lung and Blood Inst., 1977-79; vis. scientist Carlsberg Labs., Copenhagen, 1952-53, Nat. Inst. Med. Research, London, 1960-61, Rockefeller U., 1981; pres. Lipid Research Inc., 1961-64, adv. bd., 1964-73; prof. medicine, head div. metabolic disease Sch. Medicine, U. Calif., San Diego and La Jolla; also program dir. basic scis. medicine Sch. Medicine, U. Calif., 1968—. Former editor Jour. Lipid Research; mem. editorial bd. Jour Clin. Investigation, 1969-74, Jour. Biol. Chemistry, 1980-84, Arteriosclerosis, 1980—; exec. editor Analytical Biochemistry, 1978-80; contbr. articles to profl. jours. Bd. dirs. Found. Advanced Edn. in Scis., 1959-68, pres., 1956-62, 65-67. Served to capt. M.C. AUS, World War II. Mem. Nat. Acad. Scis., AAAS, Am. Acad. Arts and Scis., Am. Heart Assn. (mem. exec. com. coun. on arteriosclerosis 1960-63, 65-73, chmn. coun. arteriosclerosis 1967-69), Fedn. Am. Scientists (exec. com. 1957-58), Am. Soc. Biol. Chemists, Am. Soc. Clin. Investigation, Assn. Am. Physicians, Am. Fedn. Clin. Rsch., European Atherosclerosis Discussion Group, Alpha Omega Alpha. Home: 7742 Whitefield Pl La Jolla CA 92037-3810 Office: U Calif San Diego Dept Medicine 0682 9500 Gilman Dr La Jolla CA 92093-5003

STEINBERG, DAVID, comedian, author, actor; b. Winnipeg, Man., Can., Aug. 9, 1942; s. Jacob and Ruth S.; married; 2 children: Sasha, Rebecca. Student, Hebrew Theol. Coll., U. Chgo. Writer, actor Second City, Chicago; actor: Broadway appearances include Carry Me Back to Morningside Heights, Little Murders, (TV shows) Music Scene, The David Steinberg Show; dir.: (films) Paternity, 1981, Going Berserk, 1983, also The Richard Belzer Show, (TV shows) Newhart, Designing Women, Seinfeld, It Had To Be You, (comls.) Pizza Hut (with Roseanne Barr, Clio award 1987), NCR (with Dom deLuise), Jell-O (with Bill Cosby), Bartles & Jaymes; author spl. Return of Smothers Bros; rec. David Steinberg Disguised as a Normal Person; starred in film Something Short of Paradise, 1979. Office: care William Morris Agy Inc 151 S El Camino Dr Beverly Hills CA 90212-2704

STEINBERG, DAVID ISAAC, economic development consultant, educator; b. Cambridge, Mass., Nov. 26, 1928; s. Naaman and Miriam (Goldberg) S.; m. Isabel Maxwell, 1951 (div. 1962); 1 child, Christopher; m. Ann Myongsook Lee, May 15, 1964; children: Alexander L., Eric D. BA, Dartmouth Coll., 1950; MA, Harvard U., 1955; DLitt (hon.), Sungkunkwan U., Seoul, Republic of Korea. Analyst Nat. Security Coun., Washington, 1951-53; program officer Asia Found., N.Y.C., 1956-58; asst. rep. Asia Found., Burma, 1958-62, Hong Kong, 1962-63; rep. Asia Found., Republic of Korea, 1963-68, Washington, 1968-69; cons., sr. fgn. svc. officer AID, Washington and Bangkok (Thailand), 1969-86; ret., 1986; pres. Mansfield Ctr. for Pacific Affairs, Helena, Mont., 1986-87, Sr. Resources Internat., 1989-94; disting. prof. Korea Studies Georgetown U., Washington, 1990-94; rep. The Asia Found., Seoul, Republic of Korea, 1994—; pvt. cons., Washington, 1987—, World Bank, 1987—, Woodrow Wilson Ctr. for Scholars of the Smithsonian Instn., Dept. of State and the Agy. for Internat. Devel., the Can. Internat. Devel. Agy., Devel. Assocs., Inc., and others; founding mem. Burma Studies Found., De Kalb, Ill., 1987. Author: Burma's Road Toward Development, 1981, Burma, 1982, The Republic of Korea Economic Transformation and Social Change, 1988, The Future of Burma, 1990. 1st lt. U.S. Army, 1953-55. Fellow Lingnan U., Canton, China, 1948, Dartmouth Coll., 1950; named Disting. Prof. of Korea Studies, Georgetown U. Mem. Assn. Asian Studies, Oriental Ceramic Soc., Asia Devel. Roundtable (chmn. 1984-86, 87—), Siam Soc., Royal Asiatic Soc. (life Korea br.), Burma Rsch. Soc. (life), Asia Soc. (cons. 1988—), Cosmos Club, Royal Bangkok (Thailand) Sports Club. Home: 6207 Goodview St Bethesda MD 20817 Office: The Asia Found, KPO Box 738, Seoul 110-607, Republic of Korea

STEINBERG, DAVID JOEL, academic administrator, historian, educator; b. N.Y.C., Apr. 5, 1937; s. Milton and Edith (Alpert) S.; m. Sally Levitt (div.

Dec., 1986); children: Noah, Jonah; m. Joan Diamond, Aug. 28, 1987. BA magna cum laude, Harvard U., 1959, MA, 1963, LittD, 1964; LittD, Kyung Hee U., Seoul, Korea, 1989; LLD (hon), Keimyung U., Daegu, Korea. Prof. history U. Mich., 1964-73; exec. asst. to pres. Brandeis U., Waltham, Mass., 1973-77, v.p., univ. sec., 1977-83; pres. L.I. U., Brookville, N.Y., 1985—; testified before Com. on Fgn. Affairs, U.S. Ho. of Reps., Fgn. Affairs Com. of U.S. Senate; cons. The Ford Found., UN Fund for Population Activities. Author: Philippine Collaboration in World War II, 1967 (Univ. Press award 1969), The Philippines: A Singular and a Plural Place, 1982, rev. edit., 1994; author (with others) In Search of Southeast Asia: A Modern History, 1970, rev. edit., 1987, Asia in Western and World History: A Guide for Teaching, 1993. Trustee Commn. Ind. Colls. and Univs.; bd. dirs. L.I. Assn.; past pres. Cambridge (Mass.) Ctr. for Adult Edn., chmn. L.I. Group. English Speaking Union Exchange scholar, Malvern Coll., NDEA scholar, Fulbright Found. exchange scholar. Mem. Council Fgn. Relations, Assn. Asian Studies (chmn. fin. com.), Phi Beta Kappa. Democrat. Jewish. Club: Harvard (N.Y.C.). Office: LI U Northern Blvd Greenvale NY 11548

STEINBERG, HOWARD ELI, lawyer, holding company executive, public official; b. N.Y.C., Nov. 19, 1944; s. Herman and Anne Rudel (Sinnreich) S.; m. Judith Ann Schucart, Jan. 28, 1968; children: Henry Robert, Kathryn Jill. A.B., U. Pa., 1965; J.D., Georgetown U., 1969. Bar: N.Y. 1970, U.S. Dist. Ct. (so. and ea. dists.) N.Y. 1973, U.S. Ct. Appeals (2d cir.) 1976. Assoc. Dewey, Ballantine, Bushby, Palmer & Wood, N.Y.C., 1969-76, ptnr., 1977-83; sr. v.p., gen. counsel, corp. sec. Reliance Group Holdings Inc., N.Y.C., 1983—; chmn. N.Y. State Thruway Authority, 1996—. Editor case notes: Georgetown Law Jour., 1968-69. Bd. dir. Puerto Rican Legal Def. and Edn. Fund. Inc., 1993-95; bd. overseers U. Pa. Sch. Arts and Scis., 1989—. Capt. JAGC, USAR, 1972-74. Mem. ABA, N.Y. State Bar Assn., Assn. of Bar of City of N.Y. (com. on securities regulation 1984-87, com. on corp. law 1987-90, com. on fed. legis. 1990-93, chair ad hoc com. on Senate Confirmation Process 1991-92), Univ. Club. Jewish. Office: Reliance Group Holdings Inc 55 E 52nd St New York NY 10055-0002 also: NY State Thruway Authority 200 Southern Blvd Albany NY 12209

STEINBERG, JACK, lawyer; b. Seattle, Jan. 6, 1915; s. Solomon Reuben and Mary (Rashall) S.; widower; children: Roosevelt, Mary Ann Steinberg Shulman, Quentin. BA, U. Wash., 1936, JD, 1938. Bar: Wash. 1938, U.S. Dist. Ct. (we. dist.) Wash. 1938, U.S. Ct. Appeals (9th cir.) 1938. Ptnr. Steinberg & Steinberg, Seattle, 1938—. Former editor and pub. The Washington Examiner; contbr. numerous articles to legal jours. Judge pro tem Seattle Mcpl. Ct., Seattle, 1952; past pres. Emanuel Congregation, Seattle, Seattle chpt. Zionist Orgn. Am. Recipient Scrolls of Honor award (3) The State of Israel. Mem. Assn. Trial Lawyers Am., Am. Judicature Soc., Wash. Bar Assn., Wash. Assn. Trial Lawyers, Seattle-King County Bar Assn. Jewish Orthodox. Avocation: outdoor activities. Office: Steinberg & Steinberg 1210 Vance Bldg Seattle WA 98101

STEINBERG, JAMES IAN, marketing executive; b. N.Y.C., Oct. 2, 1957; s. S. Sherman and Marian Steinberg; m. Andrea F.C. Hacquoil, Feb. 28, 1984. Student, U. London, 1978; BA, Columbia Coll., 1979; MBA, NYU, 1984. Account exec. Grey Advt., N.Y.C., 1984-86; sr. product mgr. Sterling Drug Co., N.Y.C., 1986-91; mktg. dir. Revlon Consumer Products, N.Y.C., 1991-93; bus. devel. Gannett Corp., N.Y.C., 1995—. Mem. Am. Mktg. Assn., Columbia Club. Avocation: squash. Home: 4 River House Irvington NY 10533-1540

STEINBERG, JANET ECKSTEIN, journalist; b. Cin.; d. Charles and Adele (Ehrenfeld) Eckstein; m. Irvin S. Silverstein, Oct. 22, 1988; children: Susan Carole Steinberg Somerstein, Jody Lynn Steinberg Lazarow. BS, U. Cin., 1964. Free-lance writer; guest appearances Braun and Co., Sta.-WLW-TV, Sta. WMKV-TV; guest lectr. Tri State Travel Sch., 1994—; travel cons., 1994—; Contbr. numerous articles to newspapers, mags. and books, U.S., Can., Singapore, Australia, N.Z.; travel columnist Cin. Post, 1978-86, Ky. Post, 1978-86, Cin. Enquirer, 1986-94; travel editor S. Fla. Single Living, 1988-92; contbr. Singles Scene and Cin. Mag., 1980—; travel columnist Eastside Weekend Mag., 1994—; contbg. editor Travel Agt., 1986-88, Birnbaum Travel Guides, 1988—, The Writer, 1988-92, Entree, 1986—; travel columnist Northeast mag., 1986-88, South Fla. Single Living, 1984-92. Recipient Lowell Thomas travel journalism award, 1985, 86, 91, Henry E. Bradshaw Travel Journalism award, 1st place, best of show, 1988, Buckeye Travel award Ohio Divsn. Travel & Tourism, 1992. Mem. Am. Soc. Journalists and Authors, Soc. Am. Travel Writers (1st place award for best newspaper story 1981, 3d place award for best mag. story 1981, 91, 1st place award for best newspaper article award 1984, 91, best mag. article 1985, 2d place award best pathos article, 1984, 88, 2d place award specific category, 1989), Midwest Travel Writers Assn. (Best Mag. Story award 1981, 95, Best Series award 1981, 84, 94, 96, Cipriani award 1981, 1st place award best article 1989, 2d place award for best article 1982-84, 89, 95, 3d place award best article 1992, Mark Twain award 1992), Am. Soc. Journalists and Authors, Soc. Am. Travel Writers, Midwest Travel Writers Assn., Soc. Profl. Journalists, Losantiville Country Club, Travelers Century Club, Circumnavigators Club. Home: 900 Adams Crossing # 9200 Cincinnati OH 45202-1666

STEINBERG, JOAN EMILY, retired middle school educator; b. San Francisco, Dec. 9, 1932; d. John Emil and Kathleen Helen (Montgomery) S. BA, U. Calif.-Berkeley, 1954; EdD, U. San Francisco, 1981. Tchr., Vallejo (Calif.) Unified Sch. Dist., 1959-61, San Francisco Unified Sch. Dist., 1961-93, elem. tchr., 1961-78, tchr. life and phys. sci. jr. high sch., 1978-85, 87-93, sci. cons., 1985-87; lectr. elem. edn. San Francisco State U., 1993-94; ind. sci. edn. cons., 1993—. Contbr. articles to zool. and edn. books and profl. jours. Fulbright scholar U. Sydney (Australia), 1955-56; recipient Calif. Educator award, 1988, Outstanding Educator in Teaching award U. San Francisco Alumni Soc., 1989. Mem. ASCD, San Francisco Zool. Soc., Exploratorium, Astron. Soc. Pacific, Am. Fedn. Tchrs., Calif. Acad. Scis., Calif. Malacozool. Soc., Nat. Sci. Tchrs. Assn., Elem. Sch. Sci. Assn. (sec. 1984-85, pres. 1986-87, newsletter editor 1994—), Calif. Sci. Tchrs. Assn., Sigma Xi. Democrat.

STEINBERG, JONATHAN ROBERT, judge; b. Phila., Jan. 3, 1939; s. Sigmund Hopkins and Hortense B. (Gottlieb) S.; m. Rochelle Helene Schwartz, May 30, 1963; children: Andrew Joshua, Amy Judith. BA, Cornell U., 1960; LLB cum laude, U. Pa., 1963. Bar: D.C. 1963, U.S. Ct. Appeals (D.C. cir.) 1964. Law clk. to judge U.S. Ct. Appeals (D.C. cir.), 1963-64; atty. advisor, then dep. gen. counsel Peace Corps, Washington, 1964-69; com. on labor and pub. welfare, counsel subcom. on vets. affairs, U.S. Senate, 1969-71, counsel subcom. on R.R. retirement, 1971-73, counsel spl. subcom. on human resources, 1972-77, chief counsel com. on vets. affairs, 1977-81, minority chief counsel and staff dir. com. on vets. affairs, U.S. Senate, 1981-87, chief counsel and staff dir. com. on vets. affairs, 1987-90; assoc. judge U.S. Ct. of Vets. Appeals, 1990—. Contbr. to legal jours. Bd. dirs. Bethany West Recreation Assn., Bethany Beach, Del., 1973-84, 86-90. Mem. aba, D.C. Bar Assn., Order of Coif. Democrat. Jewish. Home: 11204 Hawhill End Potomac MD 20854-2039 Office: US Ct Vets Appeals 625 Indiana Ave NW Ste 900 Washington DC 20004-2901

STEINBERG, JOSEPH SAUL, investment company executive; b. Chgo., Feb. 5, 1944; s. Paul S. and Sylvia (Neikrug) S.; child from previous marriage, Sarah Aliza; m. Diane L. Heidt, 1987; children: Paul Steven, Rachel Catherine. A.B., NYU, 1966; M.B.A., Harvard U., 1970. Vol. Peace Corps, Kingston, Jamaica, 1966-68; v.p. Carl Marks & Co., Inc. (investment bankers), N.Y.C., 1970-78; pres. Leucadia Nat. Corp., N.Y.C., 1979—; also bd. dirs.; bd. dirs. Empire Ins. Group. Trustee NYU. Clubs: Harvard, Nat. Arts (N.Y.C.). Office: Leucadia Nat Corp 315 Park Ave S New York NY 10010-3607

STEINBERG, LAWRENCE EDWARD, lawyer; b. Dallas, Nov. 25, 1935; s. Oscar J. and Pearl L. (Soloman) S.; children: Adam Joseph, Ilana Sara. B.B.A., U. Tex., 1958; J.D., So. Methodist U., 1960. Bar: Tex. 1960. Since practiced in Dallas; partner firm Steinberg Soloman & Meer, 1971-88, Johnson & Steinberg, Dallas, 1988-93; of counsel Jenkins & Gilchrist, Dallas, 1994—. Mem. Urban Rehab. Stds. Bd., Dallas, 1975-76; mem. adv. com. affirmative action program Dallas Ind. Sch. Dist., 1974-76; regional bd. chmn. Anti-Defamation League of B'nai Brith, 1974-77, nat. exec. com., 1977—, nat. law com., 1974-87; trustee Edna Gladney Home, 1975-92, Shelton Sch., 1987-90; bd. dirs. Jewish Fedn. Greater Dallas, 1984-87, 91-94; trustee Temple Emanu-El. 2d lt. U.S. Army, 1958-59. Mem. Lincoln City Club, Columbian Club, Masons (Shriner), Zeta Beta Tau., Phi Delta Phi, Beta Gamma Sigma, Pi Tau Pi (nat. Pres.). Home: 10131 Hollow Way Rd Dallas TX 75229-6634 Office: 1445 Ross Ave Ste 3200 Dallas TX 75202

STEINBERG, LEO, art historian, educator; b. Moscow, July 9, 1920; came to U.S., 1945; s. Isaac N. and Anna (Esselson) S. PhD, NYU Inst Fine Arts, 1960; PhD (hon.), Phila. Coll. Art, 1981, Parsons Sch. Design, 1986, Mass. Coll. Art, 1987, Bowdoin Coll., 1995. Assoc. prof. art history Hunter Coll., CUNY, N.Y.C., 1961-66, prof., 1966-75; prof. Grad. Ctr. CUNY, 1969-75; Benjamin Franklin prof. art. history U. Pa., Phila., 1975-91, prof. emeritus, 1991—; Charles Eliot Norton lectr. Harvard U., 1995-96. Author: Other Criteria, 1972, Michelangelo's Last Paintings, 1975, Borromini's San Carlo alle Quattro Fontane, 1977, The Sexuality of Christ in Renaissance Art and Modern Oblivion, 1983, 2d enlarged edit., 1996. Recipient award in lit. Am. Acad. and Inst. Arts and Letters, 1983; fellow Am. Acad. Arts and Scis., 1978, Univ. Coll., London U., 1979, MacArthur Found., 1986; recipent Frank Jewett Mather award, 1956, 84. Mem. Coll. Art Assn. Am. Home: 165 W 66th St New York NY 10023-6508

STEINBERG, LOIS JOYCE RABINOWITZ, psychologist; b. Newark, Dec. 7, 1937; d. Nathan Aaron and Edythe Mary (Kruger) Rabinowitz; m. Richard Mark Steinberg, Dec. 22, 1957; children: Russel Allen, Dina Ann Steinberg Del Amo. BS, Douglass Coll., 1959; postgrad., Seton Hall U., 1959-60; MA, Montclair State Coll., 1973; postgrad., Jersey City State Coll., 1982-83; PhD, Yeshiva U., 1983; advanced cert., CCNY, 1984. Lic. psychologist, N.J., Penn., sch. psychologist, N.J., N.Y., learning disability tchr.-cons., N.J., supr., N.J., tchr. of handicapped, N.J., elem. tchr., N.J. Tchr. Bd. Edn., Elizabeth, N.J., 1959-60; substitute tchr., home instr., supplemental instr. Bd. Edn., various cities, N.J., 1960-72; learning cons. Bd. Edn., Caldwell/West Caldwell, N.J., 1972-73; learning cons., coord. Child Help and Mainstreaming Project, sch. psychologist New Providence (N.J.) Pub. Schs., 1973-85; psychologist, sr. clinician St. Clare's-Riverside Med. Ctr., Denville, N.J., 1986-88; cons. psychologist Assn. for Retarded Citizens of Essex County, Inc., 1988—; pvt. practice Denville and Millburn, N.J., 1985—; adj. faculty Montclair State Coll., Upper Montclair, N.J., 1974; speaker Unitarian House, Summit, N.J., 1993, New Providence Parents of Classified Children, 1991, Parents of Young Children, 1993; mem. adv. com. Family Svcs., Livingston, 1989-92; mem. profl. svcs. coun. N.J. Dept. Edn., 1992—; psychologist Provide Assessments and Consultation to Child Study Team(s), New Providence and Butler, N.J., 1990-94; faciliator, panelist and workshop leader in field. Contbr. articles to profl. jours. Supr. of facilitators Project GRO Self-Help Groups, Nat. Coun. Jewish Women Ctr. for Women, Livingston, 1989—; active Met. Opera Guild, Friends of N.Y. Philharm., Smithsonian Instn., Friends of Zimmerle Art Mus.; mem. adv. com. Am. Cancer Soc., 1994. Mem. NOW, APA, Soc. Psychologists in Pvt. Practice, Assn. for Advancement of Family Therapy in N.J., N.J. Assn. Learning Consultants, N.J. Assn. Women Therapists, N.J. Acad. Psychology (Psychologists Recognition award 1991, 92), N.J. Psychol. Assn. (chair psychology in the schs. com., coun. on legis. affairs, child, youth and family com.), Psi Chi. Avocations: classical music, opera, gardening, fine arts, food and wine. Office: 25 Orchard St Ste 204 Denville NJ 07834-2160

STEINBERG, MALCOLM SAUL, biologist, educator; b. New Brunswick, N.J., June 1, 1930; s. Morris and Esther (Lerner) S.; children—Jeffery, Julie, Eleanor, Catherine; m. Marjorie Campbell, 1983. B.A., Amherst Coll., 1952; M.A., U. Minn., 1954, Ph.D., 1956. Postdoctoral fellow dept. embryology Carnegie Instn., Washington, 1956-58; asst. prof. Johns Hopkins, Balt., 1958-64; assoc. prof. Johns Hopkins, 1964-66; prof. biology Princeton U., 1966-90, Henry Fairfield Osborn prof. biology, 1975—, prof. molecular biology, 1990—; instr.-in-charge embryology course Marine Biol. Lab., 1967-71, trustee, 1969-77; chmn. Gordon Research Conf. on Cell Contact and Adhesion, 1985; appointed to NAS/NRC Bd. on Biology, 1986-92. Mem. editorial bd. Bioscience, 1976-82; contbr. articles to profl. jours. Fellow AAAS; mem. AAUP, Am. Soc. Zoologists (program officer divsn. developmental biology 1966-69, chmn. elect, then chmn. 1982-85), Am. Soc. Cell Biology, Internat. Soc. Developmental Biologists, Internat. Soc. Differentation (bd. dirs. 1995—), Soc. Developmental Biology (trustee, sec. 1970-73), Sigma Xi. Home: 86 Longview Dr Princeton NJ 08540-5642

STEINBERG, MARCIA IRENE, science foundation program director; b. Bklyn., Mar. 7, 1944; d. Solomon and Sylvia (Feldman) S.; 1 child, Eric Gordon. BS, Bklyn. Coll., 1964, MA, 1966; PhD, U. Mich., 1973. Rsch. scientist Meth. Hosp. Bklyn. Dept. Pathology, Bklyn., 1966-67, U. Mich. Dept. Surg. Rsch., Ann Arbor, Mich., 1967-68; post doctoral fellow Syracuse U. Dept. Biology, Syracuse, N.Y., 1973-76; from post doctoral fellow to assoc. prof. SUNY, Syracuse, N.Y., 1976-89; with NSF, Washington, 1990—; reviewer NATO fellowship NSF, San Francisco, 1988, Ad Hoc NSF, Syracuse, N.Y., manuscripts in field; vis. scientist Weizmann Inst. Renal Rsch. Fund, Weizmann Inst., Israel, 1987, 1988. Contbr. articles to profl. jours. Recipient Wellcome Rsch. Travel Grant, Wellcome Found. Cambridge U., U.K., 1985, Regents scholarship SUNY Bd. Regents, Bklyn., 1960-64. Mem. AAAS, Am. Soc. Biochemistry Molecular Biology, Assn. Women Sci.

STEINBERG, MARSHALL, toxicologist; b. Pitts., Sept. 18, 1932; s. Harry Lionel and Eva (Goldstein) S.; m. Patricia Louise Zobac, Nov. 3, 1962; children: Leslie Renee, Michael Allan, Maureen Sara. BS, Georgetown U., 1954; MS, U. Pitts., 1956; PhD, U. Tex., 1966. Commd. U.S. Army, 1956, advanced through grades to col., 1957-74, ret., 1976; prin. investigator Tracor Jitco, Rockville, Md., 1977, v.p., chief ops., 1977-78; v.p., dir. life scis. Hazleton Labs. Am., Vienna, Va., 1978-83; v.p., sci. dir. Hazleton Labs. Corp., Vienna, Va., 1983-87, v.p. Asian ops., 1987-90; v.p. health and environment Hercules, Inc., Wilmington, Del., 1990—; chmn. safety panel Fed. Working Group on Pest Mgmt., Washington, 1973-74; cons. Office of Pesticide Programs; EPA, Washington, 1975-77; mem. expert in pharmacology and toxicology French Govt., 1985-90; chmn. safety com. Internat. Pharm. Excipients Coun., 1990—, also bd. dirs.; bd. dirs. Global Environ. Svcs., Inc. Author articles, govt. reports. book chpts. Bd. dirs. Del. chpt. Am. Lung Assn.; trustee Health Environ. Scis. Inst.; mem. sci. adv. bd. Digene, 1986-89. Decorated Legion of Merit. Mem. Soc. Toxicology (sec. 1983, 85), Am. Coll. Toxicology (pres. 1986), Am. Indsl. Hygiene Assn., Toxicology Lab. Accredidation Bd. (sec. 1985-91), Acad. Toxicological Scis. (fellow, councillor 1982-85, v.p. 1990-91), Royal Soc. Medicine, Internat. Soc. Regulatory Toxicology and Pharmacology, Brandywine Valley Assn. (bd. dirs.). Jewish. Avocation: hunting. Office: Hercules Inc Hercules Plz Wilmington DE 19894

STEINBERG, MELVIN ALLEN, lieutenant governor, lawyer; b. Balt., Oct. 4, 1933; s. Irvin and Julia (Levenson) S.; m. Anita Akman, 1958; children: Edward Bryan, Susan Renee, Barbara Ellen. AA, U. Balt., 1952, JD, 1955. Bar: Md. 1955. Ptnr. Steinberg Lichter Coleman & Rogers, Towson, Md., 1978-86, Levin Gann & Hankin, Towson, 1986—; atty. with Rifkin, Livingston, Levitan & Silver, Baltimore; mem. Md. State Senate, 1967-87, vice chmn. jud. process, 1975-79; chmn. fin. com., 1979-82, pres. of senate, 1983-87, lt. gov., Md., 1987—. Del. Dem. Nat. Conv., 1968. Mem. Am. Judicature Soc., ABA, Md. Bar Assn., Balt. Bar Assn., Nu Beta Epsilon. Democrat. Jewish. Lodges: B'nai B'rith, Masons. *

STEINBERG, MEYER, chemical engineer; b. Phila., July 10, 1924; s. Jacob Louis and Freda Leah S.; m. Ruth Margot Elias, Dec. 24, 1950; children: David Martin, Jay Louis. BSChemE, Cooper Union, 1944; MSChemE, Bklyn. Poly. Inst., 1949. Registered profl. engr. N.Y. Jr. chem. engr. Manhattan dist., Kellex Corp., Oak Ridge, Los Alamos, 1944-46; asst. chem. engr. Deutsch & Loonam, 1947-50; chem. engr. Guggenheim Brothers, Mineola, N.Y., 1950-57; head process sci. div. Brookhaven Nat. Lab., Upton, N.Y., 1957—; expert in fossil and nuclear energy. Contbr. articles to profl. jours. Served with AUS, 1944-46. Recipient IR-100 award, 1970; Wasson award Am. Concrete Inst., 1972, Engr. of Year award, 1985, Ind. award Quest, 1985. Fellow Am. Nuclear Soc., Am. Inst. Chem. Engrs. (dir. L.I. sect.); mem. Am. Chem. Soc., AAAS, Am. Concrete Inst., Inst. Assos. Hydrogen Energy, Sigma Xi. Democrat. Jewish. Research on nuclear and fossil energy. Home: 15 Alderfield Ln Melville NY 11747-1724 Office: Brookhaven Nat Lab Upton NY 11973

STEINBERG, MICHAEL, music critic, educator; b. Breslau, Germany, Oct. 4, 1928; came to U.S., 1943, naturalized, 1950; s. Siegfried and Margarethe (Cohn) S.; m. Jane Bonacker, July 26, 1953 (div. 1983); children: Peter Sebastian, Adam Gregory; m. Jorja Fleezanis, July, 1983. A.B., Princeton U., 1949, M.F.A., 1951; Mus. D. (hon.), New Eng. Conservatory Music, 1966. Free-lance writer, 1952—; head history dept. Manhattan Sch. Music, N.Y.C., 1957-64; music critic Boston Globe, 1964-76; dir. publs. Boston Symphony Orch., 1976-79; artistic adviser San Francisco Symphony, 1979-89, program annotator, lectr., 1989—; artistic adviser Minn. Orch., 1989-92; artistic dir. Minn. Sommerfest, 1990-92; program annotator, lectr. N.Y. Philharmonic, 1995—; vis. mem. faculty Hunter Coll., 1954, U. Sask. (Can.), 1959, Smith Coll., 1964, Brandeis U., 1964-65; faculty New Eng. Conservatory Music, 1968-71, Wellesley Coll., 1971-72, Brandeis U., 1971-72, Mass. Inst. Tech., 1973; disting. vis. prof. McMaster U., Hamilton, Ont., 1982; cons. NEH, Nat. Endowment for Arts, Mass. Council of Arts and Humanities, Calif. Arts Council, Rockefeller Found. Author: The Symphony: A Listener's Guide, 1995. Served with U.S. Army, 1955-57. Recipient Sang prize for criticism in arts, 1969; citation for Excellence in Criticism Am. Guild Organists, 1972. Mem. Am, Internat. musicological socs. Home: 6828 Valley View Rd Minneapolis MN 55439-1646 Office: Davies Symphony Hall San Francisco CA 94102

STEINBERG, MICHAEL, department store executive. Pres., chief exec. officer Foley's, Houston, 1988—; chmn., chief exec. officer Macy's West, San Francisco, 1992—. Office: Macy's West PO Box 7888 San Francisco CA 94108*

STEINBERG, MORTON M., lawyer; b. Chgo., Feb. 13, 1945; s. Paul S. and Sylvia (Neikrug) S.; m. Miriam C. Bernstein, Aug. 25, 1974; children: Adam Michael, Shira Judith. AB with honors U. Ill., 1967; JD, Northwestern U., 1971. Bar: Ill. 1971, U.S. Dist. Ct. (no. dist.) Ill. 1971, U.S. Ct. Appeals (7th cir.) 1971, U.S. Supreme Ct. 1974; DC, 1994, Colo. 1995. Assoc. Caffarelli & Wiczer, Chgo., 1971-73; assoc. Arnstein, Gluck, Lehr, Barron & Milligan, Chgo., 1974-76, ptnr., 1977-86; ptnr., Rudnick & Wolfe, 1986—; speaker in field. Sr. editor Jour. Criminal Law and Criminology, Northwestern U., 1969-71; Bd. dirs. Camp Ramah in Wis., Inc., Chgo., 1974—, sr. v.p., 1992-94, pres., 1994—; bd. dirs., v.p. Camp Ramah in Wis. Endowment Corp., 1993—; bd. dirs. North Suburban Synagogue Beth-El, Highland Park, Ill., 1978—, corp. sec., 1983-87, pres. 1989-91, chmn. bd. trustees, 1991-93, trustee, 1991—; mem. Nat. Ramah Commn., 1987—, v.p. 1994—; bd. dirs. Found. Conservative Judaism in Israel, 1985-90; Midwest region bd. dirs. United Synagogue of Conservative Judaism, 1989-91, 94—; charter mem. U.S. Holocaust Meml. Mus., 1992. Served with USAR, 1969-75. Recipient Youth Leadership award Nat. Fedn. Jewish Men's Clubs, N.Y.C., 1963; cert. of merit U.S. Dist. Ct. Fed. Defender Program, Chgo., 1969. Mem. ABA, Internat. Wine Lawyers Assn., Ill. State Bar Assn., Chgo. Bar Assn., D.C. Bar. Jewish. Home: 1320 Lincoln Ave S Highland Park IL 60035-3459 Office: Rudnick & Wolfe 203 N La Salle St Chicago IL 60601-1210

STEINBERG, ROBERT M., holding company executive; b. Bklyn., 1942; married. Student, N.C. State U., 1964. Asst. v.p. Ideal Rubber Co., 1964-65; with Reliance Group Inc., N.Y.C., 1965—, salesman, 1965-67, asst. dir. corp. devel., 1967-68, asst. v.p. computer svcs., 1968-69, v.p. adminstrn., 1969-74, sr. v.p. adminstrn., 1974-78, exec. v.p., 1978-81, pres., chief oper. officer, 1981—, also dir.; also pres., chief oper. officer, dir. Reliance Group Holdings Inc., N.Y.C.; pres., chief oper. officer Leasco Corp.; chmn., chief exec. officer Reliance Ins. Co.; dir. Empire Inc., Zenith Nat. Ins., Days Inn Corp., Frank B. Hall & Co., Telemundo Group, Inc. Bd. dirs. Jewish Guild for Blind. Office: Reliance Group Holdings Inc 55 E 52nd St New York NY 10055-0002*

STEINBERG, ROBERT PHILIP, lawyer; b. Danville, Ill., Apr. 4, 1931; s. Frederick Philip and Beulah Iona (Olmsted) S.; m. Doris Elizabeth Blank, May 10, 1958; children: Susan Elizabeth, Mary Louise. BA, DePauw U., 1953; LLB, N.Y. U., 1956. Bar: N.Y. 1956, Pa. 1959. Assoc. Shearman & Sterling, N.Y.C., 1956; assoc. Drinker Biddle & Reath, Phila., 1958-65, ptnr., 1965—, chmn., 1992-94. V.p. Germantown Hist. Soc., Phila., 1991-95, The Phila. Theatre Co., 1992—. Mem. Phila. Bar Assn. (treas. 1970-72). Home: 3906 W Netherfield Rd Philadelphia PA 19129-1014 Office: Drinker Biddle & Reath Phila Nat Bank Bldg 1345 Chestnut St Philadelphia PA 19107-3426

STEINBERG, SAUL PHILLIP, holding company executive; b. N.Y.C., Aug. 13, 1939; s. Julius and Anne (Cohen) S.; m. Barbara Herzog, May 28, 1961 (div. 1977); children: Laura, Jonothan, Nicholas; m. Laura Sconocchia, Dec. 21, 1978 (div. Dec. 1983); 1 child, Julian; m. Gayfryd McNabb, Jan. 22, 1984; children: Rayne, Holden. BS, Wharton Sch., U. Pa., 1959. Founder, chmn., chief exec. officer, dir. Reliance Group Holdings Inc., N.Y.C.; bd. dirs. Symbol Techs. Inc., Zenith Nat. Ins. Corp. Chmn. bd. overseers Wharton Sch. U. Pa.; mem. bd. overseers Cornell U. Med. Coll., N.Y.C.; trustee Jewish Med. Ctr., N.Y.C., U. Pa., N.Y. Pub. Libr.; bd. dirs. N.Y.C. Partnership. Mem. Glen Oaks Club. Jewish. Home: 740 Park Ave New York NY 10021-4251 Office: Reliance Group Holdings Inc 55 E 52nd St New York NY 10055-0002

STEINBERG, STEPHEN ARTHUR, information systems executive; b. Hartford, Conn., June 15, 1944; s. Morris and Irene (Lebon) S.; m. Lois Shapiro, Apr. 21, 1974; children: Beth, Meredith, Genna. B Elec. Engring., Rensselaer Poly. Inst., 1966; MBA, U. Chgo., 1968. Sr. systems cons. Mobil Oil Corp., N.Y.C., 1968-71; v.p. systems and tech. Citibank, N.A., N.Y.C., 1972-88; v.p., dir. info. systems Capital Markets Assurance Corp., N.Y.C., 1989—. Mem. IEEE Computer Soc. Avocation: jazz drummer. Office: Capital Markets Assurance Corp 885 3rd Ave New York NY 10022-4834

STEINBERG, WARREN LINNINGTON, school principal; b. N.Y.C., Jan. 20, 1924; s. John M. and Gertrude (Vogel) S.; student U. So. Calif., 1943-44, UCLA, 1942-43, 46-47, BA, 1949, MEd, 1951, EdD, 1962; m. Beatrice Ruth Blass, June 29, 1947; children: Leigh William, James Robert, Donald Kenneth. Tchr., counselor, coach Jordan High Sch., Watts, Los Angeles, 1951-57; tchr. athletic coordinator Hamilton High Sch., Los Angeles, 1957-62; boys' vice prin. Univ. High Sch., Los Angeles, 1962-67, Crenshaw Hig Sch., Los Angeles, 1967-68; cons. Ctr. for Planned Change, Los Angeles City Sch., 1968-69; instr. edn. UCLA, 1965-71; boys' vice prin. LeConte Jr. High Sch., Los Angeles, 1969-71, sch. prin., 1971-77; adminstrv. cons. integration, 1977-81, adminstr. student to student interaction program, 1981-82; prin. Gage Jr. High Sch., 1982-83, Fairfax High Sch., 1983-90. Pres. Athletic Coordinators Assn., Los Angeles City Schs., 1959-60; v.p. P-3 Enterprises, Inc., Port Washington, N.Y., 1967-77, Century City (Calif.) Enterprises, 1966-88. V.p. B'nai B'rith Anti-Defamation League, 1968-70; mem. adv. com. Los Angeles City Commn. on Human Relations, 1966-71, 72-76, commr., 1976—, also chmn. edn. com.; pres. Los Angeles City Human Relations Commn., 1978-87; mem. del. assembly Community Relations Conf. of So. Calif., 1975-91; mem. citizens adv. com. for student integration Los Angeles Unified Sch. Dist., 1976-79; chmn. So. Calif. Drug Abuse Edn. Month com., 1970. Bd. dirs. DAWN, The Seedling, 1993-95. Served with USMCR, 1943-46. Recipient Beverly Hills B'nai B'rith Presdl. award, 1965, Pres.'s awardCommunity Rels. Conf. So. Calif., 1990; commended Los Angeles City Council, 1968, 88. Mem. West Los Angeles Coordinating Council (chmn. case conf., human relations), Beverly-Fairfax C. of C. (bd. dirs. 1986-88). Lodges: Lions (dir. 1960-62), Kiwanis. Contbr. articles on race relations, youth behavior to profl. jours. and newspapers. Home: 2737 Dunleer Pl Los Angeles CA 90064-4303

STEINBOCK, JOHN T., bishop; b. L.A., July 16, 1937. Student, Los Angeles Diocesan sems. Ordained priest Roman Cath. Ch., 1963. Aux. bishop Diocese of Orange, Calif., 1984-87; bishop Diocese of Santa Rosa, Calif., 1987-91; titular bishop of Midila, 1984; bishop Diocese of Fresno, Calif., 1991—. Office: Diocese of Fresno 1550 N Fresno St Fresno CA 93703-3788

STEINBRENNER, GEORGE MICHAEL, III, professional baseball team executive, shipbuilding company executive; b. Rocky River, Ohio, July 4, 1930; s. Henry G. and Rita (Haley) S.; m. Elizabeth Joan Zieg, May 12, 1956; children: Henry G. III, Jennifer Lynn, Jessica Joan, Harold Zeig. BA, Williams Coll., 1952; postgrad., Ohio State U., 1954-55. Asst. football coach Northwestern U., 1955, Purdue U., 1956-67; treas. Kinsman Transit Co.,

Cleve., 1957-63; pres. Kinsman Marine Transit Co., Cleve., 1963-67, dir., 1965—; pres., chmn. bd. Am. Ship Bldg. Co., Cleve., 1967-78, chmn. bd., 1978—; prin. owner N.Y. Yankees, Bronx, 1973-90, 93—; limited ptnr. N.Y. Yankees, 1990-93; owner Bay Harbor Inn, Tampa, Fla., 1988—; bd. dirs. Gt. Lakes Internat. Corp., Gt. Lakes Assocs., Cin. Sheet Metal & Roofing Co., Nashville Bridge Co., Nederlander-Steinbrenner Prodns. Mem. Cleve. Little Hoover Com., group chmn., 1966; chmn. Cleve. Urban Coalition; vice chmn. Greater Cleve. Growth Corp., Greater Cleve. Jr. Olympic Found.; founder Silver Shield Found., N.Y.C.; chmn. Olympic Overview Commn.; v.p. U.S. Olympic Com., 1989—. Served to 1st lt. USAF, 1952-54. Named Outstanding Young Man of Yr. Ohio Jr. C. of C., 1960, Cleve. Jr. C. of C., 1960; Chief Town Crier, Cleve., 1968; Man of Yr., Cleve. Press Club, 1968. Mem. Greater Cleve. Growth Assn. (bd. dirs.). Office: NY Yankees Yankee Stadium E 161st St & River Ave Bronx NY 10451*

STEINBRINK, WILLIAM H., lawyer; b. Richmond, Ind., Oct. 4, 1942. AB, Wittenberg U., 1964; LLB, Duke U., 1967. Bar: Ohio 1967. Ptnr. Jones, Day, Reavis & Pogue, Cleve.; pres. Laurel Industries, 1994—. Mem. ABA (chair com. law firms bus. law sect. 1989—), Order of Coif. Office: Jones Day Reavis & Pogue North Point 901 Lakeside Ave E Cleveland OH 44114-1116 Office: Laurel Industries 30195 Chagrin Blvd Cleveland OH 44124*

STEINBRONN, RICHARD EUGENE, lawyer; b. Chgo., Oct. 16, 1941; s. Eugene Frederick and Harriet (Slominski) S.; m. Patricia Burckell, June 13, 1964; children: Jeanne L., Nanette C., Richard Eugene Jr. BA in Philosophy, St. John's U., Collegeville, Minn., 1963; LLB, U. Notre Dame, 1966. Bar: Ind. 1966, U.S. Dist. Ct. (no. dist.) Ind. 1969, U.S. Ct. Appeals (7th cir.) 1969. Assoc. Thornburg, McGill & Deahl, Elkhart, Ind., 1968-72; ptnr. Thornburg, McGill & Deahl, Elkhart, 1973-81; ptnr. Barnes & Thornburg, Elkhart, 1982-85, Ft. Wayne, Ind., 1986—. Rsch. editor Notre Dame Lawyer (law rev.), 1965-66. Chmn. United Way, Elkhart, 1978-85; bd. dirs., pres. Jr. Achievement Elkart County, 1971-85; adv. bd. Leadership Ft. Wayne, 1991—. Capt. U.S. Army, 1963-68. Mem. ABA, Nat. Health Lawyers Assn., Ind. Bar Assn. (bd. dirs. litigation sect. 1984-86), Elkhart County Bar Assn. (chmn. com. 1968-85), Allen County Bar Assn. (bd. dirs. 1986-88, jud. selection com. 1987-88, sec. 1988-89), Def. Rsch. Inst., Greater Ft. Wayne C. of C. (bd. dirs.), Rotary (dist. 6540 youth exch. com. Ft. Wayne club 1986-91, chmn. internat. affairs 1991, dist. chmn. 1992-95, dir. ctrl. states youth exch. inc. exec. 1994—), Anthony Wayne Rotary Club (bd. dirs., pres. 1996—). Republican. Roman Catholic. Avocations: Civil War history, fly fishing. Office: Barnes & Thornburg 1 Summit Sq Ste 600 Fort Wayne IN 46802

STEINDLER, HOWARD ALLEN, lawyer; b. Cleve., June 12, 1942; s. Sidney and Lois Jean (Rosenberg) S.; m. Shirley Weinstein, Oct. 26, 1973; children: Rebecca, Allison, Daniel. B.S., Miami U.-Oxford, Ohio, 1964; J.D., Ohio State U., 1967. Bar: Ohio 1967. Mem. firm Benesch, Friedlander, Coplan & Aronoff, Cleve., 1967—. Pres. bd. trustees Cleve. Scholarship Program, 1987—. Office: Benesch Friedlander Coplan & Aronoff 2300 BP America Bldg 200 Public Sq Cleveland OH 44114-2301

STEINDLER, MARTIN JOSEPH, chemist; b. Vienna, Austria, Jan. 3, 1928; came to U.S., 1938; s. J.P. and M.G. S.; m. Joan Long, Aug. 16, 1952; children: M.H., T.P. PhB, U. Chgo., 1947, BS, 1948, MS, 1949, PhD, 1952. Chemist Argonne (Ill.) Nat. Lab., 1953-74, sr. chemist, 1974—, assoc. dir. div. chem. engring., 1978-84, dir. chem. tech. div., 1984-93, sr. tech. advisor, 1993—; mem. adv. com. on nuclear waste NRC, Washington, 1988—, chmn. 1995; adminstrv. judge ASLBP, 1973-90. Contbr. articles to profl. publs.; patentee in field. Pres. Matteson-Park Forest (Ill.) Sch. Bd., 1959-78. Recipient Disting. Performance medal U. Chgo., 1992. Mem. AAAS, Am. Nuclear Soc., Am. Inst. Chem. Engrs. (Robert E. Wilson award 1990), Sigma Xi. Office: Argonne Nat Lab 9700 Cass Ave Argonne IL 60439-4803

STEINEM, GLORIA, writer, editor, lecturer; b. Toledo, Mar. 25, 1934; d. Leo and Ruth (Nuneviller) S. BA, Smith Coll., 1956; postgrad. (Chester Bowles Asian fellow), India, 1957-58; D. Human Justice, Simmons Coll., 1973. Co-dir., dir. ednl. found. Ind. Rsch. Svc., Cambridge, Mass. and N.Y.C., 1959-60; contbg. editor Glamour Mag., N.Y.C., 1962-69; co-founder, contbg. editor New York Mag., 1968-72; feminist lectr., 1969—; co-founder, editor Ms. Mag., 1971-87, columnist, 1980-87, cons. editor, 1987—; Active various civil rights and peace campaigns including United Farmworkers, Vietnam War Tax Protest, Com. for the Legal Def. of Angela Davis (treas., 1971-72); active polit. campaigns of Adlai Stevenson, Robert Kennedy, Eugene McCarthy, Shirley Chisholm, George McGovern; Co-founder, bd. dirs. Women's Action Alliance, 1970—; convenor, mem. nat. adv. com. Nat. Women's Polit. Caucus, 1971—; co-founder, pres. bd. dirs. Ms. Found. for Women, 1972—; founding mem. Coalition of Labor Union Women, 1974; mem. Internat. Women's Year Commn., 1977; editorial cons., Conde Nast Publications, 1962-69, Curtis Publishing, 1964-65, Random House Publishing, 1988—, McCall Publishing. Author: The Thousand Indias, 1957, The Beach Book, 1963, Wonder Woman, 1972, Outrageous Acts and Everyday Rebellions, 1983, Marilyn: Norma Jeane, 1986, Revolution from Within: A Book of Self-Esteem, 1992, Moving Beyond Words, 1994; contbg. corr. NBC Today Show, 1987-88; contbr. to various anthologies. Pres. Voters for Choice, 1979—. Recipient Penney-Missouri Journalism award, 1970, Ohio Gov.'s award for Journalism, 1972, Bill of Rights award ACLU of So. Calif., 1975; named Woman of the Yr. McCall's mag., 1972; Woodrow Wilson Internat. Ctr. for Scholars fellow, 1977; inducted into Nat. Women's Hall of Fame, 1993. Mem. NOW, AFTRA, Nat. Press Club, Soc. Mag. Writers, Authors' Guild, Phi Beta Kappa. Office: Ms Magazine 230 Park Ave Fl 7 New York NY 10169-0799*

STEINER, BARBARA S., lawyer; b. Highland Park, Ill., June 14, 1949. BA with high honors, U. Mich., 1970, JD with honors, 1974. Bar: Ill. 1974. Ptnr. Jenner & Block, Chgo. Mem. ABA, Ill. State Bar Assn. (mem. antitrust and unfair competition coun. 1984-92, sec. 1989, vice chmn. 1990, chair 1991). Office: Jenner & Block One IBM Plz Chicago IL 60611*

STEINER, CHARLES HARRIS, sports broadcaster, journalist; b. N.Y.C., July 17, 1949; s. Howard Stanley and Gertrude (Harris) S. Student, Bradley U., Peoria, Ill., 1967-71. News dir. WAVZ Radio, New Haven, 1972-73, All-News WPOP Radio, Hartford, Conn., 1973-77, All-News WERE Radio, Cleve., 1977-78; sports broadcaster WOR Radio, N.Y.C., 1978-86; sports dir. RKO Radio Network, N.Y.C., 1980-86; play-by-play announcer N.Y. Jets WABC Radio, N.Y.C., 1986-88; anchorman ESPN, Bristol, Conn., 1988—. Recipient Emmy award Nat. Acad. TV Arts and Scis., 1993, Cable Ace award Nat. Acad. Cable Programming, 1994, Clarion award Women in Comm., 1993; named to Bradley U. Hall of Fame, 1995. Office: ESPN ESPN Pla Bristol CT 06010

STEINER, DONALD FREDERICK, biochemist, physician, educator; b. Lima, Ohio, July 15, 1930; s. Willis A. and Katherine (Hoegner) S. BS in Chemistry and Zoology, U. Cin., 1952; MS in Biochemistry, U. Chgo., 1956, MD, 1956; D Med. Sci. (hon.), U. Umea, 1973, U. Ill., 1984, Technische Hochschule, Aachen, 1993, U. Uppsala, 1993. Intern King County Hosp., Seattle, 1956-57; USPHS postdoctoral research fellow, asst. medicine U. Wash. Med. Sch., 1957-60; mem. faculty med. sch. U. Chgo., 1960—, chmn. dept. biochemistry, 1973-79, A.N. Pritzker prof. biochemistry, molecular biology and medicine, 1985—, sr. investigator Howard Hughes Med. Inst., 1986—; Jacobaeus lectr., Oslo, 1970; Luft lectr., Stockholm, 1984. Co-editor: The Endocrine Pancreas, 1972, discoverer proinsulin. Recipient Gairdner award Toronto, 1971, Hans Christian Hagedorn medal Steensen Meml. Hosp., Copenhagen, 1970, Lilly award, 1969, Ernst Oppenheimer award, 1970, Diaz-Cristobal award Internat. Diabetes Fedn., 1973, Banting medal Am. Diabetes Assn., 1976, Banting medal Brit. Diabetes Assn., 1981, Passano award, 1979, Wolf prize in medicine, 1985, Frederick Conrad Koch award Endocrine Soc., 1990. Mem. Nat. Acad. Scis., Am. Soc. Biochemists and Molecular Biologists, AAAS, Am. Diabetes Assn. (50th Anniversary medallion 1972), European Assn. Study Diabetes, Am. Acad. Arts and Scis., Sigma Xi, Alpha Omega Alpha. Home: 2626 N Lakeview Ave Apt 2508 Chicago IL 60614-1821

STEINER, DUANE, religious administrator. Mgr. Ch. of the Brethren Annual Conf. Office: Church of The Brethern 1451 Kundee Ave Elgin IL 60120

STEINER, GEOFFREY BLAKE, lawyer; b. El Paso, Tex., Aug. 28, 1952; s. LeRoy Marshall Steiner and Rosemary (Thurman) Milligan; m. Maria del Rosario Serrano, Dec. 24, 1975 (div. Jan. 1988); children: Karen Alexander, Xavier Oliver; m. Rosemarie Sylvia Erb, May 5, 1990; 1 child, Geoffrey Blake Jr. AB, Washington U., St. Louis, 1978; JD, Samford U., 1981. Bar: Fla. 1983, U.S. Dist. Ct. (mid. dist.) Fla. 1983, U.S. Ct. Appeals (11th cir.) 1985. Asst. pub. defender Office Pub. Defender, 13th Jud. Cir., Tampa, Fla., 1982-84; assoc. Hamilton & Douglas, P.A., Tampa, 1984-86, Mulholland and Anderson, Tampa, 1986-87, Limberopolous, Steiner & Cardillo, Tampa, 1987-89; pres. Geoffrey B. Steiner, P.A., Tampa, 1989—. Co-author: Florida Rules of Juvenile Procedure Annotated, 1982. Mem. Fla. Bar (bd. cert. civil trial lawyer Bd. of Specialization and Certification), Hillsborough County Bar Assn., Assn. Trial Lawyers Am., Acad. Fla. Trial Lawyers, Hunter's Green Country Club, Masons (32d degree), Shriners, Delta Theta Phi, Beta Theta Pi. Methodist. Avocations: golf, tennis. Office: 2529 W Busch Blvd Ste 100 Tampa FL 33618-4514

STEINER, GEORGE (FRANCIS STEINER), author, educator; b. Paris, Apr. 23, 1929; s. Frederick George and Elsie (Franzos) S.; m. Zara Shakow, 1955; children—David Milton, Deborah Tarn. BA, U. Chgo., 1949; MA, Harvard U., 1950; PhD, Oxford U., 1955; DLitt (hon.), Trinity Coll., Dublin, 1996; LittD (hon.), Louvain U., 1980, Mount Holyoke Coll., 1983, Durham U., 1995; D honoris causa, U. Bristol, 1989; DLitt (hon.), U. Glasgow, 1990, U. Liége, 1990, U. Ulster, 1993, U. Durham, 1995, Kenyon Coll., 1996. Mem. staff Economist, London, 1952-56; mem. staff Inst. Advanced Study Princeton (N.Y.) U., N.J., 1956-58, Gauss lectr., 1959-60; Massey lectr., 1974; First Lord Weidenfeld prof. Comp. Lit. Oxford U., 1994—; cons. and lectr. in field; Maurice lectr. U. London, 1984, Leslie Stephen lectr. Cambridge U., 1985, W.P. Ker lectr. U. Glasgow, 1986; lectr. Page-Barbour Lectures U. Va., 1987, Gifford lectr., 1990; vis. prof. Coll. France, 1992; First Lord Weidenfeld vis. prof. comparative lit., Oxford U., 1994—. Author: Tolstoy or Dostoevsky, 1958, The Death of Tragedy, 1960, Anno Domini, 1964, Language and Silence, 1967, Extraterritorial, 1971, In Bluebeard's Castle, 1971, The Sporting Scene: White Knights in Reykjavik, 1973, After Babel, 1975 (adapted for TV as The Tongues of Men, 1977), Heidegger, 1978, On Difficulty and Other Essays, 1978, The Portage to San Cristobal of A.H., 1981, Antigones, 1984, George Steiner: A Reader, 1984, Real Presences, 1989, Proofs and Three Parables, 1992, Homer in English, 1996, No Passion Spent, 1996, The Deeps of the Sea, 1996; editor: The Penguin Book of Modern Verse Translation, 1966, Homer: A Collection of Critical Essays (with Robert Flagles), 1962. Decorated chevalier de la Legion d'Honneur (France); Churchill Coll. fellow, 1961—; Hon. fellow Balliol Coll., Oxford, Eng., 1995; Fulbright prof., 1958-69; recipient O. Henry Short Story award, 1958, Guggenheim fellowship, 1971-72, Zabel award Nat. Inst. Arts and Letters, U.S., 1970, King Albert medal Royal Belgian Acad., 1982, P.E.N. Internat. Fiction prize, 1993; Faulkner Fiction grantee P.E.N., 1983; Le Prix du Souvenir, 1974. Mem. Am. Acad. Arts and Scis. (hon.), English Assn. (pres. 1975), German Acad. Lit. (corr.). Office: Churchill Coll, Cambridge England

STEINER, GILBERT YALE, political scientist; b. Bklyn., May 11, 1924; s. Isidor Aaron and Fannie (Gelbtrunk) S.; m. Louise King, July 27, 1950; children: Charles King, Daniel Tod, Paula Amy. A.B., Columbia U., 1945; A.M., 1948; Ph.D., U. Ill., 1950. Faculty U. Ill., Urbana, 1950-66; prof. govt., pub. affairs U. Ill., 1959-66; asst. dean U. Ill. (Grad. Coll.), 1956-58; dir. Inst. Govt. and Pub. Affairs, 1958-66; sr. fellow Brookings Instn., Washington, 1966—; dir. govtl. studies Brookings Instn., 1968-76, acting pres., 1976-77; staff dir. Chgo. Home Rule Commn., 1954-55; research dir. Northeastern Ill. Local Govt. Area Commn., 1957-63; vis. prof. polit. sci. U. Calif.-Berkeley, 1964-65; Kimball lectr. Brigham Young U., 1985; study dir. Commn. to Recommend Plan for Pub. Higher Edn. in, Ill., 1960; spl. asst. to gov., Ill., 1961-63; cons. Bush Found., Edna McConnell Clark Found. Author: The Congressional Conference Committee, 1951, Legislation by Collective Bargaining, 1951, (with others) Chicago's Government, 1954, (with S.K. Gove) Legislative Politics in Illinois, 1960, Social Insecurity, 1966, The State of Welfare, 1971, The Children's Cause, 1976, The Futility of Family Policy, 1981, Constitutional Inequality, 1985; editor: The Abortion Dispute and the American System, 1983. Bd. dirs. Found. for Child Devel., Manpower Demonstration and Research Corp., Governance Inst. Served with AUS, 1943-46. Social Sci. Research Council fellow, 1957; Ford Found. fellow, 1961-62. Home: 5408 Center St Chevy Chase MD 20815-7101 Office: Brookings Institute Washington DC 20036

STEINER, HENRY JACOB, law and human rights educator; b. Mt. Vernon, N.Y., 1930; s. Meier and Bluma (Henigson) S.; m. Pamela Pomerance, Aug. 1, 1982; stepchildren: Duff, Jacoba. BA magna cum laude, Harvard U., 1951, MA, 1955, LLB magna cum laude, 1955. Bar: N.Y. 1956, Mass. 1963. Law clk. to Hon. John M. Harlan, U.S. Supreme Ct., 1957-58; assoc. Sullivan and Cromwell, N.Y.C., 1958-62; asst. prof. sch. law Harvard U., Cambridge, Mass., 1962-65, prof., 1965—, Jeremiah Smith, Jr. prof. law, 1986—, founder, dir. law sch. Human Rights Program, 1984—; chair Human Rights Studies Com., Harvard U., 1994—; vis. prof. CEPED, Rio de Janeiro, Brazil, 1968-69; vis. prof. Yale U., New Haven, 1972-73, Stanford U., 1965; cons. AID, 1962-64, Ford Found., 1966-69. Co-author: (textbook) Transnational Legal Problems, 4th edit., 1994, Tort and Accident Law, 2d edit., 1989, International Human Rights in Context: Law, Politics, Morals, 1996; author: Moral Argument and Social Vision in the Courts, 1987, Diverse Partners: Non-Governmental Organizations in the Human Rights Movement, 1991; author, editor: Ethnic Conflict and the UN Human Rights System, 1996; former devels. editor Harvard Law Rev.; contbr. articles to profl. jours. Office: Harvard Law Sch Cambridge MA 02138

STEINER, HERBERT MAX, physics educator; b. Goeppingen, Germany, Dec. 8, 1927; came to U.S., 1939, naturalized, 1944; s. Albert and Martha (Epstein) S. B.S., U. Calif., Berkeley, 1951, Ph.D., 1956. Physicist Lawrence Berkeley Lab., Berkeley, Calif., 1956—; mem. faculty U. Calif., Berkeley, 1958—, prof. physics, 1966—, William H. McAdams prof. physics, chmn. dept., 1992-95; vis. scientist European Center Nuclear Research, 1960-61, 64, 68-69, 82-83, Max Planck Inst. Physics and Astrophysics, Munich, 1976-77; vis. prof. Japanese Soc. Promotion Sci., 1978; vis. prof. physics U. Paris, 1989-90; vis. scientist Deutsches Electron Synchrotron Lab., 1995-96. Author articles in field. Served with AUS, 1946-47. Recipient Sr. Am. Scientist award Alexander von Humboldt Found., 1976-77; Guggenheim fellow, 1960-61. Fellow Am. Phys. Soc. Office: U Calif Berkeley Dept Physics Berkeley CA 94720

STEINER, JEAN LOUISE, agroclimatologist, researcher; b. Red Cloud, Nebr., Dec. 9, 1951; d. Robert Jacob and Kathleen Rose (Rice) S.; m. Robert Lynn Allen, May 14, 1988. BA, Cornell Coll., Mt. Vernon, Iowa, 1974; MS, Kans. State U., 1979, PhD, 1982. Rsch. scientist Commonwealth Sci. and Indsl. Rsch. Orgn., Griffith, N.S.W., Australia, 1982-83; rsch. soil scientist USDA/Agrl. Rsch. Svc., Bushland, Tex., 1983-84, Watkinsville, Ga., 1994—. Mem. AAAS, Am. Soc. Agronomy (assoc. editor jour. Madison, Wis. 1989-95, chair women in agronomy com. 1991—), Soil and Water Conservation Soc., Coun. for Agrl. Sci. and Tech. Achievements include research in evapotranspiration prediction in dryland and irrigated cropping, prediction of crop residue impacts on evaporation, crop growth model validation and application, soil water balance model testing and application to agricultural water management, modeling temperature and moisture effects on crop residue decomposition for prediction of wind erosion hazard. Office: USDA/Agrl Rsch Svc 1420 Experiment Station Rd Athens GA 30606

STEINER, JEFFREY JOSEF, industrial manufacturing company executive; b. Vienna, Austria, Apr. 3, 1937; came to U.S., 1958; s. Beno and Paula (Bornstein) S.; m. Claude Angel, Apr. 11, 1957 (div. 1972); children: Eric, Natalia, Thierry; m. Linda Schaller, Mar. 6, 1976 (div. June 1983); children: Benjamin, Alexandra; m. Irja Bonnier, Mar. 19, 1987. Student textile design, U. London, 1956; student textile mfg., Bradford Inst. Tech., London, 1957; HHD (hon.), Yeshiva U., 1994. Mgmt. trainee Metals and Controls div. Tex. Instruments, Attleborough, Mass., 1958-59, mgr. internat., 1959-60; pres. Tex. Instruments, Argentina, Brazil, Mex., Switzerland, France, 1960-66, Burlington Tapis, Paris, 1967-72; chmn., pres. Cedec S.A. Engring. Co., Paris, 1973-84; chmn., CEO Fairchild Corp., N.Y.C., 1985—, Banner Aerospace, 1993—; bd. dirs. Copley Fund, Fall River, Mass., Franklin Corp., N.Y.C. Trustee Montefiore Med. Ctr., N.Y.C.; bd. dirs. Israel Mus., Yeshiva U. Bus. Sch. Decorated Knight of the Arts (France), Knight Indsl. Merit of France, Chevalier de L'ordre des Arts et des Lettres, 1990, Chevalier de L'order National du Merite, 1992; recipient City of Paris medal Mayor Jacque Chirac, 1990. Mem. City Athletic Club, Racing Club, Polo Club. Jewish. Avocations: tennis, sailing. Office: Fairchild Corp 110 E 59th St 31st Fl New York NY 10022

STEINER, KAREN RUTH, physician's assistant; b. Milw., Nov. 25, 1953; d. Carl Gustav Martin and Lois Pauline Edna (Koch) S.; m. Christian Joseph Nichols, Sept. 15, 1990. AA in Sci., Glendale Community Coll., 1974; cert. of surg. tech., Maricopa County Tech. Coll., 1976; AA physician asst. pgrm., Essex Community Coll., Balt., 1980. Registered physician asst., Ariz.; lic. phys. asst., Mich.; cert. Nat. Commn. Cert. Physician's Assts. and Nat. Bd. Examiners. Operating room technician Maricopa County Gen. Hosp., Phoenix, 1976-77, Greater Balt. Med. Ctr., 1977-78; resident dept. surgery Franklin Square Hosp., Balt., 1980-811; physician's asst. urgent care unit Ariz. Health Plan, Phoenix, 1981-82; physician's asst. family practice unit CIGNA Healthplan, Tempe, Ariz., 1982-83; physician's asst. cardiac-thoracic surgery dept. Henry Ford Hosp., Detroit, 1983-87, Thoracic Surgeon's Assocs., Grand Rapids, Mich., 1987-88; physician's asst. surg. White Mountain Hosp., 1988-89; physicians asst. Grace Hosp., Detroit, 1989-91, St. John Hosp., 1991—, Women's Health Ctr., Clarkston, Mich., 1993, Livonia (Mich.) Family Physicians, 1994—. Choral Mem. Ariz. State U., Tempe, 1977, 82, Balt. Choral Arts Soc., 1978, White Mtn. Chorale, 1988. Fellow Am. Acad. Physician's Assts., Assn. Physician Assts. in Cardiovascular Surgery, Mich. Acad. Physician Assts. Democrat. Lutheran. Avocations: music, playing guitar, cats, antiques, gardening.

STEINER, KENNETH DONALD, bishop; b. David City, Nebr., Nov. 25, 1936; s. Lawrence Nicholas and Florine Marie (Pieters) S. B.A., Mt. Angel Sem., 1958; M.Div., St. Thomas Sem., 1962. Ordained priest Roman Catholic Ch., 1962, bishop, 1978; asso. pastor various parishes Portland and Coos Bay, Oreg., 1962-72; pastor Coquille Ch., Myrtle Point, Powers, Oreg., 1972-76, St. Francis Ch., Roy, Oreg., 1976-77; aux. bishop Diocese of Portland, Oreg., 1977—; vicar of worship and ministries and personnel dir. clergy personnel Portland Archdiocese. Democrat. Office: 2838 E Burnside St Portland OR 97214-1830

STEINER, LEE NATHAN, lawyer; b. Newark, Nov. 10, 1922; s. Joseph and Jeanette (Stamler) S.; m. Roslyn Roth, June 28, 1948; children: Terry, Catherine Steiner Adair, Nancy Steiner-Fraiman. BA, Lafayette Coll., 1943; JD, U. Pa., 1949. Bar: N.Y. 1950, U.S. Dist. Ct. (so. dist.) N.Y. 1950, U.S. Supreme Ct. Assoc. Weil, Gotshal & Manges, N.Y.C., 1950-56; ptnr. Loeb & Loeb, N.Y.C., 1965-90; bd. dirs. Carnegie Hall, N.Y.C., 1975—. Mem. Found. For Friends of South Pacific, 1973—. Lt. Comdr. USNR, 1943-46, PTO. Mem. Cousteau Soc. (bd. dirs. 1970—), Sunningdale Country Club (pres. 1974-78). Avocation: golf. Office: Loeb & Loeb 345 Park Ave New York NY 10154-0004*

STEINER, PAUL ANDREW, retired insurance executive; b. Woodburn, Ind., Feb. 17, 1929; s. Eli Gerig and Emma Mae (Yaggy) S.; m. Ruth Edna Henry, Sept. 1, 1950; children: Mark, Nancy, Jonathan, David. AB, Taylor U., 1950. C.P.C.U. Owner feed and grain, lumber and constrn. firms, Bluffton, Ohio, 1951-64; home office rep. Brotherhood Mut. Ins. Co., Ft. Wayne, Ind., 1964-65, dir. claims, 1966-71, v.p., treas., 1968-71, pres., 1971-94, chmn. bd., 1974—. Past treas., Nat. Assn. Evangels., bd. trustees Am. Bible Soc.; past chmn. Summit Christian Coll.; trustee Taylor U. Named Layman of Yr., Nat. Assn. Evangelicals, 1977. Mem. Nat. Assn. Mut. Ins. Cos. (past chmn. bd.; Merit award 1973), DEVCO Mut. Assn. (past chmn.) Conf. Casualty Ins. Cos. (past pres.), Mut. Ins. Cos. Assn. Ind. (past pres.), Soc. C.P.C.U.s (past nat. ethics com. past pres. No. Ind. chpt.), Ft. Wayne Rotary (past pres.). Republican. Evang. Mennonite. Club: Christian Bus. Men's Com. (Ft. Wayne). Home: 1825 Florida Dr Fort Wayne IN 46805-5036 Office: Brotherhood Mut Ins Co 111 E Ludwig Rd Ste 100 Fort Wayne IN 46825-4240

STEINER, PETER OTTO, economics educator, dean; b. N.Y.C., July 9, 1922; s. Otto Davidson and Ruth (Wurzburger) S.; m. Ruth E. Riggs, Dec. 20, 1947 (div. 1967); children: Alison Ruth, David Denison; m. Patricia F. Owen, June 2, 1968. A.B., Oberlin Coll., 1943; M.A., Harvard, 1949, Ph.D., 1950. Instr. U. Calif., Berkeley, 1949-50, asst. prof. econs., 1950-57; assoc. prof. U. Wis., Madison, 1957-59, prof., 1959-68; prof. econs. and law U. Mich., Ann Arbor, 1968-91, prof. emeritus, 1991—, chmn. dept. econs., 1971-74, dean Coll. Lit., Sci. and Arts, 1981-89; vis. prof. U. Nairobi, Kenya, 1974-75; Cons. U.S. Bur. Budget, 1961-62, Treasury Dept., 1962-63, various pvt. firms, 1952—. Author: An Introduction to the Analysis of Time Series, 1956, (with r. Dorfman) The Economic Status of the Aged, 1957, (with R.G. Lipsey) Economics, 10th edit., 1993, On the Process of Planning, 1968, Public Expenditure Budgeting, 1969, Mergers: Motives, Effects, Policies, 1975, Thursday Night Poker: Understand, Enjoy and Win, 1996; contbr. articles to profl. publs. Served to lt. USNR, 1944-46. Social Sci. Research Council Faculty Research fellow, 1956; Guggenheim fellow, 1960; Ford Faculty Research fellow, 1965. Mem. Am. Econ. Assn., Econometric Soc., AAUP (chmn. com. Z 1970-73, pres. 1976-78). Home: 502 Heritage Dr Ann Arbor MI 48105-2556 Office: U Mich Law Sch 625 S State St Ann Arbor MI 48109-1215

STEINER, RICHARD RUSSELL, conglomerate executive; b. Chgo., Feb. 26, 1923; s. Frank Gardner and Ruth (Cowie) S.; m. Colleen M. Kearns, Dec. 6, 1949; children—Robert C., Kevin K., Sheila M. B.A., Dartmouth Coll., 1948. With Steiner Corp., Salt Lake City, 1948—; divisonal dir., v.p. Steiner Corp., 1951-59, pres., 1959—; dir. Am. Uniform Co. Served with USAAF, 1942-46. Decorated D.F.C. Mem. Phi Beta Kappa. Clubs: Alta, Salt Lake Country. Office: 505 E South Temple Salt Lake City UT 84102-1004

STEINER, ROBERT FRANK, biochemist; b. Manila, Philippines, Sept. 29, 1926; came to U.S., 1933; s. Frank and Clara Nell (Weems) S.; m. Ethel Mae Fisher, Nov. 3, 1956; children: Victoria, Laura. A.B., Princeton U., 1947; Ph.D., Harvard U., 1950. Chemist Naval Med. Research Inst., Bethesda, Md., 1950-70; chief lab. phys. biochemistry Naval Med. Research Inst., 1965-70; prof. chemistry U. Md., Balt., 1970—, chmn. dept. chemistry, 1974—; prof. emeritus, 1996—; dir. grad. program in biochemistry U. Md., Balt., 1985, prof. emeritust, 1995—; mem. biophysics study sect. NIH, 1976. Author: Life Chemistry, 1968, Excited States of Proteins and Nucleic Acids, 1971, The Chemistry of Living Systems, 1981, Excited States of Biopolymers, 1983; editor Jour. Biophys. Chemistry, 1972—, Jour. Fluorescence, 1991; contbr. more than 160 articles to profl. jours. Served with AUS, 1945-47. Recipient Superior Civilian Achievement award Dept. Def., 1966; NSF rsch. grantee, 1971-77, NIH, 1973-93. Fellow Washington Acad. Sci., Japan Soc. for Promotion Sci.; mem. Am. Soc. Biol. Chemists. Club: Princeton (Washington). Achievements include development of fluorescence techniques for studying proteins. Home: 2609 Turf Valley Rd Ellicott City MD 21042-2021 Office: 5401 Wilkens Ave Baltimore MD 21228-5329

STEINER, ROBERT LISLE, language consultant; b. Tehran, Iran, May 21, 1921; s. Robert Lisle and Lois (Foresman) S.; m. Margaret S. Sherrard, June 4, 1944; children—Patricia Jean, Robert Lisle III, William Sherrard, John Scott. Grad., Mercersberg (Pa.) Acad., 1938; B.A., Wooster (O.) Coll.; M.I.A., Columbia, 1948. Cons. Commn. Chs. on Internat. Affairs, 1948-49; cultural attache Am. embassy, Iran, 1950-52; educationist U.S. Office Edn., 1952-54; program dir. Am. Friends of Middle East, 1954-59; v.p. Vershire Co., Vt., 1959-62; dir. Peace Corps, Kabul, Afghanistan, 1962-66; regional dir. North Africa, Near East and South Asia, 1966-69; dir. Washington office Devel. & Resources Corp., 1969-70; dir. Ctr. for Cross-Cultural Tng. and Research, adviser to univ. pres. on internat. affairs U. Hawaii, Honolulu, 1971-72; dir., gen. mgr. Hawaii Pub. Broadcasting Authority, 1972-73; exec. dir. N.J. Edn. Consortium, Princeton, 1973-78; pres. InterLink Lang. Ctrs., Princeton, 1979-91, chmn., 1992—; tchr. U. Kansas City, Mo., 1957, Bradford (Vt.) Acad., 1961; poultry cons. Middle East Tech. U., Ankara, Turkey, 1963. Councilman, v.p. Shanks Village Assn., Orangeburg, N.Y., 1948; chmn. Kabul Sch. Bd., 1965. Served as pilot USNR, 1943-46. Mem. Princeton Mid. East Soc. (sec. 1986-88, treas. 1993-95). Democrat. Presbyterian. Home: 1898 Villa Ct Lancaster PA 17603 Office: Interlink Lang Ctrs 1898 Villa Ct Lancaster PA 17603

STEINER, ROGER JACOB, linguistics educator, author, researcher; b. South Byron, Wis., Mar. 27, 1924; s. Jakob Robert and Alice Mildred (Cowles) S.; m. Ida Kathryn Posey, Aug. 7, 1954 (dec. May 1992); children: David Posey, Andrew Posey. BA, Franklin & Marshall Coll., 1945; MDiv, Union Theol. Sem., 1947; MA, U. Pa., 1958, PhD, 1963. Ordained to ministry, Meth. Ch., 1947. Clergyman United Meth. Ch., N.Y., Wis., Pa., 1945-61; lectr. U. Bordeaux, France, 1961-63; instr. dept. langs. & lit. U. Del., Newark, 1963-64, asst. prof., 1964-71, assoc. prof., 1971-80, prof., 1980-85; prof. dept. linguistics U. Del., Newark, 1985-96; cons. Charles Scribner's Sons, N.Y.C., 1972-75, Larousse, N.Y.C., 1981-84, Houghton-Mifflin, Boston, 1981-84, Macmillan, 1994—. Author: Two Centuries of Spanish and English Bilingual Lexicography (1590-1800), 1970, New College French and English Dictionary, 1972, rev. 2nd edit. 1988. Recipient fellowship Am. Philos. Soc., Phila., 1971, Lilly Found., Phila., 1979-81. Mem. MLA (founder lexicography group 1974-75, chmn. 1976, 77, 80, 85), Dictionary Soc. N.Am., Del. Coun. for Internat. Visitors (brochure chmn.), Phi Beta Kappa (pres. chpt. 1975-76). Republican. Avocations: languages, photography. Office: U Del Dept Linguistics Newark DE 19716-2551

STEINER, STUART, college president; b. Balt., July 24, 1937; s. Louis and Lillian (Block) S.; m. Rosalie Weiner, Sept. 12, 1962; children—Lisa, Susan, David, Robyn. AA, Balt. Jr. Coll., 1957; B.S., U. Md., 1959; grad. cert., Fla. State U., 1962; M.S.W., U. Pa., 1963; J.D., U. Balt., 1967; M.A., Tchrs. Coll., Columbia U., 1972; EdD, Columbia U., 1987. Caseworker, then supr. and dir. juvenile ct. services Balt. Dept. Social Services, 1960-64; dir. referral center Health and Welfare Council Met. Balt., 1964; dir. admissions and placement Harford Jr. Coll., Bel Air, Md., 1965-67; dean of students Genesee Community Coll., Batavia, N.Y., 1967-68; dean of coll. Genesee Community Coll., 1968-75, pres., 1975—; pres. SUNY West; mem. coun. of pres.'s SUNY, acting dep. to chancellor for community colls., 1985, pres. of assn. Pres. of Pub. Community Colls. Contbr. articles to profl. jours. Bd. dirs. St. Jerome Hosp., Genesee County Community Chest, Health Sci. Agy., Western N.Y., N.Y. Spl. Olympicsd Com., Girl Scouts Genesee Valley, 1989-90; trustee Villa Maria Coll.; trustee, v.p. N.Y. Chiropractic Coll.; pres. Genesee County United Way, Community Coll. of Balt. Hall of Fame. Heisler scholar, 1960-61; Kellogg fellow, 1971-72; Sigma Delta scholar, 1958-59. Mem. Am. Assn. Higher Edn., Assn. Pres. Pub. C.C.s (pres.), Pvt. Indsl. Coun. (bd. dirs.). Home: 33 Woodcrest Dr Batavia NY 14020-2721 Office: Genesee Community Coll One College Rd Batavia NY 14020

STEINER, ULRICH ALFRED, chemist; b. Bombay, India, Mar. 26, 1922; came to the U.S., 1957; s. Jakob Alfred and Mathilde (Gass) S.; m. Ingebord Maria Lauber, June 2, 1949 (dec. 1959); children: Gabriele Gertsch, Beat Ulrich; m. Claire Beula Koss, Jul. 15, 1961. Diploma in chemistry, Federal Inst. Tech., Zurich, Switzerland, 1946, Dr. SC, 1948. Rsch. chemist Emser Werke, Domat/Ems, Switzerland, 1948-53, asst. dept. head, 1953-57; rsch. chemist Union Carbide, Boundbrook, N.J., 1957-86; rsch. assoc. Amoco Performance Products, Inc., Boundbrook, N.J., 1986-91; ret. Patentee in field. Recipient Thomas Alva Edison Patent award R&D Coun. N.J., 1992. Home: 237 Jefferson Ave North Plainfield NJ 07060

STEINER-HOUCK, SANDRA LYNN, interior designer; b. Columbia, Pa., May 29, 1962; d. Howard Jr. and Mary Louise Steiner; m. Paul Harry Houck, Sept. 14, 1990; children: Brandon Paul, Brittany Leigh. AA in Interior Design, Bauder Fashion Coll., 1981. Cert. kitchen designer. Designer Bob Harry's Kitchen Ctr., Inc., York, Pa., 1982-87, Leggett, Inc., Camp Hill, Pa., 1987-90, Mother Hubbard's Kitchen Ctr., Mechanicsburg, Pa., 1990-93; owner ind. design svc., 1994—. Designer: Bath Industry Technical Manuals Vol.3, 1993; contbr. designs to profl. jours. Recipient 1st pl. award and Best of Show Resdl. Bath Design, 1986, Showroom Design, 1989, 3d pl. award Resdl. Kitchen, 1992, Resdl. Bath Design, 1992, Heritage Custom Kitchens Mfr.'s Design award, 1986, 94, 3 Nat. Design. awards Resdl. Kitchen, 1994. Mem. Am. Soc. Interior Design, Soc. Cert. Kitchen Designers. Home and Office: 515 Mockingbird Dr Columbia PA 17512

STEINERT-THRELKELD, THOMAS MILLER, editor, journalist; b. Glen Ridge, N.J., June 20, 1954; s. Aubrey Miller and Elizabeth (Morgan) Threlkeld; m. Kayte Steinert, Aug. 16, 1953; children: Zachary and Shane. BJ, U. Mo., 1976; MBA, Harvard U., 1979. Bus. writer Ft. Worth Star-Telegram, 1979-82, bus. columnist, 1987-88; rsch. dir. electronic pub. Capital Cities Comm., Ft. Worth, 1980-81, dir. new tech., 1981-82; owner, pres. The Info. Companies, Azle, Tex., 1982-86; editor-in-chief Interactive Week, Garden City, N.Y., 1995—. Recipient John Hancock award for excellence in bus. journalism, 1982, AP Mng. Editors award for bus. writing, 1989, Headliners award, Headliners Club, 1990. Avocation: long distance cycling. Home and Office: 6710 Landover Hills Ln Arlington TX 76017

STEINFELD, JEFFREY IRWIN, chemistry educator, consultant, writer; b. Bklyn., July 2, 1940; s. Paul and Ann (Ravin) S. B.Sc., MIT, 1962; PhD, Harvard U., 1965. Postdoctoral fellow U. Sheffield, Yorkshire, Eng., 1965-66; asst. prof. chemistry MIT, Cambridge, 1966-70; assoc. prof. MIT, 1970-79, prof., 1980—; mem. sci. adv. bd. Lasertechnics, Inc., Albuquerque, 1982—. Author: Molecules & Radiation, 1974; co-author: Chemical Kinetics and Dynamics, 1989; editor: Laser and Coherence Spectroscopy, 1977, Laser-Induced Chemical Processes, 1981; co-editor: Spectrochimica Acta, 1983—; contbr. articles to profl. jours. Treas. Ward 2 Democratic Com., Cambridge, 1972-73. NSF fellow Harvard U., Cambridge, 1962-65; NSF fellow Sheffield U., 1965-66; Alfred P. Sloan Found. research fellow MIT, 1969-71; Guggenheim fellow, 1972-73. Fellow Am. Phys. Soc.; mem. AAAS, Fedn. Am. Scientists, Sigma Xi, Phi Lambda Upsilon. Jewish. Office: MIT Room 2-221 Cambridge MA 02139

STEINFELD, MANFRED, furniture manufacturing executive; b. Josbach, Germany, Apr. 29, 1924; s. Abraham and Paula (Katten) S.; m. Fern Goldman, Nov. 13, 1949; children: Michael, Paul, Jill. Student U. Ill., 1942; BS in Commerce, Roosevelt U., 1948. Research analyst State of Ill., 1948-50; v.p. Shelby Williams Industries, Inc., Chgo., 1954-63, pres., 1964-72; chmn. bd., 1973-96, chmn. exec. com., 1996—; bd. dirs. Amalgamated Trust & Savs. Bank. Mem. adv. bd. Sch. Human Ecology, U. Tenn., 1981-87, devel. council, 1982-87; mem. adv. bd. dept. interior design Fla. Internat. U., 1981-85. Life trustee Roosevelt U., Chgo.; past pres. Roosevelt U. Bus. Sch. Alumni Council; hon. governing mem. Art Inst. Chgo., mem. com. 20th century decorative art; bd. dirs. Jewish Fedn. Chgo., 1986-90; gen. chmn. Jewish United Fund, 1987; nat. vice chmn. United Jewish Appeal, 1988-94. Served to 1st lt. AUS, 1942-45, 50-52. Decorated Bronze Star, Purple Heart; named Small Bus. Man of Yr., Central Region, 1967; established Manfred Steinfeld Hospitality Mgmt. Program at Roosevelt U., Chgo., 1988; established Fernand Manfred Steinfeld Chair Judaic Studies U. Tenn., Knoxville, 1995; recipient Horatio Alger award of disting. Ams., 1981, Outstanding Bus. Leader award Northwood Inst., 1983. Mem. Horatio Alger Assn. (bd. dirs. 1986-92), Standard Club, Bryn Mawr Country Club, Bocaire Country (Boca Raton, Fla.), Beta Gamma Sigma. Home: 1300 N Lake Shore Dr Apt 34D Chicago IL 60610-2195 Office: Mdse Mart Rm 11-111 Chicago IL 60654 also: Shelby Williams Industries Inc 150 Shelby Williams Dr Morristown TN 37813

STEINFELD, RAY, JR., food products executive; b. Portland, Oreg., Nov. 21, 1946; s. Ray and June Catherine (Cox) S.; m. Janis Bowen, Nov. 11, 1978; children: Erik, Blair. Student, Wheaton Coll., 1964-66, Drew U., 1967; BS in Polit. Sci., Lewis & Clark Coll., 1968. Sales rep. Continental Can Co., L.A., 1969-72; CEO Steinfeld's Products Co., Portland, Oreg., 1972—; chmn. Oreg. Mus. Sci. in Industry, 1992-94. Treas., bd. dirs. Portland Recycling Team, Portland, 1973—; pres. exec. bd. Stop Oreg. Litter and Vandalism, 1973-92, pres., 1976; chmn., exec. com. Oreg. Landmark of Quality, 1985-87; pres. exec. com. William Temple House, 1985-91; vestry mem. Trinity Episcopal Ch., 1987-90; chmn. Oreg. Strategic Plan Agrl. Dept., 1988, World Trade West, Portland, 1989; mem. Gov. Robert's Task Force, Salem, Oreg., 1991-92; bd. dirs. Oreg. Enterprise Forum, 1992—, chmn., 1995. Mem. Pickle Packers Internat. (mdse. com. chmn.). Democrat. Espiscopalian. Avocations: tennis, golf, bridge, handball. Office: 10001 N Rivergate Blvd Portland OR 97203-6526

STEINFELD, THOMAS ALBERT, publisher; b. N.Y.C., June 17, 1917; s. Albert and Marjorie (Lesser) S.; m. Joan Rollinson, July 29, 1945 (dec. Nov. 1973); children: Geoffrey T., Jill R.; m. Viviane Barkey, June 20, 1977. Student, G. Phillips Exeter Acad., 1934, Harvard U., 1934-35. Salesman John Orr Products, N.Y.C., 1935-36; asst. advt. mgr. Bloomingdale's, N.Y.C., 1936-37; with Playbill mag., N.Y.C., 1937—; pub. Playbill mag., 1962-65, pres., 1962-68; now v.p., nat. sales dir. Playbill. Served to capt. AUS, 1942-46, CBI. Mem. English Speaking Union, Aspetuck Valley Country Club (Weston, Conn.), The Wings Club (N.Y.C.). Home: 83 W Meadow Rd Wilton CT 06897-4722 Office: 52 Vanderbilt Ave New York NY 10017-3808

STEINFELS, PETER FRANCIS, newspaper correspondent, writer; b. Chgo., July 15, 1941; s. Melville Philip and Margaret Mary (Hollahan) S.; m. Margaret Mary O'Brien, Aug. 31, 1963; children: Gabrielle, John Melville. AB, Loyola U., 1963; MA, Columbia U., 1964, PhD, 1976. Editorial asst. Commonweal Mag., N.Y.C., 1964-65, asst. editor, 1965-67, assoc. editor, 1967-71, exec. editor, 1978-84, editor, 1984-88; sr. religion corr. N.Y. Times, 1988—; assoc. for humanities Inst. of Soc., Ethics and Life Scis., Hastings-on-Hudson, N.Y., 1972-77; co-editor (with Margaret O'Brien Steinfels) Hastings Ctr. Report, Hastings-on-Hudson, 1973-77. Author: The Neoconservatives, 1979; editor (with Robert M. Veatch) Death Inside Out, 1975. Roman Catholic. Home: 924 W End Ave New York NY 10025-3534 Office: NY Times 229 W 43rd St Fl 3 New York NY 10036-3913

STEINFINK, HUGO, chemical engineering educator; b. Vienna, Austria, May 22, 1924; s. Mendel and Malwina (Fiderer) S.; m. Cele Intrator, Mar. 21, 1948; children: Dan E., Susan D. BS, CCNY, 1947; MS, Columbia U., 1948; PhD, Bklyn. Poly. Inst., 1954. Rsch. chemist Shell Devel. Co., Houston, 1948-51, 53-60; T. Brockett Hudson prof. chem. engring. U. Tex., Austin, 1960—. Contbr. articles to profl. jours. With AUS, 1944-46. Fellow Am. Mineral Soc.; mem. AIChE, Am. Chem. Soc., Am. Crystallographic Assn. (pres.-elect 1994, pres. 1995, past pres. 1996), Materials Rsch. Soc., Phi Beta Kappa, Sigma Xi, Phi Lambda Epsilon. Home: 3811 Walnut Clay Dr Austin TX 78731-4011 Office: U Tex Coll Engring Austin TX 78712

STEINFORT, JAMES RICHARD, university program director; b. Grand Rapids, Mich., Oct. 1, 1941; s. Gerald Gene and Harriett Lois (Stauffer) S.; m. Elizabeth Ann O'Laughlin, Mar. 14, 1964; children: Dawn, Robin, Susan, Troy, Ginger. AA in Computer Sci., San Jacinto Coll., Pasadena, Tex., 1973; BS in Tech. Mgmt. cum laude, Regis Coll., 1987. Chartered cons., Am. Cons. League. Customer engr. Control Data Corp., Mpls., 1964-65; computer engr. GE, Phoenix, 1965-69; tech. analyst Manned Spacecraft Ctr., Houston, 1969-73, systems analyst, 1973-75; tech. support mgr. Ohio Med. Products, Houston, 1975-79; prodn. regional mgr. Johnson & Johnson Co., Denver, 1979-83; prin., internat. cons. J.R. Steinfort & Assocs., Boise, Idaho, 1983-90; dir. TIES (Tech. and Indsl. Ext. Svc.) Boise State U., 1990-95; exec. dir. Idaho Mfg. Alliance, 1995—. Author: (non-fiction) Conspiracy in Dallas, 1975, rev. edit., 1992; (tech. manuals) Medical/EDP Design Applications, 1985, Factory Quality Audit, 1991; editor newsletter Industry TIES, 1992-94, ISO-9000 Guidelines & Checklist, 1994. Chmn. subcom. Gov.'s Prayer Breakfast Commn., Boise, 1988-92; v.p. Full Gospel Businessman's Internat., Boise, 1990. With USAF, 1960-64. Univ. Ctr. grantee Econ. Devel. Adminstrn., Boise, 1990-92. Mem. Am. Soc. for Quality Control (sr.), Nat. Assn. Mgmt. and Tech. Assistance Ctrs. (bd. dirs. 1990—), Am. Mgmt. Assn., Am. Cons. League (chartered cons.), Idaho Total Quality Inst. (bd. dirs. 1991—, trustee 1995—, Idaho Quality award), Tech. Transfer Soc. Avocations: hiking, camping, photography, writing, hunting. Home: 11934 Ginger Creek Dr Boise ID 83713-3677 Office: Boise State Univ 1910 University Dr Boise ID 83725-0001

STEINGRABER, FREDERICK GEORGE, management consultant; b. Mpls., July 7, 1938; s. Frederick F. and Evelyn (Luger) S.; m. Veronika Agnes Wagner, Aug. 9, 1974; children—Karla, Frederick. B.S., Ind. U., 1960; MBA, Beta Gamma Sigma, U. Chgo., 1964. Cert. mgmt. cons. Internat. banker Harris Trust, Chgo., 1960-61; with comml. loan and credit No. Trust Co., Chgo., 1963; assoc. A.T. Kearney, Chgo., 1964-69, prin., 1969-72, officer/ptnr., 1972—, pres., chief ops. officer, 1981, chief exec. officer, 1984—, chmn. bd., CEO, treas., 1986—; also bd. dirs.; bd. dirs. Lawter Internat., Mercury Fin. Co.; mem. Inst. for Ill., 1986; bd. dirs. Maytag Corp., Southeastern Thrift & Bank Fund, The Conf. Bd. Chief Crusader United Way-Crusade of Mercy, Chgo., 1983-90, div. chmn., 1988; bd. dirs. Ill. Coalition, 1989, Northwestern Healthcare Network, 1989—, fin. rsch. and adv. com. City of Chgo., 1989—; mem., past chmn. dean's adv. coun. Ind. U., 1985—, bd. dirs. Ind. U. Found.; mem. coun. of Grad. Sch. Bus. U. Chgo.; mem. Northwestern U. Assocs.; bd. dirs. Children's Meml. Hosp., Chgo., 1985—; exec. com. Mid.-Am. Com., 1985—. Mem. NAM (bd. dirs.), Inst. Mgmt. Cons., Chgo. Coun. Fgn. Rels. (bd. dirs.), Ill. State C. of C. (bd. dirs. 1982-88, exec. com. 1984-88, chmn. Ill. Alliance for Econ. Initiatives), Exec. Club Chgo., Acad. Alumni Fellows Ind. U. (award), Chgo. Club, Econ. Club (bd. dirs.), Comml. Club, Northwestern U. Assn., Met. Club, Glenview Club, others. Home: 615 Warwick Rd Kenilworth IL 60043-1149 Office: AT Kearney Inc 222 W Adams St Chicago IL 60606-5307*

STEINGRABER, LARRY LEE, structural engineer; b. Manawa, Wis., June 5, 1954; s. Clarence M. and Viann M. (Vaughn) S.; m. Kathleen L. Rein, Aug. 12, 1978; 1 child, Daniel J. BS in Archtl. and Bldg. Constrn. Engring, Milw. Sch. Engring., 1980. Registered profl. engr., Wis. Engr. Inryco-Milcor, Milw., 1980-85, Inryco-Bldg. Panels, Milw., 1985-87, BCI Burke Co., Inc., Fond du Lac, Wis., 1988—. mem. ASTM, Nat. Recreation and Parks Assn., NSPE, Soc. Mfg. Engrs., Wis. Soc. Profl. Engrs., Corvair Soc. Am. Lutheran. Achievements include patent for enclosed rubber spring. Home: 279 Hartford Rd Slinger WI 53086-9545 Office: BCI Burke Co Inc 660 Van Dyne Rd Fond Du Lac WI 54937-1447

STEINHARDT, HENRY, photographer; b. N.Y.C., Nov. 15, 1920; s. Maxwell and Ruth (Davis) S.; m. Elizabeth Smith, 1946 (dec. 1955); children: Elizabeth, Maxwell; m. Helene Fleck, Feb. 1, 1958; 1 child, Henry III. AB, Harvard U., 1942, MArch, 1949. Registered architect. Office mgr. R.H. Cutting, Architect, N.Y.C., 1951-53; ptnr., architect Steinhardt & Thompson, Architects, N.Y.C., 1953-61; architect The Cerny Assocs., St. Paul, 1961-63, John Graham & Co., Seattle, 1963-67, Morse/Kirk, Seattle, 1967-68, N.G. Jacobson & Assocs., Seattle, 1968-69; pvt. practice Mercer Island, Wash., 1969-75; architect USN, Bremerton, Wash., 1975-78; photographer Mercer Island, 1979—. Prin. works exhibited at Washington, Seattle and Andover, Mass.; contbr. articles to fgn. archtl. jours. 1st lt. U.S. Army, 1943-46; capt. USAF, 1950-52. Recipient Design award Progressive Architecture, 1959, Archtl. award Fifth Ave. Assn., 1960. Fellow AIA. Democrat. Home and Office: 7825 SE 63rd Pl Mercer Island WA 98040-4813

STEINHARDT, PAUL JOSEPH, physics educator, consultant; b. Washington, Dec. 25, 1952; s. Charles Sidney and Helen (Danuff) S.; m. Nancy Riva Shatzman, July 1, 1979; children: Charles Louis, Joseph Solomon, William Martin, Cynthia Rose. BS, Calif. Inst. Tech., 1974; MA, Harvard U., 1975, PhD, 1978. Jr. fellow Soc. Fellows Harvard U., Cambridge, Mass., 1978-81; asst. prof. physics U. Pa., Phila., 1981-83, assoc. prof., 1983-85, prof., 1985—, Mary Amanda Wood chair physics, 1989—; cons. IBM Rsch., Yorktown Heights, N.Y., 1978-90, Mitre Corp., McLean, Va., 1987-92; vis. lectr. Phi Beta Kappa, 1989-90; Monell fellow Inst. for Advanced Study, Princeton, 1989-90, Dyson fellow, 1995; Harvard Loeb lectr., 1990; Welsh lectr. U. Toronto, 1996; lectr. Can. Inst. for Theoretical Astrophysics, 1996. Author: Physics of Quasicrystals, 1988, Quasicrystals: The State of the Art, 1991; patentee quasiperiodic screens, quasiperiodic patterns, quasicrystals. Recipient 1st prize Gravitational Rsch. Essay Competition, 1993, 2d prize, 1990; Sloan Found. fellow, 1982-85, Guggenheim fellow, 1994-95; U.S. Dept. Energy grantee, 1982. Fellow Am. Phys. Soc.; mem. Am. Astron. Soc., Materials Rsch. Soc., Sigma Xi. Democrat. Jewish. Home: 1000 Cedargrove Rd Wynnewood PA 19096-2006 Office: U Pa Dept Physics 33D Walnut St Philadelphia PA 19144

STEINHARDT, RALPH GUSTAV, III, law educator; b. Bethlehem, Pa., July 28, 1954; s. Ralph Gustav Jr. and Mary Etzler (Hawks) S.; m. Donna Scarboro, Oct. 23, 1982; children: Ruth Jackson Steinhardt, Ralph Gustav IV. BA summa cum laude, Bowdoin Coll., 1976; JD, Harvard U., 1980. Bar: D.C. 1980, U.S. Dist. Ct. D.C. 1981, U.S. Ct. Appeals (D.C. and 9th cirs.) 1983, U.S. Supreme Ct. 1984. Assoc. Patton Boggs & Blow, Washington, 1980-85; prof. law Nat. Law Ctr. George Washington U., Washington, 1985—; co-dir. Oxford-GW Summer Inst. in Internat. Human Rights Law, 1994—; litigation advisor Internat. Human Rights Law Group, Washington, 1985—; mem. coun. advisors UN High Commr. for Refugees, Washington, 1987—. Contbg. author: Testimonial Privileges, 1983, World Justice? U.S. Courts and International Human Rights, 1991, United Nations Legal Order, 1994; contbr. articles to profl. jours. Pro bono counsel in field; bd. dirs. Hancock Point (Maine) Village Improvement Soc., 1988-92. Recipient Pro Bono Atty. award Internat. Human Rights Law Group, 1987; finalist for Trial Lawyer of Yr., 1989; Henry Luce Found. scholar, 1976-77; Fulbright scholar Faculty of Law, Univ. Coll., Galway, Ireland, 1995-96. Mem. Am. Soc. Internat. Law (exec. com. 1994), Phi Beta Kappa. Mem. Soc. of Friends. Avocations: musical composition, sailing. Office: George Washington U Nat Law Ctr 720 20th St NW Washington DC 20006-4306

STEINHART, RONALD G., banker; b. Beaumont, Tex., June 15, 1940; s. Werner and Marga (Steinhart); m. Phyllis Yonet; children: David Alan, Kenneth Jason, Barry Joel. BBA, U. Tex., MBA. Pres. Dallas Bank & Trust, 1965-69; chmn. bd. Town North Nat. Bank, Dallas, 1972-75, Dallas/Fort Worth Airport Bank, 1972-75; pres. Main Street Nat. Bank, Dallas, 1969-77; chmn. bd. Equitable Bank, Dallas, 1979-80; pres. Valley View Bank, Dallas, 1977-80; vice chmn. InterFirst Corp., Dallas, pres., chief operating officer, 1980-86; vice chmn. First RepublicBank Corp., Dallas, 1986-88; formerly prin. RepublicBank Assn., Dallas; pres., COO Banc One Tex. Corp. (formerly Deposit Guaranty Bank), Dallas, 1988—; prin. rep. Assn. Bank Holding Cos.; chmn., chief exec. officer Tex.-Op Bancshares Inc. Mem. Edwin L. Cox Sch. Bus. assoc. bd. So. Meth. U.; mem. exec. bd., chmn. 1983 and 1984 Scout show Circle Ten council Boy Scouts Am.; sec./treas. Dallas Citizens Council; dir. Jewish Welfare Fedn. Found., Dallas Zoolog. Soc., State Fair of Tex., United Way of Dallas; mem. Cotton Bowl Council. Served with USAF, 1958-68, with res. Mem. Tex. Bankers Assn., Tex. Assn. Bank Holders Cos., Dallas Clearing House Assn. (dir.), Tex. Soc. C.P.A.s, Assn. Res. City Bankers, Young Pres. Orgn. Office: Banc One Tex Corp 1717 Main St Dallas TX 75201-4605*

STEINHAUER, BRUCE W., health facility administrator. CEO Lahey Hitchcock Clinic formerly Lahey Clinic, Burlington, Mass., 1992—. Office: Lahey Clinic Medical Ctr 41 Mall Rd Burlington MA 01805-0001*

STEINHAUS, JOHN EDWARD, physician, medical educator; b. Omaha, Feb. 23, 1917; s. Emil F. and Pearl (Haynie) S.; m. Mila Jean Pinkerton, Feb. 21, 1943; children: Kathryn, Carolyn, Barbara, William, Elizabeth. B.A., U. Neb., 1940, M.A., 1941; M.D., U. Wis., 1945, Ph.D., 1950. Diplomate: Am. Bd. Anesthesiologists. Pvt. practice specializing in anesthesiology Madison, Wis., 1951-58, Atlanta, 1958—; faculty U. Wis., 1951-58; mem. faculty Emory U., Atlanta, 1958—; prof. anesthesiology Emory U., 1959-87, prof. emeritus, 1987—, chmn. dept., 1959-85; chief anesthesiology service Grady Meml. Hosp., 1959-77, Emory U. Hosp., 1958-85. Author: Medical Care Divided; contbr. articles to profl. jours. Pres. Anesthesia Found. Mem. Am. Soc. Anesthesiologists (past pres., Disting. Service award 1982), So. Soc. Anesthesiologists (past pres.), AMA, AAAS, Assn. U. Anesthetists (past pres.), Anesthesiology History Assn. (pres), Soc. Pharm. Exptl. Therapeutics, Phi Beta Kappa, Sigma Xi, Alpha Omega Alpha. Home and Office: 836 Castle Falls Dr NE Atlanta GA 30329-4114

STEINHOFF, HAROLD WILLIAM, retired research institute executive; b. Ft. Morgan, Colo., Mar. 9, 1919; s. Lawrence Henry and Helen Grace (Morse) S.; m. Marian Andelea Towne, Jan. 19, 1944; children: Richard Terrell, David Lee. BS in Forestry, Colo. A&M Coll., 1941; MS in Forest Zoology, Syracuse U., 1947, PhD in Wildlife Biology, 1957. Grad. teaching asst. Syracuse (N.Y.) U., 1941-42, 46-47; timber estimator U.S. Forest Svc., Ft. Collins, Colo., 1944; ranger U.S. Nat. Park Svc., Estes Park, Colo., 1947; prof. Colo. State U., Ft. Collins, 1947-74, Centennial prof., 1970—, regional adminstr., 1974-77, dist. dir., 1977-81; project leader Four Corners Rsch. Inst., Durango, Colo., 1977—, pres., 1981-92; cons. Devel. Rsch. Assocs., Denver, 1971, Stanford Rsch. Inst., Menlo Park, Calif., 1971; project leader Huddelston & Buck, Denver, 1972. Author: Wildlife Ecology, 1961, Ecosystem Biology, 1976; editor: Ecological Impact of Snowpack Augmentation, 1976; contbr. The Values of the Wildlife Resource, 1987. Dean Teaching Inst. Ft. Collins Coun. Chs., 1952-56; chmn. environ. com. Durango C. of C., 1977; chmn. LaPlata County Energy Coun., Durango, 1977, Durango Uranium Tailings Task Force, 1978-91. Capt. C.E. U.S. Army, 1942-46, ETO. Recipient Oliver Pennock Disting. Svc. award Colo. State U., 1968. Mem. The Wildlife Soc. (coun. 1966-71), Coll. Forestry Alumni Assn. (pres. 1964-64, Honor Alumnus award 1976), Soc. Am. Foresters, Am. Inst. Biol. Sci., Nat. Wildlife Fedn., Toastmasters (pres. Durango chpt. 1980-81), Phi Kappa Phi (pres. Ft. Collins 1965). Avocations: photography, home construction. Home: 2705 N College Dr Durango CO 81301-4410

STEINHORN, IRWIN HARRY, lawyer, educator, corporate executive; b. Dallas, Aug. 13, 1940; s. Raymond and Libby L. (Miller) S.; m. Linda Kay Shoshone, Nov. 30, 1968; 1 child, Leslie Robin. BBA, U. Tex., 1961, LLB, 1964. Bar: Tex. 1964, U.S. Dist. Ct. (no. dist.) Tex. 1965, Okla. 1970, U.S. Dist. Ct. (we. dist.) Okla. 1972. Assoc. Oster & Kaufman, Dallas, 1964-67; ptnr. Parness, McQuire & Lewis, Dallas, 1967-70; sr. v.p., gen. counsel LSB Industries, Inc., Oklahoma City, 1970-87; v.p., gen. counsel USPCI, Inc., Oklahoma City, 1987-88; ptnr. Hastie & Steinhorn, Oklahoma City, 1988-95; mem., officer, dir. Conner & Winters, Oklahoma City, 1995—; adj. prof. law Oklahoma City U. Sch. Law, 1979—; lectr. in field. Mem. adv. com. Okla. Securities Commn., 1986—. Served to capt. USAR, 1964-70. Mem. ABA, Tex. Bar Assn., Okla. Bar Assn. (bus. assn. sect., sec.ptreas. 1986-87, chmn. 1988-89), Com. to Revise Okla. Bus. Corp. Act, Oklahoma City Golf and Country Club, Rotary, Phi Alpha Delta. Republican. Jewish. Home: 6205 Avalon Ln Oklahoma City OK 73118-1001 Office: Conner & Winters City Bank Twr Leadershp Sq 211 N Robinson Ste 1700 Oklahoma City OK 73102

STEINKAMP, FREDRIC, film editor. Editor: (films) The Adventures of Huckleberry Finn, 1960, Where the Boys Are, 1960, Two Loves, 1961, All Fall Down, 1962, Period of Adjustment, 1962, It Happened at the World's Fair, 1963, Sunday in New York, 1963, Quick, Before It Melts, 1964, The Unsinkable Molly Brown, 1964, Once a Thief, 1965, Duel at Diablo, 1966, Grand Prix, 1966 (Academy award best film editing 1966), Mister Buddwing, 1966, Doctor, You've Got to Be Kidding, 1967, Charly, 1968, The Extraordinary Seaman, 1969, The Shoot Horses, Don't They?, 1969 (Academy award nomination best film editing 1969), (with Marjorie Fowler and Roger J. Roth) The Strawberry Statement, 1970, The Marriage of a Young Stockbroker, 1971, (with Donald Guidice) A New Leaf, 1971, Nightmare Honeymoon, 1972, (with Michael McLean) Freebie and the Bean, 1974, (with Guidice) Three Days of the Condor, 1975, (with Thomas Stanford and Guidice) The Yakuza, 1975, (with David Bretherton and Guidice) Harry and Walter Go to New York, 1976, Bobby Deerfield, 1977, Fedora, 1979, (with Karl F. Steinkamp) Bound by Honor, 1993; (films; with William Steinkamp) Hide in Plain Sight, 1980, Tootsie, 1982 (Academy award nomination best film editing 1982), Against All Odds, 1984, (also with Pembroke Herring and Sheldon Kahn) Out of Africa, 1985 (Academy award nomination best film editing 1985), White Nights, 1985, Adventures in Babysitting, 1987, Burglar, 1987, Scrooged, 1988, Havana, 1990, The Firm, 1993. Office: care Lawrence A Mirisch The Mirisch Agency 10100 Santa Monica Blvd Ste 700 Los Angeles CA 90067

STEINKAMP, ROBERT THEODORE, lawyer; b. St. Louis, Sept. 11, 1945; s. William P. and Leona M. (Kraus) S.; m. Cheryl Sue Dunlop, Aug. 19, 1967; children: Theodore Bewick, Rebecca Anne. BA, William Jewell Coll., Liberty, Mo., 1967; JD, U. Mo., Kansas City, Mo., 1971; postgrad., U. Mo., Kansas City, 1971-72. Bar: Mo. 1971, U.S. Dist. Ct. (we. dist.) Mo. 1971, U.S. Tax Ct. 1971, U.S. Ct. Appeals (8th cir.) 1971. Assoc. Morris, Foust, Moudy & Beckett, Kansas City, 1971-76; ptnr. Morris, Foust & Beckett, Kansas City, 1976-78, Beckett & Steinkamp, Kansas City, 1978-90; v.p., gen. counsel, sec. Applebee's Internat., Inc., Kansas City, 1990—. Mem. Downtown, Inc., Kansas City, 1978-84, Friends of Art, Nelson Art Gallery, Kansas City, 1985—, Nat. Hist. Preservation Found., 1985—; bd. dirs., committeeman Kappa Alpha Order Nat. Fraternity Housing Corp., Lexington, Va., 1984-92; bd. dirs., pres. ADKASHA, Liberty, Mo., 1977—; bd. dirs. Liberty Symphony Orch., Inc., 1982-87, pres. 1984-86; Clay County Fine Arts Coun., 1991-93; sec. Heartland Franchising Assn., 1991-93; nat.

co-chmn. William Jewell Coll., Ann. Fund. 1995-96. Mem. ABA (forum on franchising, corp. and tax sects.), Kansas City Bar Assn. (co-chmn. bus. law com.), Lawyer's Assn. Kansas City, Mo. Bar Assn., Clay County Bar Assn., Kans. City Club, Liberty Hills Country Club (bd. dirs. 1985-87). Republican. Methodist. Avocations: golf, tennis, reading, travel. Office: Applebees Internat Inc 4551 W 107th St Ste 100 Overland Park KS 66207-4037

STEINKAMP, WILLIAM, film editor. Editor: (films) King of the Mountain, 1981, The Fabulous Baker Boys, 1989 (Academy award nomination best film editing 1989), (with Michael Tronick and Harvey Rosenstock) Scent of a Woman, 1992, Man Trouble, 1992; (films; with Fredric Steinkamp) Hide in Plain Sight, 1980, Tootsie, 1982 (Academy award nomination best film editing 1982), Against All Odds, 1984, (also with Pembroke Herring and Sheldon Kahn) Out of Africa, 1985 (Academy award nomination best film editing 1985), White Nights, 1985, Adventures in Babysitting, 1987, Burglar, 1987, Scrooged, 1988, Havana, 1990, The Firm, 1993. Office: care Motion Picture Editors 7715 W Sunset Blvd Ste 220 Los Angeles CA 90046-3912

STEINKE, BETTINA, artist; b. Biddeford, Maine, June 25, 1913; d. William and Alice Mary (Staples) S.; m. Don Blair, Mar. 21, 1946. Student, Sch. Fine Arts, Newark, 1930, Cooper Union, 1931-33, Phoenix Art Sch., 1934-35. Represented in permanent collections Indpls. Mus., Ft. Worth Mus., Nat. Cowboy Hall of Fame and Western Heritage; artist original drawings of Toscanini, 1938, Paderewski, 1939 (both now in Smithsonian Inst.); charcoal portraits NBC book on Toscanini and Orch., 1938; many portraits of well known personalities; retrospective shows Palm Springs Desert Mus., Gilcrease Mus., Tulsa, Okla., Nat. Cowboy Hall of Fame, 1995; subject of biography Bettina. Pres. bd. dirs. Harwood Found. U. N.Mex.; exec. bd. Nat. Cowboy Hall of Fame and Western Heritage. Recipient Gold and Silver medals Nat. Cowboy Hall of Fame, Oklahoma City, 1973-89, Gold medal award for Outstanding Contbn. to Painting, 1995, N.Mex. Gov.'s award, 1996, John Singer Sargant award Portrait Soc. (East Coast), 1996, others; scholar Phoenix Art Sch., N.Y.C., 1934-35. Mem. Nat. Acad. Western Artists (Prix de West award, Cowboy Hall of Fame). Home: PO Box 2342 Santa Fe NM 87504-2342

STEINMAN, LISA MALINOWSKI, English literature educator, writer; b. Willimantic, Conn., Apr. 8, 1950; d. Zenon Stanislaus and Shirley Belle Malinowski; m. James A. Steinman, Apr. 1968 (div. 1980); m. James L. Shugrue, July 23, 1984. BA, Cornell U., 1971, MFA, 1973, PhD, 1976. Asst. prof. English Reed Coll., Portland, Oreg., 1976-82, assoc. prof., 1982-90, prof., 1990—, Kenan prof. English lit. and humanities, 1993—; cons. NEH, Washington, 1984-85. Author: Lost Poems, 1976, Made in America, 1987, All That Comes to Light, 1989, A Book of Other Days, 1992; editor Hubbub Mag., 1983—; editl. bd. Williams Rev., 1991—, Stevens Jour., 1994—; contbr. articles to profl. jours. Fellow Danforth Found., 1971-75, NEH, 1983, 96, Oreg. Arts Commn., 1984-84, Nat. Endowment for Arts, 1984; Rockefeller Found. scholar, 1987-88; recipient Pablo Neruda award, 1987, Oreg. Inst. Lit. Arts award, 1993. Mem. MLA, Poets and Writers, PEN (N.W. chpt., co-founder, officer 1989-93). Home: 5344 SE 38th Ave Portland OR 97202-4208 Office: Reed Coll Dept English 3203 SE Woodstock Blvd Portland OR 97202-8138

STEINMAN, ROBERT CLEETON, accountant; b. Phila., June 11, 1931; s. George Curtis and Kathryn Agnes (Johnstone) S.; m. Nancy Badri Pourian, Sept. 24, 1960; children: Shirley Kathryn, Susan Soraya, Robert Mark. B.Sc. in Bus. Adminstrn, Drexel U., 1954, M.B.A., 1970. C.P.A., Pa. Accountant Main Lafrentz & Co. (C.P.A.'s), Phila., 1956-58; asst. treas. Ostheimer and Co., Inc., Phila., 1958-62; controller Biol. Abstracts, Inc., Phila., 1962-64; budget, cost and fin. analysis mgr. PQ Chems. Co., 1964-70; v.p., group controller 1st Pa. Bank, Phila., 1970-78; sr. v.p., comptroller Phila. Savs. Fund Soc., 1978-87; controller Kravco Co., 1987-88, spl. asst. to the pres., 1988-91; chief fin. officer Lorel Mktg. Group Inc., King of Prussia, Pa., 1991-92; adj. asso. prof. Grad. Sch., Drexel U., Phila. Co-founder Briarlin Civic Assn., 1969, treas., 1969-72, pres., 1975—; Bd. dirs. Sigma Pi Nat. Found., treas. frat. Served with AUS, 1954-56. Mem. Pa. Bankers Assn. (faculty trust tng. sch.), Fin. Execs. Inst., Pa. Inst. CPAs, Sigma Rho, Sigma Pi, Overbrook Golf Club. Republican. Methodist. Home: 804 Lawrence Ln Newtown Square PA 19073-2610

STEINMETZ, DAVID CURTIS, religion educator, publisher, minister; b. Columbus, Ohio, June 12, 1936; s. Walter Curtis and Lucy Margaret (Binderbasen) S.; m. Virginia Ruth Verploegh, June 20, 1959; children: Claire Elise, Matthew Eliot. BA with highest honor, Wheaton Coll., 1958; BD summa cum laude, Drew U., 1961; postgrad., U. Goettingen, Federal Republic of Germany, 1964-65; ThD, Harvard U., 1965. Ordained to ministry United Meth. Ch., 1959. Asst. and assoc. prof. Lancaster (Pa.) Theol. Sem., 1966-71; prof. Duke U., Durham, N.C., 1971-88, Amos Ragan Kearns prof. history of Christianity, 1988—; pres., pub. The Labyrinth Press, Inc., 1981—; vis. prof. Harvard U., 1977; adv. coun. Interpretation, Richmond, Va., 1979-84, 87-92. Autohr: Misericordia dei, 1968, Reformers in the Wings, 1971, Luther and Staupitz, 1980, Luther in Context, 1986, Calvin in Context, 1995; mem. editorial bd. Archiv für Reformationsgeschichte, 1977-93, Duke U. Monographs in Medieval and Renaissance Studies, 1972—, Brill Studies in Medieval and Reformation Thought, Leiden, Netherlands, 1981—. Named Scholar-Tchr. of Yr. Duke U., 1986; Rockefeller doctoral fellow Rockefeller Found., 1964-66, faculty fellow Assn. Theol. Schs., 1970, 77-78, Guggenheim fellow Guggenheim Found., 1977-78, NEH summer fellow, 1990. Mem. Medieval Acad. Am., Am. Soc. Ch. History (pres. 1985), Renaissance Soc. Am., Soc. for Reformation Rsch., Soc. for Scholarly Pub. Office: Duke U Div Sch Durham NC 27706

STEINMETZ, DEBORAH SUSAN, interior designer; b. New Orleans, Nov. 29, 1951; d. Donald Frederick and Estelle Margaret (Ulmer) Tossell; B.F.A., La. State U., 1973; m. Robert Steinmetz, Dec. 29, 1973. Interior designer David Grinnell Architect, 1973-75; interior design cons., Columbus, Ga., 1975-77; designer Dameron-Pierson, New Orleans, 1977-79; v.p. interior design Interior Environments, Inc., New Orleans, 1979-83; pres., owner Steinmetz & Assocs., 1983—; mem. interior design curriculum com. Dominican Coll., New Orleans, 1981-82; mem. interior design adv. com. Delgado Community Coll., New Orleans, 1982—; chmn. membership Preservatin Resource Ctr., 1988. Mem. visual arts com. Contemporary Art Center, 1980-81; dir. profl. devel. Nat. Coun. Interior Design Qualification, 1994-95. Mem. Am. Soc. Interior Designers (Presdl. citation; chmn. New Orleans assn. 1980-81, dir. La. chpt. 1982—, newsletter editor La. Chpt. 1982, chain membership/admissions La. chpt. 1984, treas. 1985-87, sec. 1988, nat. dir. 1993-94), Internat. Interior Design Assn., Nat. Trust Hist. Preservation, La. Landmarks Soc., La. State Bd. Interior Design Examiners, Interior Designers of La. (treas. 1987), La. State Interior Design Alumni (sec. 1987). Roman Catholic. Home: 2850 Annunciation St New Orleans LA 70115-1002 Office: 225 Baronne St Ste 207 New Orleans LA 70112-1704

STEINMETZ, JOHN CHARLES, geologist, paleontologist; b. St. Paul, Sept. 26, 1947; s. Charles Leonard and Ruth Naomi (Osteraas) S.; m. Sarah Cook Tristán, May 29, 1982; children: Katherine Ruth, Elizabeth Margaret. BS, U. Ill., 1969, MS, 1975; PhD, U. Miami, 1977. Asst. prof. U. South Fla., St. Petersburg, 1977-82; advanced rsch. geologist Marathon Oil Co., Littleton, Colo., 1982-86, sr. geologist, 1986-90, advanced sr. geologist, 1990-94; dir. state geologist Mont. Bur. of Mines and Geology, 1994—. Mem. bd. advisors Micropaleontology Press, N.Y.C., 1986—. Trustee Paleontol. Rsch. Instn., Ithaca, N.Y., 1990—, v.p., 1992-94, pres. 1994-96. Mem. Assn. Am. State Geologists, Am. Assn. Petroleum Geologists, Geol. Soc. Am., Internat. Nannoplankton Assn. (U.S. treas. 1982-92), Mont. Geol. Soc., Paleontol. Soc., Soc. Econ. Paleontologists and Mineralogists.

STEINMETZ, JON DAVID, mental health executive, psychologist; b. N.Y.C., June 4, 1940; s. Lewis I. and Rose (Josefsberg) S.; m. Jane Audrey Hilton, Dec. 24, 1964; children: Jonna Lynn, Jay Daniel. BA, NYU, 1962; MA, Bradley U., 1963. Lic. psychologist, Ill. Intern in psychology Galesburg (Ill.) State Rsch. Hosp., 1963-64; staff psychologist Manteno (Ill.) State Hosp., 1964-68, program dir., 1968-70, asst. dir., 1970-72; dep. dir. Manteno Mental Health Ctr., 1972-80, Tinley Park (Ill.) Mental Health Ctr., 1980-88; dir. Chgo. Read Mental Health Ctr., 1988-91; ret., 1991; clin. dir. Jane Addams Hull House Assn., 1992—. Trustee Village of Park Forest, Cook and Will Counties, Ill.; officer, bd. dirs. various civic orgns., Park Forest. Home: 200 Hickory St Park Forest IL 60466-1016

STEINMETZ, RICHARD BIRD, JR., lawyer; b. Orange, N.J., Mar. 27, 1929; s. Richard Bird and Charlotte (Quinby) S.; m. Merriam Holly Miller, June 9, 1956; children: Richard Blair, Jonathan Bird, Edward Quinby. BA, Yale U., 1950; JD, Harvard U., 1955. Bar: N.Y. 1955. Assoc. Chadbourne and Parke, N.Y.C., 1955-59; with Anaconda Co., N.Y.C., 1959-79, v.p., gen. counsel, 1971-79; v.p. Colt Industries Inc., N.Y.C., 1979-82; v.p., gen. counsel Pittston Co., Greenwich, Conn., 1982-84; exec. v.p. Case, Pomeroy and Co., N.Y.C., 1984-94; bd. dirs. Case, Pomeroy and Co. Served to capt. USMC, 1950-52. Mem. ABA, Assn. of Bar of City of N.Y., Assn. of Gen. Counsel. Republican. Episcopalian. Home: 78 Zaccheus Mead Ln Greenwich CT 06831-3752

STEINMETZ, ROBERT CHARLES, architect; b. Charleston, W.Va., Oct. 16, 1951; s. Charles and Bernadine Steinmetz; m. Deborah Susan Toselle, Dec. 29, 1974. BArch, La. State U., 1974. Architect Pound Flower & Dedyler, Columbus, Ga., 1974-75, David Allan Grinnell, Atlanta, 1975, Maxwell & Lebreton, New Orleans, 1975-77; architect, assoc. Mathes Group, New Orleans, 1977-84; architect, prin. Steinmetz & Assocs., New Orleans, 1984—; value added reseller computers, software Integrated Facility Systems Corp., New Orleans, 1991—. Mem. New Orleans Mus. Art, New Orleans Preservation Res. Ctr., Nat. Trust for Hist. Preservation. Mem. AIA (chair interiors com. 1995), La. Architecture Assn., La. Landmarks Soc., Nat. Coun. Archtl. Registration Bds. (cert.), Internat. Facility Mgmt. Assn. Office: 225 Baronne St Ste 1720 New Orleans LA 70112-1710

STEINMETZ, SOL, lexicographer, publishing company editor; b. Velki-Bockov, Slovakia, July 29, 1930; came to U.S., 1948; s. Philip and Lea (Zwiebel) S.; m. Tzipora Mandel, June 26, 1955; children: Jacob J., Abraham A., Steven B. BA, Yeshiva Coll., N.Y.C., 1952; DD, Yeshiva U., N.Y.C., 1956. Asst. editor G. & C. Merriam Co., Springfield, Mass., 1957-61; gen. editor Barnhart Books, Bronxville, N.Y., 1962-89; exec. editor dictionaries Random House, Inc., N.Y.C., 1990-94, editl. dir., 1995—. Co-author: Barnhart Dictionary of New English, 1973, Second Dictionary of New English, 1980, Thhird Dictionary of New English, 1990; author: Yiddish and English: A Century of Yiddish in America, 1986. Mem. Am. Dialect Soc., Dictionary Soc. N.Am., League of Yiddish, Religious Zionists Am., Rabbinic Alumni Yeshiva U. Avocations: reading, travel, writing, studying. Home: 1273 North Ave New Rochelle NY 10804-2702 Office: Random House Inc 201 E 50th St New York NY 10022-7703

STEINMILLER, JOHN F., professional basketball team executive; b. Mt. Prospect, Ill.; m. Corinne Steinmiller; children: John Henry, Mary Kate. V.p. bus. ops. Milw. Bucks, 1977—. Bd. dirs. M.W. Athletes Against Childhood Cancer Fund, Milw. Big Bros.-Big Sisters, Metro Milw. YMCA; mem. Greater Milw. Com. Recipient Contardi Commitment award MACC Fund, 1991. Mem. Milw. Pen and Mike Club (pres.). Office: Milw Bucks 1001 N 4th St Milwaukee WI 53203-1314

STEINRUCK, CHARLES FRANCIS, JR., management consultant, lawyer; b. Phila., Apr. 25, 1908; s. Charles Francis and Laura (Crutchley) S.; m. Esther Sophia Schramm, June 1, 1936 (dec. Oct. 1962); children—Carol, Lisa.; m. Alice Bignell Marchese, Nov. 22, 1967. Student, U. Pa., 1925-28; LL.B., South Jersey Law Sch. (now Rutgers U.), 1937, J.D., 1972. Bar: D.C. bar 1938. Accountant J.S. Timmons, Inc., Phila., 1926-28; merged with Philco Corp., 1928, asst. to sec., 1937-41, asst. sec., 1941-42, sec., 1942-61; asst. sec. Philco-Ford Corp., 1962-68; cons., 1962—; resident v.p. Togotechnique, S.A.R.L., Republique Togolaise, 1979—. Author: An Anecdotal History, 1988. Mem. John W. Westcott Law Soc., Night Watch Sr. Soc. (U. Pa.), Am. Bar Assn., Sigma Kappa Phi, Delta Sigma Pi. Republican. Presbyterian. Clubs: Germantown Cricket (Phila.); Seaview Country (Absecon, N.J.). Home: 614 E Mcdevitt Dr Absecon NJ 08201-6000

STEINWACHS, DONALD MICHAEL, public health educator; b. Boise, Idaho, Sept. 9, 1946; s. Don Peter and Emma Bertha (Weisshaupt) S.; m. Sharon Kay Carlson, Aug. 25, 1972. MS, U. Ariz., 1970; PhD, Johns Hopkins U., 1973. Asst. prof. health svcs. adminstrn. Johns Hopkins U., Balt., 1973-79, assoc. prof. health policy and mgmt., 1979-86, dir. Health Svcs. Rsch. & Devel. Ctr., 1982—, prof. health policy and mgmt., 1986—, chairperson health policy and mgmt., 1994—; sec. adv. com. Dept. Vets. Affairs, Washington, 1991-92; mem. inst. Medicine, NAS, Washington, 1993—; bd. dirs. Health Outcomes Inst., Inc., Mathematica Policy Rsch., Inc. Contbr. articles to profl. jours. Mem. Gov.'s Commn. on Health Policy Rsch. and Fin., Md., 1988-90. Capt. U.S. Army, 1973. Grantee NIMH, Agy. for Health Care Policy and Rsch., Robert Wood Johnson Found. Mem. Ops. Rsch. Soc. Am., Assn. Health Svc. Rsch. (bd. dirs., pres.), Found. for Health Svc. Rsch. (bd. dirs., pres.). Achievements include development of methods for using management information systems to examine patterns of medical care, costs, and indicators of the quality of care. Office: Johns Hopkins U 624 N Broadway Baltimore MD 21205-1901*

STEIR, PAT IRIS, artist; b. Newark, Apr. 10, 1940. Studies, Pratt Inst., 1956-58, 60-62; BFA, Boston U., 1961, studies, 1958-60; DFA (hon.), Pratt Inst., 1991. Art dir. Harper & Row, N.Y.C., 1968-69; tchr. Calif. Art Inst., 1973-75. One woman shows include Terry Dintenfass Gallery, N.Y., 1964, Bienville Gallery, N.Y., 1969, Graham Gallery, N.Y., 1971, Fourcade, Droll, Inc., N.Y., 1975, John Doyle Gallery, Paris, 1975, Galerie Farideh Cadot, Paris, 1976, 78, 79, 80, Morgan Thomas Gallery, Santa Monica, Calif., 1976, Otis Art Inst., L.A., 1976, Xavier Fourcade, Inc., N.Y., 1976, Carl Solway Gallery, Cin., 1977, Galeria Marilena Bonomo, Bari, Italy, 1978, Galerie d'Art Contemporain, Geneva, 1980, Art Mus. U. So. Fla., Tampa, 1990, Galerie Montenay, Paris, 1990, N.J. Ctr. for Visual Arts, Summit, 1990, Musée d'Art Contemporain, Lyon, France, Victoria Miro Gallery, London, 1990, Dennis Ochi Gallery, Sun Valley and Boise, Idaho, 1990, Robert Miller Gallery, N.Y.C., 1990, Landfall Press, Chgo., 1990, Gallerie Thaddeus Ropac, Paris, 1990, Tate Gallery, London, 1990, Linda Cathcart Gallery, Santa Monica, Calif., 1991, Galerie Franck & Schulte, Berlin, 1991, MacKenzie Art Gallery, Regina, Can., 1991, K. Kimpton Gallery, San Francisco, 1991, Bellas Artes, Sante Fe, 1991, Thaddeus Ropac, Salzburg, Austria, 1991, Whitney Mus. N.Y.C., 1991, Nina Freudenheim Gallery, Buffalo, 1991, The Bklyn. Mus., 1992, Documenta IX, Kassel, Germany, 1992; installation show Le Magazine, Grenoble, Switzerland, 1990; group exhbns. include Ben Shahn Gallery William Patterson Coll., Wayne, N.J., 1990, Ecole Des Beaux Arts, Tourcoing, France, 1990, 91, Mus. Art R.I. Sch. Design, 1990, Marc Richards Gallery, L.A., 1990, Louver Gallery, N.Y., 1990, Norah Haime Gallery, N.Y., 1990, Nat. Gallery of Art, Washington, 1990; represented in permanent collections including Kunstmuseum, Bern, Switzerland, Walker Art Ctr., Mpls., Bklyn. Mus., Musee d'art Contemporain, Lyons, France, Met. Mus. Art, N.Y., Mus. Modern Art, N.Y., Nat. Gallery, Washington, Nat. Mus. Am. Art, Washington, Whitney Mus. Am. Art, N.Y. Studio: c/o Robert Miller Gallery 41 E 57th St New York NY 10022-1908

STEISS, ALAN WALTER, research administrator, educator; b. Woodbury, N.J., Feb. 15, 1937; s. Walter and Martha (Schreoder) S.; m. Patricia Foster McClintock, June 13, 1959; children: Carol Jean, Darren C., Todd A. BA in Sociology and Psychology, Bucknell U., 1959; MA in Urban Planning, U. Wis., 1966, PhD, 1969. Statewide planning dir. State of N.J., Trenton, 1960-65; mem. faculty Va. Poly. Inst. and State U., Blacksburg, 1967-69, program chmn. environ. and urban systems, 1969-78, assoc. dean architecture, 1974-78, assoc. dean rsch. div., 1978-83, assoc. provost, 1983-88; dir. div. rsch. devel. and adminstrn. U. Mich., Ann Arbor, 1988—, prof. urban planning, prof. pub. health, 1988—; cons. various state and local govts., 1960—, Trust Territory of the Pacific, Micronesia, 1968. Author numerous book including: Management Control in Government, 1982, Governmental Accounting and Control, 1984, Strategic Management and Organizational Decision Making, 1985, Financial Management in Public Organizations, 1989, Management Planning and Control, 1991. Chair Montgomery (Va.) Pub. Svc. Authority, 1978-83; bd. dirs. Mich. Pub. Health Inst., 1990-95; mem. policy and planning bd. Mich. Consortium for Enabling Tech., 1991-95; hon. chair region V United Way Campaign, 1991-92. Univ. fellow U. Wis., 1959-60, NDEA fellow, 1966-67. Mem. AAUP, ASPA, Am. Inst. of Planners (prog. chmn. 1964), Assn. Collegiate Schs. of Planning (mem. exec. com. 1970-71, sec. 1971-73), Assn. Collegiate Schs. in Architecture, Nat. Assn. Schs. Pub. Affairs and Adminstrn. (inst. rep. 1975-76), Coun. of Univ. Insts. for Urban Affairs, N.J. Fed. of Planning Officials (sec. 1960-64), Urban America Inc., Nat. Urban Coalition, Psi Chi, Tau Sigma Delta, Lambda Alpha. Home: 4419 Corey Cir Ann Arbor MI 48103-9414 Office: U Mich Div Rsch Devel & Adminstrn 3003 S State ST Ann Arbor MI 48109-1274

STEITZ, ELLA EMMA ANTPUSAT, artist, educator; b. Bklyn.; d. August and Anna (Pimat) Antpusat; children: Lanning Dennis, Judith Lynn Weis. Art cert., Maironius Art Acad., Kaunas, Lithuania; student, Pratt Inst., Bklyn., Nassau C.C., 1988. Pub. rels. speaker Nat. Bank N.Am., West Hempstead, N.Y., 1962-75; instr. art Village of Lynbrook, N.Y., 1981-85, City of Glen Cove, N.Y., 1987-90, Rockville Centre (N.Y.) Recreation Dept., 1976—; spkr., demonstrator Nat. Coun. State Garden Clubs, 1965—, master flower show judge, 1970—. Author: Pressing Flowers for Fun and Profit, 1970; exhibited in group shows in Southampton (N.Y.) Gallery, 1976, Lever House Gallery, N.Y.C., 1984, 96, Hutchins Gallery, Greenvale, N.Y., 1986; pvt. collections, U.S. Chair Civic Beautificatoin Com., Garden City, N.Y., 1985—; master gardener Cornell Coop. Ext., Plainview, N.Y., 1989—; sec. Salvation Army, Garden City, 1965-82. Recipient Grumbacher award Ind. Art Soc., 1980, Creativity award Federated Garden Clubs, 1985, numerous awards from flower and art shows. Mem. Tri-County Art League (A. Roos Meml. award 1986), Art League Nassau County (Excellence award 1980), Floral Park Art League (Best in Show award 1985, 87), Village Art Club (Winsor and Newton award, Newton award 1986), Village Garden Club (pres. 1973-75, Tri Color award 1965). Avocations: organic gardening, photography, travel. Home and Studio: 127 Oxford Blvd Garden City NY 11530-2715

STEITZ, JOAN ARGETSINGER, biochemistry educator; b. Mpls., Jan. 26, 1941; d. Glenn D. and Elaine (Magnusson) Argetsinger; m. Thomas A. Steitz, Aug. 20, 1966; 1 child, Jonathan Glenn. B.S., Antioch Coll., 1963; Ph.D., Harvard U., 1967; D.Sc. (hon.), Lawrence U., Appleton, Wis., 1982, Rochester U. Sch. Medicine, 1984, Mt. Sinai Sch. Medicine, 1989, Bates Coll., 1990; DSc (hon.), Trinity Coll., 1992, Harvard U., 1992. Postdoctoral fellow MRC Lab. Molecular Biology, Cambridge, Eng., 1967-70; asst. prof. molecular biophysics and biochemistry Yale U., New Haven, 1970-74; assoc. prof. Yale U., 1974-78, prof. molecular biophysics and biochemistry, 1978—; investigator Howard Hughes Med. Inst., 1986—. Recipient Young Scientist award Passano Found., 1975, Eli Lilly award in biol. chemistry, 1976, U.S. Steel Found. award in molecular biology, 1982, Lee Hawley, Sr. award for arthritis rsch., 1984, Nat. Medal of Sci., 1986, Dickson prize for Sci. Carnegie-Mellon U., 1988, Warren Triennial prize Mass. Gen. Hosp., 1989, Christopher Columbus Disc. award in biomed. rsch., 1992, Weizmann Women and Sci. Awd., 1994, NY Acad. of Scis. Fellow AAAS; mem. Am. Acad. Arts and Sci., Nat. Acad. Arts and Sci., Am. Phil. Soc., NY Acad. of Scis., (Weizmann Women & Sci. Awd, 1994). Home: 45 Prospect Hill Rd Branford CT 06405-5711 Office: Yale U Sch Medicine Dept Biochem & Biophysics 295 Congress Ave New Haven CT 06519-1418

STEJSKAL, JOSEPH FRANK, JR., carbohydrate chemist; b. Oak Park, Ill., Jan. 16, 1932; s. Joseph Frank and Bertha Helen (Urban) S.; m. Dorothy May Milas, Nov. 28, 1953; children: Patricia Anne, Joseph Frank III. BS, Wheaton Coll., 1953. Chemist Corn Products Refining Co., Argo, Ill., 1953-89; phys. sci. asst. U.S. Army Food Container Inst., Chgo., 1955-57; chemist Am. Maize Products Co., Hammond, Ind., 1987—. Brookfield (Ill.) Hist. Commn., 1993—; elder, treas. Presbyn. Ch. USA, gen. assembly del., 1951—, nat. del. 1970); instnl. rep. Boy Scouts Am., 1961-90, cmty. svc. award 1978, silver beaver award 1987. Mem. Hollywood Citizens Assn. (historian). Republican. Presbyn. Holder patents in field. Avocations: golf, chess, local history, church and community activities. Home: 3611 Rosemear Ave Brookfield IL 60513-1738 Office: Am Maize Products 1100 Indianapolis Blvd Hammond IN 46320-1019

STELCK, CHARLES RICHARD, geology educator; b. Edmonton, Alta., Can., May 20, 1917; s. Robert Ferdinand and Florella Maud (Stanbury) S.; m. Frances Gertrude McDowell, Apr. 24, 1945; children—David, Brian, Leland, John (dec.). B.Sc., U. Alta., 1937, M.Sc., 1941; Ph.D., Stanford U., 1951. Registered prof. geologist, Alta. Field geologist B.C. Dept. Mines, Victoria, Can., 1939-41; field geologist Canol Project, Norman Wells, N.W.T., Can., 1941-43, Imperial Oil Co., Calgary, Alta., 1943-49; from lectr. to prof. emeritus geology U. Alta., Edmonton, 1946—. Contbr. numerous articles principally on biostratigraphy of Cretaceous to sci. publs. Fellow Royal Soc. Can.; mem. Assn. Profl. Engrs., Geologists and Geophysicists Alta. (Centennial award 1979), Geol. Assn. Can. (Logan medal 1982), Geol. Soc. Am., Can. Soc. Petroleum Geologists (Douglas medal 1994). Conservative. Office: U Alta, Dept Earth/Atmospheric Scis, Edmonton, AB Canada T6G 2E3

STELL, LANCE KEITH, philosophy educator; b. Galesburg, Ill., Dec. 18, 1943; s. Kenneth Phillip and Esther (Dethmers) S.; m. Susan Kathleen Stell, Aug. 19, 1967; children: Dean, Virginia, Audrey. AB cum laude, Hope Coll., 1966; AM, U. Mich., 1969, PhD, 1974. Asst. prof. philosophy Hope Coll., Holland, Mich., 1969-71; instr. Albion (Mich.) Coll., 1971-72; asst. prof. Ill. State U., Normal, 1972-75; vis. scholar U. Iowa, Iowa City, 1975-76; from asst. prof. to assoc. prof. Davidson (N.C.) Coll., 1976-85, acting chair, 1983-85, prof., chair, 1985—, Charles A. Dana prof., 1991—; prof. clin. ethics dept. internal medicine Carolinas Med. Ctr., Charlotte, N.C., 1990—; bd. dirs. Bioethics Resource Group Ltd.; mem. Am. Bd. Forensic Examiners. Fellow Danforth Teaching, 1967, Ctr. for Chinese Studies, 1967, NEH, 1975-76, Mellon Found. Summer Rsch., 1978, 80, Nat. Humanities Ctr., 1982-83, grantee Liberty Fund, 1980, Health Svcs. Found., 1991-93; Title VI Chinese Lang. fellow NDFL, 1968, biotechnology summer fellow Alfred Slone Found., 1985, teaching/rsch. med. ethics. fellow Carolinas Med. Ctr., 1989-90. Mem. Am. Philos. Assn., Am. Soc. Law and Medicine, Soc. Health and Human Values, Am. Coll. Forensic Examiners. Office: Davidson Coll PO Box 1719 Davidson NC 28036-1719

STELL, WILLIAM KENYON, neuroscientist, educator; b. Syracuse, N.Y., Apr. 21, 1939; arrived in Can., 1980; dual citizenship with Can., 1992; s. Henry Kenyon and Edith Doris (Lawson) S.; m. Judith Longbotham, June 27, 1974 (div. 1996); children: Jennifer Susan, Sarah Ruth; m. Kathie L. Roller, 1996. B.A. in Zoology with high honors, Swarthmore Coll., 1961; Ph.D. in Anatomy, U. Chgo., 1966, M.D. with honors (E. Gellhorn prize 1967), 1967. Staff fellow, then sr. staff fellow Nat. Inst. Neurol. Diseases and Stroke, NIH, 1967-72; asso. prof., then prof. ophthalmology and anatomy UCLA Med. Sch., 1972-80; assoc. dir. Jules Stein Eye Inst., UCLA, 1978-80; prof. anatomy U. Calgary (Can.) Faculty Medicine, 1980—, prof. surgery/ophthalmology, 1992—, head dept., 1980-85, prof. surgery and ophthalmology, 1992—; dir. Lions Sight Ctr., Calgary, 1980—; guest rschr. in physiology Lab. Physiologie Nerveuse, Ctr. Nat. de la Recherche Scientifique, Gif-sur-Yvette, France, 1985-86; vis. fellow Vision Scis. Ctr. Rsch. Sch. Biol. Scis. Australian Nat. U., Canberra, 1996. Served with USPHS, 1967-69. Grantee USPHS, Med. Rsch. Coun. Can., Alta. Heritage Found. Med. Rsch., Natural Scis. and Engring. Rsch. Coun. Can., NATO, Human Frontier Sci. Program; William and Mary Greve Internat. research scholar, 1979-80. Mem. Assn. Rsch. in Vision and Ophthalmology, Soc. Neurosci. Home: 2020 17th Ave NW, Calgary, AB Canada T2M 0S6 Office: Univ of Calgary, 3330 Hospital Dr NW, Calgary, AB Canada T2N 4N1

STELLA, FRANK DANTE, food service and dining equipment executive; b. Jessup, Pa., Jan. 21, 1919; s. Facondino and Chiara (Pennoni) S.; m. Martha Theresa Yetzer (dec. Apr. 1994); children: Daniel (dec.), Mary Anne, William J., Philip J., Marsha, James C., Stephen P. Student, U. Detroit, 1937-41, Washington and Lee, 1944; D in Bus. and Industry (hon.), Gentium Pacem U., Rome, 1979; D in Sci. and Bus. Adminstn. (hon.), Cleary Coll., 1985. Pres., chmn., CEO F.D. Stella Products Co., Detroit, 1946—; founding ptnr. The Fairlane Club (sold to Club Corp. Am., 1979); chmn. bd., CEO Stella Internat., N.Y.C.; mem. Mich. Higher Edn. Facilities Commn., Area-Wide Water Quality Bd., Fed. Statis. Commn., White House Fellows Commn. and others; chmn. Detroit Income Tax Rev. Bd.; instr. orgn. and mgmt. small bus. U. Detroit; vice chmn., bd. dirs. Met. Realty Corp.; bd. dirs. Fed. Home Loan Bank Indpls., Computer Bus. Solutions Inc. Bd. dirs. March of Dimes Mich., 1976, mem. exec. com., 1984; corp. bd. dirs. Boys Club Met. Detroit, 1979; bd. dirs., exec. com. Orchestra Hall, 1974, vice chmn., 1979-82, chmn. 1982—; trustee U. Detroit, 1971-80, 82—, exec. com. 1971-77, chmn. devel. com. 1971-80, chmn. nominating com. 1971-78; chmn. Nat. Vol. Commn., Nat. Rep. Heritage Council, 1985—, chmn. 1991—; trustee Sacred Heart Rehab. Ctr., 1981—, St. Gabriel Media, Inc., 1980—; group chmn. food and drug div. United Found., 1978-79; mem. adv. bd. dirs. Bishop Borgess High Sch., 1984-88; bd. dirs. Ctr. for Ind. Living, Detroit Rehab. Inst., 1977-82, New Detroit Inc., Detroit Econ. Growth Corp., 1983, Detroit Econ. Growth Fund, 1983, Mich. Opera Exec. Com.; mem. St. John's Hosp. Guild, Friend of the Folger Libr., Washington, 1978-80; vice chmn. Detroit Symphony Orch. Hall Bd.; mem. divisional bd. trustees Mt. Carmel Mercy Hosp., 1979-90; founding chmn. 1979-82, mem. exec. com. 1979—; mem. exec. com. Nat. Rep. Com. 1985—; active Mich. Rep. Com.; apptd. Presdl. Commn. on Fed. Stats.; chmn. Nat. Vol. Svc. Comm.; presdl. commn. White House fellows; apptd. by Gov. Mich. Higher Edn. Facilities Commn.; mem. Area-wide Water Quality Bd., founding pres. Legatus Mich. chpt., internat. bd. dirs.; chmn. bd. Mercy Hosp. Detroit and Health Svcs., 1987-90; Nat. Italian Am. Found., Washington, 1992; former mem. Detroit Renaissance, Inc.; appointed by Gov. John Engler to chair Mich. Christopher Columbus Quincentenary Commn., 1991; appointed by President George Bushto Christopher Columbus Presdl. Quincentenaery Jubilee Commn., 1991; chmn. Nat. Rep. Heritage Groups Coun., 1991; bd. dirs. Oakland Children's Svcs., 1992, Metro Detroit Juvenile Diabetes, 1991, Complete Bus. Solutions, Inc., 1993; mem. bd. trustees Merrill Palmer Inst. Wayne State U., chmn. 1996. Recipient over 35 awards from local, nat. and internat. civic and profl. orgns. including Ellis Island medal of Honor, 1995. Mem. Alliance for Mich. (bd. dirs. 1984—), Detroit Ctrl. Bus. Dist. Assn., Nat. Comml. Refrigerator Sales Assn. (bd. dirs., pres. 1953-54, adv. bd. 1954—), Nat. Assn. Wholesaler-Distbrs. (del. 1982—), Wholesale Distbrs. Assn. (bd. dirs. 1973—, v.p. 1976, pres. 1977-79), Bus. Edn. Alliance (various offices), Mich. Restaurant Assn., Food Svc. Execs. Assn., Italian-Am. C. of C. Mich., Nat. Italian-Am. Found. (charter, bd. dirs., exec. com., pres. 1979—), Hispanos Organized to Promote Entrepreneurs (bd. dirs. 1976-81), Econ. Club Detroit (bd. dirs. 1982—), Air Force Assn. (charter), Am. Soc. Legion Merit, Greater Detroit C. of C. (chmn. 1980-81, bd. dirs.), Wayne County C.C. Found. (pres.), Young Pres.'s Orgn., Detroit Club, Detroit Athletic Club, Detroit Golf Club, The Fairlane Club, Capitol Hill Club, Skyline Club (Southfield). Home: 19180 Gainsborough Rd Detroit MI 48223-1344 Office: 7000 Fenkell St Detroit MI 48238-2052

STELLA, JOHN ANTHONY, investment company executive; b. Jessup, Pa., Feb. 3, 1938; s. John Anthony and Alda (Parri) S.; m. Aurelia M. Arre, Feb. 20, 1965; children—John C., Matthew A., Krista R. B.S., U. Detroit, 1960; M.B.A., NYU, 1965. Bus. evaluation cons. Allied Chem. Co., N.Y.C., 1965-70; treas. Spinnerin Yarn Co., Hackensack, N.J., 1970-72, Penn-Dixie Cement Corp., N.Y.C., 1972-74; v.p. finance Halecrest Co., 1974-76; treas. Rsch.-Cottrell, 1976-84, v.p., contr./treas., 1984-88; pres. John A. Stella & Assocs., Plainfield, N.J., 1988-91; sr. v.p. Investment Support Systems, Inc., Bloomfield, N.J., 1991-95; pres. State Tax Auditing and Rsch., Inc., Plainfield, 1993—. Served with AUS, 1960. Office: State Tax Auditing & Rsch Inc 925 Madison Ave Plainfield NJ 07060

STELLA, VALENTINO JOHN, pharmaceutical chemistry educator; b. Melbourne, Victoria, Australia, Oct. 27, 1946; came to U.S., 1968; s. Giobatta and Mary Katherine (Sartori) S.; m. Mary Elizabeth Roeder, Aug. 16, 1969; children: Catherine Marie, Anne Elizabeth, Elise Valentina. B of Pharmacy, Victorian Coll. Pharmacy, Melbourne, 1967; PhD, U. Kans., 1971. Lic. pharmacist, Victoria. Pharmacist Bendigo (Victoria) Base Hosp., 1967-68; asst. prof. Coll. Pharmacy U. Ill., Chgo., 1971-73; from asst. prof. to assoc. prof. to prof. Sch. Pharmacy U. Kans., Lawrence, 1973-90, Univ. disting. prof., 1990—; dir. Ctr. for Drug Delivery Rsch.; cons. to 15 pharm. cos., U.S, Japan, Europe. Co-author: Chemical Stability of Pharmaceuticals, 2d edit., 1986; co-editor: Prodrugs as Novel Drug Delivery Systems, 1976, Directed Drug Delivery, 1985, Lymphatic Transport of Drugs, 1992; author numerous papers, revs., abstracts. Fellow AAAS, Am. Assn. Pharm. Scientists, Am. Acad. Pharm. Scientists. Roman Catholic. Achievements include 11 U.S. patents; rsch. in application of phys./organic chemistry to the solution of pharm. problems. Home: 1324 Lawrence Ave Lawrence KS 66049-2938 Office: U Kans Dept Pharm Chemistry 3306 Malott Hall Lawrence KS 66045

STELLER, ARTHUR WAYNE, educational administrator; b. Columbus, Ohio, Apr. 12, 1947; s. Fredrick and Bonnie Jean (Clark) S. BS, Ohio U., 1969, MA, 1970, PhD, 1973. Tchr., Athens (Ohio) City Schs., 1969-71; curriculum coord., tchr. Belpre (Ohio) City Schs., 1971-72; prin. elem. schs., head tchr. learning disabilities South-Western City Schs., Grove City, Ohio, 1972-76; dir. elem. edn. Beverly (Mass.) Pub. Schs., 1976-78; adj. prof. Lesley Coll., Cambridge, Mass., 1976-78; coord. spl. projects and systemwide planning Montgomery County Pub. Schs., Rockville, Md., 1978-80; asst. supt. Shaker Heights (Ohio), 1980-83; supt. schs. Mercer County Pub. Schools., Princeton, W. Va., 1983-85; supt. schs. Oklahoma City Pub Schs., 1985-92; supt. schs. Cobb County, Ga., 1992-93; dep. supt. Boston Pub. Schs., 1993-95, acting supt., 1995—; adj. faculty Harvard U., 1992-93. Author: Educational Planning for Educational Success, Effective Schools Research: Practice and Promise; editor: Effective Instructional Management; cons. editor, book rev. editor Jour. for Ednl. Pub. Rels.; mem. editl. bd. Jour. for Curriculum & Supervision; contbr. articles to profl. jours. Bd. govs. Kirkpatrick Ctr.; mem. Oklahoma City Com. for Econ. Devel.; founding bd. dirs. Oklahoma Alliance Against Drugs, Oklahoma Zool. Soc. Inc.; selected for Leadership Okla. City, 1986; bd. dirs. Leadership Oklahoma City, ARC; bd. dirs. Okla. Centennial Sports Inc.; mem. Oklahoma Acad. for State Goals, State Supt.'s Adv. Coun.; mem. clin. experiences adv. com. U. Okla. Coll. Edn.; trustee Arts Coun. Oklahoma City, Omniplex Sci. and Arts Mus., Oklahoma City Area Vocat.-Tech. Dist. 22 Found.; mem. Urban Ctr. Ednl. Adv. Bd., U.S. Dept. Edn. Urban Supt. Network, Coun. Great City Schs. Bd., Urban Edn. Clearing House Adv. com., U. Okla. Adminstrn. cert. program com., Cmty. Literacy Coun. Bd.; chmn. bd. dirs. Langston U.; chairperson United Way Greater Okla., Sch. Mgmt. Study Group, Okla. Reading Coun. (Okla. literacy coun. reading award 1989), Okla. City PTA; bd. dirs. Oklahoma County chpt. ARC, Jr. Achievement Greater Oklahoma City Bd., Oklahoma State Fair Bd., Horace Mann League Bd., Last Frontier Coun. Bd. Charles Kettering Found. IDEA fellow, 1976, 78, 80; Nat. Endowment Humanities fellow, Danforth Found., 1987-88; recipient Silver Beaver award Boy Scouts Am., 1990, Amb. award Horace Mann League, 1995. Mem. ASCD (exec. coun., pres.-elect 1993-94, pres. 1994-95), Nat. Orgn. Legal Problems in Edn., Nat. Policy Bd. Ednl. Adminstrn., Am. Assn. Sch. Adminstrs. (life, Leadership for Learning award, 1991, Coll. Bd. Advanced Placement Spl. Recognition award 1991), Nat. Assn. Elem. Sch. Prins. (life), Nat. Assn. Edn. Young Children (life), Nat. Sch. Pub. Rels. Assn. (Honor award 1991), Internat. Soc. Ednl. Planning, Nat. Soc. Study Edn., Nat. Planning Assn., Coun. Basic Edn., Am. Edn. Fin. Assn., Ohio Assn. Elem. Sch. Adminstrs., Buckeye Assn. Sch. Adminstrs., Ohio ASCD, Ohio U. Coll. Edn. (disting. alumnus award 1991), Okla. ASCD (Publ. award 1989), Okla. Assn. Sch. Adminstrs., Mass. Assn. Sch. Adminstrs., Mass. ASCD, Okla. Coalition for Pub. Edn., Okla. Commn. for Ednl. Leadership, Urban Area Supts. (Oklahoma br.), Ohio U. Alumni Assn. (nat. dir. 1975-78, pres. Cen. Ohio chpt. 1975-76, pres. Mass. chpt. 1976-78, life mem. trustee's acad.), World Future Soc. (life), Greater Oklahoma City C. of C. (exec. bd. dirs.), South Oklahoma City C. of C. (bd. dirs.), Oklahoma Heritage Assn., Heritage Hills Assn. (bd. dirs.), Victorian Soc. (New England chpt.), Nat. Eagle Scout Assn., Aerospace Found. (hon. bd. dirs.), Am. Bus. Card Club, Coca Cola Collectors Club, Internat. Club, Rotary (Boston), Mgmt. Consortium (bd. advisors), Tau Kappa Epsilon Alumni Assn. (regional officer Mass. 1976-78, named Alumni Nat. Hall of Fame 1986, Nat. Alumnus of Yr. 1993, Excellence in Edn. award 1993), Kappa Delta Pi (life, advisor Cen. Okla. chpt., nat. publs. com.), Phi Delta Kappa (life). Methodist. Home: 30 Carruth St Dorchester MA 0214-4923

STELLER, HERMANN, neurobiologist, educator; b. Bad Nauheim, Germany, Apr. 25, 1957; came to U.S., 1985; s. Horst and Gisela (Opper) S.; m. Bettina Zirnheld, June 18, 1982; 1 child, Nicolas Sebastian. Diploma in biology, U. Frankfurt, Fed. Republic Germany, 1981; PhD, U. Heidelberg, Fed. Republic Germany, 1984; postgrad., U. Calif., Berkeley, 1985-87. Predoctoral fellow European Molecular Biology Lab., Heidelberg, 1981-84; postdoctoral fellow U. Calif., Berkeley, 1985-87; asst. prof. MIT, Cambridge, Mass., 1987-92, assoc. prof. neurobiology, rschr., 1992—; assoc. investigator Howard Hughes Med. Inst., Chevy Chase, Md., 1993—; mem. sci. adv. bd. IDUN Pharms., San Diego, 1993—, NIH, ACS, 1992—; asst. neurobiologist Mass. Gen. Hosp., Boston, 1990—. Searle scholar Chgo. Cmty. Trust, 1988, Pew Charitable Trust scholar, 1989. Mem. AAAS, Genetics Soc. Am., Soc. for Neurosci. Avocations: fly fishing, hiking, skiing. Office: MIT E25-436 Dept of Brain & Cognitive 77 Massachusetts Ave Cambridge MA 02139-4301

STELLWAGEN, ROBERT HARWOOD, biochemistry educator; b. Joliet, Ill., Jan. 6, 1941; s. Harwood John and Alma Dorothy (Handorf) S.; m. Joanne Kovacs, June 15, 1963; children: Robert Harwood, Alise Anne. AB, Harvard U., 1963; PhD, U. Calif.-Berkeley, 1968. Staff fellow NIH, Bethesda, Md., 1968-69; postdoctoral scholar U. Calif.-San Francisco, 1969-70; asst. prof. biochemistry U. So. Calif., L.A., 1970-74, assoc. prof., 1974-80, prof., 1980—, chmn. dept., 1981-86, vice chmn. dept., 1993—; vis. scientist Nat. Inst. for Med. Research, Mill Hill, Eng., 1979. Contbr. articles to profl. jours. Recipient Henderson prize Harvard U., 1963; NSF fellow, 1963-67; NIH grantee, 1971-84. Mem. AAAS, Am. Soc. Biochemistry and Molecular Biology, Sierra Club, Phi Beta Kappa. Democrat. Office: U So Calif 2011 Zonal Ave Los Angeles CA 90033-1034

STELMACK, GLORIA JOY, elementary education educator; b. Chgo., Oct. 1, 1933; d. Raymond Thomas and Bess (Henneberry) Ibison; m. Carl Francis McGarrity, Feb. 7, 1953; children: Maureen, Thomas, Stephen, John; m. Stephen Stanley Stelmack, Dec. 22, 1979. BA with honors, U. Ill., 1972; MA in Reading, Northeastern Ill. U., 1977. Cert. tchr., Ill. Tchr., reading specialist St. Pius Sch., Chgo., 1972-82, St. Jane de Chantal Sch., Chgo., 1982—; adv. com. St. Jane de Chantal Sch., Chgo., 1986—; v.p. Nat. Coun. of Tchrs. of English, Chgo., 1980-81. Nominated for Golden Apple award, 1990. Avocations: travel, reading, flower arranging, golf. Office: Saint Jane de Chantal Sch 5201 S Mcvicker Ave Chicago IL 60638-1424

STELPSTRA, WILLIAM JOHN, minister; b. Paterson, N.J., Nov. 1, 1934; s. Duke and Nellie (Stapert) S.; m. Anna Rizkovsky, Sept. 6, 1958; 1 child, Linda Mae. BA, Alma White Coll., 1957; B. of Religion, Zarephath Bible Sem., 1958. Ordained to ministry Pillar of Fire Ch., 1954. Pastor Pillar of Fire Ch., Little Falls, N.J., 1956-60; evangelist Wesleyan Meth. Ch., 1960-64; founder, dir. Bethel Children's Home, Paterson, N.J., 1964-71, Bethel Ranch Rehab. for Men, West Milford, N.J., 1971—; founder, pres. World for Christ Crusade, Inc., N.J., Fla., 1960—; dir. fgn. missions World for Christ Crusade, Inc., Haiti, Ghana, India, 1980—; adminstr. Fellowship House, Bloomfield, N.J., 1979—, Bright Side Manor, Teaneck, N.J., 1978—. Mem. Ocean Grove C. of C. Republican. Wesleyan Ch. Avocations: painting with oils, swimming, boating, travel, gardening. Home: 1005 Union Valley Rd West Milford NJ 07480-1220 Office: World for Christ Crusade 1005 Union Valley Rd West Milford NJ 07480-1220

STELZEL, WALTER TELL, JR., accountant, financial company executive; b. Chgo., Aug. 23, 1940; s. Walter Tell and Kathryn (Evans) S.; m. Sarah Rauen, Jan. 5, 1963; children: William, Susan, Michael. BSBA, Xavier U., 1962; MBA, U. Chgo., 1983. CPA, Ill. Sr. acct. Ernst & Ernst, 1962-69; contr. U.S. Reduction Co., 1969-74; asst. corp. contr. Am. Nat. Can. Co. (formerly Nat. Can. Corp.), Chgo., 1974-76, corp. contr., 1976-78, v.p., contr., 1978-81, v.p., asst. to pres., 1981-84, exec. v.p. fin., 1984-93, sr. exec. v.p., bd. mem., CFO, 1993—. 1st lt. U.S. Army, 1962-65, Germany. Office: Am Nat Can Co 8770 W Bryn Mawr Ave Chicago IL 60631

STEM, CARL HERBERT, business educator; b. Eagleville, Tenn., Jan. 30, 1935; s. Marion Ogilvie and Sara Elizabeth (Jones) S.; m. Linda Marlene Wheeler, Dec. 28, 1963; children: Anna Elizabeth, Susan Kathleen, John Carl, David Leslie. BA, Vanderbilt U., 1957; AM (Woodrow Wilson fellow, Harvard scholar), Harvard U., 1960, PhD, 1969. Internat. fin. economist, bd. govs. Fed. Res. System, Washington, 1963-70; prof. econs. Tex. Tech. U., Lubbock, 1970-73; prof. internat. fin., chmn. area of fin., adminstr. grad. programs, assoc. dean, dean Coll. Bus. Adminstrn. Tex. Tech U., Lubbock, 1970—; sr. econ. adviser Office Fgn. Direct Investments, U.S. Dept. Commerce, Washington, 1973-74; cons. U.S. Dept. Treasury, 1974-75; mem. faculty Grad. Sch. Credit and Fin. Mgmt., Lake Success, N.Y., 1974-87; adj. scholar Am. Enterprise Inst. Public Policy Rsch., Washington, 1974-88; treas. Mission Jour., Inc., 1969-88. Editor (with Makin and Logue) Eurocurrencies and The Interational Monetary System; contbr. articles to profl. jours. Trustee St. Mary Plains Hosp., Lubbock, Tex., 1987-92, chmn., 1992; v.p. Tex. Coun. of Collegiate Edn. for Bus., 1977-78, pres., 1978-79. Capt. Security Agy. AUS, 1961-62. Fulbright scholar U. Reading, Eng., 1957-58. Mem. Southwestern Bus. Adminstrn. Assn. (pres. 1982-83), Nat. Assn. Bus. Economists, So. Bus. Adminstrn. Assn. (v.p. 1985-86, pres. 1986-87), Lubbock Econ. Coun. (pres. 1973), Am. Assembly Collegiate Schs. Bus. (standards com. 1981-84, bd. dirs. 1993-96), Lubbock Club (pres. 1986-87), Phi Beta Kappa, Omicron Delta Kappa, Phi Kappa Phi, Beta Gamma Sigma, Tau Kappa Alpha. Mem. Ch. of Christ. Home: 6218 Louisville Dr Lubbock TX 79413-5429 Office: Tex Tech U Bus Adminstrn Lubbock TX 79409 *Most important to me are the ever timely values of our Judeo-Christian heritage- faith in God and appreciation for the inherent value of man. These values have underpinned my aspirations and sustained me through disappointments. They have generated the perseverance and continual hope so vital to me as I have worked for self-growth and to make a contribution to the institutions and people with which I have been associated in various periods of my life.*

STEMBERG, THOMAS GEORGE, retail executive; b. Newark, Jan. 18, 1949; s. Oscar Michael and Erika (Ratzer) S.; m. Dola Davis Hamilton, Sept. 24, 1988. Student, Am. Internat. Sch., Vienna, 1962-67; AB, Harvard U., 1971, MBA, 1973. With Jewel Cos., Star Market, Cambridge, Mass., 1973-82, v.p. sales and merchandising, 1982; sr. v.p. sales and merchandising First. Nat. Supermarkets, Hartford, Conn., 1982-83, pres., 1983-84; pres. Staples, Inc., Newton, Mass., 1986-88, chmn., 1988—. Baker scholar Harvard Bus. Sch., 1973; R.H. Macy fellow Harvard Bus. Sch., 1973. *

STEMBRIDGE, VERNIE A(LBERT), pathologist, educator; b. El Paso, Tex., June 7, 1924; s. Vernie Albert and Anna Marie (Lawless) S.; m. Aileen Cofer Marston, June 14, 1944; children—Shirley (Mrs. J.P. Watkins), Ann (Mrs. Donald M. Connell), Vivian (Mrs. Lance E. Porter). B.A., U. Tex. at El Paso (formerly Tex. Coll. Mines), 1943; M.D., U. Tex., Galveston, 1948. Diplomate: Am. Bd. Pathology (trustee 1969-80, sec. 1976-79, pres. 1980). Intern U.S. Marine Hosp., Norfolk, Va., 1948-49; resident in pathology Med. Br., U. Tex., Galveston, 1949-52; asst. prof. pathology Med. Br., U. Tex., 1952-54, asso. prof., 1954-56; asso. prof. Southwestern Med. Sch., Dallas, 1959-61; prof. Southwestern Med. Sch., 1961—, Ashbel Smith prof., 1991—, chmn. dept. pathology, 1966-88; chmn. emeritus Southwestern Med. Sch., Dallas, 1992—; interim dean Sch. Allied Health Scis. U. Tex. Southwestern Med. Sch., 1988-91; assoc. dir. clin. labs. U. Tex. Med. Br. Hosps., 1952-56; sr. pathologist, chief aviation pathology sect. Armed Forces Inst. Pathology, Washington, 1956-59; dir. pathology labs. Parkland Hosp., Dallas, 1966-85; cons. VA Hosp., Dallas; cons. to surgeon gen. USAF; civil air surgeon FAA; chmn. sci. adv. bd. Armed Forces Inst. Pathology; mem. State of Tex. Radiation Adv. Bd., 1987-94. Contbr. articles to med. jours. Served with USAF, 1956-59. Decorated Legion of Merit; named Outstanding Alumnus U. Tex. at El Paso, 1978, Hon. Alumnus, U. Tex. Southwestern Med. Sch., 1964, Ashbel Smith outstanding alumnus U. Tex. Med. Br., 1982; recipient Joint Disting. Service award Am. Soc. Clin. Pathologists/Coll. Am. Pathologists, 1987. Mem. Internat. Acad. Pathology (counselor 1970-73), Am. Soc. Clin. Pathologists (bd. dirs. 1973-79, pres. 1977-78, bd. registry, gov. 1983-90, Ward Burdick award for outstanding contbns. 1981, Bd. Registry Disting. Svc. award 1995), AMA (residency rev. com. of pathology 1972-78, chmn. 1977-78, residency rev. com. nuclear medicine 1972-78), Intersoc. Pathology Coun. (sec. 1979-84), Coll. Am. Pathologists, Am. Assn. Pathologists, Assn. Pathology Chairmen (mem. coun., pres. 1979, Disting. Svc. award 1996), Am. Assn. Blood Banks, Tex. Soc. Pathologists (pres. 1966, Caldwell award 1967), Tex. Med. Assn. (ho. of dels. 1966-86), Dallas County Med. Soc. (pres. 1985, Max Cole Leadership award 1991), Am. Registry Pathology (bd. dirs. 1986-91, chmn. 1989-90), Phi Rho Sigma, Mu Delta, Alpha Omega Alpha. Home: 10424 Marsh Ln Dallas TX 75229-5223 Office: 5323 Harry Hines Blvd Dallas TX 75235-9072

STEMMLER, EDWARD JOSEPH, physician, retired association executive, retired academic dean; b. Phila., Feb. 15, 1929; s. Edward C. and Josephine (Heitzmann) S.; m. Joan C. Koster, Dec. 27, 1958; children: Elizabeth, Margaret, Edward C., Catherine, Joan. B.A., La Salle Coll., Phila., 1950, Sc.D. (hon.), 1983; M.D., U. Pa., 1960; Sc.D. (hon.), Ursinus Coll., 1977, Phila. Coll. Pharmacy and Sci., 1989; L.H.D. (hon.), Rush U., 1986, Med. Coll. Pa., 1994; ScD (hon.), SUNY, Syracuse, 1994. Diplomate Am. Bd. Internal Medicine. Intern U. Pa. Hosp., 1960-61, med. resident, 1961-63, fellow in cardiology, 1963-64, chief med. resident, 1964-65, chief med. outpatient dept., 1966-67; chief of medicine U. Pa. Med. Svc., VA Hosp., Phila., 1967-73; mem. deans com. VA Hosp., 1974-88; instr. medicine Grad. Div. Medicine, U. Pa., 1964-66, NIH postdoctoral rsch. trainee, dept. physiology, 1965-67, assoc. in medicine, 1966-67; assoc. in physiology Grad. Div. Medicine, 1967-72, asst. prof. medicine, 1967-70, assoc. prof., 1970-74, prof., 1974—, Robert G. Dunlop prof., 1981-91, prof. emeritus, 1991—; assoc. dean Univ. Hosp. (Sch. Medicine), 1973, assoc. dean student affairs, 1973-75, acting dean, 1974-75, dean, 1975-88, dean emeritus, 1989—; exec. v.p. U. Pa. Med. Ctr., 1986-89; exec. v.p. Assn. Am. Med. Colls., 1990-94, sr. adv. to pres., 1994-95; mem. Nat. Bd. Med. Examiners, 1974-76, nominating and ad hoc governance coms., 1985, vice chmn., 1987-89, treas., 1989-91, chmn., 1991-95; mem. exec. com.; mem. ednl. policy com. Nat. Fund for Med. Edn., 1975-77; mem. deans com. VA Hosp., 1974-89; bd. dirs. Rhone-Poulence Rorer, Inc.; trustee Dorothy Rider Pool Healthcare Trust, 1991—, Ursinus coll., 1991—. Contbr. articles to profl. jours. Chmn. Pa. Deans Com., 1976-87; bd. govs. Mid-Ea. Regional Med. Libr. Svcs., 1977-81, chmn., 1978-81; bd. visitors U. Pitts. Sch. Medicine, 1980-85, U. Md. Sch. Medicine, 1991-94; mem. bd. overseers Dartmouth Med. Sch. and C. Everett Koop Inst., 1992—; mem. adv. com. dept. medicine U. Ala., Birmingham, 1985-89; mem. vis. com. Tufts U. Sch. Medicine, 1990-94, U. Calif., Davis, 1993—. Decorated Commendation medal; recipient Frederick A. Packard award, 1960, Albert Einstein Med. Ctr. staff award, 1960, Roche award, 1960. Master ACP (treas., chmn. investment com. 1975-80, Laureate award Ea. Pa. region 1986); mem. AMA (health policy agenda), Med. Soc. D.C., Am. Fedn. for Clin. Rsch., Inst. Medicine NAS, Assn. Am. Med. Colls. (ad hoc external exam. rev. com. 1980—, exec. coun. 1980—, coun. of deans adminstrv. bd. 1980—, chmn. 1983-84, nat. chmn.-elect 1985-86, chmn. assembly 1986-87), Coll. of Physicians of Phila. (bd. censors 1979-85, coun. 1979-85, 90-92), Am. Clin. and Climatological Soc., Alpha Omega Alpha. Republican. Mem. Christian Ch. Home: Rt #1 Box 676 Roseland VA 22967

STEMPEL, ERNEST EDWARD, insurance executive; b. N.Y.C., May 10, 1916; s. Frederick Christian and Leah Lillian S.; m. Phyllis Brooks (dec. Mar. 1993); children: Diana Brooks Bergquist, Calvin Pinkcomb, Neil Frederick, Robert Russell. A.B., Manhattan Coll., 1938; LL.B., Fordham U., 1946; LL.M., NYU, 1949, D.J.S., 1951; LL.D. (hon.), Manhattan Coll., 1986. Bar: N.Y. 1946. With Am. Internat. Underwriters Corp., N.Y.C., 1938-53; v.p., dir. Am. Internat. Co. Ltd., Hamilton, Bermuda, 1953-63, chmn. bd., from 1963; chmn., dir. Am. Internat. Assurance Co. (Bermuda) Ltd., Am. Internat. Reins. Co. Ltd., Bermuda, Philippine Am. Life Ins. Co., Manila, Australian Am. Assurance Co., Ltd., Am. Internat. Assurance Co., Ltd., Hong Kong, AIG Life Ins. Co., Del. Am. Life Ins. Co., Wilmington, Del., Am. Internat. Life Assurance Co. of N.Y.; pres., dir. Starr Internat. Co. Inc.; vice-chmn.-life div., mem. exec. com., dir. Am. Internat. Group Inc.; dir. C.V. Starr & Co. Inc., N.Y.C., Am. Life Ins. Co., Wilmington, Seguros Interamericana (S.A.), Mexico, Mt. Mansfield Co., Inc., Stowe, Vt., Seguros Venezuela (C.A.), Caracas, dir. Am. Internat. Underwriters (Latin Am.), Inc., Bermuda, Am. Internat. Underwriters Mediterranean, Inc., Bermuda, Pacific Union Assurance Co., Calif., Underwriters Adjustment Co., Panama. Served to lt. (s.g.) USNR, 1942-46. Mem. Am. Bar Assn., N.Y. State Bar. Clubs: Marco Polo (N.Y.C.), Royal Bermuda Yacht (Bermuda), Mid-Ocean (Bermuda), Coral Beach & Tennis Club (Bermuda), Riddell's Bay Golf and Country (Bermuda). Office: Am Internat Co Ltd, PO Box HM 152, Hamilton HM AX, Bermuda

STEMPEL, GUIDO HERMANN, III, journalism educator; b. Bloomington, Ind., Aug. 13, 1928; s. Guido Hermann Jr. and Alice Margaret (Menninger) S.; m. Anne Elliott, Aug. 30, 1952; children: Ralph Warren, Carl William, Jane Louise. Student, Carnegie Tech., 1945-46; AB in Journalism, Ind. U., 1949, AM in Journalism, 1951; PhD in Mass Communication, U. Wis., 1954. Sports editor Frankfort (Ind.) Times, 1949-50; instr., asst. prof. Sch. Journalism, Pa. State U., University Park, 1955-57; from assoc. prof. to prof. Dept. Journalism, Cen. Mich. U., Mt. Pleasant, 1957-65; assoc. prof. Sch. Journalism, Ohio U., Athens, 1965-68, prof., 1968-82, Disting. prof., 1982—, dir., 1972-79; rsch. cons. Ohio Newspaper Assn., Columbus, 1985—; chmn. rsch. com. Coll. Media Advisors, 1963-69, 79-84; mem. adv. bd. dept. comm. arts U. West Fla., 1987—; survey coord. Scripps Howard News Svc., 1992—. Co-author: The Media in the 1984 and 1988 Presidential Campaigns, 1991; assoc. editor: Newspaper Rsch. Jour., 1992—; editor, co-author: The Practice of Political Communication, 1994; co-editor, co-author: Research Methods in Mass Communications, 1981, 2d edit., 1989; editor: Journalism Quar., 1972-89; contbr. articles to profl. jours. Mem. bd. visitors Def. Info. Sch., Ft. Meade, 1985-96. Recipient Chancellor's award U. Wis., 1977. Mem. Assn. for Edn. in Journalism and Mass Communication (chmn. rsch. com. 1968-71; Eleanor Blum award 1989), Soc. Profl. Journalists, Rotary (pres. Athens unit 1984-85). Democrat. Methodist. Home: 7 Lamar Dr Athens OH 45701-3730 Office: Ohio Univ Sch of Journalism Athens OH 45701

STEMPLE, JOEL GILBERT, computer company executive; b. Bklyn., Feb. 3, 1942; s. Max David and Helen (Nechamkin) S.; m. Sharon Claire Schneider, Apr. 6, 1968; children—Tracy, Allyson. BS, Bklyn. Coll., 1962; MA, Yale U., 1964, PhD, 1966. Asst. prof. Queens Coll., Flushing, N.Y., 1966-70, assoc. prof. math., 1970-82; v.p. Manchester Equipment Co. Inc., Hauppauge, N.Y., 1982—. Office: Manchester Equipment Co Inc 50 Marcus Blvd Hauppauge NY 11788-3730

STEMPLER, JACK LEON, government and aerospace company executive; b. Newark, Oct. 30, 1920; s. Morris and Ida (Friedman) S.; m. J. Adelaide Williams, Oct. 28, 1950; children: Mark N., Sandra J., Carrie B. B.A., Montclair (N.J.) State Coll., 1943; LL.B., Cornell U., 1948. Bar: N.Y., D.C. 1949. Atty. com. uniform code mil. justice Dept. Def., 1948-49, atty. adviser legis. div., 1949-50; asst. counsel Munitions Bd., 1950-53; counsel Armed Forces Housing Agy., 1952-54, Advanced Research Projects Agy., 1958-65; asst. gen. counsel logistics Dept. Def., 1953-65, asst. to sec. def. for legislative affairs, 1965-70; gen. counsel Dept. Air Force, 1970-77; asst. to sec. of def. for legis. affairs, 1977-81; v.p. legis. affairs LTV Aerospace, Washington, 1982-92; ret., 1992; cons. in field. Served to 1st lt. USMCR, 1942-46, PTO. Recipient Outstanding Civilian Performance award Dept. Def., 1959, Distinguished Civilian Service award, 1965, Distinguished Civilian Service award with palm, 1969, with 2d bronze palm, 1970; Exceptional Civilian Service award USAF, 1973, 75, 77; awarded Presdl. rank of Disting. Exec., 1980; recipient Disting. Public Service award Dept. Def., 1981. Mem. Fed., D.C. bar assns., Cornell Law Sch. Assn., Air Force Aid Soc. (trustee). Home: 4701 Newcomb Pl Alexandria VA 22304-1506

STENBERG, CARL W(ALDAMER), III, academic program director, educator; b. Pitts., July 8, 1943; s. Carl W. and Mildred (Baggs) S.; m. Kirstin D. Thompson; children: Erik Anders, Kerry Cathryn, Kaameran Baird. BA, Allegheny Coll., 1965; MPA, SUNY, Albany, 1966, PhD, 1970. Research asst. N.Y. State Div. Budget, Albany, 1967; analyst, then sr. analyst U.S. Adv. Commn. on Intergovtl. Relations, Washington, 1968-77, asst. dir. for policy implementation, 1977-83, acting exec. dir., 1982; exec. dir. Council of State Govts., Lexington, Ky., 1983-89; prof., dir. Weldon Cooper Ctr. for Pub. Svc. U. Va., Charlottesville, 1989-95, Disting. prof. pub. svc., 1991-95; prof., dean Yale Gordon Coll. Liberal Arts U. Balt., 1995—; mem. Am. Part Program USIA, 1987; adj. prof. George Washington U., 1971, 81, Am. U., 1972-80, 82, U. Md., 1976, U. So. Calif., 1984-87; v.p. Bureaucrat Inc., Washington, 1973-77, mng. editor, 1973-77. Feature editor Pub. Mgmt. Forum Pub. Adminstrn. Rev., 1977-83, editor U. of Va. newsletter, 1994-95. Pres. Reston Home Owners' Assn., Va., 1973-74; mem. U.S. del. Ad Hoc Group on Urban Problems, OECD, 1980-82. Vivien Stewart vis. fellow Cambridge U., Eng., 1980; recipient Disting. Alumni award Polit. Sci. Dept. Rockefeller Coll., 1985. Mem. Am. Soc. Pub. Adminstrn. (pres. 1990-91, Marshall E. Dimock and Louis Brownlow awards), Va. Alliance for the Pub. Svc. (pres. 1991-92). Home: 501 Edgevale Rd Baltimore MD 21210 Office: Univ Baltimore U Balt 1420 N Charles St Baltimore MD 21201-5779

STENBERG, DONALD B., state attorney general; b. David City, Nebr., Sept. 30, 1948; s. Eugene A. and Alice (Kasal) S.; m. Susan K. Hoegemeyer, June 9, 1971; children: Julie A., Donald B. Jr., Joseph L., Abby E. BA, U.

Nebr., 1970; MBA, Harvard U., 1974, JD cum laude, 1974. Bar: Nebr. 1974, U.S. Dist. Ct. Nebr. 1974, U.S. Ct. Appeals (fed. cir.) 1984, U.S. Ct. Claims 1989, U.S. Ct. Appeals (8th cir.) 1989, U.S. Supreme Ct., 1991. Assoc. Barlow, Watson & Johnson, Lincoln, Nebr., 1974-75; ptnr. Stenberg and Stenberg, Lincoln, 1976-78; legal counsel Gov. of Nebr., Lincoln, 1979-82; sr. prin. Erickson & Sederstrom, Lincoln, 1983-85; pvt. practice law Lincoln, 1985-90; atty. gen. State of Nebr., Lincoln, 1991—. Mem. Phi Beta Kappa. Republican. Office: Office of Atty Gen 2115 State Capitol Lincoln NE 68509

STENCHEVER, MORTON ALBERT, physician, educator; b. Paterson, N.J., Jan. 25, 1931; s. Harold and Lena (Suresky) S.; m. Diane Bilsky, June 19, 1955; children: Michael A., Marc R., Douglas A. A.B., NYU, 1951; M.D., U. Buffalo, 1956. Intern Mt. Sinai Hosp., 1956-57; resident obstetrics and gynecology Columbia-Presbyn. Med. Center, N.Y.C., 1957-60; asst. prof., Oglebey research fellow Case-Western Res. U., Cleve., 1962-66; asso. prof. dept. reproductive biology Case-Western Res. U., 1967-70, dir. Tissue Culture Lab., 1965-70, coordinator Phase II Med. Sch. program, 1969-70; prof., chmn. dept. obstetrics-gynecology U. Utah Med. Sch., Salt Lake City, 1970-77, U. Wash. Sch. Medicine, Seattle, 1977—; test com. chmn. for Ob-Gyn Nat. Bd. Med. Examiners, 1979-82. Author: Labor: Workbook in Obstetrics, 1968, 2d edit., 1993, Human Sexual Behavior: A Workbook in Reproductive Biology, 1970, Human Cytogenics: A Workbook in Reproductive Biology, 1973, Introductory Gynecology: A Workbook in Reproductive Biology, 1974; co-author: Comprehensive Biology, 1974; co-author: Comprehensive Gynecology, 1987, 2d edit., 1992, Caring for the Older Woman, 1991, 2d edit., 1996, Health Care for the Older Woman, 1996, Office Gynecology, 1992, 2d edit., 1996; assoc. editor Ob-Gyn., 1986—, Ob-Gyn. Survey; mem. editorial bd. Western Jour. Medicine; contbr. articles to profl. jours. Served to capt. USAF, 1960-62. Fellow Am. Coll. Obstetricians and Gynecologists (com. on residency edn. 1974-80, learning resource commn. 1980-86, vice chmn. 1982-83, chmn. prolog self-assessment program 1982-86, vice chair com. health care for the underserved women 1995—), Am. Assn. Obstetricians and Gynecologists, Am. Gynecol. Soc., Am. Soc. Ob-Gyn., Pacific Coast Ob-Gyn. Soc.; mem. AAAS, AMA, Assn. Profs. Gynecology and Obstetrics (chmn. steering com. teaching methodis in ob-gyn. 1970-79, v.p. 1975-76, pres. 1983-84, v.p. Found. 1986-87, pres. Found. 1987-91), Pacific N.W. Ob-Gyn. Soc., Wash. State Med. Assn., Seattle Gynec. Soc. (v.p. 1981, pres.-elect 1982, pres. 1982-83), Pacific Coast Ob-Gyn. Soc., Am. Soc. Human Genetics, Ctrl. Assn. Ob-Gyn., Soc. Gynecologic Investigation, Wash. State Obstet. Soc., Tissue Culture Assn., N.Y. Acad. Sci., Utah Ob-Gyn. Soc., Utah State Med. Assn., Teratology Soc., Am. Fertility Soc., Am. Bd. Ob-Gyn. (bd. dirs. 1988—, v.p. 1990-92, treas. 1992—, mem. resident rev. com. Ob-Gyn. 1993—, chmn. divsn. urogynecology of reconstructive pilvic surgery). Home: 8301 SE 83rd St Mercer Island WA 98040-5644 Office: U Wash Dept Ob-Gyn 1959 NE Pacific St Seattle WA 98195-0004

STENDAHL, KRISTER, retired bishop; b. Stockholm, Sweden, Apr. 21, 1921; came to U.S., 1954, naturalized, 1967; s. Olof and Sigrid (Ljungquist) S.; m. Brita Johnsson, Sept. 7, 1946; children: John, Anna, Daniel. Teol. kand., U. Uppsala, Sweden, 1944, teol. lic., 1949, teol.dr., 1954; Litt. D. (hon.), Upsala Coll., 1963; D.D., St. Olaf Coll., 1971, Harvard U., 1985, St. Andrews U., 1987, Calif. Luth. U., 1995; LL.D., Susquehanna U., 1973; L.H.D. (hon.), Hebrew Union Coll./Jewish Inst. Religion, 1980, Brandeis U., 1981, Loyola U., New Orleans, 1992. Ordained priest Ch. of Sweden, 1944. Chaplain to students Uppsala U., 1948-50, instr. O.T., N.T. exegesis, 1951-54, docent, 1954; asst. prof. N.T. Shalom Hartman Inst., 1954-56; asso. prof. Harvard U. Div. Sch., 1956-58, John H. Morison prof. N.T. studies, 1958-63, Frothingham prof. Bibl. studies, 1963-68, dean, John Lord O'Brian prof. div., 1968-79, Andrew W. Mellon prof. div., 1981-84; pastor Luth. Ch. Am., 1968-84; bishop of Stockholm Ch. of Sweden, 1984-88; Robert and Myra Kraft and Jacob Hiatt Disting. prof. Christian studies Brandeis U., 1991-93; moderator consultation on ch. and Jewish people World Council Chs., 1975-85; co-dir. Osher Ctr. for Tolerance and Pluralism Shalom Hartman Inst., 1994—. Author: The School of St. Matthew, 1954, 2d edit., 1968, The Bible and the Role of Women, 1966, Holy Week, 1974, Paul Among Jews and Gentiles, 1976, Meanings, 1984, Energy for Life, 1990, Final Account, 1995. Recipient Disting. Service award Assn. Theol. Schs., 1988. Fellow Am. Acad. Arts and Scis.; mem. Nathan Soederblom Soc.

STENDELL, REY, ecological research director. Dir. Midcontinent Ecol. Sci. Ctr., Fort Collins, Colo. Office: Midcontinent Ecol Sci Ctr 4512 Mcmurray Ave Fort Collins CO 80525-3400

STENEHJEM, LELAND MANFORD, banker; b. Arnegard, N.D., May 25, 1918; s. Odin N. and Lillie (Moe) S.; m. Judith H. Johnson, July 21, 1944; children—Leland Manford, Stephen Leslie, Joan Marie. B.S., N.D. State U., 1941; grad., U. Wis. Grad. Sch. Banking, 1948. With First Internat. Bank, Watford City, N.D., 1943—; exec. v.p. First Internat. Bank, 1961-66, pres., 1966—; chmn. bd. dirs. First Internat. Bank and Trust, 1992—; chmn First Nat Bank of Fessenden, N.D., 1983—; Mem. N.D. Banking Bd., 1958-63; mem. N.D. adv. council Farmers Home Adminstrn., 1957-60; bd. dirs. N.D. State U. Found. Pres. Good Shepherd Home, 1963—; bd. dirs. N.D. State U. Alumni Assn.; pres., bd. trustees First Luth. Ch. 2d lt. USMCR World War II. Recipient Singular Achievement award Greater N.D. Assn. Mem. Am. Bankers Assn. (past mem. exec. coun.), N.D. Bankers Assn. (past pres.), Ind. Bankers Assn. Am. (past pres.), Watford City Assn., Commerce Club (pres.), Viking Club (Mesa, Ariz.; pres.), Masons, Shriners, Elks, Lions (pres. Watford City), Rotary (pres.), Alpha Tau Omega. Lutheran. Lodges: Mason, Elk, Lion (pres. Watford City), Rotarian (pres.), Shriners. Home: 100 4th St SW Watford City ND 58854-7146 Office: 100 N Main St Watford City ND 58854-7100

STENEHJEM, WAYNE KEVIN, state senator, lawyer; b. Mohall, N.D., Feb. 5, 1953; s. Martin Edward and Marguerite Mae (McMaster) S.; m. Tama Lou Smith, June 16, 1978 (div. Apr. 1984); 1 child, Andrew; m. Beth D. Bakke, June 30, 1995. AA, Bismarck (N.D.) Jr. Coll., 1972; BA, U. N.D., 1974, JD, 1977. Bar: N.D. 1977. Ptnr. Kuchera & Stenehjem, Grand Forks, N.D., 1977—; spl. asst. atty. gen. State of N.D., 1983-87; mem. N.D. Ho. Reps., 1976-80, N.D. State Senate, 1980—; chmn. Senate Com. on Social Svcs., 1985-86, Senate Com. on Judiciary, Interim Legis. Judiciary Com., 1995—, Legis. Coun., 1995—; mem. Nat. Conf. Commrs. on Uniform State Laws, 1995—; mem. Gov.'s Com. on Juvenile Justice. Chmn. Dist. 42 Reps., Grand Forks, 1986-88; bd. dirs. N.D. Spl. Olympics, 1985-89, Christus Rex Luth. Ch., pres., 1985-86. Named Champion of People's Right to Know, Sigma Delta Chi, 1979, Outstanding Young Man of N.D., Grand Forks Jaycees, 1985, N.D. Friend of Psychology, N.D. Psychol. Assn., 1990; recipient Excellence in County Govt. award N.D. Assn. Counties, 1991, Legis. Svc. award State Bar Assn. N.D., 1995. Mem. N.D. State Bar Assn. (Legis. Svc. award), Grand Forks County Bar Assn., Mental Health Assn. (bd. dirs.). Home: 2204 12th Ave N Grand Forks ND 58203-2251 Office: Kuchera Stenehjem & Walberg PO Box 6352 212 S 4th St Grand Forks ND 58206-6352

STENGEL, ROBERT FRANK, mechanical and aerospace engineering educator; b. Orange, N.J., Sept. 1, 1938; s. Frank John and Ruth Emma (Geidel) S.; m. Margaret Robertson Ewing, Apr. 8, 1961; children: Brooke Alexandra, Christopher Ewing. SB, MIT, 1960; MS in Engring., Princeton U., 1965, MA, 1966, PhD, 1968. Aerospace technologist NASA, Wallops Island, Va., 1960-63; tech. staff group leader C.S. Draper Lab., Cambridge, Mass., 1968-73, Analytic Scis. Corp., Reading, Mass., 1973-77; assoc. prof. Princeton (N.J.) U., 1977-82, prof. mech. and aerospace engring., 1982—, assoc. dean engring., 1994—; cons. GM, Warren, Mich., 1985-94; mem. com. strategic tech. U.S. Army NRC, 1989-92; vice chmn. Congl. Aero. Adv. Com., Washington, 1986-89; mem. com. on trans-atmospheric vehicles USAF Sci. Adv. Bd., 1984-85; mem. com. on low altitude wind shear and its hazard to aviation Nat. Rsch. Coun., 1983. Author: Stochastic Optimal Control: Theory and Application, 1986, reprinted as Optimal Control and Estimation, 1994; N.Am. editor Cambridge Aerospace Series, 1993—, Cambridge Univ. Press, 1993—; contbr. over 100 tech. papers to profl. publs.; patentee wind probing device. Lt. USAF, 1960-63. Recipient Apollo Achievement award NASA, 1969, Cert. of Commendation, MIT, 1969. Fellow IEEE; mem. AIAA (assoc. fellow), Soc. Automotive Engrs. (mem. aerospace guidance and control systems com.). Avocations: photography, music, bicycling. Home: 329 Prospect Ave Princeton NJ 08540-5330 Office: Princeton U D202 Engineering Quadrangle Princeton NJ 08544

STENGEL, RONALD FRANCIS, management consultant; b. Lock Haven, Pa., Oct. 18, 1947; s. Elmer S. and Elizabeth (Heivley) S.; m. Margaret Linda Dezack, Aug. 23, 1969. BSME, U. Pa., 1969, MBA, 1976. Mfg. engr. Control Data Corp., Valley Forge, Pa., 1969-70; mgr. mfg. svcs. Knoll Internat., East Greenville, Pa., 1970-75; ptnr. mgmt. cons. Touche Ross & Co., Phila., 1976-85; pres. RF Stengel & Co. Inc., Valley Forge, 1985—.

STENGER, JUDITH ANTOINETTE, middle school educator; b. Camp Blanding, Fla., Dec. 20, 1942; d. Jack Joseph DiSalvo and Judith Lorraine (Donnelly) DiSalvo-Kohser; m. Harry Richard Stenger, Feb. 4, 1967; children: Scott Joseph, Christopher Richard. BS in Art Edn., Indiana U. Pa., 1965; postgrad., Trinity Coll., 1983-84, Western Md. Coll., 1983-84. Tchr. art elem. sch. Elizabethtown (Pa.) Schs., 1965, Freedom (Pa.) Area Schs., 1966; tchr. art elem. and mid. schs. Carroll County (Md.) Schs., 1967-69; spl. educator Montgomery County (Md.) Schs., 1980-92, tchr. art mid. sch., 1992—; co-leader Md. Student Assistance Program (drug intervention), Rockville, 1995—, mem., 1993—. Represented in 17 group shows. Named Outstanding Tchr. Coun. Exceptional Children, 1986. Mem. NEA, Md. State Tchrs. Assn., Montgomery County Tchrs. Assn., Nat. Art Edn. Assn., Md. Art Edn. Assn. Avocations: printmaking, sculpture, painting. Office: Montgomery County Pub Schs Parkland Mid Sch 4610 W Frankfort Dr Rockville MD 20853-2721

STENGER, VERNON ARTHUR, analytical chemist, consultant; b. Mpls., June 11, 1908; s. Laurence Arthur and Effie Harriet (Dahlberg) S.; m. Ruth Luella Day, Aug. 2, 1933 (dec. Oct. 1994); children: Robert, Emilie, Alan, Gordon, David. BS, U. Denver, 1929, MS, 1930; PhD, U. Minn., 1933; DSc (hon.), U. Denver, 1971. Chemist Eastman Kodak Co., Rochester, N.Y., 1929-30, N.W. Rsch. Inst., U. Minn., Mpls., 1933-35; chemist Dow Chem. Co., Midland, Mich., 1935-40, tech. expert, 1940-53, asst. lab. dir., 1954-61, rsch. scientist, 1961-73, cons., 1973—; chmn. subcom. on magnesium alloy analysis ASTM, Phila., 1941-54. Author: (with I.M. Kolthoff) Volumetric Analysis, Vol. I, 1942, Vol. II, 1947, (with Kolthoff and R. Belcher) Volumetric Analysis, Vol. III, 1957; contbr. 10 encyclopedia articles, 6 chpts. to books and articles to profl. jours. Bd. mem. Midland (Mich.) Symphony Orch., hon. mem. 1990—. Recipient Anachem award Soc. Analytical Chemists, Detroit, 1970. Fellow Am. Inst. Chemists, N.Y. Acad. Sci.; mem. Am. Chem. Soc. (chmn. com. on analytical reagts. 1967-73, mem. adv. bd. Analytical Chemistry 1953-56, Midland sect. award 1979), Geochem. Soc., Sigma Xi. Baptist. Achievements include patent for apparatus for instrumental determination of total organic carbon (TOC), widely used in water analysis, various analytical methods in industry. Home: 1108 E Park Dr Midland MI 48640-4275

STENHOLM, CHARLES W., congressman; b. Stamford, Tex., Oct. 26, 1938; m. Cynthia Ann Watson (div.); children: Chris, Cary, Courtney Ann. Grad., Tarleton State Jr. Coll., 1959; B.S. in Agrl. Edn., Tex. Tech U., 1961, M.S. in Agrl. Edn., 1962; LL.D. (hon.), McMurry Coll., 1983, Abilene Christian U., 1991. Farmer Tex.; past pres. Rolling Plains Cotton Growers and Tex. Electric Coops.; mem. 96th-103rd Congresses from 17th Tex. dist., Washington, D.C., 1979—; apptd. deputy whip 96th-102d Congresses from 17th Tex. dist., 1989—; former mem. state Dem. Exec. Com.; dep. whip Washington, 1989—; mem. agrl. subcom. Budget Com., Conservative Dem. Forum; founder, co-chmn. Congl. Leaders United for a Balanced Budget; founder Dem. Congl. Campaign Commn.; speaker's appt. to bd.; Dem. Caucus adv. group and task force on economy; com. on orgn. study and rev. of Dem. Caucus; ranking minority mem. Gen. Farm Commodities subcom.; mem. of Subcom. for Resource Conservation, Rsch. Forestry. Active Bethel Luth. Ch., Ericksdahl, Tex.; charter trustee Cotton Producer Inst. Recipient Gerald W. Thomas Outstanding Agriculturalist award Tex. Tech U., 1979, Am. Farmer Degree Future Farmers Am., 1979, Disting. Alumnus award Tarleton State U., 1979, Pres. Coun. award Tex. Future Farmers Am., 1981, Disting. Alumnus award Tex. Tech U., 1987, MORE Common Sense Sound Dollar awards, 1988, 90, Guardian of Small Bus. awards, 1980-92, Watchdogs of the Treasury awards, 1980-92, Legis. award Nat. Rural Health Assn., 1991, Disting. Svc. award Tex. Soc. Biomed. Rsch., 1993, Disting. Svc. award Tex. Med. Assn., 1993; named Legislator of Yr. Chem. Prodrs. and Distbrs. Assn., 1992, Man of Yr. Progressive Farmer, 1993. Mem. Tex. State Soc. (Washington, past pres.), Tex. Breakfast Club (Washington, past pres.), Rolling Plains Cotton Growers (past pres.), Stamford C. of C. (past pres.). Democrat. Lutheran. Office: 1211 Longworth Bldg Washington DC 20515-0004*

STENHOUSE, EVERETT RAY, clergy administrator; b. Minco, Okla., May 15, 1931; s. George E. and Jessie Loraine (Dean) S.; m. Alice Irene English, Aug. 22, 1948; children: Brenda Jones, Judy Lundberg, Stephen, Andrew. Student, U. Calif. Berkeley, U. Athens, 1969-71. Ordained to ministry Assemblies of God, 1955. Pastor Wayside Chapel, Bakersfield, Calif., 1955-59, Bethel Temple, Bakersfield, 1960-63; dist. dir. youth So. Calif. Dist. Assemblies of God, Costa Mesa, Calif., 1963-67; assoc. pastor 1st Assembly of God, San Diego, 1968-69; missionary Assemblies of God Fgn. Missions, Athens, Greece, 1969-73; pastor Bethany Ch., Alhambra, Calif., 1974-79; supt. So. Calif. Dist., Assemblies of God, Costa Mesa, 1979-85; asst. gen. supt. Gen. Coun. Assemblies of God, Springfield, Mo., 1986-94; bd. adminstrn. Nat. Assn. Evangs., Wheaton, Ill., 1986-94, Pentecostal Fellowship of No. Am., Ont., Can., 1986-94; chmn., bd. dirs. Assemblies of God Theol. Sem., Springfield, 1991-94, Ministers Benefit Assn., Springfield, 1986-94. Contbr. articles to various mags. Home: 19 Durango Cir Rancho Mirage CA 92270-4801

STENNETT, WILLIAM CLINTON (CLINT STENNETT), radio/TV station executive, state senator; b. Winona, Minn., Oct. 1, 1956; s. William Jessie and Carole Lee (Halsey) S. BA in Journalism, Idaho State U., 1979. Gen. mgr. Wood River Jour., Hailey, Idaho, 1979-85, pres., pub., 1985-87; pres. Sta. KWRV-TV, Ketchum, Idaho, Sta. KSKI-FM, Sun Valley, Idaho; mem. Idaho Ho. of Reps., Boise, 1990-94, state senator, 1995—. Recipient Gen. Excellence award Idaho Newspaper Assn., 1985, 96, 97; named Legislator of the Yr. Idaho Soil Conservation Dists., 1994, Idaho Wildlife Found., 1996. Mem. Idaho Broadcasters (bd. dirs.), Ketchum Sun Valley C. of C. (bd. dirs. 1990-95), Rotary. Democrat.

STENT, GUNTHER SIEGMUND, molecular biologist, educator; b. Berlin, Germany, Mar. 28, 1924; came to U.S., 1940, naturalized, 1945; s. George and Elizabeth (Karfunkelstein) S.; m. Inga Loftsdottir, Oct. 27, 1951; 1 son, Stefan Loftur. BS, U. Ill., 1945, PhD, 1948; DSc (hon.), York U., 1984. Research asst. U. Ill., 1945-48; research fellow Calif. Inst. Tech., 1948-50, U. Copenhagen, Denmark, 1950-51, Pasteur Inst., Paris, France, 1951-52; asst. research biochemist U. Calif., Berkeley, 1952-56; faculty U. Calif., 1956—, prof. molecular biology, 1959-94; prof. emeritus, 1994—; prof. arts and scis. U. Calif., 1967-68, chmn. molecular biology, 1980-86, chmn. molecular and cell biology, 1987-92, dir. virus lab., 1980-86; document analyst U.S. Field Info. Agy. Tech., 1946-47; mem. genetics panel NIH, 1959-64, NSF, 1965-68; fellow Inst. Advanced Studies, Berlin, 1985-90. Author: Papers On Bacterial Viruses, 2d edit., 1966, Molecular Biology of Bacterial Viruses, 1963, Phage and the Origin of Molecular Biology, 1966, The Coming of the Golden Age, 1969, Function and Formation of Neural Systems, 1977, Morality as a Biological Phenomenon, 1978, Paradoxes of Progress, 1978, Molecular Genetics, 2d edit., 1978; mem. editl. bd. Jour. Molecular Biology, 1965-68, Genetics, 1963-68, Zeitschrift für Vererbungslehre, 1962-68, Ann. Revs. Genetics, 1965-69, Ann. Revs. Microbiology, 1966-70, Jour. Neurosci., 1988-96; contbr. numerous sci. papers to profl. lit. Merck fellow NRC, 1948-54; sr. fellow NSF, 1960-61; Guggenheim fellow, 1969-70; Fogarty Resident Scholar NIH, 1990-92. Mem. NAS, Am. Acad. Arts and Scis., Soc. Neurosci., Am. Philos. Soc., Acad. Scis. and Lit. of Mainz (Germany), European Acad. Scis. and Arts, Cosmos Club. Home: 145 Purdue Ave Kensington CA 94708-1032

STENZEL, KURT HODGSON, physician, nephrologist, educator; b. Stamford, Conn., Nov. 3, 1932; s. Alfred B. and Aurelie C. (Hodgson) S.; m. Carolyn Briggs, Dec. 21, 1957; children—Matthew, Jennifer, Mary. BA magna cum laude, N.Y. U., 1954; M.D., Cornell U., 1958. Intern Bellevue Hosp., N.Y.C., 1958-59; resident, 1959-60, 62-63; asst. in medicine Cornell U. Med. Coll., N.Y.C., 1959-60; asst. prof. medicine Cornell U. Med. Coll., 1965-68, asso. prof. biochemistry and surgery, 1969-75, prof. biochemistry, medicine and surgery, 1976—, chief div. nephrology (medicine), 1979-92, dir. Rogosin Kidney Ctr., 1970—; attending physician, surgeon N.Y. Hosp., N.Y.C., 1976—; Diplomate Am. Bd. Internal Medicine and Nephrology. contbr. articles to profl. publs. Served to lt., M.C. USNR, 1960-62. Recipient Nat. Kidney Found. Hoenig award for excellence in renal medicine. Fellow ACP; mem. Am. Soc. Biol. Chemists, Am. Soc. Nephrology, Transplantation Soc., Am. Fedn. Clin. Research, Am. Assn. Immunologists, Am. Soc. for Artificial Internal Organs, Phi Beta Kappa. Research on cell biology, cellular immunology, transplantation and dialysis. Office: The Rogosin Inst 505 E 70th St New York NY 10021

STENZEL, WILLIAM A., consulting services executive; b. Cambridge, Mass., Jan. 21, 1923; s. Herman Rheinhold and Helen (Proskurniak) S.; m. Pallie Jean Bottorff, July 25, 1952; children: Jeffrey Rheinhold, Anne Virginia, Peter Deane, Christopher James. B.A. cum laude, Harvard U., 1944, M.B.A., 1948. Advt. mgr. Waltham Watch Co., Mass., 1948-54; v.p. Tracer Lab. Inc., Waltham, 1954-62; sr. v.p. Premier Indsl. Corp., Cleve., 1962-85, Mex. Info. and Cons. Svcs., Inc., 1985—; v.p. Edn. Techs. and Cons., Inc. Bd. dirs. Greater Cleve. chpt. ARC, 1983-86, bd. dirs., mem. exec. com. Orange City chpt., Calif.; fundraiser Cleve. Orch., 1977-81; trustee Mid Town Corridor, 1985-87, Dunham Tavern Mus., 1985-87; bd. dirs., mem. fin. devel. com. Orange City chpt. ARC; bd. dirs. Blood, tissue svcs. So. Calif. region ARC, 1992-95. With U.S. Army, 1942-45. Fellow Rowfant Club, 1985—. Clubs: Harvard Bus. Sch., Rowfant (Cleve.). Home and Office: 124 Avenida Cota San Clemente CA 92672-3327

STEORTS, NANCY HARVEY, international management consultant; b. Syracuse, N.Y., Nov. 28, 1936; d. Frederick William and Josephine Elizabeth (Jones) Harvey; 1 dau., Deborah Joan. BS, Syracuse U., 1959. Asst. buyer, public relations coordinator Woodward & Lothrop, Washington, 1958-61; home economist Washington Gas Light Co., 1961-64; sales assoc. real estate Summit, N.J., 1967-68; survey specialist Dept. Agr., Washington, 1968-69; chmn. U.S. Consumer Product Safety Commn., Washington, D.C., 1981-85; pres., CEO Nancy Harvey Steorts & Assocs., Dallas, 1985-88, Nancy Harvey Steorts Internat., Washington and Dallas, 1988—; cons. Exec. Reorgn. Govt., Washington, 1971; nat. dir. women's speakers' bur. Com. Re-elect Pres., Washington, 1971-72; dir. candlelight dinners Presdl. Inaugural Commn., 1972-73, 81; expns. dir. Dept. Commerce, Washington, 1973; spl. asst. for consumer affairs to sec. agr., 1973-77; pres. Nancy Harvey Steorts & Assocs., 1977-81; disting. lectr., Strom Thurmond Inst. Govt. and Pub. Affairs, Clemson U.; mem. adv. coun. to bd. dirs., Adolph Coors Co.; mem. U.S. Dept. of Commerce Nat. Adv. Com. Tex., Nat. Adv. Com., Dist. Export Coun. Tex., Nat. Adv. Com. Export Now; mem. working com. on standards between U.S. and Russia; U.S. del. NAFTA Com. on environ. standards; bd. govs. Nat. Consumers adv. com. Fed. Reserve, 1990-93; U.S. del. to COPOLCO, Am. Nat. Standards Inst., The Hague, The Netherlands, NAFTA Del. on Environ. Standards; dir. People to People Trade Mission to Spain, 1987; del. Japan-Tex. Trade Mission, Tokyo, Osaka, Japan, Moscow, Kiev, Leningrad, U.S.-Russia Bus. Devel. Com. on Stds.; chmn. Dallas del. to meet with Prince Charles; mem. nat. consumer adv. coun. Fed. Res. Bd.; official U.S. rep. to 4th Pub. Health, Med. Equipment and Drugs Expn. Moscow USSR; speaker U.S. Seminar Soviet Health Care Exhbn., Moscow; bd. dirs., corp. adv. bd. Sch. Mgmt., Syracuse U.; mem. nat. consumer adv. com. Am. Nat. Standards Inst., nat. bd. dirs., exec. com.; bd. dirs. Mission Investment Trust Co., Tuscon; chmn. U.S. Delegation to COPOLCO, Geneva; chmn. consumer interest coun. Am. Nat. Inst.; official U.S. Delegation on Standards to ASEAN countries; internat. lectr. and keynote speaker in field. Producer, host syndicated TV show spl. Trustee Food Safety Council Conf. Consumer Orgn.; bd. dirs. Women's Inst. Am. U.; bd. advisers Coll. Human Devel., Alumnae Assn., Syracuse U., nat. bd. dirs.; commr. Montgomery County Commn. Women; pres. Welcome Wagon Clubs from 1986, Dallas Citizens Council, 1986—; bd. dirs. Council of Better Bus. Burs.; bd. adv. Am. U. Women's Inst.; bd. dirs. Med. Coll. Pa., Tex. Women's Alliance; bd. dirs., vice-chmn. regional devel. Nat. Assn. Women Bus. Owners; mem. internat. com. Com. 2000; bd. dirs. Jr. Achievement, United Way, Dallas, Goals of Dallas, Internat. Mayor's Ball; internat. del. 1st Women's Internat. Trade Mission to Europe for Women Entrepeneurs; chairwoman Trade Mission of Women Leaders to Taiwan, 1988; del. to USSR Internat. Women's Forum Mission; mem. adv. coun. to So. Meth. U. Dept. Economics; co-chmn. fundraising, Dallas Symphony; nat. dir., coord. bicentennial presdl. inaugural dinners, 1989; pres. Dallas Citizens' Coun., 1986-88; chmn. Afternoon with Oprah Winfrey Fundraising Benefit; chmn. Women Leaders Delegation to Taiwan; mem. corp. bd. dirs. Ariz. Rehab. Systems; mem. nat. bd. overseers U.S. Dept. Commerce; mem. Am. Nat. Standards Inst., chmn.; Nat. Consumer Adv. Coun.; chmn. Mayor's Glass Ceiling Commn., Dallas; bd. dirs. Nat. Women's Econ. Alliance Found., I Have a Dream Found.; chmn. Dallas Glass Ceiling Commn.; bd. overseers Tex. Quality Bd.; consumer safety expert TV network news shows; host Nat. Consumer Safety, satellite cable show. Recipient George P. Arents Pioneer medal Syracuse U., 1979, spl. award for consumer concern Nat. Diet Workshop, Malcolm Baldridge award, Bd. of Overseers; named one of five outstanding pub. servants Gallagher Report, 1984. Mem. Nat. Bd. Dirs., Am. Home Econs.ssn., AAUW, Nat. Consumers League, Am. Women in Radio and TV, Exec. Women in Govt. (chmn.), Nat. Conf. Consumer Orgns., Syracuse U. Alumni Assn. (bd. dirs.). Office: 4689 S Versailles Ave Dallas TX 75209-6017

STEP, EUGENE LEE, retired pharmaceutical company executive; b. Sioux City, Iowa, Feb. 19, 1929; s. Harry and Ann (Keiser) S.; m. Hannah Scheuermann, Dec. 27, 1953; children—Steven Harry, Michael David, Jonathan Allen. BA in Econs., U. Nebr., 1951; MS in Acctg. and Fin., U. Ill., 1952. With Eli Lilly Internat. Corp., London and Paris, 1964-69; dir. Elanco Internat. Eli Lilly Internat. Corp., Indpls., 1969-70, v.p. marketing, 1970-72, v.p. Europe, 1972; v.p. mktg. Eli Lilly and Co., Indpls., 1972-73, pres. pharm. div., 1973-86, exec. v.p., 1986—, also dir.; bd. dirs. Scios-Nova Cell-Genesys, Medco Rsch. Pathogenesis, Guidant Corp., GMIS Inc. 1st lt. U.S. Army, 1953-56. Mem. Pharm. Mfrs. Assn. (bd. dirs. 1980-92), Internat. Pharm. Mfrs. Assn. (pres. 1991-92). Home: 741 Round Hill Rd Indianapolis IN 46260-2917

STEPAN, FRANK QUINN, chemical company executive; b. Chgo., Oct. 24, 1937; s. Alfred Charles and Mary Louise (Quinn) S.; m. Jean Finn, Aug. 23, 1958; children: Jeanne, Frank Quinn, Todd, Jennifer, Lisa, Colleen, Alfred, Richard. A.B., U. Notre Dame, 1959; M.B.A., U. Chgo., 1963. Salesman Indsl. Chems. div. Stepan Chem. Co., Northfield, Ill., 1961-63, mgr. internat. dept., 1964-66, v.p. corporate planning, 1967-69, v.p., gen. mgr., 1970-73, pres., 1973-84; pres., chmn., chief exec. officer Stepan Co., Northfield, Ill., 1984—, also bd. dirs. Mem. liberal arts council Notre Dame U., South Bend, Ind., 1972—; bd. dirs. Big Shoulders, Chgo. Served to 1st lt. AUS, 1959-61. Mem. Chem. Mfrs. Assn. (bd. dirs.), Soap and Detergent Assn. (bd. dirs.), Ill. Bus. Roundtable, Econ. Club Chgo., Exmoor Country Club, Bob O'Link Golf Club, Everglades Club. Home: 200 Linden St Winnetka IL 60093-3862 Office: Stepan Co Edens & Winnetka Rds Northfield IL 60093

STEPANIAN, IRA, banking executive; b. Cambridge, Mass., Nov. 14, 1936; s. Sarkis H. and Armenoohi (Kupelian) S.; m. Jacquelynne McLucas, Aug. 6, 1961; children: Philip, Alisa, Steven. B.A., Tufts U., 1958; M.B.A., Boston Coll., 1971. Credit investigator Dun & Bradstreet, Boston, 1958-59; rsch. assoc. Ernst Assocs., Inc., Arlington, Mass., 1959-63; with First Nat. Bank Boston, 1963—, exec. v.p., 1980, vice chmn., from 1981, pres., from 1983, now chmn., chief exec. officer, dir.; vice chmn. Bank of Boston Corp., from 1981, pres., from 1983, chief oper. officer, dir., 1983-87, chief exec. officer, 1987—, now also chmn., dir.; bd. dirs. Liberty Mut. Ins. Co., NYNEX-New Eng., Fed. Res. Bank Boston. Trustee emeritus Tufts U., Medford, Mass.; trustee Boston Mus. Sci., Boston Mus. Fine Arts, Gen. Hosp.; bd. dirs. Mass. Bus. Roundtable, Internat. Monetary Conf. Mem. Bankers Roundtable. Office: First Bank of Boston 100 Federal St PO Box 2016 Boston MA 02106-2016*

STEPANIAN, LEO MCELLIGOTT, lawyer; b. Butler, Pa., Nov. 12, 1929; s. Steven A. and Edith Marion (McElligott) S.; m. Dec. 26, 1953 (div. 1980); children: Leo II, Leanne, Joshua, Jonathan. BA cum laude, Notre Dame, South Bend, Ind., 1952; LLB, Pitts. Law Sch., 1955; JD, 1968. Bar: Pa., 1958; U.S. Dist. Ct. (we. dist.) Pa., U.S. Ct. Appeals (3rd cir.), U.S. Supreme Ct. Washington. Sr. ptnr. Stephanian & Muscatello, Butler, Pa., 1958—;

chmn. bd. trustees Slippery Rock U.; pres. Butler County Mental Health Assn.; dir. Pa. Mental Health Assn., Butler County Luth. Family Counseling Svc., Butler Area Hall of Fame, Butler Quarterback Club; divsn. chmn. Butler County United Way, WQED Fund, Cancer Crusade, Heart Fund; commr. Butler Bantam Baseball League. Editor, co-founder: Butler County Legal Journal, 1970—. Co-founder Pa. Bar Assn. Section of County Legal Jours.; bd. dirs. St. Fidelis Coll. With U.S. Army, 1955-58. Recipient U.S. News and World Report award; named Am. Legionaire of Yr., 1986. Mem. Butler Moose Lodge, Knights of Columbus, Dirken Ritzert Post of Am. Legion, Professionalism Com. Pa. Bar Assn., Golden Tornado Found. (steering com.). Avocations: boating, travel, gardening, sports. Office: Stepanian & Muscatello 228 S Main St Butler PA 16001

STEPANICH, FRED CHARLES, civil and water resources engineer; b. Neodesha, Kans., Aug. 4, 1931; arrived in The Philippines, 1972; s. Joe and Agnes (Sustar) S. BSCE cum laude, U. Notre Dame, 1959; MSCE, Colo. State U., 1963. Cons. engr. Henningson Durham Richardson, Taipei, Taiwan, 1966, Seoul, Korea, 1967-68; cons. engr. Camp Dresser McKee, Bangkok, 1969-70, Manila, 1974-75; cons. engr. Harza Engring., Jakarta, Indonesia, 1971-72, Daniel Mann Johnson Mendenhall, Manila, 1974, United Rice Mills, San Juan, P.R., 1978, King and Gavaris, Kuala Lumpur, Malaysia, 1980; cons. engr. Engring. Sci. Engrs., Madras, India, 1976-77, Cairo, 1978, Aleppo, Syria, 1980, Kota Kinabalu, Malaysia, 1981, Colombo, Sri Lanka, 1982, Aqaba, Jordan, 1986; cons. engr. Internat. Fund for Agrl. Devel., Rome, 1987; cons. engr. Aquaculture Hatcheries, Manila, 1988, Bangkok, 1989; cons. engr. Asian Devel. Bank, Manila, Pakistan, 1973, Khushab, Pakistan, 1989, Lahore, Pakistan, 1990; cons. engr. dept. pub. works and hwys. Asian Devel. Bank, Manila, 1991-94; cons. engr. Bur. Cen. d'Etudes pour les Equipments d'Outre Mer Engrs., Jatiluhur, Indonesia, 1990-91, Berger Internat. Engrs., Jakarta, Indonesia, 1991; cons. Asian Devel. Bank, Thimpu, Bhutan, 1984, Lahore, Pakistan, 1982, Engring. Sci. Engrs., Medan, Indonesia, 1983, Manila, 1982, Henningson Durham Richardson, Taipei, Taiwan, 1966, Seoul, Korea, 1967-68, Camp Dresser McKee, Bangkok, 1969-70, Manila, 1974-75, Harza Engring., Jakarta, Indonesia, 1971-72, King and Gavaris, Kuala Lumpur, Malaysia, 1980, Daniel Mann Johnson Mendenhall, Manila, 1974, United Rice Mills, San Juan, P.R., 1978, Madras, India, 1976-77, Cairo, 1978, Aleppo, Syria, 1980, Kota Kinabalu, Malaysia, 1981, Colombo, Sri Lanka, 1982. Contbr. articles to profl. jours. Charitable activity mem. Am. Legion, Manila, 1988. With USN, 1951-54. Fellow ASCE; mem. Am. Water Resources Assn., Internat. Commn. for Irrigation & Drainage, Soc. Am. Mil. Engrs., Am. Legion. Roman Catholic. Avocations: computers, sports, choir and chorus groups. Office: PO Box 1546, Manila 1099, The Philippines

STEPANSKI, ANTHONY FRANCIS, JR., computer company executive; b. Jersey City, N.J., June 29, 1941; s. Anthony Francis and Gertrude Stepanski; m. Jane Ellen Schuler, Sept. 5, 1965; children—Matthew A.W., Melinda Kate. B.A., Clark U., 1963. Sales rep. IBM Corp., N.Y.C., 1964-68; from sales rep. to sr. v.p. AGS Computers, Inc., N.Y.C. and Mountainside, N.J., 1968-82; exec. v.p. AGS Computers, Inc., Mountainside, 1982—; pres., chief exec. officer AGS Info. Services, Inc., Mountainside, 1986—; also bd. dirs. AGS Computers, Inc., a NYNEX Co., Mountainside; now exec. v.p., Keane, Inc., Clark, N.J. Trustee Clark U., Worcester, Mass., 1987, Children's Specialized Hosp. Found., Mountainside, 1989; bd. dirs. Westchester Artificial Kidney Ctr., Valhalla, N.Y., 1982, Westfield Symphony Orch., N.J., 1983. Served with USAR, 1965-66. Office: Origin Tech 430 Mountain Ave New Providence NJ 07974*

STEPHAN, ALEXANDER F., German language and literature educator; b. Lüdenscheid, Fed. Republic Germany, Aug. 16, 1946; came to U.S., 1968; s. Eberhard and Ingeborg (Hörnig) S.; m. Halina Konopacka, Dec. 15, 1969; 1 child, Michael. MA, U. Mich., 1969; PhD, Princeton U., 1973. German instr. Princeton U., N.J., 1972-73; asst. prof. German UCLA, 1973-77, assoc. prof., 1977-83, prof., 1983-85; prof. German U. Fla., Gainesville, 1985—, chmn., 1985-93. Author: Christa Wolf, 1976, 4th edit., 1991, Die deutsche Exilliteratur, 1979, Christa Wolf (Forschungsbericht), 1981, Max Frisch, 1983, Anna Seghers im Exil, 1993, Im Visier des FBI, 1995; editor: Peter Weiss, Die Ästhetik des Widerstands, 1983, 3d edit., 1990, Exilliteratur und die Kunste, 1990, Exil-Studien, 1993—, Christa Wolf: The Author's Dimension, 1993, 1995; co-editor: Studies in GDR Culture and Society, 1981-90, Schreiben im Exil, 1985, (TV documentary) Im Visier des FBI, 1995; editl. bd. Germanic Rev., Humanities Monograph Series, U. Fla., 1985-93. Peter Weiss Jahrbuch, 1994—; fellow Humboldt Found., 1988, 94, Guggenheim Found. fellow, 1989, VG Wort fellow, 1992, UCLA faculty fellow, 1984, U. Fla., 1986, 92; grantee Internat. Rsch. and Exchs. Bd., 1993, German Acad. Exch. Svcs., 1993, NEH, 1974, 84, Am. Coun. Learned Socs., 1976, 77, 84, Sch. Theory and Criticism, 1978, Am. Philos. Soc., 179, 81, 92. Mem. Internat. Vereinigung fur Germanische Sprach und Literaturwissenschaften, Am. Assn. Tchrs. German, Soc. for Exile Studies, Gemran Studies Assn., German PEN, Soc. for German-Am. Studies, Internat. Anna Seghers Soc. (founding). Home: 2402 NW 27th Terr Gainesville FL 32605-2829 Office: U Fla Dept Germanic & Slavic Langs/Lit 263 Dauer Gainesville FL 32611

STEPHAN, CHARLES ROBERT, retired ocean engineering educator, consultant; b. N.Y.C., Sept. 30, 1911; s. Charles Albert and Ella (Wallendorf) S.; m. Eleanor Grace Storck, Feb. 14, 1937 (dec. July 1992); children: Yvonne Stephan Brown, Joan Stephan Cathcart, Charles Royal, Robert W. BS in Engring., U.S. Naval Acad., 1934; D Engring. (hon.), Fla. Atlantic U., 1978. Commd. ensign U.S. Navy, 1934, advanced through grades to capt.; served various capacities including WWII, South Pacific and Korean war areas U.S. Navy, various locations, 1941-52; ret. U.S. Navy, 1963; prof. ocean engring. Fla. Atlantic U., Boca Raton, 1964-76; prof. emeritus Fla. Atlantic U., 1976—; assoc. prof. naval sci., Rensselaer Poly. Inst., Troy, N.Y., 1944-46. Contbr. articles to various publs. Bd. dirs. Legion of Valor of U.S.A., 1985-92, membership chair, 1985-93, nat. comdr., 1995—. Decorated Navy Cross, 2 Bronze Star medals. Fellow Marine Technology Soc.; mem. U.S. Naval Inst., U.S. Navy League (v.p. Delray Beach coun.), Pearl Harbor Survivors (pres. Fla. Gold Coast chpt.), Kiwanis. Republican. Lutheran. Avocations: photography, travel, swimming, bowling. Home and Office: 1136 York Ln Virginia Beach VA 23451-3816

STEPHAN, EDMUND ANTON, lawyer; b. Chgo., Oct. 7, 1911; s. Anton Charles and Mary Veronica (Egan) S.; m. Evelyn Way, July 3, 1937; children: Miriam, Edmund Anton, Martha (Mrs. Robert McNeill), Donald, Christopher, Evelyn, Gregory, Joan (Mrs. David Nelson). A.B., U. Notre Dame, 1933; LL.B., Harvard, 1939. Bar: N.Y. 1940, Ill. 1945. Assoc. firm Carter, Ledyard & Milburn, N.Y.C., 1939-42; atty. charge N.Y. office U.S. Alien Property Custodian, 1943-45; assoc. firm Mayer, Brown & Platt (and predecessors), Chgo., 1945-47; partner Mayer, Brown & Platt (and predecessors), 1947-90, of counsel, 1991—; dir. (hon.) Brunswick Corp., Marsh & McLennan Cos. Emeritus chmn. bd. trustees U. Notre Dame. Mem. Am., Ill., Chgo. bar assns. Roman Catholic. Clubs: Legal (Chgo.), Mid-Day (Chgo.), Chicago (Chgo.), Law (Chgo.); Michigan Shores (Wilmette, Ill.), Westmoreland Country (Wilmette, Ill.); Harvard (N.Y.C.); Bob-O-Link Golf (Highland Park, Ill.). Home: 1410 Sheridan Rd Wilmette IL 60091-1840 Office: Mayer Brown & Platt 190 S La Salle St Chicago IL 60603-3410

STEPHAN, JOHN JASON, historian, educator; b. Chgo., Mar. 8, 1941; s. John Walter and Ruth (Walgreen) S.; m. Barbara Ann Brooks, June 22, 1963. B.A., Harvard U., 1963, M.A., 1964; Ph.D., U. London, 1969. Research assoc. Social Sci. Center, Waseda U., Tokyo, 1969-70; mem. faculty U. Hawaii, Honolulu, 1970—; prof. history U. Hawaii, 1977—, chmn. E. Asian studies program, 1973-74, dir. program on Soviet Union in Pacific-Asia region, 1986-88; rsch. prof. Japan Found.; fellow U. Hokkaido, 1976-77; vis. prof. Inst. of Far East, Moscow, 1982, Inst. Econ. Rsch., Khabarovsk, USSR, 1982-83, Stanford U., 1986, Kennan Inst. for Advanced Studies, 1987; adj. rsch. assoc. East-West Ctr., 1988-92; Sanwa disting. lectr. Fletcher Sch. of Law & Diplomacy Tufts U., 1989. Author: Sakhalin: A History, 1971, The Kuril Islands: Russo-Japanese Frontier in the Pacific, 1974, The Russian Fascists, 1978, Hawaii Under the Rising Sun, 1984, Soviet-American Horizons on the Pacific, 1986, The Russian Far East, 1994. Sr. assoc. mem. St. Antony's Coll., Oxford (Eng.) U., 1977; Bd. dirs. Library Internat. Relations, Chgo., 1976-87; Hawaii rep. U.S.-Japan Friendship Commn., 1980-83. Fulbright fellow, 1967-68; Asia Found. grantee, 1974. Mem. AAUP, Am. Hist. Assn., Am. Assn. Advancement Slavic Studies, Assn. Asian Studies, Authors Guild, Internat. House of Japan, Can. Hist. Assn. Address: 4334 Round Top Dr Honolulu HI 96822-5021

STEPHAN, ROBERT TAFT, lawyer, former state attorney general; b. Wichita, Kans., Jan. 16, 1933; s. Taft and Julia S.; m. Marilyn Stephan; children: Dana, Lisa, Constance, Kimberly, Keith. BA, Washburn U., 1954, JD, 1957; postgrad., U. Pa., 1967. Bar: Kans. 1957. Pvt. practice law, 1957-63, 95—; judge Wichita (Kans.) Mcpl. Ct., 1963-65, Kans. Dist. Ct., 18th Jud. Dist., 1965-78; atty. gen. State of Kans., 1979-95; chmn. Kans. Jud. Conf., 1977, Kans. Sentencing Commn., 1993-95; mem. adv. bd. Shawnee County Ct.-Appointed Spl. Adv. Program. Hon. crusade chmn. Kans. div. Am. Cancer Soc., 1979-81; mem. adv. com. Kans. Spl. Olympics, chmn. Corp. Giving Club, 1985-86; mem. adv. coun. Kans. Tchrs. of Tomorrow; bd. trustees Leukemia Soc. Am., Kans. chpt.; bd. dirs. Victory in the Valley. Named Kans. Trial Judge of Yr. Kans. Trial Lawyers Assn., 1977, Big Bros. of Yr., 1984, Outstanding Big Bros. Midwest, 1985; recipient Disting. Svc. award Washburn U., 1985; Allied Profl. award Nat. Orgn. for Victim Assistance, 1993. Mem. Am. Judges Assn., Am. Judicature Soc., ABA (mem. adv. commn. youth alcohol and drug problems), Nat. Assn. Attys. Gen. (past pres., chmn. commn. car rental guidelines, mem. fed. trade commn. working group), Wagonmasters Club, Elks, Moose, Masons, Shriners. Republican. Office: 14243 W 84th Ter Lenexa KS 66215*

STEPHANI, NANCY JEAN, social worker, journalist; b. Garden City, Mich., Feb. 19, 1955; d. Ernest Helmut Schulz and Margaret Mary Fowler Thompson; m. Edward Jeffrey Stephani, Aug. 29, 1975; children: Edward J., Margaret J., James E. AA, Northwood Inst., Midland, Mich., 1975; student in theology, Boston Coll., 1991; BS summa cum laude, Lourdes Coll., Sylvania, Ohio, 1992; MSW, Ohio State U., 1995. Lic. social worker. Profl. facilitator Parents United, Findlay, Ohio, 1989-94; contbg. writer Cath. Chronicle, Toledo, 1988-95; mem. ministry formation faculty Cath. Diocese of Toledo, 1992-96, mem. accreditation com., ministry formation program, 1996-97; crisis intervention specialist John C. Hutson Ctr., 1994—; social work clinician Family Svc. Hancock County, Blanchard Valley Home Health Social Svc.; trustee, bd. dirs. Hope House for the Homeless, Findlay, 1990—, v.p. 1996-97; adult edn. coord. St. Michael Parish, Findlay, 1986-93, mem. strategic plan core com., 1989-91, v.p., pres. parish coun., 1985-89; program planning com. Family Life Conf., Cath. Diocese, 1994-95, mem. accreditation com. ministry formation dept.; profl. facilitator Hope Plus Program through Hancock County Common Pleas Ct., 1996—. Founder Food Coop., MPBA, Findlay, 1981; founding mem. Chopin Hall, Findlay, 1983; mem. Hancock County AIDS Task Force, 1994—; strategic planning com. mem., co-chair goal setting com. Findlay Pub. Schs., 1994. Nat. Inst. Food Svcs. grantee, 1974; Diocese of Toledo grantee, 1991; Ohio State U. Coll. Social Work grantee, 1994. Mem. NOW, NASW, Am. Assn. on Child Abuse, Transpsychol. Assn., Friends of Creation Spirituality, Cognitive/Behavioral Profl. Soc., Call to Action, Pax Christi. Avocations: jogging, hiking, cooking, travel. Home: 2615 Goldenrod Ln Findlay OH 45840-1025

STEPHANOPOULOS, GEORGE ROBERT, federal official; b. Fall River, Mass., Feb. 10, 1961; s. Robert and Nikki C. Stephanopoulos. AB Polit. Sci. summa cum laude, Columbia U., 1982; M Theology, Oxford U., 1986. Adminstrv. asst. rep. Edward Feighan, Washington; dep. comm. dir. Dukakis Bentsen campaign, 1988; exec. floor mgr. to House Majority leader Gephardt, Washington; dir. comm. Clinton/Gore campaign, Little Rock; dir. comm. The White House, Washington, sr. advisor to the Pres. of U.S., 1993—. Recipient medal of Excellence Columbia U., 1993; Rhodes scholar Oxford U. Mem. Phi Beta Kappa. Democrat. Greek Orthodox. Office: The White House 1600 Pennsylvania Ave NW Washington DC 20502

STEPHANOPOULOS, GREGORY, chemical engineering educator, consultant, researcher; b. Kalamata, Greece, Mar. 10, 1950; came to U.S., 1973; s. Nicholas and Elizabeth (Bitsanis) S.; m. Maria Flytzani; children—Nicholas-Odysseas, Alexander, Rona-Elisa. BS, Nat. Tech. U., Athens, Greece, 1973; MS, U. Fla., Gainesville, 1975; PhD, U. Minn., Mpls., 1978. Registered profl. engr., Greece. Asst. prof. chem. engring. Calif. Inst. Tech., Pasadena, 1978-83, assoc. prof. chem. engring., 1983-85; prof. chem. engring. MIT, Cambridge, 1985—. Editor: Kinetics and Thermodynamics of Biological Systems, 1983. Mem. editorial bd. Mathematical Biosciences, 1984—, Biotech. Progress, 1984—. Contbr. articles to profl. jours. Dreyfus Tchr. scholar Camille and Henry Dreyfus Found., 1982; recipient Pres. Young Investigator award NSF, 1984; NSF grantee, 1980—. Mem. Am. Inst. Chem. Engrs. (programming coordinator 1983, Computing in Chem. Egring. award 1993), Am. Chem. Soc. Greek Orthodox. Avocations: chess; music; travel. Office: Mass Inst Tech Dept Chem Engring 66-552 77 Massachusetts Ave Cambridge MA 02139-4301*

STEPHANY, JAROMIR, artist, educator. AAS, Rochester Inst. Tech., 1956, BFA, 1958; MFA, Ind. U., 1960. Co-lectr. history of photography Rochester (N.Y.) Inst. Tech., 1961-66; assoc. prof. Md. Inst., Balt., 1966-73, chmn. dept. photography and film, 1968-73; assoc. prof. U. Md., Baltimore County, 1973—, chmn. visual arts dept., 1976-77; mem. staff George Eastman House (now Internat. Mus. Photography), 1961-66;photographer-in-residence Skidmore Coll., 1969; vis. assoc. prof. U. Del., Newark, 1976; lectr. and cons. in field. Author: The Developing Image, 1979; editor: (newsletter) The Annapolis Power Squadron, 1990—; contbr. articles to profl. jours.; one-man shows include Foto Gallery, N.Y.C., 1975, Greater Reston Art Ctr., Va., 1977; exhibited in group shows at Fells Point Gallery, Balt., 1976, G.H. Dalsheimer Gallery, Balt., 1982, Franklin Inst. Sci. Mus., 1983, IBM Gallery Sci. and Art, N.Y.C., 1984, Rehoboth Art Ctr., 1985, U. Md., Baltimore County, 1988, 90, 92; represented in permanent collection St. Petersburg (Fla.) Mus. of Art. Grantee Union Ind. Art Colls., 1971-72, U. Md., 1982, 91, U.S. Power Squadron, 1993. Mem. Nat. Soc. Photographic Edn. (bd. dirs. 1973-74), Md. Coun. Arts Media (com. 1973), Soc. Photographic Edn. (lectr., nat. conv., 1st chmn. 1974-80, editor newsletter). Home: 786 Creek View Rd Severna Park MD 21146-4209

STEPHEN, GARY S., insurance company executive; b. 1951. CPA, N.Y. Acct. Peat Marwick Mitchell & Co., N.Y.C., 1972-78; acct. Booz Allen Hamilton Co., N.Y.C., 1978-85; treas. Buck Consultants Inc., 1985—; also bd. dirs. Office: Buck Consultants Inc 2 Penn Plz Fl 23 New York NY 10121*

STEPHEN, JOHN ERLE, lawyer, consultant; b. Eagle Lake, Tex., Sept. 24, 1918; s. John Earnest and Vida Thrall (Klein) S.; m. Gloria Yzaguirre, May 16, 1942; children: Vida Leslie Stephen Renzi, John Lauro Kurt. JD, U. Tex., 1941; postgrad., Northwestern U., 1942, U.S. Naval Acad. Postgrad. Sch., Annapolis, 1944; cert. in internat. law, U.S. Naval War Coll., Newport, R.I., 1945; cert. in advanced internat. law, U.S. Naval War Coll., 1967. Bar: Tex. 1946, U.S. Ct. Appeals (D.C. cir.) 1949, U.S. Tax Ct. 1953, U.S. Supreme Ct. 1955, U.S. Dist. Ct. D.C. 1956, U.S. Ct. Appeals (2nd cir.) 1959, U.S. Ct. Appeals (7th cir.) 1964, U.S. Dist. Ct. (so. dist.) N.Y. 1964, D.C. 1972, U.S. Dist. Ct. (no. dist.) Ill. 1974, U.S. Dist. Ct. (we. dist.) Wash. 1975, Mich. 1981, U.S. Dist. Ct. (we. dist.) Mich. 1981, U.S. Dist. Ct. (so. dist.) Tex. 1981. Gen. mgr., corp. counsel Sta. KOPY, Houston, 1946; gen. atty., exec. asst. to pres. Tex. Star Corp. and affiliated cos., Houston, 1947-50; ptnr. Hofheinz & Stephen, Houston, 1950-57; v.p., gen. counsel TV Broadcasting Co., Tex. Radio Corp., Gulf Coast Network, Houston, 1953-57; spl. counsel, exec. asst. Mayor, City of Houston, 1953-57; spl. counsel Houston C. of C., 1953-56; v.p., gen. counsel Air Transp. Assn. Am., Washington, 1958-70, Amway Corp. and affiliated cos., Ada, Mich., 1971-82; counsellor, cons. Austin, Tex., 1983—; chief protocol City of Houston, 1953-56; advisor Consulates Gen. of Mex., San Antonio, Houston, New Orleans, Washington, 1956-66; mem. adv. bd. Jour. of Air Law and Commerce, 1966-72; vis. lectr. Harvard Bus. Sch., Pacific Agribus. Conf., Southwestern Legal Found., Inter-Am. Law Conf.; apptd. by Pres. legal advisor, del. U.S. Diplomatic Dels. to Internat. Treaty Confs., Paris, London, Rome, Tokyo, Madrid, Bermuda, Guadalajara, Dakar, 1961-71, Internat. Air-Rte. Dels. to U.K., France, Spain, Portugal, Belgium, The Netherlands, Japan, Rep. of Korea, Mex., Australia, Argentina, Soviet Union, and Brazil, 1960-70; legal advisor, del. U.S. dels. to United Nations Specialized Orgns., Montreal, Geneva, 1964-71; U.S. rep. Internat. Conf. on Aircraft Noise, London, 1967; hon. faculty mem. sch. of law, sch. of bus., U. Miami, 1968—; accredited corr. United Nations, Rep. and Dem. Nat. Convs. Author, editor in field. Chmn. legal com. Nat. Aircraft Noise Abatement Coun.; bd. dirs. Houston Mus. Fine Arts, 1953-57, Contemporary Arts Assn., 1952-57, Tex. Transp. inst., 1964-72. Comdr. USNR, 1941-46, PTO and S.E. Asia; mem. staff Supreme Allied Command, NATO, 1952. Recipient Jesse L. Lasky award RKO Pictures-CBS, Hollywood, Calif., 1939, H.J. Lutcher Stark award U. Tex., 1940, 41, Walter Mack award Pepsico, U. Tex., 1941, Best U.S. Pub. Svc. Broadcasts award CCNY, 1946. Mem. ABA (past chmn., mem. coun. sect. pub. utility, comms. and transp. law, standing com. on aero. law), Am. Law Inst., World Peace Through Law Ctr. Geneva (past chmn. internat. aviation law com.), Fed. Bar Assn. (exec. com. transp. coun., comms. coun.), D.C. Bar, State Bar Tex., State Bar Mich., Fed. Comms. Bar Assn., Assn. ICC Practitioners, Am. Judicature Soc., Washington Fgn. Law Soc. (vis. lectr. 1967-68), Japanese Air Law Soc. (hon. mem. 1966—), Venezuelan Air and Space Law Soc. (hon.), Internat. Club (Washington), Explorers (Washington), Houston Polo Club, Lakeshore Club (Chgo.), Nat. Aviation Club (Washington), Saddle & Cycle Club (Chgo.), Breakfast Club (Houston), Execs. (Houston), Ky. Cols., Ark. Travelers, Tex. Adms. Home: 6904 Ligustrum Cv Austin TX 78750-8352

STEPHEN, MICHAEL ANTHONY, insurance company executive; b. Saint John, N.B., Can., Jan. 17, 1929; m. Beatrice Bourque. B.A., U. Montreal, Que., Can., 1951; grad. Advanced Mgmt. Program, Harvard U., 1983. Agt. London Life, Saint John, 1955-60; br. mgr. London Life, Halifax, N.S., Can., 1960-69; dir. agys. Sun Life, Montreal, 1969-74; v.p. life div. Aetna Can., Toronto, Ont., Can., 1974-81, exec. v.p. ins. ops., 1981-83, exec. v.p., chief oper. officer, 1983-85, pres., chief oper. officer, 1985-87, pres., chief exec. officer, 1987-92; pres. Aetna Internat., Inc., Hartford, Conn., 1992—, vice chmn., chief ops. property and casualty, 1995—, also bd. dirs.; bd. dirs. Aetna Life Ins. Co. Can., Aetna Internat. Chile S.A., Seguros Monterrey Aetna S.A. Bd. dirs. Toronto Symphony. Mem. Harvard U. Alumni Assn. (Toronto), Bd. Trade, Toronto Club, York Club. Office: Aetna Internat 151 Farmington Ave Hartford CT 06156-0001

STEPHENS, ALBERT LEE, JR., federal judge; Judge U.S. Dist. Ct. (cen. dist.) Calif., Los Angeles. Office: US Dist Ct 312 N Spring St Los Angeles CA 90012-4701*

STEPHENS, BART NELSON, former foreign service officer; b. Norfolk, Va., May 29, 1922; s. Bart Dannelly and Lura Lee (Cannon) S.; m. Barrett Krausz, Jan. 7, 1950; children: Tracey Rainier, Schuyler Barrett, Holly Cannon, Sinah Kendall Lee. A.B., Duke, 1943; A.M., Harvard, 1947; lang. tng., Fgn. Service Inst., 1962, 66, 76. Divisional asst. Greece-Turkey-Iran sect., pub. affairs overseas program staff Dept. State, 1948-49; asst. pub. affairs officer Thessaloniki, Greece, 1950; asst. info. officer Athens, 1950-51; pub. affairs officer Patras, Greece, 1951-54 and, Thessaloniki, 1954; dir. Amerika Haus, Nuernberg, Germany, 1955-59; mem. cultural council City of Nuernberg, 1958-59; mgmt. analyst USIA, Washington, 1959-61; cultural attache Am. Embassy, Warsaw, Poland, 1963-65; dir. Am. Cultural Center, Saigon, Vietnam, 1967-68; 1st sec., regional projects officer Am. Embassy, Vienna, Austria, 1968-70; consul, pub. affairs officer Am. consulate gen. Stuttgart, Germany, 1970-73; area coordinator (Europe) USIA, Washington, 1973; seminar-conf. Programming officer USIA, 1973-74; dep. dir. Office Internat. Arts Affairs, Dept. State, 1974-76; counselor cultural affairs officer Am. Embassy, Bangkok, 1977-82; counselor Sr. Fgn. Service. Contbr. articles to profl. jours. Vice chmn., bd. dirs. Thailand-U.S. Ednl. Found., 1977-82; bd. dirs. John F. Kennedy Found., Thailand, 1977-82, John E. Peurifoy Found., 1979-82, Lynchburg Symphony Orch., 1992-93; exec. sec. Eisenhower Exch. Fellowship Selection Com., Thailand, 1977-82; mem. winter forums com. Sweet Briar Coll., 1990-96. Lt. (j.g.) USNR, 1944-46, PTO. Decorated Bronze Star with combat V, Purple Heart; recipient Meritorious Svc. award USIA, 1956, medal for civilian service in Vietnam, 1968, Civilian award U.S. European Command, 1973. Mem. Am. Fgn. Svc. Assn., Soc. Lees of Va., Siam Soc., Westwood Country Club (Vienna, Va.), Boonsboro Country Club, Phi Beta Kappa, Omicron Delta Kappa, Phi Eta Sigma, Pi Kappa Phi. Home: 201 St James Pl Lynchburg VA 24503-4226 *Personal responsibility should be an essential principle for all of us, in the family, job and community. My 34 years in the U.S. Foreign Service gave me a wonderfully stimulating and rewarding career and a profound belief: the diplomatic service is America's first line of defense.*

STEPHENS, BOBBY GENE, college administrator, consultant; b. Glendale, S.C., Mar. 8, 1935; s. Dewey and Bertha Cordelia (Mott) S.; m. Sandra Elizabeth White, June 27, 1957; children: Elaine, Ward, Todd, Adam. B.S., Wofford Coll., 1957; M.S., Clemson U., 1961, Ph.D., 1964; LHD (hon.), MacMurray Coll., 1987. Textile chemist Reeves Bros., Fairforest, S.C., 1957-58; grad. asst. Clemson (S.C.) U., 1960-63; instr. chemistry Wofford Coll., Spartanburg, S.C., 1963-64, asst. prof., 1964-67, assoc. prof., 1967-72, prof., v.p. acad. affairs, 1972-80; pres. MacMurray Coll., Jacksonville, Ill., 1980-86; v.p. research and enrollment Wofford Coll., Spartanburg, S.C., 1986-91, v.p. sci. and tech., 1991—; project dir. Howard Hughes Med. Inst., 1992—; cons. colls. and industry. Contbr. articles to sci. jours.; inventor extractions with propylene carbonate, 1975; producer: TV series The Psychology of Interpersonal of Interpersonal Behavior, 1974. Co-chmn. Daniel Morgan Restoration Com., 1986-88; vice chmn. Spartanburg County Pollution Control Authority, 1970-74; bd. dirs. S.C. Lung Assn., Spartanburg, 1970-75, Communications Svcs., Inc., 1977-80; sect. maj. United Way, 1975-77. 1st lt. U.S. Army, 1958-60. Recipient Jefferson award S.C. Acad. Sci., 1969; recipient 1st prize graphics div. 2d Edit. Art Contest, 1971, 2d and 3d prizes Lawson's Fork Creek Photography Contest, 1978; USPHS grantee; NSF grantee. Mem. Am. Chem. Soc., Nat. Assn. Gifted Children, Assn. Ednl. Communications and Tech., Phi Beta Kappa. Methodist. Home: 131 Henry Ct Spartanburg SC 29306-6901 Office: Wofford College 429 N Church St Spartanburg SC 29303-3663

STEPHENS, BOBBY WAYNE, nursing home administrator; b. Booneville, Ark., Dec. 4, 1944; s. Cecil L. and Estella L. Stephens; m. Mary Beth Carolan, Nov. 27, 1966; children: Travis Wayne, Matthew Samuel. BS in Bus. Adminstrn., U. Ark., 1969; postgrad., Yale U., 1986, 89, U. Pa., 1984. Acct. Beverly Enterprises, central div., Ft. Smith, Ark., 1969-71, v.p., 1971-75, exec. v.p., 1975-80, pres., 1980-89, sr. v.p., ex. v.p., 1989—; bd. mem. Nat. Coun. Health Care Facilities, Washingotn, 1982-85, Tex. Nursing Home Assn., Austin, 1982-84, Ark. Nursing Home Assn., Little Rock, 1980-82, Ark. Health Care Assn., Little Rock, 1989; advisor Health Care Steering Com., Congressman Beryl Anthony, Washington, 1987. Bd. mem. Ark. Gerontol. Soc., Little Rock, 1985-88, Project Compassion, Ft. Smith, 1985-87, Mgmt. Dept. Adv. Bd. U. Ark., Fayetteville, 1986-89, Ark. Devel. Fin. Authority, Little Rock, 1985—. Recipient Corp. Humanitarian award Ark. Office Volunteerism, Little Rock, 1984, Extra Mile award Central Ark. Area on Aging, Little Rock, 1986. Mem. Fort Smith C. of C. (bd. mem. 1984-86), Hardscrabble Country Club, Town Club. Republican. Presbyterian. Avocations: water and snow skiing, jogging, reading, golf. Home: 3700 Free Ferry Rd Fort Smith AR 72903 Office: Beverly Enterprises 5111 Rogers Ave Ste 40 - A Fort Smith AR 72919*

STEPHENS, DONALD JOSEPH, retired architect; b. Albany, N.Y., Apr. 29, 1918; s. Arthur Everett and Evangeline (Cosgrave) S.; m. Jean E. Brown Clausen, Apr. 15, 1950; children—Christian, Linda, Suzanne, Marc, Paul, Thomas. B.Arch., Rensselaer Polytechnic Inst., 1940. Archtl. engr. Watervliet Arsenal, 1941-44; assoc. architect Henry L. Blatner, Albany, 1946-56; pres. Stephens Assocs. P.C., Architects, Albany, 1956-84; mng. architect C.T. Male Assocs PC, 1985-87; mem. N.Y. State Bd. Architecture, 1976-85. Chmn. Taconic Valley Planning Assn., 1967-72; chmn. Town of Berlin (N.Y.) Planning Bd., 1960-79; pres. bd. edn. Berlin Central Sch. Dist., 1971-72. Served with USN, 1944-46, PTO. Fellow AIA (regional dir. 1974-76); mem. N.Y. State Assn. Architects (Matthew Del Gaudio award 1971). Home: PO Box 301 Berlin NY 12022-0301

STEPHENS, DONALD R(ICHARDS), banker; b. San Francisco, June 28, 1938; s. Donald Lewis and Anona Marie (O'Leary) S.; m. Christina Brinkman, Sept. 11, 1971 (div. 1996); children: Lane B., Justin H., Nicholas W., Adam H. BS, U. So. Calif., 1961; JD, Hastings Coll., 1969. Pres. Campodonico & Stephens, San Francisco, 1963-65; pres., owner Union Investment Co., San Francisco, 1966-69; assoc. Law Offices of Louis O. Kelso, 1969-72; individual practice law, San Francisco Co., 1972-77; pres. D.R. Stephens & Co., San Francisco, 1976—; chmn., CEO Bank of San Francisco Co., 1978-91, also bd. dirs.; chmn. N.Am. Trust REIT, also bd. dirs.; bd. dirs. Charles Schwab Family of Funds Inc., Skouras Pictures. Bd. dirs. Bay Area Coun.; trustee St. Francis Meml. Hosp., San Francisco, 1976-82; mem.

policy adv. bd. U. Calif., 1985—. Mem. Urban Land Inst., World Bus. Coun., Bohemian Club, Calif. Club. Republican. Presbyterian. Avocations: tennis, golf.

STEPHENS, DOUGLAS KIMBLE, chemical engineer; b. Monticello, Ark., June 22, 1939; s. Vardeman King and Lila Belle (McMurtery) S.; m. Mary Joan John, Dec. 4, 1957; children: Kenneth R., David B. BSChemE, U. Ark., 1962. Registered profl. engr., Tex.; cert. safety profl. Sr. engr., safety supt. Monsanto Co., Alvin, Tex., 1967-73, mfg. supt., 1973-78; ptnr. Robert T. Bell & Assocs., Houston, 1978-80; v.p. Tech. Inspection Svcs., Inc., Houston, 1980-84, Bell & Stephens Labs., Inc., Houston, 1980-84; pres. Stephens Engring. Labs., Inc., Webster, Tex., 1984—; pres., CEO N.Am. Environ. Coalition, Inc., Webster, 1993—; project dir./chief engr. enviroGuard enviroFoam Project, 1994—. Contbr. articles to profl. publs. Capt. U.S. Army, 1962-67, Vietnam. Decorated Bronze Star, Air medal. Mem. ASTM (mem. coms., cons.), Am. Inst. Chem. Engrs. (sect. chmn. 1976-77), Am. Soc. Safety Engrs. (cons.), Tex. Soc. Profl. Engrs. (chpt. chmn. 1991-92, pres. 1990-91, Engr. of Yr. 1992), Nat. Assn. Corrosion Engrs. (mem. com. 1978-93, cons.), Nat. Assn. Environ. Profls., Am. Bd. Forensic Examiners. Methodist. Achievements include development of ethylene cracking furnaces decoking process, waste oil recovery process, propylene storage process, depropanizer computor control process, differential thermal analysis methods for fusion bond epoxy coatings extent of cure. Home: 1116 Deats Rd Dickinson TX 77539-4426 Office: 100 E Nasa Blvd Ste 203 Webster TX 77598-5330

STEPHENS, EDWARD CARL, communications educator, writer; b. L.A., July 27, 1924; s. Carl Edward and Helen Mildred (Kerner) S.; children: Edward, Sarah, Matthew. AB, Occidental Coll., 1947; MS, Northwestern U., 1955. Advt. exec. Dancer-Fitzgerald-Sample Inc., N.Y.C., 1955-64; prof. Medill Sch. Journalism, Northwestern U., Evanston, Ill., 1964-76; prof., chmn. dept. advt. S.I. Newhouse Sch. Pub. Communications, Syracuse U., N.Y., 1976-80, dean, 1980-89; prof. comms. S.I. Newhouse Sch. Pub. Comms. Syracuse U., 1990-92, prof. emeritus, 1992—; cons. Foote, Cone & Belding Communications. Author: (novels) A Twist of Lemon, 1958, One More Summer, 1960, Blow Negative!, 1962, Roman Joy, 1965, A Turn in the Dark Wood, 1968, The Submariner, 1974, (nonfiction) Submarines, 1960. Mem. George Polk Awards Com. With USN, 1943-46, 1950-53. Capt. USNR (ret.). Decorated Purple Heart. Mem. Am. Acad. Advt. (pres. 1976-77), Assn. Edn. Journalism and Mass Communication, Authors League, Century Club of Syracuse, Alpha Tau Omega. Episcopalian.

STEPHENS, ELTON BRYSON, bank executive, service and manufacturing company executive; b. Clio, Ala., Aug. 4, 1911; s. James Nelson and Clara (Stuckey) S.; m. Alys Varian Robinson, Nov. 28, 1935; children: James Thomas, Jane Stephens Comer, Elton Bryson Jr., Dell Stephens Brooke. B.A., Birmingham-So. Coll., 1932, LLD (hon.), 1977; LL.B., U. Ala., 1936, LHD (hon.), 1990; grad., Advanced Mgmt. Program, Harvard U., 1960; LHD (hon.), Faulkner U., 1992. Bar: Ala. 1936. Regional dir. Keystone Readers Service, Birmingham, 1937-43; partner, then founder and pres. Mil. Service Co., Inc. (predecessor of EBSCO Industries, Inc.), Birmingham, 1943-58; founder EBSCO Industries, Inc., and affiliates, 1958; since pres., chmn. bd. EBSCO Industries, Inc., and affiliates, Birmingham; now chmn. bd., CEO EBSCO Industries, Inc. and affiliates, Birmingham; bd. dirs. R.A. Brown Ins. Agy. Ltd., 1966—; chmn. EBSCO Investment Svc., Inc., 1959—, Canebsco Subscription Svc., Toronto, Ont., Can., 1972—; founder, chmn. Ala. Bancorp divsn. The Citizens Bank Leeds, The Fort Deposit Bank, Highland Bank; founder EBSCO Savs. and Profit Sharing Trust, Ala. Bancorp Savs. and Profit Sharing Trust. Mem. fin. and investment com., past chmn. bd. trustees, chmn. exec. com. Birmingham-So. Coll.; trustee So. Research Inst.; former pres., chmn. bd. trustee Birmingham Met. YMCA; mem. bd., chmn. econ. pension com. Tenn.-Tombigbee Waterway Authority; founder % Clubs of Ala., founder United Art Fund/Met. Arts Council; vice chmn., bd. dirs., hon. chmn.; vice chmn. Am. Coun. Arts, 1990-95. Elton B. Stephens Expressway named in his honor, 1970, Elton B. Stephens Library, Clio, 1979. Mem. Birmingham C. of C. (bd. dirs.), The Club, Birmingham Press Club, Summit Club, Mountain Brook Country Club (Ala.), Rotary (pres. Homewood, Ala. 1979-80, Paul Harris fellow), Ala. Symphonic Assn. (chmn., CEI, prin. fund raiser), Ala. Acad. Honor, Alpha Tau Omega (past chmn. nat. found.), Omicron Delta Kappa, Phi Alpha Delta. Methodist. *Invest/reinvest earnings to create employment/profits for growth/expansion. Support worthwhile projects including but not limited to: education, health, religion, needy, cultural, arts, boys/girls clubs, law enforcement, conservation, nature, water resources. Share profits and protect the welfare and health of your employees with a major catastrophic medical program. These philosophies built a company I started in 1943 with capital of $5,000 and sales under $1,000,000 with under 20 employees to annual sales of over $860,000,000 and 3400 employees with adequate capital from earnings and borrowing to continue growth. EBSCO operates world wide.*

STEPHENS, FREDERICK OSCAR, surgeon and educator; b. Sydney, N.S.W., Australia, Aug. 7, 1927; s. Hedley Loxton and Dorys Louise (Reed) S.; m. Alison Barclay Lipp, Dec. 24, 1959 (div.); children: Jennifer Louise, Robert Bruce Henry, Gillian Dorys Janet, Frederick William Peter, Katriona Alison. M.B.B.S., U. Sydney, 1951, MD, M. Surgery, 1970. Med. and surg. intern U. Sydney Teaching Hosps., 1951-53; surg. resident Met. Hosp., London, 1954-55; prosector in anatomy Royal Coll. Surgeons, London, 1955-56; registrar, sr. registrar in surgery profl. unit Royal Infirmary, Aberdeen, Scotland, 1957-60; Welcome traveling fellow, Joyce rsch. fellow U. Oreg. Med. Sch., Portland, 1960-61; assoc. prof. surgery U. Sydney Teaching Hosps., 1961-88, prof. and head dept. surgery, 1988-94; cons. in surg. oncology and melanoma surgery Royal Prince Alfred Hosp./Sydney Hosp., 1994—; Fulbright fellow and vis. prof. surgery U. Calif., San Francisco, 1969-70; past bd. dirs. Cancer Therapy; past chmn. Kanematsu Rsch. Labs., Royal Prince Alfred Hosp.; surger to H.M. The Queen, The Prince of Wales, The Duke of Edinburgh, U.S. Pres. Johnson, Shah of Persia, The Crown Prince of Japan, The King and Queen of Nepal during their visits to Australia, 1966, 71, 73, 77; vis. prof./vis. lectr. numerous internat. and nat. meetings throughout the world. Mng. editor Internat. Jour. Regional Cancer Treatment, 1988—; contbr. over 200 articles to profl. jours. Mem. Order of Australia, H.M. the Queen, 1992. Fellow ACS, Royal Coll. Surgeons of Edinburgh, Royal Australiasian Coll. Surgeons, Internat. Soc. for Regional Cancer Therapy (pres. 1991-95); mem. Surg. Rsch. Soc. Australasia (pres. 1971-72), Sydney Hospitallers (pres. 1977-78). Mem. Uniting Ch. of Australia. Avocations: horseback riding and sports, long-distance running, carpentry, inventing. Home: 16 Inkerman St, Mosman Sydney NSW 2088, Australia Office: University of Sydney, Dept of Surgery, Sydney NSW 2006, Australia

STEPHENS, GEORGE EDWARD, JR., lawyer; b. Lawrence, Kans., Mar. 26, 1936; s. George Edward and Mary Helen (Houghton) S.; m. Gretel Geiser, Dec. 31, 1965; children: Thaddeus Geiser, Edward Houghton, Mary Schoentgen. Student, U. Colo., Boulder, 1954-57, U. Colo. Sch. Medicine, Denver, 1957-59; LLB, Stanford U., 1962. Bar: Calif. 1963, U.S. Dist. Ct. (cen. dist.) Calif. 1963, U.S. Ct. Appeals (9th cir.) 1971. Law clk. to judge U.S. Dist. Ct., Los Angeles, 1962-64; assoc. ptnr. Pollock & Palmer, Los Angeles, 1964-69; ptnr. Gates, Morris, Merrill & Stephens, Los Angeles, 1969-72, Paul, Hastings, Janofsky & Walker, Los Angeles, 1972—; Mem. Coordinating Coun. on Lawyer Competence, Conf. Chief Justices, 1983-86; chmn. probate sect. L.A. County Bar Assn., 1979-80. Nat. chmn. Stanford (Calif.) U. Law Fund Quad Program, 1980-87; mem. bd. visitors Stanford Law Sch., 1982-85; founder mus. Contemporary Art, L.A., 1982; bd. dirs. Pacific Oaks Coll., 1990—. Recipient Stanford Assocs. award, 1982. Fellow Am. Bar Found., Am. Coll. Trust and Estates Counsel, Internat. Acad. Probate and Trust, Fellows of Contemporary Art (bd. dirs. 1991-92); mem. ABA (chmn. standing com. specialization 1979-82, standing com. lawyer referral svcs., 1969-76, consortium delivery legal svcs. and the pub., 1979-82), Stanford Law Soc. (pres. 1972-73). Episcopalian. Clubs: Chancery (Los Angeles), Annandale Golf (Pasadena, Calif.), Valley Hunt (Pasadena). Office: Paul Hastings Janofsky & Walker 555 S Flower St Fl 23D Los Angeles CA 90071-2300

STEPHENS, GERALD D., insurance company executive; b. Peoria, Ill., June 17, 1932; m. Helen Marie Davis. BBA, with honors in Ins., U. Wis., 1955. V.p. H.O. Stephens & Sons, Inc., Peoria, 1958-65; pres., dir. RLI Ins. Co., Peoria, 1965—; bd. dir. numerous businesses and ins. agys, Jefferson TR& Savs. Bank. Bd. dir. adv. bd. St. Francis Hosp., 1983—; bd. dirs. Peoria Econs. Devel. Commn. 2d lt. U.S. Army, 1955-58. Mem. Peoria C. of C., Nat. Soc. CPCU (past pres. Cen. Ill. chpt.), Creve Coeur (Ill.) Club, Country Club of Peoria, Beta Theta Pi. Home: 493 E High Point Dr Peoria IL 61614 Office: R L I Corp 9025 N Lindbergh Dr Peoria IL 61615*

STEPHENS, JACKSON THOMAS, investment executive; b. Prattsville, Ark., Aug. 9, 1923; s. Albert Jackson and Ethel Rebecca (Pumphrey) S.; children: Jackson Thomas, Warren Amerine. Grad., Columbia Mil. Acad., Tenn., 1941; student, U. Ark., 1941-43; B.S., U.S. Naval Acad., 1946. Pres. Stephens, Inc., Little Rock, from 1957; chmn. Stephens, Inc., 1986—. Trustee U. Ark., 1948-57. Office: Stephens Inc PO Box 3507 111 Center St Little Rock AR 72201*

STEPHENS, JAMES LINTON, mechanical engineer; b. Stamford, Conn., Nov. 1, 1956; s. James Regis and Beatrice Helen (Johnson) S.; m. Laura Lynn Holmes, Sept. 6, 1980; children: Mark Linton, Jaimee Lee, Matthew James. BS in Mech. Engring., BS in Biomed. Engring., Northwestern U., 1980. Registered profl. engr., Wis. Mfg. engr. Parker Hannifin Corp., Des Plaines, Ill., 1980-81, St. Mary's, Ohio, 1981-84; mfg. engr. Ohmeda divsn. BOC Group, Madison, Wis., 1984-91, sr. mfg. engr. Ohmeda divsn., 1991-95; sr. engr. Case Corp., Racine, Wis., 1995—. Mem. steering com. for engring. profl. devel. program U. Wis., Madison, 1994. Ill. State scholar, 1975. Mem. Soc. Mfg. Engrs. (treas. Madison chpt. 1984-85, 2d vice chmn. 1985-86, 1st vice chmn. 1986-87, chmn. 1987-88, certification chmn. 1988—, fundraiser 1987—, seminar and workshop leader 1987—, Chmn. plaque 1988). Avocations: swimming, tennis, reading science fiction. Office: Case Corp 7000 Durand Ave Racine WI 53406

STEPHENS, JAMES T., publishing executive; b. 1939; married. BA in Bus. Adminstrn., Yale U., 1961; MBA, Harvard U., 1964. With Ebsco Industries Inc., Birmingham, Ala., 1961—, asst. v.p., 1966-67, v.p., 1967-70, exec. v.p., from 1970, now pres., also bd. dirs. Office: Ebsco Industries Inc PO Box 1943 Top of Oak Mountain Hwy 280 Birmingham AL 35201

STEPHENS, JAY B., lawyer; b. Akron, Iowa, Nov. 5, 1946; s. Lyle R. and Marie (Borchers) S. BA magna cum laude, Harvard U., 1968, JD cum laude, 1973. Bar: D.C. 1973. Assoc. Wilmer, Cutler & Pickering, Washington, 1973-74; asst. spl. prosecutor Watergate Spl. Prosecution Force, Washington, 1974-75; assoc. gen. counsel Overseas Pvt. Investment Corp., Washington, 1976-77; asst. U.S. atty. Dept. Justice, Washington, 1977-81, spl. counsel to asst. atty. gen., 1981-83, dep. assoc. atty. gen., 1983-85, assoc. dep. atty. gen., 1985-86; dep. counsel to Pres. Reagan, 1986-88; U.S. atty. for D.C. Office U.S. Atty., 1988-93; ptnr. Pillsbury Madison & Sutro, Washington, 1993—. Contbr. articles to profl. publs. Knox fellow Oxford, Eng., 1968-69. Mem. D.C. Bar Assn., Supreme Ct. Bar Assn., Asst. U.S. Atty. Assn., Phi Beta Kappa. Republican. Presbyterian. Home: 8312 Simsbury Pl Alexandria VA 22308-1563 Office: Pillsbury Madison & Sutro 1050 Connecticut Ave NW Washington DC 20036-5303

STEPHENS, JENNIFER SUE, law librarian; b. Denton, Tex., June 5, 1964; d. Elvis Clay and Joyce (Perkins) S. BBA, U. North Tex., 1986; MLS, Tex. Woman's U., 1990. Clk. Voertmans, Inc., Denton, Tex., 1985-86, U. North Tex., Denton, 1986-87; student asst. libr. Tex. Woman's U., Denton, 1988-89, grad. asst. libr., 1989-90; law libr. Dresser Industries, Inc., Dallas, 1990—. Mem. Am. Assn. Law Librs., Dallas Assn. LAw Librs. (chair tech. sect. 1993-95), Southwestern Assn. Law Librs. Independent. Methodist. Avocations: computers, books, music, woodwork, bicycling.

STEPHENS, JERRY WAYNE, librarian, library director; b. Birmingham, Ala., Sept. 10, 1949; s. William Larkin and Odell (Kerr) S.; m. Lisa Brown, June 2, 1972; children—Jeramy Wayne, Elizabeth Ashley, John Larkin. B.S. in Acctg., U. Ala.-Birmingham, 1974, M.B.A., 1976; M.L.S., U. Ala., 1977, Ph.D. in Adminstrn. Higher Edn., 1982. Svc. mgr. Hammond Organ Studios, Birmingham, 1973-74; acct. Mervyn Sterne Libr., U. Ala., Birmingham, 1974-75, asst. to dir., 1975-76, asst. dir., 1976-85, libr., dir., 1985—; interim fiscal officer Univ. Coll. U. Ala., Birmingham, 1982, interim asst. v.p. for acad. affairs, 1989-91; v.p. for acad. affairs, 1989-91; vice chmn. Network Acad. Librs., 1985-86, 95-96, chmn., 1986-88; cons. Birmingham Pub. Libr., 1977—; cons. Southeastern Libr. Assn., Atlanta, 1979-80; bd. dirs. Southeastern Libr. Network, treas., 1992-93, chmn., 1993-94. Contbr. articles to profl. publs. Sponsored exec. United Way, Birmingham, 1978, sr. exec., 1982; foster parent Dept. Pensions and Securities, Birmingham, 1982-83; elder Homewood Cumberland Presbyn. Ch., Birmingham, 1982-84, 88-90. With USN, 1972-73. Named one of Outstanding Young Men Am., U.S. Jaycees, 1978, 79. Mem. ALA, SE Libr. Assn., Ala. Libr. Assn. (treas. 1977-78), Am Mgmt. Assn. Avocations: camping; softball. Home: 2621 Kemp Ct Birmingham AL 35226-1982 Office: U Ala-Birmingham Mervyn H Sterne Libr University Station Birmingham AL 35294

STEPHENS, JOE ALAN, investigative reporter; b. Mariemont, Ohio, July 26, 1959; s. Ken and Wilma (Vanover) S.; m. Dru Sefton. Student, De Pauw U., 1977-78; BA in English, Miami U., Oxford, Ohio, 1981. Editor-in-chief Clermont Sun, Batavia, Ohio, 1981-83; investigative reporter State Jour.-Register, Springfield, Ill., 1983-87; investigative and spl. projects reporter Kansas City (Mo.) Star, 1987—. Recipient George Polk award L.I. U., 1994, Fred Moen Sweepstakes award Mo. Assoc. Press Mng. Editors Assn., Columbia, 1994, Pub. Svc. award Soc. Profl. Journalists, 1993. Mem. Investigative Reporters and Editors. Achievements include investigation of public corruption, organized crime, building safety, charity fraud and child abuse. Home: 102 E 69th Ter Kansas City MO 64113 Office: Kansas City Star 1729 Grand Blvd Kansas City MO 64108

STEPHENS, JOHN FRANK, association executive, researcher; b. Malone, N.Y., Nov. 9, 1949; s. J. Frank and Marjorie (Drew) S.; m. Smaroula Georgina Paraskevoudakis, Sept. 1, 1989; 1 child, Georgina Elizabeth. B.A., Harpur Coll., 1971; M.A., SUNY-Binghamton, 1973, Ph.D., 1977. Research assoc. Fernand Braudel Ctr., SUNY-Binghamton, 1977; asst. to provost U. Md., College Park, 1978; vis. instr. St. Mary's Coll. Md., St. Mary's City, 1978-79; dir. Alexandria Regional Preservation Office, Va., 1980-83; exec. dir. Am. Studies Assn., College Park, Md., 1983—; cons. (in field); reviewer U.S. Dept. Interior, NEH, HEW, USIA, PBS, Washington, 1983—. Author: (with Immanuel Wallerstein) Libraries and Our Civilizations, 1978, (with others) Archaeology in Urban America: A Search for Pattern Process, 1982. Exec. bd. dirs. Nat. Humanities Alliance, 1992—. Fulbright-Hays fellow, 1974-75; Spanish Govt. fellow, 1974-75. Mem. Am. Studies Assn., Fulbright Assn. Home: 4631 Bettswood Dr Olney MD 20832-2042 Office: Am Studies Assn 1120 19th St Ste 301 Washington DC 20036

STEPHENS, LAURENCE DAVID, JR., linguist, financial executive; b. Dallas, July 26, 1947; s. Laurence D. Sr. and Amy Belle (Schickram) S.; m. Susan Leigh Foutz, Apr. 16, 1988; 1 child, Laurence David III. MA, Stanford U., 1972, PhD, 1976. Vis. fellow Yale U., New Haven, Conn., summer 1979; rsch. fellow U. S.C., Columbia, 1980; asst. prof. U. N.C., Chapel Hill, 1982-88, assoc. prof., 1989—; CEO Stephens and Family Investments, Dallas, 1994—. Co-author: Two Studies in Latin Phonology, 1977, Language and Metre, 1984, The Prosody of Greek Speech, 1994; editor ann. vol. L'Année Philologique, 1987-92; contbr. over 70 articles to profl. jours. Mem. Univ. Pk. Cmty. League, Park Cities Hist. Soc., Nat. Trust for Hist. Preservation, Washington, 1989—, Dallas Opera Guild, 1992—, The Dallas Symphony Assn. Ann. Fund, Metro. Opera Guild, N.Y.C., 1992—. Recipient L'Année Philologique, NEH, 1987-89, 89-91, 91-93. Mem. Am. Inst. Archaeology, Am. Philol. Assn., Greek and Latin Linguistic Assn. (chmn. 1987-92), Linguistic Soc. Am., N.Y. Acad. Scis., Indogermanische Gesellschaft, Société Internationale de Bibliographie Classique, Sigma Xi. Achievements include discovery of language university regularities concerning labiovelar phonemes, laws of palatalization, the law of catathesis in Greek (pitch lowering), and grammatical and semantic constraints on discontinuous constituency; co-developer of Justeson-Stephens probability distribution for chance cognates between unrelated languages, Justeson-Stephens probability distribution of the numers of vowels, consonants, and total phonological inventory size in the languages of the world; research on the law of the quantitative form of diachronic polysemy growth, sematic universals of aspect and modality, universals of writing systems and their evolution. Home: 3319 Greenbrier Dr Dallas TX 75225-4818 Office: Univ NC Chapel Hill Dept Classics CB # 3145 212 Murphey Hall Chapel Hill NC 27599 Address: Stephens Family Investments 4020 Colgate Ave Dallas TX 75225-5425

STEPHENS, LOUIS CORNELIUS, JR., insurance executive; b. Dunn, N.C., Dec. 19, 1921; s. Louis Cornelius and Agnes (Warren) S.; m. Mary Adams, Sept. 6, 1952; children: Michael W., Mary A., Louis Cornelius III, Anne M., Suzanne G., Joan R., Melanie L., Peter W. B.S., U. N.C., 1942; M.B.A., Harvard U., 1947. With Pilot Life Ins. Co., Greensboro, N.C., 1949-86; v.p., treas. Pilot Life Ins. Co., 1965-68, sr. v.p., 1968-70, exec. v.p., 1970-71, pres., chief adminstrv. officer, 1971-73, pres., chief exec. officer, 1973-86, also dir.; pres., dir. JP Investment Mgmt. Co.; v.p., dir. Jefferson-Pilot Corp.; dir. Jefferson-Pilot & So. Fire & Casualty Cos., Jefferson-Pilot Title Ins. Co.; treas. JP Growth Fund, Inc. Past pres. United Cmty. Svcs.; bd. dirs. Excellence Fund U. N.C. at Greensboro, N.C. Leadership Inst., Research Triangle Inst., Salem Coll. and Acad., Ecumenical Inst. Belmont Abbey Coll.; chmn. Research Triangle Found.; vice-chmn. The Duke Endowment. Served with USNR, World War II. Office: Jefferson-Pilot Corp PO Box 21008 Greensboro NC 27420

STEPHENS, MARJORIE JOHNSEN, lawyer; b. Dallas, Aug. 29, 1949; d. Joseph Cornelius Stephens and Marjorie Marie Johnsen; m. Andrew N. Meyercord, Dec. 27, 1971 (div. Oct. 1985); children: Andrew J., Ben, Lee. BA, Tufts U., Medford, Mass., 1971; JD, So. Meth. U., Dallas, 1974, LLM in Taxation, 1981. Bar: Tex. 1974; bd. cert. in estate planning and probate, 1981, 83, 93. Assoc. litigation and taxation Akin Gump Strauss Hauer & Feld, Dallas, 1974-79; ptnr. estate planning and tax Meyercord, Stephens & Bartholow, Dallas, 1979-83; assoc. Copeland & Almquist, Dallas, 1984-86; pvt. practice Dallas, 1986-87, 88—; head tax sect. Smith, Underwood & Hunter, Dallas, 1987-88; law instr. Stanley Kaplan CPA Rev. Course, Dallas, 1992-94; presenter Fed. tax workshops in estate planning, divorce, taxation and forensic acctg., Dallas, 1992; lectr. Dallas chpt. CPAs, 1988-95. Mem. ABA, Tex. Bar Assn., Dallas Bar Assn. Office: 5956 Sherry Ln # 1413 Dallas TX 75225

STEPHENS, MARTHA FOSTER, advertising executive; b. Lansing, Mich., Dec. 4, 1961; d. Richard Bailey and Gretchen (Meyer) Foster; m. Mark Burgis Stephens, Apr. 11, 1987; children: Emily Kaitlynn, Matthew Foster. BA in English, Mich. State U., 1984; postgrad., Wayne State U. Mem. editorial staff Better Investing, Royal Oak, Mich., 1986-88; with communications Holtzman and Silverman, Farmington Hills, Mich., 1988-89; tech. writer, intern Unisys, Plymouth, Mich., 1989; dir. corp. svcs. and advt. Nat. Assn. Investors Corp., Royal Oak, 1989—. Mem. Nat. Investor Rels. Inst. (sec. 1991-92, v.p. mem. 1992-93, v.p. programs 1993-94, pres. 1994-95, bd. dirs. 1995—). Avocations: computer layout and design, running. Office: Nat Assn Investors Corp PO Box 220 Royal Oak MI 48068-0220

STEPHENS, MARTHA LOCKHART, art educator; b. Corpus Christi, Tex., Jan. 3, 1940; d. Hugh Rairdon and Amelia Virginia (McRee) Lockhart; m. David George Hmiel, June 10, 1961 (div. Oct. 1969); m. William Melvin Stephens Jr., June 2, 1971. BA in English Lit., Colo. Coll., 1961; MA in English Lit., U. Ariz., 1967; BFA in Drawing, U. Tex., San Antonio, 1989. Cert. tchr., Tex. English tchr. Colo., Ala., N.Y., Va. and Calif. pub. schs., 1961-68, San Antonio Ind. Sch. Dist., 1968-73; English tchr. North East Ind. Sch. Dist., San Antonio, 1973-82, level chmn. English, 1974-82, chmn. English lit. selection com., 1977, art and creative writing tchr., 1981-85, art tchr., head dept., 1986-94; presenter in field; cons., tour guide, presenter workshops San Antonio Mus. Art, 1983-86; cons., docent McNay Art Mus., San Antonio, 1987; mem. adv. bd. San Antonio Coun. Tchrs. English, 1980. One woman show Art Ctr. Gallery, 1988; two person show at Chapman Grad. Ctr., Trinity U., 1979; numerous group exhbns., including Tex. Soc. Sculptors, 1979, NOW Art Show, San Antonio, 1980, Alternate Space Gallery, San Antonio, 1983, United Bank of Austin, 1985, U. Tex., San Antonio, 1986, N.E. Ind. Sch. Dist., 1986, others; authorized biographer Dorothy Dehner; contbr. articles to profl. publs. Sponsor/recipient Gold Crown award Columbia Sch. Press Assn., 1992, citation for excellence Scholastic Art and Writing Awards, 1992, State Champion award Tex. H.S. Press Assn., 1990, 91, 92. Mem. NEA, Tex. State Tchrs.' Assn. (pres. Tchrs. of English sect. region 10 1979), North East Tchrs.' Assn., Nat. Art Edn. Assn., Tex. Art Edn. Assn. (regional rep. 1989-93, Merit award 1986, rep. region V 1989-93, capt. region V 1991-93), San Antonio Art Edn. Assn. (pres. 1990-92, Svc. award 1993, adv. bd. 1988-93). Democrat. Episcopalian. Avocations: painting, writing, gardening, cooking, computers. Home: 10935 Whisper Valley St San Antonio TX 78230-3617

STEPHENS, MICHAEL DEAN, hospital administrator; b. Salt Lake City, May 1, 1942; married. B, Columbia U., 1966, MHA, 1970. Adminstrv. resident Mt. Sinai Med. Ctr., N.Y.C., 1969-70; asst. administr. Greenville (S.C.) Gen. Hosp., 1970-71, assoc. adminstr., 1971-72, adminstr., 1972-75; pres. Hoag Meml. Hosp.-Presbyn., Newport Beach, Calif., 1975—. Mem. Am. Coll. Healthcare Execs. Home: 900 Alder Pl Newport Beach CA 92660-4121 Office: Hoag Meml Hosp Presbyn PO Box 6100 Newport Beach CA 92658-6100*

STEPHENS, NORVAL BLAIR, JR., marketing consultant; b. Chgo., Nov. 20, 1928; s. Norval Blair and Ethel Margaret (Lewis) S.; m. Diane Forst, Sept. 29, 1951; children: Jill E., John G., Sandra J. (dec.), Katherine B., James N. BA, DePauw U., 1951; MBA, U. Chgo., 1959. Asst. to v.p. ops. Walgreen Drug Co., Chgo., 1953-56; with Needham, Harper Worldwide (formerly Needham, Harper & Steers), Chgo., 1956-86; v.p. Needham, Harper Worldwide (formerly Needham, Harper & Steers), 1964-70, sr. v.p., 1970-72, exec. v.p. internat., 1972-74; exec. v.p., mng. dir. Needham, Harper Worldwide (formerly Needham, Harper & Steers), N.Y.C., 1974-75; exec. v.p. Chgo. office Needham, Harper & Steers, 1975-82, exec. v.p. internat., 1982-86; also dir.; pres. Deltacom, N.Y.C., 1971-76; pres. Norval Stephens Co., 1987—. Bd. advisors Barrington Area Arts Coun., 1985-86, bd. dirs., 1987-89; bd. dirs. N.W. Cmty. Hosp. Found., Arlington Heights, 1976-89, vice chmn., 1987-89; bd. dirs. Harper Coll. Ednl. Found., Palatine, Ill., 1977-86, pres., 1980-86; bd. dirs. Barrington Area Devel. Coun., 1978—, pres., 1994—; bd. visitors, dir. alumni bd. DePauw U., 1979-83, pres., 1981-83, trustee, 1983—, vice chmn., 1995—. With USMCR, 1951-53. Named Young Man of Yr., Arlington Heights Jaycees, 1964; recipient Rector award DePauw U., 1976, Old Gold Goblet award for outstanding svc. DePauw U., 1994. Mem. Internat. Advt. Assn. (v.p. Midwest chpt. 1986-87), Am. Mgmt. Assn., Am. Mktg. Assn., Internat. Fedn. Advt. Agys. (exec. dir. 1988—), U. Chgo. Alumni Assn., DePauw Alumni Assn. (pres. 1977-79), Phi Beta Kappa, Delta Tau Delta (bd. dirs. edn. found. 1987—, vice chmn. 1994-95, chmn. 1995—, 2d v.p. Arch chpt. 1988-90, 1st v.p. 1990-92, pres. 1992-94). Republican. Methodist. Home: 107 Fox Hunt Trl Barrington IL 60010-3418 Office: 1450 American Ln Ste 1400 Schaumburg IL 60173-4973 *I view my life not as a passage but a daily renewing challenge: to be better; to be a better father, husband, brother, son; to return each day an honest day's work; to bear witness to my beliefs and my faith; to serve my fellowman. I seek a whole life and a life of rewarding parts, each a lesson and an experience.*

STEPHENS, OLIN JAMES, II, naval architect, yacht designer; b. N.Y.C., N.Y., Apr. 13, 1908; s. Roderick and Marguerite (Dulon) S.; m. Florence Reynolds, Oct. 21, 1930; children: Olin James III, Samuel R. Student, MIT, 1926-27; M.S. (hon.), Stevens Inst. Tech.; M.A. (hon.), Brown U.; D laurea ad honorem in Arch., Universario Architetura, Venice, Italy. Draftsman Henry J. Gielow, N.Y.C., 1927-28; draftsman P.L. Rhodes, N.Y.C., 1928; formed with Drake H. Sparkman firm of Sparkman & Stephens, 1928, Inc., 1929, chief designer, 1929-78; faculty mem. Royal Designers for Ind., London. Yachts designed include Dorade, 1930, Stormy Weather, 1934, Lulu, Ranger, (with W. Starling Burgess), 1937, Baruna, Blitzen, Goose, 1938, Vim, Gesture, 1939, Llanoria, 1948, Finisterre, 1954, Columbia, 1958, Constellation, 1964, Intrepid, 1967, Charisma, Morning Cloud, 1971, Courageous, 1974, Enterprise, 1977, Freedom, 1979, others; design agt. U.S. Navy, 1939—. Recipient David Taylor medal Soc. Naval Architects & Marine Engrs., 1959, Beppe Crowe award Internat. Yacht Racing Union, 1992, Gibbs Bros. medal NAS, 1993. Fellow Soc. Naval Architects and Marine Engrs. (David W. Taylor medal 1959); mem. Nat. Acad. Engring., Am. Boat and Yacht Coub. (pres. 1959, 60), N.Am. Yacht Racing Union, Offshore Racing Coun. (chmn. internat. tech. com. 1967-73, 76-69), N.Y. Yacht (tech. com. 1989—), Manhassett Bay Club (hon.), Cruising Club of Am. (tech. com. 1989—), Royal Ocean Racing Club (Eng.), Royal Thames

Yacht Club (London). Home: 80 Lyme Rd Apt 160 Kendal at Hanover Hanover NH 03755 Office: Sparkman and Stephens Inc 529 Fifth Ave New York NY 10017

STEPHENS, RICHARD BERNARD, natural resource company executive; b. Cambridge, Mass., Dec. 24, 1934; s. Theron Walter and Emma Marie (Bernard) S.; m. Anne Monique Devant, Oct. 18, 1958; children: Ann Marie, Claire Elizabeth, Jennifer Leslie. BA in Econs., Rice U., 1956; grad. exec. program bus. adminstrn., Columbia U., 1974. Landman Tenneco Oil Co., Lafayette, La., 1960-65; v.p. La. Land and Exploration Co., New Orleans, 1965-80; pres. Freeport Oil Co., New Orleans, 1980-84, McMoRan Oil and Gas Co., New Orleans, 1984-86; sr. v.p., dep. to chmn. Freeport-McMoRan, Inc., New Orleans, 1986—, office of the chmn., 1992-93; ret.; sr. advisor to chmn. Freeport, McMoran, Inc., New Orleans, 1993—. Mem. exec. bd., exec. com. New Orleans Boy Scouts Am., 1984—; trustee Mercy Hosp. New Orleans, 1977-81, La. Nature and Sci. Ctr., New Orleans, 1985-88; pres. Dad's Club St. Martin Protestant Episc. Sch., Metairie, La., 1975-76, sch. trustee, 1976-80; vice chmn. United Way New Orleans, 1976-77; dir. Eisenhower Ctr. U. New Orleans, 1989—, World Trade Ctr., 1992—; 1st lt. C.E., U.S. Army, 1956-60. Decorated The Sovereign Mil. Hospitaler Order of St. John of Jerusalem of Rhodes and of Malta, The Mil. and Hospitaler Order of St. Lazarus of Jerusalem. Mem. Nat. Gas Supply Assn. (steering com. 1982-86), Mid-Continent Oil and Gas Assn. (exec. com. 1984-88), Am. Petroleum Inst. (exec. com. 1985-88), La. Assn. Ind. Producers and Royalty Owners (dir. 1977-79), New Orleans Geol. Soc., Am. Assn. Petroleum Landmen, French-Am. C. of C., Assn. Rice Alumni (exec. bd. 1983-86, pres.-elect 1995—), Mil. Order World Wars, Rice Assocs., Brown Soc., Metairie Country Club, New Orleans Petroleum Club (bd. dirs. 1980-83), Commanderie Bordeaux sous Commanderie la Nouvelle Orleans, Pickwick Club, Laipro Wildcatters Club, Boston Club. Republican. Roman Catholic. Avocations: wildfowl wood collecting, long distance jogging, tennis, golf. Home: 800 Rue Bourbon Metairie LA 70005-3421 Office: Freeport-McMoRan Inc Box 611190004 1615 Poydras St New Orleans LA 70161

STEPHENS, ROBERT F., state supreme court chief justice; b. Covington, Ky., Aug. 16, 1927. Student, Ind. U.; LL.B., U. Ky., 1951. Bar: Ky. 1951. Asst. atty. Fayette County, Ky., 1964-69; judge Fayette County, 1969-75; atty. gen. Ky. Frankfort, 1976-79; justice Supreme Ct. Ky., Frankfort, 1979—, chief justice, 1982—; pres. Conf. of chief justices, 1992-93; chmn. Nat. Ctr. for State Ct., 1992-93. Staff: Ky. Law Jour. Bd. dirs. Nat. Assn. Counties, 1973-75; 1st pres. Ky. Assn. Counties; 1st chmn. Bluegrass Area Devel. Dist.; chmn. Ky. Heart Assn. Fund Drive, 1976-78. Served with USN, World War II. Named Outstanding Judge of Ky. Ky. Bar Assn., 1986, Outstnding County Judge, 1972; recipient Herbert Harley award Am. Judicature Soc. Mem. Order of Coif. Democrat. Office: Ky Supreme Ct 231 Capital Bldg 700 Capital Ave Frankfort KY 40601*

STEPHENS, STEVE ARNOLD, real estate broker; b. Irby, Cheshire, Eng., May 25, 1945; came to U.S., 1983; s. Harold Dennis George and Hilda Leonora (Howell) S.; m. Lynn Williams, Apr. 14, 1983. Student, Manchester U., Eng., 1967-69. Lic. pvt. detective, Ill. From cadet to detective Cheshire (Eng.) Police, 1961-69; acting detective sgt. Merseyside (Eng.) Police, 1969-75; acting sgt. Hampshire (Eng.) Police, 1975-77; retail store owner Horsham, West Sussex, Eng., 1977-79; pvt. detective Carratu Internat., London, 1979-83, D.A.C. Stephens, Aurora, Ill., 1983-86; broker Primus Coml., Oswego, Ill., 1986—. Bd. dirs. Aurora Crimestoppers, pres., 1995—. Recipient Republican Legion of Merit award. Mem. Nat. Assn. Realtors (CCIM), Comml. Investment Real Estate Inst. (cert., bd. dirs. Ill. CCIM chpt. 1992——, sec.-treas. 1994, v.p. 1995, pres. 1996), No. Ill. Comml. Assn. Realtors (dir. 1995—), Internat. Assn. Chiefs of Police, Ill. Assn. Realtors, Greater Aurora C. of C., Aurora Country Club. Avocations: travel, literature, golf. Home: 7 Saddlewood Ct Aurora IL 60506 Office: Primus Comml Real Estate 13 W Merchants Dr Oswego IL 60543-9456 *Work hard. Tell the truth and shame the Devil!.*

STEPHENS, STEVIE MARIE, psychotherapist; b. San Diego, Feb. 24, 1959. Student, Calif. State U., Fullerton, 1978-80; BA in Sociology with distinction, San Diego State U., 1983; M of Social Welfare, U. Calif., Berkeley, 1988. Lic. clin. social worker, Calif. Homefinder Indian Child Welfare Consortium, Escondido, Calif., 1986; alcoholism counselor, social work intern Harriet Street Ctr., San Francisco, 1986-87; social work intern psychiatry dept. San Francisco Gen. Hosp., 1988; social worker Adult Protective Svcs., Inc., San Diego, 1989-90, Naval Hosp., San Diego, 1990-91; psychotherapist, adminstr. in pvt. practice San Diego, 1993—. Vol. Learning Disabilities Assn. of Calif., San Diego, 1992-93, Battered Women's Svcs., San Diego, 1985-86; pres. coll. chpt. Am. Advt. Fedn., 1979; mem. Comms. Student Activities Coun., Fullerton, 1979. Recipient various naval awards; Kappa Kappa Gamma scholar. Mem. NASW, Calif. Soc. for Clin. Social Work, Am. Mensa, Ltd., Alpha Kappa Delta. Address: PO Box 98 La Jolla CA 92038-0098

STEPHENS, THOMAS M(ARON), education educator; b. Youngstown, Ohio, June 15, 1931; s. Thomas and Mary (Hanna) S.; m. Evelyn Kleshock, July 1, 1955. BS, Youngstown Coll., 1955; MEd, Kent State U., 1957; EdD, U. Pitts., 1966. Lic. psychologist, Ohio. Tchr. Warren (Ohio) public schs., 1955-57, Niles (Ohio) public schs., 1957-58; psychologist Montgomery County, Ohio, 1958-60; dir. gifted edn. Ohio Dept. Edn., Columbus, 1960-66; assoc. prof. edn. U. Pitts., 1966-70; prof. edn. Ohio State U., 1970—, chmn. dept. exceptional children, 1972-82, chmn. dept. human services edn., 1982-87, assoc. dean Coll. Edn., 1987-92, prof., 1987-92, prof. emeritus, 1992—; clin. prof. edn. U. Dayton, Ohio, 1993—; exec. dir. Sch. Study Coun. Ohio, Columbus, 1993—; mem. Higher Edn. Consortium for Spl. Edn., chmn., 1976-77; pub., pres. Cedars Press, Inc. Author: Directive Teaching of Children with Learning and Behavioral Handicaps, 2d edit, 1976, Implementing Behavioral Approaches in Elementary and Secondary Schools, 1975, Teaching Skills to Children with Learning and Behavioral Disorders, 1977, Teaching Children Basic Skills: A Curriculum Handbook, 1978, 2d edit., 1983, Social Skills In The Classroom, 1978, 2d edit., 1991, Teaching Mainstreamed Students, 1982, 2d edit., 1988, Social Behavior Assessment Scale, 1991; dir.: Jour. Sch. Psychology, 1965-75, 80—; exec. editor: The Directive Tchr.; assoc. editor: Spl. Edn. and Tchr. Edn., Techniques, Behavioral Disorders, Spl. Edn. and Remedial Edn.; contbr. articles to profl. jours. U.S. Office of Edn. fellow, 1964-65. Mem. APA, NASP (charter), State Dirs. for Gifted (pres. 1962-63), Coun. for Exceptional Children (gov., Tchr. Educator of Yr. tchr. edn. divsn. 1985), Coun. Children with Behavioral Disorders (pres. 1972-73). Home: 551 E Cooke Rd Columbus OH 43214 Office: Sch Study Coun of Ohio 665 E Granville Dublin Rd Columbus OH 43229

STEPHENS, WANDA BREWER, social services administrator, investor; b. Bolckow, Mo., Nov. 6, 1932; d. Perry Clark and Mary Carolyn (Fisher) Brewer; m. Lloyd Wesley Stephens, June 19, 1954; children: Ruth Ann, Susie Jo, John Allen, Donna Lynn. BS in home econs., U. Ark., 1954, MS, 1958. Cert. secondary edn. Home economics tchr. West Fork (Ark.) High Sch., 1954-58; pres. Devel. Child Care Assn., Fayetteville, Ark., 1971-74; pres., founding bd. Infant Devel. Ctr., Fayetteville, Ark., 1972-75, treas., 1975-81; pres. AAUW, Fayetteville, Ark., 1975-77; state treas. AAUW, 1996-98; edn. chmn., fin. com., admin. bd. Cen. United Meth. Ch., Fayetteville, Ark., 1976-79; pres. League of Women Voters, Fayetteville, Ark., 1979-83, Nat. Orgn. Women, Fayetteville, Ark., 1983-89; state legis. v.p. NOW, Fayetteville, 1985-90, 93-96; state pres. Nat. Orgn. Women Ark., Fayetteville, 1991-93; bd. sec., headstart Econ. Opportunity Agy., Fayetteville, 1969-70; treas. Mama's Milk Investment Club, 1970-72. Co-author: Bylaws for Economic Opportunity Agy., 1969; co-editor: Washington County, Ark., 1982. Fundraiser United Fund, 1972-75; polit. organizer NOW, 1986; treas. Washington County Dem. Women, 1990-92; organizer/staff/fund Women's Libr., 1982-91; cons./organizer Ctrl. Child Care Ctr., 1977-78. Recipient Internat. 4-H Youth Exch., 1953-54, Infant Devel. Ctr. Founders Plaque Univ. Ark., 1987; named Lay Person of Yr., Ctrl. United Meth. Ch., 1977. Mem. Mental Health Assn. (Community Svc. award 1972), AAUW (Edn. Found. fellowship 1984), ACLU (Susan B. Anthony award 1985), Ark. Women's Polit. Caucus (Uppity Woman award 1987, 92). Democrat. Methodist. Avocations: genealogy, reading, investing, producing cmty. access TV. Home: 1177 E Ridgeway Dr Fayetteville AR 72701-2612

STEPHENS, WARREN A., banking executive. BA, Washington & Lee U., 1979; MBA, Wake Forest U., 1981. V.p. corp. fin. dept. Stephens Inc., Little Rock, 1981-86, pres., CEO, 1986—; also bd. dirs. Stephens Inc. Office: Stephens Inc Stephens Bldg 111 Center St PO Box 3507-72203 Little Rock AR 72201-4402*

STEPHENS, WILLIAM RICHARD, college president emeritus; b. Ashburn, Mo., Jan. 2, 1932; s. George Lewis and Helen S.; m. Arlene Greer, June 28, 1952; children—Richard, Kendell, Kelli. B.S., Greenville Coll., Ill., 1953; M.Ed., U. Mo., 1958; Ed.D., Washington U., St. Louis, 1964. Tchr. Sturgeon High Sch., Mo., 1955-57; asst. prof. then assoc. prof. edn. Greenville Coll., 1957-61, dir. NCATE self-study, 1960-61; spl. instr. Washington U. St. Louis, 1961-64; mem. faculty Ind. State U., 1964-70; vis. prof. Ind. U., Bloomington, 1969-70; prof. history and philosophy of edn. Ind. U., 1970-71; v.p. acad. affairs, dean of faculty Greenville Coll., 1971-77, acting pres., 1977, pres., 1977-93; pres. emeritus, 1993—; chmn., bd. dirs. Fedn. Ind. Ill. Coll. and Univs., 1991-92. Author: Social Reform and the Origins of Vocational Guidance, 1890-1925, 1970; Education of American Life (with William Van Til), 1972; also curriculum materials, reports; editor procs. ednl. meetings. Vice-chmn. Kingsbury Park Dist., Greenville, 1972-77; mem. edn. com. Bond County Mental Health Assn., 1974. Served with U.S. Army, 1953-55. Recipient Merit award Nat. Vocat. Guidance Assn., 1973; fellow Acad. Achievers, Ctrl. Coll., 1994. Mem. History of Edn. Soc. (chmn. nominating com. 1969), Midwest History of Edn. Soc. (pres. 1971-72), Philosophy of Edn. Soc., Ohio Valley Philosophy of Edn. Soc. (sec.-treas. 1967-70), Soc. Profs. Edn. (assoc. editor publs. 1968-70), Central States Faculty Colloquium (chmn. 1969—), John Dewey Soc. (pres.-elect 1978-80, pres. 1980-82, editor Insights 1973-78), North Central Assn., Assn. Free Methodist Ednl. Instns. (pres. 1980—). Office: Greenville Coll 315 E College Ave Greenville IL 62246-1145

STEPHENS, WILLIAM THOMAS, forest products manufacturing company executive; married. BS, U. Ark., 1965, MS, 1966. Various mgmt. positions Manville Forest Products Corp., from 1963; asst. to pres., then sr. v.p., pres. forest products group Manville Corp., Denver, exec. v.p. fin. and adminstrn., from 1984, now pres., chief exec. officer, chmn., bd. dirs. Office: Manville Corp 717 17th St Denver CO 80202*

STEPHENS, WOODFORD CEFIS (WOODY STEPHENS), horse trainer, breeder; b. Stanton, Ky., Sept. 1, 1913; s. Lewis and Helen (Welch) S.; m. Lucille Elizabeth Easley, Sept. 11, 1937. Ed., Ky. Pub. Schs. Began as exercise boy, then trainer thoroughbred horses Ky., 1929—; jockey, 1931-40, profl. trainer thoroughbred horses, 1940—. Subject of biography: Guess I'm Lucky, 1985. Recipient profl. horse racing awards including: N.Y. Turf Writers Assn. Outstanding Trainer award, 1982, 83, Nat. Turf Writers Mr. Fitz award, 1982, Turf Publicists of Am. for outstanding sporting deeds benefiting horse racing, 1982, Silver Horseshoe award Ky. Derby Festival, 1983, Red Smith Good Guy award, Eclipse award for tng. of horse Swale, 1984, Gold Cup award N.Y., 1986, 87, C.V. Whitney Spl. Achievement award, 1993, 70th Ann. award N.Y. Turf Writers, 1993, Lifetime Achievement award Hialeah, 1989, others; named to Thoroughbred Racing's Hall of Fame, 1976, Horseperson of Yr. award, Fla., 1981, Legend in All Star Events, Fla., 1988, Caesars Legends of Racing, Atlantic City, 1988, Trainer of Decade AP, N.Y. Turf Writers, 1990, N.Y. Sports Mus. Hall of Fame, 1990; Ky. Col., 1963; trainer of more than 300 stake race winners, icnluding 2 Ky. Derbys, 1 Preakness, 5 Belmont Stakes; inducted into Hall of Fame, 1976, Saratoga, Hall of Fame, L.I.; Woody's Corner erected Belmont RAce Track, 1992; inducted into the Hialeah Park Classic Club, 1994; 150 silver trophies. Mem. United Thoroughbred Trainers Am., Turf and Field Club (N.Y.), Thoroughbred Club Am., Sky Island Club. Winner of 5 consecutive Belmont Stakes ranks as one of horse racings most outstanding accomplishments; life-size sculpture erected in hometown of Stanton; donated items pertinent to achievements associated with Ky. Derby and other Triple Crown races to Ky. Derby Museum, 1995. Home: 15534 Cairnryan Ct Hialeah FL 33014-2092 Office: Belmont Race Track Hempstead Elmont NY 11003 *Doing what I like best - hard work, being loyal, and I love my work, with animals.*

STEPHENSON, ALAN CLEMENTS, lawyer; b. Wilmington, N.C., Nov. 7, 1944; s. Abram Clements and Ruth (Smith) S.; m. Sherri Jean Miller, Dec. 19, 1970; children: Edward Taylor, Anne Baldwin. AB in Hist., U. N.C., 1967; JD, U. Va., 1970. Bar: N.Y. 1971. Assoc. Cravath, Swaine & Moore, N.Y.C., 1970-78, ptnr., 1978-88; mng. dir. Wasserstein, Perella and Co. Inc., N.Y.C., 1988-92; ptnr. Cravath, Swaine & Moore, N.Y.C., 1992—; bd. dirs. Victim Svcs., Inc., N.Y.C. Morehead scholar John M. Moorehead Found., 1963. Mem. N.Y. State Bar Assn., Assn. of Bar of City of N.Y., The Brook Club, The Links Club, Tuxedo Club, Union Club, Phi Beta Kappa. Home: 1107 Fifth Ave New York NY 10128-0145 Office: Cravath Swaine & Moore 825 8th Ave New York NY 10019-7416

STEPHENSON, ARTHUR EMMET, JR., investment company executive, banker; b. Bastrop, La., Aug. 29, 1945; s. Arthur Emmet and Edith Louise Stephenson; m. Toni Lyn Edwards, June 17, 1967. BS in Fin. magna cum laude, La. State U., 1967; MBA (Ralph Thomas Sayles fellow), Harvard U., 1969. Chartered fin. analyst. Adminstrv. aide to U.S. Sen. Russell Long of La., Washington, 1966; security analyst Fidelity Funds, Boston, 1968; chmn. bd., pres. Stephenson & Co., Denver, Stephenson Mcht. Banking Inc., Circle Corp.; sr. ptnr. Stephenson Ventures, Stephenson Properties; chmn. bd. Gen. Comm., Inc., Globescope Corp., Starpak Inc.; co-founder Pub. Network, Inc.; underwriting mem. Lloyd's of London, 1978-92; founder Charter Bank and Trust, chmn., 1980-91; bd. dirs. Danaher Corp.; mem. adv. bd. First Berkshire Fund, Capital Resources Ptnrs., L.P.; pub. Law Enforcement Product News, Colo. Book, Pub. Safety Product News. Mem. assocs. coun. Templeton Coll. at Oxford U., Eng.; nat. trustee Nat. Symphony Orch. at John F. Kennedy Ctr. for Performing Arts; mem. nat. steering com. Norman Rockwell Mus., Stockbridge, Mass.;; past mem. Colo. small bus. coun.; del. White House Conf. Recipient Hall of Fame award Inc. mag. Mem. Harvard U. Bus. Sch. Assn. (internat. pres. 1987-88), CEO's Orgn., World Pres.'s Orgn., Young Pres.'s Orgn. (Calif. Inland Empire chpt. chmn. 1992-93, area coun. mem.), Colo. Investment Advisors Assn. (treas., bd. dirs. 1975-76), Fin. Analysts Fedn., Denver Soc. Security Analysts (bd. dirs. 1975-77), Colo. Press Assn., Colo. Harvard Bus. Sch. Club (pres. 1980-81, chmn. 1981-82), Omicron Delta Kappa, Phi Kappa Phi, Beta Gamma Sigma, Kappa Sigma, Delta Sigma Pi. Office: 100 Garfield St Denver CO 80206-5550

STEPHENSON, BETTE MILDRED, physician, former Canadian legislator; b. Aurora, Ont., Can., July 31, 1924; d. Carl Melvin and Clara Mildred (Draper) S.; grad. Earl Haig Coll. Inst.; MD, U. Toronto, 1946; m. Gordon Allan Pengelly, 1948; children: J. Stephen A., Elizabeth Anne A., C. Christopher A., J. Michael A., P. Timothy A., Mary Katharine A. Mem. med. staff Women's Coll. Hosp., 1950-90, chief dept. gen. practice, dir. outpatient dept., 1956-64; mem. med. staff N.Y. Gen. Hosp., 1967-89; elected Ont. Legislature for York Mills, 1975, 77, 81, 85; minister labor, 1975-78; minister edn., minister colls. and univs., 1978-85, treas. and dep. premier, 1985; pres. Gwillimbury Found. Post Secondary Edn.; dir. Can. Inst. Advanced Rsch., dir. edn. quality and accountability, Ontario; dir. Women's Coll. Hosp. Fellow Coll. Family Physicians Can. (chmn. nat. coordinating com. on edn. 1961-64, chmn. confs. on edn. for gen. practice 1961, 63), Acad. Med. Toronto (hon.); mem. Ont. Med. Assn. (dir. 1964-72, pres. 1970-71), Can. Med. Assn. (dir. 1968-75, pres. 1974-75), Art Gallery Ont., Royal Ont. Mus., Order of Can. (officer), Order of St. John (officer).

STEPHENSON, C. GENE, academic administrator. Pres. U. Ozarks, Clarksville, Ark. Office: Univ Ozarks Office of President 415 N College Ave Clarksville AR 72830-2880

STEPHENSON, DONALD GRIER, JR., government studies educator; b. DeKalb County, Ga., Jan. 12, 1942; s. Donald Grier and Katherine Mason (Williams) S.; m. Ellen Claire Walker, Aug. 15, 1967; children: Todd Grier, Claire Walker. AB, Davidson Coll., N.C., 1964; MA, Princeton U., 1966, PhD, 1967. Research assoc. Nat. War Coll., Washington, 1968-70; asst. prof. govt. Franklin and Marshall Coll., Lancaster, Pa., 1970-73, assoc. prof. govt., 1973-81, prof. govt., 1981—, Charles A. Dana prof., 1989—; mem. adv. coun. to dean of the chapel Princeton U., 1974-85; Commonwealth lectr. Pa. Humanities Coun., Phila., 1987-88, 90, 92-95. Co-author: American Constitutional Development, 1977, American Government, 1992, 94, American Constitutional Law, 1996; author: The Supreme Court and the American Republic, 1981, An Essential Safeguard, 1991; contbr. articles to profl. jours. Elder, mem. session First Presbyn. Ch., Lancaster, 1973-76, 96—; judge Pa. constl. competition Dickinson Coll., 1988—. Capt. U.S. Army, 1968-70. Woodrow Wilson fellow, 1964-65, 66-67; Nat. Endowment for Humanities grantee, 1972, 85-89. Mem. Am. Polit. Sci. Assn. (Corwin award com. 1978, nominating com. Law and Courts sect. 1995), Pa. Polit. Sci. Assn. (editl. bd. Polity 1972-78), Supreme Ct. Hist. Soc. (editl. award 1990). Presbyterian. Home: 62 Oak Ln Lancaster PA 17603-4762 Office: Franklin and Marshall Coll PO Box 3003 Lancaster PA 17604-3003

STEPHENSON, DONNAN, lawyer, former state supreme court justice; b. LaHarpe, Kans., Nov. 21, 1919; s. Ralph Duane and Zoe B. (Donnan) S.; m. Patricia Marie Ledyard, May 14, 1942; children: Mark Donnan, Bruce Ledyard. B.S. in Bus. Adminstrn., U. Kans., 1941, LL.B., 1948. Bar: Kans. 1948, N. Mex. 1949. With TWA, 1948; practice law Santa Fe, 1958-70; ptnr. Bigbee & Stephenson, Santa Fe, 1949-62, Stephenson & Olmsted, 1962-66, Stephenson, Campbell & Olmsted, 1966-70; justice N. Mex. Supreme Ct., Santa Fe, 1971-76; sr. ptnr. Bigbee, Stephenson, Carpenter, Crout & Olmsted, Santa Fe, 1976-81, of counsel, 1982-88. Established and endowed Stephenson Lectures in Law and Govt. Kans. U. Law Sch. Served to lt. USNR, WWII. Decorated Bronze Star; recipient Kans. U. Law Sch. Disting. Alumnus, 1981. Fellow N.Mex. Bar Assn. Home: 1014 Bishops Lodge Rd Santa Fe NM 87501-1009

STEPHENSON, DOROTHY GRIFFITH See GRIFFITH, DOTTY

STEPHENSON, FRANK ALEX, environmental engineer, consultant; b. Helena, Mont., May 4, 1940; s. Alex Banning and Phyllis Jean (Smith) S.; m. Lorann Marcella Berg, July 9, 1962 (div. Aug. 1970); children: Patty Jo, Scott Alex; m. Brenda Mae Vitales, June 21, 1986; 1 child, Jennifer Jean. BS in Civil Constrn. Engring., Mont. State U., 1967; MS in Sanitary Engring., Delft U., 1973; PhD in Environ. Engring., Exeter U., 1975. Registered profl. engr., Ariz., Mont., S.D., Colo., N.Mex., Wyo., Kans. Constrn. engr. Al Johnson Co., Mpls., 1967-70; sr. engr. Stearns Roger Inc., Denver, 1975-79; ptnr. Thomas Group Inc., San Jose, Calif., 1979-85; sr. engr. CH2M Hill Inc., San Jose, Calif., 1985-87; dir. engring. western div. Dames & Moore, Phoenix, 1987-93; dir. techs. Terranext, Phoenix, 1993—. Mem. Rep. Nat. Com., 1996; mem. NAFTA Com., Ariz., 1994. Recipient Ernest Cook Rsch. fellowship Royal Acad. Sci., London, 1973. Mem. AIChE, Hazardous Waste Soc. Presbyterian. Achievements include development of technology for on-line total organic carbon analysis using ultraviolet light and resistivity changes; design and installation of first reverse osmosis unit used in a nuclear (electric power) reactor. Avocations: model railroading, fishing, swimming. Home: 1702 E Aurelius Ave Phoenix AZ 85020 Office: Terranext 9230 S 51st St Phoenix AZ 85044

STEPHENSON, HOWARD H., banker; b. Wichita, Kans., July 15, 1929; s. Herman Horace and Edith May (Wayland) S.; m. Virginia Anne Ross, Dec. 24, 1950; children: Ross Wayland, Neal Bevan, Jann Edith. BA, U. Mich., 1950; JD with distinction, U. Mo., Kansas City, 1958, LLD (hon.), 1993. Bar: Kans. 1958. With City Nat. Bank, Kansas City, Mo., 1952-54, City Bond & Mortgage Co., Kansas City, 1954-59, Bank of Hawaii, Honolulu, 1959-94; ret., 1994; now chmn. bd., CEO Bancorp Hawaii Inc. and subs. Bank Hawaii, Banque de Tahiti; bd. dirs. Banque de Nouvelle-Caledonie, Pacific Basin Econ. Coun. U.S. Mem. Com, Bancorp Hawaii, Inc., Bank Hawaii, bancorp Hawaii Charitable Found., Bank of Hawaii Internat. Inc., Hawaiian Trust Co. Bd. dirs. Honolulu Symphony, Maunalani Found., Aloha United Way, Pacific Fleet Submarine Meml. Assn., Pacific Basin Econ. Coun. U.S. Mem. Com.; co-chmn. Ellison Onizuka Meml. Scholarship Fund Com.; chmn. bd. regents U. Hawaii. With U.S. Army, 1950-52. Mem. ABA, Am. Bankers Assn. (past chmn. exec. com. housing and real estate fin. div., dir. 1976-77, mem. governing coun. 1976-77, mem. govt. rels. coun. 1986-89), Kans. Bar Assn., Hawaii Bankers Assn. (pres. 1991-92), U.S.-Japan Bus. Coun., Pacific Asia Travel Assn. (Hawaii chpt., assoc.), Navy League of U.S., Hawaii Bus. Roundtable, Pacific Forum/CSIS (bd. govs.), Assn. Res. City Bankers, U.S.-Korea Bus. Coun., Kappa Sigma, Pi Eta Sigma, Oahu Country Club, Pacific Club, Waialae Country Club, Rotary. Office: Bank of Hawaii PO Box 2900 Honolulu HI 96846*

STEPHENSON, HUGH EDWARD, JR., retired physician, educator; b. Columbia, Mo., June 1, 1922; s. Hugh Edward and Doris (Pryor) S.; m. Sarah Norfleet Dickinson, Aug. 15, 1964; children—Hugh Edward III, Ann Dunlop. AB, BS, U. Mo., 1943; MD, Washington U., St. Louis, 1945. Diplomate Am. Bd. Surgery, Am. Bd. Thoracic Surgery. Mem. faculty U. Mo. Sch. Medicine, Columbia, 1953—, prof. surgery, 1956—, chmn. dept. surgery, 1956-60, chief div. gen. surgery, 1976-87, chief staff, 1982-94, John Growdon Disting. prof. surgery emeritus, 1987—, interim dean, 1988-89, assoc. dean, 1989-92, dist. prof. surgery emeritus, 1993; Markle scholar acad. medicine, 1954-60. Author: Immediate Care of the Acutely Ill and Injured, 2d edit, 1974, Cardiac Arrest and Resuscitation, 4th edit., 1975, The Kicks That Count; Contbr. articles to profl. jours. Named one of Outstanding Young Men of Nation, Nat. Jr. C. of C., 1956, James IV Surg. Traveler Gt. Britain, 1962, Dist. Faculty award, 1989. Mem. ACS, AMA (del., chmn. coun. on med. edn. 1994-95, co-chmn. liaison com. on med. edn. 1995, pres. surgical caucus 1996), Vascular Surgery Soc., Soc. Thoracic Surgeons, So. Thoracic Surgery Assn., So. Med. Assn. (coun.), Mo. Med. Assn. (chmn. jud. coun. 1986—, v.p. 1986-87), Beta Theta Pi (trustees, v.p., pres. gen. frat. 1978-81). Baptist. Home: 5 Danforth Cir Columbia MO 65201-3509 Office: U Mo Sch Medicine 1 Hospital Dr Columbia MO 65201-5276

STEPHENSON, IRENE HAMLEN, biorhythm analyst, consultant, editor, educator; b. Chgo., Oct. 7, 1923; d. Charles Martin and Carolyn Hilda (Hilgers) Hamlin; m. Edgar B. Stephenson, Sr., Aug. 16, 1941 (div. 1946); 1 child, Edgar B. Author biorhythm compatibilities column Nat. Singles Register, Norwalk, Calif., 1979-81; instr. biorhythm Learning Tree Open U., Canoga Park, Calif., 1982-83; instr. biorhythm character analysis 1980—; instr. biorhythm compatibility, 1982—; owner, pres. matchmaking svc. Pen Pals Using Biorhythm, Chatsworth, Calif., 1979—; editor newsletter The Truth, 1979-85, Mini Examiner, Chatsworth, 1985—; researcher biorhythm character and compatibility, 1974—, biorhythm columnist Psychic Astrology Horoscope, 1989-94, True Astrology Forecast, 1989-94, Psychic Astrology Predictions, 1990-94, Con Artist types, 1995, Pedophile (child molester) types, 1995, Personality types, 1996; author: Learn Biorhythm Character Analysis, 1980, Do-It-Yourself Biorhythm Compatibilities, 1982, Con Artist Types, 1995, Pedophile (child molester) Types, 1995, Personality Types, 1996; contbr. numerous articles to mags.; frequent guests clubs, radio, TV. Office: PO Box 3893-ww Chatsworth CA 91313 *To be happy, you have to be what is natural for you, not what someone else wants you to be.*

STEPHENSON, JAN LYNN, professional golfer; b. Sydney, Australia, Dec. 22, 1951; d. Francis John and Barbara (Green) S.; m. Eddie Vossler, 1982. Student, Australian schs. Profl. golfer, 1972—; mem. Australian Ladies Profl. Golf Assn. tour, 1972-73, U.S. Ladies Profl. Golf Assn. tour, 1974—. Winner New South Wales (Australia) Jr. Championship, 1963-69; winner Australian Jr. Championship, 1968-71, Australian Title, 1973, Sarah Coventry Championship, 1976, Birmingham Championship Ala., 1976, Women's Internat., 1978, Sun City Classic, 1980, Peter Jackson Classic, 1981, Mary Kay Classic, 1981, United Va. Bank Classic, 1981, Ladies Profl. Golf Assn. Championship, 1982, Women's Tucson Open, 1983, Women's U.S. Open, 1983, Lady Keystone Open, GNA Tournament, 1985, French Open, 1985, Santa Barbara Open, 1987, Safeco Seattle Classsic, 1987, Konica San Jose Classic, 1987, 1st LPGA Skins Game, Frisco, Tex., 1990; named Rookie of Yr., U.S. Profl. Golfers Assn., 1974; Sportsman of Yr., Sportswriters Assn., Australia, 1976. Office: 7601 Della Dr # 276 Orlando FL 32819-7233*

STEPHENSON, MASON WILLIAMS, lawyer; b. Atlanta, May 29, 1946; s. Donald Grier and Katherine Mason (Williams) S.; m. Linda Frances Partee, June 13, 1970; children: Andrew Mason, Walter Martin. AB cum laude, Davidson Coll., 1968; JD, U. Chgo., 1971. Bar: Ga. 1971, U.S. Dist. Ct. (no. dist.) Ga. 1985. Assoc. Alston, Miller & Gaines, Atlanta, 1971-76, ptnr., 1976-77; ptnr. Trotter, Bondurant, Griffin, Miller & Hishon, Atlanta, 1977-82, Bondurant, Miller, Hishon & Stephenson, Atlanta, 1982-85, King & Spalding, Atlanta, 1985—. Mem. fin. com. Atlanta Olympic Organizing Com., 1988-90. Mem. ABA (real property, probate and trust sect.), Am. Coll. Real Estate Lawyers, State Bar Ga. (exec. com., real property law sect. 1989—), Atlanta Bar Assn. (chair real estate sect. 1981-82), Burge Hunting

Club, Causeway Club, Capital City Club, Phi Delta Phi. Avocations: sailing, skiing, jogging. Office: King & Spalding 191 Peachtree St NE Atlanta GA 30303-1740

STEPHENSON, MICHELE, photojournalist. Picture editor Time Mag., N.Y.C. Office: c/o Time Time & Life Bldg Time-Life Bldg Rockefeller Ctr New York NY 10020-1393*

STEPHENSON, ROBERT BAIRD, energy company executive; b. Washington, Jan. 20, 1943; s. Orlando Worth and Martha Ann (Kostelak) S.; m. Sheryl Ann Fish, Jan. 10, 1967; children: Brie Danielle, Eric Baird. BS in Mech. Engring., Purdue U., 1965; MS in Nuclear Engring., U. Mich., 1970, MBA, 1972. Engr. Jersey Nuclear Co., Inc., Boston, 1972-74; engr., mgr. Exxon Nuclear Co., Inc., Richland, Wash., 1974-80; mng. dir. Exxon Nuclear GmbH, Lingen, Fed. Rep. Germany, 1980-83; mktg., sales staff Exxon Nuclear Co., Inc., Bellevue, Wash., 1983-85, v.p. adminstn., 1986; v.p. comml. div. Exxon Nuclear Co., Inc., Bellevue, 1987; pres., chief exec. officer, chmn. EPID, Inc., San Jose, Calif., 1985-86; pres., chief exec. officer Advanced Nuclear Fuels Corp., Bellevue, Wash., 1988-91; pres. CEO Siemens Nuclear Power Corp., Bellevue, 1991-92; pres., CEO, Siemens Power Corp., Milw., 1992—, also bd. dirs. Bd. regents Milw. Sch. Engring. Lt. USN, 1965-70. Mem. Am. Nuclear Soc. Avocations: sailing, boating, golf. Office: Siemens Power Corp 1040 S 70th St Milwaukee WI 53214

STEPHENSON, ROBERT CLAY, commercial real estate developer; b. Meadville, Pa., Sept. 21, 1938; s. LeRoy Vernon and Martha Louise (Clay) S.; m. Judith Regina Trohaugh, Jan. 19, 1963; children: Robert Scott, Eric Thomas, Cynthia Lynn. BA, Allegheny Coll., 1962. Group sales rep. Conn. Gen. Life Ins., Detroit, 1962-64; salesman, broker Donovan Co., Pitts., 1964-73; v.p. Oliver Realty, Inc., Pitts., 1974-81; ptnr. Liberati/Davenport/Stephenson, Pitts., 1981, DeBartolo LDS Assocs., Pitts., 1981-85; pres. Carnegie Properties, Inc., Pitts., 1985-86; v.p. office/indsl. properties The Edward J. DeBartolo Corp., Youngstown, Ohio, 1986-94, v.p. asset mgmt., 1994-95; owner RCS Realty Co., Pitts., 1996—. Session ruling elder Bower Hill Presbyn. Ch.; twp. committeeman Rep. Party Mt. Lebanon Twp.; troop committeeman Boy Scouts Am., Bethel Park, Pa.; real estate cons. The Children's Mus., Pitts.; treas. Ducks Unltd., Washington County, Pa.; community amb. to Eng. Expt. in Internat. Living, Putney, Vt. Mem. Nat. Assn. Realtors, Pa. Assn. Realtors, Realtors Assn. Met. Pitts. (mem. vigilance/ethics com. 1967-69, mem. long range planning com. 1976-78, chmn. 1977-78, mem. R-day conf. com. 1981, mem. pub. rels. com. 1982, mem. Realtors of Yr. com. 1982—), Nat. Assn. Indsl. and Office Parks (mem. we. Pa. chpts. 1978—, pres. 1981-82, bd. dirs. 1993-96, mem. nat. com. project analysis 1985), Soc. Indsl. and Office Realtors (mem. we. Pa. chpt, pres. 1983, 84, 90, chmn. ann. dinner com. 1982, 89, mem. govt. rels. nat. com. 1982-83, mem. nat. com. office mktg. 1987-88), Nat. Assn. Corp. Real Estate Execs. (mem. Pitts. chpt., pres. 1982), Inst. Real Estate Mgmt., St. Clair Country Club, Bally's Scandinavian Spa, Phi Kappa Psi. Presbyterian. Avocations: fishing, snow skiing, scuba diving, golf, hunting. Home: 1895 Tilton Dr Upper St Clair PA 15241-2636 Office: RCS Realty Company 1895 Tilton Dr Pittsburgh PA 15241-2636

STEPHENSON, ROSCOE BOLAR, JR., state supreme court justice; b. Covington, Va., Feb. 22, 1922. A.B., Washington and Lee U., 1943, J.D., 1947, LL.D. (hon.), 1983. Bar: Va. 1947. Ptnr. Stephenson & Stephenson, Covington, 1947-52; commonwealth's atty. Alleghany County, Va., 1952-64; ptnr. Stephenson, Kostel, Watson, Carson and Snyder, Covington, 1964-73; judge 25th Jud. Cir. Ct. Commonwealth Va., Covington, 1973-81; justice Va. Supreme Ct., Richmond, 1981—. Recipient Covington Citizen of Yr. award, 1973; recipient Outstanding Alumni award Covington High Sch., 1973. Fellow Am. Coll. Trial Lawyers; mem. Va. State Bar (council 1969-73), Va. Bar Assn., Va. Trial Lawyers Assn., Order of Coif. Home: North Ridge Hot Springs VA 24445 Office: Va Supreme Ct 100 N 9th St Richmond VA 23219-2335 also: 214 W Main St Covington VA 24426-1543

STEPHENSON, SAMUEL EDWARD, JR., physician; b. Bristol, Tenn., May 16, 1926; s. Samuel Edward and Hazel Beatrice (Walters) S.; m. Janet Sue Spotts, May 16, 1970; children: Samuel Edward III, William Douglas, Dorothea Louise, Judith Maria. BS, U. S.C., 1946; MD, Vanderbilt U., 1950. Intern Butterworth Hosp., Grand Rapids, Mich., 1950-51; instr. to asso. prof. surgery Vanderbilt U., 1955-67; prof. surgery U. Fla., 1967-95, emeritus prof. clin. surgery, 1995—; chmn. dept. surgery Univ. Hosp., Jacksonville, 1967-78. Asst. editor So. Med. Jour., 1968-88; contbr. articles to profl. jours. Co-chmn. Fla. Burn and Trauma Registry, 1974-77. Served with USNR, 1944-45. Fellow A.C.S.; mem. Am. Coll. Chest Physicians. Mason. Club: University (Jacksonville). Home: 10553 Scott Mill Rd Jacksonville FL 32257-6227 Office: 1501 San Marco Blvd Jacksonville FL 32207-2905

STEPHENSON, TONI EDWARDS, publisher, investment management executive; b. Bastrop, La., July 23, 1945; d. Sidney Crawford and Grace Erleene Little; BS, La. State U., 1967; grad. owner/pres. mgmt. program Harvard Bus. Sch.; m. Arthur Emmet Stephenson, Jr., June 17, 1967; 1 dau., Tessa Lyn. ; pres., dir. Gen. Communications, Inc., Denver; sr. v.p., founder Stephenson & Co., Denver, 1971—; gen. ptnr. Viking Fund; ptnr. Stephenson Properties, Stephenson Ventures, Stephenson Mgmt. Co.; bd. dirs. Starpak Internat., Inc., Starpak, Inc., Startek Internat., Inc.; founder Charter Bank & Trust. Pub., Law Enforcement Product News, Pub. Safety Product News, Globescope Corp.; sec., HBS/OPM16, former dir. The Children's Hosp., St. Joseph's Hosp. Past pres. Children's Hosp. Assn. Vols. Mem. Harvard Bus. Sch. Club of Colo., DAR, Delta Gamma. Clubs: Rancho Mirage (Calif.), Annabel's (London), Thunderbird Country, Glenmoor Country Club, Denver Petroleum.

STEPHENSON, WILLIAM BOYD, JR., life insurance executive; b. St. Louis, Feb. 27, 1933; s. William Boyd and Edna (Gore) S.; BBA, U. Okla., 1954; postgrad. Dartmouth Inst., 1984; CLU, CPCU. Salesman, Pillsbury Co., Dallas, 1957-59; with Fidelity Union Life Ins. Co., Dallas, 1959-73, v.p., dir. coll. sales, 1962-67, exec. v.p., 1967-73; dir. coll. marketing Aetna Life & Casualty Co., Hartford, Conn., 1973-76, dir. individual ins. sales, 1976-78, regional v.p., 1978-85, v.p. mktg., 1986-90; pres. Donald F. Smith & Assoc., 1990—. Capt. USAF, 1954-57. Mem. Nassau Club, Delta Upsilon, Beta Gamma Sigma. Home: 45 Governors Ln Princeton NJ 08540-3670 Office: 3120 Princeton Pike Trenton NJ 08648-2306

STEPLER, RICHARD LEWIS, magazine editor; b. Norfolk, Va., Aug. 15, 1945; s. Richard Lewis and Mary Ann (Beard) S.; m. Janet Sarah Froelich, Sept. 13, 1981; children: Jesse Benjamin, Rebecca Ann. BA, NYU, 1969. From sr. editor to editor Popular Sci., N.Y.C., 1975-95; editor-in-chief Boating Mag., N.Y.C., 1996—. Mem. Nat. Assn. Sci. Writers, Am. Soc. Mag. Editors, Internat. Motor Press Assn. (v.p. 1984-91). Office: Boating Mag 1633 Broadway New York NY 10019

STEPNOSKI, MARK MATTHEW, professional football player; b. Erie, Pa., Jan. 26, 1967. Student, U. Pitts. Center Dallas Cowboys, 1989-95, Houston Oilers, 1995—; player NFC Championship Game, 1992, Super Bowl XXVII, 1992, Super Bowl XXVIII, 1993. Named to Pro Bowl Team, 1992, 93. Office: Dallas Cowboys One Cowboys Pkwy Irving TX 75063

STEPONAITIS, VINCAS PETRAS, archaeologist, anthropologist, educator; b. Boston, Aug. 10, 1953; s. Vincas and Elena (Povydis) S.; m. Laurie Cameron, Dec. 31, 1976; children: Elena Anne, Lillian Kazimiera. AB in Anthropology magna cum laude, Harvard U., 1974; MA in Anthropology, U. Mich., 1975, PhD in Anthropology, 1980. From lectr. to assoc. prof. dept. anthropology SUNY, Binghamton, 1979-87; assoc. prof. U. N.C., Chapel Hill, 1988-94, prof., 1995—, dir. Rsch. Labs. Anthropology, 1988—; guest worker Nat. Bur. Standards, 1979; adj. lectr. dept. anthropology SUNY, Binghamton, 1979; invited lectr. univs. U.S., Europe, 1980—. Author: Ceramics, Chronology, and Community Patterns, An Archaeological Study at Moundville, 1983; editor Southeastern Archaeology, 1984-87; regional editor Investigations in Am. Archaeology, 1987-91; mem. edit. bd. Southern Cultures, 1992—; mem. edit. adv. bd. Prehistory Press, 1990—; contbr. articles to profl. jours.; presenter papers profl. meetings, seminars; pub. book reviews; abstracts. Smithsonian Instn. fellow, 1978-79; grantee NSF, 1978-80, 83, 89-92, 94, Wenner-Gren Found., 1981, 86-88, Nat. Geographic Soc., 1987-88, Z. Smith Reynolds Found., 1992-94. Fellow Am. Anthrop. Assn.; mem. Soc. Am. Archaeology (Presdl. Recognition award 1993-94, exec. com. 1983-84, treas. 1992-94, pres.-elect 1996), Southeastern Archaeol. Conf. (editor 1984-87, pres. 1990-92), N.C. Archaeol. Soc. (exec. sec. 1988-91, sec. 1991—), N.C. Archaeol. Coun. (exec. com. 1988-92), Archaeol. Soc., S.C., Ala. Archaeol. Soc., Miss. Archaeol. Soc., La. Archaeol. Soc., Tenn. Anthrop. Assn. Office: U NC Rsch Labs Anthropology Alumni Bldg CB 3120 Chapel Hill NC 27599-3120

STEPP, LAURA SESSIONS, journalist; b. Ft. Smith, Ark., July 27, 1951; d. Robert Paul Sessions and M. Rae Barnes; m. Carl Sessions Stepp; children: Ashli, Amber, Jeffrey. BA, Earlham Coll., 1973; MA, Columnia U., 1974. Reporter Palm Beach Times, West Palm Beach, Fla., 1974; MA Columbia U., Phila., 1975; projects editor The Charlotte (N.C.) Observer, 1979-81, asst. editorial page editor, 1981-82; Md. editor The Washington Post, 1982-86, religion editor, 1987-92, writer Style sect., 1992—. Bd. advisors U. Md. Casey Journalism Ctr. Children and Families, College Park. Recipient Nat. Reporting award Religion Writers Am., Feature Writing award AAUW, 1994. Mem. Investigative Reporters and Editors (bd. dirs. 1986-90). Office: Washington Post Co 1150 15th St NW Washington DC 20071-0001

STEPPLER, HOWARD ALVEY, agronomist; b. Morden, Man., Can., Nov. 8, 1918; s. Alvey Morden and Sophia (Doern) S.; m. Phyllis Ivy Parsonage, May 10, 1945; 1 child, Glenn. B.S., U. Man., 1941; M.Sc., McGill U., 1948, Ph.D., 1955. Research scientist Agr. Can. Research, 1948-49; asst. prof. agronomy McGill U., 1949-57, prof., 1957-84, prof. emeritus, 1984—, chmn. agronomy dept., 1955-70, chmn. dept. plant sci., 1976-84; agrl. advisor Can. Internat. Devel. Agy., 1970-71; trustee Centro Internacional Agricultura Tropical Colombia, 1972-78, Internat. Svc. Nat. Agrl. Rsch., The Hague, 1980-84, Agrl. Devel. Coun. N.Y., 1977-85, Internat. Livestock Ctr. for Africa, Ethiopia, 1984-89; trustee Internat. Coun. Rsch. in Agroforestry, 1983-91, chmn. bd., 1984-91; interim dir. gen. Internat. Coun. for Rsch. in Agroforestry, Nairobi, 1980-81; trustee Internat. Rice Rsch. Inst., 1988-93; founding bd. dirs. So. African Ctr. Coordination in Agrl. Rsch., Botswana, 1984-85. Capt. arty. Royal Can. Arty., 1942-46. Internat. Devel. Research Centre sr. Research fellow, 1973-74. Fellow Agrl. Inst. Can. (pres. 1964-65, Internat. Agrl. Recognition award 1994); mem. Am. Soc. Agronomy, Crop Sci. Soc. Am., Can. Soc. Agronomy (pres. 1957-58, Disting. Agronomist award 1993), Rotary. Office: 21111 Lakeshore Rd, Sainte Anne de Bellevue, PQ Canada H9X 3V9

STEPTO, ROBERT CHARLES, physician, educator; b. Chgo., Oct. 6, 1920; s. Robert Louis and Grace Elvie (Williams) S.; m. Ann Burns, Sept. 13, 1942; children: Robert Burns, Jan Kristin. B.S., Northwestern U., 1938-41; M.D., Howard U., 1944; Ph.D., U. Chgo., 1948. Intern Provident Hosp., Chgo., 1945; resident in obstetrics and gynecology Provident Hosp., 1946-48, trustee, 1986-88; resident Chgo. Lying-In Hosp., 1946-48; USPHS fellow Michael Reese Hosp., Chgo., 1948-51; asst. prof. Loyola U., Chgo., 1953-56, U. Ill., Chgo., 1956-60; asso. prof. U. Ill., 1960-69; prof., chmn. dept. obstetrics and gynecology Chgo. Med. Sch., 1970-75; prof. Rush Med. Coll., Chgo., 1975-79; prof. U. Chgo., 1979-90, prof. emeritus, 1990—; dir. Ob-gyn. dept. Cook County Hosp., 1972-75, chmn. ob-gyn., 1990-93, emeritus, 1993—; mem. Chgo. Bd. Health, 1964-89, v.p., 1982—, pres., 1988-89; sec. Chgo. Health Rsch. Found., Family Planning Coordinating Coun. Met. Chgo.; pres., bd. dirs. emeritus Nat. Med. Fellowships. Bd. dirs. Chgo. Urban League, 1960-63, Mus. Contemporary Art, Lyric Opera; trustee Ill. Children's Home and Aid Soc., 1967-71. Served to capt. AUS, 1951-53. Fellow ACS, Internat. Coll. Surgeons (pres. 1978, corp. sec. 1982, sec. N.Am. 1984-85), Am. Coll. Obstetrics and Gynecology (life), Inst. of Med.; mem. Am. Urogynecol. Soc., Am. Soc. Colpscopy (emeritus), AMA, Nat. Med. Assn., Central Assn. Obstetrics and Gynecology (life), Chgo. Gynecol. Soc. (life, v.p. 1969, pres. 1982), Chgo. Pathol. Soc., Assn. Chgo. Gynecol. Oncologists (pres. 1982). Clubs: Quadrangle, Carlton, Wayfarers (Chgo.). Home: 5201 S Cornell Ave Chicago IL 60615-4207 Office: U Chgo 5841 S Maryland Ave Chicago IL 60637-1463

STEPTOE, PHILIP P., III, lawyer; b. Washington, Nov. 13, 1951. AB, Princeton U., 1973; JD, U. Va., 1976. Bar: Va. 1976, Ill. 1976. Ptnr. Sidley & Austin, Chgo. Mem. ABA (sect. pub. utility 1988—), Chgo. Bar Assn. (sect. pub. utility 1976—). Office: Sidley & Austin 1 First Nat Plz Chicago IL 60603*

STERBAN, RICHARD ANTHONY, singer; b. Camden, N.J., Apr. 24, 1943; s. Edward Joseph and Victoria Marie (Giordano) S.; children: Richard Alan, Douglas Scott, Christopher Patrick. Student, Trenton State Coll. co-owner Silverline-Goldline Music Pub. Cos.; partner Nashville Sounds, Greensboro Hornets, baseball teams. Mem. gospel singing groups; mem. Stamps Quartet, bass singer, ptnr., Oak Ridge Boys, 1972—; albums include Y'All Come Back Saloon, 1977, Room Service, 1978, Oak Ridge Boys Have Arrived, 1979, Together, 1980, Greatest Hits, 1980, Fancy Free, 1981, Bobbie Sue, 1982, Oak Ridge Boys Christmas, 1982, American Made, 1983, Deliver, 1984, Greatest Hits II, 1984, Step On Out, 1985, Seasons, 1986, Christmas Again, 1986, Where The Fast Lane Ends, 1987, Heartbeat, 1987, Monongahela, 1988, Unstoppable, 1991, The Long Haul, 1992, Back to Back, 1994. Recipient with group: Grammy awards, Am. Music award for Country Group of Yr., 1982, Best Country Video award , Everday, 1985; named Best Vocal Group Acad. Country Music, 1977, 79, Best Country Group of Yr. AGVA, 1981, Number One Country Group Billboard mag., 1978, 80, Vocal Group of the Yr. Country Music Assn., 1978. Mem. Country Music Assn., AFTRA, Nat. Acad. Rec. Arts and Scis., Acad. Country Music. Office: care Oak Ridge Boys Jim Halsey Co 3225 S Norwood Ave Tulsa OK 74135-5400

STERGIOS, PETER DOE, lawyer; b. Derry, N.H., Jan. 24, 1942; s. William G. and Ruthmary (Doe) S.; m. Leonides Conde, Aug. 29, 1971; children: Irene, Cathy. BA with distinction, Brown U., 1964; JD, Harvard U., 1972; sr. ptnr. Bar: N.Y. 1973, U.S. Dist. Ct. (so. and ea. dists.) N.Y. 1974, U.S. Ct. Appeals (2d cir.) 1974, U.S. Supreme Ct. 1977. Assoc. Shea & Gould, N.Y.C., 1972-80, ptnr., 1980-87; ptnr. Epstein Becker & Green, P.C., N.Y.C., 1987—. Contbr. articles to profl. jours. Capt. U.S. Army, 1964-68, Vietnam. Mem. ABA (internat. labor rels. law com.), Fed. Bar Assn., Am. Arbitration Assn. (panel of arbitrators), N.Y. State Bar Assn., N.Y. County Lawyers Assn., Assn. Bar City N.Y., Harvard Club, Govs. Island Officers Club, Am. Legion. Office: Epstein Becker & Green PC 250 Park Ave New York NY 10177

STERLING, DAVID MARK, graphic designer; b. Okla., Apr. 28, 1951; s. Paul J. and Roberta Myrtice (Rousseau) S. BA, Oklahoma City U., 1973; MFA, Cranbrook Acad. Art, Bloomfield Hills, Mich., 1978. Exhibit designer Omniplex, Oklahoma City, 1973-76; art dir. Indsl. Design Mag., N.Y.C., 1979-81; prin. Doublespace, N.Y.C., 1982-94; founder, prin. World Studio and World Studio Found., N.Y.C., 1992—; graphic design faculty Sch. of Visual Arts, N.Y.C., 1992—. Pub. mags. Fetish, 1979-81, Sphere, 1994—; works included in books: Graphic Style: From Victorian to Post-Modern, 1988, New American Design, 1988, Low Budget/High Quality Design, 1990, Cranbrook Design: The New Discourse, 1990, Contemporary Graphic Design, 1991; represented in permanent collections at Cranbrook Acad. Art, Libr. of Congress, Michael C. Rockefeller Arts Ctr., Cooper Hewitt Nat. Design Mus., Smithsonian Instn. Recipient Am. Inst. Graphic Arts awards for Cover Show, N.Y., 1984, for Comm. Graphics, N.Y., 1986, 90; recipient Type Dirs. Club award, 1990, 92; Best of Category award Design Rev., N.Y., 1986, Am. Assn. of Mus., 1986, 88, Am. Ctr. for Design, 1990, Indsl. Design Rev. award, 1985, 86, 88, 93, N.Y. Festival awards, Featured Internat. Design Mag., ID40, 1996. Recipient Am. Inst. Graphic Arts awards for Cover Show, N.Y., 1984, for Comm. Graphics, N.Y., 1986, 90; recipient Type Dirs. Club award, 1990, 92, Best of Category award Design Rev., N.Y., 1986, Am. Assn. of Mus., 1986, 88, Am. Ctr. for Design, 1990, Indsl. Design Rev. award, 1985, 86, 88, 93, N.Y. Festival awards. Democrat. Office: World Studio Ste 602 19 W 21 New York NY 10010

STERLING, DONALD EUGENE, civil engineer; b. Rootville, Pa., May 30, 1939; s. Blanche Marie (Phelps) Vanik; m. Janet Leigh Wotring, Apr. 23, 1983. A in Engring., Pa. State U., 1966; BSCE, W.Va. Inst. Tech., 1981; MS in Engring., W.Va. Coll. Grad. Studies, Charleston, 1987. Cert. engr. technician. Hwy. drafting technician W.Va. Dept. Transp., Charleston, 1965-67, hwy. engr. technician, 1967-82, design rev. engr., 1982-89, sr. rev. engr., 1989-94; civil engr. Woolpert Cons., Charleston, W.Va., 1994—. Tutor Charleston Dist. Outreach Ministries, 1981-83, counselor Camp For Under Privileged Children, 1982; treas., v.p. Kanawha City Midget Football Team, 1978. Sgt. USAF, 1959-63, with Pa. Nat. Guard, 1956-59. Recipient certs. Appreciation Kanawha City Midget Football Team, 1978, Charleston Dist. Outreach Ministries, 1981-83. Mem. ASCE (W.Va. sect. pres. 1990-91, v.p. 1989-90; pres. Charleston Br. 1988-89, sec., treas. 1987-88; corr. mem. nat. com. on employment conditions 1989-91). Democrat. Methodist. Home: 821 Scenic Dr Charleston WV 25311-1522 Office: Ste 400 606 Virginia St E Charleston WV 25301

STERLING, DONALD JUSTUS, JR., retired newspaper editor; b. Portland, Oreg., Sept. 27, 1927; s. Donald Justus and Adelaide (Armstrong) S.; m. Julie Ann Courteol, June 7, 1963; children: Sarah, William, John. A.B., Princeton U., 1948; postgrad. (Nieman fellow), Harvard U., 1955-56. Reporter Denver Post, 1948-52; news staff mem. Oreg. Jour., Portland, 1952-82; editor Oreg. Jour., 1972-82; asst. to pub. The Oregonian, 1982-92, ret., 1992. Pres. Tri-County Community Coun., 1972-73. Recipient Izaak Walton League Golden Beaver award, 1969, Edith Knight Hill award, 1978, Jessie Laird Brodie award Planned Parenthood Assn., 1983, McCall award Women in Communications, 1987, Roger W. Williams Freedom of Info. award Oreg. Newspaper Pubs. Assn., 1989; English-Speaking Union traveling fellow, 1959. Mem. Oreg. Hist. Soc. (pres. 1977-79), Mazamas, Lang Syne Soc., City Club (Portland, pres. 1973-74), Multnomah Athletic, Dial, Elm. Cannon (Princeton). Home: 1718 SW Myrtle St Portland OR 97201-2300

STERLING, DONALD T., professional basketball team executive; b. Chgo.. Lawyer L.A. (formerly San Diego) Clippers, Nat. Basketball Assn., owner, also chmn. bd. Office: care LA Clippers LA Meml Sports Arena 3939 S Figueroa St Los Angeles CA 90037-1207*

STERLING, KEIR BROOKS, historian, educator; b. N.Y.C., Jan. 30, 1934; s. Henry Somers and Louise Noel (de Wetter) S.; BS, Columbia U., 1961, M.A., 1963, Profl. Diploma, 1965, PhD, 1973; m. Anne Cox Diller, Apr. 3, 1961; children: Duncan Diller, Warner Strong, Theodore Craig. Asst. to dean Sch. Gen. Studies, Columbia U., N.Y.C., 1959-65, rsch. grantee, Eng., 1965-66; instr. in history Pace U., N.Y.C. and Pleasantville, N.Y., 1966-71, asst. prof., 1971-74, assoc. prof., 1974-77, adj. prof., 1977—; ordnance br. historian U.S. Army Ordnance Ctr. and Sch., Aberdeen Proving Ground, Md., 1983-94, U.S. Army Combined Arms Support Command, Ft. Lee, Va., 1994—; lectr. in gen. counselling Bklyn. Coll., City U. N.Y., 1967-68; asst. acad. dean, adj. asst. prof. history, coord. Am. studies program, dir. summer session Marymount Coll., Tarrytown, N.Y., 1968-71; asst. dean Rockland C.C., SUNY, Suffern, 1971-73; vis. prof. Mercy Coll., Westchester C.C., King's Coll., Nyack Coll., U. Wis., 1971, 75, 78-80, 83, Harford (Md.) C.C., 1987-94; adj. instr. Army Logistics Mgmt. Coll., Ft. Lee, Va., 1995—; co-project dir. Am. Ornithologists Union Centennial Hist. Project, 1976-89; cons. Arno Press, Inc., 1973-78, Coun. State Colls. of N.J., 1974-75, NSF, 1983—, Am. Trust for Brit. Libr., 1986-89; active Columbia U. Seminar on History and Philosophy of Sci., 1976—; archivist, historian mem. steering com. sect. mammalogy Internat. Union Biol. Scis., 1985—. Served with U.S. Army, 1954-56. Grantee Theodore Roosevelt Meml. Fund, Am. Mus. Natural History, 1967, Nat. Geog. Soc., 1977, NSF/Am. Soc. Mammalogists, 1978, NSF, 1981-82, IREX, 1982, mem. Archives and 75th Anniversary Coms. Mem. Am. Soc. Mammalogists, Am. Ornithologists Union (co-chmn. Centennial Hist. Com., mem. Archives Com., grantee, 1976, 77), Am. Soc. Environ. History (sec., mem. governing bd., editor newsletter), Rhinebeck (N.Y.) Hist. Soc. (trustee, pres. 1980-83), Harford County Com. of Md. Hist. Trust, Harford County Hist. Dist. Commn. (v.p. 1987-94), Hist. Soc. Harford County (bd. dirs. 1989-94), Assn. Bibliography of History (mem. coun. 1994—), Phi Alpha Theta, Sigma Tau Delta, Phi Delta Kappa. Democrat. Episcopalian. Author: Last of the Naturalists: The Career of C. Hart Merriam, 1974, 77; editor: Notes on the Animals of North America (B.S. Barton), 1974; assoc. editor Am. Nat. Biog., 1989—; editor, contbr.: Natural Sciences in America, 1974, 68 vols., 1974, Biologists and Their World, 1978, 77 vols.; gen. editor, contbr.: The International History of Mammalogy, 1987—; sr. editor, contbr. (with R. Harmond, G. Cevasco and L. Hammond) Biographical Dictionary of American and Canadian Naturalists and Environmentalists, 1996; editor, contbr. to numerous works in history Am. natural scis. and Am. mil. history. Home: 7104 Wheeler Rd Richmond VA 23229-6939 Office: 3901 A Avenue Ste 100 Fort Lee VA 23801-1807

STERLING, KENDALL WILLS, medical editor, writer, small business owner; b. Radford, Va., July 22, 1957; d. Willie Blanton and Myrtle Ross (Nolen) Wills; m. William Edward Sterling, Sept. 3, 1983. BA summa cum laude, U. Richmond, 1979; specialty cert. in Editing/Writing and Pharm. Writing, Am. Med. Writers Assn., 1992. Manuscript editor C.V. Mosby Co., St. Louis, 1980-81; editor, freelance coord. William Byrd Press, Richmond, Va., 1981-89; pres., mng. editor Sterling Comm. Svcs., Richmond, 1989—; cons. Schering-Plough, Madison, N.J., 1993. Editor: (report to U.S. Congress) The Contribution of Pharmaceutical Cos.: What's at Stake for America, 1993; 60 medical or allied health books including: Alzheimer's Disease: Treatment and Management, The Breast: Comprehensive Management of Benign and Malignant Diseases, Atlas of Pediatric Surgery, Cutaneous Surgery, Pediatric Arrhythmias: Electrophysiology and Pacing; article and issue editor: 25 med. and tech. jours including: Current Therapeutics Rsch., Am. Jour. Hosp. Pharmacy, Trauma Quarterly, Clin. Therapeutics. Mem. steering com. Campaign for Richmond, U. Richmond, 1991-93. Recipient David E. Howard Journalism scholarship U. Richmond, 1978-79. Mem. Am. Med. Writers Assn., Bd. Editors in Life Scis. (cert. editor in life scis., subcom. on member and pub. rels. 1992—), Coun. Biology Editors (authors editors com. 1993-95), European Assn. Sci. Editors, N.Y. Acad. Scis., Soc. Tech. Comm. Avocations: reading, fitness tng., hiking. Home and Office: Sterling Comm Svcs 2605 Mallards Xing Richmond VA 23233-2163

STERLING, NORMAN W., Canadian provincial official; b. Feb. 19, 1942. BA in Econs., Denison U., 1972; M Mgmt. in Hosp. and Health Adminstrn., Northwestern U., 1974. Asst./assoc. adminstr. for support svcs. Ohio State U. Hosps., Columbus, 1974-81, assoc. adminstr. profl. svcs., 1981-83; assoc. adminstr. profl. svcs. Vanderbilt U. Hosp., Nashville, 1983-84; interim CEO, interim CO Med. Coll. Va. Hosps., 1985-86; CFO, 1984-94; gen. dir. U. Minn. Hosp. and Clinic, Mpls., 1994—. Office: U Minn Hosp and Clinic Box 502 UMHC 420 Delaware St SE Minneapolis MN 55455

STERLING, RAYMOND LESLIE, civil engineering educator, researcher, consultant; b. London, Apr. 19, 1949; came to U.S., 1966; s. Richard Howard and Joan Valeria (Skinner) S.; m. Linda Lee Lundquist, Aug. 8, 1970 (div. Sept. 1982); children: Paul, Juliet, Erika; m. Janet Marie Kjera, Aug. 20, 1983; 1 child, Zoey. B in Civil and Structural Engring. with 1st class honors, U. Sheffield, Eng., 1970; MS in Geol. Engring., U. Minn., 1975, PhDCE, 1977. Registered civil engr., Minn.; chartered structural engr., Eng. Engr. trainee Met. Water Bd., London, 1968; civil engr. Egil Wefald and Assocs., Cons. Engrs., Mpls., 1969-71; structural engr. Husband and Co., Cons. Engrs., Eng., 1971-73; rsch. asst. U. Minn., Mpls., 1973-77, dir. Underground Space Ctr., 1977-95, asst. prof. dept. civil and mineral engring., 1977-83, assoc. prof., 1983-95; project. coord., structural engr. Setter, Leach and Lindstrom, Inc., Mpls., 1976-77; prin. cons. Itasca Cons. Group, Inc., Mpls., 1981-94; prof. civil engring. La. Tech. U., Ruston, 1995—, dir. Trenchless Tech. Ctr., 1995—; vice-chmn. U.S. Nat. com. on tunneling tech. NRC, NAS, 1990-91, chmn. 1992-94, mem. com. on infrastructure, 1991-93, mem. bd. infrastructure and the constructed environment, 1994-96; acting co-dir. Minn. Cold Climate Bldg. Rsch. Ctr. U. Minn., 1987-89, co-dir. Bldg. Energy Rsch. Ctr., 1986, mem. speaker's bur., active numerous other u. coms.; mem. energy adv. com. Legis. Com. on Minn. Resources, 1989-95; mem. com. on moisture control in bldgs. U.S. Bldg. Thermal Envelope Coordinating Coun., 1985-86; mem. program planning com. on bldg. founds. U.S. Dept. Energy, 1985-95; mem. adv. bd. for energy efficient residence demonstration project Nat. Assn. Home Builders, 1980; mem. Gov's. Exxon Oil Overcharge Adv. Task Force, 1986, Mpls. Energy Future Com., 1980-81, Scientist's Inst. for Pub. Info., N.Y.; cons. U.S. Army Corps. Engrs., UN, N.Y., Opus Corp., Mpls., Dames & Moore Internat., London, City of Mpls., Larson Engring., White Bear, Minn., Pilsbury Co., Mpls., Colgate Divsn.

Sch., Rochester, N.Y., many others; adv. prof. Chongqing Inst. Architecture and Engring., Sichuan, People's Republic China, 1985—; vis. rschr. Nat. Inst. Pollution and Resources MITI, Japan, 1991; vis. prof. U. Mo., Rolla, 1979; Shimizu prof. civil and mineral engring., U. Minn., 1988-95; mem. eminent speaker program Instn. Engrs., Australia, 1993; lectr., presenter numerous profl. meetings. Author: Earth Sheltered Housing Design: Guidelines, Examples and References, 1978, transl. into Chinese, French, Spanish and Russian, 2d. edit., 1985, (with others) Earth Sheltered Community Design: The Design of Energy-Efficient Residential Communities, 1980 (award for Best Book in Architecture and Urban Planning Profl. and Scholarly div. Assn. Am. Pubs. 1981), transl. into Spanish, 1981, Underground Building Design, 1983, translated into Japanese and Russian, others, Building Foundation Handbook, 1988, Underground Space Design, 1993, others; editor: (with others) Key Questions in Rock Mechanics: Proc. 29th U.S. Symposium on Rock Mechanics, 1988; contbr. articles to profl. jours. including Jour. Agrl. Engring., Internat. Jour. Rock Mechanics and Mining Scis., Exptl. Mechanics, many others. Recipient Young Engr. of Yr. award Minn. Fedn. Engring. Soc., 1982, Applied Rsch. award in rock mechanics NRC; elected fgn. mem. Acad. Engring. of Russian Fedn., 1993; grantee Shimizu Constrn. Co., 1987-93, Nat. Assn. Homebuilders, 1989, U.S. Dept. Energy, 1989-90, NSF, 1991, Minn. Dept. Transp., 1991, ASHRAE, 1991-92, many others. Fellow ASCE (pres. Minn. sect. 1990-91, bd. dirs. 1985-92, Young Civil Engr. of Yr. award 1982), Instn. Civil Engrs., Inst. Structural Engrs., Royal Soc. Arts, Mfrs. & Commerce; mem. NSPE, Am. Underground Space Assn., Internat. Tunneling Assn. (coordinating editor jour. 1986—, vice animateur working group on costs/benefits of subsurface utilization), N.Am. Soc. Trenchless Tech., Mpls. Engrs. Club. Achievements include research in rground construction, underground space utilization, trenchlen technology, rock mechanics, and energy use in buildings. Office: Trenchless Technology Ctr Louisiana Tech U PO Box 10348 Ruston LA 71272

STERLING, RICHARD LEROY, English and foreign language educator; b. Atlantic City, Feb. 18, 1941; s. Richard Leroy and Anne (Bass) S. BA, Am. U., 1968; MA, Cath. U., 1971; PhD, Howard U., 1990. Tchr. French and English, adult and continuing edn. D.C. Pub. Schs., Washington, 1969-71, 76-83; instr. French Howard U., Washington, 1973-76, grad. teaching asst., 1983-85, instr., lectr. in French, 1985-89; tchr. English Community-Based Orgns., D.C. Pub. Schs., Washington, 1989-91; asst. prof. French and English Bowie (Md.) State U., 1991—; tchr. summer enrichment program for gifted children Sch. Edn., Howard U., summers 1985, 86; tchr. ESL, D.C. Pub. Schs., summer, 1989, 94; vice chmn. World Centennial Conf.; French, Am. and Planetary Dimensions of Saint-John Perse, U. D.C., 1987; mem. adv. coun. Northeast Conf. Teaching Fgn. Langs. Author: The Prose Works of Saint-John Perse: Towards an Understanding of His Poetry, 1994; author articles and book reviews. Active Assn. Democratique des Francais a L.Etranger, 1988—, Senegal friendship com. Office Cmty. and Tehnic Affairs, Prince George's County Govt., Md., 1993-94, Assn. Inst. for Hatian Cultural and Sci. Affairs, 1992-94, local arrangements com. Conf. Coll. Composition and Communication, Washington, 1995; membership com. and outreach com. St. John's Ch., Washington, 1993, ch. growth com., 1995. With U.S. Army, 1964-66. Mem. MLA, Coll. Lang. Assn., Middle Atlantic Writers Assn. (chmn. essay contest com. 1995—), Samuel Beckett Soc., Societe des Professeurs Francais et Francophones d'Amerique, Zora Neale Hurston Soc., Am. Assn. Tchrs. French (sec.-treas. Washington chpt. 1986-90), Friends Superior Ct. Washington D.C. (bd. dirs.), Pi Delta Phi, Sigma Tau Delta. Democrat. Episcopalian. Avocations: classical music, history, travel. Home: 4235 Alton Pl NW Washington DC 20016-2017 Office: Bowie State U Dept English & Modern Langs Bowie MD 20715

STERMER, DUGALD ROBERT, designer, illustrator, writer, consultant; b. Los Angeles, Dec. 17, 1936; s. Robert Newton and Mary (Blue) S.; m. Jeanie Kortum; children: Dugald, Megan, Chris, Colin, Crystal. B.A., UCLA, 1960. Art dir., v.p. Ramparts mag., 1965-70; freelance designer, illustrator, writer, cons. San Francisco, 1970—; founder Pub. Interest Communications, San Francisco, 1974; pres. Frisco Pub Group Ltd.; chmn. illustration dept. Calif. Coll. Arts and Crafts, 1994—; bd. dirs. Am. Inst. Graphic Arts; chair illustration dept. Calif. Coll. Arts and Crafts, 1994—. Cons. editor: Communication Arts mag., 1974-90; designer: Oceans mag., 1976-82; editor: The Environment, 1972, Vanishing Creatures, 1980; author: The Art of Revolution, 1970, Vanishing Creatures, 1980, Vanishing Flora, 1994, Birds and Bees, 1994; designer 1984 Olympic medals; illustration exhbn. Calif. Acad. Scis., 1986. Mem. Grand Jury City and County San Francisco, 1989; bd. dirs. Delancey St. Found., 1990—. Recipient various medals, awards for design and illustration nat. and internat. competitions. Office: 600 The Embarcadero # 204 San Francisco CA 94107

STERN, ARTHUR PAUL, electronics company executive, electrical engineer; b. Budapest, Hungary, July 20, 1925; came to U.S., 1951, naturalized, 1956; s. Leon and Bertha (Frankfurter) S.; m. Edith M. Samuel; children: Daniel, Claude, Jacqueline. Diploma in Elec. Engring., Swiss Fed. Inst. Tech., Zurich, 1948; MSEE, Syracuse U., 1955. Mgr. electronic devices and applications lab. Gen. Electric Co., Syracuse, N.Y., 1957-61; dir. engring. Martin Marietta Corp., Balt., 1961-64; dir. ops. Bunker Ramo Corp., Canoga Park, Calif., 1964-66; v.p., gen. mgr. advanced products div. Magnavox, Torrance, Calif., 1966-79, pres. Magnavox Advanced Products and Systems Co., Torrance, 1980-90; vice chmn., bd. dirs. Magnavox Govt. and Indsl. Electronics Co., Ft. Wayne, Ind., 1987-90; pres. Ea. Beverly Hills Corp., 1991—, Calif.-Israel C. of C., 1994—; non-resident staff mem. MIT, 1956-59; instr. Gen. Elec. Bus. Mgmt., 1955-57. Chmn. engring. div. United Jewish Appeal, Syracuse, 1955-57; mem. adv. bd. dept. elec. engring. U. Calif., Santa Barbara, 1980-92; mem. Sch. Engring. Adv. and Devel. Council Calif. State U., Long Beach, 1985-90. Co-author: Transistor Circuit Engineering, 1957, Handbook of Automation, Computation and Control, 1961; also articles; U.S., fgn. patentee in field. Fellow AAAS, IEEE (pres. 1975, bd. dirs., officer 1970-77, guest editor spl. issue IEEE Trans. on Circuit Theory 1956, invited guest editor spl. issue Procs. IEEE on Integrated Electronics 1964, Centennial medal 1984). Jewish.

STERN, CARL LEONARD, former news correspondent, federal official; b. N.Y.C., Aug. 7, 1937; s. Hugo and Frances (Taft) S.; m. Joy Elizabeth Nathan, Nov. 27, 1960; children: Lawrence, Theodore. A.B., Columbia U., 1958, M.S., 1959; J.D., Cleve. State U., 1966, J.D. (hon.), 1975; J.D. (hon.), New Eng. Coll. Law, 1977. Bar: Ohio 1966, D.C. 1968, U.S. Supreme Ct. 1969. Law corr. NBC News, Washington, 1967-93; dir. Office of Pub. Affairs U.S. Dept. Justice, Washington, 1993—; lectr. Nat. Jud. Coll.; adj. prof. George Washington U., Stanford U. Editorial bd.: The Dist. Lawyer. Recipient Peabody award, 1974, Emmy award, 1974, Gavel award, 1969, 74, Headliner Club award, 1991. Mem. ABA (vice chmn. criminal justice sect. com. on criminal justice and the media, gov., forum com. on communications law, working group intelligence requirements and criminal code reform), AFTRA (nat. exec. bd. 1984-86, first v.p. Washington, Balt. chpt. 1985-87). Home: 2956 Davenport St NW Washington DC 20008-2165 Office: US Dept Justice Rm 1228 10th St & Constitution Ave NW Washington DC 20530

STERN, CARL WILLIAM, JR., management consultant; b. San Francisco, Mar. 31, 1946; s. Carl William and Marjorie Aline (Gunst) S.; m. Karen Jaffe, Sept. 7, 1966 (div. Mar. 1972); 1 child, David; m. Holly Drick Hayes, Mar. 21, 1985; 1 child, Matthew. BA, Harvard U., 1968; MBA, Stanford U., 1974. Cons. Boston Cons. Group, Inc., Menlo Park, Calif., 1974-77, mgr., 1977-78; mgr. Boston Cons. Group, Inc., London, 1978-80; v.p. Boston Cons. Group, Inc., Chgo., 1980-87, sr. v.p., 1987—. Lt. USNR, 1968-71. Office: Boston Consulting Group Inc 200 S Wacker Dr Chicago IL 60606-5802

STERN, CHARLES, foreign trade company executive; b. Germany, Dec. 2, 1920; came to U.S., 1940, naturalized, 1943; s. Julius and Else (Br) S.; m. Eve Hamburger, Sept. 20, 1947 (dec. Apr. 1980); children—Enid S., June M. Matriculation, U. London, 1937. With J. Gerber & Co., Inc., N.Y.C., 1940—; asst. v.p. J. Gerber & Co., Inc., 1960-63, v.p., 1963-68, exec. v.p., 1968-74, pres., chief exec. officer, 1974-88, chmn., 1986-89, chmn. emeritus, 1989—, cons. Served with AUS, World War II. Mem. ASTM, Am. Inst. Imported Steel (past pres.).

STERN, CLAUDIO DANIEL, medical educator; b. Montevideo, Uruguay, Feb. 9, 1954. BS with honors, U. Sussex, 1975, DPhil, 1978; MA, U. Oxford, 1985, DS, 1994. Asst. prof. anatomy dept. Cambridge (England) U., 1984-85; assoc. prof. dept. human anatomy O. Oxford (England), 1985-93; prof., chmn. dept. genetics and devel. Coll. Physicians and Surgeons Columbia U., N.Y.C., 1994—. Contbr. articles to profl. jours.; mng. editor Mechanisms of Devel.; mem. editorial adv. bd. Devel.; mem. editorial bd. Internat. Jour. Devel. Biology. Rsch. fellow U. Coll. London, 1978-84, fellow Oxford U., 1985-93. Office: Columbia U Dept Genetics & Devel 701 W 168th St New York NY 10032

STERN, DANIEL, author, executive, educator; b. N.Y.C., Jan. 18, 1928; s. Morris and Dora (Hochman) S.; m. Gloria Shapiro, Nov. 9, 1963; 1 son, Eric Branfman. Sr. v.p., mng. dir., mem. bd. mgmt. McCann-Erickson Advt., Inc., N.Y.C., 1964-69; v.p. advt. and publicity worldwide, also dir. Warner Bros., 1969-72; v.p., dir. mktg. Longchamps, Inc., N.Y.C., 1972-73; v.p., creative dir. Lubar-Southard, Inc., N.Y.C., 1973; fellow Ctr. for Humanities, Wesleyan U., 1969, vis. prof. letters and English, 1976-79; v.p. promotion East Coast CBS Entertainment, N.Y.C., 1979-86; pres. entertainment divsn. McCaffrey & McCall, Advt., N.Y.C., 1986; prof. English and creative writing U. Houston, 1992—, Cullen disting. prof. English, 1993—; dir. Humanities, 92nd St. YMHA, 1988. Author: Girl with Glass Heart, 1953, The Guests of Fame, 1955, Miss America, 1959, Who Shall Live, Who Shall Die, 1963 (Internat. Remembrance award for fiction Bergen Belsen Assn. 1973), After the War, 1967, The Suicide Academy, 1968, The Rose Rabbi, 1971, Final Cut, 1975, An Urban Affair, 1980, Twice Told Tales, 1989 (Richard and Hinda Rosenthal Fiction award AAAL 1990), Twice Upon a Time, 1992. With U.S. Army, 1946-47. Mem. PEN, Nat. Book Critics Circle, Author's League.

STERN, DANIEL, actor; b. Bethesda, Md., Aug. 28, 1957. TV movies include Samson & Delilah, Weekend War, The Court-Martial of Jackie Robinson; TV series Hometown, 1985, (narrator) The Wonder Years, 1988-93; films: Breaking Away, 1979, Starting Over, 1979, A Small Circle of Friends, 1980, Stardust Memories, 1980, It's My Turn, 1980, One-Trick Pony, 1980, Honky Tonk Freeway, 1981, I'm Dancing As Fast As I Can, 1982, Diner, 1982, Blue Thunder, 1983, Frankenweenie, 1984, Get Crazy, 1983, C.H.U.D., 1984, Key Exchange, 1985, The Boss' Wife, 1986, Hannah and Her Sisters, 1986, Born in East L.A., 1987, D.O.A., 1988, The Milagro Beanfield War, 1988, Leviathan, 1989, Little Monsters, 1989, Friends, Lovers and Lunatics, 1989, Coupe de Ville, 1990, My Blue Heaven, 1990, Home Alone, 1990, City Slickers, 1991, Home Alone 2, 1992, (also dir.) Rookie of the Year, 1993, City Slickers II: The Legend of Curley's Gold, 1994, (also prodr.) Tenderfoot, 1995. Office: CAA 9830 Wilshire Blvd Beverly Hills CA 90212-1804*

STERN, DANIEL ALAN, business management consultant; b. Bklyn., Aug. 28, 1944; s. William Joseph and Rita (Winegarten) S.; m. Gail Lynn Eddy, June 28, 1978. BS, Cornell U., 1965, PhD, 1971; MS, U. So. Calif., 1967. Cert. coll. teaching credential, Calif. Mem. sr. staff Hughes Aircraft Co., Culver City, Calif., 1965-73; mgr. digital signal processing TRW, Redondo Beach, Calif., 1973-79; pres. Martin & stern, Inc., Manhattan Beach, Calif., 1979-83; v.p. corp. devel. ROCKCOR, Inc., Redmond, Wash., 1983-85; v.p. advanced systems Rockcor group Olin Corp., Redmond, 1985-87; v.p. advanced def. systems Olin Corp., East Alton, Ill., 1987-89, v.p. tech., 1989-90; v.p. parent co. Olin Corp., Stamford, Conn., 1990-92, chief scientist, 1991-92; ind. cons., 1992—; bd. dirs. Secure Trans., Inc., Ponoma, Calif.; cons. Merctec, 1985—, United Technologies, 1993—; mem. bd. advisors U. Conn. Advanced Materials Inst., Storrs, 1991-92; mem. tech. coun. Conf. Bd. N.Y., 1992. Councilman City of Manhattan Beach, 1990-91, mayor pro tem, 1991-92, mayor, 1992-93; bd. dirs. Congregation Tifereth Jacob. Hughes fellow Hughes Aircraft Co., 1966. Mem. IEEE, Assn. U. S. Army, Assn. Old Crows, League Calif. Cities. Republican. Jewish. Avocations: motorcycle riding, shooting. Home and Office: 473 32nd St Manhattan Beach CA 90266-3928

STERN, DAVID JOEL, basketball association executive; b. N.Y.C., Sept. 22, 1942; s. William and Anna (Bronstein) S.; m. Dianne Bock, Nov. 27, 1963; children: Andrew, Eric. B.A., Rutgers U., 1963; LL.B., Columbia U., 1966. Bar: N.Y. 1963. Assoc. Proskauer Rose Goetz & Mendelsohn, N.Y.C., 1966-74, ptnr., 1974-78; gen. counsel Nat. Basketball Assn., N.Y.C., 1978-80, exec. v.p. bus. and legal affairs, 1980-84, commr., 1984—. Trustee Beth Israel Med. Ctr., 1985—, Rutgers U. Found., 1987—, Columbia U., 1992—; mem. Martin Luther King, Jr. Fed. Holiday Commn., 1988—, White House Conf. for a Drug-Free Am., 1988; bd. dirs. NAACP, 1990-93. Mem. ABA, N.Y. State Bar Assn., Assn. Bar City N.Y. (chmn. com. on entertainment and sports 1983-86). Office: NBA Olympic Tower 645 5th Ave New York NY 10022-5910*

STERN, EDWARD ABRAHAM, physics educator; b. Detroit, Sept. 19, 1930; s. Jacob Munich and Rose (Kravitz) S.; m. Sylvia Rita Sidell, Oct. 30, 1955; children: Hilary, Shari, Miri. BS, Calif. Tech., 1951, PhD, 1955. Post-doctoral fellow Calif. Tech., Pasadena, 1955-57; asst. prof. U. Md., College Park, 1957-61, assoc. prof., 1961-64, prof., 1964-65; prof. U. Wash., Seattle, 1965—. Contbr. over 200 articles to profl. jours.; editor; three books. Recipient B. Warren award Am. Crystallography Assn., 1979; named Guggenheim fellow, Cambridge, Eng., 1963-64, NSF Sr. Post-doctoral fellow, Haifa, Israel, 1970-71, Fulbright fellow, Jerusalem, Israel, 1985-86. Fellow AAAS, Am. Physical Soc. Achievements include patent for x-ray focusing device; development of x-ray absorption fine structure techniques; research on surface plasmons, nonlinear reflection from surfaces, electronic properties of alloys, structural phase transition. Office: U Wash Physics Dept FM-15 Box 351560 Seattle WA 98195-1560

STERN, ERNEST, science research executive, electrical engineer; b. Wetter, Hesse, Germany, June 5, 1928; came to U.S., 1938; s. Albert and Hilda (Katz) S.; m. Shola Jackson, May, 1955 (dec. Dec. 1960); children: Jessica, Sara; m. Phoebe M. Salten, Sept., 1962 (div. 1971); children: Hilary, Jennifer; m. Marcia Brown, May 16, 1971. BSEE, Columbia U., 1953; postgrad., Cornell U., 1953-55. Sr. engr. Sperry Gyroscope, L.I., N.Y., 1955-58; sr. researcher electronics lab. GE, Liverpool, N.Y., 1958-60; v.p. rsch. Microwave Chems. Lab., N.Y.C., 1961-64; assoc. divsn. head, sr. staff mem. MIT Lincoln Lab., Lexington, Mass., 1964-95, dir. Strategic Def. Initiative study of laser radars, 1984-85; cons., 1995—; mem. sci. and engring. adv. group to Strategic Def. Initiative Orgn., Washington, 1985-88. Co-inventor X-Ray Lithography, 1973 and ultrasonic, gyromagnetic and flat panel imaging devices. With USN, 1946-48. Fellow IEEE (sonics and ultrasonics adminstrn. com. 1980-84); mem. AAAS, Am. Phys. Soc., Appalachian Mountain Club. Democrat. Jewish. Avocations: mountain hiking, music, ballet, reading. Office: MIT Lincoln Lab PO Box 73 244 Wood St Lexington MA 02173-6499

STERN, FRITZ RICHARD, historian, educator; b. Breslau, Germany, Feb. 2, 1926; came to U.S., 1938, naturalized, 1947; s. Rudolf A. and Catherine (Brieger) S.; m. Margaret J. Bassett, Oct. 11, 1947 (div. 1992); children: Frederick P., Katherine Stern Brennan; m. Elisabeth Niebuhr Sifton, Jan. 1, 1996. B.A., Columbia U., 1946, M.A., 1948, Ph.D., 1953; D.Litt. (hon.), Oxford U., 1985. Lectr., instr. Columbia U., 1946-51, faculty, 1953—, prof. history, 1963—, Seth Low prof. history, 1967-92, univ. prof., 1992—, provost, 1980-83; acting asst. prof. Cornell U., 1951-53; tchr. Free U. Berlin, 1954, Yale U., 1963; permanent vis. prof. U. Konstanz, West Germany, 1966—; sr. adviser U.S. Embassy, Bonn, 1993-94; Élie Halévy prof. U. Paris, spring 1979; Phi Beta Kappa vis. scholar, 1979-80; Tanner lectr. Yale, 1993. Author: The Politics of Cultural Despair, 1961, The Failure of Illiberalism-Essays in the Political Culture of Modern Germany, 1972, rev. edit., 1992, Gold and Iron: Bismarck, Bleichroeder and the Bldg. of the German Empire, 1977 (recipient Lionel Trilling award Columbia U.), Dreams and Delusions: The Drama of German History, 1987; editor: The Varieties of History, 1956, 71, (with L. Krieger) The Responsibility of Power, 1967; mem. editorial bd. Foreign Affairs, 1978-92; contbr. articles to profl. jours.; reviewer Fgn. Affairs, 1963-95. Trustee German Marshall Fund, 1981—, Aspen Inst. of Berlin, 1983—; senator Deutsche Nationalstiftung, 1994—; mem. Trilateral Commn., 1983-90. Decorated Officer's Cross Order of Merit Fed. Republic of Germany; fellow Center Advanced Behavioral Scis., 1957-58; fellow Social Sci. Research Council, 1960-61; fellow Am. Council Learned Socs., 1966-67; fellow Netherlands Inst. Advanced Study, 1972-73; mem. Nuffield Coll., Oxford, 1966-67, Inst. Advanced Study Princeton, 1969-70; Guggenheim fellow, 1969-70; Ford Found. grantee, 1976-77; vis. scholar Russell Sage Found., 1989, spring 1993; recipient Leopold-Lucas-prize Evang. Faculty U. Tübingen, 1984. Mem. Am. Hist. Assn., AAAS, Am. Philos. Soc., Coun. Fgn. Rels., Deutsche Akademie für Sprache und Dichtung (corr.), Berlin Brandenburgische Akademie der Wissenschaften (corr.), Orden Pour le Mérite, Germany, Phi Beta Kappa (senator-at-large 1973-78). Club: Century (N.Y.C.). Home: 15 Claremont Ave New York NY 10027-6814

STERN, GAIL FRIEDA, historical association director; b. Atlantic City, May 18, 1950; d. Herbert and Faith (Beldegreen) Stern; m. Irwin Allen Popowsky (div.); m. Shawn Paul Aubitz, Sept. 20, 1987; 1 child, Jonathan. Student, Brown U., 1972; postgrad., U. Pa., 1973. Asst. in decorative arts Phila. Mus. Art, 1972-75; asst. curator Wheaton Mus. Glass, Millville, N.J., 1973-74; assoc. dir. Pa. Humanities Coun., Phila., 1976-79; mus. curator The Balch Inst. for Ethnic Studies, Phila., 1979-83, mus. dir., 1984-93; dir. Hist. Soc. Princeton, N.J., 1993—; chair State Task Force on Folk Arts and Culture, 1981-82; vice chmn. crafts panel Pa. Coun. on the Arts, Harrisburg, 1988-89; chair cultural conservation com., Pa. Heritage Affairs Commn., Harrisburg, 1990-92; participant Internat. Partnership in Mus., Singapore, 1991. Mem. Mus. Coun. Phila. (v.p. 1982-83), Am. Assn. Mus./Internat. Coun. Mus. (bd. dirs.), N.J. Mus. Assn. (mem. bd. dirs.), Am. Assn. for State and Local History Awards (N.J. chair 1994-95). Home: 131 E Maple Ave Morrisville PA 19067-6235 Office: Hist Soc Princeton 158 Nassau St Princeton NJ 08542-7077

STERN, GARDNER, television writer and producer. Writer TV series, including Capital News, 1990, WIOU, 1991, Sisters, 1992; co-prodr. TV series N.Y.P.D. Blue, 1992— (Emmy award for outstanding drama series 1995). Office: care ICM 8942 Wilshire Blvd Beverly Hills CA 90211

STERN, GEOFFREY, lawyer, disciplinary counsel; b. Columbus, Ohio, Nov. 29, 1942; s. Leonard J. and Anastasia (Percin) S.; m. Barbara Shnider; children: Emily, Elizabeth; stepchildren: Courtney, Jennifer, Brian Feuer. Student, Williams Coll., 1960-63; BA cum laude, Ohio State U., 1965, JD summa cum laude, 1968. Bar: Ohio 1968. Assoc. Alexander, Ebinger, Holschuh & Fisher, Columbus, Ohio, 1968-72; ptnr. Folkerth, Calhoun, Webster, Maurer & O'Brien, Columbus, Ohio, 1972-80, Arter & Hadden, Columbus, Ohio, 1980-93; disciplinary counsel Supreme Ct. of Ohio, 1993—; nat. coordinating counsel for asbestos litigation Combustion Engring. Inc. and Basic, Inc., 1985-93; lectr. on legal ethics; mem. Spl. Commn. to Review Ohio Ethics Rules, 1995—, Spl. Commn. on Legal Edn., 1995—. Sr. editor Ohio State Law Jour., 1967-68. Pres. Bexley (Ohio) City Coun., 1977-80, mem., 1973-80, mem. Bexley Civil Svc. Commn., 1983-85; v.p., trustee Creative Living, Columbus, 1981-89, Ohio Citizens Com. for Arts, Columbus, 1982-88; mem. Nat. Def. Com. on Asbestos in Bldgs. Litigation, 1986-92; pub. mem. Ohio Optical Dispensers Bd., Columbus, 1978-82. Recipient Am. Jurisprudence Evidence award Ohio State U. Coll. Law, 1967. Fellow Am. Bar Found., Columbus Bar Found., Ohio State Bar Found.; mem. Ohio State Bar Assn. (com. on legal ethics and profl. conduct, sec. 1981-90, vice chmn. 1990-92, chmn. 1992-93), Columbus Bar Assn. (profl. ethics com. 1975-86, 90-93), Order of Coif, Phi Beta Kappa, Pi Sigma Alpha. Home: 278 Crossing Creek N Columbus OH 43230-6108 Office: Disciplinary Counsel of Ohio Supreme Ct 175 S 3d St Ste 280 Columbus OH 43215-5196

STERN, GERALD DANIEL, poet; b. Pitts., Feb. 22, 1925; s. Harry and Ida (Barach) S.; m. Patricia Miller, Sept. 12, 1952 (div.); children: Rachel, David. BA, U. Pitts., 1947; MA, Columbia U., 1949. English tchr., prin. Lake Grove (N.Y.) Sch., 1951-53; English tchr. Victoria Dr. Secondary Sch., Glasgow, Scotland, 1953-54; English instr. Temple U., Phila., 1956-63; assoc. prof. English Indiana (Pa.) U. of Pa., 1963-67; prof. English Somerset (N.J.) County Coll., 1968-82; prof. English, Writers' Workshop, U. Iowa, Iowa City, 1982—; lectr. Douglas Coll., New Brunswick, N.J., 1968; vis. poet Sarah Lawrence Coll., Bronxville, N.Y., 1978, U. Pitts., 1978; vis. prof. Columbia U., N.Y.C., 1980, bucknell U., Lewisburg, Pa., 1988, NYU, 1989, 91, Princeton U., 1989; Fanny Hurst prof. Washington U., St. Louis, 1985; coal chair creative writing U. Ala., Tuscaloosa, 1984. Author: (poetry) Pineys, 1971, The Naming of Beasts, 1972, Rejoicings: selected Poems 1966-72, 1973, Lucky Life, 1977 (Lamont Poetry selection 1977, Nat. Book Critics Cir. award for poetry nominee 1978), The Red Coal, 1981 (Melville Caine award Poetry Soc. Am. 1982), Paradise Poems, 1984, Lovesick, 1987, Two Long Poems, 1990, Leaving Another Kingdom: Selected Poems, 1990, Bread Without Sugar, 1992, Odd Mercy, 1995, (essays) Selected Essays, 1988. Guggenheim fellow, 1980, Am. Acad. Poets fellow, 1993; NEA grantee to be master poet for Pa. 1973-75, Creative Writing grantee, 1976, 81, 87, State of Pa. Creative Writing grantee, 1979; recipient Gov. award for excellence in arts State of Pa., 1980, Bess Hokin award Poetry, 1980, Bernard F. Connor's award Paris Rev., 1981, Am. Poetry Rev. award, 1982, Jerome J. Shestack Poetry prize Am. Poetry Rev., 1984. Office: U Iowa 436 EPB Iowa City IA 52242

STERN, GERALD DANIEL, lawyer; b. N.Y.C., May 16, 1933; s. Solomon Stern and Stella Schoen; m. Doris Gittelman Mar. 21, 1960; children: Nelson M., Andrew L., Teri H. BA, NYU, 1954, LLB, 1957. Bar: N.Y. 1957, Calif. 1988, U.S. Ct. Appeals (2d cir.) 1959, U.S. Dist. Ct. (no. dist.) N.Y. 1965, U.S. Dist. Ct. D.C. 1969, U.S. Ct. Appeals (D.C. cir.) 1969, U.S. Dist. Ct. Md. 1970, U.S. Supreme Ct. 1970, U.S. Tax Ct. 1971, U.S. Ct. Appeals (9th cir.) 1987, U.S. Ct. Appeals (fed. cir.) 1987, U.S. Dist. Ct. (no. dist. Calif. 1987, so. dist. 1988). Assoc. Paul, Weiss, Rifkind, Wharton & Garrison, N.Y.C., 1957-67, ptnr., 1967-87; ptnr. Irell and Manella, Menlo Park, Calif., 1987-89, Brown & Bain, Palo Alto, Calif., 1989-91, Davis & Schroeder, Monterey, Calif., 1991-92; adj. prof. law NYU, 1983-87. Author: The Naked First Lady — A Humorous History of Monterey Peninsula, 1992, Fog City Follies, 1996, Was it Worth Twenty-Four Dollars?, 1996, Waiting for the Tidal Curve, 1996, Grants in Gold Grapes, 1996, Laughing at the Lawyers, 1996. Chmn. legal com., trustee Westchester Reform Temple, Scarsdale, N.Y., 1983-87. Mem. ABA, Beach Point Club, Boca West Club, Chamisol Tennis Club. Home and Office: 25493 Paseo De Cumbre Monterey CA 93940-6637

STERN, GERALD JOSEPH, advertising executive; b. Chgo., Nov. 1, 1925; s. Abraham and Mary (Spivak) S.; m. Sally R. Welham, May 28, 1950; children: Larry S., David J. B.S. in Journalism, U. Ill., 1949. Subscription sales promotion Esquire Mag., Chgo., 1949-50; v.p., creative dir. Marvin Gordon & Assos., Chgo., 1950-54; pres., chief exec. officer Stern, Walters/Earle Ludgin, Inc. (advt.), Chgo., Beverly Hills, Calif. and Ft. Lauderdale, Fla., from 1954, formerly chmn. bd., chief exec. officer, now ret.; bd. dir. Advance Leasing Corp., Ted Bates Adv. Inc.; mem. Nat. Com. Improving Advt. Bd. dirs. Off-the-St. Club. Served with USAAF, 1943-46. Mem. Am. Assn. Advt. Agys. (treas. Chgo. div. 1973), Nat. Advt. Rev. Bd., Chgo. Advt. Club. Club: Twin Orchard Country (dir.). Home: 726 Raleigh Rd Glenview IL 60025-4326

STERN, GERALD MANN, lawyer; b. Chgo., Apr. 5, 1937; s. Lloyd and Fannye (Wener) S.; m. Linda Stone, Dec. 20, 1969; children: Eric, Jesse, Maia. B.S. in Econs., U. Pa., 1958; LL.B. cum laude, Harvard, 1961. Bar: D.C. 1961, Calif. 1991, U.S. Supreme Ct. 1971. Trial atty. civil rights div. U.S. Dept. Justice, 1961-64; assoc. firm Arnold & Porter, Washington, 1964-68; ptnr. Arnold & Porter, 1969-76; founding ptnr. Rogovin, Stern & Huge, Washington, 1976-81; exec. v.p., sr. gen. counsel Occidental Petroleum Corp., Washington, 1981-82, L.A., 1982-92; spl. counsel fin. instn. fraud and health care fraud U.S. Dept. Justice, Washington, 1993-95; ind. legal cons. pvt. practice, Washington, 1995—. Author: The Buffalo Creek Disaster, 1976; co-author: Southern Justice, 1965. Mem. ABA. Home and office: 3322 Newark St NW Washington DC 20008-3330

STERN, GRACE MARY, former state legislator; b. Holyoke, Mass., July 10, 1925; d. Frank McLellan and Marguerite M. (Nason) Dain; m. Charles H. Suber, June 21, 1947 (div. 1959); children: Ann, Peter, Thomas, John; m. Herbert L. Stern, May 13, 1962; stepchildren: Gwen, Herbert III, Robert. Student, Wellesley Coll., 1942-45; LLD (hon.), Shimer Coll., 1984. Asst. supr. Deerfield Twp., Lake County, Ill., 1967-70; county clk. Lake County, Ill., 1970-82; mem. Ill. Ho. of Reps., Springfield, 1984-92, Ill. State Senate, 1993-95. Author: With a Stern Eye, 1967, Still Stern, 1969. Candidate lt. gov. State of Ill., 1982. Democrat. Presbyterian. Home: 291 Marshman Ave Highland Park IL 60035-4732 Office: 540 W Frontage Rd Ste 1000 Northfield IL 60093-1201

STERN, GUY, German language educator, writer; b. Hildesheim, Germany, Jan. 14, 1922; came to U.S., 1937, naturalized, 1943; s. Julius and Hedwig (Silberberg) S.; m. Judith Owens, June 16, 1979; 1 child, Mark. B.A. in Romance Langs., Hofstra Coll., 1948; M.A. with honors in Germanic Langs., Columbia U., 1950, Ph.D. with honors, 1953. Grad. asst., then instr. Columbia U., 1948-55; asst. prof., then asso. prof. Denison U., Granville, Ohio, 1955-63; prof. German, dept. head U. Cin., 1964-73, dean univ., 1973-76; prof., chmn. Germanic and Slavic dept. U. Md., College Park, 1976-78; v.p., provost Wayne State U., Detroit, 1978-80; disting. prof. German Wayne State U., 1980—; guest prof. Goethe Inst., Freiburg U., summers 1963-66, 84, Frankfurt U., 1993; adv. editor langs. and linguistics Dover Publs. Co-author: Brieflich Erzaehlt, 1956, Listen and Learn German, 1957, Say It in German, 1958, Uebung macht den Meister, 1959, An Invitation to German Poetry, 1960, Hints on Speaking German, 1961, Quick Change Pattern Drills, vol. I, 1962, vol. II, 1963, Hoer zu und Rat mit, 1964; author: Efraim Frisch: Zum Verstaendnis des Geistigen, 1964, War, Weimar and Literature, 1971, Alfred Neumann (anthology with biography), 1979, Literatur im Exil, 1989, Nazi Book Burning and the American Response, 1989; editor: Konstellationen: Die besten Erzaehluhgen des Neuen Merkur, 1964; co-editor: Nelly Sachs Ausgewaehlte Gedichte, 1968; assoc. editor: Lessing Yearbook, 1970-72, edit. bd. 1972—; sr. editor, 1979-81; contbr. articles on 18th and 20th century German lit. to profl. jours., also chpts. to books. Bd. dirs. Kurt Weill Found., sec., 1990—; bd. dirs. Leo Baeck Inst., 1967—, mem. exec. bd., 1978—; bd. dirs., chair acad. adv. com. Holocaust Meml. Mus. Greater Detroit; co-founder, pres. Lessing Soc., 1975-77; bd. dirs. Detroit Am. Jewish Com., 1988—. With AUS, 1942-45. Decorated Bronze Star; Fulbright Rsch. grantee U. Munich, 1961-63; recipient Order of Merit 1st Class, 1968, Friendship award, 1983, Germany, 1987, Grand Order of Merit, Festschrift in Honor of Guy Stern; Exile and Enlightment, 1987, Goethe medal, 1989, Presdl. award for Excellence in Teaching, 1992, Disting. Alumni award Hofstra U., 1993. Mem. Am. Assn. Tchrs. German (pres. 1970-72, Disting. Germanist of Yr. 1985, hon. mem. 1989), AAUP, Internat. PEN Club, MLA, South Atlantic MLA, Soc. for Exile Studies (v.p. 1981—). Home: 20672 Knob Woods Dr Southfield MI 48076-4033

STERN, HERBERT JAY, lawyer; b. N.Y.C., Nov. 8, 1936; s. Samuel and Sophie (Berkowitz) S.; children: Jason Andrew and Jordan Ezekiel (twins), Samuel Abraham, Sarah Kathrine. B.A., Hobart Coll., 1958; J.D. (Ford Found. scholar), U. Chgo., 1961; LL.D. (hon.), Seton Hall Law Sch., 1973, Hobart Coll., 1974; L.H.D. (hon.), Newark State Coll., 1973; D.C.L. (hon.), Bloomfield Coll., 1973; Litt.D. (hon.), Montclair State Coll., 1973. Bar: N.Y. 1961, N.J. 1971. Asst. dist. atty. New York County, 1962-65; trial atty. organized crime and racketeering sect. Dept. of Justice, 1965-69; chief asst. U.S. atty. Dist. of N.J., Newark, 1969-70; U.S. atty. Dist. of N.J., 1971-74, U.S. dist. judge, 1974-87; ptnr. Stern & Greenberg, Roseland, N.J., 1990—; mem. adv. com. U. Chgo. Law Sch. Author: Judgment in Berlin, 1984 (Valley Forge award Freedoms Found. 1984, Torch of Learning award Am. Friends of Hebrew U. 1987), Trying Cases to Win, Vol. I, 1991, Vol. II, 1992, Vol. III, 1993, Vol. IV, 1995. Named One of America's 10 Outstanding Young Men U.S. Jr. C. of C., 1971; Swartzer scholar U. Chgo. Law Sch., 1985; recipient Dean's Club award U. Akron Sch. Law, 1986, medal of excellence Hobart Coll., 1990. Fellow ABA, Am. Law Inst. (Clarence Darrow award), Internat. Platform Assn.; mem. ABA, N.J. Bar Assn., Fed. Bar Assn. (past pres. Newark chpt., recipient William J. Brennan, Jr. award 1987), Essex County Bar Assn., Am. Judicature Soc., Phi Alpha Delta. Subject of book Tiger in the Court, 1973. Office: 75 Livingston Ave Roseland NJ 07068-3701

STERN, HOWARD ALLAN, radio disc jockey, television show host; b. Roosevelt, N.Y., 1954; s. Ben and Ray S.; m. Alison Berns, 1978; children: Emily, Debra, Ashley Jade. BA in Comm., Boston U., 1976. Disc jockey Sta. WRNW, Briarcliff Manor, N.Y., 1976-78, Sta. WCCC, Hartford, Conn., 1978-79, Sta. WWWW, Detroit, 1979-80, Sta. WWDC, Washington, 1980-82, Sta. WNBC, N.Y.C., 1982-85, Sta. WXRK, N.Y.C., 1985—, numerous other markets, 1986—. Author: Private Parts, 1993, Miss America, 1995; TV shows include The Howard Stern Show (WOR-TV), 1990-92, The Howard Stern Interview (E!), 1992-93, The Howard Stern Show (E!), 1994—; recordings include 50 Ways To Rank Your Mother, 1982, Crucified by the FCC, 1991; pay-per-view spls./videos include: Howard Stern's Neglige and Underpants Party, U.S. Open Sores, Butt Bongo Fiesta, The Miss Howard Stern New Year's Eve Pageant. Libretarian candidate for gov. State of N.Y., 1994. Rest Stop on I-295 in N.J. named in his honor, 1995. Address: The Howard Stern Show WXRK-FM 600 Madison Ave New York NY 10022-1615 also: c/o Don Buchwald & Associates 10 E 44th St New York NY 10017-3606*

STERN, ISAAC, violinist; b. Kreminiecz, Russia, July 21, 1920; came to U.S., 1921; s. Solomon and Clara S.; m. Nora Kaye, Nov. 10, 1948; m. Vera Lindenblit, Aug. 17, 1951; children: Shira, Michael, David. Student, San Francisco Conservatory, 1930-37; numerous hon. degrees including, Dalhousie U., 1971, U. Hartford, 1971, Bucknell U., 1974, Hebrew U., Jerusalem, 1975, Yale U., 1975, Columbia U., 1977, Johns Hopkins U., 1979, U. Md., 1983, Tel Aviv U., 1983, NYU, 1989, U. Ill., 1992, Harvard U., 1992. Recital debut San Francisco, 1934; orchestral debut San Francisco Symphony Orch. (Pierre Monteux condr.), 1936; N.Y. debut, 1937; Carnegie Hall recital debut, 1943; N.Y. Philharm. debut (Arthur Rodzinski condr.), 1944; participated Prades Festival with Pablo Casals, 1950-52; soloist for first orchestral and recital performances at Kennedy Ctr., Washington; first Am. to perform in USSR after World War II, 1956; mem. Istomin-Rose-Stern trio, 1962-83 (Beethoven cycle w/Istomin & Rose 1970-71); performed in China at invitation of Chinese govt., 1979; performed world premieres of violin works by Bernstein, Dutilleux, Hindemith, Maxwell Davies, Penderecki, Rochberg and Schuman; has played with major orchestras, given countless recitals and performed at important festivals in the U.S., Europe, Israel, Far East, Australia and S. Am. Over 100 records, cassettes and CD's for CBS Masterworks, named Artist Laureate 1984 CBS Masterworks; made soundtrack for motion pictures Humoresque (Warner Bros.) and Fiddler on the Roof (United Artists); starred in soundtrack Tonight We Sing (20th Century Fox) and Journey to Jerusalem with Leonard Bernstein; documentary film From Mao to Mozart-Isaac Stern in China (Academy award 1981, Cannes Film Festival Special Mention), Carnegie Hall: The Grand Reopening, 1987 (Emmy award), Isaac Stern-A Life, 1991. Chmn. bd. Am.-Israel Cultural Found.; chmn., founder Jerusalem Music Ctr.; originating mem. Nat. Endowment for the Arts; pres. Carnegie Hall, N.Y.C., 1960—. Decorated comdr. Order de la Couronne, comdr. Legion d'Honneur; comdr.'s cross (Order of Dannebrog (Denmark); recipient numerous Grammy awards, Grammy Lifetime Achievement award, 1987, Nat. medal of Honor, 1991, Presdl. medal of Freedom, 1992, numerous local city awards; named Musician of Yr., ABC/Musical Am., 1986; Felllow of Jerusalem, 1986. Office: care ICM Artists Ltd 40 W 57th St New York NY 10019-4001

STERN, JAMES ANDREW, investment banker; b. N.Y.C., Oct. 1, 1950; s. Arthur and Lenore (Oppenheimer) S.; m. Jane Yusem, April 13, 1975; children: Peter, David. BS, Tufts U., 1972; MBA, Harvard U., 1974. Assoc. Lehman Bros. Inc., N.Y.C., 1974-79, v.p., 1979-82, mng. dir., 1982-94; chmn. The Cypress Group, N.Y.C., 1994—; dir. K & F Industries, Inc., N.Y.C., R.P. Scherer Corp., N.Y.C., Noel Group, Inc., N.Y.C., Lear Seating Corp., N.Y.C., Infinity Broadcasting Corp., N.Y.C., Anemark U.S.A., Inc. Trustee Tufts U., Medford, Mass., 1982—. Clubs: Quaker Ridge Golf (Scarsdale, N.Y.), Beach Point (Mamaroneck, N.Y.). Avocations: golf, reading. Office: The Cypress Group Inc 65 E 55th St New York NY 10022

STERN, JAMES COPER, sales executive; b. N.Y.C., Dec. 12, 1925; s. George Charles and Ruth (Coper) S.; m. Judith Vinson, Oct. 31, 1963 (div. Mar. 1974); children: Hillary Anne, Renee Jean; m. Ruth Nussbacker Szold, Aug. 22, 1982. BA, NYU, 1949. Trainee, exec. asst. Gardner Advt. Co., N.Y.C., 1949-50; advt. mgr. NOPCO Chem. Co., Harrison, N.J., 1950-53; account exec. Ziv TV Programs, N.Y.C., 1954-56; sales rep. United Artists Associated, N.Y.C., 1957-61; v.p., sales mgr. Allied Artists TV, N.Y.C., 1961-70; exec. v.p., gen. sales mgr. ITC Entertainment, Inc., Studio City, Calif., 1970-89; pres. JCS Syndication Svcs., L.A., 1990—. Cpl. U.S. Army, 1944-46, ETO. Mem. Internat. Radio and TV Soc., Nat. Assn. TV Program Execs., Ind. TV Program Execs. Republican. Jewish. Avocations: watercolor painting, skiing, golf, art. Home: 8455 Fountain Ave Apt 515 Los Angeles CA 90069-2543 Office: JCS Syndication Svcs 8455 Fountain Ave Apt 515 Los Angeles CA 90069-2543

STERN, JEANNETTE ANNE, secondary school educator; b. Bklyn., June 13, 1948; d. Samuel and Rosalie (Presler) Beckerman; m. William D. Stern, Aug. 10, 1974; children: Susan Rachel, Diana Lynne. BA, SUNY, Albany, 1970; MA, Hofstra U., 1972; MEd, Tchrs. Coll., N.Y.C., 1993, EdD, 1994. Cert. tchr. social studies 7-12, Spanish 7-12, adminstrn. and supervision. Tchr. Spanish Wantagh (N.Y.) Pub. Schs., 1970-73, tchr. social studies, 1973-92, chmn. dept. social studies, 1992—; regional dir. N.Y. State Middle Sch. Assn., 1990—; cons. in field. Contbr. articles to profl. jours. Chairperson sch. bd. Congregation B'nai Israel, Freeport, N.Y., 1989—. Recipient Faculty Svc. award Am. Legion, 1983, PTA Svc. award, Wantagh, 1988. Mem. Nat. Middle Sch. Assn., Wantagh United Tchrs., Am. Fedn. Tchrs., SUNY at Albany Alumni Assn. (bd. dirs. 1970-73), Holocaust Mus. (charter), Phi Delta Kappa. Avocations: knitting, crochet, travel. Home: 17 Florence Ave Freeport NY 11520-5823 Office: Wantagh Pub Schs 3301 Beltagh Ave Wantagh NY 11793-3365

STERN, JOAN NAOMI, lawyer; b. Phila., Mar. 7, 1944; d. Clarence J. and Diana D. (Goldberg) S. BA, U. Pa., 1965; JD, Temple U., 1977. Bar: Pa. 1977. Assoc. Blank, Rome, Comisky & McCauley, Phila., 1977-83, ptnr., 1983—, co-chair pub. fin. group, 1983-92, chair pub. fin. group, 1993, chair pub. fin. dept., 1994—; cons. counsel Phila. Charter Commn., 1993-94. Contbr. articles to profl. jours. Mem. Sch. Dist. Task Force on Regulatory Reform, Phila., 1987, Tax Policy and Budget Com., Phila., 1989, Phila. Mayor's Fiscal Adv. Com., 1990; chair Sch. Dist. of Phila. Task Force on Alternate Financing Strategies, 1995; bd. mgrs. Moore Coll. Art and Design, Phila., 1993—, vice chair bd. mgrs., 1995—; bd. dirs. Police Athletic League, Phila., 1994—. Fellow Am. Bar Found.; mem. ABA, Nat. Assn. Bond Lawyers, Phila. Bar Assn., Phila. Bar Assn. (chmn. mcpl. govt. com. 1983—), Pa. Assn. Bond Lawyers. Office: Blank Rome Comisky & McCauley 4 Penn Center Plz Philadelphia PA 19103-2521

STERN, JOSEPH A., lawyer; b. Cleve., Dec. 7, 1949; s. Arthur J. and Thelma (Arnold) S. BA, Yale U., 1972, JD, 1976. Assoc. Winthrop Stimson, N.Y.C., 1976-79; assoc. Fried Frank Harris Shriver & Jacobson, N.Y.C., London, 1979-84, ptnr., 1984—. Vice chair, dir. Mex. Am. Legal Defense and Edn. Fund, L.A., 1991-95; dir. Am. Friend Chamber Music of Europe, N.Y.C., 1986—. Mem. ABA, City Bar N.Y. Office: Fried Frank Harris 1 New York Plz New York NY 10004

STERN, JOSEPH SMITH, JR., former footwear manufacturing company executive; b. Cin., Mar. 31, 1918; s. Joseph S. and Miriam (Haas) S.; m. Mary Stern, June 14, 1942; children: Peter Joseph, William Frederick, Peggy Ann Graeter. AB, Harvard U., 1940, MBA, 1943; HHD (hon.), Xavier U., 1988; DSc(hon.), U. Cin., 1989. With R. H. Macy & Co., N.Y.C., 1940-41; with U.S. Shoe Corp., Cin., 1941-68; v.p. U.S. Shoe Corp., 1951-65, pres., 1965-66, chmn. bd., chief exec. officer, 1966, chmn. exec. com., 1966-68, dir., 1956-70; prof. bus. policy emeritus U. Cin. Pres. bd. trustees Cin. and Hamilton County Pub. Libr.; chmn. Cin. Bicentennial Com., Greater Cin. Tall Stacks Commn.; trustee Cin. Music Hall Assn., Cin. Hist. Soc., Children's Hosp. Med. Center, Cin. Symphony Orch., Cin Country Day Sch., 1956-72, Family Svc., Cin., 1964-82; trustee, pres. Cin. Mus. Festival Assn.; pres. bd. trustees Children's Convalescent Hosp., Cin., 1972-75; bd. overseers vis. com. univ. libr. Harvard U. Served to lt. USNR, 1943-46. Recipient Disting. Community Svc. award NCCJ, 1986, Great Living Cincinnatian award Cin. C. of C., 1989, Disting. Svc. award U. Cin. Coll. Bus., 1992. Mem. Am. Footwear Industries Assn. (life; dir.). Jewish (past pres. temple). Clubs: Literary (Cin.), Harvard (Cin.) (pres. 1965), Queen City (Cin.), Queen City Optimists, Harvard (N.Y.C.). Home: 3 Grandin Pl Cincinnati OH 45208-3402

STERN, LEO G., lawyer; b. Mpls., Apr. 10, 1945; s. Philip J. and June I. (Monasch) S.; m. Christine E. Lamb, June 29, 1968; children: Alison M., Zachary A. BA, U. Calif., Davis, 1967; JD cum laude, U. Minn., 1970. Bar: Minn. 1970, U.S. Dist. Ct. Minn. 1971, Calif. 1971, U.S. Ct. Appeals (6th, 7th and 8th cirs.) 1985, U.S. Supreme Ct. 1993; cert. mediator and arbitrator, Minn. Ptnr. Cox, King & Stern, Mpls., 1970-77, Wright, West & Diessner, Mpls., 1977-84, Fredrikson & Byron, P.A., Mpls., 1984—. Mem. Minn. Bar Assn. (governing coun. environ. and natural resources law sect. 1989-95, governing coun. litigation sect. 1995—), Am. Arbitration Assn. (arbitrator, mediator). Avocations: sailing, jogging. Home: 4331 Fremont Ave S Minneapolis MN 55409-1720 Office: Fredrikson & Byron PA 1100 International Ctr 900 2nd Ave S Minneapolis MN 55402-3314

STERN, LEONARD BERNARD, television and motion picture production company executive; b. N.Y.C., Dec. 23, 1923; s. Max and Esther (Marton) S.; m. Gloria Jane Stroock, Aug. 12, 1956; children: Michael Stroock, Kate Jennifer. Student, NYU, 1944. Dir. TV L.A., 1946-53; writer, dir., producer Jackie Gleason Show/Honeymooners, Sergeant Bilko, Steve Allen Show N.Y.C., 1953-60; founder Price-Stern-Sloan, L.A., 1959-64, v.p., 1964-69; dir. Price-Stern-Sloan, 1969—; pres. Heyday Prodns., L.A., 1962-69, 75—; v.p. Talent Assocs./Norton Simon, L.A. and N.Y.C., 1965-75. Author: (with Roger Price) Mad Libs, 1958, What Not to Name the Baby, 1960, Dear Attila the Hun, 1985; (with Roger Price and Larry Sloan) The Baby Boomer Book of Names, 1985, (with Diane L. Robison) A Martian Wouldn't Say That, 1994; writer, dir.: (motion pictures) Just You and Me, Kid, 1979, Target, 1985, Missing Pieces, 1990; creator, writer, dir. 21 TV series, including Get Smart, McMillan and Wife and He and She, 1953-89; media editor Dialogue newsletter. Mem. adv. coun. Sch. of Arts, NYU; bd. dirs. Nat. Coun. for Families and TV, Inst. for Mental Health Initiatives. Recipient Peabody award U. Ga., Writers Guild award 1956, 66, Nat. Assn. TV Arts and Scis. award 1956, 66-67, Emmy award 1956, 1966. Mem. Writers Guild Am., Dirs. Guild Am., Caucus for Producers, Writers and Dirs. (co-chmn., Mem. of Yr award 1987, Disting. Svc. award 1987), Producers Guild Am. (pres.), Bd. Motion Picure and TV Fund Found. Office: 5th flr east 11835 W Olympic Blvd Los Angeles CA 90064-5001

STERN, LEONARD NORMAN, pet supply manufacturing company executive; b. N.Y.C., Mar. 28, 1938; s. Max and Hilda (Lowenthal) S.; m. Allison Maher; children: Emanuel Theodore, Edward Julius, Andrea Caroline. B.S. cum laude, NYU, 1956, M.B.A., 1957. Formerly pres., dir., now chmn., chief exec. officer Hartz Group, Inc., 1959—; pres., chmn. bd. Hartz Mountain Industries, pub. Village Voice; mem. adv. bd. Chem. Bank, N.Y.C., 1970—; active real estate constrn., devel. Bd. dirs. Manhattan Day Sch., Jewish Ctr., N.Y.C.; founder Albert Einstein Coll. Medicine, 1958; mem. N.Y.C. Holocaust Meml. Comm.; founder Homes for the Homeless; trustee, chmn. fin. com. NYU. Office: Hartz Mountain Industries 667 Madison Ave New York NY 10021-8029*

STERN, LEWIS ARTHUR, lawyer; b. Pitts., Apr. 28, 1934; s. John C. and Belle (Maretsky) S.; m. Chris Ertel; children: Isobel, Gillian, Emily, Thomas. B.A., Yale U., 1955, LL.B., 1958. Bar: N.Y. 1959. Law clk. to chief judge U.S. Ct. Appeals (2d cir.), N.Y.C., 1958-59; assoc. Fried, Frank, Harris, Shriver & Jacobson, N.Y.C., 1959-67, ptnr., 1967—. Office: Fried Frank Harris 1 New York Plz New York NY 10004

STERN, LOUIS WILLIAM, marketing educator, consultant; b. Boston, Sept. 19, 1935; s. Berthold Summerfield Stern and Gladys (Koch) Cohen; m. Rhona L. Grant; children: Beth Ida, Deborah Lynn. A.B., Harvard U., 1957; M.B.A. in Mktg, U. Pa., 1959; Ph.D. in Mktg, Northwestern U., 1962. Mem. staff bus. research and consumer mktg. sects. Arthur D. Little, Inc., Cambridge, Mass., 1961-63; asst. prof. bus. orgn. Ohio State U., Columbus, 1963-64; assoc. prof. mktg. Ohio State U., 1966-69, prof. mktg., 1970-73; prof. mktg. Northwestern U., Evanston, Ill., 1973-75; A. Montgomery Ward prof. mktg. Northwestern U., 1975-83, chmn. dept. mktg., 1977-80, John D. Gray disting. prof. mktg., 1984—; on leave as exec. dir. Mktg. Sci. Inst., Cambridge, Mass., 1983-85; Thomas Henry Carroll Ford Found. vis. prof. Harvard U. Grad. Sch. Bus. Adminstrn., 1984-85; mem. staff Nat. Commn. on Food Mktg., Washington, 1965-66; vis. assoc. prof. bus. adminstrn. U. Calif., Berkeley, 1969-70; guest lectr. York U., U. Minn., U. Ky., UCLA, Ohio State U., U. N.C., Duke U., U. Wis., U. Pitts., U. Chgo., MIT, U. Mich., U. Pa., Cornell U., U. Mo., Norwegian Sch. Econs. and Bus. Adminstrn.; faculty assoc. Hernstein Inst., Vienna, Austria, 1976-77, Mgmt. Centre Europe, 1988—; faculty assoc. Gemini Cons. Inc., Montvale, N.J., 1977—, mem. midwest adv. bd., 1989—; Xerox research prof. Northwestern U., 1981-82; cons. to FTC, 1973, 80. Author: Distribution Channels: Behavioral Dimensions, 1969, (with Frederick D. Sturdivant and others) Managerial Analysis in Marketing, 1970, Perspectives in Marketing Management, 1971, (with John R. Grabner, Jr.) Competition in the Marketplace, 1970, (with Adel I. El-Ansary) Marketing Channels, 5th edit., 1996, (with Thomas L. Eovaldi) Legal Aspects of Marketing Strategy: Antitrust and Consumer Protection Issues, 1984; (with Adel I. El-Ansary and James R. Brown) Management in Marketing Channels, 1989; mem. edit. bd. Jour. Mktg. Rsch., 1976-82, Jour. Mktg., 1979-83, Mktg. Letters, 1988-94; contbr. articles on mktg. to profl. jours. Mem. exec. com. Northwest Area Council on Human Relations, Columbus, 1971-72. Rsch. grantee: Ohio State U., 1964-73, Mktg. Sci. Inst., 1976-77, 88-90, 92—; recipient Harold H. Maynard award best article Jour. Mktg., 1980; named Mktg. Educator of Yr. Sales and Mktg. Execs. Internat., 1989, also Chgo. chpt. 1990, Outstanding Profl. of Yr. award, 1992, and named one of Top 6 Profs. in Kellogg Sch., Northwestern U., Grad. Mgmt. Assocs., 1984—, (named 6 times Outstanding Prof. Exec. Masters Program), one of Top 12 Tchrs. in U.S., Bus. Week. Mem. AAUP, Am. Mktg. Assn. (mem. program com. educators conf. 1971, chmn. com. 1978, Paul D. Converse award 1986, Richard D. Irwin Disting. Mktg. Educator of Yr. 1994), Hellenic Inst. Mktg. (hon.), Beta Gamma Sigma. Home: 724 Sheridan Rd Wilmette IL 60091-1960 Office: Northwestern U JL Kellogg Grad Sch Mgmt Dept Mktg Evanston IL 60208

STERN, MADELEINE BETTINA, rare books dealer, author; b. N.Y.C., July 1, 1912; d. Moses Roland and Lillie (Mack) S. BA, Barnard Coll., 1932; MA, Columbia U., 1934. Tchr. English N.Y.C. High Schs., 1934-43; ptnr. Leona Rostenberg Rare Books, N.Y.C., 1945—, Leona Rostenberg and Madeleine B. Stern Rare Books, N.Y.C., 1980—; lectr. history of book, feminism, pub. history, lt. Author: The Life of Margaret Fuller, 1942, Louisa May Alcott, 1950, new edit., 1996, Purple Passage: The Life of Mrs. Frank Leslie, 1953, Imprints on History: Book Publishers and American Frontiers, 1956, We the Women: Career Firsts of Nineteenth Century America, 1962, new edit., 1994, So Much in a Lifetime: The Story of Dr. Isabel Barrows, 1965, Queen of Publishers' Row: Mrs. Frank Leslie, 1966, The Pantarch: A Biography of Stephen Pearl Andrews, 1968, Heads and Headlines: The Phrenological Fowlers, 1971, Books and Book People in 19th-Century America, 1978, Antiquarian Bookselling in the United States: A History from the Origins to the 1940s, 1985, Nicholas Gouin Dufief of Philadelphia Franco-American Bookseller, 1776-1834, 1988, The Life of Margaret Fuller: A Revised Second Edition, 1991; (with Leona Rostenberg) Old and Rare: Forty Years in the Book Business, 1974, rev. edit. 1988, Between Boards: New Thoughts on Old Books, 1978, Bookman's Quintet: Five Catalogues about Books, 1980, Quest Book-Guest Book: A Biblio-Folly, 1993, Connections: Our Selves-Our Books, 1994; editor: Women on the Move, 4 vols., 1972, Victoria Woodhull Reader, 1974, Louisa's Wonder Book-An Unknown Alcott Juvenile, 1975, Behind a Mask: The Unknown Thrillers of Louisa May Alcott, 1975, new edit., 1995, Plots and Counterplots: More Unknown Thrillers of Louisa May Alcott, 1976, Publishers for Mass Entertainment in 19th-Century America, 1980, A Phrenological Dictionary of 19th-Century Americans, 1982, Critical Essays on Louisa May Alcott, 1984, A Modern Mephistopheles and Taming a Tartar by Louisa May Alcott, 1987, Louisa May Alcott Unmasked: Collected Thrillers, 1995, Modern Magic: Five Stories by Louisa May Alcott, 1995The Feminist Alcott: Stories of a Woman's Power, 1996; co-editor: Selected Letters of Louisa May Alcott, 1987, A Double Life: Newly Discovered Thrillers of Louisa May Alcott, 1988, The Journals of Louisa May Alcott, 1989, Louisa May Alcott: Selected Fiction, 1990, (co-editor) Freaks of Genius: Unknown Thrillers of Louisa May Alcott, 1991, From Jo March's Attic: Stories of Intrigue and Suspense, 1993 (Victorian Soc. award), The Lost Stories of Louisa May Alcott, 1995. Guggenheim fellow, 1943-45; recipient Medalie award Barnard Coll., 1982, Victorian Soc. award. Mem. Antiquarian Booksellers Assn. Am. (gov. 1966-68, 78-80), Internat. League Antiquarian Booksellers, MLA, Am. Printing History Assn. (co-recipient award 1983), Authors League, Manuscript Soc. (former trustee), Phi Beta Kappa. Jewish. Home: 40 E 88th St New York NY 10128-1176 Office: Rare Books 40 E 88th St New York NY 10128-1176

STERN, MARC IRWIN, financial services executive; b. Vineland, N.J., Apr. 17, 1944; s. Albert B. and Sylvia (Goodman) S.; m. Eva Suzanne Kuhn, Aug. 14, 1966; children: Adam Bryan, Suzanne Rona. BA cum laude in Polit. Sci., Dickinson Coll., Carlisle, Pa., 1965; MA, Columbia U., 1966, JD magna cum laude, 1969. Bar: N.Y. 1969, N.H. 1975. Law clk. U.S. Ct. Appeals 2d Circuit, 1969-70; assoc. Debevoise & Plimpton, 1970-74; v.p., gen. counsel Wheelabrator-Frye Inc., Hampton, N.H., 1974-80, sr. v.p., 1980-83; sr. v.p. adminstrn. The Signal Cos., Inc., La Jolla, Calif., 1983-85, Allied-Signal Inc., Morristown, N.J., 1985-86; mng. dir., chief adminstrv. officer The Henley Group, Inc., N.Y.C. and La Jolla, 1986-88; pres. SunAmerica, Inc., L.A., 1988-90, The TCW Group, Inc., L.A., 1992—; chmn. bd. TCW Ams. Devel., Inc., 1990—, TCW Funds, Inc., 1990—, TCW London Internat., Ltd.., 1993, TCW Asia, Ltd., 1993; bd. dirs. Qualcomm, Inc. Trustee Salk Inst. for Biol. Studies, La Jolla, Dickinson Coll., Carlisle, Pa., UCLA Med. Ctr.; bd. dirs. L.A. Music Ctr. Opera. Home: 10247 Century Woods Dr Los Angeles CA 90067-6312 Office: The TCW Group Inc 865 S Figueroa St Ste 1800 Los Angeles CA 90017-2543 also: 200 Park Ave Ste 2200 New York NY 10166-0005

STERN, MARILYN BETH, picture editor, photographer, writer; b. Detroit, Nov. 8, 1953; d. Julian and Phyllis S. BA, Brown U., 1976. Photographer's asst. N.Y.C., 1976-82, freelance photographer, 1976—; tchr. photography pvt. practice, N.Y.C., 1980-83; freelance writer N.Y.C., 1985—; picture editor Across the Board mag., N.Y.C., 1990—. Photographer/organizer: (book) Masked Culture: The Greenwich Village Halloween Parade, 1994; author/photographer: Kval! Die Waldanger der Lofoten, 1990; represented in permanent collection Detroit Inst. Arts. Travel Study grantee Royal Norwegian Consulate to Norway in the U.S., 1987, Am.-Scandinavian Found., 1986. Jewish. Avocations: Go, Irish music, birding, drawing. Office: The Conference Bd 845 3rd Ave New York NY 10022-6679

STERN, MARVIN, management consultant; b. Bklyn., Jan. 5, 1923; s. David and Regina (Harnik) S.; m. June Bronstein Wittlin, Mar. 24, 1945; children—Ellis Roy, Richard Keith; m. Patricia Wolberg, June 17, 1955; children—Valerie Ann, Gary Allen, Jody Amanda. B.S. in Mech. Engring., CCNY, 1943; M.S., NYU, 1947, Ph.D. in Math, 1954. Corp. staff exec. rsch. and devel. Gen. Dynamics Co., 1958-60; asst. dir. strategic weapons Office Sec. Def., Washington, 1960-61; dep. dir. def. rsch. and engring., weapons systems Office Sec. Def., 1961-62; v.p. rsch. and engring. N.Am. Aviation, Inc., El Segundo, Calif., 1962-63; mgmt. cons. L.A., 1963-64; pres. aero. systems div. Gen. Precision, Inc., Wayne, N.J., 1964-66; v.p. Rand Corp., Santa Monica, Calif., 1967-68; pres. Laird Systems, L.A., 1968-70, Marvin Stern, Inc., Santa Ynez, Calif., 1970—; sr. fellow UCLA Ctr. for Internat. and Strategic Affairs, 1990-92; cons. Office Sec. Def., Sec. Transp., Pres.'s Sci. Adv. Com., CIA; Def. Sci. Bd., Naval Res. Adv. Com. Author: (with George Gamow) Puzzle Math, 1958; editor: (with Morton Alperin) Vistas in Astronautics, 1958. Trustee Lycée Français de Los Angeles. Recipient Meritorious Civilian Service medal Sec. Def., 1962. Address: 4001 Long Valley Rd Santa Ynez CA 93460-9721

STERN, MARVIN, psychiatrist, educator; b. N.Y.C., Jan. 6, 1916; s. Jacob and Mary (Kappel) S.; m. Libby Rifkin, Jan. 18, 1942; children: Carol S., Robert M., Theodore A. B.S., CCNY, 1935; M.D., NYU, 1939. Diplomate Am. Bd. Psychiatry and Neurology. Intern in medicine and surgery Bellevue Hosp., N.Y.C., 1939-40, resident in medicine and psychiatry, 1940-42, fellow in psychiatry, 1946-47; practice medicine specializing in psychiatry N.Y.C., 1947—; asst. prof. psychiatry NYU Med. Ctr., N.Y.C., 1948-55, assoc. prof., 1955-62, prof., 1962-79, Menas S. Gregory prof. psychiatry, 1979-86, prof., 1986-95; prof. emeritus, 1995—; prof. emeritus NYU Med. Ctr., N.Y.C., 1995—, exec. chmn. dept. psychiatry, 1976-86; mem. staff NYU Hosp., Bellevue Hosp.; cons. psychiatrist VA Hosp.; cons. psychiatrist emeritus Brookdale Hosp. Served to maj. AUS, 1942-46. Fellow Am. Psychiat. Assn. (sec. dist. br. 1956-63, pres. dist. br. 1964, area chmn. 1962-63); mem. Am. Psychosomatic Assn., N.Y.C. Acad. Medicine, Harvey Soc., NYU Med. Alumni Assn. (pres. 1979-80), Phi Beta Kappa, Sigma Xi, Alpha Omega Alpha. Home: 300 E 33rd St Apt 12C New York NY 10016-9415 Office: NYU Sch Medicine 550 1st Ave New York NY 10016-6481

STERN, MILTON, chemical company executive; b. Boston, Apr. 20, 1927; s. Morris and Lily (Colton) S.; m. Roberta L. Navisky, July 10, 1949;

children—Mark, Lawrence, Brian. B.S., Northeastern U., 1949; M.S. (Alcoa fellow), MIT, 1950, Sc.D. (Alcoa fellow), 1952. Postdoctoral fellow in metallurgy MIT, 1952-54; with Union Carbide Corp., N.Y.C., 1954-73; v.p. electronics div. Union Carbide Corp., 1968-69, exec. v.p. mining and metals div., 1969-73; v.p. exploration Kennecott Corp., N.Y.C., 1973-76; sr. v.p. Kennecott Corp., 1976-78, exec. v.p., 1978-82, also dir.; sr. exec. v.p. Stauffer Chem. Co., Westport, Conn., 1982-84; vice chmn. Stauffer Chem. Co., 1984—, also dir. Contbr. numerous articles in electrochemistry and metallurgy to tech. jours. Mem. vis. com. M.I.T., 1972-75; mem. corp. Northeastern U.; mem. White House Task Force on Am. Indian, 1966; bd. dirs. Assn. Am. Indian Affairs. Served with USNR, 1945-46. Recipient Nuodex award Northeastern U., 1949; Sears B. Condit award, 1949. Mem. AIME, Nat. Assn. corrosion Engrs. (Willis R. Whitney award 1963), Am. Soc. Metals, Electrochem. Soc. (Young Authors award 1955, 58, jour. div. editor 1958-61), PGA Nat. Club, Sigma Xi, Tau Beta Pi. Patentee in field.

STERN, MORT(IMER) P(HILLIP), journalism and communications educator, academic administrator, consultant; b. New Haven, Feb. 20, 1926; s. Bernard and Louise Eleanor (Spiro) S.; m. Patricia Ruth Freeman, Jan. 10, 1946; children: Susan C., Margaret L. AB, U. Ark., 1947; MS, Columbia U., 1949; postgrad., Harvard U., 1954-55; PhD, U. Denver, 1969. Reporter S.W.-Am., Ft. Smith, Ark., 1946-47; night bur. mgr. UPI, Little Rock, 1947-48; reporter, polit. writer, state editor Ark. Gazette, Little Rock, 1949-51; reporter, rewrite man Denver Post, 1951-53, night city editor, 1953-54, asst. editor Rocky Mountain Empire sect., 1955-56, mng. editor, 1956-58, assoc. editor, 1958, editorial page editor, 1958-65, asst. to pub., 1965-70, editorial page editor, 1971-73; dean Sch. Pub. communication U. Ala., 1973-74; dean Sch. Journalism U. Colo., Boulder, 1974-77; lectr. journalism U. Denver, 1953-54, adj. prof., 1970, exec. dir. pub. affairs, 1977-78, exec. asst. to chancellor, 1978-84; prof., chmn. dept. journalism and mass communication U. No. Colo., Greeley, 1985-90; pres. P. Paty & Co., Georgetown, Colo., 1989—; Atwood prof. journalism U. Alaska, Anchorage, 1981-82. With USAAF, 1944-45. Nieman fellow Harvard U., 1954-55. Mem. Assn. for Edn. in Journalism, Phi Beta Kappa, Omicron Delta Kappa, Sigma Delta Chi. Baptist. Home: PO Box 549 Georgetown CO 80444-0549

STERN, PAULA, international trade advisor; b. Chgo., Mar. 31, 1945; d. Llooyd and Fan (Wener) Stern; m. Paul A. London; children: Gabriel Stern London, Genevieve Stern London. BA, Goucher Coll., 1967; MA in Middle Eastern Studies, Harvard U., 1969; MA in Internat. Affairs, Fletcher Sch. of Law and Diplomacy, 1970, MA in Law and Diplomacy, 1970, PhD, 1976; D of Comml. Sci. (hon.), Babson Coll., 1985; LLD (hon.), Goucher Coll., 1985. Legis. asst., then sr. legis. asst. U.S. Sen. Gaylord Nelson, Washington, 1972-74, 1976; guest scholar Brookings Inst., Washington, 1975-76; policy analyst Pres. Carter-V.P. Mondale Transition Team, Washington, 1977-78; internat. affairs fellow Council on Fgn. Relations, Washington, 1977-78; commr. Internat. Trade Commn., Washington, 1978-87, chairwoman, 1984-86; sr. assoc. Carnegie Endowment for Internat. Peace, Washington, 1986-88; pres. The Stern Group, 1988—; sr. fellow The Progressive Policy Inst., 1993—; bd. dirs. Westinghouse Corp., Harcourt Gen., Duracell Internat., Wall-Mart; holder Howard W. Alkire chair in internat. bus. and econs. Hamline U., 1994—; sr. adviser to Clinton campaign; mem. Pres.'s Adv. Com. for Trade Policy and Negotiations; chair adv. com. U.S. Export-Import Bank, working chair transatlantic adv. com. on stds., cert. and regulatory policy; mem. Trilateral Commn., Commn. for Econ. Devel. Author: Water's Edge--Domestic Politics and the Making of American Foreign Policy, 1979; author numerous articles and chpts. on internat. affairs. Recipient Journalism award Alicia Patterson Found., 1970-71. Mem. Coun. Fgn. Rels., Inter-Am. Found. (bd. dirs. 1980-81). Democrat. Jewish. Avocations: sculpture, tennis, ballet. Office: The Stern Group Inc 3314 Ross Pl NW Washington DC 20008

STERN, RALPH DAVID, lawyer; b. Longview, Tex., June 20, 1943; children: Eric, Justin. AB, Bucknell U., 1963; JD, U. Chgo., 1966. Bar: D.C. 1967, Ill. 1967, Calif. 1970, U.S. Supreme Ct. 1970. Law clk. Ill. Appellate Ct., Chgo., 1966-67; assoc. Ressman & Tishler, Chgo., 1968-70; exec. asst. Orange County Bd. Suprs., Santa Ana, Calif., 1970-71; gen. counsel San Diego City Schs., 1971-83; ptnr. Whitmore, Kay & Stevens, Palo Alto, Calif., 1983-88, Stern & Keebler, San Mateo, Calif., 1988-90; gen. counsel Schs. Legal Counsel, Hayward, Calif., 1990—; chmn. Nat. Coun. Sch. Attys., 1982-83; pres. Leagal Aid Soc. San Diego, 1976-79, Nat. Orgn. on Legal Problems of Edn., 1981-82. Editor: Law and the School Principal, 1978; contbr. articles to profl. jours. Mem. exec. bd., county membership chair Boy Scouts Am., San Diego, 1979-81; vice chmn. Laurels for Leaders, San Diego, 1980-83; mem. ednl. adminstrn. adv. com. U. San Diego, 1981-86.; mem. adv. com. West's Ednl. Law Reporter, 1981-85. Named Outstanding Young Citizen, San Diego Jaycees, 1977. Office: Schs Legal Counsel 313 W Winton Ave Rm 372 Hayward CA 94544-1136

STERN, RAYMOND, principal. Prin. Hebrew Acad. Indpls. Recipient Elem. Sch. Recognition award U.S. Dept. Edn., 1989-90. Office: Hebrew Acad of Ind 6602 Hoover Rd Indianapolis IN 46260-4119

STERN, RICHARD DAVID, investment company executive; b. New Rochelle, N.Y., Nov. 5, 1936; s. Leo and Grace Marjorie (Phillips) S.; m. Phyllis Marlene Edelstein, Nov. 20, 1966; children: Marjorie Anne, Andrew Howard. AB, Princeton U., 1958; MBA, Harvard U., 1962. CFA. First v.p. Newburger, Loeb & Co., N.Y.C., 1962-74, also dir., 1969-74; sr. investment officer Central Trust Co., Cin., 1974-76, owner bus. valuation cons. co., 1976-78; v.p. Gt. Western Bank & Trust Co. (now Norwest Bank Ariz. NA), Phoenix, 1978-84; pres. Stern, Ludke & Co. (now Stern Investment Mgmt. Co.), Phoenix, 1984—. Co-author: Air Cushion Vehicles, 1962. Trustee endowment trust Phoenix Chamber Music Soc., 1982-91, v.p., 1986-90, bd. dirs., 1982-91, 93-94; pres. Ctrl. Ariz. chpt. Arthritis Found., 1982-84, chmn. planned giving com., 1986-91, mem. nat. planned giving com., 1987-89; chmn. endowments and trusts com. Temple Beth Israel, Phoenix, 1980-83; dir., investment com. Endowment Found., Temple Solel, Paradise Valley, 1990—; pres. Am. Jewish Com., Phoenix, 1983-84, bd. dirs., 1980-84, adv. bd., 1985—; bd. dirs. Asian Arts Coun., Phoenix Art Mus., 1987-93, v.p., 1989-90, pres., 1990-92; trustee Ariz. Theatre Co., 1990—, chmn. regional nominating com., 1995—. Mem. Phoenix Soc. Fin. Analysts (chmn. profl. conduct com. 1980-83, membership com. 1990-91, bd. dirs.), Anti-Defamation League of B'nai B'rith (dir. Ctrl. Ariz. chpt. 1986—, exec. bd. 1989—, chair nominating com. 1990-94, chair bd. devel. 1993-94, treas. 1994—), Princeton Alumni Assn. No. Ariz. (alumni schs. com. 1992—), Univ. Club (Phoenix, bd. dirs. 1990-92, fin. com. 1990-91), Harvard Bus. Sch. Club Ariz. (bd. dirs. 1991—, pres. 1993-95), Assn. for Corp. Growth (Ariz. chpt.). Republican. Home: 6013 E Donna Cir Paradise Vly AZ 85253-1730 Office: 2930 E Camelback Rd Ste 195 Phoenix AZ 85016-4412

STERN, RICHARD GUSTAVE, author, educator; b. N.Y.C., Feb. 25, 1928; s. Henry George and Marion (Veit) S.; m. Gay Clark, Mar. 14, 1950 (div. Feb. 1972); children: Christopher Holmes, Kate Macomber, Andrew Henry, Nicholas Clark; m. Alane Rollings, Aug. 9, 1985. B.A., U. N.C., 1947; M.A., Harvard U., 1950; Ph.D., State U. Iowa, 1954. Mem. faculty U. Chgo., 1955—, prof. English, 1965—, Helen Regenstein prof. English, 1990—. Author: Golk, 1960, Europe and Up and Down with Baggish and Schreiber, 1961, In Any Case, 1962, Teeth, Dying and Other Matters, 1964, Stitch, 1965, 1968: A Short Novel, An Urban Idyll, Five Stories and Two Trade Notes, 1970, The Books in Fred Hampton's Apartment, 1973, Other Men's Daughters, 1973, Natural Shocks, 1978, Packages, 1980, The Invention of the Real, 1982, A Father's Words, 1986, The Position of the Body, 1986, Noble Rot: Stories, 1949-88, 1989 (book of yr. award Chgo. Sun-Times 1990), Shares and Other Fictions, 1992, One Person and Another, 1993, A Sistermony, 1995 (Heartland award, nonfiction book of year); editor: Honey and Wax, 1966. Recipient Longwood Found. award, 1960, Friends of Lit. award, 1963, fiction award Nat. Inst. Arts and Letters, 1968; Nat. Coun. Arts and Humanities fellow, 1967-68, Carl Sandburg award for fiction, 1979, Arts Coun. awards, 1979, 81, Am. Acad. and Inst. of Arts and Letters medal of Merit for Novel, 1985; Rockefeller fellow, 1965, Guggenheim fellow, 1973-74. Mem. Am. Acad. Arts and Scis. Office: Dept English U Chgo Chicago IL 60637

STERN, ROBERT ARTHUR MORTON, architect, educator; b. N.Y.C., May 23, 1939; s. Sidney S. and Sonya (Cohen) S.; m. Lynn G. Solinger, May [illegible], 1966 (div. 1977); 1 child, Nicholas S.G. BA, Columbia U., 1960; MArch, Yale U., 1965. Registered architect, Calif., Colo., Conn., Fla., Hawaii, Ill., Ind., Maine, Mass., Mich., N.H., N.J., Ohio, S.C., Tex., N.Y., D.C. Program dir. Archtl. League N.Y., 1965-66; designer Office Richard Meier, Architect, N.Y.C., 1966; cons. Small Parks Program, Dept. Parks, N.Y.C., 1966-70; urban designer, asst. to asst. adminstr. housing and devel. adminstrn. N.Y.C., 1967-70; ptnr. Robert A.M. Stern & John S. Hagmann, Architects, N.Y.C., 1969-77; prin. Robert A.M. Stern, Architects, 1977-89, prin. ptnr., 1989—; cons. Eye on New York TV documentary, CBS-TV, 1966-67; mem. architecture com. Whitney Mus. Am. Art, 1970-76, adv. commn., archtl. sect. Venice Biennale, 1980; lectr. architecture Columbia U., 1970-72, asst. prof. 1973-77, assoc. prof., 1977-82, prof. 1982—; vis. fellow Inst. for Architecture and Urban Studies, 1974-76, trustee, 1983-85; dir. Temple Hoyne Buell Ctr. for Study Am. Architecture, 1984-88, acting dir. Hist. Preservation Program, 1991—; vis. lectr. Yale U., 1972, 73; vis. critic R.I. Sch. Design, 1976, U. Pa., 1977, N.C. State U., Raleigh, 1978; William Henry Bishop vis. prof. architecture Yale U., fall 1978; editorial cons. Archtl. History Found., 1979-83. Author: New Directions in American Architecture, 1969, rev. edit., 1977, George Howe: Toward a Modern American Architecture, 1975, (with Deborah Nevins) The Architect's Eye, 1979, (with John M. Massengale) The Anglo-American Suburb, 1981, (with Thomas Catalano) Raymond Hood, 1982, East Hamptons Heritage, 1982, (with John M. Massengale and Gregory Gilmartin) New York 1900, 1983, Pride of Place, 1986, (with Gregory Gilmartin and Thomas Mellims) New York 1930, 1987, (with Raymond Gastil) Modern Classicism, 1988, The House That Bob Built, 1991, The American Houses of Robert A.M. Stern, 1991, (with Thomas Mellins and David Fishman) New York 1960, 1995. Mem. N.Y.C. Mayor's Task Force on Urban Design, 1966-67, architects selection com. N.Y. Conv. Ctr., 1979; trustee Am. Fedn. Arts, 1967-79, Inst. for Architecture and Urban Studies, 1983-85; v.p. Cunningham Dance Found., 1969-73; bd. dirs. Preservation League N.Y., 1984—. Recipient numerous awards for archtl. works including Nat. Hon. awards of AIA, 1980, 85, 90, John Jay award Columbia Coll., 1991. Fellow AIA (bd. dirs. N.Y. chpt. 1976-78, Disting. archtl. award N.Y. chpt. 1982, 84, 85, 87, medal of honor 1984), Soc. Archtl. Historians (bd. dirs. 1975-78), Archtl. League N.Y. (pres. 1973-77, exec. com. 1977—), N.Y. State Assn. Architects (excellence in design cert. 1985), Am. Architecture Found. (bd. regents 1989-91), Skidmore, Owings and Merrill Found. (bd. dirs. 1984-90), Chgo. Inst. for Architecture and Urbanism (bd. dirs. 1990-93), Century Assn., Coffee House Club. Office: 460 W 34th St Fl 18 New York NY 10001-2320

STERN, ROBERT D., publishing executive; b. N.Y.C., Sept. 30, 1929; s. Morris and Jean (Gordon) S.; m. Natalie Greenberg, Sept. 5, 1952 (div. 1978); children: Mitchell, Bradley; m. Roslyne Paige, June 5, 1978. BA, Syracuse U., 1950; JD, NYU, 1953, LLM, 1958. Bar: N.Y. 1955, U.S. Dist. Ct. (D.C. cir.) 1953, U.S. Supreme Ct. 1967. Assoc. Fink, Weinberger, Levin & Gottschalk, N.Y.C., 1957-59, ptnr., 1959-72; chmn. Rudor Consol. Industries, N.Y.C., 1972—; chmn. Dance Mag., Inc., N.Y.C., 1985—, now pres.; chmn. AGC/Sedgwick Inc., Princeton, N.J., 1990—; bd. dirs. Ctr. for Graphic Comms. Mgmt. and Tech., NYU, N.Y.C., 1979—; chmn. bd. dirs. AGC Sedgwick, Princeton, N.J., Rudor Consol. Ind. Inc.; pub. Stern's Performing Arts Directory, 1989—. Bd. dirs. YMCA, N.Y.C., 1987-90;. Mem. ABA, N.Y. State Bar Assn., Sheldrake Yacht Club (Mamaroneck, N.Y.), Birchwood Country Club (Westport, Conn.). Avocations: tennis, skiing, sailing. Home: 2 Imperial Lndg Westport CT 06880-4934 Office: 33 W 60th St New York NY 10023-7905

STERN, ROBERT LOUIS, lawyer; b. N.Y.C., Sept. 18, 1908; s. Albert Louis and Alma (Hays) S.; m. Terese Marks, Oct. 16, 1936 (dec. Jan. 1990); children: Lawrence R., Kenneth M., Allan H.; m. Helen Klemperer, Dec. 1, 1990. A.B., Williams Coll., 1929; LL.B., Harvard U., 1932. Bar: N.Y. 1933, Ill. 1954, D.C. 1954. Assoc. Henry F. Wolff, N.Y.C., 1932-33; atty. Petroleum Adminstrn. Bd., Dept. Interior, Washington, 1933-34, Antitrust div. Justice Dept., 1934-41; with Office Solicitor Gen., Justice Dept., 1941-54, 1st asst., 1950-54, acting solicitor gen., 1952-54; mem. firm Mayer, Brown & Platt, Chgo., 1954-93; of counsel, 1993—; vis. prof. U. Ariz. Coll. Law, 1972; mem. Fed. Adv. Com. on Appellate Rules, 1963-68, Ill. Supreme Ct. Rules Com., 1963-94; mem. study group on caseload Supreme Ct., 1972. Author: Appellate Practice in the United States, 2d edit., 1989; co-author: Supreme Court Practice, 7th edit., 1993, Supreme Court Rules: The 1995 Revisions. Chmn. Winnetka Community Chest, 1961-62; mem. Winnetka Caucus, 1965-67. Mem. ABA (Ross prize essay 1955, mem. various coms., chmn. amicus curiae com. 1981-87), Am. Law Inst., Am. Bar Fellows (Rsch. award 1983), 7th Fed. Cir. Bar Assn., Chgo. Bar Assn., Am. Bar Found. (past dir., rsch. com.), Law Club Chgo., 49ers Country Club (Tucson). Home (summer): 706 Waukegan Rd Glenview IL 60025-4368 also (winter): 2631 E Ave de Posada Tucson AZ 85718 Office: Mayer Brown & Platt 190 S La Salle St Chicago IL 60603-3410

STERN, ROBERT MORRIS, gastrointestinal psychophysiology researcher, psychology educator; b. N.Y.C., June 18, 1937; s. Irving Dan and Nellie (Wachstetter) S.; m. Wilma Olch, June 19, 1960; children—Jessica Leigh, Alison Rachel. A.B., Franklin and Marshall Coll., 1958; M.S., Tufts U., 1960; Ph.D., Ind. U., 1963. Research assoc. dept. psychology Ind. U., 1963-65; asst. prof. psychology Pa. State U., 1965-68, assoc. prof., 1968-73, prof., 1973—, disting. prof., 1992—, head dept., 1978-87. Author: (with W.J. Ray) Biofeedback, 1977, (with W.J. Ray and C.M. Davis) Psychophysiological Recording, 1980, (with K.L. Koch) Electrogastrography, 1985; contbr. articles to profl. jours. Recipient Nat. Media award Am. Psychol. Found., 1978. Mem. Am. Psychol. Soc., Aerospace Med. Assn., Soc. Psychophysiol. Rsch., Am. Gastroent. Assn. Home: 1360 Greenwood Cir State College PA 16803-3232 Office: Pa State U 512 Moore Bldg University Park PA 16802-3105

STERN, ROSLYNE PAIGE, magazine publisher; b. Chgo., May 26, 1926; d. Benjamin Gross and Clara (Sniderman) Roer; m. William E. Weber, May 3, 1944 (div. Mar. 1956); m. Richard S. Paige, June 28, 1958 (div. Apr. 1978); children: Sandra Weber Porr, Barbara Paige Kaplan, Elizabeth Paige (dec.); m. Robert D. Stern, June 5, 1978. Cert., U. Chgo., 1945. Profl. model, singer, 1947-53; account exec. Interstate United, Chgo., 1955-58; sales mgr. Getting To Know You Internat., Great Neck, N.Y., 1963-71, exec. v.p., 1971-78; pub. After Dark Mag., N.Y.C., 1978-82; assoc. pub. Dance Mag., N.Y.C., 1978-85, pub., 1985—; pres., 1996—; bd. dirs. Rudor Consol. Industries, Inc., N.Y.C., AGC/Sedgwick, Inc., Princeton, N.J. Founding pres. Dance Mag. Found., N.Y.C., 1984-86; life mem. nat. women's com. Brandeis U., Waltham, Mass., 1958—. Mem. Pub. Relations Soc. Am., LWV, Am. Theatre Wing, Nat. Arts Club. Democrat. Jewish. Avocations: dance, theater, opera, visual arts, travel. Home: 2 Imperial Lndg Westport CT 06880-4934 Office: Dance Mag Inc 33 W 60th St 10th Fl New York NY 10023-7905

STERN, SAMUEL ALAN, lawyer; b. Phila., Jan. 21, 1929. A.B., U. Pa., 1949; LL.B., Harvard U., 1952. Bar: Mass. 1952, D.C. 1958. Ptnr. Wilmer, Cutler & Pickering, Washington, 1962-88, Dickstein, Shapiro & Morin, Washington, 1988-92; pvt. practice law and bus. Washington and St. Petersburg, Russia, 1992-94; counsel Rogers & Wells, Washington, N.Y.C., 1994—; vis. prof. law Harvard U., Cambridge, Mass., 1976; dir. Internat. Law Inst., Georgetown U., 1971—, adj. prof. law, 1979-92; asst. counsel Warren Commn., 1964; cons. UN, 1974—; bd. dirs. Ninth Moon Inc., ADEC, Inc., Stern & Co., Norandina Holdings A.V.V., Custom Software L.L.C., Megapoint Sys. Inc., Utilitrol Corp. Contbr. articles to legal jours. Adv. bd. Fishman-Davidson Ctr. for Study of Svc. Sector, Wharton Sch. Bus., U. Pa.; bd. dirs. Internat. Sci. Tech. Inst., Internat. Ctr., Washington, Sri Lanka-U.S. Bus. Forum, Washington; steering com. U.S.-Vietnam Trade Coun. Mem. ABA, Am. Law Inst., Am. Soc. Internat. Law, Internat. Bar Assn., D.C. Bar Assn. Home: 2336 California St NW Washington DC 20008-1637 Office: 607 14th St NW Washington DC 20005-2007

STERN, SHERRY ANN, journalist; b. Paterson, N.J., June 27, 1954; d. Richard Norman and Norma (Davidowitz). BA, U. S. Calif., Los Angeles, 1876; MS, Northwestern U., Evanston, 1982. Reporter Ariz. Daily Star, Tucson, 1976-79, TV critic, 1979-81; news editor The Morning Press, Vista, Calif., 1982-83, mng. editor, editor in chief, 1983-84; copy editor The Orange County Register, Calif., 1984-85; asst. features news editor The Orange County Register, Santa Ana, Calif., 1985-86; features news editor Orange County Register, Santa Ana, Calif., 1986--; journalism instr. Mira Costa Coll., Oceanside, 1983-84. Vol. Lit. Vols. of Am., Huntington Beach, 1988--. Named Best Headling Portfolio Orange County Press Club, 1985, Best Student Feature Los Angeles Press Club. Mem. Orange County, Press Club. Democrat. Jewish. Office: The Orange County Register 625 N Grand Ave Santa Ana CA 92701-4347

STERN, SOLOMON H., management consultant; 1 child. BA Econs., Bklyn. Coll. V.p. adminstrv. fin. Universal Automotive PartsDistbr., Miami, 1965-68; asst. v.p. corp. banking Marine Midland Bank, N.Y.C. and L.I., 1968-76; v.p., mgr., sr. mem. credit comms. Bank Hapoalim, N.Y.C., 1976-77; v.p. and spl. asst. to chmn. Eisenberg & Co. Worldwide Group, N.Y.C., 1977-80; major cons. to Union Specialist Corp., Chgo., 1980-81, TD Penarroya SA, Noyelles-Godault, France, 1981-88, Metaleurop, SA & PPM, France and Germany, 1987—, 89-92, Minimet, Inc., Stanford, Conn., 1980-94; bd. dirs., chmn. Govt. L.I. Assn. of Commerce and Trade, Fgn. Trade Zone Task Force; panel mem. arbitrators Am. Arbitrary Assn., N.Y.C.; chmn. bd. govt. World Trade Club, L.I.; spkr., lectr. in field. Contbr. articles to profl. jours. Mem. Inst. Mgmt. Cons., Sales and Mktg. Assn., Nat. Assn. Corp. Dirs., L.I. Assn. Commerce and Industry, Nat. Com. on U.S./China Rels., U.S./Mex. C. of C., Nat. Com. on Am. Fgn. Policy, Assocs. in Dispute Resolution. Avocations: golf, tennis, skiing, swimming, chess, music. Office: SST Internat Enterprises 521 Fifth Ave 7th Flr New York NY 10017

STERN, STEPHEN JEFFREY, lawyer; b. L.A., Dec. 31, 1940; s. M.E. and Jane (VanDement) S.; m. Betsy Stern, June 16, 1962 (div. 1974); children: Christopher, Jeffrey; m. Sheila Stern, Apr. 23, 1976. BS in Econs., U. Calif., 1962; JD, U. San Francisco, 1965. Bar: Calif., N.Y. Ptnr. O'Melveny & Myers, L.A., 1966—; lectr., chmn. N.Y. Law Jour., Calif. League of Cities, Mcpl. Fin. Officers Assn. Mem. ABA, Calif. State Bar Assn., Nat. Assn. Bond Lawyers, Bel Air Bay Club. Office: O'Melveny & Myers 400 S Hope St Los Angeles CA 90071-2801*

STERN, T. NOEL, political scientist, educator; b. Pitts., July 7, 1913; s. Leon Thomas (LeFevre) and Elizabeth Gertrude (Limburg) S.; m. Katherine Frances Kirk, Dec. 28, 1940; children: S. Yolanda, Roland Craig, Ellen Cornog, Joan Thrush. B.A. with honors, Swarthmore Coll., 1934; postgrad., U. Lyons, France, 1934-35; M.A. in Polit. Sci. U. Pa., 1940, Ph.D. in Polit. Sci, 1942. Tchr. Lycée des Garçons, Roanne, France, 1934-35; prof., acting chmn. dept. govt. Boston U., 1945-53; Fulbright prof. U. Rennes, U. Strasbourg, 1952; dir. Fondation des Etats-Unis, U. Paris, France, 1953-56; acting chief UN Pub. Adminstrn. Mission to Ethiopia, 1956-57; dir. research and stats. Pa. Dept. Revenue, 1957-60; pres. West Chester State Coll., Pa., 1960-61; research prof. govt. African Studies program Boston U., 1962-63; also chief pub. adminstrn. team Boston U./US Aid, Guinea, West Africa; prof., past chmn. dept. polit. sci. U. Mass., Dartmouth, 1964-69, prof., 1969-85, prof. emeritus, 1985—, also past chmn. acad. coun.; frequent guest on radio, Boston, 1948-53, New Bedford, Fall River and Providence, 1964—. Author: Secret Family, 1988, Your Guide to Dartmouth Town Government, 1991; past mem. editl. bd. Internat. Rev. History and Polit. Sci., Revue de la Cité, Paris; contbr. to Boston U. Law Rev., Sch. and Society, New Republic, Progressive mag., Christian Sci. Monitor, Friends Jour., Quaker Life, Quaker History, Boston Globe, Providence Jour.-Bull, New Bedford Standard-Times, U. Pa. Gazette, also others; collective writings deposited in Archieves of Friends Hist. Libr., Swarthmore Coll. and Libr. U. Mass., Dartmouth. Mem. permanent bd. New Eng. Yearly Mtg. of Friends; past mem. Dartmouth Arts Coun.; past mem. exec. com. Friends Gen. Conf., Phila.; past mem. adminstrv. bd. William Penn House, Washington; past clk. North Dartmouth Friends Mtg., past presiding clk. Sandwich Quar. Mtg. of Friends; trustee, chmn. Dartmouth Town Librs., 1992—; bd. dirs. Cmty. Ctr. for Non-Violence, New Bedford, Mass., 1994—. Mem. AAUP (past pres. U. Mass.-Dartmouth chpt.), Am. Polit. Sci. Assn., LWV (acting pres. New Bedford-Fall River area 1990-91). Home: 875 Smith Neck Rd South Dartmouth MA 02748-1511

STERN, TODD DAVID, lawyer; b. Chgo., May 4, 1951; s. Richard James and Judith (Cowen) S. BA, Dartmouth Coll., 1973; JD, Harvard U., 1977. Staff atty. criminal appeals bur. Legal Aid Soc., N.Y.C., 1977-79; assoc. Paul, Weiss, Rifkin, Wharton & Garrison, N.Y.C., 1979-85; gen. counsel Assoc. Mills-Pollenex, Chgo., 1985-87; dep. rsch. dir. Dukakis-Bentsen Presdl. Campaign, Boston, 1987-88; v.p. Podesta Assocs., Washington, 1989-90; sr. counsel subcom. on tech. and law Senate Judiciary Com., Washington, 1990-93; dep. asst. to pres., dep. staff sec. The White House, Washington, 1993—.

STERN, WALTER EUGENE, neurosurgeon, educator; b. Portland, Oreg., Jan. 1, 1920; s. Walter Eugene and Ida May (McCoy) S.; m. Elizabeth Naffziger, May 24, 1946; children: Geoffrey Alexander, Howard Christian, Eugenia Louise, Walter Eugene III. AB cum laude, U. Calif., MD, 1943. Diplomate: Am. Bd. Neurol. Surg. (vice chmn. 1975-80). Surg. intern, asst. resident surgery and neurol. surgery U. Calif. Hosp., 1943-46, asst. resident neurol. surgery and neuropathology, 1948; clin. clk. Nat. Hosp. Paralyzed and Epileptic, London, Eng., 1948-49; Nat. Research fellow med. sci. Johns Hopkins, 1949-50; asst. resident, resident U. Calif. Service, 1951; NIH spl. fellow univ. lab. physiology Oxford U., 1961-62; clin. instr. U. Calif., 1951; asst. prof. neurosurgery UCLA, 1952-56, assoc. prof., 1956-59, prof., 1959-87, now emeritus, chief div. neurosurgery, 1952-85, chmn. dept. surgery, 1981-87; cons. neurosurgery, Wadsworth VA Hosp. Former mem., chmn. editorial bd. Jour. Neurosurgery; contbr. articles to sci. jours., chpts. in books. Lt. to capt. M.C. AUS, 1946-48. Fellow ACS (sec.); mem. AMA, Am. Surg. Assn., Pacific Coast Surg. Assn., L.A. Surg. Soc. (pres. 1978), Am. Assn. Neurol. Surgeons (pres. 1979-80, Cushing medalist, 1992), James IV Assn. Surgeons, Western Neurosurg. Soc. (past pres.), Soc. Neurol. Surgeons (past pres.), Neurosurg. Soc. Am., Am. Neurol. Assn., Soc. Univ. Surgeons, Soc. Brit. Neurol. Surgeons (hon.), Phi Beta Kappa, Sigma Xi, Alpha Omega Alpha. Republican. Episcopalian. Home: 435 Georgina Ave Santa Monica CA 90402-1909 Office: U Calif Sch Medicine Los Angeles CA 90024

STERN, WALTER PHILLIPS, investment executive; b. N.Y.C., Sept. 26, 1928; s. Leo and Marjorie (Phillips) S.; m. Elizabeth May, Feb. 12, 1958; children: Sarah May, William May, David May. AB, Williams Coll., 1950; MBA, Harvard U., 1952. With Lazard Freres & Co., N.Y.C., 1953-54; assoc. Burnham & Co., Inc. (predecessor firm to Drexel Burnham Lambert Group, Inc.), N.Y.C., 1954-60, ptnr., 1960-71, sr. exec. v.p., 1972-73; vice chmn., mng. dir. Ea. ops. Capital Rsch. Co., 1973-95; chmn. bd. New Perspective Fund, Inc., 1973—, Fundamental Investors Inc., 1978—; chmn. Europacific Growth Fund, Inc., 1984—; chmn. bd. dirs. Emerging Markets Growth Fund, Income Fund Am., Inc., Growth Fund Am., Am. Balanced Fund; bd. dirs. Capital Group Internat., Inc., Temple-Inland, Inc.; past mem. pub. bd. Mcpl. Securities Rulemaking Bd., 1984-87; trustee Fin. Analysts Rsch. Found.; chmn. bd. trustees Hudson Inst.; instr. investment mgmt. and fin. NYU, 1956-62, 70-73; dir. Birla Advantage Fund, Birla Capital Internat. AMC Ltd., Bombay, 1994—; mem. adv. bd. South African Growth Fund, 1996. Contbr. articles to profl. jours. Dir. Jewish Cmty. Rels. Coun. N.Y.; mem. Coun. Fgn. Rels.; chmn. fin. adv. com. Haddassah; trustee Am. Jewish Com., Tel Aviv U., Jaffee Inst. Strategic Studies, Tel Aviv;mem. publ. com. The Commentary, 1995—; dir. Am.-Israel Friendship League, 1996—; gov. Anti-Defamation League; bd. dirs. Am. Friends of Tel Aviv U.; mem. adv. bd. Competitiveness Ctr. of Hudson Inst.; v.p., mem. exec. com. Washington Inst. Near East Policy; pres. bd. dirs. Rsch. Project on Energy and Econ. Policy; chmn. Am. steering com. Freedom Trade with Israel. Mem. N.Y. Soc. Security Analysts (bd. dirs.), Fin. Analysts Fedn. (pres. 1971-72, bd. dirs.), Inst. Chartered Fin. Analysts (pres. 1976-77, bd. dirs.), Assn. Investment and Mgmt. Rsch. (bd. dirs., exec. com. 1990—), Harvard Club, Williams Club, Econ. Club, Sunningdale Country Club, Calif. Club, Phi Beta Kappa. Jewish. Home: 450 Forthill Rd Scarsdale NY 10583-2413 Office: Capital Group Inc 53 W 36 New York NY 10111-0001 also: Capital Group Inc 333 S Hope St Los Angeles CA 90071-1406

STERN, WILLIAM LOUIS, botanist, educator; b. Paterson, N.J., Sept. 10, 1926; s. Abram and Rose (Chrisman) S.; m. Floraet Selma Tanis, Sept. 4, 1949; children: Susan Myra, Paul Elihu. BS, Rutgers U., 1950; MS, U. Ill., 1951, PhD, 1954. Instr., then asst. prof. Yale Sch. Forestry, 1953-60; curator div. plant anatomy Smithsonian Inst., 1960-64, chmn. dept botany, 1964-67; prof. botany U. Md., College Park, 1967-79, U. Fla., Gainesville, 1979—;

chmn. dept. U. Fla., 1979-85; Forestry officer FAO, 1963-64; mem. sci. adv. bd. Nat. Tropical Bot. Garden, 1969-83; mem. sci. adv. com. Winterthur Mus., 1973-86 ; vis. com. Arnold Arboretum of Harvard U., 1971-77; vice chmn. Arnold Arboretum of Harvard U. 1973-76; asesor cientifico U. de los Andes, Merida, Venezuela, 1975; program dir. systematic biology NSF, 1978, 79. Editor: Tropical Woods, 1953-60, Plant Sci. Bull., 1962-64, Biotropica, 1968-73; asso. editor: BioSci, 1963-65, Econ. Botany, 1966-75; mem. editorial com.: Am. Jour. Botany, 1967-69. Bd. dirs. Fairchild Tropical Garden, 1980-86; trustee Kampong Fund, 1985—. Served with USNR, 1944-46, PTO. Fellow Linnean Soc. of London; mem. Bot. Soc. Am. (pres. 1984-86), Am. Inst. Biol. Scis. (bd. dirs. 1987-89), Internat. Assn. Wood Anatomists (hon., council), Am. Soc. Plant Taxonomists (pres. 1981), Soc. Econ. Botany (treas. 1988-91), Bot. Soc. Am. (Cert. Merit 1987), Torrey Bot. Club (editor Memoirs 1971-75), Washington Bot. Soc. (pres. 1972), Internat. Soc. Tropical Foresters, Soc. Advancement Research (Philippines), Assn. for Tropical Biology, Internat. Wood Collectors Soc. (life), Phi Beta Kappa, Sigma Xi, Delta Phi Alpha, Phi Kappa Phi, Phi Sigma. Office: U Fla Dept Botany Gainesville FL 32611-8526

STERNBERG, DANIEL ARIE, musician, conductor, educator; b. Lwow, Poland, Mar. 29, 1913; came to U.S., 1939, naturalized, 1946; s. Philipp and Eva (Makowska) S.; m. Felicitas Gobineau, July 29, 1936. Baccalaureate, Realgymnasium, Vienna, 1931; student, U. Vienna, 1931-35; diploma of condr., Vienna State Acad. Music, 1935; composition study with Karl Weigl, 1931-35, conducting with Fritz Stiedry, 1935-36. Lectr., Vienna Volkshochschule, 1933-34; head piano dept. Hockaday Inst. Music, Dallas, 1940-42; dean Sch. Music, Baylor U., Waco, Tex., 1942-81; Ben H. Williams disting. prof. Sch. Music, Baylor U., 1981-82; lectr. mus. subjects. Condr. Vienna Vets. Orch., 1934-35; asst. condr. Leningrad Philharm. and Kirov Opera, 1935-36; guest condr. Leningrad and Moscow radio orchs., 1936, Dallas Symphony Orch., 1952, 65; music dir. Tbilisi (USSR) State Symphony Orch., 1936-37; mus. dir., condr. Waco Symphony Orch., 1962-87; concert accompanist. Recipient Abrams Meml. award for composition Dallas Symphony, 1948. Mem. Phi Mu Alpha, Omicron Delta Kappa. Home: 3108 Robin Rd Waco TX 76708-2275

STERNBERG, HARRY, artist; b. N.Y.C., July 19, 1904; s. Simon and Rose (Br) S.; m. Mary Elizabeth Gosney, 1939; 1 child, Leslie Louise. Student, Art Students League, N.Y.C. tchr. Art Students League, N.Y.C.; formerly head art dept. Idyllwild Sch. Music and Art, UCLA, U. So. Calif., Idyllwild (Calif.) Arts Found., 1956-63; tchr. graphics San Diego State Coll., 1967-68; artist-in-residence Palomar Coll., San Marcos, Calif.; adj. prof. painting U. Calif., Idyllwild Sch. Music and Art. Exhibited 25 Year Retrospective show, ACA and Gorezick Galleries, 1953; one-man shows ACA Gallery, N.Y.C., 9 shows 1956-82, Brigham Young U., 58, 62, 75, Gorelick Gallery, 58, Nat. Inst. Arts and Letters, 1961, Utah State U., 1962, Salt Lake Art Ctr., Salt Lake City, 1962, Heritage Gallery, L.A., 1964, Gray Gallery, Escondido, 1970, Ulrich Mus., Art Students League, N.Y.C., 1982, Galaria Palomas, San Juan, P.R., 1982-83, Deicas Gallery, La Jolla, Calif., 1983, San Diego Print Club, 1983, Mary Ryan Gallery, N.Y.C., 1984, 89, Idyllwild Sch. Art, 1985, Todd Gallery, Idyllwild, Calif., 1985-86, 89, (graphic exhbn.) Tobey Moss Gallery, L.A., 1986, Susan Teller Gallery, N.Y.C., 1989, 90, 92, Sragow Gallery, N.Y.C., 1990, graphics retrospective Art Students League, N.Y.C., 1992, Athenium, San Diego, 1992, Susan Teller Gallery, N.Y.C., 1993; woodcut exhibition Brighton Press, San Diego, 1992; traveling show Art in the Labor Movement: West Berlin, 1983, Hamburg, Fed. Republic of Germany, 1984, Stockholm, 1985, Rome, 185, England, 1985, Midtown Gallery, N.Y.C., 1991, Worcester Art Mus., 1991, Boston Mus. Fine Art, 1991, Palomar Coll. Gallery, Vista, Calif., 1993; retrospective exhbns. Walker Art Centre, Mpls., 1973, Wichita State U., 1975, Art Students League, N.Y.C., Assoc. Am. Artists, N.Y.C., Art and Design Gallery-Bonsall, 1976, Bethesda (Md.) Art Gallery, 1980, New Vistas Gallery, Vista, Calif., 1980, Libr. of Congress, 1983, Bethesda Gallery, (Md.), Midtown Gallery, N.Y.C., 1988, 89, Avonca Internat., Rancho Bernardo, Calif., 1988, Nat. Acad. Design, 1988, Associated Am. Gallery, N.Y.C., 1989, Art Students League, N.Y.C., 1994, San Diego Mus. Art, 1994, 95; represented in permanent collections Mus. Modern Art, Met. Mus., Whitney Mus., Bklyn., Cleve., Phila. museums, Library Congress, Victoria and Albert Mus., London, Bibliothique Nationale, Paris, Syracuse U., H. de Young Meml. Mus., Wichita (Kans.) State Mus., San Francisco, Fogg Mus., Boston, Addison Gallery Am. Art, Boston, Syracuse U. Mus., Library Congress, Washington, N.Y. Pub. Library, U. Minn., Nat. Portrait Gallery, Washington, Nat. Mus., Tel Aviv, N.Z. Mus. Art, St. Lawrence U., Roberson Art Centre, Binghamton, N.Y., Cleve. Mus. Art, Ulrich Mus., Thorne Mus., Keene State Coll., Hirshorn Mus., Washington, Roanoke Mus. Fine Arts, Bklyn. Mus., 1986, La Jolla Mus. Art, San Diego, 1988, Nat. Acad. Design, 1988, Associated Am. Artists, N.Y.C., 1988, Wolfsonian Mus., Miami, Fla., San Diego Mus. Art, Susan Teller Gallery, N.Y.C., Brighton Press, Calif., U. Judaism; producer, dir.: motion pictures The Many Worlds of Art, 1960, Art and Reality, 1961; author: Silk Screen Color Printing, 1942, Modern Methods and Materials of Etching, 1949, Compositions, 1957, Modern Drawing, 1958, Woodcut, 1962, Short Shots and Rituals With Woodcuts, 1990, A Life, an autobiography in woodcuts, 1992. Recipient Guggenheim fellowship, 1936, 1st prize Phila. Print Club, 1942; Living Arts Found., grantee, 1960; recipient graphic prize Audubon Artists, 1955, purchase award Nat. Inst. Arts and Letters, 1972. Mem. Art Students League of N.Y.C. (hon.), Artists Equity, Artists Guild of Fine Arts Gallery (San Diego), Nat. Acad. Design, Nat. Acad. Design (N.Y.C.). Home: 2234 Hilton Head Gln Escondido CA 92026-1071 Studio: 1718 E Valley Pky Escondido CA 92027-2548

STERNBERG, PAUL, retired ophthalmologist; b. Chgo., Dec. 18, 1918; s. David M. and Sarah (Kopeka) S.; m. Dorie Betty Feitler, Dec. 24, 1949; children—Daniel P., Patricia F., Paul, Susan P., David. B.S., Northwestern U., 1938, M.D., 1940. Intern Michael Reese Hosp., Chgo., 1940-41; resident ophthalmology Michael Reese Hosp., Ill. Eye & Ear Infirmary U. Ill.; spl. fellow ophthalmology Cornell U. Med. Center, N.Y. Hosp., Wilmer Inst. Johns Hopkins, 1941-44; practice medicine, specializing in ophthalmology Chgo., from 1945; attending ophthalmologist Cook County Hosp., Michael Reese Hosp., Highland Park (Ill.) Hosp., Louis Weiss Meml. Hosp.; prof. ophthalmology Chgo. Med. Sch. Contbr. sci. articles to med. and ophthal. jours. Fellow A.C.S.; mem. Assn. for Research in Ophthalmology, Am. Assn. Ophthalmology, Am. Acad. Ophthalmology, Chgo. Ophthal. Soc., Pan-Am. Congress Ophthalmology. Clubs: Standard (Chgo.); Lake Shore Country (Glencoe, Ill.). Home: 359 Surfside Pl Glencoe IL 60022-1723 Office: 225 W Washington St Ste 2150 Chicago IL 60606-3418

STERNBERG, PAUL J., lawyer; b. Nyack, N.Y., July 14, 1933; s. Paul and Helen Louise (Butler) S.; m. Barbara Patricia Boyle, Sept. 3, 1955; children: Lucinda Abbott, Alicia Boyle, Amanda Butler (dec.). AB, Harvard U., 1954; LLB, Columbia U., 1957. Bar: N.Y. 1958, Iowa 1981. Assoc. Choate, Reynolds, Huntington & Hollister, N.Y.C., 1958-61; mng. counsel The Singer Co., N.Y.C., 1963-79; sr. v.p., gen counsel, sec. Bandag Inc., Muscatine, Iowa, 1979-86; spl. counsel Hinman, Howard, and Kattell, Binghamton and Norwich, N.Y., 1986-89; v.p., gen. counsel, sec. Raymond Corp., Greene, N.Y., 1989—; bd. dirs. G.N. Johnston Equipment Co., Ltd., Dockstocker Corp., Corp. Raymond de Mex., Legal Aid for Broome and Chenango, Inc. Capt. U.S. Army, 1961-62. Mem. ABA, Assn. of Bar of City of N.Y., N.Y. State Bar Assn., Harvard Club N.Y.C., Manursing Island Club. Office: The Raymond Corp S Canal St Greene NY 13778

STERNBERG, ROBERT JEFFREY, psychology educator; b. Newark, Dec. 8, 1949; s. Joseph Sternberg and Lilliam Myriam (Politzer) Weingast; children: Seth, Sara; m. Alejandra Campos, 1991. BA summa cum laude, Yale U., 1972; PhD, Stanford U., 1975; D honoris causa, Complutense U., 1994. Mem. faculty dept. psychology Yale U., New Haven, 1975—; prof. psychology Yale U., 1983-86, IBM prof. psychology and edn., 1986—. Editor-in-chief Ency. of Human Intelligence, Psychol. Bull., 1991—; cons. editor Learning and Individual Differences, 1992—, Intelligence, 1977—, Devel. Rev., 1987-91, Jour. Personality and Social Psychology, 1989-91, Psychol. Rev., 1989-91 author: Intelligence, Information Processing and Analogical Reasoning, 1977, Beyond IQ, 1985, The Triarchic Mind, 1988, Metaphors of Mind, 1990, In Search of the Human Mind, 1995, (with T. Lubart) Defying the Crowd, 1995, Successful Intelligence, 1996. Recipient award for Excellence Mensa Edn. and Rsch. Found., 1989; Guggenheim Found. fellow, 1985-86. Fellow APA (past pres. divsns. 1 and 15, McCandless Young Scientist award divsn. devel. psychology 1982, Disting. Sci. award for early career contbn. 1981), AAAS, Am. Acad. ARts and Scis.; mem. Am. Ednl. Rsch. Assn. (Rsch. Rev. award 1986, Outstanding Book award 1987, Sylvia Scribner award 1996), Soc. Multivariate Exptl. Psychology (Cattell award 1982), Nat. Assn. Gifted Children (Disting. Scholar award 1985), Phi Beta Kappa. Avocations: physical fitness, travel, reading. Home: 105 Spruce Bank Rd Hamden CT 06518-2233 Office: Yale Univ Dept Psychology PO Box 208205 New Haven CT 06520-8205

STERNBERGER, LUDWIG AMADEUS, neurologist, educator; b. Munich, Germany, May 26, 1921; s. Hugo and Emy (Welinger) S.; m. Nancy Jeanne Hoy, Dec. 13, 1961. B.A., Am. U. Beirut, 1941, M.D., 1945. Fellow Sloan Kettering Meml. Cancer Ctr., N.Y.C., 1948-50; sr. med. biochemist N.Y. State Dept. Health, Albany, 1950-54; asst. prof. medicine Northwestern U., Chgo., 1954-55; chief basic scis. div. Med. Research Labs., Edgewood Arsenal, Md., 1957-78; prof. brain research U. Rochester Med. Ctr. (N.Y.), 1978-86; prof. neurology, pathology and anatomy U. Md., Balt., 1986-92; sci. co-dir., treas. Sternberger Monoclonals, Inc., Balt., 1992—. Author: Immunocytochemistry, 1974, 3d edit, 1986; mem. editoral bd. Cell and Tissue Research, Histochemistry, Jour. Histochemistry and Cytochemistry, Jour. Neurosci. Methods, Jour. Neuroimmunology, Histochem. Jour., Electron Microscopy in Biology. Served to maj. M.C., U.S. Army, 1955-57. Recipient Paul A. Siple prize, 1972; recipient Humboldt prize for sr. U.S. scientists, 1980, Classic Author citation Inst. Sci. Info., 1983; Senator Jacob K. Javits neurosci. investigator award, 1984; 25th most frequently cited author in sci. lit. of 1984; author of one of 17 Newcomer Superstar papers among 100 most cited of all time. Mem. Histochem. Soc. (pres. 1977-78), Am. Soc. Neurochemistry (program com. 1983-84), Am. Assn. Immunologists, Endocrine Soc., Am. Acad. Allergy, Am. Assn. Neuropathologists. Lutheran. Home: 10 Burwood Ct Lutherville Timonium MD 21093-3502

STERNE, BOBBIE LYNN, city council member; b. Ohio, Nov. 27, 1919; m. Eugene Sterne (dec.); children: Lynn, Cindy. Student, Akron U., 1941-42; student, U. Cin., 1946-47. RN, Ohio. City coun. mem. City of Cin., 1971—, mayor, 1976, 79; chair human resources com., City Coun. Cin., 1987-89, cmty. devel., housing zoning and environ. com.; mem., past chair fin. and labor com.; vice chair, past chair pub. works and traffic safety com.; chair intergovtl. affairs and environ. com., 1990—; past chair urban devel. com., housing com., human resources com.; vice chair fin. com., health social and childrens svcs. com.; mem. pub. works and utilities com., law and pub. safety com., select com. on spl. projects; past mem., past chair planning commn., retirement bd.; trustee City of Cin. Retirment Sys., 1989—. Bd. dirs. YWCA Alice Paul House, Charles P. Taft Meml. fund Com., Drug and Poison Info. Ctr., Friends of the William Howard Taft Birthplace, Greater Cin. Coalition People with Disabilities, Greater Cin. and No. Ky. Women's Sports Assn., Shawn Womack Dance Project, Ohio United Way; chmn. Emergency Svcs. Coalition; exec. com. Cmty.; adv. bd. Coun. on Child Abuse, First Step Home, State Cmty. Svc., U. Cin. Long Term Care Cmty., U. Cin. Clinical Ctr. Women's Health Initiative; govt. rels. com. Cmty. Chest; mem. sch. bd. Price Hill Cmty. Recipient Coun. Jewish Women Hannah G. Solomon award 1972, Citizens Com. on Youth's Most Valuable Citizen award, Achievement award Greater Cin. Beautiful Com., 1982, Anniversary award for work with Housing for Older Ams., Inc. Better Housing League, 1982, Orchid award Tri-State Air Com., 1982, Citizen's award Ohio Assn. for the Edn. Young Children, Advocate award Women in Communications, 1983, Betty Blake Award for Tourism, 1985, Others award Salvation Army, 1986. Home: 4033 Rose Hill Ave Cincinnati OH 45229-1524

STERNE, JOSEPH ROBERT LIVINGSTON, newspaper editor; b. Phila., Apr. 25, 1928; s. Robert Livingston and Edith Eisner (Heymann) S.; m. Barbara Adele Greene, Feb. 10, 1951; children—Robert Greene, Paul Livingston, Edward Joseph, Adam Heymann, Lee Winslow Greene. B.A. cum laude, Lehigh U., 1948; M.S., Columbia, 1950. Reporter Salt Lake Telegram, Salt Lake City, 1948-49, Wall Street Jour., N.Y.C., 1950-51, Dallas Morning News, 1951-53; reporter Balt. Sun, 1953-72, editorial page editor, 1972—. Mem. Am. Soc. Newspaper Editors, Center Club, Hamilton Street Club, Phi Beta Kappa. Home: 215 Melanchton Ave Lutherville Timonium MD 21093-5321 Office: Baltimore Sun Baltimore MD 21278

STERNER, FRANK MAURICE, industrial executive; b. Lafayette, Ind., Nov. 26, 1935; s. Raymond E. and Maudelene M. (Scipio) S.; m. Elsa Y. Rasmusson, June 29, 1958; children: Mark, Lisa. BS, Purdue U., 1958, MS, 1959, PhD, 1962. Sr. staff specialist Gen. Motors Inst., Flint, Mich., 1962-63; dir. personnel and orgnl. research Delco Electronics, Milw., 1963-66; dir. personnel devel. and research Delco Electronics, 1966-68; partner Nourse & Sterner, Inc., Milw., 1968-69; pres., 1969-73; assoc. dean, prof. Krannert Grad. Sch. of Mgmt., Purdue U., West Lafayette, Ind., 1973-79; v.p. human resources mgmt. Johnson Controls, Inc., Milw., 1979-89; pres., chief exec. officer E.R. Wagner Mfg. Co., 1989—; pres., owner Ridgeway Devel. Inc., Milw., 1993—; bd. dirs. Wasau Homes, Inc., E.R. Wagner Mfg. Co., Children's Hosp. Health Sys. Wis., Ridgeway Devel. Inc., Am. Lung Assn. Wis., Inroads/Wis., Inc., River Edge Nature Ctr., Inc. Contbr. articles to profl. jours. Club: Reamer. Home: 1440 E Standish Pl Milwaukee WI 53217-1958 Office: ER Wagner Mfg Co 4611 N 32nd St Milwaukee WI 53209-6023

STERNER, MICHAEL EDMUND, international affairs consultant; b. N.Y.C., Dec. 26, 1928; s. Harold Walther and Leonie (Knoedler) S.; m. Courtenay Read, Mar. 30, 1957; children: Lucian, Marcellin. AB, Harvard Coll., 1951. Govt. rels. rep. Arabian-Am. Oil Co., Dhahran, Saudi Arabia, 1951-54; joined Fgn. Svc., 1956; vice consul Aden, 1957-58; polit. officer Cairo, 1960-64; desk officer Near Eastern Affairs Dept. State, 1964-70, dir. Egyptian affairs, 1970-74; amb. to United Arab Emirates Abu Dhabi, 1974-76; dep. asst. sec. state for Near East and South Asian affairs, 1977-81; mng. dir. The IRC Group, Inc., 1982—. Mem. bd. govs. Mid. East Inst. With AUS, 1954-56. Mem. Coun. Fgn. Rels. Home: 2712 36th St NW Washington DC 20007-1421 Office: 1835 K St NW Washington DC 20006-1203

STERNHAGEN, FRANCES, actress; b. Washington, Jan. 13, 1930. Student, Vassar Coll., Perry-Mansfield Sch. of Theatre; studied with Sanford Meisner, N.Y. Tchr. Milton Acad., Mass.; actress Arena Stage, Washington, 1953-54. Debut Thieves Carnival, N.Y., 1955; plays include The Carefree Tree, The Admirable Bashville (Clarence Derwent award, Obie award), Ulysses in Night Town, Red Eye of Love, Misalliance, The Return of Herbert Bracewell, Laughing Stock, The Displaced Person, The Pinter Plays (Obie award); Broadway shows include The Skin of Our Teeth, Viva Madison Avenue, Great Day in the Morning, The Right Honorable Gentleman, The Cocktail Party, Cock-a-Doddle Dandy, Playboy of the Western World, The Sign in Sidney Brustein's Window, The Good Doctor (Tony award 1973), Equus, Angel, On Golden Pond (Drama League award), The Father, Grownups, Summer, You Can't Take It With You, Home Front, Driving Miss Daisy, Remembrance, A Perfect Ganesh, The Heiress (Tony award 1995); actress films including Up The Down Staircase, Starting Over, Outland, Independence Day, Romantic Comedy, Bright Lights, Big City, See You in the Morning, Communion, Misery, Doc. Hollywood, Raising Cain; (TV series) Love of Life, The Doctors, Secret Storm, Cheers, Golden Years, Under One Roof, The Road Home; (TV movies) Who Will Save Our Children?, Prototype, Resting Place, Follow Your Heart, She Woke Up, Labor of Love; The Arlette Schweitzer Story, Reunion, Tales from the Crypt, Outer Limits.

STERNITZKE-HOLUB, ANN, elementary school educator; b. Oklahoma City, Okla., May 5, 1952; d. James Francis and Doris Josephine (Lahr) Sternitzke; m. James Robert Holub, Apr. 4, 1987. AA, Golden West Coll., Huntington Beach, Calif., 1972; BS, Calif. State U., Fullerton, 1975, postgrad., 1976. Cert. secondary multiple subject, phys. edn. and English tchr. grades kindergarten-12, Calif.; life cert. educator Calif. Cmty. Colls. Phys. edn. and fencing instr. Fullerton Coll., 1976-82; fencing instr. Golden West Coll., Huntington Beach, 1977-83, Calif. State U., Fullerton, 1983-86; elem. phys. edn. specialist Placentia-Yorba Linda (Calif.) Unified Sch. Dist., 1989-93, elem. tchr. Bryant Ranch Sch., 1993—; puppeteer Adventure City Amusement Park, Anaheim, Calif. Mem. support staff 1984 Olympics, Long Beach, 1984; entertainer Stagelight Family Prodns., Brea, Calif., 1993—. Grantee Disneyland, 1993, 94, 95, 96. Mem. AAHPERD, U.S. Fencing Assn., U.S. Olympic Soc., U.S. Fencing Coaches Assn., Calif. State U. Alumni Assn. Republican. Avocations: dance, musical theatre, puppetry, fencing, costuming. Office: Bryant Ranch Sch 24695 Paseo De Toronto Yorba Linda CA 92687-5116

STERNLICHT, BENO, research and development company executive; b. Nowy Sacz, Poland; came to U.S., 1949, naturalized, 1950; s. Hugo Charles and Helena (Anisfield) S.; m. Lisa Spilberg; children—Mark David, Eric Alan, Joshua Hugh, Aaron Jonathan. B.S., Union Coll., Schenectady, N.Y., 1950; M.S., Columbia U., 1951, Ph.D., 1954, D.Sc. (hon.), 1970. Staff engr. thermal power systems, gen. engring. lab. Gen. Electric Co., 1951-54, specialist applied mechanics, 1954-58, cons. engr., 1958-61; co-founder, 1961; since chmn. bd., tech. dir. Mech. Tech., Inc., Latham, N.Y.; pres. Benjosh Mgmt. Assn., N.Y., 1983, Ameast Distbrs. Corp., N.Y.C., 1981—, 1720 E 13th St., 1215 Ave. M, 420 Shore Rd., N.Y.C., 1981—, 172 E. 4th St. Corp., N.Y.C., 1956—; dir. Small Diesels Ltd., India, New Eastern India Ltd.; chmn. com. energy tech. and space propulsion NASA, 1969-72, mem. research adv. council, 1970-72; Pres. Vols. Internat. Tech. Assistance, 1965-71, chmn. bd., 1971-73; Mem. Nat. Energy Task Force, 1981; advisor to Pres. Carter on Innovation and Energy, to Pres. Reagan and Pres. Bush on Energy; cons. to PRC, Israel. Author. Fellow ASME (Machine Design award 1966); mem. AIAA, Nat. Acad. Engring., Am. Soc. Lubrication Engrs., NavyLeague, Sigma Xi, Tau Beta Pi. Patentee in field. Address: 123 Partridge Run Schenectady NY 12309-1321

STERNLICHT, SANFORD, English and theater arts educator, writer; b. N.Y.C., Sept. 20, 1931; s. Irving Stanley and Sylvia (Hilsenroth) S.; m. Dorothy Hilkert, June 4, 1950 (dec. 1977); children: David, Daniel. BS, SUNY, Oswego, 1953; MA, Colgate U., 1955; PhD, Syracuse U., 1962. Instr. SUNY, Oswego, 1959-60, asst. prof., 1960-62, prof. and dir. grad. studies in English, 1962-72, chmn. dept. theater, 1972-84; adj. prof. English Syracuse (N.Y.) U., 1984—; Leverhulme vis. prof. English U. of York, Eng., 1965-66. Author: Gull's Way, 1961, The Blue Star Commodore, 1961, Love in Pompeii, 1967, John Webster's Imagery and the Webster Canon, 1972, John Masefield, 1977, McKinley's Bulldog, 1977 (Mil. Book Club award, Saturday Evening Post Book Club award), C.S. Forester, 1981, Padraic Colum, 1985; (with E.M. Jameson) The Black Devil of the Bayous, 1971; (with E.M. Jameson) U.S. F. Constellation: Yankee Racehorse, 1981, John Galsworthy, 1986, R.F. Delderfield, 1988, Stevie Smith, 1990, Stephen Spender, 1992, Siegfried Sassoon, 1993, All Things Herriot: James Herriot and His Peaceable Kingdon, 1995; editor: The Selected Short Stories of Padraic Colum, 1985, The Selected Plays of Padraic Colum, 1986, The Selected Poems of Padraic Colum, 1988, The Selected Poems of Padraic Colum, 1988, In Search of Steview Smith, 1991. Lt. (j.g.) USN, 1955-59, comdr. USNR, ret. Recipient New Poets award Writer mag., 1960, Chancellor's award SUNY, 1974; fellow Poetry Soc. Am., 1964; rsch. grantee SUNY, 1963-70; named Tchr. of Yr. Syracuse U., 1986. Mem. MLA, NAACP, PEN, Shakespeare Assn. Am., Am. Conf. Irish Studies. Democrat. Jewish. Home: 128 Dorset Rd Syracuse NY 13210-3048 Office: Syracuse U Dept English Syracuse NY 13244

STERNLIGHT, PETER DONN, economist, retired banker; b. N.Y.C., May 21, 1928; s. Morris Henry and Pearl (Donn) S.; m. Lenore Frane, Oct. 14, 1956; children: Jean Renee, Judith Ann. B.A., Swarthmore Coll., 1948; M.A., Harvard U., 1950, Ph.D., 1960. With Fed. Res. Bank N.Y., 1950-65; aide to under sec. treasury, 1961, asst. v.p. open market ops., 1964, dep. under sec. treasury monetary affairs, 1965-67; with Fed. Res. Bank N.Y., 1967-92, v.p. open market ops., 1968-77, sr. v.p., dep. mgr. system account for domestic ops., 1977-79, mgr. system account for domestic ops., 1979-92, exec. v.p., 1982-92; retired, 1992. Served with AUS, 1950-52. Recipient Exceptional Svc. award Treasury Dept., Disting. Achievement award for 1988 Money Marketers of NYU, William F. Butler award for Excellence in Bus. Econs. N.Y. Assn. Bus. Economists, 1994. Mem. Am. Econ. Assn., Am. Finance Assn., Phi Beta Kappa. Home: 301 Garfield Pl Brooklyn NY 11215-2351

STERNMAN, JOEL W., lawyer; b. N.Y.C., Oct. 20, 1943; s. Abraham and Sarah (Simon) S.; children: Mark S., Cheryl A.; m. Barbara E. Shiers, March 31, 1985; children: Matthew S., Julia S. AB, Dartmouth Coll., 1965; LLB, Yale U., 1968. Bar: N.Y. 1970, U.S. Dist. Ct. (so. and ea. dists.) N.Y. 1971, U.S. Ct. Appeals (2d cir.) 1972, U.S. Supreme Ct. 1984, U.S. Ct. Appeals (6th cir.) 1985, U.S. Ct. Appeals (9th cir.) 1994. Law clk. to judge U.S. Dist. Ct., New Haven, 1968-69; assoc. Rosenman Colin Freund Lewis & Cohen, N.Y.C., 1969-77; ptnr. Rosenman & Colin, N.Y.C., 1977—. Editor Yale Law Jour., New Haven, 1966-68. Mem. Phi Beta Kappa. Office: Rosenman & Colin 575 Madison Ave New York NY 10022-2511

STERNS, JOEL HENRY, lawyer; b. N.Y.C., Apr. 13, 1934; s. Barney and Yvetta S.; m. Joanne Glickman, Nov. 19, 1961; children: Racel, Leslie, David. B.S. in Journalism, 1956; M.P.A., Princeton U., 1958; J.D., N.Y. U., 1967. Bar: N.J., D.C. Exec. asst. to commr., acting commr. N.J. Dept. Conservation and Econ. Devel., 1958-61; exec. asst. to adminstr. Bur. Security and Consular Affairs, Dept. State, 1961-62; regional programs coordinator Alliance for Progress, 1962-64; exec. asst. to pres. Export-Import Bank U.S., 1964; dep. commr. N.J. Dept. Cmty. Affairs, 1967-68; counsel to gov. N.J., 1968-70; pres. firm Sterns, Herbert & Weinroth (P.A.), Trenton, N.J., 1970-88; mem. exec. com., compensation com. and mktg. com. Sterns, Herbert & Weinroth (merged with Hannoch-Weisman 1988), Roseland, N.J., 1988-91; pres. Hannoch-Weisman, Roseland, 1991-93, Sterns & Weinroth, Trenton, 1994—; mem. lawyers adv. com. U.S. Dist. Ct. N.J., 1995—. Mem. ABA, Am. Law Inst., Am. Judicature Soc., N.J. Bar Assn. (trustee), Mercer County Bar Assn., Assn. Princeton U. Grad. Alumni (trustee 1975-77), NYU Alumni Assn. N.J. (Disting. Alumni award 1987). Home: PO Box 307 RD 1 River Rd Titusville NJ 08560 Office: Sterns & Weinroth PO Box 1298 50 W State St Ste 1400 Trenton NJ 08607

STERNSTEIN, ALLAN J., lawyer; b. Chgo., June 7, 1948; s. Milton and Celia (Kaganove) S.; m. Miriam A. Dolgin, July 12, 1970 (div. July 1981); children—Jeffery A., Amy R.; m. Beverly A. Cook, Feb. 8, 1986; children: Cheryl L., Julia S. B.S., U. Ill., 1970; M.S., U. Mich., 1972; J.D., Loyola U., 1976. Bar: Ill. 1977, U.S. Dist. Ct. (no. dist.) Ill. 1977, U.S. Dist. Ct. (no. dist.) Ohio 1977, U.S. Dist. Ct. (ea. dist) Mich. 1986, U.S. Dist. Ct. (we. dist.) Mich. 1990, U.S. Ct. Customs and Patent Appeals 1978, U.S. Ct. Appeals (7th cir.) 1979, U.S. Ct. Appeals (Fed. cir.) 1982. Patent agent Sunbeam Corp., Oak Brook, Ill., 1972-76; ptnr. Neuman, Williams, Anderson & Olson, Chgo., 1976-84; div. patent counsel Abbott Labs., North Chgo., Ill., 1984-87; ptnr. Willian Brinks Hofer Gilson & Lione, Chgo., 1987—; adj. prof. of law John Marshall Law Sch., 1989-90, DePaul Univ., 1990-92, Univ. Ill., 1992—. Legal advisor Legal Aid Soc., Chgo., 1974-76, Pub. Defender's Office, Chgo., 1974. Teaching fellow U. Mich., 1971-72; research grantee U. Mich., U.S. Air Force, 1971-72. Mem. ABA, Chgo. Bar Assn., Patent Law Assn. of Chgo. (com. chmn. 1982), Am. Intellectual Property Law Assn., Licensing Execs. Soc., Tau Beta Pi, Sigma Tau, Sigma Gamma Tau, Phi Eta Sigma. Jewish. Office: Willian Brinks Hofer Gilson & Lione 455 N Cityfront Plaza Dr Chicago IL 60611-5503

STERRETT, JAMES KELLEY, II, lawyer; b. St. Louis, Nov. 26, 1946; s. James Kelley and Anastasia Mary (Holzer) S.; 1 child, Brittany. AB, San Diego State U., 1968; JD, U. Calif., Berkeley, 1971; LLM, U. Pa., 1973. Bar: Calif. 1972, U.S. Dist. Ct. (so. dist.) Calif. 1972. From assoc. to ptnr. Gray, Cary, Ames & Frye, San Diego, 1972-83; ptnr. Lillick, McHose & Charles, San Diego, 1983-90, Pillsbury, Madison & Sutro, San Diego, 1991—. Contbr. articles to profl. jours. Bd. dirs. Holiday Bowl, San Diego, 1980—, Mus. Photog. Arts, San Diego, 1985-88, San Diego Internat. Sports Coun., 1980—, pres., 1990, chmn., 1992. Capt. USAFR, 1972. Fellow U. Pa. Ctr. Study Fin. Instns., 1971-72. Mem. ABA, Calif. Bar Assn., San Diego County Bar Assn. Republican. Episcopalian. Club: Fairbanks Ranch Country (Rancho Santa Fe) (bd. dirs. 1985-87). Avocations: golf, college football, hiking. Office: Pillsbury Madison & Sutro 101 W Broadway Ste 1800 San Diego CA 92101-8219

STERRETT, JAMES MELVILLE, accountant, business consultant; b. Chicago, Dec. 25, 1949; s. James McAnlis and Antoinette (Galligan) S.; m. Joyce Mieko Motoda, Sept. 1, 1989; 1 child, Victoria Hanako. BS in Acctg., Chaminade U., Honolulu, 1988; MBA, Chaminade U., 1991. CPA, Hawaii. Cons. Profitability Cons., Honolulu, 1985-87; pres. Sterrett Cons. Group, Honolulu, 1987-88; auditor Deloitte & Touche, Honolulu, 1988-90; acct., cons. pvt. practice, Honolulu, 1990—. Mem. Nat. Soc. Pub. Accts., Nat. Assn. Tax Practitioners, Hawaii Soc. CPA's, Delta Epsilon, Sigma. Office: 1314 S King St Ste 650 Honolulu HI 96814-1941

STERRETT, SAMUEL BLACK, lawyer, former judge; b. Washington, Dec. 17, 1922; s. Henry Hatch Dent and Helen (Black) S.; m. Jeane McBride, Aug. 27, 1949; children: Samuel Black, Robin Dent, Douglas McBride. Student, St. Albans Sch., 1933-41; grad., U.S. Mcht. Marine Acad., 1945; BA, Amherst Coll., 1947; LLB, U. Va., 1950; LLM in Taxation, NYU, 1959. Bar: D.C. 1951, Va. 1950. Atty. Alvord & Alvord, Washington, 1950-56; trial atty. Office Regional Counsel, Internal Revenue Service, N.Y.C., 1956-60; ptnr. Sullivan, Shea & Kenney, Washington, 1960-68; municipal cons. to office vice pres. U.S., 1965-68; judge U.S. Tax Ct., 1968-88, chief judge, 1985-88; ptnr. Myerson, Kuhn & Sterrett, Washington, 1988-89; of counsel Vinson & Elkins, Washington, 1990—. Bd. mgrs. Chevy Chase Village, 1970-74, chmn., 1972-74; 1st v.p. bd. trustees, mem. exec. com. Washington Hosp. Center, 1969-79, chmn. bd. trustees, 1979-84; chmn. bd. trustees Washington Healthcare Corp., 1982-87; chmn. bd. trustees Medlantic Healthcare Group, 1987-89; mem. Washington Cathedral chpt., 1973-81; mem. governing bd. St. Albans Sch., 1977-81; trustee Louise Home, 1979-89. Served with AUS, 1943; Served with U.S. Mcht. Marine, 1943-46. Fellow Am. Bar Found.; mem. ABA, Fed. Bar Assn., D.C. Bar Assn., Am. Coll. Tax Counsel, Soc. of the Cincinnati, Coun. for Future, Am. Inns. of Ct., Chevy Chase Club (bd. govs. 1979-84, pres. 1984), Met. Club, Lawyers Club, Alibi Club, Alfalfa Club, Ch. of N.Y. Club, Beta Theta Pi. Episcopalian. Office: Vinson & Elkins 1455 Pennsylvania Ave NW Washington DC 20004-1008

STERZER, FRED, research physicist; b. Vienna, Austria, Nov. 18, 1929; came to U.S., 1947, naturalized, 1952; s. Karl and Rosa (Trumer) S.; m. Betty Distel, Sept. 5, 1964 (dec.). B.S. in Physics, CCNY, 1951; M.S. in Physics, NYU, 1952, Ph.D. in Physics, 1955. With RCA, 1954-87, RCA Labs., David Sarnoff Research Center, Princeton, N.J., 1956-87; dir. microwave tech. center RCA Labs., David Sarnoff Research Center, 1972-87; dir. microwave research lab. David Sarnoff Research Ctr., 1987-88; pres. MMTC, Inc., Princeton, 1988—; Herbert J. Kayser research prof., City Coll., CUNY, 1986-87. Contbr. numerous articles to profl. publs. Fellow IEEE; mem. Am. Phys. Soc., Nat. Acad. Engring., Sigma Xi, Phi Beta Kappa. Condr. research on optical components, microwave solid-state devices and circuits, med. microwave tech. Home: 4432 Province Line Rd Princeton NJ 08540-4368 Office: MMTC Inc 12 Roszel Rd Princeton NJ 08540-6234

STETLER, C. JOSEPH, retired lawyer; b. Wapaconeta, Ohio, May 13, 1917; s. Clarence Henry and Mary Frances (Kavanaugh) S.; m. Mary Norine Delaney, Aug. 16, 1941; children: Joseph James, David John, Mary Catherine, Julia Anne, Norine Teresa and Kathleen Frances (twins). LL.B., Cath. U. Am., 1938, LL.M., 1940; postgrad., Benjamin Franklin Sch. Accounting, Washington, 1940-41; D.Sc. (hon.), Mass. Coll. Pharmacy, 1978. Bar: D.C. 1940, Ill. 1951. With various agys. U.S. Govt., 1935-51; with AMA, 1951-63; gen. counsel, dir. legal and socio-econ. div., 1951-63; exec. v.p., gen. counsel Pharm. Mfrs. Assn., Washington, 1963-65; pres. Pharm. Mfrs. Assn., 1965-79, 84-85; ptnr. Munsey, Samuel & Stetler, 1979-81, Dickstein, Shapiro & Morin, 1981-84; pvt. practice Washington, 1984-86; of counsel Royer, Shacknai & Mehle, Washington, 1986-88, Hyman, Phelps & McNamara, Washington, 1988-93; ret., 1995. Author: (with Alan Moritz) Doctor Patient and the Law, 1962, Handbook of Legal Medicine, 1964, (with Wm. Cray) Patients in Peril, The Stunning Generic Drug Scandal, 1991. Mem. staff 2d Hoover Commn., 1953-54; mem. Reagan-Bush Health Adv. Com., 1980-81, Social Security Adv. Coun., 1983. Capt. AUS, 1942-46, PTO. Mem. ABA, D.C. Bar Assn. Roman Catholic. Home: 5906 Maplewood Park Pl Bethesda MD 20814-1744

STETLER, DAVID J., lawyer; b. Washington, Sept. 6, 1949; s. C. Joseph and Norine (Delaney) S.; m. Mary Ann Ferguson, Aug. 14, 1971; children: Brian, Christopher, Jennifer. BA, Villanova U., 1971, JD, 1974. Bar: U.S. Supreme Ct. 1978, Ill. 1988, U.S. Ct. Appeals (7th cir.) 1988, U.S. Ct. Appeals (3d cir.) 1992, U.S. Dist. Ct. (ctrl. dist.) 1994, U.S. Ct. Appeals (8th cir.) 1994. Atty. IRS, Washington, 1974-79; spl. atty. tax divsn. Dept. Justice, Washington, 1975-79; asst. atty. U.S. Atty.'s Office, Chgo., 1979-88, dep. chief spl. prosecutions div., 1985-86, chief criminal receiving and appellate divsns., 1986-88; ptnr. McDermott, Will & Emery, Chgo., 1988—; lectr. Atty. Gen. Trial Advocacy Inst., Washington, 1977—. Mem. ABA (chmn. midwest subcom. White Collar Crime com. 1991-93). Office: McDermott Will & Emery 227 W Monroe St Chicago IL 60606-5096

STETLER, RUSSELL DEARNLEY, JR., private investigator; b. Phila., Jan. 15, 1945; s. Russell Dearnley and Martha Eleanor (Schultz) S. B.A. with honors in Philosophy, Haverford (Pa.) Coll., 1966; postgrad., New Sch. Social Research, 1966-67. Research asst. to Bertrand Russell, 1967; lectr. Hendon Coll., London, 1968-69; pres. Archetype, Inc., Berkeley, Calif., 1971-78; pub. Westworks, Berkeley, 1977-80; pvt. investigator, 1980-90; chief investigator Calif. Appellate Project, 1990-95; dir. of investigations N.Y. State Capital Defender Office, N.Y.C., 1995—; cons., dir. Ramparts Press, Palo Alto, 1971-80; editorial cons. Internews, Berkeley, 1973-78; faculty Caribbean Sch., Ponce, P.R., 1978-80. Author: The Battle of Bogside, 1970; co-editor: The Assassinations: Dallas and Beyond, 1976. Research grantee Atlantic Peace Found., 1969-70. Mem. Calif. Assn. Lic. Investigators, Nat. Assn. Legal Investigators, Calif. Soccer Referees Assn.-North (treas. Marin County chpt. 1982-90), Amigos de las Americas (pres. Marin chpt. 1985-88). Clubs: Mill Valley Soccer (dir. 1981), Albany-Berkeley Soccer (pres. 1977-78). Office: Capital Defender Office 80 Centre St Rm 266 New York NY 10013

STETSON, DANIEL EVERETT, museum director; b. Oneida, N.Y., Jan. 3, 1956; s. Robert Everett and Barbara Elizabeth (Gray) S.; m. Catherine Marie Smith; children: Kellee, Natalie, Philip. BA in Art History, Potsdam Coll. Arts and Scis., 1978; MFA in Museology, Syracuse U., 1981. Teaching asst. fine arts dept. Potsdam (N.Y.) Coll. Arts and Scis., 1977-78; grad. asst. Syracuse (N.Y.) U. Art Collections, 1979-80; acting dir. Picker Art Gallery and Colgate U. Art Collections, Colgate U., Hamilton, N.Y., 1980-81; dir. Gallery of Art U. No. Iowa, Cedar Falls, 1981-87; dir. Davenport (Iowa) Mus. Art, 1987-91; exec. dir. Austin (Tex.) Mus. Art (formerly Laguna Gloria Art Mus.), 1991—, founding exec. dir., 1994; guest curator Joe and Emily Lowe Art Gallery, Syracuse U., 1980; mem. Inter Mus. Conservation Lab., Oberlin, 1987-91; mem. design adv. com. Iowa Capitol, Des Moines, 1989-91; panel cons. Arts Midwest/Affiliated States Art Assns. of Upper Midwest, Mpls., 1983, 88; bd. dirs. Iowa Arts Coalition, 1990-91; chair Tex. Commn. on the Arts Visual Arts Review Panel, 1994; mem. planning com. Tex. Assn. of Mus., 1994; mem. art in pub. pls. com. Austin Airport, 1995. Author/curator: (exhbn. catalog) José de Creeft (1884-1982), 1983, Contemporary Icons and Explorations, 1988, (exhbn. catalog) Philip Perlstein-Painting to Watercolors, 1983, Walter Dusenbery Classical Echoes, 1985, Jaune Quick-to-See Smith and George Longfish: Personal Symbols, 1986, Reuban Nakian: Leda and The Swan, 1983, Focus 1 Michael Boyd: Paintings, 1980, 89, Focus 2 Photo Image League, 1989, Focus 3 The Art of Haiti: A Sense of Wonder, 1989, Focus 6—Contemporary Devel. in Glass, 1990, Peter Dean: Landscapes of the Mind, 1981, Joseph Raffael, 1987, Born in Iowa-The Homecoming, 1986, Stieglitz and 40 Other Photographers—The Development of a Collection, 1991-92, New Works (Austin and Central Texas Artists), 1992, 94, Companions in Time: The Paintings of William Lester & Everett Spruce Catalogue Essay, 1993, Human Nature, Human Form Catalogue Essay, 1993, Sources and Collaborations: The Making of the Holocaust Project by Judy Chicago and Donald Woodman tour and catalog, 1994—. Bd. mem. arts coun. Cedar Arts Forum, Black Hawk County, Iowa, 1983-85; curriculum com. Leadership Investment for Tomorrow, Cedar Falls-Waterloo, Iowa, 1985-86; mem. adv. com. MBA Course of Study Styles and Strategies Non-Profit Orgns. St. Ambrose U., 1989-91, Austin BCA Arts Week Poster and Awards, 1993; mem. City of Austin Funding Process Rev. Com., 1992; Facilities Team Austin Comprehensive Arts Plan, 1991-93; mem. adv. panel Tex. Commn. Arts Visual Arts, 1993; field reviewer Inst. Mus. Svcs.-Gen. Operating Support Grant Field Reviewer, 1993; mem. arts com. Downtown Mgmt. Assn., 1995; mem. arts sub-com. Downtown Commn. Fellow N.E. Mus. Conf., Rochester, N.Y., 1979; grantee Iowa Arts Coun., Tex. Commn. Arts, NEA advancement program grant phase I & II, 1993-95; recipient mus. scholarship Am. Law Inst. ABA, Atlanta, Phila., 1984, 93. Mem. Am. Assn. Mus., Midwest Mus. Conf., Iowa Mus. Assn. (chair steering com. exhbn. workshop 1984-86, legis. action com. and indemnification com. 1981-90, bd. dirs. 1983-85), Tex. Assn. Mus. (program com., resources sharing com., 1992-94, Art Mus. Affinity Group) Davenport Rotary (cultural affairs com. 1987-91). Avocations: books, music, bike riding, visual world and media. Home: 5912 Brown Rock Trl Austin TX 78749-3306 Office: Austin Mus Art Laguna Gloria PO Box 5568 Austin TX 78763-5568

STETSON, EUGENE WILLIAM, III, film producer; b. Norwalk, Conn., Mar. 31, 1951; s. Eugene William Jr. and Grace Stuart (Richardson) S.; m. Jane White Watson, June 14, 1993. AB, Harvard U., 1982, postgrad. in Sch. Arts and Scis., 1986. Assoc. exec. dir. Conn. River Watershed Coun., Easthampton, Mass., 1978-81; v.p. Fairhill Oil & Gas Corp. (Fairhill Oil Ltd.-Can.), N.Y.C., Calgary, Alta., Can., 1981-84; pres. Fairhill Oil & Gas Corp. (Fairhill Oil Ltd.-Can.), N.Y.C., Calgary, 1984-92; film and TV writer and producer, 1991—; bd. dirs. Piedmont Fin. Co., Greensboro, N.C., 1978-80, Chisolm Mgmt. Corp., N.Y.C., 1983—; supr. Ottauquechee Conservation Dist., Woodstock, Vt., 1978-82; pres. Boatwright Found., N.Y.C., 1981—; exec. com. Westminster Sch., Simsbury, Conn., 1984-86; gov. Smith Richardson Found., N.Y., 1984—; trustee Proctor Acad., Andover, N.H., 1985—; co-founder River Watch Network, Montpelier, Vt., 1987—. Mem. Vt. Gov.'s Coun. of Environ. Advisors, 1992—, Vt. Gov.'s Coun. on Bus. and the Environment, 1994—. Mem. Harvard-Radcliffe Club Vt. (v.p. 1994—), Harvard Club N.Y.C., Hasty Pudding Club. Home: 139 Elm St Norwich VT 05055

STETSON, JOHN BATTERSON, IV, construction executive; b. Phila., Dec. 21, 1936; s. John Batterson Stetson III and Winifred (Walton) Todd; m. Solveig Weiland, Nov. 23, 1963; children: John Batterson V, Eric Weiland, Scott Walton. BA, Yale U., 1959, MArch, 1966; postgrad., U. Pa., 1969-73. Registered architect, Pa. Staff architect Bower & Fradley, Architects, Phila., 1966-68, Young & Exley, Architects, Phila., 1968-69; project architect Day & Zimmerman Assocs., Phila., 1969-71; mgr. tech. staff Day & Zimmerman Assocs. (div. MDC Systems Corp.), Phila., 1974-76, sr. v.p. cons. services div., 1985—; project mgr. Schnadelbach & Braun, Phila., 1971-74; project exec. Bldg. Scis., Inc., Balt., Kinshasa, Zaire, 1976-77; project mgr. Bldg. Scis., Inc., Balt., 1977-78; sr. cons., v.p., pres. MDC Systems Corp., Phila., 1978—. Active Haverford (Pa.) Civic Assn., 1981—. Comdr. USNR, 1959-81. Mem. Constrn. Mgmt. Assn. Am. (bd. dirs. 1986—), Am. Arbitration Assn., Constrn. Specifications Inst., Haverford Sch. Akumni Assn. Republican. Club: Merion Cricket (Haverford). Avocations: music, sailing. Home: 533 Waters Edge Newtown Square PA 19073 Office: Day & Zimmerman 1818 Market St Philadelphia PA 19103*

STETSON, PETER BRAILEY, astronomer; b. Middleboro, Mass., Aug. 30, 1952; s. George Robert and Estelle Marie (Ives) S.; m. Frances Eileen Bogucki, Aug. 5, 1979; children: Whitney Ann, Brailey Marie, Garrett Wilson, Leete Anthony. BA, Wesleyan U., 1974, MA, 1974; MS, Yale U., 1975, PhD, 1979. Postdoctoral astronomy dept. Yale U., New Haven, Conn., 1979-80; Carnegie fellow Mt. Wilson and Las Campanas Obs., Pasadena, Calif., 1980-83; rsch. assoc. Dominion Astrophys. Obs., Victoria, B.C., Can., 1983-84, asst. rsch. officer, 1984-86, assoc. rsch. officer, 1986-89, sr. rsch. officer, 1989—. Contbr. articles to Astron. Jour., Publ. Astron. Soc. of Pacific. Recipient R.M. Petrie prize lectr. Can. Astronomical Soc., 1991, Gold medal Sci. Coun. B.C., 1994. Office: Dominion Astrophys Obs, 5071 W Saanich Rd, Victoria, BC Canada V8X 4M6

STETTLER, STEPHEN F., performing company executive; b. Phila., May 1, 1952; s. Wallace Frederick and Catherine Sue (Brill) S. AB summa cum laude, Kenyon Coll., 1974; MFA in Directing, Cath. U. Am., 1982; MLitt in Theatre, Lincoln Coll., Oxford, Eng., 1983. Dir. dramatics Westminster Sch., Simsbury, Conn., 1975-80; acting coach Hartke Conservatory Cath. U., Washington, 1982; chair drama dept. St. Albans and Nat. Cathedral Schs., Washington, 1980-84; dir., instr. acting Nat. Theatre Inst. O'Neill Theater Ctr., Waterford, Conn., 1984—; artistic dir. TNT/New Theatre Bklyn., 1987-90; producing dir. Weston (Vt.) Playhouse, 1988—; lit. asst. Arena Stage Co., Washington, 1983-84; site evaluator theatres Nat. Endowment for Arts, Washington, 1990—; panelist project grants com. Vt. Coun. Arts, Montpelier, 1993-94; mem. capital grants com. N.Y.C. Dept. Cultural Affairs, 1989; cons. various ind. schs., 1986—; guest instr. directing Teatret Vart, Norway; ednl. theatre cons., guest artist Mercersburg (Pa.) Acad., Pa. Wyoming Seminar, Pa. Dir. Dancing at Lughnasa, Loot, Animal Fair, Rough Crossing, Sunday Promenade, Nora, Donkeys' Years, Into the Woods, Hay Fever, A Life in the Theatre, Spring Awakening, Mother Courage, A Midsummer Night's Dream (best play award Folger Shakespeare Libr. competition). Mem. Phi Beta Kappa. Office: Weston Playhouse PO Box 216 Weston VT 05161-0216

STETZNER, LEAH MANNING, lawyer, utilities executive; b. Hettinger, N.D., Aug. 11, 1948; d. Joseph Edward and Hazel Irene (Seymour) Manning; m. L.C. Stetzner, Mar. 20, 1970 (div. 1987); children: Autumn Lorraine, Prairie Lee. BA, U. N.D., 1970, MA, 1973; JD, U. Minn., 1977. Bar: Minn. 1977, Kans. 1985, U.S. Ct. Appeals (8th cir.) 1985, Ill. 1991. Atty. Burlington No. R.R., St. Paul, 1977-80; asst. gen. counsel Compmy and Burlington, Ft. Worth, 1981; asst. sec. No. Inc., Overland Park, Kans., 1981-84, assoc. gen. counsel, 1985, counsel, 1989; gen. counsel, corp. sec. Ill. Power Co., Decatur, 1989—. Bd. dirs. Easter Seals Soc., Decatur, 1990—. Mem. ABA (bus. law com.). Office: Ill Power Co 500 S 27th St Decatur IL 62521-2200*

STEUBEN, NORTON LESLIE, lawyer, educator; b. Milw., Feb. 14, 1936; s. Benjamin and Ria (Beerman) S.; m. Judith Ann Dickens, June 21, 1958; children: Sara Ann, Marc Nelson. A.B., U. Mich., 1958, J.D. with distinction, 1961. Bar: N.Y. 1962, Colo. 1975. Assoc., then ptnr. Hodgson, Russ, Andrews, Woods & Goodyear, Buffalo, 1961-68; mem. faculty U. Colo. Law Sch., Boulder, 1968—, prof. law, 1974—; of counsel Ireland, Stapleton, Pryor & Pascoe, Denver, 1980—; lectr. Law Sch., SUNY, Buffalo, 1961-68; officer Buffalo-Niagara Indsl. Devel. Corp., 1963-68, Buffalo Opportunities Devel. Corp., 1966-68; vis prof. law U. Puget Sound. Sch. Law, 1992-93. Author: Cases and Materials on Real Estate Planning, 1974, 3d edit., 1989; co-author: Problems in the Fundamentals of Federal Income Taxation, 1985, 3d edit. 1994, Problems in the Federal Income Taxation of Partnerships and Corporations, 1985, 3d edit., 1996; co-editor: Bittker, Fundamentals of Federal Income Taxation, 1983; editor Jour. Affordable Housing & Cmty. Devel. Law, 1994—; contbr. articles to profl. jours. Mem. Boulder Human Rights Commn., 1969-72, chmn., 1972-74; mem. Boulder Landlord-Tenant Com., 1973-74; trustee Boulder Open Space Bd., 1976-81, vice chmn., 1978-79, chmn., 1979-81; trustee Congregation Har Ha-Shem, Boulder, 1978-79, v.p., 1979-81, pres., 1982-84; mem. Boulder Housing Authority, 1982-89, vice chmn., 1984-85, chmn., 1985-88. Recipient S.I. Goldberg award Alpha Epsilon Pi, 1957, Disting. Svc. to Community award Buffalo Area C. of C., 1966, John W. Reed award U. Colo. Law Sch., 1970; Teaching Recognition award U. Colo.-Boulder, 1972, Teaching Excellence award, 1982; Presdl. Teaching scholar, U. Colo., 1989. Mem. ABA, N.Y. State Bar Assn., Colo. Bar Assn., Boulder County Bar Assn., Am. Law Inst., AAUP, Scribes (officer, editor Scrivener 1975-76, dir. 1979-82), Barristers Soc., Order of Coif, Tau Epsilon Rho. Democrat. Home: 845 8th St Boulder CO 80302-7408 Office: U Colo 418 Fleming Law Bldg Boulder CO 80309

STEUER, RICHARD MARC, lawyer; b. Bklyn., June 19, 1948; s. Harold and Gertrude (Vengar) S.; m. Audrey P. Forchheimer, Sept. 9, 1973; children: Hilary, Jeremy. BA, Hofstra U., 1970; JD, Columbia U., 1973. Bar: N.Y. 1974, U.S. Dist. Ct. (ea. and so. dists.) N.Y. 1974, U.S. Ct. Appeals (2d cir.) 1974, U.S. Dist. Ct. (no. dist.) N.Y. 1984, U.S. Ct. Appeals (3d cir.) 1987, U.S. Ct. Appeals (5th cir.) 1995, U.S. Supreme Ct. 1979. Ptnr. Kaye, Scholer, Fierman, Hays & Handler LLP, N.Y.C., 1973—; adj. assoc. prof. law NYU, 1985; lectr. various orgns.; neutral evaluator U.S. Dist. Ct. Ea. Dist., N.Y., 1994—. Author: A Guide to Marketing Law: Law and Business Inc., 1986; contbr. articles to profl. jours. Fellow Am. Bar Found.; mem. ABA (lectr. 1978, 85, 89, 96, editorial bd. antitrust devel. vol. 1984-86, chmn. monograph com. refusals to deal and exclusive distributorships 1983, various others, vaice chmn. program com. 1988-91, chmn. spring meeting program com. 1991-92, Sherman Act sect. 1 com. 1991-93, coun. sect. antitrust law 1993-96), Assn. Bar City N.Y. (antitrust and trade regulation, internat. trade, lectures and CLE coms., lectr. 1983-94, chmn. antitrust and trade regulation 1995—). Office: Kaye Scholer Fierman Hays & Handler LLP 425 Park Ave New York NY 10022-3506

STEVASON, JOHN C., lawyer; b. Bklyn., May 18, 1946. AB in Physics, Princeton U., 1967; JD, NYU, 1973. Bar: N.Y. 1974, Oreg. 1975, U.S. Ct. Appeals (4th and 9th cirs.). Law clk. U.S. Ct. Appeals, 4th Cir., Richmond, Va., 1973-74; assoc. Lane Powell Spears Lubersky, Portland, Oreg., 1975-81, ptnr., 1982—. Mem. bd. ops. com. YMCA, Columbia Willamette, Portland, 1992—; vice chmn. human resources com., Am. Heart Assn., Oreg. chpt. Portland, 1990—. Mem. Computer Law Assn., Oregon State Bar Assn. (exec. bd. computer law sect., mem. labor rels., civil rights coms.). Office: Lane Powell Spears Lubersky 520 SW Yamhill St Ste 800 Portland OR 97204-1331

STEVEN, DONALD ANSTEY, dean, educator; b. Montreal, Que., Can.; s. Ivan Campbell and Margaret Jane (Anstey) S.; m. Margaret Ann MacKenzie, May 1, 1976; children: James, Denise. BMus in Composition with honors, McGill U., Montreal, 1972; MFA, Princeton (N.J.) U., 1975. Lectr. U. Western Ont., London, 1975-76; asst. prof. McGill U., Montreal, 1976-83, assoc. prof., 1983, chair dept. of performance, 1986-92, prof., 1991-92; with Purchase Coll., SUNY, dean of music, 1992—, prof., 1992—; exec. coun. Can. League of Composers; nat. bd. dirs. Can. Music Ctr.; served on many juries. Composer: In the Land of Pure Delight, 1991, That Other Shore, 1989, Full Valleys, 1989, Orbits, 1989, Art Thou Weary, Heavy Laden, 1988, Love Where the Nights Are Long, 1987, The Breath of Many Flowers, 1986, Sapphire Song, 1986, Pages of Solitary Delights, 1985, Straight on Till Morning, 1985, Just a Few Moments Alone, 1984, Ordre Sans Ordre, 1984, Bert in Nether-Nether Land, On the Down Side, 1982, Nordring Festival Music, 1981, Wired, 1981, Night Suite, 1979, Rainy Day Afternoon, 1979, For Madmen Only, 1978, Images-Refractions of Time and Space, 1977, The Transient, 1975, Crossroads, 1974, The Gossamer Cathedral-Five Surrealistic Frescoes, 1972, Illusions, 1971, Harbinger, 1969. Advisor to vis. com. on musical instruments N.Y. Met. Mus. of Art. Recipient Gov. Gen.'s award for Chamber Music, JUNO award, Grand Prix du Disque du Canada Can. Music Coun., 1978, Broadcast Music Inc. award, 1970. Mem. N.Y. State Assn. of Coll. Music Programs (bd. dirs., sec., treas. 1992-95), Coll. Music Program, Am. Music Ctr., Can. Music Ctr. (assoc. composer). Office: Purchase Coll SUNY 735 Anderson Hill Rd Purchase NY 10577-1400

STEVENS, ALICE MARIE, educational consultant; b. Colorado Springs, Colo., Jan. 18, 1954; d. Charles C. and Gladys Marie (Craft) S. BS, S.W. Bapt. U., 1976; MEd, U. Mo., 1983; postgrad., Purdue U., 1991—. Cert. tchr. reading, learning disabilities, Mo. Sci. tchr. Lincoln County R-IV Schs., Winfield, Mo., 1976-78; sci. instr. Ricks Inst., Monrovia, Liberia, West Africa, 1978-79; learning specialist Total Learning Clinic, Columbia, Mo., 1982-89; homebound instr. Rusk Rehab. Ctr., Columbia, Mo., 1988-91; instr. Columbia Coll., Columbia, Mo., 1989, 91; learning disabilities specialist Columbia (Mo.) Pub. Schs., 1989-91; tchr., rsch. asst. Purdue U., West Lafayette, Ind., 1991—; ednl. cons. West Lafayette, Ind., 1991—. Asst. dir. Cerebral Palsy Assn. Greater Lafayette, 1993-94. Mem. ASCD, Nat. Sci. Tchrs. Assn. (conf. presenter 1993), Coun. for Exceptional Children (conf. presenter tchr. edn. divsn. 1992), Nat. Head Injury Found. Office: Purdue U Liberal Arts And Edn B West Lafayette IN 47907

STEVENS, ART, public relations executive; b. N.Y.C., July 17, 1935; m. Eva Sandberg, Mar. 19, 1972. B.A., CCNY, 1957. Pub. relations dir. Prentice Hall, Inc., Englewood Cliffs, N.J.; account exec. William L. Safire Public Relations Inc., N.Y.C., 1966-69; v.p. William L. Safire Public Relations Inc., 1967-68, pres., 1968-69; pres. Lobsenz-Stevens Inc., N.Y.C., 1970—; instr. Fairleigh Dickinson U.; weekly humor commentator WINK-TV, Ft. Myers, Fla. Author: The Persuasion Explosion, 1985, Sanibel Shell Shocked, 1992; weekly columnist Sanibel-Captiva (Fla.) Islander; contbr. articles to profl. jours. Bd. dirs. United Way of Putnam County, N.Y.; trustee Gotthelf Lupus Rsch. Inst. Mem. Publicity Club N.Y. (Disting. Service award 1969), Public Relations Soc. Am. (pub. rels. com., exec com., chmn. elegibility com., counselors acad. sect.). Club: Gipsy Trail (Carmel, N.Y., pres.). Home: 201 E 21st St New York NY 10010-6401 Office: Lobsenz-Stevens Inc 460 Park Ave S New York NY 10016-7301 *Life is not an accident. The events in one's life are not accidents either. When I look back at what I have done and the lives that have been interwined with mine, it's as though it's all been scripted by a higher power.*

STEVENS, ARTHUR WILBER, JR., English literature educator, writer, editor; b. Bklyn., Aug. 16, 1921; s. Arthur Wilber and Isabella Ellen (MacGibbon) S.; m. Marjorie Athene Rogers, Feb. 15, 1955 (dec. Feb. 1979); children: Arthur Wilber III, Christopher Rivers; m. Joan Cutuly, Mar. 6, 1992. AB, Brown U., 1942; MA, U. Wash., 1956, PhD, 1957. Teaching fellow, assoc., then instr. U. Wash., Seattle, 1944-54; vis. lectr., then asst. prof. Idaho State U., Pocatello, 1954-60; assoc. prof., chmn. dept. English, 1961-64; Fulbright prof. Am. and English lit. U. Mandalay (Burma) and U. Chulalongkorn, Thailand, 1956-57; Fulbright prof. Am. lit. U. Brazil, Rio de Janeiro, 1959; prof., chmn. dept. lit. Park Coll., Parkville, Mo., 1964-66; prof. English, chmn. Center Lang. and Lit. Studies; Prescott (Ariz.) Coll., 1966-69, provost, 1968-71, dir. Prescott Coll. Press., 1968-73, prof. English and comparative lit., 1972-73; prof. English and humanities U. Nev., Las Vegas, 1973-94, prof. emeritus, 1994—; dean Coll. Arts and Letters U. Nev., 1973-75, chmn. Asian Studies program, 1980-88; vis. prof. Ariz. State U., Tempe, summer 1968, SUNY, Buffalo, summer 1971, Utah Shakespeare Festival, 1972, Baylor U., summer 1976; vis. prof. U. Pa., 1983, 84; dramatic and music critic Billboard, 1947-54, Intermountain, 1954-64, Seattle Home News, 1947-53, Prescott Courier and The Paper, 1966-73, Las Vegas Rev.-Jour., 1973-77, Las Vegas Sun, 1977-84, Sta. KLAV-Radio, The Las Vegan. Author, editor: Poems Southwest, 1967, Stories Southwest, 1973; author: Pocatello; The World in Going to End Up in Burma, 1989, From the Still Empty Grave, 1995; co-editor: Indian Poetry in English, 1988, Seven Nevada Poets, Desert Wind: Anthology of Nevada Poets, 1991; contbr. poems and articles to profl. jours. and anthologies; editor, founder lit. mag. Interim, 1944-55, 85—; theatre critic Las Vegas Rev. Jour., 1984-94. Del. Theatre Libr. Assn. UNESCO Conf., San Francisco, 1957; mem. Nev. Humanities Com., 1982-88, Internat. James Joyce Found. Recipient Spanos Disting. Teaching award U. Nev., Las Vegas, 1986, Exemplary Svc. award Nev. Humanities Com., 1992; Frances Wayland scholar, 1940-42; inductee Nev. Writers Hall of Fame, Friends of Libr., U. Nev., Reno, 1992. Mem. MLA, Rocky Mountain MLA (pres. 1971), Conf. Christianity and Lit., Music Critics Assn. Am., Philol. Assn. Pacific Coast (exec. bd. 1978-80), Burma Studies Group, Am. Theatre Critics Assn., Renaissance Soc. Am., F. Scott Fitzgerald Soc., Theatre Libr. Assn., Brown Club (N.Y.C.), Princeton Club (N.Y.C.), Phi Kappa Phi, Beta Theta Pi. Home: 3770 Forestcrest Dr Las Vegas NV 89121-4909

STEVENS, BERTON LOUIS, JR., data processing manager; b. Chgo., Apr. 4, 1951; s. Berton Louis Sr. and Mary Cover (Kochavaris) S.; m. Janet Alene Madenberg, May 20, 1990. Student, Ill. Inst. Tech., Chgo., 1969-73. Systems and applications programmer Judge & Dolph, Ltd., Elk Grove Village, Ill., 1978-91, mgr. data processing, 1991—; instr. Adler Planetarium and Astron. Mus., Chgo., 1980-86. Editor and author newsletter Bert's Bull., 1987-90; editor newsletter No. Lights, 1990—. Recipient Regional award North Ctrl. Region Astron. League, 1989. Mem. Nat. Assn. Sys. Programmers, Internat. Occultation Timing Assn. (sec. 1975-78), Chgo. Computer Soc., Chgo. Astron. Soc. (pres. 1977, 80, 84), Racine Astron. Soc. (pres. 1979), Astron. League (exec. sec. 1993-95).

STEVENS, C. GLENN, judge; b. Rockford, Ill., Oct. 29, 1941; s. Robert W. and Mary Louise (Shaughnessy) S.; m. Suzanne Ruth Corkery, July 4, 1967; children: Robert W., Angela M. BS, St. Louis U., 1964, JD, 1966. Bar: Ill. 1966, Mo. 1966, U.S. Dist. Ct. (so. dist.) Ill. 1966, U.S. Dist. Ct. (ea. dist.) Ill. 1968. Law clk. to judge U.S. Dist. Ct. (so. dist.) Ill., Springfield, Ill., 1966-67; instr. St. Louis U., 1967-68; assoc. Pope & Driemeyer, Belleville, Ill., 1967-74; ptnr. Pope & Driemeyer, Belleville, 1974-77; judge State of Ill., Belleville, 1977—. Bd. editors St. Louis U. Law Rev., 1965-66. Arbitrator Am. Arbitration Assn., St. Clair County, Ill, 1970-77. With U.S. Army, 1958-66. Mem. Mo. Bar Assn., Ill. Judges Assn., Am. Judges Assn., Ill. State Bar Assn., St. Clair County Bar Assn., East St. Louis Bar Assn., Phi Delta Phi (pres. Murphy Inn 1965-66). Democrat. Roman Catholic. Avocations: antique cars, soccer coach. Office: Saint Clair County Courthouse Public Sq Belleville IL 62220

STEVENS, CLYDE BENJAMIN, JR., property manager, retired naval officer; b. Denver, Oct. 10, 1908; s. Clyde Benjamin and Maybelle Olive (Boot) S.; m. Lucile Lillian-Louise Kip, May 5, 1933; children: Jane Stevens

White, Donald Kip, Patricia Louise Stevens Schley. BS, U.S. Naval Acad., 1930; postgrad., U.S. Naval Postgrad. Sch., Annapolis, Md., 1939, U.S. Naval War Coll., Newport, R.I., 1947. Registered profl. engr. Commd. ensign USN, advanced through grades to rear adm., 1959; comdg. officer USS R-20, S-33 Plaice and Platte, 1950-52; comdr. officer USS Platte 50-52 Destroyer Squad 6, 1954-55; with torpedo prodn. and undersea weapons div. Bur. Ordnance, Washington, 1947-59; with USS Platte, 1950-52, Destroyer squad., 1955-56; program dir. Bur. Ordnance, Washington, 1952-55, 56-59; ret., 1959; product mgr. TRW, Inc., Cleve., 1959-65; rsch. engr. Boeing Co., Seattle, 1965-74, torpedo cons., 1985; apt. owner and mgr. Seattle, 1965—; torpedo cons. Goodyear Aerospace Co., Akron, Ohio, 1965. Patentee automobile generator. Decorated Navy Cross, Silver Star with oak leaf cluster. Mem. Seattle Apt. Assn. (bd. dirs. 1967-91), Army and Navy Club, Rainier Club. Republican. Episcopalian. Home and Office: 2339 Franklin Ave E Seattle WA 98102-3342

STEVENS, CONNIE, actress, singer; b. Bklyn., Aug. 8, 1938; d. Peter and Eleanore (McGinley) Ingolia; m. Maurice Elias; m. Edwin Jack Fisher (div.); children: Joely, Tricia Leigh. Grad. high sch. Show bus. debut as vocalist with, The Three Debs, Hollywood, at age 16; appeared in: Finians Rainbow for Hollywood Repertory Co.; numerous motion pictures, including Way, Way Out, Scorchy, Eighteen and Animals, Young and Dangerous, Drag Strip Riot, Rock-a-bye Baby, Parish, Susan Slade, Palm Springs Weekend, The Grissom Gang, Never Too Late, Grease II, 1983, Back to the Beach, 1987, Bring Me the Head of Dobie Gillis, 1988; starred in TV series Wendy and Me and TV series Hawaiian Eye, 1959-62, TV films for ABC-TV Movie-of-the-Week; Call Her Mom, 1972, Playmates, Mister Jericho, Cole Porter in Paris, The Sex Symbol, 1974; guest star on TV with, Bob Hope, Red Skelton, Englebert Humperdinck, Tom Jones, Perry Como and Laugh-In; TV appearance comedy spl. Harry's Battles; headliner at Flamingo Hotel, Las Vegas, also, Hilton Internat., Sands Hotel, Desert Inn, Aladdin, MGM, Sahara, 1969-76; stage appearances include The Wizard of Oz at Carousel Theatre in So. Calif., Any Wednesday at Melodyland, Anaheim, Calif.; made Broadway debut in Star Spangled Girl, 1967; accompanied Bob Hope around world on his Christmas tour, 1969, Persian Gulf Christmas tour, 1987. Bd. dirs. Ctr. for Plastic and Reconstructive Surgery, South Vietnam.

STEVENS, DAVID, economics educator; b. Burbank, Calif., Jan. 26, 1926; s. Frederick and Alpheus (Perkins) S.; 1 child, David Fancher. B.A., Whitman Coll., 1947; M.B.A., Stanford U., 1949; LLD (hon.), Whitman Coll., 1994. Asst. prof. Okla. State U., 1949-51; asst. prof. econs. Whitman Coll., Walla Walla, Wash., 1951-54; asso. prof. Whitman Coll., 1954-56, prof., 1956-67, Roger and David Clapp prof. of econ. thought, 1958-91, prof. emeritus, 1991—, dean adminstrn., 1954-64, chmn. faculty, 1982-85; vis. prof. Glasgow U., Scotland, 1964-66, sr. research fellow, 1980—; instr. Am. Inst. Banking. Author: Adam Smith and the Colonial Disturbances, 1976; Editor: The Wedderburn Manuscript In Adam Smith: Correspondence, 1977. Commr. Regional Planning Commn., Walla Walla County, 1960-64; chmn. Walla Walla County chpt. ARC, 1961-63, 75-77. Served to lt. J.G. U.S. Navy, 1943-46. Mem. Am. Econ. Assn., Western Econ. Assn., History of Econ. Soc. Episcopalian. Home: 602 Boyer Ave Walla Walla WA 99362-2381 Office: Whitman Coll Economics Dept Walla Walla WA 99362

STEVENS, DIANA LYNN, elementary education educator; b. Waterloo, Iowa, Dec. 12, 1950; d. Marcus Henry and Clarissa Ann (Funk) Carr; m. Paul John Stevens; 1 child, Drew Spencer. BS, Mid Am. Nazarene Coll., 1973; M in Liberal Arts, Baker U., 1989. Elem. tchr. Olathe (Kans.) Sch. Dist. #233, 1975—. Artwork appeared in traveling exhibit ARC/Nat. Art Edn. Assn., 1968. Mem. Cedarhouse Aux., Olathe, 1986—; pres. Artists' League, Olathe, 1990—. Mem. NEA, Kans. Edn. Assn., Olathe Edn. Assn. (social com.), Nat. Art Edn. Assn., Delta Kappa Gamma (profl. affairs com. mem.), Coll. Ch. of the Nazarene. Avocations: portrait art, reading biographies, power walking, exhibiting artwork. Home: 217 S Montclaire Dr Olathe KS 66061-3828

STEVENS, DONALD KING, aeronautical engineer, consultant; b. Danville, Ill., Oct. 27, 1920; s. Douglas Franklin and Ida Harriet (King) S.; BS with high honors in Ceramic Engring., U. Ill., 1942; MS in Aeros. and Guided Missiles, U. So. Calif., 1949; grad. U.S. Army Command and Gen. Staff Coll., 1957, U.S. Army War Coll., 1962; m. Adele Carman de Werff, July 11, 1942; children: Charles August, Anne Louise, Alice Jeanne Stevens Kay. Served with Ill. State Geol. Survey, 1938-40; ceramic engr. Harbison-Walker Refractories Co., Pitts., 1945-46; commd. 2d lt. U.S. Army, 1942, advanced through grades to col., 1963; with Arty. Sch., Fort Bliss, Tex., 1949-52; supr. unit tng. and Nike missile firings, N.Mex., 1953-56; mem. Weapons Systems Evaluation Group, Office Sec. of Def., Washington, 1957-61; comdr. Niagara-Buffalo (N.Y.) Def., 31st Arty. Brigade, Lockport, N.Y., 1963-65; study dir. U.S.A. ballistic missile def. studies DEPEX and X-66 for Sec. Def., 1965-66; chief Air Def. and Nuclear br. War Plans div. 1965-67, chief strategic forces div. Office Dep. Chief Staff for Mil. Ops., 1967-69; chief spl. weapons plans, J5, U.S. European Command, Fed. Republic Germany, 1969-72, ret., 1972; guest lectr. U.S. Mil. Acad. 1958-59; cons. U.S. Army Concepts Analysis Agy., Bethesda, Md., 1973-95; cons. on strategy Lulejian & Assocs., Inc., 1974-75; cons. nuclear policy and plans to Office Asst. Sec. of Def., 1975-80, 84-93; cons. Sci. Applications, Inc., 1976-78; Asst. camp dir. Piankeshaw Area coun. Boy Scouts Am., 1937; mem. chancel choir, elder First Christian Ch., Falls Church, Va., 1957-61, 65-69, 72—; elder, trustee Presbyn. Ch., 1963-65. Decorated D.S.M., Legion of Merit, Bronze Star. Mem. Am. Ceramic Soc., Assn. U.S. Army, U. Ill. Alumni Assn., U. So. Calif. Alumni Assn., Keramos, Sigma Xi, Sigma Tau, Tau Beta Pi, Phi Kappa Phi, Alpha Phi Omega. Clubs: Niagara Falls Country; Ill. (Washington); Terrapin, Rotary. Contbr. articles to engring. jours.; pioneer in tactics and deployment plans for Army surface-to-air missiles. Address: 5916 5th St N Arlington VA 22203-1010

STEVENS, DWIGHT MARLYN, educational administrator; b. Wheeler, Wis., May 13, 1933; s. Clifford and Alva Orpha (Follensbee) S.; children: Patricia Lee Stevens Vanden Heuvel, Jacqueline Ann Stevens Kreuger, Cynthia May Stevens Manthey, Robert Louis. B.S., Eau Claire (Wis.) State U., 1957; M.S., U. Wis., 1959, Ph.D., 1972. High sch. speech tchr. Ft. Atkinson, Wis., 1957-61; high sch. prin. Oostburg, Wis., 1961-64; prin. Arrowhead High Sch., Hartland, Wis., 1964-66; dist. adminstr. Arrowhead Sch. Dist., 1966-73; dep. state supt. Wis. Dept. Pub. Instrn., Madison, 1973-81; supt. schs. Stevens Point, Wis., 1982-93; faculty U. Wis.-Whitewater, 1971, U. Wis.-Superior, 1985, U. Wis.-Stevens Point, 1988-92, 93—. Author: (with Eye, Netzer and Benson) Strategies for Instructional Management, 1980. Dir. Ford Found., Community Planning Project for Chippewa Indians, 1970-71, Nat. Validation Team, Title III, Elementary Secondary Edn. Act; cons. HEW Workshops on Innovation, Eagle River, Wis.; chmn. Wis. sch. dist. adminstrn., 1992. Served with U.S. Army, 1953-55. Recipient Outstanding Citizenship award Waukesha County, Wis., 1974; Ford fellow John Hay Fellowship in Humanities, Williams Coll., 1963; Kettering fellow Nat. Seminar on Innovation, Honolulu, summer 1967, Outstanding Adminstrv. Practitioner award U. Wis.-Stevens Point, 1991; Disting. Alumni award U. Wis., 1980. Mem. Cen. Wis. C. of C. (pres. 1986-87), Acad. Letters and Scis. (v.p. 1987—, pres. 1988-90), Phi Delta Kappa (v.p. 1985-87), Pi Kappa Delta. Home: 3323 Echo Dells Ave Stevens Point WI 54481-5118

STEVENS, EDWARD, public relations executive; b. Cleve., Feb. 24, 1941. BA, John Carroll U., 1963. Asst. mgr., adv. constrn. dept. divsn. Warner & Swasey, 1966-69; A/E Cleve. office Dix & Eaton, 1969-71, A/E Erie office, 1971-74, v.p., gen. mgr. Erie office, 1974-79, group v.p., 1979-80, sr. v.p., gen. mgr. Erie office, 1980—, group pres., 1982; bd. dirs. PRSA, Cleve. Ad. Club. Recipient Erie Ad Person of the Yr. award, 1985, George Mead award, 1987. Office: Dix & Eaton/Public Rels 1301 E 9th St Ste 1300 Cleveland OH 44114-1800

STEVENS, EDWARD FRANKLIN, college president; b. Newcastle, Wyo., Sept. 7, 1940; s. Edward Downey and Esther Elizabeth (Watt) S.; m. Linda Elaine Loewenstein, June 3, 1962; children: Carla Sue, Cathy Lynne. Student, U. Denver, 1959-60; BA in Edn., Physics, Chemistry cum laude, Nebr. Wesleyan U., 1963; MA in Ednl. Psychology, Stats. and Measurement, U. Nebr., 1967; PhD in Higher Edn., Mktg., Mgmt., U. Minn., 1983; postdoctoral, Harvard U., 1991. Tchr., head basketball coach Alvo-Eagle (Nebr.) High Sch., 1963-64, Madison (Nebr.) High Sch., 1964-65; asst. basketball coach U. Nebr., Lincoln, 1965-67; head basketball coach, asst. prof. edn. Augustana Coll., Sioux Falls, S.D., 1967-71; v.p., gen. mgr. tng. Iseman divsn. U.S. Inds., Sioux Falls, 1971-74; chief devel. and instl. advancement officer Sioux Falls Coll., 1974-79, asst. prof. to prof., 1980-83; from exec. v.p. to exec. asst. pres. Kearny (Nebr.) State Coll. Found., 1979-80; pres. George Fox U., Newberg, Oreg., 1983—. Chmn. campaign Yamhill County United Way, Newberg, 1988; bd. commrs. Newberg Community Hosp., 1988-91. NDEA fellow, 1965; recipient Young Alumni Achievement award, Nebr. Wesleyan U., 1973, Leadership Fellows award, Bush Found., St. Paul, 1976. Mem. Am. Assn. Pres. Indep. Colls. and Univs., Nat. Christian Coll. Consortium (chmn. 1987-88), Nat. Assn. Intercollegiate Athletics (council pres., exec. com. 1988-92, chmn. 1992), Nat. Assn. Evangelicals (Christian higher edn. com.), Nat. Assn. Indep. Colls. and Univs., Oreg. Ind. Colls. Assn. (bd. dirs. 1983-92, chmn. 1986-87), Oreg. Ind. Colls. Found. (bd. dirs. 1983-92, vice chmn. 1993), Coun. of Ind. Colls. (bd. dirs. 1990), N.W. Assn. Schs. and Colls. (commn. on colls.), Internat. Assn. Univs. Pres., New Life 2000 (internat. com. reference), Rotary. Republican. Mem. Soc. Friends. Office: George Fox U Office of Pres 414 N Meridian St Newberg OR 97132-2625

STEVENS, EDWARD IRA, information systems educator; b. York, Pa., Oct. 13, 1937; s. Francis DeHaven and Myra Jane (Foust) S.; m. Marjorie Eleanor Bisson, Aug. 29, 1959 (div. Oct. 1978); children: Mark Edward, Whitney Lynne, Kimberly Lauren; m. Kathleen Susan Berg, May 30, 1983. AB, Davidson (N.C.) Coll., 1959; MDiv, Harvard U., 1962; PhD, Vanderbilt U., 1965. Asst. prof. psychology, then assoc. prof. Eckerd Coll. (formerly Fla. Presbyn. Coll.), St. Petersburg, 1965-69, dir. research and ednl. services, 1969-73, dir. planning, exec. asst. to pres., 1977-84, from assoc. prof. info. sys. to prof., 1984—, dir. instl. rsch. and planning, 1993—, acting dir. libr. svcs., 1995—; dean acad. affairs Northland Coll., Ashland, Wis., 1973-75, v.p., 1974-75; pres. Lyndon State Coll., Lyndonville, Vt., 1975-77; v.p. research St. Clair Software Systems, Inc., Clearwater, Fla., 1985-87; cons. and lectr. in field. Contbr. articles to profl. jours. Am. Council Edn. fellow, Washington, 1969-70; Fund for Improvement Post-Secondary Edn. grantee, Washington, 1976-78. Mem. Am. Assn. Higher Edn., Acad. Mgmt., Assn. Instl. Rsch., Assn. for Computer Machinery, Phi Beta Kappa. Presbyterian. Avocations: art, antiques, photography. Home: 15501 Eastbourn Dr Odessa FL 33556-2853 Office: Eckerd Coll 4200 54th Ave S Saint Petersburg FL 33711-4744

STEVENS, ELISABETH GOSS (MRS. ROBERT SCHLEUSSNER, JR.), writer, journalist; b. Rome, N.Y., Aug. 11, 1929; d. George May and Elisabeth (Stryker) Stevens; m. Robert Schleussner, Jr., Mar. 12, 1966 (dec. 1977); 1 child, Laura Stevens. B.A., Wellesley Coll., 1951; M.A. with high honors, Columbia U., 1956. Editorial assoc. Art News Mag., 1964-65; art critic and reporter Washington Post, Washington, 1965-66; free-lance art critic and reporter Balt., 1966—; contbg. art critic Wall Street Jour., N.Y.C., 1969-72; art critic Trenton Times, N.J., 1974-77; art and architecture critic The Balt. Sun, 1978-86. Author: Elisabeth Stevens' Guide to Baltimore's Inner Harbor, 1981, Fire and Water: Six Short Stories, 1982, Children of Dust: Portraits and Preludes, 1985, Horse and Cart: Stories from the Country, 1990, The Night Lover: Art & Poetry, 1995; contbr. articles, poetry and short stories to jours., nat. newspapers and popular mags. Recipient A.D. Emmart award for journalism, 1980, Critical Writing citation Balt.-Washington Newspaper Guild, 1980, fiction awards Md. Poetry Rev., 1992, 92, 94, 2d prize Lite Circle, 1994, 1st prize fiction Lite Circle, 1995, award Balt. Writers Alliance, 1994, Balt. Writers Alliance Play Writing Contest award, 1994; Art Critics' fellow NEA, 1973-74, fellow MacDowell Colony, 1981, Va. Ctr. for Creative Arts, 1982-85, 88-90, 92, 93, 95, Ragdale Found., 1984, 89, Yaddo, 1991, Villa Montalvo, 1995; Work-in-Progress grantee for poetry Md. Art Coun., 1986, Creative Devel. grantee for short fiction collection Balt. Mayor's Com. on Art and Culture, 1986. Mem. Nat. Press Club Washington, Coll. Art Assn., Balt. Bibliophiles, Authors Guild, Am. Studies Assn., Poetry Soc. Am. Home: 6604 Walnutwood Cir Baltimore MD 21212-1213

STEVENS, GARVIN L., college dean. Exec. dean U. N.D., Williston. Office: UND at Williston Office Exec Dean Williston ND 58801

STEVENS, GARY, professional jockey. Top money winner, 1991. Winner Breeder's Cup Turf Race, 1990, Breeder's Cup Juvenile, 1993, Breeder's Cup Distaff, 1994.

STEVENS, GEORGE, JR., film and television producer, writer, director; b. Calif., Apr. 3, 1932; s. George Cooper and Yvonne (Shevlin) S.; m. Elizabeth Guest, July, 1965; children: Caroline, Michael, David. B.A., Occidental Coll., 1953. Asst. to George Stevens, Sr., 1951-53, motion picture prodn. asst., 1956, assoc. producer, 1957-60, TV dir., 1957-61; dir. Motion Picture Service, USIA, 1962-64, Motion Picture and TV service, USIA, 1964-67; founding dir., chief exec. Am. Film Inst., 1967-80, now co-chmn. bd.; pres. New Liberty Prodns., 1980—; founding chmn. D.C. Arts Commn., 1969; chmn. U.S. del. Internat. Film Festivals at Moscow, Cannes, Venice, Berlin, 1963-66. Motion pictures include John F. Kennedy, Years of Lightning Day of Drums, 1964, Nine From Little Rock (Acad. award), 1965, America at the Movies, 1976; creator, prodr., writer Am. Film Inst. Life Achievement Award shows, 1973-95, TV series including AFI: A Salute to James Cagney (Emmy award), The Stars Salute America's Greatest Movies, 1977, America Entertains Vice Premier Deng Tsio Peng, 1979; creator, co-prodr., writer Kennedy Ctr. Honor series, 1978-94, (4 Emmy awards, George Foster Peabody award); creator, exec. prodr. Christmas in Washington series, 1982-94; writer, prodr., dir. George Stevens: A Filmmaker's Journey, 1985 (award Nat. Bd. of Rev. of Motion Pictures, 1986, WGA award for ABC broadcast 1988); prodr., co-writer (TV miniseries) The Murder of Mary Phagan, 1988 (Emmy award, Christopher award, George Foster Peabody award), George Stevens: D-Day To Berlin (Emmy awards for writing and narration); co-exec. prodr., dir., writer (TV miniseries) Separate But Equal, 1991 (Christopher award, Emmy award). Trustee Occidental Coll., 1980-82. Served to 1st lt. USAF, 1954-56. Named to Ten Outstanding Young Men in Fed. Govt., 1963, Ten Outstanding Young Men in U.S., 1964; recipient Jury prize Chgo. Internat. Film Film Fest., 1985, Paul Selvin award Writers Guild of Am., 1991, NAACP Legal Def. Fund award. Office: Kennedy Ctr Washington DC 20566

STEVENS, GEORGE ALEXANDER, realtor; b. Loma, Mont., Nov. 10, 1923; s. Otto Oliver and Josephine (Dale) S.; m. Martha Evie Fultz, Sept. 16, 1944 (div. 1978); children: Gary, Kathleen, Arlene, Tina; m. Arleen Dorothea Largent, Nov. 14, 1978. A in Bus Adminstrn., SUNY, 1992. Prin. George Stevens Farm, Loma, Mont., 1946-93, George Stevens, Realtor, Loma, Mont., 1957-93; pres. George A. Stevens COrp., Loma, 1976-93, Gold and Silver Realty, Inc., Great Falls, Mont., 1993—. Trustee Sch. Dist. # 32, Loma, 1947-50; election judge Precinct # 7, Loma, 1953-88. With USN, 1944-46, PTO. Mem. Nat. Assn. Realtors, VFW (life), Am. Legion (life), Elks (life), Eagles Lodge. Democrat. Lutheran. Home: 810 8th Ave N Great Falls MT 59401-1036

STEVENS, GEORGE RICHARD, business consultant, public policy commentator; b. Chgo., Sept. 6, 1932; s. George and Irene (Kaczmarek) S.; m. Jeanne E. Sowden, Aug. 2, 1957; children: Stacey, Samantha, Pamela. B.S. with honors, Northwestern U., 1954. C.P.A., Ill. With Arthur Andersen & Co., 1954-78; mng. ptnr. Arthur Andersen & Co., Brussels, Belgium, 1957-71; partner Arthur Andersen & Co., Chgo., 1971-78; pres. Daubert Industries, Oak Brook, Ill., 1978-80, G.R. Stevens Group, 1981—; founder, pres. Stevens Center for Public Policy Studies, 1981—; Mem. Chgo. Com., 1979—; commr. Ill. Ednl. Facilities Authority, 1989—. Commr. Ill. State Scholarship Commn., 1981-87; vice chmn. Ill. Ind. Higher Edn. Loan Authority, 1982-88. Mem. Better Govt. Assn. (dir. 1972-80). Home and Office: 22615 N Las Lomas Ln Sun City West AZ 85375-2022

STEVENS, GERALD D., secondary education educator, consultant; b. Seattle, Apr. 9, 1941; s. James Edward and Olga Rubina (Olsen) S.; m. Michele Christine Hayek, June 16, 1973; children: Heather Corrine, Wendy Jeannette, Gerald Michael. Student, U. Wash., 1963-65; BA in Polit. Sci., Calif. State U., L.A., 1989; MA, U. So. Calif., 1995, postgrad., 1995—. Cert. tchr., Calif. Bank auditor Nat. Bank Commerce, Seattle, 1965-72; pvt. practice GEMIC L.A., 1972-86; tchr. L.A. Unified Sch. Dist., 1986—; cons. model schs. program Fgn. Policy Assn., Washington, 1990; presenter coalition essential schs. L.A. Unified Sch. Dist., 1990-91. Author: Redistributive Econ. Justice, 1993. Vol. C.L.A.R.E. Found., Santa Monica, 1989-91. With USMC, 1960-63, PTO. Mem. So. Calif. Social Sci. Assn. (bd. dirs. 1990-94, v.p.), United Tchrs. L.A., Sierra Club. Avocations: songwriting, ceramic art. Home: Unit 2 2101 Ocean Ave Santa Monica CA 90405-2228 Office: LA Unified Sch Dist 450 N Grand Ave Los Angeles CA 90012-2100

STEVENS, GLADSTONE TAYLOR, JR., industrial engineer; b. Brockton, Mass., Dec. 16, 1930; s. Gladstone Taylor and Blanche Ruth S.; m. Jane A. Crouch, July 20, 1953; children—Robert, Bartlett. B.S.M.E., U. Okla., 1956; M.S.M.E., Case Inst. Tech., 1962; Ph.D. in Indsl. Engring, Okla. State U., 1966. Registered profl. engr., Tex., Okla. Project engr. E.I. duPont, Orange, Tex., 1956-59; research engr. Thompson-Ramo-Wooldridge, Cleve., 1960-62; asst. prof. mech. and indsl. engring. Lamar U., Beaumont, Tex., 1962-64; asst. prof. to asso. prof. indsl. engring. Okla. State U., Stillwater, 1966-75; prof., chmn. dept. indsl. engring. U. Tex., Arlington, 1975—. Author: (with J.E. Shamblin) Operations Research: A Fundamental Approach, 1974, Economic and Financial Analysis of Capital Investments, 1993; Engineering Economy, 1983. Served with AUS, 1948-52. Recipient E.L. Grant award, 1974, AMOCO Teaching award, 1979, Wellington award, 1992. Mem. Am. Inst. Indsl. Engrs. (sr.), Sigma Xi, Alpha Pi Mu (nat. pres.), Tau Beta Pi, Sigma Tau, Omicron Delta Kappa. Home: 3611 Shady Park Dr Arlington TX 76013-5706 Office: U Tex Indsl Engring Arlington TX 76019

STEVENS, HERBERT FRANCIS, lawyer, law educator; b. Phila., Nov. 19, 1948; s. Herbert F. and Lois Marie (Kenna) S.; m. Jane Pickard, 1994; children: Sarah, Ben. SB, MIT, 1970; JD, Catholic U. Am., 1974; ML in Tax., Georgetown U., 1983. Bar: D.C. 1975, U.S. Supreme Ct. 1980. Law clk. to presiding justice Md. Ct. of Spl. Appeals, 1974-75; assoc. Morgan, Lewis & Bockius, Washington, 1975-78; ptnr. Lane & Edson, P.C., Washington, 1984-89; ptnr. Kelley Drye & Warren, Washington, 1989-93, Peabody & Brown, Washington, 1993—; adj. prof. Georgetown U. Law Ctr., 1983—; spkr. nat. confs., seminars, TV. Editor: Real Estate Aspects of the 1984 Tax Law, 1984; author: Real Estate Taxation: A Practitioner's Guide, 1986, A Developer's Guide to Low Income Housing Tax Credit, 1992, 2nd edit., 1994. Chmn. bd. dirs. Ctr. for Mental Health, Inc., 1987-94; mem. exec. com., bd. dirs. Nat. Fund for U.S. Botanic Gardens, 1992—. Mem. ABA, D.C. Bar Assn. Democrat. Methodist. Home: 8301 Hackamore Drive Potomac MD 20854 Office: Peabody & Brown 1255 23rd St NW Washington DC 20037-1125

STEVENS, JAMES M., food processing executive; b. 1947. With Nabisco, Bethlehem, Pa., 1968, Pepsi Cola Bottling Group, Purchase, N.Y., 1969-76; sr. v.p. Great Waters France Inc., Greenwich, Conn., 1977-81; with Premium Products Sales Corp., Greenwich, 1981-86; COO Coca Cola Enterprises, Atlanta, 1986-92; pres. Suntory Water Group Inc., Atlanta, 1992—. Office: Suntory Water Group Inc 280 Interstate North Pky NW Atlanta GA 30339-2409

STEVENS, JOHN PAUL, United States supreme court justice; b. Chgo., Apr. 20, 1920; s. Ernest James and Elizabeth (Street) S.; m. Elizabeth Jane Sheeren, June 7, 1942; children: John Joseph, Kathryn Stevens Jedlicka, Elizabeth Jane Stevens Sesemann, Susan Roberta Stevens Mullen; m. Maryan Mulholland, Dec. 1979. A.B., U. Chgo., 1941; J.D. magna cum laude, Northwestern U., 1947. Bar: Ill. 1949. Practiced in Chgo.; law clk. to U.S. Supreme Ct. Justice Wiley Rutledge, 1947-48; assoc. firm Poppenhusen, Johnston, Thompson & Raymond, 1949-52; asso. counsel sub-com. on study monopoly power, com. on judiciary U.S. Ho. of Reps., 1951; ptnr. firm Rothschild, Stevens, Barry & Myers, 1952-70; U.S. circuit judge, 1970-75; asso. justice U.S. Supreme Ct., 1975—; lectr. anti-trust law Northwestern U. Sch. Law., 1952-54, U. Chgo. Law Sch., 1955-58; mem. Atty. Gen.'s Nat. Com. to Study Anti-Trust Laws, 1953-55. Served with USNR, 1942-45. Decorated Bronze Star. Mem. Chgo. Bar Assn. (2d v.p. 1970), Am., Ill., Fed. bar assns., Am. Law Inst., Order of Coif, Phi Beta Kappa, Psi Upsilon, Phi Delta Phi. *

STEVENS, JOSEPH CHARLES, psychology educator; b. Grand Rapids, Mich., Feb. 28, 1929; s. Joseph, Jr. and Anne Katheryn (Ghysels) S. A.B., Calvin Coll., Grand Rapids, 1950; M.A., Mich. State U., 1953; Ph.D., Harvard U., 1957. Instr., then asst. prof. psychology Harvard U., 1957-66; fellow John B. Pierce Found. Lab., also sr. research scientist Yale U., 1966—; cons. in field. Author: Laboratory Experiments in Psychology, 1965; co-editor: Sensation and Measurement, 1974; mem. editorial bds. profl. jours.; contbr. numerous articles to profl. jours. Grantee NSF; Grantee NIH; Grantee Air Force Office Sci. Research. Fellow AAAS, Am. Psychol. Soc., N.Y. Acad. Scis.; mem. Acoustical Soc. Am., Optical Soc. Am., Soc. Neurosci., Eastern Psychol. Assn., Gerontol. Soc. Am. Office: 290 Congress Ave New Haven CT 06519-1403

STEVENS, JOSEPH EDWARD, JR., federal judge; b. Kansas City, Mo., June 23, 1928; s. Joseph Edward and Mildred Christian (Smith) S.; m. Norma Jeanne Umlauf, Nov. 25, 1956; children: Jennifer Jeanne, Rebecca Jeanne. B.A., Yale U., 1949; J.D., U. Mich., 1952. Bar: Mo. 1952, U.S. Supreme Ct. 1973. Assoc. Lombardi, McLean, Slagle & Bernard, Kansas City, Mo., 1955-56; assoc. then ptnr. Lathrop, Koontz, Righter, Clagett & Norquist, Kansas City, Mo., 1956-81; judge U.S. Dist. Ct. (we. dist.) Mo., Kansas City, 1981—, chief judge, 1992-95; mem. adv. com. on Fed. Rules of Civil Procedure, Washington, 1987-92; bd. trustees Harry S. Truman Scholarship Found., 1995—. Bd. govs. Citizens Assn. Kansas City, 1959-70; bd. dirs., exec. com. Truman Med. Ctr., Kansas City; trustee Central United Methodist Ch., Kansas City, 1978—, Barstow Sch., Kansas City, 1978-87. Served with USNR, 1952-55. Recipient Lon O. Hocker Meml. Trial Lawyer award Mo. Bar Found., 1963, Spurgeon Smithson award, 1987, Charles E. Whittaker award Kansas City Lawyers Assn., 1996. Mem. ABA (ho. dels. 1982-88), Kansas City Met. Bar Assn., Lawyers Assn., Mo. Bar (pres. 1980-81, bd. govs. 1976-82, Pres.'s award 1995), Univ. Club, Carriage CLub, Vanguard Club, Mercury Club, Beta Theta Pi, Man-of-Month Fraternity. Office: US Dist Ct 811 Grand Blvd Ste 404 Kansas City MO 64106-1909

STEVENS, KENNETH NOBLE, electrical engineering educator; b. Toronto, Ont., Can., Mar. 23, 1924; came to U.S., 1948, naturalized, 1962; s. Cyril George and Catherine (Noble) S.; m. Phyllis Fletcher, Jan. 19, 1957 (div. 1979); children: Rebecca, Andrea, Michael Hugh, John Noble; m. Sharon Manuel, Jan. 14, 1994. B.A.Sc., U. Toronto, 1945, M.A.Sc., 1948; Sc.D., MIT, 1952. Inst. U. Toronto, 1946-48; faculty MIT, Cambridge, 1948—; prof. elec. engring. MIT, 1963—, Clarence J. Lebel prof., 1977—; Vis. fellow Royal Inst. Tech., Stockholm, 1962-63; cons. to industry, 1952—; vis. prof. phonetics U. Coll., London, 1969-70; mem. Nat. Adv. Council on Neurol. and Communicative Disorders and Stroke NIH, 1982-86. Author: (with A.G. Bose) Introductory Network Theory; Contbr. articles to profl. jours. Trustee Buckingham Browne and Nichols Sch., 1974-80. Recipient Quintana award Voice Found., 1992, medal European Speech Comm. Assn., 1995; Guggenheim fellow, 1962. Fellow IEEE, Acoustical Soc. Am. (exec. com. 1963-66, v.p. 1971-72, pres.-elect 1975-76, pres. 1976-77, gold medal 1995), Am. Acad. Arts and Scis.; mem. NAE. Home: 51 Montrose St Somerville MA 02143-1212 Office: MIT 77 Massachusetts Ave Cambridge MA 02139-4301

STEVENS, KEVIN MICHAEL, professional hockey player; b. Brockton, Mass., Apr. 15, 1965. Student, Boston Coll. With L.A. Kings, 1983; left wing Pitts. Penguins, 1983—; mem. NHL All-Star team, 1991-92, Stanley Cup championship teams, 1991, 92; player NHL All-Star games, 1991, 92, 93. Named to NCAA All-Am. East 2nd Team, 1986-87, Sporting News All-Star 2nd Team, 1990-91, 92-93, NHL All-Star 1st Team, 1991-92. Office: Pitts Penguins Civic Arena Gate # 9 Pittsburgh PA 15219*

STEVENS, LEOTA MAE, retired elementary education educator; b. Waverly, Kans., Mar. 27, 1921; d. Clinton Ralph and Velma Mae (Kukuk) Chapman; m. James Oliver Stevens, Nov. 7, 1944 (dec.); children: James Harold, Mary Ann Hooker Tibbit. BA, McPherson Coll., 1954; MS, Emporia U., 1964, postgrad., 1969-77; postgrad., Wichita U., 1977. Educator Pleasant Mound Sch., Waverly, 1940-41; prin. educator Halls Summit Sch., Waverly, 1941-42; educator Waverly Grade Sch., 1942-43, Ellinwood (Kans.) Jr. H.S., 1943-45, Hutchinson (Kans.) Grade Sch., 1945-48, Lincoln Sch., Darlow, Kans., 1948-49; educator prin. Mitchell-Yaggy Consol. Sch., Hutchinson, 1949-57; educator elem. Hutchinson Sch. Dist. 308, 1957-85, ret.,

1985; v.p. Reno County Tchrs. Assn. Hutchinson, 1956-57, pres. Assn. Childhood Edn. Internat., 1978-79. Author of numerous poems; compiler The Alexander-Kukuk Descendants: 1754 to 1990. Mem. Worker ARC Blood Mobile, 1986—, Hutchinson Cmty. Concerts 1970—; ch. sch. tchr. Trinity United Meth. Ch., 1959-71. (attendance chair, 1994); historian Women's Civic Ctr., 1988-92, art com. chmn., 1992-96; den mother Cub Scouts, 1963-66, leader Girl Scouts Ellinwood, 1944-45. Mem. AAUW (news reporter 1984-87, legis. chmn. program com. 1991—, 2d v.p., 1994—), Ret. Nation State and Local Edn. Assn., Reno County Tchrs. Assn. (v.p. 1956-57), Assn. Childhood Edn. Internat. (pres. 1978-79), Reno County Extension Homemaker Coun. (rep. 1987—), Rainbow Extension Club (pres. 1986-92), Hutchinson Area Ret. Tchrs. Assn. (historian 1996—), Am. Legion Aux., Friends of Preservation, Delta Kappa Gamma (sec., v.p. 1972-80, grant chmn. 1980-88, publicity com. 1990-93, legis. chmn. 1994—). Republican. Avocations: art, music, traveling, gardening, camping. Home: 805 W 23rd Ave Hutchinson KS 67502-3765

STEVENS, LINDA LOUISE HALBUR, addiction counselor; b. Huron, S.D., Oct. 28, 1960; d. Alvin LeRoy and Esther Louise (Schroeder) Halbur; m. Lowell Eugene Stevens, July 26, 1980 (div. 1995); children: Lowell John, Tracie Lynn. BSW, U. N.D., 1991; MEd, N.D. State U., 1993. Lic. social worker, N.D.; lic. addiction counselor, N.D. Tracker Luth. Soc. Svcs., Hillsboro, N.D., 1990-94; addiction counselor Heartland Med. Ctr., Fargo, N.D., 1993-94, S.E. Human Svc. Ctr., Fargo, 1994—; dual diagnosis Off Main Program, Fargo, 1995. Local/state officer N.D. Women of Today, Hillsboro, 1982-87. Recipient Presdl. award of excellence N.D. women of Today, 1986, 87. Mem. NASW, Am. Counseling Assn. Avocations: golf, sewing, pets. Home: 1717 40th St S Apt 114 Fargo ND 58103-4445 Office: SE Human Svc Ctr Off Main 9 9th St S Fargo ND 58103

STEVENS, LISA GAY, minister, choral director; b. Okla. City, Mar. 30, 1952; d. Charles Alton and Betty Lou (Johnson) Landrum; m. Thomas Lynn Taylor, Dec. 11, 1971 (div. 1983); children: Jason Ryan, Joel Shane; m. James Hervey Stevens Jr., Apr. 29, 1984. Student, Friends U., 1970-72; BA in Music, U. Mo., Kansas City, 1983-87; MDiv with gerontology specialization, St. Paul Sch. Theology, 1987-90. Ordained deacon United Meth. Ch., 1989, elder, 1992. Adminstrv. asst./cashier McLiney and Co., Kansas City, Mo., 1978-80; choral dir. Hickman Mills Christian Community, Kansas City, 1979-82; adminstrv. asst. Hokanson, Lehman & Stevens Creative Planning, Inc., Kansas City, 1981-88; choral dir. Crossroads Reformed Ch., Shawnee Mission, Kans., 1983-84, St. Paul Sch. Theology, Kansas City, 1988-89; chaplain St. Luke's Hosp., Kingswood Manor Health Ctr., Kansas City, 1988; pastor The Belvidere United Meth. Ch., Kansas City, 1988-90, Va./Passaic United Meth. Chs., Butler, Mo., 1990-93, North Cross United Meth. Ch., Kansas City, Mo., 1993-95, Ctrl. United Meth. Ch., Kansas City, 1995—; adj. faculty praxis team leader St. Paul Sch. Theology, 1990-93; mem. fin. and adminstrn. com. Mo. West United Meth. Conf., 1993—, subcom. health ins. com., 1993—, dist. supts.' salary com., 1994—, Kansas City north dist. supts.' com., 1994-95, conf. counseling edler, 1993—. Solo flutist Sr. Wichita Youth Orchestra, 1969-70. Pres. Life Ins. Office Mgrs. Assn. Kansas City, 1985, chairperson pub. rels, 1984; bd. trustees Shepherd's Ctr. of Northland, 1994-95, mem. funding/fin. com., 1994—. Mem. Butler Ministerial Alliance; Butler Chaplains Assn. (chaplain, 1991-93). Methodist. Avocations: flutist, train enthusiast, music, artist. Office: North Cross United Meth Ch 1321 NE Vivion Rd Kansas City MO 64118-5934

STEVENS, LORRAINE GERTRUDE, nurse anesthetist; b. Charleston, W.Va., June 12, 1942; d. James Wendel and Edna Mae (Brooks) Bennett; m. Arlen Lee Stevens, Sept. 26, 1964. Grad. in nursing, St. Mary's Hosp., Huntington, W.Va., 1964; BS, U. Cin., 1974, MS, 1976, EdD, 1981. RN, Ohio; registered nurse anesthetist, nurse practitioner ANCC. Nurse VA Hosp., Huntington, 1964-66; didactic and clin. instr. Univ. Hosp., U. Cin. Med. Ctr., 1969-72; mem. bd. admissions for nurse anesthetists Sch. Anesthesia, U. Cin. Med. Ctr., 1970-72; chief nurse anesthetist, dept. mgr. Queen City Anesthesia Assoc., Inc./Providence Hosp., Cin., 1972—; chief nurse 311th Sta. Hosp., USAR, Sharonville, Ohio, 1985-88; mem. adv. bd. nurse anesthetists masters program U. Cin. Coll. Nursing and Health, 1993—. Vol. Pro-Srs. Orgn., Cin., 1990-92. Col. USAR, 1972—. Named Outstanding Black Female in Medicine, NIP mag. Mem. Am. Assn. Nurse Anesthetists, Ophthalmic Anesthesia Assn., Ohio Assn. Nurse Anesthetists, Fla. Nurses Assn. Baptist. Avocations: reading, travel, summer water sports, working with the elderly. Office: Queen City Anesthesia Assoc PO Box 85155 Cincinnati OH 45201

STEVENS, LYDIA HASTINGS, community volunteer; b. Highland Park, Ill., Aug. 2, 1918; d. Rolland T.R. and Ruth Shotwell (Beebe) Hastings; m. George Cooke Stevens, Nov. 2, 1940; children: Lydia Stevens Gustin, Priscilla Stevens Goldfarb, Frederick S., Elizabeth Stevens MacLeod, George H., Ruth Stevens Stellard. BA, Vassar Coll., 1939. State rep. 151st Dist. of Conn., Greenwich, 1988-92; cons. Nat. Exec. Svc. Corps, N.Y.C., 1985. Pres. Greenwich YWCA, 1971-74, Greenwich Housing Coalition, 1982-86; v.p. planning Greenwich United Way, 1973-76; sr. warden Greenwich Christ Episcopal Ch., 1981-86; chmn. rev. commn. Episcopal Diocese of Conn., 1985-87; bd. dirs. Greenwich Libr., 1985-93; chmn. Greenwich Commn. Aging, 1986-88; pres., bd. dirs. Greenwich Broadcasting Corp., 1977-79; bd. dirs. Fairfield County Cmty. Found., 1992—. Recipient Golden Rule award J.C. Penney, 1987, President's award Greenwich YWCA, 1992. Republican. Episcopalian. Avocations: sailing, organic gardening.

STEVENS, M. ALLEN, geneticist, administrator; b. Mt. Carmel, Utah, Aug. 12, 1935; s. Joseph Merwin and Virginia (Tait) S.; m. Hermese Maw, June 6, 1960; children: Kent, Lance, Jennifer. BS, Utah State U., 1957, MS, 1961; PhD, Oreg. State U., 1967. Rsch. assoc. Campbell Soup Co., Camden, N.J., 1967-70; asst. geneticist U. Calif., Davis, 1970-74, assoc. geneticist, 1974-79, prof. geneticist, 1979; regional mgr. Campbell Soup Co., Camden, N.J., 1979-81; v.p. Campbell Inst. Agrl. Rsch., 1981-87, v.p. agrl. rsch., 1987-89; v.p. rsch. Petoseed Co., Inc., Woodland, Calif., 1989-95; sr. v.p. rsch. Seminis Vegetable Genetics, Woodland, Calif., 1996—; lectr. sci. Inst. Food Tech., 1970-73; adj. prof. U. Calif., Davis, 1979-82; vis. prof. Hebrew U., Rehovot, Israel, 1977; bd. dirs. Genetic Resources Comm. Sys., Washington, 1986—, Am. Seed Rsch. Found., 1993—; sci. liaison officer Asian Vegetable R & D Ctr., Tainan, Taiwan, 1983-88, bd. dirs., 1990-93; mem. Nat. Plant Genetic Resources Bd., Washington, 1987-91; mem. exec. com. Internat. Food Biotech. Coun., 1987-90. Contbr. numerous articles to books and sci. jours. Mem. coord. com. Tomato Genetics Coop., 1980-90. 1st lt. U.S. Army, 1957-59. Recipient Citation of Performance U. Calif., Davis, 1992, award of Distinction, 1995; named Vol. of Yr. Coll. Agrl. and Environ. Sci. U. Calif., Davis, 1991. Fellow AAAS, Am. Soc. Horticultural Sci. (pres. 1992-93, Nat. Canners Assn. award 1968, 1977, Asgrow award 1971, 78, Campbell award 1973, Nat. Food Processors Assn. award 1980, Homer C. Thompson award 1983). Achievements include development of tomato varieties UC82, UC204. Home: 2 Ridgeview Pl Woodland CA 95695-6823 Office: Seminis Vegetable Genetics 37437 State Highway 16 Woodland CA 95695-9353

STEVENS, MARILYN RUTH, editor; b. Wooster, Ohio, May 30, 1943; d. Glenn Willard and Gretchen Elizabeth (Ihrig) Amstutz; BA, Coll. Wooster (Ohio), 1965; MAT, Harvard U., 1966; JD, Suffolk U., 1975; m. Bryan J. Stevens, Oct. 11, 1969; children: Jennifer Marie, Gretchen Anna. Bar: Mass. 1975. Tchr., Lexington (Mass.) Public Schs., 1966-69; in various editorial positions Houghton Mifflin Co., Boston, 1969—, editorial dir. sch. depts., 1978-81, editorial dir. math. and scis. Sch. Div., 1981-84, mng. editor sch. pub., 1984—. Mem. LWV, Mass. Bar Assn. Office: Houghton Mifflin 222 Berkeley St Boston MA 02116-3748

STEVENS, MARTIN BRIAN, publisher; b. N.Y.C., Dec. 29, 1957; s. David Robert and Shirley (Marcus) S.; m. Sheri Doscher, Dec. 30, 1979. Grad. high sch. Advt. artist Unitron Pubs., N.Y.C., 1977, Westchester Publs., Elmsford, N.Y., 1978; pub. Marketers Forum, Centerport, N.Y., 1981—, Swap Meet mag., Centerport, 1990—; Pub. 8 bus. directories, rep. 6 bus. book pubs.; founder Rodeo Dr. Limousine Svc., 1990-93, Mercedes-Benz Limousine Svc., 1990-93. Named Top Mail Order Dealer, Nat. Mail Dealers Counsel, 1978. Mem. Mail Order Bus. Bd. (pres. 1978-80), Better Bus. Bur., Nat. Assn. Self-Employed, Nat. Assn. Desktop Pub., [illegible] Assn., Can. Direct Mail Assn. Avocations: weight training, reading. [illegible] Forum Pub Co 383 E Main St Centerport NY 11721-1538

STEVENS, MAY, artist; b. Boston, June 9, 1924; d. Ralph Stanley and Alice Margaret (Dick) S.; m. Rudolf Baranik, June 5, 1948; 1 child, Steven. BFA, Mass. Coll. Art, 1946; postgrad., Academie Julian, Paris, 1948-49, Art Students League, 1948. Mem. faculty Sch. Visual Arts, N.Y.C., 1964—, Skowhegan Sch. Painting and Sculpture, 1992; lectr. Royal Coll. Art, London, 1981, U. Wis.-Racine, 1973, Coll. Art Assn., Washington, 1975. One-woman shows: Terry Dintenfass Gallery, N.Y.C., 1971, Cornell U., 1973, Douglass Coll., Rutgers U., 1974, Lerner-Heller Gallery, N.Y.C., 1975, 76, 78, 81, Clark U., 1982, Boston U. Art Gallery, 1984, Frederick S. Wight Gallery, UCLA, 1985, U. Md., College Park, 1985, Real Art Ways, Hartford, Conn., 1988, New Mus. Contemporary Art, 1988, Orchard Gallery, Derry, No. Ireland, 1988, Kenyon Coll., Gambier, Ohio, 1988, Greenville County (S.C.) Art Mus., 1991, Herter Gallery, U. Mass., Amherst, 1991, U. Colo., Boulder, 1993; exhibited in group shows: Inst. Contemporary Arts, London, 1980, Gemeente Mus., The Hague, 1979, Whitney Mus., 1970, Gedok, Kunsthaus, Hamburg, Germany, 1972, Everson Mus., Syracuse, N.Y., 1976, Clocktower, N.Y.C., 1986, Guerrilla Girls Exbn. at Palladium, N.Y.C., 1985, One Penn Pla., 1985, Pentonville Gallery, London, 1986, Heckscher Mus., N.Y., 1987, Univ. Art Mus., Berkeley, Calif., 1987, Mus. Modern Art, 1988, Exit Art, N.Y.C., 1988, Sao Paulo (Brazil) Mus. Modern Art, 1989, Blum Helman Gallery, N.Y.C., 1989, Univ. Art Mus., Long Beach, Calif., 1990, Angels Gate, San Pedro, Calif., 1990, Newark Mus., 1990, Städtliche Kunsthalle, Düsseldorf, Germany, 1990, DeCordova Mus., Lincoln, Mass., 1991, Exit Art, N.Y.C., 1994, Mary Delahoyd Gallery, N.Y.C., 1995, Mary Ryan Gallery, N.Y.C., 1995, Gwenda Jay Gallery, Chgo., 1995, Lizardi Harp Gallery, L.A., 1995, ACA Galleries, N.Y.C., 1996; represented in permanent collections: Metropolitan Mus. of Art, N.Y.C., Mus. Modern Art, N.Y.C., Moca, L.A., San Francisco Mus. Art, New Mus. Contemporary Art, Whitney Mus., Bklyn. Mus., Herbert F. Johnson Mus., Cornell U., Mus. Fine Arts Boston, De Cordova Mus., Lincoln, Mass.; contbr. articles to various mags. Recipient Childe Hassam Purchase awards Nat. Inst. Arts and Letters, 1968, 69, 75, N.Y. State Coun. on Arts award, 1974; MacDowell Colony fellow, 1971, 72, 74, 75, 81, 82, 84, Bunting Inst. fellow Radcliffe Coll., 1988-89; grantee NEA, 1983, Guggenheim, 1986; honoree Women's Caucus for Art, 1990. Mem. Coll. Art Assn.

STEVENS, NORMAN DENNISON, retired library director; b. Nashua, N.H., Mar. 4, 1932; s. David P. and Ruth (Ackley) S.; m. Nora Bennett, Jan. 16, 1959; children: David P., Sara, Elizabeth. BA, U. N.H., 1954; MLS, Rutgers U., 1957, PhD, 1961. Acting dir. univ. librs. Howard U., Washington, 1961-63; assoc. libr. Rutgers U., New Brunswick, N.J., 1963-68; assoc. univ. libr. U. Conn., Storrs, 1968-75, univ. libr., 1975-87, dir. univ. librs., 1987-94, dir. emeritus univ. librs., 1994—, acting dir. Thomas J. Dodd Rsch. Ctr., 1995-96; exec. dir. The Molesworth Inst., Storrs, 1959—; condr. librs. N. Am. Sch. for the Artsy, White Bear Lake, Minn., 1988—; pres. The Bibliosmiles, 1993—; acting dir. Thomas J. Dodd Rsch. Ctr., 1995-96. Author: A Guide to Collecting Librariana Communications Throughout Libraries, 1983; editor: Library Humor, 1971, The Librarian, 1976, Postcards in the Library, 1995. Mem. ALA, Phi Beta Kappa, Phi Kappa Phi, Pi Sigma Alpha. Avocations: collecting library memorabilia, library humor, profl. writing. Home: 143 Hanks Hill Rd Storrs Mansfield CT 06268-2315

STEVENS, PAUL EDWARD, lawyer; b. Youngstown, Ohio, July 22, 1916; s. Raymond U. and Mary Ann (Pritchard) S.; m. Janet L. Weisert, Mar. 9, 1946; 1 son, Mark O. LL.B., Ohio State U., 1941. Bar: Ohio 1941. Practiced in Youngstown, 1941—; ptnr. Green, Schiavoni, Murphy & Stevens, 1962-71, Burdman, Stevens & Gilliland, 1971-75, Stevens & Toot, 1976-77, Paul E. Stevens Co., 1977—; prof. law Youngstown Coll. Sch. Law, 1946-60; gen. counsel Animal Charity League of Ohio, 1965—; sec.-treas. CASTLO Community Improvement Corp., 1986—. Trustee Poland Twp., Ohio, 1960-69; Republican candidate for U.S. Congress, 1959; dist. adminstrv. asst. Congressman Charles J. Carney, 19th Ohio dist., 1970-80; pres. Welsh Nat. Gymanfa Ganu Assn., 1988-90. With AUS, 1942-46. Mem. ABA, Ohio Bar Assn. (chmn. membership com. 1955), Mahoning County Bar Assn. (pres. 1953-54), Mahoning County Planning Assn. (chmn. 1990—). Unitarian. Home: 7191 N Lima Rd Youngstown OH 44514-3749 Office: 780 Boardman Canfield Rd Youngstown OH 44512-4344 *To be allowed to practice law is an honor. Therefore, an attorney must be fair and honest, but most of all, he must have respect for and love his fellow man.*

STEVENS, PAUL IRVING, manufacturing company executive; b. Lawrence, Kans., Mar. 22, 1915; s. Ira F. and Ida M. S.; m. Artie Faye Womack, Nov. 10, 1935; children: Richard Irving, Constance Irene. Student bus. adminstrn., Pasadena (Calif.) Coll., 1933-35. Indsl. engr. Consol. Aircraft Co., San Diego, 1940-49; founder, prin. stockholder, pres. United Machine Co., Ft. Worth, 1950-61; exec. v.p. Clary Corp., San Gabriel, Calif., 1962-65; pres., owner Stevens Corp., Ft. Worth, 1965-69; pres., chief exec. officer Waltham Industries, N.Y.C., 1969-71, Stevens Industries, La Jolla, Calif., 1972—, Campbell Industries, San Diego, 1976-79; chmn., pres. Stevens Air Systems, El Cajon, Calif., 1974-81; pres. Womack Motors, Inc., El Centro, Calif., 1982-90; chmn. bd. dirs., CEO Stevens Graphics Corp., Ft. Worth, 1986-95; bd. dirs. Rancho Santa Fe Nat. Bank, Calif., 1982-85. Mem. Nat. Mgmt. Assn. (exec. com.), Presidents Assn., Civic Round Table, La Jolla Country Club, Colonial Country Club, Canyon Country Club, University Club, Ft. Worth Club, Shady Oaks Country Club. Republican. Methodist. Home: 2585 Calle Del Oro La Jolla CA 92037-2005 Office: PO Box 950 La Jolla CA 92038-0950

STEVENS, PAUL TRACY, nuclear engineer, naval officer; b. Buffalo, Sept. 7, 1961; s. Clair W. and Dorothy G. (Garska) S. BSME, Clarkson U., 1983; MSME, U. Mich., 1990; MA, Naval War Coll., 1995. Registered profl. engr., Mich. Commd. ensign USN, 1983, advanced through grades to lt. comdr., 1994; instr. Naval Nuclear Power Plant, Ballston Spa, N.Y., 1984-86; combat systems officer nuclear submarine U.S.N., San Diego, 1986-88; instr. elec. engring. history Naval ROTC, U. Mich., Ann Arbor, 1988-90; chief engr. nuclear attack submarine U.S.N., Norfolk, Va., 1991-94. Mem. Nat. Soc. Profl. Engrs., Mich. Soc. Profl. Engrs., Tau Beta Pi, Pi Tau Sigma.

STEVENS, RAYMOND DONALD, JR., chemical company executive; b. Buffalo, Feb. 17, 1927; s. Raymond Donald and Annette (Wells) S.; m. V. Aline Larkin, Aug. 20, 1949; children—Raymond Donald III, Larkin Edgeworth, Courtney Curtis, Hunter Hubbard. Grad., Nichols Sch., Buffalo, 1945; B.S. in Econs, Wharton Sch. U. Pa., 1951. With Pierce & Stevens Chem. Corp., Buffalo, 1951-96; exec. v.p. Pierce & Stevens Chem. Corp., 1970-96, pres., 1963-70, chmn. bd., 1970—; also dir.; exec. v.p. Pratt & Lambert, Inc., Buffalo, 1967-70; pres., chief exec. officer Pratt & Lambert, Inc., 1970-89, chmn., 1970-96; bd. dirs. Mfrs. and Traders Trust Co., First Empire State Corp. Hon. trustee Buffalo Gen. Hosp. Served with USNR, 1945-47. Mem. Nat. Paint and Coatings Assn. (pres. 1977-78, dir., exec. com. 1977—), Am. Legion (past post comdr.), Nova Internat. Paint Club (past pres.), Friars Sr. Soc., Phi Kappa Sigma. Club: Saturn (Buffalo). Home: 81 Hallam Rd Buffalo NY 14216-3519 Office: 11 Summer St Buffalo NY 14209

STEVENS, ROBERT BOCKING, lawyer, educator; b. U.K., June 8, 1933; naturalized, 1971; s. John Skevington and Enid Dorthy (Bocking) S.; m. Katherine Booth, Dec. 23, 1985; 1 child, Robin; children by previous marriage: Carey, Richard. BA, Oxford U., 1955, BCL, 1956, MA, 1959, DCL, 1984; LLM, Yale U., 1958; LLD (hon.), N.Y. Law Sch., 1984, Villanova U., 1985, U. Pa., 1987; D.Litt. (hon.), Haverford Coll., 1991. Barrister-at-law London, 1956; tutor in law Keble Coll. Oxford U., 1958-59; asst. prof. law Yale U., 1959-61, assoc. prof., 1961-65, prof., 1965-76; provost, prof. law and history Tulane U., 1976-78; pres. Haverford Coll., 1978-87; chancellor, prof. history U. Calif., Santa Cruz, 1987-91; of counsel Covington and Burling, Washington and London, 1991—; master Pembroke Coll., Oxford, 1993—; vis. prof. U. Tex., 1961, U. East Africa, 1962, London Sch. Econs., 1963, Stanford U., 1966, U. Coll. London, 1991-94; cons. UN, HEW, U.S. Dept. State. Author: The Restrictive Practices Court, 1965, Lawyers and the Courts, 1967, In Search of Justice, 1968, Income Security, 1970, Welfare Medicine in America, 1974, Law and Politics, 1978, The Law School, 1983, The Independence of the Judiciary, 1993. Grantee Rockefeller Found., 1962-64, Ford Found., 1962-64, 73-74, Russell Sage Found., 1967-68, NEH, 1973-74, Nuffield Found., 1975; named Hon. fellow Keble Coll. Oxford U., 1985, Socio-Legal Ctr., 1992. Mem. Marshall Aid Meml. Commn. (chair), Rsch. com., Am. Bar Found. Home: Masters Lodgings, Pembroke Coll, Oxford OX1 1DW, England Office: Covington and Burling, Leconfield House Curzon St, London W1Y 8AS, England

STEVENS, ROBERT DAVID, librarian, educator; b. Nashua, N.H., Aug. 11, 1921; s. David Philip and Ruth (Ackley) S.; m. Helen Medora Conrad, Jan. 16, 1943; children: Ruth Wilson Robertson, Hope Conrad. A.B. magna cum laude, Syracuse U., 1942; B.S. in L.S. with honors, Columbia, 1947; M.A., Am. U., 1955, Ph.D., 1965. With Library of Congress, Washington, 1947-64; coordinator pub. law 480 programs Library of Congress, 1962-64; dir. Library East West Center, Honolulu, 1964-65; dean Grad. Sch. Library Studies U. Hawaii, Honolulu, 1966-75; chief cataloging div. Copyright Office, 1975-80, coordinator copyright collections, 1980; lectr. grad. Sch. Library Studies, U. Hawaii, 1981—; chief exec. officer Molesworth Inst. West, Inc., 1984-91, chmn., 1991-96; Fulbright lectr. U. Indonesia, 1971; U.S. del. Intergovtl. Conf. Planning Nat. Libraries Infrastructures, 1974. Author: Role of the Library of Congress in International Exchange of Government Publications, 1955, Toshokan Kyoryoku, 1970, Documents of International Organizations, 1974, Japanese and U.S. Research Libraries at the Turning Point, 1977, Short History of the School of Library and Information Studies, 1991; contbr. articles to profl. publs. Served to lt. USNR, 1943-46. Mem. Hawaii Library Assn. (pres. 1966-67), ALA (mem. council 1967-70, mem. U.S.-Japan adv. com. 1972—, chmn. 1974-76, Rlms policy and research com. 1977-81), Assocs. U. Hawaii Library (vice chmn. 1981-84), Japan Library Assn., Hui Dui, Phi Beta Kappa, Pi Sigma Alpha. Club: 15 (Honolulu). Home: 3265 Paty Dr Honolulu HI 96822-1449

STEVENS, ROBERT EDWIN, bank executive, former insurance company executive; b. Hartford, Feb. 12, 1927; s. Horace and Anna E. (Lauritzen) S.; m. Betty L. Hippler, June 30, 1951; children—Paul, Lynn, Peter. B.A., Wesleyan U., 1949. Various positions bond and common stock divs. Conn. Mut. Life Ins. Co., Hartford, 1951-71; v.p., treas. Conn. Mut. Life Ins. Co., 1972-74, sr. v.p., 1974-76, exec. v.p., 1976-89; pres. Conn. Mut. Investment Accounts, Inc., 1980-89; chmn. bd. dirs. Liberty Bank, Middletown, Conn., 1989-95; bd. dirs. Freedom Fin. Svcs. Bd. dirs. Hartford Hosp.; trustee Jacob L. and Lewis Fox Scholarship Found.; trustee emeritus Wesleyan U.; corporator Middlesex Hosp. With USNR, World War II. Mem. Hartford Soc. Fin. Analysts (past pres.). Home: 46 Keighley Pond Rd PO Box 361 Cobalt CT 06414 Office: Liberty Bank Middletown CT

STEVENS, ROBERT JAY, magazine editor; b. Detroit, July 25, 1945; s. Jay Benjamin and Louise Ann (Beyreuther) S.; m. Dahlia Jean Conger, Aug. 15, 1970; children—Sandra Lee, Julie Ann. Student, Huron (S.D.) Coll., 1963-66, Wayne State U., 1968-71. Sr. staff writer Automotive News, Detroit, 1968-71; editor Excavating Contractor mag.; Cummins Pub. Co., Oak Park, Mich., 1971-78, Chevrolets, Pro Jour., Sandy Corp., Southfield, Mich., 1978-79; editor Cars and Parts mag. Amos Press, Sidney, Ohio, 1979—; truck editor Automotive Design & Devel. mag., 1971-78; lectr., speaker in field. Author articles, poems. Served with AUS, 1966-68, Vietnam. Decorated Air medal, Bronze Star, Commendation medal; recipient Alphomega Publs. award, 1965—, Robert F. Boger Meml. award for outstanding constrn. journalism, 1975, U.L.C.C. nat. editorial award Am. Pub. Works Assn., 1978. Mem. Detroit Auto Writers (past dir.), Internat. Motor Press Assn., Soc. Automotive Historians, Antique Automobile Club Am. Republican. Presbyterian. Home: 653 Ridgeway Dr Sidney OH 45365-3432 Office: PO Box 482 911 Vandemark Rd Sidney OH 45365

STEVENS, ROGER LACEY, theatrical producer; b. Detroit, Mar. 12, 1910; s. Stanley and Florence (Jackson) S.; m. Christine Gesell, Jan. 1, 1938; 1 child, Christabel. Student, Choate Sch., 1928, U. Mich., 1928-30; DHL, U. Mich., 1964; HHD (hon.), Wayne State U., 1960; DHL, Tulane U., 1960; LLD, Amherst Coll., 1968; hon. degrees, Skidmore Coll., 1969, U. Ill., 1970, Boston U., 1970, Am. U., 1979, Boston U., 1979, Miami U., 1983, Phila. Coll. Art, 1986. Former real estate broker specializing in hotels and investment properties, 1934-60; spl. asst. to the Pres. on the arts, 1964-68; chmn. Nat. Coun. on the Arts, 1965-69, Nat. Endowment for the Arts, also trustee; pres. Nat. Inst. for Music Theater; chmn. Am. Film Inst., 1969-72; chmn. adv. com. Nat. Book Award, 1970-75, 1988-89; mem. Coun. for Arts, Mass. Inst. Tech.; chmn. Fund for New Am. Plays, 1986—; mem. Pres.'s Com. on Arts and Humanities, 1982-93. Producing partner in more than 200 theatrical prodns. including Old Times, West Side Story, Cat on a Hot Tin Roof, Bus Stop, The Visit, Mary, Mary, A Man for all Seasons, The Best Man, Deathtrap, Death of a Salesman; Kennedy Ctr. prodns. include Annie, First Monday in October, On Your Toes, Mass, Jumpers, Night and Day, Wings, Texas Trilogy, Bedroom Farce, Cocktail Hour, Love Letters, Metamorphosis, A Few Good Men, Artist Descending a Staircase, Shadowlands, She Loves Me. Chmn. fin. com. Dem. Party, 1956; chmn. bd. trustees John F. Kennedy Ctr. Performing Arts, 1961-88; trustee Am. Shakespeare Theater and Acad., Choate Sch., 1982-93; bd. dirs. Met. Opera Assn., 1958—, Ballet Theatre Found., 1977—, Nat. Symphony Orch., 1981-93, Filene Ctr./Wolf Trap Farm Park for Performing Arts, 1969-92, The Washington Opera, 1988-94, Peabody Conservatory, 1979-82, Folger Libr., Acad. Am. Poets. Decorated knight comdr. Brit. Empire; Royal Order of Vasa, Sweden; grand ufficiale Order of Merit Italy; comdr.'s cross Order of Merit Fed. Republic Germany; recipient award contbn. theatre Nat. Theater Conf., 1970, , Presdl. Medal of Freedom, 1988, Nat. Medal of Arts, 1988; Kennedy Ctr. honoree, 1988. Fellow Royal Soc. Arts; mem. ANTA (exec. com.), Phi Gamma Delta. Clubs: Bohemian (San Francisco); Racquet and Tennis (N.Y.C.), Century Assn. (N.Y.C.), Pilgrims (N.Y.C.). Office: JFK Ctr Performing Arts Washington DC 20566

STEVENS, RON A., lawyer, public interest organization administrator; b. Indpls., Sept. 4, 1945; s. Granville Thomas and Charlotte May (Wheeler) S.; m. Judy Rohde, June 15, 1968; children: Samuel Thomas, Alison Elizabeth. BA, Okla. State U.; JD with honors, Ill. Inst. Tech., 1976. Bar: Ill. 1976. Staff atty. Legal Assistance Found. Chgo., 1976-79; staff atty., dir. housing agenda Bus. and Profl. People for Pub. Interest, Chgo., 1979-81; chief housing div. Office of Cook County State's Atty., Chgo., 1981-82; campaign coord. north lakefront Washington for Mayor, Chgo., 1982-83; program officer The Joyce Found., Chgo., 1983-86; pres. Citizens for a Better Environment, Chgo., 1986-89; exec. dir. United Way Santa Fe County, 1989—; adv. bd. state support ctr. on environ. hazards Nat. Ctr. for Policy Alternatives, Washington, 1987-89; chair Local Bd. EFSP, 1989—, chair Santa Fe Affordable Housing Roundtable, 1992—; bd. dirs. No. N.Mex. Grantmakers Assn. Mem. bldg. code enforcement com. Mayor's Transition Team Housing Task Force, Chgo., 1983, steering com. Chgo. Ethics Project, 1986-88; founder, chmn. Progressive Chgo. Area Network, 1981-84; bd. dirs. Uptown Recycling Sta., Chgo., 1987-89; mem. South Ctrl. Regional Coun., United Way of Am. Mem. Chgo. Coun. Lawyers (chmn. housing com. 1978-81, bd. govs. 1981-83, bd. dirs. Fund for Justice, 1986-88), Chgo. Area Runners Assn. (founder, v.p. 1977-81). Home: 739 Gregory Ln Santa Fe NM 87501-4257 Office: United Way Santa Fe County PO Box 261 Santa Fe NM 87504-0261

STEVENS, ROSEMARY A., academic dean, public health and social history educator; b. Bourne, Eng.; came to U.S., 1961, naturalized, 1968; d. William Edward and Mary Agnes (Tricks) Wallace; m. Robert B. Stevens, Jan. 28, 1961 (div. 1983); children: Carey, Richard; m. Jack D. Barchas, Aug. 9, 1994. BA, Oxford (Eng.) U., 1957; Diploma in Social Adminstrn., Manchester (Eng.) U., 1959; MPH, Yale U., 1963, PhD, 1968. Various hosp. adminstrv. positions Eng., 1959-61; rsch. assoc. Med. Sch. Yale U., 1962-68, asst. prof. Med. Sch., 1968-71, assoc. prof. Med. Sch., 1971-74, prof. pub. health Med. Sch., 1974-76; master Jonathan Edwards Coll., 1974-75; prof. dept. health systems mgmt. and polit. sci. Tulane U., New Orleans, 1976-78; chmn. dept. health systems mgmt. Tulane U., 1977-78; prof. history and sociology of sci. U. Pa., Phila., 1979—, chmn. dept., 1980-83, 86-91, UPS Found. prof., 1990-91, dean Sch. Arts and Scis., Thomas S. Gates prof., 1991—; vis. lectr. Johns Hopkins U., 1967-68; guest scholar Brookings Instn., Washington, 1967-68; acad. visitor London Sch. Econs., 1962-64, 1973-74. Author: Medical Practice in Modern England: The Impact of Specialization and State Medicine, 1966, American Medicine and the Public Interest, 1971, In Sickness and in Wealth: American Hospitals in the Twentieth Century, 1989, (with others) Foreign Trained Physicians and American Medicine, 1972, Welfare Medicine in America, 1974, Alien-Doctors: Foreign Medical Graduates in American Hospitals, 1978. Bd. dirs. Milbank Meml. Fund, Ctr. for Advancement of Health. Fellow Am. Acad. Arts and Scis.; mem. Inst. Medicine of Nat. Acad. Sci., History of Sci. Soc., Am. Assn. for

History of Medicine, Coll. Physicians of Phila., Cosmopolitan Club. Home: # 18 A 1900 Rittenhouse Sq # 18 A Philadelphia PA 19103-5735 Office: U Pa Office of Dean 116 College Hall Philadelphia PA 19104-6377

STEVENS, ROY W., sales and marketing executive; b. Ottumwa, Iowa, Oct. 28, 1924; s. Manley O. and Ruth (Worrell) S.; m. Donna R. Borman, June 7, 1952 (dec. Jan. 1973); children: Katharine Anne Stevens Dillon, Thomas W., John M.; m. Beth A. Murphy, Apr. 20, 1974; children: Carrie Theresa, Elizabeth Mary. B.S.C., U. Iowa, 1948. With Coca-Cola Co., 1948-54, Gen. Foods Corp., 1954-67; exec. v.p. Riviana Foods, Houston, 1967-73; v.p. mktg. Hiram Walker Inc., Detroit, 1973-75; pres. Hiram Walker Inc., 1975-80, Maidstone Wine & Spirits Inc., L.A., 1980-91, Kahlua Group (Allied Domecq), 1987-91; exec. v.p. The Century Coun., Los Angeles, 1991—. Bd. dirs., past chmn. Detroit Met. YMCA; bd. dirs. L.A. Met. YMCA. Lt. (j.g.) USN, 1943-46. Mem. Sigma Alpha Epsilon, Jonathan Club, Annandale Golf Club (Pasadena, Calif.). Episcopalian. Home: 1221 San Marino Ave San Marino CA 91108-1228 Office: The Century Coun 550 S Hope St Ste 1950 Los Angeles CA 90071-2604

STEVENS, SANDY (AMANDA STEVENSON), document examiner; b. Bklyn., Oct. 24, 1943; d. Haakon and Grace Svendsen; m. James W. Moseley, 1962 (div. 1965); children: Elizabeth B. Moseley, Lawrence Harmon. Grad., Bay Ridge H.S., Bklyn., 1961. Cert. document examiner. Pvt. practice Pitts., 1967—; lectr. Jersey City State Coll., John Jay Coll. of Criminal Justice, N.Y.C., Mcpl. Credit Union, N.Y.C.; cons. numerous lawfirms. Co-author: How to Raise an Emotionally Health, Happy Child, 1964; designer forms for document examination; composer, librettist (mus.) Nellie Bly. Mem. AEA, Dramatists Guild, Songwriters Guild. Mem. Nat. Assn. Document Examiners. Democrat. Unitarian. Avocations: chess, music, stamps, pen pals. Home and Office: 1473 Mervin Ave Pittsburgh PA 15216-2028

STEVENS, SHANE, novelist; b. N.Y.C.; s. John and Caroline (Royale) S. MA, Columbia U. mem. numerous writers confs. including Bread Loaf, Santa Barbara Writers Conf. Author: Go Down Dead, Way Uptown in Another World, Dead City, Rat Pack, By Reason of Insanity, The Anvil Chorus; (as J.W. Rider) Jersey Tomatoes (Best Novel award), Hot Tickets; contbr. articles to pubs. including N.Y. Times, Life, Washington Post; screenwriter: By Reason of Insanity, The Me Nobody Knows. Mem. Authors Guild, Writers Guild Am. Office: William Morris Agy 1325 Avenue Of The Americas New York NY 10019

STEVENS, SHEILA MAUREEN, teachers union administrator; b. Glendale, Calif., Nov. 1, 1942; d. Richard Chase and Sheila Mary (Beatty) Flynn; m. Jan Whitney Stevens, Sept. 12, 1964; children: Ian Whitney, Bevin Michelle. AA in Liberal Arts, Monterey Peninsula Coll., Calif., 1963; BA in Anthropology, Calif. State U., Long Beach, 1969; postgrad. studies in Edn., U. Guam, 1976-77. Tchr. U.S. Trust Territory of the Pacific, Koror, Palau Island, 1968-72, Kolonia, Ponape Island, 1972-76; tchr. Dept. Edn., Agana, Guam, 1976-79; newspaper editor Pacific Daily News (Gannett), Agana, 1979-83; comm. dir. Guam Fedn. of Tchrs., Agana, 1983-84, exec. dir., 1984-85; exec. dir. Alaska Fedn. Tchrs., Anchorage, 1985-87; labor rels. specialist N.Y. State United Tchrs., Watertown, 1987-93; regional staff dir. N.Y. State United Tchrs., Potsdam, 1993—; mem. Gov.'s Blue Ribbonn Panel on Edn., Agana, Guam, 1983-85; leadership devel. coord. Am. Fedn. Tchrs., Washington, 1983—; trainer positive negotiations program Situation Mgmt. Sys., Hanover, Mass., 1988—. Author, editor: Pacific Daily News, 1981-83 (Guam Press Club awards 1981, 82, 83); contbr. articles to mag. and jours. Mem. task force on labor policy, com. on self determination, Govt. of Guam, Agana, 1984-85, Adult Basic Edn. Planning Com., 1985; mem. labor studies adv. bd., Anchorage, Alaska, 1989, regional compact coalition N.Y. State Edn. Dept., Albany, 1994. Named Friend of Edn., Carthage (N.Y.) Tchrs. Assn., 1990. Mem. NOW, ACLU, ASCD, Am. Fedn. Tchrs. Comm. Assn. (Best Editorial award 1984). Democrat. Methodist. Avocations: travel, reading, free-lance writing, cross-country skiing. Office: NY State United Tchrs 12 Elm St Potsdam NY 13676-1812

STEVENS, STANLEY DAVID, local history researcher, retired librarian; b. San Francisco, Nov. 10, 1933; s. David Franklyn and Ellen Myrtle (Wixson) S.; m. Carli Ann Lewis, Sept. 3, 1960; adopted children: Alexander Lewis, Nikolas Harriman, Brooke Cayton Stevens Rich. BA, San Jose State U., 1959. Conf. officer polit. and security com. 14th Gen. Assembly, UN, N.Y.C., 1959; map libr. U. Calif., Santa Cruz, 1965-93, ret., 1993, coord. Hihn-Younger Archive, Univ. Libr., 1994—; mem. Cartographic Users Adv. Coun., 1976-86, chmn., 1982-86; presenter in field, 1971—; adj. prof. libr. sci. San Jose (Calif.) State U., 1989, 91. Author: Catalog of aerial photos by Fairchild Aerial Surveys, Inc. now in the collections of the Department of Geography, University of California at Los Angeles, 1982; editor, Santa Cruz County History Journal, 1994-95; also 8 others related to Hihn-Younger Archive; contbr. over 100 articles and book revs. to profl. jours. Mem. adv. com. archaeol. program Cabrillo Coll., Aptos, Calif., 1985—; bd. dirs. Santa Cruz County Hist. Soc., 1985-94, chmn. publs. com., 1985-96, mem. programs adv. coun., 1994-95; mem. Santa Cruz Orgn. for Progress and Euthenics, 1987—; bd. dirs. Friends of U. Calif.-Santa Cruz Libr., 1994—; mem. U. Calif.-Santa Cruz Emeriti Group. With U.S. Army, 1954-56; mem. collections adv. com. Santa Cruz City Mus. Natural History, 1995—. Recipient honors award geography and map div. for outstanding achievement in map librarianship Spl. Librs. Assn., 1981, cert. of commendation Santa Cruz Hist. Soc., 1986, appreciation cert. for svcs. Assn. Info. and Image Mgmt., 1989; grantee Librs. Assn. U. Calif., 1981-82, rsch. grantee Office of Pres., U. Calif., 1985-86. Mem. ALA (publs. com. Map and Geography Round Table 1986-86, editl. bd. Meridian 1989-92, honors award Map and Geography Round Table 1992), Western Assn. Map Librs. (hon. life, founding pres. 1967-68, treas. 1968-89, editor Info. Bull. 1969-84, Exec. com. award 1984), Calif. Hist. Soc., Calif. Map Soc., Pajaro Valley Hist. Assn., Santa Cruz County Geneal. Soc., Capitola Hist. Soc., El Paso de Robles Hist. Soc. (life). Democrat. Avocations: researching local history, listening to jazz and classical music. Home: 231 13th Ave Santa Cruz CA 95062-4831 Office: U Calif Map Collection Dean E McHenry Libr Santa Cruz CA 95064

STEVENS, STEPHEN EDWARD, psychiatrist; b. Phila.; s. Edward and Antonia S.; BA cum laude, LaSalle Coll., 1950; MD, Temple U., Phila., 1954; LLB, Blackstone Sch. Law, 1973; m. Isabelle Helen Gallacher, Dec. 27, 1953. Intern, Frankford Hosp., Phila., 1954-55; resident in psychiatry Phila. State Hosp., 1955-58; practice medicine specializing in psychiatry Woodland Hills, Calif., 1958-63, Santa Barbara, Calif., 1970-77; asst. supt. Camarillo (Calif.) State Hosp., 1963-70; cons. ct. psychiatrist Santa Barbara County, 1974-77; clin. dir. Kailua Mental Health Ctr., Oahu, Hawaii, 1977—. Author: Treating Mental Illness, 1961. Served with M.C., USAAF. Diplomate Am. Bd. Psychiatry and Neurology. Decorated Purple Heart. Fellow Am. Geriatrics Soc. (founding); mem. Am. Acad. Psychiatry and Law, AMA, Am. Psychiat. Assn., Am. Legion, DAV (Oahu chpt. 1), Caledonia Soc., Am. Hypnosis Soc., Am. Soc. Adolescent Psychiatry, Hawaiian Canoe Club, Honolulu Club, Elks, Aloha String Band (founder and pres.). Home: PO Box 26413 Honolulu HI 96825-6413 Office: 2333 Kapiolani Blvd Honolulu HI 96826-4485

STEVENS, THEODORE FULTON, senator; b. Indpls., Nov. 18, 1923; s. George A. and Gertrude (Chancellor) S.; m. Ann Mary Cherrington, Mar. 29, 1952 (dec. 1978); children—Susan B., Elizabeth H., Walter C., Theodore Fulton, Ben A.; m. Catherine Chandler, 1980; 1 dau.; Lily Irene. B.A., U. Calif. at Los Angeles, 1947; LL.B., Harvard U., 1950. Bar: Calif., Alaska, D.C., U.S. Supreme Ct. bars. Pvt. practice Washington, 1950-52, Fairbanks, Alaska, 1953; U.S. atty. Dist. Alaska, 1953-56; legis. counsel, asst. to sec., solicitor Dept. Interior, 1956-60; pvt. practice law Anchorage, 1961-68; mem. Alaska Ho. of Reps., 1965-68, majority leader, speaker pro tem, 1967-68; U.S. senator for Alaska, 1968—, asst. Rep. leader, 1977-85; chmn. Senate Rules Com. Served as 1st lt. USAAF, World War II. Mem. ABA, Alaska Bar Assn., Calif. Bar Assn., D.C. Bar Assn., Am. Legion, VFW. Lodges: Rotary, Pioneers of Alaska, Igloo #4. Home: PO Box 100879 Anchorage AK 99510-0879 Office: US Senate 522 Hart Senate Bldg Washington DC 20510*

STEVENS, THOMAS CHARLES, lawyer; b. Auburn, N.Y., Oct. 17, 1949; s. Alice (Kerlin) S.; m. Christine Eleanor Brown, June 2, 1973; children: Erin, Leigh, Timothy. BA, SUNY, Albany, 1971; JD, Duke U., 1974. Bar: Ohio 1974. Mng. ptnr. Thompson, Hine & Flory, Cleve., 1991—. Bd. trustees Greater Cleve. Growth Assn., 1993—, Greater Cleve. Roundtable, 1993—; active Leadership Cleve., 1992-93. Mem. ABA, Cleve. Bar Assn., Nisi Prius. Office: Thompson Hine & Flory 3900 Key Center 127 Public Sq Cleveland OH 44114-3003

STEVENS, WARREN, actor; b. Clark's Summit, Pa., Nov. 2, 1919; s. Albert Clifford and Helen Dodd (Blakeslee) S.; m. Barbara Helen Fletcher, Sept. 9, 1969; children—Adam Fletcher, Matthew Dodd; 1 son by previous marriage, Laurence Blakeslee. Student, U.S. Naval Acad., 1939-40. Appeared on: New York stage in Gallileo, 1947, Sundown Beach, 1948, Smile of the World, 1949, Detective Story, 1949; appeared in numerous motion pictures, since 1950, including, Barefoot Contessa, Forbidden Planet; appeared on: numerous television shows, including Richard Boone Rep. With USN, 1937-40; with USAAF, 1942-46.

STEVENS, WENDELL CLAIRE, anesthesiology educator; b. Mason City, Iowa, June 28, 1931; s. Lloyd Leroy and Amy Luella (Hodson) S.; m. Lola C. Claycomb, July 27, 1958; children: Amy P., Eric C., Mitchell L. AA, Mason City Jr. Coll., 1951; MD, U. Iowa, 1956. Diplomate Am. Bd. Anesthesiology. Intern City Hosp., Cleve., 1956-57; resident in gen. surgery U. Iowa Hosp., Iowa City, 1957-58, 60-61, resident in anesthesia, 1961-63; assoc. in anesthesia U. Iowa Coll. Medicine, Iowa City, 1963, asst. prof. anesthesia dept., 1963-67; asst. prof. U. Calif. Sch. Medicine, San Francisco, 1967-72, assoc. prof., 1972-77, prof., 1977; prof., chmn. anesthesia dept. U. Iowa Coll. Medicine, Iowa City, 1978-82; prof., chmn. anesthesia dept. Oregon Health Scis. U., Portland, 1982-92, prof., 1992—. Contbr. papers and book chpts. to profl. publs. Lt. USNR, 1958-60. Recipient anesthesiology rsch. grant U. Calif., San Francisco NIH, 1969-78. Mem. Oreg. Soc. Anesthesiologists, Am. Soc. Anesthesiologists, Oreg. Med. Assn., AMA, Christian Med. Soc. Republican. Baptist. Avocations: church related activities. Office: Oreg Health Scis Ctr Dept of Anesthesiology 3181 SW Sam Jackson Park Rd Portland OR 97201-3011

STEVENS, WILBUR HUNT, accountant; b. Spencer, Ind., June 20, 1918; s. John Vosburgh and Isabelle Jane (Strawser) S.; m. Maxine Dodge Stevens, Sept. 28, 1941; children: Linda Maxine Piffero, Deborah Anne Augello. BS, U. Calif., Berkeley, 1949, MBA, 1949. CPA, Calif.; cert. fraud examiner. Staff acct. McLaren, Goode, West & Co., San Francisco, 1949-52; mng. ptnr. Wilbur H. Stevens & Co., Salinas, Calif., 1952-70; regional ptnr. Fox & Co., CPAs, Salinas, 1970-73; nat. dir. banking practice Fox & Co., CPAs, Denver, 1973-80; pres., chmn. Wilbur H. Stevens, CPA, PC, Salinas, 1980-94; chmn. Stevens, Sloan & Shah, CPAs, 1994—; adj. prof. acctg. U. Denver, 1975-78; faculty mem. Assemblies for Bank Dirs., So. Meth. U., Dallas, 1976-81, Nat. Banking Sch., U. Va., Charlottesville, 1979-87; chmn., dir. Valley Nat. Bank, 1963-71. Editor Issues in CPA Practice, 1975; contbr. articles to profl. jours. Capt. AUS, 1942-53. Decorated Bronze Star, China Svc. medal, China War Meml. medal, China Victory medal with five campaign stars; Frank G. Drum fellow U. Calif., Berkeley, 1949; Paul Harris fellow Rotary Internat., Evanston, Ill., 1978. Mem. AICPAs (v.p. 1971), Am. Acctg. Assn., Am. Assembly Collegiate Schs. Bus. (accreditation coun. 1975-78, 81-84), Nat. Assn. State Bds. Accountancy (pres. 1976-77), Calif. Soc. CPAs (pres. 1968-69, Disting. Svc. award 1988), Acctg. Rsch. Assn. (pres. 1973-75), Assn. Cert. Fraud Examiners, Burma Star Assn., CBI Vets. Assn., 14 AF Assn., Hump Pilots Assn., Acad. Acctg. Historians, Commonwealth Club Calif., Masons (master 1992, grand lodge com. taxation), Knight Templar, 32 degree Scottish Rite, Nat. Sojourners (pres. Monterey Bay chpt. 1996), Salinas High Twelve Club (pres. 1995), QCCC, London, Rotary (dist. gov. 1983, chmn. internat. fellowship accounts), Phi Beta Kappa, Beta Gamma Sigma (v.p. 1949), Beta Alpha Psi. Republican. Methodist. Home: 38 Santa Ana Dr Salinas CA 93901-4136 Office: 975 W Alisal St Ste D Salinas CA 93901-1148

STEVENS, WILLIAM DOLLARD, consulting mechanical engineer; b. Bayonne, N.J., Aug. 4, 1918; s. William B. and Beatrice (Dollard) S.; m. Mary E. King, Oct. 12, 1940; children: Sandra A. (Mrs. Jeffrey N. Melin), Barbara E. (Mrs. Dennis Gallagher), William K. B.Mech. Engring., Rensselaer Poly. Inst., 1940; postgrad., Case Inst. Tech., 1958; D.Sc. (hon.), N.J. Inst. Tech., 1986. Various engring. and mgmt. positions Babcock & Wilcox Co., N.Y.C., 1940-62; v.p. equipment div. Foster Wheeler Corp., Livingston, N.J., 1962-73, sr. v.p., 1972-74, exec. v.p., 1974-78, chmn. bd., 1978-81, dir., 1974-86, dir. emeritus, 1986-90; bd. of dir. Am. Soc. for Macro Engring., 1992—; instr. Pratt Inst., 1946-47; bd. overseers N.J. Inst. Tech., 1978-94. Contbr. articles to profl. jours.; patentee in field. Chmn. fund drive ARC, Hackensack, N.J., 1956; planning commr., Hackensack, 1955-58; trustee Bergen County Mental Health Consultation Ctr., 1955-58; bd. dirs. Metals Properties Coun.; mem. coun. Rensselaer Polytech. Inst., 1983—. Lt. USNR, 1943-45. Fellow ASME; mem. Nat. Acad. Engring., Sigma Xi, Tau Beta Pi, Phi Kappa Tau, Pi Tau Sigma. Methodist. Home and Office: 4 Stonybrook Dr North Caldwell NJ 07006

STEVENS, WILLIAM FREDERICK, III, software engineer; b. Paducah, Ky., Aug. 13, 1954; s. William Frederick Jr. and Imogene (Outland) S. Student, Case Western Res. U., 1973-77. Software engr. Allen Bradley Co., Cleve., 1977-80; sr. analyst Mark Bus. Systems, Cleve., 1980-82, Datacomp Corp., Cleve., 1982-84; sr. cons. GE, Cleve., 1984-87; sr. engr. Micro Dimensions Inc., Cleve., 1987-94, Codonics, Inc., Middleburg Heights, Ohio, 1994—; bd. dirs., pres. N.E. Ohio Apple Corps. Mem. Assn. for Computing Machinery, Maths. Assn. of Am. Avocations: science fiction, computers, theater. Home: 50 S Rocky River # 505 Berea OH 44017

STEVENS, WILLIAM JOHN, management consultant, former association executive; b. Dusseldorf, Germany, Aug. 23, 1915; arrived in U.S., 1923, naturalized, 1931; s. Peter and Margaret (Kaumanns) S.; student McCall Sch. Printing, 1933; student assn. mgmt. Northwestern U., 1947; grad. Chadwick Univ., 1993; m. Dorothy V. Santangini, Feb. 14, 1937 (dec.). With Ruttle, Shaw & Wetherill, Phila., 1931-34; partner New Era Printing Co., Phila., 1934-37; plant mgr. Marcus & Co., Phila., 1937-41; supt. Edward Stern & Co., Phila., 1941-46; exec. sec. Nat. Assn. Photo-Lithographers, N.Y.C., 1946-50, exec. v.p., 1961-64, pres., 1964-71; pres., COO NPEA Exhibits, Inc., 1971-80; owner Dorval Co., pub.; pres. Opinion-3 Graphic Arts Rsch. Agy.; exec. sec. Met. Lithographers Assn., N.Y.C., 1946-50; asst. to v.p. Miehle Co., N.Y.C., 1950-56, mgr. Phila. dist., 1956-61; cons. Sales Devel. Inst., Phila., 1960-89; mem. Am. Bd. Arbitration, 1962—; chmn. adv. commn. on graphic arts N.Y.C. Tech. Coll., 1972-95; bus. adminstr. St. Joseph's Parish, 1980-85. Named Industry Man of Yr. Nat. Assn. Photo-Lithographers, 1954, Man of Yr., N.Y. Litho Guild, 1962; recipient Mktg. award North Am. Pub. Co., 1967, B'nai B'rith award, 1968, N.Y. Navigators award, 1969, N.Y. Printing Craftsman Achievement award, 1989; laureate N.Y. Printers Hall of Fame, 1980, NAPL-Soderstrom award, 1984, recipient Gold Founders medal N.Y.C. Tech. Coll., 1987, . Mem. Am. Soc. Assn. Execs., Graphic Arts Assn. Execs. (pres. 1969), Nat. Assn. Litho Clubs (founder, pres. 1947, Industry award 1947, 79, sec. 1964-71), N.Y. Club Printing House Craftsmen, Gamma Epsilon Tau. Clubs: Phila. Litho (pres. 1945); N.Y. Litho (N.Y.C.). Mem. Writers Inst. Author: How To Prepare Copy for Offset Lithography, 1948, Building Construction and Floor Plans for Installing Web Offset Presses; under author: Basic Facts for Creating Effective Art/Design, Advertising, and Printing, 1995; columnist for daily press; contbr. editor articles to trade publs. Inventor Hiky-Picker, Quik-Match Color File for selection paint color samples, Stevens Foto Sizing System, Steve-O-Heat Printing Ink Dryer, "Travelr" security pocket, "Mar-Too-Nee" salad dressing. Home and Office: 4575 Barclay Cres Lake Worth FL 33463-6037

STEVENS, WILLIAM KENNETH, lawyer; b. Chgo., Apr. 19, 1917; s. Ernest James and Elizabeth (Street) S.; m. Anne Hughes, Jan. 4, 1943; children: Anne Elizabeth Stevens Fishman, William Hughes, Mary Carol Stevens Williams, Martha Street Stevens Gingrich. AB cum laude, U. Calif., Berkeley, 1938; MA, U. Chgo., 1940; JD, Harvard U., 1948. Bar: Ill. 1948, Fla. 1977. With First Nat. Bank Chgo., 1948-74, asst. v.p., 1958-61, v.p., 1961-74; ptnr. McDermott, Will & Emery, Chgo., 1974-85, Myers Krause & Stevens, Naples, Fla., 1986—. Author: Illinois Estate Administration, 1968. Chmn. Ill. Inst. Continuing Legal Edn., 1971-72; pres. Hinsdale (Ill.) Pub. Libr., 1977-79. Lt. USNR, 1941-45. Recipient Disting. Svc. award Chgo. Estate Planning Coun., 1981. Fellow Am. Coll. Trust and Estate Counsel; mem. ABA, Am. Law Inst., Chgo. Bar Assn., Ill. Bar Assn., Fla. Bar Assn. (bd. cert. estate planning and probate lawyer), Internat. Acad. Estate and Trust Law. Clubs: Mid-Day, Hinsdale Golf; Chikaming Country (Lakeside, Mich.), The Club at Pelican Bay (Naples). Home: 314 S Lincoln St Hinsdale IL 60521-4008 Office: 5811 Pelican Bay Blvd Ste 600 Naples FL 33963-2711

STEVENS, WILLIAM LOUIS, bishop; b. Yuba City, Calif., Jan. 12, 1932; s. Ralph Fremont and Elsie Mae (Schultz) S.; B.A., San Francisco State Coll., 1953; M.Div. Gen. Theol. Sem., 1956. Ordained priest, Episcopal Ch.; curate St. Luke's Ch., San Francisco; sr. curate St. Savior's, London, Order of the Holy Cross, N.Y.; rector St. Benedict's Ch., Plantation, Fla. to 1980; bishop Episcopal Diocese of Fond du Lac (Wis.), 1980—. Trustee, Nashotah Ho. Sem.; bishop visitor Sisterhood of the Holy Nativity; mem. Nat. Right to Life Com. Office: Diocese of Fond du Lac Grafon Hall 39 N Sophia PO Box 149 Fond Du Lac WI 54936-0149

STEVENS, YVETTE MARIE See KHAN, CHAKA

STEVENSON, A. BROCKIE, artist; b. Montgomery County, Pa., Sept. 24, 1919; s. Alfred Brockie and Caroline Lansdale (Sill) S.; m. Jane Merriman Mackenzie, Dec. 23, 1978. Student, Pa. Acad. Fine Arts, 1940-41, 46-50, Barnes Found., 1946-48, Skowhegan Sch., Maine, 1950. Instr. Sch. Fine Arts, Washington U., St. Louis, 1960-62; head dept. painting and drawing Corcoran Sch. Art, 1965-81, assoc. prof. to prof. design and watercolor, 1965—. One-man shows War Paintings, London and Salisbury, Eng., 1944, Instituto Cultural Peruano-Norteamericano, Lima, Peru, 1953, Art Center, Miraflores, Lima, 1958, 60, Association Cultural Peruano-Britanica, Lima, 1959, Mickelson Gallery, Washington, 1970, Pyramid Galleries Ltd., Washington, 1973, No. Va. Community Coll., 1974, Fendrick Gallery, Washington, 1978, 84, 88; group shows include, Nat. Gallery Art, London, 1944, Pa. Acad. Fine Arts, Phila., 1948, 49, 50, 51, Sociedad Bellas Artes del Peru, Lima, 1953, 54, 55, 56, SUNY at Potsdam and Albany, 1971, Columbia (S.C.) Mus. Art, 1971, EXPO '74, Spokane, Wash., 1974, Corcoran Gallery, Washington, 1980; represented in permanent collections Corcoran Gallery Art, Washington, Dept. Def., Washington, Nat. Mus. Am. Art, Washington, , Phillips Collection, Washington, Fed. Res. Bank Richmond, Va., Woodward Found., Washington, Ogunquit (Maine) Mus. Art, Brown U. Libr. Milit. Coll., Providence, R.I. Served as artist corr. U.S. Army, 1941-45, ETO. Home: 6106 Yale Ave Glen Echo MD 20812-1122 Office: Corcoran Sch Art 17 and New York Ave NW Washington DC 20006

STEVENSON, ADLAI EWING, III, lawyer, former senator; b. Chgo., Oct. 10, 1930; s. Adlai Ewing and Ellen (Borden) S.; m. Nancy L. Anderson, June 25, 1955; children: Adlai Ewing IV, Lucy W., Katherine R., Warwick L. Grad., Milton Acad., 1948; A.B., Harvard U., 1952, LL.B., 1957. Bar: Ill. 1957, D.C. 1957. Assoc. firm Mayer, Brown & Platt, Chgo., 1958-66; ptnr. Mayer, Brown & Platt, 1966-67, 81-83, of counsel, 1983-91; treas. State of Ill., 1967-70; U.S. senator from Ill., 1970-81; chmn. SC&M Internat. Ltd., Chgo., 1991-95, pres., 1995-96. Mem. Ill. Ho. of Reps., 1965-67; Dem. candidate for gov. of Ill., 1982, 86. Capt. USMCR, 1952-54. Office: 225 W Wacker Dr Chicago IL 60606-1002

STEVENSON, BEN, artistic director; b. Portsmouth, Eng., Apr. 4, 1936; came to U.S., 1968; s. Benjamin John and Florence May (Gundry) S.; m. Joan Toastivine, Jan. 6, 1968. Grad., Arts Ednl. Sch., London, 1955. Dir. Houston Ballet Acad.; mem. dance panel Tex. Commn. Arts, 1977; guest tchr. Am. Ballet Theatre, Joffrey Ballet, Royal Ballet, London, Beijing Dance Acad. Dancer Theatre Arts Ballet, London, 1952-54, Sadler's Wells Theatre Ballet, 1955-56, Royal Ballet, 1956-60, London Festival Ballet, 1960-62; appearances in Wedding in Paris, 1954-55, Music Man, London, 1962-63, Half a Sixpence, also, Boys in Syracuse, London, 1964; prin. dancer, ballet master, London Festival Ballet, 1964-68; artistic dir. Harkness Ballet Youth Dancers, 1968-71, Chgo. Ballet, 1974-75, Houston Ballet, 1976—; co-dir. Nat. Ballet, Washington, 1971-74; prin. ballets choreographed include Three Faces of Eve, 1965, Cast Out, 1966, Sleeping Beauty (full length), 1967, 71, 76, 78, Fervor, 1968, Three Preludes, 1968, Forbidden, 1969, Cinderella (full length), 1969, 71, 73, 74, 76, Bartok Concerto, 1970, Nutcracker (full length), 1972, 76, Symphonetta, 1972, Courant, 1973, Swan Lake (full length), 1977, L, 1978, Britten Pas de Deux, 1979, Four Last Songs, 1979, Space City, 1980, Peer Gynt (full length), 1981, Zheng Ban Qiao, 1982, The Prince of Pagodas, 1986. Recipient 1st prize London Choreographic competitions, 1965, 66, 67, 1st prize modern ballet choreography Internat. Ballet Competition, Varna, Bulgaria, 1972, Gold medal for choreography Internat. Ballet Competition, 1982. Asso. mem. Royal Acad. Dancing (Adeline Genee Gold medal 1955). Office: Houston Ballet PO Box 130487 Houston TX 77219-0487

STEVENSON, BETTY JEAN, retired teacher and vocational coordinator; b. Raritan, Ill., Jan. 4, 1920; speaker in field.; d. Willis Othal and Reva Marie (Mustain) Adams; m. William Frank Stevenson, Aug. 1, 1937; 1 child, Susan Amelia. BS in Edn., We. Ill. U., 1960; MEd, U. Ill., 1967. Cert. tchr. Insp. Silas Mason Co., Middletown, Iowa, 1952-53; bookkeeper Golden Food Svc. Corp., Middletown, 1954-55; asst. dir. Grote Hall We. Ill. U., Macomb, 1956; elem. tchr. Belmont Elem. Sch. Dist., Little York, Ill., 1957-59; home econs. and gen. sci. tchr. Unit Dist. 103, Media, Ill., 1961-72; tchr., career edn. coord. Unit Dist. 120, Stronghurst, Ill., 1972-77; comprehensive employment and tng. act field rep. Ill. Farmers Union, Galesburg, 1977-78; tchr., vocat. coord. Union Sch. Dist. 115, Biggsville, Ill., 1978-83; speaker in field. Author instructional materials and articles. Mem. Nat. Com. to Preserve Social Security and Medicare, Washington, 1993; bd. dirs. Henderson County Health Dept., 1978-94; v.p., bd. dirs. Western Ill. Area Agy. on Aging, 1990-95; mem. State of Ill. Adv. Coun. on Adult, Vocat. and Tech. Edn., chair, 1978. Mem. Ill. Vocat. Home Econs. Tchrs. Assn. (pres. 1968-69), Ill. Vocat. Assn. (bd. dirs., treas., pres.), Ill. Edn. Assn., Am. Assn. Ret. Persons, Friends of Lane Evans Com. Avocations: travel, oil painting, gardening, sewing.

STEVENSON, BRYAN ALLEN, lawyer, administrator; b. Milton, Del., Nov. 14, 1959; s. Howard Carlton and Alice Gertrude (Golden) S. BA, Eastern Coll., St. Davids, Pa., 1981; MPP, Kennedy Sch. Govt., Cambridge, Mass., 1985; JD, Harvard U., 1985. Bar: Ga. 1985, U.S. Dist. Ct. (no. dist.) Ga. 1985, U.S. Dist. Ct. (mid. dist.) Ga. 1986, Ala. 1987, U.S. Dist. Ct. (no. dist.) Ala. 1987, U.S. Dist. Ct. (mid. dist.) Ga. 1987. Staff atty. So. Prisoners Def. Com., Atlanta, 1985—; exec. dir. Ala. Capital Representation Resource Ctr., Montgomery, 1989—. Contbr. articles to publs. Recipient Nat. Human Rights award Reebol Human Rights Found., 1989, ACLU Medal of Liberty, 1991, ABA Wisdom Award for Pub. Svc., 1991; Harvard Law Sch. Pub. Interest fellow, 1985. Avocations: music, piano and keyboards.

STEVENSON, CANDACE J., museum director. Exec. dir. N.S. Mus., Halifax, N.S., Can. Office: NS Mus, 1747 Summer St, Halifax, NS Canada B3H 3A6

STEVENSON, DAVID JOHN, planetary scientist, educator; b. Wellington, New Zealand, Sept. 2, 1948; came to U.S., 1971; s. Ian McIvor and Gwenyth (Carroll) S. BSc, Victoria U., New Zealand, 1971; PhD, Cornell U., 1976. Rsch. fellow Australian Nat. U., Canberra, Australia, 1976-78; asst. prof. UCLA, L.A., 1978-80; assoc. prof. Calif. Inst. Tech., Pasadena, 1980-84, prof., 1984—, George van Osdol prof., 1995—; chmn. divsn. geol. & planetary scis. Calif. Inst. Tech., 1989-94. Contbr. about 100 articles to profl. jours. Named Fulbright scholar, USA, 1971-76. Fellow Am. Geophysical Union, Royal Soc. London, 1993; mem. AAAS, Am. Astron. Soc. (Urey prize 1984). Office: Calif Inst Tech 1201 E California Blvd Pasadena CA 91125-0001

STEVENSON, EARL, JR., civil engineer; b. Royston, Ga., May 8, 1921; s. Earl and Compton Helen (Randall) S.; B.S. in Civil Engring., Ga. Inst. Tech., 1953; m. Sue Roberts, Apr. 25, 1956; children—Catherine Helen, David Earl. Engr., GSA, Atlanta, 1959-60; engr., pres. Miller, Stevenson & Steinichen, Inc., Atlanta, 1960—; sr. v.p. Stevenson & Palmer, Inc., Camilla, 1984—; dir. Identification & Security Products, Inc., Atlanta. Served with USAAF, 1944-45. Registered profl. engr., Ga., Ala., S.C., Miss. Mem. Ga. Soc. Profl. Engrs., Water Pollution Control Fedn. Methodist. Home: 3163 Laramie Dr NW Atlanta GA 30339-4335 Office: 2430 Herodian Wa Smyrna GA 30080-2906

STEVENSON, ELIZABETH, author, educator; b. Ancon, Panama, C.Z., June 13, 1919; d. John Thurman and Bernice (Upshaw) S. B.A. magna cum laude, Agnes Scott Coll., 1941. With war time agys. U.S. Govt., Atlanta, 1942-47; order asst. Atlanta Pub. Library, 1948-56; asst. to coll. dean Emory U., Atlanta, 1960-74; from research assoc. to Candler prof. Grad. Inst. Liberal Arts, Emory U., Atlanta, 1974-87. Author: The Crooked Corridor: A Study of Henry James, 1949, Henry Adams, 1955 (Bancroft prize 1956), Lafcadio Hearn, 1961, Babbitts and Bohemians, 1967, Park Maker: A Life of Frederick Law Olmsted, 1977, Figures in a Western Landscape: Men and Women of the Northern Rockies, 1994; editor: A Henry Adams Reader, 1958. Guggenheim fellow, 1950-51, 58-59; grantee Rockefeller Found., 1958-59, Am. Coun. Learned Socs., 1975; recipient Faculty Rsch. Fund award Emory U., 1960s, 70s, summer stipend NEH, 1974. Mem. Authors Guild, Phi Beta Kappa. Democrat. *Whether as a product of the era or an irritant to it, the underlying assumption is that every single life is a drama worth exploring. Biography is bound by the facts, but it is also an art, a difficult art.*

STEVENSON, ERIC VAN CORTLANDT, mortgage banker, real estate executive, lawyer; b. N.Y.C., June 27, 1926; s. Harvey and Winifred (Worcester) S.; m. Judith Kittredge Herrick, Nov. 13, 1955; children: Jonathan Herrick, Michael Kirkham, Anne Kittredge, Margaret Low, Philip Eric. B.A., Yale U., 1947, LL.B., 1950. Bar: D.C. 1951, Conn. 1954. With NLRB, 1951; practice in Hartford, Conn., 1954-55, Norwich, Conn., 1957-61; with Electric Boat Co., 1956-57; rsch. assoc. Inst. Def. Analyses, 1961-63; with Labor Dept., 1963-65; rsch. dir. George Washington U., 1965-66; gen. counsel Peace Corps, 1966-68; dir. urban affairs Life Ins. Assn. Am., N.Y.C., 1969-72; mortgage banker Sonnenblick-Goldman Corp., Washington, 1973-74, Boykin Corp., 1974-82, Stevenson and Kittredge, Inc., 1978-82; sr. v.p. Mortgage Bankers Assn. Am., Washington, 1982-91; housing specialist Commn. Mental Health Svcs., Washington, 1992-95, Office Housing, HUD, Washington, 1995—; cons. Ford Found., 1963, Conn. Housing Investment Fund, 1968-69, Carnegie Corp., 1972, HUD, 1976-77, 78-80. Served with USNR, 1944-46, 51-53. Home: 3502 36th St NW Washington DC 20016-3150 Office: US Dept HUD 451 7th St SW Washington DC 20410

STEVENSON, HAROLD WILLIAM, psychology educator; b. Dines, Wyo., Nov. 19, 1924; s. Merlin R. and Mildred M. (Stodick) S.; m. Nancy Guy, Aug. 23, 1950; children: Peggy, Janet, Andrew, Patricia. BA, U. Colo., 1947; MA, Stanford U., 1948, PhD, 1951; ScD (hon.), U. Minn., 1996. Asst. prof. psychology Pomona Coll., 1950-53; asst. to asso. prof. psychology U. Tex., Austin, 1953-59; prof. child devel. and psychology, dir. Inst. Child Devel., U. Minn., Mpls., 1959-71; prof. psychology, fellow Center for Human Growth and Devel., U. Mich., Ann Arbor, 1971—; dir. program in child devel. and social policy U. Mich., 1978-93; adj. prof. Tohoku Fukushi Coll., Japan, 1989—, Peking U., 1990—, Inst. Psychology Chinese Acad. Scis.; mem. tng. com. Nat. Inst. Child Health and Human Devel., 1964-67; mem. personality and cognition study sect. NIMH, 1975-79; chmn. adv. com. on child devel. Nat. Acad. Scis.-NRC, 1971-73; exec. com. div. behavioral scis. NRC, 1969-72; mem. del. early childhood People's Republic of China, 1973, mem. del. psychologists, 1980; mem. vis. com. Grad. Sch. Edn., Harvard U., 1979-86; fellow Center Advanced Studies in Behavioral Scis., 1967-68, 82-83, 89-90. Recipient J.M. Cattell Fellow award in applied psychology Am. Psychol. Soc., 1994, William James Fellow award, 1995, Quest award Am. Fedn. Tchrs., 1995. Fellow Am. Acad. Arts and Scis., Nat. Acad. Edn.; mem. APA (pres. divsn. devel. psychology 1964-65, G. Stanley Hall award 1988), Soc. Rsch. Child Devel. (mem. governing coun. 1961-67, pres. 1969-71, chmn. long-range planning com. 1971-74, mem. social policy com. 1977-85, mem. internat. affairs com. 1991-94, Disting. Rsch. award 1993), Internat. Soc. Study Behavioral Devel. (mem. exec. com. 1972-77, pres. 1987-91), Phi Beta Kappa, Sigma Xi. Home: 1030 Spruce Dr Ann Arbor MI 48104-2847

STEVENSON, HOWARD HIGGINBOTHAM, business educator; b. Salt Lake City, June 27, 1941; s. Ralph Shields and Dorothy Dee (Higginbotham) S.; m. Fredericka O'Connell; children: William, Charles, Andrew. BS, Stanford U., 1963; MBA, Harvard U., 1965, DBA, 1969. Asst. prof. bus. Harvard U., Cambridge, Mass., 1968-72, assoc. prof., 1972-78, Sarofim Rock prof., 1982—, sr. assoc. dean for fin. adminstrn., 1991-94; v.p. Simmons Assocs., Boston, 1970-72; v.p. fin. adminstrn. Preco Corp., West Springfield, Mass., 1978-81; dir. Landmark Comms., Norfolk, Va., Camp Dresser and McKee Inc., Cambridge, Gulf States Steel, Gadsden, Ala., The Baupost Group, Inc., Cambridge, Sheffield Steel, Waltham, Mass., Quadra Capital Ptnrs., L.P., Commonwealth Capital Ptnrs. Co-author: Policy Formation and Administration, 1984, New Business Ventures and the Entrepreneur, 1985, 89, 4th edit., 1994, Entrepreneurial Ventures, 1992. Trustee Rural Land Found., Lincoln, Mass., 1973-78, Boston Ballet, Suffield Land Conservancy, Conn., 1978-82, Sudbury Valley Trustees. IBM Nat. Merit scholar, 1959; Ford Found. fellow, 1965. Mem. Fin. Execs. Inst., Acad. Mgmt., Urban Land Inst. Club: Harvard (N.Y.C.), Longwood Cricket. Office: Baker Libr 366 Harvard U Boston MA 02163

STEVENSON, IAN, psychiatrist, educator; b. Montreal, Que., Can., Oct. 31, 1918; s. John Alexander and Ruth Cecilia (Preston); m. Octavia Reynolds, Sept. 13, 1947 (dec. Nov. 1983); m. 2d, Margaret H. Pertzoff, Nov. 29, 1985. Student, U. St. Andrews, Scotland; BS, McGill U., 1942, MD, CM, 1943. Cert. Am. Bd. Psychiatry, 1953. Asst. prof. psychiatry La. State U., New Orleans, 1949-52, assoc. prof. psychiatry, 1953-57; prof. psychiatry, chmn. U. Va. Sch. Medicine, Charlottesville, 1957-67, Carlson prof. psychiatry, head div. of personality studies, 1967—; assoc. mem. Darwin Coll., U. Cambridge, 1981—. Author: The Diagnostic Interview, 1960, Twenty Cases Suggestive of Reincarnation, 1966, 10 other books; contbr. 250 articles to profl. jours. Fellow Am. Psychiat. Assn. (life); mem. AAAS, Am. Anthropol. Assn., Soc. for Psychical Rsch. London (coun. mem. and pres. 1988-89), Am. Soc. for Psychical Rsch., Soc. for Sci. Exploration (founding com.), Colonnade Club (U. Va.), United Oxford and Cambridge Univ. Club (London). Office: U of Va Health Sci Ctr PO Box 152 Charlottesville VA 22908

STEVENSON, JAMES RICHARD, radiologist, lawyer; b. Ft. Dodge, Iowa, May 30, 1937; s. Lester Lawrence and Esther Irene (Johnson) S.; m. Sara Jean Hayman, Sept. 4, 1958; children: Bradford Allen, Tiffany Ann, Jill Renee, Trevor Ashley. BS, U. N.Mex., 1959; MD, U. Colo., 1963; JD, U. N.Mex. 1987. Diplomate Am. Bd. Radiology, Am. Bd. Nuclear Medicine, Am. Bd. Legal Medicine, 1989; Bar: N.Mex. 1987, U.S. Dist. Ct. N.Mex. 1988. Intern U.S. Gen. Hosp., Tripler, Honolulu, 1963-64; resident in radiology U.S. Gen. Hosp., Brook and San Antonio, Tex., 1964-67; radiologist, ptnr. Van Atta Labs., Albuquerque, 1970-88, Radiology Assocs. of Albuquerque, 1988—, pres., 1994—; radiologist, ptnr. Civerolo, Hansen & Wolf, Albuquerque, 1988-89; adj. asst. prof. radiology U. N.Mex., 1970-71; pres. med. staff AT & SF Meml. Hosp., 1979-80, chief of staff, 1980-81, trustee, 1981-83. Author: District Attorney manual, 1987. Participant breast screening, Am. Cancer Soc., Albuquerque, 1987-88; dir. profl. div. United Way, Albuquerque, 1975. Maj. U.S. Army 1963-70, Vietnam; col. M.C. USAR, 1988—. Decorated Bronze Star. Allergy fellow, 1960. Med.-Legal Tort Scholar award, 1987. Fellow Am. Coll. Radiology (councilor 1980-86, mem. med. legal com. 1990—), Am. Coll. Legal Medicine, Am. Coll. Nuclear Medicine, Radiology Assn. of Albuquerque; mem. AMA (Physicians' Recognition award 1969—), Am. Soc. Law & Medicine, Am. Arbitration Assn., Albuquerque Bar Assn., Am. Coll. Nuclear Physicians (charter), Soc. Nuclear Medicine (v.p. Rocky Mountain chpt. 1975-76), Am. Inst. Ultrasound in Medicine, N.Am. Radiol. Soc. (chmn. med. legal com. 1992-95), N.Mex. Radiol. Soc. (pres. 1978-79), N.Mex. Med. Soc. (chmn. grievance com.), Albuquerque-Bernalillo County Med. Soc. (scholar 1959), Nat. Assn. Health Lawyers, ABA (antitrust sect. 1986—), N. Mex. State Bar, Albuquerque Bar Assn., Sigma Chi. Republican. Methodist. Club: Albuquerque Country. Lodges: Elks, Masons, Shriners. Home: 3333 Santa Clara Ave SE Albuquerque NM 87106-1530 Office: Van Atta Imaging Ctr A-6 Med Arts Sq 801 Encino Pl NE Albuquerque NM 87102-2612

STEVENSON, JOHN REESE, lawyer; b. Chgo., Oct. 24, 1921; s. John A. and Josephine R. S.; m. Patience Fullerton, Apr. 10, 1943 (dec. 1982); children: Elizabeth F., Sally H. Stevenson Fischer, John R. Jr., Patience Stevenson Scott; m. Ruth Carter Johnson, May 21, 1983. AB summa cum laude, Princeton U., 1942; LL.B., Columbia U., 1949, D.J.S., 1952. Bar: N.Y. 1949, D.C. 1971, U.S. Supreme Ct. 1964. Assoc. Sullivan & Cromwell, N.Y.C., 1950-55, ptnr., 1956-69, 75-87; chmn., sr. ptnr. Sullivan & Cromwell, 1979-87, counsel, 1987-92; legal adv. with rank of asst. sec. U.S. Dept. State, 1969-72, chmn. Adv. Com. on Pub. Internat. law, 1986-90, mem. com. 1993—, U.S. Dpet. State; adviser U.S. del. Gen. Assembly UN, 1969-74; chmn. U.S. del. Internat. Conf. on Air Law, The Hague, 1970; mem. U.S. del. Internat. Conf on Law of Treaties, Vienna, 1969; amb., spl. rep. of Pres. Law of the Sea conf., 1973-75; U.S. mem. Permanent Ct. of Arbitration, The Hague, 1969-79, 84-90; U.S. rep. Internat. Ct. Justice Namibia (S.W. Africa) case, 1970; spl. counsel U.S. del. Delimitation of Martime Boundary in Gulf of Maine (Can. vs. U.S.A.), 1984; mem. OAS Inter-Am. commn. on Human Rights, 1987-90; dir. Ctr. for Strategic and Internat. Studies; prin. Ctr. Excellence in Govt.; bd. dirs. Americas. Soc. Author: The Chilean Popular Front, 1952; editor-in-chief Columbia Law Rev.; contbr. articles to legal and State Dept. jours. Fellow ABA (hon.); mem. Am. Soc. Internat. Law (pres. 1966-68, hon. v.p. 1968-92, 93—, hon. pres. 1992-93), N.Y. State Bar Assn. (chmn. com. on internat. law 1963-65), Internat. Law Assn., Institut de Droit Internat. (v.p. 1987-89), Assn. Bar City N.Y. (chmn. com. on internat. law 1958-61), Am. Arbitration Assn. (bd. dirs. 1984-92, exec. com., chmn. internat. sect. law com.), Coun. Fgn. Rels., Am. Law Inst., Links Club (N.Y.C.), Met. Club (Washington), Chevy Chase Club, Burning Tree Club, Phi Beta Kappa. Home: 1200 Broad Ave Fort Worth TX 76107 Office: Ste 800 1701 Pennsylvania Ave NW Washington DC 20006-5805

STEVENSON, KATHERINE H., federal agency administrator; b. Jan. 20, 1948; d. Jacob W. and Sheila Holler; m. Donald Stevenson, aug. 14, 1982; 2 children. BA, Skidmore Coll., 1969; MA, U. Del., 1971. Researcher Nat. portrait Gallery, Smithsonian Inst., Washington, 1971; with Nat. Park Svc., Washington, 1972-80, Denver, 1980-87, Phila., 1987-95; with Nat. Trust for Historic Preservation, Washington, 1995—. Recipient Meritorious Svc. award Dept. Interior, 1994. Office: Nat Park Svc Cultural Resource 1849 C St NW Washington DC 20240*

STEVENSON, KENNETH LEE, chemist, educator; b. Ft. Wayne, Ind., Aug. 1, 1939; s. Willard Henry and Luella Marie (Meyer) S.; m. Virginia Grace Lowe, Dec. 26, 1959 (dec. Mar. 1991); children: Melinda Anne, Jill Marie; m. Carmen Ramona Kmety, May 9, 1992. B.S., Purdue U., 1961, M.S., 1965; Ph.D., U. Mich., 1968. Tchr. Ladoga High Sch., Ind., 1961-63; tchr. Central High Sch., Pontiac, Mich., 1963-65; prof. chemistry Ind.-Purdue U., Ft. Wayne, 1968—, chmn. dept. chemistry, 1979-86, 87—, acting dean Sch. Sci. and Humanities, 1986-87; sabbatical visitor Solar Energy Research Inst., Golden, Colo., 1980; vis. faculty N.Mex. State U., Las Cruces, 1975-76. Author: Charge Transfer Photochemistry of Coordination Compounds, 1993, also numerous rsch. papers. Mem. Am. Chem. Soc. (chmn. Northeastern Ind. sect. 1978-79, Chemist of Yr. 1979, 93), Inter-Am. Photochem. Soc., Phi Kappa Phi, Sigma Xi. Office: Ind U-Purdue U Dept Chemistry Fort Wayne IN 46805

STEVENSON, NIKOLAI, medical association executive; b. N.Y.C., Apr. 20, 1919; s. Milivoy Stoyan Stanoyevich and Beatrice Louise Stevenson; m. Shirley Gray, Jan. 20, 1951; children: Nanette, Matthew, Julie. BA, Columbia U., 1940. Sales mgr. Nat. Sugar Refining Co., N.Y.C., 1947-54; v.p. Olavarria & Co., N.Y.C., 1954-66; founder, sr. ptnr. Stevenson, Montgomery and Clayton, N.Y.C., 1966-82; pres. Assn. for Macular Diseases, N.Y.C., 1980—; condr. ednl. seminars in field; bd. dirs. Harper's Mag. Lectr. and contbg. author Harper's Mag., Am. Heritage, Atlantic Monthly. Col. USMCR, 1940-46. Decorated Silver Star, Bronze Star. Mem. Soc. Mayflower Descendants, John Jay Assocs. of Columbia U., Sugar Club, Manhasset Bay Yacht Club, City Midday Club, Phi Gamma Delta. Episcopalian. Home: 18 Sands Ct Port Washington NY 11050 Office: Assn for Macular Diseases 210 E 64th St New York NY 10021-7480

STEVENSON, PAUL MICHAEL, physics educator, researcher; b. Denham, Eng., Oct. 10, 1954; came to U.S., 1983; s. Jeremy and Jean Helen (Jennings) S. BA, Cambridge (Eng.) U., 1976; PhD, Imperial Coll., London, 1979. Rsch. assoc. U. Wis., Madison, 1979-81, 1983-84; fellow European Orgn. for Nuclear Rsch., Geneva, 1981-83; sr. rsch. assoc. Rice U., Houston, 1984-86, asst. prof. physics, 1986-89, assoc. prof., 1989-93; prof. physics, 1993—. Contbr. articles to profl. jours. Avocation: music.

STEVENSON, PHILIP DAVIS, lawyer; b. Canton, Republic of China, Sept. 15, 1936; s. Donald Day and Lois (Davis) S.; m. Carol Rusch, June 14, 1958 (div. 1975); children: Katherine, Ross; m. Joan Ann Lukey, Oct. 8, 1976. BA, Yale U., 1958, LLB, 1961. Assoc. Robbins, Noyes & Jansen, Boston, 1961-69; assoc. Hale and Dorr, Boston, 1969-71, jr. ptnr., 1971-75, sr. ptnr., 1975—, chmn. real estate dept., 1984-90. Contbr. articles on Mass. continuing legal edn. Mem. Weston (Mass.) Planning Bd., 1968-73, chmn., 1973. Mem. ABA, Am. Coll. Real Estate Lawyers, Mass. Bar Assn., Boston Bar Assn., N.H. Bar Assn., Abstract Club. Democrat. Unitarian. Avocations: sailing, skiing. Office: Hale & Dorr 60 State St Boston MA 02109-1803

STEVENSON, RAY, health care investor; b. Marion, Ohio, July 25, 1937; s. Ray and Hazel (Emmelhainz) S.; children: Jeffrey Parker, Kirk Andrew; m. Ellyn Gareleck, Feb. 8, 1985. BS, Ohio State U., 1959, MBA, 1967. Asst. adminstr. Children's Hosp., Columbus, Ohio, 1963-67; adminstr. Martin Meml. Hosp., Mt. Vernon, Ohio, 1967-71; sr. v.p. Hosp. Affiliates, Nashville, 1971-77; exec. v.p. Charter Med. Corp., Macon, Ga., 1977-79, pres., 1979-85; pres. R.S. Operators Inc., Atlanta, 1985—, R.S. Investors Inc., Atlanta, 1985—; chmn. bd. Am. Med. Trust, 1990—; bd. dirs. Atlanta Filmworks, Inc. Past chmn., bd. dirs. numerous hosps. and health-related orgns. Mem. Am. Coll. Hosp. Adminstrs., Fedn. Am. Hosps. (bd. dirs. 1979-81), Nat Assn. Psychiat. Hosps. Home: One NE Lagoon Island Ct Stuart FL 34996

STEVENSON, ROBERT EDWIN, microbiologist, culture collection executive; b. Columbus, Ohio, Dec. 2, 1926; s. Arthur Edwin and Mary Lucille (Beman) S. BS, Ohio State U., 1947, MS, 1950, PhD, 1954. Cert. Am. Bd. Microbiology. Virologist USPHS, Cin., 1954-58; head cell culture sect., Tissue Bank U.S. Naval Med. Sch., Bethesda, Md., 1958-60; head cell culture and tissue material sect. Nat. Cancer Inst., Bethesda, 1960-63, chief viral carcinogenesis br., 1963-67; mgr. biolog. scis., corp. devel. dept. Union Carbide Corp., Tarrytown, N.Y., 1967-72; v.p., gen. mgr., Frederick (Md.) div. Litton Bionetics, 1972-80; dir. Am. Type Culture Collection, Rockville, Md., 1980-93; dir. emeritus, 1993; dir. Large Scale Biology, Inc., Rockville, 1984—; chmn. biotech. adv. com. Dept. Commerce, Washington, 1985-93. With USN, 1944-45. Fellow Inst. for Soc., Ethics & Life Scis.; mem. Tissue Culture Assn. (pres. 1988-90), World Fedn. Culture Collections, U.S. Fedn. Culture Collections (pres. 1988-90), Am. Soc. Micrbiology, Cosmos Club (Washington). Episcopalian. Avocations: painting, cross country skiing. Home: 126 B Kearney St Santa Fe NM 87501

STEVENSON, ROBERT EVERETT, oceanography consultant; b. Fullerton, Calif., Jan. 15, 1921; m. Jeani M. Wetzel, June 20, 1988; children: Michael G., Robert K. AA, Fullerton Jr. Coll., 1941; AB, UCLA, 1946, AM, 1948; PhD, U. So. Calif., 1954. Tchg. asst. UCLA, 1946; instr. Compton (Calif.) Coll., 1947-49; lectr. U. So. Calif., L.A., 1949-51, dir. inshore rsch. Hancock Found., 1953-59, 60-61; spl. rsch. oceanographer U.S. Office Naval Rsch., London, 1959; rsch. scientist dept. oceanography and meteorology Tex. A&M U., College Station, 1961-62, dir. marine lab., prof. Grad. Sch., 1963-63; rsch. scientist Oceanographic Inst., assoc. prof. Fla. State U., Tallahassee, 1963-65; acting asst. lab. dir. Bur. Comml. Fisheries Biol. Lab., Galveston, Tex., 1965-66, asst. lab. dir., 1966-70, acting lab. dir., 1969; sci. liaison officer Office Naval Rsch., Scripps Instn. Oceanography, La Jolla, Calif., 1970-88, dep. dir. space oceanography, 1985-88; oceanography cons., Del Mar, Calif., 1988—; vis. scientist Am. Geophys. Union, 1963; disting. lectr. Am. Assn. Petroleum Geologists, 1969-72. Contbr. articles to sci. jours. With USAAF, 1942-45, ETO; capt. USAF, 1951-53. Decorated DFC, Air medal with four oak leaf clusters; recipient numerous awards Office Naval Rsch. and NASA. Fellow Geol. Soc. Am., Internat. Assn. for Phys. Scis. of Ocean (dep. sec. gen. 1985-87, sec. gen. 1987-95, emeritus sec. gen. 1995—), Marine Luftschiffer Kamradschaft (hon.), Order of Decibel, Sigma Xi. Home and Office: PO Box 689 Del Mar CA 92014-0689

STEVENSON, ROBERT MURRELL, music educator; b. Melrose, N.Mex., July 3, 1916; s. Robert Emory and Ada (Ross) S. AB, U. Tex., El Paso, 1936; grad., Juilliard Grad. Sch. Music, 1938; MusM, Yale, 1939; PhD, U. Rochester, 1942; STB cum laude, Harvard U., 1943; BLitt, Oxford (Eng.) U.; Th.M., Princeton U.; DMus honoris causa, Cath. U. Am., 1991; LHD (honoris causa), Ill. Wesleyan U., 1992; Litt honoris causa, Universidade Nova de Lisboa, 1993. Instr. music U. Tex., 1941-43, 46; faculty Westminster Choir Coll., Princeton, N.J., 1946-49; faculty research lectr. UCLA, 1981, mem. faculty to prof. music, 1949—; vis. asst. prof. Columbia, 1955-56; vis. prof. Ind. U., Bloomington, 1959-60, U. Chile, 1965-66, Northwestern U., Chgo., 1976, U. Granada, 1992; cons. UNESCO, 1977; Louis Charles Elson lectr. Libr. of Congress, Washington, 1969. Author: Music in Mexico, 1952, Patterns of Protestant Church Music, 1953, La musica en la catedral de Sevilla, 1954, 85, Music Before the Classic Era, 1955, Shakespeare's Religious Frontier, 1958, The Music of Peru, 1959, Juan Bermudo, 1960, Spanish Music in the Age of Columbus, 1960, Spanish Cathedral Music in the Golden Age, 1961, La musica colonial en Colombia, 1964, Protestant Church Music in America, 1966, Music in Aztec and Inca Territory, 1968, Renaissance and Baroque Musical Sources in the Americas, 1970, Music in El Paso, 1970, Philosophies of American Music History, 1970, Written Sources for Indian Music Until 1882, 1972, Christmas Music From Baroque Mexico, 1974, Foundations of New World Opera, 1973, Seventeenth Century Villancicos, 1974, Latin American Colonial Music Anthology, 1975, Vilancicos Portugueses, 1976, Josquin in the Music of Spain and Portugal, 1977, American Musical Scholarship, Parker to Thayer, 1978, Liszt at Madrid and Lisbon, 1980, Wagner's Latin American Outreach, 1983, Spanish Musical Impace Beyond the Pyrenees, 1250-1500, 1985, La Música en las catedrales españolas del Siglo de Oro, 1993; contbg. editor: Handbook Latin Am. Studies, 1976—; editor Inter-Am. Music Rev., 1978—; contbr. to New Grove Dictionary of Music and Musicians, 17 other internat. encys. Served to capt. U.S. Army, 1943-46, 49. Decorated Army Commendation ribbon; fellow Ford Found., 1953-54, Gulbenkian Found., 1966, 81, Guggenheim Found., 1962, NEH, 1974, Comité Conjunto Hispano-Norteamericano (Madrid), 1989; recipient Fulbright rsch. awards, 1958-59, 64, 70-71, 88-89, Carnegie Found. tchg. award, 1955-56, Gabriela Mistral award OAS, 1985, Heitor Villa Lobos Jury award OAS, 1988, OAS medal, 1986, Cert. Merit Mexican Consulate San Bernardino, Calif., 1987, Silver medal Spanish Ministry Culture, 1989, Gold medal Real Conservatorio Superior, 1994. Mem. Am. Musicol. Soc. (hon. life, Pacific SW chpt.), Real Academia de Bellas Artes, Hispanic Soc. Am., Am. Liszt Soc. (cons. editor), Heterofonia (cons. editor), Brazilian Musicol. Soc. (hon.), Portuguese Musicol. Soc. (hon.), Argentinian Musicol. Soc. (hon.), Orden Andrés Bello, Primera Clase, Venezuela, 1992. Avocation: playing piano. Office: UCLA Dept Music 405 Hilgard Ave Los Angeles CA 90024-1301 *American achievements are as nothing unless they are written about and remembered. My mission has been to rescue the musical past of the Americas. Present-day composers are too busy making their own music to worry about their predecessors. As a result, every new generation of composers thinks that they are the first ones to descry Mount Olympus. Not so. The past is a succession of musical and artistic glories.*

STEVENSON, ROBERT W., technologies company executive, financial officer. BA in Econs., Stanford U., 1961; MBA, U. Pa., 1963. Analyst fin. forecasting Boeing Co., 1963, supr. accounts receivable, 1963-64, mgr. fin. statements and planning, 1964-67, project fin. mgr., 1967-68; asst. contr. Criton Techs., 1968, contr., 1968-70, asst. v.p., contr., 1970-72, asst. v.p., sec., 1972-73, asst. v.p., sec. treas., 1973-75, sr. v.p., CFO, 1985-87, exec. v.p., CFO, 1987-89; exec. v.p., CFO Esterline Techs. Corp., Bellevue, Wash., 1987—. Mem. Fin. Execs. Inst. Office: Esterline Techs Corp 10800 NE 8th St Fl 6 Bellevue WA 98004-4429*

STEVENSON, ROGER E., geneticist; b. Neeses, S.C., 1940. MD, Bowman Gray Sch. of Medicine, Winston Salem, S.C., 1966. Office: 1 Gregor Mendel Cir Greenwood SC 29646-2307*

STEVENSON, RUSSELL B., JR., lawyer; b. 1941. B.M.E., Cornell U., 1964; J.D., Harvard U., 1969. Bar: D.C. 1970. Assoc. Surrey, Karasik, Greene & Hill, Washington, 1969-71; project dir. Environ. Law Inst., Washington, 1971; assoc. prof. George Washington U. Law Ctr., Washington, 1971-75, prof., 1975-81; dep. gen. counsel SEC, Washington, 1981-83; of counsel Hale and Dorr, Washington, 1984-86, ptnr. 1886-89; ptnr. Pepper, Hamilton & Scheetz, Washington, 1989-93; now mem. Ballard, Spahr, Andrews & Ingersoll, Wash.; vis. assoc. prof. Cornell U., 1974; vis. prof., Fulbright lectr. U. Paris-I, 1977-78; chmn. City at Peace Inc.; mem. exec. com. Washington Lawyers Com. for Civil Rights Under Law; dir. D.C. Law Students in Ct. Served to lt. j.g. USN, 1964-66. Mem. ABA, Internat. Law Assn., Washington Council Lawyers (pres.). Co-author: Environmental Improvement through Economic Incentives, 1977; Corporations: Law and Policy, 1982; author: Corporations and Information: Secrecy, Access and Disclosure, 1980; former mng. editor Harvard Civil Rights-Civil Liberties Law Rev. Office: Ballard Spahr Andrews & Ingersoll 555 13th St NW Washington DC 20004-1109

STEVENSON, THOMAS RAY, plastic surgeon; b. Kansas City, Mo., Jan. 22, 1946; s. John Adolph and Helen Ray (Clarke) S.; m. Judith Ann Hunter, Aug. 17, 1968; children: Anne Hunter, Andrew Thomas. BA, U. Kans., 1968, MD. Diplomate Am. Bd. Plastic and Reconstructive Surgery, Am. Bd. Surgery. Resident in gen. surgery U. Va., Charlottesville, 1972-78; resident in plastic surgery Emory U., Atlanta, 1980-82; asst. prof. surgery U. Mich., 1982-88, assoc. prof. surgery, 1988—; chief plastic surgery Ann Arbor VA Hosp., 1982—. Served to maj. USAR, 1978-80. Fellow ACS; mem. Am. Soc. Plastic and Reconstructive Surgery.

STEVENSON, WARREN HOWARD, mechanical engineering educator; b. Rock Island, Ill., Nov. 18, 1938; s. Joseph Howard and Camilla Irene (Darnall) S.; m. Judith Ann Fleener, June 7, 1959; children: Kathleen, Kevin, Kent. BSME, Purdue U., 1960, MSME, 1963, PhD, 1965. Engr. Martin Co., Denver, 1960-61; rsch. asst., instr. Purdue U., West Lafayette, Ind., 1961-65, asst. prof., 1965-68, assoc. prof., 1968-74, prof., 1974—, asst. dean engring., 1992—; guest prof. U. Karlsruhe, Germany, 1973-74; vis. prof. Ibaraki U., Hitachi, Japan, 1993; mem. tech. conf. coms. various profl. groups. Editor: Laser Velocimetry and Particle Sizing, 1979; mem. editorial bd. Jour. Laser Applications, 1988—; contbr. articles to profl. jours.; patentee in field. U.S. sr. scientist Alexander von Humboldt Found., Fed. Republic Germany, 1973. Fellow Laser Inst. Am. (bd. dirs. 1984—, pres. 1989); mem. ASME, Optical Soc. Am. Avocations: sailing, photography. Office: Purdue U Sch Mech Engring Applied Optics Lab West Lafayette IN 47907

STEVENSON, WILLIAM ALEXANDER, retired justice of Supreme Court of Canada; b. Edmonton, Alta., Can., May 7, 1934; s. Alexander Lindsy and Eileen Harriet (Burns) S.; m. Patricia Ann Stevenson; children: Catherine, Kevin, Vivian, James. BA, U. Alta., Edmonton, 1956, LLB, 1957; LLD (hon.), U. Alta., 1992. Called to Alta. bar, 1958. Ptnr. Hurlburt Reynolds Stevenson & Agrios, Edmonton, 1957-68; prof. U. Alta., 1968-70; ptnr. Reynolds Stevenson & Agrios, Edmonton, 1970-75; judge Dist. Ct. Alta., Edmonton, 1975-79; justice Ct. of Queens Bench Alta., Edmonton, 1979-80, Ct. of Appeal Alta., Edmonton, 1980-90, Supreme Ct. Can., Ottawa, Ont., 1990-92. Co-author: Civil Procedure Guide, 1995. Mem. Can. Bar Assn., Can. Inst. for Administrn. Justice (pres. 1983-85, hon. dir.), Nat. Jud. Inst. (hon. dir.). Home: 7 Laurier Pl, Edmonton, AB Canada T5R 5P4

STEVENSON, WILLIAM ALEXANDER, architect; b. Wilmington, Del., Nov. 17, 1940; s. Beverly Payne and Sarah (Cobb) S.; m. Roberta Louise Porcello, Feb. 8, 1969; children: Alexander William, Christopher James. BArch, Cornell U., 1963. Registered architect Mich., Ind., Ill., Ohio, N.Y., Conn. Architect Greiner Inc., Grand Rapids, Mich., 1969-74; architect Daverman, Grand Rapids, Mich., 1974-78, v.p., dir. design, 1978-82; v.p., dir. mktg. Greiner Inc., Grand Rapids, 1982-86; sr. v.p. Greiner Engring. Inc., Grand Rapids, 1986—. Designs include Lake Hills Elem. Sch. (AIA design award 1980), Calder Plaza Office Bldg (AIA design award 1980), Ledyard Bldg. (AIA Hist. award 1987), Penn H.S. (AASA Walter Taylor award 1992), Rockford H.S. Bd. dirs. Camp Blodgett for Underprivileged Children, 1984-89, Goodwill Industries, 1988-94, Opera Grand Rapids, 1990—. Mem. AIA (svc. chmn. com. on architecture for edn.).

Republican. Episcopalian. Avocations: skiing, running, gardening, cooking. Office: Greiner Inc 3950 Sparks Dr SE Grand Rapids MI 49546-6146

STEVENSON, WILLIAM HENRI, author; b. London, June 1, 1924; s. William and Alida (Deleporte) S.; m. Glenys Rowe, July 28, 1945; children: Andrew, Jacqueline, Kevin, Sally. Student, Royal Navy Coll., 1942. Fgn. corr. Toronto (Ont., Can.) Star, 1948-58; Toronto Globe & Mail, 1958-63, Ind. TV News, London, Eng., 1964-66, CBC, 1966-77; ind. writer, broadcaster, 1977—. Author: Travels In and Around Red China, 1957, Rebels in Indonesia, 1964, Chronicles of the Israeli Air Force, 1971, A Man Called Intrepid, 1976, Ninety Minutes at Entebbe, 1976, The Ghosts of Africa, 1981; producer: TV documentaries; movie screenplays include The Bushbabies, 1970. Served as aviator Royal Navy, 1942-45. Mem. Assn. Naval Aviation U.S.A., Authors Guild, Royal Overseas League (London). Mem. Progressive Conservative Party Can. Mem. Church of England. Clubs: Royal Bermuda Yacht, Royal Hong Kong Yacht. Office: care Paul Gitlin Agy 7 W 51st St New York NY 10019-6910

STEVER, DONALD WINFRED, lawyer; b. Altoona, Pa., Jan. 25, 1944; s. Donald Winfred and June Lily (Bargfrede) S.; m. Betsy Jean Seaman, May 28, 1968 (div. Oct. 1975); 1 child, Heather Elene; m. Margo Leaman Taft, July 30, 1976; children: David Whittaker, James Taft. BA, Lehigh U., 1965; JD, U. Pa., 1968. Bar: Conn. 1968, N.H. 1969, D.C. 1983, N.Y. 1983, U.S. Dist. Ct. N.H. 1969, U.S. Dist. Ct. Conn. 1986, U.S. Dist. Ct. (so. dist.) N.Y. 1985, U.S. Dist. Ct. (no. and we. dists.) N.Y. 1990, U.S. Ct. Appeals (1st cir.) 1974, U.S. Ct. Appeals (10th cir.) 1980, U.S. Ct. Appeals (5th, 11th and Fed. cirs.) 1982, U.S. Ct. Appeals (2d cir.) 1990, U.S. Supreme Ct. 1972. Atty. Aetna Life & Casualty co., Hartford, Conn., 1968-69, Office of N.H. Atty. Gen., Concord, 1969-72; asst. atty. gen., chief environ. protection Office of N.H. Atty. Gen., 1972-77; atty. pollution control sect. U.S. Dept. Justice, Washington, 1978-79, chief pollution control sect., 1979-80; chief environ. def. sect. U.S. Dept. Justice, 1980-82; prof. Pace U. Sch. Law, White Plains, N.Y., 1982-87; adj. prof. environ. law Pace U. Sch. Law, 1987-92; ptnr. Sidley and Austin, N.Y.C., 1987-93, Dewey Ballantine, N.Y.C., 1993—; bd. dirs. Environ. Law Inst., Washington, chmn., 1996-97, Hudson Valley Writers Ctr. Inc., Tarrytown, N.Y. Author: Seabrook and The Nuclear Regulatory Commission, 1980; Law of Chemical Reation and Hazardous Waste, 1986; editor: Environmental Law & Practice, 1992; co-editor Environmental Law & Practice, 1992. Bd. dirs. Biddeford Pool (Maine) Improvement Assn., 1989-93; mem. adv. com. North Tarrytown (N.Y.) Conservation, 1989—. Mem. Biddeford Pool Yacht Club (treas. 1989-92, sec. 1992—), Sleepy Hollow Country Club, Abenakee Club, Mill Reef Club. Avocations: golf, tennis, sailboat racing, early music. Home: 157 Millard Ave North Tarrytown NY 10591-1412 Office: Dewey Ballantine 1301 Avenue Of The Americas New York NY 10019-6022

STEVER, HORTON GUYFORD, aerospace scientist and engineer, educator, consultant; b. Corning, N.Y., Oct. 24, 1916; s. Ralph Raymond and Alma (Matt) S.; m. Louise Risley Floyd, June 29, 1946; children: Horton Guyford, Sarah, Margarette, Roy. A.B., Colgate U., 1938, Sc.D. (hon.), 1958; Ph.D., Calif. Inst. Tech., 1941; LL.D., Lafayette Coll., U. Pitts., 1966, Lehigh U., 1967, Allegheny Coll., 1968, Ill. Inst. Tech., 1975; D.Sc., Northwestern U., 1966, Waynesburg Coll., 1967, U. Mo., 1975, Clark U., 1976, Bates Coll., 1977; D.H., Seton Hill Coll., 1968; D.Engring., Washington and Jefferson Coll., 1969, Widener Coll., Poly. Inst. N.Y., 1972, Villanova U., 1973, U. Notre Dame, 1974; D.P.S., George Washington U., 1981. Mem. staff radiation lab. MIT, Cambridge, 1941-42; asst. prof. MIT, 1946-51, asso. prof. aero. engring., 1951-56, prof. aero. and astro., 1956-65, head depts. mech. engring., naval architecture, marine engring., 1961-65, asso. dean engring., 1956-59, exec. officer guided missiles program, 1946-48; chief scientist USAF, 1955-56; pres. Carnegie-Mellon U., Pitts., 1965-72; dir. NSF, Washington, 1972-76; sci. adviser, chmn. Fed. Council Sci. and Tech., 1973-76; dir. Office Sci. and Tech. Policy, sci. and tech. adviser to Pres., 1976-77, sci. cons., corp. trustee, 1977—; mem. secretariat guided missiles com. Joint Chiefs of Staff, 1945; sci. liaison officer London Mission, OSRD, 1942-45; mem. guided missiles tech. evaluation group Research and Devel. Bd., 1946-48; mem. sci. adv. bd. to chief of staff USAF, 1947-69, chmn., 1962-69; mem. steering com. tech. adv panel on aeros. Dept. Def., 1956-62; chmn. spl. com. space tech. NASA, chmn. research adv. com. missile and spacecraft aerodynamics, 1959-65; mem. Nat. Sci. Bd., 1970-72, mem. ex-officio, chmn. exec. com., 1972-75; mem. Def. Sci. Bd., 1962-68; mem. adv. panel U.S. Ho. Reps. Com. Sci. and Astronautics, 1959-72; mem. Pres.'s Commn. on Patent System, 1965-67; chmn. U.S.-USSR Joint Commn. Sci. and Tech. Cooperation, 1973-77, Fed. Council Arts and Humanities, 1972-76; Pres. com. Nat. Sci. medal, 1973-77. Author: Flight, 1965; Contbr. articles to profl. publs. Past trustee Colgate U., Shady Side Acad., Sarah Mellon Scaife Found., Buckingham Sch.; truste Univ. Rsch Assn., 1977—, pres., 1982-85; trustee Woods Hole Oceanographic Inst., 1980—, Univ .Corp. for Atmospheric Rsch., 1980-83; bd. dirs. Saudi Arabia Nat. Ctr. for Sci. and Tech., 1978-81; bd. govs. U.S. Israel Binat. Sci. Found., 1972-76, chmn., 1972-73; mem. Carnegie Commn. on Sci., Tech. and Govt., 1988-93. Recipient Pres.'s Cert. of Merit, 1948, Exceptional Civilian Svc. award USAF, 1956, Scott Gold medal Am. Ordinance Assn., 1960, Disting. Pub. Svc. medal Dept. Def., 1969, NASA, 1988, Nat. Medal of Sci., 1991; comdr. Order of Merit Poland. Fellow AIAA (hon., pres. 1960-62), AAAS, Royal Aero. Soc., Am. Acad. Arts and Scis., Royal Soc. Arts, Am. Phys. Soc.; mem. NAS (chmn. assembly engring. 1979-83), NAE (chmn. aero. and space engring. bd. 1967-69, fgn. sec. 1984-88), Acad. Engring. of Japan (fgn. mem.), Royal Acad. of Engring. of Great Britain (fgn. mem.), Cosmos Club, Bohemian, Phi Beta Kappa, Sigma Xi, Sigma Gamma Tau, Tau Beta Pi. Episcopalian. Office: 588 Russell Ave Gaithersburg MD 20877

STEVES, GALE C., editor-in-chief; b. Mineola, N.Y., Dec. 20, 1942; d. William Harry and Ruth (May) S.; m. David B. Stocker, Mar. 31, 1972 (div. Apr. 1978); m. Philip L. Perrone, Aug. 14, 1983. BS, Cornell U., 1964; MA, NYU, 1966. Editorial asst. Ladies Home Jour., N.Y.C., 1966-69; seafood consumer specialist U.S. Dept. Commerce, N.Y.C., 1969-73; editor food Homelife mag., N.Y.C., 1973-74; editor food and equipment Co-Ed mag., N.Y.C., 1974-76, Am. Home mag., N.Y.C., 1976-78; editor kitchen design and equipment Woman's Day mag., N.Y.C., 1979-83; editor-in-chief Woman's Day Spls., N.Y.C., 1983-91, Home Mag. Group, N.Y.C., 1991—; bd. dirs. Les Dames d'Escoffier, N.Y.C., Council of Sr. Ctrs. and Services of N.Y.C.; mem. editorial bd. Sr. Summary, N.Y.C., 1982-88. Author: Game Cookery, 1974, The International Cook, 1980, Creative Microwave Cooking, 1981, (with Lee M. Elman) Country Weekend Cooking. Mem. alumni adv. bd. Coll. Human Ecology, Cornell U. Mem. NAFE, Internat. Furnishings and Design Assn., Am. Soc. Mag. Editors, Garden Writers Assn. Am., Elec. Woman's Round Table. Office: Home Magazine Group 1633 Broadway New York NY 10019-6708

STEWARD, H. LEIGHTON, oil company executive; b. Fairfield, Tex., Dec. 1, 1934; s. Hugh Birt and Lucille (Riley) S.; m. Lynda Brady, June 6, 1959; children: Leighton Brady, Blake Worth. BS in Geology, So. Meth. U., 1958, MS in Geology, 1960. Chief exploration ops. Shell Oil Co., Houston, 1977-79; v.p. energy and minerals Burlington No. Inc., Billings, Mont., 1979-81; exec. v.p., chief ops. office Kilroy Co. of Tex., Houston, 1981-82; sr. v.p., then exec. v.p. La. Land & Exploration Co., New Orleans, 1982-84, pres., chief operating officer, 1984-88, chmn. CEO, 1989—; chmn. LL&E Petroleum Mktg. Inc., LL&E Pipeline Corp., LL&E (U.K.) Inc. Served to capt. USAF, 1959-62. Mem. Am. Assn. Petroleum Geologists, Am. Petroleum Inst. (bd. dirs. 1985-86), Mid Continent Oil and Gas Assn. Republican. Clubs: New Orleans Country Club; New Orleans Petroleum.

STEWARD, JAMES BRIAN, lawyer, pharmacist; b. Cleve., Mar. 25, 1946; s. Louis Fred and Helen Elaine (Goodwin) S.; m. Betty Kay Krans, Dec. 14, 1968; children: Christina Lynn, Brian Michael. BS in Pharmacy, Ferris State Coll., 1969; JD, U. Mich., 1973. Bar: Mich. 1973, U.S. Dist. Ct. (we. dist.) Mich. 1979, U.S. Cir. Ct. (6th Cir.) 1980, U.S. Supreme Ct. 1986. Pharmacist Revco Pharmacies, Grand Rapids, Mich., 1969-70, Coll. Pharmacy, Ypsilanti, Mich., 1970-73; assoc. Bridges & Collins, Negaunee, Mich., 1973-80; ptnr. Steward, Peterson, Sheridan & Nancarrow, Ishpeming, Mich., 1980-94, Steward & Sheridan, Ishpeming, 1995—. Mem., chmn. Negaunee Commn. on Aging, 1974-86; mem., chmn., sec. Marquette County Commn. on Aging, 1976-82; trustee, v.p., pres. Negaunee Bd. Edn., 1984-88, 91-95; adv. bd. trustee Ishpeming Area Cmty. Fund, 1995—. Mem. Mich. Bar Assn., Marquette County Bar Assn. (sec.- treas., v.p., pres.), Am. Soc. for Pharmacy Law, Ishpeming Cross County Ski Club, Wawonowin Country Club, Phi Delta Chi, Rho Chi. Avocations: cross country ski racing, downhill and water skiing, running, biking, classic cars. Office: Steward & Sheridan 205 S Main St Ishpeming MI 49849-2018

STEWARD, OSWALD, neuroscience educator, researcher; b. Sept. 12, 1948; m. Kathy L. Pyle; children: Jessica, Oswald IV. BA in Psychology magna cum laude, U. Colo., 1970; PhD in Psychobiology, U. Calif., Irvine, 1974. Asst. prof. neurosurgery and physiology U. Va. Sch. Medicine, Charlottesville, 1974-79, assoc. prof., 1979-84, prof., 1984-86, acting chmn. neurosci. dept., 1986-88, chmn., 1988—. Author: Principles of Cellular, Molecular, and Developmental Neuroscience, 1989; contbr. about 125 articles and revs. to profl. publs. Predoctoral fellow NIMH, Bethesda, Md., 1971-74; rsch. career devel. grantee NIH, 1978-83, Jacob Javitts neurosci. grantee NIH, 1987-94. Mem. Soc. for Neurosci. (chmn. chpts. com. 1985-87). Office: U Va Sch Medicine PO Box 5148 Charlottesville VA 22908

STEWARD, WELDON CECIL, architecture educator, architect, consultant; b. Pampa, Tex., Apr. 7, 1934; s. Weldon C. and Lois (Maness) S.; m. Mary Jane Nedbalek, June 9, 1956; children: Karen A., W. Craig. Cert. in architecture and planning, Ecole des Beaux Arts, Fontainebleu, France, 1956; B.Arch., Tex. A&M U, 1957; M.S. in Architecture, Columbia U., 1961; LHD (hon.), Drury Coll., 1991. Registered architect, Tex., Nebr. Designer Perkins & Will, Architects, White Plains, N.Y., 1961-62; asst. prof. architecture Tex. A&M U., College Station, 1962-67, assoc. chmn. Sch. Architecture, 1966-69, assoc. dean, prof. Coll. Environ. Design, 1969-73; dean, prof. Coll. Architecture U. Nebr., Lincoln, 1973—; ednl. cons. People's Republic of China, 1979; project dir. Imo State U. Planning, Nigeria, 1981-88; vis. prof. Tong ji U., Shanghai, 1984; hon. prof. N.W. Inst. Architects Engrs., Xian, 1989; specialist Design USA, USSR, 1990; co-chmn. nat. coordination com. AIA Nat. Coun. Archtl. Registration Bd. Intership, Washington, 1980-81; bd. visitors Drury Coll., 1980—, Coll. Arch. U. Miami, Fla., 1993—; mem. nat. design rev. bd. GSA, Washington, 1994—; mem. founding bd. dirs. East/West Pacific Arch., U. Hawaii, 1995—; vice chmn. Design Futures Coun., Reston, Va., 1995—. Designer, Quinnipiac Elem. Sch., New Haven, Conn., 1961 (Am Assn. Sch. Adminstrs. Exhibit 1969), J.J. Buser Residence, Bryan, Tex., 1969, Steward Urban Residence, Lincoln, Nebr., 1994. Mem. Lincoln Architects, Engrs. Selection Bd., 1979-88; mem. Nat. Com. for U.S.-China Rels., N.Y.C., 1981—, Nebr. Capitol Environ. Commn., 1989—; bd. dirs. Downtown Lincoln Assn., 1996—; profl. adviser nat. design competition Wick Alumni Ctr., Lincoln, 1981; steering com. Internat. Coun. Tall Bldgs., 1982-95. Grad. fellow Columbia U., 1960. Fellow AIA (pres. Brazos chpt. 1969, chmn. profl. devel. com. 1979, bd. dirs. 1979-90, dir. Cen. States 1987-90, nat. pres. 1991-92); mem. Nebr. Soc. Architects (bd. dirs. 1977—), Archtl. Found. Nebr. (bd. dirs. 1981-94, treas. 1981-94), Assn. Collegiate Schs. Architecture (bd. dirs. 1975-79), Nat. Archtl. Accrediting Bd. (bd. dirs. 1986-89, pres. 1988-89), Kazakhstan Union Architecture, Assn. Siamese Architects (hon.), Royal Inst. Canadian Architects, Fedn. Mexican Achitects, Japan Inst. Architects, Tau Sigma Delta, Phi Kappa Phi, Phi Beta Delta. Home: 125 N 11th St Lincoln NE 68508-3605 Office: U Nebr Coll Architecture Lincoln NE 68588

STEWART, ALBERT CLIFTON, college dean, marketing educator; b. Detroit, Nov. 25, 1919; s. Albert Queely and Jeanne Belle (Kaiser) S.; m. Colleen Moore Hyland, June 25, 1949. BS, U. Chgo., 1942, MS, 1948; PhD, St. Louis U., 1951. Chemist Sherwin Williams Paint Co., Chgo.; rsch. asst. dept. chemistry U. Chgo., 1947-48; instr. chemistry St. Louis U., 1949-51; exec. Union Carbide Corp., Danbury, Conn., 1951-84; prof. mktg. Western Conn. State U., Danbury, 1984—, dean Sch. of Bus., 1987-90, 94-95; cons. Ford Found., 1963-69, Union Carbide Corp., 1984-94; bd. dirs. Exec. Register, Inc., Danbury, 1985-90; assoc. Execom, Darien, Conn., 1986-90. Patentee in field. Bd. dirs. Am. Mus. Natural History, N.Y.C., 1976-85, N.Y.C. Philharm., 1975-80; arbiter Am. Arbitration Assn., N.Y.C., Danbury; active town Coun., Oak Ridge, Tenn., 1953-57. Lt. (j.g.) USNR, World War II. Recipient Cert. of Merit Soc. Chem. Professions, Cleve., 1962. Mem. Am. Mktg. Assn., Sigma Xi. Club: Rotary (Cleve., N.Y.C.). Home: 28 Hearthstone Dr Brookfield CT 06804-3006 Office: Western Conn State U 181 White St Danbury CT 06810-6845

STEWART, ALBERT ELISHA, safety engineer, industrial hygienist; b. Urbana, Mo., Dec. 20, 1927; s. Albert E. and Maurine (Lighter) S.; m. Elizabeth O. Tice, May 31, 1958 (div.); children: Sheryl E., Mical A. BA, U. Kans., 1949; MS, U. Mo., 1958, MBA, 1970; PhD, Western States U., 1984. Registered profl. engr., Calif., cert. safety engr., cert. indsl. hygenist. Sales engr. Kaiser Aluminum and Chem. Co., Toledo, 1949-56; tchr. Kansas City (Mo.) Pub. Schs., 1959-65; indsl. hygienist Bendix Corp., Kansas City, 1960-65; safety adminstr. Gulf R&D, Merriam, Kans., 1968-71; sr. indsl. hygienist USDOL-OSHA, Kansas City, 1971-77; pres. Stewart Indsl. Hygiene, Kansas City, 1977—; adj. prof. Cen. Mo. State U. Mem. Boy Scouts Am. With U.S. Army, 1950-53. Mem. Am. Indsl. Hygiene Assn., Am. Chem. Soc., Am. Acad. Indsl. Hygiene, Am. Soc. Safety Engrs., Am. Welding Soc., Nat. Mgmt. Assn., Nat. Sci. Tchrs. Assn., Adminstrv. Govt. Soc., Am. Legion Post 596, DAV, ARC, Alpha Chi Sigma. Episcopalian. Avocations: fishing, golf, travel. Office: 8019 Brooklyn Ave Kansas City MO 64132-3516

STEWART, ALEC THOMPSON, physicist; b. Windthorst, Sask., Can., June 18, 1925; s. Arthur and Nelly Blye (Thompson) S.; m. Alta Aileen Kennedy, Aug. 4, 1960; children—A. James Kennedy, Hugh D., Duncan R. B.Sc., Dalhousie U., Halifax, N.S., Can., 1946, M.Sc., 1949, LL.D. (hon.), 1986; Ph.D., Cambridge U., Eng., 1952. Research officer Atomic Energy Can., Chalk River, Ont., Can., 1952-57; assoc. prof. Dalhousie U., Halifax, 1957-60; assoc. prof. to prof. U. N.C., Chapel Hill, 1960-68; head physics Queen's U., Kingston, Ont., 1968-74, prof. physics, 1968—; vis. prof. various univs., Can., Europe, Japan, China, Hong Kong. Author 2 books; contbr. over 100 articles to profl. jours. Recipient CAP medal for achievement in physics, 1992, Canada 125 medal, 1992. Fellow Am. Phys. Soc., Royal Soc. Can. (pres. Acad. Sci. 1984-87), Japan Soc. for Promotion Sci.; mem. Can. Assn. Physicists (pres., other offices 1970-74). Achievements include research in solid state physics, behavior of phonons, electrons, positrons and postronium in crystals and liquids, public service: nuclear reactor safety, possible hazards of power frequency electric and magnetic fields. Office: Queens U, Dept Physics, Kingston, ON Canada K7L 3N6

STEWART, ALEXANDER CONSTANTINE, medical technologist; b. N.Y.C., Nov. 3, 1957; s. Dudley Constantine and Lillian Eunice (Mills) S.; m. Shirlene Denise Keys, June 22, 1985; children: Shechianh Faith, Akilah Danielle, Omari Joseph Constantine. Student, Herbert H. Lehman Coll., 1975-77; BS in Med. Tech., U. Kans., 1979; BTh, Northgate Bible Coll., 1989. Cert. med. technologist Am. Soc. Clin. Pathologists; cert. clin. lab. supr. Nat. Cert. Agy. Med. Lab. Pers. Chemistry technologist White Plains (N.Y.) Med. Ctr., 1979-89, Mt. Vernon (N.Y.) Hosp., 1987-89; chemistry supr. St. Agnes Hosp., White Plains, 1989-92, Westchester Sq. Med. Ctr., Bronx, N.Y., 1992-93; med. technologist Richland Meml. Hosp., Columbia, S.C., 1993—; instr. William Lee Bonner Sch. Bible & Theology, 1995—. Asst. historian Ch. of Our Lord Jesus Christ, 1989—; deacon Refuge Temple, Ch. of Our Lord Jesus Christ, 1993—. Mem. NAACP, Soc. Pentecostal Studies (editl. com. 1992—), Pentecostal Hist. Soc. Democrat. Pentecostal. Avocations: research and storage of African American Pentecostal materials. Home: 1000 Watermark Pl Apt 911 Columbia SC 29210-8209 also: Refuge Temple 4450 Argent Ct Columbia SC 29203 also: 4159 Grace Ave Bronx NY 10466-2015

STEWART, ALEXANDER DOIG, bishop; b. Boston, Jan. 27, 1926; s. Alexander Doig and Catherine Muir (Smith) S.; m. Laurel Gale, June 5, 1953. A.B. cum laude, Harvard U., 1948, M.B.A., 1961; M.Div. cum laude, Union Theol. Sem., N.Y.C., 1951; D.D. (hon.), Gen. Theol. Sem., N.Y.C. Ordained priest Episcopal Ch., 1951; asst. (Christ Ch.), Greenwich, Conn., 1950-52; priest-in-charge (St. Margaret's Parish), Bronx, N.Y., 1952-53; rector (St. Mark's Episc. Ch.), Riverside, R.I., 1953-70; bishop Episc. Diocese Western Mass., Springfield, 1970-83; exec. for adminstrn. Episcopal Ch., N.Y.C., 1983-86, exec. v.p., mgr. pension fund, 1987-91, part-time cons., 1992—; mem. faculty Barrington Coll., 1955-70; Mem. budget and program com. Episc. Ch. U.S.A.; bd. dirs. Ch. Ins. Co., Ch. Life Ins. Co., Ch. Hymnal Corp. Author: Science and Human Nature, 1960 (Wainwright House award), The Shock of Revelation, 1967; also articles. Chmn. Urban Renewal, E. Providence, R.I., 1967-70; vice chmn. United Fund Springfield, 1972; mem. schs. and scholarship com. R.I. chpt. Harvard Coll., 1960-70; A founder, 1959-87; mem. bd. dirs., sec. corp. Health Havens, Inc., E. Providence; trustee Barrington Coll., 1971-76, Episcopal Radio-TV Found., 1980—, Providence Country Day Sch., 1964-70, Ch. Pension Fund, N.Y.C., 1976-87; mem. corp. St. Elizabeth's Hosp., Providence, 1954-70, Springfield Hosp., 1970-84.—. Mem. Religious Research Assn., Union League (N.Y.C.), Harvard Western Club (Mass.), Colony Club (Springfield). Address: 75 Severn St Longmeadow MA 01106-1023

STEWART, ALLEN WARREN, lawyer; b. Manchester, N.H., Dec. 12, 1938; s. Ellwyn F. and Aelene W. (Harriman) S.; children: William, Paul, Geoffrey. BS, U.S. Naval Acad., 1961; MS, George Washington U., 1967; JD, U. Pa., 1970. Bar: Pa. 1970, U.S. Ct. Appeals (3d cir.) 1971, U.S. Supreme Ct. 1980. Morgan, Lewis & Bockius, Phila., 1970-77, ptnr., 1977-94; bd. dirs. Am. Sentinel Ins. Co., Conestoga Life Assurance Co., Erin Gp. Adminstrs. Editor: Reinsurance, 1991; contbr. articles to legal and ins. jours. Naval aviator, lt. comdr. USN, 1961-66. Mem. ABA, Pa. Bar Assn., Phila. Bar Assn. Club: Phila. Racquet. Avocations: sailing, fishing. Office: Conestoga Life Assurance Co 223 Willington West Chester Pike Chadds Ford PA 19317

STEWART, ARLENE JEAN GOLDEN, designer, stylist; b. Chgo., Nov. 26, 1943; d. Alexander Emerald and Nettie (Rosen) Golden; m. Randall Edward Stewart, Nov. 6, 1970; 1 child, Alexis Anne. BFA, Sch. of Art Inst. Chgo., 1966; postgrad., Ox Bow Summer Sch. Painting, Saugatuck, Mich., 1966. Designer, stylist Formica Corp., Cin., 1966-68; with Armstrong World Industries, Inc., Lancaster, Pa., 1968-96, interior furnishings analyst, 1974-76, internat. staff project stylist, 1976-78, sr. stylist Corlon flooring, 1979-80, sr. exptl. project stylist, 1980-89, sr. project stylist residential DIY flooring floor divsn., 1989-96, master stylist DIY residential tile, 1992-96; creative dir. Stewart Graphics, Lancaster, Pa., 1996—. Exhibited textiles Art Inst. Chgo., 1966, Ox-Bow Gallery, Saugatuck, Mich., 1966. Home: 114 E Vine St Lancaster PA 17602-3550 Office: Stewart Graphics 114 E Vine St Lancaster PA 17602 also: Stewart Graphics 114 E Vine St Lancaster PA 17602

STEWART, BARBARA ELIZABETH, free-lance magazine editor, artist; b. Ft. Dodge, Iowa, June 26, 1923; d. Warren Wheeler and Christine (Hubbard) Pickett; m. Charles Crombie Stewart, Sept. 2, 1943; 1 child, Charles Crombie IV. Student, Mt. Holyoke Coll., 1940-41, Wayne State U., 1941-42, So. Conn. State U., 1944-45; AA, Mercer County Community Coll., 1970; BA, Trenton State Coll., 1972. Cert, K-12 art tchr. Copywriter Fed. Dept. Stores, Goodwin's, Detroit, 1942-43; dept. coord. Sears, Roebuck & Co., Trenton, N.J., 1944; sec., writer Yale U., New Haven, Conn., 1945, 46; contbg. editor Mercer Bus. Mag., Trenton, 1980—. Oil and acrylic artist. Chmn. Stokes Sch. PTA, Trenton, 1952-58; pres. Rutgers Coop. Extension Mercer County, Trenton, 1970-82; chmn., mem. Hillcrest Civic Assn., Trenton, 1956-83; bd. dirs. Trenton YWCA, 1975-77; chmn. women's study fellowship Covenant Presbyn. Ch., Trenton, 1990-96; vol. Art Goes to Sch. program, 1992. Mem. Nat. Art Edn. Assn., N.J. Art Edn. Assn., AAUW (local chmn. 1965, 67), Torch Club (ofcl. del. 1985-88, tchr./vol. Art Goes to Sch. Programs, Pa./N.J. chpt.). Democrat. Avocations: walking, swimming, bridge, lawn bowling. Home: Pennswood Village L101 1382 Newtown-Langhorne Rd Newtown PA 18940-2401

STEWART, BARBARA LYNNE, geriatrics nursing educator; b. Youngstown, Ohio, May 10, 1953; d. Carl Arvid and Margaret (Ashton) Swanson; m. James G. Stewart, Mar. 17, 1973; children: Trevor J., Troy C. AAS, Youngstown State U., 1973, BS, 1982. Cert. gerontol. nurse, ANCC. Asst. dist. office supr. divsn. quality assurance Bureau of Healthcare Stds. and Quality; supr., dir. nursing svcs. Peaceful Acres Nursing Home, North Lima, Ohio; nurse repondent Health Sci. Ctr. U. Colo., Denver; charge nurse Westwood Rehab. Med. Ctr., Inc., Boardman, Ohio, Park Vista Health Care Ctr., Youngstown, Ohio; dir. nursing Rolling Acres Care Ctr., North Lima, Ohio; primary instr. Alliance (Ohio) Tng. Ctr., Inc.; asst. dist. office supr. Akron dist. officedivsn. of quality assurance Bureau Healthcare Stds. and Quality, Akron, Ohio. Former instr. CPR, ARC. Mem. Tri County Dir. Nurses Assn., Nat. Gerontol. Nursing Assn. (nomination com.), Youngstown State U. Alumni Assn.

STEWART, BURTON GLOYDEN, JR., banker; b. Clayton, N.C., Mar. 14, 1933; s. Burton Gloyden and Evelyn I. (Stallings) S.; m. Patricia Taylor, June 16, 1956; children: Burton Gloyden III, H. Taylor. AB, Duke U., 1955; grad. Sch. Banking of South, 1970; exec. program U. N.C., 1975. With Allstate Ins. Co., 1957-66, regional sales mgr., Charlotte, N.C., 1964-66; with Branch Banking and Trust Co., Wilson, N.C., 1966—, sr. v.p., mgr. corp. planning and mktg. div., 1972-81, mgr. corp. planning and investor rels., 1981-90; dir. investor rels., 1981—; dir. Branch Corp., 1974-82; dir. N.C. Payments System, 1980-89, v.p., 1983-86, chmn. bd. 1986-89; bd. dirs., chmn. Electronic Fin. Svcs., Inc., 1988-90. Bd. dirs. Wilson Heart Assn., 1968; bd. dirs., treas. Wilson Arts Coun., 1969-71; bd. dirs. Wilson United Way, 1974-80, 86-89, campaign chmn., 1977, pres., 1979, chmn. strategic planning com., 1986-90; mem. N.C. Gov.'s Efficiency Study Commn., 1985, N.C. Goals and Policy Bd., 1985-93. Lt. USNR, 1955-57. Mem. Nat. Investor Rels. Inst., Bank Investor Rels. Assn. (bd. dirs. 1984—, v.p. 1984-87), Am. Mgmt. Assn., N.C. Bankers Assn. (chmn. mktg. com. 1976), Wilson Country Club. Methodist. Office: 223 Nash St W Wilson NC 27893-3880

STEWART, CAMERON LEIGH, mathematics educator; b. Victoria, B.C., Can., Sept. 29, 1950; s. Ross and Greta Marie (Morris) S.; m. Ellen Papachristoforou, June 7, 1980; children: Elisa Maria, Andrew Ross. BSc, U. B.C., 1971; MSc, McGill U., Montreal, 1972; PhD, U. Cambridge, 1976. Rsch. assoc. Mathematisch Centrum, Amsterdam, 1976-77, I.H.E.S., Bures-Sur-Yvette, France, 1977-78; asst. prof. U. Waterloo, Ont., Can., 1978-82, assoc. prof., 1982-86, prof., 1986—. Contbr. articles to profl. jours. Recipient J.T. Knight prize U. Cambridge, 1974, Killam fellow Killam Estate, 1990-92. Fellow Royal Soc. Can.; mem. Can. Math. Soc., Am. Math. Soc. Avocations: golf, ice hockey. Home: 494 Heatherhill Pl, Waterloo, ON Canada N2T 1H7 Office: U Waterloo Dept Pure Math, Waterloo, ON Canada N2L 3G1

STEWART, CARL E., federal judge; b. 1950. BA magna cum laude, Dillard U., 1971; JD, Loyola U., New Orleans, 1974. Atty. Piper & Brown, Shreveport, La., 1977-78; staff atty. La. Atty. Gen. Office, Shreveport, 1978-79; asst. U.S. atty. Office U.S. Atty. (we. dist.) La., Shreveport, 1979-83; prin. Stewart & Dixon, Shreveport, 1983-85; spl. asst. dist. atty., asst. prosecutor City of Shreveport, 1983-85; judge La. Dist. Ct., 1985-91, La. Ct. Appeals (2d cir.), 1991-94, U.S. Ct. Appeals (5th cir.), 1994—; adj. instr. dept. mgmt. and mktg. La. State U., Shreveport, 1982-85. Mem. chancellor's adv. bd. La. State U., Shreveport, 1983-89, chmn., 1988-89; mem. black achievers program steering com. YMCA, 1990; active NAACP, 1988—. Capt. JAGC, 1974-77, Tex. Mem. ABA, Nat. Bar Assn., Am. Inns. of Ct. (Harry Booth chpt. Shreveport), Black Lawyers Assn. Shreveport-Bossier, La. Conf. Ct. Appeal Judges, La. State Bar Assn. (bench/bar liaison com.), Omega Psi Phi (Rho Omega chpt.). Office: US Ct Appeals 5th Cir 300 Fannin St Ste 2299 Shreveport LA 71101

STEWART, CARLETON M., banker, corporate director; b. Chgo., 1921; s. Carleton Merrill and Margaret (Lyon) S.; m. Alicia Dewar (dec.); 3 children; m. Kathryn White Stewart. Student, Stanford U., 1939-42; grad. in indsl. adminstrn., Harvard U., 1943, MBA, 1947. With Citibank, 1947-76; v.p. Citibank, N.Y.C., 1960-67, sr. v.p. in charge of Asia Pacific area, 1967-69, sr. v.p. in charge of South Asia, Middle East and Africa, 1969-73; sr. officer Citibank, London, 1973-76; dir. Grindlay's Bank Ltd., London, Banque Internat. pour L'Afrique Occidentale, Paris, 1973-76; chmn. bd., chief exec. officer Am. Security Corp. and Am. Security Bank, Washington, 1976-80; chmn. bd. Internat. Bank Miami, 1983-85; dir. Travelers Asset Mgmt. Internat. Corp., N.Y.C., 1985-87. Mayor Longboat Key, Fla., 1987-88, town commr., 1984-90, chmn. ethics commn., 1990-94; mem. Planning Commn., Sarasota County, Fla., 1990-92. Capt. AUS, 1943-46.

STEWART, CHARLES EVAN, lawyer; b. N.Y.C., Mar. 4, 1952; s. Charles Thorp and Jenifer Jennings (Barbour) S.; m. Cathleen Bacich, June 26, 1982 (div. Nov. 1986); m. Patricia A. McGlothlin, Sept. 10, 1988; 1 child, Charlotte Jenifer. BA cum laude, Cornell U., 1974, JD, 1977. Bar: N.Y. 1978, U.S. dist. ct. (so. and ea. dists.) N.Y. 1978, U.S. Ct. Appeals (

1978, U.S. Ct. Appeals (D.C. and 7th cirs.) 1980, U.S. Ct. Appeals (3d, 9th and 5th cirs.) 1981, U.S. Supreme Ct. 1981, U.S. Ct. Appeals (10th cir.) 1982, U.S. Claims Ct. 1983, U.S. Ct. Appeals (6th cir.) 1986; arbitrator NYSE, NASD. Assoc. Donovan Leisure Newton & Irvine, N.Y.C., 1977-86; 1st v.p., assoc. gen. counsel E.F. Hutton and Co., Inc., N.Y.C., 1987-88; exec. v.p., gen. counsel Nikko Securities Co. Internat., N.Y.C., 1988—; spl. asst. dist. atty. N.Y. County, 1979-80. Contbr. articles to legal jours. Chairperson Cornell U. Coun.; mem. adv. coun. Cornell U. Coll. Arts and Scis., Cornell U. Law Sch.; mem. exec. com. Westminster Sch. Alumni Assn.; trustee YWCA Nat. Bd., Am. Hist. Assn., Fed. Bar Coun. Mem. ABA, Am. Hist. Assn. (trustee), Assn. of Bar of City of N.Y. (young lawyers com. 1979-83, uniform laws com. 1984-86, corp. law dept. com. 1988-91, spl. com. on Asian affairs 1989-91), Fed. Bar Coun. (com. on 2d cir. cts. 1978-93, co-chair publs. com. 1993—, trustee), Am. Soc. Internat. Law Sec. Ind. Assn. (fed. regulation com. 1990—, lit. com. 1994—), Downtown Athletic Club, Univ. Club, Kennebunk River Club, Arundel Beach Club, Madison Beach Club, Chevy Chase Club. Republican. Episcopalian. Home: 122 E 82nd St New York NY 10028-0822 Office: Nikko Securities Co Internat 200 Liberty St Fl 29 New York NY 10281-1003

STEWART, CHARLES LESLIE, lawyer; b. Fayetteville, Ark., Aug. 12, 1919; s. Charles Leslie and Ruth (Want) S.; m. Edalee Esther Gastrock, Aug. 30, 1941; children: William Paul, Thomas Alan, Katherine Jean, Robert Edward. A.B., U. Ill., 1940; M.A., La. State U., 1941; student, George Washington U. Law Sch., 1944-45; J.D., U. Chgo., 1947. Bar: Ill. 1948, U.S. Supreme Ct. 1954. Economist, Dept. Agr., 1941-42; adminstrv. asst. OPA, 1942-43, Bd. Econ. Warfare, 1943; exec. dir. Chgo. div. ACLU, 1946-47; practiced law Chgo., 1948-91, Glencoe, Ill., 1991—; assoc. Mayer, Brown & Platt, Chgo., 1947-55, ptnr., 1956-67, 70-71, resident ptnr. charge European office, Paris, 1967-70; v.p., gen. counsel Hart Schaffner & Marx, Chgo., 1971-73, v.p., sec., gen. counsel, 1974-83; v.p., sec., gen. counsel Hartmarx Corp., Chgo., 1983-84, v.p., sec., sr. counsel, 1984, of counsel legal dept., 1985-89; arbitrator Mandatory Arbitration Program Cir. Ct., Cook County, Ill., 1990—; mem. Am. Law Inst., 1983-90. Mem. Glencoe (Ill.) Bd. Edn., 1965-66; mem. planning com. Corp. Counsel Inst., Northwestern U. Sch. Law and Ill. Inst. Continuing Legal Edn., 1981-84, vice-chmn., 1983, chmn., 1984; mem. Glencoe Union Ch. Served with OSS, AUS, 1943-45. Mem. ABA, Ill. State Bar Assn., Chgo. Bar Assn. (com. devel. of law 1977-91, vice chmn. 1984-85, chmn. 1985-86, corp. law com. 1981-91, corp. law depts. com. 1981-83, sr. lawyers com. 1987-92), Am. Soc. Corp. Secs. (adv. com. Chgo. regional group 1978-83, vice chmn. 1979-80, chmn. 1980-81, nat. dir. 1981-84, exec. com. 1983-84, corp. practices com. 1982-87, assoc. mem. 1986-91), Skokie Country Club, Delta Phi. Avocations: genealogy, history, bridge. Home and Office: 745 Vernon Ave Glencoe IL 60022-1562

STEWART, CHRISTINE SUSAN, Canadian government official; b. Jan. 3, 1941; d. Morris Alexander Leishman and Laura Anne Doherty; m. David Ian Stewart, Aug. 24, 1963; children: Douglas Alexander, John David, Catherine Anne. Ed., Neuchatel Jr. Coll., Switzerland, U. Toronto, Ont., Can. Nurse; mem. Ho. of Commons, 1988—, mem. standing com. for external affairs and internat. trade, assoc. critic for human rights; official opposition critic Can. Internat. Devel. Agy.; sec. state L.Am. and Africa Cabinet of Prime Min. Jean Chrétien, Ottawa, 1993—. Founding exec. dir. Horizons of Friendship. Liberal. Roman Catholic. Office: Parliament Bldgs, 484 Confederation Bldg, Ottawa, ON Canada K1A 0A6 Office: Fgn Affairs & Internat Trade, 125 Sussex Dr, Ottawa, ON Canada K1A 0G2

STEWART, CLAUDETTE SUZANNE, small business owner, author; b. East Orange, N.J., Jan. 23, 1948; d. Michel Fred and Helen Alberta (Margerum) Mautor; children: Shaun R., Michael B. BS, Rollins Coll., 1980. Bus. mgr. Wometco, Orlando, Fla., 1978-80; acctg. mgr. CNA, Orlando, 1980-81; fin. mgr. Martin Marietta Data Sys., Orlando, 1981-83; owner, operator Yellow Mountain Flower Farm, Leicester, N.C., 1983—; rschr., contbr. Lark Books, Asheville, N.C., 1988, 89, 91; rsch. writer Rodale Press, Emmaus, Pa., 1991. Author: Living with Potpourri, 1988, Everlasting Floral Gifts, 1990, Nature at Ground Level, 1993; author numerous poems. Vol. counselor Youth Programs, Inc., Orlando, 1981-83; vol. instr. Jr. Achievement, Orlando, 1981-83; vol. mountain search and rescue Asheville Area Rescue Squad, 1990-92; vol. Leicester Vol. Fire Dept., 1990—, Nat. Hug-A-Tree and Survive, 1996, N.C. Assn. Rescue and Emergency Med. Svcs., 1992—. Mem. N.C. Herb Assn. Avocations: etymology, ornithology, gardening. Office: Yellow Mountain Flower Farm 57 Davidson Gap Rd Leicester NC 28748

STEWART, CLINTON EUGENE, adult education educator; b. Copperas Cove, Tex., Nov. 7, 1927; s. Albert Clyde and Marjorie Lee (Jones) Stewart. BA, Baylor U., 1950, MS in Edn., 1951, MA in Biology, 1964, EdD, 1970. Cert. profl. supr., administr., supt., elem., prin., driver edn. tchr. Prof. edn. Howard Payne U., Brownwood, Tex.; dean Howard Payne U., Tex.; supt. Kopperl Independ Sch. Dist., Tex.; assoc. prof. edn. Sul Ross State U., Alpine, Tex. Lt. TNG, 1954. Mem. Phi Delta Kappa (pres. 1987), Kappa Delta Pi, Beta Beta Beta, Alpha Epsilon Delta, Alpha Chi.

STEWART, CORNELIUS JAMES, II, utilities company executive; b. Houston, June 27, 1925; s. Ross and Catherine (Rial) S.; m. Gretchen Elizabeth Braun, Nov. 28, 1947; children: Cornelius James, III, Richard Ross, David Rial, Gretchen Elizabeth Stewart Anderson, Catherine Maria Stewart Carrigan. Student, U. Tex., 1945-47. With Stewart & Stevenson Svcs., Inc., Houston, 1947—; v.p. Stewart & Stevenson Svcs., Inc., 1956-73, pres., 1973-75, chmn. bd., 1975—; chmn. bd., dir. C. Jim Stewart & Stevenson, Inc., Stewart & Stevenson Realty Corp., Stewart & Stevenson Internat. Corp., Stewart & Stevenson Transp., Inc., Stewart & Stevenson Power Inc., Machinery Acceptance; bd. dirs. Reagan Commerce Bank, 1973-76, So. State Bank, 1973—, Mchts. Bank; adv. dir. Tex. Commerce Bank, 1975—, also bd. dirs. Chmn. Houston City Planning Commn., 1974-83; bd. dirs. Better Bus. Bur. Met. Houston, 1976—, vice chmn., 1981-82, chmn., 1983-85; bd. dirs. Holly Hall, 1972-76; bd. dirs., mem. fin. devel. com. Houston chpt. ARC, 1989—; bd. dirs. Kelsey Seybold Found.; bd. dirs. Salvation Army, 1989—; chmn. Houston/Grampian Region Assn., 1978—; internat. adv. dir. Up With People, 1979—; co-chmn. Houston Fundraising, 1982; mem. engring. coun. devel. com. Tex. A&M Univ., 1989—; dir. U. Tex. med. br., Galveston, 1995. Served with USAAF, 1943-45. Mem. Nat. Assn. Mfg. (bd. dirs. 1988—), Purchasing Agts. Assn. Houston (pres. 1959-60, dir. 1961-62), U.S. C. of C. (internat. policy com. 1983—), Houston C. of C. (dir. 1969, 76, 78, 80, 82, 84, mem. aviation steering com. 1976—, chmn. bus. devel. com. 1980-81), Nat. Indsl. Conf. Bd., Newcomen Soc. Presbyterian. Clubs: Rotary (bd. dirs. Houston club 1978—, v.p. 1980, pres. 1981, pres. found. 1991-93), Breakfast, Houston (pres. 1973, pension com. 1974—), Houston Country (bd. dirs. 1974-76). Office: Stewart & Stevenson Services Inc PO Box 1637 Houston TX 77251-1637*

STEWART, C(ORNELIUS) VAN LEUVEN, lawyer; b. Balt., Sept. 22, 1936; s. Charles Morton and Lillie Emerson (Van Leuven) S.; m. Clare Wright Horsley, June 18, 1960; children: Clare Winston, Lillie Elliotte, Jenett Ten Eyck (dec.). BA, Yale U., 1958; LLB, U. Va., 1961. Bar: Md. 1962, D.C. Bar 1982. Assoc. in law U. Calif. Law Sch., Berkeley, 1961-62; assoc. Venable, Baetjer & Howard, Balt., 1962-69, ptnr., 1970-91; ptnr. Stewart, Plant & Blumenthal, Balt., 1991—. Bd. dirs., pres. Irvine Natural Sci. Ctr.; bd. overseers Balt. Sch. for the Arts; past bd. dirs. Pks. and People Found., Balt. Symphony Orch. Assn., Internat. Visitors Coun. of Balt., Roland Park Country Sch., Magic Me.; past pres. Md. Ballet Co., Met. Balt. Mental Health Assn. Mem. ABA, State Bar Assn., Balt. City Bar Assn., D.C. Bar Assn., Am. Coll. Trust and Estate Counsel (Md. chpt., state chair), Internat. Acad. of Estate and Trust Law, Balt. Estate Planning Coun. (pres. 1987). Republican. Episcopalian. Office: 7 Saint Paul St Ste 910 Baltimore MD 21202-1626

STEWART, DANIEL ROBERT, retired glass company executive; b. New Kensington, Pa., July 25, 1938; s. Daniel Joseph and Sarah Madeline (Caldwell) S.; m. Marianne Colesar, Aug. 27, 1960; children—Karen Anne, Daniel John. B.S., Pa. State U., 1960, M.S., 1962, Ph.D., 1964. Research scientist Owens-Ill., Inc., Toledo, 1964-66; chief glass sci. sect. Owens-Ill., Inc., 1967-69, dir. glass and ceramic research, 1970-71, dir. corporate research labs., 1972-73, v.p. corporate staff, dir. glass and ceramic tech., 1973-83; pres. Dura Temp Corp., Holland, Ohio, 1983-94; ret., 1994; U.S. mfg. com. Internat. Congress Glass, 1980-83. Ch. treas. Ch. of the Nazarene, 1966-83; mem. local com. Boy Scouts Am., 1975-87. PPG fellow, 1961-64. Fellow Am. Ceramic Soc. (past chmn. glass div.); mem. Nat. Inst. Ceramic Engrs. (profl. achievement in ceramic engring. award 1974), Soc. Glass Tech., Sigma Xi. Republican. Patentee in field. Office: 1750 Eber Rd Holland OH 43528-9635

STEWART, DAVID MARSHALL, librarian; b. Nashville, Aug. 1, 1916; s. David and Mary (Marshall) S.; m. Gladys Carroll, June 9, 1947; 1 son, James Marshall. B.A., Bethel Coll., 1938; B.S. in L.S, George Peabody Coll., 1939. Circulation asst. Vanderbilt U. Library, 1938-39; county librarian Ark. Library Commn., 1939-40; Tenn. supr. WPA library service projects, 1940-42; librarian Memphis State U., 1942-46; spl. asst. to chief card div. Library of Congress, Washington, 1947; librarian CIA, Washington, 1948-60; chief librarian Nashville Pub. Library, 1960-85; Instr. Peabody Library Sch., 1966-80. Bd. dirs. Council Community Agys., Nashville, Middle-East Tenn. Arthritis Found. (v.p. 1965), Friends Chamber Music Nashville, Travelers Aid Nashville. Served to lt. comdr. USNR, 1942-46. Mem. ALA, Tenn. Library Assn. (chmn. legislative com. 1961-65, v.p. 1965, pres. 1966, Honor award, 1983), Southeastern Library Assn., Pub. Library Assn. Am. (chmn. standards com. 1964-65, pres. 1966-67), Alumni Assn. Bethel Coll. (dir., Disting. Alumni award 1992). Democrat. Mem. Ch. of Christ. Clubs: Kiwanian. (Nashville), Coffee House (Nashville). Home: 6342 Torrington Rd Nashville TN 37205-3157

STEWART, DEBRA WEHRLE, university dean and official, educator; b. Petersburg, Va., May 22, 1943. BA in Philosophy and Polit. Sci., Marquette U., 1965; MA in Govt., U. Md., 1967; PhD in Polit. Sci., U. N.C., 1975. Instr. polit. sci. European divsn. U. Md., Nuremberg, Germany, 1967-69; instr. polit. sci. and pub. adminstrn. N.C. State U., Raleigh, 1974-75, asst. prof., 1975-78, assoc. prof., 1979-83, prof., 1984—, acting dir. MPA program, 1978, assoc. dean Grad. Sch., 1983-86, interim vice provost and dean Grad. Sch., 1986-88, dean Grad. Sch., 1988—, vice provost Grad. Sch., 1995—; interim chancellor U. N.C., Greensboro, 1994; mem. com. on assessment of rsch. doctorate NRC, 1992—; mem. Grad. Record Exam. Bd., 1992—, chmn.-elect, 1994-95, chmn., 1995-96; bd. dirs. Coun. Grad. Schs., 1990—, chmn.-elect, 1992-93, chmn., 1993-94; mem. Test English as Fgn. Lang. Bd., 1992-95; councilor Oak Ridge (Tenn.) Assoc. Univs., 1988-92, bd. dirs., 1993—; mem. exec. com. Coun. So. Grad. Schs., 1989-91; trustee Triangle U. Ctr. for Advanced Studies, 1989—. Author: The Women's Movement in Community Politics: The Role of Local Commissions on the Status of Women, 1980, (with G. David Garson) Organizational Behavior and Public Management, 1983, 2d edit. (with Vasu and Garson), 1990; editor: Women in Local Politics, 1980; mem. editl. bd. Rev. Pub. Pres. Adminstrn., 1981-89, Annals Pub. Adminstrn., 1982-84, Women and Politics, 1980-88, Politics and Policy, 1983-86; contbr. articles to profl. jours., chpts. to books. Recipient edn. award YWCA Acad. Women, 1988;. Mem. Nat. Assn. State Univs. and Land-Grant Colls. (bd. dirs. 1992-94, exec. com. coun. on rsch. policy and grad. edn. 1989-92, chmn. 1990-91), Am. Soc. for Pub. Adminstrn. (com. on status of women in pub. adminstrn. 1976-78, com. on profl. stds. and ethics 1980-89, chmn. com. on whistle blowing and dissent channels of profl. stds. and ethics com. 1985-86, Burchfield award 1976), So. Polit. Sci. Assn. (nominating com. 1978, coord. pub. adminstrn. sect. 1979), Women's Forum N.C., Phi Kappa Phi, Pi Sigma Alpha, Pi Alpha Alpha. Office: NC State U Grad Sch 104 Peele Hall Box 7102 Raleigh NC 27695-7102

STEWART, DORIS MAE, biology educator; b. Sandsprings, Mont., Dec. 12, 1927; d. Virgil E. and Violet M. (Weaver) S.; m. Felix Loren Powell, Oct. 8, 1956; children: Leslie, Loren. BS, Coll. Puget Sound, 1948, MS, 1949; PhD, U. Wash., 1953. Instr. U. Mont., Missoula, 1954-56, asst. prof., 1956-57; asst. prof. U. Puget Sound, Tacoma, 1957-58; head sci. dept. Am. Kiz Lisesi, Istanbul, Turkey, 1958-62; rsch. asst. prof. U. Wash., Seattle, 1963-67, rsch. assoc. prof., 1967-68; assoc. prof. Cen. Mich. U., Mt. Pleasant, 1970-72; assoc. prof. U. Balt., 1973-81, prof., 1981-95, prof. emeritus, 1995—. Contbr. numerous articles to profl. jours. Mem. Am. Physiol. Soc., Sigma Xi. Home: 1103 Frederick Rd Baltimore MD 21228-5032

STEWART, DOROTHY K., educator, librarian; b. Bristol, Conn., Sept. 28, 1928; d. Robert and Anna Esther (Schwirtz) Konopask; m. David Benjamin Stewart, Sept. 27, 1952 (div. Nov. 1979); children: Douglas Neil, Diane Alison. BA in Romance Langs. and Lit. cum laude, Boston U., 1950; MS in Libr. Sci., Cath. U. Am., 1959. Children's libr. Brookline (Mass.) Pub. Libr., 1953-55, Takoma Park (Md.) Libr., 1955-57; reference libr. U.S. Geol. Survey, 1961; libr. Washington Internat. Sch., 1979-80, Office Sea Grant NOAA, Rockville, Md., 1980-82; info. specialist Life Ring, Inc., Silver Spring, Md., 1983-84; pub. svc. libr. Urban Inst., Washington, 1984-85; user svcs. coord. ERIC Clearinghouse on Tchg. and Tchr. Edn., Washington, 1985—. Active, past pres. PTA, Rockville, Md., 1973-78; chmn., mem. com. Potomac (Md.) Libr. Adv. Com., 1975-85. Mem. Am. Ednl. Rsch. Assn., NAFE, Spl. Librs. Assn., D.C. Libr. Assn., Capital PC User Group, French lang. clubs, Phi Beta Kappa, Beta Phi Mu. Democrat. Avocations: travel, hiking, birding, microcomputers. Office: ERIC Clearinghouse on Tchgand Tchr Edn 1 Dupont Cir NW Ste 610 Washington DC 20036-1110

STEWART, DUNCAN JAMES, lawyer; b. Amsterdam, N.Y., Apr. 24, 1939; s. William James and Maybelle Veronica (Matthews) S.; m. Susan Cobb Stewart, June 18, 1966; children: Benjamin Ross, Matthew Schuyler. AB, Cornell U., 1961, LLB, 1964. Bar: N.Y. 1964, U.S. Dist. C.t (no. dist.) N.Y. 1964. Assoc. Willkie Farr & Gallagher, N.Y.C., 1964, 67-72, ptnr., 1973—. Trustee Citizens Budget Commn., N.Y.; bd. dirs. Prospect Park Alliance, Bklyn., Network for Women's Svcs., N.Y. Mem. ABA, N.Y. State Bar Assn., Assn. of Bar of City of N.Y., Cornell Club. Democrat. Presbyterian. Home: 264 Berkeley Pl Brooklyn NY 11217-3904 Office: Willkie Farr & Gallagher 1 CitiCorp Ctr 153 E 53rd St New York NY 10022-4602

STEWART, EDGAR ALLEN, lawyer; b. Selma, Ala., Sept. 1, 1909; s. Edgar A. and Irma (Mallory) S.; m. Mamie V. Packer, Oct. 15, 1938; children: Edgar Allen III (dec.), Martha M. (Mrs. Edward B. Crosland, Jr.). B.A., U. South, 1929; LL.B., U. Ala., 1932. Bar: Ala. 1932. Since practiced Selma; sr. partner Reeves & Stewart, 1947-92; spl. agt. FBI, 1942-45; ret., 1993. Contbr. articles to profl. jours. Trustee Selma Schs., 1956-67; bd. dirs., pres. Selma YMCA, 1952-68; bd. dirs. Indsl. Devel. Bd., Selma, YMCA Blue Ridge (N.C.) Assembly, 1983-85. Fellow Am. Coll. Trial Lawyers; mem. ABA, Ala. Bar Commn. (dir. 1970-76), Am. Coll. Probate Counsel, Internat. Assn. Ins. Counsel, Nat. Assn. R.R. Counsel, Am. Counsel Assn. (bd. dirs. Presbyn. Retirement Corp. 1993), Am. Judicature Soc., Phi Beta Kappa, Phi Delta Theta, Phi Delta Phi. Home: Apt 356 500 Spanish Fort Blvd Spanish Fort AL 36527-5003 Office: PO Box 457 Selma AL 36702-0457

STEWART, EUGENE LAWRENCE, lawyer, trade association executive; b. Kansas City, Mo., Feb. 9, 1920; s. Edmund Dale and Mary Elizabeth (Raef) S.; m. Jeanne Ellen Powers, Oct. 19, 1945; children—Timothy, Terence, Brian. B.S., S.S., Georgetown U., 1947, J.D., 1951. Bar: D.C. 1951, U.S. Tax Ct. 1953, U.S. Ct. of Customs and Patent Appeals 1951-82, U.S. Ct. Appeals Fed. Circuit 1982, U.S. Ct. Appeals (3d cir.) 1985, U.S. Ct. Appeals (9th cir.) 1987, U.S. Ct. Appeals (11th cir.) 1988, U.S. Ct. Appeals (D.C. cir.) 1951, U.S. Ct. Internat. Trade 1958, U.S. Supreme Ct. 1967. Assoc. Steptoe & Johnson, Washington, 1951-56, ptnr., 1956-58; ptnr. Hume & Stewart, Washington, 1958-64; pvt. practice law Washington, 1964-69, 78-83; ptnr. Lincoln & Stewart, Washington, 1969-73, Stewart & Ikenson, Washington, 1974-78; sr. ptnr. Stewart & Stewart, Inc., Washington, 1983—; adj. prof. law Georgetown U. Law Ctr., Washington, 1955-58; exec. sec. Trade Relations Council of U.S., Washington, 1962—. Contbr. articles to profl. publs. Pres., Sursum Corda, Inc. (low-income housing project), Washington, 1964-78. Served to lt. col. USAF, 1941-52; PTO. Recipient John Carroll award Georgetown U., 1966. Mem. D.C. Bar, Customs and Internat. Trade Bar Assn., Georgetown U. Alumni Assn. Inc. (pres. 1964-66). Republican. Roman Catholic. Address: Stewart & Stewart Inc 2100 M St NW Ste 200 Washington DC 20037-1207

STEWART, FRANK MAURICE, JR., federal agency administrator; b. Okalona, Miss., Apr. 1, 1939; s. Frank Maurice Stewart and Henryne Annette (Walker) Goode; m. Regina Diane Mosley, Dec. 26, 1964; children: Lisa Ann, Dana Joy. BA, Wesleyan U., 1961, MA in Teaching, 1963, diploma further study, 1963; postgrad., Am. U., 1982-84. Dir. urban edn. corps N.J. State Dept. Edn., Trenton, 1969-70; dir. urban teaching intern program Sch. Edn. Rutgers U., New Brunswick, N.J., 1970-71; staff asst. White House Conf. on Aging, Washington, 1971-73; chief program devel. U.S. Office of Equal Edn. Opportunity, Washington, 1973-74; chief policy analysis U.S. Adminstrn. on Aging, Washington, 1974-75; asst. exec. sec. U.S. HEW, Washington, 1975-77; dir. govt. programs U.S. Dept. Energy, Washington, 1977-80, dir. instnl. conservation programs, 1980-84, dir. state and local assistance programs, 1984-90, dep. asst. sec. for tech. and fin. assistance, 1990-93; acting asst. sec. for energy efficiency and renewable energy, 1993-94; mgr. Golden (Colo.) Field Office, U.S. Dept. Energy, 1994—; bd. dirs. Renewable Energy for African Devel., 1992-94; mem. U.S. Presdl. Del. on Sustainable Energy Devel. to South Africa, 1995, U.S. Del. to African-African-Am. Summit, Dakar, Senagal, 1995. Recipient Svc. Recognition award Assn. Phys. Plant Adminstrs., Washington, 1982, Svc. Appreciation award Nat. Assn. State Energy Officials, Washington, 1987; named Energy Exec. of Yr. Assn. Energy Engrs., Atlanta, 1988. Mem. Sr. Execs. Assn. Episcopalian. Home: 202 S Madison St Denver CO 80206 Office: US Dept Energy Field Office 1617 Cole Blvd Golden CO 80401

STEWART, GEORGE RAY, librarian; b. Birmingham, Ala., Aug. 19, 1944; s. DeWitt and Ann (McCain) S.; m. Nancy Ann Norton, June 5, 1964; children: Steven Ray, Jeffery Alan. B.A., Samford U., Birmingham, 1966, M.A., 1967; M.A., Emory U., 1971. Mem. staff Birmingham Pub. Libr., 1960—, assoc. dir., 1970-76, dir., 1976-93; system dir., 1993—; part-time instr. Grad. Sch. Libr. Svc. U. Ala.; bd. dirs. Southeastern Library Network, Inc., 1986-88. Editor: Birmingham Pub. Library Press. Bd. dirs. Red Mountain Mus., 1972-79, Literacy Coun. Ctrl. Ala., 1990-94; bd. dirs. Indsl. Health Coun., Birmingham, 1972-85, sec., 1979-81, pres. bd. dirs. 1982, 83. Mem. ALA, Southeastern Libr. Assn. (treas. 1985-86, v.p. 1986-88, pres. 1989-90), Ala. Libr. Assn. (scholarship 1968, pres. 1976), Ala. Hist. Assn., Birmingham Hist. Assn. Office: Birmingham-Jefferson County Libr System 2100 Park Pl Birmingham AL 35203-2744

STEWART, GEORGE TAYLOR, insurance executive; b. N.Y.C., Dec. 29, 1924; s. Fargo Calvin and Berthe Adelle (Pelleton) S.; m. Bonnie Elizabeth Myers, Sept. 14, 1946; children: Diane Barbara Stewart Carrington, Susan Gail Stewart Dupuis. A.B., Wesleyan U., Conn., 1947; LHD (hon.), Lynchburg Coll., 1994. Analyst Geyer & Co., Inc., 1948-54, Shelby Cullom Davis & Co., 1954-56; v.p. Blyth & Co., Inc., N.Y.C., 1956-65; chmn., chief exec. officer 1st Colony Life Ins. Co., Lynchburg, Va., 1965-92, chmn. fin. com., 1992—; bd. dirs. Am. Mayflower Life Ins. Co., N.Y.; chmn. Greater Lyunchburg Cmty. Trust. Author: Investing in American Business, 1964. Trustee Lynchburg Coll., Jefferson's Poplar Forest, founder. Recipient Lynchburg Bi-Centennial award, 1976, Lynchburg Pro Opera Civica award, 1982, award Navy League, 1981, Outstanding Businessman award Lynchburg Coll. Bus. Sch., 1982. Mem. N.Y. Acad. Scis., Lynchburg C. of C. (pres.), Thomas Jefferson Commemoration Commn. (presdl. apptd.), N.Y. Soc. Security Analysts, Met. Club (N.Y.C.), City Midday-Drug and Chem. Club (N.Y.C.), Calif. Club (L.A.), Boonsboro Country Club of Lynchburg (bd. dirs.), Piedmont Club, Waterfront Club. Republican. Presbyterian (elder). Office: First Colony Life Ins Co PO Box 1280 Lynchburg VA 24505-1280

STEWART, GEORGIANA LICCIONE, author; b. Mount Vernon, N.Y., May 18, 1943; d. Arthur Alfred and Grace Marie (Zuzzolo) Liccione; m. William Lawrence Stewart, July 18, 1975. BA, Columbia U., 1971; MA, Columbia Tchr.'s Coll., N.Y.C., 1973; MAT, Manhattanville Coll., 1973. Author, cons. Kimbo Ednl., Long Branch, N.J., 1970—; spl. edn. tchr. Tuckahoe (N.Y.) High Sch., 1989—; cons. NAEYC, SACUS, 1975-89, Pres.'s Coun. on Physical Fitness, 1979-81. Author 58 children's musical activity records and books including: Adaptive Motor Learning, 1982, Bean Bag Activities, 1983, Preschool Aerobic Fun, 1989, Children of the World, 1991, Multicultural Rhythm Stick Fun, 1992, Toddlerific, 1993. Mem. AAHPERD, Nat. Assn. for Edn. of Young Children, So. Assn. for Children Under Six, Assn. for Retarded Citizens, Columbia Club, Women's Nat. Rep. Club. Avocations: after school dance program, organizing local benefit programs. Home: 81 Pondfield Rd #328 Bronxville NY 10708-0625 Office: Kimbo Ednl PO Box 477 Long Branch NJ 07740-0477

STEWART, GORDON CURRAN, insurance information association executive; b. Chgo., July 22, 1939; s. Henry Stewart and Evangeline (Williams) Bolton; m. Elizabeth Knorr, June 19, 1965 (div. 1968); m. Zenne Early, Dec. 20, 1995. BA, Oberlin Coll., 1960; MA, U. Chgo., 1961; student, U. Vienna, Austria, 1963; MFA, Yale U., 1967. Instr. Amherst (Mass.) Coll., 1967-68; dir. Bus. Comm. for Arts, N.Y.C., 1969-71; exec. asst. Mayor of N.Y.C., 1971-73; dir., writer N.Y.C., L.A., U.K., 1973-78; dep. chief speechwriter President of U.S., Washington, 1978-81; instr. Bus. and Govt. Acad. forums, U.S and fgn. countries, 1981-82; v.p. AMSE, N.Y.C., 1982-89; exec. v.p. Ins. Info. Inst., N.Y.C., 1989-91, pres., 1991—; cons. Am. Bus. Conf., Washington, 1982-89, Internat. Commn. for Ctrl. Am., Washington, 1986-88, Coun. on Competitiveness, Washington, 1987-88, Def. Sci. Bd., Washington, 1988-89. Writer films: The Store, 1978, Joey, 1978, Gallery, 1978; dir. (play) The Elephant Man (1st U.S. prodn.), 1977, Jesse, 1975, Cowboy Mouth, 1976, Sleep, 1977, (films) The Blazers, 1975; condr. Beggar's Opera, 1969, West Side Story, 1970. Dir. N.Y. Urban Coalition, N.Y.C., 1984-88; dir. policy Samuels for Gov., N.Y., 1974; speechwriter numerous dem. campaigns, 1974-81; mem. fin. coun. Dem. Nat. Com., 1984-88; mem. adv. coun. Dem. Leadership Coun., 1984-90. Woodrow Wilson fellow Woodrow Wilson Found., 1961. Mem. Writers Guild Am. (west), Judson Welliver Soc. of Chief Presdl. Speechwriters (sec.-treas.), Coun. Fgn. Rels., Century Assn., Yale Club. Avocations: politics, music.

STEWART, GUY HARRY, university dean emeritus, journalism educator; b. Keyser, W.Va., Feb. 12, 1924; s. Thomas R. and Martha (Mills) S.; m. Patricia Ann Groves, Dec. 27, 1948; children: Diane, Thomas, Jeffrey. B.S.J., W.Va. U., 1948, M.A., 1949; Ph.D., U. Ill., 1957. Reporter Cumberland (Md.) Evening Times, 1941-43, Mineral Daily News-Tribune, Keyser, 1941-43; asst. editor W.Va. U., Morgantown, 1949-50, dir. grad. studies and journalism, 1960-69, dean Sch. Journalism, 1969-89; dir. pub. rels., prof. Tenn. Tech. U., Cookeville, 1950-60. Author: A Touch of Charisma, 1969. Served as ensign USNR, 1944-46, PTO. Recipient P.I. Reed Achievement award W.Va. U. Journalism ALumni Assn., 1977; named to Keyser High Sch. Legion of Honor, 1991; Guy H. Stewart Journalism Endowment Fund named in his honor. Mem. W.Va. Press Assn. (life), Assn. Edn. in Journalism and Mass Communications, Rotary (dist. gov. 1983-84), Kappa Tau Alpha (nat. pres. 1980, Top Adviser award 1987). Democrat. Methodist. Home: 525 Pocahontas Ave Morgantown WV 26505-2274

STEWART, HAROLD BROWN, biochemist; b. Chatham, Ont., Can., Mar. 9, 1921; s. John Craig and Margaret Gertrude (Brown) S.; m. Audrey Pauline Blake, Oct. 14, 1950; 1 dau., Ann Margaret. M.D., U. Toronto, 1944, Ph.D., 1950; Ph.D., Cambridge (Eng.) U., 1955. Prof. biochemistry U. Western Ont., London, 1960—; chmn. dept. biochemistry U. Western Ont., 1964-72, dean grad. studies, 1972-86, prof. emeritus, 1986—; Med. Research Council Can. vis. scientist dept. biochemistry U. Cambridge, Eng., 1971-72. Contbr. articles in biochemistry to sci. jours. Served with Royal Canadian Navy, 1945-46. Mem. Canadian, U.K. biochem. socs., Canadian Physiol. Soc., Am. Soc. Biochemistry and Molecular Biology, Coll. Physicians and Surgeons of Ont. Home: 118 Baseline Rd E, London, ON Canada N6C 2N8

STEWART, HAROLD LEROY, physician, educator, cancer investigator; b. Houtzdale, Pa., Aug. 6, 1899; s. Alexander and Lillie (Cox) S.; m. Cecelia Eleanor Finn, Sept. 30, 1929; children: Robert Campbell, Janet Eileen. Student, U. Pa., 1919-20, Dickinson Coll., 1921-22; M.D., Jefferson Med. Coll., 1926; grad., Army Med. Sch., Washington, 1929; research fellow, Jefferson Med. Coll., 1929-30, Harvard, 1937-39; Med. Sc.D. (hon.), Jefferson Med. Coll., 1964; D.Medicine and Surgery (hon.), U. Perugia, 1965, U. Turku, Finland, 1970; Doctor (hon.), Kagawa (Japan) Med. Sch., 1992. Diplomate Am. Bd. Pathology, Pan Am. Med. Assn. Intern Fitzimmons Gen. Hosp., Denver, 1926-27; instr. to asst. prof. pathology Jefferson Med. Coll., 1930-37; asst. pathologist Jefferson Med. Coll. Hosp., Phila. Gen. Hosp., 1929-37; pathologist Office Cancer Investigations Harvard, USPHS, 1937-39; chief lab. pathology Nat. Cancer Inst., USPHS, Bethesda, Md., 1939-69; chief pathologic anatomy dept. clin. ctr. NIH, 1954-69; organizer Registry Exptl. Cancers, 1970—, Sci. emeritus, 1976—; prin. investigator, head WHO Collaborating Centre for Rsch. on Tumors Lab. Animals, 1976-96; clin. prof. pathology Georgetown U., 1965—; Cons. FDA, 1969-71, Nat. Cancer Inst., 1970-76, Armed Forces Inst. Pathology, 1950—; cons., mem. study groups WHO, 1957-81, mem. expert adv. panel cancer, 1957-81; Mem. subcom. oncology NRC, 1947-65, mem. com. pathology, 1958-66, com. cancer diagnosis and therapy, 1951-57, mem. com. animal models and genetic stocks, 1972-75, chmn. com. histologic classification Lab. Animal Tumors, 1975-79; chmn. subcom. classification rat liver tumors NRC (Lab. Animal Tumors), 1976-79; chmn. U.S.A. Com. Internat. Coun. Socs. Pathology, 1957-62, 69-75; chmn. U.S. nat. com. Internat. Union Against Cancer, 1953-59, U.S. del., 1952-74; Mem. adv. bd. Leonard Wood Meml., 1961-66; mem. com. to advance world-wide fight against cancer Am. Cancer Soc., 1963-76; mem. med. rsch. coun. Referees, New Zealand, 1987. Mem. editoral bd. Cancer Rsch., 1941-49, A.M.A. Archives of Pathology, 1957-62, Jour. Toxicology Pathology, 1988; editorial adviser Jour. Nat. Cancer Inst, 1947-56; contbr. articles to profl. jours. Trustee Thomas Jefferson U., Phila., 1969-72. Served as pvt. USMC, 1918-19; lt. M.C. U.S. Army, 1926-29; from maj. to lt. col. M.C. AUS, 1942-46. Recipient Lucy Wortham James award James Ewing Soc., 1967, Alumni Achievement award Jefferson Med. Coll., 1966, Disting. Svc. award HEW, 1966, Honors award NIH, The Dirs. award NIH, 1988, Dean's medal Jefferson Med. Coll., 1994; Dedication Jour. Exptl. Pathology, Vol. 1, No. 2, 1987, Harold L. Stewart Fund for Exptl. Pathology and Harold L. Stewart Lectureship established at Uniformed Svcs. U. of Health Scis., Bethesda, Md., 1986; honored by dedication in two books. Mem. Soc. Clin. Pathologists (Ward Burdick award 1957), Am. Assn. Cancer Rsch. (pres. 1958-59), Am. Soc. Exptl. Pathology (hon., pres. 1995), Am. Assn. Pathologists (Gold-headed Cane award 1978), Coll. Am. Pathologists, Md. Soc. Pathologists (pres. 1950-51), Washington Soc. Pathologists (sec.-treas. 1947-51), Internat. Acad. Pathology (pres. 1953-55, F.K. Mostofi award 1976), Internat. Union Against Cancer (exec. com. 1952-70, v.p. 1962), Mass. Med. Soc., Internat. Coun. Socs. Pathology (pres. 1962), Internat. Soc. Geog. Pathology, Colegio Anatomico Brasilerio (hon.), Soc. Italiana di Cancerologia (hon.), Inst. Nat. de Cancerologia Mex. (hon.), Soc. Columbiana de Patologia (hon.), Soc. Belge d' Anatomie Pathologique (hon.), Soc. Peruana Cancerologia (hon.), Soc. Cryobiology, Soc. Toxicologic Pathologists (hon.), Japanese Cancer Soc. (hon.), Basic Found. Internat. Inst of Immanopathology Clin. Ctr. Humablt U., Berlin (hon. sci. dir.), Purdy Stout Surg. Pathology Soc. (hon.), others. Home: 119 S Adams St Rockville MD 20850-2315

STEWART, HARRIS BATES, JR., oceanographer; b. Auburn, N.Y., Sept. 19, 1922; s. Harris B. and Mildred (Woodruff) S.; m. Elise Bennett Cunningham, Feb. 21, 1959; children: Dorothy Cunningham, Harry Hasburgh; 2d m. Louise Conant Thompson, Dec. 22, 1988. Grad., Phillips Exeter Acad., 1941; AB, Princeton, 1948; MS, Scripps Instn. Oceanography, U. Calif., 1952, PhD, 1956. Hydrographic engr. U.S. Navy Hydrographic Office expdn. to Persian Gulf, 1948-49; instr. Hotchkiss Sch., 1949-51; research asst. Scripps Instn. Oceanography, 1951-56; diving geologist, project mgr. Geol. Diving Cons., Inc., San Diego, 1953-57; chief oceanographer U.S. Coast & Geodetic Survey, 1957-65, dept. asst. dir., 1962-65; dir. Inst. Oceanography, Environmental Sci. Services Adminstrn., U.S. Dept. Commerce, 1965-69; dir. Atlantic Oceanographic and Meteorol. Labs., NOAA, 1969-78, cons., 1978-80; prof. marine sci., dir. Center for Marine Studies, Old Dominion U., Norfolk, Va., 1980-85; adj. prof. dept. oceanography Old Dominion U., 1986—; dir. S.E. Bank of Dadeland; chmn. Fla. Commn. Marine Sci. and Tech.; mem. exec. com., earth scis. div. Nat. Acad. Scis.; chmn. adv. bd. Nat. Oceanographic Data Center, 1965-66; chmn. survey panel interagy. com. oceanography Fed. Council Sci. and Tech., 1959-67; chmn. adv. com. undersea features U.S. Bd. Geog. Names, 1964-67; mem. sci. party No. Holiday Expdn., 1951; Capricorn Expdn., 1952-53; chief scientist Explorer Oceanographic Expdn., 1960, Pioneer Indian Ocean Expdn., 1964, Discoverer Expdn., 1968, NOAA-Carib Expdn., 1972, Researcher Expdn., 1975; mem. U.S. delegation Intergovtl. Oceanographic Commn., 1961-65; mem. Gov. Calif. Adv. Commn. Marine Resources; chmn. adv. council Dept. Geol. and Geophys. Scis. Princeton; v.p. Dade Marine Inst., 1976-77, pres., 1977-79; trustee, mem. exec. com. Assoc. Marine Insts.; mem. Fisheries Mgmt. Adv. Council Va. Marine Resources Commn., 1984-85; vice chmn. adv. council Univ. Nat. Oceanographic Lab. System, 1983-85; U.S. nat. assoc. to intergovtl. oceanographic commn. UNESCO program for Caribbean, 1964-89, vice chmn., 1974. Author: The Global Sea, 1963, Deep Challenge, 1966, The Id of the Squid, 1970, Challenger Sketchbook, 1972, No Dinosaurs on the Ark, 1988, Grungy George and Sloppy Sally, 1993, Injections of Hospital Humor, 1996. Bd. dirs. Vanguard Sch., Miami, 1974-76; trustee Metro Zoo, Miami, 1991—. Served as pilot USAAF, 1942-46, PTO. Decorated comendador Almirante Padilla (Colombia); recipient Meritorious award Dept. Commerce, 1960, Exceptional Service award, 1965. Fellow AAAS, Geol. Soc. Am., Nat. Tropical Bot. Gardens, Marine Tech. Soc. (v.p.); mem. Fla. Acad. Scis. (pres. 1978-79), Va. Acad. Sci., Am. Geophys. Union, Internat. Oceanographic Found. (v.p. 1974-80), Zool. Soc. Fla. (pres. 1970-73), Maine Hist. Soc., Marine Hist. Assn., Cape Ann Hist. Assn., Marine Coun. (Miami), Explorers Club (N.Y.), Prouts Neck (Maine) Yacht Club, Cosmos Club (D.C.), Club Pelican Bay (Naples, Fla.). Presbyterian. Home (summer): 11 Atlantic Dr Scarborough ME 04074-8667 Home (winter): 720 Shadow Lake Ln Naples FL 33963-8500

STEWART, HOMER JOSEPH, engineering educator; b. Elba, Mich., Aug. 15, 1915; s. Earl Arthur and Alta Fern (Stanley) S.; m. Frieda Klassen, June 15, 1940; children—Robert Joseph, Katherine Stanley, Barbara Ellen. Student, U. Dubuque, 1932-33; B in Aero. Engring., U. Minn., 1936; PhD, Calif. Inst. Tech., 1940. Faculty Jet Propulsion Lab. Calif. Inst. Tech., Pasadena, 1938—, prof. aeros., 1949-80, prof. emeritus, 1980—, chief research analysis sect., 1945-56, chief Liquid Propulsion Systems div., 1956-58, spl. asst. to dir., 1960-62, chief Advanced Studies Office, 1963-67, advanced studies adviser, 1967-76; dir. Sargent Industries, Inc., 1964-79, Office Program Planning and Evaluation, NASA, 1958-60; mem. tech. adv. bd. Aerojet-Gen. Corp., 1956-58, 61-70; mem. tech. evaluation group guided missile com. Research and Devel. Bd., 1948-50, chmn., 1951; mem. sci. adv. bd. USAF, 1949-56, 1959-64; mem. sci. adv. com. Ballistics Research Lab., 1959-69, 73-77. Author: Kinematics and Dynamics of Fluid Flow, sect. VI Handbook of Meteorology, 1945; Contbr. articles to tech. jours. Recipient Outstanding Achievement award U. Minn., 1954, NASA Exceptional Service medal, 1970, I.B. Laskowitz award N.Y. Acad. Scis., 1985. Fellow AIAA; mem. Am. Meteorol. Soc., Internat. Acad. Astronautics, Sigma Xi, Tau Beta Pi. Home: 2393 Tanoble Dr Altadena CA 91001-2729 Office: Calif Inst Tech Advanced Studies Off Pasadena CA 91109

STEWART, ISAAC DANIEL, JR., judge; b. Salt Lake City, Nov. 21, 1932; s. Isaac Daniel and Orabelle (Iverson) S.; m. Elizabeth Bryan, Sept. 10, 1959; children: Elizabeth Ann, Shannon. BA with high honors, U. Utah, 1959, JD with high honors, 1962. Bar: Utah 1962, U.S. Dist. Ct. Utah 1962, U.S. Ct. Appeals (10th cir.) 1962, U.S. Ct. Appeals (4th cir.) 1963, U.S. Ct. Appeals (9th cir.) 1964, U.S. Ct. Appeals (8th cir.) 1965, U.S. Supreme Ct. 1965. Atty. antitrust divsn. Dept. Justice, Washington, 1962-65; asst. prof., then assoc. prof. U. Utah Coll. Law, 1965-70; ptnr. Jones, Waldo, Holbrook & McDonough, Salt Lake City, 1970-79; assoc. chief justice Utah Supreme Ct., 1979—, 1986-88, 94—; presiding judge 2nd dist. Utah Dist. Ct., Ogden, 1988—; lectr. in field; mem. Utah Bd. Oil, Gas and Mining, 1976-78, chmn., 1977-78; Utah rep. Interstate Oil Compact Commn., 1977-78, exec. com. 1978-79; mem. adv. com. rules of procedure Utah Supreme Ct., 1983-87; chmn. com. on bar-press guidelines Utah Bar. Editor-in-chief Utah Law Rev.; contbr. articles to legal jours. Chmn. subcom. on legal rights and responsibilities of youth Utah Gov's Com. on Youth, 1972; pres. Salt Lake chpt. Coun. Fgn. Rels., 1982; mem. Salt Lake City C. of C., 1974-79, mem. govtl. modernization com., 1976-78; missionary for Mormon Ch. in Fed. Republic Germany, 1953-56; bd. dirs. U. Utah Alumni Assn., 1986-89. Recipient Alumnus of Yr. award U. Utah Coll. Law, 1989. Mem. ABA, Utah Bar Assn. (com. on law and poverty 1967-69, com. on specialization 1977-78, pub. rels. com. 1968-69, chmn. com. on antitrust law 1977-78, com. on civil procedure reform 1968, mem. exec. com. bd. of appellate judges 1990—, Appellate Judge of Yr. 1986), Salt Lake County Bar Assn., Am. Judicature Soc., Order of Coif, Phi Beta Kappa, Phi Kappa Phi, Sigma Chi (Significant Sig award 1987). Office: 322 State Capital Salt Lake City UT 84114*

STEWART, J. DANIEL, air force development and test center administrator; b. Savannah, Ga., June 20, 1941; s. Benjamin F. and Bessie L. (Edenfield) S.; m. Rebecca M. Smith; children: Daniel, Laura. BS in Aero. Engring., Ga. Inst. Tech., 1963, MS in Aero. Engring., 1965, PhD in Aero. Engring., 1967; M. in Mgmt. Sci., Stanford U., 1979. Mem. tech. staff applied mechanics divsn. Aerospace Corp., El Segundo, Calif., 1967-74; br. chief tech. divsn. Air Force Rocket Propulsion Lab., Edwards AFB, Calif., 1974-78, asst. for R&D mgmt., 1979-81; divsn. chief Air Force Armament Divsn., Eglin AFB, Fla., 1981-83; dir. drone control program office 3246 Test Wing, Eglin AFB, Fla., 1983-85, joint dir. US/Allied munitions program office, 1985-86; tech. dir. rsch./devel./acquisitions Air Force Armament Divsn., Eglin AFB, Fla., 1986-88; asst. to comdr. Air Force Munitions Divsn., Eglin AFB, Fla., 1988-90; tech. dir. Air Force Devel. and Test Ctr., Eglin AFB, 1990-93, exec. dir., 1993—; mem. policy coun. Scientist and Engr. Career Program, Randolph AFB, Tex., 1994—, chmn. career devel. panel, 1994—. Bd. dirs. Internat. Found. for Telemetering, Woodland Hills, Calif., 1991—; mem. engring. adv. bd. U. Fla., Gainesville, 1988—; mem. citizens adv. com. U. West Fla., Pensacola, 1991—; mem. civilian exec. adv. bd. Air Force Materiel Command, 1990—, also former chmn.; mem. curricular adv. com. Def. Test and Evaluation Profl. Inst., 1991—. Recipient Presdl. Meritorious Rank award Pres. of U.S., 1993. Mem. Air Force Assn. (Lewis H. Brereton award 1994), Sr. Exec. Assn., Am. Def. Preparedness Assn., Internat. Test and Evaluation Assn. (Cross medal 1994), Assn. of Old Crows, Fed. Exec. Inst. Alumni, Gulf Coast Alliance for Tech. Transfer. Avocations: tennis, golf, fishing. Office: AFDTC CD 101 W D Ave Ste 117 Eglin AFB FL 32542-5490

STEWART, JAMES B., journalist. With Wall St. Jour., N.Y.C., 1983—, now editor. Author: Holy Warriors: The Abolitionists and American Slavery, The Partners: Inside America's Most Powerful Law Firms, 1984, Wendell Phillips: Liberty's Hero, 1986, The Prosecutors, 1987. Pulitzer Prize for Explanatory Journalism, 1987. Office: Wall St Jour Dow Jones & Co 200 Liberty St New York NY 10281-1003

STEWART, JAMES BREWER, historian, author, college administrator; b. Cleve., Aug. 8, 1940; s. Richard Henry and Marion Elizabeth (Brewer) S.; m. Dorothy Ann Carlson; children: Rebecca Ann, Jennifer Lynn. BA, Dartmouth Coll., 1962; PhD, Case Western Res. U., 1968. Asst. prof. history Carrol Coll., Waukesha, Wis., 1968-69; asst. prof. history Macalester Coll., St. Paul, 1969-79, James Wallace prof. history, 1979—, provost, 1986-89; cons. Am. Coun. of Learned Socs., N.Y.C., 1988-92. Author: Joshua R. Giddings & the Tactics of Radical Politics, 1970, Holy Warriors: Abolitionists & Slavery, 1976, Liberty's Hero: Wendell Phillips, 1986 (Best Biography award, Soc. Midland Authors 1986), William Lloyd Garrison and the Challenge of Emmancipation, 1992. Rsch. fellow NEH, 1973, Am. Coun. Learned Socs., 1984. Mem. Am. Hist. Assn., Orgn. Am. Historians (nom. com. 1988-92), Soc. Historians of the Early Republic (exec. com. 1987—). Avocations: camping, gardening, furniture restoration. Home: 1924 Princeton Ave Saint Paul MN 55105-1523 Office: Macalester Coll Dept Of History Saint Paul MN 55105

STEWART, JAMES GATHINGS, insurance company executive; b. Fort Wayne, Ind., Oct. 5, 1942; s. Gathings and Mary (Sieber) S.; m. Janet Kartalia, Feb. 19, 1966; children: John, David, Mitchell, Rebecca. B.A., DePauw U., 1964; M.A.S., U. Mich., 1965. Various fin. positions Conn. Gen. Life Ins. Co., Hartford, Conn., 1966-77; v.p. Conn. Gen. Life Ins. Co., 1977-82; exec. v.p., chief fin. officer CIGNA Corp., Phila., 1983—. Fellow Soc. Actuaries; mem. Am. Acad. Actuaries. Republican. Office: Cigna Corp 1 Liberty Pl PO Box 7716 1650 Market St Philadelphia PA 19192-1550*

STEWART, JAMES IAN, agricultural water scientist, cropping system developer, consultant; b. San Diego, Jan. 9, 1928; s. Castle Elmore and Myrtle Catherine (Hasty) S.; m. Robbie Nell Oliver, Mar. 23, 1975; children: Virginia Lane Stewart Carton, Ian Castle Stewart, Kevin Scott Overby. BSc, U. Calif., Berkeley, 1950; PhD, U. Calif., Davis, 1972. Farm advisor Agrl. Extension Svc., U. Calif., Stockton and Merced, 1950-61; extension expert Irrigation, Food and Agrl. Orgn. UN, Nicosia, Cyprus, 1962-66; assoc. rsch. water scientist U. Calif., Davis, 1966-77; supervisory soil scientist USDA/Office for Internat. Cooperation and Devel., Nairobi, Kenya, 1977-83; team leader, agrometeorologist USAID/Kenya Mission, 1977-83; founder, pres. Found. for World Hunger Alleviation Through Response Farming (WHARF), Davis, 1984—; cons., agrometeorology AID, USDA, World Bank, FAO/UNDP, 35 countries of Ams., Europe, Asia, Africa, Australia, 1965—; sci. convocations, internat. 14 countries worldwide, 1969—. Author: Response Farming in Rainfed Agriculture, 1988; creator (computer programs) Wharf, Wharfdat, 1990; contbr. numerous articles to profl. jours. Mem. Am. Soc. Agronomy, Crop Sci. Soc. Am., Soil Sci. Soc. Am., Internat. Soil Sci. Soc., World Assn. Soil and Water Conservation, Internat. Com. for Irrigation and Drainage (life, U.S. com.), Indian Soc. Dryland Agr. (life), Internat. Platform Assn., Sigma Xi, Phi Delta Theta. Achievements include pioneering research on soil water extraction by crops; crop water requirements; relations between crop yield and water evapotranspired; impacts of water deficits in different crop growth stages; relations between season rainfall behavior and season dates of onset. Developer of FAO world standard linear and weighted growth stage models for estimating crop yields from actual evapotranscription, and contributor to four-growth-period linear model for estimating crop water requirements. Developer of "response farming" methodology for design of dryland cropping systems based on historical rainfall behavior, and seasonal flexibility in their management based on real-time rainfall season date of onset, defined to meet crop establishment requirements. Home: 640 Portsmouth Ave Davis CA 95616-2738 Office: World Hunger Allev Through Response Farming PO Box 1158 Davis CA 95617-1158

STEWART, JAMES KEVIN, judicial administrator, management technology consultant; b. Berkeley, Calif., Nov. 28, 1942; s. Berthold and Myrle (Minson) S.; m. Marise Rene Duff, Oct. 26, 1985; children: Daphne Brooks, Andrew MacLaren, James Kevin Spencer, Mary Elizabeth Ainsley. B.S., U. Oreg., 1964; M.P.A., Calif. State U.-Hayward, 1977; grad. cert., U. Va., 1978; grad., FBI Nat. Acad., 1978. Cmmdr. criminal investigation div. Oakland Police Dept., 1976-81; instr. San Jose (Calif.) State U., 1978-81; spl. asst. atty. gen. Dept. Justice, Washington, 1981-82; dir. Nat. Inst. Justice, Washington, 1982-90, Booz, Allen & Hamilton, Inc., McLean, Va., 1990—; guest lectr. U. Calif., Berkeley, Harvard, U.; steering com. global organized crime initiative Ctr. Strategic Internat. Studies, 1994; U.S. del. Couns. of Europe, Strasborg, France, 1984; advisor DOD/DOJ Ops. Other Than War and Law Enforcement, 1994; chmn. pun. safety conf. SPTE, 1992; advisor, chmn. Dept. Justice Nat. Conf. Law Enforcement Tech., 21st Century, Washington, 1993; bd. dirs. White House Fellows Found., 1990; mem. Internat. Law Enforcement Conf., Washington, 1995. Recipient O.W. Wilson award for outstanding contbns. to law enforcement, 1986, Ennis J. Olgiati award Nat. Assn. Pre-Trial Services Agys., 1987, Predl. citation AIA, 1987, Nat. Criminal Justice Service award Nat. Criminal Justice Assn., 1988, Outstanding Nat. Contbn. to Policing Spl. award Police Exec. Research Forum, 1988, August Vollmer award Am. Soc. Criminology, 1992; White House fellow, 1981-82. Mem. Internat. Assn. Chiefs of Police (dir. 1981-82), Police Mgmt. Assn. (founder, pres. 1979-81), White House Fellows Alumni, White House Fellows Found. (bd. dirs.), FBI Nat. Acad. Assn., Internat. Homicide Investigation Assn. (charter), Nat. Inst. Corrections (bd. dirs.), Soc. for Reform of Criminal Law (planning chmn. Police Powers and Citizens Rights Conf.), Coun. For Excellence In Govt. (prin.), Delta Upsilon. Republican. Episcopalian. Club: University (Washington). Home: 6427 Lakeview Dr Falls Church VA 22041-1330 Office: Booz Allen & Hamilton Inc 8283 Greensboro Dr Mc Lean VA 22102-3838

STEWART, JAMES MAITLAND, actor; b. Indiana, Pa., May 20, 1908; s. Alexander Maitland and Elizabeth Ruth (Jackson) S.; m. Gloria McLean, Aug. 9, 1949 (dec. Feb. 1994); children: Michael, Ronald (dec.), Judy and Kelly (twins). BS in Architecture, Princeton U., 1932; hon. degree, Indiana U. of Pa., U. S.C., Chapman Coll.; 7 other hon. degrees. Appeared in N.Y.C. in: Goodbye Again, 1932, Yellow Jack, Divided by Three and Page Miss Glory, 1934; motion pictures include Mr. Smith Goes to Washington, 1939, The Philadelphia Story, 1940, It's a Wonderful Life, 1946, Rear Window, 1954, Far Country, 1955, Man from Laramie, 1955, Strategic Air Command, 1955, The Man Who Knew too Much, 1956, Night Passage, 1957 Spirit of St. Louis, 1957, Vertigo, 1958, Bell, Book and Candle, 1959, It's a Wonderful World, 1959, Anatomy of Murder, 1959, The FBI, 1959, The Mountain Road, 1960, Two Rode Together, 1961, Mr. Hobbs Takes a Vacation, 1962, How the West Was Won, 1962, Take Her, She's Mine, 1963, Cheyenne Autumn, 1964, The Rare Breed, 1966, Flight of the Phoenix, 1966, Firecreek, 1968, Bandolero, 1968, Cheyenne Social Club, 1970, Fool's Parade, 1971, That's Entertainment, 1974, The Shootist, 1976, Airport '77, 1977, The Big Sleep, 1978, The Magic of Lassie, 1978, Right of Way, 1983, TV show The Jimmy Stewart Show, 1971-72, Hawkins Murder, 1973-74; author: Jimmy Stewart and His Poems, 1989 (Recipient N.Y. Critics award for best male performance of 1939 in Mr. Smith Goes to Washington, Acad. award for performance in Philadelphia Story 1940, Berlin Film award 1962, Life Achievement award Am. Film Inst. 1980). Col. A.C., U.S. Army, World War II; brig. gen. USAFR, 1959. Decorated D.F.C. with oak leaf cluster, Air medal, Croix de Guerre with palm; recipient Lifetime Achievement award Screen Actors Guild, 1968, Disting. Performance award Drama League, 1970, Nat. Artist award Am. Nat. Acad. and Theatre, 1981, Kennedy Ctr. medal for lifetime achievement, 1983, Spl. Career Oscar, 1984, Presdl. medal of Freedom, 1985, Lifetime Achievement award Santa Barbara Film Festival, 1987, Lifetime Achievement award Monterey Film Festival, 1988, Lifetime Achievement award Am. Mus. of the Moving Image, 1988, Master Screen Artist award Dallas Film Festival, 1989, Ann. Spencer Tracy award UCLA, 1989, Woodrow Wilson medal Princeton U., 1990, Ann. Tribute N.Y. Film Soc., 1990, Ann. Tribute Film soc. of Lincoln Ctr., 1990, Career Achievement award Nat. Bd. Rev., 1991, Lifetime Achievement award Internat. Film Festival, 1992, Palm award Palm Springs Internat. Film Festival, 1992. Presbyterian.

STEWART, JAMES MONTGOMERY, banker; b. Detroit, May 31, 1939; s. Albert Edwin and Dagny Winter (Jensen) S.; m. Kathleen Williams, Sept. 27, 1940; children—Laura, Wendy, Kathleen. B.B.A., U. Mich., 1962, M.B.A., 1963. Asst. sec. Irving Trust Co., N.Y.C., 1966-68, asst. v.p., 1968-70, v.p., 1970-81, sr. v.p., 1981-86; regional gen. mgr. Copenhagen Handelsbank, 1986-90; gen. mgr. Den Danske Bank, N.Y.C., 1990—. Trustee Am. Scandinavian Found. Mem. Danish Am. C. of C. (bd. dirs.), Anglers Club, Links Club, Racquet & Tennis Club, Country Club New Canaan, Beta Gamma Sigma. Republican. Avocations: trout fishing; golf; jazz; wine. Home: 130 Ramhorne Rd New Canaan CT 06840-3007 Office: Den Danske Bank 280 Park Ave New York NY 10017-1216

STEWART, JANE, psychology educator; b. Ottawa, Ont., Can., Apr. 19, 1934; d. Daniel Wallace and Jessie Stewart; m. Dalbir Bindra, Aug. 5, 1959 (dec. 1981). BA with honours, Queen's U., Kingston, Ont., 1956; PhD, U. London, 1959; DSc (hon.), Queen's U., 1992. Sr. rsch. biologist Ayerst Labs., Montreal, Que., 1959-63; part-time instr. psychology Sir George, Montreal, 1962-63; assoc. prof. psychology Williams U., Montreal, 1963-69; prof., chmn. psychology SGW Univ. (now Concordia U.), Montreal, 1969-75; prof. psychology Concordia U., Montreal, 1975—; dir. Ctr. for Studies in Behavioral Neurobiology, Concordia U., Montreal, 1990—. Fellow AAAS, APA, Can. Psychol. Assn.; mem. Soc. for Neurosci., Corp. Psychologists Province of Que., N.Y. Acad. Sci. Office: Concordia University, 1455 de Maisonneuve Blvd W, Montreal, PQ Canada H3G 1M8

STEWART, JEFF, advertising agency executive; b. N.Y.C., May 19, 1939; s. Andrew S. and Rose (Leider) S.; m. Linda Dorr McGehee, Sept. 12, 1959; children: Charles, David, Andrea. BS, Columbia Coll., 1960. Asst. prodn. mgr. Denhard & Stewart, Inc., N.Y.C., 1960-62, art dir., 1963-66, account exec., 1966-71, pres., 1973—. Author: Trade Book Mktg., 1982. Pres. Middlesex County Young Dems., 1963-64; vol. Old Bridge Vol. Fire Dept., East Brunswick, N.J., 1963-66; scoutmaster Troop 7 Boy Scouts Am., Upper Montclair, N.J., 1970-81; elder, Presbyn. Ch., Upper Montclair, 1979-84. Mem. Commonwealth Club, Players Club. Avocations: cycling, skiing, golf, canoeing, backpacking. Home: 204 Old Beach Glen Rd Boonton NJ 07005-9525 Office: Denhard & Stewart Inc 240 Madison Ave New York NY 10016-2820

STEWART, JEFFREE ROBERT, environmental planner, artist; b. Concord, N.H., June 20, 1956; s. Robert Davison and Ruth Florence (Olney) S. BA, Evergreen State Coll., Olympia, Wash., 1983; postgrad., U. Wash., 1983-84, Inst. Creative Devel., 1989-91. River guide rafting Rio Bravo, Inc., Durango, Colo., 1981-82; forester, planner Wash. State Parks Commn., Olympia, 1983-84; fisheries biologist U. Wash., Seattle, Alaska and Aleutians, 1984-86; pub. affairs rschr. NOAA, Seattle, 1986; hazardous waste project mgr. Washington Ecology Dept., Olympia, 1987, marine waste disposal project mgr., 1988-92, interagy. liaison, facilitator policy and tech. adv. groups, 1989-90, shorelands planner, 1992—; mem. ecology art com. Ecology Dept., Olympia, 1994; mem. adv. bd. Washington Heritage Conf., Olympia, 1992; exhbns. team coord. Arts Olympia, 1993-94, mem. steering group, 1994-96. One man shows include Batdorf & Bronson, Olympia, 1989, 91, 93, 94, Colophon Cafe, Bellingham, Wash., 1987, Dancing Goats, Olympia, 1992, Hungry Moon, LaConner, 1993, Thompson Gallery, 1995; exhibited in groups shows at Janet Huston Gallery, LaConner, 1991, 92, 93, Wash. State Capitol Mus., Olympia, 1991, 92, 93, Childhoods End Gallery, 1995, 96, Evergreen State Coll., 1993, Wash. Ctr. Performing Arts, 1992, 93, 94, Valley Mus. N.W. Art, 1994, Tacoma Art Mus., 1995, also pvt. collections. Bd. trustees Evergreen State Coll., Olympia, 1981. Recipient Competent/Able Toastmaster awards Toastmasters Internat., 1989, 91, Oil Painting award of Merit Wash. State Capitol Mus., Olympia, 1993, Wash. Pub. Employees Assn. (bd. dirs. 1992-93), Meridian Toastmasters (pres., v.p. 1989-91). Mem. Arts Olympia (steering group 1994—), Profl. Geographers of Puget Sound, Wash. Planners Assn., Burke Meml. Mus., Mus. N.W. Art, Tacoma Art Mus., Belleuve Art Mus. Avocations: art collecting and curating, kayaking, freelance journalism, mountaineering. Home: PO Box 7397 Olympia WA 98507-7397 Office: Wash Ecology Dept PO Box 47609 Olympia WA 98504

STEWART, JEFFREY BAYRD, lawyer; b. Chgo., Feb. 6, 1952; s. Bruce A. and Harriet B. Stewart. A.B. magna cum laude (Rufus Choate scholar), Dartmouth Coll., 1974; J.D., Emory U., 1978. Bar: Ga. 1978, U.S. Dist. Ct. (no. dist.) Ga., U.S. Ct. Appeals (5th and 11th dists.). Ptnr., chair corp. dept., Arnall Golden & Gregory, Atlanta, 1978—. Mem. editorial bd. Emory Law Jour., 1977-78. Mem. ABA, State Bar Ga. Home: 4110 Pine Heights Dr Atlanta GA 30324 Office: Arnall Golden & Gregory 1201 W Peachtree St Atlanta GA 30309-3450

STEWART, JOANNE, secondary school educator; b. Vancouver, Wash., Mar. 10, 1944; d. Edward Charles and Claudine Marie (Meilleur) Spencer; m. William Lemley Stewart, Sept. 2, 1966 (dec. June 1983); children: Amy Diane, Nicholas William. BS, Wash. State U., 1966, MA, 1973. Cert. tchr., Mont., Idaho, Wash., Calif. Tchr. foods Seaside High Sch., Monterey, Calif., 1966-67; tchr. home econs. Marysville (Wash.) High Sch., 1967-68, Palouse (Wash.) High Sch., 1968-73, Ennis (Mont.) High Sch., 1973-76, Genesee (Idaho) High Sch., 1976-77; instr. young family Missoula (Mont.) County High Sch., 1983-84; tchr. home econs. Woodman Sch., Lolo, Mont., 1985-86; travel cons. Travel Masters, Missoula, 1984-87; ticketing mgr. Blue Caboose Travel, Missoula, 1987-91; tchr. family and consumer scis. Victor (Mont.) High Sch., 1991—. Co-pres. Lolo PTO, 1980-81; v.p. Lolo Community Ctr., 1981; sec. Lolo Mosquito Control Bd., 1988—; mem. telecommunications com. Conrad Burns & Gov. Racicot. Marysville Edn. Assn. scholar, 1962, Future Homemakers Am. scholar, 1962. Mem. AAUW (sec. 1986, program chmn. 1987), Forestry Triangle (pres. 1981, editor cookbook 1982), Future Homemakers Am. (hon. advisor), Am. Family and Consumer Scis. Assn., Mont. Family and Consumer Scis. Assn. (bylaws chair 1994, pres. 1996—, pres. elect 1995-96), Mont. Vocat. Tchrs. Assn. (returning Rookie of Yr. 1992, Am. Federated Tchrs., Mont. Vocat. Family and Consumer Scis. Tchrs. (v.p. 1993-94, pres. 1994-95). Republican. Methodist. Avocations: homemaking, swimming. Home: 1200 Lakeside Dr Lolo MT 59847-9705 Office: Victor High Sch Family and Consumer Scis 425 4th Ave Victor MT 59875-9468

STEWART, JOE J., manufacturing executive; b. 1938. BSChemE, Purdue U., 1959; MA, Kansas State U., 1961; PhD, N.C. State U., 1963; DEng (hon.), Purdue U., 1994. With Aerojet-Gen. Corp., 1966-72; with Babcock & Wilcox Co., New Orleans, 1972—, v.p., 1978; pres., COO Babcock & Wilcox Co., Barberton, Ohio, 1993; now pres. Babcock & Wilcox, govt. grp., Lynchburg, VA. Office: Babcock & Wilcox Co Government Group Mt Athos Rd Rt 726 Lynchburg VA 24504*

STEWART, JOHN DAUGHERTY, publishing company executive; b. Indiana, Pa., Oct. 16, 1915; s. Ernest Taylor and Caroline (Daugherty) S.; m.

Helen Gambrill, Sept. 23, 1940 (dec. Jan. 1964); children: Caroline Leigh Stewart Estabrook, Susan Stewart Stockard; m. 2d Margret Pahl, Feb. 18, 1967. A.B., Princeton U., 1937; postgrad., Harvard U., 1938-39. Instr. Sch. Pub. and Internat. Affairs Princeton U., 1937-38; mem. editorial staff Bur. Nat. Affairs, Inc., Washington, 1939-80; v.p. Bur. Nat. Affairs, Inc, Washington, 1947-64; pres., editor-in-chief Bur. Nat. Affairs, Inc., Washington, 1964-80, chmn. bd., 1974-94; Author: Making Employee Ownership Work, 1996; editor: The New Labor Law, 1947, The Landrum-Griffin Act, 1959. Editor: The New Labor Law, 1947, The Landrum-Griffin Act, 1959. Mem. Washington Indsl. Rels. Rsch. Assn. (pres. 1953), Swan Point Yacht and Country Club, Nat. Press Club. Home: 11280 Keokee Ct Issue MD 20645-2206 Office: Bur Nat Affairs Inc 1231 25th St NW Washington DC 20037-1157

STEWART, JOHN EZELL, educational and business consultant; b. Sand Springs, Okla., Aug. 26, 1929; m. Elsie Louise Fonville, June 18, 1954; children: Barry, Johnetta, Rhonda, Howard. BS in Vocat. Edn., Langston (Okla.) U., 1951; MS in Gen. Supervision, Calif. State U., L.A., 1964; grad. study, U. Rich., 1980, 82. Cert. collegiate profl. tchr. Staff supr. Norfolk State U.; acct. exec., v.p. Bus. Devel.; tchr., project mgr. L.A. City Unified Sch. Dist.; edn. specialist cons. Pepperdine U., L.A.; substitute tchr. Richmond City Pub. Schs.; founder, exec. dir. Va. Adolescent Adult Rehab. Agy.; founder, prin. John Ezell Stewart Sch.; grant adminstr. Steamer Co., 1991—; faculty chmn. Mary McLeod Bethune Middle Sch.; spl. projects dir. Tchr. Human rels. Workshops; pres. Pan Hellenic Coun.; founder Motivation for Success in Life Inst., 1996. Mem. Am. Fedn. Tchrs., United Tchrs. L.A., Omega Psi Phi. Democrat. Buddhist. Avocations: self-development tapes, conducting business and training seminars.

STEWART, JOHN HARGER, music educator; b. Cleve., Mar. 31, 1940; s. Cecil Tooker and Marian (Harger) S.; m. Julia Wallace, Aug. 14, 1977; children: Barbara, Cecily Bronwen. BA, Yale U., 1962; MA, Brown U., 1972; cert., New Eng. Conservatory, 1965. With various operas including Santa Fe Opera, N.Y.C. Opera, Met. Opera, U.S. and Europe, 1965—; lectr. Mt. Holyoke Coll., South Hadley, Mass., 1988-90; assoc. prof. music Washington U., St. Louis, 1990—; dir. of voice and choral program. Office: Washington U Campus Box 1032 One Brookings Dr Saint Louis MO 63130-4899

STEWART, JOHN LINCOLN, university administrator; b. Alton, Ill., Jan. 24, 1917; s. Frederick William and Hilda (Denovan) S.; m. Joan Elsdon Guthridge, Sept. 23 1939 (div. 1964); children: Leslie Cythera Stewart Chalmers, Ann Guthridge Stewart Nutt; m. Ruth Peabody Quinn, July 11, 1964; stepchildren: Geoffrey Cornelius Quinn, Andrew Dean Quinn. AB, Denison U., 1938, ArtsD (hon.), 1964; MA, Ohio State U., 1939, PhD, 1947. Teaching asst. then instr. Ohio State U., Columbus, 1939-47; instr. UCLA, 1947-49; asst. prof. then prof. English Dartmouth Coll., Hanover, N.H., 1949-64; prof. Lit. U. Calif., San Diego, 1964-87, provost John Muir Coll., 1965-87. Author: Exposition for Science and Technical Students, 1950, The Essay, 1952, John Crowe Ransom, 1962, The Burden of Time, 1965, (with others) Horizons Circled, 1974, Ernst Krenek, 1990; contbr. articles to various publs. assoc. dir. Hopkins Ctr. for Arts, 1961-64; dir. Mandeville Ctr. for Arts, 1974-76; mem. Dartmouth Community Symphony Orch., 1949-58; trustee Kinhaven Music Sch., 1960-64, Fla. West Coast Symphony, 1958; bd. dirs. Theater and Arts Found. San Diego County, 1970; pres. La Jolla (Calif.) Friends Sch. Music, 1971-73, Friends of Music, U. Calif., San Diego. Served with Aus, 1942-45. Howard Found. fellow, 1953-54, Dartmouth Coll. fellow, 1962-63. Democrat. Avocation: performer with music ensembles. Home: 9473 La Jolla Farms Rd La Jolla CA 92037-1128 Office: U Calif San Diego Off of Provost # 0106 La Jolla CA 92093

STEWART, JOHN MURRAY, banker; b. Summit, N.J., Apr. 2, 1943; s. Robert John Stewart and Mary Catherine (Grabhorn) Stewart Yoder; m. Sandra Meyers Frazier, Feb. 26, 1966; children: Jennifer Bricar, Catherine Dorothy. BA, U. Va., 1965; MBA, NYU, 1983. Trust officer, v.p. Bankers Trust Co., N.Y.C., 1965-82, Morgan Guaranty Trust Co., N.Y.C., 1982-83; mgr., pres., dir. Morgan Trust Co. Fla., Palm Beach, 1983-89; pres., dir. Bankers Trust Co. Fla., 1989-93; pres. pvt. capital group SunTrust Bank, Orlando, Fla., 1993-96; pres., dir. Harris Trust Co. Fla., West Palm Beach, 1996—. Campaign chmn. Palm Beach Cmty. Chest, 1985, 86; vestryman Bethesda By the Sea Ch., Palm Beach, 1986-89, 92-94, treas., 1986-87; treas. Cathedral Ch. of St. Luke, Orlando, 1996; bd. dirs. Orlando Opera Co., 1994-96. Mem. Fla. Bankers Assn. (chmn. trust bus. devel. com. 1989, planning commn., chmn. trust legis. com. 1990), N.Y. State Bankers Assn. (mem. trust bus. devel. com. 1978-82), N.Y. Yacht Club (N.Y.C.), Everglades Club (Palm Beach), Winter Park Racquet Club, Monmouth Boat Club (Red Bank, N.J.), Sailfish Club of Fla. (Palm Beach) (bd. govs. 1992-96), SAR (1st v.p. 1995, 96. Office: 505 S Flagler Dr West Palm Beach FL 33401

STEWART, JOHN WRAY BLACK, college dean; b. Coleraine, Northern Ireland, Jan. 16, 1936; s. John Wray and Margaret Reid (Black) S.; m. Felicity Ann Patricia Poole, Aug. 7, 1965; children: J.W. Matthew, Hannah Louise. BSc with honors, Queen's U., Belfast, Northern Ireland, 1958, B.Agr. with honors, 1959, PhD, 1963, DSc, 1988. Registered profl. agrologist. Sci. officer chem. rsch. div. Ministry of Agr., Belfast, 1959-64; asst. prof. soil sci. dept. U. Sask., Saskatoon, Can., 1966-71, assoc. prof., 1971-76, prof., 1976-81; dir. Sask. Inst. Pedology U. Sask., 1981-89; dean Coll. Agr. U. Sask., Saskatoon, 1989—; tech. expert, cons. FAO/IAEA, U.N.D.P., Vienna, Austria, 1971, 74-75; sec.-gen. Sci. Com. on Problems of Environment, Paris, 1988-92; cons. UNESCO, Paris, 1990, pres. Sci. Com. on problems of the Environment, 1992-95, past pres. 1995; trustee Internat. Inst. Tropical Agriculture, Nigeria, 1991—; mem. sci. adv. com. Inter-Am. Inst. on Global Change Res., 1994—. Contbr. articles to profl. publs., chpts. to books. Fellow Can. Soc. Soil Sci., Berlin Inst. Advanced Study, Am. Soc. Agronomy, Soil Sci. Soc. Am.; mem. Brit. Soc. Soil Sci., Brazilian Soc. Soil Sci., Internat. Soc. Soil Sci., Agrl. Inst. Can. Avocations: squash, racquet ball, tennis. Office: U Sask, Coll Agr, Saskatoon, SK Canada S7N 0W0

STEWART, JONATHAN TAYLOR, psychiatrist, educator; b. Bethpage, N.Y., Mar. 15, 1956; s. Allen Theodore and Vivian (Dreiblatt) S.; m. Linda Sue Irvin, Oct. 27, 1984; children: Jacob Zachary, Aaron Joshua. BA with honors, Rollins Coll., 1976; MD, U. South Fla., 1979. Diplomate Am. Bd. Psychiatry and Neurology, Geriatric Psychiatry, Nat. Bd. Med. Examiners. Resident in psychiatry U. Fla. Coll. Medicine, Gainesville, 1979-83, assoc. prof. psychiatry, 1983-94; asst. chief psychiatry VA Med. Ctr., Gainesville, 1987-94; prof. psychiatry U So. Fla. Coll. Medicine, 1994—; chief geropsychiatry sect. Bay Pines (Fla.) VA Med. Ctr., 1994—. Contbr. articles to profl. jours., 1985—. Mem. Head Injury Adv. Council State of Fla., 1985-90, Gov.'s Alzheimer's Disease Registry Subcom., 1987—, VA Task Force on Extended Care, Washington, 1986. Fellow Am. Psychiat. Assn.; mem. Am. Geriatrics Soc., Fla. Psychiat. Soc. Jewish. Avocations: cooking, cycling, skin diving, traveling, flying. Office: VA Med Ctr Psychiatry Service 116A Bay Pines FL 33504

STEWART, JOSEPH TURNER, JR., retired pharmaceutical company executive; b. N.Y.C., Apr. 30, 1929; s. Joseph Turner and Edna (Pride) S.; m. Carol Graham, Aug. 7, 1954; children: Lisa D., Alison D. BS with honors, U.S. Mcht. Marine Acad., 1951; MBA, Harvard U., 1954. Systems analyst Warner Lambert Co., Morris Plains, N.J., 1954-56; budget dir. internat. Warner Lambert Co., 1956-60, asst. div. controller consumer products group, 1960-62, div. controller group, 1962-66; dir. adminstrn. and fin. Proprietary Drug div. Warner Lamber Co., 1966; dir. Lactona Products div. Warner Lamber Co., 1967; controller Beech-Nut subs. Squibb Corp., N.Y.C., 1968; v.p. fin. Beech-Nut subs. Squibb Corp., 1968-71, v.p. planning, corp. staff parent corp., 1971-79, v.p. fin. and planning parent co., 1979-82, sr. v.p. corporate affairs, 1982-89; also bd. dirs.; cons. Johnson & Johnson, 1990—; bd. dirs. Gen. Am. Investment Corp., Liposome Co. Pres., mem. exec. coun. Harvard U. Bus. Sch. Assn., 1971-76, mem. vis. com. Bus. Sch., 1976-82; trustee Tax Found., 1985-89; commr. N.J. State Commn. on Income and Expenditures, 1985-88; mem. adv. com. Grad. Sch. Indsl. Adminstrn., Carnegie Mellon U., 1986-91; trustee New Sch. for Social Rsch., 1990—, U. Medicine and Dentistry of N.J. Found., 1989—; bd. dirs. Liposome Co., 1995—; vis. coun. Marine Biol. Lab., 1995—. John Hay Whitney Opportunity fellow, 1952-54. Club: Harvard (N.Y.C.). Office: Johnson & Johnson 1 Johnson Johnson Plz New Brunswick NJ 08933

STEWART, KENT KALLAM, analytical biochemistry educator; b. Omaha, Sept. 5, 1934; s. George Franklin and Grace (Sledge) S.; m. Margaret Reiber, June 10, 1956; children: Elizabeth, Cynthia, Richard, Robert. Student, U. Chgo., 1951-53; AB, U. Calif., Berkeley, 1956; PhD, Fla. State U., 1965. Guest investigator Rockefeller U., N.Y.C., 1965-67, research assoc., 1967-68, asst. prof., 1968-69; research chemist U.S. Dept. Agr., Beltsville, Md., 1970-75, lab. chief Nutrient Composition Lab., 1975-82; prof., head dept. food sci. and tech. Va. Poly. Inst. and State U., Blacksburg, 1982-85; prof. biochemistry, anaerobic microbiology, food sci./tech. Va. Poly. Inst. and State U., 1985—. Author articles and book chpts.; editor Jour. Food Composition and Analysis, also 2 books Patentee in field. Capt. USMCR, 1956-59. Fellow Inst. Food Technologist, AAAS; mem. Am. Chem. Soc., Assn. Ofcl. Analytical Chemists, Sigma Xi. Office: Dept Biochemistry Anaerobic Microbiology Va Poly Inst and State U Blacksburg VA 24061-0308

STEWART, KIRK T., public relations executive; b. 1951. BA in polit. sci., U. So. Calif., 1973; MA in public rels./journalism, 1976. Account exec. Burson-Marsteller, 1976-79; pub. affairs dir. Info. Svcs. Dir. TRW, 1979-81; group supr. Manning Selvage & Lee, 1981-82, v.p., 1982-83, exec. v.p., 1983-84; exec. v.p., mng. dir. Manning Selvage & Lee/L.A., Calif., 1984-89; pres. Manning, Selvage & Lee Inc., N.Y.C., 1989-91, pres., CEO, 1992; chmn., CEO Manning, Selvage & Lee, Inc., N.Y.C., 1993—. Office: Manning Selvage & Lee Inc 79 Madison Ave New York NY 10016-7802*

STEWART, LINDSAY D., corporate lawyer. BA, Willamette U., JD. Bar: Oreg. 1973. Corp. counsel Nike Inc., Beaverton, Oreg., 1981—. Office: Nike Inc One Bowerman Dr Beaverton OR 97005-0979

STEWART, MARGARET MCBRIDE, biology educator, researcher; b. Guilford County, N.C., Feb. 6, 1927; d. David Henry and Mary Ellen (Morrow) S.; m. Paul C. Lemon, June 1962 (div. 1968); m. George Edward Martin, Dec. 19, 1969. AB, U. N.C.-Greensboro, 1948; MA, U. N.C.-Chapel Hill, 1951; PhD, Cornell U., 1956. Instr. biology Greensboro Evening Coll. U. N.C., Greensboro, 1950-51; instr. biology Catawba Coll., Salisbury, N.C., 1951-53; extension botanist Cornell U., Ithaca, N.Y., 1954-56; asst. prof. biology SUNY, Albany, 1956-59, assoc. prof., 1959-65, prof. vertebrate biology, 1965—, Disting. Teaching prof., 1977—; faculty rsch. participant Oak Ridge Assoc. Univs., 1983. Author: (with A.H. Benton) Keys to the Vertebrates of the Northeastern States, 1964, Amphibians of Malawi, 1967; contbr. numerous articles and revs. to profl. jours. Bd. dirs. E.N. Huyck Nature Preserve, Rensselaerville, N.Y., 1976-86; bd. dirs. Ea. N.Y. chpt. Nature Conservancy, 1983-88, 90—, N.Y. State chpt., 1987-90; mem. Albany Pine Bush Commn., 1993—. Recipient Citizen Laureate award SUNY Found., 1987, Am. Philos. Soc. rsch. grantee, 1975, 81, NSF grantee, 1978-80, Oak Ridge Assocs. Univs. grantee, 1983—. Fellow Herpetologists League (bd. dirs. 1978-80); mem. Soc. for Study of Amphibians and Reptiles (pres. 1979), Am. Soc. Ichthyologists and Herpetologists (bd. govs. 1975-80, 87-90, herpetology editor 1983-85, pres. 1996), Ecol. Soc. Am., Assn. for Tropical Biologists, Soc. Study of Evolution, III World Congress of Herpetology (mem. exec. com. 1995-97), Sigma Xi, Sigma Delta Epsilon, Phi Kappa Phi. Democrat. Presbyterian. Avocations: photography, gardening, reading, travel. Office: SUNY Dept Biol Scis 1400 Washington Ave Albany NY 12222-0100

STEWART, MARILYN EPSTEIN, educational administrator, consultant; b. Balt., Jan. 27, 1950; d. Charles and Ruth (Saks) Epstein; m. Marc F. Stewart, Aug. 10, 1972; children: Benjamin, Jack. BA, U. Pitts., 1970; MEd, Goucher Coll., 1971. Cert. fund raising exec., 1983. Tchr. Calhoun Sch., N.Y.C., 1977-80, dir. mid. sch., 1980-86, dir. devel. and external affairs, 1986-93; pres. Stewart Group, N.Y.C., 1993—; ptnr. Personal Fin. Control, Waterbury, Conn., 1994; spkr. in field. Vol. fund raising cons. Housatonic Valley Assn., Cornwall Bridge, Conn., 1991-93, Ballet Manhattan, N.Y.C., 1990-93. Mem. Nat. Soc. Fund Raising Execs., Nat. Assn. Ind. Schs., Assn. Supervision and Curriculum Devel., Coun. Advancement Secondary Edn. Democrat.

STEWART, MARLENE JEAN, costume designer; b. Boston, Aug. 25, 1949; d. William Edward and Germaine (Cormier) S. BA, U. Calif., Berkeley, 1972, MA; AA, Fashion Inst. Tech., N.Y.C., 1975, Fashion Inst. Design and Mdsing., Los Angeles, 1976. Fashion designer, owner Covers Inc., Calif., 1978-84. Costume designer: (films) Body Rock, 1984, Back to the Beach, 1987, Siesta, 1987, The Women's Club, 1987, Pet Sematary, 1989, Gingerale Afternoon, 1989, Wild Orchid, 1990, Side Out, 1990, The Doors, 1991, JFK, 1991, Terminator 2: Judgement Day, 1991, Pet Sematary Two, 1992, Point of No Return, 1993, I'll Do Anything, 1994, The River Wild, 1994, True Lies, 1994, (TV movies) Pair of Aces, 1990, (videos) Material Girl, Dress You Up, Would I Lie, (concert tours) Madonna's Virgin Tour, 1985, Madonna's World Tour, 1987. Cons. wardrobe Duran Duran, Earth Wind and Fire, Eurythmics, Pointer Sisters, Madonna, Janet Jackson, Grace Jones, Sylvie Vartan, Isabella Rosellini, Michael Pare. Redipient award design, Designer Bob Mackie, 1977, best costume designer Am. Video awards, 1985. Mem. Nat. Acad. Video Arts and Scics., Nat. Orgn. Female Exec., Costume Designers Guild, Am. Film Inst. (Women Film award, 1987), Mus. Contemporary Art. Home: 1416 N Havenhurst Dr #1C Los Angeles CA 90046

STEWART, MARSHA BEACH, sales executive, entertainment executive; b. Memphis, Jan. 17, 1952; d. Bruce Charles and Marjorie Hudson (Campbell) Stewart; m. Michael G. Mushalla, Dec. 27, 1992; 1 child, Myra Grace. BBA in Internat. Bus., U. Tex., 1982; MFA in Arts Adminstrn./Dance Mgmt., Yale U., 1985. Mng. dir. Yale Cabaret, New Haven, 1984-85; agt. Columbia Artists Mgmt., Inc., N.Y.C., 1985-90; v.p., dir. sales SATRA Arts Internat. (formerly Classical Artists), N.Y.C., 1990-92; pres. Beach Internat. Enterprises, Inc., N.Y.C., 1993—; dancer with Louisville (Ky.) Ballet (formerly Civic), 1967-70, Actor's Theatre of Louisville, 1972, Arena Stage, Washington, 1972, Disney on Parade, NBC, S.Am., Europe, Africa, 1974, 75, 76, Geneva (Switzerland) Ballet Co., 1975, 76; dance chairwoman cultural entertainment com. U. Tex., Austin, 1981-82. NEA fellow, 1983, assoc., 1984. Mem. NAFE, Internat. Soc. Performing Arts Adminstrs., Assn. Performing Arts Presentors, Yale U. Alumni Assn., Yale Club of N.Y.C., Scottish Heritage Soc., N.Y. Caledonian Club, Tex. Execs. Avocations: travel, languages, ice skating.

STEWART, MARTHA KOSTYRA, editor-in-chief, lecturer, author; b. Jersey City; d. Edward and Martha (Ruszkowski) Kostyra; m. Andy Stewart, July 1, 1961 (div. 1990); 1 child, Alexis. BA in European History and Archtl. History, Barnard. Former model; former stockbroker N.Y.C.; former profl. caterer, mag. owner, editor-in-chief; mag. owner, editor-in-chief Martha Stewart Living, 1990—; lifestyle cons. for K-Mart Corp. Author: (with Elizabeth Hawes) Entertaining, 1982, Weddings, 1987; Martha Stewart Hors d'Oeurvres: The Creation and Presentation of Fabulous Finger Food, 1984, Martha Stewart's Pies and Tarts, 1985, Martha Stewart's Quick Cook Menus: Fifty-two Meals You Can Make in Under an Hour, 1988, The Wedding Planner, 1988, Martha Stewart's Gardening: Month by Month, 1991, Martha Stewart's New Old House: Restoration, Renovation, Decoration, 1992, Martha Stewart's Christmas, 1993, Martha Stewart's Menus for Entertaining, 1994, Holidays, 1994; appears in semi-monthly cooking segment on Today Show. Office: Martha Stewart Living 10 Saugatuck Ave Westport CT 06880 also: c/o Susan Magrino Agy 167 E 73rd St New York NY 10021-3510*

STEWART, MARY FLORENCE ELINOR, author; b. Sunderland, Durham, Eng., Sept. 17, 1916; d. Frederick A. and Mary Edith (Matthews) Rainbow; m. Frederick H. Stewart, 1945. BA, Durham U., 1938, MA, 1941. Asst. lectr. English Durham U., 1941-45, part-time lectr. English, 1948-56; part-time lectr. English St. Hild's Training Coll., 1948-56. Author: Madam, Will You Talk?, 1954, Wildfire at Midnight, 1956, Thunder on the Right, 1957, Nine Coaches Waiting, 1958, My Brother Michael, 1959 (Brit. Crime Writers Assn. award 1960), The Ivy Tree, 1961, The Moonspinners, 1962, This Rough Magic, 1964 (Mystery Writers Am. award 1964), Airs Above the Ground, 1965, The Gabriel Hounds, 1967, The Wind Off the Small Isles, 1968, The Crystal Cave, 1970 (Frederick Niven award 1971), The Little Broomstick, 1971, The Hollow Hills, 1973, Ludo and the Star Horse, 1974 (Scottish Arts Coun. award 1974), Touch Not the Cat, 1976, The Last Enchantment, 1979, A Walk in the Wolf Wood, 1980, The Wicked Day, 1983, Thornyhold, 1988, Frost on the Window and Other Poems, 1990, The Stormy Petrel, 1991, The Prince and the Pilgrim, 1996. Fellow Newnham Coll., Cambridge, 1986. Mem. P.E.N. Office: care William Morrow 1350 Avenue Of The Americas New York NY 10019-4702

STEWART, MELBOURNE GEORGE, JR., physicist, educator; b. Detroit, Sept. 30, 1927; s. Melbourne George and Ottilie (Tuholke) S.; m. Charlotte L. Ford, Jan. 23, 1954; children—Jill K., John H., Kevin G. A.B., U. Mich., 1949, M.S., 1950, Ph.D., 1955. Research assoc. dept. physics AEC, Ames Lab., Iowa State U., 1955-56, asst. prof., 1956-62, assoc. prof., 1962-63; prof. Wayne State U., Detroit, 1963-94, prof. emeritus, 1994—, chmn. dept. physics, 1963-73, assoc. provost for faculty relations, 1973-86; hon. research fellow Univ. Coll., London, 1986-87,93. Editorial bd.: Wayne State U. Press, 1969-73. Served with AUS, 1946-47. Mem. Am. Phys. Soc., AAAS, Sigma Xi, Phi Beta Kappa. Home: 415 Bournemouth Rd Grosse Pointe MI 48236-2817 Office: Dept Physics Wayne State U Detroit MI 48202

STEWART, MELVIN, Olympic athlete, swimmer. Olympic swimmer Barcelona, Spain, 1992. Recipient 200m Butterfly Gold medal Olympics, Barcelona, 1992. Office: US Olympic Com 1750 E Boulder St Colorado Springs CO 80909-5724*

STEWART, MILTON ROY, lawyer; b. Clovis, N.Mex., Dec. 16, 1945; s. Virgil Maurice and E. Marie (Collins) S. BA, Ind. U., 1968, JD summa cum laude, 1971. Bar: Oreg. 1971, U.S. Ct. Appeals (9th cir.) 1971, U.S. Dist. Ct. (no. dist.) Oreg. 1971. Assoc. firm Davies, Biggs, et. al., Portland, Oreg., 1971-75; v.p., gen. counsel U.S. Datacorp, Portland, 1975-77; pvt. practice, Portland, 1977-86; ptnr. Davis, Wright Tremaine and predecessor firm., Portland, 1987—, mem. exec. com., mem. mgmt. com, chmn. firmwide bus. group. Chmn. Oreg. chpt. Nat. Multiple Sclerosis Soc., 1994—; mem. pres. adv. bd. Portland State U.; bd. dirs., sec. YMCA of Columbia-Willamette, Portland, 1978-81; bd. vis. Ind. U. Sch. Law. Capt. U.S. Army, 1968-78. State Farm Found. fellow, 1970; John H. Edwards fellow Ind. U. Found., 1971. Mem. Oreg. State Bar, Multnomah Athletic Club, Astoria Golf and Country Club. Office: Davis Wright Tremaine 1300 SW 5th Ave Portland OR 97201-5667

STEWART, NORMAN LAWRENCE, university president; b. East St. Louis, Ill., June 20, 1942; s. Alfred and Helen (Grenard) S.; m. Nancy Lee Rosenthal, Aug. 28, 1966; children: Ian Andrew, Colin August, Brian Alfred. James scholar, U. Ill., 1960-61; B.A. with honors, diploma theology (asst. 1963-64), Wheaton (Ill.) Coll., 1963; honors scholarship, Near East Sch. Archaeology, Jerusalm, 1962; cert., Goethe Inst., W. Ger., 1964; fellow, U. Freiburg, W. Ger., 1964-65; honors fellow, Princeton Theol. Sem., 1966-67; M.A. (U.S. Steel Found. fellow), St. Louis U., 1971, Ph.D., 1972; Fulbright fellow, U. Bonn, W. Ger., 1971-72; LLD, Kobe U., Japan, 1987. Asst. dir. Dothan Archaeol. Expdn., Jenin, Israel, 1964; resident dir. Near East Sch. Archaeology, 1965-66; research asso. polit. archives W. German Fgn. Ministry, Bonn, 1971-72; mem. faculty Maryville Coll., St. Louis, 1972-77; asso. prof. history, asso. acad. dean Maryville Coll., 1975-77; acad. dean. Coll. Mt. St. Joseph, Cin., 1977-79; pres. Rockford (Ill.) Coll., 1979-87, Regent's Coll., London, 1984-87; CEO, Brakeley, John Price Jones, London, 1987-91, Chancery Strategies, London, 1991—; pres. Teikyo Post U., Waterbury, Conn., 1992—; co-founder Lincoln Acad., N.Y.C., 1966; bd. dirs. Rockford Devel. Corp., 1979-87. Author: Dothan Archaeological Expedition Tomb No. 1, 1964, German Relations with the Arab East, 1937-41, 1972. Trustee Kobe Coll., 1979-90, Am. Sch. in London, 1990-92; trustee Lincoln Acad., Ill., 1979-87; bd. dirs. New Am. Theatre, Rockford, 1980-86, Swedish-Am. Hosp., 1980-87; divsn. chmn. Rockford United Way, 1981; precinct committeeman, St. Clair County, Ill., 1972-73; adv. bd. St. Louis Metro Police Acad., 1976-77; bd. dirs. Vis. Nurses Assn., Cin., 1978-79. Mem. Am. Assn. Pres. Ind. Colls. and Univs., Internat. Assn. Univ. Pres., Council Ind. Colls., Archaeol. Inst. Am., Am. Hist. Assn., Phi Beta Kappa, Alpha Sigma Nu. Presbyterian.

STEWART, PAMELA L., lawyer; b. Bogalusa, La., Mar. 13, 1953; d. James Adrian and Patricia Lynn (Wood) Lloyd; m. Steven Bernard Stewart, Aug. 31, 1974 (div. July 1980); 1 child, Christopher. BA, U. New Orleans, 1986; JD, U. Houston, 1990. Intern La. Supreme Ct., New Orleans, 1984, Councilman Bryan Wagner, New Orleans, 1984-85; legal asst. Clann, Bell & Murphy, Houston, 1988-89, Tejas Gas Corp., Houston, 1989-90; atty. Law Offices of Pamela L. Stewart, Katy, Tex., 1991—. Bd. dirs. Alliance for Good Govt., New Orleans, 1983-84, Attention Deficit Hyperactivity Disorder Assn. Tex., 1989-90; vol. Houston Vol. Lawyers Program, Houston, 1992—. Innsbruck scholar, U. New Orleans, 1985. Fellow Inst. Politics; mem. ABA, Am. Bankruptcy Inst., Tax Freedom Inst., Nat. Assn. Consumer Bankruptcy Atty.'s, Houston Bar Assn., Houston Bankruptcy Conf., Nat. Assn. of Chpt. 13 Trustees (assoc.), Katy Bar Assn., Houston Assn. Debtor's Attys., Nat. Assn. Consumer Bankruptcy Attys. (co-chairperson ethics com.). Methodist. Avocations: music, cooking, swimming, politics. Home: 22415 N Rebecca Burwell Ln Katy TX 77449-2908 Office: Law Offices of Pamela L Stewart Ste 219 One West Loop South Houston TX 77027

STEWART, PAMELA PAQUET, home health administrator, consultant; b. Chgo., June 27, 1948; d. Donald and Lena (Brevard) Paquet; m. Philip James Stewart, Dec. 26, 1969. Diploma, St. Elizabeth Hosp. Sch. Nursing, Chgo., 1969; B. Nursing, Governor State U., 1978. Staff nurse emergency rm. St. Elizabeth's Hosp., Chgo., 1969-72, charge nurse emergency rm., 1973-76; staff nurse trauma Christ Hosp., Oaklawn, Ill., 1972-73; staff nurse SO Suburban Home Health, North Riverside, Ill., 1976-79, supr., 1979, dir., 1979-81; cons. home health HQR, North Riverside, 1981-82; exec. dir. Superior Care, Great Neck, N.Y., 1982—; pres. Health Care Design, Plainfield, Ill., 1984—; cons. Steuben County Pub. Health, BAth, N.Y., 1986-88, Evang. Hosp. Systems, Oakbrook, Ill., 1989-90, Midwest Home Care, Chgo., 1991-92; adv. bd. chmn. Primary Care Svcs., Chgo., 1989—. Author: Nurse, Therapists Notes and Summaries, 1981, Modual Approach, 1984, 87, Computers in Health Care and Home Care Economics, 1992, Documentation for Home Care, 1992. Mem. APHA, Ill. Home Care Coun. (reimbursement com. 1986-88, bd. dirs. and edn. chmn. 1989-91). Avocations: reading, writing, decorating, debating issues. Office: Health Care Design 1400 N Penny Ln Plainfield IL 60544-9468

STEWART, PATRICIA CARRY, foundation administrator; b. Bklyn., May 19, 1928; d. William J. and Eleanor (Murphy) Carry; m. Charles Thorp Stewart, May 30, 1976. Student U. Paris, 1948-49; BA, Cornell U., 1950. Fgn. corr. Irving Trust Co., N.Y.C., 1950-51; with Janeway Rsch. Co., N.Y.C., 1951-60, sec., treas., 1955-60; with Buckner & Co. and successor firms, N.Y.C., 1961-73, ptnr., 1962-70, v.p.-treas., 1970-71, pres.-treas., 1971-73; pres., treas. Knight, Carry, Bliss & Co., Inc., N.Y.C., 1971-73; pres., treas. G. Tsai & Co., Inc., 1973; v.p. Edna McConnell Clark Found. Inc., 1974-92; dir., vice chair Cmty. Found. Palm Beach and Martin Counties; bd. dirs. Melville Corp., Banker Trust Co., Bankers Trust N.Y. Corp., Trans World Airlines, 1973-85, Borden Inc., 1976-95, Continental Corp., 1976-95, Morton Norwich Inc., 1979-84; allied mem. N.Y. Stock Exch., 1962-73; past mem. nominating com. Am. Stock Exch., N.Y. Stock Exch., N.Y.C. Fin. Svcs. Corp.; dir. emeritus, past chmn. Investor Responsibility Rsch. Ctr. Trustee emerita, vice-chair Cornell U., bd. life overseers Cornell Med. Coll.; vis. com. Grad. Sch. Bus., Harvard U., 1974-80; bd. dirs. NOW Legal Def. and Edn. Fund, 1984-92, Women in Founds./Corp. Philanthropy 1980-86; vice chmn. Community Found. Palm Beach and Martin Counties, 1993—; v.p. fin. com. Women's Forum, 1982-90; vice chmn. CUNY, 1976-80; bd. dirs. United Way of Tri-State, 1977-81, Inst. for Edn. and Rsch. on Women and Work; voting mem. Blue Cross and Blue Shield Greater N.Y., 1975-82; trustee N.Y. State 4-H Found., 1970-76, Internat. Inst. Rural Reconstruction, 1974-79; mem. N.Y.C. panel White House Fellows, 1976-78; mem. bus. adv. coun. The Hosp. Chaplaincy. Recipient Elizabeth Cutter Morrow award YWCA, 1977, Catalyst award Women Dirs. in Corps., 1978, Trustee medal CUNY, 1983, Accomplishment award Wings Club N.Y., 1984, Women's Funding Coalition Innovators for Women$hare award, 1986, Banking Industry Achievement award Nat. Assn. Bank Women, 1987, Cert. Disting. Accomplishments Barnard Coll., 1989; named to YWCA Acad. Women Achievers. Mem. Fin. Women's Assn. N.Y., NOW (bd. dirs.), Coun. Fgn. Rels., Pi Beta Phi. Clubs: Country Club of Fla. (bd. dirs.), University (N.Y.C.); Gullane Golf (Scotland), The Glen (Scotland). Home and Office:

2613 N Ocean Blvd Delray Beach FL 33483-7367 also: Halfland Barns, North Berwick EH395PW, Scotland

STEWART, PATRICK, actor; b. Mirfield, Eng., July 13, 1940; s. Alfred and Gladys (Barraclough) S. Trained, Bristol Old Vic Theatre Sch. Performed in (theatre) Treasure Island (U.K., debut), 1959, (U.S.) A Midsummer Night's Dream (Broadway debut), 1970, A Christmas Carol, 1991, 92, 94; (TV series) Star Trek: The Next Generation, 1987-94, (mini series) I, Claudius, 1977, Tinker, Sailor, Soldier, Spy, 1979, Smiley's People, 1982, Playing Shakespeare, 1983, When the Lion Roars, 1992, (TV movies) Little Lord Fauntleroy, 1980, John Paul II, 1984, Death Train, 1993; host on Saturday Night Live, 1994; actor (films) Hennessy, 1975, Hedda, 1975, Excalibur, 1981, The Plague Dogs (voice) 1982, Dune, 1984, Lifeforce, 1985, Code Name: Emerald, 1985, Wild Geese II, 1985, The Doctor and the Devils, 1985, Lady Jane, 1986, L.A. Story, 1991, Robin Hood: Men in Tights, 1993, Gunmen, 1994, Star Trek: Generations, 1994, The Pagemaster, 1994 (voice), Jeffrey, 1995; assoc. artist with Royal Shakespeare Co., 1967—. Office: Internat Creative Mgmt 8942 Wilshire Blvd Beverly Hills CA 90211-1934*

STEWART, PATRICK, children's entertainer. Recipient Grammy award for Best Spoken Word Album for Children "Prokofiev: Peter and the Wolf", 1996. Office: Kelly Bush Pub Rels 7201 Melrose Ave Los Angeles CA 90046*

STEWART, (WILLIAM) PAYNE, professional golfer; b. Springfield, Mo., 1957; m. Tracey Stewart; children: Chelsea, Aaron. Co-champion S.W. Conf., 1979; winner Indian and Indonesian Opens, 1981, Tweed Head Classic, 1981, Magnolia Classic, 1982, Quad Cities Open, 1982, Walt Disney World Classic, 1983, Hertz Bay Hill Classic, 1987, PGA Championship, 1989, MCI Heritage Classic, 1989, 90, Byron Nelson Golf Classic, 1990, U.S. Open, 1991, Heineken Dutch Open, 1991, Morocco Open, 1992, 93, Houston Open, 1995, Skins Game Champion, 1991, 92, 93; mem. Ryder Cup U.S. team, 1987, 89, 91, 93, World Cup U.S. team, 1987, 90. Address: care PGA Tour 112 Tpc Blvd Ponte Vedra Beach FL 32082-3046

STEWART, PENNY MORRIS, secondary school educator; b. Glendale, Calif., Sept. 30, 1949; d. C. Harold and Margaret (Nelson) Morris; m. Paul D. Finocchiaro, Apr. 9, 1996; children from previous marriage: E. Pierce III, Hailey M. BA in Speech and English, Muskingum Coll., New Concord, Ohio, 1971; MA in Edn., Nat. U., Sacramento, 1991. Cert. multiple and single subject tchr., Calif. Assoc. prod. Alhecama Players, Santa Barbara (Calif.) C.C. Dist., 1972-86; docent Santa Barbara Mus. Art, 1975-86; importer Cambridge Place Corp., Santa Barbara, 1974-86; with promotions and fund raising depts. Stewart-Bergman Assocs., Nevada City, Calif., 1986-89; travel columnist The Union, Grass Valley, Calif., 1987-90; tchr. drama and English Bear River H.S., Grass Valley, 1991—, dept. chair visual and performing arts, 1993—. Art docent coord. Deer Creek Sch., Nevada City, 1986-90, pres. Parent Tchr. Club, 1987-88. Recipient award for valuable contbn. to schs. Nevada City Sch. Dist., 1990, Dir.'s award Santa Barbara C.C., 1982. Mem. Ednl. Theatre Assn., Calif. Ednl. Theatre Assn., No. Calif. Ednl. Theatre Assn. Avocations: art and antique collecting, roller-blading, skiing, biking, swimming, theatre. Home: 230 Fairmont Dr Grass Valley CA 95945-9709 Office: Bear River HS 11130 Magnolia Rd Grass Valley CA 95949-8366

STEWART, PETER BEAUFORT, retired beverage company executive; b. Montreal, Que., Can., Aug. 23, 1923; s. Harold Beaufort and Mary W. (Martin) S.; m. Yolande Winifred Powell, June 1955; children—Thomas B., Angus B. B.Comm., McGill U.; M.B.A., Harvard U. With Bldg. Products Ltd., Toronto, Ont., Can., 1947-62; dir., v.p. mktg. Molson Breweries Ltd., Montreal, 1962-66; pres. Molson Western Breweries Ltd., Calgary, Alta., Can., 1966-70; exec. v.p., pres. Molson Breweries Ltd., Montreal, 1970-75; exec. v.p. The Molson Cos. Ltd., Toronto, 1975-88.

STEWART, RICHARD ALFRED, business executive; b. Hartford, Conn., Nov. 2, 1945; s. Charles Alfred and Theresa (Procopio) S. BS, Valley Coll., 1967. Account exec. Bank Printing Inc., Los Angeles, 1967-70; pres. Carpet Closet Inc., Los Angeles, 1970-73; western sales mgr. Josten's, Los Angeles, 1973-84; pres. Western Internat. Premiums, Los Angeles, 1984-87; dir. corp. sales Tiffany and Co., Beverly Hills, Calif., 1987-90, dir. major program sales, 1990-92; dir. regional sales Tiffany and Co., N.Y.C., 1992-93, dir. major programs, 1992-93; v.p. sales mktg. and recognition divsn. Jostens, Memphis, 1993—; v.p. sales & mktg. Am. Gem Corp.; recognition cons. L.A. Olympic Com., 1983-84. Contbr. articles to profl. mags.; developer medals for 1984 summer Olympics. Chmn. bd. dirs. Athletes and Entertainers for Kids. Avocations: tennis, basketball, photography.

STEWART, RICHARD BURLESON, lawyer, educator; b. Cleve., Feb. 12, 1940; s. Richard Siegfreid and Ruth Dysert (Staten) S.; m. Alice Peck Fales, May 13, 1967; children: William, Paul, Elizabeth; m. Jane Laura Bloom, Sept. 20, 1992; 1 child, Emily. A.B., Yale U., 1961; M.A. (Rhodes scholar), Oxford (Eng.) U., 1963; LL.B., Harvard U., 1966; Dr. (hon.), Erasmus U., Rotterdam, 1993. Bar: D.C. 1968, U.S. Supreme Ct 1971. Law clk. to Justice Potter Stewart, U.S. Supreme Ct., 1966-67; assoc. Covington & Burling, Washington, 1967-71; asst. prof. law Harvard U., 1971-75, prof., 1975-82, Byrne prof. adminstrv. law,, 1982-89, assoc. dean, 1984-86; asst. atty. gen. environment and natural resources div. Dept. Justice, Washington, 1989-91; prof. law NYU Law Sch., 1992-94, Emily Kempin prof. law, 1994—; of counsel Sidley & Austin, 1992—; spl. counsel U.S. Senate Watergate Com., 1974; vis. prof. law U. Calif., Berkeley Law Sch., 1979-80, U. Chgo. Law Sch., 1986-87, Georgetown U., 1991-92, European U. Inst., 1995. Author: (with J. Krier) Environmental Law and Policy, 1978, (with S. Breyer) Administrative Law and Regulation, 1979, 3d edit., 1990, (with E. Rehbinder) Integration Through Law: Environmental Protection Policy, 1985, paper edit., 1987; editor: (with R. Revesz) Analyzing Superfund: Economics, Science, and Law, 1995. Fellow Am. Acad. Arts and Scis.; mem. ABA, Am. Law Inst. Office: NYU Law Sch 40 Washington Sq S New York NY 10012-1005

STEWART, RICHARD DONALD, internist, educator; b. Lakeland, Fla., Dec. 26, 1926; s. LeRoy Hepburn and Zoa Irene (Hachet) S.; m. Mary Leeuw, June 14, 1952; children: R. Scot, Gregory D., Mary E. AB, U. Mich., 1951, MD, 1955, MPH, 1962; MA, U. Wis. Milw., 1979, postgrad. Diplomate Am. Bd. Internal Medicine, Am. Bd. Med. Toxicology, Acad. Toxicol. Scis. Intern Saginaw (Mich.) Gen. Hosp., 1955-56; resident U. Mich. Med. Ctr., Ann Arbor, 1959-62; dir. med. rsch. sect. Dow Chem. Co., Midland, Mich., 1962-66; staff physician Midland Hosp., 1962-66; assoc. prof., prof. Med. Coll. Wis., Milw., 1966-78, 89-91, adj. prof. Dept. Pharmacology and Toxicology, 1978—; cons. Children's Hosp. Wis., 1990-93, Internal Medicine St. Mary's Hosp., Racine, Wis., 1983—, Dept. Emergency Medicine Milw. Regional Med. Ctr., 1993—, sr. attending staff, 1967—; staff Internal Medicine St. Luke's Hosp., Racine, 1983—; dir. Poison Ctr. Ea. Wis., 1989-93; corp. med. advisor S.C. Johnson & Son, Inc., Racine, 1971-78, dir., 1978-89. Mem. adv. med. staff Milw. Fire Dept., 1975—. Cadet USAF, 1945-46. Fellow ACP, Am. Coll. Occuptl. Medicine, Am. Acad. Clin. Toxicology, Acad. Toxicological Scis.; mem. AMA, Soc. Toxicology, Wis. State Med. Soc., Racine Acad. Medicine, Rotary Internat., Phi Theta Kappa, Phi Kappa Phi, Sigma Tau Delta. Avocations: history of medicine, wilderness hiking, literature, creative writing, inventing medical devices. Home and Office: 5337 Wind Point Rd Racine WI 53402-2322

STEWART, RICHARD EDWIN, insurance consulting company executive; b. Washington, Nov. 4, 1933; s. Irvin and Florence Elsie (Dezendorf) S.; m. Barbara Lewis Dickson, Oct. 29, 1993. B.A., W.Va. U., 1955; B.A. (Rhodes scholar), Oxford (Eng.) U., 1957, M.A., 1961; J.D., Harvard, 1959. Bar: N.Y. 1960. Assoc. Royall, Koegel & Rogers, N.Y.C., 1960-63; asst. counsel to Gov. of N.Y., 1963-64, 1st asst. counsel, 1965-66; supr. ins. N.Y. State Ins. Dept., 1967-70; sr. v.p., gen. counsel First Nat. City Bank, N.Y.C., 1971-72; sr. v.p., dir. Chubb & Son Inc., N.Y.C., 1973-81; sr. v.p. Chubb Corp., N.Y.C., 1973-81, chief fin. officer, 1974-81; gov. N.Y. Ins. Exchange, N.Y.C., 1979-81; chmn. Stewart Econs., Inc., N.Y.C., 1981-90, Chapel Hill, N.C., 1990—; mem. adv. com. HUD, 1968-72; mem. Adminstrv. Conf. U.S., 1970-74; bd. dirs. Am. Arbitration Assn., 1970-80; mem. UN panel experts on Transnational Bank failure, 1991. Co-author: Automobile Insurance....For Whose Benefit?, 1970, Watergate: Implications for Responsible Government, 1974, Medical Malpractice, 1977, Managing Insurer Insolvency, 1988, Insurance Insolvency Quarantees, 1990, A Brief History of Underwriting Cycles, 1991; author: Reason and Regulation, 1972, Insurance and Insurance Regulation, 1980. Trustee Coll. Ins., N.Y., 1970-78, Am. Coll. Life Underwriters, 1990-93; mem. Mayor's Com. on Taxi Regulation, 1979-82, ABA Com. to Improve Liability Ins. System, 1989; mem. panel experts on transnat. bank failure UN, 1991. Served with AUS, 1959. Mem. Nat. Acad. Pub. Adminstrn., Cosmos Club of Washington, Century Club of N.Y.C., Phi Beta Kappa Assn. Home and Office: 7601 Talbryn Way Chapel Hill NC 27516-7862

STEWART, ROBERT ANDREW, lawyer; b. Pueblo, Colo., Sept. 16, 1928; s. Robert James and Marie Anna (Biebl) S.; m. Mary Alyce Spiller, July 25, 1953; children: Alyson Marie, Anne Elizabeth, Robert James, Daniel Keating. LLB, U. Notre Dame, 1952; BA in History, U. Wash., 1972. Bar: Wash. 1953. Instr. in law U. Wash. Law Sch., Seattle, 1952-53; assoc. Bogle & Gates, P.L.L.C., Seattle, 1953-66, mem., 1966—. Chmn. bd. Am. Heart Assn. (Wash. affiliate), Seattle, 1966-68; pres. Mus. History and Industry, Seattle, 1989-91. Staff sgt. U.S. Army, 1946-47, Japan. Recipient Clint Dunagan award U.S. Jaycees, Atlanta, 1961. Fellow Am. Coll. Trust and Estate Counsel; mem. ABA (chmn. post mortem estate and tax planning com. 1987-92, chmn. marital property issues com. 1992—), Wash. Bar Assn., Seattle King County Bar Assn., Seattle Jr. C. of C. (pres. 1958), Wash. State Jr. C. of C. (pres. 1961), Wash. Athletic Club, Seattle Tennis Club. Republican. Roman Catholic. Home: 4100 E Highland Dr Seattle WA 98112-4414 Office: Bogle & Gates 5100 Two Union Sq 601 Union St Seattle WA 98101-2327

STEWART, ROBERT FORREST, JR., lawyer; b. Niagara Falls, N.Y., Oct. 25, 1943; s. Robert Forrest and Margaret Joanne (Mahoney) S.; m. Tara Campbell Mescal, Aug. 27, 1966; children: Jane Margaret, Laura Campbell, Rebecca Forrest. BS, Coll. Holy Cross, Worcester, Mass., 1965; JD, Georgetown U., 1968; LLM in Labor, Temple U., 1978. Bar: D.C. 1968, Del. 1969, Pa. 1976. Law clk. to presiding judge U.S. Dist. Ct. Del., Wilmington, 1968-69; judge adv. USAF, 1969-72; assoc. Morris, Nichols, Arsht & Tunnell, Wilmington, 1972-76; assoc. Obermayer, Rebmann, Maxwell & Hippel, Phila., 1976-80, ptnr., 1981-85; ptnr. Duane, Morris & Heckscher, Phila. and Wilmington, 1985-92; Dilworth, Paxson, Kalish & Kauffman, Phila. and Wilmington, 1992—. Author: At-Will Termination in Pennsylvania, 1983, Emerging Employee Rights, 1984, At-Will Termination in New Jersey, 1985, Legal Issues of Managing Difficult Employees in Delaware, 1988, Personnel and Employment Law in Pennsylvania/New Jersey/Delaware, 1990, Sexual Harassment, 1993. chmn. Common Cause Del., Wilmington, 1974-75, 79-80; pub. mem. coun. Del. Assn. Profl. Engrs., Wilmington, 1981-90; pres. adv. bd. Cath. Charities, Diocese of Wilmington, 1976-90; bd. dirs., vice chmn. United Way Del., 1994—; mem. N.E. regional coun. United Way Am., 1993—; bd. dirs., first vice chair Assoc. United Ways Pa., N.J. and Del., 1993—, Bayard House, 1993—; mem. adv. bd. Seton Villa and Siena Hall, 1992—. Named Vol. of Yr., United Way Del., 1984; recipient United Way Del. Fellowship award, 1993. Mem. ABA, ACLU (bd. dirs. Del. chpt. 1972-76, 92-95), Del. Bar Assn., Pa. Bar Assn., Phila. Bar Assn., Del. State C. of C. (labor advisor 1980—, chmn. com. employee rels. 1987—), Rodney Sq. Club, Holy Cross Varsity Club (bd. dirs. 1981—), Coun. Engring. and Sci. Specialty Bd. (pub. mem. 1991—). Democrat. Roman Catholic. Office: Dilworth Paxson Kalish & Kauffman 3200 Mellon Bank Ctr 1735 Market St Philadelphia PA 19103-7501

STEWART, ROBERT GORDON, former museum curator; b. Balt., Mar. 5, 1931; s. Kenneth Elsworth and Ruth (Chambers) S. Student, Gilman Sch., 1946-49; B.F.A., U. Pa., 1954. Architect Ind. Nat. Hist. Park, Phila., 1954, Nat. Park Service, Phila., 1956-57; architect, curator Jefferson Barracks Hist. Park, St. Louis, 1958-61; dir. properties Nat. Trust for Historic Preservation, Washington, 1961-64; sr. curator Nat. Portrait Gallery, Smithsonian Instn., Washington, 1964-94, sr. curator emeritus, 1994—; cons. Loyalist Homestead, St. John's, N.B., Can., 1960; vis. lectr. George Washington U., 1967-70. Author: Nucleus for a National Collection, 1965, Recent Acquisitions, 1966, A Nineteeth-Century Gallery of Distinguished Americans, 1969, Henry Benbridge (1743-1812): American Portrait Painter, 1971, Robert Edge Pine, A British Artist in America 1784-1788, 1979. Dir. Landmarks of St. Louis, 1959-61; adjudicator Jamaican Nat. Art Competition, 1971; cons. The Papers of George Washington, 1990—. Served with U.S. Army, 1954-56. Mem. Md., Dorchester County, Lewes hist. socs., Walpole Soc., Assn. of Historians of Am. Art, Zeta Psi. Episcopalian.

STEWART, ROBERT HENRY, oceanographer, educator; b. York, Pa., Dec. 26, 1941; s. Robert Henry and Mildred June (Smith) S.; m. Hedvig Susan Bagdy, June 26, 1966 (div. Dec. 1976); 1 child, Alethea Ildico Stewart; m. Tracy Ann Bertoluccci, July 19, 1986; children: Farrar Clee, Margaret Montgomery. BS, U. Tex., Arlington, 1963; PhD, U. Calif., San Diego, 1969. Asst. rsch. oceanographer Scripps Inst. Oceanography U. Calif., San Diego, 1969-78, assoc. rsch. oceanographer, 1978-79; assoc. rsch. oceanographer, assoc. adj. prof. Scripps Inst. Oceanography, U. Calif., San Diego, 1979-83, rsch. oceanographer, adj. prof., 1983-89; mem. tech. staff Jet Propulsion Lab., Calif. Inst. Tech., Pasadena, 1979-80, rsch. scientist, 1980-83, sr. rsch. scientist, 1983-89; prof. oceanography Tex. A&M U., College Station, 1989—; Topex/Poseidon project scientist Jet Propulsion Lab., 1980-88; mem. many NASA coms.; mem. coms. of Nat. Rsch. Coun., Nat. Acad. Scis.; mem. various internat. scientific coms.; cons. Univ. Corp. for Atmospheric Rsch. Author: Methods of Satellite Oceanography, 1985; editor: Radio Oceanography, 1978; contbr. articles to profl. jours. Trustee San Juan Capistrano Inst. Co-recipient Group Achievement award for Topex/Poseidon mission design NASA, 1993, NASA Pub. Svc. medal, 1994; U. Calif. Regents spl. fellow, 1963; NSF fellow, 1964. Mem. Am. Geophys. Union. Republican. Roman Catholic. Avocations: collect lepidoptera. Home: 8710 Appomattox Dr College Station TX 77845-5567 Office: Oceanography Dept Tex A&M U College Station TX 77843-3146

STEWART, ROBERT LEE, retired army officer, astronaut; b. Washington, Aug. 13, 1942; s. Lee Olin and Mildred Kathleen (Wann) S.; m. Mary Jane Murphy; children: Ragon Annette, Jennifer Lee. BS in Math., U. So. Miss., 1964; MS in Aerospace Engring., U. Tex., 1972; grad., U.S. Army Air Def. Sch., 1964, grad. advanced course, guided missile systems officers course, 1970. Commd. 2d lt. U.S. Army, 1964, advanced through grades to brig. gen., 1986, fire team leader armed helicopter platoon 101st Aviation Bn., instr. pilot Primary Helicopter Sch., 1967-69; bn. ops. officer, bn. exec. officer 309th Aviation Bn., U.S. Army, Seoul, Korea, 1972-73; exptl. test pilot Aviation Engring. Flight Activity U.S. Army, Edwards AFB, Calif., 1974-78; astronaut candidate NASA, 1978, mission specialist Space Shuttle Mission 41-B, 1984; mission specialist STS-51J, 1985; dep. comdr. U.S. Army Strategic Def. Command, Huntsville, Ala., 1987-89; dir. of plans U.S. Space Command, 1989-92. Decorated D.S.M., (2) Legion of Merit, (4) DFC, (2) Purple Hearts, Bronze star, others; recipient NASA Space Flight medal, 1984, 85; named Army Aviator of Yr., 1984. Mem. Soc. Exptl. Test Pilots, Assn. U.S. Army, Army Aviation Assn. Am., Assn. Space Explorers. Avocations: photography, woodworking, skiing. Home and Office: 815 Sun Valley Dr Woodland Park CO 80863-9013

STEWART, RODERICK DAVID, singer; b. North London, Eng., Jan. 10, 1945; m. Alana Collins, Apr. 6, 1979 (div. 1984); children: Alana, Sean; child with Kelly Emberg: Ruby Rachel; m. Rachel Hunter, Dec. 15, 1990, child, Renée. Singer with Jeff Beck Group, 1968-69, Faces, 1969-75; albums include (with Jeff Beck Group) Truth, 1968, Beck-Ola, 1969; (with Faces) The First Step, 1970, Long Player, 1971, A Nod Is As Good as a Wink...To a Blind Horse, 1971, Ooh La La, 1973, Coast to Coast/Overture & Beginners, 1973, Snakes and Ladders/The Best of Faces, 1976; (solo) An Old Raincoat Won't Ever Let You Down, 1969, Gasoline Alley, 1970, Every Picture Tells a Story, 1971, Never a Dull Moment, 1972, Sing it Again Rod, 1973, Smiler, 1974, Atlantic Crossing, 1975, The Best of Rod Stewart, 1976, The Best of Rod Stewart Vol. II, 1976, A Night on the Town, 1976, Foot Loose & Fancy Free, 1976, Blondes Have More Fun, 1978, Greatest Hits Vol. I, 1979, Tonight I'm Yours, 1981, Absolutely Live, 1981, Camouflage, 1984, (with Jeff Beck) Get Workin', 1985, Out of Order, 1988, Storyteller: The Complete Anthology 1964-1990, 1990, Downtown Train, 1990, Vagabond Heart, 1991, You Wear It Well, 1992, The Mercury Anthology, 1992, Once In A Blue Moon Vintage, 1993, Ridin High, The Rod Stewart Album, Unplugged...And Seated, 1993 (Grammy nomination, Best Pop Male Vocal for "Have I Told You Lately"). Named Rock Star of Year Rolling Stone mag., 1971; recipient British Rock and Pop Lifetime Achievement award, 1992; inducted into the Rock & Roll Hall of Fame, 1994. Office: care Warner Brothers 3300 Warner Blvd Burbank CA 91505-4632

STEWART, RONALD DANIEL, medical educator, government official; b. North Sydney, N.S., Can., Oct. 11, 1942; s. Donald Hugh and Edith Cavell (MacLellan) S. BA in Langs., Acadia U., Wolfville, N.S., Can., 1963, BSc in Biology and Chemistry, 1965, DSc (hon.), 1988; MD, Dalhousie U., Halifax, N.S., 1970. Diplomate Am. Bd. Emergency Medicine; license to practice medicine Province of N.S., 1989—; specialty cert. emergency medicine Provincial Med. Bd. N.S., 1989—. Resident emergency medicine L.A. County Med. Ctr., 1972-74; asst. prof. emergency medicine U. So. Calif./L.A. County Med. Ctr., 1974-76, assoc. prof. emergency medicine, 1976-78; dir. emergency medicine Presbyn. Univ. Hosp., Pitts., 1978-85; asst. prof. medicine U. Pitts. Sch. Medicine, 1978-81, prof. medicine, 1981-86; prof. anaesthesia Dalhousie U., Halifax, 1987—; dir. prehosp. care emergency svcs. U. Toronto/Sunnybrook Med. Ctr., 1987-89; prof. anaesthesia U. Toronto, 1987-90, prof. surgery, 1988-90; dir. dept. emergency medicine Sunnybrook Med. Ctr., 1987-89; vis. sabbatical scholar Faculty of Medicine, Dalhousie U., Halifax, 1989-90, vis. prof. anaesthesia, 1989-90; adj. prof. emergency medicine George Washington U., Washington, 1990—; adj. clin. prof. medicine U. Pitts., 1987—; ACLS provider Am. Heart Assn.-Calif. Chpt., 1975, ACLS instr., 1976; affiliate faculty Advanced Trauma Life Support, ACS, 1982-87; nat. faculty Am. Heart Assn., 1982-90. Contbr. articles to profl. jours. Mem. of the Legis. Assembly, Province of N.S., Halifax, 1993—, mem. exec. coun. Min. of Health, Province of N.S., Halifax, 1993—. Recipient award of merit The Can. Assn. Emergency Physicians, 1995, 25th Anniversary Recognition award Paramedic Programme of L.A., 1995, Centennial medallion City of San Francisco, 1995, The Ninth Annual Mulroy Meml. Lectureship, Northwestern U., Chgo., 1995. Fellow Am. Coll. Emergency Physicians, Royal Coll. Physicians Can.; mem. Am. Coll. Emergency Physicians (charter), N.S. Med. Soc., Can. Assn. Emergency Physicians, Can. Med. Assn., Assn. for Automotive Medicine, Nat. Assn. Emergency Med. Svcs. Physicians (mem. exec. com. 1985—), World Assn. for Emergency and Disaster Medicine (mem. exec. com. 1985—), Pitts. Emergency Medicine Found. (founder), Australian Ambulance Officers' Assn. (hon.), Australia and New Zealand Intensive Care Soc. (hon.). Mem. Liberal Party. Presbyterian. Avocations: music, canoeing. Office: Ministry of Health, 1670 Hollis St, Halifax, NS Canada B3J 2R8

STEWART, ROSS, chemistry educator; b. Vancouver, B.C., Can., Mar. 16, 1924; s. David Methven and Jessie (Grant) S.; m. Greta Marie Morris, Sept. 7, 1946; children—Cameron, Ian. B.A., U. B.C., 1946, M.A., 1948; Ph.D., U. Wash., 1954. Lectr. chemistry Royal Roads Coll., Victoria, B.C., 1949-52, asst. prof., 1952-54, assoc. prof., 1954-55; asst. prof. chemistry U. B.C., Vancouver, 1955-59, assoc. prof., 1959-62, prof., 1962-89, hon. prof., 1989—. Author: Oxidation Mechanisms, 1964, Investigation of Organic Reactions, 1966, The Proton: Applications to Organic Chemistry, 1985, (with J.D. Roberts & M.C. Caserio) Organic Chemistry, Methane to Macromolecules, 1970; contbr. numerous articles to profl. jours. Fellow Royal Soc. Can., Chem. Inst. Can.; mem. B.C. Thoroughbred Breeders Soc. (pres. 1972-74), Can. Thoroughbred Horse Soc. (v.p. 1974-75). Club: Point Grey Golf (Vancouver). Avocations: breeding and racing thoroughbred horses; golf; gardening. Home: 4855 Paton St, Vancouver, BC Canada V6L 2H9 Office: U BC, Dept Chemistry, Vancouver, BC Canada V6T 1Z1

STEWART, RUTH ANN, public policy analyst, adminstrator; b. Chgo., Apr. 4, 1942; d. Elmer Ashton and Ann (Mitchell) S.; m. David Levering Lewis; children: Allegra, Jason, Allison, Eric. Student, U. Chgo., 1960-61, Simmons Coll., 1963; BA, Wheaton Coll., Norton, Mass., 1963; MS, Columbia U., 1965; postgrad., Fisk U., 1970, Harvard U., 1976, John F. Kennedy Sch. Govt., 1987. Libr. Phillips Acad., Andover, Mass., 1963-64, Columbia U., N.Y.C., 1965-68; mktg. mgr. Macmillan Co., N.Y.C., 1968-70; asst. chief Schomburg Ctr. Research in Black Culture, N.Y.C., 1970-80; assoc. dir. for external svcs. N.Y. Pub. Libr., 1980-86; asst. Libr. of Congress for Nat. Programs, Washington, 1986-89; assoc. Dir. for Resource Devel., Congl. Rsch. Svc., Washington, 1989-95, sr. policy analyst, 1995—; mem. libr. vis. com. Wheaton Coll., 1975—, trustee, sec., 1980—; mem. libr. vis. com. Harvard U., 1975-88, MIT, 1986-90; bd. dirs. Nat. Park Found., Washington, 1978-84; bd. visitors Sch. Libr. and Info. Sci., U. Pitts., 1987-95; trustee Fund for Folk Culture, Santa Fe, 1991—, The Lab. Sch. of Washington, 1992-94, VOICE Internat., 1994—; bd. dirs. Women's Fgn. Policy Group, 1995—. Author: Portia, 1977. Fellow Internat. Coun. Mus. Mem. Coun. Fgn. Rels. Office: Congls Rsch Svc Libr Congress LM 320 101 Independence Ave SE Washington DC 10540

STEWART, S. JAY, chemical company executive; b. Pineville, W.Va., Sept. 18, 1938; s. Virgil Harvey and Lena Rivers (Repair) S.; m. Judith Ann Daniels, June 3, 1961; children: Julie Annette, Jennifer Amy, Steven Jay. BSChemE, U. Cin., 1961; MBA, W.Va. U., 1966. Various positions in engring., mfg., mktg. Monsanto Co., St. Louis, 1961-73; dir. mktg. Ventron Corp. subs. Morton Thiokol, Inc., Beverly, Mass., 1973-77, gen. mgr., 1977-79; pres. Dynachem Corp. subs. Morton Thiokol, Inc., Santa Ana, Calif., 1979-82; group v.p. Thiokol Corp., Newtown, Pa., 1982; group v.p. splty. chems. Morton Internat., Inc. (formerly Morton Thiokol, Inc.), Chgo., 1983-86, pres., chief oper. officer, 1986—, also chmn., bd. dirs. Mem. Anchor Cross Soc. of Rush Presbyn.-St. Luke's Med. Ctr., 1987—, Charles McMicken Soc. U. Cin. Found., Northwestern U. Assocs., 1988—; trustee Rush Presbyn.-St. Luke's Med. Ctr., Chgo., 1987—; mem. adv. bd. Nat. Found. for History of Chemistry, 1991—. Recipient Disting. Alumnus award U. Cin., 1984. Mem. Am. Chem. Soc., Am. Inst. Chem. Engrs., Chmn. Mfrs. Assn. (bd. dirs. 1984-87), Comml. Devel. Assn., Assn. Governing Bds. Univs. and Colls., Chem. Mktg. Assn. (bd. dirs. 1990), Comml. Club Chgo., The Chgo. Club, Econ. Club Chgo. Republican. Methodist. Office: Morton Internat Inc 100 N Riverside Plz Chicago IL 60606-1518*

STEWART, SALLY E., retired emergency nurse; b. Waynesboro, Miss., Feb. 2, 1932; d. Wm. Grady and Martha Pauline (Grayson) Eldridge; div.; children: Randy, Lou, Ann, Jan. Diploma, Rush Meml. Hosp., Meridian, Miss., 1955; BSN, U. Miss., 1965. Supr., head nurse Univ. Hosp., Jackson, Miss.; head nurse surg. ICU VA Hosp., Jackson, supr., staff nurse. Mem. AACN, ANA, NOVA, Emergency Dept. Nurses Assn. Baptist. Home: PO Box 47 French Camp MS 39745-0047

STEWART, SUE STERN, lawyer; b. Casper, Wyo., Oct. 9, 1942; d. Fraizer McVale and Carolyn Eliabeth (Hunt) Stewart; BA, Wellesley Coll., 1964; postgrad. Harvard U. Law Sch., 1964-65; JD, Georgetown U., 1967; m. Arthur L. Stern, III, July 31, 1965 (div.); children—Anne Stewart, Mark Alan; m. John A. Ciampa, Sept. 1, 1985 (div.). Admitted to N.Y. bar, 1968; clk. to Judges Juvenile Ct., Washington, 1967-68; mem. firm Nixon, Hargrave, Devans & Doyle, Rochester, N.Y., 1968-74, ptnr., 1975—; lectr. in field; trustee Found. of Monroe County (N.Y.) Bar, 1976-78. Sec., dir. United Community Chest of Greater Rochester, 1973-87, 92—; trustee, sec. Internat. Museum Photography at George Eastman House, Rochester, 1974—, Genesee Country Mus., Mumford, N.Y., 1976—; bd. dirs. Ctr. for Govtl. Research; trustee, chmn. United Neighborhood Ctr. of Greater Rochester Found., 1991—. Mem. Am. (chmn. task force on charitable giving, exempt orgns. com. tax sect. 1981—), N.Y. State (exec. com. tax sect., 1974-76, chmn. com. exempt orgns. 1975-76), Monroe County Bar Assn. (trustee 1974-75), BNA Portfolio, Pvt. Found. Distbns. Author: Charitable Giving and Solicitation. Office: Nixon Hargrave Devans & Doyle PO Box 1051 Clinton Sq Rochester NY 14603-1051

STEWART, TERESA ELIZABETH, elementary school educator; b. Cheverly, Md., Nov. 26, 1966; d. Richard Lynn and Sandra Lois (O'Neill) S. BS in Elem. Edn. cum laude, Bowie State U., 1988. Cert. elem. tchr., Md. Asst. tchr. Tom Thumb Day Care, Bowie, Md., 1989; elem. tchr. Berwyn Bapt. Sch., College Park, Md., 1989-95, Berkshire Elem. Sch., Forestville, Md., 1995—. Dir. vacation Bible sch., youth group leader Bowie United Meth. Ch., 1988—, sec. adminstrv. coun., 1993—, chairperson pastor parish rels. com., 1996, sec. membership com., 1993—; tchr. children's Bible class University Park Ch. of Brethren, 1990-94; instr., judge Belle-Aires Twirling Corp., Bowie, 1986—; mem. Md. Bato n Coun. Koonz, McKinney & Johnson Law Firm scholar, 1986-88. Mem. Huntington Heritage Soc.,

Kappa Delta Pi, Delta Kappa Gamma. Democrat. Avocations: camping, collecting postcards and teddy bears, twirling, choral singing. Home: 13126 11th St Bowie MD 20715-3726 Office: Berkshire Elem Sch 6201 Surrey Square Ln Forestville MD 20747

STEWART, THOMAS JAMES, JR., baritone; b. San Saba, Tex., Aug. 29, 1928; s. Thomas James and Gladys Naomi (Reavis) S.; m. Evelyn Lear, Jan. 8, 1955; children: Jan Lear, Bonni Lear. Mus.B., Baylor U., 1953; postgrad., Juilliard Sch. Music, 1953-54, Berlin Hochschule for Music, 1957-58. Appeared with, Met. Opera, Chgo. Opera, San Francisco Opera, Bayreuth Festival, Salzburg Festival, Vienna State Opera, Royal Opera Covent Garden, Grand Opera Paris, Deutsche Oper Berlin, La Scala, Milan, Budapest Opera, Prague Opera, 1960—, also major orchs., throughout the world. Served with USAF, 1945-49. Recipient Kammersaenger of Berlin, 1964; Richard Wagner medal, 1965; San Francisco Opera medal, 1985; Fulbright grantee, 1957-58.

STEWART, WARREN EARL, chemical engineer, educator; b. Whitewater, Wis., July 3, 1924; s. Earl Austin and Avis (Walker) S.; m. Jean Durham Potter, May 24, 1947; children—Marilyn, David, Douglas, Carol, Margaret, Mary Jean. B.S. in Chem. Engring, U. Wis., 1945, M.S. in Chem. Engring, 1947; Sc.D. in Chem. Engring, Mass. Inst. Tech., 1951. Project chem. engr. Sinclair Research Labs., Harvey, Ill., 1950-56; cons. Sinclair Research Labs., 1956-83; asst. prof. chem. engring. dept. U. Wis., Madison, 1956-58; assoc. prof. U. Wis., 1958-61, prof., 1961—, McFarland-Bascom prof., 1983—, chmn. dept., 1973-78; cons. Engelhard Industries, Inc., Newark, 1956-58; instr. spl. courses transport phenomena Chemstrand Corp., Pensacola, Fla., 1962, Nat. U. La Plata, Argentina, 1962, Esso Rsch. & Engring. Co., 1963, 66, Phillips Petroleum Co., 1963, Am. Inst. Chem. Engrs., 1965, 68, 69, Inst. Tec. Celaya (Mex.), 1983, Univ. Autonoma de Mex., 1985; Reilly lectr. Notre Dame U., 1993. Author: (with R.B. Bird and E.N. Lightfoot) Transport Phenomena, 1960, Special Topics in Transport Phenomena, 1965, (with R.B. Bird, E.N. Lightfoot and T.W. Chapman) Lectures in Transport Phenomena, 1969; editorial advisor: Latin Am. Applied Rsch.; editorial advisor: Computers and Chem. Engring. Served to ensign USNR, 1944-46. Recipient Benjamin Smith Reynolds teaching award, 1981, Byron Bird rsch. award, 1991. Fellow Am. Inst. Chem. Engrs. (Computing in Chem. Engring. award 1985); mem. NAE, Am. Chem. Soc. (Murphree award in indsl. and engring. chemistry 1989), Am. Soc. for Engring. Edn., (Chem. Engring. Lectureship award 1983), Phi Beta Kappa, Sigma Xi, Alpha Chi Sigma (research award 1981), Phi Eta Sigma, Tau Beta Pi, Phi Lambda Upsilon, Phi Kappa Phi. Conglist. (deacon, moderator). Home: 734 Huron Hl Madison WI 53711-2955

STEWART, WILLIAM BARTLEY, software developer; b. Alexandria, La., June 13, 1962; s. William B. Sr. and Margaret Ellen (Robertson) S. BS in Computer Sci., La. Tech. U., 1985. System operator Procter & Gamble, Tioga, La., 1986; assoc. tech. specialist Computer Scis. Corp., Herndon, Va., 1987-90, programmer, analyst, 1990—. Nat. merit scholar Dresser Harbison-Walker Found., 1980. Mem. AAAS, Assn. for Computing Machinery (spl. interest group on artificial intelligence), Planetary Soc. Republican. Home: 11653 Stone View Sq Apt 1B Reston VA 22091-2922 Office: Computer Scis Corp 3001 Centreville Rd Herndon VA 22071-3709

STEWART, WILLIAM GENE, broadcast executive; b. Winfield, Kans., Dec. 10, 1923; s. Everette Dewey and Mary Lee (Nace) S.; m. Lila Jean Bohlender, June 24, 1951; 1 child: Linda Jean. BA, Denver U., 1949. Mgr. KFKA radio, Greeley, Colo., 1951-56, KGHF radio, Pueblo, Colo., 1956-58, KWRL radio, Riverton, Wyo., 1958-59; owner KLMO radio, Longmont, Colo., 1959—, partner, 1988—. Sgt. USAF, 1943-46. Recipient numerous civic awards, 1959—. Mem. Longmont Am. Legion (life), Elks Club, Moose Lodge, Rotary Club (pres. 1984-85), Fox Hills Country Club. Republican. Avocations: golf, swimming, reading. Office: KLMO-AM PO Box 799 614 Kimbark St Longmont CO 80501-4911

STEWART, ZELMA BROWN, elementary school educator; b. St. Louis, Sept. 19, 1930; d. Floyd and Mateva (Lindsey) Brown; m. James Stewart, Sept. 21, 1948; children: James Roland, Glynis Marie. BS in Edn., Cleve. State U., 1975. Cert. tchr. religion, libr. skills, children's lit. Libr. St. Aloysius Sch., Cleve., 1965-75, tchr. grade 4, 1975-82; tchr. grade 5 St. Agatha-St. Aloysius Sch., Cleve., 1982—. Co-author: Black Christian Saints, 1987. Named Tchr. of the Yr., Cath. Diocese of Cleve., 1989, Excellence award, 1989, Cmty. Bus. Svc. Cath. Sch. award Cleve.-St. Vincent DePaul, 1989; recipient The Crystal Apple award Cleve. Plain Dealer (newspaper), 1995; established Zelma Stewart scholarship for students of St. Agatha-St. Aloysius Sch. Mem. N.E. Cath. Edn. Assn., St. Agatha-St. Aloysius Parent Tchr. Union., Cleve. Art Mus. Democrat. Roman Catholic. Avocations: reading classics, writing short stories, classical and jazz music. Office: St Agatha-St Aloysius Sch 640 Lakeview Rd Cleveland OH 44108-2606

STEYER, ROY HENRY, retired lawyer; b. Bklyn., July 1, 1918; s. Herman and Augusta (Simon) S.; m. Margaret Fahr, Feb. 21, 1953; children: Hume R., James P., Thomas F. A.B. with honors in Govt. and Gen. Studies, Cornell U., 1938; LL.B. cum laude, Yale U., 1941. Bar: N.Y. 1941, various fed. cts. from 1947, U.S. Supreme Ct. 1955. Assoc. firm Sullivan & Cromwell, N.Y.C., 1941-42, 46-52, ptnr., 1953-88, ret., 1988. Trustee N.Y.C. Sch. Vol. Program, 1974-78. Served to lt. USNR, 1943-46. Mem. Am. Coll. Trial Lawyers, ABA (chmn. com. on antitrust problems in internat. trade antitrust sect. 1959-62), N.Y. State Bar Assn., Assn. of Bar of City of N.Y. (chmn. com. on trade regulation 1962-64), Order of Coif, Century Assn., Phi Beta Kappa, Phi Kappa Phi. Home: 112 E 74th St New York NY 10021-3562

STICE, JAMES EDWARD, chemical engineer, educator; b. Fayetteville, Ark., Sept. 19, 1928; s. F. Fenner and Charlotte (Anderson) S.; m. Patricia Ann Stroner, Sept. 22, 1951; children: Susan Emily, James Clayton. BS, U. Ark., 1949; MS, Ill. Inst. Tech., 1952, PhD, 1963. Registered profl. engr., Tex., Ark. Process engr. Visking Corp., North Little Rock, Ark., 1951-53; chem. engr. Thurston Chem. Co. div. W.R. Grace & Co., Joplin, Mo., 1953-54; asst. prof. chem. engring. U. Ark., 1954-57, asso. prof., prof., 1962-68; instr. chem. engring. Ill. Inst. Tech., Chgo., 1957-62; dir. Bur. Engring. Teaching, asso. prof. chem. engring. U. Tex., Austin, 1968-73; prof. engring. edn. in chem. engring. U. Tex., 1973-85, T. Brockett Hudson prof. chem. engring., 1985-90, Bob R. Dorsey prof. engring., 1990—, dir. Ctr. for Teaching Effectiveness, 1973-89; dir. Effective Teaching Inst. U. Tex. System, summer 1970; vis. prof. U. Iberoamericana, Mexico City, summer 1977; Summer cons. E.I. duPont de Nemours & Co., Inc., Savannah River Plant, Aiken, S.C., 1955, Humble Oil & Refining Co., Baytown, Tex., 1956, Universal Oil Products Co., Des Plaines, Ill., 1957, 58, Phillips Petroleum Co., Bartlesville, Okla., 1963, Ethyl Corp., Baton Rouge, 1965, U. Wis., Eau Claire, 1970—. Author: (with B.S. Swanson) Electronic Analog Computer Primer, 1965, Computadoras Analogicas Electronicas, 1971, Expansion of Keller Plan Instruction in Engineering and Selected Other Disciplines, 1975, Developing Critical Thinking and Problem-Solving Abilities, 1987. Recipient Gen. Dynamics award for excellence in tchg., 1980, Western Electric Fund award for excellence in engring. tchg., 1981, Chester F. Carlson award for innovation in engring. tchg., 1984, Outstanding Engring. Advisor award, 1993; named Outstanding Chem. Engring. Prof., 1993, Friar Soc. Tchg. Fellow, 1993-94, Outstanding Chem. Engring. Prof., 1996, Disting. Alumnus U. Ark., 1995. Fellow Am. Soc. Engring. Edn. (life mem., elected dir. 1983-85, chmn. chem. engring. div. 1988-89, bd. dirs. 1990-92, v.p. 1991-92); mem. Am. Inst. Chem. Engrs., Instrument Soc. Am. (Jour. award 1966), Scabbard and Blade, Scholia (pres. 1989-90), Sigma Xi, Delta Sigma, Sigma Chi, Phi Eta Sigma, Pi Mu Epsilon, Alpha Chi Sigma, Tau Beta Pi, Omicron Delta Kappa, Phi Lambda Upsilon, Phi Kappa Phi. Home: 1503 W 32nd St Austin TX 78703-1409

STICH, STEPHEN PETER, philosophy educator; b. N.Y.C., May 9, 1943; s. Samuel Joseph and Sylvia Lucille (Siegel) S.; m. Judith Ann Gagnon, Dec. 20, 1971; children: Jonathan Andrew, Rebecca Elizabeth. BA summa cum laude with distinction, U. Pa., 1964; PhD, Princeton U., 1968. Teaching asst. Princton U., 1965; asst. prof. U. Mich., 1968-73, assoc. prof., 1973-78, dir. grad. studies in philosophy, 1973-74, assoc. chmn. dept. philosophy, 1975-76; assoc. prof. U. Md., 1978-81, prof., 1981-86, dir. grad. studies in philosophy, 1982-83; prof. U. Calif., San Diego, 1986-89, dir. cognitive sci. program, 1988-89; prof. philosophy and cognitive sci. Rutgers U., New Brunswick, 1989—, acting chair dept. philosophy, 1992-93; prof. Linguistic inst., Linguistic Soc. Am., summer 1982; dir. Summer Seminar for Coll. Tchrs. NEH, 1983, 89; vis. sr. lectr. U. Sydney, 1984-85; Jemison prof. humanities U. Ala., Birmingham, 1993; adj. prof. CUNY Grad. Ctr., 1994—; cons. Pres. Commn. for Nat. Priorities in the Eighties, Pres. Commn. on Ethics in Medicine and Biomed. and Behavioral Rsch.; mem. selection com. Mellon Fellowships in the Humanities, 1983-84; mem. Fulbright Selection Com., 1981-83, chair, 1983; vis. fellow Australian Nat. U., Rsch. Sch. Social Scis., 1992. Author: From Folk Psychology to Cognitive Science, 1983, The Fragmentation of Reason, 1990, Deconstructing the Mind, 1996; editor: Innate Ideas, 1975; (with others) The Recombinant DNA Debate, 1979, Philosophy and Connectionist Theory, 1991, Mental Representation, 1994; mem. editl. bd. Linguistics and Philosophy, 1984—, Mind and Language, 1985—, Cognitive Sci., 1990—, Minds and Machines, 1991—, Pragmatics and Cognition, 1991—, Philosophical Studies, 1992—, Philosophy of Sci., 1992—, Cognition, 1993—, Neural Network Modeling and Connectionism; mem. editl. adv. bd. Studies in Cognitive Sys.; contbr. articles to profl. jours., chpts. to books. Woodrow Wilson Nat. Fellowship Found. fellow, 1964-65, Woodrow Wilson dissertation fellow, 1967, Danforth grad. fellow, 1964-67, H.H. Ford fellow Princeton U., 1967, Coun. Philos. Studies Summer Inst. fellow, 1971, Am. Coun. Learned Socs. fellow, 1978-79, Rutgers U. competitive fellow; recipient fellowships NEH, 1974, 83, 96, Ctr. for Advanced Study in Behavioral Scis., Stanford, Calif., 1983; Fulbright sr. rsch. scholar, Bristol (U.K.) U., 1978-79; grantee U.S.-Israel Ednl. Found., 1979, NRC and U.S. Nat. Com. for Internat. Union of History and Philosophy of Sci., Hannover, West Germany, 1979, NSF, 1981-82. Mem. Am. Philos. Assn., Soc. for Philosophy and Psychology (pres. 1982-83, exec. com. 1980-82, 83-84, chair program com. 1979-80), Philosophy of Sci. Assn., Brit. Soc. for Philosophy of Sci., Fulbright Alumni Assn. Office: Rutgers U Philosophy Dept Davison Hall Douglass Campus New Brunswick NJ 08903

STICHT, J. PAUL, retired food products and tobacco company executive; b. Clairton, Pa., 1917. BA, Grove City Coll., 1939; postgrad., U. Pitts. With U.S. Steel Corp., 1939-44; personnel dir. Trans World Airlines, 1944-48; v.p. Campbell Soup Co., 1947-57, pres. internat., 1957-60; exec. v.p. Federated Dept. Stores, Inc., 1960-65, vice chmn., 1965-67, pres., 1967-72; chmn. exec. com., COO R.J. Reynolds Industries, Inc., Winston-Salem, N.C., 1972-73, pres., CEO, 1978-79, chmn. bd., 1979-85; chmn. RJR Nabisco, Inc., Winston-Salem, 1987-89; acting chmn., CEO RJR Nabisco, Inc. (now Castle Springs Corp.), Winston-Salem, 1989. Trustee Grove City Coll.; chmn. Caribbean/L.Am. Action; mem. bd. visitors Bowman Gray Sch. Medicine, former chmn. bd. visitors; mem. bd. visitors Fuqua Sch. Bus. Duke U. Office: Castle Springs Corp 119 Brookstown Ave Winston Salem NC 27101-5245

STICK, ALYCE CUSHING, information systems consultant; b. N.J., July 13, 1944; d. George William and Adele Margaret (Wilderotter) Cushing; m. James McAlpin Easter, July, 1970 (div. Aug. 1986); m. T. Howard F. Stick, June, 1989. AA, Colby-Sawyer Coll., 1964; student, Boston U., 1964-65, Johns Hopkins U., 1972-74; cert., Control Data Inst. and Life Office Mgmt. Assn., 1976. Claims investigator Continental Casualty Co., Phila., 1967-69; data processing coord. Chesapeake Life Ins. Co., Balt., 1970-72; sr. systems analyst Comml. Credit Computer Corp., Balt., 1972-80; v.p. Shawmut Computer Systems, Inc., Owings Mills, Md., 1980-85; pres. Computer Relevance, Inc., Gladwyne, Pa., 1985—; cons. Siani Hosp., Balt., 1982-85, AT&T, Reading, Pa., 1987-88, Dun and Brandstreet, Allentown, Pa., 1988, Arco Chem. Co., Newtown Square, Pa., 1990-91, Rohm and Haas Co., Phila., 1992-96. Designer/author: (computer software systems) Claim-Track, 1977, Property-Profiles, 1979, Stat-Model, 1989; co-designer/author: Patient-Profiles, 1983. Treas. Balt. Mus. Art, Sales and Rental Gallery, 1984. Mem. Assn. for Systems Mgmt., Data Processing Mgmt. Assn., Ind. Computer Cons. Assn., Merion Cricket Club (Haverford, Pa.). Republican. Avocations: Am. antiques, Chinese export porcelain dealer. Office: Computer Relevance Inc 1501 Monticello Dr Gladwyne PA 19035-1206

STICK, MICHAEL ALAN, lawyer; b. Elizabeth City, N.C., June 2, 1954; s. David and Phyllis (Stapells) S.; m. Debra Joan Braselton, May 22, 1993. BA, Davidson Coll., 1976; JD, U. N.C., 1981. Bar: Ill. 1981, U.S. Dist. Ct. (no. dist.) Ill. 1982, U.S. Ct. Appeals (7th cir.) 1983, U.S. Ct. Appeals (8th cir.) 1986. Assoc. Jenner & Block, Chgo., 1981-84, Butler, Rubin, Newcomer, Saltarelli & Boyd, Chgo., 1984-87; ptnr. Butler, Rubin, Saltarelli & Boyd, Chgo., 1988—. Co-author: Environmental Law Handbook, 1988, Environmental Law in Illinois, 1993; mem. staff U. N.C. Law Rev., 1979-80. Chmn. spl. gifts divsn. United Way Crusade of Mercy, Chgo., 1993-94. Me. ABA, Chgo. Bar Assn. Democrat. Methodist. Avocations: travel, skiing, art. Home: 2355 N Wayne Chicago IL 60614 Office: Butler Rubin Saltarelli & Boyd Three First Nat Pla # 1505 Chicago IL 60602

STICKEL, FREDERICK A., publisher; b. Weehawken, N.J., Nov. 18, 1921; s. Fred and Eva (Madigan) S.; m. Margaret A. Dunne, Dec. 4, 1943; children—Fred A., Patrick F., Daisy E., Geoffrey M., James E., Bridget A. Student, Georgetown U., 1939-42; BS, St. Peter's Coll., 1943. Advt. salesperson Jersey Observer daily, Hoboken, N.J., 1945-51; retail advt. salesperson Jersey Jour., Jersey City, 1951-55; advt. dir. Jersey Jour., 1955-66, publisher, 1966-67; gen. mgr. Oregonian Pub. Co., Portland, Oreg., 1967-72, pres., 1972—, publisher, 1975—. Bd. regents U. Portland; mem. adv. bd. Portland State U.; bd. dirs. Portland Rose Festival Assn., United Way Oreg.; chmn. Portland Citizens Crime Commn.; mem. adv. bd. St. Vincent's Hosp. Capt. USMC, 1942-45. Mem. Assn. for Portland Progress (dir.), Portland C. of C. (dir.), Oreg. Newspaper Pubs. Assn. (past pres.), Pacific N.W. Newspaper Assn. (pres.), Am. Newspaper Pubs. Assn., University Club, Multnomah Athletic Waverley Country Club, Arlington Club, Rotary. Office: Oregonian Pub Co 1320 SW Broadway Portland OR 97201-3469*

STICKEL, PATRICK FRANCIS, publishing executive, newspaper; b. Hoboken, N.J., Apr. 17, 1950; s. Fred A. and Margaret (Dunne) S.; m. Debra Isaak, May 10, 1986. Degree in bus. mgmt., U. Portland, 1975. With advt. dept. Jersey Jour., Jersey City, 1966-67; with Oregonian Pub. Co., Portland, 1967-68, 70-75, pressman, with retail advt. dept., 1975-77, with retail & circulation depts., 1980-86, adminstrv. asst., 1987-89, gen. mgr., 1990-94, pres., 1994—; project mgr. Times Picayune, New Orleans, 1986-87. Exec. com. Oreg. Forum, Portland. 1st lt. USMC, 1977-80. Mem. Pacific N.W. Newspapers Assn. (bd. dirs.), Waverley Country Club, Univ. Club, Multnomah Athletic Club. Avocation: golf. Office: Oregonian Pub Co 1320 SW Broadway Portland OR 97201-3469

STICKLE, DAVID WALTER, microbiologist; b. Boston, Apr. 18, 1933; s. Harold Edwards and Lucille Margaret (Magee) S.; m. Mary Elizabeth DeLong, July 29, 1972. BS in Chemistry, Biology, Tufts U., 1955; MS in Pharmacy and Health, Northeastern U., Boston, 1968; MPH, U. N.C., 1969, DrPH, 1971. Bacteriologist Mass. Dept. Pub. Health, Boston, 1959-63, supr. immunology unit, 1963-68; UNC/CDC lab. dir.'s program Ctrs. for Disease Control, Atlanta, 1968-71; chief, clin. lab. improvement program Divsn. Med. Labs./Minn. Dept. Health, Mpls., 1971-82, acting dir., 1977-78, asst. dir., 1978-88; ex-officio mem. Minn. Soc. Clin. Pathologists Exec. Com., Mpls., 1977-78; mem. Proficiency Testing Com., Minn. Acad. Family Physicians, Mpls., 1977-83; adj. asst. prof. U. Minn., Mpls., 1977-88; assoc. prof. emeritus, U. Minn., 1988—. Editor: Med. Lab. Forum periodical, 1973-88. Proctor Nat. Registry of Microbiology, Mpls. Examinations for Minn., 1987-92; instr. Edina Community Edn. Programs, Minn., 1992. With U.S. Army, 1955-57. Lab. tng. grantee Ctr. for Disease Control, HEW, Atlanta, 1977-78, 1978-80, 1979-81. Mem. Am. Soc. Microbiology, Phi Sigma, Sigma Xi. Achievements include serologic tests for systemic candidiasis which were in use for many years by the Ctrs. for Disease Control, U.S. Dept. of Health and Human Svcs.

STICKLER, DANIEL LEE, health care management consultant; b. Fairmont, W.Va., Jan. 4, 1938; s. Elmer Daniel and Ruby Lee (Ball) S.; m. Donna Lou Johnson, Apr. 16, 1960; children—Dwight Lorne, Dwayne Lee, Douglas Lynn. B.S. in Civil Engring., W.Va. U., 1960; M.P.H. in Health Adminstrn., U. Pitts., 1970. Registered profl. engr., Tex. Asst. dir. Presbyn.-Univ. Hosp., Pitts., 1970-71, assoc. dir., 1971-72, adminstr., chief operating officer, 1972-76, exec. dir., chief exec. officer, 1976-83, pres., chief exec. officer, 1983-86; pres., CEO, The Cedars Med. Ctr., Miami, Fla., 1986-91; pres. DLS Assocs., Inc., Miami, 1991—; adj. assoc. prof. Grad. Sch. Pub. Health, U. Pitts., 1976—. Fellow Am. Coll. Hosp. Adminstrn. Republican. Methodist. Clubs: LaGorce Country. Avocations: golf; gardening. Home and Office: 5803 Fairwoods Cir Sarasota FL 34243

STICKLER, FRED CHARLES, manufacturing company executive; b. Villisca, Iowa, Dec. 11, 1931; s. Donald H. and Martha E. (Reese) S.; m. Dorothy A. Frahm, July 10, 1955; children—Mark, Lisa, Kent. B.S., Iowa State U., 1953, Ph.D., 1958; M.S., Kans. State U., 1955. Research asst. Kans. State U., 1953-55, Iowa State U., 1955-58; asst. prof., then asso. prof. agronomy Kans. State U., 1958-64; with Deere & Co., Moline, Ill., 1964-87; dir. Deere & Co. (Tech. Center), 1976-80, dir. product and market planning, 1980-87, ret., 1987—; crop and soils cons., 1988—. Bd. dirs. Upper Rock Island County YMCA, 1980-87, U.S. Fed. Grain Council, 1986-89. Mem. Am. Soc. Agronomy, Crop Sci. Soc. Am., Am. Soc. Agrl. Engrs.

STICKLER, GUNNAR BRYNOLF, pediatrician; b. Peterskirchen, Germany, June 13, 1925; came to U.S., 1951, naturalized, 1958; s. Fritz and Astrid (Wennerberg) S.; m. Duci M. Kronenbitter, Aug. 30, 1956; children: Katarina Anna, George David. M.D., U. Munich, Germany, 1949; Ph.D., U. Minn., Mpls., 1957. Diplomate Am. Bd. Pediatrics, ofcl. examiner and mem., 1965-95. Resident in clin. pathology Krankenhaus III Orden, Munich, 1950; resident in pathology U. Munich, 1950-51; intern Mountainside Hosp., Montclair, N.J., 1951-52; fellow in pediatrics Mayo Grad. Sch., Rochester, Minn., 1953-56; sr. cancer research scientist Roswell Park Meml. Inst., Buffalo, 1956-57; asst. to staff Mayo Clinic, Rochester, 1957-58; cons. in pediatrics Mayo Clinic, 1959-89, head sect. pediatrics, 1969-74; prof. pediatrics, chmn. dept. pediatrics Mayo Clinic and Mayo Med. Sch., 1974-80; mem. test com. III Nat. Bd. Med. Examiners, 1973-75; vis. prof. at various univs and instns., including U. Dusseldorf (Germany) and U. Munich, 1971, Pahlavi U., Iran, 1975, Olga Hosp., Stuttgart, Germany, 1978, Martin Luther King Hosp., Los Angeles, 1979, U. Man., 1981; mem. emeritus staff Mayo Clinic, 1989. Contbr. numerous articles to med. publs.; editorial bd. Clin. Pediatrics, 1968-76, 79—, European Jour. Pediatrics, 1976-84, Pediatrics, 1983-89. Recipient Humanitarian award Chgo. region chpt. Nat. Found. Ileitis and Colitis, 1978, award for excellence of subject matter and presentation So. Minn. Med. Assn., 1978. Mem. Am. Acad. Pediatrics, Soc. Pediatric Research, Am. Pediatric Soc., Midwest Soc. Pediatric Research (council 1967-69, pres. 1970-71), N.W. Pediatric Soc. (pres. 1973-74). Achievements include description of hereditary progressive arthropthalmopathy in 1965, now called Stickler syndrome.

STICKLER, K. BRUCE, lawyer; b. Chgo., Jan. 3, 1946. BA, So. Meth. U., 1967, JD, 1970. Bar: Tex. 1970, Ill. 1972. Ptnr. Keck, Mahin & Cate, Chgo.; clin. faculty mem. dept. hosp. and health care adminstrn. Ctr. Health Care Svcs., St. Louis U., 1987—; ptnr. Stickler & Nelson, Chgo. Mem. healthcare adv. bd. DePaul U., Chgo. Mem. ABA, Am. Acad. Hosp. Attys., Ill. State Bar Assn. (chmn. labor law sect. coun. 1983), Ill. Assn. Hosp. Attys. (bd. dirs. 1991—), Chgo. Bar Assn., State Bar Tex. Office: Stickler & Nelson 333 W Wacker Dr Chicago IL 60601*

STICKNEY, JESSICA, former state legislator; b. Duluth, Minn., May 16, 1929; d. Ralph Emerson and Claudia Alice (Cox) Page; m. Edwin Levi Stickney, June 17, 1951; children: Claudia, Laura, Jeffrey. BA, Macalester Coll., St. Paul, Minn., 1951; PhD (hon), Rocky Mtn. Coll., Billings, Mont., 1986. Rep. State of Mont., 1989-92; mem. Gov.'s Commn. on Post-Sec. Edn., Mont., 1973-75. Mem. Sch. Bd. Trustees, Miles City, Mont., 1968-74; mem., chmn. zoning bd., Miles City, 1975-89; mem. Govt. Study Commn., Miles City, 1974-76, United Ch. Christ Bd. Homeland Ministries, 1975-81; chmn., conf. moderator United Ch. Christ Bd. Mont.-Northern Wyo. Conf., 1980-82; chmn. Town Meeting on the Arts, Mont., 1980; mem., chmn. Miles Community Coll. Bd., 1975-89, chmn. 1978-80. Mem. Mont. Arts Coun. (chmn. 1982-85), Western States Arts Found. (vice chmn. 1984), Nat. Assembly State Arts Agys. (bd. dirs. 1982-88), AAUW (pres. 1964-66). Democrat. Avocations: writing, sewing, painting, reading.

STIDD, LINDA MARIE, rehabilitation nurse; b. Martins Ferry, Ohio, Mar. 20, 1947; d. Stephen George and Helen Jane (Cupryk) Mularcik; m. William Leroy Stidd, May 4, 1968; 1 child, Christopher Alan. Diploma, Ohio Valley Gen. Hosp., 1968; BSN, Ohio U., 1995. CRRN; RN cert. in gerontology. Staff nurse Ohio Valley Gen. Hosp., Wheeling, W.Va., 1968-69, 73-79; supr. Woodland Acres Nursing Home, St. Clairsville, Ohio, 1971-73; staff nurse Ohio Valley Med. Ctr., Wheeling, 1973-79, head nurse rehab., 1981-91; nurse mgr. OVMC Rehab. at Woodsdale, Wheeling, 1991-92; nurse mgr. for skilled care/rehab. Peterson Rehab. Hosp. and Geriatric Ctr., Wheeling, 1991-95. Mem. Assn. Rehab. Nurses, W.Va. Assn. Rehab. Nurses, W.Va. Orgn. Nurse Execs., Nat. Disting. Svc. Registry Med. and Vocat. Rehab. Democrat. Roman Catholic. Avocations: reading, travel, drawing. Office: Peterson Rehab Hosp and Geriatric Ctr Homestead Ave Wheeling WV 26003-6697

STIDHAM, SHALER, JR., operations research educator; b. Washington, Dec. 4, 1941; s. Shaler and Gladys (Ruddick) S.; m. Carolyn Jean Noble, Apr. 6, 1968; children: Christiane Wilson, Dana Claire, Ann-Elise. BA, Harvard U., 1963; MS, Case Inst. Tech., 1964; PhD, Stanford U., 1968. Asst. prof. dept. ops. rsch. Cornell U., Ithaca, N.Y., 1968-75; assoc. prof., prof. dept. indsl. engring. N.C. State U., Raleigh, 1975-86; prof. dept. ops. rsch. U. N.C., Chapel Hill, 1986—, chmn. dept. ops. rsch., 1990-95; lektor Aarhus (Denmark) U., 1971-72; guest prof. Tech. U., Denmark, Lyngby, 1976-77; vis. fellow Statis. Lab., Cambridge (Eng.) U., 1982-83; cons. Bell Telephone Labs., 1981; vis. scholar Stanford (Calif.) U., 1975, 79; invited prof. Inst. Nat. Récherche en Informatique et en Automatique, Sophia Antipolis, France, 1991-92; keynote spkr. to profl. confs., The Netherlands, Germany, Poland, France and Japan, 1977—. Bd. dirs. Friends of Coll., Raleigh, 1979-82, chmn. program com., 1982-83; bd. dirs. N.C. Symphony Found., Raleigh, 1990—; bd. deacons Pullen Meml. Ch., 1995—; mem. faculty coun. U. N.C., Chapel Hill. Overseas fellow Churchill Coll., Cambridge, 1982—. Mem. Ops. Rsch. Soc. Am. (chmn. applied probability tech. sect. 1990-91), Inst. Mgmt. Scis. (program co-chmn. internat. meeting Osaka, Japan 1989), Sigma Xi (Young Scientist Rsch. award 1978). Home: 10428 Whitestone Rd Raleigh NC 27615-1236 Office: U NC Dept Ops Rsch Cb 3180 Smith Bldg Chapel Hill NC 27599

STIEBEL, GERALD GUSTAVE, art dealer; b. N.Y.C., Sept. 28, 1944; s. Eric and Irene (Sichel) S.; m. Judith Rudner, 1965 (div. 1975); children: Catherine Lynn, Daniel James; m. Penelope Hunter, Aug. 14, 1975; 1 son, Hunter Hans. BA, C.W. Post Coll., 1965; postgrad. Study Ctr. for Fine and Decorative Arts, London, Eng., 1965-66; MA, Columbia U., 1967. With Rosenberg & Stiebel, Inc., N.Y.C., 1966—, treas., 1968—, v.p., 1971-85, pres., 1985—; mem. faculty New Sch. Social Research, 1979-84; bd. dirs. Videodisc Pub., Inc., MUSE Film and TV; mem. art adv. panel Internal Revenue Svc., 1980-83; apptd. mem. by Pres. William Jefferson Clinton Cultural Property Adv. Com., 1995—. Mem. Nat. Antique and Art Dealers Assn. Am. (v.p. 1973-77, pres. 1977-79), Art Dealers Assn. Am. (dir. 1980-89), Internat. Confedn. Dealers in Works of Art (pres. 1981-84, permanent councillor 1990—), Syndicat National Des Antiquaires. Office: 32 E 57th St New York NY 10022-2513

STIEBER, TAMAR, journalist; b. Bklyn., Sept. 15, 1955; d. Alfred and Florence (Spector) S. Student, Rockland C.C., 1972-75, Rockland C.C., 1972-75, West London (Eng.) Coll., 1973-74; BA in Film cum laude, U. Calif., Berkeley, 1985, postgrad., 1985-86; grad. police reserve academycum laude, Napa Valley Coll., 1988. Office mgr., confidential sec. AP, San Francisco, 1981-83; stringer Daily Californian, Berkeley, Calif., 1983-84; film rsch. teaching asst. U. California, Berkeley, 1984-86; libr. and rsch. asst. Pacific Film Archive, Berkeley, 1984-86; intern San Francisco Examiner, 1984; reporter Sonoma (Calif.) Index-Tribune, 1987-88, Vallejo (Calif.) Times-Herald, 1988-89, Albuquerque Journal, 1989-94. Recipient Pulitzer prize for specialized reporting, 1990, first place pub. svc. divsn. N.Mex. Press Assn., 1990, pub. svc. award Albuquerque Press Club, 1990; first place newswriting N.Mex. Press Assn., 1991; honorable mention Assn. Press Managing Editors, 1994. Mem. Soc. Profl. Journalists, Investigative Reporters and Editors, N.M. Found. Open Govt., Internat. Platform Soc., Phi Beta Kappa. Home: PO Box 9835 Santa Fe NM 87504-9835

STIEF, LOUIS JOHN, chemist; b. Pottsville, Pa., July 26, 1933; s. Louis Norman and Dorothy Elizabeth (Bassler) S.; m. Kathleen J. Talbot, Nov. 30, 1963 (div. 1980); children—Andrew, Lorraine. B.A., La Salle Coll., 1955;

Ph.D., Catholic U. Am., 1960. Nat. Acad. Scis.-NRC postdoctoral rsch. assoc. Nat. Bur. Standards, Washington, 1960-61; NATO postdoctoral fellow, ind. researcher chemistry dept. Sheffield (Eng.) U., 1961-63; sr. scientist, sr. chemist Melpar, Inc., Falls Church, Va., 1963-68; NAS-NRC sr. postdoctoral rsch. assoc. NASA/Goddard Space Flight Ctr., Greenbelt, Md., 1968-69; astrophysicist NASA/Goddard Space Flight Ctr., 1969-76, head br. astrochemistry, 1976-90, sr. scientist, 1990—; adj. prof. chemistry Cath. U. Am. Research: numerous publs., especially in Jour. Chem. Physics and Jour. Phys. Chemistry. Recipient Alumni Achievement award Cath. U. Am., 1985; NASA fellow Queen Mary Coll., U. London, 1981-82. Fellow Washington Acad. Sci.; mem. Am. Chem. Soc., Royal Soc. Chemistry, Am. Geophys. Union, Am. Astron. Soc. (div. planetary sci.), Sigma Xi. Office: NASA Goddard Space Flight Ctr Code 690 Greenbelt MD 20771

STIEFEL, ETHAN, dancer; b. Madison, Wis.; s. Alan and Mima Stiefel. Studies under Mikhail Baryshnikov, Sch. Classical Ballet, 1987; student, Fordham U., 1995—. Guest artist Nutcracker Cavalier, 1992-93; mem. Zurich Ballet, 1992. Recipient Silver medal Prix de Lausanne, 1989, emerging dance artist grant Princess Grace Found. U.S.A., 1991-92. Office: NYC Ballet NY State Theater 20 Lincoln Ctr New York NY 10023-6966*

STIEFLER, JEFFREY E., financial services executive; b. 1946. BA, Williams Coll., 1968; MBA, Harvard U., 1970. Gen. mgr. Boise Cascade, 1971-75; pres. Mintz & Hoke, Inc., 1975-77; sr. v.p. Citicorp, 1977-82; exec. v.p. J.B. Coleman & Co., 1982-83; pres. Phila. Saving Fund Soc., 1986-87; sr. v.p. mktg. IDS Fin. Svcs., 1983-86; exec. v.p. sales and mktg. IDS Fin. Svcs., Am. Express subsidiary, 1987-90; pres. IDS Fin. Svcs., 1990-91, CEO, 1992-93; pres. Am. Express Co., N.Y.C., 1993—, also bd. dirs., 1993—; bd. dirs. Nat. Computer Sys. Office: Am Express Co Am Express Tower C World Fin Ctr New York NY 10285-9999

STIEGLITZ, PERRY JESSE, diplomat, journalist; b. Yonkers, N.Y., Apr. 18, 1920; s. Abraham Charles and Goldie (Klein) S.; m. Princess Moune Souvanna Phouma, Apr. 29, 1935; 1 child, Dara S.P. AB, NYU, 1941; postgrad., Harvard U., 1941-42, U. Lausanne, Switzerland, 1947-50. Lecturer, English Hunter Coll., N.Y.C, 1956-59; English teacher Hunter H.S., N.Y.C., 1956-59; Asst. cultural attache Am. Embassy, Paris, 1963-67; cultural attache Am. Embassy, Vientiane, Laos, 1967-68; Am. consul Am. Consulate, Marseille, France, 1968-70; cultural attache Am. Embassy, Bangkok, Thailand, 1973-76, Brussels, 1976-80; Washington Bureau chief The Bangkok Post, Thailand, 1984-85; Am. rep. Thomson Found. of Eng., London, 1986-88; dir. Gibraltar Info. Bur., Washington, 1988—. Author: In A Little Kingdom, 1990. Lt. USN, 1942-46. Fulbright grantee, Laos, 1959-60; recipient meritorious award USIA, 1967. Mem. Cercle Royal Gaulois de Bruxelles, Dacor House, Univ. Club of Washington. Office: Gibraltar Info Bureau 1156 15th St NW Washington DC 20005

STIEHL, WILLIAM D., federal judge; b. 1925; m. Celeste M. Sullivan; children: William D., Susan M. Student, U. N.C., 1943-45; LLB, St. Louis U., 1949. Pvt. practice, 1971-78; ptnrs. Stiehl & Hess, 1978-81; ptnr. Stiehl & Stiehl, 1982-86; judge, former chief judge U.S. District Court, (so. dist.) Ill., East Saint Louis, 1986—; spl. asst. atty. gen. State of Ill., 1970-73. Mem. bd. Belleville Twp. High Sch. and Jr. Coll., 1949-50, 54-56, pres., 1956-57, Clair County, Ill., county civil atty., 1956-60. Mem. ABA, Ill. Bar Assn., St. Clair County Bar Assn. Office: US Dist Ct 212 US Courthouse East Saint Louis IL 62202

STIER, ROBERT H., JR., lawyer; b. Berwyn, Ill., Dec. 19, 1952; s. Robert H. and Lois (Lindahl) S.; m. Mary Ellen FitzGerald, Aug. 11, 1979; children: Meghan, Erik, Maeve. AB, Harvard Coll., 1975; postgrad., U. Gothenburg, Sweden, 1976-77; JD, Harvard U., 1980. Bar: Md. 1980, U.S. Dist. Ct. Md. 1980, D.C. 1983, U.S. Dist. Ct. D.C. 1984, U.S. Ct. Appeals (4th and D.C. cirs.) 1985, Va. 1986, U.S. Dist. Ct. (ea. and we. dists.) Va. 1986, U.S. Ct. Appeals (fed. cir.) 1986, U.S. Supreme Ct. 1986, Maine 1988, U.S. Dist. Ct. Maine 1988. Assoc. Piper & Marbury, Balt., 1980-83, Washington, 1983-87; ptnr. Bernstein, Shur, Sawyer & Nelson, Portland, Maine, 1987—. Mem. ABA, Def. Rsch. Inst. Avocations: squash, windsurfing. Office: Bernstein Shur Sawyer & Nelson PO Box 9729 Portland ME 04104-5029

STIER, WILLIAM FREDERICK, JR., university administrator; b. Feb. 22, 1943; m. Veronica Ann Martin, 1965; children: Mark, Missy, Michael, Patrick, Willy III. BA, St. Ambrose Coll., 1965; MA, Temple U., 1966; EdD, U. S.D., 1972; postgrad. Marquette U., 1976-77, U. Wis.-Milw. Sch. Law, summer 1977. Grad. asst. Coll. Edn., Temple U., Phila., 1965-66, various faculty positions dept. health, phys. edn. and recreation, 1968-74; pres., CEO Fla. Breeders, Inc., Largo and St. Petersburg, Fla., 1974-76, treas. Charolais of Fla., Inc., St. Petersburg and Ft. Myers, 1975-76; adminstrv. asst. to v.p., dir./coordinator satellite campus Cardinal Stritch Coll., Milw., 1976-80; chmn. dept., prof. health and phys. edn., athletic dir. Ohio No. U., Ada, 1980-83; chmn., prof. phys. edn. and sports dept. SUNY, Brockport, 1983-86, dir. intercollegiate athletics, 1983-90, grad. coord. sport mgmt., 1990—, pres. faculty senate, 1992-93, grad. coord., 1994—; pres., CEO Ednl. and Sport Mgmt. Cons., N.Y. and Ohio, 1980—; chmn. bd. dirs. Kreative Kids Learning Ctrs., Inc., 1978—; bd. dirs. Creative Children Child Care Ctrs.; cons. MacMillan Pub. Co., Inc., 1981-83, Sport Fedn., Hongkong, Singapore and Malaysia, 1987, 88, Nat. coll. Sport Coaches, Mexico City, 1990; speaker numerous confs. and convs. Author and contbr. to 25 books and compendiums in field; contbr. more than 200 articles to profl. jours.; mem. editorial bd. and reviewer profl. jours. Active ARC, 1975-90, Boy Scouts Am., 1955-59; mem. Greater Milw. Regional Day Care Adv. Com., 1979-81; adv. bd. Nat. Ctr. for Exploration Human Potential, Del Mar, Calif., 1981-84; nat. basketball coach, St. Kitts-Nevis, 1984; cons. on basketball, Mex., 1982, 90. Brockport scholar, 1984-86, 93. Mem. AAHPERD (reviewer jour. 1984—), N.Y. Assn. for Health Phys. Edn. Recreation and Dance (higher edn. sect. 1983—, pres. 1985-86, 87-88), Nat. Assn. Sport and Phys. Edn., Nat. Assn. Girls and Women's Sports, Nat. Assn. Physical Edn. in Higher Edn., Nat. Assn. of Athletic, Mktg. and Devel. Dirs., Nat. Assn. Collegiate Dirs. of Athletics, Internat. Soc. on Comparative Physical Edn. and Sports, N.Am. Soc. Sport Mgmt., Eta Sigma Gamma, Phi Epsilon Kappa, Phi Kappa Phi, Phi Epsilon Omega. Office: SUNY-Brockport Dept Phys Edn and Sport Brockport NY 14420

STIERS, DAVID OGDEN, actor, conductor; b. Peoria, Ill., Oct. 31, 1942; s. Kenneth Truman and Margaret Elizabeth (Ogden) S. Diploma drama div., Juilliard Sch., 1973. Actor, Actors Workshop, 1962, Calif. Shakespeare Festival, 1963-68, mem., The Committee, 1968-70, San Francisco (revue)/ Broadway season City Center Acting Co., N.Y.C., 1974; Broadway appearances include Ulysses in Nighttown, 1974, The Magic Show, 1974-75; other stage appearances include King Lear, 1981; regular on TV series MASH 1977-83; other TV appearances include Mary Tyler Moore Show, Rhoda; TV film appearances include Charlie's Angels, 1976, A Circle of Children, 1977, A Love Affair: The Eleanor and Lou Gehrig Story, 1978, Sergeant Matlovich Vs. the US Air Force, 1978, Breaking Up Is Hard To Do, 1979, Damien: The Leper Priest, 1980, The Day the Bubble Burst, 1982, Anatomy of an Illness, 1984, The First Olympics-Athens 1896, 1984, The Bad Seed, 1985, North and South, 1985, North and South Book II, 1986, Mrs. Delafield Wants to Marry, 1986, Perry Mason: Case of the Notorious Nun, 1986, Perry Mason: Case of the Shooting Star, 1986, The Kissing Place, 1990; film appearances include: Drive, He Said, 1972, Oh God!, 1977, The Cheap Detective, 1978, Magic, 1978, The Man With One Red Shoe, 1985, Creator, 1985, Better Off Dead, 1985, The Accidental Tourist, 1988, Another Woman, 1988, Doc Hollywood, 1991, Beauty and the Beast, 1991 (2 voices), Iron Will, 1994, The Toolshed, 1994, Bad Company, 1995, Pocahontas, 1995 (voice), Steal Big, Steal Little, 1995; artistic assoc. The Acting Co., N.Y.C.; prin. guest condr. Yaquina Orch., 1989; now resident condr. Yaquina Chamber Orch.; guest condr. 70 orchs. including San Diego Symphony, Dallas Symphony Orch., Utah Symphony Orch., Chgo. Symphony Orch., Va. Symphony Orch., N.C. Symphony Philharm., Ft. Wayne Philharm., Calif. Symphony Orch., also orchs. in Honolulu, Portland, Maine, Grand Rapids, Mich., Peoria, Ill. Mem. NARAS, Conductors Guild, Am. Symphony Orch. League, Internat. Horn Soc., Magic Castle, Players Club.

STIFF, JOHN STERLING, development company executive; b. McKinney, Tex., Feb. 14, 1921; s. James Harrison and Elva (Boone) S.; m. Harriett Raschig, May 21, 1946; children—Mark, Justin. Student, Tex. A&M Coll., 1938-41; B.E., Yale U., 1947. Registered profl. engr., Tex. Mgmt. trainee City of Big Spring, Tex., 1938-39, 41-42; city engr. Abilene, Tex., 1947-51; city mgr. Irving, Tex., 1953-57; gen. mgr. Hardee-Pipkin Constrn.Co., Irving, 1957-58; city mgr. Garland, Tex., 1958-63, Amarillo, Tex., 1963-83; pres. Quail Creek Devel. Co., Amarillo, Tex., 1983-95. Pres. Amarillo Area Found., 1988; bd. dirs. Harrington Found., 1989. Served with USNR, 1942-46, 51-52. Mem. Internat. City Mgrs. Assn. (past pres.), Tex. City Mgrs. Assn. (past pres.), Panhandle Home Builders Assn. (past bd. dirs.), Garland Home Builders Assn., Amarillo Exec. Assn. (pres. 1988-89), Amarillo C. of C., Dallas C. of C., Amarillo A & M Club, Amarillo Yale Club, Rotary. Methodist. Home: Rte 8 Box 45-6 326 N Shore Dr Amarillo TX 79118-9339

STIFF, ROBERT MARTIN, newspaper editor; b. Detroit, Aug. 25, 1931; s. Martin L. and Gladys (Mathews) S.; m. Cindy Rose, Aug. 30, 1980; children: David Alan, Amy Anne, Kirsten Marie. BA in Radio and Journalism, Ohio State U., 1953. Reporter, bur. chief, city editor Painesville (Ohio) Telegraph, 1953-61; deskman, asst. city editor, sports editor, city editor, day editor, state editor, asst. mng. editor St. Petersburg (Fla.) Times, 1961-67; editor St. Petersburg Evening Ind., 1967-84; dir. St. Petersburg Times Pub. Co., 1969-84; exec. editor, v.p. Tallahassee Democrat, 1985-91; pres. Bob Stiff & Assocs., Tallahassee, 1991-95; exec. editor JMT Assocs., 1991-92, 95—; mng. editor About Florida, 1991-94; editor Lexington (N.C.) Dispatch, 1995—; dir. devel. and pub. rels. Fla. Taxwatch Inc., 1992-94; bd. dir. N.C. AP News Coun., 1995—. Bd. dirs. Cancer Svcs. Davidson County. Mem. AP Assn. Fla. (pres. 1970-71), Am. Soc. Newspaper Editors (dir. 1981-87), Am. Soc. Newspaper Editors Found. (bd. dirs., treas. 1986-90), Fla. Soc. Newspaper Editors (pres. 1975-76, dir. 1971-84, 90-93), Fla. Bar Found. (bd. dirs. 1990-92), AP Mng. Editors Assn., Sigma Delta Chi (pres. West Coast chpt. 1970-710, N.C. Press Assn., Nat. Coun. Editl. Writers, Lexington Kiwanis (bd. dirs.).

STIFFLER, JACK JUSTIN, electrical engineer; b. Mitchellville, Iowa, May 22, 1934; s. John Justin and Helen Irene (Roorda) S.; m. Ardis Ann Ackerman, Aug. 21, 1955; 1 child, Julia Alise; m. Sally Voris Burns, Apr. 20, 1989. A.B. magna cum laude in Physics, Harvard U., 1956; M.S. in E.E. Calif. Inst. Tech., 1957, Ph.D., 1962; postgrad., U. Paris, 1957-58. Engr. Hughes Aircraft Corp., Culver City, Calif., 1956-57; mem. tech. staff Jet Propulsion Lab., Pasadena, Calif., 1959-67; cons. scientist Raytheon Corp., Sudbury, Mass., 1967-81; exec. v.p. Sequoia Systems, Inc., Marlborough, Mass., 1981—; lectr. Calif. Inst. Tech., U. So. Calif., UCLA, Northeastern U. Author: Theory of Synchronous Communications, 1971; contbr. chpts. to books, articles to profl. jours. Fellow IEEE; mem. Phi Beta Kappa, Sigma Xi. Office: Sequoia Systems Inc 400 Nickerson Rd Marlborough MA 01752-4658

STIGLER, DAVID MACK, lawyer; b. Indiana, Pa., Aug. 31, 1943; s. George Joseph and Margaret Louise (Mack) S.; m. Carolyn Ann Sawko, Sept. 30, 1990; children: Zachary, Benjamin, Julie, Joanna. AB, Oberlin Coll., 1965; JD, U. Chgo., 1968. Bar: N.Y. 1969, U.S. Dist. Ct. (so. and ea. dists.) N.Y., U.S. Tax Ct., U.S. Ct. Appeals (2d and 3d cirs.). Assoc. Rogers & Wells, N.Y.C., 1968-74; asst. gen. counsel Heublein, Inc., Farmington, Conn., 1974-86, v.p., 1984-86; v.p., gen. counsel, sec. ADVO, Inc., Windsor, Conn., 1986—; sr. v.p., 1990—; staff counsel Presdl. Commn. on All-Vol. Armed Forces, Washington, 1969. Chmn. fund drive United Way, Farmington, 1980, Windsor, 1987. Mem. ABA, Am. Corp. Coun. Assn., N.Y. State Bar Assn., Am. Soc. Corp. Secs. Republican. Avocations: running, racquet sports. Office: Advo Inc 1 Univac Ln Windsor CT 06095-2629*

STIGLER, STEPHEN MACK, statistician, educator; b. Mpls., Aug. 10, 1941; s. George Joseph and Margaret (Mack) S.; m. Virginia Lee, June 27, 1964; children: Andrew, Geoffrey, Margaret, Elizabeth. BA, Carleton Coll., 1963; PhD, U. Calif., Berkeley, 1967. Asst. prof. U. Wis., Madison, 1967-71, assoc. prof., 1971-75, prof., 1975-79; prof. U. Chgo., 1979—; chmn. dept., 1986-92; Ernest DeWitt Burton Disting. Svc. prof. U. Chgo., 1992—; trustee Ctr. for Advanced Study in the Behavioral Scis., Stanford, Calif., 1986-92, 93—, chmn., 1995—. Author: The History of Statistics, 1986; contbr. articles to jours. in field. Guggenheim Found. fellow, 1976-77; Ctr. for Advanced Study in Behavioral Scis. fellow, 1978-79. Fellow AAAS, Am. Acad. Arts and Scis. (mem. coun. 1995—), Inst. Math. Stats. (Neyman lectr. 1988, pres. 1993-94), Am. Statis. Assn. (editor Jour. 1979-82, Outstanding Statistician award Chgo. chpt. 1993), Royal Statis. Soc. (Fisher lectr. 1986); mem. Internat. Statis. Inst., Bernoulli Soc., History of Sci. Soc., Brit. Soc. for History Sci., Quadrangle Club, Sigma Xi. Office: U Chgo Dept Statistics 5734 S University Ave Chicago IL 60637-1514

STIGLITZ, JOSEPH EUGENE, economic adviser to President, educator; b. Gary, Ind., Feb. 9, 1943; s. Nathaniel David and Charlotte (Fishman) S.; m. Jane Hannaway, Dec. 23, 1978; children: Siobhan, Michael, Edward, Julia. B.A., Amherst Coll., Mass, 1964; DHL (hon.), Amherst Coll., 1974; Ph.D. in Econs., MIT, 1966; M.A. (hon.), Yale U., 1970; D in Econs. (hon.), U. Leuven, 1994. Prof. econs. Cowles Found., Yale U., New Haven, 1970-74; vis. fellow St. Catherine's Coll., Oxford, Eng., 1973-74; Joan Kenney professorship Stanford U., 1974-76, 88—; Oskar Morgenstern dist. fellow Inst. Advanced Studies Math., Princeton, N.J., 1978-79; Drummond prof. polit. economy Oxford U., Eng., 1976-79; prof. econs. Princeton U., 1979-88; mem. Pres.'s Coun. Econ. Advisers, 1993-95, chmn. coun. econ. advisers, 1995—, exec. dir.; cons. World Bank, State of Alaska, Seneca Indian Nation, Bell Communications Rsch. Editor Jour. Econ. Perspectives, 1986-93; Am. editor Rev. of Econ. Studies, 1968-76; assoc. editor Am. Econ. Rev., 1968-76, Energy Econs., Managerial and Decision Econs.; mem. editl. bd. World Bank Econ. Rev. Recipient John Bates Clark award Am. Econ. Assn., 1979, Internat. prize Accademia Lincei, 1988, Union des Assurances de Paris prize, 1989; Guggenheim fellow, 1969-70. Fellow Inst. for Policy Rsch. (sr. 1991-93), Brit. Acad. (corr.); mem. Am. Econ. Assn. (exec. com. 1982-84, v.p. 1985), Am. Acad. Arts and Scis., Nat. Acad. Sci., Econometric Soc.

STIGWOOD, ROBERT COLIN, theater, movie, television and record producer; b. Adelaide, Australia, Apr. 16, 1934; came to Eng., 1956; s. Gordon and Gwendolyn (Burrows) S. Attended, Sacred Heart Coll., Adelaide. Worked as copywriter for advt. agy. Adelaide; held series of jobs, including mgr. provincial theater and halfway house for delinquents in Cambridge; opened talent agy. London, 1962; liquidated firm, 1965; became bus. mgr. for group Graham Bond Orgn.; became co-mng. dir. NEMS Enterprises, 1967; established own firm Robert Stigwood Orgn., 1967; formed RSO Records, 1973; became dir. of Polygram, 1976; co-founder (with Rupert Murdoch) R&R Films, 1979; founder Music for UNICEF. 1st ind. record producer in Eng. with release of single Johnny Remember Me; producer: films, including Jesus Christ Superstar, 1973, Bugsy Malone, Tommy, 1975, Survive, 1976, Saturday Night Fever, 1977, Grease I, 1978, Grease II, 1982, Moment By Moment, 1978, Sergeant Pepper's Lonely Hearts Club Band, The Fan, 1981, Times Square, 1980, Gallipoli, 1980, Staying Alive, 1983; stage musicals in Eng. and U.S., including, Hair, Oh! Calcutta, The Dirtiest Show in Town, Sweeney Todd, Pippin, Jesus Christ Superstar, Evita, Grease; TV producer in Eng. and U.S.; prodns. include The Entertainer (dramatic spl.); All in the Family (series), The Prime of Miss Jean Brodie (dramatic series). Bd. dirs. Police Athletic League, N.Y.C.; patron Australian Nat. Art Gallery. Recipient Tony award for best musical (Evita); named Internat. Producer of Yr. ABC Interstate Theatres, Inc., 1976, Knight of St. John of Jerusalem, Malta, 1985. Club: Royal Bermuda Yacht. Avocations: yachting, tennis. Home: East Cowes, Barton Manor Estate, Isle of Wight England

STILES, GARY LESTER, cardiologist, molecular pharmacologist, educator; b. N.Y.C., May 22, 1949; s. Robert L. and Vivian M. (Cano) S.; m. Jane V. Black, June 7, 1971; children: Heather B., Wendy A. BS in Chemistry, St. Lawrence U., 1971; MD, Vanderbilt U., 1975. Diplomate Am. Bd. Internal Medicine, sub.-bd. Cardiovascular Medicine. Resident in internal medicine Vanderbilt U., Nashville, 1975-78; fellow in cardiology Duke U., Durham, N.C., 1978-81, asst. prof. medicine, 1981-85, assoc. prof., 1986-89, chief div. cardiology, 1989—, prof. medicine, 1990—, prof. pharmacology, 1990—; mem. sci. adv. coun. Alta. Heritage Found., Edmonton, Can., 1990—; mem. pharmacology study sect. NIH, Bethesda, Md., 1988-91. Editl. bd. Jour. Biol. Chemistry, 1990-95, Molecular Pharmacology, 1991—. Recipient Katz prize Am. Heart Assn., 1983, award Am. Fedn. Clin. Rsch., 1989; grantee Am. Heart Assn., 1987-90. Fellow Am. Coll. Cardiology (award 1993); mem. Internat. Churchill Soc., Assn. Am. Physicians, Am. Soc. Clin. Investigation. Republican. Achievements include patent in field. Office: Duke U Med Ctr Div Cardiology PO Box 3681 Durham NC 27710

STILES, MARY ANN, lawyer; b. Tampa, Fla., Nov. 16, 1944; d. Ralph A. and Bonnie (Smith) S. AA, Hills Community Coll., 1973; BS, Fla. State U., 1975; JD, Antioch Sch. Law, 1978. Bar: Fla. 1978. Legis. analyst Fla. Ho. of Reps., Tallahassee, 1973-74, 74-75; intern U.S. Senate, Washington, 1977; v.p., gen. counsel Associated Industries Fla., Tallahassee, 1978-81, gen. counsel, 1981-84, spl. counsel, 1986—; assoc. Deschler, Reed & Crichfield, Boca Raton, Fla., 1980-81; founding ptnr. Stiles, Taylor & Metzler, Tampa, Fla., 1982—; shareholder and dir. Stiles Taylor & Metzler, P.A., Six Stars Devel. Co. of Fla., Inc.; shareholder First Comml. Bank of Tampa. Author: Workers' Copmenstaion Law Handbook, 1980-94 edit. Bd. dirs., sec. Hillsborough C.C. Found., Tampa, 1985-87, 94—; bd. dirs. Hillsborough Area Regional Transit Authority, Tampa, 1986-89, Boys and Girls Club of Tampa, 1986—; mem. Bay Area chpt. Nat. Women's Polit. Caucus, 1993—, The Spring, 1992-93, What's My Chance, 1992—; mem. Gov.'s Oversite Bd. on Workers' Compensation, 1989-90, Workers Comp. Ruler Com., Fla. Bar, 1990—, Workers Comp. Exec. Counsel Fla. Bar, 1990—, Jud. Nominating Commn. for Workers' Compensation Cts., 1990-93, trustee Hillsborough Cmty. Coll., 1994—. Mem. ABA, Fla. Bar Assn., Hillsborough County Bar Assn., Hillsborough Assn. Women Lawyers, Fla. Assn. Women Lawyers, Fla. Women's Alliance, Hillsborough County Seminole Boosters (past pres.). Democrat. Baptist. Club: Tiger Bay (Tampa, past pres., sec.). Avocation: reading. Office: 315 S Plant Ave Tampa FL 33606-2325 also: 111 N Orange Ave Ste 850 Orlando FL 32801-2381 also: 317 N Calhoun St Tallahassee FL 32301-7605 also: 200 E Las Olas Blvd Ste 1760 Fort Lauderdale FL 33301-2248

STILES, NED BERRY, lawyer; b. Mays Lick, Ky., Aug. 7, 1932; s. Andrew Jackson and Frances (Berry) S.; m. Patricia Pollard, Nov. 23, 1953 (div. 1959); 1 son, Michael P.; m. Lynn Shattuck, Apr. 16, 1966 (div. 1976); children: Andrew J., Peter S.; m. Deborah Fiedler, Dec. 2, 1978; 1 dau., Jessica B. A.B., Miami U., Oxford, Ohio, 1953; LL.M., U. Cin., 1958. Bar: Ohio 1958, N.Y. 1962. Staff atty. SEC, Washington, 1958-61; assoc. Cleary, Gottlieb, Steen & Hamilton, N.Y.C., 1961-67, ptnr., 1968-88, mng. ptnr., 1988—; pres., chmn. bd. Fir Tree Internat. Fund. mem., bd. eds., Cincinnati Law Review, 1957-58; co-author: The Silent Partners—Institutional Investors and Corporate Control, 1965; contbr. articles to legal publs. Pres., bd. dirs. Quogue Assn. Inc., N.Y.; treas., bd. dirs. Group for the South Fork, Southampton, N.Y.; bd. appeals Village of Quogue. Served to capt. USAF, 1953-55. Mem. ABA, Assn. Bar City N.Y. (former mem. securities regulation and corp. law coms.). Clubs: River (N.Y.C.), India House (N.Y.C.). Office: Cleary Gottlieb Steen 1 Liberty Pla New York NY 10006-1470*

STILES, PHILLIP JOHN, physicist, educator; b. Manchester, Conn., Oct. 31, 1934; married, 1956; 6 children. BS, Trinity Coll., 1956; PhD in Physics, U. Pa., 1961. Mem. rsch. staff Thomas J. Watson Rsch. Ctr. IBM, N.Y.C., 1963-70; prof. physics Brown U., 1970-93, chmn. dept. physics, 1974-80, dean Grad. Sch., dean of rsch., 1986-93; provost, vice chancellor, prof. physics N.C. State U., Raleigh, 1993—. U. Pa. fellow, 1961-62, NSF fellow, 1962-63; recipient Humboldt Sr. U.S. Sci. award, 1976, John Price Wetheral medal Franklin Inst., 1981. Fellow AAAS; mem. Am. Physics Soc. (Oliver E. Buckley prize 1988), Am. Astronomy Soc., Acoustical Soc. Am. Office: NC State U Office Provost Vice Chancellor PO Box 7101 Raleigh NC 27695-7101

STILES, THOMAS BEVERIDGE, II, investment banking executive; b. Easton, Pa., Oct. 4, 1940; s. Ezra Martin and Vivien (de Fay) S.; m. Elaine Ann Patyk, July 2, 1966 (div. Oct. 1980); children—Thomas Beveridge III, Jonathan Ezra; m. Barbara Toll Alexander, Mar. 7, 1981. B.A., Yale U., 1963; M.B.A., Harvard U., 1968. V.p. Laird, Inc., N.Y.C., 1968-73; sr. v.p., dir. Smith Barney Harris Upham and Co., Inc., N.Y.C., 1973-82; exec. v.p., dir. E.F. Hutton & Co. Inc., N.Y.C., 1982-87; chmn., chief exec. officer Shearson Lehman Advisors Asset Mgmt. Co., N.Y.C., 1988-90; chmn., chief exec. officer Bernstein Macaulay, N.Y.C., also bd. dirs., 1988-90; CEO, chmn. Greenwich Street Advisors, N.Y.C., 1990—; also mng. dir. Smith, Barney, Inc., N.Y.C.,, 1993—; bd. dirs., treas. Cedar Lawn Cemetery, Paterson, N.J., 1973—. Served to 1st lt. M.I., U.S. Army, 1963-66. Fellow Fin. Analysts Fedn.; mem. N.Y. Soc. Security Analysts. Republican. Presbyterian. Club: Spring Lake Bath and Tennis (N.J.). Avocations: political science; tennis; swimming. Office: Greenwich St Advisors 388 Greenwich St Fl 23 New York NY 10013-2375

STILL, MARY JANE (M. J. STILL), mathematics educator; b. Kingsport, Tenn., Apr. 14, 1940; d. James Charles and Allie Fair (Williams) S.; m. Michael S. Golden, 1962 (div. 1971); m. Thos L. Scruggs, 1972 (div. 1975); children: Amanda Fair, Jacob Charles. AB in English, Math., Edn-Psychology, Trevecca Nazarene Coll., 1962; MEd in Math., Statistics, Auburn U., 1969. File clk. FBI, Washington, 1958; tchr. Stratford Jr.-Sr. High Sch., Nashville, 1962-63; statistician Pub. Welfare Dept. State of Tenn., Nashville, 1963-65; math. and English tchr. Smiths Sta. High Sch., Smiths, Ala., 1965-66; math., English, psychology tchr. West Point High Sch., West Point, Ga., 1966-67; math. tchr. La Grange High Sch., La Grange, Ga., 1967-68; math. and English tchr. Townsend High Sch., Townsend, Tenn., 1968-72; math., English, physical edn. tchr. Northshore High Sch., West Palm Beach, Fla., 1974-75; prof. math. Palm Beach Community Coll., Lake Worth, Fla., 1975-78, Palm Beach Community Coll.-North Campus, Palm Beach Gardens, Fla., 1978—; cons. Fla. Power & Light Co., North Palm Beach, 1989; lectr. Palm Beach Community Coll. Speakers, Palm Beach Gardens, 1986-89. Editor, advisor: College Mathematics, 1989; textbook editor, advisor Dellen Pub., Scott Foresman Pub., 1988—, Little Brown, McGraw Hill, 1989—, Wadsworth & Prindle/Weber/Schmidt, 1992—; contbr. to textbooks and profl. jours. Scorekeeper, coach, mgr. baseball and softball leagues Palm Beach area, 1980-90; supporter Jackson polit. campaign, West Palm Beach, 1988, Children's Mus. and Turtle Soc., Juno Beach, Fla., 1986; coach, mgr., sponsor boys' baseball little league, girls' softball, ladies' softball, Lake Park, Palm Beach Gardens, Fla., 1980-92, active softball and basketball coll. and cmty. leagues. NSF math. summer fellow Northeastern U., Boston, 1988; NSF grad. scholar, Auburn, Ala., 1967-69; Shakespeare scholar Shakespearean Soc. Palm Beach, Stratford-on-Avon, Eng., 1975; NSF grantee U. Fla., 1996. Mem. NEA, Math. Assn. Am., Fla. Assn. Cmty. Colls., Am. Statis. Assn., Dreher Sci. Mus., Bus. Women North Palm Beach, Animal Rescue League (West Palm Beach, life), Audubon Soc., NOW, Hist. Soc., Rwy. Club, Consortium for Math. and its Applications. Nazarene. Avocations: artist, music, drama, sports, church work. Office: Palm Beach Community Coll N 3160 P G A Blvd West Palm Beach FL 33410-2802

STILL, THOMAS WAYNE, newspaper editor, columnist; b. Alexandria, Va., July 9, 1953; s. Claude Richmond and Margaret Louise (Stratton) S.; children: Stephanie Anne, Jason Thomas, Jessica Erin. BA in Journalism, Drake U., 1973; postgrad., U. Wis., 1980-81. Copy boy The Washington Star, 1970-71; sports reporter/copy editor The Des Moines Register, 1972-73; gen. assignment reporter The Mason City (Iowa) Globe-Gazette, 1974-76; gen. assignment reporter The Wis. State Jour., Madison, 1976-77, city hall reporter, 1977-79, chief polit. reporter, 1979-85, opinion page editor, 1985-89, assoc. editor, 1989—; polit. columnist Corp. Report/Wis., Milw., 1987-95; polit. columnist/contbr. Wis. Interest, The Wis. Policy Rsch. Inst., Milw., 1992-95; syndicated columnist "Inside Wis.", 1990-95; guest presenter/lectr. Contbr. articles to newspapers. Co-founder We the People/ Wis., Madison, 1992-93; vol. Black Hawk Girl Scout Coun., Madison, 1989-95; past vol. Big Bros./Big Sisters, PTO. Recipient Midwest Regional Emmy award Nat. Acad. TV Arts and Scis., 1993, 94, Pub. Svc. Journalism award Milw. Press Club, 1980, 93, Sweepstakes award AP Mng. Editors, 1976, edit. writing award Wis. Newspaper Assn., 1986-95, grant Pew Ctr. for Civic Journalism; named one of Most Influential, Madison Mag., 1987, 91, 94. Mem. Nat. Conf. Editl. Writers (conv. com. 1995). Avocations: men's senior baseball league, fast-pitch softball, city league basketball, reading, youth coaching. Home: 218 S Segoe Rd Madison WI 53705-4939 Office: Wis State Jour 1901 Fish Hatchery Rd Madison WI 53713

STILL, WILLIAM CLARK, JR., chemistry educator; b. Augusta, Ga., Aug. 31, 1946; s. William Clark and Ann (Smith) S. B.S., Emory U., 1969, Ph.D. in Chemistry, 1972; postgrad., Princeton U., 1972-74, Columbia U., 1974-76. Asst. prof. chemistry Vanderbilt U., Nashville, 1976-78; asst. prof. chemistry Columbia U., N.Y.C., 1978-80, assoc. prof. chemistry, 1980-81, prof. chemistry, 1981—. Contbr. numerous articles to profl. jours. Recipient Alan T. Waterman award NSF, 1981, Buchman award Calif. Inst. Tech., 1982, Cope scholar, 1987, Stieglitz award, 1984, Nagoya medal of chemistry, 1996. Mem. Am. Chem. Soc. (Computers in Chemistry award 1993), Am. Acad. Arts and Scis. Office: Columbia U Dept Chemistry New York NY 10027

STILLER, JENNIFER ANNE, lawyer; b. Washington, May 4, 1948; d. Ralph Sophian and Joy (Dancis) S. AB in Econs. and History, U. Mich., 1970; JD, NYU, 1973. Bar: Pa. 1973, U.S. Dist. Ct. (mid. dist.) Pa. 1977, U.S. Supreme Ct. 1978, Ill. 1979, U.S. Dist. Ct. (no. dist.) Ill. 1979, U.S. Dist. Ct. (ea. dist.) Pa. 1983, U.S. Ct. Appeals (3rd cir.) 1983. Dep. atty. gen. Pa. Dept. Justice, Harrisburg, 1973-75, Pa. Dept. Health, Harrisburg, 1975-78; sr. staff atty. Am. Hosp. Assn., Chgo., 1978-80, mgr., dept. fed. law, 1980-81; gen. counsel Ill. Health Fin. Authority, 1981-82; sr. assoc. Berriman & Schwartz, King of Prussia, Pa., 1983-85, Wolf, Block, Schorr & Solis-Cohen, Phila., 1985-88; sr. assoc. Montgomery, McCracken, Walker & Rhoads, 1988-90, ptnr., 1990—, chair health law group, 1991—. Contbr. health law articles to profl. jours. Mem. ABA (gov. com. Health Law Forum 1994-95), Nat. Health Lawyers Assn., Am. Acad. Hosp. Attys., Forum of Exec. Women, Pa. Soc. Healthcare Attys. (pres. 1995), Phila. Bar Assn. Avocations: gardening, bicycling, hiking, music. Office: Montgomery McCracken 3 Parkway 20th Fl Philadelphia PA 19102

STILLER, JERRY, actor; b. N.Y.C., June 8; s. William and Bella S.; m. Anne Meara, Sept. 14, 1954; children: Amy, Benjamin. BS in Speech and Drama, Syracuse U., 1950. Actor with nat. co. of Peter Pan, 1951, also at Henry St. Playhouse, 1941, Cherry Lane Theatre, N.Y.C., 1947, Billy Barnes Showboat, Chgo., 1950, Erie (Pa.) Playhouse, 1951, 52, Memphis Arena Theatre, 1952, Phoenix Theatre, 1954, 55, 56, Shakespeare Festival Theatre, Stratford, Conn., 1955, Compass Players, 1959, mem. Shakespeare Co. in Central Park, N.Y.C., 1957, 71, Two Gentlemen, 1971, Much Ado, 1988; Broadway appearances include The Golden Apple, 1954, The Ritz, 1975, Unexpected Guests, 1977, Hurleyburly, 1985, Three Men on a Horse, 1993, What's Wrong With This Picture?, 1994; "After Play", 1995-96—, (written by wife, Anne Meare), film appearances include The Taking of Pelham 1-2-3, 1974, Airport '75, 1975, The Ritz, 1976, Those Lips, Those Eyes, 1979, Nadine, 1986, That's Adequate, 1986, Hairspray, 1986, Seize The Day, 1986, Shoeshine (Acad. award nomination, short subject 1989), A Pair of Jokers, 1990, The Pickle, 1992; Off-Broadway appearances include Boubouroche, 1971, Passione, 1980, Prairie du Chien, 1985, After-Play, 1995-96; co-star: TV series Joe and Sons, 1975; mem. comedy team with wife, Anne Meara, 1961—, Ed Sullivan Show 36 appearances; night club appearances include Compass Players, St. Louis, 1957, Happy Medium, Chgo., 1960, also Village Gate, Village Vanguard, Blue Angel, Bon Soir and, Phase Two, N.Y.C., Mr. Kelly's, Chgo., Hungry I, San Francisco, The Establishment, London, The Sands, Flamingo, Las Vegas, Harrah's, Reno and Lake Tahoe, Trump Plaza; co-star: daily TV series Take Five with Stiller and Meara, 1977-78; commercials for PBS Seize the Day; (co-recipient Voice of Imagery award Radio Advt. Bur. 1975); actor TV series, Tattinger's, 1987, The Detective, The Sunset Gang, PBS, 1991, The Hollow Boy, American Playhouse, 1991, Seinfeld, 1994; commercials: Blue Nun, United Van Lines, Amalgamales Bank; video (co-host with Anne Meara): So You Want to be an Actor?. Recipient Disting. Alumnus award Syracuse U., 1973, Arents Pioneer Medal, 1979, 1st Biffy award Balt. Internat. Film Festival, Entertainment Father of Yr. award, 1977, Syracuse Walk of Stars, 1994, Syracuse U. award for Achievement in the Arts.

STILLER, SHALE DAVID, lawyer, educator; b. Rochester, N.Y., Feb. 23, 1935; s. Maurice Aaron and Dorothy (Salitan) S.; m. Ellen M. Heller; children: Lewis B., Michael J., Kenneth R.; stepchildren: William Heller, Lawrence Heller. B.A., Hamilton Coll., 1954; LL.B., Yale U., 1957; M.L.A., Johns Hopkins U., 1977. Bar: Md. 1957. Ptnr. Piper & Marbury, Balt., 1992—; lectr. U. Md. Law Sch., 1963—. Contbr. articles to profl. jours. Trustee Johns Hopkins U., Assn. Jewish Charities, Peabody Inst., Johns Hopkins Medicine, The Weinberg Found.; adv. bd. Tax Mgmt., 1972-93; chmn. Jud. Nominating Commn., Balt., 1979-83; officer, bd. dirs. Park Sch., 1973-79, pres., 1982-86; pres. Jewish Family Agy., 1972-74. Mem. ABA, Am. Law Inst., Am. Coll. Tax Counsel, Am. Coll. Trust and Estate Counsel, Order of Coif. Democrat. Jewish. Club: 14 W Hamilton St (Balt.). Home: 807 St Georges Rd Baltimore MD 21210-1408 Office: Piper & Marbury 36 S Charles St Baltimore MD 21201-3020

STILLINGER, FRANK HENRY, chemist, educator; b. Boston, Aug. 15, 1934; s. Frank Henry and Gertrude (Metcalf) S.; m. Dorothea Anne Keller, Aug. 18, 1956; children—Constance Anne, Andrew Metcalf. B.S., U. Rochester, 1955; Ph.D., Yale U., 1958. NSF postdoctoral fellow Yale U., 1958-59; with Bell Telephone Labs., Murray Hill, N.J., 1959—; head chem. physics dept. Bell Telephone Labs., 1976-79; mem. evaluation panel Nat. Bur. Stds., 1975-78; mem. adv. com. for chemistry NSF, 1980-83, mem. adv. com. for advanced sci. computing, 1984-86, mem. adv. com. material and phys. sci. directorate, 1992-94; disting. lectr. chemistry U. Md., 1981; Karcher lectr. U. Okla., 1984; Trumbull lectr. Yale U., 1984; Washburn Meml. lectr. U. Nebr., 19865; Gucker lectr. Ind. U., 1987; W.A. Noyes lectr. U. Tex., 1988; Regents lectr. UCLA, 1990; Meek indsl. lectr. Ohio State U., 1990; McElvane lectr. U. Wis., 1992; Gomberg lectr. U. Mich., 1992. Assoc. editor Jour. Stat. Physics, Jour. Chem. Physics, Phys. Rev. Contbr. articles to profl. jours. Recipient Elliott Cresson medal Franklin Inst., 1978, Hildebrand award Am. Chem. Soc., 1986, Peter J. Debye award Am. Chem. Soc., 1992; Welch Found. fellow, 1974. Fellow Am. Phys. Soc. (Langmuir award 1989); mem. AAAS, Nat. Acad. Scis. Club: Early Am. Coppers Inc. Home: 216 Noe Ave Chatham NJ 07928-1548 Office: 600 Mountain Ave New Providence NJ 07974-0636

STILLINGER, JACK CLIFFORD, English educator; b. Chgo., Feb. 16, 1931; s. Clifford Benjamin and Ruth Evangeline (Hertzler) S.; m. Shirley Louise Van Wormer, Aug. 30, 1952; children: Thomas Clifford, Robert William, Susan, Mary; m. Nina Zippin Baym, May 21, 1971. BA, U. Tex., 1953; MA (Nat. Woodrow Wilson fellow), Northwestern U., 1954; PhD, Harvard U., 1958. Teaching fellow in English Harvard U., 1955-58; asst. prof. U. Ill., Urbana, 1958-61; assoc. prof. U. Ill., 1961-64, prof. English, 1964—; permanent mem. Center for Advanced Study, 1970—. Author: The Early Draft of John Stuart Mill's Autobiography, 1961, Anthony Munday's Zelauto, 1963, Wordsworth: Selected Poems and Prefaces, 1965, The Letters of Charles Armitage Brown, 1966, Twentieth Century Interpretations of Keats's Odes, 1968, Mill: Autobiography and Other Writings, 1969, The Hoodwinking of Madeline and Other Essays on Keats's Poems, 1971, The Texts of Keats's Poems, 1974, The Poems of John Keats, 1978, Mill: Autobiography and Literary Essays, 1981, John Keats: Complete Poems, 1982, Norton Anthology of English Literature, 1986, 1993, John Keats: Poetry Manuscripts at Harvard, 1990, Multiple Authorship and the Myth of Solitary Genius, 1991, Coleridge and Textual Instability, 1994; editor Jour. English and Germanic Philology, 1961-72. Guggenheim fellow, 1964-65. Fellow AAAS; mem. MLA, Keats-Shelley Assn. Am. (bd. dirs., editorial bd. Jour., Disting. Scholar award 1986), Byron Soc., Phi Beta Kappa. Home: 806 W Indiana Ave Urbana IL 61801-4838

STILLINGS, DENNIS OTTO, research director; b. Valley City, N.D., Oct. 30, 1942; s. Harlow Cecil and Ruth Alice (Wolff) S. BA, U. Minn., 1965. Tchr. Henry (S.D.) Pub. Schs., 1965-66, Darby (Mont.) Pub. Schs., 1966-68; tech. rsch. libr., then mgr. hist. dept. Medtronic, Inc., Mpls., 1968-79; instr. humanities U. Minn., Mpls., 1970-72; founding dir., then curator Bakken Libr., Mpls., 1976-80; ind. antiquarian hist. cons. Mpls., 1979-81; project dir. Archaeus Project, Kamuela, Hawaii, 1981—, v.p., 1989—; cons. Ctr. for Sci. Anomalies Rsch., Ann Arbor, Mich., 1983—; bd. dirs. Dan Carlson Enterprises, Mpls., Hawaii Ctr. Integral Health; v.p. Waimia Coun. on Aging. Columnist Med. Progress Through Technology, 1974—; columnist Med. Instrumentation, 1973-76, guest editor, 1975; editor: Cyberphysiology: The Science of Self-Regulation, 1988, Cyberbiological Studies of the Imaginal Component in the UFO Contact Experience, 1989, The Theology of Electricity: On the Encounter and Explanation of Theology and Science in the 17th and 18th Centuries, 1990, Project 2010: On the Current Crisis in Health and Its Implications For the Hospital For the Future, 1992; founding editor: (jours.) Artifex, 1981-93, Archaeus, 1982-84, Healing Island. Bd. dirs. Hawaii Ctr. for Integral Healing. Fellow Am. Inst. Stress; mem. Assn. Sci. Study Anomalous Phenomena, Bioelectromagnetics Soc., Soc. Sci. Exploration. Avocations: Jungian psychology, golf, fishing, travel.

STILLMAN, GEORGE, artist; b. Laramie, Wyo., Feb. 25, 1921; s. Herman and Estelle (Heimlich) S.; m. Lillian Lucille Blitz, Dec. 1, 1942; children: David, Anthony. Cert. of completion, Calif. Sch. Fine Art, 1949; MFA, Ariz. State U., 1970. Prof. art U. Guadalajara, Mex., 1950-51; chief map reprodn. Inter Am. Geodetic Survey U.S. Army, Panama C.Z., 1951-58; comm. officer AID, L.Am., 1958-66; prodr. and dir. TV, Ariz. State U., Tempe, 1966-70; chmn. art dept. Columbus (Ga.) Coll., 1970-72; prof., chmn. dept. Ctrl. Wash. U., Ellensburg, 1972-88, prof. emeritus, 1988—. One-man shows include Guild Gallery, San Francisco, 1947, Lucien Labaudt Gallery, San Francisco, 1949, Ariz. State U. Mus., Tempe, 1970, Foster/White Gallery, Seattle, 1986, Ctrl. Wash. U., Ellensburg, 1991; exhibited in group shows at Palace of the Legion of Honor, San Francisco, 1947, San Francisco Mus. Art, 1949, Bklyn. Mus. Art, 1952, Ga. Artists, High Mus., Atlanta, 32d Spokane (Wash.) Ann. Nat., 1980, Art for the Parks, Jackson, Wyo., 1989, 100 Yrs. of Washington Art, Tacoma, Wash., 1990, Art Mus. Santa Cruz, Calif., 1993; represented in permanent collections Met. Mus. Art, N.Y.C., Nat. Mus. Am. Art, Smithsonian, Washington, Oakland (Calif.) Mus. Art, High Mus. Art, Atlanta, Tacoma Mus. Art, Washington State Arts Commn., British Mus. Art, London, Laguna (Calif.) Mus. Art, Worcester (Mass.) Mus. Art; contbr. chpt. to book. Recipient Bender award San Francisco Art Assn., 1949, Nat. Endowment for Arts, 1990. Mem. Coll. Art Assn., Nat. Watercolor Soc. Home: 1127 Franklin St Ellensburg WA 98926-3277

STILLMAN, HOWARD NEIL, investment analyst, consultant, writer; b. Bklyn., Oct. 29, 1935; s. Max and Betty Stillman; m. Carol Lou Panzer, Feb. 17, 1962; children: Brad, Todd. BBA, CCNY, 1957; MBA, NYU, 1964. Jr. securities analyst Fitch Investment Svcs., N.Y.C., 1957-59, Parrish & Co., N.Y.C., 1959-61; security analyst Sirota Taylor & Co., N.Y.C., 1961-66; sr. security analyst Orvis Bros., N.Y.C., 1966-67; dir. rsch. Kern Securities, N.Y.C., 1967-70; v.p. rsch. Black Stein Kimball, Paramus, N.J., 1970-73; market analyst Lustra Lighting divsn. N.Am. Phillips, East Rutherford, N.J., 1973-75; fin. advisor Prentice Hall, N.Y.C., 1975-82; dir. rsch. Phillip Appel/Muller, N.Y.C., 1983-84; ind. investment analyst, fin. specialist New Milford, N.J., 1985—; asst. prof. fin. Montclair (N.J.) State Coll., 1981-82, Fairleigh Dickinson U., Teaneck, N.J., 1976; tchr. fin. Bergen C.C., Paramus, 1969-81. With USAR, 1958-64. Mem. N.Y. Soc. Security Analysts, B'nai B'rith. Avocations: reading, music, spectator sports. Home: 2348 Terraza Ribera Carlsbad CA 92009-6632

STILLMAN, JOYCE L., artist, educator, writer, illustrator, consultant; b. N.Y.C., Jan. 19, 1943; d. Murray W. and Evelyn (Berger) Stillman. BA, NYU, 1964; student, Art Students League, 1965, Pratt Inst., 1972; MFA, L.I. U., 1975; postgrad., Calif. Inst. Integral Studies, 1994—. Tchr. N.Y.C. Pub. Schs., 1964-71; artist Cen. Hall Gallery, Port Washington, N.Y., 1974-76, Louis K. Meisel Gallery, N.Y.C., 1975-84, Tolarno Gallery, Melbourne, Australia, 1976—, Allan Stone Gallery, N.Y.C., 1990—; vis. assoc. prof. Towson State U., 1982; tchr. Women in Art, Tompkins Cortland C.C., 1988; lectr. Cornell U., 1990; founder Ithaca Women Artists Salon. One-person shows include Cen. Hall Gallery, Port Washington, 1975, Tolarno Gallery, Melbourne, 1976, Louis K. Meisel Gallery, N.Y.C., 1977, 80, 81, 82, Heckscher Mus., Huntington, N.Y., 1980, Holtzman Gallery, Towson (Md.) State U., 1982, Roslyn Oxley Gallery, Sydney, 1976, 82, Tomasulo Gallery, Union College, N.J., 1983, Stages, Keuka Coll., Keuka Park, N.Y., 1985, New Visions, Ithaca, N.Y., 1989, Herr-Chambliss, Hot Springs, Ark., 1990, Artist on the Lake, Hector, N.Y., 1992, Mus. Modern Art Christmas Card Collection, 1994; designer Mus. Modern Art Christmas Collection, 1978-81, 94, Time-Life Poster, 1978; exhibited in over 75 group shows, corp. and mus. collections. Recipient Flower Painting award Artist's Mag., 1986, Art Dir.'s Club 58th Annual Distinctive Merit award, 1979, N.Y. State Creative Artist's Pub. Svc. grant, 1979. Mem. Nat. Assn. Women Artists, Allan Stone Gallery N.Y.C. Home and Studio: PO Box 662 Montour Falls NY 14865 also: 203 S Genesse St Montour Falls NY 14865

STILLMAN, M. J., physical science rsch. administrator, biochemist; b. London, June 4, 1947; Can. citizen; BSc, U. East Anglia, 1969, MSc, 1970, PhD in Chemistry, 1973. Fellow in chemistry U. Alta., Edmonton, Can., 1973-75; from asst. prof. to assoc. prof. U. Western Ont., London, Can., 1975-86, prof. chemistry, 1986—, dir. Ctr. Chemistry and Physics, 1986—. Mem. Chem. Soc., Can. Inst. Chemistry, Am. Chem. Soc. Office: Univ Western ONCtr Chem Phys, P&A Bldg Rm 102, London, ON Canada N6A 3K7*

STILLMAN, NINA GIDDEN, lawyer; b. N.Y.C., Apr. 3, 1948; d. Melvin and Joyce Audrey (Gidden) S. AB with distinction, Smith Coll., 1970; JD cum laude, Northwestern U., 1973. Bar: Ill. 1973, U.S. Dist. Ct. (no. dist.) Ill. 1973, U.S. Dist. Ct. (ea. dist.) Wis. 1979, U.S. Dist. Ct. (no. dist. trial bar) Ill. 1983, U.S. Ct. Appeals (7th cir.) 1974, U.S. Supreme Ct. 1981, U.S. Dist. Ct. (ctrl. dist.) Ill. 1994. Assoc. Vedder, Price, Kaufman & Kammholz, Chgo., 1973-79, ptnr., 1980—; mem. adv. bd. occupational health and safety tng. program U. Mich., Ann Arbor, 1980-83; adj. faculty Inst. Human Resources and Indsl. Rels., Loyola U., Chgo., 1983-86, mem. bd. advisors, 1986—. Author: (with others) Women, Work, and Health: Challenge to Corporate Policy, 1979, Occupational Health Law: A Guide for Industry, 1981, Employment Discrimination, 1981, Personnel Management: Labor Relations, 1981, Occupational Safety and Health Law, 1988; contbr. articles to profl. jours. Legal advisor, v.p. Planned Parenthood Assn. Chgo., 1979-81; sec. jr. governing bd. Chgo. Symphony Orch., 1983. Recipient Svc. award Northwestern U., 1994. Mem. ABA (occupational safety and health law com. 1978—), Chgo. Bar Assn. (chmn. labor and employment law com. 1986-87), Human Resources Mgmt. Assn. Chgo. (officer, bd. dirs. 1986-88), Am. Inns of Ct. (v.p. Wigmore chpt. 1988-89), Northwestern U Sch. Law Alumni Assn. (pres. 1991-92), Coun. of 100, Smith Coll. Club Chgo. (pres. 1972), Law Club, Econ. Club Chgo., The Chgo. Com. Avocations: travel, reading, the arts, collecting art. Office: Vedder Price Kaufman & Kammholz 222 N La Salle St Chicago IL 60601-1003

STILLMAN, ROBERT DONALD, government official; b. Chgo., Sept. 27, 1929; s. Arthur Joseph and Grace Ellen (McLean) S.; m. Joan Ellen Caspersen, 1963 (dec. May 1993); children: Nancy, Barbara, John. BE in Chem. Engring., Yale U., 1950; MBA, Harvard U., 1952. With orgn. planning dept. FMC Corp., San Jose, Calif., 1954-57; assoc. Payson & Trask, N.Y.C., 1957-62, gen. ptnr., 1962-72; exec. v.p., treas., dir. AEA Investors Inc., N.Y.C., 1972-92; assoc. adminstr. for investment U.S. SBA, Washington, 1994-95; v.p. investment funds Overseas Pvt. Investment Corp., Washington, 1995—. Lt. USAF, 1952-54. Mem. Univ. Club (Washington and N.Y.C.), Yale Club (N.Y.C.), Tau Beta Pi, Sigma Xi, Alpha Chi Sigma. Office: Overseas Pvt Investment Corp 1100 New York Ave NW Washington DC 20527

STILLS, STEPHEN, musician, vocalist, composer; b. Dallas, Jan. 3, 1945. Vocalist, guitarist Buffalo Springfield band, 1966-68, Crosby, Stills & Nash, 1968-69, 77, 82, Crosby, Stills, Nash, & Young, 1969-71, solo career, 1971—. Albums include Stephen Stills, 1970, Stephen Stills II, 1971, Stephen Stills, 1975, Illegal Stills, 1976, Thoroughfare Gap, 1978, Right by You, 1984, (with Buffalo Springfield) Buffalo Springfield, 1967, (with Buffalo Springfield) Buffalo Springfield Again, 1967, Last Time Around, 1969, (with Crosby, Stills, Nash, & Young) Deja Vu, 1970, Four Way Street, 1972, (with Crosby, Stills, Nash, Young) So Far, 1974, American Dream, 1989, (with Crosby, Stills, Nash) Crosby, stills and Nash, 1969, Crosby, Stills and Nash, 1977, Daylight Again, Live It Up, Replay (best of), After The Storm, 1994, (with Manassas) Manassasm 1972, Down The Roadm 1973; singles include (solo) Love the One You're With, 1971, Super Session, (with Buffalo Springfield) For What It's Worth, 1967, (with Crosby, Stills, Nash, & Young) Woodstock, Ohio, Teach Your Children, 1970.

STILLWELL, G(EORGE) KEITH, physician; b. Moose Jaw, Sask., Can., July 11, 1918; came to U.S., 1947, naturalized, 1964; s. George B. and Muriel (Bolster) S.; m. Mildred Ethel Cameron, Mar. 12, 1943; children: Paul, Craig. B.A., U. Sask., 1939; M.D., Queen's U., Kingston, Ont., Can., 1942; Ph.D., U. Minn., 1954. Diplomate: Am. Bd. Phys. Medicine and Rehab. Intern Gen. Hosp., Kingston, 1942-43; resident Gen. Hosp., 1945, U. Minn., Mpls., 1947-51; pvt. practice medicine specializing in phys. medicine and rehab. Mpls., 1951-54; cons. dept. phys. medicine and rehab. Mayo Clinic, Rochester, Minn., 1954-83; chmn. dept. phys. medicine and rehab. Mayo Clinic, 1973-81; instr. U. Minn., 1950-54; instr. Mayo Grad. Sch. Medicine, 1955-60, asst. prof. phys. medicine and rehab., 1960-67, asso. prof., 1967-73; prof. Mayo Med. Sch., 1973-83; vis. prof. Ohio State U., 1970. Contbr. numerous articles to med. publs. Served with M.C., Royal Can. Army, 1943-46. Mem. AMA, Am. Acad. Phys. Medicine and Rehab. (editorial Bd. Archives Phys. Medicine and Rehab. 1960-81, chmn. editorial bd. 1972-77, bd. govs. acad. 1963-70), Am. Congress Rehab. Medicine (Gold Key award 1973), Assn. Acad. Physiatrists. Unitarian. Office: Mayo Clinic Rochester MN 55905

STILLWELL, VALORIE CELESTE, secondary school mathematics educator; b. Merced, Calif., Nov. 26, 1960; d. Wallace Dee and Frances Estelle (Cagle) Sinclair; m. William Edward Stillwell, May 27, 1990. BS in Math. with highest honors, U. Calif., Davis, 1982, BS in Human Devel. with highest honors, 1982, track coaching credential with honors, 1983; MA in Edn., U.S. Internat., 1990. Cert. gifted and talented edn. and spl. edn. educator. Asst. track coach Woodland (Calif.) and Vacaville (Calif.) H.S., 1980-83; gifted and talented edn. math tchr., head track and field coach Irvington H.S., Fremont, Calif., 1983-87; gifted and talented edn. math tchr. Mission San Jose H.S., Fremont, 1987-90; math tchr., math dept. chairperson Edna Hill Mid. Sch., Brentwood, Calif., 1990-95, math mentor tchr., 1994-96; math. dept. chairperson Bristow Mid. Sch., Brentwood, 1995—; mem. liaison com. Irvington H.S., Fremont, 1983-87; mem. safety and facilities com. Mission San Jose H.S., Fremont, 1987-90; sch. site coun. chairperson Edna Hill Mid. Sch., 1990-93, reading com. chairperson, mem. transition team, mem. dist. math. com., 1994—, salary com. co-chairperson, 1994-96. Ednl. Initiatives grantee, 1990. Mem. ASCD, Nat. Coun. Tchrs. of Math., Nat. Math. League, Calif. Math. Coun., Contra Costa County Math. (mem. adv. coun.), Diablo Math. Educators, Math Counts (peer tutor competition team). Avocations: reading, sports. Office: Bristow Sch 855 Minnesota Ave Brentwood CA 94513

STILWELL, JOHN QUINCY, lawyer; b. Columbia, S.C., Sept. 20, 1933; s. James Raymond and Edna (Douglass) S.; m. Regina Besman, Apr. 18, 1965 (div. Mar. 1977); 1 child, Laura Douglass; m. Nancy O'Neil, Mar. 20, 1987; children: William S. Rogers, Richard Blake Rogers, Stephen J. Rogers, Stewart D. Rogers. AB, U. N.C., 1954; LLB, Columbia U., 1961; MA, U. Tex., Dallas, 1988, PhD, 1994. Bar: N.Y. 1962, Tex. 1990. Assoc. atty. Winthrop, Stimson, Putnam & Roberts, N.Y.C., 1961-68; v.p., gen. counsel Total Energy Leasing Corp., N.Y.C., 1968-70, pres., 1970-72; ptnr. Gibbons, Green & Rice, N.Y.C., 1972-74; chmn. Transcable Inc., N.Y.C., 1974-77, John Stilwell Assocs., Inc., Fairfield, Conn., 1977-79; sr. v.p. Kidde, Inc., Saddle Brook, N.J., 1979-85; assoc. gen. counsel Mut. of N.Y. Life, N.Y.C., 1985-87; ptnr. Akin, Gump, Strauss, Hauer & Feld, L.L.P., Dallas, 1987—. Bd. dirs., sec. Shared Housing Ctr., Inc., Dallas, 1993—; trustee Consensus Found., Dallas, 1990. Served to lt. USN, 1954-58. Mem. Assn. Bar City N.Y., Dallas Bar Assn. Avocation: philosophy and communication theory. Home: 4808 Byron Ave Dallas TX 75205-3254 Office: Akin Gump Strauss 1700 Pacific Ave Ste 4100 Dallas TX 75201-4618

STILWELL, RICHARD DALE, baritone; b. St. Louis, May 6, 1942; s. Otho John Clifton and Tressie Fern (Parrish) S.; m. Elizabeth Louise Jencks, Mar. 21, 1967 (div.); m. Kerry M. McCarthy, Oct. 22, 1983. Student, Anderson Coll., 1960-62; MusB, Ind. U., 1966; MusD (hon.), Knox Coll., 1980. With Met. Opera Co., N.Y.C., 1970—. Appearances in major roles with Met. Opera, N.Y.C., Washington Opera Soc., Marseilles (France) Opera Co., Sante Fe Opera, San Francisco Opera Co., Paris Opera Co., Teatro Alla Scala, Covent Garden, Hamburg (Fed. Republic of Germany) State Opera, Glyndebourne Opera Festival, Eng., Vancouver (B.C.) Opera Co., Chgo. Opera Co., Tanglewood Festival, Israel Philharm., San Jose (Calif.) Opera, others; soloist with Nat. Symphony, Washington, Chgo. Symphony, Am. Symphony, Carnegie Hall, N.Y.C., St. Louis Symphony, Double Arts Chorale at Philharm. Hall, Met. Opera Studio at Tully Hall, N.Y.C., Boston Symphony, Los Angeles Philharm., Presl. dinner in honor of Apollo 11 astronauts, Los Angeles, 1969. Served with AUS, 1966-69. Recipient Nat. Soc. Arts and Letters award, 1963, Young Artist award St. Louis, 1963, Fisher Found. award Met. Opera Auditions, 1965. Mem. Am. Guild Musical Artists. Office: care Columbia Artists Mgmt Arbib Div 165 W 57th St New York NY 10019

STIMMEL, BARRY, cardiologist, internist, educator, university dean; b. Bklyn., Oct. 8, 1939; s. Abraham and Mabel (Bovit) S.; m. Barbara Barovick, June 6, 1970; children: Alexander, Matthew. BS, Bklyn. Coll., 1960; MD, SUNY, Bklyn., 1964. Diplomate: Nat. Bd. Med. Examiners, Am. Bd. Internal Medicine. Resident Mt. Sinai Hosp., N.Y.C., 1964-65, 67-69; asst. dean admissions and student affairs Mt. Sinai Sch. Medicine, CUNY, 1970-71, assoc. dean, 1971—, asst. prof. medicine, 1972-75, assoc. prof., 1975-84, prof. medicine and med. edn., 1984—, assoc. dean acad. affairs, 1975-81, dean admissions, acad. affairs and student affairs, 1981—, assoc. attending physician, 1981-94, dean grad. med. edn., 1994—, attending physician, 1984—, acting chmn. dept. med. edn., 1980-94; mem. com. planning, priorities and evaluation N.Y. Met. Regional Med. Program, 1971-73; adv. com. Nat. Ctr. Urban Problems CUNY, 1970-71; adv. com. methadone maintenance Office of Drug Abuse Svcs. State N.Y., 1976-79; sci. adv. bd. Nat. Coun. Drug Abuse, 1978-84, N.Y. State Bd. Profl. Med. Conduct, 1983—; bd. dirs. Am. Soc. Addiction Medicine, N.Y. State Coun. on Grad. Med. Edn., Greater N.Y. Hosp. Assn. Task Force on Health Manpower. Author: Heroin Dependency: Medical Social and Economic Aspects, 1975, Cardiovascular Effects Mood Altering Drugs, 1979, Pain, Analgesia, Addiction, 1982, Ambulatory Care, 1983, The Facts about Drug Use, 1991; editor Advances in Alcohol and Substance Abuse, 1980-91, Jour. Advances in Alcohol and Substance Abuse, Jour. Addictive Diseases, 1991—; assoc. editor Am. Jour. Drug and Alcohol Abuse, 1974-85; contbr. chpts. to books, articles to profl. jours. Served with M.C. USNR, 1965-67. Mem. AAUP, Am. Assn. Physicians Assts. (adv. bd. 1972-73), Am. Assn. Higher Edn., Soc. Study of Addiction to Alcohol and Other Drugs, Assn. Med. Edn. and Rsch. Substance Abuse, Inst. Study of Drug Addiction, Am., N.Y. heart assns., Am., N.Y. State socs. internal medicine, Soc. Internal Medicine County of N.Y. (dir.), Am. Coll. Cardiology, Greater N.Y. Coalition on Drug Abuse, NYS Coun. on Grad. Medical Edn., N.Y. Acad. Medicine, Nat. Coun. Alcoholism, Rsch. Soc. on Alcoholism, Am. Ednl. Research Assn., Am. Fedn. Clin. Rsch., Am. Soc. Addiction Medicine. Office: Mt Sinai Sch Med 100th St and Fifth Ave New York NY 10029

STIMPERT, MICHAEL ALAN, agricultural products company executive; b. Madisonville, La., Aug. 21, 1944; s. Warren Eugene and Louisa (Beale) S.; m. Kim Kathleen Agee, Apr. 17, 1970 (div. 1985); 1 child, Kelly Kathleen; m. Helen Marie Evans, June 27, 1987; children: Katherine Helen, Michael Adam. Student, Washburn U., 1962-64, U. Copenhagen, 1964; BA, Western Res. U., 1967; MBA, Harvard U., 1974. Asst. to group v.p. Gold Kist Inc., Atlanta, 1974, mgr. internat. div., 1975-80, dir. spl. markets and staff services, 1980-81, group v.p., 1982-86; v.p. ops. and govt. affairs Golden Peanut Co., Atlanta, 1986-89, exec. v.p., 1989-95; sr. v.p. Gold Kist Inc., Atlanta, 1996—; bd. dirs. Agri Internat., Inc., Atlanta, G.C. Properties, Atlanta, G.K. Pecans, Atlanta, Luker Inc., Augusta, Ga., GKX Inc., Agana, Guam, Global Health Action, Atlanta; chmn. Agra Trade Financing, Inc., Atlanta. Mem. adv. bd. dirs. Internat. Svc. Assn. for Health Devel. Edn. Project, 1982-91; bd. dirs. Global Health Action. Lt. (j.g.) USN, 1967-72, Vietnam. Mem. Assn. for Corp. Growth, Japan-Am. Soc. Ga., Harvard Bus. Sch. Club Atlanta, Cherokee Town and Country Club. Democrat. Roman Catholic. Office: Gold Kist Inc 244 Perimeter Center Pky Atlanta GA 30346

STIMPSON, CATHARINE ROSLYN, English language educator, writer; b. Bellingham, Wash., June 4, 1936; d. Edward Keown and Catharine (Watts) S. A.B., Bryn Mawr Coll., 1958; B.A., Cambridge U., Eng., 1960, M.A., 1960; Ph.D., Columbia U., 1967. Mem. faculty Barnard Coll., N.Y.C., 1963-80; prof. English, dean of grad. sch., vice provost grad. edn. Rutgers U., New Brunswick, N.J., 1980-92, Univ. prof., 1991—; chmn. bd. scholars Ms. Mag., N.Y.C., 1981-92; dir. fellows program MacArthur Found., 1994—. Author: Class Notes, 1979, Where the Meanings Are, 1988;

founding editor: Signs: Jour. Women in Culture and Society, 1974-81; book series Women in Culture and Society, 1981; columnist Change Mag., 1992-93. Chmn. N.Y. Council Humanities, 1984-87, Nat. Council Research on Women, 1984-89 ; bd. dirs. Stephens Coll., Columbia, Mo., 1982-85; trustee Bates Coll., 1990—. Hon. fellow Woodrow Wilson Found., 1958; Fulbright fellow, 1958-60; Nat. Humanities Inst. fellow New Haven, 1975-76; Rockefeller Humanities fellow, 1983-84. Mem. MLA (exec. coun., chmn. acad. freedom com., 1st v.p., pres. 1990), PEN, AAUP, NOW, Legal Def. and Edn. Fund (bd. dirs. 1991—), PBS (bd. dirs. 1994—). Democrat. Home: 62 Westervelt Ave Staten Island NY 10301-1432 Office: Rutgers U 172 College Ave New Brunswick NJ 08901-1157

STIMPSON, RITCHIE PLES, retired air force officer; b. Black Mountain, N.C., Mar. 22, 1917; s. David Ples and Lydia Hinson Stimpson; m. Marjorie Spruce, May 3, 1942; children: Ritchie P. Jr., David Fleming. BS in Physics, Furman U., 1940. Commd. 2nd lt. U.S. Air Force, 1941, advanced through grades to col., 1953; squadron comdr. 13th Tactical Reconnaissance Squadron, 1942-44; dir. ops. 24 Composite Wing, Borinquen Field, P.R., 1946-47; liaison officer Armed Forces Spl. Weapons Project to Strategic Air Commd., Offutt AFB, Nebr., 1950-52; dir. plans and negotiations Joint U.S. Asst. Adv. Group, Madrid, Spain, 1957-59; staff officer Joint Chiefs Staff, Washington, 1960-61, Weapons System Evaluation Group/Office of Sec. of Def., 1964-67; comdt. Air Force ROTC detachment Auburn (Ala.) U., 1967-71; ret., 1971; owner Ritch Stimpson Co., Inc., College Station, Tex., 1975-82; ind. writer, Dallas, 1982-93. Author: The Protestant Church and Bible Disregard the Truth, 1989, "Is It True?" Answers to Questions About the Bible, 1992. Decorated Commendation medals (2), Identification Badge, Outstanding Unit award. Mem. Air Force Assn., Greater Dallas Ret. Officers Assn., Greater Dallas Ret. Officers Assn. Investment Club, Oakridge Country Club, Furman U. Paladin Club. Republican. Methodist. Avocations: golf, travel, reading, bridge, gardening. Home: 2729 Laurel Oaks Dr Garland TX 75044-6939

STIMSON, FREDERICK SPARKS, Hispanist, educator; b. Newark, Ohio, Jan. 1, 1919; s. Fred Samuel and Leah Kate (Sparks) S. B.A., Ohio State U., 1940; postgrad., Harvard U., 1940-41; Jr. fellow in Archaeology, Princeton U., 1941-42; M.A., U. Mich., 1948, Ph.D. (Ford Found. grantee), 1952. Dir. Cultural Center for Dept. State, Medellin, Colombia, 1944-46; asst. public affairs officer Am. embassy, San Salvador, El Salvador, 1947; instr. to prof. dept. Spanish Northwestern U., Evanston, Ill., 1954-81; prof. emeritus Northwestern U., 1981—, chmn. dept., 1976-79. Author: Cuba's Romantic Poet, 1964, New Schools of Spanish American Poetry, 1970, Literatura de la América Hispánica, 3 vols, 1971-75, Los poemas más representativos de Plácido, 1976. Mem. MLA, Phi Beta Kappa. Home: 3300 S Ocean Blvd Apt 819C Highland Beach FL 33487

STINE, GEORGE HARRY, consulting engineer, author; b. Phila., Mar. 26, 1928; s. George Haeberle and Rhea (Matilda) (O'Neill) S.; m. Barbara Ann Kauth, June 10, 1952; children: Constance Rhea, Eleanor Anne, George Willard. B.A. in Physics, Colo. Coll., 1952. Chief controls and instruments sect., propulsion br. White Sands (N.Mex.) Proving Grounds, 1952-55; chief range ops. div. U.S. Naval Ordnance Missile Test Facility at proving grounds, 1955-57; design specialist Martin Co., Denver, 1957; chief engr., pres. Model Missiles, Inc., Denver, 1957-59; design engr. Stanley Aviation Corp., Denver, 1959-60; asst. dir. research Huyck Corp., Stamford, Conn., 1960-65; sci. cons. CBS-TV, 1969, CBC, Toronto, 1969; sci. reporter Metromedia Radio News, N.Y.C., 1968; cons. Young & Rubicam Inc., N.Y.C., also Gen. Electric Co., Valley Forge, Pa., 1966-69; lectr. Franklin Inst., Phila., 1966-72; mktg. mgr. Flow Technology, Inc., Phoenix, 1973-76; cons. curator Internat. Space Hall of Fame, 1976; cons. astronautical history Nat. Air and Space Museum, Smithsonian Instn., 1965—; cons. mktg. research and surveys Talley Industries, Inc., Mesa, Ariz., 1977; cons. mktg. and comm. Flow Tech., Inc., 1976-79; cons. Sci. Applications, Inc. 1976-81, Visions of the Future, 1982-86, McDonnell Douglas Corp., 1988-90, Sci. Applications Internat. Corp., 1990, Quest Aerospace Edn., Inc., 1992—, Aero Tech., Inc., 1991; expert witness fireworks injury cases, 1984—; pres. The Enterprise Inst., Inc., 1987—; cons., writer Discover Space Computer Program, Broderbond Software, Inc., 1992-93; moderator aviation and sport rocketry conf., Bix on-line computer network, 1986—. Freelance writer, 1951—; author more than 50 books on astronautics and sci., including The Model Rocketry Manual, 1975, The Third Industrial Revolution, 2d edit., 1979, The New Model Rocketry Manual, 1977, Shuttle Into Space, 1978, The Space Enterprise, 1980, Space Power, 1981, Confrontation in Space, 1981, The Hopeful Future, 1983, The Untold Story of the Computer Revolution, 1984, The Silicon Gods, 1984, Handbook for Space Colonists, 1985, The Corporate Survivors, 1986, Thirty Years of Model Rocketry, A Safety Report, 1988, Mind Machines You Can Build, 1991, ICBM, The Making of the Weapon That Changed the World, 1991, The Handbook of Model Rocketry 6th edit., 1994, Halfway to Anywhere, 1996; author: (as Lee Correy) sci. fiction novels and stories, including Starship Through Space, 1954, Rocket Man, 1955, Contraband Rocket, 1956, Star Driver, 1980, Shuttle Down, 1981, Space Doctor, 1981, The Abode of Life, 1982, Manna, 1984, A Matter of Metalaw, 1986, (under own name) Warbots, 1988, Operation Steel Band, 1988, The Bastaard Rebellion, 1988, Sierra Madre, 1988, Operation High Dragon, 1989, The Lost Battalion, 1989, Operation Iron Fist, 1989, Force of Arms, 1990, Blood Siege, 1990, Guts and Glory, 1991, Warrior Shield, 1992, Judgement Day, 1992, Starsea Invaders # 1, First Action, 1993, Star-sea Invaders # 2, Second Contact, 1994, Star-sea Invaders # 3, Third Encounter, 1995; contbr. numerous articles to jours. Charter mem. citizen's adv. coun. Nat. Space Policy, 1981—; mem. Ariz. Space Commn., 1992—, NASA Tech. and Commercialization Adv. Com., 1995. Recipient Silver medal Assn. U.S. Army, 1967, Spl. award Hobby Industry Assn., 1969; Paul Tissandier diploma Fedn. Aeronautique Internationale, 1985, Lifetime Space Activist award Space Access Soc., 1995. Fellow AIAA (assoc.)Explorers Club, Brit. Interplanetary Soc., Am. Rocket Soc.; mem. Nat. Assn. Rocketry (hon. trustee 1978-81, founder 1957, pres. 1957-67, trustee 1978-81, Spl. Founder's award 1967, Howard Galloway Svc. award 1978, 83, 85, 87), Nat. Fire Protection Assn. (chmn. com. pyrotechnics 1974-94, Svc. award 1993, emeritus mem. 1994), N.Y. Acad. Scis., Aircraft Owners and Pilots Assn., Ariz. Pilots Assn. (dir. 1980-93, v.p. 1981-84), L-5 Soc. (v.p. 1984). Home: 2419 W Saint Moritz Ln Phoenix AZ 85023-5041 *The most interesting data are the points that fall "off the curve" because they lead to unsuspected new discoveries. I grew up on a vanishing frontier and intend to spend my life opening new frontiers—in space, because the world is no more closed than it is flat. Because of this, we do not live in a world of limits, but a limitless universe, and have a limitless future.*

STINE, JEANNE M., mayor, educator; b. Detroit, June 18, 1929; d. William Lyle and Eleanor Laura (Abele) Goodwin; m. Cornelius Robert Powers, Oct. 3, 1952 (div. Feb. 1956); 1 child, Sheila Maureen Powers; m. John Follett Stine, Feb. 1962. BS in Edn., Wayne State U., 1960, MA in Edn., 1965. cert. K-8 Elem. edn., K-12 counseling. Telephone operator Mich. Bell, Detroit, 1946-51; clerk typist McGregor Meml. Conf., Detroit Pub. Libr., 1950-52; display advertiser Daily Tribune, Royal Oak, Mich., 1952-54; elem. sch. tchr. Guardian Angels Sch., Clawson, Mich., 1958; elem. sch. tchr. Clawson Pub. Schs., 1959-66, middle sch. counselor, 1966-92; sec. Clawson Edn. Assn., 1960-63; pres. Clawson Youth Assist., 1968-74. initiator Troy youth bur. Police Dept., 1977; pres. Troy Youth Svcs. Activities Commn., 1977-80; v.p. Troy Profl. Women's Club, 1978-84, pres. Troy Youth Svcs. Forum, 1980-84, chair Troy Consortium on Drug and Alcohol Abuse; city councilwoman City of Troy, 1976-92; pres. Troy Vol. Firefighters Women's Aux., 1989-92; mayor City of Troy, 1992—; mem. bd. dirs. Boys and Girls Club of Troy, Traffic Improvement Assn. Oakland County. Recipient Dist. Citizen award Troy C. of C., 1985, Community Svc. award Clawson-Troy Elks, 1985. Mem. Nat. League of Cities (mem. transp. steering com. 1978-86, trans. policy com. 1989-92), Am. Legion Aux., Mich. Mcpl. League (chmn. region IV transp. and pub. works 1990, meritorius svc. award 1988), Tri County Mayors Assn. (mem. steering com.), Zontas. Republican. Roman Catholic. Home: 1915 Boulan Dr Troy MI 48084-1512 Office: 500 W Big Beaver Rd Troy MI 48084-5254

STINEBRING, WARREN RICHARD, microbiologist, educator; b. Niagara Falls, N.Y., July 31, 1924; s. Clifford Thomas and Signe (Arvidson) S.; m. Delores Jean Zakes, June 12, 1948; children: Dan R., Beth E., Eric. B.A., U. Buffalo, 1948; M.S., U. Pa., 1949, Ph.D., 1951. With U. Pa., Phila., 1949-55; asso. U. Pa., 1953-55; asst. prof. U. Tex. Med. Br., Galveston, 1955-57; asso. research prof. Inst. Microbiology, Rutgers U., New Brunswick, N.J., 1957-60; asst. prof. U. Pitts. Coll. Medicine, 1960-65, asso. prof., 1965-66; prof., chmn. med. microbiology U. Calif. Coll. Medicine at Irvine, 1966-68; prof. U. Vt. Coll. Medicine, Burlington, 1968-86, prof. emeritus, 1986—; chmn. med. microbiology U. Vt. Coll. Medicine, 1968-78; sabbatical leave Royal Postgrad. Med. Sch., London, 1974-75. Served with inf. AUS, 1943-45, ETO. Decorated Purple Heart.; Recipient Golden Apple award Student AMA, 1966-67, award for outstanding research and diagnosis in brucellosis eradication in Vt. Vt. Vt. Med. Assn., 1983. Mem. AAAS, Tissue Culture Assn. (edni. com. 1970-72, chmn. 1970-72), Reticuloendothelial Soc., Am. Soc. Microbiology, Am. Soc. Mammalogy, Soc. Exptl. Biol. Medicine, Brucellosis Research Conf. (hon. patron). Research on host-parasite interactions delayed hypersensitivity, interferon stimulation by non-viral agts., brucellosis. Home: 139 N Prospect St Oberlin OH 44074-1038

STINEHART, ROGER RAY, lawyer; b. Toledo, Jan. 27, 1945; s. Forrest William and Nettie May (Twyman) S.; m. Martha Jean Goodnight, Sept. 19, 1970; children: Amanda Jean, Brian Scott. BS, Bowling Green (Ohio) State U., 1968; JD, Ohio State U., 1972. Bar: Ohio 1972. Fin. analyst Gen. Electric, Detroit, 1968-69; assoc. Gingher & Christensen, Columbus, Ohio, 1972-76, ptnr., 1976-80; sr. v.p., gen. counsel, sec. G.D. Ritzy's, Inc., Columbus, 1983-85; ptnr. Jones, Day, Reavis & Pogue, Columbus, 1980-83, 85—; adj. prof. law Capital U., Columbus, 1976-79; mem. adv. com. Ohio securities divsn. Dept. Commerce, Columbus, 1979—; fellow Columbus Bar Found., 1992—; adv. bd. The Entrepreneurship Inst., 1992-95. Contbr. Ohio State U. Coll. Law Jour., 1970-72. Gen. counsel, trustee Internat. Assn. Rsch. on Leukemia and Related Diseases, 1975—; v.p., trustee Hospice of Columbus, 1978-80; mem. Cen. Ohio chpt. Leukemia Soc. Am., Columbus, 1983-93, v.p., 1985-87; trustee Ohio Cancer Rsch. Assocs., Columbus, 1983—, v.p., 1990—. With USMCR, 1963-68. Mem. ABA (bus. law com., franchise law com.), Ohio State Bar Assn. (corp. law com., franchise law com.), Columbus Bar Assn. (securities law com., chmn. 1981-83, bus. law com., franchise law com.), Sigma Tau Delta, Beta Gamma Sigma. Home: 2155 Waltham Rd Columbus OH 43221-4149 Office: Jones Day Reavis & Pogue 1900 Huntington Ctr Columbus OH 43215

STINER, CARL WADE, army officer; b. LaFollette, Tenn., Sept. 7, 1936; s. Emmit Clyde and Hassie Delma (Bullard) S.; m. Carolyn Sue Reeves, Nov. 28, 1959; children: Carla, Laurie. BS, Tenn. Poly. Inst., 1958; MPA, Shippensburg (Pa.) State Coll., 1975. Commd. 2d lt. U.S. Army, 1958, advanced through grades to gen., 1990; inf. bn. officer, then brigade ops. officer 4th Inf. Div., Vietnam, 1967; comdr. 2d bn., 325 Airborne Inf. Rgt., div. ops. officer 82d Airborne Divsn., 1970; comdr. 1st Inf. Tng. Brigade, Ft. Benning, Ga., 1975; chief of staff Rapid Deployment Joint Task Force, 1980; asst. div. comdr. 82d Airborne Div.; asst. dep. dir. for politico-mil. affairs Joint Staff, Washington, until 1984; comdg. gen. Joint Spl. Ops. Command, Ft. Bragg, N.C., 1984-87, 82d Airborne Div., 1987-88, XVIII Airborne Corps, Ft. Bragg, 1988; comdr. of all forces Operation JUST CAUSE, Panama, 1989; comdr. in chief Hdqrs. U.S. Spl. Ops. Command, MacDill AFB, Fla.; ret. from active duty, 1993. Decorated D.S.M. with two oak leaf cluster, Def. D.S.M. with two oak leaf cluster, Legion of Merit with oak leaf cluster, Purple Heart, Def. Superior Svc. medal. Baptist. Avocations: golf, hunting, boating. Office: Holding Detachment OCSA USA Washington DC 20310-0200

STINES, FRED, JR., publisher; b. Newton, Iowa, Mar. 16, 1925; s. Fred and Nella (Haun) S.; m. Dorothy G. McClanahan, Sept. 5, 1953; children: Steven, Scott, Ann. B.C.S., U. Iowa, 1949. With Meredith Corp., Des Moines, 1949-90; sales promotion and mdse. mgr. Meredith Corp., 1955-63, advt. dir., 1963-66, pub., 1966-73, pub. dir. mag. div., 1973-76, v.p., gen. mgr. books and newspapers, 1976-83, sr. v.p., 1983-87, pres. book pub., 1986-90, corp. v.p. spl. projects, 1988-90; pres., prin. Concepts in Mktg., 1990—; cert. instr. Dale Carnegie courses, 1958-63. Bd. dirs. Des Moines Ballet Assn., North Am. Outdoor Group, Mpls., 1992-95; bd. dirs., v.p. Jr. Achievement of Ctrl. Iowa. Served with AUS, 1946-49. Named Farm Marketing Man of Year, 1972. Mem. Future Farmers Am. Found. (nat. chmn. 1971), Rotary Internat., Des Moines Golf and Country Club, Phi Gamma Delta (sect. chief 1983, nat. bd. dirs. 1985-89), Alpha Kappa Psi, Alpha Delta Sigma. Club: Des Moines Golf and Country (dir., pres. 1981).

STING (GORDON MATTHEW SUMNER), musician, songwriter, actor; b. Newcastle Upon Tyne, Eng., Oct. 2, 1951; s. Ernest Matthew and Audrey (Cowell) S.; m. Frances Eleanor Tomelty, May 1, 1976 (div. Mar. 1984); children: Joseph, Katherine; m. Trudie Styler, Aug. 22, 1992; children: Brigette Michael, Jake, Eliot Pauline. Schoolmaster Newcastle Upon Tyne, Eng., 1975-77; songwriter, singer, bass player with rock group The Police, 1977-86; mng. dir. Kaliedescope Cameras, London, from 1982. Albums recorded with The Police include Outlandos D'Amour, 1977, Reggatta De Blanc, 1979, Zenyatta Mondatta, 1980, Ghost in the Machine, 1981, Synchronicity, 1983, The Singles; Every Breath You Take, 1986; stage appearance: (Broadway) Three Penny Opera, 1989; solo albums include The Dream of the Blue Turtles, 1985, Bring On The Night, 1986, Nothing Like the Sun, 1987, The Soul Cages, 1991, Ten Summoner's Tales, 1993 (Grammy award, Best Long Form Music Video, 1994), Demolition Man (soundtrack), 1993; appeared in films Quadrophenia, 1980, The Secret Policeman's Other Ball, 1982, Brimstone and Treacle, 1982, Dune, 1984, The Bride, 1985, Plenty, 1985, Julia and Julia, 1988, Stormy Monday, 1988; rec. soundtracks for films including Brimstone and Treacle, 1982, Party, Party, 1982, The Secret Policeman's Other Ball, 1982. Recipient Grammy awards with The Police, 1980-81, 83; other Grammy awards, 1983, 87, Downbeat mag. Readers' Poll Pop/Rock Musician of Yr. award, 1989, Downbeat mag. Readers' Poll Pop/Rock group award, 1989. Mem. Performing Rights Soc. Office: SFirstars, Bugle House 21A Noel St, London W1V 3PD, England also: Firstars 3520 Hayden Ave Culver City CA 90232-2413

STINGEL, DONALD EUGENE, management consultant; b. Pitts., Jan. 31, 1920; s. Eugene E. and Ruth I. (Liddell) S.; m. Rita Marie Sweeney, June 14, 1942; children—Donald M., Scott M., Janice L. B.S., Carnegie-Mellon U., 1941. Metall. engr. Union Carbide Corp., Alloy, W.Va., 1941; metall. engr. to works mgr. Union Carbide Corp., N.Y.C., 1946-65; pres. Alloys and Carbide div. Airco, Inc., 1965-68, Pullman Swindell, Pitts., 1969-77; chmn. Rodeway Inns Internat. and Lodging Systems, Inc., 1982-83; dir. Export-Import Bank U.S., Washington, 1977-81, Wean-United, Pitts., 1981-93. Trustee Carnegie-Mellon U. Served to maj., Ordnance Dept., AUS, 1941-46; to lt. col., Transp. Corps, U.S. Army, 1950. Mem. Country Club of N.C. Republican. Home: 1600 Morganton Rd Box X-29 Pinehurst NC 28374

STINGELIN, VALENTIN, research center director, mechanical engineer; b. Basel, Switzerland, Apr. 22, 1933; s. Paul and Hulda (Tobler) S.; m. Hedwig Wagner, Oct. 18, 1963; children: Matthias, Sibylle, Thomas. Diploma, Swiss Fed. Inst. Tech. (ETH), Zurich, 1957, Ph.D. (Silver medal 1963), 1963. Sci. co-worker Swiss Fed. Inst. Tech., 1958-63; research scientist, project leader Ingersoll Rand Corp., Princeton, N.J., 1964-67; mem. staff Battelle Research Centers, Geneva, 1967—; head engrng. dept., then assoc. dir. Battelle Research Centers, 1973-75, dir. gen., 1975—; v.p. Battelle Meml. Inst., Columbus, Ohio, 1984—; v.p. indsl. bus. planning Europe and Japan Battelle Meml. Inst., 1986—; pres. Castolin & Eutectic Inst., St. Sulpice/Lausanne, Switzerland, 1986—. Mem. Swiss Soc. Physics, ASME, Swiss-Am. C. of C. (dir.). Office: Castolin & Eutectic Inst, PO Box 360, CH-1001 Lausanne Switzerland

STINI, WILLIAM ARTHUR, anthropologist, educator; b. Oshkosh, Wis., Oct. 9, 1930; s. Louis Alois and Clara (Larsen) S.; m. Mary Ruth Kalous, Feb. 11, 1950; children—Patricia Laraine, Paulette Ann, Suzanne Kay. B.B.A., U. Wis., 1960, M.S., 1967, Ph.D., 1969. Planner cost acct. Kimberly-Clark Corp., Niagara Falls, N.Y., 1960-62; asst. prof. Cornell U., Ithaca, N.Y., 1968-71, assoc. prof., 1971-73; assoc. prof. U. Kans., Lawrence, 1973-76; prof. anthropology U. Ariz., Tucson, 1976—; head dept. anthropology U. Ariz., 1980-89; panelist anthropology program NSF, 1976-78; cons. NIH, 1974—; panelist NRC/NSF Grad. Fellowship Program, 1991-95. Author: Ecology and Human Adaptation, 1975, Nature, Culture and Human History - A Biocultural Introduction to Anthropology (with Davydd J. Greenwood), 1977, Physiological and Morphological Adaptation and Evolution, 1979 (with Frank E. Poirier and Kathy B. Wreden) In Search of Ourselves: An Introduction to Physical Anthropology, 1990, 5th edit., 1994; field editor phys. anthropology The Am. Anthropologist, 1980-83; editor-in-chief Am. Jour. Phys. Anthropology, 1983-89; assoc. editor Nutrition and Cancer, 1981-95; cons. editor Collegium Antropologicum, 1985—. Mem. Gov.'s Adv. Council on Aging, State of Ariz., 1980-83. Nat. Inst. Dental Rsch. tng. grantee, 1964-68; Clark Found. grantee, Cornell U., 1973; Nat. Dairy Coun. grantee, 1985-88; Wenner-Gren Found. grantee, 1991—; fellow Linacre Coll., Oxford, 1985; vis. fellow U. London, 1991. Fellow AAAS (steering group sect. H 1987-91), Am. Anthrop. Assn., N.Y. Acad. Scis.; mem. Am. Assn. Phys. Anthropologists (exec. com. 1978-81, pres. 1989-91), Soc. for Study Human Biology, Human Biology Coun. (exec. com. 1978-81), Soc. for Study Social Biology, Am. Inst. Nutrition, Am. Soc. on Aging, Sigma Xi. Home: 6240 N Camino Miraval Tucson AZ 85718-3025 Office: U Ariz Dept Anthropology Tucson AZ 85721

STINNETT, LEE HOUSTON, newspaper association executive; b. Madisonville, Ky., Jan. 8, 1939; s. James Houston and Eolia Frances (Hutchings) S. B.A., U. Ky., 1961, M.A., 1963. Reporter Times-Picayune, New Orleans, 1963-64; med. reporter The News, Charlotte, N.C., 1965-66; devel. writer Emory U., Atlanta, 1966-67, univ. editor, 1968-69; assoc. dir. So. Newspaper Pubs. Assn. and Found., Atlanta, 1970-80; project dir. Am. Soc. Newspaper Editors, Washington, 1981-82, exec. dir., 1983—. Contbr. articles to profl. jours. Del. Arlington Civic Fedn.; active civil rights groups and polit. orgns., Washington and No. Va., Whitman-Walker Clinic, Washington; pres. Arlington Gay and Lesbian Alliance, 1989-90. Mem. Newspaper Assn. Mgrs., Four Seasons Garden (pres. 1983), ACLU of No. Va. (bd. dirs. 1992-94). Democrat. Avocations: gardening, swimming, music.

STINSMUEHLEN-AMEND, SUSAN, artist; b. Balt., Nov. 5, 1948; d. William I. and Geraldine S. (Dodds) Hamilton; m. Richard E. Amend, Nov. 27, 1987; children: Jason Stinsmuehlen, Wyatt Amend. Student, Hood Coll., U. Tex. Designer, owner Renaissance Glass Co., Austin, 1973-87; artist Impresa, Inc., L.A. and Ojai, Calif., 1987-95; mem. Art in Pub. Places Panel, Austin, 1986-87; cons. Nat. Endowment for the Arts, Washington, 1986, 87, Cmty. Redevelopment Agy., L.A., 1990-92; artist trustee Am. Craft Coun., 1988-92; lectr., lead artist Hollywood Blvd. Streetscape Team, Hollywood, Calif., 1991-94; educator in field. One-woman shows include Mattingly Baker Gallery, Dallas, 1984, Kurland Summers Gallery, L.A., 1985, 88, 90, 92, Traver Sutton Gallery, Seattle, 1986, Habatat Galleries, Detroit, 1991; exhibited in group shows at Whatcom Mus., Bellingham, Wash., 1992-94, Finegood Art Gallery, West Hills, Calif., 1993-94, Miller Gallery, N.Y.C., 1994, L.A. City Hall and UCLA Ext., Santa Monica, 1995, Philabaum Contemporary Art Glass, Tucson, 1995, The Wignall Mus., Chaffey Coll., Rancho Cucamonga, Calif., 1995, Traver Gallery, Seattle, 1995, others; represented in permanent collection The Jewish Mus., N.Y.C., The Corning (N.Y.) Mus. Glass, Detroit (Mich.) Inst. of the ARts, Leigh Yawkey Woodson Mus., Wausau, Wis., Wagga Wagga City Art Gallery, NSW, Australia, Nishida Mus., Toyoma, Japan, Pilchuck Glass Ctr., Stanwood, Wash., Am. Craft Mus., N.Y.C., L.A. (Calif.) County Mus. Art, Radisson Hotel, Austin, AT&T, Dallas, AT&T, N.Y.C., Marshall Fields Corp. Collection, Chgo., others plus numerous pvt. collections. Grantee Nat. Endowment for the Arts, Washington, 1982, 88. Mem. Glass Art Soc. (life mem., bd. dirs. 1982-86, pres. 1984-86), Mus. Contemporary Art (L.A.), L.A. County Mus. Avocations: gardening, swimming, walking, sewing.

STINSON, AVIVA JOCHEBED, psychosocial nurse; b. Jerusalem, Palestine, Mar. 21, 1933; came to U.S., 1957; d. Solomon Isaac and Sarah (Dossik) Ostrovsky; m. Lawrence William Stinson, Jan. 19, 1956; children: Teresa Louise, Lawrence William Jr., John Durant. BS, U. Wash., 1981; MS, U. Alaska, 1987; postgrad., U. Minn., 1990-91. RN, Alaska, Wash., Minn., Ill.; cert. clin. specialist in adult psychiat. and mental health nursing; cert. advanced nurse practitioner. Staff nurse Paxton (Ill.) Gen. Hosp., 1957-58; staff nurse, head nurse Mercy Hosp., Urbana, Ill., 1966-72; staff nurse Guam (Micronesia) Meml. Hosp., 1973-74, Fairbanks (Alaska) Meml. Hosp., 1975-78, Swedish Hosp., Seattle, 1980-81; supr. nurse detox Fairbanks Native Assn., 1981-83; psychosocial nurse, therapist Fairbanks Psychiatric & Neurol. Clinic, Fairbanks, 1985-94; advanced nurse practitioner, psychotherapist Fairbanks, Alaska, 1994—. Bd. dirs. Child Abuse Task Force, Fairbanks, 1982-90, Fairbanks Cmty. Mental Health Ctr., 1985-90, 92-94. Mem. ANA (pres. Dist. IV 1986-89), Alaskan Nurses Assn. Avocations: aerobics, gourmet cooking, collecting native dolls. Home: 573 Slater Dr Fairbanks AK 99701-3444 Office: 250 Cushman St Ste 5 Fairbanks AK 99701-4640

STINSON, GEORGE ARTHUR, lawyer, former steel company executive; b. Camden, Ark., Feb. 11, 1915; s. John McCollum and Alice (Loving) S.; m. Betty Millsop, May 31, 1947; children: Thomas, Lauretta, Peter, Joel. A.B., Northwestern U., 1936; J.D., Columbia U., 1939; LL.D., U. W.Va., Bethany Coll., Theil Coll., Salem Coll. Bar: N.Y. 1939. Partner Cleary, Gottlieb, Friendly & Hamilton, N.Y.C., 1951-61; spl. asst. to atty. gen., acting asst. atty. gen. tax div. Dept. Justice, 1947-48; v.p., sec. Nat. Steel Corp. (now Nat. Intergroup, Inc.), Pitts., 1961-63; pres. Nat. Steel Corp., 1963-75, bd. dirs., 1963-86, CEO, 1966-80, chmn., 1972-81; dir. Birmingham Steel Co., Pathe Techs. Inc.; trustee emeritus Mut. Life Ins. Co. N.Y. Trustee emeritus U. Pitts.; mem. Presdl. Commn. on Internat. Trade and Investment Policy, 1970-71; chmn. U.S. Indsl. Payroll Savs. Com., 1976; trustee George C. Marshall Found. Served to lt. col. USAAF, 1941-45. Decorated Legion of Merit. Mem. Am. Iron and Steel Inst. (chmn. bd. 1969-71), Internat. Iron and Steel Inst. (bd. dirs., chmn. 1975-77), Am. Law Inst., Bus. Coun., Links Club (N.Y.C.), Duquesne Club (Pitts.), Laurel Valley Golf Club (Pitts.), Phi Beta Kappa. Home: Hunting Country Rd Tryon NC 28782

STINSON, JAMES R., lawyer; b. Evanston, Ill., Mar. 21, 1952. AB, DePauw U., Ind. U., 1973; JD magna cum laude, U. Ill., 1977. Ptnr. Sidley & Austin, Chgo. Mem. ABA (vice chair sub. com. real est. ...) Order of Coif. Office: Sidley & Austin 1 First Nat Plz Chicago IL 60603*

STINSON, WILLIAM W., transportation executive; b. Toronto, Oct. 29, 1933. BA, U. Toronto, 1954; diploma in bus. adminstrn., U. Western Ont., 1955. Various positions Can. Pacific Rail, Toronto, 1950-66, supt. Toronto div., 1966-69; asst. gen. mgr. ops. and maintenance Pacific Region Can. Pacific Rail, Vancouver, 1969-71; gen. mgr. ops. and maintenance Pacific Region Can. Pacific Ltd., Vancouver, 1971, gen. mgr. ops. and maintenance Eastern Region, 1972-74; asst. v.p. ops. and maintenance Can. Pacific Rail, Montreal, 1974-76, exec. v.p., 1979-81; v.p. ops. and maintenance Can. Pacific Ltd., Montreal, 1976-79, pres., 1981-90, chief exec. officer, 1985—, chmn., chief exec. officer, 1989—; bd. dirs. Can. Pacific Enterprises Ltd., ADT Ltd., Pan Can. Petroleum Ltd., Sun Life Assurance Co., Laidlaw, Inc., Nav Can., United Dominion Industries Inc., United Dominion Industries Ltd., The Van Horne Inst.; mem. Bus. Coun. on Nat. Issues. Mem. Mt. Royal Club, Mt. Bruno Country Club. Office: Can Pacific Ltd, Succ Centre Ville PO Box 6042, Montreal, PQ Canada H3C 3E4 also: Can Pacific Ltd, 1010 de Gauchetiere St W Ste 800, Montreal, PQ Canada H3B 2N2

STIPANOVIC, ROBERT DOUGLAS, chemist, researcher; b. Houston, Oct. 28, 1939. BS, Loyola U., 1961; PhD, Rice U., 1966. Rsch. technician Stauffer Chem. Co., Houston, 1961; teaching asst. Rice U., Houston, 1961-62, rsch. asst., 1962-66; rsch. assoc. Stanford (Calif.) U., 1966-67; mem. grad. faculty Tex. A&M U., College Station, 1967—, asst. prof. chemistry, 1967-71; rsch. chemist Cotton Pathology Rsch. Unit USDA, College Station, 1971-87; rsch. leader USDA, College Station, 1987—; vis. rsch. scientist Agr. Can., Rsch. Ctr. London, Ont., 1985. Welch fellow Rice U., 1963-65, Grad. fellow, 1965-66. Mem. Sigma Xi. Home: 1103 Esther Blvd Bryan TX 77802-1924 Office: USDA Agrl Rsch Svc So Crops Rsch Lab 2765 F & B Rd College Station TX 77845-9593

STIPE, MICHAEL, musician; b. Decatur, Ga., 1960. Student, U. Ga. Singer R.E.M., 1980—; owner C-OO. Albums with R.E.M. include Chronic Town, 1982, Murmur, 1983 (Gold record, Rolling Stone Critics Poll Best Album of Yr. 1983), Reckoning, 1984 (Gold record), Fables of the Reconstruction, 1985 (Gold record), Life's Rich Pageant (Gold record), 1986, Dead Letter Office (Gold record), 1987, Document, 1987 (Platinum record), Eponymous, 1988 (Platinum record), Green, 1989 (Platinum record), Out of Time, 1991 (Platinum record, 7 Grammy nominations, Best Pop Vocals Grammy award for group 1992), Automatic for the People, 1992 (Platinum record, 4 Grammy nominations), Monster, 1994, Songs That Are Live, 1995; guest artist for following groups: 10,000 Maniacs, 1987, Indigo Girls, 1989; exec. prodr. film Desperate Angels, 1992. Recipient MTV Video Music Video of Yr. award, 1992; named Rolling Stone Critics Poll Best New

Group, 1983, Rolling Stone Group Artist of Yr., 1992, Rolling Stong Male Vocalist of Yr., 1992; MTV Best Direction, Best Editing, Best Cinematography, and Breakthrough Video awards for "Everybody Hurts", 1994. Office: Warner Bros Records 3300 Warner Blvd Burbank CA 91505-4632*

STIPE, ROBERT EDWIN, design educator; b. Easton, Pa., July 18, 1928; s. J. Norwood and Ethel M. Stipe; m. Josephine Davis Weedon, 1952; children: Daniel W. Stipe, Frederick Norwood Stipe. AB in Econ., Duke U., 1950, LLB, 1953; MRP, U. N.C., 1959. Urban planning cons. City and Town Planning Assocs., Chapel Hill, N.C., 1956-57; asst. dir., prof. pub. law and govt. U. N.C. Inst. Govt., Chapel Hill, N.C., 1957-74; sr. Fulbright rsch. fellow London U., 1968-69; dir. Divsn. Archives and History N.C. Dept. Cultural Resources, Raleigh, N.C., 1974-75; vis. prof. U. N.C., Chapel Hill, 1975-77; prof. design N.C. State U., Raleigh, 1976-89; emeritus prof. design, part time prof. design N.C. State U., 1989—; lectr. Inst. Advanced Studies, Bratislava, Slovak Republic, 1992-95; bd. trustees U.S. com. Internat. Coun. on Monuments and Sites, Preservation Action, Nat. Coun. on Preservation Edn., Hist. Preservation Fund N.C., Alliance for Preservation Hist. Landscapes, Old Salem Inc., Stagville Ctr. for Preservation Tech.; trustee Nat. Trust for Hist. Preservation; bd. counsellors Conservation Trust for N.C.; mem. bd. adv. Nat. Alliance Preservation Commn. Author, editor more than 150 articles and publs. in fields of historic preservation, landscape conservation, design, urban planning, and planning law. Mem. Chapel Hill Design Review Bd.; trustee Chapel Hill Preservation Soc.; founder, bd. mem. Chapel Hill Preservation Soc. Fellow U.S. Com. Internat. Coun. on Monuments and Sites, 1986; recipient Disting. Svc. award Ruth Coltrane Cannon award, N.C. Soc. for Preservation of Antiquities, 1973, Sec. of Interior's Disting. Conservation Svc. award, 1978, Louise DuPont Crowninshield award for Superlative Lifetime Achievement in Historic Preservation, Nat. Trust for Historic Preservation, 1988, Dist. Svc. and Profl. Leadership award Nat. Coun. for Preservation Edn., 1989. Mem. Cosmos Club (Washington), Sigma Pi Kappa (First Disting. mem. 1994), Sigma Lambda Alpha. Home: 100 Pine Ln Chapel Hill NC 27514-4331

STIPES, DAVID, special effects expert. Spl. effects expert (films) Caveman, 1981, Creepshow, 1982, Ice Pirates, 1983, Real Genius, 1985, Stuff, 1985, Night of the Demons, 1989, A Nightmare on Elm Street 5-The Dream Child, 1989, Ernest Goes to Jail, 1990, Tales from the Darkside: The Movie, 1990, Harlet Davidson and the Marlboro Man, 1991, The Lawnmower Man, 1992, (TV) Star Trek: Voyager (Emmy award for Outstanding Ind. Achievement in Spl. Visual Effects 1995). Office: 7247 Atoll Ave North Hollywood CA 91605*

STIRITZ, WILLIAM P., food company executive; b. Jasper, Ark., July 1, 1934; s. Paul and Dorothy (Bradley) S.; m. Susan Ekberg, Dec. 4, 1972; children—Bradley, Charlotte, Rebecca, Nicholas. B.S., Northwestern U., 1959; M.A., St. Louis U., 1968. Mem. mktg. mgmt. staff Pillsbury Co., Mpls., 1959-62; account mgmt. staff Gardner Advt. Co., St. Louis, 1963—; with Ralston Purina Co., St. Louis, 1963—; pres., chief exec. officer, chmn. Ralston Purina Co., 1981—; bd. dirs. Angelica Corp., Ball Corp., Boatmen's Bancshares, Inc., Gen. Am. Life Ins. Co., May Dept. Stores, S.C. Johnson & Son. With USN, 1954-57. Mem. Grocery Mfrs. Assn. (dir.). Office: Ralston Purina Co Checkerboard Sq Saint Louis MO 63164

STIRLING, ELLEN ADAIR, retail executive; b. Chgo., June 21, 1949; d. Volney W. and Ellen Adair (Orr) Foster; m. James P. Stirling, June 6, 1970; children: Elizabeth Ginevra, Diana Leslie, Alexandra Curtiss. Student, U. Chgo., 1970-71; BA, Wheaton Coll., Norton, Mass., 1971; postgrad., U. London, 1974. Pres., CEO, The Lake Forest Shop, 1986—; bd. dirs. Lake Forest Bank and Trust. Founder, v.p. aux. bd. Art Inst. Chgo., 1972-91; dir. Friends of Ryerson Woods, 1992—; mem. women's bd. Lyric Opera, Chgo., 1992—, Lake Forest Coll., 1989—; mem. costume com. Chgo. Hist. Soc. Mem. Onwentsia Club, Racquet Club. Office: The Lake Forest Shop 165 E Market Sq Lake Forest IL 60045

STIRLING, JAMES PAULMAN, investment banker; b. Chgo., Mar. 30, 1941; s. Louis James and Beverly L. (Paulman) S.; m. Ellen Adair Foster, June 6, 1970; children—Elizabeth Ginevra, Diana Leslie, Alexandra Curtiss. A.B., Princeton U., 1963; M.B.A., Stanford U., 1965. Chartered fin. analyst. Vice pres. corp. fin. Kidder, Peabody & Co. (now PaineWebber), N.Y.C. and Chgo., 1965-71, 84-86; sr. v.p. corp. fin. Kidder, Peabody & Co. (now PaineWebber), 1987—; dir. internat. investments Sears Roebuck Co., Chgo. and London, 1971-75, 77-84; asst. to sec. U.S. Dept. Commerce, Washington, 1976-77; chmn. bd. Northwestern Meml. Mgmt. Corp., Chgo., 1989—; trustee Northwestern Meml. Hosp., Chgo., 1985—. Pres. jr. bd. Chgo. Symphony, 1968-70, trustee, 1970-75; trustee Tchrs. Acad. for Math. Sci., 1991—. Mem. Investment Analysts Soc., Bond Club of Chgo., Nat. Econ. Hon. Soc. Clubs: Chicago, Racquet (Chgo.); Onwentsia (Lake Forest, Ill.). Office: PaineWebber 125 S Wacker Dr Chicago IL 60606-4402

STIRRAT, WILLIAM ALBERT, electronics engineer; b. Syracuse, N.Y., Nov. 5, 1919; s. Robert William and Doris (White) S.; m. Bernice Amelia Wilson, July 13, 1958; children: Valerie Lynne, Dorothy Grace, William Ellsworth. Student, Triuna (Yaddo) Arts of the Theater Sch., 1936, Saratoga Eastman Sch Bus., 1936-37; BS in Physics, Rensselaer Poly. Inst., 1942, postgrad., 1949-50; postgrad., Rutgers U., 1951-58, Fairleigh Dickinson U., 1971. Elecs. engr. GE, Schenectady, N.Y., 1941-44; instr. physics Clarkson Coll. Tech., 1947-49; electronic engr. rsch. and devel. U.S. Army, Fort Monmouth, N.J., 1950-87; prin. engr. Eagle Tech., Inc., Eatontown, N.J., 1987-92; pres. Stirrat Arts & Scis., Freehold, N.J., 1992—. Author: (with Alex North) Unchained Melody, 1936 (Top song of Yr., Acad. award nomination 1955), Why 3? (Army award 1985); assoc. editor IEEE Transactions on Electromagnetic Compatability, 1970-76; contbr. articles to profl. jours.; patentee in field. Chmn. pub. rels. Battleground dist. Monmouth coun. Boy Scouts Am., 1970-77; mem. Rep. Congl. Leadership Coun., 1989-91; mem. Rep. Campaign Coun., 1992-93. Mem. SAR, IEEE (editor N.J. Coast sect. Scanner 1974-75), Nat. Acad. Songwriters, Internat. Songwriters Assn., Palgrave Soc., Internat. Platform Assn., Armed Forces Comms. and Electronics Assn. Episcopalian. Achievements include development of binomial pulse. Home and Office: 218 Overbrook Dr Freehold NJ 07728-1525

STIRRATT, BETSY, artist, gallery director; b. New Orleans, Sept. 22, 1958; d. Avery and Betty Lou (Chadwick) S.; m. Jeffrey Alan Wolin, Aug. 20, 1983; children: Benjamin, Andrew. BFA, La. State U., 1980; MFA, Ind. U., 1983. Gallery dir. Fine Arts Gallery, Ind. U., Bloomington, 1987—. Exhibited works at Salon Show, Art in Gen., 1992, Meat, White, Columns, 1993, Between Mind and Body, Air Gallery, 1994, Physical Affinities, Carl Hammer Gallery, 1994, In Situ Gallery, 1995. Masters fellow Ind. Arts Commn., 1989, Arts Midwest fellow Arts Midwest, 1989, NEA fellow, 1990. Office: Fine Arts Gallery Ind Univ Bloomington IN 47405

STISKA, JOHN C., lawyer; b. Chgo., Feb. 14, 1942; s. Rudolph and Elsie Sophie (Nelson) S.; m. Janet Hazel Osuch, Aug. 8, 1964; children: Julie, Thomas, Michael, Matthew. BBA, U. Wis., 1965, JD, 1970. Bar: Wis. 1970, Calif. 1971. Assoc., ptnr. Luce, Forward, Hamilton & Scripps, San Diego, 1970-81; ptnr. Aylward, Kintz & Stiska, San Diego, 1981-86; pres., CEO Triton Group Ltd., La Jolla, Calif., 1986-88; ptnr. Brobeck, Phleger & Harrison, San Diego, 1988-90; pres., COO Intermark, Inc., La Jolla, Calif., 1990-92; pres., CEO Triton Group Ltd., 1993-94; chmn., CEO, 1994-96; sr. v.p. Qualcomm, Inc., San Diego, 1996—. 1st lt. U.S. Army, 1965-67. Mem. ABA, San Diego County Bar Assn., Calif State Bar Assn. Lutheran. Home: 5307 Soledad Rancho Ct San Diego CA 92109-1535 Office: Qualcomm Inc 6455 Lusk Blvd San Diego CA 92121-2779

STITES, ALICE GRAY, editor; b. N.Y.C., Jan. 19, 1965; d. Bowman and Katherine (Condon) Gray; m. James Walker Stites III, Nov. 21, 1992. BA in English, U. Va., 1987; MA in English, Columbia U., 1988. Asst. editor Art & Auction Mag., N.Y.C., 1988-89; assoc. editor Contemporanea Art Mag., N.Y.C., 1989-91; editor Abbeville Press, N.Y.C., 1992—. Author: Ansel Adams: The National Park Service Photographs, 1994; editor: 19th and 20th Century Painting, Living Proof: Courage in the Face of AIDS, and others, 1992-94. Mem. Phi Beta Kappa. Home and Office: 2912 Lilac Way Louisville KY 40206-2913

STITES, C. THOMAS, journalist, publisher; b. Kansas City, Mo., July 6, 1942; s. Harold Edward and Wilma Joyce (Simmons) S.; m. Helen Marie Oakey, Sept. 9, 1967 (div. 1983), children—Mary Hannah, Harold William; m. Alexandra Mezey, May 8, 1983. Student, Williams Coll., 1960-62. Night city editor Chgo. Sun-Times, 1968-70; regional editor Phila. Inquirer, 1970-72; news editor Newsday, L.I., N.Y., 1972-79; asst. nat. editor N.Y. Times, N.Y.C., 1979-1983; mng. editor Kansas City Times, Mo., 1983-85; nat. editor, assoc. mng. editor Chgo. Tribune, 1985-90; v.p. UniMedia div. Universal Press Syndicate, Kansas City, Mo., 1990—. Unitarian. Avocations: squash; music, especially jazz; reading non fiction. Office: Universal Press Syndicate 4900 Main St # 900 Kansas City MO 64112-2644

STITES, SUSAN KAY, human resources consultant; b. Colorado Springs, Colo., Sept. 20, 1952; d. William Wallace and Betty Jane (Kosley) Stites; m. Gerald Frederick Simon, Aug. 14, 1988. BA, Wichita State U., 1974; MA, Northwestern U., 1979. Benefits authorizer Social Security Adminstrn., Chgo., 1974-77; trainer Chgo. Urban Skills Inst., 1977-79; human resources mgr. Montgomery Ward, Chgo., 1979-83; mgr. tng. Lands' End, Dodgeville, Wis., 1983-87; dir. human resources Cen. Life Assurance, Madison, Wis., 1988-90; owner Mgmt. Allegories, Madison, Wis., 1987—. Author: Delegating for Results, 1992, Business Communications, 1992, Managing with a Quality Focus, 1994, Training and Orientation for the Small Business, 1994, Powerful Performance Management, 1994, Safety Management Techniques, 1995, Teaching First Aid and CPR, 1995, Alive at 25, 1995, Strategic Thinking and Planning, 1995, Teaching Alice at 25, 1996, Fundamendals of Industrial Hygiene, 1996, Recruiting, Developing, and Retaining Volunteers, 1996. Vol. tutor Japanese Students in English, Evanston, Ill., 1977-80; read to blind Chgo. Coun. for the Blind, 1974-76. Named Outstanding Woman of the Yr. Wichita State U., 1974. Mem. ASTD (chpt. pres. 1988, v.p. membership 1986, region V awards chair 1992), Soc. Applied Learning Tech., Madison Area Quality Improvement Network, Assn. for Quality and Participation, Rotary (vol. fund raiser), Mendota Yacht Club (treas. 1990-94). Avocations: sailing, boardsailing, gardening, cooking, travel. Home: 3788 Highridge Rd Madison WI 53704-6206 Office: Mgmt Allegories 3788 Highridge Rd Madison WI 53704-6206

STITH, BEVERLY JEAN, paralegal; b. Washington, Mar. 27, 1949. Assoc. Degree in Transp. Mgmt., LaSalle U., 1977; Environ. Sci. Diploma, Calif. State U., 1993, Thomas Edison State Coll., 1993; BS/MBA-Bus. Adminstrn., Chadwick U., 1995. Transp. asst. Interstate Commerce Commn., Indpls., 1977-79; paralegal specialist Interstate Commerce Commn., Washington, 1979-84; legal staff asst. Armed Svcs. Bd. of Contract Appeals, Falls Church, Va., 1987-89; paralegal specialist Mil. Sealift Command, Far East, Yokohama, Japan, 1989-94, Def. Fin. and Acctg. Svc. (former Spouse Divsn.), Cleve., 1994—. Author: Prevention of Sexual Harassment in the Workplace, 1992. Decorated Navy Unit Commendation Cert./Mil. Sealift Command, (Desert Shield/Desert Storm), Yokohoma. Mem. Nat. Paralegal Assn., Nat. Environ. Health Assn. Republican. Baptist. Avocations: golf, horseback riding, collecting antiques. Home: 5146 Arch St Maple Heights OH 44137-1506 Office: Def Fin/Acctg Svc Code L 1240 E 9th St Cleveland OH 44199-2001

STITH, CHERYL DIANE ADAMS, elementary school educator; b. Birmingham, Ala., Oct. 15, 1950; d. Mack Jones and Joan (Logan) Adams; m. Hugh P. Stith, III, Jan. 7, 1972; children: Jennifer Dawn, Kristy Michelle. BS cum laude, U. Ala., Birmingham, 1986, MA in Edn., 1992, EdS, 1994. Cert. ednl. specialist, Ala. Substitute tchr. Homewood City (Ala.) Schs., 1986-87; tchr. Robert C. Arthur Elem. Sch., Birmingham, 1987-95; instrnl. support specialist Edgewood Elem. Homewood City Schs., 1995—; mem. summer enrichment program U. Ala.-Birmingham, 1993; mem. State of Ala. Textbook Com., Montgomery, 1995; lectr. in field. Vol. Birmingham Soup Kitchens, 1988—, Habitat for Humanity, Birmingham, 1992—; spkr. Ala. Kidney Found., Birmingham, 1992—; vol. U. Ala.-Birmingham's Young Author's Conf., 1986-92; mem. Robert C. Arthur Elem. Sch. PTO. Named Tchr. of the Yr., Birmingham Pub. Schs., 1993-94, Outstanding Tchr., 1994; Beeson fellow Samford U. Writing Project, 1990; Ala. Ret. Tchrs. Found. scholar, 1994. Mem. NEA, Ala. Edn. Assn., Birmingham Edn. Assn., Internat. Reading Assn. (S.E. regional conf. presider and vol.), Ala. Reading Assn., Birmingham Reading Coun., Birmingham Tchrs. Applying Whole Lang., Nat. Coun. Tchrs. English, Phi Kappa Phi, Kappa Delta Pi. Methodist. Avocations: reading, writing, gardening. Home: 601 Turtle Lake Dr Birmingham AL 35242

STITH, FORREST CHRISTOPHER, bishop; b. Marshall, Tex., May 18, 1934; s. Forrest M. and Daisy (Haynes) S.; m. Josephine Mitchell, June 19, 1960; 1 child, Lori Crystal. BD, Drew U., 1948; BS in Edn., U. Nebr., 1955; DD, Western Md. Coll., 1979, Nebr. Wesleyan U., 1986. Pastor Douglas Meml. Ch. United Meth. Ch., Washington, from 1958; resident bishop N.Y. West Area United Meth. Ch., 1984-92, resident bishop N.Y. area, 1992—. Trustee Drew U.; pres. gen. coun. on fin. and adminstrn. United Meth. Ch.; trustee Colgate Rochester Div. Sch. Recipient Grass Roots award D.C. Fedn. Civic Assns. for Vol. Svc., 1967. Home: 9 Rosehill Ave New Rochelle NY 10804-3614 Office: 252 Bryant Ave White Plains NY 10605-2103

STITH, JEFFREY L., physical science research administrator; b. Seattle, July 15, 1950; married, 1979. BA, Western Wash. State Coll., 1971; MS, Rensselaer Poly. Inst., 1974; PhD in Atmospheric Sci., U. Wash., 1978. Rsch. scientist Meteorol. Rsch. Inc., 1978-80; rsch. assoc. atmospheric dept. U. N.D., Grand Forks, 1980-84, assoc. prof. atmospheric sci., 1984-92, chair dept. atmospheric sci., 1990—, prof. atmospheric sci., 1992—. Mem. Am. Meteorol. Soc. (cloud physics com.), Am. Geophys. Union. Office: Ctr for Aerospace Scis Univ ND PO Box 8216 Univ Station Grand Forks ND 58202*

STITH, LEAH DRAKE, legislative aide, school system administrator; b. Portsmouth, Va., Nov. 18, 1949; d. Freddie Lee Sr. and Rebecca (Greene) Drake; m. S. DeLacy Stith, Sr., Oct. 20 1979; children: Maisha Kito, S. DeLacy Jr. BS in Polit. Sci., Norfolk State U., 1985, postgrad., 1992—. Substitute tchr. Portsmouth Schs., 1985-90; asst. sr. residential counselor Pines Treatment Facility, Portsmouth, 1986-90; legis. asst. del. Gen. Assembly, Richmond, Va., 1986-90; spl. asst. to lt. gov. Va. State Govt., Richmond, 1990—; mem. sch. bd. Portsmouth Schs., 1991—; mem. adv. bd. WHRO Pub. TV, Portsmouth, 1991—; guest lectr. spl. edn. conf. Norfolk State U., 1994. Sec. Wesley Ctr. Bd., Portsmouth, 1991-92, Portsmouth Dem. Com., 1991-92; coord. Don Beyer for Lt. Gov., Portsmouth, 1989, United Negro Coll. Fund, Portsmouth, 1986. Recipient Disting. Alumnus award Norfolk State U., 1991, Sojourner Truth award Nat. Assn. Black Bus. and Profl. Women, Norfolk, 1992, Woman of Yr. award Black Women's Health Network, 1993, others. Mem. Am. Assn. Sch. Adminstrs., Va. Sch. Bd. Assn. (fin. com., Cert. of Achievement award 1991-92). Episcopalian. Avocation: politics. Home: 3604 Cedar Ln Portsmouth VA 23703-3502 Office: Office of Lt Gov 101 N 8th St Richmond VA 23219-2305

STITH-CABRANES, KATE, law educator; b. St. Louis, Mar. 16, 1951; d. Richard Taylor and Ann Carter (See) Stith; m. Jeffrey Leonard Pressman, Dec. 23, 1970 (dec. Mar. 1977); m. José Alberto Cabranes, Sept. 15, 1984; children: Alejo, Benjamin José; stepchildren: Jennifer, Amy. BA, Dartmouth Coll., 1973; MPP, J.F.K. Sch. of Govt., 1977; JD, Harvard U., 1977. Bar: D.C. 1979. Law clk. Carl McGowan/U.S. Ct. of Appeals, Washington, 1977-78, Byron White/U.S. Supreme Ct., Washington, 1978-79; staff economist Coun. of Econ. Advisers, Washington, 1979-80; spl. asst. Dept. of Justice, Washington, 1980-81; asst. U.S. atty. Dept. of Justice, N.Y.C., 1981-84; assoc. prof. Yale Law Sch., New Haven, 1985-90, prof. of law, 1990—; mem. Permanent Commn. on the Status of Women, State of Conn., Hartford, 1990-96. Trustee Dartmouth Coll., Hanover, N.H., 1989—, Women's Campaign Sch., 1994—. Mem. Am. Law Inst., Coun. Fgn. Rels., Conn. Bar Found. (bd. dirs. 1987—), New Haven Inn of Ct. (bencher 1990—). Office: Yale Law Sch 127 Wall St New Haven CT 06511-6636

STITT, DAVID TILLMAN, judge; b. St. Louis, Apr. 9, 1943; s. David Leander and Jane Wilkinson (Dupuy) S.; m. Elizabeth Celia Santino, Apr. 30, 1981; children: Rachel Elizabeth Botkin, Samuel Thornton. AB, Davidson Coll., 1964; JD, U. Tex., 1969. Assoc. Galland, Kharasch, Calkins & Brown, Washington, 1969-71; asst. corp. counsel D.C., Washington, 1971-73, asst. U.S. atty., 1973-74; asst. county atty. Fairfax County, Va., 1975-80; county atty. Fairfax County, 1980-91; ptnr. Venable, Baetjer & Howard, McLean, Va., 1991-95; judge Cir. Ct. Fairfax County, Va., 1995—. Lt. U.S. Army, 1964-66, Vietnam. Mem. Va. State Bar Coun. (exec. com. 1991-93), Local Govt. Attys. of Va. (pres. 1983-84, Disting. Svc. award 1991), Conf. of Local Bar Assn. (chmn. 1990-91), Fairfax Bar Assn. (pres. 1986-87). Presbyterian. Home: 6503 Smoot Dr Mc Lean VA 22101-4003 Office: Fairfax County Circuit Ct 4110 Chain Bridge Rd Fairfax VA 22030

STITT, DOROTHY JEWETT, journalist; b. Houston, Sept. 4, 1914; d. Harry Berkey and Gladys (Norfleet) Jewett; m. James Wilson Stitt, Feb. 14, 1939; children: James Harry, Thomas Paul. AB, Rice U., 1937; MS, Columbia U., 1938. Reporter Houston Post, 1936-38, asst. city editor, 1938; editor of publications Jewett Family of America, 1971-94; editor emeritus, 1994—; spl. asst. to pub. Jewett Genealogy Vols. III and IV, 1995—; Jewett family Dir.-for-Life, 1995—; gen. chmn. Jewett Family Reunion, 1996. Author, editor: The 100th Anniversary Yearbook and History of the George Taylor Chapter, DAR, 1895-1995, 1994, Easton Red Cross Fiftieth Anniversary Booklet an d History--Fifty Years of Service, 1967. Mem. adv. bd. Easton Salvation Army, pub. chmn., 1956—, chmn. bd., 1964, bd. treas., 1981; bd. dirs., pub. chmn. ARC, 1952-67, organizing chmn., pres. Easton JC wives, 1950-53; organizing bd. dirs. sec. and pub. chmn. Little Stone House Mus. Assn., 1974-91; bd. dirs. Easton United Cmty. Chest/United Way, 1957-60; active Easton Civil Def. Comms., 1956-60; mem. pub. bd. Montgomery County Pa. Girl Scouts USA, 1946-48, initiator and editor county newsletter; den mother cub scouts Easton Boy Scouts Am., 1948-55; mem. March School, mem. Easton PTA, 1948-57, sec., 1952-54, v.p., 1954-56, bylaws chmn., 1953, Easton H.S., 1954-61, membership chmn., 1955-57, 59-60; vol. Lehigh Valley chpt. ARC, 1995-96. Recipient plaques Salvation Army, 1982, 91, Jewett Family of Am., 1993, Cert. for Outstanding Svcs., Easton chpt. ARC, 1967, citation Hist. and Geneal. Soc. Northampton County for outstanding svc. in restoration and pub. of Little Stone House Mus., 1993, citation United Way of Easton, 1960, Molly Pitcher gold medal of appreciation, SAR, 1980. Mem. AAUW (Easton br., past treas., newsletter initiator and editor 1951-60, rep. of br. to UN N.Y.C. conf. 1961-68, internat. rels. chmn.), UDC (Jefferson Davis chpt.), DAR (George Taylor chpt. regent 1974-80, 89-95, vice regent 1980-83, historian 1971-74, 95—, pub. chmn. 1969—; Penn. state chmn. vol. svcs. 1995—), PEO (chpt. AF Houston), Easton Tavern House Soc., World Affairs Coun. Phila., Woman's Club of Easton (Outstanding Woman of Yr. 1992, Gold Medal of Honor 1992, pres. 1961-64, bd. dirs. 1959—, pub. chmn. 1952-68, 70-82, 92—, parliamentarian 1984-92. legis. cjmn. 1996—), Northampton Country Club (Niners' Golf chmn. 1957-91, Women's Golf Assn.constn. and bylaws chmn., parliamentarian 1960-92, Internat. Affairs Chmn., 1996—). Republican. Episcopalian. Avocations: antiques, historical research, golf, swimming, grandmothering. Home: 110 Upper Shawnee Ave Easton PA 18042-1356

STITT, FREDERICK HESSE, insurance broker; b. Chgo., Jan. 9, 1929; s. LeMoine Donaldson and Martha (Hesse) S.; m. Adena Fitzgerald, Dec. 23, 1950 (div. Nov. 1984); children: Rebecca Martha Hudecek, Mary Elizabeth Weeks, Barbara Anne Mistelle, Frederick Hesse Jr., Joyce Austin, Kathryn T.; m. Suzanne Boyce, Oct. 22, 1985; stepchildren: David Boyce Peyton, Jeffry Buckley Peyton. PhB, U. Chgo., 1949, MBA, 1951. CLU. Group svc. rep. Travelers Ins. Co., Peoria, Ill., 1951-52, agy. svc. rep., 1952-54; agt. Travelers Ins. Co., Chgo., 1954-59; v.p. A.W. Ormiston & Co., Chgo., 1959-80, pres., 1980—; instr. ins. Roosevelt U., 1961, 62. Contbr. articles to ins. jours. Mem. Am. Soc. CLU and ChFC (chair life ins. illustration task force 1991-93, instr. Illustration questionnaire 1992-93, mem. bd. 1992-95, pres. Chgo. chpt. 1968-69, Huebner scholar 1990), Assn. Advanced Life Underwriting (mem. bd. 1983-85), Chgo. Estate Planning Coun. (pres. 1976-77, Austin Fleming award 1984, Millard Graver Svc. award 1996). Avocations: history, writing, fly fishing.

STIVEN, ALAN ERNEST, population biologist, ecologist; b. St. Stephen, N.B., Can., Nov. 12, 1935; came to U.S., 1962, naturalized, 1977; s. Alan J. and Edith G. S.; m. Julia Ann Heeb, Aug. 18, 1972; 1 son, Alan; children by previous marriage: Terry, Kim. B.S., U. N.B., 1957; M.A., U. B.C., 1959; Ph.D., Cornell U., 1962. Asst. prof. zoology U. N.C., 1962-66, asso. prof., 1966-71, chmn. biology curriculum, 1968-70, prof., 1971—, chmn. ecology curriculum, 1971-86, chmn. dept. zoology, 1967-72, acting chmn., 1979-80, assoc. chmn. dept. biology, 1992—; mem., chmn. NRC-NSF pre-doctoral fellowship panel, 1984-86, NRC rsch. associateship panel, 1990-93, EPA Grad. fellowship panel, 1995; bd. chmn. Highlands Biol. Sta., 1987—. Editor: Ecology and Ecol. Monographs, 1967-73; editorial bd. Jour. Invertebrate Pathology, 1967-71; contbr. articles scholarly jours. Mem. Chapel Hill Bd. Adjustment, 1973-76. NSF rsch. grantee, 1962-82, NIH tng. grantee, 1966-70, U.S. Forest Svc. grantee, 1982-85, NC Wildlife Commn. grantee, 1988-94. Mem. Ecol. Soc. Am., Am. Soc. Naturalists, Soc. Study Evolution. Office: U NC Dept Biology Cb 3280 Coker Hall Chapel Hill NC 27599

STIVENDER, DONALD LEWIS, mechanical engineering consultant; b. Chgo., May 8, 1932; s. Paul Macon and Grace (Larsen) S.; m. Margaret Ann Lourim, Apr. 14, 1956; children—Anne, Robert, Carole. B.S. in Engring, U.S. Coast Guard Acad., 1954; M.S., U. Mich., 1959. Registered profl. engr., Mich. R & D engr. Rsch. Labs., GM Corp., Warren, Mich., 1959-92, sr. rsch. engr., 1968-92; owner, consulting engr. Stivender Engring. Assos., 1980—; cons. systems engring. disciplines. Contbr. articles tech. jours. on diesel, gas turbine and spark ignition engine combustion, emission, constrn. and electronic control aspects. Engring. officer USCG, 1950-58. Fellow Soc. Automotive Engrs. (Arch T. Colwell award 1968, 69, 79, governing bd. 1971-73); mem. NAS (naval studies bd. 1990-92), ASME, Combustion Inst., Sigma Xi. Achievements include invention of internal combustion engines and electronic control systems. Home: 1730 Hamilton Dr Bloomfield Hills MI 48302-0221

STIVER, PATRICIA ABARE, elementary education educator; b. Plattsburgh, N.Y., Nov. 17, 1941; d. Joseph LaBarge and Janet Marcella (Downs) Abare. BA, SUNY, Fredonia, 1964; MS, SUNY, Albany, 1988. Cert. elem. educator N.Y. Tchr. elem. Randolph (N.Y.) Ctrl. Sch., 1964-66; tchr. elem. Schoharie (N.Y.) Ctrl. Schs., 1966-86, asst. elem. math. coord., 1986—, remedial math. tchr., 1986—, coord. elem. computer assisted instrn., 1986-90. Mem. ASCD, Nat. Coun. Tchrs. Math., Assn. Math. Tchrs. of N.Y. State, N.Y. State United Tchrs. and Affiliates. Democrat. Avocations: gardening, clarinet, alto and tenor saxophone playing in bands, singing in choirs, computers, spectator sports. Home: 107 Brookside Pl PO Box 121 Schoharie NY 12157-0121 Office: Schoharie Ctrl Sch Main St Schoharie NY 12157

STIVER, WILLIAM EARL, retired government administrator; b. Madison, Ind., Mar. 30, 1921; s. John Virgil and Anna Lynne (Ryker) S.; student Hanover Coll., 1947-49; B.S., U. Calif. at Berkeley, 1951, M.B.A., 1952; m. Norma A. Cull, June 11, 1944; children—Vicki, Raymond, Gena, John. With Fed. Ser., Bur. Census, Commerce Dept., Suitland, Md., 1952-79, chief budget and finance div., 1963-73, dep. assoc. adminstr. Social and Econ. Stats. Adminstrn., 1973-75, spl. asst., assoc. dir. for adminstrn. and field ops. Bur. of Census, 1975-77, electronic data processing staff coordinator, 1977-78, ret., 1979. Served with AUS; 1942-43, 45-46. Recipient Silver medal Commerce Dept., 1969. Mem. Phi Beta Kappa, Beta Gamma Sigma. Home: 8104 Kerby Pky Ct Fort Washington MD 20744-4756

STIVERS, WILLIAM CHARLES, forest products company executive; b. Modesto, Calif., June 22, 1938; s. William P. and Helen Louise (Cummings) S.; m. Karen L. Gaspar, Aug. 6, 1961; children: William, Gregory, Michael, Kristy, Kelly, John, Jeffrey. BA, Stanford, 1960; MBA, U. So. Calif., 1963; certificate, U. Wash., 1969; grad., Advanced Mgmt. Program, Harvard U., 1977. Asst. cashier, asst. v.p., v.p. First Interstate Bank, San Francisco and Los Angeles, 1962-70; finance mgr. treas. dept. Weyerhaeuser Co., Tacoma, 1970; asst. treas. Weyerhaeuser Co., 1971, treas., 1972—, v.p., 1980-91, sr. v.p., chief fin. officer, 1991—; treas. Weyerhaeuser Real Estate Co., 1970; bd. dirs., exec. com. mem. Protection Mut. Ins. Co., Park Ridge, Ill.; bd. dirs., audit com. mem. 1st Interstate Bank; bd. dirs., chmn., pres. S&S Land and Cattle Co.; nat. adv. bd. mem. Chem. Banking Corp. Chmn. bd. trustees Franciscan Health Sys.-West, Federal Way; bd. dirs. Ctr. Study Banking and Fin. Mkts., U. Wash., Seattle; vice chmn. fin. mgmt. com. Am. Forest and Paper Assn. Mem. Financial Execs. Inst.

STIX, THOMAS HOWARD, physicist, educator; b. St. Louis, July 12, 1924; s. Ernest William and Erma (Kingsbacher) S.; m. Hazel Rosa Sherwin, May 28, 1950; children: Susan Sherwin Fisher, Michael Sherwin. B.S., Calif. Inst. Tech., 1948; Ph.D., Princeton U., 1953. Mem. staff Plasma Physics Lab. Princeton U., 1953—, co-head exptl. div., 1961-78, asst. dir. acad. affairs, 1978-80, assoc. dir. acad. affairs, 1980-93; prof. astrophys. sci., 1962—, assoc. chmn. dept. astrophys. sci., 1981-91; acting dir. Ctr. for Jewish Life Princeton U., 1994-95. Author: The Theory of Plasma Waves, 1962, Waves in Plasmas, 1992; mem. adv. bd. McGraw-Hill Advanced Physics Monograph Series, 1963-70; bd. editors: Physics of Fluids, 1966-68, Internat. Jour. Engring. Sci, 1969-77, Nuclear Fusion, 1975-80; assoc. editor: Phys. Rev. Letters, 1974-77. Chmn. Princeton United Jewish Appeal, 1954-55, 63-64, Princeton Hillel Found., 1972-76, pres., 1994-96. Served with AUS, 1942-45. Recipient award for disting. teaching Princeton U., 1991; NSF sr. postdoctoral fellow physics Weizmann Inst. Sci., Rehovot, Israel, 1960-61; Guggenheim Meml. Found. fellow, 1969-70. Fellow Am. Phys. Soc. (chmn. div. plasma physics 1962-63, com. internat. freedom of scientists 1983-87, chmn. 1985; James Clark Maxwell prize 1980); mem. AAUP, Sigma Xi, Tau Beta Pi. Home: 231 Brookstone Dr Princeton NJ 08540-2405

STOB, MARTIN, physiology educator; b. Chgo., Feb. 20, 1926; s. Cornelius and Theodora (Sluis) S. B.S., Purdue U., 1949, M.S., 1951, Ph.D., 1953. Mem. faculty Purdue U., Lafayette, Ind., 1953—, assoc. prof. animal scis., 1958-63, prof., 1963-92; ret., 1992—. Contbr. articles to profl. jours. Patentee prodn. of fermentation estrogen. Served with USN, 1944-46; ETO, PTO. Name Best Tchr. Sch. Agr., 1970, Best Counselor Sch. Agr., 1977, Best Counselor Purdue U., 1977. Fellow AAAS; mem. Am. Inst. Biol. Scis., Am. Soc. Animal Sci., Soc. Study of Reprodn., Soc. Study of Fertility. Episcopalian. Home: 6218 W Rd 75 N Lafayette IN 47906

STOBAUGH, ROBERT BLAIR, business educator, business executive; b. McGehee, Ark., Oct. 15, 1927; s. Robert B. and Helen (Parris) S.; m. Beverly Ann Parker, Oct. 18, 1947 (dec. 1990); children: Blair, Susan, William, Clay; m. June Gray Milton, Dec. 7, 1991. B.S. in Chem. Engring., La. State U., 1947; D. Bus. Adminstrn., Harvard Bus. Sch., 1968. Refinery engr. Exxon Corp., Baton Rouge and Venezuela, 1947-52; engring. mgr. Caltex Oil Co., N.Y., Bahrain, London, 1952-59; mgr. econ. evaluation Monsanto Co., Houston, 1959-65; lectr. Harvard Bus. Sch., Boston, 1967-70, assoc. prof., 1970-71, prof., 1972-83, Charles E. Wilson prof., 1984—; chmn. doctoral programs Harvard Bus. Sch., 1984-89; dir. energy project Harvard Bus. Sch., Boston, 1972-83; chmn. tech. and ops. mgmt. area Harvard Bus. Sch., 1981-83; dir. Ashland Inc., Ky., 1977—, and 8 other firms, 1971-95. Co-author: Money in the Multinational Enterprise, 1973, Energy Future (best-seller list N.Y. Times and Time mag.), 1979, How To Build an Effective Small-Company Board, 1996; author: Nine Investments Abroad and Their Impact at Home, 1976, Innovation and Competition, 1988; co-editor: Technology Crossing Borders, 1984; contbr. articles on corp. governance to profl. publs., 1992-96. Mem. bd. advisors Instituto de Estudios Superiores de la Empresa, Barcelona, Spain, 1973-80; co-chmn. The Dumbarton Oaks Symposium on Energy Efficiency, Washington, 1979; bd. dirs. Alliance to Save Energy, Washington, 1979-94; chmn. Blue Ribbon Commn. on Dir.. Compensation, Nat. Assn. Corp. Dirs., 1995; expert testimony Congress; advisor to cabinet-level depts. of White House and UN; trustee French Libr. and Cultural Ctr., Boston, 1995—. Fellow Acad. Internat. Bus. (pres. 1979-80), Council on Fgn. Relations, Am. Econ. Assn., Nat. Assn. Corp. Dirs. Episcopalian. Clubs: Belmont Hill (Mass.); Harvard (N.Y.). Office: Harvard Bus Sch Soldiers Field Rd Boston MA 02163

STOBER, WILLIAM JOHN, II, economics educator; b. Boston, Mar. 24, 1933; s. Ralph William and Marjorie Cairncross (Duthie) S.; m. Jeannine Lynn Defries, Sept. 10, 1955. B.S.c., Washington and Lee U., 1955; M.A., Duke U., 1957, Ph.D., 1965. Instr., then asst. prof. econs. N.C. State U., Raleigh, 1959-65; asst. prof., then asso. prof. La. State U., 1965-69, acting head dept. econs., 1968-69; mem. faculty U. Ky., 1969—, prof. econs., 1974—, chmn. dept., 1979-86, 90-95, dir. grad. studies, 1979-86. Mem. Am. Econs. Assn., AAUP, So. Econ. Assn. (exec. com. 1969-71), Beta Gamma Sigma. Democrat. Home: 516 Mundy's Landing Rd Rte 4 Versailles KY 40383

STOBERSKI, MICHAEL EDWARD, lawyer; b. Troy, N.Y., Oct. 18, 1966; s. John S. and Winifred A. (Boland) S.; m. Holly S. Sedarat, Oct. 21, 1994. BA, U. San Diego, 1988, JD, 1991. Bar: Calif. 1991, Nev. 1992, U.S. Dist. Ct. (so. dist.) Calif. 1991, Nev. 1992, U.S. Ct. Appeals (9th cir.) 1992. Assoc. Rawlings, Olson, Cannon, Gormley & Desruisseaux, Las Vegas, Nev., 1991—; counsel Clark County Pro Bono Project, Las Vegas, 1992—, named Rookie of Yr. 1992-93. Mem. ABA, Def. Rsch. Inst., Clark County Bar Assn. Avocations: golf, skiing, scuba diving. Office: Rawlings Olson Cannon Gormley & DesRusseaux 301 E Clark Ave Ste 1000 Las Vegas NV 89101

STOBO, JOHN DAVID, physician, educator; b. Somerville, Mass., Sept. 1, 1941. BA, Dartmouth Coll., 1963; MD, SUNY, Buffalo, 1968. Intern Osler Med. Services, Johns Hopkins, Balt., 1968-69, asst. med. resident, 1969-70, chief med. resident, 1972-73; research assoc. NIH, Bethesda, 1970-72; asst. prof. Mayo Clinic and Research Found., Rochester, Minn., 1973-76; assoc. prof. Moffitt Hosp., San Francisco, 1976-82, prof., head section rheumatology, clin. immunology, 1982-85; William Osler prof. medicine, chmn. dept. medicine John Hopkins Hosp. and Univ., Balt., 1985-94, vice dean clin. sci., assoc. v.p. medicine, 1994—; v.p. Johns Hopkins Health System, Balt., 1994—; chmn., CEO Johns Hopkins Healthcare LLC, Balt. Mem. editorial bds. Jour. Immunology, 1981-86, Jour. Lab. and Clin. Investigation, 1977-82, Arthritis and Rheumatism 1980-85, Jour. Reticuloendothelial Soc., 1982-84, Jour. Clin. Investigation, 1981-86, Jour. Clin. Immunology, 1982-87, Jour. Molecular and Cellular Immunology, 1984-86, Rheumatology Internat., 1984-86, Jour. Immunology, 1985-87; contbr. numerous articles to profl. jours. Transp. and immunobiology adv. com. NIAID, 1976-81; vice chmn. research com. Arthritis Found., 1982-84, chmn., 1984-86, sr. investigator, 1974-77; bd. scientific counselors Nat. Cancer Inst., 1982—; scientific adv. bd. exec. com. Lupus Research Inst.; research adv. bd. DuPont Co., 1987-94. Recipient Merck award 1967, Maimonides Med. Soc. award 1968; SUNY fellow, 1965-66. Fellow ACP, Am. Clin. and Climatol. Assn., Balt. City Med. Soc., Interurban Clin. Club, Md. Soc. Internal Medicine; mem. AAAS, Inst. Medicine, Am. Coll. Rheumatology (pres. 1989-90), Am. Rheumatism Assn. (sec., treas., 1st v.p. 1985-89), Am. Assn. Immunologists, Am. Assn. Physicians, Am. Fedn. Clin. Rsch., Am. Soc. Clin. Investigation, Assn. Profs. Medicine (sec.-treas. 1991-92, pres. 1994-95), Alpha Omega Alpha. Office: Johns Hopkins Outpatient Ctr 601 N Caroline St Ste 2080 Baltimore MD 21205-1809*

STOCK, DAVID EARL, mechanical engineering educator; b. Balt., Feb. 2, 1939; s. Walter E. and Minnie H. (Bauer) S.; m. Mary W. Wilford, Aug. 4, 1962; children: Joseph W., Katherine W. BS, Penn State U., 1961; MS, U. Conn., 1965; PhD, Oreg. State U., 1972. Test engr. Pratt & Whitney Aircraft, East Hartford, Conn., 1961-65; vol. Peace Corps, Ghana, 1965-68; prof. Wash. State U., Pullman, 1972—. Contbr. articles to profl. jours. Fellow ASME (chair multiphase flow com. 1988-90, Freeman scholar 1994). Office: Wash State U Dept Mech Materials Engr Pullman WA 99164-2920

STOCK, GREGG FRANCIS, retired association executive; b. Kansas City, Mo., Jan. 30, 1925; s. Arthur Robert and Verna Marie (Prawitz) S.; m. Sarah Ellen Smart, Nov. 8, 1947; children: Gregory Francis, Heidi Frances, Peter Huston. B.A. in Journalism; B.S. in Advt, U. Kans., 1948. Pres. Wayne-Fastock Equipment Co., Kansas City, Mo., 1953-65; dir. Kansas City Mus., 1971-82, dir. emeritus, 1982—; exec. dir. Old Santa Fe Assn., 1983-84, dir., 1984-87; exec. dir. Southwestern Assn. on Indian Affairs, Santa Fe, 1984-87, dir., 1987-90. Served to lt. (j.g.) USNR, 1943-46, PTO. Fellow Explorers Club. Home: 8345 Somerset Dr Shawnee Mission KS 66207-1843

STOCK, LEON MILO, chemist, educator; b. Detroit, Oct. 15, 1930; s. J.H. Frederick and Anna (Fischer) S.; m. Mary K. Elmblad, May 6, 1961; children: Katherine L., Ann V. BS in Chemistry, U. Mich., 1952; PhD in Chemistry, Purdue U., 1959. Instr. U. Chgo., 1958-61, asst. prof., 1961-65, assoc. prof., 1965-70, prof. dept. chemistry, 1970—, master Phys. Scis. Collegiate div., 1970-96, prof. emeritus dept. chemistry, 1997—, assoc. dean div. Phys. Scis., 1976-81, assoc. dean, 1976-81, chmn. dept. chemistry, 1985-88; faculty assoc. Argonne (Ill.) Nat. Lab., 1984—, joint appointment chemistry div., 1985—, dir. chemistry div., 1988-95; exploratory rsch. assoc. Elec. Power Rsch. Inst., 1989; adv. bd. Ctr. for Applied Rsch., U. Ky., 1990-95; Brown lectr. Purdue U., 1992; Given lectr. Pa. State U., 1995; cons. Westinghouse Hanford Co., 1995—, Phillips Petroleum Co., 1964-95, Amoco Oil Co., 1989-95. Recipient L.J. and H.M. Quantrell prize, 1974, H.H. Storch award Am. Chem. Soc., 1987. Mem. NAS (energy engring. bd.), Am. Chem. Soc. (com. on sci. 1990-92), Coun. of Gordon Rsch. Confs. (chmn. Gordon Conf. on Fuel Sci. 1983), NRC (mem. panel on coop. rsch. in fossil energy 1984, energy engring. bd. 1984-90, mem. panel on strategic petroleum rsch. 1985, panel on rsch. needs of advanced process tech. 1992-93), Ill. Coal Bd. (program panel 1986-90, panel on prodn. techs. for transp. fuels 1990, editl. bd. Jour. Organic Chemistry 1981-86, Energy and Fuels, 1986—). Office: U of Chicago Dept of Chemistry 5801 S Ellis Ave Chicago IL 60637-1404 also: Argonne Nat Lab Chem Div Argonne IL 60439

STOCK, STUART CHASE, lawyer; b. St. Louis, July 19, 1946; s. Sheldon Harry and Muriel Cecile (Lovejoy) S.; m. Judith Ann Stewart, July 18, 1970; 1 child, Frederick Chase. BS with highest distinction, Purdue U., 1968; JD magna cum laude, Harvard U., 1971. Bar: Mo. 1971, Ind. 1973, D.C. 1974. Law clk. to Chief Judge Henry J. Friendly U.S. Ct. Appeals 2d cir., New York, 1971-72; law clk. to Justice Thurgood Marshall U.S. Supreme Ct., Washington, 1972-73; assoc. Covington & Burling, Washington, 1974-78, ptnr., 1978—; lectr. law U. Va., Charlottesville, 1987-90. Mem. Am. Law Inst. Office: Covington & Burling PO Box 7566 1201 Pennsylvania Ave NW Washington DC 20044

STOCKAR, HELENA MARIE MAGDALENA, artist; b. Bratislava, Czechoslovakia, Mar. 22, 1933; came to the U.S., 1968; d. Arnost J. and Helen R. (Strakova) Kubasek; m. Ivo J. Stockar, Oct. 31, 1959; children: David, Laura Bates. Diploma, Graficka Skola, Prague, 1952, Music Conservatory, Prague, 1954. Piano tchr. Music Sch., Prague, 1954-68; company pianist State Ballet/Breacrest Sch., R.I., 1968-74; piano tchr. Music Tchr. Assn., R.I., 1968-86. One-woman shows include Warwick Mus., R.I., 1986, Brown U., Providence, 1987, Westerly Art Gallery, R.I., 1987, Westerly Art Gallery/Morin-Miller, 1988, 89, Galerie Horizon, Paris, 1989, others; two-woman exhibit R.I. State Com. of Nat. Mus. of Women in the Arts, Triboro Studio, R.I., 1995; exhibited in group shows at World Congress of Czechoslovak Soc. of Art and Sci., Washington, 1988, Morin-Miller Internat., N.Y.C., 1989, Ariel Gallery, Soho, N.Y.C., 1989, Art Expo N.Y.C., 1989, R.I. State Com. Nat. Mus. Women Arts, 1995, Providence Art Club, 1996, others; represented in permanent collections around the world; featured on numerous TV shows. Recipient Second prize Nat. Competition of Children's Book Illustration, Prague, 1965; named finalist Internat. Art Competition, L.A., 1984. Mem. Nat. Mus. of Women in the Arts (R.I. state com.), Czechoslovak Soc. of Art and Sci., Music Club Providence, Chopin Club Providence, Schubert Club Providence, Chaminade Club Providence. Avocations: traveling, gardening. Office: PO Box 7282 Warwick RI 02887-7282

STOCKARD, JAMES ALFRED, lawyer; b. Lake Dallas, Tex., Aug. 4, 1935; s. Clifford Raymond and Thelma Gladys (Gotcher) S.; m. Mary Sue Hogan, Aug. 17, 1956; children—Bruce Anthony, James Alfred, Paul Andrew. BA with honors, N. Tex. State U., Denton, 1956; LLB magna cum laude, So. Methodist U., 1959. Bar: Tex. 1959. Pvt. practice Dallas, 1959-62; with Employers Casualty Co., Dallas, 1962-65; v.p. Southland Life Ins. Co., Dallas, 1965-77; sr. v.p., gen. counsel, dir. Southland Life Ins. Co., 1977-87; exec. v.p., gen. counsel, sec. Southland Fin. Corp., Dallas, 1978-87; dir. Tex. Life, Accident, Health and Hosp. Svc. Ins. Guaranty Assn., 1978-84, chmn. bd., 1980-84; ptnr. Butler & Binion, Dallas, 1987—; bd. dirs. Ins. Systems Am., Atlanta; pres., bd. dir. Dallas County Municipal Utility Dist. 1, Irving, Tex.; gen. counsel, bd. dirs. Lone Star Life Ins. Co., 1988—. Contbr. legal jours. Mem. exec. com., precinct chmn. Dallas County Dem. Com., 1971. Mem. Am., Tex., Dallas Bar Assn., Assn. Life Ins. Counsel. Methodist. Home: 4300 Druid Ln Dallas TX 75205-1029 Office: 750 N Saint Paul St Ste 1800 Dallas TX 75201-3255

STOCKARD, SUSAN See **CHANNING, STOCKARD**

STOCKBURGER, JEAN DAWSON, lawyer; b. Scottsboro, Ala., Feb. 4, 1936; d. Joseph Mathis Scott and Mary Frances (Alley) Dawson; m. John Calvin Stockburger, Mar. 23, 1963; children: John Scott, Mary Staci, Christopher Sean. Student, Gulf Park Coll., 1954-55; BA, Auburn U., 1958; M in Social Work, Tulane U., 1962; JD, U. Ark., Little Rock, 1979. Bar: Ark. 1979, U.S. Dist. Ct. (ea. dist.) Ark. 1980. Assoc. Mitchell, Williams, Selig, Gates & Woodyard and predecessor, Little Rock, 1979-85, ptnr., 1985-94, of counsel, 1994—; bd. dirs., sec. Cen. Ark. Estate Planning Council, Little Rock, 1984-85, 2d v.p., 1985-86; pres. Cen. Ark. Estate Council, 1987-88. Assoc. editor U. Ark. Law Rev., 1978-79. Bd. dirs. Sr. Citizens Activities Today, Little Rock, 1983-88, treas., 1986-88; bd. dirs. Vol. Orgn. for Ctrl. Ark. Legal Svcs., 1986-91, sec., 1987-88, chmn., 1989-81, H.I.R.E. Inc., 1994—; sec. Little Rock Cmty. Mental Health Ctr., 1994-96, v.p., 1996—. Mem. ABA, Ark. Bar Assn. (chmn. probate and trust law sect. 1986-88), Pulaski County Bar Assn. (bd. dirs. 1994—), Am. Coll. Trust and Estate Counsel. Democrat. Methodist. Office: Mitchell Williams Selig Gates & Woodyard 320 W Capitol Ave Ste 1000 Little Rock AR 72201-3522

STOCKDALE, JAMES BOND, writer, research scholar, retired naval officer; b. Abingdon, Ill., Dec. 23, 1923; s. Vernon Beard and Mabel Edith (Bond) S.; m. Sybil Elizabeth Bailey, June 28, 1947; children: James Bond, Sidney Bailey, Stanford Baker, Taylor Burr. BS, U.S. Naval Acad., 1946; MA, Stanford U., 1962; LLD (hon.), Brown U., 1979; LHD (hon.), U. R.I., 1980; 9 other hon. degrees. Commd. ensign USN, 1946, advanced through grades to vice admiral, served as naval aviator, test pilot sch. instr., squadron comdr. of supersonic fighters, air wing comdr.; prisoner of war (sr. naval service POW) North Vietnam, 1965-73; pres. Naval War Coll., Newport, R.I., 1976-79; retired USN, 1979; pres. The Citadel, Charleston, S.C., 1979-80; sr. research fellow The Hoover Instn., Stanford U., 1981—; independent candidate V.P. U.S. running mate of Ross Perot, 1992. Author: A Vietnam Experience, 1985 (Freedoms Found. at Valley Forge hon. prize 1985), (with Sybil Stockdale) In Love and War, 1984, Thoughts of a Philosophical Fighter Pilot, 1995. Mem. acad. adv. bd. U.S. Naval Acad., Annapolis, 1981—. Decorated D.F.C. (2), D.S.M. (3), Silver Star (4), Medal of Honor; inducted Carrier Aviation Hall of Fame, 1993; enshrined U.S. Naval Aviation Hall of Honor, 1996. Fellow Soc. Exptl. Test Pilots (hon.); mem. Lincoln Acad. Ill. (laureate), Congl. Medal of Honor Soc., Assn. Naval Aviation, Soc. of Cincinnati, SAR, Bohemian Club (San Francisco). Episcopalian. Home: 547 A Ave Coronado CA 92118-1917 Office: Stanford U Hoover Institute Stanford CA 94305

STOCKER, ARTHUR FREDERICK, classics educator; b. Bethlehem, Pa., Jan. 24, 1914; s. Harry Emilius and Alice (Stratton) S.; m. Marian West, July 16, 1968. A.B. summa cum laude, Williams Coll., 1934; A.M., Harvard U., 1935, Ph.D., 1939. Instr. Greek Bates Coll., 1941-42; asst. prof. classics U. Va., 1946-52, assoc. prof., 1952-60, prof., 1960-84, prof. emeritus, 1984—, chmn. dept., 1955-63, 68-78, assoc. dean Grad. Sch. Arts and Scis., 1962-66; vis. asst. prof. classics U. Chgo., summer 1951. Editor: (with others) Servianorum in Vergilii Carmina Commentariorum Editio Harvardiana, Vol. II, 1946, Vol. III, 1965; assoc. editor: Classical Outlook. Served with USAAF, 1942-46; col. (ret.). Sheldon traveling fellow from Harvard, 1940-41. Mem. Va. Classical Assn. (pres. 1949-52), Mid. West and South Classical Assn. (pres. So. sect. 1960-62, pres. 1970-71), Nat. Huguenot Soc. (pres. gen. 1989-91), Am. Philol. Assn., Mediaeval Acad. Am., Poetry Soc. Va. (pres. 1966-69), S.A.R. (chpt. pres. 1972, 91), Huguenot Soc. Va. (pres. 1981-83), Raven Soc. (Raven award 1977), Phi Beta Kappa, Omicron Delta Kappa. Republican. Presbyterian (elder). Clubs: Masons, Internat. Torch, Colonnade (Charlottesville, Va.), Farmington Country (Charlottesville, Va.), Commonwealth (Richmond, Va.), Williams (N.Y.C.), Army and Navy (Washington). Home: 1434 Grove Rd Charlottesville VA 22901-3126

STOCKER, JOYCE ARLENE, retired secondary school educator; b. West Wyoming, Pa., May 13, 1931; d. Donald Arthur and Elizabeth Mae (Gardner) Saunders; m. Robert Earl Stocker, Nov. 26, 1953; children: Desiree Lee Stocker Stackhouse, Rebecca Lois Stocker Genelow, Joyce Elizabeth Stocker Scrobola. Grad. cum laude, Coll. Misericordia, Dallas, 1953; Master's equivalency diploma, Pa. Dept. Edn., 1991. Cert. tchr., Pa. Tchr. music and lang. arts West Pittston (Pa.) Sch. Dist., 1953-60; tchr. music and choral Wyoming Area Sch. Dist., Exeter, Pa., 1970-78, tchr. English composition, 1978-93, chmn. lang. arts dept., 1982-90, dir. nat. history day activities, 1982-93; state cons. Nat. History Day, 1996—. Organist, choir dir. United Meth. Ch., Wyo., 1958—; choir dir. Wyo. Centenial Choir, Wyo., 1983; mem. com., sec. Continuing Profl. Devel. Com. Pa., Exeter, 1988-93, Long Range Plan Wyo. Area Sch. Dist., Exeter, 1990-91; tutor, judge Nat. History Day; judge regional, state, and nat. events for Nat. History Day. Recipient DAR Tchr. of Yr. award, 1992-93, Wilkes U., 1990; named Outstanding Educator, Times Leader, 1993. Mem. NEA, Pa. Edn. Assn., Wyo. Edn. Assn., N.E. Pa. Writing Coun., Nat. Coun. Tchrs. English, Women Educators Internat., Orgn. Am. History, Pa. Music Educators Assn., Music Educators Nat. Coun., Nat. Coun. Social Studies, Pa. Assn. Sch. Retirees, Pa. Sch. Employees Retirement Sys., Pa. Retired Pub. Sch. Employees Assn. (Luzerne-Wyoming counties chpt.), Pa. Coun. Social Studies, Delta Kappa Gamma (recording sec. 1991—), Phi Mu Gamma. Methodist. Avocations: reading, writing, sewing, hunting, fishing. Office: Wyoming Area Sch Dist 20 Memorial St Exeter PA 18643-2659

STOCKER, JULE E(LIAS), lawyer; b. Detroit, Sept. 16, 1906; s. David R. and Hattie V. (Gerber) S.; m. Beatrice H. Klipstein, Mar. 26, 1932; children: Maida (Mrs. George S. Abrams), Michael. AB magna cum laude, Harvard U., 1926, JD magna cum laude, 1929. Bar: N.Y. 1929, U.S. Supreme Ct. 1950. Since practiced in N.Y.C.; mem. Chadbourne, Parke, Whiteside & Wolff (name changed to Chadbourne and Parke), 1950-56; assoc. counsel, law dept.-investments Equitable Life Assurance Soc. of U.S., 1956-62, 2d v.p., asso. gen. solicitor, 1962-65, v.p., asso. gen. counsel, 1965-70, v.p., gen. atty., 1970-73, cons., 1974-79, 1985—; counsel Gruber & Gruber, N.Y.C., 1977—; lectr. Practicing Law Inst., N.Y.C., 1942—; mem. adv. com. N.Y. State Commn. Estates, 1961-66; drafting cons. N.Y. State Joint Legis. Com. Revision Corp. Laws, 1960-61; project dir. N.Y. State Law Revision Com., Recodification N.Y. Ins. Law, 1979-83; cons. N.Y. State Ins. Dept., 1983-84. Author: Wills for Servicemen, 1944, Stocker on Drawing Wills, 10th edit., 1987, lead author Supplement, 1990, 11th edit. 1993; lead author codification notes McKinney's N.Y. Ins. Law, 1985; co-author Legislators Update, 1993, supplement, 1994; editor Harvard Law Rev., 1927-29. Mem. Assn. of Bar of City of N.Y. (chmn. com. real property law 1946-49), N.Y. County Lawyers Assn. (sec. com. surrogates' ct. 1946-57), Assn. Life Ins. Counsel, ABA, N.Y. State Bar Assn., Am. Law Inst. (various coms.), Am. Coun. Life Ins. (com. ins. co. fed. income tax 1972-73, legal sect. mem. emeritus), Phi Beta Kappa and Assocs. Home: 17 W 54th St New York NY 10019-5412

STOCKING, GEORGE WARD, JR., anthropology educator; b. Berlin, Dec. 8, 1928; came to U.S., 1929; s. George Ward and Dorothé Amelia (Reichhard) S.; m. Wilhelmina Davis, Aug. 19, 1949 (div. 1965); children: Susan Hallowell, Rebecca, Rachel Louise, Melissa, Thomas Shepard; m. Carol Ann Bowman, Sept. 29, 1968. BA, Harvard U., 1949; PhD, U. Pa., 1960. From. instr. to assoc. prof. history U. Calif., Berkeley, 1960-68; assoc. prof. anthropology and history U. Chgo., 1968-74, prof. anthropology, 1974—, Stein-Freiler Disting. Svc. prof., 1990—, dir. Fishbein Ctr. for History Sci. and Medicine, 1981-92; vis. prof. U. Minn., Mpls., 1974, Harvard U., Cambridge, Mass., 1977, Stanford U., Palo Alto, Calif., 1983. Author: Race, Culture and Evolution, 1968, Victorian Anthropology, 1987, The Ethnographer's Magic, 1992, After Tylor, 1995; author-editor: The Shaping of American Anthropology, 1974; editor (jour.) History of Anthropology, 1983-96. Fellow Ctr. for Advanced Study in Behavioral Scis., 1976-77, John Simon Guggenheim Meml. Found., 1984-85, Inst. for Advanced Study, 1992-93; Getty Ctr. for History of Art and Humanities scholar, 1988-89. Fellow Am. Anthropol. Assn., Am. Acad. Arts and Scis.; mem. Royal Anthropol. Inst. (Huxley medal 1993), History Sci. Soc. Avocations: gardening, needlepoint, bicycling. Office: Univ Chicago Dept Anthropology 1126 E 59th St Chicago IL 60637-1580

STOCKMAN, DAVID ALLEN, former federal official, congressman, financier; b. Ft. Hood, Tex., Nov. 10, 1946; s. Allen and Carol (Bartz) S. BA in Am. History cum laude, Mich. State U., East Lansing, 1968; postgrad., Harvard U. Div. Sch., 1968-70; fellow, Inst. Politics, 1974. Spl. asst. to Congressman John Anderson, 1970-72; exec. dir. Republican Conf., Ho. of Reps., 1972-75; mem. 95th Congress from 4th Dist. Mich., Interstate and Fgn. Commerce Com., Adminstrn. Com.; chmn. Rep. Econ. Policy Task Force, 1977-81; dir. Office of Mgmt. and Budget, Washington, 1981-85; mng. dir. Salomon Bros., N.Y.C., 1985-88; sr. mng. dir. The Blackstone Group, N.Y.C., 1988—; Mem. Nat. Commn. on Air Quality, 1978. Author: The Triumph of Politics: Why the Reagan Revolution Failed, 1986. Mem. Coun. on Fgn. Rels. Office: The Blackstone Group 345 Park Ave New York NY 10154-0004

STOCKMAN, JAMES ANTHONY, III, pediatrician; b. Phila., 1943. MD, Jeffersib Med. Coll., 1969. Diplomate Am. Bd. Pediatrics. Intern Childrens Hosp. Pa., 1969-70, resident in pediatrics, 1970-72; fellow in pediatric hematology/oncology SUNY, Syracuse, 1972-74; now cons. prof. Duke U.; also with U. N.C., Chapel Hill. Office: Am Bd Pediatrics 111 Silver Cedar Ct Chapel Hill NC 27514-1512

STOCKMAN, STEPHEN E., congressman; b. Bloomfield Hills, Mich., Nov. 14, 1956; m. Patti Stockman. BS in Acctg., U. Houston, 1990. Acct., tech. McKee Environ. Health, Inc., 1991-93; mem. 104th Congress from 9th Tex. dist., 1995—. Republican. Office: US House Reps 417 Cannon House Office Bldg Washington DC 20515-4309*

STOCKMAR, TED P., lawyer; b. Denver, May 9, 1921; s. Theodore Paul and Elda Marie (Robinson) S.; m. Suzanne Louise Harl, Feb. 14, 1947; children: Stephen Harl, John Brian, Anne Baldwin Stockmar Upton. BS in Petroleum Engring., Colo. Sch. Mines, Golden, 1943; LLB, U. Denver, 1948. Bar: Colo. 1948. Ptnr. Holme Roberts & Owen Denver, 1951-91; of counsel, 1991—. Co-author: Law of Federal Oil and Gas Leases 1964, 1984; also articles. Trustee Colo. Sch. Mines, Golden, 1948-82, bd. pres., 1970-80. 1st lt. USAF, 1943-45. Mem. Denver Bar Assn., Colo. Bar Assn., Rocky Mountain Oil and Gas Assn. (dir., exec. com. 1982-93, chmn. legal com. 1986-88), Denver Country Club, Univ. Club, Law Club, Rotary (bd. dirs. 1969-71). Republican. Avocations: bird watching; skiing; tennis; golf; reading; gardening. Home: 2552 E Alameda Ave Apt 8 Denver CO 80209-3324 Office: Holme Roberts & Owen LLC 1700 Lincoln St Ste 4100 Denver CO 80203-4541

STOCKMAYER, WALTER H(UGO), retired chemistry educator; b. Rutherford, N.J., Apr. 7, 1914; s. Hugo Paul and Dagmar (Bostroem) S.; m. Sylvia Kleist Bergen, Aug. 12, 1938; children—Ralph, Hugh,. S.B., MIT, 1935, Ph.D., 1940; B.Sc. (Rhodes scholar), Oxford U., 1937; D.Sc., U. Louis-Pasteur, Strasbourg, France, 1972; L.H.D., Dartmouth Coll., 1983; DSc, U. Mass., 1996. Instr. M.I.T., 1939-41, asst. prof., 1943-46, assoc. prof., 1946-52, prof., 1952-61; prof. chemistry Dartmouth, 1961-79, prof. emeritus, 1979—; instr. Columbia, 1941-43; cons. E.I. duPont de Nemours & Co., Inc., 1945—; vis. com. Nat. Bur. Standards, 1979-84. Contbr. articles on phys. and macromolecular chemistry to sci. jours. Recipient Nat. Medal of Sci., 1987, MCA Coll. Chemistry Tchr. award 1960, ; Guggenheim fellow, 1954-55, hon. fellow Jesus Coll., Oxford, Eng., 1976, Alexander von Humboldt fellow, 1978-79. Fellow Am. Acad. Arts and Scis., Am. Phys. Soc. (Polymer Physics prize 1975); mem. NAS, Am. Chem. Soc. (assoc. editor Macromolecules 1968-74, 76-94, chmn. polymer chem. divsn. 1968, Polymer Chemistry award 1965, Peter Debye award 1974, T. W. Richards medal 1988, polymer divsn. award 1988, Oesper award 1992), Soc. Plastics Engrs. (Internat. award 1991), Soc. Polymer Sci., Japan (hon. 1991), Appalachian Mountain Club, Sigma Xi (William Procter prize 1993). Office: Dartmouth Coll Chemistry Dept Hanover NH 03755

STOCKMEYER, NORMAN OTTO, JR., law educator, consultant; b. Detroit, May 24, 1938; s. Norman O. and Lillian R. (Hitchman) S.; m. Marcia E. Rudman, Oct. 1, 1966; children: Claire, Kathleen, Mary Frances. AB, Oberlin Coll., 1960; JD, U. Mich., 1963. Bar: Mich. 1963, U.S. Ct. Appeals (6th cir.) 1964, U.S. Supreme Ct. 1974. Legis. grad. fellow Mich. State U., 1963; legal counsel Senate Judiciary Com., Mich. Legislature, 1964; law clk. Mich. Ct. Appeals, 1965, commr., 1966-68, research dir., 1969-76; assoc. prof. law Thomas M. Cooley Law Sch., 1977-78, prof., 1978—; vis. prof. Mercer U. Sch. Law, 1986, Calif. Western Sch. Law, 1993; lectr. Mich. Judicial Inst., 1995. Editor Mich. Law of Damages, 1989; contbr. numerous articles to state and nat. legal jours. Named one of 88 Greats Lansing State Jour., 1988. Fellow Am. Bar Found. (life); mem. ABA (chmn. Mich.

membership 1972-73, lectr. Appellate Judges Conf. jud. seminars 1972-76, ho. del. 1988-92, editorial bd. Compleat Lawyer 1990—), Nat. Conf. Bar Founds. (trustee 1985-90, sec. 1988-89), Mich. State Bar Found. (pres. 1982-85, trustee 1971-92), State Bar Mich. (chmn. Young Lawyers sect. 1971-72, rep. assembly 1972-79, bd. commrs. 1985-93), Ingham County Bar Assn. (bd. dirs. 1981-85), Mich. Assn. Professions (bd. dirs. 1981-84, Profl. of Yr. 1988), Thomas M. Cooley Legal Authors Soc. (pres. 1982-83), Scribes (bd. dirs. 1994—), Delta Theta Phi (dean Christiancy Senate 1962; Outstanding Prof. 1984). Address: PO Box 13038 Lansing MI 48901-3038

STOCKSTILL, JAMES WILLIAM, secondary school educator; b. Springfield, Mo., Aug. 28, 1945; s. Arley Ian and Elma Jean Stockstill; m. Vicki Bell, Aug. 20, 1966 (div. 1970); 1 child, Michelle LaDawn; m. Meredith Jeanine Spencer, Dec. 26, 1974; 1 child, Danielle. BS in Edn., S.W. Mo. State U., 1969. Head football coach, phys. edn. tchr. Golden City (Mo.) High Sch., 1969-70; coach, tchr. Mountain View (Mo.) High Sch., 1970-71; journeyman bricklayer Fort Lauderdale (Fla.) BMPI Union, 1971-74; masonry contractor Waynesville, N.C., 1974-86; masonry contractor, master stone and brick masonry contractor Hillsborough, N.C., 1986—; masonry instr. Orange High Sch., Hillsborough, 1986—; owner Athenian Lady Fitness Ctr., Waynesville, 1984-86; gymnastics instr. Canton (N.C.) YMCA, 1976-80; pres. Trade and Industry Adv. Coun., Hillsborough, 1988-90; rep. VICA Skill Contest Orange High Sch., 1986-88. Author: A Collection of Poems, 1992, 93. Mem. Com. to Increase and Diversify Tax Base, Hillsborough, 1992. Mem. AFT. Avocations: weightlifting, karate, jogging, hiking, landscaping. Home: 2801 Canter Dr Hillsborough NC 27278-8853 Office: Orange High Sch 500 Orange High Rd Hillsborough NC 27278

STOCKTON, ANDERSON BERRIAN, electronics company executive, consultant, genealogist; b. Lithonia, Ga., Oct. 7, 1943; s. Berrian Henry and Mary Grace (Warbington) S.; m. Linda Arlene Milligan, June 9, 1963; 1 child, Christopher Lee. Cert. in cryptographic engring., USAF Acad., Wichita Falls, Tex., 1963. Supr. Western Union Telegraph Co., East Point, Ga., 1965-67; mgr. RCA Corp., Cherry Hill, N.J., 1967-72; v.p. Universal Tech., Inc., Verona, N.J., 1972-76; v.p. engring. Siemens Ag., Anaheim, Calif., 1976-84, Concorde, El Toro, Calif., 1984-85, Data Card Troy, Inc., Santa Ana, Calif., 1985-86; dir. laser engring. div. ITT, San Jose, Calif., 1986-87; v.p. S.T.A.R. Ricoh Corp., San Jose, 1988-93; v.p. mktg. QMS, Inc., Mobile, Ala., 1993-94; mng. gen. dir. IDT, Inc., Santa Clara, Calif., 1994—; cons. Hutchinson (Minn.) Tech. Corp., 1984-87, Xerox, 1993, Hewlett Packard, 1993. Author: Polled Network Communications, 1976, A Quest for the Past, 1991; patentee in field. With USAF, 1961-65. Mem. IEEE, Am. Electronics Assn. Avocations: classic car collecting, genealogical and historical research, sword, coin and stamp collecting. Home: 2086 Silence Dr San Jose CA 95148-1918 Office: IDT Inc 2972 Stender Way Santa Clara CA 95054-3213

STOCKTON, DAVID KNAPP, professional golfer; b. San Bernardino, Calif., Nov. 2, 1941; s. Gail Rufus and Audrey (Knapp) S.; m. Catherine Fay Hales, Feb. 27, 1965; children—David Bradley, Ronald Edwin. B.S. in Gen. Mgmt., U. So. Calif., 1964. Mem. Golf's All Am. Team, 1974-76. Republican. Roman Catholic. Club: Elk. Winner 11 tour tournaments including: Profl. Golf Assn., 1970, 76, Los Angeles, 1974, Hartford, 1974, Colonial, 1967, Cleve., 1968, Milw., 1968-73, Pleasant Valley, 1971, Quad Cities, 1974, Haig and Haig Open, 1968, 6 Sr. Tour tournaments, 1992 TPC Winner (sr. rookie of the yr.), 5 Sr. Tour events-Dallas Murata Reunion, Kansas City, Park City, Seattle, Transamerica at Napa; named Sr. Player of Yr. and Arnold Palmer award Dupont Cup; rep. U.S. in 2 World Cups, 1970, 76, Ryder Cup, 1971, 77; shares former record for fewest putts for 18 holes (19); U.S. Ryder Cup capt., 1991. Office: 32373 Tres Lagos St Mentone CA 92359-9611*

STOCKTON, JOHN HOUSTON, professional basketball player; b. Spokane, Wash., Mar. 26, 1962; m. Nada Stepovich, Aug. 16, 1986; 1 child, John Houston. Grad., Gonzaga U., 1984. With Utah Jazz, Salt Lake City, 1984—; mem. U.S. Olympic Basketball Team, 1992. Named to NBA All-Star team, 1989-94; holder NBA single season rec. most assists, 1991; NBA Assists leader, 1987-1992; NBA Steals leader, 1989, 92; named NBA All-Star Co-MVP, 1993, All-NBA First Team, 1994. Led NBA in most assists per gaem, 1988-93; led NBA with highest steals per game avg., 1989,1992; shares single-game playoff record for most assists, 24, 1988. Office: Utah Jazz 301 W South Temple Salt Lake City UT 84101-1216*

STOCKTON, THOMAS B., bishop; b. Winston-Salem, N.C., July 26, 1930; s. Norman V. and Emorie (Barber) S.; m. Jean Stevens, Aug. 22, 1953; children: Lisa S. Stockton Howell, Thomas B. Jr., Shannon Stockton Miller. BA, Davidson Coll., 1952; MDiv, Duke U., 1955; DD (hon.), Pfeiffer Coll., 1973. Ordained to ministry United Meth. Ch., 1956. Min. Thrift United Meth. Ch., Paw Creek, N.C., 1956-60, 1st United Meth. Ch., Reidsville, N.C., 1960-64, Dilworth United Meth. Ch., Charlotte, N.C., 1964-70, Cen. United Meth. Ch., Asheville, N.C., 1970-75, Myers Pk. United Meth. Ch., Charlotte, N.C., 1975-83, Wesley Meml. United Ch., High Point, N.C., 1983-88; bishop Va. Conf., United Meth. Ch., Richmond, 1988—. Trustee Duke U., Durham, N.C., 1981—, all United Meth. colls. and homes in Va. Ann. Conf., 1988—; mem. gen. bd. discipleship U. Meth. Ch., Nashville, 1988—. Home: 12923 Fox Meadow Dr Richmond VA 23233-2239 Office: United Meth Ch Va Conf PO Box 11367 Richmond VA 23230-1367

STOCKWELL, DEAN, actor; b. Hollywood, Calif., Mar. 5, 1936; s. Harry and Betty Veronica Stockwell; m. Millie Perkins; m. Joy Marchenko; 2 children. Performances include: (feature films) The Valley of Decision, 1945, Abbott and Costello in Hollywood, 1945, The Green Years, 1946, Home Sweet Homicide, 1946, The Mighty McGurk, 1946, The Arnelo Affair, 1947, The Romance of Rosy Ridge, 1947, Song of the Thin Man, 1947, Gentlemen's Agreement, 1947, Deep Waters, 1948, The Boy with Green Hair, 1948 (Golden Globe award), Down to the Sea in Ships, 1949, The Secret Garden, 1949, The Happy Years, 1950, Kim, 1950, Stars in my Crown, 1950, Cattle Drive, 1958, Compulsion, 1959 (Cannes Film Festival award 1959), Sons and Lovers, 1960, Long Day's Journey into Night, 1962 (Cannes Film Festival award 1961), Psych-Out, 1968, The Dunwich Horror, 1970, The Last Movie, 1971, The Loners, 1972, Tracks, 1976, Eadweard Muybridge, Zoopraxographer, 1976, Alsindo and the Condor, 1981, Wrong is Right, 1982, Human Highway, 1982, Sweet Scene of Death, 1983, Paris, Texas, 1984, Dune, 1984, The Legend of Billie Jean, 1985, To Live and Die in L.A., 1985, Blue Velvet, 1986, Gardens of Stone, 1987, Beverly Hills Cop, II, 1987, Blue Iguana, 1987, Tucker: The Man and His Dream, 1988, Married to the Mob, 1988, Limit Up, 1989, Buying Time, 1989, The Time Guardian, 1989, The Player, 1992, Chasers, 1993; (stage prodns.) Innocent Voyage, Theatre Guild, Belasco Theatre, N.Y.C., 1943, Compulsion, Ambassador Theatre, N.Y.C., 1958;(TV movies) Paper Man, 1971, The Failing of Raymond, 1971, The Adventures of Nick Carter, 1972, The Return of Joe Forrester, 1976, A Killing Affair, 1977, The Gambler III: The Legend Continues, 1991, Son of the Morning Star, 1991, Back Track, 1991, Shame, 1992, Fatal Memories, 1992, The Langoliers, 1995; appeared in TV series Quantum Leap, 1988-1993 (Emmy award nominee for best supporting actor in a drama 1993); appeared on radio shows Death Valley Days, Dr. Christian. Mem. SAG, AEA. Office: UTA 9560 Wilshire Blvd 5th fl Beverly Hills CA 90212*

STOCKWELL, ERNEST FARNHAM, JR., banker; b. Boston, Dec. 18, 1923; s. Ernest Farnham and Beatrice Burr (Beach) S.; m. Fiona Munro, May 24, 1952; children: Ernest Farnham III, Diana, Elizabeth. Grad., Phillips Acad., 1941; BA, Yale U., 1945. Asst. br. mgr. First Nat. Bank Boston, 1950-55, br. mgr., 1955-56, asst. v.p., 1956-60, v.p., 1960-71; pres. Harvard Trust Co., Cambridge, Mass., 1971-77; chief exec. officer Harvard Trust Co., 1973-77; pres. Bay Banks Assos., Inc., 1977-78; v.p. First Nat. Bank Boston, 1978-80, sr. v.p., 1980-88, ret., 1988. Bd. dirs. Yale Alumni Fund, chmn., 1980; trustee Episcopal Diocesan Investment Trust, Urban Coll. Boston. Mem. Yale Club (Boston and N.Y.C.), Dedham (Mass.) Country and Polo Club. Home: 36 Dover Rd Dover MA 02030-2020

STOCKWELL, RICHARD E., journalist, business executive; b. Neillsville, Wis., Mar. 12, 1917; s. Arthur Raymond and Ella (Stelloh) S. B.S., U. Wis., 1940; M.A., U. Minn., 1945; Nieman fellow, Harvard U., 1945-46. Farm editor Sta. WIBA, Madison, Wis., 1939-40; news staff WLW, Cin., 1940-41; program dir. Wis. Network, Wisconsin Rapids, 1941-42; asso. news editor WMT, Cedar Rapids, Iowa, 1942-43, WCCO-CBS, Mpls., 1943-45; editorial writer Mpls. Star, 1946-49; editor Aviation Age, N.Y.C., 1949-52, Monsanto Mag., Monsanto Internat. Mag., St. Louis, 1952-54; editorial dir. Am. Aviation Publs., Inc., Washington, 1954-55; cons., mgmt. information analyst Flight Propulsion Lab., Gen. Electric Co., Cin., 1956-58; group dir. pub. relations and advt., electronics, ordnance and aerostructures divs. Avco Corp., Cin., 1958-68; v.p. comml. and indsl. products group Avco Corp., Nashville, 1968-74; v.p. products and research group Avco Corp., 1974-76. Author: Soviet Air Power, 1956; also numerous mag. articles. Sta. WLW scholar, 1940. Mem. Royal, Am. econs. assns., Am. Polit. Sci. Assn. Clubs: Wings (N.Y.C.); Nat. Press (Washington). Home: Neillsville Wis. *Deceased.*

STOCKWELL, ROBERT PAUL, linguist, educator; b. Oklahoma City, June 12, 1925; s. Benjamin P. and Anna (Cunningham) S.; m. Lucy Louisa Floyd, Aug. 29, 1946; 1 child, Paul Witten. B.A., U. Va., 1946, M.A., 1949, Ph.D., 1952. Instr. English, Oklahoma City U., 1946-48; mem. linguistics staff Sch. Langs., Fgn. Service Inst., State Dept., 1952-56; mem. faculty UCLA, 1956-94, prof. English, 1962-66, prof. linguistics, 1986-94, chmn. dept., 1966-73, 80-84, prof. emeritus, 1994—; mem. com. lang. programs Am. Council Learned Socs., 1965-69. Author: (with J.D. Bowen) Patterns of Spanish Pronunciation, 1960, Sounds of English and Spanish, 1965, (with J. D. Bowen, J.W. Martin) The Grammatical Structures of English and Spanish, 1965, The Major Syntactic Structures of English, 1973, (with P.M. Schachter, B.H. Partee) Foundations of Syntactic Theory, 1977, Workbook in Syntactic Theory and Analysis, 1977; also numerous articles.; editor: (with R.S.K. Macaulay) Linguistic Change and Generative Theory, 1972, ; assoc. editor: Lang., 1973-79, Festschrift: rhetorica, Phonologica, Syntactica: A Festchrift for Robert P. Stockwell, 1989. Served with USNR, 1943-45. Am. Council Learned Socs. fellow, 1963-64. Mem. Linguistic Soc. Am. (exec. com. 1965-68), Philol. Assn. Great Britain. Home: 4000 Hayvenhurst Ave Encino CA 91436-3850 Office: UCLA Linguistics Dept Los Angeles CA 90024

STOCKWELL, VIVIAN ANN, nursing educator; b. Hardy, Ark., Apr. 26, 1943; d. Belvin L. and Armilda L. (Langston) Cooper; m. R.D. Sneed, Mar. 16, 1963 (div. Jan. 1981); m. Homer E. Stockwell, Jan. 6, 1990; 1 child, Sherilyn. Diploma, St. Luke's Sch. Nursing, Kansas City, Mo., 1964; BS in Nursing summa cum laude, Avila Coll., Kansas City, 1987. Staff nurse operating rm. North Kansas City (Mo.) Hosp., 1972-76; pvt. scrub nurse Van M. Robinson, MD, North Kansas City, 1976-81; instr. health occupations Independence (Mo.) Pub. Schs., 1981-85; instr. Park Coll., Parkville, Mo., 1987-89, asst. to dir. dept. nursing, 1989-90. Ch. sch. tchr. Independence Blvd. Christian Ch., 1976-87, deacon, 1979-88, elder, 1988—; pres. Christian Women's Fellowship, 1994—; mem. adult adv. bd. NCK Assembly, Internat. Order of Rainbow for Girls, 1983-94. Mem. Assn. Operating Rm. Nurses, Am. Vocat. Assn., Mo. Vocat. Assn., Order Eastern Star, Sigma Theta Tau, Kappa Gamma Pi, Delta Epsilon Sigma.

STODDARD, BRANDON, film and television company executive; b. Bridgeport, Conn., Mar. 31, 1937; s. Johnson and Constance (Brandon) S.; married, Feb. 1984; children: Alexandra, Brooke. B.A. in Am. Studies, Yale U., 1958; postgrad., Columbia U. Law Sch., 1963. Program asst. Batten, Barton, Durstine and Osborn, N.Y.C., 1960-61; program ops. supr. Grey Advt., N.Y.C., 1962-66; dir. daytime programs Grey Advt., 1966, v.p. in charge of radio and television programs, 1968-70; dir. daytime programs ABC-TV, 1970-72, v.p. daytime programs, 1972-74, v.p. motion pictures for television, 1974-79; pres. ABC Motion Pictures, Los Angeles, 1979-85; sr. v.p. ABC Entertainment, 1979-85, pres., 1985-89; pres. ABC Prodns., 1989—. Served with U.S. Army, 1960-61. Mem. Hollywood Radio and TV Soc., Am. Film Inst., Acad. Motion Pictures Arts and Scis. Episcopalian. Club: Bel Air Bay.

STODDARD, ELLWYN R., sociology and anthropology educator; b. Garland, Utah, Feb. 16, 1927; s. Roscoe and Mary Lloyd (Redford) S.; m. Judith Mae DeGriselles, May 10, 1951 (div. 1964); children: Ellwyn R. Jr., Michael Valin, Dawn D.; m. Elaine Kirby, Aug. 28, 1964; children: Jared Evan, Sunday, Summer; stepchildren: Laura Jane Packham, George H. Packham, R. Kirby Packham. BS, Utah State U., 1952; MS, Brigham Young U., 1955; PhD, Mich. State U., 1961. Instr. sociology Drake U., Des Moines, 1959-61, asst. prof., 1962-63, assoc. prof., 1964-65; assoc. prof. Tex. Western Coll., El Paso, 1965-69; prof. sociology and anthropology U. Tex., El Paso, 1970—; field researcher, dir. rsch. cons. numerous projects, Mich., Iowa, Tex., Nigeria, 1955—. Author: Mexican Americans, 1973, Maquila, 1987; sr. co-author: Patterns of Poverty along U.S.-Mexico Border, 1987; sr. editor: Borderlands Sourcebook, 1983 (SW Book award 1984); contbr. chpts. to books and over 100 articles to profl. jours. Scoutmaster troop 158, Boy Scouts Am., El Paso, 1965-68, asst. commr. Yucca coun., 1968-71. With USCG, 1944-46, PTO; 2d lt. arty. U.S. Army, 1952-53. Recipient Diamond Jubilee Disting. Achievement award in rsch. U. Tex., El Paso, 1990; numerous rsch. grants including U. Tex., El Paso, U.S. Army, Econ. Devel. Adminstrn., 1967-86, Tex. Com. for Humanities, 1979, Hoover Instn.-Stanford U., 1984. Mem. Assn. Borderlands Scholars (founder, pres. 1976-79, Outstanding Scholarship and Svc. award 1987), Phi Kappa Phi (chpt. charter, pres. U. Tex. 1982-84). Mem. LDS Ch. Office: U Tex El Paso Dept Sociology El Paso TX 79968-0558

STODDARD, GEORGE EARL, investment company financial executive; b. Perry, Oreg., Jan. 7, 1917; s. G. Earl and Elthira (Thomas) S.; m. Elma Skelton, Feb. 4, 1942; children—Evan, Jean, Robert, Patricia. A.B., Brigham Young U., 1937; M.B.A., Harvard U., 1939; LL.B., Fordham U., 1954. Investment analyst Central Hanover Bank & Trust Co., N.Y.C., 1939-42; v.p. investment ops. Equitable Life Assurance Soc. U.S., N.Y.C., 1945-79; chmn. fin. com. W. P. Carey & Co., N.Y.C., 1979—; also dir. W. P. Carey & Co. Bd. dirs. United Fund of Bronxville-Eastchester, N.Y., 1960-61; pres. Home Sch. Assn., Eastchester, 1962. Served to lt. USNR, 1942-45. Clubs: Harvard (N.Y.C.), Harvard Bus. Sch. (N.Y.C.), Univ. (N.Y.C.). Home: 11 Cedar Pl Eastchester NY 10709-1703 Office: 50 Rockefeller Plz New York NY 10020

STODDARD, LAURENCE RALPH, JR., retired advertising executive; b. Mt. Kisco, N.Y., Feb. 8, 1936; s. Laurence Ralph and Alice Cary (Martin) S. BA, Colgate U., 1958; postgrad., U. Calif., Berkeley, 1958. Audience research supr. NBC, N.Y.C., 1960-66; audience measurement chief Young & Rubicam, N.Y.C., 1966-69, v.p. supr.-group supr. media planning, 1969-78, v.p dir. communications service, 1978-81, sr. v.p. communication services, group supt. media planning, 1981-86; sr. v.p., dir. media research Advt. Research Found., N.Y.C., 1986-96; ret. Served with N.G., 1960. Mem. Advt. Rsch. Found.. (chmn. mag. rsch. devel. com., mem. mag. rsch. coun. and new electronic media rsch. workshop 1994, chmn. single source symposium com.), Am. Advt. Agy. Assn. (media rsch. coun.), Advt. Computer Users Assn. (media rsch. coun.), Advt. Computer Users Assn. (bd. dirs. 1988-93), market rsch. coun. 1993—). Democrat. Episcopalian. Home: 344 W 72nd St Apt 4-E New York NY 10023-2636

STODDARD, ROGER ELIOT, librarian; b. Boston, Dec. 2, 1935; s. Merton Edgar and Helen (Bonney) S.; m. Helen Louise Heckel, May 24, 1958; children—Alison Louise, Christopher Paine. A.B., Brown U., 1957. Asst. curator Harris Coll. Am. Poetry and Plays, Brown U., Providence, R.I., 1961-63, curator, 1963-65; asst. to librarian Harvard U. Houghton Library, Cambridge, Mass., 1958-61, asst. librarian, 1965-69, assoc. librarian, 1969-85; curator rare books Harvard Coll. Library, Cambridge, Mass., 1985—; lectr. English Harvard U., Cambridge, Mass., 1984-86, sr. lectr., 1986—; sec. Friends of Harvard Coll. Library, Cambridge, Mass., 1983—; faculty mem. Columbia U. Rare Book Sch., N.Y.C., 1984-85. Author: Catalogue of Books & Pamphlets Unrecorded in Wegelin's Early Am. Poetry, 1969; The Houghton Library 1942-82, 1982; Poet & Printer in Colonial & Federal America, 1983; The Parkman Dexter Howe Library, part 1: Early New England Books, 1983, Marks in Books, Illustrated and Explained, 1985 (N.E. Book Show award, 1986, Am. Library Assn. award, 1987), Put a Resolute Hart to a Steep Hill: William Gowans Antiquary and Bookseller, 1990; editor A Glance at Private Libraries, 1991; contbr. articles to profl. jours. Mem. Records and Archives Com., Concord, Mass., 1985-87; bd. dirs. Louisa May Alcott Meml. Assn., Concord, 1983—. Huntington Library fellow, San Marino, Calif., 1978; W. F. Milton fellow Harvard U. Med. Sch., Boston, 1978-80; D.W. Bryant fellow Harvard U., 1992. Mem. Bibliog. Soc. Am. (coun. mem. 1982-88, Bibliography of Am. Lit. supervisory com. chmn. 1982-91, pres. 1996—), Am. Antiquarian Soc. (coun. mem. 1989-93), Assn. Internat. de Bibliophilie, Book Club Calif., Colonial Soc. Mass. (corr. sec. 1993—), The Johnsonians, Bibliog. Soc. London (hon. sec. for Am. 1992—), Bibliog. Soc. Va., Golier Club (N.Y.C.), Harvard Club (N.Y.C.), Odd Vols. Boston Club (exec. com. 1985-87). Home: 9 Birchwood Ln Lincoln MA 01773-4907 Office: Harvard Univ Houghton Library Harvard Yard Cambridge MA 02138

STODDARD, STEPHEN DAVIDSON, ceramic engineer, former state senator; b. Everett, Wash., Feb. 8, 1925; s. Albert and Mary Louise (Billings) S.; m. Joann Elizabeth Burt, June 18, 1949 (dec. Oct. 1993); children: Dorcas Ann, Stephanie Kay; m. Barbara L. Seitz, Feb. 18, 1995. Student, Tacoma Coll., 1944, Conn. Coll., 1946; BS, U. Ill., 1950. Asst. prodn. supr., asst. ceramic engr. Coors Porcelain Co., Golden, Colo., 1950-52; ceramics-powder metallurgy sect. leader Los Alamos (N.Mex.) Sci. Lab., U. Calif., 1952-80; pres., treas. Materials Tech. Assocs., Inc., 1978-94; cons. Ceramic Age Mag., 1958-60; Cons. Nuclear Applications for Ceramic Materials, 1958-60; Jury commr. Los Alamos County, 1969; justice of peace, 1956-62; mem. Los Alamos Sch. Adv. Council, 1966; mcpl. judge, 1976-77; chmn. Los Alamos Ordinance Rev. Com., 1958; Mem. Republican County and State Central Com., 1955—; county commr. Los Alamos, N.Mex., 1966-68; mem. Los Alamos County Planning Commn., 1962-63, N.Mex. Senate, 1981-92; bd. dirs. Mountain Cmty. Bank of Los Alamos (formerly Bank of Los Alamos), 1985—, Los Alamos Econ. Devel. Corp.; mem. N.Mex. State Commn. on Nat. and Cmty. Svc., 1993—. Patentee in field. Bd. dirs. Sangre de Cristo coun. Girl Scouts U.S.A., 1965-71, N.Mex. chpt. Nature Conservancy, 1987—, v.p., 1993-94; bd. dris. Southwestern Assn. on Indian Affairs, Inc., 1987-91; active Gov.'s Commn. in Nat. & Cmty. Svc., 1993—. With AUS, 1943-46. Decorated Bronze Star, Purple Heart, Combat Infantry Badge; recipient disting. alumni award U. Ill. Coll. Engring., 1986, Leopold Conservation award N.Mex. Nature Conservancy, 1988. Fellow Am. Inst. Chemists, Am. Ceramic Soc. (treas. 1972-74, pres. 1976-77, disting. life 1984); mem. Nat. Inst. Ceramic Engrs. (PACE award 1965, Reaves Walker award 1984), Am. Soc. Metals, Los Alamos C. of C. (citizen of yr. award 1992), Masons, Shriners (pres. 1994-95), Elks (dist. dep. grand exalted ruler 1968-69), Los Alamos Golf Assn. (dir. 1964-66), Am. Legion (nat. legis. coun. 1992—), Sigma Xi, Alpha Tau Omega. Episcopalian. Home: 44 Timber Ridge Rd Los Alamos NM 87544-3528

STODDARD, WILLIAM BERT, JR., economist; b. Carbondale, Pa., Oct. 6, 1926; s. William Bert and Emily (Trautwein) S.; student Lafayette Coll., 1944-45; BS, NYU, 1950, AM, 1952; m. Carol Marie Swartz, Feb. 28, 1970; 1 child, Emily Coleman. Asst. chief acct., budget dir. Hendrick Mfg. Co., Carbondale, Pa., 1952-54, asst. dir. prodn., 1956-68, also dir.; credit corr. U.S. Gypsum Co., N.Y.C., 1954-56; investment counselor, Carbondale, 1968-73, Ridgefield, Conn., 1973—; dir. First Nat. Bank Carbondale, 1968-73; bd. dirs. Lackawanna County Mfrs. Assn., Scranton, Pa., 1960-73. Treas., trustee Aldrich Mus. Contemporary Art, Ridgefield, 1976-90; bd. dirs. Ridgefield Library and Hist. Assn., 1977-85, 87-93; trustee Ridgefield Libr. Endowment Fund Trust, 1985—. Served with U.S. Army 1946-47. Mem. Inst. Mgmt. Accts., Am. Def. Preparedness Assn., Phi Alpha Kappa, Phi Delta Theta. Republican. Methodist. Clubs: NYU (N.Y.C.), Waccabuc (N.Y.) Country, Princeton Club (N.Y.C.). Home: 59 Bridle Trl Ridgefield CT 06877-1401 Office: 23 Catoonah St Ridgefield CT 06877-4431

STODGHILL, RONALD, school system administrator; b. White Plains, N.Y., Dec. 21, 1939; s. Joseph and Marian (Wynn) Stodghill; children: Kimberly, Denise, Ronald. BS, Ea. Mich. U., 1961; MS, We. Mich. U., 1967; EdD, Wayne State U., 1981. Dir. edn. New Detroit, Detroit; deputy supt. St. Louis Pub. Schs., Mo.; supt. Wellston Pub. Schs., Mo. Mem. ASCD (sec.), Am. Assn. Advancement of Sci., Nat. Assn. Bilingual Edn. Home: 6574 Saint Louis Ave Saint Louis MO 63121-5725 Office: Wellston SD 6574 Saint Louis Ave Saint Louis MO 63121-5725

STOECKER, DAVID THOMAS, banker; b. St. Louis, June 8, 1939; s. John Garth and Marie (Zahler) S.; m. Ann E. Conrad, Aug. 18, 1962; children—Lisa Ann, Susan Jane. B.S., Ind. U., 1963. Sr. v.p. comml. loans Mercantile Trust Co. N.Am., St. Louis, 1965-80; pres. Gravois-Merc. Bank, St. Louis, 1980-87; pres., chief exec. officer Bank of South County, St. Louis, 1987—. Served to 1st lt. AUS, 1963-65. Mem. Robert Morris Assos. (pres. St. Louis 1980). Methodist. Club: Sunset Country. Office: 9100 Gravois Rd Saint Louis MO 63123-4524

STOER, ERIC F., lawyer; b. Pa., 1944. BA, U. Md., 1966, JD, 1969. Bar: Md. 1969, D.C. 1970, U.S. Supreme Ct. 1973, U.S. Ct. Appeals (3d cir.) 1976, U.S. Ct. Appeals (10th cir.) 1979, U.S. Ct. Appeals (6th cir.) 1980. Trial atty. FTC, Washington, 1969-70; ptnr. Bryan Cave, Washington. Mem. ABA (chmn. Robinson-Patman subcom. price discrimination 1973-78, mem. subcom. practice and jurisdiction 1978-80, mem. antitrust sect.), Md. State Bar Assn. Office: Bryan Cave 700 13th St NW Washington DC 20005-3960*

STOERMER, DAPHNE CAROL, physical therapist, consultant; b. Vancouver, B.C., Feb. 6, 1939; came to the U.S., 1959; d. Douglas William Walker and Thelma Ray (Kelly) Whitelaw; m. Phillip Hilary Stoermer, Apr. 28, 1962; children: Hilary Anne, Mark Andrew, Claire Marie. Student, U. B.C., 1957-59; BSc, cert. in phys. therapy, U. So. Calif., L.A., 1961; lifetime teaching credential, UCLA, 1965. Registered phys. therapist. Staff phys. therapist U. So. Calif. Med. Ctr., L.A., 1962-64, San Gabriel (Calif.) Community Hosp., 1964-72; owner Lafayette (Calif.) Phys. Therapy, 1975—, Orinda (Calif.) Sports Fitness Ctr., 1981-91; cons. Consultation By Design, Lafayette, 1984—; bd. dirs. Phys. Therapy Provider Network Inc., Woodland Hills, Calif. Telephone help worker Contact Care, Lafayette, 1991-92. Mem. Am. Phys. Therapy Assn., N.Am. Back Sch., Internat. Dance Exercise Assn., Kappa Kappa Gamma (pub. rels. Psi chpt. 1988-90). Avocations: tennis, biking, running. Office: Lafayette Phys Therapy 895 Moraga Rd Ste 10 Lafayette CA 94549-5039

STOERMER, EUGENE FILMORE, biologist, educator; b. Webb, Iowa, Mar. 7, 1934; s. Edward Filmore and Agnes Elizabeth (Ekstrand) S.; m. Barbara Purves Ryder, Aug. 13, 1960; children: Eric Filmore, Karla Jean, Peter Emil. BS, Iowa State U., 1959, PhD, 1963. Assoc. rsch. scientist, rsch. scientist U. Mich., Ann Arbor, 1965-79, assoc. prof., 1979-85, prof., 1985—; editl. advisor Jour. Paleolimonology. Contbr. over 190 articles to profl. jours. Fellow Acad. Natural Scis., Phila., 1980; recipient Darbaker prize, Bot. Soc. Am., 1993. Mem. Phycological Soc. Am. (pres. 1988-89), Internat. Assn. for Diatom Rsch. (pres. 1992-94). Home: 4392 Dexter Ave Ann Arbor MI 48103-1636 Office: U Mich Ctr for Great Lakes Ann Arbor MI 48109

STOFFA, PAUL L., geophysicist, educator; b. Palmerton, Pa., July 9, 1948; married, 1968; 2 children:. BS, Rensselaer Poly. Inst., 1970; PhD in Geophysics, Columbia U., 1974. Research assoc. marine geophysics Lamont-Doherty Geol. Observatory, 1974-81; cons. Gulf Sci. Tech., 1981—; with Inst. for Geophysics U. Tex., Austin, now Wallace E. Pratt prof. geophysics, sr. research scientist Inst. for Geophysics, from 1978; adj. asst. prof. Columbia U., 1978—. Mem. IEEE, Am. Geophys. Union, Soc., Soc. Exploration Geophysicists, Sigma Xi. Office: U Tex at Austin Inst for Geophysics 8701 N Mopac Expy Austin TX 78759

STOFFER, TERRY JAMES, advertising executive; b. Alexander, Iowa, May 28, 1946; s. Jacob John and Almeda Juanita (Roe) S.; m. Linda Rosburg, Apr. 11, 1966 (div. Mar. 1980); m. Catherine S. Jewell, Dec. 28, 1984 (div. Dec. 1990); 1 child, Alan J. BS in Journalism, Iowa State U., 1968, MS in Journalism, 1970. Instr. Iowa State U. Sch. Journalism, Ames, 1969-70; publs. mgr. Express Communications, West Des Moines, Iowa, 1970-72; sr. v.p. Creswell, Munsell, Fultz and Zirbel, Des Moines, 1972—; mktg. adv. com. Iowa State U., 1991-93; advt. adv. bd. Drake U., 1993—. Mem. Nat. Adv. Bd. Iowa State U. Sch. Journalism, Ames, 1985-88; bd. dirs. Better Bus. Bur., Des Moines, 1983. Mem. Des Moines Advt. Club (v.p. 1974-75, Cliff DePuy award 1978), Advt. Profls. of Des Moines (pres. 1982-83, Ad Person of Yr. 1980), Am. Advt. Fedn. (nat. standards com. 1984-85). Republican. Methodist. Avocations: literature, cooking. Home: 325 34th St West Des Moines IA 50265-4021 Office: Creswell Munsell Fultz & Zirbel 600 E Court Ave Des Moines IA 50309-2021

STOFFLE, CARLA JOY, university library dean; b. Pueblo, Colo., June 19, 1943; d. Samuel Bernard and Virginia Irene (Berry) Hayden; m. Richard William Stoffle, June 12, 1964; children: Brent William, Kami Ann. AA, So. Colo. State Coll., Pueblo, 1963; BA, U. Colo., 1965; MLS, U. Ky., 1969; postgrad., U. Wis., 1980. Head govt. publ. dept. John G. Crabbe Library, Eastern Ky. U., Richmond, 1969-72; head. pub. services U. Wis.-Parkside Library, Kenosha, 1972-76, exec. asst. to chancellor, 1978, asst. chancellor edn. services, 1979-85; assoc. dir. U. Mich. Library, Ann Arbor, 1985-91, dep. dir., 1986-91; mem. adv. commn. Sch. Library Sci. U. Mich., Ann Arbor, 1986-92; dean librs. U. Ariz., Tucson, 1991—; vol. Peace Corps, Barbados, W.I., 1965-67; with Bowker Libr. adv. Bd., N.Y., 1985-90; UA Press Bd. of Advisors, 1995—; OCLC Rsch. Librs. Adv. Coun., 1995—. Co-author: Administration Government Documents Collection, 1974, Materials and Method for History Research, 1979, Materials and Methods for Political Science Research, 1979; assoc. editor Collection Building, 1986-91, editorial bd., 1986-95; mem. editorial bd. The Bottom Line, 1989-95; contbr. numerous articles to profl. jours. Recipient Most Outstanding Quar. Article award Reference Svc. Press, 1986, Woman on the Move award Tucson Young Women's Christian Assn., 1992, Pres.'s award Ariz. Ednl. Media Assn., 1993, Student Honor Soc. Mortar Bd. award for Faculty Excellence, 1995; named Outstanding Alumnus, Coll. Libr. and Info. Sci., U. Ky., 1989. Mem. ALA (treas. 1988-92, exec. bd. dirs. 1985-92, councilor 1983-92), Assn. Coll. Rsch. Librs. (pres. 1982-83, Bibliographic Instrn. Libr. of Yr. 1991, Acad. Rsch. Libr. of Yr. 1992). Home: 6801 N Montezuma Dr Tucson AZ 85718-2431 Office: U Arizona Main Libr Tucson AZ 85721

STOFFT, WILLIAM A., career officer; b. Minn., May 22, 1937; s. William R. and Lorraine (Raddatz) S.; m. Pat Gates, Oct. 19, 1960; children: Bruce, Elizabeth, Pamela. BS History, U. S.D., 1959; MA History, NYU, 1969; grad., Harvard U., 1992. Command, staff assignments U.S. Army, Europe, Vietnam, U.S., 1959-79; dir. Combat Studies Inst., asst. dep. commandant Command and Gen. Staff Coll., Ft. Leavenworth, Kans., 1979-85; chief mil. history office, chief of staff U.S. Army, Washington, 1985-89, dir. mgmt. office, chief of staff, 1989-91; with U.S. Army War Coll., Carlisle Barracks, Pa., 1991-94; chmn. bd. Armed Forces Coop Assn., 1980-85. Editor America's First Battles: 1776-1965. Major gen. U.S. Army, 1991-94. Decorated D.S.M. with oak leaf cluster, Legion of Merit with oak leaf cluster, Bronze Star with V device with two oak leaf clusters. Fellow Inter-Univ. Seminar; mem. Assn. U.S. Army, Coun. on Fgn. Rels., Armor Assn. Protestant. Avocations: fishing, hunting, golf, reading, history. Home: RR 1 Box 50-F Custer SD 57730-1434

STOGNER, JAMES, airport executive. Dir. ops., safety and maintenance Atlanta City Dept. Aviation; dir. ops. and maintenance, now dep. gen. mgr William B. Hartsfield Atlanta Internat. Airport. Office: Hartsfield Atlant Internat Airpt Airport Commissioner's Office Atlanta GA 30320*

STOHR, DONALD J., federal judge; b. Sedalia, Mo., Mar. 9, 1934; s. Julius Leo and Margaret Elizabeth (McGaw) S.; m. Mary Ann Kuhlman, July 31, 1957 children: Elizabeth M., Anne M., Jane C., Sara M., Ellen R. BS, St. Louis U., 1956, JD, 1958. Bar: Mo. 1958, U.S. Dist. Ct. (ea. dist.) Mo. 1958, U.S. Ct. Appeals (8th cir.) 1966, U.S. Supreme Ct. 1969. Assoc. Hocker Goodwin & MacGreevy, St. Louis, 1958-63, 66-69; asst. counselor St. Louis County, 1963-65, counselor, 1965-66; U.S. atty. Ea. Dist. Mo., St. Louis, 1973-76; ptnr. Thompson & Mitchell, St. Louis, 1969-73, 76-92; judge U.S. Dist. Ct. (ea. dist.) Mo., St. Louis, 1992—. Mem. ABA, Mo. Bar Assn., Am. Judicature Soc., St. Louis Met. Bar Assn. Office: US Court & Custom House 1114 Market St Rm 813 Saint Louis MO 63101-2034

STOIBER, CARLTON RAY, government agency official; b. Vallejo, Calif., July 5, 1942; s. Raymond F. and Grace (Fairhurst) S.; m. Susanne Alexander, Sept. 10, 1966. BA summa cum laude, U. Colo., 1964, LLB, 1969; diploma cum laude, Hague Acad. Internat. Law, 1975. Bar: Colo.1969, D.C.1970, U.S. Supreme Ct. 1973. Atty. U.S. Dept. Justice, Washington, 1969-71, dir. Office of Indian Rights, 1972-74; asst. gen. counsel U.S. NRC, Washington, 1975-80, U.S. Arms Control and Disarmament Agy., Washington, 1980-81; dir. Office Nuclear Export Control U.S. Dept. State, Washington, 1981-85, dir. Office Nuclear Non-Proliferation Policy, 1988-91, dir. Office Nuclear Tech. and Safeguards, 1991-93; counselor U.S. Mission to UN Agys., Vienna, Austria, 1985-88; dir. Internat. Programs Internat. Programs USNRC, 1993—. Rhodes scholar, 1964, Norlin award for disting. achievement U. Colo., 1994. Mem. Reform Club, Am. Soc. Internat. Law, Phi Beta Kappa. Avocations: cartooning and caricaturing, mountaineering, birding. Office: US NRC 11555 Rockville Pike Rockville MD 20852-2738

STOICHEFF, BORIS PETER, physicist, educator; b. Bitol, Macedonia, June 1, 1924; s. Peter and Vasilka (Tonna) S.; m. Lillian Joan Ambridge, May 15, 1954; 1 child, Richard Peter. B.A.Sc., U. Toronto, 1947, M.A., 1948, Ph.D., 1950, DSc (hon.), 1994; DSc (hon.), U. Skopje, Macedonia, 1981, York U., 1982, U. Windsor, 1989. McKee-Gilchrist postdoctoral fellow U. Toronto, Ont., Can., 1950-51; postdoctoral fellow NRC Can., 1951-53, sr. research officer, 1954-64; vis. scientist MIT, 1963-64; prof. physics U. Toronto, 1964-89, Univ. prof., 1977-89, Univ. prof. emeritus, 1989—, chmn. engring. sci., 1972-77, H.L. Welsh lectr., 1984; sr. fellow Massey Coll., 1979—; exec. dir. Ont. Laser and Lightwave Rsch. Ctr., 1988-91; mem. NRC Can., 1977-83; govt. appointee to coun. Assn. Profl. Engrs. Ont., 1985-91; vis. sci. Stanford U., 1978; Walter E. Kaskan lectr. SUNY-Binghamton, 1980; Elizabeth Laird Meml. lectr. U. Western Ont., 1985; U.K./Can. Rutherford lectr., 1989; v.p. Internat. Union Pure and Applied Physics, 1994—. Contbr. numerous articles to tech. jours. Decorated officer Order of Can., 1982; I.W. Killam scholar, 1977-79; Geoffrey Frew fellow Australian Acad. Sci., 1980. Fellow Royal Soc. Can. (Henry Marshall Tory medal 1989), Royal Soc. London, Am. Phys. Soc., Optical Soc. Am. (pres. 1976, William F. Meggers award 1981, Frederic Ives medal 1983), Indian Acad. Sci. (hon.), Macedonian Acad. Sci. and Arts (hon.), Am. Acad. Arts and Scis. (fgn. hon.); mem. Can. Assn. Physicists (pres. 1984, gold medal for achievement in physics 1974). Achievements include development of techniques for high resolution Raman spectroscopy of gases and determination of geometrical structures many molecules; use of lasers in spectroscopic investigations including Brillouin and Raman scattering and two photon absorption; observation of stimulated Raman absorption and stimulated Brillouin scattering resulting in generation of intense hypersonic waves in solids; use of Brillouin spectra to measure elastic constants of rare gas crystals; generation of tunable coherent VUV radiation for use in atomic and molecular spectroscopy. Home: 66 Collier St Apt 6B, Toronto, ON Canada M4W 1L9 Office: U Toronto, Dept Physics, Toronto, ON Canada M5S 1A7

STOKELY, JOAN BARBARA, elementary school educator; b. Cleve., May 6, 1945; d. Paul Warner and Florence Leona (Sorensen) S. BS, Lamar U., 1967, M Elem. Edn., 1970. Cert. tchr., adminstr., Tex. 4th grade tchr. Vidor (Tex.) Ind. Sch. Dist., 1967-74, 88-94, 5th grade tchr., 1974-77, 7th and 8th grade tchr., 1979-88; grad. equivalency diploma tchr. Beaumont Ind. Sch. Dist., Vidor, 1977-81. Pres. Vidor Tchrs. Fed. Credit Union, 1985—; mem. troop com. Boy Scouts Am., Vidor, 1972-83; tchr. Roman Cath. Chs., Beaumont, Tex., 1967-87. Mem. AAUW, DAR, Am. Bus. Women Assn. (Vocat./Woman of Yr., chmn. 1977-78), Tex. State Tchrs. Assn. (pres. Vidor chpt. 1990-94, chmn. uniserve adv. coun. region 15 1991-92, sec. region 15 1993—), Tex. Computer Edn. Assn., Colonial Dames. Avocations: genealogy, handicrafts, writing, simple computer programs, travel. Office: Oak Forest Elem Sch 2400 Highway 12 Vidor TX 77662-3403

STOKEN, JUDITH DIANE, health education administrator; b. Little Rock, Dec. 9, 1945; d. Obie H. and Lois Bernice (Williams) Echols; children: Kimberly Cheryl, Sean Patrick Jerome. BS, Tex. Women's U., 1968; MEd, cert. of supervision, East Tex. State U., 1981, postgrad., 1982. Classroom tchr. Garland (Tex.) Ind. Sch. Dist., 1967-69, Jefferson County Sch. Dist., Louisville, 1969-76, Texarkana (Tex.) Ind. Sch. Dist., 1976-84; owner, dir. Whispering Hills Sch. Dance, Louisville, 1972-75; adminstr. Sacred Heart Cath. Sch., Texarkana, 1984-87; edn. cons. Thoth Edn. Svcs., Inc., 1987-88; in house pub. rels. developer, sr. svcs. St. Michael Hosp., Texarkana, 1988; dir. Wadley LifeSource/Wadley Regional Med. Ctr., Texarkana, 1988—; owner Great Panes Stain Glass Studio, Texarkana, 1979—; adj. faculty East Tex. State U., Texarkana, 1981-83; state accreditor Tex. Cath. Conf. Edn., Austin, 1984-87; bd. dirs. Am. Heart Assn., Texarkana chpt., Am. Lung Assn., Texarkana chpt., March of Dimes, Texarkana chpt., Cancer Soc., Texarkana chpt., Arthritis Found. Texarkana; mem. Ark.-Tex. Coun. of Govt. HIV/AIDS Consortium. Developer, coord.: (6 video tapes series) Crime Awareness for Children, 1979-80; pub.: Health Texas, 1993; contbr. articles to profl. jours. Mem. Texarkana Unite of Svc., 1978—; bd. dirs., v.p. Ctrl. Mall Mchts. Assn., Texarkana, 1989—; mem. Bowie-Cass Adult Edn. Adv. Coun., 1989—, treas.; mem. Assn. Rsch. and Enlightenment, 1981—; vice-chairperson Texarkana Civil Svc. Commr., 1992—; mem. campaign bd. United Way Texarkana, 1992—, Leadership Texarkana, 1994—. Recipient 6 Addy awards State Tex., 1989. Mem. Tex. Soc. for Hosp. Pub. Rels. and Mktg. (Tesltar award 1994), Texarkana Mus. Systems, East Tex. State U. Alumni Assn. (bd. dirs. 1991—, v.p. 1992, pres. 1993, Tex. Found. bd. vice-chmn. external affairs 1993—, Alumni Achievement award 1993), Quota Internat. (pres. 1991-92), Am. Hosp. Assn. (mgr. hosp. based ctr. 1991—), Texarkana C. of C. (tourism adv. bd. Tang Gang 1989—, Chmn.'s Coun. award 1993), Kiwanis, Alpha Delt Kappa (treas. 1985-86). Avocations: bldg. stained glass windows, reading, restoring 90 yr. old house, estoteric psychology. Office: Wadley LifeSource 57 Central Mall Texarkana TX 75503-2467

STOKER, HOWARD W., former education educator, educational administrator, consultant; b. Highland Park, Ill., July 20, 1925; s. Howard W. and Elsie (Holgate) S.; m. M. Annette Stoker, July 9, 1949; children: Joanne, Dianna, Patricia, Robert. EdB, Wis. State U., Whitewater, 1949; MA, State U. Iowa, 1950; PhD, Purdue U., 1957. H.S. tchr. Dixon (Ill.) Pub. Schs., 1950-55; prof. Fla. State U., Tallahassee, 1957-84; head instrnl. devel. and evaluation U. Tenn., Memphis, 1984-88; vis. prof. U. Tenn., Knoxville, 1988-89, rsch. prof. Coll. Edn., 1989-92; ednl. cons. H.W. Stoker, Inc., Knoxville, 1992—; sr. assoc. prof. Ednl. Testing Svc./So. Regional Office, Atlanta, 1979-80; test devel. cons. State of Tenn., 1989—; cons. in field. Editor Fla. Jour. Ednl. Rsch., 1974-83; contbr. chpts. to books and articles to profl. jours. With USN, 1944-46. Mem. Am. Edn. Rsch. Assn., Nat. Coun. on Measurement in Edn. (bd. mem.). Avocations: crafts, carving, swimming.

STOKER, THOMAS MARTIN, economics educator; b. Elmhurst, Ill., Dec. 29, 1953; s. Jerome Martin Stoker and Mary Jean (Hammersmith) Rybus; m. Deborah Jean Wahl, July 12, 1975; children: Elizabeth, Jonathan. BS in Math., U. Ariz., 1974; MS in Econs., Harvard U., 1978, PhD, 1979. Prof. applied econs. Sloan Sch. Mgmt., MIT, Cambridge, 1979—; vis. rsch. fellow Nuffield Coll., Oxford U., Eng., 1987; vis. prof. U. Bonn (West Germany), 1986-87. Contbr. articles to profl. jours. NSF grantee, 1983-96, MIT Ctr. for Energy Policy Rsch. grantee, 1984-85. Mem. Am. Econ. Assn., Am. Statis. Assn., Econometric Soc., Inst. Math. Stats., Phi Beta Kappa, Phi Kappa Phi. Avocations: fishing, woodworking. Office: Sloan Sch Mgmt MIT 50 Memorial Dr # 455 Cambridge MA 02142-1347

STOKER, WARREN CADY, university president; b. Union Springs, N.Y., Jan. 30, 1912; s. Ray W. and Dora Maude (Cady) S.; m. Ruth Eleanor Gabb, Aug. 30, 1934; children: Robert Warren, W. Lance, Lois Ruth. E.E., Rensselaer Poly. Inst., 1933, M.E.E., 1934, Ph.D., 1938. Instr. to asso. prof. elec. engring. Rensselaer Poly. Inst., 1934-51, prof., 1951—, head computer lab., 1952-55; dir. Hartford Grad. Center, 1955-57; dean Hartford Grad. Center (Grad. Center), 1957-70; asso. dean Rensselaer Poly. Inst. Grad Sch., 1957-69; v.p. Rensselaer Poly. Inst. Conn., 1961-74, pres., 1974-75, also trustee; pres. Hartford Grad. Center (formerly Rensselaer Poly. Inst. Conn.), 1975-76, pres. emeritus, 1976—, trustee, 1975—; trustee Mechanics Savs. Bank, Hartford, 1969-82, incorporator, 1969—. Fellow IEEE; mem. Sci. Rsch. Soc. Am., Newcomen Soc. N.Am., Am. Soc. Engring. Edn., Conn. Acad. Sci. and Engring., Sigma Xi, Tau Beta Pi, Eta Kappa Nu. Club: Hartford (Conn.). Home: 188 C Main St Manchester CT 06040 Office: 275 Windsor St Hartford CT 06120-2910

STOKES, (GLADYS) ALLISON, pastor, researcher, religion educator; b. Bridgeport, Conn., Aug. 17, 1942; d. Hugh Vincent and Mildred Roberta (Livengood) Allison; m. Jerome Walter Stokes, June 1, 1964 (div. 1977); children: Jonathan Jerome, Anne Jennings. BA, U. N.C., 1964; MPhil, Yale U., 1976, PhD, 1981, MDiv, 1981. Ordained to ministry United Ch. of Christ, 1981. Acting univ. min. Wesleyan U., Middletown, Conn., 1981; assoc. pastor Orange Congl. Ch., Conn., 1981-82; chaplain, asst. prof. religion Vassar Coll., Poughkeepsie, N.Y., 1982-85; assoc. univ. chaplain Yale U., New Haven, 1985-87; pastor Congl. Ch., West Stockbridge, Mass., 1987—; rsch. assoc. Hartford (Conn.) Sem., 1987-92; founding dir. Women's Interfaith Inst. in the Berkshires, 1992—; bd. dirs. Dutchess Interfaith Coun., Poughkeepsie, 1984-85; clk., bd. dirs. Gould Farm, Monterey, Mass., 1992—. Author: Ministry after Freud, 1985; co-author: Defecting in Place, 1994, Women Pastors, 1995; contbr. articles to profl. jours. Kanzer Fund Psychoanalysis and Humanities grantee, 1977; AAUW fellow, 1978, Merrill fellow Harvard Div. Sch., 1994. Mem. Am. Acad. Religion, Berkshire Conf. Women Historians, Kiwanis. Home: PO Box 422 Housatonic MA 01236-0422 Office: Conregational Church 45 Main St West Stockbridge MA 01266

STOKES, ARCH YOW, lawyer, writer; b. Atlanta, Sept. 2, 1946; s. Mack B. and Rose Stokes; m. Maggie Mead; children: Jennifer Jean, Austin Christopher, Susannah Rose, Travis, Emmarose. BA, Emory U., 1967, JD, 1970. Bar: Ga. 1970, U.S. Dist. Ct. (no. dist.) Ga. 1970, U.S. Ct. Appeals (5th cir.) Ga. 1970, U.S. Ct. Mil. Appeals 1971, U.S. Ct. Appeals (9th cir.) Ga. 1980, (2d cir.) Ga. 1990, U.S. Supreme Ct. 1981, U.S. Dist. Ct. (no. dist.) Calif. 1981, U.S. Ct. Appeals (11th cir.) Calif. 1982, U.S. Ct. Appeals (7th cir.) Calif. 1986, U.S. Ct. Appeals (1st cir.) Calif. 1992, U.S. Ct. Appeals (8th cir.) Calif. 1991, U.S. Dist. Ct. (no. dist.) N.Y. 1991, U.S. Dist. Ct. (ea. dist.) Mich. 1986. Ptnr. Stokes & Murphy, Atlanta, 1970-92, Atlanta, Pitts., L.A., 1992—. Author: The Wage & Hour Handbook, 1978, The Equal Employment Opportunity Handbook, 1979, The Collective Bargaining Handbook, 1981. Mem. bd. visitors Emory Univ., Ga. State Univ.; student rels. com. Cecil B. Day Sch. of Hospitality Adminstrn. Capt. USMC, 1971-73. Recipient Hal Holbrook award Internat. Platform Assn., 1990. Mem. ABA, ATLA, Union Internat. des Avocats, Internat. Soc. Hospitality Cons., Confrérie de la Chaîne des Rôtissuers, Am. Hotel and Motel Assn. Office: Stokes & Murphy 4751 Best Rd Ste 350 Atlanta GA 30337-5610

STOKES, ARNOLD PAUL, mathematics educator; b. Bismarck, N.D., Jan. 24, 1932; s. Joel Edward and Elizabeth (Bauer) S.; m. Gaye Teresa Wims, Oct. 19, 1957; children: Michael, Jonathan, Thomas, Katherine, Christopher, Peter. Student, St. Martin's Coll., 1949-53; B.S. (RCA scholar), U. Notre Dame, 1955, Ph.D., 1959. Mathematician Research Inst. Advanced Study, Balt., 1958-60; NSF post-doctoral fellow Johns Hopkins U., 1960-61; asst. prof. Cath. U. Am., Washington, 1961-63; asso. prof. Cath. U. Am., 1963-64; prof. Georgetown U., Washington, 1965—; chmn. math. dept. Georgetown U., 1967-70; Cons. NASA, Goddard Space Flight Center, Greenbelt, Md., 1962-67, NRC sr. research asso., 1974-75; sr. mathematician Ocean Sci. div. Sci. Applications, Inc., McLean, Va., 1979—. Trustee Consortium D.C. Univs., 1970-75. Research ordinary, functional differential equations, scattering theory, acoustic tomography. Home: 9916 Derbyshire Ln Bethesda MD 20817-1535 Office: Georgetown U Math Dept Washington DC 20057

STOKES, B. R., transportation consultant; b. Anadarko, Okla., Feb. 20, 1924; s. Robert Allan and Ethel Nan (James) S.; m. Joan Pringle, Oct. 22, 1950; children: Timothy, Leigh, Lindsey, Celia. Student, U. Okla., 1941-44; B.A., U. Calif., Berkeley, 1947. Reporter, writer Oakland (Calif.) Tribune, 1946-58; dir. info. San Francisco Bay Area Rapid Transit Dist., 1958-61, asst. gen. mgr., 1961-63, gen. mgr., 1963-74; exec. v.p. Am. Public Transit Assn., Washington, 1974-80; sr. v.p. internat. ATE Mgmt. and Service Co., Inc., 1980—; dir. gen. Saudi Arabian Public Transport Co., 1980-81. Served with USNR, 1942-46. Reid Found. fellow, 1954; Recipient Salzberg medal Syracuse U., 1975. Office: 1911 Ft Myer Dr Arlington VA 22209-1603

STOKES, CHARLES JUNIUS, economist, educator; b. Washington, Aug. 17, 1922; s. Francis Warner and Vivienne E. (Cooke) S.; m. Anne Richardson Wood, June 13, 1946; children—Kevin Barrett, Keith Warner. A.B. with honor and distinction, Boston U., 1943, A.M., 1947, Ph.D., 1950. Mem. faculty Atlantic Union Coll., South Lancaster, Mass., 1946-60, dean coll., 1954-56; Charles A. Dana prof. econs. U. Bridgeport, Conn., 1960-94, univ. prof., 1990-94; chmn. dept. U. Bridgeport, 1960-72; prof. econs. Andrews U., Berrien Springs, Mich., 1990-94; prof. Orientador Inst. Superior de Econ. e Gestão Univ. Tecnica Lisbon, Portugal, 1992—; dir. econ. rsch., region I OPS, 1951-53; dir. Latin Am. case studies Brookings Instn., 1963-64; Fulbright prof., Ecuador, 1958-59, Argentina, 1960, Peru, 1964; lectr. Inter-Am. Def. Coll., 1977-78; Staley Disting. lectr. Andrews U., 1983, founder, dir. Chan Shun Ctr. for Bus. Rsch., 1991-94; E.A. Johnson Disting. lectr., 1989; vis. prof., lectr. U. Colo., U. Conn., Clark U., Andrews U., U.S. Naval Postgrad. Sch., Yale U., Columbia U., So. Conn. State U., Atlantic Union Coll., and numerous overseas univs.; founder, dir. Conn. Small Bus. Devel. Ctr., U. Bridgeport, 1985-90; chmn., dir. Monroe Bank & Trust Co.; cons. to industry, founds. Author: Crecimiento Economico (Economic Growth), 1964, Transportation and Economic Development in Latin America, 1968, Managerial Economics: A Case Book, 1968, Managerial Economics: A Textbook, 1969, Historic Fairfield County Churches, 1969, Urban Housing Market Performance, 1975, Economics for Managers, 1978; editor: THRUST, 1978-89; columnist Christian Sci. Monitor, Internat. Bus., 1987-92; also articles to profl. jours., columns in regional newspapers. Chmn. Lancaster (Mass.) Housing Authority, 1957-61; chmn. econ. com. Greater Bridgeport Regional Planning Agy., 1961-72; asst. dir. U.S. GAO, 1972-73; mem. Instn. for Social and Policy Studies, Yale U., 1977-85; trustee Pioneer Valley Acad., 1966-69, Andrews U., 1967-72, Atlantic Union Coll., 1968-73, Conn. Grand Opera Assn., 1980-86; mem. Conn. com. Regional Plan Assn., 1977-91; bd. dirs. Greater Bridgeport Symphony Soc., 1994, Adventist Living Ctrs., Inc., Adventist Health Sys./North, 1980-85, New Eng. Trade Adjustment Assistance Ctr., Inc.; chmn. bd. dirs., CEO Geer Meml. Hosp., 1983-89; assoc. Kellogg Ctr., U. Notre Dame, 1990-94. With AUS, 1943-46. Decorated Medal of Honor Argentina; named to Collegium of Disting. Alumni Boston U. Coll. Liberal Arts, 1974; Sears Found. Fed. faculty fellow, 1972-73. Fellow New Eng. Bd. High Edn.; mem. Nat. Economists Club, Am. Econ. Assn. (pres. Conn. Valley 1966), Nat. Assn. Bus. Economists (pres. Fairfield County chpt. 1980-81), Phi Beta Kappa, Phi Kappa Phi, Phi Beta Kappa Assos., Delta Sigma Rho, Beta Gamma Sigma. Home: 264 Pepper St Monroe CT 06468-1218 Office: 14 Linden Ave Bridgeport CT 06601 *Success is fleeting. If only the good remains from what I have done, even that is not mine but God's.*

STOKES, DONALD ELKINTON, political science educator; b. Phila., Apr. 1, 1927; s. Joseph, Jr. and Frances Deborah (Elkinton) S.; m. Sybil Langbaum, May 18, 1955; children—Elizabeth Ann, Susan Carol. A.B., Princeton, 1951; Ph.D., Yale, 1958. Purser Grace Line, Inc., 1946-47; instr. polit. sci. Yale, 1952-54; prof. polit. sci. U. Mich., Ann Arbor, 1958-74; program dir. U. Mich. (Inst. Social Research), 1958-74, chmn. dept. polit. sci., 1970-71; dean U. Mich. (Grad. Sch.), 1971-74, Woodrow Wilson Sch. Pub. and Internat. Affairs Princeton U., N.J., 1974-92; prof. pub. and internat. affairs Princeton U., 1974—; vis. prof. Australian Nat. U., U. W.I., 1969. Author: Pasteur's Quadrant, 1996; co-author: The American Voter, 1960, Elections and the Political Order, 1966, Political Change in Britain, 1969. Assoc. mem. Nuffield Coll., Oxford, 1963-64; Sr. Fulbright scholar to Britain, 1963; fellow Social Sci. Rsch. Coun., 1955-57; fellow Guggenheim Found., 1964-65; vis. rsch. fellow Royal Inst. Internat. Affairs, 1980, Brookings Inst., 1987, 89. Fellow Am. Acad. Arts and Scis., AAAS, Nat. Acad. Pub. Adminstrn.; mem. Am. Polit. Sci. Assn. (Woodrow Wilson award 1970), Coun. Fgn. Rels., Am. Assn. Pub. Opinion Rsch., Phi Beta Kappa. Mem. Soc. Friends. Home: 150 Fitzrandolph Rd Princeton NJ 08540-7224 Office: Princeton Univ Woodrow Wilson Sch Pub & Internat Affairs Princeton NJ 08544

STOKES, DONALD GRESHAM, vehicle company executive; b. London, Mar. 22, 1914; s. Harry Potts and Marie Elizabeth (Yates) S.; m. Laura Elizabeth Courteney Lamb, May 25, 1939 (dec. Apr. 1995); 1 child, Michael Donald. Grad. mech. engring., Harris Inst. Tech., Preston, Eng., 1933; LL.D., U. Lancaster, 1967; Ph.D. in Tech, U. Loughborough, 1968; D.Sci., U. Southampton, 1969, U. Salford, 1971. Student apprentice Leyland Motors Ltd., London, 1930; export mgr. Leyland Motors Ltd., 1946-49, gen. sales and service mgr., 1949-53, dir., 1963-67; mng. dir., dep. chmn. Brit. Leyland Motor Corp. Ltd., 1967, chmn., mng. dir., 1968-73, chmn., chief exec., 1973-75; pres. Brit. Leyland Ltd., 1975-79; chmn. Brit. Arabian Adv. Co. Ltd., 1977-85; pres. Jack Barclay Ltd., 1980-90; Dutton-Forshaw Motor Group Ltd., 1980-90; v.p. Empresa Nacional de Autocamiones S.A., Spain, 1965-73; chmn. Reliant Group, 1990-94, Two Counties Radio Ltd., 1990-94. Dep. lt. for County Palatine of Lancashire; v.p. Inst. Sci. and Tech., U. Manchester, 1968-72, pres., 1972-75. Lt. col. R.E.M.E., 1939-45. Created knight, 1965, baron (life peer), 1969; decorated Territorial Decoration; officier de l'ordre de la Couronne Belgium; comdr. de l'Ordre de Leopold II. Fellow Inst. Mech. Engrs. (coun., v.p. 1971, pres. 1972), Inst. Road Transport Engrs., Inst. Civil Engrs., Royal Acad. Engring.; mem. Nat. Econ. Devel. Com. (chmn. electronics com. 1966-68), Soc. Motor Mfrs. and Traders (coun., pres. 1961-62), Worshipful Company Carmen. Home: Branksome Cliff, Westminster Rd, Poole BH13 6JW, England

STOKES, HARRY MCKINNEY, lawyer; b. Pitts., Jan. 1, 1942; s. Harry Emory and Eurith Elizabeth (McKinney) S.; m. Patricia Mason, Oct. 7, 1973; 1 child, Andrea Elizabeth. BS, U. Pitts., 1971; MBA, Columbia U., 1986; JD, Pace U., White Plains, N.Y., 1990. Bar: Conn. 1990, N.Y. 1991, D.C. 1992, U.S. Dist. Ct. Conn. 1991, U.S. Dist. Ct. (ea. and so. dist.) N.Y. 1991, U.S. Dist. Ct. D.C. 1992, U.S. Ct. Appeals (2d cir.) 1992, U.S. Supreme Ct. 1995. With IBM, Armonk, N.Y., 1971-90; assoc. Wiggin & Dana, Stamford, Conn., 1990—. Contbr. articles to profl. jours. Bd. dirs. Youth Continuum, New Haven, Conn. Mem. ABA (litigation sect.), Conn. Bar Assn. (CLE teaching faculty), Assn. of Bar of City of N.Y. (del. to state bar assn.), Conn. Trial Lawyers Assn., C. of C., Delta Theta Phi. Avocation: equestrian sports. Home: 49 Raemont Rd Granite Springs NY 10527 Office: Wiggin & Dana 301 Tresser Blvd Stamford CT 06901-3234

STOKES, HENRY ARTHUR, journalist; b. Jacksonville, Fla., Dec. 9, 1944; s. Henry Jasper and Waneta Marian (Lord) S.; m. Carolyn Elizabeth Morley, Aug. 6, 1966; children: Elizabeth, Virginia, Katherine. AA, St. Johns River Jr. Coll., Palatka, Fla., 1966; BS in Journalism with high honors, U. Fla., 1969. Reporter Daytona Beach (Fla.) News-Jour., 1966, Palatka (Fla.) Daily News, 1966-69; reporter Fla. Times-Union, Jacksonville, 1969-71, night city editor, 1972; various editing positions Detroit News, 1972-88; asst. mng. editor Comml. Appeal, Memphis, 1988-92, mng. editor, 1992—. Mem. Memphis Literacy Coun., 1989—, chmn., 1993, 94; bd. dirs. Friends Memphis/Shelby Co. Libr., 1991—; mem. pres.' adv. coun. LeMoyne-Owen Coll., 1992—. Recipient Emig award Coll. Journalism U. Fla., 1970. Mem. AP Mng. Editors Assn., Soc. Profl. Journalists, Investigative Reporters and Editors, The Egyptians, Rotary. Mem. Unitarian-Universalist Ch. Avocations: orinthology, fly fishing. Office: Comml Appeal 495 Union Ave Memphis TN 38103-3242

STOKES, JAMES CHRISTOPHER, lawyer; b. Orange, N.J., Mar. 19, 1944; s. James Christopher and Margaret Mary (Groome) S.; m. Eileen Marie Brosnan, Sept. 7, 1968; children: Erin Margaret, Michael Colin, Courtney Dorothy. AB, Holy Cross Coll., 1966; JD, Boston Coll., 1975. Bar: Hawaii 1975, U.S. Ct. Appeals (1st and 9th cirs.) 1976, Mass. 1977, U.S. Ct. Internat. Trade 1988. Officer USMC, 1966-72; assoc. Carlsmith, Carlsmith, Wichman & Case, Honolulu, 1975-76, Bingham, Dana & Gould, Boston, 1976-82; ptnr. Bingham, Dana & Gould, London, 1980-84, Boston, 1982—. Contbr. articles to profl. jours. Active personnel bd. Town of Wellesley, Mass., 1984-89, chmn. bd., 1988-89, town moderator, 1992—. Capt. USMC, 1966-72, Vietnam. Mem. Hawaii Bar Assn., Mass. Bar Assn., Internat. Bar Assn., Boston Bar Assn., Traveller's Club (London), Union Club (Boston), Wellesley Club, German-Am. Bus. Club (Boston) (bd. dirs.). Roman Catholic. Office: Bingham Dana & Gould 150 Federal St Boston MA 02110-1745

STOKES, JAMES SEWELL, lawyer; b. Englewood, N.J., Jan. 24, 1944; s. James Sewell III and Doris Mackey (Smith) S.; m. Esther Moger, Aug. 19, 1967; children: Jessica Neale, Elizabeth Sewell. BA, Davidson (N.C.) Coll., 1966; LLB, Yale U., 1969. Bar: Ga. 1969. Asst. to gen. counsel Office Gen. Counsel of the Army, Washington, 1969-72; assoc. Alston, Miller & Gaines, Atlanta, 1972-77; ptnr. Alston & Bird (previously Alston, Miller & Gaines), Atlanta, 1977—, lead environ. lawyer, 1978—, chmn. environ. group, 1987—, chmn. client svcs. com., 1983-85, chmn. hiring com., 1986-87, chmn. mktg. com., 1993—, mem. ptnr.'s com., 1995—; speaker on environ. matters to various seminars and meetings; mem. Gov.'s Environ. Adv. Coun., 1991—. Contbr. articles to profl. jours. Co-chmn. Spotlight on Ga. Artists V, 1986; mem. City of Atlanta Zoning Rev. Bd., 1978-85, chmn., 1984-85; bd. dirs. Brookwood Hills Civic Assn., 1975-77, pres., 1977; bd. dirs. Nexus Contemporary Arts Ctr., Atlanta, 1987-92, vice chmn. capital campaign,

1989, chmn. nominating com., 1988, chmn. fundraising com., 1987-88; bd. dirs. Butler St. YMCA N.W. br., 1973-75, Dynamo Swim Club, 1988-91, Arts Festival Atlanta, 1994—; trustee Inst. Continuing Legal Edn., Athens, 1980-81, Trinity Sch., Atlanta, 1988, Charles Loridaus Found., 1994—; mem. session Trinity Presbyn. Ch., 1986-89, clk. of session, 1988-89, chmn. cmty. concerns com., 1987-88, chmn. pers. com., 1989-90, chmn. assoc. pastor search com., 1991-92; bd. dirs. Park Pride, 1992; chmn. environ. affairs com. Ga. C. of C., Bus. Coun. Ga., 1987-92, environ. legal counsel, 1981-87; mem. spl. program Leadership Atlanta, 1979-80, Leadership Ga., 1985; mem. Ga. bd. advisors Trust for Pub. Land, 1990—. Capt. U.S. Army, 1969-72. Decorated D.S.M.; recipient Spl. award Atlanta chpt. AIA, 1988, Mayor Andrew Young, 1985. Mem. ABA (natural resources sect.), State Bar Ga. (chmn. environ. law sect. 1979-82), Atlanta Bar Assn., City of Atlanta Hist. Preservation (policy steeering com. 1989), Atlanta C. of C. (water resources task force 1982-87, solid waste task force 1989, air quality task force 1993—), Ga. Indsl. Developers Assn. (hazardous waste com. 1983-84), Phi Beta Kappa, Omicron Delta Kappa. Avocations: swimming, bird watching, community activities. Home: 129 Palisades Rd NE Atlanta GA 30309-1532 Office: Alston & Bird One Atlantic Ctr 1201 W Peachtree St NW Atlanta GA 30309-3424

STOKES, JOHN LEMACKS, II, clergyman, retired university official; b. Songdo, Korea, Aug. 23, 1908; s. Marion Boyd and Florence Pauline (Davis) S.; m. Alda Grey Beaman, June 20, 1933; children: John Lemacks III, Mary Anne (foster dau.). A.B., Asbury Coll., 1930; postgrad., Asbury Theol. Sem., 1930-31; M.Div., Duke U., 1932; Ph.D., Yale U., 1936; LL.D., Pfeiffer Coll., 1975. Ordained to ministry Meth. Ch., 1931. Pastor Meth. chs., Randleman, Franklin and Elkin, N.C., 1936-45, Rock Hill, St. John's, S.C., 1945-50; sec. religion higher edn., div. ednl. instns. Bd. Edn. Meth. Ch., Nashville, 1950-53; del. jurisdictional conf. Meth. Ch., 1952, 60, 68; pres. Pfeiffer Coll., Misenheimer, N.C., 1953-68; exec. sec. Quadrennial Emphasis, United Meth. Ch., 1968-69; asso. dir. N.C. Bd. Higher Edn., Raleigh, 1969-71; acting dir. N.C. Bd. Higher Edn., 1972; asso. v.p. U. N.C., Chapel Hill, 1972-75; spl. asst. in acad. affairs U. N.C., 1976-93; dir. numerous out-of-state programs in health professions, 1972-94; mem. Govs. Commn. Citizens for Better Schs. N.C., 1956-60, N.C. Com. on Nursing and Patient Care, 1956-64, N.C. Higher Edn. Facilities Edn., 1964-68, N.C. Com. on Drug Abuse, 1970-76, N.C. Com. on Aero. Edn., 1971-86; chmn. N.C. adv. com. Farmers Home Adminstrn., 1967-69, Marine Sci. Coun., 1969-72; dir. N.C. Inst. Undergrad. Curricular Reform, 1972-78; coordinator Fort Bragg-Pope Grad. Program, 1973-77; adv. com. Nat. Four-year Servicemens Opportunity Coll., 1973-78. Contbr. articles to religious publs. Bd. dirs. ARC, 1940-48, YMCA, 1946-50; vice chmn. Western N.C. Conf. Bd. Missions, 1960-64; trustee Asbury Coll., 1945-51. Recipient Outstanding Svc. award N.C. Optometric Assn., 1988, Merit award So. Coun. Optometrists, 1990. Mem. Aircraft Owners and Pilots Assn., U.S. Lawn Tennis Assn., Am. Assn. Higher Edn., So. Srs. Golf Assn., NEA, Nat. Christian Edn. Assn., So. Philos. Soc., Woman's Soc. Christian Service, Junaluska Country Club, Inland Greens Golf Club, Masons, Shriners, Rotary Civitan. Address: 6004 Caddy Cir Wilmington NC 28405

STOKES, LOUIS, congressman; b. Cleveland, Ohio, Feb. 23, 1925; s. Charles and Louise (Stone) S.; m. Jeanette Frances, Aug. 21, 1960; children: Shelley, Louis C., Angela, Lorene. Student, Case Western Res. U., 1946-48; JD, Cleve. Marshall Law Sch., 1953; LLD (hon.), Wilberforce U., 1969, Shaw U., Livingstone Coll., Morehouse Coll., Meharry Coll. Medicine. Bar: Ohio 1953. Mem. 91st-104th Congresses from 21st (now 11th) Ohio dist., Washington, D.C., 1969—; ranking minority mem. appropriations subcom. on Vets. Affairs, HUD & Ind. Agys.; guest lectr., 1960—. Mem. adv. council African-Am. Inst. Internat.; mem. exec. com. Cuyahoga County Democratic Party, Ohio State Dem. Party; bd. dirs. Karamu House; trustee Martin Luther King, Jr. Center for Social Change, Forest City Hosp., Cleve. State U. Served with AUS, 1943-46. Recipient numerous awards for civic activities including Distinguished Service award Cleve. br. NAACP; Certificate of Appreciation U.S. Commn. on Civil Rights. Fellow Ohio State Bar Assn.; mem. Am., Cuyahoga County, Cleve. bar assns., Nat. Assn. Def. Lawyers Criminal Cases Fair Housing (dir.), Urban League, Citizens League, John Harlan Law Club, ACLU, Am. Legion, Kappa Alpha Psi. Clubs: Masons (Cleve.), Plus (Cleve.). Office: US Ho of Reps 2365 Rayburn House Bldg Washington DC 20515

STOKES, MACK (MARION) BOYD, bishop; b. Wonsan, Korea, Dec. 21, 1911; came to U.S., 1929; s. Marion Boyd and Florence Pauline (Davis) S.; m. Ada Rose Yow, June 19, 1942; children: Marion Boyd III, Arch Yow, Elsie Pauline. Student, Seoul Fgn. High Sch., Korea; A.B., Asbury Coll., 1932; B.D., Duke, 1935; postgrad., Boston U. Sch. Theol., 1935-37, Harvard, 1936-37; Ph.D., Boston U., 1940; LL.D., Lambuth U., Jackson, Tenn., 1963; D.D., Millsaps Coll., 1974. Resident fellow systematic theology Boston U., 1936-38, Bowne fellow in philosophy, 1938-39; ordained to ministry Meth. Ch., deacon, 1938, elder, 1940; vis. prof. philosophy and religion Ill. Wesleyan U., 1940-41; prof. Christian doctrine Candler Sch. Theology, Emory U., 1941-56, asso. dean, Parker prof. systematic theology, 1956-72, chmn. exec. com. div. of religion of grad. sch., 1956-72; acting dean Candler Sch. Theology, Emory U. (Candler Sch.), 1968-69; faculty mem. Inst. Theol. Studies, Oxford U., 1958; Del. Meth. Ecumenical Conf., 1947, 52, 61, 71, Holston, Gen. confs., S.E. Jurisdictional Conf., 1956, 60, 64, 68, 72; chmn. com. ministry Gen. Conf. Meth. Ch., 1960; nat. com. Nature Unity We Seek, 1956—; mem. gen. com. ecumenical affairs theol. study com. United Meth. Ch., 1968-72, com. on Cath.-Meth. relations, 1969—, bishop, 1972—. Author: Major Methodist Beliefs, 1956, rev. 15th edit., 1990, also Chinese transl., The Evangelism of Jesus, 1960, The Epic of Revelation, 1961, Our Methodist Heritage, 1963, Crencas Fundamentals Dos Methodistas, 1964, Study Guide on the Teachings of Jesus, 1970, The Bible and Modern Doubt, 1970, Major United Methodist Beliefs, 1971, Korean transl., 1977, rev. 16th edit., 1990, The Holy Spirit and Christian Experience, 1975, Korean transl., 1985, Twelve Dialogues on John's Gospel, 1975; Jesus, The Master-Evangel, 1978, Can God See the Inside of an Apple?, 1979, Questions Asked by United Methodists, Philippine transl., 1980; The Bible in the Wesleyan Heritage, 1981, Respuestas A Preguntas Que Hacen Los Metodistas Unidos, 1983, The Holy Spirit in the Wesleyan Heritage, 1985, Spanish translation, 1992, Korean translation, 1992, Scriptural Holiness for the United Methodist Christian, 1988, Talking with God: A Guide to Prayer, 1989, Theology for Preaching, 1994. Trustee Emory U., Millsaps Coll., Rust Coll., Wood Jr. Coll. Mem. Am. Philos. Assn., Am. Acad. Religion, Metaphys. Soc. Am., Theta Phi (nat. sec.), Pi Gamma Mu. Home: Peachtree House 306 2637 Peachtree Rd NE Atlanta GA 30305 *Faith in God and basic trust in people. Knowing the direction in which to go, and moving toward it with persistence, resourcefulness, imagination and patience.*

STOKES, PATRICK T., brewery company executive; b. Washington, 1942; married. BS, Boston Coll., 1964; MBA, Columbia U., 1966. Fin. analyst Shell Oil Co., 1966-67; v.p. materials acquisitions Anheuser-Busch Cos. Inc., St. Louis, 1979-81, v.p., group exec., 1981—; pres. Anheuser-Busch Inc., St. Louis, 1990—; chief operating officer Campbell Taggart Inc. (subs. Anheuser-Busch Cos. Inc.), Dallas, 1986-90, chief exec. officer, 1990—. Served to 1st lt. U.S. Army, 1967-69. Office: Anheuser-Bush Co Inc 1 Busch Pl Saint Louis MO 63118-1849*

STOKES, PAUL MASON, lawyer; b. Miami Beach, Fla., July 16, 1946; s. Walter Johnson and Juanita (Hemperley) S.; m. Carol Crocker, Sept. 12, 1970; children: Macon Lanford, Walter Ashley, Mary Juanita. BA, Duke U., 1968; JD, U. Chgo., 1971. Bar: Fla. 1971. Law clerk to hon. Milton Pollack U.S. Dist. Ct. (so. dist.) N.Y., N.Y.C., 1971-72; assoc. Smathers and Thompson, Miami, Fla., 1972-77, ptnr., 1977-88; ptnr. Kelley Drye & Warren, Miami, 1988—; adj. prof. law U. Miami, Coral Gables, Fla., 1987—; pub. defender Miami Springs, Fla., 1974, City of Hialeah, Fla., 1974-75. Mem. Code Enforcement Bd. Miami Springs, 1990-92; trustee Trinity Internat. U., Deerfield, Ill., 1989—. Fellow Am. Coll. Trust and Estate Coun.; mem. Dade County Bar Assn. (probate and guardianship ct. com. 1988—, bd. dirs. 1989-92, 94—), Fla. Bar (cert. wills, trusts and estates). Democrat. Presbyterian. Office: Kelley Drye & Warren 201 S Biscayne Blvd Miami FL 33131-4332

STOKES, ROBERT ALLAN, science research facility executive, physicist; b. Richmond, Ky., June 25, 1942; s. Thomas Allan Stokes and Callie Mae (Ratliff) Watson; m. Elizabeth Ann Efkeman, Nov. 25, 1963 (div. 1992); m. Amy Hawthorne Carney, 1993; 1 child, Robert Curtis. BS in Physics, U. Ky., 1964; MA in Physics, Princeton U., 1966, PhD, 1968; Exec. Program, U. Mich. Bus. Sch., 1991. Asst. prof. physics U. Ky., Lexington, 1968-72, assoc. prof., 1972-76; sr. scientist Battelle, Pacific N.W. Labs., Richland, Wash., 1972-74, mgr. space scis. sect., 1974-83, assoc. mgr. geophysics rsch. and engring. dept., 1983-86, mgr. engring. physics dept., 1986-87, mgr. Applied Physics Ctr., 1987-88; dep. dir. rsch. Solar Energy Rsch. Inst., Golden, Colo., 1988-90; dep. dir. NREL, Golden, Colo., 1990—; v.p. Midwest Rsch. Inst., Kansas City, Mo., 1990—; mem. adv. bd. Geophysics Inst., U. Alaska, Fairbanks. Contbr. articles to profl. jours. Woodrow Wilson fellow, Princeton U., 1964, NASA fellow, 1966-68. Mem. Am. Phys. Soc., Am. Astron. Soc., Am. Geophys. Union, AAAS, Am. Solar Energy Soc., Phi Beta Kappa. Home: 24967 Foothills Dr N Golden CO 80401-8558 Office: Nat Renewable Energy Lab 1617 Cole Blvd Golden CO 80401

STOKES, TEREZE ANN, sales executive; b. Hyannis, Mass., July 30, 1958; d. James Thomas and Arlene Anna (Bourassa) Stokes; m. Curtis Michael Blais, Mar. 19, 1975 (div. June 1977); 1 child, James Brendon Stokes. Student, Rivier Coll., Harvard U. Cert. metallurgy. Sales rep. Diversified Resorts, Burlington, Mass., 1981-88, Edgcomb Metals, Nashua, N.H., 1988-91, Northstar Steel, Manchester, N.H., 1991—, Olympic Steel, Milford, Conn., 1992—. Mem. Nat. Pks. and Conservation Assn., Assn. Women in Metals Industry (publicity chairperson 1992—, editor, pub. newsletter 1993), Exec. Women's Golf League. Office: 1 Eastern Steel Rd Milford CT 06460-2837

STOKES, THOMAS EDWARD, librarian; b. Canton, Ohio, Oct. 17, 1942; s. Thomas Edward and Elsie Mae (Groves) S.; m. Barbara Ann Wise, Aug. 19, 1967; children—Andrew Thomas, Ian Philip. B.A., Malone Coll., 1968; M.Div., Emmanuel Sch. Religion, 1974; M.L.S., George Peabody Coll. for Tchrs., 1974. Ordained to ministry Christian Ch., 1969; youth minister Calvary Evang. United Brethren Ch., Canton, 1966-67; resident counselor Malone Coll., Canton, 1967-69; student union mgr. Milligan Coll. (Tenn.), 1969-74; library asst. George Peabody Coll. for Tchrs., Nashville, 1974-75; librarian, mem. faculty Emmanuel Sch. Religion, Johnson City, Tenn., 1975—, asst. prof., 1979-81, assoc. prof. bibliography and research, 1981-89, prof., 1989—; treas. Chaplaincy Endorsement Commn., Christian Chs. and Chs. of Christ, Johnson City, 1976—. Chaplain, Tenn. Army N.G., 1974—; scoutmaster Boy Scouts Am., Johnson City, 1983-87. Served with USNR, 1960-63. Named An Outstanding Young Man of Am., Johnson City Jaycees, 1971. Mem. ALA, Am. Theol. Library Assn., Tenn. Theol. Library Assn. (v.p. pres.-elect 1982-85, pres. 1985-87), Disciples of Christ Hist. Soc. Club: Johnson City Optimist (pres. 1979-80, 81-82, sec.-treas. 1982-83). Office: Emmanuel Sch Religion One Walker Dr Johnson City TN 37601

STOKLOS, RANDY (STOKEY STOKLOS), volleyball player; b. Pacific Palisades, Calif., Dec. 13, 1960; m. Carrie Stoklos. Student, UCLA. Profl. volleyball tour player, 1982—; mem. U.S.A. Nat. Team, 1979-80; pres. Audio Spkrs. of Am.; model, actor. Actor: Side Out, 1990; model mag. covers. Voted AVP Most Valuable Player 1988, 89, 91; named Italian, Brazilian and Australian tour Most Valuable Player, 1991. Mem. Assn. Volleyball Profls. Won Miller Lite Chgo. Open with Brian Lewis, 1993, Nestea Open with Adam Johnson, Manhattan Beach, 1994, San Francisco, 1994; placed 2d FIVB Beach Volleyball World Championships with Sinjin Smith; ranked 1st AVP Career Earnings list and 2d on Career Open Wins; registered 100th career open, 1991, 2d player to reach that mark; won World Championships during 1st yr. on tour, 1982. Office: c/o Assn Volleyball Profls 15260 Ventura Blvd Ste 2250 Sherman Oaks CA 91403-5352*

STOKSTAD, MARILYN JANE, art history educator, curator; b. Lansing, Mich., Feb. 16, 1929; d. Olaf Lawrence and Edythe Marian (Gardiner) S. BA, Carleton Coll., 1950; MA, Mich. State U., 1953; PhD, U. Mich., 1957; postgrad., U. Oslo, 1951-52. Instr. U. Mich., Ann Arbor, 1956-58; mem. faculty U. Kans., Lawrence, 1958—; assoc. prof. U. Kans., 1961-66, prof., 1966-80, Univ. Disting. prof. art history, 1980-94, Judith Harris Murphy disting. prof. art, 1994—, dir. mus. art, 1961-67, research assoc., summers 1965-66, 67, 71, 72; assoc. dean Coll. Liberal Arts and Scis., U. Kans., 1972-76; research curator Nelson-Atkins Mus. Art, Kansas City, Mo., 1969-80, consultative curator medieval art, 1980—; bd. dirs. Internat. Ctr. Medieval Art, 1972-75, 81-84, 88—, v.p., 1990-93, pres., 1993-96; cons., evaluator North Ctrl. Assn. Colls. and Univs., 1972—, commr.-at-large, 1984-89. Author: Santiago de compostela, 1978, The Scottish World, 1981, Medieval Art, 1986, Art History, 1995. Recipient Disting. Service award Alumni Assn. Carleton Coll., 1983; Fulbright fellow, 1951-52; NEH grantee, 1967-68. Fellow AAUW; mem. AAUP (nat. coun. 1972-75), Archeol. Inst. Am. (pres. Kans. chpt. 1960-61), Midwest Coll. Art Conf. (pres. 1964-65), Coll. Art Assn. (bd. dirs. 1970-80, pres. 1978-80), Soc. Archtl. Historians (chpt. bd. dirs. 1971-73).

STOKVIS, JACK RAPHAEL, urban planner and developer, government agency administrator; b. Hartford, Conn., Dec. 10, 1944; s. John and Ivette (Korda) S.; m. Evelyn Noether, May 11, 1980. A.B., Union Coll., 1967; postgrad. in bus., Boston U., 1968; M.U.P., NYU, 1973; MPhil, Columbia U., 1995. Lic. planner, N.J. Project planner Jersey City Redevel. Agy., 1970-73; sr. planner City of Jersey City, 1973-75; prin. planner City of Paterson, (N.J.), 1975-76; spl. project mgr. Gt. Falls Hist. Dist., Dept. Community Devel. City of Paterson, N.J., 1976-80; dir. Dept. Planning and Grants, East Orange, N.J., 1980-81; gen. dep. asst. sec. community planning and devel. HUD, Washington, 1981-88, asst. sec. community planning and devel., 1988-89; pres. Stokvis Assocs., Inc., Haworth, N.J., 1989—; dir. Gt. Falls Devel. Corp., Paterson, 1975-80; project dir. Revitalization of Jersey City Italian Village, 1974-79; lectr. George Washington U., Washington; adj. prof. Rutgers U. New Brunswick, N.J., Columbia U., N.Y.C., 1981—. Author numerous articles in field. Founder Friends of Paterson Parks; v.p. Jersey City Preservation and Restoration Assn. Recipient Outstanding Student of Yr. award Am. Inst. Planning, NYU; recipient Environ. Quality award U.S. Dept. Environ. Protection, N.Y.C., Outstanding Grant Recognition Program award Nat. Endowment Arts, Program Implementation award Am. Planning Assn., Princeton, N.J., Secretary's award, 1989. Mem. Am. Inst. Cert. Planners, Urban Land Inst., Am. Planning Assn., Nat. Trust Hist. Preservation. Office: PO Box 93 Haworth NJ 07641-0093

STOL, ISRAEL, welding engineer; b. Stockholm, Aug. 18, 1947; came to U.S., 1972; s. Haim Fima and Sara (Epstein) S.; m. Diane Reva Morron, Jan. 27, 1983; children: Hagye, Talia, Ilana. BS in Welding Engring., Ohio State U., 1976, MS in Welding Engring., 1977. Sr. welding rsch. engr. Westinghouse R & D Ctr., Pitts., 1977-85; sr. welding rsch. engr. Alcoa Tech. Ctr., Pitts., 1985-87, staff welding rsch. engr., 1987-89; mgr. assembly and joining tech. transfer Alcoa Automotive Structures Internat., Pitts., 1990—, plant welding sys. implementation mgr., 1990—; cons. in welding engring. Westinghouse and Alcoa, Pitts., 1977-89. Contbr. rsch. articles to profl. welding jours. Mem. Beth-El Synagogue, Pitts., 1990—. Corp. Tech. Support, 1968-69, Israel. Recipient award James Lincoln Arc Welding Found., 1986, 88. Mem. Am. Welding Soc. (A.F. Davis silver award 1990). Achievements include patents in Pressure-Differential Method for Sleeve-To-Tube Joining, Method and Apparatus for Arc Welding, Narrow Groove Welding Torch, Arc Welding Method and Electrode for Narrow Groove Welding, Corrosion Resistant Steam Generator and Method of Making the Same, High Reliability Double-Chambered Shielding System for Welding, Method and Apparatus for Controlling the Temperatures of Continuously Fed Wires, Improved Apparatus for Electrically Isolated Hot Wire Surfacing Processes, Ultrasonic Excitation of Underwater Torpedoes for Enhancing Maneuverability and others; responsibility for 140 inventions, 21 patents, and fifty corporate reports and studies in welding tech.; developed the Advanced GMA, GTA and laser welding processes; identified a new type of hydrodynamic welding instability and methods of controlling it during arc welding; developed innovative welding methods for narrow-groove GTA and GMA welding of titanium; devised new robotic GMA welding approaches. Office: Alcoa Automotive Structures Internat 425 6th Ave Pittsburgh PA 15219-1819

STOLAR, HENRY SAMUEL, lawyer; b. St. Louis, Oct. 29, 1939; s. William Allen and Pearl Minnette (Schukar) S.; m. Mary Goldstein, Aug. 26, 1962 (dec. Nov. 1987); children: Daniel Bruce, Susan Eileen; m. Suzanne Chapman Jones, June 2, 1989. AB, Washington U., 1960; JD, Harvard U., 1963. Bar: Mo. 1963, U.S. Supreme Ct. 1972. Assoc. then ptnr. Hocker, Goodwin & MacGreevy, St. Louis, 1963-69; v.p., sec., gen. counsel LaBarge Inc., St. Louis, 1969-74; v.p., assoc. gen. counsel then sr. v.p., gen. counsel Maritz Inc., St. Louis, 1974—. Sec., bd. dirs. New City Sch. Inc., St. Louis, 1968-75; mem. St. Louis Bd. Aldermen, 1969-73, Bd. Freeholders City and County St. Louis, 1987-88; bd. dirs. Ctrl. West End Assn., 1993—; sec., bd. dirs. Forest Park Forever, Inc., 1988—. Mem. ABA, Mo. Bar, Bar Assn. Met. St. Louis, Frontenac Racquet Club, Triple A Club, Phi Beta Kappa. Home: 59 Kingsbury Pl Saint Louis MO 63112-1824 Office: Maritz Inc 1375 N Highway Dr Fenton MO 63026-1929

STOLARIK, M. MARK, history educator; b. St. Martin, Slovak Republic, Apr. 22, 1943; s. Imrich and Margita (Vavro) S.; m. Anne Helene Ivanco, June 15, 1968; children: Roman Andrej, Matthew Mark. BA, U. Ottawa, 1965, MA, 1967; PhD, U. Minn., 1974. Asst. prof. history Cleve. State U., 1972-76; hist. researcher Nat. Mus. of Man., Ottawa, Ont., Can., 1977-78; pres. Balch Inst. for Ethnic Studies, Phila., 1979-91; prof. history, chair dept. Slovak history and culture U. Ottawa, Ont., Can., 1992—; cons. Harvard Ency. Ethnic Groups, Cambridge, Mass., 1976-80; advisor State Hist. Records Bd., Harrisburg, Pa., 1982-91; cons. Ency. Canada's Ethnic Groups, 1991—. Author: film documentary Vianoce-Slovak Christmas, 1978 (2d prize 1979), Slovaks in Bethlehem, Pa., 1985, The Slovak Experience, 1870-1918, 1989. Mem. Pa. adv. com. to U.S. Commn. on Civil Rights, 1985-91. Lehigh U. fellow, 1976. Mem. 1st Cath. Slovak Union, Nat. Slovak Soc., Canadian Slovak League (pres. 1994—). Roman Catholic.

STOLBERG, IRVING J., state legislator, international consultant; b. Phila., Sept. 24, 1936; s. Ralph B.; 1 son, Robert. BA, UCLA, 1958; MA, Boston U., 1964, postgrad., 1964-66; JD (hon.), U. Hartford, 1987. Internat. campus adminstr. Nat. Student Assn., Cambridge, Mass., 1958-59; program dir. Internat. Student Ctr., Cambridge, 1959-60; Midwest dir. World Univ. Service, Chgo., 1960-63; asst. prof. So. Conn. State U., New Haven, 1966-78; mem. Conn. Gen. Assembly, 1971-93; speaker Ho. of Reps., 1983-84, 87-88, minority leader, 1985, 86, speaker-at-large, 1989, 90; prin. Internat. Solutions, 1994—; del. numerous internat. disarmament and conflict resolution confs. Del. Dem. Nat. Convs. 1968, 72, 76, 84, 88, 92; founder Caucus Conn. Dems., pres. 1995—; chmn. Caucus New Eng. State Legislatures, 1985; mem. bd. overseers Regional Lab. for Edn. in New Eng. and the Islands; bd. dirs. Dem. Nat. Com., 1986-89; appointed by Pres. to U.S. Commn. for Preservation of America's Heritage Abroad, 1995. Named Conn. Caucus Dems. Outstanding Legislator, 1974; recipient Disting. Alumni award Boston U., 1984, Presdl. medal for Community Service, So. Conn. State U., 1987. Mem. Nat. Conf. State Legislators (pres. 1987, pres. Found. 1989), Nat. Assn. Jewish Legislators (pres. 1990-91), Ctr. for Policy Alternatives (bd. dirs., CPA lifetime achievement award), Conn. Tennis Found. (bd. dirs. 1991-94). Home: 50 Roydon Rd New Haven CT 06511-2807

STOLBERG, SHERYL GAY, journalist; b. N.Y.C., Nov. 18, 1961; d. Irving and Marcia Dawn (Papier) S. BA, U. Va., 1983. Reporter Providence Jour. Bulletin, 1983-87, L.A. Times, 1987—. Recipient Unity award Lincoln U., 1987. Office: LA Times Ste 1100 1875 I St NW Washington DC 20006 also: 9019 Le Velle Dr Chevy Chase MD 20815

STOLGITIS, WILLIAM CHARLES, professional society executive; b. Ware, Mass., Jan. 9, 1941; s. Vincent Charles and Doris (Dansereau) S.; m. Helen Elizabeth Dermody, Apr. 18, 1969. BS, U.S. Naval Acad., 1962; MS, U.S. Naval Postgrad. Sch., 1969; JD, Georgetown U., 1977. Bar: N.J. 1977, D.C. 1977. Commd. ensign USN, 1962, officer, 1962-82; exec. dir. Soc. Tech. Comm., Arlington, Va., 1982—; legal counsel Internat. Hydrofoil Assn., 1978—. Mem. ABA, D.C. Bar Assn., N.J. Bar Assn., Am. Soc. Assn. Execs., Am. Legion. Republican. Roman Catholic. Home: 3711 Military Rd Arlington VA 22207-4831 Office: Society for Tech Comm 901 N Stuart St Ste 904 Arlington VA 22203-1854

STOLL, HOWARD LESTER, JR., dermatologist; b. Buffalo, June 13, 1928; s. Howard L. and Margaret (Kahler) S.; m. Jacklyn Fay Straight, June, 1948; children—Shelley, Margaret, Amy, Howard III. A.B., Harvard U., 1948; M.D., U. Pa., 1952. Diplomate Am. Bd. Dermatology. Intern E.J. Meyer Hosp., Buffalo, 1952; resident in dermatology E.J. Meyer Hosp., 1953-55; sr. cancer research surgeon Roswell Park Meml. Inst., Buffalo, 1958-59, assoc. cancer research dermatologist, 1959-67, chief, sect. dermatology, 1984-92; mem. courtesy staff Mercy Hosp., Buffalo, 1958-70; asst. in dermatology E.J. Meyer Meml. Hosp., Buffalo, 1962-72; clin. assoc. prof. dermatology Sch. Medicine, SUNY-Buffalo, 1976-91, clin. prof., 1991—. Served to capt. U.S. Army, 1955-57. Mem. Am. Acad. Dermatology, Soc. Investigative Dermatology, Buffalo-Rochester Dermatologic Soc. Office: Roswell Park Meml Inst Elm & Carlto Sts 666 Elm St Buffalo NY 14263-0001

STOLL, JOHN ROBERT, lawyer, educator; b. Phila., Nov. 29, 1950; s. Wilhelm Friedrich and Marilyn Jane (Kremser) S.; m. Christine Larson, June 24, 1972; children: Andrew Michael, Michael Robert, Meredith Kirstin, Alison Courtney. BA magna cum laude, Haverford Coll., 1972; JD, Columbia U., 1975. Bar: Ind. 1975, U.S. Dist. Ct. (no. and so. dists.) Ind. 1975, U.S. Ct. Appeals (7th cir.) 1978, U.S. Dist. Ct. (no. dist.) Ill. 1980, (so. dist.) N.Y. 1993, Ill. 1981, N.Y. 1989. Atty. Barnes & Thornburg, South Bend, Ind., 1975-80, Mayer, Brown & Platt, Chgo., 1980—; adj. prof. law Northwestern U., Chgo., 1985—, DePaul U., Chgo., 1987; lectr. in bus. St. Mary's Coll., Notre Dame, Ind., 1977-78. Contbr. articles to profl. jours. Mem. ABA, Ind. State Bar Assn., Am. Bankruptcy Inst., Phi Beta Kappa. Office: Mayer Brown & Platt 190 S La Salle St Chicago IL 60603-3410

STOLL, LOUISE FRANKEL, federal official; b. N.Y.C., June 6, 1939; d. Abraham H. and Ruth C. (Flexo) Frankel; m. Marc H. Monheimer, Dec. 22, 1978; children: Miriam F., Malaika S., Abraham D. BA, MA in Philosophy with honors, U. Chgo., 1961; PhD, U. Calif., Berkeley, 1978. High sch. English tchr. Nairobi, Kenya, 1964-65; trustee Berkeley Unified Sch. Dist., 1971-78; mgr. govt. affairs Clear Water Program San Francisco, 1978-80, budget dir. Pub. Utilities Commn., 1980-85; sr. v.p., No. Calif. regional mgr. O'Brien-Kreitzberg and Assoc., Inc., San Francisco, 1985-93; CFO and asst. sec. budget and programs Office of Sec. Dept. Transp., Washington, 1993—; mem. Nat. Legal Affairs Com., Mid. East Com. of Anti-Defamation League of B'nai B'rith. Active Anti-Defamation League of B'nai B'rith. Recipient Mayor's Fiscal Adv. award, City of San Francisco, 1984. Jewish. Avocation: bicycle riding. Office: Office of Sec Dept Transp 400 7th St SW Rm 10101 Washington DC 20590

STOLL, NEAL RICHARD, lawyer; b. Phila., Nov. 7, 1948; s. Mervin Stoll and Goldie Louise (Serody) Stoll Wilf; m. Linda G. Seligman, May 25, 1972; children: Meredith Anne, Alexis Blythe. BA in History with distinction, Pa, State U., 1970; JD, Fordham U., 1973. Bar: N.Y. 1974, U.S. Dist. Ct. (ea. dist.) N.Y. 1974, U.S. Ct. Appeals (2d cir.) 1974, U.S. Ct. Appeals (11th cir.) 1982, U.S. Dist. Ct. (ea. dist.) Mich. 1983, U.S. Dist. Ct. (so. dist.) N.Y. 1974, U.S. Supreme Ct. 1986. Assoc. Skadden, Arps, Slate, Meagher & Flom, N.Y.C., 1973-81, mem., 1981—; lectr. Practicing Law-Inst., N.Y.C. Contbr. articles to profl. publs. Author: (with others) Aquisitions Under the Hart Scott Rodino Antitrust Improvements Act, 1980. Mem. Assn. Bar City of New York (mem. trade regulation com. 1983-85), ABA, N.Y. State Bar Assn. Democrat. Office: Skadden Arps Slate 919 3rd Ave New York NY 10022-3903

STOLL, RICHARD EDMUND, retired manufacturing executive; b. Dayton, Ohio, Aug. 5, 1927; s. George Elmer and Mary Francis (Zimmerle) S.; m. Vera Mae Cohagen, Sept. 2, 1950; children: Richard Edmund, Linda Ann, Donna Gail. Student in mech. engring., MIT, 1945-47; MetE, Ohio State U., 1950. Registered profl. engr. Ill., Tex. Various staff and operating positions U.S. Steel Corp., Pitts., Chgo., Houston, 1952-78; gen. mgr. metall. services U.S. Steel Corp., Pitts., 1978-84, dir. quality mgmt. program and tech., 1984-85; corp. chief metallurgist Wheeling-Pitts. Steel Corp., Wheeling, W.Va., 1985-86, v.p., gen. mgr. flat rolled steel, 1986-87, v.p., gen. mgr., interim chief ops. officer, 1987-89, exec. v.p., 1989-91, ret., 1991; cons. McElrath & Assocs., Mpls., 1984. Contbr. articles to profl. jours.; patentee in field. Served with C.E., U.S. Army, 1950-52. Fellow Am. Soc. Metals (chmn. 1963); mem. Am. Iron and Steel Inst., Am. Inst. Mining and Metallurgy (Nat. Open Hearth award 1957, bd. dirs. 1961-68), Am. Inst. Steel Engrs., Am. Soc. Metals, Dolphin Head Golf Club. Republican. Roman

Catholic. Avocation: golf. Home: 3 Kinglet Lagoon Rd Hilton Head Island SC 29926-2548

STOLL, RICHARD G(ILES), lawyer; b. Phila., Oct. 2, 1946; s. Richard Giles and Mary Margaret (Zeigler) S.; m. Susan Jane Nicewonger, June 15, 1968; children: Richard Giles III, Christian Hayes. BA magna cum laude, Westminster Coll., 1968; JD, Georgetown U., 1971. Bar: D.C. 1971, U.S. Dist. Ct. D.C. 1971, U.S. Ct. Appeals D.C. 1971, U.S. Ct. Appeals (4th cir.) 1977. Assoc. Arent, Fox, Kintner, Plotkin & Kahn, Washington, 1971-73; atty. Office of Gen. Counsel EPA, Washington, 1973-77, asst. gen. counsel, 1977-81; dep. gen. counsel Chem. Mfrs. Assn., Washington, 1981-84; ptnr. Freedman, Levy, Kroll & Simonds, Washington, 1984—; instr. environ. law and policy U. Va., Charlottesville, 1981-90. Author: Handbook on Environmental Law, 1987, 88, 89, 91, Practical Guide to Environment Law, 1987; contbr. articles to profl. jours.; moderator, panelist legal ednl. TV broadcasts and tapes ABA and Am. Law Inst. Mem. Georgetown Presbyn. Ch.; frequent panelist and moderator on environ. law TV programs. Served to capt., USAR, 1968-76. Mem. ABA (sect. natural resources, energy and environ. law; chmn. water quality com. 1980-82, hazardous waste com. 1983-85, coun. mem. 1985-88, sect. chmn. 1990-91), Washington Golf and Country Club, McLean Racquet and Health Club. Avocations: piano, golf. Office: Freedman Levy Kroll & Simonds 1050 Connecticut Ave NW Ste 825 Washington DC 20036-5303

STOLL, ROBERT W., principal. Prin. Harrison (Ohio) Elem. Sch. Recipient Elem. Sch. Recognition award U.S. Dept. Edn., 1989-90. Office: Harrison Elem Sch 600 E Broadway St Harrison OH 45030-1323

STOLL, ROGER G., health insurance company executive; b. 1942. BS, Ferris State Coll., 1965; PhD in Bio-Pharmacetics, U. Conn., 1970. With Upjohn Co., Kalamazoo, Mich., 1970-76, Am. Critical Care divsn., Baxter Internat. Inc., Deerfield, Ill., 1976-86; exec. v.p., gen. mgr. Diagnostics Bus. Group, Miles, Inc., Pitts., 1986-91; pres. Ohmeda, Liberty Corner, N.J., 1991—. Office: Ohmeda 110 Allen Rd Liberty Corner NJ 07938*

STOLL, WILHELM, mathematics educator; b. Freiburg, Germany, Dec. 22, 1923; came to U.S., 1960; s. Heinrich and Doris (Eberle) S.; m. Marilyn Jane Kremser, June 11, 1955; children: Robert, Dieter, Elisabeth, Rebecca. Ph.D. in Math, U. Tübingen, Fed. Republic Germany, 1953, habilitation, 1954. Asst. U. Tübingen, 1953-59, dozent, 1954-60, ausserplanmässiger prof., 1960; vis. lectr. U. Pa., 1954-55; temp. mem. Inst. Advanced Study, Princeton, 1957-59; prof. math. U. Notre Dame, 1960-88, Vincent J. Duncan and Annamarie Micus Duncan prof. math., 1988-94, prof. emeritus, 1994—, chmn. dept., 1966-68, co-dir. Ctr. for Applied Math., 1992; vis. prof. Stanford U., 1968-69, Tulane U., 1973, U. Sci. and Tech., Hefei, Anhui, People's Republic of China, summer, 1986; adviser Clark Sch., South Bend, Ind., 1963-68; Japan Soc. Promotion Sci. fellow, vis. prof. Kyoto U., summer 1983. Publs. in field. Research complex analysis several variables. Home: 54763 Merrifield Dr Mishawaka IN 46545-1519 Office: U Notre Dame Dept Math Notre Dame IN 46556

STOLLAR, BERNARD DAVID, biochemist, educator; b. Saskatoon, Sask., Can., Aug. 11, 1936; came to U.S., 1960; s. Percival and Rose (Direnfeld) S.; m. Carol A. Singer, Oct. 7, 1956; children: Lawrence, Michael, Suzanne. BA, U. Sask., 1958, MD, 1959. Intern U. Sask. Hosp., Saskatoon, 1959-60; postdoctoral fellow Brandeis U., Waltham, Mass., 1960-62; dep. chief divsn. biol. scis. USAF Office of sci. Rsch., Washington, 1962-64; asst. prof. dept. pharmacology Tufts U. Schs. Medicine and Dental Medicine, Boston, 1964-67, asst. prof. dept. biochemistry, 1967-68, assoc. prof. biochemistry/pharmacology, 1968-74, prof., 1974—, acting chmn. dept. biochemistry and pharmacology, 1984-86, chmn. dept. biochemistry, 1986—; vis. prof. internat. course in immunology and immunochemistry Mexico City, 1971; sr. fellow Weizmann Inst. Sci., Rehovot, Israel, 1971-71; vis. prof. chemistry Wellesley (Mass.) Coll., 1976, U. Tromsö, Norway, 1981; Dozor vis. prof. Ben-Gurion U. Sch. Medicine, Beer Sheva, Israel, 1986; cons. USAF Office Sci. Rsch., 1966-69, Seragen, Inc., 1983-88, Cetus, 1982-85, Gene-Trak, 1986-89, Alkermes, Inc., 1989—, Catalytic Antibodies, Inc., 1993—; mem. allergy/transplantation rsch. com. NIH/NIAID, 1990-94. Contbr. over 200 articles to profl. jours., chpts. to books; exec. editl. bd. Analytical Biochemistry, 1988—; editl. bd. Jour. Immunology, 1981-85, Molecular Immunology, 1980-95, Arthritis and Rheumatism, 1986-89, Jour. Immunological Methods, 1988-95. Mem. adult edn. com. Temple Reyim, Newton, Mass. Capt. USAF, 1962-64. Recipient Copland prize U. Sask. Coll. Arts and Sci., 1958, Gold medalist, Coll. of Medicine, 1959, Medalist in Medicine, Pediatrics, Obstetrics, Gynecology, 1959; decorated Air Force Commendation medal; Weizmann Inst. Sci. sr. fellow, 1971-72; named Third Ann. Alumni Lectr., U. Sask. Coll. Medicine, 1989; rsch. grantee NSF, NIH, 1964—. Mem. AAAS, Am. Assn. Immunologists, Am. Soc. Biochemistry and Molecular Biology, Am. Coll. Rheumatology, Clin. Immunology Soc. Office: Tufts Univ Sch Medicine Dept Biochemistry 136 Harrison Ave Boston MA 02111-1800

STOLLDORF, GENEVIEVE SCHWAGER, media specialist; b. Ames, N.Y., July 17, 1943; d. Herbert Blakely and Genevieve Agnes (Alessi) Schwager; m. John G. Stolldorf, June 25, 1972; 1 child, Nathan Schwager. AA, Auburn (N.Y.) C.C., 1963; BS, Murray State U., 1967; MA in Edn., Seton Hall U., 1975. Cert. libr. media specialist, social studies tchr. grades 7-12. Libr. So. Orangetown Schs., Orangeburg, N.Y., 1967-70; libr. media specialist Nanuet (N.Y.) Pub. Schs., 1970-78; tchr. social studies grade 9 Monroe (N.Y.)-Woodbury, 1978-80; libr. media specialist Nyack (N.Y.) Pub. Schs., 1981—. Reviewer Libr. Jour., 1981-90. Kykuit guide Hist. Hudson Valley, 1994—; active Friends of the Nyacks, Nyack. Mem. N.Y. Libr. Assn., N.Y. State United Tchrs., Sch. Libr. Media Specialists Southeastern N.Y., Nyack Tchr. Assn. (editor newsletter 1982-84), Tri-Town League Women Voters, C. of C. of the Nyacks (hon.). Avocations: travel, photography, gardening, reading. Office: Valley Cottage Elem Sch Lake Rd Valley Cottage NY 10989

STOLLER, CLAUDE, architect; b. N.Y.C., Dec. 2, 1921; s. Max and Esther (Zisblatt) S.; m. Anna Maria Oldenburg, June 5, 1946 (div. Oct. 1972); children: Jacob, Dorothea, Elizabeth; m. Rosemary Raymond Lax, Sept. 22, 1978. Student, Black Mountain Coll., N.C., 1942; M.Arch., Harvard U., 1949. Architect Architects Collaborative, Cambridge, Mass., after 1949, Shepley, Bulfinch, Richardson & Abbot, Boston, 1951; co-founder, partner firm Marquis & Stoller, San Francisco, 1956; pvt. practice architecture N.Y.C. and San Francisco, 1974-78; founder, partner Stoller/Partners, Berkeley, Calif., 1978, Stoller, Knoerr Archs., 1988-95; mem. faculty Washington U., St. Louis, 1955-56, U. Calif., Berkeley, 1957-91, prof. arch., 1968-92, acting chmn. dept., 1965-66, chair grad. studies, 1984-91; mem. Berkeley Campus Design Rev. Bd., 1985-91, chmn., 1992-93; commr. Calif. Bd. Archtl. Examiners, 1980-90, mem. exam. com., 1985-88; mem. diocesan commn. arch. Episcopal Diocese Calif., 1961—; vis. arch. Nat. Design Inst., Ahmedabad, India, 1963; planning commr. City of Mill Valley, 1961-66, Marin County Planning Commn., 1966-67; mem. pub. adv. panel archtl. svcs. GSA, 1969-71; citizens urban design adv. com. City of Oakland, Calif., 1968; vis. com. nat. archtl. accrediting bd. U. Minn. and U. Wis., Milw., 1971; coun. Harvard Grad. Sch. Design Assn., 1976—; mem. design rev. com. The Sea Ranch, Calif., 1990—. Prin. works include St. Francis Sq. Coop. Apts., San Francisco, 1961, Pub. Housing for Elderly, San Francisco, 1974, Learning Resources Bldg, U. Calif., Santa Barbara, 1975, Menorah Park Housing for Elderly, San Francisco, 1979, San Jose State U. Student Housing Project, 1984, Delta Airlines Terminal, San Francisco Internat. Airport, 1988. Served with AUS, 1943-46. Recipient numerous awards including AIA Honor awards, 1963, 64, AIA Bay Region Honor award, 1974, Concrete Reinforced Steel Inst. award, 1976, AIA award, 1976, CADA Site I Solar Housing award Sacramento, Calif., 1980, State of Calif. Affordable Housing award, 1981, PG&E Suntherm award, 1981, San Francisco Housing Authority award, 1983, Orchid award City of Oakland, 1989, Citation for achievement and svc. U. Calif., Berkeley, 1991, Design award Berkeley Design Advocates. Fellow AIA. Home: 2816 Derby St Berkeley CA 94705-1325 Office: Claude Stoller FAIA Arch 1818 Harmon St Berkeley CA 94703-2472

STOLLER, DAVID ALLEN, lawyer; b. Burlington, Iowa, Oct. 27, 1947; s. Richard L. and Marjorie E. (Thornton) S.; m. Nancy E. Leachman, July 14, 1973; children: Aaron J., Anne C., John D. BSBA, Drake U., 1970, JD, 1977. Bar: Iowa 1977, U.S. Dist. Ct. (so. dist.) Iowa 1978, (no. dist.) Iowa 1981, U.S. Ct. Appeals (8th cir.) 1981, N.C. 1985, U.S. Dist. Ct. (ea. dist.) N.C. 1985, U.S. Ct. Appeals (4th cir.) 1986. Assoc. city atty. City of Des Moines, 1977-81; assoc. Connolly, O'Malley, Lillis, Hansen & Olson, Des Moines, 1981-85, Ward & Smith, New Bern, N.C., 1985-89; ptnr. Dunn, Dunn & Stoller, New Bern, 1990—. Bd. dirs. Episcopal Found. of Diocese of East Carolina, Thompson's Children's Home, Inc., Charlotte, N.C.; mem., sec. standing com. Episcopal Diocese of East Carolina. Eagle Scout Boy Scouts Am., 1964. Mem. ABA (torts and ins. practice, litigation, law office mgmt. sects.), Def. Rsch. Inst., N.C. Bar Assn. (litigation sect.), N.C. State Bar (councilor 1995—), 3d Jud. Dist. Bar, N.C. Soc. Health Care Attys., Craven County Bar Assn., New Bern Golf and Country Club. Avocations: coaching youth soccer, basketball, T-ball. Home: 2432 Tram Rd New Bern NC 28562-7370 Office: Dunn Dunn & Stoller 3230 Country Club Rd New Bern NC 28562-7304

STOLLER, EZRA, photojournalist; b. Chgo., May 16, 1915; s. Max and Esther (Zistblatt) S.; m. Helen Rubin, Sept. 23, 1938; children: Erica, Evan, Lincoln. B.F.A., NYU, 1938. Guest lectr. U. Okla., U. Kans., U. Notre Dame, 1971, Ga. Inst. Tech., Va. Poly. Inst. and State U., 1972, Columbia Coll., 1974, 76, U. N.C., Smithsonian Instn., Harvard U., 1984-86, Harvard Grad. Sch. Design, 1985, 86, 88, U. Ariz., 1985, U. Pa., 1987, U. Orange Free State, 1995, Nat. Inst. Archtl. Edn., 1995. Exhbns. include, Max Protetch Gallery, N.Y.C., 1980, Bonafant Gallery, San Francisco, 1981, Bannenford Books, Toronto, 1981, Mpls. Art Inst., 1981, Nat. Gallery Johannesburg, 1983, Harvard GSD, 1991; author: Modern Architecture Photographs By Ezra Stoller, 1990. Recipient 1st medal for archtl. photography AIA, 1960. Mem. AIA (hon.), Am. Soc. Mag. Photographers (past pres., lifetime achievement award 1982), Archtl. League N.Y. (Gold medal 1955). Home: Kirby Ln N Rye NY 10580

STOLLER, MITCHELL R., non-profit organization administrator; b. Washington, Aug. 1, 1953; s. Sidney and Goldie (Berman) S.; m. Sheri Ann Stutsky, June 15, 1980; children: Betsy, Lauren. BS, Frostburg State Coll., 1975; postgrad., George Washington U., 1983. Tchr. Charles County Bd. Edn., Waldorf, Md., 1976-81; dir. devel. Ctrl. Md. chpt. Easter Seal Soc., Balt., 1981-83, March of Dimes Birth Defects Found., Balt., 1983-86; nat. dir. spl. projects and field ops. Retinitis Pigmentosa Found., Balt., 1986-88; exec. dir. Sudden Infant Death Syndrome Assn., Landover, md., 1988-91; exec. v.p., COO Sudden Infant Death Syndrome Alliance, Columbia, md., 1991-93; pres., CEO Am. Paralysis Assn., Springfield, N.J., 1993—, bd. dirs. Bd. dirs. C.J. Found. for Sudden Infant Death Syndrome Alliance, Hackensack, N.J., 1994; fundraiser Warren (N.J.) Synagogue, 1993—. Mem. Am. Soc. Assn. Execs. Avocations: golf, basketball league, coach children's soccer. Home: 11 Surrey Ln Basking Ridge NJ 07920 Office: Am Paralysis Assn 500 Morris Ave Springfield NJ 07081*

STOLLER, PATRICIA SYPHER, structural engineer; b. Jackson Heights, N.Y., Dec. 16, 1947; d. Carleton Roy and Mildred Vivian (Ferron) Sypher; m. David A. Stoller Sr.; children: Stephanie Jean, Sheri Lynn. BSCE, Washington U., St. Louis, 1975; M in Mgmt., Northwestern U., 1989. R&D engr. Amcar div. ACF Industries, St. Charles, Mo., 1972-79; project engr. Truck Axle div. Rockwell Internat., Troy, Mich., 1979-81; sr. engr. ABB Impell, Norcross, Ga., 1981-83; supervising mgr., client mgr., div. mgr. ABB Impell, Lincolnshire, Ill., 1983—; dir. bus. devel., v.p. VECTRA (formerly ABB Impell), Lincolnshire, 1991-94; pres., CEO ASC Svcs. Co., LLC, Chgo., 1994—; Author computer program Quickpipe, 1983; numerous patents in field. Mem. ASCE, NAFE, Soc. Women Engrs., Am. Nuclear Soc. (exec. bd. Chgo. sect. 1991-93). Avocations: golf, music. Office: ASC Svcs Co LLC 300 W Washington St Ste 200 Chicago IL 60606-1720

STOLLERMAN, GENE HOWARD, physician, educator; b. N.Y.C., Dec. 6, 1920; s. Maurice William and Sarah Dorothy (Mezz) S.; m. Corynne Miller, Jan. 21, 1945; children: Lee Denise Stollerman Meyburg, Anne Barbara Stollerman DiZio, John Eliot. AB summa cum laude, Dartmouth Coll., 1941; MD, Columbia U., 1944. Diplomate Am. Bd. Internal Medicine. Clin. tng. Mt. Sinai Hosp., N.Y.C, 1944-46; chief med. resident Mt. Sinai Hosp., 1948; Dazian research fellow microbiology NYU Med. Sch., 1949-50, mem. dept. medicine, 1951-55; med. dir. Irvington House for Cardiac Children, 1951-55; prin. investigator Sackett Found. Research in Rheumatic Diseases, 1955-64; asst. prof. medicine Northwestern U., 1955-57, assoc. prof., 1957-61, prof. medicine, 1961-65; prof., chmn. dept. medicine U. Tenn., 1965-81, Goodman prof., 1977-81; physician-in-chief City of Memphis Hosps., 1965-81; prof. medicine Boston U. Sch. Medicine, 1981-95, prof. pub. health, 1991-95, prof. medicine and pub. health emeritus, 1996—; chief sect. gen. internal medicine Univ. Hosp., Boston U. Med. Ctr., 1983-86; Disting. physician VA Med. Ctr., Bedford, Mass., 1986-89; assoc. chief of staff Geriatrics and Extended Care, 1989-92; clin. dir. Bedford div. Geriatric Rsch., Ednl. and Clin. Ctr., 1989-92; dir. VA Health Svcs. Rsch. Field, 1990-93; chmn. research career program com. NIAMD-NIH, 1967-70; mem. commn. streptococcal and staphylococcal diseases U.S. Armed Forces Epidemiol. Bd., 1956-74; adv. bd. immunization practices Center for Disease Control, 1968-71; expert adv. panel cardiovascular disease WHO, 1966—; mem. Am. Bd. Internal Medicine, 1967-73, chmn. cert. exam. com., 1969-73, mem. exec. com., 1971-73; chmn. Panel on Bacterial Vaccines, FDA, 1973-80; mem. nat. adv. council Nat. Inst. Allergy and Infectious Diseases, NIH, 1978-82; mem. Dept. Health & Human Services nat. vaccine adv. com.. Editor-in-chief Advances in Internal Medicine, 1968-93, Jour. Am. Geriatric Soc., 1984-88; co-editor Hosp. Practice, 1990—; contbr. chpts. to Braunwald's Textbook of Cardiology, Harrison's Textbook of Medicine, Cecil & Lobe Textbook of Medicine, others; contbr. articles to profl. jours. Served as capt. M.C., AUS, 1946-48. Recipient Bicentennial award in internal medicine Columbia U., 1967, Disting. Alumnus award Mt. Sinai Hosp., 1989, Thewlis award Am. Geriatric Soc., 1990. Master ACP (bd. regents 1978, v.p. 1984, Bruce medal for preventive medicine 1985), Am. Coll. Rheumatology; mem. Am. Heart Assn. (mem. exec. com., pres. coun. on rheumatic fever and congenital ACP disease 1965-67), Am. Fedn. Clin. Rsch., Am. Rheumatism Assn., Am. Soc. Clin. Investigation, Cen. Soc. Clin. Rsch. (v.p. 1973-74, pres. 1974-75), Assn. Profs. Medicine (pres. 1975-76), Am. Assn. Immunologists, Assn. Am. Physicians, Infectious Disease Soc. Am. (coun. 1968-70), Phi Beta Kappa, Alpha Omega Alpha.

STOLLERY, ROBERT, construction company executive; b. Edmonton, Alta., Can., May 1, 1924; s. Willie Charles and Kate (Catlin) S.; m. Shirley Jean Hopper, June 11, 1947; children: Carol, Janet, Douglas. B.Sc. Eng., U. Alta., 1949, LL.D. (hon.), 1985; hon. LL.D., Concordia U., Montreal, Que., 1986. Field engr. Poole Constrn. Ltd., Edmonton, 1949-54, project mgr., 1954-64, v.p., 1964-69, pres., 1969-81; chmn. bd. PCL Constrn. Group Inc., Edmonton, 1979-93; chmn. PCL Constrn. HOldings, Edmonton, 1993—; bd. dirs. TransCanada Pipelines, Melcor Devels. Ltd., Edmonton, Alta., Toronto Dominion Bank. Chmn. bus. adv. coun. U. Alta., gov. of trustees; chmn. Edmonton Community Found. Recipient Exec. of Yr. award Inst. Cert. Mgmt. Cons. of Alta., 1988, Can. Businessman of Yr. award U. Alta., 1993. Fellow Can. Acad. Engring.; mem. Assn. Profl. Engrs. (Frank Spragins Meml. award 1981), Engring. Inst. Can. (Julian C. Smith medal 1990), Conf. Bd. Can. (vice chmn. 1980-82), Constrn. Assn. Edmonton (pres. 1972, Claude Alston Meml. award), Can. Constrn. Assn. (v.p. 1970, Can. Businessman of the Yr. award 1993). Conservative. Mem. United Ch. of Canada. Club: Mayfair Golf and Country (Edmonton). Office: PCL Construction Group Inc, 5410 99 St, Edmonton, AB Canada T6E 3P4

STOLLEY, ALEXANDER, advertising executive; b. Coethen Anhalt, Germany, May 12, 1922; came to U.S., 1923, naturalized, 1929; s. Mihail and Tatiana (Rainich) Stolarevsky; m. Patricia Martin, June 26, 1944 (dec. Aug. 1970); children: Christopher, Peter, Laura Stolley Smith, Annabel Stolley Hetzer, Megan Stolley Berry; m. Bette Scott Vogt, June 15, 1973. M.E., U. Cin., 1948. With Cin. Milacron, Inc., 1941-50, dir. employee relations, 1948-50; with Northlich, Stolley, Inc., Cin., 1950-89, exec. v.p., 1959-67, pres., 1967-84; chmn. Northlich, Stolley, LaWarre, Inc. (formerly Northlich, Stolley, Inc.), Cin., 1984-89. Mem. exec. com. Cincinnatus Assn., 1968-73, sec., 1970-71, v.p., 1971-72, pres., 1972-73; mem. Cin. Council on World Affairs, 1969—; chmn. Contemporary Arts Center, Cin., 1966-67; mem. exec. com. Cin. Conv. and Visitors Bur., 1975, chmn. long range planning com., 1983; trustee Cin. Symphony Orch., 1969-75. Served to 1st lt. AUS, 1943-46. Mem. Bus., Profl. Advt. Assn., Greater Cin. C. of C. (exec. com. 1982-83). Clubs: Cincinnati Country, Cincinnati Tennis, University, Gyro., Literary, Gasparilla Beach, Lemon Bay Golf, Boca Bay Pass. Home: 2363 Bedford Ave Cincinnati OH 45208-2656 Home (winter): PO Box 1339 Boca Grande FL 33921-1339

STOLLEY, PAUL DAVID, medical educator, researcher; b. Pawling, N.Y., June 17, 1937; s. Herman and Rosalie (Chertock) S.; m. Jo Ann Goldenberg, June 13, 1959; children: Jonathan, Dorie, Anna. B.A., Lafayette Coll., 1957; M.D., Cornell U., 1962; M.P.H., Johns Hopkins U., 1968; M.A. hon., U. Pa., 1976. Diplomate: Am. Coll. Preventive Medicine, Am. Coll. Epidemiology. Intern U. Wis. Med. Ctr., 1962-63, resident in medicine, 1963-64; med. officer USPHS, Washington, 1964-67; asst. prof. Johns Hopkins Sch. Pub. Health, Balt., 1968-71, assoc. prof., 1971-76; Herbert C. Rorer prof. medicine U. Pa. Sch. Medicine, Phila., 1976-91; prof. and chmn. dept. epidemiology U. Md. Sch. Medicine, Balt., 1991—. Co-author: Foundations of Epidemiology, 3d edit., 1994, Epidemiology: Investigating Disease, 1995; contbg. author: Case-Control Studies, 1982; mem. editl. bd. New Eng. Jour. Medicine, 1989-93, Milbank Quar., Health and Soc., 1986—; assoc. editor Clin. Pharmacology and Therapeutics, 1987-93; contbr. articles to med. jours. Mem. Physicians for Social Responsibility, 1961—. Served to lt. comdr. USPHS, 1964-67. Fellow ACP; mem. Am. Coll. Epidemiology (pres. 1987-89), Inst. Medicine of NAS, Soc. Epidemiol. Rsch. (pres. 1982-84), Am. Epidemiol. Soc. (pres. 1994—), Internat. Epidemiol. Assn. (treas. 1982-84), Johns Hopkins Soc. Scholars. Home: Watermark Pl Apt 106 10001 Windstream Dr Columbia MD 21044 Office: Univ of Md Sch Medicine 660 W Redwood St Baltimore MD 21201-1541

STOLLEY, RICHARD BROCKWAY, journalist; b. Peoria, Ill., Oct. 3, 1928; s. George Brockway and Stella (Sherman) S.; m. Anne Elizabeth Shawber, Oct. 2, 1954 (div. 1981); children—Lisa Anne, Susan Hope, Melinda Ruth, Martha Brockway. B.S. in Journalism, Northwestern U., 1952, M.S., 1953; LL.D. (hon.), Villa Maria Coll., 1976. Sports editor Pekin (Ill.) Daily Times, 1944-46; reporter Chgo. Sun-Times, 1953; mem. staff weekly Life mag., 1953-73; bur. chief weekly Life mag., Los Angeles, 1961-64, Washington, 1964-68; sr. editor weekly Life mag., Europe, 1968-70; asst. mng. editor weekly Life mag., N.Y.C., 1971-73; mng. editor monthly Life mag., N.Y.C., 1982-86; founding mng. editor People mag., N.Y.C., 1974-82, Picture Week mag., N.Y.C., 1985-86; dir. spl. projects Time Inc., N.Y.C., 1987-89; editorial dir. Time Inc. Time Warner Inc., N.Y.C., 1989-93, sr. editl. adviser, 1993—. Introd. to Leigh A. Wiener, Marilyn: A Hollywood Farewell: The Death and Funeral of Marilyn Monroe, 1990; editor People Celebrates People: The Best of 20 Unforgettable Years, 1994. Bd. dirs. Dirksen Congl. Rsch. Ctr., Pekin, Ill.; chmn. Twins Found., Providence; bd. govs. Nat. Parkinson Found., Miami, Fla.; pres. Child Care Action Campaign, N.Y.C.; bd. trustees N.Y.C. Citizens Crime Commn. With USN, 1946-48. Recipient Alumni merit award Northwestern U., 1977, Alumni medal Northwestern U., 1994; inducted into Am. Soc. Magazine Editors' Hall of Fame, 1996. Mem. Am. Soc. Mag. Editors (pres. 1982-84), Nat. Press Club, Overseas Press Club, Century Assn., Kappa Tau Alpha, Sigma Delta Chi.

STOLLMAN, ISRAEL, city planner; b. N.Y.C., Mar. 15, 1923; s. Philip and Yetta (Strelchik) S.; m. Mary Florence Callahan, Dec. 27, 1953; children—Susan Elisabeth, Katharine Rachel, Sarah Ellen. B.S. in Social Sci, CCNY, 1947; M. City Planning, MIT, 1948. Planner Cleve. Planning Commn., 1948-51; planning dir. Youngstown, Ohio, 1951-57; prof., chmn. div. city and regional planning Ohio State U., 1957-68; exec. dir. Am. Soc. Planning Ofcls., 1968-78; exec. dir. Am. Planning Assn., Washington, 1978-93, cons., 1994—; lectr. Western Res. U., 1949-51, U. Chgo., 1968-69, U. Va., 1994—; pres. Assn. Collegiate Sch. Planning, 1966-67; chmn. Charles E. Merriam Center Pub. Adminstrn., 1977-93. Trustee Alfred Bettman Found.; bd. govs. Met. Housing and Planning Council Chgo., v.p., 1969-79. Served with USAAF, 1943-45. Mem. Am. Inst. Cert. Planners (exec. dir. emeritus), Internat. Fedn. Housing and Planning (bur. mem.), Soc. for Am. City and Regional Planning History (trustee 1996—), Lambda Alpha. Avocation: stereoscopy. Home and Office: 1708 Swann St NW Washington DC 20009-5535

STOLNITZ, GEORGE JOSEPH, economist, educator, demographer; b. N.Y.C., Apr. 4, 1920; s. Isidore and Julia (Jurman) S.; m. Monique Jeanne Delley, Aug. 26, 1976; children: Cindy, Wendy, Dia. BA, CCNY, 1939; MA, Princeton U., 1942, PhD, 1952. Statistician U.S. Bur. Census, 1940-41; rsch. assoc. Princeton U. Office of Population Rsch., 1948-56; asst. prof. Princeton U., 1953-56; prof. econs. Ind. U., Bloomington, 1956-90, prof. emeritus, 1990—; dir. Ind. U. Internat. Devel. Rsch. Ctr., Bloomington, 1967-72, Ind. U. Population Inst. for Rsch. and Tng., Bloomington, 1986-91; prin. officer Population and Econ. Devel. UN, N.Y.C., 1976-78; cons. Ford Found., U.S. Congress, Rockefeller Found., UN, U.S. Dept. Commerce, U.S. Dept. Energy, U.S. Dept. HHS, U.S. Dept. State; vis. rsch. scholar Resources for the Future, 1965-67; vis. scholar Poplulation Reference Bur., 1987-88. Author books; contbr. numerous articles in population and devel. fields, testimonies on pub. utility costs of capital. Capt. USAF, 1942-46. Nat. Sci. Found. fellow, 1959-60. Mem. Population Assn. Am. (pres. 1983), Am. Econ. Assn., Am. Statis. Assn., Econometric Soc., Internat. Union Sci. Study of Population, Cosmos Club. Home: 2636 E Covenanter Ct Bloomington IN 47401-5408 Office: Ind U Population Inst Poplars # 738 Bloomington IN 47405 *Challenges are rarely more forbidding in fact than in anticipation. Early coping often pays off; faintheartedness has higher risk of loss.*

STOLOFF, NORMAN STANLEY, materials engineering educator, researcher; b. Bklyn., Oct. 16, 1934; s. William F. and Lila (Dickman) S.; m. Helen Teresa Arcuri, May 15, 1971; children: Michael E., Linda M., David M., Stephen L. BMetE, NYU, 1955; MS, Columbia U., 1956, PhD, 1961. Metall. engr. Pratt & Whitney Aircraft, East Hartford, Conn., 1956-58; prin. rsch. scientist Ford Sci. Lab., Dearborn, Mich., 1961-65; asst. prof. materials engring. Rensselaer Polytechnic Inst., Troy, N.Y., 1965-68, assoc. prof., 1968-71, prof., 1971—; cons. Electric Boat div. Gen. Dynamics, New London, Conn., 1987-89, Martin Marietta Rsch. Labs., Balt., 1990, Rockwell Internat., Thousand Oaks, Calif., 1989, Cummins Engine Co., Columbus, Ind., 1991. Editor: (with others) High Temperature Ordered Intermetallic Alloys, 1985, Superalloys II, 1987, Physical Metallurgy and Processing of Intermetallic Compounds, 1996, others; contbr. articles to profl. jours. Recipient Fulbright Rsch. award U.S. State Dept., 1968-69, DOE Fellowship Assoc. Western U., 1995. Fellow Am. Soc. Materials Internat.; mem. The Minerals, Metals and Materials Soc., Materials Rsch. Soc. Avocations: hiking, fishing, reading. Office: Rensselaer Polytechnic Inst Materials Sci Engring Dept MRC Bldg Troy NY 12180-3590

STOLOV, JERRY FRANKLIN, healthcare executive; b. Kansas City, Mo., Jan. 31, 1946; s. I. Paul and Marion R. (Rothberg) Stolov. BA, Washington U., 1968; MPA, Roosvelt U., 1972. Adminstrv. asst. U. Ill. Chgo. Circle & Med. Sch. Campuses, Chgo., 1970-75; exec. dir. Hosp. Hill Health Svcs. Corp., Kansas City, Mo., 1976—; also bd. dirs. Hosp. Hill Health Svcs. Corp., Kansas City, 1976—; bd. dirs. Kansas City Psychoanalytic Found., 1996—; adv. dir. Mchts. Bank Corp., Kansas City, 1985-92. Leadership tng. C. of C., Kansas City, 1977-78. Mem. Assn. Am. Med. Colls. (group on faculty practice), Med. Group Mgmt. Assn., Internat. City Mgrs. Assn., Am. Soc. Pub. Health Adminstrs., Acad. Polit. Sci. (contbg. mem.). Office: Hosp Hill Health Svcs Corp 800 Hospital Hill Ctr 2310 Holmes St Kansas City MO 64108-2634

STOLOV, WALTER CHARLES, physician, rehabilitation educator; b. N.Y.C., Jan. 6, 1928; s. Arthur and Rose F. (Gordon) S.; m. Anita Carvel Noodelman, Aug. 9, 1953; children: Nancy, Amy, Lynne. BS in Physics, CCNY, 1948; MA in Physics, U. Minn., 1951, MD, 1956. Diplomate Am. Bd. Phys. Med. and Rehab., Am. Bd. Electrodiagnostic Medicine. Physicist U.S. Naval Gun Factory, Nat. Bur. Stds., Washington, 1948-49; teaching and rsch. asst. U. Minn., Mpls., 1950-54; from instr. to assoc. prof. U. Wash., Seattle, 1960-70, prof., 1970—, also chmn., 1987—; editl. bd. Archives Phys. Medicine and Rehab., 1967-78, Muscle and Nerve, 1983-89, 92-95; cons. Social Security Adminstrn., Seattle, 1975—; sec. Am. Bd. Electrodiagnostic Medicine, 1995—. Co-editor: Handbook of Severe Disability, 1981; contbr. articles to profl. jours. Surgeon USPHS, 1956-57. Recipient Townsend Harris medal CCNY, 1990. Fellow AAAS, Am. Heart Assn.; mem. Am. Acad. Phys. Medicine & Rehab. (Disting. Clinician award 1987), Am. Congress Rehab. Medicine (Essay award 1959), Assn. Acad. Physiatrists, Am. Assn. Electrodiagnostic Medicine (pres. 1987-88), Am. Spinal Cord Injury Assn. Avocations: dancing, singing. Office: U Wash Box 356490 1959 NE Pacific St Seattle WA 98195-0004

STOLPEN, SPENCER, professional sports team executive. Pres. Charlotte Hornets. Office: Charlotte Hornets 100 Hive Dr Charlotte NC 28217*

STOLPER, EDWARD MANIN, secondary education educator; b. Boston, Dec. 16, 1952; s. Saul James and Frances A. (Liberman) S.; m. Lauren Beth Adoff, June 3, 1973; children: Jennifer Ann, Daniel Aaron. AB, Harvard U., 1974; M Philosophy, U. Edinburgh, Scotland, 1976; PhD, Harvard U., 1979. Asst. prof. geology Calif. Inst. Tech., Pasadena, 1979-82, assoc. prof. geology, 1982-83, prof. geology, 1983-90, William E. Leonhard prof. geology, 1990—, chmn. divsn. geol. and planetary sci., 1994—. Marshall scholar Marshall Aid Commemoration Commn., 1974-76, recipient Newcomb Cleve. prize AAAS, 1984, F.W. Clarke medal Geochem. Soc., 1985. Fellow Meteoritical Soc. (Nininger Meteorite award 1976), Am. Geophys. Union (James B. Macelwane award 1986), Mineral Soc. Am., Am. Acad. Arts and Scis.; mem. NAS, Geol. Soc. Am., Sigma Xi. Office: Calif Inst Tech Div Geol Planetary Sci Pasadena CA 91125

STOLPER, PINCHAS ARYEH, religious organization executive, rabbi; b. Bklyn., Oct. 22, 1931; s. David Bernard and Nettie (Rosch) S.; m. Elaine Liebman, Nov. 22, 1955; children: Akiva Psachia, Michal Hadassah Cohen, Malka Tova Kaweblum. B.A., Bklyn. Coll., 1952; M.A., New Sch. for Social Research, 1971. Rabbinical ordination Chaim Berlin-Gur Aryeh Rabbinical Acad., 1956; dir. L.I. Zionist Youth Commn., 1956-57; dir. public relations, adminstrv. dean, adviser to English-speaking students Ponevez Yeshiva, Bnai Brak, Israel, 1957-59; also prin.; instr. English and Talmud Gimnazia Bnei Akiva High Sch., 1959-77; nat. dir. youth div. Union Orthodox Jewish Congregations Am., Nat. Conf. Synagogue Youth, N.Y.C., 1959-76; founder NCSY, Torah Fund, Ben Zakai Honor Soc. Union Orthodox Jewish Congregations Am., Nat. Conf. Synagogue Youth, 1959-76; editor Jewish Youth Monthly, 1967—; exec. v.p. Union Orthodox Jewish Congregations Am., 1976-94, sr. exec., 1994—; adj. prof. Jewish studies Touro Coll., N.Y., 1975—; mem. publs., Israel, campus commns., staff mem. responsible for edn., Talmud Torah, day sch. commns. Union Orthodox Jewish Congregations Am., 1965—; del. White House Conf. on Children and Youth, 1961; cons. N. Am. Jewish Youth Conf., 1967—. Author: Tested Teen Age Activities, 1961, rev. edit., 1964, Day of Delight, 1961, Tefilah, Text and Source Book, 1963, Revelation What Happened on Sinai, 1966, Prayer, The Proven Path, 1967, The Road to Responsible Jewish Adulthood, 1967, Jewish Alternatives in Love, Dating and Marriage, 1985, The Sacred Trust, Love, Dating and Marriage, The Jewish View, 1996, Beyond Belief, Revelation for the Modern Jew, 1996; contbr. numerous articles, plays, and revs. to Jewish publs.; columnist The Jewish Press, 1994. Nat. dir. Nat. Conf. Synagogue Youth, 1995—; bd. dirs. Chaim Berlin Torah Schs.-Mesivta Rabbi Chaim Berlin-Rabbinical Acad., 1965—. Recipient Alumi Amudim award Mesivta Rabbi Chaim Berlin-Gur Aryeh Inst., 1967, award Assn. Orthodox Jewish Tchrs., 1975, citation Rabbinical Coun. Am., 1984, Jabotinsky medal, 1990, Alumnus of Yr. award Flatbush Yeshiva, 1989, Joseph K. Miller Achdut Yisrael award Shaalvim Yeshiva, 1993. Mem. Rabbinical Coun. Am. Home: 954 E 7th St Brooklyn NY 11230-2706 Office: Union Orthodox Jewish Cong of Am 333 7th Ave New York NY 10001-5004

STOLPER, WOLFGANG FRIEDRICH, retired economist, educator; b. Vienna, Austria, May 13, 1912; came to U.S., 1934, naturalized, 1940; s. Gustav and Paula (Deutsch) S.; m. Marta Voegeli, Aug. 11, 1938 (dec. July 1972); children: Thomas E., Matthew W.; m. Margot Kaufmann, 1979. M.A., Harvard U., 1935, Ph.D., 1938; Dr. honoris causa, U. Saarbrücken, Grosses Verdienstkreuz, Fed. Republic Germany, 1984. Instr. Harvard U., 1936-41; asst. prof. econs. Swarthmore Coll., 1941-48, assoc. prof., 1948-49; assoc. prof. U. Mich., 1949-53, prof., 1953-82; dir. U. Mich. (Center for Research on Econ. Devel.), 1963-70; guest prof. U. Zurich, summers, 1952, 69-79; head econ. planning unit Fed. Ministry for Econ. Devel., Lagos, Nigeria., 1960-62; cons. USAID, Ford Found., IBRD, UN; vis. prof. Inst. F. Weltwirtschaft, Kiel, 1987. Author: (with P.A. Samuelson) Protection and Real Wages, 1941, The Structure of the East German Economy, 1960, Planning Without Facts, 1966, Joseph A. Schumpeter 1883-1950. The Public Life of the Private Man, 1994; contbr. articles to profl. jours. Guggenheim fellow, 1947-48; Fulbright prof. Heidelberg, 1966; recipient Bernhard Harms medal U. Kiel, 1985. Mem. Am. Econ. Assns., Internat. Schumpeter Soc. (founding pres.). Home: 1051 Lincoln Ave Ann Arbor MI 48104-3526 Office: U Mich Dept Econs Ann Arbor MI 48109

STOLTZ, ERIC, actor; b. American Samoa, 1961. Studied with Peggy Fury, William Traylor, U. So. Calif. Actor: (stage prodns.) One Flew Over the Cuckoo's Nest, 1978, Hello, Dolly!, 1979, The Seagull, 1980, The Widow Claire, 1987, Our Town, 1988 (Tony award nomination Drama Desk nomination), The American Plan, 1990, Two Shakespearean Actors, 1992, Down the Road, 1993; (feature films) Fast Times at Ridgemont High, 1981, Wild Life, 1983, Mask, 1984 (Golden Globe award nomination 1985), Lionheart, 1986, Some Kind of Wonderful, 1987, Sister, Sister, Haunted Summer, Code Name Emerald, 1988, Say Anything, 1989, Manifesto, 1989, The Fly II, 1989, Memphis Belle, 1990, Singles, 1991, The Waterdance, 1991, , Naked in New York, 1993, Killing Zoe, 1993, God's Army (renamed The Prophesy), 1993, Pulp Fiction, 1994, Little Women, 1994, Rob Roy, 1995, Fluke, 1995, Kicking and Screaming, 1995, Grace of My Heart, 1995, Inside, 1996, Two Days in the Valley, 1996; (TV movies(the Grass Is Greener, 1980, The Violation of Sarah McDavid, 1982, Thursday's Child, 1982, Paper Dolls, 1982, A Killer in the Family, 1983, Foreign Affairs, 1993, Roommates, 1994; (TV episodes) St. Elsewhere, 1983, Fallen Angels, 1994, (13 episodes) Mad About You, 1995, Partners, 1995; actor, prodr. Bodies, at Rest and Motion, 1993, Sleep With Me, 1993. Office: 9830 Wilshire Blvd Beverly Hills CA 90212-1804

STOLTZFUS, VICTOR EZRA, academic administrator; b. Martinsburg, Pa., Mar. 24, 1934; s. Ira Mark and Elsie Rebecca (Shenk) S.; m. Marie Histand Althouse, June 19, 1955; children: Kristina, Rebecca, Malinda. BA in Social Sci., Goshen Coll., 1956; BD, Goshen Bibl. Sem., 1959; MA in Sociology, Kent State U., 1964; PhD in Sociology, Pa. State U., 1970. Pastor North Lima (Ohio) Mennonite Ch., 1959-66; instr. Youngstown (Ohio) U., 1964-66, Pa. State U., University Park, 1966-70; prof. Eastern Ill. U., Charleston, 1970-81; dean Goshen (Ind.) Coll., 1981-84, pres., 1984—. Contbr. articles to profl. jours. Mem. Am. Assn. Higher Edn. Lodge: Rotary. Avocation: raquetball. Home: 305 Reservoir Pl Goshen IN 46526-5231 Office: Goshen Coll Office of Pres Goshen IN 46526

STOLTZMAN, RICHARD LESLIE, clarinetist; b. Omaha, July 12, 1942; s. Leslie Harvey and Dorothy Marilyn (Spohn) S.; m. Lucy Jean Chapman, June 6, 1976; children: Peter John, Margaret Anne. MusB summa cum laude, Ohio State U., 1964; MusM magna cum laude, Yale U., 1967; postgrad., Columbia U. Tchrs. Coll., 1967-70. Mem. faculty Calif. Inst. Arts, 1970-75; Western regional dir. Young Audiences, Inc., 1972-74, mem. nat. adv. bd. Appeared in concerts throughout U.S., Europe, Japan, Hong Kong, Australia, 1976—; rec. artist, 1974—; debut LaScala, Milan, 1981, Carnegie Hall, N.Y.C., 1982; appeared in world premiere of Einar Englund concerto Helsinki Festival, 1991, Toro Takemitsu concerto (Fantasma/Cantos) Wales BBC, 1991, U.S. premiere of Lukas Foss concerto L.A. Philharm. Orch., 1991, Copland concert, 1993 (Emmy award for best performing arts video 1993), world premiere of Leonard Bernstein sonata for clarinet and orch. Pacific Music Festival, Sapporo, Japan, 1994. Recipient Horatio Parker award Yale U., 1966, Avery Fisher prize, 1977, Martha Baird Rockefeller award, 1973, Grammy award, 1983, Avery Fisher artist award, 1986, Disting. Alumnus award Ohio State U., 1990. Home: 6 Lincolnshire Way Winchester MA 01890-3048 Office: 201 W 54th St Apt 4C New York NY 10019-5521 *Be mindful of the breath. It gives life to the sound which sends music to the soul.*

STOLWIJK, JAN ADRIANUS JOZEF, physiologist, biophysicist; b. Amsterdam, Netherlands, Sept. 29, 1927; came to U.S., 1955, naturalized, 1962; s. Leonard and Cornelia Agnes (Van Der Bijl) S.;m. Deborah Rose, 1990. B.S., Wageningen U., Netherlands, 1948, M.S., 1951, Ph.D., 1955. Biophysicist John B. Pierce Found., New Haven, 1957-61; asso. fellow John B. Pierce Found. Lab., 1961-64, fellow, 1964, asso. dir., 1974-89; instr. dept. physiology Yale U. Sch. Medicine, New Haven, 1962-63, asst. prof., 1964-68, asst. prof. epidemiology, 1968-69, asso. prof., 1969-75, prof., 1975—, dir. grad. studies, dept. epidemiology and public health, 1992—, chmn. dept. epidemiology and pub. health, 1982-89; research fellow Harvard U., 1955-56; cons. divsn. disease prevention Conn. Health Dept., 1977—; cons. vehicle inspection program Dept. Motor Vehicles, 1979-83; mem. sci. adv. bd. EPA, 1985-93; mem. tech. adv. bd. Dept. Commerce, 1972-77. Mem. Am. Physiol. Soc., Biophys. Soc., Aerospace Med. Soc., Am. Public Health Assn., AAAS, Internat. Biometeorol. Soc., Soc. Occupational and Environ. Health, Am. Conf. Govt. Indsl. Hygienists, ASHRAE, Conn. Acad. Sci. and Engring. Club: Cosmos. Home: 165 Dromara Rd Guilford CT 06437-2391 Office: PO Box 8034 60 College St New Haven CT 06520

STOLZ, BENJAMIN ARMOND, foreign language educator; b. Lansing, Mich., Mar. 28, 1934; s. Armond John and Mabel May (Smith) S.; m. Mona Eleanor Seelig, June 16, 1962; children: Elizabeth Mona, John Benjamin. A.B., U. Mich., Ann Arbor, 1955; certificat, U. Libre de Bruxelles, Belgium, 1956; A.M., Harvard U., 1957, Ph.D., 1965. Mem. faculty U. Mich., 1964—, prof. Slavic langs. and lits., 1972—, chmn. dept., 1971-85, 89-91; cons. in field. Editor: Papers in Slavic Philology, 1977; co-editor: Oral Literature and the Formula, 1976, Cross Currents, 1982-85, Language and Literary Theory, 1984, Mich. Slavic Publs., 1990—; co-editor, translator: (Konstantin Mihailovic): Memoirs of a Janissary, 1975; contbr. articles to profl. pubs. Served to lt. (j.g.) USNR, 1957-60. Recipient Orion E. Scott award humanities U. Mich., 1954, Fulbright scholar, 1955-56; Fgn. Area fellow Yugoslavia, 1963-64; Fulbright-Hays rsch. fellow Eng. and Yugoslavia, 1970-71; grantee Am. Coun. Learned Socs., 1968-70, 73, Internat. Rsch. and Exchs. Bd., 1985, 87, Woodrow Wilson Ctr., 1992. Mem. Am. Assn. Advancement Slavic Studies, Am. Assn. Tchrs. Slavic and East European Langs., Midwest MLA (pres. 1976), Huron Valley Tennis Club, Phi Beta Kappa, Phi Kappa Phi, Delta Upsilon. Democrat. Home: 1060 Baldwin Ave Ann Arbor MI 48104-3504 Office: Univ Mich 3040 Mlb Ann Arbor MI 48109

STOLZ, KATHY LYNN, public relations professional; b. Portland, Ind., Mar. 14, 1953; d. Roger Cloyce and Luetta June (Smith) Bowen; m. Dennis Lee Stolz, Aug. 13, 1972; 1 child, Elizabeth Grace. BS, Ind. U., 1975; MA, Ball State U., 1981. Cert. secondary tchr., Ind. Tchr. English/journalism Woodlan High Sch., Woodburn, Ind., 1975-77; co-owner Georgetown Clock Shop, Fort Wayne, Ind., 1975-77; G.E.D. tutor Lockyear Jr. Coll., Indpls., 1977; English tchr. Northview Jr. High Sch., Indpls., 1978; English, journalism tchr. Shelbyville (Ind.) High Sch., 1978-82; dir. alumni & parents rels. Franklin (Ind.) Coll., 1982-88; sales rep. Horace Mann Ins., Springfield, Ind., 1988; info./edn. coord. Meth. Hosp. of Ind. Cancer Ctr., Indpls., 1989-94, program devel. coord. health promotions, 1994—; cons. assoc. Pamela K. Boggs & Assocs., Indpls., 1991—. Sec., mem. City of Franklin Plan Commn., 1989-93; sec., precinct committeeman Johnson County Dem. Ctrl. Com., Franklin, 1988—; vol. Ctrl. Ind. Area Am. Cancer Soc., 1989—, United Way of Ctrl. Ind., 1993—; pres. Johnson County Lit. Coalition, Franklin, 1988, Johnson County Youth Svcs. Bur., Franklin, 1987, 88; mem. Historic Franklin, Inc., 1992—; Sunday sch. tchr. Grace United Meth. Ch., Franklin, 1987—. Recipient Cert. of Merit Cen. Ind. Area Am. Cancer Soc., 1990. Mem. Internat. Assn. of Bus. Communicators, Ind. U. Alumni Assn., Ball State U. Alumni Assn. Democrat. United Methodist. Avocations: current events, local politics, photography, movies, home renovation. Home: 51 S Edwards St Franklin IN 46131-2503 Office: Meth Hosp of Ind Inc 1701 Senate Blvd Indianapolis IN 46202-1239

STOLZENBERG, PEARL, fashion designer; b. N.Y.C., Oct. 9, 1946; d. Irving and Anna (Shenkman) S. Student, Fashion Inst. Tech., 1964-66. Textile stylist, designer Forum Fabrics Ltd., N.Y.C., 1966-68; freelance ceiling designer Maxwell's Plum, N.Y.C., 1968; dir. styling Beauknit Corp., N.Y.C., 1969-74; stylist, designer Mi-Bru-San Co., Inc., N.Y.C., 1983-84; gen. mgr. Laissez-Faire Inc., N.Y.C., 1984-85; merchandiser prodn. The Clothing Acad. Inc., N.Y.C., 1986-87; v.p. String of Pearls Knitwear, Inc., N.Y.C., 1988—; pres. Pearl's Cutting Ltd., N.Y.C., 1994—; cons. Tam O'Shanter Textile Ltd., Montreal, 1974-79, Mitsui, Osaka, Japan, 1976-79, Sergio Valente English Town Sportswear, N.Y.C., 1980-84; cons. merchandiser The Fashion Acad., Hollywood Crossing, Inc., N.Y.C.; owner Josu Cutting Inc., Bklyn. Democrat. Jewish. Avocations: fishing, animal conservation, gourmet cooking, physical fitness. Home: 8340 Austin St Apt 1E Jamaica NY 11415-1827 Office: Pearl's Cutting Ltd 410 W 16th St New York NY 10011-5891

STOLZER, LEO WILLIAM, bank executive; b. Kansas City, Mo., Oct. 14, 1934; s. Leo Joseph and Lennie Lucille (Hopp) S.; m. Eleanor Katherine Griffith, Aug. 17, 1957; children: Joan Ellen Stolzer Bolen, Mary Kevin Stolzer Giller. BS in Acctg., Kans. State U., 1957. Teller Union Nat. Bank & Trust Co., Manhattan, Kans., 1960-62, asst. cashier, 1962-63, asst. v.p., 1963-64, v.p., 1964-69, exec. v.p., 1969-72, pres., 1972-80, chmn., CEO, 1980-95; chmn., 1995—; bd. dirs. State Mut. Life Ins. Co., Commerce Bankshares Inc., Commerce Bank-Manhattan; chmn., CEO Griffith Lumber Co.; chmn. Corp. for Am. Banking. Mem. exec. com., vice chair Kans. State U. Found.; trustee Midwest Rsch. Inst.; chmn. Riley County Savs. Bond. Capt. USAF, 1957-60. Recipient Disting. Service award Manhattan Jr. C. of C., 1968, Kans. State U. Advancement award. Mem. Am. Bankers Assn. (past treas., past exec. com., past bd. dirs.), Assn. U.S. Army (bd. dirs. Ft. Riley Ctl. Kans. chpt.), Kans. U. Alumni Assn. (devel. com.), Newcomen Soc. in N.Am. (past Kans. chmn.), KC, Beta Theta Pi. Avocation: skiing. Office: Commerce Bank 727 Poyntz Ave Manhattan KS 66502-6077

STONE, ALAN, container company executive; b. Chgo., Feb. 5, 1928; s. Norman H. and Ida (Finkelstein) S.; children: Christie-Ann Stone Weiss, Joshua. B.S.E., U. Pa., 1951. Trainee, salesman Stone Container Corp., Chgo., 1951-53, dir. mktg. service, 1954-64, gen. mgr., regional mgr., 1964-72, sr. v.p. adminstrn., gen. mgr. energy div., 1972—, also dir.; pres. Atlanta St. Andrews and Bay Line R.R., 1972-94, Abbeville-Grimes R.R., 1972-94, Apache R.R., 1972-94. Pres. Jewish Vocat. Svc., Chgo., 1975-77; v.p. Sinai Temple, Chgo., 1977-84; vice chmn. Roycemore Sch., Evanston, Ill., 1982-87; trustee Brewster Acad., Wolfeboro, N.H.; vol. exec. for overseas needs Citizen's Democracy Corps; vol. cons. for non-profit agys., schs. and librs. Exec. Svc. Corps.; bd. dirs. Gastrointestinal Rsch. Found. Mem. Standard Club, Tavern Club, Bryn Mawr Country Club, Tamarisk Country Club, Long Boat Key Club, Beta Alpha Psi, Phi Eta Sigma, Zeta Beta Tau. Avocations: golf; sports; reading. Office: Stone Container Corp 150 N Michigan Ave Chicago IL 60601

STONE, ALAN A., law and psychiatry educator, psychiatrist; b. 1929. A.B., Harvard U., 1950; M.D., Yale U., 1955. Dir. resident edn. McLean Hosp., 1962-68; lectr. Harvard U., 1966-72, asst. prof. psychiatry, 1966-69, assoc. prof., 1969-72, prof. law and psychiatry, 1972—; Touroff-Glueck prof. Law and Psychiatry, 1982—; mem. adv. com. Am. Bar Found. Project on Mentally Ill, 1967-71; mem. Mass. Gov.'s Com. for Revision Criminal Code, 1968-72; mem. com. on mentally disabled ABA, 1973-77; chmn. Mass. Com. on Psychosurgery, 1974-75; fellow Ctr. Advanced Study in Behavioral Scis., Stanford U., 1980-81; Tanner lectr. Stanford U., 1982. Served as capt. M.C., U.S. Army, 1959-61. Recipient Manfred S. Guttmacher award; Isaac Ray award, 1982. Mem. Group Advancement Psychiatry, Am. Psychiat. Assn. (trustee, v.p., pres.; chmn. com. jud. action 1974-9). Author: (with Onque) Longitudinal Studies of Child Behavior, 1961; Mental Health and Law: A System in Transition, 1975; Law, Psychiatry and Morality: Essays and Analysis, 1984; editor: (with Sue Stone) Abnormal Psychiatry through Literature, 1966; Office: Harvard U Law Sch Cambridge MA 02138

STONE, ALAN JAY, college administrator; b. Ft. Dodge, Iowa, Oct. 15, 1942; s. Hubert H. and Bernice A. (Tilton) S.; m. Jonieta J. Smith; 1 child, Kirsten K. Stone Morlock. BA, Morningside Coll., 1964; MA, U. Iowa, 1966; MTh, U. Chgo., 1968, DMin, 1970; PhD (hon.), Kyonggi U., Korea, 1985; LLD, Stillman Coll., 1991, Sogong U., Korea, 1992. Admissions counselor Morningside Coll., Sioux City, Iowa, 1964-66; dir. admissions, asso. prof. history George Williams Coll., Downers Grove, Ill., 1969-73; v.p. coll. relations Hood Coll., Frederick, Md., 1973-75; v.p. devel. and fin. affairs W.Va. Wesleyan Coll., Buckhannon, 1975-77; dir. devel. U. Maine, 1977-78; pres. Aurora (Ill.) U., 1978-88, Alma (Mich.) Coll., 1988—; bd. dirs. Bank of Alma. Chmn. bd. Mich. Intercollegiate Athletic Assn.; bd. dirs. Mich. Coll. Found., Assn. Ind. Colls. and Univs. of Mich., Mich. Campus Compact, Korean Social Policy Inst., Seoul; chmn. United Way Gratiot County, Strategic Planning Group Gratiot County, Assn. Presbyn. Coll. Pres. Mem. Am. Assn. Higher Edn., Am. Assn. Colls., Renaissance Club, Alma Country Club. Home: 313 Maple Ave Alma MI 48801-2234 Office: Alma Coll Off of Pres Alma MI 48801

STONE, ALAN JOHN, manufacturing company executive, real estate executive; b. Dansville, N.Y., Sept. 9, 1940; s. Guthrie Boyd and Doris Irene (Wolfanger) S.; m. Sandra Barber, Aug. 22, 1964; children: Teri, Timothy, Michael. B.S. in Mech. Engring., Rochester Inst. Tech., 1963; M.B.A., U. Pitts., 1964. Engring. aide Xerox Corp., Webster, N.Y., 1960-63; gen. mgr. plastic component div. Stone Conveyor Co., Inc., Honeoye, N.Y., 1964-67, v.p. sales, 1968; co-founder, chief exec. officer Stone Constrn. Equipment Inc., Honeoye, 1969-86, also com., bd. dirs., 1969—; founder, pres. Canandaigua Apts. Inc., N.Y., 1968-83; pres. Wildtrak, Inc., 1983—; founder, gen. ptnr. Stone Properties, 1986—; dir., co-founder Baker Rental Svc., Inc., 1973-75; met. adv. bd. Chase Lincoln Bank, 1981-84; co-founder, dir. Royal Lines Ltd., 1989-91; bd. dirs. Canadaigua Nat. Bank & Trust Co., chmn. 1994—. Patentee in field. Mem. Town of Richmond (N.Y.) Planning Bd., 1970-75, chmn., 1970-71; mem. Honeoye Ctrl. Sch. Bd. Edn., 1971-76, pres., 1973-74; com. chmn. pack 10 Boy Scouts Am., 1975-78; mem. Ontario County Overall Econ. Devel. Com., 1976-81; bd. dirs. F.F. Thompson Hosp., 1987-91; chmn. fin. com. United Meth. Ch., Allens Hill, 1995. Mem. Honeoye C. of C. (chmn indsl. com. 1974-82), Constrn. Industry Mfrs. Assn. (exec. mem. new bus. challenges coun. 1980-83), Honeoye Valley Assn. (dir. 1991-95, treas. 1993-95), Griswold and Cast Iron Collectors Assn. (treas. 1994—), Honeoye Area Hist. Soc. (bicentennial com. 1989), Young Pres.'s Assn., Grand Slam Club, Safari Internat., Found N.Am. Wild Sheep. Methodist. Home and Office: Box 500 5170 County Road 33 Honeoye NY 14471-0500

STONE, ANDREW GROVER, lawyer; b. L.A., Oct. 2, 1942; s. Frank B. and Meryl (Pickering) S.; divorced; 1 child, John Blair. BA, Yale U., 1965; JD, U. Mich., 1969. Bar: D.C. 1970, U.S. Dist. Ct. D.C. 1970, U.S. Ct. Appeals (D.C. cir.) 1972, Mass. 1981. Assoc. Rogers & Wells, Washington, 1969-71; atty. Bur. Competition, FTC, Washington, 1971-80; antitrust counsel Digital Equipment Corp., Maynard, Mass., 1980-83, mgr. N.E. law group, 1983-86, mgr. headquarters sales law group, 1986-88; asst. general counsel U.S. (acting), 1987, 88; corp counsel Washington, 1988-90; corp. counsel, pub. sect. mktg. Digital Equipment Corp., 1990-91; corp. counsel Thinking Machines Corp., Cambridge, Mass., 1992-95; pvt. practice Wellesley and Marblehead, Mass., 1995—. Corp. mem. Tenacre Country Day Sch., Wellesley, Mass., 1981-88. Mem. ABA (bus. law sect., sci. tech. sect., pub. contracts sect., vice-chmn. comml. products and svcs. com. 1983-84), Mass. Bar Assn. (internat. law steering com. 1993-94), Boston Bar Assn. (co-chair corp. counsel com. 1995—), Licensing Execs. Soc., Am. Arbitration Assn. (comml. arbitrator), Am. Intellectual Property Law Assn., New Eng. Corp. Counsel Assn., Assn. Ind. Gen. Counsel.

STONE, ARTHUR HAROLD, mathematics educator; b. London, Sept. 30, 1916; came to U.S., 1959; s. Aurel P. and Rosa (Schekter) S.; m. Dorothy Maharam, Apr. 12, 1942; children: David A., Ellen R. BA, Cambridge (Eng.) U., 1938, MA, 1939; PhD, Princeton U., 1941. Mem. Inst. Advanced Study, Princeton, N.J., 1941-42; instr. Purdue U., 1942-44; with Geophys. Lab., Washington, 1944-45; fellow Trinity Coll. Cambridge U., 1946-48; lectr. Manchester (Eng.) U., 1948-57, sr. lectr., 1957-61; prof. math. U. Rochester, 1961-87, prof. emeritus, 1987—; adj. prof. Northeastern U., Boston, 1988—; vis. prof. Columbia U., 1961, Yale U., 1965-66; vis. rsch. assoc. U. Calif., Berkeley, 1971-72; vis. fellow Australian Nat. U., Canberra, 1978. Mem. editorial adv. bd. Topology and Its Applications, 1971-93; mem. internat. adv. bd. Mathematica Japonica, 1991—; contbr. articles to profl. jours. Mem. AAUP, Am. Math. Soc., Math. Assn. Am., London Math. Soc. Jewish. Office: Northeastern U Dept Math Boston MA 02115

STONE, ARTHUR JOSEPH, judge; b. St. Peters, N.S., Can., 1929; s. George and Charlotte S.; m. Anna M., 1956. B.A., St. Francis Xavier U., Antigonish, N.S., 1952; LL.B., Dalhousie Law Sch., 1955; LL.M., Harvard U., 1956. Assoc., Wright & McTaggart and successor firms, 1957-83; justice Fed. Ct. Appeal, Ottawa, Ont., Can., 1983—; justice Ct. Martial Appeal Ct., Ottawa, Ont., Can., 1983—; lectr. faculty of law U. Toronto, Ont., 1971-76. Contbr. articles to profl. publs. Mem. N.S. Barristers Soc., Law Soc. of Upper Can., N.B. Barristers Soc., Law Soc. of B.C., Can. Bar Assn. (nat. exec. com. 1971-73), Can. Tax Found. (gov. 1977-79), Can. Maritime Law Assn. (pres.), Harvard U. Law Sch. Assn. Ont. (chmn. law sch. fund). Club: Toronto Marine (pres. 1977-78). Office: Fed Ct, Kent & Wellington Sts, Ottawa, ON Canada K1A 0H9

STONE, BEVERLEY, former university dean, former dean of students; b. Norfolk, Va., June 10, 1916; d. James L. and Clara (Thompson) S. B.A. in Chemistry, Randolph-Macon Woman's Coll., 1936; M.A. in Student Personnel Adminstrn, Columbia U., 1940, profl. diploma, 1956; L.H.D. (hon.), Purdue U., 1986. Tchr. Norfolk High Sch., 1936-41; instr. Tusculum Coll., 1941-43; asst. dean women U. Ark., 1946-50, assoc. dean women, 1952-54, dean women, 1954-55; asst. dean women Purdue U., 1956-67, assoc. dean women, 1967-68, dean women, 1968-74, dean students, 1974-80, ret., 1980. Author (with Barbara Cook); monograph Counseling Women, 1973. Mem. pres.'s coun. Purdue U., 1985-91; trustee Katherine S. Phillips Trust Fund, 1978-84; mem. lay bd. St. Elizabeth's Hosp., 1974-80, Salvation Army, Lafayette Art Mus., 1982-85, Crisis Ctr.; mem. Tippecanoe County Bd. Zoning Appeals, 1982-83, West Lafayette Cuty Coun., 1984-88; past mem. adminstrv. bd., found. bd., hon. steward 1st United Meth. Ch., West Lafayette. Lt. comdr. UNSR, 1943-46, 52-55. Recipient Outstanding Woman in Edn. award Coalition of Women's Orgns. in Greater Lafayette Area, 1978, Disting. Alumni award Purdue Pres.'s Coun., 1980, Disting. Woman award Purdue U., 1980; named Sagamore of the Wabash Gov. Ind., 1980, 85; Nat. Mortar Bd. Fellowship named in honor, 1994-95. Mem. AAUW (past pres. Fayetteville, Ark.), Nat. Assn. Women Deans and Counselors (treas., chmn. hdqs. adv. com. 1973-75, mem. 1975-79), Ind. Assn. Women Deans and Counselors, Mental Health Assn., Purdue Women's Club, Parlor Club, Randolph-Macon Women's Coll.. Conway Club, Mortar Bd. (nat. fellowship named in her honor 1994-95), Phi Beta Kappa, Kappa Delta Pi, Omicron Delta Kappa, Pi Lambda Theta, Alpha Lambda Delta (v.p. 1975-79), Zeta Tau Alpha. Home: 1807 Western Dr West Lafayette IN 47906-2239

STONE, DAVID BARNES, investment advisor; b. Brookline, Mass., Sept. 2, 1927; s. Robert Gregg and Bertha L. (Barnes) S.; m. Sara Cruikshank, June 16, 1951 (div. July 1976); children—David Stevenson, Benjamin Barnes, Peter Cruikshank, Jonathan Fitch, Andrew Hasbrouck; m. Ellen J. Desmond, Feb. 16, 1980; 1 son, Daniel Desmond. Grad., Milton (Mass.) Acad., 1945; A.B., Harvard, 1950, M.B.A., 1952; D.C.S. (hon.), Suffolk U., 1969; LL.D., Northeastern U., 1974; L.H.D., Curry Coll., 1981. Vice pres. Hayden, Stone Inc. (and predecessor), 1962-65, chmn. exec. com., 1965-67; pres. N.Am. Mgmt. Corp., 1968-78, chmn., 1978—; trustee Mass. Fin. Svcs. Group of Mut. Funds, 1989—; pres. Stonetex Oil Corp., Dallas. Pres. bd. trustees New Eng. Aquarium, 1959-70, chmn. bd. trustees, 1970-76; bd. overseers Boys Club Boston, 1956-61, treas., 1961-67; trustee Charles Hayden Found., 1966-92, Wellesley Coll., vice chmn. bd., 1992-95; chmn. Meml. Dr. Trust; mem. Woods Hole Oceanographic Instn. With U.S. Mcht. Marines, 1945-47. Mem. Investment Bankers Assn. (chmn. New Eng. group 1963, bd. govs. 1964-67). Clubs: Kittansett (Marion, Mass.); Country (Brookline, Mass.). Home: Great Hill Marion MA 02738 also: 282 Beacon St Boston MA 02116-1101 Office: North American Mgmt Ten Post Office Sq Ste 300 Boston MA 02109

STONE, DAVID DEADERICK, physician, educator; b. Bristol, Va., Feb. 8, 1932; s. Albert Wallace and Margaret Clifton (Deaderick) S.; children: Margaret E., Caroline A., Jennifer R., Shannon D. BA cum laude, Vanderbilt U., 1954; MD, U. Va., 1958. Diplomate Am. Bd. Internal Medicine, Am. Bd. Gastroenterology. Intern N.Y. Hosp., 1958-59, resident, 1959-61; chief resident U. Va. Hosp., Charlottesville, 1961-62; fellow in gastroenterology Barnes Hosp., St. Louis, 1962-63; inst. in internal medicine U. Va. Sch. Medicine, Charlottesville, 1963-66, asst. prof., 1966-71, assoc. prof., 1971-76, prof., 1976-85, Disting. prof., 1985—; dir. outpatient dept. U. Va. Hosp., 1968-72, pres. clin. staff, 1971-72, dir. phys. diagnosis program, 1972-75, vice chmn. dept. internat. medicine, 1979, dir. med. ICU, 1982-88, assoc. chmn. for clin. affairs, 1989. Contbr. articles to jours. in field. Recipient Robley

Danglison award U. Va. Sch. Medicine, 1972, 78. Fellow ACP; mem. Am. Gastroent. Assn., Soc. Critical Care Medicine, Alpha Omega Alpha.

STONE, DAVID KENDALL, financial executive; b. Natick, Mass., Dec. 7, 1942; s. Harold Hamilton and Mary (Perkins) S.; m. Patricia Donahue, June 12, 1965; children: Jonathan, Andrew, Timothy. AB, Franklin & Marshall Coll., 1964. CPA, N.Y. Acct. Gilfoil & McNeal, Syracuse, N.Y., 1967-69, Ernst & Whinney, Cleve., 1969-83; sr. v.p., comptroller Fiduciary Trust Co. Internat., N.Y.C., 1983-87, sr. v.p. dir. ops., 1987-92, exec. v.p., 1992—. Treas. Cerebral Palsy and Handicapped Children's Assn., Syracuse, N.Y., 1972-75. 1st lt. U.S. Army, 1964-67, Vietnam. Mem. AICPA, N.Y. State Soc. CPAs (com. on banking and savs. instns. 1983-87), Com. Banking Instns. on Taxation, N.Y. State Bankers Assn. (com. on trust ops.). Office: Fiduciary Trust Co Internat 2 World Trade Ctr New York NY 10048-0203

STONE, DAVID PHILIP, lawyer; b. N.Y.C., Sept. 11, 1944; s. Robert and Laura Stone; m. Arlene R. Stone, June 11, 1966; children: Aaron J., Rachel E. AB, Columbia U., 1967; JD, Harvard U., 1970. Bar: N.Y. 1971. Assoc. Cahill, Gordon & Reindel, N.Y.C., 1970-74, Baer & McGoldrick, N.Y.C., 1974-76; assoc. Weil, Gotshal & Manges, N.Y.C., 1976-79, ptnr., 1979—. Office: Weil Gotshal & Manges 767 5th Ave New York NY 10153

STONE, DENNIS J., chief information officer, educator; b. Sacramento, May 25, 1948; s. Edward F. and Irene V. (Johnson) S. BA, U. Calif., Berkeley, 1970, MLS, 1971; JD, U. of Pacific, 1977. Bar: Calif. 1977. Asst. law librarian McGeorge Sch. of Law, Sacramento, 1974-77, lectr., asst. law librarian, 1977-79; law librarian, asst. prof. Gonzaga Sch. of Law, Spokane, 1979-83; law librarian, assoc. prof. law U. Conn. Sch. of Law Library, Hartford, 1983—. Founder Can.-Am. Law Jour., 1983; founder, editor Trends in Law Library Mgmt. and Tech. Jour., 1987; contbr. articles to profl. jours. Mem. Am. Assn. Law Libraries (exec. bd. 1983-87), New Eng. Law Library Consortium (bd. dirs. 1983—, pres. 1986-88), Law Librarians of New Eng., So. New Eng. Law Libraries, Am. Assn. Law Libraries (spl. interest sect.). Office: Fla Coastal Sch Law 7555 Beach Blvd Jacksonville FL 32216

STONE, DON CHARLES, computer science educator; b. Passaic, N.J., Sept. 5, 1942; s. Robert Porter and Catherine Cook (Lanman) S. B Engring. Physics, Cornell U., 1965; MS in Engring., U. Pa., 1967, PhD in Instnl. Systems, 1985. Asst. prof. Glassboro State Coll. (now Rowan Coll. of N.J.), 1968-89, assoc. prof., 1989—, chair computer sci. dept., 1992—; sr. sys. analyst Intelligent Micro Sys., Inc., Narberth, Pa., 1985—. Contbr. articles to profl. jours.; patentee in field. Mem. IEEE Computer Soc., Assn. for Computing Machinery, Geneal. Computing Assn. Pa. (v.p. 1992—). Avocations: genealogy, graphic design, typography. Home: Apt 9B-28 2401 Pennsylvania Ave Philadelphia PA 19130-3034 Office: Rowan Coll of NJ Computer Sci Dept Glassboro NJ 08028

STONE, DONALD JAMES, retired retail executive; b. Cleve., Mar. 5, 1929; s. Sidney S. and Beatrice (Edelman) S.; m. Norma Fay Karchmer, Oct. 26, 1952; children—Michael, Lisa, Angela. BBA, U. Tex., Austin, 1949. With Foley's, Houston, 1949-75; v.p., gen. mdse. mgr. Foley's, 1960-75; chmn., chief exec. officer Sanger-Harris, Dallas, 1975-80; vice chmn. Federated Dept. Stores, Inc., Cin., 1980-88; bd. dirs. M Corp., Fossil, Inc., Bloom Agy., Dallas, XTEC Corp., Cin. Pres. Dallas Symphony Soc., 1980-82, 88—, chmn. Found. bd., 1989—; chmn. exec. com. Dallas Ballet, 1979; bd. dirs. Dallas Mus. Fine Art, 1979-81; mem. adv. coun. Coll. Bus. Adminstrn. U. Tex., 1981—, chmn., 1990-92; bd. dirs. Cin. Ballet, 1982-87, Cin. Symphony, 1983-88, pres., 1987; bd. Cin. overseers, chmn., 1988-92; bd. govs. Hebrew Union Coll., 1988-94; bd. dirs. Aspen Inst. Humanistic Studies, 1988—. Mem. Dallas C. of C. (chmn. cultural com. 1979-81), Assoc. Mdse. Corp. (bd. dirs., exec. com.). Democrat. Jewish. Home: 3601 Turtle Creek Blvd Dallas TX 75219-5522 Office: 3601 Turtle Creek Blvd Apt 502 Dallas TX 75219-5503

STONE, DONALD RAYMOND, lawyer; b. Madison, Wis., Mar. 6, 1938; s. Donald Meredith and June Dorothy (Graffenberger) S.; m. Dorothy Tetzlaff, June 23, 1962; children—Randall, Brian. B.S. in Physics, U. Wis., 1960, J.D., 1963. Bar: Minn. 1963, D.C. 1987, U.S. Supreme Ct. 1987. Patent atty. Honeywell, Inc., Mpls., 1963-66; patent atty. firm Burd, MacEachron, Braddock, Bartz & Schwartz, Mpls., 1966-68; with Medtronic, Inc., Mpls., 1968-87, v.p., then sr. v.p. product assurance and regulation, 1973-77, sr. v.p., sec., gen. counsel, 1977-80, sr. v.p., 1980-85, v.p., 1985-87; ptnr., mem. Burditt, Bowles & Radzius, Chartered, Washington, 1987-90; ptnr. McKenna & Cuneo, L.L.P., Washington, 1990—; condr. seminars, 1974—. Contbr. articles to profl. jours. Bd. dirs., 1st v.p. East Side Neighborhood Services, Inc., Mpls., 1976-80; bd. dirs. Guthrie Theater Found., 1979-85; mem. allocations com. United Way Mpls., 1979-86, chmn. allocations com., 1985, bd. dirs. 1985-86; mem. Citizens League of Twin Cities, 1965-86. Mem. ABA, D.C. Bar Assn., Fed. Bar Assn., Hennepin County Bar Assn., Am. Soc. Quality Control, Am. Intellectual Property Law Assn., Health Industry Mfrs. Assn. (past chmn. legal and regulatory sect., standard sect., 1975-87), Nat. Elec. Mfrs. Assn. (past chmn. med. electronics sect., 1970-76), Assn. Advancement Med. Instrumentation, Minn. State Bar Assn., Minn. Intellectual Property Law Assn. (past sec.), Minn. Corp. Counsel Assn., Regulatory Affairs. Profls. Soc., Order of Coif, Phi Delta Phi, Kappa Sigma. Episcopalian. Clubs: Mpls. Office: McKenna & Cuneo LLP 1900 K St Washington DC 20006

STONE, EDMUND CRISPEN, III, banker; b. Charleston, W.Va., Nov. 29, 1942; s. Edmund C. and Sallie Ragland (Thornhill); S.; m. Annette Margarethe Isaksen, Nov. 26, 1965; 1 child, Kristine Margarethe. BS, U.S. Mil. Acad., 1964; MBA, U. Va., 1972. V.p. Wachovia Bank, Winston-Salem, N.C., 1972-81; exec. v.p. First Am. Corp., Nashville, from 1981; vice chmn. First Am. Nat. Bank Nashville, 1988; exec. v.p. Regions Fin. Corp. (formerly First Ala. Bancshares, Inc.), Birmingham, 1988—. Contbg. author: The International Banking Handbook, 1983. Mem. export policy task force U.S. C. of C., 1980-81. With inf. U.S. Army, 1964-70, Vietnam, Iran. Decorated Bronze Star (Valor) with oak leaf cluster, Vietnamese Cross of Gallantry, others; hon. mem. Imperial Iranian Spl. Forces, 1968. Mem. Assn. of Grads. U.S. Mil. Acad. (trustee 1992-93). Republican. Avocations: sailing; hunting; fishing. Office: Regions Fin Corp PO Box 10247 Birmingham AL 35202-0247

STONE, EDWARD CARROLL, physicist, educator; b. Knoxville, Iowa, Jan. 23, 1936; s. Edward Carroll and Ferne Elizabeth (Baber) S.; m. Alice Trabue Wickliffe, Aug. 4, 1962; children: Susan, Janet. AA, Burlington Jr. Coll., 1956; MS, U. Chgo., 1959, PhD, 1964; DSc (hon.), Washington U., Saint Louis, 1992, Harvard U., 1992, U. Chgo., 1992. Rsch. fellow in physics Calif. Inst. Tech., Pasadena, 1964-66, sr. rsch. fellow, 1967, mem. faculty, 1967—, prof. physics, 1976-94, David Morrisroe prof. physics, 1994—, v.p. for astron. facilities, 1988-90, v.p., dir. Jet Propulsion Lab., 1991—; Voyager project scientist, 1972—; cons. Office of Space Scis., NASA, 1969-85, mem. adv. com. outer planets, 1972-73; mem. NASA Solar System Exploration Com., 1983; mem. com. on space astronomy and astrophysics Space Sci. Bd., 1979-82; mem. NASA high energy astrophysics mgmt. operating working group, 1976-84, NASA Cosmic Ray Program Working Group, 1980-82, Outer Planets Working Group, NASA Solar System Exploration Com., 1981-82, Space Sci. Bd., NRC, 1982-85, NASA Univ. Relations Study Group, 1983, steering group Space Sci. Bd. Study on Major Directions for Space Sci., 1995-2015, 1984-85; mem. exec. com. Com. on Space Research Interdisciplinary Sci. Commn., 1982-86; mem. commn. on phys. scis., math. and resources NRC, 1986-89; mem. adv. com. NASA/Jet Propulsion Labs. vis. sr. scientist program, 1986-90; mem. com. on space policy NRC, 1988-89; chmn. adv. panel for The Astronomers, KCET, 1989—. Mem. editl. bd. Space Sci. Instrumentation, 1975-81, Space Sci. Rev., 1982-85, Astrophysics and Space Sci., 1982—, Sci. mag. Bd. dirs. W.M. Keck Found. Recipient medal for exceptional sci. achievement NASA, 1980, Disting. Svc. medal, 1981, Disting. Pub. Svc. medal, 1985, Outstanding Leadership medal, 1986, 95, Am. Edn. award, 1981, Dryden award, 1983, Aviation Week and Space Tech. Aerospace Laureate, 1989, Sci. Man of Yr. award ARCS Found., 1991, Pres.'s Nat. medal of Sci., 1991, Am. Acad. Achievement Golden Plate award, 1992, COSPAR award for outstanding contbn. to space sci., 1992, LeRoy Randle Grumman medal, 1992, Disting Pub. Svc. award Aviation/Space Writers Assn., 1993, Internat. von Karman Wings award, 1996; Asteroid named for Edward C. Stone, 1996; Sloan Found. fellow, 1971-73. Fellow AIAA (assoc., Space Sci. award 1984), AAAS, Am. Phys. Soc. (chmn. cosmic physics divsn. 1979-80, exec. com. 1974-76), Am. Geophys. Union, Internat. Astron. Union; mem. NAS, Internat. Acad. Astronautics, Am. Astron. Soc. (divsn. planetary scis. com. 1981-84), Am. Assn. Physics Tchrs., Am. Philos. Soc. (Magellanic award 1992), Calif. Assn. Rsch. in Astronomy (bd. dirs., vice chmn. 1987-88, 91-94, chmn. 1988-91, 94—), Astron. Soc. Pacific (hon.), Nat. Space Club (bd. govs., Sci. award 1990), Calif. Coun. Sci. and Tech. Office: Jet Propulsion Lab 4800 Oak Grove Dr M/S 180-904 Pasadena CA 91109

STONE, EDWARD DURELL, JR., golf course architect; b. Norwalk, Conn., Aug. 30, 1932; s. Edward Durell and Orlean (Vandiver) S.; m. Jacqueline Marty, Dec. 15, 1954 (div.); children: Edward D. III, Patricia Marty; m. Helen S. Eccelstone, Aug. 5, 1995. B.A. in Architecture, Yale U., 1954; M.Landscape Architecture, Harvard U., 1959. Pres. Edward D. Stone, Jr., & Assos. (P.A.), Ft. Lauderdale, Fla., 1960-89, chmn., 1989—; vis. critic, lectr. Tex. A&M U., Lawrence Inst. Tech., U. Ga.; chmn. Edward D. Stone Jr. & Assocs., Ft. Lauderdale, Fka; vis. critic, lectr. U. Mich., U. Ill., U. Va., U. Tenn.; adj. prof. landscape architecture U. Miami, Fla.; cons. First Lady's Com. More Beautiful Capital, 1965-68, Fla. Gov.'s. Conf. Environ. Quality, 1968-69; mem. Commn. Fine Arts, Washington, 1971-85; Mem. vis. com. Harvard U. Sch. Design; guest lectr. Chautaqua Inst., 1989, Golf Course Europe '89, Wiesbaden, Fed. Republic Germany, 1st Internat. Resort Conf., Tokyo, 1989, Symposium on European Recreational and Leisure Devel., Opio, France, 1989. Landscape archtl. designer: Pepsico World Hdqrs, Purchase, N.Y., 1972, Bal Harbour Shops (Fla.), 1971, El Morro Resort, Puerto La Cruz, Venezuela, 1972—, Profl. Golf Assn. Hdqrs. Master Plan, Palm Beach, Fla., 1978-79, Grand Cypress Resort, Orlando, Fla., 1983, Carambola Beach and Golf Club, St. Croix, V.I., 1988, Ft. Lauderdale (Fla.) Beach Revitalization, 1989, Onagawa, Japan, 1989, Pont Royal, Aix-en-Provence, France, 1989, Treyburn, Durham N.C., 1984, Euro Disney, Marne la Vallee, France, 1990, Riverwalk, Ft. Lauderdale, FL, 1989, El Conquistador, P.R., 1990. V.p. Landscape Architecture Found.; bd. dirs. Fla. Trust for Hist. Preservation, 1985-88. Capt. USAF, 1954-57. Recipient Profl. Landscape Architecture award HUD, 1968, awards Am. Assn. Nurserymen, 1967, 69, 70, 71, 77, 83, 88, 90, 91, Fla. Nurserymen and Growers Assn., 1982, 83, 85, 86, 88, 90, 91, 92, Am. Resort and Residential Devel. Assn., 1984, 85, 88, 89, 90, 91, 92, Interior Landscape Assn., 1984, 85. Fellow Am. Soc. Landscape Architects (13 awards 1963-88, 8 awards Fla. chpt. 1981-89, awards N.C. chpt. 1987, 88, 89, 92, medal 1994). Office: Edward D Stone Jr & Assocs 1512 E Broward Blvd Ste 110 Fort Lauderdale FL 33301

STONE, EDWARD HARRIS, II, landscape architect; b. Lanesboro, Pa., Aug. 28, 1933; s. Frank Addison and Beth Lee (Brennan) S.; m. Diane Gertrude Berg, June 11, 1955; children: Randel Harris, Deborah Dee. B.S., SUNY, 1955. Landscape architect Harmon, O'Donnell & Henninger, Denver, 1955-56, U.S. Forest Service, Colo., 1958-61; regional landscape architect Alaska, 1961-64, Colo., 1964-65; chief landscape architect U.S. Forest Service, U.S. Dept. Agr., Washington, 1966-79; asst. dir. for recreation U.S. Forest Service, U.S. Dept. Agr., 1979-85; ret., 1985; with C-3 Co., Bowie, Md., 1986—. Served with AUS, 1956-57. Recipient Arthur S. Flemming award for outstanding fed. govt. service U.S. Jr. C. of C., 1969. Fellow Am. Soc. Landscape Architects (pres. 1975-76); mem. Sigma Lambda Alpha (hon.). Home and Office: 13200 Forest Dr Bowie MD 20715-4390

STONE, ELAINE MURRAY, author, composer, television producer; b. N.Y.C., Jan. 22, 1922; d. H. and Catherine (Fairbanks) Murray-Jacoby; m. F. Courtney Stone, May 30, 1944; children: Catherine Gladnick, Pamela Webb, Victoria. Student, Juilliard Sch. Music, 1939-41; BA, N.Y. Coll. Music, 1943; licentiate in organ, Trinity Coll. Music, London, 1947; student, U. Miami, 1952, Fla. Inst. Tech., 1963; PhD (hon.), World U., 1985. Organist, choir dir. St. Ingatius Episc. Ch., 1940-44; accompanist Strawbridge Ballet on Tour, N.Y.C., 1944; organist All Saints Episc. Ch., Ft. Lauderdale, 1951-54, St. John's Episc. Ch., Melbourne, Fla., 1956-59, First Christian Ch., Melbourne, 1962-63, United Ch. Christ, Melbourne, 1963-65, piano studio, Melbourne, 1955-70; editor-in-chief Cass Inc., 1970-71; dir. continuity radio Sta. WTAI, AM-FM, Melbourne, 1971-74; mem. sales staff Engle Realty Inc., Indialantic, Fla., 1975-78; v.p. pub. relations Consol. Cybertronics Inc., Cocoa Beach, Fla., 1969-70; writer, producer Countdown News, Sta. KXTX-TV, Dallas, 1978-80; assoc. producer Focus News, Dallas, 1980; host producer TV show, Focus on History, 1982-94, Epsic. Digest, 1984-90; judge Writer's Contest sponsored Brevard Cmty. Coll., 1987; v.p. Judges Fla. Space Coast Writer's Conf., 1985—, chmn., 1987. Author: The Taming of the Tongue, 1954, Love One Another, 1957, Menéndez de Avilés, 1968, Bedtime Bible Stories, Travel Fun, Sleepytime Tales, Improve Your Spelling for Better Grades, Improve Your Business Spelling, Tranquility Tapes, 1970, The Melbourne Bi-Centennial Book, 1976, Uganda: Fire and Blood, 1977, Tekla and the Lion, 1981 (1st Place award Nat. League Am. PEN Woman), Brevard County: From Cape of the Canes to Space Coast, 1988, Kizito, Boy Saint of Uganda, 1989 (2nd Place award Nat. League Am. PEN Woman 1990), Christopher Columbus: His World, His Faith., His Adventures, 1991 (1st Place award Nat. League Am. PEN Woman 1992), Elizabeth Bayley Seton: An American Saint, 1993 (3d Place award Nat. League Am. PEN Women 1994), Dimples The Dolphin, 1994 (1st Place award Fla. Space Coast Writer's Guild, 1994), Brevard at The Edge of Sea and Space, 1995, Carter G. Woodson Father of Black History, 1996, Maximilian Kolbe: Saint of Auschwitz, 1996; composer: Christopher Columbus Suite, 1992 (1st Place award PEN Women Music Awards 1992, 2d Place award 1993), Florida Suite for cello and piano, 1993; contbr. articles to nat. mags., newspapers including N.Y. Herald Tribune, Living Church, Christian Life; space corr. Religious News Service, Kennedy Space Ctr., 1962-78. Mem. exec. bd. Women's Assn., Brevard Symphony, 1967—; mem. heritage com. Melbourne Bicentennial Commn.; mem. Evangelism Commn. Episc. Diocese Cen. Fla., 1985-94; v.p. churchwomen group Holy Trinity Episcopal Ch., Melbourne, 1988-89, Stephen minister, 1988—, pres. churchwomen group, 1989—; bd. dirs. Fla. Space Coast Council Internat. Visitors, Fla. Space Coast Philharm., 1989—, Aid for the Arts, 1994. Recipient 1st place for piano Ashley Hall, 1935-39, S.C. State Music Contest, 1939, 1st place for piano composition Colonial Suite, Constitution Hall, Washington 1987, 88, 89, 3d place for vocal composition, 1989, honorable mention for article, 1989, 2nd place for piano composition, 1989, award lit. contest Fla. AAUW, 1989, 1st place award Fla. State PEN Women, 1990, 1st Place award Nat. Black History Essay Contest, 1990, Disting. Author or Yr. plaque Fla. Space Coast Writers Guild, 1992; numerous other awards. Mem. AAUW, ASCAP, Nat. League Am. PEN Women (1st place awards Tex. 1979, v.p. Dallas br. 1978-80, organizing pres. Cape Canaveral br. 1969, pres. 1988-90), Women Communications, DAR (Fla. state chmn. music 1962-63), Colonial Dames Am. (organizing pres. Melbourne chpt. 1994), Nat. Soc. DAR (organizing regent Rufus Fairbanks chpt. 1981-85, vice regent 1987—, historian 1989—), Children Am. Revolution (past N.Y. state chaplain), Am. Guild Organists (organizing warden Ft. Lauderdale), Space Pioneers, Fla. Press pisc. Home: 1945 Pineapple Ave Melbourne FL 32935-7656

STONE, ELIZABETH WENGER, retired dean; b. Dayton, Ohio, June 21, 1918; d. Ezra and Anna Bess (Markey) Wenger; m. Thomas A. Stone, Sept. 14, 1939 (dec. Feb. 1987); children: John Howard, Anne Elizabeth, James Alexander. A.B., Stanford U., 1937, M.A., 1938; M.L.S., Catholic U. Am., 1961; Ph.D., Am. U., 1968. Tchr. pub. schs. Fontana, Calif., 1938-39; asst. state statistician State of Conn., 1939-40; libr. New Haven Pub. Librs., 1940-42; dir. pub. relations, asst. to pres. U. Dubuque, Iowa, 1942-46; substitute libr. Pasadena (Calif. Pub. Libr. System), 1953-60; instr. Cath. U. Am., 1962-63, asst. prof., asst. to chmn. dept. libr. sci., 1963-67, assoc. prof., asst. to chmn., 1967-71, prof., asst. to chmn., 1971-72, prof., chmn. dept., 1972-80, dean Sch. Libr. and Info. Scis., 1981-83, prof. and dean emeritus, 1983—, lectr., 1990; libr. cons. U.S. Inst. of Peace, 1988-90; libr. Nat. Presbyn. Ch., Washington, 1991—, archivist, 1994—; founder, exec. dir. Continuing Libr. Edn. Network and Exchange, 1975-79; founder Nat. Rehab. Info. Ctr., 1977, project mgr., 1977-83; co-chmn. 1st World Conf. on Continuing Edn. for the Libr. and Info. Sci. Professions, 1984-85, 2nd World Conf., Barcelona, 1993. Author: Factors Related to the Professional Development of Librarians, 1969, (with James J. Kortendick) Job Dimensions and Educational Needs in Librarianship, 1971, (with R. Patrick and B. Conroy) Continuing Library and Information Science Education, 1974, Continuing Library Education as Viewed in Relation to Other Continuing Professional Movements, 1975, (with F. Peterson and M. Chobot) Motivation: A Vital Force in the Organization, 1977, American Library Development 1600-1899, 1977, (with others) Model Continuing Education Recognition System in Library and Information Science, 1979, (with M.J. Young) A Program for Quality in Continuing Education for Information, Library and Media Personnel, 1980, (with others) Continuing Education for the Library Information Professions, 1985, The Growth of Continuing Education, 1986, Library Education: Continuing Professional Education, 1993, (with others) ALA World Encyclopedia of Library and Information Science, 3d edit., 1993; author, editor: Continuing Professional Education for Library and Information Science Personnel: Papers from Seminar at Matica Slovenska, Martin Czechoslovakia, 1989; editor: D.C. Libraries, 1964-66; contbr. articles to profl. jours. Mem. Pres.'s Com. on Employment of Handicapped, 1972-88, Establishment of Elizabeth W. Stone Lectureship Cath. U. Am., 1990; pres. D.C. chpt. Am. Mothers, Inc., 1984-86, nat. v.p., 1989-91. Recipient Presdl. award Cath. U. Am., 1982, Spl. Librs. Profl. award, 1988, DCLA Ainsworth Rand Spofford Pres.'s award, 1990, Hon. Life Mem. 1994, Alumni Achievement award in libr. and info. sci. Cath. U. Am., 1990; named D.C. Mother of Yr., 1980. Mem. ALA (coun. 1976-83, v.p. 1980-81, pres. 1981-82, chmn. Nat. Libr. Week, 1983-85; founder ALA Nat. Ptnrs. for Librs. and Literacy 1984, Lippincott award 1986, Hon. Life award 1986), Assn. Libr. Info. and Sci. Edn. (pres. 1974), Am. Soc. Assn. Execs., Am. Assn. Adult and Continuing Edn., Internat. Fedn. Libr. Assns. and Instns. (chmn. Continuing Profl. Edn. Roundtable 1986—), D.C. Libr. Assn. (hon. life, pres. 1966-67, hon. chair centennial com. 1992-94, hon. life 1994), Spl. Librs. Assn. (hon. life, pres. D.C. chpt. 1973-74), Cath. Libr. Assn. (hon. life), Continuing Profl. Edn. Libr. and Info. Sci. Pers., Soc. Am. Archivists, Cosmos Club, Phi Sigma Alpha, Beta Phi Mu, Phi Lambda Theta. Presbyterian. Home: 4000 Cathedral Ave NW # 15B Washington DC 20016-5249 Office: Cath U Am Sch Lib & Info Scis Washington DC 20064

STONE, F. L. PETER, lawyer; b. Wilmington, Del., Feb. 24, 1935; s. Linton and Lorinda (Hamlin) S.; m. Therese Louise Hannon, Apr. 7, 1969; 1 child, Lisa Judith. AB, Dartmouth Coll, 1957; LLB, Harvard U., 1960. Bar: Del. Supreme Ct. 1960, U.S. Ct. Appeals (3d cir.) 1964, U.S. Supreme Ct. 1965, U.S. Ct. Appeals (fed. cir.) 1983. Assoc. Connolly, Bove & Lodge, Wilmington, 1960-64; dep. atty. gen. State of Del., Wilmington, 1965-66; atty. Del. Gen. Assembly, Dover, 1967-68; counsel Gov. Del., Dover, 1969; U.S. atty. Dist. of Del., Wilmington, 1969-72; ptnr. Connolly, Bove, Lodge, & Hutz, Wilmington, 1972—; mem. Del. Agy. to Reduce Crime, 1969-72, Del. Organized Crime Commn., 1970-72, State Drug Abuse Coun., 1990-93, State Judicial Nominating Commn., 1991-93, State Coun. Corrections, 1992—; co-founder, adj. prof. criminal justice progra, West Chester (Pa.) U., 1975-79; chmn. Gov.'s Harness Racing Investigation Com., 1977, Del. Jai Alai Commn., 1977-78, Corrections Task Force, 1986-88. Author numerous articles. Chmn. UN Day, Del., 1989; Rep. candidate for atty. gen. Del., 1990; mem. Del. Gov.'s Task Force in Prison Security, 1994-95; trustee Leukemia Soc. Am., N.Y.C., 1972-74, Marywood Coll., Scranton, Pa., 1974-79, Ursuline Acad., Wilmington, 1974-80. Mem. Port of Wilmington Maritime Soc. (bd. dirs. pres 1996), Wilmington Country Club, Rodney Square Club, Lincoln Club Del. (pres. 1994), Wilmington Rotary (bd. dirs. 1995—). Roman Catholic. Avocations: hiking/mountaineering, tennis, music. Office: Connolly Bove Lodge & Hutz PO Box 2207 1220 Market St Wilmington DE 19899 *My major accomplishment has been establishing and maintaining a close relationship with my family, first and foremost, regardless of what activities and accomplishments were pursued in my professional, political and community life.*

STONE, FRANZ THEODORE, retired fabricated metal products manufacturing executive; b. Columbus, Ohio, May 11, 1907; s. Julius Frederick and Edna (Andress) S.; m. Katherine Devereux Jones, Feb. 23, 1935; children: Franz Theodore, Thomas Devereux Mackay, Raymond Courtney (dec.), Catherine Devereux Diebold. AB magna cum laude, Harvard U., 1929; hon. degrees, Canisius Coll., 1975, Ohio State U., 1976. Chmn. bd. Columbus McKinnon Corp., Amherst, N.Y., 1935-86. Chmn. emeritus Arts Council in Buffalo and Erie County, 1973-86; pres. Buffalo Philharmonic Orch. Soc., 1959-61, also life dir.; chmn. emeritus Studio Arena Theatre, Buffalo, 1968-86; Nat. Conf. of Christian and Jews Brother Sisterhood citation, 1986; First Arts award Arts Council and Greater Buffalo C. of C. Recipient Gold Key award Buffalo YMCA, 1966, Red Jacket award Buffalo & Erie County Hist. Soc., 1976, Disting. Citizen award SUNY, Buffalo, 1985, Conductor's award Buffalo Philharm. Orch., 1993. Mem. Gulfstream Bath & Tennis Club, Ocean Club of Fla., Boca Raton Country Club, Pundits Club, The Greenbrier Club (W. Va.), Buffalo Country Club, Buffalo Club, Saturn Club (Buffalo), The Little Club (Gulfstream). Home: 1171 N Ocean Blvd Apt 4CS Gulf Stream FL 33483

STONE, FRED MICHAEL, lawyer; b. Bklyn., Jan. 20, 1943; s. Nathan and Rose (Silverman) S.; m. Bonnie B. Dobkin, Aug. 14, 1965; children—Jonathan, Jennifer. A.B. cum laude, Bklyn. Coll., 1964; J.D., Harvard U., 1967; LL.M., N.Y. U., 1971. Bar: N.Y. 1968. Assoc. Cadwalader, Wickersham & Taft, N.Y.C., 1967-69; asst. gen. counsel Standard & Poor's/Intercapital, Inc., N.Y.C., 1969-71; v.p., gen. counsel Neuwirth Funds, 1971-73, Mocatta Metals Corp., N.Y.C., 1973-76; sr. v.p., gen. counsel Am. Stock Exchange, Inc., N.Y.C., 1976-86; exec. v.p., gen. counsel Jamie Securities Co., Caronan Ptnrs., N.Y.C., 1986-88; sr. v.p., gen. counsel, sec. M.D. Sass Assocs., Inc., N.Y.C., 1989—; chmn. exec. com. Amex Commodities Exch., 1980-81; dir. Am. Gold Coin Exchange, Inc., 1981-85; exec. v.p., dir. Revere Copper and Brass, Inc., 1986-88; dir. Ea. Electric Motor Co., Inc., 1987-88; ofcl. adv. Drafting Com. to Revise Uniform Securities Act of Nat. conf. Uniform State Law Commrs., 1981-85; chmn. options and futures regulation subcom. of fed. regulation of securities com. ABA, 1989-91, mem. task force on Hedge Funds, 1994—; lectr. various legal seminars; sec. rules com. Investment Co. Inst., 1989-92; sec., treas. steering com. Taxable Mcpl. Bondholders Protective Com., 1990-95. Mem. Manalapan (N.J.) Twp. Zoning Bd. Adjustment, 1975-86; vice-chmn. Manalapan Dem. Com., 1988—; Dem. candidate for Manalapan Twp. Com., 1989, 93; mem. N.J. regional exec. com. Anti-Defamation League of B'nai Brith, 1991—. Mem. ABA, Assn. of Bar of City of N.Y. (mem. corp. law dept. comm. 1995—), Harvard U. Law Sch. Assn., Am. Stock Exch., Inc. (arbitrator 1986—), Nat. Assn. Securities Dealers Inc. (arbitrator 1986—), Nat. Futures Assn. (nominating com. 1986-88). Democrat. Jewish. Home: 15 Kingsley Dr Manalapan NJ 07726-3134

STONE, GAIL SUSAN, gifted, talented education educator; b. Elmhurst, Ill., Aug. 22, 1944; d. Harold Frederick Lopatka and May Anna (Lippert) Lopatka Wickham; m. Ronald Eugene Stone, Dec. 26, 1971; children: Andrew, Susanna. BA in Edn., Elmhurst Coll., 1966; M in Arts/Edn., Nat. Louis U., 1975. Cert. elem. edn. and supr. adminstrn. Tchr. first grade Shc. Dist. 89, Glen Ellyn, Ill., 1966-70; tchr. learning disability and gifted resource, kindergarten Sch. Dist. 94, North Riverside, Ill., 1972-81; gifted program coord. Sch. Dist. 102, La Grange, Ill., 1984-87, Sch. Dist. 96, Riverside, Ill., 1987-88; substitute tchr. Sch. Dist. 181, Hinsdale, Ill., 1988-92; tchr. gifted resources/spl. edn. aide Sch. Dist. 92, Broadview, Ill., 1992-93; coord. gifted program Sch. Dist. 103, Lyons, Ill., 1993—. Mem. Salt Creek Area AAUW (v.p. mem. 1986, v.p. program 1992-94), Ill. Coun. Gifted (v.p. 1979), Nat. Assn. Gifted, Children with Attention Deficit Disorder, Alpha Xi Delta, Phi Delta Kappa. Avocations: swimming, reading, needlework. Home: 329 N Stone Ave La Grange IL 60525

STONE, GEOFFREY RICHARD, law educator, lawyer; N.Y.C.; b. Jan. 20, 1946; s. Robert R. and Shirley (Weliky) S.; m. Nancy Spector, Oct. 8, 1977; children: Julie, Mollie. BS, U. Pa., 1968; JD, U. Chgo., 1971. Bar: N.Y. 1972. Law clk. to Hon. J. S. Kelly Wright, U.S. Ct. Appeals (D.C. cir.), 1971-72; law clk. to Hon. William J. Brennan, Jr., U.S. Supreme Ct., 1972-73; asst. prof. U. Chgo., 1973-77, assoc. prof., 1977-79, prof., 1979-84, Harry Kalven Jr. disting. svc. prof., 1984-93; dean Law Sch., 1987-93, provost, 1994—. Author: Constitutional Law, 1986, 3d edit., 1996, The Bill Of Rights In The Modern State, 1992; editor The Supreme Ct. Rev., 1991—; contbr. articles to profl. jours. Bd. dirs. Ill. div. ACLU, 1978-84; bd. advisors Pub. Svc. Challenge, 1989. Fellow AAAS; mem. Chgo. Coun. Lawyers (bd. govs. 1976-77), Assn. Am. Law Schs. (exec. com. 1990-93), Legal Aid Soc. (bd. dirs. 1988), Order of Coif. Office: U Chgo 5801 S Ellis Ave Chicago IL 60637-1404

STONE, HARRY H., business executive; b. Cleve., May 21, 1917; s. Jacob and Jennie (Kantor) Sapirstein; m. Lucile Tabak, Aug. 10, 1960; children: Phillip, Allan, Laurie (Mrs. Parker), James Rose, Douglas Rose. Student, Cleve. Coll., 1935-36. With Am. Greetings Corp., Cleve., 1936—, v.p., 1944-

58, exec. v.p., 1958-69, vice chmn. bd., chmn. finance com., chmn audit com., 1969-78, now dir.; mem. Ofcl. U.S. Mission to India and Nepal, 1965; cons. U.S. Dept. Commerce, U.S. Dept. State; adviser U.S. del. 24th session UN Econ. Commn. for Asia and Far East, Canberra, Australia, 1968; cons. Nat. Endowment for Arts, Nat. Council on Arts. Treas. Criminal Justice Coordinating Council., 1968-82; trustee emeritus Brandeis U., also univ. fellow. Mem. Rotary. Home: Suite 9D Bratenahl Pl # 2 Cleveland OH 44108-1183 Office: The Courtland Group Inc 1540 Lander Rd Cleveland OH 44124-3337

STONE, HERBERT MARSHALL, architect; b. N.Y.C., July 12, 1936; s. Irving and Rose (Gelb) S.; m. Linda Ann Baskind, May 30, 1960; children: Ian Howard, Matthew Lloyd. BArch, Pratt Inst., N.Y.C., 1958, postgrad., 1958-59. Registered architect, N.Y., Iowa, Kans., Ill., Wis., Minn. Designer Henry Dreyfuss Indsl. Design, N.Y.C., 1960-63; architect Max O. Urbahn Architect, N.Y.C., 1963-66; project architect Brown Healey Bock, P.C., Cedar Rapids, Iowa, 1966-73; ptnr. Brown Healey Stone & Sauer, Cedar Rapids, Iowa, 1973—; guest lectr. U.S. Inst. Theatre Tech., Seattle, 1978; speaker on design of pub. librs. ALA Nat. Conv., Miami, Fla., 1994. Prin. works include Strayer-Wood Theatre, 1978, KUNI radio sta. U. No. Iowa, 1978, Cedar Rapids Pub. Libr., 1984, Greenwood Terr. Sr. Citizen Housing, 1986, Iowa State Hist. Mus., 1988, Nat. Hot Air Balloon Mus., 1988 (Spectrum Ceramic Tile Grand award 1989), Student Ctr. Grinnell Coll., 1992, Hall of Pride, I.H.S.A.A., 1995. Pres. Cedar Rapids Trust for Hist. Preservation, 1981—; bd. dirs. Art in Pub. Places Com., Cedar Rapids, 1988, Cedar Rapids/Marion Arts Coun., 1988, Jane Boyd Community House, Cedar Rapids, 1988. Mem. AIA, Am. Mus. Assn., Greater Downtown Assn. Cedar Rapids. Avocations: bicycling, skiing, reading, ceramics. Home: 3730 Terrace Hill Dr NE Cedar Rapids IA 52402-2846 Office: Brown Healey Stone & Sauer PC 800 1st Ave NE Cedar Rapids IA 52402-5002

STONE, HOWARD LAWRENCE, lawyer; b. Chgo., Sept. 16, 1941; s. Jerome Richard Stone and Ceale (Perlik) Stone Tandet; m. Susan L. Saltzman, June 2, 1963; children—Lauren, David. Student U. Ill., 1960-61; B.S.B.A., Roosevelt U., 1963; J.D., DePaul U., 1972. Bar: Ill. 1972, U.S. Dist. Ct. (no. dist.) Ill. 1972, U.S. Tax Ct. 1972, U.S. Supreme Ct. 1982; C.P.A., Ill. Agt. IRS, Chgo., 1964-72; spl. asst. U.S. atty. and chief fin. auditor and investigator No. Dist. Ill., Dept. Justice, Chgo., 1972-76; sr. ptnr. Stone, McGuire & Benjamin, Chgo., 1976—; lectr. in taxation. Author: Defending the Federal Tax Case: What To Do When the IRS Steps In, 1978; Client Tax Fraud—A Practical Guide to Protecting Your Rights, 1984. Co-editor, co-author: Handling Criminal Tax Cases: A Lawyers Guide, 1982, 87; co-author: Federal Civil Tax Law, 1982, 88; co-author: Negotiating to Win, 1985. Bd. dirs. Israel Bonds, Chgo., 1982, U. Chgo.; chmn. U. Ill. Found. Fund for Gerontology Rsch., 1984—; bd. dirs. Gastro Intestinal Research Found. U. Chgo., 1978—. Mem. Chgo. Bar Assn., Ill. State Bar Assn., Fed. Bar Assn., ABA, Decalogue Soc. Lawyers, Am. Inst. C.P.A.s, Ill. C.P.A. Found., Am. Assn. Atty.-C.P.A.s, Ill. C.P.A. Soc. (resident lectr. in tax fraud 1976-84, 90, 91, chmn. Investment Advisers Act task force 1983-84, co-chair accts. liability annual conf.). Jewish. Lodges: B'nai B'rith, Shriners. Office: Altschuler Melvoin & Glasser 30 Wacker St Ste 2600 Chicago IL 60606*

STONE, HUBERT DEAN, editor, journalist; b. Maryville, Tenn., Sept. 23, 1924; s. Archie Hubert and Annie (Cupp) S.; student Maryville Coll., 1942-43; B.A., U. Okla., 1949; m. Agnes Shirley, Sept. 12, 1953 (dec. Mar. 1973); 1 son, Neal Anson. Sunday editor Maryville-Alcoa Daily Times, 1949; mng. editor Maryville-Alcoa Times, 1949-78, editor, 1978—; v.p. Maryville-Alcoa Newspapers, Inc., 1960-90; pres. Stonecraft, 1954—. Photographer in field. Vice-chmn., chmn. Tenn. Great Smoky Mountains Park commn.; co-chmn. 175th anniversary com. Maryville Coll.; mem. mayor's adv. com. City of Maryville; mem. air service adv. com. Knoxville Met. Airport Authority; bd. dirs. United Fund of Blount County, 1961-63, 74-76, vice chmn. campaign, 1971-72, chmn. campaign, 1973, v.p., 1974, pres., 1975; vice chmn. bd. dirs. Maryville Utilities Bd.; bd. dirs. Sam Houston Meml. Assn., Alcoa City Sch. Found., Blount County Hist. Trust, Nat. Hillbilly Homecoming Assn., Friendsville Acad., 1968-73, Alkiwan Crafts, Inc., 1970-73, Middle East Tenn. Regional Tourism Group; dir. Foothills Land Conservancy, Smoky Mountains Passion Play Assn., Blount County History Mus.; mem. adv. com. Blount County Alternative Center for Learning, Overlook Center, Inc., Sr. Citizens Home Assistance Svcs.; chmn. Blount County Long Range Planning for Sch. Facilities; mem. adv. bd. Harrison-Chilhowee Bapt. Acad, mem. Leadership Knoxville; co-founder, vice pres., pres. Leadership Blount County; founder, chmn. Townsend-in-the-Smokies Art Show/Sale, 1984—; mem. bd. govs. Maryville-Alcoa C.C. Orch. Soc; trustee, pres. bd. trustees, deacon, chmn. evangelism, fin. & pers. coms. Bapt. Ch.; mem. Blount County Bicentennial com., State of Tenn. Hist. commn. Served from pvt. to staff sgt. AUS, 1943-45. Decorated Bronze Star; named Outstanding Sr. Man of Blount County, 1970, 77, Hon. Order Ky. Cols., Commonwealth of Ky.; recipient Pride of Tenn. award for vol. work, 1993, Outstanding Leadership award Maryville Ch. of Christ, First Tourism Pioneer award Smoky Mount. Vis. Bur. and Blount C. of C., 1994. Mem. VFW, Profl. Photographers of Am., Internat. Post Card Distbrs. Assn., Great Smoky Mountains Natural History Assn., State of Tenn. Hist. Commn., Ft. Loudoun Assn., Tenn. Jaycees (editor 1954-55, sec.-treas. 1955-56), Blount County Arts/ Crafts Guild, Jr. Chamber Internat. (senator) Maryville-Alcoa Jaycees (life mem., pres. 1953-54), Blount County (v.p. 1971, 76, pres. 1977), Townsend C. of C. (dir. 1969-71, 83-85, pres. 1983), Tenn. AP News Execs. Assn. (v.p. 1973, pres. 1974), AP Mng. Editors Assn., Tenn. Profl. Photographers Assn., Am. Legion, Foothills Pkwy. Assn. (v.p., pres.), Chilhowee Bapt. Assn. (chmn. history com.) U. Okla. Alumni Assn. (life mem., pres. East Tenn. chpt. 1954-55), Sigma Delta Chi (life, dir. E. Tenn. chpt.), Mason, Kiwanian (pres. Alcoa 1969-70); Club: Green Meadow Country. Contbr. articles to profl. publs. Home: 1510 Scenic Dr Maryville TN 37803-5634 Office: 307 W Harper Ave Maryville TN 37804-4723

STONE, IRVING I., greeting card company executive; b. Cleve., Apr. 5, 1909; s. Jacob and Jennie (Canter) Sapirstein; m. Helen K. Sill, Dec. 12, 1976; children: Hensha (Mrs. Hirsch Gansbourg), Neil, Myrna (Mrs. Harold Tatar), Judith (Mrs. Morry Weiss). Student, Case-Western Res. U., Cleve. Inst. Art. With Am. Greetings Corp., Cleve., 1923—, pres., 1960-78, chmn. bd., 1978—, chief exec. officer, 1978-87, also chmn. exec. com. Chmn. bd. Hebrew Acad. Cleve.; bd. dirs. Cleve. Inst. Art, Young Israel of Cleve., Yeshiva U.; trustee Simon Wiesenthal Ctr. for Holocaust Studies; 1st v.p. Telshe Yeshiva; life mem. bd. dirs. Jewish Community Fedn. of Cleve.; v.p. Am. Assn. for Jewish Edn., Bur. Jewish Edn., Cleve., Am. Friends of Boys Town Jerusalem; founder Kiryat Telshe Stone, Israel. Office: Am Greetings Corp 1 American Rd Cleveland OH 44144-2301*

STONE, JACK, religious organization administrator. Gen. sec., hdqs. ops. officer Ch. of the Nazarene, Kansas City, Mo. Office: Ch Nazarene 6401 Paseo Blvd Kansas City MO 64131-1213

STONE, JAMES HOWARD, management consultant; b. Chgo., Mar. 4, 1939; s. Jerome H. and Evelyn Gertrude (Teitelbaum) S.; m. Carole Marlen David, Apr. 21, 1972; children: Margaret Elisa, Emily Anne, Phoebe Jane. AB cum laude, Harvard U., 1960, MBA, 1962. Cert. mgmt. cons., CMC, 1977. Staff analyst Stone Container Corp., Chgo., 1962-64, gen. mgr., Kansas City Div., 1964-66, asst. treas., 1966-68, dir., 1969—, with exec. com., 1983—; founder, owner, CEO Stone Mgmt. Cons., 1969—; mem. strategic alliance Boston Cons. Group, 1990—, trustee, sec., exec. com. Roosevelt U., Chgo., 1983—, exec. com. edn. alliance, 1994—; co-chmn. commn. fgn. and domestic affairs Northwestern U., Evanston, Ill., 1981-85, bus. plan judge Kellog Grad. Sch. Mgmt., 1994—; mem. vis. com. libr. U. Chgo., 1980—, The Chgo. Com., 1986—, Mid-Am. Com., Chgo., 1993—; bd. overseers IIT Stuart Sch. Bus., 1994—; bd. dirs. Fullerton Metals Corp., 1986—, Berteau Corp. Mem. Chgo. Coun. Fgn. Rels., 1967, bd. dirs., 1974-78; bd. dirs., mem. exec. com. NCCJ, Chgo., 1985, presiding co-chmn., 1990—; trustee Hadley Sch. Blind, Winnetka, Ill., 1985, chmn. planning com., 1989—. Mem. Warehousing Edn. and Rsch. Coun., Inst. Mgmt. Cons. (pres. Chgo. chpt. 1981-83, regional dir. 1983-86), Coun. Logistics Mgmt. (dir. Roundtable-Chgo. 1990-94), Assn. of Corp. Growth, The Exec. Club Chgo., Econs. Club, Harvard Club Chgo., Harvard Bus. Sch. Assocs. Chgo. (dir. 1992), Traffic Club Chgo., Standard Club, Northmoor Country Club. Avocations: family-centered activities, reading, golf, travel, coaching girls' softball. Home: 83 Woodley Rd Winnetka IL 60093-3746 Office: Stone Mgmt Corp 208 S La Salle St Chicago IL 60604-1003

STONE, JAMES J., photographer; b. Los Angeles, Dec. 2, 1947; s. Charles S. and Sylvia S. S.B. in Arch, M.I.T., 1970; M.F.A. in Photography, R.I. Sch. Design, 1975. Mem. faculty R.I. Sch. Design, Providence, 1975-78, 93—, Boston Coll., Chestnut Hill, Mass., 1973-88. Author: A User's Guide to the View Camera, 1987, Stranger Than Fiction, 1993; editor: Darkroom Dynamics, 1979; one-man shows Anchorage Fine Arts Mus., 1977, Polaroid Gallery, Cambridge, Mass., 1978, Carl Siembab Gallery, Boston, 1979, Wesleyan U., Middletown, Conn., 1980, Visual Studies Workshop, Rochester, N.Y., 1986, San Francisco Camera Work, 1985, Robert Klein Gallery, 1987, Mitchell Mus., 1989, Huntington Mus. Art, 1990, Rice U., Houston, 1992; exhibited in group shows De Cordova Mus., Lincoln, Mass., 1972, Fogg Art Mus., Cambridge, 1974, 76, Corcoran Gallery Art, Washington, 1978-79, Mpls. Inst. Arts, 1987, Phila. Mus. Art, 1987, Nat. Mus. Am. Art, 1992; represented in permanent collection Nat. Mus. Am. Art, Washington, Corcoran Gallery Art, Fogg Art Mus., George Eastman House, Rochester, L.A. County Mus. Art, Mus. Modern Art, N.Y.C. Pres. bd. dirs. Photog. Resource Ctr., Boston. Mass. Artists Found. artists fellow, 1976, 88, New Eng. Found. for the Arts/NEA Regional Artists' fellow, 1993; artist-in-residence Alaska State Arts Coun., 1977; NEA photographic survey grantee, 1980. Office: care Robert Klein Gallery 38 Newbury St Boston MA 02116-3210

STONE, JAMES MICHAEL, medical educator; b. Oct. 30, 1952. BS in Psychology magna cum laude, U. Ill., 1974; MD, Northwestern U., Chgo., 1978. Diplomate Nat. Bd. Med. Examiners, Am. Bd. Surgery, Am. Bd. Colon and Rectal Surgery; lic. physician, Calif. Intern surgery Michael Reese Hosp. & Med. Ctr., Chgo., 1978-79, resident, 1979-83, adminstrv. chief resident, 1982-83; trauma rsch. fellow U. Calif.-San Francisco, San Francisco Gen. Hosp., 1980-81; asst. prof. surgery U. Ill., 1983-85; attending surgeon, co-dir. hyperalimentation svc. Cook County Hosp., Chgo., 1983-85; clin. asst. prof. Stanford U. Med. Ctr., 1986-89, asst. prof. surgery, divsn. surg. oncology, 1990—, chief divsn. trauma, 1992—; chief gen. surgery Palo Alto VA Med. Ctr., 1986-89; med. fellow dept. colon and rectal surgery U. Minn., 1989-90; mem. staff U. Ill. Hosp. and Clinics, Cook County Hosp., 1983-85, Stanford U. Med. Ctr., Palo Alto VA Med. Ctr., 1985-89, U. Minn. Med. Ctr., 1989-90, Stanford U. Med. Ctr., 1990—. Contbr. articles to profl. jours., chpts. to books. James scholar U. Ill., Urbana, 1970-74, Paul M. Cherementa award Paralyzed Vets. Am., 1988, grant Spinal Cord Rsch. Found., 1988-90. Mem. Phi Beta Kappa, Phi Kappa Phi. Home: 40 Willow Park Menlo Park CA 94025

STONE, JAMES ROBERT, surgeon; b. Greeley, Colo., Jan. 8, 1948; s. Anthony Joseph and Dolores Concetta (Pietrafeso) S.; m. Kaye Janet Friedman, May 16, 1970; children: Jeffrey, Marisa. BA, U. Colo., 1970; MD, U. Guadalajara, Mex., 1976. Diplomate Am. Bd. Surgery, Am. Bd. Surg. Critical Care. Intern Md. Gen. Hosp., Balt., 1978-79; resident in surgery St. Joseph Hosp., Denver, 1979-83; practice medicine specializing in surgery Grand Junction, Colo., 1983-87; staff surgeon, dir. critical care Va. Med. Ctr., Grand Junction, 1987-88; dir. trauma surgery and critical care, chief surgery St. Francis Hosp., Colorado Springs, Colo., 1988-91; pvt. practice Kodiak, Alaska, 1991-92; with South Denver Surg. Cons., Englewood, Colo., 1992-93, Summit Surg. Assocs., 1993—; asst. clin. prof. surgery U. Colo. Health Sci. Ctr., Denver, 1984—; pres. Stone Aire Cons., Grand Junction, 1988—; owner, operator Jjnka Ranch, Flourissant, Colo.; spl. advisor CAP, wing med. officer, 1992—; mem. advisor med. com. unit, 1990-92; advisor Colo. Ground Team Search and Rescue, 1994—. Contbr. articles to profl. jours.; inventor in field. Bd. dirs. Mesa County Cancer Soc., 1988-89, Colo. Trauma Inst., 1988-91. Colo. Speaks out on Health grantee, 1988; recipient Bronze medal of Valor Civil Air Patrol. Fellow Denver Acad. Surgery, Southwestern Surg. Congress, Am. Coll. Chest Physicians, Am. Coll. Surgeons (trauma com. Colo. chpt.), Am. Coll. Critical Care; mem. Am. Coll. Physician Execs., Soc. Critical Care (task force 1988—). Roman Catholic. Avocations: horse breeding, hunting, fishing.

STONE, JEFFREY JAY, film critic, journalist, writer; b. Toronto, Ont., Can., Oct. 2, 1946; s. Philip Maurice and Mildred (Walton) S.; m. Sandra Patricia Ridob, May 2, 1970; children: Benjamin Matthew, Laura Noelle. Editor The Record-News, Smith Falls, Ont., 1972-73; reporter, columnist The Brampton (Ont.) Times, 1973-76; copy editor The Ottawa (Ont.) Citizen, 1976-80, asst. sports editor, 1980-81, asst. city editor, 1981-84, design editor, 1984-85, entertainment editor, 1985-90, entertainment columnist, 1990-94, film critic, 1994—. Patron Coun. for Arts in Ottawa, 1994. Mem. Variety Club of Can., Laurentian Jr. Music Club, Elvis Sighting Soc. Avocations: bridge, reading, chess. Office: The Ottawa Citizen, 1101 Baxter Rd, Ottawa, ON Canada K2C 3M4

STONE, JEREMY JUDAH, professional society administrator; b. N.Y.C., Nov. 23, 1935; s. I.F. and Esther (Roisman) S.; m. Betty Jane Yannet, June 16, 1957. B.S. magna cum laude, Swarthmore Coll., 1957, LL.D. (hon.), 1985; Ph.D., Stanford U., 1960. Research mathematician Stanford Research Inst., 1960-62; mem. profl. staff Hudson Inst., Croton-on-Hudson, 1962-64; research asso., arms control and disarmament Harvard Ctr. Internat. Affairs, 1964-66; asst. prof. math., lectr. polit. sci. Pomona Coll., Claremont, Calif., 1966-68; CEO Fedn. Am. Scientists, Washington, 1970—. Author: Containing the Arms Race; Some Concrete Proposals, 1966, Strategic Persuasion, 1967. Recipient award for pub. svc. Forum on Physics and Soc., Am. Phys. Soc., 1979, Fedn. of Am. Scientists Pub. Svc. award, 1994; Social Sci. Rsch. Coun. fellow in econs. Stanford U., 1968-69, Coun. Fgn. Rels. internat. affairs fellow, 1969-70. Mem. Coun. Fgn. Rels., Internat. Inst. Strategic Studies, Phi Beta Kappa. Home: 5615 Warwick Pl Bethesda MD 20815-5503 Office: Fedn Am Scientists 307 Massachusetts Ave NE Washington DC 20002-5701

STONE, JERRY DUANE, packaging engineer; b. Mt. Pleasant, Mich., Feb. 13, 1943; s. James A. and Vera L. (Watson) S.; m. Karen L. Budner, Oct. 27, 1983; 1 child, Kim D. BS in Packaging Engring., Mich. State U., 1965. Cert. profl. in packaging. Packaging engr. and advisor nat. classification com. Am. Trucking Assns., Alexandria, Va., 1970-85, packaging cons., 1970—; lectr. in field. Contbr. articles to profl. jours. Mem. Nat. Inst. Packaging Profls., Inst. Packaging, Handling and Logistic Engrs., Internat. Safe Transit Assn., Am. Mgmt. Assn. (packaging coun.). Avocation: antique automobile restoration. Home: 7826 Mulberry Bottom Ln Springfield VA 22153-2313

STONE, JOE ALLAN, economics educator; b. Seminole, Tex., Mar. 17, 1948; s. Richard Elick and Ivy Lillian (Childs) S.; m. Crystal Lee Barnes, Aug. 30, 1969; children: Christopher Dylan, Elizabeth Ivy. BA, U. Tex., El Paso, 1970; MA, Mich. State U., 1974, PhD, 1977. Research economist U.S. Bur. Labor Stats., Washington, 1977-79; asst. prof. U. Oreg., Eugene, 1979-82, assoc. prof., 1982-84, W.E. Miner prof. econs., 1985—, head dept., 1988-92, assoc. dean Coll. Arts and Scis., 1992—; sr. economist Pres.' Council Econ. Advisors, Washington, 1984-85; vis. scholar Fed. Res. Bank Cleve., 1986. Author: (with others) Unions and Public Schools, 1984, Wage and Employment Adjustment in Local Labor Markets, 1992; contbr. articles to profl. jours. Served with U.S. Army, 1970-72. Mem. AAUP (pres. U. Oreg. chpt. 1986-87), Am. Econ. Assn., Western Econ. Assn., So. Econ. Assn., Indsl. Rels. Rsch. Inst. Episcopalian. Home: 3820 Onyx St Eugene OR 97405-4515 Office: U Oreg Dept Econs Eugene OR 97403

STONE, JOHN FLOYD, soil physics researcher and educator; b. York, Nebr., Oct. 13, 1928; s. Harry Floyd and Anastasia (Klima) S.; m. Carol Ottilie Youngson, Aug. 2, 1953; children: Mary, Margaret, David, Jana. BS, U. Nebr., 1952; MS, Iowa State U., 1955, PhD, 1957. Lab. technician U. Nebr., 1944-53; from rsch. asst. to rsch. assoc. Iowa State U., 1953-57; from asst. to assoc. prof. Okla. State U., Stillwater, 1957-69, prof. soil physics, 1969-94; prof. emeritus, 1994—; mem. adv. agrl. panel U.S. Dept. Def., 1977-78; mem. grant evaluation panel Water Quality Grant Program, USDA, 1989, Small. Bus. Initiative Rsch. Grant Program, 1990. Editor: Plant Modification for More Efficient Water Use, 1975, Plant Production and Management under Drought Conditions, 1983; contbr. chpts. to books, rsch. articles to profl. jours.; co-patentee apparatus for measuring water content of soil; co-discoverer Nova-Cygni, 1975. Commr. Stillwater City, 1974-75; mem. Stillwater Housing Appeals Bd., 1975-79; com. mem. troop 14 Boy Scouts Am., 1976-83, merit badge counselor, 1974—; del. to jurisdictional conf. United Meth. Ch., 1968, alt. del. to gen. conf., 1968. Grantee USDA, 1980, 83, 89, 90, 91, 92, NSF, 1961, U.S. Dept. Interior, 1968, 73, 79, 89, 91, Okla. Dept. Commerce, 1988, Okla. Coun. for Applied Sci. and Tech., Energy Efficient Irrigation, 1990. Fellow Am. Soc. Agronomy (editl. bd., assoc. editor Agronomy jour. 1982-85); mem. ASCE (com. on irrigation water requirements 1979-95, chmn. task com. on calibration and use of neutron moisture meters 1990-94, State-of-the-Art of Civil Engring. award 1992), Internat. Soil Sci. Soc., Am. Geophys. Union (vis. scientist lectr. 1972), Sigma Xi, Am. Radio Relay League, Stillwater Amateur Radio Club. Democrat. Methodist. Avocations: photography, amateur astronomy, music, amateur radio.

STONE, JOHN HELMS, JR., admiralty advisor; b. Andalusia, Ala., Dec. 3, 1927; s. John Helms and Ruth May (Barker) S.;m. Mary Ham, July 24, 1950; children: Malcolm, Mary Ruth, Ronald, John T. Student Ga. Mil. Coll., U.S. Merchant Marine Sch., 1945; student, Tulane U., 1975. Master mariner, USCG. Master capt. Sea-Land Steamship, Port Newark, N.J., 1947-60; Lt. (jg) USNR, 1948-62; sr. pilot Panama Canal Co., Balboa Canal Zone, 1960-73; chief of transit op. Panama Canal Commn., Balboa Canal Zone, 1973-76; chmn. bd. local inspection Panama Canal Commn., Balboa, Republic of Panama, 1976-85; admiralty cons. John H. Stone & Assocs., Boulder, Colo., 1985—, Am. Registry Arbitrators, 1994—; admiralty advisor Phelps-Dunbar, New Orleans, 1958-79, Fowler White, Tampa, Fla., 1984, Terriberry & Assocs., New Orleans, 1992. County treas. Dem. Party, Boulder, 1989. Mem. NRA (v.p. 1970, master pistol and rifle shot), Master, Mates and Pilots Union (v.p. 1970-72). Presbyterian. Avocation: stock market. Home: 3795 Wild Plum Ct Boulder CO 80304-0460

STONE, JOHN MCWILLIAMS, JR., electronics executive; b. Chgo., Nov. 4, 1927; s. J. McWilliams and Marion (Jones) S.; m. Cheryl Johansen Cullison, Dec. 18, 1976; children: Jean Stone Savanyu, Lee Stone Nelson, John III, Michael (dec.), Shannon, Tammy. BA, Princeton U., 1950. Salesman A.B. Dick Co., Milw., 1950-51; prodn. supr. Dukane Corp., St. Charles, Ill., 1951-56, exec. v.p., 1956-62, pres., 1962-70, pres., chmn. bd., 1970—, chmn. bd., chief exec. officer, 1991—; bd. dirs. Harris Bank St. Charles. Trustee The Elgin (Ill.) Acad. (recipient Elgin medal 1984, emeritus 1985—), Phillips Exeter (N.H.) Coun., 1985—, Three Rivers Coun. Boy Scouts Am., St. Charles; mem. Delnor Cmty. Hosp. Men's Found., St. Charles. Named Exec. of Yr. Valley chpt. Profl. Secs. Internat., Aurora, 1981. Mem. Commonwealth Club of Chgo., Econ. Club of Chgo., Princeton Club of Chgo., Execs. Club of Chgo., Dunham Woods Riding Club (pres. 1967-68, 78-79, 89-90). Republican. Episcopalian. Avocation: tennis. Home: PO Box 755 Wayne IL 60184-0755 Office: Dukane Corp 2900 Dukane Dr Saint Charles IL 60174-3348

STONE, JOHN TIMOTHY, JR., writer; b. Denver, July 13, 1933; s. John Timothy and Marie Elizabeth (Briggs) S.; m. Judith Bosworth Stone, June 22, 1955; children: John Timothy III, George William. Student Amherst Coll., 1951-52, U. Mex., 1952; BA, U. Miami, 1955; postgrad., U. Miami 1955, U. Colo., 1959-60. Sales mgr. Atlas Tag, Chgo., 1955-57; br. mgr. Household Fin. Corp., Chgo., 1958-62; pres. Janeff Credit Corp., Madison, Wis., 1962-72; pres. Recreation Internat., Mpls., 1972-74; pres. Continental Royal Services, N.Y.C., 1973-74; dir. devel. The Heartlands Group/Tryon Mint, Toronto, Ont., Can., 1987-89; spl. cons. Creative Resources Internat., Madison, 1988-90, Pubs Adv. Group, 1990—; spl. cons. art and antiques Treasure Hunt Assocs., 1994—; bd. dirs. Madison Credit Bur., Wis. Lenders' Exchange. Author: Mark, 1973, Going for Broke, 1976, The Minnesota Connection, 1978, Debby Boone So Far, 1980, (with John Dallas McPherson) He Calls Himself "An Ordinary Man", 1981, Satiacum, The Chief Who's Winning Back the West, 1981, Runaways, 1983, (with Robert E. Gard) Where The Green Bird Flies, 1984, The Insiders Guide to Buying Art, 1993, Anyone's Treasure Hunt, 1995; syndicated columnist The Great American Treasure Hunt, 1983-87. Served with CIC, U.S. Army, 1957-59. Mem. Sigma Alpha Epsilon. Republican. Presbyterian. Clubs: Minarani, African First Shotters. Home: 1009 Starlight Dr Madison WI 53711-2724 Office: Pubs Adv Group 1009 Starlight Dr Madison WI 53711-2724

STONE, KAREN RASMUSSEN, clinical psychologist; b. Takoma Pk., Md., Dec. 14, 1948; d. Wayne David and Marion (Fowler) Rasmussen; m. Paul Steven Stone, Sept. 13, 1975 (div. 1990); children: Katie, Kristin, Jesse; m. Michael Lee Waddell, June 26, 1993. AB magna cum laude, Harvard U., 1971; MA, Boston U., 1974, PhD, 1978. lic. psychologist, Mass. Psychology intern Beth Israel Hosp., Boston, 1974-76; teaching fellow Boston U., 1975-77; sch. psychologist Concord (Mass.) Acad., 1976-78; staff psychologist numerous instns., Mass., 1977-91; pvt. practice Marshfield, Mass., 1985-94; dir. psychol. svcs. Women's Health Ctr., Bridgewater, Mass., 1991-94; mentor Radcliffe Mentor Program, 1991-92. Mem. Harvard Schs. and Scholarship com., 1992-94. Mem. APA, Mass. Psychol. Assn. Democrat. Home: 153 Boles Rd Marshfield MA 02050-1765 Office: Women's Health Ctr 65 Forest St Marshfield MA 02050-2818

STONE, LAWRENCE, historian; b. Epsom, Surrey, Eng., Dec. 4, 1919; came to U.S., 1963, naturalized, 1970; s. Lawrence Frederick and Mabel Julia Annie (Read) S.; m. Jeanne Caecilia Fawtier, July 24, 1943; children: Elizabeth Caecilia, Robert Lawrence Fawtier. Student, U. Paris-Sorbonne, 1938; BA, MA, Christ Church, Oxford (Eng.) U., 1946; LHD, U. Chgo., 1979, U. Pa., 1986; LittD, U. Edinburgh, 1983, U. Glasgow, 1993; Oxford U., 1994; LittD, Princeton U., 1995. Bryce research student Oxford U., 1946-47; lectr. Oxford U. (Univ. Coll.), 1947-50; fellow Wadham Coll., 1950-63; mem. Inst. Advanced Study, Princeton, 1960-61; Dodge prof. history Princeton, 1963-90, chmn. dept. history, 1967-70; dir. Shelby Cullom Davis Ctr. Hist. Studies, 1968-90. Author: Sculpture in Britain: The Middle Ages, 1955, An Elizabethan: Sir Horatio Palavicino, 1956, The Crisis of the Aristocracy, 1558-1641, 1965, The Causes of the English Revolution 1529-1642, 1972, rev. edit., 1986, Family and Fortune: Studies in Aristocratic Finance in the Sixteenth and Seventeenth Centuries, 1973, Family, Sex and Marriage in England 1500-1800, 1977, The Past and the Present, 1981, An Open Elite? England 1540-1880, 1985, The Past and the Present Revisited, 1987, Road to Divorce: England 1530-1987, 1990, Uncertain Unions: Marriage in England 1660-1753, 1992, Broken Lives: Marital Separation and Divorce in England 1660-1857, 1993, also numerous articles; mem. editl. bd. Past and Present, 1959—. Served as lt. Royal Naval Vol. Res., 1940-45. Fellow Am. Acad. Arts and Scis.; Corr. mem. Brit. Acad.; mem. Am. Philos. Soc. Home: 266 Moore St Princeton NJ 08540-3476

STONE, LAWRENCE MAURICE, lawyer, educator; b. Malden, Mass., Mar. 25, 1931; s. Abraham Jacob and Pauline (Kurtz) S.; m. Anna Jane Clark, June 15, 1963; children: Abraham Dean, Ethan Goldthwaite, Katharine Elisheva. AB magna cum laude, Harvard U., 1953, JD magna cum laude, 1956. Bar: Mass. 1956, Calif. 1958. Rsch. asst. Am. Law Inst., Cambridge, Mass., 1956-57; assoc. Irell and Manella, L.A., 1957-61, ptnr., 1963, 79—; internat. tax coordinator U.S. Treasury Dept., Washington, 1961-62, tax. legis. counsel, 1964-66; prof. law U. Calif., Berkeley, 1966-78; vis. prof. law Yale U., New Haven, 1969, Hebrew U. Jerusalem, 1973-74, U. So. Calif., L.A., 1984; mem. adv. group to commr. IRS, Washington, 1973-74; mem. President's Adv. Commn. on Tax Ct. Appointments, Washington, 1976-80; tax advisory bd. Little Brown Co., 1994—. Author: (with Doernberg) Federal Income Taxation of Corporations and Partnerships, 1987, (with Klein, Bankman and Bittker) Federal Income Taxation, 1990; bd. editors Harvard Law Rev., 1955-56. Fellow Am. Coll. Tax Counsel; mem. ABA, Am. Law Inst., Internat. Fiscal Inst., Am. Arbitration Assn., Phi Beta Kappa. Office: Irell & Manella 1800 Avenue Of The Stars Los Angeles CA 90067-4211

STONE, LEON, banker; b. Rockdale, Tex., Feb. 27, 1914; s. Harley J. and Ella (Strelsky) S.; m. Bess Northington, Aug. 19, 1939; children—Pebble Stone Moss, Cherry J. Stone Wallin. Student, Blinn Coll., Brenham, Tex, 1932, Sul Ross Coll., Alpine, Tex., 1934, U. Tex., 1935, Rutgers U., 1954. With Brown & Root, Houston, 1936-37; Guggenheim-Goldsmith, Austin, Tex., 1937-38; with Austin Nat. Bank, 1938—, pres., 1963-84; also dir.; bd. dirs. First State Bank, Burnet, Tex.; chmn. Southwestern Grad. Sch. Banking, So. Meth. U. Dallas. Vice chmn. Tchr. Retirement System Tex., 1956-77; Bd. dirs. Presbyn. Theol. Sem., 1958—, Seton Hosp., 1966—, Mental Health and Mental Retardation Assn., 1965—. Served to lt. col. U.S. Army, ETO. Named Boss of Year, Credit Women of Austin, 1966. Mem. Am. Bankers Assn. (regional v.p. 1965—, exec. com. 1966—), Tex. Bankers Assn. (pres. 1973), Am. Inst. Banking (past pres.), Austin C. of C. (pres.

1968), Tex. Taxpayers Assn. (pres.). Clubs: Rotarian, Mason, Shriner (Jester). Office: Nations Bank PO Box 908 Austin TX 78781

STONE, LEWIS BART, lawyer; b. Bklyn., Mar. 5, 1938; s. Michael and Sylvia (Silberling) S.; m. Gretchen E. Haug, Dec. 23, 1964; children: Pamela Kendall, Lewis Bart. B.Ch.E., Rensselaer Poly. Inst., 1958; LL.B., Harvard U., 1962 Bar: N.Y. 1963, U.S. Dist. Ct. (so. dist.) N.Y. 1964, U.S. Dist. Ct. (ea. dist.) N.Y. 1964, U.S. Ct. Appeals (5th and 2d cirs.) 1964, U.S. Supreme Ct. Assoc., Strasser, Spiegelberg, Fried & Frank, N.Y.C., 1962-65; assoc. Valicenti, Leighton Reid & Pine, N.Y.C., 1965-67; asst. counsel to gov. of N.Y., Albany, 1967-71; spl. asst. to gov., 1971; assoc. Carb, Luria, Glassner, Cook & Kufeld, N.Y.C., 1972-75, ptnr., 1975-83; ptnr. Rogers & Wells, N.Y.C., 1983—; bd. dirs. Brooks Brothers Inc. Treas. N.Y. Rep. Party, 1986—; sec., counsel citizens budget commn., 1987—. Mem. Am. Coll. Real Estate Lawyers, Sky Club, Sigma Xi, Tau Beta Pi, Phi Lambda Upsilon, Lambda Alpha. Republican. Office: Rogers & Wells 200 Park Ave Ste 5200 New York NY 10166-0005

STONE, MARVIN JULES, physician, educator; b. Columbus, Ohio, Aug. 3, 1937; s. Roy J. and Lillian (Bedwinek) S.; m. Jill Feinstein, June 29, 1958; children: Nancy Lillian, Robert Howard. Student, Ohio State U., 1955-58; SM in Pathology, U. Chgo., 1962, MD with honors, 1963. Diplomate Am. Bd. Internal Medicine, (Hematology, Med. Oncology). Intern ward med. svc. Barnes Hosp., St. Louis, 1963-64, asst. resident, 1964-65; clin. assoc. arthritis and rheumatism br. Nat. Inst. Arthritis and Metabolic Diseases, NIH, Bethesda, Md., 1965-68; resident in medicine, ACP scholar Parkland Meml. Hosp., Dallas, 1968-69; fellow in hematology-oncology, dept. internal medicine U. Tex. Southwestern Med. Sch., Dallas, 1969-70, instr. dept. internal medicine, 1970-71, asst. prof., 1971-73, assoc. prof., 1974-76, clin. prof., 1976—, chmn. bioethics com., 1979-81; mem. faculty and steering com. immunology grad. program, Grad. Sch. Biomed. Scis., U. Tex. Health Sci. Ctr., Dallas, 1975, adj. mem., 1976—; dir. Charles A. Sammons Cancer Ctr., chief oncology, dir. immunology, co-dir. divsn. hematology-oncology, attending physician Baylor U. Med. Ctr., Dallas, 1976—; v.p. med. staff Parkland Meml. Hosp., Dallas, 1982. Contbr. chpts. to books, articles to profl. jours. Chmn. com. patient-aid Greater Dallas/Ft. Worth chpt. Leukemia Soc. Am., 1971-76, chmn. med. adv. com., 1978-80, bd. dirs., 1971-80; mem. v.p. Dallas unit Am. Cancer Soc., 1977-78, pres., 1978-80; mem. adv. bd. Baylor U. Med. Ctr. Found. With USPHS, 1965-68. Named Outstanding Full Time Faculty Mem. Dept. Internal Medicine, Baylor U. Med. Ctr., 1978, 87. Fellow ACP (gov. No. Tex. 1993—); mem. AMA, Am. Assn. Immunologists, Am. Soc. Hematology, Internat. Soc. Hematology, Coun. Thrombosis, Am. Heart Assn. (established investigator 1970-75), Am. Soc. Clin. Oncology, Am. Osler Soc., Am. Assn. for Cancer Rsch., So. Soc. Clin. Investigation, Tex. Med. Assn., Dallas County Med. Soc., Clin. Immunology Soc., Phi Beta Kappa, Sigma Xi, Alpha Omega Alpha. Office: Baylor U Med Ctr Charles A Sammons Cancer Ctr 3500 Gaston Ave Dallas TX 75246-2045

STONE, MARVIN LAWRENCE, journalist, government official; b. Burlington, Vt., Feb. 26, 1924; s. Samuel and Anita (Abrams) S.; m. Sydell Magelaner, Nov. 20, 1949; children—Jamie Faith, Stacey Hope, Torren Magelaner. Student, Emory and Henry Coll., 1943, U. Vt., 1948; B.A., Marshall Coll., 1947; M.S., Columbia U., 1949; Litt.D., Marshall U., 1968; LL.D., Emory and Henry Coll., 1981; D.H.L., Elon Coll., 1982. Assignment reporter Huntington (W.Va.) Herald-Dispatch, 1941-43, 46-48; European corr. Internat. News Service, 1949-52, Far Eastern dir., 1952-58; Sloan Found. fellow in sci. Columbia U., 1958-59; cons. chief army research and devel., 1959-60; assoc. editor U.S. News & World Report mag., 1960-66, gen. editor, 1966-68, asso. exec. editor, 1969-70, sr. asso. exec. editor, 1971-72, exec. editor, 1973-76, v.p., editor-in-chief, 1976-85, chmn. bd., 1984-85; chmn. bd. Madana Realty Co., 1984-85; dep. dir. USIA, 1985-89; U.S. commr. gen. Seville '92' Expo, 1989-90; mem. adv. com. U.S. Patent Office, 1976-78; adj. fellow Coun. on Strategic and Internat. Studies, 1989-90; mem. adv. bd. Univ. Pubs., 1989-92, Corp. for Pub. Broadcasting program adv. bd., 1992; chmn., pres., Internat. Media Fund, 1990-95. Author: Man in Space. Trustee, v.p., bd. dirs. Washington Opera; chmn. bd. dirs. USN Meml. Found., 1981-82, vice chmn., 1983-94, bd. dirs., 1991-95; mem. nat. adv. bd. Am. U.; bd. dirs. Pub. Diplomacy Found., Am. News Women's Found., 1991. Lt. (j.g.) USNR, 1943-46. Recipient Columbia Journalism 50th Anniversary Honor award, 1963, Marshall U. Disting. Alumnus award, 1973, Nat. Disting. Alumnus award Am. Assn. State Colls. and Univs., 1977, Freedoms Found. award, 1978, 79, 80, 81, Legion of Honor Chapel of Four Chaplains, 1980, Am. Eagle award, 1983, Silver Gavel award ABA, 1983, Gold Mercury Internat. award, Rome, Nat. Communication award Boys Clubs Am., Gill Robb Wilson award U.S. Air Force Assn., Disting. Honor award USIA; named to Washington Journalists' Hall of Fame, 1990; Pulitzer traveling fellow, Columbia, Austria, 1950, Knight fellowship, 1995. Fellow Ctr. for Security and Internat. Studies (adj.); mem. White House Corrs. Assn., Am. Soc. Mag. Editors (exec. com. 1985), Nat. Press Club, Omicron Delta Kappa, Sigma Delta Chi. Clubs: Fgn. Corrs. of Japan (pres. 1956-57); Internat. (Washington), Cosmos (Washington), Caribao (Washington). Home: 6318 Crosswoods Circle Lake Barcroft Falls Church VA 22044

STONE, MATTHEW PETER, lawyer; b. L.A., Sept. 21, 1961. BA in English, UCLA, 1985; JD, Loyola U., L.A., 1988. Bar: Calif. 1989, Ga. 1992, U.S. Dist. Ct. (ctrl. dist.) Calif. 1989, U.S. Dist. Ct. (no., mid. and so. dists.) Ga. 1992. Litigation assoc. Seligmann, Slyngstad & Wright, L.A., 1988-90, Musick, Peeler & Garrett, L.A., 1990-92; asst. atty. gen. Ga. Dept. of Law, Atlanta, 1992-95; litig. assoc. Casey, Gilson & Williams P.C., Atlanta, 1995—. Chmn. Law Day and Liberty Bell com. younger lawyers sect. State Bar of Ga., 1993—, co-chair Law Day com., 1995—, mem. intrastate moot ct. com. younger lawyers sect., 1994—; panel judge Ga. Intrastate Moot Ct. Competition, 1994—, ABA Nat. Appellate Advocacy Competition, S.E. Regional, 1994; chmn. Parks Project Hands on Atlanta Day, 1994; vol. Hands on Atlanta Day, 1993, 95; mem. ethical action com. Univ. Synagogue, L.A., 1990-92; participant Bet Tzedek Legal Svcs., L.A., 1986; participant, vol. Income Tax Assistance, L.A., 1988. Avocations: fishing, automobiles, physical fitness. Office: Casey Gilson Williams PC 211 Perimeter Ctr Pkwy Ste 1000 Atlanta GA 30346-9003

STONE, MERRILL BRENT, lawyer; b. Jersey City, N.J., Aug. 16, 1951; s. Leonard and Claire (Orlean) S.; m. Geri Ellen Satkin, Nov. 24, 1976; children: Jacqueline Blair, Erica Lauren. AB summa cum laude, Rutgers U., 1973; JD, Columbia U., 1976. Bar: N.J. 1976, N.Y. 1977, Fla. 1981, U.S. Dist. Ct. N.J. 1976, U.S. Dist. Ct. (so. dist.) N.Y. 1977, U.S. Dist. Ct. (so. dist.) Fla. 1983. Assoc. Kelley, Drye & Warren, N.Y.C., 1976-84; resident Kelley, Drye & Warren, Miami, 1983-85; ptnr. Kelley, Drye & Warren, N.Y.C., 1985-92, mng. ptnr., 1992—. Editor: (comments section) Columbia Human Rights Law Rev., N.Y.C., 1975-76. Trustee Greater Miami C. of C., 1984-85. Named Harlan Fiske Stone Scholar, Columbia Law Sch., N.Y.C., 1975-76. Mem. ABA (bus. bankruptcy com. sect. on bus. law, banking law com.), Am. Soc. Corp. Secs., Fla. Bar Assn., Club 101, Weston Field Club, Phi Beta Kappa, Pi Sigma Alpha. Office: Kelley Drye & Warren 101 Park Ave New York NY 10178

STONE, MINNIE STRANGE, retired automotive service company executive; b. Palatka, Fla., Mar. 10, 1919; d. James Arrious and Pansy (Thomas) Strange; student Massey Bus. Coll., 1938-39; m. Fred Albion Stone, Nov. 30, 1939; children: Fred Albion, James Thomas, Thomas Demere. Sec., bookkeeper Sears, Roebuck & Co., Jacksonville, Fla., 1939-41; fin. sec. U.S. Army, Macon, Ga., 1941, Atlanta, 1942; sec., bookkeeper Raleigh Spring & Brake Sv., Inc. (name changed to Stone Heavy Vehicle Specialist) (N.C.), 1953-84, sec.-treas. corp., 1960-84, dir., sec. Vol. Wake County Mental Health, 1970-80; pres. YWCA, Wake County, 1973-76, bd. dirs., 1966-76; bd. dirs. Urban Ministry Ctr. Raleigh, 1983-89, mem. adv. bd., 1989—; bd. trustees Bapt. Children's Homes N.C.; former mem. subcom. Gov. Coun. Older Adult Fitness. Mem. N.C. Mus. of History Assocs., N.C. Art Soc., Monthly Investors Club, Coley Forest Garden Club. Republican. Baptist. Home: 920 Runnymede Rd Raleigh NC 27607-3108

STONE, OLIVER WILLIAM, screenwriter, director; b. N.Y.C., Sept. 15, 1946; s. Louis and Jacqueline (Goddet) S. Student, Yale U., 1965; B.F.A., NYU Film Sch., 1971. Tchr. Cholon, Vietnam, 1965-66; wiper U.S. Mcht. Marine, 1966; taxi driver N.Y.C., 1971. Screenwriter, dir.: Seizure, 1973, Midnight Express, 1978 (Acad. award for screenplay, Writers Guild Am. for screenplay), The Hand, 1981, (with John Milius) Conan, the Barbarian, 1982, Scarface, 1983, (with Michael Cimino) Year of the Dragon, 1985, (with David Lee Henry) 8 Million Ways to Die, 1986, (with Richard Boyle) Salvador, 1986, Platoon (also dir.), 1986 (Acad. award, Dirs. Guild award, British Acad. award); co-writer, dir.: Wall Street, 1987, Talk Radio, 1988, The Doors, 1991; screenwriter, prodr., dir.: Born on the Fourth of July, 1989 (Acad. award, 1990), JFK, 1991, Heaven & Earth, 1993, Natural Born Killers, 1994, Nixon, 1995 (Acad. award nominee for best screenplay with Stephen J. Rivele and Christopher Wilkinson 1996); prodr.: South Central, 1992, Zebrahead, 1992, The New Age, 1994, The Joy Luck Club, 1993, (TV mini-series) Wild Palms, 1993; exec. prodr. Killer: A Journal of Murder, 1995, (HBO) Indictment: The McMartin Preschool, 1995 (Emmy award). Served with inf. U.S. Army, 1967-68, Vietnam. Decorated Purple Heart with oak leaf cluster, Bronze Star. Mem. Writers Guild Am., Dirs. Guild Am., Acad. Motion Picture Arts and Scis. Office: Ixtlan 201 Santa Monica Blvd Fl 6 Santa Monica CA 90401-2214

STONE, PETER, playwright, scenarist; b. Los Angeles, Feb. 27, 1930; s. John and Hilda (Hess) S.; m. Mary O'Hanley, Feb. 17, 1961. BA, Bard Coll., 1951, DLitt, 1971; MFA, Yale U., 1953. Ind. stage and screen writer, 1961—. Author: (musical comedies) Kean, 1961, Skyscraper, 1965, 1776, 1969 (Tony award Best Musical Book, 1969, N.Y. Drama Critics Circle award 1969, London Plays and Players award 1969, Drama Desk award Best Musical book writer 1969), Two by Two, 1970, Sugar, 1972, Woman of the Year, 1981 (Tony award Best Musical book 1981), My One and Only, 1983, Grand Hotel, 1989, The Will Rogers Follies, 1991 (Tony award Best Musical 1991, N.Y. Drama Critics Circle award Best New Musical 1991, Grammy award 1991), (play) Full Circle, 1973, (films) Charade, 1963 (Writers Guild award Best Comedy Film 1964, Mystery Writers Am. award Best Mystery film 1964), Father Goose, 1964 (Acad. award Best Original Screenplay 1964), Mirage, 1965, Arabesque, 1966, Secret War of Harry Frigg, 1968, Sweet Charity, 1969, Skin Game, 1971, 1776, 1972 (Christopher award for Best Film), Taking of Pelham 123, 1974, Silver Bears, 1978, Who is Killing the Great Chefs of Europe?, 1978, Why Would I Lie?, 1980, Just Cause, 1995, (TV spl.) Androcles and the Lion, 1968; (TV episodes) Studio One, 1956, Brenner, 1959, Witness, 1961, Asphalt Jungle, 1961, The Defenders, 1961-62 (Emmy award 1962), The Benefactors, 1962, Espionage, 1963, Adam's Rib, 1973-74, Ivan the Terrible, 1976, Baby on Board, 1988, Grand Larceny. Mem. Dramatists Guild (pres.), Authors League, Writers Guild Am. Home: 160 E 71st St New York NY 10021-5119 also: Stony Hill Rd Amagansett NY 11930

STONE, PETER GEORGE, lawyer, publishing company executive; b. N.Y.C., July 29, 1937; s. Leo and Anne S.; m. Rikke Linde, Dec. 26, 1974; children: Adam, Rachel. BS in Econs., U. Pa., 1959; JD, Columbia U. 1962. Bar: N.Y. 1963. Assoc. Ballon Stoll & Itzler, N.Y.C., 1963-65, Raphael, Searles & Vischi, N.Y.C., 1965-67; v.p., counsel Firedoor Corp. Am., N.Y.C., 1967-69; ptnr. Cahill, Stone & Driscoll, N.Y.C., 1969-75; v.p. fin. and law, gen. counsel Ottaway Newspapers, Inc., Campbell Hall, N.Y., 1975—; lectr., columnist on media law numerous univs. including Jud. Coll. U. Nev., Hartwick Coll., Bucknell U., U. N.C., Western Conn. State U., SUNY. Bd. dirs., trustee, treas. Daily Pennsylvanian Alumni Assn. With USAR, 1962-63. Mem. ABA (forum com. on comm. law), N.Y. State Bar Assn. (ct. and cmty., pub. events and edn., pub. info. through TV coms., com. media law), N.Y. Bar Found., N.Y. State Fair Trial Free Press Assn., Newspaper Assn. Am. (com. on employee rels., chmn. com. on legal affairs, del. 1st amendment congress, com. on pub. policy), Am. Arbitration Assn., Soc. Human Resource Mgmt., Internat. Newspaper Fin. Execs., Newspaper Pers. Rels. Assn. (chmn. legal task force, bd. dirs.), Penn Club. Office: PO Box 401 Campbell Hall NY 10916-0401

STONE, RANDOLPH NOEL, law educator; b. Milw., Nov. 26, 1946; s. Fisher and Lee Della Stone; children: Sokoni, Rahman. BA, U. Wis., Milw., 1972; JD, Madison, 1975. Bar: D.C., 1975, Wis. 1975, Ill. 1977. Staff atty. Criminal Def. Consortium of Cook County, Chgo., 1976-78; clin. fellow U. Chgo. Law Sch., 1977-80; ptnr. Stone & clark, Chgo., 1980-83; staff atty., dep. dir. Pub. Defender Svc. for D.C., Washington, 1983-88; pub. defender Cook County Pub. Defender's Office, Chgo., 1988-91; lectr. U. Chgo. Law Sch., 1990, clin. prof. law, dir. Mandel Legal Aid Clinic, 1991—; adj. prof. Ill. Inst. Tech. Chgo.-Kent Coll. Law Sch., 1991, bd. overseers, 1990; lectr. law Harvard U., 1991—; mem. Ill. Bd. Admissions to the Bar, 1994—; bd. dirs. The Sentencing Project, 1986—; instr. trial advocacy workshop Harvard Law Sch., 1985-89. Adv. bd. Neighborhood Defender Svc. (Harlem), N.Y.C. Reginald Heber Smith fellow Neighborhood Legal Svcs. Program, Washington, 1975-76. Mem. ABA (sect. criminal justice coun. 1989-95, chair 1993), Ill. State Bar Assn. (sect. criminal justice coun. 1989-92), Chgo. Bar Assn. (bd. dirs. 1990-92), Nat. Legal Aid and Defender Assn. (def. com.). Office: U Chgo Law Sch Mandel Legal Aid Clinic 6020 S University Ave Chicago IL 60637-2704

STONE, RICHARD JAMES, lawyer; b. Chgo., Apr. 30, 1945; s. Milton M. and Ruth Jean (Manaster) S.; m. Lee Lawrence, Sept. 1, 1979; children: Robert Allyn, Katherine Jenney, Grant Lawrence. B.A. in Econs., U. Chgo., 1967; J.D., UCLA, 1970. Bar: Calif. 1971, Oreg. 1994. Assoc., O'Melveny & Myers, L.A., 1971-77; dep. asst. gen. counsel U.S. Dept. Def., Washington, 1978-79; asst. to sec. U.S. Dept. Energy, Washington, 1979-80; counsel Sidley & Austin, L.A., 1981, ptnr., 1982-88; ptnr., head litigation dept. Milbank, Tweed, Hadley & McCloy, 1988-94; mng. ptnr., Zelle & Larson, L.A., 1994—; gen. counsel and staff dir. Study of L.A. Civil Disturbance for Bd. Police Commrs., 1992. Mem. Pub. Sector Task Force, Calif. State Senate Select Com. on Long Range Policy Planning, 1985-86, U.S. del. Micronesian Polit. Status Negotiations, 1978-79; mem. adv. panel Coun. Energy Resource Tribes, 1981-85; mem. Bishop's com. St. Aidan's Episcopal Ch., 1990-93; dir. Legal Aid Found., 1991—, officer 1994—. Recipient Amos Alonzo Stagg medal and Howell Murray Alumni medal U. Chgo., 1967; honoree Nat. Conf. Black Mayors, 1980; recipient spl. citation for outstanding performance Sec. Dept. Energy, 1981. Fellow Am. Bar Found.; mem. ABA, Calif. Bar Assn., Oreg. Bar Assn., L.A. County Bar Assn. (trustee 1986-88), Assn. Bus. Trial Lawyers, Phi Gamma Delta. Editor-in-chief UCLA Law Rev., 1970. Office: Zelle & Larson 10990 Wishire Blvd 15th Fl Los Angeles CA 90024

STONE, ROBERT A., airport administrator. Mgr. Greater Buffalo Internat. Airport. Office: Greater Buffalo Internat Airport Genesee St Buffalo NY 14225*

STONE, ROBERT ANTHONY, author; b. N.Y.C., Aug. 21, 1937; s. C. Homer and Gladys Catherine (Grant) S.; m. Janice G. Burr, Dec. 11, 1959; children: Deidre M., Ian A. Student, N.Y. U., 1958-59; Stegner fellow, Stanford, 1962. Editorial asst. N.Y. Daily News, N.Y.C., 1958-60; former actor New Orleans; former advt. copywriter N.Y.C.; writer Nat. Mirror, N.Y.C., 1965-67; novelist, 1960—; mem. faculty Johns Hopkins U., Balt., 1993-94, Yale U., 1994—; free-lance writer London, Hollywood, Calif., South Vietnam, 1967-71; writer-in-residence Princeton U., 1971-72; faculty Amherst Coll., 1972-75, 77-78, Stanford U., 1979, U. Hawaii-Manoa, 1979-80, Harvard U., 1981, U. Calif.-Irvine, 1982, NYU, 1983, U. Calif.-San Diego, 1985, Princeton U., 1985. Author: (novels) A Hall of Mirrors, 1967, Dog Soldiers, 1974 (Nat. Book award 1975), A Flag for Sunrise, 1981, Images of War, 1986, Children of Light, 1986, Outerbridge Reach, 1992, (screenplays) WUSA, 1970, (with Judith Rascoe) Who'll Stop the Rain, 1978; contbg. author: Best American Short-stories, 1970, 88. Served with USN, 1955-58. Recipient William Faulkner prize, 1967, John Dos Passos prize for lit., 1982; award in lit. Am. Acad. and Inst. Arts and Letters, 1982, grantee, 1988-92; Guggenheim fellow, 1971, NEH fellow, 1983. Mem. PEN (exec. bd.). Address: PO Box 967 Block Island RI 02807*

STONE, ROBERT CHRISTOPHER, computer scientist, educator; b. Norman, Okla., Aug. 19, 1964; s. Robert Joseph and Billie Dee (Combs) S.; m. Yvette Marie Hewes, May 2, 1983; children: Katherine Angelica Stone, Nicholas Christopher Stone. BS in Psychology, Regents Coll., 1989; DO, U. North Tex. Health Sci. Ctr., Ft. Worth, 1995; cert. med. asst., Western Coll., San Leandro, Calif., 1987. Cert. med. asst., ACLS. Psychiat. counselor CareUnit, Ft. Worth, 1985-86; med. office nurse Bay Area Health, San Francisco, 1986-88; guest lectr. U. North Tex., Denton, 1989-92; rschr. U. North Tex. Health Sci. Ctr., 1989—, instr., 1992—; chief exec. officer Edn. Rsch. Labs., Inc., Ft. Worth, 1993—; also chmn. bd. dirs. Edn. Rsch. Labs., Inc.; v.p. Exec. Edn. Rsch., Inc., Ft. Worth, 1990—; v.p. edn. CyberMed, Ft. Worth, 1994—; edn. cons. Diocese of S.W., Dallas, 1993—; presenter in field. Author: (electronic editions) DSM-IV, Diagnostic Criteria, Little Black Book of Primary Care Pearls and References, Current Clinical Strategies Series, Lexi-Comp Seris; contbr. articles to profl. jours. Pres. parish coun. St. Barbara's Orthodox Ch., Ft. Worth, 1994, choir dir., 1992—. Recipient tchg. fellowship U. North Tex. Health Sci. Ctr., 1992-95; computer adaptive testing grantee Found. for the Improvement of Post Secondary Edn., Washington, 1993—. Mem. AMA, Am. Osteo. Assn., Soc. for Acad. Emergency Medicine, Undergrad. Acad. Osteopathy, Emergency Medicine Club (v.p.). Republican. Russian Orthodox. Avocations: classical music, theater, travel, cooking.

STONE, ROBERT ELDRED, small business owner, museum director; b. Chester, N.H., July 26, 1929; s. Harold I. and Anna L. (Ahlberg) S.; m. Dorothy Harriette Fullonton, Feb. 3, 1951 (div. 1977); children: Dennis Wayne, Kathy Ann. Electronic Technician, USCG Tng. Ctr., Groton, Conn., 1952; A. in Electronic Engring., Merrimac Coll., Andover, Mass., 1957. Crew chief N.H. Permastone Corp., Londonderry, 1948, 49; quality assurance technician Western Elec. Corp. (AT&T), Lawrence, Mass., 1953-57, assoc. engr., 1957-83; owner, pres. America's Stonehenge, North Salem, N.H., 1957—. Coach, Little League Basketball, Derry, N.H.; chmn. Cub Scouts, Derry; past mem. vestry Episc. Ch. of Transfiguration, Derry, past chmn. fin. com. With USCG, 1949-52. Mem. N.H. Archaeol. Soc., New England Antiquities Rsch. Assn. (founder, pres. 1964-76, rsch. dir. 1976-78), The Gungywamp Soc. Avocations: archaeology, history, acrylic painting, reading, TV documentaries. Office: Am's Stonehenge PO Box 84 North Salem NH 03073-0084

STONE, ROBERT RYRIE, financial executive; b. Toronto, Mar. 25, 1943; s. Frank R. and Norah I. (Varey) S.; m. Jacqueline P. Cogan, July 8, 1966; children: Charlie, Tracy. BSc, U. Toronto, 1964. Chartered acct., Can Inst. Chartered Accts. Treas., dir. fin. Gt. No. Capital Corp., Toronto, 1969-73; various positions Cominco Ltd., Vancouver, B.C., Can., 1973-78, treas., 1978-80, v.p. fin., chief fin. officer, 1980—, also bd. dirs.; bd. dir. Agrium Inc., Highland Valley Copper, Union Bank of Switzerland; chmn. Global Stone Corp.; mem. adv. bd. Allendale Ins. Bd. dirs. Jr. Achievement Can. Mem. B.C. Inst. Chartered Accts., Fin. Execs. Inst. (pres. 1983-84). Office: Cominco Ltd, 200 Burrard St # 500, Vancouver, BC Canada V6C 3L7

STONE, ROGER DAVID, environmentalist; b. N.Y.C., Aug. 4, 1934; s. Patrick William and Kathleen Mary Stone; married; 1 child. BA in English, Yale U., 1955. Asst. to pub. Time Mag., 1959-61; corr., news bur. chief Time Mag., San Francisco, Rio, Paris, 1961-68; asst. to pres. Time Inc., N.Y.C., 1968-70; v.p. internat. dept. Chase Manhattan Bank, N.Y.C., 1970-74; pres. Ctr. for Inter-Am. Rels., N.Y.C., 1975-82; v.p. World Wildlife Fund, 1982-86, sr. fellow, 1986-90; vis. fellow, cons. on environ. issues Coun. on Fgn. Rels., 1990-92; vice chmn. ECO Inc., Washington, 1992—; pres. Sustainable Devel. Inst., Washington, 1993—; vis. lectr. Yale Ctr. for Internat. and Area Studies, 1994-95. Author: Dreams of Amazonia, 1985, The Voyage of the Sanderling, 1990, Wildlands and Human Needs, 1991, The Nature of Development: Reports from the Rural Tropics on the Quest for Sustainable Economic Growth, 1992, Fair Tide: Sailing Toward Long Island's Future, 1996; contbr. chpts. to books; contbr. articles to Time, Life, Life en Espanol, Fgn. Affairs, N.Y. Times, Internat. Herald Tribune, Christian Sci. Monitor, Harvard Bus. Rev., USA Today Mag., Cruising World, Conservation Found. Letter, numerous others. Bd. dirs. Asian Inst. of Tech. Found., Caribbean Conservation Corp., Cintas Found., Armand G. Erpf Fund, Scenic Hudson, Inc.; former bd. dirs. U. Andes Found.; former bd. dirs. and exec. com. World Wildlife Fund-U.S., Ctr. for Inter-Am. Rels., Ams. Found., Accion Internat., Arts Internat., others. Lt. (j.g.) USN, 1956-59. Mem. Coun. on Fgn. Rels., Century Assn. Democrat. Episcopalian. Avocation: sailing. Home and Office: 3403 O St NW Washington DC 20007-2817

STONE, ROGER WARREN, container company executive; b. Chgo., Feb. 16, 1935; s. Marvin N. and Anita (Masover) S.; m. Susan Kesert, Dec. 24, 1955; children: Karen, Lauren, Jennifer. BS in Econs., U. Pa., 1957. With Stone Container Corp., Chgo., 1957—, dir., 1968-77, v.p., gen. mgr. container div., 1970-75, pres., chief operating officer, 1975-79, pres., chief exec. officer, 1979—, chmn. bd., chief exec. officer, 1983—; bd. dirs. Morton Internat., McDonald's Corp., Option Care, Inc. Past trustee Glenwood (Ill.) Sch. for Boys; trustee Chgo. Symphony Orch. Assn.; fellow Lake Forest (Ill.) Acad.; mem. bd. overseers Wharton Sch. Bus., U. Pa.; mem. adv. coun. Econ. Devel. Named Best or Top CEO in firm's industry Wall Street Transcript, 1981-86; recipient Top CEO award in Forest and Paper Specialty Products Industry, Fin. World Mag., 1984, Bronze award in Paper and Packaging Category, 1996. Mem. Am. Forest and Paper Assn. (chmn. bd. 1985-86, bd. dirs), Chief Execs. Orgn., Corrugated Industry Devel. Corp. (past pres.), Inst. Paper Sci. and Tech. (former trustee), The Chgo. Com., Mid-Am. Com., Chgo. Coun. Fgn. Rels., Standard Club, Tavern Club, Comml. Club, Econ. Club, Lake Shore Country Club. Republican. Office: Stone Container Corp 150 N Michigan Ave Chicago IL 60601

STONE, RUSSELL A., sociology educator; b. Medicine Hat, Alta., Can., Feb. 8, 1944; came to U.S., 1966; s. Ben and Clara G. (Gibbs) S.; m. S. Rala Stollar, Aug. 18, 1965; children: Peter H., Mira Beth. BA, McGill U., Montreal, Que., Can., 1965; PhD, Princeton U., 1971. Asst. to assoc prof. sociology SUNY, Buffalo, 1970-84, prof., 1984-91, chmn. dept. sociology, 1985-88; prof. sociology Am. U., Washington, 1991—, assoc. dean for grad. affairs, 1991-96; vis. rsch. assoc. Israel Inst. Applied Social Rsch., Jerusalem, 1977-78; vis. assoc. prof. Ben Gurion U. of the Negev, Beersheba, Israel, 1978; vis. prof. Hebrew U., Jerusalem, 1977-78. Author: Social Change in Israel: Attitudes and Events, 1982; co-author: Political Elites on Arab North Africa, 1982; editor: OPEC and the Middle East, 1977; co-editor: Change in Tunisia, 1976, Critical Essays on Israeli Social Issues and Scholarship, 1994; chmn. editorial bd. SUNY Press, 1987-90, series editor; contbr. articles to profl. jours. Mem. Am. Sociol. Assn., Middle East Studies Assn., World Future Soc., Assn. for Israel Studies (sec., treas. 1989-93). Office: Am U Dept Sociology 4400 Massachusetts Ave NW Washington DC 20016-8072

STONE, SAMUEL BECKNER, lawyer; b. Martinsville, Va., Feb. 4, 1934; s. Paul Raymond and Mildred (Beckner) S.; m. Shirley Ann Gregory, June 18, 1955; children: Paul Gregory, Daniel Taylor. BSEE, Va. Polytech. Inst. & State U., 1955; JD, George Wash. U., 1960. Bar: Md. 1960, Calif. 1963, Patent and Trademark Office. Patent examiner, 1955-58; patent advisor Naval Ordinance Lab., Silver Spring, Md., 1958-59; assoc. Thomas & Crickenberger, Washington, 1959-61, Beckman Instruments Inc., Fullerton, Calif., 1961-65; assoc. Lyon & Lyon, L.A., 1965-72, ptnr., 1972; mng. ptnr. Lyon & Lyon, Costa Mesa, Calif., 1982—; judge Disneyland Com. Svc. Awards, Anaheim, Calif., 1987. Mem. Orange County Bar Assn. (bd. dirs. 1988-91, travel seminar chair 1986-92), Orange County Patent Law Assn. (pres. 1987, bd. exec. com. 1987-90), Calif. Bar Assn. (intellectual property sect. bd. 1987-90), Am. Electronics Assn. (lawyers com. 1988—), Orange County Venture Group (dir. 1985—, pres. 1996), Rams Booster Club (dir. 1984-90), Pacific Club (chair legal adv. com. 1989-92). Republican. Avocations: tennis, waterskiing, music. Home: 1612 Antigua Way Newport Beach CA 92660 Office: Lyon & Lyon Ste 1200 3200 Park Center Dr Costa Mesa CA 92626

STONE, SHARON, actress; b. Meadville, Pa., Mar. 10, 1958; d. Joe and Dorothy S; m. Michael Greenburg, 1984 (div. 1987). Student, Edinboro U. Model Eileen Ford Modeling Agy. Appeared in films Stardust Memories, 1980, Deadly Blessing, 1981, Irreconcilable Differences, 1984, King Solomon's Mines, 1985, Allan Quatermain and the Lost City of Gold, 1986, Cold Steel, 1987, Police Academy 4, 1987, Action Jackson, 1988, Above the Law, 1988, Total Recall, 1990, He Said/She Said, 1991, Scissors, 1991, Basic Instinct, 1991, Where Sleeping Dogs Lie, 1992, Sliver, 1993, Intersection, 1994, The Specialist, 1994, The Quick and the Dead, 1995, Casino, 1995 (Golden Globe award for best actress in film 1996, Acad. award nominee for best actress 1996); TV appearances include Not Just Another Affair, 1982, Bay City Blues, 1983, Calendar Girl Murders, 1984, The Vegas Strip Wars, 1984, War and Remembrance, 1988, (guest) The Larry Sanders Show, 1994; narrator: Harlow: The Blond Bombshell, 1993. Office: c/o ICM 8942 Wilshire Blvd Beverly Hills CA 90211-1934*

STONE, STEVEN MICHAEL, sports announcer, former baseball player; b. Cleve., July 14, 1947. BS in Edn., Kent State U. Baseball player San Francisco Giants, 1971-72, Chgo. Cubs, 1974-76, Chgo. White Sox, 1977-78, Balt. Orioles, 1979-82; baseball announcer WGN Continental Broadcasting Co., Chgo., 1982—; owner restaurant Scottsdale, Ariz. Recipient Cy Young award Am. League, 1980. Mem. Am. League All-Star Team, 1980. Office: WGN TV 2501 W Bradley Pl Chicago IL 60618-4701

STONE, SUSAN BLANKENSHIP, grants writer, public policy consultant; b. Evansville, Ind., Nov. 1, 1962; d. Sammy Delano and Shirley Elaine (Morlock) B.; m. Lucas Stone, Aug. 11, 1984. BA, Murray State U., 1984; MPA, U. Ky., 1987. Cert. probation officer, Ind. Staff asst. McCloskey for Congress, Bloomington, Ind., 1988; probation officer Monroe County Probation Dept., Bloomington, 1989-91; rsch. asst./assoc. Coun. of State Govts., Lexington, Ky., 1992-93; grants writer MDK Assocs., Inc., Lexington, 1993—; county cons. juvenile jail removal project Monroe County Probation Dept., Bloomington, 1990-91; cons. SBCS, Inc., Mt. Vernon, Ind., 1993—. Contbr. book chpt.: Intermediate Sanctions: Sentencing in the 90s, 1994; co-author: (jour.) Perspectives, 1993, (mag.) Corrections Today, 1993, also papers, tng. manuals and reports. Named Ky. State Epée champion, 1981. Buddhist. Avocations: running, dogs, cooking. Office: MDK Assocs Inc 277 E High St Lexington KY 40507-1450

STONE, THOMAS EDWARD, defense consultant, retired rear admiral; b. Selfridge, Mich., Oct. 21, 1939; m. Lucy Lee, June 9, 1962. BS, U.S. Naval Acad., 1962; MS in Elec. Engring., Naval Postgrad. Sch., 1968; postgrad., Destroyer Dept. Head Sch., 1969. Advanced through grades to rear adm. USN, 1990, ops. officer USS Sampson, 1970; aide, flag sec. to commdr. Attack Carrier striking Force /CTF 77, 7th Fleet Vietnam, 1971-72; communications/ops. officer to comdr. in chief U.S. Naval Forces, Europe, 1972-75, exec. officer USS Mitscher, 1976-78, asst. chief of staff for communications, comdr. Naval Surface Force Atlantic, 1978-80; comdg. officer USS Preble, 1980-82; surface ops. officer, staff of comdr. Cruiser Destroyer Group 12, 1982-83; dir. Space, Command and Control Devel. Div. USN, 1984-85; comdr. U.S. Naval Communications Master Sta., Western Pacific, Guam, Marianas Island, 1985-87; comdr. Naval Telecommunications Command, 1988-90; dir. Naval Commns. info systems of Naval opers. staff, 1990-91; dir. communication programs Space & Naval Warfare Systems Command, 1991-93. Decorated Legion of Merit with three gold stars. Roman Catholic. Office: American Systems Corp 14200 Park Meadow Dr Chantilly VA 22021-2219

STONE, VOYE LYNNE, women's health nurse practitioner; b. Grandfield, Okla., Apr. 17, 1941; d. Clint Voy and Mattie Evelyn (Averyt) Wynn; m. Don Dale Stone, Dec. 19, 1964; children: Melinda Anne Stone Phelps, Tari Elisabeth. Student, Bapt. Hosp. Sch. Nursing, Oklahoma City, 1965; diploma in nursing, U. Okla., Oklahoma City, 1965; BS, St. Joseph's Coll., North Windham, Maine, 1985; grad. women health care nursing program, U. Tex., Dallas, 1990; postgrad., U. Okla. Cert. women's health nurse. Dietary cons. Frederick Meml. Hosp., 1967; pub. health nurse Dept. Health, State of Okla., Frederick, 1985; insvc. educator Frederick Meml. Hosp.; women's health nurse practitioner Dept. Health, State of Okla., Oklahoma City, 1990. Vol., unit pres. Am. Cancer Soc.; vol. ARC; pres. adv. coun. 4-H Club; pres. local PTA. Named one of Outstanding Young Women of Am., 1970. Mem. AWHONN, Am. Acad. Nurse Practitioners, ANA, Okla. State Nurses Assn., Okla. Pub. Health Assn., Okla. Mental Health Assn., PEO, Beta Sigma Phi (various offices, Girl of Yr. 1976, 77, 78). Home: RR 1 Box 121 Frederick OK 73542-9721

STONE, WARREN R., book publishing executive. Chmn., ceo. Addison-Wesley Pub. Co. Inc., Reading, Mass. Office: Addison-Wesley Pub Co Inc 1 Jacob Way Reading MA 01867-3932

STONE, WILLIAM EDWARD, association executive; b. Peoria, Ill., Aug. 13, 1945; s. Dean Proctor and Katherine (Jamison) S.; m. Deborah Ann Duncan; children: Jennifer, Allison, Molly. A.B., Stanford U., 1967, M.B.A., 1969. Asst. dean Stanford U., 1969-71, asst. to pres., 1971-77; exec. dir. Stanford Alumni Assn., 1977-90, pres., chief exec. officer, 1990—; pres., dir. Alpine Chalet, Inc., Alpine Meadows, Calif., 1987—; dir. Coun. Alumni Assn. Execs., 1989-93, v.p., 1990-91, pres., 1991-92; trustee Coun. for Advancement and Support of Edn., 1988-91; bd. dirs. Univ. ProNet, Inc., chmn., 1990-92. Bd. dirs. North County YMCA, 1975-76; bd. dirs., chmn. nominating com. faculty club Stanford U., 1979-81; trustee Watkins Discretionary Fund, 1979-82; mem. community adv. bd. Resource Ctr. for Women. Recipient K.M. Cuthbertson award Stanford U., 1987, Tribute award Coun. for Advancement and Support of Edn., 1991. Mem. Stanford Hist. Soc., Stanford Assocs. Club: Stanford Faculty. Home: 1061 Cathcart Way Stanford CA 94305-1048 Office: Stanford Alumni Assn Inc 416 Santa Teresa St Stanford CA 94305-2203

STONE, WILLIAM HAROLD, geneticist, educator; b. Boston, Dec. 15, 1924; s. Robert and Rita (Scheinberg) S.; m. Elaine Morein, Nov. 24, 1947; children: Susan Joy, Debra M.; m. Carmen Maqueda, Dec. 22, 1971; 1 son, Alexander R.M. A.B., Brown U., 1948; M.S., U. Maine, 1949; Ph.D., U. Wis., 1953; Sc.D. (hon.), U. Cordoba, Spain, 1984. Research asst. Jackson Meml. Lab., Bar Harbor, Maine, 1947-48; faculty dept. genetics U. Wis., Madison, 1949-83; prof. U. Wis., 1961-83, prof. med. genetics, 1964-83; Cowles Disting. prof. dept. biology Trinity U., San Antonio, 1983—; staff scientist S.W. Found. for Biomed. Research, San Antonio, 1983—; adj. prof. Cellular and Structural Biology U. Tex., San Antonio, 1983—; mem. panel blood group experts FAO, 1962-67, program dir. immunogenetics rsch., Spain, 1971-74; adj. prof. dept. cellular and structural biology, U. Tex. Health Sci. Ctr., San Antonio, 1983—; mem. Cmty. Health Svcs. Rsch. Adv. Com., 1987—, Coun. Inst. Lab. Animal Resources, NRC; mem. competitive rsch. grants panel USDA; bd. dirs. and v.p. So. Tex. Blood and Tissue Ctr., 1986—, v.p. bd., 1989-92, pres. 1995—; bd. dirs. Tex. Rsch. and Tech. Found., 1986-90, Mind Sci. Found., 1988—, Winston Sch., 1989-91, Bexar County Women's Ctr., Inst. Lab. Animal Sci., 1977-89; mem. rev. panel NSF; mem. primate study sect. Comparative Medicine Program NIH; mem. adv. com. Harvard Med. Sch. Regional Primate Rsch. Ctr.; mem. Armstrong Lab. awards com. Author: Immunogenetics, 1967; contbr. articles to profl. jours. Bd. dirs. Bexar County Women's Ctr., Alamo Theatre Arts Coun., S. A. Libr. Assn., 1994. Recipient I.I. Ivanov medal USSR, 1974, Disting. Tex. Geneticist award, 1992; Calif. Inst. Tech. NIH fellow, 1960-61. Mem. NRC, AAAS, Am. Inst. Biol. Scis., Assembly Life Scis., Am. Soc. Immunologists, Am. Genetics Assn., Am. Aging Soc., Tex. Genetics Soc. (editor newsletter, pres. elect 1995, pres. 1996), Am. Soc. Human Genetics, Rsch. Soc. Am., Internat. Soc. Transplant, Am. Soc. Animal Sci., Internat. Soc. Devel. Comparative Immunology, Internat. Primatological Soc., Am. Soc. Primatology, Internat. Soc. Immunology Reproduction, Fedn. Am. Soc. Exptl. Biology, Soc. Devel. and Comparative Immunology (pub. affairs com.), Sigma Xi, Gamma Alpha, Beta Beta Beta. Office: Trinity U Dept Biology San Antonio TX 78212 *Some things are better never than late. We need more education and less legislation. I can't believe I get paid for something I have so much fun doing. In science you don't know what the truth is until you have read what you have written. Quite often, bad luck is really good luck gone unrecognized.*

STONE, WILLIAM LYNDON, retired minister; b. Detroit, Mar. 1, 1926; s. Paul Lyndon and Johnnie (Graham) S.; m. Gladys Helen Farley, Aug. 9, 1948; children: William Paul, John Wesley, Beth Ann. AB, Taylor U., 1948; MDiv., Garrett-Evang. Theol. Sem., 1957. Lic. local preacher, 1944; ordained deacon, 1952, elder, 1957; cert. rural chaplain, 1991. Min. Meth. Ch., Napoleon, Mich., 1948-53, Am. Bapt. Ch., Norvell, Mich., 1948-52, Meth. Ch., Constantine, Mich., 1953-57, Court St. Meth. Ch., Flint, Mich., 1957-58; min. to students Wesley Found., Flint, 1958-60; min. Atherton Meth. Ch., Flint, 1958-63, 1st Meth. Ch., Mt. Morris, Mich., 1963-68, Met. Meth. Ch., Detroit, 1968-69, United Meth. Ch., Oscoda, Mich., 1969-76; supr. Oscoda Indian Mission, Oscoda, Mich., 1969-76; min. Wilber United Meth. Ch., East Tawas, Mich., 1980-83, United Meth. Ch., Harrisville and Lincoln, Mich., 1983-90, First Presbyn. Ch. of Maple Ridge, 1992—; mem. Detroit Conf. United Meth. Ch., Hispanic Initiative Com., Town and Country Com. Trustee Charter Twp. of Oscoda, 1978-92, planning commn., 1986-92; chmn. planning commn. City of Mt. Morris, 1966-68, domestic action program Wurtsmith AFB, Mich., 1969-72; dir., founder Hotline of Oscoda, 1970-95, Oscoda Area Non-Profit Housing Corp., 1970-75; former bd. dirs. Child and Family Svcs., Northeast Mich. Housing Corp., E. Cen. Mich. Housing Com., Au Sable Valley Cmty. Mental Health Bd., Mich Assn. Cmty. Mental Health Bds.; bd. dirs. Wurtsmith Re-Use Com., Charter Twp. Oscoda, 1978-92; chaplain CAP, 1978—; mem. exec. com. Iosco County Rep. Com., precinct del., 1984-92; chmn. Oscoda Twp. Dept. Pub. Works, Oscoda Twp. Roads and Grounds Commn.; mem. Oscoda Safety Com.; initiated into Chippewa Tribe, 1975; past mem. Bd. Edn., Bd. Christian Social Concerns, Camp Commn. and Planning Rsch. com. Named to Honorable Order Ky. Cols., 1983; recipient Vandenberg award, 1983, Medal of Merit, 1983, 85, 87, Exceptional Svc. medal, 1990, Presdl. Citation award, 1991. Mem. Mich. Twps. Assn. (bd. dirs. 1989-93), Air Force Assn. (life, pres. state chpt. 1986-91, Huron chpt. 1980-83, 93—, Traverse City chpt. 1990-93), Mich. Air Force Assn. (Hoyt S. Vandenberg trophy 1983), Iosco County Twps. Assn. (chmn. 1984-87), Aerospace Edn. Found. (life), Mich. Aviation Hall of Fame (charter, life). Avocations: music, singing, piano, organ, photography. Home: 7357 Lakewood Dr Oscoda MI 48750-9751

STONE, WILLIARD EVERARD, accountant, educator; b. Phila., Aug. 28, 1910; s. Theodore Williard Jr. and Blanche (Patton) S.; m. Louise Cousins Harder, May 19, 1934; children: Theodore Williard III, Donald Edwin, Richard Patton. A.B., Pa. State U., 1933; M.A., U. Pa., 1950, Ph.D., 1957. C.P.A., Pa. Auditor Pa. Liquor Control Bd., 1934-43, U.S. comptroller gen., 1943-47; partner Stone & Fisher (C.P.A.'s), Phila., 1947-50; asst. prof. accounting U. Pa. Wharton Sch. Finance and Commerce, Phila., 1951-57; assoc. prof. U. Pa. Wharton Sch. Finance and Commerce, 1957-60; prof. U. Fla., Gainesville, 1960-80; head dept. accounting U. Fla., 1960-74; bd. mgrs. U. Fla. Press, 1961-80; vis. prof. U. New South Wales, 1966; Carman G. Blough chair of acctg. U. Va., 1972-73; vis. prof. U. Port Elizabeth, 1975, Va. Poly. Inst. and State U., 1977, U. Ky., 1980-81; cons. editor Chilton Book div. Chilton Co., Phila., 1957-61, Holt, Rinehart & Winston, Inc., 1961-70; cons. to U.S. Comptr. Gen., 1963-69. Author: (with MacFarland, Ayars) Accounting Fundamentals, 1957; Co-editor: Accounting Historian's Jour.; Contbr. articles to profl. jours. Gordon Fellow Deakin U., Australia, 1981. Mem. Nat. Assn. Accountants (dir. Phila. 1954-55), Am. Inst. C.P.A.'s, Fla. Inst. C.P.A.'s, Pa. Inst. C.P.A.'s (dir. 1954-55), Am. Accounting Assn. (v.p. 1963), Acad. Accounting Historians (editor Acctg. Historians Jour. 1974-79), Beta Alpha Psi (past pres), Beta Gamma Sigma. Home: 1717 NW 23rd Ave # Pha Gainesville FL 32605-3031

STONECIPHER, DAVID A., insurance company executive; b. 1941. Degree, Vanderbilt U.; M Agrl. Sci., Ga. State U., 1967. With Life Ins. Co. Ga., Altanta, 1967-92; also pres. Ga. U.S. Corp., Altanta, until 1992; pres., CEO Jefferson-Pilot Corp., Greensboro, N.C., 1992—, also bd. dirs. Office: Jefferson-Pilot Corp 100 N Greene St Greensboro NC 27401*

STONECIPHER, HARRY CURTIS, manufacturing company executive. BS, Tenn. Polytech Inst., 1960. With GE, 1960-61, 62-86, Martin Aircraft Co., 1961-62; exec. v.p. Sundstrand Corp., 1987, pres., chief operating officer, 1987-88, pres., chief exec. officer, 1988-94, chmn., 1991-94, also past bd. dirs.; pres. McDonnell-Douglas Corp., St. Louis, 1994—. Office: McDonnell-Douglas Corp McDonnell Blvd at Airport Rd Berkeley MO 63134*

STONEHILL, ERIC, lawyer; b. Rochester, N.Y., Feb. 27, 1950. BA with distinction, Northwestern U., 1970; JD, Cornell U., 1973, MBA, 1981, cert. hosp. and health svc. adminstrn., 1981. Bar: N.Y. 1974, D.C. 1981, U.S. Dist. Ct. (we. dist.) N.Y. 1974, U.S. Dist. Ct. (no. dist.) N.Y. 1976. Assoc. Harris, Beach & Wilcox, Rochester, 1973-81, ptnr., 1982—. Contbr. articles to profl. jours. Bd. dirs. Rochester Eye and Human Parts Bank, 1983-91, 92—, pres., 1987-90. Mem. Nat. Health Lawyers Assn., Am. Soc. Hosp. Attys., N.Y. State Bar Assn. (mem. health law sect., exec. com., chair health care systems design com.), D.C. Bar Assn., Monroe County Bar Assn., Sloan Alumni Assn., Phi Beta Kappa. Office: Harris Beach & Wilcox Granite Building 130 Main St E Rochester NY 14604-1620

STONEHILL, LLOYD HERSCHEL, gas company executive, mechanical engineer; b. South Bend, Ind., May 20, 1927; s. Charles Myers and Louise Mary (Reed) S.; m. Jean Carole Herzer, Dec. 30, 1961; children: Mark, Bill, John, Rob. BS in Mech. Engring., Purdue U., 1949. Registered profl. engr., La. Chief engr. Rothschild Boiler & Tank Works, Shreveport, La., 1949-54; chmn. bd. Frankfort (Ind.) Bottle Gas, Inc., 1956—. Patentee in field. Founding prs. Clinton County Hosp. Authority, Frankfort, 1974; membership chmn. Clinton County Hosp. Found., Frankfort, 1982-83, 89. With U.S. Army, 1954-56. Recipient Heroism award Elks Lodge, Frankfort, 1959. Mem. Nat. Propane Gas Assn. (mktg. awards 1986, 87), Am. Legion LFW, Purdue Alumni Assn. (Clinton County chpt., mem. pres.' coun.), Hudson Inst., Rotary (sec. 1963-65, Paul Harris fellow), Lambda Chi Alpha (sec. 1946-47). Republican. Mem. Christian Ch. Avocations: collecting old violins, sailing, reading. Home: 1258 Forest Dr Frankfort IN 46041-3230 Office: Frankfort Bottle Gas Inc 1555 McKinley Ave Frankfort IN 46041-1805

STONEHILL, ROBERT MICHAEL, federal agency administrator; b. N.Y.C., Oct. 29, 1949; s. Frederick and Olga (Berkowitz) S.; m. Ilene Laven, June 1, 1975 (div. Nov. 1983); 1 child, David; m. Camille Recchia, Oct. 12, 1985; children: Eric, Elizabeth, Matthew. BA, CUNY, Queens, 1971; MA, U. Colo., 1973, PhD, 1976. Teaching and rsch. asst. U. Colo., Boulder, 1972-76; evaluation specialist U.S. Office Edn., Washington, 1976-83; acting dir. state and local grants div. U.S. Dept. Edn., Washington, 1984-86, dir. Ednl. Resources Info. Ctr., 1987-94, dir. state and local svcs. divsn., 1995—; del. Fed. Libr. Pre-Conf., The White House Conf. on Librs. and Info. Scis., 1990. Mem. editorial adv. bd. various jours., contbr. articles. Regents scholar, 1966-70. Mem. Am. Ednl. Rsch. Assn., Am. Soc. for Info. Sci., Nat. Coun. for Measurement in Edn. Jewish. Avocations: skiing, popular cultural history. Office: US Dept Edn ORAD/OERI State and Local Svcs Divsn 555 New Jersey Ave NW Washington DC 20208-5644

STONEHOUSE, JAMES ADAM, lawyer; b. Alameda, Calif., Nov. 10, 1937; s. Maurice Adam and Edna Sigrid (Thuesen) S.; m. Marilyn Jean Kotkas, Aug. 6, 1966; children: Julie Aileen, Stephen Adam. AB, U. Calif., Berkeley, 1961; JD, Hastings Coll. Law, U. Calif., San Francisco, 1965. Bar: Calif. 1966; cert. specialist probate, estate planning & trust law.. Assoc. Hall, Henry, Oliver & McReavy, San Francisco, 1966-71; ptnr. firm Whitney, Hanson & Stonehouse, Alameda, 1971-77; pvt. practice, Alameda, 1977-79; ptnr. firm Stonehouse & Silva, Alameda, 1979—; judge adv. Alameda council Navy League, 1978—. Founding dir. Alameda Clara Barton Found., 1977-80; mem. Oakland (Calif.) Marathon-Exec. Com., 1979; mem. exec. bd. Alameda council Boy Scouts Am., 1979—, pres., 1986-88; mem. Nat. council Boy Scouts Am., 1986—; trustee Golden Gate Scouting, 1986-95, treas. 1989-91, v.p. 1991-92, pres. 1993-95, v.p. area III western region, 1990-95, bd. dirs. western region, 1991—; bd. dirs. Lincoln Child Ctr. Found., 1981-87, 94—, pres., 1983-85; sch. bd. mem. St. Joseph Notre Dame, 1994—. Recipient Lord Baden-Powell Merit award Boy Scouts Am., 1988, Silver Beaver award, 1991; named Boss of Yr. Alameda Jaycees, 1977; Coro Found. fellow in pub. affairs, 1961-62. Mem. ABA, State Bar Calif., Alameda County Bar (vice chmn. com. office econs., 1977-78). Republican. Roman Catholic. Club: Commonwealth. Lodges: Rotary (dir. club 1976-78, trustee Alameda Rotary Found. 1991—, treas., 1994—), Elks (past exalted ruler, all state officer 1975-76, all dist. officer 1975-77, 78-79, Alameda). Home: 2990 Northwood Dr Alameda CA 94501-1606 Office: Stonehouse & Silva 512 Westline Dr Ste 300 Alameda CA 94501-5870

STONEMAN, SAMUEL SIDNEY, cinema company executive; b. Boston, Dec. 18, 1911; s. David and Anne (Fleisher) S.; m. Miriam Helpern, Sept. 2, 1934; children: Jane Stein, Elizabeth Deknatel. A.B., Dartmouth Coll., 1933; J.D., Harvard U., 1936. Bar: Mass. 1936. Ptnr. Singer, Stoneman & Kirland, Boston, 1936-42; pres. Bretton Woods Co., (N.H.), 1946-56; vice chmn. bd. Gen. Cinema Corp., Chestnut Hill, Mass., 1969-84, also dir.; vice-chmn. Harcourt Gen.; dir. Shawmut Bank of Boston, N.A., Purity Supreme, Inc., Billerica, Mass., Donlevy's Inc., Boston. Vice pres., trustee Boston Symphony Orch., 1970-83; bd. overseers Hopkins Ctr. and Hood Mus., Dartmouth Coll., 1982-88; trustee Dana-Farber Cancer Inst., Boston, 1978; pres. Combined Jewish Philanthropies, 1964-66, Beth Israel Hosp., 1970-73; mem. Dartmouth Coll. Alumni Council, 1963-66; bd. dirs. Massachusetts Bay United Fund, 1966-77, Community Found. Palm Beach and Martin Counties, Fla., Kravis Performing Arts Centre, Palm Beach; mem. adv. bd. St. Mary's Hosp., Palm Beach; regional co-chmn. NCCJ, Boston, 1969-73. Served to maj. Q.M.C. AUS, 1942-46. Fellow Brandeis U., 1956—; recipient Brotherhood Human Relations citation NCCJ, 1968, Alumni award Dartmouth Coll., 1972, Disting. Grad. award Noble and Greenough Sch., 1982. Home: 200 Via Pelicano Palm Beach FL 33480-5017 Office: 1 Post Office Sq Ste 3730 Boston MA 02109

STONEMAN, WILLIAM, III, physician, educator; b. Kansas City, Mo., Sept. 8, 1927; s. William and Helen Louise (Bloom) S.; m. Elizabeth Johanna Wilson, May 19, 1951; children: William Laurence, Sidney Camdon (dec.), Cecily Anne Erker, Elizabeth Wilson, John Spalding. Student, Rockhurst Coll., 1944-46; B.S., St. Louis U., 1948, M.D., 1952. Diplomate: Am. Bd. Surgery, Am. Bd. Plastic Surgery. Intern Kansas City Gen. Hosp., 1952-53; resident in surgery St. Louis U., 1953-57, resident in plastic surgery, 1957-59, mem. faculty, 1959—, assoc. prof. surgery, assoc. prof. community medicine, 1975-84, prof. surgery, community medicine, 1984-94, prof. surgery, community medicine emeritus, 1994, assoc. dean Sch. Medicine, 1973-76; exec. assoc. dean St. Louis U. (Sch. Medicine), 1976-82, dean, 1982-95, dean emeritus, 1995—, assoc. v.p. med. ctr., 1983-95; mem. adj. faculty Washington U. Sch. Medicine, St. Louis, 1968-74; chief exec. officer Bi-State Regional Med. Program, 1968-74; bd. dirs. St. Louis Office Mental Retardation/Developmentally Disabled Resources, 1980-82, Combined Health Appeal of Mo., 1990-94. Editor: Parameters, 1976-94 ; contbr. articles on plastic surgery, health care delivery planning to profl. jours. Served with AUS, 1946-47. Fellow ACS; mem. AMA (chmn. sect. on med. schs. 1987-88, sect. alt. del. 1989-91, del. 1992-94), Mo. Med. Assn., Mem. St. Louis Met. Med. Soc., St Louis Surg. Soc., Am. Soc. Plastic and Reconstructive Surgeons, Midwestern Assn. Plastic Surgeons. Roman Catholic. Club: Racquet. Office: St Louis U Sch Medicine 1316 Carr Lane Ave Saint Louis MO 63104-1011

STONEMAN, WILLIAM HAMBLY, III, professional baseball team executive; b. Oak Park, Ill., Apr. 7, 1944; s. William Hambly Jr. and Kathryn Jane (Hennessey) S.; m. Diane Falardeau, Dec. 6, 1969; children: Jill Helene, Jeffrey Alan. BS in Edn., U. Idaho, 1966; MEd, Okla. U., 1969. Baseball player Chgo. Cubs, 1967-68, Montreal (Que., Can.) Expos, 1969-73, Calif. Angels, 1974; mktg. mgr. Royal Trust Corp., Montreal and Toronto, Ont., Can., 1975-79, br. mgr., 1980-82; asst. to pres. Montreal Expos, 1983, v.p., 1984—; now v.p. baseball ops. Mem. All-Star Team Nat. League, 1972; no-hit games vs. Phila. Phillies, 1969, N.Y. Mets, 1972. Home: 17 Willow, PO Box 386, Hudson, PQ Canada J0P 1H0 Office: Montreal Baseball Club Inc, Olympic Stadium, Montreal, PQ Canada H1V 3N7*

STONER, JAMES LLOYD, retired foundation executive, clergyman; b. Point Marion, Pa., Apr. 23, 1920; s. Martin Clark and Bess (Hare) S.; m. Janice Faller Evans, Aug. 28, 1943; children: Thomas Clark, James Douglas and Geoffrey Lloyd (twins). B.S., Bethany Coll., 1941, D.D. (hon.), 1958; B.D., M.A., Yale U., 1944. Ordained to ministry Christian Ch., 1943; minister in Hamden, Conn., 1942-44; assoc. exec. sec. U. Tex., YMCA, 1944-45; dir. Student Christian Fellowship, Bowling Green State U., 1945-47, Univ. Christian Mission, Fed. Council Ch. and Nat. Council Chs., 1947-56; minister North Christian Ch., Columbus, Ind., 1956-66; asst. gen. sec. for exec. operations Nat. Council Chs., 1966-72; sr. minister Central Christian Ch., Austin, Tex., 1972-80; dep. exec. dir. Found. for Christian Living, Pawling, N.Y., 1980-83, exec. dir., 1983-87; chmn. com. recommendations Internat. Conv. Christian Chs., 1962-65; bd. mgrs. United Christian Missionary Soc., 1956-63; mem. adv. bd. Am. Bible Soc., 1966-72; life mem. coun. Christian Unity, Christian Ch.; a founder, 1st pres. LINK Award, Ridgewood, N.J., 1966-72; mem. Austin Conf. Chs., pres., 1973-75; rep. Tex. Conf. Chs., 1976-80; mem. goals com. Austin Tomorrow; mem. adv. bd. 1st Comml. Bank of Lakeway, Austin, Tex., 1990-95. Contbr. articles to profl. publs. A founder, bd. dirs. Fellowship Christian Athletes, Kansas City, Mo., 1956-68; trustee Tougaloo (Miss.) Coll., 1968-74; v.p., mem. exec. com. Ecumenical Center Continuing Edn., Yale, 1966-72; mem. exec. com. Boy Scouts Am., Austin, 1980, Dutchess County council, 1981-82; bd. mgrs. New Milford Hosp., 1983-88; bd. dirs. Holiday Hills YMCA, 1983-87; com. mem. Town of Pawling 200th Anniversary, 1985-88, Lakeway Ecumenical Ch. Mem. Pawling C. of C. (exec. com. 1984-87), Fellowship of Christian Athletes (nat. adv. bd. 1994—), Masons (32 degree), Pawling Rotary Club (pres. 1983-84, dist. gov.-elect 1991-92, dist. gov. 1992-93, Paul Harris fellow), Shriners, Austin Rotary Club (spl. lifetime mem.), Lake Travis/Lakeway Rotary Club (hon.), Alpha Psi Omega, Beta Theta Pi. Home: 1134 Challenger Austin TX 78734-3802 *Fill every day with rainbow colors, and punctuate life with a positive outlook... Even the Cross of Christ is a positive sign.*

STONER, JOHN RICHARD, federal government executive; b. Ypsilanti, Mich., May 11, 1958; s. Richard P. and Marjorie G. Stoner; m. Diane Leslie Snow. BA in Govt., B in Music Edn., Lawrence U., 1981. Staff asst. Senator Robert Kasten Jr., Washington, 1981-82; staff assoc. Wis. Office Fed.-State Rels., Washington, 1982-83; intergovtl. rels. officer U.S. Dept. Transp., Washington, 1983-86, congl. rels. officer, 1989-91; dir. Office of Program and Policy Support, Rsch. and Spl. Programs Adminstrn., Dept. Transp., Washington, 1991-93; exec. dir. Republican Nat. Lawyers Assn., 1993—; rep. Primerica Fin. Svcs., 1993—; state govt. rels. mgr. Am. Trucking Assn., Inc., Alexandria, Va., 1986-88; researcher George Bush for Pres. Com., 1988; staff asst. Office of Pres.-Elect, Washington, 1988-89. Admissions contact Washington area Lawrence U., 1986-87; softball team mgr. Montgomery County Recreation League. Recipient Eagle Scout award Boy Scouts Am., 1972; Mortar Bd. scholar, 1980; Senate Rep. Policy Com. Legis. fellow, 1993—. Republican. Mem. Ch. of Christ, Scientist. Avocation: water skiing, organ. Home: 10409 Brunswick Ave Silver Spring MD 20902-4845 Office: Rep Nat Lawyers Assn 310 1st St SE Washington DC 20003-1801

STONER, PHILIP JAMES, hospital administrator; b. Brookline, Mass., Mar. 5, 1943; s. Philip and Beatrice Margaret (Murphy) S.; m. Allison Fern Leighton, Aug. 28, 1971; children: Jennifer Marie, Andrew Leighton. AS in Engring., Wentworth Inst., Boston, 1963; BS in Indsl. Engring., Millikin U., 1966; MS, Northeastern U., 1973; MBA, Western New Eng. Coll., 1980. Prodn. mgr. Goodwill Industries, Boston, 1971-72; indsl. engr. Ea. Air Lines, Boston, 1973-74; mgmt. engr. Baystate Med. Ctr., Springfield, Mass., 1974-80; v.p. for profl. svcs. Farren Meml. Hosp., Turners Falls, Mass., 1980-85; adminstr. Taylor Hosp., Bangor, Maine, 1985-87, Massena (N.Y.) Meml. Hosp., 1987-89, Falls Meml. Hosp., International Falls, Minn., 1990-93; CEO Tyrone (Pa.) Hosp., 1993—; mem. adv. bd. Rainy River Community Coll., International Falls, 1990-93. Author: (monograph) Resource Based Relative Value System, 1991. Capt. USMC, 1966-69, Vietnam. Fellow Am. Coll. Healthcare Execs.; mem. Inst. Indsl. Engrs. (sr.). Avocations: reading, jogging, making bread, boat building. Home: RR 5 Box 287A Tyrone PA 16686-9751 Office: Tyrone Hosp 1 Hosp Dr Tyrone PA 16686

STONER, R(ICHARD) B(URKETT), manufacturing company executive; b. Ladoga, Ind., May 15, 1920; s. Edward Norris and Florence May (Burkett) S.; m. Virginia B. Austin, Feb. 22, 1942; children—Pamela T., Richard Burkett, Benjamin Austin, Janet Elizabeth, Rebecca Lee, Joanne Jeannea. BS, Ind. U., 1941; JD, Harvard U., 1947; LLD, Butler U., 1975, Ind. U., 1994. With Cummins Engine Co., Inc., Columbus, Ind., 1947—, various adminstrv., exec. positions, 1947-66, exec. v.p., corporate gen. mgr., 1966-69, vice. chmn. bd., 1969-88, vice chmn. emeritus, 1989—; dir. Cummins Engine Found. Dem. nat. committeeman for Ind.; del. Dem. Nat. Conv., 1956-92; pres., bd. dirs. Irwin-Sweeney-Miller Found.; bd. dirs. Christian Found., Columbus, Ind. U. Found., 1975—; trustee Ind. U., 1971-92 (pres. bd. trustees, 1980-92). Capt. AUS, 1942-46. Mem. Ind. C. of C. (dir.). Office: Cummins Engine Co Inc Box 3005 MC-60909 Columbus IN 47202

STONESIFER, RICHARD JAMES, retired humanities and social science educator; b. Lancaster, Pa., June 21, 1922; s. Paul Tobias and Esther (Wittlinger) S.; m. Nancy Jane Weaver, June 28, 1947; 1 dau., Pamela Ann. A.B., Franklin and Marshall Coll., 1946; M.A., Northwestern U., 1947; Ph.D., U. Pa., 1953. Mem. faculty Franklin and Marshall Coll., 1947-63, assoc. prof. English, 1954-63, asst. to dean, 1957-60, asst. pres., 1960-63; asst. to provost, also dir. coll. gen. studies U. Pa., 1963-65; assoc. prof. communications Annenberg Sch. Communications, 1963-65; dean. Coll. Liberal Arts, prof. English Drew U., Madison, N.J., 1965-71; pres. Monmouth U., West Long Branch, N.J., 1971-79; Woodrow Wilson prof.

humanities and social sci. Monmouth U., 1979-82; moderator TV discussion series, 1954-60. Author: W.H. Davies: A Critical Biography, 2d edit, 1965, also articles in profl. jours.; newspaper columnist and commentator weekly; free lance journalist. Mem. Pa. Adv. Com. Ednl. Broadcasting, 1963-65; Bd. dirs. Harrisburg Area Center Higher Edn., 1963-65; trustee N.J. Cancer Inst., 1975—. Served with USAAF, 1943-46. Mem. Phi Beta Kappa. Home: PO Box 906 306 Sanders St Mullins SC 29574-4214 *My life has been devoted to higher education, and to keeping the liberal arts at the center of the enterprise, even as of necessity we put new emphases on professional and career matters. In teaching and in administration I take as fundamental guidance the teaching from ancient Greece: moderation in all things.*

STONICH, TIMOTHY WHITMAN, financial executive; b. Evanston, Ill., July 30, 1947; s. Joseph and Joyce (Whitman) S.; m. Joy Anne Harrison, June 14, 1969 (dec. Apr. 1986); m. Tamara L. Tierney, Nov. 13, 1987. B.A. in Econs., Denison U., 1969; M.B.A. in Fin., U. Chgo., 1972. Comml. banking officer Harris Bank, Chgo., 1969-74; asst. treas. Pullman Inc., Chgo., 1974-77, treas. Pullman Standard div., 1977-80; v.p. fin. Pullman Leasing Co., Chgo., 1977-80; v.p., gen. mgr. Pullman Leasing Co. Pullman Inc., 1980-83; treas. The Marmon Group, 1984-86; sr. v.p. fin. Lease Investment Corp., 1986-87; sr. v.p. fin., CFO U.S. Can Co., Oakbrook, Ill., 1987-91, exec. v.p., 1991—. Office: US Can Co 900 Commerce Dr Oak Brook IL 60521-1967

STONIER, DARYLE L., agricultural supplies company executive; married. Vice-chmn. Growmark, Inc., Bloomington, Ill., 1980—, also dir.; vice-chmn. bd. Ill. Grain Corp. Served with USN, 1953-57. Mem. Ill. Agrl. Auditing Assn. (bd. dirs.). Office: Growmark Inc 1701 N Towanda Ave Bloomington IL 61701*

STOODT, BARBARA DERN, education educator, magazine editor; b. Columbus, Ohio, June 12, 1934; d. Millard Fissel and Helen Lucille (Taes) Dern; divorced; children: Linda Stoodt Neu, Susan Stoodt Price. BS in Edn., Ohio U., 1956; MA in Edn., Ohio State U., 1965; PhD, 1970; postgrad., U. Chgo., 1967. Tchr. North Charleston (S.C.) Schs., 1956-57, Cleveland Heights (Ohio) U., 1957-58, Mansfield (Ohio) Bd. Edn., 1958-59, 65-68; dir. reading, 1968; teaching assoc. Ohio State U., 1968-70; prof. edn. U. Akron, Ohio, 1970-77, U. N.C., Greensboro, 1977—; vis. prof. No. Ky. U. and U. Cin. Author: Reading Instruction, 1981, 2d edit., 1989, Teaching Language Arts, 1988; co-author: Secondary School Reading Instruction, 1987, 5th edit., 1994, Children's Literature: Discovery for a Lifetime, 1996, Riverside Reading Program. U.S. Office Edn. research grantee, 1970. Mem. Nat. Conf. on Research in English, Internat. Reading Assn. (Outstanding Dissertation award), Am. Ednl. Research Assn., Nat. Council Tchrs. English (outstanding research award 1971), Assn. for Supervision and Curriculum Devel., Assn. for Childhood Edn. Internat. Methodist. Avocations: gardening, travel, golf. Home: PO Box 9630 Cincinnati OH 45209-0630 Office: Learning Mag 1607 Battleground Ave Greensboro NC 27408-8005

STOOKEY, GEORGE KENNETH, research institute administrator, dental educator; b. Waterloo, Ind., Nov. 6, 1935; s. Emra Gladison and Mary Catherine (Anglin) S.; m. Nola Jean Meek, Jan. 15, 1955; children—Lynda, Lisa, Laura, Kenneth. A.B. in Chemistry, Ind. U., 1957, M.S.D., 1962, Ph.D. in Preventive Dentistry, 1971. Asst. dir. Preventive Dentistry Research Inst., U. Ind., Indpls., 1968-70; assoc. dir. Oral Health Research Inst., U. Ind., 1974-81, dir., 1981—; assoc. prof. preventive dentistry Sch. of Dentistry, Ind. U., 1973-78, prof., 1978—, assoc. dean research, 1987—; cons. USAF, San Antonio, 1973—, ADA, Chgo., 1972—, Nat. Inst. Dental Rsch., Bethesda, Md., 1978-82, 91-95. Author: (with others) Introduction to Oral Biology and Preventive Dentistry, 1971, Preventive Dentistry for the Dental Assistant and Dental Hygienist, 1977, Preventive Dentistry in Action, 1972, 80 (Meritorious award 1973); contbr. articles to profl. jours. Mem. Internat. Assn. for Dental Research, European Orgn. Caries Research, Am. Assn. Lab. Animal Sci. Republican. Office: Oral Health Research Inst 415 Lansing St Indianapolis IN 46202-2855

STOOKEY, LAURENCE HULL, clergyman, theology educator; b. Belleville, Ill., Apr. 8, 1937; s. Loyd Leslie and Gladys E. (Hull) S.; m. Peggy Ann Reynolds, June 8, 1963 (div. 1990); children: Laura, Sarah. B.A., Swarthmore Coll., 1959; STB. magna cum laude, Wesley Theol. Sem., Washington, 1962; Th.D. with honors, Princeton Theol. Sem., 1971. Ordained to ministry United Meth. Ch., 1962. Pastor Peninsula-Del. Ann. Conf., United Meth. Ch., 1962-67, 71-73; instr. preaching and worship Princeton (N.J.) Theol. Sem., 1967-71; mem. faculty Wesley Theol. Sem., Washington, 1973—, Hugh Latimer Elderice prof., 1979—; guest lectr. Union Theol. Sem., Richmond, Va., McCormick Theol. Sem., Duke U. Div. Sch., Garrett-Evangel. Theol. Sem., Shenandoah (Va.) U.; vis. prof. U. Auckland, New Zealand, Melbourne Coll. Divinity; mem. Nat. Lutheran-United Meth. Bi-Lateral Theol. Dialogue, 1977-80; bd. dirs. Ctr. for Art and Religion, 1983-87, Liturgical Conf., 1983-91; officer Hymnal Revision Com. United Meth. Ch., 1984-88; cons. in field. Author: Living in a New Age: Sermons for the Season of Easter, 1978, Baptism-Christ's Act in the Church, 1982; co-author: Handbook of the Christian Year, 1986, rev. edit., 1992, Eucharist-Christ's Feast with the Church, 1993, Calendar: Christ's Time for the Church, 1996; mem. editorial bd. Homiletic, 1974-86; contbr. articles to profl. jours. Fellow Assn. Theol. Schs. in U.S. and Can., 1979-80. Fellow N. Am. Acad. Liturgy, Acad. Homiletics; mem. Fellowship United Methodists in Worship, Music and Other Arts (officer 1981-83). Home: 13500 Justice Rd Rockville MD 20853-3268 Office: 4500 Massachusetts Ave NW Washington DC 20016-5690 *The pursuit of happiness can be dangerous. To ask ourselves whether we are happy may only fasten our attention upon those demons of discontent and frustration that plague us all. The proper query is, "How best can we contribute to the welfare of others?" Individuals-and nations-do well to abandon both oppressive practices of dependency and the destructive illusion of absolute independence. True happiness comes only with the discovery that we are designed to be constructively interdependent.*

STOOKEY, NOEL PAUL, folksinger, composer; b. Balt., Dec. 30, 1937; s. George William and Dorothea (St. Aubrey) S.; m. Mary Elizabeth Bannard, Sept. 4, 1963; children: Elizabeth Drake, Katherine Darby, Anna St. Aubrey. Student, Mich. State U., 1955-58; HHD (hon.), Husson Coll., 1978. prodn. mgr. Cormac Chem. Corp., 1959-60. Released album of songs Birds of Paradise, 1954; sang professionally, master ceremonies events, Mich. State U., 1955-58; profl. singer, Greenwich Village, N.Y.C., 1960-61; mem. folksinging group, Peter, Paul and Mary, 1961—; solo rec. artist for Warner Bros., 1971-74; producer folk albums for Scepter Records, Verve/Folkway Records; founder, Neworld Media, rec. studio Neworld Records, 1977-81; rec. artist: Paul And, 1971, One Night Stand, 1972, Real to Reel, 1976, Something New and Fresh, 1978, Band and Bodyworks, 1979, Wait'll You Hear This, 1982, There is Love, 1985, State of the Heart, 1985, In Love Beyond Our Lives, 1990, Peter Paul and Mommy Too, 1993, Lifelines, 1995. Mem. AFTRA, Screen Actors Guild, ASCAP, Delta Upsilon. Club: St. Botolph's (Boston). Home: Rt 175 Blue Hill Falls ME 04615

STOOP, NORMA MCLAIN, editor, author, photographer; b. Panama, C.Z., July 20, 1910; b. Harry Edward and Gladys (Brandon) McLain; student Penn Hall Jr. Coll., Carnegie Inst. Tech., New Sch., N.Y. U.; m. William J. Stoop, Jr., Sept. 20, 1932. Contbg. editor Dance Mag., N.Y.C., 1969-71, assoc. editor, 1971-79, sr. editor, 1979-91, contbg. editor, 1991-92; sr. editor After Dark, 1978-82, also feature writer; also photographer, theater, ballet and film critic; entertainment editor sr. edit. Sta. WNYC-AM, 1980-83; chief film critic Manhattan Arts, 1983-89, mem. editors panel Antioch U. summer writers workshop, 1988, 89, spl. guest for dialogue sessions, 1990. Mem. Poetry Soc. Am., Acad. Am. Poets, TV Acad. Arts and Scis., Overseas Press Club, Deadline Club, Sigma Delta Chi. Contbr. poems to Tex. Quar., Chgo. Rev., Plains Poetry Jour., Arts in Society, Quest, Atlantic Monthly, Puerto Del Sol, The Quarterly, Md. Poetry Rev., others, short stories to Portland Monthly, others, 1958—, essays to Book Week in N.Y. Herald Tribune; represented in Best Poems of 1973, Exhibit of Dance Photography, Harvard U., Tufts Coll., 1975, featured in 1990 Poet's Market; MacNeil Lehrer News, 1988. Recipient award Dance Tchrs. Club Boston, 1977, Eve of St. Agnes Competition award, 1993

STOORZA GILL, GAIL, corporate professional; b. Yoakum, Tex., Aug. 28, 1943; d. Roy Otto and Ruby Pauline (Ray) Blankenship; m. Larry Stoorza, Apr. 27, 1963 (div. 1968); m. Ian M. Gill, Apr. 24, 1981; 1 child, Alexandra Leigh. Student, N. Tex. State U., 1961-63, U. Tex., Arlington, 1963. Stewardess Cen. Airlines, Ft. Worth, 1963; advt. and acctg. exec. Phillips-Ramsey Advt., San Diego, 1963-68; dir. advt. Rancho Bernardo, San Diego, 1968-72; dir. corp. communications Avco Community Developers, San Diego, 1972-74; pres. Gail Stoorza Co., San Diego, 1974—, Stoorza, Ziegaus & Metzger, San Diego, 1974—; CEO Stoorza, Ziegaust, Metzger, Inc., 1993—; chmn. Stoorza/Smith, San Diego, 1984-85, Stoorza Internat., San Diego, 1984-85; CEO ADC Stoorza, San Diego, 1987—, Franklin Stoorza, San Diego, 1993—. Trustee San Diego Art Found.; bd. dirs. San Diego Found. for Performing Arts, San Diego Opera, Sunbelt Nursery Groups, Dallas. Names Small Bus. Person of Yr. Selest Com. on Small Bus., 1984, one of San Diego's Ten Outstanding Young Citizens San Diego Jaycees, 1979; recipient Woman of Achievement award Women in Communications Inc., 1985. Mem. Pubs. Soc. Am., Nat. Assn. Home Builders (residential mktg. com.), COMBO. Methodist. Clubs: Chancellors Assn. U. Calif. (San Diego), Pub. Relations, San Diego Press. Home: PO Box 490 Rancho Santa Fe CA 92067-0490 Office: Franklin Stoorza 225 Broadway Ste 1800 San Diego CA 92101*

STOPHER, PETER ROBERT, civil and transportation engineering educator, consultant; b. Crowborough, Eng., Aug. 8, 1943; came to U.S., 1968; s. Harold Edward and Joan Constance (Salmon) S; m. Valerie Anne Alway, Apr. 11, 1964 (div. Feb. 1989); children: Helen Margaret Anne, Claire Elizabeth; m. Catherine Coville Jones July 7, 1990. BSCE, U. Coll., London, 1964, PhD, 1967. Research officer Greater London Council, London, 1967-68; asst. prof. transp. planning, applied statistics, math. modeling Northwestern U., Evanston, Ill., 1968-70, from assoc. prof. to prof., 1973-79, vis. prof., 1980-81; asst. prof. McMaster U., Hamilton, Ontario, 1970-71; assoc. prof. Cornell U., Ithaca, N.Y., 1971-73; tech. v.p. Schimpeler Corradino Assoc., Miami, Fla., and Los Angeles, 1980-84, v.p., 1984-87; dir., CFO Evaluation and Tng. Inst., 1987-90; prin., co-founder Applied Mgmt. and Planning Group, 1988-90; prof. civil engring. La. State Univ., Baton Rouge, 1990—, dir. La. Transp. Rsch. Ctr., 1990-93; co-founder, ptnr. PlanTrans, 1994—; spl. advisor Nat. Inst. Transp. and Rd. Research, Pretoria, S. Africa, 1976-77; vis. prof. U. Syracuse, N.Y., 1971-73, U. Louvain, Belgium, 1980. Co-author Urban Transportation Planning and Modeling, 1974, Transportation Systems Evaluation, 1976, Survey Sampling and Multivariate Analysis, 1978; contbr. articles to profl. jours. Active Stephen Ministry. Recipient Fred Burgraaf prize Hwy. Research Bd., 1968, Jules Dupuit prize World Conf. on Transp. Rsch., 1992. Mem. ASCE, Am. Stats. Assn., Transp. Rsch. Bd. (com. chmn. 1970-77, 95—), Transp. Rsch. Forum (Joyce E. Yaeger Intermodel Rsch. Paper award 1994), Inst. Transp. Engrs. Democrat. Methodist. Avocations: working out, gardening, photography, reading, classical music. Home: 3533 Granada Dr Baton Rouge LA 70810-1142 Office: La State U Dept Civil and Environ Engring Baton Rouge LA 70803-6405

STOPPARD, TOM (TOMAS STRAUSSLER), playwright; b. Zlin, Czechoslovakia, July 3, 1937; s. Eugene and Martha (Stoppard) Straussler; m. Jose Ingle, 1965 (div.); m. Miriam Moore-Robinson, 1972; 4 children. MLitt (hon.), U. Bristol, Eng., 1979, Brunel U., Eng., 1979, U. Sussex, Eng., 1980. Journalist Western Daily Press, Bristol, Eng., 1954-58, Evening World, Bristol, 1958-60; free-lance reporter, 1960-63; bd. dirs. Royal Nat. Theatre, London, 1989—. Author: (plays) The Gamblers, 1965, Rosencrantz and Guildenstern Are Dead, 1966 (Plays and Players Best Play award 1967, Best Play Tony award 1968), Enter a Free Man, 1968, The Real Inspector Hound, 1968, Albert's Bridge, 1969 (Prix Italia 1968), If You're Glad I'll Be Frank, 1969, After Magritte, 1970, Dogg's Our Pet, 1971, Jumpers, 1972 (Evening Standard Best Play award 1972, Plays and Players Best Play award 1972), Travesties, 1974 (Evening Standard Best Play award 1974, Best Play Tony award 1976), Dirty Linen and New-Found-Land, 1976, Every Good Boy Deserves Favor, 1974, Night and Day, 1978 (Evening Standard Best Play award 1978), Dogg's Hamlet, Cahoot's Macbeth, 1979, The Real Thing, 1982 (Evening Standard Best Play award 1982, Best Play Tony award 1984, Best Fgn. Play Tony award 1984), Hapgood, 1988, Artist Descending a Staircase, 1988, Arcadia, 1993 (Evening Standard Best Play award 1993, Oliver award 1994), Indian Ink, 1995; (play adaptations) Tango by Slawomir Mrozek, 1966, The House of Bernarda Alba by Federico Garcia Lorca, 1973, Undiscovered Country (based on Das Weite Land by Arthur Schnitzler), 1979, On the Razzle (based on Einen Jux will er sich machen by Johann Nestroy), 1981, Rough Crossing (based on The Play's the Thing by Ferenc Molnar), 1984, Dalliance (based on Liebelei by Arthur Schnitzler), 1986; (radio plays) The Dissolution of Dominic Boot, 1964, M is for Moon Among Other Things, 1964, If You're Glad I'll Be Frank, 1966, Albert's Bridge, 1967, Where Are They Now?, 1970, Artist Descending A Staircase, 1972, The Dog It Was That Died, 1982, In the Native State, 1991, also episodes of radio serials The Dales, 1964, A Student's Diary, 1965; (screenplays) The Romantic Englishwoman, 1975, Despair, 1978, The Human Factor, 1980, (with Terry Gilliam and Charles McKeown) Brazil, 1985 (Best Screenplay Acad. award nominee 1985, Best Screenplay L.A. Critics Circle award 1985), Empire of the Sun, 1987, The Russia House, 1990; (author, dir.) Rosencrantz and Guildenstern Are Dead, 1990 (Grand prize Venice Film Festival 1990), Billy Bathgate, 1991; (teleplays) A Walk on the Water, 1963, A Separate Peace, 1966, Teeth, 1967, Another Moon Called Earth, 1967, Neutral Ground, 1968, The Engagement (based on his radio play The Dissolution of Dominic Boot), 1970, One Pair of Eyes, 1972, (with Clive Exton) Boundaries, 1975, Three Men in a Boat, 1975, Professional Foul, 1977, Squaring the Circle: Poland 1980-81, 1985; (translator) Largo Desolato by Vaclav Havel, 1987; (novel) Lord Malquist and Mr. Moon, 1966; contbr. short stories to Introduction 2, 1964. Decorated comdr. Order Brit. Empire; Ford Found. grantee, 1964; recipient John Whiting award Arts Coun. Great Britain, 1967, Evening Standard Most Promising Playwright Drama award, 1972, Shakespeare prize Hamburg, Germany, 1979. Fellow Royal Soc. Literature. Office: Peters Fraser Dunlop, The Chambers 5th fl, Lots Rd, London SW10 OXF, England

STOPPLEMOOR, CHERYL See LADD, CHERYL

STORANDT, MARTHA, psychologist; b. Little Rock, June 2, 1938; d. Farris and Floy (Montgomery) Mobbs; m. Duane Storandt, Dec. 15, 1962; 1 child, Eric. AB, Washington U., St. Louis, 1960, PhD, 1966. Lic. psychologist, Mo. Staff psychologist VA, Jefferson Barracks, Mo., 1967-68; asst. prof. to prof. Washington U., St. Louis, 1968—; mem. nat. adv. council on aging Nat. Inst. on Aging, 1984-87; editor-in-chief Jour. Gerontology, 1981-86. Author: Counseling and Therapy with Older Adults, 1983; co-author: Memory, Related Functions and Age, 1974; co-editor: The Clinical Psychology of Aging, 1978, The Adult Years: Continuity and Change, 1989, Neuropsychological Assessment of Dementia and Depression in Older Adults: A Clinician's Guide, 1994. Recipient Disting. Service award Mo. Assn. Homes for the Aging, 1984, Disting. Sci. Contbn. award Am. Psychol. Assn. div. Adult Devel. and Aging, 1988. Fellow Am. Psychol. Assn. (pres. div. 20 1979-80, council rep. 1983-84, 86-88), Gerontol. Soc. Am. Office: Washington U Dept Psychology Saint Louis MO 63130

STORARO, VITTORIO, cinematographer; b. Rome, June 24, 1940; s. Renato and Teodolinda (Laparelli) S.; m. Antonia Cafolla, Dec. 29, 1962; children: Francesca, Fabrizio, Giovanni. Student, Duca D'Aosta, Rome, 1951-56, Centro Italiano Addestramento Cinematografico, Rome, 1956-58; Degree in Cinematography, Centro Sperimentale di Cinematografia, Rome, 1958-60. Cinematographer Titanus, 1968, Paramount, 1970, 81, 87, United Artist, 1972, 76-77, 20th Century Fox, 1976, 78, Columbia, 1981, 84-86, Cronard Communications, 1982, Warner Bros., 1983, NBC, 1984-85. Cinematographer films including Youthful Youthful, 1968, The Bird With The Crystal Plummage, 1970, The Conformist, 1970, Last Tango in Paris, 1972, Nineteen Hundred, 1976, Scandalo Submission, 1977, Luna, 1978, Apocalypse Now, 1979 (Academy Award, 1980), Reds, 1981 (Acad. award 1982), One From the Heart, 1981, Wagner, 1982, Lady Hawke, 1983, Peter the Great, 1985, Ishtar, 1986, The Last Emperor, 1987 (Acad. award 1988), Tucker, 1987, New York Stories, 1988, Dick Tracy, 1990, The Sheltering Sky, 1990, Little Buddha, 1994. Recipient Best Cinematography award N.Y. Film Critics, 1971. Mem. Acad. Motion Picture Arts and Scis., Italian Assn. of Cinematographers (pres.). Home: Via Divino Amore 2, 00040 Rome Italy

STORCH, ARTHUR, theater director; b. Bklyn., June 29, 1925; s. Sam and Bessie (Goldner) S.; children: Max Darrow, Alexander English, Bess Martin. B.A., New Sch. Social Research, 1949. Actor in Broadway prodns. End as a Man, 1953, Time Limit, 1955, Girls of Summer, 1956, Look Homeward, Angel, 1957, Night Circus, 1958, The Long Dream, 1960, The Best Man, 1961; motion pictures The Strange One, 1956, Girls of the Night, 1959, The Exorcist, 1974; dir. off-Broadway Two by Saroyan, 1961, Three by Three, 1962, Talking to You (London debut), 1962, The Typists and the Tiger, 1963, The Owl and the Pussycat, 1964, The Impossible Years, 1965, The Local Stigmatic, 1970, Under the Weather, 1965, Golden Rainbow, 1967, The Chinese and Dr. Fish, 1969, Promenade All, 1970, 42 Seconds from Broadway, 1973, Tribute, 1978, Twice Around the Park, 1982, Clarence, 1986; Of Mice and Men, 1988; dir. nat. tour The King and I, 1989; dir. Syracuse Stage Waiting for Lefty, Noon, Of Mice and Men, 1974, 75, La Ronde, The Butterfingers Angel. Mornings at Seven, Dynamo, 1975-76, A Quality of Mercy, The Seagull, 1976-77, 1976-77; dir. Love Letters on Blue Paper, End of the Beginning, 1977-78, Loved, 1978, Naked, 1979, The Comedy of Errors, 1980, The Impromptu of Outremont, 1982, The Double Bass, 1984, Arms and the Man, Handy Dandy, Cyrano de Bergerac, Romeo and Juliet, 1986, Of Mice and Men, N.Y.C., 1987, Fugue, 1988, Seven By Beckett, 1988, Look Homeward Angel, Wait Unitl Dark, Dangerous Corner, 1990, A Walk in the Woods, 1989, Finding Donis Ann, 1990, Androcles and the Lion, 1991; Lend Me a Tenor, 1992, Awake and Sing, 1993; dir., actor Love Letters, 1992; founder, producing artistic dir. Syracuse Stage; chmn. drama dept. Syracuse U., 1974-92, Arthur Storch Theatre, 1992; artistic dir. Berkshire Theatre Festival, Stockbridge, Mass., 1995—. Home: 231 E 48th St New York NY 10017-1538 Office: Berkshire Theatre Festival Stockbridge MA 01262

STOREN, THOMAS, JR. See DOHERTY, TOM

STORER, JOHN W., lawyer, consultant; b. Washington, June 22, 1922; s. John W. and Nellie Grace (Mudd) S.; m. Harriet S. Trembecki, Oct. 2, 1945; children: Margaret, John III, Mark, Susan. JD, Loyola U., Chgo., 1949. Bar: Ill. 1949, U.S. Dist. Ct. (no. dist.) Ill. 1950, U.S. Supreme Ct. 1956. Atty. Continental Gas Co., Chgo., 1949-54, Law Offices Wyatt Jacobs, Chgo., 1954-60; founding, sr. ptnr. McKenna Storer et al., Chgo., 1960-84; mng. ptnr. McKenna Storer, Chgo., 1970-84; of counsel McKenna Storer Rowe White & Farrug, Chgo., 1984—; founder, faculty mem. transp. law inst. U. Denver, 1969; lectr. in field. Contbr. articles to profl. jours. Founder, dir. Timber Lakes (Ill.) Civic Assn., 1956; pres. Wildwood Community Assn., Chgo., 1960; organizer, past pres. Edgebrook Civic Orch.; former trustee sch. bd. St. Mary Woods Ch. Lt. AC, USN, 1942-46, PTO. Fellow Am. Bar Found.; mem. ABA (chair sr. lawyers divsn. 1990), Am. Arbitration Assn. (comml. arbitrator), Am. Soc. Metals, Am. Mgmt. Assn., Ill. State Bar (chair law practice mgmt. 1954—), Ill. Assn. Def. Counsel, Chgo. Bar Assn. (chair law practice mgmt., arbitration, 1954—, aviation law 1976—), Aviation Ins. Assn., Internat. Assn. Def. Counsel (dir., sec., treas. 1975-81, organizing advisor alternative dispute resolution com.), Transp. Lawyers Assn. (Disting. Svc. award 1989), Def. Rsch. Inst., Soc. Trial Lawyers, Trial Lawyers Club, Ridgemoor Country Club (pres. 1967), Rio Verde Country Club (gen. counsel 1990—), Attic Club (bd. dirs. 1986-92), Rotary. Home: 26231 N Tonto Trl Rio Verde AZ 85263-7276 Office: McKenna Storer Row Shite & Farrug 200 N La Salle St Ste 3000 Chicago IL 60601-1014*

STORER, MARYRUTH, law librarian; b. Portland, Oreg., July 26, 1953; d. Joseph William and Carol Virginia (Pearson) Storer; m. David Bruce Bailey, Jan. 1, 1981; children: Sarah, Allison. BA in History, Portland State U., 1974; JD, U. Oreg., 1977; M in Law Librarianship, U. Wash., 1978. Bar: Oreg. 1978. Assoc. law librarian U. Tenn., Knoxville, 1978-79; law librarian O'Melveny & Myers, Los Angeles, 1979-88; dir. Orange County Law Library, Santa Ana, Calif., 1988—. Mem. Am. Assn. Law Libraries, So. Calif. Assn. Law Libraries (pres. 1986-87), Coun. Calif. County Law Librs. (sec.-treas. 1990-94, pres. 1994—). Democrat. Episcopalian. Office: Orange County Law Library 515 N Flower St Santa Ana CA 92703-2354

STORER, NORMAN WILLIAM, sociology educator; b. Middletown, Conn., May 8, 1930; s. Norman Wyman and Mary Emily (House) S.; m. Ada Joan Van Valkenburg, Aug. 19, 1951; children: Martin Wilson, Thomas Wyman; m. Mary Ashton Pott Hiatt, Mar. 7, 1975. A.B., U. Kans., 1952, M.A., 1956; Ph.D., Cornell U., 1961. Lectr., asst. prof. Harvard U., Cambridge, Mass., 1960-66; staff assoc. Social Sci. Research Council, N.Y.C., 1966-70; prof. sociology CUNY-Baruch Coll., N.Y.C., 1970-88; prof. emeritus CUNY-Baruch Coll., 1989—; dept. chmn. CUNY-Baruch Coll., N.Y.C., 1970-85, chmn. faculty senate, 1981-84. Author: The Social System of Science, 1966, Focus on Society, 1973, 2d edit., 1980, A Leer of Limericks, 1990, (with William Flores) Domestic Violence in Suburban San Diego, 1994; editor: The Sociology of Science, 1973; column editor San Diego Writers' Monthly, 1992-94. Served to sgt. AUS, 1953-55. Mem. AAAS, Phi Beta Kappa, Sigma Xi. Democrat. Home: 1417 Van Buren Ave San Diego CA 92103-2339

STORER, THOMAS PERRY, lawyer; b. Washington, July 14, 1944; s. Morris Brewster and Gretchen Geuder (Schneider) S.; m. Julia Manganip Owek, Dec. 22, 1966; children: Lingbawan Frederick, Allinnawa Elizabeth, Gessingga Nathaniel. BA in Math., Harvard U., 1965, JD, 1979; MPA, Woodrow Wilson Sch. Pub. and Internat. Affairs, 1969. Bar: Mass. 1979, U.S. Dist. Ct. Mass. 1979. Program officer U.S. Peace Corps, Kuala Lumpur, Malaysia, 1969-72; analyst, unit chief Bur. of Budget State of Ill., Springfield, 1972-74, dep. dir. Dept. Pub. Aid, 1974-76; cons. Mass. Medicaid Program, Boston, 1976-79; assoc. Goodwin, Procter & Hoar, Boston, 1979-87, ptnr., 1987—. Vol. U.S. Peace Corps, Bontoc, Mountain Prov., Philippines, 1965-67; elder Newton (Mass.) Presbyn. Ch., Mass., 1987—. Mem. ABA, Mass. Bar Assn. Avocations: music, computers. Home: 114 Waban Hill Rd N Chestnut Hill MA 02167-1026 Office: Goodwin Procter & Hoar Exchange Pl Boston MA 02109

STORETTE, RONALD FRANK, lawyer; b. N.Y.C., June 20, 1943; m. Monique Storette; 1 child, Ronald. BA summa cum laude, U. Va., 1966; JD, Harvard U., 1969; Diploma of Internat. Law, Stockholm Faculty of Law, 1970. Bar: D.C. 1973, U.S. Ct. Appeals (D.C. cir.) 1976, U.S. Supreme Ct. 1976, U.S. Dist. Ct. (so. and ea. dists.) N.Y. 1977, U.S. Dist. Ct. D.C. 1977, U.S. Ct. Appeals (2d cir.) 1978, U.S. Ct. Internat. Trade. 1978. Lectr. law Stockholm Faculty of Law, 1970-71; assoc. Jean-Pierre De Bandt, Brussels, 1971-73; chief legal counsel Textron Atlantic S.A., Brussels, 1973-75; assoc. Donovan, Leisure, Newton & Irvine, N.Y.C., 1975-79; ptnr. Fragomen, Del Rey & Bernsen, P.C., N.Y.C., 1979-88, Baker & McKenzie, N.Y.C., 1988-91, Proskauer Rose Goetz & Mendelsohn, N.Y.C., 1991—. Author: The Politics of Integrated Social Investment; An American Study of the Swedish LAMCO Project in Liberia, 1971, The Administration of Equality; An American Study of Sweden's Bilateral Development Aid, 1972; also articles. Cassal Found. fellow U. Stockholm, Sweden, 1969. Mem. ABA, N.Y. State Bar Assn., Assn. of Bar of City of N.Y., Am. Immigration Lawyers Assn., Phi Beta Kappa. Office: Proskauer Rose Goetz & Mendelsohn 1585 Broadway New York NY 10036-8200

STOREY, BOBBY EUGENE, JR., electrical engineer, engineering consultant; b. Bainbridge, Md., Jan. 26, 1958; s. Bobby E. Sr. and Rebecca J. (Seagraves) S.; m. Lynn M. Miller, May 24, 1976 (div. June 1988); 1 child, Christopher David; m. Mary H. Freeman, Feb. 14, 1992. AA in Math., Gordon Jr. Coll., 1986; BS in Applied Physics, Ga. Inst. Tech., 1988, M in Applied Physics, 1989. Engr. instrumentation and controls Va. Power Co., Mineral, 1982-85; engr. electro optics GEC Avionics, Norcross, Ga., 1988; pres. E&H Enterprises, Inc., 1994—; v.p. EnerSci Inc., Norcross, 1989-95; product engr. LXE, Inc., Norcross, 1988-94; pres. E & H Enterprises, Inc., Duluth, Ga., 1994-96; sr. program mgr. Sci. Atlanta, Inc., Norcross, Ga., 1995—. With USN, 1976-82. Mem. Internat. Orgn. Electrical and Electronic Engrs. Republican. Avocations: coins, woodworking, target shooting. Home: 2820 Bluebird Cir Duluth GA 30136-3908 Office: Sci Atlanta Inc 4386 Park Dr Norcross GA 30092

STOREY, BRIT ALLAN, historian; b. Boulder, Colo., Dec. 10, 1941; s. Harold Albert and Gladys Roberta (Althouse) S.; m. Carol DeArman, Dec. 19, 1970; 1 child, Christine Roberta. AB, Adams State Coll., Alamosa, Colo., 1963; MA, U. Ky., 1965, PhD, 1968. Instr. history Auburn (Ala.) U., 1967-68, asst. prof., 1968-70; dep. state historian State Hist. Soc. Colo., Denver, 1970-71, acting state historian, 1971-72, rsch. historian, 1972-74; hist. preservation specialist Adv. Coun. on Hist. Preservation, Lakewood,

Colo., 1974-88; sr. historian Bur. Reclamation, Lakewood, 1988—. Contbr. articles to profl. publs. Mem. Fed. Preservation Forum (pres. 1990-91), Nat. Coun. Pub. History (sec. 1987, pres.-elect 1990-91, pres. 1991-92), Orgn. Am. Historians (com. 1983-86, chmn. 1985-86), Victorian Soc. Am. (bd. dirs. 1977-79), Western History Assn. (chmn. com. 1982-86), Colo.-Wyo. Assn. Mus. (sec. 1974-76, pres. 1976-77), Cosmos Club (Washington). Avocations: fishing, birding. Home: 7264 W Otero Ave Littleton CO 80123-5639 Office: Bur Reclamation D 5300 Bldg 67 Denver Fed Ctr Denver CO 80225-0007

STOREY, CHARLES PORTER, lawyer; b. Austin, Tex., Dec. 4, 1922; s. Robert Gerald and Frances Hazel (Porter) S.; m. Helen Hanks Stephens, Oct. 14, 1950; children: Charles Porter, Harry Stephens, Frederick Schatz. BA, U. Tex., 1947, LLB, 1948; LLM, So. Methodist U., 1952. Bar: Tex. 1948. Pvt. practice law Dallas, 1948—; with Storey Armstrong Steger & Martin P.C. Pres. Dallas Day Nursery Assn., 1958, Greater Dallas Coun. Chs., 1970-71; chmn. Internat. Com. YMCA, 1969-71; nat. bd. dirs. U.S. YMCA, 1964-75; pres. Children's Devel. Ctr., Dallas, 1959; trustee Baylor Coll. Dentistry, 1981-90, Hillcrest Found.; trustee Southwestern Legal Found., chmn. 1980-90. 1st lt., pilot USAAF, 1943-45, ETO. Decorated Air medal. Master Dallas Inn of Ct. (pres. 1991-93); fellow Am. Coll. Trial Lawyers, Am. Bar Found., Tex. Bar Found.; mem. ABA, Tex. Bar Assn. (bd. dirs. 1976-79), Dallas Bar Assn. (pres. 1975), Philos. Soc. Tex., Dallas Country Club, Crescent Club, Idlewild Club, Phi Delta Phi, Phi Delta Theta. Mem. Christian Ch. (Disciples of Christ). Home: 4400 Rheims Pl Dallas TX 75205-3627 Office: 4600 Fountain Pl 1445 Ross Ave Dallas TX 75202-2812

STOREY, FRANCIS HAROLD, business consultant, retired bank executive; b. Calgary, Alberta, Can., June 20, 1933; s. Bertwyn Morrell and Hilda Josephine (Masters) S.; m. Willomae Saiter, Apr. 25, 1954; children: Daryl, Elizabeth, Brian, Shelley. Student, Gonzaga U., 1953, Pacific Coast Bankers Sch., 1974-76. Designated Certified Profl. Cons. Bank trainee Wash. Trust Bank, Spokane, 1950-56; owner Storey & Storey, Spokane, 1956-64; agt. Bankers Life Nebr., Spokane, 1964-67; sr. v.p. Old Nat. Bank, Spokane, 1967-87, U.S. Bank of Wash., Spokane, 1987-90; pvt. practice cons. Spokane, 1990—; bd. dirs. Alloy Trailers Inc., Output Tech. Corp. Bd. dirs. Spokane Bus. Incubator, 1985-96, United Way of Spokane, 1987-95; bd.dirs., treas., fin. chair, gen. conv. dep. Episc. Diocese Spokane Dep., 1969—; trustee Spokane Symphony Soc., 1986-93, Spokane Area Econ. Devel. Coun., 1982-89; mem. adv. bd. Intercollegiate Ctr. Nursing Edn., chair, 1996. Mem. Acad. Profl. Cons. and Advisors, Inland N.W. Soc. Cons. Profls., Spokane Rotary, Spokane Country Club. Episcopalian. Avocations: golf, reading, travel. Home: 214 E 13th Ave Spokane WA 99202-1115

STOREY, JAMES MOORFIELD, lawyer; b. Boston, Apr. 12, 1931; s. Charles Moorfield and Susan Jameson (Sweetser) S.; m. Adair Miller, Aug. 28, 1954 (div. 1973); children: Barbara Sessums Storey McGrath, Mary Sweetser Storey Meley, Susan Adair Storey Frank, Eliza Allison Tebo Storey Anderson, Alice Leovy Storey Thorpe; m. Isabelle Helene Boeschenstein, May 17, 1973. A.B., Harvard U., 1953, LL.B., 1956. Bar: Mass. 1956. Atty. SEC, Washington, 1956-57, legal asst. to chmn., 1957-59; assoc. Gaston, Snow, Motley & Holt, Boston, 1959-62; ptnr. Gaston, Snow, Motley & Holt (name changed to Gaston Snow & Ely Bartlett), Boston, 1962-87; ptnr. Dechert Price & Rhoads, Boston, 1987-94, ret., 1994, profl. trustee, corp. dir., 1994—; trustee Mt. Auburn Cemetery, Cambridge, Mass., 1980—. Mem. ABA, Boston Bar Assn., Tavern Club Boston (pres. 1985-87), City Club Corp. (pres. 1987-89), Century Assn. of N.Y. Unitarian. Home: 89A Mount Vernon St Boston MA 02108-1330 Office: Room 1239 10 Post Office Sq S 12th Fl Boston MA 02109

STOREY, KENNETH BRUCE, biology educator; b. Taber, Alta., Can., Oct. 23, 1949; s. Arthur George and Madeleine Una (Mawhinney) S.; m. Janet Margaret Collicutt, June 6, 1975; children: Jennifer, Kathryn. BSc with honors, U. Calgary, Alta., 1971; PhD, U. B.C., Vancouver, Can., 1974. Asst. prof. Duke U., Durham, N.C., 1975-79; assoc. prof. Carleton U., Ottawa, Ont., Can., 1979-85, prof., 1985—; invited lectr. at various confs., univs. Mem. editl. bd. Cryo-Letters, 1983—, Jour. Comparative Physiology, 1995—, Am. Jour. Physiology, 1994—; contbr. over 300 articles to profl. jours. Recipient E.W.R. Steacie award Nat. Sci. and Engring. Rsch. Coun. Can., 1984-86, Killam sr. rsch. fellow, 1993—; Killam fellow Can. Coun., Sheffield, Eng., 1975-77. Fellow Royal Soc. Can.; mem. Am. Soc. Biol. Chemists, Can. Biochem. Soc. (Ayerst award 1989), Can. Soc. Zoology, soc. Cryobiology. Avocations: movies, music, Renaissance art. Office: Carleton U Dept Biology, 1125 Colonel By Drive, Ottawa, ON Canada K1S 5B6

STOREY, NORMAN C., lawyer; b. Miami, Fla., Oct. 11, 1943. BA cum laude, Loyola U., L.A., 1965; JD, U. Ariz., 1968. Bar: Ariz. 1968. Law clk. to Hon. James A. Walsh U.S. Dist. Ct. Ariz.; ptnr. Squire, Sanders & Dempsey, Phoenix. Mem. ABA (corp., banking and bus. law, real property, probate, trust law sects., task force pub. rels.), State Bar Ariz., Maricopa County Bar Assn., Am. Arbitration Assn. (panelist). Office: Squire Sanders & Dempsey 40 N Central Ave Ste 2700 Phoenix AZ 85004-4424*

STOREY, ROBERT DAVIS, lawyer; b. Tuskegee, Ala., Mar. 28, 1936; s. Dewitt Herald and Katie Pearl (Johnson) S.; m. Juanita Kendrick Cohen, May 9, 1959; children: Charles Kendrick, Christopher Robert Ransom, Rebecca Kate. AB, Harvard U., 1958; JD, Case Western Res. U., 1964. Bar: Ohio, 1964. Atty. East Ohio Gas Co., Cleve., 1964-66; asst. dir. Legal Aid Soc., Cleve., 1966-67; assoc. Burke, Haber & Berick, Cleve., 1967-70, ptnr., 1971-93; ptnr. Thompson, Hine & Flory, P.L.L., Cleve., 1994—; bd. dirs. GTE Corp., Stamford, Conn., Procter & Gamble Co., Cin., May Dept. Stores Co., St. Louis, Bank One, Cleve.; trustee The Kresge Found., Case Western Res. U., Spelman Coll., Univ. Sch., Great Lakes Sci. Ctr.; trustee Cleve. State U., 1971-80, chmn., 1979-80; trustee Phillips Exeter Acad., 1968-83; overseer Harvard U., 1978-84; dir. Fed. Res. Bank Cleve., 1987-90, Louisville Courier-Jour., 1984-86. Served to capt. USMC, 1958-61. Recipient Charles Flint Kellog award Assn. Episcopal Colls., 1984; named Chief Marshal, 25th Reunion, Harvard Class of 1958, 1983. Mem. Soc. Benchers, Union Club, Rowfant Club, Univ. Club, Ponce de Leon Club. Episcopalian. Home: 2385 Coventry Rd Cleveland Hts OH 44118-4074 Office: Thompson Hine & Flory LLP 3900 Society Ctr 127 Public Sq Cleveland OH 44114

STORHOFF, DONALD C., agricultural products company executive; b. 1935; married. Supr. Meadowland Dairy, 1953-69; asst. plant mgr. Associated Milk Producers Inc., 1969-72; plant mgr. Wis. Dairies Coop., Baraboo, 1972-74, product mgr., 1974-77, mgr., 1977-84, pres., 1984—; also bd. dirs. Wis. Dairies Coop. (name now Foremost Farms USA), Baraboo; pres. Wis. Fedn. Coop. Dairy Div. & Whey Products Inst.; bd. dirs. Am. Dry Milk Inst., Nat. Milk Producers Fedn., Nat. Cheese and Butter Inst. Office: Foremost Farms USA E10-889A Penny Lane Baraboo WI 53913*

STORIN, MATTHEW VICTOR, newspaper editor; b. Springfield, Mass., Dec. 24, 1942; s. Harry Francis and Blanche Marie S.; m. Keiko Takita, Aug. 1, 1975; 1 child, Kenyatta; children by previous marriage: Karen, Aimee, Sean. BA, U. Notre Dame, 1964. Reporter Springfield Daily News, 1964-65, Griffin-Larrabee News Bur., Washington, 1965-69; Washington corr., city editor, Asian corr., nat. editor, asst. mng. editor, dep. mng. editor, mng. editor Boston Globe, 1969-85; dep. mng. editor U.S. News & World Report, Washington, 1985-86; editor, sr. v.p. Chgo. Sun-Times, 1986-87; editor The Maine Times, Topsham, 1988-89; mng. editor N.Y. Daily News, 1989-91, exec. editor, 1991-92; exec. editor Boston Globe, 1992-93, editor, 1993—. Recipient Disting. Polit. Reporting award Am. Assn. Polit. Sci., 1969. Home: 1501 Beacon St Brookline MA 02146-4626 Office: The Boston Globe 135 Morrissey Blvd Boston MA 02107

STORING, PAUL EDWARD, foreign service officer; b. Ames, Iowa, Oct. 24, 1929; s. James Alvin and Edith Nora (Ryg) S.; children: Mimi Storing Harlan, Felice Storing Kite. Student, U Oslo, Norway, 1950-51; B.A., Allegheny Coll., 1952; M.A. with honors, Colgate U., 1956; postgrad., U. Wis., Madison, 1955-59. Fgn. service officer Dept. State, Washington, Mex. and Scandinavia, 1960-80; spl. asst. U.S. Sect. Internat. Boundary and Water Commn. U.S. And Mex., Washington, 1980—. Contbr. articles to profl. jours. Served to cpl. U.S. Army, 1953-55. Fellow U. Wis., 1957-58; Fulbright fellow U. Oslo, 1959-60. Mem. Am. Fgn. Svc. Assn., Fulbright Assn., Phi Beta Kappa, Delta Tau Delta (pres. 1949-50). Baptist. Avocations: swimming; tennis; travel. Office: Office of Mex Affairs Dept of State Rm 4258 Washington DC 20520-0001

STORK, DONALD ARTHUR, advertising executive; b. Walsh, Ill., June 17, 1939; s. Arthur William and Katherine Frances (Young) S.; m. Joanna Gentry, June 9, 1962; 1 child, Brian Wesley. BS, So. Ill. U., 1961; postgrad. St. Louis U., 1968-69. With Naegele Outdoor Advt., Mpls., St. Louis, 1961-63; account exec. Richard C. Lynch Advt., 1963-64; media exec. Gardner Advt. Co., 1964-69; v.p. mktg. Advanswers Media/Programming divsn. Wells Rich Greene, N.Y.C., 1975-79; pres. Advanswers divsn. WRG/BDDP, N.Y.C., 1979—. Bd. dirs. Trailblazers, Inc.; pres. Signal Hill Sch. Assn. Parents Tchrs. Recipient Journalism Alumnus of Yr. award So. Ill. U., 1971, Alumni Achievement award, 1983. Served to capt. USAFR, 1961-67. Mem. St. Louis Advt. Club, Mensa, Mo. Athletic Club, St. Clair Country Club, Alpha Delta Sigma (Aid to Advt. Edn. award 1971). Home: 27 Symonds Dr Belleville IL 62223-1905 Office: Advanswers Media/Programming 10 S Broadway Saint Louis MO 63102-1712 also: 1740 Broadway New York NY 10019-4315

STORK, GILBERT (JOSSE), chemistry educator, investigator; b. Brussels, Belgium, Dec. 31, 1921; s. Jacques and Simone (Weil) S.; m. Winifred Stewart, June 9, 1944 (dec. May 1992); children: Diana, Linda, Janet, Philip. B.S., U. Fla., 1942; Ph.D., U. Wis., 1945; D.Sc. (hon.), Lawrence Coll., 1961, U. Paris, 1979, U. Rochester, 1982, Emory U., 1988, Columbia U., 1993. Sr. research chemist Lakeside Labs., 1945-46; instr. chemistry Harvard U., 1946-48, asst. prof., 1948-53; assoc. prof. Columbia U., N.Y.C., 1953-55, prof., 1955-67, Eugene Higgins prof., 1967-92, prof. emeritus, 1992—, chmn. dept., 1973-76; plenary lectr. numerous internat. symposia, named Lectureships in U.S. and abroad; cons. several cos.; chmn. Gordon Steroid Conf., 1958-59. Recipient Baekeland medal, 1961, Harrison Howe award, 1962, Edward Curtis Franklin Meml. award Stanford, 1966, Gold medal Synthetic Chems. Mfrs. Assn., 1971, Nebr. award, 1973, Roussel prize in steroid chemistry, 1978, Edgar Fahs Smith award, 1982, Willard Gibbs medal Chgo. sect. Am. Chem. Soc., 1982, Nat. Medal of Sci., 1982, Linus Pauling award, 1983, Tetrahedron prize, 1985, Remsen award, 1986, Cliff S. Hamilton award, 1986, Mony Ferst award Sigma Xi, 1987, George Kenner award, 1992, Chem. Pioneer award Am. Inst. Chemistry, 1992, Welch Found. Award in Chemistry, 1993, Allan R. Day award Phila. Chemists Club, 1994, Wolf prize, 1996; Guggenheim fellow, 1959. Fellow NAS (award in chem. sci. 1982), French Acad. Scis., Am. Acad. Arts and Scis., Am. Philos. Soc.; mem. Am. Chem. Soc. (chmn. organic chemistry divsn. 1967, award in pure chemistry 1957, award for creative work in synthetic organic chemistry 1967, Nichols medal 1980, Arthur C. Cope award 1980, Roger Adams award in organic chemistry 1991), Royal Soc. Chemistry (hon., London), Pharm. Soc. Japan (hon.), Chemists Club (hon.). Home: 459 Next Day Hill Dr Englewood NJ 07631-1921 Office: Columbia U Dept of Chemistry Chandle Hall New York NY 10027

STORK, WILLIAM WILLIS, secondary education educator; b. Toledo, May 25, 1940; s. Willis and Helen (Baldwin) S.; children: Christina, Willis W. III. BA, Yale U., 1962; MAT, Brown U., 1966; MA, Bowdoin Coll., 1969; postgrad., U. So. Calif., L.A. Cert. tchr., Calif., R.I. Dept. head history, instr. Brimmer & May Sch., Chestnut Hill, Mass., 1963-65; asst. dean of students, master St. George's Sch., Newport, R.I., 1965-71; dir. studies, instr. Marlborough Sch., L.A., 1971-83; dept. head math. Polytechnic Sch., Pasadena, Calif., 1983—, acting head of upper sch., 1985, dir. summer session, 1987; vis. scholar Cambridge (Eng.) U., 1991. Author: Linear Programming and Matrix Games, 1970, Social Change in Rural China, 1980. Pres. Friends of the Pasadena (Calif.) Pub. Libr., 1987; committeeman Pasadena Tournament of Roses, 1973—, mem. cmty. rels. com., 1988-90, mem. float entries com., 1990-92, mem. formation area com., 1992-94. Fulbright scholar, 1978. Mem. Assn. Yale Alumni (sec., bd. govs. 1992—, sec. 1992—, internat. and nat. coord. 1990-92, exec. com. 1990—, among others), Yale Club of So. Calif. (pres. 1987-89). Home: 1586 Oakdale St Pasadena CA 91106-3563 Office: Polytechnic Sch 1030 E California Blvd Pasadena CA 91106-4042

STORM, JONATHAN MORRIS, television critic; b. N.Y.C.; s. Thomas Walton and Martha Louise (Morris) S.; m. Kathleen Jo Pottick, Oct. 13, 1979. BA, Williams Coll., 1969. Reporter, city editor Rutland (Vt.) Herald, 1970-76; copy editor, assoc. editor Detroit Free Press, 1976-82; copy editor, feature editor Phila. Inquirer, 1982-89, TV critic, 1989—. Recipient Benjamin Franklin award Nat. Press Found., 1987. Mem. Hopewell Valley Golf Club, Soc. Profl. Journalists (treas. Phila. chpt. 1993—). Office: Phila Inquirer 400 N Broad St Philadelphia PA 19130-4015

STORMDANCER, ROWAN EHLENFELDT, traditional herbalist, management consultant; b. Terre Haute, Ind., July 7, 1952; d. John Nelson and Phyllis Inez (White) Turnbloom; m. Earl J. Chidester, Jan. 18, 1971 (div. 1976) 1 child, John; m. Rollin Sakeeta, Apr. 29, 1989; children: Brendan Lorithian, Allayne Carson. AA in English, Contra Costa Coll., 1978. Tutor English and trigonometry Contra Costa Coll., San Pablo, Calif., 1976-78; sales rep., asst. mgr. Avon, Richmond, Calif., 1977-78; sales mgr. C-Shor Sales, San Leandro, Calif., 1978-80; exec. sec. C.N. Petsas, CPA, Richmond, 1980-81; mgr., designer Jan's Attic, Bamberg, Germany, 1982-85; writing team Jovialis, Austin, Tex., 1988-89; pres., CEO Arcane Attic Ltd., Colorado Springs, Colo., 1988-95; owner Fairy Spirit, Arlington, Tex., 1989—; CEO North Star Metaphys. Enterprises, Inc., Arlington, Tex., 1995—; herbal cons. North Star Gardens, Arlington, Tex., 1990—; mng. dir. Pagan Merchant Coop., Arlington, Tex., 1992—. Author: Cyclopedia Talislanta, Vol. 3, 1989, Cyclopedia Talislanta, Vol. 5, 1990. Organizer Fairy Spirit and Friends Metaphys. Faire, Colorado Springs. Mem. North Circle Circle (chairperson 1988—), Gaianauts. Avocations: herbal rsch., collecting antiques, camping, writing. Office: PO Box 201253 Arlington TX 76006-1253

STORMER, HORST LUDWIG, physicist; b. Frankfurt-Main, Fed. Republic Germany, Apr. 6, 1949; came to U.S., 1977; s. Karl-Ludwig and Marie (Ihrig) S.; m. Dominique A. Parchet, 1982. Ph.D., U. Stuttgart, 1977. Mem. tech. staff AT&T Bell Labs., Murray Hill, N.J., 1977-83, head dept., 1983-91, dir. phys. rsch. lab., 1992—. Recipient Otto Klung prize Fed. Republic of Germany, 1985; Bell Labs. fellow, 1983. Fellow Am. Phys. Soc. (Buckley prize 1984), Am. Acad. Arts and Scis. Office: Lucent Technologies 700 Mountain Ave New Providence NJ 07974

STORMES, JOHN MAX, instructional systems developer; b. Manila, Oct. 7, 1927; s. Max Clifford and Janet (Heldring) S.; m. Takako Sanae, July 29, 1955; children: Janet Kazuko Stormes-Pepper, Alan Osamu. BS, San Diego State U., 1950; BA, U. So. Calif., 1957, MA, 1967. Cert. secondary and community coll. tchr. Editing supr. Lockheed Propulsion Co., Redlands, Calif., 1957-61; proposals supr. Rockwell Internat., Downey, Calif., 1961-62; publs. dir. Arthur D. Little, Inc., Santa Monica, Calif., 1962-63; publs. coord. Rockwell Internat., Downey, 1963-68; project dir. Gen. Behavioral Systems, Inc., Torrance, Calif., 1969-73; tng. and comm. cons. Media Rsch. Assocs., Santa Cruz, Calif., 1973—; tng. support svc. supr. So. Calif. Gas Co., L.A., 1985—; lectr. Calif. State U., Northridge, 1991—; tng. cons. Nat. Ednl. Media, Chatsworth, Calif., 1966-81, communications cons. Opinion Rsch. Calif., Long Beach, 1974—. Co-author: TV Communications Systems For Business and Industry, 1970. Curriculum adv. bd. communications dept. Calif. State U., Fullerton, 1964-78. Sgt. U.S. Army, 1953-55, Japan. Mem. Soc. Tech. Communication (sr. mem., 2nd v.p. Orange County chpt. 1962-63), Nat. Soc. Performance and Instruction (v.p. L.A. chpt. 1989, pres. 1990). Democrat. Episcopal. Avocations: photography, sailing. Home: 9140 Brookshire Ave Apt 207 Downey CA 90240-2963 Office: So Calif Gas Co ML 15H1 Box 3249 Los Angeles CA 90051-1249

STORMONT, RICHARD MANSFIELD, hotel executive; b. Chgo., Apr. 4, 1936; s. Daniel Lytle and E. Mildred (Milligan) S.; m. Virginia Louellen Walters, Nov. 21, 1959; children: Stacy Lee Freeman, Richard Mansfield, John Frederick. B.S., Cornell U., 1958. Cert. hosp. adminstrn.; cert. hosps. industry profl. Food cost analyst, sales rep. Edgewater Beach Hotel, Chgo., 1957-58; asst. sales mgr. Marriott Hotels, Inc., Washington, 1962-64; dir. sales Marriott Hotels, Inc., Atlanta, 1964-68; resident mgr. Marriott Hotels, Inc., 1969-71; gen. mgr. Marriott Hotel, Dallas, 1971-73, Phila., 1973-74, Atlanta, 1974-79; pres. Hardin Mgmt. Co., 1979-80; v.p. Marriott Franchise div. Marriott Corp., Washington, 1981-83, v.p. ops. Courtyard by Marriott, 1981-83; pres. The Stormont Cos. Inc., Atlanta, 1984-92; chmn. bd. dirs. Stormont Trice Corp., Atlanta, 1993—; dir. Walters & Co. Cons. to Mgmt., 1975-82. Pres. Atlanta Conv. and Visitors Burs., 1975-76, chmn. bd., 1976-77, vice chmn., 1996-97; bd. dirs. Better Bus. Bur.; exec. com. Ctrl. Atlanta Progress, 1979-80; exec. coun. Boy Scouts Am. Lt. (j.g.) USNR, 1959-62. Recipient Disting. Salesman of Yr. award Marriott, 1967, Obi T. Brewer award for Decade of Outstanding Svc., 1979. Mem. Sales and Mktg. Execs. (exec. v.p. 1969-70, pres. Atlanta 1970-71), Am. Hotel-Motel Assn. (exec. com., bd. dirs. 1993-95), Ga. Hospitality and Travel Assn. (founder, bd. dir., pres. 1989-90, chmn. bd. 1991-92, Hotelier of Yr. award 1977, Ga. Bus. and Industry Assn. (bd. dirs.), Atlanta Hotel Assn. (pres. 1976), So. Innkeepers Assn., Atlanta C. of C. (v.p. 1978-79), Gwinnett C. of C. (bd. dirs.), Cornell Soc. Hotelmen (pres. Ga. chpt. 1976, regional v.p. 1989-91). Home: 2980 Nancy Creek Rd NW Atlanta GA 30327-2000 Office: 3350 Cumberland Cir NW Ste 1800 Atlanta GA 30339-3340

STORMS, CLIFFORD BEEKMAN, lawyer; b. Mount Vernon, N.Y., July 18, 1932; s. Harold Beekman and Gene (Pertak) S.; m. Barbara H. Grave, 1955 (div. 1975); m. Valeria N. Parker, July 12, 1975; children: Catherine Storms Fischer, Clifford Beekman. BA magna cum laude, Amherst Coll., 1954; LLB, Yale U., 1957. Bar: N.Y. 1957. Assoc. Breed, Abbott & Morgan, N.Y.C., 1957-64; with CPC Internat., Inc., Englewood Cliffs, N.J., 1964—, v.p. legal affairs, 1973-75, v.p., gen. counsel, 1975-88, sr. v.p., gen. counsel, 1988—; bd. dirs. Atlantic Legal Found.; mem. N.J. Alternate Dispute Resolution panel Ctr. for Pub. Resources. Trustee Food and Drug Law Inst.; bd. dirs. CPC Ednl. Found. Mem. ABA (com. on corp. law depts.), Assn. Gen. Counsel (pres. 1992-94), Assn. Bar City N.Y. (sec., com. on corp. law depts. 1979-81), Indian Harbor Yacht Club, Econ. Club N.Y., Sky Club, Yale Club, Phi Beta Kappa. Home: 19 Burying Hill Rd Greenwich CT 06831-2604 Office: CPC Internat Inc Box 8000 International Plz Englewood Cliffs NJ 07632-1300

STORMS, LOWELL HANSON, psychologist; b. Schenectady, Feb. 14, 1928; s. Charles Arba and Afton Miriam (Hanson) S.; children: Chris, Karen, Bruce; m. Joan McEvoy Endres, Nov. 21, 1993. B.A. in Biostats, U. Minn., 1950, M.S., 1951, Ph.D. in Psychology, 1956. Clin. psychologist Hastings (Minn.) State Hosp., 1954-56; mem. faculty Neuropsychiat. Inst., UCLA, 1957-71, prof. psychiatry, 1970-71, supervising psychologist, 1963-71; prof. psychiatry Sch. Medicine, U. Calif., San Diego, 1971—; head med. psychology Sch. Medicine, U. Calif., 1971-80; v.p., dir. Clin. Psychol. Services, L.A., 1972—. Program chmn. Westwood Dem. Club, 1962-65. Served with U.S. Army, 1946-48. Fulbright grantee, 1956-57. Fellow Am. Psychol. Assn., AAAS; mem. Western Psychol. Assn., Calif. Psychol. Assn., Sigma Xi. Discoverer priming effect in verbal assns.; co-developer theory of schizophrenic behavioral disorganization. Office: 2022 Camino Del Rio N San Diego CA 92108-1508 *I try to live with full respect for the depth, richness, beauty and power of nature and with love and respect for my fellow creatures who share with me the human condition.*

STORR, ROBERT, curator painting and sculpture, artist, writer; b. Portland, Maine, Dec. 28, 1949; s. Richard J. and Virginia V. Storr; m. Rosamund Helen Morley, Sept. 1, 1979; children: Katharine, Susannah. BA, Swarthmore Coll., 1972; postgrad., Sch. Art Inst. of Chgo., 1975-78; MFA, Skowhegan (Maine) Sch. Painting and Sculpture, 1978. Assoc. dean N.Y. Studio Sch., N.Y.C., 1987-88; asst. prof. Tyler Sch. Art, Phila., 1989—; Avery prof. Bard Coll., Annandale On Hudson, N.Y., 1990-91; curator painting and sculpture Mus. Modern Art, N.Y.C., 1991—; vis. artist Cooper Union, N.Y.C., 1988-89; vis. artist, critic R.I. Sch. Design, Providence, 1988; lectr. art mus., univs. and art schs. in U.S. and abroad; coordinating curator at Moma, 1995. Author: Philip Guston, 1986; co-author: Chuck Close, 1987, (with Lars Hitue) Susan Rothenberg 15 Years a Survey, 1990, (with Kirk Varnedois) From Bauhaus to Pop: Masterworks Given By Phillip Johnson, 1996; also exhbn. catalogues; contbg. editor Art in Am.; mem. editorial bd. Art Jour.; contbr. articles to profl. jours.; exhibitions include Inst. Contemporary Art Phila., 1991, Moma, 1991, 93, 94, 95, 96. Penny McCall Found. grantee, 1988, Peter Norton Family Found. grantee, 1990. Mem. Internat. Assn. Art Critics. Office: Mus Modern Art 11 W 53rd St New York NY 10019-5401

STORRER, WILLIAM ALLIN, consultant; b. Highland Park, Mich., Mar. 22, 1936; s. Fredrick Ray and Margaret Ann (Pitts) S.; m. Carol A. Tuthill, Nov. 6, 1964 (div. June 1969); 1 child, Kirsten; m. Patricia Alice Whalley, Dec. 30, 1976. Student, Albion Coll., 1954-56; AB in Engring. Scis., Harvard U., 1959; MFA in Theatre Arts, Boston U., 1962; PhD in Comparative Arts, Ohio U., 1968. Electronics engr. Raytheon Co., Wayland, Mass., 1958-60; tech. dir. small stage Boston Arts Festival, 1961, 62; dir. dramatics Melrose (Mass.) H.S., 1962-63; dir. playhouse and repertory theatre, instr. drama-speech Hofstra U., 1963-66, instr. opera, 1965; asst. prof. theatre, dir. univ. theatre, U. Toledo, 1968-69; assoc. prof. theatre and film, dir. Southampton Coll., L.I. U., 1969-73; asst. prof. cinema studies and still photography Ithaca (N.Y.) Coll., 1973-76; assoc. prof. media arts U. S.C., Columbia, 1976-82; pres. MINDaLIVE Creative Mind Enhancement, Newark, 1980—; assoc. prof. theater and speech World Campus Afloat, Chapman Coll., 1972; edn. media specialist Newark Bd. Edn., 1990-94, Linden Bd. Edn., 1994-95, Harrison Bd. Edn., 1995—. Author: The Architecture of Frank Lloyd Wright, 1974, The Frank Lloyd Wright Companion, 1993; contbr. articles to popular mags. and profl. jours. Grantee Graham Found. for Advanced Studies in Fine Arts, 1987, 94. Home and Office: 289 Highland Ave Newark NJ 07104-1301

STORRS, ALEXANDER DAVID, astronomer; b. Idaho Falls, Idaho, May 30, 1960; s. Charles Lysander and Betty Lou (Wood) S.; m. Jean Elizabeth Seitzer, Nov. 4, 1989; 1 child, Matthew. BS, MIT, 1982; MS, U. Hawaii, 1985, PhD, 1987. Postdoctoral fellow NASA/Goddard Space Flight Ctr., Greenbelt, Md., 1987-89, U. Tex., Austin, 1989-91; assoc. scientist Space Telescope Sci. Inst., Balt., 1991—. Mem. AAAS, Am. Astron. Soc. (divsn. planetary scis.), Smithsonian Air and Space Mus. Office: Space Telescope Sci Inst 3700 San Martin Dr Baltimore MD 21218-2410

STORRS, ELEANOR EMERETT, research institute consultant; b. Cheshire, Conn., May 3, 1926; d. Benjamin Porter and Alta Hyde (Moss) S.; m. Harry Phineas Burchfield, Jr., Nov. 29, 1963; children: Sarah Storrs, Benjamin Hyde. B.S. with distinction in Botany, U. Conn., 1948; M.S. in Biology, NYU, 1958; Ph.D. in Chemistry, U. Tex., 1967. Asst. biochemist Boyce Thompson Inst. for Plant Research, Yonkers, N.Y., 1948-62; research scientist Clayton Found. Biochem. Inst., U. Tex., Austin, 1962-65; biochemist Pesticides Research Lab., USPHS, Perrine, Fla., 1965-67; dir. dept. biochemistry Gulf South Research Inst., New Iberia, La., 1967-77; adj. prof. chemistry U. Southwestern La., Lafayette, 1974-77; research prof. biology, dir. comparative mammalogy lab. Fla. Inst. Tech., Melbourne, 1977-94; ret., cons. on leprosy-armadillo programs, 1975-94, mem. Faculty Senate, 1979-84; cons. in rehab. and prevention deformities leprosy Pan Am. Health Orgn., WHO, Venezuela, Argentina, Brazil, Mex., 1972-90; dep. v.p. Coll. Hansenology in Endemic Countries, 1980-85. Author: (with H.P. Burchfield) Biochemical Applications of Gas Chromatography, 1962, (with Burchfield, D.E. Johnson) Guide to the Analysis of Pesticide Residues, 2 vols, 1965; also articles, book chpts. Grantee NIH, 1968-88, CDC, 1969-73, WHO, 1973-93, Leprosy Program, 1978-93, German Leprosy Relief Assn., 1973-78, Nat. Coun. Episc. Ch., 1975-77, Brit. Leprosy Relief Assn., 1981-88; recipient plaque La. Health Dept., 1972, Disting. Alumni award U. Conn., 1975, Gold award Am. Coll. Pathologists and Am. Soc. Clin. Pathologists, 1974, Gerard B. Lambert award for spl. recognition, 1975. Fellow AAAS, N.Y. Acad. Scis.; mem. AAUW, Interant. Leprosy Assn., Am. Soc. Mammalogy, Am. Assn. Lab. Animal Sci. (Charles A. Griffin award 1975), East Coast Zool. Soc. (bd. dirs. 1989-92), Am. Recorder Soc., Early Music Assn., Sigma Xi. Episcopalian (vestryman). Clubs: Appalachian (Boston); Green Mountain (Bear Mountain, N.Y.); Mystik Krewe of Iberians (mem. ct. 1972, queen 1974). Pioneer devel. leprosy in exptl. animal (armadillo) reproduction. Home: 72 Riverview Ter Melbourne FL 32903-4640 *Children display interests early in their lives, and in my life, this early interest - in animals, and the beauty of nature - is one which I have never lost, but one which seems to become more important now with the passing of years. Parents can help mold a child, but should mold the child in the child's interests as my parents did, not in a mold designed by them.*

STORRY, JUNIS OLIVER, retired engineering educator; b. Astoria, S.D., Mar. 16, 1920; s. Ole Jensen and Betsey (Ruttum) S.; m. Laurel Helen Davis,

June 15, 1950; children: Cheryl Ann, David Junis. B.S. in Elec. Engring., S.D. State U., 1942, M.S., 1949; Ph.D., Iowa State U., 1967. Registered profl. engr., S.D. Engr. trainee Westinghouse Electric Co., 1942; elec. engr. Bur. Ships, Navy Dept., 1942-46, Reliance Electric Co., Cleve., 1946; mem. faculty S.D. State U., Brookings, 1946-85; prof. elec. engring. S.D. State U., 1955-85, Amdahl Disting. prof. engring., 1982-85, dean engring., 1972-82, prof., dean emeritus, 1985—; mem. S.D. Elec. Bd., 1972-77. Mem. founding bd. Assn. Christian Chs. S.D., 1972-73. NSF Sci. Faculty fellow, 1964-65. Mem. IEEE (life sr. mem.), NSPE, Am. Soc. Engring. Edn., S.D. Engring. Soc. Lutheran. Home: 105 Sunnyview 3132 Sunnyview Dr Brookings SD 57006-4281

STORSTEEN, LINDA LEE, librarian; b. Pasadena, Jan. 26, 1948; d. Oliver Matthew and Susan (Smock) Storsteen. AB cum laude in History, UCLA, 1970, MA in Ancient History, 1972, MLS, 1973. Librarian, L.A. Pub. Library, 1974-79; city librarian Palmdale City Library (Calif.), 1979—. Adv. bd. So. Calif. Inter-Library Loan Network, L.A., 1979-80; commr. So. Calif. Film Circuit, L.A., 1980—; council South State Coop. Library System, 1981—, chmn., 1982-83, 85-86, 87-88, 89-90, 92-93; pres. So. Calif. Film Circuit, 1985-86; rec. sec. So. Antelope Valley Coordinating Council, Palmdale, 1983-84. Mem. ALA, Calif. Library Assn., Pub. Libraries Exec. Assn. So. Calif., Am. Saddle Horse Assn., Pacific Saddlebred Assn., So. Calif. Saddle Bred Horse Assn. (bd. dirs.), Chinese Shar-Pei Club of Am. Home: PO Box 129 Palmdale CA 93590-9971 Office: Palmdale City Libr 700 E Palmdale Blvd Palmdale CA 93550-4742

STORY, JAMES EDDLEMAN, lawyer; b. Calvert City, Ky., June 7, 1928; s. William Arthur and Estella (Harper) S.; m. Barbara Owens, Oct. 11, 1953; children: Paul, Margaret, Virginia Lee, Sara Jane, Betty Ann, James Arthur. BS, Murray State Coll., 1952; JD, U. Louisville, 1958. Bar: Ky. 1958. Tchr. Jefferson County Bd. Edn., Louisville, 1954-58; assoc. prof. U. Ky. C.C., Paducah, 1958-64; county atty. Lyon County, Eddyville, Ky., 1962-74; pub. defender Lyon County, Princeton, Ky., 1974-82; pvt. practive Eddyville, 1974—; atty. Lake Barkley Project, U.S. Army Corp Engrs., Cadiz, Ky., 1960-62. With U.S. Army, 1946-48. Mem. ATLA, Ky. Trial Lawyers Assn., Ky. Assn. Criminal Def. Lawyers, Ky. Bar Assn., Sierra Club, Wilderness Club, Kentuckians for the Commonwealth, Am. Legion, Lions. Avocations: tennis, swimming, hunting, water skiing, boxing. Office: PO Box 216 Eddyville KY 42038-0216

STORY, JIM LEWIS, neurosurgeon, educator; b. Alice, Tex., July 30, 1931; s. Edwin Booth and Martha (Williams) S.; m. Joanne Beverly Nessly, Dec. 31, 1958; children: Kristin Kae, Mary Elizabeth, Jane Martha, James Durward. BS, Tex. Christian U., 1952; MD, Vanderbilt U., 1955. Diplomate Am. Bd. Neurol. Surgery. Intern in surgery U. Minn. Hosps., 1955-56; resident in neurosurgery U. Minn. Grad. Sch. Medicine, 1956-61; instr., asst. prof. neurosurgery div. U. Minn. Med. Sch., 1961-67; prof., head div. neurosurgey U. Tex. Health Sci. Ctr., San Antonio, 1967-95; pvt. practice San Antonio, 1996—. Contbr. articles to profl. publs. Mem. Am. Acad. Neurol. Surgery (v.p. 1988-89), Soc. Neurol. Surgery (chmn. membership adv. com. 1981, v.p. 1990—), Am. Assn. Neurol. Surgery (profl. practice com. 1979), Neurosurg. Soc. Am. (sec. 1978-82, pres. 1985-86), Soc. Univ. Neurosurgeons (pres. 1968-69), Congress Neurol. Surgeons (v.p. 1975-76). Office: Lone Star Neurosurgery 315 N San Saba Ste 1240 San Antonio TX 78207

STOSICH, DAVIDJOHN, company executive; b. Idaho Falls, Idaho, May 24, 1938; s. Vaughn T. and Esther (Smith) S.; m. Adeana Marshall, Aug. 28, 1962; children: Jennifer Lynne, Jacquelyn, Bryan, Jill, Jon, Anthony, Vaughndavid, Jelair, Hartman, Jeanne. BS, Brigham Young U., 1964; BPA in Profl. Illustrator, Art Ctr. Coll. Design, L.A., 1967. Graphic support Computer Scis. Corp., El Segundo, Calif., 1967-68; corp. communications staff Geotech, Salt Lake City, 1968-69; asst. to pres. Computer Update, Salt Lake City, 1969-70; corp. communications staff Omnico, Salt Lake City & Tacoma, 1970-71; support staff Big Sky of Mont., Big Sky, Mont., 1972-73; art dir. Artcraft, Bozeman, Mont., 1973-75; owner Stosich Advt., Idaho Falls, 1975-78; pres. Worldwide Achievements, Idaho Falls, 1980-81, Hive Systems, Idaho Falls, 1982-92; pres. Stosich Woodlock, Inc., Idaho Falls, 1986-94, CEO. Graphic designer Tour Guide to Europe, 1988; sculptor woodlock wood sculptures. Graphic designer Crapo for U.S. Congress, Boise, 1992; active Idaho Falls Arts Coun., Exch. Club Am.; missionary to Switerland LDS Ch., 1958-61. Mem. Art Guild (Pocatello, Idaho). Republican. Avocations: drawing, woodwork, gardening, horses, hunting. Home: 2300 S Charlotte Dr Idaho Falls ID 83402-5675

STOSKOPF, MICHAEL KERRY, educator; b. Garden City, Kans., Mar. 21, 1950; s. Cleve William and Doris Janet (Griffis) S.; m. Suzanne Kennedy, May 30, 1981. BS, Colo. State U., 1973, DVM, 1975; PhD, Johns Hopkins Sch. Hygiene and Pub. Health, 1986. Staff vet. Overton Park Zoo and Aquarium, 1975-77; instr. divsn. comparative medicine Johns Hopkins U., 1977-79; staff vet. Balt. Zool. Soc., 1977-81; biochemist JFK Inst., Balt., 1986-88; asst. prof. divsn. comparative medicine Johns Hopkins U., 1979-87; chief medicine Nat. Aquarium Balt., 1981-88; assoc. prof. dept. radiology Johns Hopkins U., 1986-89, assoc. prof. divsn. comparative medicine, 1987-89; dept. head, prof. companion animal & spl. species medicine N.C. State U. Coll. Vet. Medicine, 1989-93, prof. aquatic and wildlife medicine, 1989—; adj. prof. dept. biology Memphis State U., 1976-77; adj. prof. pathology U. Md., 1982-89; adj. prof. radiology and comparative medicine Johns Hopkins U., 1989-91; rsch. assoc. Smithsonian Inst., Washington, 1986—; coord. environ. medicine consortium N.C. State U., 1993—. Author: A Diagnostic Pathologist's Introduction to Fish, 1989, (with S. Citino) Marine Tropical Fish Medicine, 1987; editor: Tropical Fish Medicine, 1988, Fish Medicine, 1992; contbr. articles to profl. jours. Recipient AAZK Nat. award for Edn., 1978, Mark Morris Found. award, 1974, AAZV Pres.'s Svc. award, 1990; U. Helsinki Jalanka medal, 1993. Mem. AVMA, Am. Assn. Zoo Vets. (edn. com. 1989—, editl. bd. 1979-93, sect. editor 1987-93, chmn. coms. 1979-87), Am. Coll. Zool. Medicine (v.p. 1993-95, pres. 1995-97, sec. 1991-93, chmn. 1986-87), Am. Fisheries Soc., Am. Assn. Wildlife Vets., European Assn. Aquatic Mammals, Internat. Assn. Aquatic Animal Medicine (pres. 198-89, bd. dirs. 1985-90, newsletter editor 1987-89), Acad. Zoo Medicine (chmn. 1979-85), Soc. Study of Reptiles and Amphibians (Rsch. award 1985), Marine Mammal Soc., Wildlife Disease Assn. Avocations: painting, photography, sculpture, water sports. Office: NC State Universtiy College of Veterinary Med 4700 Hillsborough St Raleigh NC 27606-1428

STOSSEL, JOHN, news analyst. BA in Psychology, Princeton U., 1969. Prodr., reporter Sta. KGW-TV, Portland, Oreg.; consumer editor WCBS-TV, N.Y.C., Good Morning Am.; consumer corr. 20/20, 1981—; weekly consumer reporter ABC Radio Info. Network,. Recipient 19 Emmy awards, 5 awards for Excellence in Consumer Reporting Nat. Press Club, award Nat. Environment Devel. Assn., award Retirement Rshc. Found., George Polk award Outstanding Local Radio and Television Reporting. Office: 20/20 147 Columbus Ave Fl 10 New York NY 10023-5900

STOSSEL, THOMAS PETER, medical educator, medical research director; b. Chgo., Sept. 10, 1941; married 1965. AB, Princeton U., 1963; MD, Harvard U., 1967; MD (hon.), U. Linkoping, Sweden, 1989. Diplomate Am. Bd. Internal Medicine. House staff medicine Mass. Gen. Hosp., Boston, 1967-69, chief hematology-oncology, 1976-90; staff assoc. NIH, Bethesda, Md., 1967-71; fellow to sr. assoc. Med. Ctr. Children's Hosp., Boston, 1971-76; chief hematology and oncology unit Mass. Gen. Hosp., 1976-91; prof. medicine Harvard Med. Sch., Boston, 1982—; chief divsn. exptl. medicine Brigham & Women's Hosp., Boston, 1991—; dir. exptl. medicine Brigham Women's Hosp., Boston, 1991—; fellow Harvard Med. Sch., 1971-78; sci. bd. Biogen Corp., 1987—; clin. rsch. prof. Am. Cancer Soc., 1987—. Author: (with B. Babior) Hematology, A Pathophysiological Approach, 1984, 90, 94; contbr. articles to profl. jours.; editor: (with R. Hanon & S. Lux) Blood, Principles & Practice of Hematology, 1995; inventor 4 U.S. patents. Lt. comdr. USPHS, 1969-71. Mem. Am. Fedn. Clin. Rsch., Am. Soc. Clin. Investigation (pres. 1987), Am. Soc. Hematology (Damashek prize 1983, Thomas prize 1993), Am. Soc. Cell Biology, Assn. Am. Physicians, Am. Assn. Immunology, Am. Acad. Arts and Scis. Office: Brigham & Womens Hosp 221 Longwood Ave Boston MA 02115

STOTHERS, JOHN B., chemistry educator; b. London, Ont., Can., Apr. 16, 1931; s. John Cannon and Florence L. (Sleigh) S.; m. Catherine Ruth Smith, June 6, 1953; children—Marta L., Margot E. B.Sc., U. Western Ont., 1953, M.Sc., 1954; Ph.D., McMaster U., 1957. Research chemist Imperial Oil Ltd., Sarnia, Ont., 1957-59; lectr. U. Western Ont., London, 1959-61, asst. prof. dept. chemistry, 1961-64, assoc. prof., 1964-67, prof., 1967-96, prof. emeritus, 1996—. Author: 13C NMR Spectroscopy, 1972; also over 200 research articles. Recipient award Merck, Sharpe & Dohme, 1971; Royal Soc. Can. fellow, 1976. Fellow Chem. Inst. Can.; mem. Am. Chem. Soc. Club: Sunningdale (London). Avocations: golf; traditional jazz. Home: 45 Mayfair Dr, London, ON Canada

STOTLER, ALICEMARIE HUBER, judge; b. Alhambra, Calif., May 29, 1942; d. James R. and Loretta M. Huber; m. James Allen Stotler, Sept. 11, 1971. BA, U. So. Calif., 1964, JD, 1967. Bar: Calif. 1967, U.S. Dist. Ct. (no. dist.) Calif. 1967, U.S. Dist. Ct. (cen. dist.) Calif. 1973, U.S. Supreme Ct., 1976; cert. criminal law specialist. Dep. Orange County Dist. Atty.'s Office, 1967-73; mem. Stotler & Stotler, Santa Ana, Calif., 1973-76, 83-84; judge Orange County Mcpl. Ct., 1976-78, Orange County Superior Ct., 1978-83, U.S. Dist. Ct. (cen. dist.) Calif., L.A., 1984—; assoc. dean Calif. Trial Judges Coll., 1982; lectr., panelist, numerous orgns.; standing com. on rules of practice and procedure U.S. Jud. Conf., 1991—, chair, 1993-96; mem. exec. com. 9th Cir. Jud. Conf., 1989-93, Fed. State Jud. Coun., 1989-93, jury com., 1990-92, planning com. for Nat. Conf. on Fed.-State Judicial Relationships, Orlando, 1991-92, planning com for We. Regional Conf. on State-Fed. Judicial Relationships, Stevens, Wash., 1992-93; chair dist. ct. symposium and jury utilization Ctrl. Dist. Calif., 1985, chair atty. liason, 1989-90, chair U.S. Constitution Bicentennial com., 1986-91, chair magistrate judge com., 1992-93; mem. State Adv. Group. on Juvenile Justice and Delinquency Prevention, 1983-84, Bd. Legal Speciliazations Criminal Law Adv. Commn., 1983-84, victim/witness adv. com. Office Criminal Justice Planning, 1980-83, U. So. Calif. Bd. Councilors, 1993—; active team in tng. Leukemia Soc. Am., 1993, 95; legion lex bd. dir. U. So. Calif. Sch. Law Support Group, 1981-83. Winner Hale Moot Ct. Competition, State of Calif., 1967; named Judge of Yr., Orange County Trial Lawyers Assn., 1978, Most Outstanding Judge, Orange County Bus. Litigation Sect., 1990; recipient Franklin G. West award Orange County Bar Assn., 1985. Mem. ABA (jud. adminstrn. divsn.and litigation sect. 1984—, nat. conf. fed. trial judges com. on legis. affairs 1990-91), Am. Law Inst., Am. Judicature Soc., Fed. Judges Assn. (bd. dirs. 1989-92), Nat. Assn. Women Judges, U.S. Supreme Ct. Hist. Soc., Ninth Cir. Dist. Judges Assn., Calif. Supreme Ct. Hist. Soc., Orange County Bar Assn. (mem. numerous coms., Franklin G. West award 1984), Calif. Judges Assn. (mem. com. on judicial coll. 1978-80, com. on civil law and procedure 1980-82, Dean's coll. curriculum commn. 1981), Calif. Judges Found. Office: US Dist Ct PO Box 12339 751 W Santa Ana Blvd Santa Ana CA 92701-4509

STOTLER, EDITH ANN, grain company executive; b. Champaign, Ill., Oct. 11, 1946; d. Kenneth Wagner and Mary (Odebrecht) S. Student, Mary Baldwin Coll., 1964-66; BA, U. Ill., 1968. Asst. v.p. Harris Trust and Savs. Bank, Chgo., 1969-83; mgr. Can. Imperial Bank of Commerce, Chgo., 1983, sr. mgr., 1983-85, asst. gen. mgr. group head, 1985-88, v.p., dir. utilities, 1988-90; ptnr. Stotler Grain Co., Champaign, Ill., 1990—; pres. Homer Grain Co., 1990—; bd. dirs., mem. exec. compensation com., nominating com. Southeastern Mich. Gas Enterprises, Inc. Mem. investment com. 4th Presbyn. Ch.; past pres. liberal arts and scis. constituent bd. U. Ill., mem. pres.' coun.; mem. Friends of Libr. Bd., U. Ill. Mem. U. Ill. Found., Champaign Country Club, Art Club. Avocations: needlepoint, reading, tennis, golf, cooking. Home: 900 N Lake Shore Dr Apt 2106 Chicago IL 60611-1523

STOTT, BRIAN, software company executive; b. Eccles, Eng., Aug. 5, 1941; came to U.S., 1983; s. Harold and Mary (Stephens) S.; m. Patricia Ann Farrar, Dec. 3, 1983. BSc, Manchester U., 1962, MSc, 1963, PhD, 1971. Asst. prof. Middle East Tech. U., Ankara, Turkey, 1965-68; lectr. Inst. Sci. and Tech., U. Manchester (Eng.), 1968-74; assoc. prof. U. Waterloo (Ont., Can.), 1974-76; cons. Electric Energy Rsch. Ctr. Brazil, Rio de Janeiro, 1976-83; prof. Ariz. State U., Tempe, 1983-84; pres. Power Computer Applications Corp., Mesa, Ariz., 1984—; cons. in field. Contbr. numerous articles to rsch. publs. Fellow IEEE. Office: Power Computer Applications 1921 S Alma School Rd Ste 207 Mesa AZ 85210-3038

STOTT, DIANA ELLEN, social services advocate; b. Cedarville, Calif., Apr. 14, 1934; d. I.A. and Lois A. (Tyeryar) Barber; m. Norman K. Stott, June 29, 1956; children: Charlotte, Russell. BA, U. Calif., Berkeley, 1956; BS in Metaphysics, Am. Inst. Holistic Theology, Berkeley, 1996, Am. Inst. Holistic Theology, 1996. Cert. pre-sch., elem., adult edn. Tchr. Tsuda Sch., Tokyo, 1956, Colegio Americano, Durango, Mex., 1968, Mt. Diablo Schs., Concord, Calif., 1964-74; founder, owner Sunbonnet Sue Templates, Willits, Calif., 1970-89; owner, operator 3T Sheep Ranch, Willits, 1974-89; founder, dir. Animal Crackers PreSch., Willits, 1979-89; dir. of shelter svcs. CATRL, Kimberling City, Mo., 1992—; co-founder Harbor Lights Shelter Svcs., Stone County, Mo., 1994; com. Mo. Coalition Against Domestic Violence, 1992—, Nat. Coalition Against Domestic Violence; sch./cmty. organizer for drug and alcohol prevention, 1993—. Editor newsletter The Quilting Room, 1974-80. Patron Friends of the Libr., Kimberling City, Mo., 1989-94; legis. chmn. Bus. & Profl. Women, Tri-Lakes Area, 1993-94; publicity chmn. Welcome Wagon, Tri-Lakes Area, 1992. Recipient quilting awards Guild of Quilters, 1975-76, Premium Wool award Mendocino County Fair, 1986-88. Mem. AAUW (founder, chmn. Tri-Lakes 1993-94), Bus. and Profl. Women's Club (Woman of Yr. 1996), Kimberling Area C. of C. (rep. 1993-96), Phi Mu, Pi Lambda Theta. Mem. Unity Ch. Avocations: square dancing, writing, herbs. Address: PO Box 488 Kimberling City MO 65686-0488 Office: Christian Assocs of Table Rock Lake Country Club Shopping Ctr Kimberling City MO 65686

STOTT, GRADY BERNELL, lawyer; b. Bailey, N.C., Sept. 19, 1921; s. William Willard and Zettie Harriett (Bissette) S.; m. Mays Beal, May 9, 1952; children: Sue J., Caroline Beal. A.B., Duke U., 1947, J.D., 1952. Bar: N.C. 1952. Dist. atty. 27th Jud. Dist., Gastonia, N.C., 1957-62; partner firm Stott, Hollowell, Palmer & Windham, Gastonia, 1960—. Served with USMC, 1943-48. Fellow Am. Bar Found., Am. Coll. Trial Lawyers; mem. N.C. State Bar (pres. 1978-79), Am. Bar Assn. (del. 1980), N.C. Bar Assn., Assn. Ins. Attys. Democrat. Methodist. Club: Masons. Office: 110 W Main Ave Gastonia NC 28052-2306

STOTT, JAMES CHARLES, chemical company executive; b. Portland, Oreg., Sept. 5, 1945; s. Walter Joseph and Rellalee (Gray) S.; m. Caroline Loveriane Barnes, Dec. 7, 1973; children: William Joseph, Maryann Lee. BBA, Portland State U., 1969. Ops. mgr. Pacific States Express, Inc., Portland, 1970-73; bus. mgr. Mogul Corp., Portland, 1974-80; v.p. Market Transport, Ltd., Portland, 1980-85; pres., founder, chmn. bd. dirs. Chem. Corp. Am., Portland, 1985—, also bd. dirs.; chmn. bd. dirs. Carolina Industries, Portland. Mem. TAPPI. Republican. Roman Catholic. Club: University (Portland). Avocations: golf, outdoors. Home: 3842 Wellington Ct West Linn OR 97068-3651 Office: Chem Corp Am 2525 SE 9th Ave Portland OR 97202-1048

STOTT, PETER WALTER, forest products company executive; b. Spokane, Wash., May 26, 1944; s. Walter Joseph and Rellalee (Gray) S. Student Portland State U., 1962-63, 65-68, U. Americas, Mexico City, 1964-65. Founder, chmn. bd. dirs. Market Transport Ltd., Portland, Oreg., 1969—; bd. dirs., pres., CEO, prin. Crown Pacific. Bd. dirs. Sunshine divsn. Portland Police Bur. (hon.), Liberty Northwest; assoc. mem. adv. bd. Pacific Crest Outward Bound Sch.; mem. pres.'s adv. bd. for athletics Portland State U. With USAR, 1966-72. Mem. Nat. Football Found. and Hall of Fame, Oreg. Sports Hall Fame (lifetime), Oreg. Trucking Assn., Arlington Club, Astoria Golf and Country, Mazamas Club, Multnomah Athletic Club, Portland Golf Club, Univ. Club. Republican. Roman Catholic. Office: Crown Pacific 121 SW Morrison St Ste 1500 Portland OR 97204-3139

STOTT, THOMAS EDWARD, JR., engineering executive; b. Beverly, Mass., May 14, 1923; s. Thomas Edward and Mildred (Ayers) S.; m. Mary Elizabeth Authelet, Feb. 26, 1944; children: Pamela, Randi, Wendy, Thomas E., Diana. BS, Tufts U., 1945. Design engr. Bethlehem Steel, Quincy, Mass., 1956-59; project engr. Bethlehem Steel, 1959-64, sr. engr. basic ship design, 1960-63, project coordinator, 1963-64; pres. Stal-Laval, Inc., Elmsford, N.Y., 1964-84, Thomas Stott & Co., Cummaquid, Mass., 1984-88; ret., 1988. Bd. dirs., treas. Friends of Prisoners, Inc.; deacon West Parish Barnstable, Mass., 1994—. With USNR, 1944-46. Fellow ASME (chmn. marine com., chmn. gas turbine div. exec. com., chmn. nat. nominating com., exec. sec. gas turbine div., Centennial medal 1980, R. Tom Sawyer award 1981, Dedicated Svc. award 1989), Soc. Naval Architects and Marine Engrs. Republican. Home: 51 Kates Path Yarmouth Port MA 02675

STOTT, WILLIAM ROSS, JR., retired college executive; b. Paterson, N.J., July 20, 1935; s. William Ross and Irene (Kearns) S.; m. Margaret Ann Lawler, July 25, 1959; children—William III, Stasia, Christopher, Rachel, Alexa. BSS in English Lit. and Philosophy, Georgetown U., 1957, LHD (hon.), 1985; MA, Columbia U., 1963; DHL (hon), Fisk U., 1994. Faculty Fordham U., N.Y.C., 1964-73, asst. dean Coll. Arts and Scis., 1973-77; dean of students Georgetown U., Washington, 1977-80, v.p., dean of student affairs, 1980-85; pres., trustee Ripon (Wis.) Coll., Wis., 1985-95; bd. dirs. Cornell Lab. Ornithology; professorial lectr. Georgetown U., 1995—; Donald C. Faber Disting. scholar-in-residence Miami U., Oxford, Ohio, 1996. Contbr. poetry to various publs., chpt. to book; art works exhibited and pub. Served to lt. USN, 1959-62. Recipient teaching award Fordham U., 1973, Project Quill award Am. Assn. Colls., 1978. Fellow Explorers Club (nat. br.); mem. Nat. Audubon Soc., Am. Birding Assn. (bd. dirs.), Defenders of Wildlife (bd. dirs.), Am. Bird Conservancy (bd. dirs.), Kaytee Avian Found. (bd. dirs.), Urner Ornithology Club Newark. Avocations: ornithology, poetry, drawing.

STOTTER, DAVID W., marketing executive; b. Chgo., May 17, 1904; s. Max and Lena (Wolfson) S.; m. Lucille Guild, Nov. 28, 1930; 1 child, Michael David. Student, U. Chgo., 1925. Advt. writer Campbell-Ewald Co., Detroit, 1929-34; sr. writer Lord & Thomas, Chgo., 1935-42; v.p., copy dir. MacFarland, Aveyard & Co., Chgo., 1942-51; account exec. MacFarland, Aveyard & Co., 1951-62, sr. v.p., 1959-62; pres., dir. Drewrys Ltd. U.S.A., Inc., S. Bend, Ind., 1962-64; marketing dir. Campbell-Mithun, Inc., Chgo., 1964-65; v.p. Arthur Meyerhoff Assos., Inc., Chgo., 1965—. Bd. dirs. Jewish Welfare Fund Chgo., 1954-61, Alfred Adler Inst., Chgo., 1975—; chmn. pub. relations com. Jewish United Fund, 1969. Home: 2960 N Lake Shore Dr Apt 2303 Chicago IL 60657-5661 Office: 410 N Michigan Ave Chicago IL 60611-4211

STOTTER, HARRY SHELTON, banker, lawyer; b. N.Y.C., Aug. 28, 1928; s. Jack and Adele (Sgel) S.; m. Marilyn H. Knight, Nov. 7, 1954; children: Jeffrey Craig, Cheryl dee. Student, L.I. U., 1948-49; JD, St. John's U., 1952; postgrad., N.Y. U. Law Sch., 1956-57. Bar: N.Y. 1952, N.J. 1974. Pvt. practice in N.Y.C., 1952-53, 54-56; atty. Dept. Def., 1953; with trust div. Bank of N.Y., 1956-63; exec. v.p., sr. mgmt. com. United Jersey Bank, Hackensack, 1963-84; div. exec. v.p. Chase Manhattan Bank, N.Y.C., 1984-94; dir., vice chmn. Chase Manhattan Trust Co. Fla., Palm Beach, Fla., 1984-87; pvt. trust and estates law practice N.J., 1974—; former mem. probate com. N.J. Supreme Ct. Jud. Conf. Mem. N.Y.C. and Bergen County estate planning couns.; former pres. bd. dirs. Bergen County coun. Girl Scouts Am.; bd. dirs., pres., chief exec. officer Bergen County United Way; treas. 2d Century Fund, Hackensack Hosp.; bd. dirs. Holy Name Hosp., Teaneck, N.J. With USN, World War II; brig. gen. Army N.G. Mem. ABA (co-chmn. nat. conf. lawyers and corp. trustees 1991-93), Am. Bankers Assn. (chmn. trust counsel com. 1991-93), N.Y. Bar Assn., N.J. Bar Assn., N.Y. County Lawyers Assn., Bergen County Bar Assn. (former trustee, former chmn. probate and estate planning com.), Fed. Bar Assn., N.Y. Militia Assn.

STOTTER, LAWRENCE HENRY, lawyer; b. Cleve., Sept. 24, 1929; s. Oscar and Bertha (Lieb) S.; m. Ruth Rapoport, June 30, 1957; children: Daniel, Jennifer, Steven. BBA, Ohio State U., 1956, LLB, 1958, JD, 1967. Bar: Calif. 1960, U.S. Supreme Ct. 1973, U.S. Tax Ct. 1976. Pvt. practice San Francisco, 1963—; ptnr. Stotter and Coats, San Francisco, 1981—; mem. faculty Nat. Judicial Coll.; mem. Calif. Family Law Adv. Commn., 1979-80. Editor in chief: Am. Bar Family Advocate mag, 1977-82; TV appearances on Phil Donahue Show, Good Morning America. Pres. Tamalpais Conservation Club, Marin County, Calif.; U.S. State Dept. del. Hague Conf. Pvt. Internat. Law, 1979-80; legal adv. White House Conf. on Families, 1980—. Served with AUS, 1950-53. Mem. ABA (past chmn. family law sect.), Am. Acad. Matrimonial Lawyers (past nat. v.p.), Calif. State Bar (past chmn. family law sect.), San Francisco Bar Assn. (past chmn. family law sect.), Calif. Trial Lawyers Assn. (past chmn. family law sect.). Home: 2244 Vistazo St E Tiburon CA 94920-1970 Office: # 200 1255 Columbus Ave San Francisco CA 94133

STOTTLEMYER, DAVID LEE, government official; b. Waynesboro, Pa., June 1, 1935; s. Omar Samuel and Miriam (Noll) S.; m. Jane Ann Hembree, Aug. 26, 1961; children: Todd Andrew, Kristen Elizabeth, Kathryn Ann. A.B., Miami U., Oxford, Ohio, 1959; M. Pub. and Internat. Affairs (NDEA fellow), U. Pitts., 1964, also postgrad. Program and budget analyst Exec. Office of Pres., Office of Mgmt. and Budget, Washington, 1964-69; sr. mgmt. officer UN, N.Y.C., 1969-70; adviser internat. orgn. affairs U.S. Mission to UN, N.Y.C., 1971-72; counsellor internat. orgn. affairs U.S. Mission to UN, 1973-75, counsellor UN resources mgmt., 1976-77; also mem. U.S. del. 26th-31st gen. assemblies, mem. UN Com. on Contbns., 1971; mem. UN Adv. Com. on Adminstrv. and Budgetary Questions, 1973-77; dir. policy mgmt. staff Bur. Internat. Orgn. Affairs, U.S. Dept. State, Washington, 1977-80; exec. asst. to asst. sec. of state for internat. orgn. affairs Bur. Internat. Orgn. Affairs, U.S. Dept. State, 1980; mem. staff Office of Vice-Pres., Washington, 1981-83; dir. adminstrv. mgmt. service UN, N.Y.C., 1984-85; exec. asst., dir. Office of Under-Sec.-Gen. for Adminstrn. and Mgmt., UN, N.Y.C., 1986-87; pvt. practice as cons., 1987-90; dir. industry rels. NASA, Washington, 1990-91, dir. office nat. svc., 1992-93; retired, 1993; cons. pvt. practice, 1993—. Served with AUS, 1953-56. Recipient Superior Honor award State Dept., 1975. Mem. Am. Fgn. Svc. Assn. Home and Office: 5920 Sherborn Ln Springfield VA 22152-1035

STOTZKY, GUENTHER, microbiologist, educator; b. Leipzig, Germany, May 24, 1931; came to U.S., 1939; s. Moritz Stotzky and Erna (Angres) Kester; m. Kayla Baker, Mar. 17, 1958; children: Jay, Martha, Deborah. BS, Calif. Poly. State U., 1952; MS, Ohio State U., 1954, PhD, 1956. Spl. sci. employee Argonne Nat. Lab. USAEC, Lemont, Ill., 1955; rsch. assoc. Dept. Botany U. Mich., Ann Arbor, 1956-58; head soil microbiology Cen. Rsch. Labs. United Fruit Co., Norwood, Mass., 1958-63; chmn., microbiologist Kitchawan Rsch. Labs. Bklyn. Botanic Garden, Ossining, N.Y., 1963-68; assoc. prof. Dept. Biology NYU, 1967-70, prof., 1970—, chmn., 1970-77. Editor: Soil Biochemistry, 1990—; series editor Marcel Dekker, Inc., 1986-92; contbr. over 250 articles to profl. jours. and chpts. to books. With USCG, 1957. Recipient Selman A. Waksman Hon. Lecture award Theobald Smith Soc., 1989, Honored Alumnus of Yr. award Calif. Poly. State U., 1992; named Disting. Vis. Scientist, U.S. EPA, 1986-89. Fellow AAAS, Am. Acad. Microbiology, Am. Soc. Microbiology (Fisher Co. award for applied and environ. microbiology 1990, Excellence in Tchg. award N.Y.C. br. 1994), Am. Soc. Agronomy, Soil Sci. Soc. Am. Jewish. Avocations: fishing, reading, music. Office: NYU Dept Biology 1009 Main New York NY 10003

STOUFER, RUTH HENDRIX, community volunteer; b. Pitts., June 21, 1916; d. Walter Willits and Frances (Ponbeck) Hendrix; m. William Kimball Stoufer, Sept. 8, 1937 (dec.); children: Walter Hendrix, Frances Elizabeth Stoufer Waller (dec.). BS, Iowa State U., 1937. Trustee Marcus J. Lawrence Meml. Hosp., 1989—; devel. chairperson Sedona-Verde Valley Am. Heart Assn., 1988-91; mem. adv. bd. L.A. chpt. Freedom's Found., 1965-78; mem. coord. med. adv. bd. U. Ariz., 1986—; founding chairperson Muses of the Mus. No. Ariz., 1984-85, pres., 1986-87, mem. Sinagua Soc., 1983—; bd. dirs. Nat. Charity League, L.A., 1963, Found. for Children, L.A., 1964, 65, 66; pres. Panhellenic adv. bd. U. So. Calif., 1964; key adv. U. So. Calif. chpt. Beta Alpha of Gamma Phi Beta, 1960-63. Named Woman of Yr., Inter-city Coun., Gamma Phi Beta, 1963. Avocations: Southwestern U.S. history, bridge, piano, reading. Home: 87 Doodlebug Knoll Sedona AZ 86336-6422

STOUGHTON, W. VICKERY, healthcare executive; b. Peoria, Ill., Mar. 1, 1946; s. Warner Vickery and Mary Olive (McNamara) S.; m. Christine Mary Kreder, Aug. 9, 1969; children: Zachary Benjamin, Samantha. B.S., St. Louis U., 1968; M.B.A., U. Chgo., 1973. Asst. dir. Boston Hosp. for Women, 1973-74; asst. dir. Peter Bent Brigham Hosp., Boston, 1975-77, dir., 1978-80; pres. The Toronto Hosp., Ont., Can.; asst. prof. U. Toronto, 1982-

90, assoc. prof., 1991; vice chancellor health affairs, chief exec. officer Duke U. Hosp., Durham, N.C., 1991-92; pres. Smithkline Beecham Clin. Labs., Collegeville, Pa., 1992-95, Smithkline Beecham Diagnostic Systems, King of Prussia, Pa., 1996—; bd. dirs. Sun Life Assurance Co. Bd. dirs. Toronto Symphony, 1983-86, Toronto United Way, 1988-91. Served to capt. AUS, 1969-72. Fellow Am. Coll. Hosp. Adminstrs. Home: 7 Harford Ln Radnor PA 19087-4529 Office: Smithkline Beecham Diagnostic Systems POB 1539 709 Swedeland Rd King Of Prussia PA 19406

STOUP, ARTHUR HARRY, lawyer; b. Kansas City, Mo., Aug. 30, 1925; s. Isadore and Dorothy (Rankle) S.; m. Kathryn Jolliff, July 30, 1948; children—David C., Daniel P., Rebecca Ann, Deborah E. Student, Kansas City Jr. Coll., Mo. 1942-43; BA, U. Kansas City, 1950; JD, U. Mo., Kansas City, 1950. Bar: Mo. 1950, D.C. 1979. Pvt. practice law Kansas City, Mo., 1950—; prin. Arthur H. Stoup & Assocs., P.C., adr; chmn. U.S. Merit Selection Com. for Western Dist. Mo., 1981. Chmn. com. to rev. continuing edn. U. Mo., 1978-79; mem. U. Mo. Law School search com., 1994-95; trustee U. Mo.-Kansas City Law Found., 1972—, pres., 1979-82; trustee U. Kansas City, 1979—. With USNR, 1942-45. Fellow Internat. Soc. Barristers (state mem. chmn.), Am. Bar Found. (life mem.); mem. ABA (ho. dels. 1976-80), Kansas City Met. Bar Assn. (pres. 1966-67, Litigation Emeritus award 1991), Mo. Bar (bd. govs. 1967-76, v.p. 1972-73, pres. elect 1973-74, pres. 1974-75), Lawyers Assn. Kansas City Mo., Mo. Assn. Trial Attys. (sustaining), Assn. Trial Lawyers Am. (sustaining), So. Conf. Bar Pres.'s (life), Mobar Research Inc. (pres. 1978-86), Phi Alpha Delta Alumni (justice Kansas City area alumni 1955-56). Lodges: Optimists (pres. Ward Pkwy. 1961-62, lt. gov. Mo. dist. internat. 1963-64), Sertoma, B'nai B'rith. Home: 9002 Western Hills Dr Kansas City MO 64114-3566 Office: 1710 Mercantile Tower 1101 Walnut St Kansas City MO 64106-2122

STOUT, ANTHONY CARDER, publisher; b. N.Y.C., May 20, 1939; s. Harry Howard and Maxine (Carder) S.; m. Julie Jeppson, May 24, 1965 (div. 1986); children: Craig Fitzhugh, Carder Jeppson, Antonia Armstrong, Julie Shellabarger. B.A., Williams Coll., 1961; LL.B., Harvard U., 1964. Bar: N.Y. 1966. Assoc. Milbank, Tweed, Hadley & McCloy, N.Y.C., 1965-69; pres. Ctr. for Polit. Research, Washington, 1969-72; chmn. Govt. Pub. Corp./Nat. Jour., Washington, 1972-89; pres. Govt. Investment Mgmt. Corp., Washington, 1990—; dir. World Affairs Coun., Washington, 1981-89, Nat. Press Found., 1981-89; pres. The Battle of Normandy Found., 1985-94. Trustee St. Paul's Sch., Concord, N.H., 1980-86. Mem. Phi Beta Kappa. Clubs: Brook (N.Y.); Metropolitan (Washington), Chevy Chase (Washington). Office: Govt Investment Mgmt Corp 1730 Rhode Island Ave NW Washington DC 20036-3101

STOUT, DONALD EVERETT, real estate developer, environmental preservationist; b. Dayton, Ohio, Mar. 16, 1926; s. Thorne Franklin and Lovella Marie (Sweeney) S.; m. Gloria B. McCormick, Apr. 10, 1948; children: Holly Sue, Scott Kenneth. BS, Miami U., 1950. Mgr. comml.-indsl. div. G.P. Huffman Realty, Dayton, 1954-58; leasing agt., mgr. Park Plaza, Dayton, 1959-71; pres. various real estate groups; developer 1st transp. ctr. for trucking in Ohio; pres. The Falls Estates, Wright Gate Tech. Ctr., Edglo Land Recycle, pres. Donald E. Stout, Inc. Contbr. articles to profl. jours. Served with U.S. Army 1944-45, USN 1945-46. Named Outstanding Real Estate Salesman in Dayton, Dayton Area Bd. Realtors, in Ohio, Ohio Bd. Realtors, 1961. Lic. real estate broker, Ohio, U.S. V.I.; cert. gen. appraiser, Ohio. Mem. Dayton Area Bd. Realtors (founder, 1st pres. salesman div., gen. appraiser), Nat. Assn. Real Estate Bds., Appraisal Inst., Sr. Residential Appraiser, Soc. Indsl. Office Realtors, Res. Officers Assn., Masons (32 degree), Shriners, Phi Delta Theta. Office: 1344 Woodman Dr Dayton OH 45432-3442

STOUT, ELIZABETH WEST, foundation administrator; b. San Francisco, Mar. 4, 1917; d. Claudius Wilson and Sarah (Henderson) West; m. Bruce Churchill McDonald, Mar. 19 1944 (dec. 1952); children: Douglas, Anne; m. Charles Holt Stout, Oct. 27, 1958 (dec. 1992); stepchildren: Richard, George (dec.), Martha Stout Gilweit. Student, U. Nev., 1934-37; grad., Imperial Valley Coll., 1990. Cashier, acct. N.Y. Underwriters, San Francisco, 1937-42; sec. supply and accounts USN, San Francisco, 1942-44. Contbr. articles to profl. jours. Mem. adv. bd. Anza-Borrego Desert, Natural History Assn., 1974-84; founder Stout Paleontology Lab., Borrego Springs, Calif., 1982; found. trustee Desert Rsch. Inst., Reno, 1989—; active Black Rock Desert Project, 1989, Washoe Med. Ctr. League, 1953—, St. Mary's Hosp. Guild, 1953—. Named Disting. Nevadan U. Nev., 1993. Mem. Anza-Borrego Desert Natural History Assn. (dir. emeritus 1984), Soc. Vertebrate Paleontology, De Anza Desert Country Club, Kappa Alpha Theta. Republican. Episcopalian. Avocations: travel, writing, reading, golf.

STOUT, GLENN EMANUEL, retired science administrator; b. Fostoria, Ohio, Mar. 23, 1920. AB, Findlay U., 1942, DSc, 1973. Sci. coord. NSF, 1969-71; asst. to chief Ill. State Water Survey, Champaign, 1971-74; prof. Inst. Environ. Studies, Urbana, Ill., 1973-94, dir. task force, 1975-79; dir. Water Resources Ctr. U. Ill., Urbana, 1973-94; rsch. coord. Ill.-Ind. Sea Grant Program, 1987-94; emeritus, 1994—; Mem. Ill. Gov.'s Task Force on State Water Plan, 1980-94; bd. dirs. Univ. Coun. Water Resources, 1983-86, chmn. internat. affairs, 1989-92; mem. nomination com. for Stockholm Water Prize, 1994—. Contbr. articles to profl. jours. Mem. Am. Water Resources Assn., Internat. Water Resources Assn. (sec. gen. 1985-91, v.p. 1992-94, exec. dir. 1984-95, pres. 1995—), Am. Meteorol. Soc., Am. Geophys. Union, N.Am. Lake Mgmt. Soc., Ill. Lake Mgmt. Assn. (bd. dirs. 1985-88), Internat. Assn. Rsch. Hydrology, Am. Water Works Assn., Kiwanis (pres. local club 1979-80, lt. gov. 1982-83), Sigma Xi (pres. U. Ill. chpt. 1985-86). Home: 920 W John St Champaign IL 61821-3907 Office: Intl Water Resource Assn 1101 W Peabody Dr Urbana IL 61801-4723

STOUT, GREGORY STANSBURY, lawyer; b. Berkeley, Calif., July 27, 1915; s. Verne A. and Ella (Moore) S.; m. Virginia Cordes, Apr. 23, 1948; 1 son, Frederick Gregory. A.B., U. Calif., 1937, LL.B., 1940. Bar: Calif. 1940. Practice law San Francisco, 1946, 52—; asst. dist. atty., 1947-52; mem. Penal Code Revision Commn. Calif.; chmn. com. State Bar Calif. Contbr. articles to profl. jours. Served to master sgt. AUS, 1942-45. Fellow Am. Coll. Trial Lawyers, Am. Bar Found.; mem. ABA, Fed. Bar Assn., Am. Bd. Trial Advocates, Nat. Assn. Criminal Def. Lawyers (sec. 1958-59, pres. 1962-63). Democrat. Episcopalian. Club: Bohemian. Home and Office: 100 Thorndale Dr San Rafael CA 94903-4501

STOUT, JAMES DUDLEY, lawyer; b. Lawrence County, Ill., June 22, 1947; s. Donald K. and Myrtle Irene (Pullen) S.; m. Susan A. West, Jan. 3, 1976 (div. Feb. 1985); children: Lindsey Diane, Kristi Lynn. BA, So. Ill. U., 1969; JD, U. Ill., 1974. Bar: Tex. 1974, U.S. Dist. Ct. (so. dist.) Tex. 1974, Ill. 1978, U.S. Dist. Ct. (cen. dist.) Ill. 1979, U.S. Dist. Ct. (so. dist.) Ill. 1986. Sole practice Humble, Tex., 1974-78; assoc. Law office Robert W. Dodd, Champaign, Ill., 1978-79; ptnr. Dodd, Stout, Martinkus, et al, Champaign, 1979-81, Zimmerly, Gadau, Stout, Selin & Otto, Champaign, 1981-85, Correll and Stout, Bridgeport, Ill., 1985-86; sole practice Bridgeport, 1986—. Served with U.S. Army, 1969-71. Mem. Assn. Trial Lawyers Am., Ill. Bar Assn., Tex. Bar Assn. Lodges: Elks, Shriners. Avocations: golf, tennis, reading. Office: 324 N Main St Bridgeport IL 62417-1524

STOUT, JUANITA KIDD, judge; b. Wewoka, Okla., Mar. 7, 1919; d. Henry Maynard and Mary Alice (Chandler) Kidd; m. Charles Otis Stout, June 23, 1942. BA, U. Iowa, 1939; JD, Ind. U., 1948, LLM, 1954; LLD (hon.), Ursinus Coll., 1965, Ind. U., 1966, Lebanon Valley Coll., 1969, Drexel U., 1972, Rockford (Ill.) Coll., 1974, U. Md., 1980, Roger Williams Coll., 1984, Morgan State U., 1985, Russell Sage Coll., 1966, Fisk U., 1988, Del. State Coll., 1990. Bar: D.C. 1950, Pa. 1954. Tchr. pub. schs. Seminole and Sand Springs, Okla., 1939-42; tchr. Fla. A&M U., Tallahassee, 1949, Tex. So. U., Houston, 1949; adminstrv. asst. to judge U.S. Ct. Appeals (3d cir.), Phila., 1950-54; pvt. practice law Turner & Stout, Phila., 1954-55; chief of appeals Dist. Atty.'s Office City of Phila., 1955-59, judge mcpl. ct., 1959-69; judge Ct. Common Pleas, Phila., 1969-88, sr. judge, 1989—; justice Supreme Ct. Pa., Phila., 1988-89; sitting as sr. judge Ct. Common Pleas. Recipient Jane Addams medal Rockford Coll., 1966, Disting. Svc. award U. Iowa, 1974, MCP/Gimbel award for humanitarianism, 1988, 89—, John Peter Zenger award John Peter Zenger Soc., 1994; named to Hall of Fame of Okla., Okla. Heritage Soc., 1981, Disting. Svc. award U. Okla. Alumni Assn. and U. Okla., 1995; Disting. Alumni svc. award Ind. U., Bloomington, 1992; named Disting. Dau. of Pa., 1988. Mem. ABA, Pa. Bar Assn., Phila. Bar Assn. (Sandra Day O'Connor award 1994), Nat. Assn. Women Judges, Nat. Assn. Women Lawyers. Democrat. Episcopalian. Home: Logan Sq E # 1803 2 Franklin Town Blvd Philadelphia PA 19103-1231

STOUT, LOWELL, lawyer; b. Tamaha, Okla., July 23, 1928; s. Charles W. and Rosetta (Easley) S.; m. Liliane Josue, Nov. 29, 1952; children: Georgianna, Mark Lowell. Student, Northeastern State Coll., Tahlequah, Okla., 1946-49, U. Okla., 1949-51; LLB, U. N.Mex., 1952. Bar: N.Mex. 1952. Ptnr. Easley, Quinn & Stout, Hobbs, N.Mex., 1954-58, Girand & Stout, Hobbs, 1958-60; pvt. practice Hobbs, 1960-80; ptnr. Stout & Stout, Hobbs, 1980—. Cpl. U.S. Army, 1952-54. Fellow Am. Coll. Trial Lawyers; mem. Assn. Trial Lawyers Am., State Bar N.Mex., N.Mex. Trial Lawyers Assn., Lea County Bar Assn. Home: 218 W Lea St Hobbs NM 88240-5110 Office: Stout & Stout PO Box 716 Hobbs NM 88241-0716

STOUT, WILLIAM JEWELL, department store executive; b. Bloomington, Ind., Dec. 14, 1914; s. Selatie Edgar and Frances M. (Blodgett) S.; m. Harriet Cracraft, June 15, 1940; children—David Bruce, Karen Louise. A.B., Ind. U., 1937. With L.S. Ayres & Co., Indpls., 1937-78, v.p., 1958-64, v.p. operation, 1964-65, exec. v.p., 1965-78; pres., dir. Citizens Gas & Coke Utility. Mem. Ind. Personnel Bd., 1952-66; dir. devel. Wabash Coll., Crawfordsville, Ind., 1978-84, cons. capital fund drives; chmn. United Fund drive, 1953; pres., bd. dirs. Flanner House; bd. dirs. St. Vincent Hosp. Found., pres., 1972-73; bd. dirs. St. Richard's Day Sch. Served to lt. comdr. USNR, 1942-46. Mem. Indpls. Personnel Assn. (past pres.), Nat. Retail Mchts. Assn., Indpls. Mchts. Assn. (pres. 1970-72), Ind., Indpls. chambers commerce. Home: 1903 Seaport Dr Indianapolis IN 46240-2832

STOUT-PIERCE, SUSAN, marketing specialist; b. Denver, June 6, 1954; d. Joseph Edward and Esther Mae (Miller) Hull; m. Lee Stout, Nov. 3, 1979 (div. Aug. 1984); m. Gary Myron Pierce, Nov. 21, 1987. AS, Denver Community Coll., 1975; BS, Met. State Coll., 1986. Cert. Radiologic Technologist, Calif., Am. Registry Radiologic Technologists. Radiologic technologist The Swedish Med. Ctr., Englewood, Colo., 1975-79, The Minor Emergency Clinic, Lakewood, Colo., 1979-80, The Children's Hosp., Denver, 1980-86, Merit Peralta Med. Ctr., Oakland, Calif., 1986-87, Am. Shared Hosp. Svcs., Oakland, 1987, HCA South Austin (Tex.) Med. Ctr., 1987-88, U. Calif., San Francisco, 1988-89; clin. imaging specialist OEC-Diasonics, Salt Lake City, 1989-92; software applications specialist Cemax, Inc., Fremont, Calif., 1992-93; mktg. specialist ADAC Healthcare Info. Systems, Houston, Tex., 1993—. Mem. NAFE, Am. Bus. Women's Assn. Avocations: photography, downhill skiing, bicycling. Home: 264 Rachael Pl Pleasanton CA 94566-6228

STOVALL, CARLA J, state official, lawyer; b. Hardner, Kans., Mar. 18, 1957; d. Carl E. and Juanita Jo (Ford) S. BA, Pittsburg (Kans.) State U., 1979; JD, U. Kans., 1982. Bar: Kans. 1982, U.S. Dist. Ct. Kans. 1982. Pvt. practice, Pittsburg, 1982-85; atty. Crawford County, Pittsburg, 1984-88; gov. Kans. Parole Bd., Topeka, 1988-94; attorney general State of Kansas, Topeka, 1995—; lectr. law Pittsburg State U. 1982-84; pres. Gilston Internat. Mktg., Inc., 1988—. Bd. dirs., sec. Pittsburg Family YMCA, 1983-88. Mem. ABA, Kans. Bar Assn., Crawford County Bar Assn. (sec. 1984-85, v.p. 1985-86, pres. 1986-87), Kans. County and Dist. Attys. Assn., Nat. Coll. Dist. Attys., Pittsburg State U. Alumni Assn. (bd. dirs. 1983-88), Pittsburg Area C. of C. (bd. dirs. 1983-85, Leadership Pitts. 1984), Bus. and Profl. Women Assn. (Young Careerist 1984), Kans. Assn. Commerce and Industry (Leadership Kans. 1983), AAUW (bd. dirs. 1983-87). Republican. Methodist. Avocations: travel, photography, tennis. Home: 3561 SW Mission Ave Topeka KS 66614-3637 Office: Atty Gen Office Kansas Judicial Ctr 2nd Fl Topeka KS 66612*

STOVALL, JERRY (COLEMAN STOVALL), insurance company executive; b. Houston, July 31, 1936; s. Clifford Coleman and Maxine (Lands) S.; m. Elsie Hostetter, June 20, 1959; 1 child, Brent Allen. BBA, U. Houston, 1968. Home office adminstr. Am. Gen. Life, Houston, 1955-63, agt., agy. mgr., 1963-66, agy. mgr., regional dir. agys., regional v.p., 1969-74; sr. brokerage cons. Conn. Gen. Life, Houston, 1966-69; sr. v.p., dir. mktg. Capitol Life Ins. Co., Denver, 1974-78; v.p., dir. mktg. Integon Life Ins. Corp., Winston-Salem, N.C., 1978-81; pres. Life of Mid-Am. Ins. Co., Topeka, 1981-85; pres. Victory Life Ins. Co., Topeka, 1981-85, chmn., pres., chief exec. officer, 1981-87; pres., retired chief exec. officer Integon Life Ins. Co., Winston-Salem, N.C., 1987-91, Winston-Salem.; vice-chmn. Mktg. One Inc.; bd. dirs., vice-chmn. Ga. Internat. Life; pres., Lamar Life Ins. Co., 1992-95, ret. 1995. Bd. dirs. Winston-Salem Symphony, Jr. Acievement Miss. Inc., Andrew Jackson Coun., Boy Scouts Am.; mem. Miss. Econ. Coun.; bd. govs. Univ. Club. With U.S. Army, 1955-57. Mem. Nat. Assn. Life Cos., Nat. Assn. Life Underwriters, Am. Soc. CLUs (Gold Key Soc.), ACI Exec. Round Table (chmn. 1995). The Country Club of Jackson, Rotary Club Jackson, Rotary Internat. Home: 115 Winged Foot Cir Jackson MS 39211-2528 Office: Lamar Life Ins Co 317 E Capitol St Jackson MS 39201-3405

STOVALL, ROBERT H(ENRY), money management company executive; b. Louisville, 1926; s. Harold Samuel and Agnes C. (Hinkle) S.; m. Inger Bagger; children: Sten Torben, Harold Samuel II, Inger Benedikte, Robert Henry. B.S. in Econs., U. Pa., 1948; postgrad. in polit. economy, U. Copenhagen, 1948-49; M.B.A., N.Y. U., 1957. With E. F. Hutton & Co., 1953-67; mgr. dept. investment research E. F. Hutton & Co., N.Y.C., 1958-60, gen. partner responsible for research, 1961-67, chmn. com. investment policy, 1966-68; research dir. Nuveen Corp., N.Y.C., 1968-69; partner in mktg. and research Reynolds & Co., N.Y.C., 1969; dir. research Reynolds & Co., 1970-73; sr. v.p., dir. investment policy Dean Witter Reynolds Inc. (merger Reynolds & Co. and Dean Witter & Co., acquired by Sears, Roebuck and Co. 1981), N.Y.C., 1978-85, pub. comments on market column, 1961-85; pres. Stovall/Twenty-First Advisers, Inc., 1985—; lectr., tchr. in field; commentator Nat. Pub. Radio, 1982—; prof. fin. NYU, 1985—; regular commentator Bus. Morning, Turner Broadcasting System, 1985-88, "This Morning's Business", CBS-TV, 1988-91, "Market Wrap", Sta. CNBC/FNN-TV; governing mem. Com. on Developing Am. Capitalism, Fairfield, Conn. Columnist Forbes, 1968-76, Fin. World, 1979—; contbr. articles to profl. pubs.; panelist: Wall St. Week, Public Broadcasting System, 1977—, Hall of Fame, 1995. Bd. overseers Grad. Sch. Bus. Adminstrn. NYU, 1984-90, U. Pa. Librs., 1992—; chmn. Security Industry Inst., 1986-88, life trustee, 1989—, trustee St. Clare's-Riverside Health Care Ctr. Found., Denville, N.J., 1980-93, Wayne County (Pa.) Meml. Hosp.; mem. found. bd. 1989—; bd. overseers Seton Hall Prep. Sch., West Orange, N.J., 1985-93; bd. sponsors Loyola Coll. in Md. Schs. Bus., 1990-95, 1991—; dir. Sarasota Opera Assn., 1993—. With U.S. Army, WWII, Italy. Mem. Inst. Chartered Fin. Analysts (CFA), N.Y. Soc. Security Analysts (past dir., vice chmn. program com.), Mensa, Sarasota Univ. Club, Union League (N.Y.C.), S.R., Kentuckians of N.Y. (pres. 1988-90), Sons of Confederate Vets., Beta Gamma Sigma. Home: 888 Boulevard Of The Arts Sarasota FL 34236-4871 Office: Stovall/Twenty-First Advisers Inc 780 3rd Ave New York NY 10017-2024

STOVER, CARL FREDERICK, foundation executive; b. Pasadena, Calif., Sept. 29, 1930; s. Carl Joseph and Margarete (Müller) S.; m. Catherine Swanson, Sept. 3, 1954; children: Matthew Joseph, Mary Margaret Stover Marker, Claire Ellen; m. Jacqueline Kast, Sept. 7, 1973. BA magna cum laude, Stanford U., 1951, MA, 1954. Instr. polit. sci. Stanford U., 1953-55; fiscal mgmt. officer Office Sec. Dept. Agr., 1955-57; asso. dir. conf. program pub. affairs Brookings Instn., 1957-59, sr. staff mem. govtl. studies, 1960; fellow Center Study Democratic Instns., Santa Barbara, Calif., 1960-62; asst. to chmn. bd. editors Ency. Brit., 1960-62; sr. polit. scientist Stanford Research Inst., 1962-64; dir. pub. affairs fellowship program Stanford U., 1962-64; pres. Nat. Inst. Pub. Affairs, Washington, 1964-70, Nat. Com. U.S.-China Relations, 1971-72; pres., dir. Federalism Seventy-Six, Washington, 1972-74; dir. cultural resources devel. Nat. Endowment Arts, 1974-78; pres., dir. Cultural Resources, Inc., Washington, 1978-85; bd. dirs. H.E.A.R. Found., 1976-86, treas., 1976-80, pres., 1980-86; bd. dirs. Ctr. for World Lit., pres., 1987-90, chmn., 1990-92; pvt. profl. cons., 1970—; scholar-in-residence Nat. Acad. Pub. Adminstrn., 1980-82; cons. to govt., 1953—. Author: The Government of Science, 1962, The Technological Order, 1963; Founding editor: Jour. Law and Edn., 1971-73; pub. Delos mag., 1987-92. Treas. Nat. Com. U.S.-China Rels., 1966-71, 82-87, 89-94, bd. dirs.; bd. dirs. Coord. Coun. Lit. Mags., 1966-68; trustee Inst. of Nations, 1972-76, Nat. Inst. Pub. Affairs, 1967-71, Kinesis Ltd., 1972-78; vol. Nat. Exec. Svc. Corps, 1984-89. Fellow AAAS; mem. Am. Soc. Pub. Adminstrn., Fedn. Am. Scientists, Soc. Internat. Devel., Jordan Soc. (dir. 1982-84), Nat. Acad. Pub. Adminstrn. (hon.), Md. U. Club, Internat. Soc. Panetics (pres. 1991-95, chmn. 1996—, founding mem. 1991—), Phi Beta Kappa Assocs. (hon., lectr. 1972-87), Phi Beta Kappa. Democrat. Presbyterian. Home and Office: 4109 Metzerott Rd College Park MD 20740-2082

STOVER, CAROLYN NADINE, middle school educator; b. Martinsburg, W.Va., May 30, 1950; d. Norman Robert and Garnet Agnes (Zombro) Whetzel; m. James Stenner Stover Sr., Nov. 20, 1971; children: Heather N., James S. Jr. BA in Home Econs., Shepherd Coll., 1972; cert. in advanced studies, W.Va. U., 1978; cert. in tchg. methods, Marshall U., 1973; cert. in spl. edn., Shippensburg Coll., 1972. Cert. tchr., W.Va., N.Mex.; reg. EMT. Substitute tchr. Berkeley County Schs., Martinsburg, W.Va., 1972, adult edn. instr., 1972-77, home econs. instr., 1973-83; substitute tchr. Ruidoso (N.Mex.) Mcpl. Schs., 1984-90, child find coord. Region 9 edn. coop., 1990, life skills and at-risk educator, 1991—, coord. coun., 1991-93, mem. budget com., 1993. Elder First Presbyn. Ch., Ruidoso, 1984-90, 94—; sponsor Acad. Booster Club, Ruidoso, 1993—; instr. CPR, 1980. Named Outstanding Young Women of Am., 1981. Mem. NEA, Nat. Middle Sch. Assn., Ruidoso Edn. Assn., Rotary (youth leadership councilor 1991—). Democrat. Avocations: cross-stitching, needlework, family, sports, youth. Home: Box 7837 1007 Hull Rd Ruidoso NM 88345 Office: Ruidoso Mid Sch 100 Reese Dr Ruidoso NM 88345-6016

STOVER, DAVID FRANK, lawyer; b. Phila., May 15, 1941; s. Emory Frank and Beatrice Norah (Spinelli) S. A.B., Princeton U., 1962; J.D., U. Pa., 1965. Bar: D.C. 1966, U.S. Ct. Appeals (D.C. cir.) 1968, U.S. Ct. Appeals (9th cir.) 1969, U.S. Ct. Appeals (4th cir.) 1972. Atty. FPC, Washington, 1965-71, Tally & Tally, Washington, 1972-75; asst. gen. counsel Postal Rate Commn., Washington, 1975-79, gen. counsel, 1979-92, regulatory cons. 1992—. Author: (with Bierman, Lamont, Nelson) Geothermal Energy in the Western United States, 1978. Mem. Fed. Bar Assn. Episcopalian. Home and Office: 2970 S Columbus St # 1-B Arlington VA 22206-1450

STOVER, HARRY M., corporate executive; b. 1926; married. BS, U. So. Calif., 1947. Engr. Stone & Webster Corp., 1947-48; chief engr. Raymond Internat., 1948-51, Standard Vacuum Corp., 1951-54; with A.P. Green Refractories, 1954-76, pres., 1972-76, chief exec. officer, 1974-76, chmn., 1976; group v.p. USG Corp., 1976-79; exec. v.p. USG Corp., Chgo., 1979-85, vice chmn., 1985; chmn., chief exec. officer A.P. Green Industries Inc., Mexico, Mo., 1988-93. Served to ensign USN, 1944-46. Office: A P Green Industries Inc Green Blvd Mexico MO 65265-2980

STOVER, JAMES HOWARD, real estate executive; b. Forest Hill, W.Va., Oct. 20, 1911; s. Charles William and Zora (Goode) S.; m. May Simmons, Oct. 21, 1939 (dec.); children: Ann, Robert Bruce; m. Elizabeth J. Cobb, Dec. 27, 1977 (dec.). Student, Benjamin Franklin U., 1936-38; grad., Advanced Mgmt. Program, Harvard U., 1959, Exec. Devel. Program Ind. U., 1960, Inst. Mgmt. Northwestern U., 1960. Asst. purchasing agt. Woodward & Lothrop, Washington, 1932-35; asst. chief field supervision div., central accounts office Bur. Accounts Treasury Dept., 1935-41, asst. chief Treasury Budget sect., 1941-42, fiscal acct. Office Commr. Pub. Debt, 1946-51, chief treasury mgmt. analysis staff, 1951-63, dir. Office Mgmt. and Orgn., 1963-66, regional commr. customs Miami Region IV, 1966-72; real estate sales assoc., mgmt. cons., 1972-75; pres. Bay Realty of Fla., Inc., 1975—; Chmn. Interagy. Mgmt. Analysis Conf., 1958-59; mem. orgn. and mgmt. adv. com. Dept. Agr. Grad. Sch., 1956-63. Chmn. adv. coms. orgn. and procedure and legislative program Arlington (Va.) County Bd., 1958-63; pres. Tuckahoe Recreation Club, 1957; chmn. Greater Miami Fed. Exec. Coun., 1968-69; mem. exec. adv. coun. Coll. Bus. and Pub. Adminstrn., Fla. Atlantic U., 1969-80. 2d lt. to maj. AUS, 1942-46. Recipient Rockefeller Pub. Svc. award, 1959, Spl. Svc. award Treasury Dept., 1963, Exceptional Svc. award, 1965, other treasury awards, 1969, 70, 71, 72. Home: 707 Vilabella Ave Coral Gables FL 33146-1733 Office: 2335 Biscayne Blvd Miami FL 33137-4513

STOVER, JOHN FORD, railroad historian, educator; b. Manhattan, Kans., May 16, 1912; s. John William and Maud (Ford) S.; m. Marjorie Ellen Filley, Aug. 21, 1937; children: John Clyde, Robert Vernon (dec.), Charry Ellen Stover Olin. AB, U. Nebr., 1934, MA, 1937; PhD, U. Wis., 1951. Instr. social studies Arcadia (Nebr.) High Sch., 1936-37; instr. history and govt. Bergen (N.J.) Jr. Coll., 1937-41; grad. asst. history U. Wis., 1941-42, 46-47, Univ. fellow, 1946; from instr. to assoc. prof. Purdue U., Lafayette, Ind., 1947-59, prof. history, 1959-78, prof. emeritus, 1978—; Purdue Research Found. XL grantee Purdue U., summer 1957, 59, fellow in Coll.-Bus. Exchange Program, I.C. R.R., summer 1962; chmn. Pres.'s adv. coun. on retirement Purdue U., 1981-82. Author: The Railroads of the South, 1865-1900, 1955, American Railroads, 1961, A History of American Railroads, 1967, Turnpikes, Canals and Steamboats, 1969, The Life and Decline of the American Railroad, 1970, Transportation in American History, 1970, History of Illinois Central Railroad, 1975, Iron Road To The West, 1978, Sixty-Five Years of Kiwanis in Indiana, 1981, History of the Baltimore & Ohio Railroad, 1987, Seventy-Five Years of Kiwanis of Indiana, 1990; contbr. to hist. jours., books, numerous encys. and biog. works. Chmn. edn. com., mem. exec. com. Ind. Sesquicentennial Commn., 1962-67; hon. mem. Indiana Am. Revolution Bicentennial commn., 1972-82; mem. adv. council Centennial History of Ind. Gen. Assembly, 1979-83; pres. Lafayette Kiwanis Found., 1977-78. Served to capt. USAAF, 1942-46; Res., ret. George F. Hixson fellow, 1996; named Sagamore of the Wabash Gov. Ind., 1978; recipient Alumni Achievement award U. Nebr., 1985. Fellow Soc. Am. Historians; mem. Ind. Acad. Social Scis., Western History Assn., Bus. History Conf. (trustee 1973-76), Am. Hist. Assn., So. Hist. Assn. (com. on library), Nebr. Hist. Assn., Tippecanoe County Hist. Assn. (pres. 1972-74), Lexington Group (r.r. historians), AAUP, Ind. History Tchrs. Assn. (pres. 1958-59), Orgn. Am. Historians, Newcomen Soc. N.Am., Ry. and Locomotive Hist. Soc. (editorial adv. bd. for Railroad History jour., 1970-94, Sr. Achievement R.R. History award 1983), Soc. Ind. Pioneers, Civil War Round Table of Nebr., Nat. Ry. Hist. Soc., Phi Beta Kappa (hon.), Phi Alpha Theta, Delta Sigma Rho. Republican. Methodist. Club: Fortnightly, Lincoln Open Forum. Lodge: Kiwanis (local pres. 1973-74, disting. lt. gov. 1978-79, historian Ind. dist. 1980-81, 83-90, 91-92). Avocations: golf, model railroading, stamps. Home: 2114 Heritage Pines Ct Lincoln NE 68506-2866

STOVER, LEON (EUGENE), anthropology educator, writer, critic; b. Lewistown, Pa., Apr. 9, 1929; s. George Franklin and Helen Elizabeth (Haines) S.; 1 dau. by previous marriage, Laren Elizabeth; m. 2d Takeko Kawai, Oct. 12, 1956. BA, Western Md. Coll., 1950, LittD (hon.), 1980; MA, Columbia U., 1952, PhD, 1962. Instr. Am. Museum Natural History, N.Y.C., 1955-57; asst. prof. Hobart and William Smith Colls., Geneva, N.Y., 1957-63; vis. asst. prof. Tokyo U., 1963-65; assoc. prof. Ill. Inst. Tech., Chgo., 1966-74, prof. anthropology, 1974-94, prof. emeritus, 1995—; founder, 1st chmn. John W. Campbell Meml. Award, 1972; guest lectr. Brit. Film Inst., 1986; humanities cons. Champaign (Ill.) Pub. Library H.G. Wells Traveling Exhbn., 1986; commd. as Robert A. Heinlein's authorized biographer, 1988. Author: La Science Fiction Americaine, 1972, The Cultural Ecology of Chinese Civilization, 1974, China: An Anthropological Perspective, 1976, The Shaving of Karl Marx, 1982, The Prophetic Soul: A Reading of H.G. Wells's "Things to Come", 1987, Robert A. Heinlein for Twayne's United State Authors Series, 1987, Harry Harrison for Twayne's United States Authors Series, 1990, The Annotated H.G. Wells: The Tiem Machine, 1996, The Annotated H.G. Wells: The Island of Doctor Moreau, 1996; sr. author: Stonehenge: The Indo-European Heritage, 1979; co-author: Stonehenge: Where Atlantis Died, 1983; sr. editor: Apeman, Spaceman, 1968; co-editor: Above the Human Landscape, 1972; sci. editor: Amazing, Stories, 1967-69; cons. editor: Contemporary Authors, 1987. Recipient Chris award for best edn. film, 1974; recipient Cine award Internat. Council Non-Theatrical Events, 1973; named Disting Faculty Lectr. Sigma Xi, 1978; honored with Stover Day Western Md. Coll., 1981. Mem. H.G. Wells Soc., Sci. Fiction Writers Am. Home: 3100 S Michigan Ave Apt 602 Chicago IL 60616-3825

STOVER, MATTHEW JOSEPH, communications executive; b. Palo Alto, Calif., May 5, 1955; s. Carl Frederick and Catherine (Swanson) S.; m. Elizabeth Biddle Richter, Apr. 27, 1985; children: Katharine Elizabeth, Madeleine Westbrook. BA, Yale U., 1976; postgrad., U. Va., 1987. Gen. mgr. K&S Assocs., Beltsville, Md., 1977-78; dir. outreach programs U.S. Office Personnel Mgmt., Washington, 1978-81; exec. asst. to chmn. Fed. Maritime Commn., Washington, 1981; exec. dir. STN Computer Services, Inc., Alexandria, Va., 1981-82; dir. corp. communications Norton Simon, Inc., N.Y.C., 1982-83; dist. mgr. corp. communications N.Y. Telephone Co., N.Y.C., 1983-86, dist. mgr. customer services, 1986-87; v.p. corp. communications Am. Express Co., N.Y.C., 1987-90, sr. v.p. communications, 1990; v.p. pub. affairs and corp. communications NYNEX Corp., White Plains, N.Y., 1990-92; pres., CEO AGS Computers, Inc., 1993-94, NYNEX Info. Resources Co., Middleton, Mass., 1994—; bd. dirs. Infoseek Corp., Nat. Assn. Mfrs., Yellow Pages Pubs. Assn., Computer and Comm. Industry Assn.; trustee Com. for Econ. Devel. Editor, pub.: (lit. mag.) Buffalo Stamps, 1971-74. Mem. Nat. Com. U.S.-China Rels. Coun. for Excellence in Govt., Nat. Advt. Rev. Bd., Arthur W. Page Soc., Yale Club (N.Y.C.). Office: NYNEX Info Resources Co 35 Village Rd Middleton MA 01949-1202

STOVER, PHIL SHERIDAN, JR., investment consultant; b. Tulsa, Jan. 23, 1926; s. Phil Sheridan and Noma (Smith) S. Student, Yale, 1943-44, Denison U., 1944-45; B.S., U. Pa., 1948. With Nat. Bank Tulsa, 1948-70, v.p., 1956-64, sr. v.p., 1964-65, sr. v.p., cashier, 1965-70; owner Phil Stover & Assocs., Tulsa, 1970—; pres., treas. Tulsalite, Inc. (mag. pubs.), 1973-79; vice chmn., dir. Tulsa Oiler Baseball Club, 1975-82, Springfield (Ill.) Redbirds Baseball Club; pres. Macon (Ga.) Baseball Club, 1980; dir. Redbirds Baseball Club, Louisville, 1982-86; ptnr. A Hotel, The Frenchmen, New Orleans, 1982-94. Chmn. Tulsa County chpt. Nat. Found., 1956-59, Tulsa Met. Water Authority, 1961-70; vice chmn. Tulsa Utility Bd., 1957-70; Treas. adv. bd. Salvation Army. Served with USNR, 1944-46. Named Okla. Jr. C. of C. Outstanding Young Man, 1954. Republican. Presbyterian.

STOVER, W. ROBERT, temporary services executive; b. Phila., June 26, 1921; s. Robert William Stover and Jane Horton; m. Joan Cote; children: Stephen R., Susan J., Amy J. BS, Waynesburg Coll., 1942, LHD (hon.), 1991; postgrad., U. Ill., 1942-43, U. Pa., 1946. Founder, chief exec. officer Western Temporary Svcs., Walnut Creek, Calif., 1948—, also chmn. bd. dirs.; dir., past chmn. Presbyn. Lay Com., Phila.; mem. Latin Am. Missions Gen. Coun., Miami, Fla., Luis Palau Adv. Com., Portland, Oreg.; past chmn. Oakland Billy Graham Crusade. Former chmn. Fuller Theol. Sem., Pasadena, Calif., African Enterprise, L.A.; life mem., former nat. chmn. Young Life Campaign, Colorado Springs. Lt. USN, WWII. Office: Western Staff Svcs Inst 301 Lennon Ln Walnut Creek CA 94598-2418

STOWE, ALEXIS MARIANI, accountant, consultant; b. Binghamton, N.Y., May 3, 1950; d. Albert Joseph and Gilda Ann (DiNardo) Mariani; m. Dennis James Stowe, June 3, 1972 (dec. Nov. 1988); children: Cort Andrew, Derek Anthony, Jilda Ann. Student, Le Moyne Coll., 1968-70; BS in Acctg., SUNY, Buffalo, 1972; MS in Acctg., SUNY, Albany, 1974; MS in Taxation, Southeastern U., 1980. CPA, N.Y., Va.; cert. fraud examiner; cert. govt. fin. mgr., cert. info. sys. auditor. In-charge acct. Ernst & Young, CPA's, Buffalo, 1973-74; sr. corp. acct. Moog, Inc., East Aurora, N.Y., 1974-76; auditor U.S. Gen. Acctg. Office, Washington, 1976-78, 79-80; tax law specialist IRS, Washington, 1978-79; pvt. practice CPA Woodbridge, Va., 1980-87; v.p., contr. M.T. Hall, Ltd., Woodbridge, 1987-91; audit mgr. U.S. Dept. Health and Human Svcs., Washington, 1991-93; oversight mgr. Resolution Trust Corp., Washington, 1993-94; v.p., prin. Gardiner, Kamya, CPA's, Washington, 1994—; trustee pension plan M.T. Hall, Ltd., Woodbridge, 1987-90; team leader CFO task force Pres.'s Coun. on Integrity and Efficiency, Washington, 1991-93; instr. Inspector Gen. Auditor Tng. Inst., Ft. Belvoir, Va., 1992—; mem. task force on grants Govtl. Acctg. Stds. Bd., Norwalk, Conn., 1992—; mem. faculty Assn. Cert. Fraud Examiners, 1995—. Contbr. articles to profl. jours. N.Y. Regents scholar, 1968-72. Mem. AICPA, Va. Soc. CPAs, Assn. Govt. Accts. (vice chair publs. 1994—, Author's award 1991), Assn. Cert. Fraud Examiners, Info. Sys. Audit Control Assn., Cath. Daus. of Am., Chi Omega, Beta Gamma Sigma. Roman Catholic. Home: 6013 Wheeler Ln Broad Run VA 22014-2201 Office: Gardiner Kamya & Assocs CPA 1717 K St NW Ste 601 Washington DC 20006-1501

STOWE, BRUCE BERNOT, biology educator; b. Neuilly-sur-Seine, France, Dec. 9, 1927; came to U.S., 1935; s. Leland and Ruth Florida (Bernot) S.; m. Elizabeth Louise Kwasny, June 23, 1951 (dec. June 1983); children: Mark Kwasny, Eric Bernot. BSc, Calif. Inst. Tech., 1950; MA, Harvard U., 1951, PhD, 1954; MA (hon.), Yale U., 1971. Instr. biology Harvard U., Cambridge, Mass., 1955-58, tutor biochem. scis., 1956-58, lectr. botany, 1958-59; asst. prof. Yale U., New Haven, 1959-63, assoc. prof., 1963-71, prof. biology and forestry, 1971—, dir. bot. garden, 1975-78; rsch. professor Japan Soc. Promotion Sci. U. Osaka Prefecture, 1973; vis. investigator Nat. Inst. for Basic Biology, Okazaki, Japan, 1985-86. Mem. editorial bd. Plant Physiology, Waltham, Mass., 1965-89; mem. editorial com. Ann. Rev. Plant Physiology, Palo Alto, Calif., 1968-73; cons. editor Am. Scientist, New Haven, 1985-90; contbr. sci. papers to Nature, Biochem. Jour., Analytical Biochemistry, others. With U.S. Army, 1946-47. Predoctoral fellow Atomic Energy Commn. Harvard U., 1951-53, postdoctoral fellow NSF, U. Coll. North Wales, 1954-55, fellow John Simon Guggenheim Found., 1965-66; travel grantee U. Adelaide, Waite Inst., South Australia, 1972-73. Fellow AAAS; mem. AAUP, Am. Assn. Plant Physiologists (sec. 1963-65, trustee 1970-72, 75), Bot. Soc. Am., Am. Soc. Biol. Chemistry, Phytochem. Soc., N.Am. Phytochem. Soc., Société Française de Physiologie Végétale, Conn. Acad. Arts and Scis. (chair publs. com. 1992-94). Democrat. Achievements include research in analysis and metabolism of plant hormones, lipid activation of plant hormone action, biochemistry of secondary plant products. Home: 161 Grand View Ave Hamden CT 06514-3518 Office: Yale U Dept Biology PO Box 208103 New Haven CT 06520-8103

STOWE, DAVID HENRY, arbitrator; b. New Canaan, Conn., Sept. 10, 1910; s. Ansel Roy Monroe and Marjorie (Henry) S.; m. Mildred Walker, June 7, 1932; children—David H., Richard W. Student, Washington and Lee U., 1927-30; A.B., Duke, 1931, M. Ed., 1934. Tchr. N.C., 1931-37; asst. state dir. N.C. state Employment Service, 1937-41; chief examiner Bur. Budget, Washington, 1943-47; dep. to asst. to Pres. U.S., 1947-49; adminstrv. asst. to Pres., 1949-53; arbitrator Washington, 1953-70; mem. Nat. Mediation Bd., 1970-79, chmn., 1972-75, 78; mem. atomic energy-labor mgmt. relations panel, 1962—; pub. mem. Pres.'s Missile Sites Labor Commn., 1961-67; mem. bd. Harry S. Truman Library Inst., 1981—. Recipient distinguished service award Dept. Labor, 1965. Mem. Nat. Acad. Arbitrators, Lambda Chi Alpha, Alpha Kappa Psi. Democrat. Episcopalian. Home: 717 Maiden Choice Ln Apt 417 Catonsville MD 21228-6115

STOWE, DAVID HENRY, JR., agricultural and industrial equipment company executive; b. Winston-Salem, N.C., May 11, 1936; s. David Henry and Mildred (Walker) S.; m. Lois Burrows, Nov. 28, 1959; children: Priscilla, David Henry. BA in Econs., Amherst Coll., 1958. V.p. First Nat. Bank Boston, 1961-68; mgr. Deere & Co., Moline, Ill., 1968-71; dir. Deere & Co., Moline, 1971-77, v.p., 1977-82, sr. v.p., 1982-87, exec. v.p., 1987-90, pres., COO, 1990-96; ret., 1996. Home: 4510 5th Ave Moline IL 61265-1904

STOWE, DAVID METZ, clergyman; b. Council Bluffs, Iowa, Mar. 30, 1919; s. Ernest Laewllyn and Florence May (Metz) S.; m. Virginia Ware, Nov. 25, 1943; children: Nancy F. (Mrs. Charles Hambrick-Stowe), Priscilla B., David W. BA, UCLA, 1940; BD, Pacific Sch. Religion, 1943, ThD, 1953, DD (hon.), 1966; postgrad., Yale U., 1945-46. Ordained to ministry Congl. Ch., 1943; assoc. min. Congl. Ch., Berkeley, Calif., 1943-45, 51-53; missionary, univ. prof. Peking, China, 1947-50; chaplain, chmn. dept. religion Carleton Coll., 1953-56; ednl. sec. Am. Bd. Commnrs. and United Ch. Bd. World Ministries, 1956-62; prof. theology Beirut, 1962-63; exec. sec. div. fgn. missions Nat. Coun. Chs., 1963-64, assoc. gen. sec. overseas ministries, 1965-70; also bd. govs.; exec. v.p. United Ch. Bd. for World Ministries, 1970-85; cons. mission and religion China, 1985—; adj. prof. Andover Newton Theol. Sch., 1987—; mem. exec. coun. World Conf. on Religion and Peace, 1988—; bd. dirs. Congl. Christian Hist. Soc.; del. 2nd, 3rd and 4th Assemblies of World Coun. of Chs.; mem. Divsn. of World Mission & Evangelism, 1963-75. Author: The Churches' Mission in the World, 1963, When Faith Meets Faith, 1963, Ecumenicity and Evangelism, 1970; also articles in religious books and periodicals. Mem. Am. Soc. Missiology (sec.-treas. Ea. fellowship 1986—), Internat. Assn. Mission Studies, Nat. Soc. Values in Higher Edn., Phi Beta Kappa, Pi Gamma Mu, Blue Key. Home: 54 Magnolia Ave Tenafly NJ 07670-2120

STOWE, LELAND, journalist, writer; b. Southbury, Conn., Nov. 10, 1899; s. Frank Philip and Eva Sarah (Noe) S.; m. Ruth F. Bernot, Sept. 27, 1924; 1 son, Bruce B.; m. Theodora F. Calauz, June 17, 1952. A.B., Wesleyan U., Conn., 1921, M.A. (hon.), 1936, LL.D., 1944; M.A. (hon.), Harvard U., 1945; LL.D., Hobart Coll., 1946. Reporter Worcester Telegram, 1921-22, N.Y. Herald, 1922-24; fgn. editor Pathe News, 1924-26; Paris corr. N.Y. Herald Tribune, 1926-35; roving reporter in N.Y. Herald Tribune, North and South Am., 1936-39; reporter (League of Nations' councils and assemblies), 1927-31, (World Disarmament Conf. Geneva), 1932, (World Econ. Conf.), London, 1933, (Reichstag fire trial), Germany, 1933, (end of Spanish dictatorship and founding of Spanish Republic), 1929-31, (Spanish Civil War), 1937-38, (Pres. Roosevelt's visit to Brazil and Argentina and Inter-American Peace Conf.), Buenos Aires, 1936, (Pan-Am. Conf. at Lima), Peru, 1938; war corr. Chgo. Daily News, from, London, 1939; war corr. Chgo. Daily News, in Finland throughout Russo-Finnish war, 1939-40, Norway, 1940, Hungary, Yugoslavia, Rumania, Bulgaria and Turkey, 1940, Greece and Albania, 1940-41, Malaya, Thailand, Indo-China and China, 1941, Burma, 1942, Russia, 1942; commentator Am. Broadcasting Co., 1944-45; war corr. in France, Belgium, Germany, 1944, Italy and Greece, 1945; radio commentator A.B.C. and M.B.S., 1945-46; fgn. editor The Reporter Magazine, 1949-50; dir. News and Information Service of Radio Free Europe, Munich, 1952-54; roving editor Reader's Digest, 1955-76; prof. journalism U. Mich., 1956-69, prof. emeritus, 1989—. Lectr., free-lance writer, 1947-48; Author: Nazi Means War, 1933, No Other Road to Freedom, 1941, They Shall Not Sleep, 1944, While Time Remains, 1946, Target: You, 1949, Conquest by Terror: The Story of Satelite Europe, 1952, Crusoe of Lonesome Lake, 1957, The Last Great Frontiersman; The Remarkable Adventures of Tom Lamb, 1982. Recipient Pulitzer prize for coverage of Paris (1929) Reparations Com. and formation of Young Plan and Bank for Internat. Settlements, 1930; Legion of Honor France, 1931; U. of Mo. Sch. of Journalism medal for outstanding war correspondence, 1941; Sigma Delta Chi medal and award for 1940 dispatches revealing German conquest of So. Norway, 1941; awarded Mil. Cross of Greece, 1945; Wesleyan U.'s James L. McConaughy Meml. award, 1963.

STOWE, MADELEINE, actress; b. L.A., Aug. 18, 1958; m. Brian Benben. Films: Stakeout, 1987, Worth Winning, 1989, Revenge, 1990, The Two Jakes, 1990, Closetland, 1991, Unlawful Entry, 1992, The Last of the Mohicans, 1992, Another Stakeout, 1993, Short Cuts, 1993, China Moon, 1993, Blink, 1994, Bad Girls, 1994; TV movies: The Gangster Chronicles: An American Story, The Nativity, Beulah Land, Black Orchid (miniseries). Office: c/o UTA 9560 Wilshire Blvd Fl 5 Beverly Hills CA 90212-2401*

STOWE, ROBERT ALLEN, catalytic and chemical technology consultant; b. Kalamazoo, July 26, 1924; s. Allen Byron Stowe and Doris Alfreda (Wood) Stowe Weber; m. Dorothea May Davis, Aug. 23, 1947 (div. 1973); children: Michael, Randall, Catherine, Robert; m. Marion June Smith, Oct. 20, 1973 (div. 1980). AB, Kalamazoo Coll., 1948; PhD, Brown U., 1953. Phys. chemist Dow Chem. Co., Midland, Mich., 1952-58; rsch. chemist Dow Chem. Co., Ludington, Mich., 1958-64, sr. rsch. chemist, 1964-69; sr. rsch. chemist Dow Chem. Co., Midland, 1969-72, assoc. scientist, 1972-88; ret., 1988; pres. Bobcat Techs. Ltd., Cross Village, Mich., 1988—; sr. consulting assoc. Omnitech Internat. Ltd., Midland, 1989—; bd. dirs., mem. oper. bd., chief scientist Van Tek Corp. (formerly VF Sales), 1990—; chief exec. scientist Environ. Assessments Ltd., Midland, 1990—. Contbr. articles to sci. jours.; numerous patents in U.S. and fgn. countries. Treas. Ludington Bd. Edn., 1960-63, pres., 1963-68. With USAAF, 1943-45; mem. Nat. Ski Patrol. Recipient Victor J. Azbe award Nat. Lime Assn., 1964. Fellow Am. Inst. Chemists (cert. profl. chemist); mem. Am. Chem. Soc. (program sec. divsn. indsl. and engrng. chemistry 1972-82, chmn. 1982-83, councilor 1986—, sec. gen. Catalysis Secretariat 1990, 94, Joseph P. Stewart award 1984), N.Am. Catalysis Soc., N.Am. Thermal Analysis Soc., Mich. Catalysis Soc. (sec.-treas. 1987-88, pres. 1988-89). Avocations: tennis, skiing, sailing. Home and Office: Box 173 5680 Chippewa Dr Cross Village MI 49723-0173

STOWE, WILLIAM WHITFIELD, English language educator; b. New Haven, Dec. 7, 1946; s. Arthur Clifford Jr. and Barbara (Borst) S.; m. Karin Ann Trainer, May 8, 1976. BA magna cum laude, Princeton U., 1968; MPhil, Yale U., 1977, PhD, 1978; MA ad eundem gradum, Wesleyan U., 1992. Tchr. Coleytown Jr. High Sch., Westport, Conn., 1968-73; lectr. Princeton (N.J.) U., 1976, 77; instr. Rutgers U., New Brunswick, N.J., 1977; asst. prof. Wesleyan U., Middletown, Conn., 1979-84, assoc. prof., 1984-90, prof., 1990—, chair English dept., 1992-95; vis. lectr. Yale U., New Haven, 1978; vis. asst. prof. Wesleyan U., 1978-79. Author: Balzac, James and the Realistic Novel, 1983, Going Abroad: European Travel in Nineteenth-Century American Culture, 1994; editor: The Poetics of Murder, 1983 (Edgar Allen Poe award nominee 1983); contbr. articles to profl. jours. Yale U. fellow, 1973-77. Home: 50 Miller Rd Middlefield CT 06455-1229 Office: Wesleyan U Dept English Middletown CT 06459

STOWELL, CHRISTOPHER R., dancer; b. N.Y.C., June 8, 1966; s. Kent and Francia (Russell) S. Student, Pacific N.W. Ballet Sch., 1979-84, Sch. Am. Ballet, 1984-85. Entered corps de ballet San Francisco Ballet, 1986, promoted to soloist, 1987, prin., 1990—; guest artist Ballet Met, Ohio, Pacific N.W. Ballet, Seattle, and with Jean Charles Gil, Marseilles, France. Created leading roles in Handel-A Celebration, Con Brio, The Sleeping Beauty, New Sleep, Connotations, Pulcinella, Meistens Mozart; other roles include Calcium Light Night, Rubies, The Sons of Horus, The Four Temperaments, Hearts, Tarantella, Flower Festival, La Fille Mal Garde, Haffner Symphony, Forgotten Land, The End, Agon, In the Middle Somewhat Elevated, Le Quattro Stagioni, Swan Lake, Job, Company B, Tchaikousky Pas de Deux, Maelstrom, Mercutio in Romeo and Juliet, The Dance House, Stars and Stripes; performed in Reykjavik Arts Festival, Iceland, 1990, San Francisco Ballet at the Paris Opera Garnier, 1994. Avocations: cooking, reading, camping. Office: San Francisco Ballet 455 Franklin St San Francisco CA 94102-4438

STOWELL, JOSEPH, III, academic administrator. Head Moody Bible Inst., Chgo. Office: Moody Bible Inst 820 N La Salle Dr Chicago IL 60610-3214 Office: Sta WKES-FM PO Box 8888 Saint Petersburg FL 33738-8888

STOWELL, KENT, ballet director; b. Rexburg, Idaho, Aug. 8, 1939; s. Harold Bowman and Maxine (Hudson) S.; m. Francia Marie Russell, Nov. 19, 1965; children: Christopher, Darren, Ethan. Student, San Francisco Ballet Sch., Sch. Am. Ballet; Lead dancer San Francisco Ballet, 1957-62, N.Y.C. Ballet, 1962-68; ballet dir., ballet master Frankfurt (Fed. Republic Germany) Opera Ballet, 1973-77; artistic dir. Pacific N.W. Ballet, Seattle, 1977—; prof. dance Ind. U., Bloomington, 1969-70; bd. dirs. Dance/USA, Washington, 1986—. Choreographer: Cinderella, Carmina Burana, Coppelia, Time & Ebb, Faurè Requiem, Hail to the Conquering Hero, Firebird, Over the Waves, Nutcracker, The Tragedy of Romeo and Juliet, Delicate Balance, Swan Lake, Time and Ebb, Through Interior Worlds, Quaternary, Orpheus. Bd. dirs. Sch. of Am. Ballet, N.Y.C., 1981—; mem. Goodwill Games Arts Com., Seattle, 1987—; chmn. dance panel NEA, 1981-85. Grantee NEA, 1980, 85; fellow NEA, 1979. Recipient Arts Service award King County Arts Commn., 1985, Outstanding Contbn. to Pacific N.W. Ballet State of Was., 1987, Best Dance Co. award The Weekly Newspaper, Seattle, 1987, Gov. Arts award, 1988. Office: Pacific NW Ballet 301 Mercer St Seattle WA 98109-4600

STOWELL, ROBERT EUGENE, pathologist, retired educator; b. Cashmere, Wash., Dec. 25, 1914; s. Eugene Francis and Mary (Wilson) S.; m. Eva Mae Chambers, Dec. 1, 1945; children: Susan Jane, Robert Eugene Jr. Student, Whitman Coll., 1932-33; BA, Stanford U., 1936, MD, 1941; PhD, Washington U., 1944. Fellow in cytology Wash. U. Sch. Medicine, St. Louis, 1940-42; rsch. fellow Barnard Free Skin and Cancer Hosp., St. Louis, 1940-42, rsch. assoc., 1942-48; asst. resident in pathology Barnes, McMillan, St. Louis Children's Hosps., St. Louis, 1942-43, resident in pathology, 1943-44, asst. pathologist, 1944-48; instr. in pathology Washington U. Sch. Medicine, St. Louis, 1943-45; asst. prof. Washington U. Sch. Medicine, St. Louis, 1945-48; assoc. prof. Washington U. Sch. Medicine, St. Louis, 1948; advanced med. fellow Inst. for Cell Rsch., Stockholm, 1946-47; chmn. dept. oncology U. Kansas Med. Ctr., Kansas City, Kans., 1948-51, prof. pathology and oncology, dir. cancer rsch., 1948-59, chmn., 1951-59; sci. dir. Armed Forces Inst. Pathology, Washington, 1959-67; chmn. dept. pathology Sch. of Medicine U. Calif., Davis, 1967-69, asst. dean Sch. Medicine, 1967-72, prof. pathology Sch. Medicine, 1967-82, prof. emeritus, 1982—; dir. div. pathology Sacramento (Calif.) Med. Ctr., 1967-69; vis. prof. U. Md. Sch. Medicine, Balt., 1960-67; acting dir. Nat. Ctr. for Primate Biology, U. Calif., Davis, 1968-69, dir., 1969-71; cons. U.S. Atomic Energy commn., Los Alamos, N.Mex., 1949-54, NIH, 1949-74, Cancer Control Div. USPHS, 1949-59, others; mem. adv. med. bd. Leonard Wood Meml. found., Washington, 1965-67, numerous univs.; prin. investigator, chmn. Expert Panel on Assessment of the Practical risk to Human Health from Nitrilotriacetic Acid in Household Laundry Product, 1984-85. Contbr. 120 articles, 30 abstracts to jours. in field; editor 32 biomed. books, monographs and conf. reports, 1941-88; mem. editorial bd. Cancer Rsch., 1949-59, Lab. Investigation, 1952-71, editor, 1967-71. Recipient Meritorious Svc. award Dept. Army, 1963, Exceptional Civilian Svc. award Dept. Army, 1965, Disting. Svc. award U. Calif. Sch. Medicine, 1988; Robert E. Stowell ann. lectureship established U. Calif. Sch. Medicine, 1991 and Am. Registry of Pathology, Washington, 1991. Mem. AMA, Am. Registry of Pathology (bd. dirs. 1976-83, exec. com. 1976-82, v.p. 1976-78, pres. 1978-79, Disting. Svc. award 1995), Am. Assn. Cancer Rsch., Am. Assn. Pathologists (Gold-headed Cane award 1990), Am. Assn. Pathologists and Bacteriologists (councilor 1965-72, v.p. 1969-70, pres. 1970-71), Am. Soc. Clin. Pathologists, Am. Soc. Exptl. Pathology (councilor 1962-66, v.p. 1963-64, pres. 1964-65), Calif. Med. Soc., Calif. Soc. Pathologists, Binford-Dammin Soc. Infectious Disease Paahologists, Coll. Am. Pathologists, Histochem. Soc., Internat. Acad. Pathology (councilor 1954-61, pres.-elect 1958-59, pres. 1995-60, Disting. Svc. award 1970, Diamond Jubilee award 1981, Stowell-Orbison award established 1982—), Soc. Cryobiology (bd. govs. 1968-71), Soc. Exptl. Biology and Medicine, U.S. and Can. Acad. Pathology, Yolo County Med. Soc., Assn. Mil. Surgeons U.S. (sustaining membership award 1965), Univs. Associated for Rsch. and Edn. in Path. (bd. dirs. 1975-90, sec.-treas. 1978-82, hon. dir. 1990—), Sigma Xi, Alpha Omega Alpha. Office: Univ of Calif Sch Medicine Dept of Pathology Davis CA 95616

STOWERS, CARLTON EUGENE, writer; b. Brownwood, Tex., Apr. 14, 1942; s. Ira Milton and Fay Eloise (Stephenson) S.; m. Patricia Ann Folks, Mar. 2, 1981; children: Anson, Ashley. Student, U. Tex., Austin, 1961-63. Sportswriter Abilene (Tex.) Reporter News, 1963-64; sports editor Roswell (N.Mex.) Daily Record, 1964-65; sportswriter Lubbock (Tex.) Avalanche Jour., 1965-67; sports editor Amarillo (Tex.) Globe News, 1967-72; reporter, columnist Dallas Morning News, 1972-81; freelance writer Cedar Hill, Tex., 1981—; contbg. editor Dallas Observer, 1986—; editor Dallas Cowboys Weekly, 1985-89. Author: (non-fiction) The Randy Matson Story, 1971, Spirit, 1973, (with E.B. Hughes) Doc, 1976, (with Trent Jones) Where the Rainbows Wait, 1978, pub. softcover as Terlingua Teacher, 1982, (with Wilbur Evans) Champions, 1978, The Overcomers, 1978, (with Roy Rogers and Dale Evans) Happy Trails, 1979 (book clubs awards, Christian Herald Family Bookshelf main selection, selected for talking book program Nat. Library Svc. for Blind and Handicapped), The Unsinkable Titanic Thompson, 1982, softcover, 1988, Journey to Triumph, 1988 (also in Spanish), (with Steve Perkins and Greg Aiello) Dallas Cowboys Bluebook III, 1982 (Spanish lang. edit. 1982), Partners in Blue: The 100-Year History of the Dallas Police Department, 1983, Friday Night Heroes, 1983, Just One Kiss Baby, 1983, (with Greg Aiello) Dallas Cowboys Bluebook IV, 1983 (Spanish lang. edit. 1983), (with Billy Olson) Reaching Higher, 1984, The Dallas Cowboys: The First 25 Years, 1984, The Cowboy Chronicles, 1984, (ghosted for Ralph Carmichael) He's Everything To Me, 1986, (ghosted for Pam Lontos) Don't Tell Me It's Impossible Until I've Already Done It, 1988, Careless Whispers, 1986 (Edgar Allen Poe award Mystery Writers Am. 1986, Oppie award S.W. Booksellers Assn. 1986, other awards and included in talking book program), The Cotton Bowl: The First 50 Years, 1986, (with Jarret Bell) Dallas Cowboys Bluebook IX, 1988, (with William C. Dear) Please...Don't Kill Me: The True Story of the Milo Murder, 1989 (Literary Guild selection), (with Larry Wansley) The FBI Undercover: The True Story of Special Agent 'Mandrake', 1989, Innocence Lost, 1990, (childrens book) A Hero Named George, 1991, (childrens book) Hard Lessons, 1994, Open Secrets, 1994, Sins of the Son, 1995; gen. editor series 8 collections sports columns Sportswriters' Eye Series, 1988, 89; writer, producer 79-week, 30 minute news feature show Countdown to '84, official show of U.S. Olympic Com., documentary African Stars '84 for African Nat. TV., football halftime feature Greatest of the Great; writer cable TV show Polaroid's Sports Camera Internat.; co-producer TV show Texas by Land: The Story of the Sesquicentennial Wagon Train; script writer syndicated radio shows Faith Made Them Great, Inside the NFL. Bd. dirs. Cedar Hill (Tex.) Libr. Assn., 1989-92; mem. adv. bd. Kevin Curnutt Found. for Brain Injury Rsch., Arlington, Tex., 1988-89. Recipient Katie awards Dallas Press Club, 1985-92, Oppie award S.W. Booksellers, 1986, Edgar Allen Poe award for best fact crime book Mystery Writers Am., 1986, Stephen Philben awards Dallas Bar Assn., 1987-92, other journalism awards Tex. HEadliners Club, William Randolph Hearts Found., UPI, other; named Best Local Writer in the 1988's, reader's poll Dallas Observer. Mem. Authors Guild Am., Mystery Writers Am., Internat. Assn. Crime Writers, Profl. Football Writers Am., Tex. Sportswriters Assn. Home: 1015 Randy Rd Cedar Hill TX 75104-3035 Office: care Janet W Manus Lit Agy Inc 417 E 57th St Ste 5D New York NY 10022

STOWERS, JAMES EVANS, JR., investment company executive; b. Kansas City, Mo., Jan. 10, 1924; s. James Evans Sr. and Laura (Smith) S.; m. Virginia Ann Glasscock, Feb. 4, 1954; children: Pamela, Kathleen, James Evans III, Linda. A.B., U. Mo., 1946, B.S. in Medicine, 1947. Pres. Twentieth Century Svcs., Kansas City, 1956—, Survivors Benefit Ins. Co., Kansas City, 1956-80, 20th Century Investors, Inc., Kansas City, 1957—, Investors Research Corp., Kansas City, 1958—, Twentieth Century Cos. Inc., Kansas City, 1984—; chmn. bd., CEO Twentieth Century Svcs., 20th Century Investors, Investors Rsch. Group, Twentieth Century Cos. Inc., Kansas City, 1993—. Author: Why Waste Your Money on Life Insurance, 1967, Principles of Financial Consulting, 1971, Yes, You Can....achieve financial independence, 1992. Co-founder, pres. Stowers Inst. for Med. Rsch., Kansas City, 1995—. Capt. USAAF, 1943-45; with USAFR, 1945-57. Mem. Kansas City C. of C., Sigma Chi. Republican. Office: Twentieth Century Svcs 4500 Main St Kansas City MO 64111-1800

STOY, JOSEPH FRANK, chemical engineer, consultant; b. Clifton, N.J., Apr. 10, 1926; s. Joseph and Mary (Sudol) S.; m. Mayfa Reep, June 1, 1952; children: Joseph III, Joanne, Jerrold. BSChemE, Washington U., 1950; postgrad., NYU, U. Houston, U. Cin., 1950-56. Lic. profl. engr. N.Y., N.J., La. Va. Tex., Utah, Ill., Wis., Ohio, Kans. With tech. sales dept. Belco Indsl. Co., Paterson, N.J., 1950-53; project engr. Chem. & Indsl., Cin., 1953-57; sr. project engr. Foster Wheeler, Livingston, N.J., 1957-64; project mgr. M.W. Kellogg, N.Y.C., 1964-69; asst. mgr. constrn. Chem. Constrn., N.Y.C., 1969-74; project dir. C.E. Lummus, The Hague, The Netherlands, 1974-81; dir. projects Petrochem. Industries, Kuwait, 1981-87. Contbr. (book) Project Management: Reference for Professionals, 1989. Mem. AIChE, Tau Beta Pi, Sigma Xi, Axe. Home: 6408 Dougherty Dr Charlotte NC 28213

STOYANOV, MILAN, lumber products company executive; b. 1933. BA, U. Oreg., 1955. With Oreg. Pacific Forest Products Corp., Portland, 1964-70, Am. Internat. Forest Products Inc., Beaverton, Oreg., 1970-74; with Buckeye Pacific Corp., 1974-86, pres.; pres. Forest City Trading Group Inc., Portland, 1986—, also bd. dirs. Served to 1st lt. USAF, 1955-58. Office: Forest City Trading Group PO Box 4209 Portland OR 97208-4209*

STRAATSMA, BRADLEY RALPH, ophthalmologist, educator; b. Grand Rapids, Mich., Dec. 29, 1927; s. Clarence Ralph and Lucretia Marie (Nicholson) S.; m. Ruth Campbell, June 16, 1951; children: Cary Ewing, Derek, Greer. Student, U. Mich., 1947; MD cum laude, Yale U., 1951; DSc (hon.), Columbia U., 1984. Diplomate Am. Bd. Ophthalmology (vice chmn. 1979, chmn. 1980). Intern New Haven Hosp., Yale U., 1951-52; resident in ophthalmology Columbia U., N.Y.C., 1955-58; spl. clin. trainee Nat. Inst. Neurol. Diseases and Blindness, Bethesda, Md., 1958-59; assoc. prof. surgery/ophthalmology UCLA Sch. Medicine, 1959-63, chief div. ophthalmology, dept. surgery, 1959-68, prof. surgery/ophthalmology, 1963-

68, prof. ophthalmology, 1968—, dir. Jules Stein Eye Inst., 1964-94, chmn. dept. ophthalmology, 1968-94; ophthalmologist-in-chief UCLA Med. Ctr., 1968-94; lectr. numerous univs. and profl. socs. 1971—; cons. to surgeon gen. USPHS, mem. Vision Research Tng. Com., Nat. Inst. Neurol. Diseases and Blindness, NIH, 1959-63, mem. neurol. and sensory disease program project com., 1964-68; chmn. Vision Research Program Planning Com., Nat. Adv. Eye Council, Nat. Eye Inst., NIH, 1973-75, 75-77, 85-89; mem. med. adv. bd. Internat. Eye Found., 1970-79; mem. adv. com. on basic clin. research Nat. Soc. to Prevent Blindness, 1971-87; mem. med. adv. com. Fight for Sight, 1960-83; bd. dirs. So. Calif. Soc. to Prevent Blindness, 1967-77, Ophthalmic Pub. Co., 1975—, v.p. 1990-93, Pan-Am. Ophthalmol. Found., 1985—; chmn. sci. adv. bd. Ctr. for Partially Sighted, 1984-87; mem. nat. adv. panel Found. for Eye Research, Inc., 1984—; mem. cons. com. Palestra Oftalmologica Panamericana, 1976-81; coord. com. Nat. Eye Health Edn. Program, 1989; mem. sci. adv. bd. Rsch. to Prevent Blindness, Inc., 1993—; mem. Internat. Coun. Opthalmology, 1993—. Editor-in-chief Am. Jour. Ophthalmology, 1993—; mem. editorial bd. UCLA Forum in Med. Scis., 1974-82, Am. Jour. Ophthalmology, 1974-91, Am. Intra-Ocular Implant Soc. Jour., 1978-79, EYE-SAT Satellite-Relayed Profl. Edn. in Ophthalmology, 1982-86; mng. editor von Graefe's Archive for Clin. and Exptl. Ophthalmology, 1976-88; contbr. over 400 articles to med. jours. Trustee John Thomas Dye Sch., Los Angeles, 1967-72. Served to lt. USNR, 1952-54. Recipient William Warren Hoppin award N.Y. Acad. Medicine, 1956, Univ. Service award UCLA Alumni Assn., 1982, Miguel Aleman Found. medal, 1992, Benjamin Boyd Humanitarian award Pan Am. Assn. Ophthalmology, 1991, Lucian Howe medal, Am. Ophthalmological Soc., 1992. Fellow Royal Australian Coll. Ophthalmologists (hon.); mem. Academia Ophthalmologica Internationales, Am. Acad. Ophthalmology (bd. councillors 1981), Found. of Am. Acad. Ophthalmology (trustee 1989, chmn. bd. trustees 1989-92), Am. Acad. Opthalmology and Otolaryngology (pres. 1977), Am. Soc. Cataract and Refractive Surgery, AMA (asst. sec. ophthalmology sect. 1962-63, sec. 1963-66, chmn. 1966-67, council 1970-74), Am. Ophthalmol. Soc. (coun. 1985-90, v.p. 1992, pres. 1993), Assn. Research in Vision and Ophthalmology (Mildred Weisenfeld award 1991), Assn. U. Profs. of Ophthalmology (trustee 1969-75, pres.-elect 1973-74, pres. 1974-75), Assn. VA Ophthalmologists, Calif. Med. Assn. (mem. ophthalmology adv. panel 1972-94, chmn. 1974-79, sci. bd. 1973-79, ho. of dels. 1974, 77, 79), Chilean Soc. Ophthalmology (hon.), Columbian Soc. Ophthalmology (hon.), Glaucoma Soc. Internat. Congress of Ophthalmology (hon.), Heed Ophthalmic Found. (chmn., bd. dirs. 1990—), Hellenic Ophthalmol. Soc. (hon.), Internat. Coun. Ophthalmology (bd. dirs. 1993—), Los Angeles County Med. Assn., Los Angeles Soc. Ophthalmology, The Macula Soc., Pacific Coast Oto-Ophthalmol. Soc., Pan-Am. Assn. Ophthalmology (council 1972—, pres. elect 1985-87, pres. 1987-89), Peruvian Soc. Ophthalmology (hon.), The Retina Soc. Republican. Presbyterian. Clubs: Internat. Intra-Ocular Implant, The Jules Gonin, West Coast Retina Study. Avocations: music, tennis, scuba diving. Home: 3031 Elvingeles CA 90049-1107 Office: UCLA Jules Stein Eye Inst 100 Stein Pla Los Angeles CA 90024-7000

STRACHAN, DAVID E., trade association executive; b. Pitts., June 3, 1947; s. Edward Adam and Helen Joanna (Beatty) S.; m. Judith Mary Squires, Mar. 14, 1970; children: Sarah Duff, Matthew Squires. BS, W.Va. U., 1969. Cert. assn. exec. Fin. asst. SEC, Washington, 1970-71; fin. analyst Fed. Deposit Ins. Corp., Washington, 1971-72; assoc. dir. Am. Bankers Assn., Washington, 1972-78; exec. v.p. Nat. Assn. Pers. Cons., Washington, 1978-83, D.C. Assn. Realtors, Washington, 1983-89; pres. Am. Wholesale Marketers Assn., Washington, 1989—; pres. Mgmt. and Svcs. Corp., Washington, 1991—. Contbr. articles to mags. Pres. Dist. Edn. Found., Washington, 1990—. Mem. Am. Soc. Assn. Execs., Nat. Assn. Wholesale Distbrs. Republican. Presbyterian. Avocations: boat bldg., fishing. Office: Am Wholesale Marketers 1128 16th St NW Washington DC 20036-4802

STRACHAN, GLADYS, executive director; b. N.Y.C., Dec. 10, 1929; d. Jacob Allen and Annie Mae (Alston) McClendon; m. Eugene S. Callender (div. 1963); 1 child, Renee Denise; m. John R. Strachan (dec. 1982). Student, NYU, 1947-49. Dep. asst. Presbyn. Ch. of East Africa, Nairobi, Kenya, 1964-67; assoc. for women's program Presbyn. Ch. of U.S., N.Y.C., 1970-83; exec. United Presbyn. Women, N.Y.C., 1983—; cons. Peace Corps, Nairobi, 1964-67, Operation Crossroads Africa, Nairobi, 1964-67, Afro-Am. Ednl. Inst., Teaneck, N.J., 1977-79, various women's orgns. in Asia, Australia, Europe, Africa. V.p. Addicts Rehab. Ctr. Bd., N.Y.C., 1957—; mem. N.Y. Coalition of 100 Black Women, N.Y.C., 1972—; v.p., bd. dirs. La. Internat. Cultural Ctr. Recipient Cert. of citation borough pres. N.Y.C., 1977, Harlem Peacemaking award Harlem Peacemaking Com., 1983. Mem. La. C. of C., River City Assn. Bus. and Profl. Women. Avocations: music, reading, travel, needlepoint, theater. Office: Presbyn Women 100 Witherspoon St Louisville KY 40202-1396

STRACHAN, GRAHAM, pharmaceutical company executive; b. Dundee, Scotland, Sept. 12, 1938; arrived in Can., 1968; s. Roualyn and Ellen Strachan. BSc, Glasgow U., 1961, MA, 1963. Registered patent and trade agt. Licensing officer Schering Inc., Switzerland, 1963-66; v.p. bus. devel. John Labatt Ltd., Can., 1967-82; pres., chief exec. officer Allelix Biopharms., Inc., Mississauga, Ont., Can., 1982—; chmn. Nat. Biotech. Adv. Com. Patentee in field. Fellow Patent and Trademark Inst. Can.; mem. Am. Chem. Soc., Licensing Execs. Soc., Indsl. Biotech. Assn. Can. (bd. dirs.), Assn. Biotech. Cos. (bd. dirs. 1985—, past pres.). Achievements include several patents relating to biotechnology. Home: 40 Deane Wood crescent, Etobicoke, ON Canada M9B 3B1 Office: Allelix Biopharmaceuticals Inc, 6850 Goreway Dr, Mississauga, ON Canada L4V1P1

STRACHER, ALFRED, biochemistry educator; b. Albany, N.Y., Nov. 16, 1930; s. David and Florence (Winter) S.; m. Dorothy Altman, July 4, 1954; children: Cameron, Adam, Erica. BS in Chemistry, Rensselaer Poly. Inst., 1952; MA in Chemistry, Columbia U., 1954, PhD in Chemistry, 1956. Asst. prof. SUNY Health Sci. Ctr. at Bklyn., 1959-62, assoc. prof., 1962-68, prof. biochem., 1968—, chmn. dept., 1972—, assoc. dean for research and devel., 1982-88; cons. Nat. Inst. Neurol. Communicative Disorders and Stroke NIH, 1981-84, 85-89. Editor: Muscle and Non-Muscle Motility, 1983; editorial bd. 3 jours.; editor-in-chief: Drug Targeting and Delivery; contbr. 95 articles to profl. jours. Fellow Nat. Found. for Infantile Paralysis Rockefeller Inst. for Med. Rsch., 1956-58 and Carlsberg Lab., 1958-59, Commonwealth Fund Kings Coll. U. London, 1966-67, Guggenheim Found. Oxford U., 1973-74; career scientist grantee Health Rsch. Coun. N.Y., 1962-69. Fellow AAAS; mem. Am. Soc. for Biochemistry and Molecular Biology, Harvey Soc. (treas. 1978-83), Marine Biol. Labs. (corp. 1968—). Avocations: tennis, travel. Home: 47 The Oaks Roslyn NY 11576-1704 Office: SUNY Health Sci Ctr Bklyn 450 Clarkson Ave Brooklyn NY 11203-2012

STRACK, HAROLD ARTHUR, retired electronics company executive, retired air force officer, planner, analyst, author, musician; b. San Francisco, Mar. 29, 1923; s. Harold Arthur and Catheryn Jenny (Johnsen) S.; m. Margaret Madeline Decker, July 31, 1945; children: Carolyn, Curtis, Tamara. Student, San Francisco Coll., 1941, Sacramento Coll., 1947, Sacramento State Coll., 1948, U. Md., 1962, Indsl. Coll. Armed Forces, 1963. Commd. 2d lt. USAAF, 1943; advanced through grades to brig. gen. USAF, 1970; comdr. 1st Radar Bomb Scoring Group Carswell AFB, Ft. Worth, 1956-59; vice comdr. 90th Strategic Missile Wing SAC Warren AFB, Cheyenne, Wyo., 1964; chief, strategic nuclear br., chmn. spl. studies group Joint Chiefs of Staff, 1965-67, dep. asst. to chmn. for strategic arms negotiations, 1968; comdr. 90th Strategic Missile Wing SAC Warren AFB, Cheyenne, 1969-71; chief Studies, Analysis and Gaming Agy. Joint Chiefs Staff, Washington, 1972-74, ret., 1974; v.p., mgr. MX Program v.p. strategic planning Northrop Electronics Divsn., Hawthorne, Calif., 1974-88; ret., 1988. 1st clarinetist, Cheyenne Symphony Orch., 1969-71. Mem. Cheyenne Frontier Days Com., 1970-71. Decorated D.S.M., Legion of Merit, D.F.C., Air medal, Purple Heart; mem. Order Pour le Merite. Mem. Inst. Nav., Am. Def. Preparedness Assn., Air Force Assn. (nat. dir.), Aerospace Edn. Found., Am. Fedn. Musicians, Cheyenne Frontier Days "Heels". Home: 707 James Ln Incline Village NV 89451-9612 *The precepts which have guided me recognize the dignity of the individual and human rights. I believe that living by the Golden Rule contributes to the quality of life by making us better and more useful citizens while favorably influencing others. Integrity, ideals, and high standards reinforce one's own character. While taking pride in accomplishment, show gratitude for opportunity and humility for success. Lead by example and always do your best. Service to humanity and country is the highest calling, and the satisfaction of a job well done, approbation, respect and true friendship are one's greatest rewards.*

STRACK, J. GARY, hospital administrator; b. Orlando, Fla., Aug. 1, 1945; married. Bachelors degree, U. Fla., 1967, masters degree, 1969. Adminstrv. rschr. Va. Med. Ctr., Gainesville, Fla., 1969; program mgr. Fla. Regional Med. Program, Gainesville, 1969-70; asst. prof. program in hosp. adminstrn. U. Fla., Gainesville, 1970-74; assoc. dir. Holiday Hosp., Orlando, 1974-77; assoc. exec. dir. Orlando Regional Med. Ctr., 1977-80; pres., CEO Orlando Regional Healthcare System, 1980—. Contbr. articles to profl. jours. Mem. AHA, Fla. Hosp. Assn. (bd. dirs. 1979-80). Home: 6305 Gibson Dr Orlando FL 32809-6148 Office: Orlando Regional Healthcare System 1414 Kuhl Ave Orlando FL 32806-2008*

STRADER, JAMES DAVID, lawyer; b. Pitts., June 30, 1940; s. James Lowell and Tyra Fredrika (Bjorn) S.; m. Ann Wallace, Feb. 8, 1964; children: James Jacob, Robert Benjamin. BA, Mich. State U., 1962; JD, U. Pitts., 1965. Bar: Pa. 1966, U.S. Dist. Ct. (we. dist.) Pa. 1966, U.S. Dist. Ct. (ea. dist.) Pa. 1973, U.S. Dist. Ct. (mid. dist.) Pa. 1985, U.S. Ct. Appeals (4th and 5th cirs.) 1977, U.S. Ct. Appeals (3d and 11th cirs.) 1981, U.S. Supreme Ct. 1982, W.Va. 1996. Assoc. Peacock, Keller & Yohe, Washington, 1967-68; atty. U.S. Steel Corp., Pitts., 1968-77, gen. atty. workman's compensation, 1977-84; assoc. Caroselli, Spagnolli & Beachler, Pitts., 1984-87; ptnr. Dickie, McCamey & Chilcote, Pitts., 1987—. Del. Dem. Mid-Yr. Conv., 1974; mem. Dem. Nat. Platform Com., 1976; commr. Mt. Lebanon Twp., Pa., 1974-78. Served to capt. U.S. Army, 1965-67. Mem. ABA (sr. vice-chmn. worker's compensation com. 1978-94), Pa. Bar Assn. (chair worker's compensation com. 1978-94), Pa. Bar Assn. (chair worker's compensation law sect. 1994-95), State Bar W.Va., Allegheny County Bar Assn., Valley Brook Country Club. Democrat. Presbyterian. Office: Dickie McCamey & Chilcote 2 Ppg Pl Ste 400 Pittsburgh PA 15222-5402

STRAFFON, RALPH ATWOOD, urologist; b. Croswell, Mich., Jan. 4, 1928; s. Lloyd Atwood and Verle R. (Rice) S.; m. Cary Arden Higley, Feb. 13, 1954; children: David, Daniel, Jonathan, Peter, Andrew; m. Shirley Louise Gilmore, June 20, 1987; children: Scott, Leslie. M.D., U. Mich., 1953. Diplomate: Am. Bd. Urology. Intern, then resident in surgery Univ. Hosp., Ann Arbor, 1953-56, resident in urology, 1956-59; mem. staff Cleve. Clinic, 1956—, head dept. urology, 1963-83, chmn. div. surgery, 1983-87, vice chmn. bd. govs. and chief of staff, 1987—; practice medicine specializing in urology Cleve., 1959—. Contbr. articles to med. jours. Served with AUS, 1946-48. Fellow A.C.S.; mem. Am. Assn. Genitourinary Surgeons, AMA, Am. Urol. Assn., Cleve. Acad. Medicine, Cleve. Urol. Assn., Clin. Soc. Genitourinary Surgeons, Soc. Univ. Urologists, Frederick A. Coller Surg. Soc., Am. Soc. Nephrology, Transplantation Soc., Soc. Pelvic Surgeons, Soc. Pediatric Urology, Am. Fertility Soc., Am. Assn. Clin. Urologists, Soc. Internat. d'Urologie, Am. Surg. Assn, Royal Coll. Surgeons Edinburgh (hon. fellow), Coll. Medicine South Africa (hon. fellow). Home: 19701 Shelburne Rd Cleveland OH 44118-4959 Office: 9500 Euclid Ave Cleveland OH 44195-0001

STRAHILEVITZ, MEIR, inventor, researcher, psychiatry educator; b. Beirut, July 13, 1935; s. Jacob and Chana Strahilevitz; m. Aharona Nattiv, 1958; children: Michal, Lior. MD, Hadassah Hebrew U. Med. Sch., 1963. Diplomate Am. Bd. Psychiatry and Neurology, Royal Coll. Physicians and Surgeons Can. Asst. prof. Washington U. Med. Sch., St. Louis, 1971-74; assoc. prof. So. Ill. U., Springfield, 1974-77, U. Chgo., 1977, U. Tex. Med. Br., Galveston, 1978-81; chmn. dept. psychiatry Kaplan Hosp., Rehovot, Israel, 1987-88; clin. assoc. prof. U. Wash., Seattle, 1981-88; prof. U. Tex. Med. Sch., Houston, 1988-92. Contbr. articles to profl. jours. Fellow Am. Psychiat. Assn., Royal Coll. Physicians and Surgeons Can. Achievements include patents for immunological methods for removing species from the blood circulatory system, for treatment methods for psychoactive drug dependence, for immunological methods for treating mammals; invention of use of antibodies to receptors and their fragments as drugs, of immunoadsorption treatment of hyperlipidemia, cancer, autoimmune disease and coronary artery disease; discovery of the protective effects of Nitric Oxide (NO) on psychiatric patients. Office: PO Box 190 Hansville WA 98340-0190

STRAHM, SAMUEL EDWARD, veterinarian; b. Fairview, Kans., Feb. 9, 1936; s. Silas Tobias and Martha Mary (Beyer) S.; m. Barbara Jean Wenger, June 1, 1958; children: Gregory Lee, Bryan Scott, Andrea Marie Enloe. BS, DVM, Kansas State U., 1959. Diplomate Nat. Acad. Practice. Owner, ptnr. Osage Animal Clinic Inc., Pawhuska, Okla., 1959—, pres., 1985—; bd. 1st Nat. Bank, Pawhuska, Okla.; mem. bd. cons. Profl. Exam Svc., 1990—; mem. adv. bd. USDA Users, 1991—; mem. adv. com. Pew Nat. Health Profession Vet. Medicine, 1991. Mem. Okla. State Sch. Bd. Assn., 1977-94, 2d v.p., 1993, 1st v.p., 1994, pres., 1996; mem. Okla. All-State Sch. Bd., 1993; mem. Pawhuska Sch. Bd., 1974—, pres., 1991-94; mem. Pawhuska Planning Commn., 1965-70; mem. Okla. State U. Centennial Commn., Stillwater, 1986-91; chmn. Am. Vet. Med. Found., 1995—; chmn. western region Nat. Sch. Bds. Assn. 1996, bd. dirs., 1996—. Recipient Disting. Alumni award Coll. Vet. Medicine Kans. State U., 1994. Mem. Am. Vet. Med. Assn. (pres. elect 1988-89, pres. 1989-90, AVMA award 1986, Coun. on Govt. Affairs, 1992—), Am. Assn. Theriogenealogy, Am. Assn. Bovine Practitioners, Am. Assn. Vet. State Bds., Nat. Bd. Vet. Med. Examiners, Okla. Vet. Med. Assn. (all offices from 1959, Veterinarian of Yr. 1990), Kans. Vet. Med. Assn., Okla. Bd. Vet. Med. Examiners (pres.), Pawhuska C. of C. (pres. 1968), Pawhuska Jaycees (all offices 1959-69), Toastmasters Club. Republican. Baptist. Avocations: gardening, fishing, flying. Home: PO Box 1256 Pawhuska OK 74056-1256 Office: Osage Animal Clinic Inc PO Box 1209 Pawhuska OK 74056-1209

STRAIGHT, JAMES WESLEY, secondary education educator; b. Ely, Nev., Jan. 3, 1930; s. James Wesley Sr. and Mary Elizabeth (Hunter) S.; m. Gloria Frances Roysum, Aug. 22, 1954; children: James W. Jr., Elizabeth Straight Stevenson, Kathryn Straight Hernandez, Douglas Scott. BS in Geol. Engring., U. Nev., Reno, 1954. Cert. secondary tchr., Calif. Geol. engr. Kennecott Copper Corp., McGill, Nev., 1954-57; soil engr. John F. Byerly, Bloomington, Calif., 1967-82; foreman Eagle-Picher, Lovelock, Nev., 1957-61, Kaiser Steel, Fontana, Calif., 1962-67; tchr. indsl. arts Fontana Unified Schs., 1967-92; tchr. prospecting class Rialto (Calif). Unified Schs., 1969—; tchr. prospecting class U. Calif., Riverside, 1976. Author, pub.: Follow the Drywashers, 1988, vol. 2, 1990, vol. 3, 1993, Magnificent Quest, 1990; contbg. editor mags. Popular Mining, Treas. Found., Western and Ea. Treas., Treas. Gold and Silver, Treas. Seekers. Treas. San Bernadino (Calif.) Area Assn. for the Retarded, 1972. 1st lt. U.S. Army C.E., 1955-57. Mem. Masons. Republican. Episcopalian. Avocation: amature radio. Home and Office: 19225 Mesa St Rialto CA 92377-4558

STRAIGHT, RICHARD COLEMAN, photobiologist; b. Rivesville, W.Va., Sept. 8, 1937. BA, U. Utah, 1961, PhD in Molecular Biology, 1967. Asst. dir. radiation biology summer inst. U. Utah, 1961-63; supervisory chemist med. svc. VA Hosp., 1965—; dir. VA Venom Rsch. Lab., 1975—; adminstrv. officer rsch. svc. VA Ctr., 1980—; dir. Dixon laser inst. U. Utah, Salt Lake City, 1985-90; pres. Western Inst. for Biomed. Rsch., Salt Lake City, 1990—; dir. Utah Ctr. for Photo Medicine, Salt Lake City, 1993—. Assoc. editor Lasers in Surgery and Medicine, 1990-95, Jour. Biomed. Optics, 1995—. Mem. AAAS, Am. Chem. Soc., Am. Soc. Photobiology, Biophysics Soc., Am. Soc. for Laser Medicine and Surgery, Utah Life Sci. Industries Assn. (charter). Achievements include research in photodynamic action on biomonomers and biopolymers, tumor immunology, effect of antigens on mammary adenocarcinoma of C3H mice, biochemical changes in aging, venom toxicology, mechanism of action of photoactive drugs, optical imaging and spectroscopy. Office: VAMC/Univ of Utah Western Inst Biomed Rsch 500 Foothill Dr Salt Lake City UT 84148-0001

STRAIN, DOUGLAS CAMPBELL, precision instrument company executive; b. Spokane, Wash., Oct. 24, 1919; s. Clayton Preston and Edith (Crockatt) S.; m. Leila Cleo Karicofe, June 10, 1943; children: James Douglas, Barbara Joanne, Gordon Campbell. BSEE, Calif. Inst. Tech., 1948; PhD (hon.), Internat. Coll. of the Cayman Islands, 1979. Registered profl. engr., Oreg. Design engr. Nat. Tech. Labs. Beckman Instruments, South Pasadena, Calif., 1948-49; v.p. research and engring. Brown Electro Measurements Corp., Portland, Oreg., 1949-53; pres. Electro Sci. Industries, Inc., Portland, 1953-80, chmn. bd., 1953-85, vice chmn. bd., 1985—; pres. Sunset Sci. Park, Inc., Portland, 1963-70; bd. dirs. Org. Software Inc., Portland, U.S. Bancorp/U.S. Nat. Bank, Portland, Optical Data, Inc., Lattice, Portland, Oreg. Grad. Ctr.; bd. overseers The Org. Health Sci. U. Portland. Patentee optical and electronic devices. Chmn. Tri-County Colls. for Oreg.'s Future, 1964-68, treas., 1968—; mem. Gov.'s Adv. Council for Oreg. Tech. Services, 1966-70; chmn. adv. panel to electricity div. Nat. Bur. Standards, Nat. Acad. Sci., 1971-74; mem. nat. metric adv. panel Commerce Dept., 1969-70; trustee Internat. Coll. of Caymans, 1971—, Scis. of Tomorrow, Pacific U., past pres.; assoc. Calif. Inst. Tech., 1975—; chmn. Oreg. Alumni Fund, 1975—; bd. dirs. Vols. Internat. Tech. Assistance. Recipient Bausch and Lomb Sci. award, 1938, Reed Coll. award, 1975, Wildhack award Nat. Conf. Standards Labs., 1977, Disting. Alumni award Calif. Inst. Tech., 1986; Menninger Found. fellow. Fellow Instrument Soc. Am. (nat. pres. 1970-71); mem. IEEE (sr.), Sci. Apparatus Makers Assn. (chmn., indsl. instrument sect. 1966-68, bd. dirs. 1973-76), Nat. Mgmt. Assn. (pres. Portland chpt. 1956-57, v.p. West Coast 1962-63), AAAS, Western Electronic Mfrs. Assn. (bd. dirs. 1956-57), Nat. Soc. Profl. Engrs., Precision Mgmt. Assn. (sr.), Electron Microscope Soc. Am. Clubs: City (research bd.), Multnomah (Portland). Home: PO Box 749 729 Shadow Mountain Lane Grand Lake CO 80447 Office: Electro Scientific Industries Inc 13900 NW Science Park Dr Portland OR 97229-5411

STRAIN, JAMES ELLSWORTH, pediatrician, retired association administrator; b. Lincoln, Nebr., Apr. 23, 1923; s. Elmer Ellsworth and Tessa Elizabeth (Stevens) S.; m. Ruby Lee Shepard; children: James A., John D., Janet M. Strain McKinney, Jeffrey Lee Phillips-Strain. AB, Phillips U., Enid, Okla., 1945; MD, U. Colo., Denver, 1947. Diplomate Am. Bd. Pediatrics (examiner 1984-89, mem. 1989-93, emeritus mem. 1993—). Intern Mpls. Gen. Hosp., 1947-48; resident in pediatrics Denver Children's Hosp., 1948-50, pres. med. staff, 1964, dir. genetic unit, 1982-86; pvt. practice specializing in pediatrics, Denver, 1950-86; exec. dir. Am. Acad. Pediatrics, Elk Grove Village, Ill., 1986-93, ret., 1993; pres. med. bd. Colo. Gen. Hosp., 1969-70; clin. prof. pediatrics U. Colo. Med. Ctr., 1969-86, 93—, U. Chgo., 1987-93; mem. Colo. Med. Adv. Coun. for Title 19, 1968-75, chmn., 1968-71; mem. Task Force on Iowa Health Care Stds. Project, 1984-85; presenter numerous profl. confs. Mem. editorial bd. Pediatrics in Rev.; reviewer Jour. Pediatrics; contbr. articlest to profl. publs. Mem. Colo. Commn. on Children and Youth, 1971-75; trustee Phillips U., 1974—. Capt. U.S. Army, 1953-55. Recipient Disting. Alumnus award Phillips U., 1974, Florence Sabin award U. Colo., 1984, Excellence in Pub. Svc. award U.S. Surgeon Gen., 1988, Abraham Jacobi award AMA and Am. Acad. Pediatrics, 1994; James E. Strain Child Advocacy award established in his name Denver Children's Hosp., 1983. Fellow Am. Acad. Pediatrics (numerous offices and com. memberships at chpt., dist. and nat. level, including pres. 1982-83, Clifford Grulee award 1985); mem. APHA, AMA (mem. coun. sect. pediatrics 1971-93, chmn. coun. 1974-79, sect. del. 1978-79), Colo. Med. Soc. (mem. coun. dels. 1964-80), Denver Med. Soc. (mem. coun. dels. 1964-80), Can. Pediatric Soc., Ambulatory Pediatric Assn., Inst. Medicine, Alpha Omega Alpha. Republican. Mem. Disciples of Christ. Avocations: fishing, sports, reading.

STRAIN, LINDA ROGERS, elementary art educator; b. Greensburg, Ind., Sept. 10, 1943; d. Horace Sterling Rogers and Marguerite Coombs Caldwell; m. Harold Trenton Strain, Feb. 13, 1976; 1 child, Roger Lee. AA, Hinds Jr. Coll., Raymond, Miss., 1963; BA, Miss. Coll., Clinton, 1965. Art resource tchr. Jacksonville (Fla.) Pub. Schs., 1966-67; art tchr. Hapeville H.S., Atlanta, 1967-68, Nortan Elem. Sch., Louisville, 1968-71; elem. tchr. Gardendale Elem. Sch., Merritt Island, Fla., 1971-73; Congl. appointee Washington, 1973-75; art tchr. Clinton Jr. H.S., 1975-79, Pillow Acad., Greenwood, Miss., 1981-85, Warren (Ark.) H.S., 1985-86, Brown Elem. Sch., Star City, Ark., 1986—; tchr. liaison At The Arts and Sci. Ctr., Pine Bluff, Ark., 1992—; mem. Ark. Arts Coun., Little Rock, 1994—; reader Winthrop Rockefeller Found., Little Rock, 1993—. Author: Jefferson County Art Curriculum Guide, 1970. Recipient award for patriotic svc. U.S. Savs. Bonds, 1994; Rockefeller grantee, 1992. Mem. DAR, Ark. Art Educators (newsletter editor 1991—, named Elem. Art Educator for Ark. 1992, Ark. Art Educator 1996), Ark. Edn. Assn. Democrat. Baptist. Avocations: reading, travel. Home: 303 Marie Dr Warren AR 71671-3435 Office: Brown Elem Sch 201 Ashley Star City AR 71667

STRAIT, GEORGE, country music vocalist; b. Pearsall, Tex., 1952; m. Norma. Degree in Agr., S.W. Tex. State U. Albums include Easy Come, Easy Go, Right or Wrong, Strait from the Heart, Strait Country, Does Ft. Worth Ever Cross Your Mind, 1985 (Country Music Assn. Album of Yr. 1985), Pure Country, 1986, No. 7, Something Special, 1986, Ocean Front Property, 1987, If You Aint Lovin' (You Aint Livin'), 1988, Beyond the Blue Neon, 1989, Livin' It Up, 1990, Ten Strait Hits, 1991, Chill of An Early Fall, 1991, Greatest Hits Volume I, II, Lead On, other platinum albums; #1 country hits include Fool Hearted Memory, 1982, Amarillo By Morning, 1983, You Look So Good in Love, 1984, The Chair, 1986, Baby Blue, 1989, Beyond the Blue Moon, 1989, Baby's Gotten Good At Goodbye, 1989, Love Without End, Amen, 1990, I've Come to Expect It From You, 1990, Chill of An Early Fall, 1991, If I Know Me, 1991, The Big One, 1995; (movie) Pure Country, 1992. Served with U.S. Army, until 1975. Recipient Entertainer of Yr. award Country Music Assn., 1989, 90, Entertainer of Yr. award Acad. Country Music, 1990; named Male Vocalist of Yr. Country Music Assn., 1985, 86, Male Vocalist of Yr. Acad. Country Music, 1984, 85, 89, SRO Touring Artist of Yr., 1990, Top Country Vocalist Am. Music Awards, 1991.

STRAIT, VIOLA EDWINA WASHINGTON, librarian; b. El Paso, Tex., Aug. 29, 1925; d. Leroy Wentworth and Viola Edwina (Wright) Washington; m. Freeman Adams, Mar. 6, 1943; 1 child, Norma Jean (Mrs. Louis Lee James); m. Clifford Moody, Jan. 8, 1950; 1 child, Viola Edwina III (Mrs. Paul M. Cunningham); m. Amos O. Strait, Dec. 9, 1972. Bus. cert., Tillotson Coll., 1946, BA, 1948; MS in Libr. Sci., U. So. Calif., 1954. Substitute tchr. El Paso Pub. Schs., 1948; sec., bookkeeper U.S.O.-YWCA, El Paso, 1948-50; libr. asst. Spl. Svcs. Libr., Ft. Bliss, Tex., 1950-53, libr., 1954-71; equal employment opportunity officer Ft. Bliss, 1971-72; dep. equal employment opportunity officer Long Beach (Calif.) Naval Shipyard, 1972-85; with Temporary Job Mart, Torrance, Calif., 1986-87; substitute tchr. Ysleta Ind. Sch. Dist., 1988-89; profl. libr. Eastwood Hts. Elem. Sch., 1989-90; sec. Shiloh Bapt. Ch., El Paso, 1991-92; br. mgr. El Paso Pub. Libr., 1992—. Sec. Sunday sch. Bapt. Ch., 1956-66, min. music, 1958-72, supr. young adult choir, 1966-72, pres. sr. choir, 1969-71; disc jockey Sta. KELP, El Paso, 1970-72; host radio show Sta. KTEP, U. Tex., El Paso, 1994—. Mem. Am. Libr. Assn., Border Region Libr. Assn. (chmn. scholarship com. 1970), Fed. Bus. Assn., Equal Opportunity Assn., Toastmasters Internat., NAACP, Alpha Kappa Alpha, Order Ea. Star. Democrat. Baptist. Avocations: playing the piano and organ, public speaking, reading, ocean view dining. Home: 1667 Nancy Lopez Ln El Paso TX 79936-5410 Office: El Paso Pub Libr Vets Park Br 5303 Salem Dr El Paso TX 79924-1801

STRAITON, ARCHIE WAUGH, electrical engineering educator; b. Arlington, Tex., Aug. 27, 1907; s. John and Jeannie (Waugh) S.; m. Esther McDonald, Dec. 28, 1932; children: Janelle (Mrs. Thomas Henry Holman), Carolyn (Mrs. John Erlinger). BSEE, U. Tex., 1929, MA, 1931, PhD, 1939. Engr. Bell Telephone Labs., N.Y.C., 1929-30; from instr. to assoc. prof. Tex. Coll. Arts and Industries, 1931-41, prof., 1941-43, head dept. engring., 1941-43; faculty U. Tex., Austin, 1943—; prof. U. Tex., 1948-63, dir. elec. engring. research lab., 1947-72, Ashbel Smith prof. elec. engring., 1963-89, Ashbel Smith prof. emeritus, 1989—, chmn. dept., 1966-71, acting v.p., grad. dean, 1972-73. Contbr. articles to profl. jours. Fellow IEEE (Thomas A. Edison medal 1990); mem. NAE, Sigma Xi, Tau Beta Pi, Eta Kappa Nu. Home: 4212 Far West Blvd Austin TX 78731-2804

STRAITS, BEVERLY JOAN, gynecologist; b. Aurora, Ill., Jan. 29, 1939; d. Ernest Joseph and Mildred Betty (Shobe) S.; children: Kell Donald, Jill Elizabeth. BA, Carleton Coll., 1961; MD, Northwestern U., 1965. Diplomate in gynecology and obstetrics. Intern Passavant Hosp., Chgo., 1965-66; residency Lutheran Hosp., Milw., 1966-69; pvt. practice Wheat Ridge, Colo., 1969—. Fellow Am. Coll. Obstetrics & Gynecology. Avocations: skiing, camping. Office: 7855 W 38th Ave Wheat Ridge CO 80033-6109

STRAKA, LASZLO RICHARD, publishing consultant; b. Budapest, Hungary, June 22, 1934; came to U.S., 1950, naturalized, 1956; s. Richard J. and

Elisabeth (Roeck) S.; m. Eva K. von Viczian, Jan. 20, 1962 (div. May 1981); children: Eva M., Monika E., Viktoria K. B.A. cum laude, NYU, 1959. Acct. Greatrex Ltd., N.Y.C., 1952-53; pres. Maxwell Macmillan Internat. Pub. Group, N.Y.C., 1991-92; with Pergamon Press, Inc., Elmsford, N.Y., 1954-90, v.p., 1964-68, exec. v.p., treas., 1968-74, pres., 1974-75, 80-88, chmn. bd., 1975-77, 88-90, vice chmn. bd., 1977-80, 88-89, also dir.; vice chmn. bd. Pergamon Books Ltd., Oxford, Eng., 1986-88; group v.p. Macmillan Inc., N.Y.C., 1989-91; pub. cons., 1992—; treas. Brit. Book Centre, Inc., N.Y.C., 1956-67; pres. Pergamon Holding Corp., 1981-86; chmn. bd. Microforms Internat., Inc., 1971-87. d. dirs., sec. Szechenyi Istvan Soc., N.Y.C., 1967-80, 89-93. Mem. Phi Beta Kappa. Club: K.C. Home and Office: 80 Radnor Ave Croton On Hudson NY 10520-2610

STRALEM, PIERRE, retired stockbroker; b. Chappaqua, N.Y., Oct. 17, 1909; s. Casimir Ignace and Edithe (Neustadt) S.; m. Nancy Lou D.A. Coffyn, June 11, 1936 (dec. Aug. 1995). A.B., Princeton, 1932. With Hallgarten & Co. (mems. N.Y. Stock Exchange), 1933—, partner, 1941-74; v.p., dir. Moseley Hallgarten Estabrook & Weeden Inc., 1974-79. Bd. dirs. George Jr. Republic. Mem. Court Club (Princeton, N.J.), Princeton Club (N.Y.C.). Home: 651 Bering Dr Houston TX 77057-2133

STRALING, PHILLIP FRANCIS, bishop; b. San Bernardino, Calif., Apr. 25, 1933; s. Sylvester J. and Florence E. (Robinson) S. BA, U. San Diego, 1963; MS in Child and Family Counseling, San Diego State U., 1971. Ordained priest Roman Catholic Ch., 1959, consecrated bishop, 1978. Mem. faculty St. John Acad., El Cajon, Calif., 1959-60, St. Therese Acad., San Diego, 1960-63; chaplain Newman Club, San Diego State U., 1960-72; mem. faculty St. Francis Sem., San Diego, 1972-76; pastor Holy Rosary Parish, San Bernardino, 1976-78; bishop Diocese of San Bernardino, 1978-95; pub. Inland Cath. newspaper, 1979-95; chmn. com. on lay ministry U.S. Cath. Conf./Nat. Cath. Conf. Bishops, 1993—; bishop of Reno, Nev., 1995—; bd. dirs. Calif. Assn. Cath. Campus Mins., 1960s; exec. sec. Diocesan Synod II, 1972-76; Episcopal vicar San Bernardino Deanery, 1976-78. Mem. Nat. Cath. Campus Ministries Assn. (bishop rep. 1992—). Office: PO Box 1211 Reno NV 89504-1211

STRAM, HANK LOUIS, former professional football coach, television and radio commentator; b. Chgo., Jan. 3, 1923; s. Henry L. and Nellie (Boots) S.; m. Phyllis Marie Pesha, Nov. 27, 1953; children: Henry Raymond, Dale Alan, Stuart Madison, Julia Anne, Gary Baxter, Mary Nell. Grad., Purdue U., 1948. Offensive football coach, head baseball coach Purdue U., 1948-55; offensive football coach So. Meth. U., 1956, Notre Dame U., 1958, U. Miami, 1959; head football coach Kansas City Chiefs, 1960-74, New Orleans Saints, 1976-77; color commentator CBS Sports, N.Y.C., 1978—, CBS Radio Football Broadcasts, 1978-85. Served with USAAF, 1943-46. Recipient Big 10 medal for athletes and scholarship Big 10 Conf., 1948; named Profl. Football Coach of Year Knute Rockne Club Am. and Ft. Lauderdale Touchdown Club, 1962. Office: care CBS Sports 51 W 52nd St New York NY 10019-6119*

STRANAHAN, ROBERT PAUL, JR., lawyer; b. Louisville, Oct. 29, 1929; s. Robert Paul and Anna May (Payne) S.; m. Louise Perry, May 12, 1956; children: Susan Dial, Robert Paul, Carol Payne. A.B., Princeton U., 1951; J.D., Harvard U., 1954. Bar: D.C. 1954, Md. 1964. Assoc. Wilmer & Broun, Washington, 1957-62; ptnr. Wilmer, Cutler & Pickering, Washington, 1963-94, of counsel, 1995—; professorial lectr. Nat. Law Ctr., George Washington U., 1969-72. Served to 1st lt. USMCR, 1954-57. Mem. ABA, D.C. Bar Assn., Met. Club (Washington), Gridiron Club (Washington), Chevy Chase (Md.) Club. Home: 5316 Cardinal Ct Bethesda MD 20816-2908 Office: Wilmer Cutler & Pickering 2445 M St NW Washington DC 20037-1435

STRAND, MARION DELORES, social service administrator; b. Kansas City, Mo., Dec. 19, 1927; d. Henry Franklin and Julia Twyman (Noland) Pugh; m. Robert Carmen Scipioni, Aug. 2, 1947 (dec. 1984); children: Mark, Brian, Roberta, Laura, Steven, Mary,Angela, Julie, Victor, Robert, Lawrence; m. Donald John Strand, Sept. 1, 1985. BA, U. Kans., 1948; MS, SUNY, Brockport, 1975. Counselor N.Y. Dept. Labor, Rochester, 1971-75, 77-79; regulatory adminstr. N.Y. Dept. Social Svcs., Rochester, 1976-77, 79-81; pres. Greater Rochester Svcs., Inc. (doing bus. as Scribes & Scripts), 1982—; founder Ctr. for Law Access and Document Preparation. Columnist, local newspaper. Active polit. campaigns for women candidates, 1981—; UN envoy Unitarian Ch., Rochester, 1988-92; fin. chair William Warfield Scholarship Com., Rochester, 1988-90; chair bd. govt. affairs Genesee Valley Arthritis Found., Rochester, 1988-90; mem. parade com. 95/75 Celebration of Monroe County, 1995; mem. Lyell Av. Revitalization Com. Mem. NOW (pres. child care com. Greater Rochester sect. 1987-88, chair family issues task force), AAUW (bd. dirs., cmty. rep. Greater Rochester br.), DAR (Irondequoit chpt.), Greater Rochester C. of C. (legis. com., small bus. com. 1987—, bd. dirs. women's coun. 1981-91, pres. 1989-90), Susan B. Anthony Rep. Women's Club (program com., 1st v.p. 1994, co-chair Greater Rochester Coalition for Choice 1994-95) Golden Girls Investment Club (founder), Phi Beta Kappa, Psi Chi. Avocations: tennis, golf, art, organ playing. Home and Office: Greater Rochester Svcs Inc 105 Elmwood Ter Rochester NY 14620-3703

STRAND, MARK, poet; b. Summerside, P.E.I., Can., Apr. 11, 1934; came to U.S., 1938.; s. Robert Joseph and Sonia (Apter) S.; m. Antonia Ratensky, Sept. 14, 1961 (div. June 1973); 1 dau., Jessica; m. Julia Rumsey Garretson, Mar. 15, 1976; 1 son, Thomas Summerfield. BA, Antioch Coll., 1957; BFA, Yale, 1959; MA, U. Iowa, 1962. Instr. English U. Iowa, 1962-65; asst. prof. Mt. Holyoke Coll., 1967; assoc. prof. Bklyn. Coll., 1971-72; Bain-Swiggett lectr. Princeton, 1973; Hurst prof. poetry Brandeis U., 1974-75; prof. U. Utah, 1981-93; U.S. poet laureate Library of Congress, Washington, 1990-91; prof. Johns Hopkins U., 1994—; Fulbright lectr. U. Brazil, Rio de Janeiro, 1965-66; adj. assoc. prof. Columbia U., 1969-72; vis. prof. U. Wash., 1968, 70, U. Va., 1977, Wesleyan U., 1979, Harvard U., 1980; vis. lectr. Yale, 1969-70, U. Va., 1976, Calif. State U., Fresno, 1977, U. Calif., Irvine, 1979. Author: Sleeping with One Eye Open, 1964, Reasons for Moving, 1968, Darker, 1970, The Story of Our Lives, 1973 (Edgar Allan Poe award Acad. Am. Poets 1974), The Sargeantville Notebook, 1974, The Monument, 1978, Elegy for My Father, 1978, The Late Hour, 1978, Selected Poems, 1980, The Planet of Lost Things, 1982, The Night Book, 1983, Mr. and Mrs. Baby and Other Stories, 1985, Rembrandt Takes a Walk, 1986, William Bailey, 1987, The Continuous Life, 1990, Dark Harbor, 1993, Hopper, 1994; editor: The Contemporary American Poets, 1968, New Poetry of Mexico, 1970, 18 Poems from Quechua, 1971, The Owl's Insomnia, 1973, The Best American Poetry 1991, The Golden Ecco Anthology, 1994; co-editor: Another Republic: Seventeen European and South American Writers, 1976, The Art of the Real, 1983, Traveling in the Family, 1987; translator: Souvenir of the Ancient World, 1976. Recipient award Am. Acad. and Inst. Arts and Letters, 1975, Utah Gov.'s award in arts, 1992, Bobbitt Nat. prize for poetry, 1992, Bollingen prize for poetry Yale Univ. Libr., 1993; Fulbright scholar in Italy, 1960-61; Ingram Merrill Found. grantee, 1966; Nat. Endowment for Arts grantee, 1967-68, 78-79, 86-87; Rockefeller Found. grantee, 1968-69; Guggenheim fellow, 1975-76; Acad. Am. Poets fellow, 1979; MacArthur Found. fellow, 1987. Fellow Acad. Am. Poets; mem. Am. Acad. and Inst. Arts and Letters. Office: c/o Harry Ford Knopf Publishers Inc 201 E 50th St New York NY 10022-7703

STRAND, RAY WALTER, general contractor; b. Seattle, July 23, 1924; s. Arvid O. and Antonia (Sjogren) S.; m. Luella Oak, Oct. 1948 (div. 1959); m. Ruby Good, Jan. 8, 1960; children: Timothy Ray, Donald Brent. Student, U. Wash., 1945-48. Ptnr. Strand & Sons, Seattle, 1939-54; CEO, pres. Strand Inc., Seattle and Bellevue, Wash., 1954-92; chmn., CEO Strand Hunt Constrn., Kirkland, Wash., 1992-94. Staff sgt. U.S. Army Air Corps, 1943-45. Republican. Congregational. Avocations: golf, fishing, hunting. Office: Strand Trust 5800 Princeton Ave NE Seattle WA 98105-2134

STRAND, ROGER GORDON, federal judge; b. Peekskill, N.Y., Apr. 28, 1934; s. Ernest Gordon Strand and Lisabeth Laurine (Phin) Steinmetz; m. Joan Williams, Nov. 25, 1961. AB, Hamilton Coll., 1955; LLB, Cornell U., 1961; grad., Nat. Coll. State Trial Judges, 1968. Bar: Ariz. 1961, U.S. Dist. Ct. Ariz. 1961, U.S. Supreme Ct. 1980. Assoc. Fennemore, Craig, Allen & McClennen, Phoenix, 1961-67; judge Ariz. Superior Ct., Phoenix, 1967-85, U.S. Dist. Ct. Ariz., Phoenix, 1985—; assoc. presiding judge Ariz. Superior Ct., 1971-85; lectr. Nat. Jud. Coll., Reno, 1978-87. Past pres. cen. Ariz. chpt. Arthritis Found. Lt. USN, 1955-61. Mem. ABA, Ariz. Bar Assn., Maricopa County Bar Assn., Nat. Conf. Fed. Trial Judges, Phi Delta Phi, Aircraft Owners and Pilots Assn. Lodge: Rotary. Avocations: computer applications, golf, fishing. Home: 5825 N 3rd Ave Phoenix AZ 85013-1537 Office: US Dist Ct Courthouse and Fed Bldg 230 N 1st Ave Ste 3013 Phoenix AZ 85025-0002

STRANDBERG, JOHN DAVID, comparative pathologist; b. Alexandria, Minn., Aug. 28, 1939; s. Winfred Carl and Evelyn Joyce (Studlien) S. AB, Johns Hopkins U., 1960; DVM, Cornell U., 1964, PhD, 1968. Diplomate Am. Coll. Vet. Pathologists. USPHS-NIH postdoctoral fellow Cornell U., Ithaca, N.Y., 1964-67; fellow, resident in pathology Sch. Medicine, Johns Hopkins U., Balt., 1966-67; instr. dept. pathology/divsn. animal medicine Sch. Medicine Johns Hopkins U., Balt., 1967-68, asst. prof. pathology/divsn. lab. animal medicine, 1968-75, dir. comparative pathology tng. program Sch. Medicine, 1973—, asst. prof. pathobiology Sch. Hygiene and Pub. Health, 1974-77, acting dir. divsn. lab. animal medicine Sch. Medicine, 1974-76, assoc. prof. pathology and comparative medicine, 1975—, assoc. prof. pathobiology Sch. Hygiene and Pub. Health, 1977—, dir. divsn. comparative medicine Sch. Medicine, 1983—; vis. scientist Marine Biol. Lab., Woods Hole, Mass., 1993; cons., panelist, presenter in field; mem. peer rev. group Nat. Zool. Park, 1987, 88, 90; chmn. Md. Coun. on Sci. Use of Animals, 1989—; mem. adv. con. Nat. Ctr. for Rsch. Resources NIH, 1991—; mem. adv. bd. Nat. Aquarium in Balt., 1986—, Ctr. for Alternatives to Animal Testing, Balt., 1985—. Mem. editorial rev. bd. The Biomedical Investigator's Handbook, 1987; contbr. articles to profl. publs. V.p. Balt. Zool. Soc., 1978-82, chmn. med. com., 1973-86. Mem. AAAS, AMVA, Am. Coll. Vet. Pathologists (com. on tng. programs 1976-82), U.S. and Can. Acad. Pathology, Am. Assn. Pathologists, Md. State Vet. Med. Assn. (com. on liaison to humane orgns. 1986-88, com. on registration of vet. technicians 1977—), Am. Soc. Microbiology, Electron Microscopy Soc. Am., Med. Zool. Soc., Wildlife Disease Assn., Am. Soc. Lab. Animal Practitioners, Phi Beta Kappa, Phi Kappa Phi, Phi Zeta.

STRANDBERG, MALCOM WOODROW PERSHING, physicist; b. Box Elder, Mont., Mar. 9, 1919; s. Malcom and Ingeborg (Riestad) S.; m. Harriet Elisabeth Bennett, Aug. 2, 1947 (dec.); children—Josiah R.W., Susan Abby, Elisabeth G., Malcom B. S.B., Harvard Coll., 1941; Ph.D., M.I.T., 1948. Research asso. M.I.T., Cambridge, 1941-48; asst. prof. physics M.I.T., 1948-53, asso. prof., 1953-60, prof., 1960—. Author: Microwave Spectroscopy, 1954. Fellow Am. Phys. Soc., Am. Acad. Arts and Scis., IEEE, AAAS; mem. Am. Assn. Physics Tchrs. Episcopalian. Patentee in field. Home: 82 Larchwood Dr Cambridge MA 02138-4639 Office: Mass Inst Tech 26-353 Cambridge MA 02139

STRANDBERG, REBECCA NEWMAN, lawyer; b. Ft. Smith, Ark., Apr. 22, 1951; d. Russell Lynn and Doris Jean (Lindsey) Newman; m. Jeffrey Eugene Strandberg, Nov. 23, 1979; children: Lindsey Katherine, Russell Jeffrey. BA, Tex. Christian U., 1973; JD, So. Meth. U., 1976. Bar: Tex. 1976, Md. 1981, D.C. 1983. Field atty. NLRB, New Orleans, 1976-79; legis. asst. Senator Dale Bumpers, Washington, 1979-81; pvt. practice, Montgomery County, Md., 1981-92; ptnr. Carlin & Strandberg PA, Bethesda, Md., 1992—. Vice-pres. bd. dirs. Share-A-Ride Corp., Montgomery County, 1984; bd. mgrs. Woodside Meth. Ch., 1989-92; mem. Holy Cross Community Hosp Quality Evaluation Com., 1989—; CLE chmn. Montgomery County Bar: Am. Inns of Ct., 1990-92. Named Chmn. of Yr. Montgomery County Bar, 1992-93. Mem. ABA (litigation, labor and employment law sect. 1985—), Md. State Bar (bd. govs. 1992—, spl. com. devel. guidelines for prevention of sexual harassment 1994—, co-chair centenial pub. svc. project subcom.), Silver Spring C. of C., Montgomery County Women's Bar Assn. (chmn. membership 1982-83), Md. Women's Bar Assn., Silver Spring Bus. and Profl. Women (pres. 1984-85), SBA Women in Bus. (advocate 1982), Women's Bar D.C. Office: Carlin & Strandberg PA 4405 E West Hwy Ste 603 Bethesda MD 20814-4537

STRANDJORD, PAUL EDPHIL, physician, educator; b. Mpls., Apr. 5, 1931; s. Edphil Nels and RuBelle Pearl (Corneliusen) S.; m. Margaret Thomas, June 27, 1953; children: Thomas Paul, Scott Nels. BA, U. Minn., 1951, MA, 1952; MD, Stanford U., 1959. Intern U. Minn., Mpls., 1959-60; resident U. Minn., 1960-63, dir. div. chemistry, dept. lab. medicine, 1963-69, asso. dir. clin. labs. dept. lab. medicine, 1967-69; asso. prof. lab. medicine U. Wash., 1969, prof., chmn. dept. lab. medicine, 1969—; prof. emeritus, 1994—; cons. VA Hosps. Author: (with E.S. Benson) Multiple Laboratory Screening, 1969, (with G. Schmer) Coagulation-Current Research and Clinical Applications, 1973. Pres. U. Wash. Physicians. With USN, 1952-55. Recipient Borden award Stanford U., 1959, Watson award U. Minn., 1962, Gerald T. Evans award Acad. Clin. Lab. Physicians and Scientists, 1976. Fellow Am. Soc. Clin. Pathologists; mem. AAAS, Acad. Clin. Lab. Physicians and Scientists (pres.), Am. Assn. Clin. Chemistry, Am. Chem. Soc., Am. Fedn. Clin. Research, Internat. Acad. Pathology, Assn. Pathology Chmn. Home: 9410 Lake Washington Blvd NE Bellevue WA 98004-5409 Office: U Wash Dept Lab Medicine SB-10 Seattle WA 98195

STRANDNESS, DONALD EUGENE, JR., surgeon; b. Bowman, N.D., Sept. 22, 1928; s. Donald Eugene and Merinda Clarine (Peterson) S.; m. Edith Victoria Olund, June 30, 1957; children: Erik, Tracy, Jill, Sandra. B.A., Pacific Luth. U., 1950; M.D., U. Wash., 1954. Rotating intern Phila. Gen. Hosp., 1954-55; resident U. Wash. Sch. Medicine Integrated Program, 1955-57, 59-62; research fellow Nat. Heart Inst., 1959-60; clin. investigator VA Hosp., Seattle, 1962-65; NIH Career Devel. awardee VA Hosp., 1965-68; pvt. practice medicine specializing in surgery Seattle, 1962—; instr. surgery Sch. Medicine, U. Wash., Seattle, 1962-63, asst. prof., 1963-66, assoc. prof., 1966-70, prof., 1970—, head peripheral vascular divsn., 1971-95; mem. VA Merit Rev. Com. in Surgery, 1984; mem. cardiology com. Nat. Heart, Lung Blood Inst., 1985. Author: Duplex Scanning in Vascular Disorders, 1990; co-author: Hemodynamics for Surgeons, 1975, Ultrasonic Techniques in Angiology, 1975, Selected Topics in Venous Disease, 1981; editor: Collateral Circulation in Clinical Surgery, 1969, Peripheral Arterial Disease--A Physiologic Approach, 1969; co-editor: Vascular Diseases, 1987, Duplex Ultrasound, 1989; assoc. editor: Jour. Vascular Surgery, 1979, Handbook of Clinical Ultrasound, 1978, Noninvasive Diagnostic Techniques in Vascular Disease, 1978, 85, Haimovici's Vascular Surgery, 1995; editor: Duplex Scanning in Vascular Disorders, 1990, 93; co-editor: Vascular Diseases: Surgical and Interventional Therapy, 1993; mem. editl. adv. bd. Vascular Diagnosis and Therapy, 1980; mem. editl. bd. Jour. Vascular Surgery, 1983, Jour. Clin. Physiology, 1981, VASA, 1983, Jour. Vascular Medicine and Biology, 1989, Stroke, 1985; sect. editor Echocardiography, 1985; adv. editor Jour. Cardiovasc. Surgery, 1984, Circulation, 1991; exec. editor: Jour. Vascular Investigation, 1995—; editor-in-chief: Vascular Surgery, 1995—. Served with USAF, 1957-59. Recipient Alumnus award Pacific Luth. U., 1980, Cid Dos Santos prize, 1980, Merit award Nat. Heart, Lung and Blood Inst., 1987, Albion O. Bernstein award N.Y. State Med. Assn., 1995. Fellow ACS; mem. Interat. Soc. Thrombosis and Haemostasis, Am. Surg. Assn., North Pacific Surg. Assn., Soc. for Vascular Surgery (pres. 1988), Western Vascular Soc. (pres. 1988), Am. Venous Forum (pres.-elect 1996), Soc. Univ. Surgeons, Intnerat. Cardiovascular Soc., Am. Inst. Ultrasound in Medicine (bd. govs. 1990-92), Will C. Sealy Surg. Soc. (hon.), So. Assn. for Vascular Surgery (hon.). Home: 105 Cedar Crest Ln Bellevue WA 98004-6725 Office: U Wash Sch Medicine 1959 NE Pacific St Seattle WA 98195-0004

STRANDQUIST, JOHN HERBERT, social services administrator; b. Menominee, Mich., June 29, 1929; s. John H. and Mary A. (Van Calligan) S.; m. Mary Gabrielle Thomas, Nov. 22, 1952; children: John H. III, Mark J., Michael T., Julie P. Headland, Bridget M. Mills, Blaise R., Skye M. Kirby, Peter S. BA, George Washington U., 1968. Cert. assn. exec., Am. Soc. Assn. Execs.; sr. profl. in human resources, Soc. Human Resource Mgmt. Enlisted USMC, 1948, advanced through ranks to lt. col., 1967, retired, 1973; asst. v.p. George Washington U., Washington, 1973-77; sr. v.p. Soc. for Human Resource Mgmt., Alexandria, Va., 1977-90; pres. Am. Assn. of Motor Vehicle Adminstrs., Arlington, Va., 1990—, also bd. dirs.; bd. dirs. AAMVAnet, Inc., IRP, Inc., Arlington. Mem. Belle Haven Country Club, Rotary (Paul Harris fellow 1992). Avocations: golf, sailing. Office: Am Assn Motor Vehicle Admns 4301 Wilson Blvd Ste 400 Arlington VA 22203

STRANG, CHARLES DANIEL, marine engine manufacturing company executive; b. Bklyn., Apr. 12, 1921; s. Charles Daniel and Anna Lincoln (Endner) S. B.M.E., Poly. Inst. Bklyn., 1943. Mem. mech. engring. staff MIT, 1947-51; v.p. engring., exec. v.p. Kiekhaefer Corp. div. Brunswick Corp., Fond du Lac, Wis., 1951-64; v.p. marine engring. Outboard Marine Corp., Waukegan, Ill., 1966-68; exec. v.p. Outboard Marine Corp., 1968-74, pres., gen. mgr., 1974-80, pres., CEO, 1980-82, chmn. bd., CEO, 1982-90, chmn., 1990-93; bd. dirs., chmn. mgmt. rev. com. Outboard Marine Corp., Waukegan, 1993—. Patentee engine design and marine propulsion equipment; contbr. research papers to sci. publs. Bd. dirs. Poly. Inst. N.Y. Served with USAAF, 1944-47. Mem. Am. Power Boat Assn. (past pres.), Soc. Automotive Engrs., Union Internat. Motorboating (continental v.p. N.Am.), Sigma Xi. Club: Waukegan Yacht. Home: 25679 W Florence Ave Antioch IL 60002-8734

STRANG, JAMES DENNIS, editor; b. Ashtabula, Ohio, June 23, 1945; s. Delbert Devoe and Mildred Edith (Green) S.; m. Margaret Florence Littell, Aug. 25, 1974; children: Megan Lisbeth, Amy Colleen, Benjamin Jefferson. BS in Journalism, Kent State U., 1969. Cert. firearms instr. Reporter The Star-Beacon, Ashtabula, Ohio, 1966, The Record-Courier, Kent, Ohio, 1966-69, The Cleve. Press, 1969-71; cons. Tom Rall & Assocs., Washington, 1971-72; reporter, editor The Plain Dealer, Cleve., 1973—; instr. journalism Lorain County C.C., Elyria, Ohio, 1973-74. Recipient Nat. Comdrs. award DAV, 1980, Best Editorial award AP Soc. Ohio, 1988. Mem. Nat. Conf. Editorial Writers, Soc. Profl. Journalists, Nat. Rifle Assn. (life). Unitarian-Universalist. Avocation: shooting sports. Office: The Plain Dealer 1801 Superior Ave E Cleveland OH 44114-2107

STRANG, RUTH HANCOCK, pediatric educator, pediatric cardiologist, priest; b. Bridgeport, Conn., Mar. 11, 1923; d. Robert Hallock Wright and Ruth (Hancock) S. BA, Wellesley Coll., 1944, postgrad., 1944-45; MD, N.Y. Med. Coll., 1949; MDiv, Seabury Western Theol. Sem., 1993. Diplomate Am. Bd. Pediat.; ordained deacon Episc. Ch., 1993, priest, 1994. Intern Flower and Fifth Ave. Hosp., N.Y.C., 1949-50, resident in pediatrics, 1950-52; mem. faculty N.Y. Med. Coll., N.Y.C., 1952-57; fellow cardiology Babies Hosp., N.Y.C., 1956-57, Harriet Lane Cardiac Clinic, Johns Hopkins Hosp., Balt., 1957-59, Children's Hosp., Boston, 1959-62; mem. faculty U. Mich., Univ. Hosp., Ann Arbor, 1962-89, prof. pediatrics, 1970-89, prof. emeritus, 1989—; priest-in-charge St. Johns Episcopal Ch., Howell, Mich., 1994—; dir. pediatrics Wayne County Gen. Hosp., Westland, Mich, 1965-85; mem. staff U. Mich. Hosps.; mem. med. adv. com. Wayne County chpt. Nat. Cystic Fibrosis Rsch. Found., 1966-80, chmn. med. adv. com. nat. found., Detroit, 1971-78; cons. cardiology Plymouth (Mich.) State Home and Tng. Sch., 1970-81. Author: Clinical Aspects of Operable Heart Disease, 1968; contbr. numerous articles to profl. jours. Mem. citizen's adv. coun. to Juvenile Ct., Ann Arbor, 1968-76; mem. med. adv. bd. Ann Arbor Continuing Edn. Dept., 1968-77; mem. Diocesan Com. for World Relief, Detroit, 1970-72, Am. Heart Assn. Mich. (v.p. 1989, pres. 1991); trustee Episcopal Med. Chaplaincy, Ann Arbor, 1971—; mem. bishop's com. St. Aidan's Episc. Ch., 1966-69, sec., 1966-68, vestry, 1973-76, 78-80, 84-86, 90-91, sr. warden, 1975, 76, 78, 80, 86, 90; del. Episc. Diocesan Conv., 1980, 91; bd. dirs. Livingston Cmty. Hospice, 1995—. Mem. AMA, Am. Acad. Pediatrics, Am. Coll. Cardiology, Mich. Med. Soc., Washtenaw County Med. Soc., N.Y. Acad. Medicine, Am. Heart Assn., Women's Rsch. Club (membership sec. 1966-67), Ambulatory Pediatric Assn., Am. Assn. Child Care in Hosps., Am. Assn. Med. Colls., Assn. Faculties of Pediatric Nurse Assn./Practitioners Programs (pres. 1978-81, exec. com. 1981-84), Episc. Clergy Assn. Mich., Northside Assn. Ministries (pres. 1975, 76, 79-80). Home: 4500 E Huron River Dr Ann Arbor MI 48105-9335

STRANG, SANDRA LEE, airline official; b. Greensboro, N.C., Apr. 22, 1936; d. Charles Edward and Lobelia Mae (Squires) S.; BA in English, U. N.C., 1960; MBA, U. Dallas, 1970. With American Airlines, Inc., 1960—, mgr. career devel. for women, N.Y.C., 1972-73, dir. selection and tng., 1974-75, sr. dir. selection, tng. and affirmative action, 1975-79, sr. dir. compensation and benefits, Dallas/Ft. Worth, Tex., 1979-84, dir. passenger sales tng. and devel., 1984—; regional sales mgr. Rocky Mountain Region, Denver, 1985—; pres. The SLS Group, Inc., (DBAs) Sales Leadership Seminars, Inc., Sr. Leadership Svcs., Inc., Svc. Leadership Seminars, Inc., Speakers, Lectrs., and Seminars, Inc, 1988—. AARP, Mem. Am. Mgmt. Assn., Assn. Advancement of Women into Mgmt., Am. Soc. Tng. and Devel., Am. Compensation Assn., Internat. Platform Assn. Home: 3493 E Euclid Ave Littleton CO 80121-3663

STRANG, STEPHEN EDWARD, magazine editor, publisher; b. Springfield, Mo., Jan. 31, 1951; s. A. Edward and Amy Alice (Farley) S.; m. Joy Darlene Ferrell, Aug. 19, 1972; children: Cameron Edward, Chandler Stephen. BS in Journalism, U. Fla., Gainesville, 1973; LittD (hon.), Lee Coll., 1995. Reporter Orlando Sentinel Star, Fla., 1973-76; editor Charisma mag. Calvary Assembly, Winter Park, Fla., 1976-81; pres. Strang Comm. Co., Lake Mary, Fla., 1981—; owner Creation House Books, 1986, Christian Retailing mag., 1986. Founding editor Charisma mag., 1975, Ministries Today mag., 1983; founding pub. CharismaLife Learning Resources, 1990, New Man mag., 1994. Mem. steering com. N.Am. Renewal Svcs. Com., 1985—; trustee Internat. Charismatic Bible Ministries, 1986—; pres. Christian Life Missions, 1991—. Recipient First Place award Nat. Writing Championship, William Randolph Hearst Found., 1973, Alumnus of Distinction award U. Fla. Coll. of Journalism and Comm., 1994, Industry of Yr. award for Seminole County, Fla., Econ. Devel. Commn. of Mid-Fla., 1994. Mem. Internat. Pentecostal Press Assn., Christian Booksellers Assn., Fla. Mag. Assn. (pres. 1979-80), Evang. Christian Pubs. Assn., Evang. Press Assn. Republican. Mem. Assemblies of God. Avocations: racquetball, golf. Office: Strang Comm Co 600 Rinehart Rd Lake Mary FL 32746-4872

STRANG, WILLIAM GILBERT, mathematician, educator; b. Chgo., Nov. 27, 1934; s. William Dollin and Mary Catherine (Finlay) S.; m. Jillian Mary Shannon, July 26, 1958; children—David, John, Robert. S.B., MIT, 1955; B.A. (Rhodes scholar), Oxford (Eng.) U., 1957; Ph.D. (NSF fellow), UCLA, 1959. Asst. prof. mathematics MIT, 1959-63, assoc. prof., 1963-66, prof., 1966—; pres. Wellesley-Cambridge Press; hon. prof. Xian Jiaotong U., People's Republic of China, 1980. Author: An Analysis of the Finite Element Method, 1973, Linear Algebra and Its Applications, 1976, Introduction to Applied Mathematics, 1986, Calculus, 1990, Introduction to Linear Algebra, 1993, Wavelets and Filter Banks, 1995. Recipient Chauvenet prize Math. Assn. Am., 1977; Sloan fellow, 1966-67; Fairchild scholar, 1981. Home: 7 Southgate Rd Wellesley MA 02181-6606 Office: MIT Math Dept Rm 2-240 Cambridge MA 02139

STRANGE, CURTIS NORTHROP, professional golfer; b. Norfolk, Va., Jan. 30, 1955; s. Thomas Wright Strange Jr. and Nancy (Ball) Neal; m. Sarah Jones; children: Thomas Wright III, David Clark. Student, Wake Forest U., 1974-76. Winner of Southeastern Amateur, 1973, NCAA, 1974, Western Amateur, 1974, Eastern Amateur, 1975, 76, North and South Amateur, 1975, 76, Va. State Amateur, 1976, World Amateur Cup, 1975, Walker Cup, 1974, Pensacola Open, 1979, Michelob-Houston Open, Mfrs. Hanover Westchester Classic, 1980, Panama Open, 1980, Sammy Davis Jr.-Greater Hartford Open, 1983, LaJet Classic, 1984, Honda Classic, Panasonic-Las Vegas Invitational, Canadian Open, 1985, Houston Open, 1986, Canadian Open, Fed. Express-St. Jude Classic, NEC World Series of Golf, 1987, Ind. Ins. Agent Open, Meml. Tournament, U.S. Open, 1988, 89, Nabisco Championships, 1988. Named to Collegiate Golf Hall of Fame, 1987, Wake Forest Hall of Fame, 1988, PGA Player-of-the-Yr., 1988; recipient Golf Writers Player-of-the-Yr. award, 1985, 87, 88, ABC Cup Japan, 1986, PGA Leading Money Winner 1985, 87-88. Avocation: hunting, fishing. Office: care IMG 1 Erieview Plz Ste 1300 Cleveland OH 44114-1715*

STRANGE, DONALD ERNEST, health care company executive; b. Ann Arbor, Mich., Aug. 13, 1944; s. Carl Britton and Donna Ernestine (Tenney) S.; m. Lyn Marie Purdy, Aug. 3, 1968; children: Laurel Lyn, Chadwick Donald. BA, Mich. State U., 1966, MBA, 1968. Asst. dir. Holland (Mich.) City Hosp., 1968-72, assoc. dir., 1972-74; exec. dir. Bascom Palmer Eye Inst./Anne Bates Leach Eye Hosp., U. Miami, Fla., 1974-77; v.p. strategic planning and rsch. Hosp. Corp. Am., Nashville, 1977-80; group v.p. Hosp. Corp. Am., Boston, 1980-82, regional v.p., 1982-87; chmn., chief exec. officer HCA Healthcare Can., 1985-87; exec. v.p. Avon Products, Inc., 1987-89;

chmn. Sigecom, Ltd., 1989-94, U.S. HomeCare Corp., 1990-91; exec. v.p., COO, dir. EPIC Healthcare Group, Dallas, 1991-93; chmn, CEO TransCare Corp., Dallas, 1993—; bd. dirs. Access Radiology, Inc., Boston, Bon Secours Health System, Balt. Author: Hospital Corporate Planning, 1981. Mem. Harvard Club (Boston), Nat. Arts Club (N.Y.). Republican. Episcopalian. Office: TransCare 3232 Mckinney Ave Ste 1160 Dallas TX 75204-2470

STRANGE, GARY R., medical educator; b. Mammoth Cave, Ky., Jan. 16, 1947. BS Biology and Chemistry summa cum laude, Western Ky. U., 1966, MA in Secondary Edn., 1968; postgrad. in pharmacology, Vanderbilt U., 1967-68; postgrad. in edn., U. Ky., 1968-69, MD, 1974. Diplomate Am. Bd. Emergency Medicine. Intern in ob-gyn. Letterman Army Med. Ctr., San Francisco, 1974-75; resident in emergency medicine U. So. Calif. Med. Ctr., L.A., 1977-79; attending staff emergency medicine various hosps., Calif., 1978-79, Grayson Cmty. Hosp., Leitchfield, Ky., 1979-81; dir. emergency medicine Ireland Army Cmty. Hosp., Ft. Knox, Ky., 1979-81; attending staff emergency medicine Hardin Meml. Hosp., Elizabethtown, Ky., 1980-81, various hosps., Ill., 1981—; dir. emergency medicine Mercy Hosp. and Med. Ctr., Chgo., 1981-86, assoc. dir. emergency medicine, 1986-90; chief emergency svc. U. Ill. Hosp., Chgo., 1990—; dir. U. Ill. Affiliated Hosps. Emergency Medicine Residency, Chgo., 1986-93; head dept. emergency medicine U. Ill. Coll. Medicine, 1990—, assoc. prof. emergency medicine, 1991—. Contbr. articles to profl. jours. Mem. adv. bd. on emergency med. svcs. for children Ill. Dept. Pub. Health, 1994—; mem. panels Agency for Health Care Policy/Rsch., 1994, 95; regional coord. Yr. of the Child Nat. Campaign, 1990-91; com. on pediatric emergency med. svcs. Nat. Rsch. Coun. Inst. Medicine, 1991-93. Hubbell scholar 1971-72; recipient Lange Med. Publs. award 1971-72. Fellow Am. Coll. Emergency Physicians (councillor 1987-92, coun. steering com. 1991-93, chmn. course devel. task force mktg. and diversification 1986-87, infant and childhood emergencies com. 1983—, chmn. pediatric emergencies com. 1988-90, chmn. sect. pediatric emergency medicine 1990-91, sects. task force 1992—, core content task force, Chgo., 1993); mem. AMA, Am. Bd. Emergency Medicine (bd. examiner panel 1987—), Ill. chpt. Am. Coll. Emergency Physicians (bd. dirs. 1985—, chmn. med. econs. com. 1984-87, edn. com. 1982-84, product devel. com. 1988—, various other coms.), Soc. Tchrs. Emergency Medicine (chmn. ednl. resources com. 1982-86), Soc. Acad. Emergency Medicine (chmn. edn. com. 1989-93, program com. 1989-93, task force on developing residencies in traditional med. schs. 1991-93, injury prevention com. 1991—), Ill. Med. Soc., Chgo. Heart Assn. (ACSL Affiliate Faculty 1986-91, 92—), Chgo. Med. Soc. (diagnostic and therapeutic tech. assessment panel 1991). Office: Univ Illinois Dept Emergency Medicine Univ Illinois Hospital Chicago IL 60612

STRANGE, HENRY HAZEN, judge; b. Oleary, N.B., Can., July 26, 1939; s. Henry Hazen and Marion Yvonne (Copp) S.; m. Heather Susan Carson, July 30, 1966; children: Elizabeth Marion, Jennifer Jody. BBA, U. N.B., Fredericton, 1961, BA, 1963, B in Civil Laws, 1964. Pvt. practice barrister, solicitor N.B., 1964-66; spl. asst. to dir. of pub. rels. Centennial Commn., N.B., 1966-67; crown prosecutor Dept. Justice, Ottawa, Ont., Can., 1967-71; dir. pub. prosecutors Dept. Justice, N.B., 1971-81; judge Provincial Ct., N.B., 1981—, chief judge, 1987—. Apptd. as Queen's Counsel, Min. of Justice/Atty. Gen., N.B., 1977. Mem. Can. Coun. Chief Judges (chmn. 1995). Avocations: salmon fishing, sports. Home: 664 Woodstock Rd, Fredericton, NB Canada E3B5N7 Office: Provincial Ct, PO Box 94, Oromocto, NB Canada E2V2G4

STRANGE, J. LELAND, computer company executive; b. Dallas, May 15, 1941; s. James Alton and Ola (Johnson) S.; m. Jane Hendrix Strange, Aug. 28, 1965; children—Mark, Cary, Ryan. BS Indsl. Mgmt., Ga. Tech. U., 1965, MBA, Ga. State U., 1968. Gen. mgr. Colonial Film & Equipment Co., Atlanta, 1967-69; pres. Cheese Villa Stores, Inc., 1969-74, Quadram Corp., 1981-83, Intelligent Systems Corp., 1983—(all Atlanta); prof. mktg. Mercer U., 1976-83; bd. dirs. Healthdyne Corp., Atlanta, Intelligent Systems Corp., Wave Air Corp, IQ Software Corp. Republican. Baptist. Office: Intelligent Systems Corp 4355 Shackleford Rd Norcross GA 30093-2931

STRANGWAY, DAVID WILLIAM, university administrator, geophysicist; b. Can., June 7, 1934. BA in Physics and Geology, U. Toronto, 1956, MA in Physics, 1958, PhD, 1960; DLittS (hon.), Victoria U., U. Toronto, 1986; DSc (hon.), Meml. U. Nfld., 1986, McGill U., Montreal, Que., Can., 1989, Ritsumeikan U., Japan, 1990; D.Ag.Sc. (hon.), Tokyo U. Agr., 1991; DSc (hon.), U. Toronto, 1994. Sr. geophysicist Dominion Gulf Co. Ltd., Toronto, 1956; chief geophysicist Ventures Ltd., 1956-57, sr. geophysicist, summer 1958; research geophysicist Kennecott Copper Corp., Denver, 1960-61; asst. prof. geology U. Colo., Boulder, 1961-64; asst. prof. geophysics MIT, Cambridge, Mass., 1965-68; mem. faculty U. Toronto, 1968-85, prof. physics, 1971-85, chmn. dept. geology, 1972-80, v.p., provost, 1980-83, pres., 1983-84; pres. U. B.C., 1985—; chief geophysics br. Johnson Space Ctr., NASA, Houston, 1970-72, chief physics br., 1972-73, acting chief planetary and earth sci. divsn., 1973; vis. prof. geology U. Houston, 1971-73; interim dir. Lunar Sci. Inst., Houston, 1973; vis. com. geol. scis. Brown U., 1974-76, Meml. U. St. John's Newfoundland, 1974-79, Princeton U., 1981-86; v.p. Can. Geosci. Coun., 1977; chmn. proposal evaluation program Univs. Space Rsch. Assocs., 1977-78, Ont. Geosci. Rsch. Fund, 1978-81; Pahlavi lectr. Govt. Iran, 1978; cons. to govt. and industry, mem. numerous govt. and sci. adv. and investigative panels; hon. prof. Changchun Coll. Geology, People's Republic China, 1985, Guilin Coll. Geology, China, 1987; fellow Green Coll. Oxford U., Eng.; hon. advisor Urasenke Found., Kyoto, Japan; hon. alumnus U. B.C.; bd. dirs. MacMillan Bloedel Ltd., Echo Bay Mines, Ltd., BC Gas Ltd., Corp.-Higher Edn. Forum, Internat. Inst. for Sustainable Devel. Author numerous papers, reports in field. Recipient Exceptional Sci. Achievement medal NASA, 1972; named Kil-Sly, Haida Nation (West Coast Indians of Can.), 1993. Fellow Royal Astron. Soc., Royal Soc. Can., Geol. Assn. Can. (pres. 1978-79, Logan Gold medal 1984); mem. AAAS, Soc. Exploration Geophysicists (Virgil Kauffman Gold medal 1974), Can. Geophys. Union (chmn. 1977-79, J. Tuzo Wilson medal 1987), Am. Geophys. Union (planetology sect. 1978-82), European Assn. Exploration Geophysicists, Soc. Geomagnetism and Geolectricity (Japan), Can. Geosci. Coun. (pres. 1980), Can. Soc. Exploration Geophysicists, Soc. Exploration Geophysics (hon.), Can.-Japan Soc. (founding dir.), Internat. House Japan, Inc.

STRANKS, REGINALD JOHN, packaging company executive; b. Revelstoke, B.C., Can., June 5, 1930; s. Charles R. and Olive A. (Howe) S.; m. Lydia Plesco, Nov. 7, 1953; children: David R., Robert D., Timothy A. Student, Okanagan Coll., 1949. Mktg. mgr. Bank of Montreal, Toronto, Ont., Can., 1971-74; v.p. Bank of Montreal, Winnipeg, Man., Can., 1974-76, B.C., Can., 1976-86; pres., CEO Gemini Packaging Ltd., Vancouver, B.C., 1986—, Sierra Products Ltd., Vancouver, 1986—; bd. dirs. Internat. Northair Mines Ltd., Vancouver, Tenajon Mines Ltd., Vancouver. Mem. Royal Vancouver Yacht Club, Vancouver Club. Office: Gemini Packaging Ltd, 9251 Van Horne Way, Richmond, BC Canada V6X 1W2

STRASBAUGH, WAYNE RALPH, lawyer; b. Lancaster, Pa., July 20, 1948; s. Wayne Veily and Jane Irene (Marzolf) S.; m. Carol Lynne Taylor, June 8, 1974; children: Susan, Wayne T., Elizabeth. AB, Bowdoin Coll., 1970; AM, Harvard U., 1971, PhD, 1976, JD, 1979. Bar: Ohio 1979, Pa. 1983, U.S. Tax Ct. 1980, U.S. Ct. Fed. Claims 1980, U.S. Ct. Appeals (fed. cir.) 1982, U.S. Dist. Ct. (no. dist.) Ohio 1979, U.S. Dist. Ct. (ea. dist.) Pa. 1983. Assoc. Jones Day Reavis & Pogue, Cleve., 1979-82, Morgan Lewis & Bockius, Phila., 1982-84; assoc. Ballard Spahr Andrews & Ingersoll, Phila., 1984-88, ptnr., 1988—. Mem. ABA (tax sect., chair com. 1992-94), Phila. Bar Assn. (tax sect., chair fed. tax com. 1992, coun. mem. 1995, sec.-treas. 1996—). Episcopalian. Office: Ballard Spahr Andrews & Ingersoll 1735 Market St Philadelphia PA 19103-7599

STRASBURGER, JOSEPH JULIUS, retired lawyer; b. Albia, Iowa, Aug. 29, 1913; s. Joseph and Elsa (Gottlieb) S.; m. Lucile C. Lapidus, Oct. 11, 1957; 1 dau., Susan A. (dec. Jan. 1970). A.B., Knox Coll., 1934; J.D., Harvard, 1937. Bar: Ill. 1937. Assoc. firm Moses, Kennedy, Stein & Bachrach, Chgo., 1938-39; asso. gen. counsel's office Middle West Service Co., Chgo., 1939-44; ptnr. Altheimer & Gray (and predecessor firms), Chgo., 1944-87; Chmn. lawyer's handbook editorial com. Jewish Fedn. Chgo., 1968-73; mem. adv. council Ill. Inst. Continuing Legal Edn., 1970-76, exec. com., 1971-76, chmn., 1974-75; lectr. probate and tax subjects. Contbr. articles to legal jours. Mem. devel. com. Knox Coll., 1964-70, trustee, 1982-87, life trustee, 1987—; trustee Latin Sch. Chgo., 1978-84. Fellow Am. Bar Found.; mem. ABA, Ill. Bar Assn., Chgo. Bar Assn. (chmn. probate practice com. 1960-61, chmn. continuing legal edn. com. 1968-69, chmn. legal edn. com. 1972-73), Chgo. Estate Planning Council (pres. 1975-76), Phi Beta Kappa, Delta Sigma Rho, Beta Theta Pi. Jewish. Clubs: Tavern (Chgo.), Harvard (Chgo.). Home: 1335 N Astor St Chicago IL 60610-2152 Office: 10 S Wacker Dr Chicago IL 60606-7407

STRASFOGEL, IAN, stage director; b. N.Y.C., Apr. 5, 1940; s. Ignace and Alma (Lubin) S.; m. Judith Hirsch Norell, Feb. 15, 1973; children: Daniella Elizabeth, Gabrielle Sandra. BA, Harvard U., 1961. Adminstrv. asst. N.Y.C. Opera Co., 1962-64, stage dir., 1964—; tchr. music Julliard Sch. Music, N.Y.C., 1965-66, Augusta (Ga.) Coll., 1967-68; founder, previous artistic dir. Augusta Opera Co., from 1967; chmn. dept. opera New Eng. Conservatory, Boston, 1968-72; prof. opera U. Mich., Ann Arbor, 1980; stage dir. Balt. Civic Opera, Kansas City Lyric Theatre, Netherlands Opera Co., 1973—, N.Y.C. Opera, San Francisco Opera, Stuttgart Opera, Alte Oper Frankfurt, Edinburgh Festival, Aix-en-Provence Festival, Aspen Music Festival; dir. music theatre project Tanglewood Festival, Lenox, Mass., 1971-73; gen. dir. Opera Soc. Washington, 1972-75; artistic cons. Phila. Lyric Opera, 1973; dir. New Opera Theatre, Bklyn. Acad. Music, 1976-79. Author: Il Musico (music by Larry Grossman), 1990-91; editor: Ba-Ta-Clan, 1970. Served with AUS, 1966-68. Henry Russell Shaw travelling fellow, 1961-62; Ford Found. internship in performing arts, 1962-64; Internat. Inst. Edn. grantee, 1965. Mem. Phi Beta Kappa. Home: 915 W End Ave New York NY 10025-3535 Office: Sardos Artist Mgmt Corp 180 W End Ave New York NY 10023-4902

STRASMA, JOHN DRINAN, economist, educator; b. Kankakee, Ill., Mar. 29, 1932; s. Roy and Charlotte Wilkins (Deselm) S.; m. Judith Feaster, Mar. 18, 1956 (div. 1983); children: Anne, Patricia, Susan, Kenneth, Mary; m. Anne Corry, July 21, 1984. AB, DePauw U., 1953; AM, Harvard U., 1958, PhD, 1960. Research asst. Fed. Res. Bank of Boston, 1958-59; prof. Econs. Inst., U. Chile, Santiago, 1959-72; economist UN Secretariat, 1964-65; advisor Ministry of Economy and Fin., Lima, Peru, 1970; prof. econs. and agrl. econs. U. Wis., Madison, 1972—; cons. in field; v.p., dir. Latin Am. Scholarship Program of Am. Univs., 1970-74; chmn. fin. com. Wesley Found. of Wis., 1978-87; public mem. Wis. Legis. Council Com. on Mining, 1975-90. Author: State and Local Taxation of Manufacturing Industry, 1969, Agrarian Reform in El Salvador, 1982, Agricultural Land Taxation in Developing Countries, 1987, Land Tax Reform Alternatives in Zimbabwe, 1990, Options for Redistributing Land in the New South Africa, 1993, Market-Based Land Redistribution in the New South Africa, 1993, Resolving Land Conflicts in Necaragua, 1996. Served with U.S. Army, 1954-56. Danforth fellow, 1956-60; Recipient Outstanding Public Service award Wis. Environ. Decade, 1978. Mem. Am. Econs. Assn., Am. Agrl. Econs. Assn., Internat. Agrl. Econs. Assn., Latin Am. Studies Assn., Soc. Internat. Devel. Methodist. Office: U Wis 427 Lorch St Madison WI 53706-1513

STRASSBURGER, JOHN ROBERT, academic administrator; b. Sheboygan, Wis., Apr. 6, 1942; s. J. Robert and Elizabeth (Mathewson) S.; m. Gertrude Hunter Mackie, Aug. 24, 1968; children: Sarah Electa, Gertrude Hunter. BA, Bates, 1964; Honours degree, Cambridge (Eng.) U., 1966; PhD, Princeton U., 1976. Faculty Hiram (Ohio) Coll., 1970-82; program officer NEH, Washington, 1982-84; prof. history, v.p. acad. affairs, exec. v.p., dean Coll., Knox Coll., Galesburg, Ill., 1984-94; pres. Ursinus Coll., Collegeville, Pa., 1995—. Contbr. articles to profl. jours. Dir. Knox Galesburg Symphony. Mem. Am. Conf. Acad. Deans (chair 1990-91), Associated Coll. of the Midwest (chair deans adv. coun. 1989-90), Ill. State Hist. Soc. (bd. dirs. 1988-91), Sunday Breakfast Club (Phila.). Office: Ursinus Coll Office of Pres Collegeville PA 19426-1000

STRASSER, GABOR, priest, management consultant; b. Budapest, Hungary, May 22, 1929; s. Rezso and Theresa (Seiler) S.; m. Linda Casselman Pemble, Aug. 16, 1958 (div. 1976); children: Claire Margaret, Andrew John; m. Joka Verhoeff, Feb. 2, 1978; children: Steven Verhoeff, Tessa Christina. BCE, City Coll. N.Y., 1954; MS, U. Buffalo, 1959; PMD, Harvard, 1968; MDiv, Va. Theol. Sem., 1992. Research engr. Bell Aircraft Co., Buffalo, 1956-61; project leader Boeing Airplane Co., Seattle, 1961-62; dept. head Mitre Corp., Bedford, Mass., Washington, 1962-68; v.p. Urban Inst., Washington, 1968-69; tech. asst. to pres.'s sci. adviser White House, 1969-71, exec. sec. pres.'s sci. and tech. policy panel, 1970-71; dir. planning Battelle Meml. Inst., Columbus, Ohio, 1971-73; pres. Strasser Assocs., Inc., Washington, 1973-92; priest Va. Diocese, 1992—. Author, editor: Science and Technology Policies-Yesterday, Today, Tomorrow, 1973; Contbr. articles to profl. jours. Served to 1st lt., C.E. USAR. Recipient 1st nat. award Gravity Research Found., 1952. Mem. Am. Inst. Aeros. and Astronautics, IEEE, AAAS (chmn. indsl. sci. sect. 1974), Sigma Xi. Clubs: Cosmos (Washington), Harvard (Washington).

STRASSER, WILLIAM CARL, JR., retired college president, educator; b. Washington, Feb. 4, 1930; s. William Carl and Minnie Elizabeth (Saxton) S.; m. Jeanne Carol Peake, Sept. 17, 1954 (div.); children: Sheryl Lynn, Keith Edward, Robert Carl; m. Jane Ann Gunn, Nov. 25, 1978. BA with first honors, U. Md., 1952, MA, 1954; PhD, 1961; Carnegie postdoctoral fellow in coll. adminstrn, U. Mich., 1961-62. High sch. tchr. Cin. and Balt., 1955-57; v.p. W.C. Strasser Co., Inc., 1957-59; pub. info. specialist Balt. County (Md.) Pub. Schs., 1960-61; asst. dean, asst. prof. Sch. Edn., State U. N.Y. at Buffalo, 1962-64; rsch. asst. U.S. Office Edn., 1959-60; specialist ednl. adminstrn. U.S. Office Edn., Washington, 1964-65; asst. dir. profl. personnel Montgomery County (Md.) Pub. Schs., 1965-66; acting pres., exec. dean Montgomery Community Coll., Rockville, Md., 1966-67, pres., 1967-79, prof., 1978-86, pres. emeritus, prof. emeritus, 1986—; vis. scholar U. Calif., Berkeley, 1977-79; vice pres. Md. Council Community Coll. Presidents, 1971-72, 75-77; pres., v.p. Jr. Coll. Council Middle Atlantic States, 1969-72; founder Council Chief Exec. Adminstrs., 1973-75; mem. exec. com. Pres.'s Acad., 1975-77; mem. Gov.'s Adv. Council, Md. Higher Edn. Facilities, 1977-79; Del. UNESCO Conf. on Africa, 1961; participant 50th Anniversary Conf. Fgn. Policy Assn. U.S., 1968; mem. Congl. Internship Adv. Com., 1969-78; chmn. Montgomery County Community White Ho. Conf. on Aging, 1971; cons. Middle States Assn. Colls. and Secondary Schs., 1975—. Author: For The Community: Continuing General Education, 1979, A College For a Community, 1988; co-author: Dual Enrollment in Public and Non-Public Schools, 1965; contbr. poetry and articles to jours. Served with AUS, 1954-55. Recipient Gov. Md. Cert. Disting. Citizenship, 1979; Danforth Found. study grantee, 1972; Ford Found. grantee, 1974-75; Silver medallion for Outstanding Service, Bd. Trustees of Montgomery Coll., 1986. Mem. Am. Assn. Jr. Colls. (chmn. nat. commn. on instrn. 1969-71, mem. nat. assembly 1973, founder Pres. Acad. 1973-77), AAUP, Am. Assn. Higher Edn., Am. Mgmt. Assns., Nat. Soc. Sons. and Daus of the Pilgrims, Montgomery County C. of C. (Disting. Svc. award 1979), Rotary, Phi Kappa Phi, Omicron Delta Kappa, Pi Delta Epsilon, Phi Eta Sigma, Phi Delta Kappa. Democrat. Unitarian-Universalist. Home: 3011 Stoney Rd Shepherdstown WV 25443

STRASSMANN, W. PAUL, economics educator; b. Berlin, July 26, 1926; s. Erwin Otto and Ilse (Wens) S.; m. Elizabeth Marsh Fanck, June 27, 1952; children—Joan, Diana, Beverly. B.A. magna cum laude, U. Tex., Austin, 1949; M.A., Columbia U., 1950; Ph.D., U. Md., 1956. Econ. analyst Dept. Commerce, 1950-52; instr. U. Md., 1955; mem. faculty Mich. State U., East Lansing, 1956—, assoc. prof. econs., 1959-63, prof., 1963—; sr. research dir. ILO, Geneva, 1969-70, 73-74; cons. World Bank, AID. Author: Risk and Technological Innovation, 1959, Technological Change and Economic Development, 1968, The Transformation of Housing, 1982, (with Jill Wells) The Global Construction Industry, 1988. Served with USN, 1944-46. Mem. Am. Econ. Assn., Latin Am. Studies Assn., Phi Beta Kappa. Office: Mich State Univ Dept Econs East Lansing MI 48824

STRASSMEYER, MARY, newspaper columnist; b. Cleve., Aug. 5, 1929; d. Frederick H. and Katherine (Mullally) S. A.B., Notre Dame Coll., 1951; postgrad., Toledo U., 1952; J.D., Cleve. Marshall Coll. Law, Cleve. State U., 1981. Bar: Ohio 1983. Reporter Cleve. News, 1956-60; contbr. Cleve. Plain Dealer, 1957-60, feature writer, 1960-65, beauty editor, 1963-65, travel writer, 1963—, society editor, 1965-77, 85—; columnist, 1977—; co-creator syndicated cartoon Sneakers; co-owner Gerry's Internat. Travel Agy., Cleve., 1991—. Author: Coco: The Special Delivery Dog, 1979. Mem. Soc. Am. Social Scribes (founder, 1st pres.), Notre Dame Coll. Alumnae Assn., Women in Comm. Club: Press (Cleve.) (inducted into Hall of Fame 1994). Home: 2059 Broadview Rd Cleveland OH 44109-4145 Office: The Plain Dealer 1801 Superior Ave E Cleveland OH 44114-2107

STRATAS, TERESA (ANASTASIA STRATAKI), opera singer, soprano; b. Toronto, Ont., Can., May 26, 1938. Student, of Irene Jessner, 1956-59; grad., Faculty Music, U. Toronto, 1959; LLD (hon.), McMaster U., 1986, U. Toronto, 1994. Winner Met. Opera auditions, 1959; major roles in opera houses throughout world include: Mimi in La Bohème; Tatiana in Eugene Onegin; Susanna in The Marriage of Figaro; Nedda in Pagliacci; Marenka in The Bartered Bride; Three Heroines in Il Trittico; Violetta in La Traviata; title role in Rusalka; Jennie in Mahagonny; created title role in completed version of Lulu (Alban Berg), Paris Grand Opera, 1979; film appearances Kaiser von Atlantis, Seven Deadly Sins; Zefirelli's La Traviata, Salome, Lulu, Paganini, Zarewitsch, Eugene Oregin; Broadway debut in Rags, 1986; creator the role of Marie Antoinette Ghosts of Versailles world premiere Met. Opera, 1992; sang both female leading roles Il Tabarro, Pagliacci double bill opening Met. Opera, 1994, numerous recs. including Richard Strauss' Salomé, Songs of Kurt Weill. Decorated Order of Can.; recipient 3 Grammy awards, Emmy award, Drama Desk award, 1986, 3 Grammy nominations, Tony nomination, 1986, Tiffany award, 1994; named Performer of Yr., Can. Music Council, 1979. Office: care Met Opera Co Lincoln Center Plz New York NY 10023 also: Vincent & Farrell Associates 157 W 57th St Ste 502 New York NY 10019-2210

STRATFORD, RAY PAUL, electrical engineer, consultant; b. Pocatello, Idaho, Feb. 26, 1925; s. Ray Percy and Olive Eudora (Jenson) S.; m. Claire Elizabeth Dennery, Sept. 2, 1949 (div. July 1969); children: Bruce Ballentyne, James Lowell, Susanne Dennery; m. Nancy Lorraine Long, Apr. 24, 1974; 1 child, Heather Lyn; stepchildren: Deborah Lorraine, David Paul. Student, Idaho State U., 1946-47; BSEE, Stanford U., 1950. Registered profl. engr., N.Y. Test engr. GE, Schenectady, N.Y., 1950-52; application GE, Schenectady, 1954-62, project mgr., 1963-73, cons. engr., 1974-85; proposal engr. GE, Phila., 1952-54, application engr., 1962-63; pvt. cons. Island Park, Idaho, 1991—; adj. prof. Rensselaer Poly. Inst., Troy, N.Y., 1988, 90. Co-author: Handbook of Industrial and Commercial Electric Power System Designs, 1995; contbr. articles to profl. jours. Mem. bldg. com. LDS Sch., Schenectady, 1962-64, coord. phys. facilities, 1980-84; mem. bldg. com. Burnt Hills Sch. Bd., Glenville, N.Y., 1963-64, YMCA, Schenectady, 1965. Fellow IEEE (life mem., chairperson static power converter com. 1972, chairperson task force standard 1973-84, co-chairperson task force standard 1984-92, contbg. author Red Book 1993, Best Paper award 1981, Outstanding achievement award 1994), Rotary Internat. Avocations: woodworking, family, travel. Office: PO Box 186 Island Park ID 83429-0186

STRATHAIRN, DAVID, actor; b. San Francisco, CA, 1949. numerous stage appearances including: I'm Not Rappaport, Salonika, A Lie of the Mind, The Birthday Party, Danton's Death, Mountain Language, L'Atelier, A Moon for the Misbegotten, Temptation; television appearances include:Miami Vice, 1985, The Equilizer, 1988, The Days and Nights of Molly Dodd, 1988-91, Day One, 1989, Son of the Morning Star, 1991, Heat Wave, 1990, Judgment, 1990, Without Warning: The James Brady Story, 1991, O Pioneers!, 1992, The American Clock, 1993; films include: Return of the Secaucus Seven, 1980, Lovesick, 1983, Silkwood, 1983, The Brother From Another Planet, 1984, Iceman, 1984, Enormous Changes at the Last Minute, 1985, When Nature Calls, 1985, At Close Range, 1986, Matewan, 1987, Eight Men Out, 1988, Stars and Bars, 1988, Dominick and Eugene, 1988, Call Me, 1988, The Feud, 1989, Memphis Belle, 1990, City of Hope, 1991, Big Girls Don't Cry...They Get Even, 1992, Bob Roberts, 1992, Shadows and Fog, 1992, A League of Their Own, 1992, Sneakers, 1992, Passion Fish, 1992, Lost in Yonkers, 1993, The Firm, 1993, A Dangerous Woman, 1993, The River Wild, 1994, Dolores Claiborne, 1995, Losing Isaiah, 1995. *

STRATING, SHARON L., elementary school educator, college instructor; b. Jamestown, N.D., Jan. 20, 1949; d. Walter and Evelyn Darlene (Lang) Remmick; m. Rick Donald Strating, Dec. 24, 1978; children: Heather Dawn, Amber Nicole, Ashley Renee. BS in Secondary Edn., So. Mo. State U., 1971; MEd in Sci. Edn., N.W. Mo. State U., 1992. Cert. elem. tchr., Mo. Tchr. Cassville R-III Schs., 1971-76, Savannah R-III Sch. System, Mo., 1976-91; instr. 4th grade Horace Mann Lab. Sch., Maryville, Mo., 1991—; facilitator for Environ. Edn. Pilot Project Kans. U., Lawrence; co-chair EPA Pollution Prevention Adv. Task Force; mem. biol. sci. curriculum study Elem. Tchr. Module Project, 1993; instr. for coll. practicum students; Map 2000 Sr. Leader for performance-based assessment sys., Mo., 1994—. Author: Living the Constitution Through the Eyes of the Newspaper, 1987, Tabloid Teaching Tool, 6 edits., 1986-91. Chairperson March of Dimes, 1972-76, Cystic Fibrosis, 1972-78; scout leader Brownies, 1976-77; exec. bd. dirs. PTA, 1976-82, fund raising chairperson, 1976-83; program chairperson presch. PTA, 1976-80;chairperson community environ. activities, 1976—, Adopt a Hwy. Program, 1976-91; mem. Mo. Stream Team Effort, 1976—. Recipient Nat. Pres. Environ. Youth award, 1988, 89, Presdl. award State of Mo., 1992, 93, Nat. Presdl. award, 1992-93; named Mo. State Tchr. of Yr., 1990-91, Disney Salutes the Am. Tchr. award, 1995. Mem. Nat. Hist. Soc., Internat. Reading Assn., Nat. Bd. for Profl. Tching. Standards and Mid.-Age Child in Sci., Nat. Sci. Tchrs. Assn., Nat. Assn. Lab. Schs. (sec. 1994-95), Sci. Tchrs. Mo. Lutheran. Avocations: travel, ecology, creative writing, motivational speaking, arts and crafts. Office: Northwest Mo State U Horace Mann Lab Sch Brown Hall Rm 108 Maryville MO 64468

STRATMAN, FRANK HERMAN, travel company executive; b. Louisville, Oct. 6, 1920; s. Dominic Herman and Mary Ann (Wolf) S.; m. Lynne M. Fawnsworth, Nov. 6, 1947 (div. Aug. 1977); children: Frank H., Teri L. Revilla, Deborah L. Burke, Cynthia G. Savage. B of Chem. Engring., U. Louisville, 1942. Gen. mgr. Process Equipment div. GATX, Chgo., 1946-61; pres. Infilco, Inc. subs. GATX, Tucson, 1961-67; gen. mgr. Process div. Chgo. Bridge and Iron, Oak Brook, Ill., 1967-75; pres. Reclasource, Inc., Chgo., 1975-82, BEPEX, Inc., Chgo., 1970-82; chmn. bd. Dynasty Travel, Inc., Arlington Heights, Ill., 1982—. Lt. USNR, 1942-46, PTO. Decorated Bronze Star. Roman Catholic. Avocations: golf, history, travel. Home: 400 Ascot Dr Park Ridge IL 60068-3684 Office: Dynasty Travel Inc 1780 W Algonquin Rd Arlington Heights IL 60005-3405

STRATMAN, JOSEPH LEE, petroleum refining company executive, consultant, chemical engineer; b. Louisville, Oct. 15, 1924; s. Dominic Herman and Mary Ann (Wolf) S.; m. Elizabeth Jewell Doyle, July 1, 1950; children—Joseph Lee, Mary Elizabeth, Sharon Ann, Judith Ann. BChemE, U. Louisville, 1947. Registered profl. engr., Tex. Chem. engr. Pan Am. Refining Corp. (doing bus. as Amoco Oil Co.), Texas City, Tex., 1947-55, operating supr., 1955-61; mgr. Texas City Refining, Inc., Texas City, Tex., 1961-69, v.p., 1969-80, sr. v.p., 1980—. Bd. dirs., mem. exec. com., treas., chmn. Galveston County ARC, 1966-73; bd. dirs., mem. exec. com., chmn. Texas City Jr. Achievement, 1966-73; treas. Texas City Refining Good Govt. Fund., 1983-88. Served with USNR, 1945-46. Mem. Am. Inst. Chem. Engrs. Roman Catholic.

STRATON, JOHN CHARLES, JR., investment banker; b. Warwick, N.Y., Apr. 18, 1932; s. John Charles and Helen (Sanford) S.; m. Sally M. Strawhand (div. Mar. 1970); children: John Charles III, Sara; m. Marion S. Holder, Feb. 18, 1974; 1 child, Ashley Holder Straton. B.A., U. Va., 1954. With Jas. H. Oliphant and Co., N.Y.C., 1956—; gen. ptnr. Jas. H. Oliphant and Co., 1962—, 1st v.p., 1972-75; v.p. Spencer Trask & Co., Inc., N.Y.C., 1975-77, Hornblower, Weeks, Noyes & Trask, N.Y.C., 1977-78, Loeb Rhoades, Hornblower & Co., 1978-79, Shearson Loeb Rhoades, 1979-81; v.p., fin. cons. Shearson Lehman Bros., N.Y.C., 1981-93; sr. v.p. Smith Barney, N.Y.C., 1993—; assessor Village of Tuxedo Park, 1963-70. Vestryman St. Mary's in Tuxedo. Served to maj. AUS, 1954-56; ret. Mem. U. Va. Alumni Assn. N.Y. (pres., treas. 1973-90), Mil. Order Fgn. Wars (comdr. 1981-86, treas. 1986—), Pilgrims of U.S., Tuxedo Pk. Club, Sigma Phi Epsilon. Home: Ledge Rd Tuxedo Park NY 10987 Office: 250 Park Ave New York NY 10177

STRATOS, KIMARIE ROSE, lawyer, sports agent; b. Miami, Fla., Aug. 24, 1960; d. Jack Sloshower and Charmaine (McDougal) S. BS with high honors, U. Fla., 1981, JD with honors, 1984. Bar: Fla. 1985, U.S. Dist. Ct. (so. and mid. dist.) Fla. 1987. Ptnr. Shutts & Bowen, Miami, 1984-85, 86—; chair sports law dept., law clk. to judge U.S. Dist. Ct. for So. Dist. Fla., Miami, 1985-86; bd. dirs. Fla. Sports Found., 1992—, vice chmn., 1995—. Co-author, asst. editor: Facility Development and the Sports Authority, Law of Professional and Amateur Sports; asst. editor: Clark Boardmen, 1990; contbr. articles to profl. jours. Mem. ABA, Fla. Bar (bd. govs. young lawyers sect. 1987-93, exec. coun. entertainment, arts and sports law sect. 1988—), Fla. Assn. Women Lawyers, Sports Lawyers Assn. (nat. v.p. 1988-90, 93—, bd. dirs. 1990—). Avocation: running, travel. Office: Shutts & Bowen 100 Chopin Plz Ste 1500 Miami FL 33131-2305

STRATT, RICHARD MARK, chemistry researcher, educator; b. Phila., Feb. 21 1954; s. Stanford Lloyd and Florence Clair (Sussman) S. SB in Chemistry, MIT, 1975; PhD, U. Calif.-Berkeley, 1979. Postdoctoral rsch. assoc. U. Ill., Champaign, 1979-80, NSF postdoctoral research assoc., 1980; asst. prof. chemistry Brown U., Providence, 1981-85, assoc. prof., 1986-88, prof., 1988—. Contbr. articles to profl. jours. Alfred P. Sloan fellow, 1985-89; Fulbright scholar Oxford U., 1991-92. Mem. Am. Phys. Soc., Am. Chem. Soc., Sigma Xi, Phi Lambda Upsilon. Office: Brown U Dept Chemistry Providence RI 02912

STRATTON, FRANCES RUTH, retired bookkeeper; b. Island Falls, Maine, Dec. 7, 1925; d. William Joseph and Sarah Verna (Grant) Morin; m. Walter Donald Webb, Dec. 23, 1943 (div. 1982); m. Richard Earle Stratton, Oct. 1, 1982. Student, Husson Coll., Bangor, Maine, 1980-82. Office mgr. Summers Fertilizer Co., Inc., Bangor, Maine, 1955-65; office mgr. Corenco Fertilizer Co., Bangor, 1966-76, McAuley Textile, Bangor, Maine, 1976-77; sr. bookeeper Bangor Hydro Electric Co., Maine, 1977-88, retired, 1988; founder, owner, curator John E. and Walter D. Webb Mus. Vintage Fashion, Island Falls, 1983—. Co-author: (with Richard E. Stratton) My Life on the Line, 1985; rsch. cons. Surviving: an Acadian Chronicle, 1990. Loaned exec. Penobscot Valley United Way, 1986-87, 88-89; pres. Bangor Mgmt. Club, 1984-85. Mem. Maine Assn. Mus., Mo. Katahdin Valley Regional C. of C., Hampden Hist. Soc., Island Falls Hist. Soc., Costume Soc. Am., R.S.v.P., Aroostook County Maine, Vashti Rebekah Lodge # 35, Women's Ten Pin Bowling (pres. Bangor-Brewer Assn. 1965-69, pres. Maine 1967-69). Home: John E & Walter D Webb Mus PO Box 18 Hampden ME 04444-0018

STRATTON, FREDERICK PRESCOTT, JR., manufacturing executive; b. Milw., May 25, 1939; married. B.S., Yale U.; M.B.A., Stanford U., 1963. With Arthur Andersen & Co., 1963-65, Robert W. Baird & Co., Inc., 1965-73; with Briggs & Stratton Corp., Wauwatosa, Wis., 1973—, asst. service mgr., 1973-75, asst. sales mgr., 1975-76, group sales and service adminstrn., 1976-77, v.p. adminstrn., 1977; formerly pres. Briggs & Stratton Corp., Wauwatosa, to 1987; chmn. bd., chief exec. officer Briggs & Stratton Corp., Wauwatosa, Wis., 1987—, chmn. bd. dirs.; bd. dirs. Banc One Corp., Columbus, Ohio, Wis. Energy Corp., Milw., Weyenberg Shoe Man Co., Milw. Office: Briggs & Stratton Corp PO Box 702 Milwaukee WI 53201*

STRATTON, GREGORY ALEXANDER, computer specialist, administrator, mayor; b. Glendale, Calif., July 31, 1946; s. William Jaspar and Rita Phyllis (Smith) S.; m. Yolanda Margot Soler, 1967 (div. 1974); 1 child, Tiffany; m. Edith Carter, Sept. 27, 1975; stepchildren: John Henkell, Paul Henkell, D'Lorah Henkell Wismar. Student, Harvey Mudd Coll., 1964-65; BS in Physics, UCLA, 1968; MBA, Calif. Luth. U., 1977. Elec. engr. Naval Ship Weapon System Engrng. Sta., Port Hueneme, Calif., 1968-73; sr. staff mem. Univac, Valencia, Calif., 1973-74; v.p. Digital Applications, Camarillo, Calif., 1974-75; cons. Grumman Aerospace, Point Mugu, Calif., 1975-76; F-14 software mgr. Pacific Missle Test Ctr., Pt. Mugu, 1976-84; software mgr. Teledyne Systems, Northridge, Calif., 1984-92, dir. engrng. software dept., 1992-93; dep. dir. software engrng. Teledyne Electronic Systems, Northridge, Calif., 1993-94; software mgr. Litton Guidance and Controls, Northridge, Calif., 1995—. Mem. City Coun., City of Simi Valley, Calif., 1979-86, mayor, 1986—; alt. Rep. County Cen. Com., Ventura County, 1986-88; mem. Rep. State Cen. Com., Calif., 1990—; bd. dirs. Simi Valley Hosp., 1987—. Mem. Assn. Ventura County Cities (chair 1990-91), Rotary (Paul Harris award Simi Sunrise chpt. 1989), Jaycees (pres. Simi Valley chpt. 1974-75, nat. bd. dirs. 1975-76, v.p. Calif. state 1976-77). Republican. Lutheran. Home: 254 Goldenwood Cir Simi Valley CA 93065-6771 Office: Office of Mayor 2929 Tapo Canyon Rd Simi Valley CA 93063-2199

STRATTON, MARGARET MARY, art educator; b. Seattle, Nov. 12, 1953; d. Harold Wesley and Veronica Margaret (Weber) S. BA in Media Studies, Evergreen State Coll., Olympia, Wash., 1977; MA in Photography, U. N.Mex., 1983, MFA in Photography, 1985. Tchr. U. N.Mex., Albuquerque, 1983-85; artist-in-residence Wash. State Arts Commn., U. Puget Sound, Tacoma, 1985, Yakima (Wash) Elem. Sch. Dist., 1985; staff adj. faculty Evergreen State Coll., Olympia, 1985-86; asst. prof. art U. Iowa, Iowa City, 1986-92, assoc. prof., 1993—; vis. prof. Cornish Coll. Art, Seattle, 1991-92, Art Inst. Chgo., 1992-93; advisor NEA regional Intermedia Arts/Minn., Mpls., 1991; juror Women in Drs. Chair, Chgo., 1993. Videomaker: (film festivals) Berlin Film Festival, 1995, Black Maria Film Festival (dir. award 1995); contbr.: New Feminist Photographies, 1995; one-woman shows at New Image Gallery, James Madison U., Harrisonburg, Va., 1989, Sushi Inc., San Diego, 1990, Coll. of Pacific, Stockton, Calif., 1990, Intermedia Arts Gallery, Mpls., 1991, Cornish Coll. Arts, Seattle, 1991; exhibited in group shows at Rice U., Houston, 1989, Mid-Hudson Arts and Sci. Ctr., Poughkeepsie, N.Y., 1989, Arts Ctr. Gallery, Coll. DuPage, Glen Ellyn, Ill., 1989, N.A.M.E., Gallery, Chgo., 1989, Randolph St. Gallery, Chgo., 1989, Moore Coll. Art, Phila., 1989, Union Square Gallery, N.Y.C., 1989, U. Iowa Mus. Art, Iowa City, 1990, D.C. 37 Gallery, N.Y.C., 1990, Camerawork, San Francisco, 1990, 91, 93, 94, 911 Media Arts Ctr., Seattle, 1991, Kohler Art Ctr., Wis., 1991, Rena Bransten Gallery, San Francisco, 1991, Eye Gallery, San Francisco, 1992, 93,Port Angeles (Wash.) Fine Arts Ctr., 1992, Davenport (Iowa) Art Mus., 1992, Atlanta Gallery of Photography, 1992, U. Calif., Davis, 1992, Greg Kuchera Gallery, Seattle, 1992, Henry Gallery, U. Wash., Seattle, 1992, Valparaiso (Ind.) U., 1993, Gallery N.S.W., Sydney, Australia, 1993, Allied Arts Gallery/Hanford Nuclear Complex, Richland, Wash., 1993, Mus. Contemporary Photography and State Ill. Art Gallery, Chgo., 1993, The Harvard Archive, Cambridge, Mass.,1994, Portable Works Collection, Seattle Ctr. Pavilion, 1994, Women's U. Tex., Denton, 1994, Houston Ctr. Photography, 1994, Smithsonian Instn., Washington, 1994, Berlin Film and Video Festival, 1995. Recipient Regional Visual Fellowship award Nat. Endowment for Arts, 1987, Interdisciplinary Arts award, Intermedia Arts Nat. Endowment for Arts/Rockefeller Found., 1988, Individual fellowship in photography Nat. Endowment fo Arts, Washington, 1990, Pub. Art awards Seattle Arts Commn., 1992, Film and Video Prodn. Regional Grant Nat. Endowment for Arts/Jerome Found., Mpls., 1993, Individual fellowship in new Genres Nat. Endowment for the Arts, Washington, 1995, fac. scholar award U. Iowa, 1996. Mem. Soc. Photographic Edn. (bd. dirs. 1991-95), Coll. Art Assn. (1st chair Gay Caucus 1990-93). Achievements include research on the effects of media on stereotypes in United States/TV/Film. Home: 1611 E Court St Iowa City IA 52245 Office: U Iowa Art Dept Riverside Dr Iowa City IA 52242

STRATTON, MARIANN, retired naval nursing administrator; b. Houston, Apr. 6, 1945; d. Max Millard and Beatrice Agnes (Roemer) S.; m. Lawrence Mallory Stickney, nov. 15, 1977 (dec.). BSN, BA in English, Sacred Heart Dominican Coll., 1966; MA in Mgmt., Webster Coll., 1977; MSN, U. Va., 1981. Cert. adult nurse practitioner. Ensign USN, 1966, advanced through grades to rear adm., 1991; patient care coord. Naval Regional Med. Ctr., Charleston, S.C., 1981-83; nurse corps plans officer Naval Med. Command, Washington, 1983-86; dir. nursing svcs. U.S. Naval Hosp., Naples, Italy, 1986-89, Naval Hosp., San Diego, 1989-91; chief pers. mgmt. Bur. Medicine & Surgery, Washington, 1991-94; dir. USN Nurse Corps, Washington, 1991-94; ret. Oct. 1, 1994 USN, 1994. Decorated Disting. Svc. medal, Meritorious Svc. medal with two stars, Naval Achievement medal. Mem. ANA, Assn. Mil. Surgeons of U.S., Interagy. Inst. of Fed. Health Car Execs.

STRATTON, RICHARD JAMES, lawyer; b. Sandwich, Ill., May 17, 1946; s. James L. and Dorothy (Olson) S.; m. Michele Disario, June 13, 1970; children: Matthew A., Laura D. AB, Harvard U., 1968, JD, 1972; MS, London Sch. of Econs., 1969. Bar: Calif. 1972, U.S. Dist. Ct. (no. dist.) Calif. 1972, U.S. Ct. Appeals (9th cir.) 1972, U.S. Dist. Ct. (cen. dist.) Calif. 1978, U.S. Dist. Ct. (so. and ea. dists.) Calif. 1979, U.S. Supreme Ct. 1979. Assoc. Bronson, Bronson & McKinnon, San Francisco, 1972-79, ptnr., 1980—; early neutral evaluator, mediator U.S. Dist. Ct. Co-author: Real Property Litigation, 1994. Trustee San Francisco Day Sch., 1987-94; bd. dirs. Legal Aid Soc. of San Francisco, 1989—. Fellow Am. Bar Found.; mem. ABA, Bar Assn. of San Francisco (bd. dirs. 1988-90), Calif. Bar Assn., Def. Rsch. Inst. (chmn. subcom. real estate brokers and agts. 1986-87), No. Calif. Assn. Def. Counsel, No. Calif. Assn. Bus. Trial Lawyers, San Francisco Barristers Club (pres. 1980), City Club, Harvard Club (San Francisco). Office: Bronson Bronson & McKinnon 505 Montgomery St San Francisco CA 94111-2552

STRATTON, ROBERT, electronics company executive; b. Vienna, Austria, Aug. 14, 1928; came to U.S., 1959, naturalized, 1966; s. Kenneth Kurt and Eugenie (Schwatzer) S.; m. Elfriede Karlberger, Jan. 11, 1980; children: David Alexander, Valerie Pam. B.Sc. in Physics, Manchester U., 1949, Ph.D. in Theoretical Physics, 1952. Rsch. physicist Met. Vickers Elec. Co., Manchester, Eng., 1952-59; with Tex. Instruments, Inc., Dallas, 1959-94; dir. physics rsch. lab. Tex. Instruments, Inc., 1959-94, assoc. dir. cen. rsch. labs., 1971-72, dir. semiconductor R & D, 1972-75, dir. cen. rsch. labs., 1975-77, asst. v.p., dir. cen. rsch. labs., 1977-82, v.p. corp. staff, dir. cen. rsch. labs., 1982-94; dir. Indsl. Outreach Elec. Materials Sci. and Tech. Ctr., Engrng. and Tech. Inst. U. Tex., Austin, 1994—. Contbr. articles to profl. jours. Bd. dirs. Indsl. Rsch. Inst., 1985-88, Coun. on Superconductivity for Am. Competitiveness, 1987-90; adv. bd. dirs. Tex. Ctr. for Superconductivity, 1989—. Fellow IEEE, Inst. Physics (U.K.), Am. Phys. Soc.; mem. NAE. Office: JJ Pickle Rsch Ctr U Tex MER 1 606J Austin TX 78758

STRATTON, THOMAS OLIVER, investment banker; b. Los Angeles, Feb. 14, 1930; s. Oliver Clarke and Ethel (Savage) S.; m. Carol Joyce Wilson, Feb. 21, 1953; children: Brentley Clarke, James Morris, Thomas Oliver Jr. Student, Taft Sch., 1946-48, Stanford, 1948-50; B.S., U. Calif. at Los Angeles, 1956; M.B.A., Boston U., 1960. With Security Pacific Nat. Bank, Los Angeles, 1955-56; security analyst New Eng. Mut. Life Ins. Co., Boston, 1956-60; exec. v.p., dir. Bankers Leasing Corp., Boston, 1960-64; treas. Montgomery Ward & Co., Chgo., 1964-67; pres. Investco Assoc., Inc., 1967-75, Monterey Capital, Inc., 1975—; bd. dirs. MCI Securities, Inc. Served with AUS, 1952-55. Republican. Congregationalist. Clubs: Old Capital (Monterey); Beach and Tennis (Pebble Beach); World Trade (San Francisco). Home: PO Box 3713 Carmel CA 93921-3713 Office: PO Box 7370 Carmel CA 93921-7370

STRATTON, WALTER LOVE, lawyer; b. Greenwich, Conn., Sept. 21, 1926; s. John McKee and June (Love) S.; children: John, Michael, Peter (dec.), Lucinda; m. DeAnna Weinheimer, Oct. 1, 1994. Student, Williams Coll., 1943; A.B., Yale U., 1948; LL.B., Harvard U., 1951. Bar: N.Y. 1952. Assoc. Casey, Lane & Mittendorf, N.Y.C., 1951-53; assoc. Donovan, Leisure, Newton & Irvine, N.Y.C., 1956-63; ptnr. Donovan, Leisure, Newton & Irvine, 1963-84, Gibson, Dunn & Crutcher, 1984-93; ptnr. Andrews & Kurth, N.Y.C., 1993-95, of counsel, 1996—; asst. U.S. atty. So. Dist. N.Y., N.Y.C., 1953-56; lectr. Practising Law Inst. Served with USNR, 1945-46. Fellow Am. Coll. Trial Lawyers; mem. ABA, Fed. Bar Coun., N.Y. State Bar Assn. Clubs: Indian Harbor Yacht, Colo. Arlberg, Yale (N.Y.C.). Home: 434 Round Hill Rd Greenwich CT 06831-2639 Office: Andrews & Kurth 425 Lexington Ave New York NY 10017-3903

STRATTON-CROOKE, THOMAS EDWARD, financial consultant; b. N.Y.C., June 28, 1933; s. Harold and Jeanne Mildred (Stifft); children: Karen, John Ryland; m. Suzanne Williams, Oct. 21, 1989. Student, Hunter Coll., 1951-52; BS in Marine Engrng. and Transp., U.S. Maritime Acad., 1952-56; student, Washington U., St. Louis, 1961; MBA in Internat. Mktg., Banking and Fin., NYU, 1967. Commd. ensign USN, 1956, advanced through grades to lt., 1967; with Goodyear Internat. Corp., Akron, Ohio, 1956-58, Esso Internat., N.Y.C., 1958-60; dir. market info. and devel. Hotel Corp. Am., Boston, 1960-63; with Continental Grain Co., N.Y.C., 1960-64; dir. charter contracts Conoco, Stamford, Conn., 1969-70; cons. A. T. Kearney, Cleve., 1970-81; investment banker E. F. Hutton, Cleve., 1981-83, AG Edwards and Sons, Inc., Cleve., 1983-89; sr. fin. cons., registered investment adviser Merrill Lynch, Cleve., 1989-95, asst. v.p., sr. fin. cons., 1995—; chmn. Indsl. Devel. Resch. Coun., Atlanta, 1970, Indsl. Devel. Resch. Coun., Snow Mass, Colo., 1971; lectr. bus. U. R.I., Kingston, 1968-70, tchr. Bus. Coll. Internat., 1986-89. Contbr. articles to profl. jours. Mem. Findley Lake (N.Y.) Hist. Soc.; mem. Nat. Task Force Reps. for Pres. Reagan, Cleve., 1982—. Mem. Naval Res. Officers Assn., Great Lakes Hist. Soc., Soc. Naval Architects/Engrs., Navy League, U.S. Coast Guard Club (Cleve.), Univ. Club, Circumnavigators Club (life), Internat. Shipmasters Assn., Propeller Club, Army Club, Navy Club, French Creek Hist. Soc., Town Club (Jamestown, N.Y.), Masons, Shriners, Cleve. City Club. Avocations: sailing, skiing, bird watching, gardening, sports car enthusiast. Office: Merrill Lynch 1 Cleveland Ctr 1375 E 9th St Cleveland OH 44114-1724

STRATTON-WHITCRAFT, CATHLEEN SUE, critical care, pediatrics nurse; b. Jackson, Mich., Jan. 14, 1964; d. Ronald Alfred and Shirley Anne (Wickham) Stratton; m. David R. Whitcraft, Aug. 14, 1988. BSN magna cum laude, SUNY, Brockport, 1985. Cert. critical care nurse, ACLS. Student clin. asst. Yale-New Haven Hosp., 1984; charge nurse Walter Reed Army Med. Ctr., Washington, 1990; clin. nurse, critical care med. ICU and pediatric ICU SRT-Med. Staff Agy., Springfield, Va., 1985-88; asst. head nurse Sinai Hosp., Balt., 1988-90; charge nurse surg. SICU ICU VA Med. Ctr., Balt., 1991—. 1st lt. U.S. Army Nurse Corps, 1985-88, Res., 1988-93. Recipient Cert. of Achievement, Elizabeth Dole.

STRAUB, CHESTER JOHN, lawyer; b. Bklyn., May 12, 1937; s. Chester and Ann (Majewski) S.; m. Patricia Morrissey, Aug. 22, 1959; children: Chester, Michael, Christopher, Robert. AB, St. Peter's Coll., 1958; JD, U. Va., 1961. Bar: N.Y. State 1962, U.S. Dist. Ct. (so. and ea. dists.) N.Y. 1963, U.S. Ct. Appeals (2d cir.) 1967, U.S. Supreme Ct. 1978. Assoc. Willkie Farr & Gallagher, N.Y.C., 1963-71; ptnr. Willkie Farr & Gallagher, 1971—; mem. N.Y. State Assembly, 1967-72, N.Y. State Senate, 1973-75, Dem. Nat. Com., 1976-80; mediator U.S. Dist. Ct. (so. dist.) N.Y.; neutral evaluator U.S. Dist. Ct. (ea. dist.) N.Y.; chmn. N.Y. State statewide jud. screening com., 1988-94, first dept. jud. screening com., 1983-94; mem. Senator Moynihan's jud. selection com., 1976—. Mem. Cardinal's Com. of Laity for Cath. Charities N.Y.; trustee Lenox Hill Hosp., Collins Found. With U.S. Army, 1961-63. Mem. Am. Bar Assn., N.Y. State Bar Assn., Assn. of Bar of City of N.Y., Kosciuszko Found., Assn. Sons of Poland. Home: 35 Prescott Ave Bronxville NY 10708-1727 Office: Willkie Farr & Gallagher 1 Citicorp Ctr 153 E 53rd St New York NY 10022-4602

STRAUB, CHESTER JOHN, JR., government official; b. Charlottesville, Va., Oct. 4, 1960; s. Chester John and Patricia (Morrisey) S.; m. Erin Mary Norton, Apr. 21, 1990. BA, Tufts U., 1982. Asst. to exec. dir. Friends of Mario M. Cuomo, Inc., N.Y.C., 1986; dep. exec. dir. N.Y. State Dem. Com., N.Y.C., 1987-89, exec. dir., 1989-90; corp. sec. Battery Park City Authority, N.Y.C., 1990-93; dep. asst. sec. Econ. Devel. Adminstrn., Washington, 1993—. Dir. campaign ops. Clinton/Gore Coordinated Campaign, N.Y.C., 1992. Democrat. Roman Catholic. Home: 716 Queen St Alexandria VA 22314 Office: Econ Devel Adminstrn Rm 7824 14th St and Constitution Washington DC 20230

STRAUB, PETER FRANCIS, novelist; b. Milw., Mar. 2, 1943; s. Gordon Anthony and Elvena (Nilsestuen) S.; m. Susan Bitker, Aug. 27, 1966; children: Benjamin Bitker, Emma Sydney Valli. BA, U. Wis., 1965; MA, Columbia U., 1966. English tchr. Univ. Sch., Milw., 1966-68. Author: Marriages, 1973, Julia, 1975, If You Could See Me Now, 1977, Ghost Story, 1979, Shadow Land, 1980, Floating Dragon, 1983, Lesson Park and Belsize Square, 1984, Wild Animals, 1984, Blue Rose, 1985, Koko, 1988, Mystery, 1989, Houses Without Doors, 1990, Mrs. God, 1991, The Throat, 1993, The Hell Fire Club, 1996; (with Stephen King) The Talisman, 1984; editor: Peter Straub's Ghosts, 1995. Recipient Brit. Fantasy award, August Derleth award, 1983, World Fantasy awards World Fantasy Conv., 1989, 93. Mem. PEN, Mystery Writers Am., Horror Writers Assn (award 1994). Avocations: jazz, opera, classical music.

STRAUB, PETER THORNTON, lawyer; b. St. Louis, Mar. 27, 1939; s. Ralph H. and Mary Louise (Thornton) S.; m. Wendy B. Cubbage, Dec. 29, 1964; children: Karl Thornton, Philip Hamilton, Ellen Elizabeth. A.B., Washington and Lee U., 1961, LLD, 1964. Bar: Mo. 1964, Va. 1964, U.S. Dist. Ct. (ea. dist.) Mo. 1967, U.S. Circuit Ct. Appeals (8th cir.) 1969, U.S. Supreme Ct. 1970. U.S. Circuit Ct. Appeals (D.C. cir.) 1971, Ct. Mil. Appeals 1970, U.S. Tax Ct. 1971, U.S. Bankruptcy Ct. 1991. Assoc. Evans & Dixon, St. Louis, 1966-68; asst. pub. defender St. Louis County, St. Louis, 1968-69; asst. U.S. Atty. St. Louis, 1969-71; trial atty. internal security div. Dept. Justice, Washington, 1971-72; atty.-adviser office of dep. atty. gen. Dept. Justice, 1972-73, dir. office criminal justice, 1974; minority counsel com. on judiciary U.S. Ho. of Reps., Washington, 1973-74; gen. counsel SSS, Washington, 1974-76; sole practice Alexandria, Va., 1976—. Pres., gov. bd. Alexandria Cmty. Mental Health Ctr., 1982-95; mem. No. Va. Estate Planning Coun., 1981—; mem. pres.'s coun. Trinity Coll., Washington, 1980-87; bd. dirs. Parc Frank Condominium, 1990—, sec., 1992—; mem. adv. bd. Am. Heart Assn., Alexandria, 1991-92, Salvation Army, 1991—, v.p., 1994-96; chmn. Alexandria Cmty. Shelter Adv. Bd., 1995—; Va. escheat atty., City of Alexandria, 1994—. Capt. USAR, 1964-66. Recipient certificate of award Dept. Justice, 1970, certificate of appreciation Law Enforcement Assistance Adminstrn. Dept. Justice, 1974, Silver Beaver award Boy Scouts Am., Washington , 1987. Mem. ABA, Fed. Bar Assn., Va. Bar Assn., Bar Assn. Met. St. Louis, Mo. Bar Assn., Alexandria Bar Assn., Va. Trial Lawyers Assn., Nat. Eagle Scout Assn., Nat. Lawyers Club, Optimists (bd. dirs., pres. Alexandria chpt. 1984, lt. gov. Nat. Capitol Va. Dist. 1987-89), Sigma Nu. Republican. Congregationalist. Avocations: scouting, reading, bicycling. Office: 1225 Martha Custis Dr Alexandria VA 22302-2017

STRAUBER, DONALD I., lawyer; b. Bklyn., Dec. 28, 1936; s. Jacob N. and Hannah (Lebedinsky) S.; m. Rachel Leah Sklaroff, Aug. 14, 1960; 1 child, Jocelyn Emily. A.B., U. Pa., Phila., 1957; LL.B., Harvard U., 1960. Bar: N.Y. 1961, U.S. Supreme Ct. 1965. Law clk. to Judge William Herlands U.S. Dist. Ct., So. Dist. N.Y., N.Y.C., 1960-61; assoc. Cravath, Swaine & Moore, N.Y.C., 1962-70; ptnr. Chadbourne & Parke and predecessor, N.Y.C., 1971—. Mem. ABA, N.Y. State Bar Assn., Assn. of Bar of City of N.Y. Home: 1160 Park Ave New York NY 10128-1212 Office: Chadbourne & Parke 30 Rockefeller Plz New York NY 10112

STRAUCH, GERALD OTTO, surgeon; b. Three Rivers, Mich., July 26, 1932; s. Gerald Otto and Helen Jeanette (Zierle) S.; m. Margaret Mary Spindler, Aug. 20, 1955; children—David Mark, Susan Mary, Jean Ellen. Grad., U. Mich., M.D., 1957. Diplomate: Am. Bd. Surgery. Intern R.I. Hosp., Providence, 1957-58; resident in surgery, 1958-62; practice medicine specializing in surgery Stamford, Conn., 1964-79; chief of surgery New Britain (Conn.) Gen. Hosp., 1979-87; clin. prof. surgery N.Y. Med. Coll., 1979-80; prof. surgery U. Conn. Sch. Medicine, 1980-87; clin. prof. surgery Uniformed Svcs. Univ. Health Scis., 1984—, U. Chgo., 1988—; dir. trauma and assembly depts. Am. Coll. Surgeons, 1988—; adj. prof. surgery Northwestern U., 1988—. Contbr. numerous articles to profl. jours. Served to capt. AUS, 1962-64. Fellow ACS; mem. New Eng. Surg. Soc., Frederick A. Coller Surg. Soc., Soc. for Surgery of Alimentary Tract, Collegium Internationale Chirurgiae Digestivae, Conn. Soc. Am. Bd. Surgeons, Am. Assn. Surgery of Trauma, Ctrl. Surgery Assn., Chgo. Surg. Soc., Assn. Advancement Automotive Medicine, Shock Soc., Corr. Soc. Surgeons (editor), Sociedad de Cirujanos de Chile (hon.), Assn. Mejicana de Cirujanos Generales (hon.), Assn. Française de Chirurgie (hon.), Hellenic Surg. Soc. (hon.). Republican. Roman Catholic. Clubs: Wee Burn Country. Home: 633 Sheridan Rd Winnetka IL 60093-2323 Office: Am Coll Surgeons 55 E Erie St Chicago IL 60611-2731

STRAUCH, JOHN L., lawyer; b. Pitts., Apr. 16, 1939; s. Paul L. and Delilah M. (Madison) S.; m. Gail Lorraine Kohn, Dec. 5, 1991; children: Paul L., John M., Lisa E. BA, U. Pitts., 1960; JD magna cum laude, NYU Sch. Law, 1963. Law clk. to Judge Sterry Waterman U.S. Ct. Appeals (2d cir.), St. Johnsbury, Vt., 1963-64; assoc. Jones, Day, Reavis & Pogue, Cleve., 1964-70, ptnr., 1970—, mem. adv. com., partnership com., chmn. litigation group; mem. Statutory Com. on Selecting Bankruptcy Judges, Cleve., 1985-88; mem. lawyers com. Nat. Ctr. for State Cts. Editor-in-chief: NYU Law Rev., 1962-63. Pres., trustee Cleve. Task Force on Violent Crimes, 1985-88; trustee Legal Aid Soc., Cleve., 1978, Cleve. Greater Growth Assn., 1985-86, Citizens Mental Health Assembly, 1989-90, lawyers com. Nat. Ctr. for State Cts., 1989—. Fellow Am. Coll. Trial Lawyers (life); mem. ABA, Ohio Bar Assn., Cleve. Bar Assn. (trustee 1980-83, pres. 1985-86), Fed. Bar Assn. (trustee Cleve. chpt. 1978-79, v.p. Cleve. chpt. 1979-80), Sixth Fed. Jud. Conf. (life), Ohio Eighth Jud. Conf. (life), Order of Coif, Inns of Ct., Oakmont Club, Cleve. Racquet Club, 13th St. Racquet Club, The Country Club, Phi Beta Kappa. Home: 28149 N Woodland Rd Cleveland OH 44124-4522 Office: Jones Day Reavis & Pogue N Point 901 Lakeside Ave E Cleveland OH 44114-1116

STRAUCH, KARL, physicist, educator; b. Germany, Oct. 4, 1922; came to U.S., 1939, naturalized, 1944; s. Georg and Carola (Bock) S.; m. Maria Gerson, June 10, 1951; children—Roger A., Hans D. A.B. in Chemistry and Physics, U. Calif. at Berkeley, 1943, Ph.D. in Physics, 1950. Jr. fellow Soc. Fellows, Harvard U., 1950-53; asst. prof. Harvard U., Cambridge, Mass., 1953-57, assoc. prof., 1957-62, prof., 1962-76; dir. Cambridge Electron Accelerator, 1967-74, George Vasmer Leverett prof. physics, 1976-93, George Vasmer Leverett prof. emeritus, 1993—; researcher in high energy physics. Contbr. articles to profl. jours. Served with USNR, 1944-46. Mem. Am. Phys. Soc., Am. Assn. Physics Tchrs., Am. Acad. Arts and Scis., Phi Beta Kappa, Sigma Xi. Home: 81 Pleasant St Lexington MA 02173-6116 Office: Harvard U Dept Physics Cambridge MA 02138

STRAUGHAN, WILLIAM THOMAS, engineering educator; b. Shreveport, La., Aug. 2, 1936; s. William Eugene and Sara Chloetilde (Harrell) S.; m. Rubie Ann Barnes, Aug. 20, 1957; children: Donna Ann, Sara Arlene, Eugene Thomas. BS, MIT, 1959; MS, U. Tex., 1986; PhD, Tex. Tech. U., 1990. Registered profl. engr., Fla., Ill., Iowa., La., Tex., Wash. Project engr. Gen. Dynamics Corp., Chgo., 1959-60; chief project, design engr. Gen. Foods Corp., Kankakee, Ill., 1960-64; mgr. plant engrng. Standard Brands Inc., Clinton, Iowa, 1964-66; regional mgr. Air Products & Chems., Inc., Creighton, Pa., 1966-68; gen. mgr. Skyline Corp., Harrisburg, N.C., 1968-70; cons. Charlotte, N.C., 1970-72; dir. engrng. and Fla. ops. Zimmer Homes Corp., Pompano Beach, 1972-73; v.p. engrng. and mfg. Nobility Homes, Inc., Ocala, Fla., 1973-78, Moduline Internat., Inc., Lacey, Wash., 1978-85; rsch. engr. U. Tex., Austin, 1985-86; lectr., rschr. Tex. Tech. U., Lubbock, 1987-90; assoc. prof. U. New Orleans, 1990-92; asst. prof. dept. civil engrng. La. Tech. U., Ruston, 1992—; cons. in field, Dubach, La., 1992—; condr. workshops in field; apptd. spokesman Mfrd. Housing Industry before U.S. Congress. Contbr. articles to profl. jours. Vol. engrng. svcs. Lubbock Fire Safety House, 1990; judge sci. fair Ben Franklin H.S., New Orleans, 1990. Recipient T.L. James Svc. award La. Tech. U., 1994; grantee Urban Waste Mgmt. and Rsch. Ctr., New Orleans, 1991, Shell Devel. Co., 1993, La. Edn. Quality Support Fund, Insituform Techs., Inc., Trenchless Tech. Ctr., PABCO, Inc., InLiner USA, Inc., 1995, and numerous others. Mem. ASME (life), ASCE (Student chpt. Tchr. of Yr. award 1995), NSPE, Am. Soc. Engrng. Edn., Phi Kappa Phi, Sigma Xi, Chi Epsilon. Achievements include: designed, constructed and managed first plant for the prodn. of intermediate moisture pet food (Gainesburgers) in the world. Organized and directed all activities to allow Clinton, Iowa plant with a 1 mile shoreline to continue ops. during the greatest flood of the upper MIss. River in 1965. Avocations: flying, skiing, backpacking, golf, photography. Home: 199 Sellers Rd Dubach LA 71235

STRAUGHN, LAURA HAMILTON, special education educator; b. LaGrange, Ky., Nov. 11, 1961; d. Bruce Ross and Hilda Ann (King) Hamilton; m. Leonard Ray Straughn, Dec. 27, 1986. Student, Eastern Ky. U., 1979-81; BA, U. Ky., Lexington, 1983; Masters, U. Louisville, 1990. Cert. spl. edn. tchr., Ind., Ky. Tchr. spl. edn. Oldham County Schs., 1984-89; edn. specialist Jefferson (Ind.) Hosp., 1989-93; state cons. Ky. Dept. of Edn., Frankfort, 1993; cons. Floyd County Schs., New Albany, Ind., 1993-94, spl. edn. tchr., 1994—; presenter Floyd County Schs. and Jefferson Hosp., 1990—, Ky. Dept. Edn., Frankfort, 1993—; mem. task force on emotional behavioral disability Ky. Dept. Edn., Frankfort, 1993. presenter Floyd County Schs. and Jefferson Hosp., 1990—, Ky. Dept. Edn., Frankfort, 1993—; mem. tasl force on emotional behavioral disability Kt. Dept. Edn., Frankfort, 1993; adj. instr. Ind. U., 1996. Mem. ASCD, Coun. for Exceptional Children, Coun. for Children with Behavior Disorders (v.p. 1994). Avocations: antiques, horse-back riding. Home: 7425 W Highway 524

Westport KY 40077-9705 Office: New Albany HS 1020 Vincennes St New Albany IN 47150-3148

STRAUMANIS, JOHN JANIS, JR., psychiatry educator; b. Riga, Latvia, Apr. 22, 1935; came to U.S., 1950; s. Janis and Ella (Fredrichson) S.; m. Carol A. Sharar, Aug. 8, 1959; children: John, Susan. BA, U. Iowa, 1957, MD, 1960, MS, 1964. Intern Georgetown U. Hosp., Washington, 1960-61; resident U. Iowa, Iowa City, 1961-64; asst. prof. Temple U., Phila., 1966-71, assoc. prof., 1971-77, prof., 1977-85; prof. psychiatry La. State U., Shreveport, 1985-92; prof. psychiatry, dir. rsch. Tulane U. Med. Sch., New Orleans, 1992—; cons. Camden County Hosp., Blackwood, N.J., 1967-85, VA Hosp., Shreveport, 1985-92, VA Hosp., New Orleans, 1992—. Contbr. articles to profl. jours. Lt. comdr. USN, 1964-65. Rsch. Career Devel. award NIMH, 1966. Fellow Am. Psychiat. Assn.; mem. ACP, Am. Psychopathol. Assn., Soc. Biol. Psychiatry, Am. EEG Assn., Phi Eta Sigma, Phi Beta Kappa, Alpha Omega Alpha. Avocations: travel, music, photography. Office: Tulane U Med Ctr Dept Psychiatry & Neurology 1430 Tulane Ave New Orleans LA 70112-2699

STRAUS, ALAN GORDON, lawyer; b. Washington, Nov. 1, 1952; s. Richard and Elaine (Scharroff) S.; m. Katherine Way Schoonover, June 16, 1979. BA with honors, U. Wis., 1974; JD, NYU, 1977. Bar: N.Y. 1978. Assoc. Skadden, Arps, Slate, Meagher & Flom, N.Y.C., 1977-84, 85-88, ptnr., 1988—; ptnr. Brown, Raysman & Milstein, N.Y.C., 1984-85. Co-author: Federal Regulation of Campaign Finance and Political Activity, 1982. Office: Skadden Arps Slate Meagher 919 3rd Ave New York NY 10022*

STRAUS, DAVID A., architectural firm executive; b. Medford, Oreg., 1943; m. Sherry Straus, 1974; 2 children. BArch, U. Oreg., 1967. Registered architect, Oreg. Founding ptnr. Skelton, Straus & Seibert, Medford, 1989—. Past bd. dirs. Medford YMCA, Rogue Valley Art Assn.; past pres. Medford Arts Commn., Arts Coun. So. Oreg.; coach Rogue Valley Soccer Assn.; leader Boy Scouts Am.; bd. dirs., past pres. Schneider Mus. Art SOSC. Ret. lt. USNR, Vietnam. Mem. AIA (past pres. So. Oreg. chpt.), Archtl. Found. Oreg. (bd. dirs.), Univ. Club Medford (past pres.), Oreg. Club So. Oreg. (past pres.), U. Oreg. Alumni Assn., Medford/Jackson County C. of C. (bd. dirs.), Rotary. Office: Skelton Straus & Seibert Arch 26 Hawthorne St Medford OR 97504-7114

STRAUS, DONALD BLUN, retired company executive; b. Middletown, N.J., June 28, 1916; s. Percy S. and Edith (Abraham) S.; m. Elizabeth Allen, Sept. 7, 1940; children: David Allen, Robert Beckwith, Sara Elizabeth. A.B., Harvard U., 1938, M.B.A., 1940. Exec. dir. labor relations panel AEC, 1948-53; v.p. Health Ins. Plan of Greater N.Y., 1953-61; pres. Am. Arbitration Assn., 1963-72, pres. research inst., 1972-81; cons. Internat. Inst. of Applied Systems Analysis, 1982-85; mem. N.Y. State Bd. Mediation, 1956-59. Chmn. bd. Planned Parenthood Fedn. Am., 1962-65; emeritus bd. dirs. Internat. Council Comml. Arbitration, Population Resources Commn., Soc. Human Ecology; emeritus trustee Carnegie Endowment for Internat. Peace, Inst. Advanced Study, Princeton, Coll. of Atlantic. Mem. Coun. Fgn. Rels. Clubs: Century Assn., Knickerbocker, Harvard of N.Y.C., Pot and Kettle (Bar Harbor, Maine). Home: 1 E 66th St New York NY 10021-5852

STRAUS, HELEN LORNA PUTTKAMMER, biologist, educator; b. Chgo., Feb. 15, 1933; d. Ernst Wilfred and Helen Louise (Monroe) Puttkammer; m. Francis Howe Straus II, June 11, 1955; children: Francis Howe III, Helen E., Christopher M., Michael W. AB magna cum laude, Radcliffe Coll., 1955; MS in Anatomy, U. Chgo., 1960, PhD in Anatomy, 1962. With U. Chgo., 1964—, asst. prof. anatomy, 1967-73, dean of students, 1971-82, assoc. prof., 1973-87, dean of admissions, 1975-80, prof. anatomy and biol. scis., 1987—; bd. govs. U. Chgo. Internat. House, 1987—. Trustee Radcliffe Coll., Cambridge, Mass., 1973-83. Recipient Quantrell Award for Excellence in teaching, U. Chgo., 1970, 87, Silver medal Case Outstanding Tchr. Program, 1987. Mem. AAAS, NCAA (acad. requirements com. 1986-92, chmn. 1990-92, rsch. com. 1996—), Nat. Sci. Tchrs. Assn., Am. Assn. Anatomists, Harvard U. Alumni Assn. (bd. dirs. 1980-83), Phi Beta Kappa (sec., treas. U. Chgo. chpt. 1984—). Avocations: gardening, crafts, travel. Home: 5642 S Kimbark Ave Chicago IL 60637-1606 Office: U Chgo 5845 S Ellis Ave Chicago IL 60637-1404

STRAUS, IRVING LEHMAN, public relations executive; b. N.Y.C., Apr. 1, 1921; s. Nathan and Helen (Sachs) S.; m. Anna M. Straus, Jan. 27, 1977; children: Daniel, William. Student, Amherst Coll. (Mass.), 1939-41. Ptnr. Ralph E. Samuel & Co., N.Y.C., 1954-65; v.p. Energy Fund Inc., N.Y.C., 1958-65; pres., founder Straus Assocs., Inc., N.Y.C., 1965-80; ptnr. Fin. Rels. Board Inc., N.Y.C., 1980-88, sr. cons., 1986—; dir. Arnold Constable Corp., N.Y.C., 1979-88; chmn. bd. Straus Corp. Comm., N.Y.C., 1989—; founder, pres. Mut. Fund Coun., 1989—, Westchester Aquarium, Inc., White Plains, N.Y., 1947-55; pres. Inst. Systems Corp., N.Y.C., 1983—. With USN, 1942-45. Decorated Air medal. Mem. Pub. Rels. Soc. Am. (Silver Anvil 1979), Intrepid Mus. Pilot's Assn. (chmn. N.Y.C. chpt. 1985-89). Office: Straus Corp Comm 1501 Broadway New York NY 10036

STRAUS, KENNETH HOLLISTER, former retail store executive; b. N.Y.C., Feb. 18, 1925; s. Jack Isidor and Margaret (Hollister) S.; m. Elizabeth Browne, Apr. 14, 1945 (dec. 1991); children: Melinda Straus Schwartz, Timothy; m. Brenda Newbauer Murphy, June 28, 1993. Grad., Milton Acad., 1943; student, NYU Sch. Retailing, 1945-46; grad. advanced mgmt. program, Harvard Bus. Sch., 1957. With R.H. Macy & Co., Inc., N.Y.C., 1947-85, v.p. men's and boy's wear, 1963-67, sr. v.p. domestic and internat. corp. buying, 1967-78, pres. corp. buying, 1978-80, chmn., chief exec. officer corp. buying, 1980-85, also dir., ret., 1985; cons. Nat Exec. Svc. Corp., 1985—. Hon. dep. commr., 1985-93, trustee, hon. commr. 1993—, honor emergency fund N.Y.C. Fire Dept., 1966—, chair, hon. officer adv. com., 1988—; bd. dirs. N.Y. Fire Safety Found., 1984—; pres. Fire Found. of N.Y. Inc., 1968—; mem. adv. bd. John Jay Coll. Criminal Justice, 1987—; mem. pub. safety com. The Partnership, 1987-89; bd. dirs. Police Found. 1987—, chair crime stoppers program, 1987—; vestryman St. James' Ch., 1988-94, chmn. bldgs. and grounds com., 1988-94, grants com., Michel Fund com., 1989-90; trustee St. Luke's/Roosevelt Hosp. Ctr., 1988—, mem. exec. com., 1994—; trustee, v.p. Bd. Fgn. Parishes, 1988—, exec. com., 1989—; mem. coun. Episcopal Diocese of N.Y., 1988-91, chair comm. task force, 1989-90; bd. dirs. Episcopal Mission Soc., 1989-91, Crime Stoppers Internat., 1993—; v.p., bd. dirs. Eastside Community Ctr., Inc., 1988-91. With AUS, 1943-45. Decorated Order of Crown (Belgium); recipient Good Scout award Boy Scouts Am., 1965; named to Soc. St. John Jerusalem, 1987—. Mem. Piping Rock Club, Union Club, Harvard Club, Honor Legion FDNY (hon. 1992—). Home: 60 E End Ave Apt 40-c New York NY 10028

STRAUS, LEON STEPHAN, physicist; b. Takoma Park, Md., May 29, 1943; s. Sidney and Ruth Straus; m. Cheryl Sarran Straus, Apr. 4, 1970; children: Jonathan, Jennifer. BS in Physics, Antioch Coll., Yellow Springs, Ohio, 1965; M Physics, Georgetown U., 1970, PhD in Physics, 1971. Mem. rsch. staff Ctr. Naval Analyses, Alexandria, Va., 1973-75; field rep. CTF 69 Ctr. Naval Analyses, Naples, Italy, 1975-77; project mgr. Ctr. Naval Analyses, Alexandria, 1977-79; field rep. CTF 69 and CTF 66/67 Ctr. Naval Analyses, Naples, Italy, 1979-82; assoc. dep. dir. Ctr. Naval Analyses, Alexandria, 1982-85; field rep. CTF 72 Ctr. Naval Analyses, Kamiseya, Japan, 1985-87; program mgr. Ctr. Naval Analyses, Alexandria, 1987-90; field rep. COMSIXTHFLT Ctr. Naval Analyses, Gaeta, Italy, 1990-92; project mgr. Ctr. Naval Analyses, Alexandria, 1992-95, dir. spl. projects, 1995—; asst. AEC, Germantown, Md., 1968-71. Contbr. articles to profl. jours. Vol. Jewish lay leader USN, Naples, 1975-77, 79-82. Recipient Fellowship Georgetown U., Washington, 1965-68. Mem. Acoustical Soc. Am., Navy Submarine League. Jewish. Achievements include planning, evaluating and documenting tests/exercises associated with U.S. Navy and joint strategy, tactics, comm. and tech. Office: Ctr Naval Analyses 4401 Ford Ave Alexandria VA 22302-1432

STRAUS, OSCAR S., II, foundation executive; b. N.Y.C., Nov. 6, 1914; s. Roger Williams and Gladys (Guggenheim) S.; m. Marion Miller Straus, 1941 (div. 1982); 1 child, Oscar S. III.; m. Joan Sutton, 1982. A.B., Princeton U., 1936; postgrad., U. Dijon, summer 1936, Sch. Bus. Adminstrn. Harvard U., 1938. Pvt. sec. Internat. Labor Office, Geneva, Switzerland, 1937-38; U.S. fgn. service officer, 1940-42; divisional asst. Dept. State, 1942-43, 44-45; treas., dir., v.p., chmn. finance com. Am. Smelting & Refining Co., 1945-59; partner Guggenheim Bros., 1959-83; pres., dir. Guggenheim Exploration Co., Inc., 1963-73; gen. ptnr. Straus Minerals, 1973-88; pres., bd. dirs. Daniel and Florence Guggenheim Found., N.Y.C.; pres., bd. dirs. Fred L. Lavanburg Found.; bd. dirs. Mutual of Omaha, Companion Life Ins. Co., United of Omaha. Trustee emeritus Am. Mus. Natural History, Mystic Seaport, Conn.; hon. chmn. Rensselaerville (N.Y.) Inst.; trustee Congregation Emanu-El. Mem. Coun. Fgn. Rels., Royal Nova Scotia Yacht Squadron Club, Cruising Club Am., River Club, Megantic Fish and Game Club, Doubles Club, Knickerbocker Club, L.I. Wyandanch Club Inc. Jewish. Home: 7 Gracie Sq New York NY 10028-8030 Office: Daniel & Florence Guggenheim Found 950 3rd Ave Fl 30 New York NY 10022-2705

STRAUS, R. PETER, communications company executive, broadcasting executive; b. N.Y.C., Feb. 15, 1923; s. Nathan and Helen (Sachs) S.; m. Ellen Louise Sulzberger, Feb. 6, 1950; children: Diane (Mrs. Carll Tucker), Katherine (Mrs. Blair Caple), Jeanne (Mrs. Richard Tofel), Eric. B.A. cum laude, Yale U., 1943. Chief sec. manpower div. U.S. Office Mil. Govt., Berlin, 1946-47; pub. relations exec. Edward L. Bernays, N.Y.C., 1947-48; program dir. spl. features radio sta. WMCA, N.Y.C., 1948-50; exec. asst. to dir. gen. ILO, Geneva, 1950-55; dir. U.S. office, 1955-58; pres. Straus Broadcasting Group, 1958-67; asst. adminstr. for Africa AID, 1967-69; pres. Straus Communications Inc., 1970-77, chmn., 1979—; chmn. Radio Sta. WMCA, N.Y.C., 1979-87, Radio Sta. WFTR, Front Royal, Va., 1980—, Radio Sta. WELV, Ellenville, N.Y., 1982—; pub. Advertiser Group Newspapers, Monroe, N.Y., 1986—, Pointer View, West Point, N.Y., Sparta (N.J.) Independent, 1988—; dir. Voice of Am., 1977-79; pres. Straus Comm., Inc., Stas. WELV-AM, WWWK-Fm, Ellenville, N.Y., 1993—; mem. faculty Johns Hopkins U. Sch. Advanced Internat. Studies, Washington, 1979-80; pub. Straus Editor's Report, 1970-72, Cranford (N.J.) Citizen and Chronicle, 1976-78; Spl. cons. USIA, 1966; Co-chmn. Interracial Council Bus. Opportunity N.Y., 1966-67; chmn. Com. Constl. Issues, N.Y., 1966-67; mem. N.Y.C. Commn. on State-City Relations, 1972-73; advisory com. Ministry of Tourism, Israel, 1972-75, N.Y.C. Aux. Policeman, 1974-77; lectr. Boston U. Sch. Pub. Communication, 1975-76; host internat. radio program Hotline, 1974-77; vis. prof. Woodrow Wilson Sch., Princeton U., 1981-82; moderator Aspen Inst. Exec. Seminar, 1982-83; founder, chmn. Com. Decent Unbiased Campaign Tactics Conduct, 1982—. Author: How To Keep Albany from Milking The City Dry, 1968, Is The State Department Color Blind, 1971, The Buddy System in Foreign Affairs, 1973, The Father of Anne Frank, 1975, The Risks and Rewards of Candor, 1979. Chmn. N.Y. State Democratic Campaign Com., 1964; N.Y. del. Nat. Dem. Convs., 1960, 64; mem. fgn. affairs task force Dem. Nat. Com., 1975-77; bd. govs. Am. Jewish Com., 1982—, pres. N.Y. chpt., 1984-87; founding mem. Black/Jewish Coalition, 1983—; v.p. Jewish Community Relations Council N.Y., 1987—; adv. bd. Nat. Inst. Against Prejudice and Violence, 1987—; bd. dirs. Golda Meir Assn., 1987—; mem. The Ctr. for Excellence in Govt.; pres. Jewish Edn. in Media, 1990. Served to 1st lt. USAAF, 1943-45. Decorated Air medal with 5 oak leaf clusters; recipient award Harlem Lawyers Assn., 1964. Mem. Council Fgn. Relations, N.Y. State Broadcasters Assn. (pres. 1964), Assn. for Edn. in Journalism and Mass Communication. Clubs: Federal City (Washington), Nat. Press (Washington); Yale (N.Y.C.). Office: Straus Communications 22 N Main St Ellenville NY 12428-1019*

STRAUS, ROBERT, behavioral sciences educator; b. New Haven, Jan. 9, 1923; s. Samuel Hirsh and Alma (Fleischner) S.; m. Ruth Elisabeth Dawson, Sept. 8, 1945; children: Robert James, Carol Martin, Margaret Dawson, John William. BA, Yale U., 1943, MA, 1945, PhD, 1947. Asst. prof. Yale U., 1948-51, research asso. applied psychology, 1951-53; acting dir. Conn. Child Study and Treatment Home, New Haven, 1952-53; assoc. prof. preventive medicine SUNY Upstate Med. Center, 1953-56; prof. med. sociology U. Ky., Lexington, 1956-59; prof. dept. behavioral sci. Coll. Medicine, also chmn. dept. U. Ky., 1959-87; dir. for sci. devel. Med. Rsch. Inst. San Francisco, 1991-93; vis. fellow Yale U., 1968-69; vis. prof. U. Calif., Berkeley, 1978, 86; sec. Com. Med. Sociology, 1955-57; chmn. Coop. Com. Study Alcoholism, 1961-63; chmn. Nat. Adv. Com. on Alcoholism, 1966-69; mem. Nat. Adv. Coun. on Alcohol Abuse and Alcoholism, 1984-87; trustee Med. Rsch. Inst. San Francisco, 1988-93; mem. Calif. Pacific Med. Ctr. Rsch. Coun., 1993. Author: Medical Care for Seamen, 1950 (with S.D. Bacon), Drinking in College, 1953, Alcohol and Society, 1973, Escape From Custody, 1974; A Medical School is Born, 1996; co-editor: Medicine and Society, 1963; mem. editorial bd.: Jour. Studies on Alcohol. Pres., Bluegrass R.R. Mus., 1980. Mem. Inst. Medicine NAS, Am. Sociol. Assn. (chmn. med. sociology sect. 1967-68), Assn. Behavioral Scis. and Med. Edn. (pres. 1974), Am. Pub. Health Assn. (lifetime achievement award sect. on alcohol, tobacco and other drugs 1993), Acad. Behavioral Medicine Rsch., Phi Beta Kappa, Sigma Xi. Home: 656 Raintree Rd Lexington KY 40502-2874

STRAUS, R(OBERT) JAMES, lawyer; b. New Haven, Aug. 17, 1946; s. Robert and Ruth (Dawson) S.; m. Donna Craig, Dec. 27, 1968; children—Leigh Elisabeth, Amanda Craig, Emily Dawson, Robert Benjamin. B.A. cum laude, Yale U., 1968; J.D., U. Chgo., 1974. Bar: Ky. 1974, U.S. Dist. Ct. (we. dist.) Ky. 1974. Assoc., Brown, Todd & Heyburn, Louisville, Ky., 1974-79, ptnr., 1979—. Chmn. Legal Aid Soc., Inc., Louisville, 1981-85. Served to capt. USMC, 1968-71; Vietnam. Mem. Louisville Bar Assn., Ky. Bar Assn., ABA. Democrat. Presbyterian. Clubs: Jefferson, Louisville Boat. Home: 2517 Top Hill Rd Louisville KY 40206-2830 Office: 3200 Providian Ctr Louisville KY 40202-3363

STRAUS, ROGER W., JR., publishing company executive; b. N.Y.C., Jan. 3, 1917; s. Roger Williams and Gladys (Guggenheim) S.; m. Dorothea Liebmann, June 27, 1938; 1 son, Roger W. III. Student, Hamilton Coll., 1935-37; B.J., U. Mo., 1939, Litt.D. (hon.), 1976. Reporter Daily Reporter, White Plains, N.Y., 1936; feature writer Daily Reporter, 1939-40; editorial writer, reporter Columbia Missourian, 1937-39; editor, pub. Asterisk, 1939; editorial asst. Current History, 1940, assoc. editor, 1940-45; assoc. editor Forum, 1940-45; pres. Book Ideas, Inc., 1943-46; founder Farrar, Straus & Co., Inc. (now Farrar, Straus & Giroux, Inc.), 1945; pres. Farrar, Straus & Giroux, Inc., N.Y.C., 1987—; chmn. adv. bd. Partisan Rev. mag., 1959-69. Co-editor: The Sixth Column, 1941, War Letters from Britain, 1941, The New Order, 1941; Chmn. publ. bd.: Am. Judaism mag, 1955-65. Vice pres. Fred L. Lavanburg Found., 1950-80, Daniel and Florence Guggenheim Found., 1960-76; bd. dirs. Harry Frank Guggenheim Found., Manhattanville Coll., 1970-76, John Simon Guggenheim Found.; fellow N.Y. Inst. for Humanities. Served to lt. USNR, 1941-45. Mem. P.E.N., Union Am. Hebrew Congregations (pub. com. 1955-65), Sigma Delta Chi. Clubs: Lotos, Westchester Country, Players. Office: Farrar Straus & Giroux Inc 19 Union Sq W New York NY 10003-3307

STRAUS, ROGER W, III, book publishing executive, photographer; b. N.Y.C., Nov. 13, 1943; s. Roger Williams and Dorothea (Leibman) S.; m. Nina Pelikan, June 4, 1965; children: Laura, Rachel, Tamara; m. Doris Ann Borowski, Mar. 3, 1987. BA, Columbia Coll., 1967. Dir. sales, mktg. Farrar, Straus & Giroux, N.Y.C., 1967-75; dir. mktg. Harper & Row, N.Y.C., 1976-79, editorial dir., 1979-81, assoc. pub., 1981-82; dir. sales Times Books, N.Y.C., 1982-84; exec. editor Avon Books, N.Y.C., 1984-85; mng. dir. Farrar, Straus & Giroux, 1986—; dir. Beacon Press, Boston, The Godine Press, Boston. Democrat. Jewish. Avocation: kayaking. Home: 730 King Ave Bronx NY 10464-1115 Office: Farrar Straus & Giroux Inc 19 Union Sq W New York NY 10003-3307

STRAUSBAUGH, SCOTT DAVID, Olympic athlete, canoeist. Olympic slalom doubles canoeist Barcelona, Spain, 1992. Recipient Gold medal canoe slalom doubles Olympics, Barcelona, 1992. Address: PO Box 114 Hartford TN 37753

STRAUSER, BEVERLY ANN, education educator; b. Dunkirk, N.Y., July 19, 1956; d. Henry Frank and Agnes Frances (Bielat) Rutkowski; m. Edward Britton Strauser, Oct. 9, 1982; children: Nicholas, Douglas, Thomas. BS, Regents Coll., Albany, N.Y., 1985; MS, SUNY, Fredonia, 1990. Cert. tchr. early childhood, bus. adminstrn., N.Y. Tchr. gifted edn. and computer literacy North Collins (N.Y.) Ctrl. Sch., 1986-87; tchr. pre-sch. St. Anthony's Sch., Fredonia, 1988-91; asst. prof. edn. Armstrong State Coll., Savannah, Ga., 1992—; cons. Jamestown (N.Y.) Cmty. Schs., 1989-91, Jewish Ednl. Allance, Savannah, 1991-92, Meth. Daysch. of Richmond Hill, Ga., 1992-93; presenter in field. Recipient Key award Jamestown Cmty. Schs., 1990. Mem. Nat. Assn. for the Edn. of Young Children, Ga. Assn. on Young Children (bd. dirs., sr. dist. rep. 1992-94), Internat. Reading Assn., Assn. Childhood Edn. Internat. Avocations: travel, reading. Home: 264 Boyd Dr Richmond Hill GA 31324-9400 Office: Armstrong State Coll 11935 Abercorn St Savannah GA 31419-1909

STRAUSER, EDWARD B., psychologist, educator; b. Dunkirk, N.Y., June 6, 1953; s. Fredrick Edward and Lucille Ruth (Mayott) S.; m. Beverly Ann Rutkoswki; children: Nicholas, Douglas, Thomas. BS, SUNY, Fredonia, 1975; MS, Canisius Coll., 1980; EdD, SUNY, Buffalo, 1986. 4th-9th grade tchr. Pioneer Mid. Sch., Yorkshire, N.Y., 1977-82; sch. psychologist BOCES, Orchard Park, N.Y., 1982-91; asst. prof. Pembroke (N.C.) State U., 1987-88; asst. prof., then assoc. prof. Armstrong State Coll., Savannah, Ga., 1991—; cons. ACT/PEP Test Svc., Albany, N.Y., 1988, SUNY, Fredonia, 1988-89, Cleve. City Schs., 1992. Contbr. chpts. to books and articles to profl. jours. Mem. exec. bd. Erie County Spl. Olympics, Orchard Park, 1983-84; bd. dirs. N.Y. Assn. Sch. Psychologists, 1990. Recipient Citation of Appreciation for Profl. Contbn., Nat. Mid. Sch. Assn., 1988. Mem. AAUP, Am. Assn. Tchg. and Curriculum, Nat. Assn. Sch. Psychologists, N.Y. State Tchrs. of Handicapped, Ga. Mid. Level Educators, Phi Delta Kappa. Avocation: travel. Home: 264 Boyd Dr Richmond Hill GA 31324-9400 Office: Armstrong State Coll 11935 Abercorn St Savannah GA 31419-1909

STRAUSER, ROBERT WAYNE, lawyer; b. Little Rock, Aug. 28, 1943; s. Christopher Columbus and Opal (Orr) S.; m. Atha Maxine Tubbs, June 26, 1971 (div. 1991); children: Robert Benjamin, Ann Kathleen. BA, Davidson (N.C.) Coll., 1965; postgrad., Vanderbilt U., Nashville, 1965-66; LLB, U. Tex., 1968. Bar: Tex. 1968, U.S. Ct. Mil. Appeals 1971. Staff atty. Tex. Legis. Coun., Austin, 1969-71; counsel Jud. Com., Tex. Ho. of Reps., Austin, 1971-73; chief counsel Jud. Com., Tex. Constl. Conv., Austin, 1974; exec. v.p. and legis. counsel Tex. Assn. Taxpayers, Austin, 1974-85; assoc. Baker & Botts, Austin, 1985-87; ptnr. Baker & Botts, 1988—. Assoc. editor Tex. Internat. Law Jour., 1968. Mem. Tex. Ho. Speakers Econ. Devel. Com., Austin, 1986-87; mem. Austin Coun. Fgn. Affairs, 1987—; dir. McDonald Obs. Bd. Visitors, 1988—; mem. adv. bd. Sch. of Social Work, U. Tex. Lyceum Assn., 1980-81, 84-88; mem. Dean's Roundtable, U. Tex. Law Sch.; elder Presbyn. Ch.; mem. exec. com. Austin Symphony Orch. Soc., 1985—, v.p., 1993-94. Capt. USNR, ret. Named Rising Star of Tex., Tex. Bus. Mag., 1983. Mem. State Bar of Tex. (coun. mem. tax sect.), Travis County Bar Assn., Headliners Club (Austin). Home: 3312 Gilbert St Austin TX 78703-2102 Office: Baker & Botts 1600 San Jacinto Blvd Austin TX 78701

STRAUSFELD, NICHOLAS JAMES, neurobiology and evolutionary biology researcher, educator; b. Claygate, England, Oct. 22, 1942. BSc in Zoology, U. Coll. London, 1965, PhD in Neurophysiology, 1968; PhD in Neurophysiology, Habilitation, Frankfurt, Germany, 1985. Prof. U. Ariz., Tucson. Author: (books) Atlas of an Insect Brain, 1976, Functional Neuroanatomy, 1983. John Simon Guggenheim fellow, 1984, MacArthur fellow, 1995. Office: U Arizona Rsch Labs Divsn Neurobiology Tucson AZ 85721

STRAUSS, ALBRECHT BENNO, English educator, editor; b. Berlin, May 17, 1921; came to U.S., 1940; s. Bruno and Bertha (Badt) S.; m. Nancy Grace Barron, July 30, 1978; 1 child, Rebecca Ilse; stepchildren: Carolyn, Kathryn. BA, Oberlin Coll., 1942; MA, Tulane U., 1948; PhD, Harvard U., 1956. Instr. English Brandeis U., 1951-52; teaching fellow gen. edn. Harvard U., 1952-55; instr. English Yale U., 1955-59; asst. prof. English U. Okla., Norman, 1959-60; asst. prof. English U. N.C., Chapel Hill, 1960-64, assoc. prof., 1964-70, prof., 1970-91, prof. emeritus, 1991—. Editor Studies in Philology, 1974-80; sec. editorial com. Yale Edit. of Works of Samuel Johnson, 1975—; mem. editorial com. Ga. edit. works of Tobias Smollett, 1973—; contbr. articles to lit. publs. Served with U.S. Army, 1942-46. Recipient Tanner Teaching award U. N.C., 1966; Fulbright fellow, Germany, 1983-84. Mem. MLA, South Atlantic MLA, Am. Soc. Eighteenth-Century Studies (pres. Southeastern group 1980-81), Coll. English Assn., Johnsonians. Republican. Jewish. Home: 396 Lakeshore Ln Chapel Hill NC 27514-1728 Office: U NC 401 Greenlaw Bldg Chapel Hill NC 27599

STRAUSS, AUDREY, lawyer; b. Phila., Oct. 7, 1947; m. John R. Wing; children: Carlin, Matthew. AB, Barnard Coll., 1968; JD, Columbia U., 1971. Bar: N.Y., 1972, U.S. Dist. Ct. (so. and ea. dists.) N.Y. 1972, U. S. Ct. Appeals (2d cir.) N.Y. 1972. Law clk. to Hon. Lawrence W. Pierce, N.Y.C., 1971-72; asst. atty. U.S. Atty.'s Office (So. Dist of N.Y.), N.Y.C., 1975-82, chief appellate atty., 1977-78, chief, Fraud Unit, 1980-82; assoc. counsel Office of Independent Counsel, 1987-89; ptnr. Fried, Frank, Harris, Shriver & Jacobson, N.Y.C., 1990—. James Kent Scholar Columbia U., 1970-71, Harlan Fiske Stone Scholar, Columbia U., 1968-69. Fellow Am. Coll. Trial Lawyers. Office: Fried Frank Harris Shriver & Jacobson One NY Plz 24th Fl New York NY 10004

STRAUSS, DAVID, Vice Presidential Office official; b. Fargo, N.D., Apr. 2, 1950. BA in Sociology, Moorhead State U., 1973, BS Polit. Sci. and Edn. magna cum laude, 1973; postgrad., Harvard U., 1992. Exec. dir. N.D. Dem. Party, 1975-76; dir. N.D. Agrl. Stblzn. and Conservation Svc., 1977-81; adminstrv. asst. Senator Quentin Burdick of N.D., 1981-88; staff dir. U.S. Senate Com. on Environment and Pub. Works, Washington, 1988-92; chief of staff U.S. Senator Jocelyn Birch Burdick of N.D., Washington, 1992, Senator John Breaux of La., Washington, 1993; dep. chief of staff Office of Vice Pres., Washington, 1993. Office: Vice Pres Old Executive Office NW Bldg Washington DC 20501

STRAUSS, DAVID J., lawyer; b. Chgo., Jan. 26, 1943. BBA, U. Iowa, 1964, JD, 1967. Bar: Iowa 1967, Ohio 1967. Ptnr. Baker & Hostetler, Cleve. Mem. Phi Delta Phi, Order of Coif. Office: Baker & Hostetler 3200 Nat City Ctr 1900 E 9th St Cleveland OH 44114-3485*

STRAUSS, DOROTHY BRANDFON, marital, family, and sex therapist; b. Bklyn.; d. Marcus and Beatrice (Wilson) Brandfon; widowed; 1 child, Josette E. MacNaughton. BA, Bklyn. Coll., 1932; MA, NYU, 1937, PhD, 1963. Diplomate Am. Bd. Sexology. Instr. Hunter Coll. CUNY, 1960-63; prof. Kean Coll., Union, N.J., 1963-77; pvt. practice and clin. supervision Bklyn. and, N.J., 1970—; clin. assoc. prof. psychiatry Downstate Med. Ctr., SUNY, Bklyn., 1974—; assoc. dir. Ctr. for Human Sexuality, 1974-82; mem. NIMH rsch. team U. Pa., 1973-82. Contbr. articles on gerontology and sexual dysfunctions to profl. jours. Fellow Am. Assn. Clin. Sexologists (founding); mem. Am. Psychol. Assn., Am. Assn. for Marital and Family Therapy (clin. mem. 1971—, supr. 1981—), Am. Assn. Sex Therapists, Counselors and Educators (chairperson task force on supervision 1984-86, chairperson supr. cert. com. 1986-93, chair cert. steering com. 1992—), Kappa Delta Pi. Home and Office: 1401 Ocean Ave Brooklyn NY 11230-3971

STRAUSS, EDWARD ROBERT, carpet company executive; b. Jersey City, June 14, 1942; s. Abraham and Elsie Alice (Goldstein) S.; m. Martha Ann Patmore, Oct. 30, 1966; children: Jeffrey Aaron, Craig Michael. BSBA, Rutgers U., 1973. Dept. systems mgr. Port of N.Y. Authority, N.Y.C., 1961-68; account exec. Steiner Rouse & Co., N.Y.C., 1968-70; purchasing mgr. N.Y. State Urban Devel. Corp., N.Y.C., 1970-73; sales mgr. Siracco's Staten Island, N.Y., 1973-76; carpet and TV buyer Hahnes Dept. Stores, Newark, 1976-80; sales mgr. Clodan Carpets, N.Y.C., 1980-83; regional mgr. Deans Carpets, Manchester, N.H., 1983-85; pres. Carpet Contractors Inc., N.Y.C., 1985-95; v.p. contact sales Simon Manges/Patterson Flynn Martin & Manges, N.Y.C., 1995—. Bd. dirs. Marlboro (N.J.) Little League, 1979-87, Marlboro Pop Warner Football, 1979-83. Mem. Free Sons of Israel (trustee, v.p.), Marlboro Mcpl. Swim Club (bd. dirs. 1989-91), Free and Accepted Masons (Menorah lodge # 249 1966—, master 1978). Jewish. Avocations: electric trains, sports. Office: Simon Manges Patterson Flynn The D&D Bldg Martin & Manges 979 3rd Ave New York NY 10022

STRAUSER, ELLIOTT BOWMAN, economic development consultant, retired naval officer; b. Washington, Mar. 15, 1903; s. Joseph and Mary (Sweitzer) S.; m. Beatrice Phillips, Feb. 12, 1951; children by previous marriage: Elliott MacGregor, Armar Archbold, Lydia S. (Mme. Delaunay); 1 child, Christopher Joseph. B.S., U.S. Naval Acad., 1923; student, Imperial Def. Coll., London, 1948. Commd. ensign USN, 1923, advanced through grades to rear adm., 1955; assigned ships at sea, 1923-30, 32-35; asst. naval attache London, 1935-37; staff comdr. Atlantic Squadron, 1937-40; spl. naval observer London, 1941; staff Chief Brit. Combined Ops., 1942-43; U.S. ops. officer Allied Naval Comdr.-in-Chief for Normandy Invasion, 1944; comdr. Attack Transport, Pacific, 1944-45; naval adviser 1st Gen. Assembly UN, staff Mil. Staff Com., UN, 1946; comdg. officer USS Fresno, 1946-47; staff div. strategic plans Office Chief Naval Ops., 1948-51; comdr. Destroyer Flotilla 6, 1951-52; dir. def. programs div. Office Spl. Rep. in Europe, Dept. Def. rep. econ. def., 1952-55; ret., 1955; dir. engring. Bucknell U., 1956-57; dir. U.S. ops. Mission to Tunisia, 1957-60; spl. asst. to dir. ICA, 1960; dir. AID Missions to Madagascar, 1961-63; pub. mem. Fgn. Service Inspection Corps, 1965; assoc. Laidlaw & Co., N.Y.C., 1963-66; econ. devel. cons. Gen. Electric Co., 1966-69; chmn. bd. Interplan Corp., 1969-81; rep. overseas of Interplan.; cons. Dept. State, 1970. Author profl. and newspaper articles. Bd. dirs. Am. Econ. Found.; chmn. Naval Hist. Found. Decorated Bronze Star; comdr. Order Brit. Empire; Croix de Guerre with palm France). Mem. U.S. Naval Inst., English Speaking Union (nat. bd. dirs.), Order of St. John of Jerusalem (assoc.). Mem. Ch. of England. Clubs: The Pilgrims; Army-Navy (Washington), Chevy Chase (Washington), Metropolitan (Washington); New York Yacht. Home: 2945 Garfield Ter NW Washington DC 20008-3507

STRAUSS, HARLEE SUE, environmental consultant; b. New Brunswick, N.J., June 19, 1950; d. Robert Lemuel and Helene (Marcus) S. BA, Smith Coll., 1972; PhD, U. Wis., 1979. Postdoctoral fellow dept. biology MIT, Cambridge, 1979-81; congrl. sci. fellow U.S. House of Reps., Washington, 1981-83; spl. asst. Am. Chem. Soc., Washington, 1983-84; spl. cons. Environ. Corp., Washington, 1984-85; rsch. assoc. Ctr. for Tech., Policy and Indsl. Devel. MIT, Cambridge, 1985-86, rsch. affiliate, 1986—; sr. assoc. Gradient Corp., Cambridge, 1986-88; pres. H. Strauss Assocs., Inc., Natick, Mass., 1988—; pres., exec. dir. Silent Spring Inst., Inc., 1994-95; adj. assoc. prof. Sch. Pub. Health, Boston U., 1990-94; lectr. Sch. Medicine, Tufts U., Boston, 1988—; mem. steering com. Boston Risk Assessment Group, 1986-95. Co-editor, author: Risk Assessment in Genetic Engineering, 1991; author: Biotechnology Regulations, 1986; author book chpts. in field. Active Instl. Biosafety Com., Army Rsch. Lab., Natick, 1989—, Army Sci. Bd., 1994—. Mem. AAAS, Am. Chem. Soc., Am. Soc. Microbiology, Assn. for Women in Sci. (chmn. com. New England chpt. 1986-88, co-chmn. legis. com. 1985—), Biophys. Soc. (chmn. com. 1983-84, Congl. Sci. fellow 1981-83), Soc. for Risk Analysis (pres. New England chpt. 1991-92). Jewish. Avocations: travel, hiking. Office: H Strauss Assocs Inc 21 Bay State Rd Natick MA 01760-2942

STRAUSS, HERBERT LEOPOLD, chemistry educator; b. Aachen, Germany, Mar. 26, 1936; came to U.S., 1940, naturalized, 1946; s. Charles and Joan (Goldschmidt) S.; m. Carolyn North Cooper, Apr. 24, 1960; children: Michael Abram, Rebecca Anne, Ethan Edward. A.B., Columbia U., 1957, M.A., 1958, Ph.D., 1960; postgrad, Oxford U., 1960-61. Mem. faculty U. Calif., Berkeley, 1961—, prof. chemistry, 1973—, vice chmn. dept. chemistry, 1975-81, 92-95, asst. dean. Coll. Chemistry, 1986-92, assoc. dean, 1995—; vis. prof. Indian Inst. Tech., Kanpur, 1968-69, Fudan U., Shanghai, 1982, U. Tokyo, 1982, U. Paris du Nord, 1987; chmn. IUPAC Commn. I, 1994—. Author: Quantum Mechanics, 1968; assoc. editor Ann. Rev. Phys. Chemistry, 1976-85, editor, 1985—. Recipient Bomen-Michaelson award Coblentz Soc., 1994, Ellis Lippincott award Optical Soc. Am., 1994; Alfred P. Sloan fellow, 1966-70. Fellow Am. Phys. Soc., AAAS; mem. Am. Chem. Soc., Sigma Xi, Phi Beta Kappa, Phi Lambda Upsilon. Achievements include research in elucidation of vibrational spectra associated with large amplitude molecular motion in gases, liquids and solids. Home: 2447 Prince St Berkeley CA 94705-2021 Office: U Calif Dept Chemistry Berkeley CA 94720-1460

STRAUSS, JEROME MANFRED, lawyer, banker; b. Milw., Nov. 7, 1934; s. Emanuel and Loraine (Goetz) S.; m. Mary Beth Johnson, June, 1959 (div. Nov. 1964); 1 child, Martha Lynn; m. Susan Jean Kauffman, Dec. 30, 1967; children: Jared Lee, David Aaron. BA with honors, Ind. U., 1956; JD, NYU, 1959. Bar: Ind. 1959, U.S. Dist. Ct. (so. dist.) Ind. 1959, U.S. Tax Ct. 1965, U.S. Ct. Appeals (7th cir.) 1969. Assoc. Ice Miller Donadio & Ryan, Indpls., 1959-69, ptnr., 1969-93; sr. v.p. and regional trust mgr. Merrill Lynch Trust Co., 1993-95; with Dunwody, White & Landon, Naples, 1995—. Co-author: Marital Deduction Trusts, 1963, Real Estate in an Estate, 1963; contbr. articles to profl. jours., proc., others. Bd. dirs. Orton Soc., Indpls., 1970-72, Indpls., 1970-72, Indpls. Hebrew Congregation, 1979-85, Planned Giving Group of Ind., Indpls., 1988-95, Ind. Continuing Legal Edn. Forum, 1989-94. Fellow Am. Coll Trust and Estate Counsel; mem. ABA (vice chmn. marital deductin com. real estate property, probate and trust sect. 1988-93), Internat. Acad. Estate and Trust Law (academician 1987—), Ind. State Bar Assn. (sec. 1979-80, chmn. probate, trust and real property sect. 1970-71), Ind. Estate Planning Coun. (pres. 1970-71), Skyline Club, Columbia Club, Collier Athletic Club. Home: 1056 Diamond Lake Cir Naples FL 33961 Office: Dunwody White and Landon Ste 395 4001 N Tamrami Dr Naples FL 33940

STRAUSS, JOHN, public relations executive; b. N.Y.C., Apr. 2, 1913; s. Nathan and Bertha Dorothy (Heineman) S.; m. Renee Valensi, Oct. 15, 1947; children: Susan Strauss Koenig, John Jay. Grad., Phillips Exeter Acad., 1931; BA, Yale U., 1935. Securities analyst Mabon & Co., N.Y.C., 1935-41; sales rep. Warner Bros. Pictures, Buffalo, 1941-45; publicist Warner Bros. Studios, Burbank, Calif., 1945-46, Columbia Studios, Hollywood, Calif., 1946-48; founder, pres. Cleary, Strauss & Irwin, 1948-64; pres. McFadden, Strauss & Irwin, Inc., 1964-75, ICPR, L.A., 1975-80, Communifax, Inc., L.A., 1980—. Trustee Oakwood Schs., 1967-70, Acad. TV Arts, 1967-70, Columbia Coll., L.A., 1979-83. Mem. Acad. Motion Picture Arts and Scis. Home and Office: 4205 Stansbury Ave Sherman Oaks CA 91423-4233

STRAUSS, JOHN STEINERT, dermatologist, educator; b. New Haven, July 15, 1926; s. Maurice Jacob and Carolyn Mina (Ullman) S.; m. Susan Thalheimer, Aug. 19, 1950; children—Joan Sue, Mary Lynn. B.S., Yale U., 1946; M.D., 1950. Intern U. Chgo., 1950-51; resident in dermatology U. Pa., Phila., 1951-52, 54-55; fellow in dermatology U. Pa., 1955-57, instr., 1956-57; mem. faculty Boston U. Med. Sch., 1958-78, prof., 1966-78; prof., head dept. dermatology U. Iowa, Iowa City, 1978—. Mem. editorial bd. Archives of Dermatology, 1970-79, Jour. Am. Acad. Dermatology, 1979-89, Jour. Investigative Dermatology, 1977-82; contbr. articles to profl. jours. Served with USNR, 1952-54. James H. Brown jr. fellow, 1947-48; USPHS fellow, 1955-57; USPHS grantee. Fellow Am. Acad. Dermatology (pres.); mem. Soc. Investigative Dermatology (sec.-treas., pres.), Dermatology Found. (pres.), Am. Bd. Dermatology (bd. dirs., pres.), Am. Dermatol. Assn. (sec., pres.), Assn. Am. Physicians, Central Soc. Clin. Rsch., Am. Fedn. Clin. Rsch., Coun. Med. Splty. Socs. (pres.), 18th World Congress Dermatology (pres.), Internat. League Dermatol. Socs. (pres. 1992—), Internat. Com. Dermatology (pres. 1992—), others. Research in sebaceous glands and pathogenesis of acne. Office: U Iowa Hosp & Clinics Dept of Dermatology 200 Hawkins Dr # Bt2045 1 Iowa City IA 52242-1009

STRAUSS, JON CALVERT, medical research administrator; b. Chgo., Jan. 17, 1940; s. Charles E. and Alice C. (Woods) S.; m. Joan Helen Bailey, Sept. 19, 1959 (div. 1985); children: Susan, Stephanie; m. Jean Anne Sacconaghi, June 14, 1985; children: Kristoffer, Jonathon. BSEE, U. Wis., 1959; MS in Physics, U. Pitts., 1962; PhD in E.E., Carnegie Inst. Tech., 1965. Assoc. prof. computer sci., elec. engring. Carnegie Mellon U., Pitts., 1966-70; dir. computer ctr., prof. computer sci. Tech. U. Norway, Trondheim, Norway, 1970; vis. assoc. prof. elec. engring. U. Mich., Ann Arbor, 1971; assoc. prof. computer sci. Washington U., St. Louis, Mo., 1971-74, dir. computing facilities, 1971-73; dir. computing activities U. Pa., Phila., 1974-76, faculty master Stouffer Coll. House, 1978-80, prof. computer, info. scis., prof. decision sci. Wharton Sch., 1974-81, exec. dir. Univ. Budget, 1975-78, v.p. for budget, fin., 1978-81; prof. elec. engring. U. So. Calif., Los Angeles, 1981-85; sr. v.p. adminstrn. U. So. Calif., 1981-85; pres. Worcester Poly. Inst., Mass., 1985-94; v.p., chief fin. officer Howard Hughes Med. Inst., Chevy Chase, Md., 1994—; cons. Electronics Assocs., Inc., 1965, IBM Corp., 1960-64, Westinghouse Elec. Corp., 1959-60; bd. dirs. Wyman Gordon Co., Computervision Corp. Contbr. articles on computer systems and university mgmt. to profl. jours.; co-holder patent. Bd. dirs. Presbyn.-U. Pa. Med. Ctr., Phila., 1980-81, U. So. Calif. Kenneth Norris Jr. Cancer Hosp., L.A., 1981-85, Med. Ctr. of Ctrl. Mass., 1986-94, Worcester Acad., 1986-91, Mass. Biotech. Rsch. Inst., 1985-94. Mem. New. Eng. Assn. Schs. and Colls., Inc., Commn. on Instns. of Higher Edn., Nat. Collegiate Athletic Assn. (pres.'s commn. 1990-94). Avocations: rowing, running, sailing, swimming. Office: Howard Hughes Med Inst 4000 Jones Bridge Rd Chevy Chase MD 20815-6789

STRAUSS, JUDITH FEIGIN, physician; b. N.Y., Mar. 7, 1942; d. Milton M. and Blanche (Tobias) Feigin; m. Harry William Strauss, June 14, 1964; children: Cheryl, Marcy. BS, Cornell U., Ithaca, 1963; MD, SUNY, 1967. Pediatrics. Pediatric resident SUNY, N.Y.C., 1976-68, Sinai Hosp., Balt., 1968-69; fellow pediatrics and psychiatry Johns Hopkins Hosp., Balt., 1969-70; pvt. practice in pediatrics Sacramento; cons. in pediatrics Bur. of Disability Ins. Social Security, Balt., 1973-74; pediatrician East Balt. Med. Plan, 1974-76; dir. pediats. USPHS Hosp., Boston, 1976-80; pvt. practice in pediatrics Boston, 1980-87; dir. med. svcs. Mediqual Systems, 1988-92; pres. Strauss Healthcare Consulting, Skillman, N.J., 1992-94; v.p. med. affairs Sutter Health Bay Region, 1995; chief med. officer Calif. Advantage, Inc., San Francisco, 1995—. Fellow Am. Acad. of Pediatrics; mem. Mass. Med. Soc., Am. Med. Women's Orgn., Alpha Lamda Delta. Home: 45 Summit Ridge Pl Redwood City CA 94062

STRAUSS, PETER, actor; b. Croton-on-Hudson, N.Y., Feb. 20, 1947; m. Nicole S.; children: Justin, Tristen. Student, Northwestern U. Performances include (films) debut in Hail Hero, 1969, Soldier Blue, 1970, The Trial of the Catonsville Nine, The Last Tycoon, 1976, Spacehunter, 1983; (TV dramas) Rich Man, Poor Man, 1976, Rich Man, Poor Man-Book II, 1976-77, Masada, 1981, Tender is the Night, 1985, Kane and Abel, 1986; (TV spls.) The Man Without a Country, 1973, A Whale for the Killing, 1981; (TV movies) The FBI Story: The FBI Vs. the Ku Klux Klan, 1975, Attack on Terror, 1975, Young Joe, the Forgotten Kennedy, 1978, The Jericho Mile, 1979 (Emmy award), Angel on My Shoulder, 1980, Heart of Steel, 1983, Under Siege, 1986, Penalty Phase, 1986, The Proud Men, 1987, Brotherhood of the Rose, 1989, Peter Gunn, 1989, 83 Hours Till Dawn, 1990, Flight of the Black Angel, 1991, Fugitive Among Us, 1992, Trial: The Price of Passion, 1992, Men Don't Tell, 1993, The Yearling, 1994. Office: care William Morris Agy care Robert Lee 151 S El Camino Dr Beverly Hills CA 90212-2704*

STRAUSS, PETER L(ESTER), law educator; b. N.Y.C., Feb. 26, 1940; s. Simon D. and Elaine Ruth (Mandle) S.; m. Joanna Burnstine, Oct. 1, 1964; children: Benjamin, Bethany. AB magna cum laude, Harvard U., 1961; LLB magna cum laude, Yale U., 1964. Bar: D.C. 1965, U.S. Supreme Ct., 1968. Law clk. U.S. Ct. Appeals D.C. Cir., 1964-65, U.S. Supreme Ct., 1965-66; lectr. Haile Selassie U. Sch. Law, Addis Ababa, Ethiopia, 1966-68; asst. to solicitor gen. Dept. Justice, Washington, 1968-71; assoc. prof. law Columbia U., 1971-74, prof., 1974—, Betts Prof., 1985—, vice dean, 1996; gen. counsel NRC, 1975-77, Adminstrv. Conf. U.S., 1984-95; Byrne vis. prof. Sch. Law Harvard U., Cambridge, Mass., 1994. Adv. bd. Lexis Electronic Author's Press, 1995—. Recipient John Marshall prize Dept. Justice, 1970, Disting. Svc. award NRC, 1977. Mem. ABA (chair sect. adminstrv. law and regulatory practice 1992-93, Disting. Scholarship award 1988), Am. Law Inst. Author: (with Abba Paulos, translator) Fetha Negast: The Law of the Kings, 1968; (with others) Administrative Law Cases and Comments, 1995; Introduction to Administrative Justice in the United States, 1989; (with Paul Verkuil) Administrative Law Problems, 1983; contbr. articles to law revs. Office: Columbia U Law Sch 435 W 116th St New York NY 10027-7201

STRAUSS, ROBERT C., manufacturing executive; b. Chgo., June 1, 1941; s. Henry K. and Clara (Santi) S; children: Jennifer, Morgan. BS in Engring. and Physics, U. Ill., 1963; NS in Physics, U. Idaho, 1965. Systems analyst Eastman Kodak Co., Rochester, N.Y., 1965-68, GE, Phila., 1968-73; mgr. mgmt. consulting Touche Ross & Co., Phila., 1973-79; sr. v.p. fin. Pantry Pride Inc., Ft. Lauderdale, Fla., 1979-83; pres., CEO Cordis Corp., Miami Lakes, Fla., 1983—, also dir. Bd. dirs. U. Miami Venture Coun. Forum, 1989—, Coral Gables, Miami Children's Hosp., 1990—; mem. campaign com. United Wade Dade County; chmn. biomed. devices subcom. under rsch. com. Fla. High Tech. and Industry Coun., 1989—; trustee U. Miami, 1991—. Avocations: sailing, running. *

STRAUSS, ROBERT DAVID, lawyer; b. Cambridge, Mass., Oct. 20, 1951; s. Walter Adolf and Lilo (Teutsch) S.; m. Deborah Mackall, Feb. 15, 1986; 1 child, Benjamin Walter. BA, Emory U., 1973, JD, 1976. Bar: Ga. 1976. Assoc. Gambrell & Russell, Atlanta, 1976-81; ptnr. Smith, Gambrell & Russell, Atlanta, 1981-89, Trotter Smith & Jacobs, Atlanta, 1989-92, Troutman Sanders, Atlanta, 1992—. Contbr. articles to profl. jours. Mem. ABA (chmn. leasing subcom. 1988-94, uniform comml. code com.), State Bar of Ga., Equipment Leasing Assn. Am. Home: 1159 Morningside Pl NE Atlanta GA 30306-3061 Office: Troutman Sanders 5200 NationsBank Plz 600 Peachtree St NE Atlanta GA 30308-2220

STRAUSS, ROBERT PHILIP, economics educator; b. Cleve., May 11, 1944; s. Harry and Carrie S.; m. Celeste G. Meade, Jan. 11, 1980; children—Sarah Elizabeth, David Anthony, Elena Nicole. A.B. in Econs., U. Mich., 1966; M.A., U. Wis., 1968, Ph.D. in Econs., 1970. Fellow Inst. Research on Poverty, 1968-69; asst. prof. econs. U. N.C., Chapel Hill, 1969-73, assoc. prof., 1973-79; econ. policy fellow Brookings Instn., Washington, 1971-72; economist U.S. Congress Joint Com. Taxation, 1975-78; prof. econs. and pub. policy Carnegie-Mellon U., Pitts., 1979—, assoc. dean Sch. Urban and Pub. Affairs, 1981-83, dir. Ctr. for Pub. Fin. Mgmt., 1984-91; dir. research Pa. Tax Commn., 1979-81; vis. prof. econs. and pub. policy U. Rochester, 1992-94. Mem. Pa. Local Tax Reform Commn., 1987; sec. faculty Carnegie-Mellon U., 1991-92. Recipient Exceptional Service award U.S. Treasury, 1972, Disting. Service award Pitts. Tax Execs. Inst., 1987; grantee NSF, U.S. Dept. Labor, U.S. Treasury, HUD, Social Security Adminstrn. Mem. Am. Econ. Assn., Econometric Soc., Am. Statis. Assn., Nat. Tax Assn., Pub. Choice Soc., Assn. for Pub. Policy and Mgmt., Am. Soc. for Pub. Adminstrn., Am. Acctg. Assn. Club: Cosmos. Home: 2307 Country Pl Export PA 15632-9059 Office: 5000 Forbes Ave Pittsburgh PA 15213-3816

STRAUSS, SIMON DAVID, manufacturing executive; b. Lima, Peru, July 24, 1911; s. Lester W. and Bertha (Miller) S.; m. Elaine Ruth Mandle, Sept. 1, 1936 (dec.); children: Peter Lester, Susan Dee (Mrs. Samuel Carson Orr); m. Janet McCloskey Robbins, Dec. 19, 1982. Student, Mackay Sch., Valparaiso, Chile, 1919-21, Townsend Harris Hall, N.Y.C., 1924-27; LL.D., U. Ariz., 1981. Asst. editor Engring. and Mining Jour., 1927-32; editor Madison Eagle, N.J., 1932-34; economist Standard Statistics Co., 1935-41; asst. to dep. adminstr. Fed. Loan Agy., 1941; asst. v.p., v.p. Metals Res. Co., 1942-45; sales dept. Asarco, Inc., 1946; sales mgr. Am. Smelting & Refining Co., 1947-71, v.p., 1949-71, exec. v.p., 1971-77, vice chmn., 1977-79, also dir., 1953-81; cons. indsl. firms, 1981—; gov. N.Y. Commodity Exchange Inc., 1947-63; dir., mem. exec. com. Zinc Inst., 1953-77, pres., 1957-59, 73-75; cons. Def. Materials Procurement Agy., 1951-52, Office Def. Moblzn., 1954-55; mem. adv. coms. Munitions Bd.; mem. adv. com. Nat. Growth Policies, 1976, vis. lectr. MIT, 1977-84, Columbia U., 1988; lectr. Pa. State U., 1978, Poly. Inst. N.Y., 1978, U. Ariz., 1979, 80, Columbia U., 1982, U. Calif., Berkeley, 1986. Author: (with L.H. Sloan) Two Cycles of Corporation Profits, 1936, (with E.H. Robie) Mineral Economics, 1959, (with W.H. Vogeley), 1976, Trouble in the Third Kingdom, 1986; contbr. articles on mining to trade jours. Trustee Manhattan Sch. Music, 1958-79, v.p., 1966-79; bd. dirs. Internat. Copper Research Assn.; mem. bd. govs. Nat. Mining Hall of Fame and Mus., Leadville, Colo., 1987—. Mem. Lead Industries Assn. (pres. 1964-66, exec. com., dir., v.p. 1967-69, pres. 1970-71), Silver Inst. (dir., pres. 1971-73, chmn. bd. 1974-76), Am. Bur. Metal Stats. (chmn. 1975-77), Copper Club (pres. 1967-68), Mining and Metall. Soc. Am. (Gold medal 1984), Am. Inst. Mining and Metall. Engrs. (hon.), Council Fgn. Relations. Clubs: Mining, Stockbridge Golf.

STRAUSS, SIMON WOLF, technical consultant; b. Bedzin, Keltz, Poland, Apr. 15, 1920; came to U.S., 1929; s. Israel Calvin and Anna (Hops) S.; m. Mary Jo Boehm, Dec. 27, 1957; children: Jack Calvin, Ruth Ann. BS in Chemistry, Polytech. Inst. of Bklyn., 1944, MS in Chemistry, 1947, PhD in Chemistry, 1950. Rsch. chemist Nat. Bur. Standards, Washington, 1951-55; from phys. chemist to head chem. metallurgy sect. Naval Rsch. Lab., Washington, 1955-63; sr. staff scientist Air Force Systems Command, Washington, 1963-80; ind. tech. cons. Washington, 1980—; mem. bd. civil svc. examiners for sci. and tech. pers. U.S. Naval Dist. of Washington, 1959-63; co-chair com. on career planning and appraisal of sci. and engrs. Air Force Sys. Command, Washington, 1966-67; chair rsch. steering com. Air Force Dir. of Sci. Tech., Washington, 1976-80; mem., chair editorial adv. com. Acad. Jour., 1983-87, chair com. on scholarly activities, 1984-88. Prin. compiler 75 Years of Scientific Thought, 1987; contbr. articles to profl. jours. Recipient Air Force Decoration for Exceptional Civilian Svc., 1980, first Disting. Career in Sci. award Wash. Acad. Scis., 1988, Disting. Svc. award, 1990. Fellow AAAS, Wash. Acad. Scis. (first Disting. Scholar-in-Residence 1984-89, pres. 1986-87, life mem. fund trustee 1988—), Am. Inst. Chemists, Cosmos Club, Air Force Meterials Lab. (hon. life mem.), Sigma Pi Sigma, Phi Lambda Upsilon, Sigma Xi. Achievements include 3 patents for electrodeposition of Cadmium on high strength steel; research and development of advanced composites technology; the development of equations for the estimation of surface tensions, viscosities and densities of liquid metals as a function of temperature. Home: 4506 Cedell Pl Temple Hills MD 20748-3805

STRAUSS, STANLEY ROBERT, lawyer; b. N.Y.C., June 3, 1915; s. Maurice M. and Blanche Anna (Danciger) S.; m. Margaret Inglis Forbes, Mar. 13, 1944 (div. 1950); m. Helen Anne Cummings, Dec. 31, 1975 (dec. 1980). BA cum laude, Williams Coll., 1936; LLB, Columbia U., 1940. Bar: N.Y. 1941, D.C. 1964, U.S. Ct. Appeals (1st cir.) 1977, U.S. Ct. Appeals (3d cir.) 1986, U.S. Ct. Appeals (4th cir.) 1974, U.S. Ct. Appeals (5th cir.) 1970, U.S. Ct. Appeals (6th cir.) 1977, U.S. Ct. Appeals (8th cirs.) 1975, U.S. Supreme Ct. 1965. Assoc. Howard Henig, N.Y.C., 1940-41; atty. NLRB, Washington, 1946-52, supervising atty., 1953-59, chief counsel, 1959-63; assoc. Vedder, Price, Kaufman & Kammholz, Washington, 1963-65, ptnr., 1965-90; of counsel Ogletree, Deakins, Nash, Smoak & Stewart, Washington, 1990—. Co-author: Practice and Procedure Before the National Labor Relations Board, 3d edit., 1980, 4th edit., 1987, 5th edit., 1996. Officer U.S. Army, 1941-45, PTO. Decorated Bronze Star; Horn scholar Columbia U. Law Sch., 1937-40. Mem. ABA, Fed. Bar Assn., D.C. Bar Assn., Kenwood Country Club. Avocations: golf, tennis. Home: 4956 Sentinel Dr Bethesda MD 20816-3594 Office: Ogletree Deakins Nash 2400 N St NW Washington DC 20037-1153

STRAUSS, ULRICH PAUL, educator, chemist; b. Frankfurt, Germany, Jan. 10, 1920; s. Richard and Marianne (Seligmann) S.; m. Esther Lipetz, June 20, 1943 (dec. Sept. 1949); children—Dorothy, David; m. Elaine Greenbaum, Nov. 23, 1950; children—Elizabeth, Evelyn. A.B., Columbia U., 1941; Ph.D., Cornell U., 1944. Sterling fellow Yale U., 1946-48; faculty Rutgers U., New Brunswick, N.J., 1948—, prof. phys. chemistry, 1960-90, prof. emeritus, 1990—; also dir. Sch. Chemistry, 1965-71, chmn. dept. chemistry, 1974-80; prof. emeritus Rutgers U., 1990—. Mem. editorial bd. Macromolecules, 1990-93; contbr. articles to profl. jours. Recipient Sci. achievement award Johnson Wax Co., 1986; NSF sr. fellow Nat. Center Sci. Research, Strasbourg, France, 1961-62; Guggenheim fellow U. Oxford, Eng., 1971-72. Fellow N.Y. Acad. Scis.; mem. Am. Chem. Soc. (chmn. phys. chemistry group N.J. sect. 1956, councillor 1961-72, honored by 1-day symposium at nat. meeting N.Y.C. 1986, Excellence in Edn. award N.J. sect. 1994). Home: 227 Lawrence Ave Highland Park NJ 08904-1837 Office: Rutgers U Dept Chemistry New Brunswick NJ 08903

STRAUSZ-HUPÉ, ROBERT, ambassador, author; b. Vienna, Austria, Mar. 25, 1903; emigrated to U.S., 1923, naturalized, 1938; s. Rudolph and Doris (Hedwig) Strausz-H.; m. Eleanor deGraff Cuyler, Apr. 26, 1938 (dec. 1976); m. Mayrose Ferreira Nugara, Aug. 22, 1979. A.M., Ph.D., U. Pa., 1944. Investment banker, 1927-37; assoc. editor Current History, 1939-41; assoc. prof. polit. sci. U. Pa., 1946-52, former prof.; spl. lectr., 1940-46; dir. Fgn. Policy Rsch. Inst., 1955-69; U.S. amb. Ceylon, 1970-72, Belgium, 1972-74, Sweden, 1974-76, NATO, 1976-77, Turkey, 1981-89; disting. fellow U.S. Inst. Peace, 1992-93. Author: The Russian-German Riddle, 1940, Axis-America, 1941, Geopolitics, 1942, The Balance of Tomorrow, 1945, International Relations, 1950, The Zone of Indifference, 1952, Power and Community, 1956, Democracy and American Foreign Policy, 1995, (with Kintner, Cottrell, Dougherty) Protracted Conflict, 1959, (with W. Kintner, Stefan Possony) A Forward Strategy for America, 1961, (with others) Building the Atlantic World, 1963, In My Time, 1967, Dilemmas Facing the Nation, 1979; editor: The Idea of Colonialism, 1958, Orbis, 1957-69. Lectr. Air War Coll., 1953. Served to 1st col. AUS. Mem. Coun. Fgn. Rels., Merion Cricket Club, Met. Club, Knickerbocker Club. Lutheran. Address: White Horse Farm 864 Grubbs Mill Rd Newtown Square PA 19073-1210

STRAVALLE-SCHMIDT, ANN ROBERTA, lawyer; b. N.Y.C., Jan. 2, 1957. Grad. cum laude, Phillips Exeter Acad., 1975; student, Occidental Coll., 1975-78, Oxford Coll., Eng., 1976-77; BS cum laude, Boston Coll., 1980; JD, Boston U., 1987. Bar: Conn. 1987, U.S. Dist. Ct. Conn. 1988, U.S. Supreme Ct. 1993. Consulting staff Arthur Andersen, Boston, 1980-82; supr. CID ops. Aetna Life & Casualty, Hartford, Conn., 1982-84; summer intern U.S. Atty.'s Office, Boston, 1985; jud. clk. Hon. Judge Thayer III N.H. Supreme Ct., 1987-88; trial lawyer Day, Berry & Howard, Hartford, 1988-91; sr. lawyer comml. litigation and appellate practice Berman & Sable, Hartford, 1991—; brief judge Nat. Appellate Advocacy Competition, 1996. Mem. editorial bd. Conn. Bar Jour., 1990—; contbr. articles to profl. jours. Mem. Hebron Dem. Town Com.; mem. Hebron Bd. Fin., 1995—. Mem. ABA, Conn. Bar Assn. (founder, chair appellate practice com. litigation sect. 1994—, mem. exec. com. litigation sect.), Hartford Bar Assn., Hartford Assn. Women Attys. Home: 51 Elizabeth Dr Hebron CT 06248 Office: Berman & Sable 100 Pearl St Hartford CT 06103-4500

STRAVINSKA, SARAH, dance educator; b. Pitts., Nov. 12, 1940; d. Robert Edwin Williams and Alice Elizabeth Markey Hildebold; m. George Lawrence Denton, May 10, 1959 (div. 1973); children: Kathryn, Michael, Laura, David. BFA in Dance, Fla. State U., 1977, MFA in Dance, 1979; Cert. in Ballet, Vaganova Inst., Leningrad, Russia, 1990; Cert., Raoul Gelabert Kinesiology Ins, N.Y.C., 1980. Dancer Ballet Russe, N.Y.C., 1957-58; dance choreographer Dutchess County Ballet, Beacon, N.Y., 1960-65; instr. Brevard C.C., Cocoa, Fla., 1969-73; chair dept. dance Randolph/Macon Woman's Coll., Lynchburg, Va., 1979-84; asst. prof. dance U. So. Miss., Hattiesburg, 1984-86; prof. and coord. dance U. Southwestern La., Lafayette, 1986—; dir. State of La. Danse Project, Lafayette, 1991-94. Choreographer original dance works: Mama! Stop the Bombs, 1989, The Yellow Wallpaper, 1990; reconstructor of classical ballets: Les Sylphides, 1991, Giselle, 1992, Swan Lake, 1993, Raymonda, Pas de Quatre, 1994. Dir. concerns for children La Danse with Acadiana Arts Coun., Lafayette, 1987-93; mem. Arts in Edn. Program, Lafayette, 1987—. Mellon Found. grantee, 1982, U. So. Miss. faculty devel. grantee, 1986. Mem. Am. Coll. Dance Festival Assn. (bd. dirs., festival coord. 1989-91), Dance History Scholars, Phi Kappa Phi. Episcopalian. Avocations: writing, music, reading, biking. Office: Univ of Southwestern La Dept Performing Arts Box 43850 Lafayette LA 70504

STRAWBRIDGE, FRANCIS REEVES, III, department store executive; b. Bryn Mawr, Pa., Dec. 14, 1937; s. Francis Reeves Strawbridge Jr. and Elizabeth Ann (Schwarz) Strawbridge Grange; m. Patricia Webb, Jan. 13, 1962 (div. 1967); children: Cynthia, Pamela; m. Mary Jo Beatty, Jan. 25, 1969; children: Elisabeth, Margaret. A.B., Princeton U., 1959. With exec. tng. program Bloomingdale's, N.Y.C., 1960-61; with Strawbridge & Clothier, Phila., 1961—, chmn. bd., 1984—; dir. Mellon Bank, Phila.; chmn. bd. trustees Princeton U. Store, 1978—. Vice chmn. bd. mgrs. Germantown Hosp., Pa., 1975—. Served to pfc. U.S. Army, 1959-60. Mem. Nat. Retail Merchants Assn. (bd. dirs. 1976—), Am. Retail Fedn. (bd. dirs. 1984—), Associated Merchandising Corp. (bd. dirs. 1984—), Greater Phila. C. of C. (bd. dirs. 1985—). Republican. Quaker. Office: Strawbridge & Clothier 801 Market St Philadelphia PA 19107-3109*

STRAWBRIDGE, PETER S., department store executive; b. Phila., 1938; married. B.A., Hamilton Coll., 1960. Exec. trainee Abraham & Straus, Bklyn., 1960-61; with Strawbridge & Clothier, Phila., 1961—, buyer men's sportswear, 1963-68; mgr. Neshaminy Br. Store-Strawbridge & Clothier, Phila., 1968-69; v.p., gen. mgr. Clover Store div. Strawbridge & Clothier, Phila., 1969-76, corp. exec. v.p. mdse. and publicity, 1976-79, pres., 1979—, dir.; bd. dirs. Associated Merchandising Corp., CoreStates Fin. Corp., Greater Phila. First Corp. Mem. bd. mgrs. Pa. Hosp., 1971-94; bd. dirs. Phila. Orch. Assn., 1990—. Office: Strawbridge & Clothier 801 Market St Philadelphia PA 19107-3199

STRAWDERMAN, WILLIAM E., statistics educator; b. Westerly, R.I., Apr. 25, 1941; s. Robert Lee and Alida Browning (Dow) S.; m. Susan Linda Grube; July 20, 1985; children: Robert Lee, William Edward, Heather Lynne. BS, U. R.I., 1963; MS, Cornell U., 1965, Rutgers U., 1967; PhD, Rutgers U., 1969. Mem. tech. staff Bell Telephone Labs., Holmdel, N.J., 1965-67; prof. Stanford (Calif.) U., 1969-70; instr. Rutgers U., New Brunswick, N.J., 1967-69, prof. stats., 1970—. Contbr. over 90 articles to profl. jours. Fellow Inst. Math. Stats., Am. Statis. Assn. Office: Rutgers U Statistics Dept Hill Ctr-Busch Campus New Brunswick NJ 08903

STRAWN-HAMILTON, FRANK, jazz musician, folksinger, composer and arranger, educator; b. N.Y.C., Aug. 3, 1934; s. Frank Strawn and Gladys (Bley) Hamilton; m. Sheila Lofton, Nov. 7, 1954 (div. Nov. 1971); children: Cameron, Auguste, Evan Baird, Liam Christopher, Heather Alexa; m. Deeanne Lee Walter, May 5, 1972 (div. Oct. 1980); m. Mary Doyle, Jan. 15, 1983. Student, Los Angeles City Coll., 1952-53, Chgo. Mus. Coll., 1959-62, L.A. Valley Coll., 1963-64. Organizer, head teaching staff, v.p. Old Town Sch. Folk Music, Chgo., 1957-62; ho. musician Gate of Horn, Chgo., 1959-61; mem. The Weavers, 1962-63; founder The Hot Club of Atlanta, 1995. Appeared Asheville (N.C.) Folk Festival, 1953, Newport Folk Festival, 1959; motion picture appearance in Subterraneans, 1958; performed with trio Meridian for spl. children's programs Young Audiences in Atlanta Pub. Sch. System, 1987-94; rec. artist Folkways, Vanguard records; devel. method annotation folk guitar and 5 string banjo; film score: A Time Out of War, 1952; TV score: Survival. Mem. Irish Arts Atlanta. Mem. ACLU, UN Assn., Dramatist Guild, Chgo. Hist. Soc. (hon.). Home: 852 Cinderella Ct Decatur GA 30033-5812

STRAYER, BARRY LEE, federal judge; b. Moose Jaw, Sask., Can., Aug. 13, 1932; s. Carl John and Nina Naomi (Carr) S.; m. Eleanor Lorraine Staton, July 2, 1955; children: Alison Lee, Jonathan Mark Staton, Colin James. BA, U. Sask., Can., 1953, LLB, 1955; BCL, Oxford U., Eng., 1957; SJD, Harvard U., 1966. Bar: Sask., 1959. Crown solicitor Gov. Sask., Regina, 1959-62; prof. law U. Sask., 1962-68; dir. constitutional rev. Gov. Can., Ottawa, 1968-72, dir. constitutional law, 1972-74, asst. dep. minister justice, 1974-83; judge Fed. Ct. Can., Ottawa, 1983—; jud. mem. Competition Tribunal Can., Ottawa, 1986-93; judge Fed. Ct. Appeal of Can., 1994—; chief justice Ct. Martial Appeal Ct. of Can., 1994—; sessional lectr. U. Ottawa, 1973-78; constitutional advisor Rep. Seychelles, Victoria, 1979; adviser Hongkong Govt. Bill of Rights, 1989. Author: Judicial Review of Legislation, 1968, Canadian Constitution and the Courts, 1983, 3d edit., 1988; contbr. articles to profl. jours. Mem. Internat. Bar Assn., Internat. Commn. Jurists, Rideau Club, Larrimac Golf Club. Office: Fed Ct, Kent & Wellington Sts, Ottawa, ON Canada K1A 0H9

STRAYHORN, RALPH NICHOLS, JR., lawyer; b. Durham, N.C., Feb. 16, 1923; Ralph Nichols and Annie Jane (Cooper) S.; m. Donleen Carol MacDonald, Sept. 10, 1949; children: Carol Strayhorn Rose, Ralph Nichols III. BS in Bus. Adminstrn., U. N.C., 1947, LLB/JD, 1950. Bar: N.C. 1950, U.S. Dist. Ct. (mid. and ea. dists.) N.C. 1950, U.S. Ct. Appeals (4th cir.) 1950. Assoc. Victor S. Bryant, Sr., Durham, 1950-55; ptnr. Bryant, Lipton, Strayhorn & Bryant, Durham, 1956-62; sr. ptnr. Newson, Graham, Strayhorn & Hedrick, Durham, 1962-78; gen. counsel Wachovia Corp., Wachovia Bank and Trust Co., N.A., Winston-Salem, N.C., 1978-88; of counsel Petree Stockton Winston-Salem, N.C., 1988—; mem. legal adv. com. to N.Y. Stock Exch., 1986-89; adv. dir. Wachovia Bank and Trust Co., Durham, 1973-78; chmn. bd. 1st Fed. Savs. & Loan Assn., Durham, 1976-78; mem. N.C. Gen. Assembly, 1959-61; bd. of visitors U. N.C., Wake Forest U. Law Sch. Lt. comdr. USNR, 1943-46. Fellow Am. Coll. Trial Lawyers, Am. Bar Found., Internat. Assn. Def. Counsel; mem. ABA, N.C. Bar Assn. (pres. 1971-72), Newcomen Soc. of U.S., 4th Jud. Conf. Episcopalian. Clubs: Old Town Club (Winston-Salem). Office: Petree Stockton 1001 W 4th St Winston Salem NC 27101-2410

STRAYTON, ROBERT GERARD, public communications executive; b. Bklyn., Aug. 4, 1935; s. George Andrew and Kathryn Loretta (Monahan) S.; m. Patricia Cecelia Hand, Aug. 16, 1958 (div. Aug. 1972); children—Jennifer Anne, Melissa Marie, Robert Hand, Bruce Andrew; m. Jayne Helene Kramer, Mar. 4, 1983. B.A. in English, Villanova U., 1957. Accredited in pub. relations. Account exec. Carl Byoir & Assocs., Inc., N.Y.C., 1962-65; dir. pub. relations and advt. EDP div. Honeywell Inc., Wellesley, Mass., 1966-69; pres. Strayton Corp., Wellesley, Mass., 1969-84; pres., chief operating officer Gray Strayton Internat., Waltham, Mass., 1984-86; exec. v.p., vice chmn. bd. dirs. Gray and Co., Washington; exec. v.p., mng. dir. Advanced Technology div. Hill and Knowlton, Inc., 1986-89; pres. The Strayton Group Inc., 1990—. Mem. NCCJ, Boston, 1984—; trustee Bacon Free Libr., 1994—. Lt. (j.g.) USNR, 1958-61. Fellow Pub. Rels. Soc. Am. (Silver Anvil award 1968, 89, counselor, mem. exec. com. Counselors Acad. 1983-84, disting. svc. award 1984); mem. Nat. Investors Rels. Inst., Assn. Nat. Advertisers, Advt. Club Boston (trustee 1982-87), Trout Unltd. (v.p., dir. 1984-93), Atlantic Salmon Task Force (bd. dirs. 1988—), Blue Water Sailing Club (bd. govs. 1995—), Red Brook Harbor Yacht Club, Wellesley Country Club, Flycasters Club. Republican. Roman Catholic. Avocations: sailing; flyfishing; tennis; golf. Home: 18 Phillips Pond Rd Natick MA 01760-5643 Office: The Strayton Group Inc 8 Pleasant St Natick MA 01760

STRAZZELLA, JAMES ANTHONY, law educator, lawyer; b. Hanover, Pa., May 18, 1939; s. Anthony F. and Teresa Ann (D'Alonzo) S.; m. Judith A. Coppola, Oct. 9, 1965; children: Jill M., Steven A., Tracy Ann, Michael P. AB Villanova U., 1961; JD, U. Pa., 1964. Bar: Pa. 1964, U.S. Ct. Appeals (3d cir.) 1964, D.C. 1965, U.S. Dist. Ct. D.C. 1965, U.S. Ct. Appeals (D.C. cir.) 1965, U.S. Dist Ct. (ea. and mid. dist.) Pa. 1969, U.S. Supreme Ct. 1969, U.S. Ct. Appeals (4th cir.) 1983. Law clk. to Hon. Samuel Roberts Pa. Supreme Ct., 1964-65; asst. U.S. atty. dept. chief appeals, spl. asst. to U.S. Atty., Washington, D.C., 1965-69; vice dean, asst. prof. law U. Pa., Phila., 1969-73; faculty Temple U., Phila., 1973—, James G. Schmidt Chair in law, 1989—, acting dean, 1987-89; chief counsel Kent State investigation Pres.'s Commn. Campus Unrest, 1970; chmn. Atty. Gen.'s Task Force on Family Violence, Pa., 1985-89; mem., chmn. justice ops. Mayor's Criminal Justice Coordinating Commn., Phila., 1983-85; Pa. Joint Council Criminal Justice, 1979-82; Com. to Study Pa.'s Unified Jud. System, 1980-82; Jud. Council Pa., 1972-82; chmn. criminal procedural rules com. Pa. Supreme Ct., 1972-85; mem. task force on prison overcrowding, 1983-85, rsch. adv. com. ,1988, Pa. Commn. on Crime and Delinquency; chmn. U.S. Magistrate Judge Merit Selection Com., 1991, mem., 1989, 90, 91; co-chair Mayor's Transition Task Force on Pub. Safety, Phila., 1992; designate D.C. Com. on Adminstrv. Justice Under Emergency Conditions, 1968. Mem. adv. bd. dirs., past pres. A Better Chance in Lower Merion; dir. Hist. Fire Mus., Phila.; dir. Neighborhood Civic Assn. Bala-Cynwyd, Pa., 1984-87. Recipient Lindback Found. award for disting. teaching, 1983, Atty. Gen.'s Advancement of Justice award, 1989, Disting. Pub. Svc. award Assn. State and County Detectives, 1989, Spl. Merit award Pa. Assn. Police Chiefs, 1989, significant contbn. to legal scholarship and edn. Beccaria award, 1995. Fellow Am. Bar Found.; mem. Am. Law Inst., ABA (faculty appellate judges' seminars 1977—, various coms., acad. advisor appellate judges edn. com. 1993—), Fed. Bar Assn. (Phila. Crim. Law com. adv. bd. 1988-93, chmn. nat. criminal law com. 1991-92), Pa. Bar Assn. (commn. profl. standards 1981-84, chmn. criminal law sect., 1986-88, Spl. Merit award 1987), Phila. Bar Assn. (criminal justice sect., appellate cts. com.), del. D.C. Jud. Conf. 1985, Order of the Coif (exec. bd. U. Pa.), St. Thomas More Soc. (pres., 1985-86, past dir. Phila. area, St. Thomas More award 1996). Roman Catholic. Contbr. articles to legal jours. Home and Office: 100 Maple Ave Bala Cynwyd PA 19004-3017 also: Temple U Law Sch 1719 N Broad St Philadelphia PA 19122-2504

STREAM, ARNOLD CRAGER, lawyer, writer; b. N.Y.C.; s. Mervyn and Sophia (Hyams) S.; m. Barbara Bloom, Oct. 1, 1967; children by previous marriages: Jane, Abigail. BA, CCNY, 1936; LLD, St. Lawrence U., 1940. Bar: N.Y. 1940, D.C. 1942. Asst. U.S. Atty. N.Y.Dist., 1940-43; ptnr. Amen, Weisman & Butler, N.Y.C., 1948-55; exec. v.p., gen. counsel C & C TV Corp., 1955-60, Hazel Bishop, Inc., 1955-60; trial lawyer, 1960-91; sr. ptnr. Monasch, Chazen & Stream, N.Y.C., 1973-82, Blum, Gersen & Stream, N.Y.C., 1982-93; ret., 1993; former trial counsel Gulfstream Aerospace Corp., Twentieth Century-Fox Film Corp., French Embassy, N.Y.C.; spl. counsel to TV industry; vis. lectr. Tauro Coll. Law; spkr. on lit. topics for Gt. Neck Libr.; archivist Palace of the Govs., Sante Fe; tutor lit. and bus. law Santa Fe C.C. Author: (novels) The Third Bullet, Until Proven Guilty, Nemo; (short story) Sudi, others; contbr. book revs., tax series, series on constl. law, articles to profl. jours. Served to lt. col. JAGD, AUS, 1943-46. Mem. Bar of Assn. of City of N.Y. *A lawyer standing in the courtroom provides the ultimate balance between excess government and excess liberty.*

STREAN, BERNARD M., retired naval officer; b. Big Cabin, Okla., Dec. 16, 1910; s. Ralph Lester and Maude (Hopkins) S.; m. Janet Lockey, June 12, 1935; children: Bernard M., Richard Lockey, Judy (Mrs. William S. Graves). B.S., U.S. Naval Acad., 1933; grad., Armed Forces Staff Coll., 1949, Nat. War Coll., 1958. Commd. ensign USN, 1933, advanced through grades to vice adm., 1965, designated naval aviator, 1935, assigned USS Pennsylvania, 1933-35; assigned Naval Air Sta. USN, Pensacola, Fla., 1935-36; assigned USS Saratoga USN, 1936-38, assigned San Diego Naval Sta., 1938-39; assigned Pearl Harbor Naval Air Sta. USN, Hawaii, 1939-40; assigned Naval Air Sta. USN, Jacksonville, Fla., 1940-42; comdr. Fighter Squadron 1, USS Yorktown USN, 1943-44, comdr. Air Group 98, 1944-45, comdr. Air Group 75, 1945-46, head tech. tng. program sect. Office Chief Naval Ops., 1950-51, comdg. officer Air Transp. Squdaron 8, 1951-54, comdg. officer Pre-Flight Sch., 1954-56, comdg. officer USS Kenneth Whiting, 1956-57, comdg. officer USS Randolph, 1958-59, chief staff, aide to comdr. Naval Air Force, U.S. Atlantic Fleet, 1959-60, comdr. Fleet Air Whidbey, 1960-61, comdr. Patrol Force 7th Fleet, also U.S. Taiwan Patrol Force, 1961-62, asst. chief naval ops. for fleet ops., 1962-64, comdr. Carrier Div. 2, Atlantic Fleet, 1964-65, comdr. World's 1st All-Nuclear Naval Task Force, 1964, comdr. round the world cruise; dep. asst. chief for pers., Bur. Naval Pers. Dept. Navy, Washington, 1965-68; chief naval air tng. Naval Air Sta. Dept. Navy, Pensacola, Fla., 1968-71; ret., 1971; v.p. O.S.C. Franchise Devel. Corp., 1971-75; chmn. bd. Solaray Corp., 1975-80; v.p. Huet-Browning Corp., Washington. Bd. dirs. U.S. Olympic Com., 1965-68; trustee No. Va. Community Colls., 1978-82. Decorated Navy Cross, (2) D.F.C. with 2 gold stars, Air medal with 7 gold stars, Legion of Merit, D.S.M., numerous area and campaign ribbons; Disting. Svc. medal (Greece); medal of Pao-Ting (Republic of China). Mem. Mil. Order World Wars, Loyal Order Carabao, Early and Pioneer Naval Aviators Assn. (pres. 1977-79), Arlington County Tax Assn. (vice chmn. 1978-80), Md. Aviation Hist. Soc. (founder, bd. dirs. 1978-82), U.S. Naval Acad. Alumni Assn. (pres. Class 1933, 1973-88), Army Navy Club (Washington), N.Y. Yacht Club, Washington Golf and Country Club (Arlington), L.A. Country Club. Address: 1200 N Nash St Apt 846 Arlington VA 22209-3615 also: 804 N Camden Dr Beverly Hills CA 90210-3026

STREAR, JOSEPH D., public relations executive; b. N.Y.C., Nov. 5, 1933; s. Morris and Betty (Birenbaum) S. B.A., CCNY, 1955. Pres. AC&R Pub. Relations, Inc., N.Y.C., 1972-82; mng. ptnr. Kanan, Corbin, Schupak & Aronow, Inc., N.Y.C., 1982-84; pres. Strear, David & Mitchell, Inc., N.Y.C., 1984-91; now prin. Joseph Strear Pub. Rels., N.Y.C. Served to 1st lt. U.S. Army, 1955-57. Mem. Pub. Relations Soc. Am. Avocation: sports. Office: 408 W 57th St New York NY 10019-3053

STREATOR, EDWARD, diplomat; b. N.Y.C., Dec. 12, 1930; s. Edward James and Ella (Stout) S.; m. Priscilla Craig Kenney, Feb. 16, 1957; children: Edward James, III, Elinor Craig, Abigail Merrill. AB, Princeton U., 1952. Commd. fgn. service officer Dept. State, 1956; assigned ICA, 1956-58; 3d sec. embassy Addis Ababa, Ethiopia, 1958-60; 2d sec. embassy Lome Togo, 1960-62; intelligence research specialist Office Research and Analysis for Africe, Dept. State, Washington, 1962-63, staff asst. to sec. state, 1964-66, chief polit.-mil. affairs unit, 1966-67; dep. dir. polit.-mil. affairs Office Polit.-Mil. Affairs, 1967-68; dep. dir. polit. affairs U.S. Mission to NATO, 1968-69; dep. dir. Office NATO and Atlantic Polit.-Mil. Affairs, Dept. State, 1969-73; dir. office, 1973-75, dep. U.S. permanent rep. to NATO, dep. chief U.S. Mission to NATO, 1975-77; minister, dep. chief of mission Am. embassy, London, 1975-84; ambassador, U.S. rep. OECD Paris, 1984-87; bd. dirs. South Bank. U.S. dels. NATO and OECD Ministerial Meetings, 1964, 66, 69-75, 85-87; mem. 10th SEATO Coun. Min. Meeting, 1965; 2d spl. Inter-Am. Conf., 1965, Conf. Security and Coop., Europe, 1973; mem. Coun., Royal United Svcs. Inst., 1987-91, v. patron, 1991—; exec. com. The Pilgrims, Internat. Inst. Strategic Studies; gov. Ditchley Found., English Speaking Union, 1988-94; pres. Am. C. of C., U.K., 1988-94; chmn. European Coun. Am. C. of C., 1992-94; bd. dirs. Brit-Am. Arts Assn.; dir. Brit. Mus. Natural History Internat. Found.; adv. bd. Inst. U.S. Studies-U. London; coun. mem. Oxford Inst. Am. Studies; adv. com. Fulbright Commn., 1995—. U.S. dels. NATO and OECD Ministerial Mtgs., 1964, 66, 69-75, 85-87; active 10th SEATO Coun. Min. Mtg., 1965, Coun. Royal United Svc. Inst., 1987-91, vice-patron, 1993—; 2d spl. Inter-Am. Conf., 1965, Conf. Security and Coop., Europe, 1973. Recipient Presdl. Meritorious Svc. award, 1986, Wilbur Carr award Dept. of State, 1987, Benjamin Franklin medal Royal Soc. Arts, 1992. Mem. Met. Club (Washington), Beefsteak Club, Garrick Club, White's Club (London), Mill Reef Club (Antigua). Episcopalian. Address: 9 St Albans Mansion, Kensington Court Pl, London W8 5QH, England also: Chateau de St Aignan, 32480 La Romieu France

STRECKER, IGNATIUS J., archbishop; b. Spearville, Kans., Nov. 23, 1917; s. William J. and Mary B. (Knoeber) S. Student, St. Benedict's Coll., Atchison, Kans., 1931-37, Kenrick Sem., St. Louis, 1937-42, Cath. U. Am., 1944-45. Ordained priest Roman Cath. Ch., 1942; aux. chaplain USAAF, Great Bend, Kans., 1942-44; chancellor Diocese Wichita, 1948-62; bishop Diocese Springfield-Cape Girardeau, Mo., 1962-69; archbishop Archdiocese of Kansas City, Kans., 1969—; retired archbishop Archdiocese of Kansas City. Office: Chancery Office 12615 Parallel Ave Kansas City KS 66109-3718

STRECKFUSS, JAMES ARTHUR, lawyer, historian; b. Cin., Apr. 28, 1951; s. Arthur James and Ruby Carolyn (Meyer) S.; m. Sharon Lynn Betz, Nov. 18, 1977; 1 child, Erich. BA in Polit. Sci., U. Cin., 1973; JD, Woodrow Wilson Coll. Law, 1981. Bar: Ind. Field rep. Ohio Lottery Commn., Cin., 1974-78; adminstrv. staff Powell, Goldstein, Frazer & Murphy, Atlanta, 1979-80; bailiff U.S. Ct. Appeals 11th Cir., Atlanta, 1980-81; spl. asst. Congressman Thomas Luken, Cin., 1982-84; job svc. employer com. staff State of Ohio, Cin., 1984—. Contbr.: The United States in the First World War: An Encyclopedia, 1995; mng. editor Over the Front, 1986—. Chmn. Progressive Young Dems., Cin., 1974-75. Mem. Ind. State Bar Assn., League of W.W. I Aviation Historians (pres. 1993—), Cross and Cockade Internat. Home: 3127 Penrose Pl Cincinnati OH 45211-6719

STREEB, GORDON LEE, diplomat, economist; b. Windsor, Colo., Dec. 24, 1935; s. Gerhard O. and Amelia (Martin) S.; m. Alice Junette Thomas, Aug. 11, 1962; children: Kurt, Kent, Kerry-Lynn. BSBA, U. Colo., 1959, BSChemE, 1959; PhD in Econs., U. Minn., 1978. Fgn. service officer U.S. Dept. State, Berlin, 1963-65; vice consul Am. Consulate, Guadalajara, Mex., 1965-67; instr. econs. U. Minn., 1968; examiner Bd. Examiners, 1972-73; internat. economist for trade policy Bur. Econ. and Bus. Affairs, Washington, 1973-77; econ. counselor U.S. mission European Office of the UN and other internat. orgns., Geneva, 1977-80; exec. asst. to undersec. of state on econ. affairs Washington, 1980-81; dep. asst. sec. state for econ. and social affairs Bur. Internat. Orgn. Affairs, Washington, 1981-84; dep. chief mission Am. Embassy, New Delhi, India, 1984-88; sr. inspector Dept. State, Washington, 1988-90; amb. to Zambia Am. Embassy, Lusaka, 1990-93; diplomat-in-residence The Carter Ctr., Atlanta, 1994-95; dir. Sustainable Devel. Program The Carter Ctr., 1995—. Home: 2680 Churchwell Ln Tucker GA 30084-2402 Office: The Carter Ctr One Copenhill Atlanta GA 30307

STREEP, MERYL (MARY LOUISE STREEP), actress; b. Madison, N.J., June 22, 1949; d. Harry Jr. and Mary W. Streep; m. Donald J. Gummer, 1978. BA, Vassar Coll., 1971; MFA, Yale U., 1975, DFA (hon.), 1983; DFA (hon.), Dartmouth Coll., 1981. Appeared with Green Mountain Guild, Woodstock, Vt.; Broadway debut in Trelawny of the Wells, Lincoln Center Beaumont Theater, 1975; N.Y.C. theatrical appearances include 27 Wagons Full of Cotton (Theatre World award), A Memory of Two Mondays, Henry V, Secret Service, The Taming of the Shrew, Measure for Measure, The Cherry Orchard, Happy End, Wonderland, Taken in Marriage, Alice in Concert (Obie award 1981); movie appearances include Julia, 1977, The Deer Hunter, 1978 (Best Supporting Actress award Nat. Soc. Film Critics), Manhattan, 1979, The Seduction of Joe Tynan, 1979, Kramer vs. Kramer, 1979 (N.Y. Film Critics' award, Los Angeles Film Critics' award, both for best actress, Golden Globe award, Acad. award for best supporting actress), The French Lieutenant's Woman, 1981 (Los Angeles Film Critics award for best actress, Brit. Acad. award, Golden Globe award 1981), Sophie's Choice, 1982 (Acad. award for best actress, Los Angeles Film Critics award for best actress, Golden Globe award 1982), Still of the Night, 1982, Silkwood, 1983, Falling in Love, 1984, Plenty, 1985, Out of Africa, 1985 (Los Angeles Film Critics award for best actress 1985), Heartburn, 1986, Ironweed, 1987, A Cry in the Dark, 1988 (named Best Actress N.Y. Film Critics' Circle, 1988, Best Actress Cannes Film Festival, 1989), She-Devil, 1989, Postcards From the Edge, 1990, Defending Your Life, 1991, Death Becomes Her, 1992, The House of the Spirits,1994, The River Wild, 1994, The Bridges of Madison County, 1995 (Acad. award nominee for best actress 1996); TV film The Deadliest Season, 1977; TV mini-series Holocaust, 1978 (Emmy award); TV dramatic spls. Secret Service, 1977, Uncommon Women and Others, 1978;TV (narrator) The Velveteen Rabbit, 1985, A Vanishing Wilderness, 1990. Recipient Mademoiselle award, 1976, Woman of Yr. award B'nai Brith, 1979, Woman of Yr. award Hasty Pudding Soc., Harvard U., 1980, Best Supporting Actress award Nat. Bd. of Rev., 1979, Best Actress award Nat. Bd. of Rev., 1982, Star of Yr. award Nat. Assn. Theater Owners, 1983, People's Choice award, 1983, 85, 86, 87. Office: Creative Artists Agy 9830 Wilshire Blvd Beverly Hills CA 90212-1804

STREET, CECILIA REGINA, elementary school educator, administrator; b. Mobile, Ala., June 18, 1935; d. Joseph Monroe and Regina (Cain) S. BA in Elem. Edn., Mt. St. Agnes Coll., 1958; MRE, Cath. U. Am., 1968; M in Elem. Adminstrn., U. South Ala., 1977, M in Counseling, 1991. Tchr. 1st grade St. Mary Sch., Rockville, Md., 1958-59, St. Joseph Sch., Macon, Ga., 1959-62; tchr. 1st and 2d grades St. Mary Sch., Mobile, 1962-65; adminstr. St. Joseph Sch., Mobile, 1965-67, St. Mary Sch., Huntsville, Ala., 1967-69, St. Aloysius Sch., Bessemer, Ala., 1969-71, Corpus Christi Sch., Mobile, 1971-90; tchr. Meadowlake Sch., Mobile, 1990-91; adminstr. Palmer Pillans Mid. Sch., Mobile, 1991-92; founder, dir. Parish Day Care Ctr., Mobile, 1983-87, Corpus Christi Day Ctr., Mobile, 1983-87; adminstr. Meadowlake Elem. Sch., Mobile, 1992-95. Dir. parish religious edn. Corpus Christi Ch., 1971-82. Named Career Woman of the Yr. Gayfer Career Club, Mobile, 1993; recipient Blue Ribbon plaque Nat. Fedn. Elem. Sch. Prins., Mobile, 1990. Roman Catholic. Home: 1151 Cody Rd S # 19 Mobile AL 36695-4401

STREET, DANA MORRIS, orthopedic surgeon; b. N.Y.C., May 7, 1910; s. William Dana and Elizabeth (Clark) S.; m. Elna Alice Clare, June 18, 1940; children: Rosalyn Clare (Mrs. David R. Sprague), Dana Clark, Steven Morris, William Milo. B.S., Haverford Coll., 1932; M.D., Cornell U., 1936. Diplomate: Am. Bd. Orthopaedic Surgery. Intern pathology Duke Hosp., 1936-37, Duke Hosp. (orthopedics), 1937-38; asst. resident phys. medicine Albany (N.Y.) Hosp., 1938-39; fellow Nemour Found., 1939-40; intern orthopedics Boston City Hosp., 1940; asst. resident surgery Albany Hosp., 1940-41; intern, asst. resident orthopedics Johns Hopkins Hosp., 1941-42; fellow N.Y. Orthopaedic Hosp., 1942; chief orthopedic sect. Kennedy VA Hosp., Memphis, 1946-59; prof. surgery, chief orthopedic div. U. Ark., 1959-62; prof. surgery in residence UCLA, 1962-75; head orthopedic div. Harbor Gen. Hosp., Torrance, Calif., 1962-75, Riverside (Calif.) Gen. Hosp., 1975-77; chief orthopedic sect. Jerry L. Pettis Meml. VA Hosp., Loma Linda, Calif., 1977-80; prof. orthopedics Loma Linda U., 1975-80, emeritus, 1980—. Author: (with others) Science and Practice of Intramedullary Nailing, 1995; contbr. aricles on medullary nailing and joint replacement to med. jours.; also book chpts. Served to maj. M.C. USAAF, 1942-46. Mem. AMA, Am. Acad. Orthopaedic Surgeons, Am. Orthopaedic Assn., Calif. Med. Assn., Calif. Orthopaedic Assn., Western Orthopedic Assn., Assn. Bone and Joint Surgeons (treas. 1953-56, v.p. 1956-58, pres. 1959), Am. Fracture Assn. Presbyn. (elder, deacon, clk. sessions). Home: 44201 Village 44 Camarillo CA 93012-8935

STREET, DAVID HARGETT, investment company executive; b. Oklahoma City, Dec. 4, 1943; s. Bob Allen and Elizabeth Anne (Hargett) S.; m. Betty Ann Nichols, Oct. 1, 1966; children: Elizabeth Ann, Randall Hargett, Jeffrey David. BA in English, U. Okla., 1965; MBA in Fin., U. Pa., 1970. Vice pres. SEI Corp., 1970; v.p., prin. Street & Street, Inc., N.Y.C., 1970-74; v.p., mgr. San Francisco regional office First Nat. Bank Chicago, 1974-78; sr. v.p., CFO, treas. Bangor Punta Corp., Greenwich, Conn., 1978-84; v.p., treas. Penn Cen. Corp., Greenwich, 1984-86, v.p. fin., 1986-87; sr. v.p. fin. Penn Cen. Corp., Cin., 1987-92; exec. v.p. Gen. Cable Corp., Highland Heights, Ky., 1992-94, also bd. dirs.; pres., CEO Street Capital Group, Cin., 1994—; mem. adv. bd. Mfrs. Hanover Trust Co., 1982-88. Vice chmn. bd. dirs. Greenwich Acad. for Girls, 1984-87, chmn. bd. trustees, treas., 1987-88; trustee Cin. County Day Sch., 1990-91; mem. cmty. bd. Sta. WGUC-FM, 198-94; trustee Bethesda Hosp., Inc., 1993—; trustee Cin. Classical Pub. Radio, Inc., 1994—, Cmty. Chest Cin. Area, Inc., 1993—, treas., 1994-95; trustee John Austin Cheley Found., 1995—, Fountain Valley Sch., 1995—. 1st lt. M.I. U.S. Army, 1966-67. Mem. Greenwich Country Club. Republican. Presbyterian. Home and Office: 3425 Oyster Bay Ct Cincinnati OH 45244

STREET, JOHN CHARLES, linguistics educator; b. Chgo., Apr. 3, 1930; s. Charles Larrabee and Mary Louise (Rouse) S.; m. Eve Elizabeth Baker, June 4, 1975. BA, Yale, 1951, MA, 1952, PhD, 1955. Asst. prof. English Mich. State U., 1957-59; asst. prof. linguistics and Mongolian langs. Columbia, 1959-62; vis. asst. prof. linguistics U. Wash., 1962-63; assoc. prof. linguistics U. Wis., Madison, 1963-65; prof. linguistics U. Wis., 1965-92; prof. emeritus U. Wis., Madison, 1992—. Author: The Language of the Secret History of the Mongols, 1957, Khalkha Structure, 1963, The Journal of Oliver Rouse, 1983, An Ellis Family of Devon and Newfoundland, 1994. Research asso. Am. Council Learned Socs., 1959-62. Served with AUS, 1955-57.

STREET, PICABO, Olympic athlete; b. Triumph, Idaho, 1971. Silver medalist, women's downhill alpine skiing Olympic Games, Lillehammer, Norway, 1994; downhill skier U.S. Ski Team, 1994—. Named World Cup Downhill Women's Champion, 1995. Office: US Olympic Com 1750 E Boulder St Colorado Springs CO 80909-5724

STREET, ROBERT LYNNWOOD, civil and mechanical engineer; b. Honolulu, Dec. 18, 1934; s. Evelyn Mansel and Dorothy Heather (Brook) S.; m. Norma Jeanette Ensminger, Feb. 6, 1959; children: Brian Clarke (dec.), Deborah Lynne, Kimberley Anne. Student, USN ROTC Program, 1952-57; M.S., Stanford U., 1957, Ph.D. (NSF grad. fellow 1960-62), 1963. Mem. faculty sch. engring. Stanford U., 1962—, prof. civil engring., assoc. chmn. dept., 1970-72, chmn. dept., 1972-80, 94-95, prof. fluid mechanics and applied math., 1972—, dir. environ. fluid mechanics lab., 1985-91, assoc. dean research, 1971-83, vice provost for acad. computing and info. systems, 1983-85, vice provost and dean of research and acad. info. systems, 1985-87, v.p. for info. resources, 1987-90, acting provost, 1987, v.p. librs. and info. resources, 1990-92; vice provost, dean of librs. and info. resources Stanford U., 1992-94; vis. prof. U. Liverpool, Eng., 1970-71; vis. prof. mech. engring. James Cook U., Australia, 1995; trustee Univ. Corp. Atmospheric Rsch., 1983-94, chmn. sci. programs evaluation com., 1981, treas. corp., 1985, vice chmn. bd., 1986, chmn. bd., 1987-91; bd. dirs., sec.-treas. UCAR Found., 1987-91; bd. govs. Rsch. Libr. Group, 1990-91; chmn. Com. Preservation Rsch. Libr. Materials, Assn. Rsch. Librs., 1993; mem. higher edn. adv. bds. computer corps., 1983-94; mem. basic energy sci. adv. com. U.S. Dept. Energy, 1993—; bd. dirs. Stanford U. Bookstore, Inc. vis. prof. U. Liverpool, Eng., 1970-71; vis. prof. mech. engring. James Cook U., Australia, 1995; trustee Univ. Corp. Atmospheric Rsch., 1983-94, chmn. sci. programs evaluation com., 1981, treas. corp., 1985, vice chmn. bd., 1986, chmn. bd., 1987-91; bd. dirs., sec.-treas. UCAR Found., 1987-91; bd. govs. Rsch. Libr. Group, 1990-91; chmn. Com. Preservation Rsch. Libr. Materials, Assn. Rsch. Librs., 1993; mem. higher edn. adv. bds. computer corps., 1983-94; mem. basic energy sci. adv. com. U.S. Dept. Energy, 1993-96; bd. dirs. Stanford U. Bookstore, Inc. With C.E.C., USN, 1957-60. Sr. postdoctoral fellow Nat. Center Atmospheric Research, 1978-79; sr. Queen's fellow in marine sci., Australia, 1985; fellow N.E. Asia-U.S. Forum on Internat. Policy at Stanford U., 1985-89. Fellow AAAS; mem. ASCE (chmn. publs. com. hydraulics divsn. 1978-80, Walter Huber prize 1972), ASME (R.T. Knapp award 1986), Am. Geophys. Union, Oceanographic Soc., Am. Phys. Soc., Phi Beta Kappa, Sigma Xi, Tau Beta Pi. Office: Environ Fluid Mechs Lab Dept Civil Engring Stanford U Stanford CA 94305-4020

STREET, STEPHANIE, federal official. Dep. asst. to pres., co-dir. scheduling and advance Exec. Office of the Pres., Washington, 1995—. Office: Scheduling and Advance Exec Office of Pres 1600 Pennsylvania Ave NW Washington DC 20500

STREET, WILLIAM MAY, beverage company executive; b. Louisville, 1938. Grad., Princeton U., 1960; MBA, Harvard U., 1963. V.p. Brown-Forman Corp., Louisville, 1969, dir., mem. exec. com., 1971, sr. v.p., 1977, vice chmn., 1983—; pres., COO Brown-Forman Beverage Co. Divsn., Louisville, 1986—; pres., CEO Brown-Forman Beverages Worldwide Divsn., 1994—; vice chmn. Brown-Forman Corp., 1983—. Office: Brown-Forman Beverages Worldwide PO Box 1080 850 Dixie Hwy Louisville KY 40210-1091

STREETER, HENRY SCHOFIELD, lawyer; b. N.Y.C., May 2, 1920; s. Thomas Winthrop and Ruth (Cheney) S.; m. Mary Ann Dexter, May 16, 1959; children—Frank Sherwin, Cornelia Van Rensselaer, Natalie Thayer. B.A., Harvard U., 1942, J.D. magna cum laude, 1949. Bar: Mass. Law clk. Judge A.N. Hand, N.Y.C., 1950-51; mem. firm Ropes & Gray, Boston, 1949—. Chmn. Bd. Appeals, Wenham, Mass., 1983—; trustee, v.p. Peabody Mus. Salem, 1968—; corporator Mass. Gen. Hosp., 1976, Beverly Hosp., 1972. Served to lt. USNR, 1941-46. Mem. Mass. Hist. Soc., Am. Antiquarian Soc. (trustee 1972), Club of Odd Volumes (pres.), Somerset Club, Myopia Hunt Club, Cruising of Am. Club, Walpole Soc., Tobique Salmon Club (pres.), St. Andrew Lodge. Episcopalian. Avocations: sailing; shooting; fishing. Home: Old Farm Maple St Wenham MA 01984 Office: Ropes and Gray 1 International Pl Boston MA 02110-2600

STREETER, RICHARD BARRY, academic official; b. Albany, N.Y., Aug. 6, 1940; s. Lyle Tyler and Marion Downey S.; m. Janet Grace Marsteller, July 31, 1971; children—Jonathan Lyle, Stephanie Lyn. BA, U. Fla., 1962, MEd, 1963; EdD, U. Miami, 1972. Assoc. dir. fin. aid U. Miami, Coral Gables, Fla., 1970-73; dir. fin. aid Portland (Oreg.) State U., 1973-76, asst. dean grad. studies, dir. sponsored research, 1976-80; dir. office of research Lehigh U., Bethlehem, Pa., 1980-90; asst. v.p. rsch., dir. U. South Fla., Tampa, 1990—; dir. USDOE/USF Tech. Deployment Ctr., 1994—; bd. trustees Northampton County Area C.C., 1986-90; del. to Pa. Fed. of C.C. Trustees; mem. Easton area Sch. Bd. 1984-90; bd. dirs. Oak Ridge Associated Univs. Bus. mgr. Quality of Life Maintenance Orgn., 1976-80. Mem. AAAS, Nat. Coun. Univ. Rsch. Adminstrs., Soc. Rsch. Adminstrs., Coun. on Rsch. and Tech. (rsch. policy com., commercialization task force), Archontes, Omega, Phi Delta Kappa. Republican. Presbyterian. Home: 507 Cliff Dr Temple Ter FL 33617-3807 Office: U South Fla 4202 E Fowler Ave Tampa FL 33620-9951

STREETER, RICHARD EDWARD, lawyer; b. Mpls., Aug. 6, 1934; s. Donald Stivers and Beatrice Louise (Gibbs) S.; m. Charlotte Mae Tharp; children—Christopher A., Joanna G., Matthew J., Jonathan R. B.A., Yale U., 1956; LL.B., Yale Law Sch., 1959. Bar: Ohio 1960, D.C. 1964, U.S. Supreme Ct. 1964. Assoc. Thompson, Hine and Flory, Cleve., 1960-63, 65-68, ptnr., 1968—; atty. State Dept. Legal Advisors Office, Washington, 1963, Justice Dept. Antitrust Div., Washington, 1964; asst. gen. counsel Senate Democratic Policy Com., Washington, 1964-65. Contbr. article to profl. jour. Mem. Leadership Cleve., 1981; v.p. Youth Opportunities Unltd., Cleve., 1983—; pres. Fedn. Commty. Planning, Cleve., 1980-82, Cleve. Legal Aid Soc., 1974-76, Plan of Action for Tomorrow's Housing, Cleve., 1987-88; chmn. Ctr. for Human Svcs., 1990-93; trustee City Club, Cleve., 1987-91, St. Vincent Quadrangle Inc., 1991—, Lake Erie Coll., 1993—; bd. dirs. United Way Svcs. Cleve., 1992-96. Recipient Cleve. 10 Outstanding Young Men award Jr. C. of C., 1968. Mem. ABA, Bar Assn. Greater Cleve. (trustee 1971-74, chmn. securities law sect. 1979-80, chmn. corps. banking and bus. law sect. 1983-85), Ohio State Bar Assn. (corp. law com.). Home: 472 Greenhaven Dr Chagrin Falls OH 44022-3323 Office: Thompson Hine & Flory PLL 3900 Society Ctr 127 Public Sq Cleveland OH 44114-1216

STREETER, TAL, sculptor; b. Oklahoma City, Aug. 1, 1934; s. Paul Waller and Pauline Viola (Roberts) S.; m. Dorothy Ann Romig Sheets, June 26, 1957; 1 child, Lissa. B.F.A., U. Kans., 1956, M.F.A., 1961. Prof. SUNY, Purchase, 1973—; fellow Ctr. for Advanced Visual Studies MIT, 1988—, vis. prof., 1991—; curator exhbn. The Art of the Japanese Kite, Japan Soc., N.Y.C., 1980, Ice and Air Show NEA/N.Y. Arts Coun., Lake Placid, 1983, Dayton Art Inst., 1990; Fulbright lectr., Korea, 1971; conferee Internat. Design Conf., Aspen, Colo., 1979. Exhibited in group and one-man shows N.Y. World's Fair, 1965, Whitney Mus., N.Y.C., 1965, Larry Aldrich Mus., Ridgefield, Conn., 1968, 70, Sheldon Art Mus., Lincoln, Nebr., 1970, Sculpture in Environment, Parks Dept., N.Y.C., 1970, Minami Gallery, Tokyo, 1971, Neuberger Mus., Purchase, N.Y., 1977, U. Ky. Mus., 1982, Bruckner Festival, Linz, Austria, 1982, Dayton Art Inst., 1982, AG Mus., Munich, 1983, Cleve. Art Mus., Eng., 1985, Milton Avery Mus., Bard Coll., N.Y., 1985, Citicorp Plz., Queens, N.Y., 1991, MIT Mus., 1994; represented in permanent collections Mus. Modern Art, N.Y.C., San Francisco Mus. Contemporary Art, Wadsworth Atheneum, Newark Mus., Neuberger Mus., Purchase, N.Y., Contemporary Arts Mus., Houston, Smith Coll. Mus. Art, High Mus., Atlanta, Storm King Art Center, Ark. Art Ctr., Little Rock, Milw. Art Ctr.; vis. artist-in-residence Dartmouth Coll., 1963, Bennett Coll., 1964-70, U. N.C., 1970, 72, 73, Queens Coll., N.Y.C., 1973, Penland Sch. of Crafts, 1974, 75, 76, Arcosanti Festival, Phoenix, 1978, 80, 81, Artpark, 1978, Lakefront Festival, Milw., 1981, Sun Valley Arts Ctr., Idaho, 1986, Walker Art Ctr., Minn., 1986; commns.: Morris Coll., N.J., 1981, N.J. State Library for Blind, 1982-84, Nat. Mus. Contemporary Art, Seoul (Republic of Korea) Olympics, 1988, Gyewon Coll. of Arts, Seoul, 1991, Total Contemporary Art Mus., Seoul, 1992; author: The Art of the Japanese Kite, 1974; co-editor: Art That Flies, 1991, A Kite Journey Through India, 1996; also articles; contbr. to Ency. of Japan, 1981, Grove/ Macmillan Dictionary of Art, 1996; profiled in Arts Mag., Dec., 1977, U & lc Mag., Nov., 1984, An American Portrait, CBS TV, 1986, Sky, Moon, Dragons, Kites and Smiles: Tal Streeter, An American Artist in Asia, 1994, From the Place at the Far End of the Sky, 1994. Collaborations in Art, Sci. and Tech./N.Y. State Coun. on Arts grantee, 1978.

STREETMAN, BEN GARLAND, electrical engineering educator; b. Cooper, Tex., June 24, 1939; s. Richard E. and Bennie (Morrow) S.; m. Lenora Ann Music, Sept. 9, 1961; children: Paul, Scott. BS, U. Tex., 1961, MS, 1963, PhD, 1966. Fellow Oak Ridge Nat. Lab., 1964-66; asst. prof. elec. engring. U. Ill., 1966-70, asso. prof., 1970-74, prof., 1974-82; rsch. prof. Coordinated Sci. Lab., 1970-82; prof. elec. engring. U. Tex., Austin, 1982—, dir. Microelectronics Rsch. Ctr., 1984—, Dula D. Cockrell Centennial chair engring., 1989—; cons. in field. Author: Solid State Electronic Devices, 4th edit., 1995. Recipient Frederick Emmons Terman award Am. Soc. Engring. Edn., 1981, AT&T Found. award Am. Soc. Engring. Edn., 1987. Fellow IEEE (Edn. medal 1989), Electrochem. Soc.; mem. NAE, Tau Beta Pi, Eta Kappa Nu, Sigma Xi. Home: 3915 Glengarry Dr Austin TX 78731-3835 Office: U Tex Microelectronics Rsch Ctr PRC/MER R9900 Austin TX 78758

STREETMAN, JOHN WILLIAM, III, museum official; b. Marion, N.C., Jan. 19, 1941; s. John William, Jr. and Emily Elaine (Carver) S.; children: Katherine Drake, Leah Farrior, Burgin Eaves. BA in English and Theatre History, Western Carolina U., 1963; cert. in Shakespeare studies, Lincoln Coll., Oxford (Eng.) U., 1963. Founding dir. Jewett Creative Arts Ctr., Berwick Acad., South Berwick, Maine, 1964-70; exec. dir. Polk Mus. Art, Lakeland, Fla., 1970-75; dir. Mus. Arts and Sci., Evansville, Ind., 1975—; chmn. mus. adv. panel Ind. Arts Commn., 1977-78. Mem. Am. Assn. Museums, Assn. Ind. Museums (bd. dirs.). Episcopalian. Office: Evansville Mus Arts & Scis 411 SE Riverside Dr Evansville IN 47713-1037

STREETT, WILLIAM BERNARD, university dean, engineering educator; b. Lake Village, Ark., Jan. 27, 1932; s. William Bernard and Marie Louise (Pfeffer) S.; m. Jackie Lou Heard, June 8, 1955; children—Robert Stuart, David Alexander, Kathleen Ann, Michael Richard. B.S., U.S. Mil. Acad., 1955; M.S., U. Mich., 1961, Ph.D., 1963. Commd. 2d lt. U.S. Army, 1955; founder, first dir. Sci. Research Lab. U.S. Mil. Acad., West Point, N.Y., 1968-78; asst. dean U.S. Mil. Acad., West Point, N.Y., 1968-78, ret. col., 1978; sr. research assoc. Cornell U., Ithaca, 1978-81, prof. chem. engring., 1981-95, dean engring., 1984-93; v.p. Impact-Echo Consultants, Ithaca, 1995—. Contbr. articles to profl. jours. Postdoctoral fellow NATO, 1966, Guggenheim fellow Oxford U., 1974. Mem. ACI, Tau Beta Pi, Sigma Xi. Home: 105 Oak Hill Pl Ithaca NY 14850-2323 Office: Cornell U Coll Engring Hollister Hall Ithaca NY 14850

STREFF, WILLIAM ALBERT, JR., lawyer; b. Chgo., Aug. 12, 1949; s. William Albert Streff Sr. and Margaret (McKeough) Streff Fisher; m. Kathleen Myslinski, Sept. 29, 1984; children: Amanda, William III, Kimberly. BSME, Northwestern U., 1971, JD cum laude, 1974. Bar: Ill. 1974, U.S. Dist. Ct. (no. dist.) Ill. 1974, U.S. Dist. Ct. (no. dist.) N.Y. 1987, U.S. Dist. Ct. (no. dist.) Calif. 1988, U.S. Ct. Appeals (7th cir.) 1980, U.S. Ct. Appeals (9th cir.) 1988, U.S. Ct. Appeals (fed. cir.) 1982. Legal writing instr. Law Sch. Northwestern U., Chgo., 1973-74; assoc. Kirkland & Ellis, Chgo., 1974-80, ptnr., 1980—; lectr. Ill. Inst. Continuing Legal Edn., 1984; adj. prof. Northwestern U. Law Sch., 1992-94. Contbr. articles to profl. jours. Mem. adv. bd. Ill. Inst. Tech./Chgo.-Kent, 1983-86; trustee Northwestern U., Evanston, 1984-86, mem. vis. com. Law Sch., Chgo., 1988-94. Mem. ABA. Office: Kirland & Ellis 200 E Randolph St # 6100 Chicago IL 60601-6436

STREIBEL, BRYCE, state senator; b. Fessenden, N.D., Nov. 19, 1922; s. Reinhold M. and Frieda I. (Broschat) S.; m. June P. Buckley, Mar. 23, 1947; 1 child, Kent. Attended U. N.D., Grand Forks; BS, San Francisco State Coll., 1947. Engr. U.S. Govt., Napa, Calif., 1943-46; dir. Martin Funeral Home, Stockton, Calif., 1946-55; owner Streibel Twin Oaks Farm, Fessenden, N.D., 1955—; state sen. State of N.D., Bismarck, 1981—, pres. pro tempore, 1995, state rep., 1957-75. Author: Pathways Through LIfe, 1983. Chmn. N.D. Legis. Coun., Bismarck, 1969-75; councilman Town of Fessenden, 1976-84; former pres. 20-30 Internat. Group, Sacramento, trustee, 1952-54; dir. World Coun., Sacramento, 1951-53; bd. dirs. U. N.D. Fellows, Grand Forks, 1982-86; pres. Fessenden Airport Authority, 1980—; mem. N.D. Bd. Higher Edn., 1977-81; chmn. N.D. adv. commn. U.S. Commn. on Civil Rights, 1988-93. Recipient Sioux award U. N.D. Alumni Assn., 1976, Benefactor award U. N.D. Found., 1982, William Budge award, 1983, Outstanding Svc. award Jaycees, 1988; named Outstanding Alumnus Theta Chi, 1987. Mem. Masons (Master), Elks, Kiwanis, Shriners, Farm Bur. Republican. Baptist. Avocations: golf, philately. Home and Office: 226 2nd St N Fessenden ND 58438-7204 Office: PO Box 467 Fessenden ND 58438-0467

STREIBICH, HAROLD CECIL, lawyer; b. Baton Rouge, June 19, 1928; s. Frederick Franklin and Margaret Rose (Foley) S.; m. Theresa Ann Grimes, Apr. 25, 1973; 1 dau. by previous marriage, Margaret Ann; stepchildren: John B. Snowden, IV, Kathryn Snowden. BA, U. Tenn., 1949; LLB, U. Va., 1953; Spl. Honors, U. Memphis, 1972. Bar: Miss. 1954, Tenn. 1960. Ptnr. Streibich & Seale and predecessor firms, Memphis, 1960—; vis. lectr. Vanderbilt U. Sch. Law, 1968-74, Brigham Young U., summer 1971, Harvard U. Law Sch., 1979, 92; prof. music, prof. entertainment law U. Memphis, 1973-91; pres. Am. Rec. Inst., 1979—. Chmn. Tenn. Athletic Commn., 1970, 74. Served with U.S. Army, 1945-47, 50-52; ret. brig. gen. Tenn. N.G., 1980. Recipient World Boxing Assn. award as outstanding commr., 1972, various civic awards for Easter Seal, Heart Fund. Mem. ABA, NARAS (nat. v.p. 1980-81, bd. dirs., treas. 1978-79, pres. 1979-80, Gov.'s award Nashville chpt. 1972, Memphis chpt. 1976), Tenn. Bar Assn. (ho. of dels. 1978-83, v.p., bd. govs. 1983-85, chmn. copyright, entertainment and sports law sect. 1979), Miss. Bar Assn., Memphis Bar Assn. (bd. dirs. 1975-76), Am. Coll. Intellectual Property Law (pres. 1994—), Am. Judicature Soc., Internat. Assn. Music Pubs., Summit Club, Rotary, Phi Kappa Phi, Kappa Sigma, Omega Delta Kappa, Phi Delta Phi. Home: 5475 Crescent Ln Memphis TN 38120-2449 Office: Bryton Tower Ste 101 1271 Poplar Ave Memphis TN 38104-7265

STREICHER, JAMES FRANKLIN, lawyer; b. Ashtabula, Ohio, Dec. 6, 1940; s. Carl Jacob and Helen Marie (Dugan) S.; m. Sandra JoAnn Jennings, May 22, 1940; children: Cheryl Ann, Gregory Scott, Kerry Marie. BA, Ohio State U., 1962; JD, Case Western Res. U., 1966. Bar: Ohio 1966, U.S. Dist. Ct. (no. dist.) Ohio 1966. Assoc., Calfee, Halter & Griswold, Cleve., 1966-71, ptnr., 1972—; bd. dirs. The Mariner Group Inc., Ft. Myers, Fla., Spectra-Tech Inc., Stamford, Conn., Cuyahoga Bolt & Screw, Cleve.; mem. Div. Securities Adv. Bd., State of Ohio; lectr. Case Western Res. U., Cleve. State U.; mem. pvt. sector com. John Carroll U. Trustee Achievement Ctr. for Children; mem. corp. coun. Cleve. Mus. Art. Mem. ABA, Fed. Bar Assn., Ohio State Bar Assn., Assn. for Corp. Growth, Ohio Venture Assn., Greater Cleve. Bar Assn., Ohio State U. Alumni Assn., Case Western Res. U. Alumni Assn., Newcomen Soc., Bluecoats Club (Cleve.), Mayfield Country (bd. dirs. 1985-89), Tavern Club, Union Club, Rotary, Beta Theta Pi, Phi Delta Phi. Roman Catholic. Republican. Home: 50 Windrush Dr Chagrin Falls OH 44022-6841

STREICHLER, JERRY, exec. director internl. honorary prof. tech.; b. N.Y.C., Dec. 8, 1929; s. Samuel and Mirel (Waxman) S.; m. Rosalind Fineman, Feb. 25, 1951; children: Stuart Alan, Seth Ari, Robin Cheryl. Spl. courses cert., Newark Coll. Engring., 1951; BS magna cum laude, Kean Coll. N.J., 1956; MA, Montclair State Coll., 1958; PhD, NYU, 1963. Cons. machine designer to materials handling and auto wash cos., Montclair, N.J., 1950-67; mem. faculty dept. indsl. edn. Montclair (N.J.) State Coll., 1958-65, Trenton (N.J.) State Coll., 1965-67; prof., chmn. dept. indsl. edn. and tech. Bowling Green (Ohio) State U., 1967-78, dir. Sch. Tech., 1978-85, dean Coll. Tech., 1985-91; trustee prof., 1992, dean emeritus, trustee prof. emeritus, 1993—; pres. Tng. and Edn. Mgmt. Cons. Group, 1993—; vis. prof. S.I. Community Coll., CCNY, 1965, Rutgers U., 1967, U. Mo., 1967, U. Mich., Saginaw, 1971; cons., tchr. Newaygo Vocat. Ctr., Saginaw Career Opportunities Ctr., 1971; cons. indsl. tng., pub. schs., colls.; cons. human resource tng. and quality scis., 1984—; disting. vis. dean, spl. cons. to pres. Calif. State U., San Marcos, 1991. Asst. editor: Jour. Indsl. Tchr. Edn., 1968-70; co-editor: The Components of Teacher Education, 20th Yearbook Am. Council on Indsl. Arts Tchr. Edn.; editor: Jour. of Technology studies; contbr. articles to profl. jours. Founding com. chmn. Ohio Coun. on Indsl. Arts Tchr. Edn., 1968-69; dir. Homeowners Assn., 1993-95. With USAF, 1951-52. Univ. honors scholar, 1963. Mem. NEA, Internat. Tech. Edn. Assn., Am. Vocat. Assn., Am. Tech. Edn. Assn., Am. Soc. Engring. Edn., Nat. Assn. Indsl. Tech., Miss. Valley Indsl. Tchr. Edn. Conf., Epsilon Pi Tau, Laureate citation 1972, Disting. Svc. citation 1989), Omicron Delta Kappa, Phi Delta Kappa, Kappa Delta Pi. Office: TeMac Training & Edn Mgmt Cons PO Box 12332 La Jolla CA 92039-2332

STREICKER, JAMES RICHARD, lawyer; b. Chgo., Nov. 9, 1944; s. Seymour and De Vera (Wolfson) S.; m. Mary Stowell, Mar. 11, 1989; children: David, Sarah. AB, Miami U., 1966; JD, U. Ill., 1969. Bar: Ill. 1969, U.S. Dist. Ct. (no. dist.) Ill. 1970, U.S. Ct. Appeals (7th cir.) 1971, U.S. Supreme Ct. 1980, U.S. Dist. Ct. (ea. dist.) Wis., (no. dist.) Ind. 1986. Asst. atty. gen. State of Ill., 1970-71, asst. appellate def., 1971-75; dep. appellate def. First Dist. Ill., 1975; asst. U.S. atty. No. Dist. Ill., 1975-80; chief criminal receiving and appellate div. U.S. Attys. Office, Ill., 1979-80; ptnr. Cotsirilos, Stephenson, Tighe & Streicker, Chgo., 1980—; instr. Trial Adv. John Marshall Law Sch., 1979-80, U.S. Atty. Gens. Adv. Inst. 1978-80, Nat. Inst. for Trial Adv. 1981—; lectr. Ill. Inst. Continuing Legal Edn., Sentencing, New Techniques and Attitudes, 1986. Mem. ABA, Nat. Assn. Criminal Def. Lawyers, Am. Coll. Trial Lawyers, Am. Bd. Criminal Lawyers, Ill. State Bar Assn., Chgo. Bar Assn. Office: Cotsirilos Stephenson Tighe & Streicker 33 N Dearborn St Chicago IL 60602-3102

STREIFF, ARLYNE BASTUNAS, business owner, educator; b. Sacramento, Calif., Nov. 4; d. Peter James and Isabel (Gemnas) Bastunas; children: Peter Joshua, Joshua Gus. BS, U. Nev., 1965; postgrad., U. Calif., Davis, 1965-68, Calif. State U., Chico, 1968, 71. Cert. elem. tchr., Calif., Nev. Tchr. reading, lang. and kindergarten Enterprise Elem. Sch. Dist., Redding, Calif., 1965-95, tchr. kindergarten, 1988-95; owner, pres. Arlyne's Svcs., Redding, Calif., 1990—. Author: Niko and His Friends, 1989, Niko and the Black Rottweiler, 1995, Color-Talk-Spell. Mem. Rep. Women, Five County Labor Coun., Redding, 1976-93, Calif. Labor Fedn., 1974-93, AFL-CIO, 1974-93. Named Tchr. of Yr., Enterprise Sch. Dist., 1969. Mem. AAUW, Am. Fedn. Tchrs., Calif. Tchrs. Assn. (bargaining spokesperson 1968-72, exec. bd. dirs.), United Tchrs. Enterprise (pres. 1979-80, chmn. lang. com.), Calif. Reading Assn., Enterprise Fedn. Tchrs. (pres. 1974), Calif. Fedn. Tchrs. (v.p. 1974-78), Redding C. of C., Women of Moose, Elks. Avocations: home interior design, real estate, construction, creative writing, educational advancement. Home: 1468 Benton Dr Redding CA 96003-3116 Office: Arlynes Svcs 1468 Benton Dr Redding CA 96003-3116

STREILEIN, J. WAYNE, research scientist; b. Johnstown, Pa., June 19, 1935; s. Jacob and Mina Alma (Krouse) S.; m. Joan Elaine Stein, June 15, 1957; children: Laura Anne, William Wayne, Robert Dietrich. BA in Chemistry, Gettysburg Coll., 1956; MD, U. Pa., 1960. Asst. prof., assoc. prof. genetics U. Pa. Sch. Medicine, Phila., 1965-71; prof. cell biology Southwestern Med. Sch., Dallas, 1971-84; prof., chair microbiology and immunology U. Miami, Fla., 1984-93; prof. ophthalmology and dermatology Harvard Med. Sch., Boston, 1993—; pres., dir. rsch. Schepens Eye Rsch. Inst., Boston, 1993—. Capt. USAR, 1961-67. Recipient award Alcon Rsch. Inst., 1984, Merit award Nat. Eye Inst., 1990; Markle Found. scholar, 1967. Mem. Assn. Rsch. in Vision and Ophthalmology (Procter award 1996), Am. Assn. Immunologists (chair pub. rels. 1988-93), Soc. Investigative Dermatology, Transplantation Soc. Achievements include elucidation of cellular and molecular basis of immune privilege in eye, genetic basis of effects of ultraviolet B light on cutaneous immunity, microenvironmental factor effects on tissue-restricted antigen presenting cells. Home: 1501 Beacon St Apt 1901 Brookline MA 02146-4606 Office: Schepens Eye Rsch Inst 20 Staniford St Boston MA 02114-2508

STREISAND, BARBRA JOAN, singer, actress, director; b. Bklyn., Apr. 24, 1942; d. Emanuel and Diana (Rosen) S.; m. Elliott Gould, Mar. 1963 (div.); 1 son, Jason Emanuel. Grad. high sch., Bklyn.; student, Yeshiva of Bklyn. N.Y. theatre debut Another Evening with Harry Stoones, 1961; appeared in Broadway musicals I Can Get It for You Wholesale, 1962, Funny Girl, 1964-65; motion pictures include Funny Girl, 1968, Hello Dolly, 1969, On a Clear Day You Can See Forever, 1970, The Owl and the Pussy Cat, 1970, What's Up Doc?, 1972, Up the Sandbox, 1972, The Way We Were, 1973, For Pete's Sake, 1974, Funny Lady, 1975, The Main Event, 1979, All Night Long, 1981, Nuts, 1987; star, prodr. film A Star is Born, 1976; prodr., dir., star Yentl, 1983, The Prince of Tides, 1991; exec. prodr.: (TV movie) Serving in Silence: The Margarethe Cammermeyer Story, 1995; TV spls. include My Name is Barbra, 1965 (5 Emmy awards), Color Me Barbra, 1966; rec. artist on Columbia Records; Gold record albums include People, 1965, My Name is Barbra, 1965, Color Me Barbra, 1966, Barbra Streisand: A Happening in Central Park, 1968, Barbra Streisand: One Voice, Stoney End, 1971, Barbra Joan Streisand, 1972, The Way We Were, 1974, A Star is Born, 1976, Superman, 1977, The Stars Salute Israel at 30, 1978, Wet, 1979, (with Barry Gibb) Guilty, 1980, Emotion, 1984, The Broadway Album, 1986, Til I Loved You, 1989; other albums include: A Collection: Greatest Hits, 1989, Just for the Record, 1991, Back to Broadway, 1993, Concert at the Forum, 1993, The Concert Recorded Live at Madison Square Garden, 1994, The Concert Highlights, 1995. Recipient Emmy award, CBS-TV spl. (My Name Is Barbra), 1964, Acad. award as best actress (Funny Girl), 1968, Golden Globe award (Funny Girl), 1969, co-recipient Acad. award for best song (Evergreen), 1976, Georgie award AGVA 1977, Grammy awards for best female pop vocalist, 1963, 64, 65, 77, 86, for best song writer (with Paul Williams), 1977, 2 Grammy nominations for Back to Broadway, 1994; Nat. Acad. of Recording Arts & Sciences Lifetime Achievement Award, 1994. Office: Creative Artists Agy care Fred Spector 9830 Wilshire Blvd Beverly Hills CA 90212-1804*

STREITWIESER, ANDREW, JR., chemistry educator; b. Buffalo, June 23, 1927; s. Andrew and Sophie (Morlock) S.; m. Mary Ann Good, Aug. 19, 1950 (dec. May 1965); children—David Roy, Susan Ann; m. Suzanne Cope Beier, July 29, 1967. A.B., Columbia U., 1949, M.A., 1950, Ph.D., 1952; postgrad. (AEC fellow), MIT, 1951-52. Faculty U. Calif., Berkeley, 1952-92, prof. chemistry, 1963-92, prof. emeritus, 1993—; researcher on organic reaction mechanisms, application molecular orbital theory to organic chemistry, effect chem. structure on carbon acidities; cons. to industry, 1957—. Author: Molecular Orbital Theory for Organic Chemists, 1961, Solvolytic Displacement Reactions, 1962, (with J.I. Brauman) Supplemental Tables of Molecular Orbital Calculations, 1965, (with C.A. Coulson) Dictionary of Pi Electron Calculations, 1965, (with P.H. Owens) Orbital and Electron Density Diagrams, 1973, (with C.H. Heathcock and E.M. Kosower) Introduction to Organic Chemistry, 4th edit., 1992; also numerous articles; co-editor: Progress in Physical Organic Chemistry, 11 vols., 1963-74. Recipient Humboldt Found. Sr. Scientist award, 1976, Humboldt medal, 1979, Berkeley citation, 1993. Fellow AAAS; mem. NAS, Am. Chem. Soc. (Calif. sect. award 1964, award in Petroleum Chemistry 1967, Norris award in phys. organic chemistry 1982, Cope scholar award 1989), Am. Acad. Arts and Scis., German Chem. Soc., Bavarian Acad. Scis. (corr.), Phi Beta Kappa, Sigma Xi. Office: U Calif Dept Chemistry Berkeley CA 94720-1460

STREITWIESER, FRANZ XAVER, musician, museum director; b. Laufen, Bayern, Germany, Sept. 16, 1939; came to U.S., 1963; s. Simon and Cacilia (Auer) S.; m. Katherine Dulcinea Schutt, July 20, 1963 (dec. Mar. 1993); children: Erik, Charles, Bernhard, Christiane; m. Katharine L. Bright, Sept. 4, 1994. Diploma, Mozarteum Akademie, Salzburg, Austria, 1961; postgrad., Julliard Sch. Music, 1963-65; MusM, U. S.D., 1985. Asst. trumpeter Camerata Academica Orch., Salzburg, 1957-62; 1st trumpet coordinator Stadt-Theater Trier Philharm. Orch., Mosel, Fed. Republic Germany, 1963-72; prin. trumpeter Philharm. Orch., Freiburg, Fed. Republic Germany, 1965-72; assoc. prof. trumpet U. Freiburg, Fed. Republic Germany, 1972-75; prin. trumpeter Del. Symphony, Wilmington (Del.) Opera, 1973-75; asst. prof. music Tchrs. Coll. U. of Freiburg, 1975-78; founder, pres. Streitwieser Found. Trumpet Mus., Pottstown, Pa., 1979—; founder Del. Trumpet Ensemble, West Chester, Pa., 1973; asst. trumpeter Pottstown Symphony and Chamber Orch., 1982—; 1st trumpeter All-Am. Cornet Band, West Chester, 1983—; founding mem., condr. Sudelendeubohe Ostermusik-Tage Regensburg, 1980—. Author: Das Waldhorn in Böhmen und Mähren, 1981; inventor Clarinhorn, 1977. Founder Freiburg Munsterblaser, 1965; bd. dirs. Cornerstone of the Arts, Pottstown, 1980-82, 91—; dir. for life Sheitwieser Found. Internat. Brass Mus. Schloss Kremsegg in Kremsmünster, Austria, 1995. Recipient Adalbert Stifter Preis medal Musikpreis Musikforschung, Regensburg, Fed. Republic Germany, 1981. Mem. Internat. Trumpet Guild (pres. German sect. 1976-78), Internat. Horn Soc., Internat. Trombone Assn., Tuba Soc., Antroposophical Soc., Phi Mu Alpham, Tri-M, Rotary. Republican. Avocations: collecting antiques, skiing, swimming, mountain climbing. Home and Office: Streitwieser Found Vaughan Rd Fairway Far Pottstown PA 19464

STREJCEK, ELIZABETH GEIERMAN, reading specialist, educator; b. Chgo., Dec. 7, 1948; d. Aloysius Herman and Lillian Elizabeth (Cowan) Geierman; m. George Joseph Strejcek, Jan. 27, 1971; children: James Edwin, Theodore Eliot. BA in History, U. Ill., Chgo., 1971, MA in Ednl. Leadership, 1981. Cert. reading specialist, Ill. Subs. tchr. pub. schs., Berwyn, Ill., 1972-74; tchr. reading grades 5-8 South Berwyn Pub. Sch., Berwyn, 1974-77; tchr. reading lab. grades 9-12 Bolinbrook (Ill.) High Sch., 1979-83; tchr. reading grades 7-8 Westview Mid. Sch., Romeoville, Ill., 1983-84, tchr. grades 6-8, 1984-85; chpt. I reading tchr. grades K-5 Northview Elem. Sch., Bolingbrook, 1985-91; tchr. grades 9-10 Morton East H.S., Cicero, 1991—, tchr. spl. program on attendance, chpt. I-title I tchr., 1991, 94, tchr. truancy and attendance program, 1993—, mem. various coms., 1991—; presenter lectures, demonstrations on reading and writing and using technology in classroom, 1989—. Mem. AAUW, Internat. Reading Assn., Ill. Reading Coun. (bd. dirs. 1994-95), Ill. Computing Educators, Nat. Coun. Tchrs. English, Vlasta Vraz chpt. Czechoslovak Nat. Coun. Am., Secondary Reading League (pres. 1993-95). Avocations: pottery/ceramics, computer applications, reading, drawing. Office: J Sterling Morton HS 2423 S Austin Blvd Cicero IL 60650-2627

STREKOWSKI, LUCJAN, chemistry educator; b. Grabowo, Poland, June 21, 1945; came to U.S., 1981; s. Antoni and Janina (Chrapowicz) S.; m. Alewtina Smirnova, Oct. 14, 1967; children: Rafal, Anna. BS in Polymer Chemistry with distinction, Mendeleev Inst. Chemistry, Moscow, 1967; PhD in Organic Chemistry, Polish Acad. Scis., 1972; DSc in Chemistry, Adam Mickiewicz U., Poznan, Poland, 1976. Instr. organic chemistry Adam Mickiewicz U., Poznan, 1971-72, asst. prof. dept. chemistry, 1972-78, assoc. prof. dept. chemistry, 1978-81; rsch. assoc. dept. chemistry U. Fla., Gainesville, 1981-84; asst. prof. dept. chemistry Ga. State U., Atlanta, 1984-89, assoc. prof. dept. chemistry, 1989-96, prof. dept. chem., 1996—; vis. prof. U. Fla., Gainesville, 1979-80, 81, Australian Nat. U., 1980, U. Kans., Lawrence, 1972-73. Editor: Pyridine-Metal Complexes, Vol. 14, Part 6, 1985; contbr. more than 150 articles to profl. jours.; patentee in field. Recipient award Polish Ministry Sci., 1977, Polish Chem. Soc., 1973, Polish Acad. Scis., 1972, Ga. State U., 1993; grantee Am. Chem. Soc.-Petroleum Rsch. Fund, 1985—, Solvay Pharms., 1992-93, Nat. Diagnostics, 1991-93, NIAID/NIH, 1988—,

Rohm and Hass Co., 1988, Am. Cancer Soc., 1987-89, Rsch. Corp., 1985-94, Milheim Found. Cancer Rsch., 1985-86, numerous others. Mem. Am. Chem. Soc., Internat. Soc. Heterocyclic Chemistry, Internat. Acad. Scis. of Nature and Soc. (mem. presidium). Avocation: classical music. Office: Ga State Univ Dept Chemistry Atlanta GA 30303

STRELAU, RENATE, historical researcher, artist; b. Berlin, Feb. 1, 1951; came to U.S., 1960; d. Werner Ernst and Gerda Gertrud (Bargel) S. BA, U. Calif., Berkeley, 1974; cert. Arabic lang. proficiency, Johns Hopkins U., 1976; MA, Am. U., 1985, MFA, 1991. Rsch. asst. Iranian Embassy, Washington, 1976-80. One-woman shows include Cafe Espresso, Berkeley, Calif., 1973, Riggs Bank, Arlington, Va., 1994-95; represented in permanent collections at C. Law Watkins Meml. Collection, Am. U. Mem. Am. Hist. Assn., Orgn. Am. Historians, Soc. for Historians Am. Fgn. Rels. (life). Home: 1021 Arlington Blvd Apt E-1041 Arlington VA 22209-2212

STRELZER, MARTIN, retired religious organization administrator; b. N.Y.C., Oct. 17, 1925; s. Samuel Strelzer and Sadie Rothman; m. Florence Moskowitz, Jan. 30, 1947; children: Stuart, Amy. BBS, NYU, 1953. Pres. Harry D. Spielberg, Inc., N.Y.C., 1967-70, Amstrel Textiles, Inc., N.Y.C., 1970-83, Temple Beth-El, Closter, N.J., 1971-83; pres. N.J. West Hudson Valley region Union of Am. Hebrew Congregations, Paramus, N.J., 1976-80; trustee Union of Am. Hebrew Congregations, N.Y.C., 1976-83, mem. exec. com., 1982-83, chmn. new congregations com., 1979-83; N.Am. dir. World Union for Progressive Judaism, N.Y.C., 1984-95; arbitrator Am. Arbitration Assn., N.Y.C., 1970-83. Chmn. Israel Bonds Campaign, Bergen County, N.J., 1971-72, United Jewish Appeal campaign, No. Valley, N.J., 1973-74, Community Rels. Com., Bergen County, 1980-81. Recipient Circle of Light Israel Bonds Testimonial Closter, N.J., 1980. Democrat. Office: World Union for Progressive Judaism 838 5th Ave New York NY 10021-7012

STRENA, ROBERT VICTOR, research laboratory manager; b. Seattle, June 28, 1929; s. Robert Lafayette Peel and Mary Oliva (Holmes) S.; m. Rita Mae Brodovsky, Aug. 1957; children: Robert Victor, Adrienne Amelia. AB, Stanford U., 1952. Survey mathematician Hazen Engring., San Jose, Calif., 1952-53; field engr. Menlo Sanitary Dist., Menlo Park, Calif., 1954-55; ind. fin. reporter Los Altos, Calif., 1956-59; asst. dir. Hansen Labs. Stanford U., 1959-93, asst. dir. emeritus Ginzton Lab., 1993—; ind. fin. cons., Los Altos, 1965—; bd. mem. Rehab. Adv. Bd., Moffett Fed. Airfield, 1994—. Active Edn. System Politics, Los Altos, 1965-80, local Boy Scouts Am., 1968-80; mem. restoration adv. bd. Moffett Fed. Airfield. Maj. USAR, 1948-70. Mem. AAAS, Soc. Rsch. Adminstrs., Mus. Soc., Big X (Los Altos). Republican. Avocations: golf, sailing. Home: 735 Raymundo Ave Los Altos CA 94024-3139 Office: Ginzton Lab Stanford Univ Stanford CA 94305

STRENG, WILLIAM PAUL, lawyer, educator; b. Sterling, Ill., Oct. 17, 1937; s. William D. and Helen Marie (Conklen) S.; m. Louisa Bridge Egbert, July 8, 1967; children: Sarah, John. BA, Wartburg Coll., 1959; JD, Northwestern U., 1962. Bar: Iowa 1962, Ill. 1962, Ohio 1964, Tex. 1975. Law clk. to U.S. circuit judge Lester L. Cecil, Cin., 1963-64; asso. firm Taft, Stettinius & Hollister, Cin., 1964-70; atty.-advisor Office Sec. Tax Policy, Office Tax Legis. Counsel, Dept. Treasury, Washington, 1970-71; dep. gen. counsel Export-Import Bank U.S., Washington, 1971-73; prof. law Sch. Law, So. Methodist U., Dallas, 1973-80; vis. prof. Coll. Law Ohio State U., Columbus, 1977; partner firm Bracewell & Patterson, Houston, Washington and London, 1980-85; Vinson & Elkins prof. of law U. Houston Law Ctr, 1985—; vis. prof. Rice U., NYU Law Sch., 1990; disting. vis. prof. U. Hong Kong Law Faculty, 1992; Fulbright prof. U. Stockholm Law Faculty, 1993; vis. fellow law faculty Victoria U., Wellington, New Zealand, 1996; cons. Bracewell & Patterson, 1985—; lectr. various confs. Am. Law Inst., Practicing Law Inst., World Trade Inst., Internat. Fiscal Assn., ABA, Tex. State Bar. Author: International Buinsess Transactions-Tax and Legal Handbook, 1978, Estate Planning, 1991, International Business Planning: Law and Taxation, 6 vols., 1982, 95, 96, Tax Planning for Retirement, 1989, 93, 94, 95, Doing Business in China, 1990, 93, 94, 95, 96, Federal Income Taxation of Corporations and Shareholders--Forms, 1995, 96, Choice of Entity, 1994, U.S. International Estate Planning, 1996; contbr. articles to profl. jours. Served with USMC, 1962. Lutheran. Home: 1903 Dunstan Rd Houston TX 77005-1619 Office: U Houston Law Ctr Houston TX 77204-6372

STRENGTH, DANNA ELLIOTT, nursing educator; b. Texarkana, Ark., Aug. 20, 1937; d. Clyde Olin and Willie (Stephens) Elliott; m. Vernon E. Strength, Dec. 27, 1960. BSN, Tex. Christian U., 1959; MSN, Washington U., 1968; DNSc, Cath. U. of Am., 1986. Instr. The Cath. Univ. of Am., Washington; asst. prof. Georgetown Univ., Washington, Tex. Christian Univ., Fort Worth; edn. leader Acad. Seminars Internat.; edn. cons. Trnascultrual Edn. Corp.; med. com. Ft. Worth Sister Cities Internat., Budapest, Hungary, and Bandung, Indonesia. Contbr. articles to profl. jours. Recipient Edn. in a Global Soc. award to study health care in Indonesia and Scandinavia, 1992-94. Mem. ANA, Tex. Nurses' Assn., Am. Assn. for History of Nursing, Lucy Harris Linn Inst., Sigma Theta Tau (Beta Alpha rsch. award). Home: 305 Birchwood Ln Fort Worth TX 76108-4601

STRENGTH, ROBERT SAMUEL, manufacturing company executive; b. Tullos, La., May 14, 1929; s. Houston Orion and Gurcie Dean (Cousins) S.; BS in Indsl. Mgmt., Auburn U., 1956; m. Janis Lynette Grace, Sept. 12, 1954; children: Robert David (dec.), James Steven (dec.), Stewart Alan, James Houston (dec.). Engr., supr. plant safety Monsanto Co., 1956-74, engring. stds. mgr. Corporate Fire Safety Center, St. Louis, 1974-78, mgr. product safety and acceptability Monsanto Polymer Products Co. (formerly Monsanto Plastics and Resins Co.), St. Louis, 1978-82, mgr. product safety, Monsanto Chem. Co., 1982-87; founder, pres. Product Safety Mgmt., Inc., 1987—. mem. com. on toxicity of materials used in rapid rail transit, NRC, 1984-87. Pres. Greenwood (S.C.) Citizens Safety Coun., 1966-68; U.S. del. Internat. Electrotech. Commn. With USAF, 1948-52. Recipient S. C. Outstanding Svc. to Safety award Nat. Safety Coun., 1968; registered profl. engr., Calif.; cert. safety profl. Mem. Am. Soc. Safety Engrs., Nat. Safety Coun. (pres. textile sect. 1966), So. Bldg. Code Congress, Internat. Conf. of Bldg. Ofcls., Bldg. Ofcls. and Code Adminstrs. Internat., Nat. Fire Protection Assn. (mem. code making panel 7 nat. electrical code), ASTM Fire Test Com. (chmn. fire hazard & risk assessment sub-com., mem. exec. com. fire test com.), Nat. Inst. Bldg. Scis., Plastic Pipe and Fittings Assn. ASHRAE, Soc. Plastics Ind. (past chmn. coordinating com. on fire safety 1985-87), Nat. Acad. Scis., Cherry Hills Country Club, Raintree Plantation Golf and Country Club, Tiger Point Country Club. Republican. Methodist. Editor textile sect. newsletter Nat. Safety Coun., 1961-62. Home and Office: 3371 Edgewater Dr Gulf Breeze FL 32561-3309

STRENSKI, JAMES B., communications executive; b. Jan. 2, 1930; m. Jane E.; 5 children. Grad., Marquette U. Pub. info. officer USN, NATO; with Pub. Communications Inc., Chgo.; chmn., chief exec. officer Pub. Communications Inc, Tampa, Fla.; cons. to nonprofit, health care and social agys., pub. and pvt. corps., fin. and acad. instns.; lectr. to industry groups, trade assns., bus. orgns. Contbr. more than 70 articles on pub. rels. to jours. in field. Mem. Tampa Jesuit High Sch. Found., Tampa Downtown Partnership Bd., Hillsborough County Affordable Housing Com., Bus. Adv. Coun., Coll. of Journalism of Marquette U.; bd. dirs. Chgo. Leadership Coun. for Met. Open Communities, Tampa Goodwill Industries-Suncoast; program chmn. Tampa Pkwy. Assn.; pub. rels. chmn. Paint Your Heart Out, Tampa, U. Tampa Bd. Fellows. Mem. Worldcom Group, Inc. (founder, exec. com.). Office: Public Communications Inc 35 E Wacker Dr Chicago IL 60601*

STRETCH, JOHN JOSEPH, social work educator, management and evaluation consultant; b. St. Louis, Feb. 24, 1935; s. John Joseph and Theresa Carmelita (Fleming) S.; children: Paul, Leonmarie, Sylvan, Adrienne, Sharonalice; m. Barbara Ann Stewart, Mar. 16, 1985; children: Margaret, Thomas. AB, Maryknoll Coll., Glen Ellyn, Ill., 1957; MSW, Washington U., St. Louis, 1961; PhD, Tulane U., 1967; MBA, St. Louis U., 1980. Lic. clin. social worker, 1990. Instr. Tulane U., 1962-67, asst. prof., 1967-69; mem. faculty St. Louis U., 1969—, prof. social work, 1972—, asst. dean Sch. Social Service, 1976-87, dir. doctoral studies, 1976-94, dir. M.S.W. program, 1985-86; dir. rsch. Social Welfare Planning Coun. Met. New Orleans, 1962-69; cons. to United Way Met. St. Louis, Cath. Charities of Archdiocese of St. Louis, Cath. Svcs. for Children and Youth, Full Achievement, Mo. Province of S.J., Cath. Family Svcs., Youth Emergency Svcs., Mo. State Dept. Social Svcs., U. Mo. Extension Svc., St. Joseph's Home for Boys, Marian Hall Ctr. for Adolescent Girls, Boys Town, A World of Difference, Anti Defamation League of B'nai Brith, Prog. Youth Ctr.; expert witness on homeless U.S. House Select Com. on Families, Children and Youth, 1987; mem. resource spl. task force on homeless Office of Sec. U.S. Dept. Housing and Urban Devel., 1989; survey design cons. U.S. Office of The Insp. Gen., 1990; methodology expert on homelessness U.S. Census Bur., 1989; expert homeless policy General Acctg. Office hearings, 1992; chair Mo. Assn. for Social Welfare Low Income Housing; mem. Comprehensive Housing Affordabiltiy Strategies (CHAS) Mo. Statewide Planning Group, Missouri Housing Devel. CHAS citizen's com., Missouri Inst. of Psychiatry, Univ. City sch. dist.; mgmt. cons. People's Issues Task Force Agricultural div. Monsanto Chemical Inc., Nat. Conf. of Christians and Jews, regional office; vis. prof. Nat. Catholic U. of Am. Sch. of Soc. Svcs., 1991, 92, U. Bristol, England, 1992, U. Calif. Sch. of Pub. Health, Berkeley, 1990; cons. Mo. Speaker of the Ho. statewide legislative task force, 1990-92; statewide grant project reviewer emergency shelter grant program Mo. Dept. of Social Svcs., 1989—; homeless svcs. grant reviewer City of St. Louis, 1994—. Editl. bd. Social Work, 1968-74, Health Progress, 1988—; manuscript referee Jour. Social Svc. Rsch., 1977—; mgmt. and evaluation content referee Wadsworth Press, Human Svcs. Press, Allyn and Bacon Press; contbr. articles profl. jours. and books. Bd. dirs. Ecumenical Housing Prodn. Corp., 1985—, pres. bd. dirs., 1993-95; mem. Mo. Assn. Social Welfare, 1980—, Dunbourg Soc. of St. Louis U.; mem. Salvation Army Family Haven, 1987, mem. adv. bd., 1988-92; chmn. United Way of Greater St. Louis venture grant com., 1988-91, mem. allocation com., 1985-95, mem. process and rev. com., 1991-93, inter-orgnl. priorities com., 1991-93; organizer Mo. State Nat. Coalition for the Homeless; appointee St. Louis U. Instl. Representation nat. Jesuits social Concern Group, 1993—; mem. exec. and support tng. group, St. Louis U., 1987—. NIMH Career Leadership Devel. fellow, 1965-67; recipient Scholar of Yr. award Sch. Social Svc., St. Louis U., 1987; named Vol. of Yr. Ecumenical Prodn. Corp., 1990; Presdl. scholar Sch. Social Svc., 1992. Mem. AAUP (St. Louis U. chpt. exec. com. 1990—, pres. 1994—), ACLU, Acad. Cert. Social Workers (charter mem.), Nat. Assn. Social Workers, Mo. Assn. for Social Welfare (bd. dirs., Outstanding State-Wide Mem. of Yr. 1987), Coun. on Social Work Edn., Common Cause, Amnesty Internat., Nat. Com. on Vital and Health Stats. (subcom. on health stats. for minorities and other spl. populations of U.S. 1988—). Democrat. Roman Catholic. Home: 9100 Litzsinger Rd Saint Louis MO 63144-2214 Office: 3550 Lindell Blvd Saint Louis MO 63103-1021 *My entire professional life has been in the field of social work. My personal and professional values are derived from a dual commitment to empower the uniqueness of individuals and to enhance the development of caring communities. These goals have organized and directed my professional practice, teaching and writing. I believe that the profession of social work has a unique and singular mission in society. That mission is to advocate for and consciously bring about the social development of all people.*

STRETTON, ROSS, ballet dancer; b. Canberra, Australia; came to U.S., 1979.; Student, Australian Ballet Sch. Mem. corps de ballet Australian Ballet, 1972-74, soloist, 1974-78, prin. dancer, 1978-79; with Joffrey Ballet, 1979-81; joined No. Ballet Theatre, Manchester, Eng.; guest artist Am. Ballet Theatre, 1980-81, soloist, 1981-83, prin. dancer, 1983-90, asst to the dirs., 1990-91, regisseur, 1991-93, asst. dir., 1993—. Created role in Martine van Hamel's Amnon V'Tamar; other repertoire includes: Bach Partita, La Bayadere, Bouree Fantastique, Giselle, Duets, Pillar of Fire, La Sylphide, The Wild Boy, Cinderella, Don Quixote, The Nutcracker, Swan Lake, The Sleeping Beauty, others. Office: care Am Ballet Theatre 890 Broadway New York NY 10003-1211

STREVER, MARTHA MAY, mathematics educator; b. Rhinebeck, N.Y., Oct. 27, 1939; d. Louis Grant and Marguerite Hazel (Irwin) S. BS, New Paltz (N.Y.) State U., 1961, MS, 1966. Cert. tchr. math. and sci., N.Y. Tchr. math. and sci. Red Hook (N.Y.) Ctrl. Sch., 1961-72, tchr. math., 1961—, chairperson dept. math., 1972—, jr. high computer coord., 1984-92, math/computer instrn. dept. chair, 1992—. Mem. choir, sec.-treas. Rhinebeck (N.Y.) Ref. Ch., 1974—, deacon and elder, 1976-80, Women's Guild edn. chmn., various yrs., pres., 1984-86, 89-90, 92-95, sec., 1996—. Summer Math and Sci. scholar New Paltz State U., 1962. Mem. ASCD, N.Y. State United Tchrs., Dutchess County Math. Tchrs. Assn., Nat. Coun. Tchrs. Math., N.Y. Assn. Math. Suprs., Assn. of Math. Tchrs. N.Y. State, Agonian Alumni Assn., Internat. Soc. for Tech. in Edn., N.Y. State Assn. for Computers and Tech. in Edn., Kappa Delta Pi, Delta Kappa Gamma, Alpha Zeta (1st v.p. 1978-80, pres. 1980-82, music chmn. 1982—). Avocations: playing electronic keyboard, accordian and organ, spoon collecting, stamp collecting, postcard collecting, photography. Home: 940 NY Route 9G Hyde Park NY 12538 Office: Red Hook Ctrl H S 63-73 West Market St Red Hook NY 12571

STREVEY, TRACY ELMER, JR., army officer, surgeon; b. Shorewood, Wis., Apr. 24, 1933; s. Tracy Elmer and Margaret (Rees) S.; m. Victoria Crowley (div.); children: Virginia Ann, Tracy Elmer III, Andrew Victor; m. Elizabeth Sommers. Student, Pomona Coll., 1951-54; MD, U. So. Calif., 1958; student, Armed Forces Staff Coll., 1970-71, U.S. Army War Coll., 1977-78. Diplomate Am. Bd. Surgery, Am. Bd. Thoracic Surgery. Intern Los Angeles County Gen. Hosp., 1958-59; commd. officer U.S. Army, 1959, advanced through grades to maj. gen., 1983; resident in gen. surgery Letterman Gen. Hosp., San Francisco, 1962-66; resident in thoracic and cardiovascular surgery Walter Reed Gen. Hosp., Washington, 1968-70; comdg. officer 757 Med. Detachment OA, Ludwigsburg, Fed. Republic Germany, 1959-61; ward officer orthopaedic svc. 75th Sta. Hosp., Stuttgart, Fed. Republic Germany, 1961-62; chief profl. svc., chief surgery 85th Evacuation Hosp., Qui Nhon, Vietnam, 1967; comdg. officer 3d Surg. Hosp., Dong Tam, Vietnam, 1967-68; asst. chief thoracic and cardiovascular surgery service Fitzsimons Army Med Ctr., Denver, 1971-73, chief thoracic and cardiovascular surgery service, 1973-75; asst. dir. med. activities and dir. Profl. Edn. Gorgas Hosp., Panama Canal Zone, 1975-77; chief dept. surgery Walter Reed Army Med. Ctr., Washington, 1978-81; comdr. Brooke Army Med. Ctr., Ft. Sam Houston, Tex., 1981-83, Tripler Army Med. Ctr., Hawaii, 1983-86, U.S. Army Health Svcs. Command, San Antonio, 1986-88; ret. U.S. Army, 1988; CEO Nassau County Med. Ctr., 1988-93; pres., CEO N.Y. Hosp Med. Ctr. Queens, N.Y.C., 1993-94; v.p. N.Y. Hosp. Care Network, N.Y.C., 1994-95; v.p. for med. affairs Sisters of Mercy Health Sys., St. Louis, 1995—; asst. clin. prof. surgery U. Colo. Med. Ctr., Denver, 1973-75; prof. surgery Uniformed Services U. Health Scis., Bethesda, 1978—, vice chmn. dept. surgery, 1978-81. Contbr. articles to profl. jours. Decorated D.S.M., Legion of Merit, Meritorious Service medal with 2 oak leaf clusters, Purple Heart, Army Commendation Medal for Valor, Vietnam Cross of Gallantry with Palm; recipient Outstanding Service award U. So. Calif. Med. Alumni Assn., 1983. Fellow ACS, Am. Coll. Chest Physicians, Am. Coll. Cardiology, Am. Coll. Physician Execs. (disting.); mem. Assn. Mil. Surgeons U.S., Soc. Thoracic Surgeons, Western Thoracic Surg. Assn., Am. Assn. Thoracic Surgery, Am. Cancer Soc., Bexar County Med. Soc., ARC (bd. dirs. 1984-86), Honolulu-Pacific Fed. Exec. Bd., Masons, Rotary. Avocations: ham radio; scuba diving; golf; computer science. Home: 1509 Woodgate Dr Frowtewac MO 63131 Office: 2039 N Geyer Rd Saint Louis MO 63131

STREW, SUZANNE CLAFLIN, choreographer, dance educator; b. Canton, Ohio, May 31, 1935; d. William Jenney and Mildred Mae (McClellan) Claflin; m. Rudolph John Strew, Aug. 15, 1964. BS, Bowling Green (Ohio) State U., 1957; postgrad., U. Wis., summer 1962; MEd, Kent (Ohio) State U., 1964; postgrad., Ohio State U., summer 1967. Tchr. Deerfield Beach (Fla.) Pub. Sch., 1959-60; instr. dance Baldwin-Wallace Coll., Berea, Ohio, 1957-59, prof., dir., choreographer, 1961—, chairperson divsn., 1992—; choreographer Berea Summer Theatre, 1965—; dir. dance concert Baldwin-Wallace Coll., 1961—. Choreographer numerous prodns. including The Sound of Music, Cleve. Opers, 1992, and over 100 prodns. Advisor Laurels Hon. Soc. Recipient Cleve. Critics Circle award Cleve. Critics Circle, 1980, 81, 83, 84. Mem. AAHPERD (nat. dance sect.), Ohio Dance, Mortar Board, Chi Omega, Omicron Delta Kappa. Office: Baldwin-Wallace Coll Berea OH 44017

STRICKLAND, ANITA MAURINE, retired business educator, librarian; b. Groom, Tex., Sept. 24, 1923; d. Oliver Austin and Thelma May (Slay) Pool; m. LeRoy Graham Mashburn, Aug. 12, 1945 (dec. Mar. 1977); 1 child, Ronald Gene; m. Reid Strickland, May 27, 1978. BBA, West Tex. State U., 1962, MEd, 1965; postgrad. in library sci., Tex. Women's U., 1970. Cert. tchr., Tex.; cert. librarian. Employment interviewer Douglas Aircraft Co., Oklahoma City, 1942-45; cashier, bookkeeper Southwestern Pub. Services, Groom and Panhandle, Tex., 1950-58; acct. Gen. Motors Outlet, Groom, 1958-62; tchr. bus., lang. arts Groom Pub. Schs., 1962-68; bus. tchr., librarian Amarillo (Tex.) Pub. Schs., 1968-81. Vol. Amarillo Symphony, 1980—, Amarillo Rep. Com., 1981—, Lone Star Ballet, 1981-92; docent Amarillo Mus. Art, 1987—, sec., 1987-90, 93-94, Amarillo Art Alliance, 1989-93; vol. Amarillo Alliance, 1989—, sec., 1989-90. Mem. AAUW (legis. com. 1986-88, sec. 1989-90, bd. dirs. 1989-91), Amarillo C. of C. (vol. women's divsn. 1981-86), Amarillo Christian Women's Club (asst. prayer advisor 1989-90, treas. 1995-96). Baptist. Avocations: piano, reading, swimming, tennis. Home: 6513 Roxton Dr Amarillo TX 79109-5120

STRICKLAND, ARVARH EUNICE, history educator; b. Hattiesburg, Miss., July 6, 1930; s. Eunice and Clotiel (Marshall) S.; m. Willie Pearl Elmore, June 17, 1951; children: Duane Arvarh, Bruce Elmore. BA, Tougaloo Coll., 1951; MA, U. Ill., 1953, PhD, 1962. Tchr. Hattiesburg Schs., 1951-52; instr. Tuskegee Inst., 1955-56; prin. supr. Madison County Schs., Canton, Miss., 1956-59; asst. prof. history Chgo. State U., 1962-65, assoc. prof. history, 1965-68, prof., 1968-69; prof. U. Mo., Columbia, 1969-96, prof. emeritus, 1996—, chmn. dept. history, 1980-83, interim dir. black studies program, 1994-96, sr. faculty assoc., Office of V.P. acad. affairs, 1987-88, assoc. v.p. acad. affairs, 1989-91. Author: History of the Chicago Urban League, 1966, (with Reich and Biller) Building the United States, 1971, (with Reich) The Black American Experience to 1877, 1974, The Black American Experience since 1877, 1974; editor: Working with Carter G. Woodson, the Father of Black History: A Diary, 1928-1933, (Lorenzo J. Greene), 1989. Commr. Planning and Zoning, Columbia, Mo., 1977-80, Boone County Home Rule Charter, 1982, Mo. Peace Officers Standards and Tng. Commn., 1988-89; co-chmn. Mayors Com. to Commemorate Contbns. of Black Columbians, Columbia, 1981; mem. exec. subcom. Mayor's Ad Hoc Election '82 Com., 1982; bd. dirs. Harry S. Truman Library Inst., 1987—. Recipient Disting. Svc. award Ill. Hist. Soc., 1957, Byler Disting. Prof. award U. Mo., 1994, St. Louis Am.'s Educator of Yr. award, 1994, Disting. Faculty award U. Mo.-Columbia Alumni Assn., 1995, Tougalloo Coll. Alumni Hall of Fame, 1995. Mem. Orgn. Am. Historians, Am. Hist. Assn., Assn. Study Afro-Am. Life and History, So. Hist. Assn., State Hist. Soc. Mo., Kiwanian, Alpha Phi Alpha, Phi Alpha Theta (internat. v.p. 1991-93, pres. 1994-95, chair adv. bd. 1996—). Democrat. Methodist. Home: 4100 Defoe Dr Columbia MO 65203-0252 Office: U Mo Dept History 101 Read Hall Columbia MO 65211

STRICKLAND, BONNIE RUTH, psychologist, educator; b. Louisville, Nov. 24, 1936; d. Roy E. and Billie P. (Whitfield) S. B.S., Ala. Coll., 1958; M.S., Ohio State U., 1960, Ph.D. (USPHS fellow), 1962. Diplomate: clin. psychology Am. Bd. Examiners in Profl. Psychology. Research psychologist Juvenile Diagnostic Center, Columbus, Ohio, 1958-60; from asst. to asso. prof. psychology Emory U., Atlanta, 1962-73; dean of women Emory U., 1964-67; prof. psychology U. Mass., Amherst, 1973—; chmn. dept. psychology U. Mass., 1976-77, 78-82, assoc. to chancellor, 1983-84; mem. adv. coun. NIMH, 1984-87; Sigma Xi nat. lectr., 1991-93. Adv. editor numerous psychology jours., acad. pub. houses; contbg. author texts personality theory.; contbr. of numerous articles on social personality and clin. psychology to profl. jours.; contbg. author of two citation classics. Recipient Outstanding Faculty award Emory U., 1968-69; Chancellor's medal disting. service U. Mass., 1983. Fellow APA (pres. divsn. clin. psychology 1983, chmn. bd. profl. affairs 1980-83, chmn. policy and planning bd. 1983-85, pres. 1987, bd. dirs. 1986-87, Outstanding Leadership award 1992), Am. Psychol. Soc. (founder 1988, bd. dirs. 1989-93), Am. Assn. Applied and Preventive Psychology (founder 1990, bd. dirs. 1990-94, pres. 1992-94), Acad. Clin. Psychology, Coun. Grad. Depts. Psychology (chmn. 1982-83). Home: 558 Federal St Belchertown MA 01007-9754 Office: U Mass Dept Psychology Amherst MA 01003-7710

STRICKLAND, GEORGE THOMAS, JR., physician, researcher, educator; b. Goldsboro, N.C., Apr. 20, 1934; s. George Thomas and Flora Ross (Bridgers) S.; m. Anne Belle Garst, Feb. 13, 1960; children: George Thomas III, Paul Garst, James Kelly. BA in History, U. N.C., 1956, MD, 1960; DCMT, London Sch. Hygiene and Tropical Medicine, Eng., 1971, PhD in Parasitology, 1974. Diplomate Am. Bd. Internal Medicine. Head dept. immunoparasitology Naval Med. Rsch. Inst., Bethesda, Md., 1972-74, program mgr. infectious diseases rsch., naval med. R&D com., 1974-76; prof., dir. rsch. and edn., dept. medicine Uniformed Svcs. U. Health Scis., Bethesda, 1976-81; staff pathologist Armed Forces Inst. Pathology, Washington, 1981-82; dir. Internat. Health Program, Sch. Medicine U. Md., Balt., 1982—, prof. microbiology, medicine, epidemiology and preventive medicine Sch. Medicine, 1982—; dir. Internat. Ctr. Med. Rsch. and Tng., Lahore, Pakistan, 1983-85; chmn., vice-chmn. Nat. Coun. Internat. Health, Washington, 1977-80; Am. co-investigator Egyptian Schistosomiasis Rsch. Project, 1990—; prin. investigator rsch. project on Lyme disease, Md., 1993—, hepatitis C, Egypt, 1995—. Editor: Hunter's Tropical Medicine, 6th edit., 1984, 7th edit., 1991. Capt. USN, 1960-82. Fellow ACP, Infectious Diseases Soc. Am., Am. Coll. Tropical Medicine Hygiene, Royal Coll. Tropical Medicine Hygiene. Democrat. Avocations: tennis, gardening, travel, classical music. Home: 220 Hawthorne Rd Baltimore MD 21210-2504

STRICKLAND, HATTIE DENE, medical/surgical nurse, rehabilitation nurse, home health care nurse; b. Statesville, N.C., Sept. 10, 1944; d. Benton Ozzie and Magdlene (Teague) S.; children: Cindy, Jeffrey, Teri. Diploma, Bowman Grey Sch. of Nursing, Winston-Salem, N.C., 1967. RN, N.C.; cert. child devel. nurse. Staff RN, float Rex Hosp., Durham, N.C.; RN, surgical High Point (N.C.) Hosp., Thomasville (N.C.) Hosp.; pvt. duty nurse High Point, 1984—; home health owner, operator Home Care, High Point, 1995—. Home and Office: 1010 N Rotary Dr High Point NC 27262-3610

STRICKLAND, HUGH ALFRED, lawyer; b. Rockford, Ill., May 3, 1931; s. Hugh and Marie (Elmer) S.; m. Donna E. McDonald, Aug. 11, 1956; children: Amy Alice, Karen Ann. A.B., Knox Coll., 1953; J.D., Chgo. Kent Coll. Law, 1959. Bar: Ill. 1960. Partner firm McDonald, Strickland & Clough, Carrollton, Ill., 1961—; asst. atty. gen. Ill., 1960-67, spl. asst. gen., 1967-69; pres. McDonald Title Co. Mem. Greene County Welfare Svcs. Com., 1963—, Ill. Heart Assn., 1961-65; trustee Thomas H. Boyd Meml. Hosp., 1972-95. With AUS, 1953-55. Recipient award for meritorious service Am. Heart Assn., 1964. Fellow Ill. Bar Found. (charter); mem. ABA, Ill. Bar Assn., Greene County Bar Assn. (past pres.), Southwestern Bar Assn. (past pres.), Ill. Def. Counsel, Am. Judicature Soc., Def. Rsch. Inst., Elks Club, Westlake Country Club (v.p. 1968-70, dir.), Big Sand Lake Country Club, Phi Delta Theta, Phi Delta Phi. Methodist. Home: 827 7th St Carrollton IL 62016-1421 Office: 524 N Main St Carrollton IL 62016

STRICKLAND, MARSHALL HAYWARD, bishop; b. Rome, Ga., Oct. 8, 1933; s. Albert A. Strickland and Elzie Greer Strickland Morton; 1 child, Marshall H. 2d. BA, Livingstone Coll., 1951; PhD, St. Mary's Theol. Sem., Balt.; MDiv, Hood Theol. Sem., 1955, DD (hon.); DD (hon.), Allen U. Ordained deacon AME Ch. Pastor Patten Meml. AME Zion Ch., Chattanooga, David Stan AME Zion Ch., Lancaster, S.C., Hood Meml. AME Zion Ch., Bristol, Tenn., Big Zion AME Ch., Mobile, Ala., Pa. Ave. AME Zion Ch., Balt.; bishop AME Ch.; bd. bishops AME Zion Ch., chmn. commn. judiciary, chmn. Am. Bible Soc., 1st vice chair brotherhood pension svc., 1st vice chair Christian edn., 2d vice chair bicentennial commn., trustee Livingstone Coll.; past mem. Ala. Consultation Ch. Union; guest pastor Gen. Conf. AME Ch., St. Paul Cathedral, others; speaker in field; guest on various radio and TV stas. Author: William E. Fine: Kennedy-The Dreamer, Church and Stae: Not Separate, Our Heritage is Our Religion, The Black Church: Black America's Salvation, The Black Church: Solving Black America's Crisis, Health Care: Preaching Prevention from the Pulpit, Rebuilding Our Cities in Partnership with the Black Church: A Master Plan; contbr. articles to profl. jours. Former chmn. bd. dirs. Mobile Community Action Authority; past mem. Commn. Organic Union; founder Zion Outreach Ctr., Balt. Recipient Humanitarian award Zion Outreach Svcs. Associated Black Charities, Econ. Devel. award HUB, Flood Relief Support award Jamaican Assn. Md. Mem. NAACP (past pres. Bristol chpt., Recognition awards Bristol and Balt. chpts.). Office: 2000 Cedar Circle Dr Baltimore MD 21228-3743

STRICKLAND, NELLIE B., library program director; b. Belmont, Miss., Dec. 12, 1932. BS, Murray State U., 1954; MLS, George Peabody Coll., 1971. Ref. libr. Murray State Coll., Murray, Ky., 1954; asst. libr. Dept. Army, Ft. Stewart, Ga., 1955-56; field libr. U.S. Army, Japan, 1957-59; area libr. U.S. Army, Europe, 1960-66; staff libr. U.S. Army So. Command, C.Z., 1966-67; area libr. U.S. Army, Vietnam, 1967-68, staff libr., 1971-72; chief libr. U.S. Army, Ft. Benning, Ga., 1970-71; dir. library program U.S. Army Pacific, 1973-74; dir. Army libr. program Washington, 1974-94. Recipient Outstanding Performance award Ft. Benning, 1970, Armed Forces Achievement citation, 1982, 94, Order of the White Plume; Dept. of Army

Tng. grantee, 1971; Dept. of Army decoration for Exceptional Civil Svc., 1994. Mem. ALA, Kappa Delta Phi, Alpha Sigma Alpha. Home: 203 S Yoakum Pky Apt 614 Alexandria VA 22304-3716

STRICKLAND, ROBERT LOUIS, business executive; b. Florence, S.C., Mar. 3, 1931; s. Franz M. and Hazel (Eaddy) S.; m. Elizabeth Ann Miller, Feb. 2, 1952; children: Cynthia Anne, Robert Edson. AB, U. N.C., 1952; MBA with distinction, Harvard U., 1957. With Lowe's Cos., Inc., North Wilkesboro, N.C., 1957—, sr. v.p., 1970-76, exec. v.p., 1976-78, chmn. bd., 1978—, chmn. exec. com., 1988—, mem. office of pres., 1970-78, also bd. dirs.; founder Sterling Advt., Ltd., 1966; v.p., mem. adminstrv. com. Lowe's Profit-Sharing Trust, 1961-87, chmn. ops. com., 1972-78; mgmt. com. Lowe's ESOP Plan, 1978—; bd. dirs. T. Rowe Price Assocs., Balt., Hannaford Bros., Portland; paenlist investor rels. field, 1972—; spkr., panelist employee stock ownership, 1978—; spkr. on investor rels., London, Edinburgh, Glasgow, Paris, Zurich, Frankfurt. Author: Lowe's Cybernetwork, 1969, Lowe's Living Legend, 1970, Ten Years of Growth, 1971, The Growth Continues, 1972, 73, 74, Lowe's Scoreboard, 1978, also articles. Mem. N.C. Ho. of Reps., 1962-64, Rep. Senatorial Inner Circle, 1980-95; exec. com. N.C. Rep. Com., 1963-73; trustee U. N.C., Chapel Hill, 1987-95, chmn. bd., 1991-93; dir., dep. chmn. Fed. Res. Bank of Richmond, 1996—; com. on bus. laws and the economy N.C., 1994—; dir. U.S. Coun. Better Bus. Burs., 1981-85; bd. dirs., v.p. Nat. Home Improvement Coun., 1972-76; bd. dirs. N.C. Sch. Arts Found., 1975-79, N.C. Bd. Natural and Econ. Resources, 1975-76; bd. dirs., govt. affairs com. Home Ctr. Inst.; trustee, sec. bd. Wilkes C.C., 1964-73; chmn., pres. bd. dirs. Do-It-Yourself Rsch. Inst., 1981-89; pres. Hardware Home Improvement Coun. City of Hope Nat. Med. Ctr., L.A., 1987-89. With USN, 1952-55, lt. Res. 1955-62. Named Wilkes County N.C. Young Man of Yr., Wilkes Jr. C. of C., 1962; recipient Bronze Oscar of Industry award Fin. World, 1969-74, 76-79, Silver Oscar of Industry award, 1970, 72-74, 76-79, Gold Oscar of Industry award as best of all industry, 1972, 87, Excellence award in corp. reporting Fin. Analysts Fedn., 1970, 72, 74, 81-82, cert. of Distinction Brand Names Found., 1970, Retailer of Yr. award, 1971, 73, Disting. Mcht. award, 1972, Spirit of Life award City of Hope, 1983, Free Enterprise Legend award Students Free Enterprise, 1994; named to Home Ctr. Hall of Fame, 1985. Mem. Nat. Assn. Over-Counter Cos. (bd. advisers 1973-77), Newcomen Soc., Employee Stock Ownership Assn. (pres. 1983-85, chmn. 1985-87), Twin City Club, Forsyth Country Club, Piedmont City Club, Hound Ears Club (Blowing Rock, N.Y.), Elk River Club (Banner Elk, N.C.), Roaring Gap Club (N.C.), Ponte Vedra Inn and Club (Fla.), Scabbard and Blade, Phi Beta Kappa, Pi Kappa Alpha. Clubs: Forsyth Country, Piedmont City (Winston-Salem, N.C.); Hound Ears (Blowing Rock, N.C.); Elk River (Banner Elk, N.C.); Roaring Gap (N.C.); Ponte Vedra Inn and Club (Ponte Vedra Beach, Fla.). Home: 226 N Stratford Rd Winston Salem NC 27104 Office: Lowes Cos Inc 604 Two Piedmont Plz Winston Salem NC 27104

STRICKLAND, SANDRA JEAN HEINRICH, nursing educator; b. Tucson, Sept. 18, 1943; d. Henry and Ada (Schmidt) Heinrich; B.S., U. Tex. Sch. Nursing, 1965; M.S. in Nursing (fellow), U. Md., 1969; Dr.P.H., U. Tex., 1978; m. William C. Strickland, Aug. 18, 1973; children—William Henry, Angela Lee. Clin. instr. U. Tex. Sch. Nursing, Galveston, 1965-66; staff nurse Hidalgo County Health Dept., Edinburg, Tex., 1966-67; supr. nursing Tex. Dept. Health Tb Control, Austin, 1969-70; instr. St. Luke's Hosp. Sch. Nursing, Houston, 1971-72, Tex. Women's U. Sch. Nursing, Houston and Dallas, 1972-73; dir. nursing Dallas City Health Dept., 1974-80; assoc. prof. community health nursing grad. program Tex. Woman's U., Dallas, 1980-87, U. Incarnate Word, 1987—; mem. profl. adv. com. Dallas Vis. Nurse Assn., 1978-83, Santa Rosa Home Health Agy., 1991-94; mem. health adv. bd. Dallas Ind. Sch. Dist., 1976-84; chmn. nursing and health services Dallas chpt. ARC, 1984-86, bd. dirs. San Antonio chpt., 1990; Tex. Lung Assn., 1991—, bd. dirs. San Antonio Chpt., Tex. Public Health Assn. fellow, 1977. Mem. Tex. Public Health Assn., Am. Public Health Assn., Sigma Theta Tau. Methodist. Home: 508 US Highway 90 E Castroville TX 78009-5230

STRICKLAND, THOMAS JOSEPH, artist; b. Keyport, N.J., Dec. 27, 1932; s. Charles Edward and Clementine Maria (Grasso) S.; m. Ann DeBaun Browne, Apr. 28, 1992. Student, Newark Sch. Fine and Indsl. Arts, 1951-53, Am. Art Sch., 1956-59, Nat. Acad. Sch. Fine Arts with Robert Philipp, 1957-59. Judge local and nat. art shows; TV guest; instr. painting and pastels Grove House; lectr. Exhibited in one man shows at, Hollywood (Fla.) Art Mus., 1972-76, Elliott Mus., Stuart, Fla., 1974, others; exhibited in group shows at, Am. Artists Profl. League, N.Y.C., 1958, 61, Parke-Bernet Galleries, N.Y.C., 1959, 61, 64, Exposition Intercontinentale, Monaco, 1966-68, Salon Rouge du Casino Dieppe, 1967, 7e Grand Prix Internat. de Peinture de la Cote d'Azur, Cannes, 1971, Hollywood Art Mus., 1972-76, Art Guild of Boca Raton, 1973, Stagecoach Gallery, 1973, Am. Painters in Paris, 1975; represented in permanent collections, St. Vincent Coll., Elliott Mus., Martin County Hist. Soc., Hollywood Art Mus., Salem Coll., Winston-Salem, N.C., St. Hugh Catholic Ch., Fla.; (Recipient Digby Chandler prize Knickerbocker Artists 1965, Best in Show Blue Dome Art Fellowship 1972, 1st Place, Fine Arts League, La Junta, Colo. 1973, Blue Ribbon award Cape Coral Nat. Art Show 1973, 1st prize Hollywood Art Mus. 1973, Charles Hawthorne Meml. award Nat. Arts Club Exhbn. 1977, 1st prize Miami Palette Club 1978, others.); Contbr. articles to profl. jours. With AUS, 1953-55. Mem. Blue Dome Art Fellowship, Pastel Soc. Am., Nat. Soc. Lit. and Arts, Grove House, Miami Palette Club. Roman Catholic. Home: 2595 Taluga Dr Miami FL 33133-2433 *My aim in life has been to find, capture, and communicate the beauty I see in the world to others by means of painting in my Impressionistic style. To achieve this goal I have developed my talent, been dedicated to art and its disciplines. I have been uncompromising in my choice of what I paint as I paint only what I want to, preferring people and always striving to do my best.*

STRICKLAND, WILLIAM JAMES, air force officer, research psychologist; b. Boston, Apr. 12, 1948; s. Harry Gunnard and Barbara Anne (Rusk) S.; m. Martha Cecile Williams, Sept. 11, 1971; children: Adam Gregory, Aaron Christopher. BS, USAF Acad., 1970; MA, Ohio State U., 1971, PhD, 1979. Commd. 2d lt. U.S. Air Force, 1970, advanced through grades to col., 1992; test constrn. psychologist USAF Occupational Measurement Ctr., Lackland AFB, Tex., 1971-74; chief instnl. rsch. div. USAF Acad., Colorado Springs, Colo., 1980-83; chief pers. testing policy USAF Hdqrs., Pentagon, Washington, 1983-87; comdr. 3568 USAF Recruiting Squadron, Ft. Douglas, Utah, 1987-90; chief rsch. and market analysis USAF Recruiting Svc., Randolph AFB, Tex., 1990-92; dir. human resources rsch. Air Force Armstrong Lab., Brooks AFB, Tex., 1992—. Assoc. editor Jour. Mil. Psychology, 1987—; mem. editorial bd. Pers. Psychology, 1985-90. Vol. mediator Bexar County Dispute Resolution Ctr., San Antonio, 1991—. Grad. fellow Mershon Ctr. for Nat. Security, 1970, NSF, 1970. Mem. APA, Soc. for Indsl. and Orgnl. Psychology, Alamo Area Mediators Assn. Home: 15502 Cloud Top San Antonio TX 78248 Office: Armstrong Lab AL/HR 7909 Lindbergh Dr Brooks AFB TX 78235-5352

STRICKLAND, WILLIAM JESSE, lawyer; b. Newport News, Va., Mar. 21, 1942. BSBA, U. Richmond, 1964, JD, 1970. Bar: Va. 1969, U.S. Dist. Ct. (ea. and we. dists.) Va., U.S. Ct. Claims, U.S. Tax Ct., U.S. Ct. Appeals (4th cir.). Exec. com. coord. dept., mng. ptnr. McGuire, Woods, Battle & Boothe, Richmond, Va., 1969—; bd. dirs. Cableform Inc., Zion Crossroads, Va., Va. Coll. Bldg. Authority. Capt. USMC 1964-67, Vietnam. Mem. ABA, Va. Bar Assn., Richmond Bar Assn., Nat. Assn. Bond Lawyers, Va. Govt. Fin. Officers Assn., Local Govt. Attys. Assn., Va. Bond Club. Office: McGuire Woods Battle & Boothe 1 James River Plz Richmond VA 23219-3229

STRICKLER, HOWARD MARTIN, physician; b. New Haven, Conn., Oct. 26, 1950; s. Thomas David and Mildred Laing (Martin) S.; m. Susan Hunter, May 2, 1982; children: Hunter Gregory, Howard Martin Jr. BA, Berea Coll., 1975; MD, Univ. Louisville, 1979. Diplomate Am. Bd. Family Practice. Resident Anniston (Ala.) Family Practice Residency, 1979-82; pvt. practice Monteagle, Tenn., 1982-85; fellow in addictive diseases Willingway Hosp., Statesboro, Ga., 1985-86; faculty devel. fellow Univ. N.C., Chapel Hill, 1985-86; pvt. practice Birmingham, Ala., 1986-90; pres. Employers Drug Program Mgmt., Inc., Birmingham, 1990—; med. dir. Am. Health Svcs., Inc., 1993—; med. dir. Bradford Facilities, Birmingham, 1987-90, New Life Clinic, Bessemer, ala., Physicians Smoke Free Clinic, Birmingham, 1988-90, Am. Health Svcs., Inc., 1993—; chmn. dept. family practice and emergency medicine Bessemer Carraway Med. Ctr., 1993-95. With U.S. Army, 1969-72, Vietnam. Decorated Bronze Star, 1971, Vietnam Campaign medal, Vietnam Svc. medal 3 Stars, 1971. Fellow Am. Acad. Family Physicians; mem. Am. Soc. Addiction Medicine (cert.), Am. Coll. Occupl. and Environ. Medicine, Am. Assn. Med. Rev. Officers (cert.), Med. Assn. State of Ala., Am. Bd. Forensic Examiners, Phi Kappa Phi. Methodist. Avocations: flying, tennis, golf. Home: 868 Tulip Poplar Dr Birmingham AL 35244-1633 Office: 616 9th St S Birmingham AL 35233-1113

STRICKLER, IVAN K., dairy farmer; b. Carlyle, Kans., Oct. 23, 1921; s. Elmer E. and Edna Louise (James) S.; m. Madge Lee Marshall, Aug. 7, 1949; children—Steven Mark, Thomas Scott, Douglas Lee. B.S., Kans. State U., 1947. Owner, mgr. dairy farm Iola, Kans., 1947—; tchr. farm tng. to vets. World War II, 1947-54; judge 1st and 2d Nat. Holstein Show, Brazil, 1969-70, Internat. Holstein Show, Buenos Aires, 1972, Nat. Holstein Show, Ecuador, 1978, 10th Nat. Holstein Show, Brazil, 1980; judge Holstein Show, Australia, Mex. and Argentina, 1981, Lang Lang, 1984; judge Adelaide (Australia) Royal Show, 1987; pres Mid-America Dairymen, Inc., Springfield, MO, 1981—; appointed chmn. Nat. Dairy Bd., 1985-90; dairy leader 4-H Club, 1962-75; dir. Iola State Bank; rep. U.S. Internat. Dairy Symposium, 1994, Belo Horinzote, Brazil. Trustee Allen County Community Jr. Coll.; mem. agr. edn. and rsch. com. Kans. State U., U.S. Agrl. Trade and Devel. Mission, Algeria and Tunisia, 1989. With USN, 1942-46, PTO. Recipient Silver award Holstein Friesian Assn. Brazil, 1969, Top Dairy Farm Efficiency award Ford Found., 1971, Master Farmer award Kans. State U. and Kans. Assn. Commerce and Industry, 1972, Gold award Holstein Friesian Assn. Argentina, 1972, Richard Lynng award Nat. Dairy Bd., 1990, award of merit Gamma Sigma Delta, 1987; named Man of Yr. World Dairy Exposition, 1978; portrait in Dairy Hall of Fame Kans. State U., 1974; Guest of Hon. Nat. Dairy Shrine, 1985. Mem. Mid Am. Dairymen (sec. corporate bd. 1971-81, pres. 1981—), Holstein Friesian Assn. Am. (nat. dir. 1964-72), Dairy Shrine (nat. dir. 1971-81), United Dairy Industry Assn. (dir. 1971—), Nat. Holstein Assn. Am. (pres. 1979-80), Alpha Gamma Rho. Mem. Christian Ch. (elder, bd. dirs.). Club: Nat. Dairy Shrine (pres. 1978). Home: PO Box 365 Iola KS 66749-0365 Office: Mid America Dairymen Inc 3253 E Chestnut Expy Springfield MO 65802-2540

STRICKLER, JAMES CALVIN, JR., banker; b. N.Y.C., Sept. 14, 1956; s. James Calvin and Margaret Jane (Wallick) S.; m. Elizabeth Anne Warren, June 25, 1962; 1 child, Zachary Warren. AB, Duke U., 1979; MBA, U. Chgo., 1983. Registered securities prin. Assoc. Citibank, N.Y.C., 1983-85, Morgan Stanley Co., N.Y.C., 1985-88; v.p. asset securitization Chem. Bank, N.Y.C., 1988—. Office: Chemical Bank 277 Park Ave Fl 9 New York NY 10172-0099

STRICKLER, JEFF, newspaper movie critic. Movie critic Mpls Star Tribune. Office: Minneapolis Star Tribune 425 Portland Ave Minneapolis MN 55488-0001

STRICKLER, MATTHEW M., lawyer; b. Bryn Mawr, Pa., June 27, 1940; s. Charles S and Mary Webster (Cornman) S.; m. Margaret Renshaw, Sept. 3, 1966; children: Matthew David, Andrew Kellogg, Timothy Webster, Edward Charles. AB, Haverford Coll., 1962; JD, Harvard U., 1965. Bar: Pa. 1965, U.S. Supreme Ct. 1975. Assoc. Ballard, Spahr, Andrews & Ingersoll, Phila., 1965-74, ptnr., 1974—; lectr. in law Temple U. Sch. Law, Phila., 1993—. Editor: Representing Health Care Facilities, 1981. Bd. dirs. Phila. chpt. Girl Scouts Am., 1978—, v.p., 1984-90, 94—. Mem. Union League Phila. Office: Ballard Spahr Andrews & Ingersoll 51st Fl 1735 Market St Fl 51 Philadelphia PA 19103-7501

STRICKMAN, ARTHUR EDWIN, retired retail executive; b. N.Y.C., July 12, 1924; s. Samuel W. and Lee (Light) S.; m. Rosemary C. Lawson, Sept. 13, 1947; children: Ellen Sue, Wendy Lee, Nancy Ann. B.A. in Bus. Adminstrn., Duke U., 1945. Exec. tng., asst. buyer Bloomingdales, 1946-47; sr. buyer Bond Stores, N.Y.C., 1948-50; pres. Sandra Post, N.Y.C., 1951-58; with Lerner Stores, N.Y.C., 1959-85; v.p. mdse. Lerner Stores, 1973-74, exec. v.p., 1975-81, pres., 1982-85, chmn. bd., chief exec. officer, 1982-85. Bd. trustees Eisenhower Med. Ctr., Rancho Mirage, Calif., 1996; chmn. bd. dirs. Eisenhower Med. Ctr. Found. Officer USN, 1942-46, PTO. Home: 136 Yale Dr Rancho Mirage CA 92270-3677

STRICKON, HARVEY ALAN, lawyer; b. Bklyn., Nov. 9, 1947; s. Milton and Norma (Goodhartz) S.; m. Linda Carol Meltzer, July 2, 1972; children: Joshua Andrew, Meredith Cindy, Erica Stacey. BBA, CCNY, 1968; JD, NYU, 1971. Bar: N.Y. 1972, U.S. Dist. Ct. (so. and ea. dists.) N.Y. 1973, U.S. Ct. Appeals (2d cir.) 1973, U.S. Supreme Ct. 1975, U.S. Dist. Ct. (no. dist.) N.Y. 1980, U.S. Dist. Ct. (we. dist.) N.Y. 1981, U.S. Dist. Ct. Ariz. 1991. Law clk. U.S. Dist. Ct. (ea. dist.) N.Y., Bklyn., 1971-73; assoc. Moses & Singer, N.Y.C., 1973-80; from assoc. to ptnr. Kaye, Scholer, Fierman, Hays & Handler, N.Y.C., 1980-91; ptnr. Paul, Hastings, Janofsky & Walker, N.Y.C., 1991—; mem. complaint mediation panel, departmental disciplinary com. appellate div., 1st dept. Supreme Ct. State N.Y. Mem. Nassau County Rep. Com., Great Neck, N.Y., 1982—; chmn. bd. dirs. Flushing Community Vol. Ambulance Corps. Inc., N.Y., 1981-86, vice chmn., 1987-92. Mem. ABA, N.Y. State Bar Assn., Assn. Bar City N.Y. (chmn. complaint mediation panel com. on profl. discipline), Am. Judicature Soc., Assn. Comml. Fin. Attys., N.Y. Law Inst., Bankruptcy Lawyers Bar Assn., (bd. govs. 1987-89, corr. sec. 1989—), Am. Bankruptcy Inst. Republican. Jewish. Home: 11 West Brook Rd Great Neck NY 11024-1219 Office: Paul Hastings Janofsky & Walker 399 Park Ave New York NY 10022-4697

STRIDER, MARJORIE VIRGINIA, artist, educator; b. Guthrie, Okla.; d. Clifford R. and Marjorie E. (Schley) S. BFA, Kansas City Art Inst., 1962. Mem. faculty Sch. Visual Arts, N.Y.C., 1970—; artist-in-residence City U. Grad. Ctr. Mall, N.Y.C., 1976, Fabric Workshop, Phila., 1978, Grassi Palace, Venice, Italy, 1978. One-woman shows of sculpture, drawings and/or prints include Pace Gallery, N.Y.C., 1963-64, Nancy Hoffman Gallery, N.Y.C., 1973-74, Weather Spoon Mus., U.N.C., Chapel Hill, 1974, City U. Grad. Center Mall, 1976, Clocktower, N.Y.C., 1976, Sculpture Center, N.Y.C., 1983, Steinbaum Gallery, N.Y.C., 1983, 84, Andre Zarre Gallery, 1993, 95; one-woman travelling shows to numerous mus. across USA; exhibited in group shows The Sculpture Center, N.Y.C., 1981, Drawing Biennale, Lisbon, Portugal, 1981, Newark Mus., 1984, William Rockhill Nelson Mus., Kansas City, 1985, Danforth Mus., Framingham, Mass., 1987, Delahoyd Gallery, N.Y.C., 1992; represented in permanent collections Guggenheim Mus., N.Y.C., U. Colo., Boulder, Albright-Knox Mus., Buffalo, Des Moines Art Center, Storm King (N.Y.) Art Center, Larry Aldrich Mus., Ridgefield, Conn., City U. Grad. Center, N.Y.C., Hirschhorn Mus. and Sculpture Garden, Washington, Santa Fe (N. Mex.) Mus. of Art, also pvt. collections. Nat. Endowment for Arts grantee, 1973, 80, Longview Found. grantee, 1974, Pollock-Krasner Found. grantee, 1990, Florsheim Art Fund grantee, 1991; Va. Ctr. for Creative Arts fellow, 1974, 92, Millay Colony for Arts fellow, 1992, Yaddo Colony, 1996.

STRIDSBERG, ALBERT BORDEN, advertising consultant, educator, editor; b. Wyoming, Ohio, July 22, 1929; s. Carl Alexander Herbert and Edith Vivian (Farley) S. BA with honors, Yale U., 1950; Diplome D'Etudes Franc., U. of Poitiers, Tours, France, 1951; postgrad., Am. U. Beirut, Lebanon, 1953-54; diploma, Direct Mktg. Inst., 1986. Copywriter Howard Swink Advt., Inc., Marion, Ohio, 1955-58; acct. supr. McCann-Erickson, Co., Brussels, 1958-60, J. Walter Thompson Co., Amsterdam, The Netherlands, 1960-63; asst. to internat. exec. v.p. J. Walter Thompson Co., N.Y.C., 1963-67, internat. cons. spl. projects, acquisitions and diversifications, 1969-73; cons., coord. Internat. Markets Advt. Agy., Inc., N.Y., London, 1967-69; editor-in-chief Advt. World mag., N.Y.C., 1975-77; lectr. in mktg. NYU, N.Y.C., 1978-84; lectr. in advt. Marist Coll., Poughkeepsie, N.Y., 1984-94; U.S. features editor Media Internat. Mag., London, 1984-90; assoc. prof. NYU, 1966-78; ind. cons., freelance writer on advt. and mktg. issues, N.Y.C., 1972—; seminar leader, Lagos, Nigeria, 1991. Author: Effective Advertising Self-Regulation, 1974, Progress Toward Advertising Self Regulation, 1976, Controversy Advertising, 1977, Advertising Self-Regulation, 1980. With U.S. Army, 1951-53. Fulbright fellow U. Poitiers, 1950-51, Ford. Found. fellow Beirut U., 1953-54. Mem. Internat. Advt. Assn. (cons., project coord. 1974-80), Am. Mktg. Assn., Advt. Rsch. Found., Direct Mktg. Assn., Am. Acad. Advt., Yale Club N.y.C., Elizabethan Club New Haven. Democrat. Episcopalian. Office: PO Box 1675 South Rd Sta Poughkeepsie NY 12601-0675

STRIEFSKY, LINDA A(NN), lawyer; b. Carbondale, Pa., Apr. 27, 1952; d. Leo James and Antoinette Marie (Carachilo) S.; m. James Richard Carlson, Nov. 3, 1984; children: David Carlson, Paul Carlson, Daniel Carlson. BA summa cum laude, Marywood Coll., 1974; JD, Georgetown U., 1977. Bar: Ohio 1977. Assoc., Thompson, Hine and Flory, Cleve., 1977-85, ptnr., 1985—. Loaned exec. United Way of Northeast Ohio, Cleve., 1978; trustee Cleve. Music Sch. Settlement. Mem. Am. Bar Found., ABA (mem. real estate fin. com. 1980—, vice-chair lender liability com. 1993—), Am. Coll. Real Estate Lawyers bd. govs. 1994—), Internat. Coun. of Shopping Ctrs., Nat. Assn. Office and Indsl. Parks, Urban Land Inst., Cleve. Real Estate Women, Ohio State Bar Assn. (bd. govs. real property sect. 1985—), Greater Cleve. Bar Assn. (chmn. bar applicants com. 1983-84, exec. coun. young lawyers sect. 1982-85, chmn. 1984-85, mem. exec. coun. real property sect. 1980-84, Merit Svc. award 1983, 85), Pi Gamma Mu. Democrat. Roman Catholic. Home: 2222 Delamere Dr Cleveland OH 44106-3204 Office: Thompson Hine and Flory PLL 3900 Society Ctr 127 Public Sq Cleveland OH 44114-1216

STRIEGEL, PEGGY SIMSARIAN, advertising executive; b. Phila., July 12, 1941; d. Robert Ernest Samuel and Margaret (Miller) Thompson; m. James P. Simsarian, Sept. 4, 1965 (div. Sept. 1976); children: Catherine Ann, Sheila Thompson; m. Louis E. Striegel, Sept. 14, 1976 (div. June 1984); m. Andrew H. Schmeltz Jr., Dec. 4, 1991. BA, Sarah Lawrence Coll., 1963. Asst. editor Oxford U. Press, N.Y.C., 1963-64; picture editor Western Pub. Co., N.Y.C., 1964-66; art editor Houghton-Mifflin, Inc., Boston, 1966-68; pres. Peggy's Graphics, McLean, Va., 1968-78, Striegel Advt. and Graphics, Inc., Broken Arrow, Okla., 1978—. Lower Merion (Pa.) area coord. Shapp for Congress, Phila., 1970; area coord. and graphic designer Phillips for U.S. Congress, McLean, 1972; pres. bd. dirs. Gatesway Found., Broken Arrow, 1987-89; chair, Cmty. Playhouse Broken Arrow, 1979-81; mktg. bd. chair Tulsa Philharmonic, 1985-95, exec. com., bd. dirs. 1993—; active internet radio talk show Women of the Roundtable. Recipient numerous advt. awards including several Addies and citations Tulsa Advt. Club, 1990-91, Gold Quill, 1990, cert. Merit Printing Industries Am., 1983, award of Excellence Am. Inst. Graphic Arts, 1983, Am. Corp. Identity Graphics award, 1994. Mem. Advt. Fedn. Tulsa, Bus. and Profl. Advt. Assn. (Gold Ring award 1986, 87), Women in Communications (prog. chmn. 1991), Met. Tulsa C. of C., Broken Arrow C. of C., Bus. Profl. Advt. Assn., Jr. Achievement of Tulsa (bd. dirs. 1990-94). Democrat. Presbyterian. Club: Art Directors. Avocations: tennis, swimming, sailing, jogging. Home: 6110 S 221st East Ave Broken Arrow OK 74014-2017 Office: 716 S Main St Broken Arrow OK 74012-5527

STRIER, KAREN BARBARA, anthropology educator; b. Summit, N.J., May 22, 1959; d. Murray Paul and Arlene Strier. BA, Swarthmore Coll., 1980; MA, Harvard U., 1981, PhD, 1986. Lectr. anthropology Harvard U., Cambridge, Mass., 1986-87; asst. prof. Beloit (Wis.) Coll., 1987-89; asst. prof. U. Wis., Madison, 1989-92, assoc. prof. anthropology, 1992-95, prof., 1995—; dept. chair, 1994-96; panel mem. U.S. Dept. Edn., Washington, 1989-92. Author: Faces in the Forest, 1992; mem. editorial bd. Internat. Jour. Primatology, 1990—, Primates, 1991—. Recipient Presdl. Young Investigator award NSF, 1989—. Fellow Am. Anthropol. Assn.; mem. AAAS, Am. Assn. Phys. Anthropologists, Internat. Primatological Soc., Animal Behavior Soc. Office: U Wis Dept Anthropology 5440 Social Sci Bldg 1180 Observatory Dr Madison WI 53706-1320

STRIER, MURRAY PAUL, chemist, consultant; b. N.Y.C., Oct. 19, 1923; s. Jack and Rose (Goldman) S.; m. Arlene Schimmel, Feb. 12, 1955; children: Sheri Jeanette, Karen Barbara, Robin Joy. BChemE, CCNY, 1944; MS, Emory U., 1947; PhD, U. Ky., 1952. Rsch. chemist Reaction Motors Inc. (named changed to Thiokol Co.), Denville, N.J., 1952-56; sect. head Air Reduction, Inc., Murray Hill, N.J., 1956-58; chief chemist Fulton-Irgon Corp. (now Inc. with Lithium Corp.), Lake Denmark, N.J., 1958-59; supr. Rayonier, Inc., Whippany, N.J., 1959-61; rsch. chemist McGraw Edison Co., West Orange, N.J., 1961-64; sr. rsch. scientist McDonnell Douglas Corp., Newport Beach, Calif., 1964-69; rsch. assoc. Hooker Rsch. Ctr., Grand Island, N.Y., 1969-71; phys. scientist EPA, Washington, 1972-86; cons. Rockville, Md., 1986-94, Houston, 1994—; instr. analytical chem. Upsala Coll., East Orange, N.J., 1963-64; cons. electroplating NSF, Washington, 1973-75. Contbr. articles to Jour. Am. Chem. Soc., Jour. Electrochem. Soc., Jour. Environ. Sci. & Tech. Commr. sci. and tech. commn. City of Rockville, 1985-91; vol. office consumer affairs Montgomery County, Rockville, 1989-90, dept. environ. protection, 1989-90. With USNR, 1944-46. Recipient Gold medal EPA, Washington, 1979. Fellow Am. Inst. Chemists (cert.); mem. AAAS, ASTM, Am. Chem. Soc., Electrochem. Soc. Achievements include patents on advanced solid rocket propellants, new high energy density batteries and fuel cells, improved methods for removal of toxic chemicals from water by electrochemical methods; development of less toxic dielectrics for capacitors and more facile methods for evaluation, optimal treatment methods, for removal of toxic chemicals from waters by use of chemical structure-activity approach. Home and Office: 4114 Meadow Edge Sugar Land TX 77479

STRIFLER, VIVIAN ELSIE, health facilities nursing consultant; b. Port-of-Spain, Trinidad and Tobago, Mar. 30, 1938; came to U.S., 1960; d. John and Mary Apple (Ward) Joseph; m. Harold C. Strifler, Dec. 20, 1969; children: Indra Lynn, Rakesh Lance. BSN, Avila Coll., 1969, cert. mgmt., 1981; MS, Kans. State U., 1981; instr./examiner/nurse asst., Sch. Dist. Kansas City, 1987. Cert. gerontol. nurse, RN, Mo., RNC in gerontology. Charge and staff nurse St. Joseph Hosp., Kansas City, Mo., 1969-73; dir. shift ops. Truman Med. Ctr., Kansas City, 1977-83; assoc. dir. nursing svcs. Swope Ridge Health Care, Kansas City, 1983-87; dir. nursing svcs. Wornal Health Care, Kansas City, 1987-88, Plaza Manor SNF, Kansas City, 1988-89; ind. nursing cons. Prairie Village, Kans., 1989-90; health facilities nursing cons. State of Mo. Dept. Health, Jefferson City, 1990—; past v.p. Kansas City Assn. DON in longterm care, 1987-88. Mem. NAFE, AAUW, Am. Bus. Women's Assn. (past pres. High Achiever chpt. 1986-87, Woman of Yr. High Achiever chpt. 1986-87), Nat. League for Nursing, Mo. League for Nursing, Inc. (scholarship com., program com. 1992-95), Women's C. of C. of Greater Kansas City. Democrat. Roman Catholic. Avocations: plants, gardening, fishing, learning stock market. Home: 613 W 112th St Kansas City MO 64114-5201 Office: Mo Dept Health Bur Hosp Licenseship/Cert 2014 Williams St Jefferson City MO 65102

STRIGHT, I. LEONARD, educational consultant; b. Mercer, Pa., May 7, 1916; s. Fred L. and Martha (Dight) S.; m. Virginia Minser, July 24, 1940; children—Suzanne (Mrs. L. David York), Robert, William (dec.). B.A., Allegheny Coll., 1935, M.A., 1938, LL.D., 1978; Ph.D., Case-Western U., 1946; postgrad., U. Chgo., 1963. Math. tchr. Freedom (Pa.) High Sch., 1935-39, Indiana (Pa.) Joint High Sch., 1939-42; prof. math. Baldwin-Wallace Coll., Berea, Ohio, 1942-46, No. Mich. U., Marquette, 1946-47, Indiana (Pa.) U., 1947-57; dean Indiana (Pa.) U. (Grad. Sch.), 1957-71; acad. v.p. Ohio No. U., 1971-78; cons. in higher edn., 1978—; adj. prof. Gettysburg (Pa.) Coll., Shippensburg (Pa.) U. Contbr. articles profl. jours. Mem. Nat. Council Tchrs. Math., Am. Assn. U. Profs., N.E.A., S.A.R., Phi Delta Kappa, Phi Kappa Phi, Delta Tau Delta. Methodist. Clubs: Kiwanian (pres. 1960), Mason. Home: C-224 300 Willow Valley Lakes Dr Willow Street PA 17584

STRIKER, CECIL LEOPOLD, archaeologist, educator; b. Cin., July 15, 1932; s. Cecil and Delia (Workum) S.; m. Ute Stephan, Apr. 27, 1968. BA, Oberlin Coll., 1956; MA, NYU, 1960, PhD, 1968; MA (hon.), U. Pa., 1972. Instr., asst. prof. Vassar Coll., 1962-68; assoc. prof. U. Pa., Phila., 1968-78; prof. history of art U. Pa., 1978—, chmn. dept. history of art, 1980-87; field archaeologist Dumbarton Oaks Center for Byzantine Studies, 1966—, fellow, 1972-73; dir. survey and excavation, Myrelaion, Istanbul, 1965-66; co-dir. Kalenderhane Archaeol. Project, Istanbul, 1966-78, Aegean Dendrochronology Project, 1977-88; gen. archaeol. cons. Istanbul Metro and Bosphorus Tunnel Project, 1985-87; dir. Archtl. Dendrochronology Project, 1988—; cons. Integrated Study of Hagia Sophia Structure, 1991-95. Mem. editorial bd. Architectura: Zeitschrift für Geschichte der Architektur, 1986—. Mem. adv. bd. Ctr. for Advanced Study in the Visual Arts, 1986-88, Samuel H. Kress Found. Art History Fellowship Program, 1986-87. Served with U.S.

Army, 1954-57. Fulbright grantee in Germany, 1960-62; art historian in residence Am. Acad. in Rome, 1973; NEH grantee, 1985-86. Mem. Archaeol. Inst. Am., Coll. Art Assn., Am. Research Inst. in Turkey (fellow 1965-66, pres. 1978-84), Council Am. Overseas Research Ctr. (chmn. 1980-84), Soc. of Archtl. Historians, Turkish Studies Assn., U.S. Nat. Com. for Byzantine Studies, Koldewey Gesellschaft, German Archaeol. Inst. (corr.), Oriental Club of Phila.

STRIKER, GARY E., scientist, research institution administrator; b. Mar. 7, 1934; m. Liliane Zeligson. MD, U. Seattle, 1959. Diplomate Am. Bd. Pathology, Nat. Bd. Med. Examiners (pathology test com. 1980-83). Rotating intern U. Wash. Hosp., Seattle, 1959-60; pathology resident UCLA, Wadsworth Gen. Hosp., VA Ctr., 1960-62; postdoctoral trainee in exptl. pathology, dept. pathology U. Wash., Seattle, 1962-64, asst. prof. dept. pathology, 1966-71, assoc. prof., 1971-75, prof., 1975-84, dean for curriculum Sch. Medicine, 1971-77; dir. div. kidney, urologic and hematologic diseases Nat. Inst. Diabetes, and Digestive and Kidney Diseases, NIH, Bethesda, Md., 1984—; attending physician Univ. Hosps. of U. Wash., 1966-84, VA Hosp., Seattle, 1969-84; cons. Children's Orthopedic Hosp., Seattle, 1966-84, Madigan Hosp., Tacoma, 1971-84, Clin. Ctr. NIH, 1985—; conf. chmn. exptl. pathology sect. U. Pierre and Marie Curie, Paris, 1981-82; guest reviewer for NSF, Juvenile Diabetes Found., VA; chmn. or mem. of multiple site visits for Nat. Inst. Gen. Med. Scis., and Nat. Heart, Lung and Blood Inst.; lectr. various univs., med. orgns., sci. meetings, confs., worldwide. Mem. editorial bd. Lab. Investigation, Am. Jour. Kidney Diseases, Am. Jour. Pathology, Am. Jour. Nephrology, Clin. Nephrology, Nephron, Diabetes and Metabolism Revs.; guest reviewer Kidney Internat., In Vitro, Am. Jour. Physiology, Jour. Clin. Investigation, Jour. Clin. Immunology and Immunopathology, Infection and Immunity, Diagnostic Immunology, Diabetes Care; contbr. numerous articles to profl. jours. With M.C., U.S. Army, 1964-66. Recipient Disting. Leadership award Am. Urol. Assn., 1987, Louis Pasteur award U. Strasbourg; fellow Macy Found., Fogarty Internat.; grantee NIH, 1975-88. Mem. AAAS, Nat. Kidney Found. (Sci. Leadership award 1986), Am. Assn. Physicians, Am. Assn. Pathologists, Am. Fedn. Clin. Rsch., Am. Soc. Nephrology, Internat. Soc. Nephrology, Am. Soc. Cell Biology, Am. Heart Assn., King County Med. Soc., Wash. State Med. Soc., Italian Soc. Nephrology (hon.).

STRIKER, GISELA, philosophy educator; b. Gütersloh, Germany, 1943; came to the U.S., 1986; Student, Tübingen U., 1962, Hamburg U., 1962-64, Göttingen U., 1964-69, Oxford U., 1966-67; PhD, Göttingen U., 1969, Habilitation for philosophy, 1978. Asst. prof. philosophy Göttingen (Germany) U., 1971-83, prof. philosophy, 1983-86; prof. philosophy Columbia U., N.Y.C., 1986-89; prof. philosophy Harvard U., Cambridge, Mass., 1989—, George Martin Lane prof. philosophy and the classics, 1990—; vis. asst. prof. philosophy Stanford (Calif.) U., 1974; vis. assoc. prof. philosophy Princeton (N.J.) U., 1979; Nellie-Wallace-lectr. Oxford U., 1984; vis. prof. philosophy Harvard U., 1985; Tanner lectr. Stanford U., 1987. Author: Essays on Hellenistic Epistemology and Ethics, 1996; contbr. articles to profl. jours.; pub. papers and monographs. Rsch. fellow Deutsche Forschungsgemeinschaft, 1970-71, 82-84, fellow Wissenschaftskolleg zu Berlin, 1990-91. Mem. Am. Philos. Assn., Am. Acad. Arts and Scis., N.Y. Acad. Scis. Office: Harvard U Dept Philosophy Cambridge MA 02138

STRIMBU, VICTOR, JR., lawyer; b. New Philadelphia, Ohio, Nov. 25, 1932; s. Victor and Veda (Stancu) S.; m. Kathryn May Schrote, Apr. 9, 1955; children: Victor Paul, Michael, Julie, Sue. BA, Heidelberg Coll., 1954; postgrad. Western Res. U., 1956-57; JD, Columbia U., 1960. Bar: Ohio 1960, U.S. Supreme Ct. 1972. With Baker & Hostetler, Cleve., 1960—, ptnr., 1970—. Bd. dirs. North Coast Health Ministry; mem. Bay Village (Ohio) Bd. Edn., 1976-84, pres., 1978-82; mem. indsl. rels. adv. com. Cleve. State U., 1979—, chmn., 1982; mem. Bay Village Planning Commn., 1967-69; life mem. Ohio PTA; mem. Greater Cleve. Growth Assn.; bd. trustees New Cleve. Campaign, 1987—, North Coast Health Ministry, 1989—. With AUS, 1955-56. Recipient Service award Cleve. State U., 1980. Mem. ABA, Ohio Bar Assn., Greater Cleve. Bar Assn., Ohio Newspaper Assn. (minority affairs com. 1987—), Ct. of Nisi Prius Club, Cleve. Athletic Club, The Club at Soc. Ctr. Republican. Presbyterian. Office: Baker & Hostetler 3200 National City Ctr 1900 E 9th St Cleveland OH 44114-3401

STRINER, HERBERT EDWARD, economics educator; b. Jersey City, Aug. 16, 1922; s. Harry and Pearl (Strynar) S.; m. Erma Steinert, Dec. 9, 1943 (div. 1970); children: Richard Alan, Deborah Jane; m. Iona V. Meredith. A.B., Rutgers U., 1947, M.A., 1948; Ph.D. (Maxwell fellow 1949-50), Syracuse U., 1951. Asst. prof. Syracuse U., 1951; economist Interior Dept., 1951-54; program dir. NSF, 1954-55, Nat. Planning Assn., 1955-57; sr. analyst Operations Research Office, Johns Hopkins, 1957-59; program dir. Brookings Inst., 1959-61, Stanford Research Inst., 1961-62; dir. Upjohn Inst., Washington, 1962-69; dean Coll. Continuing Edn. Am. U., Washington, 1969-73; dean Coll. Bus. Am. U., 1974-81, prof. econs. and mgmt., 1981-89; cons. Los Alamos Nat. Lab., 1990-91; chief planning and policy NIH, 1972-73; pres. U. Research Corp., 1973-74. Author: Toward a Fundamental Program for the Training, Employment and Economic Equality of the American Indian, 1968, Continuing Education as a National Capital Investment, 1972, Regaining The Lead: Policies for Economic Growth, 1984; co-author: Local Impact of Foreign Trade, 1960, Civil Rights, Employment and the Social Status of American Negros, 1966; Contbr. profl. jours. Mem. rev. panel Pres.'s Cabinet Com. Juv. Delinquency, 1961-63, D.C. Youth Employment Com., 1963, Pres.'s Task Force Am. Indians, 1967, White House Conf. Aging, 1971; bd. dirs. Opportunities Industrialization Ctr., NAACP, Washington. Officer inf. U.S. Army, 1943-46. Decorated Govt. China medal of merit, 1945. Home: 4979 Battery Ln Bethesda MD 20814-2634

STRINGER, GRETCHEN ENGSTROM, consulting volunteer administrator; b. Pitts., Feb. 25, 1925; d. Birger and Gertrude Anne (Schuchman) Engstrom; m. Loren F. Stringer, Oct. 3, 1953 (dec. Sept. 1992); children: Lizbeth Stringer Coffman, Pamela, William E., Frederick E. BA, Oberlin Coll., 1946; Cert. in Teaching, U. Pitts., 1951, SUNY, Buffalo, 1964; M, SUNY, Buffalo, 1996. Cert. vol. adminstr. Owner, founder, pres. Vol. Cons., Clarence, N.Y., 1979—; owner, founder, officer Non Profit Mgmt. Ctr., Buffalo, 1995—; Founding pres., bd. dirs. Ctrl. Referral Svc. Author: The Board Manual Workbook, 1980, rev., 1993, The Instructors Guide, 1982, A Magical Formula, 1980; contbr. articles to profl. jours. Exec. dir. Vol. Action Ctr., United Way Buffalo and Erie County, 1978-81; founding vice chair Erie County Commn. on Status of Women, 1989-93; pres. Girl Scout Coun. of Buffalo and Erie County, chair, gen. mgr. cadette encampment; bd. dirs. Clarence Ctrl. Sch. Dist., 1976-86; chair, gen. mgr. Buffalo and Erie County Bicentennial Parade, 1976, Erie County Ski Swap; active Longview Protestant Home for Children Bd., Millard Fillmore Jr. Bd., Prevention is Primary, N.Y. Bd. State Foster Care Youth Ind. Project, others; Cmty. Hero Torch Bearer Summer Olympics, 1996. Recipient Pinny Wilson Vol. award Buffalo and Erie County, 1981, Continuing Svc. award Mass. Mutual, 1987, Girl Scouts Thanks Badge, 1983, Susan Reid Greene Russell award Jr. League of Buffalo, 1994. Mem. N.Y. Assn. Vol. Ctrs. (founding exec. bd.), Vol. Adminstrs. Western N.Y. (founding pres. 1980), Buffalo Ambassadors of C. of C. (bd. dirs.), Jr. League Buffalo, Inc., Assn. Vol. Adminstrn. (chair, gen. mgr. nat. conf. 1986, nat. trainer, re-cert. chair, subcom. vol. adminstrn. higher edn.). Office: Non Profit Mgmt Ctr 707 Cayuga Creek Rd Buffalo NY 14227

STRINGER, JOHN, materials scientist; b. Liverpool, Eng., July 14, 1934; came to U.S., 1977; s. Edward Gitchen and Isobel (Taylor) S.; m. Audrey Lancaster, Feb. 4, 1957; children: Helen Caroline, Rebecca Elizabeth. BS in Engring., U. Liverpool, 1955, PhD, 1958, D in Engring., 1974. Chartered engr., U.K. Lectr. Univ. Liverpool, Eng., 1957-63; fellow Battelle Columbus (Ohio) Labs., 1963-66; prof. materials sci. Univ. Liverpool, 1966-77; sr. project mgr. Electric Power Rsch. Inst., Palo Alto, Calif., 1977-81; sr. program mgr. Electric Power Rsch. Inst., Palo Alto, 1981-87, dir. tech. support, 1987-91, dir. applied rsch., 1991-95, tech. exec. Applied Sci. and Tech., 1995—; chmn. Sci. and Tech. Edn., Merseyside, Liverpool, 1971-74; pres. Corrosioin and Protection Assn., London, 1972. Editorial bd.: Oxidation of Metals Jour., 1971—; author: An Introduction to the Electron Theory of Solids, 1967; editor: (book) High Temperature Corrosion of Advanced Materials, 1989, Chlorine in Coal, 1991, Applied Chaos, 1992; contbr. over 300 articles to profl. jours. Recipient U.R. Evans award Inst. Corrosion, U.K., 1993, Campbell Meml. Lectr. of ASM Internat., 1995. Fellow AAAS, NACE Internat., AIME, Inst. Energy, Royal Soc. Arts; mem. ASM Internat., Materials Rsch. Soc. Office: Electric Power Rsch Inst 3412 Hillview Ave Palo Alto CA 94304-1395

STRINGER, L.E. (DEAN STRINGER), lawyer; b. Sayre, Okla., June 22, 1936; s. Rex Herman and Bessie (Morris) S.; m. Carol Ann Woodson, Aug. 31, 1963; children: Craig Woodson, Laura DeAnn. BA, Okla. State U., 1958; LLB, Harvard U., 1961. Bar: Okla. 1961, U.S. Ct. Appeals (10th cir.) 1962, U.S. Dist. Ct. (we. dist.) 1963, U.S. Supreme Ct. 1972. Assoc. Crowe, Boxley, et al (now Crowe & Dunlevy), Oklahoma City, 1961-68, mem., dir., 1968—; pres. Crowe & Dunlevy, P.C., 1979-81, chmn. litigation dept., 1987—. Bd. regents Okla. State U. and A&M Colls., Stillwater, 1986-94, vice chmn., 1989-90, chmn., 1990-91; chmn. Okla. State U. Found., Stillwater, 1982-85; dir. Okla. Heritage Assn., 1995—. Maj. Okla. N.G., 1961-71. Recipient Disting. Alumnus award Okla. State U., 1979. Fellow Am. Bar Found.; mem. ABA, Okla. Bar Assn., Okla. County Bar Assn., Internat. Assn. of Def. Counsel, Okla. Assn. Def. Counsel. Democrat. Methodist. Home: 325 NW 17th St Oklahoma City OK 73103-3424 Office: Crowe & Dunlevy 20 N Broadway Ave Oklahoma City OK 73102-8202

STRINGER, MARY EVELYN, art historian, educator; b. Huntsville, Mo., July 31, 1921; d. William Madison and Charity (Rogers) S. A.B., U. Mo., 1942; A.M., U. N.C., Chapel Hill, 1955; Ph.D. (Danforth scholar), Harvard U., 1973. Asst. prof. art Miss. State Coll. for Women (now Miss. U. for Women), Columbus, 1947-58; asso. prof. Miss. State Coll. for Women (now Miss. U. for Women), 1958-73, prof. emeritus, 1973—; regional dir. for Miss., Census of Stained Glass Windows in Am., 1840-1940. Bd. dirs. Mississippians for Ednl. Broadcasting; mem. Miss. com. Save Outdoor Sculpture, 1992-93. Fulbright scholar W.Ger., 1955-56; Harvard U. travel grantee, 1966-67; NEH summer seminar grantee, 1980. Mem. AAUW, Coll. Art Assn., Southeastern Coll. Art Conf. (dir. 1975-80, 83-89, Disting. Svc. award 1992, Miss. Hist. Soc. (award of merit, 1995), Internat. Ctr. Medieval Art, Audubon Soc., The Nature Conservancy, Sierra Club, Phi Beta Kappa, Phi Kappa Phi. Democrat. Episcopalian. Office: Dept Art Miss U for Women Columbus MS 39701

STRINGER, PATRICIA ANNE, retired secondary educator; b. Mpls., Mar. 17, 1935; d. Raphael Clarence and Marie Christine (Kwakenat) S. BS, U. Minn., 1960, MA, 1967. Cert. tchr., Minn. Tchr. Sunrise Park Jr. High Sch., White Bear Lake, Minn., 1960-72; tchr., coach Mariner High Sch., White Bear Lake, 1972-84, White Bear Lake High Sch., 1984-91; mem. adv. bd. Minn. State High Sch. League, 1973-77; cons. in phys. edn., Minn., Wis., Mont., 1978-82; dept. chair White Bear Lake Schs., 1962-91, athletic coord., 1972-82; mem. Minn. State Coaching Cert. Com., 1980. Contbr. articles to profl. jours. Named to Minn. Softball Coaches Hall of Fame, 1992, Regional Coach of Yr., 1980, 90, Minn. Softball Hall of Fame Amateur Softball Assn. Am., 1982. Mem. AAHPERD, Minn. Assn. Health, Phys. Edn., Recreation and Dance (Secondary Phys. Edn. Tchr. of Yr. 1990), Ctrl. Dist. Assn. for Health, Phys. Edn., Recreation and Dance (Secondary Phys. Edn. Tchr. of Yr. 1991), Nat. Assn. for Sports and Phys. Edn. Avocations: golf, fishing, travel. Home: 24338 Dawnridge Ct Eden Valley MN 55329

STRINGER, WILLIAM JEREMY, university official; b. Oakland, Calif., Nov. 8, 1944; s. William Duane and Mildred May (Andrus) S.; BA in English, So. Meth. U., 1966; MA in English, U. Wis., 1968, PhD in Ednl. Adminstrn., 1973; m. Susan Lee Hildebrand; children: Shannon Lee, Kelly Erin, Courtney Elizabeth. Dir. men's housing Southwestern U., Georgetown, Tex., 1968-69; asst. dir. housing U. Wis., Madison, 1969-73; dir. residential life, asso. dean student life, adj. prof. Pacific Luth., Tacoma, 1973-78; dir. residential life U. So. Calif., 1978-79, asst. v.p., 1979-84, asst. prof. higher and post-secondary edn., 1980-84; v.p. student life Seattle U., 1984-89, v.p. student devel., 1989-92, assoc. provost, 1989-95, assoc. prof. edn., 1990—, chair educational leadership, 1994—. Author: How to Survive as a Single Student, 1972, The Role of the Assistant in Higher Education, 1973. Bd. dirs. N.W. area Luth. Social Services of Wash. and Idaho, pres.-elect, 1989, pres., 1990-91. Danforth Found. grantee, 1976-77. Mem. AAUP, Am. Assn. Higher Edn., Nat. Assn. Student Pers. Adminstrs. (bd. dirs. region V 1985—, mem. editl. bd. Jour. 1995—), Am. Coll. Pers. Assn., Phi Eta Sigma, Sigma Tau Delta, Phi Alpha Theta. Lutheran. Home: 4553 169th Ave SE Bellevue WA 98006 Office: Seattle U Seattle WA 98122

STRINGFELLOW, GERALD B., engineering educator; b. Salt Lake City, Apr. 26, 1942; s. Paul Bennion and Jean (Barton) S.; m. Barbara Farr, June 9, 1962; children: Anne, Heather, Michael. BS, U. Utah, 1964; PhD, Stanford U., 1968. Staff scientist Hewlett Pacakrd Labs., Palo Alto, Calif., 1967-70, group mgr., 1970-80; prof. elec. engring., materials sci. U. Utah, Salt Lake City, 1980—; chmn., 1994—; adj. prof. physics U. Utah, Salt Lake City, 1988—; cons. Tex. Instruments, Dallas, 1995—, AT&T-Bell Labs., Holmdel, N.J., 1986-90, Brit. Telecom., London, 1989-92; editor-in-chief Phase Diagrams for Ceramics, Vol. IX. Author: Organometallic Vapor Phase Epitaxy, 1989; editor: Metal Organic Vapor Phase Epitaxy, 1986, American Crystal Growth, 1987, Alloy Semiconductor Physics and Electronics, 1989, Phase Equilibria Diagrams-Semiconductors and Chalcogenides, 1991, High Brightness LEDs, 1996; U.S. sr. editor Jour. Crystal Growth; letters editor Jour. Electronic Materials; contbr. over 300 articles to profl. jours. Recipient U.S. Sr. Scientist award Alexander von Humboldt Soc., Bonn, Germany, 1979; guest fellow Royal Soc., London, 1990. Fellow IEEE; mem. Am. Phys. Soc., Electronic Materials Com. (pres. 1985-87). Achievements include pioneering development of organometallic vapor phase epitaxy, development of theories of thermodynamic properties of alloy semiconductors; discovery of phenomenon of compositional latching in alloy semiconductor layers grown by epitaxial techniques. Home: 960 Donner Way Salt Lake City UT 84108-2167 Office: Dept Materials Sci Univ Utah 304 EMRO Salt Lake City UT 84112

STRINGFIELD, CHARLES DAVID, hospital administrator; b. Nashville, May 11, 1939; s. Ernest Jake Stringfield and Lucille (Lovelace) Birthright; m. Ruth Dvorak, Aug. 25, 1962; children—David Fisher, John Lovelace. B.A., Vanderbilt U., 1961; cert. tchr., George Peabody Coll., 1962, M.A. in Sch. Adminstrn., 1964; M.A. in Hosp. Adminstrn., Washington U., St. Louis, 1966. Tchr. Sch. Dist. No. 11, Colorado Springs, Colo., 1962-64; adminstrv. asst., adminstrv. resident Milwaukee County Instns., Milw., 1965-66; exec. dir. Tenn. Nursing Home Assn., Nashville, 1966-67; asst. dir. Tenn. Hosp. Assn., Nashville, 1966-68; adminstrv. dir. Bapt. Hosp., Inc., Nashville, 1968-70, exec. v.p., 1970-82, exec. v.p., chief exec. officer, 1981-82, pres., chief exec. officer, 1982—; pres. dedication of C. David Springfield Bldg. to Bapt. Hosp.; mem. governing bd. Mid.-Tenn. Eye Bank Found.; bd. dirs. NationaBank/Ctrl. South, Nashville Health Care Mgmt. Found./Comprehensive Care Ctr., 1993. Author: Hospital Administrator - Physician Relationships. Recipient 1st Ann. Arthritis Foun. Tribute, 1989, C. David Stringfield Dedicatory plaque Bapt. Women's Pavillion East at Mid. Tenn. Med. Ctr., Disting. Svc. award Tenn. Secondary Sch. Athletic Assn., 1993; named one of Nashville's 100 Most Influential Leaders, SOURCEBOOK, 1991, 92, one of Nashville's 100 Most Powerful People, Bus. Nashville, 1994, 95, 96. Fellow Am. Coll. Hosp. Adminstrs.; mem. Am. Hosp. Assn., Am. Nursing Home Assn., Southeastern Hosp. Assn., Vol. Hosps. of Am. (bd. dirs.). Lodge: Kiwanis. Office: Bapt Hosp 2000 Church St Nashville TN 37236-0001

STRINGFIELD, HEZZ, JR., contractor, financial consultant; b. Heiskell, Tenn., Oct. 4, 1921; s. Hezz and Cecil Willie (Williams) S.; m. Helen Louise Hinton, Mar. 20, 1939; children—Carolyn Mae Joyce (Mrs. James M. Corum), Don Wayne, Gail Louise (Mrs. John D. Gamble), Debra June (Mrs. Patrick T. Cassidy). Grad. bus. adminstr., Draughon Coll., 1939; student finance and bus., U. Tenn. Fin. and bus. adminstrn. exec. Clinton Engr. Works, E.I. duPont de Nemours & Co., 1943-44; Manhattan Dist. metall. project U. Chgo., 1944-45, Monsanto Chem. Co., 1945-48; nuclear div. Union Carbide Corp., 1948-77; ind. bldg. contractor, real estate developer, 1946—, cons. gen. bus., real estate financing, 1946—; pres. FBF, Inc., 1977—; with U.S. AID Mission to Middle East; cons. with industry, govt. and edn. in developing nations, 1965; bd. dirs. Found. Mgmt. Edn., Advanced Mgmt. Council, Council for Internat. Progress in Mgmt., Inc., Found. for Internat. Progress in Mgmt.; mem. Adv. Council Univs. and Colls. Fellow Soc. Advancement Mgmt. (Profl. Mgr. citation 1963, v.p. 1958-62, exec. v.p. 1962-63, pres. 1963-64, chmn. bd. 1964-65); mem. Am. Mgmt. Assn., Am. Inst. Accountants. Baptist. Home: 921 Laurel Hill Rd Knoxville TN 37923-2024 Office: 1201 Hilton Rd Knoxville TN 37921-5902

STRINGHAM, LUTHER WINTERS, economist, administrator; b. Colorado Springs, Colo., Dec. 14, 1915; s. Luther Wilson and Fern (Van Duyn) S.; m. Margret Ann Pringle, Dec. 1, 1942; 1 child, Susan Jean. B.A. summa cum laude, U. Colo., 1938, M.A. in Econs, 1939; Rockefeller fellow pub. adminstrn., U. Minn., 1939-40, Nat. Inst. Pub. Affairs, 1940-41. Economist Dept. Commerce, also OPA, 1941-43; intelligence officer Def. Dept., 1946-55; program analysis officer Office of the Sec. HEW, 1956-63, chmn. sec.'s com. mental retardation, 1961-63; exec. dir. Nat. Assn. for Retarded Children, 1963-68; intergovtl. relations officer HEW, 1968-77; planning dir. Central Va. Health Systems Agy., 1977-83. Dir. TV series Healthy Virginians, 1981-83. Mem. Pres.'s Com. Employment Handicapped, 1963-68; pres. Music for People, Inc., 1971-74; lectr. CUNY, 1971-76; mem. nat. coun. Boy Scouts Am., 1963-83; co-founder Older Virginians for Action, 1983-84; bd. dirs. Capital Area Agy. Aging, 1984-87; Midlothian Dist. rep. Keep Chesterfield Clean Corp., 1992-94; mem. Quality Coun. Greater Richmond, 1993-94. Capt. AUS, 1943-46; lt. col. USAFR, 1946-56. Mem. Am. Econ. Assn., Phi Beta Kappa, Pi Gamma Mu, Delta Sigma Rho. Home: 3101 Mount Hill Dr Midlothian VA 23113-3932

STRINGHAM, RENÉE, physician; b. Mpls., July 16, 1940; d. Clifford Leonard and Helen Pearl (Marcineak) Heinrich; children: Lars Eric, Leif Erik, Lance Devon. BS, St. Lawrence U., 1962; MD, U. Ky., 1972. Diplomate Am. Bd. Family Practice. Intern U. Fla., Gainesville, 1972-73; physician Lee County Coop. Clinic, Marianna, Ark., 1973-74; pvt. practice Coastal Health Practitioners, Lincoln City, Oreg., 1975-84; county health officer Lincoln County Health Dept., Newport, Oreg., 1986-90; pvt. practice, 1984-90; student health Miami U., Oxford, Ohio, 1991-93; cons. student health Willamette U., 1994—; contract physician West Salem Clinic, 1994; trustee Coast Home Nursing, Lincoln County, 1984-86; expert witness EPA, 1980—. Facilitator Exceptional Living, 1984-86. Fellow Am. Acad. Family Practice; mem. Lincoln County Med. Soc. (pres. 1984), Oreg. Med. Assn. Avocations: spontaneous music, folk dancing, sailing.

STRINGILE, MARIE ELIZABETH, educational administrator; b. Bayonne, N.J., May 13, 1954; d. Orlando Salvatore and Amelia Mary (Prisco) S. BA in edn., Jersey State Coll., 1976; MA in adminstrn., St. Peter's Coll., 1988. Cert. elem. tchr., prin./supr., sch. adminstr., N.J. Tchr. St. James Sch., Newark, N.J., 1976-79; remedial math tchr. Ind. Child Study Teams, Jersey City, N.J., 1979-88, assoc. dir., 1988-90, adminstr., 1990—; data documentation monitor Ind. Child Study Teams, Jersey City, 1990—, testing and curriculum specialist, 1990—, staff inservices, 1990—, data collection on all eligible remedial students, 1990—; cons. Devel. Remedial Math. Curriculum, 1993, resource room, 1985-88. Bd. dirs. O.L. Assumption Sch. Bd., 1991-93. Mem. ASCD, Sisters of St. Joseph of Peace (assoc.), Nat. Coun. Tchrs. Math., Disabled Vets. Am., Medic Alert Found., Handyman Club Am., Black Seal Boiler Operator. Avocations: carpentry, gardening, reading, mechanics, educational research. Home: 133 W 25th St Bayonne NJ 07002-1715 Office: Ind Child Study Teams Inc 377 Danforth Ave Jersey City NJ 07305-1904

STRIP, CAROL ANN, gifted education specialist, educator; b. Jackson, Mich., July 3, 1945; d. Harold Don and Marion Estelle (Diemer) Gillespie; m. Asriel Strip, June 15, 1978 (div. Dec. 1992); 1 child, Julie Kay. BS, Western Mich. U., 1966, MA, 1969; PhD, Ohio State U, 1994. Cert. elem. prin., Mich.; cert. supr., ednl. specialist, Ohio. Kindergarten tchr. Kalamazoo (Mich.) Pub. Schs., 1967-74, primary tchr., 1974-75, 76-78, title 1-B adminstr., 1975-76; 4th grade tchr. Westerville (Ohio) City Schs., 1978-83; enrichment specialist Dublin (Ohio) City Schs., 1983-88, gifted edn. coord., 1988-94, gifted edn. specialist, 1988-94, gifted edn. specialist, tchr., 1994—; adv. bd. mem. Ohio Wesleyan Jr. League, Delaware, 1987—, Dublin Arts Coun., 1989—; workshop presenter. Contbr. articles to profl. jours. Bd. dirs. Friends of the Libr., Columbus, 1978-83; com. mem. Ohio State Fair Orphans Day Com., Columbus, 1983-90. Recipient Master of Comms. award Ednl. Facilities Ctr., 1975, Golden Apple Achiever award Ashland Oil, 1993, Silver Anvil award AMA, 1972; named Ctrl. Mich. Tchr. of Yr., 1976. Fellow ASCD, Ohio Assn. Supervision Curriculum Devel., Sch. Study Coun. of Ohio, Ctrl. Ohio Coord. of Gifted, Alpha Chi Omega; mem. NEA, Ohio Ednl. Assn., Nat. Ret. Tchrs. Assn., Ohio Assn. of Gifted Children (regional rep. 1994, Outstanding Educator of Yr. 1994), Gifted Coord. of Ctrl. Ohio (pres. 1992-93), Alpha Delta Kappa. Republican. Avocations: reading, travel, music, theatre, museums. Home: 8929 Turin Hill Dublin OH 43017 Office: Dublin City Schs 7030 Coffman Rd Dublin OH 43017-1068

STRISIK, PAUL, artist; b. Bklyn., Apr. 21, 1918; s. Abraham Roger and Reine Rose (Rehbock) S.; m. Nancy Susan Samaras, Nov. 16, 1968; children: Peter, John Catherine, Ellen. Student, Art Students League, N.Y.C., 1946-48. Tchr. workshops, lectr. throughout, U.S. and, Europe; tchr. Scottsdale (Ariz.) Artists Sch., Nov. 1986, 88; mng. dir. Hall Line Co., Highland Mills, N.Y., 1937-40; dir. Empire Twine & Yarn Co., N.Y.C., 1945-69. Author: The Art of Landscape Painting, 1980, Capturing Light in Oils, 1995; One-man exhbns. include, Grand Central Art Galleries, N.Y.C., 1971-84, Doll & Richards, Boston, 1965, 76, Rockport (Mass.) Art Assn., 1964-69, 75, Andover (Mass.) Gallery Fine Arts, 1969, Gordon Coll., Wenham, Mass., 1972, Johnson-Welch Gallery, Kansas City, Mo., 1978, Francesca Anderson Gallery, Boston, 1986, Dodson Gallery, Oklahoma City, 1990, So. Vt. Art Ctr., Manchester, 1994; group exhbns. include, Nat. Acad. Art, 1955-93, Allied Artists Am., N.Y.C., 1971-94, Salmagundi Club, N.Y.C., 1962-88, Knickerbocker Artists, N.Y.C., 1963-95, Am. Watercolor Soc., N.Y.C., 1963-91, Rockport Art Assn., 1956-95, North Shore Arts Assn., Gloucester, Mass., 1956-95, Am. Artists Profl. League, N.Y.C., 1960-95, Cowboy Hall of Fame, Oklahoma City, 1978-95, Artists of Am., Denver, 1981-95, NAD, 1970-93, Catto Gallery, London, 1992, Royal Watercolor Soc., London, 1992; rep. permanent collections, Parrish Mus. Art, Southampton, N.Y., Percy H. Whitney Mus., Fairhope, Ala., Mattatuck Mus., Conn., Utah State U., Peabody Mus., Salem, Mass.; appeared on NBC Today Show (TV), July, 1987. Bd. govs. Rockport Bd. Trade, 1958-60. Served with USN, 1941-45. Recipient over 170 awards, including 15 gold medals; Windsor and Newton award Knickerbocker Artists, 1965; medal of merit, 1972; FAS award Allied Artists Am., 1965; Lehrer Meml. award, 1970; Wick award Salmagundi Club, 1967; Chandler award, 1967; AWS award, 1970; Salmagundi award, 1970-73; gold medal Marsh ann. exhbn., 1967, 71; gold medal Rockport Art Assn., 1967, 72, 87, 90; Best in Show award Am. Artists Profl. League grand. nat., 1968, 72; A. Dedn award Am. Watercolor Soc., 1969; Lehman award, 1970; gold medal Hudson Valley Art Assn., 1970, Bohnert award, 1989; Ray Jones Gold medal Am. Vets. Soc. Artists, 1970; Watercolor prize Nat. Arts Club, 1970; bronze medal, 1960; Obrig prize Nat. Acad., 1972; silver medal Arts Atlantic, Mass., 1972; Gold medal Franklin Mint Gallery Am. Art, 1974; Arthur T. Hill Meml. award Salmagundi Club, 1974; Helen Gould Kennedy award Acad. Artists Ann., 1974; Claude Parsons Meml. award Am. Artists Profl. League, 1975; Grumbacher award Acad. Artists, 1975; Philip G. Shumaker award Rockport Art Assn., 1975; honored by Rockport Art Assn., 1988; Elizabeth Schlemm award, 1975; Canelli Gold Medal for oils, 1975; Isabel Steinschneider Meml. award Hudson Valley Art Assn., 1980, also Dumond award 1990; spl. tribute to Paul Strisik Hudson Valley Art Assn., 1982, 88; Silver medal Acad. Artists Assn., Springfield, Mass., 1980, Rockport Art Assn., 1993; Gold medal Academic Artists Assn., 1986, Frank Vincent Dumond Meml. award Hudson Valley Art Assn., N.Y., 1990, 94, Frank Vincent Dumond $1,000 award Hudson Valley Art Assn., N.Y., 1995; named Artist of Yr. Santa Fe, N.Mex. Rotary, 1986, over 170 awards including 15 Gold medals. Mem. NAD (academician), Nat. Acad. Western Art (gold medal 1981, 84), Oil Painters Am., Rockport Art Assn. (pres. 1968-71), Am. Watercolor Soc., Allied Artists Am., Knickerbocker Artists, Internat. Soc. Marine Painters, Am. Artists Profl. League (award 1980), Am. Acad. Taos, N. Shore Arts Assn., Santa Fe Watercolor Soc., Rockport C. of C. Club: Salmagundi. Home: 123 Marmion Way Rockport MA 01966-1928

STRITTMATTER, PETER ALBERT, astronomer, educator; b. London, Eng., Sept. 12, 1939; came to U.S., 1970.; s. Albert and Rosa S.; m. Janet Hubbard Parkhurst, Mar. 18, 1967; children—Catherine D., Robert P. B.A., Cambridge U., Eng., 1961, M.A., 1963, Ph.D., 1967. Staff scientist Inst. for Astronomy, Cambridge, Eng., 1967-70; staff scientist dept. physics U. Calif.-San Diego, La Jolla, 1970-71; assoc. prof. dept. astronomy U. Ariz.,

Tucson, 1971-74, prof. dept. astronomy, 1974—, Regent's prof., 1994—; dir. Steward Observatory, Tucson, 1975—; mem. staff Max Planck Inst. Radioastronomy, Bonn, W. Germany, 1981—. Contbr. articles to profl. jours. Recipient Sr. award Humboldt Found., 1979-80. Fellow Royal Astron. Soc.; mem. Am. Astron. Soc., Astronomische Gesellschaft. Office: U Ariz Steward Observatory Tucson AZ 85721

STROBEL, DARRELL FRED, planetary science, physics and astronomy educator; b. Fargo, N.D., May 13, 1942; married, 1968; 2 children. BS, N.D. State U., 1964; AM, Harvard U., 1965, PhD in Applied Physics, 1969. Rsch. assoc. planetary astronomer Kitt Peak Nat. Obs., 1968-70, ast. physicist, 1970-72, assoc. physicist, 1972-73, rsch. physicist, 1973-76; supr. rsch. physicist Naval Rsch. Lab., 1976-84; prof. planetary sci., earth sci., physics and astronomy Johns Hopkins U., Balt., 1984—; mem. space sci. bd. NAS-NRC. Mem. AAAS, Am. Astron. Soc., Am. Geophys. Union, Am. Meteorol. Soc., Internat. Astron. Union. Achievements include research in chemistry, dynamics, and physics of planetary atmospheres; planetary aeronomy; planetary physics; planetary magetosphers. Office: Johns Hopkins/ Ctr Astrophys Sci 3400 N Charles St Baltimore MD 21218-2608*

STROBEL, MARTIN JACK, motor vehicle and industrial component manufacturing and distribution company executive; b. N.Y.C., July 4, 1940; s. Nathan and Clara (Sorgen) S.; m. Hadassah Orenstein, Aug. 15, 1965; children: Gil Michael, Karen Rachel. BA, Columbia U., 1962; JD, Cleve. Marshall Law Sch., 1966; completed advanced bus. mgmt. program, Harvard U., 1977. Bar: Ohio bar 1966. Counsel def. contract adminstrn. services region Def. Supply Agy., Cleve., 1966-68; with Dana Corp., Toledo, 1968—; gen. counsel Dana Corp., 1970—, dir. govt. relations, 1970-71, asst. sec., 1971—, v.p., 1976—, sec., 1982—. Mem. ABA, Fed. Bar Assn., Machinery and Allied Products Inst., Ohio Bar Assn., Toledo Bar Assn. Office: Dana Corp PO Box 1000 Toledo OH 43697-1000

STROBEL, PAMELA B., lawyer; b. Chgo., Sept. 9, 1952. BS highest honors, U. Ill., 1974, JD cum laude, 1977. Bar: Ill. 1977, U.S. Dist. (ctrl. and no. dists.) Ill. 1977, U.S. Ct. Appeals (7th cir.) 1981, U.S. Claims Ct. 1983, U.S. Ct. Appeals (fed. cir.) 1985. Ptnr. Sidley & Austin, Chgo. Mem. Kappa Tau Alpha (staff 1975-77). Office: Commonwealth Edison Co PO Box 767 Chicago IL 60690-0767*

STROBEL, RUSS M., lawyer; b. N.Y.C., May 2, 1952. BA, Northwestern U., 1974; JD magna cum laude, U. Ill., 1977. Bar: Ill. 1977. Ptnr. Jenner & Block, Chgo. Mem. ABA, Ill. State Bar Assn., Chgo. Bar Assn. Office: Jenner & Block 1 E IBM PLz Chicago IL 60611

STROBER, MYRA HOFFENBERG, education educator, consultant; b. N.Y.C., Mar. 28, 1941; d. Julius William Hoffenberg and Regina Scharer; m. Samuel Strober, June 23, 1963 (div. Dec. 1983); children: Jason M., Elizabeth A.; m. Jay M. Jackman, Oct. 21, 1990. BS in Indsl. Rels., Cornell U., 1962; MA in Econs., Tufts U., 1965; PhD in Econs., MIT, 1969. Lectr., asst. prof. dept. econs. U. Md., College Park, 1967-70; lectr. U. Calif., Berkeley, 1970-72; asst. prof. grad. sch. bus. Stanford (Calif.) U., 1972-86, assoc. prof. sch. edn., 1979-90, prof., 1990—, assoc. dean acad. affairs, 1993-95, interim dean, 1994; organizer Stanford Bus. Conf. Women Mgmt., 1974; founding dir. ctr. rsch. women Stanford U., 1974-76, 79-84, dir. edn. policy inst., 1984-86, dean alumni coll., 1992, mem. policy and planning bd., 1992-93, chair program edn. adminstrn. and policy analysis, 1991-93, chair provost's com. recruitment and retention women faculty, 1992-93, chair faculty senate com. on coms., 1992-93; mem. adv. bd. State of Calif. Office Econ. Policy Planning and Rsch., 1978-80; mem. Coll. Bd. Com. Develop Advanced Placement Exam. Econs., 1987-88; faculty advisor Rutgers Women's Leadership Program, 1991-93. Author: (with others) Industrial Relations, 1972, Sex, Discrimination and the Division of Labor, 1975, Changing Roles of Men and Women, 1976, Women in the Labor Market, 1979, Educational Policy and Management: Sex Differentials, 1981, Women in the Workplace, 1982, Sex Segregation in the Workplace: Trends, Explanations, Remedies, 1984, The New Palgrave: A Dictionary of Economic Theory and Doctrine, 1987, Computer Chips and Paper Clips: Technology and Women's Employment, Vol. II, 1987, Gender in the Workplace, 1987; editor: (with Francine E. Gordon) Bringing Women Into Management, 1975, (with others) Women and Poverty, 1986, (with Sanford M. Dornbusch) Feminism, Children and the New Families, 1988; mem. bd. editors Signs: Jour. Women Culture and Soc., 1975-89, assoc. editor, 1980-85; mem. bd. editors Sage Ann. Rev. Women and Work, 1984—; mem. editorial adv. bd. U.S.-Japan Women's Jour., 1991—; assoc. editor Jour. Econ. Edn., 1991—; contbr. chpt. to book. Mem. rsch. adv. task force YWCA, 1989—; chair exec. bd. Stanford Hillel, 1990-92; bd. dirs. Resource Ctr. Women, Palo Alto, Calif., 1983-84; pres. bd. dirs. Kaider Found., Mountain View, Calif., 1990—. Fellow Stanford U., 1975-77, Schiff House Resident fellow, 85-87. Mem. NOW (bd. dirs. legal def. and edn. fund 1993—), Am. Econ. Assn. (mem. com. status of women in the profession 1972-75), Am. Ednl. Rsch. Assn., Indsl. Rels. Rsch. Assn. Office: Stanford U School of Education Stanford CA 94305

STROBER, SAMUEL, immunologist, educator; b. N.Y.C., May 8, 1940; s. Julius and Lee (Lander) S.; m. Linda Carol Higgins, July 6, 1991; children: William, Jesse; children from previous marriage: Jason, Elizabeth. AB in Liberal Arts, Columbia U., 1961; MD magna cum laude, Harvard U., 1966. Intern Mass. Gen. Hosp., Boston, 1966-67; resident in internal medicine Stanford U. Hosp., Calif., 1970-71; rsch. fellow Peter Bent Brigham Hosp., Boston, 1962-63, 65-66, Oxford U., Eng., 1963-64; rsch. assoc. Lab. Cell Biology, Nat. Cancer Inst., NIH, Bethesda, Md., 1967-70; instr. medicine Stanford U., 1971-72, asst. prof., 1972-78, assoc. prof. medicine, 1978-82, prof. medicine, 1982—, Diane Goldstone Meml. lectr., John Putnam Merrill Meml. lectr., chief div. immunology and rheumatology, 1978—; investigator Howard Hughes Med. Inst., Miami, Fla., 1976-81. Assoc. editor Jour. Immunology, 1981-84, Transplantation, 1981-85, Internat. Jour. Immunotherapy, 1985—, Transplant Immunology, 1992—; contbr. articles to profl. jours. bd. dirs. La Jolla Inst. for Allergy and Immunology; founder Activated Cell Therapy, Inc. Served with USPHS, 1967-70. Recipient Leon Reznick Meml. Research prize Harvard U., 1966. Mem. Am. Assn. Immunology, Am. Soc. Clin. Investigation, Am. Rheumatism Assn., Transplantation Soc. (councilor 1986-89), Am. Soc. Transplantation Physicians, Western Soc. Medicine, Am. Assn. Physicians, Clin. Immunology Soc. (pres. 1996), Alpha Omega. Home: 435 Golden Oak Dr Menlo Park CA 94028-7734 Office: Stanford U Sch Medicine 300 Pasteur Dr Palo Alto CA 94305

STROBERT, BARBARA, principal. Prin. Watchung Sch., Montclair, N.J. Recipient Elem. Sch. Recognition award U.S. Dept. Edn., 1989-90. Office: Watchung Sch 14 Garden St Montclair NJ 07042-4116

STROCK, ARTHUR VAN ZANDT, architect; b. Los Angeles, Sept. 14, 1945; s. Arthur and Eileen (Cortelyou) S.; m. Hallie vonAmmon, Mar. 22, 1969. BArch, U. Calif., Berkeley, 1971. Registered profl. architect. Asst. dean Sch. Architecture and Fine Arts U. So. Calif., Los Angeles, 1970-71; designer Allied Architects, Long Beach, Calif., 1971-73; architect Langdon and Wilson, Newport Beach, Calif., 1973-77, Lee & Strock Architects, Newport Beach, 1978-82, Strock Architects, Inc., Newport Beach, 1982-91, Pacmar Strock Group, Newport Beach, Calif., 1992—, Strock Group; guest lectr. U. Calif., Irvine; guest speaker Pacific Coast Deisgn Conf., Monterey, Calif.; mng. ptnr., head design team Shantou World Trade Ctr., Racetrack Ctr. Prin. works include I.R.W.D. Bldg., 1979 (Merit award 1982), Newport/Irvine Ctr., 1980 (Merit award 1982), Bay Corp. Ctr., 1982 (Merit award 1984), Scripps Ctr., 1985, Long Beach Airport Bus. Park, 1986, Orange County Register Hdqrs., 1986. Pres. Beacon Bay Cmty. Assn., Newport Beach, 1985-86; bd. dirs. Nat. History Found. of Orange County, 1982; bd. dirs. Bowers Mus., 1987—, pres., 1988-90, chmn., 1991-94. Fellow AIA; mem. Assn. Univ. Related Rsch. Pks., Urban Land Inst.(internat. coun.), Newport Harbor yacht Club, Sigma Chi, U.S. Sailing (sr. judge). Republican. Avocations: yachting, fishing, tennis. Home: 23 Beacon Bay Newport Beach CA 92660-7218 Office: Strock Group 23 Beacon Bay Newport Beach CA 92660

STROCK, GERALD E., school system administrator. Supt. Hatboro-Horsham (Pa.) Sch. Dist. State finalist Nat. Supt. Yr., 1993. Office: Hatboro-Horsham Sch Dist 229 Meetinghouse Rd Horsham PA 19044-2119

STROCK, HERBERT LEONARD, motion picture producer, director, editor, writer; b. Boston, Jan. 13, 1918; s. Maurice and Charlotte Ruth (Nesselroth) S.; m. Geraldine Pollinger, Dec. 25, 1941; children: Leslie Carol, Genoa Ellen, Candice Dell. B.A., U. So. Calif., 1941, M.A., 1942. Asst. editor Metro-Goldwyn-Mayer, Culver City, Calif., 1941-42; producer IMPPRO, Culver City, 1946-51; film editor Hal Roach Studios, Culver City, 1951-53; dir., film editor Ian Tors Prodns., Culver City, 1951-58; dir. ZIV Prodns., Hollywood, Calif., 1956-61, Warner Bros., Burbank, Calif., 1958-63; ind. dir., pres. Herbert L. Strock Prodns., Hollywood, Calif., 1963—; pres., chmn. bd. Hollywood World Films Inc., lectr. U. So. Calif. Producer, dir.: I Led Three Lives, Mr. District Attorney, Favorite Story, Corliss Archer, Science Fiction Theater, Highway Patrol, Dr. Christian, Man Called X, Harbor Command, 1954; dir. Battle Taxi; assoc. producer, dir.: Tom Swift series,(TV shows) Mann of Action, Red Light and Siren Sky King; Maverick, Alaskans, Colt 45, Bronco, Cheyenne, 77 Sunset Strip, Bonanza, Hans Brinker Spl., Decisions-Decisions, (feature pictures) Perfect World of Rodney Brewster, I Was a Teenage Frankenstein, Blood of Dracula, How to Make a Monster, Rider on a Dead Horse, Strike Me Deadly, Search the Wild Wind, Magnetic Monster, Riders to the Stars, Gog - Storm Over Tibet; editor, dir.: The Crawling Hand, One Hour of Hell; editorial supr. Shark; writer, dir. Brother on the Run; editor: So Evil My Sister, Chamber-Mades; co-producer Small Miracle; editor, dir. (documentary) They Search for Survival; supervising film editor Hunger Telethon; editor (spl.) The Making of America, co-writer, film editor Hurray for Betty Boop; dir., chief prodn. coordinator for Miss World, 1976; editor (documentary) UFO Journals, UFO Syndrome, Legends, all 1979; co-dir., film editor Witches Brew, 1979; writer, film editor (TV series) Flipper, 1981. Editor post prodn. services: China--Mao to Now, Eucatastrophe, Tibet, El Papa, Night Screams, King Kung Fu; dir., editor Deadly Presence; producer, writer, dir. (med. documentary) A New Lease on Life; editor Snooze You Lose, Olympic Legacy, Water You Can Trust, Directions, Fish Outta Water; dir., editor Gramma's Gold; co-editor Infinity, Peaceful Sabbath; producer, writer, dir. (fund raising documentary) Combined Federal Campaign; co-dir., film editor Gramma's Gold; editor Detour; editor (experimental film) This Old Man..., Sidewalk Motel; dir. Electric God. Served with U.S. Army, 1940-41. Mem. Acad. Motion Picture Arts and Scis., Dirs. Guild Am., Am. Cinema Editors (dir., bd. mem. 1984-85), Motion Picture Editors Guild, Delta Kappa Alpha (pres. 1941-65), Film and Videotape Editors Guild. Democrat. Avocation: photography. Office: Herbert L Strock Prodns 6311 Romaine St Los Angles CA 90038-2600

STROCK, JAMES MARTIN, state agency administrator, lawyer, conservationist; b. Austin, Tex., Aug. 19, 1956; s. James Martin Strock Sr. and Augusta (Tenney) Mullins. AB, Harvard U., 1977, JD, 1981; postgrad, New Coll. Oxford U., 1981-82. Bar: Colo. 1983. Teaching fellow dept. govt. Harvard U., 1980-81; spl. cons. to majority leader U.S. Senate, Washington, 1982-83; spl. asst. to adminstr. EPA, Washington, 1983-85, asst. adminstr. for enforcement, 1989-91; spl. counsel U.S. Senate Com. on Environment and Pub. Works, Washington, 1985-86; environ. atty. Davis, Graham & Stubbs, Denver, 1986-88; acting dir., gen. counsel U.S. Office Pers. Mgmt., Washington, 1988-89; sec. for environ. protection State of Calif., Sacramento, 1991—; mem. bd. advisors CALSTART, 1993—, The Environ. Tech. Export Coun., 1993—, Toxics Law Reporter, 1987-89, Greenwire, 1991—; mem. Intergovtl. Policy Adv. Com., rep. U.S. Trade, 1991—. Contbr. articles to profl. jours.; moderator, producer Lay It On The Line, Sta. WDSU-TV, New Orleans, 1973-74. Bd. dirs. Youth Svc. Am., Washington, 1988-89, Environ. Law Inst., 1992—; nat. chair Bush Campaign Environ. Coalition, 1992. Capt. JAGC USAR, 1987-96. Recipient Retsie Arco Future award, 1992, Ross Essay award ABA, 1985, Environ. Leadership award Calif. Environ. Bus. Coun., 1994; Charles Joseph Bonaparte scholar Harvard U., 1976, Rotary Internat. scholar, 1981-82. Mem. Coun. on Fgn. Rels., Phi Beta Kappa. Republican. Office: 555 Capitol Mall Ste 525 Sacramento CA 95814-4503

STRODE, DEBORAH LYNN, English language educator; b. Ft. Dodge, Iowa, June 18, 1948; d. Franklin Max and Helen (Crook) S. BS in Speech and Theater, Parsons Coll., 1971; teaching cert., Boise State U., 1977; MS in Edn., So. Oreg. State U., 1985; adminstrv. cert., U. Alaska, Anchorage, 1986. Cert. tchr. Alaska, cert. adminstr., Nev. Tchr. U.S. Peace Corps., Liberia, West Africa, 1971-73; tchr., adminstr. North Slope Borough Sch. Dist., Barrow, Alaska, 1976-90; adminstr. fed. programs Iditarod Area Sch. Dist., McGrath, Alaska, 1990-91; vis. tchr. English Nishinomiya (Hyogo, Japan) Mcpl. Edn. Bd., 1993—; dir. childrens receiving home North Slope Borough Health Dept., Barrow, summer 1978. Supporting mem. Friends of Liberia, Washington; counselor McLaughlin Youth Detention Ctr., summer 1975; counselor Long and Short House Alaska Children's Svcs., 1974; treas. Barrow PTA; sponsor Internat. Thespian Soc.; active Fairfax County Pub. Access TV. Mem. NEA, Alaska Arts in Edn., Am. Theater Assn., Returned Peace Corps Vol. Assn., North Slope Adminstrn. Assn., North Slope Edn. Assn. (v.p.), Secondary Theater Assn., Childrens Theater Assn.

STRODE, GEORGE K., sports editor; b. Amesville, Ohio, Nov. 10, 1935; s. Mac and Edith M. (Murphey) S.; m. Jennifer Lanning (div. 1973); m. Ruth E. Wingett, July 15, 1973. BJ, Ohio U., 1958. Sports editor Zanesville (Ohio) Times Reporter, 1958, Athens (Ohio) Messenger, 1958-62; sports reporter Dayton (Ohio) Daily News, 1962-63, Columbus (Ohio) Citizen Jour., 1963-69; Ohio sports editor AP, Columbus, 1969-85; sports editor Columbus Dispatch, 1985—. Mem. Ohio AP Sports Writers Assn. (v.p. 1984—), U.S. Golf Writers Assn., U.S. Harness Writers Assn. (pres. Ohio chpt. 1968-69). Republican. Methodist. Avocations: golfing, horse racing. Office: Columbus Dispatch 34 S 3rd St Columbus OH 43215-4201

STRODE, WILLIAM HALL, III, photojournalist, publisher; b. Louisville, Aug. 6, 1937; s. William Hall and Margaret (Diehl) S.; m. Elizabeth Ann Wheeler, Nov. 26, 1960 (div. 1973); children: Alissa Michelle, Erin Hall; m. Hope Powel Alexander, Nov. 12, 1977; children: Hope Ives, Charlotte Alexander. BS, Western Ky. U., 1959. News photographer Courier Jour. and Louisville Times, 1960-64, asst. dir. photography, 1968-75; photographer Courier Jour. mag., 1964-77; formed William Strode Assocs., photog. and pub. co., Louisville, 1978—, Harmony House pubs., 1984—. Author 16 books; exhbns. include Fine Arts III, 1961, Profile in Poverty, Smithsonian Instn., 1966, Documerica, in Corcoran Gallery, Washington, 1972, 73, Picture of the Year Travelling Exhibits; one man show includes Speed Mus. Active local Boy Scouts Am.; founder Nat. Press Photographers Found., 1975. Served with AUS, 1959. Recipient Headliners best photojournalism award, 1965; award for excellence for best mag. photog. reporting Overseas Press Club, 1967; co-recipient Pulitzer Prize for pub. service Courier Jour., 1967, for feature photography, 1976; Art Dirs. Gold medal, 1980, World Press Photog. Arts and Scis. award, 1985. Mem. Nat. Press Photographers Assn. (nat. ednl. chmn. 1966-68, v.p. 1973, pres. 1974, Photographer of Yr. 1966, Newspaper Mag. Picture Editor of Yr. 1968), Am. Soc. Mag. Photographers, Soc. Profl. Journalists, Sigma Chi, Kappa Alpha Mu. Methodist. Home and Office: 1008 Kent Rd Goshen KY 40026-9768

STRODEL, ROBERT CARL, lawyer; b. Evanston, Ill., Aug. 12, 1930; s. Carl Frederick and Imogene (Board) S.; m. Mary Alice Shonkwiler, June 17, 1956; children: Julie Ann, Linda Lee, Sally Payson. BS, Northwestern U., 1952; JD, U. Mich., 1955. Bar: Ill. 1955, U.S. Supreme Ct. 1970; diplomate Am. Bd. Profl. Liability Attys., Am. Bd. Forensic Examiners; cert. civil trial specialist Am. Bd. Trial Advocacy. Mem. firm Davis, Morgan & Witherell, Peoria, Ill., 1957-59; sole practice Peoria, 1959-69; prin. Strodel, Kingery & Durree Assoc., Peoria, Ill., 1969-92, Law Offices of Robert C. Strodel, Ltd., Peoria, 1992—; asst. state's atty. Peoria, 1960-61; instr. bus. law Bradley U., Peoria, 1961-62; lectr. Belli seminars, 1969-87; lectr. in trial practice; mem. U.S. Presdl. Commn. German-Am. Tricentennial, 1983. Author books and articles in med.-legal field. Gov. appointee Ill. Dangerous Drugs Advisory Council, 1970-73; gen. chmn. Peoria-Tazewell Easter Seals, 1963, Cancer Crusade, 1970; pres. Peoria Civic Ballet, 1969-70; mem. Mayor's Commn. on Human Relations, 1962-64; chmn. City of Peoria Campaign Ethics Bd., 1975; Peoria County Rep. Sec., 1970-74; campaign chmn. Gov. Richard Ogilvie, Peoria County, 1972, Sen. Ralph Smith, 1970; treas. Michel for Congress, 1977—, campaign coordinator, 1982; bd. dirs. Crippled Children's Center, 1964-65, Peoria Symphony Orchestra, 1964-68. Served with AUS, 1956-57. Decorated Officer's Cross of Order of Merit (Fed. Republic Germany), 1984; named Outstanding Young Man Peoria Peoria Jr. C. of C., 1963. Mem. Assn. Trial Lawyers Am. (bd. govs. 1987—), Ill. Trial Lawyers Assn. (bd. mgrs. 1985—), ABA, Ill. Bar Assn. (Lincoln awards for legal writing 1961, 63, 65), Am. Coll. Legal Medicine, Am. Soc. Law and Medicine, Am. Inns of Ct. (charter master of bench, Lincoln Inn-Peoria, Ill.). Club: Mason (Shriner). Home: 3908 N Pinehurst Ct Peoria IL 61614-7246 Office: Commerce Bank Bldg Ste 927 Peoria IL 61602 *The pursuit of professional excellence has been a lifetime goal, coupled with contributions to public, political and civic affairs. He who takes from his community must also contribute to it.*

STROEMPLE, RUTH MARY THOMAS, social welfare administrator; b. Cleve., Jan. 31, 1923; d. Daniel William and Jeanette Alexandria (Webb) Thomas; m. Robert Theodore Stroemple, July 27, 1944 (dec. July 1991); children: Susan, George, Janet, Gayle. BA in Child Devel., Marylhurst Coll., 1981. Specialist infant care Oreg. Health Scis. U., Portland, 1976-85, Emanuel Hosp., Portland, 1986-87; mem. failure to thrive rsch. team Doernbecher Hosp., Portland, 1978-85; founder, dir. Newborn Connection, Portland, 1986-90; founder, dir. Med. Foster Parent Program Childrens' Svcs. Divsn., Portland, 1976-94; specialist infant assessment Foster Parent Program, Childrens' Svcs. Divsn., Portland, 1990-94, cons., trainer, 1991-94; team leader sensory stimulation program Infant Dystrophy Ctr., Romania; cons. in field. Author: (booklet) Infant Sensory Stimulation, 1986, (manual) Newborn Connection Hospital, 1986, (tng. manual) Medical Foster Parent Handbook, 1990. Ctr. Child Abuse & Neglect grantee, 1991; recipient Golden Rule award J.C. Penny, Portland, 1993. Mem. Infant Devel. Edn. Assn. (cert. instr.), Infant Massage Assn. (cert. instr.), Foster Parent Assn. Avocations: gardening, reading, hiking, family activities. Home: 12535 SW Tooze Rd Sherwood OR 97140-8442

STROESENREUTHER, GEORGE DALE, financial executive; b. Milw., Aug. 13, 1954; s. George Dale and Alice Marie (Raisler) S.; m. Karen Lee Daniels, Aug. 29, 1981 (div. Oct. 1984); 1 child, Jason Dale; m. Lynn Louise Lloyd, Feb. 2, 1985 (div. Apr. 1995); children: Timothy George, Steven Douglas; m. LiLi Xin, Apr. 13, 1995; 1 child, George Dale III. BBA, U. Wis., 1976. CPA, Wis., N.C., Ill. Internal auditor Allis Chalmers Corp., Milw., 1977-79, sr. fin. analyst, 1979-80, mgr. cost acctg., inventory control, 1980-82; supr. cost acctg. Abbott Labs., Rocky Mount, N.C., 1982, bus. unit controller, 1982-84; sr. div. analyst Abbott Labs., North Chicago, Ill., 1984-85, plant controller, materials mgr., 1985-87; dir. internal audit Outboard Marine Corp., Waukegan, Ill., 1987-88, Asea Brown Boveri, Inc., New Berlin, Wis., 1988-90; v.p. fin., CFO ABB Process Automation, Inc., Columbus, Ohio, 1990-91, ABB Traction Inc., Elmira Heights, N.Y., 1991; fin. contr. Ams.-Pacific and Far East, Cleve., 1992-95; contr., CFO Bailey Fischer & Porter of Elsag Bailey Process Automation, Cleve., 1995; CFO US Assist Inc., Bethesda, Md., 1996—; dir. Harbor West Assn., Rocky Mount, 1983-84. Treas. Students for an Accessible Soc., Whitewater, 1976-78. Mem. AICPA, Il. CPA Soc. (industry com. 1986-88), Ohio Soc. CPAs (industry com. 1991), Inst. Internal Auditors. Republican. Lutheran. Avocations: fishing, golf, volleyball. Office: US Assist Inc 6903 Rockledge Dr Ste 800 Bethesda MD 20817 *There is a lot of truth to the statement "The only thing constant in life is change". Those that recognize this fact and respond accordingly are best prepared to meet the challenges of the future.*

STROH, PETER WETHERILL, brewery executive; b. Detroit, Dec. 18, 1927; s. Gari Melchers and Suzanne (Suddards) S.; m. Nicole Elizabeth Fauquet-Lemaitre, June 30, 1964; children—Pierre Alexander, Frederic Charlton. B.A., Princeton U., 1951. Asst. to pres. Stroh Brewery Co., Detroit, 1952-65, v.p., 1965-66, dir. ops., 1966-68, pres., 1968-82, chmn., chief exec. officer, 1982—, also bd. dirs.; dir. NBD Bancorp., Inc.; chmn. Detroit Renaissance, Inc., Atlantic Salmon Fedn.; vice chmn. Detroit Econ. Growth Corp.; trustee New Detroit, Inc., Solomon Guggenheim Found. With USN, 1945-46. Mem. Nat. Audubon Soc. (bd. dirs.), Conservation Internat. (bd. dirs.), Econ. Alliance Mich. (bd. dirs.). Clubs: Detroit; Country of Detroit (Grosse Pointe Farms, Mich.), Grosse Pointe; Yondotega; Anglers of N.Y.; Island of Hobe Sound (Fla.). Office: Stroh Brewery Co 100 River Place Dr Detroit MI 48207-4295*

STROH, RAYMOND EUGENE, personnel executive; b. Bloomington, Ill., Aug. 13, 1942; s. Harry William and Felcie Cleo (Weaver) S.; m. Peggy Jane Whitacre, June 12, 1966; children: Rebecca Jane, David Ray. BA, So. Ill. U., 1966, U. Ill., 1977. Pers. technician Ill. Dept. Mental Health, Springfield, Ill., 1966-67; pers. officer Andrew McFarland Mental Health Ctr., Springfield, 1967-68, Manteno (Ill.) State Hosp., 1968-69; chief pers. officer Ill. Dept. Law Enforcement, Springfield, 1969-75, Ill. Dept. Revenue, Springfield, 1975-81, Ill. Dept. Mental Health, Springfield, 1981-82; pers. exec. Ill. Dept. Cen. Mgmt. Svcs., Springfield, 1982—; state govt. chmn. U.S. Savs. Bond Campaign, Springfield, 1978-82. Bd. dirs. Consumer Credit Counseling Svc., Springfield, 1988-94, sec., 1994; coun. exec. bd. Boy Scouts Am., Springfield, 1987—, v.p., 1987-94, 96—, dist. commr., 1979-86, unit commr., 1970-79; bd. dirs. Ill. State Employees Credit Union, 1984-85. Recipient Patriotic Svc. awards U.S. Treasury Dept., 1979-82, Silver Beaver award Boy Scouts Am., 1987, Dist. award of merit, 1981, Area Pres. awards, 1985, 86, Scouters Key award, 1976. Mem. NRA, U. Ill. Alumni Assn., So. Ill. U. Alumni Assn., Exptl. Aircraft Assn., Aircraft Owners and Pilots Assn., Ponce De Leon Inlet Lighthouse Assn., Nat. Geog. Soc., Cornell U. Lab. of Ornithology Project Feederwatch, Abraham Lincoln Gun Club, Appalachian Trail Conf., Union County (Tenn.) Hist. Soc., Bass Anglers Sportsman Soc., Lionel Railroader Club, Wabash R.R. Hist. Soc., Theta Delta Chi. Republican. Lutheran. Avocations: aviation, hunting, fishing, bird watching, model railroading. Home: 2111 Warwick Dr Springfield IL 62704-4147 Office: Ill Dept Cen Mgmt Svcs 501 Stratton Ofc Bldg Springfield IL 62706

STROHBEHN, EDWARD ALLEN, investment company executive; b. Madison, Wis., Nov. 13, 1952; s. Bernhard Edward and Helen Lorraine (Evans) S. BS, Bob Jones U., 1974; postgrad., Clemson U., 1974-77. Instr. math. Bob Jones U., Greenville, S.C., 1974-77; rsch. dir. PCA Internat., Charlotte, N.C., 1977-81; v.p. Merrill Lynch, Pierce, Fenner & Smith, Inc., N.Y.C., 1981-91; mgr. Riyad (Saudi Arabia) Bank, 1987-89; sr. v.p. Oppenheimer & Co., Inc., N.Y.C., 1991-92; pres. Strohbehn & Co., Inc., N.Y.C., 1992—. Mem. Internat. Trade Com., Bklyn., 1992—. Mem. C. of C. Baptist. Avocations: golf, cello. Home: 245 96th St Apt B9 Brooklyn NY 11209 Office: Strohbehn & Co Inc 53 Wall St New York NY 10005-2834

STROHBEHN, JOHN WALTER, engineering science educator; b. San Diego, Nov. 21, 1936; s. Walter William and Gertrude (Powell) S.; children from previous marriage: Jo, Kris, Carolyn; m. Barbara Ann Brungard, Aug. 30, 1980. BS, Stanford U., 1958, MS, 1959, PhD in Elec. Engring., 1964. Assoc. prof. engring. sci. Dartmouth Coll., Hanover, N.H., 1968-73, prof., 1973-94, assoc. dean, 1976-81, adj. prof. medicine, 1979-90, Sherman Fairchild prof., 1983-91, acting provost, 1987-89, provost, 1989-93; provost, prof. biomed. engring. Duke U., Durham, N.C., 1994—; disting. lectr. IEEE Antennas and Propagation Soc., 1979-82; vis. fellow Princeton (N.J.) U., 1993-94. Editor: Laser Propagation in the Clear Atmosphere, 1978; assoc. editor Trans. Ant and Propagation, 1969-71, Trans. Biomed. Engring., 1981-87; contbr. articles to profl. jours. Scoutmaster Boy Scouts Am., Norwich, Vt., 1971-73; bd. dirs. Norwich Recreation and Conservation Council. Fellow AAAS, IEEE, Optical Soc. Am., Am. Inst. Med. Biol. Engring. (founding); mem. Radiation Rsch. Soc., Bioelectromagnetics Soc. (bd. dirs. 1982-85), N.Am. Hyperthermia Group (pres. 1986). Avocations: jogging; hiking; skiing. Home: 3806 Chippenham Rd Durham NC 27707 Office: Duke U Provost's Office 220 Allen Durham NC 27708

STROHM, ROBERT DEAN, publications executive; b. Chgo., Oct. 14, 1945; s. John Louis and Lillian Ann (Murphy) S.; m. Patricia Ann Quincannon, July 10, 1976; children: John Wilson, Charles Quincannon. BS, U. Ill., 1968. Assoc. editor Nat. Wildlife Fedn., Washington, 1968-73, mng. editor, 1973-81, exec. editor, 1981-88, editor-in-chief, 1989—; v.p. publs. Nat. Wildlife Fedn., 1996—. Mem. Am. Soc. Mag. Editors. Democrat. Roman Catholic. Office: Nat Wildlife Fedn 8925 Leesburg Pike Vienna VA 22184

STROHMEYER, JOHN, writer, former editor; b. Cascade, Wis., June 26, 1924; s. Louis A. and Anna Rose (Saladunas) S.; m. Nancy Jordan, Aug. 20, 1949; children: Mark, John, Sarah. Student, Moravian Coll., 1941-43; A.B., Muhlenberg Coll., 1947; M.A. in Journalism, Columbia, 1948; L.H.D. (hon.), Lehigh U., 1983. With Nazareth Item, 1940-41; night reporter Bethlehem (Pa.) Globe-Times, 1941-43, 45-47; investigative reporter Providence Jour.-Bull., 1949-56; editor Bethlehem Globe-Times, 1956-84, v.p., 1961-84, dir., 1963-84; African-Am. journalism tchr. in Nairobi, Freetown, 1964; Atwood prof. journalism U. Alaska Anchorage, 1987-88, writer-in-residence, 1989—. Author: Crisis in Bethlehem: Big Steel's Struggle to Survive, 1986, Extreme Conditions: Big Oil and The Transformation of Alaska, 1993. Lt. (j.g.) USNR, 1943-45. Pulitzer Traveling fellow, 1948; Nieman fellow, 1952-53; recipient Comenius award Moravian Coll., 1971; Pulitzer prize for editorial writing, 1972; Alicia Patterson Found. fellow, 1984, 85. Mem. Am. Soc. Newspaper Editors, Pa. Soc. Newspaper Editors (pres. 1964-66), Anchorage Racquet Club. Home: 6633 Lunar Dr Anchorage AK 99504-4550

STROIK, DUNCAN GREGORY, architect, architectural design educator; b. Phila., Jan. 14, 1962; s. John Stephen and Mary Eugenia (Dorsey) S.; m. Ruth Valeria Engelhardt, Aug. 29, 1987; children: Gabrielle Marie, Raffaella Maria. BS in Architecture, U. Va., 1984; MArch, Yale U., 1987. Registered arch., Ill. Tchg. asst. Yale U. Sch. Architecture, New Haven, Conn., 1985-87; arch. Allan Greenberg, Arch., Washington, 1987-90; asst. prof. U. Notre Dame (Ind.) Sch. Architecture, 1990—; arch. Duncan Stroik, Arch., South Bend, Ind., 1990—; chmn. lectr. com. U. Notre Dame, Ind., 1990—, mem. undergrad. com., 1992—, com. on internat. studies, 1993-94; chmn. jury Ind. Concrete Masonry Assn., Ind., 1994. Arch., author: Building Classical, 1993; exhbns. include: U. Steubenville, 1995, N.Y. Acad. of Art, 1994, Yale U. Sch. Architecture, 1995, Chgo. Cultural Ctr., 1995, others; contbr. articles to profl. jours. With East Rock Pavilion-Design and Constrn., Yale U. Sch. Architecture, New Haven, 1985; active Habitat for Humanity, New Haven, 1987, U. Notre Dame chpt. faculty adv.; fundraiser Diocesan Bishops Appeal, Ft. Wayne/South Bend, 1993; active Carraige Hills Assn., South Bend; parish coun. mem. Cathedral St. Matthew, 1995—. Palladio and Vitruvius grantee Graham Found. for Advanced Studies, 1991, Student Rsch. grantee Promote Women and Minorities Grad. Studies, U. Notre, Dame, 1993; C.L.V. Meeks Meml. scholar Yale U., New Haven, 1987. Mem. Assn. Collegiate Schs. Architecture, Classical Architecture League, Classical Am., Nat. Trust for Hist. Preservation. Roman Catholic. Avocations: classical music, philosophy, hiking, painting. Home: 52488 Briarcliff Ln South Bend IN 46635-1104 Office: Univ Notre Dame Sch Architecture Notre Dame IN 46556

STROKE, HINKO HENRY, physicist, educator; b. Zagreb, Yugoslavia, June 16, 1927; came to U.S., 1943, naturalized, 1949; s. Elias and Edith (Mechner) S.; m. Norma Bilchick, Jan. 14, 1956; children: Ilana Lucy, Marija Tamar. BEE, N.J. Inst. Tech., 1949; MS, MIT, 1952, PhD, 1954. Rsch. asst. Princeton (N.J.) U., 1954-57, rsch. assoc., 1957; mem. rsch. staff Lab. Electronics MIT, 1957-63; asso. prof. physics NYU, N.Y.C., 1963-68, prof., 1968—, dept. chmn., 1988-91; prof. associ248 U. Paris, 1969-70, Ecole Normale Supérieure, 1976; vis. scientist Max Planck Inst. für Quantenoptik, Garching, U. Munich, 1977-78, 81, 82, 93; cons. Atomic Instrument Co., MIT Sci. Translation Svc., Tech. Rsch. Group, Cambridge Air Force Rsch. Ctr., Am. Optical Corp., ITT Fed. Labs., NASA, others; mem. com. on line spectra on elements NAS-NRC, 1976-82; sci. assoc. CERN, Geneva, 1983—. Contbg. author: Nuclear Physics, 1963, Atomic Physics, 1969, Hyperfine Interactions in Excited Nuclei, 1971, Francis Bitter: Selected Papers, 1969, Atomic Physics 3, 1973, Nuclear Moments and Nuclear Structure, 1973, A Perspective of Physics, Vol. 1, 1977, Atomic Physics 8, 1983, Lasers in Atomic, Molecular, and Nuclear Physics, 1989; editor: Comments on Atomic and Molecular Physics, The Physical Review-The First Hundred Years. Mem. Chorus Pro Musica, Boston, 1951-54, 57-63, Münchener Bach-Chor, Munich, 1977-82, 92; Choeur pro Arte, Lausanne, 1983-92; mem. Collegiate Chorale, N.Y., 1964-94, Dessoff Choirs, 1994—. With AUS, 1946-47. Recipient Sr. U.S. Scientist award Alexander von Humboldt Found., 1977; NATO sr. fellow in sci., 1975. Fellow Am. Phys. Soc. (publs. oversight com. 1991-93), Optical Soc. Am.; mem. AAAS, IEEE, European Phys. Soc., Société Française de Physique, Sigma Xi, Tau Beta Pi, Omicron Delta Kappa. Home: 271 Old Army Rd Scarsdale NY 10583-2619 Office: NYU Dept Physics 4 Washington Square New York NY 10003-6621

STROM, BRIAN LESLIE, internist, educator; b. N.Y.C., N.Y., Dec. 8, 1949; s. Martin and Edith (Singer) S.; m. Elaine Marilyn Moskowitz, June 4, 1978; children: Shayne Lee, Jordan Blair. BS, Yale U., 1971; MD, Johns Hopkins U., 1975; MPH, U. Calif., Berkeley, 1980. Diplomate Am. Bd. Internal Medicine, Am. Bd. Epidemiology. Intern in medicine U. Calif., San Francisco, 1975-76; resident in medicine U. Calif., 1976-78, research fellow in clinical pharmacology, 1978-80; from asst. prof. to assoc. prof. medicine and pharmacology U. Pa., Phila., 1980-93, prof. medicine, 1993—, prof. biostatistics & epidemiology, 1995—; adj. asst. prof. clin. pharmacy Phila. Coll. of Pharmacy and Sci., 1981-90, adj. assoc. prof., 1990-93, adj. prof., 1993—; mem. U. Pa. Cancer Ctr., 1981—; attending staff Hosp. U. Pa., 1980—, co-dir Clin. Epidemiology Unit, 1980-91, dir., 1991—; dir. Clin. Pharmacology Cons. Svc., 1981-82; dir. Ctr. for Clin. Epidemiology and Biostats., 1993—, chair dept. biostats. and epidemiology, 1995—; lectr. in field; cons. CDC, 1981, Coun. for Internat. Orgn. of Med. Scis., Geneva, Switzerland, 1981-83, Office of Tech. Assessment, Congress of U.S., 1980-81, Aging Rev. Com., Nat. Inst. Aging, 1982, Ministry of Pub. Health, State of Kuwait, 1982, Royal Tropical Inst., Amsterdam, 1983, others. Editl. cons. Johns Hopkins U. Press, J.B. Lippincott; referee Annals of Internal Medicine, Archives of Internal Medicine, Clin. Pharmacology and Therapeutics, Digestive Diseases and Sci., Internat. Jour. Cardiology, Internat. Jour. Epidemiology, Jour. AMA, Jour. Gen. Internal Medicine, Med. Care, Primary Care Tech., Sci.; assoc. editor Jour. Gen. Internal Medicine; mem. editl. bd. 7 jours.; contbr. numerous articles to profl. jours. Nat. Acad. Scis. grantee, Rockefeller Found. grantee, NIH grantee, many others. Fellow ACP, Am. coll. Epidemiology, Am. Epidemiology Soc.; mem. Am. Fedn. Clin. Rsch., Am. Pub. Health Assn., Am. Soc. Clin. Pharmacology and Therapeutics, Am. Soc. Clin. Investigation, Assn. of Tchrs. of Preventive Medicine, Internat. Epideliol. Assn., Soc. for Clin. Trials, Soc. for Epidemiologic Rsch., Soc. Group Internal Medicine. Democrat. Jewish. Avocations: hiking, biking, camping, skiing. Home: 332 Hidden River Rd Narberth PA 19072-1111

STROM, J. PRESTON, JR., prosecutor; b. May 21, 1959; s. Grace and J.P. Sr. S.; m. Donna Savoca, Oct. 5, 1985; 1 child, Margaret. BA, U. S.C., 1981, JD, 1984. Bar: S.C. 1984, U.S. Dist. Ct. S.C., 1984, U.S. Ct. Appeals (4th cir.) 1984. Asst. solicitor 5th Jud. Cir., S.C., 1985-86; ptnr. Leventis, Strom & Wicker, 1986-88, Harpootlian & Strom, 1988-90, Bolt, Popowski, McCulloch & Strom, 1990-93; acting U.S. atty. Office U.S. Atty., S.C., 1993, U.S. atty., 1993—; chmn. Law Enforcement Coord. Com.; chmn. juvenile justice and child support enforcement subcom. U.S. Dept. Justice; active Atty. Gen. Adv. Com. Mem. S.C. Bar, S.C. Trial Lawyers Assn., Richland County Bar Assn. (chmn. criminal law sect.). Office: US Attys Office 1441 Main St Ste 500 Columbia SC 29201-2848

STROM, LYLE ELMER, federal judge; b. Omaha, Nebr., Jan. 6, 1925; s. Elmer T. and Eda (Hanisch) S.; m. Regina Ann Kelly, July 31, 1950; children: Mary Bess, Susan Frances, Amy Claire, Cassie A., David Kelly, Margaret Mary, Bryan Thomas. Student, U. Nebr., 1946-47; AB, Creighton U., 1950, JD cum laude, 1953. Bar: Nebr. 1953. Assoc. Fitzgerald, Brown, Leahy, Strom, Schorr & Barmettler and predecessor firm, Omaha, 1953-60, ptnr., 1960-63, gen. trial ptnr., 1963-85; judge U.S. Dist. Ct. Nebr., Omaha, 1985-87, chief judge, 1987-95, sr. judge, 1995—; adj. prof. law Creighton U., 1959-95, prof., 1996—; mem. com. pattern jury instrns. and practice and proc. Nebr. Supreme Ct., 1965-91; spl. legal counsel Omaha Charter Rev. Commn., 1973. Mem. exec. com Covered Wagon Coun. Boy Scouts Am., 1953-57, bd. trustees and exec. com. Mid-Am. Coun., 1988—; chmn. bd. trustees Marian High Sch., 1969-71; mem. pres. coun. Creighton U., 1990—. Ensign USNR and with U.S. Maritime Svc., 1943-46. Fellow Am. Coll. Trial Lawyers, Internat. Acad. Trial Lawyers; mem. ABA, Nebr. Bar Assn. (ho. of dels. 1978-81, exec. coun. 1981-87, pres. 1989-90), Omaha Bar Assn. (pres. 1980-81), Am. Judicature Soc., Midwestern Assn. Amateur Athletic Union (pres. 1976-78), Alpha Sigma Nu (pres. alumni chpt. 1970-71). Republican. Roman Catholic. Lodge: Rotary (pres. 1993-94). Office: US Dist Ct PO Box 607 Omaha NE 68101-0607

STROM, MILTON GARY, lawyer; b. Rochester, N.Y., Dec. 5, 1942; s. Harold and Dolly (Isaacson) S.; m. Barbara A. Simon, Jan. 18, 1975; children: Carolyn, Michael, Jonathan. BS in Econs., U. Pa., 1964; JD, Cornell U., 1967. Bar: N.Y. 1968, U.S. Dist. Ct. (we. dist.) N.Y. 1968, U.S. Ct. Claims 1969, U.S. Ct. Mil. Appeals 1969, U.S. Ct. Appeals ((D.C. cir.) 1970, U.S. Supreme Ct. 1972, U.S. Dist. Ct. (so. dist.) N.Y. 1975. Atty. SEC, Washington, 1968-71; assoc. Skadden, Arps, Slate, Meagher & Flom, N.Y.C., 1971-77, ptnr., 1977—. Served with USCGR, 1967-68. Mem. ABA, N.Y. State Bar Assn. (corp. law sect.), Assn. of Bar of City of N.Y. Republican. Jewish. Club: Beach Point, Marco Polo. Avocations: tennis, skiing. Office: Skadden Arps Slate Meagher & Flom 919 3rd Ave New York NY 10022

STROM, TERRY BARTON, physician, immunologist; b. Chgo., Nov. 30, 1941; s. David and Sylvia (Abelson) S.; m. Margot Stern, Aug. 2, 1964; children: Adam, Rachel. Student U. Ill.-Chgo./Urbana, 1959-62; M.D., U. Ill. Coll. Medicine, Chgo., 1966; MA (hon.) Harvard U., 1989; DSc (hon.) Hahnemann U., 1990. Diplomate Am. Bd. Internal Medicine. Intern/jr. resident U. Ill. Hosp., Chgo., 1966-68; sr. resident in internal medicine Beth Israel Hosp., Boston, 1970-71; research fellow in medicine Peter Bent Brigham Hosp. and Harvard Med. Sch., Boston, 1971-73; asst. prof. medicine Harvard Med. Sch., 1974-78, assoc. prof. medicine, 1978-88, prof. medicine, 1988—; med. dir. renal transplant svc. Peter Bent Brigham Hosp., 1973-83, assoc. dir. lab. immunogenetics and transplantation; sr. physician Beth Israel Hosp., med. dir. renal transplant service, 1983—, dir. div. clin. immunology, 1983—; Lilly lectr. Royal Coll. Physicians, London, 1991; Clarke lectr. U. Pa., 1995; Billingham vis. prof. Vanderbilt U., 1990; Bernard Pimstone vis. prof. U. Capetown, 1995. Author: 4 books, contbr. 400 articles to profl. jours.; also holder 3 patents. Campaign worker polit. campaigns and peace orgns.; mem. U.S. Congl. Task Force on Transplantation, 1985-87, adv. panel for allergy and transplantation NIAID, 1988-91, NIH; cons. FDA, 1993—. Served to capt. USAF, 1968-70. Ill. State Scholar, 1959-56; recipient Rsch. Career Devel. award NIH, 1976-81; Acad. Honors Day award U. Ill., 1959-61; Ill. State scholar, 1959-66. Mem. Internat. Soc. Nephrology (councillor), Assn. Am. Immunologists, Internat. Transplant Soc., Am. Soc. Clin. Investigation, Am. Soc. Transplant Physicians (founding past pres. 1981), Assn. Am. Phys., Clin. Immunol. Soc. (pres. 1990), Inter Urban Clin. Club. Democrat. Jewish. Office: Beth Israel Hosp 330 Brookline Ave Boston MA 02215-5400

STROMAN, SUSAN, choreographer; d. Charles and Frances S. Grad., U. Del. Dancer: Chicago, 1977-78, Whoopee!, 1979, Richard III, 1980, Peter Pan, 1983; asst. dir., asst. choreographer: (off-Broadway) Musical Chairs, 1980; co-conceiver: Trading Places, Equity Library Theatre Informals, 1983; dir., co-conceiver: (off-Broadway) Living Color, 1986; choreographer: (off-Broadway) Broadway Babylon, 1984, Sayonara, 1987, Flora, the Red Menace, 1987, Shenandoah, 1988, Slasher, 1988, Rhythm Ranch, 1989, The Roar of the Greasepaint-The Smell of the Crowd, 1990, Gypsy, 1991, And the World Goes 'Round, 1991 (Outer Critics' Circle award 1991), A Christmas Carol, 1994; (Broadway) Crazy for You, 1992 (Tony award best choreography 1992, Drama Desk award 1992, Outer Critics' Circle award 1992, Laurence Olivier award 1993), Picnic, 1993, Show Boat, 1994 (Tony award best choreography 1995, Astaire award Theatre Development Fund 1995); (New York City Opera) Don Giovanni, 1989, A Little Night Music, 1990, 110 in the Shade, 1992; (other) Liza Minnelli: Stepping Out at Radio City Music Hall, 1991 (Emmy award nomination for HBO presentation), (mus.) Big Broadway, 1996; dir.: (TV spl.) A Evening with the Boston Pops-A Tribute to Leonard Bernstein, 1989; co-conceiver, choreographer: (TV spl.) Sondheim-A Celebration at Carnegie Hall, 1992.

STROMBERG, ARTHUR HAROLD, retired professional services company executive; b. Los Angeles, July 17, 1928; s. Walter John and Ingfrid Christine (Olsen) S.; m. Fredna B. Copeland, Aug. 29, 1953. B.A. in Econs, U. So. Calif., 1952. Broker Francis I. duPont & Co., San Francisco, 1953-59; ptnr. Glore Forgan & Co., Chgo., San Francisco, 1959-67; v.p., dir. Eaton & Howard, San Francisco, 1967-70; chief exec. officer, chmn. bd. Thortec Internat., San Mateo, Calif., 1970-89; chmn. bd. URS Internat., Arlington, Va., 1986-91. Served with USNR, 1945-48. Mem. Bohemian Club, Burlingame Country Club. Republican.

STROMBERG, CLIFFORD DOUGLAS, lawyer; b. N.Y.C., June 1, 1949; s. George M. and Greta (Netzow) S.; m. Ava S. Feiner, June 25, 1972; children: Kimberly, Eric. BA summa cum laude, Yale U., 1971; JD, Harvard U., 1974. Bar: N.Y. 1975, D.C. 1975, U.S. Dist. Ct. (so. and ea. dists.) N.Y. 1975, U.S. Ct. Appeals (D.C. cir.) 1975, U.S. Ct. Appeals (2nd cir.) 1975, U.S. Supreme Ct. 1980. Law clk. to judge U.S. Dist. Ct. (ea. dist.) N.Y., 1974-75; assoc. Arnold & Porter, Washington, 1975-78, 80-83; dep. exec. sec. HHS, Washington, 1978-80; cons. FTC, Washington, 1980; ptnr. Dorsey & Whitney, Washington, 1983-84, Hogan & Hartson, Washington, 1984—; adj. asst. prof. emergency medicine George Washington U. Sch. Medicine, 1991—. Co-author: Mental Health and Law: A System in Transition, 1975, Alternatives to the Hospital: Ambulatory Surgery Centers and Emergicenters, 1984, Entrepreneurial Health Care: How to Structure Successful New Ventures, 1985, The Psychologist's Legal Handbook, 1988, Access to Hospital Information: Problems and Strategies: 4 Frontiers of Health Services Management 3-33, 1987, Healthcare Provider Networks: Antitrust Issues and Practical Considerations in devels. in antitrust law; editorial bd. Harvard Law Rev., 1972-73; editor in chief Healthspan: The Report of Health Business and Law, 1984-87; contbr. articles to profl. jours. Bd. dirs. Nat. Children's Eye Care Found., Washington, 1985-87. Teaching fellow in govt. Harvard U., 1973-74. Fellow Am. Bar Found.; mem. ABA (chair working group health care reform 1993—, state membership chmn. 1984, forum com. health lawk 1987-90, adv. com. govt. affairs 1993—, governing bd., individual rights and responsibilities sect., exec. coun., 1980-90, sec. 1984-87, chair-elect 1987-88, chair 1988-89, legal aid and indigent defendants com. 1982-87), Nat. Health Lawyers Assn., Phi Beta Kappa. Office: Hogan & Hartson 555 13th St NW Washington DC 20004-1109

STROMBERG, GREGORY, printing ink company executive; b. Milw., Feb. 10, 1948; s. Clifford Norman and Margaret Betty (Hoover) S.; m. Gail Elizabeth Steinbach, Aug. 22, 1970; children: Christopher, Brian, Ellen. BS, Marquette U., Milw., 1970. Office contact salesman Continental Can Co., Milw., 1970-78; sales rep. Sun Chem. Co., Milw., 1978-82; v.p., gen. mgr. Acme Printing Ink Co., Milw., 1982—; exec. v.p. Can. op. Acme Printing Ink Can. Ltd., 1985—, pres., 1990—; bd. dirs. Can. Ops. Acme Inks of Can.; pres. Toobee Internat., Inc., Milw., 1981—; v.p., dir. mktg. and internat. sales INX Internat. Ink Co., 1991—. Author: Toobee Air Force Flight Training Manual, 1983. Advisor Milw. Jr. Achievement, 1974; sponsor Muscular Dystrophy, 1983; asst. com. mem. Toys for Tots, Children's Hosp., Milw., 1983; active United Meth. Men. Mem. Am. Mktg. Assn., Sales and Mktg. Execs. of Milw., Am. Mgmt. Assn., Am. Soc. Quality Control Milw., Nat. Metal Decorators Assn., Nat. Assn. Printer and Lithographers, Nat. Assn. Printing Equipment and Suppliers. Home: N69w23448 Donna Dr Sussex WI 53089-3245

STROMBERG, ROLAND NELSON, historian; b. Kansas City, Mo., July 5, 1916; s. Clarence Rol and Harriet (Ridgell) S.; m. Mary R. Gray, June 10, 1939; children: Eric, Juliet. AB, U. Kansas City, 1939; MA, Am. U., 1946; PhD, U. Md., 1952. With U.S. Dept. Justice, 1940-45; instr., then asst. prof., asso. prof., prof. U. Md., College Park, 1949-66; prof. So. Ill. U., Carbondale, 1966-67; prof. history U. Wis., Milw., 1967—; acting chmn. dept. art history U. Wis., 1977-78. Author: Collective Security and American Foreign Policy, 1963, An Intellectual History of Modern Europe, 1966, European Intellectual History Since 1789, 1966, 6th edit., 1994, After Everything, 1975, Religious Liberalism in Eighteenth Century England, 1954, Heritage and Challenge of History, 1971, 2d edit., 1989, Arnold J. Toynbee, 1972, Europe in the Twentieth Century, 1979, 4th edit., 1996, Redemption by War: The European Intellectuals and the 1914 War, 1982, Five Twentieth Century Thinkers, 1990, Men, Women, and History, 1994, Democracy, A Short History, 1996, others. Rockefeller Found. grantee, 1957-58; recipient Disting. Alumnus award U. Mo., Kansas City, 1966; fellow Woodrow Wilson Internat. Center for Scholars, 1974. Mem. History of Sci. Soc., Soc. Historians of Am. Fgn. Relations. Home: 7033 N Fairchild Cir Milwaukee WI 53217-3851 Office: U Wis Holton Hall Milwaukee WI 53201 *It would be more edifying to say that, as historian, I have sought an understanding of the past in order to help mankind master its future. It is probably truer to say that I have simply been fascinated by the amazing record of human actions and thoughts and by the problem of making sense of them.*

STROMBERG, ROSS ERNEST, lawyer; b. Arcata, Calif., May 5, 1940; s. Noah Anders and Anne Laura (Noyes) S.; m. Toni Nicholas, Dec. 16, 1961; m. Margaret Telonicher, Oct. 3, 1965; children: Kristin, Matthew, Gretchen, Erik. BS, Humboldt State U., 1962; JD, U. Calif., Berkeley, 1965. Bar: Calif. 1966, U.S. Dist. Ct. (no. dist.) Calif. 1966, U.S. Ct. Appeals (9th cir.) 1966. Assoc. Hanson Bridgett, San Francisco, 1965-70, ptnr., 1970-85; ptnr. Epstein Becker Stromberg & Green, San Francisco, 1985-90, Jones Day Reavis & Pogue, L.A., 1990—; chmn. Jones Day's Healthcare Specialized Industry Practice. Author: Economic Joint Venturing, 1985, Acquisition and Enhancement of Physician Practices, 1988. Pres. East Bay AHEC, Oakland, Calif., 1984-87; bd. dirs. Am. Cancer Soc., Oakland, 1984—; bd. dirs. U.S.-China Ednl. Inst., San Francisco, 1985—, chmn., 1988—; pres. Am. Acad. Hosp. Attys. of Am. Hosp. Assn., Chgo., 1978. Mem. Health Fin. Mgmt. Assn., Nat. Health Lawyers Assn., Am. Acad. Hosp. Attys., World Trade Club, Ingomar Club. Democrat. Office: Jones Day Reavis & Pogue 555 W 5th St Ste 4600 Los Angeles CA 90013-3002

STROME, STEPHEN, distribution company executive; b. Lynn, Mass., June 20, 1945; s. David and Rose (Cantor) S.; m. Phyllis Ruth Fields, Jan. 14, 1967; children: Michael, Rochelle. BA, Hillsdale (Mich.) Coll., 1967; MBA, Wayne State U., 1968. Trainee KMart Corp., Detroit, 1968-69; mgr. work measurement KMart Corp., Troy, Mich., 1970-73; mgr. tng., edn. Fruehauf Corp., Detroit, 1974-76, regional mgr. labor relations, 1976-78; dir. ops. Handleman Co., Clawson, Mich., 1978-80, account exec., 1980-82; v.p. computer software div. Handleman Co., Troy, 1983-85, pres. computer software/video div., 1986-87, exec. v.p., 1987-89, exec. v.p., chief oper. officer, 1990, pres., CEO, 1991—. Home: 4597 Kiftsgate Bnd Bloomfield Hills MI 48302-2331 Office: Handleman Co 500 Kirts Dr Troy MI 48084-5225

STROMINGER, JACK LEONARD, biochemist; b. N.Y.C., Aug. 7, 1925. AB, Harvard U., 1944; MD, Yale U., 1948; DSc (hon.), Trinity Coll., Dublin, 1975, Washington U., 1988. From asst. prof. to prof. pharmacology sch. med. Washington U., St. Louis, 1955-61, prof. pharmacology and microbiology, 1961-64; prof. pharmacology and chem. microbiology med. sch. U. Wis., Madison, 1964-68; prof. biochemistry Harvard U., 1968-83, chmn. dept. biochemistry and molecular biology, 1970-73, Higgins prof. biochemistry, 1983—; head tumor virol. divsn. Dana-Farber Cancer Inst., Boston, 1977—. Recipient John J. Abel award, 1960, Paul-Lewis Lab award, 1962, Rose Payne award Am. Soc. Histocompat. & Immunogen., 1986, Hoechst-Roussel award, 1990, Pasteur medal, 1990, Albert Lasker Award for Basic Med. Rsch., 1995; named Passano Found. laureate, 1993. Mem. NAS (mem. inst. medicine, Microbiology award 1968, Selman Waxman award 1968), AAAS, Am. Soc. Biol. Chemists, Am. Soc. Pharmacology & Exptl. Therapeutics, Am. Assn. Immunologists, Am. Soc. Microbiologists, Am. Chem. Soc., Am. Acad. Arts & Sci., European Molecular Biol. Orgn., Sigma Xi. Office: Dana Farber Cancer Inst Dept of Biochem 44 Binney St Boston MA 02115-6013

STROMMEN, CLIFFORD H., headmaster; b. Gilby, N.D., May 2, 1935; m. Bette Ann Freeman, Dec. 22, 1963; children: Clint K., Emily A. BS in English, Moorhead State U., 1958; MEd in Ednl. Administrn., U. Houston, 1975, EdD in Ednl. Administrn., 1981. Cert. Eng. tchr., superintendent, dist. administr., N.Y., tchr. English, Phys. Edn., Calif. Tchr. English various sr. and jr. high schs., 1958-70; dir. athletics Seaside High Sch., Monterey, Calif., 1968; dir. dormitories Am. Internat. Sch., New Delhi, India, 1970-72, vice-prin., 1971-72; dir. Am. Embassy Sch. (formerly Am. Internat. Sch.), New Delhi, India, 1972-74; supt. Internat. Sch. Lusaka, Zambia, 1976-84, Escola Graduada de São Paulo, Brazil, 1984-90; headmaster Internat. Sch. Nido de Aguilas, Santiago, Chile, 1990—. Recipient Nat. Superintendent of the Yr. awd., Overseas, Am. Assn. of School Administrators, 1993. Mem. Assn. Am. Sch. Administrs. (Internat. Superintendent of Yr. 1993), Assn. Advancement of Internat. Edn. (bd. dirs. 1983-84, 87-89, v.p. 1991-92, pres. 1993-94), Assn. Am. Schs. Brazil (treas. 1984-88, pres. 1989-90), Assn. Am. Schs. S.Am.(treas. 1985-86, v.p. 1986-87, pres. 1987-88), So. Assn. Colls. and Schs. (Latin Am. com. 1993), Assn. Internat. Schs. Africa (v.p. 1976, pres. 1976-78). Office: Internat Sch Nido de Aguilas, Casilla 16211 Correo 9, Santiago Chile

STRONACH, CAREY ELLIOTT, physicist, educator; b. Boston, Aug. 8, 1940; s. Ralph Howard and Frances Burns (Maynard) S.; m. Joan Alice Louise Venner, Aug. 20, 1966; children: John Maynard, Howard Stanley. BS, U. Richmond, Va., 1961; MS, U. Va., 1963; PhD, Coll. William and Mary, Williamsburg, Va., 1975. Instr. physics Va. State U., Petersburg, 1965-66, asst. prof., 1966-71, 72-76, assoc. prof., 1976-78, 79-80, prof., 1980—, dir. Muon Spin Rotation Rsch. Program, 1977—, dir. Solid State Physics Rsch.Inst., 1983-87, radiation safety officer, 1983-87, dir. Superconducting Materials Rsch. Program, 1988—; dir. Galactic Cosmic Radiation Rsch. Program, 1993—; dir. U.S.- France Joint Muon Spin Rotation Rsch. Program, 1985-91; vis. assoc. prof. U. Alta., 1978-79; guest scientist Brookhaven Nat. Lab.; mem. organizing com. Internat. Symposium on the Electronic Structure and Properties of Hydrogen in Metals, 1982, Internat. Symposium on the Physics and Chemistry of Small Clusters, 1986, From Clusters to Crystals, 1991, The Sci. and Tech. of Atomically Engineered Materials, 1995; mem. sci. adv. com. European Workshop on the Spectroscopy of Subatomic Species in Non-Metallic Solids, 1985, govs. com on Superconducting Supercollider, 1987; TV physics lectr., 1991—. Contbr. 94 articles to publs. in field; playwright. Pres. Petersburg area chpt. Va. Coun. Human Rels., 1965-67; mem. Petersburg Commn. Community Rels. Affairs, 1974-77; corr. sec. Petersburg Dem. Com., 1974-77, mem., 1972-78, 79-85, vice chmn., 1981-85; mem. long-range transp. adv. com. City of Petersburg, 1994—. Fellow duPont Corp. 1961-63, NSF, 1971-72, NASA, 1976. Mem. AAAS, Am. Phys. Soc., Am. Assn. Physics Tchrs., AAUP (chpt. pres. 1968-70), Va. Acad. Sci. (sec. astronomy, math. and physics sect. 1983-84, chmn. 1984-85), Southeastern Univs. Rsch. Assn. (site selection com. 1980-81, materials sci. com. 1983-86, trustee 1983—, sci. and tech. com. 1986-88, rules com. 1988-92, edn. com. 1992-94, new projects com. 1994-95, CEBAF com. 1995—), High Speed Rail/Maglev Assn. (govt. rels. com. 1992—, Maglev Task Force, 1994—), Coun. Dem. and Secular Humanism (assoc.), Los Alamos Meson Physics Facility Users' Group, Continuous Electron Beam Accelerator Facility User's Group, Tri-Univ. Meson Facility Users Group, Va. Computer Networking Com., N.Y. Acad. Scis., Phi Beta Kappa, Sigma Xi (chpt. sec. 1977-78, chpt. pres. 1980-84, 87-88), Sigma Pi Sigma, Pi Mu Epsilon. Achievements include development (with others) of low-energy muon beam line at the AGS of Brookhaven Nat. Lab.; research in pion-nucleus interactions, muon spin rotation studies of high-temperature superconductors and related materials, fullerenes, heavy-fermion materials, ferromagnetic metals, metal hydrides, fatigue in metals and other materials; participation in the establishment of the Southeastern Universities Research Association and the Thomas Jefferson National Accelerator facility; discovery of formation of muonium and muonated radicals in Buckminster-Fullerene. Home: 2241 Buckner St Petersburg VA 23805-2207 Office: Va State U Box 9325 Petersburg VA 23806

STRONACH, FRANK, automobile parts manufacturing executive. Chmn., dir. Magna Internat. Inc., Markham, Ont., Can., 1971—. Founder The Fair Enterprise Inst. Office: Magna Internat Inc, 36 Apple Creek Blvd, Markham, ON Canada L3R 4Y4

STRONE, MICHAEL JONATHAN, lawyer; b. N.Y.C., Feb. 26, 1953; s. Bernard William and Judith Semel (Sogg) S.; m. Andrea Nan Acker, Jan. 27, 1979; children: Noah Gregory, Joshua Samuel. BA cum laude, Colby Coll., 1974; JD, Fordham Law Sch., 1978. Bar: N.J. 1978, N.Y. 1979, U.S. Ct. Appeals (2d and 3d cirs.) 1979, U.S. Dist. Ct. (so. and ea. dists.) N.Y. 1979, U.S. Dist. Ct. N.J. 1979, Conn. 1988. Assoc. Ratheim Hoffman et al, N.Y.C., 1978-80, Botein Hays et al, N.Y.C., 1980-84; v.p., assoc. gen. counsel, asst. sec. GE Investment Corp., Stamford, Conn., 1984—; v.p., asst. sec. GE Investment Mgmt. Inc., 1988—; v.p., gen. counsel Gindoff Enterprises Inc., 1985-90. Bd. dirs. N.Y. chpt. Juvenile Diabetes Found., N.Y.C., 1981-89, vice chmn., 1981-88; mem. fin. com. Juvenile Diabetes Found. Internat., 1981-86; asst. prin. bassist Westchester Symphony Orch., Scarsdale, N.Y., 1982—, pres., 1982-87, chmn. bd., 1982-90, exec. mng. dir., 1990-93; vice-chmn. ann. dinner NCCJ, 1987; bd. dirs. Parkinson's Disease Found., 1989—, v.p., 1991—; active steering com. Parkinson's Disease Soc. Am., 1991—, merger com., 1991—; bd. dirs. Parkinson's Action Network, 1994—; trustee Jewish Cmty. Ctr. of Harrison, 1996—. Mem. ABA (chmn. pension plan investments 1989-91, chmn. asset mgmt., 1992-94, 95—, significant legis. coms. 1985-92, chmn. subcom. on joint ventures 1988-90), Am. Coll. Real Estate Lawyers, The Corp. Bar Assn., Internat. Assn. Atty's and Execs. in Corp. Real Estate, Nat. Assn. of Real Estate Investment Mgrs. (mem. sr. legal officers adv. com. 1993—), Colby Coll. Alumni Coun. (nominating com. 1994—, chair fin. com. 1995—), Netsuke Kenkyukai Soc. Republican. Jewish. Home: 10 Genesee Trail Harrison NY 10528-1802 Office: Gen Electric Investment Corp 3003 Summer St Stamford CT 06905-4316

STRONG, CHARLES ROBERT, waste management administrator; b. Bklyn., Aug. 9, 1935; s. Charles Stanley and Ida May (Brower) S.; m. Melba Janice Cochran, July 8, 1961; children: William Charles, Colin Brower. BSME, Yale U., 1957. Registered profl. engr., Tex. Equipment engr. Remington Arms Co., Bridgeport, Conn., 1957-60; prodn. supr. Johnson & Johnson, Decatur, Ill., 1960; prodn. and maintenance dept. mgr. Johnson & Johnson, New Brunswick, N.J., 1961-66; maintenance supt. Johnson & Johnson, Chgo., 1966-70; from maintenance & engr. plant mgr. to facility engring. mgr Johnson & Johnson, Sherman, Tex., 1970-80; cons. engr. Acurex Solar Corp., Mountainview, Calif., 1980-83; tech. v.p. Young-Montenay, Inc., Sherman, Tex., 1983-85, Metro Energy Co., Miami, 1985-86; pres. Airko Svc. Co., Miami, 1986-87; v.p., adminstr. Montenay Power Corp., Miami, 1987—. Contbr. articles to profl. jours. Dir. Greater Texoma Utility Dist., Sherman, 1982-85; pres. Texoma Valley Coun. Boy Scouts Am., Sherman, 1980-82, Salvation Army, Sherman, 1983; chmn., bd. dirs. 1st United Meth. Ch., Sherman, 1982-84; bd. dirs. United Meth. Ch., Plantation, Fla. Recipient Silver Beaver award Boy Scouts Am., 1982. Mem. ASME, N.W. Dade Hialeah, Miami Springs C. of C. (bd. dirs., trustee 1995, 96), Rotary (program chmn. 1976-85). Republican. Methodist. Avocations: watching sports, financial planning, home projects, exercising. Office: Montenay Power Corp 6990 NW 97th Ave Miami FL 33178-2500 *Whether it be athletics or in industry, I have found that hard work and developing a good team lead to success, satisfaction and self-confidence. This then will lead to the desire for continued success.*

STRONG, DAVID F., university administrator; b. Botwood, Nfld., Can., Feb. 26, 1944; s. Cyril and Ruby Strong; m. Lynda Joan Marshall; children: Kimberley, Joanna. B.Sc., Meml. U. Nfld., 1965; M.Sc., Lehigh U., 1967; PhD, U. Edinburgh, 1970. NRC postgrad. scholar U. Edinburgh, Scotland, 1970-72; assoc. prof. teaching and rsch. Meml. U. Nfld., 1972-74, prof., acting dept. head, 1974-75, E.W.R. Steacie fellow, 1975-77, prof. dept. earth scis. univ. rsch., 1985-90, spl. adv. to pres., 1985-87, v.p. (acad.), 1987-90; W.F. James prof. pure and applied scis. St. Francis Xavier U., N.S., 1981-82; pres., vice-chancellor U. Victoria, B.C., Can., 1990—; Swiney lectr. U. Edinburgh, 1981; mem. rsch. coun. Can. Inst. Advanced Rsch., 1986—. Editor or co-editor several books; contbr. more than 200 papers to sci. lit. Recipient Atlantic Provinces Young Scientist award (Frazer medal), 1973; NRC Can. E.W.R. Steacie fellow, 1975-77; Fgn. Exch. fellow to Japan, 1976, France, 1976-77. Fellow Geol. Assn. Can. (Past Pres.'s medal 1980), Geol. Soc. Am., Royal Soc. Can.; mem. Can. Inst. Mining and Metallurgy (Disting. Svc. award 1979, Disting Llctrs. award 1983-84), Soc. Econ. Geologists. Office: U Victoria, PO Box 1700, Victoria, BC Canada V8W 2Y2

STRONG, GARY EUGENE, librarian; b. Moscow, Idaho, June 26, 1944; s. Authur Dwight and Cleora Anna (Nirk) S.; m. Carolyn Jean Roetker, Mar. 14, 1970; children: Christopher Eric, Jennifer Rebecca. BS in Edn., U. Idaho, 1966; AMLS, U. Mich., 1967. Adminstrv. and reference asst. U. Idaho, 1963-66; extension librarian Latah County Free Library, Moscow, 1966; head librarian Markeley Residence Library, U. Mich., 1966-67; library dir. Lake Oswego (Oreg.) Public Library, 1967-73, Everett (Wash.) Public Library, 1973-76; asso. dir. services Wash. State Library, Olympia, 1976-79; dep. state librarian Wash. State Library, 1979-80; state librarian Calif. State Library, Sacramento, 1980-94; dir. Queens Borough Pub. Libr., Jamaica, 1994—; dir. emeritus Calif. State Library Found., 1994—; chief exec. Calif. Libr. Svcs. Bd., 1980-94; founder, bd. dirs. Calif. State Libr. Found., 1982-94, Calif. Literacy Campaign, 1984-94, Calif. Rsch. Bur., 1992; bd. dirs. No. Regional Libr. Bd., 1983-94, Queens Libr. Found., 1994—; mem. adv. bd. Ctr. for Book in Libr. of Congress, 1983-86; mem. nat. adv. com. Libr. of Congress, 1987-89; chmn. adv. bd. Calif. Libr. Constrn. and Renovation Bond Act Bd., 1989-94; vis. lectr. Marylhurst Coll., Oreg., 1968, Oreg. Divsn. Continuing Edn., 1972, San Jose State U. Sch. Libr. Svc., 1990; lectr. and cons. in field. Host, producer: cable TV Signatures Program, 1974-76, nationwide videoconfs. on illiteracy, censorship, 1985; author: On Reading-in the Year of the Reader, 1987; editor Calif. State Library Found. Bull., 1982-94 (H.W. Wilson Periodical award 1988), Western Americana in the Calif. State Library, 1986, On Reading-In The Year of the Reader, 1987, Chinatown Photographer: Louis J. Stellman, 1989, Local History Genealogical Resources, 1990, Literate America Emerging, 1991; contbr. articles to profl. jours.; editor, designer and pub. of various books. Bd. dirs., v.p. Pacific N.W. Bibliog. Ctr., 1977-80; bd. dirs. Thurston Mason County Mental Health Ctr., 1977-80, pres., 1979-80; bd. dirs. Coop. Library Agy. for Systems and Services, 1980-94, vice chmn., 1981-84; bd. dirs. Sr. Services Snohomish County, 1973-76, HISPANEX (Calif. Spanish lang. database), 1983-86; bd. govs. Snohomish County Hist. Assn., 1974-76; mem. Oreg. Coun. Pub. Broadcasting, 1969-73; mem. psychiat. task force St. Peters Hosp., Olympia, 1979-80; co-founder Calif. Ctr. for the Book, bd. dirs., 1987-94; mem. adv. bd. Calif. State PTA, 1981-86, Gov.'s Tech. Conf., 1993-94; mem. adv. com. Sch. Libr. Sci., UCLA, 1991-94, Sch. Libr. and Info. Studies, U. Calif., Berkeley, 1991-94; mem. Calif. Adult Edn. Steering Com., 1988-94; chmn. collaborative coun. Calif. State Literacy Resource Ctr., 1993-94; bd. dirs. Queens coun. Boy Scouts of Am., 1994—. Recipient Disting. Alumnus award U. Mich., 1984, Disting. Svc. award Calif. Literacy Inc., 1985, Spl. Achievement award Literacy Action, 1988, Assn. Specialized and Coop. Libr. Agys. Exceptional Achievement award, 1992, Gov.'s Award of Achievement Govt. Tech. Conf., 1994, Advancement of Literacy award Pub. Libr. Assn., 1994, John Cotton Dana award Libr. Adminstrn. and Mgmt. Assn., 1994; named Libr. of Yr. Calif. Assn. Libr. Trustees and Commrs., 1994; Oreg. Libr. scholar, 1966. Mem. ALA (legis. com. 1980-82, 95—, chair intellectual property subcom. 1995—, Commn. on Freedom and Equality of Access to Info. 1983-86), Libr. Adminstrn. and Mgmt. Assn. (bd. dirs. 1980-88, pres. 1984-85), N.Y. Libr. Assn., Oreg. Libr. Assn. (hon. life mem., pres. 1970-71), Pacific N.W. Libr. Assn. (hon. life mem., pres. 1978-79), Calif. Libr. Assn. (govt. rels. com. 1980-94), Chief Officers of State Libr. Agys. (pres. 1984-86), Western Coun. State Librs. (pres. 1989-91), Assn. Specialized and Coop. Libr. Agys., Queens County C. of C. (bd. dirs. 1996—), Greater Jamaica Devel. Corp., Everett Area C. of C. (bd. dirs. 1974-76), METRO (bd. dirs. 1995—), Book Club of Calif., Sacramento Book Collectors Club, Roxburghe Club, The Book Collectors Club Grolier Club. Office: Queens Borough Pub Libr 89-11 Merrick Blvd Jamaica NY 11432-5200

STRONG, HENRY, foundation executive; b. Rochester, N.Y., Oct. 6, 1923; s. L. Corrin and Alice (Trowbridge) S.; m. Malan Swing, June 30, 1951; children: Sigrid Anne, Barbara Kirk, Dana Elizabeth, Henry Lockwood. A.B., Williams Coll., 1949. Joined Fgn. Service, 1950; with State Dept., 1950-51; vice consul The Hague, 1951-54, Washington, 1954-55; 2d sec. U.S. Embassy, Copenhagen, 1955-58, State Dept., 1958-62, Djakarta, Indonesia, 1962-64; resigned, 1968; chmn. bd., pres. Hattie M. Strong Found., 1968—. Mem. D.C. Commn. Arts, 1968-75; mem. D.C. Bd. Higher Edn., 1973-76; vice chmn. bd. trustees J.F. Kennedy Ctr. for Performing Arts, 1975-90, hon. trustee, 1991—; bd. dirs. Nat. Symphony Orch., Pomfret Sch., Fed. City Coun., M.M. Post Found. D.C., Community Found. of Greater Washington, 1974-91, Mt. Vernon Coll., 1969-88, 91—, Nat. Capital chpt. ARC, 1994—. Republican. Episcopalian. Clubs: Chevy Chase; Metropolitan (Washington); Gibson Island (Md.). Home: 5039 Overlook Rd NW Washington DC 20016-1911 Office: Hattie M Strong Found 1620 I St NW Ste 700 Washington DC 20006-4005

STRONG, JAMES THOMPSON, financial/management/security consultant, executive search; b. Boca Raton, Fla., Oct. 26, 1945; s. Earl William and Mary Joe (Thompson) S.; m. Lenore Jean Stager, Feb. 2, 1974; 1 child, Daria Nicole. BA in Polit. Sci., U. Calif., Riverside, 1973; MS in Strategic Intelligence, Def. Intelligence Coll., Washington, 1982. Factoring specialist. Commd. USAF, 1968, advaned through grades to maj., ret., 1990; faculty Def. Intelligence Coll., Washington, 1982-86; dir. translations USAF, 1986-88, dir. info. svcs., 1988-90; proprietary security mgr. McDonnell-Douglas Technologies, San Diego, 1990-92; owner Employment Svcs. for Bus., San Diego, 1995—. Author: The Basic Industrial Counter-Espionage Cookbook, 1993, The Government Contractor's OPSEC Cookbook, 1993; co-author: The Military Intelligence Community, 1985; mem. bd. editors Internat. Jour. Intelligence and Counterintelligence, 1986—; contbr. articles to profl. jours. Recipient Disting. EEO award USAF, 1987, Def. Meritorious Svc. medal 1986, Meritorious Svc. medal, 1981, 90, Joint Svc. Commendation medal Def. Intelligence Agy./NATO, 1982, 85. Mem. Nat. Mil. Intelligence Assn. (bd. dirs. 1984—, chpt. pres. 1989, 94), Ops. Security Profls. Soc. (chpt. chair 1993, 94), Nat. Cargo Security Coun., San Diego Roundtable (exec. coord. 194, 95), Assn. Former Intelligence Officers, Am. Soc. for Indsl. Security, Air Force Assn., San Diego Soc. for Human Resource Mgmt. Republican. Avocations: bridge, golf, reading. Home: 13785 Quinton Rd San Diego CA 92129-3202 Office: Employment Svcs for Bus 13785 Quinton Rd San Diego CA 92129-3202

STRONG, JOHN DAVID, insurance company executive; b. Cortland, N.Y., Apr. 12, 1936; s. Harold A. and Helen H. S.; m. Carolyn Dimmick, Oct. 26, 1957; children: John David Jr., Suzanne. BS, Syracuse U., N.Y., 1957; postgrad, Columbia U., 1980. With Kemper Group, 1957-90, Kemper Corp., 1990-96, Empire div. sales mgr., 1972-74, exec. v.p. Fed. Kemper Ins. Co., Decatur, Ill., 1974-79, pres., bd. dirs., 1979-93, CEO, 1988-93, chmn. bd., 1989-93; vice chmn. Millikin Assocs., 1993-96, chmn., 1996—; exec. v.p., dir. Facilitators, Inc., 1995—; bd. dirs. First of Am. Bank, Decatur, 1994. Mem. adv. council Sch. Bus. Millikin U., 1975-79, 84—; bd. dirs. United Way of Decatur and Macon County, Ill., 1976-83, campaign chmn., 1978-79, pres. bd. dirs., 1979-81; pres. United Way of Ill., 1981-83; bd. dirs. DMH Commn. Svcs. Corp., 1985—, chmn., 1988-90; bd. dirs. Decatur-Macon County Econ. Devel. Found., 1983-88, DMH Health Systems, 1987-94, Richland C.C. Found., 1987-90, Symphony Ord. Guild of Decatur, 1992-96, DMH Found., 1988—; bd. dirs. Ill. Ednl. Devel. Found., 1983-90, pres., 1986-87; bd. dirs. Decatur Meml. Hosp., 1985-94, vice-chmn., 1988, chmn. 1990-92; bd. dir. Ctrl. Ill. Health Assocs., Inc., 1994, vice chmn. 1994-96; mem. steering com. Decatur Advantage, 1981-93, pres., 1988-93. Capt. USAR, 1958-69. Mem. Metro Decatur C. of C. (bd. dirs. 1977-80, 2d vice chmn. 1981-82, 1st vice chmn. 1982-83, chmn. 1983-84), Alpha Kappa Psi. Club: Decatur (bd. dirs. 1980-83, pres. 1983), Country of Decatur (bd. dirs. 1993—, pres. bd. 1995—). Office: Ste 366 First Am Ctr 250 N Water Decatur IL 62523

STRONG, JOHN SCOTT, finance educator; b. Phila., Aug. 28, 1956; s. John S. and Thelma J. (Willard) S. BS, Washington & Lee U., 1978; M of Pub. Policy, Harvard U., 1981, PhD in Bus. Econs., 1986. Rsch. fellow Harvard U., Cambridge, Mass., 1983-85, 89-90, 93, vis. asst. prof. econs., 1989-90; assoc. prof. fin. Coll. William and Mary, Williamsburg, Va., 1985-96, prof., 1996—; cons. on econs. and fin. Republic of Indonesia, 1987—, MITI, Japan, 1988-89, European Bank for Reconstruction and Devel., 1993, Govt. of Bolivia, 1994. Author: Why Airplanes Crash: Aviation Safety in a Changing World, Moving to Market: Restructuring Transport in the Former Soviet Union, 1996; co-author 2 books on airline deregulation; contbr. articles to profl. jours. Fulbright scholar, 1978-79; grad. fellow NSF, 1979-82. Office: Coll William & Mary Sch Bus Williamsburg VA 23187

STRONG, JOHN WILLIAM, lawyer, educator; b. Iowa City, Aug. 18, 1935; s. Frank Ransom and Gertrude Elizabeth (Way) S.; m. Margaret Waite Cleary, June 16, 1962; children—Frank Ransom, Benjamin Waite. B.A., Yale U., 1957; J.D., U. Ill., 1962; postgrad, U. N.C., 1966-67. Bar: Ill. 1963, Oreg. 1976. Assoc. firm LeForgee, Samuels, Miller, Schroeder & Jackson, Decatur, Ill., 1963-64; asst. prof. law U. Kans., 1964-66; assoc. prof. Duke U., 1966-69; prof. U. Oreg., 1969-75; legal counsel Oreg. Task Force on Med. Malpractice, 1976; prof. U. Nebr., 1977-84, dean, 1977-82, vice chancellor for acad. affairs, 1981-84; Rosenstiel Disting. prof. law U. Ariz., 1984—; nat. sec.-treas. Order of the Coif, 1992—; cons. Nat. Judicial Coll. Author: (with others) Handbook on Evidence, 4th edit., 1992. Served with U.S. Army, 1957-59. Mem. Ill. Bar Assn., Oreg. Bar Assn., ABA, Am. Law Inst., Phi Delta Phi. Republican. Congregationalist. Home: 3220 E 3rd St Tucson AZ 85716-4233 Office: U Ariz Coll Law Tucson AZ 85721

STRONG, ROBERT S., banker; b. N.Y.C., Jan. 27, 1949; s. Henry William and Ida Anna (Krone) S.; m. Virginia Hala, June 11, 1994; children: Lauren, Jennifer, Tracy, Emily. BA in Econs., Columbia U., 1971; MBA in Fin., NYU, 1977. Lending officer Chase Manhattan Corp., N.Y.C., 1973-77; v.p. Chase Manhattan Bank, N.Y.C., 1977-88, sr. v.p., 1988-91, sector exec., 1991—, exec. v.p., 1993—; chief credit officer Chase Manhattan Corp., N.Y.C., 1995—. Episcopalian. Office: Chase Manhattan Corp 270 Park Ave New York NY 10017

STRONG, SARA DOUGHERTY, psychologist, family and custody mediator; b. Phila., May 30, 1927; d. Augustus Joseph and Orpha Elizabeth (Dock) Dougherty; m. David Mather Strong, Dec. 21, 1954. BA in Psychology, Pa. State U., 1949; MA in Clin. Psychology, Temple U., 1960, postgrad., 1968-72; cert. in Family Therapy, Family Inst. Phila., 1978. Lic. psychologist, Pa. Med. br. psychologist Family Ct. Phila., 1960-85, asst. chief psychologist, 1985-88, chief psychologist, 1988-92; retired, 1992; pvt. practice Phila., 1992—; cons. St. Joseph's Home for Girls, Phila., 1963-84, Daughters of Charity of St. Vincent De Paul, Albany, N.Y., 1965-90. Mem. APA (assoc.), Am. Assn. Marriage and Family Therapists, Pa. Psychol. Assn., Nat. Register of Health Svc. Providers in Psychology, Family Inst. Phila. Democrat. Avocations: reading, dramatic productions, writing, Yoga.

STRONG, WILLIAM L., III, investment executive; b. Plainfield, N.J., Nov. 27, 1932; s. William Lord Jr. and Elizabeth (Burke) S.; m. Beverly Carter Brand, Sept. 17, 1955; children: William L. IV, Peter B., Catherine B. BA, Yale U., 1955; postgrad., NYU, 1958-61. Security analyst Franklin Cole & Co., N.Y.C., 1958-64; investment officer Fiduciary Trust Internat., N.Y.C., 1965-67, asst. v.p., 1967-69, v.p., 1969-71, sr. v.p., 1971—. Bd. dirs. Muhlenberg Hosp., Plainfield, 1969-74; trustee Oceanic Free Libr., Rumson, N.J. Republican. Episcopalian. Office: Fiduciary Trust Internat 2 World Trade Ctr New York NY 10048-0203

STRONG, WINIFRED HEKKER, educational counselor, consultant; b. Passaic, N.J., May 16, 1923; d. Frank T. and Wilhelmine (Bohack) Hekker; divorced; 1 child, Frank R. Bush; m. Fred N. Strong, June 21, 1969. BA, Marymount Coll., 1945; MA, NYU, N.Y.C., 1948; postgrad. counseling, Calif. State U., Long Beach, 1958-62, 72, 73. Cert. counselor U.S., Calif. State Bd. Edn. Tchr. Marymount Acad., Tarrytown, N.Y., 1945-46; instr. Fairleigh Dickinson U., Rutherford, N.J., 1950-57; tchr. Long Beach Unified Sch. Dist., 1957-60, sch. counselor, 1960-80, cons. counseling svcs., 1980-90; cons. Calif. Acad. Math. and Sci., Dominguez Hills, 1990-93; pvt. practice Laguna Hills, Calif., 1990—; mem. profl. adv. bd. Learning Disabilities Assn. Calif., San Leandro, 1990—; part-time instr. U. La Verne, Calif., 1991-92; chair profl. devel. com. Calif. Assn. for Counseling and Devel., Fullerton, Calif., 1993—. Author: (elem. career awareness program) Color Me Successful, 1988; contbr. handbook Caution - Crisis Ahead, 1994. Mem. League Women Voters, Long Beach, 1982—. Recipient Counseling Program award Dept. of Edn. Los Angeles County, 1988, Adminstr. Recognition award Calif. Sch. Counselor Assn., 1990, Cmty. Contbn. citation Delta Kappa Gamma, 1990. Mem. AAUW (com. edn. found. 1993—), Am. Assn. Adult Devel. and Aging (exec. coun. 1993—), Am. Counseling Assn., Nat. Learning Disabilities Assn., Learning Disabilities Assn. Calif., Calif. Assn. Counseling & Devel. (Clarion model award 1990), Calif. Assn. for Adult Devel. & Aging (pres. 1991-92), Long Beach C. of C. (bd. dirs. women's coun. 1987-89), Nat. Bd. Cert. Counselors. Avocations: travel, reading, needlework, swimming. Home and Office: 5216 Elvira Laguna Hills CA 92653-1817

STRONGIN, THEODORE, journalist; b. N.Y.C., Dec. 10, 1918; s. Isadore and Ida (Slevin) S.; m. Ruth Klein, Aug. 13, 1947 (dec. 1954); children: Deborah, Daniel Otto; m. Harriet Stern Rosenberg, Oct. 4, 1969 (dec. 1991). Student, Harvard, 1935-37; A.B., Bard Coll., 1941; postgrad., Juilliard Sch. Music, summers 1940, 41, fall 1946, Columbia, 1947-49. Dir. music East Woods Sch., Oyster Bay, N.Y., 1947-54; mem. music faculty Bennington (Vt.) Coll., 1954-56, Dartmouth, spring 1955; arts editor Chattanooga Times, 1957-61, Albany (N.Y.) Knickerbocker News, 1961-63; music critic, reporter, record reviewer N.Y. Times, 1963-65, music critic, reporter, recs. editor, 1965-71; columnist East Hampton (N.Y.) Star, 1972-77; Cons. Music in Our Time series, N.Y.C., 1972-73, N.Y. State Council on Arts, 1970, various art instns., 1971-77. Composer: Suite for Unaccompanied Cello, 1951, Quartet for Oboe and Strings, 1952; author: Casals, 1966. Mem. Amagansett Village Improvement Soc., 1974-86; mem. Amagansett Residents Assn., 1975-86, bd. dirs., pres., 1975-77; dir. pub. relations Ind. Voters of East Hampton, 1971. Served to capt. AUS, 1941-46. Recipient Broude Publ. prize for piano piece, 1948. Democrat. Address: 204 Woodland Dr Osprey FL 34229-9551

STRONG-TIDMAN, VIRGINIA ADELE, marketing and advertising executive; b. Englewood, N.J., July 26, 1947; d. Alan Ballentine and Virginia Leona (Harris) Strong; m. John Fletcher Tidman, Sept. 23, 1978. BS, Albright Coll., Reading, Pa., 1969; postgrad. U. Pitts., 1970-73, U. Louisville, 1975-76. Exec. trainee Pomeroy's div. Allied Stores, Reading, 1969-70; mktg. rsch. analyst Heinz U.S.A., Pitts., 1970-74; new products mktg. mgr. Ky. Fried Chicken, Louisville, 1974-76; dir. Pitts. office M/A/R/C, 1976-79; assoc. rsch. dir. Henderson Advt., Inc., Greenville, S.C., 1979-81; sr. v.p., dir. rsch. Bozell, Jacobs, Kenyon & Eckhardt, Inc., Dallas, 1981-86, sr. v.p., dir. rsch. and strategic planning Atlanta, 1986-88; sr. v.p., dir. mktg. svcs. Bozell, Inc., Atlanta, 1988-91; sr. v.p., mng. ptnr. Henderson Adv., Inc., 1991-95; prin. Ender-Ptnr., Inc., 1995-96; v.p. mktg. Booth Rsch. Svcs., Inc., 1996—; cons. mktg. rsch. Greenville Zool. Soc., 1981; adj. prof. So. Meth. U., 1984-85. Mem. Am. Mktg. Assn. (Effie award N.Y. chpt. 1982). Republican. Episcopalian. Home: 1835 Johnson Ferry Rd Atlanta GA 30319-1922

STRONSKI, ANNA MARIA NIEDŹWIEDZKA, language professional; b. Starachowice, Poland, Aug. 17, 1940; came to U.S., 1954; d. Antoni Niedzwiedzki and Wanda Gluszkiewicz; divorced; 1 child, Alexandra Joanna Paszkowski. BA, Wayne State U., 1963, MA, 1972. Cert. secondary edn. tchr., Mich. Tchr. French and Spanish Ford Mid. Sch., Highland Park, Mich., 1965-66; tchr. fgn. lang. dept. Highland Park Cmty. H.S., 1966—, head fgn. lang. dept., 1968-70, 73-78, lang. arts facilitator, 1991-94; owner, founder Horizons-Internat., Grosse Pointe Park, Mich., 1993—; dist.-wide lang. cons./coord. Highland Park Pub. Schs., 1994—; ind. contractor/cons. Langs. and Svcs. Agy., 1993—; assessor, field study, tchr. performance lang. arts Nat. Bd. Profl. Tchg. Stds., Mich., 1994; scorer writing proficiency assessments Mich. Dept. Edn., 1994-95, trainer of tchrs., 1995; mem. instrnl./profl. devel. task force Mid. Cities Assn., Lansing, Mich., 1995—; mem. North Ctrl Accreditation Evaluations Teams, 1970—. Advisor: (high sch. yearbook) Polar Bear, 1985-86 (Big E award Josten's Printing Divsn. 1986); editor: (newsletter) Happenings, 1977-79, Mich. Writing Assessment News, 1994—. Bd. dirs. French Inst. Mich., Southfield, 1985—, Friends of Polish Art, Mich., 1995—. Recipient cert. appreciation for participation in Classrooms of Tomorrow program, Mich. Gov., 1990. Mem. Alliance Francaise: Detroit/Grosse Pointe, AAUW. Roman Catholic. Avocations: travel, sailing, skiing, literature, music. Home: 790 Middlesex Blvd Grosse Pointe MI 48230-1742 Office: Horizons Internat 790 Middlesex Blvd Grosse Pointe Park MI 48230-1742

STROOCK, DANIEL WYLER, mathematician, educator; b. N.Y.C., Mar. 20, 1940; s. Alan Maxwell and Katherine (Wyler) S.; m. Lucy Barber, Nov. 21, 1962; children: Benjamin, Abraham. AB, Harvard Coll., 1962; PhD, Rockefeller U., 1966. Vis. mem. Courant Inst., N.Y. U., 1966-69, asst. prof., 1969-72; asso. prof. math. U. Colo., Boulder, 1972-75; prof. U. Colo., 1975-84, chmn. dept. math, 1979-81; prof. math. MIT, 1984—; adj. prof. U. Colo., Beijing Normal U. Author: (with S.R.S. Vanadhan) Multidimensional Diffusion Processes, 1979, (with J.D. Deutschel) Large Deviations, 1989, Probability Theory, An Analytic View, 1993; editor Math. Zeitschrift, 1992—, Ill. Jour. Math., 1976-82, Transactions of Am. Math. Soc., 1974-80, Annals of Probability, 1988-93, Advances in Math., 1995—, Jour. Functional Analysis, 1994—; contbr. articles on probability theory to profl. jours. Guggenheim fellow, 1978-79. Mem. Am. Acad. Arts and Scis., Nat. Acad. Scis. Democrat. Jewish. Home: 55 Frost St Cambridge MA 02140-2247 Office: MIT Dept Math Cambridge MA 02139

STROOCK, MARK EDWIN, II, public relations company executive; b. N.Y.C., Nov. 6, 1922; s. Irving Sylvan and Blanche (Loeb) S.; m. Hanna Marks Eiseman, June 24, 1945; children—Mark E., Carolyn E. B.A., Bard Coll., 1947. Reporter The New York Journal of Commerce, 1947-50; writer Barrons, N.Y.C., 1950-51; mng. editor Fairchild Publication, N.Y.C., 1952-53; bus. editor World Mag., N.Y.C., 1953-54; contbg. editor Time Mag., N.Y.C., 1954-56; with Young & Rubicam Inc., N.Y.C., 1956-87, sr. v.p., dir. corporate rels., cons., 1987—. Bd. trustee N.Y. Urban League, 1971-78, Alvin Ailey Dance Theatre, N.Y.C., 1977-84, Friends of the Theatre Mus. City N.Y., 1977-85; vice chmn. Covenant House, N.Y.C., 1978-90; exec. com., mktg. and communications com. Anti-Defamation League, 1992—. Served with U.S. Army, 1943-46. Democrat. Jewish. Home: 50 Park Ave New York NY 10016-3000 Office: Young & Rubicam Inc 285 Madison Ave New York NY 10017-6401

STROOCK, THOMAS FRANK, business executive; b. N.Y.C., Oct. 10, 1925; s. Samuel and Dorothy (Frank) S.; m. Marta Freyre de Andrade, June 19, 1949; children: Margaret, Sandra, Elizabeth, Anne. BA in Econs., Yale U., 1948; LLB (hon.) U. Wyo., 1995. Landman Stanolind Oil & Gas Co., Tulsa, 1948-52; pres. Stroock Leasing Corp., Casper, Wyo., 1952-89, Alpha Exploration, Inc., 1980-89; ptnr. Stroock, Rogers & Dymond, Casper, 1960-82; dir. Wyo. Bancorp., Cheyenne, First Wyo. Bank, Casper; mem. Wyo. Senate, 1967-69, 71-75, 79-89, chmn. appropriations com. 1983, co-chmn. joint appropriations com., 1983-89, mem. mgmt. and audit com. P; mem. steering com. Edn. Commn. of States; amb. to Guatemala, Govt. of U.S., 1989-92; pres. Alpha Devel. Corp., 1992—; prof. pub. diplomacy U. Wyo., Casper, 1993—. Rep. precinct committeeman, 1950-68; pres. Natrona County Sch. Bd., 1960-69; pres. Wyo. State Sch. Bds. Assn., 1965-66; chmn. Casper Community Recreation, 1955-60; chmn. Natrona County United Fund, 1963-64; chmn. Wyo. State Republican Com., 1975-78, exec. com. 1954-60; delegate Rep. Nat. Convetion, 1956, 76; regional coord. campaign George Bush for pres., 1979-80, 87-88; chmn. Western States Rep. Chmn. Assn., 1977-78; chmn. Wyo. Higher Edn. Commn., 1969-71; mem. Nat. Petroleum Council, 1972-77; chmn. trustees Sierra Madre Found. for Geol. Research, New Haven; chmn. Wyo. Nat. Gas Pipeline Authority 1987-88; bd. dirs. Ucross Found., Denver; mem. Nat. Pub. Lands Adv. Council, 1981-85; chmn. Wyo. Health Reform Commn., 1993-95. Served with USMC, 1943-46. Mem. Rocky Mountain Oil and Gas Assn., Petroleum Assn. Wyo. Republican. Unitarian. Lodge: Kiwanis. Clubs: Casper Country; Casper Petroleum; Denver. Home and Office: PO Box 2875 Casper WY 82602-2875

STROPNICKY, GERARD PATRICK, theater director, consultant; b. Teaneck, N.J., Aug. 25, 1953; s. John F. and Elizabeth M. (Novotny) S.; m. Kathleen Horkay Baas, Aug. 16, 1987; children: Diane, William. BSc in Speech, Northwestern U., 1976. Founding mem. Bloomsburg (Pa.) Theatre Ensemble, 1978—; cons. Fedapt, N.Y.C., 1984-89; cons. theatre design Bristol (Pa.) Riverside Theatre, 1986-87, F.M. Kirby Ctr., Wilkes Barre, Pa., 1988; guest dir. Fla. Shakespeare Festival, Coral Gables, 1986-87, Touchstone Theatre, Bethlehem, Pa., 1989, 91. Pa. Playwright fellow, 1991. Mem. Theatre Assn. Pa. (bd. dirs. 1991-94), Bucknell Univ. Assn. Arts (bd. dirs. 1989—). Office: Bloomsburg Theatre Ensemble 226 Center St Bloomsburg PA 17815-1752

STROSAHL, WILLIAM AUSTIN, artist, art director; b. N.Y.C., June 11, 1910; s. William August and Margaret Theresa (Peterson) S.; m. Rosemary Rachel Jordan, May 28, 1949 (dec. Dec. 1989); children: Timothy, Brian, William, Jordan, Margaret. Student, Parsons Sch. Design, 1926-27. Cub cartoonist N.Y. Evening Graphic, N.Y.C., 1927-28; art dir. Ohio Match Co., N.Y.C., 1928-29, Lindsay Assoc. Artists, N.Y.C., 1929-30; asst. art dir. J. Walter Thompson, N.Y.C., 1930-32, art dir., 1932-42; exec. art dir. William Esty Co., N.Y.C., 1942-55, creative dir., exec. v.p., 1956-69, watercolor painter, 1969—. Recipient Gold medal Allied Artist Am., 1965, 88; recipient Hallmark Audubon Artists, 1959, Gold and Silver medal Audubon Artists, 1980, Nat. Acad. Design, John Pike Meml. award, 1985, Ogden Pleisner Meml. award, 1987, William A. Paton Meml. prize, 1988, Creative Watercolor awards, 1990-91, 200 Yrs. Watercolor Painting award Met. Mus. Art, N.Y.C., 58 other awards for watercolor painting, 1946-90. Fellow Dolphin Fellowship; mem. Am. Watercolor Soc. (v.p. 1950), Am. Watercolor Soc. (hon. pres. 1983—), Nat. Art Dirs. Assn. (v.p. 1954), Nat. Acad. Design, Academician 1994—, Silvermine Guild, Allied Artists Am., Audubon Artists. Republican. Home: 301 Haviland Rd Stamford CT 06903-3324

STROSCIO, MICHAEL ANTHONY, physicist, educator; b. Winston-Salem, N.C., June 1, 1949; s. Anthony and Norma Lee (Sidbury) S.; children: Elizabeth de Clare, Charles Marshall Sidbury, Gautam Dutta. BS, U. N.C., 1970; MPhil in Physics, Yale U., 1972, PhD in Physics, 1974. Physicist Los Alamos Sci. Lab., N.Mex., 1975-78; sr. staff mem. Johns Hopkins U. Applied Physics Lab., Laurel, Md., 1978-80; prof. mgr. for electromagnetic research Air Force Office of Sci. Research, Washington, 1980-83; spl. asst. to research dir. Office of Under Sec. Def., Washington, 1982-83; policy analyst White House Office of Sci. and Tech. Policy, Washington, 1983-85; prof. dir. for microelectronics, prin. scientist U.S. Army Research Office, Research Triangle Park, N.C., 1985—; adj. prof. depts. physics and elec. and computer engring. N.C. State U., Raleigh, 1985—; adj. prof. depts. elec. engring. and physics Duke U., Durham, 1986—; vis. prof. dept. of elec. engring. U. Va., Charlottesville, 1990-95, U. Md., College Park, 1996—; mem. Congrl. Coun., 1989-91; lectr. UCLA, 1987, U. Mich., 1988; cons. U.S. Dept. Energy, Washington, 1985—; vice chmn. White House Panel on Sci. Communication, Washington, 1983-84; chmn. Dept. Def. Rsch. Instrumentation Com., Washington, 1982; assoc. mem. Adv. Group on Electron Devices, 1985-91, liaison Nat. Laser Users Facility, Rochester, N.Y., 1984; liaison Panel on Sci. Comm. and Nat. Security, NAS, 1982, Panel on Materials for High-Density Electron Packaging, 1987-90; U.S. Army liaison to JASON, 1991—; mem. U.S. Govt. coord. com. on Semiconductor Rsch. Corp., 1992—. Author: Positronium: A Review of the Theory, 1975, Onslow Families, 1977; reviewer NSF, Office of Naval Rsch., Dept. Commerce and the Natural Scis., Engring. Rsch. Coun. Can., 1981—; referee jours.; contbr. articles to profl. jours.; patentee in field. Served to capt. USAF, 1974-75. Los Alamos Sci. Lab. grantee, 1977. Fellow IEEE (exec. com. for plasma sci. 1983—), Yale Sci. and Engring. Assn. (exec. bd. dirs. 1983—); mem. Am. Phys. Soc., Phi Beta Kappa, Nat. Geneal. Soc. Home: 206 E Woodridge Dr Durham NC 27707-2842 Office: US Army Research Office PO Box 12211 Durham NC 27709-2211

STROSS, JEOFFREY KNIGHT, physician, educator; b. Detroit, May 2, 1941; s. Julius Knight and Molly Ellen (Fishman) S.; m. Ellen Nora Schwartz, May 22, 1965; children: Wendy, Jonathan. BS in Pharmacy, U. Mich., 1962, MD, 1967. Diplomate Am. Bd. Internal Medicine. Intern Univ. Mich. Hosp., Ann Arbor, 1967-68, resident in internal medicine, 1971-73; instr. internal medicine U. Mich., Ann Arbor, 1973-74, asst. prof., 1974-79, assoc. prof., 1979-87, prof., 1987—; cons. Merck Sharp Dohme Co., West Point, Pa., 1982—, U.S. Dept. State, Washington, 1976—. Contbr. numerous articles to med. jours. Served to maj. USAF, 1969-71. Nat. Heart, Lung and Blood Inst. grantee, 1975—. Fellow ACP; mem. Soc. for Gen. Internal Medicine (regional chmn. 1984-86). Jewish. Home: 3541 Larchmont Dr Ann Arbor MI 48105-2853 Office: Univ of Mich Med Sch 246 Med Inn Bldg Ann Arbor MI 48109

STROSSEN, NADINE, law educator, human rights activist; b. Jersey City, Aug. 18, 1950; d. Woodrow John and Sylvia (Simicich) S.; m. Eli Michael Noam, Apr. 25, 1980. AB, Harvard U., 1972, JD magna cum laude, 1975. Jud. clk. Minn. Supreme Ct., St. Paul, 1975-76; assoc. Lindquist & Vennum, Mpls., 1976-78, Sullivan & Cromwell, N.Y.C., 1978-83; prof. clin. law, supervising atty. Civil Rights Clinic, Sch. Law, NYU, 1984-88; prof. law N.Y. Law Sch., N.Y.C., 1988—. Editor Harvard Law Rev., 1975; contbr. book chpts., articles to profl. jours.; author: In Defense of Pornography: Free Speech and the Fight for Women's Rights, 1995. Bd. dirs. The Fund for Free Expression, 1990—. Recipient Outstanding Young Person award Jaycees Internat., 1986, Outstanding Contbn. to Human Rights Jour. Human Rights, N.Y. Law Sch., 1989; named one of Ten Outstanding Young Ams., U.S. Jaycees, 1986. Mem. ACLU (exec. com. 1985—, gen. counsel 1986-91, pres. 1991—), Nat. Coalition Against Censorship (bd. dirs. 1989—), Coalition to Free Soviet Jews (bd. dirs. 1984—), Human Rights Watch (exec. com. 1989-91), Asia Watch (vice chair 1989-91), Mid. East Watch (bd. dirs. 1989-91), Harvard Club (N.Y.C.). Avocations: travel, skiing, singing. Home: 450 Riverside Dr # 51 New York NY 10027-6821 also: Sedgewood Club RR 12 Carmel NY 10512-9812 Office: NY Law Sch 57 Worth St New York NY 10013-2926*

STROTE, JOEL RICHARD, lawyer; b. N.Y.C., Apr. 19, 1939; s. Jack and Fortuna (Benezra) S.; children: Jared, Noah, Sebastian; m. Elisa Ballestas, Dec. 14, 1991. BA, U. Mich., 1960; JD, Northwestern U., 1963. Bar: N.Y. 1964, D.C. 1965, Calif. 1967, U.S. Dist. Ct. (cen. dist.) Calif. 1967, U.S. Supreme Ct. 1971. Assoc. Damman, Blank, Hirsh & Heming, N.Y.C., 1964-65, ICC, Washington, 1965-66, Capitol Records, Hollywood, Calif., 1966-67; ptnr. Strote & Whitehouse, Beverly Hills, Calif., 1967-89; of counsel Selvin, Weiner & Ruben, Beverly Hills, Calif., 1989-94; ptnr. with Cohen, Strote & Young, 1992-94; sole practice law, 1994—; judge pro tem L.A. County Mcpl. Ct., 1973—; probation monitor Calif. State Bar Ct., L.A., 1985—; pres. Liberace Found., Las Vegas, Nev., 1987—; bd. chmn. Tuesday's Child, L.A., 1989-91. Cpl. USMC, 1963-64. Mem. Calif. State Bar Assn., L.A. County Bar Assn., L.A. Copyright Soc., Beverly Hills Bar Assn., Assn. Internat. Entertainment Lawyers, Internat. Fedn. of Festival Orgns. Democrat. Jewish. Avocations: swimming, bicycling, hiking, opera, travel. Office: Joel R Strote Profl Corp 21700 Oxnard St Ste 340 Woodland Hills CA 91367-3665

STROTHMAN, JAMES EDWARD, editor; b. Pitts., Mar. 27, 1939; s. Edward Charles and Harriet Hope (Jones) S.; m. Eleanor Shawfield Jacobs, Sept. 9, 1961; children—Joseph, Jill, Stuart. B.A. in Journalism, Pa. State U., 1961. Asst. city editor, city hall reporter Williamsport Grit, Pa., 1961-64; with Miami Herald, Fla., 1964-67; aerospace writer AP, Cape Kennedy, Fla., 1967-69; reporter Los Angeles bur. Electronic News, 1969-71, sr. editor computer news sect., 1971-73, mng. editor, 1973; sr. info. rep. corp. hdqrs., then program adminstr. data processing div. hdqrs. IBM Corp., 1973-77, mgr. eastern area communications data processing div., 1977-79, field communications mgr. data processing div., 1979-81, mgr. communications research div., 1981; free-lance writer and cons. Strothman Assocs., 1981-82; editor-in-chief MIS Week, N.Y.C., 1982-88; free-lance writer, cons., 1988-89; editor-in-chief Computer Pictures, Chappaqua, N.Y., 1989—; sr. editor Intech Mag. Instrument Soc. Am., Research Triangle Park, N.C., 1994—. Episcopalian.

STROTHMAN, WENDY JO, book publisher; b. Pitts., July 29, 1950; d. Walter Richard and Mary Ann (Hodtum) S.; m. Mark Kavanaugh Metzger, Nov. 25, 1978; children: Andrew Richard, Margaret Ann. Student, U. Chgo., 1979-80; AB, Brown U., 1972. Copywriter, mktg. U. Chgo. Press, 1973-76, editor, 1977-80, gen. editor, 1980-83, asst. dir., 1983; dir. Beacon Press, Boston, 1983-95; v.p., pub. adult, trade and reference Houghton-Mifflin, Boston, 1995-96, exec. v.p. trade and reference divsn., 1996—; trustee Brown U., 1990—. Edtl. adv. bd. Scholarly Pub., 1993-94; bd. editors Brown Alumni Monthly, 1983-89; chmn., 1986-89. Bd. dirs. Editorial Project for Edn., trustee, 1987-91, treas., 1988-90. Mem. Renaissance Soc. (bd. dirs. 1980-83), Assn. Am. Pubs. (Freedom to Read com.), Pubs. Lunch Club (N.Y.C.), PEN New Eng. (adv. bd.), Examiner Club, NacRe Reins. Corp. (bd. dirs.). Office: Houghton Mifflin Co 222 Berkeley St Boston MA 02116

STROUD, JAMES STANLEY, 419; b. Wimbledon, N.D., Jan. 26, 1915; s. Herbert Montgomery and Amanda Getchell (Longfellow) S.; m. Marjorie Marsh Hovey, Sept. 11, 1940; children: Jay Stanley, Steven Hovey. AB, Jamestown Coll., 1936; JD, U. Chgo., 1939. Bar: Ill. 1939, U.S. Supreme Ct. 1945, D.C. 1972. Counsel Ill. Mcpl. Code Commn., Chgo., 1939-40; bill drafter Ill. Legis. Ref. Bur., Springfield, 1941; from assoc. to ptnr. Mayer, Brown & Platt, Chgo., 1941-71; ptnr.-in-charge Mayer, Brown & Platt, Washington, 1972-80. Bd. dirs. Chgo. Community Renewal Found., 1962-70; mem. adminstrv. bd. Nat. United Meth. Ch., Washington, 1982-84; coord. Extended Family Program, 1981-82. Capt. AUS, 1943-46. Home: Cottage 304 3300 Darby Rd Haverford PA 19041-1063

STROUD, JOE HINTON, newspaper editor; b. McGehee, Ark., June 18, 1936; s. Joseph Hilliard and Marion Rebecca (McKinney) S.; m. Janis Mizell, Aug. 21, 1957; children: Rebecca McKinney, Joseph Scott, Alexandra Jane.; m. Kathleen M. Fojtik, Nov. 1, 1981; children: Jonathan Rudolph, Anna Marion. BA, Hendrix Coll., Conway, Ark., 1957; MA, Tulane U., 1959; LLD (hon.), Eastern Mich. U., 1977, Kalamazoo Coll., 1984, Adrian Coll., 1985; D Communicating Arts (hon.), Cen. Mich. U., 1986; LittD (hon.), Mich. State U., 1987, Olivet Coll., 1995. Reporter, then editor editorial page Pine Bluff (Ark.) Comml., 1959-60; editorial writer Ark. Gazette, Little Rock, 1960-64; editorial writer then editor editorial page Winston-Salem (N.C.) Jour.-Sentinel, 1964-68; assoc. editor Detroit Free Press, 1968-73, editor, 1973—, sr. v.p., 1978—. Mem. gen. bd. publs. United Meth. Ch., 1975-76; adv. bd. Mich. Christian Advocate, 1975-79; bd. govs. Cranbrook Inst. Sci., 1978—; trustee Cranbrook Ednl. Community, 1989—; bd. dirs. S.E. Mich. chpt. ARC, 1972-88, Detroit Symphony, 1978-83; chmn. adv. com. Svc. to Mil. Families, 1974-77, chmn. program evaluation com. 1978-80; bd. assocs. Adrian Coll., 1985—; trustee Starr Commonwealth Schs., 1989—. Recipient N.C. Sch. Bell award, 1967; Mich. Sch. Bell award, 1973; William Allen White award Inland Daily Press Assn., 1973, 76, 77; citation Overseas Press Club, 1974; Paul Tobenkin award Columbia U., 1976; Disting. Service award Mich.'s Women's Commn., 1984; Laity award Detroit Ann. Conf. United Meth. Ch., 1985. Mem. Am. Soc. Newspaper Editors, Nat. Conf. Editorial Writers (program chmn. 1978, v.p. 1987-88, pres. 1988-89), Detroit Econ. Club, Detroit Com. Fgn. Relations, Sigma Delta Chi. Clubs: Detroit, Renaissance, Nat. Press. Office: Detroit Free Press 321 W Lafayette Blvd Detroit MI 48226-2705

STROUD, JOHN FRANKLIN, engineering educator, scientist; b. Dallas, June 29, 1922; s. Edward Frank and Ethel A. Stroud; m. Dorcas Elizabeth Stroud, Feb. 4, 1944; children: Kevin, Karen, Richard. BSME, Stanford (Calif.) U., 1949, postgrad., 1949-53; cert. in fin. mgmt. for sr. execs., U. Pa., 1984. Aero. rsch. scientist NASA Ames Rsch. Lab., Moffett Field, Calif., 1949-53; thermodynamics engr. Lockheed, Burbank, Calif., 1953-55, group engr. propulsion, 1955-63, dept. engr. propulsion, 1963-70, from dept. engr. to divsn. engr. propulsion, 1970-83, chief engr. flight scis., 1983-85, divsn. engr., 1985-90, ret., 1990; cons. spl. studies in econs. and engring. sci., 1990—; mem. ad hoc adv. congrl. subcom. on high tech wind tunnels, 1985. Contbr. articles to profl. jours.; author and speaker in field. Charity fund raiser United Way, 1970-80, others. Lt., naval aviator USN, 1942-45, ETO. Decorated Battle of Atlantic. Fellow AIAA (assoc., airbreathing propulsion com. 1966-68, 80-83, chmn. many sessions 1970—); mem. Soc. Automotive Engrs. (aviation div. air transport com., propulsion com., chmn. many sessions nat. confs. 1970—, co-chmn. AIAA/SAE nat. propulsion conf. 1978). Achievements include patent for low drag external compression supersonic inlet; design and development of integrated F-104A inlet and air inductions system, integrated inlet/air induction system into the total propulsion system and airframe; management of team that developed, designed, and integrated the aeropropulsion systems on the L1011 commercial transport; devised new theory for turbulent boundary layers in adverse pressure gradients; numerous other patents pending.

STROUD, JOHN FRED, JR., state supreme court justice; b. Hope, Ark., Oct. 3, 1931; s. John Fred and Clarine (Steel) S.; m. Marietta Kimball, June 1, 1958; children: John Fred III, Ann Kimball, Tracy Steel. Student, Hendrix Coll., 1949-51; BA, U. Ark., 1959, LLB, 1960. Bar: Ark. 1959, Tex. 1988, U.S. Supreme Ct. 1963. Ptnr. Stroud & McClerkin, 1959-62; city atty. City of Texarkana (Ark.), 1961; legislative asst. to U.S. Senator John L. McClellan, 1962-63; ptnr. Smith, Stroud, McClerkin, Dunn & Nutter, 1963-79, 1981—; assoc. justice Ark. Supreme Ct., Little Rock, 1963-79; judge Ark. Ct. Appeals, Little Rock, 1996—. Chmn. Texarkana Airport Authority, 1966-67, Texarkana United Way Campaign, 1988; pres. Caddo area coun. Boy Scouts Am., 1971-73; former trustee Ark. Nature COnservancy; former bd. dirs. Ark. Cmty. Found.; former pres. Red River Valley Assn.; former commr. Red River Compact Commn.; past vice chmn. Ark. Water Code Study Commn.; chmn. bd., chmn. coun. ministries Meth. Ch. Lt. col. USAF, 1951-56, Res. ret. Recipient award of exceptional accomplishment Ark. State C. of C., 1972, 86, Silver Beaver and Disting. Eagle awards Boy Scouts Am.; named Outstanding Young Man of Texarkana, 1966, One of Five Outstanding Young Men of Ark., 1967, Outstanding Alumnus of U. Ark. Law Sch., 1980. Fellow Am. Bar Foun.; mem. ABA, Ark. Bar Assn. (chmn. exec. coun. 1979-80, pres. 1987-88), Four States Area Estate Planning Coun. (past chmn.), State Bar Tex., Miller County Bar Assn. (past pres.), Texarkana Bar Assn. (pres. 1982-83), Ark. Bar Found. (chmn. 1974-75), Am. Coll. Trust and Estate Counsel (chmn. Ark. chpt. 1986-91), S.W. Ark. Bar Assn., N.E. Tex. Bar Assn., Texarkana C. of C. (pres. 1969, C.E. Palmer award 1979), Texarkana Country Club (pres. 1990-92), Rotary (pres. Texarkana 1965-66). Democrat. Avocations: tennis, golf, hunting, fishing. Office: Ark Ct Appeals Box 8030 Ste 6 625 Marshall Little Rock AR 72201

STROUD, JUNIUS BRUTUS, III, mathematics educator; b. Greensboro, N.C., June 9, 1929; s. Junius Brutus Jr. and Rachel (Witherington) S.; m. Ruby Lee Masincup, Aug. 27, 1955; children: Timothy Brion, Jonathan McIver, Cynthia Lee. BS cum laude, Davidson (N.C.) Coll., 1951; MA, U. Va., 1962, PhD in Math., 1965. Instr./coach Fishburne Mil. Sch., Waynesboro, Va., 1953-57; tchr./coach Robert E. Lee High Sch., Staunton, Va., 1957-58; instr. math. Davidson (N.C.) Coll., 1960-63, asst. prof. math., 1965-67, assoc. prof. math., 1967-76, prof. math., 1976-85, chmn. dept. math., 1983-89, Richardson prof. math., 1985-94; Richardson prof. emeritus math., 1994—; lectr. N.C. Gov.'s Sch., Winston-Salem, 1983, 85; vis. prof. Dartmouth Coll., 1973, St. Andrews U., Scotland, 1987. 1st lt. U.S. Army, 1951-53. Decorated Army Commendation medal; Danforth Found. grantee, 1963, NSF Sci. Faculty fellow, 1964, Smithsonian fellow, 1979; Thomas Jefferson award, Davidson Coll., 1987. Mem. Math. Assn. Am., N.C. Council Tchrs. Math., Scabbard and Blade, Sigma Xi, Sigma Pi Sigma, Phi Beta Kappa. Democrat. Presbyterian. Avocations: travel, reading, furniture repair and restoration. Home: 207 Pine Rd PO Box 94 Davidson NC 28036-9048

STROUD, RICHARD HAMILTON, aquatic biologist, scientist, consultant; b. Dedham, Mass., Apr. 24, 1918; s. Percy Valentine and Elizabeth Lillian (Kimpton) S.; m. Genevieve Cecelia DePol, Dec. 20, 1943; children: William DePol, Jennifer Celia Trivett. BS, Bowdoin Coll., 1939; MS, U. N.H., 1942; postgrad., Yale U., 1947-48, Boston U. Sch. Edn., 1948-49. Asst. aquatic biologist N.H. Fish and Game Dept., Concord, 1940-41; jr. aquatic biologist TVA, Norris, Tenn., 1942, asst. aquatic biologist, 1946-47; chief aquatic biologist Mass. Div. Fisheries and Game, Boston, 1948-53; asst. exec. v.p. Sport Fishing Inst., Washington, 1953-55, exec. v.p., 1955-81, editor monthly bull.; sr. scientist Aquatic Ecosystems Analysts, Fayetteville, Ark., 1983-88; founder., mng. v.p., trustee Sport Fishery Rsch. Found., Washington, 1967-88; cons. aquatic resources, 1981-89, cons. editor fish sci. publs., 1982-95; rsch. adv. bd. Sport Fishing Inst. Fund, 1988-94; Pentelow lectr. U. Liverpool, England, 1975. Author Fisheries Report for Massachusetts Lakes, Ponds, and Reservoirs, 1955; editor (ann. series) Marine Recreational Fisheries Symposia, 1982-95, Nat. Leaders of American Conservation, 1985, World Angling Resources and Challenges, 1985, Fish Culture in Fisheries Management, 1986, Multi-Jurisdictional Management of Marine Fisheries, 1986, Management of Atlantic Salmon, 1988, Planning the Future of Billfishes, Part 1, 1989, Part 2, 1990, Stemming The Tide of Coastal Fish Habitat Loss, 1991, Fisheries Management and Watershed Development, 1992, Conserving America's Fisheries, 1994; co-editor The Biological Significance of Estuaries, 1971, Black Bass Biology and Management, 1975, Predator Prey Systems in Fisheries Management, 1979; contbr. articles to various publs. Bd. dirs. Nat. Coalition Marine Conservation, 1977—; treas. Natural Resources Coun. Am., 1961-68, chmn., 1969-71, hon. mem., 1981—. Served with U.S. Army, 1942-46. Decorated Croix de Guerre with cluster.; recipient Conservation Achievement award Nat. Wildlife Fedn., 1975, 81, SOAR award Boy Scouts Am., 1972; named to Nat. Fishing Hall of Fame, 1984. Fellow Am. Inst. Fishery Research Biologists (emeritus, Outstanding Achievement award 1981), Am. Fisheries Soc. (pres. 1979-80, hon. life mem., Outstanding Achievement award 1990); mem. Internat. Fish and Wildlife Agys., Freshwater Biol. Assn. (U.K.), Fisheries Soc. Brit. Isles, Moore County Wildlife Club, Country Club (Pinehurst, N.C.). Office: PO Box 1772 Pinehurst NC 28374-1772

STROUD, ROBERT EDWARD, lawyer; b. Chester, S.C., July 24, 1934; s. Coy Franklin and Leila (Caldwell) S.; m. Katherine C. Stroud, Apr. 8, 1961; children: Robert Gordon, Margaret Lathan. AB, Washington and Lee U., 1956, LLB, 1958. Bar: Va. 1959, U.S. Ct. Appeals (4th cir.) 1967. Assoc. McGuire, Woods, Battle & Boothe LLP, Charlottesville, Va., 1959-64; ptnr. McGuire, Woods, Battle & Boothe, LLP, Charlottesville, Va., 1964—, mem. exec. com., 1978-89; lectr. math. Washington and Lee U., 1957-59; lectr. bus. tax Grad. Bus. Sch., U. Va., Charlottesville, 1969-87, lectr. corp. taxation law sch., 1985-91; lectr. to legal edn. insts., lectr. in corp. law Washington and Lee Law Sch., 1984. Co-author: Buying, Selling and Merging Businesses, 1975; editor-in-chief Washington and Lee Law Rev., 1959; editor: Advising Small Business Clients, Vol. 1, 1978, 4th edit., 1994, Vol. 2, 1980, 3d edit., 1990; contbr. articles to profl. jours. Pres. Charlottesville Housing Found., 1968-73; mem. mgmt. coun. Montreat Conf. Ct., N.C., 1974-77; trustee Presbyn. Found., 1972-73, Union Theol. Sem., Va., 1983-91; bd. dirs. Presbyn. Outlook Found., 1974—, pres., 1985-88; mem. governing coun. Presbyn. Synod of the Virginias, 1973-78, moderator, 1977-78; trustee, v.p. Va. Tax Found., 1984-95; adv. bd. Westminster Orgn. Concert Series, 1989-93; adv. bd. Ashlawn-Highland Summer Festival, 1989—, pres., 1994—; mem. gov. coun. Presbyn. Presbytery of the James, 1993—, moderator of coun., 1995—. Capt. inf. U.S. Army, 1958, with res. 1958-70. Fellow Am. Bar Found., Va. Bar Found.; mem. ABA, Va. State Bar, Va. Bar Assn., Nat. Tax Inst., Am. Judicature Soc., Washington and Lee Law Sch. Assn. (governing coun. 1974-80, pres. 1979-80), Redland Club, Bull and Bear Club, Phi Deta Sigma, Omicron Delta Kappa, Phi Delta Phi. Democrat. Home: 345 Terrell Ct Charlottesville VA 22901-2171 Office: McGuire Woods Battle PO Box 1288 Bldg Charlottesville VA 22902-1288

STROUP, ELIZABETH FAYE, librarian; b. Tulsa, Mar. 25, 1939; d. Milton Earl and Lois (Buhl) S. BA in Philosophy, U. Wash., 1962, MLS, 1964. Intern Libr. of Congress, Washington, 1964-65; asst. dir. North Cen. Regional Libr., Wenatchee, Wash., 1966-69; reference specialist Congl. Reference div. Libr. of Congress, Washington, 1970-71, head nat. collections Div. for the Blind and Physically Handicapped, 1971-73, chief Congl. Reference div., 1973-78, dir. gen. reference, 1978-88; city libr., chief exec. officer Seattle Pub. Libr., 1988—; cons. U.S. Info. Svc., Indonesia, Feb. 1987. Mem. adv. bd. KCTS 9 Pub. TV, Seattle, 1988—; bd. visitors Sch. Librarianship, U. Wash., 1988—; bd. dirs. Wash. Literacy, 1988—. Mem. ALA (pres. reference and adult svcs. div. 1986-87, div. bd. 1985-88), Wash. Libr. Assn., D.C. Libr. Assn. (bd. dirs. 1975-76), City Club, Ranier Club. Avocations: gardening, mountain climbing, reading. Office: Seattle Pub Libr 1000 4th Ave Seattle WA 98104-1109

STROUP, KALA MAYS, state education official. BA in Speech and Drama, U. Kans., 1959, MS in Psychology, 1964, PhD in Speech Comm. and Human Rels., 1974. V.p. acad. affairs Emporia (Kans.) State U., 1978-83; pres. Murray State U., Ky., 1983-90, S.E. Mo. State U., Cape Girardeau, 1990-95; commr. of higher edn. State of Mo., Jefferson City, 1995—; pres. Mo. Coun. on Pub. Higher Edn.; mem. pres.'s commn. NCAA; cons. Edn. Commn. of States Task Force on State Policy and Ind. Higher Edn.; adv. bd. NSF Directorate for Sci. Edn. Evaluation; adv. com. Dept. Health, Edn. and Welfare, chair edn. com.; citizen's adv. coun. on state of Women U. S. Dept. Labor, 1974-76. Mem. nat. exec. bd. Boy Scouts Am., nat. exploring com., former chair profl. devel. com., mem. profl. devel. com., exploring com., Young Am. awards com., 1986-87, north ctrl. region strategic planning com., bd. trustees, nat. mus. chair; mem. Gov.'s Cabinet, Gov.'s Coun. on Workforce Quality, State of Mo.; bd. dirs. Midwestern Higher Edn. Commn.; chair ACE Leadership Commn.; mem. bd. visitors Air U.; v.p. Missourians for Higher Edn.; mem. bd. St. Francis Med. Ctr. Found., 1990-95, Cape Girardeau C. of C., 1990-95, U. Kans. Alumni Assn.; pres. Forum on Excellence, Carnegie Found.; adv. bd. World Trade Ctr., St. Louis; mem. Mo. Higher Edn. Loan Authority, 1995—, depts. econ. devel. & agrl. Mo. Global Partnership, 1995—, Mo. Tng. & Employment Coun., 1995—, Concordia U. Sys. Advancement Cabinet, State Higher Edn. Exec. Officers; bd. govs. Heartland Alliance Minority Participation, 1995—. ACE fellow; recipient Alumni Honor Citation award U. Kans. and U. Kans. Womans Hall of Fame. Mem. Am. Assn. State Colls. and Univs. (past bd. dirs., mem. Pres.'s Commn. on Tchr. Edn., Task Force on Labor Force Issues and Implications for the Curriculum), Mortar Board, Phi Beta Kappa, Omicron Delta Kappa, Phi Kappa Phi, Rotary (found. Ednl. awards com.). Office: Southeast Missouri State Univ 1 University Plz Cape Girardeau MO 63701

STROUP, RICHARD LYNDELL, economics educator, writer; b. Sunnyside, Wash., Jan. 3, 1943; s. Edgar Ivan and Inez Louise (Kellet) S.; m. Sandra Lee Price, Sept. 13, 1962 (div. Sept. 1981); children—Michael, Craig; m. Jane Bartlett Steidemann Shaw, Jan. 1, 1985; 1 child, David. Student, MIT, 1961-62; B.A., M.A., U. Wash., 1966, Ph.D. in Econs., 1970. Asst. prof. econs. Mont. State U., Bozeman, 1969-74; assoc. prof. econs. Mont. State U., 1974-78, prof. econs., 1978—; dir. Office Policy Analysis, Dept. Interior, Washington, 1982-84; vis. assoc. prof. Fla. State U., Tallahassee, 1977-78; sr. assoc. Polit. Economy Research Ctr., Bozeman, 1980—/lectr. summer univ., U. Aix (France), 1985—. Co-author: Natural Resources, 1983, Economics: Private and Public Choice, 7th edit., 1995, Basic Economics, 1993, What Everyone Should Know About Economics and Prosperity, 1993; also articles, 1972—; mem. editorial adv. bd. Regulation, 1993—. Adj. scholar Cato Inst., 1993—. Mem. Am. Econ. Assn., Western Econ. Assn. (exec. com. 1985-88), So. Econ. Assn., Mont Pelerin Soc., Phila. Soc., Pub. Choice Soc. Episcopalian. Home: 9 W Arnold St Bozeman MT 59715-6127 Office: PERC 502 S 19th Ave Ste 211 Bozeman MT 59715-6827

STROUP, SHEILA TIERNEY, columnist; b. Aurora, Ill., Nov. 28, 1943; d. Lawrence Clifford and Dorothy (Vilven) Tierney; m. Merwin F. Stroup, Sept. 4, 1965; children: Keegan, Shannon, Claire. BA in Liberal Arts, U. Ill., 1965; MA in English, Southeastern La. U., 1982. Cert. secondary tchr., La. Tchr. English Great Mills (Md.) High Sch., 1966-69; feature writer St. Tammany News, Covington, La., 1974-75; grad. asst. Southeastern La. U., Hammond, 1981-82, instr. English, 1982-85; ednl. cons. Custom Computer Systems, Hammond, 1985-86; tchr. English William Pitcher Jr. High, Covington, 1987; community news writer Times-Picayune, New Orleans, 1988-90; met. page columnist New Orleans Times-Picayune, 1990—; free-lance writer, Covington, La., 1986-88; speaker and workshop leader in field. Author newspaper column Sheila Stroup, 1990 (1st Pl. award La. Press Assn. 1990); author adult and juvenile short stories included in Woman's World, Cricket, Reader's Digest, others. Recipient 1st Pl. award Deep South Writers Competition, 1979, 2d Pl. award, 1987-90; 1st Pl. award for column New Orleans Press Club, 1989, 93. Fellow AAUW (bd. dirs. 1978-88, various chairwoman positions); mem. Nat. Soc. Newspaper Columnists (v.p. 1991-93, pres. 1994—). Avocations: bike riding, reading, loves animals. Office: The Times-Picayune 1001 N Highway 190 Covington LA 70433-8962

STROUP, STANLEY STEPHENSON, lawyer, educator; b. Los Angeles, Mar. 7, 1944; s. Francis Edwin and Marjory (Weimer) S.; m. Sylvia Douglass, June 15, 1968; children—Stacie, Stephen, Sarah. A.B., U. Ill., 1966; J.D., U. Mich., 1969. Bar: Ill. 1969, Calif. 1981, Minn. 1984. Atty. First Nat. Bank Chgo., 1969-78, asst. gen. counsel, 1978-80, v.p., 1980; sr. v.p., chief legal officer Bank of Calif., San Francisco, 1980-84; sr. v.p., gen. counsel Norwest Corp., Mpls., 1984-93, exec. v.p., gen. counsel, 1993—; mem. adj. faculty Coll. Law, William Mitchell Coll., St. Paul, 1985—. Mem. ABA, Ill. Bar Assn., State Bar Calif., Minn. Bar Assn. Office: Norwest Corp 6th & Marquette Sts Minneapolis MN 55479-1026

STROUPE, CYNTHIA KAY, secondary school counselor, educator; b. Cleve., Dec. 22, 1942; d. Fred Richard and Florence Crockett (Hart) S. BA in History, Queens Coll., 1964; MA in Guidance and Counseling, Rollins Coll., 1982. Cert. tchr., guidance and counseling, history, social sci., Fla. Clerical staff acctg. ops. office IBM Corp.-Cleve., 1964-66; tchr. Andrews Sch. for Girls, Willoughby, Ohio, 1966-67, North Iredell High Sch., Statesville, N.C., 1967-70; tchr. Winter Haven (Fla.) Sch., 1970-82, counselor, 1982—; mem. scholarship selection com. Polk C.C., Winter Haven, 1991—, Polk EDn. Found., Bartow, Fla., 1990—; dir., sec., pres. Polk County Scholarship Fund, Inc., Lakeland, Fla., 1983—. Sec. Rep. Women of Greater Polk, Winter Haven, 1991-93. Mem. NEA, Fla. Edn. Assn., Polk Edn. Assn., Fla. Counseling and Devel. Assn., So. Assn. Coll. Admissions Advisors, Delta Kappa Gamma (2d v.p. 1994—). Presbyterian. Avocations: travel, showing Abyssinian cats, Scottish heritage games, speed walking, cross-word puzzles. Office: Winter Haven High Sch 600 6th St SE Winter Haven FL 33880-3737

STROUPE, HENRY SMITH, university dean; b. Alexis, N.C., June 3, 1914; s. Stephen Morris and Augie (Lineberger) S.; m. Mary Elizabeth Denham, June 2, 1942; children—Stephen Denham, David Henry. Student, Mars Hill Jr. Coll., 1931-33; B.S., Wake Forest Coll., 1935, M.A., 1937; Ph.D., Duke U., 1942. Faculty Wake Forest U., Winston-Salem, N.C., 1937—; assoc. prof. history Wake Forest U., 1949-54, prof., 1954-84, prof. emeritus, 1984—, chmn. dept. history, 1954-68, dir. evening classes, 1957-61, dir. div. grad. studies, 1961-67, dean grad. sch., 1967-84, dean emeritus,

1984—; Vis. prof. history Duke, summer 1960. Author: The Religious Press in the South Atlantic States, 1802-1865: An Annotated Bibliography with Historical Introduction and Notes, 1956; Mem. editorial bd.: N.C. Hist. Rev, 1963-69. Mem. N.C. Civil War Centennial Commn., 1959-60. Served from ensign to lt. USNR, 1943-46. Recipient Christopher Crittenden award N.C. Lit. and Hist. Assn., 1982. Mem. Am. Hist. Assn., N.C. Hist. Soc. (pres. 1965), N.C. Lit. and Hist. Assn. (pres. 1974), Phi Beta Kappa, Omicron Delta Kappa. Democrat. Baptist. Home: 2016 Faculty Dr Winston Salem NC 27106-5221

STROUT, SEWALL CUSHING, JR., humanities educator; b. Portland, Maine, Apr. 19, 1923; s. Sewall Cushing and Margaret Deering S.; m. Jean Philbrick, June 12, 1948; children: Nathaniel Cushing, Benjamin Philbrick, Nicholas Lockey. B.A., Williams Coll., Williamstown, Mass., 1947; M.A., Harvard U., 1949, Ph.D., 1952. Instr. English and history Williams Coll., 1949-51; instr. history Yale U., 1952-56, asst. prof., 1956-59; asso. prof. humanities Calif. Inst. Tech., 1959-62, prof., 1962-64; faculty Cornell U., 1964-89, Ernest I. White prof. Am. studies and humane letters, 1975-89, emeritus. Author: The Pragmatic Revolt in American History: Carl L. Becker and Charles A. Beard, 1958, The American Image of the Old World, 19632, The New Heavens and New Earth: Political Religion in America, 1974, The Veracious Imagination: Essays on American History, Literature, and Biography, 1981, Making American Tradition: Visions and Revisions from Ben Franklin to Alice Walker, 1990. Served with U.S. Army, 1943-46. Morse fellow, 1956-57; Am. Philos. Soc. grantee, 1961; Fulbright fellow, spring 1967; Soc. Humanities fellow, 1971-72; resident scholar Rockefeller Study and Conf. Center, Bellagio, Italy, 1978; Nat. Humanities Ctr. fellow, 1984-85. Mem. Am. Studies Assn., Tocqueville Soc., Phi Beta Kappa. Home: 204 Cayuga Heights Rd Ithaca NY 14850-2155 Office: Cornell University Dept Am Studies Ithaca NY 14853

STROUTH, BARON HOWARD STEVEN, geologist, mining engineer; b. Frankfurt, Germany, Sept. 28, 1919; arrived in U.S., 1941; s. Baron Karl Siegfried and Ida (Morch) von Strauss; m. Penelope Ann Creamer-Osteen, Nov. 8, 1951. BSc, U. Sorbonne, 1939; PhD in Engring., Bretton Woods U., 1965; PhD in Engring. (hon.), Rochedale U., Can., 1970. Asst. mgr. Drexel Bros. Ltd., N.Y.C., 1941-43; pres. Std. Mining, N.Y.C., 1951-58, Stanleigh Uranium Mine, Toronto, Can., 1954-61; mng. dir. Norsul Oil and Mining Quito, Ecuador, 1961-71; dir., officer Mining and Oil Cos., various locations; founder, operator Stanleigh Uranium and Norsul Oil; sr. trustee Weinguster Baron K. S. von Strauss, Erben Trust, Vaduz, 1954—; dir. Pharmed Dr. Liedtke, Munich, 1993—. Translator: The Cornet (Rilke), 1950; author: A Window to the Morrow, 1963, A Sonata for Frankfurt, 1987, Cities of the Break of Dawn, 1988; patentee in mining and oil porcesses. Maj. USAR, 1943-69, ret. Recipient Conspicuous Svc. Cross, Gov. Dewey, 1947, French, Czech, Cambodian decorations. Fellow Explorers Club; mem. Can. Inst. Mining Engrs. (life), Am. Inst. Mining Engrs. (sr.), St. James Club (London), Ontario Club Toronto. Avocations: collector, antique books, pre-Colombian art, antique maps.

STROYD, ARTHUR HEISTER, lawyer; b. Pitts., Sept. 5, 1945; s. Anne (Griffiths) S.; m. Susan Fleming, July 21, 1973; 1 child, Elizabeth. AB, Kenyon Coll., 1967; JD, U. Pitts., 1972. Bar: Pa. 1972, U.S. Dist. Ct. (we. dist.) Pa. 1972, U.S. Ct. Appeals (3d cir.) 1972. Law clk. to judge U.S. Ct. Appeals (3d cir.), Phila., 1972-75; ptnr., head litigation group Reed, Smith, Shaw & McClay, Pitts., 1975—; mem. Nat. Adv. Council on Child Nutrition, U.S. Dept. Agriculture, 1984-85. Treas. Mt. Lebanon Zoning Hearing Bd., 1978-81; pres. bd. dirs. Mt. Lebanon Sch. dist., 1981-87; solicitor Allegheny County Rep. Com., 1988-95; pres. bd. dirs. Ctr. for Theatre Arts, Pitts., 1984-93; participant Leadership Pitts., 1991-92; chair bd. dirs. Mt. Lebanon Hosp. Authority, 1993—; coun. U. Pitts. Cancer Inst., 1993—; mem. alumni coun. Kenyon Coll., 1996—. Lt. USNR, 1969-71. Mem. Pa. Bar Assn., Allegheny County Bar Assn., Acad. Trial Lawyers (bd. govs.), Duquesne Club. Episcopalian. Avocations: skiing. Home: 17 St Clair Dr Pittsburgh PA 15228-1830 Office: Reed Smith Shaw & McClay 435 6th Ave Pittsburgh PA 15219-1809

STROZESKI, MICHAEL WAYNE, director research; b. McKinney, Tex., Aug. 19, 1944; s. Edwin Guy and Margaret K. (Orr) Parchman; m. Sandra S. Samples, June 9, 1967. BS, U. North Tex., 1966, MEd, 1970, PhD, 1980. Cert. tchr. sci. secondary, prin., supt. Tchr. sci. Grapevine (Tex.) Ind. Sch. Dist., 1966-70; tchr. physics and biology Ft. Worth Country Day Sch., 1970-78; tchg. fellow U. North Tex., Denton, 1978-79; evaluator, exec. dir. planning, research and evaluation Garland (Tex.) Ind. Sch. Dist., 1979—; adv. mem. grad. program U. North Tex., Denton, 1985—; dir., CEO Strozeski Enterprises Consulting, Garland, 1985—. Bd. dirs. Garland YMCA. Mem. Am. Evaluation assn. (charter), Am. Edn. Rsch. Assn., Am. Assn. Sch. Adminstrs., Nat. Coun. on Measurement in Edn., Nat. Assn. Test Dirs. (pres. 1988), Garland Rotary Club (pres. 1993-94, Paul Harris fellow 1994). Avocations: camping, climbing, snowmobiling, reading, computers. Home: PO Box 462306 Garland TX 75046-2306 Office: Garland Ind Sch Dist 720 Stadium Dr Garland TX 75046

STRUBBE, THOMAS R., diagnostic testing industry executive; b. Ft. Wayne, Ind., Mar. 30, 1940; s. Rudolph C. and Maverne E. (Wagoner) S.; children: Tracy Lynn, Patrick Thomas, Christina Lee. B.S., Ind. U., 1962; J.D., Tulane U., 1965. Bar: Ind. 1965, Ill. 1969. Atty. Lincoln Nat. Life Ins. Co., Ft. Wayne, 1965-66; asst. counsel Lincoln Nat. Life Ins. Co., 1967-68; with Washington Nat. Corp., Evanston, Ill., 1968-90; gen. counsel Washington Nat. Corp., 1973-79, sec., 1970-84, v.p., 1975-79, sr. v.p., 1979-83, exec. v.p., 1983-84, pres., 1984-90, also bd. dirs., mem. exec. com.; pres., chief exec. officer Osborn Labs. Inc., Olathe, Kans., 1990—, also bd. dirs. Trustee Glencoe (Ill.) Union Ch., 1984-87; v.p., bd. dirs., exec. com. Chgo. chpt. Epilepsy Found. Am., 1975-79; bd. dirs. Assn. Retarded Citizens Ill., 1985-89, Northlight Theater, 1984-89. Lt. USNR, 1965-71. Lincoln Found. grantee, 1964. Mem. ABA, Assn. Life Ins. Counsel, Nat. Investor Rels. Inst., Am. Soc. Corp. Secs., Home Office Life Underwriters Assn., Ind. Bar Assn., Ill. Bar Assn., Skokie Country Club (Ill.), Shadow Glen Golf Club (Kans.), Hideaway Beach Club (Fla.). Office: Osborn Labs Inc PO Box 2920 Shawnee Mission KS 66201-1320

STRUBEL, RICHARD PERRY, manufacturing company executive; b. Evanston, Ill., Aug. 10, 1939; s. Arthur Raymond and Martha (Smith) S.; m. Linda Jane Freeman, Aug. 25, 1961 (div. 1974); children: Douglas Arthur, Craig Tollerton; m. Ella Doyle G'sell, Oct. 23, 1976. B.A., Williams Coll., 1962; M.B.A., Harvard U., 1964. Assoc. Fry Cons., Chgo., 1964-66, mng. prin., 1966-68; with N.W. Industries, Inc., Chgo., 1968-83, v.p. corp. devel., 1969-73, group v.p., 1973-79, exec. v.p., 1979-83, pres., 1983; chmn. bd., pres. Buckingham Corp., N.Y.C., 1972-73; pres., chief exec. officer Microdot Inc., Chgo., 1983-94; mng. ptnr. Tandem Ptnrs. Inc., Chgo., 1991—; trustee Benchmark Funds and various mutual funds of Goldman Sachs Asset Mgmt. Trustee U. Chgo.; bd. dirs. Children's Meml. Hosp., Children's Meml. Med. Ctr.; chair vis. com. Divinity Sch., U. Chgo. Presbyterian. Clubs: Mid-Day, Casino, Chicago, Comml., Racquet of Chgo., Commonwealth (Chgo.). Office: Tandem Ptnrs Inc 70 W Madison St Ste 1400 Chicago IL 60602-4206

STRUBLE, DEAN L., agricultural research administrator; b. Wawota, Sask., Can., Aug. 29, 1936; married, 1957; 3 children. BA, U. Sask., 1961, MA, 1962, PhD in Chemistry, 1966. Devel. chemist DuPont Can., Ont., 1962-63; fellow organic chemistry U. Adelaide, Australia, 1966-67; rsch. scientist Lethbridge, 1968-89; dir. Agr. Can. Vancouver (B.C.) Rsch. Sta., 1989—; adj. prof. Simon Fraser U., Burnaby, B.C., 1987. Contbr. to numerous publs.; patentee in field. Fellow Entomol. Soc. Can., Chem. Inst. Can. Achievements include research in identification and synthesis of sex pheromones of lepidopterans, primarily cutworm species; development of practical application of synthetic pheromones for monitoring abundance of major cutworm species. Office: Agr Can Rsch Sta, 6660 NW Marine Dr, Vancouver, BC Canada V6T 1X2*

STRUBLE, DONALD EDWARD, mechanical engineer; b. Oakland, Calif., Oct. 10, 1942; s. Donald Edward and Marjorie E. (Griffin) S.; m. Allison Florence Dietrick, Dec. 20, 1964; children: Lisa Kathleen, Donald Lyman, John Dietrick. BS, Calif. Poly., 1964; MS, Stanford U., 1965; PhD, Ga. Inst. Tech., 1972. Asst. prof. Calif. Poly. State U., San Luis Obispo, Calif., 1970-74; sr. v.p. Minicars, Inc., Goleta, Calif., 1974-81; pres. Dynamic Sci., Inc., Phoenix, 1981-83; sr. engring. assoc. Cromack Engring. Assoc., Tempe, Ariz., 1983-85; cons. engr. Donald E. Struble, PhD, Phoenix, 1985-87; sr. engr. Collision Safety Engring., Phoenix, 1987—. Author: Fundamentals of Aerospace Structural Analysis, 1972; contbr. articles to profl. jours. Mem. Soc. Automotive Engrs., Assn. Advancement Automotive Medicine, Sigma Xi. Democrat. Episcopalian. Achievements include patent for Inflatable Restraint for Side Impactcs; research in experimental safety vehicles. Home: 564 W Moon Valley Dr Phoenix AZ 85023-6231 Office: Collisions Safety Engring 2320 W Peoria Ave Ste B145 Phoenix AZ 85029-4766

STRUCHTEMEYER, CAROL SUE, elementary education educator; b. Kansas City, Mo., Apr. 21, 1954; d. Olin Carl and Anna Christine (Skou) Brookshier; m. Leland Leonard Struchtemeyer, May 26, 1973; children: Rhonda Sue, Thomas Leland. BS in Edn., Ctrl. Mo. State U., 1975, MS in Edn., 1981; edni. resource tchr. tng., U. Mo., 1977. Cert. elem. tchr., spl. edn. tchr. Tchr. elem. Mayview (Mo.) R-7 Sch. Dist., 1975-76; tchr. learning disabilities Odessa (Mo.) R-5 Sch. Dist., 1976-78; tchr. 5th grade Lexington (Mo.) R-5 Sch. Dist., 1978—; sec. Leslie Bell Intervention Team, Lexington, 1992-94. Mem. Trinity United Ch. of Christ, Lexington, 1990—, Lexington Athletic Boosters, 1992—, Lexington Fine Arts Club, 1992—. Mem. NEA, Nat. Coun. Tchrs. Math., Mo. Edn. Assn., Mo. Coun. Tchrs. Math., Lexington Cmty. Tchrs. Assn. (sec. 1983-84, treas. 1985-86). Avocations: reading, sewing, gardening. Home: PO Box 58 501 Roncelli Rd Lexington MO 64067

STRUDLER, ROBERT JACOB, real estate development executive; b. N.Y.C., Sept. 22, 1942; m. Ruth Honigman, Aug. 29, 1965; children: Seth, Keith, Craig. BS in Indsl. and Labor Relations, Cornell U., 1964; LLB, Columbia U., 1967. Bar: N.Y. 1967, Fla. 1973. Assoc. firms in N.Y.C., 1967-71; v.p., chmn. operating com. U.S. Home Corp., Clearwater, Fla., 1972-76, v.p. legal affairs, 1976-77, v.p. ops., 1977-79; sr. v.p. ops. U.S. Home Corp., Houston, 1979-81, sr. v.p. acquisitions, 1981-84, pres., chief operating officer, 1984-86, chmn., chief exec. officer, 1986—. Pres., trustee Sch. for Young Children; mem. pres.' adv. coun. U. St. Thomas. Corecipient Builder of Yr. award Profl. Builder Mag., 1994, Bronze award Wall Street, 1995. Mem. ABA, N.Y. State Bar Assn., Fla. Bar Assn., Cornell Real Estate Coun., Nat. Assn. Homebuilders (chmn. high prodn. coun. 1991-93). Home: 11110 Greenbay St Houston TX 77024-6729 Office: US Home Corp 1800 West Loop S Houston TX 77027-3210

STRUEBING, ROBERT VIRGIL, retired oil company executive; b. Winfield, Kans., Nov. 8, 1919; s. Walter Charles and Jettie Marie (Hetherington) S.; m. Helen L. Harrington, Aug. 19, 1943; children: Gloria Struebing West, Steven R., William S. B.S. in Chem. Engring, U. Nebr., 1949. With Skelly Oil Co., El Dorado, Kans., 1949-76, refinery mgr., 1971-76; mgr. gas plants Getty Oil Co., Tulsa, 1977-80, v.p. mfg., 1980-85; sr. v.p. mfg. Getty Refining & Mktg. Co., Tulsa, 1980-85; ret., 1985. Mem. El Dorado Bd. Edn., 1965-75, pres., 1967-68. Served to capt. USAAF, 1940-45. Mem. Sigma Tau. Club: Cedar Ridge Country.

STRUELENS, MICHEL MAURICE JOSEPH GEORGES, political science educator, foreign affairs consultant; b. Brussels, Belgium, Mar. 10, 1928; m. Godelieve de Wilde, Aug. 2, 1949; children: Alain, Patricia, Brigitte, Bernard, Jean Paul (dec.). B.A., Coll. St. Pierre, Brussels, 1944; M.A., Antwerp U., Belgium, 1949; Ph.D., Am. U., Washington, 1968. Insp. econ. affairs Congo Govt., Leopoldville, 1950-54, chief insp. econ. affairs, 1954-55, dep. commr. transp., 1955-57; dir. Info. and Public Relations Office for Congo, Brussels, 1957-58, Congo Tourism Pavillion, Internat. World's Fair, Brussels, 1958-59; dir. gen. Belgian Congo and Ruanda Urundi Tourist Office, Congo, 1959; chmn. African Commn. Internat. Union Ofcl. Travel Orgns., Geneva, 1959-60; ofcl. Katanga rep. in U.S., N.Y.C., 1960-63; dir. gen. Internat. Inst. for African Affairs in Can., 1963-64; spl. asst. to prime minister Democratic Republic Congo; fgn. affairs minister, adviser to Congo UN del., adviser Congo embassy Democratic Republic Congo, Washington, N.Y.C., 1964-66; dir. Eurafrica, Consultants on Fgn. Affairs, Washington, 1966—; prof. polit. sci., French, internat. bus. Am. U., 1968-93; prof. emeritus, 1993; dir. Ctr. Rsch and Documentation on European Community Am. U., 1971—, chmn. faculty rels. com., 1986-87, chmn. grad. studies com., SIS, 1989-90; dir. E.C. Inst. in Europe, 1978-93, U. Antwerp Exchange Program, 1979-83; dir. EPSCI/ESSEC (France) Exchange Program, 1980-84, chmn. internat. bus. dept., 1980-84; dir. exchange program Bus. Sch. of Poly., U. Madrid, 1981-84; investment adviser, 1977—; adminstr. French Parish, Ctr. Studies on Internat. Relations, Econs. and Bus., La Rochelle, France, 1987—; exec. v.p. Eglise St. Louis Corp., French-Speaking Union, Washington, 1974-75; mgr. by agreement with European Communities, European Documentation Ctr. (CERDEC), accessing by satellite EC Data Banks, 1985— and providing through WCL Libr. of Am. U., On Line Pub. Access Cataloging, 1991—. Author: (with Inforcongo) Congo Belge et Ruanda-Urundi, 1958; monograph Le Canada à l'Heure de l'Afrique, 1964; The United Nations in the Congo - or ONUC and International Politics, 1976. Recipient Internat. Union Ofcl. Travel Orgns. Poster award Brussels, 1958, Etoile de Service en Argent King of Belgium, 1956; chevalier de l'Ordre Royal du Lion, 1957; Faculty award for outstanding contbn. to acad. program devel. Coll. Bus. Adminstrn., Am. U., 1979; Faculty award for outstanding teaching, 1980, 82, 84; Faculty award for outstanding service to Am. U., 1981. Mem. Golden Key, Phi Sigma Alpha. Clubs: Cosmos (Washington); Bukavu Royal Sports (founder 1950, pres. 1951-54, hon. pres. 1957) (Congo). Lodge: Rotary. Home: 1374 Woodside Dr Mc Lean VA 22102-1536 *"Ad Augusta per Angusta". Using Latin, French writer Victor Hugo said it all! Nothing comes easy and "success," a very personal perception indeed, requires a great deal of luck, perseverance and hard work. True success, though, is directly related to the pursuit of happiness, which in turn is a state of mind. If and when I reach eternity, I'll then be able to tell how successful I was during my passage on earth.*

STRUGGLES, JOHN EDWARD, management consultant; b. Wilmette, Ill., Nov. 29, 1913; s. William George and Sarah Adell (Chambers) S.; m. Dorothy Eloise Goetz, Oct. 23, 1937; 1 child, John Kirk. Student, Miami U., Oxford, Ohio, 1932-34. Supt. Consol. Biscuit Co., Chgo., 1934-37; sales rep. Pillsbury Mills, Chgo., 1937-41; various personnel and operating positions Montgomery Ward & Co., Chgo., Kansas City, Denver, 1941-50; v.p. personnel Montgomery Ward & Co., 1950-53; co-founder, co-chmn. Heidrick & Struggles, Inc., Chgo., 1953—. With USNR, World War II. Republican. Home: 505 Sheridan Rd Winnetka IL 60093-2639 Office: Heidrick Struggles Inc 125 S Wacker Dr Chicago IL 60606-4402

STRUIF, L. JAMES, lawyer; b. Alton, Ill., Sept. 18, 1931; s. Leo John and Clara Lillie (Bauer) S.; m. Shirley Ann Spatz, Mar. 24, 1965; children: Scott B., Jamie Lynn, Susan Marie, Jeffrey James. BS, Northwestern U., 1953; JD, U. Ill., Champaign, 1960. Bar: Ill. 1960, U.S. Dist. Ct. (so. Dist.) Ill. 1960. Gen. counsel So. Ill. U., 1960-64; pvt. practice Struif Law Offices, Alton, Ill., 1964—; lectr. So. Ill. U., Edwardsville, 1960-65. Author: Guide to Law for Laymen, 1987, Field Guide to 150 Prairie Plants of S.W. Ill., 1989. Scoutmaster Boy Scouts Am., Alton, 1966-69; active civil rights worker, Miss., 1964. With USN, submarines 1953-57, Pacific. Recipient Chmns. award Madison County Urban League, 1989, Blazing Star award The Nature Inst., 1990. Mem. Assn. Trial Lawyers Am., Ill. Trial Lawyers Assn., Ill. Bar Assn. Democrat. Mem. United Ch. of Christ. Avocations: nature, gardening, science, piano. Office: The Struif Law Offices 2900 Adams Pky Alton IL 62002-6535

STRUL, GENE M., communications executive, former television news director; b. Bklyn., Mar. 25, 1927; s. Joseph and Sally (Chartoff) S.; student journalism U. Miami (Fla.), 1945-47; m. Shirley Dolly Silber, Aug. 7, 1949 (dec.); children: Ricky, Gary, Eileen. News dir. Sta. WIOD AM-FM, Miami, 1947-56; assignment editor, producer Sta. WCKT-TV, Miami, 1956-57, news dir., 1957-79; dir. broadcast news Miami News, 1957; free-lance writer newspapers and mags.; cons. dept. comm. U. Miami, 1979, dir. public relations, 1979-80; v.p. Hernstadt Broadcasting Corp., 1980-81; dir. corp. comm. Burnup & Sims, 1981-90; dir. comm. Printing Industry of South Fla., 1990-92, Printing Assn. Fla., 1992—. Comm. dir. United Way of Dade County, 1981. Served with AUS, 1945. Recipient Peabody award, 1975; Preceptor award Broadcast Industry conf., San Francisco State U.; Abe Lincoln awards (2) So. Baptist Radio-TV Conf.; Nat. Headliners awards (5); led Sta. WSVN (formerly WCKT) to more than 200 awards for news, including 3 Peabody awards, Emmy award. Mem. Nat. Acad. Television Arts and Scis. (past gov. Miami chpt.), Radio-TV News Dirs. Assn., Fla. AP Broadcasters (past pres.), Greater Miami C. of C., Nat. Broadcast Editorial Assn., Sigma Delta Chi (2 nat. awards). Home: 145 SW 49th Ave Miami FL 33134-1228

STRULL, GENE, technology consultant, retired electrical manufacturing company executive; b. Chgo., May 15, 1929; s. Albert and Helen (Wolf) S.; m. Joyce Landsbaum, July 6, 1952; children—David Jay, Brian Lee. B.S.E.E., Purdue U., 1951; M.S., Northwestern U., 1952, Ph.D. in Elec. Engring, 1954. With Westinghouse Electric Corp., 1954-93; supervisory engr., adv. engr., mgr. solid state tech.-aerospace Westinghouse Electric Corp., Balt., 1958-68; mgr. sci. and tech. systems devel. div., mgr. advanced tech. labs. Westinghouse Electric Corp., 1968-78, dep. gen. mgr. systems devel. div., 1979-81, gen. mgr. advanced tech. div., 1981-93, exec. dir. tech., 1987-93; cons. Army Sci. Bd., 1981-83, NRC-NAS, 1980-82, Def. Sci. Bd., 1981-83, NSF, 1992-95; cons. NASA, 1967-87, com. chmn., 1976-78; adv. com. panel USNR, 1989. Contbg. author: Integrated Electronic Systems, 1970, Integrated Circuit Technology, 1967; contbr. articles to profl. jours.; patentee in field. Gene Strull Tech. Ctr. at Westinghouse Electric Corp. Advanced Tech. Labs. named in his honor, Balt., 1993; named Outstanding Elec. Engr. award Purdue U., 1994. Fellow IEEE (life, Govt. Industry Svc. award 1987, Frederik Philips award 1991); mem. Md. Acad. Scis. (chmn. 1978-80). Home: One Gristmill Ct # 606 Baltimore MD 21208

STRUM, BRIAN J., real estate executive; b. Bklyn., Nov. 27, 1939; s. Max J. and Beatrix (Galitzky) S.; m. Mickey Weiss, Nov. 19, 1966; children: Ira, Howard, Beth. BA, Bklyn. Coll., 1960; LLB, NYU, 1963. Bar: N.Y. 1964, N.J. 1969; CLU; counselor of real estate. Atty. Gilbert, Segall and Young, N.Y.C., 1963-65; assoc. res. atty. Prudential Ins. Co. Am., N.Y.C., 1965-67, various positions, law dept., 1967-75, v.p. real estate investments, 1975-86; chmn. Prudential Property Co., Newark, 1986-92; CEO Prudential Realty Group, Newark, 1992-94; Silverstein chair of real estate devel. NYU, 1995—; pres., trustee Prudential Realty Trust, 1985-94; mem. adv. bd. Chgo. Title & Trust Co., N.Y.C., 1982—. Editor: Financing Real Estate in the Inflationary Eighties, 1981; contbr. articles to profl. jours. With USAR, 1963-69. Recipient Disting. Cmty. Svc. award Brandeis U., 1983, Urban Leadership award NYU, 1990, Good Scout award N.Y.C. coun. Boy Scouts Am., 1991, Nat. Achievement awrd D.A.R.E. Am., 1993. Fellow Anglo Am. Real Property Inst. (charter); mem. ABA (chmn. real property, probate and trust law sects. 1984-85), N.Y. State Bar Assn. (chmn. real property sect. 1975-76), Urban Land Inst. (coun. mem.), Am. Coll. Real Estate Lawyers (charter), Am. Soc. Real Estate Counselors. Office: NYU 11 W 42d St New York NY 10036-8002

STRUM, JAY GERSON, lawyer; b. N.Y.C., July 6, 1938; s. John and Dorothy (Chaikind) S.; m. Patricia Ann Burtis, Jan. 25, 1969; children: Daniel, Jennifer. BA in polit. sci. magna cum laude, CCNY, 1959; LLB, Harvard U., 1962. Bar: N.Y. 1963, U.S. Dist. Ct. (so. and ea. dists.) N.Y. 1963, U.S. Ct. Appeals (2d cir.) 1965, U.S. Supreme Ct. 1979. Trial atty. SEC, N.Y.C., 1963-65; ptnr. Coon, Dubow, Kleinberg & Strum, N.Y.C., 1965-67; assoc. Kaye, Scholer, Fierman, Hays & Handler, N.Y.C., 1967-70, ptnr., 1971—. Mem. ABA, Assn. of Bar of City of N.Y., Phi Beta Kappa. Club: Harvard (N.Y.C.). Office: Kaye Scholer Fierman Hays & Handler 425 Park Ave New York NY 10022-3506

STRUNK, BETSY ANN WHITENIGHT, education educator; b. Bloomsburg, Pa., May 28, 1942; d. Mathias Clarence and Marianna (Naunas) Whitenight; children: Robert J. Jr., Geoffrey M. BS in Edn., Bloomsburg U., 1964; MEd, West Chester U., 1969; cert. mentally/physically handicapped, Pa. State U., 1981; postgrad., Wilkes U., Joseph's U., Drexel U., Western Md. Coll. Cert. elem. edn., spl. edn. Tchr. Faust Sch., Bensalem (Pa.) Twp., 1964, Eddystone (Pa.) Elem. Sch., 1964-66, Lima Elem. Sch., Rose Tree Media Sch. Dist., 1966-69, Rose Tree Media (Pa.) Sch. Dist., 1977—; adj. prof. Wilkes Coll., Wilkes-Barre, Pa., 1981-86; instr. Delaware C.C., Media, 1986; instr., dir. ground sch. edn. Brandywine Airport, West Chester, Pa., 1986-88; instr. Drexel U., Phila., 1989—, Performance Learning Systems, Inc., Emerson, N.J. and Nevada City, Calif., 1981—; rep. FAA, Phila., 1986-88; spl. edn. resource rm. specialist, tchr. cons. Media Elem. Sch., Rose Tree Media Sch. Dist., spl. edn. supervisory selection com.; curriculum designer pvt. pilot ground sch.; instr. introduction to flying and pilot companion course; chairperson profl. devel. com. Rose Tree Media Sch. Dist., 1992; mem. Insvc. Coun. of Delaware County, 1992—; mem. educator's adv. com. Phila. Franklin Inst., 1990-92, 95—; cons. edni. programs, 1988—; owner, designer Betsy's Belts, Del., N.J., Pa., 1970-74; mem. gov. bd. Southeastern Tchr. Leadership Ctr. West Chester (Pa.) U.; learning support tchr. Glenwood Elem. Sch., Media, Pa., 1994—; presenter State of Pa. Lead Tchr. Conf., 1994, Ind. Sch. Tchrs. Assn., 1995; project dir. video documentary Performance Learning Sys., Calif., 1994. Program dir. video documentaries including Learning Through Live Events, 1995; contbr. articles to profl. jours. Mem. Middletown Free Libr. Bd., 1977-79; officer Riddlewood Aux. to Riddle Meml. Hosp., Media, 1973-78; chairperson Lima (Pa.) Christian Nursery Sch., 1973, March of Dimes, Middletown, 1973; pres. Roosevelt PTG (Elem. Sch.), Media, 1982; com. person, v.p. Middletown Twp. Dem. Com., 1974; capt. March of Dimes, Media, 1987-91, Diabetes Assn., Media, 1989-91; mem. Vietnamese refugee com. Media Presbyn. Ch., 1975, mem., 1967—; vol. Tyler Arboretum, Middletown Twp., 1980-82. Recipient 1st Pl. Color Divsn. Photography award Pa. Colonial Plantation PLS 500 Club award, 1st pl. Color Divsn. in Photography Bloomsburg State Fair, 1994; Fine Arts in Spl. Edn. grantee Pa. Dept. Edn., 1993-94. Mem. NEA, ASCD, Pa. ASCD, Rose Tree Media Edn. Assn. (profl. devel. com. chairperson 1992-93, profl. devel. com. rep. 1990-93, Exceptional Svc. award), Pa. State Edn. Assn., Nat. Staff Devel. Coun., Aircraft Owners and Pilots Assn., Tyler Arboretum, Media Soc. Performing Arts, Phila. Zoo. Democrat. Avocations: reading, writing, interior decorating, nature walking, antiquing. Home: 203 Cohasset Ln West Chester PA 19380-6507 Office: Rose Tree Media Sch Dist Glenwood Elem Sch Pennell Rd Media PA 19063

STRUNK, ORLO CHRISTOPHER, JR., psychology educator; b. Pen Argyl, Pa., Apr. 14, 1925; s. Orlo Christopher and Katherine Elizabeth (Glasser) S.; m. Mary Louise Reynolds, July 3, 1947; children: Laura Louise, John Christopher. Certificate, Churchman Bus. Coll., Easton, Pa., 1948; A.B., W. Va. Wesleyan Coll., Buckhannon, 1953; S.T.B., Boston U., 1955, Ph.D., 1957. Exec. sec. Inst. Pastoral Care, Mass. Gen. Hosp., 1955-57; grad. asst. Boston U., 1955-57, instr. psychology of religion, 1956; instr. Boston U. (Sch. Theology), 1957-58, 62; assoc. prof. psychology W. Va. Wesleyan Coll., 1957-60, dean, prof. psychology, 1959-69; prof. psychology of religion Boston U., 1969-86; also faculty counselor, supr. Albert V. Danielsen Inst.; part-time faculty Webster U., 1994—; pastoral psychotherapist The Coastal Samaritan Ctr., Myrtle Beach, S.C., 1986—; assoc. dir., staff psychologist Ecumenical Counseling Svc., Inc., Melrose, Mass.; rsch. cons. Religion in Edn. Found., Calif. Author: Readings in the Psychology of Religion, 1959, Religion: A Psychological Interpretaton, 1962, Mature Religion: A Psychological Study, 1965, The Choice Called Atheism, 1969, The Psychology of Religion, 1971, Dynamic Interpersonalism for Ministry, 1973, The Secret Self, 1976, Privacy: Experience, Understanding, Expression, 1983; mng. editor: Jour. Pastoral Care. Served with USAAF, 1943-46. Decorated Air medal with five oak leaf clusters. Fellow Am. Psychol. Assn.; mem. W.Va. Assn. Acad. Deans (pres.). Methodist (elder). Home: 1068 Harbor Dr SW Calabash NC 28467-2300 *It is my conviction that life is a mystery to be lived more than it is a problem to be solved. As such, I have tried to develop a style of life which permits me to be open to a wide range of experiences guided by a simple principle which requires me to do battle with all those conditions which disrupt my and others freedom to live an authentic life of openness and continuous growth. The central principle guiding the openness to life is found in the spirit of Jesus Christ which includes love of Self, others, and my God. The task of working out these abstractions in a concrete manner is difficult and mysterious - but never, never dull.*

STRUNK, ROBERT CHARLES, physician; b. Evanston, Ill., May 29, 1942; s. Norman Wesley and Marion Mildred (Ree) S.; m. Alison Leigh Gans, Apr. 3, 1971; children: Christopher Robert, Alix Elizabeth. BA in Chemistry, Northwestern U., 1964, MS in Biochemistry, 1968, MD, 1968. Lic. MD, Ariz., Colo., Mass., Mo. Resident in pediatrics Cin. Children's Hosp., 1968-70; pediatrician Newport (R.I.) Naval Hosp., 1970-72; rsch. fellow in pediatrics Harvard Med. Sch., Boston, 1972-74; asst. prof. pediatrics U. Ariz. Health Sci. Ctr., Tucson, 1974-78; dir. clin. svcs. Nat. Jewish

Ctr. for Immunology and Respiratory Med., Denver, 1978-87; sabbatical leave Boston Children's Hosp., 1984-85; dir. divsn. allergy and pulmonary medicine Children's Hosp., St. Louis, 1987--; pediatrician Barnes and Allied Hosp., St. Louis, 1987--; prof. pediatrics Sch. Medicine Washington U., St. Louis, 1987--. Recipient Allergic Disease Acad. award Nat. Inst. Allergy and Infectious Disease of NIH. Mem. Am. Acad. Allergy and Immunology, Am. Thoracic Soc. Office: Washington U Sch Med Dept Pediatrics 400 S Kingshighway Blvd Saint Louis MO 63110-1014

STRUPP, DAVID JOHN, lawyer; b. Terre Haute, Ind., Feb. 28, 1938; s. Fares John and Mary (Stark) S.; m. Elizabeth Ann Sullivan, Aug. 22, 1959; children: Sally Katherine, David John Jr. BS, Ind. U., 1960; JD, U. Mich., 1963; LLM in Taxation, NYU, 1968. Bar: N.Y. 1964. Mem. firm Shearman & Sterling, N.Y.C., 1963-73, ptnr., 1973-81; pres. Shorenstein Co., San Francisco, 1981-82; ptnr. Davis Polk & Wardwell, N.Y.C., 1982—; bd. dirs. MEPC Am. Properties Inc., European Investors Inc. Chmn. South St. Seaport Corp., N.Y.C., 1987; trustee South St. Seaport Mus., N.Y.C., 1985—, Miriam Osborne Home Assn., Rye, N.Y., 1973-81. Served to capt. U.S. Army, 1963-65. Avocations: sailing, golf, tennis. Office: Davis Polk & Wardwell 450 Lexington Ave New York NY 10017-3911*

STRUPP, HANS HERMANN, psychologist, educator; b. Frankfurt am Main, Germany, Aug. 25, 1921; came to U.S., 1939, naturalized, 1945; s. Josef and Anna (Metzger) S.; m. Lottie Metzger, Aug. 19, 1951; children: Karen, Barbara, John. AB with distinction, George Washington U., 1945, AM, 1947, PhD, 1954; MD (hon.), U. Ulm, Fed. Republic of Germany, 1986. Diplomate in clin. psychology Am. Bd. Profl. Psychology; lic. clin. psychologist, Tenn. Research psychologist Human Factors Ops. Research Labs., Dept. Air Force, Washington, 1949-54; supervisory research psychologist, personnel research br. Adj. Gen.'s Office, Dept. of Army, Washington, 1954-55; dir. psychotherapy research project Sch. Medicine, George Washington U., Washington, 1955-57; dir. psychol. services, dept. psychiatry U. N.C. Sch. Medicine, Chapel Hill, 1957-64; asso. prof. psychology U. N.C. Sch. Medicine, 1957-62, prof., 1962-66; prof. dept. psychology Vanderbilt U., Nashville, 1966-76, dir. clin. tng., dept. psychology, 1967-76, disting. prof., 1976-94, disting. prof. emeritus, Harvie Branscomb disting. prof., 1985-86; disting. prof. emeritus, 1994—. Mem. editorial adv. bd. Psychotherapy: Theory, Research and Practice, 1963—, Jour. Cons. and Clin. Psychology, 1964—, Jour. Nervous and Mental Disease, 1965—, Jour. Am. Acad. Psychoanalysis, 1972—, Jour. Contemporary Psychotherapy, 1972-86, Psychiatry Research, 1979-86, Jour. Profl. Psychology, 1976-89, others; contbr. chpts. to books, articles and revs. to profl. jours. Recipient Helen Sargent meml. prize Menninger Found., 1963; Alumni Achievement award George Washington U., 1972; Disting. Profl. Achievement award Am. Bd. Profl. Psychology, 1976, Disting. Profl. Contbns. to Knowledge award Am. Psychol. Assn., 1987; others. Fellow Am. Psychol. Assn. (mem. exec. council 1964, exec. bd. 1969-72, council of reps. 1970-73, chmn. com. on fellows div. psychotherapy 1970-74, pres. div. clin. psychology 1974-75, recipient Disting. Profl. Psychologist award 1973, Disting. Scientist award 1979), Tenn. Psychol. Assn., AAAS; mem. Eastern Psychol. Assn., Southeastern Psychol. Assn., Am. Psychopathol. Assn., Soc. for Psychotherapy Research (pres. 1972-73, Career Contbr. award 1986), Psychologists Interested in Advancement of Psychoanalysis, Phi Beta Kappa, Sigma Xi. Home: 4117 Dorman Dr Nashville TN 37215-2404 Office: Vanderbilt U Dept Psychology Nashville TN 37240 *Scientific and professional work is a very personal endeavor. It is the pursuit of meaning and the search for answers to the existential questions that have occupied mankind through the ages. Thus, the motivation to do one's best within one's limited powers is nothing altruistic although it counts as a great reward to kindle a spark in others. As a refugee from Nazi Germany, I remain deeply grateful for the opportunities my adopted country has provided me.*

STRUPP, JACQUELINE VIRGINIA, professional business manager; b. Montevideo, Uruguay, July 24, 1963; d. Gunther and Silvia (Klemens) S.; children: Matias, Mercedes. BA with hons. cum laude, NYU, 1986. Customer svc. mgr. Games Mag./Mail Order, N.Y.C., 1984-86; treas., property mgr., asst. to chief exec. officer Hudson Properties, Lyndhurst, N.J., 1986-90; sales assoc. Bloomingdale's, Palm Beach Gardens, Fla., 1990-91, staff tng. supr. and pers. asst., 1991-92; legal asst., bookkeeper Gov.'s Bank and Bruce W. Keihner, Palm Beach, Fla., 1993; assoc. Ideas & Things, 1994—; freelance bus. mgr., 1994—, personal and bus. coach, 1994—.

STRUTIN, KENNARD REGAN, lawyer, educator; b. Bklyn., Dec. 1, 1961; s. Fred and Estelle (Brodzansky) S. BA summa cum laude, St. John's U., Jamaica, N.Y., 1981; JD, Temple U. Sch. Law, Phila., 1984; MLS, St. John's U., 1994. Bar: N.Y. 1986, U.S. Dist. Ct. (ea. and so. dists.) N.Y. 1990, U.S. Dist. Ct. (no. and we. dists.) N.Y. 1991, U.S. Ct. Appeals (2d cir.) 1990, U.S. Ct. Appeals (fed. cir.) 1991, U.S. Tax Ct. 1991, U.S. Ct. Mil. Appeals 1991, U.S. Supreme Ct. 1990. Atty. pvt. practice, West Hempstead, N.Y., 1986; trial atty. Nassau County Legal Aid Soc., Hempstead, N.Y., 1987-88, Orange County Legal Aid Soc., Goshen, N.Y., 1988-90; atty. pvt. practice, West Hempstead, N.Y., 1990-91; staff atty. N.Y. State Defenders Assn., Albany, N.Y., 1991-93; adjunct asst. prof. St. John's U., Jamaica, N.Y., 1993—; small claims tax assessment hearing officer Supreme Ct., Nassau, Suffolk, N.Y., 1993—; spkr. lawyer in classroom Nassau County Bar Assn., Mineola, N.Y., 1987-94; spkr. pre-release program Correctional Facilities, Lower Hudson Valley, N.Y., 1989-94. Contbr. articles to profl. jours. Recipient Gold Key in History award, 1981, Cert. Achievement in History award, 1980, Cert. Acad. Excellence, St. John's U., 1994, Orange County Exec. Recognition award, 1990, 93. Mem. ABA, Am. Assn. Law Librs., Beta Phi Mu.

STRUTTON, LARRY D., newspaper executive; b. Colorado Springs, Colo., Sept. 12, 1940; s. Merril and Gladys (Sheldon) S.; m. Carolyn Ann Croak, Dec. 3, 1960; children—Gregory L., Kristen. A.A. in Electronics Engring., Emily Griffith Electronics Sch., 1968; B.S. in Bus. Mgmt. and Systems Mgmt., Met. State Coll., 1971; diploma in Advanced Mgmt. Program, Harvard U., 1988. Printer Gazette Telegraph, Colorado Springs, Colo., 1961-64; prodn. dir. Rocky Mountain News, Denver, 1964-80, pres., 1990, pres. and CEO, 1991—; exec. v.p. ops. and advt. Detroit Free Press, 1981-83; v.p. ops. Los Angeles Times, 1983-85, exec. v.p. ops., 1986-90. Mem. adv. com. Rochester Inst. Tech., 1984—. Mem. Am. Newspaper Pubs. Assn. (chmn. 1987, chmn. TEC com. 1985-86), R&E Council (research and engring. council of the Graphic Arts Industry Inc.). Club: Lakeside Golf (Los Angeles). Home: 50 Glenmoor Cir Englewood CO 80110-7121 also: Rocky Mountain News 400 W Colfax Ave Denver CO 80204

STRUTZ, WILLIAM A., lawyer; b. Bismarck, N.D., May 13, 1934; s. Alvin C. and Ina Vee (Minor) S.; m. Marilyn Seagly, Aug. 31, 1957; children: Heidi Jane Mitchell, Colin Christopher, Nathaniel Paul. Student, Drake U., 1952-53; BA, N. Cen. Coll., 1956; postgrad., Washington and Lee U., 1956-57; JD, U. N.D., 1959. Bar: N.D. 1959, U.S. dist. Ct. N.D. 1959, U.S. Ct. Appeals (8th cir.) 1961. Atty., pres. Fleck, Mather & Strutz, Ltd., Bismarck, N.D., 1959—; mem. grievance com. N.D. Supreme Ct., Bismarck, 1974-77, chmn. supreme ct. svcs. com., 1979—. Bd. dirs. Vets. Meml. Pub. Libr., Bismarck, Shiloh Christian Sch., Bismarck, 1978—. Recipient Herbert Harley award Am. Judicature Soc., 1991. Mem. ABA, Am. Bd. Trial Advocates (advocate), Lions Club. Methodist. Avocations: reading, rare book collecting, music, sports. Home: 1238 W Highland Acres Rd Bismarck ND 58501-1259 Office: Fleck Mather Strutz Ltd 400 E Broadway Ave Bismarck ND 58501-4038

STRUVE, GUY MILLER, lawyer; b. Wilmington, Del., Jan. 5, 1943; s. William Scott and Elizabeth Bliss (Miller) S.; m. Marcia Mayo Hill, Sept. 20, 1986; children: Andrew Hardenbrook, Catherine Tolstoy, Frank Leroy Hill, Guy Miller, Beverly Marcia Wise (dec.), Elena Wise Struve-Hill. A.B. summa cum laude, Yale U., 1963; LL.B. magna cum laude, Harvard U., 1966. Bar: N.Y. 1967, D.C. 1986, U.S. Dist. Ct. (so. dist.) N.Y. 1970, U.S. Dist. Ct. (ea. dist.) N.Y. 1973, U.S. Dist. Ct. (no. dist.) Calif. 1979, U.S. Dist. Ct. D.C. 1987, U.S. Ct. Appeals (2d cir.) 1969, U.S. Ct. Appeals (D.C. cir.) 1973, U.S. Ct. Appeals (8th cir.) 1976, U.S. Ct. Appeals (9th cir.) 1979, U.S. Supreme Ct. 1971, U.S. Dist. Ct. (we. dist.) N.Y. 1991. Law clk. Hon. J. Edward Lumbard, Chief Judge United States Ct. Appeals for 2d Circuit, 1966-67; assoc. firm Davis Polk & Wardwell, 1967-72, ptnr., 1973—; ptnr. Ind. Counsel's Office, 1987-94. Mem. ABA, N.Y. State Bar Assn., Assn. of Bar of City of N.Y. (chmn. com. antitrust and trade regulation, 1983-86), Am. Law Inst. Home: 116 E 63rd St New York NY 10021-7343 Office: Davis Polk & Wardwell 450 Lexington Ave New York NY 10017-3911

STRUYK, ROBERT JOHN, lawyer; b. Sanborn, Iowa, May 17, 1932; s. Arie Peter and Adriana (VerHoef) S.; m. Barbara Damon, Sept. 7, 1963; children: Arie Franklin, Damon Nicholas, Elizabeth Snow. BA, Hope Coll., 1954; MA, Columbia U., 1957; LLB, U. Minn., 1961. Bar: Minn., U.S. Dist. Ct. Minn. Secondary tchr. Indianola (Iowa) Pub. Schs., 1957-58; assoc., then ptnr. Dorsey & Whitney, Mpls., 1961—. Episcopalian. Clubs: Mpls., Minikahda. Office: Dorsey & Whitney 220 S 6th St Minneapolis MN 55402-4502

STRYER, LUBERT, biochemist, educator; b. Tientsin, China, Mar. 2, 1938. B.S. with honors, U. Chgo., 1957; M.D. magna cum laude, Harvard U., 1961; DS (hon.), U. Chgo., 1992. Helen Hay Whitney fellow Harvard U., also Med. Research Council Lab., 1961-63; from asst. prof. to assoc. prof. biochemistry Stanford U., 1963-69; prof. molecular biophysics and biochemistry Yale U., 1969-76; Winzer prof. neurobiology Stanford U. Sch. Medicine, 1976—, chmn. dept. structural biology, 1976-79; chmn. sci. adv. bd. Affymetrix, Inc., 1993—; cons. NIH, NRC; pres., sci. dir. Affymax Rsch. Inst., Palo Alto, Calif., 1989-90; mem. sci. adv. bd. Jane Coffin Childs Fund, 1982-90, Rsch. to Prevent Blindness, 1984-93, Pew Scholars Profs. in Biomed. Scis.; chmn. sci. adv. bd. Affymetrix, Inc., 1993—; bd. dirs. Aurora Bioscis. Corp., 1996—. Mem. editorial bd.: Jour. Molecular Biology, 1968-72, Jour. Cell Biology, 1981—; assoc. editor: Annual Revs. Biophysics and Bioengineering, 1970-76. Recipient Am. Chem. Soc. award in biol. chemistry Eli Lilly & Co., 1970, Alcon award in vision Alcon Rsch. Inst., 1992. Fellow AAAS (Newcomb Cleveland prize 1992), Am. Acad. Arts and Scis.; mem. NAS, Am. Chem. Soc., Am. Soc. Biol. Chemists, Biophys. Soc., Phi Beta Kappa. Office: Stanford Sch Medicine Fairchild Ctr D133 Stanford CA 94305

STRYKER, JAMES WILLIAM, automotive executive, former military officer; b. Grand Rapids, Mich., Apr. 20, 1940; s. John Alvin and Marian (Anderson) S.; m. Eleanor Marie Finger, Sept. 26, 1964; children: James William II, Marian Marie, Kathryn Alison Greenbauer. BS, U.S. Mil. Acad., 1963; MA, U. Mich., 1972; postgrad., U.S. Army Command and Gen. Staff Coll., 1978. Commd. 2d lt. U.S. Army, 1963; battery exec. officer 6th/20th field arty. U.S. Army, Ft. Carson, Colo., 1964-65; advisor U.S. Army, Vietnam, 1965-66; battery comdr. 4th/3d field arty. U.S. Army, Ft. Hood, Tex., 1967-68; advisor U.S. Army, Thailand, 1969-70; S-3 ops. officer 1st/7th F.A., Ft. Riley, Kans., 1972-73; assoc. prof. history U.S. Mil. Acad., West Point, N.Y., 1973-77; chief nuclear ops. Ctrl. Army Group NATO, Heidelberg, Germany, 1978-81; dir., project mgr. tank-automotive command U.S. Army, Warren, Mich., 1981-86; ret. U.S. Army, 1986; program mgr. military vehicles operation GMC Truck, Pontiac, Mich., 1987-95; cross brand portfolio mgr. Pontiac-GMC Divsn. GM Corp., Pontiac, Mich., 1996—. Author: (with others) Encyclopedia of Southern History, 1977; co-author: Early American Wars, 1978. Decorated Legion of Merit, Bronze Star medal, Def. Meritorious Svc. medal, Meritorious Svc. medal with oakleaf cluster, Army Commendation medal with oakleaf cluster, U.S. Army/Vietnamese Cross of Gallantry with palm and gold star. Mem. NRA (life), Am. Def. Preparedness Assn. (dir. Detroit chpt. 1991-92, 94—, 2d v.p. 1995, 1st v.p. 1995-96, pres. 1996—), Assn. U.S. Army (dir. Detroit chpt. 1990-95), Gordon Setter Club Am., Nodrog Setter Club Mich. Avocations: hunting, skeet shooting, trout fishing, field training English and Gordon Setters. Home: 168 First St Romeo MI 48065-5000 Office: Pontiac-GMC Divsn 31 E Judson St MC 3103-12 Pontiac MI 48342-2230 Office: Pontiac GMC Divsn Gen Motors Corp MC 3103-12 31 E Judson St Pontiac MI 48342-2230

STRYKER, SHELDON, sociologist, educator; b. St. Paul, May 26, 1924; s. Max and Rose (Moskevitz) S.; m. Alyce Shirley Agranoff, Sept. 7, 1947; children: Robin Sue, Jeffrey, David, Michael, Mark. B.A. summa cum laude, U. Minn., 1948, M.A., 1950, Ph.D., 1955. Mem. faculty Ind. U., 1951—, prof. sociology, 1964—, disting. prof. sociology, 1985—; dir. Inst. Social Research, 1965-70, 89-94, chmn. dept. sociology, 1969-75; co-dir. Ctr. for Social Rsch., 1989-94; cons. in field; mem. social scis. research rev. com. NIMH, 1974-79, chmn., 1976-79, mem. research scientist devel. award com., 1981-85. Editor: Sociometry, 1966-69, Rose Monograph Series of Am. Sociol. Assn., 1971-73, Am. Sociol. Rev., 1982-85; assoc. editor: Social Problems, 1957-59; author books, monographs, articles, chpts. in books. Served with AUS, 1943-46. Fellow Social Sci. Research Council, 1959-60, Ctr. Advanced Behavioral Scis., 1986-87; Fulbright research scholar Italy, 1966-67. Mem. Am. Sociol. Assn. (nat. coun. 1965-67, 80-81, chmn. social psychology sect. 1978-79, chmn. publs. com. 1991-93, Cooley-Mead award), Ohio Valley Sociol. Soc. (coun. 1965-67), North Ctrl. Sociol. Assn. (pres. 1978-79), Sociol. Rsch. Assn. (coun. 1978-84, pres. 1983-84), Phi Beta Kappa. Home: 3710 Saint Remy Dr Bloomington IN 47401-2418

STRYKER, STEVEN CHARLES, lawyer; b. Omaha, Oct. 26, 1944; s. James M. and Jean G. (Grannis) S.; m. Bryna Dee Litwin, Oct. 20, 1972; children: Ryan, Kevin, Gerrit, Courtney. BS, U. Iowa, 1967, JD with distinction, 1969; postgrad., Northwestern Grad. Sch. Bus., 1969-70, DePaul U., 1971. Bar: Iowa 1969, Tex. 1986; CPA, Ill., Iowa. Sr. tax acct. Arthur Young & Co., Chgo., 1969-72; fed. tax mgr. Massey Ferguson, Des Moines, 1972-74; fed./state tax mgr FMC Corp., Chgo., 1974-78; gen. tax atty. Shell Oil Co., Houston, 1978-81, asst. gen. tax counsel, 1981-83, gen. mgr., 1983-86, v.p., gen. tax counsel, 1986—. Mem. ABA, Texas Bar Assn., Iowa Bar Assn., Am. Inst. CPA's, Ill. Soc. CPA's, Iowa Soc. CPA's., Tax Execs. Inst., Am. Petroleum Inst. Republican. Home: 10819 Everwood Ln Houston TX 77024-5416 Office: Shell Oil Co 1 Shell Plz Ste 4570 Houston TX 77001

STUART, ANNE ELIZABETH, journalist, freelance writer, educator; b. Lansing, Mich., Nov. 5, 1956. BA in English and Journalism with honors, Mich. State U., 1979; MS in Journalism, Columbia U., N.Y.C., 1986. Reporter, editor Star-Gazette/Sunday Telegram, Elmira, N.Y., 1980-83; reporter Knickerbocker News, Albany, N.Y., 1983-85; intern Newsday, Long Island, N.Y., 1985; freelance writer N.Y.C. and Boston, 1985-87; reporter The Patriot Ledger, Quincy, Mass., 1987-90, AP, Boston, 1990-94; sr. editor CIO, WebMaster Mags., Framingham, Mass., 1994—; instr. adult edn. programs, Boston, Brookline, Mass., Cambridge, Mass.; instr. Northeastern U., 1990-91, Emerson Coll., 1989. Contbr. chpts. to books; contbr. articles to Boston mag., Boston Woman Mag., Women's Day, Mass. Health Care, Boston Herald, Newsday, Seventeen, Northeastern Mag., and other publs.; mng. editor Mich. State U. newspaper The State News, 1978-79, other State News reporting and eiditng, 1975-78. Knight Found. for Specialized Journalism fellow, 1988; Brookdale Inst. scholar, Scripps-Howard Found. Jacqueline Radin Newsday scholar, 1985-86, recipient nat. 1st pl. in-depth reporting Sigma Delta Chi Mark of Excellence Competition, 1986, 1st pl. in-depth reporting and feature writing, 1986, statewide 3d pl. N.Y. State Assn. Press Competition Am. Acad. Family Physicians, 1983, Nat. Well-Done award Gannett Co., 1982, statewide 2d pl. in news Detroit Press 1979, La Nacion Press award, 1990. Office: CIO Communications 492 Old Conn Path Framingham MA 01701

STUART, BEN R., manufacturing company executive. Sr. v.p. Dresser Industries Inc.; chmn. Dresser-Rand, Corning, N.Y.; pres. and ceo, 1995—. Office: Dresser Rand Co One Baron Steuben Pl Corning NY 14830*

STUART, CAROLE, publishing executive; b. N.Y.C., Feb. 22, 1941; d. Frank and Sally (Stern) Rose; m. Lyle Stuart, Feb. 4, 1982; 1 child, Jennifer Susan Livingston. Student, Bklyn. Coll. Pub. Lyle Stuart, Inc., Secaucus, N.J.; assoc. pub. Carol Pub. Group, N.Y.C.; pub. Barricade Books, Inc., N.Y.C. Author: Why Was I Adopted?, To Turn You On, 39 Sex Fantasies for Women, (with Claire Ciliotta), Why Am I Going to the Hospital?, I'll Never Be Fat Again, How To Lose 5 Pounds Fast, The Affair. Mem. Authors Guild, Women's Media Group, Wine and Food Soc. N.Y., Emily's List. Home: 1530 Palisade Ave Apt 6L Fort Lee NJ 07024-5421 Office: Barricade Books 150 5th Ave New York NY 10011-4311

STUART, CHARLES EDWARD, electrical engineer, oceanographer; b. Durham, N.C., Feb. 9, 1942; s. Charles Edward and Wilma Kelly Stuart; m. Margaret Ann Robinson, Jan. 9, 1982; children: Marjorie Kelly, Heather Alison. BSEE, Duke U., 1963. Engr. Westinghouse Electric Corp., Balt., 1963-65; sr. engr. Booz Allen Hamilton, Chevy Chase, Md., 1966-68; rsch. dir. B-K Dynamics Inc., Huntsville, Ala., 1969-78; oceanographer Office of Naval Rsch., Arlington, Va., 1979-84; dir. maritime system office Advanced Rsch. Projects Agy., Arlington, 1985—. Contbr. 12 papers on ocean acoustics to profl. jours. Recipient Am. Def. Preparedness Assn. award, Bushnell award for career contbns. to undersea warfare. Mem. IEEE (sr., ad. com. 1991-93), Assn. Unmanned Vehicle Systems (trustee 1989-93), Acoustical Soc. Am. Methodist. Achievements include leading work in development of unmanned undersea vehicle technology. Home: 4718 17th St N Arlington VA 22207-2031 Office: Advanced Rsch Projects Agy 3701 Fairfax Dr Arlington VA 22203-1700

STUART, DAVID EDWARD, anthropologist, author, educator; b. Calhoun County, Ala., Jan. 9, 1945; s. Edward George and Avis Elsie (Densmore) S.; B.A. (Wesleyan Merit scholar 1965-66), W.VA. Wesleyan Coll., 1967; M.A. in Anthropology, U. N.Mex., 1970, Ph.D., 1972, postdoctoral student, 1975-76; m. Cynthia K. Morgan, June 14, 1971. Research assoc. Andean Center, Quito, Ecuador, 1970; continuing edn. instr. anthropology U. N.Mex., 1971, research archeologist Office Contract Archeology, 1974, research coordinator, 1974-77, asst. prof. anthropology, 1975-77, assoc. prof. anthropology, 1984—, asst. v.p. acad. affairs, 1987-95, assoc. v.p. academic affairs, 1995—; asst. prof. Eckerd Coll., St. Petersburg, Fla., 1972-74; cons. archeologist right-of-way div. Pub. Service Co. N.Mex., Albuquerque, 1977-78; cons. anthropologist Bur. Indian Affairs, Albuquerque, 1978, Historic Preservation Bur. N.Mex., Santa Fe, 1978-81, Nat. Park Service, 1980, Albuquerque Mus., 1981; sr. research assoc. Human Systems Research, Inc., 1981-83, Quivira Research Center, Albuquerque, 1984-86; bd. dirs. Table Ind. Scholars, 1979-83, pres., bd. dirs. Rio Grande Heritage Found., Albuquerque and Las Cruces, 1985-87; advisor Human Systems Research, Inc., Tularosa, N.Mex., 1978-80, Albuquerque Commn. on Hist. Preservation, 1984-86. Grantee Eckerd Coll., 1973, Historic Preservation Bur., 1978-80. Essayist award N.Mex. Humanities Council, 1986. Mem. Am. Anthrop. Assn., Royal Anthrop. Inst. Gt. Britain, N.Mex. Archeol. Council, Albuquerque Archeol. Soc. (pres. 1986-88), Descs. Signers Declaration Independence, Sigma Xi, Phi Kappa Phi. Presbyterian. Co-author: Archeological Survey: 4 Corners to Ambrosia, N.Mex., 1976, A Proposed Project Design for the Timber Management Archeological Surveys, 1978, Ethnoarcheological Investigations of Shepherding in the Pueblo of Laguna, 1983; Author: Prehistoric New Mexico, 1981, 2d edit., 1984, 3d edit., 1988, Glimpses of the Ancient Southwest, 1985, The Magic of Bandelier National Monument, 1989, Power and Efficiency in Eastern Anasazi Architecture, 1994, others; columnist New Mexico's Heritage, 1983-87, others. Editor: Archeological Reports, No. 1, 1975, No. 2, 1981. Office: U NMex Rm 263 Student Svcs Ctr Albuquerque NM 87131 *Personal philosophy: In academics, as in life, reliability, integrity and compassion are far more precious than mere intellectual brilliance.*

STUART, FRANK ADELL, county official; b. Tahoka, Tex., Dec. 18, 1928; s. John Franklin and Mary Elizabeth (Reed) S.; m. Mary Louise Wheat Crelia, Feb. 2, 1962; children: Rita, Donna, Franklin, Burce, Susan, Mary, Chris. BBA, Tex. Tech U., 1979. Asst. cashier Am. State Bank, Lubbock, Tex., 1949-52, Citizen Nat. Bank, Lubbock, 1953-59; acct. in pvt. practice Lubbock, 1960-63; asst. mgr. Gibson Discount Ctr., Lubbock, 1964-77; tax. assessor and collector Lubbock County, Lubbock, 1979-94, ret., 1994. Served to lt. col. Tex. State Guard, 1988—. Mem. Tax Assessor-Collectors Assn. Tex., Lubbock C. of C., Masons, YorkRite, Scottish Rite, Shriners, Yellow House Lodge, Daylight Lodge. Baptist. Home: 2704 57th St Lubbock TX 79413-5605

STUART, GARY MILLER, railroad executive; b. Normal, Ill., May 8, 1940; s. Henry Woodward and Ruth Amy (Miller) S.; m. Sylvia Georgeades, Oct. 10, 1965; children: David, Peter, Paul, Michael. BS, MIT, 1962; MA, Harvard U., 1965. With Ford Motor Co., Dearborn, Mich., 1965-74, Gen. Foods Corp., White Plains, N.Y., 1974-81; dir. operational rsch. Union Pacific Corp., Bethlehem, Pa., 1981-83, asst. treas., 1983-87, treas., 1987-89, v.p., treas., 1990—; bd. dirs. ACE Ltd., Hamilton, Bermuda, 1988—, Union Pacific Resources Group, Ft. Worth, 1995—. Bd. govs. Lehigh Valley Cmty. Found., 1992—; bd. dirs. Sta. WLVT-TV/Lehigh Valley Pub. TV, 1992-94. NSF fellow, 1962-65, Hon. Woodrow Wilson fellow, 1962. Mem. Fin. Execs. Inst., Assn. Am. Railroads (chmn. treas. div. 1992-93). Office: Union Pacific Corp 8th & Eaton Aves Bethlehem PA 18018

STUART, GERARD WILLIAM, JR., investment company executive, city official; b. Yuba City, Calif., July 28, 1939; s. Gerard William and Geneva Bernice (Stuke) S.; student Yuba Jr. Coll., 1957-59, Chico State Coll., 1959-60; A.B., U. Calif., Davis, 1962; M.L.S., U. Calif., Berkeley, 1963; m. Lenore Frances Loroña, 1981. Rare book librarian Cornell U., 1964-68; bibliographer of scholarly collections Huntington Library, San Marino, Calif., 1968-73, head acquisitions librarian, 1973-75; sec.-treas., dir. Ravenstree Corp., 1969-80, pres., chmn. bd., 1980—; pres., chmn. bd. William Penn Ltd., 1981—. Councilman City of Yuma, 1992-96, also dep. mayor, 1995; bd. dirs. Ariz. Humanities Coun., 1993—. Lilly fellow Ind. U., 1963-64. Mem. Bibliog. Soc. Am., Phi Beta Kappa, Alpha Gamma Sigma, Phi Kappa Phi. Clubs: Rolls-Royce Owners; Grolier (N.Y.C.); Zamorano (Los Angeles). Office: 204 S Madison Ave Yuma AZ 85364-1421

STUART, HAROLD CUTLIFF, lawyer, business executive; b. Oklahoma City, July 4, 1912; s. Royal Cutliff and Alice (Bramlitt) S.; m. Joan Skelly, June 6, 1938 (dec. 1994); children: Randi Stuart Wightman, Jon Rolf; m. Frances Langford, Nov. 18, 1994. J.D., U. Va., 1936. Bar: Okla. 1936, D.C. 1952. Ptnr. Stuart, Biolchini, Turner & Givran, Tulsa; judge Common Pleas Ct., 1941-42; asst. sec. air force, 1949-51; chmn. bd. 1st Stuart Corp., radio, oil, real estate and investments, Tulsa; dir. Lowrance Electronics, Inc., Tulsa; spl. cons. to sec. Air Force, 1961-63; mem. Okla. Hwy. Commn., 1959-63; bd. dirs. Great Empire Broadcasting Inc., Wichita, Kans. Trustee emeritus Lovelace Found., Albuquerque; trustee N.Am. Wildlife Fedn; mem. Nat. Eagle Scout Coun. Boy Scouts Am., Disting. Eagle Scout; past pres. Air Force Acad. Found., chmn. bd. Served from 1st lt. to col. USAAF, 1942-46, ETO. Decorated Bronze Star (U.S.); comdr. Order of St. Olav; King Haakon 7th Victory medal; medal of Liberation (Norway); Croix de Guerre (Luxembourg); named to Okla. Aviation and Space Hall of Fame, Okla. Hall of Fame. Mem. Am., Okla., D.C. bar assns., Air Force Assn. (dir., nat. pres., chmn. bd. 1951-52), Tulsa C. of C., Tulsa Headliner, Falcon Found. (vice chmn.), Ducks Unltd. (trustee), Delta Kappa Epsilon. Democrat. Clubs: Southern Hills Country, The Boston (Tulsa); Burning Tree (Washington), Willoughby Golf, The Amb. (Stuart, Fla.). Home: PO Box 96 Jensen Beach FL 34958 also: 4590 E 29th St Tulsa OK 74114-6208

STUART, JAMES, banker, broadcaster; b. Lincoln, Nebr., Apr. 11, 1917; s. Charles and Marie (Talbot) S.; m. Helen Catherine Davis, July 24, 1940; children: Catherine, James, William Scott. BA, BS, U. Nebr., 1940, HHD (hon.), 1990; HHD (hon.), U. Nebr., 1990, DHL (hon.), 1990. Chmn. bd. Stuart Mgmt. Co.; mng. ptnr. Stuart Enterprises; chmn. exec. com., bd. dirs. Nat. Bank Commerce, Lincoln; pres. Stuart Found. Founder, trustee Nebr. Human Resources Rsch. Found., 1948—; trustee Bryan Meml. Hosp., 1952-58, U. Nebr. Found., 1956—, Nebr. U. Endowment Fund for Disting. Tchrs.; mem. Lincoln Found., 1955—, Lincoln Sch. Bd., 1961-64, pres., 1964; chmn. bd. trustees 1st Plymouth Ch., Lincoln, 1956; pres. Lincoln Community Chest, 1960. With AUS, 1942-45. Recipient Disting. Svc. award U. Nebr., 1961, Alumni Achievement award, 1980. Mem. U. Nebr. Alumni Assn. (past pres.), Lincoln U. Club, Country Club of Lincoln, Gitchigami Club (Duluth, Minn.), Sunrise Country Club (Rancho Mirage, Calif.), Thunderbird Country Club. Home: 2801 Bonacum Dr Lincoln NE 68502-5723 Office: 852 Nbc Ctr Lincoln NE 68508

STUART, JAMES FORTIER, musician, artistic director; b. Baton Rouge, Dec. 22, 1928; s. Evander Morgan and Jeanne (Fortier) S. Mus.B., La. State U., 1950, B.Music Edn., 1950, Mus.M., 1954; Mus.D., U. Rochester, 1968. Asst. prof. voice, dir. opera Boston U.; also Boston Conservatory, 1964-68; prof. music, dir. opera Kent (Ohio) State U., 1968—; founder, artistic dir. Kent Light Opera Co., 1969—, Nat. Light Opera Co., 1977—; artistic dir. Ohio Light Opera Co., Wooster, 1979—; pres. Stuart Prodns., Ltd., Cleve., 1974—; mus. cons. Internat. Hospitality Mgmt., Inc., Cleve., 1974. Tenor soloist maj. opera cos. and symphonies, N.Y.C., Boston, Phila., Atlanta and New Orleans, 1950-70; leader tenor Am. Savoyards, 1956-60, Martyn Green Gilbert and Sullivan Co., 1961-67; translator into English from original French text: Auber's Fra Diavolo, 1988, Lecocq's Fille de Madame Angot,

1989, Ciboulette (Reynaldo Hahn), 1990. Recipient Significant Sig Outstanding Achievement in Lyric Theatre award Sigma Chi, 1995; inducted Coll. of Fellows of Am. Theatre, 1996. Office: Ohio Light Opera Wooster Coll Wooster OH 44691 *A man's greatest contribution to society is developing himself to the fullest. Only after he has accomplished this can he be of service to his fellow human beings.*

STUART, JOHN MCHUGH, JR., public relations consultant, retired foreign service officer; b. Albany, N.Y., Apr. 21, 1916; s. John McHugh and Marie (Fitzgerald) S.; m. Ruth Sherman, June 24, 1944 (dec. May 1977). Student, U. Santa Clara, 1934-35; B.A., Georgetown U., 1939; M.A., George Washington U., 1966; grad., Air War Coll., 1966. Reporter, editor, 1938-44; fgn. service officer Office Mil. Govt. U.S., Germany, 1945-50, USIA, 1954-71; press attache Am. embassy, New Delhi, 1962-65; pub. affairs officer U.S. Mission in Geneva, 1956-61; fgn. corr. Voice of Am., Korea and Germany, 1950-56; press counselor Am. embassy, Saigon, 1966-67; sr. adviser pub. affairs U.S. Mission to UN, N.Y.C., 1967-71; spl. adviser U.S. del. 26th UN Gen. Assembly, 1971; spokesman U.S. del. conf. on human environment, Stockholm, 1972; adviser 31st Gen. Assembly, 1976, 3d UN Law of Sea Conf., N.Y., 1977, VIth and Xth Spl. Gen. Assemblies on Disarmament, 1978, 82; now cons. internat. pub. affairs N.Y.C., also Washington; adviser European Security Conf., USIA, 1973, Agri-Energy Roundtable, Geneva, 1981. Served with SHAEF, World War II. Mem. Nat. Press Club. Home and Office: 180 West End Ave Apt 27L New York NY 10023-4919

STUART, JOSEPH MARTIN, art museum administrator; b. Seminole, Okla., Nov. 9, 1932; s. Arch William and Lillian (Lindsey) S.; BFA in Art, U. N.Mex., 1959, MA in Art, 1962; m. Signe Margaret Nelson, June 18, 1960; 1 dau., Lise Nelson Stuart. Dir., Roswell (N.Mex.) Museum and Art Center, 1960-62; curator U. Oreg. Mus. Art, 1962-63; dir. Boise (Idaho) Gallery Art, 1964-68, Salt Lake (City) Art Ctr., 1968-71, S.D. Art Mus., Brookings, 1971-93; prof. art S.D. State U., 1971-93; represented in permanent collections: Coll. Idaho, Eureka Coll., Salt Lake Art Ctr., Sioux City (Iowa) Art Ctr., U. N.Mex. Art Mus., West Tex. State U. With USN, 1951-55. Mem. Am. Assn. Museums, Artists Equity, Coll. Art Assn., Phi Kappa Phi. Unitarian. Author: Index of South Dakota Artists, 1974; Art of South Dakota, 1974, The South Dakota Collection, 1988; author numerous exhbn. catalogs.

STUART, JUANITA RYAN, recreation facility executive; b. Cullman, Ala., Aug. 9, 1937; d. Stacy Carlton and Unie Mae (Hopkins) Ryan; m. Roy A. Stuart, Dec. 20, 1962 (div. Sept. 1964); 1 child, Dean Trent. Student, Alverson Draughn, Cleve., 1955-56. Cert. club mgr. Asst. mgr. Vestavia (Ala.) Country Club, 1964-75, Indian Hills Country Club, Tuscaloosa, Ala., 1975-78; gen. mgr. Mountain Brook Club, Birmingham, Ala., 1978—. Chairperson Taste of Birmingham, 1981—. Recipient Deanie Vacalis award Ala. Restaurant and Food Svc. Assn., 1987, Who's Who of Birmingham award C. of C., 1989, 90. Mem. CMAA (Ala. chpt., pres., bd. dirs.), Ala. Restaurant Assn. (pres., bd. dirs., Restauranteur of Yr. 1987, Salut Au Restauranteur of Yr. 1987), Birmingham-Jefferson Restaurant Assn. (pres., bd. dirs.), Ala. Sheriff's Boys and Girls Ranch (bd. dirs.), U. Ala. Alumni Assn. (life). Republican. Baptist. Avocations: reading, football, travel, grandchildren. Office: Mountain Brook Club 19 Beechwood Rd Birmingham AL 35213-3955

STUART, KENNETH D., plant research administrator, microbiologist; b. Boston, 1940; married; 3 children. BA, Northeastern U., 1963; MA, Wesleyan U., 1965; PhD in Zoology, U. Iowa, 1969. Rsch. biochemist Nat. Inst. Med. Rsch., London, 1969-71, SUNY, Stony Brook, 1971-72; rsch. biologist U. San Francisco, 1972-76; dir. Seattle Biomed. Rsch. Inst., 1982—; affiliate prof. microbiology U. Wash., Seattle, 1984—. Fellow AAAS; mem. Am. Soc. Microbiology, Am. Soc. Parasitology, Am. Soc. Cell Biology, Am. Soc. Advancement Sci. Office: Seattle Biomed Rsch Inst 4 Nickerson St Seattle WA 98109-1651*

STUART, LAWRENCE DAVID, JR., lawyer; b. Temple, Tex., June 23, 1944; s. Lawrence David Sr. and SueLee (Dean) S.; m. Janey Pharr, Nov. 24, 1966 (div. Nov. 1982); children: Susan J., Lawrence David III; m. Venise Notias, May 7, 1983; 1 child, Marcus Stephen. BA in Econs., So. Meth. U., 1966, JD, 1969. Bar: Tex. 1969. Assoc. Rain, Harrell, Emery, Young & Doke, Dallas, 1969-74; ptnr. Johnson & Gibbs, P.C., Dallas, 1974-89; mng. ptnr. Weil, Gotshal & Manges, Dallas, 1989—. Mem. ABA, State Bar Tex. (ad hoc venture capital com. sect. of bus. law), Dallas Bar Assn., Tex. Bus. Law Found. Avocations: skiing, scuba diving, jogging, reading, tennis. Office: Weil Gotshal & Manges 100 Crescent Ct # 1300 Dallas TX 75201-6900

STUART, LILLIAN MARY, writer; b. Chgo., Nov. 7, 1914; d. Ira and Katherine (Tries) Daugherty; m. Robert Graham Stuart, Aug. 7, 1936 (dec. Sept. 1969); 1 child, Mary Leone. Asst. to pres. Weisberger Bros., South Bend, 1933-42; head TWX distbn. Davis-Monthan AFB, Tucson, 1946-48; artist and music tchr., 1945-55; interviewer-counselor Ariz. State Employment Commn., Tucson, 1955-70; residence dir. YWCA, Tucson, 1970-71; tax preparer Tucson, 1971-72; U.S. census taker U.S. Govt., N.Mex., 1976, 80; mng. Luna County Rep. Party, Deming, 1976; tchr. YWCA, Tucson, 1969, El Paso Coll. Bus., 1972; tutor math, English, 1981; travel lectr. various civic groups and clubs; radio reader Lighthouse for the Blind, El Paso, 1983-89; spkr. Internat. Women's Day Celebration, 1996. Contbr. stories to The Quarterly; author: (series of biographies) Lighthouse for the Blind; actress Studebaker Players, South Bend, 1936-42, South Bend Theatre, 1936-42, (film) Extreme Prejudice, 1986; writer Centennial Mus. at U. Tex., El Paso, 1992-95. Counselor, vol. Crisis Ctr., Deming, 1975-77. Recipient plaques and prizes for various pieces of writing. Mem. Mensa, Rosicrucians, Sisters in Crime. Episcopalian. Avocations: travel, art. Address: 2710 W Ashby Pl Apt 323 San Antonio TX 78201-5380

STUART, LYLE, publishing company executive; b. N.Y.C., Aug. 11, 1922; s. Alfred and Theresa (Cohen) L.; m. Mary Louise Strawn, Sept. 26, 1946; children: Sandra Lee, Rory John.; m. Carole Livingston, Feb. 4, 1982; 1 dau., Jenni. Student pub. schs., N.Y.C.; PhD (hon.), State of Calif. Reporter Internat. News Service, 1945, Variety, 1945-46; script writer Dept. State, Voice of Am., 1946; editor Music Bus. mag., 1946-48; founder Expose, 1951; pub. The Independent, 1951-75; bus. mgr. MAD mag., 1952-54; pres. Citadel Press, 1970-89; founder Lyle Stuart, Inc., 1956; pres. University Books, Inc., 1983—, Hot News, 1983, Barricade Books, 1990—; Founder North Bergen (N.J.) Pub. Library. Prodr. Chinese Festival of Music, 1952-62; author: God Wears A Bowtie, 1949, The Secret Life of Walter Winchell, 1953, Mary Louise, 1970, Casino Gambling for the Winner, 1978, Lyle Stuart on Baccarat, 1983, 2d edit., 1995, Map of Life, 1996, Winning at Casino Gambling, 1995. Served with AUS, 1942-44. Mem. Am. Booksellers Assn., Silurians, Nat. Acad. TV Arts. and Scis., N.Y. Zool. Soc., Soc. Ky. Cols. Home: 1530 Palisade Ave Apt 6L Fort Lee NJ 07024-5421 Office: Barricade Books Inc 150 5th Ave New York NY 10011-4311

STUART, MARIE JEAN, physician, hematologist, researcher; b. Bangalore, India, Sept. 11, 1943; came to U.S., 1967; d. Norman and Dorothy (Dias) S. BS, Madras (India) U., MB. Asst. prof. pediatrics SUNY Health Sci. Ctr., Syracuse, 1972-76, assoc. prof., 1976-81, prof. pediatrics, 1981-87; prof. chief hematology and oncology div. St. Christophers Hosp. for Children and Temple U., Phila., 1987—; prof. thrombosis rsch. Temple U., 1987—; mem. nat. child health com. Nat. Inst. Child Health and Human Devel., Bethesda, Md., 1982-86; mem. nat. heart, lung and blood rsch. tng. com., NIH, Bethesda, 1993—. Contbr. articles to profl. jours.; contbr. book chpts. Mem. Am. Fedn. Clin. Research. Am. Pediatric Soc., Soc. for Pediatric Research. Mem. Christian Ch. Avocations: music, art. Home: 10B W Society Hill Towers Philadelphia PA 19106 Office: St Christophers Hosp Children Div Hematolog Philadelphia PA 19134

STUART, MARTY, country music singer, musician, songwriter; b. Philadelphia, Miss., Sept. 30, 1958; m. Cindy Cash (div.). With The Sullivan Family, 1970, Lester Flatt & the Nashville Grass, 1972-79, Johnny Cash, 1980-86; studio musician on albums with Willie Nelson, Emmylou Harris, Neil Young, Billy Joel, Bob Dylan, George Jones others; co-prodr. album A Joyful Noise, 1991; albums include Marty, With A Little Help From My Friends, 1977, Busy Bee Cafe, 1982, Marty Stuart, 1986, Hillbilly Rock, 1989, Tempted, 1991, This One's Gonna Hurt You, 1992, Let There Be Country, 1992, Love & Luck, 1994, Marty Party Hit Park, 1995, Honky Tonkin's What I Do Best, 1996. Recipient (with Travis Tritt) Grammy award for The Whiskey Ain't Workin', 1993, Country Music Assn. Vocal Event of Yr. (with Travis Tritt), with Asleep at the Wheel 1994 Grammy for Instrumental Performance "Red Wing." Office: 119 17th Ave S Nashville TN 37203-2707

STUART, MARY, actress; b. Miami, Fla., July ; d. Guy M. and Mary (Stuart) Houchins; m. Richard Krolik, Aug. 1, 1951 (div.); children: Cynthia, Jeffrey M.; m. Wolfgang Neumann, 1986. Student pub. schs., Tulsa. Appears in leading role: Search For Tomorrow, NBC-TV, N.Y.C., 1951-86; songwriter, singer, Columbia Records, 1956, Bell Records, 1973; Author: (autobiography) Both of Me, 1980 (Lit. Guild selection). Mem. Actors Equity Assn., AFTRA, Screen Actors Guild, ASCAP. Episcopalian.

STUART, NORTON ARLINGTON, JR., data processing manufacturing executive; b. Cin., Feb. 5, 1935; s. Norton A. and Olga I. (Hess) S.; m. Julia Ann (Sue) Sullivan, June 29, 1957; children: Norton A. III, Douglas S., Mark S. BBA, U Mich., 1957; postgrad., U. Ga., 1960. Account rep. IBM, Atlanta, 1961-65; industry mgr. EDS, Dallas, 1966-67; regional sales mgr., v.p. Recognition Equipment, Chgo., 1967-70; internat. sales v.p. Recognition Equipment, Frankfurt, Fed. Republic of Germany, 1971-72; industry group v.p. Recognition Equipment, Dallas, 1972-73; industry v.p., mktg. v.p., exec. v.p. Docutel Corp., Dallas, 1973-84; sr. v.p., exec. v.p. BancTec Inc., Dallas, 1984-87, pres., chief operating officer, 1987—. Served to lt. USN, 1957-60. Mem. Am. Mgmt. Assn., Am. Mktg. Assn., Am. Electonic Assn. Republican. Presbyterian. Avocations: tennis, golf, fishing, travel. Office: Banctec Inc 4435 Spring Valley Rd Dallas TX 75244-3704*

STUART, RAYMOND WALLACE, lawyer; b. Chattanooga, Feb. 13, 1941; s. Raymond Newton and Mary Vance (Wallace) S.; m. Peggy Woodward, Dec. 19, 1965; children: Raymond Warren, Laura Wallace. BS in Physics, U. Cin., 1963, JD, 1972. Bar: Ohio 1972. Pvt. practice Cin., 1972-74; atty. USIA, Washington, 1975-89, dep. gen. counsel, 1989—. Exec. editor Univ. Cin. Law Review, 1971-72. Capt. U.S. Army Spl. Forces, 1963-69. Avocations: hunting, fishing, reading. Home: 9894 Becket Ct Fairfax VA 22032-2412 Office: USIA Office of Gen Counsel 301 4th St SW Washington DC 20547-0009

STUART, ROBERT, container manufacturing executive; b. Oak Park, Ill., Aug. 3, 1921; s. Robert S. and Marie (Vavra) Solinsky; m. Lillian C. Kondelik, Dec. 5, 1962 (dec. May 1978); m. Lila Winterhoff Peters, May 21, 1982. BS, U. Ill., 1943. Sec.-treas., gen. mgr. Warren Metal Decorating Co., 1947-49; asst. to gen. mgr. Cans, Inc., 1950-52; asst. to v.p., then v.p. Nat. Can Corp., Chgo., 1953-59, exec. v.p., 1959-63, pres., 1963-69, chief exec., 1966-69, chmn. bd., chief exec. officer, 1969-73, chmn. bd., 1973-83, chmn. fin. com., 1983, mem. corp. devel. com., until 1986, chmn. emeritus, 1986—; past pres., bd. dirs. Corp. Responsibility Group of Greater Chgo. Past pres., bd. dirs. Chgo. Crime Commn.; dir. Nat. Crime Prevention Coun.; founding chmn. Nat. Minority Supplier Devel. Coun., 1972-73, Lloyd Morey Scholarship fund; Freedoms Found. at Valley Forge, trustee; bd. assocs. Chgo. Theol. Sem.; trustee Ill. Masonic Med. Ctr.; mem. adv. bd. Salvation Army, Broader Urban Involvement and Leadership Devel.; chmn. emeritus World Federalist Assn.; past pres., past trustee, chmn. Cen. Ch. Chgo. Congregationalist; chmn. Assn. to Unite the Democracies; numerous other civic activities. Capt. AUS, 1943-46. Mem. Pres.'s Assn. of Ill. (founding chmn. 1972-73), Naples Yacht Club, Capitol Hill Club (Washington), Chgo. Club, Econ. Club, Comml. Club, Yacht Club, Met. Club, Little Ship Club (London), Mason (32 degree), Rotary (past pres. Chgo. club, past dist. gov.), Alpha Kappa Lambda (past nat. pres.). Home: Apt 3810 400 E Randolph St Chicago IL 60601-7329 Office: Ste 6B 400 E Randolph St Chicago IL 60601-7329

STUART, ROBERT CRAMPTON, economics educator; b. Chemainus, B.C., Can., Oct. 22, 1938; s. Alexander Graham Robert and Olive C. (Chalk) S.; m. Beverly Joy, June 12, 1964; children: Craig Robert, Andrea Joy. B of Commerce in Econs., U. B.C., Vancouver, 1961; MSc in Econs., U. Wis., 1961, cert. in Russian studies, 1965, PhD in Econs., 1969. Vis. prof. econs. Princeton U., 1978-93; prof. econs. Rutgers U., 1976—; dir. grad. studies, 1985-86; chmn. dept. Rutgers U., 1986-89; vice chair dept., 1995—. Mem. Assn. Comp. Econ. Studies (exec. bd.), Mid Atlantic Slavic Conf. (pres.), Am. Assn. Advancement of Slavic Studies, Miata Club of Am., Photographic Soc. Am. Democrat. Avocations: antique auto collecting, photography. Home: 34 Sturwood Dr Belle Mead NJ 08502-3124 Office: Rutgers U Dept Of Econs New Brunswick NJ 08403

STUART, SANDRA KAPLAN, federal official; b. Greensboro, N.C.; d. Leon and Renee (Myers) Kaplan; children: Jay Jr., Timothy. BA, U. N.C., Greensboro; JD, Monterey Coll. Law. Chief legis. asst. Rep. Robert Matsui, Washington, 1979-81; legis. dir., assoc. staff Ho. of Appropriations and Budget Coms., Washington, 1981-87; adminstrv. asst. Rep. Vic Fazio, Washington, 1987-89, chief of staff, 1990-93; asst. sec. def. legis. affairs Dept. Def., The Pentagon, Washington, 1993—. Office: Office Legis Affairs Dept Def The Pentagon Washington DC 20301-1300

STUART, WALKER DABNEY, III, poet, author, English language educator; b. Richmond, Va., Nov. 4, 1937; s. Walker Dabney Jr. and Martha (vonSchilling) S.; m. Sandra Westcott, Jan. 20, 1983; children—Martha, Nathan vonSchilling, Darren Wynne. A.B., Davidson Coll., 1960; A.M., Harvard U., 1962. Instr. Coll. William and Mary, Williamsburg, Va., 1961-65; prof. English Washington and Lee U., Lexington, Va., 1965—, S. Blount Mason Jr. prof. English, 1991—; vis. prof. Middlebury (Vt.) Coll., 1968-69, Ohio U., Athens, 1975, U. Va., Charlottesville, 1981-83. Author: The Diving Bell, 1966, A Particular Place, 1969, The Other Hand, 1974, Friends of Yours, Friends of Mine, 1974, Round and Round, 1976, Nabokov: The Dimensions of Parody, 1978, Rockbridge Poems, 1981, Common Ground, 1982, Don't Look Back, 1987, Narcissus Dreaming, 1990, Sweet Lucy Wine, 1992, Light Years: New and Selected Poems, 1994, Second Sight: Poems for Paintings by Carroll Cloar, 1996, Long Gone, 1996. Recipient Dylan Thomas prize Poetry Soc. Am., 1965, Gov.'s award State of Va., 1979; Nat. Endowment for Arts lit. fellow, 1975, 82; Guggenheim fellow, 1987-88. Mem. Authors Guild Am., Poetry Soc. Am. Avocations: food, travel. Home: 30 Edmondson Ave Lexington VA 24450-1904 Office: Washington and Lee U Dept English Lexington VA 24450

STUART, WALTER BYNUM, III, banker; b. Baton Rouge, Oct. 5, 1922; s. Walter Bynum and Rosa (Gauthreaux) S.; m. Rita Kleinpeter, May 20, 1944; children—Walter Bynum IV, Robert, Douglas, Ronald, Scott. B.S., La. State U., 1943. Adminstrv. mgr. Kaiser Aluminum & Chem. Corp., 1946-63; v.p. First Nat. Bank Commerce, New Orleans, 1963-65, sr. v.p., 1965, exec. v.p., 1965-73; vice chmn. bd., dir. 1st Nat. Bank Commerce, New Orleans, 1973-78; exec. v.p. 1st Commerce Corp., New Orleans, 1972-73, pres., 1973-75, vice-chmn. bd., 1975-78, dir., 1973-78; pres. Am. Bank & Trust Co., Lafayette, La., 1978-86, cons.; assoc. dir., mem. faculty Sch. Banking La. State U., 1973-75, dir., 1975-78; mem. Faculty Assemblies for Bank Dirs. Campaign group chmn. industry com., mem. United Fund for Greater New Orleans Area, 1974; mem. research com. Pub. Affairs Research Council La., 1973-76, v.p., trustee, 1973-76; bd. dirs. Bur. Govtl. Research, 1973-77, Council Better La., 1975—; pres. New Orleans Indsl. Devel. Bd., 1973-75. Served to lt. (j.g.) USNR, 1943-46. Mem. C. of C. of Greater New Orleans Area (v.p. 1973-75, bd. dirs.), Am. Bankers Assn., La. Bankers Assn. (pres. 1977), Am. Mgmt. Assn., Kappa Alpha, Delta Sigma Pi, Beta Gamma Sigma. Democrat. Roman Catholic. Office: Jefferson at Lee Lafayette LA 70501 *Recognizing that life is the experiencing of reality, and that reality is simply a continuing series of problems, I long ago decided that I would treat a problem as an opportunity. Every incident of difficulty has always invited my intense interest as a challenge, and my thoughts have been immediately marshalled for positive effort. My life has been most rewarding because I believe that "a problem is an opportunity!".*

STUART, WALTER BYNUM, IV, lawyer; b. Grosse Tete, La., Nov. 23, 1946; s. Walter Bynum III and Rita (Kleinpeter) S.; m. Lettice Lee Binnings May 18, 1968; children: Courtney Lyon, Walter Burke V. Student Fordham U., 1964-65; BA, Tulane U., 1968, JD, 1973. Bar: La. 1973, U.S. Dist. Ct. (ea. and we. dists.) La. 1974, U.S. Tax Ct. 1974, U.S. Supreme Ct. 1981, U.S. Dist Ct. (so. dist.) Colo. 1987, U.S. Dist. Ct. (so. dist.) Tex. 1989. Ptnr. Stone, Pigman, Walther, Wittman and Hutchinson, New Orleans, 1973-78, Singer Hutner Levine Seeman and Stuart, New Orleans, 1978-81, Gordon, Arata, McCollam and Stuart, New Orleans, 1981-88, Vinson & Elkins, Houston, 1988—; instr. Tulane U. Law Sch., 1978-82; mem. faculty Banking Sch. of the South; bd. dirs. Inst. Politics; mem. adv. bd. City Atty.'s Office, New Orleans, 1978-79. Bd. dirs., gen. counsel Houston Grand Opera, 1992—. Mem. ABA, La. Bar Assn., Tex. Assn. Bank Counsel (pres. 1994-95), La. Bankers Assn. (chmn. bank counsel com.). Office: Vinson & Elkins 2500 First City Tower 1001 Fannin St Houston TX 77002-6760

STUART, WILLIAM CORWIN, federal judge; b. Knoxville, Iowa, Apr. 28, 1920; s. George Corwin and Edith (Abram) S.; m. Mary Elgin Cleaver, Oct. 20, 1946; children: William Corwin II, Robert Cullen, Melanie Rae, Valerie Jo. BA, State U. Iowa, 1941, JD, 1942. Bar: Iowa 1942. Pvt. practice Chariton, 1946-62, city atty., 1947-49; mem. Iowa Senate from, Lucas-Wayne Counties, 1951-61; justice Supreme Ct. Iowa, 1962-71; judge U.S. Dist. Ct., So. Dist. of Iowa, Des Moines, 1971-86, sr. judge, 1986—. With USNR, 1943-45. Recipient Outstanding Svc. award Iowa Acad. Trial lawyer, 1987, Iowa Trial Lawyers Assn., 1988, Spl. award Iowa State Bar Assn., 1987, Disting. Alumni, U. Iowa Coll. Law, 1987. Mem. ABA, Iowa Bar Assn., Am. Legion, All For Iowa, Order of Coif, Omicron Delta Kappa, Phi Kappa Psi, Phi Delta Phi. Presbyterian. Club: Mason (Shriner). Home: 216 S Grand St Chariton IA 50049-2139 Office: US Dist Ct 103 US Courthouse E 1st & Walnut Sts Des Moines IA 50309

STUBBERUD, ALLEN ROGER, electrical engineering educator; b. Glendive, Mont., Aug. 14, 1934; s. Oscar Adolph and Alice Marie (LeBlanc) S.; m. May B. Tragus, Nov. 19, 1961; children: Peter A., Stephen C. B.S. in Elec. Engring, U. Idaho, 1956; M.S. in Engring, UCLA, 1958, Ph.D., 1962. From asst. prof. to assoc. prof. engring. UCLA, 1962-69; prof. elec. engring. U. Calif., Irvine, 1969—; assoc. dean engring. U. Calif., 1972-78, dean engring., 1978-83; chair elec. and computer engring., 1993—, acting dean engring., 1994—; chief scientist U.S. Air Force, 1983-85; dir. Elec. Communications and Systems Engring. divsn. NSF, 1987-88; chair dept. elec. and computer engring. U. Calif., Irvine, 1993—, acting dean engring., 1994—. Author: Analysis and Synthesis of Linear Time Variable Systems, 1964, (with others) Feedback and Control Systems, 2d edit., 1990, (with others) Digital Control System Design, 2d edit., 1994; contbr. articles to profl. jours. Recipient Exceptional Civilian Svc. medal USAF, 1985, 90. Fellow IEEE (Centennial medal 1984), AIAA, AAAS; mem. Ops. Research Soc. Am., Sigma Xi, Sigma Tau, Tau Beta Pi, Eta Kappa Nu. Home: 19532 Sierra Soto Rd Irvine CA 92715-3841 Office: U Calif Dept Elec Engring & Computer Sci Irvine CA 92717

STUBBINS, HUGH A(SHER), JR., architect; b. Birmingham, Ala., Jan. 11, 1912; s. Hugh Asher and Lucile (Matthews) S.; m. Diana Hamilton Moore, Mar. 3, 1938 (div. 1960); children: Patricia, Peter, Hugh Asher III, Michael; m. Colette Fadeuilhe, Sept. 1960 (dec. 1992); m. June M. Kootz, 1994. BS in Architecture, Ga. Inst. Tech., 1933; MArch, Harvard U., 1935. Pvt. practice Boston, 1935-38, 41—; formed partnership, 1938-40; pvt. practice Birmingham, 1940; assoc. prof. Grad. Sch. Design Harvard U., 1946-52, chmn. dept. architecture, 1953, mem. vis. com. Grad. Sch. Design, 1958-72; pres. Hugh Stubbins & Assocs., Inc., 1957-83, also chmn. bd. dirs., 1983-92; vis. critic-in-residence, Yale U., 1948-49, U. Oreg., 1950; sec. Rotch traveling Scholarship, 1971-80; Thomas Jefferson prof. architecture U. Va., 1979; mem. adv. coun. Sch. Architecture, Princeton U., 1962-65; mem. Harleston Parker Medal Com., 1973. Designer Berlin Congress Hall, 1957, Countway Libr. Medicine, Harvard U., Fed. Res. Bank, Boston, U. Va. Law Sch., Citicorp Ctr., N.Y.C., St. Peter's Ch., N.Y.C., Fifth Ave. Pl., Pitts., 1988, Bank One, Indpls., 1989, Landmark Tower, Minoto-Mirai 21, Yokohama, Japan, 1989, Ronald Reagan Presdl. Libr., 1990, numerous other bldgs.; exec. architect Phila. Stadium. Hon. mem. Boston Archtl. Ctr.; chmn. design adv. com. Boston Redevel. Authority, 1964-76; mem. design rev. panel Worcester Redevel. Authority, 1966-70; mem. adv. com. Office Fgn. Bldgs. Ops., U.S. Dept. State, 1979-82; bd. dirs. Benjamin Franklin Found.; mem. arts and archtl. com. Kennedy Meml. Libr.; mem. Fgn. Bus. Coun., Commonwealth of Mass., 1978-79; mem. nat. adv. bd. Ga. Inst. Tech., 1978-81; trustee Tabor Acad., 1974-78; mem. adv. bd. Whitney Libr. Design, 1976-78. Recipient Alpha Rho Chi medal, 1933, 3d prize at competition Nat. Smithsonian Gallery of Art, 1939, Progressive Architecture 1st Design award, 1954, Arcadia Achievement award, 1957, Rodgers and Hammerstein award, 1961, award Am. Inst. Steel Constrn., 1970, award Archtl. Record, 1971, award Prestressed Concrete Inst., 1971, award of merit Inst. So. Affairs and So. Acad. Letters, Arts and Scis., 1973, citation Am. Assn. Sch. Adminstrs., 1974, award for environ. design, 1975, award of merit Libr. Bldgs. award for Nathan Marsh Pusey Libr., Harvard U./AIA/ALA, 1976, Spl. Energy award for Shiraz Tech. Inst., Am. Assn. Sch. Adminstrs./AIA, N.E. Regional Coun. award Fed. Res. Bank, 1979, Thomas Jefferson Meml. medal U. Va., 1979, R.S. Reynolds Meml. award Citicorp, 1981, numerous other awards. Fellow AIA (v.p. 1964-65, jury fellows 1974-75, chmn. Nat. Honor award com. 1966, 79, 80, award of merit 1970, honor award 1979, firm award 1967), Mexican Soc. Archs. (hon.), AAAS; mem. NAD (academician), Mass. Assn. Archs., Boston Soc. Archs. (;res. 1969-70, award of honor 1988), Archl. League N.Y. (silver medal 1958), Harvard Club, Laurel Brook Club, Mahogan Yacht Club, The Little Club (Gulf Stream, Fla.), Century Club (N.Y.C.), Soc. Four Arts (Palm Beach), Beta Theta Pi, Omicron Delta Kappa. Home: 6110 N Ocean Blvd Boynton Beach FL 33435 Home (summer): 199 Brattle St Cambridge MA 02138-3345

STUBBLEFIELD, DANA WILLIAM, professional football player; b. Cleve., Nov. 14, 1970. Student, U. Kans. Defensive tackle San Francisco 49'ers, 1993—. Selected to Pro Bowl, 1994. Achievements include member San Francisco 49'ers Super Bowl XXIX Champions, 1994. Office: San Francisco 49'ers 4949 Centennial Blvd Santa Clara CA 95054

STUBBLEFIELD, PAGE KINDRED, banker; b. Bloomington, Tex., Aug. 28, 1914; s. Edwin Page and Vinnye L. (Kindred) S.; m. Dorothea Mock, July 7, 1940; children—Edwin Mark, Bob Lynn. Student, Southwestern U., Georgetown, Tex., 1931; B.B.A., U. Tex., Austin, 1936. Mgr. Page Stubblefield Gen. Mdse., 1936-42; owner-operation P.K. Stubblefield Ins. Agy., 1946-51; asst. v.p. pub. relations Victoria (Tex.) Bank & Trust Co., 1951-52, v.p., 1952-58, sr. v.p., 1958-69, pres., 1969-81, chmn. bd., from 1977, chmn. bd. dirs., 1984-88; pres. Victoria Bankshares, Inc., 1974-84; past chmn. bd. dirs. Victoria Bankshares, Inc., curren bd. dirs.; past chmn. bd. dirs. Victoria Bank and Trust Co., current bd. dirs. Hon. mem. U. Tex. Centennial Commn. With fin. dept. USAAF, 1942-45. Mem. Am. Bankers Assn., Tex. Bankers Assn., Plaza Club, Victoria Country Club. Home: 2402 N De Leon St Victoria TX 77901-4814 Office: 120 S Main St Ste 414 Victoria TX 77901-8144

STUBBLEFIELD, THOMAS MASON, agricultural economist, educator; b. Taxhoma, Okla., Apr. 16, 1922; s. Temple Roscoe and Martha Lacy (Acree) S.; BS, N.Mex. State U., 1948; MS, A. and M. Coll. Tex., 1951, PhD, 1956; postgrad. U. Ariz., 1954; m. Martha Lee Miller, Mar. 7, 1943; children: Ellen (Mrs. Richard Damron), Paula (Mrs. James T. Culbertson), Thommye (Mrs. Gary D. Zingsheim). Specialist cotton mktg. N.Mex. State Coll., 1948; extension economist, then asst. agrl. economist U. Ariz., Tucson, 1951-58, from assoc. prof. to prof., 1958-64, prof. and agrl. economist, 1964-83, emeritus prof., 1983—, acting asst. dir. agrl. expt. sta., 1966-68, asst. to dir. sta., 1973-74, chief party Brazil contract, 1968-70. Mem. Pima Council Aging, 1974-77, 80-90; chmn. adv. com. Ret. Sr. Vol. Program, Pima County, 1974-77, 80-90, mem. 1974-96. Chmn. bd. Saguaro Home Found., 1980-85. With AUS, 1942-45. Author bulls. Home: 810 W Calle Milu Tucson AZ 85706-3925

STUBBS, BARBARA JOAN, secondary education educator; b. Salem, N.J., Apr. 19, 1945; d. Joseph and Mary Eleanor (Conrad) Prochazka; m. William E. Thorp, Sept. 22, 1972 (div. 1981); 1 child, Joanna Denise; m. John L. Stubbs, Feb. 11, 1982; 1 child, Jill L. Washington. BA, Rutgers U., 1967; MA, Rowan Coll., 1995; postgrad., U. Sarasota. With sales dept. Pan Am. World Airways, San Francisco, 1968-70, Phila., 1970-75; owner Eastern Seaboard Stone, Marlton, N.J., 1976-85, Delsea Marble & Granite, Clayton, N.J., 1981-90; tchr. Clearview Regional Sch. Dist., Mullica Hill, N.J., 1990—; learning cons., N.J. Bd. dirs., treas. Nazarene Ch., Vineland, N.J., 1984-90. Mem. Coun. for Exceptional Children, ASCD. Home: RR 3 Box 92 Monroeville NJ 08343-9102

STUBBS, DANIEL GAIE, labor relations consultant; b. Charleston, S.C., Nov. 13, 1940; s. Daniel Hamer and Esther Virginia (Garlow) S.; m. Sherrill Ann Sloan, July 8, 1984; children: Kimberly, Allison, Don; student U. Fla., 1959-60; BA, W.Va. U., 1965; postgrad. Temple U., 1965-67. Tchr., Sch. Dist. of Phila., 1965-67; rep. Am. Fedn. Tchrs., Washington, 1967; exec. sec. Calif. State Coll. Coun., Am. Fedn. Tchrs., AFL-CIO, L.A., 1967-68; rep. Am. Fedn. Tchrs., AFL-CIO, L.A., 1968-69, dir. orgn. Balt. Tchrs. Union, 1969-70; employee relations specialist Calif. Nurses Assn., L.A., 1971-72; exec. dir. United Nurses Assn. Calif., L.A., 1972-74; labor rels. cons. Social Svcs. Union, Svc. Employees Internat. Union, Local 535, AFL-CIO, L.A., 1974-76; exec. dir. Met. Riverside UniServ Unit, Calif. Tchrs. Assn., 1976-79, exec. dir. San Bernardino/Colton Uniserv Unit, 1979-80; gen. svcs. adminstr. Housing Authority, City of L.A., 1980-82; cons. Blanning & Baker Assocs., Tujunga, Calif., 1983-84; asst. exec. dir. adminstrv. svcs. L.A. Housing Authority, 1984-86; labor rels. cons., L.A., 1986—; lectr. in field. With U.S. Army, 1961-62. Recipient W.Va. U. Waitman Barbe Prize for creative writing, 1965. Mem. So. Calif. Indsl. Rels. Rsch. Assn., Orange County Indsl. Relations Research Assn., Indsl. Rels. Rsch. Assn., UCLA Inst. Indsl. Rels. Assn., Soc. of Profls. in Dispute Resolution, Town Hall Club of Calif. Presbyterian. Home: 3200 Fairesta St Apt 11 La Crescenta CA 91214-2681

STUBBS, DONALD CLARK, secondary education educator; b. Providence, Mar. 6, 1935; s. Edward J. and Margaret Eleanor (Clark) S.; m. Lorraine Alice Thivierge, Apr. 3, 1969 (dec. Jan. 1986); 1 child, Derek C.; m. Jean Elizabeth Stubbs. AB, Cath. U. Am., Washington, 1959, MS, 1966; postgrad., St. John's U., N.Y.C., 1960. Tchr. Bishop Loughlin Meml. High Sch., Bklyn., 1959-61, Bishop Bradley High Sch., Manchester, N.H., 1961-66; tchr., sci. dept. chair LaSalle Mil. Acad., Oakdale, N.Y., 1966-69, Ponaganset Regional High Sch., Glocester, R.I., 1969—. Home: 51 Woodland Ave Smithfield RI 02917-4117 Office: Ponaganset High Sch Anan Wade Rd North Scituate RI 02857

STUBBS, GERALD, biochemist, educator; b. Hobart, Australia, May 9, 1947; came to the U.S., 1976; m. Rebecca Lynn Harris; children: Andrew, Tamsin, Anneliese, Rachel. BSc, Australian Nat. U., 1968; DPhil, Oxford U., 1972. Sci. asst. Max Planck Inst., Heidelberg, Fed. Republic of Germany, 1973-76; rsch. assoc. Brandeis U., Waltham, Mass., 1976-83; asst. prof. Vanderbilt U., Nashville, 1983-87, assoc. prof., 1987-90, prof., 1990—. Contbr. articles to profl. jours. Achievements include determination of molecular structure of tobacco mosaic virus. Office: Vanderbilt U Dept Molecular Biology PO Box 1820 Nashville TN 37235-1820

STUBBS, JAMES CARLTON, retired hospital administrator; b. MaGee, Miss., Jan. 26, 1924; s. James Sylvester and Katie Lucille (Grayson) S.; m. Essie Geraldine Shows, June 17, 1949; 1 child, James Hilton. Mgr. R. & A. Appliance store, MaGee, Miss., 1950; field insp. Miss. Mental Instn. Bd., Jackson, 1950-52; dir. Miss. Eleemosynary Bd., Jackson, 1952-75, Miss. State Hosp., Whitfield, 1975-88. Chmn. Miss. Reimbursement Commn., 1965-85; pres. Jackson-Vicksburg Hosp. Coun., 1977-79, 79—; mem. Miss. Coun. on Aging; chmn. Miss. Mental Health Planning Coun., 1988—, chmn., 1988-89; bd. dirs. Goodwill Industries, 1989—; chmn. bd. dirs., 1993, elected vice chmn. Cmty. Mental Health/Mental Retardation Commn., 1995; mem. exec. com., 1991—; mem. Friends of Miss. State Hosp., 1986—, bd. dirs., 1988—, pres., 1995-96; deacon Broadnoor Bapt. Ch., 1990; torchbearer Olympic Torch Relay, Jackson, Miss., 1996. Charter mem. Sports Hall of Fame U. S. Miss. Mem. Nat. Assn. Reimbursement Officers, Miss. Mental Health/MentalRetardation Coun., Epilepsy Found., Miss. Mental Health Assn., Miss. Pub. Health Assn., Hinds County Mental Health Assn. (apptd. commr. to mental health commn. 1993—), Assn. Mental Health Adminstrs., Am. Coll. Hosp. Adminstrs., Am. Acad. Health Adminstrn., Miss. Hosp. Assn. (fin. com., dir., bd. govs. 1979-82, 85-87, chmn. 1986-87, speaker ho. of dels. 1987-88), Capital Area Mental Health Assn. (bd. dirs. 1988-90, life bd. dirs. emeritus 1994—), Colonial Country Club (bd. dirs.), Quarter Century Club, M Club, Big Gold Club, Hardwood Club (U. So. Miss.). Home: 5430 Pine Lane Dr Jackson MS 39211-4016

STUBBS, JAN DIDRA, retired travel industry executive, travel writer; b. Waseca, Minn., June 19, 1937; d. Gordon Everett and Bertha Margaret (Bertsch) Didra; m. James Stewart Stubbs, Nov. 24, 1962; children: Jeffrey Stewart, Jacqueline Didra. BA in Speech/English, U. Minn., 1961; cert. travel counselor, Inst. Cert. Travel Agts., 1988. Sales agt. United Airlines, Mpls., 1961-64; interior decorator Lloyd and Assocs., St. Paul, 1964-66; v.p. Stubbs and Assocs., Textiles, St. Paul, 1966-83; account exec. Twin Cities Mag., Mpls., 1983-85; account exec. Internat. Travel Arrangers, St. Paul, 1985-86, asst. dir. sales, 1986-88; mgr. Dayton's Group Holidays, Mpls., 1988-96; writer for Mgmt. Assistance Project. V.p. Jr. Women's Assn. of Minn. Symphony Orch.; chairperson 60th anniversary Jr. League of St. Paul, sec., 1967—, sustaining mem.; deacon Ho. of Hope Presbyn. Ch., St. Paul, 1970; mem. Unied Way adv. bd. corporate giving Dayton Hudson Corp. Named Outstanding Alumni, Coll. Liberal Arts, U. Minn., 1995. Mem. AAUW, Inst. Cert. Travel Agts., Am. Soc. Travel Agts., Minn. Exec. Women in Tourism (publicity com. 1987-88, by-laws chmn. 1989-90, sec. 1988-89, 90, fedn. dir. 1990—, v.p., 1993, pres. 1993-94), Internat. Fedn. Women in Travel (alt. gov. Mid-Am. region, standing com. dir. historian, gov. mid-Ams. area I 1994, 95), Jr. Assistance League, St. Paul Pool and Yacht Club, Alpha Omicron Pi (pres. 1958-59, alumni pres. 1962), Whitefish Chain Yacht Club (sec.), U. Minn. Alumni Assn. Republican. Avocations: reading, water sports, travel, photography, cooking, skiing, classical music, writing. Home: 1575 Boardwalk Ct Saint Paul MN 55118-2747 Office: Dayton's Group Holidays 320 Plymouth Bldg 12 S 6th St Minneapolis MN 55402-1508

STUBBS, KENDON LEE, librarian; b. Washington, Apr. 6, 1938; s. Donald Harrison and Rosalee Adelia (Brown) S.; m. Patricia Townsend, June 3, 1961; children—Christopher, Peter, Timothy. B.A., St. John's Coll., Annapolis, Md., 1960; M.A., U. Va., 1964; M.S., Columbia U., 1965. Sr. asst. in manuscripts U. Va. Library, Charlottesville, 1965, reference librarian, 1966-76, acting acquisitions librarian, 1967-68, assoc. univ. librarian, 1976-87, assoc. univ. libr. for pub. svcs., 1987-92; acting univ. libr., 1993, assoc. univ. libr., 1994—; cons. U.S. Dept. Edn., Washington, 1982-84. Author: Quantitative Criteria for Academic Research Libraries, 1984; editor: Cumulated Assn. Research Libraries Statistics, 1981, Rsch. Libr. Statistics, 1990, ARL Statistics, 1992-95, Japanese Text Initiative on World Wide Web, 1995—; contbr. articles on library stats., rsch. to profl. publs., Internet. Mem. Am. Stats. Assn., Assn. of Rsch. Librs. (mem. stats. com., vis. program officer 1995—), Bibliog. Soc. U. Va. (pres. 1975-78, v.p. 1978—). Office: Alderman Libr U Va Charlottesville VA 22903

STUBBS, THOMAS HUBERT, company executive; b. Americus, Ga., Aug. 16, 1944; s. Hubert F. and Elizabeth (Askew) S.; m. Mary Louise Quarles, Mar. 19, 1965; children: Thomas C., Chad P. BS, Auburn U., 1966. CPA, Ala., Ga., Miss. Sr. acct. Peat, Marwick, Mitchell and Co., Birmingham, Ala., 1966-72; supr. L. Paul Kassauf and Co., CPA's, Birmingham, 1972-73; staff mem. Snow, Stewart and Bradford, Birmingham, 1973-75; v.p. Cen. Computer Svcs., Inc., Birmingham, 1975-79, Cen. Bancshares of the South, Birmingham, 1979-81; ptnr. Bradford and Co., CPA's, Gulf Shore, Ala., 1981-82; v.p., trust officer Deposit Guaranty Nat. Bank, Jackson, Miss., 1983; treas. Data Supplies, Inc., Norcross, Ga., 1983-88; treas. Stevens Graphics, Inc., Atlanta, 1988-89, v.p., 1989-90, pres. bus. products div., 1990-93, CFO, 1994—. Served with USNG, 1966-72. Mem. Am. Inst. CPA's, Ala. Soc. CPA's, Ga. Soc. CPA's, Miss. Soc. CPA's. Republican. Presbyterian. Avocations: tennis, jogging, golf. Home: 2875 Towne Village Dr Duluth GA 30155-7610 Office: 713 RD Abernathy Blvd SW Atlanta GA 30310

STUBER, CHARLES WILLIAM, genetics educator, researcher; b. St. Michael, Nebr., Sept. 19, 1931; s. Harvey John and Minnie Augusta (Wilks) S.; m. Marilyn Martha Cook, May 28, 1953; 1 child, Charles William Jr. BS, U. Nebr., 1952, MS, 1961; PhD, N.C. State U., 1965. Vet., agrl. instr. Broken Bow (Nebr.) H. S., 1956-59; research asst. U. Nebr., Lincoln, 1959-61; research geneticist Agrl. Rsch. Svc., USDA, Raleigh, N.C., 1962-75, supervisory research geneticist, research leader, 1975—; prof. genetics & crop sci. N.C. State U., Raleigh, 1975—. Assoc. editor Crop Sci. Jour., 1979-82, tech. editor, 1984-86, editor, 1987-89; contbr. over 190 articles to profl. jours., chpts. to books. Chmn. coun. on ministries and numerous offices Highland United Meth Ch., Raleigh. Lt. USN, 1952-56. Named Outstanding Scientist of Yr., USDA-ARS, 1989; recipient Genetics and Plant Breeding award Nat. Coun. Comml. Plant Breeders, 1995. Fellow Am. Soc. Agronomy, Crop Sci. Soc. Am. (editor-in-chief 1987-91, pres. 1992-93, Crop Sci. Rsch. award 1995); mem. AAAS, Genetics Soc. Am., Am. Genetic Assn. (sec. 1984-86), Sigma Xi, Phi Kappa Phi. Avocations: windsurfing, water skiing, sailing. Home: 1800 Manuel St Raleigh NC 27612-5510 Office: USDA-ARS NC State U Dept Genetics PO Box 7614 Raleigh NC 27695

STUBER, JAMES ARTHUR, lawyer; b. Warren, Ohio, July 17, 1948; s. Andrew Frederick and Betty Jane (Long) S.; m. Carol Lee Burr, Apr. 22, 1989 (div. Sept. 1995); stepchildren: Jason Burr, Anisa Burr. BA, U. Pa., 1970; MA, Columbia U., 1973; JD, Georgetown U., 1976. Bar: Fla. 1977, D.C. 1978, U.S. Dist. Ct. (D.C. dist.) 1979, U.S. Ct. Appeals (11th cir.) 1983. Legis. asst. U.S. Congressman Paul Rogers, Washington, 1972-78; assoc. Hogan & Hartson, Washington, 1979-82; ptnr. Sang & Stuber, Palm Beach, Fla., 1983-84; pvt. practice law Palm Beach, 1984-89; ptnr. Stuber & Finley, West Palm Beach, 1990-91; shareholder Carlton, Fields et al, West Palm Beach, 1992-93; pvt. practice law West Palm Beach, 1993—; mem. Federal Caribbean Basin Bus. Adv. Coun., Washington, 1985-89; internat. adv. bd. Nova U. Sch. Bus., Ft. Lauderdale, 1989-91. Mem. Palm Beach County Land Use Bd., West Palm Beach, 1984-85. Mem. Internat. Bar Assn., Am. Immigration Lawyers Assn., The Fla. Bar Assn. (bd. cert. in immigration & naturalization 1995), Palm Beach County Bar Assn. (cultural & civic activities award 1988). Democrat. Episcopal. Avocations: sailing, travel. Office: 777 S Flagler Dr # 800W West Palm Beach FL 33401

STUCK, WANDA MARIE, special education educator; b. Schoolcraft, Mich., Oct. 25, 1934; d. Glen Robert and Luella Esther (Porter) Shearer; m. Paul Revere Stuck, June 15, 1958; children: Pamela Joyce, Lauri Linn, Jeffry Paul. BS, Western Mich. U., 1968, MA, 1978. Tchr. spl. edn. Vicksburg, Mich., 1968-90; tchr. adult edn. sewing Cunningham Fabrics, Vicksburg, Mich., 1982-88; tchr. adult edn. computers Edwardsburg (Mich.) Sch., 1994—, tchr. spl. edn., home econs., 1991—; prof. seamstress, Schoolcrest, Mich., 1953—; clk. Fields Fabric, Kalamazoo, Mich., 1991—. mem. bd. dirs. Meth. Ch., Schoolcraft, 1994—; mem. Ladies Libr., Schoolcraft, 1969—. Mem. AAUW, Coun. Exceptional Children, Learning Disabilities Assn. Mich., Order of Ea. Star, Order of Eagles. Methodist. Avocations: sewing, reading, quilting. Home: 16101 S 2nd St Schoolcraft MI 49087-9728 Office: Edwardsville Mid Sch 69410 Section St Edwardsburg MI 49112-9655

STUCKEMAN, HERMAN CAMPBELL, architectural engineer; b. Pitts., Aug. 7, 1914; s. Herman Sydney and Alma (Campbell) S.; m. Margaret Eleanor Rockwell, Aug. 28, 1940; children: Ellen Campbell, Alan Rockwell, Joyce Thayer. B.S. in Architecture, Sch. Engring. Pa. State U., 1937. Architect Edward B. Lee, Pitts., 1938-39, Gen. State Authority, Harrisburg, Pa., 1940-41, Prack & Prack, Texarkana, Tex. and Pitts., 1941-42; ptnr. Delta Mfg. Co., Milw., 1942-45; gen. mgr. Delta Mfg. Co., 1945-50; v.p. Rockwell Mfg. Co., Pitts., 1950-73; dir. real estate Rockwell Internat. Corp. (merger Rockwell Mfg. Co. and N.Am. Rockwell), 1973-75; chmn. Precise Corp., 1975—. Clubs: Duquesne, Pittsburgh Athletic, Longue Vue (Pitts.). Lodge: Rotary. Home: 300 Fox Chapel Rd Pittsburgh PA 15238-2331 *Be fair with those with whom you work and associate. At all times, be honest and truthful. Give credit for work well done. Develop enthusiasm in the organization and set the goals high. Set an example by working hard. Get the work done on time.*

STUCKEY, HELENJEAN LAUTERBACH, counselor educator; b. Bushnell, Ill., May 17, 1929; d. Edward George and Frances Helen (Simpson) Lauterbach; m. James Dale Stuckey, Sept. 30, 1951; children: Randy Lee, Charles Edward, Beth Ellen. BFA, Ill. Wesleyan U., 1951; MEd, U. Ill., 1969. Cert. art tchr., guidance, psychology instr.; lic. clin. profl. counselor, Ill. Display designer Saks Fifth Ave., Chgo., 1951; interior designer Piper City, Ill., 1953-63; art tchr. Forrest (Ill.)-Strawn-Wing Schs., 1967-68; tchr., counselor Piper City Schs., 1969-74; counselor, art tchr. Ford Cen. Schs., Piper City, 1974-85; psychiatric counselor Community Resource Counseling Ctr., Ford County, Ill., 1985-87; history tchr., counselor Iroquois West High Sch., Gilman, Ill., 1987-88; spl. needs coord. Livingston County Vocat., Pontiac, Ill., 1988-93; ret., 1993; clin. profl. counselor, pvt. practice Piper City, 1995—. Job skills coord. Livingston Area Edn. for Employment, 1994. Mem. AACD, Am. Vocat. Assn., Ill. Counseling Assn., Ill. Vocat. Assn., Ill. Mental Health Counselors Assn., Ill. Assn. Vocat. Spl. Needs Pers. (membership com.), Ill. Ret. Tchrs., Delta Kappa Gamma (v.p., sec., program chmn., pres.). Presbyterian. Avocations: skiing, reading, travel, sewing, playing flute. Home: 2667 N 1700E Rd Piper City IL 60959-7032

STUCKWISCH, CLARENCE GEORGE, retired university administrator; b. Seymour, Ind., Oct. 13, 1916; s. William Henry and Clara Sophia (Benter) S.; m. Esther Elizabeth Ebert, Dec. 19, 1942; children: William, Stephen, David, Deborah, Stephanie. B.A. magna cum laude, Ind. U., 1939; Ph.D., Iowa State U., 1943. Mem. faculty U. Wichita, Kans., 1943-60; prof. chemistry U. Wichita, 1958-60; prof., chmn. dept. N.Mex. Highlands U., Las Vegas, 1960-64; prof., exec. officer dept. chemistry SUNY, Buffalo, 1964-68; prof., chmn. dept. U. Miami, Coral Gables, Fla., 1968-72; asso. v.p. advanced studies and research, dean Grad. Sch. U. Miami, 1972-81, exec. v.p., provost, 1981-82; ret.; mem. council Oak Ridge Assn. Univs. Contbr. articles to profl. jours. Mem. AAAS, Am. Chem. Soc., Lions, Phi Beta Kappa, Sigma Xi, Phi Kappa Phi. Democrat. Lutheran. Patentee in chem. intermediates and pharms.

STUCKY, KEN, clergy member, religious publication editor, church organization administrator. Dir. Stewardship of the Missionary Church, Fort Wayne, Ind.; editor Priority. Office: The Missionary Ch PO Box 9127 3811 Vanguard Dr Fort Wayne IN 46899-9127

STUCKY, SCOTT WALLACE, lawyer; b. Hutchinson, Kans., Jan. 11, 1948; s. Joe Edward and Emma Clara (Graber) S.; m. Jean Elsie Seibert, Aug. 18, 1973; children: Mary-Clare, Joseph. BA summa cum laude, Wichita State U., 1970; JD, Harvard U., 1973; MA, Trinity U., 1980; LLM with highest honors, George Washington U., 1983; postgrad. Nat. War Coll., 1993. Bar: Kans. 1973, U.S. Dist. Ct. Kans. 1973, U.S. Ct. Appeals (10th cir.) 1973, U.S. Ct. Mil. Appeals 1974, U.S. Supreme Ct. 1976, D.C. 1979, U.S. Ct. Appeals (D.C. cir.) 1979. Assoc. Ginsburg, Feldman & Bress, Washington, 1978-82; chief docketing and service br. Nuclear Regulatory Commn., Washington, 1982-83; legis. counsel U.S. Air Force, Washington, 1983—; lectr. bus. law Maria Regina Coll., Syracuse, N.Y., 1977; congressional fellow Office Senator John Warner, 1986; res. judge adv. U.S. Air Force Res., Washington, 1982—; col. Appellate Mil. Judge, USAF Ct. Criminal Appeals, 1991-95; sr. reservist USAF Judiciary, 1995—. Served to capt. USAF, 1973-78. Decorated Air Force Meritorious Svc. medal with two oak leaf clusters, Commendation medal with oak leaf cluster. Mem. Fed. Bar Assn., Judge Advs. Assn. (bd. dirs. 1984-88), Res. Officers Assn., Wichita State U. Alumni Assn. (pres. chpt. 1981-86, nat. bd. dirs. 1986-92), Phi Delta Phi, Phi Alpha Theta, Phi Kappa Phi, Omicron Delta Kappa, Sigma Phi Epsilon. Republican. Episcopalian. Club: Army and Navy (Washington). Lodge: Mil. Order of Loyal Legion of U.S. (state comdr. and recorder 1984-92, nat. treas. 1987-89, nat. vice comdr. 1989-93, nat. comdr.-in-chief 1993-95), Sons of Union Vets. of Civil War (chpt. vice comdr. 1986-88). Contbr. articles to profl. jours. Home: 4404 Burlington Pl NW Washington DC 20016-4422 Office: Hdqrs USAF/JAG Washington DC 20330-1420

STUCKY, STEVEN (EDWARD), composer; b. Hutchinson, Kans., Nov. 7, 1949; s. Victor Eugene and Louise Doris (Trautwein) S.; m. Melissa Jane Whitehead, Aug. 22, 1970; children: Maura Catharine, Matthew Steven. MusB, Baylor U., 1971; MFA, Cornell U., 1973, DMA, 1978. Vis. asst. prof. Lawrence U., Appleton, Wis., 1978-80; prof. Cornell U., Ithaca, N.Y., 1980—, chmn. dept. music, 1992—; composer-in-residence L.A. Philharm. Orch., 1988—. Author: Lutoslawski and His Music, 1981 (Deems Taylor award ASCAP 1982); composer: Voyages, 1984, Boston Fancies, 1985, Dreamwaltzes, 1986, Concerto for orch., 1987, Son et Lumière, 1988, Angelus, 1990, Impromptus, 1991, Four Poems of A.R. Ammons, 1992, Ancora, 1994, Double Flute Cto., 1994, Fanfares and Arias, 1994, Pinturas de Tamayo, 1995; received commn. from Nat. Endowment for Arts, 1982, Koussevitzky Found., 1991, Meet the Composer, 1995. Bd. advisors Barlow Endowment, 1993—; bd. dirs. MacDowell Colony, 1993-95. Fellow Guggenheim Found., Nat. Endowment for the Arts. Avocation: gardening. Office: Theodore Presser Co Care One Presser Pl Bryn Mawr PA 19010

STUDDS, GERRY EASTMAN, congressman; b. Mineola, N.Y., May 12, 1937; s. Eastman and Beatrice (Murphy) S. B.A., Yale U., 1959, M.A.T., 1961. Fgn. service officer State Dept., Washington, 1961-63; exec. asst. to presdl. cons. for a nat. service corps White House, 1963; legis. asst. to Sen. Harrison Williams U.S. Senate, 1964; tchr. St. Paul's Sch., Concord, N.H., 1965-69; mem. 93d-97th Congresses from 12th Mass. dist., 1973-83, 98th-103rd Congresses from 10th Mass. dist., 1983-96; chmn. com. Merchant Marine and Fisheries, 1993; mem. commerce com., resources com., ranking minority of Fisheries, Wildlife and Oceans subcomm. Candidate for U.S. Congress from 12th Dist. Mass., 1970; del. Democratic Nat. Conv., 1968. Office: US House of Reps 237 Cannon House Office Bureau Washington DC 20515

STUDE, EVERETT WILSON, JR., rehabilitation counselor, educator; b. Fresno, Calif., Dec. 27, 1939; s. Everett Wilson and Vera Mae (Williams) S.; m. Mary-Ann Meadows, June 11, 1960; children: Susan, Sandra. B.A., Pasadena (Calif.) Coll., 1961; M.S., Calif. State U., Los Angeles, 1963; cert. psychiat. intern, U. Oreg. Med. Sch., 1965; Ed.D., U. So. Calif., 1972. Counseling psychol. trainee VA Hosp., Long Beach Calif., 1963; rehab. counselor Calif. Dept. Rehab., Pasadena, 1963-66; asst. to regional adminstr. Calif. Dept. Rehab., Los Angeles, 1966-67; vocat. rehab. coordinator, dir. tng. Rehab Research and Tng. Center, U. So. Calif. Sch. Medicine, 1967-71, instr., fieldwork coordinator Sch. Edn. rehab. counseling masters degree program, 1967-71; mem. faculty Calif. State U., Fresno, 1971—; prof. rehab. counseling Calif. State U., 1976, program coordinator, 1980-92; vocat. expert, social security disability ins. program Bur. Hearing and Appeals, 1972—; contract rehab. counselor VA, 1981-85; vocat. econ. analyst Vocat. Econs., Inc., 1990—. Author: Ethics and the Counselor, 1975; also articles. Chmn. Pasadena Jaycees Jr. Golf Tournament, 1964; bd. dirs. Day Care Center, Friends Community Ch., Fresno, 1976-77, mem. ministry and cousel, 1977-80, chmn., 1980. Recipient numerous grants; selected to give First Ann. Andrew F. Marrin Meml. lecture, 1978. Mem. Am. Coun. Assn. (senator 1975-78, chmn., treas. Western Region br. assembly, 1979-81, bd. dirs. 1981-84, mem. Ethical Stds. and Practice Com. 1985-88), Nat. Rehab. Assn. (exec. bd. So. Calif. 1969-71, pres. San Joaquin Valley chpt. 1978-79), Calif. Rehab. Counselors Assn. (pres. 1971-72, 1985-86, newsletter editor 1975-77, 1986-93, Outstanding Contbn. to Profession award 1977, Citation Merit 1978), Calif. Assn. for Coun. and Devel. (pres. 1973-74, mem. Profl. Stds. and Ethical Practices com. 1987-92, mem. editorial bd. 1990-94), Nat. Coun. on Rehab. Edn. (mem. editorial bd. 1987—, 2d v.p. 1989-90, 1st v.p. 1990-91, pres. 1991-92, past pres. 1992-93). Address: 2727 W Bluff Ave Apt 117 Fresno CA 93711-7014

STUDEBAKER, IRVING GLEN, engineering educator, researcher; b. Ellensburg, Wash., July 22, 1931; s. Clement Glen and Ruth (Krause) S.; (widowed); children: Ruth, Betty, Raymond, Karl, Donna. BS in Geol. Engring., U. Ariz., 1957, MS in Geology, 1959, PhD in Geol. Engring., 1977. Registered profl. engr., Wash., Nev., Ariz., Colo., Mont. Geophys. engr. Mobil, 1959-61; civil engr. City of Yakima, Wash., 1964-66; instr. Yakima Valley Coll., 1962-67; sr. rsch. geologist Roan Selection Trust, Kalulushi, Zambia, 1967-72; sr. mining engr. Occidental Oil Shale, Grand Junction, Colo., 1974-81; prof. Mont. Coll. Mining Sch., Butte, 1982—; cons. in field. Sgt. U.S. Army, 1951-54, Korea. Mem. N.W. Mining Assn., Geol. Soc. Am., Soc. for Mining and Metall. Engring., Soc. Econ. Geologists, Mont. Mining Assn., Sigma Xi (pres. Mont. tech. chpt. 1990-91). Avocations: golf, travel. Home: 5 Cedar Lake Dr Butte MT 59701-4337 Office: Mont Tech Mining Dept West Park Butte MT 59701

STUDEBAKER, JOHN MILTON, utilities engineer, consultant, educator; b. Springfield, Ohio, Mar. 31, 1935; s. Frank Milton and Monaruth (Beatty) S.; m. Virginia Ann Van Pelt, Mar. 12, 1960; 1 child, Jacqueline Ann Allcorn. MS, PhD in Indsl. Engring.; BS in Law, LaSalle U., Chgo., 1969, LaSalle U., Chgo., 1969; MS and PhD in Indsl. Engring., Columbia Pacific U., San Rafael, Calif., 1984. Cert. plant engr. Am. Inst. Plant Engrs., profl. cons. Acad. Profl. Cons. & Advisors. Indsl engr. Internat. Harvest Co., 1957-60, supr. indsl. engring., 1960-66, gen. supr. body assembly, 1967-68, mgr. indsl. engring., 1968-70; mgr. manufacturing engring. Lamb Electric Co., 1970-72, Cascade Corp., 1972-78; engring. mgr. Bundy Tubing Corp., Winchester and Cynthia, Ky., 1978-84; utility cons. engr., 1989—; instr. numerous univs. including Boston U., Clemson U., Cornell U., Harvard U., Duquesne U., U. Ala., U. Ill., U. Wis., Ga. State U., James Madison U., Tex. Tech. U., U. Calif., Calif. State U., Pacific Lutheran U., Fairleigh Dickinson U., San Francisco State U.; instr. Am. Mgmt. Assn., Rochester Inst. Tech., Ctr. for Profl. Advancement. Author: Slashing Utility Costs Handbook, 1992, Natural Gas Purchasing Handbook, 1993, Electricity Purchasing Handbook, 1995, Electricity Retail Wheeling Handbook, 1995, Energy Service Handbook, 1995. Mem. NSPE, Am. Inst. Plant Engrs. (cert.), Assn. Energy Engrs. (instr.), Doctorate Assn. N.Y. Educators. Republican. Office: Studebaker Group Inc Ste 106 5285 Shawnee Rd Alexandria VA 22312

STUDEMAN, WILLIAM OLIVER, retired naval officer; b. Brownsville, Tex., Jan. 16, 1940; s. Oliver Jennings and Gail (McDavitt) S.; m. Gloria Diane Jeans, Sept. 12, 1964; children: Kimberly, Michael, Kate. BA, U. of S. Sewanee, 1962; student, Def. Intelligence Sch., 1966-67; M in Internat. Affairs, George Washington U., 1973; postgrad., Naval War Coll., 1973, Nat. War Coll., 1981; DSc in Strategic Intelligence (hon.), Def. Intelligence Coll., 1987. Commd. ensign USN, 1963, advanced through grades to admiral, 1992; analyst Naval Intelligence Support Ctr., Washington, 1974-75; exec. asst. Office Naval Intelligence, Washington, 1975-76; officer in charge FOSIC Norfolk, CINLANTFLT, Norfolk, Va., 1976-78; asst. chief of staff COMSIXTHFLEET, Gaeta, Italy, 1978-80; exec. asst. Office of VCNO, Washington, 1981-82; comdg. officer Navy Operational Intel Command, Washington, 1982-84; dir. long range planning USN, Washington, 1984-85; dir. Naval Intelligence, Washington, 1985-88, Nat. Security Agy., MD, 1988-92; dep. dir. CIA, Washington, 1991-95; ret., 1995. Decorated Legion of Merit with two gold stars, Naval and Intelligence D.S.M.; recipient President's Nat. Security medal. Mem. Armed Forces Comm. and Electronics Assn., Nat. Mil. Intelligence Assn., Naval Intelligence Profls., Assn. Former Intelligence Officers. Episcopalian. Avocations: sailing, rebuilding cars. Office: Dep Dir Ctrl Intelligence CIA Washington DC 20505*

STUDER, WILLIAM ALLEN, county official; b. Chgo., July 27, 1939; s. William Gotlieb and Annette Elizabeth (Bruzek) S.; m. Donna Barnes Bray, Dec. 26, 1961; children: Scott, Shannon. BS in Indsl. Mgmt., Ga. Inst. Tech., 1961; MS in Guidance and Counseling, Troy State U., 1975, MS in Mgmt., 1978; student, Air War Coll., Maxwell AFB, Ala., 1980-81. Commd. 2d lt. USAF, 1961, advanced through grades to maj. gen., 1989; legis. liaison U.S. Senate, Washington, 1981-83; dir. fighter ops./tng. USAF Hdqrs. Europe, Ramstein AB, Fed. Republic Germany, 1983-84; vice comdr. 10th Tactical Reconnaissance Wing RAF USAF, Alconbury, Eng., 1984-85, comdr. 10th Tactical Reconnaissance Wing RAF, 1985-86; cmdr. 81st Tactical Fighter Wing RAF USAF, Bentwaters, Eng., 1986-87; comdr. 316th Air Div/Kaiserslautern USAF, Ramstein AB, Fed. Republic Germany, 1987-88; vice comdr. 12th Air Force/U.S. So. Command USAF, Bergstrom AFB, Tex., 1988-90; comdr. 13th Air Force USAF, Clark AFB, The Philippines, 1990-91; dir. ops. CENTCOM/J-3, MacDill AFB, Fla., 1992-94; ret. USAF, 1994; dir. pub. safety dept. Hillsborough County, Tampa, Fla., 1994—. Decorated D.S.M., Legion of Merit with oak leaf cluster, DFC with three oak leaf clusters, Bronze Star, Air medal with 35 oak leaf clusters; Legion of Honor, Bronze Cross medal (The Philippines). Mem. Daedalians, Quiet Birdmen, Rotary. Avocations: golf, reading. Home: 5312 W Crescent Dr Tampa FL 33611-4126 Office: Hillsborough County Pub Safety Dept Tampa FL 33601

STUDER, WILLIAM JOSEPH, library director; b. Whiting, Ind., Oct. 1, 1936; s. Victor E. and Sarah G. (Hammersley) S.; m. Rosemary Lippie, Aug. 31, 1957; children: Joshua E., Rachel Marie. B.A., Ind. U., 1958, M.A., 1960, Ph.D. (Univ. fellow), 1968. Grad. asst. div. Library Sci., Ind. U., 1959-60, reference asst., 1960-61; spl. intern Library of Congress, 1961-62, reference librarian, sr. bibliographer, 1962-65; dir. regional campus libraries Ind U., Bloomington, 1968-73; assoc. dean univ. libraries Ind. U., 1973-77; dir. libraries Ohio State U., Columbus, 1977—; mem. Library Services and Constrn. Act Adv. Com. of Ind., 1971-76, Adv. Coun.on Fed. Library Programs in Ohio, 1977-85, chmn., 1980-81; mem. ARL Office Mgmt. Studies Adv. Com., 1977-81, ARL Task Force on Nat. Library Network Devel., 1978-83, chmn., 1981-83, com. on preservation, 1985-88, vice-chmn.,

1989-90, chmn., 1991-92, task force on scholarly communication, 1983-87, bd. dirs., 1981-84, com. stats. and measurement, 1993—; mem. network adv. com. Library of Congress, 1981-88; mem. library study com. Ohio Bd. Regents, 1986-87; mem. steering com. Ohio Library and Info. Network (Ohio Link), 1987-90; bd. dirs. Ctr. Rsch. Librs., 1989—, vice-chmn., 1993-94, chmn., 1994-95, sec., chmn. membership com., 1990-93; mem. adv. coun. Ohio Link Libr., 1990—, chmn., 1991-92, policy adv. coun., governing bd., 1991-92. Contbr. articles to profl. jours. Trustee On Line Computer Libr. Ctr. Inc., 1977-78; del. On Line Computer Libr. Ctr. Users Coun., 1983-91; mem. rsch. librs. adv. com. OnLine Computer Libr. Ctr., 1989-95, vice chair, chair-elect, 1993-94, chair, 1994-95; bd. dirs. Ohio Network of Librs. Ohionet, 1977-87, chmn., 1980-82, 86-87, treas., 1983-86; mem. Columbia U. Sch. Library Svc. Conservation Programs, vis. com., 1987-90; mem. nat. adv. coun. to commn. on preservation and access, 1989-92; treas. Monroe County (Ind.) Mental Health Assn., 1968-76; active Mental Health Social Club, 1971-73; budget rev. com. United Way, 1975-77; bd. dirs. Mental Health Assn. Recipient citation for participation MARC Insts., 1968-69; Louise Maxwell award Ind. U., 1978. Mem. ALA, Ohio Libr. Assn. (bd. dirs. 1980-83), Assn. Coll. and Rsch. LIbrs. (bd. dirs. 1977-81, com. on activities model for 1990, 1981-82, chmn. libr. sch. curriculum task force 1988-89), Acad. Libr. Assn. Ohio, Torch Club (pres. 1993-94), Phi Kappa Phi (pub. rels. officer 1982-83, sec. 1983-85), Phi Eta Sigma, Alpha Epsilon Delta, Beta Phi Mu. Home: 724 Olde Settler Pl Columbus OH 43214-2924 Office: Ohio State U William Oxley Thompson Meml Libr 1858 Neil Ave Columbus OH 43210-1225

STUDLEY, JAMIENNE SHAYNE, lawyer; b. N.Y.C., Apr. 30, 1951; d. Jack Hill and Joy (Cosor) S.; m. Gary J. Smith, July 14, 1984. BA magna cum laude, Barnard Coll., 1972; JD, Harvard U., 1975. Bar: D.C. 1975, U.S. Dist. Ct. D.C. 1978. Assoc. Bergson, Borkland, Margolis & Adler, Washington, 1976-80; spl. asst., sec. U.S. HHS, 1980-81; assoc. Weil, Gotshal & Manges, Washington, 1981-83; assoc. dean law sch. Yale U., New Haven, 1983-87; lectr. law, 1984-87; syndicated columnist Am. Lawyer Media, 1990-91; exec. dir. Nat. Assn. for Law Placement, Washington, 1987-90, Calif. Abortion Rights Action League, 1992-93; dep. gen. counsel U.S. Dept. Edn., 1993—; vis. scholar adj. faculty U. Calif., Berkeley, 1990-93. Pres. Conn. Women's Ednl. and Legal Fund, Hartford, 1986-87; mem. bd. advisors Nat. Assn. Pub. Interest Law Pub. Svc. Challenge. Mem. ABA (commn. on women in the profession 1991-94, chair editl. bd. Perspectives, coord. coun. legal edn. 1995—), D.C. Bar Assn., Bar Assn. San Francisco, Women's Bar Assn., Assn. Alumnae Barnard Coll. (bd. dirs. 1978-81), Barnard in Washington (pres. 1977-78), Phi Beta Kappa. Home: 5349 MacArthur Blvd Washington DC 20016 Office: Office of the Gen Coun Dept of Edn 600 Independence Ave SW Washington DC 20202-0004

STUDWELL, THOMAS W., lawyer; b. New Haven, Conn., Aug. 12, 1949. BA with honors, Haverford Coll., 1971; JD magna cum laude, U. Ill., 1977. Bar: Ill. 1978. Ptnr. Baker & McKenzie, Chgo. Office: Baker & McKenzie 1 Prudential Plz 130 E Randolph St Chicago IL 60601*

STUEART, ROBERT D., university information services director, educator. B.A., So. Ark. U., 1956; cert. Russian lang., 1958; M.S.L., La. State U., 1962; library sci. advanced cert., U. Pitts., 1969, Ph.D., 1971. Library asst. in reference and cataloging So. State Coll., Magnolia, Ark., 1953-56; librarian, tchr. Desha County (Ark.) Public Schs., 1956-57; library asst. microforms room, serials and Russian cataloging La. State U. Library, 1960-62; with U. Colo. Libraries, 1962-66, head circulation dept., 1964-65, instr., adminstrv. asst. to dir. libraries, 1965-66; asso. prof. library sci., asst. dir. libraries for systems and processes Pa. State U., 1966-68; vis. lectr. U. Pitts. Grad. Sch. Library and Info. Scis., 1968-71, Coll. Librarianship Wales, 1971-72; asso. prof., asst. dean U. Denver Grad. Sch. Librarianship, 1972-74; dean, prof. library and info. sci. Simmons Coll. Grad. Sch. Library and Info. Sci., Boston, 1974-94; prof., exec. dir. CLAIR Asian Inst. Tech., Bangkok, 1994—; cons., speaker in field. Author: The Area Specialist Bibliographer: An Inquiry Into His Role, 1972, (with John T. Eastlick) Library Management, 1975, 3d edit, 1987, (with Barbara Moran) Library and Information Center Management, 4th edit., 1993, Michelle My Chelle, 1987, (with Maureen Sullivan) Performance Appraisal and Evaluation, 1991; editor: (with George Miller) Collection Development, 1980, (with Richard Johnson) New Horizons for Academic Libraries, 1979; Academic Librarianship, 1982, Information Needs of the 80s, 1982; gen. editor Founds. of Library and Info. Sci., 1979-87; contbr. articles and revs. to profl. publs. Mem. Mass. Gov.'s Planning Com. for White Ho. Conf. on Librs., 1976-79, Mass. Br. Libr. Commrs., 1989—, chair, 1993-94; mem. ALA Internat. Rels. Roundtable, China Programs com., United Bd. for Christian Higher Edn. in China; chair U.S.-USSR Commn. on Libr. Cooperation, 1987-92, US-CIS/BALTIC Com. on Archives and Librs. Recipient Melville Dewey medal, 1980, Blackwell NA award, 1980, Disting. Alumni award So. Ark. U., 1984, Disting. Grad. award U. Pitts., 1985, ALISE Svc. award 1987, Beta Phi Mu award, 1990, Outstanding Alumni award La. State U., 1991; John F. Kennedy Found. fellow, 1991-92, Humphrey OCLC Forrest Press Internat. award, 1994. Mem. ALA (coun. 1978-81, 84-91, exec. bd. 1987-91, chmn. pub. com. 1983-84, chmn. internat. rels. com. 1991-92), Assn. Libr. and Info. Sci. Edn. (pres. 1983-84, Assn. Coll. and Rsch. Librs. (editl. bd. Coll. and Rsch. librs. 1973-74), Libr. Adminstrn. and Mgmt. Assn. (chmn. stats. com. for libr. edn. 1978-81, Libr. Edn. Divsn. pres. 1977-78), Rsch. Roundtable, Am. Soc. Info. Scis., Spl. Librs. Assn., New Eng. Libr. Assn., Mass. Libr. Assn. (Libr. Advocate award 1994), Internat. Fedn. Libr. Assns. (standing com. on libr. edn. 1986-90, mem. exec. bd. 1991—), New Eng. Hist. Geneal. Soc. (bd. dirs.). Office: Asian Inst Tech, P O Box 2754, Bangkok 10505, Thailand

STUEBNER, JAMES CLOYD, real estate developer, contractor; b. Phila., Dec. 15, 1931; s. Erwin A. and Frances (Quinn) S.; children: Kathleen, Stephen, James, Susan, Elizabeth; m. Susan Rae Peterson, June 16, 1990. BA, Dartmouth Coll., 1953. Sales engr. Rohm & Haas Co., Phila., 1956-69; pres. Structural Plastics Corp., Mpls., 1961-69; pres., gen. ptnr. Stuebner Properties, Mpls., 1969—; pres. Northland Inn and Exec. Conf. Ctr., 1988—. Mem. Minn. Conv. Ctr. Commn., St. Paul, 1988; commr. Minn. Econ. Devel. Commn., St. Paul, 1985; bd. dirs. Bach Soc. of Minn., Mpls., 1986—, Minn. Orchestral Assn., Mpls., 1988-91. Sgt. U.S. Army, 1953-55. Mem. Nat. Assn. Office and Indsl. Parks (bd. dirs. Minn. chpt. 1976-85, 81-90, pres. 1978-80, 92-93, nat. pres. 1983-84, v.p. 1981-81, Developer of Yr. award 1987, Minn. Bus. Person of Yr. award 1990, vice chmn. indsl. devel. forum 1996). Avocations: sailing, running, singing. Office: Five Star Rental and Development Co 7000 Northland Dr N Minneapolis MN 55428-1502

STUEHRENBERG, PAUL FREDERICK, librarian; b. Breckenridge, Minn., Mar. 14, 1947; s. Henry Ernest Frederick and Marian Violet (Sandberg) S.; m. Suzanne Elaine Draper, June 14, 1969 (div. Apr. 1982); m. Carole Lee DeVore, Aug. 1, 1983. BA, Concordia Sr. Coll., 1968; MDiv, Concordia Sem., 1972; STM, Christ Sem., 1974; MA, U. Minn., 1978, PhD, 1988. Asst. libr. U. Minn., Mpls., 1974-82; monographs libr. Yale Divinity Libr., New Haven, 1982-91, div. libr., 1991—; adj. assoc. prof. in theol. lit. Yale Divinity Sch., New Haven, 1993—; asst. pastor Christ Meml. Luth. Ch., Plymouth, Minn., 1974-82; adj. pastor Bethesda Luth. Ch., New Haven, 1984—; sec. Luth. Student Found., Mpls., 1978-81. Contbr. articles to profl. jours. Sec. North Haven (Conn.) Libr. Bd., 1989—. Mem. Am. Theol. Libr. Assn., Soc. Bibl. Lit., Am. Acad. Religion, North Haven Meml. Libr. Assn. Home: 280 Bayard Ave North Haven CT 06473-4307 Office: Yale U Div Sch Libr 409 Prospect St New Haven CT 06511-2167

STUELAND, DEAN THEODORE, emergency physician; b. Viroqua, Wis., June 24, 1950; s. Theodore Andrew and Hazel Thelma (Oftedahl) S.; m. Marlene Ann McClurg, Dec. 30, 1972; children: Jeffrey, Michael, Nancy, Kevin. BSEE, U. Wis., 1972, MSEE, 1973, MD, 1977. Diplomate Am. Bd. Internal Medicine, Am. Bd. Geriatric Medicine, Am. Bd. Emergency Medicine; cert. in addictions medicine, cert. med. rev. officer. Resident Marshfield (Wis.) Clinic, 1977-80, emergency physician, dir. emergency svc., 1981-93; emergency physician Riverview Hosp., Wisconsin Rapids, Wis., 1980-81; med. dir. Nat. Farm Medicine Ctr., Marshfield, 1986—, alcohol and other drug abuse unit St. Joseph's Hosp., Marshfield, 1988—; exec. com. Marshfield Clinic, 1989-91, 93-95, treas., 1993-95, ACLS state affiliate faculty Am. Heart Assn., 1984—, nat. faculty, 1992—; mem. emergency med. svcs. adv. bd. State of Wis., 1994—. Contbr. articles to profl. jours. Charter mem., pres. Hewitt (Wis.) Jaycees, 1984; bd. dirs. Northwood County chpt. ARC, 1988-95, Wood County Partnership Coun., 1993—. Fellow ACP, Am. Coll. Emergency Physicians (bd. dirs. Wis. chpt. 1984-90, v.p. 1990-91, pres. 1991-92, counselor 1993—), Am. Coll. Preventive Medicine; mem. Biomed. Engring. Soc. (sr. mem.), Am. Soc. Addictions Medicine. Mem. Missionary Alliance Ch. (bd. govs., treas. 1991—). Office: Marshfield Clinic 1000 N Oak Ave Marshfield WI 54449-5703

STUENKEL, WILLIAM C., airport administrator. Dir. engring. and ops. Pitts. Internat. Airport; dir. engrng. and ops. Broward County Aviation Dept., Ft. Lauderdale, Fla., 1994—. Office: Broward County Aviation Dept. 1400 Lee Wagner Blvd Fort Lauderdale FL 33315*

STUFFLEBEAM, DANIEL LEROY, education educator; b. Waverly, Iowa, Sept. 19, 1936; s. LeRoy and Melva Stufflebeam; m. Carolyn T. Joseph; children: Kevin D., Tracy Smith, Joseph. BA, State U. Iowa, 1958; MS, Purdue U., 1962, PhD, 1964; postgrad., U. Wis., 1965. Prof., dir. Ohio State U. Evaluation Ctr., Columbus, 1963-73; prof. edn., dir. Western Mich. U. Evaluation Ctr., Kalamazoo, 1973—. Author monographs and 15 books; contbr. chpts. to books, articles to profl. jours. Served with U.S. Army, 1960. Recipient Paul Lazersfeld award Evaluation Rsch. Soc., 1985. Mem. Am. Ednl. Rsch. Assn., Nat. Coun. on Measurement in Edn., Am. Evaluation Assn. Baptist. Office: Western Michigan Univ The Evaluation Ctr Kalamazoo MI 49008-5178

STUHAN, RICHARD GEORGE, lawyer; b. Braddock, Pa., July 1, 1951; s. George and Pauline Madeline (Pavlocik) S.; m. Mary Ann Cipriano, Aug. 23, 1975; children: Brendan George, Sara Katherine, Brian Christopher, Caitlin Emily. BA summa cum laude, Duquesne U., 1973; JD, U. Va., 1976. Bar: Va. 1976, D.C. 1977, U.S. Ct. Appeals (D.C. cir.) 1977, U.S. Ct. Appeals (4th cir.) 1977, U.S. Claims Ct. 1979, U.S. Supreme Ct. 1980, U.S. Ct. Appeals (3d cir.) 1981, U.S. Ct. Appeals (11th cir.) 1982, U.S. Dist. Ct. (no. dist.) Ohio 1985, Ohio 1986. Assoc. Arnold & Porter, Washington, 1976-84; of counsel Jones, Day, Reavis & Pogue, Cleve., 1984-86, ptnr., 1987—. Mem. Va. Law Review, 1974-76. Recipient Gold Medal for Gen. Excellence, Duquesne U., 1973,. Mem. Order of Coif. Democrat. Roman Catholic. Avocations: tennis, swimming, basketball, home repair. Home: 2865 Falmouth Rd Shaker Heights OH 44122-2838 Office: Jones Day Reavis & Pogue 901 Lakeside Ave Cleveland OH 44114-1116

STUHL, OSKAR PAUL, scientific and regulatory consultant; b. Wilhelmshaven, Fed. Republic Germany, Dec. 23, 1949; s. Johannes Alexander and Johanna Wilhelmine (Hoelling) S. Dipl. Chem., U. Duesseldorf, 1976, Dr.rer.nat., 1978. Tutor, Institut fuer Organische Chemie, U. Dusseldorf, 1975-76, sci. assoc., 1976-79; mgr. product devel. Drugofa GmbH, Cologne, Fed. Republic Germany, 1980; mgr. sci. rels. RJRN, Cologne, 1981-88, mgr. sci. svcs., 1989-94; cons. in field, 1995—. Mem. editl. bd. Beitraege zur Tabakforschung Internat. Mem. Dusseldorf Museums Verein, Verein der Freunde des Hetjens-Museums, Verein der Freunde und Foerderer der U. Dusseldorf, Verein der Freunde des Stadtmuseums Dusseldorf, Met. Mus. Art (N.Y.C.), Friends Royal Acad. Arts, London, Art Soc. of Rheinlande and Westfalen, Gesellschaft der Freunde der Kunstammlung NRW; Gesellschaft der Freunde und Foerderer der Univ. Dusseldorf; Zuercher Kunstgesellschaft; Freundeskreis Theatermuseum, Dusseldorf; Foerderverein NRW-Stiftung; Forum fuer Film (Duesseldorf); Deutsch-Japanische-Gesellschaft. Mem. Gesellschaft Deutscher Chemiker, Gesellschaft Deutscher Naturforscher und Aerzte, Max-Planck-Gesellschaft, Deutsche Gesellschaft fuer Arbeits hygiene, Am. Chem. Soc. (including various divs.), Chem. Soc. Japan, N.Y. Acad. of Scis., Royal Soc. Chemistry, Am. Pharm. Assn., Acad. Pharm. Rsch. and Sci., AAAS, Internat. Union Pure and Applied Chemistry, Am. Soc. Pharmacognosy, Fedn. Internat. Pharmaceutic, Christlich Demokratische Union, CDU-Mittelstaudf and Wirtschoftsvereinigung. Roman Catholic. Clubs: Vereinigung AC Dusseldorf; PCL (London); KDStV Burgundia-Leipzig (Zu Dusseldorf) im CV, Golf Club Velbert. Contbr. articles to profl. jours.; patentee in field. Office: PO Box 140544, D-40075 Düsseldorf Germany

STUHLINGER, ERNST, physicist; b. Niederrimbach, Germany, Dec. 19, 1913; came to U.S., 1946, naturalized, 1955.; s. Ernst and Pauline (Werner) S.; m. Irmgard Lotze, Aug. 1, 1950; children: Susanne, Tilman, Hans Christoph. PhD, U. Tuebingen, Germany, 1936. Asst. prof. Technische Hochschule, Berlin, Germany, 1936-41; guidance and control equipment rocket Devel. Center, Peenemuende, Germany, 1943-45; with Guided Missile Devel. Office, Ft. Bliss, Tex., 1946-50; physicist Ordnance Missile Labs., Huntsville, Ala., 1950-56, Army Ballistic Missile Agy., 1956-60; dir. Space Scis. Lab., George C. Marshall Space Flight Center, NASA, Huntsville, Ala., 1960-68; assoc. dir. for sci. George C. Marshall Space Flight Center, NASA, 1968-76; sr. research scientist, adj. prof. U. Ala. at Huntsville, 1976-84; sr. research assoc. Teledyne Brown Engring. Corp., Huntsville, 1984-88; cons. aerospace cos.; vis. scientist Tech. U. Munich, W. Germany, 1978, Max Planck Inst. Nuclear Physics, Heidelberg, 1983-85; cons. Teledyne-Brown Engring., 1984-90. Author: Ion Propulsion for Space Flight, 1964; co-author: Skylab, A Guidebook, 1973, Project Viking, 1976, Aufbruch in Den Weltraum, 1992, Wernher von Braun, Crusade for Space, 1994. Served with German Army, 1941-43, Russian Campaign. Fellow Am. Astronautical Soc., Am. Rocket Soc. (dir.), AIAA (tech. dir.), Brit. Interplanetary Soc.; mem. Internat. Acad. Astronautics, Von Braun Astron. Soc. (dir.), Austrian Astron. Soc. (hon.), Am. Optical Soc., Deutsche Roentgengesellschaft (hon.), Deutsche Physikalische Gesellschaft, Deutsche Gesellschaft Fuer Luft und Raumfahrt (hon.), Hermann Oberth Gesellschaft (hon.), Sigma Xi. Rsch. cosmic rays, nuclear physics, 1934-41, electric space propulsion, 1947—, studies on manned missions to Mars, 1954—. Home: 3106 Rowe Dr SE Huntsville AL 35801-6151

STUHR, DAVID PAUL, business educator, consultant; b. Ridgewood, N.J., Oct. 10, 1938; s. Edward Philip and Theresa Alma (Cherny) S. B Engring., Yale U., 1960; MS, Rensselaer Poly. Inst., 1962; PhD, NYU, 1972. Research fellow Fed. Res. Bank of N.Y., N.Y.C., 1968-69, cons. economist, 1969-92; assoc. in bus. Columbia U. Grad. Sch. Bus. Adminstrn., N.Y.C., 1969-72, asst. prof. fin., 1972-73; assoc. prof. fin. Rutgers U. Grad. Sch. Bus. Adminstrn., Newark, N.J., 1973-77; assoc. prof. fin. Fordham U., Faculty of Bus., N.Y.C., 1977—, acting dean faculty, 1984-85; assoc. dean Fordham U. Coll. Bus. Adminstrn., Bronx, N.Y., 1980-83, dean, 1983-87; pres. faculty senate Fordham U., Bronx, N.Y., 1994-95, assoc. v.p. for acad. affairs, 1995—; mem. bus. faculty com. Regents Coll. degrees SUNY, Albany, 1987—. Contbr. articles to profl. jours. Mem. Exec. bd. Bergen coun. Boy Scouts Am., 1979-95; mcpl. chmn. Ho-Ho-Kus (N.J.) Rep. Com., 1968—; chair fin. com. St. Gabriel the Archangel Ch., Saddle River, N.J., 1986—. Mem. Am. Econ. Assn. (life), Am. Fin. Assn. (life), Fin. Mgmt. Assn., Phila. Soc. (founding mem., trustee 1977-80, treas. 1979—). Republican. Roman Catholic. Avocations: backpacking, camping, skiing. Office: Fordham Univ Dept Fin Bronx NY 10458

STUHR, WALTER M., seminary educator, clergyman; b. Mpls., June 4, 1932; s. Walter M. and Norma (Bodenschatz) S.; m. Barbara Jean Gordon, June 13, 1953; children—Deborah Jean, Rebecca Ann, Philip Martin. B.A., Yale U., 1954; B.D., Pacific Lutheran Sem., 1958; M.A., U. Chgo., 1965, Ph.D., 1970. Ordained to ministry United Lutheran Ch. Am. 1958. Pastor Luth. Ch. of our Redeemer, Sacramento, Calif., 1958-63; interim pastor various chs., Chgo., 1963-67; prof. ethics Pacific Luth. Theol. Sem., Berkeley, Calif., 1967—, pres., 1979-88. Mem. Richmond-Shimada Sister City Program, Calif., 1975—. Mem. Soc. Christian Ethics. Democrat. Office: Pacific Luth Theol Sem 2770 Marin Ave Berkeley CA 94708-1530*

STUIVER, MINZE, geological sciences educator; b. Vlagtwedde, Groningen, The Netherlands, Oct. 25, 1929; came to U.S., 1959; s. Albert and Griet (Welles) S.; m. Annie Hubbelmeyer, July 12, 1956; children: Ingrid, Yolande. D.Sc. in Physics, U. Groningen, 1953, Ph.D. in Biophysics, 1958. Research assoc. Yale U., New Haven, 1959-62; sr. research assoc., dir. Radiocarbon Lab. Yale U., 1962-69; prof. geol. sci. and zoology U. Wash. Seattle, 1969-82, prof. geol. sci. and quaternary scis., 1982—, dir. Quaternary Isotope Lab, 1972—. Editor: Radiocarbon, 1976-88; mem. editorial bd.: Quaternary Research, 1974—, Isotope Geoscience, 1983—. Named Alexander von Humboldt sr. scientist Fed. Republic Germany, 1983. Mem. Geol. Soc. Am., Am. Quaternary Assn. Office: U Wash Box 351360 Seattle WA 98195-1360

STUKEL, JAMES JOSEPH, academic administrator, mechanical engineering educator; b. Joliet, Ill., Mar. 30, 1937; s. Philip and Julia (Mattivi) S.; m. Mary Joan Helpling, Nov. 27, 1958; children: Catherine, James, David, Paul. B.S. in Mech. Engring, Purdue U., 1959; M.S., U. Ill., Champaign-Urbana, 1963, Ph.D., 1968. Research engr. W.Va. Pulp and Paper Co., Covington, Va., 1959-61; mem. faculty U. Ill., 1968—, prof. mech. engring., 1975—, dir. Office Coal Research and Utilization, 1974-76, dir. Office Energy Research, 1976-81, dir. pub. policy program Coll. Engring., 1981-84, assoc. dean Coll. Engring. and dir. Expt. Sta., 1984-85; dean Grad. Coll., vice chancellor for research U. Ill. at Chgo., 1985-86, exec. vice chancellor, vice chancellor academic affairs, 1986-91, interim chancellor, 1990-91, chancellor, 1991-95, pres., 1995—; v.p. Chgo. Tech. Park Corp., 1985-88. pres., 1990-91; exec. sec. midwest Consortium Air Pollution, 1972-73, chmn. bd. dirs., 1973-75; mem. adv. bd. regional studies program Argonne (Ill.) Nat. Lab., 1975-76; adv. com. Energy Resources Commn., 1976; chmn. panel on dispersed electric generating techs. Office Tech. Assessment, U.S. Congress, 1980-81; chmn. rev. adv. bd. tech. rev. dist. heating and combined heat and power systems Internat. Energy Agy, OECD, Paris, 1982-83; cons. in field. Contbr. articles to profl. jours. Pres. parish council Holy Cross Roman Cath. Ch., Urbana, 1967-68. Mem. ASCE (State-of-the-Art of Civil Engring. award 1975), ASME, AAAS, Sigma Xi, Phi Kappa Phi, Pi Tau Sigma. Home: 2650 N Lakeview Ave Apt 1610 Chicago IL 60614-1819 Office: PO Box 4348 2833 Univ Hall M/C 105 Chicago IL 60680-4348

STULC, JAROSLAV PETER, surgeon, educator; b. Teplitz, Czechoslovakia, Sept. 14, 1947; came to U.S., 1948; s. Jaroslav Pavel and Emilie Vanca Stulc; m. Diana Susan Minassian, Dec. 27, 189; children: Alexan Christopher, Evan Thomas. BA, Cornell Coll., Mt. Vernon, Iowa, 1969; MD, U. Iowa, 1973. Diplomate Am. Bd. Surgery. Intern SUNY, Syracuse, 1973-75; resident in surgery Georgetown U., Washington, 1975-80, instr. surgery, 1979-80; instr. surgery, fellow transplant surgery Loyola U., Chgo., 1980-83; fellow surg. oncology Roswell Park Cancer Inst., Buffalo, 1983-85, attending surgeon, 1985-90; asst. prof. surgery SUNY, Buffalo, 1988-91; chief surgery VA Hosp., Buffalo, 1990-91; attending surgeon Trover Clinic Found., Madisonville, Ky., 1991—; clin. faculty U. Louisville, 1991—; co-dir. Mahr Cancer Ctr., Madisonville, 1992—. Editor Ky. Med. Jour., Physician Focus; contbr. articles and abstracts to publs. Vis. lectr. outreach program Am. Cancer Soc., bd. dirs. Ky. chpt., 1993—. Capt. USNR, 1987—. Fellow ACS (cert. advanced trauma life support), Internat. Coll. Surgeons; mem. AMA, AAAS, Am. Soc. Gastrointestinal Endoscopy, Am. Soc. Abdominal Surgeons, Am. Soc. Clin. Oncology, Soc. Am. Gastrointestinal Surgeons, Nat. Surg. Adjuvant Breast and Bowel Protocl, Ea. Coop. Oncology Group, Iowa Jr. Acad. Sci., Chgo. Assn. Immunologists, Roswell Park Surg. Soc., Buffalo Surg. Soc., Acad. Surg. Rsch., Assn. Acad. Surgery, Adrian Kantrowitz Surg. Rsch. Soc., Tri Beta. Presbyterian. Home: 1200 College Dr Madisonville KY 42431-9182 Office: Trover Clinic Found 435 N Kentucky Ave Madisonville KY 42431-1768

STULCE, MIKE, Olympic athlete, track and field. Olympic track and field participant Barcelona, Spain, 1992. Recipient Shotput Gold medal Olympics, Barcelona, 1992. Office: US Olympic Com 1750 E Boulder St Colorado Springs CO 80909-5724*

STULL, DEAN P., chemical company executive; b. Denver, Jan. 18, 1950; s. Donald Gordon and Dorothy Alice (Pilcher) S.; m. Nora Jo Nesbitt, June 11, 1971; children: Rebecca Lucile, Valerie Jo. BS in Chemistry, Colo. State U., Ft. Collins, 1972; MS in Organic Chemistry, U. Colo., 1974, PhD in Phys. Chemistry, 1976. Chief chemist Hauser Labs, Boulder, Colo., 1976—; chief exec. officer Hauser Chem. Research, Boulder, Colo., 1983—; vis. asst. prof. organic chemistry U. Colo., Boulder, 1981. Contbr. papers presented to sci. meetings and conventions. Mem. Am. Chem. Soc., Rocky Mountain Chromatography Discussion Group, Rocky Mountain Soc. of Applied Spectroscopy, Am. Soc. Lubrication Engrs., Fedn. Socs. Coatings Tech., Steel Structures Painting Council. Home: 6225 Niwot Rd Longmont CO 80503-8755 Office: Hauser Chem Rsch Inc 55555 Airport Blvd Boulder CO 80301-2339*

STULL, DONALD LEROY, architect; b. Springfield, Ohio, May 16, 1937; s. Robert Stull and Ruth Branson; m. Patricia Ann Ryder, Dec. 29, 1959 (div. Dec. 1985); children: Cydney Lynn, Robert Branson, Gia Virginia. BArch, Ohio State U., 1961; MArch, Harvard U., 1962. Registered arch., Calif., Conn., Fla., Ky., Maine, Md., Mass., Mich., Mo., N.H., N.J., N.Y., Pa., R.I., Tenn., Tex., Va., D.C. Pres. Stull Assocs., Inc., Boston, 1966-83; pres. Stull and Lee, Inc., Boston, 1983—; mem. Loeb fellowship com. Harvard Grad. Sch. Design, Cambridge, 1969-80; mem. adv. bd. Boston Archtl. Ctr., 1972-80, Mus. Nat. Ctr. of Afro-Am. Artists, Boston, 1978—, Ohio State U. Sch. Architecture, 1980—; design prof. Harvard Grad. Sch. Design, 1974-81; mem. vis. design studio, Rice University, Houston, Tex., spring 1993; bd. dirs. Mus. of Afro-Am. History, Boston, 1975-85; mem. vis. com. Yale Sch. Art and Architecture, New Haven, Conn., 1972-76, William Henry Bishop chair Yale Sch. Architecture, 1975; mem. nat. presdl. design award jury Nat. Endowment for Arts, 1984, 88. Trustee Shaw U., 1973-75, Boston Found. for Architecture, 1992—; mem. design adv. panel, Balt., 1976-80; chmn. Mass Art Commn., Boston, 1978-80; commr. Boston Art Commn., 1980-92; mem. Design Adv. Group, Cambridge, 1980-90, 94—; commr. Boston Civic Design Commn., 1987—; adv. com. Suffolk Sch. Bus. Mgmt., 1989-95; bd. dirs Historic Boston, 1990—; trustee Mass. Coll. Art, 1995—. Recipient Presdl. Design award Nat. Endowment for Arts, 1988; named one of Outstanding Young Men Boston, 1969, Outstanding Young Men Am., 1970, Centennial Yr. Outstanding Alumnus Ohio State U., 1970. Fellow AIA (nat. design com. 1972-84); mem. Boston Soc. ARchitects (bd. dirs. 1969, AIA Regional Design award 1975, 80, 89), Mass. Soc. Architects (bd. trustees Mass. 1995). Office: Stull and Lee Inc 38 Chauncy St Ste 1100 Boston MA 02111-2301

STULL, FRANK WALTER, elementary school educator; b. Easton, Pa., June 4, 1935; s. George Washington and Minnie Elizabeth S.; m. Darlene Joy Hunsicker, Aug. 2, 1958; children: James, Ronald, Wendy. BS, East Stroudsburg State Coll., 1956; MEd, Lehigh U., 1966. Cert. tchr., N.J. Tchr. Korea Heung-Up Bank, Seoul, Korea, 1957-58, Howell Twp. Elem. Sch., Freehold, N.J., 1958-59, Holland Twp. Elem. Sch., Milford, N.J., 1959-91; lectr. Friends of U.S. Navy, 1992—. Bd. dirs., sec., treas., mgr. Hunterdon County Sch. Employees Fed. Credit Union, Phillipsburg, N.J., 1969-87, mem.adv. com., 1995; merit badge counselor Boy Scouts Am., 1970-84, cubmaster, 1971-72; active Friends of USN, 1992—; treas., mem. Hist. Preservation Commn. Holland Twp., 1993—. With U.S. Army, 1956-58, Korea. Recipient Meritorious Svc. award N.J. Credit Union League, 1988, Tchr. Recognition award State N.J. Gov., 1987, Disting. Achievement award for rsch. and preservation of history of Holland Twp. and surrounding areas; named Outstanding Elem. Tchr. Am., 1972; Experienced Tchr. in Geography fellow Pa. State U., 1967. Mem. NEA, Holland Twp. Edn. Assn., Hunterdon County Edn. Assn., N.J. Edn. Assn., Phi Delta Kappa (chartered mem. Zeta Gamma chpt.). Avocations: photography, travel. Home and Office: 806 Rugby Rd Phillipsburg NJ 08865-2033

STULL, G. ALAN, health professions educator, administrator; b. Easton, Pa., Jan. 26, 1933; s. George Washington and Minnie Elizabeth (Walter) S.; m. Joan Carolyn Gittings, July 30, 1955 (div. 1981); children—Bobbi Ann, John David; m. Jeanine Joosten, Nov. 23, 1984. Student, Lafayette Coll., Easton, Pa., 1950-51; B.S., East Stroudsburg U., 1955; M.S., Pa. State U., 1957, Ed.D., 1961. From instr. to asst. prof. Pa. State U., State College, 1958-66; from assoc. prof. to prof. U. Md., College Park, 1966-72; prof., assoc. dean U. Ky., Lexington, 1972-77; prof., dir. U. Minn., Mpls., 1977-85; prof., dean Sch. Allied Health Professions U. Wis., Madison, 1985-88; prof., dean Sch. Health Related Professions SUNY, Buffalo, 1988—. Co-author: Statistical Principles and Procedures with Applications for Physical Education, 1975; editor: Ency. of Physical Education, Fitness, and Sports, 1980; contbr. articles to profl. jours. Served with U.S. Army, 1956-58. Recipient Disting. Alumni Svc. award East Stroudsburg U., 1974; recognition award Am. Corrective Therapy Assn., 1981. Fellow Am. Acad. Kinesiol. Phys. Edn. (sec.-treas. 1982-84, pres. 1985-86), Am. Coll. Sports Medicine (chmn. position stands 1979-81); mem. AAHPERD (pres. rsch. consortium 1981-82, honor award 1981), Nat. Assn. Phys. Edn. in Higher Edn. (chmn. rsch. com. 1976-77), Assn. for Rsch., Adminstrn., Profl. Couns. and Socs. (pres. 1976-77, honor award 1980), Assn. Schs. Allied Health Professions, Phi Epsilon

Kappa. Republican. Methodist. Avocations: athletics; photography; travel; boating; fishing. Office: SUNY Sch Health Related Professions 435 Stockton Kimball Tower Buffalo NY 14214

STULTS, LAURENCE ALLEN, airline pilot; b. Evanston, Ill., Nov. 2, 1940; s. Allen Parker and Elizabeth Van Horne; m. Karen Frashure, Feb. 13, 1965 (div. 1986); m. Takako Yajima, Mar. 25, 1986; children: Rex Allen, Mark Edwin. AB in Econs., Colgate U., 1962; MS, George Washington U., 1978; postgrad., Cath. U., 1977; cert. in Japanese Lang., U. Guam, Maniglao, 1991. Commd. 2d lt. U.S. Marine Corps, 1962, fighter pilot, 1962-83; flight instr., 1965-68, 74-75; test pilot, mgr. fighter Naval Air Test Ctr., 1971-74; advanced through grades to lt. col. commdg. officer USMC, 1980; capt. Continental Air Micronesia, 1984-91; chief pilot World Fish and Agriculture, 1991; capt. B-727 Continental Airlines, Denver, 1991-94; capt. B-757 Continental Airlines, Newark, 1994—; cons. real estate sales, Honolulu, 1983-86; gen. ptnr. Transpac Translations, 1987—; cons. aviation transportation matters, 1991—. Pres. Mariners Ridge Homeowners, Honolulu, 1980-86, Tumon View (Guam) Homeowners, 1987-91; active Boy Scouts Am. Decorated disting. flying cross, bronze star, cross of gallantry, , meritorious svc. medal, Navy achievement medal; recipient Eagle Scout award Boy Scouts Am. Mem. Soc. Exptl. Test Pilors, Ind. Assn. Continental Pilots, Continental Ops. Group, Marine Corps Assn., Order of Arrow, Hash-House Harriers, AARP, The Ret. Officers Assn., Sigma Nu. Republican. Congregationalist. Avocations: sailing, running, bicycling, tennis, golf. Home: Redondo Vista Apt 204 28602 16th Ave S Federal Way WA 98003-3134 Office: 5300 Riverside Dr Cleveland OH 44135

STULTS, WALTER BLACK, management consultant, former trade organization executive; b. Hightstown, N.J., Oct. 25, 1921; s. C. Stanley and Nettie M. (Black) S.; m. Ann D. Haynes, June 28, 1947; children: Andrew Haynes, Thomas Stanley. BA, Williams Coll., 1943; MA (Woodrow Wilson fellow), Princeton U., 1949. Teaching asst. Princeton (N.J.) U., 1946-49; legis. asst. to U.S. Senator Robert Hendrickson, Washington, 1949-50; staff dir. U.S. Senate Small Bus. Com., Washington, 1950-61; pres. Nat. Assn. Small Bus. Investment Cos., Washington, 1961-86; prin. W.B. Stults, Cons., Chapel Hill, N.C., 1979—; dir. Pardee & Curtin Lumber Co., Pardee Resources Co., Phila.; chmn. Coun. Small and Ind. Bus. Assns., 1976-81. Pres. Carol Woods Residents Assn.; dir. Carol Woods Retirement Comty. With USAAF, 1943-46. Mem. Am. Soc. Assn. Execs. Republican. Congregationalist. Clubs: The Exchequer, Masons, Chapel HIll Country.

STULTZ, NEWELL MAYNARD, political science educator; b. Boston, June 13, 1933; s. Irving Washburn and Marjorie May (MacEachern) S.; m. Elizabeth Petronella Olckers, Apr. 6, 1958; children: Elliot Andries, Amy Elizabeth. A.B., Dartmouth Coll., 1955; M.A., Boston U., 1960, Ph.D., 1965; M.A. hon., Brown U., 1968. Fulbright exchange scholar U. Pretoria, South Africa, 1955-56; asst. prof. polit. sci. Northwestern U., Evanston, Ill., 1964-65; asst. prof. to prof. polit. sci. Brown U., Providence, 1965—, assoc. grad. dean, 1970-74, assoc. dean of faculty, 1993—; vis. fellow Yale U.-South African Research Program, 1977; vis. prof. U. South Africa, Pretoria, 1980; James Gathings lectr. Bucknell U., Lewisburg, Pa., 1980. Author: Afrikaner Politics in South Africa, 1974, Who Goes to Parliament?, 1975, Transkei's Half Loaf, 1979, (bibliography) South Africa, 1989, 2d edit., 1993; co-author: South Africa's Transkei, 1967; co-editor: Governing in Black Africa, 1970, 2d edit., 1986. V.p. World Affairs Council R.I., 1983. Served as lt. (j.g.) USN, 1956-59. Fulbright fellow, 1955-56; NDEA grantee, 1959-62; Ford Found. fellow, 1962-64; Rockefeller Found. fellow, 1976-77. Unitarian. Home: 371 New Meadow Rd Barrington RI 02806-3729 Office: Brown U Dept Polit Sci PO Box 1844 Providence RI 02912-1844

STULTZ, THOMAS JOSEPH, newspaper executive; b. Ironton, Ohio, July 28, 1951; s. Riley Frederick and Mary (Leslie) S.; m. Patricia Ann Conley, Dec. 18, 1971; children: Leslie Faye, Jessica Kristin. Student, Ohio U., 1969-71, Marshall U., 1971, U. N.C., Chapel Hill. Reporter Ashland (Ky.) Daily Ind., 1970-73, Orlando (Fla.) Sentinel, 1973; owner/pub. Greenup County Sentinel, Greenup, Ky., 1973-80; editor, writer Bob Jones U., Greenville, S.C., 1980; advt. dir. Daily Adv., Greenville, 1980-81; dir. community publs. Anderson (S.C.) Ind. Mail, 1981-84; v.p., gen. mgr. Leader Newspapers, Inc., Charlotte, N.C., 1984-86; mktg. dir. Suburban Newspapers Greater St. Louis, 1986-88; v.p. Multimedia Newspaper Co., Greenville, 1988-96; pres. pub. divsn. Gray Comms. Systems, Inc., Albany, Ga., 1996—; pres., owner Internat. Employment Gazette, Greenville, 1989—. Deacon, tchr. Temple Bapt. Ch., Flatwoods, Ky., 1978-80. Republican. Avocations: golf, travel, reading, church and missions activities. Home: 6 Titleist Ct Taylors SC 29687-6651 Office: 6 Titleist Ct Taylors SC 29687

STUMP, BOB, congressman; b. Phoenix, Apr. 4, 1927; s. Jesse Patrick and Floy Bethany (Fields) S.; children: Karen, Bob, Bruce. B.S. in Agronomy, Ariz. State U., 1951. Mem. Ariz. Ho. of Reps., 1957-67; mem. Ariz. Senate, 1967-76, pres., 1975-76; mem. 95th-104th Congresses from 3rd Dist.Ariz., 1976—; mem. Nat. Security Com. With USN, 1943-46. Mem. Am. Legion, Ariz. Farm Bur. Republican. Seventh-day Adventist. Office: 211 Canon House of Representatives Washington DC 20515-0303 also: 230 N 1st Ave Rm 5001 Phoenix AZ 85025-0230*

STUMP, JOHN EDWARD, veterinary anatomy educator, ethologist; b. Galion, Ohio, June 3, 1934; s. Clarence Willard and Mabel Katherine (Pfeifer) S.; m. Patricia Anne Auer, Aug. 7, 1955; children—Karen, James. D.V.M. summa cum laude (Borden award for acad. excellence 1958), Ohio State U., 1958; Ph.D., Purdue U., 1966. Pvt. practice vet. medicine Bucyrus, Ohio, 1958-61; mem. faculty Purdue U., West Lafayette, Ind., 1961-91; prof. vet. anatomy Purdue U., 1976-91, prof. emeritus vet. anatomy, 1991; vis. prof. dept. physiol. scis. Sch. Vet. Medicine, U. Calif.-Davis, fall 1980; vis. prof. Coll. Vet. Medicine, Tex. A&M U., spring 1981. Recipient Autotutorial Excellence award Student AVMA, 1974, Amoco Found. Purdue undergrad. teaching award, 1979, Norden Disting. Tchr. award Purdue U., 1977, Outstanding Tchr. award Purdue U. Alumni Found., 1978; named Outstanding Tchr. Freshman Vet. Students, Purdue U., 1987. Mem. AVMA, Ind. Vet. Med. Assn., Ind. Acad. Vet. Medicine, World Assn. Vet. Anatomists, Am. Assn. Vet. Anatomists (pres. 1977-78), Am. Assn. Anatomists, Am. Vet. Soc. Animal Behavior, Assn. Am. Vet. Med. Colls. (Purdue del. to council of educators 1982-84), Ind. Acad. Sci., Sigma Xi, Phi Zeta, Gamma Sigma Delta. Republican. Presbyterian. Club: Tecumseh Kiwanis (pres. 1973).

STUMP, JOHN SUTTON, lawyer; b. Clarksburg, W.Va., Aug. 7, 1929; s. John Sutton and Helen (Mannix) S.; m. Elaine Claire Scammahorn, Sept. 14, 1968; children—John Sutton IV, James Felix. Student, Washington and Lee U., 1946-47, LL.B., 1957; B.S. in Commerce, U. N.C., 1951. Bar: W.Va. 1957, Va. 1957. Assoc. Jackson, Kelly, Holt & O'Farrell, Charleston, W.Va., 1957-58, Boothe, Dudley, Koontz & Boothe, Alexandria, Va., 1958-61, Boothe, Dudley, Koontz & Blankingship, Fairfax and Alexandria, Va., 1962-63; ptnr. Boothe, Dudley, Koontz, Blankingship & Stump, Fairfax and Alexandria, 1963-71, Boothe, Prichard & Dudley, 1971-87, McGuire, Woods, Battle & Boothe, 1987—. Served to lt. comdr. USNR, 1951-54, 61-62. Fellow Am. Coll. Trial Lawyers; mem. Am. Law Inst. Home: 8329 Weller Ave Mc Lean VA 22102-1717 Office: 8280 Greensboro Dr Mc Lean VA 22102-3807

STUMP, T(OMMY) DOUGLAS, lawyer, educator; b. Cushing, Okla., Jan. 7, 1957; s. Thomas Burl and Lindsey L. (Laffoon) S.; children: Kelli Jo and Matthew Douglas. BA in English, E. Ctrl. U., Ada, Okla., 1979; JD, Oklahoma City U., 1982. Bar: Okla. 1983, U.S. Dist. Ct. (we. dist.) Okla. 1983, U.S. Ct. Appeals (10th cir.) 1983, U.S. Dist. Ct. (ea. and no. dists.) Okla. 1986, U.S. Ct. Appeals (5th cir.) 1986, U.S. Supreme Ct. 1986. Assos. Winningham & Assocs., Oklahoma City, 1983-90; founding atty. T. Douglas Stump & Assocs., Oklahoma City, 1990—; adj. prof. law Oklahoma City U., asst. project coord. Okla./Am. Immigration Lawyers Assn. Pro Bono Amnesty Appeals Project, 1987-89; mem. pro bono panel (immigration) Legal Aid of Western Okla.; lectr. various continuing legal edn. programs, immigration seminars, 1983-94. Author: General Information Concerning United States Immigration Laws, 1989, Intracompany Transfers, 1995, Employment Based Immigration Law, 1995. Bd. dirs. Lyric Theater, mem. exec. com., co-sponsor various prodns., 1992—, Oklahoma City Econ. Roundtable, founder and provider Focus on Success Scholarship Fund, Drumright H.S., Oklahoma City, 1993—. Fellow Okla. Bar Found., mem. ABA (young lawyers divn. delegate 1988, 1989, exec. mem. young lawyers divsn. com. on immigration law), Am. Immigration Lawyers Assn. (Okla., Tex., N.M. chptrs., chmn. com. on nonimmigrant visas 1986-88, Oklahoma City sect. chmn. 1987-91, chmn. membership com. 1988-90, treas. 1991-92, vice chmn. 1992-93, Okla. City INS liaison 1995—), Okla. Bar Assn. (com. on legal specialization 1987-91, spl. com. on Unauthorized Practice of Law 1988-90, House Counsel Sect. 1988—, Com. on Legal Ethics 1990-92, Com. on Civil Procedure 1991-94, Solo and Small Firm Task Force 1993—, Young Lawyers Divsn., dir. 1986-90, dir. com. on Alien/Refugee Assistance 1986-89, chmn. com. on Alien/Refugee Assistance 1986-90, recipient Outstanding Dir. award 1987, treas. 1988, sec. 1989); Oklahoma County Bar Assn (Law Day com. 1983-84, Ask A Lawyer programs 1986-91, dir. Young Lawyers Assn. 1987, mem. fee grievance com. 1990-91), Oklahoma City U. Law Sch. Alumni Assn. (bd. dirs. 1989-94, pres. 1992-94, recipient Outstanding Law School Alumni award 1993). Republican. Office: 50 Penn Pl Ste 1320 Oklahoma City OK 73118

STUMPE, WARREN ROBERT, scientific, engineering and technical services company executive; b. Bronx, N.Y., July 15, 1925; s. William A. and Emma J. (Mann) S.; children: Jeffrey, Kathy, William. B.S., U.S. Mil. Acad., 1945; M.S., Cornell U., 1949; M.S. in Indsl. Engring, N.Y. U., 1965; grad., Command and Gen. Staff Coll., 1972, Army War Coll., 1976; Ph.D. (hon.), Milw. Sch. Engring., 1982. Registered profl. engr., N.Y., Fla., Wis. Commd. 2d lt., C.E. U.S. Army, 1945, advanced through grades to capt., 1954; with (65th Engr. Bn.), 1945-48; asst. prof. mechanics U.S. Mil. Acad., 1951-54; resigned, 1954; from capt. to col. Res., 1958-79; dep. gen. mgr., gen. engring. div. AMF, Stamford, Conn., 1954-63; exec. v.p. Dortech, Inc., Stamford, 1963-69; dir. systems mgmt. group Mathews Conveyor div. REX, Darien, Conn., 1969-71; dir. research and devel. Rexnord, Inc., Milw., 1971-73, v.p. corp. research and tech., from 1973, v.p. bus. devel. sector, 1981-83, v.p., chief tech. officer, 1983-86; pres. Rexnord Techs., Milw., 1986-87; v.p. Radian Corp., Milw., 1987-90; civilian aide to sec. army for State of Wis., 1981-85; mem. adv. bd. technology transfer program U. Wis.-Whitewater. Contbr. articles to profl. jours. Founder, pres. No. Little League, Stamford, 1965-69; pres. Turn of River Jr. High Sh. PTA, 1967-68; vice chmn. for Wis. Dept. Def., Nat. Com. Employer Support Guard and Res.; bd. regents Milw. Sch. Engring.; mem. liaison coun. Coll. Engring., U. Wis., also mem. indsl. adv. coun.; mem. adv. coun. Marquette U.; mem. Wis. Gov.'s Task Force on Energy, Coun. Great Lakes Govs.' Regional Econ. Devel. Commn., 1987-88; bd. dirs. MRA-Inst. Mgmt., Inc. Mem. Am. Water Pollution Control Fedn., Indsl. Rsch. Inst. (pres., dir.), Wis. Assn. Rsch. Mgrs. (founder), West Point Soc. Wis., Tau Beta Pi, Phi Kappa Phi. Clubs: Wis., Ozaukee Country.

STUMPF, DAVID ALLEN, pediatric neurologist; b. L.A., May 8, 1945; s. Herman A. and Dorothy F. (Davis) S.; children: Jennifer F., Kaitrin E.; m. Elizabeth Dusenbery, Feb. 2, 1989; stepchildren: Todd Coleman, Shilo Walker. BA, Lewis and Clark Coll., 1966; MD cum laude, U. Colo., 1972, PhD, 1972. Pediatric intern Strong Meml. Hosp., Rochester, N.Y., 1972-73, resident, 1973-74; neurology resident Harvard Med. Sch., Boston, 1974-77; dir. pediatric neurology U. Colo. Health Sci. Ctr., Denver, 1977-85; chief neurology Children's Meml. Hosp., Chgo., 1985-89; chmn. neurology, Benjamin and Virginia T. Boshes Prof. Northwestern U., 1989—; mem. sci. adv. co. Muscular Dystrophy Assn., 1981-87. Editorial bd. Neurology, 1982-87; contbr. articles to sci. jours. NIH grantee, 1979-84; Muscular Dystrophy Assn. grantee, 1977-89; March of Dimes grantee, 1983-85; recipient Lewis and Clark Coll. Disting. Alumni award, 1991. Fellow Am. Acad. Neurology; mem. Child Neurology Soc. (counsellor 1982-84, pres. 1985-87), Am. Neurol. Assn., Am. Pediatric Soc., Soc. Pediatric Rsch. Presbyterian. Home: 540 Judson Ave Evanston IL 60202-3084 Office: 233 E Erie St Ste 614 Chicago IL 60611-2906

STUMPF, HARRY CHARLES, lawyer; b. New Orleans, May 1, 1944; s. John Frederick and Amy Ruth (Lynch) S.; m. Mary Frances Henricks, Aug. 27, 1966 (div. Dec. 3, 1992); children: Ashley Frances Stumpf Borges, Piper Lynch, Harry Charles Jr. BBA, Tulane U., 1967, JD, 1968. Bar: La. 1968, U.S. Dist. Ct. (ea. dist.) La. 1968, U.S. Ct. Appeals (5th cir.) 1968, U.S. Supreme Ct. 1995. Assoc./of counsel Knight, D'Angelo & Knight, Gretna, La., 1968-83; ptnr. Stumpf, Dugas, LeBlanc, Papale & Ripp, Gretna, La., 1983—. Lector/commentator St. Anthony Ch., Gretna, 1970—; trustee La. Cystic Fibrosis, New Orleans, 1975-78. Recipient Outstanding Svc. award West Jefferson Levee Dist., 1994. Fellow La. Bar Found.; mem. Jefferson Bar Assn., Westbank Rotary (dir. 1970—), Semreh Club. Avocations: golf, boating, skiing, computers. Office: Stumpf Dugas LeBlanc Papale & Ripp 901 Derbigny St Ste 200 Gretna LA 70053

STUMPF, MARK HOWARD, lawyer; b. Chgo., Jan. 25, 1947; s. Samuel Enoch and Jean (Goodman) S.; m. Elizabeth Bruce, Nov. 18, 1972; children: Nicholas, Anna, Lawrence, Gillian. AB, Harvard U., 1969, JD, 1972. Bar: N.Y. 1973, D.C. 1977, U.S. Dist. Ct. (so. and ea. dists.) N.Y. 1973. Assoc. Paul, Weiss, Rifkind, Wharton & Garrison, N.Y.C., 1972-76; assoc. Arnold & Porter, Washington, 1976-80, ptnr., 1981-92, sr. ptnr., 1993—; bd. dirs. Martha's Table, Washington. Co-author: Shark Repellents and Golden Parachutes; author: (with others) Latin American Sovereign Debt Management, 1990. Decorated Order of Generalissimo Francisco de Miranda, 1st Class (Republic of Venezuela) 1991. Mem. ABA, Harvard Club N.Y.C. Democrat. Episcopalian. Home: 3820 Jocelyn St NW Washington DC 20015-1920 Office: Arnold & Porter 555 12th St NW Washington DC 20004

STUMPF, PAUL KARL, biochemistry educator emeritus; b. N.Y.C., N.Y., Feb. 23, 1919; s. Karl and Annette (Schreyer) S.; married, June 1947; children: Ann Carol, Kathryn Lee, Margaret Ruth, David Karl, Richard Frederic. AB, Harvard Coll., 1941; PhD, Columbia U., 1945. Instr. pub. health U. Mich., Ann Arbor, 1946-48; faculty U. Calif., Berkeley, 1948-58, prof., 1956-58; prof. U. Calif., Davis, 1958-84, prof. emeritus, 1984—; chief scientist Competitive Rsch. Grants Office USDA, Washington, 1988-91; cons. Palm Oil Rsch. Inst., Kuala Lumpur, Malaysia, 1982-92; mem. sci. adv. bd. Calgene, Inc., Davis, 1990-93; mem. sci. adv. panel Md. Biotech. Inst., 1990-92. Co-author: Outlines of Enzyme Chemistry, 1955, Outlines of Biochemistry, 5th edit., 1987; co-editor-in-chief Biochemistry of Plants, 1980; exec. editor Archives of Biochemistry/Biophysics, 1965-88; contbr. over 250 articles to profl. jours. Mem. planning commn. City of Davis, 1966-68. Guggenheim fellow, 1962, 69; recipient Lipid Chemistry award Am. Oil Chemists Soc., 1974, Sr. Scientist award Alexander von Humboldt Found., 1976, Superior Svc. Group award USDA, 1992. Fellow AAAS; mem. NAS, Royal Danish Acad. Scis., Am. Soc. Plant Physiologists (pres. 1979-80, chmn. bd. trustees 1986-90, Stephen Hales award 1974, Charles Reid Barnes Life Membership award 1992), Yolo Fliers Country Club (Woodland, Calif.). Avocation: golf. Home: 764 Elmwood Dr Davis CA 95616-3517 Office: Univ of Calif Molecular/Cellular Biology Davis CA 95616

STUMPF, SAMUEL ENOCH, philosophy educator; b. Cleve., Feb. 3, 1918; s. Rev. Louis and Elizabeth (Jergens) S.; m. Jean Goodman, July 3, 1943; children—Paul Jergens, Mark Howard, Samuel Enoch. B.S., U. Calif. at Los Angeles, 1940; B.D., Andover Newton Theol. Sch., 1943; postgrad., Columbia, 1946; Ph.D., U. Chgo., 1948. Asst. prof. ethics Vanderbilt U., 1948-49, asso. prof., 1949-52, prof. philosophy, chmn. dept., 1952-67, prof. philosophy emeritus, 1984—; vis. prof. med. ethics Vanderbilt U. (Med. Sch.), 1973-74; research prof. jurisprudence Vanderbilt U. (Law Sch.), 1974-77; research prof. med. philosophy Vanderbilt U. (Med. Sch.), 1974—, prof. law, 1977-84, prof. law emeritus, 1984—, also asst. to chancellor, 1966-67; pres. Cornell Coll., Mt. Vernon, Iowa, 1967-74; Gates lectr. Grinnell Coll., 1951; Keese lectr. U. Chattanooga, 1962; Decell lectr. Millsaps Coll., 1963; Louttit-George lectr. Washington Coll., 1967; Willson lectr. Southwestern U., 1970. Author: Philosophical Problems; Elements of Philosophy, A Democratic Manifesto, Socrates to Sartre, Morality and the Law, Philosophy: History and Problems; Contbr. articles to profl. jours. Trustee Food Safety Coun., 1976-80, Food and Drug Law Inst., 1978—. Lt. USNR, 1943-46. Carnegie research grantee, 1949; Ford fellow Harvard, 1955-56; Rockefeller fellow Oxford (Eng.) U., 1958-59. Mem. Am. Council on Legal and Polit. Philosophy, Am. Philos. Assn., Phi Beta Kappa. Home: 424 Page Rd Nashville TN 37205-4244

STUMPF, WALTER ERICH, cell biology educator, researcher; b. Oelsnitz, Sachsen, Germany, Jan. 10, 1927; came to U.S., 1963; m. Ursula Emily Schwinge, May 20, 1961; children: Andrea, Martin, Carolin, Silva. MD summa cum laude, Humboldt U., Berlin, 1952; PhD, U. Chgo., 1967; D in Biol. Humanities (hon.), U. Ulm, Germany, 1987. Resident in neurology and psychiatry Humboldt U., Berlin, 1954-57; resident in neurology and psychiatry U. Marburg, 1957-61, resident in radiobiology, 1961-62; rsch. assoc. U. Chgo., 1963-67, asst. prof., 1967-70; assoc. prof. U. N.C., Chapel Hill, 1970-73, prof., 1973-95, mem. labs. for reproductive biology and neurobiology program, mem. Cancer Rsch. Ctr., Carolina Population Ctr., mem. curriculum in toxicology; vis. psychiatrist Maudsley Hosp., London, 1959; vis. prof. Max-Planck Inst. for Cell Biology, Wilhelmshaven, Germany, 1975, U. Ulm, 1981; rsch. advisor Chugai Pharm. Co., Ltd., Tokyo, 1992-95; cons. Harris Mfg. Co., North Billerica, Mass., Rsch. Triangle Inst., Chemistry and Life Scis. Divsn., Rsch. Triangle Park, N.C., Merck Sharp and Dome , Westpoint, Pa.; exec. com. NRC, Inst. of Lab. Animal Resources, Nat. Acad. Scis., 1979-81, coun. Inst. of Lab. Animal Res., 1978-81, com. Soc. for Exptl. Biology and Medicine, 1987-92, founder Internat. Inst. Drug Distbn. Cytopharmacology and Cytoxicology, Chapel Hill, N.C., 1995—. Editor: Autoradiography of Diffusible Substances, 1969, Anatomical Neuroendocrinology, 1975, Autoradiography and Correlative Imaging, 1995; mem. editl. bd. Neuroendocrinology Letters, 1979-87, Exptl. Aging Rsch., 1975-85, Jour. Histochemistry and Cytochemistry, 1982-90, Cell and Tissue Rsch., 1982—, Molecular and Cellular Neurosci., 1989-94, Biomed. Rsch., 1991-94, Histochemistry, 1992-96; contbr. numerous articles to profl. jours. Recipient Humboldt Found. award, 1989. Mem. AAAS, Am. Assn. Anatomists, N.Y. Acad. Scis., Soc. for Exptl. Biology and Medicine, Soc. for Neurosci., Endocrine Soc., Internat. Brain Rsch. Orgn., Am. Soc. Zoologists, Histochem. Soc. (coun. 1977-81), Histochem. Gesellschaft (Feulgen lectureship 1982), Internat. Soc. Xenobiotics (charter), Internat. Inst. Drug Distbn. Cytopharmacology and Cytotoxicology (founder). Home: U NC Sch Medicine 2612 Damascus Church Rd Chapel Hill NC 27516 Office: Internat Inst Drug Distribution Cytopharmacology & Cytotoxicology Chapel Hill NC 27516

STUMPFF, ROBERT THOMAS, academic administrator; b. Lewistown, Pa., June 25, 1945; s. Harry Clarence and Marjorie Louise (Bossinger) S.; m. Sylvia Simmons, Apr. 22, 1972; children: Robert Dale, Cherie Lynn Stumpff Zimmer. BS, U. Md., 1968; cert., U. Ky., 1978. Adminstrv. asst. to dir. athletics U. Md., College Park, 1968-69, asst. dir. Md. student union, 1969-72, assoc. dir. Md. student union, 1973-80, acting dir. Md. student union, 1974-75, bus. mgr. athletics, 1980-81, asst. athletic dir., 1982-88, mgr. gen. svcs. phys. plant, 1988—; cons. U.S. Naval Acad. Athletic Assn., Annapolis, Md., 1984. Author, editor: Maryland Wrestling, 1964-65, 68-69 (Nation's Best award); asst. editor: Maryland Football Guide, 1965-69, Maryland Basketball, 1964-65, 68-69. Mem. ch. coun. Abiding Savior Lutheran Ch., Columbia, Md., 1986-87. Mem. Am. Pub. Works Assn., Solid Waste Assn. Am. (cert. mcpl. solid waste mgr., bd. dirs. Mid-Atlantic chpt. 1992-94), Nat. Solid Wastes Mgmt. Assn., Md.-Del. Solid Waste Assn., Assn. Phys. Plant Adminstrs., Md. Ednl. Found., U. Md. Alumni Assn. (life), Terrapin Club, U. Md. M Club Found. (life, bd. dirs. 1970—, past pres., chmn. outstanding awards banquet 1990, Outstanding Wrestling Publ. award 1968), Omicron Delta Kappa (Sigma Cir., faculty sec.-treas. 1972-76, faculty advisor 1976-91, faculty coord. 1991—). Avocations: reading, sight-seeing. Home: 8206 Bubbling Spring Laurel MD 20723-1079 Office: Univ Md Phys Plant Svc Bldg College Park MD 20742

STUNDZA, THOMAS JOHN, journalist; b. Lawrence, Mass., Mar. 4, 1948; s. John Anthony and Matilda (Stanulonis) S. BA, Merrimack Coll., 1970; MA, Valparaiso U., 1975. Reporter Eagle-Tribune, Lawrence, 1968-70, Post-Tribune, Gary, Ind., 1970-73; bus. editor Post-Tribune, Gary, 1974-78; steel editor Am. Metal Market, Pitts., 1978-80; news editor Am. Metal Market, N.Y.C., 1981-83; sr. editor Purchasing mag., Boston, 1984-94, exec. editor, 1995—; editor Purchasing's Buying Strategy Forecast newsletter, Boston, 1988—; editor audiotape news programming Purchasing's MetalsWatch!, 1994—; instr. journalism Valparaiso (Ind.) U., 1976, U. Pitts., 1980. Pres. Porter County (Ind.) Youth Svc. Bur., 1976-78. Recipient Honor Roll award U.S. Izaak Walton League, 1973, Paul Tobenkin award Columbia U., 1974; Pub. Affairs Reporting award Am. Polit. Sci. Assn., 1971, Ind. Reporting award AP Mng. Editors, 1976, Newswriting awards Ind. Pub. Health Assn., 1972-74, Amos Tuck Media award Dartmouth Coll., 1977. Mem. Soc. Am. Bus. and Econ. Writers, Soc. Profl. Journalists. Home: 144 Shore Dr Winthrop MA 02152-1286 Office: 275 Washington St Newton MA 02158-1646

STUNKARD, ALBERT JAMES, psychiatrist, educator; b. N.Y.C., Feb. 7, 1922; s. Horace Wesley and Frances (Klank) S. BS, Yale U., 1943; MD, Columbia U., 1945; MD (hon.), U. Edinburgh, 1992. Intern in medicine Mass. Gen. Hosp., Boston, 1945-46; resident physician psychiatry Johns Hopkins Hosp., 1948-51, rsch. fellow psychiatry, 1951-52; rsch. fellow medicine Columbia U. Svc., Goldwater Meml. Hosp., N.Y.C., 1952-53; Commonwealth rsch. fellow, then asst. prof. medicine Cornell U. Med. Coll., 1953-57; mem. faculty U. Pa., 1957-73, 76—, prof. psychiatry, 1962-73, 76—, Kenneth Appel prof. psychiatry, 1968-73, chmn. dept., 1962-73; prof. psychiatry Med. Sch., Stanford U., 1973-76. Contbr. articles on psychol., physiol., sociol. and genetic aspects of obesity to profl. jours. Capt. M.C., AUS, 1946-48. Ctr. for Advanced Study in Behavioral Scis. fellow, 1971-72, Dist. Service award Am. Psychiatric Association, 1994. Mem. Inst. Medicine of NAS, Am. Assn. of Chmn. of Depts. of Psychiatry (past pres.), Acad. Behavioral Medicine Rsch. (past pres.), Am. Psychosomatic Soc. (past pres.), Assn. Rsch. in Nervous and Mental Diseases (past pres.), Soc. Behavioral Medicine (past pres.). Achievements include contributions to the behavioral and pharmacological treatment of obesity and to understanding of sociological, physiological, psychological and genetic contributions to the disorder. Office: U Pa Sch Medicine Dept Psychiatry 3600 Market St Ste 734 Philadelphia PA 19104-2611

STUNTEBECK, CLINTON A., lawyer; b. Hibbing, Minn., May 25, 1938; s. Robert F. and S. Mary (Conti) S.; m. Mary Joan Carmody, Nov. 23, 1963; children: Robin, M. Alison, Susan, John, William. BA in Psychology, U. Minn., 1960; LLB, U. Maine, 1968. Bar: Pa. 1969, U.S. Dist. Ct. (ea. dist.) Pa. 1969. Ptnr. Schnader, Harrison, Segal & Lewis, Phila., 1968—; bd. dirs. Markel Corp., Greater Phila. First Partnership for Econ. Devel.; lectr. corp. and securities law. Contbr. articles to profl. jours. Pres. Radnor (Pa.) Twp. Bd. Commn., 1981-83, 92—; trustee Cabrini Coll. Capt. USAF, 1960-65. Mem. ABA, Am. Law Inst., Pa. Bar Assn., Phila. Bar Assn., Securities Industry Assn. (law and compliance com.), U. Maine Law Alumni Assn. (pres. 1974-76), Union League Phila., Phila. Country Club, Sunday Breakfast Club, Corinthian Yacht Club. Avocations: sailing, skiing, golf, tennis. Home: 371 Rose Glen Dr Wayne PA 19087-4410 Office: Schnader Harrison Segal 1600 Market St Ste 3600 Philadelphia PA 19103-7240

STUPAK, BART T., congressman, lawyer; b. Feb. 29, 1952; m. Laurie Ann Olsen; children: Ken, Bart Jr. AA in Criminal Justice, Northwestern Mich. C.C., Traverse City, 1972; BS in Criminal Justice, Saginaw Valley State Coll., 1977; JD, Thomas M. Cooley Law Sch., 1981. Patrolman Escanaba City Police Dept., 1972-73; state trooper Mich. Dept. State Police, 1973-84; instr. State Police Tng. Acad., 1980-82; atty., 1981-84, Hansley, Neiman, Peterson, Beauchamp, Stupak, Bergman P.C., 1984-85; ptnr. Stupak, Bergman, Stupak P.C., 1985-88; mem. Mich. Ho. of Reps., 1989-90; prin. Bart T. Stupak P.C., 1991—; mem. 103rd-104th Congresses from 1st Mich. dist., 1993—; mem. commerce subcom. on health & environment. Nat. committeeman Boy Scouts Am., coach Menominee Youth Baseball Assn., Little League; active Wildlife Unltd., Menominee Woods and Streams Assn., Menominee County Hist. Soc.; adv. com. Bay Pines Juv. Detection Ctr. Mem. Nat. Rifle Assn., Sons of the Am. Legion, Knights of Columbus, Elks Club, State Employees Retirees Assn., fin. com. Holy Spirit Catholic Ch. Democrat. Office: US Ho of Reps 317 Cannon Ho Ofc Bldg Washington DC 20515*

STURDEVANT, WAYNE ALAN, data processing executive, educator; b. Portland, Oreg., Apr. 3, 1946; s. Hervey Sturdevant and Georgia (Rawls) Bright; m. Helen F. Radbury, Sept. 24, 1976; children: Wayne Alan Jr., Stephen Thomas, John Howard; children from previous marriage: Brian Alan, Daniel Robert. BS in Edn., So. Ill. U., 1980. With USAF, 1964-85, supt. Air Force on the job tng. adv. svc., 1978-82; chief USAF On-Job-Tng., 1982-85; ret., 1985; lead engr. instl. tech. McDonnell Douglas Corp., St. Louis, 1985-88; mgr., instr. sys. design Southeastern Computer Cons., Inc., Austin, 1988—; developed advanced concepts in occupational edn. and computer-based tng. design, innovations in support of ISO 9000. Contbr. articles on mgmt. and tng. innovations in the work place to profl. jours.

Bishop LDS Ch., 1983-84, mem. stake presidency, 1990—; mem. exec. bd. Boy Scouts Am., 1986—. Recognized for leadership in multi-nat. programs; recipient Citation of Honor Air Force Assn., 1980, Award of Merit Boy Scouts Am., 1996. Mem. Internat. Orgn. for Standardization. Republican. Avocations: reading, camping. Home: 9214 Independence Loop Austin TX 78748-6312

STURDIVANT, FREDERICK DAVID, consultant, business educator; b. Whitewright, Tex., Oct. 17, 1937; s. Wyatt A. and Juanita P. (Phillips) S.; m. Patricia A. Robinson, Dec. 22, 1959 (div. 1981); children—Kaira, Lisha, Brian.; m. Teresa A. Mobley, Feb. 3, 1982. B.S., San Jose State Coll., 1959; M.B.A., U. Oreg., 1960; Ph.D., Northwestern U., 1963. Asst. prof. U. So. Calif., 1964-67; assoc. prof. U. Tex. at Austin, 1967-70, Harvard U., 1970-72; M. Riklis prof. bus. and its environment Ohio State U., Columbus, 1972-84; mng. dir. Gemini Mgmt. Consulting, San Francisco, 1984-96; dir. Progressive Corp., Cleve., 1973-81, State Savs., Columbus, 1975-86, Actmedia, N.Y.C., 1977-80, Fel-Pro, Inc., Chgo., 1987—; bd. trustees Mktg. Sci. Inst., Cambridge, Mass., 1992—; mem. Task Force on Mktg. and Low-Income Consumers, Nat. Mktg. Adv. Com., Dept. Commerce, 1967-70; cons. Office Calif. Atty. Gen., 1966, Sen. Charles Percy, 1968; mem. adv. coun. on urban affairs to lt. gov., Tex., 1969-70; dir. rsch. Robert N. Shamansky of Ohio Congl. Campaign, 1980. Author: (with others) Competition and Human Behavior, 1968, The Ghetto Marketplace, 1969, Managerial Analysis in Marketing, 1970, Growth Through Serivce: The Story of American Hospital Supply Corporation, 1970, Perspectives in Marketing Management, 1971 (with O. Smalley) The Credit Merchants: A History of Spiegel, Inc, 1973 (with A. Andreasen) Minorities and Marketing: Research Challenges, 1977, Business and Society: A Managerial Approach, 4th edit, 1990, The Corporate Social Challenge, 5th edit., 1994; contbr. articles to profl. jours. Recipient CBA Teaching Excellence award, 1968, Jack G. Taylor Teaching Excellence award, 1969, Cactus Teaching Excellence award, 1970. Mem. Am. Mktg. Assn., Assn. for Consumer Research, Southwestern Social Sci. Assn., Bus. and Society Initiative Council, Acad. of Mgmt., Beta Gamma Sigma. Democrat. Home: 10130 Oakwood Cir Carmel CA 93923-8004 Office: Gemini Mgmt Consulting 1 Montgomery St Fl 17 San Francisco CA 94104-4505

STURGE, MICHAEL DUDLEY, physicist; b. Bristol, Eng., May 25, 1931; came to U.S., 1961, naturalized 1991; s. Paul Dudley and Rachel (Graham) S.; m. Mary Balk, Aug. 21, 1956; children: David Mark, Thomas Graham, Peter Daniel, Benedict Paul. BA in Engring. and Physics, Gonville and Caius Coll., Cambridge, Eng., 1952; PhD in Physics, Cambridge U., Eng., 1957. Mem. staff Mullard Rsch. Lab. (now Philips), Redhill, Eng., 1956-58; sr. rsch. fellow Royal Radar Establishment, Malvern, Eng., 1958-61; mem. tech. staff Bell Labs., Murray Hill, N.J., 1961-83, Bellcore, Red Bank, N.J., 1984-86; prof. dept. physics Dartmouth Coll., Hanover, N.H., 1986—; rsch. assoc. Stanford U., 1965, U. B.C., Vancouver, Can., 1969; vis. prof. Technion, Haifa, Israel, 1972, 76, 81, 85, Williams Coll., Williamstown, Mass., 1982, 84, Trinity Coll., Dublin, 1989, 93, U. Fourier, Grenoble, France, 1989, 91; exch. scientist Philips Rsch. Lab., Eindhoven, The Netherlands, 1973-74; vis. scholar U. Sheffield, Eng., 1996. Contbr. over 100 papers in solid state physics to profl. publs.; co-editor: Excitons, 1982; editor Jour. of Luminescence, 1984-90. Fellow Am. Phys. Soc.; mem. Am. Assn. Physics Tchrs. Office: Dartmouth Coll Dept Physics Wilder Lab Hanover NH 03755-3528

STURGEN, WINSTON, photographer, printmaker, artist; b. Harrisburg, Pa., Aug. 27, 1938; s. George Winston and Gladys Erma (Lenker) S.; m. Nancy Kathryn Otto, Jan. 23, 1959 (div. 1981); 1 child, Bruce Eugene Sturgen; m. Jessica Sheldon, Mar. 15, 1988. BS in Forestry, Pa. State U., 1960; postgrad., U. N.H., 1961-62; M of Forestry, Pa. State U., 1964; postgrad., U. Oreg., 1966-68. Cert. profl. photographer. Devel. engr. Weyerhaeuser Co., Longview, Wash., 1964-66; mgr. Wickes Lumber Co., Elkhorn, Wis., 1968-70; dir. ops. Wickes Wanderland, Inc., Delavan, Wis., 1970-72; owner, mgr. Sturgen's Cleaners, Delavan, 1972-80, Images by Sturgen, Delavan, 1980-84; instr. photography continuing edn. dept. Western N.Mex. U., 1988-90; juror numerous orgns., 1982—. One-man shows include Artesia (N.Mex.) Mus. and Art Ctr., 1992, Delavan Art Mus., 1984, Donnell Libr., N.Y.C., 1992; exhibited in group shows at Carlsbad (N.Mex.) Mus., 1992, Sister Kenny Inst., 1992, (3rd Pl.), 93 (1st Pl.), 94, Deming Ctr. for the Arts, N.Mex., 1991, Shellfish Collection, Silver City, N.Mex., 1989, 90, 91, 92, 93, Thompson Gallery, U. N.Mex., 1989, Profl. Photographers Assn. of N.Mex., 1985, 86, 87, 88 (awards), Union Gallery, U. N.Mex., 1987, Gallery Sigala, Taos, N.Mex., 1986, World Trade Ctr., N.Y.C., 1992, 93, 94, Internat. Exposition of Photography, 1983, 84, 85, 87, Beyond Photography Touring Exhibit, 1991-92, An Am. Collection Touring Exhibit, San Francisco, Washington, Brussels, Tokyo, 1993-95, Sapporo (Japan) Internat. Print Biennial, 1993, Very Spl. Arts/N.Mex. Touring Exhibit, 1993-94, Ctr. Contemporary Art, St. Louis, 1994 (Purchase award), many others; pub. poetry, numerous articles in field. Founder, chmn. Winter Arts Festival, Silver City, N.Mex., 1988-90; com. mem. Taos Fall Arts Festival, 1985; com. chair Oktoberfest, Delavan, 1976-80. Residency grant Wurlitzer Found., 1987, 89. Mem. Very Spl. Artists N.Mex., Very Spl. Artists Washington, Enabled Artists United, Fuller Lodge Art Ctr. Avocations: painting, printmaking, photography. Home: C 116 Henderson Creek Dr Naples FL 33961

STURGEON, CHARLES EDWIN, management consultant; b. Cherryvale, Kans., May 30, 1928; s. William Charles and Lucile Myrtle (Gill) S.; children by previous marriage: Carol Ann, John Randolph, Richard Steven; m. Karen B. Riggan, May 21, 1988. A.A., Independence Jr. Coll., 1948; B.S., U. Kans., 1951; postgrad., U. Tulsa Grad. Sch., 1953-56; grad., Advanced Mgmt. Program, Harvard Bus. Sch., 1977. Research engr. Stanoline Oil and Gas, Tulsa, 1953-56; production supr. Vulcan Materials Co., Wichita, Kans., 1956-62; maintenance supt. Vulcan Materials Co., 1962-64, mgr. tech. services, 1964-69; plant mgr. Vulcan Materials Co., Newark, N.J., 1970-71; gen. mktg. mgr., v.p. mktg. Vulcan Materials Co., Wichita, 1971-73; v.p. mfg. Vulcan Materials Co., Birmingham, Ala., 1974-77, pres. chem. div., 1977-87, pres., sr. v.p., 1987-90; prin. CESCO Cons. Co., Birmingham, 1990—, Birmingham, Ala., 1990. Adv. U. Kans. Sch. Chem. Engring. Served with U.S. Army, 1951-53. Mem. Am. Inst. Chem. Engrs., Nat. Mgmt. Assn., Chlorine Inst. (bd. dirs.), Chem. Mfg. Assn., Soc. Chem. Industries, Soc. of Materials, The Club Inc., Tau Theta Pi, Tau Beta Pi, Sigma Tau. Republican. Presbyterian. Office: CESCO Cons Co 2628 Apollo Cir Birmingham AL 35226-2664

STURGES, HOLLISTER, III, museum director; b. Kingston, N.Y., July 1, 1939; s. Hollister Jr. and Elizabeth (Betz) S.; m. Caroline Berg (div.); children: Kimberly, William Steele.; m. Judith Layson; 1 child, Elizabeth Layson. BA in Comparative Lit., Cornell U., 1962; MA in Art History, U. Calif., Berkeley, 1969, MPh in Art History, 1972. Cert. tchr., Calif. Tchr. English Placer High Sch., Auburn, Calif., 1963-66; instr. U. Mo., Kansas City, 1972-80; curator European art Joslyn Art Mus., Omaha, 1980-84; chief curator Indpls. Mus. Arts, 1984-87; dir. Springfield (Mass.) Mus. Fine Arts, 1988—, George Walter Vincent Smith Art Mus., 1988-95; exec. dir. Bruce Mus., Greenwich, Conn., 1995—; Panelist NEA, 1982, 86, 90; organizer art exhbns. Author: (exhbn. catalogue) Angels and Urchins: Images of Children at the Joslyn, 1980, (exhbn. catalogue) Jules Breton and the French Rural Tradition, 1982, (exhbn. catalogue) New Art from Puerto Rico, 1990; co-author: (exhbn. catalogue) Art of the Fantastic: Latin America, 1920-87, 1987; author, editor: The Rural Vision: France and Americans in the late Nineteenth Century, 1987; author, co-editor: (mus. catalogue) Joslyn Art Museum Paintings and Sculptures from the Permanent Collections, 1987, (mus. handbook) Indianapolis Museum of Art: collections handbook, 1988. Bd. dirs. World Affairs Coun., 1989. Kress Found. fellow, 1974. Mem. Coll. Art Assn., Am. Assn. Mus., New Eng. Mus. Assn. Avocations: squash, canoeing, chess. Office: Bruce Museum 1 Museum Dr Greenwich CT 06830

STURGES, JOHN SIEBRAND, consultant; b. Greenwich, Conn., Feb. 12, 1939; s. Harry Wilton and Elizabeth Helen (Niewenhous) S.; AB, Harvard U., 1960; MBA, U. So. Calif., 1965; cert. EDP, N.Y.U., 1972; cert. exec. program. Grad. Sch. Bus., U. Mich., 1982. Cert. sr. profl. in human resources, mgmt. cons.; m. Anastasia Daphne Bakalis, May 6, 1967; children: Christina Aurora, Elizabeth Athena. With Equitable Life Assurance Soc. U.S., N.Y.C., 1965-79, mgr. systems devel., 1965-70, dir. compensation and benefits, 1971-75, v.p., personnel and adminstrv. svcs., 1975-79; sr. v.p. personnel Nat. Westminster Bank U.S.A., N.Y.C., 1979-82; corp. sr. v.p. adminstrn. and human resources Willis-Corroon Corp., N.Y.C., 1982-84; mng. dir. human resources Marine Midland Bank, N.Y.C., 1984-87; mng. dir. Siebrand-Wilton Assocs., N.Y.C., 1986-87, pres., 1987—. Lay reader St. Peters Episcopal Ch., Freehold, N.J., 1972—. Lt. USNR, 1960-65. Mem. Internat. Found. Employee Benefit Plans, Commerce Assocs., Soc. for Human Resource Mgmt. (dir. 1979—), Am. Compensation Assn., Human Resources Planning Soc., Inst. Mgmt. Cons. (bd. dirs. 1992—), Employment Mgmt. Assn. (bd. dirs. 1993—), Monmouth-Ocean Devel. Coun. (dir. 1989-95), Beta Gamma Sigma (dir. N.Y. 1978—), Phi Kappa Phi. Republican. Clubs: India House, Harvard (N.Y.C., Boston, Princeton, N.J., dir. 1991—), Nassau Club. Office: Siebrand-Wilton Assocs Inc PO Box 2498 New York NY 10008-2498

STURGES, SHERRY LYNN, recording industry executive; b. Long Beach, Calif., Dec. 11, 1946; d. Howard George and Alice Myrtle (Waymire) Fairbairn; m. Jeffery Alan Sturges, Dec. 30, 1969; children: Allisun Malinda, Jay. Grad. high sch., Las Vegas, Nev. V.p. Soultime, Inc., Las Vegas, 1968-69, Universe, Inc., Las Vegas, 1971-76; co-developer, owner Fun Trax Music Video and Audio Recording Studios, Westwood, Calif., 1986—; creative cons. John Debella Show, 1990, M.T.V., L.A., 1990, KCET-TV, L.A., 1990, KTLA-TV, L.A., 1991. Officer PTA, Woodland Hills, Calif., 1977-86, pres., 1984-86; vol. Connie Stevens Charity Orgn., Beverly Hills, Calif., 1980-84; vol. Crossroads Sch. for Arts and Sci., Westwood Meth. presch., West L.A. Bapt. Sch., Northridge United Meth. Ch., St. Vincent's Parents Coun., St. Joseph the Worker Sch., Chatsworth H.S., Sepulveda Nursery Sch., Nat. Neurofibromatosis Found., Life Steps Found., Westwood Village Assn. Recipient Outstanding Contribution award L.A. Unified Sch. Dist. Republican. Avocations: collecting dolls, plates and figurines. Office: Fun Trax Inc 22270 Del Valle St Woodland Hills CA 91364-1515

STURGIS, ROBERT SHAW, architect; b. Boston, July 8, 1922; s. George and Rosamond Thomas (Bennett) S.; m. Chiquita Mitchell, Dec. 20, 1947; children: Susanna Jordan, Roger Bennett, John Hanson, Ellen Shaw. Grad., St. Mark's Sch., Southboro, Mass., 1939; AB, Harvard, 1947, MArch, 1951. Architect Kilham, Hopkins, Greeley & Brodie, Boston, 1952-55, Shepley, Bulfinch, Richardson & Abbott, Boston, 1955-64, Robert S. Sturgis, Boston, 1964-68; ptnr. Feloney & Sturgis (architects), Cambridge, 1969-75, Robert Sturgis, FAIA, 1975—; head critic Boston Archtl. Ctr., 1955-66, instr., 1988—, chair edn. com., 1989-95; dir., 1971-93, 95—; vis. lectr. Va. Poly. Inst., Blacksburg, 1970, Boston U., Yale U., 1975; urban design cons. Haverhill, Lynn and Cambridge, Mass., also, Atlanta.; mem. overseers' vis. com. Sch. Design Harvard, 1965-70; chmn. Gov.'s Task Force Arts and Cultural Facilities, 1972; chmn. bd., lectr. Boston Archtl. Center, 1981-85; cons. Maine State Capitol com., 1989-90. Prin. works include Cotting House, Harvard Bus. Sch., 1968, Architects' Plan for Boston, 1961, AIA Urban Design Assistance Team Program, 1967; urban designs for, Atlanta, Haverhill, Kendall Sq., Cambridge; contbr. articles to profl. jours. Served with USAAF, 1942-45. Fellow AIA (chmn. urban planning and design com. 1970, mem. planned growth task group 1988-92, Presdl. citation 1988); mem. Boston Soc. Architects (pres. 1972, chmn. civic design com. 1959-67, chmn. regional design com. 1988—, mem. joint regional transp. com. 1994—). Home and Office: 5 Doublet Hill Rd Weston MA 02193-2304

STURLEY, MICHAEL F., law educator; b. Syracuse, N.Y., Feb. 14, 1955; s. Richard Avern and Helen Elizabeth (Fisher) S.; m. Michele Y. Deitch, July 2, 1989; 1 child, Jennifer Diane Starley. BA, Yale U., 1977, JD, 1981; BA in Jurisprudence, Oxford U., 1980, MA, 1985. Bar: N.Y. 1984, U.S. Dist. Ct. (so. and ea. dists.) N.Y. 1984, U.S. Supreme Ct. 1987. Law clk. to Judge Amalya L. Kearse, U.S. Ct. Appeals for 2d Cir., N.Y.C., 1981-82; law clk. to Justice Lewis F. Powell, Jr. U.S. Supreme Ct., Washington, 1982-83; assoc. Sullivan & Cromwell, N.Y.C., 1983-84; asst. prof. law U. Tex. Law Sch., Austin, 1984-88, prof., 1988—; vis. prof. Queen Mary and Westfield Coll., U. London, 1990, advisor Restatement (3d) of Property (servitudes), 1989—. Compiler, editor: The Legislative History of the Carriage of Goods by Sea Act and the Travaux Préparatoires of The Hague Rules, 3 vols., 1990; mem. editl. bd. Jour. Maritime Law and Commerce, 1989—, book rev. editor, 1993—; contbg. author: Benedict on Admiralty, 1990—; contbr. articles to legal jours. Mem. Am. Law Inst., Maritime Law Assn. (proctor). Office: U Tex Sch Law 727 E 26th St Austin TX 78705-3224

STURM, NICHOLAS, biological sciences educator, author; b. Meriden, W.Va., Dec. 19, 1931; s. Henry Earl and Beulah Agnes (Coffman) S. BS, W.Va. Wesleyan Coll., 1952; MS, Purdue U., 1955; postgrad., U. Tex., 1956-59. Head sci. dept. S.W. Tex. Jr. Coll., Uvalde, 1959-61; instr. Amarillo (Tex.) Coll., 1961-64; asst. prof. Youngstown (Ohio) U., 1964-67; prof. biol. scis. Youngstown State U., 1967-95, prof. emeritus, 1995—; cons. on edn. texts various pubs., 1969-90; field editor various pubs., 1972-86; cons. on computer applications S&S Software, Youngstown, 1986-95, Philippi, 1995—. Author: Exploring Life, 1972, 3d edit., 1986, (computer software) Natural Selection, 1992. Mem. Am. Fern. Soc. (life), Brit. Lichen Soc., Antiquus Mysticusque Orda Rosae Cruris. Avocations: photography, local history, nature study, computer programming, multimedia design. Office: Youngstown State U 410 Wick Ave Youngstown OH 44555-0001

STURMAN, LAWRENCE STUART, health research administrator; b. Detroit, Mar. 13, 1938; married, 1959; 4 children. BS, Northwestern U., 1957, MS, MD, 1960; PhD in Virology, Rockefeller U., 1968. Intern Hosp. Univ. Pa., 1960-61; staff assoc. virology Nat. Inst. Allergy and Infectious Disease, 1968-70; rsch. physician virology Wadsworth Ctr. N.Y. State Dept. Health, 1970-92, dir. divsn. clin. sci., 1989-92, dir., 1992—; asst. prof. microbiology and immunology Albany Med. Coll., 1979-93; chmn., prof. dept. biomed. sci. Sch. Pub. Health N.Y. State U., Albany, 1985—. Mem. AAAS, Am. Soc. Microbiology, Am. Soc. Virology, N.Y. Acad. Sci., Sigma Xi. Achievements include research in viral pathogenesis; public health, scientific basis of public health practice; biomedical research and public policy; laboratory regulation/quality assurance; graduate education in biomedical sciences; viral disease. Office: NY State Dept Health Wadsworth Ctr Labs & Rsch Albany NY 12201*

STURROCK, THOMAS TRACY, botany educator, horticulturist; b. Havana, Cuba, Dec. 9, 1921; s. David and Ruth Esther (Earle) S. (parents U.S. citizens); m. Jeanne Norquist, June 30, 1948; children—Nancy Elizabeth, John David, Barbara Jeanne Sturrock Morris, Catherine Ann Sturrock Hilliard, Robert Charles. B.S. in Agr. with honors, U. Fla., Gainesville, 1943, M.S. in Agr, 1943, Ph.D., 1961. Ptnr. Sturrock Tropical Fruit Nursery, 1946-56; insp. Fla. State Plant Bd., 1956-57; tchr. Palm Beach (Fla.) High Sch., 1957-58; research asst. U. Fla., 1958-60; instr. Palm Beach Jr. Coll., 1960-64; asst. prof. botany Fla. Atlantic U., 1964-68, assoc. prof., 1968-74, prof., 1974-89, prof. emeritus, 1989—, asst. dean Coll. Sci., 1971-89. Pres. West Palm Beach Jaycees, 1951-52; scoutmaster Gulf Stream council Boy Scouts Am., 1946-55, cubmaster, 1960-62, dist. chmn., 1961-63, exec. bd., 1961—, v.p., 1969-70, 80—. Served with USAAF, 1943-46. Recipient Silver Beaver award, 1951, Disting. Eagle Scout award Boy Scouts Am., 1989. Mem. Fla. Hort. Soc., Fla. Acad. Scis., Sigma Xi. Presbyterian. Home: 1010 Camellia Rd West Palm Beach FL 33405-2408

STURTEVANT, BRERETON, retired lawyer, former government official; b. Washington, Nov. 24, 1921; d. Charles Lyon and Grace (Brereton) S. B.A., Wellesley Coll., 1942; J.D., Temple U., 1949; postgrad., U. Del., 1969-71. Bar: D.C. 1949, Del. 1950. Research chemist E.I. duPont DeNemours & Co., 1942-50; law clk. Del. Supreme Ct., 1950; gen. practice law Wilmington, Del., 1950-57; partner Connolly, Bove & Lodge, Wilmington, 1957-71; examiner-in-chief U.S. Patent and Trademark Office Bd. Appeals, Washington, 1971-88; Adj. prof. law Georgetown U., 1974-79. Trustee Holton-Arms Sch., Bethesda, Md., 1977—, chmn. or mem. all coms., mem. trustee com. and bldgs./grounds com., 1994—. Mem. Am., Del. bar assns., Exec. Women in Govt. (charter mem., chmn. 1978-79). Episcopalian. Clubs: Wellesley College, Washington-Wellesley (pres. 1982-84). Home: 1227 Morningside Ln Alexandria VA 22308-1042

STURTEVANT, JULIAN MUNSON, biophysical chemist, educator; b. Edgewater, N.J., Aug. 9, 1908; s. Edgar Howard and Bessie Fitch (Skinner) S.; m. Elizabeth Reihl, June 8, 1929; children: Ann Sturtevant Ormsby, Bradford. AB, Columbia U., 1927; PhD, Yale U., 1931; ScD (hon.), Ill. Coll., 1962; Sc.D. (hon.), Regensberg U., 1978. Instr. chemistry Yale U., New Haven, 1931-39, asst. prof., 1939-46, assoc. prof., 1946-51, prof., 1951-77, sr. research scientist, 1977—; staff mem. Radiation Lab., MIT, Cambridge, 1943-46; vis. prof. U. Calif.-San Diego, 1966-67, 69-70; vis. fellow Battelle Seattle Research Ctr. and U. Wash., 1972-73, Stanford U., 1976-77. Contbr. numerous articles to profl. jours. Recipient Huffman award Calorimetry Conf. U.S.A., 1964; William DeVane award Yale U., 1978; Innovator in Biochemistry award Med. Coll. Va., 1984, Wilbur Cross medal Yale U., 1987; Guggenheim fellow Cambridge U., 1955-56; Fulbright scholar U. Adelaide, Australia, 1962-63; vis. scholar, Stanford U., 1975-76; Alexander von Humboldt sr. scientist award, 1978-79. Fellow AAAS, Am. Acad. Arts and Scis.; mem. Nat. Acad. Sci., Am. Chem. Soc., Am. Soc. Biol. Chemists, Conn. Acad. Sci. and Tech.

STURTEVANT, PETER MANN, JR., television news executive; b. Northampton, Mass., Feb. 27, 1943; s. Peter Mann and Katharine Bryan (Hobson) S.; m. Anne Elizabeth Fitzpatrick, July 12, 1969 (div. Dec. 1984); 1 child, Amanda Hadden; m. Toni E. Siegel, Apr. 14, 1985; 1 child, Gillian Lee. BA, Wilmington Coll., 1965; MA, U. Iowa, 1967. Assoc. prodr. CBS News, Washington, 1967-71; bur. chief Viet Nam CBS News, Saigon, 1971-73; nat. news editor CBS News, N.Y.C., 1974-80, asst. v.p. spl. events, 1981-83, producer 60 Minutes, 1984-85; exec. news editor CNN, N.Y.C., 1985-86; prodr. Today's Bus. Buena Vista TV, N.Y.C., 1987; dir. news coverage CNBC, N.Y.C., 1988-90; v.p., mng. editor CNBC, Ft. Lee, N.J., 1991-94; sr. v.p. Internat. Bus. News NBC, 1994—. Named Disting. Alumnus, Wilmington Coll., 1975; named to Journalism Hall of Fame, U. Iowa Sch. Journalism, 1988. Mem. Nat. Acad. Cable Programming (nominated ACE award 1992, 93, 94), Soc. Profl. Journalists, Deadline Club N.Y., The Asia Soc. Episcopalian. Avocations: racquet sports, landscaping, travelling, philately, parenting. Home: 90 Riverside Dr New York NY 10024-5306 Office: NBC 30 Rockefeller Plz New York NY 10112

STURTZ, DONALD LEE, physician, naval officer; b. Coshocton, Ohio, Apr. 18, 1933; s. Walter Raymond and Helene Josephine (Kubic) S.; m. Alice Marie McGuire, June 11, 1955; children: Jimalee, Janel. BS, U.S. Navel Acad., Annapolis, Md., 1955; MD, U. Pa., 1965. Diplomate Am. Bd. Surgery. Surg. resident USN, Phila., 1965-70; ship's surgeon USN, 1970-71; staff surgeon Bethesda Naval Hosp., USN, 1971-80; chief of surgery San Diego Naval Hosp., USN, 1980-84; exec. officer Oakland (Calif.) Naval Hosp., USN, 1984-85; prof. clin. surgery USN, Bethesda, Md., 1985-87; commd. Naval Med. Command USN, 1987-88; fleet surgeon USN, Norfolk, Va., 1989-91; surgeon USUHS, Bethesda, Md., 1991—. Contbr. articles to profl. jours. Recipient B.D. Larrey award for Surgical Excellence, Surgical Dept. USUHS, Bethesda, 1988. Fellow ACS (gov. 1985-88); mem. Am. Assn. for Surgery of Trauma, Assn. Mil. Surgeons, USN Inst. Republican. Methodist. Avocations: travel, antiquing, music, reading. Office: USUHS Dept Surgery 4301 Jones Bridge Rd Bethesda MD 20814-4712

STUTZMAN, THOMAS CHASE, SR., lawyer; b. Portland, Oreg., Aug. 1, 1950; s. Leon H. and Mary L. (Chase) S.; B.A. with high honors, U. Calif., Santa Barbara, 1972; J.D. cum laude, Santa Clara U., 1975; m. Wendy Jeanne Craig, June 6, 1976; children: Sarah Ann, Thomas ChaseJr. Bar: Calif. 1976, cert. Family Law Specialist, 1992; individual practice law, San Jose, Calif., 1976-79; pres., sec., CFO Thomas Chase Stutzman, P.C., San Jose, 1979—; legal counsel, asst. sec. Cen. Valley Cirs., Inc., Cypress Human Resources, Inc., EPACK, Inc., DMJ Pro Care, Inc., Sparacino's Foods, Inc., Tax Firm, Inc., United Charities, Marina Assocs. Inc., Midnight Fraction Mine Inc., Forbord Enterprises, D.A.M. Good Engring./Mfg., Inc., E.M.I. Oil Filtration Systems, Inc., China Villa, Inc., Creative Pacifica, Inc., Am. West Furniture Mfg., Inc., Cody Electronics, Inc., Advanfab Corp., Am. First Tech., Analog Engring., Inc., AVS Seating & Fixture Co., Inc.Excel-Law Video, Inc., First Am. Real Estate Financing Co., Hoffman Industries, Inc., Info. Scan Tech., Inc., PRD Construction Mgmt. Svcs., Unifed Homes, Inc.; instr. San Jose State U., 1977-78. Bd. dirs. Santa Cruz Campfire, 1978-80, Happy Hollow Park, 1978-80, 83-86, Pacific Neighbors, pres., 1991-92. Mem. Calif. Bar Assn., Santa Clara County Bar Assn. (chmn. environ. law com. 1976-78, exec. com. family law, exec. com. fee arbitration com.), Assn. Cert. Law Specialist, San Jose Jaycees (Dir. of the Year 1976-77), Almadon Valley Rotary Club, Phi Beta Kappa. Congregationalist. Lodges: Lions (dir. 1979-81, 2d v.p. 1982-83, 1st v.p. 1983-84, pres. 1984-85), Masons, Scottish Rite. Office: 1625 The Alameda Ste 309 San Jose CA 95126-2223

STUTZMAN, WARREN LEE, electrical engineer, educator; b. Elgin, Ill., Oct. 22, 1941; s. James Earl and Christina Louise (Steidinger) S.; m. Claudia Janeanne Morris, Dec. 20, 1964; children: Darren Morris, Dana Lynn. BEE, U.Ill., 1964, AB in Math., 1964; MEE, Ohio State U., 1965, PhD in Elec. Engring., 1969. Asst. prof. Va. Poly. Inst. and State U., Blacksburg, 1969-74, assoc. prof., 1974-79, prof., 1979—, Thomas Phillips prof. engring., 1992—. Author: (with G. Thiele) Antenna Theory and Design, 1981, Polarization in Electromagnetic Systems, 1993. Fellow IEEE. Office: Va Poly Inst & State U Elec Engring Dept Blacksburg VA 24061-0111

STUTZMANN, NATHALIE, classical vocalist; b. Paris. Student piano, bassoon and chamber music, Ecole de l'Opéra de Paris. Performer: (operatic prodns.) Debussy's Pelleas et Mélisande, Florence and Bonn, Mussorgsky's Boris Godunov at the Liceu, Barcelona, Bordeaux, Gounod's Romeo et Juliette, Zurich, Mozart's Die Zauberflöte, Opéra de Paris Bastille, Aix-en-Provence Festival; apperances in recitals include: London Wigmore Hall, Amsterdam Concertgebouw, Salle Gaveau, St. Denis Festival, Alte Oper; vocal performances include: Mahler Third Symphony, Weisbaden, (with Gary Bertini) Knaben Wunderhorn, Stuttgart, Kindertotenlieder, Paris, Lugano, (with Nicolas Harnoncourt) Bach's St. Matthew's Passion, (with Maestro Wolfgang Sawallisch) Bach's St. John's Passion, Italy, Ombra Felice, London Symphony Orchestra; participated in numerous audio and video recordings. Recipient Deutsche Schallplattenkritik prize for Schumann recording, 1993. Office: care Herbert H Breslin Inc 119 West 57th St Rm 1505 New York NY 10019

STUVER, FRANCIS EDWARD, former railway car company executive; b. Greenville, Pa., Aug. 22, 1912; s. Willard Seeley and Anna Katherine (Henry) S.; m. Jessie Lucile Bright, Jan. 26, 1938; children: Robert Edward, Nancy (Mrs. Randolph Patrick Mutdosch). Grad. high sch. With Greenville Steel Car Co. (subsidiary Pitts. Forgings Co.), 1937—, chief accountant, 1944-46, asst. treas., 1946-54, asst. sec., 1948-56, treas., 1956-61, v.p., 1956-61, exec. v.p., 1961-75, ret., 1975; pres. Greenville Savs. & Loan Assn., 1977-83, dir., 1949-83; dir. Greenville Steel Car Co., 1961-74, Pitts. Forgings Co., 1975-80. Bd. dirs. Municipal Authority Borough Greenville, 1946-74, treas., 1946-73; bd. dirs., mem. exec. com. Mercer County br. Pa. Economy League, 1949-64; bd. dirs., treas., chmn. finance com. Greenville Hosp., 1953-59. Mem. Am. Ry. Car Inst. (dir. 1964-75). Clubs: Masons, Elks, Moose, KP, Greenville Country. Home: 46 Chambers Ave Greenville PA 16125-1856 Office: Greenville Steel Car Co Foot of Union St Greenville PA 16125

STUZIN, CHARLES BRYAN, savings and loan association executive; b. Miami, Fla., 1942. Grad., Univ. Fla., 1964, postgrad., 1967. With Stuzin and Camner, Miami, 1973—; pres. Citizens Savs. and Fin. Corp. (CSF Holdings Inc.), Miami, 1980—, chmn., 1982—, also chief exec. officer, bd. dirs.; now pres. S.F. Inc.; chmn. Citizens Mortgage Corp.; chmn., pres. Citizens Fed. Savs. and Loan; chmn., chief exec. officer Loan Am. Fin. Corp.; v.p., sec. Moore Ins. Agy.; ptnr. Webster Park Assocs., Sarasota Properties. Office: S.F. Inc 1221 Brickell Ave Miami FL 33131-3200*

STWALLEY, WILLIAM CALVIN, physics and chemistry educator; b. Glendale, Calif., Oct. 7, 1942; s. Calvin Murdoch and Diette Clarice (Hanson) S.; m. Mauricette Lucille Frisius, June 14, 1963; children—Kenneth William, Steven Edward. B.S., Calif. Inst. Tech., 1964; Ph.D., Harvard U., 1968. Asst. prof. U. Iowa, Iowa City, 1968-72, assoc. prof., 1972-75, prof. dept. chemistry, 1975-93, prof. dept. physics and astronomy, 1977-93, dir. Iowa Laser Facility, 1979-93, dir. Ctr. for Laser Sci. and Engring., 1987-89, George Glockler prof. physical scis., 1988-93; program dir. NSF, Washington, 1975-76 (leave of absence); prof. and head dept. physics, prof. chemistry U. Conn., Storrs, 1993—; program chmn. Internat. Laser Sci. Conf., 1985, co-chmn., 1986, chmn., 1987; lectr. Chinese Acad. Scis., 1986. Editor books in field; contbr. more than 240 articles to profl. pubs. Japan Soc. for Promotion of Sci. fellow, 1982; Sloan fellow, 1970-72; numerous grants in field, 1970—. Fellow Am. Phys. Soc. (sec.-treas. div. chem. physics 1984-90, vice chair/chair/past chair Topical Group on Laser Sci. 1989-92), Optical Soc. Am.; mem. AAAS, Am. Chem. Soc. Democrat. Avocations: comic books and cartoons, philately. Home: 21 Britainy Dr Mansfield Center CT 06250-1647 Office: Dept Physics U-46 U Conn Storrs CT 06269-3046

STYAN, JOHN LOUIS, English literature and theater educator; b. London, July 6, 1923; came to U.S., 1965; s. Louis and Constance Mary (Armstrong) S.; m. Constance W. M. Roberts, Nov. 17, 1945; children: Leigh, Day Campbell, Kim, Valentina Ebner. B.A., Cambridge (Eng.) U., 1947, M.A., 1948. Staff tutor lit., drama U. Hull, Eng., 1950-63; sr. staff tutor U. Hull, 1963-65; prof. English U. Mich., Ann Arbor, 1965-74, chmn. dept. English, 1973-74; Andrew Mellon prof. English U. Pitts., 1974-77; Franklyn Bliss Snyder prof. English lit. Northwestern U., 1977-87, prof. emeritus, 1987—, prof. theater, 1984-87, prof. theater emeritus, 1987—; chmn. acad. coun. Shakespeare Globe Theatre Ctr. (N.A.), 1981-87. Author: The Elements of Drama, 1960, The Dark Comedy, 1962, The Dramatic Experience, 1965, Shakespeare's Stagecraft, 1967, Chekhov in Performance, 1971, The Challenge of the Theatre, 1972, Drama Stage and Audience, 1975, The Shakespeare Revolution, 1977, Modern Drama in Theory and Practice, 3 vols, 1981, Max Reinhardt, 1982, All's Well That Ends Well, Shakespeare in Performance series, 1984, The State of Drama Study, 1984, Restoration Comedy in Performance, 1986. Served to lt. Royal Arty., 1941-45, Eng. Recipient Robert Lewis medal for lifetime achievement in theatre rsch. Kent State U., 1995; sr. rsch. fellow NEH, 1978-79, Guggenheim Found. fellow, 1983. Mem. Guild Drama Adjudicators, Brit. Drama League, MLA, Internat. Shakespeare Assn., Royal Over-Seas League. Home: Oak Apple Cottage, Barnes Ln, Milford on Sea Hampshire S041 0RP, England

STYCOS, JOSEPH MAYONE, demographer, educator; b. Saugerties, N.Y., Mar. 27, 1927; s. Stravos and Clotilda (Mayone) S.; m. Maria Nowakowska, Nov. 25, 1964; children: Steven Andrew, Christina Mayone (by previous marriage), Marek. AB, Princeton U., 1947; PhD, Columbia U., 1954. WithBur. Applied Social Rsch. Columbia U., 1948-50, lectr. sociology, 1951-52; project co-dir. U. P.R., 1952-53; postgrad. PC fellow U. N.C., 1954-55; assoc. prof. sociology St. Lawrence U., 1955-57; faculty Cornell U., Ithaca, N.Y., 1957—, prof. sociology, 1963—, chmn. dept., 1966-70, dir. Latin Am. program, 1962-66, dir. internat. population program, 1962-88, prof. rural sociology, 1987—, dir. population and devel. program, 1988-92; Fulbright-Hayes Disting. prof. U. Warsaw, Poland, 1979; external examiner U. Ife, Nigeria, 1973; Cons. AID, 1962-64; sr. cons. Population Council, 1963-74, 77-79; cons. Airlie Found., 1972-73, Inst. for Research in Social Behavior, 1974, Clapp & Mayne, Inc., 1974, Ford-Rockefeller Population Program, 1977, Nat. U. Costa Rica, 1979, U. P.R., 1979; trustee Population Reference Bur., 1964-68, cons., 1968-74; mem. exec. com. Internat. Planned Parenthood Fedn., West Hemmis, 1965-71, cons., 1971-77; adv. com. population and devel. OAS, 1968-70; mem. bd. Population Assn. Am., 1968-71, editorial cons. demography, 1965-69; adv. panel population Nat. Inst. Child Health and Human Devel., Dept. Health, Edn. and Welfare, 1969; co-chmn. population task force U.S. Nat. Commn. for UNESCO, 1972-73; adv. council, interdisciplinary communications program Smithsonian Instn., 1974-76; cons. Pan Am. Health Orgn., WHO, 1975; cons. steering com., acceptability task force WHO, 1978-85; cons. UNESCO, 1978-79, UN Fund for Population Activities, 1979-82, WHO, 1987-90; co-dir. Spanish family life project U. Complutense de Madrid, 1978-80; Fulbright-Hayes prof. Nat. U. Costa Rica, spring 1986; chmn. U.S. Census Adv. Com. on Population Stats., 1983-84; mem. Fulbright-Hays program Nat. Screening Com. Cen. Am., 1989-92. Author: (with Hussein Abdel Aziz Sayed, Roger Avery and Samuel Firdman) Community Development and Family Planning: An Egyptian Experiment, 1988; mem. editl. bd. Human Orgn., 1962-64; gen. editor Irvington Population and Demographic Series, 1974-78; cons. editor Studies in Family Planning, 1977—; editor: Demography as an Interdiscipline, 1989. Mem. council Cornell U., 1969-70. Mem. Rural Sociological Soc. Home: 28 Twin Glens Rd Ithaca NY 14850-1041 Office: Cornell U Population & Devel Program Warren Hall Ithaca NY 14853-7801

STYER, ANTOINETTE CARDWELL, middle school counselor; b. Martinsville, Va.; d. John E. Cardwell and I. Lois Cardwell Shelton; children: Yvette D., Christopher P. BA in Liberal Arts, Temple U., 1975; MEd in Elem./Secondary Sch. Counseling, Antioch U., Phila., 1980. cert. sec. prin., 1994. Sec. Edward S. Cooper, M.D., Phila., 1960-66; rsch. asst. Temple U., Phila., 1971-73; confidential sec. Sch. Dist. Phila., 1967-71, sec., 1974-76, social worker Child Care Ctr., 1976-86, sch. counselor elem. edn., 1986-89; secondary edn. counselor Sch. Dist. Phila. Roosevelt Mid. Sch., Phila., 1989—; sch. evaluator Mid. States Assn. of Colls. and Schs.; organizer Project Exposure: Bus.; chaperone student visit to colls., Atlanta; interviewee Nat. Opinion Rsch. Ctr., Phila., 1971-72; mgmt. trainee GSA divsn. U.S. Govt., Phila., 1987; del. leader People to People Student Amb. Programs, Australia, 1993, Russia and the Baltic States, 1994, U.K. and Ireland, 1995. Past chair 75th anniversary com. Pinn Meml. Bapt. Ch., scholarship com., new mem. com., aides to first lady and women's support group; mem. bd. dirs. Day Care Com.; ann. vol. United Negro Coll. Fund Telethon, mem. small bus. fundraising com. Mem. Nat. Coun. Negro Women, Pa. Sch. Counselors Assn., Delta Sigma Theta (life, chpt. journalist, chair May Week, del. to regional conv., mem. scholarship com.), Phi Delta Kappa. Home: 925 E Roumfort Rd Philadelphia PA 19150-3215 Office: Sch Dist Phila Roosevelt Mid Sch Washington Ln Musgrave St Philadelphia PA 19144

STYLES, BEVERLY, entertainer; b. Richmond, Va., June 6, 1923; d. John Harry Kenealy and Juanita Russell (Robins) Carpenter; m. Wilbur Cox, Mar. 14, 1942 (div.); m. Robert Marascia, Oct. 5, 1951 (div. Apr. 1964). Studies with Ike Carpenter, Hollywood, Calif., 1965—; student, Am. Nat. Theatre Acad., 1968-69; studies with Paula Raymond, Hollywood, 1969-70; diploma, Masterplan Inst., Anaheim, Calif., 1970. Freelance performer, musician, 1947-81; owner Beverly Styles Music, Joshua Tree, Calif., 1971—; v.p. spl. programs Lawrence Program of Calif., Yucca Valley, Calif.; talent coord., co-founder Quiet Place Studio, Yucca Valley, 1994. Composer: Joshua Tree, 1975, I'm Thankful, 1978, Wow, Wow, Wow, 1986, Music for the Whispering, 1994, Worl of Dreams, 1996, Thank You God, 1996; (compositions) Color Cords and Moods, 1995, (with lyricist Betty Curtis), Desert Nocturne Piano Arrangement, 1996; records include The Perpetual Styles Of Beverly, 1978; albums include The Primitive Styles Of Beverly, 1977; author: A Special Plan To Think Upon, The Truth As Seen By A Composer, 1978, A Special Prayer To Think Upon, 1983. Mem. ASCAP (Gold Pin award), Profl. Musicians Local 47 (life), Internat. Platform Assn. Republican. Avocation: creating abstract art. Office: PO Box 615 Joshua Tree CA 92252-0615

STYLES, RICHARD GEOFFREY PENTLAND, retired banker; b. Regina, Sask., Can., Dec. 3, 1930; s. Alfred G. and C. Ila (Pentland) S.; m. Jacqueline Joyce Frith, Oct. 31, 1959; children: Leslie Diane, David Patrick. B. in Commerce, U. Sask., 1951; Program for Mgmt. Devel., Harvard U., 1964. With Royal Bank Can., 1951-87, various domestic and internat. positions; vice chmn. Royal Bank Can., Toronto, Ont., until 1987; ret., 1987; formerly involved with Orion Royal Bank and bank's internat. subs., London, 1961-64; chmn., bd. dirs. Grosvenor Internat. Holdings Ltd., Drivers Jonas (Can.) Ltd.; bd. dirs. Echo Bay Mines Ltd., Fairwater Capital Corp., The Geon Co., Onex Corp., ProSource Distbn. Svcs., The Royal Trust Co., Scott's Hospitality Inc., Working Ventures Can. Fund Inc. Chmn. Toronto Symphony Found.; bd. govs. Mt. Sinai Hosp. Mem. Toronto Club, Rosedale Golf Club. Office: Royal Bank Plz Ste 3115, Toronto, ON Canada M5J 2J5

STYNE, DENNIS MICHAEL, physician; b. Chgo., July 31, 1947; s. Irving and Bernice (Coopersmith) S.; m. Donna Petre, Sept. 5, 1971; children: Rachel, Jonathan, Juliana, Aaron. BS, Northwestern U., 1969, MD, 1971. Diplomate Am. Bd. Pediats. Intern in pediatrics U. Calif., San Diego, 1971-72, resident in pediatrics, 1972-73; resident in pediatrics Yale U., New Haven, 1973-74; fellow in pediatric endocrinology U. Calif., San Francisco, 1974-77, asst. prof. pediatrics, 1977-83; assoc. prof. U. Calif., Davis, 1983-90; prof., 1990—, chair pediatrics, 1989—. Author numerous book chpts., contbr. articles to profl. jours. Mem. Endocrine Soc., Soc. Pediat. Rsch., Am. Pediat. Soc., Am. Acad. Pediats., Lawson Wilkins Soc. for Pediat. Endocrinology. Avocations: sailing, music. Office: U Calif Dept Pediatrics Davis CA 95616

STYNES, STANLEY KENNETH, retired chemical engineer, educator; b. Detroit, Jan. 18, 1932; s. Stanley Kenneth and Bessie Myrtle (Casey) S.; m. Marcia Ann Meyers, Aug. 27, 1955; children: Peter Casey, Pamela Kay, Suzanne Elizabeth. B.S., Wayne State U., 1955, M.S., 1958; Ph.D., Purdue U., 1963. Lab. asst. U. Chgo., 1951; instr. Purdue U., 1960-63; asst. prof. chem. engring. Wayne State U., Detroit, 1963-64, assoc. prof., 1964-71, prof., 1971-92, dean engring., 1972-85, prof. emeritus, 1992—; dir. Energy Conversion Devices, Inc., Troy, Mich.; cons. Schwayder Chem. Metallurgy Co., 1965; chemistry dept. Wayne State U., 1965-66, Claude B. Schneible Co., Holly, Mich., 1968. Contbr. engring. articles to profl. jours. Mem. coun. on environ. strategy S.E. Mich. Coun. Govts., 1976-81; bd. dirs. Program for Minorities in S.E. Mich.; sec.-treas. Mich. Ednl. Rsch. Info. Triad; bd. dirs. Sci. and Engring. Fair of Met. Detroit, pres., 1983; bd. dirs. Midwest Program for Minorities in Engring., Sci. Ctr. Met. Detroit. Ford Found. fellow, 1959-63; DuPont fellow, 1962-63; Wayne State U. faculty research fellow, 1964-65. Fellow AIChE (past chmn. Detroit sect.), Engring. Soc. Detroit (past bd. dirs.), Mich. Soc. Profl. Engrs. (pres. 1987-88); mem. AAAS, Am. Chem. Soc., Engring. Sci. Devel. Found. (pres. 1992-94), Argonne Univs. Assn. (del.), Adult Learning Inst. (bd. dirs. 1994—), Sigma Xi, Tau Beta Pi, Omicron Delta Kappa, Phi Lambda Upsilon. Presbyterian. Home: 20161 Stamford Dr Livonia MI 48152-1246 Office: Coll Engring Wayne State U Detroit MI 48202

STYRON, WILLIAM, writer; b. Newport News, Va., June 11, 1925; s. William Clark and Pauline Margaret (Abraham) S.; m. Rose Burgunder, May 4, 1953; children: Susanna Margaret, Paola Clark, Thomas, Claire Alexandra. Student, Christchurch Sch., Davidson Coll.; Litt.D., Davidson Coll., 1986; A.B., Duke U., 1947, Litt.D., 1968. Fellow Am. Acad. Arts and Letters at Am. Acad. in Rome, 1953; fellow Silliman Coll., Yale, 1964—; jury pres. Cannes Film Festival, 1983. Author: novels Lie Down in Darkness, 1951, The Long March, 1953, Set This House on Fire, 1960, The Confessions of Nat Turner, 1967 (Pulitzer prize 1968, Howells medal Am. Acad. Arts and Letters 1970), Sophie's Choice, 1979 (Am. Book award 1980), In the Clap Shack (play), 1972, This Quiet Dust, 1982, Darkness Visible, 1990, A Tidewater Morning, 1993; also articles, essays, revs.; editor: Best Stories from the Paris Rev., 1959; adv. editor: Paris Rev., 1953—; mem. editorial bd. The Am. Scholar, 1970-76. Decorated Commandeur de l'Ordre des Arts et des Lettres, Commandeur Legion d'Honneur (France); recipient Duke U. Disting. Alumni award, 1984, Conn. Arts award, 1984, Prix Mondial del Duca, 1985, Elmer Holmes Bobst award for fiction, 1989, Edward MacDowell medal for excellence in the arts, 1988, Nat. Mag. award, 1990, Nat. medal of Arts, 1993, Medal of Honor, Nat. Arts Club, 1995, Common Wealth award, 1995. Mem. Am. Acad. Arts and Scis., Am. Acad. Arts and Letters, Soc. Am. Historians, Signet Soc., Harvard, Académie Goncourt, Phi Beta Kappa. Democrat.

STYSLINGER, LEE JOSEPH, JR., manufacturing company executive; b. Birmingham, Ala., June 28, 1933; s. Lee Joseph and Margaret Mary (McFarl) S.; m. Catherine Patricia Smith, Apr. 30, 1960; children—Lee Joseph III, Jon Cecil, Mark Joseph. Student, U. Ala., 1952. Pres., chief exec. officer Altec Industries, Inc. and predecessors, truck equipment mfrs., Birmingham, 1956-89, chief exec. officer, chmn. bd., 1989-92, chmn., 1992—; bd. dirs. Regions Fin., Mead Corp., So. Rsch. Tech., Inc., Jemison Investment Co., Birmingham, Ala., Children's Harbor, Electronic Healthcare Systems, So. Rsch. Inst. Pres. cabinet U. Ala., Tuscaloosa; bd. dirs. St. Vincent's Hosp. Mem. Nat. Assn. Mfrs., Newcomen Soc., Operation New Birmingham, U.S. C. of C., Birmingham C. of C., Bus. Coun. Ala., Country Club Birmingham, Mountain Brook Club, Shoal Creek Club, Willow Point Golf and Country Club, Rotary. Roman Catholic. Home: 3260 E Briarcliff Rd Birmingham AL 35223-1305 Office: 210 Inverness Center Dr Birmingham AL 35242-4808

STYVE, ORLOFF WENDELL, CRE, electrical engineer; b. Winnebago, Minn., Feb. 1, 1936; s. Orloff Wendell and Katharine (Drake) S.; m. Jane Carol Meister, Feb. 25, 1961 (div. 1981); children: Elizabeth Anne, David John, Robert Peter, Susan Katharine. BEE, U. Minn., 1959. Registered profl. engr., Wis. Dist. distbn. engr. Wis. Electric Power Co., Menomonee Falls, 1959-69; div. distbn. engr., then svc. ctr. engring. supr. Wis. Electric Power Co., West Bend, 1969-73; planning engr. Wis. Electric Power Co., Milw., 1973-76, sr. underground dist. engr., 1976-84, elec. engr. underground dist., 1984-94; cons. elect. distbn. engr. Slinger (Wis.) Utilities, 1995-96, utility mgr., 1996—; dir. WPPI, 1996—; mem. elec. bd., West Bend, 1972-94; dir. WPPI, 1996—. Mem. IEEE (voting mem. 1993, insulated conductors com. 1991—), Assn. of Edison Illuminating Cos. (cable engring. sect. 1991-94), Am. Nat. Stds. Inst. (distbn. transformer stds. com. 1985-88), Masons, Scottish Rite (com. stage properties & elec. effects com. 1986—, Wis. Player's award Valley of Wis. 1989, Svc. award 1991), Shriners (potentate's aide emeritus Tripoli Shrine 1986), Nat. Honor Soc. Avocations: amateur theater, camping. Office: Slinger Utilities PO Box 227 Slinger WI 53086-0227

SU, HELEN CHIEN-FAN, research chemist; b. Nanping, Fujian, China, Dec. 26, 1922; came to U.S. 1949; d. Ru-chen and Sieu-Hsien (Wong) Su. BA, Hwa Nan Coll., China, 1944; MS, U. Nebr., Lincoln, 1951; PhD, U. Nebr., 1953. Cert. profl. chemist. Asst. instr. in chemistry Hwa Nan Coll., Fuzhou, Fujian, China, 1944-49; prof. chemistry Lambuth Coll., Jackson, Tenn., 1953-55; rsch. asst. Auburn Rsch. Found., Auburn, Ala., 1955-57; sr. chemist, project ldr. Borden Chem. Co., Phila., 1957-63; scientist Lockheed-Ga. Rsch. Lab., Marietta, Ga., 1963-67; rsch. chemist Agrl. Rsch. Svc., USDA, Savannah, Ga., 1968-90. Contbr. numerous articles to profl. jours., chpts. in books; patentee in field. Recipient IR-100 award, Indsl. Research Mag., 1966. Fellow Am. Inst. Chemists, Ga. Inst. Chemists; mem. ACS, AAAS, N.Y. Acad. Sci., Entomol. Soc. Am., Ga. Entomol. Soc., Sigma Xi, Sigma Delta Epsilon. Methodist. Avocations: reading, gardening. Home: 5978 Robin Hood Ln Norcross GA 30093-3804 Office: USDA-ARS 3401 Edwin Ave Savannah GA 31405-1607

SU, JUDY YA HWA LIN, pharmacologist; b. Hsinchu, Taiwan, Nov. 20, 1938; came to U.S., 1962; d. Ferng Nian and Chiu-Chin (Cheng) Lin; m. Michael W. Su; 1 child, Marvin. BS, Nat. Taiwan U., 1961; MS, U. Kans., 1964; PhD, U. Wash., 1968. Asst. prof. dept. biology U. Ala., Huntsville, 1972-73; rsch. assoc. dept. anesthesiology U. Wash., Seattle, 1976-77, acting asst. prof. dept. anesthesia, 1977-78, rsch. asst. prof., 1978-81, rsch. assoc. prof., 1981-89, rsch. prof., 1989—; mem. surg. anesthesiology & trauma study sect. NIH, 1987-91; vis. scientist Max-Planck Inst. Med. Rsch., Heidelberg, West Germany, 1982-83; vis. prof. dept. anesthesiology Mayo Clinic, Rochester, Minn., Med. Coll. Wis., 1988; editorial bd. cons. Jour. Molecular & Cellular Cardiology, London, 1987—, European Jour. Physiology, Berlin, Germany, Muscle & Nerve, Kyoto, Japan, 1989—, Anesthesiology, Phila., 1987—, Molecular Pharmacology, 1988—, Jour. Biol. Chemistry, 1989—, Am. Jour. Physiology, 1990—; mem. rsch. study com. Am. Heart Assn., 1992-95. Contbr. articles to profl. jours. Grantee Wash. Heart Assn., 1976-77, 1985-87, Pharm. Mfrs. Assn. Found., Inc., 1977, Lilly Rsch. Labs, 1986-88, Anaquest, 1987—, NIH, 1978—; recipient Rsch. Career Devel. award NIH, 1982-87; rsch. fellowship San Diego Heart Assn., 1970-72, Max-Planck Inst., 1982-83. Mem. AAAS, Biophys. Soc., Am. Soc. for Pharmacology and Exptl. Therapeutics, Am. Physiol. Soc., Am. Soc. Anesthesiologists. Home: 13110 NE 33rd St Bellevue WA 98005-1318 Office: U Wash Dept Anesthesiology Box 356540 Seattle WA 98195-6540

SU, KENDALL LING-CHIAO, engineering educator; b. Fujian, China, July 10, 1926; came to U.S., 1948; s. Ru-chen and Sui-hsiong (Wang) S.; m. Jennifer Gee-tsone Chang, Sept. 10, 1960; children: Adrienne, Jonathan. BEE, Xiamen U., Peoples Republic China, 1947; MEE, Ga. Inst. Tech, 1949; PhD, Ga. Inst. Tech., 1954. Jr. engr. Taiwan Power Co., Taipei, Republic China, 1947-48; asst. prof. Ga. Inst. Tech., Atlanta, 1954-59, assoc. prof., 1959-65, prof., 1965-70, Regents prof., 1970-94, Regents' prof. emeritus, 1994—; mem. tech. staff Bell Labs., Murray Hill, N.J., 1957. Author: Active Network Synthesis, 1965, Time-Domain Synthesis of Linear Networks, 1969, Fundamentals of Circuits, Electronics, and Signal Analysis, 1978, Handbook of Tables for Elliptic-Function Filters, 1990, Fundamentals of Circuit Analysis, 1993, Analog Filters, 1996; mem. sci. adv. com. Newton Graphic Sci. mag., 1987—. Fellow IEEE (life); mem. Sigma Xi (pres. Ga. Inst. Tech. chpt. 1968-69, 72-73, Faculty Rsch. award 1957), Phi Kappa Phi, Eta Kappa Nu. Methodist. Office: Ga Inst Tech Sch Elec & Comp Engring Atlanta GA 30332-0250

SU, SHIAW-DER, nuclear engineer; b. Tainan, Republic of China, Jan. 20, 1945; came to U.S., 1969; s. Hsin-Chun and King-New (Chen) S.; m. Shi-Ju Wang, June 30, 1968; children: Eastor Y., Wesley Y. BS, Nat. Tsing Hua U., Republic of China, 1968; MS, Purdue U., 1971. Registered profl. nuclear engr., Calif. Engr. Burns & Roe Inc., Oradell, N.J., 1971-72; prin. Gen. Atomics, San Diego, Calif., 1972-95; pres. China Nuclear Corp., Taiwan, 1990-91, Peak Engring., San Diego, Calif., 1995—. Mem. Am. Nuclear Soc., Chinese Inst. Engrs. (life). Avocations: tennis, swimming, ping-pong, bridge. Home: 5093 Zimmer Cv San Diego CA 92130-2756 Office: Peak Engring PO Box 910472 San Diego CA 92191

SUARD, PIERRE HENRI ANDRE, power company executive; b. Lons le Saunier, Jura, France, Nov. 9, 1934; s. Gaston and Jeanne (Gaillard) S.; m. Michele Sender, Aug. 22, 1959; children: Brigitte, Bruno. Diploma in engring., Ecole Polytechnique, Paris, 1954, Ecole Ponts & Chaussees, Paris, 1959. With Min. Pub. Works, Paris, 1960-63; dir. ops. Paris Airport Authority, 1963-70; ceo Setec Economie & Informatique, Paris, 1971-73, Sogelerg-Sedim, Paris, 1973-76, Cables de Lyon, Paris, 1976-84; from mng. dir. to vice chmn. Cit Alcatel, Paris, 1984-85; chmn., ceo Alcatel NV, 1987—, Alcatel Alsthom, Paris, 1986—, Alcatel U.S.A. Corp., N.Y.C., 1985—; now chmn. Alcatel USA Corp., N.Y.C.; bd. dirs. Credit Commercial de France, Paris, 1987—, Societe Generale, 1987—, La Farge Coppee—, Compagnie General des Eaux—, Fiat S.P.A. Named Chevalier de la Legion d'Honneur, French Govt., 1987. Office: Alcatel Alsthom Co Gen d'Electricite, 54 rue de la Boetie, 75382 Paris Cedex 08, France*

SUAREZ, ROBERTO, retired newspaper publishing executive; b. Havana, Cuba; came to U.S., 1961; m. Pitucha Campuzano; children: 7 sons, 5 daughters. Student, Colegio de Belén, Cuba; grad., Villanova Coll., 1949. Various postions in real estate, constrn., fin. Havana, 1950-60; from part-time mailer to contr. The Herald's subs., 1962-72; contr. Knight Pub. Co., Charlotte, N.C., 1972-78; v.p., gen. mgr. The Miami (Fla.) Herald, 1978-86, pres., 1986—; pub. El Nuevo Herald Knight Ridder Pub. Co., 1986-96. Past pres. Art and Sci. Coun., Spirit Sq. Arts Ctr., Charleston; chair Kids Voting/Dade County; bd. dirs. United Way. Recipient Gold medal Knight-Ridder Pub. Co., 1989, Heritage award HIspanic Alliance, 1990, Leadership award ASPIRA, 1991, Marion Guastella award Asociacion de Publicitarios Latinoamericanos, 1993. Mem. Inter Am. Press Assn. (pres. exec. com.), N.C. Press Assn. (former treas.), Interam. Businessmen Assn.

SUAREZ, XAVIER LOUIS, lawyer, former mayor; b. Las Villas, Cuba, May 21, 1949; m. Rita Suarez; 4 children. BE, Villanova U., 1971, hon. degree, 1988; M of Pub. Policy, JD, Harvard U., 1975. Bar: Fla. 1975. Instr. bus. law Biscayne Coll., 1977-78; mayor City of Miami, 1985-93; ptnr. Jorden, Schulte & Burchette, Miami, 1988-93, Shutts & Bowen, Miami, 1993—; mem. criminal justice coun. Dade County, Miami, Fla., 1980. Chmn. Miami Affirmative Action Bd., 1981, Downtown Devel. Authority, 1985—; chmn. bd. regents Cath. Univ., 1988-89; bd. advisors Harvard U. Kennedy Sch. Govt. Inst. Politics, Cambridge, Mass., St. Thomas U. Sch. Law. Mem. Fla. Bar Assn., Cuban Bar Assn. Office: Shutts and Bowen 1500 Miami Ctr 201 S Biscayne Blvd Miami FL 33131-4332*

SUAREZ-MURIAS, MARGUERITE C., retired language and literature educator; b. Havana, Cuba, Mar. 23, 1921; came to U.S., 1935, naturalized, 1959; d. Eduardo R. and Marguerite (Vendel) S.-M. A.B., Bryn Mawr Coll., 1942; M.A., Columbia U., 1953, Ph.D., 1957. Lectr. in Spanish Columbia U., 1954-56; pub. relations officer med. div. Johns Hopkins U., 1957-58; asst. prof. Spanish and French Sweet Briar Coll., 1958-59, Hood Coll., 1960-61; lectr. Cath. U., 1960-63, asst. prof., summers 1960-62, asso. prof., summers 1964-66; asst. prof. dept. langs. and linguistics Am. U., 1961-63, asso. prof., 1963-66; prof. dept. classical and modern langs. Marquette U., Milw., 1966-68; prof. Spanish and Portuguese U. Wis., Milw., 1968-83; chmn., 1972-75; guest prof. U. South Africa, Pretoria, 1980. Author: La novela romántica en Hispanoamérica, 1963, Antología estilística de la prosa moderna española, 1968, Essays on Hispanic Literature/Esnayos de literatura hispana, 1982; contbr. articles to profl. jours.; editor: Gironella's Los cipreses creen en Dios, 1969; designed built homes, 1987-93. Mem. Nat. Trust for Historic Preservation. Roman Catholic. Home: 1315 Cold Bottom Rd Sparks MD 21152-9518

SUAREZ RIVERA, ADOLFO ANTONIO, cardinal; b. Jan. 9, 1927. Archbishop of Monterrey Mex. Office: Calle Porfirio Barba Jacob, 66450 San Nicolas de Garza Mexico

SUAREZ RIVERA, ADOLFO ANTONIO, archbishop; b. San Cristobal de las Casas, Mexico, Jan. 9, 1927. Ordained priest Roman Cath. Ch., 1952; bishop of Tepic, 1971-80, Tlalnepantla, 1980-83; archbishop of Monterrey, 1984—. Office: Porfirio Barba Jacob No 906, Col Anahuac, CP 66450 San Nicolas de Garza Nuevo Leon, Mexico also: Zuazua # 10o Sur con Ocampo, Apartado Postal 7, CP 64000 Monterrey Mexico

SUBA, ANTONIO RONQUILLO, surgeon; b. Philippines, Apr. 25, 1927; came to U.S., 1952, naturalized, 1961; s. Antonio Mesina and Valentina Cabais (Ronquillo) S.; m. Sylvia Marie Karl, June 16, 1956; children—Steven Antonio, Eric John, Laurinda Ann, Gregory Karl, Timothy Mark, Sylvia Kathleen. M.D., U. St. Thomas, Philippines, 1952. Diplomate: Am. Bd. Surgery. Intern St. Anthony's Hosp., St. Louis, 1952-53; resident St. Louis County Hosp., St. Louis, 1953-57; trainee Nat. Cancer Inst., Ellis Fischel State Cancer Hosp., Columbia, Mo., 1957-59; chief surg. services U.S. Army, Bremerhaven, Germany, 1959-61; practice medicine specializing in gen. and hand surgery St. Louis, 1961-89; ret., 1989; pres., prin. ARS (P.C.), 1971-84. Contbr. feature articles to Philippine pubis., 1946-51, articles to med. jours. Fellow A.C.S.; mem. AMA, Pan-Pacific, Mo. surg. assns., St. Louis Surg. Soc., Am. Assn. Hand Surgery. Club: K.C. Home: 12085 Heatherdane Dr Saint Louis MO 63131-3119

SUBAK, JOHN THOMAS, lawyer; b. Trebic, Czechoslovakia, Apr. 19, 1929; came to U.S., 1941, naturalized, 1946; s. William John and Gerda Maria (Subakova) S.; m. Mary Corcoran, June 4, 1955; children—Jane, Kate, Thomas, Michael. BA summa cum laude, Yale U., 1950, LLB, 1956. Bar: Pa. 1956. From assoc. to ptnr. Dechert, Price & Rhoads, Phila., 1956-76, v.p., gen. counsel, dir., 1976-77; group v.p., gen. counsel, dir. Rohm and Haas Co., Phila., 1977-93; counsel Dechert Price & Rhoads, Phila., 1994—; bd. dirs. Newport Corp. Editor: The Bus. Lawyer, 1982-83. Bd. dirs. Am. Cancer Soc., 1982-95; trustee Smith Coll. Lt. (j.g.) USN, 1950-53. Mem. ABA (chmn. corp. and bus. law sect. 1984-85), Am. Law Inst. (coun. mem.), Defender Assn. of Phila. (v.p., bd. dirs. 1982-95), Merion Cricket Club, Lemon Bay Club. Democrat. Roman Catholic. Office: Dechert Price & Rhoads 1717 Arch St Philadelphia PA 19103-2713

SUBAK-SHARPE, GERALD EMIL, electrical engineer, educator; b. Vienna, Austria, June 15, 1925; came to U.S., 1959, naturalized, 1967; s. Robert and Nelly (Brull) S.; m. Genell Jackson, Nov. 23, 1963; children: David, Sarah and Hope (twins). BS with 1st class honors, Univ. Coll., London, 1951; PhD, U. London, 1965; ScD, Columbia U., 1969. Rsch. engr. Brit. Telecommunications Rsch., Taplow, Eng., 1951-58; mem. tech. staff Bell Labs., Murray Hill, N.J., 1959-64, cons., 1977-78; assoc. prof. elec. engring. Manhattan Coll., Bronx, N.Y., 1966-68; prof. elec. engring. CCNY, N.Y.C., 1968—; v.p. G.S. Sharpe Communications Inc., 1981—. Author: (with A.B. Glaser) Integrated Circuit Engineering, 1978; contbr. articles on network structure and semicondr. theory to profl. jours. Served as lt. Royal Warwickshire Regt., 1944-47. Recipient Prof. of Yr. award Eta Kappa Nu/CCNY, 1985-86. Fellow Instn. Elec. Engrs. (London); mem. IEEE (sr.), N.Y. Acad. Scis., Nat. Trust for Historic Preservation. Home: 606 W 116th St Apt 71 New York NY 10027-7024 Office: CCNY Dept Elec Engring Convent Ave New York NY 10027 also: Knollcroft New Concord NY 12060

SUBER, ROBIN HALL, former medical, surgical nurse; b. Bethlehem, Pa., Mar. 14, 1952; d. Arthur Albert and Sarah Virginia (Smith) Hall; m. David A. Suber, July 28, 1979; 1 child, Benjamin A. BSN, Ohio State U., 1974. RN, Ariz., Ohio. Formerly staff nurse Desert Samaritan Hosp., Mesa, Ariz. Lt. USN, 1974-80. Mem. ANA, Sigma Theta Tau.

SUBLER, EDWARD PIERRE, advertising executive; b. Shelby, Ohio, Mar. 24, 1927; s. Leo John and Dorotha (Armstrong) S.; m. Alice Ellen Carpenter, Sept. 8, 1956; children: Leo, Scott, Dorotha. B.A., Denison U., 1950; grad. advanced mgmt. course, Emory U. Mgr. product advt. Westinghouse Electric Co., Mansfield, Ohio, 1950-65; mgr. advt. and sales promotion Bell & Howell Co., Chgo., 1965-69; v.p. mdsg. Westinghouse Consumer Products Co., 1969-76; sr. v.p. Ketchum Advt., Pitts., 1976-92, ret., 1992. Served with USN, 1945-46. Mem. Am. Mktg. Assn., Am. Assn. Advt. Agencies (regional chmn.), Catawba Island Club. Presbyterian. Home: 2881 N Firelands Blvd Port Clinton OH 43452-3028

SUBLETT, CARL CECIL, artist; b. Johnson County, Ky., Feb. 4, 1919; s. Tandy and Beulah (Fitzpatrick) S.; m. Helen C. Davis, Aug. 20, 1942; children: Carol, Eric. Student, Western Ky. U., 1938-40, Univ. Center, Florence, Italy, 1945, U. Tenn., 1955-56. Indsl. engr., draftsman Enterprise Wheel & Car Corp., Bristol, Va., 1946-49; staff artist Bristol Va.-Tennesean & Herald Courier, 1950-52; artist, asst. mgr. Bristol Art Engravers, 1952-54; art dir. Advt., Knoxville, Tenn., 1954-65; prof. art U. Tenn., Knoxville, 1966-82; juror Watercolor Soc. Ala., Birmingham, 1979, Jacksonville U. Ann., 1980; juror Bristol Art Guild 8th ann. juried exhbn., 1993. Artist prize-winning watercolors, 1964, drawing Soc. Nat. Exhbn., 1965, Artists U.S.A., 1971-72, 73-74, 74-75; one-man shows in oil and watercolors, 1995—; numerous exhbns. art in embassies program, 1964—; numerous exhbns. featured in publs. Taipei Fine Arts Inst. including Allied Publs. Inc.; numerous exhbns. in catalogs Tenn. State Mus., Nashville, Artist U.S.A., others; retrospective exhbn. Knoxville Mus. Art, 1991; invitational show Hampton III Gallery, Ltd., Taylors, S.C., 1992, Union U., Jackson, Tenn., 1991, Collector's Gallery, Nashville, 1960, 93, 96, Bennett Galleries, Knoxville, 1992-93, 95. Hon. mem. Oak Ridge Tenn.Community Art Ctr. Served with U.S. Army, 1943-45. Recipient Purchase Mead Corp. Painting of Yr., Atlanta, 1963, Grumbacher Washington Watercolor Club, 1964, Rudolph Leach Am. Watercolor Soc., N.Y.C., 1972, Purchase Watercolor U.S.A., Springfield, Mo., 1975, Lifetime Achievement award Knoxville Arts Coun. and Knoxville Mus. of Art, 1994. Mem. NAD (Alfred Easton poor prize 1995), Bristol Art Guild (treas. 1951-54), Tenn. Watercolor Soc. (gold medal 1973, award of merit 1974, 75, 77, 78, 81, 84, 85), Knoxville Watercolor Soc., Port Clyde (Maine) Arts and Crafts Soc., Watercolor USA Soc., Knoxville Mus. Art. Methodist. Home and Studio: 2104 Lake Ave Knoxville TN 37916-2802 *We are creatures of history; credit your helpers, share your successes, and the future will reward your time.*

SUBLETTE, JULIA WRIGHT, music educator, performer, adjudicator; b. Natural Bridge, Va., Sept. 13, 1929; d. Paul Thomas and Annie Belle (Watkins) Wright; m. Richard Ashmore Sublette, Oct. 18, 1952; children: C. Mark, Carey P., Sylvia S. Bennett, Wright D. BA in Music, Furman U., 1951; MusM, Cin. Conservatory, 1954; postgrad., Chautauqua Inst., N.Y., 1951-52; PhD, Fla. State U., 1993. Ind. piano tchr., 1953—; instr. music and humanities Okaloosa-Walton C.C., Niceville, Fla., 1978—; panelist Music Tchr. Nat. Conv., Milw., 1992. Editor Fla. Music Tchr., 1991—; contbr. articles to profl. music jours. Mem. AAUW, Music Tchrs. Nat. Assn. (cert., chmn. so. divsn. jr. high sch. piano/instrumental contests 1986-88), Fla. State Music Tchrs. Assn., So. Assn. Women Historians, Southeastern Hist. Keyboard Soc., Friday Morning Music Club, Colonial Dames of 17th Century Am., Pi Kappa Lambda. Avocations: reading, travel, herb gardening. Home: 217 Country Club Rd Shalimar FL 32579-2203

SUBY, JOHN F., accountant, diversified financial services exec; b. 1935. CPA. Pres. Suby, Von Haden & Assocs., 1972—. Office: Suby, Von Haden & Assocs 1221 John Q Hammons Dr Madison WI 53717

SUCHENEK, MAREK ANDRZEJ, computer science educator; b. Warsaw, Poland, May 2, 1949; came to U.S., 1986; s. Tadeusz Aleksander and Barbara Krystyna (Zych) S.; m. Ewa Aleksandra Czerny, July 30, 1974 (div. 1991). MSc in Math. Engring., Warsaw Tech. U., 1973, PhD in Tech. Scis. with distinction, 1979. Instr. Warsaw (Poland) Tech. U., 1973-79, asst. prof., 1979-88; vis. asst. prof. Wichita (Kans.) State U., 1986-88; assoc. Nat. Inst. for Aviation Rsch., Wichita, 1987-90; vis. asst. prof. Wichita (Kans.) State U., 1986-88, assoc. prof., 1988-89, assoc. prof., chair, 1989-90; prof. Calif. State U.-Dominguez Hills, Carson, 1990—; mem. organizing com. Internat. Symposium on Methodologies for Intelligent Sys., 1989-90; program com. Ann. Ulam Math. Conf., 1990-91, Internat. Conf. on Computing and Info., 1992—; referee NSF, 1990—, Annals of Math. and Artificial Intelligence, 1992—, Jour. Logic Programming, 1992—; presenter in field. Author: (with Jan Bielecki) ANS FORTRAN, 1980, (with Jan Bielecki) FORTRAN for Advanced Programmers, 1981, 2d edit., 83, 3d edit., 88 (Minister of Sci. Higher Edn. and Techs. prize 1982); reviewer Zentralblatt fur Mathematik, 1980-89, Math. Reviews, 1989-91; mem. editorial bd.: Ulam Quarterly, 1990—; contbr. articles to profl. jours. Recipient rsch. grants Polish Govt., 1974-76, 85-86, FAA, 1988-90. Mem. AAUP, The Assn. for Logic Programming, Computer Soc. IEEE, Assn. Symbolic Logic, Sigma Xi (chpt. pres.). Avocations: travel, modern music, cats, collectibles, target shooting. Home: 830 N Juanita Ave #4 Redondo Beach CA 90277-2229 Office: Calif State Univ Dominguez Hills 1000 E Victoria St Carson CA 90747-0001

SUCHKOV, ANATOLY, astronomer; b. Kalai-Khumb, USSR, May 14, 1944; came to the U.S., 1991; s. Alexander and Anna (Nazarenko) S.; m. Galina (Sidorenko) Soutchkova, Jan. 4, 1965; children: Svetlana, Vera. Candidate of sci., Tajik State U., 1970; DSc, Moscow State U., 1980. Scientist Inst. Astrophysics, Dushanbe, Tajikistan, 1965-69, sr. scientist, 1969-72; prof. astrophysics Rostov (USSR) State U., 1972-80, head dept. astrophysics, 1980-93; planning scientist Space Telescope Sci. Inst., Balt., 1993-94, assoc. scientist, 1994—; vis. scientist Space Telescope Sci. Inst., 1991-93; head space rsch. and astronomy divsn. North Caucasus Sci. Ctr., Rostov-on-Don, USSR, 1980-91. Author: The Milky Way Galaxy, 1995, Galaxies: Familiar and Puzzling, 1988, The Galaxy, 1984; contbr. articles to profl. jours. Mem. Am. Astron. Soc. Achievements include discovery of the discreteness of the metallicity distribution of the stellar populations of the galaxy; formulation of the theory of active phases of the evolution of the galaxy; determination of the parameters of the spiral structure of the galaxy; revealing of the two-dimensional age-metallicity relation for the nearby stars; discovery of the absence of a dependence of the main sequence of F stars on heavy element abundance. Home: 8 Deaven Ct Baltimore MD 21209 Office: Space Telescope Sci Inst 3700 San Martin Dr Baltimore MD 21218

SUCHODOLSKI, RONALD EUGENE, publishing company executive; b. Bklyn., May 17, 1946; s. John Florence Burke; m. Carolyn Cortese, Dec. 4, 1977; children: Keith, Craig. BA, CUNY, 1973, MA, 1975. Dir. product mktg. Holt, Rinehart & Winston, N.Y.C., 1973-80; dir. mktg. product devel. Instructo/McGraw-Hill, Malvern, Pa., 1980-83; dir. sch. div. Childcraft, Edison, N.J., 1984-89; pres. Judy/Instructo div. Paramount Publs. Inc., Eden Prairie, Minn., 1989-93; sr. v.p. mktg. sales Paramount Supplemental Educ., Morristown, N.J., 1993—. Sgt. U.S. Army, 1966-67, Vietnam. Mem. Nat. Sch. Supply and Equipment Assn., Ednl. Dealers and Suppliers Assn. Home: 15 Lance Rd Lebanon NJ 08833-5007

SUCKIEL, ELLEN KAPPY, philosophy educator; b. Bklyn., June 15, 1943; d. Jack and Lilyan (Banchefsky) Kappy; m. Joseph Suckiel, June 22, 1973. A.B., Douglass Coll., 1965; M.A. in Philosophy, U. Wis., 1969, Ph.D. in Philosophy, 1972. Lectr. philosophy U. Wis., Madison, 1969-71; asst. prof. philosophy Fla. State U., Tallahassee, 1972-73; asst. prof. philosophy U. Calif., Santa Cruz, 1973-80, assoc. prof., 1980-95, prof., 1995—, provost Kresge Coll., 1983-89. Author: The Pragmatic Philosophy of William James, 1982, Heaven's Champion: William James's Philosophy of Religion, 1996, also articles, book introductions and chpts. Mem. Am. Philos. Assn., Soc. for Advancement Am. Philosophy. Office: U Calif Cowell Coll Santa Cruz CA 95064

SUCKLING, ROBERT MCCLEARY, architect; b. Hollidaysburg, Pa., Feb. 27, 1932; s. Melvin E. and Rosanna B. (McCleary) S.; m. MaryLou Morris, Feb. 12, 1956; children: Dawn Morden, Kevin, Scott, Lisa Cronin. BArch, Carnegie-Mellon U., 1955. Registered architect, Pa., Ohio, N.Y., W.Va., N.C., Md., Ky., Va. Designer, job capt. Hayes Large Architects, Altoona, Pa., 1957-61, Nicholas J. Fiore, AIA, Altoona, 1861-62; designer, project mgr. N. Grant Nicklas, AIA, Altoona, 1962-64; project architect Pietrolungo & Kimball, Ebensburg, Pa., 1964-66; project coord. and mgr. Hayes Large Architects, Altoona, 1966-74, ptnr., 1974-94; ret., 1995; dir.-at-large Coun. Ednl. Facility Planners, Phoenix, 1987—. Neighborhood commr. Boy Scouts Am., Altoona; pres. 1st Luth. Ch., Altoona, 1984-85. Served to 1st lt. U.S. Army, 1955-57. Recipient Disting. Svc. award CEFPI, 1993. Mem. Rotary, Masons, Shriners, Order Ea. Star, Alpha Phi Omega. Republican. Avocations: travel, photography, reading. Home: 2500 Walton Ave Altoona PA 16602-3375 Office: Hayes Large Architects PO Box 1784 Logan Blvd and 5th Ave Altoona PA 16603

SUDAK, HOWARD STANLEY, physician, psychiatry educator; b. Cleve., Nov. 13, 1932; s. Sol and Leona (Simms) S.; m. Diane M. Ressler, Dec. 25, 1955 (dec.); children: Ellen, Nancy, Janet, David; m. Donna M. Miller, Mar. 25, 1995. AB in Chemistry magna cum laude, Case Western Res. U., 1954, MD, 1958. Diplomate Am. Bd. Psychiatry and Neurology (sr. examiner 1991—). Intern in medicine Univ. Hosps. Cleve., 1958-59, resident in psychiatry, 1959-62; clin. assoc. NIMH, Bethesda, Md., 1962-64; chief psychiatry Cleve. VA Med. Ctr., 1964-84; asst. prof. psychiatry Case Western Res. U., Cleve., 1964-74, assoc. prof., 1974-82, prof., 1982—, vice dean Med. Sch., 1985-92; chmn. dept. psychiatry The Pa. Hosp., Phila., 1992—; psychiatrist-in-chief Inst. of Pa. Hosp., Phila., 1992—; clin. prof. psychiatry U. Pa. Sch. Medicine, 1993-94; prof. psychiatry, vice chmn. psychiatry/human behavior Thomas Jefferson U., Phila., 1994—; mem. profl. adv. coun. Youth Suicide Nat. Ctr., Washington, 1986—; com. mem. Ctrs. for Disease Control, Atlanta, 1990-91. Editor: Suicide in the Young, 1984, Clinical Psychiatry, 1985; cons. editor Suicide and Life Threatening Behavior, 1988—; contbr. numerous articles to profl. jours., chpt. to books. Dir. Inst. for Urban Health, Cleve., 1990-92. Grantee NIMH, 1972-73, 83-86. Fellow Am. Psychiat. Assn., Am. Coll. Psychiatrists, Am. Coll. Psychoanalysts; mem. Am. Assn. Suicidology (trustee 1988-90), Am. Suicide Found. (trustee 1987—, pres. 1989-91), Phi Beta Kappa, Alpha Omega Alpha. Avocations: biking, sailing, reading, tennis, jazz and classical music. Home: 321 Lawrence St Philadelphia PA 19106 Office: Inst of Pa Hosp 111 N 49th St Philadelphia PA 19139-2718

SUDAN, RAVINDRA NATH, electrical engineer, physicist, educator; b. Chineni, Kashmir, India, June 8, 1931; came to U.S., 1958, naturalized, 1971; s. Brahm Nath and Shanti Devi (Mehta) S.; m. Dipali Ray, July 3, 1959; children: Rajani, Ranjeet. B.A. with first class honors, U. Punjab, 1948; diploma, Indian Inst. Sci., 1952, Imperial Coll., London, 1953; Ph.D., U. London, 1955. Engr., Brit. Thomson-Houston Co., Rugby, Eng, 1955-57; Engr. Imperial Chem. Industries, Calcutta, India, 1957-58; research assoc. Cornell U., Ithaca, N.Y., 1958-59; asst. prof. elec. engring. Cornell U., 1959-63, assoc. prof., 1963-68, prof., 1968-75, IBM prof. engring., 1975—, dir. Lab. Plasma Studies, 1975-85, dep. dir. Cornell Theory Ctr., 1985-87; cons. Lawrence Livermore Lab., Los Alamos Sci. Lab., Sci. Applications Inc., Physics Internat. Co.; vis. research asso. Stanford U., summer 1963; cons. U.K. Atomic Energy Authority, Culham Lab., summer 1965; vis. scientist Internat. Center Theoretical Physics, Trieste, Italy, 1965-66, summers 1970, 73, Plasma Physics Lab. Princeton U., 1966-67, spring 1989, Inst. for Advanced Study, Princeton, N.J., spring 1975; head theoretical plasma physics group U.S. Naval Research Lab., 1970-71, sci. adviser to dir., 1974-75; chmn. Ann. Conf. on Theoretical Aspects of Controlled Fusion, 1975, 2d Internat. Conf. on High Power Electron and Ion Beam Research and Tech., 1977. Mem. edit. bd. Physics of Fluids, 1973-76, Comments on Plasma Physics, 1973, Nuclear Fusion, 1976-84, Physics Reports, 1990—; co-editor Handbook of Plasma Physics; contbr. over 220 articles to sci. jours. Recipient Gold medal Acad. Scis. of the Czech Republic, 1993. Fellow IEEE, AAAS, Am. Phys. Soc. (Maxwell prize 1989), Nat. Rsch. Coun. (chmn. Plasma Sci. com. 1993—). Achievements include patents (with S. Humphries, Jr) intense ion beam generator. Office: Cornell Univ 369 Upson Hall Ithaca NY 14853-7501

SUDARSKY, JERRY M., industrialist; b. Russia, June 12, 1918; s. Selig and Sara (Ars) S.; m. Mildred Axelrod, Aug. 31, 1947; children: Deborah, Donna. Student, U. Iowa, 1936-39; B.S., Poly. U. Bklyn., 1942; D.Sc. (hon.), Poly. U. N.Y., 1976. Founder, chief exec. officer Bioferm Corp., Wasco, Calif., 1946-66; cons. to Govt. of Israel, 1966-67; founder, chmn. Israel Chems., Ltd., Tel Aviv, Israel, 1967-72; chmn. I.C. Internat. Cons., Tel Aviv, 1971-73; vice chmn., bd. dirs. Daylin, Inc., Los Angeles, 1972-76; pres., chmn. J.M.S. Assocs., Los Angeles, 1976-82; vice chmn. bd. Jacobs Engring. Group Inc., Pasadena, Calif., 1982-94; chmn., CEO Health Sci. Properties, Inc., Pasadena, 1994—. Patentee in field of indsl. microbiology. Bd. govs. Hebrew U., Jerusalem; trustee Polytechnic U. N.Y., 1976—; bd. dirs. Arthritis Found., L.A., 1989-94, Mgmt. Edn. Assn., UCLA, 1990—. Served with USNR, 1943-46. Mem. AAAS, Am. Chem. Soc., Sigma Xi. Clubs: Brentwood Country (Los Angeles). Office: Health Sci Properties Inc 251 S Lake Ave Pasadena CA 91101-3003

SUDBRINK, JANE MARIE, sales and marketing executive; b. Sandusky, Ohio, Jan. 14, 1942; niece of Arthur and Lydia Sudbrink. BS, Bowling Green State U., 1964; postgrad. in cytogenetics Kinderspital-Zurich, Switzerland, 1965. Field rep. Random House and Alfred A. Knopf Inc., Mpls., 1969-72, Ann Arbor, Mich., 1973, regional mgr., Midwest and Can., 1974-79, Can. rep., mgr., 1980-81; psychology and ednl. psychology adminstrv. editor Charles E. Merrill Pub. Co. div. Bell & Howell Corp., Columbus, Ohio, 1982-84; sales and mktg. mgr. trade products Wilson Learning Corp., Eden Prairie, Minn., 1984-85; fin. cons. Merrill Lynch Pierce Fenner & Smith, Edina, 1986-88; sr. editor Gorsuch Scarisbrick Pubs., Scottsdale, Ariz., 1988-89; regional mgr. Worth Publs., Inc. - von Holtzbrinck Pub. Grp., N.Y.C., 1988—. Lutheran. Home and Office: 3801 Mission Hills Rd Northbrook IL 60062-5729

SUDBURY, JOHN DEAN, religious foundation executive, petroleum chemist; b. Natchitoches, La., July 29, 1925; s. Herbert J. and Mary Flora S.; m. Jean Elizabeth Jung, July 18, 1947; children: John Byron, James Vernon (dec.), Linda Gail. BS, U. Tex., Austin, 1943, MA, 1947, PhD, 1949. Registered profl. engr., Okla. With Conoco Inc., various locations, 1949-83; asst. to v.p. tech. Conoco Inc., N.Y.C., 1970-72; v.p. coal research Conoco Coal Devel. Co. subs. Conoco Inc., Pitts., 1972-83; pres. Ea. European Mission & Bible Found., Houston, 1983—. Author: Oil Well Corrosion, 1956; contbr. articles to profl. jours. Mem. Ponca City (Okla.) Sch. Bd., 1965-67; trustee Okla. Christian Coll., 1968—. Served with USN, 1943-45. Recipient Frank Newman Speller award Nat. Assn. Corrosion Engrs., 1967. Mem. Am. Chem. Soc., N.Y. Acad. Scis., AAAS, Sigma Xi. Republican. Mem. Ch. of Christ. Club: Woodlands Country (Tex.). Patentee in energy field. Home: 42 Cascade Springs Pl Spring TX 77381-3101 Office: PO Box 90755 Houston TX 77290-0755

SUDDICK, PATRICK JOSEPH, defense systems company executive; b. London, Ont., Can., Sept. 27, 1923; s. Percy Edward and Eva Isobel (Jones) S.; m. Mary Agnes Walsh, July 7, 1951; children: Paul, Peter, Michael Jane Suddick Reynolds, Mark. BA in Sci., U. Toronto, 1949. With Honeywell Ltd., 1953-84; project mgr. comml. div. Honeywell Ltd., Scarborough, Ont., Can., 1953-57, asst. mgr. mil. products, 1957-58, market mgr. EDP div., 1958-65, gen. mgr. EDP div., 1965-68; v.p. EDP div. Honeywell Ltd., Willowdale, Ont., Can., 1968-70, v.p. and dir., 1970-84. Served with Can. Arty., 1942-46. Mem. Assn. Profl. Engrs. Ont., NATO Indsl. Adv. Group. Roman Catholic. Address: 25 Austin Dr Ste 419, Unionville, ON Canada L3R 8H4

SUE, ALAN KWAI KEONG, dentist; b. Honolulu, Apr. 26, 1946; s. Henry Tin Yee and Chiyoko (Ohata) S.; m. Ginger Kazue Fukushima, Mar. 19, 1972; 1 child, Dawn Marie. BS in Chemistry with honors, U. Hawaii, 1968; BS, U. Calif., San Francisco, 1972, DDS, 1972. Film editor, photographer Sta. KHVH-TV ABC, Honolulu, 1964-71; staff dentist Strong-Carter Dental Clinic, Honolulu, 1972-73; dentist Waianae Dental Clinic, Honolulu, 1972-73; pvt. practice Pearl City, Hawaii, 1973—; chief exec. officer Dental Image Specialists, Pearl City, 1975—; dental dir. Hawaii Dental Health Plan, Honolulu, 1987—; dental cons. Calif. Dental Health Plan, Tustin, 1987—, Pacific Group Med. Assn., The Queen's Health Care Plan, Honolulu, 1993—; dental cons. Pacific Group Med. Assn., 1994—; cons. Hawaii Mgmt. Alliance Assn., 1996—; bd. dirs. Kula Bay Tropical Clothing Co.; mem. exec. bd. St. Francis Hosp., Honolulu, 1976-78, chief dept. dentistry, 1976-78; mem. expert med. panel Am. Internat. Claim Svc., 1995—. Mem. adv. bd. Health Svcs. for Sr. Citizens, 1976—; mem. West Honolulu Sub-Area Health Planning Coun., 1981-84; mem. dental task force Hawaii Statewide Health Coordinating Coun., 1980, mem. plan devel. com., 1981-84; vol. oral cancer screening program Am. Cancer Soc.; v.p. Pearl City Shopping Ctr. Merchants Assn., 1975-84, 92-93, pres., 1994—. Regents' scholar U. Calif., San Francisco, 1968-72. Fellow Pierre Fauchard Acad., Acad. Gen. Dentistry; mem. ADA, Acad. Implants and Transplants, Am. Acad. Implant Dentistry, Hawaii Dental Assn. (trustee 1978-80), Honolulu County Dental Soc. (pres. 1982), Am. Acad. and Bd. Head, Facial, Neck Pain and TMJ Orthopedics, Intertel, Internat. Platform Assn., Mensa, Porsche Club, Pantera Owners Club, Mercedes Benz Club. Democrat. Avocations: cars, tennis, photography, gardening. Office: Dental Image Specialists 850 Kam Hwy Ste 116 Pearl City HI 96782-2603

SUEDFELD, PETER, psychologist, educator; b. Budapest, Hungary, Aug. 30, 1935; emigrated to U.S., 1948, naturalized, 1952; s. Leslie John and Jolan (Eichenbaum) Field; m. Gabrielle Debra Guterman, June 11, 1961 (div. 1980); children: Michael Thomas, Joanne Ruth, David Lee; m. Phyllis Jean Johnson, Oct. 19, 1991. Student, U. Philippines, 1956-57; B.A., Queens Coll., 1960; M.A., Princeton U., 1962, Ph.D., 1963. Research assoc. Princeton U.; lectr. Trenton State Coll., 1963-64; vis. asst. prof. psychology U. Ill., 1964-65; asst. prof. psychology Univ. Coll. Rutgers U., 1965-67, assoc. prof., 1967-71, prof., 1971-72, chmn. dept., 1967-72; prof. psychology U. B.C., Vancouver, 1972—; head dept. U. B.C., 1972-84, dean faculty grad. studies, 1984-90; cons. in field; chmn. Can. Antarctic Rsch. Program. Author: Restricted Environmental Stimulation: Research and Clinical Applications, 1980; editor: Attitude Change: The Competing Views, 1971, Personality Theory and Information Processing, 1971, The Behavioral Basis of Design, 1976, Psychology and Torture, 1990, Restricted Environmental Stimulation: Theoretical and Empirical Developments in Flotation REST, 1990, Psychology and Social Policy, 1991; editor Jour. Applied Social Psychology, 1975-82; assoc. editor Environment and Behavior, 1992—; contbr. articles to profl. jours. Served with U.S. Army, 1955-58. Recipient Antarctica svc. medal, 1994, Donald O. Hebb award, 1996; grantee NIMH, 1970-72, Can. Coun., 1973—, Nat. Rsch. Coun. Can., 1973-90, NIH, 1980-84. Fellow Royal Soc. Can., Can. Psychol. Assn., Am. Psychol. Assn., Am. Psychol. Soc., Acad. Behavioral Medicine Research, Soc. Behavioral Medicine, N.Y. Acad. Scis.; mem. AAAS, Psychonomic Soc., Soc. Exptl. Social Psychology, Phi Beta Kappa, Sigma Xi. Office: U BC, Dept Psychology, Vancouver, BC Canada V6T 1Z4

SUELFLOW, AUGUST ROBERT, historian, educator, archivist; b. Rockfield, Wis., Sept. 5, 1922; s. August Henry and Selma Hilda (Kressin) S.; m. Gladys I. Gierach, June 16, 1946; children: August Mark, Kathryn Lynn Du Bois. BA, Concordia Coll., Milw., 1942; BDiv, MDiv, Concordia Sem., St. Louis, 1946, fellow, 1947, STM, 1947; DivD, Concordia Sem., Springfield, Ill., 1967. Asst. curator Concordia Hist. Inst., St. Louis, 1946-48, dir., 1948-95, cons., 1995—; guest lectr. Concordia Sem., St. Louis, 1952-69, 74-75, adj. prof., 1975—; asst. pastor Luther Meml. Ch., Richmond Heights, Mo., 1948-56, Mt. Olive, St. Louis, 1958-75; archivist Western Dist. Luth. Ch.-Mo. Synod, 1948-66, archivist Mo. Dist., 1966-87, 88-95; instr. Washington U., St. Louis, 1967-82. Inst. Mem. Am. Assn. Museums, Nat. Trust for Hist. Preservation, Soc. Am. Archivists, Orgn. Am. Historians, Western History Assn., Luth. Hist. Conf. Lutheran. Author: A Preliminary Guide to Church Records Depositories, 1969, Religious Archives: An Introduction, 1980, Heart of Missouri, 1954; cons., contbr. Luth. Cyclopedia, 1975; contbr. Moving Frontiers, 1964, Ency. of the Luth. Ch., 1965, The Luths. in N.Am., 1975, C.F.W. Walther: The American Luther, 1987; mng. editor Concordia Hist. Inst. Quar., 1950-95, assoc. editor., 1950—; Archives & History: Minutes and Reports, 1952-89; editor: Directory of Religious Hist. Depositories in America, 1963, Microfilm Index and Bibliography, vol. I, 1966, vol. II, 1978, Luth. Hist. Conf. Essays and Reports, 1964-92; series editor: Selected Writings of C.F.W. Walther, 6 vols., 1981; vol. editor, translator: Walther's Convention Essays, vol. III, 1981; sec., mem. editorial com. Concordia Jour., 1976-81; mem. editorial/adv. com. Luth. Higher Edn. in N.Am., 1980; mem. editorial com., contbr. Moving Frontiers, 1964. Office: Concordia Hist Inst 801 De Mun Ave Saint Louis MO 63105-3168

SUELTENFUSS, SISTER ELIZABETH ANNE, academic administrator; b. San Antonio, Apr. 14, 1921; d. Edward L. and Elizabeth (Amrein) S. BA in Botany and Zoology, Our Lady of Lake Coll., San Antonio, 1944; MS in Biology, U. Notre Dame, 1961, PhD, 1963. Joined Sisters of Divine Providence, Roman Catholic Ch., 1939; tchr. high schs. Okla. and La., 1942-49; mem. summer faculty Our Lady of Lake U. (formerly coll.), 1941-49, mem. full-time faculty, 1949-59, chmn. biology dept., 1963-73, pres., 1978—; mem. adminstrv. staff to superior gen. Congregation Divine Providence, 1973-77. Author articles in field. Bd. dirs. Am. Cancer Soc., San Antonio chpt. ARC, Mind Sci. Found., YWCA, Alamo Pub. Telecomm. Bd., S.W. Rsch. Found., I Have a Dream Found., Inst. Ednl. Leadership, Trim and Swim, San Antonio Edn. Partnership; bd. dirs., chmn. San Antonio Pub. Libr. Recipient Achievement and Leadership awards U. Notre Dame, 1979, Svc. to Community award, 1991, Headliner award Women in Comms., 1980, Good Neighbor award NCCJ, 1982, Brotherhood award, 1992, Today's Woman award San Antonio Light, 1982, Outstanding Women award San Antonio Express-News, 1983, Spirit of Am. Woman award J.C. Penney, 1992, Lifetime Achievement award, 1993, Svc. to Edn. awrd Ford Found., 1993; named to San Antonio Women's Hall of Fame, 1985. Mem. AAUP, AAUW, San Antonio 100 Tex. Women's Forum, San Antonio Women's C. of C., Hispanic Assn. Colls. and Univs., Greater San Antonio C. of C. (past vice chmn.), San Antonio Coun. Pres. (past pres.), San Antonio Women's Hall of Fame (past pres.). Home and Office: Our Lady of the Lake U Office of Pres 411 SW 24th St San Antonio TX 78207-4689

SUELTO, CONSUELO QUILAO, nursing educator; b. The Philippines, June 27, 1924; d. Catalina Pamplona; m. Anacleto T. Suelto, Apr. 28, 1952; children: Ramona, Anacleto T. Jr. Diploma, U. Philippines Sch. Nursing, Manila, 1949; BS in Nursing Edn., Philippine Women's U., Manila, 1955, EdD, 1983; MA in Nursing, U. Philippines, Quezon City, 1960; EdD, P.W. U., 1983. Staff nurse U. Philippines-Philippine Gen. Hosp., 1949-50, instr. Sch. Nursing, 1950-61; adminstrv. officer, asst. dean Philippine Women's U., 1961-68; prin. St. Jude Sch. Nursing, Manila, 1968-73, Lipa City (The Philippines Sch. Nursing, 1976-80; dean Lipa City Coll. Nursing, 1980-84, Golden Gate Coll. Coll. Nursing, Batangas City, The Philippines, 1980-84; coord., instr. St. James Mercy Hosp. Sch. Nursing, Hornell, N.Y., 1973-75, 84-94. Mem. adv. bd. PNA of Fla., 1995. Mem. Philippines Nurses Assn. (life, bd. dirs.), Nurses Assn. of the Am. Assn. of Ob-Gyn. Home: 175 Brittain Dr # 5 Tallahassee FL 32310

SUEN, CHING YEE, computer scientist and educator, researcher; b. Chung Shan, Kwang Tung, China, Oct. 14, 1942; s. Stephen and Sin (Kan) S; m. Sheung Ling Chan, May 12, 1970; children: Karwa, Karnon. BSc in Engring., U. Hong Kong, 1966, MSc in Engring., 1968; M.A.Sc., U. B.C., 1970, PhD, 1972. Asst. prof. computer sci. Concordia U., Montreal, Can., 1972-76, assoc. prof., 1976-79, prof., 1979, chmn., 1980-84, dir. Centre for Pattern Recognition and Machine Intelligence, 1988—, assoc. dean faculty engring. and computer sci., 1993—; vis. scientist Rsch. Lab. of Electronics, MIT, Cambridge, 1975, 76, 78-79; invited prof. Ecole Polytechnique Fédérale de Lausanne, Switzerland, 1979, Institut de Recherche d'Informatique et d'Automatique, Rocquencourt, France, 1976, 78, 79; co-founder, co-chmn. Internat. Conf. on Document Analysis and Recognition, St.-Malo, France, 1991, Tsukuba Sci. City, Japan, 1993, chmn., Montreal, Can., 1995; founder, chmn. Internat. Workshop on Frontiers in Handwriting Recognition, Montreal, 1990; organizer numerous confs. Author: Computational Analysis of Mandarin, 1979, Computational Studies of the Most Frequent Chinese Words and Sounds, 1986, (with Z.C. Li, T.D. Bui, Y.Y. Tang) Computer Transformation of Digital Images and Patterns, 1989; editor: (with R. De Mori) Computer Analysis and Perception Vol. 1, Visual Signals, 1982, Computer Analysis and Perception Vol. 2, Auditory Signals, 1982, (with R. De Mori) New Systems and Architectures for Automatic Speech Recognition and Synthesis, 1985, (with R. Plamondon and M.L. Simner) Computer Recognition and Human Production of Handwriting, 1989, Frontiers in Handwriting Recognition, 1990, Operating Expert System Applications in Canada, 1992, (with P.S.P. Wang) Thinning Methodologies for Pattern Recognition, 1994; assoc. editor Signal Processing, 1979—, Pattern Recognition Letters, 1982—, Pattern Recognition, 1983—, IEEE Transactions on Pattern Analysis and Machine Intelligence, 1986-89, Internat. Jour. Pattern Recognition and Artificial Intelligence, 1986—; founder, editor-in-chief Computer Processing of Chinese and Oriental Langs., 1982-93; adviser IEEE Transactions on Pattern Analysis and Machine Intelligence, 1989—; author more than 300 publs.; patentee in field. Recipient award Fedn. Chinese Can. Profls., 1988; Swire scholar U. Hong Kong, 1967, ITAC/NSERC award Info. Tech. Assn. Can. and Natural Scis. and Engring. Rsch. Coun. Can., 1992. Fellow IEEE (advisor Computer Soc.), Royal Soc. Can., Internat. Assn. for Pattern Recognition (gov.); mem. Chinese Lang. Computer Soc. (pres. 1990-93, award 1988), Can. Image Processing and Pattern Recognition Soc. (pres. 1984-90). Office: Concordia U Dept Computer Sci, 1455 Maisonneuve W Ste GM-606, Montreal, PQ Canada H3G 1M8

SUEN, JAMES YEE, otolaryngologist, educator; b. Dermott, Ark., Oct. 9, 1940; s. Yee Gow and Mary (Chaing) S.; m. Karen Hannahs; children: Brent, Tiffany, Bradley, Brennan. BA in Zoology, U. Tex., 1962; BS, MD, U. Ark., 1966. Diplomate Am. Bd. Otolaryngology. Rotating intern San Francisco Gen. Hosp., 1966-67; resident in gen. surgery U. Ark. Med. Ctr., Little Rock, 1969-70, resident in otolaryngology, 1970-73; advanced sr. fellow M.D. Anderson Hosp. and Tumor Inst., Houston, 1973-74, faculty assoc., 1974; asst. prof. U. Ark. Coll. Medicine, Little Rock, 1974-76, assoc. prof., 1976-78, prof. otolaryngology, 1978—, chief div. otolaryngology, 1974-78, chmn. dept. otolaryngology and head and neck surgery, 1978—. Author, editor: Cancer of the Head and Neck, 1981, 3d edit., 1996, Emergencies in Otolaryngology, 1986. Capt. USAF, 1967-69. Recipient Disting. Alumnus award U. Tex., M.D. Anderson Cancer Ctr., 1995; named Chinese Man of Yr., Chinese Soc. Ark., 1983, Disting. Citizen of Yr. Gov. Ark., 1991. Fellow ACS, Am. Acad. Otolaryngology and Head and Neck Surgery, Am. Soc. Head and Neck Surgery (pres. 1993-94, coun. 1988-92); mem. Soc. Univ. Otolaryngologists. Methodist. Avocation: sculpturing. Office: U Ark Coll Medicine 4301 W Markham St Little Rock AR 72205-7101

SUER, MARVIN DAVID, architecture, consultant; b. Phila., Apr. 4, 1923; m. Gertrude Litvin, 1947; children: Marsha Suer Clark, Sharon, Deborah Suer Berman. BArch, U. Pa., 1950. Registered architect, N.J., Pa. Ptnr. Suer & Livingston, 1961-62, Suer, Livingston & Demas, 1962-69; dir. tech. prodn. Eshbach, Pullinger, Stevens & Bruder, Phila., 1969-74; assoc. Ballinger, Phila., 1974-79, Bartley Long Mirenda, Phila., 1979-85, S.T. Hudson Internat., Phila., 1986-95; archtl. cons., 1996—. Archtl. works include State Hosp. for Crippled Children addition, 1964, Huey Elem. Sch., Phila., 1964, Dist. No. 4 Health Ctr., Phila., 1967, Stephen Smith Towers, 1969, Foxchase Br. Libr., 1969. Chmn. bd. trustees Phila. Found. for Architecture, 1980-81. With C.E., AUS, 1943-46. Fellow AIA (pres. Phila. chpt. 1968, 125th Yr. citation 1982); mem. Tau Sigma Delta. Home: 305 Overlook Ave Willow Grove PA 19090-2806

SUERO, JOSÉ AGUSTIN, company executive; b. Santo Domingo, Dominican Republic, May 3, 1947; s. Justiniano Vasquez and Amelia Suero; m. Josefina Cuello, Mar. 19, 1972; children: Juan Carlos, Arlene Suero Cuello. Student, Mahatmagandy, Santo Domingo, 1967-68, Corp. Argentina de Production, Buenos Aires, 1970, NYU, 1983, 84, Ctrl. Ednl. Caribe, N.Y.C., 1987. Mgr. prodn. Super Maquet Domincano, Santo Domingo, 1966-71; pres. adminstrn. Products Gaucho, Santo Domingo, 1971-76; mgr. meat Fedco Foods, Bronx, N.Y., 1976-82, Pioneer Super Marquet, 1982-84, Associated Super Marquet, 1984-87, Read Apple Super Marquet, N.Y.C., 1987—. Bd. mem. Esperanza Ctr., 1974-94, Dominican Parade, 1981-84, La Gran Parade of Bronx, 1990; v.p. Ceduca Centro Ednl. Caribe, 1976-90, 34 Police Precinct coun., 1989-92; active Presdl. Commn. Am. Agenda. Mem. U.S. Families of Am., Lions Club. Republican. Roman Catholic. Home: 580 W 161st St Apt 26 New York NY 10032-6210 Office: High Power Coalition 580 W 161st St Apt 26 New York NY 10032-6210

SUESS, JEFFREY KARL, lawyer; b. Carbondale, Ill., May 27, 1960; s. Raymond Karl and Maryloy (Ronat) S.; m. Karen Elizabeth Mason, Oct. 17, 1987; children: Matthew Karl, Alexandra Margret, Mason Robert. BA in Polit. Sci., Washington U., St. Louis, 1982, JD, 1985. Bar: Mo. 1985, Ill. 1986. Assoc. Evans & Dixon, St. Louis, 1985-92, ptnr., 1993—. Contbr. chpts. to book: Civil Procedure: Missouri Bar CLE, 1988, 90, 94. Trustee First Presbyn. Ch., St. Louis, 1990-93, pres. bd. deacons, 1987-89; commr. University City (Mo.) Arts and Letters Commn., 1994—, treas. Mem. ABA, Mo. Orgn. Def. Lawyers, Mo. Bar Assn. (civil procedure com.), St. Louis County Bar Assn., Vol. Lawyers Assn., Sigma Chi (sec. 1980), Phi Delta Phi (pres. 1983-84). Avocations: golf, hockey, soccer, raising children. Office: Evans & Dixon 200 N Broadway Ste 1200 Saint Louis MO 63102

SUGAR, PETER FRIGYES, historian; b. Budapest, Hungary, Jan. 5, 1919; s. Peter S. and Margit (Pongor) S.; m. Sally Bortz, June 18, 1955; children: Steven P., Klari A., Karen L. B.A., CCNY, 1954; M.A., Princeton, U., 1956, Ph.D., 1959. Instr. history Princeton U., 1957-59; asst. prof. history U. Wash., Seattle, 1959-63; assoc. prof. U. Wash., 1963-69, prof., 1969-89, now prof. history emeritus; assoc. dir. U. Wash. (Inst. Comparative and Foreign Area Studies.). Author: The Industrilization of Bosnia-Hercegovina, 1878-1919, 1963, Southeastern Europe under Ottoman Rule, 1354-1804, 1977, A History of Hungary, 1990, Eastern European Nationalism in the Twentieth Century, 1995, and others. Guggenheim Found. fellow, 1964-65; Woodrow Wilson fellow, 1954-55; Fulbright fellow, 1984. Mem. Am. Hist. Assn., Am. Assn. Advancement of Slavic Studies, Western Slavic Assn., Am. Assn. Study of Hungarian History. Home: 11737 12th Ave NE Seattle WA 98125-5007 Office: U Wash Dept History Seattle WA 98195

SUGAR, SANDRA LEE, art consultant; b. Balt., May 18, 1942; d. Harry S. and Edith Sarah (Levin) Pomerantz; children: Gary Lee, Terry Lynn. BS in Edn. and English, Towson State U., 1965; MS in Edn. and Applied Behavioral Scis., Johns Hopkins U., 1986. Chairperson arts exhibit Balt. Arts Festival, 1979; med. interviewer Johns Hopkins Sch. of Hygiene, Balt., 1980-82; copy writer Concepts & Communications, Balt., 1984; instr. art history and world cultures Catonsville Community Coll., Balt., 1981-85; instr. English Community Coll. of Balt., 1981-85; instr. English and math. Info. Processing Tng. Ctr., Balt., 1985; info. specialist Info. of Md. New Directions for Women, Balt., 1986; trainer, job developer Working Solutions, Balt., 1987-88; art gallery dir. Renaissance Fine Arts Gallery, Bethesda, Md., 1988-93; art cons. Bethesda, 1994—; judge nat. high sch. sci. fiction contests. Author poetry collection, juried exhibition, 1979, 80; editor mus. guides' newsletter Guidelines, 1978; painter juried exhibitions, 1979, 80. Docent Balt. Mus. of Art, 1973-86; festival coordinator Internat. Brass Quintet Festival, Balt., 1986; chairperson spl. events Balt. PTA, 1978-82; bd. dirs. Citizens Planning and Housing Assn., Balt., 1980-82; mem. women's com., ctr. stage hand Balt. Ballet, 1979-84, Balt. Symphony, 1979-80. Recipient F.J. Bamberger scholarship, Johns Hopkins U., 1985, Mayoral Vol. of Yr. award Balt. Mus. Art, 1979.

SUGARBAKER, EVAN R., nuclear science research administrator; b. Mineola, N.Y., Nov. 17, 1949; married, 1985; 1 child. BA, Kalamazoo Coll., 1971; PhD in Physics, U. Mich., 1976. Rsch. assoc. nuclear structural rsch. lab. U. Rochester (N.Y.), 1976-68; vis. asst. prof. physics U. Colo., 1978-80; asst. prof. physics Ohio State U., Columbus, 1981-86, assoc. prof. physics, 1986—; co-prin. investigator NSF grant, 1981-88, prin. investigator, 1988—. Mem. AAAS, Am. Phys. Soc., Am. Assn. Physics Tchrs. Office: Dept Physics Ohio State U 1302 Kinnear Rd Columbus OH 43212*

SUGARMAN, ALAN WILLIAM, educational administrator; b. Boston, Sept. 26, 1924; s. Henry and Dorothy (Adams) S.; m. Alice Mulhall, 1974; children: Michael, Susan, Ellen, William, Jane, James. BS, Boston U., 1948; MA, Columbia U., 1949, EdD, 1967; postgrad., SUNY, Albany, 1954-56. Entrance examiner Boston U., 1947-48; tchr. Public Schs. Hudson, N.Y., 1950-54; prin. jr. high sch. Public Schs. Hudson, 1954-56, prin. sr. high sch., 1956-61; prin. Spring Valley (N.Y.) Sr. High Sch., 1961-67; dir. secondary edn. Ramapo Central Sch. Dist. No. 2, Spring Valley, 1967-69; asst. supt. instrn. Ramapo Central Sch. Dist. No. 2, 1969-73; prin. Ramapo Sr. High Sch., Spring Valley, 1969; supt. schs. Connetquot Central Sch. Dist. Islip, Bohemia, N.Y., 1973-80, Ft. Lee (N.J.) Sch. Dist., 1980—; adj. prof. N.Y. U., N.Y.C., U. P.R., Rio Piedras, Hofstra U., 1967—; prof. Fordham U., N.Y.C., 1969. Athletic dir. East River Day Camp, N.Y.C., summer 1949; group worker St. John's Guild, summer 1950; asst. dir. Tenn. Work Camp, Unitarian Service Com., summer 1951; dir. spl. activities Hudson Youth Bur., Hudson, N.Y., summer 1952; exec. dir. Jewish Community Center, Hudson, 1953-56; chmn. vis. coms. Middle States Commn. Colls. and Secondary Schs., 1958-76; chmn. county leadership tng. com., mem. Rockland County exec. council Boy Scouts Am., 1956; bd. dirs. Bergen County Red Cross; corr. sec. Rockland County Negro Scholarship Fund, Inc.; pres. Spring Valley Youth Activities Com., 1956-58; bd. dirs., past campaign co-chmn. Greater Hudson Community Chest; bd. dirs., 2d v.p. Hudson Youth Recreation Center, 1958-61; bd. dirs. Rockland County br. Am. Cancer Soc., 1958-61, Columbia Meml. Hosp., 1959-61; chmn. Town of Islip Health Usage Com., 1973; bd. dirs. Am. Heart Assn. N.J. affiliate, 1993—. Served with AUS, 1944-46, ETO. Recipient Disting. Svc. award Hudson Jr. C. of C., 1960, Ft. Lee Citizen of Yr. award VFW, Bergen County Citizen of Yr. award VFW, 1989, N.J. State Elks Alcohol and Drug Prevention award, 1989, St. Michael's award, 1992, PBA Silver Life Card award, 1993, EIA award Greek Orthodox Archdiocese, 1993; named Adminstr. of Yr., Fordham U., 1990, B'nai Brith Man of Yr., 1995. Mem. Nat. Honor Soc. Secondary Schs. (hon.), Nat. PTA (hon. life), Am. Assn. Sch. Adminstrs., Assn. Supervision and Curriculum Devel., Nat. Sch. Public Relations Assn., Assn. Sch. Bus. Ofcls., Nat. Soc. Study Edn., DAV, VFW, Jewish War Vets., Rotary (bd. dirs.), Phi Delta Kappa (Adminstr. of Yr. award 1990), Kappa Delta Pi, Pi Gamma Mu. Jewish (bd. edn.). Home: Shelter Bay Club 1225 River Rd Apt 7B Edgewater NJ 07020-1461 Office: 255 Whiteman St Fort Lee NJ 07024-5629

SUGARMAN, IRWIN J., lawyer; b. Dayton, Ohio, June 17, 1943; s. Nathan and Esther (Goldstein) S.; 1 child, Alexander David Skigen Sugarman. BA, Rutgers U., New Brunswick, N.J., 1965; JD, Rutgers U., Newark, 1968. Bar: N.Y. 1968. Law clk. to Judge Edmund Palmieri U.S. Dist. Ct. for So. Dist. N.Y., N.Y.C., 1968-69; assoc. Debevoise Plimpton Lyons & Gates, N.Y.C., 1969-79; ptnr. Schulte Roth & Zabel, N.Y.C., 1979—. Bd. dirs. Santa Fe Opera, 1989-94. Office: Schulte Roth & Zabel 900 3rd Ave New York NY 10022-4728

SUGARMAN, JULE M., children's services consultant, former public administrator; b. Cin., Sept. 23, 1927; s. Melville Harty and Rachel Wolf (Meyer) S.; m. Sheila Mary Shanley, May 20, 1956 (dec.); children: Christopher, Maryanne, Jason, James; m. Candace Sullivan, Apr. 2, 1989. Student, Western Res. U., 1945-46; A.B. with highest distinction, Am. U., 1951. Dir. Head Start, 1965-69; adminstr. Human Resources Adminstrn., N.Y.C., 1970-73; chief adminstrv. officer City of Atlanta, 1974-76; vice chmn. CSC, Washington, 1977-78; dep. dir. Office Personnel Mgmt., 1979-81; mng. dir. Human Service Info. Ctr., 1981-83; v.p. Hahnemann U., 1983-86; sec. Wash. State Dept. Social and Health Services, 1986-89; exec. dir. Spl. Olympics Internat., Washington, 1989-91; chmn. Ctr. on Effective Svcs. for Children, Washington, 1991—. Served with U.S. Army, 1946-48. Recipient Meritorious Service award Dept. State, 1963, Alumni Service award Am. U., 1977, Disting. Pub. Svc. award Nat. Acad. Pub. Adminstrn., 1988. Home: 2555 Pennsylvania Ave NW Washington DC 20037-1613 Office: PO Box 27412 Washington DC 20038-7412*

SUGARMAN, MATTHEW S., historic site adminstrator. Park ranger trainee Golden Gate Area Calif. State Parks, 1972, patrol resource ranger Montane Area, 1972-76, supervising ranger campground ops. Pt. Mugu Area, 1976-77, from tng. supervisor to supervising ranger Santa Monica Mtn., 1977-81, supervising ranger vis. svcs. Klamath Dist. South Sector, 1981-85; park supt. Gold Rush Dist. Marshall Gold Discovery, State Hist. Park, 1985—. Mem. El Dorado County Sesquicentennial Commn. Mem. El Dorado County Recreation Profls., El Dorado County Law Enforcement Adminstrs., El Dorado County C. of C. (bd. dirs.). Office: Marshall Gold Discovery State Hist Pk PO Box 265 Coloma CA 95613-0265 Office: c/o Marshall Gold Discovery PO Box 265 Coloma CA 95613

SUGARMAN, MYRON GEORGE, lawyer; b. San Francisco, Nov. 7, 1942; s. Irving Carden and Jane Hortense (Weingarten) S.; m. Cheryl Ann Struble, June 8, 1968 (div. 1993); children: Andrew, Amy, Adam; m. Cynthia Wilson Woods, Apr. 16, 1994. BS, U. Calif., Berkeley, 1964, JD, 1967. Assoc. Cooley, Godward, Castro, Huddleson & Tatum, San Francisco, 1972-77, ptnr., 1977—. Served to capt. U.S. Army, 1968-71. Fellow Am. Coll. Trust and Estate Counsel, Am. Coll. Tax Counsel, Am. Bar Found.; mem. U. Calif. Alumni Assn. (bd. dirs. 1985-88), San Francisco Tax Club (pres. 1990), San Francisco Grid Club. Avocations: skiing, tennis. Office: Cooley Godward Castro Huddleson & Tatum 1 Maritime Plz San Francisco CA 94111-3404

SUGARMAN, PAUL RONALD, lawyer, educator, academic administrator; b. Boston, Dec. 14, 1931; m. Susan J. Sugarman; children: Amy J., Ellen J. AA, Boston U., 1951, JD cum laude (Law Week award 1954, asso. editor law rev. 1952-54), 1954; LLD (hon.), Suffolk U., 1989. Bar: Mass. 1954, U.S. Supreme Ct. 1965. Ptnr. Sugarman & Sugarman, Boston, 1967-90, 94—; prof. law, dean Suffolk U. Law Sch., Boston, 1990-94; mem. Atty. Gen. Mass. Hwy. Law Study Commn., 1965, Mass. Gov.'s Select Com. on Jud. Needs, 1976; bd. bar overseers Supreme Jud. Ct., 1984-88, chmn., 1985-88; advocate Am. Bd. Trial Advocates; spl. master, commr. Boston Mcpl. Ct. Report Supreme Jud. Ct. of Mass., 1990. Trustee Mass. Bar Found., 1980-81. Served as officer AUS, 1955-58. Recipient Courageous Adv. award, Mass. Acad. Trial Attys., 1984, William O. Douglas First Amendment Freedom award, Anti-Defamation League, 1986, Silver Shingle award for svc. to legal profession Boston U. Sch. Law, 1989, Jurisprudence award Am. Orgn. for Rehab. through Tng. Fedn., 1991, Civil Justice award Am. Bd. trial Adv., 1993. Fellow Am. Coll. Trial Lawyers, Am. Bar Found., Mass. Bar Found., Internat. Soc. Barristers; mem. Am. Bar Assn., Mass. Bar Assn. (pres. 1976-77, chmn. com. on recall of ret. judges 1982-86, Gold Medal award 1991), Am. Trial Lawyers Assn. (gov. 1966-68, pres. Mass. chpt. 1968-70), Boston Bar Assn., Boston U. Sch. Law Alumni Assn. (pres. 1979-80). Office: Sugarman and Sugarman PC One Beacon St Boston MA 02108

SUGARMAN, PAUL WILLIAM, lawyer; b. Cambridge, Mass., July 31, 1947; s. Louis Edward and Natalie (Waldman) S.; m. Susan Lee Richard, July 16, 1978; children: Sarah, Emily, Hannah. BA, Harvard U., 1969; JD, Yale U., 1975. Bar: Calif. 1976, U.S. Dist. Ct. (no. dist.) Calif. 1976, U.S. Ct. Appeals (9th cir.) 1976. Law clk. to judge U.S. Dist. Ct. (no. dist.) Calif., San Francisco, 1975-76; assoc. Heller, Ehrman, White & McAuliffe, San Francisco, 1976-81, ptnr., 1982—. Vol. U.S. Peace Corps, Ethiopia, 1969-72. Mem. ABA, Calif. Bar Assn., San Francisco Bar Assn., Phi Beta Kappa. Home: 907 Longridge Rd Oakland CA 94610-2444 Office: Heller Ehrman White & McAuliffe 333 Bush St Ste 3100 San Francisco CA 94104-2806*

SUGARMAN, ROBERT GARY, lawyer; b. Bronx, N.Y., Sept. 3, 1939; s. Eugene Leonard and Frances (Solomon) S.; m. Brenda Harrison, Sept. 8, 1963 (div. 1984); children: Dana, Alison; m. Surie Rudoff, June 16, 1985; children: Amanda, Jason. BA, Yale U., 1960, LLB, 1963. Bar: N.Y. 1963, Fla. 1963, U.S. Supreme Ct. 1971, U.S. Dist. Ct. (so. dist.) N.Y. 1966, U.S. Dist. Ct. (ea. dist.) N.Y. 1982, U.S. Ct. Appeals (2d cir.) 1970, U.S. Ct. Appeals (10th cir.) 1971. Assoc. Sugarman, Kuttner & Fuss, N.Y.C., 1966, Sullivan & Cromwell, N.Y.C., 1966-72; assoc. Weil, Gotshal & Manges, N.Y.C., 1972-75, ptnr., 1975—. Author: (with others) Litigation Strategy and Tactics , 1979, Deposition Strategy Law and Forms, 1980, Masters of Trial Practice, 1988; contbr. articles on intellectual property law to profl. jours. Assoc. counsel N.Y. State Constl. Conv., Albany, N.Y., 1967; pres. Hillel of N.Y., 1986-88. Served to capt. U.S. Army, 1963-65. Fellow Am. Coll. Trial Lawyers; mem. Assn. of Bar of City of N.Y. (chmn. comm. and media law com. 1989-92), B'nai Brith (internat. bd. govs. 1975-85), Anti-Defamation League (nat. commn. 1981—, nat. exec. com. 1988—, vice-chmn. 1990-92, chmn. intergroup rels. com. 1992-94, chmn. civil rights com. 1994—). Democrat. Jewish. Office: Weil Gotshal & Manges 767 Fifth Ave New York NY 10022

SUGARMAN, ROBERT JAY, lawyer; b. Meriden, Conn., May 29, 1938; s. Lester Holman and Ruth Frieda (Kalman) S.; m. Kathleen A. Knoppel; children: Karen Elizabeth, Kenneth John, Jane Alexandra, Lily Anna. A.B., Brown U., 1960; postgrad. (Ford Found. fellow), Stanford U., 1960-61; LL.B. magna cum laude, Harvard U., 1964. Law clk. to Hon. Abraham L. Freedman, U.S. Ct. Appeals, Phila., 1965-66; ptnr. Dechert Price and Rhoads, Phila., 1964-65, 66-78, Sugarman & Assocs., Phila., 1982—; lectr. in environ. law, adj. prof. planning; legal cons. Nat. Water Quality Commn. Author: (with T. Reiner) The Crosstown Expressway: A Case Study, 1970, (with D. DeVaul and T. Keating) Trading in Power, 1985; editor: Harvard Law Rev, 1963-64; contbr. articles to profl. jours. U.S. chmn. Internat. Joint Commn., U.S. and Can., Washington, 1978-81. Office: Sugarman & Assocs 100 N 17th St Fl 7 Philadelphia PA 19103-2736

SUGARMAN, SAMUEL LOUIS, retired oil transportation and trading company executive, horse breeder; b. Montague, Mass., Apr. 18, 1927; s. Julius William and Minnie S.; m. Marlene Rodenz, Mar. 3, 1958; children—Jord Ann, Shawn, Jay Scott, Robin. B.S., U.S. Merchant Marine Acad., 1947; postgrad., N.Y. State Sch. Indsl. and Labor Relations, Cornell U., 1950; M.B.A. with distinction, Harvard U., 1953. Dir. market research and spl. projects Gulf Oil U.S., Houston, 1968-70; mgr. new venture investments Gulf Oil Corp., Pitts., 1972-74; exec. v.p. Gulf Trading & Transp. Co., Pitts., 1974-86; sr. v.p. Gulf Exploration and Prodn. Co., Houston; pres. Gulf Overseas Commodities Ltd. Served with USNR, 1953-55.

SUGG, JOHN LOGAN (JACK SUGG), advertising executive; b. Hillsboro, Ill., June 2, 1914; s. Norman J. and Clythera (McDavid) S.; m. Jean Ellen Morrison, Feb. 7, 1942; children: Michael L., Patrick M., Terry Jean. B.A., Lake Forest Coll., 1938. Engaged in newspaper work, 1938-41; with Cole & Weber, Inc., 1946—, pres., 1968-72, chmn. bd., 1972-76, chmn. exec. com., 1976-80; ret., 1981; pres. Assoc. Oreg. Industries, 1968-69. Bd. dirs. Emanuel Med. Center Found.; chmn. bd. dirs. Portland Better Bus. Bur., 1975—. Served to lt. comdr. USN, 1941-45. Named Oreg. Advt. Man of Year, 1965. Mem. Portland C. of C. (dir.), Am. Assn. Advt. Agys. (chmn. Western region 1970-71). Clubs: Arlington (pres. 1975—), Multnomah Athletic, Portland Golf. Home: 2415 SW Timberline Dr Portland OR 97225-4129 *When young people seek my advice concerning careers in the advertising agency field, this is what I tell them: "Advertising can be rich and rewarding for one who has an understanding of human motivation, basic skills in communication, capacity for plain hard work and the ability to shrug off disappointment. But if you're not confident that you can achieve management status by age 40, go into another field. Advertising's daily firing-line is for the young and venturesome.".*

SUGG, ROBERT PERKINS, former state supreme court justice; b. Eupora, Miss., Feb. 21, 1916; s. Amos Watson and Virgie Christian (Cooper) S.; m. Elizabeth Lorraine Carroll, June 23, 1940; children: Robert Perkins, Charles William, John David. Student, Wood Jr. Coll., 1933-34, Miss. State U., 1935-37, Jackson Sch. Law, 1939-40. Bar: Miss. Practice law, 1940-51, chancery judge, 1951-71; asso. justice Miss. Supreme Ct., 1971-83; county pros. atty. Webster County, Miss., 1949-50; spl. chancery judge Hinds, Scott and Jasper counties, Miss., 1989, sr. judge, 1990—; mem. adv. council Nat. Ctr. for State Cts., 1973-79. Bd. govs. Miss. Jud. Coll., 1973-80; literacy missions assoc. Home Mission Bd. of So. Bapt. Conv., 1983—. Served with USAAF, 1942-43. Named Outstanding Citizen, Eupora Jr. C. of C., 1970, Alumnus of Year, Wood Jr. Coll., 1973; recipient Service to Humanity award Miss. Coll., 1976. Mem. Miss. State Bar, Am. Judicature Soc., CAP (Miss. Wing, squadron comdr. 1974-76), Am. Legion (post comdr. 1950). Democrat. Baptist (chmn. bd. deacons 1964). Home: 1067 Meadow Heights Dr Jackson MS 39206-6021

SUGGARS, CANDICE LOUISE, special education educator; b. Pitts., Jan. 16, 1949; d. Albert Abraham and Patricia Louise (Stepp) S. BS in Elem. Edn., W.Va. U., 1972; MS in Spl. Edn., Johns Hopkins U., 1979, Cert. Advanced Studies, 1986. Clin. supr./head tchr. The Kennedy Kreiger Inst., Balt., 1974-80, inpatient coord., 1980-83, ednl. evaluator, 1980-85, spl. educator/pediatric rehab. team, 1985-86; spl. edn. cons. Charleston County (S.C.) Sch. Dist., 1986-90, spl. edn. pre-sch. tchr., 1990-95; pvt. tutor children with spl. needs and disabilities, Charleston, 1995—; spl. needs cons. U. S.C., 1996—; mem. adv. bd. S.C. Accelerated Schs. Project, Charleston, 1994-95. Contbg. author: Disadvantaged Pre-School Child, 1979, Leisure Education for the Handicapped Curriculum, 1984. Exhibitor ann. conv. S.C. State Sch. Bd. Assn., 1994. Mem. Coun. for Exceptional Children (hospitality chair 1987-89, publicity chair 1989-90), Nat. Assn. for Edn. of Young Children. Avocations: singing, reading, travel, tennis. Home: 29 Savage St Apt B Charleston SC 29401-2409

SUGGS, JAMES C., publishing executive. Pres. Christian Bd. Publ. (CBP), St. Louis. Office: Christian Bd Publication PO Box 179 1316 Convention Plaza Dr Saint Louis MO 63166

SUGGS, JOSEPHINE GREENWAY, controller; b. Lula, Ga., Dec. 19, 1946; d. Marvin W. and Lucille (Echols) Greenway; m. Ray M. Suggs, May 31, 1969; children: Jeffrey Ray, Martin Ryan. Cert. in computer programming, Lanier Tech. Inst., 1979; AA, Am. Inst. Profl. Bookkeepers, 1989. Contr. Hilb, Rogal & Hamilton Co., Gainesville, Ga., 1988—. Vol. ARC, 1979—, N.E. Ga. Med. Aux., 1993—. Mem. NAFE, Am. Bus. Women, Am. Inst. Profl. Bookkeepers, Nat. Assn. Ins. Women, Ins. Women Gainesville. Baptist. Avocation: community involvement. Home: 5906 Homer Hwy PO Box 364 Lula GA 30554

SUGGS, MARION JACK, minister, college dean; b. Electra, Tex., June 5, 1924; s. Claude Frank and Lottie Maye (Gibson) S.; m. Ruth Barge, Nov. 13, 1943; children: Adena Ruth Suggs Beck, James Robert, David Nathan. BA, U. Tex., 1946; BD, Tex. Christian U., 1949; PhD, Duke U., 1954. Ordained to ministry Christian Ch. (Disciples of Christ), 1948. Min. First Christian Ch., Gladewater, Tex., 1948-50, Wendell Christian Ch., N.C., 1950-52; asst. prof. Brite Div. Sch. Tex. Christian U., Ft. Worth, 1952-54, assoc. prof., 1954-56, prof., 1956-89, dean Brite Div. Sch., 1977-89; emeritus dean and prof. Tex. Christian U., Fort Worth, 1989—; mem. com. on ministry Christian Ch. in S.W., 1976-89; chmn. coun. on theol. edn. Div. Higher Edn., 1987-88, mem. ch. fin. coun., 1985-89, bd. dirs.; mem. gen. bd. Christian Ch. (Disciples of Christ), 1986-87; lectr. min.'s week Tex. Christian U., 1961, Lexington Theol. Sem., 1966, S.W. Mo. State U., 1977; mem. Disciples-Roman Cath. Internat. Bilateral Conv., 1978-87. Author: The Layman Reads His Bible, 1957, The Gospel Story, 1960 (Adult Book of Yr. Christian Lit. Com. 1960), Wisdom, Christology and Law in Matthew's Gospel, 1970 (Christian Rsch. Found. award 1967); also articles ; co-editor: Studies in the History and Text of the New Testament, 1967, New English Bible: Oxford Study Edition, 1976 (Religious Book award 1977), The Oxford Study Bible, Revised English Bible, 1992. Bd. dirs. Granville T. Walker Found. G.H. Kearns fellow, 1951, Am. Coun. Learned Socs. fellow, 1963-64, Assn. Theol. Schs. fellow, 1963-64; recipient Disting. Alumnus award Tex. Christian U., 1973. Mem. Soc. Bibl. Lit., Studiorum Novi Testamenti Societas, Internat. Greek N.T. Project, Phi Beta Kappa, Alpha Kappa Delta, Pi Gamma Mu, Theta Phi. Democrat. Home: 5605 Winifred Dr Fort Worth TX 76133-2501

SUGGS, MICHAEL EDWARD, lawyer; b. Conway, S.C., Nov. 9, 1962; s. Edward and Rebecca S. BSBA, U. S.C., 1985, JD, 1992. Bar: S.C. 1992. Asst. pub. defender Def. Corp. Horry County, Conway, S.C., 1993—. Troop 847 com. Boy Scouts Am., Loris, S.C., 1985—; coun. City of Loris, 1994—. Recipient Eagle Scout award Boy Scouts Am., 1977. Mem. ABA, S.C. Assn. Criminal Def. Lawyers, Horry County Bar Assn., Loris C. of C. Methodist. Home: 4932 Circle Dr Loris SC 29569-3146 Office: Def Corp Horry County PO Box 1666 114 Laurel St Conway SC 29526

SUGHRUE, ROBERT NORMAN, financial analyst; b. N.Y.C., June 20, 1949; s. Henry Gordon and Ann Catherine (Klein) S.; m. Beverly K. Kachurik, Jan. 21, 1977; children: Shannon S., Valerie L. BSBA, Duquesne U., 1971. Staff acct. LTV Steel Corp., Pitts., 1973-76, staff auditor, 1976-78; staff auditor Blue Cross Western Pa., Pitts., 1979-81, sr. auditor, 1981-84, mgr. payroll svcs., 1984-86; mgr. fiscal affairs Pitts. Rsch. Inst., 1986-95; grants adminstr. Duquesne U., Pitts., 1995—; cons. in field, Pitts., 1986—; pub. arbitrator Nat. Assn. Securities Dealers, N.Y.C., 1990—. Co-author: Qualifying as a Nonprofit Tax-Exempt Organization, 1991. Pres. Allegheny County Transit Coun., Pitts., 1989-91, v.p., 1988-89. Mem. Inst. Mgmt. Accts. Republican. Roman Catholic. Avocations: camping, reading, volunteering for community work. Home: 837 Fredericka Dr Bethel Park PA 15102-3736

SUGIHARA, KENZI, publishing executive; b. Kearny, N.J., Oct. 4, 1940; s. Kyuichi and Shinobuko (Yamaguchi) S.; m. Roslyn Forbes, Dec. 1966 (div. Mar. 1981); children: Kenichi, Takeo, Akira, Fumio; m. Nancy Elizabeth Kirsh, June 8, 1981; 1 child, Toshiro. BA, NYU, 1963. Supr. McGraw Hill, Inc., N.Y.C., 1965-67; assoc. dir. coll. product dept. Harcourt Brace Jovanovich Inc., N.Y.C., 1978-82, dir. electronic pub., 1982-83; v.p., pub. Bantam Electronic Pub. div., pub. Bantam Reference Books, Bantam Profl. Books, Bantam Doubleday Dell, N.Y.C., 1983-93; v.p., pub. Random House Reference & Electronic Pub. (Random House Inc.), 1993-95; pres. Sugihara and Rose, 1995—. Democrat. Presbyterian. Home: 585 W End Ave # 15D New York NY 10024-1715

SUGIKI, SHIGEMI, ophthalmologist, educator; b. Wailuku, Hawaii, May 12, 1936; s. Sentaro and Kameno (Matoba) S.; AB, Washington U., St. Louis, 1957, M.D., 1961; m. Bernice T. Murakami, Dec. 28, 1958; children: Kevin S., Boyd R. Intern St. Luke's Hosp., St. Louis, 1961-62, resident ophthalmology, Washington U., St. Louis, 1962-65; chmn. dept. ophthalmology Straub Clinic, Honolulu, 1965-70, Queen's Med. Ctr., Honolulu, 1970-73, 80-83, 88-90, 93—; assoc. clin. prof. ophthalmology Sch. Medicine, U. Hawaii, 1973—. Served to maj. M.C., AUS, 1968-70. Decorated Hawaiian NG Commendation medal, 1968. Fellow ACS; mem. Am., Hawaii med. assns., Honolulu County Med. Soc., Am. Acad. Ophthalmology, Contact Lens Assn. Opthalmologists, Pacific Coast Oto-Ophthal. Soc., Pan-Pacific Surg. Assn., Am. Soc. Cataract and Refractive Surgery, Am. Glaucoma Soc., Internat. Assn. Ocular Surgeons, Am. Soc. Contemporary Ophthalmology, Washington U. Eye Alumni Assn., Hawaii Ophthal. Soc., Rsch. To Prevent Blindness. Home: 2398 Aina Lani Pl Honolulu HI 96822-2024 Office: 1380 Lusitana St Ste 714 Honolulu HI 96813-2449

SUGINTAS, NORA MARIA, scientist, veterinarian, medical company executive; b. Evergreen Park, Ill., Mar. 12, 1956; d. George and Mary (Navickas) S. BS in Biol. Scis. with highest distinction, U. Ill., Chgo., 1978; DVM, U. Ill., 1982. Lic. veterinarian, Ill. Profl. hosp. specialist Abbott Labs., Detroit, 1983-87; anes./crit. care patient monitoring equipment acct. exec. Shiley, Inc., Detroit, 1987-91; anesthesia and critical care monitoring equipment sales exec. and cons. Ohmeda, Detroit, 1991-94; regional mgr. Criticare Systems, Detroit, 1994-95, nat. acct. dir., 1995—. Journalist The Lithuanian World-Wide Daily Newspaper, 1975; author: The Production S-Adenosylmethionine by Saccharomyces cerevisiae and Candida utilis. Troop leader Girl Scouts Lithuanian, Chgo., 1972-77, camp dir., 1977. Recipient Louis Pasteur award for Academic Excellence in the Biol. Scis. and Ind. Rsch. U. Ill., 1978. Mem. NAFE, Econ. Club Detroit, Phi Beta Kappa. Republican. Avocations: hiking, nature preservation, photography, internat. politics. Office: 6284 Aspen Ridge West Bloomfield MI 48322-4433

SUGIOKA, KENNETH, anesthesiologist educator; b. Hollister, Calif., Apr. 19, 1920; s. Seigiro and Kameno (Takeda) S.; m. Mary Trabue Hinternhoff, June 18, 1966; children—Stephanie, Colin, Kimi (by previous marriage), Nathan, Brian. B.S., U. Denver, 1945; M.D., Washington U., St. Louis, 1949. Intern, resident U. Iowa, 1949-52, instr. anesthesiology, 1952; asst. prof. surgery N.C. Meml. Hosp., Chapel Hill, 1954-62, assoc. prof. surgery, 1962-64; prof. surgery, chmn. div. anesthesiology U. N.C., 1964-69, prof., chmn. dept. anesthesiology, 1969-83; prof. anesthesiology and physiology Duke U., 1985—; vis. prof. Physiol. Inst., U. Göttingen, Fed. Republic of Germany, 1963, Kings Coll. Med. Sch., London, Max-Planck Inst. Physiology, Dortmund, Fed. Republic of Germany, 1976-77; vis. prof. Royal Coll. Surgeons, Eng., 1983-84; dir. Morgan Creek Land Co.; mem. adv. com. on anesthetic and life support drugs FDA; bd. alumni U. Denver. Author textbook of clin. anesthesiology; contbr. articles to profl. jours. Pres. Triangle Opera Theater. Served to capt., M.C. USAF, 1952-54. Recipient spl. research fellowship NIH, 1961-62. Fellow Faculty Anaesthesiologists Royal Coll. Surgeons (Eng.) (hon.); mem. Soc. Acad. Anesthesia Chairmen (past pres.). Home: 319 Bayberry Dr Chapel Hill NC 27514-9116

SUH, DAE-SOOK, political science educator; b. Hoeryong, Korea, Nov. 22, 1931; came to U.S., 1952; s. Chang-Hee and Chong-Hee (Paek) S.; m. Yun-Ok Park, Oct. 29, 1960; children: Maurice, Kevin. BA, Tex. Christian U., 1956; MA, Ind. U., 1958; PhD, Columbia U., 1964. Asst. prof. U. Houston, 1965-67, assoc. prof., 1968-71; prof. polit. sci., dir. Ctr. for Korean Studies, U. Hawaii, Honolulu, 1972-95; prof. policy studies Korea Found., 1994—. Author: The Korean Communist Movement, 1967, Documents of Korean Communism, 1970, Korean Communism, 1980, Kim Il Sung, 1988. Mem. Conv. Ctr. Authority, Honolulu, 1989-94. Grantee Social Sci. Rsch. Coun.-Am. Coun. Learned Socs., 1963, East-/West Ctr., Columbia U., 1971, The Wilson Ctr. for Scholars, 1985, Fulbright, 1988. Mem. Am. Polit. Sci. Assn. (life), Assn. for Asian Studies. Avocations: tennis, golf. Home: 7122 Niumalu Loop Honolulu HI 96825-1635 Office: U Hawaii at Manoa Ctr Korean Studies 1881 E West Rd Honolulu HI 96822-2322

SUH, NAM PYO, mechanical engineering educator; b. Seoul, Apr. 22, 1936; came to U.S., 1954, naturalized, 1963; s. Doo Soo and Joon Joo (Lee) S.; m. Young Ja Surh; children: Mary M., Helen H., Grace J., Caroline Y. SB, MIT, 1959, SM, 1961; PhD, Carnegie-Mellon U., 1964; D of Engring. (hon.), Worcester Poly. Inst., 1986; LHD (hon.), U. Mass., Lowell, 1988. Devel. engr. Guild Plastics Inc., Cambridge, Mass., 1958-60; sr. research engr., project mgr. USM Corp., Beverly, Mass., 1961-65; asst. prof. U. S.C., Columbia, 1965-68, assoc. prof., 1968-69; assoc. prof. mech. engring. MIT, Cambridge, 1970-75, prof., 1975—, Ralph E. and Eloise F. Cross prof., 1989—, head dept. mech. engring., 1991—, dir. Lab. Mfg. and Productivity, 1977-84, dir. industry polymer processing program, 1973-84, dir. Mfg. Inst., 1989—; asst. dir. for engring. NSF, Washington, 1984-88; bd. dirs. Trexell, Inc. (formerly Axiomatics Corp.), Woburn, Mass., SVG Industries, SVG, Inc.; former chmn. bd. Sutek Corp., Hudson, Mass.; tech. advisor Daewoo Group; cons. Lawrence Livermore Nat. Lab.; former mem. sci. and tech. rev. bd. Idaho Nat. Engring. Lab.; mem. NRC rev. panel Nat. Engring. Lab., 1986-90; mem. vis. com. (statutory) Nat. Inst. Stds. and Tech., 1990-94; mem. tech. adv. com. Alcan Aluminum Corp., 1989-90; editor advanced mfg. series Oxford U. Press. Author: (with A.P.L. Turner) Mechanical Behavior of Solids, 1975, Tribophysics, 1986, The Principles of Design, 1990, (with others) Manufacturing Engineering, 1990; editor: (with N. Saka) Fundamentals of Tribology, 1980, (with N. Sung) Science and Technology of Polymer Procs., 1979, The Delamination Theory of Wear, 1977, (with B.M. Kramer) University: Industry Cooperation, 1982; former co-editor-in-chief Robotics and Computer Aided Mfg.; contbr. over 200 articles to profl. jours.; holder 40 U.S. patents. Former chmn. bd. Korean-Am. Soc. New Eng., 1979. USM Corp. fellow, 1962-63; recipient Best Paper award Soc. Plastics Engrs., 1981, citation Classic Inst. for Sci. Info., 1981, F.W. Taylor Research award Soc. Mfg. Engrs., 1986, Disting. Svc. award NSF, 1988, Mainstream Am. award, 1991; named Fed. Engr. of Yr., NSF/NSPE, 1987. Fellow ASME (Gustus L. Larson Meml. award 1976, Blackall award 1982, W.T. Ennor Mfg. Tech. award 1993, Best Tribology Paper award 199); mem. AAAS, Am. Soc. for Engring. Edn. (Centennial medal 1993), Internat. Instn. for Prodn. Engring., Royal Swedish Acad. Engring. Sci. (fgn.), Sigma Xi, Pi Tau Sigma, Phi Kappa Phi. Office: MIT Rm 3-174 Dept of Mechanical Engineering Cambridge MA 02139

SUHL, HARRY, physics educator; b. Leipzig, Fed. Republic Germany, Oct. 18, 1922; s. Bernhard and Klara (Bergwerk) S.; widowed. BSc, U. Wales, 1943; PhD, U. Oxford, 1948, DSc (hon.), 1970. Temp. exptl. officer British Admiralty, England, 1943-46; mem. tech. staff Bell Labs., Murray Hill, N.J., 1948-60; prof. physics U. Calif.-San Diego, La Jolla, 1961—. Editor (with others) book series: Magnetism, 1961-74. Guggenheim fellow, 1968-69, NSF fellow, 1971. Fellow Am. Phys. Soc., Am. Acad. Arts and Scis.; mem. NAS. Office: U Calif Dept Physics 9500 Gilman Dr La Jolla CA 92093-5003

SUHR, PAUL AUGUSTINE, lawyer; b. Sonwunri, Chonbuk, Korea, Jan. 20, 1940; came to U.S. 1966; s. Chong-ju and Oksuk (Pang) So; m. Angeline M. Kang Suhr; 1 child, Christopher. BA, Campbell Coll., Buies Creek, N.C., 1968; MA, U. N.C., Greensboro, 1970; MS, U. N.C., Chapel Hill, 1975; JD, N.C. Cen. U., 1988. Bar: N.C. 1989, U.S. Dist. Ct. (ea. and mid. dist.) N.C. 1989, U.S. Dist. Ct. D.C. 1990, U.S. Ct. Appeals (4th cir.) 1992. Bibliographer N.C. Div. of State Libr., Raleigh, 1975-78; dir. Pender County Pub. Libr., Burgaw, N.C., 1978-80; libr. Tob. Lit. Svc., N.C. State U., Raleigh, 1980-85; pvt. practice law Law Office of Paul A. Suhr, Raleigh & Fayetteville, 1989—. Author short stories and novelettes various lit. mags., jours. and revs. Mem. Human Resources and Human Rels. Adv. Commn., City of Raleigh, 1990-95, chmn., 1994-95. N.C. Humanities Com. grantee, 1979-80; recipient Presdl. award President of Korea, 1992. Mem. ABA, ATLA, N.C. Bar Assn., N.C. Trial Lawyers Assn., Wake County Bar Assn. (bd. dirs.), D.C. Bar Assn. Democrat. Roman Catholic. Avocations: gardening, fishing, writing. Office: 1110 Navaho Dr Ste 605 Raleigh NC 27609-7322

SUHRBIER, KLAUS RUDOLF, hydrodynamicist, naval architect; b. Gnoien, Germany, Sept. 12, 1930; arrived in U.K., 1966; s. Ulrich Julius and Dora Auguste (Elsaesser) S.; m. Inge Ursula Koepke, Oct. 1, 1955; children: Andreas, Karin. Dipl. Ing., U. Rostock, Germany, 1955; Dr. Ing., Tech. U., Berlin, 1995. Chartered engr. Hydrodynamicist Institut fuer Schiffbau, Berlin, 1955-60, Versuchsanstalt fuer Binnenschiffbau e.V., Duisburg, Fed. Republic of Germany, 1960-63; sci. officer Inst. fuer Schiffbau U. Hamburg, Fed. Republic of Germany, 1963-66; sr. hydrodynamicist Vosper Ltd., Portsmouth, Eng., 1966; chief hydrodynamicist Vosper Thornycroft (U.K.) Ltd., Portsmouth, Eng., 1966-92; cons. ship hydrodynamics, 1992—; mem. cavitation com. 16th and 17th Internat. Towing Tank Conf., Leningrad, USSR, 1978-81, Gothenburg, Sweden, 1981-84; chmn. cavitation com. 18th Internat. Towing Tank Conf., Kobe, Japan, 1984-87; chmn. high speed marine vehicles com. Internat. Towing Tank Conf., Madrid, 1987-90. Co-author: (book) Dhows to Deltas, 1971; inventor reduction of cavitation erosion, 1974, 92; contbr. numerous articles and papers to profl. jours. and procs. Fellow Royal Soc. Naval Architects; mem. Soc. Naval Architects and Marine Engrs., Schiffbautechnische Ges. e.V. Avocations: sailing, skiing, history. Home and Office: 30A Beach Rd, Emsworth Hampshire PO10 7HR, England

SUHRE, WALTER ANTHONY, JR., retired lawyer and brewery executive; b. Cin., Jan. 17, 1933; s. Walter A. and Elizabeth V. (Heimbuch) S. B.S. in Bus. Adminstrn., Northwestern U., 1956; LL.B. with honors, U. Cin., 1962. Bar: Ohio 1962, Mo. 1982. Assoc. Taft, Stettinius & Hollister, Cin., 1962-65; with Eagle-Picher Industries, Inc., Cin., 1965-82, v.p., gen. counsel, 1970-82; v.p., gen. counsel Anheuser-Busch Cos., Inc., St. Louis, 1982-94; ret., 1993. Served with USMC, 1956-59. Mem. Old Warson Country Club. Republican. Presbyterian. Home: 48 Woodcliffe Rd Saint Louis MO 63124-1336

SUHRHEINRICH, RICHARD FRED, federal judge; b. 1936. BS, Wayne State U., 1960; JD cum laude, Detroit Coll. Law, 1963, LLM, 1992; LLM, U. Va., 1990. Bar: Mich. Assoc. Moll, Desenberg, Purdy, Glover & Bayer, 1963-67; asst. prosecutor Macomb County, 1967; ptnr. Rogensues, Richard & Suhrheinrich, 1967; assoc. Moll, Desenberg, Purdy, Glover & Bayer, 1967-68; ptnr. Kitch, Suhrheinrich, Saurbier & Drutchas, 1968-84; judge U.S. Dist. Ct. (ea. dist.) Mich., Detroit, 1984-90, U.S. Ct. Appeals (6th Cir.), Detroit, 1990—. Mem. State Bar Mich., Ingham County Bar Assn. Office: US Ct Appeals 6th Cir Rm 241 USPO & Fed Bldg 315 W Allegan St Lansing MI 48933-1514

SUHRSTEDT, TIM, cinematographer. Films include: Forbidden World, 1982, Android, 1982, The House on Sorority Row, 1983, Suburbia, 1984, Teen Wolf, 1985, City Limits, 1985, Space Rage, 1985, Stand Alone, 1985, Mannequin, 1986, Critters, 1986, Feds, 1988, Mystic Pizza, 1988, Split Decisions, 1988, Doin' Time on Planet Earth, 1988, Bill and Ted's Excellent Adventure, 1989, Men at Work, 1990, Noises Off, 1992, Don't Tell Mom the Babysitter's Dead, 1992, Traces of Red, 1992, Getting Even with Dad, 1993; TV films include: The Ratings Game, 1984, And the Children Shall Lead, 1985, Dead Solid Perfect, 1988, She Knows Too Much, 1989, The Cover Girl and the Cop, 1989, Man Against the Mob: The Chinatown Murders, 1990, Pair of Aces, 1990; (TV series) Chicago Hope (Emmy award for Outstanding Individual Achievement in Cinematography for a Series 1995). Office: care Spyros Skouras Sanford Skouras Gross & Assocs 1015 Gayley Ave Fl 3 Los Angeles CA 90024-3424*

SUINN, RICHARD MICHAEL, psychologist; b. Honolulu, May 8, 1933; s. Maurice and Edith (Wong) S.; m. Grace D. Toy, July 26, 1958; children: Susan, Randall, Staci, Bradley. Student, U. Hawaii, 1951-53; B.A. summa cum laude, Ohio State U., 1955; MA in Clin. Psychology, Stanford U., 1957, PhD in Clin. Psychology, 1959. Lic. psychologist, Colo.; diplomate Am. Bd. Profl. Psychology. Counselor Stanford (Calif.) U., 1958-59, rsch. assoc. Med. Sch., 1964-66; asst. prof. psychology Whitman Coll., Walla Walla, Wash., 1959-64; assoc. prof. U. Hawaii, Honolulu, 1966-68; prof. Colo. State U., Ft. Collins, 1968—, head dept. psychology, 1972-93; cons. in field; psychologist U.S. Ski Teams, 1976, Olympic Games, U.S. Women's Track and Field, 1980 Olympic Games, U.S. Ski Jumping Team, 1988, U.S. Shooting Team, 1994; mem. sports psychology adv. com. U.S. Olympic Com., 1983-89; reviewer NIMH, 1977-80, 94—. Author: The Predictive Validity of Projective Measures, 1969, Fundamentals of Behavior Pathology, 1970, The Innovative Psychological Therapies, 1975, The Innovative Medical-Psychiatric Therapies, 1976, Psychology in Sport: Methods and Applications, 1980, Fundamentals of Abnormal Psychology, 1984, 88, Seven Steps to Peak Performance, 1986, Anxiety Management Training, 1990; editorial bd.: Jour. Cons. and Clin. Psychology, 1973-86, Jour. Counseling Psychology, 1974-91, Behavior Therapy, 1977-80, Behavior Modification, 1977-78, Jour. Behavioral Medicine, 1978-83, Behavior Counseling Quar., 1979-83, Jour. Sports Psychology, 1980—, Clin. Psychology: Science and Practice, 1994—, Professional Psychology, 1994—; author: tests Math. Anxiety Rating Scale, Suinn Test Anxiety Behavior Scale, Suinn-Lew Asian Self-identity Acculturation Scale. Mem. City Council, Ft. Collins, 1975-79, mayor, 1978-79; mem. Gov.'s Mental Health Adv. Council, 1983, Colo. Bd. Psychologist Examiners, 1983-86. Recipient cert. merit U.S. Ski Team, 1976, APA Career Contbn. to Edn. award, 1995; NIMH grantee, 1963-64; Office Edn. grantee, 1970-71. Fellow APA (chmn. bd. ethnic minority affairs 1982-83, chmn. edn. and tng. bd. 1986-87, policy and planning bd. 1987-89, publs. bd. 1993—, bd. dirs. 1990-93), Behavior Therapy and Rsch. Soc. (charter); mem. Assn. for Advancement Psychology (trustee 1983-86), Assn. for Advancement Behavior Therapy (sec.-treas. 1986-89, pres. 1992-93), Asian Am. Psychol. Assn. (bd. dirs. 1983-88), Am. Bd. Behavior Therapy (bd. dirs. 1987—), Phi Beta Kappa, Sigma Xi. Home: 808 Cheyenne Dr Fort Collins CO 80525-1560 Office: Colo State U Dept Psychology Fort Collins CO 80523

SUITER, JOHN WILLIAM, industrial engineering consultant; b. Pasadena, Calif., Feb. 16, 1926; s. John Walter and Ethel May (Acton) S.; B.S. in Aero. Sci., Embry Riddle U., 1964; m. Joyce England, Dec. 3, 1952; children—Steven A., Carol A. Cons. indsl. engr., Boynton Beach, Fla., 1955—. Instr. U. S.C. Tech. Edn. Center, Charleston, 1967-69. Served as pilot USAF, 1944-46. Registered profl. engr., Fla. Mem. Am. Inst. Indsl. Engrs., Soc. Mfg. Engrs. (sr.), Computer and Automated Systems Assn., Methods-Time Measurement Assn. (assoc.), Soc. Quality Control. Home: PO Box 5262 Englewood FL 34224-0262

SUITS, BERNARD HERBERT, philosophy educator; b. Detroit, Nov. 25, 1925; s. Herbert Arthur and Helen Dorothy (Carlin) S.; m. Nancy Ruth Berr, July 3, 1952; children—Mark, Constance. B.A., U. Chgo., 1944, M.A., 1950; Ph.D., U. Ill., 1958. Investigator venereal disease USPHS, 1950-51; personnel officer Detroit Civil Service Commn., 1952-54; instr. philosophy U. Ill., Urbana, 1958-59; asst. prof. Purdue U., 1959-66; asso. prof. U. Waterloo, Ont., 1966-72; prof. philosophy, chmn. dept. U. Waterloo, 1972—, asso. dean arts for grad. affairs, 1981—; vis. prof. U. Lethbridge, Alta., Can., 1980, U. Bristol, Eng., 1980. Author: The Grasshopper: Games, Life, and Utopia, 1978, paper, 1990; Contbr. to profl. jours. and books. Served with USNR, 1944-46. Mem. Canadian, Am. philos. assns., Philos. Soc. for Study of Sport (pres. 1975—). Office: U Waterloo, Dept Philosophy, Waterloo, ON Canada

SUITS, DANIEL BURBIDGE, economist; b. St. Louis, June 27, 1918; s. Hollis Emerson and Dorothy Dandridge (Halyburton) S.; m. Adelaide Evens Boehm, Feb. 14, 1942; children—Evan Halyburton, Holly Boehm Suits Kazarinoff. A.B. in Philosophy, U. Mich., 1940, M.A. in Econs, 1942, Ph.D. in Econs, 1948. Asst. prof. econs. dept. U. Mich., 1950-55, assoc. prof., 1955-59, prof., dir. research seminar in quantitative econs., 1959-69; dir. Am. Studies Ctr., Kyoto, Japan, 1958; prof. econs. U. Calif., Santa Cruz, 1969-74; prof. econs. Mich. State U., East Lansing, 1974-86, prof. emeritus, 1986—; vis. prof. People's U., Beijing, 1985, Fudan U., Shanghai, 1987, Swarthmore Coll., 1988; disting. vis. prof. Kalamazoo Coll., 1989; cons. to various state and fed. agys.; rsch. assoc. Ctr. Econ. Rsch., Athens, Greece, 1962-63. Author: Statistics: An Introduction to Quantitative Economic Research, 1963, Theory and Application of Econometric Models, 1963, Principles of Economics, 1970, rev. edit., 1973; originator Suits Index tax progressivity; contbr. articles to tech. jours. Served alt. mil. duty 1942-46. Recipient Disting. Faculty award Mich. State U., 1980; sr. fellow East-West Population Inst., 1978—. Fellow Econometric Soc., Am. Statis. Assn.; mem. Am. Econ. Assn. Mem. Soc. of Friends. Home: 1446 Karlin Ct East Lansing MI 48823-2333 Office: Mich State U Econs Dept East Lansing MI 48824

SUKIENNIK, LEOPOLD JONAH, civil, structural engineer, consultant; b. Odessa, Ukraine, Mar. 20, 1936; cames to U.S., 1966; s. Chaim and Gita (Vinokurova) S.; m. Judith Bloch, 1962 (div. 1964); 1 child, Robert Daniel; m. Adelaida Reno Weir, 197 (separated 1991); children: Esther Olga, Lana Rachel. BCE, Politechnika Wroclawska, Poland, 1960, MCE, 1961; MCE, U. Pitts., 1985. Registered profl. engr., Pa., Ohio, registered fallout shelter analyst. Various design engring. positions, 1961-68; sr. bridge engr. Sanders and Thomas, Consulting Engrs., Pitts., 1968-70, project bridge engr., 1974-76; design engr. Jacob Engring. Co., Inc., Pitts., 1971-73; asst. prof. engring. Pa. State U., New Kensington, 1976-79; chief structural engr. Westmoreland Engring. Co., Inc., Monessen, Pa., 1982-83; chief engr. Sukiennik Engring. Co., Inc., Swissvale, Pa., 1983-88; sr. bridge engr. Rackoff Engrs., Inc., Mt. Lebanon, Pa., 1988-89; primary civil, structural engr. Davy, Dravo, Comstock, Pitts., 1989-92; sr. structural engr. U.S. Filter Corp., 1992-93. Mem. Squirrel Hill Urban Coalition, Pitts. Mem. NSPE, Pa. Soc. Prof. Engrs., Am. Concrete Inst., Am. Inst. Steel Constrn., Assn. Bridge Constrn. and Design, Assn. Iron and Steel Engrs., U.S. Chess Fedn., Pitts. Ski Club, Pitts. Chess Club. Democrat. Jewish. Avocations: chess, skiing, skating, tennis, swimming. Home: 1646 Denniston Ave Pittsburgh PA 15217-1458

SUKO, LONNY RAY, judge; b. Spokane, Wash., Oct. 12, 1943; s. Ray R. and Leila B. (Snyder) S.; m. Marcia A. Michaelsen, Aug. 26, 1967; children: Jolynn R., David M. BA, Wash. State U., 1965; JD, U. Idaho, 1968. Bar: Wash. 1968, U.S. Dist. Ct. (ea. dist.) Wash. 1969, U.S. Dist. Ct. (we. dist.) Wash. 1978, U.S. Ct. Appeals (9th cir.) 1978. Law clk. U.S. Dist. Ct. Ea. Dist. Wash., 1968-69; assoc. Lyon, Beaulaurier & Aaron, Yakima, Wash., 1969-72; ptnr. Lyon, Beaulaurier, Weigand, Suko & Gustafson, Yakima, 1972-91, Lyon, Weigand, Suko & Gustafson, P.S., 1991-95; U.S. magistrate judge, Yakima, 1971-91, 95—. Mem. Phi Beta Kappa, Phi Kappa Phi, Phi Eta Sigma. Office: PO Box 2726 Yakima WA 98907-2726

SULC, DWIGHT GEORGE, investment advisor; b. Oklahoma City, May 25, 1948; s. George Bennett and Hedvika (Kyzivat) Shultz. BA, U. Tex., 1971; JD, Tuebingen U., Germany, 1979, LLD, 1983. Cert. securities and exch. commn., Paris, U.S. Investment advisor Paris, Berlin, London, 1974-83, Oklahoma City, 1984—; strategic planning advisor cmty. orgns., Oklahoma City, 1989. Author: A National Neighborhood Association System for America, 1991, Building A Volunteer Neighborhood Watch Patrol, A Civic Leadership Training Manual of the Council of Confederated Neighborhoods of America,1996. Chmn. strategic planning com. Federally Employed Women Assn., Tinker AFB, 1990; founder The Coun. of Confederated Neighborhoods of Am. Inc., Oklahoma City, 1991, The Internat. Soc. for the Arts, Praha, Czechoslovakia/London/Oklahoma City, 1994; pres. Mil. Park chpt. Coun. Confederated Neighborhoods of Am., 1992. Rsch. grantee Fulbright, Berlin, 1980, Brusselles, 1981. Mem. Nat. Assn. Parliamentarians (pres. 1994). Presbyterian. Avocation: music. Home: 3321 N Virginia Ave Oklahoma City OK 73118-3044

SULC, JEAN LUENA (JEAN L. MESTRES), lobbyist, consultant; b. Worcester, Mass., Mar. 17, 1939; d. Emilio Beija and Julia (Bulan) Luena; m. Lee Gwynne Mestres, Oct. 9, 1965 (div. Dec. 1973); m. Lawrence Bradley Sulc, Nov. 4, 1983. BS in Psychology, Tufts U., 1961; M in Urban and Regional Planning, U. Colo., 1976. Lic. real estate, Va.; lic. pvt. pilot. Mem. staff U.S. fgn. svc. Dept. State, Washington, 1962-65; intern Adams County Planning Dept., Brighton, Colo., 1974-75; cons. office policy analysis City and County of Denver, 1976; program dir. Coun. Internat. Urban Liaison, Washington, 1976-79; asst., dir. internat. Cities Svc. Oil & Gas Corp., Washington, 1980-81; govt. affairs rep. Cities Svc., OXY USA Inc., Washington, 1982-89; mgr. fed. rels. OXY USA Inc., Washington, 1990-95; pres. EdgeSystem.XXI, Washington, 1996—; chmn. govt. affairs com. L.P. Gas Clean Fuel Coalition, Irvine, Calif., 1990-92. Author, editor: (newsletter) Dayton Climate Project, 1979-80; contbr. articles to newsletters. Vol. Reagan/Bush and Bush/Quayle Presdl. Campaigns and Inaugural Coms., Washington, 1984-89; pres. Hale Found., Nathan Hale Inst., Washington, 1984-85; mem. nat. panel consumer arbitrators Better Bus. Burs., Va., 1991—. Recipient Presdl. citation Nat. Propane Gas Assn., 1992; Minority Intern grantee Denver Regional Coun. Govts., 1974-76. Mem. ASTD, ABA (assoc., arbitration sect.), Am. League Lobbyists (chmn. energy sect., bd. dirs. 1994—, sec. 1996—), Women in Govt. Rels., Assn. Image Cons. Internat., Psi Chi. Episcopalian. Avocations: skiing, fitness, dancing, sports shooting, gourmet cooking. Office: EdgeSystem.XII 927 15th St NW Ste 1000 Washington DC 20005

SULCER, FREDERICK DURHAM, advertising executive; b. Chgo., Aug. 28, 1932; s. Henry Durham and Charlotte (Thearle) S.; m. Dorothy Wright, May 2, 1953; children—Thomas W., Ginna M., David T. BA, U. Chgo., 1949, MBA, 1963. Reporter UP Assn., Chgo., 1945-46; reporter AP, 1947; with Needham, Harper & Steers Advt., Chgo., 1947-78, dir., 1965-78, sr. account dir., 1965-66, mem. exec. com., 1966-78, exec. v.p., 1967, dir. N.Y. div., 1967-78; pres. N.Y. div. Needham, Harper & Steers Advt., 1974-75; chmn. bd. NH & S Internat., 1975-76; pres. Sulcer Communication Co., Inc., 1977-78; group exec., dir. Benton & Bowles (advt.), 1978-85; dir. bus. devel. D'Arcy Masius Benton & Bowles, advt., N.Y.C., 1985-90; vice-chmn. bd. dirs. DDB Needham Worldwide, N.Y.C., 1990-95; founder, prin. The Persuasion Group, N.Y.C., 1995—; Schering-Plough disting. vis. prof. corp. comm. Fairleigh Dickinson U., Madison, N.J., 1993-96. Served to capt. C.E. AUS, 1950-53. Mem. Am. Assn. Advt. Agys. (bd. govs. N.Y. chpt.), Internat. Advertisers Assn., Alpha Delta Phi. Home and Office: The Persuasion Group 350 W 50th St Ste PH 1-D New York NY 10019-6664

SULEYMANIAN, MIRIK, biophysicist; b. Chartar, Karabagh, Armenia, Jan. 20, 1948; s. Avanes and Gohar (Hakopian) S.; m. Nelia Agababian, Mar. 24, 1973; children: Hovanes, Gagik. Diploma, Yerevan (Armenia) State U., 1973; PhD, Inst. Exptl. Biology, Yerevan, 1981, DS, 1990. Rsch. worker Acad. Scis. Armenia, Yerevan, 1975-81, sr. rsch. worker, 1981-88, leading rsch. worker, 1988-92; rsch. assoc. dept. physiology Va. Commonwealth U., Richmond, 1992—. Contbr. over 50 articles to profl. jours. Mem. Biophys. Soc. U.S.A., Internat. Soc. Heart Rsch. Avocations: sports, music. Office: Va Commonwealth U Sanger Hall 1101 E Marshall Richmond VA 23298

SULG, MADIS, corporation executive; b. Tallinn, Estonia, May 25, 1943; came to U.S., 1950; s. Hand Eduard and Erika (Turk) S.; m. Mary Diane Detellis, Dec. 30, 1967; children: Danielle Marie, Michaella Erika. SB in Indsl. Mgmt., MIT, 1965, SM in Mgmt., 1967. Cons. Barss, Reitzel & Assocs., Cambridge, Mass., 1970-71; mgr. planning and research Converse Rubber Co., Wilmington, Mass., 1971-75; dir. bus. planning and devel. AMF, Inc., Stamford, Conn., 1975-79; sr. v.p. planning and devel. Bandag, Inc., Muscatine, Iowa, 1978-88; pres. Prime Investments, 1988—, Muscatine Natural Resources Corp., 1981-88; chmn., chief exec. officer Sieg Auto Parts, Davenport, Iowa, 1989-93; COO Hammer's Plastic Recycling, Iowa Falls, Iowa, 1994, Purethane, Inc., West Branch, Iowa, 1994—. With U.S. Army, 1968-70. Presbyterian. Avocations: bridge; jogging; swimming. Home: 4855 Rambling Ct Bettendorf IA 52722-5839 Office: Purethane Inc One Purethane Pl West Branch IA 52358

SULGER, FRANCIS XAVIER, lawyer; b. N.Y.C., Sept. 3, 1942; s. John J. and Regina (Slawkowska) S.; m. Helga Nelsen, July 23, 1968; children: Derek N., Justin D. BA, Fordham U., 1964; JD, Harvard U., 1967. Bar: N.Y. 1970, U.S. Dist. Ct. (so. dist.) N.Y. 1979. Atty. F.I. duPont & Co., N.Y.C., 1968-70; assoc. Townsend & Lewis, N.Y.C., 1970-73, Thacher Proffitt & Wood, N.Y.C., 1973-78; ptnr. Thacher Proffitt & Wood, 1978—. Trustee Wildcliff Mus., New Rochelle, N.Y., 1970-74; mem. U.S. Olympic Rowing Com., Colorado Springs, Colo., 1980-84. Mem. U.S. Rowing Assn. (bd. dirs. 1979-84), N.Y. Athletic Club (rowing chmn. 1979-95), Larchmont (N.Y.) Yacht Club. Avocations: rowing, collecting antiques, computers. Home: 10 Meadow Ln Greenwich CT 06831-3709 Office: Thacher Proffitt & Wood 2 World Trade Ctr New York NY 10048-0203

SULIK, DORIE, realtor, marketing professional; b. Cleve., Apr. 11, 1942; d. Howard Anthony and Henrietta (Schulhauser) Nieberding; divorced; children: Jodie Frydl, Rob. Grad. high sch., Euclid, Ohio. Realtor Hilltop

Realty, Cleve., 1977-82, residential sales agt., 1982-90; from adminstr. mktg. and sales to dir. devel. mktg. HGM-Hilltop Condominium Assocs., Cleve.; from mktg. mgr. to dir. sales and mktg. new homes dept. Realty One, Cleve.; dir. builder mktg. Smythe Cramer Co., Cleve., 1990—. Mem. Cleve. Bldg. Industry Assn. (chmn. assoc. adv. coun. 1994, chmn. sales and mktg. coun. 1990—, Assoc. of Yr. 1991, 94, Outstanding Mktg. Person of Yr. 1993), Builder Mktg. Soc. (trustee 1992—), Nat. Sales and Mktg. Coun. of Nat. Assn. Home Builders (trustee 1992-94), Inst. Residential Mktg. (trustee 1996). Roman Catholic. Avocations: boating, skiing, reading, walking, travel. Home: 8501 Waterside Dr Sagamore Hills OH 44067 Office: Smythe Cramer Co 5800 Lombardo Ctr Ste 200 Cleveland OH 44131-2550

SULIK, EDWIN (PETE SULIK), health care administrator; b. Bryan, Tex., Feb. 1, 1957; s. Edwin Peter and Bonny Jo (Robertson) S.; m. Kolleen Marie Stevens, Aug. 8, 1981; 1 child, Laine Sheridan. Student, Blinn Jr. Coll., 1977-78, U. Tex., 1977, Tex. A&M U., 1977-83; BBA, Ky. Western. U., 1990; MBA, Ky. Western U., 1994. Lic. long term care adminstr.; cert. preceptor. Sr. v.p. ops. Sherwood Health Care, Inc., Bryan, 1976-90, pres., 1990—; sec.-treas. Sherwood Health Care, Inc., Lubbock, Tex., 1987-89; pres. Sherwood Health Care, Inc., Bryan, 1990, Lubbock, 1990; pres., owner Brazos Mgmt. Health Care, Inc., Bryan, 1991; owner Sherwood Forest Children's Ctr., 1991; pres. Sherwood Gardens Adult Day Health Care, 1996. Mem. Lt. Gov. Bullock's Nursing Home Work Group, 1991-92; participant state debate with Lt. Gov. Hobby, Austin, Tex., 1987; mem. Legis. Oversight Com.; active St. Joseph Sch. Bd. Fellow Am. Coll. Health Care Adminstrs., Am. Health Care Assn., Tex. Health Care Assn. (bd. dirs. 1987-90, chair, chpt. pres. 1987-88, facility stds. com. 1987—, payment for svcs. com. 1987—, Medicare com. 1989—, Omnibus Budget Reconciliation Act of 1987 com. 1987—, patient admission screening and resident rev. com. 1989—, legis. com. 1987-89, co-chair budget and fin. com. 1990-91, automation com. 1990-91, pilot project site NHIC automation 1990-91, nursing home quality and case mix demonstration pilot project 1995—), Bryan Coll. C. of C. Inner Cir., Am. Assn. Ret. Persons (Medicare/Medicaid steering com.), Tex. A&M U. Century Club, KC, Elks. Republican. Roman Catholic. Avocations: racquetball, golf, bowling, bow fishing, water skiing. Home: PO Box 3553 Bryan TX 77805-3553 Office: Sherwood Health Care Inc 1401 Memorial Dr Bryan TX 77802-5218

SULIMIRSKI, WITOLD STANISLAW, banker; b. Lwow, Poland, May 18, 1933; came to U.S., 1957; s. Tadeusz and Olga (Lepkowska) S.; m. Teresa Maria Boniecka, Dec. 28, 1957; children: Elizabeth Sulimirski Blakeslee, Adam, Edward. BA with honors, Cambridge U., 1953, MA, 1957. With Irving Trust Co., N.Y.C., 1957-89, exec. v.p., 1986-89; pres. Servus Assocs., Inc., N.Y.C., 1989—; chmn. exec. com. Intercap Investments, Inc., N.Y.C., 1989—; chmn. Am. Bank in Poland, Warsaw, 1989-91, LBS Bank N.Y., 1990—; exec. dir. Am. Investment Initiative in Poland, Warsaw, 1992-94; bd. dirs. Bank Pekao SA, Warsaw, 1993-95, 12th Nat. Investment Fund, Warsaw,, Bank Gdanski. Treas. Polish Inst. Arts and Scis., Inc., N.Y.C., 1976—; vice chmn. Kosciuscko Found., Inc., N.Y.C., 1983—; chmn. Polish Assistance, Inc., N.Y.C., 1984-92; bd. dirs. Middle East Policy Coun., Washington, 1984—, Nat. U.S.-Arab C. of C., Washington, 1987-93. Mem. Bronxville Field Club, Knights of Malta. Roman Catholic. Office: Intercap Investments Inc 430 Park Ave Fl 10 New York NY 10022-3505

SULKIN, HOWARD ALLEN, college president; b. Detroit, Aug. 19, 1941; s. Lewis and Vivian P. (Mandel) S.; m. Constance Annette Adler, Aug. 4, 1963; children—Seth R., Randall K. PhB, Wayne State U., 1963; MBA, U. Chgo., 1965, PhD, 1969; LHD (hon.), De Paul U., 1990. Dir. program rsch., indsl. rels. ctr. U. Chgo., 1964-72; dean Sch. for New Learning, De Paul U., Chgo., 1972-77; v.p. De Paul U., Chgo., 1977-84; pres. Spertus Inst. Jewish Studies, Chgo., 1984—; St. Paul's vis. prof. Rikkyo U., Tokyo, 1970—; cons., evaluator North Central Assn., Chgo., 1975—. Contbr. articles to profl. jours. Sec.-treas. Grant Park Cultural and Ednl. Cmty., Chgo., 1984—; bd. dirs. Chgo. Sinai Congregation, 1972—, pres., 1980-83; bd. dirs. S.E. Chgo. Commn., 1980—, United Way, 1984—, Crusade of Mercy United Way, 1990—; bd. dirs., chmn. Parliament of World's Religions, 1989—. Mem. Adult Edn. Assn. U.S.A., Acad. Internat. Bus. Club: Cliff Dwellers (Chgo.). Office: Spertus Inst. of Jewish Studies 618 S Michigan Ave Chicago IL 60605-1901

SULLENBERGER, ARA BROOCKS, mathematics educator; b. Amarillo, Tex., Jan. 3, 1933; d. Carl Clarence and Ara Frances (Broocks) Cox; m. Hal Joseph Sullenberger, Nov. 2, 1952; children: Hal Joseph Jr., Ara Broocks Sullenberger Switzer. Student, Randolph-Macon Woman's Coll., 1951-52, So. Meth. U., 1952, U. Tex., Arlington, 1953, Amarillo Coll., 1953-54; BA in Math., Tex. Tech. U., 1955, MA, 1958; postgrad., Tex. Christian U., 1963-67, U. N. Tex., 1969-80, Tarrant Jr. Coll., Fort Worth, Tex., 1972-83. Cert. tchr., Tex. Math. tchr. Tom S. Lubbock (Tex.) High Sch., 1955-56; instr. math. Tex. Tech U., Lubbock, 1956-63; teaching fellow math. Tex. Christian U., Ft. Worth, 1963-64; chmn. dept. math. Ft. Worth Country Day Sch., 1964-67; instr. math. Tarrant County Jr. Coll.-South, Ft. Worth, 1967-70, asst. prof. math., 1970-74, assoc. prof. math., 1974-95; prof. emeritus, 1995—, ret., 1995; cons. Project Change, Ft. Worth, 1967-68; math. scis. advisor Coll. Bd., Princeton, N.J., 1979-83; math. book reviewer for vaarious pub. cos. including Prentice-Hall, McGraw Hill, D.C. Health, Prindle, Weber & Schmidt, MacMillan, Harcourt, Brace Jovanovich, West, Worth, Saunders, Wadsworth. Contbr. article, book revs. to profl. publs.; author book supplement to Intermediate Algebra, 1990. Active mem. Jr. League of Ft. Worth, 1954-73, sustaining mem., 1973—; editor newsletter Crestwood Assn., Ft. Worth, 1984, 86, 91, membership sec., 1985, 90, 91, 95, pres., 1988-89, crime patrol capt., 1993, v.p., 1993, treas. 1987, 96. Recipient award for excellence in teaching Gen. Dynamics, 1968. Mem. Math. Assn. Am. (life), Nat. Coun. Tchrs. Math. (life), Am. Math. Assn. Two-Yr. Colls. (life), Tex. Math. Assn. Two-Yr. Colls. (charter), Tex. Jr. Coll. Tchrs.' Assn., Pi Beta Phi. Republican. Episcopalian. Avocations: grandchildren, reading, pets, walking, writing. Home: 600 Eastwood Ave Fort Worth TX 76107-1020

SULLENBERGER, DONALD SHIELDS, air force officer, business executive; b. Knoxville, Tenn., Sept. 30, 1940; s. Archibald Jack and Rebecca Pauline (Myers) S.; m. Karen Sue Long, June 10, 1961; children: Douglas, Robert, Erik. BA magna cum laude, U. Nebr., Omaha, 1966; MBA, U. Mont., Missoula, 1979; MS summa cum laude, Golden Gate U., 1990, Marymount U., 1995. Lic. comml. airline pilot. Commd. 2d lt. USAF, 1962, advanced through grades to col., 1984; dir. tng. and evaluation USAF, Da Nang AFB, Vietnam, 1971-73; dir. ICBM ops./tng. USAF, Great Falls, Mont., 1973-76; several posts USAF, Madrid, 1976-79; comdr. USAF, Moody AFB, Ga., 1979-84; dep. comdr. for maintenance USAF, Myrtle Beach AFB, S.C., 1984-85; base comdr. USAF, Homestead AFB, Fla., 1985-87; div. and gen. mgr. Holloman Support div. Dyncorp, Alamogordo, N.Mex., 1987-91; corp. v.p. Dyncorp, Reston, Va., 1991-95; pres. Apogee Cons. Inc., Knoxville, Tenn., 1995—; ind. cons., Washington, 1995—. Bd. dirs. United Way, Alamogordo, 1989-91; bd. dirs. Vision 2000 of Homestead City Coun., 1985-87; mem. Reston Quality Roundtable, 1991-94. Decorated Legion of Merit, DFC, Bronze Star, Air medal (10), Meritorious Svc. medal (4), Joint Svc. Commendation medal. Mem. VFW, Am. Soc. Quality Control, Quality Productivity and Mgmt. Assn., Am. Mgmt. Assn., Am. Legion. Avocations: running, conditioning, flying. Home: 5212 Hickory Hollow Rd Knoxville TN 37919 Office: Apogee Cons Inc 600 Tedlo Knoxville TN 37920

SULLENDER, JOY SHARON, elementary school educator; b. Bloomington, Ind., Apr. 9, 1932; d. Fred Laymond and Edith (Parrish) Medaris. BS, Ind. U., 1959, MS, 1965; postgrad., Ind. U./Purdue U., Indpls., 1991. Cert. tchr. elem. edn. 1-8. Tchr. Monroe Sch., Salem, Ind., 1952-55, Pekin (Ind.) Sch., 1955-61, Highland Park (Ill.) Sch., 1961-62, George Julian Sch. #57, Indpls., 1962—; mem. prin.'s adv. coun. Indpls. Pub. Schs., 1985-95, supts. adv. coun., 1982-90; state mentor student tchrs., 1969—. Author col.: Let's Be Informed, 1993—. Class sponsor Best Friends, Indpls., 1990—; vol. Toys for Foster Children, Indpls., 1991—; workshop presenter Alpha Epsilon Staet, Anderson, South Bend, 1994, 95. NSF grantee, 1971. Mem. PTA (tchr. rep. 1993-95), Ind. Sch. Women's Club (v.p. 1989-91, pres. 1992-94), Delta Kappa Gamma (pres. 1978-80, state com. 1989—). Republican. Baptist. Avocations: reading, collecting antiques, volunteer work, decorating, shopping. Home: 3134 N Richardt Ave Indianapolis IN 46226-6385 Office: George Julian School 5435 E Washington St Indianapolis IN 46219-6411

SULLIVAN, ADÈLE WOODHOUSE, organization official; b. Trenton, N.J.; d. William and Adaline Dearth (Fox) Woodhouse; m. Harold E. Erb, May 27, 1929 (dec. Nov. 1957); m. William H. Sullivan, Jr., Mar. 17, 1960 (dec. Dec. 1985); 1 child, Nancy Elizabeth (Mrs. Joseph P. Thorne). Student, Rider Coll., 1925-27; LHD, Lincoln Meml. U., 1968. Mem. DAR, 1931—; state regent DAR, N.Y., 1953-56, hon. state regent for life, 1956—, nat. rec. sec. gen., 1956-59, 1st v.p. gen., 1959-62, nat. pres. gen., 1965-68, hon. pres. gen. for life, 1968—, organizing chmn. Centennial Jubilee, 1983-89; founder, pres. Nat. DAR Exec. Club, 1962-64; pres. Nat. DAR Officers Club, 1978-80; past trustee DAR Schs. Kate Duncan Smith, Grant, Ala., Tamassee, S.C., Crossnore, N.C.; sec. Air Corps office Keystone Aircraft Corp., 1927-29; sec., treas. Power Machinery Corp., N.Y.C., 1961-65. Pres. Woodhull Day Sch. PTA, Hollis, N.Y., 1942-44; chmn. student loan fund women's aux. ASME, 1946-48; v.p. N.Y. colony New Eng. Women, 1963-65; mem. Women's Nat. Adv. Commn. for Nixon, 1968; chmn. N.Y. Women for Buckley, 1970, Women's Nat. Rep. Campaign Com., 1972; mem. nat. adv. bd. Am. Security Coun..; vis. U.S. Troops, Vietnam, Jan., 1968; bd. dirs. Nat. Symphony Orch. Assn., 1965-68, Friends of Historic St. George's Ch., Hempstead, L.I., 1960-67; bd. dirs., exec. v.p. nat. affairs Cultural Laureat Found., Inc., 1973-77 ; mem. awards jury Freedoms Found., 1966-67; mem. nat. honors com. Women's Hall of Fame, Inc.; program chmn. Women's Soc., Scarsdale Community Bapt. Ch., 1977-80, trustee, 1980-86. Recipient commendation award U.S. Navy for work with DAR, World War II. award for outstanding svc. to nation Am. Coalition Patriotic Socs., 1967, Freedom Found. medal of honor, 1967, Gold medal Nat. Soc. New Eng. Women, 1969, Nat. Capital USO Disting. Svc. cert., 1968. Mem. Am. Friends of Lafayette (exec. coun.), Hon. Soc. Ky. Cols., Ams. for Patriotism, Inc. (organizing past pres.). Home and Office: 10 Scarsdale Ave Scarsdale NY 10583-4045 *To aid in promoting a sense of responsible citizenship through education. To do each task undertaken to the best of my ability. To endeavor to do unto others as I would have them do unto me. To have the satisfaction of having a young woman say she had been favorably influenced by me.*

SULLIVAN, ALFRED DEWITT, academic administrator; b. New Orleans, Feb. 2, 1942; s. Dewitt Walter and Natalie (Alford) S.; m. Marilyn Janie Hewitt, Sept. 1, 1962 (div. May 1989); children: Alan, Sean; m. Dorothy Madeleine Hess, Apr. 1993. BS, La. State U., 1964, MS, 1966; PhD, U. Ga., 1969. Asst. prof. Va. Poly. Inst. and State U., Blacksburg, 1969-73; assoc. prof., then prof. Miss. State U., Starkville, 1973-88; dir. Sch. Forest Resources Pa. State U., University Park, 1988-93; dean coll. natural resources U. Minn., St. Paul, 1993—. Contbr. articles to profl. jours. Fellow Am. Coun. on Edn., 1987-88, NDEA fellow U. Ga., 1966-69; assoc. Danforth Found., 1981. Mem. Soc. Am. Foresters. Office: U Minn 235 Natural Resources Adminstrn Bldg 2003 Upper Buford Cir Saint Paul MN 55108-6146

SULLIVAN, ALLEN TROUSDALE, securities company executive; b. Nashville, Dec. 16, 1927; s. William Albert and Eleanor (Allen) S.; m. Barbara Oman, Nov. 12, 1955; children: Merida, Louise. Mgr. Ralph Nichols Co., Nashville, 1949-56; ptnr. J.C. Bradford & Co., Nashville, 1956—. Bd. dirs. Loves & Fishes, Monroe Harding Children's Home. With USN, 1943-46. Mem. Nashville Security Dealers Assn. (pres. 1989). Clubs: Belle Meade (Nashville), Nashville City (Nashville). Home: 7 Valley Frg Nashville TN 37205-4725 Office: JC Bradford & Co 330 Commerce St Nashville TN 37201-1805

SULLIVAN, ANNE DOROTHY HEVNER, artist; b. Boston, Mar. 17, 1929; m. James Leo Sullivan, Jan. 20, 1951; children: Maura, Mark, Lianne, Christopher. Student, Northeastern U., 1973-75; BA, U. Mass., Lowell, 1977; postgrad., De Cordova Mus., Lincoln, Mass., 1978-81. Art dir., instr. Whistler House Mus., Lowell, Mass., 1971-73; art instr., dir. alternatives for individual devel. program U. Mass., Lowell, 1976-84; incorporator Depot Square Artists Gallery, Lexington, Mass., 1981-84; dir., art cons. Abbey Art Gallery, Boston, 1987-88; juried artist Emerson Umbrella Ctr. for Arts, Concord, Mass., 1989-92, Brush with History Gallery, Lowell, Mass., 1992—; juror, lectr., demonstrator, tchr. to art groups and assns., 1971—. Exhibited in juried group shows at Fed. Res. Gallery, Boston, 1990-94, Brush With History Gallery, Boston, 1990, Lowell Urban Nat. Pk., 1990, Midwest Mus. of Am. Art, Elkhardt, Ind., 1991, Cahoon Mus., Cotuit, Mass., 1991, Sumner Mus., Washington, 1992, Whistler Mus., 1992, Duxbury Mus., 1992, Attleboro (Mass.) Mus., 1992, C.L. Wolfe Art Club, N.Y.C., 192, N.E. Ctr.-U. N.H., 1992, Emerson Umbrella at Fed. Res. Boston, 1993, Bentley Coll., Waltham, Mass., 1993, Fitchburg (Mass.) Mus., 1994, U. Mass. Med. Sch., Worcester, 1994, Whistler Mus. Invitational Exhibit of Paintings, Lowell, 1995, Fuller Mus. - Printmakers' Monotype Exhibit, Brockton, Mass., 1995, Nat. Assn. Women Artists 107th Ann., N.Y.C., 1996, N.Am. Open Compeition, Boston, 1996; represented in permanent collections at Neil Sulier Art Collection, Lexington, Ky., The New Eng. Bank, Shawmut Bank, Bay Banks, Concord Nat. Bank, Amoskeag Banks, N.H., 1st Capital Bank of Concord, N.H., Sheraton Corp., Boston, Calif., New Orleans; artist: watercolor series/abstracts. Bd. dirs. Human Svcs. Corp., Lowell, 1971-72; v.p. Whistler Mus. Art, 1972-73; chmn. Lowell Arts Coun., 1980-81; mem. Mass. Arts Advocacy Coun., Boston, 1982. Recipient M.M. Rines award for outstanding contemporary painting N.Am. Open Competition, Fed. Res. Gallery, Boston, 1994, Catharine Lorillard Wolfe Art Club, Inc. award, 1992, hon. mention All New Eng. Competition, 1989, Fitchburg Mus. 59th Ann., 1994, 2d prize Cahoon Mus., 1991. Mem. Nat. Assn. women Artists (Martha Reed Meml. award 1988, Leila Sawyer Meml. award 1994), New Eng. Watercolor Soc. (bd. dirs. 1984-92), Monotype Guild New Eng. (pres. 1992-93), Nat. League Am. Penwomen (award of excellence 1990), Copley Soc. (Copley Artist award). Home: 28 Rindo Park Dr Lowell MA 01851-3413 Studio: Brush Gallery & Studio Urban Nat Park 256 Market St Lowell MA 01852-1856

SULLIVAN, AUSTIN PADRAIC, JR., diversified food company executive; b. Washington, June 26, 1940; s. Austin P. Sullivan and Janet Lay (Patterson); m. Judith Ann Raab, June 8, 1968; children: Austin P. III, Amanda, Alexander. AB cum laude, Princeton U., 1964. Spl. asst. to dep. dir. N.J. Office Econ. Opportunity, Trenton, 1965-66; prof. staff mem. Com. on Edn. and Labor, U.S. Ho. of Reps., Washington, 1967-71, legis. dir., 1971-76; dir. govt. relations Gen. Mills, Inc., Mpls., 1976-78,, 1977-78, v.p., corp. dir. govt. relations, 1978-79, v.p. pub. affairs, 1979-93, v.p. corp. comms. and pub. affairs, 1993-94, sr. v.p. corp. rels., 1994—; lectr. fed. labor market policies Harvard U., 1972-76, Boston U., 1972-76. Bd. dirs., exec. com. Guthrie Theatre, Mpls., 1978-84, Minn. Citizens for the Arts, 1980-83, Mpls. Cmty. Bus. Employment Alliance, 1982-84, Urban Coalition Mpls., 1978-80; chmn. Pub. Affairs Coun., 1993-94—; chmn. Mpls. Pvt. Industry Coun.,1983-87; mem. nat. Commn. on Employment and Tng., 1979-81; chmn. Gov.'s Coun. on Employment and Tng., 1976-82; 1, co-chmn. gov's Commn. on Dislocated Workers, 1988-89; mem. steering com. Minn. Meeting, 1982-94; bd. advisors Dem. Leadership Coun., 1986—; Minn. C. of C., bd. dirs. 1993—; prin. the Coun. for Excellence inGovt., 1988—; With USMC, 1957-59. Eleanor Roosevelt fellow in interracial relations, 1964-65. Mem. conf. bd., Coun. of Pub. Affairs Execs. (chmn. 1989-90) Grocery Mfrs. Assn. (chmn. state govt. task force 1989-90, govt. affairs coun. 1991—), Bus. Roundtable (pub. info. com. 1987—), Greater Mpls. C. of C. (bd. dirs. and exec. com., 1980-86, 90-93). Home: 17830 County Rd 6 Minneapolis MN 55447-2905 Office: Gen Mills Inc One Gen Mills Blvd Minneapolis MN 55426

SULLIVAN, BARBARA, publishing company executive. Pres. Reed Info. Svcs., New Providence, N.J. Office: Reed Info Svcs 121 Chanlon Rd New Providence NJ 07974*

SULLIVAN, BARBARA BOYLE, management consultant; b. Scranton, Pa., Apr. 12, 1937; d. Edmund F. and Mary R. (O'Connell) Boyle; m. John L. Sullivan Jr. BS in Bus. Adminstrn., Drexel U., 1958; PhD (hon.), Newton Coll., 1975, Gwynedd Mercy Coll., 1975. With IBM, 1959-72; systems engrng. mgr. Ea. and Cen. Europe IBM, Vienna, Austria, 1967-70; mgmt. devel. mgr. IBM, 1970, mgr. spl. programs, 1970-71, sales mgr., asst. br. mgr., 1971-72; pres. Boyle/Kirkman Assocs., N.Y.C., 1972-88; mng. ptnr. Innovation Assocs., Framingham, Mass., 1988-92; bd. dirs. Equitable Resources, Inc., 1974—, chair compensation com., 1989-92, nominating com., 1991, mem. audit, pension trust, and compensation com.; cons. major corps. on human resource devl. programs, organizational change programs, changing work force; condr. exec. leadership and visionary and strategic planning awareness seminars Harvard Bus. Sch., Internat. Mgmt. Conf. Trustee Drexel U.; mem. Pres.'s adv. com. Gwynedd Mercy Coll., adv. com. Drexel U. Coll. Bus. Adminstrn.; vice chmn. bd. trustee Marymount Manhattan Coll., N.Y., bd. regents Mt. St. Mary's Coll., L.A., 1982-88. Featured in numerous mags., books, radio and TV programs, including CBS 60 Minutes; named Bus. Person of Yr. St. Johns U., 1973, One of 50 Leaders for Future, Time mag., 1979. Mem. AAUW, Women's Forum, Weston Womens' League, Boston Club. Home: PO Box 505 Weston MA 02193-0003

SULLIVAN, BARRY, lawyer, educator; b. Newburyport, Mass., Jan. 11, 1949; s. George Arnold and Dorothy Bennett (Furbush) S.; m. Winnifred Mary Fallers, June 14, 1975; children: George Arnold, Lloyd Ashton. AB cum laude, Middlebury Coll., 1970; JD, U. Chgo., 1974. Bar: Mass. 1975, Ill. 1975, Va. 1995, U.S. Dist. Ct. (no. dist.) Ill. 1976, U.S. Ct. Appeals (7th cir.) 1976, U.S. Ct. Appeals (10th cir.) 1977, U.s. Supreme Ct. 1978, U.S. Ct. Appeals (11th cir.) 1986, U.S. Ct. Appeals (5th and 9th cirs.) 1987, U.S. Ct. Appeals (fed. cir.) 1993, U.S. Ct. Appeals (D.C. cir.) 1994. Law clk. to judge John Minor Wisdom U.S. Ct. Appeals (5th cir.), New Orleans, 1974-75; assoc. Jenner & Block, Chgo., 1975-80; asst. to solicitor gen. of U.S. U.S. Dept. of Justice, Washington, 1980-81; ptnr. Jenner & Block, Chgo., 1981-94; dean, prof. law Washington and Lee U., Lexington, Va., 1994—; spl. asst. atty. gen. State of Ill., 1989-90; lectr. in law Loyola U., Chgo., 1978-79; adj. prof. law Northwestern U., Chgo., 1990-92, 93-94, vis. prof., 1992-93; Jessica Swift Meml. lectr. in constnl. law Middlebury Coll., 1991. Assoc. editor U. Chgo. Law Rev., 1973-74; contbr. articles to profl. jours. Trustee Cath. Theol. Union at Chgo., 1993—; mem. vis. com. U. Chgo. Divinity Sch., 1987—. Yeats Soc. scholar, 1968; Woodrow Wilson fellow, Woodrow Wilson Found., 1970. Mem. ABA (chmn. coord. com. on AIDS 1988-94, mem. standing com. on amicus curiae briefs 1990—, mem. coun. of sect. of individual rights and responsibilities 1993—, mem. sect. of legal edn. com. on law sch. adminstrn. 1994—), Va. Bar Assn., Bar Assn. 7th Fed. Cir. (vice chmn. adminstrv. justice com. 1985-86), Am. Law Inst., Law Club Chgo., Phi Beta Kappa. Democrat. Roman Catholic. Home: 201 Jackson Ave Lexington VA 24450-2007 Office: Washington and Lee U Sch Law Lewis Hall Lexington VA 24450

SULLIVAN, BILL, church administrator. Dir. Church Growth Division of the Church of the Nazarene, Kansas City, Mo. Office: Church of Nazarene 6401 Paseo Blvd Kansas City MO 64131-1213

SULLIVAN, BRENDAN V., JR., lawyer; b. Providence, Mar. 11, 1942. AB, Georgetown U., 1964, JD, 1967. Bar: R.I. 1967, D.C. 1970, U.S. Dist. Ct. D.C. 1970, U.S. Ct. Appeals (D.C. cir.) 1970, U.S. Supreme Ct. 1972, U.S. Dist. Ct. Md. 1974, U.S. Ct. Appeals (4th cir.) 1978, U.S. Ct. Appeals (3d cir.) 1979. Mem. Williams & Connolly, Washington; lectr. Practicing Law Inst., 1981—, Md. Inst. for Continuing Profl. Edn. of Lawyers, Inc., 1979—, D.C. Criminal Practice Inst., 1975-81. Author: Grand Jury Proceedings, 1981, Techniques for Dealing with Pending Criminal Charges or Criminal Investigations, 1983, White Collar Criminal Practice Grand Jury, 1985. Fellow Am. Coll. Trial Lawyers; mem. ABA, R.I. Bar Assn., D.C. Bar. Office: Williams & Connolly 725 12th St NW Washington DC 20005-5901

SULLIVAN, CHARLES, university dean, educator, author; b. Boston, May 27, 1933; s. Charles Thomas and Marion Veronica (Donahue) S.; divorced; children: Charles Fulford, John Driscoll, Catherine Page. BA in English, Swarthmore Coll., 1955; MA, NYU, 1968, PhD in Social Psychology, 1973; MPA, Pa. State U., 1978. Predoctoral fellow NYU, 1964-68; postdoctoral fellow Ednl. Testing Svc., Princeton, N.J., 1973-74; asst. prof. psychology Ursinus Coll., Collegeville, Pa., 1973-78; mgmt. cons., 1978-86; adj. prof. Pa. State U., Radnor, Pa., 1978-80; prof., head dept. pub. adminstrn., dir. student svcs. Southeastern U., Washington, 1986-89; asst. dean Grad. Sch. Arts and Scis. Georgetown U., Washington, 1989-92, assoc. dean Grad. Sch. Arts and Scis., 1992—, professorial lectr., dept. psychology, 1994—; exec. dir. Doylestown Found., Doylestown, Pa., 1958-73; adj. prof. social and behavioral scis. U. Md., 1984—; lectr., spkr. on lit. and art Cooper-Hewitt Mus., N.Y.C., Nat. Soc. Arts and Letters, Washington, Martin Luther King Jr. Libr., Washington, Met. Mus. Art, N.Y.C., Smithsonian Instn., Washington, Children's Book Fair, N.Y.C., Nat. Mus. Women in Arts, Lombardi Cancer Rsch. Ctr., Georgetown U., Arts Club of Washington, Phillips Collection, Corcoran Gallery of Art. Author: Alphabet Animals, 1991, The Lover in Winter, 1991, Numbers at Play, 1992, Circus, 1992, Cowboys, 1993, A Woman of A Certain Age, 1994. Out of Love, 1996; editor: America in Poetry, 1988, 2d edit., 1992, 3d edit., 1996, Imaginary Gardens, 1989, Ireland in Poetry, 1990, Children of Promise, 1991, Loving, 1992, American Beauties, 1993, Here Is My Kingdom, 1994, Fathers and Children, 1995, Imaginary Animals, 1996. Mem. bd. trustees Folger Poetry Bd., 1988-92; Nat. Soc. Arts and Letters, 1992-94, Am. Acad. Liberal Edn., 1995—. Mem. Am. Poetry Soc., Am. Found. for Arts (pres. 1995—), Acad. Am. Poets, Cosmos Club. Office: Georgetown U Grad Sch 302 Intercultural Ctr Washington DC 20057

SULLIVAN, CHARLES A., food products executive. BBA, U. Toledo, 1959. With Seven-Up Co., Los Angeles, 1966-70; v.p. strategic planning Pepsi-Cola Co., Los Angeles, 1966-70; pres. Seven Up of Ind.; with Westinghouse Electric Corp., 1970-79; pres. Can. Dry of New Eng. subs. Norton Simon Co., 1979-82; sr. v.p. pres. Merita div. Am. Bakeries Co. subs. BCA Corp., N.Y.C., 1982-86; exec. v.p. BCA Corp., N.Y.C.; pres., exec. v.p. Merita div. Am. Bakeries Co., 1986-89; pres., chief exec. officer Interstate Bakeries Corp., 1989—; pres., chief oper. officer Interstate Brands Corp. Office: Interstate Brands Corp PO Box 419627 Kansas City MO 64141-6627*

SULLIVAN, CHARLES BERNARD, hospital administrator; b. Darby, Pa., Jan. 5, 1945; married. BA, Manhattan Coll., 1966; MA, L.I.U., 1969; MHA, Columbia U., 1971. Adminstrv. resident Montefiore Med. Ctr., Bronx, N.Y., 1970-71; asst. adminstr. Mt. Sinai Med. Ctr., Milw., 1971-73, assoc. adminstr., 1973-75; exec. v.p. Reading (Pa.) Hosp. and Med. Ctr., 1975-86, pres., CEO, 1986—. Contbr. articles to profl. jours. Recipient awards. Office: Reading Hosp & Med Ctr 6th Ave Spruce St Reading PA 19603*

SULLIVAN, CLAIRE FERGUSON, marketing educator; b. Pittsburg, Tex., Sept. 28, 1937; d. Almon Lafayette and Mabel Clara (Williams) Potter; m. Richard Wayne Ferguson, Jan. 31, 1959 (div. Jan. 1980); 1 child, Mark Jeffrey Ferguson; m. David Edward Sullivan, Nov. 2, 1984. BBA, U. Tex., 1958, MBA, 1961; PhD, U. North Tex., 1973; grad., Harvard Inst. Ednl. Mgmt., 1991. Instr. So. Meth. U., Dallas, 1965-70; asst. prof. U. Utah, Salt Lake City, 1972-74; assoc. prof. U. Ark., Little Rock, 1974-77, U. Tex., Arlington, 1977-80, Ill. State U., Normal, 1980-84; prof., chmn. mktg. Bentley Coll., Waltham, Mass., 1984-89; dean sch. bus. Met. State Coll. Denver, 1989-92, prof. mktg., 1992—; cons. Denver Partnership, 1989-90, Gen. Tel. Co., Irving, Tex., 1983, McKnight Pub. Co., Bloomington, Ill., 1983, dental practitioner, Bloomington, 1982-83, Olympic Fed., Berwyn, Ill., 1982, Denver Partnership Econ. Devel. Adv. Coun., 1989-91; mem. African-Am. Leadership Inst. Gov. Bd. Contbr. mktg. articles to profl. jours. Direct Mktg. Inst. fellow, 1981; Ill. State U. rsch. grantee, 1981-83. Mem. Am. Mktg. Assn. (faculty fellow 1984-85), Beta Gamma Sigma. Republican. Methodist. Home: 408 E 10th Ave Salt Lake City UT 84103 Office: Met State Coll Dept Mktg MSCD Box 79 PO Box 173362 Denver CO 80217-3362

SULLIVAN, CONNIE CASTLEBERRY, artist, photographer; b. Cin., Jan. 8, 1934; d. John Porter and Constance (Alf) Castleberry; m. John J. Sullivan, June 6, 1959; children: Deirdre Kelly, Margaret Graham. BA, Manhattanville Coll., 1957. spl. lectr. Cin. Contemporary Art Ctr., 1984, Toledo Friends of Photography, 1991, U. Ky. Art Mus., 1993, Dennison U. Sch. Art, 1993, El Instituto de Estudios Norte Americanos, Barcelona, 1994. One-woman shows include Contemporary Art Ctr. Cleve., 1982, Cin. Contemporary Arts Ctr., 1983, Fogg Art Mus., Cambridge, Mass., 1983, 90, Camden Arts Ctr., London, 1987, Jean-Pierre Lambert Galerie, Paris, 1988,

96, David Winton Bell Gallery, Brown U., Providence, 1989, Toni Burckhead Gallery, Cin., 1989, Rochester Inst. Tech., 1991, Fotomus. im Münchner Stadtmus., Munich, 1992, U. Ky. Art Mus., Lexington, 1993, Internat. Photography Hall, Kirkpatrick Mus. complex, Oklahoma City, 1993, Institut d'Estudios Fotografics de Catalunya, Barcelona, Spain, 1994, Cheekwood Art Mus., Nashville, 1994, Museo Damy di Fotografia Contemporanea, Brescia, Italy, 1995, Photography Gallery U. Notre Dame, Ind., 1995, Louisville Visual Art Assoc., Watertower, Louisville, KY, 1995; exhibited in numerous group shows including Dayton (Ohio) Art Inst., 1987, J.B. Speed Art Mus., Louisville, 1988, Ohio U., Athens, 1989, Centre Nat. Photographie, Paris, 1989, Cleve. Ctr. for Contemporary Art, 1991, Tampa Mus. Art, 1991, 93, Images Gallery, 1991, Dayton Art Inst./Mus. Contemporary Art Wright State U., Dayton, 1992, Bowling Green State U. Sch Art, 1992, Carnegie Arts Ctr., Covington, Ky., 1993, Cin. Art Mus., 1993, POLK Mus. Art, Lakeland, Fla., 1993, Tampa (Fla.) Mus. Art, 1993, Adams Landing Fine Art Ctr., Cin., 1995, Checkwood Mus. Art, Nashville, 1995, Photo Forum Gallery, 1995, Jean-Pierre Galerie, 1996, Soros Ctr. Contemporary Art, Kiev, Ukraine, 1996, Dom Khudozhnikiv, Kharkiv, Ukraine, 1996; represented in numerous permanent collections Tampa Mus. of Art, Mûnchner Stadt Mus., Munich, Germany, Museo Damy, Brescia, Italy, Ctr. Creative Photography, Tucson, Detroit Inst. Arts, Biblioteque National, Paris, Internat. Photography Hall of Fame and Mus., Kirkpatrick Ctr. Mus. Complex, Okla. City, Nelson Gallery-Atkins Mus., Kansas City, Ctr. for Photography, Bombay, Milw. Art Mus., Mus. Photography Arts, San Diego, Musee Nat. D'Art Modern, Centre Georges Pompidou, Paris, Denver Art Mus., Boston Mus. Fine Arts, Stanford U. Mus. Art, Palo Alto, Indpls. Art Mus., New Orleans Mus. Art, Fogg Mus., Cambridge, Mass., numerous others; also pvt. collections; author: Petroglyphs of the Heart, Photographs by Connie Sullivan, 1983; work represented in numerous publs. Trustee Images Ctr. for Fine Photography, Cin., 1986-94. Arts Midwest fellow NEA, 1989-90; recipient award Toledo Friends Photography Juried Show, 1986, Best of Show award, 1988, Images Gallery, 1986, Pres.'s Coun. for Arts award Manhattanville Coll., 1991; Treasure of the Month award Mus. Fine Arts St. Petersburg, Fla., 1995; Aid to Individual Artists grantee Summerfair, 1987; named Hyde Park Living Person of Yr., 1996. Mem. McDowell Soc. Avocations: travel, reading, gardening, music. Home and Studio: 9 Garden Pl Cincinnati OH 45208-1056

SULLIVAN, CORNELIUS FRANCIS, JR., banking executive; b. Plainfield, N.J., Aug. 16, 1960; s. Cornelius Francis and Ruth Theresa Sullivan. AB, Duke U., 1982, MBA, 1985. Youth campaign coord. Jim Johnson for Congress, Madison, 1982; founder, ptnr. Raleigh Sports Venture, Durham, N.C., 1985-86; corp. planning analyst Midlantic Banks Inc., Edison, N.J., 1986-87, corp. planning officer, 1988-89, asst. v.p., 1990-93; v.p. corp. fin. and comm. Midlantic Corp., Edison, 1993-95; sr. v.p. corp. fin. and comm. PNC Bank, East Brunswick, N.J., 1995-96; chief adminstrv. officer PNC Bank Comml. Fin., 1996—. Press chmn. LPGA Charity Golf Tournament, N.J., 1978-89; asst. press sec. Bo Sullivan for Gov., Fairfield, 1981; mem. zoning bd. of adjustment Town of Westfield, 1994, councilman, 1995—, mem. planning bd., 1996—. Mem. S.R., Duke U. Fuqua Sch. of Bus. Alumni Coun. Home: 335 Sycamore St Westfield NJ 07090-1645 Office: Midlantic Corp 499 Thornall St Edison NJ 08837-2235

SULLIVAN, CORNELIUS WAYNE, marine biology educator, research foundation administrator; b. Pitts., June 11, 1943; s. John Wayne and Hilda Sullivan; m. Jill Hajjar, Oct. 28, 1966; children: Shane, Preston, Chelsea. BS in Biochemistry, Pa. State U., 1965, MS in Microbiology, 1967; PhD in Marine Biology, U. Calif., San Diego, 1971. Postdoctoral fellow Scripps Inst. Oceanography, La Jolla, Calif., 1971-74; asst. prof. marine biology U. So. Calif., L.A., 1974-80, assoc. prof., 1980-85, prof., 1985—, dir. marine biology sect., 1982-91; dir. Hancock Inst. Marine Studies, L.A., 1991-93; dir. Office of Polar Programs Nat. Sci. Found., Washington, 1993—; vis. prof. U. Colo., Boulder, 1981-82, MIT, Cambridge, 1981-82, U.S. Army Cold Regions Rsch. & Engring. Lab., Hanover, 1989, Goddard Space Flight Ctr., Greenbelt, Md., 1990; field team leader Sea Ice Microbial Communities Studies, McMurdo Sound, Antarctica, 1980-86; chief scientist/cruise coord. Antartic Marine Ecosystem Rsch. at the Ice Edge Zone Project, Weddell Sea, 1983, 86, 88; mem. BIOMASS Working Party on Pack-Ice Zone Studies, 1983-86, ecol. rsch. rev. bd. Dept. Navy, 1982-85; So. Ocean Ecology Group Specialist Sci. Com. on Antarctic Rsch.; chmn. SCOR working group 86 "Sea Ice Ecology" sci. com. on oceanic rsch.; mem. polar rsch. bd. NAS, 1983-86, chmn. com. to evaluate polar rsch. platforms Nat. Rsch. Coun., 1985—; mem. dir. policy group NSF, 1993—. Mem. editl. bd. Jour. Microbiol. Methods, 1982-85, Polar Biology, 1987—; contbr. over 100 articles to profl. jours. Mem. U.S. Delegation Antarctic Treaty, 1993—. With USPHS, 1969-71. Fellow USPHS, 1969-71; recipient Antarctic Svc. medal of U.S., NSF, 1981. Fellow AAAS. Office: NSF 4201 Wilson Blvd Ste 755 Arlington VA 22230-0001

SULLIVAN, DANIEL J., artistic director; b. Wray, Colo., June 11, 1940; s. John Martin and Mary Catherine (Hutton) S.; children: Megan, John, Rachel M. BA, San Francisco State U. Actor, Actor's Workshop, San Francisco, 1963-65; actor, dir. Lincoln Center Repertory, N.Y.C., 1965-73; dir. (broadway) I'm Not Rappaport, also numerous regional theatres, 1973-79; resident dir. Seattle Repertory Theater, 1979-81, artistic dir., 1981—. Recipient Drama Desk award N.Y. Theatre Critics, 1972. Mem. Nat. Endowment for Arts. Democrat. Office: Seattle Repertory Theatre 155 Mercer St Seattle WA 98109-4639

SULLIVAN, DANIEL JOSEPH, journalist; b. Worcester, Mass., Oct. 22, 1935; s. John Daniel and Irene Ann (Flagg) S.; m. Helen Faith Scheid, 1965; children: Margaret Ann, Benjamin, Kathleen. AB, Holy Cross Coll., 1957; postgrad., U. Minn., 1957-59, U. So. Calif., 1964-65, Stanford U., 1978-79. Reporter Worcester Telegram, Mass., 1957; reporter Red Wing Republican Eagle, Minn., 1959, St. Paul Pioneer Press, 1959-61; music and theater critic Mpls. Tribune, 1961-64; comedy writer Dudley Riggs' Brave New Workshop, 1961-64; music writer/theater reviewer N.Y. Times, 1965-68; theater critic L.A. Times, 1969-90; dramaturge Eugene O'Neill Theatre Ctr., Waterford, Conn., 1972-73, 93-95; instr. Nat. Critics Inst., Waterford, 1977-92, assoc. dir., 1993—; adj. prof. U. Minn., Mpls., 1990—; juror theater panel Nat. Endowment for Arts, 1983; juror Pulitzer Prize for Drama, 1985, 89, 92; pres. L.A. Drama Critics Circle, 1970-71, Ctr. for Arts Criticism, St. Paul, 1992-95. Mem. Am. Theater Critics Assn. (founding mem.).

SULLIVAN, DANNY, professional race car driver; b. Mar. 9, 1950; 1 child, Driscoll. Winner Indpls. 500, 1985. Office: 434 E Cooper St Ste 201 Aspen CO 81611-1859

SULLIVAN, DENNIS JAMES, JR., public relations executive; b. Jersey City, Feb. 23, 1932; s. Dennis James and Mary Theresa (Coyle) S.; m. Constance Rosemary Shields, Jan. 31, 1953; children: Denise Sullivan Morrison, Mary Agnes Sullivan Wilderotter, Colleen Sullivan Bastkowski, Andrea Sullivan Doelling. AB, St. Peters Coll., 1953; postgrad., U. Md., 1955; MBA, U. Pa., 1973. Various line and staff positions N.J. Bell, 1955-61, N.Y. Telephone Co., 1961-64, 67-68; various line and staff positions AT&T, N.Y.C., 1964-67, 68-76, dir. mktg., 1972-74, asst. v.p., 1974-76; v.p. mktg. Ohio Bell Telephone Co., Cleve., 1976-78; v.p. consumer info. services AT&T-Am. Bell, Parsippany, N.J., 1978-83; exec. v.p. Cin. Bell Telephone Co., 1983-84, pres., 1984-87, also bd. dirs.; exec. v.p., chief fin. officer Cin. Bell Inc., 1987-93; ret., 1993; bd. dirs. Fifth Third Bancorp & Bank; vice chmn. Associated Ins. Cos., Inc., Access Corp. Author: Videotex, IEE Nat. Conf., 1981. Bd. dirs. Boy Scouts, Cin. Bd. Edn., 1993—; gen. chmn. United Way, 1990—. Lt. (j.g.) USN, 1953-55, ret. comdr. USNR, 1976. Mem. Commonwealth Club, Cin. Country Club, Queen City Club, Bankers Club. Roman Catholic. Office: DP Pub Relsc Hist Cable House 2245 Gilbert Ave Cincinnati OH 45206-1872

SULLIVAN, DONALD, college president; b. Bklyn., Oct. 22, 1930; s. John T. and Catherine (Lane) S. B.S., Fordham U.; M.A., N.Y. U.; Ph.D., St. John's U.; LittD, St. Francis Coll., 1979. Former asst. prof., dean students St. Francis Coll., Bklyn.; now pres. St. Francis Coll.; mem. Commn. Ind. Colls. and Univs.; bd. dirs. Ridgewood Savs. Bank. Trustee Helen Keller Svcs. for the Blind. Mem. C. of C. (dir.), Downtown Bklyn. Dirs. Assn. (bd. dirs.). Clubs: Brooklyn. Office: St Francis Coll 180 Remsen St Brooklyn NY 11201-4398

SULLIVAN, DONALD BARRETT, physicist; b. Phoenix, June 13, 1939. BS, Tex. Western Coll., 1961; MA, Vanderbilt U., 1963, PhD in Physics, 1965. Rsch. assoc. physics Vanderbilt U., 1965; physicist, br. chief radiation physics br. U.S. Army Nuclear Def. Lab., 1965-67; Nat. Rsch. Coun. assoc. Nat. Bur. Stds., 1967-69, physicist, chief cryoelectronic metrol. sect., 1969-84, chief time and frequency divsn., 1984—. Mem. Am. Phys. Soc. Office: Nat Inst of Stds Tech Physics Lab Time Frequency Divsn 4036 Radio Bldg 325 Broadway Boulder CO 80303

SULLIVAN, EDWARD JOSEPH, lawyer, educator; b. Bklyn., Apr. 24, 1945; s. Edward Joseph and Bridget (Duffy) S.; m. Patte Hancock, Aug. 7, 1982; children: Amy Brase, Molly Elsasser, Mary Christine. MA, St. John's U., 1973; JD, Willamette U., 1969; MA, cert. Urban Studies, Portland State U., 1974, Cert. in Urban Studies, 1974; LLM, Univ. Coll., London, 1978; diploma in law, Univ. Coll., Oxford, 1984. Bar: Oreg. 1969, D.C. 1978, U.S. Dist. Ct. Oreg. 1970, U.S. Ct. Appeals (9th cir.) 1970, U.S. Supreme Ct. 1972. Counsel Washington County, Hillsboro, Oreg., 1969-75; legal counsel Gov. of Oreg., Salem, 1975-77; ptnr. O'Donnell, Sullivan & Ramis, Portland, Oreg., 1978-84, Sullivan, Josselson, Roberts, Johnson & Kloos, Portland, Salem and Eugene, Oreg., 1984-86, Mitchell, Lang & Smith, Portland, 1986-90, Preston Gates & Ellis, Portland, 1990—; bd. dirs., pres. Oreg. Law Inst. Contbr. numerous articles to profl. jours. Chmn. Capitol Planning Commn., Salem, 1975-77, 78-81. Mem. ABA (local govt. sect., com. on planning and zoning, adminstrv. law sect.) Oreg. State Bar Assn., D.C. Bar Assn., Am. Judicature Soc., Am. Polit. Sci. Assn. Democrat. Roman Catholic. Office: Preston Gates & Ellis 111 SW 5th Ave Ste 3200 Portland OR 97204-3635

SULLIVAN, EMMET G., judge; b. Washington, June 4, 1947; s. Emmet A. and Eileen G. Sullivan; m. Nan Sullivan; children, Emmet, Erik. BA in Polit. Sci., Howard U., 1968, JD, 1971. Law clk. to Hon. James A. Washington, Jr. Superior Ct. D.C.; from assoc. to ptnr. Houston and Gardner, 1973-80; ptnr. Houston, Sullivan & Gardner, 1980-84; judge Superior Ct. D.C., 1984-92; assoc. judge U.S. Ct. Appeals (D.C. cir.), 1992—. Reginald Heber Smith fellow. Office: 6th Fl 500 Indiana Ave NW Fl 6 Washington DC 20001-2131

SULLIVAN, EUGENE JOHN JOSEPH, manufacturing company executive; b. N.Y.C., Nov. 28, 1920; s. Cornelius and Margaret (Smith) S.; m. Gloria Roesch, Aug. 25, 1943; children: Eugene John Joseph, Edward J., Robert C., Elizabeth Ann Hansler. B.S., St. John's U., 1942, D.Commerce, 1973; M.B.A., N.Y. U., 1948. With chem. div. Borden, Inc., N.Y.C., 1946—; beginning as salesman, successively asst. sales Borden, Inc., 1957-58, exec. v.p., 1958-64; pres. Borden Chem. Co. div. Borden, Inc.; v.p. Borden, Inc., 1964-67, exec. v.p., 1967-73, pres., chief operating officer, 1973-79, chmn., pres., chief exec. officer, 1979-86; former adj. prof., now prof. St. John's U., 1987—; bd. dirs. W.R. Grace & Co.; chmn. bd. dirs. Hamilton Fund; trustee Atlantic Mut. Ins. Co. Trustee, vice chmn., past sec. St. John's U.; trustee N.Y. Med. Coll., Cath. Health Assn.; chmn. Commn. on Cath. Health Care. Served as lt. USNR, 1942-46; lt. Res. Mem. Coun. Fgn. Rels., Knights of Malta, Knights of Holy Sepulchre, Knights of St. Gregory, Univ. Club, Plandome Country Club, Westhampton Country Club. Office: Borden Inc 277 Park Ave New York NY 10172-0099

SULLIVAN, EUGENE JOSEPH, food service company executive; b. Phila., Sept. 30, 1943; s. Eugene Joseph and Helen Patricia (Gartland) S.; m. Judith Ann Heller, June 12, 1965; children: Christine, Kimberly, Gregg. BS in Acctg., U. Scranton, 1965. Mgr. Swift & Co., 1965-72; with Dobbs Houses, Inc., Memphis, 1972-85, v.p., gen. mgr., 1977-82, sr. v.p., 1982-84, pres., 1984-85; pres. CKG Enterprises, Inc., Memphis, 1986—. Office: CKG Enterprises Inc 1642 E Shelby Dr Memphis TN 38116-7228

SULLIVAN, EUGENE RAYMOND, federal judge; b. St. Louis, Aug. 2, 1941; s. Raymond Vincent and Rosemary (Kiely) S.; m. Lis Urup Johansen, June 18, 1966; children—Kim, Eugene II. BS, U.S. Mil. Acad., 1964; JD, Georgetown U., 1971. Bar: Mo. 1972, D.C. 1972. Law clk. to judge U.S. Ct. Appeals (8th cir.), St. Louis, 1971-72; assoc. Patton Boggs & Blow, Washington, 1972-74; asst. spl. counsel The White House, Washington, 1974; trial counsel U.S. Dept. of Justice, Washington, 1974-82; dep. gen. counsel U.S. Air Force, Washington, 1982-84; gen. counsel U.S. Air Force, 1984-86; gov. Wake Island, 1984-86; judge U.S. Ct. Appeals (Armed Forces), Washington, 1986-90, 95—, chief judge, 1990-95; mem. Fed. Commn. To Study Honor Code at West Point, 1989-90. Trustee U.S. Mil. Acad., 1989—. Decorated Bronze Star, Air medal, airborne badge, ranger badge, others. Republican. Roman Catholic. Home: 6307 Massachusetts Ave Bethesda MD 20816-1139 Office: US Ct Appeals (Armed Forces) 450 E St NW Washington DC 20442-0001

SULLIVAN, FRANK, JR., state supreme court justice; b. Mar. 21, 1950; s. Frank E. and Colette (Cleary) S.; m. Cheryl Gibson, June 14, 1972; children: Denis M., Douglas S., Thomas R. AB cum laude, Dartmouth Coll., 1972; JD magna cum laude, Ind. U., 1982. Bar: Ind. 1982. Mem. staff Office of U.S. Rep. John Brademas, 1974-79, dir. staff, 1975-78; with Barnes & Thornburg, Indpls., 1982-89; budget dir. State of Ind., 1989-92; exec. asst. Office of Gov. Evan Bayh, 1993; assoc. justice Ind. Supreme Ct., 1993—. Mem. ABA, Ind. State Bar Assn., Indpls. Bar Assn. Home: 6153 N Olney St Indianapolis IN 46220-5166 Office: State House Rm 311 Indianapolis IN 46204-2728

SULLIVAN, F(RANK) VICTOR, retired dean; b. Wichita, Kans., Mar. 5, 1931; s. Frank Townsend and Olive Mae (Kinseley) S.; m. Mary-Kate Larson, June 2, 1956; children: Mark Kenneth, Olive Louise. BS, Friends U., 1953; MA, U. No. Colo., 1957; EdD, U. Ill., 1964. Tchr. indsl. arts Minneha Pub. Schs., Wichita, 1953-56; instr. indsl. arts Friends U., Wichita, 1956-60; instr. U. Ill. H.S., 1960-63; rsch. assoc. Illini Blind Project, U. Ill., 1963-64; asst. prof. Sch. Tech. Pitts. State U., 1964-66, assoc. prof., 1966-68; prof. Sch. Tech., 1968-96; chair dept. tech. studies Pitts. State U., 1978-85, interim dean Sch. Tech. and Applied Sci., 1980-82, dean Sch. Tech. and Applied Sci., 1985-96; prof. and dean emeritus Pitts. (Kans.) State U., 1996—; bd. dirs. Am. Inst. Design and Drafting, Bartlesville, Okla., Kans. Tech. Enterprise Corp., Topeka. Mem. ESEA (dir./author secondary exploration of tech. project III 1971-74, dir. curriculum from contemporary industry summer 1967), Am. Soc. for Engring. Edn., Phi Delta Kappa (coord. Kans. area 3-B 1974-79, bd. dirs. dist. III 1979-85). Mem. ESEA (dir./author secondary exploration of tech. project III 1971-74, dir. curriculum from contemporary industry summer 1967), Am. Soc. for Engring. Edn. Home: 510 Thomas St Pittsburg KS 66762-6526 Office: Pittsburg State Univ Wilkerson Alumni Ctr Pittsburg KS 66762

SULLIVAN, G. CRAIG, chemical executive; b. 1940. BS, Boston Coll., 1964. With Proctor & Gamble Co., 1964-69, Am. Express Co., 1969-70; regional sales mgr. Clorox Co., Oakland, Calif., 1971-76, v.p. mktg., 1976-78, mgr. food svc. sales devel., mgr. bus. devel., 1978-79, gen. mgr. food svc. products divsn., 1979-81, v.p. food svc. products divsn., 1981, v.p. household products, 1981-89, group v.p. household products, 1989-92, chmn. bd., pres., CEO, 1992—. Office: The Clorox Co PO Box 24305 Oakland CA 94623-1305*

SULLIVAN, GEORGE EDMUND, editorial and marketing company executive; b. N.Y.C., Feb. 3, 1932; s. Timothy Daniel and Helen Veronica (Danaher) S.; m. Carole Ann Hartz, Sept. 4; 1954; children—Patricia Lynn, George Edmund, Michael Frank. B.A., Iona Coll., 1957; M.Ed., Rutgers U., 1961; Ph.D., Walden U., 1980. Tchr. English Holmdel Twp. and Keyport (N.J.) Pub. Schs., 1957-62; field mgr. regional mktg. Harcourt, Brace & World, Inc., N.Y.C., 1962-69; v.p. sales Noble & Noble, Publishers, Inc., 1969-72, sr. v.p., chief exec. officer, 1972-78; pres. Sullivan Ednl. Assos., Inc., Scottsdale, Ariz., 1978—; cons. to pub. and pvt. schs. on improving writing instruction and scholastic aptitude test scores. Author numerous books on English lang., writing and map reading skills. Served with USAF, 1950-52. Mem. Assn. Am. Publishers (ofcl. rep. 1972-82), Keyport Edn. Assn. (pres. 1960-62), Am. Mgmt. Assn. Home: 7714 E 1st Ave Scottsdale AZ 85251-4602 *The world is full of people who don't really care. Any person who chooses a worthy activity and really cares about doing it the right way, the best way, the most perfect way despite all adversity, will succeed. Really caring is the fuel that generates miracles.*

SULLIVAN, GEORGE EDWARD, author; b. Lowell, Mass., Aug. 11, 1927; s. Timothy Joseph and Cecilia Mary (Shea) S.; m. Muriel Agnes Moran, May 24, 1952; 1 son, Timothy. B.S., Fordham U., 1952. Pub. relations mgr. Popular Library, N.Y.C., 1952-55; pub. relations dir. AMF, N.Y.C., 1955-63; adj. prof. Fordham U. Author: numerous books including: The Supercarriers, 1981 (Jr. Lit. Guild selection), The Gold Hunter's Handbook, 1981 (Outdoor Life book club and Popular Sci. book club selections), The Art of Base Stealing, 1982 (Jr. Lit. Guild selection), Great Imposters, 1982, Quarterback, 1982, Indise Nuclear Submarines, 1982, Anwar el-Sadat: The Man Who Changed Mid-East History, 1982, Pope John Paul: The People's Pope, 1984, Mr. President, 1984, Work When You Want to Work, 1985, The Thunderbirds, 1986, Work Smart, Not Hard, 1987, How the White House Really Works, 1988, Mikhail Gorbachev, 1988, The Day Man Walked on the Moon, 1989, All About Basketball, 1990, The Day They Bombed Pearl Harbor, 1991, Racing Indy Cars, 1992, Matthew Brady, His Life and Photographs, 1993, The Day Women Got the Vote, 1994, Black Artists in Photography, 1995, Alamo!, 1996. Served with USN, 1945-48. Mem. PEN, Authors Guild, Am. Soc. Journalists and Authors. Roman Catholic.

SULLIVAN, GEORGE MURRAY, transportation consultant, former mayor; b. Portland, Oreg., Mar. 31, 1922; s. Harvey Patrick and Viola (Murray) S.; m. Margaret Eagan, Dec. 30, 1946; children: Timothy M., Harvey P., Daniel A., Kevin Shane, Colleen Marie, George Murray, Michael J., Shannon Margaret, Casey Eagan. Student pub. schs.; D.P.A. (hon.), U. Alaska, 1981. Line driver Alaska Freight Lines, Inc., Valdez-Fairbanks, 1942-44; U.S. dep. marshal Alaska Dist., Nenana, 1946-52; mgr. Alaska Freight Lines, 1952-56; Alaska gen. mgr. Consol. Freightways Corp. of Del., Anchorage, 1956-67; mayor of Anchorage, 1967-82; exec. mgr. Alaska Bus. Council, 1968; sr. cons. to pres. Western Air Lines Inc., 1982-87; former legis. liaison for Gov. of Alaska; now cons.; past mem. Nat. Adv. Com. on Oceans and Atmosphere, Joint Fed.-State Land Use Planning Commn.; past chmn. 4-state region 10 adv. com. OEO; mem. Fairbanks City Council, 1955-59, Anchorage City Council, 1965-67, Greater Anchorage Borough Assembly, 1965-67, Alaska Ho. of Reps., 1964-65. Trustee U. Alaska Found.; chmn. Anchorage Conv. and Visitors Bur.; bd. dirs. Western council Boy Scouts Am., 1958-59. Served with U.S. Army, 1944-46. Mem. Nat. Def. Transp. Assn. (life mem., pres. 1962-63), Nat. League Cities (dir.), Pioneers of Alaska, Alaska Mcpl. League (past pres.), Anchorage C. of C. (exec. com. 1963-65, treas. 1965-66, dir.), Alaska Carriers Assn. (exec. com.), Alaska Transp. Conf. (chmn.), U.S. Conf. Mayors (exec. com.), VFW (comdr. Alaska 1952). Club: Elks. Office & Home: George M Sullivan Co 1345 W 12th Ave Anchorage AK 99501-4252 *America is truly the land of opportunity, and I feel that the success with which God has blessed my life attests to this fact. I have been blessed four times. Not only was I born in America, but I have lived my life in Alaska. My other two blessings are my wonderful and supportive wife and our nine healthy children.**

SULLIVAN, GORDON R., retired career officer; b. Boston, Sept. 25, 1937; s. Russsell Edgar and Penuel Edith (Gordon) S.; m. Miriam Gay Loftus, June 20, 1965; children: John, Mark, Elizabeth. BA in History, Norwich U., 1959, D Mil. Sci. (hon.), 1991; MA in Polit. Sci., U. N.H., 1974. Commd. 2d lt. U.S. Army, 1959, advanced through grades to gen., 1990; student Armor Officer Basic Course U.S. Army Armor Sch., Ft. Knox, Ky., 1959-60; platoon leader Co. B, 1st Medium Tank Bn., 66th Armor, 2d Armored Div., Ft. Hood, Tex., 1960; student Armor Communication Class U.S. Army Armor Sch., Ft. Knox, 1960; communications officer 1st Medium Tank Bn., 66th Armor, 2d Armored Div., Ft. Hood, 1960-61; comdr. Co. A, 1st Medium tank Bn., 66th Armor,. 2d Armored Div., Ft. Hood, 1961; bn. communications officer 3d Medium Tank Bn. (Patton), 40th Armor, U.S. Army Pacific, Republic of Korea, 1961-62; platoon leader Co. A 3d Medium Tank Bn., 40th Armor, U.S. Army Pacific, Korea, 1962; asst. civil guard/self def. corps advisor 21st Inf. Div., Mil. Assistance Adv. Group, Vietnam, 1962-63; adminstrv. officer, later exec. asst. Office of Asst. Chief of Staff, J2 Div., Mil. Assistance Command, Vietnam, 1963-64; student Armor Officer Advanced Course U.S. Army Armor Sch., Ft. Knox, 1964-65; S-4 (Logistics) 3d Bn., 32d Armor, 3d Armored Div., U.S. Army Europe, 1965-66; comdr. Co.A, 3d Bn., 32d Armor, 3d Armored Div., U.S. Army Europe, 1966; assignment officer, later staff officer Combat Arms Sect., Mil. Pers. Div., Office of Dep. Chief of Staff for Pers., U.S. Army Europe, 1966-68; student U.S. Army Command Gen. Staff Coll., Ft. Leavenworth, Kans., 1968-69; pers. svcs. officer Plans and Ops. Div., G-1, Hdqrs., I Field Force, Vietnam, 1969-70; pers. mgmt. officer Pers. Actions Sect., Armor Br., Office of Pers. Ops., Washington, 1970-73; student Internat. Rels. U. N.H., Durham, 1973-74; comdr. 4th Bn., 73d Armor, 1st Inf. Div. (Forward), U.S. Army Europe, 1975-76; chief of staff 1st Inf. Div. (Forward), U.S. Army Europe, 1976-77; student U.S. Army War Coll., Carlisle Barracks, Pa., 1977-78; asst. chief of staff G-3 (Ops.)/Dir. Plans and Tng., 1st Inf. Div. and Fort Riley, Kans., 1978-79, G-3 (Ops.), VII Corps, U.S. Army Europe, 1980-81; comdr. 1st Brigade, 3d Armored Div., U.S. Army Europe, 1981-83; chief of staff 3d Armored Div., U.S. Army Europe, 1983; asst. comdt. U.S. Army Armor Sch., Ft. Knox, 1983-85; dep. chief of Staff for support Cen. Army Group, Europe, 1985-87; dep. comdt. U.S. Army Command and Gen. Staff Coll., Ft. Leavenworth, 1987-88; comdg. gen. 1st Inf. Div. (Mechanized), Ft. Riley, 1988-89; dep. chief of staff for ops. and plans U.S. Army/Army Sr. Mem., Mil. Staff Com., UN, Washington, 1989-90; vice chief of staff Office of the Chief of Staff, U.S. Army, Washington, 1990-91; chief of staff U.S. Army, Washington, 1991-95. Editor: Portrait of an Army, 1991. Decorated D.S.M., Def. Superior Svc. medal, Legion of Merit, Bronze Star, Purple Heart, Meritorius Svc. medal with oak leaf cluster, Joint Svc. Commendation medal, Army Commendation medal with oak leaf cluster, Army Achievement medal, Combat Infantryman badge. Mem. Assn. of U.S. Army, Armor Assn. Home: Quarters One Fort Myer VA 22211 Office: Chief of Staff Army 200 Army Pentagon Washington DC 20310-0200*

SULLIVAN, GREGORY PAUL, secondary education educator; b. Buffalo, June 13, 1957; s. Jerome Patrick and Gloria Mae (Struble) S.; m. Sarah Davis Houston, May 17, 1986; 1 child, Patrick Benjamin. BS in Indsl. Edn., State U. Coll., Oswego, N.Y., 1979; MA in Indsl. Edn., Ball State U., 1983. postgrad. collegiate profl. teaching cert. Grad. asst. mfg. lab. Ball State U., Muncie, Ind., 1982-83; tchr. tech. edn. John Rolfe Mid. Sch., Richmond, Va., 1979-86, Horton Mid. Sch., Pittsboro, N.C., 1986-88, Dunbar Mid. Sch., Lynchburg, Va., 1988-93; supr. career-tech. programs Lynchburg City Schs., 1993—; coord./judge regional and nat. mfg. contest Tech. Edn. and Collegiate Assn., 1988—; coord. Eisenhower Grant, 1991-92; presenter in field. Asst. dir. Camp Minnehaha, Minnehaha Springs, W.Va., 1979-88. Named Va. Tchr. of Yr., Va. Dept. Edn., 1993. Mem. Soc. Mfg. Engrs. (internat. edn. com. career guidance 1984, 91), Internat. Tech. Edn. Assn. (mem. editl. rev. bd. The Tech. Tchr., delphi com. critical issues and concerns tech. edn. 1992), Coun. Tech. Tchr. Edn. (student svcs. com. 1991), Va. Tech. Edn. Assn., Phi Delta Kappa, Epsilon Pi Tau, Kappa Delta Pi. Avocations: intramural sports, golf, tennis, running. Home: 724 Sanhill Dr Lynchburg VA 24502-4924 Office: Lynchburg City Schs 10th and Court Sts PO Box 1599 Lynchburg VA 24505-1599

SULLIVAN, JAMES F., physicist, educator; b. Cin., Mar. 7, 1943; s. James E. and Alma L. (Lienesch) S.; m. Sylvia J. Kasselmann, Aug. 16, 1969; 1 child, Robert L. BS, Xavier U., 1965, MS, 1969. Instr. physics Brebeuf Prep. Sch., Indpls., 1965-67; instr. physics OMI Coll. Applied Sci., U. Cin., 1968-71, asst. prof. physics, 1971-77, assoc. prof. physics, 1977-88, prof. physics, 1988—; summer faculty researcher Solar Energy Rsch. Inst., Golden, Colo., 1980; mem. high sch. evaluation team N. Ctrl. Assn., Cin., 1983, 84, 85. Author: Technical Physics, 1988; Co-author: Laboratory Manual for General Physics, 1973, 83, 90, 92, Physics for Technology Laboratory Manual, 1995. Organizer of events St. Xavier H.S. Alumni, Cin., 1983—; vol. examiner Am. Radio Relay League for U.S. Fed. Comm. Commn., Newington, Conn., 1984—; judge physics category Ohio State Sci. Fair, Delaware, Ohio, 1986—; chief negotiator faculty and librs. U. Cin., 1995. Named Faculty Mem. of Yr., Gamma Alpha chpt. Tau Alpha Phi, 1983. Mem. AAUP (v.p. U. Cin. chpt. 1994-96), Am. Assn. Physics Tchrs. (founder, past pres., assoc. sec. So. Ohio sect. 1993—, com. on instrnl. media 1994—, chief organizer and presenter Fundamentals of Radio workshop Toronto, Ont., Can. 1985, Columbus, Ohio 1986, Bozeman, Mont. 1987, Orono, Maine 1992, Boise, Idaho 1993, South Bend, Ind. 1994, College Park, Md. 1996), Am. Soc. Engring. Edn., Ohio Acad. Sci. Achievements include supervising successful attempt of OMI Coll. Applied Sci. contact of shuttle

Challenger during STS-51F mission, 1985. Office: Univ Cin 2220 Victory Pkwy Cincinnati OH 45206-2839

SULLIVAN, JAMES FRANCIS, university administrator; b. Pitts., Sept. 15, 1930; s. Francis P. and Leona C. (Patterson) S.; m. Carol Rea, Sept. 10, 1955; children—Leslie Ann, Daniel Paul. B.A., Dartmouth Coll., 1953; M.S., U. Colo., 1956; Ph.D., U. Pitts., 1965. Asst. city mgr. Monterey, Calif., 1957-60; city mgr. Ojai, Calif., 1960-62; asst. prof. U. Pitts., 1965-66; vice-chancellor U. Calif. at Riverside, 1966-74; assoc. prof. Grad. Sch. Adminstrn., 1970-78; assoc. dir. Dry Lands Research Inst., 1974-78; vice chancellor U. Calif. at Davis, 1978-91, dean univ. extention, 1980-91; vice chancellor U. Calif., Santa Cruz, 1995—. Served with USAF, 1954-55. Home: 1005 Rodeo Rd Pebble Beach CA 93953-2720

SULLIVAN, JAMES GERALD, business owner, postal letter carrier; b. Bad Axe, Mich., Sept. 13, 1935; s. John Thomas and Frances Eugena (O'Henley) S.; m. Florence Marie Tack, Sept. 12, 1959; children: Kevin Michael, Kathleen Marie. Student, U. Detroit, 1957-58, Highland Park Coll., 1959-60. Owner Jerry's Barber Shop, Kinde, Bad Axe, Mich., 1963-66, 79—; purchasing agt. Thumb Elec. Coop., Ubly, Mich., 1966-79, Walbro Corp., Cass City, Mich., 1979-80; sales rep. Thumb Blanket, Bad Axe, Mich., 1980-81, Sta. WLEW, Bad Axe, 1981-82; sr. regional mgr. Pri Am. Fin. Svcs., Bad Axe, 1985—; treas. Colfax Twp., Bad Axe, 1979-90; rural letter carrier PO, Bad Axe, 1982—; loss clk., Toplis & Harding Wagner & Gliddon, Detroit, 1959-61; inventory control clk., Carrick Products Co., Royal Oak, Mich., 1957-59. pres., Huron County (Mich.) Twp. Assn., 1988-90; leader Boy Scouts Am., Bad Axe,1975-77. Served in U.S. Army, 1954-56. Mem. Huron County Rural Letter Carriers Assn. (pres. 1990—), Armed Forces Vets. Club of the Nat. Rural Letter Carriers Assn. (Mich. divsn.), Am. Legion, 4-H Club (pres. 1948-50), Lions (pres. 1979-80), Cmty. Club (pres. 1976-77), KC (mem. coun. #1546), Ushers Club Sacred Heart Ch. Republican. Roman Catholic. Avocations: gardening, golf, swimming, snowmobiling, fishing. Home: 122 W Richardson Rd Bad Axe MI 48413-9108

SULLIVAN, JAMES KIRK, forest products company executive; b. Greenwood, S.C., Aug. 25, 1935; s. Daniel Jones and Addie (Brown) S.; m. Elizabeth Miller, June 18, 1960; children: Hal N., Kim J. BS in Chemistry, Clemson U., 1957, MS, 1964, PhD, 1966; postgrad. program for sr. execs., MIT, 1975; DSc (hon.), U. Idaho, 1990. Prodn. supr. FMC Corp., South Charleston, W.Va., 1957-62; tech. supt. FMC Corp., Pocatello, Idaho, 1966-69; mktg. mgr. FMC Corp., N.Y.C., 1969-70; v.p. govtl. and environ. affairs Boise (Idaho) Cascade Corp., 1971—; bd. dirs. Key Bank Idaho, chmn. trust and investment com., 1983-90, exec. com., 1983—; bd. dirs., chmn. audit com. Key Trust Co. of the West; chmn. adv. bd. U. Idaho Coll. Engring., 1966-70, 80-87, centennial campaign, 1987-89, rsch. found., 1980-82; mem. Accreditation Bd. Engring. and Tech., Inc., 1994—. Contbr. articles to profl. jours.; patentee in field. Mem. Coll. of Forest and Recreation Resources com. Clemson U., Idaho Found. for Pvt. Enterprise and Econ. Edn., Idaho Rsch. Found., Inc., Idaho Task Force on Higher Edn.; bd. dirs. Idaho Found. for Excellence in Higher Edn., Exptl. Program to Stimulate Competitive Rsch. NSF, N.W. Nazarene Coll., 1988-90; mem. Len B. Jordan Pub. Affairs Symposium; trustee Idaho Children's Emergency Fund, 1984—; bd. trustees Bishop Kelly H.S., 1987-89; chmn. Bishop Kelly Found., 1972-79, 85-89; chmn. adv. bd. U. Idaho Coll. Engring., Am. Forest and Paper Assn., Govtl. Affairs Com., Environ. Com., Future Options Group; pub. affairs com. NAM; mem. Idaho Found. Pvt. Enterprise and Econ. Edn., 1988—; chmn. centennial campaign U. Idaho, U. Idaho Found., others; mem. environ. com. Future Options Group; bd. dirs. Boise Master Chorale, 1995—. 1st lt. U.S. Army, 1958-59. Recipient Presdl. Citation U. Idaho, 1990. Mem. AIChE, Am. Chem. Soc., Bus. Week Found. (chmn. Bus. Week 1980), Am. Forest and Paper Assn. (environ. and health coun., product and tech. com., solid waste task force), Bus. Roundtable (environ. com.), Idaho Assn. Commerce and Industry (past chmn. bd. dirs.), C. of C. of U.S. (pub. affairs com.). Republican. Home: 5206 Sorrento Cir Boise ID 83704-2347 Office: Boise Cascade Corp 1111 W Jefferson St PO Box 50 Boise ID 83728

SULLIVAN, JAMES LENOX, clergyman; b. Silver Creek, Miss., Mar. 12, 1910; s. James Washington and Mary Ellen (Dampeer) S.; m. Velma Scott, Oct. 22, 1935; children: Mary Beth (Mrs. Bob R. Taylor), Martha Lynn (Mrs. James M. Porch, Jr.), James David. B.A., Miss. Coll., 1932, D.D., 1948; Th.M., So. Bapt. Theol. Sem., 1935. Ordained to ministry of Baptist Ch., 1930; pastor Baptist Ch., Boston, Ky., 1932-33, Beaver Dam, Ky., 1933-38, Ripley, Tenn., 1938-40, Clinton, Miss., 1940-42; pastor First Bapt. Ch., Brookhaven, Miss., 1942-46, Belmont Heights, Nashville, 1946-50, Abilene, Tex., 1950-53; exec. sec., treas. Bapt. Sunday Sch. Bd., Nashville, 1953-73; pres. Bapt. Sunday Sch. Bd., 1973-75; exec. sec. Broadman Press, 1953-75, Convention Press, 1955-75; pres. So. Bapt. Conv., 1977. Author: Your Life and Your Church, 1950, John's Witness of Jesus, Memos for Christian Living, Reach Out, Rope of Sand with Strength of Steel, God Is My Record, Baptist Polity As I See It, Southern Baptist Polity at Work in a Church; also articles and manuals. Trustee Union U., Cumberland U., So. Bapt. Theol. Sem., Hardin-Simmons U., Midstate (Tenn.) Bapt. Hosp., Hendrick Meml. Hosp., Tex. Recipient E.Y. Mullins Denominational Service award, 1973; named Miss. Bapt. Clergyman of Century. Mem. Baptist World Alliance (exec. com. 1953-80, v.p. 1970-75). Clubs: Rotary (Ripley, Tenn.); Lions (Brookhaven, Miss.); Kiwanis (Abilene, Tex.).

SULLIVAN, JAMES LEO, organization executive; b. Somerville, Mass., Dec. 11, 1925; s. James Christopher and Anna Agnes (Kilmartin) S.; m. Anne Dorothy Hevner, Jan. 20, 1951; children: Maura, Mark, Lianne, Christopher. BS in History and Govt. cum laude, Boston Coll., 1950, MEd in Adminstrn. and Fin., 1958; DCS (hon.), Suffolk U., 1990. Asst. town mgr. Arlington, Mass., 1957-62; town mgr. Watertown, Conn., 1962-65; chief adminstrv. officer Town of Milton, Mass., 1965-68; city mgr. Cambridge, Mass., 1968-70, 74-81, Lowell, Mass., 1970-74; sr. research asst. MIT, 1970-71; pres. Greater Boston C. of C., 1981-91, H.M.S. Mktg., Boston, 1991—; chmn. Mass. Gov.'s Local Govt. Adv. Com., 1978; del. to Orgn. Econ. and Cooperative Devel., Paris, 1979; chmn. New Eng.-Can. Bus. Coun., 1983; pres. Careers for Later YEars, 1983; bd. dirs. Input-Output Computer Svcs., Imugen Inc., Mass. Bus. Devel. Corp. Trustee Emerson Coll., 1984-88, mem. fin. and investment com., 1985-88; bd. dirs. Bunker Hill Community Coll. Found., 1988—; mem. Adv. Com. on Reorgn. of Mass. Ct. System, 1991—, chmn. budget subcom. 1991—; bd. overseers Univ. Hosp. Boston. With USN, 1943-46. Mem. Mass. League of Cities and Towns (pres. 1978), Mass. Mayors Assn., Internat. City Mgmt. Assn., Nat. League Cities, Am. C. of C. Execs. (bd. dirs. 1988—). Club: World Trade (bd. govs. 1986—). Office: HMS Mktg 65 Franklin St Boston MA 02110-1303

SULLIVAN, JAMES N., fuel company executive; b. San Francisco, 1937. Student, U. Notre Dame, 1959. Formerly v.p. Chevron Corp., until 1988, now vice chmn., dir., 1988—. Office: Chevron Corp 575 Market St San Francisco CA 94105*

SULLIVAN, JAMES STEPHEN, bishop; b. Kalamazoo, July 23, 1929; s. Stephen James and Dorothy Marie (Bernier) S. Student, St. Joseph Sem.; BA, Sacred Heart Sem.; postgrad., St. John Provincial Sem. Ordained priest, Roman Cath. Ch., 1955, consecrated bishop, 1972. Assoc. pastor St. Luke Ch., Flint, Mich., 1955-58; assoc. pastor St. Mary Cathedral, Lansing, Mich., 1958-60, sec. to bishop, 1960-61; assoc. pastor St. Joseph (Mich.) Ch., 1961-65, sec. to bishop, 1965-69; assoc. pastor Lansing, 1965, vice chancellor, 1969-72; aux. bishop, vicar gen. Diocese of Lansing, 1972-85, diocesan consultor, 1971-85; bishop Fargo, N.D., 1985—. Mem. Nat. Conf. Cath. Bishops (bishop's liturgical commn.). Office: Chancery Office PO Box 1750 1310 Broadway Fargo ND 58107-4419*

SULLIVAN, JAMES THOMAS, printing company executive; b. N.Y.C., Jan. 9, 1939; s. James A. and Mary Sullivan; m. Hildegard Reif, Apr. 6, 1959; children—Kathleen, Sean Michael. Student, U. Md., 1959-62; A.M.P., Harvard U., 1985. With R.R. Donnelley & Sons, 1969—; sales rep. N.Y.C., 1969-74, sales mgr., 1974-75, v.p., 1975-76, sr. v.p., 1976-79, pres. book group, 1980-83, pres. mag. group, 1983-86; pres., CEO Maxwell Communications, 1986-88; chmn., CEO Sullivan Comm., Stamford, Conn., 1988—. Served with U.S. Army, 1956-62. Mem. Union League Club (N.Y.C.), Richland Country Club (Nashville). Republican. Congregationalist. Home: 160 Round Hill Rd Greenwich CT 06831-3746 Office: Sullivan Graphics 225 High Ridge Rd Stamford CT 06905-3000*

SULLIVAN, JAY MICHAEL, medical educator; b. Brockton, Mass., Aug. 3, 1936; s. William Dennis and Wanda Nancy (Kelpsh) S.; m. Mary Suzanne Baxter, Dec. 30, 1964; children: Elizabeth, Suzanne, Christopher. B.S. cum laude, Georgetown U., 1958, M.D. magna cum laude, 1962. Diplomate Nat. Bd. Med. Examiners, Am. Bd. Internal Medicine. Med. intern Peter Bent Brigham Hosp., Boston, 1962-63; resident Peter Bent Brigham Hosp., 1963-64, 66-67, chief resident, 1969-70, fellow in cardiology, 1964-66, dir. hypertension unit, 1970-74; Nat. Heart Inst. fellow, 1964, Med. Found. research fellow, 1967; preceptorship in biol. chemistry Harvard U. Med. Sch., Boston, 1967-69; asst. prof. medicine Harvard U. Med. Sch., 1970-74; dir. med. services Boston Hosp. for Women, 1973-74; prof. medicine, chief div. cardiovascular diseases U. Tenn. Coll. Medicine, Memphis, 1974—; vice-chmn. dept. medicine U. Tenn. Coll. Medicine, 1982-85; mem. staff Regional Med. Ctr., Memphis, VA, Bapt. Meml. hosps., U. Tenn. Medical Center-Wm. F. Bowld Hosp., Le Bonheur Children's Hosp., Saint Jude Children's Rsch. Hosp.; fellow Council for High Blood Pressure Research; cons. Nat. Heart, Lung and Blood Inst., 1974—, VA, 1983—. Contbr. articles to sci. jours. Served with M.C., U.S. Army, 1963-70. Fellow ACP, Am. Coll. Cardiology (bd. govs., pres. Tenn. chpt.); mem. AAAS, Am. Heart Assn. (fellow coun. on circulation, chpt. pres. 1982-83, affiliate pres. 1994-95), Assn. Univ. Cardiologists, Assn. Profs. Cardiology, Internat. Soc. Hypertension, Am. Fedn. Clin. Rsch., Racquet Club Memphis, Sigma Xi, Alpha Omega Alpha, Alpha Sigma Nu. Roman Catholic. Home: 6077 Maiden Ln Memphis TN 38120-3104 Office: Univ TN Divsn Cardiovascular Diseases 951 Court Ave Rm 353D Memphis TN 38103-2813

SULLIVAN, BROTHER JEREMIAH STEPHEN, former college president; b. Boston, June 25, 1920; s. John Joseph and Bridget Claire (Quirke) S. BA, Cath. U. Am., 1943, STL, 1957, STD, 1959; MA in Classics, Manhattan Coll., 1950; MA in Philosophy, Boston Coll., 1955; LLD (hon.), La Salle U., 1979; LHD (hon.), Coll. Mt. St. Vincent, 1987. Tchr. St. Peters High Sch., S.I., N.Y., 1943-48, St. Marys High Sch., Waltham, Mass., 1948-53; instr. theology and classics De La Salle Coll., Washington, 1953-59; asst. prof. theology Manhattan Coll., N.Y.C., 1959-63, assoc. prof., 1963, acad. v.p., 1963-70, exec. v.p., provost, 1970-75, pres., 1975-87; La Salle provincialate, dir. devel. programs Christian Bros. Acad., Lincroft, N.J., 1988—. Contbr. articles to profl. jours. Chmn. N.Y.C. com. on Ind. Colls. and Univs., 1978-79; chmn. com. on Sci. and Tech., 1981; trustee African Med. Rsch., LaSalle U.; bd. dirs., chmn., FSC Found. Mem. Coll. Theology Soc. (dir., nat. treas. 1960-71), Cath. Theol. Soc. Am., Cath. Bibl. Assn., Nat. Cath. Ednl. Assn., Nat. Cath. Devel. Coun., AAUP, Phi Beta Kappa, Delta Mu Delta. Address: Christian Bros Acad Lincroft NJ 07738

SULLIVAN, JIM, artist; b. Providence, Apr. 1, 1939; s. James Henry, Jr. and Frances Winifred (Welch) S.; m. Marie-Louise Paulson. B.F.A., R.I. Sch. Design, 1961; postgrad., Stanford, 1962-63. Prof. emeritus art Bard Coll., Annandale-on-Hudson, N.Y., 1966-95, prof. emeritus, 1995—. One-man shows Paley and Lowe Gallery, N.Y.C., 1971, 73, Henri Gallery, Washington, 1974, Fischback Gallery, N.Y.C., 1974, Willard Gallery, N.Y.C., 1978, Nancy Hoffman Gallery, N.Y.C., 1980, 82, 84, 86, 88, Foker Skulima Gallery, Berlin, Germany, Anne Jaffe Gallery Bay Harbor Islands, Fla. 1990; exhibited in group shows including, Whitney Mus., Mus. Modern Art, Columbus Gallery Fine Arts, Worcester Art Mus., Corcoran Gallery Art, Washington; pub. collections including Met. Mus., Whitney Mus., Albany State Mus., Wadsworth Atheneum, Philip Morris INc., Owens Corning Coll., Amerada Hess. Recipient Hinda and Richard Rosenthal award Am. Acad. Arts and Letters, 1973; Stanford grantee, 1962-63; R.I. Sch. Design European Honors program Rome, 1960-61; Fulbright fellow, Paris; Fulbright fellow, 1961-62; Guggenheim fellow, 1972-73; grantee Nat. Endowment for Arts, 1982. Home: 59 Wooster St New York NY 10012-4349 Office: Bard Coll Dept Art Annandale On Hudson NY 12504

SULLIVAN, JOHN FOX, publisher; b. Phila., Oct. 19, 1943; s. Neil Joseph S. and Mary (Fox) Cullumbine; m. Beverly Knight Lilley, June 10, 1978; stepchildren: Buchanan, Brooke, Whitman, Justin Lilley. BA, Yale U., 1966; MBA, Columbia U., 1968. Staff econ. analyst U.S. Dept. Def., Washington, 1968-69; asst. to pub. Newsweek Internat., N.Y.C., 1970-73, asst. mng. dir., 1974-75; pres., pub. Nat. Jour. Inc., Washington, 1975—. Mem. editl. adv. bd. Who's Who. Bd. dirs. Arena Stage, Times Mirror Found., Nat. Gallery Cartoon Art; trustee Monterey Inst. Internat. Studies. Episcopalian. Clubs: 1925 F Street; Yale (N.Y.C.). Home: 1412 28th St NW Washington DC 20007-3145 Office: Nat Jour 1501 M St NW Washington DC 20005-1700

SULLIVAN, JOHN LAWRENCE, III, psychiatrist; b. Scranton, Pa., Nov. 24, 1943; s. John Lawrence and Jane Marie (Hoppel) S.; m. Paula Ann DeRemer, Mar. 3, 1979; 1 child, John Bradley. BA, Duke U., 1965; MD, Johns Hopkins U., 1969. Diplomate Am. Bd. Psychiatry and Neurology. Asst. prof. psychiatry Duke U., Durham, N.C., 1973-78, assoc. prof. of psychiatry, 1978-81; dep. dir. med. rsch. Dept. Vet. Affairs Cen. Office, Washington, 1981-83; chmn. dept. psychiatry Richard L. Roudebush VA Med. Ctr., Indpls., 1985—; prof. psychiatry and of neurobiology Ind. U., Indpls., 1985—; mem. Nat. Coun. on Health Care Tech., Washington, 1981-82; rschr. Pres.'s Task Force on Drug Abuse, 1982-83' rep. to AAAS for Am. Psychiat. Assn., 1983-86. Co-editor: Foundations of Biochemical Psychiatry, 1976; editor: Biomedical Psychiatric Therapeutics, 1984; contbr. articles to profl. jours. Sr. fellow Duke U. Ctr. for Study of Aging and Human Devel., Durham, 1975; recognition for Disting. Pub. Svc. Dept. of Vet. Affairs, Washington, 1984. Fellow Am. Psychiat. Assn.; mem. Soc. Biol. Psychiatry, AAAS, Acad. Psychosomatic Medicine, Sigma Xi. Achievements include rsch. interests in the neurobiology of monoamine oxidase and alcoholism, and med. psychiatry. Office: RL Roudebush VA Med Ctr 1481 W 10th St Indianapolis IN 46202-2803

SULLIVAN, JOHN LOUIS, JR., retired search company executive; b. Macon, Ga., Aug. 27, 1928; s. John Louis and Elizabeth (Macken) S.; m. Barbara Boyle, Aug. 17, 1974; children: John, Katherine, Betsy, Ted. A.B. in Econs., Duke U., 1950; M.B.A., U. Pa., 1957; postgrad. Advance Mgmt. Program, Harvard U., 1975. Br. mgr. IBM, Phila., 1962-63; mgr. edn. IBM, Endicott, N.Y., 1963-64; asst. to pres. Data Procesing Div. IBM, White Plains, N.Y., 1965-67; dist. mgr. Data Processing Div. IBM, Washington, 1967-69; mgr. eastern and fed. regions Memorex Corp., 1969-71; v.p. mktg. Infonet div. Computer Sci. Corp., El Segundo, Calif., 1971-75; exec. v.p. Fin. Service Group-ADP Inc., Clifton, N.J., 1975-77; sr. v.p. Heidrick & Struggles Inc., San Francisco and Los Angeles, 1977-82, dir., 1977-82, office mgr., 1979-82; v.p., mng. dir. Korn-Ferry Internat., Los Angeles, 1982-87; v.p., mng. ptnr. Korn-Ferry Internat., Boston, 1987-94; ret., 1994. Bd. dirs., mem. exec. com. March of Dimes, Los Angeles County; bd. regents Mount St. Mary's Coll., Los Angeles. Served to lt. (j.g.) USN, 1950-53. Mem. Harvard U. Bus. Sch. Alumni Assn. (dir.). Democrat. Clubs: Regency (Los Angeles), Bankers (San Francisco), Atheneum (Pasadena), Mission Hills (Rancho Mirage), Calif. Yacht (Los Angeles), Harvard (Boston). Office: Korn Ferry Internat 101 Federal St Boston MA 02110-1800 also: Korn Ferry Internat 1800 Century Park E Los Angeles CA 90067-1501

SULLIVAN, JOSEPH B., retired judge; b. Detroit, May 30, 1922; s. Joseph A. and Winifred R. (Bruin) S.; m. Mary Sullivan, June 6, 1946; children: Kathleen (Mrs. Thomas Lewand), Timothy. PhB, U. Detroit, 1947, JD, 1957. Bar: Mich. 1958. Mem. firm Sullivan, Sullivan, Ranger & Ward, Detroit, after 1958; head criminal div. Atty. Gen.'s Office State of Mich., 1963-64; exec. sec. to mayor City of Detroit, 1962, commr. purchasing, 1967-69; clk. Wayne County, 1970-74; judge Wayne County Cir. Ct., 1975-86, Mich. Ct. Appeals, 1986-93; ret., 1993. Mem. Detroit Charter Revision Com., 1970-73, past bd. dirs. Mercy Coll., Detroit. With AUS, 1943-46. Mem. Soc. Irish-Am. Lawyers, Mich. Bar Assn., U. Detroit Alumni Assn., Cath. Lawyers Assn. Democrat. Home: 842 Park Ln Grosse Pointe MI 48230-1853 Office: 900 First Federal Bldg Detroit MI 48226

SULLIVAN, JOSEPH M., bishop; b. Bklyn., Mar. 23, 1930. Ed. Immaculate Conception Sem., Huntington, N.Y., also, Fordham U. Ordained priest Roman Catholic Ch., 1956; consecrated titular bishop of Suliana and aux. bishop of Bklyn., 1980—. Office: Diocese of Bklyn 378 Clermont Ave Brooklyn NY 11238-1002*

SULLIVAN, JOSEPH PATRICK, agricultural product company executive; b. Newton, Mass., Apr. 10, 1933; s. Joseph Patrick and Ruth Ann (Kelter) S.; m. Jeanne Marie Baldi, Oct. 19, 1957; children: Deirdre, Barbara, Mark. B.A. cum laude, Harvard U., 1954, M.B.A., 1956. With Swift & Co., Chgo., 1959-73; pres. Swift Chem. Co., 1972-73, Estech Inc., Chgo., 1973-80; pres., chief exec. officer Swift & Co., Chgo., 1980-83; chmn. bd. Vigoro Industries Inc., Fairview Heights, Ill., 1983—; dir. Vigoro Industries Inc.; chmn. exec. com. IMC Global (merged with Vigoro), Chgo., 1996—; mem. bus. adv. com. Coll. Commerce and Bus. Adminstrn., U. Ill. Bd. dirs. Chgo. Opera Theater, Am. Refugee Com.; trustee Mundelein Coll., Chgo. Acad. Scis.; trustee, mem. fin. com. Farm Found., Oak Brook, Ill.; past pres. trustees Latin Sch., Chgo., 1977—; co-chmn. Emergency Task Force for Indochinese Refugees. Served with AUS, 1956-59. Mem. Presidents Assn. Roman Catholic. Clubs: Chicago (Chgo.), Economic (Chgo.), Union League (Chgo.), Saddle and Cycle (Chgo.), Harvard (Chgo.); Harvard (Boston). Home: 6145 N Sheridan Rd Chicago IL 60660-2803 Office: Vigoro Corp 225 North Michigan Ave Ste 2500 Chicago IL 60601*

SULLIVAN, JOSEPH PETER, insurance broker; b. Boston, Sept. 8, 1939; s. Joseph Francis and Mary Anna S.; m. Rachael Anne Cullen, Dec. 22, 1974; children: Philip, Sandra, Susan, Frederick. B Gen. Studies, U. Nebr., 1968; MA, U. No. Colo., 1973, Cen. Mich. U., 1976. Sr. acct. exec. Arkwright Ins., Greenwich, Conn., 1977-83; v.p. Frenkel & Co., N.Y.C., 1983-84; sr. account exec. Republic Hogg Robinson, N.Y.C., 1984-85; v.p. Alexander & Alexander, N.Y.C., 1985-92, Hugh Wood Inc., N.Y.C., 1992-93, Thomas Howell Group, N.Y.C., 1993—; assoc. Miller-Heiman Internat., 1986—; instr. Dale Carnegie and Assocs., 1980-87; ajd. prof. ins. The Coll. of Ins., N.Y.C., 1991—. Mem. membership com. Met. Rep. Club; bd. advisors The Salvation Army. With U.S. Army, 1956-77, ETO, Korea and Vietnam. Decorated Bronze Star. Mem. Soc. Human Resource Mgmt., Assn. Former Intelligence Officers (life), Ret. Officers Assn. (bd. dirs. Knickerbocker chpt.), Soc. CPCU's, Am. Soc. CLU's, Nat. Assn. Health Underwriters, Profl. Liability Underwriting Soc., N.Y. Soc. Security Analysts, Soc. Competitive Intelligence Profls., Advt. Club N.Y., Toastmasters, N.Y. Athletic Club, Rotary, Masons, Shriners. Republican. Roman Catholic. Avocations: American history, photography, collecting old photographic prints and antique photographic equipment. Home: 105 Oldfield Rd Fairfield CT 06430-6660 Office: Thomas Howell Group 17 State St New York NY 10004-1501

SULLIVAN, JOSEPH THOMAS, chemical executive, chemical engineer; b. Monroe County, Iowa, Mar. 10, 1940; s. James Leo and Mary Cecelia (Barron) S.; m. Marcia Jean Uttley, May 22, 1965; children: Michael, Paul, Daniel. BS in Chem. Engring., Iowa State U., 1962; PhD, U. Minn., 1966. Tech. supr. Exxon Chem., Linden, N.J., 1966-68; engring. devel. mgr. Gen. Mills Inc., Mpls., 1968-71; with Ciba-Geigy Corp., St. Gabriel, La., Cranston, R.I., Toms River, N.J. and Ardsley, N.Y., 1971-86; sr. v.p. prodn. and tech. services Ciba-Geigy Corp., Ardsley, 1986—; also bd. dirs., now sr. v.p.; chmn. bd. dirs. Ilford Inc., Paramus, N.J., 1987—. Home: 49 Bittersweet Trl Wilton CT 06897-3902 Office: Ciba-Geigy Corp 520 White Plains Rd Tarrytown NY 10591*

SULLIVAN, KAREN LAU, real estate company executive, campaign consultant, federal commissioner; b. Honolulu, Jan. 21, 1948; d. Ralph Karn Yee and Beatrice (Loo) Lau; m. Paul Dennis Sullivan, Apr. 24, 1976. BA, Whittier Coll., 1970; MA, U. Hawaii, 1987. Staff asst. to Congresswoman Patsy Mink U.S. Ho. Reps., Washington, 1974, staff asst. subcom. mines and mining, 1975-77, legis. asst. to Congressman Cec. Heftel, 1977-79; spl. asst. to asst. to Pres. for policy and women's affairs The White House, Washington, 1979; spl. asst. office of sec. of transp. U.S. Dept. Transp., Washington, 1979-81; regional dir. mid-Atlantic states Mondale-Ferraro Presdl. Campaign, Washington, 1984; dep. nat. field dir. Paul Simon Presdl. Campaign, Washington, 1987-88; Ill. dir. forum inst. Martin & Glantz Polit. Cons., San Francisco, 1988; regional dir. western states Clinton-Gore Presdl. Campaign, Little Rock, 1992; dep. dir. for pub. outreach Office of Pres.-Elect Bill Clinton, Little Rock/Washington, 1992-93; v.p. Hoaloha Ventures, Inc., Honolulu, 1981—. U.S. alt. rep. South Pacific Commn., 1995-96. Mem. Carter/Mondale Alumni Fund, The Carter Ctr. Avocations: downhill skiing, auto racing. Home and Office: 810-K N Kalaheo Ave Kailua HI 96734

SULLIVAN, LAURA PATRICIA, lawyer, insurance company executive; b. Des Moines, Oct. 16, 1947; d. William and Patricia (Kautz) S. BA, Cornell Coll., Iowa, 1971; JD, Drake U., 1972. Bar: Iowa 1972. Various positions Ins. Dept. Iowa, Des Moines, 1972-75; various legal positions State Farm Mut. Auto Ins. Co., Bloomington, Ill., 1975-81, sec. and counsel, 1981-88, v.p., counsel and sec., 1988—; v.p., sec., dir. State Farm Cos. Found., 1985—; sec. State Farm Lloyd's, Inc., 1987—; v.p., counsel and sec. State Farm Fire and Casualty Co., 1988—; v.p., counsel and sec. State Farm Gen. Ins. Co., 1988—, also bd. dirs.; v.p. counsel, sec., dir. State Farm Life and Accident Assurance Co.; v.p. counsel, sec. State Farm Annuity and Life Assurance Co., State Farm Life Ins. Co.; dir. State Farm Indemnity Co., Bloomington, Ill., 1995—; bd. dirs. Ins. Inst. for Hwy. Safety, Nat. Conf. Ins. Guaranty Funds, chmn., 1995—. Trustee John M. Scott Indsl. Sch. Trust, Bloomington, 1983-86, bd. dirs. Scott Ctr., 1983-86, Bloomington-Normal Symphony, 1980-85, YWCA of McLean County, 1993-95; chmn. Ins. Inst. for Hwy. Safety, 1987-88. Mem. ABA, Iowa State Bar Assn., Am. Corp. Counsel Assn., Am. Soc. Corp. Secs. Office: State Farm Mut Automobile Ins Co 1 State Farm Plz Bloomington IL 61710-0001

SULLIVAN, LEON HOWARD, clergyman; b. Charleston, W.Va., Oct. 16, 1922; m. Grace Banks, Aug. 1945; children—Howard, Julie, Hope. B.A., W.Va. State U., 1943, H.H.D. (hon.), 1956; student, Union Theol. Sem., N.Y.C., 1943-45; M.A. in Religion, Columbia U., 1947; D.D. (hon.), Va. Union U., 1956, Dartmouth Coll., 1968, Princeton U., 1969, Yale U., 1971; D.H.L. (hon.), Del. State Coll., 1966; D.Social Scis. (hon.), Villanova U., 1968; LL.D. (hon.), Beaver Coll., 1967, Swarthmore Coll., 1968, Bowdoin Coll., 1968, Denison U., 1968, Gannon Coll., 1969, Temple U., 1969; Ed.D. (hon.), Judson Coll., 1967. Ordained to ministry Bapt. Ch., 1941. Pastor Zion Bapt. Ch., Phila., 1950-88, now pastor emeritus; founder, chmn. bd. Zion Home for Ret., 1960—, Opportunities Industrialization Ctrs. Am., 1964—, Zion Investment Assocs., Inc., Progress Aerospace Inc.; dir. Girard Bank Phila., Gen. Motors Corp. Pres. Internat. Found. for Edn. and Self-Help, 1984—. Named One of Ten Outstanding Young Men Am., U.S. Jr. C. of C., 1955; One of 100 Outstanding Young Men Am., Life mag., 1963; recipient Freedom Found. award, 1960; Russwurm award Nat. Pubs. Assn., 1963; Edwin T. Dalhberg award Am. Bapt. Conv., 1968; Am. Exemplar medal, 1969; Phila. Book award; Phila. Fellowship Commn. award; Presdl. Medal of Freedom, 1991; Disting. Svc. award Pres. Cote d'Ivoire, 1991.

SULLIVAN, LOUIS WADE, former secretary health and human services, physician; b. Atlanta, Nov. 3, 1933; s. Walter Wade and Lubirda Elizabeth (Priester) S.; m. Eve Williamson, Sept. 30, 1955; children: Paul, Shanta, Halsted. B.S. magna cum laude, Morehouse Coll., Atlanta, 1954; M.D. cum laude, Boston U., 1958. Diplomate: Am. Bd. Internal Medicine. Intern N.Y. Hosp.-Cornell Med. Ctr., N.Y.C., 1958-59, resident in internal medicine, 1959-60; fellow in pathology Mass. Gen. Hosp., Boston, 1960-61; rsch. fellow Thorndike Meml. Lab. Harvard Med. Sch., Boston, 1961-63; instr. medicine Harvard Med. Sch., 1963-64; asst. prof. medicine N.J. Coll. Medicine, 1964-66; co-dir. hematology Boston U. Med. Ctr., 1966; assoc. prof. medicine Boston U., 1968-74; dir. hematology Boston City Hosp., 1973-75; also prof. medicine and physiology Boston U., 1974-75; dean Sch. Medicine, Morehouse Coll., Atlanta, 1975-89, pres., until 1989, 1993—; sec. Dept. of Health and Human Svcs., Washington, 1989-93; non-exec. dir. GM, 1993—; mem. sickle cell anemia adv. com. NIH, 1974-75; ad hoc panel on blood diseases Nat. Heart, Lung Blood Disease Bur., 1973, Nat. Adv. Rsch. Coun., 1977; mem. med. adv. bd. Nat. Leukemia Assn., 1968-70, chmn., 1970; researcher suppression of hematopoiesis by ethanol, pernicious anemia in childhood, folates in human nutrition. John Hay Whitney Found. Opportunity fellow, 1960-61; recipient Honor medal Am. Cancer Soc., 1991. Mem. Am. Soc. Hematology, Am. Soc. Clin. Investigation, Inst. Medicine, Phi Beta Kappa, Alpha Omega Alpha. Episcopalian. Office: Morehouse Sch Medicine Office of the Pres 720 Westview Dr SW Atlanta GA 30310-1495

SULLIVAN, LYNN DAVIS, special education educator; b. San Benito, Tex., Sept. 27, 1952; d. Clark Gilbert and Joan Ruth (Cox) Davis; m. Mark

W. Sullivan, Mar. 16, 1985. BA, Tex. A&I U., 1973; MEd, Tex. Woman's U., 1982. Cert. elem. tchr., early childhood, handicapped, lang. and learning disabilities; cert. supr. all levels. Ct. liaison Tex. Dept. Human Resources, Fort Worth; specialist spl. edn. Edn. Svc. Ctr., Reg. XI, Fort Worth. Profl. staff coord. Tarrant County Parents United; mem. 1st Tex. Coun. of Camp Fire (Blue Ribbon Vol. award, 1993), Campaign for Children, Child Care Tng. Network, 1990-95; mem. Cmty. Adv. Com. United Cerebral Palsy of Tarrant County, 1994-95. Mem. Assn. Tex. Profl. Educators (local unit pres. 1990-91), Coun. Exceptional Children (state organizing com. divsn. early childhood, sec. Tex. divsn. for early childhood 1987-88, pres. 1994—). Home: 3508 Western Ave Fort Worth TX 76107-6238

SULLIVAN, MARCIA WAITE, lawyer; b. Chgo., Nov. 30, 1950; d. Robert Macke and Jacqueline (Northrop) S.; m. Steven Donald Jansen, Dec. 20, 1975; children: Eric Spurlock, Laura Macke, Brian Northrop. BA, DePauw U., 1972; JD, Ind. U., 1975. Assoc. Arnstein, Gluck, Weisenfeld & Minow, Chgo., 1975-76; ptnr. Greenberger and Kaufmann, Chgo., 1976-86, Katten Muchin & Zavis, Chgo., 1986—; adj. prof. Kent Coll. Law, Ill. Inst. Tech., Chgo., 1991-94. Mem. ABA, Ill. Bar Assn., Chgo. Bar Assn., Am. Land Title Assn. (mem. lender's coun.). Avocations: bicycling, cross country skiing, gardening, camping. Office: Katten Muchin & Zavis 525 W Monroe St Ste 1600 Chicago IL 60661-3629

SULLIVAN, SISTER MARIE CELESTE, health care executive; b. Boston, Mar. 18, 1929; d. Daniel John and Katherine Agnes (Cunniff) S. BBA, St. Bonaventure U., 1965. Joined Order Franciscan Sisters Roman Cath. Ch., 1952; bus. mgr. St. Joseph's Hosp., Providence, 1954-62; asst. adminstr. St. Joseph's Hosp., Tampa, Fla., 1965-70, adminstr., 1970-83, chief exec. officer, 1983-93; pres., chief exec. officer Allegany Health Sys., Tampa, Fla., 1994—; coord. health affairs Diocese of St. Petersburg, 1980-93; mem. Fla. Cancer Control and Research Adv. Bd., 1980-90; bd. dirs. First Fla. Bank, N.A., Barnett Bank of Tampa; gen. councillor Franciscan Sisters of Allegany, 1984-92. Contbr. articles to profl. jours. Trustee St. Francis Med. & Health Ctr., Miami Beach, Fla., 1986-92; bd. dirs. local chpt. Am. Cancer Soc. Recipient Humanitarian award Judeo-Christian Health Clinic, Tampa, 1977, Athena award Fla. West Coast chpt. Women in Communications, 1978, Exec. Woman of Yr. award Tampa Bay chpt. Network Exec. Women, 1987. Fellow Am. Coll. Health Care Execs. (life); mem. Fla. Hosp. Assn. (trustee 1983-87), Am. Mgmt. Assn., Greater Tampa C. of C. (bd. govs. 1982-87). Democrat. Club: Centre (Tampa) (founding bd. govs.). Home: 2924 W Curtis St Tampa FL 33614-7102 Office: Allegany Health Sys 6200 Courtney Campbell Causeway Tampa FL 33607 *I believe success is guaranteed when there is dedication to high standards, when there is respect for the dignity and worth of the human person, and when one believes in the goodness of God.*

SULLIVAN, MARTIN EDWARD, museum director; b. Troy, N.Y., Feb. 9, 1944; s. John Francis and Helen Edna (Lynch) S.; m. Katherine Mary Hostetter, May 9, 1981; children: Abigail, Bethany. BA in History, Siena Coll., 1965; MA in History, U. Notre Dame, 1970, PhD in History, 1974. Exec. dir. Ind. Commn. for Humanities, Indpls., 1972-75; dir. pub. programs NEH, Washington, 1976-81; pres. Inst. on Man and Sci., Rensselaerville, N.Y., 1981-83; dir. N.Y. State Mus., State Edn. Dept., Albany, N.Y., 1983-90, The Heard Mus., Phoenix, 1990—; trustee Am. Indian Ritual Object Repatriation Found., N.Y.C., 1992—; chair U.S. Govt. Cultural Property Adv. Com., 1995—. Author: Museums, Adults and the Humanities, 1981, Inventing the Southwest: The Fred Harvey Company and Native American Art, 1996; contbr. articles to profl. jours. Trustee Phoenix Cmty. Alliance, 1991—, Am. Fedn. Arts, 1994—; mem. Native Am. Repatriation Act Adv. Com., 1992—. Served in U.S. Army, 1966-68. Mem. Am. Assn. Mus. (v.p. 1990-93, mem. exec. com. internat. com. 1992—). Democrat. Home: 4601 E Solano Dr Phoenix AZ 85018-1280 Office: The Heard Mus 22 E Monte Vista Rd Phoenix AZ 85004-1480

SULLIVAN, MARY JANE, elementary school educator; b. Mason City, Iowa, Nov. 23, 1947; d. Lawrence Wesly and Elizabeth Barbara (Steinbach) Kohler; m. Mark Jay Sullivan, June 26, 1993. BS, Mankato (Minn.) State U., 1970; MS, Iowa State U., 1982. Cert. tchr. K-9, coach K-12, Iowa. Tchr. 5th grade Keokuk (Iowa) Cmty. Sch., 1970-77, West Bend (Iowa) Cmty. Sch., 1977-80; tchr. 6th grade North Mahaska Cmty. Sch., New Sharon, Iowa, 1980—. Author: (poetry teaching book) Poetry Pals, 1982. Mem. Regional telecomms. Coun., Des Moines, 1994—; treas. New Sharon Activities Com., 1988—; mem. Iowa Pub. TV, Des Moines, Iowa Heritage Assn., Des Moines. Named County Sci. Tchr. of Yr., Mahaska County Conservation Bd., Oskaloosa, Iowa, 1992; sci. grantee Ctrl. Coll., Iowa Dept. Edn. Mem. NEA, ASCD, Iowa State Edn. Assn. (exec. bd. negotiations), Nat. Staff Devel. Coun. (mem. 1st acad.), Kappa Delta Pi, Phi Delta Kappa (v.p. 1990-91). Roman Catholic. Avocations: reading, cross stitch, walking, gardening. Office: N Mahaska Elem Sch 204 W Maple New Sharon IA 50207

SULLIVAN, MARY JEAN, elementary school educator; b. Cambridge, Mass., May 13, 1956; d. Joseph Leo and Jean Marie (Isaac) S. BA, Flagler Coll., 1978; postgrad., U. No. Fla., 1980—, Fla. State U., 1992, Okla. State U., 1992. Cert. elem. educator, Fla. Tchr. grade 2 St. Agnes Sch., St. Augustine, Fla., 1978-79; tchr. grades 1 through 5 Evelyn Hamblen Elem. Sch., St. Augustine, 1979-91; tchr. grade 5 Osceola Elem. Sch., St. Augustine, 1991—, chair math./ sci.; adv. Sci. Club; chairperson, St. John's County Tchr. Edn. Coun., 1985—, SACS Evaluation Team, Duval County Schs., 1988, 89, 90; rep. tchr. edn. coun.; sch. improvement co-chair, 1994-95; trainer coll. intern students. Developer tchr. edn. coun. tng. handbook for State of Fla. Active PTO, past pres., Cub Scouts Am., past asst. program dir., Cathedral-Basilica Ch., United Child Care After Sch. Program, 1988-89; coord. summer recreation Evelyn Hamblen Sch., St. Augustine, 1987-90; dir. tournament Pam Driskell Meml. Paddle Tennis Scholarship Fund, 1986, 87, 88, 89. Grantee Fla. Coun. Elem. Edn., 1981-82, Summer Enhancement, 1988-89, Fla. Inst. Oceanography, 1994, St. John's County Horizon award mini-grantee, 1994, Fla. Assn. for Computer Edn., 1994, Fla. Humanities Coun., 1995; recipient Human Rels. award State of Fla., 1992, NEWEST award, 1992, award Geography Summer Inst., 1992; named Kiwanis Tchr. of Month, 1993. Mem. NEA, Nat. Sci. Tchrs. Assn., Fla. Teaching Profession, Fla. Assn. Staff Devel., Fla. Geographic Alliance, Fla. Assn. Computer Edn., St. John's Educator Assn., Fla. Assn. for Sci. Tchrs., ASCD. Office: Osceola Elem Sch 1605 Osceola Elem Sch Rd Saint Augustine FL 32095

SULLIVAN, MARY ROSE, English language educator; b. Boston, May 13, 1931; d. John Joseph and Elinor Mary (Crotty) Sullivan. BA, Emmanuel Coll., Boston, 1952; MA, Cath. U. Am., 1957; PhD, Boston U., 1964. Tchr. Woburn Pub. Schs., Mass., 1957-60; faculty Emmanuel Coll., Boston, 1960-66; prof. English U. Colo., Denver, 1966-96; mem. book reviewing staff San Diego Mag., 1980-90. Author: Browning's Voices in the Ring and the Book, 1969; co-editor: (3 vols.) letters of E.B. Browning to M.R. Mitford, 1836-54, 1983, Women of Letters: Selected Letters of E.B. Browning to M.R. Mitford, 1987, Crime Classics, 1990, Elizabeth Barrett Browning: Selected Poetry and Prose, 1993; editl. bd. English Lang. Notes, 1970-96. Served to capt. USNR, 1952-83. Am. Council Learned Socs. fellow, 1973. Mem. Browning Inst., Boston Browning Soc., Mystery Writers of Am., Denver Woman's Press Club, P.E.N. West U.S.A.

SULLIVAN, MICHAEL DAVID, state supreme court justice; b. Hattiesburg, Miss., Dec. 2, 1938; s. Curran W. and Mittie (Chambers) S.; m. Catherine Ainsworth Carter; children: David Paul, Rachel Michel, Margaret Elizabeth, Sarah Catherine. BS, U. So. Miss., 1960; JD, Tulane U., 1966; LLM in Jud. Process, U. Va., 1988. Atty. Hattiesburg, Miss., 1967-75; chancellor Miss. Chancery Ct. Dist. 10, 1975-84; justice Miss. Supreme Ct., Jackson, 1984—. Office: Miss Supreme Ct PO Box 117 Jackson MS 39205-0117

SULLIVAN, MICHAEL JOACHIM, financial executive; b. Offenbach, Germany, Apr. 30, 1954; s. Donald and Eleanor (Denver) S.; m. Marianne Murphy, July 7, 1990. BA, LeMoyne Coll., 1976; MS, Syracuse U., 1980, MBA, 1993. Counselor County of Onondaga, Syracuse, N.Y., 1976-79, rsch. tech. 1, 1979, rsch. tech. 2, 1980-81, adminstrv. planning and funding coord., 1982-85, budget analyst 3, 1985, budget analyst 4, 1985-86, dep. dir. mgmt. and budget, 1986-87, dir. mgmt. and budget, 1988-92, commr. of fin., CFO, 1992-95; chief fiscal officer Loretto, Inc., N.Y., 1995—. Bd. dirs. Lourdes Camp, Inc., Syracuse, 1980—, Syracuse Opera, 1994—; mem. fin. com. Interreligious Coun., Syracuse, 1993—; mem. Thursday morning roundtable Univ. Coll., Syracuse, 1991—; mem. fin. com. ARC, 1994—, St. Michael's Ch., 1994—. Mem. N.Y. State Govt. Fin. Officers Assn. (chmn. ctrl. region 1993-95, bd. dirs. 1993-95), Govt. Fin. Officers Assn. (Disting. Budget award 1988-92), N.Y. State Assn. Counties, Beta Gamma Sigma. Roman Catholic. Avocations: sailing, reading. Home: 4644 Bloomsbury Dr Syracuse NY 13215-2326 Office: Loretto Inc 710 E Brighton Ave Syracuse NY 13205

SULLIVAN, MICHAEL PATRICK, marine officer; b. L.A., Aug. 22, 1933; s. Charles Gardner and Ann (May) S.; m. Nicole Marie St. Germaine; children: Steven, John, Byron. BA, San Diego State U., 1971; MS, Coll. Naval Warfare, 1976. Commd. 2d lt. USMC, 1956, advanced through grades to maj. gen.; comdg. officer VMFA-323 and MAWTU USMC, El Toro, Calif., 1973-75, comdg. officer Marine Aircraft Group II, 1980-83; with Group 3A 1st Marine Aircraft Wing USMC, Okinawa, Japan, 1976-77; AVN evaluator Combat Readiness Evaluation System USMC, Washington, 1977-80; comdg. officer Marine Aircraft Group-41, Dallas, 1983-85; comdg. gen., asst. wing comdr. 2d Marine Aircraft Wing MCAS, Cherry Point, N.C., 1985-88; dep. comdr. War Fighting Ctr. Marine Corps Combat Devel. Command Devel. Command, Quantico, Va., 1988-90; dep. comdr. Fleet Marine Force, Atlantic Norfolk, Va., 1990-91; asst. v.p. First Citizens Bank, N.C. Mem. Marine Corps Aviation Assn. (A.A. Cunninghamaward, Aviator of Yr. 1974, Silver Hawk award 1990), Marine Corps. Assn., Marine Corps Mustang Assn., Golden Eagles.

SULLIVAN, MICHAEL PATRICK, food service executive; b. Mpls., Dec. 5, 1934; s. Michael Francis and Susan Ellen (Doran) S.; m. Marilyn Emmer, June 27, 1964; children: Katherine, Michael, Maureen, Bridget, Daniel, Thomas. BS, Marquette U., 1956; JD, U. Minn., 1962. Bar: Minn. 1962, U.S. Dist. Ct. Minn. 1962, U.S. Supreme Ct. 1975, U.S. Ct. Appeals (8th cir.) 1978. Assoc., Gray, Plant, Mooty, Mooty & Bennett, Mpls., 1962-67, ptnr., 1968-87, mng. ptnr., 1976-87; pres., chief exec. officer Internat. Dairy Queen, Inc., 1987—; bd. dirs. The Valspar Corp., Allianz Life Ins. Co. N.Am., Opus U.S. Corp.; instr. U. Minn. Law Sch., 1962-67; lectr. continuing legal edn.; spl. counsel to atty. gen. Minn., 1971-79, 82-84. Contbr. articles to profl. jours. Bd. dirs. Legal Aid Soc. Mpls.; bd. trustees Fairview Hosps., St. Paul Sem; bd. govs. Children's Miracle Network; bd. dirs. Met. Mpls.YMCA; pres. Uniform Law Commn., 1987-89. Served with USN, 1956-59. Mem. ABA (ho. of dels., 1984-89), Minn. Bar Assn. (gov. 1974-86), Hennepin County Bar Assn. (pres. 1978-79), Am. Bar Found., Am. Law Inst., Order of Coif. Roman Catholic. Office: Internat Dairy Queen 7505 Metro Blvd Minneapolis MN 55439-3020

SULLIVAN, MORTIMER ALLEN, JR., lawyer; b. Buffalo, Sept. 19, 1930; s. Mortimer Allen Sr. and Gertrude (Hinkley) S.; m. Maryanne Calella, Nov. 20, 1965; children: Mark Allen, Michael John. BA, U. Buffalo, 1954. Bar: N.Y. 1964, U.S. Dist. Ct. (we. dist.) N.Y. 1966, U.S. Dist. Ct. (no. dist.) N.Y. 1967, U.S. Supreme Ct. 1970. Counsel liability claims Interstate Motor Freight System, Grand Rapids, Mich., 1964-82; v.p. J.P.M. Sullivan, Inc., Elmira, N.Y., 1959-67; govt. appeal agt. U.S. Selective Service System, 1967-71; dep. sci. div. Erie County (N.Y.) Sheriff's Office, 1971—, lt., 1986—. Inventor (with others) in field; creator, dir. video depiction JudiVision, 1969; composer High Flight, 1983. Chmn. com. on Constn. and canons Episcopal Diocese of Western N.Y., 1975—; bd. dirs. Erie County Sheriff's Found., Inc., 1987—; bd. dirs. Orchard Park (N.Y.) Symphony Orch., 1975—, v.p., 1977-79, 91-94. With USAF, 1954-57; spl. agt. Air Force Office of Spl. Investigations, 1972-87, col. res. ret. Decorated Legion of Merit. Mem. N.Y. State Bar Assn., Erie County Bar Assn. (chmn. law and tech. com. 1970-81), Transp. Lawyers Assn., Kappa Alpha Soc. Republican. Clubs: Saturn (Buffalo); Wanakah (N.Y.) Country. Avocation: aviation. Home: 19 Knob Hill Rd Orchard Park NY 14127 Office: 88 S Davis St PO Box 1003 Orchard Park NY 14127-1003

SULLIVAN, NEIL MAXWELL, oil and gas company executive; b. McKeesport, Pa., May 25, 1942; s. Thomas James and Jane Mason (Ginn) S.; m. Holly Abolt; children: Margaret Blair, Mason Pedrick. BS, Dickinson Coll., 1970; MS, Tulane U., 1994; postgrad., U. S.C., 1992—. Exploration geologist Bass Enterprises, Midland, Tex., 1976-77; dist. geologist ATAPCO, Midland, 1977-78, Anadarko Prodn. Co., Midland, 1978-79, chief geologist, 1979-80, v.p. exploration, regional mgr., Houston, 1980-82; exploration ops. mgr. Valero Producing Co., San Antonio, 1982-85, v.p. exploration, New Orleans, 1985-87; pres. Bluebonnet Petroleum Co., New Orleans, 1987—; mem. Dept. Interior Outer Continental Shelf Com. adv. bd., 1985-87. Editor: Petroleum Exploration in Thrust Belts and Their Adjacent Forelands, 1976, Ancient Carbonate Reservoirs and Their Modern Analogs, 1977, Guadalupian Delaware Mountain Group of West Texas and Southeast New Mexico, 1979, Deep Water Sands in the Gulf Coast Region, 1988, Offshore Louisiana Geology: An Onshore Exploration Model, 1988, Risk: Evaluation and Management, 1989, Volga-Ural Basin Analysis, 1993, Northern Marginal Zone of the Pricaspian Basin, 1996. Bd. dirs. Permian Basin Grad. Ctr., Midland, 1979; com. chmn. Mus. of S.W., Midland, 1978. Served with USAF, 1964-68. Mem. Geol. Soc. Am., Am. Assn. Petroleum Geologists (cert. petroleum geologist), New Orleans Geol. Soc. (chmn. continuing edn. com. 1987-89), South Tex. Geol. Soc. (nominating com. chmn. 1985), Soc. Econ. Paleontologists and Mineralogists (pres. Permian Basin sect. 1979), Am. Inst. Profl. Geologists (cert. profl. geologist). Lodge: Elks. Home: 2813-8 Shadblow Ln Springdale SC 29170

SULLIVAN, NICHOLAS G., science educator, speleologist; b. Phila., Dec. 20, 1927; s. Edward James and Florence (Delaney) S. BS, Cath. U. Am., 1950; MSc, U. Pitts., 1954; PhD, U. Notre Dame, 1961. Asst. prof. U. Notre Dame (Ind.), 1961-63; asst. prof., assoc. prof., prof. La Salle Coll., Phila., 1963-78, asst. to pres., 1972-74; prof. sci. Manhattan Coll., Riverdale, N.Y., 1979—; vis. prof. U. Alaska, Anchorage, 1961, U. NSW, Sydney, Australia, 1963; chmn. U.S. Deep Caving Team. Author: Speleology, the Study of Caves, 1962; contbr. over 200 articles on speleology to profl. jours. Trustee Gwynedd (Pa.) Mercy Coll., 1963-75, Nat. Speleological Found., Washington, 1978-84, Charles Lindberg Found., 1989—. Fellow Nat. Speleological Soc. (hon. life, trustee 1955-79, pres. 1957-63), Royal Geog. Soc., AAAS, N.Y. Acad. Scis., Explorers Club (pres. 1989-92, trustee 1968—, Explorer's medal Phila. chpt. 1978, Sweeney medal 1979); mem. Sydney Speleogical Soc. (hon. life), South African Speleogical Soc. (hon. life), Rittenhouse Club, Bankstown Sports Club (Sydney).

SULLIVAN, PAUL WILLIAM, communications specialist; b. Brockton, Mass., Dec. 7, 1939; s. Augustus Henry and Pearl Irene (Chisholm) S.; children: Todd Andrew, Geoffrey Scott, Dustin Raymond; m. Frances Tina Brown, Jan. 23, 1989. BA cum laude, Yale U., 1961; MA, U. Fla., 1971; PhD, So. Ill. U., 1977. Gen. mgr. Chronicle Pub. Co., Stoughton, Mass., 1962-67; editor Easton Bull., N. Easton, Mass., 1963-70; pub., editor Associated Weekly Newspapers, Stoughton, 1967-70; instr. dept. mass comm. Moorhead (Minn.) State U., 1971-73; assoc. prof., chmn. dept. comm. U. Evansville, Ind., 1973-78; prof., chmn. dept. journalism Temple U., Phila., 1978-87; pvt. practice comm. cons., sales tng. cons. Indian Rocks Beach, Fla., 1986-92; pvt. practice comm. and fin. cons. Sullivan Comms., Indian Rocks Beach, 1992—; mng. gen. ptnr. Atlantis Adventure Ltd. Partnership, Largo, Fla., 1996—; mem. rev. panel Harry S Truman Scholarship Found., 1981-86. Author: The Modern Free Press Fair Trial Precedent, 1987, monograph News Piracy, 1978; co-author, editor: The Teaching of Graphic Arts, 1977, The Art of Consulting, 1989; contbr. articles to profl. jours. Mem. Gov.'s Commn. for Pa. Lottery, 1981. Mem. Assn. for Edn. in Journalism and Mass Communications, Soc. Profl. Journalists, Pa. Soc. Newspaper Editors (bd. dirs. 1980-87), Phila. Bar Assn. (media rels. com. 1982-87), ACLU. Avocations: photographer, landscape gardening. Office: PO Box 1049 Indian Rocks Beach FL 34635-1049 *Never underestimate the power of a liberal education to keep opening doors into the future. That education coupled with what I learned from my father and keep learning from my wife has made all the difference.*

SULLIVAN, PEGGY (ANNE), librarian; b. Kansas City, Mo., Aug. 12, 1929; d. Michael C. and Ella (O'Donnell) S. A.B., Clarke Coll., 1950; M.S. in L.S, Cath. U. Am., 1953; Ph.D. (Tangley Oaks fellow, Higher Edn. Act Title II fellow), U. Chgo., 1972. Children's public librarian Mo., Md., Va., 1952-61; sch. library specialist Montgomery County (Md.) public schs., 1961-63; dir. Knapp Sch. Libraries Project, ALA, 1963-68, Jr. Coll. Library Info. Ctr., 1968-69; asst. prof. U. Pitts., 1971-73; dir. Office for Library Personnel Resources, ALA, Chgo., 1973-74; dean of students, assoc. prof. Grad. Library Sch., U. Chgo., 1974-77; asst. commr. for extension services Chgo. Public Library, 1977-81; dean Coll. Profl. Studies, No. Ill. U., DeKalb, 1981-90; dir. univ. librs. No. Ill. U., 1990-92; exec. dir. ALA, 1992-94; assoc. Tuft & Assocs., 1995—; dean Grad. Sch. Libr. and Info. Sci. Rosary Coll., 1995—; instr. several grad. libr. edn. programs, 1958-73, UNESCO cons. on sch. librs., Australia, 1970; trustee Clarke Coll., 1969-72; sr. ptnr. Able Cons., 1987-92. Author: The O'Donnells, 1956, Impact: The School Library and the Instructional Program, 1966, Many Names for Eileen, 1969, Problems in School Media Management, 1971, Carl H. Milam and the American Library Association, 1976, Opportunities in Library and Information Science, 1977, Realization: The Final Report of the Knapp School Libraries Project, 1968; (with others) Public Libraries: Smart Practices in Personnel, 1982. Mem. ALA, Cath. Libr. Assn. Roman Catholic. Home: 2800 N Lake Shore Dr Apt 816 Chicago IL 60657-6202 Office: Rosary Coll Grad Sch Libr and Info Sci 7900 W Division St River Forest IL *Opportunities to use my abilities in a variety of public services have enriched my life, as I hope the results have enriched and empowered others.*

SULLIVAN, PETER M., lawyer; b. Evanston, Ill., Nov. 9; s. Harold W. and Mildred (Dolan) S.; m. Michele H. Chermak, Aug. 30, 1986. BA, U. Notre Dame, 1980; JD, Loyola U., 1983. Assoc. atty. Hinshaw, Culbertson, Moelmann, Hoban & Fuller, Chgo., 1983—; litigation ptnr Gibson Dunn & Crutcher, L.A., CA. Contbr. articles to profl. jours. Mem. ABA, Ill. State Bar Assn. Roman Catholic. Office: Gibson Dunn & Crutcher 333 S Grand Ave Los Angeles CA 90071*

SULLIVAN, ROBERT EDWARD, lawyer; b. San Francisco, May 18, 1936; s. Edward C. S. and Mary Jane (Sullivan); m. Maureen Lois Miles, June 14, 1958 (dec. 1972); children: Teresa Ann, Andrew Edward, Edward Braddock. BS, U. San Francisco, 1958; LLB, U. Calif-Berkeley, 1961. Bar: Calif. 1962. Assoc. Pillsbury, Madison & Sutro, San Francisco, 1963-70, ptnr., 1971—; lectr. bus. law Calif. Continuing Edn. Bar and Practicing Law Inst.; v.p., treas., dir. MPC Ins., Ltd., 1986-93. Contbr. articles to profl. jours. Bd. dirs., exec. com. mem., sec. San Francisco Opera Assn., 1993—. 1st lt. U.S. Army, 1961-63. Mem. ABA, State Bar Calif. (com. corps. 1979-82, chmn. 1981-82, mem. exec. com. bus. law sect. 1982-85, vice chmn. 1983-84, chmn. 1984-85, advisor 1985-86, mem. partnership com. 1990-92, chmn. ltd. liability co. drafting com. 1992-93), San Francisco Bar Assn., Bankers Club San Francisco (bd. dirs.). Democrat. Roman Catholic. Office: Pillsbury Madison & Sutro 235 Montgomery St San Francisco CA 94104-2902

SULLIVAN, RUTH ANNE, librarian; b. Portland, Maine, Jan. 15, 1955; d. Lawrence P. and Mary Louise (Gilman) S.; m. Charles H. Sullivan, May 1, 1982; children: Nora J., Ian J. BA, Wheaton Coll., 1979; MLS, U. Ariz., 1980. Serials ref. Mass. Bay Community Coll., Wellesley, 1980-81; asst. dir. Bristol Community Coll., Fall River, Mass., 1981-86, chief libr., 1986—. Office: Bristol Community Coll 777 Elsbree St Fall River MA 02720-7307

SULLIVAN, SELBY WILLIAM, lawyer, business executive; b. Houston, Oct. 8, 1934; s. John Francis and Lois Blanch (Selby) S.; m. Diane Pace; children: Selby William, Tricia, Lisa, Terry, Jack. B.A., Rice U., 1956; postgrad., Stanford U., 1956-57; LL.B. with honors, U. Tex., 1963. Bar: Tex. 1963, Fla. 1971. Ptnr. Andrews, Kurth, Campbell & Jones, Houston, 1963-72; pres. Fla. Gas Co., 1973-79, chief exec. officer, 1974-79, chmn. bd., 1977-79; exec. v.p., chief fin. and adminstrv. officer, dir., mem. exec. office Continental Group Inc., N.Y.C., 1979-80; ptnr. Maguire Vooris & Wells, Orlando, Fla., 1982-83; owner, chmn., chief exec. officer Hubbard Constrn. Co., 1984-89; chmn. bd. Orange Paving and Constrn. Co., 1984-89, Orlando Paving Co., 1984-89; owner, chmn., pres. Diamond S. Ranch, Inc., Meridian Homes, 1989—; chmn., pres. Summit Land Co., 1989—, Sullivan Investments, 1989—; dir. Sun Banks of Fla., Electric Fuels Corp., Fla. Progress Corp. Bd. dirs. Orange Bowl Com., Rice U., Fla. Bus. Forum, 1974-80; chmn. Rollins Coll. Sch. Bus., 1985-88; vice chmn. bd. dirs. Fla. Coun. 100. Mem. ABA, Fla. Bar Assn., Tex. Bar Assn., Interstate Natural Gas Assn. Am. (dir. 1975-79), Am. Natural Gas Assn. (bd. dirs. 1978-79), So. Gas Assn. (bd. dirs. 1976-79), Fla. C. of C., Interlachen Country Club (chmn., pres., bd. dirs. 1984—), Blind Brook Club, River Club, Country club of the Rockies (bd. dirs.), Eldorado Country Club (bd. dirs.), Eagle Springs Golf Club, Plantation Country Club. Home: PO Box 1740 Eagle CO 81631-1740

SULLIVAN, STEVE JOSEPH, editor, journalist; b. St. Louis, Nov. 9, 1954; s. Donald R. and Ruth (Maiers) S. BA, George Mason U., 1978. Legis. asst. Congressman Moris Udall, Washington, 1975-76; freelance writer Network News, Inc., Washington, 1979-82; researcher, writer Record Rsch., Inc., Washington, 1982-85; reporter Land Devel. Inst., Washington, 1985-87; mng. editor Land Devel., Inc., Washington, 1987—. Author: Pop Memories: The History of American Popular Music, 1890-1954, 1985, A Practical Guide to FIRREA, 1989, VaVaVoom, 1995; co-author: The New Work Out Game, 1991; contbr. articles to mags. Avocations: popular culture research, music. Office: Land Devel Inc 1401 16th St NW Washington DC 20036-2201

SULLIVAN, STUART FRANCIS, anesthesiologist, educator; b. Buffalo, July 15, 1928; s. Charles S. and Kathryn (Duggan) S.; m. Dorothy Elizabeth Faytol, Apr. 18, 1959; children: John, Irene, Paul, Kathryn. BS, Canisius Coll., 1950; MD, SUNY, Syracuse, 1955. Diplomate Am. Bd. Anesthesiology. Intern Ohio State Univ. Hosp., Columbus, 1955-56; resident Columbia Presbyn. Med. Ctr., 1958-60; instr. anesthesiology Columbia U. Coll. Physicians and Surgeons, N.Y.C., 1961-62, assoc., 1962-64, asst. prof., 1964-69, assoc. prof., 1969-73; prof. dept. anesthesiology UCLA, 1973-91, vice chair anesthesiology, 1974-77, exec. vice chair, 1977-90, acting chmn., 1983-84, 87-88, 90-91, prof. emeritus, 1991—. Served to capt. M.C., USAR, 1956-58. Fellow NIH, 1960-61; recipient research career devel. award NIH, 1966-69. Mem. Assn. Univ. Anesthetists, Am. Physiol. Soc., Am. Soc. Anesthesiologists. Home: 101 Foxtail Dr Santa Monica CA 90402-2047 Office: UCLA Sch Medicine Dept Anesthesiology Los Angeles CA 90024

SULLIVAN, TERESA ANN, law and sociology educator, academic administrator; b. Kewanee, Ill., July 9, 1949; d. Gordon Hager and Mary Elizabeth (Finnegan) S.; m. H. Douglas Laycock, June 14, 1971; children: Joseph Peter, John Patrick. BA, Mich. State U., 1970; MA, U. Chgo., 1972, PhD, 1975. Asst. prof. sociology U. Tex., Austin, 1975-76, assoc. prof. sociology, 1981-87, dir. women's studies, 1985-87, prof. sociology, 1987—, prof. law, 1988—, assoc. dean grad. sch., 1989-90, 1992—, chair dept. sociology, 1990-92, vice provost, 1994-95, v.p., grad. dean, 1995—; asst. prof. sociology U. Chgo., 1977-81; pres. Southwestern Sociol. Assn., 1988-89; mem. faculty adv. bd. Hogg Found. Mental Health, 1989-92; mem. sociology panel NSF, 1983-85. Author: Marginal Workers Marginal Jobs, 1978; co-author: As We Forgive Our Debtors, 1989 (Silver Gavel 1990), Social Organization of Work, 1990, 2d edit. 1995; contbr. articles and chpts. to profl. jours. Bd. dirs. Calvert Found., Chgo., 1978, CARA, Inc., Washington, 1985; mem. U.S. Census Bur. Adv. Com., 1989-95, chmn., 1991-92; mem. sociology panel NSF, 1983-85. Grantee NSF, 1983-95, U.S. Dept. Labor, 1983-85, Leadership Tex. 1994. Fellow AAAS (liaison to Population Assn. Am. 1989-91, chair sect. K 1996), Sociol. Rsch. Assn., Am. Sociol. Assn. (sec. 1995—, editor Rose Monograph Series 1988-92), Soc. Study of Social Problems (chair fin. com. 1986-87), Population Assn. Am. (bd. dirs. 1989-91, chair fin. com. 1990-91). Roman Catholic. Avocations: volkssporting, sci. fiction. Office: U Tex Office Grad Studies Main Bldg 101 Austin TX 78712

SULLIVAN, TERRANCE CHARLES, lawyer; b. Neptune, N.J., Mar. 23, 1950; s. John Joseph and Marilyn Anne (DiBlasi) S.; m. Kathy Lavonne Collett, June 21, 1980; children: Jennifer Collett, Michael Charles, Cynthia Grace, Philip Gregory. BA, U. Ga., 1972; JD, U. Va., 1975. Bar: Ga. 1975. Assoc. Swift, Currie, McGhee & Hiers, Atlanta, 1975-77; assoc., ptnr. Phillips, Hart & Mozley, Atlanta, 1977-82; sr. ptnr. Hart & Sullivan, P.C., Atlanta, 1982-89, Sullivan, Hall, Booth & Smith, P.C., Atlanta, 1989—; bd. dirs. Atlanta Coun. Younger Lawyers, 1975-77. Contbr. articles on legal edn. to profl. jours. Capt. USAF Res., 1972-80. Fellow Am. Coll. Trial Lawyers, Am. Bd. Trial Advocate's; mem. ABA, State Bar Ga., Atlanta Bar Assn., Nat. Inst. Trial Advocacy, Atlanta Inst. Trial Advocacy (co-dir. 1986-88), Def. Rsch. Inst., Atlanta Lawyers Club, Commerce Club, Trial Lawyers Assn. Am. (conf. speaker 1988). Roman Catholic. Home: 3986 Fernway Ct

NE Atlanta GA 30319-1667 Office: Sullivan Hall Booth & Smith 1360 Peachtree St NE Atlanta GA 30309-3214

SULLIVAN, TERRY T., newspaper publishing executive; b. Cedar Rapids, Iowa; married; 5 children. BS in Bus., Skidmore Coll. With Gannett Co. Inc., Arlington, Va., 1980-83; human resources dir. Gannett West, Reno, Nev., 1983-85; divsn. v.p. USA Today, Arlington, 1985—. Past bd. mem. United Way, Arlington County, Va., Vol. Clearinghouse Washington, Skidmore Coll. Alumni Assn.; past mem. Employer's Com. Pres.'s Com. Employment People with Disabilities. Mem. Newspaper Pers. Rels. Assn. (past pres., Catalyst award 1991), Human Resources Planning Soc., Soc. Human Resource Mgmt., Sr. Pers. Execs. Forum (Washington), Washington Human Resources Forum. Office: USA Today 1000 Wilson Blvd Arlington VA 22229

SULLIVAN, THOMAS CHRISTOPHER, coatings company executive; b. Cleve., July 8, 1937; s. Frank Charles and Margaret Mary (Wilhelmy) S.; m. Sandra Simmons, Mar. 12, 1960; children: Frank, Sean, Tommy, Danny, Kathleen, Julie. B.S., Miami U., Oxford, Ohio, 1959. Div. sales mgr. Republic Powdered Metals, Cleve., 1961-65; exec. v.p. Republic Powdered Metals, 1965-70; pres., chmn. bd. RPM, Inc., Medina, Ohio, 1971-78; chmn. bd. RPM, Inc., 1978—; bd. dirs. Pioneer Standard Electronics, Inc., Cleve., Nat. City Bank, Cleve., Cleve. Clinic Found., Huffy Corp., Dayton, Ohio. Trustee Culver (Ind.) Ednl. Found., Cleve. Tomorrow; bd. dirs. Urban Community Sch., Cleve., Malachi House, Cleve., bd. dirs., adv. com. May Dugan Ctr. Cleve. Lt. (j.g.) USNR, 1959-60. Mem. Nat. Paint and Coatings Assn. (bd. dirs., exec. com.), Nat. Assn. Securities Dealers (bd. govs. 1986-88, long-range strategic planning com.). Roman Catholic. Office: RPM Inc 2628 Pearl Rd Medina OH 44256-7623

SULLIVAN, THOMAS JOHN, communications company executive; b. Jersey City, N.J., Apr. 11, 1935; s. Patrick J. and Angel (Minihane) S.; m. Frances D. Gibbons, Oct. 28, 1961; children: Kelly Ann, Thomas J. B.S. in Acctg., St. Peter's Coll., 1957; J.D., Seton Hall U., 1969. With Merck & Co., Inc., Rahway, N.J., 1957-65; mgr. fin. systems McGraw-Hill Info. Systems Co., N.Y.C., 1965-67, budget dir., 1967-68; controller McGraw-Hill Info. Systems, 1968-71, sr. v.p. product devel., 1971-73; v.p. planning systems McGraw-Hill Inc., N.Y.C., 1973-76, v.p. fin. analysis, 1976-77, sr. v.p. corp. planning, 1977-83, sr. v.p., asst. to pres., 1983-86, exec. v.p. adminstrn., 1986—. Mem. N.J. Bar Assn., ABA, Fin. Execs. Inst., Nat. Assn. Accts. Office: McGraw-Hill Inc 1221 Ave Of The Americas New York NY 10020-1001

SULLIVAN, THOMAS PATRICK, academic administrator; b. Detroit, July 8, 1947; s. Walter James and Helen Rose (Polosky) S.; m. Barbara Jean Fournier, Aug. 9, 1968; children: Colleen, Brendan. BA in English, U. Dayton, 1969; M. Edn. and Adminstrn., Kent State U., 1971; postgrad., U. Mich., 1988. Tchr. Resurection Elem. Sch., Dayton, Ohio, 1968-69; administr. residence hall Kent (Ohio) State U., 1969-71; program mgr. residence hall Ea. Mich. U., Ypsilanti, 1971-73, adminstrv. assoc., 1973-76, dir. housing, 1976-83; assoc. provost Wayne County Community Coll., Belleville, Mich., 1983-84; dir. budget and mgmt. devel. Wayne County Community Coll., Detroit, 1984-85, sr. v.p. acad. affairs, acting provost, 1985-86; acting exec. dean Wayne County Community Coll., Belleville, 1986-88; dir. budget and mgmt. devel. Wayne County Community Coll., Detroit, 1988-89; pres. Cleary Coll., Ypsilanti, 1989—; part-time instr. English and math. Schoolcraft Coll., Livonia, Mich., 1980-90. Home: 44954 Patrick Dr Canton MI 48187-2551 Office: Cleary Coll 2170 Washtenaw Rd Ypsilanti MI 48197-1744

SULLIVAN, THOMAS PATRICK, lawyer; b. Evanston, Ill., Mar. 23, 1930; s. Clarence M. and Pauline (DeHaye) S.; divorced; children: Margaret Mary, Timothy Joseph, Elizabeth Ann; m. Anne Landau. Student, Loras Coll., Dubuque, Iowa, 1947-49; LL.B. cum laude, Loyola U., Chgo., 1952. Bar: Ill. 1952, Calif. 1982. Asso. firm Jenner & Block, Chgo., 1954-62; partner Jenner & Block, 1963-77, 81—; U.S. atty. for No. Dist. Ill., Chgo., 1977-81. Contbr. articles to profl. jours. Served with U.S. Army, 1952-54. Decorated Bronze Star.; Recipient medal of excellence Loyola U. Law Sch., 1965; Ill. Pub. Defender Assn. award, 1972. Fellow Am. Coll. Trial Lawyers; mem. Am., Ill., Fed. Seventh Circuit, Chgo. bar assns., Fed. Bar Assn., Am. Law Inst., Am. Judicature Soc., Chgo. Council Lawyers. Office: Jenner & Block 1 E Ibm Plz Chicago IL 60611

SULLIVAN, TIMOTHY, lawyer; b. Detroit, May 16, 1948; s. Paul Gilmary and Virginia (Rosier) S.; m. Marsha Rosenberg Sullivan, June 19, 1971; children: Eileen A., Hugh V. BA Journalism, U. Mich., 1970; JD, Georgetown U., 1975. Bar: Va. 1975, D.C. 1976. Contract negotiator CIA, Washington, 1973-75; assoc. Fried, Frank, Harris, Shriver & Kampelman, Washington, 1975-78; ptnr. Capell, Howard, Knabe & Cobbs P.A., Washington, 1978-83, Dykema Gossett, Washington, 1983-95; lectr. in field. Narrator (audio cassette) How to Negotiate Government Contracts, 1986. Citizen mem. Alexandria Commn. Persons with Disabilities, Va., 1992—. Sgt. U.S. Army, 1970-73. Mem. ABA, Nat. Contract Mgmt. Assn., Univ. Club Washington, Congl. Country Club (bd. govs.). Roman Catholic. Avocations: reading, sports. Office: Adduci Mastriani & Schaumberg, L.L.P. Ste 250 1140 Connecticut Ave NW Washington DC 20036

SULLIVAN, TIMOTHY JACKSON, law educator, academic administrator; b. Ravenna, Ohio, Apr. 15, 1944; s. Ernest Tulio and Margaret Elizabeth (Caris) S.; m. Anne Doubet Klare, Jan. 21, 1973. AB, Coll. William and Mary, 1966; JD, Harvard U., 1969; LLD (hon.), U. Aberdeen, Scotland, 1993. Asst. prof. law Coll. William and Mary, Williamsburg, Va., 1972-75, assoc. prof., 1975-78, prof., 1978-85, Bryan prof. law, dean, 1985-92, pres., 1992—; exec. asst. for policy Office of Gov. Charles S. Robb, Richmond, Va., 1982-85; atty. Freeman, Drapers' Co., London, 1992; vis. prof. law U. Va., Charlottesville, 1981; exec. dir. Gov.'s Commn. on Va.'s Future, Richmond, 1982-84; vice-chmn. Gov.'s Commn. on Fed. Spending, Richmond, 1986; mem. Gov.'s Fellows Selection Com., 1985-90, Gov.'s Commn. on Sexual Assault and Substance Abuse on the Coll. Campus (chmn. enforcement subcom.), 1991-92; counsel Commn. on Future of Va.'s Jud. System, 1987-89. Mem. Va. State Bd. Edn., Richmond, 1987-92; chair Gov.'s Task Force on Intercollegiate Athletics, 1992-93. Decorated Bronze Star. Fellow Am. Bar Fedn., Va. Bar Fedn.; mem. ABA, Va. State Bar, Va. Bar Assn., Bull and Bear Club, Phi Beta Kappa, Omicron Delta Kappa, Univ. Club (N.Y.C., Washington). Democrat. Avocations: wine, swimming, reading. Home: Pres House Williamsburg VA 23185 Office: Coll William & Mary PO Box 8795 Williamsburg VA 23187-8795

SULLIVAN, TIMOTHY PATRICK, ophthalmologist; b. Bklyn., Aug. 17, 1950; s. Timothy and Johanna (Gaine) S.; m. Karen Cioffi, Aug. 6, 1977; children: Brian, Meghan, Michael. BS, Manhattan Coll., 1973; MS, Columbia U., N.Y.C., 1974; MD, SUNY, Bklyn., 1978; ed. numerous continuing edn. courses, 1980-94. Diplomate Am. Bd. Ophthalmology; lic. physician, Iowa, N.Y., Pa., Conn., N.J. Intern St. Vincent's Hosp., N.Y.C., 1978-79; resident in ophthalmology N.Y. Hosp.-Cornell U. Med. Ctr., N.Y.C., 1979-81, chief resident, 1981-82; fellow in cornea-external disease N.Y. Eye and Ear Infirmary, N.Y.C., 1982-83, asst. attending ophthalmologist, 1982-89; pvt. practice N.Y.C., 1982-83; asst. attending ophthalmologist Manhattan Eye, Ear, Nose and Throat Hosp., N.Y.C., 1982-88; asst. attending ophthalmologist, clin. instr. Cornell Med. Coll., N.Y.C., 1982-90; asst. attending ophthalmologist Southampton (N.Y.) Hosp., 1983-93; pvt. practice Hampton Eye Physicians & Surgeons, P.C., Southampton, 1983-93, Wolfe Clinic, P.C., Marshalltown, Iowa, 1993-94; ptnr. White and Sullivan, MD, P.A., Basking Ridge, N.J., 1994—; asst. attending ophthalmologist, clin. inst. U. Med. and Dentistry of N.J., 1995—. Fellow ACS, EBBA Paton Soc. (sustaining); mem. AMA, Am. Coll. Eye Surgeons, N.J. State Med. Soc., Am. Acad. Ophthalmology, Contact Lens Soc. Ophthalmologists, Somerset County Med. Soc., Castroviejo Soc., Downstate Alumni Assn., Manhattan Coll. Alumni Assn., Rotary (bernardsville and Southampton chpts.). Home: 71 Landau Rd Basking Ridge NJ 07920 Office: Somerset Hills Eye Care Ctr 40 Morristown Rd Bernardsville NJ 07924

SULLIVAN, WALTER FRANCIS, bishop; b. Washington, June 10, 1928; s. Walter Francis and Catherine Jeanette (Vanderloo) S. B.A., St. Mary's Sem. U., Balt., 1947; S.T.L., St. Mary's Sem. U., 1953; J.C.L., Catholic U. Am., 1960. Ordained priest Roman Catholic Ch., 1953; asst. pastor St. Andrews Ch., Roanoke St. Mary's, Star of Sea, Ft. Monroe, 1956-58; sec. Diocesan Tribunal, 1960-65; chancellor Diocese of Richmond, Va., from 1965; rector Sacred Heart Cathedral, Richmond, from 1967; ordained aux. bishop of Richmond, 1970, bishop of Richmond, 1974—. Office: Chancery Office 811 Cathedral Pl Ste B Richmond VA 23220-4801*

SULLIVAN, WALTER J., school system administrator. Supt. Skaneateles (N.Y.) Ctrl. Sch. Recipient Nat. Superintendent of the Yr. awd., New York, Am. Assn. of School Administrators, 1993. Office: Skaneateles Ctrl Sch 49 E Elizabeth St Skaneateles NY 13152-1337

SULLIVAN, WALTER LAURENCE, writer, educator; b. Nashville, Jan. 4, 1924; s. Walter Laurence and Aline (Armstrong) S.; m. Jane Harrison, Aug. 30, 1947; children: Pamela Sullivan Chenery, Walter Laurence, John Harrison. BA, Vanderbilt U., 1947; MFA, U. Iowa, 1949; Litt.D., Episc. Theol. Sem., Lexington, Ky., 1973. Instr. dept. English Vanderbilt U., Nashville, 1949-52, asst. prof., 1952-57, assoc. prof., 1957-63, prof., 1963—; lectr. on pub. TV. Author: Sojourn of a Stranger, 1957, The Long, Long Love, 1959, Death by Melancholy: Essays on Modern Southern Fiction, 1972, A Requiem for the Renascence: The State of Fiction in the Modern South, 1976, In Praise of Blood Sports and Other Essays, 1990, Allen Tate: A Recollection, 1988, A Time to Dance, 1995, The War the Women Lived, 1995; coauthor: Southern Fiction Today: Renascence and Beyond, 1969, Southern Literary Study: Problems and Possibilities, 1975, Writing From the Inside, 1983; writer, narrator film for pub. TV; contbr. articles to publs. 1st lt. USMC, 1943-46. Ford Found. fiction fellow, 1951-52; Rockefeller Found. fiction fellow, 1957-58. Fellow Fellowship of So. Writers. Roman Catholic. Home: 6104 Chickering Ct Nashville TN 37215-5002 Office: Vanderbilt U Dept English Nashville TN 37235

SULLIVAN, WILLIAM COURTNEY, retired communications executive; b. Webster Groves, Mo., Aug. 26, 1928; s. William J. and Corinne (Courtney) S.; m. Valerie Blaes, June 20, 1953; children: William C. Jr., Kathleen M., Margaret M. Stonecipher. Student, St. Louis U., 1946-49, J.D. cum laude, 1952. Atty. Southwestern Bell Telephone Co., St. Louis, 1956-58, atty. Mo.-Ill. area, 1958-64, gen. atty. Kans. area, 1964-70, gen. atty. Mo.-Ill., 1970-74, gen. solicitor Mo.-Ill., 1974-75, gen. solicitor gen. headquarters, 1975-84, v.p., assoc. gen. counsel, 1984-91;, 1991. Bd. dirs. Sea & Sky Found., Miami, 1985—. Town and Country Police Commn., Mo., 1986—, Corp. Disputes Resolution, Inc., 1990—. Capt. USAF, 1952-55. Mem. ABA, Mo. Bar Assn., Kans. Bar Assn., St. Louis Bar Assn., Bellerive Country Club, The Club, Pelican Bay Country Club. Roman Catholic. Avocations: golf, tennis, reading, sailing, travel.

SULLIVAN, WILLIAM FRANCIS, lawyer; b. San Francisco, May 6, 1952; s. Francis Michael and Jane Frances (Walsh) S.; m. Joanne Mary Nebeling; children: Matthew, Meghan, Kathleen. AB, U. Calif., Berkeley, 1974; JD, UCLA, 1977. Bar: Calif. 1977, U.S. Dist. Ct. (no. dist.) Calif. 1977, U.S. Ct. Appeals (9th cir.) 1977, U.S. Dist. Ct. (ea. dist.) Calif. 1978, U.S. Ct. Appeals (D.C. cir.) 1979, U.S. Ct. Appeals (fed. cir.) 1985, U.S. Dist. Ct. (so. dist.) Calif. 1986, U.S. Dist. Ct. (cen. dist.) Calif. 1990, U.S. Supreme Ct. 1986. Assoc. Chickering & Gregory, San Francisco and Washington, 1977-81; assoc. Brobeck, Phleger & Harrison, San Diego and San Francisco, 1981-84, ptnr., 1984—; mng. ptnr. Brobeck, Phleger & Harrison, San Diego, 1992-96; firmwide mng. ptnr. Brobeck, Phleger & Harrison, 1996—; panelist Calif. Continuing Edn. Bar; instr. Fed. Practice Program, U.S. No. Dist., chair Litigation sect., 1992, U.S. Dist. Ct. (no. dist.) Calif., 1980; instr. Coll. of Advocacy, Hastings Law Sch.; adv. bd. AMICUS Info. Svcs. Mem. ABA, Assn. Bus. Trial Lawyers (bd. govs. San Diego chpt. 1993-95), Calif. Bar Assn. (litigation sect.), San Francisco Bar Assn., San Diego Bar Assn., Barristers Club San Francisco (bd. dirs. 1984-86, pres. 1985), Calif. Young Lawyers Assn. (bd. dirs. 1986-89, sec. 1987-99, 1st v.p. 1988-89). Democrat. Roman Catholic. Office: Brobeck Phleger & Harrison 550 W C St Ste 1300 San Diego CA 92101-3532

SULLIVAN, WILLIAM HALLISEY, JR., professional football team executive; b. Lowell, Mass., Sept. 13, 1915; s. William H. and Vera F. (Sullivan); m. Mary K. Malone, Dec. 29, 1941; children: Charles W., Kathleen Marie, Mary Jeannie, Nancie Vera, William Hallissey III, Patrick Jerome. A.B., Boston Coll., 1937, postgrad., 1938-39; postgrad., Harvard U. (summer 1938). Publicity dir. Boston Coll., 1938-40; spl. asst. to dir. athletics U. Notre Dame, 1941-42; with U.S. Naval Aviation Tng. Program, 1942-45; dir. pub. relations U.S. Naval Acad., 1946, Boston Braves, 1946-52; owner All Star Sports, Inc., 1952-55; asst. to pres. Met. Coal & Oil Co., Dorchester, Mass., 1955-56; v.p. Met. Coal & Oil Co., 1956-58, pres., 1958-76; group v.p. Met. Petroleum Co., 1977-84; owner New Eng. Patriots Football Club, 1975-88; pres. U.S. Naval Aviation Tng. Program; pres. Am. Football League, 1963-65; chmn. TV com., merger com. Nat. and Am. football leagues; bd. dirs. Brynwood Ptnrs., Air Express Internat., Dana-Farber Inst.; chmn. bd. NFL Properties, Inc.; incorporator Union Savs. Bank. Chmn. Greater Boston Stadium Authority, 1962-64; chmn. Christmas Seal campaign Mass. TB Assn., 1963-64; bd. dirs. Cath. Counseling Svc., Mass. Eye Rsch. Corp., Stonehill Coll.; mem. Pres.'s Coun. Boston Coll. With USNR, 1942-46. Mem. New Eng. Fuel Dealers Assn., Knight of Malta. Clubs: Indian Creek Country, Hundred of Mass. (dir.), Algonquin (Boston), Woodland Golf, Vesper Country, Fort Hill, Oyster Harbors, Atlantis Country Club (Fla.). Office: care New England Patriots Sullivan Stadium RR 1 Foxboro MA 02035

SULLIVAN, WILLIAM JAMES, university president; b. Freeport, Ill., Dec. 20, 1930; s. Arlend Eugene and Bessie (Burton) S. B.A. in Philosophy, St. Louis U., 1954, M.A. in Philosophy, 1956, Ph.L., 1956; S.T.L., Faculté de Theologie, Lyons, France, 1962; M.A., Yale U., 1966, M.Phil. in Religious Studies, 1967, Ph.D. in Religious Studies, 1971; D.D. (hon.), Concordia Sem. in Exile, 1977. Joined S.J., Roman Cath. Ch. Tchr. classical lang. Creighton Prep. Sch., 1955-58; asst. prof. theology Marquette U., 1967-71; dean Sch. Div., St. Louis U., 1971-75; provost Seattle U., 1975-76, pres., 1976—; bd. dirs. Internat. Fedn. Catholic Univs., 1978-88, Maryville Coll., 1972-75, Am. Council Edn., 1978-81, U. San Francisco, 1976-84; founder, bd. dirs. Wash. Student Loan Guaranty Assn.; trustee Carnegie Found. Advancement of Teaching, 1985—; mem. Wash. State Higher Edn. Facilities Authority, 1984—, Wash. State Math. Coalition, co-chair with Gov. Gardner, 1990—, Wash. State Coalition for Student Svc., 1990—; bd. dirs. U.S. Bank of Wash. Contbr. articles on theology, edn. and cultural topics to profl. jours., popular publs. Bd. dirs. World Without War Coun., Seattle, 1978-81, Seattle United Way, 1979-81, Creighton U., 1982-86, Loyola U. Chgo., 1983-87, Seattle Found.; chmn. host com. 1990 Goodwill Games, 1986-90. Recipient Edmund Campion award Campion High Sch., 1970; Pope John XXIII award Viterbo Coll., 1979; Brotherhood award NCCJ, 1981; Torch of Liberty award Anti-Defamation League, B'nai Brith; named Seattle First Citizen, 1990. Mem. Assn. Cath. Colls. and Univs. (bd. dirs. 1986—), Nat. Assn. Ind. Colls. and Univs. (bd. dirs. 1983-86), Assn. Jesuit Colls. and Univs. (bd. dirs. 1986—), Wash. Friends Higher Edn., Ind. Colls. Wash., Seattle C. of C. (dir. 1979-82, 88—). Catholic. Clubs: Rainier, Seattle Yacht, Columbia Tower (bd. dirs.), University (Seattle). Lodge: Rotary (Seattle). Office: Seattle U Broadway and Madison Seattle WA 98122

SULLOWAY, FRANK JONES, historian; b. Concord, N.H., Feb. 2, 1947; s. Alvah Woodbury and Alison (Green) S.; 1 child, Ryan. AB summa cum laude, Harvard U., 1969, AM in History of Sci., 1971, PhD History of Sci., 1978. Jr. fellow Harvard U. Soc. Fellows, 1974-77; mem. Sch. Social Sci. Inst. for Advanced Study, Princeton, N.J., 1977-78; rsch. fellow Miller Inst. for Basic Rsch. in Sci., U. Calif., Berkeley, 1978-80; rsch. fellow MIT, Cambridge, 1980-81, vis. scholar, 1989—; postdoctoral fellow Harvard U., Cambridge, 1981-82, vis. scholar, 1984-89; rsch. fellow Univ. Coll., London, 1982-84; Vernon prof. biography Dartmouth Coll., Hanover, N.H., 1986. Author: Freud, Biologist of the Mind, 1979 (Pfizer award History Sci. Soc. 1980), Born to Rebel, 1996; contbr. numerous articles on Charles Darwin and Sigmund Freud to profl. jours. Fellow NEH, 1980-81, NSF, 1981-82, John Simon Guggenheim Meml. Found., 1982-83, MacArthur Found., 1984-89. Fellow AAAS (mem. electorate nominating com. sect. L 1988-91, 94—); mem. History of Sci. Soc. (fin. com. 1987-92, com. on devel. 1988-92). Home: 18 Traymore St Cambridge MA 02140-2214 Office: MIT Bldg E51-128 Cambridge MA 02139

SULTAN, TERRIE FRANCES, curator; b. Asheville, N.C., Oct. 28, 1952; d. Norman and Phyllis Ellen (Galumbeck) Sultan; m. Christopher French, June, 1988. BFA, Syracuse U., 1973; MA, John F. Kennedy U., 1985. Exhbn. dir. Source Gallery, San Francisco, 1982-83; adj. curator Oakland (Calif.) Mus., 1984-85; dir. pub. affairs and pub. programs New Mus. Contemporary Art, N.Y.C., 1986-88; curator contemporary art Corcoran Gallery of Art, Washington, 1988—. Author: Representation and Text in the Work of Robert Morris, 1990, Redefining The Terms of Engagement: The Art of Louise Bourgeois, 1944; also exhbn. catalogues. Mem. Am. Assn. Museums, Coll. Art Assn., ArTable. Democrat. Office: The Corcoran Gallery Art 17th St New York Ave NW Washington DC 20006

SULTANA, NAJMA, psychiatrist; b. Nirmal, Andhra, India; July 22, 1948; came to U.S. 1973; d. Khaja Moinuddin and Mujib (Unnisa) Begum; m. Khaja Mohiuddin, July 8, 1971 (div. 1978); m. M. Rashid Chaudhry, Oct. 16, 1981. M.B.B.S. Gandhi Med. Coll., Hyderaba, India, 1973. Resident in psychiatry SUNY/Kings County Hosp. Ctr., Bklyn., 1976-78, fellow child psychiatry, 1978-80; asst. clin. physician S. Beach Psychiat. Ctr., S.I., N.Y., 1980-81; asst. clin. prof. SUNY Downstate Med. Ctr., N.Y.C., 1981-94; attending psychiatrist King's County Hosp., Bklyn., 1981-94, Creedmoile Psychiatric Ctr., 1994—. Exec. bd. mem. Balkan Rape Response Team; co-pres. Coalition for Intervention Against Genocide in Bosnia; pres. Am. Fedn. of Muslims from India, v.p.; founding mem. G.O.P.I.O.; bd. dirs. T.O.U.C.H. Recipient Non-Resident Indian Internat. Women's award, 1992. Mem. Am. Psychiat. Assn. Democrat. Muslim.

SULTANIK, KALMAN, professional society administrator; b. Miechow, Poland, Apr. 12, 1916; came to U.S., 1952, naturalized, 1966; s. Samuel and Gitla (Wechadlowski) S.; m. Broniz Burganski, Jan. 28, 1947; children: Aaron, Samuel. Student, Sch. Econs., Tel aviv, 1949-51, columbia U., 1954-57; LL.B., Columbia U., 1976. Leader Hanoar Hatzioni, Poland, 1935-39; co-founder Ichud Movement, Postwar Poland; active Aliyah Bet, 1946-48; del. 22d Zionist Congress, Basel, Switzerland, 1946; mem. Central Com. Liberated Jews, Munich, Germany, 1947; with World Confedn. United Zionists, N.Y.C., 1948—, exec. co-pres., 1972—; chmn. Thedor Herzl Found., 1975—; sponsor monthly lit. publ. Midstream and Herzl Press, 1974—. Author: The World Confederation of General Zionists: Its Aims, Program and Achievements, 1974; editor: The Zionist Movement in the New Era, 1955, Zionism for Our Day, 1960; contbr. articles to profl. jours. V.p. World Jewish Congress, 1977—; bd. dirs. United Israel Appeal, 1973; mem. U.S. Holocaust Meml. Council, 1980—; sec.-gen. Gen. Zionist Constructive Fund, 1948—; head orgn. dept. World Zionist Orgn., 1981. Home: 120 E 81st St New York NY 10028-1428 Office: 30 E 60th St New York NY 10022-1008

SULTZER, BARNET MARTIN, microbiology and immunology researcher; b. Union City, N.J., Mar. 24, 1929; s. Moses Joseph and Florence Gertrude (Fischer) S.; m. Judith Ray Moreinis, Aug. 26, 1956; 1 child, Steven Bennett. BS, Rutgers U., 1950; MS, Mich. State U., 1951, PhD, 1958. Rsch. assoc. Princeton (N.J.) Labs., Inc., 1958-64; from asst. prof. to prof. microbiology SUNY, Bklyn., 1964-94, prof. emeritus, 1994—, interim chmn. dept. microbiology, 1980-82; vis. scientist Karolinska Inst., Stockholm, 1971-72; vis. prof. Pasteur Inst., Paris, 1979-80; adj. prof. Fels Inst. of Cancer Rsch. and Molecular Biology, Temple U., Phila., 1995—. Assoc. editor Jour. of Immunology, 1983-86; contbr. book chpts. and over 50 articles to profl. jours. on microbiology and immunology; mem. editl. bd. Infection and Immunity, 1980-94. Pres. Tenants Assn. Gateway Plz., Manhattan, N.Y., 1990-92; mem. Cmty. Bd. #1, Manhattan, 1989-94. 1st lt. USMC, 1952-55. Pres.'s fellow Am. Soc. Microbiology, 1957; grantee USPHS, NIH, Office of Naval Rsch., 1967-94. Mem. AAAS, Am. Soc. Microbiology, Am. Assn. Immunologists, N.Y. Acad. Sci., Harvey Soc., Internat. Endotoxin Soc., Reticuloendothelial Soc., Sigma Xi. Achievements include patent for chemical detoxification of endotoxins and discovery of the genetic basis for mammalian responses to endotoxins including immunological and pathophysiological effects; developed first commercial immunological pregnancy test. Office: SUNY Health Sci Ctr 450 Clarkson Ave Brooklyn NY 11203-2012

SULYK, STEPHEN, archbishop; b. Balnycia, Western Ukraine, Oct. 2, 1924; s. Michael and Mary (Denys) S. Student, Ukrainian Cath. Sem. of Holy Spirit, Fed. Republic Germany, 1945-48, St. Josaphat's Sem., 1948-52; Licentia in Sacred Theology, Cath. U. Am., 1952. Ordained priest Ukrainian Cath. Ch., 1952. Assoc. pastor Omaha, 1952; assoc. pastor Bklyn., 1953, Minersville, Pa., 1954, Youngstown, Ohio, 1955; pastor Ch. Sts. Peter and Paul, Phoenixville, Pa., 1955, St. Michael's Ch., Frackville, Pa., 1957-61, Assumption of Blessed Virgin Mary Ch., Perth Amboy, N.J., 1962-81; sec. Archeparchy Chancery, 1956-57; adminstr. St. Nicholas, Phila., 1961; archbishop Met. of Ukraine-Rite Catholics of Archeparchy, Phila., 1981—; vice chmn. Priests Senate, 1977-78; bd. dirs. Diocesan Adminstrn., 1972-79; pres. Ascension Manor, Inc.; archbishop Ukranian Rite Caths. Archeparchy Phila., Met. Ukranian-Rite Caths. U.S.A.; chmn. Priest's Senate; chmn. ad-hoc inter-rite com. Nat. Cath. Conf. Bishops/U.S. Cath. Conf., 1991. Mem. Providence Assn. Am. (Supreme Protector), Coll. Bishops of Roman Cath. Ch., Presidium of Synod of Ukranian Cath. Bishops (treas.). Office: Archdiocese of Philadelphia 827 N Franklin St Philadelphia PA 19123-2004*

SULZBERGER, ARTHUR OCHS, newspaper executive; b. N.Y.C., Feb. 5, 1926; s. Arthur Hays and Iphigene (Ochs) S.; m. Barbara Grant, July 2, 1948 (div. 1956); children: Arthur Ochs, Karen Alden; m. Carol Fox, Dec. 19, 1956 (dec. Aug. 1995); 1 child, Cynthia Fox; 1 adopted child, Cathy; m. Allison Stacey Cowles, Mar. 9, 1996. B.A., Columbia, 1951; LL.D., Dartmouth, 1964, Bard Coll., 1967; L.H.D., Montclair State Coll., 1972, Tufts U.; LLD (hon.), U. Scranton; L.H.D., Columbia U., 1992. With N.Y. Times, N.Y.C., 1951—; asst. treas. N.Y. Times, 1958-63, pres., 1963-79, pub., 1963-92, chmn., chief exec. officer, 1963—, also bd. dirs.; dir. Times Printing Co., Chattanooga. Trustee emeritus Columbia U.; trustee Met. Mus. Art, chmn. bd. trustees, 1987—. Served to capt. USMCR, World War II. Mem. SAR, Overseas Press Club, Explorers Club, Met. Club (Washington). Office: NY Times Co 229 W 43rd St New York NY 10036-3913

SULZBERGER, ARTHUR OCHS, JR., newspaper publisher; b. Mt. Kisco, N.Y., Sept. 22, 1951; s. Arthur Ochs Sulzberger and Barbara Winslow Grant; m. Gail Gregg, May 24, 1975; children: Arthur Gregg, Ann Alden. BA, Tufts U., 1974; postgrad., Harvard U. Bus. Sch., 1985. Reporter The Raleigh (N.C.) Times, 1974-76; corr. AP, London, 1976-78; Washington corr. N.Y. Times, 1978-81, city hall reporter, 1981, asst. metro editor, 1981-82, group mgr. advt. dept., 1983-84, sr. analyst corp. planning, 1985, prodn. coordinator, 1985-87, asst. pub., 1987-88, dep. pub., 1988-92, pub., 1992—; bd. dirs. Times Square Business Improvement Dist. Bd. dirs. N.Y.C. Outward Bound Ctr., N.Y.C., 1988, chmn. 1992. Mem. Newspaper Assn. of Am. Office: The NY Times 229 W 43rd St New York NY 10036-3913

SUMANTH, DAVID JONNAKOTY, industrial engineer, educator; b. Machilipatnam, India, Jan. 28, 1946; came to U.S., 1972; s. John Devraj and Nancy (David) Jonnakoty; m. Chaya J. Victor, June 26, 1974; children: John J., Paul J. B in Mech. Engring., Osmania U., India, 1967, M in Mech. Engring., 1969; MS in Indsl. Engring., Ill. Inst. Tech., 1974, PhD in Indsl. Engring., 1979. Teaching/research asst. Ill. Inst. Tech., Chgo., 1973-78, instr., 1979; asst. prof. indsl. engring. U. Miami, Coral Gables, Fla., 1979-83, founding dir. productivity research group, 1979—, dir. grad. studies, 1980-83, assoc. prof. indsl. engring., 1983-88, Coll. Engring. coordinator MBA/MSIE, 1984-93; prof. indsl. engring. U. Miami, Coral Gables, 1988—; chmn. 1st and 2d Internat. Conf. on Productivity Rsch., 3d, 4th, 5th Internat. Conf. on Productivity and Quality Rsch. Author: Productivity Engineering and Management, 1984, internat. student edit., 1985, Spanish edit., 1990, Indian edit., 1990, coll. custom series edit., 1994, also instrs. manual, (script) Total Productivity Management, 1985; editor: Productivity Management Frontiers-I, 1987, II, 1989, Productivity and Quality Management Frontiers III, 1991, IV, 1993, V, 1995. Recipient over 60 honors, awards and recognitions including YMCA Edn. Gold medal, 1969, Freedoms Found., 1987; fellow U. Miami Eaton Honors Coll., 1986, fellow World Acad. Productivity Sci., 1989; gov.'s appointee as sr. judge Fla. Sterling award, 1992-93, judge, 1993-94, 94-95. Mem. Am. Inst. Indsl. Engrs. (sr. mem., pres. Miami chpt. 1982-83, bd. dirs. 1983-84, nat. asst. dir. productivity mgmt. 1984—, chairperson rsch. com. 1987, Outstanding Indsl. Engr. of Yr. Miami chpt. 1983, 84); Productivity Ctr. (trustee 1985-89), Internat. Soc. for Productivity and

Quality Rsch. (founder 1993, founding pres. 1993-95, chmn. 1995—). Republican. Baptist. Avocations: reading, writing, people. Office: U Miami Productivity Rsch Group Coral Gables FL 33124

SUMICHRAST, JOZEF, illustrator, designer; b. Hobart, Ind., July 26, 1948; s. Joseph Steven and Stella Sumichrast; m. Susan Ann Snyder, June 22, 1972; children—Kristin Ann, Lindsey Ann. Student, Am. Acad. Art, Chgo. Illustrator Stevens Gross, Chgo., 1971-72; illustrator Eaton & Iwen, Chgo., 1972-73, Graphique, Chgo., 1973-74; pres. Jozef Sumichrast, Deerfield, Ill., 1975—. Author, illustrator: Onomatopoeia, Q is For Crazy; exhbns. include: 200 Years of Am. Illustration, N.Y. Hist. Soc. Mus., Chgo. Hist. Soc., Finland Lath Mus., Library of Congress, Los Angeles County Mus. Art, Md. Inst. Graphic Art, State Colo. Community Coll., Tokyo Designers Gakiun Coll.; represented in permanent collections: Soc. Illustrators, Chgo. Hist. Soc., Milw. Art Dirs. Club, Phoenix Art Dirs. Club, Columbia Coll., U. Tex., contbr. numerous articles to profl. periodicals. Recipient award for children's book Chgo. Book Clinic, 1978; Gold medal Internat. Exhibition of Graphic Arts, Brazil, 1981; Gold medal Chgo. Artist Guild, 1980, 81; Silver medal N.Y. Art Dirs. Club, 1983; numerous others. Mem. Soc. Illustrators.

SUMME, GREGORY LOUIS, management consultant; b. Ft. Mitchell, Ky., Nov. 25, 1956; s. James Augustine and Mary Elizabeth (McQueen) S.; m. Susan Louise Stevie, Aug. 1, 1981; children: Heather, Erin. BSEE, U. Ky., 1978; MS, U. Cin., 1980; MBA with distinction, U. Pa., 1983. Design engr. Mostek Corp., Dallas, 1980-81; mktg. specialist Gen. Electric Plastics Europe, The Netherlands, 1982; ptnr. McKinsey & Co. Inc., Atlanta and Hong Kong, 1983-90; gen, mgr., comml. motors GE, 1991-93; sr. v.p. and gen. mgr. Allied Signal Avionics, 1993—; pres. Allied Signal Engine, Phoenix. Contbr. articles to profl. jours. Alex Proudfoot fellow Wharton Sch., U. Pa., 1981-83. Mem. IEEE, Eta Kappa Nu. Roman Catholic. Avocations: running, squash, golf. Office: Allied Signal Engine Mail Stop 301222 PO Box 52181 Phoenix AZ 85072-2181*

SUMMERALL, PAT (GEORGE ALLAN SUMMERALL), sportscaster; b. Lake City, Fla., May 10, 1931; m. Katherine Summerall; children: Susan, Jay, Kyle. Degree in Education, U. Ark., M. in Russain History. Football player Detroit Lions, 1952-53, Chgo. Cardinals, 1953-57, N.Y. Giants, 1958-61; played briefly in St. Louis Cardinals baseball orgn.; with CBS Sports, 1962-94; dir. sports Sta. WCBS-Radio, N.Y.C., 1964-71; host morning program Sta. WCBS-TV, 1966-67; sportscaster early news Sta. WCBS-TV, N.Y.C.; with CBS Radio Network; sportscaster Sports Time, Predictions, Profiles; host CBS Sports Spectacular.; lead play-by-play announcer NFL Football coverage CBS Sports, anchor golf and tennis coverage; sports commentator, football analyst Fox Network, 1994—. Named Sportscaster of Yr., 1977. Office: care FOX Network PO Box 900 Beverly Hills CA 90213-0900

SUMMERFIELD, JOHN ROBERT, textile curator; b. St. Paul, Feb. 21, 1917; s. Isaac and Irene (Longini) S.; m. Anne Benson, July 14, 1945. S.B. in Mech. Engring., MIT, 1938; M.B.A., U. Calif.-Berkeley, 1947, Ph.D. in Econs., 1954. Asst. prof. Sloan Sch. Mgmtg., MIT, 1952-54; br. chief CIA, Washington, 1954-56; project leader The Rand Corp., Santa Monica, Calif., 1956-62; corp. economist Douglas Aircraft Co., Santa Monica, 1962-66; v.p. econ. planning Western Airlines, Los Angeles, 1966-70; staff v.p. econ. planning Pan Am. Airways, N.Y.C., 1970-71; pres. Summerfield Assocs., Pacific Palisades, Calif., 1972-92; vis. curator Fowler Mus. Cultural History, UCLA, 1993—. Co-curator exhbns. of antique Minangkabau ceremonial textiles from West Sumatra, Textile Mus., Washington, 1990-91, Santa Barbara (Calif.) Mus. Art, 1991, Bellevue (Wash.) Art Mus., 1992, Utah Mus. Fine Art, 1992. Served to lt. USNR, 1942-45.

SUMMERFIELD, MARTIN, physicist; b. N.Y.C., Oct. 20, 1916; s. Jacob and Augusta (Tobias) S.; m. Eileen Budin, Aug. 31, 1945; 1 dau., Jacqueline. B.S., Bklyn. Coll., 1936; M.S., Calif. Inst. Tech., 1938, Ph.D., 1941. Asst. chief Air Corps Jet Propulsion Project, Calif. Inst. Tech., 1940-43, chief, rocket research div., 1945-49; chief, rocket devel. div. Aerojet Engring. Corp., Azusa, Calif., 1943-45; mem. subcom. on fuels NACA, 1948-49, subcom. on combustion, 1949-50; prof. jet propulsion Princeton U., 1951-78, prof. emeritus, 1978—; Astor prof. applied sci. N.Y. U., 1978-80; tech. dir. Project Squid, 1949-51; chief scientist Flow Industries Inc., 1975-78; pres. Princeton Combustion Research Labs., 1978-94; editor Aeros. Publ. Program, 1949-52; editor in chief Jour. Am. Rocket Soc., 1951-57; editor Jet Propulsion; also tech. editor Astronautics, 1957-63; editor in chief AIAA series on Progress in Astronautics and Aeros., 1960-90, mem. editorial bd., 1990—; editor in chief Astronautica Acta, 1964-69; cons. U.S. Army Rsch. Office, 1968-71; mem. adv. com. chem. propulsion NASA, 1968-71, Inst. of Aerospace and Astronautics, Cheng-Kung Univ., Tainan, Taiwan, 1985—; chmn. com. on toxicity hazards of materials NRC, 1984-86, mem. com. on energetic materials, 1984-87. Patentee on rocket motors and related devices. Recipient Pendray award, 1954; Wyld award, 1977. Fellow AAAS, AIAA (v.p. 1963-65), Am. Rocket Soc. (pres. 1962-63), Inst. of Advanced Tech., U. Texas, 1991—; mem. Inst. Aeronautics and Astronomy, Internat. Acad. Astronautics, Nat. Acad. Engring., ASME (Heat Transfer award 1978), Internat. Astronautical Fedn. (v.p. 1963-65), Sigma Xi. Office: Martin Summerfield Assoc Inc 6 Marvin Ct Trenton NJ 08648

SUMMERFORD, BEN LONG, retired artist, educator; b. Montgomery, Ala., Feb. 3, 1924; s. Ben Long and Ollie Jo (Gilchrist) S.; m. Christene Morris, Jan. 30, 1951; children: Jeffrey(dec.), Rebecca, James. Student, Birmingham-Southern Coll., 1942-43; B.A., Am. U., 1948, M.A., 1954; student, Ecole des Beaux Arts., Paris., 1949-50. Staff art dept. Am. U., 1950-88, chmn. dept., 1957-66, 70-86, prof., 1960-88; prof. emeritus, 1988—; artist in residence Dartmouth Coll., 1993. One-man shows include, Balt. Mus. Art, Goucher Coll., Franz Bader Gallery, Washington, Jefferson Place Gallery, Washington; one-man show include Phillips Collection, Washington; represented in permanent collection, Watkins Gallery, Phillips Gallery Art, Corcoran Gallery Art, all Washington, numerous group shows of paintings. Served to ensign USNR, 1943-46. Fulbright fellow, France, 1949-50; J. Paul Getty scholar, Phillips Collection, 1990-91. Home: PO Box 2086 Shepherdstown WV 25443-2086 Office: Am U Dept Art Washington DC 20016

SUMMERLIN, GLENN WOOD, advertising executive; b. Dallas, Ga., Apr. 1, 1934; s. Glenn Wood and Flora (Barrett) S.; student Ga. Inst. Tech., 1951-52; BBA, Ga. State U., 1956, MBA, 1967; m. Anne Valley, Oct. 16, 1971; 1 child, Wade Hampton; children by previous marriage: Glenn Wood III, Edward Lee. Prodn. mgr. Fred Worrill Advt., Atlanta, 1956-65; v.p. sales Grizzard, Atlanta, 1965-74, pres., 1974-94, vice chmn., 1994—. Vice chmn. Polaris dist. Boy Scouts Am., 1967. Vice chmn. Ga. State U. Found., 1974; chmn. distributive edn. adv. com. DeKalb Coll., 1974-76; bd. founders Geo. M. Sparks Scholarship Fund; bd. dirs. Atlanta Humane Soc., 1971—, treas., 1973, 81-82, 84-86, asst. treas. for capital devel., 1987—; mem. steering com. Com. to Honor Hank Aaron, 1982; lay rep. animal care com. Emory U., 1984-85; mem. adv. bd. Families in Action, 1985-86, Soc. Nonprofit Orgns.; bd. dirs. Travelers Aid Metro. Atlanta, 1989-90; mem. Atlanta Sr. Marketers Coun. 100; chmn.'s coun., mem. mktg. adv. com. Crow Canyon Archeol. Ctr., 1993-95. Recipient C.S. Bolen award So. Council Indsl. Editors, 1967; named Outstanding Young Man in DeKalb County, DeKalb Jaycees, 1967, Alumnus of Year, Ga. State U., 1973; recipient Direct Mail Spokesman award Direct Mktg. Assn., 1973. Mem. Mail Advt. Svc. Assn. (pres. N.Ga. chpt. 1959-60), Ga. Assn. Bus. Communicators (pres. 1966-67), Am. Mktg. Assn. (pres. Atlanta chpt. 1973-74), Ga. State U. Alumni Assn. (pres. 1971-72, dir. 1966-78), Sales and Mktg. Execs. Atlanta (dir. 1969-71), Ga. Bus. and Industry Assn. (bd. govs. 1974-76), Asso. Mail Advt. Agys. (pres. 1975-77), Nat. Soc. Fund Raising Execs. (bd. dirs. Ga. chpt. 1984, cert. 1983), Ga. Arms Collectors Assn. (dir. 1974-76, Pres.'s award 1973), Southeastern Antique Arms Collectors (charter; bd. dirs. 1978—), Tenn. Gun Collectors Assn., Tex. Gun Collectors Assn., Assn. Am. Sword Collectors (charter), Mid-Am. Antique Arms Soc. (charter), Mensa, Soc. Animal Welfare Adminstrs., Travelers Aid of Atlanta (bd. dirs. 1989-90), Am. Humane Assn., Omicron Delta Kappa. Home: 1133 Ragley Hall Rd NE Atlanta GA 30319-2511 Office: Grizzard 1144 Mailing Ave SE Atlanta GA 30315-2500

SUMMERS, ANDY (ANDREW JAMES SOMERS), popular musician; b. Poulton-Fylde, England, Dec. 31, 1942; m. Kate Unter (div.); 1 child, Layla. Attended, UCLA, 1969-73. Performed with Zoot Money's Big Roll Band, Dantalion's Chariot, The Soft Machine, The Animals; worked in bands led by Neil Sedaka, Kevin Coyne, Kevin Ayers, Strontium 90; lead guitarist The Police, 1977-84; solo artist, 1984—; albums: (with The Police) Outlandos D'Amour, 1978, Reggatta De Blanc, 1979, Zenyatta Mondatta, 1980, Ghost in the Machine, 1981, Synchronicity, 1983, The Singles; Every Breathe You Take, 1986; (with Robert Fripp) I Advance Masked, 1982, Bewitched, 1984; (solo) XYZ, 1987, Mysterious Barricades, 1988, The Golden Wire, 1989, Charming Snakes, 1990, World Gone Strange, 1991; film soundtracks: Down & Out in Beverly Hills, 1986, Out of Time, 1988, End of the Line, 1988, Weekend at Bernies, 1989.

SUMMERS, ANITA ARROW, public policy and management educator; b. N.Y.C., Sept. 9, 1925; d. Harry I. and Lillian (Greenberg) Arrow; m. Robert Summers, Mar. 29, 1953; children: Lawrence H., Richard F., John S. BA, Hunter Coll., 1945, DHL (hon.), 1995; MA, U. Chgo., 1947. Sr. econ. analyst Standard Oil Co. N.J., N.Y.C., 1947-54; asst. in econs. Yale U., New Haven, Conn., 1956-59; lectr. dept. econs. Swarthmore (Pa.) Coll., 1965-71; sr. economist Fed. Res. Bank Phila., 1971-75, research officer, 1975-79; adj. prof. pub. policy U. Pa., Phila., 1979-82, prof. pub. policy and mgmt., 1982—, dept. chair, 1983-88, co-dir Wharton Urban Decentralization Project, 1987—, sr. scholar Nat. Ctr. on the Edn. Quality of the Workforce, 1991—; expert witness schs. fin. Md., Mass., Va., 1980-85, Md., 1996, bd. dirs. Meridian Bancorp Inc., Reading, Pa., William Penn Found., Phila.; chair bd. dirs. Mathematica Policy Rsch., inc., Princeton, N.J. Author: Economic Report on the Philadelphia Metropolitan Area, 1985, Economic Development within the Philadelphia Metropolitan Area, 1986, Local Fiscal Issues in the Philadelphia Metropolitan Area, 1987; editor: Urban Change in the United States and Western Europe, 1992; contbr. articles to profl. jours. Chair econ. subcom. Pa. Three Mile Island Commn., Harrisburg, 1979; pres. Lower Merion (Pa.) LWV, 1963-65; mem. Mayor's Econ. Roundtable, Phila., 1984-88; mem. rsch. policy coun., 1992—, Com. for Econ. Devel.; chmn. bd. dirs. Math. Policy Rsch. Inc., 1993—; bd. dirs. William Penn Found., 1993—. Rockefeller Found. resident scholar, Bellagio, Italy, 1986. Mem. Am. Econ. Assn., Assn. for Pub. Policy and Mgmt. (policy coun. 1986), Phi Beta Kappa. Avocations: needlepoint, cooking. Home: 641 Revere Rd Merion Station PA 19066-1007 Office: U Pa Wharton Sch Dept Pub Policy and Mgmt Philadelphia PA 19104

SUMMERS, CAROL, artist; b. Kingston, N.Y., Dec. 26, 1925; s. Ivan Franklin and Theresa (Jones) S.; m. Elaine Smithers, Oct. 2, 1954 (div. Aug. 1967); 1 son, Kyle; m. Joan Ward, May 6, 1974. B.A., Bard Coll., 1951, D.F.A. (hon.), 1974. Tchr. Hunter Coll., Sch. Visual Arts, Haystack Mountain Sch. Crafts, Bklyn. Mus. Art Sch., Pratt Graphic Art Ctr., Chelterham Twp. Art Ctr., Valley Stream Community Art Ctr., U. Pa., Columbia Coll., U. Calif., Santa Cruz, San Francisco Art Inst., U. Utah, Logan, Art Study Abroad, Paris, Casa de Espiritus Allegres Marfil, Mex., USIS workshop tour, India, 1974, 79. Represented in permanent collections at, Mus. Modern Art, Bklyn. Mus., N.Y. Pub. Libr., Libr. of Congress, Nat. Gallery, Victoria and Albert Mus., London, Bibliotheque Nationale, Paris, Kinstmuseum, Basil, Lugan (Switzerland) Art Mus. Grenchen (Switzerland) Art Mus., Malmo (Sweden) Mus., Los Angeles County Mus., Phila. Mus., Balt. Mus., Seattle Mus., Boston Mus., Art Inst. Chgo., Am. embassies in Russia, Can., India, Thailand, Fed. Republic Germany and Eng.; traveling exhibit, Mus. Modern Art, 1964-66; retrospective exhbn. Brooklyn Mus., 1977, Nassau County Mus. Art, 1990, Belles Artes, San Miquel de Allende, Mex., 1992, Miami U. Art Mus., Oxford, Ohio, 1995. Served with USMCR, 1944-48, PTO. Italian govt. study grantee, 1954-55; Louis Comfort Tiffany Found. fellow, 1955, 60; John Simon Guggenheim Found. fellow, 1959; Fulbright fellow, Italy, 1961; Coun. for Internat. Exch. Scholars rsch. grantee, India, 1993-94. Mem. NAD, Calif. Soc. Printmakers. Address: 2817 Smith Grade Santa Cruz CA 95060-9764

SUMMERS, CLYDE WILSON, law educator; b. Grass Range, Mont., Nov. 21, 1918; s. Carl Douglas and Anna Lois (Yontz) S.; m. Evelyn Marie Wahlgren, Aug. 30, 1947; children: Mark, Erica, Craig, Lisa. B.S., U. Ill., 1939, J.D., 1942; LL.M., Columbia, 1946, J.S.D., 1952; LL.D., U. Leuven, Belgium, 1967, U. Stockholm, 1978. Bar: N.Y. 1951. Mem. law faculty U. Toledo, 1942-49, U. Buffalo, 1949-56; prof. law Yale U., 1956-66, Garver prof. law, 1966-75; Jefferson B. Fordham prof. law U. Pa., 1975-90; prof. emeritus, 1990—; Hearing examiner Conn. Commn. on Civil Rights, 1963-71. Co-author: Labor Cases and Material, 1968, 2d edit., 1982, Rights of Union Members, 1979, Legal Protection for the Individual Employee, 1989, 2d edit., 1995; co-editor: Labor Relations and the Law, 1953, Employment Relations and the Law, 1959, Comparative Labor Law Jour., 1984—. Chmn. Gov.'s Com. on Improper Union Mgmt. Practices N.Y. State, 1957-58; chmn. Conn. Adv. Council on Unemployment Ins. and Employment Service, 1960-72; mem. Conn. Labor Relations Bd., 1966-70, Conn. Bd. Mediation and Arbitration, 1964-72. Guggenheim fellow, 1955-56; Ford fellow, 1963-64; German-Marshall fellow, 1977-78; NEH fellow, 1977-78, Fullbright fellow, 1984-85. Mem. Nat. Acad. Arbitrators, Am. Arbitration Assn. (nat. chmn.), Internat. Soc. Labor Law and Social Legislation. Congregationalist. Home: 753 N 26th St Philadelphia PA 19130-2429 Office: U Pa Sch Law 3400 Chestnut St Philadelphia PA 19104-6204

SUMMERS, FRANK WILLIAM, librarian; b. Jacksonville, Fla., Feb. 8, 1933; s. Frank Wesley and Kathleen (Gilreath) S.; 1 son, William Wesley. B.A., Fla. State U., 1955; M.A., Rutgers U., 1959, Ph.D., 1973. Libr. Jacksonville Pub. Libr., 1955, 57; sr. libr. Linden (N.J.) Pub. Libr., 1958-59; dir. Cocoa (Fla.) Pub. Libr., 1959-61; assoc. libr. Providence Pub. Libr., 1961-65; libr. Fla. State Libr., 1965-69; research fellow Rutgers U., New Brunswick, N.J., 1969-70; asst. dean, prof. Coll. Librarianship, U. S.C., 1971-76, dean, 1976-85; dean Sch. Libr. and Info. Studies Fla. State U., Tallahassee, 1985-94, prof., 1994—; lectr. Libr. Sch. U. R.I., 1964-95; libr. surveys in Fla., Ohio, N.Y., S.C., N.C., Ky., Tex. Contbr. profl. jours. Mem. R.I. Bd. Library Commrs., 1964-65. Served to lt. (j.g.) USNR, 1955-57. Mem. ALA (exec. bd., v.p., pres.-elect 1987-88, pres. 1988-89), R.I. Libr. Assn. (pres.), S.C. Libr. Assn. (pres.), Assn. Am. Libr. Schs. (pres.), Beta Phi Mu (exec. sec. 1996—). Home: 505 Live Oak Plantation Rd Tallahassee FL 32312-2335 Office: Fla State Univ Sch Libr & Info Studies 2048 Tallahassee FL 32306-2048

SUMMERS, HARDY, state supreme court justice; b. Muskogee, Okla., July 15, 1933; s. Cleon A. and Fern H. Summers; m. Marilyn, Mar. 16, 1963; children: Julia Clare, Andrew Murray. BA, U. Okla., 1955, LLB, 1957. Asst. county atty. Muskogee County, 1960-62; pvt. practice law Muskogee, 1962-76; dist. judge 15th dist. Okla. Dist. Ct., 1976-85; justice Okla. Supreme Ct., Oklahoma City, 1985—. Sec. Muskogee County Election Bd., 1965-72. Capt. JAGC, USAF, 1957-62. Mem. ABA, Okla. Bar Assn., Okla. Jud. Conf. (pres. 1984). Avocations: fishing, hunting, classical music. Office: Okla Supreme Ct 242 State Capital Bldg Oklahoma City OK 73105*

SUMMERS, JAMES IRVIN, retired advertising executive; b. Lexington, Mo., July 10, 1921; s. William E. and Elizabeth (Hoeflicker) S.; m. Priscilla Barstow West, Jan. 15, 1948 (div. 1985); children: Susanne Cornelia, Elizabeth Barstow, James Irvin, Daniel Edward; m. Jane Browning Beckwith, Oct. 4, 1986. With Harold Cabot & Co. Inc., Boston, 1946-86, exec. v.p., 1960-77, pres., chief exec. officer, dir., chmn. exec. com., 1977-86; mem. editorial bd. Sta. WEEI, Boston, 1985-90, also bd. dirs. Mem. exec. com., bd. dirs., v.p., chmn. Pub. Info. Com., Mass. Bay United Way, 1979-84; chmn. Swampscott Rep. Fin. Com., 1964-75; trustee, bd. mgrs., exec. com. Mass. Eye & Ear Infirmary; trustee Family Svc. Assn. Greater Boston, 1952-62; bd. dirs. Mass. Taxpayers Com., 1984-87; pres. Lit. Vols. Mass., 1987-88; pub. rels. bd. USS Constn. Mus., 1988-91. With USAAF, 1941-45. Decorated Bronze Star. Mem. Greater Boston Advt. Club (bd. dirs. 1984-86), Internat. Fedn. Advt. Agys. (bd. dirs. 1985-86), Am. Assn. Advt. Agys. (bd. dirs., treas. 1985-86), New. Eng. Broadcasters Assn. (bd. dirs. 1985-86), Bay Club, Madison Square Garden Club, Tedesco Country Club, Boca Raton Resort and Club. Home: Boca Highlands 4748 S Ocean Blvd PH 3 Highland Beach FL 33487

SUMMERS, JOSEPH FRANK, author, publisher; b. Newnan, Ga., June 26, 1914; s. John Dawson and Anne (Blalock) S.; B.A. in Math., U. Houston, 1942; profl. cert. meteorology, U. Calif. at L.A., 1943, U. Chgo., 1943; postgrad., U. P.R., 1943-44; M.A. in Math., U. Tex. at Austin, 1947; postgrad. Rice U., 1947-49; m. Evie Margaret Mott, July 8, 1939 (dec. May 1989); children: John Randolph, Thomas Franklin, James Mott. With Texaco Inc., Houston, 1933-42, 49-79, mgr. data processing, 1957-67, asst. gen. mgr. computer svcs. dept., 1967-79, automation cons., 1979-83; pres. Word Lab Inc., Houston, 1983—; instr. math. AAC, Ellington Field, Tex., 1941-42, U. Tex. at Austin, 1946-47. Pres. Houston Esperanto Assn., 1934-39; vol. tutor Thousand Points of Light, 1991—. Capt. AAC, 1942-46. Rice U. fellow, 1947-49. Mem. Assn. Computing Machinery (pres. 1956-58), Nat. Assn. Accts. (past bd. dir.), Am. Petroleum Inst. (mem. data processing and computing com. 1955-59). Author: Mathematics for Bombadiers and Navigators, 1942, Wholly Holey Holy, An Adult American Spelling Book, 1984. Contbg. author: American Petroleum Institute Drilling and Production Practices. Home and Office: 5517 Tilbury Dr Houston TX 77056-2017

SUMMERS, LAWRENCE, deputy secretary treasury department; b. New Haven, 1954; m. Victoria Summers; 2 daughters (twins), 1 son. SB, MIT, 1975; PhD, Harvard U., 1982. Faculty MIT, 1979-82; domestic policy economist Pres'. Coun. Econ. Advisors, 1982-83; Nathaniel Ropes prof. Harvard U., Cambridge, Mass., 1983-93; v.p. devel. econs., chief economist World Bank, 1991-93; under sec. for internat. affairs dept. U.S. Dept. Treasury, Washington, 1993-95, dep. se., 1995—. Author Understanding Unemployment; co-author Reform in Eastern Europe; editor series Tax Policy and the Economy; contbr. numerous articles to profl. jours. Recipient John Bates Clark medal, 1993, Alan Waterman award NSF. Fellow Econometric Soc., Am. Acad. Arts and Scis. Office: US Dept Treasury Office of Dep Sec 1500 Pennsylvania Ave NW Washington DC 20220*

SUMMERS, LAWRENCE H., federal agency administrator; b. New Haven, Conn., Nov. 30, 1954; s. Robert and Anita Arrow S.; m. Victoria Perry; children: Pamela A. and Ruth P., Harry Charles. SB, MIT, 1975; PhD, Harvard, 1982. Prof. econs. MIT, Cambridge, Mass., 1979-82; domestic policy economist Pres. Coun. Econ. Advisors, Washington, 1982-83; Nathaniel Ropes prof. Harvard U., Cambridge, 1983-91; v.p., chief econ. World Bank, Washington, 1991-93; under sec. for internat. affairs U.S. Treasury Dept., Washington, 1993-95, dep. sec., 1995—. Author: (book) Understanding Unemployment, 1990; co-author: (book) Reform in Eastern Europe, 1991; editor: (series) Tax Policy & the Economy, 1987-90, (jour.) Quarterly Jour. of Econs., 1984-90. Recipient Alan Waterman award NSF, 1987, John Bates Clark medal Am. Econs. Assn., 1993. Fellow: Am. Acad. Arts & Scis., Econometric Soc. Office: US Dept Treas 15th & Pennsylvania Ave NW Washington DC 20220

SUMMERS, LORRAINE DEY SCHAEFFER, librarian; b. Phila., Dec. 14, 1946; d. Joseph William and Hilda Lorraine (Ritchey) Dey; m. F. William Summers, Jan. 28, 1984. B.A., Fla. State U., 1968, M.S., 1969. Extension dir. Santa Fe Regional Library, Gainesville, 1969-71; pub. library cons. State Library of Fla., Tallahassee, 1971-78, asst. state librarian, 1978-84; dir. adminstrv. services Nat. Assn. for Campus Activities, Columbia, S.C., 1984-85; asst. state librarian State Library of Fla., Tallahassee, 1985—; cons. in field. Contbr. articles to profl. jours. Del. Pres.'s Com. on Mental Retardation Regional Forum, Atlanta. 1975; del. Fla. Gov.'s Conf. on Library and Info. Services, 1978, 90. Mem. ALA (orgn. com. 1979-83, council 1982-84, 93—, resolutions com. 1983-85, mem. legislation com. 1993-95, nominating com. 1996), Assn. Specialized and Coop. Library Agys. (dir. 1976-82, chmn. planning and orgn. com. 1976-80, chmn. nominating com., 1980-81, chmn. by laws com. 1985-86, exec. bd. state library agy sect. 1983-86, pres. 1987-88, chmn. standards rev. com. 1990-92), Southeastern Library Assn. (exec. bd. 1976-80, v.p., pres.-elect 1994-96, pres. 1996—), Fla. Library Assn. (sec. 1978-79, dir., 1976-80), Zonta (dir. 1992-95). Democrat. Methodist. Office: State Library Fla Ra Gray Bldg Tallahassee FL 32399

SUMMERS, MAX (DUANNE), entomologist, scientist, educator; b. Wilmington, Ohio, June 5, 1938; s. John Williams Summers and Helen Jane (Rolfe) Summers Kantner; children, Mark William, Keith Dwayne; m. Sharon Braunagel, Dec. 28, 1991. AB magna cum laude, Wilmington Coll., 1962; PhD, Purdue U., 1968. Asst. prof. U. Tex., Austin, 1969-73, assoc. prof., 1973-75; prof. entomology Tex. A&M U., College Station, 1977-83, Disting. prof., 1983—, chair agrl. biotech., dir. Ctr. for Advanced Invertebrate Molecular Scis., Inst. Bioscis. and Tech., 1988—; vis. prof. U. Calif., Berkeley, 1976. Editor Virology Jour., 1983—; exec. editor Protein Expression and Purification; contbr. more than 200 articles to profl. jours.; patentee baculovirus expression vector system. Recipient J.V. Osmun Profl. Achievement award, 1988, President's award of honor Tex. A&M U., 1988, Alumni award Wilmington Coll., 1988; Alumni award Purdue U., 1989, Disting. Alumni award, 1992. Fellow AAAS, Am. Acad. Microbiology; mem. NAS, Am. Soc. for Virology (councilor 1982-85, pres. 1991-92), Am. Soc. Microbiology (lectr. Found. for Microbiology 1986-87), Soc. for Invertebrate Pathology, Genetics Soc. Am., Internat. Com. on Taxonomy of Viruses (exec. com., chair invertebrate virus subcom. 1988-93), Am. Soc. for Biochemistry and Molecular Biology, Entomol. Soc. of Am., Am. Acad. Microbiology, Sigma Xi. Home: 1908 Streamside Way Bryan TX 77807-2715 Office: Tex A&M U Dept Entomology 324 Minnie Belle Heep College Station TX 77843-2475

SUMMERS, ROBERT, economics educator; b. Gary, Ind., June 20, 1922; s. Frank and Ella (Lipton) Samuelson; m. Anita Arrow, Mar. 29, 1953; children: Lawrence Henry, Richard Fredric, John Steven. B.S., U. Chgo., 1943; Ph.D., Stanford, 1956; postgrad. (Social Sci. Research Council fellow), King's Coll., U. Cambridge, Eng., 1951-52. Instr. Stanford, 1949-50; mem. faculty Yale, 1952-59, asst. prof., 1956-59; staff mem. Cowles Found., 1955-59; economist RAND Corp., Santa Monica, Calif., 1959-60; cons. RAND Corp., 1960-80; mem. faculty U. Pa. Wharton Sch., 1959—, prof., 1967—, chmn. grad. group in econs., 1967-70, 73-76. Author: (with Lawrence R. Klein) The Wharton Index of Capacity Utilization, 1966, (with others) Strategies for Research and Development, 1967, (with others) A System of International Comparisons of Gross Product and Purchasing Power, 1975, International Comparisons of Real Product and Purchasing Power, 1978, (with others) World Product and Income, 1982; contbr. articles to profl. jours. Served with AUS, 1944-46. Ford Found. faculty rsch. fellow London Sch. Econs., 1966-67; NSF grantee 1957-59, 63-66, 80-82, 86-88, 89-91, 92-94, 94—; resident scholar Rockefeller Found. Study Ctr., 1986. Fellow Econometric Soc.; mem. AAUP, Am. Econs. Assn., Am. Statis. Assn. Home: 641 Revere Rd Merion Station PA 19066-1007 Office: U Pa Dept Econ Philadelphia PA 19104-6297

SUMMERS, ROBERT SAMUEL, lawyer, author, educator; b. Halfway, Oreg., Sept. 19, 1933; s. Orson William and Estella Bell (Robertson) S.; m. Dorothy Millicent Kopp, June 14, 1955; children: Brent, William, Thomas, Elizabeth, Robert. BS in Polit. Sci., U. Oreg., 1955; postgrad. (Fulbright scholar), U. Southampton, Eng., 1955-56; LLB, Harvard U., 1959; postgrad. rsch., Oxford U., 1964-65, 74-75, 81-82, 88-89; LLD (hon.), U. Helsinki, Finland, 1990, U. Göttingen, Germany, 1994. Bar: Oreg. 1959, N.Y. 1974. Asso. King, Miller, Anderson, Nash and Yerke, Portland, Oreg., 1959-60; asst. prof. law U. Oreg., 1960-63, asso. prof., 1964-68; vis. asso. prof. law Stanford U., 1963-64; prof. U. Oreg., 1968-69; prof. Cornell U., 1969-76, McRoberts prof. law, 1976—; summer vis. prof. Ind. U., 1969, U. Mich., 1974, U. Warwick, Eng., 1975, Australia Nat. U., U. Sydney, Australia, 1977; vis. Fulbright prof. U. Vienna, Austria, 1985; Goodhart vis. prof. Cambridge U., Eng., 1991-92; H. Hurst Eminent vis. scholar U. Fla., 1995; rsch. fellow Merton Coll., oxford U., 1981-82, Exeter Coll., Oxford U., 1988-89; cons. Cornell Law Project in publ. schs., N.Y., 1969-74, Law in Am. Soc. project Chgo. Bd. Edn., 1968-69; instr. Nat. Acad. Jud. Edn., 1976—; mem. faculty Salzburg Seminar in Am. Studies, 1990; ofcl. advisor Drafting commn. on New Civil Code for Russian Fedn., 1994-96. Author: Law, Its Nature, Functions and Limits, 1986; (with Hubbard and Campbell) Justice and Order Through Law, 1973; (with Bozzone and Campbell) The American Legal System, 1973; (with Speidel and White) Teaching Materials on Commercial Transactions, 1987, Collective Bargaining and Public Benefit Conferral-A Jurisprudential Critique, 1976, The Uniform Commercial Code, 1988, 4th edit., 1995; (with White) Het Pramatisch Instrumentalisme, 1981, Instrumentalism and American Legal Theory, 1982, Lon L. Fuller-Life and Work, 1984; (with Atiyah) Form and Substance in Anglo-American Law, 1987; (with Hillman) Contract and Related Obligation, 1987; (with MacCormick and others) Interpreting Statutes-A Comparative Study, 1991, Nature of Law and Legal Reasoning, 1993; contbr. book revs. and articles to profl. jours.; editor: Essays in Legal Philosophy, vol. 1, 1968, vol. 2, 1971. Social Sci. Research Council fellow, 1964-65. Mem. Am. Law Inst., Assn. Am. Law Schs. (chmn. sect. jurisprudence 1972-73), Am. Soc. Polit. and

Legal Philosophy (v.p. 1976-78), Internat. Acad. Comp. Law, Internat. Assn. of Legal and Social Philosophy Am. Soc. (pres. 1989-91), Austrian Acad. of Scis., Phi Beta Kappa. Republican. Congregationalist. Office: Cornell U Sch Law Myron Taylor Hall Ithaca NY 14853

SUMMERS, THOMAS CAREY, lawyer; b. Frederick, Md., Feb. 9, 1956; s. Harold Thomas and Doris Jean (Culler) S.; m. Robin Ann Stalnaker, May 12, 1990; children: Kristin, Heather, Lindsay. BA, Dickinson Coll., 1978; JD, U. Balt., 1981. Bar: Md. 1981, U.S. Dist. Ct. Md. 1981, D.C. 1986. Assoc. Ellin & Baker, Balt., 1979-89, Peter G. Angelos, Towson, Md., 1989—. Mem. ABA, Md. State Bar Assn., Md. Trial Lawyers Assn. Democrat. Lutheran. Avocation: golf. Office: Law Offices of P G Angelos 300 E Lombard St 18th Fl Baltimore MD 21202

SUMMERS, WILLIAM KOOPMANS, neuropsychiatrist, researcher; b. Jefferson City, Mo., Apr. 14, 1944; s. Joseph S. and Amy Lydia (Koopmans) S.; m. Angela Forbes McGonigle, Oct. 2, 1972(div. Apr. 1985); children: Elisabeth Stuart, Wilhelmina Derek. Student, Westminster Coll., Fulton, Mo., 1962-64; BS, U. Mo., 1966; MD, Washington U., St. Louis, 1971. Internal medicine intern Barnes Hosp-Washington U., St. Louis, 1971-72; resident in internal medicine Jewish Hosp., St. Louis, 1972-73; resident in psychiatry Rsch. Hosp., St. Louis, 1973-76; asst. prof. U. Pitts., 1976-78, U. So. Calif., L.A., 1978-82; asst. clin. prof. rsch. UCLA, 1982-88; rschr. Arcadia, Calif., 1988-92, Albuquerque, 1992—. Patentee in field. Mem. AMA, ACP, Am. Psychiat. Assn., Soc. Neurosci., N.Y. Acad. Scis., Am. Fedn. Clin. Rsch. Episcopalian. Avocation: gardening. Office: 201 Cedar St SE Ste 404 Albuquerque NM 87106

SUMMERSELL, FRANCES SHARPLEY, organization worker; b. Birmingham, Ala.; d. Arthur Croft and Thomas O. (Stone) Sharpley; m. Charles Grayson Summersell, Nov. 10, 1934. Student U. Montevallo, Peabody Coll.; LHD (hon.) U. Ala., 1996. Ptnr., artist, writer Assoc. Educators, 1959—. Vice chmn. Ft. Morgan Hist. Commn., 1959-63; active DAR, Magna Charta Dames, U. Women's Club (pres. 1957-58), Daus. Am. Colonists (organizing regent Tuscaloosa 1956-63). Recipient Algernon Sidney Sullivan award U. Ala., 1994. Mem. Tuscaloosa County Preservation Soc. (trustee 1965-78, svc. award 1975), Birmingham-Jefferson Hist. Soc., Ala. Hist. Assn. (exec. bd. Ala. Review 1991—), Omicron Delta Kappa, Iota Circle, Anderson Soc. Clubs: University (Tuscaloosa). Co-author: Alabama History Filmstrips, 1961; Florida History Filmstrips, 1963; Texas History Filmstrips, 1965-66; Ohio History Filmstrips, 1967 (Merit award Am. Assn. State and Local History 1968); California History Filmstrips, 1968; Illinois History Filmstrips, 1970. Home: 1411 Caplewood Dr Tuscaloosa AL 35401-1131

SUMMERTREE, KATONAH See WINDSOR, PATRICIA

SUMMITT, (WILLIAM) ROBERT, chemist, educator; b. Flint, Mich., Dec. 6, 1935; s. William Fletcher and Jessie Louise (Tilson) S.; m. Nancy Jo Holland, Apr. 2, 1956; children: Elizabeth Louise, David Stanley. A.S., Flint Jr. Coll., 1955; B.S. in Chemistry, U. Mich., 1957; Ph.D., Purdue U., 1961. Research asso., instr. chemistry Mich. State U., 1961-62, asst. prof. metallurgy, mechs. and materials, 1965-68, asso. prof., 1968-73, chmn. dept. metallurgy mechs. and materials sci., 1972-78, prof., 1973-92, prof. emeritus, 1992; research chemist Corning Glass Works, 1962-65; cons. in field. NRC Sr. Research asso. Air Force Materials Lab., Fairborn, Ohio, 1974-75. Research, publs. in corrosion, failure analysis, optical properties of materials, spectroscopy, and color sci. Mem. ASTM, Am. Chem. Soc., Am. Phys. Soc., Am. Soc. Metals, Nat. Assn. Corrosion Engrs., Sigma Xi. Home: RR4 8535 Clough Dr Grayling MI 49738 Office: Dept Materials Sci & Mechs Michigan State Univ East Lansing MI 48824

SUMMITT, ROBERT LAYMAN, pediatrician, educator; b. Knoxville, Tenn., Dec. 23, 1932; s. Robert Luther and Mary Ruth (Layman) S.; m. Joyce Ann Sharp, Dec. 23, 1955; children: Robert Layman Jr., Susan Kelly Summitt Pridgen, John Blair. Student, Davidson Coll., 1950-51; MD, U. Tenn., 1955, MS in Pediatrics, 1962. Diplomate Am. Bd. Pediatrics, recert. in pediatrics, 1983, 92, Am. Bd. Med. Genetics (bd. dirs. 1985-89). Rotating intern U. Tenn. Meml. Research Ctr. and Hosp., Knoxville, 1956; asst. resident in pediatrics U. Tenn. Coll. Medicine and City of Memphis Hosp., 1959-60, chief resident, 1960-61; USPHS fellow in pediatric endocrinology U. Tenn. Coll. Medicine, Memphis, 1961-62; fellow in med. genetics U. Wis.-Madison, 1963; asst. prof. pediatrics, child devel. U. Tenn., Memphis, 1964-68, assoc. prof., 1968-71, prof. pediatrics and anatomy, 1971—, dean Coll. Medicine, 1981—, provost, 1988-91; cons. President's Commn. on Mental Retardation, 1979-80; CEO U. Tenn. Med. Group, 1983-93, chmn., 1983—; mem. Coun. on Grad. Med. Edn., 1990—. Lt. M.C., USN, 1957-59, rear admiral USNR, ret. 1992. NIH grantee, 1965—; recipient Alumni Pub. Service award U. Tenn. Alumni Assn., 1980-81, U. Tenn. Coll. Medicine Student Body Disting. Tchr. award, 1981-82, 82-83, 83-84, 84-85, 85-86, Outstanding Alumnus award U. Tenn. Coll. of Medicine, 1984. Fellow Am. Coll. Med. Genetics, Am. Acad. Pediatrics; mem. AMA (rep. to accreditation coun. on grad. med. edn. 1995—), Tenn. Med. Assn., Memphis-Shelby County Med. Soc. (bd. dirs. 1994—), Am. Soc. Human Genetics, Soc. Pediatric Rsch., Coun. Deans of AAMC, Jour. Rev. Club (Memphis). Office: U Tenn Coll Medicine 800 Madison Ave Memphis TN 38103-3400

SUMMITT, ROBERT MURRAY, circuit judge; b. Sweetwater, Tenn., Jan. 14, 1924; s. Murray Dyer and Vina Mae (Brakebill) S.; m. Florence Varnell, May 14, 1955; children: Virginia Anne Sharber, Robert M. Jr., Laura Stephens, Martin Dyer. JD, U. Tenn., 1949; postgrad., Nat. Jud. Coll., 1972, 79, 82, Am. Acad. Jud. Edn., 1974, 75, 76, 77, U. Tenn., 1978. Bar: Tenn. 1949, U.S. Supreme Ct. 1956. Pvt. practice Chattanooga, 1949-68; cir. judge Tenn. Jud. 1st Div. 11th Jud. Dist. Ct., Tenn., 1968—; served on Tenn. Supreme Ct., 1990; pres. Tenn. Jud. Conf., 1980, ec., v.p., exec. com. mem., 1980-84, past chmn. nominating com., continuintg edn. com., past chmn.; mem. Tenn. Ct. of the Judiciary; past chmn. ad hoc fed. diversity com. National Conf. State Trial Judges, past chmn. task force on jud. support, past chairman State Jud. Assn., chmn. fin. and budget com., Tenn. rep. to nat. conf. Author: (with others) Tenn. Trial Judges Benchbook; contbr. articles to profl. jours. State chmn., nat. rep., Inner City com. chmn., Boy Scouts Am. (Silver Beaver award 1976); bd. dirs. Salvation Army; mem. Freedom's Found.; bd. dirs., trustee, past Sunday Sch. tchr. First Centenary United Meth. Ch. Decorated Red Cross of Constantine; recipient Nat. Heritage award Downtown Sertoma Club, 1984; named Young Man of Yr., Jaycees, 1959. Mem. ABA (past chmn. Nat. Conf. State Trial Judges 1991-92, mem. judicial adminstrn. divsn. coun., judicial coun. House of Dels.), Tenn. Bar Assn., Chattanooga Bar Assn. (bd. govs.), Am. Judicature Soc., Am. Judges Assn., Internat. Acad. Trial Judges, Silver Falcon Assn., Air Force Assn., Res. Officers Assn., Retired Res. Officers Assn., U. Tenn. Alumni Assn. Century Club, Order of the Arrow, City Farmers Club, Half-Century Club, SAR (chancellor), Mason, Royal Order Jesters, Royal Order Scotland, Eastern Star, Alhambra Temple, Rotary, Phi Delta Phi, Sigma Alpha Epsilon. Avocations: gardening, beekeeping, hunting. Home: 957 Ravine Rd Signal Mountain TN 37377-3054 Office: 11th Jud Dist Hamilton County Courthouse Chattanooga TN 37402-1401

SUMNER, DANIEL ALAN, economist, educator; b. Fairfield, Calif., Dec. 5, 1950. B.S. in Agrl. Mgmt., Calif. State Poly. U., 1971; M.A. in Econs., Mich. State U., 1973; M.A. in Econs., U. Chgo., 1977, Ph.D., 1978. Post-doctoral fellow, labor and population group, econ. dept. Rand Corp., Santa Monica, Calif., 1977-78; asst. prof. N.C. State U., Raleigh, 1978-83, assoc. prof., 1983-87, prof. 1987-92; resident fellow, Resources for the Future, Washington, 1986-87; sr. economist Pres.'s Council of Econ. Advisers, 1987-88; dep. asst. sec. for econs. USDA, 1990-91, asst. sec. for econs., 1992-93. Frank H. Buck Jr. prof. dept. agrl. econs. U. Calif., Davis, 1993—. Author and editor books and monographs; contbr. chpts. to books, articles in profl. jours. Named Alumnus of Yr., Calif. State Poly. U., 1991. Mem. Am. Econ. Assn., Econometric Soc., Am. Agrl. Econs. Assn., Internat. Assn. Agrl. Economists. Office: U Calif Davis Dept Agrl Econ Davis CA 95616

SUMNER, DAVID SPURGEON, surgery educator; b. Asheboro, N.C., Feb. 20, 1933; s. George Herbert and Velna Elizabeth (Welborn) S.; m. Martha Eileen Sypher, July 25, 1959; children: David Vance, Mary Elizabeth, John Franklin. BA, U. N.C., 1954; MD, Johns Hopkins U., 1958. Diplomate Am. Bd. Surgery; cert. spl. qualification gen. vascular surgery, 1983, 93. Intern in surgery Johns Hopkins Hosp., Balt., 1958-59, resident in gen. surgery, 1960-61; resident in gen. surgery U. Wash. Sch. Medicine, Seattle, 1961-66; clin. investigator in vascular surgery VA Hosp., Seattle, 1967, 70-73; asst. surgery U. Wash. Sch. Medicine, Seattle, 1961-66, instr. surgery, 1966-70, asst. prof. surgery, 1970-72, assoc. prof. surgery, 1972-75; prof. surgery, chief sect. peripheral vascular surgery So. Ill. U. Sch. Medicine., Springfield, 1975-84, Disting. prof. surgery, chief sect. peripheral vascular surgery, 1984—; staff surgeon Seattle VA Hosp., 1973-75, Univ. Hosp., Seattle, 1973-75, St. John's Hosp., Springfield, 1975—, Meml. Med. Ctr., Springfield, 1975—; mem. VA Merit Review Bd. Surgery, 1975-78; mem. vascular surgery rsch. award com. The Liebig Found., 1990-95, chmn., 1994; bd. dirs. Am. Venous Forum Found.; vis. prof. Cook County Hosp., Chgo., 1971, Washington U., St. Louis, 1976, U. Tex., San Antonio, 1978, Wayne State U., Detroit, 1978, U. Ind., Indpls., 1979, Ea. Va. Med. Sch., Norfolk, 1979, Case-Western Res. U., Cleve., 1980, U. Chgo., 1981, U. Manitoba, Winnipeg, Can., 1983, and others to present; dist. lectr. Yale U., 1982; guest examiner Am. Bd. Surgery, St. Louis, 1982, assoc. examiner, 1989, certifying examination gen. vascular surgery, 1993, 94; lectr. in field. Author: (with D.E. Strandness Jr.) Ultrasonic Techniques in Angiology, 1975, Hemodynamics for Surgeons, 1975, (with R.B. Rutherford, V. Bernhard, F. Maddison, W.S. Moore, M.O. Perry) Vascular Surgery, 1977, (with J.B. Russell) Ultrasonic Arteriography, 1980, (with F.B. Hershey, R.W. Barnes) Noninvasive Diagnosis of Vascular Disease, 1984, (with R.B. Rutherford, G. Johnson Jr., R.F. Kempczinski, W.S. Moore, M.O. Perry, G.W. Smith) Vascular Surgery, 3d edit., 1989, (with A.N. Nicolaides) Investigation of Patients With Deep Vein Thrombosis and Chronic Venous Insufficiency, 1991, (with R.B. Rutherford, G. Johnson, K.W. Johnston, R.F. Kempczinski, W.C. Krupski, W.S. Moore, M.O. Perry, A.J. Comerota, R.H. Dean, P. Gloviczki, K.H. Johansen, T.S. Riles, L.M. Taylor Jr.) Vascular Surgery, 4th edit., 1995; author 150 chpts. to books; editor Vascular Surgery, 1984; mem. editl. adv. bd. Vascular Diagnosis and Therapy, 1980-84; mem. editl. bd. advisors Appleton Davies, Inc., 1983—; mem. editl. review bd. Jour. Soc. of Non-Invasive Vascular Tech., 1987—; mem. editl. bd. Jour. Vascular Surgery, 1987—; series editor Introduction to Vascular Tech., 1990—; mem. exec. editl. com. Phlebology, 1987-91; mem. Internat. Editl. Adv. Bd., 1991; mem. editl. com. Internat. Angiology, 1992—; contbr. over 140 articles to profl. jours. Lt. col. U.S. Army, 1967-70. Recipient fellowship in surg. rsch. Johns Hopkins U. Sch. Medicine, 1959-60, fellowship Am. Cancer Soc., Inc., 1965-66, Appleton-Century Crofts Scholarship award, 1956, Mosby Scholarship award, 1958. Fellow Am. Coll. Surgeons (Wash. chpt. 1971-75, Ill. chpt. counselor 1981-83), Cyprus Vascular Soc. (hon.); mem. AMA, Soc. Univ. Surgeons, Soc. Vascular Surgery (constn. and by-laws com. 1983, Wiley Fellowship com. 1990), Internat. Soc. Cardiovascular Surgery (N.Am. chpt. program com. 1985-88), Am. Surg. Assn., Am. Heart Assn. (stroke coun., cardiovascular surgery coun. 1978), Soc. Noninvasive Vascular Tech. (hon.), Vascular Surgery Biology Club, Am. Venous Forum (organizing com. 1987, founding mem. 1988, chmn. membership com. 1988-91, treas. 1992—), Cardiovascular Sys. Dynamics Soc., Internat. Soc. Surgery, Vascular Soc. So. Africa (hon.), North Pacific Surg. Assn., Ctrl. Surg. Assn. (local arrangements com. 1990), Midwestern Vascular Surg. Soc. (counselor 19es.-elect 1980-81, pres. 1981-82), Ill. Heart Assn., Ill. State Med. Soc., Ill. Surg. Soc., Chgo. Surg. Soc., Seattle Surg. Soc., Sangamon County Med. Soc., Henry N. Harkins Surg. Soc., Harbinger Soc., Phi Eta Sigma, Phi Beta Kappa, Alpha Omega Alpha, Sigma Xi. Presbyterian. Achievements include research in surgical hemodynamics and noninvasive methods for diagnosing peripheral vascular disease. Avocations: painting, sailing, history, computers. Home: Southern Illinois U Sch Med Dept Surgery 2324 West Lake Dr Springfield IL 62707 Office: So Ill U Sch Medicine 800 N Rutledge St Springfield IL 62781

SUMNER, GORDON, electronics research executive. Treas BNR, Inc., Research Triangle Park, N.C., 1987—; v.p., gen. auditor Northern Telecom, Mississauga, Canada. Office: BNR inc 35 Davis Rd Durham NC 27709*

SUMNER, GORDON, JR., retired military officer; b. Albuquerque, July 23, 1924; s. Gordon and Esstella (Berry) S.; m. Frances Fernandes, May, 1991; children: Ward T., Holly Rose. AS, N.Mex. Mil. Inst., 1943; BA, La. State U., 1955; MA, U. Md., 1963. Commd. 2d. lt. U.S. Army, 1944, advanced through grades to lt. gen., 1975, ret., 1978; founder, chmn. Cypress Internat., 1978-96; chmn. La Mancha Co., Inc., 1981-89, Sumner Assoc.; cons. U.S. Depts. State and Def; amabassador at large for Latin Am.; spl. advisor U.S. Dept. State; nat. security advisor Pres.' Bi-Partisan Commn. Cen. Am.; vis. staff mem. Los Alamos Nat. Lab. Contbr. articles to profl. jours. Decorated D.S.M., Silver Star, Legion of Merit with three oak leaf clusters, Disting. Flying Cross with 13 oak leaf clusters, Bronze Star, Army Commendation medal with oak leaf cluster, Purple Heart. Mem. Phi Kappa Phi, Pi Sigma Alpha. Office: La Mancha Co 100 Cienega St Ste D Santa Fe NM 87501-2003

SUMNER, GORDON MATTHEW See STING

SUMNER, WILLIAM MARVIN, anthropology and archaeology educator; b. Detroit, Sept. 8, 1928; s. William Pulford Jr. and Virginia Friel (Umberger) S.; m. Frances Wilson Morton, June 21, 1952 (div. 1975): children: Jane DeVault, William Morton; m. Kathleen A. MacLean, Apr. 7, 1989. Student, Va. Mil. Inst., 1947-48; B.S., U.S. Naval Acad., 1952; Ph.D., U. Pa., 1972. Dir. Am. Inst. Iranian Studies, Tehran, Iran, 1969-71; asst. prof. Ohio State U., Columbus, 1971-73, assoc. prof., 1974-80, prof. anthropology, 1981-89, prof. emeritus, 1989—; dir. Oriental Inst., prof. Near Eastern langs. and civilizations U. Chgo., 1989—; dir. excavations at Tal-e Malyan (site of Elamite Anshan) sponsored by Univ. Mus., U. Pa., 1971—; v.p. Am. Inst. Iranian Studies, 1983-86. Contbr. chpts. to books, articles and essays to profl. jours. Served to lt. comdr. USN, 1952-64. Grantee NSF, 1975, 76, 79, NEH, 1988. Office: Univ Chgo Oriental Inst 1155 E 58th St Chicago IL 60637-1540

SUMPTER, SONJA KAY, elementary school educator; b. Weston, W.Va., Aug. 12, 1948; d. Glen A. and Sarah R. (White) Wade; m. Charles Fredrick Sumpter, Mar. 25, 1967; children: Lisa Marie Sumpter Pethtel, Charles Fredrick II. BS in Elem. Edn., Glenville (W.Va.) State Coll., 1984; MS in Edn., W.Va. Wesleyan Coll., 1993; postgrad., W.Va. U., 1994. Cert. tchr. elem. edn. 1-6, math. 5-8. Tchr. Weston (W.Va.) Jr. H.S., 1984-92; tchr. Robert Bland Mid. Sch., Weston, 1992—, team leader, 1992-94. Mem. Nat. Coun. Tchrs. Math., Order Ea. Star. Republican. Baptist. Avocations: singing, walking, macrame. Home: RR 4 Box 297 Weston WV 26452-9517 Office: Robert Bland Middle School 358 Court Ave Weston WV 26452-2008

SUMRALL, HARRY, journalist; b. Palestine, Tex., Oct. 15, 1950; s. Harry Glenn and Sherea Sue (Selden) S.; m. Leslie Leizear, Dec. 19, 1954; 1 child, Samuel Harry. BA, George Mason U., 1974. Writer, critic The Washington Post, 1978-81; contbg. writer The New Republic, Washington, 1979; assoc. editor Rock Concert Mag., Washington, 1979; music writer San Jose (Calif.) Mercury News/Knight Ridder News Svc., 1982—; advisor New Music Am., Washington, 1983; lectr., guest San Francisco State U., 1991; guest critic Sta. KGO, San Francisco, 1991—. Author: Pioneers of Rock and Roll, 1994, Giants of Country Music, 1995; contbg. author: New Grove Dictionary of American Music, 1983; broadcaster: (radio program) Rockology, 1989. Paneslist Chatauquas for Congress, Washington, 1979. Fellow New Music Am., 1980. Office: San Jose Mercury News 750 Ridder Park Dr San Jose CA 95131-2432

SUMRELL, GENE, research chemist; b. Apache, Ariz., Oct. 7, 1919; s. Joe B. and Dixie (Hughes) S. BA, Eastern N.Mex. U., 1942; BS, U. N.Mex., 1947, MS, 1948; PhD, U. Calif., Berkeley, 1951. Asst. prof. chemistry Eastern N.Mex. U., 1951-53; sr. rsch. chemist J. T. Baker Chem. Co., Phillipsburg, N.J., 1953-58; sr. organic chemist Southwest Rsch. Inst., San Antonio, 1958-59; project leader Food Machinery & Chem. Corp., Balt., 1959-61; rsch. sect. leader El Paso Natural Gas Products Co. (Tex.), 1961-64; project leader So. utilization research and devel. div. U.S. Dept. Agr., New Orleans, 1964-67, investigations head, 1967-73, rsch. leader Oil Seed and Food Lab., So. Regional Rsch. Ctr., 1973-84, collaborator, 1984— . Contbr. numerous papers to profl. jours. Served from pvt. to staff sgt. AUS, 1942-46. Mem. AAAS, Am. Chem. Soc., N.Y. Acad. Scis., Am. Inst. Chemists, Am. Oil Chemists Soc., Am. Assn. Textile Chemists and Colorists, Rsch. Soc. Am., Phi Kappa Phi, Sigma Xi. Achievements include patents in field. Home: PO Box 24037 New Orleans LA 70184-4037 Office: 1100 Robert E Lee Blvd New Orleans LA 70124-4305

SUN, WEIDONG, molecular biologist; b. Beijing, China, May 2, 1959; s. Jinghao Sun and Yinglan Chen; m. Xiaoli, May 17, 1989; children: Michael Sun, James Sun. MD, Beijing Med. U., 1983, MS, 1986; PhD, Med. Coll. Pa., 1993. Rsch. assoc. Med. Coll. Pa., Phila., 1989-93; rsch. scientist Sch. of Med. U. Pa., Phila., 1993—; vis. scientist Sch. of Med. Boston U., 1986-89; vis. prof. Beijing Med. U., 1995-97; pres. BBB Internat. Inc., Phila., 1993—. Grantee Muscular Dystrophy Assn., Ariz., 1995-96. Mem. Am. Soc. Cell Biology, Am. Soc. Biophysics, AAAS. Achievements include cloning of neuronal myosin heavy chain. Office: U Pa Inst for Human Gene Therapy BRB-1 Rm 409 422 Curie Blvd Philadelphia PA 19104

SUNAMI, JOHN SOICHI, designer; b. N.Y.C., June 10, 1949; s. Soichi and Suyeko (Matsushima) S.; m. Marialyce Norman, Apr. 21, 1973; children: Christopher Andrew, Jennifer Kiyoko. BA, CCNY, 1969. Cert. Gemological Inst. Am. Vol. Peace Corps, Jamaica, W.I., 1969-71; jeweler N.Y.C. and Columbus, Ohio, 1971-82; dir. mktg. Knight's Inn/Cardinal Industries, Columbus, 1982; founder, exec. designer Nimbus, Columbus, 1983—. Designer/sculptor pub. artwork IntroCenter, 1990; designer logo identities for various cos.; exhibited paintings and sculpture; author poems and essays. Bd. dirs. William H. Thomas Gallery, Columbus, 1992-93; v.p., bd. dirs. South Side Settlement House, Columbus, 1982-93; mem. cultural diversity outreach com. United Way of Franklin County, 1993—. Recipient 1st prize Macworld Gallery/Macworld Mag., 1985. Mem. Columbus C. of C., Columbus Art League. Avocations: music, travel. Home: 419 Fairwood Ave Columbus OH 43205-2202 Office: Nimbus 413 Fairwood Ave Columbus OH 43205-2202

SUND, JEFFREY OWEN, publishing company executive; b. Bklyn., June 19, 1940; children: Catherine, Meredith. BA, Dartmouth Coll., 1962. Sales rep. Prentice-Hall, Englewood Cliffs, N.J., 1967-73; sales rep. Houghton Mifflin, Boston, 1973-74, coll. div. editor, 1974-77, editor-in-chief, 1977-86, v.p., editorial dir., 1986-89; pres., chief exec. officer Richard D. Irwin, Burr Ridge, Ill., 1989—. Lt. USN, 1962-66. Office: Richard D Irwin 1333 Burr Ridge Pky Burr Ridge IL 60521-6489

SUND, KELLY G., public health science administrator; b. Northridge, Calif., Oct. 22, 1966; d. Donald C. and Evelyn M. (Miller) S. BS in Biol. Scis., Stanford U., 1988, MS in Biol. Scis., 1989. Rsch. assoc. Health & Environ. Scis. Group, Ltd., Washington, 1990-92, assoc. dir. rsch., 1992-95, dir. GLP-Lab., 1994-95, dir. rsch., 1995—; sci. outreach coord. Wireless Tech. Rsch., Washington, 1994-95, ongoing surveillance coord., 1996— occpl., environ.health tchr. George Washington U., Washington, 1995—; presenter in field. Contbr. articles to profl. jours. Big sister Big Bros./Big Sisters, Palo Alto, Calif., 1985-89; counselor D.C. AIDS Info. Line, Washington, 1990—; spkr. AIDS Edn. Spkrs. Bur., Washington, 1991. Recipient U.S. Achievement Acad. Nat. award. Mem. Soc. for Risk Analysis (comm. working group leader 1992-93), Met. Washington Mensa (spl. interest group leader 1990-96, area coord. 1993, scrivener 1993-94, testing coord. 1994—, proctor 1995—). Avocations: dancing, languages. Office: Health & Environ Scis Group Ltd 1711 N St Ste 200 Washington DC 20036-2811

SUNDARESAN, MOSUR KALYANARAMAN, physics educator; b. Madras, India, Sept. 2, 1929; parents Mosur Ramanathan and Kanakavalli Kalyanaraman; m. Bharathy Sundaresan, June 7, 1957; children: Sudhir, Sujata. BSc with honors, Delhi U., 1947, MSc, 1949; PhD, Cornell U., 1955. With Atomic Energy Establishment, Bombay, 1955-57; postdoctoral fellow NRC, Can., 1957-59; reader in physics Punjab U., Chandigarh, India, 1959-61; prof. physics Carleton U., Ottawa, Can., Can., 1961-95; hon. disting. rsch. prof. physics Carleton U., Ottawa, 1995—. Mem. Can. Assn. Physicists, Am. Phys. Soc., Am. Assn. Physics Tchrs., Inst. Particle Physics Can.

SUNDBERG, ALAN CARL, former state supreme court justice, lawyer; b. Jacksonville, Fla., June 23, 1933; s. Robert Carl and Gertrude Harriet (Rudd) S.; children: Allison, Angela, Laura, Alan, William. BS, Fla. State U., 1955; LLB, Harvard U., 1958; LLD (hon.), Stetson U., 1977. Bar: Fla. 1958. Practiced in St. Petersburg, 1958-75; justice Supreme Ct. Fla., 1975-82, chief justice, 1980-82; sr. atty. Carlton, Fields, Ward, Emmanuel, Smith & Cutler, P.A., Tallahassee, 1982—; com. mem. on rules of practice and procedure of Judicial Conf. of U.S. Author: Process and Appearance, Civil Practice Before Trial, 1963. Mem. Salvation Army Adv. Bd.; chmn. bd. trustees Canterbury Sch. Fla., Inc.; bd. dirs. Fla. Gulf Coast Symphony, St. Petersburg Symphony; trustee Pinellas County Law Library; mem. Fla. Sentencing Guidelines Commn., 1982-89; chmn. Fla. Bench Bar Commn. Mem. ABA, Fla. Bar Found. (past 2d v.p.), St. Petersburg Bar Assn., Fla. Bar Assn. (spl. commn. referall contingency fees), Pinellas Trial Lawyers Assn., Internat. Acad. Trial Lawyers, Am. Coll. Trial Lawyers, Best Lawyers in Am., Phi Beta Kappa, Phi Kappa Phi, Omicron Delta Kappa, Phi Delta Phi, Dragon, Suncoasters. Democrat. Episcopalian. Office: Carlton Fields Ward Emmanuel Smith & Cutler PC PO Box 190 Tallahassee FL 32302-0190

SUNDBERG, CARL-ERIK WILHELM, telecommunications executive, researcher; b. Karlskrona, Sweden, July 7, 1943; came to U.S., 1984; s. Erik Wilhelm and Martha Maria (Snaar) S. MEE, U. Lund, Sweden, 1966, PhD, 1975. Tchr., rsch. asst., lectr. U. Lund, 1966-75, rsch. prof. (docent), 1977-84; rsch. fellow European Space Agy., Nordwijk, The Netherlands, 1975-76; disting. mem. tech. staff AT&T Bell Labs., Murray Hill, N.J., 1984-96, Lucent Technologies, Bell Labs., 1997—; cons. L.M. Ericsson, Gothenburg, Sweden, 1976-77, Bell Labs., Crawford Hill, N.J., 1981-82; instr. Carl Cranz Gesellschaft, Oberpfaffenhofen, Fed. Republic Germany, 1990-93. Co-author: Digital Phase Modulation, 1986, Source-Matched Mobile Communications, 1995; contbr. articles to profl. jours.; patentee in field. Served in Swedish Navy, 1968. Fellow IEEE (Best Paper award 1986, guest editor Jour. on Selected Areas in Comm. 1988-89), IEE Marconi Premium (Best Paper award 1989); mem. Swedish Union Radio-Scientifique Internationale, Svenska Electric Engrs., Riksförening (Sweden), CF Civil Engrs. förbundet (Sweden). Lutheran. Avocations: travel, history, photography. Home: 25 Hickory Pl Apt A11 Chatham NJ 07928-1465 Office: Lucent Technologies Bell Labs RM 2C-480 600 Mountain Ave New Providence NJ 07974-2008

SUNDBERG, R. DOROTHY, physician, educator; b. Chgo., July 29, 1915; d. Carl William and Ruth (Chalbeck) S.; m. Robert H. Reiff, Dec. 24, 1941 (div. 1945). Student, U. Chgo., 1932-34; B.S., U. Minn., 1937, M.A., 1939, Ph.D., 1943, M.D., 1953. Diplomate Am. Bd. Pathology. Instr., asst. prof. anatomy U. Minn., 1939-53, assoc. prof., 1953-60, prof., 1960-63, prof. of lab. medicine and anatomy, 1963-73, prof. lab. medicine, pathology and anatomy, 1973-84, emeritus prof., 1984—; hematologist, dir. Hematology Labs., 1945-74, hematologist, co. dir., 1974-84. Editorial bd.: Soc. Exptl. Biology and Medicine, until 1975; mem. editorial bd.: Blood, 1960-67; assoc. editor, 1967-69. Recipient Lucretia Wilder award for research in anatomy, 1943. Mem. Am. Assn. Anatomists, Internat., European Soc. Hematology, Sigma Xi. Home: 1255 Shenandoah Ct Marco Island FL 33937-5023 also: 2618 158th Ave NE Ham Lake MN 55304

SUNDBERG, RICHARD JAY, chemistry educator; b. Sioux Rapids, Iowa, Jan. 6, 1938; s. Ernest Julius and Rosa Paulina Christina (Christensen) S.; m. Lorna Swift, 1962 children—Kelly, Jennifer. B.S., U. Iowa, 1959; Ph.D., U. Minn., 1962. Mem. faculty dept. chemistry U. Va., Charlottesville, 1964—, prof., 1974—. Author monograph: Chemistry of Indoles, 1970; author (with F. A. Carey) Advanced Organic Chemistry, 1990. Served to 1st lt. U.S. Army, 1962-64. Mem. Am. Chem. Soc., Internat. Soc. Heterocyclic Chemistry. Lutheran. Home: 2001 Greenbrier Dr Charlottesville VA 22901-2916 Office: U Va Dept Chemistry Mccormick Rd Charlottesville VA 22904

SUNDBY, SCOTT EDWIN, law educator; b. Aurora, Ill., Oct. 24, 1958; s. Elmer Arthur and Marilyn Edruth (Koeller) S.; m. Katie Louise Rees, June 15, 1980; children: Russell Taylor, Christopher Scott, Kelsey Kathleen. BA, Vanderbilt U., 1980; JD, Cornell U., 1983. Bar: Calif. 1985, U.S. Dist. Ct. (no. dist.) Calif. 1985. Law clk. to judge U.S. Ct. Appeals for llth Cir., Savannah, Ga., 1983-84; prof. law U. Calif. Hastings Coll. Law, San

Francisco, 1984-92; prof. Washington and Lee U., Lexington, Va., 1992—; spl. asst. U.S. Atty. (so. dist.), Fla., 1994-95. Editor-in-chief Cornell Law Rev., 1982-83. Mem. Order of Coif, Phi Beta Kappa. Office: Washington and Lee Univ Sch Law Lexington VA 24450

SUNDEL, MARTIN, social work educator, psychologist; b. Bronx, N.Y., Sept. 22, 1940; s. Louis and Pauline (Brotman) S.; m. Sandra Stone, Aug. 22, 1971; children: Adam Daniel, Jenny Rebecca, Ariel Pauline. B.A. cum laude, St. Mary's U., 1961; M.S.W., Worden Sch. Social Service, 1963; M.A., U. Mich., 1968, Ph.D., 1968. Social group work supr. Valley Cities Jewish Community Ctr., Van Nuys, Calif., 1963-65; asst. prof. U. Mich. Sch. Social Work, Ann Arbor, 1968-71; postdoctoral fellow Harvard U. Lab. Community Psychiatry, Boston, 1971-72; dir. research and evaluation River Region Mental Health-Mental Retardation Bd., Louisville, 1972-77; adj. prof. Kent. Sch. Social Work-U Louisville, 1972-77, assoc. clin. prof. dept. psychiatry and behavioral scis., 1974-77, assoc. in psychology, 1975-77; sr. research assoc. The Urban Inst., Washington, 1977-80; pvt. practice psychology Dallas; Dulak Disting. prof. U. Tex., Arlington, 1980-89, prof., 1980-95; prof. Fla. Internat. U., North Miami, Fla., 1995—; mental health cons. UN High Commn. for Refugees in Cyprus, 1993—; mem. profl. adv. coun. Dallas Geriatric Rsch. Inst., 1980-89; mem. long-range planning com. Dallas Jewish Coalition for the Homeless, 1986-95; mem. coordinating com. Arlington Human Svcs. Project, 1981-90, Mayor's Forum on Human Svc. Needs Assessment, Ft. Worth, 1983-86; vis. prof. U. So. Calif. Sch. Social Work, spring 1985. Author: (with Sandra Stone Sundel) Behavior Modification in the Human Services, 1975, 3d edit., 1993; Be Assertive, 1980; co-editor: Assessing Health and Human Service Needs, 1983, Individual Change Through Small Groups, 2d edit., 1985, Midlife Myths, 1989; mem. editorial bds. and cons. to profl. jours. Mem. APA, Nat. Assn. Social Workers (mem. futures commn. 1979-85, mem. steering com. Dallas 1986-90), Behavior Therapy and Rsch. Soc. (charter clin. fellow), Assn. Advancement of Behavior Therapy, Acad. Cert. Social Workers, Coun. Social Work Edn., Internat. Soc. for the Sys. Scis. Home: 3804 Barbados Ave Cooper City FL 33026 Office: Fla Internat U Sch Social Work North Miami Campus ACI-234 Miami FL 33181

SUNDELOF, JON GRENVILLE, microbiologist; b. Washington, Nov. 28, 1944; s. Herbert G. W. and Mabel doris (Ferger) S.; m. Joan Elizabeth Ely, Sept. 13, 1967; children: Deborah Jean, Jeffrey Eric. BA, Rutgers U., 1976. LPN, N.J. Lab. technician Gulton Industries, Metuchen, N.J., 1963-64; technician Merck & Co. Inc., Rahway, N.J., 1964-67, jr. scientist, 1971-85, sr. scientist, 1985—. County committeeman Middlesex Rep. Party, 1988-94. With U.S. Army 1967-71. Decorated Bronze star. Mem. AAAS, VFW, Am. Soc. for Microbiology, Am. Legion. Avocations: golf, bowling, private pilot. Home: 517 Willow Ave Piscataway NJ 08854 Office: Merck & Co Inc (R80T-100) PO Box 2000 Rahway NJ 07065

SUNDERLAND, RAY, JR., retired insurance company executive; b. N.Y.C., Nov. 12, 1913; s. Ray and Rose (Goehl) S.; m. Melva Joyce Mace, June 13, 1943; 1 son, Joel Wayne. Grad., Sch. Profl. Accountancy Practice, Pace Coll., 1948, Sch. Bus. Adminstrn., Columbia U., 1968. CPA, N.Y. With comptroller's dept. Brown Bros. Harriman & Co., N.Y.C., 1934-40; sr. auditor Price Waterhouse & Co., N.Y.C., 1940-50; with N.Y. Life Ins. Co., N.Y.C., 1950-79; gen. auditor N.Y. Life Ins. Co., 1969-71, comptroller, 1971-79, v.p., 1971-75, sr. v.p., 1975-79; comptroller N.Y. Life Fund, Inc., 1972-79. Author and publisher: The Descendants of William Sunderland and Allied Families, 1988. Pres. community scholarship fund local sch. dist., Locust Valley, N.Y., 1958-62, pres. parents club, 1958-62; bd. dirs. Vis. Nurse Assn. L.I., N.Y., 1982-93, Vis. Nurse Assn. of Oyster Bay-Glen Cove, N.Y., 1982-92; mem. Locust Valley Libr. (long range planning com. 1992, nominating com. for bd. trustee mems. 1992-93). Served to capt. USAAF, 1942-45; active duty USAR, 1946-52. Fellow Am. Coll. Genealogists (v.p. N.Y. area 1990—); mem. NRA (life), SAR (Huntington, N.Y. chpt.), Am. Coun. Life Ins. (fin. reporting principles com. 1977-78), Nat. Geneal. Soc., Geneal. Soc. Southwestern Pa., Locust Valley Hist. Soc. (N.Y.). Home: 3 Wood Ln Locust Valley NY 11560-1628

SUNDERLAND, ROBERT, cement company executive; b. Omaha, Dec. 21, 1921; s. Paul and Avis Marie (Peters) S.; m. Terri Reed, Nov. 21, 1959; children—Sharon Marie, Lori Diane. B.S. in Bus. Adminstrn, Washington U., St. Louis, 1947; LL.D. (hon.), Bethany Coll., Lindsborg, Kans., 1980. With Ash Grove Cement Co., Overland Park, Kans., 1947—; sec., asst. treas. Ash Grove Cement Co., 1953-57, treas., 1957-61, v.p., treas., 1961-67, chmn. bd., 1967-91, hon. chmn., 1992—. Trustee Lester T. Sunderland Found., Kansas City. Served with USAAF, 1942-46, Philippines. Mem. Kansas City Club, Shadow Glen Golf Club, Sigma Chi. Republican. Presbyterian. Office: Ash Grove Cement Co 8900 Indian Creek Pky Ste 600 Shawnee Mission KS 66210-1513

SUNDERMAN, DUANE NEUMAN, chemist, research institute executive; b. Wadsworth, Ohio, July 14, 1928; s. Richard Benjamin and Carolyn (Neuman) S.; m. Joan Catherine Hoffman, Jan. 31, 1953; children: David, Christine, Richard. BA, U. Mich., 1949, MS, 1954, PhD in Chemistry, 1956. Researcher Battelle Meml. Inst., Columbus, Ohio, 1956-59; mgr. Battelle Meml. Inst., Columbus, 1959-69, assoc. dir., 1969-79, dir. internat. programs, 1979-84; sr. v.p. Midwest Rsch. Inst., Kansas City, Mo., 1984-90, exec. v.p., 1990-94; exec. v.p. Midwest Rsch. Inst., Golden, Colo., 1990-94; dir. Nat. Renewable Energy Lab., Golden, Colo., 1990-94, dir. emeritus, 1994—. Contbr. numerous articles to profl. jours. Bd. dirs. Mid-Ohio chpt. ARC, 1982-83, U. Kansas City, 1985-90, Mo. Corp. for Sci. and Tech., Jefferson City, 1986-90. Mem. AAAS, Am. Chem. Soc., Am. Mgmt. Assn. Republican. Presbyterian. Avocation: computers.

SUNDERMAN, FREDERICK WILLIAM, physician, educator, author, musician; b. Altoona, Pa., Oct. 23, 1898; s. William August and Elizabeth Catherine (Lehr) S.; m. Clara Louise Baily, June 2, 1925 (dec. 1972); children: Louise (dec.), F. William, Joel B. (dec.); m. Martha-Lee Taggart, May 3, 1980. BS, Gettysburg Coll., 1919, ScD (hon.), 1952; MD, U. Pa., 1923, MS, 1927, PhD, 1929. Diplomate Am. Bd. Internal Medicine, Am. Bd. Pathology (v.p. 1944-50 life trustee 1950—), Nat. Bd. Med. Examiners. Intern, then resident Pa. Hosp., 1923-25; assoc. rsch. med. U. Pa., Phila., 1925-48; assoc. in chem. divsn. William Pepper Lab. U. Pa. Hosp., Phila., 1929-48; physician U. Pa. Hosp., 1929-48; med. dir. Office of Sci. R & D, 1943-46; physician, hon. pathologist Pa. Hosp., 1988—; mem. faculty U. Pa. Sch. Medicine, Phila., 1925-47; assoc. prof. research medicine, also lectr. U. Pa. Sch. Medicine; acting head med. dept. Brookhaven Nat. Lab., Upton, N.Y., 1947-48; chief chem. div. William Pepper Lab. Clin. Medicine, U. Pa. Med. Sch., 1933-47; prof. clin. pathology, dir. Temple U. Lab. Clin. Medicine, 1947-48; med. dir. govt. explosives lab. Carnegie Inst. Tech. and Bur. Mines, 1943-46; head dept. clin. pathology Cleve. Clinic Found., 1948-49; dir. clin. research M.D. Anderson Hosp. Cancer Research, Houston, 1949-50; dir. clin. labs. Grady Meml. Hosp., Atlanta, 1949-51; prof. clin. medicine Emory U. Sch. Medicine, 1949-51; chief clin. pathology Communicable Disease Center, USPHS, 1950-51; med. adviser Rohm & Haas Co., 1947-71; med. cons. Redstone Arsenal, U.S. Army Ordnance Dept., Huntsville, Ala., 1947-49; cons. clin. pathology St. Joseph's Hosp., Tampa, Fla., 1965-66; attending physician Jefferson Hosp., Phila., 1951—, dir. div. metabolic research, clin. prof. medicine, 1951-67, clin. prof. medicine, 1951-74, hon. clin. prof. medicine, 1975—; dir. Inst. Clin. Sci., 1965—; prof. pathology Hahnemann U. Med. Coll., 1970—, co-chmn. dept. lab. medicine, 1970-75, prof. emeritus, 1989; med. adviser and cons. bus. and industry, 1947—; dir. internat. seminars on clin. chemistry and pathology, 1947—; guest lectr. Beijing (People's Republic of China) Med. U., 1989. Author, editor 36 books on clin. chemistry and pathology; author: Our Madeira Heritage, 1979, Musical Notes of a Physician, 1982, Painting with Light, 1993; editor-in-chief Annals Clin. Lab. Sci., 1970—; mem. editl. bd. Am. Jour. Clin. Pathology, 1939-87, Am. Jour. Indsl. Medicine, 1979-85; cons. editor Am. Jour. Occupl. Medicine, 1979-85; also over 350 articles. Trustee Gettysburg Coll., 1967-89, chmn. bd. trustees, 1972-74, hon. life trustee, 1986—; bd. dirs. Mus. Fund Soc. Phila., 1938—, hon. life bd. dirs., 1993—; bd. dirs. Dwight D. Eisenhower Soc., 1984—, German Soc. Pa., 1986—, Geog. Soc. Phila., 1995; violin soloist Chautauqua Summer Series, Ea. U.S., 1919-20; guest soloist Concerto Soloists Pa., 1979, 83, 84, Pa. String Tchrs. Assn., Gettysburg, 1959, Westchester, 1962, 63, 67, 68, Trenton (N.J.) Tchrs. Coll. Orch., 1965; Internat. String Conf. soloist World Congress on Arts and Medicine, Carnegie Hall, N.Y.C., 1992. Recipient Naval Ordnance Devel. award, 1946, cert. appreciation War Dept., 1947, Honor medal Armed Forces Inst. Pathology, 1964; recipient Meritorious Svc. award, 1979, Honor award Latin Am. Assn. Clin. Biochemistry, 1976, Disting. Svc. award Am. Soc. Clin. Pathology-Coll. Am. Pathologists, 1988, Life-time Achievement award in clin. chemistry Joint Congresses of IX Congresso Nacional de la Sociedad Espanola de Quimica Clin., 2d Internat. Congress Therapeutic Drug Monitoring and Toxicology, and 4th Internat. Congress on Automation and New Tech., Spain, 1990, John Gunther Reinhold award Phila. Sect. Am. Assn. for Clin. Chemistry, 1991, Jacob Ehrenzeller award Res. Assn. Pa. Hosp., 1993; named Disting. Alumnus Gettysburg Coll., 1963; Sunderman Seminar Rm. dedicated at Bermuda Biol. Sta. for Rsch., 1992; 1st ann. F. William Sunderman award for Disting. Community Svc. and Excellence in a ChoField of Endeavor established by Rho Deuteron chpt. Phi Sigma Kappa, Gettysburg Coll; recipient Nat. Phi Sigma Kappa Disting. Alumnus award, 1995. Fellow ACP (life), Royal Soc. Medicine (hon., life), Royal Soc. Health Great Britain (life); mem. Am. Assn. History Medicine, Am. Diabetes Assn., AMA, Am. Soc. Clin. Investigation, Royal Soc. Health, AAUP, Endocrine Soc., Am. Assn. Biol. Chemistry, AAAS, Am. Chem. Soc., Internat. Union Pure and Applied Chemistry (nickel subcom. Commn. on Toxicology), Inst. Occupational Health (Finland), Outokumpu Oy (Finland), Am. Assn. Clin. Chemists (award for outstanding efforts in edn. and tng. 1981, John Gunther Reinhold award 1991), Coll. Am. Pathologists (founding gov., Pathologist of Yr. award 1962, Pres.'s Honor award 1984), Am. Soc. Clin. Pathology (pres. 1951, archives com. 1977—, intersoc. pathology coun. 1976—, interpathology soc. coun. 1976—, Ward Burdick award 1975, Continuing Edn. Distinguished Service award 1976), Assn. Clin. Scientists (pres. 1957-59, dir. edn. 1959—, diploma honor 1960, ann. goblet award 1964, Gold-headed cane 1974), Coll. Physicians of Phila. (sec. 1946-48, hon. pres. arts medicine sect. 1995, Disting. Service award 1980, 85, 90, 95), Knight of Order of St. Vincent of Portugal (Disting. Svc. cross, Order of merit, (das Verdienstkreuz), Bundesrepublik Deutschland, 1989), Am. Indsl. Hygiene Assn., Am. Occupational Medicine Assn., Med. Soc. Pa., Nat. Soc. Med. Research, Nat. Acad. Clin. Biochemistry, Pan Am. Med. Assn., Pa. Assn. Clin. Pathology, Philadelphia County Med. Soc., Mus. Fund Soc. Phila. (hon. life), Soc. Toxicology, Brit. Assn. Clin. Biochemists (hon.), Soc. Pharm. and Environ. Pathologists (hon.), Internat. Union Pure and Applied Chemistry, Inst. Occupational Health Finland (nickel subcom. commn. toxicology), Phi Beta Kappa, Sigma Xi, Alpha Omega Alpha, Phi Sigma Kappa (1st annual F. William Sunderman award for Cmty. Svc Rho Deuteron chpt. Gettysburg Coll. 1995, Nat. Disting. Alumnus award grand chpt. 1995), Alpha Kappa Kappa. Lutheran. Spl. symposium given in honor for lifetime achievement, Internat. Union Pure and Applied Chemistry, Finland, 1988. Home: 1833 Delancey Pl Philadelphia PA 19103-6606 Office: Pa Hosp Inst for Clin Sci 301 S 8th St Duncan Bldg 3A Philadelphia PA 19106-4014

SUNDLUN, BRUCE, governor; b. Providence, R.I., Jan. 19, 1920; s. Walter I. and Jane Z. (Colitz) S.; m. Marjorie G. Lee, Dec. 15, 1985; children by previous marriage: Tracy, Stuart, Peter, Mark Santelia, Kimberly Gerrie, Kara Hewes. BA, Williams Coll., 1942; LLB, Harvard U., 1949; student, Air Command and Staff Sch., 1948; DSBA (hon.), Bryant Coll., 1980; DBA (hon.), Roger Williams Coll., 1980; LLD (hon.), Johnson and Wales U., 1993, Williams Coll., 1993. Bar: R.I. and D.C. 1949. Asst. U.S. atty., Washington, 1949-51; spl. asst. to U.S. atty. gen., Washington, 1951-54; pvt. practice Washington and Providence, R.I., 1954-76; v.p., gen. counsel, dir. Outlet Co., Providence, 1960-76, pres., CEO, 1976-84, chmn. bd., CEO, 1984-88; gov. of R.I., 1990-92, 92—; pres. Exec. Jet Aviation, Inc., Columbus, Ohio, 1970-76, chmn. bd., 1976-84; incorporator, bd. dirs. Communications Satellite Corp., 1962-92; chmn. Round Hill Devel. Ltd., 1989-90. Mem. adv. group Nat. Aviation Goals, 1961; chmn. Inaugural Medal Com., Washington, 1961, 65; vice chmn. Inaugural Parade Com., 1961; bd. visitors USAF Acad., 1978-80; mem. R.I. Capital Center Commn., 1980, R.I. Legis. Pay Commn., 1980; vice chmn. Providence Rev. Com., 1981, chmn., 1982-85; mem. Providence Sch. Bd., 1985-90; mem. Providence Housing Authority, 1987, chmn. 1987-90; del. Dem. Nat. Conv. 1964, 68, 80, 88, 92, R.I. Constl. Conv., 1985; Dem. candidate for gov. R.I., 1986, 88, 90, 92; mem. exec. com. Dem. Gov. Assn., 1990-94; vice chmn. CONEG, 1992-94, chmn., 1994, chmn., vice chmn. Com. on Economy Nat. Gov. Assn., 1992-94, chmn. N.E. Gov. Assn., 1994; pres. Washington Internat. Horse Show, 1970-75, trustee, 1975-90; pres. Providence Performing Arts Ctr., 1978-90; bd. dirs. Touro Synagogue, Newport, R.I., 1979—, Miriam Hosp., 1985-90; bd. dirs. Temple Beth El, Providence, 1979-84, v.p., 1984-88, pres., 1988-91; bd. dirs. Trinity Repertory Theater, 1980-89, chmn., 1984-89; trustee R.I. Philharm. Orch., 1981-90; trustee Providence Preservation Soc., 1981-90, v.p., 1987-90; trustee Newport Art Mus., 1985, pres., 1987-91; pres. Providence Found., 1985-86; pres. R.I. C. of C. Fedn., 1981-84, bd. dirs., 1977-81; pres. Greater Providence C. of C., 1978-81, bd. dirs. 1976-85; bd. dirs. New Eng. Coun., 1978, vice chmn., 1980-81, chmn., 1981-83; trustee Bryant Coll., 1989—. Capt. USAAF, 1942-45; col. USAFR, ret., 1980. Decorated D.F.C., Air medal with oak leaf cluster, Purple Heart; chevalier Legion d'Honneur (France); Prime Minister's medal (Israel). Mem. Hope Club, Univ. Club, Spouting Rock Beach Assn., Clambake Club, Ida Lewis Club, Yacht Club (R.I.), 1925 F Street Club (Washington), Delta Upsilon. Home: Seaward Cliff Ave Newport RI 02840 Office: Office of the Governor State House Providence RI 02903

SUNDQUIST, DONALD KENNETH (DON SUNDQUIST), governor, former congressman, sales corporation executive; b. Moline, Ill., Mar. 15, 1936; s. Kenneth M. and Louise (Rohren) S.; m. Martha Swanson, Oct. 3, 1959; children: Tania, Andrea, Donald Kenneth. BA, Augustana Coll., 1957. Div. mgr. Josten's, Inc., 1961-72; exec. v.p. Graphic Sales of Am., Memphis, 1972, pres., 1973-82; mem. 98th-103rd Congresses from 7th Tenn. dist., Washington, 1983-94; gov. State of Tenn., Nashville, 1995—; vice chmn. bd. Bank of Germantown, Tenn. Past mem. White House Commn. Presdl. Scholars; past chmn. Jobs for High Sch. Grads. of Memphis; chmn. Congl. Steering Com. George Bush for Pres., 1988, 92; nat. campaign mgr. Howard Baker for Pres., 1979; dir. com. ops., alt. del. Republican Nat. Conv., 1980; chmn. Shelby County Rep. Party, 1975-77; alt. del. Rep. Nat. Conv., 1976; exec. com. Rep. Nat. Com., 1971-73; nat. chmn. Young Rep. Nat. Fedn., 1971-73; sec. Bedford County Election Commn., 1968-70; chmn. Tenn. Young Rep. Fedn., 1969-70; dir. Mid-South Coliseum, Am. Council Young Polit. Leaders, 1972-74, U.S. Youth Council, 1972-75; bd. govs. Charles Edison Meml. Youth Fund; nat. adv. bd. Distributive Edn. Clubs Am.; mem. U.S. del. study tour, People's Republic of China, 1978, study tour, USSR, 1975. Served with USN, 1957-59. Lutheran. Lodge: Kiwanis. Office: Office of Gov State Capitol Bldg Nashville TN 37243-0001*

SUNDQUIST, ERIC JOHN, American studies educator; b. McPherson, Kans., Aug. 21, 1952; s. Laurence A. and Frances J. (Halene) S.; m. Tatiana Kreinine, Aug. 14, 1982; children: Alexandra, Joanna, Ariane. BA, U. Kans., 1974; MA, Johns Hopkins U., 1976, PhD, 1978. Asst. prof. English Johns Hopkins U., Balt., 1978-80; asst. prof. English U. Calif., Berkeley, 1980-82, assoc. prof., 1982-86, prof. English, 1986-89; prof. English UCLA, 1989—, chair dept. English, 1994—; vis. scholar U. Kans., 1985, dir. Holmes grad. seminar, 1993; dir. NEH Summer Seminar for Coll. Tchrs., U. Calif., Berkeley, 1986, 90, UCLA, 1994; cons. Calif. Coun. for Humanities, 1986-87; prof. Bread Loaf Sch. English, Middlebury (Vt.) Coll., 1987, 89, Sante Fe, 95; mem. fellowship com. Newberry Libr., 1987, 88, 92; dir. NEH Summer Seminar for Secondary Sch. Tchrs., Berkeley, 1988; vis. prof. UCLA, 1988; Andrew Hilen vis. prof. U. Wash., 1990; Lamar Meml. lectr. in so. states Mercer U., 1991; Gertrude Conaway Vanderbilt prof. English Vanderbilt U., Nashville, 1992-93; mem. fellowship cons. Nat. Humanities Ctr., 1992, 93; acad. specialist in Am. studies Tel Aviv U., 1994; mem. adv. bd. Colloquium for the Study of Am. Culture, Claremont (Calif.) Grad. Sch. & Huntington Libr., 1994—. Author: Home as Found: Authority and Genealogy in Nineteenth-Century American Literature, 1979 (Gustave Arlt award Coun. Grad. Schs. in U.S. 1980), Faulkner: The House Divided, 1983, The Hammers of Creation: Folk Culture in Modern African-American Fiction, 1992, To Take the Nations: Race in the Making of American Literature, 1993 (Christian Gauss award Phi Beta Kappa 1993, James Russell Lowell award MLA 1993, Choice Outstanding Acad. Book 1994); co-author: Cambridge History of American Literature, Vol. II, 1995; editor: American Realism: New Essays, 1982, New Essays on Uncle Tom's Cabin, 1986, Frederick Douglass: New Literary and Historical Essays, 1990, Mark Twain: A Collection of Critical Essays, 1994, Cultural Contexts for Ralph Ellison's Invisible Man, 1995, Oxford W.E.B. DuBois Reader, 1996; mem. adv. bd. Studies in Am. Lit. and Culture, 1987-90, gen. editor, 1991—; mem. editl. bd. Am. Lit. History, 1987—, Ariz. Quar., 1987—; assoc. editor Am. Nat. Biography, 1990—; cons. The Libr. of Am., 1992—; consulting reader African-Am. Rev., 1992—; contbr. articles to profl. jours. Am. Coun. Learned Socs. fellow, 1981, NEH fellow, 1989-90, Guggenheim fellow, 1993-94 (declined). Mem. MLA (chair adv. coun. Am. lit. sect. 1994, mem. exec. com. divsn. 19th Century Am. lit. 1994—), Am. Studies Assn. (chair John Hope Franklin Prize com. 1993, mem. nat. coun. 1994—, mem. fin. com. 1995—, and other coms.), Am. Lit. Assn., Orgn. Am. Historians, So. Hist. Assn., So. Am. Studies Assn. (mem. exec. com. 1993—), Phi Beta Kappa. Office: Dept English UCLA Los Angeles CA 90077

SUNDQUIST, JAMES LLOYD, political scientist; b. West Point, Utah, Oct. 16, 1915; s. Frank Victor and Freda (Carlson) S.; m. Beth Ritchie, Dec. 25, 1937 (dec. 1982); children: Erik L., Mark L., James K.; m. Geraldine Coote, Dec. 3, 1983. Student, Weber Coll., 1932-34, HHD (hon.), 1990; student, Northwestern U., 1934-35; BS, U. Utah, 1939; MS in Pub. Adminstrn, Syracuse U., 1941; DDS (hon.), Carthage Coll., 1987. Reporter Salt Lake Tribune, 1935-39; adminstrv. analyst U.S. Bur. Budget, 1941-47, 49-51; reports and statistics officer Office Def. Moblzn., 1951-53; dir. mgmt. control European Command, U.S. Army, Berlin, 1947-49; asst. to chmn. Democratic Nat. Com., 1953-54; asst. sec. to gov. N.Y. State, 1955-56; asst. to U.S. Senator Clark, 1957-62; dep. under sec. agr., 1963-65; sr. fellow Brookings Instn., 1965-85, emeritus, 1985—, dir. govtl. studies, 1976-78; adj. prof. Smith Coll., 1975-78; Sec. platform com. Dem. Nat. Conv., 1960, 68. Author: Politics and Policy: The Eisenhower, Kennnedy and Johnson Years, 1968, Making Federalism Work, 1969 (Louis Brownlow award for best pub. adminstrn. book), Dynamics of the Party System, 1973 2d edit., 1983, Dispersing Population: What America Can Learn form Europe, 1975, The Decline and Resurgence of Congress, 1981 (Hardeman prize for best book on Congress), Constitutional Reform and Effective Government, 1986, 2d edit., 1992; editor Internat. Rev. Adminstrv. Scis., 1980-89, Beyond Gridlock?, 1993, Back to Gridlock?, 1995. Mem. Gov.'s Commn. on Va.'s Future, 1983-84. Recipient Exceptional Civilian Service award War Dept., 1945, Lifetime Achievement award Maxwell Sch. (Syracuse U.) Alumni Assn., 1994; sr. Research fellow U. Glasgow, Scotland, 1972-73. Mem. Nat. Acad. Pub. Adminstrn., Am. Soc. Pub. Adminstrn., Am. Polit. Sci. Assn. (treas. 1980, Charles E. Merriam award 1985), Am. Acad. Arts and Scis. Home: 3016 N Florida St Arlington VA 22207-1808 Office: 1775 Massachusetts Ave NW Washington DC 20036-2188

SUNDQUIST, JOHN A., religious organization executive. Exec. dir. Internat. Ministries Am. Bapt. Chs. U.S.A., Valley Forge, Pa.; chair internat. mission, gen. coun. Secs. of Bapt. World Alliance. Trustee No. Bapt. Sem., Lombard, Ill., Internat. Bapt. Sem., Prague. Office: Am Bapt Chs Internat Ministries PO Box 851 Valley Forge PA 19482-0851

SUNDQUIST, LEAH RENATA, physical education specialist; b. El Paso, Tex., July 22, 1963; d. Dominic Joseph and Patricia Ann (Manley) Bernardi; m. David Curtis Sundquist, June 23, 1990. AA, N.Mex. Mil. Inst., 1983; BS, U. Tex., El Paso, 1986; MEd in Curriculum & Instrn., City U., Bellevue, Wash., 1996. Field exec. Rio Grande Girl Scout Coun., El Paso, 1983-84; customer teller M-Bank, El Paso, 1984-85; soccer coach St. Clements Sch., El Paso, 1985; substitute tchr. El Paso Sch. Dist., 1986; commd. 2nd lt. U.S. Army, 1983, advanced through grades to capt., 1990-91; plans/exercise officer U.S. Army, Ft. Lewis, Wash., 1990; ops. officer U.S. Army, Ft. Lewis, 1990-1991; comdr. HHC 141st SPT BN U.S. Army Nat. Guard, 1996—; dir. Childrens World Learning Ctr., Federal Way, Wash., 1992-94; phys. edn. specialist, tchr. K-6 Kent (Wash.) Elem. Sch., Kent, Wash., 1995—. Coord. Nat. Conf. Christians and Jews, El Paso, 1979-81; v.p. Jr. Achievement, El Paso, 1980-81; adult tng. vol. Girl Scout Coun., bd. dirs. Pacific Peaks coun., 1993—, chair nominating com., 1996, jr. troop Girl Scout leader totem Girl Scout Coun., 1996; bd. dir. Jr. League Tacoma, 1993, 94. 3rd Res. Officer Tng. Corps scholar, 1981-83, H.P. Saunder scholar, 1982; recipient Humanitarian Svc. medal Great Fires of Yellowstone, U.S. Army, 1988, Gold award Girl Scouts U.S.A., 1981; decorated Nat. Def. Svc. medal Desert Storm; meritorious Svc. medal, 1991. Mem. NEA, Wash. Edn. Assn., Assn. U.S. Army, Air Def. Artillery Assn., Zeta Tau Alpha (sec. 1983-85, house mgr. 1984-86), Fellowship of Christian Athletes. Republican. Roman Catholic. Avocations: soccer, fishing, hunting, skydiving, rafting. Home: 2905 N 14th St Tacoma WA 98406-6905

SUNDQUIST, MARIA ALEXANDRA, diplomat; b. Buenos Aires, Argentina, Feb. 4, 1943; came to U.S., 1962; d. Alberto Oscar and Filomena (Cacciavillani) Garcia; m. Ralph H. Gunther, Oct. 10, 1964 (div. 1970); m. Erik Lindon Sundquist, Mar. 1, 1975; 1 child, Karin Alexandra. BA, Smith Coll., 1964; MA in Econs., NYU, 1969. Economist Chase Manhattan Bank, N.Y.C., Chem. Bank, N.Y.C.; asst. comml. attache Am. Embassy, Jeddah, Saudi Arabia, 1980-82; 1st sec. Am. Embassy, Paris, 1982-86; econ. officer U.S. Dept. of State, Washington, 1986-90; legis. asst. U.S. Senate, Washington, 1990-91; consul gen. U.S. Dept. of State, Bordeaux, France, 1991-94. Pearson fellow, 1990-91. Avocations: history, mysteries, opera, gastronomy. Office: US Dept State 2201 C St NW Rm 1252 Washington DC 20520-0001

SUNDSTROM, HAROLD WALTER, public relations executive; b. Chgo., Jan. 26, 1929; s. Elmer A. and Rosalind Lillian (Busse) S.; m. Mary Olin, Oct. 1, 1955; children: Geoffrey Lee, Lori Lynn, Deborah Barron. AA, Wright Jr. Coll., 1949; BA, Mich. State U., 1952, MA, 1954. Fgn. svc. info. officer USIA, Tokyo, Jakarta, Seoul, 1955-61; sr. pub. rels. assoc. Eli Lilly and Co., Indpls., 1962-66; v.p., dir. pub. rels. Eisenhower People to People Program, Kansas City, Mo., and Copenhagen, 1966-68; govt. and pub. affairs rep. North Ctrl. States Automobile Mfrs. Assn., Kansas City, 1968-69; speechwriter, pub. rels. cons. Commdr.-in-Chief U.S. Pacific Forces, Aiea, 1969-75; pres. No. Ariz. Comm., Inc., Flagstaff, 1975-79; asst. sec., dir. pub. affairs U.S. Internat. Trade Commn., Washington, 1977-87; v.p. pub. affairs and publs. Export-Import Bank U.S., Washington, 1987-89; pres. Halamar, Inc., Manassas, Va. and Easley, S.C., 1983—; freelance writer and poet. Author: The American West, 1956, Garuda, Introducing Indonesia, 1957, Politics and Nationalism in Indonesia, 1962, Faces of Asia: Korea, 1965, The Northern Arizona Scene, 1976, American Collie Champions, Vol. I, 1979, Vol. II, 1980, Vol. III, 1987, Collies - A Complete Pet Owners Manual, 1994, Pedigree Points, 1996; editor, pub. Hawaiian Dog Rev., 1972-76, Collie Cues, The Alaska Cir., The Arizona Cir., Internat. Lhasa Apso Rev., Sandwich Isles Dog Gazette, Travel Writer, Honolulu Sun Press, 1972-76. With US Army, 1947-48, 52-53, Tokyo. Recipient People to People Disting. Svc. award, 1967, George Washington Honor medal Freedam Found., 1968, Silver Beaver award, Aloha coun. Boy Scouts Am., 1975. Fellow Japan Soc. N.Y.; mem. Pub. Rels. Soc. Am. (past pres. Hawaii chpt., Silver Anvil award 1973), Dog Writers Assn. Am. (pres. 1984-92, Disting. Svc. award 1993), Dog Writers Ednl. Trust (vice chmn.), Collie Club Am. Found. (pres. 1990-92), Am. Kennel Club (del. 1986—), Pi Sigma Alpha, Phi Kappa Sigma. Republican. Avocations: pure-bred dog breeding and showing, power boating, travel, photography. Home and Office: 401 Watson Rd Easley SC 29642-8357

SUNDT, HARRY WILSON, construction company executive; b. Woodbury, N.J., July 5, 1932; s. Thoralf Mauritz and Elinor (Stout) S.; m. Dorothy Van Gilder, June 26, 1954; children: Thomas D., Perri Lee Sundt Touche, Gerald W. BS in Bus. Adminstrn., U. Ariz., 1954, postgrad., 1957-59. Salesman ins. VanGilder Agys., Denver, 1956-57; apprentice carpenter M.M. Sundt Constrn. Co., Tucson, 1957-58, estimator, 1958-59; adminstrv. asst. M.M. Sundt Constrn. Co., Vandenberg AFB, 1959-62; sr. estimator M.M. Sundt Constrn. Co., Tucson, 1962-64, div. mgr., 1964-65, exec. v.p., gen. mgr., 1965-75, pres., chmn., 1975-79; pres., chmn. Sundt Corp., Tucson, 1980-83, chmn., chief exec. officer, 1983—; bd. dirs. Tucson Electric Power Co., Nations Energy Co. Pres. Tucson Airport Authority, 1982; bd. dirs. U. Ariz. Found. 1981. 1st lt. U.S. Army, 1954-56. Recipient Disting. Citizen award U. Ariz., 1982, Centennial Medallion award, 1989. Mem. Tucson Country Club. Republican. Episcopalian. Avocation: tennis. Home: 6002 E San Leandro Tucson AZ 85715-3014 Office: Sundt Corp PO Box 26685 4101 E Irvington Rd Tucson AZ 85714-2118

SUNDY, GEORGE JOSEPH, JR., engineering executive; b. Nanticoke, Pa., Apr. 22, 1936; s. George Joseph Sr. and Stella Mary (Bodurka) S.; m. Stella Pauline Miechur, May 21, 1966; children: Sharon Ann, George Joseph III. BS, Pa. State U., 1958. Rsch. engr. Bethlehem (Pa.) Steel Corp., 1959-85; reliability engr. Flo-Con Systems, Inc. (name now Vesuvius USA), Champaign, Ill., 1985-90; reliability mgr., 1990—. Patentee in field. Mem.

Am. Soc. Materials, Am. Ceramics Soc., Iron and Steel Soc. AIME, Keramos, Sigma Tau. Democrat. Roman Catholic. Home: 604 E South Mahomet Rd Mahomet IL 61853-3602 Office: Vesuvius USA 1404 Newton Dr Champaign IL 61821-1069

SUNELL, ROBERT JOHN, retired army officer; b. Astoria, Oreg., June 5, 1929; s. Ernest and Grace L. S.; m. JoAnn L. Toikka, Dec. 29, 1951; children—Perry Sunell Peterson, Patti Sunell Sigl, Robert P. Student, U. Oreg., 1949-53; B.E., U. Nebr., 1963; M.S., Shippensburg State Coll., 1973. Commd. U.S. Army, 1953, advanced through grades to maj. gen., 1983, ret., 1987; exec. officer 1st Brigade, 4th Inf. div. U.S. Army, Vietnam, 1966-67, comdr. 2d Bn., 8th Inf., 4th Inf. div., 1969-70; chief Bn. and Brigade Tactical Ops. div. Armor Sch. U.S. Army, Ft. Knox, Ky., 1973-74, dep. dir. Armored Reconnaissance Scout Vehicle Task Force, 1974-76; dep. program mgr. XM1 Tank Systems U.S. Army, Warren, Mich., 1976-78; comdr. 11th Armored Cav. Regt. U.S. Army, Germany, 1978-79; comdr. Army Tng. Support Ctr. U.S. Army, Ft. Eustis, Va, 1980-83; program mgr. Tank Systems U.S. Army, Warren, Mich., 1983-86; dir. Armored Family of Vehicles Task Force, Fort Eustis, Va., 1986-87; apptd. adv. bd. dirs. Land Combat Com., Assn. of U.S. Army, 1995; cons. U.S. Army Sci. Bd. Decorated Silver Star, Legion of Merit, Bronze Star, Meritorious Service award, Disting. Service medal. Mem. U.S. Army Assn., Armor Assn. Republican.

SUNG, CHIEH-YUAN FRED, petro-chemical company executive; b. Tao-Yuan, China, Dec. 16, 1946; came to U.S., 1970; s. Fu-Ying and Chin-Mei (Wu) S.; m. Ann Sho-chu wu, Sept. 1, 1973; children: Kevin, Erwin. BSChemE, Nat. Taiwan U., Taipei, 1969; MSChemE, Clarkson U., 1972, PhChemE, 1974. Process engr. USI Chems. Co., N.Y.C., 1974-78, sr. prcoess engr., 1978-80, group leader process engring., 1980-84; mgr. process engring. USI Chems. Co., Cin., 1984-86, tech. dir., 1986-87; dir. process engring. Quantum Chem. Corp., Cin., 1987—; Patentee in field. Mem. AICE. Republican. Avocations: electronics, computers, travelling, tennis, photography. Home: 7005 Plumwood Ct Cincinnati OH 45241-1092

SUNG, NAK-HO, science educator; b. Seoul, Republic of Korea, Sept. 30, 1940; s. K.Y. and B.S. (Lee) S.; m. Chong Sook Paik, May 13, 1972; 1 child, Andrew J. BS, Seoul Nat. U., 1964; MS, U. Chgo., 1967; ScD, MIT, 1972. Process engr. Hanil Nylon Industry, Republic of Korea, 1963-66; teaching asst. U. Chgo., 1966-67; rsch. asst. MIT, Cambridge, Mass., 1967-72, rsch. assoc., 1972-74, asst. prof., 1974-78; asst. prof. Tufts U., Medford, Mass., 1978-80, assoc. prof., 1980-85, prof., 1985—; dir. Lab. for Materials Interfaces Lab. for Materials and Interfaces, Medford, Mass., 1989—; vis. prof. Chengdu (China) U. Sci. and Tech., 1985, U. Conn., Storrs, 1985; cons. Sunkyong Group, Seoul, 1976—, U.S. Army Material and Mech. Rsch. Ctr., Watertown, Mass., Johnson and Johnson, W.R. Grace; pres. northeast chpt. Korean Scientists and Engrs. Assn. in Am., Boston, 1977-78. Editor: Science and Technology of Polymer Processing, 1979; also over 80 publs. and one patent. Bd. dirs. JNG Internat. Inc., Korean Lang. Sch., Lexington, Mass., Korean Am. Soc. New Eng. Mem. Am. Chem. Soc., Am. Phys. Soc., Soc. Plastic Engrs., Adhesion Soc., Am. Inst. Chem. Engrs. Office: Tufts Univ Lab for Materials Interfaces Dept Chem Engring Medford MA 02155

SUNIA, TAUSESE, government official. Lt. gov. Pago Pago, AS. Office: Lieutenant Gov's Office Pago Pago AS 96799*

SUNLEY, EMIL MCKEE, economist; b. Morgantown, W.Va., July 30, 1942; s. Emil McKee and Nelle Berniece (Traer) S.; m. Judith Evelyn Steere, Dec. 23, 1966; children: Rachel Anne, Gillian Traer, Neil Steere. B.A., Amherst Coll., 1964; M.A., U. Mich., 1965, Ph.D., 1968. Economist office tax analysis Dept. Treasury, Washington, 1968-73; assoc. dir. office tax analysis Dept. Treasury, 1973-75, dep. asst. sec. for tax policy, 1977-81; sr. fellow Brookings Instn., Washington, 1975-77; dir. tax analysis Deloitte & Touche, Washington, 1981-92; asst. dir. fiscal affairs dept. Internat. Monetary Fund, 1992—. Mem. editl. bd. Nat. Tax Jour., 1992-95. Mem. Commn. on RR Retirement Reform, 1987-90. Mem. Am. Econ. Assn., Nat. Tax Assn. (pres. 1995-96), Tax Analysts (bd. dirs. 1982-93). Episcopalian. Office: Internat Monetary Fund Rm IS3-210 Fiscal Affairs Dept Washington DC 20431

SUNSTEIN, CASS ROBERT, law educator; b. Salem, Mass., Sept. 21, 1954. AB, JD, Harvard U. Bar: D.C. 1980. Law clk. for Thurgood Marshall, U.S. Supreme Ct., Washington, 1979-80; atty.-adviser U.S. Dept. Justice, Washington, 1980-81; prof. law U. Chgo. Sch. Law, 1981—; co-dir. Ctr. on Constitutionalism in Eastern Europe, 1992—. Author: After the Rights Revolution, 1990, The Partial Constitution, 1993, Democracy and the Problem of Free Speech, 1993 (Goldsmith Book award Harvard U.), Legal Reasoning and Political Conflict, 1996. Office: U Chgo Sch Law 1111 E 60th St Chicago IL 60637-2702

SUOJANEN, WAINO W., management educator; b. Maynard, Mass., Jan. 12, 1920; s. Waino I. and Milma (Lindroos) S.; m. Doris G. Stinson, Dec. 24, 1948; children—Wayne William, James Norman. BS, U. Vt., 1942; MBA, Harvard U., 1946; PhD, U. Calif. at Berkeley, 1955. Chief acct. UARCO Inc., Oakland, Calif., 1947-49; div. acct. Chris-Craft Corp., Salem, Oreg., 1949-50; Asst. prof. Sch. Bus. Adminstrn., U. Calif. at Berkeley, 1950-59; assoc. prof. U.S. Naval Postgrad. Sch., Monterey, Calif., 1959-61; dir. research and devel. mgmt. program Air Proving Ground Center, Eglin AFB, Fla., 1961-64; prof., chmn. dept. mgmt. U. Miami, Fla., 1964-70; prof. mgmt. Ga. State U., Atlanta, 1970-90, prof. emeritus, 1990—; adv. editor Chandler Pub. Co., 1965-71; mem. mgmt. adv. panel NASA, 1968-71; cons. U.S. Army Mgmt. Engring. Tng. Activity, 1954-89, U.S. Office Pers. Mgmt., 1964-84; fin. mgmt. cons. to comtr. Office Asst. Sec. Def., 1957-61; cons. in logistics mgmt. tng. Office Assn. Sec. Def. for Installations and Logistics, 1964-66; cons. in mgmt. edn. and tng. Office Asst. Sec. Def. for Manpower, 1966-67; lectr. mgmt. Royal Victorian Chamber Mfrs., Melbourne, Australia, summer 1968; bd. dirs. Russian-Am. Tech. Assocs., 1992. Author: The Dynamics of Management, 1966, (with others) The Operating Manager-An Integrative Approach, 1974, Perspectives in Job Enrichment and Productivity, 1975, Management and the Brain: An Integrative Approach to Organizational Behavior, 1983. Treas. Alameda County Mental Health Assn., 1953-56; bd. dirs. Vol. Atlanta, 1971-76. With Vt. Nat. Guard, 1937-40; capt. AUS, 1942-46; lt. col. USAF, ret., 1980. Recipient McKinsey Found. Book award, 1966. Mem. Acad. Mgmt, AAAS, Phi Beta Kappa, Alpha Kappa Psi, Beta Alpha Psi, Beta Gamma Sigma, Pi Gamma Mu, Sigma Iota Epsilon. Home: 1270 Mayflower Ave Melbourne FL 32940-6722

SUPPES, PATRICK, statistics, education, philosophy and psychology educator; b. Tulsa, Mar. 17, 1922; s. George Biddle and Ann (Costello) S.; m. Joan Farmer, Apr. 16, 1946 (div. 1970); children: Patricia, Deborah, John Biddle; m. Joan Sieber, Mar. 29, 1970 (div. 1973); m. Christine Johnson, May 26, 1979; children: Alexandra Christine, Michael Patrick. B.S., U. Chgo., 1943; Ph.D. (Wendell T. Bush fellow), Columbia U., 1950; LL.D., U. Nijmegen, Netherlands, 1979; Dr. honoris causa, Académie de Paris, U. Paris V, 1982. Instr., Stanford U., 1950-52, asst. prof., 1952-55, assoc. prof., 1955-59, prof. philosophy, statistics, edn. and psychology, 1959-92, prof. emeritus; founder, chief exec. officer Computer Curriculum Corp., 1967-90. Author: Introduction to Logic, 1957, Axiomatic Set Theory, 1960, Sets and Numbers, books 1-6, 1966, Studies in the Methodology and Foundations of Science, 1969, A Probabilistic Theory of Causality, 1970, Logique du Probable, 1981, Probabilistic Metaphysics, 1984, Estudios de Filosofia y Metodologí de la Ciencia, 1988, Language for Humans and Robots, 1991, Models and Methods in the Philosophy of Science, 1993; (with Davidson and Siegel) Decision Making, 1957, (with Richard C. Atkinson) Markov Learning Models for Multiperson Interactions, 1960, (with Shirley Hill) First Course in Mathematical Logic, 1964, (with Edward J. Crothers) Experiments on Second-Language Learning, 1967, (with Max Jerman and Dow Brian) Computer-assisted Instruction, 1965-66, Stanford Arithmetic Program, 1968, (with D. Krantz, R.D. Luce and A. Tversky) Foundations of Measurement, Vol. 1, 1971, (with M. Morningstar) Computer-Assisted Instruction at Stanford, 1966-68, 1972, (with B. Searle and J. Friend) The Radio Mathematics Project: Nicaragua, 1974-75, 1976 (with D. Krantz, R.D. Luce and A. Tversky) Foundations of Measurement, Vol. 2, 1989, Vol. 3, 1990, (with Colleen Crangle) Language and Learning for Robots, 1994. Served to capt. USAAF, 1942-46. Recipient Nicholas Murray Butler Silver medal Columbia, 1965, Disting. Sci. Contbr. award Am. Psychol. Assn., 1972, Tchrs. Coll. medal for disting. service, 1978, Nat. medal Sci. NSF, 1990; Center for Advanced Study Behavioral Scis. fellow, 1955-56; NSF fellow, 1957-58. Fellow AAAS, Am. Psychol. Assn., Am. Acad. Arts and Scis., Assn. Computing Machinery; mem. NAS, Math. Assn. Am., Psychometric Soc., Am. Philos. Assn., Am. Philos. Soc., Assn. Symbolic Logic, Am. Math Soc., Académie Internationale de Philosophie des Scis. (titular), Nat. Acad. Edn. (pres. 1973-77), Am. Psychol. Assn., Internat. Inst. Philosophy, Finnish Acad. Sci. and Letters, Internat. Union History and Philosophy of Sci. (div. logic, methodology and philosophy of sci., pres. 1975-79), Am. Ednl. Research Assn. (pres. 1973-74), Croatian Acad. Scis. (corr.), Russian Acad. Edn. (fgn.), Norwegian Acad. Sci. and Letters (fgn.), European Acad. Scis. and Arts, Chilean Acad. Scis., Sigma Xi.

SUPPLE, JEROME H., academic administrator; b. Boston, Apr. 27, 1936; m. Catherine Evans; 3 children. BS in Chemistry, Boston Coll., 1957, MS in Organic Chemistry, 1959; PhD in Organic Chemistry, U. New Hampshire, 1963. Asst. prof. chemistry SUNY Coll., Fredonia, 1964-69, assoc. prof., 1969-76, prof., 1976-78, acting dept. chair, 1975-76, assoc. dean for arts and scis., 1972-73, assoc. v.p. for acad. affairs, 1973-78, acting v.p. for acad. affairs, 1977, dean for gen. and spl. studies, 1977-78; assoc. provost for undergrad. edn. SUNY Cen. Adminstrn., 1974-75; prof. chemistry, v.p. for acad. affairs SUNY Coll., Plattsburgh, acting pres., 1978-89, on leave 1988-89; acting provost, v.p. for acad. affairs SUNY Coll., Postsdam, 1988-89; prof. chemistry, pres. S.W. Tex. State U., San Marcos, 1989—; Faculty fellow NSF, vis. rsch. faculty U. East Anglia, Norwich, Eng., 1970-71. Author books; contbr. numerous articles to profl. jours. Mem. Tex. Gov.'s total quality mgmt. steering com. Eastman Kodak rsch. fellow. Mem. AAAS, Am. Chem. Soc., Am. Assn. Higher Edn., Am. Assn. State Colls. and Univs., Am. Coun. on Edn. (mem. commn. on govtl. rels.), So. Assn. Colls. and Schs. Commn. on Colls., Tex. Coun. on Econ. Edn. (bd. dirs.), Tex. Coun. Pub. Univ. Pres. and Chancellors (state affairs and exec. com.), Tex. Assn. Coll. Tchrs., Tex. Higher Edn. Master Plan Adv. Com., San Marcos C. of C. Econ. Devel. Coun., San Marcos Rotary, Golden Key, Sigma Xi (past pres. Fredonia club), Phi Eta Sigma (hon.), Omicron Delta Kappa (hon.). Office: SW Tex State U Office of Pres 1020 J C Kellam Bldg San Marcos TX 78666

SUPUT, RAY RADOSLAV, librarian; b. Columbus, Ohio, May 13, 1922; s. Elias and Darinka (Balac) S.; m. Mary Grace Hansen, May 23, 1953 (dec. Nov. 1980); children: David Ray, Dorothy Mary; m. Milana Preradov, July 12, 1986. B.A., Ohio State U., 1950; M.S.L.S., Case Western Res. U., 1951, Ph.D., 1972; M.A., U. Chgo., 1955. Librarian Northwestern U., Evanston, Ill., 1951-52; reference and circulation librarian Law Library, U. Chgo., 1952-54, cataloger, 1954-57; asso. librarian Garrett-Evang. Theol. Sem., Evanston, 1957-58; head librarian Garrett-Evang. Theol. Sem., 1958-64; asst. dir. libraries and adj. lectr. dept. Slavic and E. European langs. Sch. Library Sci. Case Western Res. U., Cleve., 1964-67; acting dir. libraries Case Western Res. U., 1967-68; adj. instr. Case Western Res. U. (Sch. Library Sci.), 1965-69; librarian Case Western Res. U. (Freiberger Library), 1968-69; dir. univ. library, head dept. and prof. library sci. Ball State U., Muncie, Ind., 1969-78; univ. librarian, head dept. and prof. library service Ball State U., 1978-81, prof. library service, also adj. prof. library sci., 1981-82, chmn. dept. library and info. sci., prof. library sci., 1982-87, prof. library sci., info. sci. emeritus, 1987—. Contbr. articles to profl. jours. Nat. Endowment for Humanities and Council on Library Resources Inc. grantee. Mem. ALA, AAUP, African Violet Soc. Am., Am. Theol. Libr. Assn., Serb Nat. Fedn., Ohio Hist. Soc. Eastern Orthodox.

SURACI, CHARLES XAVIER, JR., retired federal agency administrator, aerospace education consultant; b. Washington, Feb. 10, 1933; s. Charles Xavier and June Celcia (Hunter) S.; m. Florence Patricia De Mino, May 23, 1970. Cadet, Penn Mil. Coll. (now Widener U.), 1951-53; grad., Nat. Acad. Broadcasting Sch., Washington, 1959; student, Columbia Union Coll., 1962-63, 72, Catholic U., 1969; grad. extension course, CAP Staff Coll., 1974; BA, Calif. Christian Coll., 1977, HHD (hon.), 1977; grad., USAF Inspectors Gen. Sch., Eglin AFB, Fla., 1982; also grad. numerous other govt. schs. and courses. Served with USAF, 1953-57; enlisted CAP, 1957, commd. 1st lt., 1961; advanced through ranks to Col. CAP USAF Aux, 1974; co-founder Wheaton-Silver Spring Cadet Squadron; comdr. Nat. Capital Wing, 1973-76; dep. chief of staff cadet activities Middle East region, 1977-79, dir. cadet tng., 1979-82, insp. gen., 1982—; with Harry Diamond Lab., U.S. Army, Adelphi, Md., 1963—, material publs. asst., 1963-68, later asst. to motor transp. officer, now supply specialist, logistics sect. Mem. youth com. YMCA, Silver Spring, Md., 1962-69, mem. bd. mgmt., 1967—; bd. dirs. Am. Youth Com.; mem. Commn. on Children and Youth Bd. Montgomery County, Md.; mem. Montgomery County Juvenile Ct. Com., 1978-86; choir mem. Blessed Sacrament Cath. Ch., Washington; co-chmn. Right to Life Com. K.C.-Rosensteel Coun.; mem. bd. dirs. Pregnancy Aid Ctr., College Park, Md. Recipient Leader and Svc. award Silver Spring YMCA, 1968, 69, CAP Meritorious Svc. award Dept. Def., 1969, 1977, cert. of commendation from Pres. Richard Nixon, 1970, CAP Exceptional Service award Congressman Lester Wolff of N.Y., 1972, award Montgomery County C. of C., 1973, commendation Gov. of Tenn., 1975, letter of commendation Washington Mayor Walter Washington, 1977, Dept. Outstanding Patriotic Civilian Service award, 1977, Md. Vol. Cmty. honor award Montgomery County, 1981, Vol. Activist award, 1984, George Washington Honor medal Valley Forge Freedom Found., 1995, Patrick Henry medal for patriotic achievement Military Order of the World Wars, 1995; named Air Man of Month USAF, 1956; grand marshall Rockville, Md., Meml. Day parade, 1971; honored by Md. Ho. Dels., 1974, D.C. Govt., 1977; recipient numerous AF and CAP ribbons and medals, Dept. of Army Spl. Act or Svc. award, Dept.of the Army Superior Performance award, 1987, Pres.'s Vol. Action award nomination Pres. of the U.S., 1988, 1991, Cmty. Svc. award Wheaton-Kensington News, Bethesda Chevy Chase Current, Montgomery County Press Assn., 1990, Outstanding support Aviation Career Day Tuskegee Airmen and Commdg. Gen. of D.C. Air Nat. Guard, 1992, spl. award State of Md. for training over 1000 youth cadets in the CAP in 31 yrs., 1986, plaque name displayed at U.S. Army-Harry Diamond Lab, Adelphi, Md., Pro-Life award Knights of Columbus-Rosensteel Coun., 1992, Frank G. Brewer Meml. Aerospace award-CAP Middle East Region HQ, 1984, 1991, 1992, CAP-U.S. Air Force Auxiliary Meritorious Svc. award Middle East Region HQ, 1993, Man of the Year award State of Md. Air Force Assn., 1993, Cert. Appreciation Md. Air Force Assn. Aerospace Edn., 1993-95, Exceptional Svc. award U.S. Air Force Auxiliary, 1994-95. Mem. Air Force Assn. (bd. dirs., v.p. aerospace edn. Thomas W. Anthony chpt. Andrews AFB, Md., medal of Merit 1990, Exceptional svc. award 1991, 94, Disting. Svc. as Inspector Gen. 1991), Nat. Aerospace Assn., Navy League, Army Aviation Assn., Fed. Ret. Employees Assn., Tuskegee Airmen Inc., Mil. Order of World Wars, Nat. Officers Assn., Md. Press Assn. Montgomery County, Md. Private Industry Coun. (bd. dirs. Opportunity Skyway program), Knights of Columbus (chmn. Pro-Life Father Rosensteel coun., Outstanding Leadership Pro-Life activities 1990-91, Outstanding Svc. award 1993-94), Alumni Assn. Widener U. Democrat. Club: Andrews AFB Officers (Md.). Lodge: KC. 2 plaques in his name displayed at Columbia Union Coll., Takoma Park, Md., Widener U. (formerly Pa. Mil. Coll.), Chester. me: Rock Creek Hills 9817 La Duke Dr Kensington MD 20895-3156 Office: USAF Aux CAP Mid East Region Hdqrs Office of Insp Gen 9817 La Duke Dr Kensington MD 20895-3156

SURATT, PAUL MICHAEL, physician, researcher; b. Ft. Lewis, Wash., Jan. 5, 1944; s. Theodore Paul and Ruth (Habink) S. BA, Columbia U., 1966; MD, Case Western Res. U., 1970. Diplomate Am. Bd. Internal Medicine. Intern, then resident in internal medicine U. Va. Sch. Medicine, Charlottesville, 1970-75, asst. prof. internal medicine, 1975-80, assoc. prof., 1980-88, prof., 1988—; organizer 1st Internat. Symposium on Sleep Apnea, 1989, 2d, 1991. Contbr. articles to med. jours. Maj. Va. N.G., 1971-77. Fellow Am. Coll. Internal Medicine, Am. Coll. Chest Physicians; mem. Am. Thoracic Soc., Am. Sleep Apnea Assn. (pres. 1989-93). Avocations: hiking, cycling, skiing, reading. Office: U Va Health Sci Ctr PO Box 546 Charlottesville VA 22902-0546

SURBECK, LEIGHTON HOMER, retired lawyer; b. Jasper, Minn., Oct. 8, 1902; s. James S. and Kathryn (Kilpatrick) S.; m. Margaret H. Packard, 1976. B.S., S.D. State Sch. Mines, 1924; J.D. magna cum laude, Yale, 1927; L.H.D., S.D. Sch. Mines and Tech., 1957; LL.D., Central Coll., 1973; D.Humanitarian Services, Northwestern Coll., Iowa, 1980; LL.D., Hope Coll., 1986; DHL (hon.), Judson Coll., Elgin, Ill., 1995. Bar: N.Y. 1929. Law sec. to Chief Justice Taft, 1927-28; assoc. Hughes, Schurman & Dwight, N.Y.C., 1928-34; mem. firm Hughes, Schurman & Dwight, 1934-37; mem. firm Hughes, Hubbard & Reed, N.Y.C., 1937-70, counsel, 1981-70. Author: Success on the Job, 1957, The Success Formula that Really Works, 1986. Trustee Pacific Sch. Religion, Berkeley, Calif., 1962-80, Golden Gate U., San Francisco, 1979-91, Central Coll., Pella, Iowa, 1966-78, Collegiate Boy's Sch., N.Y.C., 1975-78; chmn. Yale Law Sch. Fund, 1971-75. Served as col. AUS, 1942-45; chief econ. br. M.I. 1944-45. Recipient Yale medal Yale Alumni, 1975, Distinguished Service award Yale Law Sch., 1976; Horatio Alger award, 1977; named Centennial Alumnus State of S.D., 1989. Mem. ABA, N.Y. State Bar Assn., N.Y. County Bar Assn., Assn. of Bar of City of N.Y., Siwanoy Country Club, Univ. Club (N.Y.C.), Menlo Country Club (Woodside, Calif.), Masons, Order of Coif, Sigma Tau., Delta Theta Phi. Mem. Marble Collegiate Ch. (elder 1962-78). Home: 88 Faxon Rd Atherton CA 94027-4046 *Every honest, best effort prayerfully and with enthusiasm toward noble purposes useful beyond self always pays off handsomely, often at the most unexpected time, in the most unexpected ways and from the most unexpected sources.*

SURBER, EUGENE LYNN, architect; b. Hagerstown, Md., May 15, 1938; s. Eugene Wicker and Kathryn Gertrude (Hunt) S.; m. Margaret Ann Sparks, May 7, 1983; 1 child, James Eugene. BArch, Ga. Inst. Tech., 1964. Registered architect, Ga. Intern architect Edwards & Portman Architects, Atlanta, 1964-65, J. Robert Carlton & Assocs., Richmond, Va., 1965-66; assoc. architect Jova/Daniels/Busby Architects, Atlanta, 1966-71; prin. Surber & Barber Architects, Inc., Atlanta, 1971—; mem. bldg com. Cath. Archdiocese Atlanta, 1990-95, chmn., 1994-95. Prin. works include N.E.-Intown YWCA (Ga. Trust award 1992), Peachtree Presbyn. Ch. (Ga. Trust award 1992), The Buggyworks (Fulton Cty Devel. award 1987), The Castle (Atlanta Urban Design award 1991), Wade Hampton Clubhouse and Cottages (So. Home awards 1990), Hillcrest Chapel (Ga. Trust award 1991), Byron Depot (Ga. Trust award 1991), Upson House (Ga. Trust award 1980), Franklin House (Ga. Trust award 1986), Acad. of Medicine (Ga. Assn. AIA award 1983, Ga. Trust award 1985). Past chmn. Ga. Nat. Register Rev. Bd., 1990; trustee Ga. Trust for Historic Preservation, 1989-95, chmn. restoration com. Lt. USN, 1961-64. Fellow AIA (sec. Atlanta chpt. 1989-90, v.p. 1990-91, Hist. Preservation award 1986, Ivan Allen Sr. award 1992, Silver medal Atlanta chpt. 1993, Bronze medal 1974), Ga. Assn. AIA (state preservation coord. 1986—, Bronze medal 1993). Avocation: gardening. Office: Surber & Barber Archs Inc 1389 Peachtree St NE Ste 350 Atlanta GA 30309-3038

SURBER, REGINA BRAMMELL, early childhood education educator, administrator; b. Grayson, Ky., Apr. 3, 1952; d. Jack D. and Opal (Mullins) Brammell; m. Thomas Jerry Surber, Dec. 18, 1976; 1 child, Jerry David. BA in Elem. Edn., Berea Coll., 1974; MA in Early Childhood Edn., Ea. Ky. U., 1975; MA in Child Care Administrn., Nova U. Cert. K-8 grade tchr., ky., Tenn. Kindergarten tchr. Carter County Bd. Edn., Grayson, Ky.; presch. tchr. Oak Ridge Nursery Sch., Tenn.; elem. tchr. Anderson County Bd. Edn., Clinton, Tenn.; dir. daycare Roane State Community Coll., Harriman, Tenn., 1989-90; exec. dir. Knox Assn. on Young Children, Knoxville, Tenn., 1993—. Dir. weekday sch. programs 1st Meth. Ch., Oak Ridge, 1990-93. Mem. ASCD, Nat. Assn. for Edn. Young Children, Tenn. Assn. on Young Children, Anderson Area Assn. on Young Children (pres.).

SURDAM, ROBERT MCCLELLAN, retired banker; b. Albany, N.Y., Oct. 28, 1917; s. Burke and LeMoyne (McClellan) S.; m. Mary Caroline Buhl, July 8, 1946; children—Peter Buhl, Robert McClellan, Mary Caroline. B.A. cum laude, Williams Coll., 1939. With Nat. Bank Detroit, 1947-88, exec. v.p., 1964-66, pres., 1966-72, chmn. bd., 1972-82, also bd. dirs., 1966-88. Served to lt. comdr. USNR, 1941-46. Mem. Detroit Club, Country Club of Detroit, Yondotega Club, Jupiter Island Club (Hobe Sound, Fla.), Little Traverse Yacht Club (Harbor Springs, Mich.), Rolling Rock Club (Ligonier, Pa.), Hobe Sound Yacht Club. Home: 396 Provencal Rd Grosse Pointe MI 48236-2959 Office: 333 W Fort St Detroit MI 48226-3134

SURDOVAL, DONALD JAMES, accounting and management consulting company executive; b. N.Y.C., Aug. 26, 1932; s. Donald J. and Catherine A. (Slevin) S.; m. Patricia Fitzpatrick, May 28, 1955; children: Donald, Lisa, John, Catherine, Brian. B.B.A., Manhattan Coll., 1954. C.P.A., N.Y., N.J. Mgr. Touche Ross & Co., 1956-63; treas. Mohican Corp., 1963-65; asst. controller, then v.p., controller Litton Industries, 1965-68; v.p., controller Norton Simon Inc., N.Y.C., 1968-81; owner Donald J. Surdoval, C.P.A. and Mgmt. Cons. Co., Waldwick, N.J., 1982—; dir. Fuller O'Brien Paint Co. Bd. dirs. Calvary Hosp., N.Y.C., Our Lady of Mercy Hosp. Served to 1st lt. USMCR, 1954-56. Mem. Fin. Execs. Inst., Hackensack Golf Club, Saddle River Valley Lions (treas.). Home: 12 Warewoods Rd Saddle River NJ 07458-2713 Office: 20 Franklin Tpke Waldwick NJ 07463-1749

SURGENT, SUSAN PEARL, benefits consultant; b. Binghamton, N.Y., Jan. 6, 1963; d. Victor J. and Joan A. (Linville) Courtney; m. David M. Surgent, Sept. 7, 1985. AAS in Bus., Broome C.C., Binghamton, 1982; BS in Applied Social Sci magna cum laude, Binghamton U., 1993. Notary pub., N.Y. Mktg. asst. Johnson Camping, Inc., Binghamton, 1982-84; employment asst. CAE-Link Corp., Binghamton, 1984-85, adminstr. facility benefits, 1985-90, adminstr. corp. benefits, 1990-94; regional sales mgr. Prepaid Health Plan, Binghamton, N.Y., 1994—. Vol. educator Sch. and Bus. Alliance, Broome and Tioga counties, 1992—. Mem. Internat. Soc. Employee Benefit Profls., Golden Key, Phi Theta Kappa. Democrat. Episcopalian. Avocations: travel, collectibles, antiques. Home: 93 Albany Ave Johnson City NY 13790-1503 Office: Prepaid Health Plan 49 Court St Binghamton NY 13901-3236

SURH, YOUNG-JOON, medical educator; b. Seoul, Korea, Sept. 26, 1957; came to the U.S., 1985; s. Jung-Chun and Kyung-Ok (Yoon) S.; m. Young-Kyu Lee, Jan. 10, 1983; 1 child, Jee-Hyuk. BS, Seoul (Korea) Nat. U., 1981, MS, 1983; PhD, U. Wis., 1990. Tchg. staff Seoul (Korea) Nat. U., 1983-85; rsch. asst. U. Wis., Madison, 1985-90, tchg. asst., 1988; rsch. assoc. Harvard Med. Sch., Boston, 1990; postdoctoral assoc. MIT, Cambridge, Mass., 1991-92; asst. prof. Yale Sch. Medicine, New Haven, 1992—; adv. bd. Soc. Biomed. Rsch., Rockville, Md., 1994—. Author: Adv. Exp. Medicine Biol., 1991, Advances in Pharmacology, 1994, Handbook Exp. Pharmacol., 1994. 2d lt., 1983-84, Korea. Recipient Best Paper award U. Ill., Urbana, 1989, Spl. Interest Rsch. award Am. Cancer Soc., 1992. Mem. Internat. Soc. for the Study Xenobiotics, Am. Assn. for Cancer Rsch. (assoc.), N.Y. Acad. Scis. (acting), Sigma Xi. Achievements include first demonstration of formation of a covalently bound adduct between vitamin C and an ultimate electrophilic and carcinogenic metabolite; first demonstration of DNA adduct formation in vivo from electrophilic sulfate esters. Avocations: baseball, hiking. Home: 12131 Town Walk Dr Hamden CT 06518-3728 Office: Yale U Sch Medicine 400 LEPH 60 College St New Haven CT 06510-3210

SURJAATMADJA, JIM BASUKI, research engineer; b. Malang, Indonesia, Apr. 17, 1945; came to U.S., 1971; s. Rudolph and Gwat Nio (Oei) S.; m. Agnes Irmawati Said, Aug. 26, 1971; children: Sylvia Michelle, Amy Lynn. MS, Inst. Technol. Bandung, Bandung, Indonesia, 1970, Okla. State U., 1972; PhD, Okla. State U., 1976. Registered profl. engr., Okla. System engr. IBM, Jakarta, Indonesia, 1970-71; rsch. asst. Okla. State U., Stillwater, 1972-76; project engr. Fluid Power Rsch., Stillwater, 1972-76; from engr. to prin. engr. Halliburton Energy Svcs., Duncan, Okla., 1976—. Author: Introduction to Fluid Logic, 1976; contbr. more than 36 articles to profl. jours. and confs. Recipient Young Engrs. award S.W. region Okla. Soc. Profl. Engrs., 1979, Okla. Soc. Profl. Engrs., 1980. Fellow ASME; mem. Soc. Petroleum Engrs. (chmn.), U.S. Water Jet Tech. Assn. Achievements include 29 patents in area of fluid systems, automated systems, artificial intelligence, laboratory instruments, oil well-related tools, and industrial cleaning tools. Home: 1105 Timbercreek Dr Duncan OK 73533-1143 Office: Halliburton Energy Svcs 2600 S 2d Duncan OK 73536

SURKIN, ELLIOT MARK, lawyer; b. Phila., Apr. 22, 1942; s. Hersh M. and Minnie (Shore) S.; m. Carol E. Foley, May 26, 1973; 1 child, Jennifer Dykema. A.B., Princeton U., 1964; LL.B., Harvard U., 1967. Bar: Mass. 1967. Assoc. Hill & Barlow, Profl. Corp., Boston, 1967-73; mem. Hill & Barlow, Profl. Corp., 1973—, chmn. mgmt. com., 1988-92; lectr. law Harvard U., 1975-96; vis. lectr. MIT, Ctr. for Real Estate, 1996—. Chmn. bd. Boston Ctr. Arts, 1972-81, dir., mem. exec. com., 1981-83, hon. dir., 1983—; trustee, mem. exec. com., clk. Wang Ctr. for Performing Arts, Boston, 1980—; mem. New Eng. com. Legal Def. Fund NAACP, 1976-93;

mem. Chappaquiddick local com. Trustees of Reservations, 1982—, chmn. local com. 1986—, trustee 1985—, mem. adv. coun. 1988-94, mem. standing com. 1994—, mem. exec. com. 1996—; dir. Sheriff's Meadow Found., 1994—. Mem. ABA, Am. Law Inst., Am. Coll. Real Estate Lawyers, Mass. Bar Assn., Boston Bar Assn., St. Botolph Club, Harvard Club of Boston, Edgartown Yacht Club, Country Club of Brookline, Mass. Home: 1784 Beacon St Newton MA 02168-1434 Office: Hill & Barlow PC One International Place Boston MA 02110

SURKS, MARTIN I., medical educator, endocrinologist; b. N.Y.C., May 21, 1934. A.B., Columbia U., 1956; M.D., NYU, 1960. Diplomate Nat. Bd. Med. Examiners, Am. Bd. Internal Medicine, Am. Bd. Endocrinology and Metabolism; lic. physician, N.Y. State. Intern Montefiore Hosp., N.Y.C., 1960-61, jr. asst. resident in medicine, 1961-62; sr. asst. resident VA Hosp., Bronx, 1962-63; postdoctoral research fellow Nat. Inst. Arthritis and Metabolic Diseases, 1963-64; assoc. in medicine Albert Einstein Coll. Medicine, Bronx, 1967-69, asst. prof. medicine, 1969-72, assoc. prof., 1972-78, prof., 1978—, assoc. prof. lab. medicine, 1978-85, prof., 1985—, prof. pathology, 1994—; co-dir. endocrine rsch. lab. Montefiore Hosp., Bronx, 1969-76, head div. endocrinology and metabolism, 1976—, attending, 1981—; attending N. Cen. Bronx Hosp., 1976—; Van Meter lectr. Am. Thyroid Assn., Seattle, 1973; mem. merit rev. bd. VA, 1976-79; mem. endocrine study sect. NIH, 1981-85. Editorial bd. Endocrinology, 1974-78, Endocrine Research Communications, 1974—, Am. Jour. Physiology: Endocrinology and Metabolism, 1982-85, Jour. Clinical Endocrinal Metabolism, 1991-95; assoc. editor Endocrinology, 1986-87. Contbr. articles to profl. jours. Served to capt. M.C., U.S. Army, 1964-66. Grantee U.S. Army, Am. Cancer Soc., USPHS, Nat. Cancer Inst.; Schering fellow, 1968. Fellow ACP; mem. Am. Thyroid Assn. (Van Meter prize, 1973; program com. 1975-77, 3d v.p. 1976-77, chair membership com. 1977-78, 80-81, dir. 1982-83, 87-90, nominating com. 1982-85, chair awards and prizes com. 1983-84, dir. 1988-92, sec. 1993—), Endocrine Soc. (manpower liaison com. 1983-86, fin. com. 1995—, internat. endocrine congress com. 1995—), N.Y. Zool. Soc., Am. Fedn. Clin. Rsch., Am. Bd. of Internal Medicine (sect. of endocrinology and metabolism 1987-95, chmn. 1991-95, bd. dirs. 1991-95), Harvey Soc., Am. Physiology Soc., AAAS, Am. Soc. Clin. Investigation, European Thyroid Assn. (corr.), Assn. Am. Physicians, Am. Soc. Cell Biology, Interurban Clin. Club (councillor 1987-89), Phi Beta Kappa, Alpha Omega Alpha. Office: Montefiore Med Ctr 111 E 210th St Bronx NY 10467-2490

SURLES, CAROL D., university president; b. Pensacola, Fla., Oct. 7, 1946; d. Elza Allen and Versy Lee Smith; divorced; children: Lisa Surles, Philip Surles. BA, Fisk U., 1968; MA, Chapman Coll., 1971; PhD, U. Mich., 1978. Personnel rep. U. Mich., Ann Arbor, 1973-78; vice chancellor-adminstrn. U. Mich., Flint, 1987-89; exec. asst. to pres., assoc. v.p. for human resources U. Ctrl. Fla., Orlando, 1978-87; v.p. acad. affairs Jackson State U., Miss., 1989-92; v.p. adminstrn. and bus. Calif. State U., Hayward, 1992-94; pres. Tex. Woman's U., Denton, Dallas, Houston, 1994—. Trustee Pub. Broadcasting Ch. 24, Orlando, 1985-87; bd. dirs. First State Bank, Denton, Tex., Tex.-N.Mex. Power Co., TNP-Enterprise. Recipient Outstanding Scholar's award Delta Tau Kappa, 1983. Mem. AAUW, Am. Assn. Colls. and Univs., Golden Key Honor Soc., Mortar Bd. Soc., Dallas Citizens' Coun., Dallas Women's Found., Coun. of Pres. (Austin, Tex.), Phi Kappa Phi, Alpha Kappa Alpha. Methodist. Avocation: playing piano and oboe.

SURLES, RICHARD HURLBUT, JR., law librarian; b. Norfolk, Va., Mar. 28, 1943; s. Richard H. and Elda Florine (Belvin) S.; m. Judith Louise Coffin, May 29, 1964; children—Stephanie Anne, Richard H. B.A., Tex. A&M U., 1963; J.D., U.Houston, 1967; M.L.L., U.Wash., 1969. Bar: Colo. 1971. Asst. to law librarian U. Houston, 1966-68; asst. to law librarian King county Law Library, Seattle, 1968-69; dir. of law library, prof. law U. Denver, 1969-71, U. Tenn., Knoxville, 1971-76, U. Oreg., Eugene, 1976-81; dir. of law library, prof. law U. Ill., Champaign, 1981—, prof. libr. adminstrn., 1991. Author: Legal Periodical Management Data, 1977. Mem. Am. Assn. Law Libraries. Republican. Office: Ill Coll of Law 504 E Pennsylvania Ave Champaign IL 61820-6909

SURLS, JAMES, sculptor; b. Terrell, Tex., 1943. BS, Sam Houston State Coll., 1965; MFA, Cranbrook Acad. Art, 1969. instr. sculpture So. Meth. U., Dallas, 1970-75; assoc. prof. U. Houston, 1975-83. Commd. works include Pine Flower Buford TV Inc., Tyler, Tex., 1979, The Brazos Flower Brazos Ctr. and Arena/Pavilion Complex, Bryan, Tex., 1986, There Used to be a Lake (with Robert Creeley), Poets Walk, Citicorp Plz., L.A., 1988, Points of View Market Sq. Park Project, Houston, 1991, To the Point GTE Telephone Operators World Hdqrs. Hidden Ridge, Irving, Tex., 1991; exhibited in group shows at San Francisco Mus. Modern Art, 1975, 82, Solomon R. Guggenheim Mus., N.Y., 1977, Whitney Mus. Am. Art, 1979, 83, 84, 85, Fine Art for Fed. Bldgs., 1972-79, Smithsonian Instn., Washington, 1980, Mus. Fine Arts Houston, 1983, Art Inst. Chgo., 1986, Albright-Knox Art Gallery, Buffalo, N.Y., 1987; one-man shows include Arthur Roger Gallery, New Orleans, 1989, Barry Whistler Gallery, Dallas, 1989, 92, Hiram Butler Gallery, Houston, 1989, 92, Jan Weiner Gallery, Kansas City, Mo., 1990, 92, Contemporary Mus. Honolulu, 1991, Marlborough Gallery, N.Y.C., 1988, Gerald Peters Gallery, Dallas, 1988, Dallas Art Mus., 1991, Braustein/Quay Gallery, San Francisco, 1992, Allen Ctr. Gallery, Houston, 1992. Fellow Nat. Endowment Arts, 1979; named Tex. Artist of Yr. Houston Area Art League, 1991. *

SURMA, JANE ANN, secondary education educator; b. Chgo., Dec. 11, 1947; d. John James and Genevieve (Buettner) S. BS, Barry U., Miami, Fla., 1969; MST, U. Ill., 1974. Tchr. phys. edn. Little Flower H.S., Chgo., 1969-72; tchr. English, phys. edn. and health, coach Oak Lawn (Ill.) Cmty. H.S., 1974—. Named Coach of Yr. Southtown Economist, 1992, Boy's Volleyball Ill. State Championship Coach, 1994, Fred Parks Coach of Yr., 1995. Mem. AAHPERD, Ill. H.S. Coaches Assn., Ill. H.S. Assn., Nat. Coun. Tchrs. English. Roman Catholic. Office: Oak Lawn Cmty HS Oak Lawn IL 60453

SUROVELL, EDWARD DAVID, real estate company executive; b. Washington, Mar. 20, 1940; s. Samuel and Florence Deborah (Starfield) S.; m. Barbara Ann Bartelmes, Apr. 26, 1958 (div. Jan. 1974); children: David Alexander, Claire Katherine. AB, Columbia U., 1962; postgrad., U. Mich., 1968-71. Lic. real estate broker, Mich. Copy editor Harcourt, Brace & World, Inc., N.Y.C., 1963-65; editor Princeton (N.J.) U. Press, 1965-67, Scott, Foresman Co., Glenview, Ill., 1967-68, U. Mich., Ann Arbor, 1970-73; real estate agt. Fletcher & Klein, Inc., Ann Arbor, 1973-75; sales mgr. Charles Reinhart Co., Ann Arbor, 1975-82; pres. Edward Surovell Co., Realtors, Ann Arbor, 1982—. Chmn. Ann Arbor City Planning Commn., 1988; active Downtown Devel. Authority, Ann Arbor, 1991-95, vice chair, 1994-95; trustee Ann Arbor Dist. Libr., 1996—. Mem. Nat. Assn. Realtors (bd. govs. RB coun. 1987-91), Mich. Bd. Profl. Cmty. Planners, Hist. Soc. Mich. (trustee 1992—), Ann Arbor Bd. Realtors (v.p. 1984, pres. 1985, Realtor of Yr. 1990), Univ. Mus. Soc. (bd. dirs. 1992—). Democrat. Jewish. Avocations: book collecting, arts philanthropy. Home: 2024 Vinewood Blvd Ann Arbor MI 48104-3614 Office: Edward Surovell Co/Realtors 1886 W Stadium Blvd Ann Arbor MI 48103-7007

SUROWIECKI, JERZY, pharmaceutical executive; b. Dabrowka, Radom, Poland, Jan. 14, 1934; s. Jozef and Jadwiga (Kurkowska) W.; m. Bozenna Bronislawa Jamrozek, Nov. 6, 1959; 1 child, Robert J. MS, Med. Acad., Warsaw, Poland, 1956; PhD, Jagiellonian U., Cracow, Poland, 1970. Pharm. diplomate. Asst. Pharm. Industry Inst., Warsaw, 1957-59, head applied pharmacy, 1965-70; Family Planning Securitas Family Planning Securities, Warsaw, 1960-64; UN expert UNIDO, Accra, Ghana, 1971-75; tech. and sci. mgr. Union Pharm. Industry, Warsaw, 1976-77; mng. dir. Polfa-Nigeria Ltd., Lagos, 1978-83; dep. gen. Tgn. Trade Orgn., Warsaw, 1984-86; gen. mgr. Upjohn Co., Warsaw, 1987-95; pres. Pharmacia and Upjohn Inc. Mkt. Co., Warsaw, Poland, 1996—; cons. Ctr. for Strategic and Internat. Studies, Warsaw, 1992, Am. C. of C., Warsaw, 1993—. Contbr. numerous articles to profl. jours. 2d lt. Polish Univ. Mil. Svc., 1952-56. Recipient Dow Leadership award Hillsdale (Mich.) Coll., 1990. Mem. Pharm. Assn., Pharm. Industry Rep. Assn. (chmn. 1994—), N.Y. Acad. Scis. Avocations: tennis, bridge, books. Home: Filtrowa 81 m 40, 02 032 Warsaw Poland Office: Upjohn, Jakuba Kubickiego 21, 02 594 Warsaw Poland

SURPRISE, JUANEE, chiropractor, nutrition consultant; b. Gary, Ind., Apr. 28, 1944; d. Glenn Mark and Willia Ross (Vasser) Surprise; m. Peter E. Coakley, Feb. 12, 1966 (div. Jan. 1976); children: Thaddeus, Mariah, Darius; m. Robert T.Howell, Feb. 24, 1984. RN, Phila. Gen. Hosp. Sch. Nursing, 1965; DrChiropractic summa cum laude, Life Chiropractic Coll, Marietta, Ga., 1981. Diplomate Nat. Bd. Chiropractic Bd. Nutrition, Am. Acad. Pain Mgmt.; cert. clin. nutritionist; cert. in acupuncture, Thompson technique, Nimmo receptor tonus technique. Staff nurse Children's Hosp., Balt., 1966-67; charge nurse Melrose (Mass.)-Wakefield Hosp., 1967-68; hosp. adminstr. Animal Hosp. of Wakefield, Mass., 1967-79; chiropractor Chiropractic Clinic of Greenville, N.C., 1982-84, Chiropractice Rehab. Clinic, Denton, Tex., 1984—. Mem., chmn. Cmty. Planning Commn., North Reading, Mass., 1976-79; chmn. bldg. com. Immaculate Conception Ch., Denton, 1987-90, parish coun., 1990-92. Mem. ACA Coun. on Nutrition (sec.-treas.), Internat. and Am. Assns. Clin. Nutritionists, Internat. Assn. Pain Mgmt., Am. Chiropractic Assn., Am. Chiropractic Bd. on Nutrition (pres.), Tex. Chiropractic Assn., Tex. Chiropractic Assn. Coun. on Nutrition (sec.-treas.), Pi Tau Delta. Republican. Roman Catholic. Avocations: health education, camping, equine events. Office: Chiropractic Rehabs Clinic 1100 Dallas Dr Denton TX 76205-5153

SURREY, MILT, artist; b. N.Y.C., Mar. 18, 1922; s. Leopold and Pauline (Zipper) Schleifer; m. Eleanor Gallant, Sept. 15, 1946; children—Elaine, Robert, David. Student, Coll. City N.Y., 1939-42. Represented in permanent collections, Allentown (Pa.) Art Mus., Butler Inst. Am. Art, Youngstown, Ohio, Cin. Art Mus., Coll. Mus. Hampton (Va.) Inst., Columbia (S.C.) Mus. Art, Davenport (Iowa) Mus., Detroit Inst. Arts, Evansville (Ind.) Mus. Art, Hickory (N.C.) Mus. Art, Jacksonville (Fla.) Art Mus., Lowe Art Center, Syracuse (N.Y.) U., Massillon (Ohio) Mus., Miami (Fla.) Mus. Modern Art, Springfield (Mo.) Art Mus., Telfair Acad. Arts and Scis., Savannah, Ga., Holyoke (Mass.) Mus. Natural History, Theodore Lyman Wright Art Center, Beloit (Wis.) Coll., Treat Gallery, Bates Coll., Lewiston, Maine. Served with AUS, 1942-45. Mem. Am. Fedn. Arts. Home: 425 E 58th St New York NY 10022-2300

SURRIDGE, STEPHEN ZEHRING, lawyer, writer; b. N.Y.C., Dec. 12, 1940; s. Robert George and Florence Elizabeth (Zehring) S.; m. Helen Frances McKenna, Mar. 15, 1969; children: Christopher S., Jonathan R., Matthew W., Martha H. BA magna cum laude, Yale U., 1962; MBA, JD, U. Mich., 1969. Bar: Wis. 1969, Mich. 1969. Assoc. Quarles & Brady, Milw., 1969-76, ptnr., 1977-89; freelance writer, 1990—. Author: (monograph) Seven Thunders of Revelation, 1985, Revelation Revisited, 1995. 1st lt. U.S. Army, 1963-65. Mem. Phi Beta Kappa. Mem. Christian Ch. Home: 4480 N Ardmore Ave Shorewood WI 53211-1418

SURSA, CHARLES DAVID, banker; b. Muncie, Ind., Nov. 5, 1925; s. Charles Vaught and Ethel Fay (Schukraft) S; m. Mary Jane Palmer, Feb. 2, 1947; children: Ann Elizabeth, Janet Lynne, Charles Vaught, Laura Jane. BSChemE, Purdue U., 1946; MBA, Harvard, 1948. Executive NBD Bank N.A. (formerly Summit Bank, Indsl. Trust & Savings), Muncie, Ind., 1946-51, pres., 1951-80; chmn. bd., pres. NBD Bank N.A. (formerly Summit Bank, Indsl. Trust & Savings), Muncie, 1980-88, chmn. bd., CEO, 1988-90, chmn. bd., 1990-94, chmn. emeritus, 1994—; bd. dirs. Old Rep. Life Ins. Co., Chgo., Home Owners Life Ins. Co., Chgo., Old Rep. Internat. Corp., Chgo., Ball Meml. Hosp., Inc., Old Rep. Ins. Co., Greensburg, Pa., Old Rep. Life Ins. Co. N.Y.C., Am. Bus. & Merc. Ins. Group, Chgo., Am. Bus. & Merc. Reassurance Co., Chgo., bd. dirs., pres. Com. Svcs. Coun. of Del. County, 1973-74. Treas. Muncie Symphony Assn., 1949-62, pres., 1962-72, 2d v.p., 1978-80, dir., 1991—; bd. dirs., pres. The Community Found. of Muncie and Del. County, Inc., 1985—. Recipient Outstanding Young Man award Ind. Jr. C. of C., 1956, Hon. Jaycees award, 1974. Mem. Ind. Banker's Assn., Ind. Pres.'s Orgn. (treas. 1980-86), Ind. Soc. of Chgo., Internat. Wine and Food Soc., Delaware County C. of C., Ind. State C. of C., Muncie C. of C. (pres. 1959-60), Rotary (pres. 1964-65), Delaware Country Club (pres., bd. dirs. 1964), Elks, Phi Gamma Delta. Republican. Presbyterian. Home: 3410 W University Ave Muncie IN 47304-3970 Office: NBD Bank NA 220 Walnut Plz Muncie IN 47305-2804

SURWILL, BENEDICT JOSEPH, JR., college dean, educator; b. Chgo., Oct. 8, 1925; s. Benedict Joseph and Emily (Zemgolis) S.; m. Frances May Welling, Oct. 16, 1948; children: Thomas, Benedict, Robert, Patricia; m. Charlene R. McClintock, Feb. 17, 1990; 1 child, Michael McClintock. BS in Edn., Ariz. State Coll., 1951, MS in Edn., 1954; EdD, U. Colo., 1962. Elem. tchr. Winnetka (Ill.) Pub. Schs., 1958-61; jr. high sch. prin. Champaign (Ill.) Pub. Schs., 1961-63; dir. Campus Sch. SUNY, Buffalo, 1963-68; dean. Sch. Edn. Ea. Mont. Coll., Billings, 1968-88, asst. to pres., 1988-91, dean Sch. Edn., prof. edn. emeritus, 1991—; chmn. dean's coun. Mont. Univ. System, 1974; mem. Mont. Supts. Adv. Com. on Tchr. Edn. and Cert., 1969-76, chmn., 1972-73; mem. ednl. forum State Supt. Pub. Instrn., 1977-83, Mont. Rural Youth Adv. Coun., Billings, 1979-81; lectr. in field. Editor: A Critical Examination of American Education, 1985; mem. editorial bd., contbg. editor Jour. Creative Behavior, 1966-93. Co-chmn. cancer drive Billings chpt. Am. Cancer Soc., 1988-89, Mont. State Cancer Crusade, 1989. With inf. U.S. Army. Recipient Am. Assn. of Coll. for Tchr. Edn. award, 1972, Presdl. citation Ill. Assn. Sch. Adminstrs., 1973. Mem. Nat. Coun. Accreditation Tchr. Edn. (mem. standards com., mem. multicultural edn. com. 1977, bd. appeals 1980-83, bd. examiners 1988-90), Elks, Yellowstone Country Club, Phi Delta Kappa, Kappa Delta Pi. Home: 5864 Sam Snead Trl Billings MT 59106-1021

SURWIT, RICHARD SAMUEL, psychology educator; b. Bklyn., Oct. 7, 1946; s. David and Ethel (Turetsky) S.; m. Sandra E. Cummings, May 23, 1982; children: Daniel Alan, Sarah Jeanne. AB, Earlham Coll., 1968; PhD, McGill U., Montreal, Que., Can., 1972; postgrad., Harvard U., Boston. Postdoctoral fellow Harvard Med. Sch., 1972-74, instr., 1974-76, asst. prof., 1976-77; assoc. prof. psychiatry Duke U. Med. Ctr., Durham, N.C., 1977-83, prof., 1980, 83—, vice chmn., 1993—; prof. psychology Duke U., 1991-96; CEO Healthware Corp., Chapel Hill, N.C., 1983—; pres., CEO Healthware Corp. Author: Fear and Learning To Cope, 1978, Behavioral Approaches to Cardiovascular Diseases, 1982. Recipient rsch. devel. award NIMH, 1980, rsch. scientist award NIMH, 1993. Fellow APA, Soc. Behavioral Medicine (pres. 1994), Acad. Behavioral Medicine. Home: 3804 Sweeten Creek Rd Chapel Hill NC 27514-9706 Office: Duke U Med Ctr PO Box 3842 Durham NC 27710

SUSANKA, SARAH HILLS, architect; b. Bromley, Kent, England, Mar. 21, 1957; d. Brian and Margaret (Hampson) Hills; m. Lawrence A. Susanka, July 4, 1980 (div. May 1984); m. James Robert Larson, Sept. 4, 1988. BArch, U. Oreg., 1978; MArch, U. Minn., 1983. Registered architect. Prin. Mulfinger, Susanka, Mahady & Ptnrs., Mpls., 1983—; Contbr. articles to profl. jours. Mem. AIA Minn. Avocation: writing. Home: 70 Upper Afton Ter Saint Paul MN 55106 Office: Mulfinger Susanka & Mahady Archs 43 Main St SE Minneapolis MN 55414-1029

SUSCHITZKY, PETER, cinematagrapher. Cinematographer: (films) It Happened Here, 1962, The War Game, 1966, Privilege, 1967, A Midsummer Night's Dream, 1968, Charlie Bubbles, 1968, Leo the Last, 1970, Melody/Swalk, 1971, The Pied Piper, 1972, Henry VIII and His Six Wives, 1972, That'll Be the Day, 1974, All Creatures Great and Small, 1975, Lisztomania, 1975, The Rocky Horror Picture Show, 1976, Valentino, 1977, The Empire Strikes Back, 1980, Krull, 1983, Falling in Love, 1984, Dead Ringers, 1988, Where the Heart Is, 1990, Naked Lunch, 1992, The Public Eye, 1992, The Vanishing, 1993, M. Butterfly, 1993. Office: Sandra Marsh Mgt 9150 Wilshire Blvd Ste 220 Beverly Hills CA 90212-3429

SUSKIND, DENNIS A., investment banker; b. Staten Island, N.Y., Dec. 13, 1942; s. Morris and Ida (Levine) S.; m. Cynthia Ann Leverenz, Sept. 14, 1968; children—Brian, John Paul, Pamela Claire, Audrey Elizabeth. Student, Pace Coll., N.Y.C. Vice pres. J. Aron & Co., N.Y.C., 1962-81; ptnr. Goldman Sachs & Co., N.Y.C., 1981—; bd. dirs. Merc. Exchange, 1972-80, Gold Inst., Washington, 1980-90; bd. dirs. Commodity Exchange, Inc., N.Y.C., 1980-87, 1st vice chmn., 1989-91; lectr. Fin. Times Conf., 1983, 84, 86—. Bd. dirs. Mt. Sinai Hosp. Assocs., N.Y.C., East End chpt. Nature Conservancy, Arthur Ashe Inst. for Urban Youth; trustee Collegiate Sch., N.Y.C. Mem. AIME, Silver Inst., Futures Industry Assn. (bd. dirs.),Southampton Golf Club, Atlantic Golf Club (Bridgehampton, N.Y., bd. dirs.). Home: 136 E 79th St New York NY 10021-0328 Office: Goldman Sachs & Co 85 Broad St New York NY 10004-2434

SUSKIND, RAYMOND ROBERT, physician, educator; b. N.Y.C., Nov. 29, 1913; s. Alexander and Anna (Abramson) S.; m. Ida Blanche Richardson, Dec. 27, 1944; children: Raymond Robert, Stephen Alexander. AB, Columbia U., 1934; student medicine, Edinburgh, Scotland, 1938-39; MD, SUNY, Bklyn., 1943. Intern Cin. Gen. Hosp., 1944, resident in dermatology, 1944-46, 48-49; research fellow in indsl. health U. Cin., 1948-50; research asst. bacteriology N.Y. U., 1934-36; research asst. pharmacology, 1936-37; practice medicine specializing in dermatology Cin., 1949-62; mem. faculty U. Cin., 1948-62, asso. prof. dermatology, 1952-62, dir. dermatol. research program Kettering Lab., 1948-62, Jacob G. Schmidlapp prof., chmn. dept. environ. health, dir. Kettering Lab., 1969-85, Jacob G. Schmidlapp prof. emeritus Inst. Environ. Health, 1985—, prof. medicine and dermatology, 1969-85, prof. emeritus medicine and dermatology, 1985—; attending physician U. Hosps., Cin., 1969—; dir. environ. and occupational dermatology program Ctr. for Occupational Health, U. Cin. Hosp., Cin., 1985—; prof., head divsn. environ. medicine, prof. dermatology U. Oreg. Med. Sch., 1962-69; chmn. stds. adv. com. on cutaneous and eye hazards OSHA, 1978; Gehrmann lectr. Am. Acad. Occupl. Medicine, 1977; founding mem. certifying bd. Am. Bd. Toxicology, 1978-83; mem. nat. air quality adv. com. EPA, 1970-73; mem. com. on health related effects of herbicides VA, 1979-83; cons. on Agt. Orange studies; mem. panel on human health effects of stratospheric change NAS, 1977-85; trustee Dermatology found., 1975-80; master, trustee Fernald Settlement Fund Program, Long Term Health Effects of Ionizing Radiation Exposure from Nuclear Fuel Processing Plant, 1989—; cons. Accreditation Coun. for Grad. Med. Edn.; advisor Sch. of Pub. Health, Mahidol U., Bangkok; vis. prof. dermatology Columbia U., 1996. Contbg. editor Am. Jour. Indsl. Medicine, 1979-89, now reviewer; mem. editorial bd. Annals Internal Medicine, 1983-86, Chemosphere, 1987—; reviewer Archives Internal Medicine, Jour. AMA, Am. Jour. Pub. Health; contbr. articles to profl. jours., chpts. to books. Mem. Cin. Air Pollution Bd., 1972-76, chmn., 1974-75; bd. dirs. Cin. Chamber Music Soc. Served to capt. M.C. AUS, 1946-48. Recipient award Project Hope, 1984, Robert A. Kehoe award of merit Am. Acad. Occupational Medicine, 1987, Presdl. citation for outstanding contbns. to occupational medicine Am. Acad. Dermatology, 1988, Daniel Drake medal U. Cin., 1985, Disting. Alumni Achievement award SUNY Coll. Medicine, 1993; fellow U. Cin. Grad. Sch., 1971—. Fellow A.C.P.; mem AMA (adv. panel on toxicology council sci. affairs 1980-85), Am. Occupational Med. Assn. (chmn. dermatology com. and policy group 1958-66, dir. 1969-75, Health Achievement in Industry award 1977), Soc. Investigative Dermatology (dir., v.p., hon. mem. 1984—), Am. Acad. Dermatology (chmn. edn. com.), N.Y. Acad. Scis., Am. Indsl. Hygiene Assn., Soc. for Occupational and Environ. Health (councillor), AAAS, Am. Dermatol. Assn., Japanese Dermatol. Assn. (hon.), Chilean Dermatol. Soc. (hon.), Sigma Xi, Alpha Omega Alpha. Achievements include first description of inhibiting effect of ultraviolet radiation on allergic skin reactions; research on cutaneous toxicology, on effects of exposure to chlorinated dioxins, on effects of ionizing radiation on populations living in the vicinity of nuclear fuel processing plants. Office: Dept Environ Health U Cin Coll Medicine 3223 Eden Ave Cincinnati OH 45267-0001

SUSKIND, RONALD STEVEN, journalist; b. Kingston, N.Y., Nov. 20, 1959; s. Walter Burton and Shirley Lila (Berman) S.; m. Cornelia Kennedy, May 4, 1986; children: Walter Kennedy, Harry Owen. BA in Govt. and Fgn. Affairs, U. Va., 1981; MS in Journalism, Columbia U., 1983. No. Va. field coord. Charles Robb for Gov., Alexandria, Va., 1981; campaign mgr. John Downey for U.S. Senate, New Haven, 1982; news asst., interim reporter The New York Times, 1983-85; city/state reporter The St. Petersburg (Fla.) Times, 1985-86; sr. editor Boston Bus. Mag., 1987-88, editor, 1988-90; staff reporter The Wall Street Jour., Boston, 1990-93; sr. nat. affairs writer The Wall Street Jour., Washington, 1993—; instr. advanced journalism Harvard U., Cambridge, Mass., 1987-93; mag. cons. Big Ideas, Inc., Boston, 1988-90; commentator Sta. WBUR, Boston, 1989-93. Recipient Pulitzer prize for feature writing, 1995, Benjamin Fine award Nat. Assn. Secondary Sch. Prins., 1995, Nat. Writing award Ball State U., 1995. Office: The Wall Street Jour 1025 Connecticut Ave NW Washington DC 20036

SUSKIND, SIGMUND RICHARD, microbiology educator; b. N.Y.C., June 19, 1926; s. Seymour and Nina Phillips S.; m. Ann Parker, July 1, 1951; children: Richard, Mark, Steven. A.B., NYU, 1948; Ph.D., Yale U., 1954. Research asst. biology div. Oak Ridge Nat. Lab., 1948-50; USPHS fellow NYU Med. Sch., N.Y.C., 1954-56; mem. faculty Johns Hopkins U., Balt., 1956—; prof. biology Johns Hopkins U., 1965—, Univ. prof., 1983—, Univ. ombudsman, 1988-91, dean grad. and undergrad. studies, 1971-78, dean Sch. Arts and Scis., 1978-83; head molecular biology sect. NSF, 1970-71; cons. NIH, 1966-70, Coun. Grad. Schs., Mid States Assn. Colls. and Secondary Schs., 1973—, NSF, 1986; vis. scientist Weizmann Inst. of Sci., Israel, 1985; trustee Balt. Hebrew U., 1985-93; mem. adv. bd. La. Geriatric Ctr., 1990—. Author: (with P.E. Hartman) Gene Action, 1964, 69, (with P.E. Hartman and T. Wright) Principles of Genetics Laboratory Manual, 1965; editor: (with P.E. Hartman) Foundations of Modern Genetics series, 1964, 69; mem. sci. editorial bd. Johns Hopkins U. Press, 1973-76, 88-91. With USNR, 1944-46. NIH grantee, 1957-76. Fellow AAAS; mem. Am. Soc. Microbiology, Genetics Soc. Am., Am. Assn. Immunology, Am. Soc. Biol. Chemistry and Molecular Biology, Coun. Grad Schs., Assn. Grad. Schs., Northeastern Assn. Grad. Schs. (exec. com. 1975-76, pres. 1977-78). Research in microbial biochemical genetics and immunogenetics. Office: Johns Hopkins U Dept Biology and McCollum-Pratt Inst 34th and Charles Sts Baltimore MD 21218

SUSKO, CAROL LYNNE, lawyer, accountant; b. Washington, Dec. 5, 1955; d. Frank and Helen Louise (Davis) S. BS in Econs. and Acctg., George Mason U., 1979; JD, Cath. U., 1982; LLM in Taxation, Georgetown U., 1992. Bar: Pa. 1989, D.C. 1990; CPA, Va., Md. Tax acct. Reznick Fedder & Silverman, P.C., Bethesda, Md., 1984-85; sr. tax acct. Pannell Kerr Forster, Alexandria, Va., 1985; tax specialist Coopers & Lybrand, Washington, 1985-87; supervisory tax sr. Frank & Co., McLean, Va., 1987-88; editorial staff Tax Notes Mag., Arlington, Va., 1989-90; adj. faculty Am. U., Washington, 1989—; tax atty. Marriott Corp., Washington, 1993-94; tax mgr. Host Marriott Inc., Washington, 1994—. Mem. ABA, AICPAs, Va. Soc. CPAs, D.C. Soc. CPAs, D.C. Bar Assn., Women's Bar Assn. of D.C., Am. Assn. Atty.-CPAs. Office: Host Marriott Dept 910 Dept 72/92469 10400 Fernwood Rd Washington DC 20058

SUSLICK, KENNETH SANDERS, chemistry educator; b. Chgo., Sept. 16, 1952; s. Alvin and Edith (Paul) S.; m. Adele Mazurek; 1 child, Benjamin Adam. BS with honors, Calif. Inst. Tech., 1974; PhD, Stanford U., 1978. Rsch., teaching asst. Stanford (Calif.) U., 1974-78; chemist Lawrence Livermore (Calif.) Lab., 1974-75; asst. prof. U. Ill., Urbana, 1978-84, assoc. prof., 1984-88, prof. of chemistry, 1988—, Alumni Rsch. Scholar prof., 1995—; prof. Beckman Inst. for Advanced Sci. and Tech., Urbana, 1989-92; prof. of materials sci. and engring. U. Ill., Urbana, 1993—; vis. fellow Balliol Coll., Inorganic Chemistry Lab., Oxford U., Eng., 1986; bd. dirs. Ney Ultrasonics, Inc., 1993—; sci. bd. dirs. VivoRx, Inc., 1994—; cons. in field. Editor: High Energy Processes in Organometallic Chemistry, 1987, Ultrasound: Its Chemical, Physical and Biological Effects, 1988, Comprehensive Supramolecular Chemistry, vol. 5, 1996; editl. bd. Ultrasonics, 1992—; patentee isotope separation by photochromatography, protein microspheres, drug delivery, blood substitutes; contbr. articles to profl. jours. Fellow DuPont Found., 1979-80, Sloan Found., 1985-87; recipient Rsch. Career Devel. award NIH, 1985-90, NSF Spl. Creativity award 1992-94, Material Rsch. Soc. medal, 1994. Fellow AAAS, Am. Acoustical Soc. Royal Soc. Arts, Mfrs. and Commerce (Silver medal 1974); mem. Am. Chem. Soc. (chmn. sect. 1987-89, Nobel Laureate Signature award 1994). Avocations: sculpting, folk music. Office: U Ill Dept Chemistry 505 S Mathews Ave Urbana IL 61801-3617

SUSMAN, MILLARD, geneticist, educator; b. St. Louis, Sept. 1, 1934; s. Albert and Patsy Ruth S.; m. Barbara Beth Fretwell, Aug. 18, 1957; children: Michael K., David L. A.B., Washington U., St. Louis, 1956; Ph.D., Calif. Inst. Tech., 1962. With microbial genetics research unit Hammersmith Hosp., London, 1961-62; asst. prof. genetics U. Wis., Madison, 1962-66, assoc. prof., 1966-72, prof., 1972—, chmn. lab. genetics, 1971-75, 77-86, assoc. dean med. sch., 1986-95, acting dean Sch. Allied Health Professions, 1988-90, vice dean med. sch., 1994-95; spl. advisor to the dean Sch. Allied Health Professions, 1995; dir. Ctr. for Biology Edn., Madison, 1996—; phage course instr., Cold Spring Harbor, N.Y., 1965. Co-author: Life on Earth, 2d edit., 1978, Human Chromosomes: Structure, Behavior, Effects, 3d edit., 1992; contbr. articles to sci. jours. Mem Genetics Soc. Am., AAAS, Sigma Xi, Phi Beta Kappa, Phi Eta Sigma, Omicron Delta Kapp. Home: 2707 Colgate Rd Madison WI 53705-2234 Office: U Wis Med Sch 1220 Medical Science Ctr Madison WI 53706

SUSMAN, MORTON LEE, lawyer; b. Detroit, Aug. 6, 1934; s. Harry and Alma (Koslow) S.; m. Nina Meyers, May 1, 1958; 1 child, Mark Lee. BBA, So. Meth. U., 1956, JD, 1958. Bar: Tex. 1958, U.S. Dist. Ct. (so. dist.) Tex. 1961, U.S. Ct. Appeals (5th cir.) 1961, U.S. Supreme Ct. 1961, U.S. Ct. Appeals (11th cir.) 1981, D.C. 1988, U.S. Ct. Appeals (D.C. cir.) 1988, N.Y. 1990, Colo. 1996. Asst. U.S. atty., Houston, 1961-64, 1st asst. U.S. atty., 1965-66, U.S. atty., 1966-69; ptnr. Weil, Gotshal & Manges and predecessor firm Susman & Kessler, Houston, 1969—. Lt. USNR, 1958-61. Fellow Am. Coll. Trial Lawyers, Tex. Bar Found.; mem. ABA, Fed. Bar Assn. (dir., Younger Fed. Lawyer award 1968), Tex. Bar Assn., Houston Club, Houstonian Club, Crescent Club. Democrat. Jewish. Home: 3238 Ella Lee Ln Houston TX 77019-5924 Office: Weil Gotshal & Manges 700 Louisiana St Ste 1600 Houston TX 77002-2722

SUSMAN, STEPHEN DAILY, lawyer; b. Houston, Jan. 20, 1941; s. Harry and Helene Gladys (Daily) S.; m. Karen Lee Hyman, Dec. 26, 1965; children: Stacy Margraeta, Harry Paul. B.A. magna cum laude, Yale U., 1962; LL.B. summa cum laude, U. Tex. Austin, 1965. Bar: Tex. 1965, U.S. Supreme Ct 1960. Law clk. U.S. Ct. Appeals (5th cir.), New Orleans, 1965-66, U.S.Supreme Ct., Washington, 1966-67; ptnr. Fulbright & Jaworski, 1966-75; spl. counsel to atty. gen. Austin, Tex., 1975; sr. ptnr. Susman Godfrey, Houston, 1980—; vis. prof. law U. Tex., Austin, 1975; chmn. adv. com. on discovery Tex. Supreme Ct. Bd. dirs. Contemporary Arts Mus., Assn. Yale Alumni, Yale Devel. Fund, Southwest Legal Found., Inns of Ct. Recipient ADL Jurisprudence award, 1995; named one of Best Trial Lawyers in Am., Nat. Law Jour., 1989; subject of America's Best Trial Lawyers, 1994, The Litigators, 1994. Mem. ABA (antitrust sect., mem. coun. litigation sect., chmn. task force on fast track litigation), State Bar Tex., Am. Law Inst., Assn. Trial Lawyers Am., Houston Bar Assn., Yale Club (Houston, N.Y.C.), Houston Trial Lawyers Assn., Tex. Assn. Civil Trial Specialists, Houston Club, Houstonian Club, Century Club, Petroleum Club (Dallas), Quinnipiac Club (New Haven). Avocations: jogging, skiing. Office: 1st Interstate Bank 1000 Louisiana St Ste 5100 Houston TX 77002-5013

SUSMAN, THOMAS M(ICHAEL), lawyer, lobbyist; b. Houston, Feb. 24, 1943; s. Harry and Helene Gladys (Daily) S.; m. Julia Turitz (div. 1980); children: Tara Marie, Shana Raissa, Micah Joseph; m. Susan G. Braden, May 31, 1981; 1 child, Daily Lacey. BA, Yale U., 1964; JD, U. Tex., 1967. Bar: Tex. 1967, U.S. Ct. Appeals (D.C. cir.) 1968, D.C. 1972, U.S. Dist. Ct. D.C. 1972, U.S. Supreme Ct. 1973, U.S. Ct. Appeals (5th cir.) 1980, U.S. Ct. Appeals (1st cir.) 1982, U.S. Dist. Ct. Mass. 1982, U.S. Ct. Claims 1983, Mass. 1985. Law clk. to judge U.S. Ct. Appeals for 5th Cir., Washington, 1967-68; spl. asst. to asst. atty. gen. Office Legal Counsel, U.S. Dept. Justice, Washington, 1968-69; counsel, chief counsel subcom. on adminstrv. practice and procedure U.S. Senate, Washington, 1969-76, gen. counsel antitrust subcom., 1977-78, judiciary com., 1979-80, legis. asst. to Senator Edward Kennedy, 1980; ptnr. Ropes & Gray, Washington, 1981—; pub. mem. Adminstrv. Conf. U.S., 1980—; gen. counsel adv. coun. U.S. Ct. Claims, Washington, 1988. Contbr. numerous articles on freedom of info., antitrust and intellectual property to legal publs.; editor: The Lobbying Manual, 1993. Am. participant USIA, 1985, 88, 92. Eisenhower Found. exchange fellow, 1977. Mem. ABA (chair adminstrv. law sect. 1991-92), D.C. Bar Assn. (chmn. steering coms., Cert. of Appreciation), Am. Jewish Com. (mem. exec. bd. Washington chpt.). Jewish. Home: 3901 Argyle Ter NW Washington DC 20011-5328 Office: Ropes & Gray 1301 K St NW Ste 800-E Washington DC 20005*

SUSSE, SANDRA SLONE, lawyer; b. Medford, Ma., June 1, 1943; d. James Robert and Georgie Coffin (Bradshaw) Slone; m. Peter Susse, May 10, 1969 (div. May 1993); 1 child, Toby. BA, U. Mass., 1981; JD, Vt. Law Sch., 1986. Bar: Mass. 1986, U.S. Dist. Ct. Mass. 1988, U.S. Ct. Appeals (1st cir.) 1995. Staff atty. Western Mass. Legal Svcs., Springfield, 1986—. Mem. ABA, Mass. Bar Assn., Women's Bar Assn. Mass. Avocations: hiking, German literature, films, skating. Office: Western Mass Legal Svcs 145 State St Springfield MA 01103

SUSSENGUTH, EDWARD HENRY, computer company executive, computer network designer; b. Holyoke, Mass., Oct. 10, 1932; s. Edward Henry and Mary Frances (Murphy) S.; m. Ann Paula Coughlin, Jan. 31, 1959; children—Edward Henry III, John Andrew. A.B., Harvard U., 1954, Ph.D., 1964; M.S., MIT, 1959. Researcher IBM Corp., Poughkeepsie, N.Y., 1959-64; mem. research and devel. staff IBM Corp., Menlo Park, Calif., 1964-70; mgr. IBM Corp., Raleigh, N.C., 1970-77; div. dir. IBM Corp., White Plains, N.Y., 1977-80; fellow IBM Corp., Raleigh, 1980-91; pres. IBM Acad. Tech., 1989-91; cons., 1991—. Contbr. articles to profl. jours.; patentee in field. Bd. dirs. Wake County Hosp. System, Raleigh, 1985—. Served to lt. USN, 1954-57. Recipient Interface award Data Communications, 1988. Fellow IEEE (Simon Ramo medal, 1989); mem. NAE, Assn. Computing Machinery, Sigma Xi. Club: MacGregor Downs Country (Cary, N.C.) (gov. 1980-85), Amelia Island. Avocations: golf; photography. Home and Office: 411 Rutherglen Dr Cary NC 27511-6436

SUSSER, MERVYN WILFRED, epidemiologist, educator; b. Johannesburg, South Africa, Sept. 26, 1921; came to U.S., 1965; s. Solomon and Ida Rose (Son) S.; m. Zena Athene Stein, Mar. 28, 1949; children: Ida, Ezra, Ruth. MB, BChir, U. Witwatersrand, Union of South Africa, 1950; diploma pub. health, London Conjoint Bd., 1960; DMS (hon.), U. Witwatersrand, 1993. Med. officer, then supt. Alexandra Health Centre and Univ. Clinic, Johannesburg, 1952-55; successively lectr., sr. lectr., reader, head dept. social and preventive medicine Manchester (Eng.) U., 1957-65; also med. officer div. mental health Salford, Eng.; prof., chmn. div. epidemiology Sch. Pub. Health, Columbia U., N.Y.C., 1966-78, Gertrude H. Sergievsky prof. epidemiology, dir. Sergievsky Ctr., 1977-91; Sergievsky prof. emeritus, spl. lectr., 1992—; cons. WHO, 1962, 66-72, 79, 90, NIH, NAS. Author: (with W. Watson) Sociology in Medicine, 1962, 2d edit., 1971, (with W. Watson and K. Hopper), 3d edit., 1985, Community Psychiatry: Epidemiologic and Social Themes, 1968, Causal Thinking in the Health Sciences: Concepts and Strategies of Epidemiology, 1973, (with others) Famine and Human Development: Studies of the Dutch Hungerwinter 1944-45, 1975, (with D. Rush and Z. Stein) Diet in Pregnancy: A Randomized Controlled Trial of Nutritional Supplements, 1980, Epidemiology, Health and Society: Selected Essays, 1987, (with Jennie Kline and Zena Stein) Conception to Birth: Epidemiology of Prenatal Development, 1989; editor Am. Jour. Pub. Health, 1992—. With South African Defence Force, 1940-45. Belding scholar Assn. Aid Crippled Children, 1965-66; Guggenheim fellow, 1972; Disting. Svc. award Coll. Physicians and Surgeons, Columbia U., 1994. Fellow Royal Coll. Physicians (Edinburgh), Am. Pub. Health Assn. (John Snow award 1994), Am. Epidemiol. Soc., Am. Coll. Epidemiol., N.Y. Acad. Medicine; mem. Internat. Epidemiol. Assn., World Psychiat. Assn., Soc. Epidemiol. Rsch., Soc. Pediatric Epidemiol. Rsch., Physicians Forum. Home: 100 Pinecrest Dr Hastings Hdsn NY 10706-3702 Office: 630 W 168th St New York NY 10032-3702

SUSSEX, JAMES NEIL, psychiatrist, educator; b. Northcote, Minn., Oct. 2, 1917; s. Rollo and Florence (Bartholomew) S.; m. Margaret Ann Garty, Apr. 25, 1943; children: Margaret Eileen, Mary Patricia, Barbara Lorraine, Teresa Virginia. AB, U. Kans., 1939, MD, 1942. Diplomate: Am. Bd. Psychiatry and Neurology (dir. for child psychiatry 1966-70, dir. 1975-83, pres. 1982). Commd. lt. (j.g.), M.C. U.S. Navy, 1943, advanced through grades to comdr., 1955; intern (Naval Hosp.), Chelsea, Mass., 1942-43; resident psychiatry (Naval Hosp.), Vallejo, Calif., 1946-49; fellow child psychiatry Phila. Guild Guidance Clinic, 1949-51; asst. chief neuropsychiatry Naval Hosp., Bethesda, Md., 1951-55; resigned, 1955; mem. faculty Med. Coll. Ala., 1955-68, prof. psychiatry, chmn. dept., 1959-68; psychiatrist-in-chief U. Ala. Hosps. and Clinics, 1959-68; faculty U. Miami Sch. Medicine, Fla., 1968—; prof. psychiatry U. Miami Sch. Medicine, 1970—, chmn. dept., 1970-83, chmn. emeritus, 1983—, spl. asst. to v.p. for med. affairs for geriatric medicine program, 1983-86; mem. adv. bd. Nat. Psychiat. Residency Selection Plan, 1965—; mem. Med. Adv. Bd. Ednl. Film Prodn., 1966—; cons. Bur. Rsch., U.S. office Edn., 1966-72; dir. Ala. Planning for Mental Retardation, 1964—; mem. psychiatry tng. rev. com. NIMH; mem. exec. com. Am. Bd. Med. Spltys., 1980-83. Editor: Jour. Ala. Soc. Med. History, 1957-63; editorial bd.: Jour. Am. Acad. Child Psychiatry, 1966-70. Mem. Am. Assn. Psychiat. Svcs. for Children (coun. 1966—, pres. 1972-74), Coun. Med. Specialty Socs. (pres. 1988-89), Accreditation Coun. for Grad. Med. Edn. (exec. com. 1989-94, chmn. 1992-93), Phi Beta Kappa, Nu Sigma Nu. Home: 6950 SW 134th St Miami FL 33156-6975

SUSSKIND, CHARLES, engineering educator, author, publishing executive; b. Prague, Czech Republic; came to U.S., 1945, naturalized, 1946; s. Bruno Bronislav and Gertruda (Seger) S.; m. Teresa Gabriel, May 1, 1945; children: Pamela Susskind Pettler, Peter Gabriel, Amanda Frances. Student, City U., London, 1939-40; B.S., Calif. Inst. Tech., 1948; M.Engring., Yale U., 1949, Ph.D., 1951. Research asst. Yale U., 1949-51; research assoc. Stanford U., 1951-55, lectr., asst. dir. Microwave Lab., 1953-55; mem. faculty U. Calif., Berkeley, 1955—; prof. U. Calif., 1964-91; prof. emeritus U. Calif., Berkeley, 1991—; asst. dean Coll. Engring. U. Calif., 1964-68, also statewide adminstr., 1969-74; Vis. prof. U. London, 1961-62, U. Geneva, Switzerland, 1968-69; mem., cons. EPA Sci. Adv. Bd., 1982—; cons. electronics industry, govt., publishers; dir. San Francisco Press, Inc. Author: (with M. Chodorow) Fundamentals of Microwave Electronics, 1964, (with L. Schell) Exporting Technical Education, 1968, Understanding Technology, 1973, 74, 85 (transl. into Dutch, French, Italian, Korean, Spanish, Indian edit. in English), Twenty-Five Engineers and Inventors, 1976, (with F. Kurylo) Ferdinand Braun, 1981, (with M.E. Rowbottom) Electricity and Medicine: History of their Interaction, 1984, Janáček and Brod, 1985, Heinrich Hertz: A Short Life, 1995; eidtor: (with M. Hertz) Heinrich Hertz: Memoirs, Letters, Diaries, bilingual edit., 1977; editor-in-chief Ency. Electronics, 1962. Served with USAAF, 1942-45. Named to Hon. Order Ky. Cols. Fellow IEEE; mem. AAAS, History of Sci. Soc., Soc. for History of Tech., Instn. Elec. Engrs. (London), Yale Club of N.Y.C., Faculty Club of Berkeley (bd. dirs. 1972-73), Sigma Xi (pres. Berkeley chpt. 1972-73), Tau Beta Pi. Office: U Calif Coll Engring Berkeley CA 94720-1770

SUSSKIND, HERBERT, biomedical engineer, educator; b. Ratibor, Germany, Mar. 23, 1929; came to U.S., 1938; s. Alex and Hertha (Loewy) S.; m. E. Suzanne Lieberman, June 18, 1961; children: Helen J., Alex M., David A. BChE cum laude, CCNY, 1950; MChE, NYU, 1961. Engr., sect. supr. Brookhaven Nat. Lab., Upton, N.Y., 1950-77, biomed. engr., 1977-94, asst. to chmn. med. dept., 1989-94, rsch. collaborator, 1994—; assoc. prof. medicine SUNY, Stony Brook, 1979—. Co-inventor 3 patents in field. Co-founder, 1st pres. Huntington Twp. Jewish Forum, Huntington, N.Y., 1970-73; trustee Huntington Hebrew Congregation, 1970-78. Mem. Biomed. Engring. Soc., Soc. Nuclear Medicine, Am. Thoracic Soc., Am. Nuclear Soc. (exec. com., treas. L.I. Sect., 1978-83), Am. Inst. Chem. Engrs., CCNY Alumni Assn. (pres. 1982-84), CCNY Engring. & Architecture Alumni Assn., N.Y.C. (pres. 1963-65). Office: Brookhaven Nat Lab Box 5000 Bldg 490 Upton NY 11973-5000

SUSSKIND, LAWRENCE ELLIOTT, urban and environmental planner, educator, mediator; b. N.Y.C., Jan. 12, 1947; s. David J. and Marjorie H. (Friedman) S.; m. Miriam Mason, June 8, 1968 (div. Dec. 1982); m. Leslie Webster Tuttle, Dec. 12, 1982; children: Noah Gates, Lily Webster. A.B. in Sociology, Columbia U., 1968; M.C.P., MIT, 1970, Ph.D. in Urban Planning, 1973. Asst. prof. urban and environ. planning MIT, Cambridge, 1971-74, assoc. prof., 1974-82, prof., 1982-95, Ford prof., 1995—, head dept. 1978-82, dir. MIT-Harvard Pub. Disputes Program, 1980—; exec. dir. program on negotiation Harvard U. Law Sch., Cambridge, 1984-87; sr. fellow program on negotiation, 1988—; pres. Consensus Bldg. Inst. Author: Paternalism, Conflict and Co-Production, 1983, Proposition 1 1/2: Its Impact on Massachusetts, 1983, Resolving Environmental Regulatory Disputes, 1983, Breaking the Impasse, 1987, Environmental Diplomacy, 1994, Reinventing Congress for the 21st Century, 1995, Dealing With an Angry Public, 1996; sr. editor, founder Environ. Impact Assessment Rev., 1980—; editl. policy bd. Negotiation Jour., 1984—. Mem. Am. Inst. Cert. Planners, Soc. for Profls. in Dispute Resolution. Jewish. Home: 32 Jericho Hill Rd Southborough MA 01772-1007 Office: MIT 3-411 Cambridge MA 02139

SUSSKIND, TERESA GABRIEL, publisher; b. Watford, Eng., came to U.S., 1945, naturalized, 1948; d. Aaron and Betty (Fox) Gabriel; m. Charles Susskind, May 1, 1945; children: Pamela Pettler, Peter Gabriel, Amanda. Ed. U. London, 1938-40. Profl. libr. Calif. Inst. Tech., Pasadena, 1946-48, Yale U., New Haven, Conn., 1948-51, Stanford U., Calif., 1951-52, SRI Internat., Menlo Park, Calif., 1953; founder, pres. San Francisco Press, Inc., 1959—. With Women's Royal Naval Svc., 1943-45. Author: A Room of One's Own Revisited, 1977. Active in cultural affairs; bd. govs. San Francisco Symphony, 1986-89. Mem. Town and Gown Club (Berkeley, Calif., pres. 1984-85). Office: PO Box 426800 San Francisco CA 94142-6800

SUSSMAN, ALEXANDER RALPH, lawyer; b. Bronx, N.Y., Sept. 24, 1946; s. Herman R. and Claire (Blumenson) S.; m. Edna Rubin, Mar. 24, 1973; children: Jason, Carl, Matthew, Eric. AB cum laude, Princeton U., 1968; JD, Yale U., 1972. Bar: N.Y. 1973, U.S. Dist. Ct. (so. and ea. dists) N.Y. 1974, U.S. Ct. Appeals (2d, 3d, 5th, 6th, 8th and 10th cirs.) 1983, U.S. Supreme Ct. Law clk. to justice U.S. Dist. Ct., N.Y.C., 1972-73; assoc. Cravath, Swaine & Moore, N.Y.C., 1974-76; assoc. Fried, Frank, Harris, Shriver & Jacobson, N.Y.C., 1977-79, ptnr., 1979—. Author: (with A. Fleischer, Jr.) Takeover Defense, 2 vols., 1995. Vice pres. litigation, exec. com., bd. dirs. N.Y. Lawyers for the Pub. Interest, 1983—; bd. dirs., exec. com. Legal Aid Soc., 1987-93. Fulbright scholar U. Bordeaux, 1969. Mem. ABA, Am. Law Inst., N.Y. State Bar Assn., Assn. of Bar of City of N.Y. (fed. cts. com. 1984-87, jud. com. 1987-90, chmn. legal assistance com. 1988-91, Marden lectr. com. 1991—, chmn. mergers and acquisitions com. 1995—). Home: 20 Oak Ln Scarsdale NY 10583-1627 Office: Fried Frank Harris Shriver & Jacobson 1 New York Plz New York NY 10004

SUSSMAN, ARTHUR MELVIN, educator; b. Bklyn., Nov. 17, 1942; m. Rita Padnick; children: Eric, Johanna. BS, Cornell U., 1963; LLB magna cum laude, Harvard U., 1966. Bar: N.Y. 1967, Ill. 1970. Assoc. atty. Cahill, Gordon, Reindel & Ohl, N.Y.C., 1966-67; assoc. atty. Jenner & Block, Chgo., 1970-75, ptnr., 1975-77; univ. legal counsel So. Ill. U., Carbondale, 1977-79; gen. counsel, v.p. legal affairs and govt. rels. U. Chgo., 1979-84, gen. counsel, v.p. adminstrn., 1984-88, lectr. law Grad. Sch. Bus., 1986—, master Broadview Hall, 1986-87, resident master Woodward Ct., 1987—, bd. dirs. Lab. Schs., 1985; gen. counsel, v.p. adminstrn. Argonne (Ill.) Nat. Lab., 1988—; exec. dir. Borman Commn., U.S. Mil. Acad., 1976; chmn., bd. dirs. Ency. Birt., Inc., 1995-96; presenter in field. Contr. articles to profl. jours. Mem. Ill. Sec. of State's Com. on Not-for-Profit Corp. Act, 1984-85; chair regional selection panel Harry S. Truman Scholarship Found.; bd. dirs. Chapin Hall for Children, 1986—. Capt. JAGC, U.S. Army, 1967-70. Fulbright fellow, London, 1987. Mem. Nat. Assn. Coll. and Univ. Attys., Am. Coun. Edn. Office: U Chgo Office of Legal Counsel Office of Legal Counsel 5801 S Ellis Ave Rm 503 Chicago IL 60637-1404

SUSSMAN, BARRY, author, public opinion analyst and pollster, journalist; b. N.Y.C., July 10, 1934; s. Samuel and Esther (Rosen) S.; m. Peggy Earhart, Jan. 20, 1962; children: Seena, Shari. BA, Bklyn. Coll., 1956. Reporter Herald Courier, Bristol, Va., 1960-62, mng. editor, 1962-65; editor Washington Post, 1965-69, city editor, 1970-73, spl. Watergate editor, 1972-74, pollster, pub. opinion analyst, 1975-87; co-founder, co-dir. Washington Post-ABC News poll, 1981-87; columnist Washington Post Nat. Weekly, 1983-87; mng. editor nat. affairs UPI, Washington, 1987; ind. pub. opinion analyst and pollster, 1988—. Author: The Great Coverup: Nixon and the Scandal of Watergate, 1974, What Americans Really Think, 1988, (with Lowell P. Weicker, Jr.) Maverick, 1995. Recipient Drew Pearson award for Nat. Reporting, 1972, 1st Prize award Washington Newspaper Guild, 1973, Editor of Yr. award Washington Newspaper Guild, 1973. Mem. Am. Assn. for Pub. Opinion Rsch. (exec. coun. 1985-87). Jewish. Avocation: chess.

SUSSMAN, GERALD, publishing company executive; b. Balt., Feb. 21, 1934; s. Hyman Jacob and Sylvia (Applebaum) S.; m. Arla Ilene Ellison, Aug. 25, 1963; children: Daniel Leonard, Andrew Louis. B.A., U. Md., 1956. Co-founder, prin. Investors Service of Md., Balt., 1956-60; coll. traveller Oxford U. Press, Inc., N.Y.C., 1961-62; coll. sales mgr. Oxford U. Press, Inc., 1962-69, gen. advt. mgr., 1970-73, v.p., dir. mktg., 1974-79, sr. v.p., dir. mktg., 1979-83, sr. v.p., dir. adminstrn. and planning, 1983—. Mem. Assn. Am. Pubs. (chmn. mktg. com.), Assn. Am. Univ. Presses (chmn. mktg. com. 1980-81), Pubs. Advt. Club, Phi Alpha Theta. Democrat. Jewish. Home: 8 Opatut Ct Edison NJ 08817-2923 Office: Oxford U Press Inc 198 Madison Ave New York NY 10016-4314

SUSSMAN, LEONARD RICHARD, foundation executive; b. N.Y.C., Nov. 26, 1920; s. Jacob and Carrie (Marks) S.; m. Frances Rukeyser, May 9, 1942 (div. 1958); m. Marianne Rita Gutmann, May 28, 1958; children: Lynne, David William, Mark Jacob. A.B., NYU, 1940; M.S. in Journalism, Columbia U., 1941. Copy editor N.Y. Morning Telegraph, news editor radio sta. WQXR, 1941; cable editor San Juan (P.R.) World Jour., also corr. Business Week mag., 1941-42; editor fgn. broadcast intelligence svc. FCC, 1942; press sec. to Gov. of P.R., 1942-43; dir. info. in N.Y. for Govt. of P.R., 1946-49; regional dir., then nat. exec. dir. Am. Coun. Judaism, 1949-66; cons. pub. affairs cons. Nationwide Ins. Cos. (and indsl. subs.), 1955-57; mem. editorial com. Coun. Liberal Chs., 1956-59; exec. dir. Freedom House, 1967-88, sr. scholar in internat. communications, 1988—; evaluator Fulbright Program Bd. Fgn. Scholarships, 1990-92; exec. dir. Willkie Meml., 1970-88; adj. prof. journalsim and mass communication NYU, N.Y.C., 1990—; organizer, dir. Freedom House/Books USA, 1968-85; editor Freedom at Issue, bimonthly, 1970-81; mem. U.S. Dels. to Conf. World Communicaiton Yr./83, 1982-83; organizer acad. confs.; participant Internat. Conf. on Press Freedom, Venice, Italy, 1976, 77, Cairo, 1978, Talloires, 1981, 83, San Jose, Costa Rica, Johannnesburg, and Santiago Chile, 1987, also others; mem. panel competition in space Congl. Office Tech. Assessment, 1982-83. Author: American Press-Under Siege?, 1973, Mass News Media and The Third World Challenge, 1977, Glossary for International Communications: Warning of a Bloodless Dialect, 1983, Spanish version, 1987, Power, The Press and the Technology of Freedom: The Coming of Age of ISDN, 1990, The Culture of Freedom: The Small World of Fulbright Scholars, 1992, Good News Bad News, 1994, Can A Free Press Be Responsible? To Whom?, 1995, The Press: Pressed and Oppressed, 1995, The Journalist as Pariah: Press Freedom, 1996, The Global Airscape, 1996; editor: Three Years at the East-West Divide, 1983, Today's American: How Free?, 1986; contbr. sects. to books, articles to profl. jours. and newspapers; project dir.: Big Story-How the American Press and Television Reported and Interpreted the Crisis of Tet-1968 in Vietnam and Washington, 1977; eidtor: textbook series, also quar. mag. Issues, 1953-66; editl. bd. Polit. Comm. and Persuasion. Trustee Internat. Coun. on Future of Univ., 1973-84; bd. dirs. World Press Freedom Com., 1977—; chmn. Friends of Survey Mag. Charitable Trust, London, 1978-92; mem. U.S. Nat. Commn. for UNESCO, 1979-85, vice-chmn., 1983-85; mem. U.S. dels. to internat. conf. on space, African Aid, UNESCO, London Info. Forum. Decorated Legion of Merit; recipient Ann. First Amendment award N.Y. br. Soc. Profl. Journalists, 1988. Mem. Internat. Inst. Comm., Internat. Press Inst., Internat. Assn. Mass Comm. Rsch., Century Club. Home: 215 E 73rd St New York NY 10021-3653 Office: 120 Wall St Fl 26 New York NY 10005-4001

SUSSMAN, MARTIN VICTOR, chemical engineering educator, inventor, consultant; b. N.Y.C.; s. Samuel and Selma (Bagno) S.; m. Jeanne Fowler, Aug. 22, 1953; children: Ann M., Eve Leslie, David Fowler. B.S., CCNY; M.S., Columbia U., Ph.D., 1958. Registered profl. engr. Mass.; lic. marine engr. Instr., research assoc. chem. dept. Fordham U., N.Y.C., 1949-50; research fellow chem. engring. dept. Columbia U., 1951-53; sr. engr., research engr. Pioneering Lab., DuPont, Del., 1953-58; co-founder, 1st dept. chem. engring in Turkey Robert Coll., Istanbul, Turkey, 1958-61; prof. chem. engring. dept. Tufts U., Medford, Mass., 1961—; dept. chmn., established PhD and MS programs Tufts U., 1961-71; cons. engring. edn. US AID, Brazil and Uruguay, 1963, Ethiopia, 1965; cons. engring. edn. Ford Found., India, 1971, 72, 73, 74, 79; coord. engring. edn. NSF, New Delhi, 1967-68; vis. prof. MIT, 1976, U. Capetown, Republic South Africa, 1990; Disting. vis. scholar Va. Poly. Inst., 1980; hon. rsch. fellow U. Exeter, 1990; introduced grad. chem. engring program Tufts U.; co-founder chem. engring. dept. Robert Coll., Turkey. Author: Elementary General Thermodynamics, 1972, 89, Availability (Exergy) Analysis, 1980; patentee in field. Mem. Town Meeting, Lexington, Mass., 1971-78. Served with U.S. Maritime Service, 1945-47, U.S. Coast Guard. NIH Spl. Research fellow, 1968; AEC fellow, 1951; Fulbright Hays lectr., 1977; Erskine fellow U. Canterbury (N.Z.), 1983; Meyerhoff fellow Weizman Inst. Sci., 1984-85. Fellow Am. Inst. Chem. Engrs., Am. Inst. Chemists; mem. Am. Chem. Soc., Sigma Xi, Tau Beta Pi (eminent engr. 1974). Achievements include invention of "Incremental Draw Process" for synthetic fiber manufacture now in use by industry, "Fibra-Cel" tissue culture matrix, establishment of first modern chemical engineering department in a Turkish university, introduced graduate degree in chem. engring. program at Tufts U. Office: Tufts U Dept Chem Engring Medford MA 02155

SUSSMAN, MONICA HILTON, lawyer; b. N.Y.C., Apr. 2, 1952. BA cum laude, Syracuse U., 1973; JD, Hofstra U., 1977. Bar: Va. 1977, D.C. 1978. Legis. coun. N.Y. State Gov's. Office, Washington, 1977-79; spl. asst. to under sec. U.S. Dept. HUD, Washington, 1979-80, br. chief office State Agy. and Bond Fin. programs, 1980-82, office gen. counsel, 1982-83, also bd. dirs., 1988—, v.p., 1989—, treas. Nat. Housing Conf., 1990—, also programs and regulations dep. gen. counsel; ptnr. McDermott, Will & Emery, Washington; now ptnr. Peabody & Brown, Washington, 1996—; bd. dirs. Nat. Leased Housing Assn. Mem. ABA, Mortgage Bankers Assn. (insured project subcom.), D.C. Bar (govtl. assisted programs for real estate com. 1985—), Va. State Bar. Office: Peabody & Brown 1255 23rd St NW Ste 800 Washington DC 20037*

SUSSNA, EDWARD, economist, educator; b. Phila., Nov. 26, 1926; s. Louis and Manya (Prytzycka) S.; m. Sylvia Fishman, Mar. 8, 1953; children: Audrey Francine, Ellen Sondra. B.A., Bklyn. Coll., 1950; M.A., U. Ill., 1952, Ph.D., 1954. Instr. U. Ill., 1952-54; asst. prof. Lehigh U., 1956-57; prof. bus. adminstrn. and econs. U. Pitts., 1957—; dir. ctr. for exec. edn. Grad. Sch. Bus. U. Pitts., 1983-89; dir. mgmt. program for execs. Center for Econ. Edn., Grad. Sch. Bus., acad. dir. study program in Hong Kong and Peoples Republic China, spring 1989, 95; inaugural prof. MBA program Bratislava Sch. Econs., Slovakia, 1996; vis. Fulbright prof. U. Tehran, Iran, adviser, 1972-73; cons. Bur. of Budget, Dept. HEW, Dept. Transp., UN Indsl. Devel. Orgn., Bell Telephone Co., Alcoa, Westinghouse Corp., NSF, Pitts. Nat. Bank, Japanese Regional Bankers Assn., others; vis. prof. UCLA, 1970, Ecole Superieure des Scis. Economiques et Commerciales, Paris, 1976-77, U. East Asia, Hong Kong and Macau, winter 1986; vis. scholar Internat. Inst. Mgmt., Berlin, spring 1982. Contbr. articles to profl. jours. Served with U.S. Mcht. Marine, 1944-47; Served with AUS, 1954-56. Vis. prof. under Ford Found. fellowship Harvard, 1960-61; guest scholar under Ford Found. fellowship Brookings Instn., Washington, 1962-63. Mem. Am. Econ. Assn., Am. Fin. Assn., Strategic Mgmt. Inst., Beta Gamma Sigma, Omicron Delta. Home: 1538 S Negley Ave Pittsburgh PA 15217-1420

SUSSNA, ROBERT EARL, architect; b. Lakewood, N.J., Mar. 21, 1939; s. Harry D. and Emma (Tarshish) S.; m. Deborah Sarah Beilin, Nov. 5, 1960; 1 child, Jeffrey Eric. BArch, Cornell U., 1963. Registered architect N.Y., N.J., Pa., Va. Designer Holt, Morgan, Short & Agle, Princeton, N.J., 1966-68; architect Burton F. Weisbecker AIA, Princeton, 1968; prin. Weisbecker & Sussna AIA, Princeton, 1969-70, Robert Earl Sussna AIA, Princeton, 1970-90; pres. Sussna Architects PA, Princeton, 1990—. Prin. works include Chem. Bank, Princeton, U., Bristol-Myers Squibb, Rhone-Poulenc Inc., Trenton State Coll., Expansion of U. Medicine and Dentistry of N.J. Med. Edn. Bldg., Mobil Rsch. & Devel. TSL/Engring. Ct., Lawrenceville Sch. Circle Houses Renovation, J&J Cafeteria Renovation Design, Rahway Hosp. Emergency Ctr. Renovation, master plan design of Ambulatory Svcs. Ctr., MRI Addition Exec. Architect, Inst. for Advanced Study Facility Audit & Housing Modemization Study, Newton Meml. Hosp. Facility Audit and Master Plan & Ambulatory Svc. Ctr. Design, Exec. Square One and Two Axiom interior design, Ortho Diagnostic Systems Kitchen Renovation, numerous one-man shows for photography including Trenton State Mus., Newark Mus. and Jersey City Mus., 1974—. Mem. Hopewell (N.J.) Twp. Planning Bd., 1976. Grantee in photography N.J. Coun. on the Arts. Mem. AIA (treas. N.J. chpt. 1994), Am. Hosp. Assn., N.J. Soc. Archs. (Spl. award of merit 1988), Rotary (bd. dirs.), Nassau Club. Office: Sussna Architects PA 53 State Rd Princeton NJ 08540-1318

SUSTAR, T. DAVID, religious organization executive. Dir of youth and christian edn. Ch. of God, Cleve., Tenn. Office: Ch of God PO Box 2430 Cleveland TN 37320-2430

SUTCLIFFE, ERIC, lawyer; b. Calif., Jan. 10, 1909; s. Thomas and Annie (Beare) S.; m. Joan Basché, Aug. 7, 1937; children: Victoria, Marcia, Thomas; m. Marie C. Paige, Nov. 1, 1975. AB, U. Calif., Berkeley, 1929, LLB, 1932. Bar: Calif. 1932. Mem. firm Orrick, Herrington & Sutcliffe, San Francisco, 1943-85, mng. ptnr., 1947-78. Trustee, treas., v.p. San Francisco Law Libr., 1974-88; founding fellow The Oakland Mus. of Calif.; bd. dirs. Merritt Peralta Found., 1988; past bd. dirs. Hong Kong Bank of Calif., Friends of U. Calif. Bot. Garden, sec. Fellow Am. Bar Found (life); mem. ABA (chmn state regulation securities com. 1960-65), San Francisco Bar Assn. (chmn. corp. law com., 1964-65), San Francisco C. of C. (past treas., dir.), State Bar Calif., Pacific Union Club, Bohemian Club, Phi Gamma Delta, Phi Delta Phi, Order of Coif. Home: 260 King Ave Oakland CA 94610-1231 Office: Old Fed Reserve Bank Bldg 400 Sansome St San Francisco CA 94111-3308

SUTCLIFFE, MARION SHEA, writer; b. Washington, July 29, 1918; d. James William and Ida (Hewitt) Shea; m. James Montgomery Sutcliffe, Aug. 23, 1941; 1 child, Jill Marion. BMus, Boston Conservatory Music, 1956-60; EdM, Boston State Coll., 1969. Cert. music, English, psychology and reading tchr., Mass. Tchr. Milford (Mass.) Pub. Schs., 1966-70; tchr. music Worcester (Mass.) Pub. Schs., 1970-71; reading tchr. Natick and Newton (Mass.) Pub. Schs., 1971-73; real estate developer Sutcliffe Family Trust, South Dennis, Mass., 1969—; developer Delray Beach Club, Dennisport, Mass.; mfr. A&A Assocs., South Dennis, 1989—; dir., sec. bd. mgrs. The Soundings Resort, Dennisport, Mass., 1990—. Songwriter Diablo, 1954. Founder, mgr. Boston Women's Symphony, 1962-66. Fuller grantee New England Conservatory, 1957, grantee State Mass., 1957. Mem. AAUW, DAR, Nat. Am. Theatre Organ Soc., Ea. Mass. Am. Theatre Organ Soc. (bd. dirs. 1989-92), Organ-Aires (v.p. 1991—), West Dennis Garden Club, Amateur Organists Assn. Internat. Episcopalian. Avocations: painting, playing the organ, swimming, gardening, walking. Home: 145 Cove Rd South Dennis MA 02660-3515 Office: 60 Macarthur Rd Natick MA 01760-2938

ŠUTEJ, VJEKOSLAV, conductor; b. Rijeka, Croatia, July 31, 1951; s. Josip and Alemka (Stefanini) Š.; m. Linela Malici; 1 child Alemka. Degree, Music Acad., Zagreb, Croatia, 1975. Music dir. Opera Split, Split, Croatia, 1985-90, La Fenice, Venice, Italy, 1990-93, Orquesta Simfonica de Sevilla, Seville, Spain, 1991—, Houston Grand Opera, Houston, Tex., 1994—. Home: 510 Preston HGO Houston TX 77002-1954 Office: Houston Grand Opera 510 Preston St Houston TX 77002-1504

SUTER, ALBERT EDWARD, manufacturing company executive; b. East Orange, N.J., Sept. 18, 1935; s. Joseph Vincent and Catherine (Clay) S.; m. Michaela Sams Suter, May 28, 1966; children: Christian C., Bradley J., Allison A. BME, Cornell U., 1957, MBA, 1959. Pres., chief exec. officer L.B. Knight & Assocs., Chgo., 1959-79; v.p. internat. Emerson Electric Co., St. Louis, 1979-80, pres. motor div., 1980-87, group v.p., 1981-83, exec. v.p., 1983-87, vice chmn., 1987; pres., chief operating officer, dir. Firestone Tire & Rubber Co., Akron, Ohio, 1987-88; pres., chief operating officer Whirlpool Corp., Benton Harbor, Mich., from 1988; exec. v.p. Emerson Electric Co., St. Louis, until 1990, pres., COO, 1990-92, sr. vice chmn., COO, 1992—; bd. dirs. Boatmen's Bancshares, Inc., St. Louis U. Bd. dirs. Jr. Achievement Nat. Bd., Colorado Springs, Colo., Jr. Achievement Miss. Valley, St. Louis Sci. Ctr. Bd.; chmn. Torch div. St. Louis chpt. United Way, 1982-86. Mem. Glenview (Ill.) Country Club, St. Louis Club, Old Warson Country Club, Log Cabin Club. Republican. Episcopalian. Office: Emerson Electric Co PO Box 4100 Saint Louis MO 63136-8506

SUTER, JON MICHAEL, academic library director, educator; b. Holdenville, Okla., Oct. 30, 1941; s. Franklin Hyatt and Erma (Abee) S. BA cum laude, East Cen. State Coll., 1963; MLS, U. Okla., 1964; PhD, Ind. U., 1973. Asst. libr. East Cen. State Coll., Ada, Okla., 1964-76; assoc. libr. East Cen. U., Ada, Okla., 1976-84; dir. librs. Houston Bapt. U., 1984—; chmn. Libr. Edn. Div. Okla. Libr. Assn., 1981, Coll. Rsch. Libr. Div., Okla., 1982. Contbr. articles to profl. jours. Pres. Ada Camp Gideons Internat., 1980-82. Higher Edn. Act fellow Ind. U., 1969-71. Mem. Popular Culture Assn., Richard III Socl., Med. Acad., Renaissance Soc., Patristics Soc. Republican. Baptist. Avocations: comic books, medieval history. Home: 8271 Wednesbury Ln Houston TX 77074-2918 Office: Houston Bapt U - Moody Libr 7502 Fondren Rd Houston TX 77074-3204

SUTER, PEGGY JEAN, library director; b. Wilburton, Okla., July 18, 1937; d. Henry Paul and Violet Jessie Eads; m. James William Suter, May 15, 1954; children: Pauline Jeanette Owens, Jo Lavonne Ahlm. Grad., Hartshorne (Okla.) H.S., 1955. Cert. grade I libr., N.Mex. Piano tchr. Lovington, N.Mex., 1968-72, Eunice, N.Mex., 1973-88; kindergarten music tchr. First Meth. Ch., Lovington, 1970-73; substitute sch. tchr. Eunice Pub. Schs., 1978-81; libr. dir. Eunice Pub. Libr., 1981—. Organist First Meth. Ch., Eunice, 1982—. Mem. Am. Libr. Assn., N.Mex. Libr. Assn. (community Svc. award 1992), Lea County Libr. Assn. (v.p. 1982, pres. 1983, treas. 1984). Democrat. Methodist. Avocations: playing piano, singing, crochet. Office: Eunice Pub Libr Corner of 10th and Ave Eunice NM 88231

SUTERA, SALVATORE PHILIP, mechanical engineering educator; b. Balt., Jan. 12, 1933; s. Philip and Ann (D'Amico) S.; m. Celia Ann Fielden, June 21, 1958; children: Marie-Anne, Annette Nicole, Michelle Cecile. B.S. in Mech. Engring, Johns Hopkins, 1954; postgrad., U. Paris, 1955-56; M.S., Calif. Inst. Tech., 1955; Ph.D., Cal. Inst. Tech., 1960; M.A. (hon.), Brown U., 1965. Asst. prof. mech. engring. Brown U., Providence, 1960-65; asso. prof. Brown U., 1965-68, exec. officer div. engring., 1966-68; prof. dept. mech. engring. Washington U., St. Louis, 1968—; chmn. dept. Washington U., 1968-82, 86—; vis. prof. U. Paris VI, 1973. Assoc. editor: Jour. Biochem. Engring.; mem. editorial bd. Circulation Rsch., 1975-82. Fulbright fellow Paris, 1955. Fellow ASME, Am. Inst. of Med and Biol. Engring. (founding); mem. ASHRAE, Biomed. Engring. Soc., Am. Acad. Mechanics, Internat. Soc. Biorheology, N.Am. Soc. Biorheology (pres.-elect 1986-89, pres. 1989-90), Am. Soc. Artificial Internal Organs, Am. Soc. Engring. Edn., AAAS, AIAA (Lindbergh award St. Louis sect. 1988), Tau Beta Pi, Pi Tau Sigma. Republican. Roman Catholic. Research in fluid mechanics, heat transfer, blood flow, rheology of suspensions. Home: 830 S Meramec Ave Saint Louis MO 63105-2539

SUTHERLAND, ALAN ROY, foundation administrator; b. N.Y.C., Jan. 15, 1944; s. Arthur Abbott and Margaret Louise (Schweitzer) S. BFA, Pratt Inst., Bklyn., 1964; MPA, NYU, 1969, PhD, 1984. Personnel dir. Manhattan Psychiat. Ctr., N.Y.C., 1966-72; dep. dir. Rockland Children's Psychiat. Ctr., Orangeburg, N.Y., 1972-74; dep. dir. L.I. Devel. Ctr., Melville, N.Y., 1974-78, dir., 1978-80; personnel dir. Kiamesha (N.Y.) Concord, Inc., 1982-83; program dir. Vols. Am., N.Y.C., 1983-86; sr. staff officer Nat. Acad. Scis., Washington, 1986-88; dep. dir. U.S. Interag. Coun. on Homeless, Washington, 1988-89; exec. dir. Travelers Aid Internat., Washington, 1989-91, AIDS Ctr. of Queens County, Rego Park, N.Y., 1992—. Editor: Homlessness, Health and Human Service Needs. Recipient Citation, N.Y.C. Coun., 1986. Mem. Am. Soc. Pub. Adminstrn., N.Y. State Assn. Mental Health Adminstrs. (pres. 1975). Lutheran. Avocation: weight lifting. Home: 355 W 29th St Apt 2A New York NY 10001-4785 Office: AIDS Ctr of Queens County 97-45 Queens Blvd Ste 1220 Flushing NY 11374-2101

SUTHERLAND, BRUCE, composer, pianist; b. Daytona Beach, Fla.; s. Kenneth Francis and Norma (Williams) S.; Mus.B. cum laude, U. So. Calif., 1957, Mus.M., 1959; studies with Halsey Stevens, Ellis Kohs, Ethel Leginska, Amparo Iturbi. Harpsichord soloist with Telemann Trio in concert tour, 1969-70; tchr. master class for pianists U. Tex., Austin, 1971; dir. Bach festivals Music Tchrs. Assn. Calif., 1972-73, dir. Artists of Tomorrow Music Festivals Music Tchrs. Assn. Calif., 1984-88, competitions performed in numerous contemporary music festivals in U.S., 1957—; piano faculty Calif. State U. at Northridge, 1977—; tchr. master class for pianists UCLA, 1995—, adjudicator music competitions and auditions Nat. Guild Piano Tchrs. U. So. Calif., 1996, others; dir. Brentwood-Westwood Symphony ann. competition for young artists, 1981-88; composer: Allegro Fanfara for Orch., world premiere conducted by José Iturbi with Bridgeport Symphony Orch., 1970; Saxophone Quartet, 1971; Quintet for Flute, Strings, Piano, 1972; Notturno for Flute and Guitar, 1973; also string trio, piano and vocal works. Recipient grand prize Internat. Competition Louis Moreau Gottschalk, 1970; Stairway of Stars award Music Arts Soc., Santa Monica, 1973; named one of Los Angeles' Finest Piano Tchrs., New West Mag., 1977; honored as Dist. Tchr. of Anders Martinson, presdl. scholar in arts, 1991, Disting. Tchr. White House Commn. on Presidential Scholars, 1991; honored by Nat. Found. Advancement Arts 1989, 91, 93. Mem. Nat. Assn. Am. Composers and Condrs., Music Tchrs. Nat. Assn., Music Tchrs. Assn., Calif. Assn. Profl. Music Tchrs., Pi Kappa Lambda.

SUTHERLAND, DENISE JACKSON, ballerina; b. N.Y.C., Oct. 19, 1951; d. John Henry and Aldwyn Kepple J.; m. Donald James Sutherland, July 22, 1985; 1 child, Conor. Grad., Profl. Children's Sch., 1969; student, Am. Ballet Ctr.; studied with, Robert Joffrey, Maggie Black, David Howard. Joined Joffrey Ballet, 1969, leading ballerina; ret., 1986; artistic cons., trustee Dance Notation Bur., 1986—, Profl. Children's Sch., 1987—;cons. to dance program Nat. Endowment for Arts, 1991—; trustee Joffrey Ballet, 1986-90, bd. of Vistors N.C. Sch. Arts, 1993—. Featured in three Dance in Am. programs PBS; video dictionary of Classical Ballet, guest artist with N.Y.C. Opera, Detroit Symphony, numerous regional ballet cos., in fundraising galas Met. Opera House. Home: PO Box 154 Glen Head NY 11545-0154

SUTHERLAND, DONALD, actor; b. St. John, N.B., Can., July 17, 1935; m. Lois Hardwick; m. 2d, Shirley Douglas; children: Kiefer, Rachel; m. 3d, Francine Racette; children: Roeg, Rossif, Angus. Grad., U. Toronto, 1958. Actor: London Acad. Music and Dramatic Art, Perth Repertory Theatre, Scotland, also Nottingham, Chesterfield, Bronley, Sheffield, (plays) The Spoon River Anthology, The Male Animal, The Tempest, August for People (London debut), On a Clear Day You Can See Canterbury, The Shewing Up a Blanco Posnet, (films) The World Ten Times Over, 1963, The Castle of the Living Dead, 1964, Dr. Terror's House of Horrors, 1965, Fanatic, 1965, The Bedford Incident, 1965, Promise Her Anything, 1966, The Dirty Dozen, 1967, Sebastian, 1968, Oedipus the King, 1968, Interlude, 1968, Joanna, 1968, The Split, 1968, Start the Revolution Without Me, 1969, The Act of the Heart, 1970, M*A*S*H, 1970, Kelly's Heroes, 1970, Little Murders, 1970, Alex in Wonderland, 1971, Klute, 1971, Johnny Got His Gun, 1971, Steelyard Blues, 1972, Lady Ice, 1972, Alien Thunder, 1973, Don't Look Now, 1973, S*P*Y*S, 1974, The Day of the Locust, 1975, End of the Game, 1976, Casanova, 1976, 1900, 1976, The Eagle Has Landed, 1977, Animal House, 1978, Invasion of the Body Snatchers, 1978, The Great Train Robbery, 1979, The Kentucky Fried Movie, 1978, Murder by Decree, 1979, Bear Island, 1979, A Man, A Woman and a Bank, 1980, Nothing Personal, 1980, Ordinary People, 1980, Eye of the Needle, 1981, Gas, 1981, The Disappearance, Blood Relative, Threshold, 1983, Max Dugan Returns, 1983, Crackers, 1984, Heaven Help Us, 1985, Revolution, 1985, The Trouble with Spies, 1987, The Wolf at the Door, 1987, Apprentice to Murder, 1988, The Rosary Murders, 1988, Lock Up, 1989, Lost Angels, 1989, A Dry White Season, 1989, Backdraft, 1991, JFK, 1991, Eminent Domain, 1991, Buffy the Vampire Slayer, 1992, Younger and Younger, 1993, Shadow of the Wolf, 1993, Six Degrees of Separation, 1993, The Puppet Masters, 1994, Quicksand, Disclosure, 1994, Outbreak, 1995, Bethune: The Making of a Hero, FTA; TV shows and movies include Marching to the Sea, The Death of Bessie Smith, Hamlet at Elsinore, The Saint, The Avengers, Gideon's Way, The Champions, The Winter of Our Discontent, 1984, Ordeal By Innocence, 1985, Buster's Bedroom, Citizen X, 1995 (Emmy award). Decorated officier dans l'Ordre des Artes et des Lettres (France); officer Order of Can. Office: Creative Artists Agy Inc 9830 Wilshire Blvd Beverly Hills CA 90212-1804 also: 760 N La Cienega Blvd Los Angeles CA 90069-5231*

SUTHERLAND, DONALD GRAY, lawyer; b. Houston, Jan. 19, 1929; s. Robert Gray and Elizabeth (Cunningham) S.; m. Mary Reynolds Moodey, July 23, 1955; children: Stuart Gray, Elizabeth Dana. BS, Purdue U., 1954; LLB, Ind. U., Bloomington, 1954. Bar: Ind. 1954, U.S. Dist. Ct. (so. dist.) Ind. 1954, U.S. Tax Ct. 1956, U.S. Ct. Claims 1957, U.S. Ct. Appeals (7th cir.) 1981, U.S. Ct. Appeals (3d cir.) 1984, U.S. Ct. Internat. Trade 1987, U.S. Supreme Ct. 1987. Assoc. Ice Miller Donadio & Ryan, Indpls., 1954-64, ptnr., 1965—; practitioner in residence Ind. U. Sch. of Law, Bloomington, 1987; bd. dirs. Woodward Funds, Detroit; pres. Bison Money Market Fund., Indpls., 1982-92, chmn. bd. Contbr. articles to numerous profl. jours. Bd. dirs., v.p. Japan-Am. Soc. of Ind., Inc., Indpls., 1988—; bd. dirs. Conner Prairie Inc., Fishers, Ind., 1988—, v.p., 1989-90, chmn. bd., 1990-93; tennis ceremonies 10th Pan-Am. Games, Indpls., 1987; bd. dirs. The Children's Bur. Indpls., 1962-73, v.p., 1968-70, pres., 1970-72; bd. dirs. Orchard Country Day Sch., Indpls., 1970-73, Episc. Cmty. Svcs., Indpls., 1965-73, v.p., 1968, pres., 1969; trustee United Episc. Charities, Indpls., 1970-71, pres., 1971. Cpl. USMC, 1946-48. Mem. ABA, Internat. Bar Assn., Ind. State Bar Assn., Indpls. Bar Assn., Woodstock Club, Skyline Club, Econ. Club (bd. dirs. Ind. chpt. 1988-94). Republican. Avocations: tennis, opera. Office: Ice Miller Donadio & Ryan 1 American Sq Unit 82001 Indianapolis IN 46282-0002

SUTHERLAND, DONALD JAMES, investment company executive; b. Teaneck, N.J., Jan. 2, 1931; s. Conrad James and LaVinia Marie (Peters) S.; m. Denise Jackson, July 22, 1985; children: Paige, Donald, Shelley, Julie, Conor. A.B., Princeton U., 1953; M.B.A., Harvard U., 1958; LH.D (hon.), St. Michael's Coll., 1981. Regional sales mgr. Dahlstrom Corp., Jamestown, 1958-60; assoc. McKinsey & Co., N.Y.C., 1961-64; v.p. Laird, Inc., N.Y.C., 1965-67, New Court Securities Corp., N.Y.C., 1968-70; pres. Quincy Assocs., Inc., N.Y.C., 1970-75; pres., corp. gen. ptnr. Quincy Ptnrs., Glen Head, N.Y., 1975—; chmn. bd. Crane Hoist Engring. Corp., 1975-79, Am. Spring & Wire Splty. co., Inc., 1977-82, Muehlhausen Bros. Spring & Mfg. Co., Inc., 1977-82, Lewis Spring & Mfg. Co., Inc., 1979-82, Ohio Locomotive Crane Co., Inc., 1981-86, Water Products Co., 1988-89, Publix Shirt Co., L.P., 1979-91, Quincy Packaging Group, L.P., 1984-91, Will & Baumer, Inc., 1984-94, Quincy Spring Group, Inc., 1986-94, Quincy Techs., Inc., 1987—, PCI Group, Inc., 1987-93, Perfection Forms Corp., 1990-94, Tectron Tube Corp., 1991-95, The Lion Brewery Inc., 1993—, Cavert Wire Co., Inc., 1994—; chmn. bd., pres. Ala. Metal Products Co. Inc., 1976-77. Contbr. articles to profl. jours. Trustee Sheltering Arms Children's Svc., 1973-75, St. Michael's Coll., 1972—, Cancer Rsch. Inst., 1984—, Joffrey Ballet, 1982-91, pres. 1985-87, Barry Goldwater Scholarship and Excellence in Edn. Found., 1991—, Hofstra U., 1992—; mem. vis. com. Fordham Bus. Sch., 1987—, Villa I Tatti Coun., 1991—, The New Sch., 1992—, Muhlenberg Coll., 1992—, Nassau County (N.Y.) Planning Commn., 1965-68, Internat. Coun. of World Monuments Fund, 1991—. Lt. (j.g.) USN, 1953-56. Mem. The Creek (gov. 1987—, treas. 1991-93), Cap and Gown (trustee 1981—), The Links, Econ. Club of N.Y.C. Democrat. Roman Catholic. Office: PO Box 154 Glen Head NY 11545-0154

SUTHERLAND, DOUGLASS B., former mayor, tent and awning company executive; b. Helena, Mont., May 2, 1937; s. Chris and Marie Sutherland; m. Grace Sutherland, Sept. 5, 1986; children: Karen, Scott. B.A., Central Wash. U., 1959. Program specialist Boeing Co., Tacoma, Wash., 1960-71; owner, pres. Tacoma Tent & Awning, Inc., 1971-86; sec., pres., 1986—. Bd. dirs. Tacoma-Pierce County Bd. Health, Tacoma-Pierce County Employment and Tng. Consortium; mayor City of Tacoma, 1982-89; pres. Puget Sound Regional Coun.; chair Urban County Caucus, Wash. Assn. of Counties. Mem. Assn. Wash. Cities, Tacoma-Pierce County C. of C. Republican. Lodge: Rotary. Avocation: sailing. Office: Tacoma Tent and Awning Inc 121 N G St Tacoma WA 98403-2226 Office: Pierce County Executive Exec Ste 737 930 Tacoma Ave Tacoma WA 98402

SUTHERLAND, FRANK, publishing executive, editor; b. Mount Juliet, Tenn., May 31, 1945; s. Ernest Franklin Sr. and Fontelle (Moore) S.; m. Natilee Duning; children: Kate, Daniel. BA, Vanderbilt U., 1970. Reporter The Tennessean, Nashville, Tenn., 1963-77, zone editor, 1977-78, city editor, 1978-82, editor, 1989—; editor The Shreveport (La.) Times, 1988-89; mng. editor The Hattiesburg (Miss.) Am., 1982-86; exec. editor The Jackson (Tenn.) Sun, 1986-88. Mem. Soc. Profl. Journalists (mem. Tenn. chpt. pres. 1974-81, nat. bd. dirs. 1974, nat. treas. 1981, sec. 1982, pres.-elect 1983, pres. 1984-85), Am. Soc. Newspaper Editors (mem. steering com., reporters com. for freedom of press 1979-82). Office: The Tennessean 1100 Broadway Nashville TN 37203-3116

SUTHERLAND, GAIL RUSSELL, retired industrial equipment manufacturing company executive; b. Rush Lake, Wis., Dec. 20, 1923; s. Gail Marion and Edith (Grueb) S.; m. Leone Marie Witkowski, Mar. 10, 1945; children: Keith Allan, Glenn Elliott. BS in Agr., U. Wis., Madison, 1947, BSME, 1948, MS in Agrl. Engring., 1949. Div. engr. Deere & Co., Ottumwa, Iowa, 1949-63; mgr. product engring. Deere & Co., Des Moines, 1963-77; dir. product planning Deere & Co., Moline, Ill., 1977-80, dir. product engring. planning, 1980-83, dir. product engring., 1983-84, v.p. engring., 1984-86, v.p. engring. and tech., 1986-87. Mem. editorial adv. bd. Mfg. Engring. Mag., 1987; inventor: cotton harvester blower discharge, combine soybean header, beet harvester flail feeder, pasture renovator cutter. Served as ensign USN, 1943-46. Mem. Nat. Acad. Engring., Am. Soc. Agrl. Engrs. (Engr. of Yr. 1980, Disting. Engr. of Yr. 1983), Soc. Automotive Engrs., Am. Nat. Standards Inst. (bd. dirs. 1984-86). Republican. Home and Office: 16 Mason Ln Bella Vista Village Hiwasse AR 72739

SUTHERLAND, GEORGE LESLIE, retired chemical company executive; b. Dallas, Aug. 13, 1922; s. Leslie and Madge Alice (Henderson) S.; m. Mary Gail Hamilton, Sept. 9, 1961 (dec. Mar. 1984); children: Janet Leslie, Gail Irene, Elizabeth Hamilton; m. Carol Brenda Kaplan, Feb. 19, 1986. BA, U. Tex., Austin, 1943, MA, 1947, PhD, 1950. With Am. Cyanamid Co., various locations, 1951-87; asst. dir. research and devel. Princeton, N.J., 1969-70, dir. research and devel., agr. div., 1970-73; v.p. med. research and devel. Pearl River, N.Y., 1973-86, dir. med. research div., 1978-86, dir. chem. research div., 1980-81; v.p. corp. research tech. Pearl River, 1986-87. Served with USN, 1944-46. Mem. Assn. Research Dirs. (pres. 1975-76), AAAS, Am. Chem. Soc. Home: 42 Sky Meadow Rd Suffern NY 10901-2519

SUTHERLAND, DAME JOAN, retired soprano; b. Sydney, Australia, Nov. 7, 1926; d. McDonald S.; m. Richard Bonynge, 1954; 1 son. Student, Royal Coll. Music, London, 1951. Appeared concert and oratorio performances, Australia; appeared in: opera Judith, Syndey Conservatory of Music; debut Covent Garden in Magic Flute, 1952; Italian debut in Handel's Alcina, Teatro la Fenice, Venice, 1960, Bellini's Puritani, Glyndebourne Festival, Sussex, Eng., 1960, Bellini's Beatrice di Tenda, La Scala, 1961, Rossini's Semiramide, La Scala, 1962, Meyerbeer's Les Huguenots, La Scala, 1962, N.Y. debut, Carnegie Hall, 1961; Opera debut Lucia, 1961; opened Sutherland-Williamson Opera Co. tour, Australia, 1965; appeared: Handel's Julius Caesar, Hamburg Opera, 1969, Bellini's Norma, Met Opera, 1970, opened, Lyric Opera Chgo. with, Semiramide, 1971, San Francisco Opera with, Norma, 1972, San Francisco Opera with, Trovatore, 1975, Met. Opera with, I Puritani, 1976, Vancouver Opera with, Le Roi de Lahore, 1977; premiered new prodn., Met. Opera in, Tales of Hoffmann, 1973; 1st prodn. in Am. in 80 years Esclarmonde, Massenet, San Fancisco Opera, 1974; author: (with Richard Bonynge) The Joan Sutherland Album, 1986. Decorated Order of Merit, comdr. and dame comdr. Order Brit. Empire, 1991; Companion, Order Australia, 1991; recipient Grammy award for best classical vocal soloist, 1981. Fellow Royal Coll. Music. Office: care Ingpen & Williams, 14 Kensington Ct, London W8 5DN, England also: care Colbert Artist Mgmt 111 W 57th St New York NY 10019-2211

SUTHERLAND, JOHN BEATTIE, radiologist, health center administrator; b. Cultus Lake, B.C., Can., Apr. 21, 1932; s. George William and Annie Ethylwynne (Nicholson) S.; m. Eva Freko, Dec. 23, 1956; children: Ian Scott, Evan Michael, Karen Elaine, Eric Neil. BSc in Physics, U. Man., Winnipeg, Can., 1954, MSc in Physics, 1956, MD, 1960, postgrad. in radiology, 1966-69. Rotating intern Winnipeg Gen. Hosp., 1960-61; rsch. asst. dept. physiology U. Man., 1961-62; staff advisor Atomic Energy Control Bd., Ottawa, Ont., Can., 1962-64, rsch. officer, Pinawa, Man., 1964-66; radiology resident Winnipeg Gen. Hosp., 1966-69; head sect. nuclear medicine Health Scis. Centre, Winnipeg, 1970-82, acting head radiology, 1982-84, head radiology, 1984-90, v.p., 1990—; chmn. health scis. Med. Adv. Com., Winnipeg, 1987—. Fellow Royal Coll. Physicians and Surgeons Can. (mem. diagnostic radiology 1969, nuclear medicine 1976), Am. Coll. Radiology; mem. Can. Med. Assn., Can. Assn. Radiologists (pres. 1994—), Can. Assn. Nuclear Medicine, Radiol. Soc. N.Am., Man. Med. Assn. (pres. 1986-87, chmn. bd. dirs. 1987-89). Office: Health Scis Centre Med, 820 Sherbrook St, Winnipeg, MB Canada R3A 1R9

SUTHERLAND, KIEFER, actor; b. London, Eng., Dec. 21, 1966; s. Donald and Shirley Douglas S.; m. Camelia Kath, Sept. 12, 1986 (div.); children: Michelle Kath, Sarah. Appearances include (theater) debut in Throne of Straw, 1977, (films) Max Dugan Returns, 1983, The Bay Boy, 1984 (Genie award nominee 1984), At Close Range, 1986, Crazy Moon, 1986, Stand By Me, 1986, The Lost Boys, 1987, The Killing Time, 1987, Promised Land, 1987, 1969, 1988, Bright Lights, Big City, 1988, Young Guns, 1988, Renegades, 1989, Chicago Joe and the Showgirl, 1990, Flashback, 1990, Flatliners, 1990, The Nutcracker Prince (voice), 1990, Young Guns II, 1990, Article 99, 1991, Twin Peaks: Fire Walk With Me, 1992, A Few Good Men, 1992, The Vanishing, 1993, The Three Musketeers, 1993, The Cowboy Way, 1994; (TV movies) Trapped in Silence, 1986, Brotherhood of Justice, 1986, Last Light, 1993. *

SUTHERLAND, LEWIS FREDERICK, diversified services company executive; b. Charleston, W.Va., Jan. 1, 1952; s. Lewis Frederick and Dorothy Louise (Droddy) S.; m. Barbara Hall Hoover, Aug. 24, 1974; children—Matthew, Mark. B.S. in Physics, Duke U., 1973; M.B.A., U. Pitts., 1974. Credit trainee Chase Manhattan Bank, N.Y.C., 1974-76, asst. treas., 1976-78, 2nd v.p., 1978-80, v.p., 1980; asst. treas. Aramark Corp., Phila., 1980-83, v.p., treas., 1983-87, v.p. corp. fin. and devel., 1987-91, sr. v.p. fin. and corp. devel., 1991-93, pres. uniform svcs. group, 1993—; bd. dirs. Acme Metals Inc. Trustee People's Light and Theatre Co. Named Treas. of Yr., Cash Flow mag., 1987. Mem. Beta Gamma Sigma. Office: Aramark Corp 1101 Market St Philadelphia PA 19107-2934

SUTHERLAND, MALCOLM READ, JR., clergyman, educator; b. Detroit, Nov. 11, 1916; s. Malcolm Read and Edith Ione (Osborne) S.; m. Mary Anne Beaumont, Dec. 23, 1943; children: Malcolm Read III, Maryanne B. AB, Miami (Ohio) U., 1938; MS, Western Res. U., 1941; BD, Fed. Theol. Faculty U. Chgo., 1945; LLD, Emerson Coll., 1963; LHD, Meadville-Lombard Theol. Sch., 1975. Ordained to ministry Unitarian Universalist Assn., 1945. Dir. boys work Goodrich Social Settlement, Cleve., 1938-40; housing mgr. Cleve. Met. Housing Authority, 1940-41; regional housing supr. Farm Security Adminstrn., 1941-42; housing mgmt. supr. FPHA, 1942-43; pastor in Ill., Va., Mass., 1944-60; exec. v.p. Am. Unitarian Assn., 1959-61; Robert Collier prof. ch. and soc., pres., dean faculty Meadville Theol. Sch. of Lombard Coll., Chgo., 1960-75; minister Harvard (Mass.) Unitarian Ch., 1975-94, min. emeritus, 1994—; minister emeritus Thomas Jefferson Meml. Ch., Charlottesville, Va., 1985—; adj. prof. dept. ministry Andover Newton Theol. Sch., 1992—; exec. dir. U.S. Com. World Conf. on Religion and Peace, N.Y.C., 1980-83, internat. coun., 1984—, also v.p. U.S. exec. coun.; bd. dirs. Unitarian Universalist Svc. Com., Beacon Press; chmn. editl. adv. com. bd. Christian Register, 1955-60; field rep. Unitarian Svc. Com., Mex., 1950-51; mem. sr. secretariat World Conf. Religion and Peace, Kyoto, 1970 and del. to Louvain, 1974, Princeton, 1979, Nairobi, 1984, Melbourne, Australia, 1989, Reva del Garda, Italy, 1994, hon. pres., 1994—; cons. Niwano Peace Found., Tokyo, 1982—; lectr., del. Japan-U.S. consultation on peace Internat. Assn. for Religious Freedom, 1970; trustee Dana McLean Greeley Found. for Peace and Justice, 1986-94, trustee emeritus, 1994—; Thomas Minns lectr., Boston, 1955, Charlottesville, Va., 1978, Berry St. lectr., Boston, 1956; Harvard chair lectr. Warner Free Lectrs., 1985, 93; chmn. common. coun. Chgo. Cluster of Theol. Schs., inc., 1970-74; pres. Inst. on Religion in an Age of Sci., 1969, 75-77, hon. v.p., 1980—, acad. fellow, 1988; bd. dirs., sec. Ctr. for Advanced Study Religion and Sci., Chgo., 1965—. Author: Personal Faith, 1955, Creators of the Dawn, 1979, Star Light, Star Bright, 1993; co-chmn. publs. bd. jour. religion and sci. Zygon, 1964—; also articles. Bd. govs. Manchester Coll., Oxford U., also hon. fellow, 1974—. Recipient Disting. Svc. award Charlottesville (Va.) Jr. C. of C., 1949, Disting. Svc. award Internat. Assn. Religious Freedom, 1975, Disting. Svc.award Konko Kyo Chs. Am., 1975. Mem. Unitarian Universalist Ministers Assn., Phi Delta Theta, Phi Mu Alpha, Alpha Kappa Delta, Omicron Delta Kappa. Club: Bucks Harbor Yacht (Maine) (commodore 1979-81). Home: 21 Woodside Rd Harvard MA 01451-1616

SUTHERLAND, MICHAEL CRUISE, librarian; b. Morgantown, W.Va., Aug. 29, 1938; s. Charles Fish and Mildred (Haymond) S. BA in English, San Fernando Valley State U., 1967, postgrad., 1968-69; postgrad., UCLA, 1967, MLS, 1970. Office asst., clk. Lindsay & Hall, L.A., 1959-60; libr. asst. I, bindery clk. Biomed. Libr. UCLA, 1961-65; jr. adminstrv. asst. Dept. Pub. Works City of L.A., 1967; intermediate clk. typist San Fernando Valley State U., Northridge, Calif., 1967-69; libr. I, tchg. asst. Grad. Sch. Libr. and Info.

Sci. UCLA, 1970; spl. collections libr. Occidental Coll., L.A., 1970—; attendee numerous workshops and seminars; organizer Western Books Exhbn. at various librs. throughout the Western U.S., 1992, 96; judging organizer, 1993. Author numerous exhbn. catalog booklets; author: (with others) Encyclopedia of Library and Information Sciences, 1979, Western Books Exhibition Catalog, 1986, Striking Research Gold: Distinguished Collections in California Independent Academic Libraries, 1988; contbr. articles to profl. jours. Active Neighborhood Watch, AIDS Quilt Program. Mem. ALA (rare books and mag. divsn.), Assn. Coll. and Rsch. Librs., Rounce and Coffin Club (sec., treas.). Office: Occidental Coll Mary Clapp Libr 1600 Campus Rd Los Angeles CA 90041-3384

SUTHERLAND, RAYMOND CARTER, clergyman, English educator emeritus; b. Horse Cave, Ky., Nov. 5, 1917; s. Raymond Carter and Nellie Ruth (Veluzat) S. A.B., U. Ky., 1939, M.A., 1950, Ph.D., 1953; grad., Gen. Theol. Sem., N.Y.C., 1942; postgrad., St. John's Theol. Sem., Camarillo, Calif., 1948, Gen. Theol. Sem., N.Y.C., 1979. Ordained priest Episcopal Ch., 1942, reactivated, 1985; curate St. Luke's Ch., Anchorage, Louisville, 1942-44; prof. English U. Tenn., Knoxville, 1953-57; mem. faculty Ga. State U., Atlanta, 1957-84; prof. English Ga. State U., 1965-84, dir. English grad. studies, 1978-84, prof. emeritus, 1985—; lectr. Oriental ceramics, events in nature as prototypes for classical myths, China's dragon in Pensee; spkr., panel Ga. State U. Author: Medieval English Conceptions of Hell as Derived from Biblical, Patristic and Native Germanic Sources, 1953, The Religious Background of Swift's Tale of a Tub, 1958, The Mechanics of Verification, 1963, 64-72; author of Japanese haiku, 1960-65; contbr. articles to profl. jours. Served as chaplain AUS, 1944-47. Omicron Delta Kappa disting. prof., 1979-80. Mem. Alumni Assn. Gen. Theol. Sem., Am. Assn. Advancement Humanities, Medieval Acad. Am., MLA, New Chaucer Soc., Heraldry Soc. Eng., Oriental Ceramics Soc. Eng., Ky. Hist. Soc., Hart County Hist. Soc., Phi Kappa Phi, Omicron Delta Kappa. Office: care Episcopal Diocese of Atlanta 2744 Peachtree Rd NW Atlanta GA 30305-2937

SUTHERLAND, ROBERT L., engineering company executive, educator; b. Fellsmere, Fla., May 15, 1916; s. John Alexander and Georgia Myrtle (Legg) S.; m. Mary-Alice Reed, May 18, 1945; children: Rober Hynes (dec.), Wayne Mussy, Connie Anne, Nancy Lee, John Gary. B.S., U. Ill., 1939, M.S., 1948. Registered profl. engr., Ill., Iowa, Wyo. Devel. engr. Firestone Tire & Rubber Co., Akron, Ohio, 1939-41; research engr. Borg & Beck div. Borg-Warner Corp., Chgo, 1941; test engr. Buick Motor Div. Gen. Motors Corp., Melrose Park, Ill., 1942-43; sr. engr. research dept. Aeronca Aircraft Corp., Middletown, Ohio, 1943-45; research asso. Coll. Engring., U. Ill., 1945-48; asst., then asso. prof. mech. engring. State U. Iowa, Iowa City, 1948-58; city engr. Coralville, Iowa, 1950-53; prof. mech. engring. U. Wyo., Laramie, 1958-80; prof. emeritus U. Wyo., 1980—, head dept., 1960-70, rsch. assoc., 1989-92; pres. Skyline Engring. Co. Inc., Laramie, 1972—; research engr. Collins Radio Co., Cedar Rapids, Iowa, summer 1954, cons. engr., 1950-56; staff engr. Environ. Test Lab., Martin Co., Denver, summer 1960; dir. Hunter Mfg. Co., Iowa City, 1955-58, sec. bd., 1956-58. Author: Engineering Systems Analysis, 1958, History of the University of Wyoming College of Engineering 1893-1993, 1993; contbr. articles to profl. jours. Bus. adviser mfg. group Jr. Achievement, Middletown, 1943-44; mem. Iowa City Sch. Study Coun., 1956-58; mem. Civil Air Patrol, Chgo., 1941-43, Laramie, Wyo., 1995—; legis. fellow to Nat. Conf. State Legislatures, 1982-84. Co-recipient Richard L. Templin award ASTM, 1952. Fellow ASME (life, regional v.p. 1965-67); mem. Soc. Automotive Engrs., Sigma Xi, Sigma Tau, Pi Tau Sigma, Tau Beta Pi. Methodist (steward, chmn. ofcl. bd. 1964-65, trustee 1966-69, pres. bd. 1967-69, lay leader 1969-72, chmn. council ministries 1973-75, chmn. finance com. 1975-79). Club: Kiwanian (dir. Laramie chpt. 1963-65, 79-82, pres. 1966, dir. lt. gov. 1970-71, life mem. 1978). Home: 1420 Sanders Dr Laramie WY 82070-4710

SUTHERLAND, WILLIAM OWEN SHEPPARD, English language educator; b. Wilmington, N.C., Jan. 19, 1921; s. William Owen Sheppard and Mary Owen (Green) S.; m. Madeline Ethel Cooley, Sept. 12, 1947; children: Madeline, William, John, Thomas. A.B. in English with honors, U. N.C., 1942, M.A., 1947, Ph.D., 1950. Instr. English U. N.C., Chapel Hill, 1950-51; instr. Northwestern U., Chgo., 1951-54; asst. prof. U. Tex., Austin, 1954-58, assoc. prof., 1958-65, prof., 1965—, chmn. dept., 1983-90, faculty humanist rep. Deans of Humanities of Southwest Conf., 1980; cons. Ednl. Testing Svc. and Coll. Bd., Princeton, N.J., 1965-72, NEH, Washington, 1978—. Author: Art of the Satirist, 1965; co-editor: The Reader, 1960, Six Contemporary Novels, 1961; index An Index to 18th Century Periodicals, 1800, 1956. Served to capt. C.E. U.S. Army, 1942-45. Recipient Scarborough Excellence in Tchg. award U. Tex. Austin, 1959, Liberal Arts Pro Bene Meritis award, 1996, Pres. Assocs. Tchg. award, 1982; NEH grantee, 1978-79. Mem. MLA, South Central MLA (exec. com. 1967-69), AAUP (state v.p. 1970-71), Nat. Council Tchrs. English (dir. 1974-78). Democrat. Episcopalian. Home: 3610 Highland View Dr Austin TX 78731-4033 Office: U Tex Dept English Austin TX 78712

SUTHERLAND, YVETTE FAUSTINA, emergency room nurse; b. Biabou St. Vincent, W.I., Nov. 13, 1944; came to U.S., 1976; d. Enos Regisford and Rosilda Imelda Sutherland. BS, Coll. St. Francis, Joliet, Ill., 1985. Cert. ACLS, BLS, emergency nurse, Ill.; RN, Ind.; cert. midwife, Eng., Wales; cert. mobile intensive care nurse. Nurse Queen Victoria Hosp., Sussex, Eng., 1967-69, Farnborough Hosp., Kent, Eng., 1970-72; postgrad. psychiat. nurse St. Clement's Hosp., London, 1972; midwife Farnborough Hosp., Kent, Eng., 1973-75; emergency dept. nurse St. Andrew's Hosp., London, 1975-76; emergency dept. staff nurse Northwest Family Hosp., Gary, Ind., 1976—, acting head nurse, 1985-86; planner/presenter workshop: Child Sexual Abuse, 1985; presenter workshop: Sudden Infant Death Syndrome, 1985; lectr. in field. Hosp. rep. Sexual Abuse Task Force, Gary, 1984-86; mem. Northwest Hosp. Choir, Gary, 1988—; mem. Episcopal Cmty. Svcs., Gary, 1994; sponsor mother World Vision, Calif.-Haiti, 1986—. Mem. Emergency Nurses Assn. Avocations: reading, travel, baking, dancing. Home: PO Box 4315 Gary IN 46404-0315

SUTHERLUND, DAVID ARVID, lawyer; b. Stevens Point, Wis., July 20, 1929; s. Arvid E. and Georgia M. (Stickney) S. BA, U. Portland, 1952; JD, U. N.Mex., 1957; postgrad., U. Wis., 1957. Bar: D.C. 1957, U.S. Supreme Ct. 1961. Atty. ICC, Washington, 1957-58; counsel Am. Trucking Assn., Washington, 1958-62; assoc. and ptnr. Morgan, Lewis & Bockius, Washington and Phila., 1962-72; ptnr. Fulbright & Jaworski, Washington and Houston, 1975-83; sr. ptnr. Zwerling, Mark & Sutherlund, Washington and Alexandria, Va., 1987-91; spl. counsel LaRoe, Winn, Moerman & Donovan, Washington, 1983—; prin. Sutherlund & Assocs., Washington, 1989—; bd. dirs., gen. counsel Nat. Film Svc., 1962-75; mem. family div. panel Pub. Defender Svc. for D.C., 1972-76. Founder, chmn. bd. govs. Transp. Law Jour, 1969-74. Vice chmn. Nat. Capitol Area coun. Boy Scouts Am., 1975-78; mem. bd. regents U. Portland, 1985-91. Spl. agt. CIC, U.S. Army, 1952-54. Mem. ABA, Fed. Bar Assn., D.C. Bar Assn., Transp. Lawyers Assn., Am. Arbitration Assn. (nat. panel arbitrators 1970—), Am. Judicature Soc., Internat. Club (Washington), Primsoll Club (New Orleans), Balboa Bay Club (Newport Beach, Calif.). Office: 2600 Virginia Ave NW Ste 1000 Washington DC 20037-1905

SUTIN, NORMAN, chemistry educator, scientist; b. Ceres, Republic of South Africa; came to U.S., 1956; s. Louis and Clara (Goldberg) S.; m. Bonita Sakowski, June 29, 1958; children: Lewis Anthony, Cara Ruth. B.Sc., U. Cape Town (S. Africa), 1948, M.Sc., 1950; Ph.D., Cambridge U. (Eng.), 1953. Research fellow Durham U. (Eng.), 1954-55; research assoc. Brookhaven Nat. Lab., Upton, N.Y., 1956-57, assoc. chemist, 1958-61; chemist Brookhaven Nat. Lab., 1961-66, sr. chemist, 1966—, dept. chmn., 1988-95; affiliate Rockefeller U., N.Y.C., 1958-62; vis. fellow Weizmann Inst., Rehovoth, Israel, 1965; vis. prof. SUNY-Stony Brook, 1968, Columbia U., N.Y.C., 1968-69, Tel Aviv U., Israel, 1973-74, U. Calif.-Irvine, 1977, U. Tex. Austin, 1979. Editor: Comments on Inorganic Chemistry Jour., 1980-87; mem. editorial bd. Jour. Am. Chem. Soc., 1985-89, Inorganic Chem., 1986-89, Jour. Phys. Chem., 1987-92; contbr. articles to profl. jours. Mem. NAS, Am. Acad. Arts and Scis., Am. Chem. Soc. (recipient award for disting. svc. in advancement of inorganic chemistry 1983). Office: Brookhaven Nat Lab Dept of Chemistry Upton NY 11973

SUTMAN, FRANCIS XAVIER, university dean; b. Newark, Dec. 20, 1927; s. Joseph L. and Ella (Joyce) S.; m. Mabel Ranagan, Apr. 1, 1956; children—Frank J., Catherine J., Elizabeth A. AB, Montclair State Coll., 1949, MA, 1952; EdD, Columbia U., 1956. Instr. pub. secondary schs. N.J., 1949-55; instr. chemistry Upsala Coll., 1953-55; asst. prof. Wm. Paterson Coll., 1955-57; chmn., assoc. prof. natural scis. Inter-Am. U. P.R., 1957-58; prof. gen. edn., chmn. SUNY at Buffalo, 1958-62; prof. sci. edn., chmn. dept. secondary edn., dir. Merit Bilingual Center Temple U., 1962-82; dean Coll. Edn., Fairleigh Dickinson U., 1982-87; tech. rsch. staff Exxon Engring. & Rsch. Lab., Linden, N.J., 1955; vis. lectr. Rutgers U.; cons. India AID Project; vis. prof., scientist Hebrew U., Israel; sr. scholar Temple U., 1988—; vis. sci. educator, program dir. edn. and human resources NSF, 1989-93; exec. dir. curriculum devel. coun., Rowan Coll., N.J., 1993—; del. OAS Coun. Sci. Edn. and Culture, 1971; co-dir. Environ. Edn. Conf. Environ. Protection Svc., Jerusalem, 1975; cons. fed., state, local sch. dists.; dir. spl. tech. project Huazhong U., China, 1980-87; co-dir. chem. edn. conf. Tianjin Normal U., 1984. Author: Concepts in Chemistry, 1962, 2d edit., 1968, What Kind of Environment Will Our Children Have?, 1971, Educating Personnel for Bilingual Settings: Today and Beyond, 1979, Teaching English Through Science, 1985, Improving Language in Science and Basic Skills Among Diverse Student Populations, 1995. Active Haddonfield (N.J.) Bd. Edn., 1976-79; v.p. alumni bd. Montclair State Coll., 1988. Recipient N.J. Gov.'s Edn. award, 1987, award Hispanic Congress of Pa., 1980, Alumni Citation Montclair State Coll., 1988. Fellow AAAS; mem. NSTA, Am. Chem. Soc., Am. Assn. Colls. Tchr. Edn. (chief instnl. rep. 1968-87), Nat. Assn. Rsch. Sci. Tchg. (pres.), N.J. Gov.'s Acad., Phi Delta Kappa (5 rsch. awards). Home: 128 Stratton Ln Mount Laurel NJ 08054-3301 Office: Temple U 454 Ritter Hall Philadelphia PA 19122 also: Rowan Coll Dept Curriculum Devel Glassboro NJ 08028 *Professional success comes after one accepts the paradoxes of life: willing to accept conflict and criticism, and willing to give of one's self for a cause. But even then timing must be right.*

SUTNICK, ALTON IVAN, dean, educator, researcher, physician; b. Trenton, N.J., July 6, 1928; s. Michael and Rose (Horwitz) S.; m. Mona Reidenberg, Aug. 17, 1958; children: Amy Sutnick Plotch, Gary Benjamin Sutnick. A.B., U. Pa., 1950, M.D., 1954; postgrad. studies in biomed. math., Drexel Inst. Tech., 1961-62; postgrad. studies in biometrics, Temple U., 1969-70. Diplomate Am. Bd. Internal Medicine. Rotating intern Hosp. U. Pa., 1954-55, resident in anesthesiology, 1955-56, resident in medicine, 1956, USPHS postdoctoral research fellow, 1956-57; asst. instr. anesthesiology, then asst. instr. medicine U. Pa. Sch. Medicine, 1955-57; resident in medicine Wishard Meml. Hosp., Indpls., 1957-58; chief resident in medicine Wishard Meml. Hosp., 1960-61; resident instr. medicine Ind. U. Sch. Medicine, Indpls., 1957-58; USPHS postdoctoral research fellow Temple U. Hosp., 1961-63; instr., then assoc. in medicine Temple U. Sch. Medicine, 1962-65; mem. faculty U. Pa. Sch. Medicine, 1965-75, assoc. prof. medicine, 1971-75; clin. asst. physician Pa. Hosp., 1966-71; research physician, then assoc. dir. Inst. Cancer Research, Phila., 1965-75; vis. prof. medicine Med. Coll. Pa., Phila., 1971-74; prof. medicine Med. Coll. Pa., 1975—, dean, 1975-89, sr. v.p., 1976-89; v.p. Ednl. Commn. Fgn. Med. Grads, 1989-95; dir. clin. devel. Am. Oncologic Hosp., Phila., 1973-75; attending physician Phila. VA Hosp., 1967—, Hosp. Med. Coll. Pa., 1971—; cons. in field; mem. U.S. nat. com. Internat. Union Against Cancer, 1969-72; mem. Nat. Conf. Cancer Prevention and Detection, 1973, Nat. Cancer Control Planning Conf., 1973; vice chmn. Gov. Pa. Task Force Cancer Control, 1974-76, chmn. com. cancer detection, 1974-76; mem. health rsch. adv. bd. State of Pa., 1976-78; mem. diagnostic rsch. adv. group Nat. Cancer Inst., 1974-78; chmn. coord. com., comprehensive cancer ctr. program Fox Chase Cancer Ctr., U. Pa. Cancer Ctr., 1975; cons. WHO, Govt. of India, 1979, Govt. of Indonesia, 1980, entire S.E. Asia region, 1981, U. Zimbabwe, 1989, Minister of Health of Poland, 1992, Israel Sci. Coun., 1992, U. Autonoma de Guadalajara, Mex., 1993, Generalitat de Catalunya, Spain, 1993, Ministry of Health Russian Fedn., 1993; mem. Inst. de Pos-Graduacae Medica Carlos Chagas, 1994, U.S.-China Ednl. Inst., 1996, Georgian Postgrad. Med. Found., 1996, Instituto Universitario de Ciencias Biomedicas, Argentina, 1996, German med. schs., 1996, Ctr. for Med. Edn., Ben Gurion U., Israel, 1996. Author numerous articles in field.; Asst. editor: Annals Internal Medicine, 1972-75; editorial bd. other med. jours. Bd. dirs. Phila. Coun. Internat. Visitors, 1972-77, Israel Cancer Rsch. Fund, 1975-95; nat. bd. dirs. Am. Assocs. Ben Gurion U., 1991—, Phila. divsn., 1986—, assoc. chair, 1993-95; bd. Internat. med. Scholar Program, 1988-89, Sight Savers Internat., 1988-91; trustee Ednl. Commn. Fgn. Med. Grads., 1987-89; adv. commn. Internat. Participation Phila. '76, 1973-76. Capt. M.C. AUS, 1958-60. Recipient Arnold and Marie Schwartz award in medicine AMA, 1976, Torch of Learning award Am. Friends of Hebrew U., 1981, medal Ben Gurion U. of Negev, Israel, 1985, medal U. Cath. de Lille, France, 1987, medal U. Belgrade, Yogoslavia, 1988, Founder's award and medal Med. Coll. Pa., 1989, St. Thomas Aquinas award Santo Tomas U. Med. Alumni Assn., The Philippines, 1989, medal Kiev Med. Inst., Ukraine, 1991, Benjamin Albagli medal Inst. de Pos-Graduacao Medica Carlos Chagas, Brazil, 1993, shield Coll. Physicians and Surgeons, Pakistan, 1993, medal Ukrainian State Med. U., 1994, medal Universidad de Cantabria, Spain, 1994. Fellow ACP, Coll. Physicians Phila. (censor 1977-86 , councillor 1977-86); mem. AMA, AAAS, Am. Fedn. Clin. Research (pres. Temple U. chpt. 1964-65), Am. Assn. Cancer Research, Am. Soc. Clin. Oncology, Am. Dermatoglyphics Assn., Assn. Am. Cancer Insts., Assn. Am. Med. Colls., Northeast Consortium on Med. Edn. (treas. 1983-89, chmn. 1986-87), Council of Deans of Pvt. Free-Standing Med. Schs. (co-found nat. chmn. 1983-85), Pa. Council Deans (chmn. 1987-89), Am. Cancer Soc. (vice chmn. service com. Phila. div. 1974-76, bd. dirs. 1974-80, chmn. awards com. 1976), Am. Lung Assn., Am. Heart Assn., NAFSA-Assn. Internat. Educators, Pan Am. Med. Assn., Phila. Coop. Cancer Assn., N.Y. Acad. Scis., Pa. Heart Assn., Heart Assn. Southeastern Pa., Pa. Med. Soc., Phila. County Med. Soc. (chmn. com. internat. med. affairs 1964-72), Pa. Lung Assn., Phila. Assn. for Clin. Trials (bd. dirs. 1980-81), Health Systems Agy. Southeastern Pa. (gov. bd., exec. com. 1983-87, sec. 1985-87), Am. Assn. Ben Gurion U. (bd. dirs. 1986—), Soc. des Medecins Militaires Français, Assn. Med. Edn. in Europe, Soc. Española de Educacion Medica, Internat. Med. Sch. Affiliates Consortium (co-founder, vice chmn. 1985-87), Phi Beta Kappa, Sigma Xi, Alpha Omega Alpha (councillor 1963-65). Discovered assn. of hepatitis B surface antigen with hepatitis; performed 1st studies of pulmonary surfactant in adult human lung disease; developed cancer screening system based on risk status; pioneer in describing non-A non-B hepatitis, pioneer in showing relationship of body iron stores to cancer susceptibility and life expectancy; organized first symposium on problems of foreign medical graduates; coined word "ergasteric" for lab.-contracted disease; responsible for advances in assessment of clinical competence. Office: Sutnick Assocs 2135 St James St Philadelphia PA 19103-4804

SUTOWSKI, THOR BRIAN, choreographer; b. Trenton, N.J., Jan. 27, 1945; s. Walter X. and Kathryn (Tang) S.; m. Sonia Arova, Mar. 11, 1965; 1 dau., Ariane. Student San Diego Ballet, 1958-63, San Francisco Ballet, 1963-64, Nat. Ballet, 1964. Cert. solotanzer (solo dancer), Genossenschaft Deutscher Buhnen-Angehorigen, West Germany. Soloist, Norwegian State Opera, Oslo, 1965-70; 1st soloist Hamburgische Staatsoper, Hamburg, Ger., 1970-71; dir. San Diego Ballet, 1971-76, Ballet Ala., Birmingham, 1978-81; dir. State of Ala. Ballet, Birmingham, 1982-83; chmn. Ala. Sch. Fine Arts, Birmingham, 1976—; artistic advisor, choreographer Asami Maki Ballet, Toyko, 1976-79; choreographer Atlanta Ballet, 1980-87, resident choreographer Atlanta Ballet Co., 1987-93; dance advisor Ala. State Arts Council, Montgomery, 1977-78; advisor Tenn. Ballet Co.; dance advisor Miss. Arts Council; choreographer Ballet South and State of Ala. Ballet; mem. City of Atlanta Mayor's Review Fellowship panel, 1987; adj. prof. choreography U. Ala., Tuscaloosa, 1988—; commd. choreographer Bavarian State Ballet-State Opera, Munich, 1994. Recipient Pub. TV Emmy award, 1976; Obelisk award for Choreography, 1977, 78, 79, 80; grantee Ford Found., 1964, Nat. Endowment Arts, 1973-74. Mem. Am. Guild Mus. Artists. Republican. Lutheran.

SUTPHEN, HAROLD AMERMAN, JR., retired paper company executive; b. Verona, N.J., Feb. 13, 1926; s. Harold Amerman and Marion Esther (Mason) S.; m. Greta May Peterson, June 24, 1950; children—Judith Amerman, Peter Lehmann, Pamela Torrance. Grad., Phillips Exeter Acad., 1944; B.S. in Mech. Engring, Princeton, 1950. With Universal Oil Products Co., Chgo., 1950-51, Texaco, Inc., 1951-52; bus. research analyst Arthur D. Little, Inc., 1952-56; asst. div. mgr. adminstrn., fine papers div. W.Va. Pulp and Paper Co. (name now changed to Westvaco Corp.), 1956-60, v.p., 1967-80, sr. v.p., 1980-88, mgr. fine papers div., 1974-88, dir., 1975-88; v.p., treas. U.S. Envelope Co., Springfield, Mass., 1960-62, pres., CEO, 1962-67, chmn. bd., 1967-74; bd. dirs. Assessment Appeals, Fairfield, Conn., 1993—, chmn. Served with AUS, 1944-46. Mem. Holland Soc. N.Y., Phi Beta Kappa. Clubs: Country of Fairfield (Conn.); Weston (Conn.) Gun. Home: 33 Hill Brook Ln Fairfield CT 06430-7169

SUTTENFIELD, NANCY DEZORT, financial executive; b. Mt. Pleasant, Pa., Feb. 1, 1950; d. James Joseph and Alice Mae (Roofner) Dezort; m. Charlie W. Suttenfield, May 1, 1982. BS, Indiana U. of Pa., 1971; MA, Va. Commonwealth U., 1978. Rsch. asst. Va. Dept. Taxation, Richmond, 1973-74, asst. economist, 1975-77, economist, 1977-78, sr. economist, dep. rsch. dir., 1978-81; instr. econs. John Tyler C.C., Chester, Va., 1979-80; sr. budget analyst Va. Dept. Planning and Budget, Richmond, 1981-83, budget mgr., 1983-86; dir. office planning and budget Smithsonian Instn., Washington, 1986-90, acting under sec., 1990, CFO, 1990-96; v.p. fin. and adminstrn. Case Western Res. U., Cleve., 1996—. Contbr. articles to profl. jours. Co-founder Va. Higher Edn. Budge Officers Com.; past mem. governing bd. Nat. Postal Mus. Mem. ASPA (mem. exec. com. 1993-94), Nat. Assn. Coll. and Univ. Bus. Officers, Planning Forum (past bd. dirs. Washington chpt.), Am. Assn. Mus., Fed. Exec. Inst. Alumni Assn. Office: Case Western Reserve Univ Finance & Adminstrn 10900 Euclid Ave Cleveland OH 44106-7003

SUTTER, ELEANOR BLY, diplomat; b. N.Y.C., Oct. 21, 1945; d. Samuel M. and Sylvia Gertrude (Ferber) Bly; children: Deborah, Willis. BA, Swarthmore Coll., 1966; MA, Am. U., 1978. Instr. English Thammasat U., Bangkok and Udornthani Tchr. Tng. Coll., 1967-71, Lomonosov State U., Moscow, 1973-74; rschr. Kennan Inst. for Advanced Russian Studies, 1977-79; fgn. svc. officer Office Soviet Internal Affairs, Dept. of State, 1979-80; fgn. svc. officer U.S. Embassy, Kinshasa, 1980-82, London, 1982-85; fgn. svc. officer Office of Strategic Nuclear Policy, Dept. of State, 1986-88, Office of Soviet Union Affairs, Dept. of State, 1988-90, U.S. Embassy, Moscow, 1990-92; charge d'affaires ad interim U.S. Embassy, Bratislava, 1993, dep. prin. officer, 1993-95, dep. chief of mission, 1995—; exec. dir., exec. sec., advisor U.S. Del. to Nuclear and Space Talks, Geneva, 1987-91; teaching fellow Russian lit. The Am. U., 1976-77; escort interpreter and translator Dept. of State, 1976. Co-author: Final Report of the Kennan Institute's Soviet Research Institutes Project, 1981. Founder Camp Wocsom, Moscow, 1974. Mem. Am. Fgn. Svc. Assn. Avocations: music, folk dance. Office: Dept of State Fgn Svc Lounge Washington DC 20520

SUTTER, HARVEY MACK, engineer, consultant; b. Jennings, La., Oct. 5, 1906; s. Josiah Harvey and Effie Relief (Murray) S.; AB, U. Wichita, 1932; m. Julia Genevieve Wright, Sept. 19, 1936; children: James Houston, Robert Mack, Julia Ann Boyd, John Norman. Design and prodn. engr. Boeing Aircraft, Wichita, Kans., 1936-38; supr. arts, crafts and coop. activities Bur. Indian Affairs, U.S. Dept. of Interior, 1938-42, chief procurement br. Bur. of Reclamation, Washington, 1946-54, chief div. procurement and property mgmt., 1954-58; asst. to adminstr. Bonneville Power Adminstrn., 1958-61, asst. to chief engr., 1962-66; cons. engr., 1967—; analyst, chief prodn. service WPB, Denver, 1942-44; chief div. supply C.E., Denver, 1944-46. Mem. exec. bd. Portland area Boy Scouts Am. Recipient Silver Beaver award. Presbyterian. Mem. Nat., Western woodcarvers assns., Internat. Wood Collectors Soc., Electric of Oreg. Author or co-author books and articles on woodcarving. Home: 3803 SE Carlton St Portland OR 97202-7635

SUTTER, JOSEPH F., aeronautical engineer, consultant, retired aircraft company executive; b. Seattle, Wash., Mar. 21, 1921; m. Nancy Ann French, June 14, 1943. B.A., U. Wash., 1943. Various engring. positions Boeing Comml. Airplane Co., Seattle, 1946-65, dir. engring. for Boeing 747, 1965-71, v.p., gen. mgr. 747 div., 1971-74, v.p. program ops., 1974-76, v.p. ops. and product devel., 1976-81, exec. v.p., 1981-86, cons., 1986-87; cons. Boeing Comml. Airplane Co., 1987—; chmn. aerospace safety adv. panel NASA, 1986; mem. Challenger Accident Commn., 1986. Served to lt. j.g. USN, 1943-45. Recipient Master Design award Product Engring. mag., 1965, Franklin W. Kolk Air Transp. Progress award Soc. Aero. Aerospace Coun., 1980, Elmer A. Sperry award, 1980, Nuts & Bolts award Transport Assn., 1983, Nat. Medal Tech., U.S. Pres. Reagan, 1985, Sir Kingsford Smith award Royal Aero. Soc. in Sydney, 1980, Wright Bros. Meml. Trophy, 1986; Joseph F. Sutter professorship established in his honor at U. Wash., Boeing Co., 1992. Fellow Royal Aero Soc. (hon.), AIAA (Daniel Guggenheim award 1990); mem. Internat. Fedn. Airworthiness (pres. 1989). Office: Boeing Comml Airplane Co PO Box 3707 Mail Stop 13-43 Seattle WA 98124

SUTTER, LAURENCE BRENER, lawyer; b. N.Y.C., Feb. 5, 1944; s. Meyer and Beatrice Sutter; m. Betty A. Satterwhite, June 9, 1979. AB, Columbia Coll., 1965; JD, N.Y.U., 1976. Bar: N.Y. 1977, U.S. Dist. Ct. (so. and ea. dists.) N.Y. 1977. Assoc. Shea & Gould, N.Y.C., 1976-80, Meyer, Suozzi, English & Klein P.C., Mineola, N.Y., 1980-82; assoc. counsel publs. Gen. Media Internat., Inc., N.Y.C., 1982—. With N.Y. Army N.G., 1966-72. Mem. ABA, Assn. of Bar of City of N.Y. (mem. com. on civil rights 1986-89, mem. com. on comm. and media law 1989-92, mem. com. on copyright and lit. property 1994—). Democrat. Jewish. Avocation: music. Office: Gen Media Internat Inc 277 Park Ave Fl 4 New York NY 10172-0003

SUTTER, MORLEY CARMAN, medical scientist; b. Redvers, Sask., Can., May 18, 1933; s. Christian Benjamin and Amelia (Duke) S.; m. Virginia Frances Mary Laidlaw, June 29, 1957; children—Gregory Robert, F. Michelle, Brent Morley. M.D., U. Man., 1957, B.Sc., 1957, Ph.D., 1963. Intern Winnipeg (Man.) Gen. Hosp., 1956-57, resident, 1958-59; teaching fellow pharmacology U. Man., 1959-63; supr. Downing Coll., Cambridge U., 1963-65; asst. prof. pharmacology U. Toronto, 1965-66; asst. prof. pharmacology U. B.C., 1966-68, asso. prof., 1968-71, prof., 1971—, head dept. pharmacology, 1971-87; mem. staff Vancouver (B.C.) Hosp. & Health Sci. Ctr., St. Paul's Hosp.; mem. Minister of Health's Adv. Com. on Drugs, Province of B.C., 1971-87. Contbr. articles to sci. jours. Recipient Gov. Gen. medal, 1950; Med. Research Council of Can. fellow, 1959-63; Wellcome Found. Travelling fellow, 1963; Imperial Chem. Industries fellow, 1963-65; Med. Research Council scholar, 1966-71. Mem. Pharmacol. Soc. Can. (treas. 1969-72, sec. 1986-89), British Pharmacol. Soc., Am. Soc. Pharmacology and Exptl. Therapeutics, Can. Med. Assn., N.Y. Acad. of Scis. Office: U BC Faculty Medicine Therapeutics, 2176 Health Scis Mall/Dept Pharmacology, Vancouver, BC Canada V6T 1Z3

SUTTER, RICHARD ANTHONY, physician; b. St. Louis, July 20, 1909; s. John Henry and Molly Louisa (Schuchman) S.; m. Elizabeth Henby, June 15, 1935; children—John Richard, Jane Elizabeth; Judith Sutter Hinrichs. AB, Washington U., St. Louis, 1931, MD, 1935. Diplomate Am. Bd. of Preventive Medicine, Am. Bd. of Occupational Medicine. Intern St. Louis City Hosp., 1935-36; asst. to Otto Sutter, M.D., 1937; founder, med. dir. Sutter Clinic, St. Louis, 1947-84; mem. faculty Washington U. Sch. Medicine; apptd. physician mem. nat. adv. com. on occupational safety and health OSHA, 1971-75; med. dir. St. Louis Internat. Airport, 1964-84, emeritus med. dir., 1988—; mem. Mo. Gov.'s Council on Occupational Health and Safety, Gov's Adv. Com. on Worker's Compensation, Com. on Vocat. Rehab.; cons. Barnes/Sutter Health Care, 1984-91; hon. cons. St. Mary's Hosp. East St. Louis, Ill., 1991—; mem. staff Barnes, Lutheran, Deaconess hosps.; dir. Blue Cross/Blue Shield. Contbr. articles to med. publs. Bd. dirs. Downtown St. Louis, Inc. (hon. chmn. membership com., Leadership award 1994); past dir. Blue Cross/Blue Shield; mem. St. Louis Merc. Libr. Assn., Jefferson Nat. Expansion Commn., Commn. on Future of Washington U., mem. aviation com. Regional Commerce and Growth Assn. Served to lt. col. M.C., U.S. Army, 1941-46, ETO. Decorated Bronze Star; recipient Man of Yr. award St. Louis chpt. Beta Theta Pi, 1974; Alumni Achievement award Washington U. Med. Sch., 1985; Richard A. and Elizabeth H. Sutter chair Occupational, Indsl. and Environ. Medicine named in honor, Washington U. Sch. Medicine, 1993. Fellow APHA, Am. Coll. Occupational and Environ. Medicine (Health Achievement in Industry award 1978), Am. Coll. Preventive Medicine, Am. Indsl. Hygiene Assn. (emeritus, mem. Internat. com. occupational health); mem. AMA (coun. on occupational health, coun. on aviation and space medicine), Mo. Med. Assn. (del.), St. Louis Met. Med. Soc. (hon., pres. 1947, Dr. Robert Schlueter award for Leadership 1994), Am. Assn. Ry. Surgeons (past pres.), Cen. States Soc. Ind. Medicine and Surgery (past pres.), Univ. Club, Old Warson Country Club, Washington U.

Faculty Club, Eliot Soc. (founder, life), Yachting Club Am. (founder), Bradenton Country Club. Avocations: aviation, hunting, golf, fishing, estate management. Home and Office: 7215 Greenway Ave Saint Louis MO 63130-4126 also: Condo 321 6701 Gulf of Mexico Dr Longboat Key FL 34228-1338

SUTTER, WILLIAM PAUL, lawyer; b. Chgo., Jan. 15, 1924; s. Harry Blair and Elsie (Paul) S.; m. Helen Yvonne Stebbins, Nov. 13, 1954; children: William Paul, Helen Blair Sutter Doppelheuer. A.B., Yale U., 1947; J.D., U. Mich., 1950. Bar: Ill. 1950, Fla. 1977, U.S. Supreme Ct. 1981. Assoc. Hopkins & Sutter (and predecessors), Chgo., 1950-57; ptnr. Hopkins & Sutter (and predecessors), 1957-89, of counsel, 1989—; mem. Ill. Supreme Ct. Atty. Registration Commn., 1975-81. Contbr. articles on estate planning and taxation to profl. jours. Chmn. Winnetka Caucus Com., 1966-67; pres., trustee Lucille P. Markey Charitable Trust, 1983—; precinct capt. New Trier Twp. (Ill.) Rep. party, 1960-68; asst. area chmn. New Trier Rep. Orgn., 1968-72; trustee Gads Hill Center, pres., 1962-70, chmn., 1971-80; trustee Northwestern Meml. Hosp., 1983—; bd. dirs. Chgo. Hort. Soc., 1982—; mem. dean's coun. Sch. Medicine, Yale U., 1991—. Served to 1st lt. AUS, 1943-46. Fellow Am. Bar Found., Am. Coll. Trust and Estate Counsel (bd. regents 1977-83, exec. com. 1981-83); mem. ABA (ho. dels. 1972-81, chmn. com. on income estates and trusts, taxation sect. 1973-75), Ill. Bar Assn. (bd. govs. 1964-75, pres. 1973-74), Chgo. Bar Assn. (chmn. probate practice com. 1963-64), Am. Law Inst., Internat. Acad. Estate and Trust Law, Internat. Exec. Coun., Am. Judicature Soc., Ill. LAWPAC (pres. 1977-83), Order of Coif, Phi Beta Kappa, Phi Delta Phi, Chi Psi, Tavern Club, Mid-Day Club, Indian Hill Club, Law Club, Legal Club, Gulf Stream Golf Club, Country Club Fla., Ocean Club (Fla.) (bd. govs. 1993—, sec. 1993—). Episcopalian. Home: 96 Woodley Rd Winnetka IL 60093-3746 also: 6110 N Ocean Blvd Ocean Ridge FL 33435 Office: Hopkins & Sutter 3 First National Pla Chicago IL 60602

SUTTERLIN, JAMES S., political science educator, researcher; b. Frankfort, Ky., Mar. 15, 1922; s. Frederick J. and Agnes (Douglas) S.; m. Betty C. Berven, June 24, 1950 (dec. Jan. 1989); children: Rose E., Sabrina, Jamie Ann, James E. BA, Haverford Coll., 1943; postgrad., Harvard U., 1949, 67; hon. degree in jurisprudence, Kyung Hee U., Seoul, Korea, 1973. Vice-consul U.S. Fgn. Svc., Berlin, 1946-48; polit. officer U.S. Mission, Berlin, 1951-54; 1st sec. U.S. Embassy, Tel Aviv, 1954-56; desk officer U.S. State Dept., Washington, 1956-60; 1st sec. U.S. Embassy, Tokyo, 1960-63; counselor U.S. Embassy, Bonn, 1963-68; dir. U.S. Dept. State, Washington, 1969-72, insp.-gen., 1972-74; dir. UN, N.Y.C., 1974-87; dir. rsch. L.I. U., Bklyn., 1985-87, adj. prof., 1985—; fellow/lectr. Yale U., New Haven, 1988—. Author: Berlin—Symbol of Confrontation, 1989, UN and the Maintenance of Security, 1995. Elder Presbyn. Ch., Rye, N.Y., 1976—; chmn. Samaritan House, White Plains, N.Y., 1990—; pres. Wainwright House, Rye, 1995—; chmn. acad. coun. on the UN Brown U., 1995—. 1st lt. U.S. Army, 1945-46. Recipient Grosse Verdienstkreuz, Fed. Republic of Germany, 1974. Mem. UN Assn. of U.S.A., Am. Coun. on Germany, Coun. Fgn. Rels., Phi Beta Kappa. Avocation: gardening. Home: 17 N Chatsworth Ave Apt 6KL Larchmont NY 10538 Office: Yale U 34 Hillhouse Ave New Haven CT 06511

SUTTLE, DORWIN WALLACE, federal judge; b. Knox County, Ind., July 16, 1906; s. William Sherman and Nancy Cordelia (Hungate) S.; m. Anne Elizabeth Barrett, Feb. 1, 1939 (dec.); children: Stephen Hungate, Nancy Joanna Suttle Walker (dec.); m. Lucile Cram Whitecotton, Aug. 21, 1956; stepchildren: Fred and Frank Whitecotton. JD, U. Tex., 1928. Bar: Tex., U.S. Supreme Ct. 1960. Practiced law Uvalde, Tex., 1928-64; U.S. dist. judge Western Dist. Tex., 1964—. Democrat. Methodist. Office: US District Court 655 E Durango Blvd San Antonio TX 78206-1102

SUTTLES, WILLIAM MAURRELLE, university administrator, clergyman; b. Ben Hill, Ga., July 25, 1920; s. Wiley Maurrelle and Eddie Lou (Campbell) S.; m. Julia Lanette Lovern, Jan. 28, 1950. B Comml. Studies, Ga. State U., 1942; M Religious Edn., Emory U., 1953, ThM, 1947; MDiv, Yale U., 1946; EdD, Auburn U., 1958; DD, Mercer U., 1972; D Humanities, Tift Coll., 1978; LLD, Atlanta Law Sch., 1978. Ordained to ministry Baptist Ch., 1938. Asst. registrar Ga. State U., 1942-44, asst. prof. English and speech, 1946-55, assoc. prof. speech, 1955-57, prof., 1957—, prof. ednl. adminstrn. and higher edn., 1970—, also chmn. dept. speech, 1955-62, dean students, 1956-62, v.p. acad. affairs, 1964-69, exec. v.p., provost, 1970—, acting pres., exec. v.p., provost, 1987—; pres. emeritus, 1989; exec. asst. to Gov. Joe Frank Harris Ga., 1989-91; pastor Haralson (Ga.) Bapt. Ch., 1950—, Luthersville (Ga.) Bapt. Ch., 1951-62; v.p., pers. dir. Rich's, Inc., Atlanta, 1962-64; dir. Ga. Fed. Bank; adv. dir. First Union Nat. Bank of Ga. (ret.). Chmn. Joint Citizens Adv. Com. to Study Atlanta/Fulton County Govts., 1967-69, State Adv. Com. on Consol. Edn. Progs., 1983-90, Christmas Seal Tribute Dinner, Am. Lung Assn., 1985; mem. S.E. regional manpower adv. com. U.S. Dept. Labor, 1972-74, Ga. Adv. Coun. Edn., 1985-87; trustee John and Mary Franklin Found., Ga. State U. Found., George M. Sparks Scholarship Fund, Ga. Coun. Moral/Civic Concerns, 1981—, Christian Coun. Met. Atlanta, Ga. Bapt. Homes; dir. John Mercer Found., Ga. Bapt. Children's Homes & Families Ministries,1996—. With USN, 1944-46. Recipient medal of St. Paul, Greek Orthodox Archdiocese N. and S.Am., 1976, Community Svc. award Christian Coun. Met. Atlanta, 1985, Christmas Seal Tribute Am. Lung Assn., 1988, Gold medal award Religious Heritage Am., 1989, Medal of Honor DAR, 1990, Nat. Edn. award Am. Legion, 1992; co-recipient Abe Goldstein human rels. award Anti Defamation League B'nai Brith, 1984; named Rural Min. of Yr. for Ga., Progressive Farmer mag. and Emory U., 1959, Clergyman of Yr. for Ga., Ga. region NCCJ, 1971, One of 300 Who Have Shaped Atlanta, Atlanta mag., 1976, Ga. State U. Disting. Alumnus, 1989; selected as Exemplary Disting. Bivocational Minister in Town and Country area Nat. Coun. Bivocational Ministries, 1988. Mem. Atlanta C. of C., Ga. State U. Athletic Assn. (trustee 1982-89), Ga. State U. Alumni Assn. (pres. 1967, bd. dirs. 1963-74), Masons (33 degree, grand chaplain of grand masonic lodge of Ga. 1994-95), Shriners, Kiwanis (pres. 1966), Commerce Club, Blue Key, Mortar Bd., Phi Kappa Phi, Beta Gamma Sigma, Phi Eta Sigma, Omicron Delta Kappa, Alpha Kappa Psi, Kappa Phi Kappa, Phi Delta Kappa, Kappa Delta Pi, Sigma Pi Alpha, Sigma Tau Delta, Sigma Nu (grand chaplain 1979-82, 86-92, 94—, vice regent 1992—), Alpha Lambda Delta. Home: 2734 Piney Wood Dr East Point GA 30344-1956 Office: Ga State U Univ Plaza Atlanta GA 30303

SUTTON, BARRETT BOULWARE, former insurance company executive; b. Forsyth, Ga., July 6, 1927; s. James Phinazee and Katherine Woodward (Boulware) S.; m. Mary Terecia Wade, Sept. 1, 1948; children: Katherine (Mrs. John P. Apel), Barrett Boulware, Wade. AB, Vanderbilt U., 1949, LLB, 1950. Bar: Tenn. 1950. With Life and Casualty Ins. Co. Tenn., Nashville, 1950-85; gen. counsel Life and Casualty Ins. Co. Tenn., 1970-83, sr. v.p., 1972-85, also dir. Pres. Nashville Council Community Services, 1968-70, Nashville Travelers Aid Soc., 1970-72; chmn. Nashville U.S.O. Com., 1960-62; treas. Nashville Sr. Citizens, 1980; bd. dirs., sec. Oak Hill Sch., 1983-88, chmn., 1988-90; bd. dirs., treas. Exchange Club Charities, Inc., 1984-87. With USNR, 1945-46. Mem. Assn. Life Ins. Counsel, Order of Coif, Phi Beta Kappa. Presbyterian (elder). Clubs: Belle Meade Country, Nashville Exchange. Home: 750 Greeley Dr Nashville TN 37205-2634

SUTTON, BERRIEN DANIEL, beverage company executive; b. Axson, Ga., Jan. 24, 1926; s. Frank and Commie (Brooker) S.; m. Verda Lee Adams, June 6, 1953; 1 child, Kathryn. B.B.A., U. Ga., 1948. From traveling auditor to St. Louis dist. mgr. Coca-Cola Co., 1948-62; from v.p. sales to pres., gen. mgr. Coca-Cola Bottling Co., St. Louis, 1962-66; pres. Assoc. Coca-Cola Bottling Co., Inc., Daytona Beach, Fla., 1966-82; past mem. pres.'s adv. coun. Coca-Cola Co.; past. pres., bd. govs. Coca-Cola Bottlers Assn. Past gen. campaign chmn., v.p., dir., mem. exec. com. United Fund East Volusia County; past mem. exec. com. Civic League Halifax Area; past trustee Bethune Cookman Coll.; past mem. bd. dirs. Daytona Beach Symphony Soc. Served with USNR, 1944-46. Mem. 49ers, Young Pres. Orgn., Rotary (past bd. dirs., treas., pres. Daytona Beach club). Methodist. Home: 20 Habersham Park NW Atlanta GA 30305-2856

SUTTON, BEVERLY JEWELL, psychiatrist; b. Rockford, Mich., May 27, 1932; d. Beryl Dewey and Cora Belle (Potes) Jewell; m. Harry Eldon Sutton, July 7, 1962; children: Susan, Caroline. MD, U. Mich., 1957. Diplomate Am. Bd. Pediatrics, Am. Bd. Psychiatry and Neurology. Rotating intern St. Joseph Mercy Hosp., Ann Arbor, Mich., 1958; resident in child psychiatry Hawthorne Ctr., Northville, Mich., 1958-62; resident in pediatrics U. Hosp./U. Mich. Med. Ctr., Ann Arbor, 1959-61; resident in psychiatry Austin (Tex.) State Hosp., 1962-64, dir. children's svc., 1964-89, dir. psychitric residency prof., 1989—; cons. in field. Contbr. articles to profl. jours. Active numerous civic orgns. Recipient Outstanding Achievement award, YWCA, 1989, Jackson Day award, Tex. Soc. Child and Adolescent Psychiatry, 1989, Showcase award, Tex. Dept. Mental Health/Mental Retardation, 1990, Disting. Svc. award, Tex. Soc. Psychiatric Physicians, 1990. Fellow Am. Acad. Child and Adolescent Psychiatry, Am. Psychiatric Soc., Am. Pediatric Assn.; mem. Tex. Soc. Child and Adolescent Psychiatry (pres. 1979-80), Tex. Soc. Psychiatric Physicians, AMA, Tex. Med. Soc., Am. Genetics Soc. Office: Austin State Hospital 4110 Guadalupe St Austin TX 78751-4223

SUTTON, CHARLES RICHARD, architect, designer; b. Sand Springs, Okla., June 25, 1927; s. Charles A. and Violet L. Sutton; m. Jean Rector, Dec. 18, 1949; children: John Isaac, Adam Franklin. BArch, Okla. State U., 1950; MArch, Cranbrook Acad. Art, Bloomfield Hills, Mich., 1954. Draftsman Parr & Aderhold, Oklahoma City, 1950-53; draftsman/designer Coston, Frankfurt & Short, Oklahoma City, 1954-55; designer I.M. Pei & Assocs., N.Y.C., 1957-62; designer/office dir. John Carl Warnecke & Assocs., Washington, Honolulu, 1962-68; pres. Charles R. Sutton & Asscs. Inc., Honolulu, 1968-85; ptnr. Sutton Candia Ptnrs., Honolulu, 1985-94; pres. Sutton Candia Inc., 1995—; lectr. in design Columbia U., 1958-62; cons. Honolulu Waterfront Master Plan, 1984; mem. design rev. bd. Kaanapali Resort, Maui, Hawaii, 1985, Kapolei New Town, Oahu, Hawaii, 1991; lectr. in urban design sch. arch. U. Hawaii, 1994-96; authority engr. Hawaii Conv. Ctr., 1995-96. Archtl. designer East West Ctr., 1961, Hawaii State Capitol, 1962-68; planner designer Honolulu Capitol Dist., 1965-68; architect Aloha Tower Pla,1974-78. Founding mem., v.p. Hist. Hawaii Found.; bd. dirs. Kakaako Improvement Assn., Hawaii, 1990—. Recipient 1st prize Kalakaua Comml. Area Competition (Bishop Estate), 1971; Lloyd Warren fellow Nat. Inst. for Archtl. Edn., N.Y., Paris, 1955-56. Fellow AIA (pres. Hawaii sect. 1973, fellowship 1980); mem. Waikiki Yacht Club (commodore 1984). Mem. Christian Ref. Ch. Avocations: sailing, painting, photography. Home: 3077 Wailani Rd Honolulu HI 96813-1005

SUTTON, DANA FERRIN, classics educator; b. White Plains, N.Y., Oct. 10, 1942; s. Joseph Guy Jr. and Eleanor Sutton; m. Kathryn A. Sinkovich, Aug. 16, 1975. BA, The New Sch. for Social Rsch., N.Y.C., 1965; MA, U. Wis., 1966, PhD, 1970. Lectr. Herbert Lehman Coll., CUNY, 1969-72; postdoctoral rsch. Darwin Coll., Cambridge, Eng., 1972-74, U. Auckland, New Zealand, 1974-75; asst. prof. U. Ill., Urbana, 1975-79; prof. U. Calif., Irvine, 1979—, dept. chair., 1986-94; assoc. dir. Thesaurus Linguae Graecae Project, Irvine, 1991—. Author: The Greek Satyr Play, 1975, numerous other books and monographs; editor: William Gager: The Complete Works, 1994; contbr. articles to profl. jours. John Guggenheim fellow, 1975-76. Mem. Am. Philol. Assn., Calif. Classical Assn. Office: U Calif Dept of Classics 156 Humanities Hall Irvine CA 92717

SUTTON, DOLORES, actress, writer; b. N.Y.C.. BA in Philosophy, NYU. Appeared in plays including Man With the Golden Arm, 1956, Career, 1958, Machinal, 1960, Rhinoceros, Liliom, She Stoops to Conquer, Hedda Gabler, Anna Karenina, Eccentricities of a Nightingale, Brecht on Brecht, Young Gifted and Black, Luv, The Friends, The Web and the Rock, The Seagull, Saturday, Sunday, Monday, The Little Foxes, What's Wrong With This Picture, The Cocktail Hour, My Fair Lady (Broadway revival), 1994, My Fair Lady (nat. tour), 1993-94; films include The Trouble With Angels, Where Angels Go, Trouble Follows, Crossing Delancey, Crimes and Misdeameanors, Tales of the Darkside: TV appearances include Studio One, Hallmark Hall of Fame Prodn. An Wilderness, Theatre Guild of the Air: Danger, Suspense, Gunsmoke, Valiant Lady, General Hospital, From These Roots, As the World Turns, Edge of Night, F. Scott Fitzgerald in Hollywood, Patty Hearst Story, All in the Family, Bob Newhart Show, All My Children, others; TV writer Lady Doc, The Secret Storm, Loving; playwright: Down at the Old Bull and Bush, The Web and the Rock Company Comin', 1995, Born Yesterday, 1995, A Perfect Ganesh, 1995, Detail of a Larger Work, 1995, The Front Page, 1996. Mem. League of Profl. Theatre Women (bd. dirs.), Ensemble Studio Theatre (bd. dirs.).

SUTTON, FRANCIS XAVIER, social scientist, consultant; b. Oneida, Pa., July 7, 1917; s. Frank James and Rose Marie (Burns) S.; m. Ruth Jacqueline Young, Aug. 24, 1948; children: Peter, Sean, Philip, Elizabeth. BS, Temple U., 1938; MA, Princeton U., 1940, Harvard U., 1941; PhD, Harvard U., 1950. Jr. fellow, Soc. Fellows Harvard U., Cambridge, Mass., 1946-49, asst. prof., lectr., 1949-54; program officer, overseas rep. Ford Found., N.Y.C., 1954-67, dep. v.p., acting v.p., 1968-83; cons. Ford Found. and Harvard U., 1983-85; acting pres. Social Sci. Research Council, N.Y.C., 1985-86, also bd. dirs., chmn., 1988-92; cons. Rockefeller Found, U.S. Agy. for Internat. Devel. and World Bank, N.Y.C. and Washington, 1987-92; acting dir. Rockefeller Study and Conf. Ctr., Bellagio, Italy, 1990-92; cons. Aga Khan U., 1992—. Author: The American Business Creed, 1956; editor: A World to Make/Development in Perspective, 1989; contbr. articles to profl. jours. and chpts. to books. Pres. Am. Found. for Intellectual Freedom in Europe, N.Y.C., 1987-93; mem. bd. fgn. scholarships Dept. State, Washington, 1961-63; bd. dirs. Nat. Ctr. on Adult Literacy, U. Pa., Phila., 1990—; mem. adv. bd. Ctr. on Philanthropy, City Univ., N.Y.C., 1988—; mem. Coun. Internat. Partnerships in Sci. and Tech., N.Y. Acad. Scis., 1995—. Capt. U.S. Army Air Corps, 1941-45. Fellow AAAS; mem. Council on Fgn. Relations, African Studies Assn., Assn. for Asian Studies (disting. service award 1984). Democrat. Club: Century Assn. (N.Y.C.). Avocations: piano playing, dancing, snorkeling. Home: 80 Bellair Dr Dobbs Ferry NY 10522-3504

SUTTON, GEORGE WALTER, research laboratory executive, mechanical engineer; b. Bklyn., Aug. 3, 1927; s. Jack and Pauline (Aaron) S.; m. Evelyn D. Kunnes, Dec. 25, 1952; children—James E., Charles S., Richard E., Stewart A. B. Mech. Engring. with honors, Cornell U., 1952; M.S., Calif. Inst. Tech., 1953, Ph.D. magna cum laude, 1955. Rsch. scientist Lockheed Missile Co., 1955; rsch. engr. Space Sci. Lab. GE, 1955-61, mgr. magnetohydrodynamic power generation, 1962-63; vis. Ford prof. MIT, 1961-62; sci. adviser Hdqrs. USAF, 1963-65; with Avco Rsch. Lab., 1965-83, dir. laser devel., 1971-82, v.p., 1972-82, v.p., tech. dir. Helionetics Laser div., 1983-85; v.p. JAYCOR, San Diego, 1985-90; dir. E-O rsch. Kaman Aerospace Corp., Tucson, 1990-92; chief scientist Aero Thermal Tech., Inc., Arlington, Va., 1993-96; prin. engr. ANSER, Arlington, Va., 1996—; cons. Energy Agy., 1977-79, Arms Control Agy., 1986; lectr. magnetohydrodynamics U. Pa., 1960-63, Stanford, 1964; developer of ablation heat protection for ICBM and high energy lasers, pioneer aero-optics, missile interceptor tech. Author: (with A. Sherman) Engineering Magnetohydrodynamics, 1965, Direct Energy Conversion, 1966; editor-in-chief Jour. AIAA, 1967—; editor various procs.; contbr. some 90 articles to profl. jours. Served with USAAF, 1945-47. Recipient Arthur Flemming award for outstanding govt. service, 1965. Fellow AIAA (chmn. plasmadynamics tech. com., Thermophysics award 1980, Disting. Svc. award 1988), ASME, AAAS, Nat. Acad. Engring. (audit com.). Avocations: tennis, travel, sailing. Office: Ste 800 1215 Jefferson Davis Hwy Arlington VA 22202 *I have been blessed with certain abilities so I strain to utilize and sharpen them to the maximum. But I do the right thing - always. Love of my family and my desire to do best for them have led to situations wher my values could have been compromised. I still do the right thing. It has usually worked out best for my family and myself.*

SUTTON, GREGORY PAUL, obstetrician-gynecologist; b. Tokyo, Dec. 12, 1948; (parents Am. citizens); s. Vernon S. And Vonna Lou (Streeter) S.; m. Judith Craigie Holt, June 26, 1977; children: Anne Craigie, James Streeter. BS in Chemistry with honors, Ind. U., 1970; MD, U. Mich., 1976. Diplomate Am. Bd. of Ob/Gyn. Assoc. prof. and chief div. gynecologic oncology Ind. U. Sch. Medicine, Indpls., 1983—. Cancer Clin. fellow Am. Cancer Soc., Phila., 1981-83; recipient Career Devel. award Am. Cancer Soc., 1986-89. Fellow Am. Coll. Obstetrics and Gynecology; mem. Gynecologic Oncology Group (cert. Spl. Competence in Gynecologic Oncology 1985), Marion County Med. Soc., Ind. State Med. Soc., Bayard Carter Soc., Soc. of Gynecologic Oncologists, Gynecologic Oncology Group, Hoosier Oncology Group. Avocations: swimming, cycling, woodworking. Office: Ind U Hosp 926 W Michigan St Indianapolis IN 46202-5203

SUTTON, HARRY ELDON, geneticist, educator; b. Cameron, Tex., Mar. 5, 1927; s. Grant Edwin and Myrtle Dovie (Fowler) S.; m. Beverly Earlene Jewell, July 7, 1962; children: Susan Elaine, Caroline Virginia. B.S. in Chemistry, U. Tex., Austin, 1948, M.A., 1949; Ph.D. in Biochemistry, U. Tex., 1953. Biologist U. Mich., 1952-56, instr., 1956-57, asst. prof. human genetics, 1957-60; asso. prof. zoology U. Tex., Austin, 1960-64; prof. U. Tex., 1964—, chmn. dept. zoology, 1970-73, asso. dean Grad. Sch., 1967-70, 73-75, v.p. for research, 1975-79; mem. adv. council Nat. Inst. Environ. Health Scis., 1968-72, council sci. advs., 1972-76; mem. various coms. Nat. Acad. Scis.-NRC; cons. in field; bd. dirs. Associated Univs. for Research in Astronomy, 1975-79, Argonne Univs. Assn., 1975-79, Univ. Corp. for Atmospheric Research, 1975-79, Associated Western Univs., 1978-79. Author: Genes, Enzymes, and Inherited Disease, 1961, An Introduction to Human Genetics, 1988, Genetics: A Human Concern, 1985; editor: First Macy Conference on Genetics, 1960, Mutagenic Effects of Environmental Contaminants, 1972, Am. Jour. Human Genetics, 1964-69. Trustee S.W. Tex. Corp. Public Broadcasting, 1977-80, sec., 1979-80; bd. dirs. Ballet Austin, 1978-84; mem. Austin Arts Commn., 1991-95. Served with U.S. Army, 1945-46. Mem. AAAS, Am. Soc. Human Genetics (dir. 1961-69, pres. 1979), Genetics Soc. Am., Am. Soc. Biochem. and Molecular Biology, Am. Chem. Soc., Tex. Genetics Soc. (pres. 1979), Am. Genetic Assn., Headliners Club (Austin), Town and Gown Club. Achievements include research and publications in human genetics. Home: 1103 Gaston Ave Austin TX 78703-2507 Office: Dept Zoology Univ Tex Austin TX 78712

SUTTON, JAMES ANDREW, diversified utility company executive; b. Gary, Ind., June 29, 1934; s. Winfield Alexander and Margaret (Aulwurm) S.; m. Beverly Joan McCorkle, Aug. 27, 1955; children—James II, Susan, Stephen, Scot. BSChemE, Purdue U., 1957. V.P., gen. mgr./gas products Linde div. Union Carbide Corp., Danbury, Conn., 1978-82; sr. v.p. compressed gases UGI Corp., Valley Forge, Pa., 1982-84, exec. v.p., COO, 1984-85, pres., COO, 1985-86, pres., CEO, 1986-88, chmn., pres., CEO, 1989-94; chmn., CEO UGI Corp., Valley Forge, 1994-95; chmn., 1995—; bd. dirs. Gilbert Assocs., Inc., Reading, Pa., UGI Corp., Valley Forge, AmeriGas Propane, Inc., Valley Forge; former mem. Mellon PSFS Bd., Phila.; former mem. bd. trustees Thomas Jefferson U. Chmn. United Way Chester/Montgomery Counties Region, 1991; former mem., bd. dirs., mem. exec. com. Reading is Fundamental, Washington. Lt. U.S. Army, 1958. Mem. Phila. Country Club, Oyster Reef Country Club. Office: UGI Corp PO Box 858 Valley Forge PA 19482-0858

SUTTON, JOHN F., JR., law educator, university dean, lawyer; b. Alpine, Tex., Jan. 26, 1918; s. John F. and Pauline Irene (Elam) S.; m. Nancy Ewing, June 1, 1940; children: Joan Sutton Parr, John Ewing. J.D., U. Tex., 1941. Bar: Tex. 1941, U.S. Dist. Ct. (we. dist.) Tex. 1947, U.S. Ct. Appeals (5th cir.) 1951, U.S. Supreme Ct. 1960. Assoc. Brooks, Napier, Brown & Matthews, San Antonio, 1941-42; spl. agt. FBI, Washington, 1942-45; assoc. Matthews, Nowlin, Macfarlane & Barrett, San Antonio, 1945-48; ptnr. Kerr, Gayer & Sutton, San Angelo, Tex., 1948-50, Sutton, Steib & Barr, San Angelo, 1951-57; prof. U. Tex.-Austin, 1957-65, William Stamps Farish prof., 1965-84, A.W. Walker centennial chair, 1984—, dean Sch. Law, 1979-84. Editor: (with Wellborn) Materials on Evidence, 8th edit., 1996, (with Dzienkowski) Cases and Materials on Professional Responsibility of Lawyers, 1989, (with Schuwerk) Guideline to the Texas Disciplinary Rules of Professional Conduct, 1990; contbr. articles to profl. jours. Served to 1st lt. JAGC USAR, 1948-54. Fellow Am. Bar Found. (life), Tex. Bar Found. (life); mem. ABA (com. on ethics 1970-76), State Bar Tex. (com. on rules of profl. conduct, com. adminstrn. rules of evidence), Inter-Am. Bar Assn., Fed. Bar Assn., Philos. Soc. Tex., Order of Coif, Phi Delta Phi, San Angelo Country Club, River Club of San Angelo,. North Austin Rotary (pres. 1969). Presbyterian. Home: 3830 Sunset Dr San Angelo TX 76904-5956 Office: U Tex Sch Law 727 E 26th St Austin TX 78705-3224

SUTTON, JOHN PAUL, lawyer; b. Youngstown, Ohio, July 24, 1934; m. Jane Williamson, Aug. 20, 1958; children—Julia, Susan, Elizabeth. B.A., U. Va., 1956; J.D., George Washington U., 1963. Bar: Calif. 1965. Patent examiner U.S. Patent Office, Washington, 1956, 59-62; law clk. U.S. Ct. Customs and Patent Appeals, Washington, 1962-64; assoc. Flehr, Hohbach, Test, Albritton & Herbert, San Francisco, 1964-68; ptnr. Limbach, Limbach & Sutton, San Francisco, 1969-91; spl. counsel Heller, Ehrman, White & McAuliffe, San Francisco, 1992-95; of counsel Medlin & Carroll, San Francisco, 1995, Bryan, Hinshaw Rubin, Cohen & Barnet, San Francisco, 1996—; adj. instr. Practicing Law Inst., 1968-69; continuing edn. program Calif. State Bar, 1972, 75, U. Calif. Law Sch., Berkeley, 1975, 84. Contbr. articles to legal jours. Served with USNR, 1956-59. Mem. Calif. Patent Law Assn. (pres. 1975), San Francisco Patent Law Assn. (pres. 1976), State Bar Calif. (exec. com. patent sect. 1975-77), Am. Chem. Soc. Democrat. Episcopalian. Home: 2421 Pierce St San Francisco CA 94115-1131 Office: Bryan Hinshaw et al Medlin & Carroll San Francisco CA 94104-2806

SUTTON, JONATHAN STONE, landscape architect; b. Columbus, Ohio, July 31, 1944; s. Charles Reuel and Theodora (Stone) S.; m. Karen Marie Johnson, May 21, 1970; children—Eva Marie, Theodore Stone. B.A., Amherst Coll., 1966; M.Arch., M.Landscape Architecture, U. Pa., 1970. Draftsman Pierre Zoelly (Architect), Zurich, Switzerland, 1966; designer Weissman/Spohn, Phila., 1967; research asst., regional planning br. Delaware River Port Authority, Phila., 1969; research asst. computer applications group Center Ecol. Research in Planning Design, U. Pa., Phila., 1970; instr. landscape architecture studio Center Ecol. Research in Planning Design, U. Pa. (Grad. Sch. Fine Arts), 1972-73, dir. urban design studio, 1973-79; partner Adaptive Design, Phila., 1970; architect, landscape architect Wallace, McHarg, Roberts & Todd, Phila., 1971—; asso. partner Wallace, McHarg, Roberts & Todd, 1973—; adj. asst. prof. Drexel U. Sch. Architecture, 1976—; affiliated Wallingford Community Arts Center.; prin. Hist. Devel. Corp., 1978—, Growth Properties, Renaissance Properties, 1990, Renaissance Assets, Inc., 1993. Contbr. articles to profl. jours. Mem. Citizens Council Delaware County, Pa. Mem. Am. Soc. Landscape Architects (Brad Williams medal 1974, 76, Merit award 1971), AIA, Am. Inst. Planners. Democrat. Presbyterian. Home: 355A Plush Mill Rd Media PA 19086-6022

SUTTON, JULIA SUMBERG, musicologist, dance historian; b. Toronto, Ont., Can., July 20, 1928; d. Samuel L. and Anne R. (Rubin) Sumberg. AB summa cum laude, Cornell U., 1949; MA, Colo. Coll., 1952; PhD, U. Rochester, 1962. Instr. music history New Sch. for Social Research, 1962-63; instr. music Queens Coll., CUNY, 1963-66; chmn. dept. music history and musicology New Eng. Conservatory Music, 1971-90, chmn. faculty senate, 1971-73; prof. emerita New England Conservatory Music, 1992; vis. asst. prof. George Peabody Coll. for Tchrs., 1966-67; instr. NYU, summers 1963, 64; pvt. tchr. piano, 1949-65; lectr., rsch. dir. in musicology, music as related to the dance; presenter numerous workshops and summer insts. on Renaissance dance. Dance dir. N.Y. Pro Musica prodn. An Entertainment for Elizabeth, Caramoor, N.Y., Saratoga, N.Y., U. Ariz., Stanford U., UCLA, 1969, nationwide tours, 1970-1973; dance dir. Descent of Rhythm and Harmony, Colorado Springs, Colo., 1970, Renaissance Revisited, Phila., 1972, An Evening of Renaissance Music and Dance, York U., Toronto, 1974; author: Jean Baptiste Besard's Novus Partus 1617, 1962; editor: Thoinot Arbeau: Orchesography 1588, 1967; translator, editor: Fabritio Caroso: Nobiltà di dame 1600, 1986, rev. 1995; producer, co-dir. (tng. video) Il Ballarino, 1991; contbr. articles and book revs. to profl. jours. and encys. Mem. Am. Musicological Soc., Coun. of Rsch. in Dance, Soc. of Dance History Scholars, Phi Beta Kappa.

SUTTON, KELSO FURBUSH, publishing executive; b. Boston, Mar. 8, 1939. B.A. cum laude, Harvard U., 1961. With Time Inc., N.Y.C., 1961—; exec. v.p. Time, Inc., 1984-88, pres, chief exec. officer Mag. Group, 1985-86; pres., CEO Book div. Time Inc., 1986-93; exec. v.p. Times Inc., 1993-94. Office: Carnegie Hill Tower 40 E 94th St Apt 13E New York NY 10128-0726

SUTTON, LOUISE NIXON, retired mathematics educator; b. Hertford, N.C., Nov. 4, 1925; d. John Calhoun and Annie Mariah (McNair) Nixon. BS, N.C. A&T State U., 1946; MA, NYU, 1951, PhD, 1962. Cert. tchr.

sci. and math., N.C. Tchr. math./sci. Willis Hare H.S., Pendleton, N.C., summer 1946; tchr. math. Dudley High Sch., Greensboro, N.C., 1946-47; instr. math. N.C. A&T State U., Greensboro, 1947-57; asst. prof. math. Del. State U., Dover, 1957-62; assoc. prof. to prof. and dept. head math. Elizabeth City (N.C.) State U., 1962-87, prof. emeritus, 1987—; adv. com. math. cert. Del. State Bd. Edn., Dover, 1961-62, adv. com. cert. in math. and sci., 1959-61. Bd. dirs. Peruimans County Indsl. devel. Corp., Hertford, 1967-72; NAACP rep. adv. com. N.C. Bd. Social Svcs., Raleigh, 1969-71; mem. fin. bd. Pearson St. YWCA, Greensboro, 1954-56; AME Zion rep. Com. on Christian Edn. of Exceptional Persons, Nat. Coun. Chs., N.Y.C., 1963-65, rep. 150th Anniversary Advance, Am. Bible Soc., 1964-66; bd. dirs. Divsn. Higher Edn., N.C. Assn. Educators, 1969-72; trustee St. Paul AME Zion Ch., 1972—. Recipient Disting. Tchr. award Ea. Carolina State U. Gen. Alumni Assn., 1974, Tchr. of Yr., 1980, Woman of Yr. award NAUW, 1976. Mem. Nat. Coun. Tchrs. Math., NAACP, Order Ea. Star (grand assoc. dean 1993-95, worthy matron 1993-96), George Washington Carver Floral Club (pres. 1990—), Daus. of Isis, Delta Sigma Theta. Republican. Avocations: mini-golf, bowling, ceramics, crochet, fishing. Home: 5277 Holiday Is Hertford NC 27944-9794

SUTTON, LYNN SORENSEN, librarian; b. Detroit, July 31, 1953; d. Leonard Arthur Edward and Dorothy Ann (Steele) Sorensen; m. Richard Dale Sutton, May 2, 1981 (div. Sept. 1992); children: Elizabeth, Alexander, Derek. AB, U. Mich., 1975, MLS, 1976. Dir. Med. Libr. South Chgo. Cmty. Hosp., 1976-77; corp. dir. libr. Detroit-Macomb Hosp. Corp., Detroit, 1977-86; dir. librs. Harper Hosp., Detroit, 1987-88; dir. Sci. and Engring. Libr. Wayne State U., Detroit, 1989-95, dir. undergrad. libr., 1996—; cons. Catherine McAuley Health Sys., Ann Arbor, Mich., 1993. Contbr. articles to profl. jours. Mem. ALA, Assn. Coll. and Rsch. Librs. (co-chair membership, sci. tech. sect., comparison sci. and tech. librs. 1990—), Mich. Health Scis. Librs. Assn. (pres. 1987-88), Met. Detroit Med. Libr. Group (pres. 1983-84), Phi Beta Kappa, Beta Phi Mu. Lutheran. Office: Wayne State U Undergrad Libr Detroit MI 48202-3918

SUTTON, PAT LIPSKY, artist, educator; b. N.Y.C., Sept. 21, 1941; d. Bernard G. and Bernice D. (Brown) S.; children: David Lipsky, Jonathan Lipsky. BFA, Cornell U., 1963; attended, Bklyn. Mus. Art Sch., 1960, 61; postgrad., Art Student's League, 1963; MA, Hunter Coll., 1968. Mem. faculty Fairleigh Dickinson U., 1968-69, Hunter Coll., 1972, San Francisco Art Inst., 1974; assoc. prof. U. Hartford, 1983—; guest lectr. Hirshhorn Mus., 1975, Va. Commonwealth U., Bennington Coll., 1977, U. Pitts., 1974, NYU, 1983, SACI, Florence, 1986, Springfield Mus., 1987, 88, U. Miami, 1992, Pollock-Krasner House and Study Ctr., East Hampton, L.I., N.Y., 1995; guest lectr. Parsons Sch. Design, 1990, lectr., 1982-83, 90; instr. SUNY, Purchase, 1980-81; mem. adv. coun. Cornell U. Coll. Art and Architecture, 1988—. One-woman shows include Andre Emmerich Gallery, N.Y.C., 1970, 72, 74, 75, Deichter O'Reilly Gallery, 1976, Medici-Berenson Gallery, 1976, Everson Mus., 1970, Gloria Luria Gallery, Miami, 1988, Slater-Price Gallery, N.Y.C., 1986, Hartell Gallery Cornell U., 1989, Andre Zarre Gallery, 1991, Virginia Miller Gallery, Coral Gables, Fla., 1994; exhibited in group shows at Whitney Mus. Am. Art, 1971, Hirshhorn Mus. and Sculture Garden, 1975, Promenade Galelry, Hartford, 1984, U. Mass. Art Gallery, Amherst, 1987, Gloria Luria Gallery, 1988, 92, Andre Zarre Gallery, 1990, 95, Denise Renè Gallery, Paris, 1993, Gallery One, Toronto, Can., 1996; represented in permanent collections Herbert Johnson Mus., Itaca, N.Y., Witney Mus., Hisrhhorn Mus., Walker Art Ctr., Hunter Coll., Fogg Art Mus., Harvard U., San Francisco Mus. Art, Bklyn. Mus., Wadsworth Atheneum, Hartford; stage designer (play) Custody, Westbeth Theatre, N.Y.C., 1991. Grantee N.Y. State Coun., 1972, N.Y. Found. Arts, 1992, Winsor and Newton Paint Co., 1992; fellow Va. Ctr. for Creative Arts, 1986, 93, Tyrone Guthurie Centre, Co., Moneghan, Ireland, 1996. Home: 11 Riverside Dr New York NY 10023-2504

SUTTON, PETER ALFRED, archbishop; b. Chandler, Que., Can., Oct. 18, 1934. BA, U. Ottawa, 1960; MA in Religious Edn, Loyola U., Chgo., 1969. Ordained priest Roman Catholic Ch., 1960, bishop, 1974; oblate of Mary Immaculate; high sch. tchr. St. Patricks, Ottawa, Ont., 1961-63, London (Ont.) Cath. Cen. Sch., 1963-74; bishop of Labrador-Schefferville, Que., Can., 1974—; archbishop Missionary Diocese of Keewatin-Le Pas, Man., 1986, apptd. coadjustor archbishop, 1986—, archbishop, 1986—; mem. Can. Conf. Cath. Bishops, Western Cath. Conf. of No. Bishops, Man. Bishops; accompanying Bishop L'Arch Internat. (homes for mentally handicapped), 1983—. Contbr. religious articles to newspapers. Address: PO Box 270, 108 1st St W, The Pas, MB Canada R9A 1K4

SUTTON, RAYMOND L., JR., lawyer; b. Detroit, Oct. 4, 1951. BA, U. Mich., 1973; JD, U. Colo., 1976; LLM, U. Denver, 1979. Bar: Mich. 1976, Colo. 1978. Ptnr. Baker & Hostetler, Denver; adj. prof. law U. Denver, 1980-81, vis. asst. prof. law, 1981-82. Editor: Colo. Lawyer, 1984-86; contbr. articles to profl. jours. Fellow Am. Coll. Trust and Estate Coun.; mem. ABA, Colo. Bar Assn., State Bar Mich. Office: Baker & Hostetler 303 E 17th Ave Ste 1100 Denver CO 80203-1264*

SUTTON, RICHARD LAUDER, lawyer; b. Dover, Del., July 4, 1935; s. Richard and Anna Kimber (Massey) S.; m. Violette Witwer, June 25, 1960; children: Jane Valentine, Richard Mohler. A.B. with distinction, U. Del., 1957; LL.B., Yale U., 1960. Bar: Del. 1961. Law clk. to Judge Edwin D. Steel, U.S. Dist. Ct., Wilmington, Del., 1960-61; assoc. firm Morris Nichols Arsht & Tunnell, Wilmington, 1961-65; ptnr. Morris Nichols Arsht & Tunnell, 1966—; v.p., sec. Prodair Corp.; mem. antitrust and trade regulation com. U.S. C. of C., 1976-80, mem. council on governance, 1980-82. Chmn. Del. Gov.'s Higher Edn. Commn., 1976; treas., bd. dirs., mem. exec. com. Greater Wilmington Devel. Coun., 1970-82; trustee Wilmington Pub. Libr., 1974-96; bd. dirs. Grand Opera House, Inc., 1976-92, Am. Judicature Soc., U. Del. Libr. Assocs.; chmn. William H. Heald Scholarship Fund. Mem. ABA, Am. Law Inst., Del. Bar Assn., Confrererie des Chevaliers du Tastevin Soc. Colonial Wars, The Brook Wilmington Club, Wilmington Country Club, Pine Valley Golf Club, Vicmead Hunt Club, The Seminole, U.S. Srs. Golf Assn., Royal and Ancient Golf Club, Phi Beta Kappa, Phi Kappa Phi, Omicron Delta Kappa, Phi Delta Phi. Home: 10 Barley Mill Dr Wilmington DE 19807-2218 Office: PO Box 1347 Wilmington DE 19899-1347

SUTTON, ROBERT EDWARD, investment company executive; b. Burlington, Vt., July 3, 1943; s. Rollin Robert and Blanche Margaret (Deforge) S.; m. Julie Robin Levine, Feb. 1, 1975; children: Katherine Vanessa, David Robert. BA in Econs., St. Michaels Coll., 1962-66. V.p. Compretic, Inc., Beverly Hills, Calif., 1967-70; brokerage cons. Conn. Gen. Life Ins. Co., Denver, 1970-74; pres. The Core Corp., Denver, 1975-80; mng. dir. Willshire Investments & Holding Co., Denver, 1981-91; pres., chmn. Gen. Capital, Inc., Denver, 1991-93; pres, CEO WK Capital Advisors, Inc., Denver, 1993—; dir. NAt. Assn. Indep. Contr., Denver. 1991—, Nat. Endowment Trust, Denver, 1990—, Tri Corp, Denver, 1980-89, Nat. Acceptance Corp., L.A., 1991—, Nat. Investment Holdings, L.A., 1990—. Mem. Nat. Rep. Eagles, Washington, 1986-90, Inner Circle, Washington, 1985-90, Denver Ctr. Performing Arts, 1976-86. Mem. Am. Cancer League, Glenmoor Country Club. Home: 57 Glenmoor Cir Cherry Hl Vlg CO 80110-7121 Office: WK Capital Advisors Inc Ste 650 3773 Cherry Creek Dr Denver CO 80209

SUTTON, RONNIE NEAL, lawyer, state legislator; b. Pembroke, N.C., June 17, 1941; s. Willie French and Vergie Mae (Oxendine) S.; m. Genny Chavis, June 19, 1967; children: Ronette, Fonda Lynn. BA, U. West Fla., 1970; MS, Naval War Coll., 1977; MA, Ctrl. Mich. U., 1979; JD, U. N.C., 1985. Commd. ensign USN, 1958, advanced through grades to comdr., ret., 1982; atty. Locklear, Jacobs, Sutton & Hunt, Pembroke, 1985-94; rep. N.C. Ho. of Reps., Raleigh, 1993—; bd. dirs. Lumber River Legal Svcs., Pembroke, N.C. Cancer Inst., Lumberton; bd. found. dir. Pembroke State U., 1992—. Chmn. Robeson County Dem. Party, Lumberton, 1991-92. Mem. Pembroke Kiwanis Club (pres. 1991-92, Kiwanian of Yr. 1992). Democrat. Home: RR 1 Box 154 Pembroke NC 28372-9721 Office: NC Ho of Reps Jones St Raleigh NC 27601

SUTTON, ROYAL KEITH, marketing professional; b. Tomah, Wis., Feb. 18, 1932; s. Rollin E. Sutton and Anna M. (Doebel) S.; m. Kathryn E. Bennett, April 7, 1957; children: Patricia Petite, Gregg Bennett, Margaret Mary. Student, Omaha U., 1958-59, Luzerne Community Coll. Lic. ins. salesperson, real estate salesperson. Photographer Rinehart-Marsden Studio, Omaha, 1953-72; salesperson N.Y. Life Ins. Co., Scranton, Pa., 1972-75, Educators Mut. Life Ins. Co., Scranton, 1975-83; mgr. time-share resort Ski Side Village, Tannersville, Pa., 1983-84; dir. mktg. Coachman's Beach Club, Cape May, N.J., 1984-86; owner 1898 Mktg., Dallas, Pa., 1987—; mgmt. cons. Coachman's Motor Inn, Cape May. Author: Faces of Courage, 1972. Served with USAF, 1951-55. Republican. Methodist. Avocation: travel. Office: 1898 Marketing 62 Dallas s/c #303 Dallas PA 18612

SUTTON, SAMUEL J., lawyer, educator, engineer; b. Chgo., July 21, 1941; s. Samuel J. and Elaine (Blossom) S.; m. Anne V. Sutton, Aug. 28, 1965; children: Paige, Jean, Leah, Jepson. BA in History and Philosophy, U. Ariz., 1964, BSEE, 1967; JD, George Washington U., 1969. Bar: Ariz. 1969, D.C. 1970, U.S. Ct. Appeals (fed. cir.) 1983. Patent atty. Gen. Electric Co., Washington, Phoenix, 1967-70; ptnr. Cahill, Sutton & Thomas, Phoenix, 1970—; prof. law Ariz. State U., Tempe, 1975—; expert witness Fed. Dist. Cts., 1983—; trial cons. to numerous lawyers, 1972—; v.p. engring. Shintech, Inc., 1991—; arbitrator Am. Arbitration Assn., Phoenix, 1971—. Author: Patent Preparation, 1976, Intellectual Property, 1978, Art Law, 1988, Law, Science and Technology, 1991, Licensing Intangible Property, 1994, Commercial Torts, 1995; exhibited in group shows at Tanner Sq., Phoenix, Tucson Art Inst., Mobil Corp., Mesa, Ariz., Cox Devel. Co., Tempe, Ariz., Downtown Phoenix, Desert Bot. Garden, Phoenix, Gateway Ctr., Phoenix, Sedona Sculpture Garden, Construct Gallery, Phoenix. Chmn. air pollution hearing bd. City of Phoenix, 1970-85. Recipient Patent prize Patent Resources Group, 1979, Publ. award IEEE, 1967, Genematus award U. Ariz., 1964, Disting. Achievement award Ariz. State U., 1980, Construct Sculpture prize, 1989. Avocation: large scale steel sculpture. Office: Cahill Sutton & Thomas 2141 E Highland Ave Ste 155 Phoenix AZ 85016-4737

SUTTON, THOMAS C., insurance company executive; b. Atlanta, June 2, 1942; m. Marilyn Sutton; children: Stephen, Paul, Matthew, Meagan. BS in Math. and Physics, U. Toronto, 1965; postgrad., Harvard U., 1982. With Pacific Mut. Life Ins. Co., Newport Beach, Calif., 1963—, actuarial asst., 1966-69, successively asst. actuary, assoc. actuary, asst. v.p., 2d v.p., v.p. individual ins., 1969-80, successively v.p. individual fin., sr. v.p. corp. devel., exec. v.p. individual ins., 1980-87, pres., from 1987, now chmn. bd., chief exec. officer, also bd. dirs.; mem. affiliates adv. bd. U. Calif. Irvine Grad. Sch. Mgmt. Trustee South Coast Repertory; bd. dirs. Ind. Colls. So. Calif. Fellow Soc. of Actuaries (mem. numerous coms.); mem. Am. Acad. Actuaries (com. on dividend prins. and practices, 1978), Pacific States Actuarial Club, L.A. Actuarial Club (sec. 1974-75, pres. 1978-79). Office: Pacific Mut Life Ins Co 700 Newport Center Dr Newport Beach CA 92660-6307*

SUTTON, WALTER, English educator; b. Milw., Jan. 25, 1916; s. Walter Evender and Maud (Farrington) S.; m. Vivian Irene Ryan, Dec. 22, 1941; 1 dau., Catherine S. Penner. B.A., Heidelberg Coll., 1937; M.A., Ohio State U., 1938, Ph.D., 1946. Instr. English U. Rochester, 1946-47; successively asst. prof., asso. prof., prof. English, dir. grad. studies, chmn. dept. English Syracuse (N.Y.) U., 1948—, now distinguished prof. humanities, 1971—; Vis. prof. U. Minn., summer 1960; vis. prof., sr. vis. fellow Council Humanities Princeton, 1960-61; vis. prof. U. Wash., summer 1966, Colgate U., 1967, U. Hawaii, summer 1968; Mem. com. examiners advanced lit. test Grad. Record Exam., 1962-72. Author: The Western Book Trade, 1961, Modern American Criticism, 1963, American Free Verse: The Modern Revolution in Poetry, 1973; Editor: Ezra Pound: A Collection of Critical Essays, 1963, (with Richard Foster) Modern Criticism: Theory and Practice, 1963, (with Vivian Sutton) Plato to Alexander Pope: Backgrounds of Modern Criticism, 1966, (with others) American Literature: Tradition and Innovation, 1969-74, Pound, Thayer, Watson and The Dial: A Story in Letters, 1994; editorial bd.: (with others) Am. Lit., 1973-76. Served with USCGR, 1942-45. Recipient Ohioana Book award, 1963; Howald fellow Ohio State U., 1947-48. Mem. AAUP, Am. Soc. Aesthetics, Am. Studies Assn., Modern Lang. Assn. Am. Office: Dept English 401 HL Syracuse U Syracuse NY 13244

SUTTON, WILLIAM BLAYLOCK, pastor; b. Little Rock, Aug. 10, 1942; s. Richard Otto and Bettye (Blaylock) S.; m. Martha Davis, Apr. 19, 1968; children: Blake, Bryan, Stephen. BBA, Baylor U., 1964; BD, Southwestern Bapt. Theol. Sem., Ft. Worth, 1967; ThM, Internat. Theol. Sem., Orlando, Fla., 1982, DD, 1984. Ordained to ministry So. Bapt. Conv., 1965. Pastor North Hopkins Bapt. Ch., Sulphur Springs, Tex., 1965-67, 1st Bapt. Ch. Pine Hills, Orlando, 1969-77, Windsor Park Bapt. Ch., Ft. Smith, Ark., 1977-86; assoc. pastor Dauphin Way Bapt. Ch., Mobile, Ala., 1968-69; pastor 1st Bapt. Ch., McAllen, Tex., 1986—; v.p. Fla. Bapt. Pastors Conf., Orlando, 1973; pres. Ark. Bapt. Pastors Conf., Ft. Smith, 1983; trustee fgn. mission bd. So. Bapt. Conv., Richmond, Va., 1990—. Bd. visitors Criswell Coll., Dallas, 1991. Office: 1st Bapt Ch 1200 Beech Ave Mcallen TX 78501-4606

SUTTON, WILLIS ANDERSON, JR., sociology educator; b. Atlanta, July 18, 1917; s. Willis Anderson and Louneal (Walton) S.; m. Dorothy Rebecca Drake, Dec. 22, 1941; children: Willis Anderson III, Franklin Drake, Sarah Sutton Haggard. Student, Young Harris Jr. Coll., 1934-36; B.A., U. N.C., 1939, M.A., 1941, Ph.D., 1952. Project dir. WPA, Ga., 1940-41; instr. Emory U., Atlanta, 1948-52; asst. prof. U. Ky., Lexington, 1952-58; asso. prof. U. Ky., 1959-68, prof. sociology, 1968-82, chmn. dept., 1976-82. Author: Village Level Workers and Their Work, 1962. Served to 2d lt. U.S. Army, 1941-45. Ford Found. fellow India, 1959-60. Mem. Am. Sociol. Assn., Soc. Study Social Problems, Soc. Study Symbolic Interaction, Soc. Sociol. Soc., North Central Sociol. Soc. Democrat. Presbyterian.

SUTTON-STRAUS, JOAN M., journalist; b. Mimico, Ont., Can., Nov. 30, 1932; d. Frederick Edward and Anna May (Taylor) Treble; m. Walter J. Sutton, Feb. 1955 (div. 1979); children: Walter John, Deborah Anne.; m. Oscar S. Straus, Mar. 1982. Student, U. Toronto, 1951-53. Fashion editor Toronto Telegram, 1972; lifestyle editor, daily columnist Sutton's Place, Toronto Sun, 1972-79; daily commentator Sta. CFRB, Toronto, 1974-77; columnist Toronto Star, 1979; agt. gen. to U.S. Ont., 1990-91; columnist Toronto, Calgary, Edmonton and Ottawa Sun. Fin. Post, 1992—; dir. Personal Ins. Co. Author: Lovers and Others, 1974, Once More with Love, 1975, Clothing and Culture, 1975, Lovelines, 1979, All Men are not Alike. Former mem. adv. bd. Peggy Guggenheim Mus.; former trustee Am. Acad. Dramatic Arts; nat. gov. The Shaw Festival; trustee Am. Friends of Can.; dir. Citizens Com. for N.Y.C., Soc. Meml. Sloan-Kettering Cancer Ctr. Recipient Judy award Garment Salesmen Ont., 1964, Canada medal, 1993; named Can. Woman of Yr., N.Y.C., 1990; honored with Freedom of City of London. Home: 7 Gracie Sq New York NY 10028

SUUBERG, ERIC MICHAEL, chemical engineering educator; b. N.Y.C., Nov. 23, 1951; s. Michael and Aino (Berg) S.; m. Ina Inara Vatvars, Apr. 26, 1987; 1 child, Alessandra Anna. BSChemE, MIT, 1974, MSChemE, 1974, BS in Bus. Mgmt., 1974, MS in Bus. Mgmt., 1976, ScD in Chem. Engring., 1978. Asst. prof. chem. engring. Carnegie-Mellon U., Pitts., 1977-81; asst. prof. engring. Brown U., Providence, 1981-84, assoc. prof. engring., 1984-90, prof. engring., 1990—, rep. exec. com. fluids, thermal and chem. processes group, 1991—; vis. scientist Centre National de la Recherche Scientifique, Mulhouse, France, 1988; invited lectr. Ministry Edn., Monbusho, Japan, 1991, 93. Mem. internat. editorial bd. Fuel, 1988—; mem. editorial adv. bd. Energy and Fuels, 1990-93; contbr. over 75 articles to profl. jours. Elected mem. Estonian Am. Nat. Coun., N.Y.C., 1984—. Vice Chancellor's Rsch. Best Practice fellow U. Newcastle, Australia, 1995. Mem. AIChE, Combustion Inst., Am. Chem. Soc. (chmn. divsn. fuel chemistry 1991, bd. dirs.-at-large 1995-97). Office: Brown Univ Divsn Engring Box D Providence RI 02912

SUWYN, MARK A., paper company executive; b. Denver, Aug. 12, 1942. BS in Chemistry, Hope Coll., Holland, Mich., 1964; PhD in Inorganic Chemistry, Wash. State U., 1967. From R&D to gen. mgmt. positions DuPont Co., 1967-91, sr. v.p. imaging and med. products, 1989-91; exec. v.p. Internat. Paper, Purchase, N.Y., 1991—; CEO Louisianna Pacific Corp., Portland. Office: Louisianna Pacific Corp 111 SW 5th Ave Portland OR 97204*

SUYCOTT, MARK LELAND, naval flight officer; b. Riverside, Calif., Oct. 3, 1956; s. Morgan L. Suycott and Dixie L. (Drury) Bobbitt; m. Lisa Lyn Brammer, Oct. 1, 1983. BSCE, U. Mo., 1979; MS in Aero. Engring., Naval Postgrad. Sch., Monterey, Calif., 1987; test flight officer, U.S. Naval Test Pilot Sch., Patuxent River, Md., 1987; student, Def. Sys. Mgmt. Coll., Ft. Belvoir, Va., 1994. Commd. ensign USN, 1979, advanced through grades to comdr., 1995; aviation armament divsn. officer Fighter Squadron Thirty Three, Virginia Beach, Va., 1981-84; flight test project officer Pacific Missile Test Ctr., Point Mugu, Calif., 1987-89; air ops. officer Comdr. U.S. 7th Fleet, Yokosuka, Japan, 1989-91; ops./maintenance officer Fighter Squadron 11, San Diego, 1992-93; dep. asst. program mgr. Naval Air Sys. Command, Arlington, Va., 1994—. Decorated Meritorious Svc. medal. Mem. AIAA (sr.), Soc. Flight Test Engrs., Assn. Naval Aviation, Nat. Eagle Scout Assn., Masons (master mason), Omicron Delta Kappa, Tau Beta Pi, Chi Epsilon, Alpha Phi Omega (life). Avocations: running, sailing, skiing. Office: Naval Air Sys Command 1421 Jefferson Davis Hwy Arlington VA 22243-0001

SUYDAM, PETER R., clinical engineer, consultant; b. Jersey City, Apr. 1, 1945; s. Stedman Mills and Winifred M. (Murphy) S.; m. Patricia Cunniff, Feb. 2, 1970 (dec. 1976); m. Jaimy Slifka, Feb. 11, 1978; children—Rycken Stedman, Stephen Michael. Student in engring. Rensselaer Poly. Inst.; student in pre-medicine, psychology, U. Rochester; B.S. in Bio-Engring., U. Ill.-Chgo., 1975. Cert. clin. engr.; cert. health care safety profl. Dir. clin. engring. Rush-Presbyn.-St. Luke's Med. Ctr., Chgo., 1975-81; pres. Syzygy, Inc., Chgo., 1978-81; lead auditor quality assurance Callaway Nuclear Power Plant, Union Elec. Co., St. Louis, 1981-84; sr. cons. Ellerbe Assocs., Inc., Mpls., 1984-86; div. mgr. CH Health Technologies, Inc., St. Louis, 1986—; project mgr. Landmark Contract Mgmt., Inc., 1988-89; dir. healthcare tech. planning The Cannon Corp., 1989-91; tech. advisor New V.I.P. Hosp., Riyadh, Saudi Arabia, 1991-92; dir. mid. east ops. E.C.R.I., 1992—; staff cons. Joint Commn. on Accreditation for Hosps., Chgo., 1978-81; mem. tech. com. Safe Use of Electricity in Patient Care Areas of Health Care Facilities; mem. Bd. Examiners for Clin. Engring. Cert., 1980-85; com. mem. Midwest Med. Group Standards, Chgo. Hosp. Council, 1976-81. Contbr. articles to profl. jours. Served with USN, 1967-73. Mem. Assn. Advancement Med. Instrumentation (elec. safety com. 1980—), AAAS, IEEE (chpt. chmn. group on engring. in medicine and biology), Instrument Soc. Am., Am. Nat. Standards Inst., Am. Hosp. Assn., Nat. Fire Protection Assn. (health care, elec. and engring. sects.), Am. Soc. Hosp. Engrs., Am. Soc. Quality Control. Current work: Biotechnology applications in medicine and industry; quality assurance-all fields. Subspecialties: Biomedical engineering; Clinical engineering. Office: 5200 Butler Pike Plymouth Meeting PA 19462

SUZIEDELIS, VYTAUTAS A., engineering corporation executive; b. Kaunas, Lithuania, June 22, 1930; s. Simas and Antanina S. B.S., Northeastern U., 1954; M.S., N.Y. U., 1955. With Stone & Webster Engring. Corp., Boston, 1956-90, chief power engr., 1972-74, v.p., 1974-76, sr. v.p., 1976-79, exec. v.p., 1979-87, dir., 1975-87, cons., 1987-90; pres. Vasair Corp., Brockton, Mass., 1977-91. Mem. ASME, Aircraft Owners and Pilots Assn., Pi Tau Sigma (hon.). Republican. Roman Catholic. Home: 6101 Pelican Bay Blvd Apt 1205 Naples FL 33963-7111

SUZUKI, BOB H., university president. Formerly v.p. acad. affairs Calif. State Univ., Northridge; pres. Calif. State Poly. Univ., Pomona, 1991—. Office: Calif State Polytech Univ Office of Pres 3801 W Temple Ave Pomona CA 91768-2557

SUZUKI, FUJIO, immunologist, educator, researcher; b. Chiba, Japan, June 25, 1946; came to U.S., 1980; s. Takeshi and Kimie Suzuki; m. Katsuko Eda, Oct. 4, 1969; children: Emi, Sumihiro. BA in English Lit., Tohoku-Gakuin U., Sendai, Japan, 1968; PhD in Bacteriology, Sch. Medicine Tohoku U., Sendai, 1975. Postdoctoral fellow U. Tex. Med. Br., Galveston, 1980-82, asst. prof., 1982-84, assoc. prof., 1987-91, prof., 1991—; mem. sci. staff Shriners Burns Inst., Galveston, 1987—. Contbr. articles to profl. jours. Pres. Japanese Alumni Assn. Galveston, 1990—. Recipient Nohagi Rsch. award Tohoku U., 1972, James W. McLaughlin award U. Tex. Med. Br., 1980. Mem. Am. Soc. Microbiology, Am. Assn. Cancer Rsch., Internat. Soc. Antiviral Rsch., Soc. Leukocyte Biology, N.Y. Acad. Scis., Soc. Japanese Virologists, Japanese Soc. Immunology, Japanese Cancer Assn., Japanese Bacteriol. Soc. Republican. Buddhist. Achievements include discovery that type 2 T cells and suppressor macrophages are generated by the stimulation of thermal injury, that interferon-gamma is produced by the adminstration of various immunomodulators into man and animals, that opportunistic herpes virus infections are developed through type 2 cytokines (IL-4, IL-10, IL-13) released from type 2 cells (Th 2 cells, CD8+ type 2T cells), others and that an alkaroid benzoilmesaconine protects individuals infected with various intracellular pathogens through the induction of new CD4+ anti-type 2 T cells. Home: 7714 Chantilly Cir Galveston TX 77551-1629 Office: U Tex Med Br 200 University Blvd Rm 730 Galveston TX 77555

SUZUKI, HIDETARO, violinist; b. Tokyo, June 1, 1937; came to U.S., 1956; s. Hidezo and Humi (Sakai) S.; m. Zeyda Ruga, May 16, 1962; children: Kenneth Hideo, Nantel Hiroshi, Elina Humi. Diploma, Toho Sch. Music, Tokyo, 1956, Curtis Inst. Music, 1963. Prof. violin Conservatory Province Que., Quebec, 1963-79, Laval U., Quebec, 1971-77, Butler U., Indpls., 1979—. Concertmaster Que. Symphony Orch., 1963-78, Indpls. Symphony Orch., 1978—; performed as concert violinist Can., U.S., Ea. and Western Europe, Cuba, Japan, S.E. Asia, 1951—, formerly performed in USSR; guest condr. orchs. in numerous concerts, broadcasts, 1968—; mem. jury Mont. Internat. Competition, 1979, Internat. Violin Competition, 1979, Internat. Violin Competition of Indpls., 1982, 86, 90, 94; artistic dir. Suzuki and Friends chamber music series, 1980—; rec. artist. Office: Indpls Symphony Orch 45 Monument Cir Indianapolis IN 46204-2907

SUZUKI, HOWARD KAZURO, retired anatomist, educator; b. Ketchikan, Alaska, Apr. 3, 1927; s. Goerge K. and Tsuya S.; m. Tetsuko Fujita, Sept. 12, 1952; children: Georganne, Joan, James, Stanley. BS, Marquette U., 1949, MS, 1951; PhD, Tulane U., 1955. Instr. anatomy Yale U. Sch. Medicine, 1955-58; asst. prof. anatomy U. Ark. Med. Center, Little Rock, 1958-62; asso. prof. U. Ark. Med. Center, 1962-67, prof., 1967-70; prof. anatomy, asso. dean health related professions U. Fla., Gainesville, 1970-71; prof. anatomy U. Fla. (Coll. Medicine), 1970-71; dean U. Fla. (Coll. Health Related Professions), 1971-79; prof. anatomy U. Fla. (Coll. Medicine and Health Related Professions), 1979-90, ret., 1990; cons. NIH, VA, NASA; vis. research prof. U. Utah Sch. Medicine, 1962. Contbr. articles to profl. jours. Bd. dirs. Civitan Regional Blood Bank, 1977—; regional v.p. Fla. Retarded Citizens Assn., 1974-76; mem. Fla. Adv. Council on Vocat. Edn., 1978-86, chmn., 1981; active United Way. Fellow AAAS; mem. Soc. Exptl. Biol. Medicine, Am Assn. Anatomists, Am. Soc. Allied Health Professions, Am. Soc. Marine Artists, Sigma Xi. Episcopalian. Home: 4331 NW 20th Pl Gainesville FL 32605-3436

SUZUKI, ISAMU, microbiology educator, researcher; b. Tokyo, Aug. 4, 1930; emigrated to Can., 1962; s. Jisaku and Michie (Baba) S.; m. Yumiko Kanehira, May 16, 1962; children: Kenji, Miyo, Kohji. B.Sc.Agr., U. Tokyo, 1953; Ph.D., Iowa State U., 1958. NIH postdoctoral fellow Western Res. U., 1958-60; instr. Inst. Applied Microbiology, U. Toyko, 1960-62; asst. prof. mcirobiology U. Man., Winnipeg, Can., 1964-66, assoc. prof., 1966-69, prof., 1969—, head. dept., 1972-85. Contbr. articles on chemoautotrophic bacteria, mechanism of inorganic oxidation to sci. jours. NRC of Can. postdoctoral fellow, 1962-64. Mem. AAAS, Can. Soc. Microbiologists, Can. Biochem. Soc., Am. Soc. Microbiology, Sigma Xi. Office: U Manitoba Dept Microbiology, Winnipeg, MB Canada R3T 2N2

SUZUKI, JON BYRON, dean, periodontist, educator; b. San Antonio, July 22, 1947; s. George K. and Ruby (Kanaya) S. BA in Biology, Ill. Wesleyan U., 1968; PhD magna cum laude in Microbiology, Ill. Inst. Tech., 1971; DDS magna cum laude, Loyola U., 1978. Med. technologist Ill. Masonic Hosp. and Med. Ctr., Chgo., 1966-67; instr. lab. in histology and parasitology Ill. Wesleyan U., Bloomington, 1967-68; med. technologist Augustana Hosp., Chgo., 1968-69; rsch. assoc., instr. microbiology Ill. Inst. Tech., Chgo., 1968-71; clin. rsch. assoc. U. Chgo. Hosps., 1970-71; clin. microbiologist St. Luke's Hosp. Ctr., Columbia Coll., Physicians and Surgeons, N.Y.C., 1971-73; assoc. med. dir. Paramed. Tng. and Registry, Vancouver, B.C., Can., 1973-74; dir. clin. labs. Registry of Hawaii, 1973-74; chmn. clin. labs. edn. Kapiolani Community Coll., U. Hawaii, Honolulu, 1974; lectr. periodontics, oral pathology Loyola U. Med. Ctr., Maywood, Ill., 1974-90; lectr. stomatology Northwestern U. Dental Sch., Chgo., 1982-90; NIH rsch. fellow depts. pathology and periodontics Ctr. for Rsch. in

Oral Biology, U. Wash.-Seattle, 1978-80; prof. dept. periodontics and microbiology U. Md. Coll. Dental Surgery, Balt., 1980-90; mem. attending faculty divsn. dentistry and oral and maxillofacial surgery The Johns Hopkins Med. Inst., Balt., 1985—; practice dentistry specializing in periodontics Balt., Pitts.; dean Sch. Dental Medicine, U. Pitts., 1989—; cons. Dentsply Internat., York, Pa., U.S. Army, Walter Reed Med. Ctr., Washington, U.S. Army, Ft. Gordon, Ga., USN, Nat. Naval Med. Command, Bethesda, The NutraSweet Co., Deerfield, Ill.; cons. Food and Drug Adminstrn., Rockville, Md.; mem. Oral Biology/medicine study sect. NIH, Bethesda, 1985-90; mem. nat. adv. dental rsch. coun. NIH/NIDR, Bethesda, 1994—; vis. scientist to Moscow State U., USSR, 1972, NASA, Houston, 1976-92; lectr. Internat. Congress Allergology, Tokyo, 1973; lab. dir. Hawaii Dept. Health. Author: Clinical Laboratory Methods for the Medical Assistant, 1974; mem. editorial bd. Am. Health Mag.; contbr. articles on research in microbiology, immunology and dentistry to sci. jours. Instr. water safety ARC, Honolulu, 1973-90. Recipient Pres.'s medallion Loyola U., Chgo., 1977; named Alumnus of Yr., Ill. Wesleyan U., 1977. Fellow Acad. Dentistry Internat., Am Coll. Dentists, Internat. Coll. Dentists, Am. Coll. Stomatognathic Surgeons; mem. AAAS, ADA (vice chair coun. sci. affairs), AAUP, Am. Acad. Periodontology (diplomate), Am. Inst. Biol. Scis., Internat. Soc. Biophysics, Internat. Soc. Endocrinologists, Ill. Acad. Sci. , Am. Internat. Assn. Dental Rsch. (pres. Md. chpt.), Am. Acad. Microbiology (diplomate), Am. Acad. Microbiology (diplomate, examiner), N.Y. Acad. Scis., Sigma XI, Omicron Kappa Upsilon (past nat. pres., exec. sec.), Beta, Beta, Beta Hon. Soc. Home: 3501 Terrace St Pittsburgh PA 15213-2523 Office: U Pitts Sch Dental Medicine Dean's Office Pittsburgh PA 15261

SUZUKI, KUNIHIKO, biomedical educator, researcher; b. Tokyo, Japan, Feb. 5, 1932; came to U.S., 1960; s. Nobuo and Teiko (Suzuki) S.; m. Kinuko Ikeda, Dec. 20, 1960; 1 child, Jun. BA in History and Philosophy of Sci., Tokyo U., 1955, MD, 1959; MA (hon.), U. Pa., 1971. Diplomate Nat. Bd. Med. Licensure Japan. Rotating intern USAF Hosp. Tachikawa, Tokyo, Japan, 1959-60; asst. resident in neurology Bronx (N.Y.) Mcpl. Hosp. Ctr.-Albert Einstein Coll. Medicine, 1960-61, resident in neurology, 1961-62, clin. fellow in neurology, 1962-64; instr. in neurology Albert Einstein Coll. Medicine, Bronx, 1964, asst. prof., 1965-68; assoc. prof. U. Pa. Sch. Medicine, Phila., 1969-71, prof. neurology and pediatrics, 1971-72; prof. neurology Albert Einstein Coll. Medicine, 1972-86, prof. neurosci., 1974-86; prof. neurology and psychiatry, faculty curriculum in neurobiology U. N.C. Sch. Medicine, Chapel Hill, 1986—; dir. Brain and Devel. Rsch. Ctr. UNC Neurosci. Ctr., Chapel Hill, 1986—; staff dept. neuropsychiatry Tokyo U. Faculty Medicine, 1960, U. Pa. Inst. Neurol. Scis., 1969-72; attending physician Bronx Mcpl. Hosp. Ctr., 1976-86, Hosp. Albert Einstein Coll. Medicine, 1977-86; vis. prof. fellowship Japan Soc. for Promotion Sci., 1980, Yamada Sci. Found., 1981; mem. neurology B study sect. NIH, 1971-75, guest scientist, 1984-85, program com. mental retardation and devel. disabilities, 1989-92; mem. basic neurosci. task force Nat. Inst. Neurol. and Communicative Disorders and Stroke, 1978, adv. panel directions and opportunities for future research, 1983, bd. sci. counselors, NIH, 1980-84; mem. adv. com. on fellowships Nat. Multiple Sclerosis Soc., 1974-77; jury St. Vincent Internat. award for Med. Sci., 1979; mem. adv. com. Eunice Kennedy Shriver Ctr., Waltham, Mass., 1974-84; med. adv. bd. Children's Assn. for Research on Mucolipidosis Type IV, 1983—; mem. U.S. Nat. Com. for Internat. Brain Research Orgn., 1985-89. Editor: Ganglioside Structure and Function, 1984; chief editor Jour. Neurochemistry, 1977-82, dep. chief editor, 1975-77; mem. editorial bd. Jour. Neuropathology and Exptl. Neurology, 1981-83, Neurosci., 1975—, Molecular Chem. Neuropathology, 1983—, Neurochem. Research, 1985—, Metabolic Brain Disease, 1985-87, Molecular Brain Research, 1985—, Jour. Molecular Neurosci., 1987—, Developmental Neurosci., 1987—, Jour. Neurosci. Rsch., 1993—; contbr. articles to profl. jours. Mem. Nat. Adv. Commn. on Multiple Sclerosis, 1973-74; mem. med. adv. bd. United Leukodystrophy Found., 1982-86, Nat. Tay-Sachs and Allied Diseases Assn., 1971—, Canavan Found., 1992—. Recipient A. Weil award Am. Assn. Neuropathologists, 1970, Saul R. Korey Lectureship, 1993, M. Moore award, 1975; Jacob K. Javits Neurosci. Investigator award NIH, 1985, 92, Humboldt Sr. Rsch. award Humboldt Found., 1990, Eminent Scientist award Inst. Phys. Chem. Rsch., Japan, 1995. Mem. NAS, AAAS, Am. Soc. for Neurochemistry (prs. 1985-87, coun. 1973-77, 87-91, Basic Neurochemistry Lectureship 1995), Internat. Soc. for Neurochemistry (coun. 1987-89, treas. 1989-93, pres. 1993-95), Soc. for Neurosci., Am. Soc. Biochemistry and Molecular Biology, Am. Acad. Neurology, Japanese Med. Soc. Am. (Disting. Scientist award 1985), Japanese Neurochem. Soc., Internat. Brain Rsch. Orgn., Am. Soc. Human Genetics, Japan Soc. Inherited Metabolic Disease (hon.). Avocations: piano, photography, bird watching, skiing. Office: U NC Chapel Hill Neurosci Ctr Campus Box 7250 Chapel Hill NC 27599-7250

SUZUKI, MICHIO, mathematics educator; b. Chiba, Japan, Oct. 2, 1926; came to U.S., 1952; s. Kyosuke and Taka (Saito); m. Naoko Akizuki, Nov. 11, 1952; 1 child, Kazuko. B.S., U. Tokyo, 1945-48, Ph.D., 1952; hon. degree, U. Kiel, Fed. Republic Germany, 1991. Asst. prof. math. U. Ill.-Urbana, 1955-57, assoc. prof., 1958, prof., 1959—, prof. Center Advanced Study, 1968—; research assoc. Harvard U., 1956; vis. prof. U. Chgo., 1960; mem. Inst. Advanced Study, Princeton, N.J., 1962, 68, 81. Recipient Acad. prize Japan Acad., 1974; Guggenheim fellow, 1962. Mem. Am. Math. Soc. (council 1962-71), Math. Soc. Japan. Home: 2406 Melrose Dr Champaign IL 61820-7607 Office: Dept Math U Ill 1409 W Green St Urbana IL 61801-2917

SUZUKI, NOBUTAKA, chemistry educator; b. Nishio, Aichi, Japan, Nov. 8, 1942; s. Kihachiro and Masayo (Miwa) S.; m. Fumiko Sato, Mar. 21, 1971; children: Mina, Kumi. B of Chemistry, Nagoya U., Japan, 1966, D of Chemistry, 1972. Asst. prof. dept. chemistry Mie U., Tsu, Japan, 1971-88, assoc. prof., 1988; sr. rschr. Biophoton project JRDC, Sendai, Japan, 1988-90; assoc. prof. Shimonoseki (Japan) Nat. U. Fisheries, 1990-92, prof., 1993—. Author: Natural Products Chemistry, 1975, 2d rev. edit., 1983, Bioluminescence of Chemiluminescence, Current Status, 1991, Oxygen Radicals, 1992, Chemistry of Functional Dyes, vol. 2, 1993, Bioluminescence and Chemiluminescence, status report, 1993, Bioluminescence and Chemiluminescence: Fundamentals and Applied Aspects, 1994, Maillard Reactions in Chem., Food, and Health, 1994; editor: (book) The Roles of Oxygen in Chemistry and Biochemistry, 1988, (book/tape) Scientific English in Fisheries, 1992, English for Science and Technological Experiments, 1994, English for Pharmacy and Medical Science, 1995, English for International Conference, 1995. Recipient Internat. Tech. Exch. Soc. award, 1995; grantee Naito Meml. Found., 1977, Tokai Sci. Rsch. Found., 1986, Agrl. Biol. Chemistry Japan, 1990, Kiei-Kai Sci. Rsch. Found., 1991-96, Skylark Rsch. Found., 1992, The Sci. and Tech. Agy., Japan, 1994-96, Internat. Tech. Exch. K-Found., 1996-97. Mem. Am. Chem. Soc., Am. Soc. for Photobiology, Agrl. Biol. Soc. Japan, Chem. Soc. Japan, Japan Soc. Sci. Fisheries, Internat. Tech. Exch. Soc. (bd. dirs. 1995—). Office: Nat U Fisheries, Yoshimi, Shimonoseki Yamaguchi 75965, Japan

SUZUKI, TAKUYA, telecommunications executive; b. Hakodate, Hokkaido, Japan, Dec. 11, 1935; parents Yoshio and Kunie (Sato) S.; m. Ryoko Suzuki, Dec. 15, 1968; children: Naomi, Scott. BS, U. Calif., L.A. Loan officer Bank of Tokyo, 1960-68; v.p. Asahi Overseas Corp., Torrance, Calif., 1968-84; exec. v.p., chief fin. officer PhoneMate, Inc., Torrance, 1984—. Notary pub. Mem. UCLA Alumnus Club, Lion's Club. Avocation: golf. Home: 2520 S Angelcrest Dr Hacienda Heights CA 91745 Office: Phonemate Inc 20665 Manhattan Pl Torrance CA 90501-1827*

SUZUKI, TSUNEO, molecular immunologist; b. Nagoya, Aichi, Japan, Nov. 23, 1931; s. Morichika and Toshiko (Kita) S.; widowed; children: Riichiro, Aijiro, Yozo. BS, U. Tokyo, 1953, MD, 1957; PhD, U. Hokkaido, 1967. Asst. prof. U. Kans. Med. Ctr., Kansas City, 1970-79, assoc. prof., 1979-83, prof., 1983—, interim chair, 1994—; mem. NIH Study Sect., Washington, 1983-87. Contbr. articles to profl. jours. Postdoctoral fellows U. Wis., 1963-66, 69-70, U. Lausanne, Switzerland, 1966-67, U Toronto, 1969; recipient Fulbright Travel award, 1962, Sr. Investigator award, U. Kans. Med. Ctr., 1990. Mem. Am. Assn. Immunologists, Am. Soc. Biological Chemists (Travel award 1988). Home: 3620 W 73rd St Prairie Vlg KS 66208-2903 Office: U Kans Med Ctr Dept Microbiology 3901 Rainbow Blvd Kansas City KS 66160-0001

SVAASAND, LARS OTHAR, electronics researcher; b. Oslo, Feb. 3, 1938; married; 4 children. MSc, Norwegian Inst. Tech., Trondheim, 1961, PhD, 1976. Rsch. scientist div. radar and electronics Norwegian Def. Rsch. Establishment, Kjeller, 1961-65; rsch. scientist div. theoretical electronics U. Trondheim, 1966-69, asst. prof., 1971-74, assoc. prof. phys. electronics, 1974-81, head dept. elec. engring. and computer sci., 1984-87; rsch. scientist Electronics Rsch. Labs., ELAB, Trondheim, 1969-71, head electro optics rsch. group, 1972-76; sci. advisor Continental Shelf and Petroleum Tech. Rsch. Inst., Iku, Norway, 1984—; prof. phys. electronics Norwegian Inst. Tech., U. Trondheim, 1982—; vis. and cons. prof. U. So. Calif. Sch. Medicine, L.A., 1989—, U. Calif., Irvine, 1990—; bd. dirs. Norwegian Inst. Tech., 1990-96, SINTEF Rsch. Group, Norway. Author books; co-editor: Lasers in Med. Sci., 1985-93. Fellow Am. Soc. Laser Medicine and Surgery; mem. Am. Phys. Soc., Am. Soc. Photobiology, Internat. Soc. Optical Engring., Inst. Elec. Engrs., Norwegian Acad. Tech. Scis., N.Y. Acad. Scis., Royal Norwegian Soc. Scis. Office: U Trondheim Inst Tech, O S Bragstads plass 4, Trondheim N-7034, Norway

SVADLENAK, JEAN HAYDEN, museum administrator, consultant; b. Wilmington, Del., Mar. 4, 1955; d. Marion M. and Ida Jean (Calcagni) Hayden; m. Steven R. Svadlenak, May 26, 1979. BS in Textiles and Clothing, U. Del., 1977; MA in History Mus. Studies, SUNY, Oneonta, 1982; postgrad., U. Calif., Berkeley, 1982. Curatorial asst. The Hagley Mus., Wilmington, 1976-77; curator of costumes and textiles The Kansas City (Mo.) Mus., 1978-82, chief curator, 1982-84, assoc. exec. dir. for collection and exhibits mgmt., 1984-86, interim pres., 1986-87, pres., 1987-89; researcher, guest curator N.Y. State Hist. Assn., Cooperstown, 1980; grant reviewer Inst. for Mus. Svcs., 1985-89; ad hoc faculty U. Kans., 1991—, U. Mo., Kansas City, 1992—. Mem. Am. Assn. Mus. (surveyor mus. assessment program 1985-89, mem. accreditation vis. com. 1990—), Am. Assn. State and Local History, Costume Soc. Am., Heritage League Kansas City (bd. dirs. 1987-89), Midwest Mus. Conf. (coun. 1992-94), Mo. Mus. Assocs. (pres. 1992-94, com. on mus. profl. tng. 1993—, 2d v.p. 1994-96). Avocations: music, sports, photography, cooking. Home: 624 Romany Rd Kansas City MO 64113-2037

SVAGER, THYRSA ANNE FRAZIER, university administrator, retired educator; b. Wilberforce, Ohio, July 16; d. G. Thurston and E. Anne Frazier; m. Aleksandar Svager. AB, Antioch Coll., Yellow Springs, Ohio, 1951; MA, Ohio State U., 1952, PhD, 1965. Statist. analyst Wright Patterson AFB (Ohio), 1952-53; instr. Tex. So. U., Houston, 1953-54; from asst. to assoc. prof. Ctrl. State U., Wilberforce, 1954-66, prof., chmn., 1966-85, v.p. acad. affairs, 1985-89, exec. v.p., provost, 1989—; adj. faculty Antioch Coll., 1964; vis. prof. Nat. Sci. Found. Inst., 1966-67; vis. faculty MIT, 1969; cons. in field. Author: Essential Mathematics, 1976, rev. edit., 1983, Compact Facts-Calculus, 1980, (workbook) Modern Elementary Algebra, 1969. NSF grantee, 1969-71, 76-79; recipient Svc. award Jack and Jill Am., 1985, Edn. award Green County Women's Hall of Fame, 1986, Edn. award Top Ladies of Distinction Wilberforce chpt., 1985, Svc. award Challenge 95 Human Needs Task Force, 1992. Mem. NAACP, Nat. Urban League, Math. Assn. Am., Nat. Assn. Math., Nat. Coun. Tchrs. of Math., Assn. Computing Machinery, Assn. Study Afro-Am. Life and History, Phi Mu Epsilon, Beta Kappa Chi, Alpha Kappa Mu, Alpha Kappa Alpha (life). Avocations: travel, tournament bridge, antique glass. Office: Ctrl State U PO Box 174 Wilberforce OH 45384-0174

SVAHN, JOHN ALFRED, government official; b. New London, Conn., May 13, 1943; s. Albert Russell and Esther Marilu (Caffero) S.; m. Jill Weber, July 12, 1977; children: Kirsten Marie, John Alfred III. B.A. in Polit. Sci, U. Wash., 1966; postgrad., U. Pacific, 1970-73, Georgetown U., 1973-74. Spl. asst. to dir. Calif. Dept. Public Works, 1968-70; chief dep. dir. Calif. Dept. Social Welfare, 1971-73, dir., 1973; acting commr. Community Services Adminstrn., HEW, Washington, 1973-74; commr. Assistance Payments Adminstrn., 1973-76; dep. adminstr. Social and Rehab. Service, 1974-75; adminstr. Social and Rehab. Svcs., 1975-76; mgr. Haskins and Sells, 1976-79; pres. John A. Svahn, Inc., Annapolis, Md., 1979-81; U.S. commr. social security Balt., 1981-83; undersec. HHS, Washington, 1983-84; assst. to Pres. for policy devel. Washington, 1984-86; chmn. Maximus Inc., Washington, 1988-94; U.S. commr. Commn. for Study of Alternatives for Panama Canal, 1987-92; exec. v.p. The Wexler Group, Washington, 1995—. Mem. Nat. Devel. Disability Adv. Council, 1975-76, Pres.'s Transition Team, 1980-81, Calif. Health Care Commn., 1972, pub. affairs com. United Way Am., 1987—; chmn. Govs. Commn. on Corrections Health Care, Md., 1990—; assoc. mem. Calif. Republican State Cen. Com., 1970-72; bd. dirs. Nat. Aquarium, Balt.; bd. dirs. Health Care Svcs. NAS Inst. Medicine, 1987-92; mem. Gov.'s Privatization Coun., 1992—. Served to lt. USAF, 1966-68. Named Outstanding Young Man in HEW, 1974; recipient Sec.'s citation, 1975, Adminstr.'s spl. citation, 1975. Mem. Phi Delta Phi, Zeta Psi. Republican. Clubs: Annapolis Yacht, Sailing of the Chesapeake. Office: 1356 Beverly Rd Mc Lean VA 22101-3625

SVALDI, KATHLEEN ALICE, elementary education educator; b. Chgo., Sept. 14, 1946; d. Albert Fred and Phyllis (Tworkowski) Sodin; m. Livio Svaldi, June 27, 1981; children: Jeffrey, Melissa, Edward. BS in Edn., Loyola U., 1968; postgrad., Nat. Louis U. Cert. Chgo. Bd. of Edn., cert. tchr., Ill., cert. archdiocese of Chgo. Cath. edn. Intermediate tchr. St. Wenceslaus Sch., Chgo., 1968-72, St. Viator Sch., Chgo., 1973-74; primary tchr. St. Wenceslaus Sch., Chgo., 1974-80; intermediate tchr. St. Joan of Arc Sch., Skokie, Ill., 1980-82; primary tchr. St. Peter Sch., Skokie, 1987—; primary unit leader St. Wenceslaus Sch., Chgo., 1975-79. Mem. ASCD.

SVANBORG, ALVAR, retired geriatrics educator; b. Umea, Sweden, Nov. 15, 1921; s. Arvid and Althea (Lindstrom) S.; m. Marianne Lindh, Dec. 11, 1948; children: Catharina, Elisabeth, Anna, Arvid. MD, Karolinska Inst., Stockholm, 1948, Phd, 1951. With U. Goteborg, Gothenburg, Sweden, 1954—, prof. geriatric and long term med. care, 1976-88, prof. emeritus geriatric and long term med. care, 1988—; sci. advisor Swedish Nat. Bd. Health & Welfare, Stockholm, 1968-88; advisor, cons. WHO, Geneva, 1970—; chmn. Fedn. Gerontology Nordic Countries, 1977-88; advisor US Govtl. Orgn., NIH, U.S. Senate and The White House. Mem. editorial bd. Jour. Clin. Exptl. Gerontology, 1977, Archives of Gerontology & Geriatrics, 1977, Comprehensive Gerontology, 1986-89. Expert Supreme Nat. Swedish Ins. Ct., Stockholm, 1969-88; Swedish del. UN, 1982; mem. expert adv. panel to dir. gen. WHO, 1984. Recipient Thureus prize U. Uppsala, Sweden, 1980, Gothenburg City Gold medal, 1983, Brookdale Fgn. award Brookdale Found., 1985, Sandoz prize Internat. Assn. Gerontology, 1987. Mem. Royal Soc. Art and Scis. of Sweden, Ill. Geriatric Soc., Am. Geriatric Soc., Gerontol. Soc. Am., Royal Bachelors Club, Alpha Omega Alpha. Home: 13 Herrgaardsgatan, S-412 74 Goeteborg Sweden Office: U Ill 840 S Wood St Chicago IL 60612-7317

SVEC, HARRY JOHN, chemist, educator; b. Cleve., June 24, 1918; s. Ralph Joseph and Lilian Josephine (Pekarek) S.; m. Edna Mary Bruno, Oct. 27, 1943; children—Mary, Peter, Katherine, Jan, Thomas, Jean, Benjamin, Daniel, Lillian. BS, John Carroll U., 1941; PhD in Phys. Chemistry, Iowa State U., 1949. Asst. chemist Iowa State U., 1941-43; research asso. Inst. Atomic Research, 1946-50, asst. prof. chemistry, 1950-55, assoc. prof., 1955-60, prof., 1960-83, emeritus prof., 1983—, Disting. prof. in scis. and humanities, 1978—; assoc. chemist Ames Lab., 1950-55; chemist Ames Lab., Dept. Energy, 1955-60, sr. chemist, 1960-85, program dir., 1974-85, assoc. scientist, 1983—; jr. chemist Manhattan Project, 1943-46; cons., lectr. in field. Author lab. manual in phys. chemistry; contbr. numerous articles to profl. publs.; founding editor: Internat. Jour. Mass Spectrometry and Ion Processes, 1968-86. NSF grantee, 1972-82; EPA grantee, 1974-81; AEC grantee, 1950-74; ERDA grantee, 1974-77; Dept. Energy grantee, 1977-87; Am. Water Works Assn. grantee, 1977-79. Fellow AAAS, The Chem. Soc., Am. Chem. Soc.; mem. ASTM, Geochem. Soc., Am. Soc. Mass Spectroscopy (charter, v.p. 1972-74, pres. 1974-76), Sigma Xi, Alpha Sigma Nu, Phi Lambda Upsilon, Alpha Chi Sigma (cons. 1985—). Roman Catholic. Home: 2427 Hamilton Dr Ames IA 50014-8203 Office: Iowa State U 1605 Gilman Hall Ames IA 50014-8203 *Success in anything we choose to do requires a commitment. The degree of one's success depends directly on the kind of commitment that is made.*

SVEDA, MICHAEL, management and research consultant; b. West Ashford, Conn., Feb. 3, 1912; s. Michael and Dorothy (Druppa) S.; m. Martha Augusta Gaeth, Aug. 23, 1936; children—Sally Anne, Michael Max. B.S., U. Toledo, 1934; Ph.D. (Eli Lilly research fellow), U. Ill., 1939. Tchr. chemistry U. Toledo, 1932-35, U. Ill., 1935-37; research, sales and product mgmt. positions E.I. du Pont de Nemours & Co., Inc., 1939-54; mgmt. counsel Wilmington, Del., 1955-59; dir. acad. sci. projects NSF, 1960-61; corp. assoc. dir. research FMC Corp., 1962-64; mgmt. and research counsel to academia, industry and govt., 1965—; lectr. univs., 1961—, fed. govt., groups, 1965—; mem. adv. com. on creativity in scientists and engrs. Rensselaer Poly. Inst., 1965—. Numerous appearances on pub. and comml. TV and radio. Named Outstanding Alumnus U. Toledo, 1954. Fellow AAAS (life); mem. Am. Chem. Soc., Sigma Xi, Phi Kappa Phi, Alpha Chi Sigma, Phi Lambda Upsilon. Patentee chems. and processes in polymers, pesticides, chem. intermediates; synthesizer, discoverer cyclamates, sweetening agts., 1937; deviser new concepts and patentee 3 dimensional models complex orgns., selection key personnel; new approach to diets, taking off human fat; new use Boolean algebra, theory of sets in people problems; active drive to have cyclamate sweeteners reinstated, 1973—. Home: Revonah Woods 228 West Ln Stamford CT 06905-3959 Office: PO Box 3086 Stamford CT 06905-0086 *Basic capacity for intelligence is given to us through inheritance. Knowledge—and stupidity—we acquire or develop. My objective has been to minimize my acquisition of, or contribution to, stupidity, while developing as much new knowledge as possible for mankind.*

SVEINSON, PAMELA J., human resources executive. BA in Sociology, Whitman Coll., 1974; M in Indsl. Rels., U. Minn., 1980. Social worker Mont. State Dept. Social & Rehab. Svcs., 1975-77; behavior therapist Spl. Tng. Exceptional People, Billings, Mont., 1977; asst. mgr. manpower planning Burlington Northern, St. Paul, 1978-80; sr. human resources planner Morrison-Knudsen Co., Inc., Boise, Idaho, 1980-83; asst. v.p. human resources 1st Bank System, 1983-84, v.p., 1984-88, sr. v.p., 1988-90; v.p. human resources Star Tribune and Cowles Media Co., Mpls., 1990—; pres. Human Resources Exec. Coun., 1995-96. Mentor Minn. 100; mem. Mpls. Inst. Arts. Mem. Nat. Human Resources Planning Soc., Minn. Human Resources Planning Soc. (bd. dirs.), Horseman's Benevolent & Protective Assn., Park Ave. Meth. Ch. Avocations: thoroughbred horse racing, swimming, skiing, private pilot, racquetball. Home: 101 Meadow Ln Golden Valley MN 55416 Office: Cowles Media Co 329 Portland Ave Minneapolis MN 55415-1112

SVEINSSON, JOHANNES, former city and county government official, building material sales engineer; b. Winnipeg, Man., Can., Nov. 30, 1912; m. M. Eleanor Lundstedt, 1938; children: Joleen Sveinsson Kinney, Kenneth J., Johannes. Student, Fresno State Coll., 1935, U. Calif.-Berkeley, 1940. With Pacific Rock & Gravel & Paving Co., Los Angeles, 1935-41; counselor Calif. Dept. Corrections, 1941-76. Bd. dirs. Anti Poverty, Monterey County, 1965-75, Monterey County Med. Assn., 1977, Sr. Citizens, Monterey County, 1982-88; v.p. Monterey Bay Govts., Monterey, Santa Cruz and San Benito Counties, 1960-83; mem. Gonzales City Council Calif., 1960-83; pres. Calif. League of Cities, Monterey Bay Div., 1976-77; mayor Gonzales, 1981-83; mem. Monterey County Grand Jury, Salinas, Calif., 1983—; mem. Monterey County Grand Jury, 1991. Served with USAAF, 1942-45. Mem. Calif. League Cities (bd. dirs. pub. safety com. 1962-74), Icelandic Assn. No. Calif. (pres. 1966), Am. Scandanavians of Calif. (pres. 1975). Democrat. Home: PO Box 9756 Yakima WA 98909-0756

SVENDSBYE, LLOYD AUGUST, college president, clergyman, educator; b. Hamlet, N.D., May 26, 1930; s. Anders A. and Gudrun J. (Birkelo) S.; m. Annelotte Frieda Erika Moertelmeyer, Dec. 20, 1958. BA, Concordia Coll., Moorhead, Minn., 1951, DD (hon.), 1983; BTh, Luther Theol.Sem., 1954; postgrad, U. Erlangen, Germany, 1954-55, Columbia U., 1959-60; ThD, Union Theol. Sem., 1966; LLD (hon.), Gettysburg Coll., 1977; LHD (hon.), Kilian C.C., 1992. Ordained to ministry, 1955; asst. pastor Our Saviours Luth. Ch., Mpls., 1955-56; adminstrv. asst. to dir. 3d Assembly Luth. World Fedn., 1956-57; asst. prof. religion Concordia Coll., 1957-59; asst. pastor Trinity Lutheran Ch., Bklyn., 1959-61; chmn. dept. religion Concordia Coll., 1962-66; editor in chief Augsburg Publ. House, Mpls., 1966-71; v.p., dean St. Olaf Coll., 1971-74; pres., prof. ch. history Luther Theol. Sem., St. Paul, 1974-82; pres. Northwestern Luth. Theol. Sem., 1976-82; pres. Luther Northwestern Theol. Sem., 1982-87, prof. ch. history, 1982-87; pres. Augustana Coll., Sioux Falls, S.D., 1987-92; v.p. Am. Luth. Ch., 1981-87; Mem. Am. Luth. Ch.-Luth. Ch. Am. coop. com., 1974-78; Luth. World Fedn. Com. on Info. Services, 1971-76; mem. Com. on Luth. Unity, 1978-82, Commn. To Form a New Luth. Ch., 1982-86. Chmn. senate dist. 49A, Dem. Farm Labor Com., 1970-71; bd. dirs. Luth. Brotherhood, 1970-95, Luth. Gen. and Health Care Sys., Park Ridge, Ill., 1981-87; trustee Luth. Deaconess Hosp., Mpls., 1970-71, Fairview-Southdale Hosp., 1975-87, Fairview Cmty. Hosps., 1979-87. Recipient Alumni Achievement award Concordia Coll., 1974. Home: 2500 Quentin Ct Saint Louis Park MN 55416-1900

SVENGALIS, KENDALL FRAYNE, law librarian; b. Gary, Ind., May 16, 1947; s. Frank Anthony and Alvida Linnea (Matheus) S.; m. Deborah Kay Andrews, May 23, 1970; children: Hillary Linnea, Andrew Kendall. BA, Purdue U., 1970, MA, 1973; MLS, U. R.I., 1975. Reference librarian Roger Williams Coll., Bristol, R.I., 1975, Providence (R.I.) Coll., 1975-77; asst. law librarian R.I. State Law Library, Providence, 1976-82, state law librarian, 1982—; adj. prof. libr. and info. studies U. R.I., 1987—. Author: The Legal Information Buyer's Guide and Reference Manual, 1996; editor: The Criv Sheet, 1988-94; contbr. articles to profl. jours. Chmn. jud. branch United Way Com. R.I., 1980. Mem. Am. Assn Law Librs. (state, ct. and county libr. spl. interest sect., recipient Connie E. Bolden significant publ. award 1993, bd. dirs. 1986-88), Law Librs. New Eng. (treas. 1983-85, v.p. 1985-86, pres. 1986-87), Com. on Rels. with Info. Vendors (editor 1988-94), New Eng. Law Libr. Consortium (v.p. 1990-92, pres. 1992-94). Republican. Lutheran. Home: 17 Mosher Dr Barrington RI 02806-1909 Office: RI State Law Libr Frank Licht Jud Complex 250 Benefit St Providence RI 02903-2719

SVENSON, CHARLES OSCAR, investment banker; b. Worcester, Mass., June 28, 1939; s. Sven Oscar and Edahjane (Castner) S.; m. Sara Ellen Simpson, Nov. 15, 1968; children: Alicia Lindall, Tait Oscar. A.B., Hamilton Coll., 1961; LL.B., Harvard U., 1964; LL.M., Bklyn. Law Sch., 1965. Bar: N.Y. 1965, U.S. Dist. Ct. (so. dist.) N.Y. 1965, U.S. Ct. Appeals (2d. cir.) 1965. Atty. Dewey, Ballantine, Bushby, Palmer & Wood, N.Y.C., 1964-68; v.p. Goldman Sachs & Co., N.Y.C., 1968-75; sr. v.p. Donaldson, Lufkin & Jenrette, N.Y.C, 1975-89; mng. dir., 1989—. Trustee Kirkland Coll., Clinton, N.Y., 1976-78; trustee Hamilton Coll., Clinton, 1979-83, 90—. Mem. ABA, N.Y. State Bar Assn., Assn. of Bar of City of N.Y. Clubs: Tuxedo (Tuxedo Park, N.Y.); Harvard (N.Y.C.). Home: 1185 Park Ave New York NY 10128-1308 Office: Donaldson Lufkin & Jenrette Securities Corp 277 Park Ave New York NY 10172

SVENSSON, LARS GEORG, cardiovascular and thoracic surgeon; b. Barbeton, Republic South Africa, Aug. 11, 1955; came to U.S., 1986; s. Karl-Georg and Marianne (Wiss) S.; m. Marion Francis Robinson, June 14, 1986. MB, BCh, U. Witwatersrand, Johannesburg, South Africa, 1978, MSc (Med.), 1983, PhD, 1986. Diplomate Gen., Vascular and Cardiothoracic Surgery. Resident in surgery Johannesburg Hosp., 1981-86; fellow cardiovascular surgery Cleve. Clinic Found., 1986-87; fellow cardiovascular surgery Baylor Coll. of Medicine, Houston, 1987-89, resident cardiothoracic surgery, 1989-91; attending surgeon Meth. Hosp., VA Med. Ctr., Houston, 1991-92; attending surgeon Lahey Clinic, Burlington, Mass., 1993—, dir. Aortic Surgery Ctr. and Marfan Syndrome Clinic, 1993—; spkr. in field. Contbr. numerous articles to profl. jours. including Jour. Vascular Surgery, Chest, Ann. Thoracic Surgery, Jour. Thoracic, Cardiovascular Surgery and Anesthesia. Recipient Good Fellowship award Treverton Coll., 1970, Cert. of Merit South African Sugar Assn., 1972, Robert Niven award 1974-76, DeBakey Heart Fund Rsch. award 1988, 89, 90, 91, V.A. Rag Rsch. Fund award 1992; Dana Fund Rsch. fellowship, 1994, David Lurie Rsch. fellowship 1985; Davis and Geck Surg. Rsch. scholarship, 1985. Fellow Am. Coll. Surgeons, Royal Coll. Surgeons, Coll. Surgeons and Physicians of South Africa, Royal Coll. Surgeons in Can. in Vascular and Cardiothoracic Surgery, Am. Coll. Cardiology; mem. AMA, Soc. Thoracic Surgeons. Achievements include animal research to find methods of intraoperatively locating the spinal cord blood supply and methods to prevent paraplegia after aortic surgery; investigation of methods to protect the brain, spinal cord and kidneys; study of hydrogren injection to localize spinal cord supply in humans, study of intrathecal papaveine in patients undergoing aortic surgery, minimizing use of homologous blood for major aortic surgery, particularly of the ascending and aortic arch; novel operations for ascending and aortic arch surgery; first reported replacement of the entire aorta from the heart to the aortic bifurcation during a single operation; (with E. Stanley Crawford) wrote the first definitive textbook on the aorta entitled Cardiovascular and Vascular Disease of the Aorta.

SVETLOVA, MARINA, ballerina, choreographer, educator; b. Paris, May 3, 1922; came to U.S. from Australia, 1940; d. Max and Tamara (Andreieff) Hartman. Studies with Vera Trefilova, Paris, 1930-36, studies with L. Egorova and M. Kschessinska, 1936-39; studies with A. Vilzak, N.Y.C., 1940-57; D honoris causa, Fedn. Francaise de Danse, 1988. Ballet dir. So. Vt. Art Ctr., 1959-64; dir. Svetlova Dance Ctr., Dorset, Vt., 1965—; prof. ballet dept. Ind. U., Bloomington, 1969-92, prof. emeritus, 1992—, chmn. dept., 1969-78; choreographer Dallas Civic Opera, 1964-67, Ft. Worth Opera, 1967-83, San Antonio Opera, 1983, Seattle Opera, Houston Opera, Kansas City Performing Arts Found. Ballerina original Ballet Russe de Monte Carlo, 1939-41; guest ballerina Ballet Theatre, 1942, London's Festival Ballet, Teatro dell Opera, Rome, Nat. Opera, Stockholm, Sweden, Suomi Opera, Helsinki, Finland, Het Nederland Ballet, Holland, Cork Irish Ballet, Paris Opera Comique, London Palladium, Teatro Colon, Buenos Aires, others; prima ballerina Met. Opera, 1943-50, N.Y.C. Opera, 1950-52; choreographer: (ballet sequences) The Fairy Queen, 1966, L'Histoire du Soldat, 1968; tours in Far East, Middle East, Europe, S.Am., U.S.; performer various classical ballets Graduation Ball; contbr. articles to Debut, Paris Opera. Mem. Am. Guild Mus. Artists (bd. dirs.), Conf. on Ballet in Higher Edn., Nat. Soc. Arts and Letters (nat. dance chmn.). Office: 2100 E Maxwell Ln Bloomington IN 47401-6119 also: 25 W 54th St New York NY 10019-5411

SVIDOR, RHONA BEVERLY, real estate broker, elementary education educator; b. Boston, May 12, 1934; d. Sydney Z. and Bella (Shapiro) Zonis; m. Leonard Svidor, May 23, 1957; 1 child, Mark Allen. AA, UCLA, 1957; BA, Calif. State U., L.A., 1959, MA in Am. Studies, 1972. Lic. real estate broker; cert. elem. and secondary edn. tchr. Tchr. Rivera Sch. System, 1956-57, Hermosa Beach Sch. System, 1958-59, L.A. City Schs., 1959-88; real estate broker Rhona Realty, San Fernando Valley, Calif., 1977—. Leader art history group Valley U. Women, 1989-94, v.p. of programs, 1994—; bd. dirs. Nat. Bd. Brandeis U. Women's Com., 1993-94; leader Greek World Through Art and French, Brandeis U. Women's Com., 1993—; program chmn. Pacific Asia Mus. Himalyan Arts Counsel, 1993; bd. dirs. Natanya chpt. Na'amat USA, events and theatre chairperson. Mem. Toastmasters (v.p. membership 1993-94, pres. 1994-95, chair 1993-94). Avocations: traveling, writing, reading, swimming.

SWACKHAMER, GENE L., bank executive; b. Frankfort, Ind., 1938. BS, Purdue U., 1960; MS, Cornell U., 1963; PhD, Purdue U., 1966. Pres. emeritus Farm Credit Bank Balt., Sparks, Md.; agrl. economist Kansas City Federal Reserve Bank, 1966-69; dep. gov. U.S. Govt. Farm Credit Adminstrn., 1970-76. Lt. USN, 1962. Office: Farm Credit Bank Balt 16429 Yeoho Rd Sparks Glencoe MD 21152

SWADOS, ELIZABETH A., composer, director, writer; b. Buffalo, Feb. 5, 1951; d. Robert O. and Sylvia (Maisel) S. B.A., Bennington Coll., 1972. Composer, mus. dir. Peter Brook's Internat. Theatre Group, Paris,, Africa, U.S., 1972-73; composer-in-residence La Mama Exptl. Theater Club, N.Y.C., 1977—; mem. faculty Carnegie-Mellon U., 1974, Bard Coll., 1976-77, Sarah Lawrence Coll., 1976-77. Author: The Girl With the Incredible Feeling, 1976, Runaways, 1979, Lullaby, 1980, Sky Dance, 1980, Listening Out Loud: Becoming a Composer, 1988, The Four of Us, 1991, The Myth Man, 1994; composer theatrical scores: Medea, 1969 (Obie award 1972), Elektra, 1970, Fragments of Trilogy, 1974, The Trojan Women, 1974, The Good Women of Setzuan, 1975, The Cherry Orchard, 1977, As You Like It, 1979, The Sea Gull, 1980, Alice in Concert, 1980, (with Garry Trudeau) Doonesbury, 1983, Jacques and His Master, 1984, Don Juan of Seville, 1989, The Tower of Evil, 1990, The Mermaid Wakes, 1991; composer, dir., adapter, mem. cast: Nightclub Cantata, 1977 (Obie award 1977); composer, adapter (with Andrei Serban) Agamemnon, 1976, The Incredible Feeling Show, 1979, Lullaby and Goodnight, 1980; composer, dir., adapter: Wonderland in Concert, N.Y. Shakespeare Festival, 1978, Dispatches, 1979, Haggadah, 1980, The Beautiful Lady, 1984-86, Swing, 1987, Esther: A Vaudeville Megillah, 1988, The Red Sneaks, 1989, Jonah, 1990; author, composer, dir.: Runaways, 1978 (Tony award nominee for best musical, best musical score, best musical book 1978); adapter: Works of Yehuda Amichi, Book of Jeremiah; composer music for films: Step by Step, 1978, Sky Dance, 1979, Too Far to Go, 1979, OHMS, 1980, Four Friends, 1982, Seize the Day, 1986, A Year in the Life, 1986, Family Sins, 1987; composer music CBS Camera Three shows, 1973-74, PBS short stories, 1979, CBS-TV and NBC-TV spls.; composer: Rap Master Ronnie, 1986; composer, dir. Swing, Bklyn. Acad. Music, 1987; performer: Mark Taper Forum, Los Angeles, 1985, Jerusalem Oratorio, Rome, 1985. Recipient Outer Critics Circle award, 1977; Creative Artists Service Program grantee, 1976; N.Y. State Arts Council playwriting grantee, 1977—; Guggenheim fellow. Mem. Broadcast Music Inc., Actors Equity. Jewish. Home: 112 Waverly Pl New York NY 10011-9109 Office: care Sam Cohn Internat Creative Mgmt Co 40 W 57th St New York NY 10019-4001

SWAGGART, JIMMY LEE, evangelist, gospel singer; b. Ferriday, La., Mar. 15, 1935; s. W. L. and Minnie Bell S.; married; 1 child. Began preaching on street corners Mangham, La., 1955; traveled throughout U.S. preaching at revival meetings, recording and marketing gospel songs, 1960's, preacher on TV and radio broadcasts; min., pastor Jimmy Swaggart Ministries, Baton Rouge. Gosepl albums include This Is Just What Heaven Means To Me, 1971, There Is A River, 1972; author: (with Robert Paul Lamb) To Cross A River, 1977. Office: 8919 World Ministry Ave Baton Rouge LA 70810-9000

SWAILS, NORMAN E., church officer; b. St. Joseph, Mo.; m. Darleen Craven; children: Tom, Jan Shannon, John. AA, Graceland Coll., 1950; BA, Mo. Valley Coll., 1952. CFP. Exec. Boy Scouts Am., 1954-78, asst. chief scout exec., nat. dir. fin., 1978-85; mem. highest fin. coun. Reorganized Ch. of Jesus Christ of Latter Day Saints, 1985-88; presiding bishop, 1988—; Reorganized Ch. of Jesus Christ of Latter Day Saints. Active Hope House. Mem. Rotary, Independence C. of C. Office: Reorganized Ch of Jesus Christ of Latter Day Saints PO Box 1059 Independence MO 64051

SWAIM, CHARLES HALL, lawyer; b. Delta, Colo., Dec. 31, 1939; s. H. Albert and Janet (Hall) S.; m. Patricia Fahey, Oct. 9,, 1976; children: Caitlin Fahey, Bryan Hall. Grad. Geophys. Engr., Colo. Sch. Mines, 1961; JD, NYU, 1964. Asst. counsel Tex. Instruments Inc., Dallas, 1964-71; assoc. Hale & Dorr, Boston, 1971-74, ptnr., 1974—. Served to capt. U.S. Army, 1965-67, Vietnam. Mem. ABA, Mass. Bar Assn., Boston Bar Assn., Comml. Law League Am. Office: Hale & Dorr 60 State St Boston MA 02109-1803

SWAIM, DAVID DEE, diversified company financial executive; b. Ft. Wayne, Ind., Aug. 12, 1947; s. Carl Edwin and Pauline E. (Johnson) S.; m. Barbara Lynn Strock, June 21, 1969; children: Emily Anne, Benjamin Dee, Thomas Ryan. BS in Acctg., Ind. U., 1969. Sr. auditor Price Waterhouse & Co., Indpls., 1970-76; controller VideoInd., Inc., Indpls., 1976-77; treas., chief fin. officer Bindley Western Industries, Inc., Indpls., 1977-90, v.p., 1979-90, sr. v.p., 1986-90; v.p., treas., bd. dirs. Bennett Mktg. Svcs., Indpls., 1990-91; pres. Ironwood Corp., 1991—; bd. dirs., officer all subs. of Bindley Western Industries, Inc. Mem. Am. Inst. CPAs, Ind. CPA Soc., Fin. Execs. Inst. Republican. Methodist. Lodge: Masons.

SWAIM, JOSEPH CARTER, JR., lawyer; b. S.I., N.Y., Jan. 15, 1934; s. J. Carter and Charlotte (Klein) S.; m. Elizabeth Lenora Owen, Aug. 2, 1958; children: Laura, Charles. BA, Oberlin Coll., 1955; JD, Columbia U., 1958. Bar: U.S. Dist. Ct. (we. dist.) Pa. 1960, Pa. 1961, U.S. Ct. Appeals (3rd cir.) 1964. Assoc. Kirkpatrick & Lockhart, Pitts., 1961-68, ptnr., 1968—. Bd. dirs. Davis and Elins (W.Va.) Coll., 1976-82; bd. pensions Presbyn. Ch. U.S.A., Phila., 1982-89; trustee, bd. sec. The Alban Inst., Inc., Bethesda, Md., 1991-94; trustee, sec.-treas. Henry C. Frick Edn. Com., Pitts., 1978-94; bd. dirs., former pres. Family Resources, Pitts., 1975—; bd. dirs., Sec. Desert Ministries, Inc., Palm Beach, Fla.; chmn. permanent jud. commn. Pitts. Presbytery, 1991—; mem. adv. com. Henry L. Frick Ednl. Fund Buhl Found., Pitts., 1994—. With U.S. Army, 1959-61. Mem. ABA, Pa. Bar Assn., Allegheny County Bar Assn. Republican. Clubs: Duquesne, Allegheny (bd. dirs., sec. 1976—) (Pitts.). Avocations: tennis, reading. Home: 740 Scrubgrass Rd Pittsburgh PA 15243-1124 Office: Kirkpatrick & Lockhart 1500 Oliver Building Bldg Pittsburgh PA 15222-2312

SWAIM, RUTH CAROLYN, secondary education educator; b. Oklahoma City, May 3, 1940; d. G. Dale and Helen H. (Meister) Arbuckle; children: Stanley Kent, Sharon Gay. BS in Edn., U. Okla., 1963. Cert. secondary edn. tchr., Calif., Okla. Math. substitute tchr. USN Mil. Dependent, Sangley Pt., Philippines, 1961-63; math. tchr. Norman (Okla.) Pub. Schs., 1963, Bartlesville (Okla.) Pub. Schs., 1963-65, Dewey (Okla.) Pub. Schs., 1965-67; math. lab. instr. L.A. City Schs., 1975-83, math. tchr., 1984—; chair All Sch. Tutorial Program Taft High Sch. Instr. first Aid ARC, 1961-67; trustee Woodland Hills Community Ch., 1989—. Recipient Cert. Merit ARC, 1965, hon. svc. award PTA, 1980; named Outstanding Math. Tchr. Tandy, 1989-90. Mem. Nat. Coun. Tchrs. Math., NEA, Calif. Tchrs. Assn., Kappa Delta Pi. Home: 4555 San Feliciano Dr Woodland Hills CA 91364-5037 Office: Taft High Sch 5461 Winnetka Ave Woodland Hills CA 91364-2548

SWAIMAN, KENNETH F., medical educator; b. St. Paul, Minn.. BA magna cum laude, U. Minn., 1952, BS, 1953, MD, 1955. Diplomat Am. Bd. Pediatrics, Am. Bd. Psychiatry and Neurology, Am. Bd. Psychiatry and Neurology with Spl. Competence in Child Neurology. Intern Mpls. Gen. Hosp., 1955-56; fellow in pediatrics to chief resident U. Minn. Hosps., 1956-58; chief pediatrics U.S. Army Hosp., Ft. McPherson, Ga., 1958-60; spl. fellow in pediatric neurology U. Minn., 1960-63; pediatric neurology attending staff Hennepin County Med. Ctr., 1963—; dir. pediatric neurology tng. program U. Minn., 1968-94, various to interim head, dept. neurology, 1994—; vis. prof. numerous univs., including Children's Hosp. of Mich., Detroi, 1990, Univ. de Concepion, Chile, 1989, Xian Med. U., China, 1989, Beijing Med. U., China, 1989, Driscoll Children's Hosp., Corpus Christi, Tex., 1986, Hong Kong Child Neurology Soc., 1995, Inst. Nacional de Pediatria, Mexico City, 1986, U. Kyushu, Shiga, Nagoya, Tokyo, 1985, U. Ind. Med. Sch., 1983, Loyola U., 1982, U. N.Mex., 1982, others; lectr. in field; cons. in field; guest worker NIH, NICHD, Bethesda, Md., 1978-79, 79-81. Contbr. articles to profl. jours. and publs. Fellow Am. Acad. Neurology, Am. Acad. Pediatrics; mem. AAAS, Am. Chem. Soc., AMA, Am. Neurol. Assn., Am. Soc. Neurochemistry, Cen. Soc. Clin. Rsch., Cen. Soc. Neurol. Rsch., Child Neurology Soc. (1st pres.), Internat. Child Neurology Assn., Internat. Soc. Neurochemistry, Midwest Soc. Pediatric Rsch., Minn. Med. Found., Profs. of Child Neurology (1st pres.), Phi Beta Kappa, numerous others. Office: Univ Minn Med Sch Box 380 UMHC 420 Delaware St SE Minneapolis MN 55455

SWAIMAN, KENNETH FRED, pediatric neurologist, educator; b. St. Paul, Nov. 19, 1931; s. Lester J. and Shirley (Ryan) S.; m. Phyllis Kammerman Sher, Oct. 1985; children: Lisa, Jerrold, Barbara, Dana. B.A. magna cum laude, U. Minn., 1952, B.S., 1953, M.D., 1955; postgrad., 1956-58; postgrad. (fellow pediatric neurology), Nat. Inst. Neurologic Diseases and Blindness, 1960-63. Diplomate: Am. Bd. Psychiatry and Neurology, Am. Bd. Pediatrics. Intern Mpls. Gen. Hosp., 1955-56; resident pediatrics U. Minn., 1956-58, neurology, 1960-63; postgrad. fellow pediatric neurology Nat. Inst. Neurologic Diseases and Blindness, 1960-63; asst. prof. pediatrics, neurology U. Minn. Med. Sch., Mpls., 1963-66; asso. prof. Nat. Inst. Neurologic Diseases and Blindness, 1966-69; prof., dir. pediatric neurology U. Minn. Med. Sch., 1969—; interim head Dept. Neurology, U. Minn. Med. Sch., 1994-96; interim head dept. neurology U. Minn. Med. Sch., 1994—, mem. internship adv. council exec. faculty, 1966-70; interim head dept. neurology, 1994—; cons. pediatric neurology Hennepin County Gen. Hosp., Mpls., St. Paul-Ramsey Hosp., St. Paul Children's Hosp., Mpls. Children's Hosp.; vis. prof. Beijing U. Med. Sch., 1989. Author: (with Francis S. Wright) Neuromuscular Diseases in Infancy and Childhood, 1969, Pediatric Neuromuscular Diseases, 1979, (with Stephen Ashwal) Pediatric Neurology Case Studies, 1978, 2d edit., 1984, Pediatric Neurology: Practice and Principles, 1989; editor: (with John A. Anderson) Phenylketonuria and Allied Metabolic Diseases, 1966, (with Francis S. Wright) Practice Pediatric Neurology, 1975, 2d edit., 1982; mem. editorial bd.: Annals of Neurology, 1977-83, Neurology Update, 1977-82, Pediatric Update, 1977-85, Brain and Devel. (Jour. Japanese Soc. Child Neurology), 1980—, Neuropediatrics (Stuttgart), 1982-92; editor-in-chief: Pediatric Neurology, 1984—; contbr. articles to sci. jours. Chmn. Minn. Gov.'s Bd. for Handicapped, Exceptional and Gifted Children, 1972-76; mem. human devel. study sect. NIH, 1976-79, guest worker, 1978-81. Served to capt. M.C. U.S. Army, 1958-60. Fellow Am. Acad. Pediatrics, Am. Acad. Neurology (rep. to nat. council Nat. Soc. Med. Research); mem. Soc. Pediatric Research, Central Soc. Clin. Research, Central Soc. Neurol. Research, Internat. Soc. Neurochemistry, Am. Neurol. Assn., Minn. Neurol. Soc., AAAS, Midwest Pediatric Soc., Am. Soc. Neurochemistry, Child Neurology Soc. (1st pres. 1972-73, Hower award 1981, chmn. internat. affairs com., 1991—, mem. long range planning com. 1991—), Internat. Assn. Child Neurologists (exec. com. 1975-79), Profs. of Child Neurology (1st pres. 1978-80, mem. nominating com. 1986—), Japanese Child Neurology Soc. (Segawa award 1986, mem. nominating com. 1986—, chair internat. affairs com. 1991—, mem. long range planning com. 1991—), Soc. de Psiquiatria y Neurologia de la Infancia y Adolescencia, Phi Beta Kappa, Sigma Xi. Home: 420 Delaware St SE Minneapolis MN 55455-0374 Office: U Minn Med Sch Dept Pediatric Neurology Minneapolis MN 55455

SWAIN, DONALD CHRISTIE, retired university president, history educator; b. Des Moines, Oct. 14, 1931; s. G. Christie and Irene L. (Alsop) S.; m. Lavinia Kathryn Lesh, Mar. 5, 1955; children: Alan Christie, Cynthia Catherine. BA, U. Dubuque, 1953; MA in History, U. Calif., Berkeley, 1958, PhD, 1961; D (hon.), U. Louisville, 1995. Asst. rsch. historian U. Calif., Berkeley, 1961-63; mem. faculty U. Calif., Davis, 1963-81, prof. history, 1970-81, acad. asst. to chancellor, 1967-68, asst. vice chancellor acad. affairs, 1971, vice chancellor acad. affairs, 1972-75; acad. v.p. U. Calif. System, Berkeley, 1975-81; pres. U. Louisville, 1981-95, pres. emeritus, 1995—, prof. history, 1981-95; ret., 1995; bd. dirs. LGE Energy, PNC Pank, Ky. Author: Federal Conservation Policy, 1921-33, 1963, Wilderness Defender: Horace M. Albright and Conservation, 1970; co-editor: The Politics of American Science 1939 to the Present, 1965. Mem. bd. govs. J.B. Speed Art Mus.; mem. exec. com. Ky. Hist. Soc. Lt. (j.g.) USNR, 1953-56. Recipient William B. Hellestine award Wis. State Hist. Soc., 1967, Disting. Tchg. award U. Calif., Davis, 1972, Wilson Wyatt award U. Louisville Alumni Assn., 1995; named Louisvillian of Yr., 1995. Democrat. Presbyterian. Home: 2506 Belknap Beach Rd Prospect KY 40059 Office: U Louisville Alumni Ctr Louisville KY 40292

SWAIN, JUDITH LEA, cardiovascular physician, educator; b. Long Beach, Calif., Sept. 24, 1948; m. Edward W. Holmes. BS in Chemistry with deptl. honors, UCLA, 1970; MD, U. Calif., San Diego, 1974. Diplomate Am. Bd. Internal Medicine, cardiovasc. disease; lic. physician Calif., Pa., N.C. Intern in medicine Duke U. Med. Ctr., 1974-75, resident in medicine, 1975-76, fellow in cardiology, 1976-80, assoc. in medicine, 1979-81, from asst. prof. medicine to assoc. prof. medicine, 1981-91, asst. prof. physiology, 1981-88, assoc. prof. microbiology & immunology, 1988-91, Herbert C. Rorer prof. med. scis., prof. genetics, 1991—, mem. molecular biology grad. group, 1991—, chief cardiovasc. divsn., 1991—; vis. asst. prof. dept. genetics Harvard Med. Sch., Boston, 1985-86; mem. search com. for dir. Ctr. for Aging, Duke U. Med. Ctr., 1991—, mem. exec. com. deptl. awards selection, 1992—, chmn. combined degree dir. search com., 1993, mem. clin. rsch. ctr. adv. com., 1993-94, mem. grad. student admissions com., 1993, mem. search com. for chief cardiovasc. surgery, 1992, dept. medicine intern selection com., 1992—; mem. instnl. rev. com. Pa. Muscle Inst., 1993; cardiology adv. com. Nat. Heart, Lung, & Blood Inst., 1989-93; dir. USA-Russia Cardiovasc. Rsch. Program, 1992—; mem. NIH Task Force on Heart Failure, 1992-93; cons. Netherlands Rsch. Initiative in Molecular Cardiology, 1993; external adv. com. Ctr. for Prevention of Cardiovasc. Disease, Harvard Sch. Pub. Health, 1993—; lectr. in field. Exec. editor: Trends in Cardiovascular Medicine, 1990-93; mem. editl. bd. Circulation Rsch., 1991—, Circulation, 1991—, Jour. Clin. Investigation, 1992—; cons. editor: Circulation, 1993—; contbr. articles to med. jours. Mem. exec. com. Coun. on Basic Sci., Am. Heart Assn., 1986-93, chmn. Katz Prize Award Com., 1989-92, rsch. rev. com., 1990-93, fellowship rsch. com., 1992—, program com., 1992—, mem. Levine Young Investigator Awards Com., Coun. on Clin. Cardiology, 1994—, mem. Basic Sci. Coun.; bd. dirs. Southeastern Pa. Heart Assn., 1992—. Recipient Bristol-Myers Squibb Cardiovasc. Achievement award, 1992, also numerous rsch. grants. Fellow Am. Coll. Cardiology (internat. edn. com. 1994—), Coll. Physicians of Phila.; mem. Assn. Univ. Cardiologists, Assn. Am. Physicians, Assn. Prof. of Cardiology, Am. Soc. Cell Biology, Am. Fedn. Clin. Rsch., Am. Soc. Clin. Investigation (pres.-elect 1994—, councilor 1991—), Internat. Soc. Heart Rsch. (councilor 1988—), Interurban Clin. Club, Clin. and Climitol. Soc., John Morgan Soc. Office: Hosp of Univ of Pa Cardiovasc Divsn 3400 Spruce St Philadelphia PA 19104

SWAIN, MELINDA SUSAN, elementary education educator; b. Sacramento, Oct. 30, 1944; d. William A. and Maxine (Wickberg) S. BA, Aurora U., 1967; MA, U. N.Mex., 1981. Cert. early adolescence/generalist Nat. Bd. Profl. Tchg. Standards, 1995. Tchr. 1st grade Crownpoint (N.Mex.) Elem. Sch., 1968-69, tchr. English as second lang., 1969-71; tchr. English as second lang. Church Rock (N.Mex.) Elem. Sch., 1971-72; tchr. kindergarten Sky City Elem. Sch., Gallup, N.Mex., 1972-73; program specialist Gallup-McKinley County Schs., 1973-82; tchr. 5th grade Lincoln Elem. Sch., Gallup, 1982—; mem. Dist. Task Force, Gallup, 1989—. Columnist N.Mex. Jour. Reading, 1991—. Recipient N.Mex. World Class Tchrs. Project award, 1994-95. Mem. N.Mex. Coun. Internat. Reading Assn. (pres. 1984, state coord. 1991—), Gallup Reading Coun. of Internat. Reading Assn. (pres., membership dir. 1977—). Avocations: mountain biking, reading, computers, RV-ing. Home: 1000 Country Club Dr Gallup NM 87301 Office: Lincoln Elem Sch 801 W Hill Ave Gallup NM 87301-6571

SWAIN, ROBERT, artist; b. Austin, Tex., Dec. 7, 1940; s. Robert O. and Beth (Brower) S.; m. Annette Carol Leibel, Oct. 4, 1969. B.A., Am.U., 1964. Prof. fine arts Hunter Coll.; vis. artist to various schs., univs., including Bklyn. Mus. Art Sch., 1975, 77, 78; dept. architecture Harvard U. Grad. Sch. Design, 1977. One-man shows, Thenan Gallery, N.Y.C., 1965, Fischbach Gallery, N.Y.C., 1968-69, Everson Art Museum, N.Y.C., 1974, Susan Galdwell Gallery, N.Y.C., 1974, 75, 78, Tex. Gallery, Houston, 1975, Columbus (Ohio) Gallery Fine Arts, 1976, Nina Freundenhein Gallery, Buffalo, 1978, group shows include, Mus. Modern Art, N.Y.C., 1968, Grand Palais, Paris, 1968, Kunsthaus, Zurich, Switzerland, 1969, Tate Gallery, London, 1969, Corcoran Gallery Art, Washington, 1969, Whitney Mus. Am. Art, N.Y.C., 1971, Albright-Knox Gallery, Buffalo, 1971, Mus. Modern Art Internat. Circulating Exhbn.-Latin Am., 1974-75; represented in permanent collections, Corcoran Gallery Art, Walker Art Center, Mpls., Va. Mus. Fine Arts, Richmond, Everson Art Mus., Columbus Gallery Fine Arts, Detroit Inst. Art, Albright-Knox Mus., works include archtl. installations, Am. Republic Ins. Co., Des Moines, 1969, N.K. Winston Corp., N.Y.C., 1969, Schering Labs., Bloomfield, N.J., 1970, Skidmore, Owings and Merrill, N.Y.C., 1970, Kahn & Mallis Assos., N.Y.C., 1972, Harris Bank, Chgo., 1977, Powell/Kleinschmidt Chgo., 1977, Travenol Labs., Deerfield, Ill., 1977, Skidmore, Owings and Merrill, Chgo., 1977. John Simon Guggenheim Meml. Found. fellow, 1969; Nat Endowment for Arts grantee, 1976. Home and Office: 57 Leonard St 4th Fl New York NY 10013

SWAIN, ROBERT EDSON, architect; b. Wareham, Mass., Apr. 19, 1946; s. Albert Hampton and Ellen Nora (Spillane) S. Urban Design Cert., Istituto Univ. di Architettura, Venice, Italy, 1970; BArch, U. Ariz., 1972. Field engr., estimator Eastern Erection Co., Woburn, Mass., 1972-73; project mgr., designer The Architects Collaborative Inc., Cambridge, Mass., 1973-76; architect in pvt. practice Cambridge, 1977-90; real estate prin. various trust properties, Cambridge, 1977—; pilot, prin. SWAIR, Cambridge, 1984-90; pres., prin., architect Swain Assocs. Inc., Cambridge, 1983-90; architect in pvt. practice Seattle, 1990—; trustee Conway (Mass.) Sch. Landscape Design, 1990-94; dir. McKinnon's Neck Conservancy, Argyle, Nova Scotia, Can., 1991—; tchr., guest critic Harvard, MIT, Boston Archtl. Ctr., Boston U., Conway Sch., U. Calif.-Berkeley, 1977—; critic-in-residence U. Nebr. Coll. Architecture, 1986. Prin. archtl. works include residence for Pres. of Boeing Co.; architect more than 350 projects including bldgs., landscapes and interiors, 1977—. Recipient Merit award Am. Sch. and Univ., Rindge, N.H., 1987, Best Office Interior award New Eng. Real Estate Dirs., Boston, 1984, others. Mem. AIA. Avocations: sailing, flying, travel, wilderness exploring, bicycling. Home and Office: PO Box 31566 Seattle WA 98103-1566

SWAIN, WILLIAM GRANT, landscape architect; b. Covington, Ky., Sept. 5, 1923; s. George Wellington and Emma Grant (Holmes) S.; m. Sybil Yvonne Harris, Mar. 30, 1946 (div. 1954); 1 son, Grant Marc; m. Marjorie Page Reno, Dec. 21, 1957; children: Margaret Page, Jill Holmes. B.Arch., Carnegie-Mellon U., 1952. Registered landscape architect, Pa., Ohio, Mich., Ga. Ptnr. Griswold, Winters, Swain & Mullin, Pitts., 1957-75; pres. GWSM Inc., Pitts., 1975-83; chmn. bd. GWSM Inc., 1983—; chmn. Interprofl. Council on Environ. Design, Washington, 1974. Author: (with Ralph E. Griswold) Opportunities in Landscape Architecture, 1978. Mem. Mayor's Com. on Community Improvement, Monroeville, Pa., 1965; bd. dirs. W. Pa. Conservancy, Pitts., 1970—, Rachel Carson Homestead Assn., Springdale, Pa., 1976—; mem. Pa. State Art Commn., Harrisburg, 1977-84, chmn., 1981-84. Served as 1st lt. U.S. Army, 1943-46, ETO. Decorated Purple Heart; recipient Service award Carnegie-Mellon U. Alumni Fedn., 1963. Fellow Am. Soc. Landscape Architects (pres. 1973-74 recipient medals), Phi Kappa Phi. Republican. Episcopalian. Club: University (dir.) (1976-82). Home: 413 Harper Dr Monroeville PA 15146-1235 Office: GWSM Landscape Architects 1101 Greenfield Ave Pittsburgh PA 15217-2930 *The central thread of my life is a sense of loyalty to those for whom I have worked or served in professional capacities. I have been motivated to do my best for all who depend on me. It remains my belief that volunteer service to one's community is an obligation.*

SWAISGOOD, HAROLD EVERETT, biochemist, educator; b. Ashland, Ohio, Jan. 19, 1936; s. Ray Weaver and Jennie (Morr) S.; m. Janet Cromwell, Sept. 15, 1956; children—Mark Harold, Ronald Ray. B.S., Ohio State U., 1958; Ph.D. in Chemistry (NIH fellow), Mich. State U., 1963. Reserach asst. Mich. State U., 1958-63; postdoctoral research asso. NIH, 1963-64; asst. prof. food sci. and biochemistry N.C. State U., 1964-67, asso. prof., 1967-72, prof., 1972-84, William Neal Reynolds prof., 1984—; vis. prof. U. Lund, Sweden, 1974, chmn. biotech. program. Editor for Ams., Comments on Agr. and Food Chemistry; mem. editorial bd. Jour. Dairy Sci, 1975—, Jour. Food Sci, 1978—, Jour. Food Biochemistry, 1983—; contbr. articles, chpts. to profl. publs. USPHS fellow, 1963-64. Fellow Am. Chem. Soc. (agriculture food chem. divsn., award advancement of application of agrl. and food chemistry sponsored by IFF 1994); mem. Am. Inst. Nutrition, Am. Soc. Biochemists and Molecular Biologists, AAAS, Am. Dairy Sci. Assn. (Borden awardee 1987), Inst. Food Technologists, Sigma Xi, Phi Kappa Phi, Gamma Sigma Delta. Democrat. Methodist. Achievements include research in protein structure, interactions, and functionality; characteristics and applications of immobilized enzymes; patents in field. Office: NC State U Dept Food Sci Raleigh NC 27695

SWALES, THOMAS G., electronics executive; b. 1936. Grad., Swarthmore Coll., 1958; postgrad. degree, Rensselaer Polytech. Inst., 1961. With GE, Troy, N.Y., 1961, Schenectady, N.Y., 1968-72; with McDonnell Douglas, St. Louis, 1961-68, Fairchild Industries, Germantown, Md., 1972-78; with Swales & Assocs., Inc., Beltville, Md., 1978—, pres. Office: Swales & Assocs Inc 5050 Powder Mill Rd Beltsville MD 20705-1913*

SWALIN, RICHARD ARTHUR, scientist, company executive; b. Mpls., Mar. 18, 1929; s. Arthur and Mae (Hurley) S.; m. Helen Marguerite Van Wagenen, June 28, 1952; children: Karen, Kent, Kristin. B.S. with distinction, U. Minn., 1951, Ph.D., 1954. Rsch. assoc. GE, 1954-56; mem. faculty U. Minn., Mpls., 1956-77, prof., head Sch. Mineral and Metall Engring., 1962-68, assoc. dean Inst. Tech., 1968-71, dean Inst. Tech., 1971-77; acting dir. Space Sci. Center, 1965; v.p. tech. Eltra Corp., N.Y.C., 1977-80; v.p. R & D Allied-Signal Corp., Morristown, N.J., 1980-84; dean Coll. Engring. and Mines U. Ariz., Tucson, 1984-87, prof., 1984-94; pres. Ariz. Tech. Devel. Corp., Tucson, 1987; prof. emeritus U. Ariz., Tucson, 1995—; guest scientist Max Planck Inst. für Phys. Chemie, Göttingen, Fed. Republic Germany, 1963, Lawrence Radiation Lab., Livermore, Calif., 1967; cons. to govt. and industry; bd. dirs. Medtronic Corp., BMC Industries; corp. adv. bd. AMP Inc., 1990-93. Author: Thermodynamics of Solids, 2d edit, 1972; Contbr. articles to profl. jours. Dir. div. indsl. coop. U. Ariz. Found., 1985-86; trustee Midwest Research Inst., 1975-78, Sci. Mus. Minn., 1973-77, Nat. Tech. U., 1983-90. Recipient Disting. Teaching award Inst. Tech., U. Minn., 1967, Leadership award U. Minn. Alumni, 1993; NATO sr. fellow in sci.,

1971. Mem. Sigma Xi, Tau Beta Pi, Phi Delta Theta, Gamma Alpha. Home: 4705 N Via De La Granja Tucson AZ 85718-7404 Office: U Ariz Ariz Materials Lab 4715 E Fort Lowell Rd Tucson AZ 85712-1201

SWALM, THOMAS STERLING, aerospace executive, retired military officer; b. San Diego, Sept. 28, 1931; s. Calvin D. and Margaret A. (Rynning) S.; m. Charlene La Vern Garner, June 26, 1954; children: Edward Steven, Lori Ann. BS, U. Oreg., 1954; MS in Pub. Adminstrn., George Washington U., 1964; grad., Air Command and Staff Coll., 1964, Nat. War Coll., 1974. Commd. USAF, 1954, advanced through grades to maj. gen., 1982; instr. fighter-interceptor weapons sch. USAF, Tyndall AFB, Fla., 1956; pilot 434th Fighter-Day Squadron USAF, George AFB, Calif., 1957-58; engrng. test pilot and flight examiner 50th Tactical Fighter Wing, 10th Tactical Fighter Squadron USAF, Toul-Rosieres AFB, France, and Hahn AFB, Fed. Republic Germany, 1958-61; hdqrs. 12th USAF, Waco, Tex., 1961-64; instr. pilot, flight examiner 4453d Combat Crew Tng. Wing USAF, Davis-Monthan AFB, Ariz., 1965-66; flight comdr. 12th Tactical Fighter Wing USAF, Cam Ranh Bay AFB, Republic Vietnam, 1966-67; comdr. air-to-air flight, instr. and chief R&D/OT&E sect. Fighter Weapons Sch., Nellis AFB, Nev., 1967-70; comdr., leader Thunderbirds USAF, 1970-73; chief fighter attack directorate USAF, Kirtland AFB, N.Mex., 1974-75, dep. dir. test and evaluation, 1975-76; from vice comdr. to comdr. 8th Tactical Fighter Wing USAF, Kunsan AFB, Republic of Korea, 1976-78; comdr. 3d Tactical Fighter Wing USAF, Clark AFB, Philippines, 1978-79; comdr. 57th Fighter Weapons Wing, comdr. fighter weapons sch. USAF, Nellis AFB, Nev., 1979-80; comdr. 833d air div. USAF, Holloman AFB, N.Mex., 1980-81; comdr. tactical air warfare ctr. USAF, Eglin AFB, Fla., 1981-86; ret. USAF, 1986; pres. T. Swalm and Assocs., Ft. Walton Beach, Fla., 1986-91; v.p. Melbourne Systems Div. Grumman Corp., 1991-95; pres. T. Swaim and Assocs., Melbourne, Fla., 1995—; v.p. Applications Group Internat., Inc., Atlanta, 1986-89; scientific adv. bd. USAF, 1994—. Mem. editorial bd. Jour. Electronic Def., 1983-86; contbr. articles to profl. jours. Hon. chmn. Heart Assn., Las Vegas, Nev., 1972; exec. dir. Boy Scouts Am., Las Vegas and Alamagordo, N.Mex., 1970-81; chmn. AFA Scholarship Found., 1989-91; active Fla. Govs. Coun. for TQM, 1992-94; bd. dirs. Jr. Achievement, Ctrl. Fla., 1992-94; mem. USAF scientific adv. bd., 1994-98. Decorated D.S.M., Legion of Merit with two oak leaf clusters, DFC, Air medal with 14 oak leaf clusters, Vietnam Service medal with three service stars, Republic Vietnam Campaign medal; recipient R.V. Jones Trophy Electronic Security Command, 1984. Mem. Air Force Assn. (exec. advisor, Jerome Waterman award 1985, Jimmy Doolittle fellow 1986), Thunderbirds Pilots Assn., Old Mission Beach Athletic Club (founder), Assn. Old Crows (editl. bd. R.V. Jones trophy 1984), Order of Daedalians (flight capt.), Melbourne C of C. (trustee 1993-95), Sigma Nu. Republican. Presbyterian. Avocations: golf, tennis, sailing.

SWAN, BARBARA, artist; b. Newton, Mass., June 23, 1922; d. Carl Lilja and Clara May (Knowlton) S.; m. Alan D. Fink, June 28, 1952; children: Aaron, Joanna. B.A., Wellesley Coll., 1943; B.F.A., Boston Mus. Sch., 1948. Faculty mem. Wellesley Coll., 1947-48, Milton (Mass.) Acad., 1952-55, Boston U., 1961-64. Exhibited one-woman shows Boston Pub. Libr., 1994, Alpha Gallery, Boston, 1970, 73, 76, 80, 83, 87, 92, Addison Gallery Am. Art, Andover, Mass., 1973; group shows Inst. Contemporary Art, Boston, 1960, Boston Mus. Fine Arts, 1976, Nat. Inst. Arts and Letters, N.Y.C., 1976, Danforth Mus., Framingham, Mass., 1981; represented permanent collections Boston Mus. Fine Arts, Phila. Mus. Art, Worcester Mus., Nat Portrait Gallery. MacDowell Colony grantee Peterborough, N.H., 1947-48; Albert Whittin traveling fellow Boston Mus. Sch., Europe, 1949-51, Bunting fellow Radcliffe Coll., 1961-63; recipient Wellesley Coll. Alumnae Lifetime Achievement award, 1996. Democrat. Address: 808 Washington St Brookline MA 02146-2122

SWAN, BETH ANN, nursing administrator; b. Phila., Nov. 11, 1958; d. John H. and Elizabeth A. Jenkins; m. Eric J. Swan, Apr. 11, 1987. BSN, Holy Family Coll., Phila., 1980; MSN, U. Pa., 1983. RN, Pa.; cert. adult nurse practitioner ANCC. Nursing dir. admission evaluation ctr. Hosp. of U. Pa., Phila. Mem. ANA, Pa. Nurses Assn., Am. Acad. Nurse Practitioners, Am. Acad. Ambulatory Nursing Adminstrn., Sigma Theta Tau.

SWAN, GEORGE STEVEN, lawyer, educator; b. St. Louis. BA, Ohio State U., 1970; JD, U. Notre Dame, 1974; LLM, U. Toronto, 1976, SJD, 1983. Bar: Ohio 1974, U.S. Dist. Ct. (so. dist.) Ohio 1975, U.S. Supreme Ct. 1987, U.S. Ct. Appeals (6th and 11th cirs.) 1993, U.S. Ct. Appeals (10th cir.) 1994; CFP; registered investment advisor U.S. Securities and Exchange Commn., 1989, Sec. of State, N.C., 1990. Asst. atty. gen. state of Ohio, Columbus, 1974-75; jud. clk. Supreme Ct. Ohio, Columbus, 1976-78; asst. prof. Del. Law Sch., Wilmington, 1980-83, assoc. prof., 1983-84; prof. law St. Thomas U. Law Sch., Miami, Fla., 1984-88; jud. clk. U.S. Ct. Appeals 7th cir., Chgo., 1988-89; assoc. prof. N.C. Agrl. & Tech. State U., Greensboro, 1989-96; vis. prof. John Marshall Law Sch., Atlanta, 1996—. Contbr. articles to law jours. Mem. Ohio State Bar Assn., Internat. Assn. for Fin. Planning, Am. Polit. Sci. Assn. Office: NC Agrl & Tech State U Sch Bus 1601 E Market St Greensboro NC 27411

SWAN, HENRY, retired surgeon; b. Denver, May 27, 1913; s. Henry and Carla (Denison) S.; m. Mary Fletcher Wardwell, June 25, 1937 (div. Jan. 25, 1964); children: Edith, Henry, Gretchen; m. Geraldine Morris Fairchild, Mar. 21, 1964. AB magna cum laude, Williams Coll., 1935, DSc (hon.), 1958; MD cum laude, Harvard U., 1939. Diplomate Nat. Bd. Med. Examiners, Am. Bd. Surgery. Pathology fellow Colo. Gen. Hosp., Denver, 1939-40; intern surgery Peter Bent Brigham Children's Hosp., Boston, 1940-42; pathology fellow Children's Hosp., Boston, 1942-43; asst. in surgery Harvard Med. Sch., Boston, 1942-43; from asst. to assoc. prof. surgery U. Colo. Med. Sch., 1946-50, prof. surgery, head dept. surgery, 1950-61, prof. surgery, rsch., 1963-82, prof. emeritus, 1985—. Author: Thermoregulation and Bioenergetics, 1974; assoc. editor Jour. Cardiovasc. Surgery, 1956-70, AMA Archives Surgery, 1956-66; contbr. articles to profl. jours. With AUS, 1943-45, ETO. Mem. ACS, AMA (Gold medal for original rsch. 1955), AAAS, Acad. Surg. Rsch. (medallion for exptl. surgery 1996), Am. Surg. Assn., Am. Assn. Thoracic Surgery, Soc. for Cryobiology, Soc. Univ. Surgeons, Soc. Vascular Surgery, Halsted Soc., Surgery Biology Club, Ctrl. Surg. Assn., Western Surg. Assn., Internat. Cardiovasc. Soc., Internat. Soc. Surgery, Assn. Surgery Costa Rica, Soc. Surgeons Chile, Soc. Cardiology Chile, Soc. Pediat. Mex., Denver Acad. Surgery, Denver Clin. and Path. Soc., Phi Beta Kappa, Alpha Omega Alpha. Republican. Episcopalian. Avocations: sailing, tennis, fly fishing, duck hunting, golf. Home: 6700 W Lakeridge Rd Lakewood CO 80227

SWAN, JUDITH, marine lawyer; b. June 8, 1944; d. William J. and Lee M. (Shannon) Lee; 1 child, Ward Swan. BA, McGill U., Montreal, 1966; LLB, U. Alta., Edmonton, 1970; LLM, U. London, 1971. Bar: Can. 1978. Lectr. law, assoc. dean U. Melbourne, Australia, 1971-75; vis. prof. law U. Toronto, Ont., Can., 1975-76; assoc. prof. law U. Ottawa, Ont., Can., 1976-80; internat. rels. officer Fisheries and Oceans Can., 1980-85; legal counsel South Pacific Forum Fisheries Agy., Honiara, Solomon Islands, 1985-90; exec. dir. Oceans Inst. of Can., Halifax, N.S., 1990-94; pres., CEO SwanSea Oceans Environment, Inc., Waverley, N.S., 1994—; cons. World Bank, 1993-95, UN Food and Agr. Orgn., Rome, 1994—, Fgn. Affairs and Internat. Trade Can., Ottawa, 1993—, Internat. Inst. for Sustainable Devel., Winnipeg, Man., 1995—, numerous other cons. positions; adj. prof. Dalhousie U.; sessional prof. dept. law Carleton U., 1975, 80, 81; rsch. dir. Ont. Commn. on Election Contbns. and Expenses, 1975; founder, Oceans Day. Contbr. articles to profl. jours., chpts. to books. Bd. dirs. Law of the Sea Inst., 1994—. Mem. Projet de Société, Cuisine Can., Law Soc. Upper Can. Avocations: metaphysics, ocean-related activities. Office: SwanSea Oceans Environment Inc, PO Box 188, Waverley, NS Canada B0N 2SO

SWAN, KENNETH CARL, surgeon; b. Kansas City, Mo., Jan. 1, 1912; s. Carl E. and Blanche (Peters) S.; m. Virginia Grone, Feb. 5, 1938; children: Steven Carl, Kenneth, Susan. A.B., U. Oreg., 1933, M.D., 1936. Diplomate: Am. Bd. Ophthalmology (chmn. 1960-61). Intern U. Wis., 1936-37; resident in ophthalmology State U. Iowa, 1937-40; practice medicine specializing in ophthalmology Portland, Oreg., 1945—; staff Good Samaritan Hosp.; asst. prof. ophthalmology State U. Iowa, Iowa City, 1941-44; asso. prof. U. Oreg. Med. Sch., Portland, 1944-45, prof. and head dept. ophthalmology, 1945-78; Chmn. sensory diseases study sect. NIH; mem. adv. council Nat. Eye Inst.; also adv. council Nat. Inst. Neurol. Diseases and Blindness. Contbr. articles on ophthalmic subjects to med. publs. Recipient Proctor Rsch. medal, 1953; Disting. Svc. award U. Oreg., 1963; Meritorious Achievement award U. Oreg. Med. Sch., 1968; Howe Ophthalmology medal, 1977; Aubrey Watzek Pioneer award Lewis and Clark Coll., 1979, Disting. Alumnus award Oreg. Health Scis. U. Alumni Assn., 1988, Disting. Svc. award, 1988; named Oreg. Scientist of Yr. Oreg. Mus. Sci. and Industry, 1959. Mem. Assn. Research in Ophthalmology, Am. Acad. Ophthalmology (v.p. 1978, historian), Soc. Exptl. Biology and Medicine, AAAS, AMA, Am. Ophthal. Soc. (Howe medal for distinguished service 1977), Oreg. Med. Soc., Sigma Xi, Sigma Chi (Significant Sig award 1977). Home: 4645 SW Fairview Blvd Portland OR 97221-2624 Office: Ophthamology Dept Oreg Health Scis U Portland OR 97201

SWAN, RICHARD ALAN, executive recruiter; b. Hollywood, Calif., May 5, 1944; s. Morris George and Mary Theresa (Fenusz) S.; m. Carol Ann Jacobs, Apr. 15, 1967; children: David Michael, Jennifer Marie, Matthew Richard. BS in Indsl. Mgmt., U. So. Calif., 1966; MS in Health Care Adminstrn., Trinity U., 1970. Adminstrv. resident Tucson (Ariz.) Med. Ctr., 1971; assoc. cons. A.T. Kearney and Co. Inc., Chgo., 1971-72; v.p. Tribrook Group Inc., Oakbrook, Ill., 1972-82; dir. program and spl. studies div. James A. Hamilton Assocs. Inc., Dallas, 1982-83; v.p. corp. devel. Vincentian Health Services, L.A., 1983-88; v.p., dir. healthcare group Boyden Internat., L.A., 1988-89; regional v.p. Kieffer Ford & Assocs., Ltd., Orange, Calif., 1989-92; ptnr. Witt/Kieffer, Ford, Hadelman & Lloyd, Irvine, Calif., 1992—. Contbr. articles to profl. jours. Served to capt. Med. Service Corps, U.S. Army, 1967-69. Fellow Am. Assn. Hosp. Cons., Am. Coll. Healthcare Execs.; mem. Soc. Hosp. Planning and Mktg., So. Calif. Soc. Hosp. Planners (charter), Health Care Execs. of So. Calif., Am. Hosp. Assn. Republican. Roman Catholic. Avocations: golfing, fishing. Office: Witt Kieffer Ford Hadelman & Lloyd 1920 Main St Ste 310 Irvine CA 92714-7235

SWAN, RICHARD GORDON, mathematics educator; b. N.Y.C., Dec. 21, 1933; s. A. Gordon and Rose (Nespor) S.; m. Erdmuthe J.D.B. Plesch-Ritz, Mar. 18, 1963; children—Adrian Alexander, Irit Alexandra. A.B., Princeton U., N.J., 1954, Ph.D., 1957. Instr. U. Chgo., 1958-60, asst. prof., 1960-62, assoc. prof., 1962-65, prof., 1965—, Louis Block prof., 1982—. Author: Theory of Sheaves, 1964, Algebraic K-Theory, 1968, K-Theory of Finite Groups and Orders, 1970; editor Am. Jour. Math., 1977-83, Jour. Algebra, 1981-95; contbr. articles to profl. jours. Alfred P. Sloan fellow, 1961-65; recipient Cole prize in Algebra Am. Math. Soc., 1970. Fellow AAAS; mem. Nat. Acad. Scis., Am. Math. Soc., Math. Assn. Am., N.Y. Acad. Scis., Sigma Xi. Avocation: music. Home: 475 Oakdale Ave Glencoe IL 60022-2180 Office: U Chgo 5734 S University Ave Chicago IL 60637-1546

SWAN, WILLIAM, actor; b. Buffalo, N.Y., Feb. 6, 1932; s. Earl B. and Irene (Hall) S. Student, Geller Workshop, L.A. Appeared in films including Lady in a Cage, Hotel, The Parallax View, Bombers B-52; more than 200 TV guest appearances including Streets of San Francisco, Quincy, Perry Mason, Felony Squad, Twilight Zone, Have Gun Will Travel, Cannon, Barnaby Jones; appeared in off-Broadway plays, including Anne of a Thousand Days, Night Fishing in Beverly Hills; appeared in regional theatres including A Delicate Balance, The Cocktail Hour, California Suite, The Middle Ages, Stained Glass, What The Butler Saw, The Price, and others; appeared in TV day-time drama, All My Children, 1982—. Trustee Berkshire Theatre Festival, Stockbridge, Mass., 1984—. Sgt. U.S. Army, 1948-49, ETO. Mem. Acad. TV Arts and Scis., The Players. Democrat. Avocation: tennis. Home: 141 E 55th St Apt 12B New York NY 10022-4036 Home: Barberry Close Monterey MA 01245

SWANBERG, EDMUND RAYMOND, investment counselor; b. Newton, Mass., Oct. 18, 1921; s. Raymond C. and Olga (Clement) S.; m. Ruth P. Mattson, May 24, 1943; children: Linda Ruth, Charles Howard, Peter Bush. BS, MIT, 1943; MBA, NYU, 1951. Chartered Investment Counselor. Assoc. Scudder, Stevens & Clark, Boston, 1946-48; assoc. Scudder, Stevens & Clark, N.Y.C., 1948-61, ptnr., sr. v.p., 1961-85, mng. dir., 1985-86, adv. mng. dir., 1987—; pres., dir. Scudder Devel. Fund, 1970-86, Scudder Capital Growth, 1982-86, Scudder Internat. Fund, 1975-86. Capt. AUS, 1943-46. Mem. Assn. for Investment Mgmt. and Rsch., N.Y. Soc. Security Analysts, Internat. Soc. Fin. Analysts, Racquet and Tennis Club (N.Y.C.), Somerset Club (Boston), Country Club of New Canaan (Conn.), Blind Brook Club (N.Y.), Mill Reef Club (Antigua), Wharf Rat Club (Nantucket), Union Club (N.Y.C.), Ekwanok Club (Conn.). Republican. Presbyterian.

SWANEY, THOMAS EDWARD, lawyer; b. Detroit, Apr. 25, 1942; s. Robert Ernest and Mary Alice (Slinger) S.; m. Patricia Louise Nash, Sept. 9, 1967; children: Julia Bay, Mary Elizabeth, David Paul. AB, U. Mich., 1963, JD, 1967; postdoctoral, London Sch. Econs., 1967-68. Bar: Ill. 1968. From assoc. to ptnr. Sidley & Austin, Chgo., 1968—; bd. dirs. Corey Steel Co., Cicero, Ill., Gertrude B. Nielsen Child Care & Learning Ctr., Northbrook, Ill., Ward C. Rogers Found., Chgo. Trustee H. Earl Hoover Found., Glencoe, Ill., 1986—, RF Found., Chgo., 1992—; officer, pres. bd. trustees 1st Presbyn. Ch., Evanston, Ill., 1984-89; bd. dirs. Lakeland Conservancy, Minocqua, Wis., 1987—. Mem. ABA, Ill. State Bar Assn., Chgo. Bar Assn., Legal Club Chgo. Office: Sidley & Austin 1 First Nat Plz Chicago IL 60603

SWANGER, STERLING ORVILLE, appliance manufacturing company executive; b. Battle Creek, Iowa, Jan. 5, 1922; s. Orville M. and Alma Louise (Messing) S.; m. Maxine O. Hindman, July 2, 1950; 1 son, Eric. B.S., Iowa State U., 1947; student U. Va., 1965. Registered profl. engr., Iowa. Indsl. engr. Maytag Co., Newton, Iowa, 1947-52, methods engr., 1952-54, asst. chief methods engr., 1954-57, chief methods engr., 1957-68, mgr. prodn. engrng., 1968-71, mgr. engrng., 1971-74, asst. v.p. mfg., 1974-75, v.p. mfg., 1975-86, sr. v.p. and chief mfg. officer, 1986-87, also dir., cons., 1987—. Mem., Newton Planning and Zoning Commn., 1966-70; trustee Newton Skiff Hosp., 1970-85, chmn., 1982-85, Progress Industries, 1987-90; chmn. Progress Industries, 1991. Served with AUS 1943-46. Mem. Nat. Soc. Profl. Engrs., Iowa Engrng. Soc., Nat. Mgmt. Assn., Am. Mgmt. Assn., Am. Ordnance Assn. Republican. Presbyterian. Clubs: Newton Country, Elks.

SWANK, EMORY COBLENTZ, world affairs consultant, lecturer; b. Frederick, Md., Jan. 29, 1922; s. George Phillip and Mary Ruth (Coblentz) S.; m. Margaret Katherine Whiting, May 12, 1949. A.B., Franklin and Marshall Coll., 1942; A.M., Harvard, 1943. With U.S. Dept. State, 1946-75; vice consul U.S. Dept. State, Shanghai, China, 1946-48, Tsingtao, China, 1948-49; 2d sec. Am. Embassy, consul U.S. Dept. State, Djakarta, Indonesia, 1950-51, Moscow, U.S.S.R., 1953-55; polit. analyst, fgn. service officer U.S. Dept. State, Washington, 1956-57; conselor of legation U.S. Dept. State, Bucharest, 1958-60; spl. asst. to sec. of state U.S. Dept. State, 1961-63; assigned Nat. War Coll., Ft. L.J. McNair, Washington, 1963-64; counselor of embassy, dep. chief of mission Am. Embassy, Vientiane, Laos, 1964-67; minister Am. Embassy, Moscow, USSR, 1967-67; dep. asst. sec. state for European affairs Am. Embassy, 1969-70; ambassador to Cambodia, 1970-73; polit. adviser to CINC, Atlantic, and Supreme Allied Comdr., NATO Atlantic Forces, 1973-75; pres., chief exec. officer Cleve. Council on World Affairs, 1977-87, hon. trustee, 1987—. Served with AUS, 1943-46. Decorated Bronze Star medal; recipient Superior Honor award Dept. of State, 1973; Alumni Citation award Franklin and Marshall Coll., 1973. Mem. Phi Beta Kappa. Address: 65 Kendal Dr Oberlin OH 44074

SWANK, ROY LAVER, physician, educator, inventor; b. Camas, Wash., Mar. 5, 1909; s. Wilmer and Hannah Jane (Laver) S.; m. Eulalia F. Shively, Sept. 14, 1936 (dec.); children: Robert L., Susan Jane (Mrs. Joel Keizer) Stephen (dec.); m. Betty Harris, May 23, 1987. Student, U. Wash., 1926-30; M.D., Northwestern U., 1935; Ph.D., 1935. House officer, resident Peter Bent Brigham Hosp., Boston, 1936-39; fellow pathology Harvard Med. Sch., 1938-39; mem. staff neurol. unit Boston City Hosp., 1945-48; asst. prof. neurology Montreal Neurol. Inst., McGill U., 1948-75; prof. emeritus Oreg. Med. Sch., 1974—; dir. Swank Multiple Sclerosis Clinic, Beaverton, Oreg., 1994—; prof. neurology, head divsn. neurology Oreg. Med. Sch., 1954-75; pres. Pioneer Filters, 1970-78. Served to maj. M.C. AUS, 1942-46. Recipient Oreg. Gov.'s award for research in multiple sclerosis, 1966. Mem. Am. Physiol. Soc., Am. Neurol. Assn., European Microcirculation Soc., Sigma Xi. Achievements include invention of micro embolic filter; research of physical chemical changes in blood after fat meals and during surgical shock, platelet-leukocyte aggregation in stored blood in hypotensive shock; low-fat diet in multiple sclerosis; research of physical chemical changes in multiple sclerosis (plasma proteins); importance of plasma proteins in multiple sclerosis; investigation of breakdown of blood-brain barrier by infused micro emboli, and by in vitro produced micro emboli due to aggregated red blood cells. Home: 789 SW Summit View Dr Portland OR 97225-6185 Office: Swank Multiple Sclerosis Clin 13655 SW Jenkins Rd Beaverton OR 97005

SWANKIN, DAVID ARNOLD, lawyer, consumer advocate; b. Boston, Jan. 18, 1934; s. Max and Anne (Rotefsky) S.; m. Jeanne Phyllis Herrick; 1 dau., Sheryl. A.B., Brandeis U., 1954; M.S., U. Wis., 1957; J.D., George Washington U., 1962. Mgmt. intern U.S. Dept. Labor, Washington, 1957-60; spl. asst. to asst. sec. labor U.S. Dept. Labor, 1961-63, dep. asst. sec. labor, 1967; dir. Bur. Labor Standards, 1967-68; exec. sec. Pres.'s Consumer Adv. Council, Washington, 1964; exec. dir. Pres's Com. on Consumer Interests, Washington, 1965-66; Washington rep. Consumer's Union, 1969-71; exec. dir. Consumer Interests Found., 1971-73; sr. partner Swankin & Turner, 1973—; pres. Regulatory Alternatives Devel. Corp., 1985—; pres. Citizen Advocacy Ctr. 1994—; cons. U.S. Dept. Labor; pres. Citizen Advocacy Ctr., 1994—. Mem. Pres.'s Council, Brandeis U., 1968-69. Served with AUS, 1954-56. Recipient Jump award U.S. Govt., 1969. Mem. Am. Bar Assn., Ombudsman Com. Home: 300 N Cherry St Falls Church VA 22046-3522 Office: 1424 16th St NW Washington DC 20036-2211

SWANN, BARBARA, lawyer; b. N.Y., Sept. 15, 1950; d. George Arthur. BA summa cum laude, Montclair State U., 1988; JD, Rutgers Law, 1992. Bar: N.J. 1992, D.C. 1994, N.Y. 1995, U.S. Dist. Ct. N.J. 1992, U.S. Ct. Appeals (3rd cir.) 1994. Correspondent The Associate Press, Newark, N.J., 1974-80; reporter, bureau chief The Hudson Dispatch, Union City, N.J., 1973-80; editorial page editor The Paterson (N.J.) News, 1980-81; v.p., acct. supr. Gerald Freeman, Inc., Clifton, N.J., 1981-86; pres. LePore Assoc., Inc., West Caldwell, N.J., 1986-89; law clk. to Hon. Robert N. Wilentz N.J. Supreme Ct., 1992-93; law clk. to Hon. Leonard I. Garth U.S. Ct. Appeals (3rd cir.), 1993-94; assoc. Cahill, Gordon & Reindel, N.Y., 1994—. Editor-in-chief: Rutgers Computer & Technology Law Jour., 1991-92. Founding trustee Ctr. for Children's Advocacy, Riverdale, N.J. 1994—. Mem. ABA, Assn. of the Bar of the City of New York, N.J. State Bar Assn., D.C. Bar Assn. Office: Cahill Gordon & Reindel 80 Pine St New York NY 10005

SWANN, BRIAN, writer, humanities educator; b. Wallsend, Northumberland, Eng., Aug. 13, 1940; came to U.S., 1963, naturalized, 1980; s. Stanley Frank and Lilyan Mary (Booth) S.; m. Roberta Metz. B.A., Queens' Coll., Cambridge U., 1962. M.A., 1965; Ph.D., Princeton U., 1970. Instr. Princeton U., 1964-65; lectr., 1968-70, asst. prof., 1970-72; instr. Rutgers U., 1965-66; asst. prof. humanities Cooper Union for Advancement Sci. and Art, N.Y.C., 1972-75, assoc. prof., 1975-80, prof., 1980—, acting dean, 1990-91; dir. Bennington Writing Workshops, 1988-91. Author: (poetry) The Middle of the Journey, 1982, Song of The Sky: Versions of Native American Song-Poems, 1993, also many other books of fiction, translations, children's books; The Plot of the Mice, 1984, A Basket Full of White Eggs, 1988; editor: Smoothing The Ground: Essays of Native American Oral Literature, 1983; (with Arnold Krupat) Recovering the Word, 1987, I Tell You Now: Autobiographical Essays by Native American Writers, 1987, Coming to Light: Contemporary Translations of the Native Literatures of North America, 1995; Essays on the Translation of Native American Literatures, 1992; editor The Smithsonian Series of Essays on Native American Literatures, 1990—. NEA fellow, 1981; Creative Arts in Pub. Service grantee, 1982. Office: Cooper Union Adv Sci & Art Faculty Humanities & Social Sci Cooper Sq New York NY 10003

SWANN, ERIC JERROD, professional football player; b. Pinehurst, N.C., Aug. 16, 1970. Student, Wake Tech. Coll. Defensive tackle Ariz. Cardinals, Phoenix, 1991—. Selected to Pro Bowl, 1995. Office: Arizona Cardinals 8701 S Hardy Phoenix AZ 85285

SWANN, JERRE BAILEY, lawyer; b. Gadsden, Ala., May 12, 1939; s. Julius Seth and Alma Nell (McCartney) S.; m. Jane Goodwillie, June 26, 1965 (div. Jan. 1977); children: Jerre B. Jr., Eliza W.; m. Cynthia Pangia, Sept. 17, 1977. BA, Williams Coll., 1961; postgrad., U. St. Andrews, Scotland, 1961-62; LLB, Harvard U., 1965. Bar: N.Y. 1966, Ga. 1968, U.S. Dist. Ct. (no. and mid. dists.) Ga., U.S. Dist. Ct. (ea. dist.) Tex., U.S. Ct. Appeals (1st, 4th, 5th, 8th, 11th cirs.). Law clk. U.S. Dist. Ct. (so. dist.) N.Y., N.Y.C., 1965-67; assoc. Kilpatrick & Cody, Atlanta, 1967-72, ptnr., 1972—. Contbr. numerous articles to profl. jours. Mem. ABA, Ga. Bar Assn., Internat. Trademark Assn. (bd. dirs. 1989-91, editor-in-chief Trademark Reporter 1988-90), Cherokee Town and Country Club, Phi Beta Kappa. Democrat. Avocation: woodworking. Home: 9905 Huntcliff Trce Atlanta GA 30350-2715 Office: Kilpatrick & Cody 1100 Peachtree St Atlanta GA 30309

SWANN, LYNN CURTIS, sportscaster, former professional football player; b. Alcoa, Tenn., Mar. 7, 1952; s. Willie and Mildred (McGarity) S. B.A., U. So. Calif., 1974. Wide receiver Pitts. Steelers Profl. Football Team, 1974-83, leading receiver in team history, 1981; commentator ABC Sports, 1976—. Entertainment and media apppearances as dancer with Twyla Tharp and Peter Martines Omnibus TV Spl., 1980, guest star Night of 100 Stars I, 1982, 100 Stars II, 1985; host and narrator Britten's Young Person's Guide to Orchestra, Wheeling Symphony Orch., 1982; host of 13 part art edn. spl. Arts Alive, PBS, 1984; major character in episodes Paper Chase, 1984, Hotel, 1984, Love American Style, 1985; other appearances on various TV shows including 20/20, Good Morning America, Merv Griffin, Hollywood Squares, others; intermittent host daily talk show Pittsburgh 2Day, 1985—. Spokesman for Big Bros./Big Sisters Assn.; trustee Pitts. Ballet Theatre, creator youth scholarship program; bd. dirs. Scott Newman Juvenile Drug and Alcohol Prevention Found.; bd. dirs. U. So. Calif. Sch. Journalism Alumni Assn. Named All Pro, 1976 77, 78, Most Valuable Player in Super Bowl X, 1976, Pitts. Multiple Sclerosis Athlete of Yr., 1980, NFL Man of Yr., 1981; holder 4 Super Bowl records, 2d in 2 categories; mem. Pitts. Steelers All-Time Team, 50th Anniv.; named to NFL Hall of Fame Team of Decade/1970's, AP, UPI, Kodak All Am. Teams, Pop Warner Hall of Fame; recipient Image award NAACP, 1979, Ebonics Soc. award, Outstanding Alumni award U. So. Calif., 1984, Oleg Cassini Competitors Fashion award, 1985. Mem. Screen Actors Guild, AFTRA. Office: Swann Inc 600 Grant St Ste 48 Pittsburgh PA 15219-2703

SWANN, RANDE NORTOF, public relations executive; b. Louisville, July 14, 1952; d. Thomas Joseph and Garrith Louise (Hines) Nortof; m. William Donald Swann, Nov. 20, 1977; children: Nicole, Amy. BA, Hollins Coll. For Women, Roanoke, Va., 1974; MS, U. Louisville, 1980. Various positions Hollins Coll. For Women, Roanoke, 1971-74; exec. dir. USO-Louisville (Ky.) Svc. Club, Inc., 1974-81; asst. campaign dir. Metro United Way, Louisville, 1981-82; pub. affairs dir. Jefferson County Pub. Schs., Louisville, 1983-89; pub. rels. dir. Regional Airport Authority of Louisville & Jefferson County, 1989—; speaker workshops and confs. in field, including Internat. Quality and Productivity Ctr., Nat. Seminar, Atlanta, 1995, ACI-NA Aviation Edn. Tour Guide Conf., St. Louis, 1995, Mtkg./Comms. Conf., Tex., 1995, Ann. Conf., Toronto, 1994, numerous others. Patron Actors Theatre Louisville; mem. pub. rels. adv. com. Metro United Way, 1987-88. Recipient numerous profl. advt. awards, including grand prize comm. contest Airport Coun. Internat.-N.Am., 1994, award Ad. Club Louisville, 1995, nat. summit awards for creativity, 1995. Mem. Internat. Assn. Bus. Communicators (Silver Quill award of excellence, award of merit, Landmarks of Excellence award 1984-88, 95), Pub. Rels. Soc. Am. (dist. award of excellence, regional award 1983-88, Landmarks of Excellence award 1995), Nat. Sch. Pub. Rels. Assn. (4 Golden Achievement awards, 2 sch. publs.-comm. awards, Nat. Award of Honor 1984-88), Airport Coun. Internat. (vice chmn. mktg. and comm. group), Ky. Assn. Govt. Communicators (Blue Pencil awards), Hollins Coll. Alumnae Club, also others. Democrat. Presbyterian. Avocations: reading, traveling. Office: Regional Airport Authority PO Box 9129 Louisville KY 40209-0129

SWANNER, LINDA ALLEN (LIN SWANNER), artist; b. Burlington, N.C., Dec. 11, 1942; d. Allen Wade Swanner and Mary Jane (Waller) Griffin; m. Eugene Miller Barnes Jr., May 24, 1969. Grad. in Printmaking, Figure Sculpture, Glassell Sch. of Art, Houston, 1979; postgrad., Ecole des Arts Decoratif, Strasbourg, France, 1979-80. Artist, 1981—. Editor (catalogue) The 1984 Show, 1984, The 1985 Show/Self-Image, 1985; artist (cover) Houston Arts Mag., 1982; one-woman shows include Little Egypt Enterprises, Houston, 1981, Meredith Long and Co., Houston, 1986, Lanning Gallery, 1991, 92; exhibited in groups shows at Galveston Art Ctr., 1984, L.A. Gallery Contemporary Art, Calif., 1985, Tex. Art Celebration '86, Houston, 1986, Celebration '87 (3d place award), San Antonio, 1987, Tex. Fine Arts Assn. Traveling Show, 1987-89, Lynn Goode Gallery, Houston, 1989, Transco Gallery (2d place award), Houston, 1991, Pink Floyd, Houston, 1994. Recipient Creative Artist award Cultural Arts Coun. Houston, 1993, Wm. A. Smith Endowment award Glassell Sch. Art, 1979, Carl Jung Sculpture award The Jung Ctr., 1978. Mem. Lawndale Art and Performance Ctr., DiverseWorks, Tex. Accts. and Lawyers for the Arts (chair artist bd. 1992, chair Brush-off 1993, chair fine arts gala 1993, Artist of Yr. 1994), Houston Women's Caucus for Art (pres. 1985, curator "Ex-Officio Exhbn." 1992), Art League Houston. Avocations: kayaking, swimming, hiking, gardening. Office: Studio Eleven 1111 East Fwy Houston TX 77002-1108

SWANSBURG, RUSSELL CHESTER, medical administrator educator; b. Cambridge, Mass., Aug. 6, 1928; s. William W. and Mary A. (Pierce) S.; m. Laurel Swansburg, Sept. 1951; children: Philip Wayne, Michael Gary, Richard Jeffrey. Diploma, N.S. Hosp. Sch. Nursing, 1950; BSN, Western Res. U., 1952; MA in Edn., Columbia U., 1961; PhD, U. Miss., 1984. CNAA. Asst. adminstr. U. of S. Ala. Med. Ctr., Mobile; v.p. U. South Ala., Mobile; prof. Auburn U., Montgomery, Ala., Med. Coll. of Ga., Augusta; mil. cons. USAF Surgeon Gen., 1972; sr. med. svc. cons., 1973-76; nurse cons. VA Med. Ctr., Tuskegee, Ala., 1987-88; mem. editl. adv. bd. Nursing Adminstrn. Manual. Author: Team Nursing: A Programmed Learning Experience, 1968, Inservice Education, 1968, The Measurement of Vital Signs, 1970, The Team Plan, 1971, Management of Patient Care Services, 1976, Strategic Career Planning and Development, 1984, The Nurse Manager's Guide to Financial Management, 1988, Management and Leadership for Nurse Managers, 1990, 2d edit. 1996, Introductory Management and Leadership for Clinical Nurses, 1993, Staff Development: A Component of Human Resource Development, 1994, Budgeting and Financial Management for Nurse Managers, 1996, (audiovisual course) Nurses & Patients: An Introduction to Nursing Management, 1980; contbr. articles to profl. publs. Bd. dirs. Air Force Village Found., Alzheimer's Care and Research Ctr. Found. Col. USAF, 1956-76. Decorated Legion of Merit. Fellow AONE, Ala. Orgn. Nurse Exec's. (past state pres.); mem. Council Grad. Edn. Adminstrn. in Nursing (sec.), Ala. Acad. Sci., Sigma Xi, Phi Kappa Phi, Sigma Theta Tau. Home and Office: 4917 Ravenswood Dr Apt 1711 San Antonio TX 78227-4356

SWANSEN, DONNA MALONEY, landscape designer, consultant; b. Green Bay, Wis., July 8, 1931; d. Arthur Anthony and Ella Marie Rose (Warner) Maloney; m. Samuel Theodore Swansen, June 27, 1959; children: Jessica Swansen Bonelli, Theodor Arthur Swansen, Christopher Currie Swansen. AS in Integrated Liberal Studies, U. Wis., 1956; AS in Landscape Design, Temple U., 1982. Bridal cons. Richard W. Burnham's, Green Bay, 1951-54, 57-58; asst., buyer Shreve Crump & Low, Boston, 1958-59; buyer Harry S. Manchester, Madison, Wis., 1959-62; ptnr. Corson Borie & Swansen, Ambler, Pa., 1976, Swansen & Borie, Ambler, 1977-82; owner, operator Donna Swansen/Design, Ambler, 1983—; v.p. Energy Islands Internat. Inc., East Troy, Wis., 1963-94. Editor: Internat. Directory Landscape Designers, 1993. Mem. search com. for chair dept. landscape architecture and horticulture Temple U., 1987, curriculum rev. com., 1993; mem. Gwynedd (Pa.) Monthly Meeting of Friends (Quakers), 1974—; Dem. candidate for judge elections, 1988; co-founder Friends of Rising Sun, Ambler, Ambler Area Arts Alliance, 1975-76; founder, 1st pres. Plant Ambler, 1973-83; mem. adv. com. Green Bay Bot. Garden, 1993—; chair Temple U. Exhibit, Do It, Dig It. Recipient Key to the Borough, Borough of Ambler, 1972; winner urban beautification project Roadside Coun. Am., Ambler, 1975, award of Distinction Assn. Profl. Landscape Designers, 1996, Athena award Wissahickon Valley C. of C., 1996; entry named Best in Show Pa. Hort. Soc., Phila., 1987. Mem. Assn. Profl. Landscape Designers (cert., co-founder, 1st pres. 1989-91, bd. dirs. 1989-95, 1st pres. Landscape Design Network Phila. 1978-85), Sigma Lambda Alpha. Avocations: putting people and plants together, encouraging women, travel, gardening. Home and Office: 221 Morris Rd Ambler PA 19002

SWANSEN, SAMUEL THEODORE, lawyer; b. Milw., June 6, 1937; s. Theodore Lawrence and Clarinda Dingwall (Crittenden) S.; m. Donna Rae Elizabeth Maloney, June 27, 1959; children: Jessica Swansen Bonelli, Theodor Arthur, Christopher Currie. AB, Dartmouth Coll., 1959; LLB, U. Wis., 1962. Bar: Wis. 1962, Pa. 1964, U.S. Supreme Ct. 1969; accredited estate planner Nat. Assn. Estate Planners and Couns. Law clk. to presiding justice Wis. Supreme Ct., Madison, 1962-63; assoc. Dechert, Price & Rhoads, Phila., 1963-68, 70-73, ptnr., 1973-93; asst. dist. atty. City of Phila. Dist. Atty.'s Office, 1968-70, chief frauds div., 1969; pvt. practice Phila., 1963—, Blue Bell, Pa., 1994—; adj. prof. law Temple U., Phila., 1970-80; lectr. Pa. Bar Inst., Nat. Bus. Inst., Ctr. Profl. Edn., 1985—. Editor, author U. Wis. Law Rev., 1960-62. Violinist, trombonist North Penn Symphony Orch., 1977—; mem. Gwynedd Monthly Meeting of Friends, 1974—; bd. dirs. Friends Rehab. Program, Inc., Phila., 1966-73, 85—, Franklin Found., Phila., 1969—; v.p., sec., bd. dirs. Foulkeways at Gwynedd, 1979—, pres., 1986—; chmn. bd. dirs. Friends Life Care at Home, Inc., 1990—, bd. dirs., 1985—; bd. dirs. Friends Retirement Concepts, Inc., Gwynedd, Pa., sec. bd. dirs., 1985-92; hon. bd. dirs. Friends Neighborhood Guild, Greater Phila. Fedn. Settlements; corp. mem. Anna T. Jeanes Found., Fox Chase, Phila., 1985-93, Associated Svcs. for Blind, Phila, 1974-91, Bach Festival of Phila., 1989—, pres. 1993—; dir., sec. Energy Islands Internat., Inc., 1963—; mem. Nat. Network of Estate Planning Atty., 1993, accredited estate planner Nat. Assn. of Estate Planners & Counselor, 1995—. Mem. ABA, Pa. Bar Assn., Phila. Bar Assn., Nat. Network Estate Planning Attys., Dartmouth Club Phila., Delta Upsilon, Phi Delta Phi. Republican. Mem. Soc. of Friends. Home: 221 Morris Rd Ambler PA 19002 Office: 640 Sentry Pky Ste 104 Blue Bell PA 19422-2317

SWANSON, ARNOLD ARTHUR, retired biochemistry educator; b. Rawlins, Wyo., Mar. 11, 1923; s. Arnold David and Gladys Fern (Murphy) S.; m. Florence P. Swanson; children: Kathleen, Kristine, Annabeth. BA, Duke U., 1948; MA, Trinity U., 1959; PhD, Tex. A&M U., 1961. Asst. prof. The U. Tex. Southwestern, 1963-66; assoc. prof. Baylor U. Coll. Medicine, 1963-66; prof. Tex. Women's U., 1963-65, Baylor U., Waco, Tex., 1966-68, Med. U. S.C., Charleston, 1968-94; ret., 1994. Contbr. over 250 articles to profl. jours. Recipient Alexander von Humboldt-Stiftung, Fed. Republic Germany, 1974-75. Mem. Am. Chem. Soc., AAAS, Sigma Xi. Republican. Methodist. Home: 726 Wildwood Rd Charleston SC 29412-9162 Office: Medical Univ South Carolina 171 Ashley Ave Charleston SC 29425-0001

SWANSON, AUGUST GEORGE, physician, retired association executive; b. Kearney, Nebr., Aug. 25, 1925; s. Oscar Valderman and Elnora Wilhelmina Emma (Block) S.; m. Ellyn Constance Weinel, June 28, 1947; children: Eric, Rebecca, Margaret, Emilie, Jennifer, August. BA, Westminster Coll., Fulton, Mo., 1951; MD, Harvard U., 1949; DSc (hon.), U. Nebr., 1979. Intern King County Hosp., Seattle, 1949-50; resident internal medicine U. Wash. Affiliated Hosps., 1953-55, neurology, 1955-57; resident neurology Boston City Hosp., 1958; dir. pediatric neurology, then dir. div. neurology U. Wash. Med. Sch., Seattle, 1958-67; assoc. dean acad. affairs U. Wash. Med. Sch., 1967-71; v.p. acad. affairs Assn. Am. Med. Colls., Washington, 1971-89, v.p. grad. med. edn., exec. dir. Nat. Resident Matching Program, 1989-91, ret., 1991; vis. fellow physiology Oxford (Eng.) U., 1963-64; cons. in field. Author articles brain function, physician edn., med. manpower. With USNR, 1943-46, 50-53. Markle scholar medicine, 1959-64; recipient Abraham Flexner awd. for Distinguished Service to Medical Education, Assn. of Am. Medical Coll., 1992. Mem. Inst. Medicine, Nat., Acad. Sci., Am. Neurol. Assn. Home: 3146 Portage Bay Pl E # H Seattle WA 98102-3878

SWANSON, AUSTIN DELAIN, educational administration educator; b. Jamestown, N.Y., June 11, 1930; s. Manley Moris and Beulah Marjorie (Waite) S.; m. Marilyn Jean Peterson, Mar. 31, 1956; children: Paul Delain, Karin Lorine Swanson Daun. BS, Allegheny Coll., 1952; MS, Columbia U., 1955, EdD, 1960. Tchr. Ramapo Cen. High Sch., Suffern, N.Y., 1955-58; rsch. assoc. Tchrs. Coll. Columbia U., N.Y.C., 1958-63; prof. ednl. adminstrn. SUNY, Buffalo, 1963—, chair dept. ednl. orgn.. adminstrn. and policy, 1991—; vis. scholar Inst. Edn. U. London, 1979, 93, Zold Inst., Israel, 1988. Author: Modernizing the Little Red School House, 1979, School Finance: Its Economics and Politics, 1991, 2d edit., 1996, Fundamental Concepts of Educational Leadership, 1995; contbr. articles to profl. jours. WiTh U.S. Army, 1952-54. Fellow Stanford U., 1969-70; Fulbright scholar U. Melbourne, Australia, 1986. Mem. Am. Ednl. Rsch. Assn., Am. Edn. Fin. Assn., Politics of Edn. Assn., Phi Delta Kappa. Republican. Lutheran. Office: SUNY Grad Sch Edn Buffalo NY 14260

SWANSON, BERNET STEVEN, consulting engineer, former educator; b. Chgo., Nov. 20, 1921; s. Bernet Stephanie and Emma (Conrad) S.; m. Lucile A. Clapham, June 12, 1948; children—Brian Bernet, David Herbert. BS, Armour Inst. Tech., 1942; MS, Ill. Inst. Tech., 1944, PhD, 1950. Mem. faculty Ill. Inst. Tech., Chgo., 1950-85; prof. chem. engring. Ill. Inst. Tech., 1960-85, head dept., 1967-85; cons. engr., 1944—. Author: Electronic Analog Computer, 1965. Mem. Am. Inst. Chem. Engrs., Instrument Soc. Am., Am. Soc. Engring. Edn., Sigma Xi, Alpha Chi Sigma, Phi Lambda Upsilon. Home: 2n151 Swift Rd Lombard IL 60148-1185 Office: 3300 S Federal St Chicago IL 60616-3732

SWANSON, CHARLES ANDREW, mathematics educator; b. Bellingham, Wash., July 11, 1929; s. Clarence Otto and Esther (Hougen) S.; m. Carolyn Marie Dennis, Aug. 5, 1957; children—Laird Randall, Denise Claire. BA, U. B.C., 1951, MA, 1953; PhD, Cal. Inst. Tech., 1957. Prof. U. B.C., Vancouver, 1957-94, prof. emeritus math., 1994—. Author: An Introduction to Differential Calculus, 1962, Comparison and Oscillation Theory of Linear Differential Equations, 1968; Contbr. articles to tech., profl. jours. Office: U British Columbia, Dept Math, Vancouver, BC Canada V6T 1Z2

SWANSON, DAVID HEATH, agricultural company executive; b. Aurora, Ill., Nov. 3, 1942; s. Neil H. and Helen J. (McKendry) S.; children: Benjamin Heath, Matthew Banford. B.A., Harvard U., 1964; M.A., U. Chgo., 1969. Account exec. 1st Nat. Bank Chgo., 1967-69; dep. mgr. Brown Bros. Harriman & Co., N.Y.C., 1969-72; asst. treas. Borden, Inc., N.Y.C., 1972-75; v.p., treas. Continental Grain Co., N.Y.C., 1975-77, v.p., CFO, 1977-79, gen. mgr. European div., 1979-81, exec. v.p. and gen. mgr. World Grain div., 1981-83, corp. sr. v.p., chief fin. and adminstrv. officer, 1983-86, group pres., 1985-86; pres., CEO Cen. Soya, Ft. Wayne, Ind., 1986-93; chmn. Premiere Agri Tech., Inc., Ft. Wayne, 1994—; chmn., CEO Explorer Nutrition Group, N.Y.C., 1995-96; pres., CEO, Countrymark Coop., Inc., Indpls., 1996—; mem. adv. bd. U.S. Export-Import Bank, 1985-86; mem. Gov.'s Agrl. Bd. Ind.; bd. dirs. Fiduciary Trust Internat., Conrail. Mem. Internat. Policy Coun. on Agr. and Trade; mem. adv. bd. Purdue U. Agr. Sch.; mem. Gov.'s Econ. Devel. Ind. Bd.; bd. govs. Exec. Coun. on Fgn. Diplomats and U.S. Agr. Libr.; gov. Found. for U.S. Constn. Mem. Coun. Fgn. Rels., Nat. Assn. Mfrs. (bd. dirs.), Ind. C. of C. (bd. dirs.), Am. Alpine Club (bd. dirs.), Links Club, Racquet and Tennis Club, Explorers Club (bd. dirs., sec., pres.). Republican. Congregationalist. Office: Countrymark Coop Inc 950 N Meridian St Indianapolis IN 46204-3909

SWANSON, DAVID H(ENRY), economist, educator; b. Anoka, Minn., Nov. 1, 1930; s. Henry Otto and Louise Isabell (Holiday) S.; m. Suzanne Nash, Jan. 19, 1952 (dec. Sept. 1990); children: Matthew David, Christopher James; m. Joanne Perkins, Feb. 1, 1991. BA, St. Cloud State U., 1953; MA, U. Minn., 1955, PhD, Iowa State U., 1987. CPCU. Economist area devel. dept. No. States Power Co., Mpls., 1955-56, staff asst., v.p. sales, 1956-57, economist indsl. devel. dept., 1957-63; dir. area devel. dept. Iowa So. Utilities Co., Centerville, 1963-67, dir. econ. R & D, 1967-70; dir. New Orleans Econ. Devel. Coun., 1970-72; div. mgr. Kaiser Aetna Texas, New Orleans, 1972-73; dir. corp. rsch. United Svcs. Automobile Assn., San Antonio, 1973-76; pres. Lantern Corp., 1974-79; adminstr. bus. devel. State of Wis., Madison, 1976-78; dir. Ctr. Indsl. Rsch. and Svc., Iowa State U., Ames, 1978-89, mem. mktg. faculty Coll. Bus. Adminstrn., 1979-85; dir. Iowa Devel. Commn., 1982-83; mem. adv. bd. Iowa Venture Capital Fund, 1985-88; dir. Applied Strategies Internat. Ltd., 1983-88; dir. econ. devel. lab. Ga. Inst. Tech., Atlanta, 1989-93; adv. bd. Nat. Tech. Transfer Ctr., 1992—; exec. on loan Nat. Inst. of Stds. and Tech., 1993—; chmn. Iowa Curriculum Assistance System, 1984-85. Mem. Iowa Airport Planning Coun., 1968-70; mem. adv. coun. office Comprehensive Health Planning, 1967-70; mem. adv. coun. Ctr. Indsl. Rsch. and Svc., 1967-70, New Orleans Met. Area Com., 1972-73; mem. Iowa Dist. Export Coun., 1978-88; mem. Atlanta Dist. Export Coun., 1989—; mem. region 7 adv. coun. SBA, 1978-88; dir. Mid-Continent R&D Council, 1980-84; chmn. Iowa del. White House Conf. on Small Bus., 1980; chmn. Gov.'s Task Force on High Tech., 1982-83; chmn. Iowa High Tech. Coun., 1983-86; adv. com. U. New Orleans, 1971-73; county fin. chmn. Rep. Party, 1966-67; bd. dirs. Greater New Orleans Urban League, 1970-73, Indsl. Policy Coun., 1984-88; mem. Iowa Gov.'s Export Coun., 1984-89; v.p. Iowa Sister State Friendship Com., 1985-87, pres. 1988; chmn. nat. adv. coun. Fed. lab. Consortium, 1985—, Ga. Tech. Faculty Assembly, 1990-92. Served with USAF, 1951-52. Mem. Am. Indsl. Ext. Alliance (pres. 1992-96), Nat. Assn. Mgmt. Tech. Assistance Ctrs. (pres. 1985, bd. dirs. 1982-86), Tech. Transfer Soc. (bd. dirs. 1984-94, v.p. 1987-90, pres.-elect 1991-92, pres. 1992-93), Oak Ridge Associated Univs. (tech. transfer adv. coun. 1992-95), Ga. Fin. Developers Assn., Ga. 2000, Profl. Developers Assn., Nat. Univ. Continuing Edn. Assn., Internat. Coun. Small Bus., Rotary (bd. dirs. 1986-88), Toastmasters (past pres.). Episcopalian. Home: 104 Hart Rd Gaithersburg MD 20878-5681 Office: Nat Inst Standards and Tech Step Program Gaithersburg MD 20899

SWANSON, DAVID PAUL, accountant; b. Everett, Wash., Nov. 27, 1945; s. Lloyd E. and Electa A. (McFarland) S.; m. Barbara J. Clough, Feb. 25, 1968 (div. Sept. 1977); children: Elizabeth, Devin; m. Linda Diane Westby, Dec. 4, 1995. BA, Western Wash. U., 1968; MBA, City U., Seattle, 1984. CPA, Wash. With Everett Trust Bank, 1968-70, Security Bank, Portland, Oreg., 1970-71; mgr. Herfys, Seattle, 1971-73, Chuckwagon Restaurant, Seattle, Aberdeen, Wash., 1973-74, Yukon Jacks, Seattle, 1974-76; acctg. specialist Data I/O, Bellevue, Wash., 1977-83; acctg. and tax mgr. Balance Sheet Acctg. Svcs. Inc., Lynnwood, Wash., 1983—; pres. Delta Pacific Securites Inc., Everett, Wash., 1989—; instr. City U., 1986-90; treas., bd. dirs. Log C Corp., Everett, 1987—; pres., bd. dirs. Delta Pacific Securities, Everett, 1989—; corp. cont. Black Mountain Escrow, San Diego, 1990—. Bd. dirs. Everett Drug Abuse Coun., 1984-87, J-Bird Ranch, Everett, 1991—; bd. dirs., pres. Evergreen Manor, 1987—; bd. dirs., treas. Big Bros. and Big Sisters, Everett, 1988-92. Mem. Nat. Fedn. Ind. Bus., Inst. Bus. Appraisers, Wash. State Soc. CPA's, Sons of Norway, South Snohomish County Chamber, Northshore C. of C. Avocations: bowling, hiking, reading, travel, biking. Office: Delta Pacific Securities Inc PO Box 2543 Everett WA 98203

SWANSON, DON RICHARD, university dean; b. L.A., Oct. 10, 1924; s. Harry Windfield and Grace Clara (Sandstrom) S.; m. Patricia Elizabeth Klick, Aug. 22, 1976; children—Douglas Alan, Richard Brian, Judith Ann. BS, Calif. Inst. Tech., 1945; MA, Rice U., 1947; PhD, U. Calif., Berkeley, 1952. Physicist U. Calif. Radiation Lab., Berkeley, 1947-52, Hughes Research and devel. Labs., Culver City, Calif., 1952-55; research scientist TRW, Inc., Canoga Park, Calif., 1955-63; prof. Grad. Library Sch., U. Chgo., 1963—, dean, 1963-72, 77-79, 86-90; mem. Sci. Info. Council, NSF, 1960-65; mem. toxicology info. panel Pres.'s Sci. Advisory Com., 1964-66; mem. library vis. com. Mass. Inst. Tech., 1966-71; mem. com. on sci. and tech. communication Nat. Acad. Scis., 1966-69. Editor: The Intellectual Founds. of Library Education, 1965, The Role of Libraries in the Growth of Knowledge, 1980; co-editor: Operations Research: Implications for Libraries, 1972, Management Education: Implications for Libraries and Library Schools, 1974; mem. editorial bd.: Library Quarterly, 1963—; Contbr.: chpt. to Ency. Brit, 1968—; sci. articles to profl. jours. Trustee Nat. Opinion Research Center, 1964-73; Research fellow Chgo. Inst. for Psychoanalysis, 1972-76. Served with USNR, 1943-46. Mem. Am. Soc. for Info. Sci. Home: 5825 S Dorchester Ave Apt 14E Chicago IL 60637-1701 Office: U Chgo Divsn Humanities 1010 E 59th St Chicago IL 60637-1512 *Problems I wish I could solve: how the universe got started, how volition arose in a heap of molecules, how to find information in a library, and how to sum up life in a sentence or two.*

SWANSON, DONALD ALAN, geologist; b. Tacoma, July 25, 1938; s. Leonard Walter and Edith Christine (Bowers) S.; m. Barbara Joan White, May 25, 1974. BS in Geology, Wash. State U., 1960; PhD in Geology, Johns Hopkins U., 1964. Geologist U.S. Geol. Survey, Menlo Park, Calif., 1965-68, 71-80, Hawaii National Park, 1968-71; sr. geologist Cascades Volcano Obs. U.S. Geol. Survey, Vancouver, Wash., 1980-90, rsch. scientist-in-charge, 1986-89; sr. geologist U.S. Geol. Survey, Seattle, 1990—; assoc. dir. Volcano Systems Ctr. U. Wash., 1993—; affiliate prof. U. Wash., 1992—; cons. U.S. Dept. Energy, Richland, Wash., 1979-83; volcanologist New Zealand Geol. Survey, Taupo, 1984; advisor Colombian Volcano Obs., Manizales, 1986. Assoc. editor Jour. Volcanology and Geothermal Rsch., 1976—, Jour. Geophys. Rsch., 1992-94; editor Bull. of Volcanology, 1985-90, exec. editor, 1995—; contbr. numerous articles to profl. jours. Recipient Superior Service award U.S. Geol. Survey, 1980, Meritorious Service award U.S. Dept. Interior, 1985; postdoctoral fellow NATO, 1964-65. Fellow Geol. Soc. Am.; mem. AAAS, Am. Geophys. Union, Sigma Xi. Avocation: hiking. Home: 7537 34th Ave NE Seattle WA 98115-4802 Office: U Washington US Geol Survey Geol Scis Box 351310 Seattle WA 98195-1310

SWANSON, DONALD FREDERICK, retired food company executive; b. Mpls., Aug. 6, 1927; s. Clayton A. and Irma (Baiocchi) S.; m. Virginia Clare Hannah, Dec. 17, 1948; children—Donald Frederick, Cynthia Hannah Lindgren, Janet Clare Webster. B.A., U. Minn., 1948. With Gen. Mills, Inc., 1949-85, div. v.p., dir. marketing flour, dessert and baking mixes, 1964-65, v.p., gen. mgr. grocery products div., 1965-68, v.p., corporate adminstrn. officer consumer foods group, fashion div., transp. and purchasing depts., advt. and marketing services, 1969, exec. v.p. craft, game and toy group, fashion group, direct marketing group, travel group, dir., 1968-76, sr. exec. v.p. consumer non-foods, 1976-85, chief financial officer, 1977-79, sr. exec. v.p. restaurants and consumer non-foods, 1980-81, vice chmn. restaurants and consumer non-foods, 1981-85; ret. chmn. bd. Soo Line Corp.; bd. dirs. Costume Jewelry Group. Served with AUS, 1946-47. Mem. Lafayette Club, Mpls. Club, Wayzata Country Club, Royal Poinciana Golf Club, Phi Kappa Psi. Home: 2171 Gulf Shore Blvd N Naples FL 34102-9999 Office: 641 Lake St E Wayzata MN 55391-1760

SWANSON, EMILY, state legislator; b. Oak Park, Ill., Jan. 12, 1947; m. Tim Swanson; 2 children. BA, Bennington Coll.; MA, U. Calif., Berkeley. Mem. Mont. Ho. of Reps. Home: 15042 Kelly Canyon Rd Bozeman MT 59715-9625 Office: Mont Ho of Reps State Capitol Helena MT 59620*

SWANSON, ERIK CHRISTIAN, museum director; b. Breckenridge, Colo., June 17, 1940; s. Glen Leonard and Eveitte Leona (Snell) S.; m. Elizabeth Jane Thompson, Aug. 22, 1976; children: Johannah Elizabeth, Nils Christian. Student, Royal U., Lund, Sweden, 1960-64; BA in History, German Lang., 1976, cert., U. No. Colo. Curator South Pk. City Mus., Fairplay, Colo., 1974-89; dir. Alma (Colo.) Fire House Mus., 1976-82; exec. dir. Cripple Creek (Colo.) Dist. Mus., 1988—. With U.S. Army, 1966-68. Mem. Odd Fellows (grand 1988-89), Masons (sr. warden Cripple Creek chpt. 1995), Elks. Republican. Home: 101 North Pine St Box #27 Alma CO 80420 Office: Cripple Creek Dist Mus PO Box 1210 Cripple Creek CO 80813

SWANSON, GILLIAN LEE, law librarian; b. Bozeman, Mont., Sept. 13, 1961; d. Garry Arthur and Betty Ellen (McIelwain) S.; m. Thomas Darryl Fox, June 23, 1990. BA in Philosophy, U. Calgary, Alta., Can., 1985; LLB, U. Western Ont., London, Ontario, Can., 1988. Bar: Ont. 1991. Student-at-law Harris, Barr, St. Catharine's, Ont., 1989-90; law libr. Banc One Corp., Columbus, Ohio, 1993—. Vol. tutor ESL Ohio State U. Students' Wives, Columbus Pub. Schs., 1991—; vol. Interfaith Refugee Svcs. Ohio, 1995—. Mem. Law Soc. Upper Can. Avocation: Canadian and American immigration and refugee legal and social issues. Home: 100 E Henderson Rd Columbus OH 43214 Office: Banc One Corp 100 E Broad St Columbus OH 43271-0152

SWANSON, KARIN, hospital administrator, consultant; b. New Britain, Conn., Dec. 8, 1942; d. Oake F. and Ingrid Lauren Swanson; m. B. William Dorsey, June 26, 1965 (div. 1974); children: Matthew W., Julie I., Alison K.; m. Sanford H. Low, Oct. 14, 1989. BA in Biology, Middlebury Coll., 1964; MPH, Yale U., 1981. Biology tchr. Kents Hill (Maine) Sch., 1964-66; laboratory instr. Bates Coll., Lewiston, Maine, 1974-78; asst. to gen. dir. Mass. Eye and Ear Infirmary, Boston, 1979-80; v.p. profl. services Portsmouth (N.H.) Hosp., 1981-83; v.p. Health Strategy Assn. Ltd., Chestnut Hill, Mass., 1983-85; v.p. med. affairs Cen. Maine Med. Ctr., Lewiston, 1986-89; health care mgmt. cons. Cambridge, Mass., 1989-91; CEO Hahnemann Hosp., Brighton, Mass., 1991-94; adminstr. Vencor Hosp., Boston, 1994-95; pres., CEO The Laser Inst. New Eng., Newton, Mass., 1996—. Mem. Phi Beta Kappa. Avocations: reading, gardening, walking. Home: 198 Glen St Natick MA 01760-5606

SWANSON, LESLIE KEATING, financial services executive; b. Wilmington, Del., Sept. 27, 1952. BS, U. Del., 1974, postgrad., 1980-83. Registered securities broker and ins. broker. Registered securities broker Merrill Lynch Pierce Fenner & Smith, Wilmington, 1984-89; corp. svcs. specialist Dean Witter Reynolds, Phila., 1989—. Avocations: tennis, skiing, painting. Home: PO Box 4046 Wilmington DE 19807-0046 Office: Dean Witter Reynolds Two Logan Sq 18th And The Pky Philadelphia PA 19103-1199

SWANSON, LLOYD OSCAR, former savings and loan association executive; b. Mpls., June 26, 1913; s. Carl G. and Ellen (Peterson) S.; m. Eileen E. Hedlof, Mar. 29, 1958; children: Marcia L. (Mrs. Joseph Massee), Paul L., J. Bradley, Craig R. Student, U. Minn., 1930-31; B.A., Gustavus Adolphus Coll., 1935, L.H.D. (hon.), 1968. Dir. admissions and pub. relations Gustavus Adolphus Coll., 1935-37; spl. agt. John Hancock Life Ins. Co., Mpls., 1937-42; gen. agt. Nat. Life Ins. Co., Mpls., 1942-62; pres. First Fed. Savs. and Loan Assn., Mpls., 1962-77; chmn. bd. First Fed. Savs. and Loan Assn., 1967-84; chmn. bd. dirs. The Security Corp., 1967-84; dir. Soderberg Optical Co., St. Paul. Former trustee, chmn. bd. trustees Gustavus Adolphus Coll., St. Peter, Minn.; trustee Greater Gustavus Fund, 1952—; former chmn. bd. pensions Luth. Ch. in Am.; former chmn. bd. trustees Fairview Cmty. Hosps. Mem. Savs. League Minn. (dir., pres. 1970), Swedish Coun. Am. (mem. bd.), Athletic Club, Interlachen Country Club (past mem. bd. govs.), Royal Poinciana Golf Club (Naples, Fla.). Home: 2171 Gulf Shore Blvd N Naples FL 33940-4694 Office: 4900 IDS Tower Minneapolis MN 55402

SWANSON, LORNA ELLEN, physical therapist, athletic trainer, researcher; b. Bridgeport, Conn., July 22, 1954; d. Harold Carl and Marna Ellyn (French) S.; m. James M. Kelley, Oct. 16, 1993; 1 child, Ellen Elizabeth Kelley. BFA in Dance, So. Meth. U., 1975, MFA in Dance, 1978; BS in Phys. Therapy, U. Tex., Dallas, 1984; PhD in Exercise Sci., U. Tenn., 1994. Lic. phys. therapist, Tenn. Mem. faculty Brookhaven Coll., Dallas, 1982-84; staff therapist St. Mary's Med. Ctr., Knoxville, Tenn., 1984-85, Ft. Sanders Regional Med. Ctr., Knoxville, 1985-86, Knoxville Sports Therapy, 1991-92; program dir., mem. faculty Roane State C.C., Harriman, Tenn., 1987-92; clin. specialist Ft. Sanders Ctr. for Sports Medicine, Knoxville, 1992-93, mgr., 1994-96; clin. specialist dir. clin. and cont. edn. Fort Sanders Therapy Ctr. West, Knoxville, 1996—; grad. asst. athletic dept. U. Tenn., Knoxville, 1989-91; reviewer Jour. Orthopedic and Sports Phys. Therapy, 1993, 94; adj. faculty mem. Pellissippi State Tech. C.C., 1994; presenter in field. Contbr. chpt. to book and articles to profl. jours. Ballet mistress Victoria Bolen Dance Theatre, Knoxville, 1986-88; mem. bd. of trust Appalachian Ballet Co. Mem. Am. Phys. Therapy Assn. (bd. content experts 1990-93), Tenn. Phys. Therapy Assn., Nat. Athletic Tng. Assn. (cert. athletic trainer), Tenn. Athletic Tng. Assn., Nat. Strength and Conditioning Assn. (cert. specialist), Neurodevel. Treatment Assn. (nominating com. 1987-89). Democrat. Lutheran. Avocations: music, sports, reading, dance, choreography. Office: Ft Sanders Therapy Ctr West 200 Fort Sanders W Blvd Ste 204 Knoxville TN 37922-3355

SWANSON, NORMA FRANCES, federal agency administrator; b. Blue Island, Ill., Oct. 24, 1923; d. Arnold Raymond and Bessie Oween (Bewley) Brown; m. George Clair Swanson, Mar. 18, 1948; 1 child, Dane Craig. AB, Asbury Coll., 1946; BS cum laude, Eastern Nazarene Coll., Wollaston, Mass., 1970; MA cum laude, Ind. Christian U., 1986. Confidential asst. dep. undersec. interagy. intergovt. affairs U.S. Dept. Edn., Washington, 1981—; pres. Window to the World, Inc., Schroon Lake, N.Y., 1985—; asst. dir. edn. Commn. Bicentennial U.S. Constn., Washington, 1987—; dir. Horizons Plus

Values Program Hampton Roads Va. Detention Homes; dir. Project Fresh Start Washington D.C. Pub. Sch., 1993-96; cons. Conf. Industrialized Nations, Williamsburg, Va., 1982, Nellie Thomas Inst. Learning, Monterey, Calif., 1981-82. Author: Dear Teenager, A Teen's Guide to Correct Social Behavior, 1987, A Constitution is Born, A Teacher's Guide to Resource Materials, 1987, Sunlights and More, Bright Beginnings, 1993, Vol. II, 1996, The Ones that Count and Other Stories with Values to Live By, 1994, A Think and Write Journal Sunlights and More Vol. II, 1996; editor: (anthology) Horizons Plus; developer ednl. materials; theorem artist Early Life mag., 1974. Bd. regents Ind. Christian U., 1986—; program dir. Tidewater (Va.) Outreach, 1992; dir. project Fresh Start, Washington Pub. Sch., 1993-94; dir. youth outreach with values program U.S. Dept. Juvenile Justice, 1992-93. Recipient J.C. Penney award for volunteerism, 1993, Precision Tune awrd for svc. tto Washington Inner-City Schs. Republican. Baptist. Avocation: theorem painting. Home: 704 D Spyglass Way Lexington Park MD 20653 also: 18047 Cross Manor Rd Saint Inigoes MD 20684

SWANSON, PATRICIA K., university official; b. St. Louis, May 8, 1940; d. Emil Louis and Patricia (McNair) Klick; 1 child, Ivan Clatanoff. BS in Edn., U. Mo., 1962; postgrad., Cornell U., 1963; MLS, Simmons Coll., 1967. Reference librarian Simmons Coll., Boston, 1967-68; reference librarian U. Chgo., 1970-79, sr. lectr. Grad. Library Sch., 1974-83, 86-88, head reference service, 1979-83, asst. dir. for sci. libraries, 1983-93, acting asst. dir. for tech. svcs., 1987-88, assoc. provost, 1993—; project dir. Office Mgmt. Svcs., Assn. Rsch. Librs., 1982-83; speaker in field; cons. on libr. mgmt., planning and space. Author: Great is the Gift that Bringeth Knowledge: Highlights from the History of the John Crerar Library, 1989; contbr. articles to profl. jours. Office: U of Chicago Office of the Provost 5801 S Ellis Ave Rm 501 Chicago IL 60637-1404

SWANSON, PAUL RUBERT, minister; b. Bakersfield, Calif., May 13, 1943; s. Roland Hilding and Myrtle Isabelle (Magnuson) S.; m. Mary Elizabeth Greene, June 18, 1967; children: Kristen Ann, Karlynn Marie, Jonathan Paul. BA, Pacific Luth. U., 1966; MDiv, Luth. Sch. Theology, 1970. Ordained minister, Luth. Ch. Pastor 1st Luth. Ch., Anaconda, Mont., 1970-76, King of Kings Luth. Ch., Milwaukie, Oreg., 1976-84; asst. to bishop Pacific N.W. Synod-Luth. Ch. in Am., Portland, Oreg., 1984-87; bishop Oreg. Synod-Evang. Luth. Ch. Am., Portland, 1987—; bd. dirs. Legacy Health System, Portland. Regent Pacific Luth. U., Tacoma, 1987—; bd. dirs. Emanuel Hosp., Portland, 1987; chmn. bd. dirs. Hearthstone, Inc., Anaconda, 1973-76; bd. dirs. Ecumenical Ministries Oreg., Portland, 1984—. Recipient Disting. Svc. award Pacific Luth. U., 1993. Avocation: golf.

SWANSON, PEGGY EUBANKS, finance educator; b. Ivanhoe, Tex., Dec. 29, 1936; d. Leslie Samuel and Mary Lee (Reid) Eubanks; m. B. Marc Sommers, Nov. 10, 1993. BBA, U. North Tex., 1957, M. Bus. Edn., 1965; MA in Econs., So. Meth. U., 1967, PhD in Econs., 1978. Instr. El Centro Coll., Dallas, 1967-69, 71-78, bus. div. chmn., 1969-71; asst. prof. econs. U. Tex., Arlington, 1978-79, asst. prof. fin., 1979-84, assoc. prof., 1984-86, chmn. dept. fin. and real estate, 1986-88, prof. fin., 1987—; expert witness various law firms, primarily Tex. and Calif., 1978—; cons. Internat. Edn. Program, 1992—; curriculum cons. U. Monterrey, Mexico, 1995. Contbr. articles to profl. jours. Vol. Am. Cancer Soc., Dallas, Arlington, 1981—, Meals on Wheels, Arlington, 1989—; mem. adv. bd. Ryan/Reilly Ctr. for Urban Land Utilization, Arlington, 1986-88. Mem. Fin. Exec. Inst. (chmn. acad. rels. 1987-88), Internat. Bus. Steering Com. (chmn. 1989-91), Am. Fin. Assn., Am. Econ. Assn., Fin. Mgmt. Assn. (hon. faculty mem. Nat. Honor Soc. 1985-86), Southwestern Fin. Assn. (program com. 1987-88), Acad. of Internat. Bus. (program com. 1992-95), Phi Beta Delta (membership com. 1987-89). Republican. Episcopalian. Avocations: tennis, gardening. Home: 4921 Bridgewater Dr Arlington TX 76017-2729 Office: U Tex at Arlington UTA Box 19449 Arlington TX 76019

SWANSON, PHILLIP DEAN, neurologist; b. Seattle, Oct. 1, 1932; s. William Dean and Kathryn C. (Peterson) S.; m. Sheila N. Joardar, Apr. 20, 1957; children: Stephen, Jennifer, Kathryn, Rebecca, Sara. B.S., Yale U., 1954; student, U. Heidelberg, 1952-53; M.D., Johns Hopkins U., 1958; Ph.D. in Biochemistry, U. London, 1964. Intern Harvard med. svc. Boston City Hosp., 1958-59; resident in neurology Johns Hopkins Hosp., Balt. City Hosp., 1959-62; asst. prof. U. Wash. Sch. Medicine, Seattle, 1964-68; assoc. prof. U. Wash. Sch. Medicine, 1968-73, prof., 1973—, head divsn. neurology, 1967-95; mem. med. adv. bd. Puget Sound chpt. Nat. Multiple Sclerosis Soc., 1967—, chmn., 1970-74; mem. com. to combat Huntington's Disease Nat. Sci. Council, 1975-84. Author: (with others) Introduction to Clinical Neurology, 1976; editor: Signs and Symptoms in Neurology, 1984; contbr. articles to profl. jours. NIH spl. fellow, 1962-64; NIH grantee. Fellow Am. Acad. Neurology; mem. Am. Neurol. Assn., Assn. Univ. Profs. Neurology (pres. 1975-76), Am. Heart Assn., Am. Soc. Neurochemistry, Internat. Soc. Neurochemistry, Biochem. Soc. (London), Am. Soc. Clin. Investigation (emeritus). Home: 6537 29th Ave NE Seattle WA 98115-7234 Office: U Wash Sch Medicine Dept Neurology Seattle WA 98195

SWANSON, RICHARD WILLIAM, statistician; b. Rockford, Ill., July 26, 1934; s. Richard and Erma Marie (Herman) S.; m. Laura Yoko Arai, Dec. 30, 1970. BS, Iowa State U., 1958, MS, 1964. Ops. analyst Stanford Rsch. Inst., Monterey, Calif., 1958-62; statistician ARINC Rsch. Corp., Washington, 1964-65; sr. scientist Booz-Allen Applied Rsch., Vietnam, 1965-67, L.A., 1967-68; sr. ops. analyst Control Data Corp., Honolulu, 1968-70; mgmt. cons., Honolulu, 1970-73; exec. v.p. SEQUEL Corp., Honolulu, 1973-75; bus. cons. Hawaii Dept. Planning and Econ. Devel., Honolulu, 1975-77, tax rsch. and planning officer Dept. Taxation, 1977-82; ops. rsch. analyst U.S. Govt., 1982-89; shipyard statistician U.S. Govt., 1989—. Served with AUS, 1954-56. Mem. Hawaiian Acad. Sci., Sigma Xi. Home: 583 Kamoku St Apt 3505 Honolulu HI 96826-5240 Office: Pearl Harbor Naval Shipyard PO Box 400 Honolulu HI 96809-0400

SWANSON, ROBERT DRAPER, college president; b. Sioux City, Iowa, Aug. 6, 1915; s. Alfred and Tida Ruth (Draper) S.; m. Roberta B. Clements, May 5, 1941 (dec. Oct. 1975); children: Sara Louise, Mark Robert; m. Dorothy B. Howe, Aug. 4, 1979. A.B., Park Coll., 1937; student, U. Iowa, 1937; B.D., McCormick Theol. Sem., 1941; D.D., James Millikin U., 1950; L.H.D., Tusculum Coll., 1966, Olivet Coll., 1971, Central Mich. U., 1979, Alma Coll., 1981; LL.D., Hillsdale Coll., 1968, Hope Coll., 1981. Dir. athletics, phys. edn. Park Coll., 1937-38; ordained to ministry Presbyn. Ch., 1941; pastor Second Presbyn. Ch., Tulsa, 1941-45; dean of students McCormick Sem., 1946-47, v.p., prof. preaching, 1948-56; pres. Alma Coll., 1956-80, pres. emeritus, 1980—; dir. Gen. Telephone Co. Mich. Served as lt. (j.g.), Chaplain's Corps USNR, 1945-46. Recipient Disting. Alumnus award McCormick Theol. Sem., 1981. Mem. Phi Beta Kappa. Club: Rotary (Alma). Home: 4105 Riverview Dr Alma MI 48801-9563

SWANSON, ROBERT KILLEN, management consultant; b. Deadwood, S.D., Aug. 11, 1932; s. Robert Claude and Marie Elizabeth (Kersten) S.; m. Nancy Anne Oyaas, July 19, 1958; children: Cathryn Lynn, Robert Stuart, Bart Killen. BA, U. S.D., 1954; postgrad., U. Melbourne, Australia, 1955. With Gen. Mills, Inc., Mpls., 1955-58, 71-79, v.p., 1971-73, group v.p., 1973-77, exec. v.p., 1977-79; with Marathon Oil Co., Findlay, Ohio, 1958-60; sr. v.p., dir. Needham, Harper & Steers, Inc., Chgo., 1961-69; joint mng. dir. S. H. Benson (Holdings) Ltd., Eng., 1969-71; pres., chief operating officer Greyhound Corp., Phoenix, 1980; chmn., chief exec. officer Del E. Webb Corp., Phoenix, 1981-87; chmn. RKS Inc., Phoenix, 1987—; bd. dirs. Am. S.W. Concepts Inc., Ariz. Desert Seguaro, Thunsley Group; chmn. Grossman's Inc., Boston, 1994—, U.S. Games, Inc., Atlanta, 1994—. Bd. dirs. Univ. S.D. Found. 2d lt. U.S. Army, 1955. Fulbright scholar, 1954-55; Woodrow Wilson scholar. Mem. U.S. Coun. Fgn. Rels., U.K. Dirs. Inst., U.S. Internat. Scholars Assn., English Speaking Union. Episcopalian. Home and Office: RKS Inc 5600 N Palo Christi Rd Paradise Valley AZ 85253

SWANSON, ROBERT LEE, lawyer; b. Fond du Lac, Wis., July 15, 1942; s. Walfred S. and Edna F. (Kamp) S.; m. Mary Ruth Francis, Aug. 19, 1967; children: Leigh Alexandra, Mitchell Pearson. BS, U. Wis., 1964; JD, Valparaiso U., 1970; LLM, Boston U., 1979. Bar: Wis. 1970, U.S. Dist. Ct. (ea. dist.) Wis. 1970, U.S. Dist. Ct. (we. dist.) Wis. 1974, U.S. Dist. Ct. (cen.) Ill. 1988, U.S. Tax Ct. 1981. Atty. Kasdorf, Dahl, Lewis & Swietlik, Milw., 1970-73; atty., ptnr. Wartman, Wartman & Swanson, Ashland, Wis., 1973-80; city atty. City of Ashland, Wis., 1976-80; atty., ptnr. DeMark, Kolbe & Brodek, Racine, Wis., 1980-95; ptnr. Hartig, Bjelajac, Swanson & Koenen, Racine, 1995—; lectr. civil rights and discrimination laws, 1980—. Columnist (legal) Burlington Std. Press, 1991—, Wis. Restaurant Assn. Mag., 1986. Vice comdr. USCG Aux. Bayfield (Wis.) Flotilla, 1975-81; v.p., bd. dirs. Meml. Med. Ctr., Ashland, 1975-80; chmn. Ashland County Rep. Party, 1976-79; vol. atty. ACLU Wis., 1975—. 1st lt. U.S. Army, 1964-66. Named one of Outstanding Young Men of Am., Jaycees, 1978; recipient Disting. Achievement in Art and Sci. of Advocacy award Internat. Acad. Trial Lawyers, 1970. Mem. Racine County Bar Assn. (bd. dirs. 1986-89), Wis. Acad. Trial Lawyers, Def. Rsch. Inst., Am. Hockey Assn. U.S. (coach, referee 1983—), Am. Legion, The Federalist Soc. Avocations: softball, volleyball, hockey. Home: 333 Hollow Creek Rd Racine WI 53402-2637 Office: Hartig Bjelajac Swanson and Koenen 601 Lake Ave Racine WI 53401-0038

SWANSON, ROBERT MCLEAN, retired business educator; b. Union City, Pa., Aug. 11, 1920; s. Peter Leonard and Mary Edna (McLean) S.; m. Marie Manda, May 25, 1946; children: Catherine, Robert Jr., Mary Ann, Christina. BS in Edn., Ind. U. of Pa., 1942; MA, Columbia U., 1949, EdD, 1953. Bus. tchr. Darlington (Pa.) Joint Schs., 1946-48; prof. bus. Thiel Coll., Greenville, Pa., 1948-52; vis. prof. Teachers Coll. Columbia U., N.Y.C., 1953; prof. bus. Ball State U., Muncie, Ind., 1954-85, head dept. bus. edn., 1961-67, prof. emeritus, 1985—. Author: (with others) Century 21 Accounting, 1967, 72, 77, 82, 87, 92, 95. Charter bd. dirs. Muncie Hosp. Hospitality House, 1983-86. Maj. U.S. Army, 1942-46, ETO. Mem. Nat. Bus. Edn. Assn., Ind. Bus. Edn. Assn., Delta Pi Epsilon. Roman Catholic. Avocations: home computer, traveling. Home: 1719 E Wexley Rd Bloomington IN 47401-4357

SWANSON, ROY ARTHUR, classicist, educator; b. St. Paul, Apr. 7, 1925; s. Roy Benjamin and Gertrude (Larson) S.; m. Vivian May Vitous, Mar. 30, 1946; children: Lynn Marie (Mrs. Gerald A. Snider), Robin Lillian, Robert Roy (dec.), Dyack Tyler, Dana Miriam (Mrs. Jon Butts). B.A., U. Minn., 1948, B.S., 1949, M.A., 1951; Ph.D., U. Ill., 1954. Prin. Maplewood Elementary Sch., St. Paul, 1949-51; instr. U. Ill., 1952-53, Ind. U., 1954-57; asst. prof. U. Minn., Mpls., 1957-61; assoc. prof. U. Minn., 1961-64, acting chmn. classics, 1963-64, prof. classics, chmn. comparative lit., 1964-65; prof. English Macalester Coll., St. Paul, 1965-67; coord. humanities program, 1966-67; prof. comparative lit. and classics U. Wis.-Milw., 1967—, prof. English, 1990—, chmn. classics dept., 1967-70, 86-89, chmn. comparative lit., 1970-73, 76-83, coord. Scandinavian studies program, 1982-96; cons. St. Paul Tchrs. Sr. High Sch. English, 1964. Author: Odi et Amo: The Complete Poetry of Catullus, 1959, Heart of Reason: Introductory Essays in Modern-World Humanities, 1963, Pindar's Odes, 1974, Greek and Latin Word Elements, 1981, The Love Songs of the Carmina Burana, 1987, Pär Lagerkvist: Five Early Works, 1989; editor Minn. Rev., 1963-67; Classical Jour., 1966-72; contbr. articles to profl. jours. With AUS, 1944-46. Decorated Bronze Star; recipient Disting. Teaching award U. Minn., 1962, Disting. Teaching award U. Wis.-Milw., 1974, 91. Mem. Am. Philol. Assn., Am. Comparative Lit. Assn., Modern Lang. Assn., Soc. for Advancement Scandinavian Study, Phi Beta Kappa (pres. chpt. 1975-76). Home: 11618 N Bobolink Ln Mequon WI 53092-2804 Office: U Wis Dept Classics & Comp Lit PO Box 413 Milwaukee WI 53201-0413

SWANSON, ROY JOEL, lawyer; b. Houston, Feb. 21, 1945; s. Roy J. and Daisy Lee (Peper) S.; m. Lynn Northway, Apr. 5, 1986; children: Emily Rebecca, Nell Cameron. BSChemE, U. Tex., 1967; MBA, Harvard U., 1972, JD, 1972. Bar: Tex. 1972. Assoc. Baker & Botts, Houston, 1972-80, ptnr., 1980—. Office: Baker & Botts 3000 One Shell Pla 910 Louisiana St Houston TX 77002

SWANSON, RUNE E., financial executive; b. Chgo., Aug. 9, 1919; s. John E. and Emma C. (Carlson) S.; m. Lenore Reed, Mar. 18, 1944; children: Deborah, Cynthia, Patricia. B.S. in Commerce (Univ. scholar), Northwestern U., 1943. Asst. contr. U.S. Gypsum Co., Chgo., 1946-56; contr. Internat. Minerals & Chem. Corp., Chgo., 1956-60, Mobil Chem. Co., N.Y.C., 1960-66; v.p. fin. Nat. Gypsum Co., Dallas, 1966-84; assoc. Swearingen Co., 1985-86; pres. Swanson Assocs., Dallas, 1986—; instr. Northwestern U. Served as lt. USNR, 1943-46, PTO. Mem. Fin. Execs. Inst., Northwood Country Club, Dallas Knife and Fork Club, Rotary, Masons, Scottish Rite, Shriners. Republican.

SWANSON, WALLACE MARTIN, lawyer; b. Fergus Falls, Minn., Aug. 22, 1941; s. Marvin Walter and Mary Louise (Lindsey) S.; m. Susan W. Swanson; children: Kristen Lindsey, Eric Munger. B.A. with honors, U. Minn., 1962; LL.B. with honors, So. Methodist U., 1965. Bar: Tex. 1965. Since practiced in Dallas; assoc. Coke & Coke, Dallas, 1965-70; ptnr. firm Johnson & Swanson, Dallas, 1970-88; prin. Wallace M. Swanson, P.C., Dallas, 1988—; chmn., CEO Ace Cash Express Inc., Irving, Tex., 1987-88, State St. Capital Corp., 1990—, Highland Park Cafeterias, Ltd., 1994—. Served with USNR, 1960-65. Mem. ABA, Tex. Bar Found., State Bar Tex. (securities com. 1972-86, chmn. 1978-80, coun. bus. law sect. 1980-86), Dallas Bar Assn., Crescent Club. Methodist. Address: 3816 Miramar Ave Dallas TX 75205-3126

SWANSON-SCHONES, KRIS MARGIT, developmental adapted physical education educator; b. Mpls., Mar. 22, 1950; d. Donald Theodore Swanson and Alice Alida (Swanson) Suhl; m. Gary Wallace Suhl, Apr. 6, 1974 (div. Aug. 1985); m. Gregory Edward Schones, Dec. 30, 1989. BA, Augsburg Coll., 1972. Cert. devel. adapted phys. edn. tchr., phys. edn. tchr., health tchr., coach/corrective therapist. Devel. adapted phys. edn. tchr. St. Paul Schs., 1972—, adapted athletic dir., 1989—; mem. adapted athletics adv. bd. Minn. State H.S. League, 1992—. Author: On the Move, 1979. Chmn. hospitality Tanbark Club, Lakeville, Minn., 1992—, mem. show cmty., 1991—; mem. outreach com. Spl. Olympics, Minn., 1989-94. Recipient Nutrition Edn. grant Fed. Govt., 1978-79, Christmas Album grant Spl. Olympics, 1989, Internat. Spl. Olympics Coach award Minn. Spl. Olympics, 1991. Mem. NEA, AAHPERD, Minn. Edn. Assn., Minn. Assn. Adapted Athletics (exec. bd. 1989—, sec. exec. bd. 1990—). Avocations: showing horses and dogs, gardening, fishing. Home: 16280 Webster Ct Prior Lake MN 55372-9772 Office: St Paul Schs Bridgeview 360 Colborne St Saint Paul MN 55102-3228

SWANSTROM, THOMAS EVAN, economist; b. Green Bay, Wis., May 17, 1939; s. Alfred Enoch and Elizabeth Nan (Thomas) S.; m. Nancy Anne Roche; children: Amy, Scott. Student, U. Notre Dame, 1957-59; B.A., U. Wis., 1962, M.A., 1963; postgrad., Am. U., 1963-66. Economist, U.S. Bur. Labor Statistics, Washington, 1963-66; dir. research Population Ref. Bur., Washington, 1966-68; economist Sears, Roebuck & Co., Chgo., 1968-70, market analyst, 1970-72, mgr. catalog research, 1972-75, asst. mgr. econ. research, 1974-80, chief economist, 1980-90; pres. Consumer Econs., Chgo., 1991—; mem. bus. research adv. council Bur. Labor Stats. Contbr. articles to industry publs. Mem. Nat. Assn. Bus. Economists, Conf. Bus. Economists.

SWANTON, SUSAN IRENE, library director; b. Rochester, N.Y., Nov. 29, 1941; d. Walter Frederick and Irene Wray S.; m. Wayne Holman, Apr. 12, 1969 (div. June 1973); 1 child, Michael; life ptnr. James Donald Lathrop; children: Kathryn, Kristin. AB, Harvard U., 1963; MLS, Columbia U., 1965. Libr. dir. Warsaw (N.Y.) Pub. Libr., 1963-64, Gates Pub. Libr., Rochester, N.Y., 1965—. Pres. Drug and Alcohol Coun., Rochester, 1985-91, mem. adv. coun., 1992-94; bd. dirs., co-chairperson info. svcs. Rochester Freenet, 1995—. Mem. Gates-Chili Coun. Rochester Met. C. of C. (pres. 1982, sec. 1990-94, Citizen of Yr. 1995), Harvard Club of Rochester (mem. adv. bd.). Office: Gates Pub Libr 1605 Buffalo Rd Rochester NY 14624-1637

SWANZEY, ROBERT JOSEPH, data processing executive; b. Bklyn., Feb. 4, 1935; s. Robert and Olivia (MacIntosh) S.; m. Marie Shannon, Nov. 23, 1957; children: Barbara Ann, Stephen. BA, Pace Coll., 1962. Teller Mfrs. Hanover Trust, N.Y.C., 1953-56; programmer N.Y. Cen. R.R., N.Y.C., 1956-64; systems analyst Schenley Industries, N.Y.C., 1964-70; v.p. systems and programming Raam Info. Services, Inc., N.Y.C., 1970-75; sr. v.p. ops. Century Bus. Credit Corp. (formerly Century Factors, Inc.), N.Y.C., 1975—. Treas. St. Patrick's Sports Programs, Bklyn., 1984-88; dir. basketball St. Patrick's Cath. Youth Orgnl. Program, Bklyn., 1976-84. Co-recipient Adult of Yr. award St. Patrick's Cath. Youth Orgn., 1983. Mem. Factors-Controllers Assn. (treas. 1983-84). Avocations: golf, music. Office: Century Bus Credit Corp 119 W 40th St New York NY 10018-2500

SWAP, WALTER CHARLES, academic dean, psychology educator; b. Seattle, Jan. 23, 1943; s. Clifford Lloyd and Edna France (Hastings) S.; m. Susan Webster McAllister, June 25, 1966 (dec.); children: Clifford John, Alison Frances. BA, Harvard U., 1965; PhD, U. Mich., 1970. Prof. psychology Tufts U., Medford, Mass., 1971-95, chmn. psychology dept., 1983-89, dean undergrad. edn., 1990-94; dean colls., 1994—. Editor, author: Group Decision Making: 1984; contbr. articles to scholarly jours. Mem. Am. Psychol. Soc., Soc. for Exptl. Social Psychology. Democrat. Unitarian-Universalist. Avocations: competitive road running, musical performing, organic gardening. Home: 9 Harrison St Winchester MA 01890-2416 Office: Tufts U Ballou Hall Medford MA 02155

SWART, ROBERT H., lawyer; b. Grand Rapids, Mich., Nov. 12, 1946. AB, U. Mich., 1968, JD cum laude, 1970. Bar: Mich. 1970, D.C. 1971. Ptnr. Mayer, Brown & Platt, Washington. Mem. ABA (mem. taxation sect.), D.C. Bar. Office: Mayer Brown & Platt Ste 6500 2000 Pennsylvania Ave NW Washington DC 20006-1812*

SWARTHOUT, MARGARET, artistic director. Grad. with honors, Royal Acad. Dancing; student, Royal Ballet Sch., London. Tchr., performance coach Marin Ballet, San Rafeal, Calif., 1975, artistic dir. tng. divsn.; mem.faculty Harkness House for Ballet Arts, N.Y.C., 1966; guest tchr. dance ctrs., competitions and festivals. Soloist Royal Ballet Co., Covent Garden; appeared in opera houses in Europe, Scandinavia, Russia, Eastern Block countries, U.S. and Can. Office: The Marin Ballet 100 Elm St San Rafael CA 94901

SWARTLING, DANIEL JOSEPH, chemistry educator, researcher; b. Black Falls, Wis., Sept. 3, 1960; s. Ronald James Swartling and Jean Marie (Welda) Trester. BS, Winona State U., 1985; PhD, U. N.D., 1989. Rsch. asst. Purdue U., West Lafayette, Ind., 1989-90; rsch. assoc. U. Chgo., 1990-92; teaching fellow S. Meth. U., Dallas, 1992-94; asst. prof. chemistry Tenn. Tech. U., Cookeville, 1994—; cons. ARCH Rsch. Corp., Chgo., 1992—. Contbr. chpt. to book; contbr. articles to prof. jours. Mem. Am. Chem. Soc., Am. Scientific Glassblowers Soc., Am. Orchid Soc., Sigma Xi. Avocations: radio, gardening, cycling, sports, music. Office: Tenn Tech U P O Box 5055 Cookeville TN 38505

SWARTWOUT, JOSEPH RODOLPH, obstetrics and gynecology educator, administrator; b. Pascagoula, Miss., June 17, 1925; s. Thomas Roswell and Marshall (Coleman) S.; m. Brandon C. Leftwich, Jan. 23, 1989. Student, Miss. Coll., 1943-44; MD, Tulane U., 1951. Intern Touro Infirmary, New Orleans, 1951-52; asst. in obstetrics and medicine Tulane U., 1952-53, instr., 1955-60; Nat. Found. fellow Harvard U., 1953-55; asst. in medicine Peter Bent Brigham Hosp., Boston, 1953-55; assoc. in obstetric rsch. Boston Lying-In-Hosp., 1953-55; asst. prof. U. Pitts., 1960-61; assoc. prof. Emory U., Atlanta, 1961-66; assoc. prof. ob-gyn. U. Chgo., 1967-80; chief ob-gyn. at Prime Health, also clin. assoc. prof. U. Kans. Sch. Medicine, 1978-80; prof. dept. ob-gyn. Mercer U. Sch. Medicine, Macon, Ga., 1980-95, prof. emeritus, 1995; dist. health dir. Dist. 5-2, Macon, Ga., 1996—; dist. dir. Ga. Divsn. Pub. Health, Macon, 1996—. Fellow Am. Coll. Obstetricians and Gynecologists, Am. Heart Assn. (coun. clin. cardiology), Am. Acad. Reproductive Medicine; mem. AAAS, AMA, APHA, Population Assn. Am., Med. Assn. Ga., Bibb County Med. Soc.

SWARTZ, B(ENJAMIN) K(INSELL), JR., archaeologist, educator; b. L.A., June 23, 1931; s. Benjamin Kinsell and Maxine Marietta (Pearce) S.; m. Cyrilla Casillas, Oct. 23, 1966; children: Benjamin Kinsell III, Frank Casillas. AA summa cum laude, L.A. City Coll., 1952; BA, UCLA, 1954, MA, 1958; PhD, U. Ariz., 1964. Curator Klamath County Mus., Oreg., 1959-61, rsch. assoc., 1961-62; asst. prof. anthropology Ball State U., Muncie, Ind., 1964-68, assoc. prof., 1968-72, prof., 1972—; vis. sr. lectr. U. Ghana, 1970-71; exch. prof. U. Yaounde, Cameroon, 1984-85; field rschr. N.Am. and West Africa; mem. exec. bd., pres. Am. Com. to Advanced Study of Petroglyphs and Pictographs and rep. to Internat. Fedn. Rock Art Orgns.; bd. dirs., sec.-treas. Coun. Conservation Ind. Archaeology; mem. adv. bd. Am. Com. for Preservation of Archaeol. Collections. Editor: Archaeological Reports; contbr. revs. and articles to profl. jours.; author books, monographs in field, including: West African Culture Dynamics, 1980, Indiana's Prehistoric Past, 1981, Rock Art and Posterity, 1991, Proceedings of 1st Internat. South African Rock Art Assn. Conf., 1991. Klamath County chmn. Oreg. Statehood Centennial, 1959. With USN, 1954-56. Fellow AAAS, Ind. Acad. Sci.; mem. Current Anthropology (assoc.), Soc. Am. Archaeology, Soc. African Archaeologists, Internat. Com. Rock Art, Ind. Fedn. Tchrs. (higher edn. trustee, exec. bd.), Sigma Xi, Lambda Alpha (nat. coun., exec. sec.). Home: 3600 W Brook Dr Muncie IN 47304-2923 Office: Ball State U Dept Anthropology Muncie IN 47306-0435

SWARTZ, DONALD EVERETT, television executive; b. Mpls., Mar. 7, 1916; s. Albert L. and Sara (Shore) S.; m. Helen Gordon, Mar. 24, 1940; children: Stuart, Lawrence, Gary. Grad. high sch. Owner Ind. Film Distbrs., 1940-53, Tele-Film Assocs., 1953-57; pres., gen. mgr. KMSP-TV, Mpls., 1957-79; pres. United TV, Inc. (subs. 20th Century Fox Film Corp. until 1981); operating KMSP-TV, KTV4, Salt Lake City, KBHK-TV, San Francisco KMOL-TV, San Antonio; CEO United Television, Inc., Mpls., 1979-85; cons. KMOL-TV, 1985—; founder Tele-Video Assocs., 1985—, Tele-Video Entertainment, 1985—; owner/mgr. Donald Investment Co., 1989—. Vice pres. Twin City Broadcast Skills Bank (scholarship program), St. Paul Arts and Sci. Inst.; pres. U. Minn. Heart Hosp.; mem. Gov.'s Commn. Bicentennial; bd. dirs. Mpls. United Jewish Fund and Council; Mem. Mpls. Inst. Arts, Mpls., St. Paul chambers commerce, Minn. Orch. Assn., Citizens League, U. Minn. Alumni Assn. Elected Minn. Pioneer Broadcaster of Yr., 1992. Mem. Press Club (Mpls.), Advt. Standard Club (Mpls.), Hillcrest Country Club (St. Paul), Variety Club, Mission Hills Country Club (Rancho Mirage, Calif.), Oak Ridge Country Club (Mpls.), B'nai B'rith. Jewish (pres. temple). Home: 2221 Youngman Ave Saint Paul MN 55116-3055 Office: 7101 York Ave S Minneapolis MN 55435-4450

SWARTZ, DONALD PERCY, physician; b. Preston, Ont., Can., Sept. 12, 1921; s. Simon Wingham and Lydia (Ethell) S.; m. Norma Mae Woolner, June 24, 1944 (dec. May 1980); children: Ian Donald, Rhonda Swartz Peterson; m. Isabelle Liz Dales, Apr. 21, 1984. B.A., U. Western Ont., 1951, M.D. cum laude, 1951, M.S. cum laude, 1953. Intern Victoria Hosp., London, Ont., 1951-52; asst. resident Westminster Hosp., London, 1953-54; resident Johns Hopkins U., Balt., 1954-58; asst. prof. ob-gyn. U. Western Ont., London, 1958-62; prof. Columbia U., N.Y.C., 1962-72; dir. ob-gyn. Harlem Hosp.; prof. dept. ob-gyn. Albany (N.Y.) Med. Coll., 1972—, chmn., 1972-79, chief sect. gen. gynecology, 1982-88, head. div. gen. gynecology, 1988—, acting chmn., 1992; vis. prof. dept. Ob-Gyn. U. Rochester, N.Y., 1981. Assoc. editor: Advances in Planned Parenthood. Vice pres., pres. Assn. Planned Parenthood Physicians, 1972-74. Served with RCAF, 1942-45. NRC Can. fellow, 1952-53; Am. Cancer Soc. fellow, 1956-57; Markle scholar, 1958-63. Fellow Royal Coll. Surgeons Can., Am. Coll. Obstetricians and Gynecologists, Am. Gynecologic Soc., Am. Gyn-Ob Soc., Am. Fertility Soc., Royal Soc. Health, Soc. Gynecologic Surgeons. Home: 24 Devon Rd Delmar NY 12054-3534 Office: Albany Med Coll 47 New Scotland Ave Albany NY 12208-3412 *It has been a privilege and a challenge to participate in the forefront of the revolutionary changes in the health care of women during the past four decades. Acceptance, initiation and implementation of positive change have been guidelines for gratifying action.*

SWARTZ, JACK, association executive; b. Dodge City, Kans., Nov. 24, 1932; s. John Ralph and Fern (Cave) S.; m. Nadine Ann Langlois, Aug. 4, 1956; children: Dana, Shawn, Tim, Jay. A.A., Dodge City Community Coll., 1953; student St. Mary of Plains Coll., 1953-55, 58; B.A. in Econs., Washburn U., 1974, B.B.A., 1973. Vice pres. D.C. Terminal Elevator Co., Dodge City, Kans., 1957-65; exec. v.p. Kans. Jaycees, Hutchinson, 1965-68, Kans. C. of C. and Industry, Topeka, 1968-82; pres. Nebr. C. of C. and Industry, Lincoln, 1982—. Past chmn., bd. regents U.S. C. of C. Inst. U. Colo. Served with U.S. Army, 1955-57. Named Outstanding Local Pres. in State, Kans. Jaycees, 1961, Outstanding Young Man of Yr., Dodge City Jaycees, 1961; Outstanding State Vice Pres., U.S. Jaycees, 1962, Outstanding Nat. Dir., 1963. Mem. Am. Soc. Assn. Execs. (cert.), Am. Chamber Commerce Execs. (bd. dirs., cert.), Nebr. Chamber Commerce Execs. (sec.-treas.), Nebr. Soc. Assn. Execs. (past pres.), Nebr. Fedn. Bus. Assns. (pres. 1986-88), Washburn U. Alum. (bd. dirs.). Republican. Roman Catholic. Lodge: Rotary. Home: 2744 Laurel St Lincoln NE 68502-5142 Office: Nebr C of C and Industry 1320 Lincoln Mall PO Box 95128 Lincoln NE 68509

SWARTZ, JON DAVID, psychologist, educator; b. Houston, Dec. 28, 1934; s. Orville Elmo and Nina June (Baker) S.; m. Carol Joseph Hampton, Oct. 20, 1966; children: Eric Jason McFarland, Sally Katherine Baker, Edward Joseph Bryson. BA, U. Tex., Austin, 1956, MA, 1961, PhD, 1969, postgrad. (fellow), 1973-74. Research and teaching asst. dept. psychology U. Tex., 1956-62, asst. prof. dept. ednl. psychology, 1969-72; assoc. prof. psychology, chmn. U. Tex.-Permian Basin, 1974-78, chmn. anthropology and sociology, 1975-78, field dir., 1962-65; asst. dir. Austin Longitudinal Research project, 1965-69, co-dir., 1969-74; research scientist Hogg Found. for Mental Health, 1972-74; prof. edn. and psychology Southwestern U., Georgetown, Tex., 1978-90, vis. prof. psychology, 1991; dir. testing and guidance Southwestern U., 1978-81, holder Brown vis. chair, 1978-82, assoc. dean for libraries and learning resources, 1981-90; coord., adminstrv. head Killeen office Cen. Counties Ctr. for MHMR Svcs., Temple, Tex., 1990-91; chief psychol. svcs. Temple, Tex., 1991—; lectr. Nat. U., Mexico, 1962. Author: (with W.H. Holtzman) Inkblot Perception and Personality, 1961, (with C.C. Cleland) Mental Retardation: Approaches to Institutional Change, 1969, Administrative Issues in Institutions for the Mentally Retarded, 1972, Exceptionalities Through the Lifespan: An Introduction, 1982, Multihandicapped Mentally Retarded, 1973, (with W.H. Holtzman, R. Diaz-Guerrero) Personality Development in Two Cultures, 1975; editor: (with C.C. Cleland, L.W. Talkington) Profoundly Mentally Retarded, 1976, (with R.K. Eyman, C.C. Cleland) Research with the Profoundly Retarded, 1978, Holtzman Inkblot Technique: An Annotated Bibliography (supplement), 1988, (with R.C. Reinehr, W.H. Holtzman) Holtzman Inkblot Technique: An Annotated Bibliography 1956-1982, 1983, SW U. Bibliographic Series, 1986-90, (with R.C. Reinehr) Handbook of Old-Time Radio, 1993; editorial assoc.: Current Anthropology, 1971-77; assoc. editor: Am. Corrective Therapy Jour, 1971-81, Exceptional Children, 1982-84; mem. editorial bd.: Texas Psychologist, 1979-83 , Phi Kappa Phi Jour./Nat. Forum, 1976-80; editorial cons.: Mental Retardation, 1972-77; book rev. editor: Jour. Biol. Psychology, 1972-80; book rev. editor for English lang. publs.: Revista Interamericana de Psicologia, 1983-89; cons. editor Jour. Personality Assessment, 1981-90; contbr. over 400 articles to profl. jours. Mem. Mayor's Drug Abuse Panel, Odessa, Tex., 1975-78; chmn. adv. bd. Human Potentials Center, Permian Basin Community Centers for Mental Health and Mental Retardation, Odessa and Midland, Tex., 1975-78; bd. govs. Mood-Heritage Mus., 1984-90. U.S. Office Edn. fellow, 1964-66; recipient Franklin Gilliam prize Humanities Research Center U. Tex., 1965; Spencer Research award Nat. Acad. Edn., 1972; Faculty Fellowship award Southwestern U., 1981. Fellow AAAS, Am. Psychol. Soc., Soc. Personality Assessment; mem. Western Rsch. Conf. on Mental Retardation, Am. Acad. Mental Retardation, Southwestern Psychol. Assn., Bell County Psychol. Assn., Sigma Xi, Psi Chi, Mu Alpha Nu, Delta Tau Kappa, Phi Kappa Phi, Phi Delta Kappa. Office: Cen Counties Ctr for MHMR Svcs 304 S 22d St Temple TX 76501 *All my life I have had teachers, in school and out, who challenged me to do more than I thought I was capable of doing. Any success I have achieved, I owe to them and their efforts in my behalf.*

SWARTZ, MALCOLM GILBERT, retail executive, restaurateur; b. N.Y.C., Nov. 4, 1931; s. Morris Baer and Ethel (Gutstein) S.; m. Marjorie Diane Rose, Nov. 27, 1955; children: Lindsay Brian, James Michael, Donna Carrie, Andrea Gail. Grad., Ont. Inst. of Chartered Accts., 1955. Ptnr. William Eisenberg and Co., Chartered Accts., Toronto, Ont., Can., 1962-69; exec. v.p. Shoppers Drug Mart, Toronto, 1969—. Author: Basic Finance, 1975, Advanced Finance, 1979, Asset Productivity, 1983, Cash Flow and Financial Planning, 1986. Mem. Inst. Chartered Accts. Ont. Club: Toronto Thoroughbred Racing (past pres.). Avocation: tennis. Office: Shoppers Drug Mart, 225 Yorkland Blvd, Willowdale, ON Canada M2J 4Y7

SWARTZ, MORTON NORMAN, medical educator; b. Boston, Nov. 11, 1923; s. Jacob H. and Janet (Heller) W.; m. Cesia Rosenberg, Sept. 18, 1956; children: Mark David, Caroline Joan. BA, Harvard Coll., 1945; MD, Harvard U., 1947; MD (hon.), U. Geneva, Switzerland, 1988. Diplomate Am. Bd. Internal Medicine (subsplty. exam. com. 1971-76, bd. govs. 1979-85). Med. intern and resident Mass. Gen. Hosp., Boston, 1947-50, chief resident in medicine, 1953-54; USPHS postdoctoral rsch. fellow Johns Hopkins U., McCollum-Pratt Inst. Enzymology, Balt., 1954-56; chief infectious disease unit Mass. Gen. Hosp., Boston, 1956-90, chief James Jackson Firm, dept. medicine, 1990—; assoc. prof. medicine Harvard Med. Sch., Boston, 1967-73, prof., 1973—; vis. assoc. prof. biochemistry, Stanford Med. Sch., Palo Alto, Calif., 1969-70. Author: (with others) Osteomyelitis, 1971; editor: Current Clinical Topics in Infectious Diseases, 1980—; assoc. editor New Eng. Jour. Medicine, 1981—; contbr. articles to profl. jours. 1st lt. U.S. Army, 1950-52. Sir MacFarlane Burnett lectr. Australasian Soc. Infectious Disease, 1981. Fellow ACP (master 1988, Disting. Tchr. award 1989); mem. Am. Soc. Biochemistry and Molecular Biology, Am. Soc. for Clin. Investigation, Assn. Am. Physicians, Infectious Diseases Soc. Am. (Bristol award 1984, Feldman award 1989), Inst. Medicine, Nat. Inst. Child Health and Devel. (bd. sci. counselors 1992—, chmn. 1995—). Jewish. Avocations: biology, bird watching. Home: 54 Shaw Rd Chestnut Hill MA 02167-3122 Office: Mass Gen Hosp 32 Fruit St Boston MA 02114-2620

SWARTZ, STEPHEN ARTHUR, banker, lawyer; b. Boston, Oct. 7, 1941; s. Norman and Frances S.; m. Karen M. McLoughlin, Aug. 18, 1992; children: Marti Anne, Nanci Beth, Lori Ellen, Stephen Arthur, Jr. BA in Polit. Sci., U. Mass., 1963; LLB, Boston U., 1966; postgrad. in fin. and mgmt, Boston Coll., 1968-70. Bar: Mass. 1967, N.Y. 1971. Asst. counsel Fed. Res. Bank Boston., 1968-70, Irving Trust Co., N.Y.C., 1970-74; counsel, asst. sec. Charter N.Y. Corp., N.Y.C., 1974-77; v.p., asst. dir. investor communications Charter N.Y. Corp., 1977-79; v.p., dir. investor communications Irving Bank Corp., N.Y.C., 1979-86; v.p. investor relations Seamen's Corp., N.Y.C., 1986-88, sr. v.p., corp. sec., 1990; sr. v.p. investor rels. H.F. Ahmanson & Co., L.A., 1990—. Served to capt. AUS, 1966-68, Vietnam. Decorated Bronze Star (2), Army Commendation medal (2), Air medal (2); Vietnamese Honor medal 1st class. Mem. ABA, Mass. Bar Assn., N.Y. State Bar Assn., Nat. Investor Rels. Inst. (former bd. dirs., treas. L.A. chpt.), Bank Investor Rels. Assn. (founder, former pres., bd. dirs., dir.), Bedford Riding Lns. Assn. Home: 2084 Liliano Dr Sierra Madre CA 91024-1557 Office: HF Ahmanson & Co 4900 Rivergrade Rd Baldwin Park CA 91706-1404

SWARTZ, THOMAS R., economist, educator; b. Phila., Aug. 31, 1937; s. Henry Jr. and Elizabeth (Thomas) S.; m. Jeanne Marie Jourdan, Aug. 12, 1961; children: Mary Butler, Karen Miller, Jennifer, Anne, Rebecca. BA, LaSalle U., 1960; MA, Ohio U., 1962; PhD, Ind. U., 1965. Asst. prof. U. Notre Dame, Ind., 1965-70, assoc. dept. chair, 1968-70, assoc. prof., 1970-78, acting dir. grad. studies, 1977-78, prof. econs., 1978—, dir. program econ. policy, 1982-85; resident dir. U. Notre Dame London Program, 1990-91; vis. prof. U. Notre Dame London Program 1982, 85; fiscal cons. Ind. Commn. State Tax, Indpls., 1965-68, also spl. tax cons., 1971-81, City of South Bend, Ind., 1972-75. Co-editor: The Supply Side, 1983, Changing Face of Fiscal Federalism, 1990, Urban Finance Under Siege, 1993, Taking Sides, 7th edit., 1995, America's Working Poor, 1995; contbr. articles to profl. jours. Bd. dirs. Forever Learning Inst., South Bend, Ind., 1988-93; mem. steering com. Mayor's Housing Forum, South Bend, 1989—; chair Com. Svcs. Block Grant, South Bend, 1985-90, Econ. Devel. Task Force, South Bend, 1985. Rsch. fellow Nat. Ctr. Urban Ethnic Affairs, 1979-85; recipient Danforth Assoc. award Danforth Found., 1972-86, Tchg. award Kanzajian Found., 1974. Democrat. Roman Catholic. Avocation: racquetball. Home: 402 Marquette Ave South Bend IN 46617-1157 Office: U Notre Dame Dept Econs 414 Decio Hall Notre Dame IN 46556-5644

SWARTZ, WILLIAM JOHN, transportation resources company executive/retired; b. Hutchinson, Kans., Nov. 6, 1934; s. George Glen and Helen Mae (Prather) S.; m. Dorothy Jean Parshall, June 5, 1956; children: John Christopher, Jeffrey Michael. BSME, Duke U., 1956; JD, George Washington U., 1961; MS in Mgmt. (Alfred P. Sloan fellow), MIT, 1967. With AT & SF Ry., 1961-78, 79—, asst. v.p. exec. dept., 1973-77, v.p. adminstrn., 1977-78, exec. v.p., 1979-83; exec. v.p. Santa Fe Industries, Chgo., 1978-79, pres., 1983-90; vice chmn. Santa Fe So. Pacific, 1983-90; pres. AT & SF Ry., 1986-89. Past bd. dirs. Chgo. Mus. Sci. and Industry; mem. Dean's Coun. Duke U. Sch. Engring. With USMC, 1956-59. Mem. Assn. Am. R.R. (past bd. dirs.). Republican. Methodist. Home: 914 Paseo del Sur Santa Fe NM 87501

SWARTZ, WILLIAM RICK, school psychologist; b. Buffalo, Dec. 27, 1951; s. William Wallace and Ruth Mae (Williams) S.; m. Saundra Kay Hess, June 21, 1980. BS in Edn., Bucknell U., Lewisburg, Pa., 1974; MS in Edn., Bucknell U., 1976; MEd, Shippensburg (Pa.) State U., 1982. Sch. psychologist Waynesboro (Pa.) Area Sch. Dist., 1976—; ednl. cons. Mont Alto Campus, Pa. State U., 1990-93. Mem. Assn. of Sch. Psychologists of Pa., Coun. for Exceptional Children. Avocations: theater, music, art. Office: Waynesboro Area Sch Dist 210 Clayton Ave # 72 Waynesboro PA 17268-2014

SWARTZBAUGH, MARC L., lawyer; b. Urbana, Ohio, Jan. 3, 1937; s. Merrill L. and Lillian K. (Hill) S.; m. Marjory Anne Emhardt, Aug. 16, 1958; children: Marc Charles, Kathleen Marie, Laura Kay. BA magna cum laude, Wittenberg Coll., 1958; LLB magna cum laude, U. Pa., 1961. Bar: Ohio 1961, U.S. Dist. Ct. (no. dist.) Ohio 1962, U.S. Claims Ct. 1991, U.S. Ct. Appeals (6th cir.) 1970, U.S. Ct. Appeals (3d cir.) 1985, U.S. Ct. Appeals (Fed. cir.) 1995, U.S. Supreme Ct. 1973. Law clk. to judge U.S. Ct. Appeals (3d cir.), Phila., 1961-62; assoc. Jones, Day, Reavis & Pogue, Cleve., 1962-69, ptnr., 1970—. Note editor U. Pa. Law Rev., 1960-61. Co-chmn. Suburban Citizens for Open Housing, Shaker Heights, Ohio, 1966; v.p. Lomond Assn., Shaker Heights, 1965-68; trustee The Dance Ctr., Cleve., 1980-83; amb. People to People Internat., 1986; chmn. legal divsn. Cleve. campaign United Negro Coll. Fund, 1989-96. Mem. ABA (litigation sect.), Fed. Bar Assn., Ohio Bar Assn., Cleve. Bar Assn., Order of Coif, Beta Theta Pi. Democrat. Club: 13th St Racquet (Cleve.). Avocations: poetry, painting, music, skiing, squash, photography. Office: Jones Day Reavis & Pogue N Point 901 Lakeside Ave E Cleveland OH 44114-1116

SWARTZENDRUBER, DALE, soil physicist, educator; b. Parnell, Iowa, July 6, 1925; s. Urie and Norma (Kinsinger) S.; m. Kathleen Jeanette Yoder, June 26, 1949; children: Karl Grant, Myra Mae, John Keith, David Mark. BS, Iowa State U., 1950, MS, 1952, PhD, 1954. Instr. sci. Goshen (Ind.) Coll., 1953-54; asst. soil scientist U. Calif., Los Angeles, 1955-56; assoc. prof. soil physics Purdue U., West Lafayette, Ind., 1956-63; prof. Purdue U., 1963-77; prof. soil physics U. Nebr., Lincoln, 1977—; vis. prof. Iowa State U., 1959, Ga. Inst. Tech., 1968, Hebrew U. Jerusalem at Rehovot, 1971, Griffith U., Brisbane, Australia, 1989-90, Centre for Environ. Mechanics, CSIRO, Canberra, Australia, 1990; vis. scholar Cambridge (Eng.) U., 1971. Contbr. articles on soil physics to profl. jours.; assoc. editor: Soil Sci. Soc. Am. Proc., 1965-70; mem. editorial bd. Geoderma (Amsterdam), 1975-93; cons. editor: Soil Sci., 1976—. Fellow Soil Sci. Soc. Am. (Soil Sci. award 1975, Editors' citation for excellence in manuscript rev. 1993), Am. Soc. Agronomy; mem. AAAS, Am. Geophys. Union, Internat. Soc. Soil Sci., Am. Sci. Affiliation, Sigma Xi. Mennonite. Achievements include research in water infiltration into soil, validity of Darcy's equation for water flow in soils, measurement of water and solid content in soils, mathematical solutions to problems of water flow in saturated and unsaturated soils. Home: 1400 N 37th St Lincoln NE 68503-2016 Office: U Nebr E Campus Dept Agronomy 133 Keim Hall Lincoln NE 68583 *Along with complete dedication and honesty in spirit and action, bring to each task a new thought, or ask the implications, should the customary or conventional wisdom not hold.*

SWARTZLANDER, EARL EUGENE, JR., engineering educator, former electronics company executive; b. San Antonio, Feb. 1, 1945; s. Earl Eugene and Jane (Nicholas) S.; m. Joan Vickery, June 9, 1968. BSEE, Purdue U., 1967; MSEE, U. Colo., 1969; PhD, U. So. Calif., 1972. Registered profl. engr., Ala., Calif., Colo., Tex. Devel. engr. Ball Bros. Rsch. Corp., Boulder, Colo., 1967-69; Hughes fellow, mem. tech. staff Hughes Aircraft Co., Culver City, Calif., 1969-73; mem. rsch. staff Tech. Svc. Co., Santa Monica, Calif., 1973-74; chief engr. Geophys. Systems Corp., Pasadena, Calif., 1974-75, staff engr. to sr. staff engr., 1975-79, project mgr., 1979-84, lab. mgr., 1985-87; dir. ind. R&D TRW Inc., Redondo Beach, Calif., 1987-90; Schlumberger Centennial prof. engring. dept. elec. and computer engring. U. Tex., Austin, 1990—; gen. chmn. Internat. Conf. Wafer Scale Integration, 1989, 11th Internat. Symposium on Computer Arithmetic, 1992; gen. chmn. Internat. Conf. Application Specific Array Processors, 1990, co-gen. chmn., 1994; chmn. 3d Internat. Conf. Parallel and Distributed Sys., Taiwan, 1993. Author: VLSI Signal Processing Systems, 1986; editor: Computer Design Development, 1976, Systolic Signal Processing Systems, 1987, Wafer Scale Integration, 1989, Computer Arithmetic Vol. 1 and 2, 1990; editor-in-chief Jour. of VLSI Signal Processing, 1989-95, IEEE Transactions on Computers, 1991-94, IEEE Transactions on Signal Processing, 1995; editor: IEEE Transactions on Computers, 1982-86, IEEE Transactions on Parallel and Distributed Systems, 1989-90; hardware area editor ACM Computing Revs., 1985—; assoc. editor: IEEE Jour. Solid-State Circuits, 1984-88; contbr. more than 150 articles to profl. jours. and tech. conf. procs. Bd. dirs. Casiano Estates Homeowners Assn., Bel Air, Calif., 1976-78, pres., 1978-80; bd. dirs. Benedict Hills Estates Homeowners Assn., Beverly Hills, Calif., 1984—, pres., 1990-95. Recipient Disting. Engring. Alumnus award Purdue U., 1989, Outstanding Elec. Engr. award Purdue U., 1992, knight Imperial Russian Order St. John of Jerusalem (Knights of Malta), 1993. Fellow IEEE; mem. IEEE Computer Soc. (bd. govs. 1987-91), IEEE Signal Proc. Soc. (bd. govs. 1992-94), IEEE Solid-State Cirs. Coun. (sec. 1992-93, treas. 1994—), Eta Kappa Nu, Sigma Tau, Omicron Delta Kappa. Office: U Tex Austin Dept Elec Computer Engring Austin TX 78712

SWARZ, JEFFREY ROBERT, securities analyst, neuroscientist; b. Newark, Nov. 9, 1949; s. Irvin Brad and Blanche S. (Marcus) S.; m. Kathy Helen Kafer, June 20, 1976. B.S. with honors, U. Calif.-Irvine, 1971; Ph.D. (NIMH trainee 1971-74, NIH fellow 1975-76), U. Rochester, 1976. Postdoctoral fellow in neurovirology Johns Hopkins U. Sch. Medicine, 1976-79; staff fellow Infectious Disease br. NIH, Bethesda, Md., 1979-80; dir. biotech. group Teknekron Research Inc., McLean, Va., 1980-81; pres. AgroBiotics, Inc., Balt., 1981-82, Urbana, Ill., 1981-82; sr. scientist Pall Corp., Glen Cove, N.Y., 1982-83, sr. mktg. mgr. biotech., 1983-85; dir. mktg. and sales, 1985-86; biotech./health care analyst Goldman Sachs & Co., 1986-92; dir. CS First Boston, N.Y.C., 1992—; cons. U.S. Senate Subcom. on Sci., Tech. and Space, 1979-80. Author: (with others) Genetic Engineering: Issues and Trends, 1982; contbr. numerous articles to profl. jours. Recipient Undergrad. Research award Bank of Am., 1970-71, Nat. Research Service award, 1976-79. Mem. Univ. Club, N.Y. Athletic Club, Neptune Boat Club. Democrat. Jewish. Office: CS First Boston 55 E 52nd St New York NY 10055-0002

SWARZ, SAHL, sculptor; b. N.Y.C., May 4, 1912; s. Samuel and Ida (Fass) S.; m. Naoco Kumasaka, May 1978. Student, Clay Club, N.Y.C., 1928-34, Art Students League, N.Y.C., 1930-31. Asso. Dir. Clay Club (and successor, Sculpture Center), 1938-54; creative sculpture in Italy, 1951-63; residence Am. Acad. in, Rome, 1955-57; lectr. sculpture Columbia U., N.Y.C., 1966-68, asst. prof., 1969-78; instr. Pratt Inst., Bklyn., 1964; instr. New Sch. for Social Rsch., 1965, 66; vis. lectr. art U. Wis., 1966; trustee Mus. Contemporary Sculpture, Tokyo. Author, illustrator: Blueprint for the Future of American Sculpture, 1943, also monograph.; one man exhbns. Sculpture Ctr., 1954, 57, 60, 62, 66, 71, 74, 78, Art Alliance, Phila., 1958, Fairweather-Hardin Gallery, Chgo., 1963, Brandeis U., Waltham, Mass., 1964, (retrospective exhbn.) Fair Lawn (N.J.) Pub. Library, 1977, Saikaya Gallery, Fujisawa, Japan, 1983, Mus. Contemporary Sculpture, Tokyo, 1985, Shonan Gallery, Fujisawa, Japan, 1985, 90, 93, (retrospective exhbn.) Toni de Rossi Gallery, Verona, Italy, 1983, 87, 91, Takashimaya Gallery, Yokohama, Japan, 1984, Atagoyama Gallery, Tokyo, 1988, 91, 94, 1st exhibition of painting Toni de Rossi Gallery, Verona, Italy, 1992, 96, Move Gallery Chigasaki, Japan, 1993; group shows include Fairmont Park Internat., Phila., 1948, Whitney Mus. Am. Art, 1948, 58, 60, 62, 64, Pa. Acad., 1948, 52, 54, 57, 60, 62, 66, Bklyn Mus., 1935, Detroit Inst. Fine Arts, 1957, San Francisco Mus., 1955, U. Ill., 1960, 62, others; represented in permanent collections Norfolk (Va.) Mus., Whitney Mus. Am. Art, Ball State Tchrs. Coll., Williams Coll. Mus., Ford Found., Mpls. Inst. Fine Arts, Va. Mus. Fine Arts, Richmond, Newark Mus., N.J. State Mus. at Trenton, Vatican Mus. Collection Modern Religious Art, Rose Art Mus., Brandeis U., Stamford (Conn.) Mus., Columbia U., others; bronze group The Guardian at Brookgreen (S.C.), Gardens Mus.; terra cotta wall sculpture, Linden, (N.J.), Post Office, sculptural designs, Fed. Courthouse, Statesville, N.C.; equestrian monument Gen. Bidwell, Buffalo; fountain commn., Spruce Run State Park, N.J.; mall sculpture, Pittsfield, Mass.; monument to Demeter in stainless steel, Fujisawa, Japan; subject of biography: Fifty Years of Sculpture by Sahl Swarz. Chmn. sculpture panel N.J. Coun. on Arts. With AUS, 1941-45. Grantee Am. Acad. Arts and Letters, 1955; Guggenheim fellow, 1955, 58. Address: Kumasaka-Swarz, 11-9 2 Chome Ishigami, Kugenuma, Fujisawa, Kanagawa 251, Japan *The essence of creativity is in the searching after the form. Search leads to revelation, understanding, knowledge. Realization of one's ignorance is the first step to the attainment of wisdom. A wise man makes a work of art out of life itself.*

SWATEK, FRANK EDWARD, microbiology educator; b. Oklahoma City, June 4, 1929; s. Clarence Michael and Bessie (Doubek) S.; m. Mary Frances Over, Jan. 28, 1951; children: Frank Edward, Lorraine Beth Butcher, Martha Lynn Bradshaw, Susan Ann Denny, Cheryl Lee. B.S. in Zoology, San Diego State Coll., 1951; M.A. in Microbiology, UCLA, 1955, Ph.D., 1956. Mem. faculty Calif. State U. at Long Beach, 1956-92, prof. microbiology, 1962-82, chmn. dept., 1960-82; cons. to industry, 1953—; cons. dept. dermatology Long Beach VA Hosp., 1956—; lectr. postgrad. medicine U. So. Calif., 1958—; adj. prof. clin. med. U. Calif., Irvine, 1980—; mem. fuel sect. Coordinating Research Council, 1961—. Author: Textbook of Microbiology, 1967, Laboratory Manual and Workbook for General Microbiology, 1969; also articles. Fellow Royal Soc. Health, Am. Acad. Microbiology; mem. Am. Soc. Microbiology (chmn. bd. edn. and tng. 1980-85, Carski Found. Disting. Teaching award 1974), Internat. Platform Assn., Sigma Xi, Lambda Xi Alpha, Phi Kappa Phi. Club: Long Beach Aquatic (pres. 1963-65). Research on med. mycology. Home: 812 Stevely Ave Long Beach CA 90815-5022

SWATSKY, BEN, church administrator. Exec. dir. Evangelical Free Church Mission, Minneapolis, Minn. Office: The Evang Free Ch Am 901 E 78th St Minneapolis MN 55420-1334

SWATT, STEPHEN BENTON, communications executive, consultant; b. L.A., June 26, 1944; s. Maurice I. and Lucille E. (Sternberger) S.; m. Susan Ruth Edelstein, Sept. 7, 1968; 1 child, Jeffrey Michael. BSBA, U. Calif., 1966, M in Journalism, 1967. Writer San Francisco Examiner, 1967; reporter United Press Internat., L.A., 1968-69; producer news Sta. KCRA-TV, Sacramento, Calif., 1969-70, reporter news, 1970-79, chief polit. and capitol corres., 1979-92; exec. v.p. Nelson-Lucas Communications, Sacramento, 1992—; guest lectr. Calif. State U., Sacramento. Contbr. articles to profl. jours. With USCG, 1966. Recipient No. Calif. Emmy NATAS, 1976-77, Pub. Svc. award Calif. State Bar, 1977, Exceptional Achievement Coun. advancement and Support of Edn., 1976, Nat. Health Journalism award Am. Chiropractic Assn., 1978. Mem. Soc. Profl. Journalists (8 awards), Capitol Corres. Assn., U. Calif. Alumni Assn., Sacramento Press Club. Avocations: hiking, jogging, fishing. Office: Nelson-Lucas Communications 1029 J St Ste 400 Sacramento CA 95814-2825

SWAYNE, DAVID EUGENE, avian pathologist, researcher; b. Yellville, Ark., Sept. 22, 1958; s. Dallas Eugene and Mary Sue (Shipman) S.; m. Anita Jane Walker, July 4, 1981; children: Rachel Miranda, Tyler Dallas, Kyle David. BSA, U. Ark., 1980; DVM, MSc in Vet. Pathology, U. Mo., 1984; PhD in Vet. Pathology, U. Ga., 1987. Diplomate Am. Coll. Vet. Pathologists, Am. Coll. Poultry Veterinarians. Asst. prof., assoc. prof. Ohio State U., Columbus, 1987-94; supervisory med. officer, lab. dir. S.E. Poultry Rsch. Lab., USDA Agr. Rsch. Svc., Athens, Ga., 1994—; adj. assoc. prof. U. Ga., Athens, 1994—. Mem. editl. bd. Avian Diseases; contbr. articles to Avian Diseases, Vet. Pathology, Infection and Immunity, Avian Pathology. Grantee USDA, 1991. Mem. AVMA, Am. Assn. Avian Pathologists (New Investigator award 1992), World Vet. Poultry Assn., Poultry Sci. Assn. Mem. Ch. of Christ. Achievements include research in avian influenza and intestinal spirochetosis. Office: USDA/ARS/SEPRL 934 College Station Rd Athens GA 30605-2720

SWAYZE, PATRICK, actor, dancer; b. Houston, Aug. 18, 1954; s. Patsy Swayze. Student, Harkness Sch., Joffrey Ballet Sch. Dancer (Broadway) Goodtime Charley, Grease; film appearances include (debut) Skatetown, U.S.A., 1979, The Outsiders, 1983, Uncommon Valor, 1983, Red Dawn, 1984, Grandview U.S.A., 1984, Youngblood, 1986, Dirty Dancing, 1987, Steel Dawn, 1987, Tiger Warsaw, 1988, Road House, 1989, Next of Kin, 1989, Ghost, 1989, Point Break, 1991, City of Joy, 1992, Father Hood, 1993, Tall Tale, 1994, To Wong Foo, Thanks for Everything, Julie Newmar, 1995, Three Wishes, 1995. Recipient Golden Apple award. Office: William Morris 151 El Camino Beverly Hills CA 90212*

SWAZEY, JUDITH POUND, institute president, sociomedical science educator; b. Bronxville, N.Y., Apr. 21, 1939; d. Robert Earl and Louise Titus (Hanson) Pound; m. Peter Woodman Swazey, Nov. 28, 1964; children: Elizabeth, Peter. AB, Wellesley Coll., 1961; PhD, Harvard U., 1966. Rsch. assoc. Harvard U., 1966-71, lectr., 1969-71, rsch. fellow, 1971-72; cons. com. brain scis. NRC, 1971-73; staff scientist neurosci. rsch. program MIT, Cambridge, 1973-74; assoc. prof. dept. socio-med. scis. and community medicine Boston U., 1974-77, prof., 1977-80, adj. prof. Schs. Medicine and Pub. Health, 1980—; exec. dir. Medicine in the Pub. Interest, Inc., Boston and Washington, 1979-82, 89-93; pres. Coll. of the Atlantic, Bar Harbor, Maine, 1982-84, Acadia Inst., Bar Harbor, 1984—; mem. Army Sci. Bd., 1987-92. Author: Reflexes and Motor Integration, the Development of Sherrington's Integrative Action Concept, 1969, (with others) Human Aspects of Biomedical Innovation, 1971, (with R. C. Fox) The Courage to Fail, a Social View of Organ Transplants and Hemodialysis, 1975, rev. edit., 1978 (hon. mention Am. Med. Writers Assn., C. Wright Mills award Am. Sociol. Assn.), Chlorpromazine in Psychiatry, a Study of Therapeutic Innovation, 1974, (with K. Reeds) Today's Medicine, Tomorrow's Science, Essays on Paths of Discovery in the Biomedical Sciences, 1978; editor: (with C. Wong) Dilemmas of Dying, Policies and Procedures for Decisions Not to Treat, 1981, (with F. Worden and G. Adelman) The Neurosciences: Paths of Discovery, 1975, (with R. C. Fox) Spare Parts, Organ Replacement in American Society, 1992; assoc. editor IRB: A Jour. of Human Subjects Rsch., 1979—; mem. editl. bd. Sci. and Engring. Ethics, 1994—; contbr. articles to profl. jours. Mem. Maine Dept. Human Svcs. Bioethics Adv. Com. (chair 1991-94); mem. Commn. on Rsch. Integrity, 1994-95; bd. dirs. Maine Bioethics Network, 1994—. Wellesley Coll. scholar, 1961; Wellesley Coll. Alumnae fellow Harvard U., 1966, NIH predoctoral fellow, 1966, Radcliffe Coll. Coll. grad. fellow, 1966. Mem. AAAS (sci. freedom and responsibility com. 1986-89), Inst. Medicine NAS (mem. health scis. policy bd. 1986-89), Grad. Record Exam. (bd. dirs. 1987-91), Sherrington Soc., Phi Beta Kappa, Sigma Xi. Office: Acadia Inst Bar Harbor ME 04609

SWEARER, DONALD KEENEY, Asian religions educator, writer; b. Wichita, Kans., Aug. 2, 1934; s. Edward Mays and Eloise Catherine (Keeney) S.; m. Nancy Chester; children: Susan Marie, Stephen Edward. AB cum laude, Princeton U., 1956, MA, 1965, PhD, 1967; BD, Yale U., 1962, STM, 1963. Instr. English dept. Bangkok Christian Coll., 1957-60; adminstrv. asst. Edward W. Hazen Found., New Haven, 1961-63; instr., then asst. prof. Oberlin (Ohio) Coll., 1965-70; assoc. prof. Swarthmore (Pa.) Coll., 1970-75, prof. Asian religions, 1975—, Eugene M. Lang Rsch. prof., 1987-92, Charles and Harriet Cox McDowell prof., 1993—, chair dept. religion, 1986-91; Numata prof. Buddhist studies U. Hawaii, 1993; adj. prof. U. Pa., Phila., 1979—, Temple U., Phila., 1991—; film. cons. ABC, 1972, BBC, 1977, WGBH, 1991-93; lectr. Smithsonian Instn., 1982—, Asia Soc. N.Y., 1982—; bd. dirs. Soc. Buddhist-Christian Studies, 1994—. Author: Wat Haripunjaya, 1976, Dialogue. The Key to Understanding Other Religions, 1977, Buddhism and Society in Southeast Asia, 1981; co-author: For the Sake of the World. The Spirit of Buddhist and Christian Monasticism, 1989; co-editor: Ethics, Wealth and Salvation. A Study in Buddhist Social Ethics, 1989, Me-and-Mine, Selected Essays of Bhikkhu Buddhadasa, 1989, The Buddhist World of Southeast Asia, 1995; mem. editl. bd. Jour. Religious Ethics, 1978-93, Jour. Ecumenical Studies, 1983—; asst. editor Jour. Asian Studies, 1978-80; book rev. editor S.E. Asia Religious Studies Rev., 1985-93; contbr. articles to various publs. Chair adult edn. Swarthmore Presbyn. Ch., 1985-87, 92-93. Asian religious study fellow Soc. Religion in Higher Edn., Sri Lanka, Thailand, Japan, 1967-68, NEH sr. fellow Thailand, 1972-73, Rockefeller Found. humanities fellow, Thailand, 1985-86, Guggenheim fellow, 1994, Fulbright fellow Dept. Energy, 1994; sr. rsch. scholar Fulbright

Found., 1989-90, 94; NEH transl. grantee, 1990-91. Mem. AAUP, Assn. Asian Studies (bd. dirs. 1977-80), Am. Acad. Religion (v.p. mid-Atlantic region 1971-72), Am. Soc. Study of Religion, Soc. Buddhist-Christian Studies (bd. dirs. 1995—), Phi Beta Kappa. Democrat. Home: 109 Columbia Ave Swarthmore PA 19081-1615 Office: Swarthmore Coll Dept Religion 500 College Ave Swarthmore PA 19081-1390

SWEARINGEN, DAVID CLARKE, physician, musician; b. Shreveport, La., Apr. 23, 1942; s. David C. and Alverne (Walker) S.; m. Marion Joan Adams; children: David, Joy. BS, Centenary Coll., 1963; MD, La. State U., 1967. Intern Confederate Meml. Med. Ctr., Shreveport, 1967-68, resident in ophthalmology, 1968-71; staff ophthalmologist U.S. Naval Hosp., Memphis, 1971-73; pvt. practice in ophthalmology Shreveport, 1973-78; jr. officer of deck USS Halsey CG23, 1979; comdr. med. corps, head dept. ophthalmology, chmn. utilization rev. com. ophthalmology, family practice resident instr. opthalmology U.S. Naval Hosp., Jacksonville, Fla., 1981-84; med. dir. Bio Blood Components, Shreveport, 1985-88; dir. phys. health support svcs. Ctrl. La. State Hosp., Pineville, La., 1991—, exec. hosp. and med. exec. com., chmn. infection control and pharmacy, therapeutics com.; chmn. infection control com., pharmacy and therapeutics com.; pres. Shreveport Eye and Ear Soc., 1973-74; med. cons. Cenla Chem. Dependency Coun., Pineville, 1989—, Work Tng. Facility, Pineville, 1989—. Prin. bassoonist Cenla Symphonic Band, Pineville, 1988—; mem. Jacksonville Fla. Concert Choral, 1978-81; vestry mem. St. Michaels Ch., Pineville; active Am. Mus. Natural History Assocs. Recipient Physician Recognition award for Continuing Med. Edn. Mem. Internat. Platform Assn., So. Med. Assn., Nat. Parks and Conservation Assn., N.Y. Acad. Scis., La. Wildlife Fedn., Wilderness Soc., Nature Conservancy, Smithsonian Assocs., Cousteau Soc., Soc. Hist. Preservation, Environ. Def. Fund, Planetary Soc., Nat. Audubon Soc., Am. Legion, Alpha Epsilon Delta, Gamma Beta Gamma, Nu Sigma Nu. Republican. Episcopalian. Avocations: organ and bassoon music, collectibles, breeding exotic birds, shipmodel building. Home: 10 Azalea Rd Pineville LA 71360-8004 Office: Ctrl La State Hosp PO Box 5031 242 W Shamrock Ave Pineville LA 71360-6439

SWEASY, JOYCE ELIZABETH, government official, military reserve officer; b. Key West, Fla., Apr. 25, 1948; d. James Alfred and Josephine Mary (Fassel) Messick. BFA, Phila. Coll. Art, 1971; A in Bus. Adminstrn., Howard County Community Coll., 1985; grad., Army Command and Gen. Staff Co, 1988. Commd. 1st lt. U.S. Army, 1978, advanced through grades to lt. col., 1996; contract specialist U.S. Army, Adelphi, 1978-84, analyst procurement Lab. Command,, 1984-85; appointed command competition adv. Sec. of the Army, Adelphi, 1985-91; dep. chief of staff procurement, 1991-92, div. chief small bus. adminstrn., 1992-94; chief constrn. and arch. engrng. contracting NIH, Bethesda, Md., 1994—; owner, operator Hand Made 'N Ellicott City, Md., 1983—; owner, gen. mgr. Data Solutions. Contbr. numerous articles to profl. jours. Mem. Font Hill Citizens Orgn., Ellicott City, 1987—. Mem. U.S. Army Res. Officers Assn, Nat. Contract Mgrs. Assn., Am. Def. Preparedness Assn. Republican. Roman Catholic. Avocations: skiing, private pilot/flying, backpacking, skydiving, writing short stories. Home: 4008 Arjay Cir Ellicott City MD 21042-5608 Office: NIH Bethesda WA 20892

SWEDA, LINDA IRENE, elementary school educator; b. Elyria, Ohio, June 16, 1951; d. Charles R. and Hattie M. (Nolan) Rogers; m. Robert D. Winnigham, Jan. 29, 19071 (div. Mar. 1988); 1 child, Ryan D.; m. Paul G. Sweda, July 2, 1993. BS in Edn. summa cum laude, Ohio U., 1976; MA in Edn. and Supervision, Ashland U., 1989. Cert. tchr., Ohio. Psychiat. technician Licking County Meml. Hosp., Newark, Ohio, 1971-72; psychiat. technician, house parent Nelsonville (Ohio) Children's Ctr., 1972-73; tchr. Elyria City Schs., 1977—, mem. tchr. mentorship com., 1990—, mem. math. coun. adv., 1991—, mem. tchr. camp intervention program, 1991—, mem. venture capital grant rsch. Jefferson Elem. Sch., 1992—; insvc. facilitator Math Manipulatives, 1993-94; spkr. Sch. Levy, Elyria, 1987, 89. Scriptwriter (video) Math Matters, 1993. Mem. adv. bd., participant Cleve. Children's Mus., 1989-91; campaign worker coun., mayors, judges, senate, house, 1994—; participant, rschr. Polit. Discussion Group, Elyria, 1989—; mem. Earth Island Inst., San Francisco, 1994; mentor Lorain County Ctr. for Leadership, 1990—. Named Martha Holden Jennings scholar, 1979. Mem. NEA, Ohio Edn. Assn., Elyria Edn. Assn. Avocations: reading, decorating, painting, swimming. Home: 989 Gulf Rd Elyria OH 44035-2961 Office: Jefferson Elem Sch 615 Foster Ave Elyria OH 44035-3328

SWEDBERG, ROBERT MITCHELL, opera company director; b. Glendale, Calif., Feb. 7, 1950; s. William Miller and Marion (Mitchell) S.; m. Melissa Ellen Libby, Aug. 4, 1954; children: Olivia Lauren, Erik Andrew. BA, BM, Calif. State U., Northridge, 1975. Dir. edn. and spl. projects, production stage mgr. Seattle Opera, 1978-82; mgr., artistic dir. N.C. Operas (now called Opera Carolina), Charlotte, 1982-87; gen. dir. Syracuse (N.Y.) Opera, 1987-90; dir. opera program Syracuse U., 1989-90; gen. dir. Orlando (Fla.) Opera, 1990—; stage dir. Anchorage Opera, 1979-81, San Francisco Opera, 1982, Greater Buffalo Opera, 1988; judge auditions Met. Opera, 1986—; cons. Nat. Endowment for Arts, 1991—. Host: Opera Hour Sta. WMFE, Orlando. Bd. dirs. arts svcs. coun. World Cup Spl. Events Com., Italian Cultural Soc., Downtown Orlando partnership; mem. Leadership Orlando, 1995, Leadership Ctrl. Fla., 1996. Recipient Tiffany award Civic Morning Mus., 1989, Jaycees award, 1990. Avocations: camping, fishing. Home: 9437 Lake Douglas Pl Orlando FL 32817-2603 Office: Orlando Opera Co 1111 N Orange Ave Orlando FL 32804-6407

SWEEBE, RICHARD DALE, lawyer; b. Akron, Ohio, Aug. 13, 1951; s. Delbert Henry and Yvonne Rose (Gray) S. BA in Polit. Sci. cum laude, Kent State U., 1975; JD, U. Akron, 1979. Bar: Ohio 1979, U.S. Dist. Ct. (no. dist.) Ohio 1980, U.S. Ct. Appeals (6th cir.) 1980. Asst. prosecutor Summit County, Akron, 1979-82; assoc. Ulmer & Berne, Cleve., 1982-88, ptnr., 1988; instr. Bur. Alcohol, Tobacco and Firearms Arson for Profit Sch.; speaker ins. and law enforcement seminars, 1980—. Mem. planning com. Ohio Arson Sch., Columbus, 1985—. Served with U.S. Army, 1970-72. Recipient commendation Akron Fire Dept., 1981, Akron Police Dept., 1982, FBI, 1981, Ohio Arson Sch. and Internat. Assn. Arson Investigators, 1984-85. Mem. ABA, Ohio Bar Assn., Greater Cleve. Bar Assn., Def. Rsch. and Trial Lawyers Assn., Nat. Soc. Profl. Ins. Investigators, Interant. Assn. Arson Investigators. Avocations: boating, snow skiing.

SWEED, PHYLLIS, publishing executive; b. N.Y.C., Dec. 6, 1931; d. Paul and Frances (Spitzer) S.; m. Leonard Bogdanoff (dec. Oct. 1975); children: Patricia Romano (dec.), James Alan. BA, NYU, 1950. Asst. buyer Nat. Bellas Hess, N.Y.C., 1950; assoc. editor Fox-Shulman Pub., N.Y.C., 1951-57; products editor McGraw-Hill Pub., N.Y.C., 1957-61; mng. editor Haire Pub., N.Y.C., 1962-66; editor-in-chief, co-pub., sr. v.p. Geyer-McAllister Pub., N.Y.C., 1966—. Editor-in-chief: (mag.) Gifts and Decorative Accessories, 1966— (Nat. Assn. Ltd. Edit. Dealers award 1993, Mag. Week Excellence award 1992, Dallas Mkt. Ctr. awards 1969, 80, 82). Bd. dirs. Frances Hook Scholarship Fund, 1989—. Recipient Editorial Excellence award Indsl. Mktg., 1964. Mem. Nat. Assn. Ltd. Ed. Dealers (assoc.), Internat. Furnishings and Design Assn. Avocations: gardening, collecting antique Belleek. Home: 505 Laguardia Pl New York NY 10012-2001 Office: Geyer-McAllister Publs 51 Madison Ave New York NY 10010-1603

SWEEDEN, THOMAS RICHARD, hospital administrator; b. Abilene, Tex., June 16, 1947; married;. BA, U. Houston, 1972; MA, Southwest Tex. State U., 1978. Asst. dir. mgmt. unit U. Tex. Med. Branch, Galveston, 1972-75; dir. unit mgmt. Scott and White Meml. Hosp., Temple, Tex., 1976-81, asst. administr. support svcs., 1981-86, administr., 1988—; interim administr. Coryell Meml. Hosp., Gatesville, Tex., 1986-88. Office: Scott & White Meml Hosp 2401 S 31st St Temple TX 76508-0001*

SWEEDLER, BARRY MARTIN, federal agency administrator; b. Bklyn., Mar. 11, 1937; s. Louis and Sadie (Bloch) S.; m. Kathryn Grace Stewart, June 26, 1988; children by previous marriage: Ian, Elizabeth. BME, CCNY, 1960; MBA, Baruch Sch., CUNY, 1966. Registered profl. engr., N.Y. Asst. and jr. engr. N.Y. State Pub. Svc. Commn., N.Y.C., 1960-66, sr. gas engr., 1966-69; chief pipeline safety div. Nat. Transp. Safety Bd., Washington, 1969-74, dep. dir. Bur. Surface Transp. Safety, 1974-76, dep. dir., acting dir. Bur. Plans and Programs, 1976-79, dep. dir. Bur. Tech., 1979-82, dir. Bur. Safety Programs, 1982-90; dir. Office of Safety Recommendations Nat. Transp. Safety Bd., 1990—; guest lectr. Inst. Gas Tech., 1973, U. Md., 1974, U. Calif., San Diego, 1986, 88-89, U. N.Mex., 1987, U. Calgary, 1988; participant Internat. Workshop on High Alcohol Consumers and Traffic, Paris, 1988; presented policy and tech. papers on alcohol and drug abuse in transp. at numerous internat. symposiums and congresses including 34th Internat. Congress on Alcoholism and Drug Dependencies, Calgary, Atla., Can., 1985, 10th Internat. Conf. on Alcohol, Drugs & Traffic Safety, Amsterdam, The Netherlands, 1986, and Internat. Symposium on Young Drivers Alcohol and Drug Impairment, Amsterdam, 1986; co-editor proc., chmn. alcohol, drugs and traffic safety program 35th Internat. Congress on Alcoholism and Drug Dependencies, Oslo, Norway, 1988, the 12th Internat. Conf. on Alcohol, Drugs and Traffic Safety, Cologne, 1992, 36th Internat. Inst. on Prevention and Treatment of Alcoholism, Stockholm, 1991, 12th World Congress of Internat. Assn. Accident and Traffic Medicine, 1992, 13th Internat. Conf. on Alcohol, Drugs and Traffic Safety, Adelaide, Australia, 1995. Author (with others) Gas Engineers Handbook, 1985; contbr. numerous articles on transp. safety to jours.; mem. editorial bd. Jour. Traffic Medicine, 1989—; numerous TV and print media interviews. Bd. dirs. Great Falls (Va.) Citizens Assn., 1980-85, Tysons Manor Home Owners Assn., Vienna, Va., 1973-77; mem. Fairfax County (Va.) oversight com. on drinking and driving, 1984—, chmn., 1986-88. Recipient Presdl. Rank of Meritorious Exec., 1987. Mem. ASME, Transp. Rsch. Bd. NAS (chmn. com. on alcohol, other drugs and transp. 1991—, com. on transp. of hazardous materials 1972-78, com. on highway/R.R. grade crossing safety 1977-86, com. on utilities 1972-79), Internat. Coun. Alcohol and Addictions (co-chmn. sect. on traffic safety 1988—), Internat. Coun. Alcohol, Drugs and Traffic Safety (sec. 1992—, co-editor coun. newsletter ICADTS Reporter 1990—), Am. Acad. Forensic Scis. (adv. mem. drugs and driving com. 1988—), Operation Lifesaver (program devel. coun. 1987—), Nat. Safety Coun. (motor vehicle occupant protection com. 1983—), Am. Pub. Works Assn. (exec. com. utility location and coordination coun. 1980-87, hon. life mem.), Internat. Transp. Safety Assn. (editor assn. newsletter ITSA Report 1994—). Jewish. Avocations: tennis, hiking, bicycling. Office: Nat Transp Safety Bd Office of Safety Recommendations 490 L'enfant Plz SW Washington DC 20594-0001

SWEEN, JOYCE ANN, sociologist, psychologist, educator; b. N.Y.C.; d. Sigfried Joseph Ellmer and Julie (Hollins) Ellmer Hutchins; children: Terri Lynn, James Michael. B.S. in Math., Antioch Coll., 1960; M.S. in Exptl. Psychology, Northwestern U., 1965, Ph.D. in Social Psychology/Evaluation Research, 1971; Univ. fellow Northwestern U., Evanston, Ill., 1960-63, dir. computer ops. Inst. Met. Studies, Northwestern U., 1965-70; asst. prof. sociology DePaul U., Chgo., 1971-74, assoc. prof., 1974-80, prof., 1980-83, prof. sociology and pub. service, 1983—; cons. Nat. Commn. on Violence, 1968; evaluator Office Adolescent Pregnancy Programs, 1988-92, Office of Substance Abuse Prevention, 1988-93, Office of Treament Improvement, 1988-93, dropout prevention program Aspira of Ill., 1984-88, Dept. of Edn., 1989-95, AIDS edn. program, Ctrs. for Disease Ctrl., 1992, Chgo. Dept. Health, 1993-95; cons. in field. NIH grantee, 1971-75, 78-81; NSF grantee, 1979-82; AMA grantee, 1991. Mem. Internat. Sociol. Assn., Am. Sociol. Assn., Am. Psychol. Assn., Am. Evaluation Assn., Midwest Sociol. Soc., AAAS, Sigma Xi. Research, publs. on fertility, African polygyny, childlessness, teen pregancy, urbanization, social effects of assassination, evaluation methodology, exptl. regression designs, sch. dropout prevention, AIDS edn., bilingual education, violence. Office: DePaul U Dept Sociology 2323 N Seminary Ave Chicago IL 60614-3211

SWEENEY, ARTHUR HAMILTON, JR., metal manufacturing executive, retired army officer; b. Charleston, W.Va., Nov. 9, 1920; s. Arthur Hamilton and Neva Pauline (Davies) S.; m. Veronica Frances Donovan, Dec. 27, 1952. S.B., MIT, 1942; M.B.A., Harvard, 1947. Commd. officer U.S. Army, advanced through grades to maj. gen.; comdg. officer U.S. Army Springfield (Mass.) Armory, 1965-67, U.S. Army Watervliet (N.Y.) Arsenal, 1967-68; dep. comdg. gen. U.S. Army Weapons Command, Rock Island, Ill., 1968-70; comdg. gen. Quinhon Support Command, Vietnam, 1970, DaNang Support Command, Vietnam, 1970-72, White Sands Missile Range, N.Mex., 1972-74, U.S. Army Materiel Mgmt. Agy., Europe, 1974-76; dep. chief of staff for logistics U.S. Army Forces Command, 1976-78; ret., 1978; corporate dir., v.p. corp. devel. Reynolds Metals Internat., Richmond, Va., 1978-91; exec. cons. Bd. of Def. Enterprise Fund, 1994. Decorated D.S.M. with oak leaf cluster, Legion of Merit with oak leaf cluster, Joint Services Commendation medal, Army Commendation medal. Home: 2956 Hathaway Rd Richmond VA 23225-1728

SWEENEY, ASHER WILLIAM, state supreme court justice; b. Canfield, Ohio, Dec. 11, 1920; s. Walter William and Jessie Joan (Kidd) S.; m. Bertha M. Englert, May 21, 1945; children: Randall W., Ronald R., Garland A., Karen M. Student, Youngstown U., 1939-42; LL.B., Duke U., 1948. Bar: Ohio 1949. Practiced law Youngstown, Ohio, 1949-51; judge adv. gen. Dept. Def., Washington, 1951-65; chief Fed. Contracting Agy., Cin., 1965-68; corp. law, 1968-77; justice Ohio Supreme Ct., Columbus, 1977—. Democratic candidate for Sec. of State Ohio, 1958. Served with U.S. Army, 1942-46; col. Res. 1951-68. Decorated Legion of Merit, Bronze Star; named to Army Hall of Fame Ft. Benning, Ga., 1981. Mem. Ohio Bar Assn., Phi Delta Phi. Democrat. Home: 6690 Drake Rd Cincinnati OH 45243-2706 Office: Ohio Supreme Ct 30 E Broad St Fl 3D Columbus OH 43215-3414

SWEENEY, CLAYTON ANTHONY, lawyer, business executive; b. Pitts., Oct. 20, 1931; s. Denis Regis and Grace Frances (Roche) S.; m. Sally Dimond, Oct. 4, 1958; children—Sharon, Lorrie, Maureen, Clayton Anthony, Tara, Megan. B.S., Duquesne U., 1957, LL.B., 1962. Bar: Pa. 1962, U.S. Supreme Ct. 1968. Supr. transp. claims H.J. Heinz Co., Pitts., 1955-57; mgr. market research Murray Corp. Am., Pitts., 1957-62; ptnr. Buchanan, Ingersoll, Rodewald, Kyle and Buerger, Pitts., 1962-78; sr. v.p. Allegheny Ludlum Industries, Inc., Pitts., 1978-81; exec. v.p., chief adminstrv. officer Allegheny Internat., Inc., Pitts., 1981-84, vice chmn., 1984-85; ptnr., mng. dir. Dickie, McCamey & Chilcote, Pitts., 1986—, also bd. dirs.; bd. dirs. Wilkinson Sword Group Ltd., U.K., Landmark Savs. and Loan Assn., Liquid Air N.Am., Halbouty Energy Co., Koppers Holding Corp., Koppers Industries, Inc., Schaefer Mfg., Inc., Schaefer Marine, Inc., Schaefer Equipment, Inc.; adj. prof. Duquesne U. Sch. Law; lectr. Pa. Bar Inst. Bd. dirs. Met. Pitts. Pub. Broadcasting, Inc., Diocesan Sch. Bd., Roman Cath. Diocese Pitts., Toner Inst., Christian Assocs. of Southwestern Pa., Wesley Inst., Inc., Jr. Achievement S.W. Pa., YMCA Western Pa.; chmn. Seton Hill Coll.; mem. St. Thomas More Sch. Bd., Bethel Park, Pa.; chmn. St. Francis Med. Ctr., St. Francis Health System; chmn. bd. DePaul Inst. With U.S. Army, 1953-55. Named one of 100 Most Disting. Living Alumni Duquesne U. Century Club, 1978. Mem. Acad. Trial Lawyers Allegheny County, ABA, Pa. Bar Assn., St. Thomas More Soc. Home: 232 Thornberry Cir Pittsburgh PA 15234 Office: Dickie McCamey & Chilcote Ste 400 2 PPG Pl Pittsburgh PA 15222-5402

SWEENEY, DANIEL THOMAS, cable television company executive; b. N.Y.C., Sept. 25, 1929; s. Daniel Thomas and Rose Marie (Delorenzo) S.; m. Anita Geraldine Madeo, Feb. 14, 1953; children: John, William, Robert, Ellen, Daniel, David. BS, N.Y. State Maritime Coll., 1952; LLB, Fordham U., 1957; LLM, NYU, 1962. Bar: N.Y. Assoc. Kirlin, Campbell and Keating, N.Y.C., 1957-62; dep. county atty. Nassau County, Garden City, N.Y., 1962-65, undersheriff, 1965-66, dep. county exec., 1966-69; chmn., chief exec. officer Mitchel Field Devel. Corp., Garden City, 1969-71; pres. Sweeney/Edman Enterprises Inc., Hempstead, N.Y., 1971-72; exec. v.p., chief oper. officer HBO, N.Y.C., 1972-73; dir. Cablevision Systems Corp., Woodbury, N.Y., 1973—; pres. Channel 21, Sta. WLIW-TV, Garden City, N.Y., 1970-74. Chmn. L.I. State Pk. and Recreation Com., Babylon, N.Y., 1976-83, Jones Beach State Pkwy. Authority, Babylon, N.Y., 1976-79. Lt. comdr. USN, 1952-54, Korea. Democrat. Roman Catholic. Home: 94 Glenlawn Ave Sea Cliff NY 11579-2038 Office: Cablevision Systems Corp 1 Media Crossways Woodbury NY 11797-2062

SWEENEY, DAVID BRIAN, lawyer; b. Seattle, June 23, 1941; s. Hubert Lee and Ann Louise (Harmon) S.; m. Janice Kay Goins, June 18, 1983; children: Stuart, Jennifer, Ann, Katharine. B.A. magna cum laude, Yale U., 1963; LL.B., Harvard U., 1967. Bar: Wash. 1968, U.S. Dist. Ct. (we. dist.) Wash., 1968, U.S. Ct. Appeals (9th cir.) 1968. Assoc. Roberts, Shefelman, Lawrence, Gay and Moch, Seattle, 1968-75; ptnr. Roberts, Shefelman, Lawrence, Gay & Moch, later Roberts & Shefelman, then Foster, Pepper and Shefelman, 1976—. Mem. Seattle-King County Bar Assn., Wash. State Bar Assn., ABA, Estate Planning Council of Seattle. Republican. Presbyterian. Clubs: College, Harbor, Columbia Tower (Seattle). Home: 2343 32nd Ave S Seattle WA 98144-5533 Office: Foster Pepper & Shefelman 1111 3rd Ave Fl 34 Seattle WA 98101-3207

SWEENEY, FRANCIS E., state supreme court justice; b. Jan. 26, 1934; married; 4 children. BSBA, Xavier U., 1956; JD, Cleve.-Marshall Law Sch., 1963. Profl. football player Ottawa Rough Riders, Ont., Can., 1956-58; mem. legal dept. Allstate Ins. Co., Cleve., 1958-63; asst. prosecuting atty. Cuyahoga County, Cleve., 1963-70; judge Cuyahoga County Ct. of Common Pleas, Cleve., 1970-88; judge (8th cir.) U.S. Ct. Appeals, Cleve., 1988-92; justice Ohio Supreme Ct., Columbus, 1992—. With U.S. Army, 1957-58. Recipient Legion of Honor award Xavier U., 1956, Outstanding Jud. Svc. award Ohio Supreme Ct., 1972-85, Alumnus of Yr. award Xavier U., 1977. Office: Ohio Supreme Ct 30 E Broad St Columbus OH 43215-3414

SWEENEY, GARNETTE GRINNELL, elementary education educator; b. Pensacola, Fla., Oct. 5, 1964; d. Robert Orlando and Diane (Dodge) Grinnell; m. John William Sweeney, Feb. 21, 1988. AD, Ctrl. Va. C.C., Lynchburg, 1985; BS, Radford U., 1987; M in Adminstrn. and Supervision, Va. Tech., 1994. Tchr. elem. Bedford (Va.) County Schs., 1989-94, tchr. mid. sch., 1994—; coach Odyssey of the Mind, Lynchburg, Va., 1991-93, 94-95, trainer, problem chpt., state judge, 1994. Named Conservation Educator of Yr. Peaks of Otter Soil and Conservation Dist., 1991-92; recipient Environ. award Jr. Women's Club Va., 1991, Hon. Mention Newsweek and Amway Environ. Awareness, 1992. Mem. ASCD, Fraternal Order Police. Republican. Avocations: skiing, travel, hiking, canoeing, reading. Office: Bedford County Pub Schs PO Box 748 Bedford VA 24523-0748

SWEENEY, JAMES LEE, engineering and economic systems educator, consultant; b. Waterbury, Conn., Mar. 22, 1944; s. James Wallace and Aletha B. Sweeney; m. Susan L. Van Every, Aug. 21, 1971; children: Erin, Ryan, Regan. BSEE, M.I.T., 1966; PhD in Engrng.-Econ. Systems, Stanford U., 1971. Dir. office energy systems, modeling and forecasting U.S. Fed. Energy Adminstrn. Washington, 1974-76; with Stanford U. 1967—, prof. engring.-econ. systems, 1971—, chmn. dept. engring.-econ. systems, 1991—; dir. Energy Modeling Forum, 1978-85, chmn. Inst. Energy Studies, 1981-84, cons. faculty Sch. of Law, 1980-82, mem. steering com. Ctr. Econ. policy Rsch., 1982—, dir., 1984-86; cons. U.S. Dept. Energy, NRC, Exxon, Charles River Assocs. Recipient Disting. Service award Fed. Energy Adminstrn., 1975. Mem. Am. Econ. Assn., Internat. Assn. Energy Econs. (past v.p. for publs.), Eta Kappa Nu, Tau Beta Pi, Rotary (past pres.), Menlo Circus Club. Co-author: Macroeconomics Impacts of Energy Shocks, 1987, Fuels to Drive Our Future, 1990; editor: Handbook of Natural Resources and Energy Economics, 1985, 93; co-editor: (jour.) Resources and Energy; contbr. numerous publs. in field to profl. jours. Home: 445 El Escarpado Stanford CA 94305 Office: Stanford U Dept Engring-Econ Systems Terman Engring Ctr Rm 312 Stanford CA 94305-4025

SWEENEY, JAMES RAYMOND, lawyer; b. Chgo., Feb. 19, 1928; s. John Francis and Mae J. (McDonald) S.; m. Rhoda W. Davis, May 15, 1987; children from previous marriage: Margaret Elizabeth, John Francis, Thomas Edward. B.S., U. Notre Dame, 1950; J.D., Northwestern U., 1956. Bar: Ill. 1956. With firm Schroeder, Hofgren, Brady & Wegner, Chgo., 1956-61; ptnr. Hofgren, Wegner, Allen, Stellman & McCord, Chgo., 1962-71, Coffee, Wetzel, Sweeney, Chgo., 1971-72, Coffee & Sweeney, 1972-76, Mason, Kolehmainen, Rathburn & Wyss, Chgo., 1976-82, McWilliams, Mann, Zummer & Sweeney, 1983-86, Mann, McWilliams, Zummer, & Sweeney, 1986-89, Lee, Mann, Smith, McWilliams & Sweeney, 1989-91, Lee, Mann, Smith, McWilliams, Sweeney & Ohlson, 1991—; commr. for disbarment matters Ill. Supreme Ct., 1963-73; mem. hearing div. Atty. Registration and Discipline Commn., 1974-77, chmn. commn. 1983-90. Bd. dirs., sec. Highland Park (Ill.) Hosp., 1972-79. Served as lt. (j.g.) USN, 1950-53; lt. comdr. Res. ret. Mem. ABA (coun. patent, trademark and copyright sect., sec. 1978-82), Ill. State Bar (assembly 1990-96), Chgo. Bar Assn. (sec. 1977-79), Bar Assn. 7th Cir., Intellectual Property Law Assn. Chgo., Patent Law Assn. Chgo. (pres. 1974), The Law Club Skokie (Ill.), Country Club, Union League Club. Home: 505 N Lake Shore Dr Chicago IL 60611-3427 Office: Lee Mann Smith McWilliams Sweeney & Ohlson 209 S LaSalle St # 410 Chicago IL 60604-1202

SWEENEY, JOHN LAWRENCE, lawyer; b. Staten Island, N.Y., Jan. 5, 1962; s. Lawrence Patrick and Lauretta (Kronen) S.; m. Karen Anne Herbank, Aug. 26, 1988; children: Conor, Lauren, Devin, Pearse. BA, Yale U., 1984; JD magna cum laude, Seton Hall U., 1990; LLM in Taxation, NYU, 1993. Bar: N.J. 1990, U.S. Dist. Ct. N.J. 1990, N.Y. 1991, U.S. Tax Ct. 1995. Assoc. Connell, Foley & Geiser, Roseland, N.J., 1990-92, Lampf, Lipkind, Prupis & Pettegrew, West Orange, N.J., 1992-93; atty. pvt. practice, Morristown, N.J., 1993—. Interview supr. Yale Alumni Schs. Com., 1991—; charter mem. Seton Hall Prep Hall of Fame Com., 1984-94. Mem. N.J. Bar Assn., N.Y. Bar Assn., Morris County Bar Assn., Yale Club Ctrl. N.J. (trustee 1991-94). Home: 102 Runnymede Pky New Providence NJ 07974 Office: 4 Maple Ave Morristown NJ 07960

SWEENEY, JOHN W., III, newspaper executive; b. Jersey City, N.J., July 11, 1946; s. John William Jr. and Rita Constance (Dillon) S.; m. Jo Ellen Cooley, Nov. 7, 1970; children: John W. IV, Jessica Elizabeth. BA in English, King's Coll., Wilkes Barre, Pa., 1968. Dealer sales Humble Oil/Exxon, Washington, 1968-69; nat. automotive mgr. Washington Post, 1969-74; advt. dir. Trenton (N.J.) Times, 1974-78, Boston Herald, 1978-80; advt. dir. Houston Chronicle, 1980-83, sales & mktg. dir., 1983-86, v.p. sales & mktg., 1986-91, v.p., gen. mgr., 1991—. Chmn. mktg. com. United Way Tex. Gulf Coast, Houston, 1985-86, 90-91; bd. dirs. Jr. Achievement, Houston, 1991—, Better Bus. Bur., Houston, 1991—; mem. adv. bd. Houston Ballet, 1988-92. Mem. Newspaper Assn. Am. (bd. govs. 1993—, mem. mktg. ops. com. 1993—). Avocations: golf, coaching youth sports. Office: Houston Chronicle 801 Texas St Houston TX 77002-2906

SWEENEY, JUDITH L., newspaper publishing executive. V.p., pres. Orange County edit. L.A. Times. Office: LA Times Times Mirror Sq Los Angeles CA 90012

SWEENEY, MARK OWEN, publisher; b. Cherryvale, Kans., Dec. 27, 1942; s. Paul Eldon and Clelia Eugenia (Bosette) S.; m. Janet Lynn Turner, July 24, 1964; children—Douglas, Jonathan. Grad., Moody Bible Inst., 1963; B.A., Pacific Coll., 1965; M.A., Wheaton Coll., Ill., 1967. Instr. history Cascade Coll., Portland, Oreg., 1967-70; editor Moody Bible Inst., Chgo., 1970-72; exec. producer Moody Corr. Sch., Moody Bible Inst. (Radio div.), 1972-74; dir. public relations Moody Bible Inst. (dir. Moody Lit. Ministries), 1974-77, mgr. publ. div., 1977-81; dir. Victor Books, Scripture Press Publs., 1981-83, v.p., 1983-90; pubr., COO Victor Books, Scripture Press Publs., Wheaton, Ill., 1990-94; corp. v.p., pub. Scripture Press Publs., Inc. and Victor Books, Wheaton, 1994-95; sr. v.p. Killion McCabe and Assocs., Dallas, 1995—. Mem. Christian Booksellers Assn., Evang. Christian Pubs. Assn. (past chmn. bd.), Nat. Assn. Evangelicals. Home: 5939 Deseret Trail Dallas TX 75252 Office: Killion McCabe and Assocs 900 Coit Central Tower 12001 North Central Expwy Dallas TX 75243-3788

SWEENEY, MICHAEL ANDREW, newspaper editor; b. York, Pa., Nov. 27, 1948; s. Felix William and Deuris C. (Ehehalt) S.; m. Linda Carol Gillam, Nov. 20, 1976; children: Barbara Catherine, Matthew Allan. BA in Communication Art, Seton Hall U., 1972; MA in Polit. Sci., Rutgers U., 1981. Reporter The Courier-News, Bridgwater, N.J., 1972-75, asst. night editor, 1975-77, night editor, 1977-78, nat. editor, 1978-79, asst. news editor, 1980-81; news editor The Advocate Southern Conn. Newspapers Inc., Stamford, Conn., 1981-83, exec. news editor, 1983-85, asst. mng. editor, 1985-88; editorial page editor Greenwich Time/So. Conn. Newspapers, Inc., 1988—, columnist, 1991—. Contbr. articles to profl. jours. Roman Catholic. Avocations: gardening, computers. Office: Greenwich Time 20 E Elm St Greenwich CT 06830-6529

SWEENEY, MICHAEL J., lawyer; b. Chgo., Feb. 17, 1953. BA with high honors, U. Ill., 1973; JD cum laude, U. Chgo., 1976. Bar: Ill. 1976, U.S. Dist. Ct. (no. dist.) Ill. 1976, U.S. Ct. Appeals (7th cir.) 1978, U.S. Ct. Appeals (3d cir.) 1986, U.S. Ct. Appeals (10th cir.) 1988. Ptnr. Sidley &

Austin, Chgo.; part-time instr. DePaul U., Chgo., 1987, 89. Office: Sidley & Austin 1 First Nat Plz Chicago IL 60603*

SWEENEY, RICHARD JAMES, economics educator; b. San Diego, Jan. 13, 1944; s. John Joseph and Catherine Scott (Spahr) S.; m. Joan Long, June 19, 1965; children: Robin Scott, Erin Michaela. BA, UCLA, 1965; PhD, Princeton U., 1972. Acting asst. prof. econs. UCLA, 1968-71; asst. prof. Tex. A&M U., College Station, 1971-73; dep. dir. office of internat. monetary research U.S. Dept. Treasury, Washington, 1973-77; Charles M. Stone prof. econs. and fin. Claremont (Calif.) McKenna Coll., 1977-89, chmn. dept. econs., 1987-89; Sullivan/Dean prof. internat. fin. Georgetown U., Washington, 1989—; vis. assoc. prof. econs. U. Va., Charlottesville, 1975; vis. prof. bus. adminstrn. Dartmouth Coll., Hanover, N.H., 1979; vis. prof. fin. Gothenburg (Sweden) Sch. Econs., 1991, 92, 93, 94, 95, 96. Author: A Macro Theory with Micro Foundations, 1974, Principles of Microeconomics, Macroeconomics, 1980, Wealth Effects and Monetary Theory, 1988, Profit-Making Speculation in Foreign Exchange Markets, 1992; author, editor: Exchange Rates, Trade and the U.S. Economy, 1985; contbr. articles to profl. jours. Fellow NSF 1966-68, Woodrow Wilson Found. 1965; grantee Gen. Electric Found., 1980, Mid.-Am. Found., 1987, Earhart Found., 1988. Mem. Western Econ. Assn. (editor Econ. Inquiry jour. 1984—), Am. Econ. Assn., Am. Fin. Assn., Western Fin. Assn., Phi Beta Kappa. Democrat. Avocations: writing, weightlifting, walking, aerobics. Office: Sch Bus Adminstrn Georgetown U Washington DC 20057

SWEENEY, THOMAS JOSEPH, JR., lawyer; b. N.Y.C., Oct. 29, 1923; s. Thomas Joseph and Johanna M. (Flynn) S.; m. Robin Virginia Thwaites, May 30, 1947; children: Thomas Joseph, III, Deidre Ann. BA, N.Y. U., 1947; JD, Columbia U., 1949. Bar: N.Y. 1949. Assoc. in law Columbia U. Law Sch., 1949-50; assoc. Cravath, Swaine & Moore, N.Y.C., 1950-62; with Morgan Guaranty Trust Co. N.Y., 1962-89, v.p., 1965-76, sr. v.p., sr. trust officer, 1976-89, chmn. instl. trust and investment com., 1989—; ptnr. Decker, Hubbard, Welden & Sweeney, N.Y.C.; bd. dirs. W.R. Kenan Fund. Trustee Pinkerton Found., Jean and Louis Dreyfus Found., Para-Educator Found. 2nd Lt. USAAF, 1943-45. Mem. N.Y. State Bar Assn. Democrat. Roman Catholic. Home: 525 Teaneck Rd Ridgefield Park NJ 07660-1127 Office: Decker Hubbard 30 Rockefeller Plz New York NY 10112-0001

SWEENY, JOHN, labor union administrator; b. Bronx, N.Y., May 5, 1934; married; children: John, Patricia. BA in Econs., Iona Coll. Contract dir. Svc. Employees Internat. Union, 1960-72, exec. bd., 1972-80, pres., 1980; v.p., chair exec. coun. coms. health care & orgn. & field svcs. AFL-CIO, Washington, pres., 1995—; mem. Nat. Com. Employment Policy, 1995, Internat. Labor Orgn., Geneva, 1984-85, 91; adv. coun. Fed. Mediation & Conciliation Svc. Co-author: Solutions for the New Work Force, 1989; co-editor: Family and Work: Bridging the Gap, 1987. Bd. dirs. Am. Arbitration Assn., ARC, Cath. Youth Orgn., Citizen-Labor Orgnl; trustee Asian-Am. Free Labor Inst., George Meany Ctr. Labor Studes, Iona Coll.; del. Dem. Nat. Conv., 1992. Office: AFL-CIO 815 16th St NW Washington DC 20002*

SWEENY, STEPHEN JUDE, academic administrator; b. N.Y.C., Sept. 15, 1943; s. Herbert Vincent and Isabel Mary (Dolan) S.; m. Barbara Mary Stasz, Aug. 7, 1976. BA in Spanish, Cath. U., 1966; MA in Theology, Manhattan Coll., 1971, MA in Psychology, 1976; PhD, NYU, 1991. Prin. Incarnation Elem. and Jr. High Sch., N.Y.C., 1969-73; dir. campus ministry Manhattan Coll., N.Y.C., 1973-76; asst. to provost Coll. of New Rochelle, N.Y., 1976-78, mem. edn. dept., 1976—, exec. asst. to pres., 1978-80, v.p. for planning, 1980-81, sr. v.p., 1981—. Vice chair bd. dirs. The Home for the Aged, New Rochelle, 1988-92; chair, bd. trustees Convent of the Sacred Heart, Greenwich, Conn., 1990—; mem. com. on goals Soc. of the Sacred Heart, St. Louis, 1990—, chair 1995—; assoc. Sisters of Charity N.Y., 1984—. Mem. Nat. League Nurses (commn. on accreditation, appeals panel on accreditation actions). Roman Catholic. Office: Coll New Rochelle 29 Castle Pl New Rochelle NY 10805-2338

SWEET, CHARLES WHEELER, executive recruiter; b. Chgo., June 11, 1943; s. Charles Wheeler and Alice Nomi (Grush) S.; m. Joy Ann Weidenmiller, Mar. 23, 1968; children: Charles III, Kimberly Ann, Rebecca Townsend. AB, Hamilton Coll., Clinton, N.Y., 1965; MBA, U. Chgo., 1968. Salesman Procter & Gamble, Chgo., 1965-67; with pers. Ford, Dearborn, Mich., 1968-69, R.R. Donnelley, Chgo., 1969-72; executive recruiter A.T. Kearney Inc. Exec. Search, Chgo., 1972—; pres. A.T. Kearney Inc. Exec. Search, 1988—; bd. dirs. First Fed. Savs., Barrington, Ill. Trustee Village Barrington Hills, Ill., 1985—; chmn. bd., exec. advisor No. Ill. U., 1979-88; bd. dirs. Rehab. Inst. Chgo., 1987—, A.T. Kearney, Inc., 1985-89, Barrington Hills Country Club, 1993—. Mem. AESC. Avocations: tennis, bridge. Home: 92 Meadow Hill Rd Barrington IL 60010-9601 Office: A T Kearney Inc 222 W Adams St Chicago IL 60606-5307

SWEET, HARVEY, theatric, scenic and lighting designer; b. Detroit, Oct. 27, 1943; s. Sam and Rose Sweet; m. Susan Perrett, Mar. 16, 1964 (div. Mar. 1975); children: Deborah Anne, Rebecca Lynn, Jason Aaron; m. Patricia Ravn, Sept. 9, 1978 (div. July 1987). BS, Ea. Mich. U., 1965; MS, U. Wis., 1967, PhD, 1974. Instr. U. N.D., Grand Forks, 1967-69; asst. prof. Boise (Idaho) State Coll., 1972-73; instr. U. Wis., Madison, 1973-74; prof. of theater arts U. No. Iowa, Cedar Falls, 1974-89; dir. lighting Landmark Entertainment Group, L.A. and Tokyo, 1989-91; tech. writer Walt Disney Imagineering, Glendale, Calif., 1992; cons. Advanced Tech., Tokyo, 1991; tech. writer Walt Disney Imagineering, Glendale, Calif., 1992; owner, operator Sweet Studios Theatrical Equipment, Cedar Falls, 1981-89; dir. theater tech. and design U. No. Iowa, 1974-87; project mgr., sr. designer, tech. writer Tru Roll, INc., Glendale, Calif., 1993—. Author: Graphics for the Performing Arts, 1982, Handbook of Scenery, Properties and Lighting I and II, 1988, 2nd edit., 1995, The Complete Book of Drawing for the Theatre, 1995; scenic designer Summer Repretory Theatre, 1988, Timberlake Playhouse, 1988-89; lighting designer, scenic designer, tech. dir. various coll. theatrical prodns., 1964-89. Mem. U.S. Inst. for Theatre Tech. (vice commr. 1979-81, commr. 1981-87, mem. graphic stds. bd. 1979-86, evaluation commr. 1983-88, mem. publs. com. 1986-89, bd. dirs. 1989). Avocations: tennis, aerobics, cooking, drawing. Office: Tru-Roll Inc 622 Sonora Ave Glendale CA 91201-2339

SWEET, LYNN D., journalist; b. Chgo., May 15, 1951; d. Jason and Ione Dover S. AB, U. Calif., Berkeley, 1973; MS in Journalism, Northwestern U., Evanston, Ill., 1975. Reporter Independent-Register, Libertyville, Ill., 1975-76; reporter Chgo. Sun-Times, 1976-93, polit. writer, bur. chief Washington bur., 1993—. Bd. dirs. Northwestern Univ.'s Medill Sch. of Journalism Alumni Bd., 1990-93. Office: 1112 National Press Building Washington DC 20045-2101

SWEET, PHILIP W. K., JR., former banker; b. Mt. Vernon, N.Y., Dec. 31, 1927; s. Philip W.K. and Katherine (Buhl) S.; m. Nancy Frederick, July 23, 1950; children—Sandra H., Philip W.K. III, David A.F. AB, Harvard U., 1950; MBA, U. Chgo., 1957. Pres., dir. The No. Trust Co., Chgo., 1975-81; chmn., chief exec. officer No. Trust Corp., 1981-84. Alderman City of Lake Forest, Ill., 1972-74; adv. com. United Negro Coll. Fund; vis. com. U. Chgo. Grad. Sch. Bus.; trustee Chgo. Zool. Soc., past chmn. 1988-93; life trustee Rush-Presbyn.-St. Luke's Med. Ctr.; vestryman Epis. Ch., 1971-74, 86-89. Mem. Soc. Colonial Wars (gov. Ill. chpt. 1978-80), Chgo. Sunday Evening Club (trustee, treas.), Econ. Club, Comml. Club, Chgo. Club, Commonwealth Club (past pres.), Old Elm Club (Highwood, Ill.), Onwentsia Club (gov.), Shoreacres Club (past pres. Lake Bluff).

SWEET, ROBERT WORKMAN, federal judge; b. Yonkers, N.Y., Oct. 15, 1922; s. James Allen and Delia (Workman) S.; m. Adele Hall, May 12, 1973; children by previous marriage—Robert, Deborah, Ames, Eliza. B.A., Yale U., 1944, LL.B., 1948. Bar: N.Y. 1949. Asso. firm Simpson, Thacher & Bartlett, 1948-53; asst. U.S. atty. So. Dist. N.Y., 1953-55; asso. firm Casey, Lane & Mittendorf, 1955-65, partner, 1957-65; counsel Interdepartmental Task Force on Youth and Juvenile Delinquency, 1958-78; dep. mayor City of N.Y., 1966-69; partner firm Skadden, Arps, Slate, Meagher & Flom, N.Y.C., 1970-77; mem. hearing office N.Y.C. Transit Authority, 1975-77; U.S. dist. judge So. Dist. N.Y., N.Y.C., 1978—; participant USIA Rule of Law Program in Albania, 1991; observer Albanian elections, 1992. Pres. Community Service Soc., 1961-78; trustee Sch. Mgmt. Urban Policy, 1970—, Taft Sch.; vestryman St. Georges Epis. Ch., 1958-63. Served to lt. (j.g.) USNR, 1943-46. Recipient Alumni citation of merit Taft Sch., 1985, various other awards, citations for service as dept mayor N.Y.C. Mem. ABA, Assn. of Bar of City of N.Y., N.Y. Law Inst., N.Y. County Lawyers Assn., State Bar Assn., Am. Legion (comdr. Willard Straight Post). Clubs: Quaker Hill Country, Century Assn., Merchants, Indian Harbor Yacht, Mid City Rep.

SWEET, WILLIAM HERBERT, neurosurgeon; b. Kerriston, Wash., Feb. 13, 1910; m. Paul Williams and Daisy Eleanor (Pool) S.; m. Elizabeth Jane Dutton, July 29, 1978; children: David Rowland, Gwendolyn Sweet Fletcher, Paula Sweet Carroll. SB, U. Wash., 1930; BSc, Oxford U., 1934, DSc, 1957; MD, Harvard U., 1936; DHC (hon.), Université Scientifique et Médicale de Grenoble, France, 1979. Diplomate Am. Bd. Psychiatry and Neurology, Am. Bd. Neurol. Surgery. Rhodes research fellow Nat. Hosp. for Nervous Disease, London, 1939; asst. in neurosurgery Mass. Gen. Hosp., Boston, 1945-47; asst. neurosurgeon Mass. Gen. Hosp., 1947-48, assoc. vis. neurosurgeon, 1948-57, vis. neurosurgeon, 1957-61, chief neurol. service, 1961-77, sr. neurosurgeon, 1977—; asst. in surgery Harvard U. Med. Sch., Boston, 1945-46; instr. surgery Harvard U. Med. Sch., 1946-47, assoc. in surgery, 1947-48, asst. prof. surgery, 1948-54, assoc. clin. prof., 1954-58, assoc. prof., 1958-65, prof., 1965-76, prof. emeritus, 1976—; cons., lectr. in field; trustee Neuro-Research Found. Inc., 1951—, pres., 1971—; trustee Neurosci. Research Found. Inc., 1961—, pres., 1961-76. Author: (with J.C. White) Pain: Its Mechanisms and Neurosurgical Control, 1955, Pain and the Neurosurgeon: A Forty Year Experience, 1969; editor books in field; contbr. articles to profl. jours., chpts. to books, monographs in medicine. Sci. trustee Assoc. Univs. Inc. (AUI), rep. Harvard U., 1958-82, hon. trustee, 1982—. Served with AUS, 1941-45. Rhodes scholar, 1932-34; Arthur Tracy Cabot fellow Harvard U. Med. Sch., 1935-36; Commonwealth Fund fellow, 1940-41, Royal Coll. Surgeons of Edinburgh hon. fellow, 1986. Mem. Am. Acad. Arts and Scis., Am. Pain Soc., AAAS, Am. Acad. Surgery, Am. Acad. Neurology, ACS, Am. Assn. Neurol. Surgeons, Am. Neurol. Assn., Am. Physiol. Assn., Am. Surg. Assn., Assn. de chirgiens Suisses (corr.), Assn. for Research in Nervous and Mental Diseases, Congress Neurol. Surgeons (hon.), Electroencephalographic Soc., Halsted Soc., Internat. Assn. for Study Pain, Internat. Brain Research Orgn., Internat. Soc. Psychiat. Surgery, Internat. Soc. Surgery, Italian Neurosurg. Soc. (corr.), New Eng. Neurosurg. Soc., Research Soc. Neurol. Surgeons, Royal Soc. Medicine, Scandinavian Neurosurg. Soc. (corr.), Societe de Neuro-Chirurgie de Langue Francaise (hon.), Soc. Brit. Neurol. Surgeons, Soc. for Neurosci., Spanish-Portuguese Neurosurg. Soc. (hon.), Soc. Neurol. Surgeons, Egyptian Soc. Neurol. Surgeons (hon.). Office: 5 Longfellow Pl Ste 211 Boston MA 02114

SWEETING, LINDA MARIE, chemist; b. Toronto, Ont., Can., Dec. 11, 1941; came to U.S., 1965, naturalized, 1979; d. Stanley H. and Mary (Robertson) S. BSc, U. Toronto, 1964, MA, 1965; PhD, UCLA, 1969. Asst. prof. chemistry Occidental Coll., L.A., 1969-70; asst. prof. chemistry Towson (Md.) State U., 1970-75, assoc. prof., 1975-85, prof., 1985—; guest worker NIH, 1976-77; program dir. chem. instrumentation NSF, 1981-82; vis. scholar Harvard U., 1984-85; contractor U.S. Army MRICD, 1991-93. Bd. dirs. Chamber Music Soc. Balt., 1985-91. Exec. com. Exptl. NMR. Conf. 1985-87, local arr. chair 1986. Mem. Md. Acad. Scis. (mem. sci. council 1975-83, 89-94), Assn. for Women in Sci. (treas. 1977-78, Woman of Yr. 1989), Am. Chem. Soc. (mem. women chemists Com. 1983-89), AAAS, Nature Conservancy, Sierra Club, Sigma Xi (sec. TSU Club 1979-81, 95—, Towson chpt. pres. 1987-88, 91-92, sec. 1995—, mid-Atlantic nominating com. 1987-90, regional dir. 1988-89, nat. nominating com. 1991-94). Office: Towson State U Dept Chemistry Baltimore MD 21204

SWEETLAND, ANNETTE FLORENCE (ANNIE SWEETLAND), special education educator; b. Dallas; d. George R. and Odessa (Donnhue) S.; children: George William Davison, James Erron Davison; m. Ralph J. Guinn. BS in Edn., U. Okla., 1988, MS in Edn., 1992. Lic. profl. counselor. Tchr. multi-handicapped students Noble (Okla.) Pub. Sch., 1988-90; child-find S.E.A.R.C.H. coord. and preschool handicap tchr. Shawnee (Okla.) Pub. Sch., 1989-93; regional coord. Sooner Start Okla. Dept. Edn., Norman, 1993-94; case mgr. II Developmental Disabilities Scv. Divsn./DHS, State of Okla., Oklahoma City, 1994-95; spl. educator Okla. Youth Ctr., 1995—; mgr. group home Able Group Homes, Norman, Okla., 1989-90; dir. returning adult program St. Gregory's Coll., Shawnee, 1990-91. Mem. ARC, ACA, Coun. for Exceptional Children, Okla. Edn. Assn.

SWEETLAND, LORAINE FERN, librarian, educator; b. Morristown Corners, Vt., Aug. 13, 1933; d. William Eric and Sylbil Bedina (Bailey) Bloomfield; m. Ronald David Sweetland, July 1, 1950; children: Kathy L. (dec.), Dale J. Bettis. BS in Elem. Edn., Columbia Union Coll., 1968; MS in Library Sci., Syracuse U., 1973. Tchr. 1st and 2d grade Beltsville (Md.) Seventh-Day Adventist Sch., 1960-67; asst. libr., cataloger Vt. Tech. Coll., Randolph Ctr., 1968-69; middle sch. libr. Barre (Vt.) City Schs., 1970-74; tchg. prin. Cen. Vt. Seventh-Day Adventist Sch., Barre, 1974-76, Brooklawn Seventh-Day Adventist Sch., Bridgeport, Conn., 1976-81; med. libr. Washington Adventist Hosp., Takoma Park, Md., 1981-85; dir. libr. svcs. Seventh-Day Adventists World Hdqs., Silver Spring, Md., 1985-95; med. libr. cons., Balt., 1983-85; pres. Oasis, 1993-94; tchr. Home Study Internat., IPS-Info. Problem Solvers. Book reviewer Libr. Jour., 1990—. Trustee Randolph (Vt.) Pub. Library, 1970-71; sec. Nat. Area Hosp. Council, Washington, 1985. Mem. Assn. Seventh-Day Adventist Librarians, Laurel Rotary Club (bulletin editor 1990-94). Republican. Avocations: gardening, photography, knitting, sewing, crocheting. Home and Office: 10182 High Ridge Rd Laurel MD 20723-1782

SWEETMAN, BEVERLY YARROLL, physical therapist; b. Phila., Apr. 8, 1939; d. Albert Henry and Theresa (Payne) Yarroll; m. Denman John Sweetman, Apr. 1, 1961; children: Denman Eric, John Albert. BA in Biology, Hood Coll., 1961; cert. phys. therapist, Hahnemann U., 1983. Rsch. technician Mass. Gen. Hosp., Boston, 1961-62, Princeton (N.J.) U., 1965-66; part owner, phys. therapist Pain & Stress Control Ctr., Allentown, Pa., 1983-85; pvt. practice Body Ease Phys. Therapy Ctr., Grants Pass, Oreg., 1985; pvt. practice, pres. Body Ease Phys. Therapy Ctr., Staunton and Charlottesville, Va., 1986—; developer and co-presenter Total Body Concept Seminars; lectr. in field; pres. VMG Med., Staunton, 1988—; cons., co-presenter seminars Lossing Orthopedic, Mpls., 1985—. Fellow Am. Back Soc.; mem. Am. Phys. Therapy Assn. Office: Body Ease Phys Therapy Ctr 409 Walnut Hills Rd Staunton VA 24401-9467

SWEETS, HENRY HAYES, III, museum director; b. Lexington, Ky., May 8, 1949; s. Henry Hayes Jr. and Elizabeth (Keith) S.; m. Nancy Riley, Jan. 28, 1984; children: Amy Louisa, Henry Hayes IV. BS in Chemistry, U. Ill., 1971, MEd., 1973; MA in History, U. Del., 1978. Tchr. Scotch Plains (N.J.)-Fanwood High Sch., 1972-74, Byron (Ill.) High Sch., 1974-76; mus. dir. Mark Twain Mus., Hannibal, Mo., 1978—. Author: A Sesquicentennial History of the Hannibal, Missouri Presbyterian Church; editor The Fence Painter. Bd. dirs. Becky Thatcher coun. Girl Scouts U.S., 1984-88; mem. bd. edn. Hannibal, Mo. Pub. Schs., 1991—. Mem. Nat. Trust for Hist. Preservation. Methodist. Office: Mark Twain Home and Mus 208 Hill St Hannibal MO 63401-3316

SWEETSER, GENE GILLMAN, quality assurance professional, state legislator; b. Burlington, Vt., Apr. 24, 1948; s. Archelaus William and Stella Ruth (Brink) S.; m. Elizabeth Ann Hannett, Apr., 1967 (div. May 1972); 1 child, Analei; m. Susan Williams, Aug. 27, 1978 (div. Feb. 1995); 1 child, Virginia Lucretia. BA Polit. Sci. and Environ. Sci., Johnson State Coll., Vt., 1978; MS in Adminstrn., St. Michael's Coll., Vt., 1993. Maintenance machinist Avdel Internat., Inc., Parsippany, N.J., 1982-84; machine shop supr. Mitec Systems, Inc., Williston, Vt., 1984-84; maintenance supr. Fonda, Inc., Albans, Vt., 1985-88; asst. quality control mgr. Chatham Precision, Hinesburg, Vt., 1988-91; state representative Vt. State Ho. of Reps., 1990—; prodn. control IBM, Essex, Vt., 1992—; mem. Bd. Civil Authority, Essex, Vt., 1988—, Justice of the Peace, 1988—; mem. com. ways and means Vt. State Ho. of Reps., 1994—. Founder, bd. dirs. paper recycling program Worcester Vol. Fire Dept., 1978-82; founder, bd. dirs. Worcester Film Soc., 1978-82, Worcester Views Newsletter, 1978-82; vice chmn. Ctrl. Ct. Regional Planning Commn., 1980-82; vol. The Holiday Project, 1987-89; coach Essex Youth Soccer, 1988, 89; player agt. for minor league Essex Little League Assn., 1990; v.p. Survivors of Crime, Inc. With USMC, 1969-72, Vt. Army nat. Guard, 1978—. Address: 28 Foster Rd Essex Junction VT 05452

SWEETSER, SUSAN W., state legislator, lawyer, advocate; b. Dec. 13, 1958; d. Robert Joseph and Lucretia Rose (Donnelly) Williams. BA in Polit. Sci./Environ. Adminstrn. with high honors, Johnson (Vt.) State Coll., 1982; JD magna cum laude, Vt. Law Sch., 1985. Bar: N.Y. 1986, Vt. 1986, U.S. Dist. Ct. Vt. 1989; CLU, ChFC. Confidential law clk. Appellate div. N.Y. Supreme Ct., Albany, 1985-86; assoc. Gravel & Shea, Burlington, Vt., 1986-90; atty. Nat. Life Ins. Co., Montpelier, Vt., 1990—; now mem. Vt. State Senate; victims rights adv. Essex Junction, Vt., 1980—; adj. prof. bus. law St. Michael's Coll., Winooski, Vt., 1991—, Johnson State Coll., 1995—; justice of peace Town of Essex, 1991-95; chair judiciary com.; former mem. Health and Welfare Com.; mem. Housing and Conservation Trust Fund Study Com., Civil Rights Study Com., Adoption Law Reform Study Com., Appropriations Com. Author articles on victims rights. Trustee Vt. State Colls., Waterbury, 1979-81, Univ. Health Ctr., 1992-94; mem. ethics com. Fanny Allen Hosp., Winooski, Vt., 1989-92; v.p. Lyric Theatre, Burlington, 1989—; mem. Vt. Rep. State Com., Montpelier, chmn. Rep. State Conv., 1988, 92; founder, pres. Survivors of Crime, Inc. Recipient Achievement award Vt. Law Enforcement Coordinating Com., 1990, Vt. Ctr. for Prevention and Treatment of Sexual Abuse and The Safer Soc. Program, 1991, Nat. recognition for victims rights work The Giraffe Project, 1991, award Nat. Found. for Improvement of Justice, 1993; named 754th Point of Light by former Pres. George Bush, 1992, Am. Heroine Ladies Home Jour., 1991, Legislator of Yr. Nat. Rep. Legislators Assn., 1995. Fellow AAUW; mem. Vt. Bar Assn., N.Y. State Bar Assn., Internat. Assn. Fin. Planners (chmn. legis. affairs Greater Vt. chpt. 1988-91). Roman Catholic. Avocations: skiing, flower gardening, running, camping, horseback riding. Office: Survivors of Crimes Inc PO Box 8304 Essex VT 05451-8304

SWEEZY, JOHN WILLIAM, political party official; b. Indpls., Nov. 14, 1932; s. William Charles and Zuma Frances (McNew) S.; BS in Mech. Engring., Purdue U., 1956; MBA, Ind. U., 1958; student Butler U., 1953-54, U. Ga., 1954-55, Ind. Cen. Coll., 1959; m. Carole Suzanne Harman, July 14, 1956; children: John William, Bradley E. Design, test engr. Allison div. GM, Indpls., 1953-57; power sales engr. Indpls. Power & Light Co., 1958-69; dir. pub. works City of Indpls., 1970-72; chmn. Marion County Rep. Cen. Com., 1972—; bd. dir. Lorco Engring., Indpls., Indpls. Industrial Products, Acme Screw & Mfg., Inc., Telnet, Inc., Landmarks Ltd.; ptnr. Arch. Products, Innovative Investment Co. Bd. dirs. Indpls. Humane Soc.; chmn. 11th Dist. Rep. Com., 1970, 73—; chmn. Nat. Assn. Urban Rep. County Chmn.; alt. del. Rep. Nat. Conv., 1968, del., 1972, 76, 80, 84, 88, 92, del., mem. credentials com., 1984, 88; mem. credentials com., 1980; mem. Rep. Nat. Com., 1984—, exec. com., 1984—; mem. Warren Schs. Citizens Screening Com., 1958-72; bd. dirs. Warren Devel. Com. With AUS, 1953-55. Mem. AMA, Mensa, Sigma Iota Epsilon. Home: 2089 S German Church Rd Indianapolis IN 46239-9620 Office: 12 N Delaware St Indianapolis IN 46204-3205

SWEEZY, MELANIE ELIZABETH, elementary school educator; b. Orlando, Fla., Nov. 16, 1952; d. Henry Marvin Goldman Jr. and Shirley Elizabeth (Daugherty) Reid. BA in Elem. Edn., U. Ctrl. Fla., 1987; M of Adminstrn. and Supervision, George Washington U., 1995. Cert. tchr., Md. Acctg. mgr. Optimum Systems, Inc., Rockville, Md., 1972-83; elem. educator Orange County Bd. Edn., Orlando, 1987, Dept. Def. Schs., Naples, Italy, 1987-90, Charles County Bd. Edn., Waldorf, Md., 1990—; cons., task writer Md. Dept. Edn., Balt., 1990-94; staff developer Charles County Bd. Edn., Waldorf, 1991-94 (Outstanding Stsff Developer award 1994, Exemplary Tchr. award 1994); com., advisor PreK-4 Integrated Curriculum Project, Washington, 1992-94; mem. Charles County Curriculum Framework Com., 1994—. Mem. Rockville Chpt. Jaycees, 1981-83; regional and state judge Odyssey of the Mind, Waldorf, Balt., 1993-94. Mem. NEA, ASCD, Nat. Coun. Social Studies, Md. Alliance of Geography. Republican. Lutheran. Avocations: golf, arts and crafts, walking, sewing. Office: JP Ryan Elem Sch 12140 Vivian Adams Dr Waldorf MD 20601-3603

SWEEZY, PAUL MARLOR, editor, publisher; b. N.Y.C., Apr. 10, 1910; s. Everett Benjamin and Caroline (Wilson) S.; m. Zirel Dowd, June 17, 1961; children by previous marriage: Samuel Everett, Elizabeth MacDougall, Martha Adams. BA, Harvard U., 1931, PhD, 1937; LittD (honoris causa), Jawaharlal Nehru U., 1983. With econs. dept. Harvard U., 1934-42; editor Monthly Rev., 1949—; vis. prof. Cornell U., Stanford U., New Sch. Social Research, U. Calif., Davis, Yale U., Hosei U., Tokyo, U. Manchester, Eng.; lectr. Cambridge (Eng.) U., 1971; pres. Monthly Rev. Found., Inc. Author or editor: Monopoly and Competion in the English Coal Trade, 1950-1850, 1938, The Theory of Capitalist Development, 1942, Socialism, 1949, The Present as History, 1953; co-author: (with Leo Huberman) Cuba: Anatomy of a Revolution, 1960, (with Paul Baran) Monopoly Capital, 1966, (with Leo Huberman) Socialism in Cuba, 1969, (with Charles Bettelheim) On the Transition to Socialism, 1971, (with Harry Magdoff) The Dynamics of U.S. Capitalism, 1972, Modern Capitalism and Other Essays, 1972, (with Harry Magdoff) The End of Prosperity, 1977, Post Revolutionary Society, 1981, (with Harry Magdoff) The Deepening Crisis of U.S. Capitalism, 1981, Four Lectures on Marxism, 1981, (with Harry Magdoff) Stagnation and Financial Explosion, 1987, (with Harry Magdoff) The Irreversible Crisis, 1988. Served with AUS, 1942-46. Decorated Bronze Star; recipient David A. Wells prize, 1938. Home: 2 Lindsley Dr Larchmont NY 10538-3808 Office: 122 W 27th St Fl 10 New York NY 10001-6227

SWEIG, MICHAEL TERRY, building services company executive, consultant; b. N.Y.C., May 31, 1946; s. Morton and Charlotte (Phillips) S. BS, NYU, 1968, MBA, 1969. V.p. sales Nat. Cleaning Group, N.Y.C., 1969-77, sr. v.p. sales, 1977-81, exec. v.p., 1981-85, pres., CEO, 1985-90; chmn., CEO, Lakeside Bldg. Co., Chgo., 1991—; bd. dirs., owner Armonk (N.Y.) Tennis Club, 1986—. Contbr. articles to profl. jours. Named Man of Yr., AFL-CIO, N.Y., 1986. Mem. Chgo. Soc. Clubs, Sports Club L.A. Republican. Avocations: skiing, flying, tennis, racquetball, golf. Home: Ste 60M3 161 E Chicago Ave Chicago IL 60611-2601 also: 2112 Century Park Ln Los Angeles CA 90067-3300 Office: Lakeside Bldg Maintenance 155 N Wacker Dr Chicago IL 60606-1717

SWENKA, ARTHUR JOHN, food products executive; b. Lone Tree, Iowa, Oct. 21, 1937; s. Samuel Joseph and Verdis Mary (Weed) S.; m. Elizabeth Simms, July 1956 (div. 1976); children: Lee Arthur, Timothy John; m. Dixie Jo Meade, Feb. 1982. Gen. equivalency diploma, U.S. Army, 1957. Truck driver U.S. Mail, Oelwein, Iowa, 1958-59, Stiles Supermarket, Oelwein, 1959-60; salesman Hoxie Inst. Wholesale Co., Waterloo, Iowa, 1960-68, slaes mgr., 1968-69, br. mgr., 1969-70; br. mgr. Hoxie Inst. Wholesale Co., Waterloo and Mason City, Iowa, 1970-72, Nobel Inc., Albuquerque, 1972-81; pres. Nobel/Sysco Food Svcs. Co., Albuquerque, 1981-84; sr. v.p. ops. Sysco Corp., Houston, 1995—; mem. Dirs. Coun., Houston, 1985—. Treas., bd. dirs. Albuquerque Conv. and Visitors Bur., 1975-80; v.p., bd. dirs. Albuquerque Internat. Balloon Festival, 1975-82; bd. dirs. New Day Home for Runaway Children, Albuquerque, 1980-89, Found. St. Joseph's Hosp., 1990—, Kodak Internat. Balloon Fiesta, Albuquerque. Republican. Roman Catholic. Avocation: hot air ballooning. Home: 7112-32 Pan American Fwy Albuquerque NM 87109 Office: Nobel/Sysco Food Svcs Co 1101 W 48th Ave Denver CO 80221-1576

SWENSEN, CLIFFORD HENRIK, JR., psychologist, educator; b. Welch, W.Va., Nov. 25, 1926; s. Clifford Henrik and Cora Edith (Clovis) S.; m. Doris Ann Gaines, June 6, 1948; children—Betsy, Susan, Lisa, Timothy, Barbara. B.S., U. Pitts., 1949, M.S., 1950, Ph.D., 1952. Diplomate Am. Bd. Profl. Psychology. Instr. U. Pitts., 1951-52; clin. psychologist VA, 1952-54; from asst. prof. to assoc. prof. U. Tenn., Knoxville, 1954-62; assoc. prof. psychology Purdue U., West Lafayette, Ind., 1962-65, prof., 1965—; dir. clin. tng. Purdue U., 1975-85; vice chair U. Senate, 1994-95; vis. prof. U. Fla., 1968-69, U. Bergen, Norway, 1976-77, 83-84; cons. VA, 1981 White House Conf. on Aging, others; Am. Psychol. Assn.-NSF Disting. Sci. lectr., 1968-69; Fulbright-Hays lectr., Norway, 1976-77. Author: An Approach to Case Conceptualization, 1968; Introduction to Interpersonal Relations, 1973; contbr. chpts. to books, articles to profl. jours. Served with USN, 1944-46. Recipient Gordon A. Barrows Meml. award for disting. contributions to psychology, 1990. Fellow APA (pres divsn. cons. psychology 1976-77), Am. Psychol. Soc. Personality Assessment, Am. Assn. Applied and Preventive Psychology, Acad. of Clin. Psychology; mem. Midwestern Psychol. Assn., Southeastern Psychol. Assn., Ind. Psychol. Assn., Gerontol. Soc., Sigma Xi, Psi Chi. Republican. Mem. Ch. of Christ. Home: 611

Hillcrest Rd West Lafayette IN 47906-2349 Office: Purdue U Dept Psychol Scis West Lafayette IN 47907

SWENSEN, LAIRD S., orthopedic surgeon; b. Provo, Utah, Oct. 5, 1944; s. Russel Brown and Beulah (Strickler) S.; m. Gloria Elaine Matoza, Sept. 23, 1973; children: Lara Ann, Christine, Russel, Tracy, Laird. BA in Chemistry, Brigham Young U., 1968; MD, George Washington U., 1972. Diplomate Am. Bd. Orthopedic Surgery; cert. added qualifications in surgery of hand, 1992. Intern San Francisco Gen. Hosp., 1972-73; resident in orthopedics U. Calif., San Francisco, 1973-77; pvt. practice orthopedic surgery Salt Lake City, 1978—; fellow in hand and microvascular surgery Jack Tupper, 1978; vice chmn. dept. surgery LDS Hosp.; chmn. divsn. orthopedics LDS Hosp., 1991-92; assoc. clin. prof. dept. orthop. surgery U. Utah, 1979, asst. clin. prof., 1990—; vol. surgeon Orthopedics Overseas, Nepal, 1988, 90, Bhutan, 1992; med. advisor Tibetan Resettlement Project, Salt Lake City. Active 4th St. Homeless Clinic, 1995. Fellow Am. Acad. Orthopedic Surgery; mem. Western Orthopedic Assn. (pres. Utah chpt. 1991), Am. Soc. Surgery of Hand, Utah State Med. Assn. Avocation: mountaineering. Office: 324 10th Ave Salt Lake City UT 84103-2853

SWENSEN, MARY JEAN HAMILTON, graphic artist; b. Laurens, S.C., June 25, 1910; d. Elvin A. and Della (Brown) Hamilton; m. Oliver Severn Swensen, Mar. 3, 1943 (dec.). BS, Columbia U., 1956, MA, 1960; Cert. Notable, U. Madrid, Spain; postgrad., Ariz. State U., 1974-80. mem. 1st USSA sr. internat. cross-country skiing team. One person shows at Colo. Fed. Savs. and Loan Assn., Denver, 1978, Panoras Gallery, N.Y.C., 1963; exhibited in group shows at Soc. Western Artist, M.H. de Young Mus., San Francisco, 1964, Nat. Art Roundup, Las Vegas, 1965, Fine Arts Bldg., Colo. State Fair, Pueblo, 1965, Duncan Gallery, Paris, 1974, Colo. Fed. Savs. & Loan Assn., Denver, 1978; graphics arts in pub. collections at Met. Mus. Art, N.Y.C., Nat. Graphic Arts Collection, Smithsonian Inst., Laurens (S.C.) Pub. Libr., N.Y.C. Pub. Libr. Assoc. Libr. of Congress, Archael. Inst. Am., Smithsonian Instn., Johns Hopkins. Recipient Duncan Gallery Prix de Paris, 1974, Notable award M.H. de Young Mus., 1964, YWCA of U.S.A. Gold Medal as most admired athlete of yr., 1977, USSA Nat. Vets. X-Country Racing Team Gold, Silver and Bronze medals for downhill, giant slalom, slalom, and cross-country sr. citizen and vet. races, 1963-79. Mem. Internat. Platform Assn., Am. Mensa, Columbia Club N.Y., Delta Phi Delta.

SWENSON, DANIEL LEE, bishop; b. Oklahoma City, Feb. 2, 1928; s. Daniel and Lillian (Twedt) S.; m. Sally Mason, June 9, 1951; children: Martha Mason, Sara Swenson Shuford, Daniel Gerald. BA, U. Minn., 1950; DD (hon.), Seabury-Western Theol Sem., Evanston, Ill., 1987. Pvt. practice bus. mgmt. St. Martin's by the Lake, Alexandria, Minn., 1952-58; asst. min. St. Martin's By the Lake, Minnetonka Beach, Minn., 1959-62; vicar St. Edward's Mission, Wayzata, Minn., 1962-65; rector St. Paul's Ch., Virginia, Minn., 1965-75; dean Cathedral of Our Merciful Saviour, Faribault, Minn., 1975-78; rector St. John in the Wilderness, White Bear Lake, Minn., 1978-86; bishop Episc. Diocese Vt., Burlington, 1986—; dean Region II, Diocese of Minn., 1972-75; chmn., Diocesan Commn. on Ministry, Minn., 1976-83; examining chaplain Diocese of Minn., 1974-86; trustee Seabury-Western Theol. Sem., Evanston, Ill., 1978-89. Vice chmn. City Human Rights Commn., Virginia, Minn., 1972-75; dist. chmn. N.E. Minn. Boy Scouts Am., 1970-73; coun. mem. Indianhead and Green Mountain Boy Scouts Am., 1975-89. With U.S. Army, 1946-48.

SWENSON, EMILY BARRON, broadcast executive; b. Boston, Feb. 9, 1954; d. William Andros and Mary Douglas (Robertson) Barron; m. Peter F. Gerrity; m. 2d. Christopher B. Swenson, Oct. 7, 1984; children: Billy, Mike, Lisa. BA, Trinity Coll., 1975; M in Pub. and Pvt. Mgmt., Yale U., 1982. Mgr. bus. planning and interactive techs. Children's Television Workshop, N.Y.C., 1982-83, asst. to pres. for fin. and adminstrn., 1983, dir. of adminstrn., 1983-84, dir. fin. and adminstrn., 1984-85, asst. v.p. corp. affairs, 1985-87, v.p. corp. affairs, 1987, sr. v.p. corp. affairs, 1987-93, exec. v.p., COO, 1993—; trustee Trinity Coll., Conn.; bd. advisors KAPOW. Recipient Salute to Women Achievers award YWCA, 1994. Office: Childrens TV Workshop 1 Lincoln Plz Fl 4 New York NY 10023-7129

SWENSON, ERIC PIERSON, publishing company executive; b. South Orange, N.J., Sept. 21, 1918; s. Svante Magnus and Dorothy Wharton (Mendelson) S.; m. Patricia Morgan, Sept. 14, 1945 (div. June 1965); children: Juliet Morgan Swenson Carter (dec.), Karen Rosamond Swenson McCollom, Dana Graham Swenson Seberg, Hilary Lloyd SwensonMoody; m. Ann Brooke Kirkland, Aug. 5, 1965; 1 child, Alexandra Brooke. Grad. magna cum laude, St. Paul's Sch., Concord, N.H., 1937; B.A. with high orations, Yale, 1941. Publicity asst., editor Pocket Books, Inc., N.Y.C., 1945-47; publicity, editor William Sloane Assos., N.Y.C., 1947-51; sr. editor, vice chmn., dir. W.W. Norton & Co., N.Y.C., 1951-91, editor emeritus, hon. bd. dirs., 1991—; bd. dirs. SMS Ranch Co., Stamford, Tex., Ctr. for Marine Conservation, Washington, Trafalger Sq. Pub. Co. Inc., North Pomfret, Vt. Author: The South Sea Shilling, 1952. With USN, 1941-45, PTO. Clubs: New York Yacht, Cruising of Am., Royal Yacht Squadron, Indian Harbor Yacht, Yale, Storm Trysail, Royal Ocean Racing, Coun. on Fgn. Rels. Home: 99 Eleven O'Clock Rd Weston CT 06883 Office: 500 5th Ave New York NY 10110

SWENSON, GEORGE WARNER, JR., electronics engineer, radio astronomer, educator; b. Mpls., Sept. 22, 1922; s. George Warner and Vernie (Larson) S.; m. Virginia Laura Savard, June 26, 1943 (div. 1970); children: George Warner III, Vernie Laura, Julie Loretta, Donna Joan; m. Joy Janice Locke, July 2, 1971. BS, Mich. Coll. Mining and Tech., 1944, E.E., 1950; MS, MIT, 1948; PhD, U. Wis., 1951. Asso. prof. elec. engring. Washington U., St. Louis, 1952-53; prof. U. Alaska, 1953-54; asso. prof. Mich. State U., 1954-56; faculty U. Ill., Urbana, 1956—, prof. elec. engring. and astronomy, 1958-88, prof. emeritus, 1988—; acting head dept. astronomy U. Ill., 1970-72, head dept. elec. and computer engring., 1979-85; dir. Vermilion River Obs., 1968-81; vis. scientist Nat. Radio Astronomy Obs., 1964-68; cons. to govt. agys. and other sci. bodies; sr. rsch. assoc. U.S. Army Constrn. Engring. Rsch. Lab., 1988-95. Author: Principles of Modern Acoustics, 1953, An Amateur Radio Telescope, 1980; co-author: Interferometry and Synthesis in Radio Astronomy, 1986; contbr. articles to profl. jours. Recipient citation for disting. service to engring. U. Wis., 1984; Guggenheim fellow, 1984-85. Fellow IEEE, AAAS; mem. NAE, Am. Astron. Soc., Internat. Sci. Radio Union (mem. U.S. nat. com. 1965-67, 80-82), Internat. Astron. Union, Sigma Xi, Eta Kappa Nu, Tau Beta Pi, Phi Kappa Phi. Achievements include chairing conceptual design group which produced the concept/proposal for the Very Large Array of National Radio Astronomy Observatory; designed and built two large innovative radio telescopes for the University of Illinois. Home: 1107 Kenwood Rd Champaign IL 61821-4718 Office: U Ill 328 CSRL 1308 W Main St Urbana IL 61801-2307

SWENSON, HAROLD FRANCIS, crisis management consultant; b. N.Y.C., Apr. 28, 1915; s. Charles Henry and Ethel Marie (Igoe) S.; A.B., Manhattan Coll., 1938; student Fordham U. Law Sch., 1938-41; m. Mildred Chandler, Dec. 31, 1943; 1 dau., Sally. Mem. law firm Root, Clark, Buckner & Ballantine, N.Y.C., 1938-41; spl. agt. FBI, 1941-47; indsl. relations exec. Gulf Oil, San Tome, Venezuela, 1947-52; employee relations and security exec. Sears, Roebuck & Co., Chgo., 1953-54; with State Dept., Washington, 1955-65, Def. Dept., Washington, 1965-68; pres., chief exec. officer, dir. Bishop's Service Inc., N.Y.C., 1969-73; v.p. surveys, mktg. and fgn. ops. Intertel Inc., Washington, 1974-78; with law dept., security exec. Chesebrough-Pond's Inc., Greenwich, Conn., 1978-86, crisis mgmt. cons. exec., 1986—. Polit. attache U.S. Embassy, Buenos Aires, Argentina, 1956-62. Served with USMC, 1944-46, PTO. Mem. Soc. Former FBI Agts., Internat. Assn. Chiefs of Police, Capital Marines, Mil. Order Carabao, U.S. Naval Inst., Mil. Order Fgn. Wars, Marine Corps. Hist. Soc., Bad Ems Golf Alumni, Air Crew Assn. of London, Epsilon Sigma Pi, Beta Sigma. Clubs: Chantilly Golf and Country (Centerville, Va.); Army-Navy (Washington); Pathfinders (London); American (Buenos Aires). also: 7337 Oak Moss Dr Sarasota FL 34241-6222

SWENSON, JAMES REED, physician, educator; b. Utah, Nov. 18, 1933; s. Reed K. and Ruth (Freebairn) S.; m. Sharon Coray, Aug. 21, 1953; children—Richard, Karen, Leslie, David, Julie. Student, Weber Coll., 1952-54; M.D., U. Utah, 1959. Intern, then resident in phys. medicine and rehab.; mem. faculty div. phys. medicine and rehab. U. Utah Sch. Medicine, Salt Lake City; chmn. div. U. Utah Sch. Medicine, 1965—, asso. prof., 1970-85, prof., 1985—. Chmn. bd. trustees U. Utah Sch. Alcoholism and Other Drug Dependencies; founder Miss Wheelchair Utah Pageant. Served to capt. M.C. U.S. Army, 1960-62. Mem. AMA, Utah State Med. Assn., Am. Acad. Phys. Medicine and Rehab., Assn. Acad. Physiatrists, Am. Spinal Injury Assn., Utah Soc. Phys. Medicine & Rehab., Am. Med. Soc. Alcoholism. Office: U Utah Med Ctr 50 N Medical Dr Salt Lake City UT 84132-0001

SWENSON, KAREN, poet, journalist; b. N.Y.C., July 29, 1936; d. Howard William and Dorothy (Trautman) S.; m. Michael Shuter, 1958 (div. 1971); 1 son, Michael. B.A., Barnard Coll., 1959; M.A., NYU, 1971. Free lance journalist; preliminary judge CAPS grants, 1975; judge Walt Whitman Award, Acad. Am. Poets, 1976, 88. Author: An Attic of Ideals, 1974, East-West, 1980, A Sense of Direction, 1989, The Landlady in Bangkok, 1994. Runner up Arvon Poetry award, Ann Stanford Poetry award, 1988; winner Nat. Poetry Series, 1993; Yaddo fellow, 1987, 89, Albee Found fellow, 1990-91. Mem. Century Assn. Home: 61 Pierrepont St Brooklyn NY 11201

SWENSON, MARY ANN, bishop. Bishop Rocky Mountain Conf., Denver. Office: Rocky Mountain Conference 2200 S University Blvd Denver CO 80210-4708*

SWENSON, ORVAR, surgeon; b. Halsingborg, Sweden, Feb. 7, 1909; s. Carl Albert and Amanda (Johnson) S.; m. Melva Criley, Sept. 11, 1941; children: Melva, Elsa, Wenda. AB, William Jewell Coll., 1933, DSc (hon.), 1979; M.D., Harvard U., 1937; Dr hc, U. Aix, Marseilles, France, 1975. Diplomate Am. Bd. Surgery. Intern Peter Bent Brigham and Children's hosps., Boston, 1939-41; chief resident Peter Bent Brigham Hosp., 1944-45; Arthur Tracy Cabot fellow Harvard Med. Sch., 1941-44; surgeon Peter Bent Brigham Hosp., 1945-50, Children's Hosp., Boston, 1947-50; surgeon-in-chief Boston Floating Hosp. Infants and Children, 1950-60; asso. surgery Harvard Med. Sch., 1947-50; prof. pediatric surgery Tufts U. Med. Sch., 1957-60; surgeon-in-chief Children's Meml. Hosp., Chgo., 1960-73; prof. surgery Northwestern U. Med. Sch., 1960-73, U. Miami, Fla., 1973-78; chmn. sect. surgery Am. Acad. Pediatrics, 1954-57; lectr. Alex Simpson Smith Lecture Inst. of Child Health, U. London, 1954, Blackfan Lecture Harvard Med. Sch., Boston Children's Hosp., 1958; spl. guest lectr. 16th Gen. Assembly, Japan Med. Congress, 1963; Felton Bequest vis. prof. surgery Univs. Sidney and Melbourne, 1959; vis. prof. U. Bombay, 1980. Author: Pediatric Surgery, 1958; mem. editorial bd. Pediatrics, 1962-68. Recipient Mead Johnson award, 1952, Ladd award Surg. sect. Am. Acad. Pediatrics, 1969, Achievement award Modern Medicine mag., 1971, Frank Billings award AMA, 1949; Swenson Vis. Professorship established in his honor Tufts U. Sch. Medicine, 1987, Swenson Chair in Pediatric Surgery established in 1990. Hon. fellow Royal Coll. Surgeons (Dublin, Ireland), Royal Coll. Physicians and Surgeons Can., Brit. Assn. Pediatric Surgeons (hon., Denis Brown medal 1979); mem. A.C.S., Am. Surg. Assn., Soc. Univ. Surgeons, Am. Pediatric Surg. Assn. (pres. 1973). Discovered cause and cure of Hirschsprung's Disease, 1948. Home: PO Box 41 Rockport ME 04856-0041 also: 172 Cabo de Lagos Fort Pierce FL 34951

SWENSON, ROBERT J., physics educator; b. Butte, Mont., Mar. 3, 1934; m. Jan Swenson; children—Johanna, Kari, Paul. B.S. in Physics, Mont. State U., 1956; M.S. in Physics, Lehigh U., 1958, Ph.D., 1961. Asst. prof. physics Temple U., Phila., 1965-67, assoc. prof., 1967-70, chmn. dept., 1967-70; chmn. dept., prof. physics Mont. State U., Bozeman, 1970—. Chmn. subcom. Mont. Gov.'s Council Sci. and Tech., 1984-85; ad hoc mem. Adv. Council Sci. and Tech., 1984-85; bd. dirs. U.S. Biathlon Assn., 1980—. NSF fellow, 1959, 61-62, 62-63; postdoctoral fellow Joint Inst. Lab. Astrophysics, 1964-65. Fellow Am. Phys. Soc., AAAS; mem. Am. Assn. Physics Tchrs., AAUP, Sigma Xi.

SWENSSON, EARL SIMCOX, architect; b. Nashville, July 28, 1930; s. Earl Ebenezer and Viola Lazelle (Simcox) S.; m. Suzanne Dickenson, June 6, 1953; children: Krista, Lin, Kurt. BS in Bldg. Design, Va. Poly. Inst. and State U., 1952, MSArch, 1953; MSArch, U. Ill., 1955. Registered architect 28 states. Founder, prin. Earl Swensson Assocs., Inc., Nashville 1961—; adj. prof. Va. Poly. Inst., Blacksburg, 1971-72, Auburn U., 1976-83; lectr. in field. Contbr. articles to profl. jours. patentee systamodule for pharmacies. Author: (with Richard L. Miller and Earl S. Swensson) New Directions in Hospital and Healthcare Facility Design, 1995. Bd. dirs. Metro Arts Commn., 1979-86, Middle Tenn. Health Systems Aug. 1973-78, Leadership Nashville Alumni Groups, 1984—; mem. bd. advisers U. Tenn. Sch. Architecture, 1982, chmn., 1985-88; mem. architecture program adv. coun. Auburn U., 1990-94. Recipient Jefferson award Am. Inst. Public Service, Nashville chpt., 1985; named Outstanding Nashvillian of Yr. Downtown Kiwanis Club, 1992. Fellow AIA. Presbyterian. Office: Earl Swensson Assocs 2100 W End Ave Ste 1200 Nashville TN 37203-5225

SWERDA, PATRICIA FINE, artist, author, educator; b. Ft. Worth, Aug. 10, 1916; d. William Emerson and Margaret Ellen (Cull) Finé; B.S. cum laude, Tex. Woman's U., 1941; grad. Ikenobo U., Tokyo, 1965-66, Ikenobo Dojo, Kyoto, Japan, 1976, 77, 81, 83, 85, 87, 91; m. John Swerda, July 7, 1941; children: John Patrick James, Susan Ann Mary Swerda Foss, Margaret Rose Swerda Kownover. Exhibited ikebana in one-woman shows including: Bon Marche, Tacoma, 1966, Seattle, 1967, 85, Gallery Kokoro, Seattle, 1972-78; exhibited in group shows including: Takashimaya Dept. Store, 1965, 76, 77, 83, 85, Matsuzakaya Dept. Store, Tokyo, 1966, Ikenobo Center, Kyoto, 1966, 77, Seattle Art Mus., 1974-80, Sangyo Kaikan, Kyoto, 1976, Burke Mus., U. Wash., ann. Cherry Blossom Festival, Seattle, Bellevue Art Mus., 1984, 85, 87, 89, 90, 91, 92, 93, 94, 95; demonstrations in field for various groups, including Greater Northwest Flower and Garden Show, Milw. Art en Fleurs, Japan Week in Bellevue. Master of Ikebana of Ikenobo Ikebana Soc., Kyoto. Pres. Bellevue Sister Cities Assn. 1985; bd. dirs. Washington State Sister Cities Coord. Com. Named Disting. Alumna class of 1941 Tex. Woman's U., 1991. Mem. N.W. Sakura Chpt. of the Ikenobo Ikebana Soc. (pres. 1960-91), Bonsai Clubs Internat., Puget Sound Bonsai Assn., G.O. Philoptochos (Charitable) Soc. Democrat. Greek Orthodox. Author: Japanese Flower Arranging: Practical and Aesthetic Bases of Ikebana, 1969; Creating Japanese Shoka, 1979; contbr. articles to mags. in field; creator Ikenobo Gardens, Redmond; numerous radio and TV appearances. *Personal philosophy: One must continue to learn, always. The mind must understand what the heart wishes to create before the hands can carry out an all-encompassing directive. This the real Kokoro. This is the basis of service to and with others.*

SWERDLOFF, MARK HARRIS, lawyer; b. Buffalo, Sept. 7, 1945; s. John and Joan (Harris) S.; m. Ileen Pollock, Dec. 24, 1967; 1 child, Jonathan Edward. BA, SUNY, Buffalo, 1967; JD, U. Conn., 1975. Bar: Conn. 1975, U.S. Dist. Ct. Conn. 1975, U.S. Ct. Appeals (2d cir.) 1983, U.S. Supreme Ct. 1985, Fla. 1977. Assoc. Wilson, Asbel & Channin, Hartford, Conn., 1975-78; ptnr. Swerdloff & Swerdloff, West Hartford, Conn., 1978—; pres. Arpus Enterprises, Old Saybrook Conn., 1993—; trial fact finder Superior Ct., Hartford, 1990—; arbitrator Dispute Resolution Inst., Hartford, 1990—. Mem. ABA, Conn. Bar Assn., Conn. Trial Lawyers Assn. Democrat. Jewish. Avocations: photography, travel, cooking. Home: 24 Linwold Dr West Hartford CT 06107-1236 Office: Swerdloff & Swerdloff 433 S Main St West Hartford CT 06110-1670

SWERDLOFF, RONALD S., medical educator, physician, researcher; b. Pomona, Calif., Feb. 18, 1938; s. Julius Lewis and Eva (Kelman) S.; children: Jonathan Nicolai, Peter Loren. BS, U. Calif., 1959, MD, 1962. Diplomate Am. Bd. Internal Medicine, Am. Bd. Endocrinology. Intern U. Wash., Seattle, 1962-63, resident, 1963-64; rsch. assoc. NIH, Bethesda, Md., 1964-66; resident UCLA Sch. Medicine, 1966-67; rsch. fellow Harbor-UCLA Med. Ctr., Torrance, Calif., 1967-69, asst. prof., 1969-72, assoc. prof. divsn. Endocrinology, 1972-78, chief divsn. Endocrinology, 1973—, prof., 1978—; dir. UCLA Population Rsch. Ctr., Torrance, Calif., 1986-92; dir. WHO Collaborating Ctr. Reprodn., Torrance; cons. WHO Geneva, 1982-90, NIH, Bethesda, 1982—, UN Fertility Planning Assn., Geneva, 1983—, Am. Bd. Internal Medicine, Phila., 1989—; inaugural lectr. Australian Soc. Reproductive Biology, Perth, 1990; mem. tech. adv. com. Contraceptive R&D Agy. (CONRAD, AID), 1992—. Contbr. 50 chpts. to books, 250 articles to profl. jours. Fellow Am. Coll. Physicians; mem. Am. Soc. Andrology (Serono award 1986, pres. 1992-93), Am. Assn. Physicians, Am. Soc. Clin. Rsch. (pres. 1972-73), Pacific Coast Fertility (Squibb award, Outstanding rsch. award 1976, 84, Wyeth award 1984, pres. 1984), Endocrinology Soc., We. Soc. Clin. Rsch. (pres. 1983-84). Office: UCLA Sch Medicine/Harbor-UCLA Med Ctr Divsn Endocrinology 1000 W Carson St Torrance CA 90502-2004

SWERDLOW, MARTIN ABRAHAM, physician, pathologist, educator; b. Chgo., July 7, 1923; s. Sol Hyman and Rose (Lasky) S.; m. Marion Levin, May 19, 1945; children—Steven Howard, Gary Bruce. Student, Herzl Jr. Coll., 1941-42; BS, U. Ill., 1945; MD, U. Ill., Chgo., 1947. Diplomate: Am. Bd. Pathology. Intern Michael Reese Hosp. and Med. Center, Chgo., 1947-48; resident Michael Reese Hosp. and Med. Center, 1948-50, 51-52, mem. staff, 1974—, chmn. dept. pathology, v.p. acad. affairs, 1974-90; pathologist Menorah Med. Ctr., Kansas City, Mo., 1954-57; asst. prof., pathologist U. Ill. Coll. Medicine, Chgo., 1957-59, assoc. prof., 1959-60, clin. assoc. prof., 1960-64, clin. prof., 1964-66, prof., pathologist, 1966-72, assoc. dean, prof. pathology, 1970-72; prof. pathology, chmn. U. Mo., Kansas City, 1972-74; prof. pathology U. Chgo., 1975-89, Geever prof., head pathology U. Ill., 1989-93, Geever prof., head pathology emeritus, 1993—; mem. com. standards Chgo. Health Systems Agy., 1976—. Served with M.C. U.S. Army, 1944-45, 50-54. Recipient Alumnus of Yr. award U. Ill. Coll. Medicine, 1973; Instructorship award U. Ill., 1960, 65, 68, 71, 72. Mem. Chgo. Pathology Soc. (pres. 1980—), Am. Soc. Clin. Pathologists, Coll. Am. Pathologists, Internat. Acad. Pathology, Am. Acad. Dermatology, Am. Soc. Dermatopathology, Inst. Medicine, AMA. Jewish. Office: U Ill Coll Medicine Dept Pathology 1819 W Polk St Chicago IL 60612-7331 *My credo these years has been to care about patients, students, colleagues, employees, my institution and the many publics I serve. Honesty and thoroughness has been a basic life style, irrespective of the cost. With all, competence is a necessity and ongoing. Continuous responsibility for my education and learning is my way of living.*

SWERN, FREDERIC LEE, engineering educator; b. N.Y.C., Sept. 9, 1947; s. Reuben Swern and Anne Lillian Goldberg; m. Gayle Regina Unger, Dec. 25, 1969; children: Lauren, Michael. BEE, City Coll., N.Y.C., 1969; MSEE, Newark Coll. Engr., 1974; PhD Engr. Sci., N.J. Inst. Tech., 1981. Registered profl. engr., N.J. Engr. Navigation and Control divsn. Bendix, Teterboro, N.J., 1969-72, UNIVAC, divsn. Sperry Rand, Morris Plains, N.J., 1972-73; sr. systems analyst Chubb & Son Inc., Short Hills, N.J., 1973-78; sr. engr. Flight Systems divsn. Bendix, Teterboro, N.J., 1978-84; cons. Swerlin Assoc., 1981—; assoc. prof. engring Stevens Inst. Tech., Hoboken, N.J., 1984—; researcher, cons., Westinghouse Elevator, Morristown, N.J., 1987, NASA Langley Rsch. Center, Hampton, Va., 1979-82, 1985-90, Hyatt Clark Industries, Clark, N.J., 1984-85, U.S. Army Armament Rsch. and Devel. Ctr., 1985-92, Gen. Motors Corp., Warren, Mich., 1983-84; reviewer Prentice-Hall, Englewood Cliffs, N.J.; cons. Gov. Commn. on Sci. and Tech., 1985-86. Contbr. to profl. jours. Mem. Inst. Elec. Electronic Engrs., Am. Soc. Mech. Engrs., Assn. Computing Machinery, Am. Inst. Aeronautics and Astronautics, Sigma Xi, Pi Tau Sigma. Achievements include Automatic Flight Control System Patent using instrument landing system information and including inertial filtering means for reduced ILS noise; Aircraft Control System Patent using inertial signals; Improved Flare Control Patent for transport aircraft. Home: 53 Village Rd Florham Park NJ 07932-2412 Office: Stevens Institute of Technology Mechanical Engring Lab Castle Point Hoboken NJ 07030

SWETMAN, GLENN ROBERT, English language educator, poet; b. Biloxi, Miss., May 20, 1936; s. Glenn Lyle and June (Read) S. BS, U. So. Miss., 1957, MA, 1959; PhD, Tulane U., 1966; m. Margarita Ortiz, Feb. 8, 1964 (div. 1979); children: Margarita June, Glenn Lyle Maximilian, Glenda Louise. Instr., U. So. Miss., 1957-58, asst. prof., 1964-66; instr. Ark. State U., 1958-59, McNeese U., 1959-61; instr. English, Univ. Coll. Tulane U., 1961-64, spl. asst. dept. elec. engring., 1961-64; assoc. prof. La. Inst. Tech., 1966-67; prof., head dept. langs. Nicholls State Coll., Thibodaux, La., 1967-69, head dept. English, 1969-71, prof., 1971-91, prof. emeritus, William Carey Coll., Gulfport, Miss., 1991—; writer in residence, prof. English William Carey Coll., Gulfport, Miss., 1991—. Ptnr., Breeland Pl., Biloxi, Miss., 1960—; stringer corr. Shreveport (La.) Times, 1966—; ptnr. Ormuba, Inc., 1975—; cons. tech. writing Union Carbide Corp., Am. Fedn. Tchrs. State v.p. Nat. Com. to Resist Attacks on Tenure, 1974—. Subdiv. coord. Rep. Party, Hattiesburg, Miss., 1964. With AUS, 1957. Recipient Poetry awards KQUE Haiku contest, 1964, Coll. Arts contest, L.A., 1966, Black Ship Festival, Yoqosuka, Japan, 1967; Green World Brief Forms award Green World Poetry Editors, 1965. Mem. MLA, S. Cen. MLA, So. Literary Festival Assn. (v.p. 1975-76, 82-83, pres. 1984-85), Coll. Writers Soc. La. (pres. 1971-72, exec. dir. 1983—), IEEE, Am. Assn. Engring. Edn., La. Poetry Soc. (pres. 1971-74, 1986—), Internat. Boswellian Inst., Nat. Fedn. State Poetry Socs. (2d v.p., nat. membership chmn. 1972-74, pres. 1976-77), Nat. Soc. Scholars and Educators (bd. dirs. 1982—, sec. exec. bd. 1986—, sec. bd. dirs. 1968—, sec. soc. 1989—), Am. Fedn. Tchrs. (chpt. pres. 1973-78), Nat. Fedn. State Poetry Socs. (1st v.p. 1975-76, exec. bd. 1972—), Phi Eta Sigma, Omicron Delta Kappa. Book reviewer Jackson (Miss.) State Times, 1961. Poems pub. in various publs. including Poet, Prairie Schooner, Trace, Ball State U. Forum, Film Quar., Poetry Australia, numerous others worldwide; (books of poems) Tunel de Amor, 1973, Deka #1, 1973, Deka #2, 1979, Shards, 1979, Concerning Carpenters, 1980, Son of Igor, 1980; A Range of Sonnets, 1981, Christmas, 1982, Poems of the Fantastic, 1990; contbr. articles (147) to encys.; cons. editor (poetry) Paon Press, 1974—, Scott-Foresman, 1975; editorial bd. Scholar and Educator, 1980—. Home: PO Box 146 Biloxi MS 39533-0146 Office: Nicholls State U Thibodaux LA 70310 also: William Carey Coll 1856 Beach Dr Gulfport MS 39507-1508

SWETNAM, DANIEL RICHARD, lawyer; b. Columbus, Ohio, Dec. 22, 1957; s. Joseph Neri and Audrey Marguerite (Mason) S.; m. Jeannette Deanna Dean, June 7, 1980; children: Jeremiah Daniel, Laura Janelle, Andrew Michael. BA, Ohio State U., 1979; JD, U. Cin., 1982. Bar: Ohio 1982, U.S. Dist. Ct. (so. dist.) Ohio 1982, U.S. Ct. Appeals (6th cir.) 1986, U.S. Supreme Ct. 1986. Assoc. Schwartz, Warren & Ramirez, Columbus, 1982-88; ptnr. Schwartz, Kelm, Warren & Rubenstein, Columbus, 1989—. Deacon Grace Brethren Ch., Worthington, Ohio, 1989—; mem. Grace Brethren Christian Schs. Commn., 1993—. Mem. ABA, Ohio State Bar Assn., Columbus Bar Assn., Comml. Law League Am., Order of Coif. Republican. Avocations: golf, tennis. Home: 2178 Stowmont Ct Dublin OH 43016-9563 Office: Schwartz Warren & Ramirez 41 S High St Columbus OH 43215-6101

SWETNAM, MONTE NEWTON, petroleum exploration executive; b. Alexandria, La., Oct. 9, 1936; s. Montreville Morris and Margaret Elizabeth (Cullison) S.; m. Elaine Adelia Taylor, Dec. 21, 1957; children: Scott David, Robert Troy. Student, Johns Hopkins, 1955-58; B.S. in Geology, U. Wyo., 1960, M.S. in Geology, 1961; M.B.A. in Bus. Adminstrn, Pepperdine U., 1978. Registered geologist, Calif. Exploration geologist Amerada Petroleum Corp., Durango, Colo., 1961-63; exploration geologist Tenneco Oil Co., Durango, 1963-65; dist. project geologist Tenneco Oil Co., Bakersfield, Calif., 1965-69; div. staff geologist Tenneco Oil Co., Bakersfield, 1969; partner Argonaut Oil & Gas Cons., Denver, 1969-71; internat. exploration mgr. Tesoro Petroleum Corp., San Antonio, 1971-73; v.p. internat. exploration Tesoro Petroleum Corp., 1973-74, sr. v.p. exploration, 1974-82; pres. Tesoro-Bolivia Petroleum Co., 1975-82, Tesoro-Algeria Petroleum Co., 1975-82; sr. v.p. exploration Natural Resource Mgmt. Corp./NRM, Dallas, 1983-86; sr. v.p. exploration and prodn. Harken Energy Corp., 1987-89, exec. v.p., 1991-93; pres. Harken Exploration Co., 1988-91, Harken Bahrain Oil Co., 1989-93; exec. v.p., chief oper. officer Giant Exploration and Prodn. Co., Farmington, N.Mex., 1994—; pres. Canyon Marinas, Inc., San Antonio. Contbr. articles to profl. jours. Mem. Am. Assn. Petroleum Geologists, Geol. Soc. Am., Sigma Xi. Republican. Clubs: Alamo Yacht, Lake Canyon Yacht. Home: 3500 Island Moorings Pky # 231 PO Box 154 Port Aransas TX 78373 Office: PO Box 2810 2200 Bloomfield Hwy Farmington NM 87499-2810

SWETS, JOHN ARTHUR, psychologist, researcher; b. Grand Rapids, Mich., June 19, 1928; s. John A. and Sara Henrietta (Heyns) S.; m. Maxine Ruth Crawford, July 16, 1949; children—Stephen Arthur, Joel Brian. B.A., U. Mich., Ann Arbor, 1950, M.A., 1953, Ph.D., 1954. Instr. psychology U. Mich., Ann Arbor, 1954-56; asst. prof. psychology M.I.T., Cambridge, 1956-60, assoc. prof. psychology, 1960-63; v.p. Bolt Beranek & Newman Inc., Cambridge, 1964-69, sr. v.p., 1969-74, gen. mgr. research, devel. and cons., dir., 1971-74; chief scientist BBN Labs., Cambridge, 1975—; lectr. dept. clin. epidemiology Harvard Med. Sch., 1985-88, dept. health care policy, 1988—; mem. corp. Edn. Devel. Ctr., Newton, Mass., 1971-75; vis. rsch. fellow Philips Labs., The Netherlands, 1958; Regents' prof. U. Calif., 1969; advisor vision com., com. on hearing and bioacoustics NAS-NRC, 1960-96; mem. Commn. on Behavioral Social Scis. and Edn., NRC, 1988-92, vice chair, 1992-93, chmn., 1993-96; sci. advisor, cons., lectr. numerous govtl. and profl. orgns. Author: Signal Detection Theory and ROC Analysis in Psychology and Diagnostics, 1996; co-author: (with D.M. Green) Signal Detection Theory and Psychophysics, 1966, (with R.M. Pickett) Evaluation of Diagnostic Systems: Methods From Signal Detection Theory, 1982; editor: Signal Detection and Recognition by Human Observers, 1964, (with L.L. Elliott) Psychology and the Handicapped Child, 1974, (with D. Druckman) Enhancing Human Performance, 1988; mem. editorial bd. Med. Decision Making, 1980-85, Psychol. Sci., 1989-94, Psychol. Rev., 1995—, Jour. Exptl. Psychology: Applied, 1995—; contbr. articles to profl. jours. Past mem. numerous civic orgns.; mem. corp. Winchester Hosp., Mass., 1981-84. Fellow AAAS (coun. 1986-89), APA (Disting. Sci. Contbn. award 1990), Am. Acad. Arts and Scis., Acoustical Soc. Am. (exec. coun. 1968-71), Soc. Exptl. Psychologists (chmn. 1986, exec. com. 1986-89, Howard Crosby Warren medal 1985), Am. Psychol. Soc.; mem. NAS (Troland award com. 1991, chmn. 1992), Psychonomic Soc., Psychometric Soc., Soc. Math. Psychology, Sigma Xi, Sigma Alpha Epsilon, Winchester Country Club. Congregationalist (moderator). Office: BBN Corp 10 Moulton St Cambridge MA 02138-1119

SWETT, ALBERT HERSEY, retired lawyer, business executive, consultant; b. Medina, N.Y., Feb. 18, 1923; s. Raymond Fuller and Marion (Hersey) S.; m. Mary Stewart, Oct. 10, 1944; children: Marion Hersey Swett Robinson, Margaret Stewart Swett Haskell, Albert Louis. Grad., The Hill Sch., 1941; B.Engring., Yale U., 1944; LL.B., Harvard U., 1949. Bar: N.Y. 1949. Assoc. Harris, Beach & Wilcox, Rochester, N.Y., 1949-56, ptnr., 1957-66; v.p., gen. counsel Xerox Corp., Stamford, Conn., 1966-75; v.p., gen. counsel Coca-Cola Co., Atlanta, 1975-78, v.p., counsel to chmn., 1978-80; ind. cons., 1980—. Trustee Practising Law Inst., 1977-83. Served with USNR, 1942-46. Mem. Assn. Gen. Counsel (emeritus), Tau Beta Pi. Republican. Methodist. Lodge: Masons. Home: PO Box 30319 River Ranch FL 33867-0319

SWETT, FRANCISCO XAVIER, economist, former congressman; b. Guayaquil, Guayas, Ecuador, Oct. 26, 1947; s. Luis Alberto and Piedad (Morales) S.; m. Natalia Crespo, June 6, 1969; children: Natasha, Frances; m. Ana Sofia G. de Ascásubi, April 27, 1988; children: Sophie, Luis Francisco. Econs. Deg., Universidad Catolica, Quito, Ecuador, 1979; M.Pub. Affairs, Princeton U., 1974; B.A. magna cum laude with high honors, Wesleyan U., 1971. Pres., Nat. Planning Bd., Quito, 1978-79; econs. counsellor Central Bank of Ecuador, Guayaquil, 1980; pres., gen. mgr. Corporacion Estudios Economicos, Guayaquil, 1980-84; minister Ministry of Fin. and Pub. Credit, Quito, 1984-86; counselor to Pres. Republic of Ecuador, Quito, 1987-88; mem. Congress of Ecuador, 1988-90; mng. dir. Noboa Orgn., 1990-93, mem. ind. econ. coun., 1994—; chief coord. unit state enterprise reform and privatization, 1995, coord. Pub. Enterprise Reform Initiative; cons. in field. Author: El Modelo de Desorrollo Agricola, 1983, La Deuda Externa del Ecuador, 1980, Financiamiento y Costo de la Educacion Ecuatoriana, 1978, Turnaround the Political Economy of Reform in Ecuador, 1989; editor: (column) Diario El Teleprafo. Clubs: Princeton, Club de la Union.

SWETT, MARGARET CHRISTINE, finance executive; b. San Francisco, Sept. 14, 1959; d. Benson Payne Swett and Helen Irene (Frey) Iddings. BA in Econ., U. Calif., Santa Barbara, 1981; MBA, San Francisco State U., 1991. Acctg. supr. Geneva Group, Menlo Park, Calif., 1981-83; mgr. acctg. Pearl Cruises, San Francisco, 1983-87; mgr. acctg. and adminstrn. Seabourn Cruise Line, San Francisco, 1987-90, dir. fin. svcs., 1990-93, v.p. fin. and adminstrn., 1993—. Mem. NAFE, Nat. Honor Soc. (life), Beta Gamma Sigma. Avocations: photography, swimming, travel, humanities, literature. Home: 1400 Jones St Apt 201 San Francisco CA 94109-3292 Office: Seabourn Cruise Line 55 Francisco St Ste 710 San Francisco CA 94133-2117

SWETT, STEPHEN FREDERICK, JR., principal, educator; b. Englewood, N.J., Sept. 14, 1935; s. Stephen Frederick and Frances (Gulotta) S.; B.A., Montclair State Coll., 1959, M.A., 1965; Ed.D. in Ednl. Adminstrn., Rutgers U., 1976, graduate North Light Art School, 1995; m. Annette Palazzolo, Nov. 18, 1961; children—Susan, Kimberly Ann, Stephen Laurence. Tchr., Long Branch (N.J.) High Sch., 1961-62, Roselle Park (N.J.) High Sch., 1962-73; research asst. Rutgers U., New Brunswick, N.J., 1973-74; instructional supr. Elmwood Park (N.J.) Schs., 1974-76, Morris Hills Regional Schs., Denville, N.J., 1976-77; asst. prin. Lawrence High Sch., Lawrenceville, N.J., 1977-79; prin. Stafford Intermediate Sch., Manahawkin, N.J., 1979-94, recreation and art cons., 1994—. participant NSF Inst. in physics, chemistry and math. Seton Hall U., 1964, Newark Coll. Engring., 1965, Stevens Inst. Tech., summers 1966-68. Served with AUS, 1959-61. Mem. Roselle Park Edn. Assn. (pres. 1971-73). Nat. Soc. Study Edn., Am. Assn. Physics Tchrs., Am. Inst. Physics, Am., N.J. assns. sch. adminstrs., Nat. Assn. Elementary and Middle Sch. Adminstrs., N.J. Assn. Elementary and Middle Sch. Adminstrs., Nat. Assn. Secondary Sch. Prins., Phi Delta Kappa (sec. Rutgers chpt. 1977-80, v.p. 1980-82, pres. 1983-84). Research on sch. fin. Home: 12 Louis St Old Bridge NJ 08857-2235

SWEZEY, CHARLES MASON, Christian ethics educator, administrator; b. Charlottesville, Va., May 16, 1935; s. Fenton Hendy and Catherine Jane (Mason) S.; m. Mary Evelyn Knight, June 16, 1960; children: Christopher Stephen, Margaret Fenton, Mary Mason. BA, Washington and Lee U., 1957; BD, Union Theol. Sem., 1961; STM, Yale U., 1962; MA, Phd, Vanderbilt U., 1974, 78. Ordained to ministry, Presbyterian Ch., 1962. Asst. minister Lexington (Va.) Presbyn. Ch., 1962-70; stated clk. Lexington Presbytery, 1967-68; vis. lectr. Mary Baldwin Coll., Staunton, Va., 1966-67, 68; asst. prof. Union Theol. Sem., Richmond, Va., 1974-80, assoc. prof., 1980-83, prof. Christian ethics, 1983—, dean of faculty, 1990-95; mem. coop. com. on examination for candidates, Presbyn. Ch. U.S.A., 1978-88. Editorial bd. Interpretation, Richmond, 1981-92; co-editor: James Gustafson's Theocentric Ethics, 1988; contbr. articles to theol. publs. Bd. dirs. Va. Blood Svcs., 1987-95; mem. Human Fetal Tissue Transplantation panel NIH, Bethesda, Md., 1988. Grantee Danforth Found., 1968-69; Woodrow Wilson Found. fellow, 1970-71. Mem. Soc. Christian Ethics. Office: Union Theol Sem 3401 Brook Rd Richmond VA 23227-4514

SWHIER, CLAUDIA VERSFELT, lawyer; b. Mineola, N.Y., Jan. 15, 1950; d. William Holly and Ruth (Gerland) Versfelt; m. Robert Dewain Swhier Jr., June 5, 1974; children: James Robert, Jeffrey William. BA in Philosophy magna cum laude, Yale U., 1972; JD cum laude, Harvard U., 1975. Bar: Ind. 1975. Assoc. Barnes & Thornburg, Indpls., 1975-82, ptnr., 1982—. Mem. editorial bd. Harvard Law Rev., 1973-75; editor Thrift Law in Rev., Banking Law in Rev., 1989—. Mem. ABA, Ind. Bar Assn., Indpls. Bar Assn. Republican. Presbyterian. Avocations: skiing, swimming, aerobics. Office: Barnes & Thornburg 1313 Mchts Bank Bldg Indianapolis IN 46204

SWIBEL, STEVEN WARREN, lawyer; b. Chgo., July 18, 1946; s. Morris Howard and Gloria S.; m. Leslie Cohen; children: Deborah, Laura. BS, MIT, 1968; JD, Harvard U., 1971. Bar: Ill. 1971, U.S. Dist. Ct. (no. dist.) Ill. 1971, U.S. Tax Ct. 1973, U.S. Ct. Appeals (7th cir.) 1981. Assoc. Sonnenschein Carlin Nath & Rosenthal, Chgo., 1971-78, ptnr., 1978-84; ptnr. Rudnick & Wolfe, 1984-93; ptnr. Schwartz, Cooper, Greenberger, Krauss Chartered, 1993—; adj. prof. taxation Ill. Inst. Tech. Kent Coll. Law, Chgo., 1989—; lectr. in field. Contbr. articles to profl. jours. Ednl. counselor MIT, 1979—; bd. dirs. MIT Alumni Fund, 1992-95, Ragdale Found., 1987—, treas. 1987-92. Recipient Lobdell Disting. Svc. award MIT Alumni Assn., 1989. Mem. ABA (com. partnerships sect. taxation), Ill. Bar Assn., Chgo. Bar Assn. (fed. taxation com., exec. subcom. 1984—, chmn. subcom. on real estate, partnerships and tax sheltered investments 1986-87, vice chmn. 1988-89, chmn. 1989-90), Met. Club, MIT Club (dir. Chgo. chpt. 1980-91, sec. 1980-87, pres. 1987-89), Sigma Xi, Tau Beta Pi, Eta Kappa Nu. Office: Schwartz Cooper Greenberger & Krauss Chartered 180 N La Salle St Ste 2700 Chicago IL 60601

SWICK, HERBERT MORRIS, medical educator, neurologist; b. Baton Rouge, Nov. 22, 1941; s. Edgar Haight and Mary Ellen (Morris) S.; m. Mary Lynne McCluggage, June 29, 1963; children: Kristin Ann, Elizabeth May, Diane Marie. BA with honors, Johns Hopkins U., 1963, MD Sch. Medicine, 1966. Cert. Am. Bd. Psychiatry and Neurology, Am. Bd. Pediatrics. Resident in pediatrics Johns Hopkins U., Balt., 1966-69; resident in neurology U. Ky., Lexington, 1971-74, asst. prof. neurology and pediatrics, 1974-75; asst. to assoc. prof. neurology and pediatrics Med. Coll. Wis., Milw., 1975-84, prof. neurology and pediats., 1984-94, asst. dean med. edn., interm chmn. dept. neurology, 1987-88, assoc. dean acad. affairs, 1988-91, sr. assoc. dean acad. affairs, 1991-93, sr. assoc. dean for acad. programs, 1993-94; prof. neurology, sr. assoc. dean acad. affairs Sch. Medicine U. Kans., Kansas City, 1994—, acting chmn. dept. history and philosophy of medicine Sch. Medicine, 1995, interim exec. dean Sch. Medicine, 1995—; chief dept. neurology Children's Hosp. Wis., Milw., 1981-87, acting chmn. dept. neurology, 1987-88; vis. prof. neurol. edn. Mayo Clinic and Found., Rochester, Minn., 1985. Contbr. numerous articles to profl. jours. Bd. dirs. Milw. Chamber Music Soc., 1982-88, pres. 1986-88. Served to lt. commdr., USN, 1969-71. Fulbright sr. scholar, 1978. Fellow Am. Acad. Neurology (edn. com., undergrad. edn. subcom. 1985-89); mem. Am. Assn. History Medicine, Child Neurology Soc. (archives and history com. 1981-88, exec. com. 1982-86, sci. selection com. 1983, 84), Columbia History of Medicine Club, Internat. Child Neurology Assn., Milw. Acad. Medicine (coun. 1993-94), Profs. of Child Neurology, Wis. Neurol. Soc. (sec.-treas. 1981-82, pres.-elect 1982-84, pres. 1984-85), Assn. Univ. Profs. in Neurology (undergrad. edn. com. 1979-86), Assn. Am. Med. Colls. (coun. deans 1995—).

SWID, STEPHEN CLAAR, business executive; b. N.Y.C., Oct. 26, 1940; s. David and Selma (Claar) S.; m. Nan Goldman, Mar. 1, 1963; children: Robin, Scott, Jill. BS, Ohio State U., 1962. Mgmt. trainee Alside Aluminum Co., Akron, Ohio, 1962-63; securities analyst Dreyfus Fund, N.Y.C., 1963-66; sr. investment officer Oppenheimer Fund, N.Y.C., 1966-67; gen. ptnr. City Assocs., 1967-69, Swid Investors, N.Y.C., 1970-78; co-chmn. bd. Gen. Felt Industries Inc., Saddle Brook, N.J., 1974-86, Knoll Internat., 1977-86; chmn. bd., chief exec. officer SBK Entertainment World, Inc., N.Y.C., 1986-89; chmn., chief exec. officer SCS Communications, N.Y.C., 1989—; chmn. strategy com., dir. Inst. for East-West Studies. Trustee Solomon Guggenheim Mus.; mem. vis. com. 20th century art Met. Mus. Art; past trustee Horace Mann Sch., N.Y.C.; former exec. vp. bd. dirs. Lenox Sch. N.Y.; chmn. Mcpl. Art Soc. Office: SCS Communications 152 W 57th St New York NY 10019-3310

SWIDEN, LADELL RAY, travel company executive; b. Sioux Falls, S.D., June 17, 1938; s. Alick and Mildred Elizabeth (Larson) S.; m. Phyllis Lorriane Enga, Sept. 10, 1961; children: David, Daniel, Shari. BSEE, S.D. State U., 1961; MBA, U. S.D., 1982. Registered profl. engr., S.D., Minn. Instrument engr. Honeywell, Mpls., 1962-67; v.p. sales Swiden Appliance and Furniture, Sioux Falls, 1967-68; engring. mgr. Raven Industries, Inc., Sioux Falls, 1968-84; v.p. engring. Beta Raven Inc., St. Louis, 1984-85; pres. Delta Systems, Inc., St. Louis, 1985-86; acting dir. Engring. and Environ. Rsch. Ctr. S.D. State U., Brookings, 1986-94, dir. univ./industry tech. svc., 1986-94; v.p. Village Travel Inc., Brookings, 1994—; bd. dirs. Brookings Econ. Devel. Ctr. Patentee in field. Chmn. Indsl. Devel. Com., Brookings, 1989-90, vice-chair, 1988-89; chmn. bldg. com. Ascension Luth. Ch., 1988-90. Mem. NSPE, Nat. Assn. of Mgmt. and Tech. Assistance Ctrs. (bd. dirs.), Instrument Soc. Am., Aircraft Owners and Pilots Assn., Exptl. Aircraft Assn., Am. Bonanza Soc., S.D. Engring. Soc. (pres. N.E. chpt. 1991-92), Rotary, Elks. Avocations: flying, travel. Home: 105 Heather Ln Brookings SD 57006-4123 Office: Village Travel Inc 1715 6th St Brookings SD 57006

SWIDLER, JOSEPH CHARLES, lawyer; b. Chgo., Jan. 28, 1907; s. Abraham and Dora (Cromer) S.; m. Gertrude Tyrna, 1944; children: Ann, Mark. Student, U. Ill., U. Fla.; Ph.B., U. Chgo., 1929, J.D., 1930. Pvt. law practice Chgo., 1930-33; asst. solicitor U.S. Dept. Interior, 1933; mem. legal dept. TVA, 1933-57; gen. counsel, sec., chmn. bd. TVA Retirement System, 1945-57; counsel Alien Property Bur., Dept. Justice, 1941, Power Div., War Prodn. Bd., 1942; pvt. practice law Knoxville and Nashville, 1957-61; chmn. FPC, 1961-65; mem. Water Resources Council, 1964-65, Swidler & Belnap, Washington, 1966-70; chmn. N.Y. State Pub. Service Commn., Albany, 1970-74; dir. Inst. Pub. Policy Alternatives, SUNY, Albany, 1974-75; ptnr. Leva, Hawes, Symington, Martin & Oppenheimer, Washington, 1975-82; counsel Swidler & Berlin, Washington, 1982—; bd. dirs. Nat. Regulatory Rsch. Inst.; mem. adv. coun. Electric Power Rsch. Inst., 1973-80, Gas Rsch. Inst. Served with USNR, 1943-45. Fellow Nat. Acad. Pub. Adminstrn. Home: 8100 Connecticut Ave Apt 1608 Bethesda MD 20815 Office: 3000 K St NW Washington DC 20007-5109

SWIECICKI, MARTIN, neurosurgeon; b. Camden, N.J., June 29, 1934; s. Martin E. and Annetta Swiecicki; m. Gloria J. Whelpley; children: Diane, Annette, Karen, Sheryl, Martin C. BA, Colgate U., 1956; MD, Hahnemann Med. Sch., 1960. Diplomate Am. Bd. Neurol. Surgery. Intern West Jersey Hosp., Camden, 1960-61; resident in neurological surgery Jefferson U., Phila., 1961-65; mem. staff in neurol. surgery West Jersey Hosp., Camden, Berlin, N.J., 1967—, chief Neurol. Surgery, 1967-89; clin. assoc prof. Neurol. Surgery Hahnemann Med. Coll., Phila., 1977—. Contbr. articles to profl. jours. Recipient N.J. Gov.'s award for Outstanding Svcs., 1970, 71, 72, 73, Award for Support and Svc. Boy Scouts Am., 1992. Fellow ACS; mem. AMA, Camden County Med. Soc. (v.p.1993, pres. 1995), West Jersey Med. Soc., N.J. State Med. Soc., N.J. Neurosurg. Soc.(sec.-treas. 978-79, pres. 1981, chmn. peer rev. com. 1983-89, mem. peer rev. com. 1977—), Camden County Med. Soc. (exec. com. 1977—, v.p. 1993, pres.- elect 1994, pres. 1995), Soc. Air Force Clin. Surgeons, Am. Assn. Neurol. Surgeons. Office: Neurosurg Assocs NJ 2301 E Evesham Rd Ste 406 Voorhees NJ 08043-4505

SWIFT, CALVIN THOMAS, electrical and computer engineering educator; b. Quantico, Va., Feb. 6, 1937; s. Thomas and Elsie (Hill) S.; m. Joanne Taylor, Sept. 5, 1959; children: Pamela, Janet. B.S., MIT, 1959; M.S., Va. Poly. Inst., 1965; Ph.D., William and Mary Coll., 1969. Research engr. N. Am. Aviation Co., Downey, Calif., 1959-62; aerospace technologist NASA, Hampton, Va., 1962-81; prof. elec. and computer engring. U. Mass., Amherst, 1981—; cons. engring., Amherst, 1981—. Editor: Transactions on Geoscience and Remote Sensing, 1980-84; assoc. editor: Jour. Oceanic Engring., 1980-84. F.L. Thompson fellow NASA, 1977. Fellow IEEE; mem. Internat. Union Radio Sci. (chmn. Commn. F 1988-91), Antennas and Propagation Soc. (adminstrv. com. 1974-77, 80-85), Geosci. and Remote Sensing Soc. (adminstrv. com. 1978-86, pres. 1985, Disting. Achievement award 1994). Office: U Mass Dept Elec & Computer Engring Amherst MA 01003

SWIFT, DAVID L., manufacturing company executive; b. Muncie, Ind., 1936. Grad., Ball State U., 1958, No. Ky. U., 1966. Former v.p., sec., gen. counsel Acme-Cleve. Corp., pres., CEO, chmn. bd. dirs., 1987—. Mem. ABA. Office: Acme-Cleve Corp 30100 Chagrin Blvd Ste 100 Pepper Pike OH 44124-5705*

SWIFT, DOLORES MONICA MARCINKEVICH, public relations executive; b. Hazleton, Pa., Apr. 3, 1936; d. Adam Martin and Anna Frances (Lizbinski) Marcinkevich; student McCann Coll., 1954-56; m. Morden Leib Swift, Dec. 18, 1966. Pub. rels. coord. Internat. Coun. Shopping Ctrs., N.Y.C., 1957-59, Wendell P. Colton Advt. Agy., N.Y.C., 1959-61, Sydney S. Baron Pub. Rels. Corp., N.Y.C., 1961-65, Robert S. Taplinger Pub. Rels., N.Y.C., 1965-66; prin. Dolores M. Swift, Pub. Rels., Chgo., 1966—. Bd. dirs. Welfare Pub. Rels. Forum, 1971-79, treas., 1975-77; mem. pub. rels. adv. com. Mid-Am. chpt. A.R.C., 1973—; mem. women's com. Mark Twain Meml., 1968-69; pub. rels. dir. N.J. Symphony, Bergen County, 1969-70, mem. pub. rels. and promotion com.; mem. Wadsworth Atheneum, 1968-69; bd. dirs. Youth Guidance, 1972-75, Camp Fire, Met. Chgo. Coun., Inc., 1990-91; mem. NCCJ Labor, Mgmt. and Pub. Interest Conf., 1977-78; mem. pub. rels. com. United Way/Crusade of Mercy, 1979-80, 83, chmn. health svcs. com., 1984, direct mail com. 1985-86. Mem. Pub. Rels. Soc. Am. (accredited, coll. of fellows, Disting. Svc. award 1988, chmn. subcom. Nat. Ctr. for Vol. Action 1971-72, pub. svcs. com. Chgo. chpt. 1971-72, dir. 1975-82, chmn. counselors sect. 1976-77, assembly del. 1976, 79-81, 84-89, sec. 1977-78, v.p. 1978-79, pres.-elect 1979-80, pres. 1980-81, Midwest dist. chmn. 1984, nat. bd. dirs. 1985-89, sec. 1987-89, host chpt. chmn. 1981 conf., chmn. Midwest Dist. Conf. 1983, chmn. ethics awareness com. 1990-92, chmn. sr. forum com. 1993-94, 95-96, chmn. past pres. coun. 1995-96, mem. sr. forum com. 1995—, edml. affairs com. 1990—, chmn., past pres. coun. 1995—), Women's Club (publs. chmn. Englewood, N.J., 1970-71), Publicity Club (chmn. pub. info. com. 1975-76). Mem. editorial bd. Public Relations Jour., 1978.

SWIFT, EDWARD FOSTER, III, investment banker; b. Chgo., Nov. 1, 1923; s. Theodore Philip I and Elizabeth (Hoyt) S.; m. Joan McKelvy, July 2, 1947; children: Theodore Philip II, Edward McKelvy, Lockhart McKelvy, Elizabeth Hoyt; m. Carol Coffey Whipple, June 21, 1968. Grad., Hotchkiss Sch., 1941; BA, Yale U., 1945. With Esmark, Inc. (formerly Swift & Co.), 1947-75, asst. to v.p. charge meat packing plants, 1958, asst. v.p., 1958-59, v.p. for provisions, fgn., casings and storage, 1959-64, exec. v.p., 1964-75; vice-chmn. Chgo. Corp., 1975-79; vice chmn. Bacon, Whipple & Co., Chgo., 1980-84; mng. dir. A.G. Becker Paribas Inc., Chgo., 1984-85; with E.F. Hutton and Co., Chgo., 1985-87; mng. dir. Shearson Lehman Hutton Inc, Chgo., 1987-92; bd. dirs. Santa Fe Pacific Pipelines, Inc. Chmn. So. Ind. chpt. United Negro Coll. Fund, 1956; trustee Northwestern U., Evanston, Ill.; bd. dirs. Northwestern Meml. Hosp., Chgo. Served to capt. U.S. Army, 1942-46. Mem. Chgo. Assn. Commerce and Industry (bd. dirs.), Scroll and Key, Chgo. Club, Racquet Club, Econ. Club, Valley Club, Comml. Club, Onwentsia Club, Old Elm ClubBirnam Wood Golf Club, Aurelian Honor Soc. Home: 1500 N Astor St Chicago IL 60610-1640 Office: 70 W Madison St Ste 1400 Chicago IL 60602-4206

SWIFT, EVANGELINE WILSON, lawyer; b. San Antonio, May 2, 1939; d. Raymond E. and Josephine (Woods) Wilson; 1 child, Justin Lee. Student So. Meth. U., 1956-59; LL.B., St. Mary's U., San Antonio, 1963. Bar: Tex. 1963, U.S. Ct. Appeals (5th cir.) 1972, D.C. 1976, U.S. Dist. Ct. D.C. 1976, U.S. Supreme Ct. 1980, U.S. Ct. Appeals (11th cir.) 1981, U.S. Ct. Appeals (10th cir.) 1982, U.S. Ct. Appeals (D.C. cir.) 1982, U.S. Ct. Appeals (fed. cir.) 1983. Atty.-adv. ICC, Washington, 1964-65; staff atty. Headstart Program, OEO, Washington, 1965; exec. legal asst. to chmn., spl. asst. to vice chmn. EEOC, Washington, 1965-71, chief decisions div., 1971-75, asst. gen. counsel, 1975-76; cons. to sec. Employment Standards Adminstrn., Dept. Labor, Washington, 1977-79; ptnr. Swift & Swift, P.C., Washington, 1977-79; gen. counsel Merit Systems Protection Bd., Washington, 1979-86, mng. dir., 1986-87, dir. policy and evaluation, 1987—; bd. govs. U.S. Ct. Appeals (fed. cir.) Bar Assn., 1984-93, treas., 1987-89, sec., 1989-90, pres. elect, 1990; Fed. Cir. Bar Assn. (pres. 1992); guest lectr. Drake U., U. Pa., MIT; mem. U.S. del. 23d Sessions UN Commn. on Status of Women, Geneva, 1970. Recipient Meritorious Service award Fed. Govt., 1967, Fed. Women's award, 1975, Performance award Merit Systems Protection Bd., 1981-86, 92, 93, 94, Gold award 1986, Presdl. CFC award, 1984, 86, 94, EEO award Merit Systems Protection Bd., 1985, 94, 96, Theodore Roosevelt award, 1988, Elmer B. Staats award NCAC, Am. Soc. Pub. Adminstrn., 1994, Mary D. Pinkard Leader in Fed. Equity award, Fed. Employed Women, 1995. Methodist. Office: Merit System Protection Bd Office of Policy and Evaluation 1120 Vermont Ave NW Washington DC 20419-0001

SWIFT, FRANK MEADOR, lawyer; b. N.Y.C., Dec. 27, 1911; s. Frank Meador and Alberta (Rankin) S.; m. Harriet Elizabeth Simpson, May 30, 1944; children: Frank Meador, Thomas Lamar. Student, Emory U., 1930-32; LL.B., U. Ga., 1935. Bar: Ga. 1935. Partner Swift, Currie, McGhee & Hiers, Atlanta, 1965-82; of counsel Swift, Currie, McGhee & Hiers, 1982—. Served to comdr. USNR, 1942-46. Mem. Am., Ga. bar assns., Lawyers Club Atlanta, Am. Judicature Soc. Republican. Presbyn. Clubs: Piedmont Driving. Home: 3150 Palisades Ct Marietta GA 30067-5130 Office: Swift Currie McGhee & Hiers 1355 Peachtree St NE Atlanta GA 30309-3269

SWIFT, HUMPHREY HATHAWAY, manufacturing executive; b. Phila., Apr. 18, 1915; s. Robert Wesselhoeft and Edith (Steel) S.; m. Dorothea Banks, Apr. 8, 1943 (dec. 1951); children: Edith S., Alexandra Swift Bigelow; m. Pamela Ann Whitney, June 6, 1953; children: Pamela Swift Tarnower, Hope S. Baker, Alison Clarke. AB, U. N.C., 1939. Salesman Swift & Anderson Inc., 1946-50; mgr. sales Standard Thermometer Inc., Boston, 1951-55, pres., 1960-70; exec. v.p. Swift Instruments Inc., Boston, 1959-68, pres., 1968—; v.p. Swift Instruments Internat. S.A., Boston, 1959-68, pres., 1968—. Mem. Hingham (Mass.) Adv. Com., 1965-66, Hingham Town Com., 1955-60; trustee Manomet Obs., 1994—, New Eng. Deaconess Hosp., 1954-73; overseer U.S. Constitution Mus., 1995—, Childrens Hosp., 1990-95, hon. overseer, 1995—. Mem. World Trade Ctr., Photog. Mktg., Nat. Sporting Good Assn., St. Anthony Club, New Bedford Yacht Club, Hingham Yacht Club, Corinthians. Republican. Episcopalian. Avocations: sailing, skiing. Office: Swift Instruments Inc 952 Dorchester Ave Boston MA 02125-1219

SWIFT, ISABEL DAVIDSON, editorial director; b. Tokyo; d. Carleton Byron and Mary Howard (Davidson) S.; m. Steven C. Phillips. BA, Harvard U., 1976. Asst. editor Pocket Books, Simon & Schuster, N.Y.C., 1979-81; assoc. editor, editor, sr. editor, editorial mgr. Silhouette Books, N.Y.C., 1981-91, editorial dir., 1991—; internat. speaker on romance genre. Contbr. articles to profl. jours. Recipient RITA award Romance Writers Am., 1992, 94. Mem. N.Y. Women's Found. Office: Silhouette Books 300 E 42nd St New York NY 10017-5947

SWIFT, JAMES WILLIAM, health care executive; b. Sheridan, Wyo., Nov. 21, 1945; s. Barney L. and Agnes S.; m. Elizabeth Ann Connors, Aug. 17, 1968; children—Courtney, Colleen, Molly, Jennifer, Michael, Matthew. B.A., St. Louis U., 1968, M.H.A., 1971, M.B.A., 1975; M.A., Central State U., Edmond, Okla., 1979. Asst. adminstr. St. John's Mercy Medical Center, St. Louis, 1971-75; exec. v.p. Mercy Health Center, Oklahoma City, 1975-78; exec. dir. Mercy Health Center, 1978-79; pres., dir. St. John's Regional Health Center, Springfield, Mo., 1979—; CEO Unity Health System, St. Louis, 1995—; dir. Empire Bank; tchr. Maryville Coll., Florissant Valley Community Coll.; chmn. task force continuing edn. Bi-State Regional Med. Program, St. Louis, 1972. Exec. com. Breech Sch. Bus., Drury Coll.; devel. bd. Cath. Sch. System; bd. dirs. Adult Edn. Council of St. Louis, 1973; treas. Alumni Assn. St. Louis U. Program in Hosp. and Health Care Adminstrn., 1975-76; vice chmn. fin. com. St. Eugene Ch. and Sch., Oklahoma City, 1978. Fellow Am. Coll. Hosp. Adminstrs.; mem. Am. Hosp. Assn., Mo. Hosp. Assn., St. Louis U. Hosp. and Health Care Adminstrn. Alumni Assn. (dir. 1978—). Roman Catholic. Office: Unity Health System 1655 Des Peres Rd Ste 301 Saint Louis MO 63131*

SWIFT, JANE MARIA, state senator; b. North Adams, Mass., Feb. 24, 1965; d. John Maynard and Jean Mary (Kent) S.; m. Charles T. Hunt III, Feb. 19, 1994. BA in Am. Studies, Trinity Coll., Hartford, Conn., 1987. Exec. mgmt. trainee G. Fox & Co., Hartford, 1987-88; adminstrv. aide Sen. Peter C. Webber, Boston, 1988-90; mem. Mass. State Senate, Boston, 1991—; 3d asst. minority leader, 1993—. Republican. Roman Catholic. Office: Massachusetts State Senate 8 Bank Row Pittsfield MA 01201

SWIFT, JILL ANNE, industrial engineer, educator; b. Memphis, Nov. 12, 1959; d. Gary Green and Sharon (Willoughby) Brown; m. Fredrick Wallace Swift, June 12, 1987; children: Andrew, Samantha. BS, Memphis State U., 1981, MS, 1982; PhD, Okla. State U., 1987. Registered profl. engr., Fla.; cert. quality engr. Design engr. DuPont Co., Glasgow, Del., 1982-83; head dept. physics Coll. Boca Raton, Fla., 1983-87; asst. prof. indsl. engring. U. Miami, Coral Gables, Fla., 1987—; vis. scholar Air Force Inst. Tech., Wright-Patterson AFB, Ohio, 1988; cons. A. T. Kearney, Amman, Jordan, 1990; quality liaison U. Miami Inst. Study of Quality in Mfg. and Svc., 1988—; cons., spkr. in field. Author: Introduction to Modern Statistical Quality Control and Management, 1995; contbr. articles to profl. publs. Mem. IIE (chpt. dir. 1988-90, Christmas toy dr. coord. 1989, 90), Am. Soc. Engring. Edn., Am. Soc. Quality Control, Phi Kappa Phi, Alpha Pi Mu (faculty adviser 1988—), Tau Beta Pi. Republican. Avocations: racquetball, water skiing, cross-stitch, reading. Office: Univ Miami 268 McArthur Bldg Coral Gables FL 33124

SWIFT, JOHN FRANCIS, health care advertising company executive; b. N.Y.C., June 15, 1935; s John F. and Mary Veronica (Kehoe) S.; m. Eleanor H. Cunniff, Oct. 10, 1964; children—John Francis, Sharon Ann. B.S. in Bus. Adminstrn, Seton Hall U., 1960, postgrad., 1960-61. Mktg. research mgr. Lederle Labs. div. Cyanamid Internat., 1960-63; account exec. Robert A. Becker Advt. Agy., N.Y.C., 1963-66; mgr. new products Chesebrough Ponds Co., N.Y.C., 1966-68; v.p. Frohlich Intercon Co., N.Y.C., 1968-72; pres., chief exec. officer Lavey/Wolff/Swift, Inc., N.Y.C., 1972-91, chmn., chief exec. officer, 1991-94; pres., chief exec. officer BBDO Health & Med.

Comms. Inc., 1977-91; chmn., chief exec. officer Health & Med. Comms. Inc., 1991—; vice chmn. Lyons Lavey Nickel Swift, Inc., 1995—. Bd. govs. Cathedral Healthcare Systems, 1991—; chmn. Cathedral Healthcare Found., 1994—. Served with USN, 1955-57. Mem. Pharm. Advt. Coun. (pres. 1979), Bio-Med. Mktg. Assn., Canoe Brook (Summit, N.J.), Skytop Club (Pa.), Boca Raton (Fla.) Country Club, N.Y. Athletic Club. Home: 32 Peppermill Rd Chatham NJ 07928-1312 also: 600 S Ocean Blvd Boca Raton FL 33432 also: 76 Bay Point Harbour Pt Pleasant NJ 08742-5509 Office: Lyons Lavey Nickel Swift Inc 488 Madison Ave New York NY 10022-5702

SWIFT, JONATHAN, educator, tenor; b. Glasgow, Scotland, Apr. 26, 1932; came to U.S., 1948, naturalized, 1954; s. John Francis and Catherine Little (McGowan) S.; M.A., Wayne State U., 1957; postgrad. Ecole Normale Superieure de St. Cloud, Paris, 1954-55; cert. Conservatoire Nat. de Musique (France), 1955; postgrad. U. Mich., 1959, Cambridge U., 1981; PhD, Mich. State U., 1983. On-camera tchr. French, Sta. WTVS, Detroit, 1955-56, Am. lit., 1960-62; instr. French, Wayne State U., Detroit, 1955-60; tchr. English, French and social studies Detroit Pub.Schs., 1957-64; tchr. English and history Glasgow Corp. Schs., 1967; tchr. English and French, Livonia (Mich.) Pub. Schs., 1967; chmn. English dept. Stevenson High Sch., Livonia, 1970-78, dir. Sch. Global Edn., 1978—; sr. lectr. Mich. State U.; cons. to U.S. Dept. Edn., 1979, NEA pub. dept., 1979, Mich. State Dept. Edn., 1978, Gale Rsch. Co., 1981, Globe Book Co., 1985, Amideast Publs.; test writer Am. Coll. Testing Program, 1975-76; Internat. Reading Assn. lectr., Philippines, 1980, Hong Kong, 1984; lectr., curriculum cons. Debut in opera as Alfredo in La Traviata, 1961; mem. adv. bd. dirs. Arab World Almanac; host PBS TV and cmty. t.v. series Global Connections, Time Out for Opera; leading tenor with Detroit Piccolo Opera Co., 1961-86, Detroit Grand Opera Assn., 1965, Mich. Opera Co., 1961-64; concert soloist with major symphonies in U.S., Can., Europe, Australia, 1961-81; appeared as tenor soloist in various radio and TV programs, 1961-81; rec. artist with Scotia and Andis (U.K.). Recipient French Govt. medal, 1954; tribute Mich. State Legislature, 1984, NEA Applegate-Dorros award, 1987, MEA Siddall Internat. award, 1987, Phila Farnsworth award alliance Cmty. Media, 1990, 94-95, Hometown award Nat. Fedn. Local Cable Programmers, 1994, Nat. TV award Nat. Assn. Telecomm.Officers and Advs., 1995; Fulbright scholar, 1954-55. Mem. NEA, Internat. Reading Assn., Nat. Coun. Tchrs. English (chmn. secondary sect. 1980-82), Assn. Tchr. Educators, Am. Assn. for Advancement of the Humanities, Nat. Coun. for Social Studies, World Coun. for Curriculum & Instrn., ASCD (internat. steering com.), Myasthenia Gravis Assn. (pres. 1968-69), Assn. of World Edn., World Future Soc., Nat. Acad. of TV, Econ. Club of Detroit, Soc. Friends of St. George, Descs. of Knights of Garter. Roman Catholic. Contbr. articles and poems to profl. and lit. jours. Office: 33500 6 Mile Rd Livonia MI 48152-3156

SWIFT, MICHAEL RONALD, physician, scientist, educator; b. N.Y.C., Feb. 5, 1935; s. Herbert Allen and Estelle (Clafter) S.; m. Ronnie Elaine Gorman, Nov. 27, 1971; children—Melissa, Amy, Laura. B.A., Swarthmore Coll., 1955; M.A., U. Calif.-Berkeley, 1958; M.D., NYU, 1962. Diplomate Am. Bd. Internal Medicine, Am. Bd. Med. Genetics. Instr., then asst. prof. NYU Sch. Medicine, N.Y.C., 1966-70; assoc. prof., then prof. U. N.C., Chapel Hill, 1972-92, also chief genetics div.; prof. pediatrics, dir. Inst. for Genetic Analysis Diseases N.Y. Med. Coll., N.Y.C., 1992—. Contbr. chpts. to books and articles to profl. jours. Mem. AAAS, Am. Assn. Cancer Rsch., Am. Soc. Human Genetics, Alpha Omega Alpha. Avocations: hiking, fishing, traveling, theatre. Office: NY Med Coll 4 Skyline Dr Hawthorne NY 10532

SWIFT, RICHARD G(ENE), composer, educator; b. Middlepoint, Ohio, Sept. 24, 1927; s. Lisle Russell and Josephine (Ladd) S.; m. Dorothy Zackrisson, Feb. 10, 1951; children: Jeremy, John, Joel. MA, U. Chgo., 1956. Assoc. prof. music U. Calif., Davis, 1956-67, prof., 1967-91, prof. emeritus, 1991—, chmn. dept., 1963-71; vis. prof. Princeton U., 1977; faculty research lectr. U. Calif., 1983. Composer: A Coronal, 1954, String Quartet I, 1956, II, 1958, III, 1964, Sonata for Clarinet and Piano, 1957, Sonata for Solo Violin, 1958, Eve, 1959, Stravaganza III for Clarinet, Violin and Piano, 1960, Concerto for Piano and Chamber Ensemble, 1961, Extravaganza for Orchestra, 1962, Domains, I, II, III, 1963, Bucolics, 1964, Concerto for Violin and Chamber Ensemble, 1967, Music for A While, 1969, Thanatopsis, 1971, Prime, 1973, Quartet IV, 1973, Specimen Days, 1976, Mein blaues Klavier, 1979, Concerto II for piano and chamber ensemble, 1980, Quartet V, 1982, Things of August, 1985, Roses Only, 1991, In Arcadia, 1994; consulting editor: 19th Century Music. Served with AUS, 1950-52. Recipient award Rockefeller Found., 1956, 68; award Fromm Found.; Composers String Quartet award, 1973; award Nat. Endowment for Arts, 1976; Inst. award Am. Acad. and Inst. Arts and Letters, 1978; Disting. Teaching award U. Calif., 1980. Fellow Inst. Creative Arts; mem. Am. Music Ctr., ASCAP, Soc. for Music Theory. Home: 568 S Campus Way Davis CA 95616-3523

SWIFT, RICHARD J., engineering company executive; b. 1944. BS, U.S. Mil. Acad., 1966; MS, Purdue U., 1972; MBA, Fairleigh Dickinson U., 1972. With TVA, 1970-72; with Foster Wheeler Corp., Clinton, N.J., 1972-76, from various mgmt. positions to pres., COO, 1977-94, chmn. bd., pres., CEO, 1994—; with Union Carbide Corp., 1976-77. Served U.S. Army, 1966-70. Office: Foster Wheeler Corp Perryville Corp Pk Clinton NJ 08809*

SWIFT, ROBERT FREDERIC, music educator; b. Ilion, N.Y., July 7, 1940; s. Frederic Fay and Ruth Eleanor (Ainslie) S.; m. Margot Sue Werme, Nov. 24, 1962; children: Jeffrey Robert, Jennifer Sue. BS, Hartwick Coll., 1962, MA, 1968; PhD, Eastman Sch. Music, Rochester, N.Y., 1970. Music instr. West Winfield (N.Y.) Cen. Sch., 1962-67, N.Y. State Music Camp, Oneonta, 1962—, Brighton High Sch., Rochester, 1970-71; asst. prof. music Eastman Sch. Music, Rochester, 1971-76; assoc. prof. music Memphis State U., 1976-79; prof. music, dept. chmn. Plymouth State Coll. of U. N.H., Plymouth, 1979—. Author: Music from the Mountains: The New York State Music Camp, 1947-96; compuser numerous musical compositions. Ch. musician Christian Sci., Presbyn., Bapt. chs. Nat. Def. Edn. Act Title IV fellow U. Rochester, 1967-70; recipient Disting. Teaching award Memphis State U., 1979, Disting. Teaching award Coll. for Lifelong Learning of U. System of N.H., 1987. Mem. N.H. Music Edn. Assn., Music Educators Nat. Conf., Am. Choral Dirs. Assn., Coll. Music Soc., Royal Sch. Ch. Music., Phi Mu Alpha Sinfonia, Kappa Delta Pi. Republican. Mem. Christian Science Ch. Home: PO Box 125 Plymouth NH 03264-0125 Office: Plymouth State Coll Dept Music And Theatre Plymouth NH 03264

SWIFT, STEPHEN JENSEN, federal judge; b. Salt Lake City, Sept. 7, 1943; s. Edward A. and Maurine (Jensen) S.; m. Lorraine Burnell Facer, Aug. 4, 1972; children: Carter, Stephanie, Spencer, Meredith, Hunter. BS, Brigham Young U., 1967; JD, George Washington U., 1970. Trial atty. U.S. Dept. Justice, Washington, D.C., 1970-74; asst. U.S. atty. U.S. Atty.'s Office, San Francisco, 1974-77; v.p., sr. tax counsel Bank Am. N.T. & S.A., San Francisco, 1977-83; judge U.S. Tax Ct., Washington, 1983—; adj. prof. Golden Gate U., San Francisco, 1978-83, U. Balt., 1990—. Mem. ABA, Calif. Bar Assn., D.C. Bar Assn. Office: US Tax Ct 400 2nd St NW Washington DC 20217-0001

SWIFT, WILLIAM CHARLES, professional baseball player, Olympic athlete; b. Portland, Maine, Oct. 27, 1961. Student, Maine. Mem. U.S. Olympic Baseball Team, 1984; with Seattle Mariners, 1984-91; pitcher San Francisco Giants, 1991-94, Colo. Rockies, 1994—. Nat. League Earned Run Average leader, 1992. Office: Colo Rockies 2850 W 20th Ave Denver CO 80211*

SWIGER, ELINOR PORTER, lawyer; b. Cleve., Aug. 1, 1927; d. Louie Charles and Mary Isabelle (Shank) Porter; m. Quentin Gilbert Swiger, Feb. 5, 1955; children: Andrew Porter, Calvin Gilbert, Charles Robinson. BA, Ohio State U., 1949, JD, 1951. Bar: Ohio 1951, Ill. 1979. Sr. assoc. Robbins, Schwartz, Nicholas, Lifton & Taylor, Ltd., Chgo., 1979—. Author: Mexico for Kids, 1971, Europe for Young Travelers, 1972, The Law and You, 1973 (Literary Guild award), Careers in the Legal Professions, 1978, Women Lawyers at Work, 1978, Law in Everday Life, 1977. Mem. Northfield Twp. (Ill.) Bd. Edn., 1976-83; mem. Glenview (Ill.) Fire and Police Commn., 1976-86; chmn. Glenview Zoning Bd. Appeals, 1987—. Mem. ABA (chmn. pub. edn. com. urban, state and local govt. sect. 1982-85), Ill. Bar Assn. (chmn. local govt. sect. 1986-87, chmn. legal edn. sect. 1991-92), Ill. Coun. Sch. Attys. (chmn.), Women Bar Assn. Ill., Chgo. Bar Assn. (chmn. legis. exec. com. 1990-92), Soc. Midland Authors. Republican. Home: 1933 Burr Oak Dr Glenview IL 60025 Office: Robbins Schwartz Nicholas Lifton & Taylor 29 S La Salle St Ste 860 Chicago IL 60603-1505

SWIGER, ELIZABETH DAVIS, chemistry educator; b. Morgantown, W.Va., June 27, 1926; d. Hannibal Albert and Tyreeca Elizabeth (Stemple) Davis; m. William Eugene Swiger, June 2, 1948; children: Susan Elizabeth Swiger Knotts, Wayne William. BS in Chemistry, W.Va. U., 1948, MS in Chemistry, 1952, PhD in Chemistry, 1964. Instr. math. Fairmont (W.Va.) State Coll., 1948-49, instr. math. and phys. sci., 1956-57, instr. chemistry, 1957-60, asst. prof. chemistry, 1960-63, assoc. prof. chemistry, 1964-66, prof. chemistry, 1966—, chmn., div. sci., math, and health careers, 1991-92; NSF fellow rsch. W.Va. U., Morgantown, 1963-64; prof. emeritus, 1992; advisor Am. Chem. Soc. student affiliates, 1965-88. Author: Morton Family History, 1984-94, Davis-Winters Family History, 1994, Civil War Letters and Diary of Joshua Winters, 1991; contbr. articles to profl. jours. Bd. dirs. Prickett's Fort Meml. Found., Fairmont, 1988—, chmn. elect, 1990-92, chair., 1992—, Blacks Chapel Meml. Found., 1993—, rep. adv. coun. to Bd. Regents, Fairmont State Coll., Charleston, 1977-78, rep. instl. bd. advisors, Fairmont, 1990-92. NSF grantee, 1963; named Outstanding Prof. W.Va. Legislature, Charleston, 1990. Mem. Am. Chem. Soc. (sec. chmn. North W. Va. 1975, 83), W.Va. Acad. Sci. (pres. 1978-79, exec. com. edn. chmn. 1990-93), The Nature Conservancy (bd. dirs. W.Va. chpt. 1970-86, chmn. 1980-82), AAUW. Republican. Methodist. Avocations: local history, genealogy, gardening, computers. Home: 1599 Hillcrest Rd Fairmont WV 26554-4807 also: 382 Laird Dr Freeport FL 32439

SWIGER, L. A., agricultural studies educator. Diploma in animal husbandry, Ohio State U., 1954, MS, 1957, PhD, 1960. Geneticist USDA, Lincoln, Neb., 1959, assoc. prof. animal sci., experiment sta. statistician; prof. animal genetics, grad. chmn/ Ohio State U.; prof. animal sci., dept. head Va. Tech, Blacksburg, 1980-86, assoc. dean rsch. Coll. Agrl. and Life Scis., 1986-92, interim dean, 1992-93, dean, 1993—. Recipient Rockefeller Prentice Meml. award Am. Soc. Animal Sci., 1984. Office: Va Tech Coll Agrl and Life Sci Blacksburg VA 24061-0402

SWIGERT, JAMES MACK, lawyer; b. Carthage, Ill., Sept. 25, 1907; s. James Ross and Pearl (Mack) S.; m. Alice Francis Titcomb Harrower, July 7, 1931 (dec. 1990); children: Oliver, David Ladd, Sally Harper (Mrs. Hamilton). Student, Grinnell Coll., 1925-27; SB, Harvard U., 1930, LLB, 1935. Bar: Ill. 1935, Ohio 1937. With Campbell, Clithero & Fischer, Chgo., 1935-36, Taft, Stettinius & Hollister, Cin., 1936—; ptnr. Taft, Stettinius & Hollister, 1948-79, sr. ptnr. and chmn. exec. com., 1979-85, of counsel, 1985—; dir., mem. exec. com. Union Cen. Life Ins. Co., 1963-79; dir., chmn. audit com. Philips Industries, 1975-82. Author articles on labor rels. and labor law. Bd. dirs. Cin. Symphony Orch., 1976-78; trustee, chmn. exec. com. Am. Music Scholarship Assn., 1987-92. Republican. Presbyterian. Clubs: Queen City (past dir.), Cincinnati Country (past v.p., dir.), Queen City Optimists (past pres.), Tennis (past pres.), Recess (past pres.), Harvard Law (past pres.) (Cin.). Home: 2121 Alpine Pl Cincinnati OH 45206-2690 Office: 1800 Star Bank Ctr Cincinnati OH 45202

SWIGGER, KEITH BOYD, dean; b. Hutchinson, Kans., Feb. 3, 1943; s. Paul Clarke and Loneta (Miller) S.; children: Jessica, Nathaniel. BA, U. Chgo., 1965, MA, 1975; MA, Ind. U., 1967; PhD, U. Iowa, 1973. Sketchwriter Marquis Who's Who, Chgo., 1963-67; teaching asst. Ind. U., Bloomington, 1967; teaching asst. U. Iowa, Iowa City, 1968-73, lectr., 1973-74, libr., 1976-77; asst. prof. East Tex. State U., Commerce, 1977-81; asst. prof. libr. scis. Tex. Woman's U., Denton, 1981-85, assoc. prof., 1985-89, prof., 1989—, interim dean Sch. Libr. Sci., 1991-92, dean Sch. Libr. and Info. Studies, 1992—. Contbr. numerous articles to profl. jours. Bd. dirs. ACLU, Denton, 1990-92, Emily Fowler Pub. Libr., Denton, 1995—. Rsch. grantee OCLC, Inc., 1990-91, Career Tng. grantee U.S. Office Edn., 1990-96; postdoctoral fellow Coun. on Libr. Resources U. Chgo., 1974-75. Mem. ALA, Tex. Libr. Assn., Young Adult Libr. Svcs. Assn., Tex. Faculty Assn., Assn. Libr. Info. Sci. Edn. Office: Tex Womans Univ Sch Libr and Info Studies PO Box 425438 Denton TX 76204-5438

SWIGGETT, HAROLD E., writer, photographer; b. Moline, Kans., July 22, 1921; s. Otho Benjamin and Mildred (Spray) S.; ed. high sch.; m. Wilma Caroline Turner, Mar. 1, 1942; children: Gerald, Vernon. Staff photographer San Antonio Express-News, 1946-67, head dept., 1955-67; freelance writer/photographer San Antonio, 1947—, full-time, 1967—; ordained minister So. Baptist Ch. Served with USAAC, World War II. Recipient 10th ann. Outstanding Am. Handgunner award, 1982, Lifetime Cicero award, 1991, St. Gabriel Possenti medal, 1991; named to Am. Handgunner Hall of Fame, 1987, Anschutz/PSI Gun Writer of Yr., 1990, Handgun Hunter Hall of Fame, 1991. Mem. NRA (life), Wildlife Unltd. (pres. chpt. 1955-58), Outdoor writers Assn. Am. (dir. 1969-72), Tex. Outdoor Writers Assn. (pres. 1967-68), Ducks Unltd., Tex. Rifle Assn. (life), Internat. Handgun Metallic Silhouette Assn. (life), Game Conservation Internat. Republican. Contbg. author books game hunting, gun-oriented paperbacks; author: Hal Swiggett on North American Deer, 1980; sr. editor Harris Publs., Guns/Hunting, Tex. Fish & Game; editor: Handguns 95; contbg. editor Gun Digest, North Am. Hunter. Home: 539 Roslyn Ave San Antonio TX 78204-2456

SWIHART, FRED JACOB, lawyer; b. Park Rapids, Minn., Aug. 19, 1919; s. Fred and Elizabeth Pauline (Judnitsch) S.; m. Edna Lillian Jensen, Sept. 30, 1950; 1 child; Frederick Jay. BA, U. Nebr., 1949, JD, 1954; M in Russian Lang., Middlebury Coll., 1950; grad., U.S. Army Command and Staff Coll., 1965. Bar: Nebr. 1954, U.S. Dist. Ct. Nebr. 1954, U.S. Ct. Appeals (8th cir.) 1977, U.S. Supreme Ct. 1972. Claims atty. Chgo. & Eastern Ill. R.R., 1954-56; atty. Assn. Amer. R.R.s, Chgo., 1956-60; assoc. Wagener & Marx, Lincoln, Nebr., 1960-61; prosecutor City of Lincoln, 1961-68; sole practice Lincoln, 1968—. Editor Law for the Aviator, 1969-71. Served to lt. col. U.S. Army, 1943-46, ETO, Korea, ret. col., USAR, 1979. Fellow Nebr. State Bar Found.; mem. ABA, Nebr. Bar Assn., Fed. Bar Assn., Assn. Trial Lawyers Am., Am. Judicature Soc., Aircraft Owners and Pilots Assn. (legis. rep.), Nebr. Criminal Def. Attys. Assn., Nat. Assn. Criminal Def. Lawyers, Mercedes Benz Club Am., Nebr. Assn. Trial Attys., Nat. Assn. Uniformed Svcs., Res. Officers Assn., Nat. Assn. Legion of Honor, Internat. Footprint Assn., Am. Legion (adm. Nebr. Navy), Mason (knight comdr. of ct. of honor), Shriners, The Cabiri. Republican. Presbyterian. Avocations: collecting art, music, pistol competition. Home: 1610 Susan Cir Lincoln NE 68506-1854 Office: 4435 O St Ste 130 Lincoln NE 68510-1864

SWIHART, H. GREGG, real estate company executive; b. San Francisco, Sept. 25, 1938; s. Lawson Benjamin and Violet Mary (Watters) S.; B.A., U. Ariz., 1958; postgrad. U. Heidelberg (W.Ger.), 1958-59, Harvard U., 1959-60; M.A., Boston U., 1961; postgrad. U. Freiburg (West Germany), 1961-65; m. Ilse Paula Rambacher, Dec. 24, 1958; children—Tatjana Etta, Brett Marc, Natascha Theda. Stock broker Walston & Co., Tucson, 1966-71; with Solot Co., Tucson, 1971-74; pres. Cienega Properties, Inc., property mgmt. and investment, Tucson, 1975-77; pres. GT Realty Assocs., Ltd., Tucson, 1977—. Mem. Tucson Com. Fgn. Relations, 1973—; pres. Forum for Greater Outdoors, 1977-79; bd. dirs. Tucson Mus. Art, 1968-74, pres. 1969-70; pres. and trustee Canelo Hills Sch., 1977-79. Cert. property mgr. Mem. Tucson Bd. Realtors, Inst. Real Estate Mgmt. (pres. Tucson-So. Ariz. chpt. 1982, mem. nat. governing council 1985-87), Inst. Real Estate Mgmt. (governing council 1985-87, Property Mgr. of Yr. award So. Ariz. chpt. 1988), Realtors Nat. Mktg. Inst. Clubs: Harvard (pres. 1973-74), Active 20-30 (pres. 1969), Downtown Tucson. Home: Tunnel Springs Ranch PO Box 555 Sonoita AZ 85637 Office: 4003 E Speedway Blvd Ste 110 Tucson AZ 85712-4555

SWIHART, JAMES W., JR., diplomat; b. Washington, DC, July 25, 1946; s. James Wilbur and Ruth (Inge) S.; m. Ellen Jane Cendo Mar. 30, 1968; children: Jennifer Anne, Christopher John. BA, Columbia Coll., 1968. Vice consul Am. Embassy, Belize, Brit. Honduras, 1970-72; 2nd sec., polit. officer Am. Embassy, Belgrade, Yugoslavia, 1972-74; ops. officer ops. ctr. Dept. State, Washington, 1974-75, country officer for Italy and the Vatican, 1975-78; polit./mil. officer for U.S. Mission Berlin Dept. State, 1978-82; officer C.S.C.E. Bur. European Affairs Dept. State, Washington, 1982-83, officer for Fed. Republic of Germany, 1983-84; consul gen., prin. officer U.S. Consulate Gen., Zagreb, Yugoslavia, 1984-1988; mem. sr. seminar Dept. State, Washington, 1988-89, dir. Bur. for Ea. European and Yugoslavia Affairs, 1989-1991; min. counselor, deputy chief of mission Am. Embassy, Vienna, Austria, 1991-94, Chargé d'Affaires ad interim, 1993; amb. to Lithuania Am. Embassy, Vilnius, 1994—. Avocations: piano, harpsichord, jogging, classical music appreciation. Home and Office: American Embassy Vilnius Dept of State Washington DC 20521-4510 Office: Am Embassy Vilnius Psc 78 # V APO AE 09723-9998

SWIHART, JOHN MARION, retired aircraft manufacturing company executive; b. New Winchester, Ohio, Dec. 27, 1923; s. Harry Miron and Fay I. (Cress) S.; m. Gail G. Carter, Nov. 8, 1986; children from previous marriages: Vicki Ann, John Richard, Thomas Marion, Mark Andrew, Karen Lee, Laurie Christine, Stacey Anne. BS in Physics, Bowling Green State U., 1947; BS in Aero. Engring., Ga. Inst. Tech., 1949, postgrad., 1951-53; postgrad., U. Va., 1951-53. Asst. group leader propulsion group NASA, 1956-58, group leader spl. projects, 1958-59, head advanced configurations group aircraft, 1959-62, chief large supersonic tunnels br., 1962; with Boeing Co., 1962-89; dep. dir. internat. sales Boeing Co., Renton, Wash., 1974-75; v.p. Japan Boeing Internat. Corp. Boeing Co., Tokyo, 1973-74; program mgr. 7X7 Boeing Co., Kent, Wash., 1975-76; dir. new airplane product devel., sales, mktg. Boeing Co., Seattle, 1976-78; dir. product devel., sales mktg. Boeing Co., 1978-79, v.p. U.S., Can. sales, 1979-83, v.p. govt. tech. liaison, 1983-85, corp. v.p. airplane market analysis, 1985; corp. v.p. internat. affairs Boeing Co., Seattle, 1985-89; ret., 1989. Contbr. over 100 articles to profl. jours. 1st lt. USAAF, 1943-45. Decorated D.F.C., Air medal with 3 oak leaf clusters; recipient Wright Bros. Meml. Lectureship award, 1987, Maurice Roy medal for internat. cooperation Internat. Coun. Aeronautical Scie., 1992. Fellow AIAA (hon., chmn. airdraft design com. Pacific N.W. sect. 1969-70, gen. chmn. aircraft sys. and design meeting 1977, pres. 1990-91), Royal Aero. Soc., Internat. Soc. for Air-Breating Engines (pres. 1993—); mem. Japan-Am. Soc. (pres. 1978-79), Wash. State China Rels. Coun. (past pres.).

SWILLING, PAT, professional football player; b. Toccoa, Ga., Oct. 25, 1964. Student, Ga. Tech. U. With New Orleans Saints, 1986-92, Detroit Lions, 1993—. Named to Pro Bowl Team, 1990-93; named outside linebacker Sporting News NFL All-Pro Team, 1991, 92; led league in sacks, 1991. Office: Detroit Lions 1200 Featherstone Rd Pontiac MI 48342-1938

SWINBURN, CHARLES, lawyer; b. Bowness on Windermere, Cumbria, Eng., Apr. 11, 1942; came to U.S., 1949; s. Joseph and Myra (Sullivan) S.; m. Carol Ann Ditzler, Dec. 16, 1972; children: Ann Elizabeth, Catherine Knowles. BA in Psychology, Princeton U., 1963; MBA, Harvard U., 1971; JD, U. Pa., 1993. Industry analyst U.S. Dept. Transp., Washington, 1971-73, chief Industry Analysis Div., 1973-76, dep. asst. sec., 1979-83; assoc. adminstr. fed. assistance Fed. R.R. Adminstrn., Washington, 1976-79; v.p. FS Rollins Environ. Svcs. Inc., Wilmington, Del., 1983-90; assoc. Morgan, Lewis & Bockius, Washington, 1993—; mem., bd. dirs. RailAmerica, Inc. Capt. USMC, 1963-69; major USMCR, 1970-75. Decorated DFC (2), Air medal (35); recipient Presdl. Disting. Exec. award, 1980, Dept. Transp. Meritorious Achievement award, 1976, 78, 81. Home: 1713 Maple Hill Pl Alexandria VA 22302-3927

SWINBURN, JOHN S., trade association administrator. BA in Social Scis. and English, U. Tex., 1975; postgrad., Sam Houston State U., 1975-76. Rsch. intern Tex. Dept. Corrections, Huntsville, 1976-77; mgr. spl. projects Birkman & Assocs., Inc., Birkman-Mefferd Rsch. Found., Houston, 1977-79; asst. tech. activities dir. Nat. Assn. Corrosion Engrs. Internat., Houston, 1979-80, tech. activities dir., 1980-82, assoc. exec. dir., 1982-85; sr. mgmt. exec. Humes & Assocs., Inc., Chgo., 1985-86; pres. Anthem Group, Inc., Chgo., 1986-88; dir. corp. comm. Bostrom Corp., Chgo., 1988-89; exec.dir. Internat. Assn. Auditorium Mgrs., Irving, Tex., 1989—. Mem. Am. Soc. Assn. Execs. (cert., mem. internat. com. 1995—), Tex. Soc. Assn. Execs. (chairperson exhbn. com. 1994-95), Dallas/Ft. Worth Soc. Assn. Execs. (v.p. 1994-95, treas. 1993-94, program chairperson Assn. Day in North Tex. 1991, instr. cert. assn. exec. study course 1990—). Office: Interest Assn Auditorium 4425 W Airport Fwy Ste 590 Irving TX 75062-5831

SWINBURNE, HERBERT HILLHOUSE, architect; b. Los Angeles, Dec. 6, 1912; s. George W. and Lucretia R. (Hillhouse) S.; m. Berenice A. Lawler, July 10, 1937; children: Herbert Hillhouse, Mary Jo, Stephen Richard, Lucretia Marie. Architect State of Nev., 1935-41; pvt. practice architecture Phila., 1947-49; ptnr. Nolen, Swinburne & Assocs., Phila., 1949-74; cons. in architecture and construction freelance, 1975—; vis. lectr. Princeton (N.J.) U., 1965-76. Prin. works include many colls. and univs., elem. and high schs., research and health scis. bldgs., office bldgs., country clubs; author: Design Cost Analysis for Architects and Engineers; contbr. articles to profl. jours. Mem. Bldg. Research Adv. Bd., 1966-73, exec. com., 1970; mem. Fed. Constrn. Council, 1966-78, chmn., 1971-73; mem. USN Design Revue Panel, 1966-68; adv. panel U.S. Bur. Standards, 1965-72; nat. adv. panel Gen. Services Adminstrn., 1967-69; bldgs. research com. Pa. State U.; trustee Illuminating Engring. Research Inst., 1972-76, Rosemont Coll. 1980-88, appointed lifetime trustee, 1989. Served with USNR, 1943-45. Recipient over 30 nat., state, and city awards for disting. design in architecture. Fellow AIA (chmn. research for architecture com., 1960-65, chmn. of two nat. conv. 1951, 71); mem. Am. Arbitration Assn. Home: 300 Cathedral Rd # L209 Philadelphia PA 19128

SWINDELL, ARCHIE CALHOUN, JR., research biochemist, statistician; b. Greenville, Tex., Sept. 26, 1936; s. Archie Calhoun and Louise Evelyn (Ellis) S.; m. Dolores Dyer Holland, Dec. 28, 1962; children: Randy Zidick, Matthew Earle. BS in Chemistry, So. Methodist U., 1958; M. Nutritional Sci., Cornell U., 1965, PhD in Biochemistry, 1968. NIH postdoctoral fellow Duke U. Med. Ctr., Durham, N.C., 1968-70; rsch. sci. positions in biochemistry, pharmacology, statis. Pfizer, Inc., Groton, Conn., 1970-95; statis. cons., 1995—. Contbr. articles on cholesterol metabolism, hormone action, cell culture, actions of drugs, data analysis, stats. to profl. jours., 1968-93. Patentee trimazosin, doxazosin as anti-atherosclerosis agt. ; mem. Town Coun., Groton, Conn., 1991—. Served with U.S. Army, 1958-61. NIH fellow Cornell U., Ithaca, N.Y., 1967. Mem. AAAS, Am. Stat. Assn., Am. Heart Assn., Am. Assn. Artificial Intelligence, Sigma Xi. Club: Shennecossett Yacht (Groton). Avocations: astronomy, woodworking. Home: 192 Monument St Groton CT 06340-3915 Office: Pfizer Inc Cen Rsch Eastern Point Rd Groton CT 06340-4947

SWINDELLS, WILLIAM, JR., lumber and paper company executive; b. Oakland, CA, 1930; married. B.S., Stanford U., 1953. With Willamette Industries, Inc., Portland, Oreg., 1953—; sr. v.p. prodn., mktg. bldg. materials Willamette Industries, Inc., until 1978, exec. v.p., 1978-80, pres. forest products div., 1980-82, pres., chief exec. officer, 1982—, also dir., chmn., 1984—; dir. Oreg. Bank, Portland. Office: Willamette Industries 1300 SW 5th Ave Portland OR 97201-5667*

SWINDLER, DARIS RAY, physical anthropologist, forensic anthropologist; b. Morgantown, W.Va., Aug. 13, 1925; s. George Raymond and Minnie Mildred (McElroy) S.; m. Kathryn Pardo, Nov. 10, 1977; children: Gary, Darece, Linda, Dana, Bruce, Geoffry, Jason. AB, W.Va. U., 1950; MA, U. Pa., 1952, PhD, 1959. Instr. Cornell Med. Sch., N.Y.C., 1956-57, W.Va. Med. Sch., Morgantown, 1957-59; asst. prof. Med. Coll. S.C., Charleston, 1959-64; assoc. prof. Mich. State U., East Lansing, 1964-68; prof. phys. anthropology, comparative primate anatomy, dental anthropology U. Wash., Seattle, 1968-91, prof. emeritus anthropology, 1991—; emeritus curator comparative primate anatomy Burke Mus., Seattle, 1991—; cons. King County Med. Examiner, Seattle, 1968—; vis. sr. scientist U. Frankfurt, Germany, 1982-83, Com. on Scholarly Commns. with Peoples Republic of China, 1987-88; vis. prof. U. Zurich, 1992; field participant Valley of Kings Expdn., Egypt., 1990-93; vis. prof. U. Padua, Italy, 1994. Author: A Racial Study of the West Nakani of New Britain, 1962, Dentition of Living Primates, 1976, Systematics, Evolution and Anatomy, Comparative Primate Biology; (with C.D. Wood) Atlas of Primate Gross Anatomy, 1973 (Gov's. award 1973), (with J. Sirianni) Growth and Development of Pigtailed Macaque, 1985. Served with USN, 1943-46. Recipient Alexander von Humboldt Sr. U.S. Scientist awrd, Germany, 1981. Fellow AAAS, Explorer's Club; mem. Am. Assn. Phys. Anthropologists (v.p. 1976-78), Dental

Anthropology Assn. (pres. 1990-92), Internat. Primatology Soc., N.Y. Acad. Sci., Italian Primatol. Assn., Sigma Xi.

SWINERTON, WILLIAM ARTHUR, retired construction company executive; b. San Francisco, Dec. 12, 1917; s. Alfred Bingham and Jane Thomas (Hotaling) S.; m. Mary Nichols Clark, June 5, 1943; children: Leslie Engelbrecht, Susan McBaine, James B., Sarah Blake. B.S., Yale, 1939; postgrad., Stanford, 1940. With Swinerton & Walberg Co., San Francisco, 1940-88, ret. Served with USMCR., 1940-46. Decorated Bronze Star. Clubs: Pacific Union, Burlingame Country. Home: PO Box 620265 Redwood City CA 94062-0265

SWING, JOHN TEMPLE, lawyer, association executive; b. London, Eng., June 7, 1929; s. Raymond Gram and Betty (Gram) S.; m. Devereux Loy Powell, June 19, 1976; children by previous marriage: Jennifer Anne, John Mead. A.B. cum laude, Harvard Coll., 1950; LL.B., Yale U., 1953. Bar: N.Y. 1955, Conn. 1956. Asso. firm Becket and Wagner, Lakeville, Conn., 1955-60; partner Becket and Wagner, 1960-61; partner firm Rorabeck and Swing, Canaan, Conn., 1961-63; dir. adminstrn. Council on Fgn. Relations, N.Y.C., 1963-67; assoc. exec. dir. Coun. on Fgn. Rels., 1967-72; v.p., sec. Council on Fgn. Relations, 1972-85, acting pres., 1985-86, exec. v.p., 1986-93; of counsel Coun. on Fgn. Rels., 1993—; pres., CEO Fgn. Policy Assn., N.Y.C., 1993-95; mem. adv. com. on law of the sea NSC, 1974-81; mem. U.S. del. to 3d UN Conf. on Law of the Sea, 1974-81, spl. adv. to del., 1977-78, alt. rep., 1978-81; expert cons. Dept. State, 1977-81; mem. adv. bd. Center for Oceans Law and Policy, U. Va. Sch. Law, 1975—; bd. dirs. Council on Ocean Law, 1980—; mem. adv. bd. Inst. for the Study of World Politics, 1971—. Contbr. articles to profl. jours. Selectman Town of Salisbury, Conn., 1959-61, 61-63; vice chmn. Salisbury Democratic Town Com., 1959-63; Dem. candidate State Senate, Conn., 1962; trustee Putney Sch. (Vt.), 1983-89, chmn., 1986-89; bd. advs. CUNY Grad. Sch. and Univ. Ctr., Grad. Study in Transl.; bd. dirs. Non-Profit Coordinating Com. of N.Y., 1984—, chmn. 1984-89, designated founding chmn., 1989. Mem. Am. Soc. Internat. Law, Internat. Law Assn., Bar Assn. of City of N.Y. (chmn. com. on lawyer's role in search for peace 1980-82, coun. on internal affairs 1987—), Fgn. Policy Assn. (bd. dirs. 1993—), Nat. Coun. World Affairs Orgn. (bd. dirs. 1993—), Coun. Fgn. Rels., Century Assn. Club (sec. 1984-86), Fishers Island Yacht Club. Home: 61 E 86th St Apt 51 New York NY 10028-1037 Office: 470 Park Ave S 2d Floor New York NY 10016-6819

SWING, MARCE, producer, publisher; b. Wichita, Kans., Dec. 3, 1943; d. Eldon Derry and Ruth (Biddle) S. Bus. mgr. Old Westport Med. Assn., Kansas City, Mo., 1972-73; dept. chmn., instr. Ft. Bragg (N.C.) Nursery and Kindergarten, 1965-66, Luth. Schs., Tex. Dist., Irving, 1966-68, Kansas City (Kans.) Sch. Dist. 500, 1973-78, Extension Dept. U. Calif., Northridge, 1979-82, Pima Coll., Tucson, 1983-84, Kinder Care, Lake Buena Vista, Fla., 1989-90; TV/motion picture exec. producer, dir., writer Swing Prodns., Orlando, Fla., 1989—; owner, pres. Swing Enterprises/Swing Prodns., Orlando, 1978—, Living for Edn., Inc., Orlando, 1994—; exec. mgmt., acctg. andmktg. cons. to major internat. corps.; lectr., seminar instr., guest speaker, anchorperson, moderator, panelist. Exec. producer, dir., writer, featured talent on-air live and taped programming for networks, network affiliates and cable, feature motion picture, TV series, mini series, 30 celebrity profiles, 36 documentaries, 14 televents, 45 pub. svc. spots, 30 minute infomat, 12-hour entertinment Christmas Eve project; developer entertainment informational, ednl. and indsl. TV programs and videos; contbr. articles to profl. jours. Corp. adminstr., TV exec. producer, dir., fundraiser nat. hdqrs. March of Dimes, White Plains, N.Y., 1984-86, Arthritis Found., Atlanta, 1985; ofcl. hostess Seattle World's Fair; mem. Nat. Task Force for Child Care, Nat. Task Force for Youth Suicide, Nat. Task Force for Child Abuse; mem. Ariz. Commn. on Arts. Recipient local, regional and nat. art and craft awards. Mem. NEA, NAFE, AAUW, Am. Mgmt. Assn., Nat. Assn. Women Artists, Profl. Assn. Producers and Dirs., Nat. Printmaker's Assn., Nat. Thespian Soc., Thousand Oaks Art Assn., Show of Hands Gallery, Nat. Youth Camps. Lutheran. Avocations: reading, writing, photography, cooking, mural painting.

SWING, WILLIAM EDWIN, bishop; b. Huntington, W.Va., Aug. 26, 1936; s. William Lee and Elsie Bell (Holliday) S.; M. Mary Willis Taylor, Oct. 7, 1961; children—Alice Marshall, William Edwin. B.A., Kenyon Coll., Ohio, 1954-58; D.Div. (hon.), Kenyon Coll., 1980; M.A., Va. Theol. Sem., 1958-61, D.Div., 1980. Ordained priest Episcopal Ch. Asst. St. Matthews Ch., Wheeling, W.Va., 1961-63; vicar St. Matthews Ch., Chester, W.Va., 1963-69, St. Thomas Ch., Weirton, W.Va., 1963-69; rector St. Columba's Episcopal Ch., Washington, 1969-79; bishop Episcopal Ch. Calif., San Francisco, 1980—; chmn. bd. Ch. Div. Sch. of the Pacific, 1983-84; founder, chmn. Episcopal Found. for Drama, 1976—. Republican. Home: 2006 Lyon St San Francisco CA 94115-1610 Office: Episcopal Ch Diocesan Office 1055 Taylor St San Francisco CA 94108-2209

SWING, WILLIAM LACY, ambassador; b. Lexington, N.C., Sept. 11, 1934; s. Baxter Dermot and Mary Frances (Barbee) S.; AB, Catawba Coll., 1956, LLD (hon.), 1980; BD, Yale U., 1960; postgrad. Oxford U., U. Tuebingen (Germany), 1961, Hofstra U.; LLD (hon.), 1994; m. Yuen Fong Cheong; children: Brian Curtis, Gabrielle. Vice consul Am. Consulate, Port Elizabeth, Republic of South Africa, 1963-66; internat. economist Bur. Econ. Affairs, Dept. State, 1966-68; consul, chief consular sect. Am. Consulate Gen., Hamburg, Germany, 1968-72; internat. rels. officer, desk officer for Federal Republic of Germany, Dept. State, Washington, 1972-74; dep. chief of mission, counselor Am. Embassy, Bangui, Central African Republic, 1974-76; fellow Center for Internat. Affairs, Harvard U., 1976-77; dep. dir. Office of Cen. African Affairs, 1977-79; ambassador to People's Republic of Congo, 1979-81; amb. to Republic of Liberia, Monrovia, 1981-85; amb. to South Africa, 1989-92; amb. to Fed. Republic of Nigeria, 1992-93; amb. to Haiti, 1993—; dir. Fgn. Svc. Career Devel. and Assignments, 1985, 87; sr. dep. asst. sec. state for pers., 1987-89. Recipient Meritorious Honor award USIA, 1971, Superior Honor award Dept. State, 1985, Presdl. Disting. Svc. award, 1985, Presdl. Meritorious Svc. award, 1987, 90, 94, Equal Employment Opportunity award Dept. State, 1988, Disting. Honor award, 1994, Valor award, 1995, Disting. Svc. award, 1996. Mem. Am. Fgn. Svc. Assn., Army and Navy Club (Washington), Yale Club (Washington and N.Y.C.), Harvard Club (Washington), Internat. Club (Washington), Lions. Co-editor: Education for Decision, 1963. Office: Am Embassy Port-Au-Prince State Dept Washington DC 20521-3400

SWINGLE, HOMER DALE, horticulturist, educator; b. Hixson, Tenn., Nov. 5, 1916; s. Edward Everett and Sarah Elizabeth (Rogers) S.; m. Gladys F. Wells, Dec. 21, 1942 (dec. June 1961); 1 child, Janet Faye Swingle Sciscioli; m. Ella Margaret Porterfield, Dec. 19, 1962. BS, U. Tenn., 1939; MS, Ohio State U., 1948; PhD, La. State U., 1966. Tchr. vocat. agr. Spring City (Tenn.) High Sch., 1939-46; hort. specialist U. Tenn., Crossville, 1946-47; from asst. prof. to prof. horticulture U. Tenn., Knoxville, 1948-79, prof. emeritus non-credit program, 1979—; cons. in plant and water rels. Oak Ridge (Tenn.) Nat. Lab., 1971-75; chmn. collaborators Vegetable Breeding Lab. USDA, Charleston, S.C., 1975. Cons. editor: Growing Vegetables and Herbs, 1984; contbr. 49 articles to sci. jours. Fellow Am. Soc. Hort. Sci. (chmn. so. sect. 1970-71); mem. Lions (life), Gamma Sigma Delta (pres. U. Tenn. chpt. 1977, teaching award of merit 1978-79). Republican. Methodist. Home: 3831 Maloney Rd Knoxville TN 37920-2823

SWINNEY, HARRY LEONARD, physics educator; b. Opelousas, La., Apr. 10, 1939; s. Leonard Robert and Ethel Ruth (Bertheaud) S.; m. Gloria Luyas, Oct. 21, 1967; 1 child, Brent Luyas (dec.). BS in Physics, Rhodes Coll., 1961; PhD in Physics, Johns Hopkins U., 1968. Vis. asst. prof. Johns Hopkins U., 1970-71; asst. prof. physics NYU, 1971-73; assoc. prof. CCNY, 1973-77, prof., 1978; prof. physics U. Tex., Austin, 1978—, Trull Centennial prof., 1984-90, Sid Richardson Found. regents chair, 1990—, dir. Ctr. Nonlinear Dynamics, 1985—; Morris Loeb lectr. Harvard U., 1982. Editor: Hydrodynamic Instabilities and the Transition to Turbulence, 1985; contbr. articles to profl. jours. Regents chair Sid Richardson Found., 1990—. Grantee NSF, Dept. Energy, NASA, Office Naval Rsch., Welch, others; Guggenheim fellow, 182-83. Fellow Am. Phys. Soc. (exec. bd. 1992-94, Fluid Dynamics prize 1995); mem. NAS, Am. Acad. Arts and Scis., Am. Assn. Physics Tchrs. Democrat. Methodist. Office: U Tex Dept Physics Ctr Nonlinear Dynamics Austin TX 78712

SWINSON, SUE WHITLOW, secondary education educator; b. Rocky Mount, Va., Apr. 14, 1939; d. Homer P. and Etholene R. (Ramsey) Whitlow; m. Arthur Pitt Burgess, 1961 (div. 1975); 1 child, Robert A.; m. William Edward Swinson, Jr., Sept. 7, 1979. AB, Coll. of William & Mary, 1961; MEd, Ga. State U., 1978. Cert. lifetime profl. DT-5. Tchr. Latin Chesterfield (Va.) County Bd. Edn., 1961-62; Army tchr. USAF I, Augsburg, Germany, 1962-64; tchr. Latin Henrico County Bd. Edn., Richmond, Va., 1965-68; tchr. Latin, English, history DeKalb County Bd. Edn., Decatur, Ga., 1974-92; tchr. Latin and English Randolph County Bd. Edn., Cuthbert, Ga., 1992—; book selection com. DeKalb County Bd. Edn., Decatur, 1983-84. Co-author, editor quar. bull. The Georgia Classicist, 1985-86; co-author: (resource guide) Ga. Advanced Latin State Dept. Resource, 1992-93; co-author: (curriculum guide) Latin Curriculum Guides. Named Ga. Latin Tchr. of Yr., Ga. Classical Assn., 1986, 92, recipient Student-Tchr. Achievement Recognition award, 1991-92. Mem. Am. Classical League, Ga. Classical Assn. (co-editor state paper 1985-86), Fgn. Lang. Assn. of Ga., Profl. Assn. Ga. Educators. Republican. Methodist. Avocations: reading, golf, fishing, gardening, bridge. Home: RR 2 Box 254-d Georgetown GA 31754-9579

SWIRE, EDITH WYPLER, music educator, musician, violist, violinist; b. Boston, Feb. 16, 1943; d. Alfred R. Jr. and Frances Glenn (Emery) Wypler; m. James Bennett Swire, June 11, 1965; 1 child, Elizabeth Swire-Falker. BA, Wellesley (Mass.) Coll., 1965; MFA, Sarah Lawrence Coll., Bronxville, N.Y., 1983; postgrad., Coll. of New Rochelle, 1984-85. Tchr. instrumental music, viola, violin The Windsor Sch., Boston, 1965-66; tchr., dir. The Lenox Sch., N.Y.C., 1967-76; music curriculum devel. The Nightingale-Bamford Sch., N.Y.C., 1966-69; head of fine arts dept. The Lenox Sch., N.Y.C., 1976-78, head of instrumental music, 1978-80; founder, dir., tchr. of string sch. Serpentine String Sch., Larchmont, N.Y., 1981—; mem. founding com. Inter Sch. Orch., N.Y.C., 1972, trustee, 1976—; panelist Nat. Assn. Ind. Sch. Conf., N.Y.C., 1977. Mem. music and worship com., Larchmont Ave. Ch., 1978-82, 88. Mem. Westchester Musicians Guild, N.Y. State Music Tchrs. Assn., Music Tchrs. Nat. Assn., Music Tchrs. Coun. Westchester (program com.), Violin Soc. Am., Wellesley in Westchester, Am. String Tchrs. Assn., The Viola Soc. of N.Y. Avocations: study of Alexander technique, chamber music, encouraging music in schools. Home and Office: 11 Serpentine Trl Larchmont NY 10538-2618

SWIRSKY, JUDITH PERLMAN, arts administrator, consultant; b. Bklyn., Oct. 31, 1928; d. Samuel and Rose (Klein) Perlman; m. Leo Jerome Swirsky, June 26, 1949; 1 child, Marjorie Ann Swirsky Zelner. BA, NYU, 1947; postgrad., Columbia U., 1947-48. Rsch. asst. The Bklyn. Mus., 1947-49, vol. coord., 1983-89; exec. dir. Grand Cen. Art Galleries Edn. Assn., N.Y.C., 1988-90; freelance curator Genest Gallery, Lambertville, N.J., 1990; dir. vol. resources, dir. spl. events Snug Harbor Cultural Ctr., S.I., 1992-95, dir. spl. events, 1994-95; dir. art sales and rental Gallery The Bklyn. Mus., 1974-77; del. Vol. Com. of Art Mus., Balt., 1973, panelist, 1979; mem., co-founder Vol. Program Adminstrs., N.Y.C., Cultural Inst., 1984—; ind. curator travelling exhbn. Relatively Speaking: Mothers and Daus. in Art, 1996, Memory and Desire, Paintings and Watercolors by Harriet Shorr. Co-author: On Exhibit, 1993, 96, The Art Lover's Travel Guide to American Museums, 1993, 94. Pres. Community Com. for the Bklyn. Mus., 1969-70; bd. dirs. Greater N.Y. Girl Scouts U.S., 1965-71; founder Children's Sch. Time Program and Women's League, Bklyn. Acad. Music, 1961-64; chmn. Bklyn. Guild for Opera, 1966-77; bd. dirs. Arthritis Found. Greater N.Y., 1969-79; trustee Bklyn. Home for Children, 1961-70, Julia Bernstein League of the Free Nurses Inst., 1952-60. Mem. Am. Assn. Mus., Assn. Vol. Adminstrn. (cert., editor region II newsletter), Am. Assn. Mus. Vols., Civitas. Avocations: travel, cooking. Home and Office: 57 Montague St Brooklyn NY 11201-3374

SWIST, MARIAN IRENE, emergency nurse; b. Pottsville, Pa., Oct. 26, 1941; d. Thomas Francis and Marian C. (Munster) Moran; m. John J. Swist, Aug. 3, 1963 (dec.); children: Christine M. Swist Mullen, Robert J. Diploma in nursing, Reading (Pa.) Hosp., 1962. RN, Pa.; cert. emergency nursing pediatric course. Staff nurse Reading Hosp. Med. Ctr., 1962-65; staff nurse emergency dept. Pottstown Meml. Med. Ctr., 1971—. Mem. Alumni Assn. Reading Hosp. Sch. Nursing.

SWIT, LORETTA, actress; b. N.J., Nov. 4, 1939. Student, Am. Acad. Dramatic Arts, Gene Frankel Repertoire Theatre, N.Y.C. Broadway appearances include Same Time Next Year, Any Wednesday, Mame, The Mystery of Edwin Drood, Shirley Valentine, Chgo. (winner Sarah Siddons award 1990); films include Stand Up and Be Counted, 1972, Freebie and the Bean, 1974, Race with the Devil, 1975, S.O.B, 1980, Beer, 1985, Whoops, 1987, Apocalypse (U.K.), 1987; star TV series M*A*S*H, 1972-83 (Emmy awards for Outstanding Supporting Actress in a Comedy series 1979-81); TV movies include Shirts/Skins, 1973, The Last Day, 1975, Mirror, Mirror, 1979, Valentine, 1979, Friendships, Secrets and Lies, 1979, Cagney and Lacey, 1981, Games Mother Never Taught You, 1982, First Affair, 1983, The Execution, 1985, Dreams of Gold: The Mel Fisher Story, 1986, My Dad Can't Be Crazy, Can He?, Hell Hath No Fury, 1992, A Killer Among Friends, 1993; star on major dramatic shows and musical variety shows, including Bob Hope Christmas Special, Perry Como, The Muppets. Mem. AFTRA, Screen Actors Guild, Actors Equity.

SWITZER, BARRY, professional football coach, former university athletic coach; b. Crossett, Ark., Oct. 5, 1937; s. Frank and Louise Switzer; m. Kay Switzer, 1963 (div. 1983); children: Greg, Kathy, Dove. BA, U. Ark., 1960. Asst. football coach U. Ark., 1960-65; asst. football coach U. Okla., 1966-72, head coach, 1973-89; head coach Dallas Cowboys, 1994—. author: Bootlegger's Boy, 1990. Served with U.S. Army. Named Coach of Year, 1973, AP/UPI Nat. Champions (shared with U. So. Calif.), 1974, consensus champions, 1975, 85. Coach winning Orange Bowl team, 1976, 79-81, 86-87, winning Super Bowl team (Super Bowl XXX), 1995. Office: Dallas Cowboys 1 Cowboys Pky Irving TX 75063-4945

SWITZER, MAURICE HAROLD, publisher; b. Toronto, Ont., Can., Mar. 28, 1945; s. Harold Switzer and Ruby (Marsden) Hicks; m. Mary Helene Pavlik; children: Andrea Zimperi, Adin, Lisa Doracka. Student, Trent U., Peterborough, Ont., 1964-65. Journalist Belleville (Ont.) Intelligencer, 1965-67, sports editor, 1967-72, mng. editor, 1972-79; mng. editor Oshawa (Ont.) Times, 1979-81; pub. Timmins (Ont.) Daily Press, 1981-86, Sudbury (Ont.) Star, 1986-92, Winnipeg (Man.) Free Press, 1992-94; ret.; owner Media Help Svcs., 1994—. Author: Bruno Cavallo a Conversation, 1991.

SWITZER, PAUL, statistics educator; b. St. Boniface, Man., Can., Mar. 4, 1939. B.A. with honors, U. Man., 1961; A.M., Harvard U., 1963, Ph.D., 1965. Mem. faculty Stanford (Calif.) U., 1965—, now prof. stats. and earth scis., chmn. dept. stats., 1979-82. Fellow Internat. Statis. Inst., Am. Statis. Assn. (editor jour. 1986-88), Inst. Math. Stats. Office: Stanford U Dept Stats Stanford CA 94305-4065

SWITZER, ROBERT LEE, biochemistry educator; b. Clinton, Iowa, Aug. 26, 1940; s. Stephen and Elva Delila (Allison) S.; m. Bonnie George, June 13, 1965; children: Brian, Stephanie. BS, U. Ill., 1961; PhD, U. Calif., Berkeley, 1966. Research fellow Lab. Biochemistry, Nat. Heart Inst., Bethesda, Md., 1966-68; asst. prof. biochemistry U. Ill., Urbana, 1968-73; assoc. prof. U. Ill., 1973-78, prof. biochemistry and basic med. scis., 1978—, dept. head, 1988-93; mem. biochemistry study sect. NIH, 1985-89, chmn., 1987-89; guest prof. U. Copenhagen, 1995. Author: (with John M. Clark) Experimental Biochemistry, 1977; mem. bd. editors Jour. Bacteriology, 1977-82, 85—, Archives Biochemistry and Biophysics, 1977—, Jour. Biol. Chemistry, 1980-85; contbr. articles to profl. jours. NSF predoctoral fellow, 1961-66; NIH postdoctoral fellow, 1966-68; Guggenheim fellow, 1975. Mem. Am. Soc. for Biochemistry and Molecular Biology, Am. Soc. Microbiology, Am. Chem. Soc., AAAS, Sigma Xi. Home: 404 W Michigan Ave Urbana IL 61801-4948 Office: U Ill Dept Biochemistry 600 S Mathews Ave Urbana IL 61801-3602

SWOAP, DAVID BRUCE, children's relief official, art gallery director; b. Kalamazoo, Aug. 12, 1937; s. Orlo Frederick and Aileen Esther (Hempy) S. B.A. in Govt. with honors, Denison U., 1959; M.A. in Govt, Claremont Grad. Sch., 1961; D.Sci. (hon.), U. Osteo. Medicine and Health Scis., Des Moines, 1981. Asst. sec. Calif. State Personnel Bd., Sacramento, 1972-73; chief dep. dir., acting dir. Calif. State Dept. Social Welfare, Sacramento, 1973; dir. Calif. State Dept. Social Welfare, 1973-74, Calif. State Dept. Benefit Payments, 1974-75; sr. research asso. Republican Study Com., U.S. Ho. of Reps., Washington, 1975-76; profl. staff mem. U.S. Senate Com. on Fin., Washington, 1976-79; legis. dir. U.S. Senator William L. Armstrong, Washington, 1979-81; dep. sec. HHS, Washington, 1981-83; sec. health and welfare State of Calif., Sacramento, 1983-85; ptnr. Franchetti & Swoap, San Francisco, 1985-90; vice chmn. Sacramento Advocates, 1991-93; chmn. bd. dirs. Hope Unltd. Internat., San Diego, 1991-96, chmn. bd. internat. advisors, 1996—; owner, dir. David Bruce Gallery, Carlsbad, Calif., 1995—; owner Mana Olana Farms, Hakalau, Hawaii. Elder Presbyn. Ch.; bd. dirs. Friends of SOS Children's Villages, 1989-91; bd. regents John F. Kennedy U., 1990-93. Rotary Club Found. fellow, 1961-62. Mem. Wycliffe Assocs., Phi Beta Kappa, Delta Upsilon. Republican. Office: Ste 207 300 Carlsbad Village Dr Carlsbad CA 92008

SWOFFORD, ROBERT LEE, newspaper editor, journalist; b. Berryville, Ark., Aug. 22, 1949; s. Andrew Madison and Verna Mae (England) S.; m. Karen King, Jan. 24, 1969 (div. 1977); children: Teri, Toby; m. Sandra Dunn, 1978 (div. 1979); m. B. Joanna Rongren, Feb. 14, 1981; 1 child, Tyler. AA, Coll. of the Sequoias, 1969; student, Calif. State U., 1969-71. Photographer, reporter, news editor The Advance-Register, Tulare, Calif., 1965-78; city editor The Record Searchlight, Redding, Calif., 1978-81; suburban editor, Neighbors editor The Sacramento Bee, 1981-86; assoc. metro. editor, community editor The Orange County Register, Santa Ana, Calif., 1986-89; exec. news editor The Press Democrat, Santa Rosa, Calif., 1989-90, mng. editor, 1990—. Mem. Assoc. Press Mng. Editors, Calif. Soc. of Newspaper Editors, Soc. of Newspaper Design. Office: The Press Democrat 427 Mendocino Ave Santa Rosa CA 95401-6313

SWOPE, CHARLES EVANS, banker, lawyer; b. West Chester, Pa., June 16, 1930; s. Charles S. and Edna (McAllister) S.; m. Stephanie Swope; 1 son., Charles E. BS, Bucknell U., 1953; JD, Washington and Lee U., U. Va., 1959; MS, Ind. Coll., 1966; attended Naval War Coll., Judge Adv. Gen. Sch., 1957, Command and Staff Coll., 1969; D of Pub. Svc. (hon.), West Chester U., 1994. Assoc. firm Gawthrop & Greenwood, Attys., West Chester, Pa., 1960; pres., chmn. bd., sr. trust officer 1st Nat. Bank, West Chester, 1965—, also chmn. bd. dirs.; pres. Eachus Dairy Co., 1970-84; pres., bd. dirs. West Chester Corp.; bd. dirs. Madison Co., Penjerdel, Penn Mut. Fire Ins. Co., 1st Nat. Bank West Chester; pres. Automobile Assn. Chester County; lectr. corp. law. Pres., West Chester Civic Assn., 1964; co-chmn. Chester County Heart Assn. Drive, West Chester Community Center Bldg. Drive, 1970-90, 175th Anniversary West Chester; mem. Nat. Football Found. and Hall of Fame; dir. Chester County council Boy Scouts Am., 1961-72; bd. dirs. Chester County Service, Swope Found. Trust; bd. dirs., v.p. West Chester U. Found.; pres. West Chester Found.; mem. Marine Corps. Scholarship Found.; chmn. Bus. and Indsl. Council of Chester County, pres., 1981; chmn. Easter Seal Soc. Chester County; mem. Com. to Restore Tun Tavern; trustee, West Chester U., 1962-72, pres. bd. trustees, 1966-72; trustee Chester County Devel. Fund, Dr. Charles S. Swope Scholarship Fund, Hatfield Home; YMCA trustee Chester County Hosp. Corp. Served to maj. USMC, 1952-55, col. Res. Decorated Legion of Merit, Nat. Def. medal, Navy Commendation medal, Meritorious Service medal; recipient Coll. Football Centennial award, 1970; Congressional Medal of Merit, 1981; Disting. Eagle Scout award Boy Scouts Am., 1983. Mem. Pa. Bankers Assn. (chmn. Legis. com. 1965, 70), U.S. Naval Inst., Assn. Univ. Trustees Pa., Am. Soc. Internat. Law, Chester County Bar Found. (v.p.), Greater West Chester C. of C. (pres. 1963), Marine Corps League Chester County (vice comdr. 1960-72), Freedoms Found., Am. Legion (life mem.), Chester County Hist. Soc., Marine Corps Res. Officer Assn. (nat. pres. 1982-83, vice chmn. bd. dirs.), Marine Corps Assn., Marine Corps League, Pa. C. of C., Navy League U.S., Washington and Lee Law Sch. Assn., Bucknell, West Chester U. alumni assns., Pa. Economy League, Brandywine Valley Assn., Maxwell Football Club, Phi Alpha Delta, Phi Kappa Psi. Republican. Methodist (ofcl. bd.). Clubs: West Chester (Pa.) Golf and Country; Union League (Phila.) Italian Social; Sky Top; Great Oaks Yacht and Country, Masons, Rotary (pres. West Chester, Pa., 1968-69, Paul Harris fellow), Elks. Home: 200 W Ashbridge St West Chester PA 19380-2371 Office: First Nat Bank 9 N High St West Chester PA 19380-3002

SWOPE, DENISE GRAINGER, lawyer, educator; b. Columbia, S.C., Apr. 27, 1966; d. Thomas Dayton and Faye (Amerson) Grainger; m. William Koatsworth Swope, May 19, 1990. BA cum laude, U. S.C., 1986, JD, 1990. Bar: S.C. Asst. solicitor Charleston County (S.C.) Solicitor, 1991-92; pvt. practice Charleston, 1992—; instr. Inst. for Legal Edn., Columbia and Greenville, S.C., 1993—, Charleston So. U., 1994—. Atty., S.C. Bar Pro Bono Program, Columbia, 1991-95. U. S.C. Sch. Law Recruitment scholar, 1987, Outstanding Handicapped Law Student scholar, 1989. Mem. ABA, S.C. Bar Assn., Golden Key. Office: 1133 Hillside Dr # 2B Charleston SC 29407

SWOPE, DONALD DOWNEY, retired banker; b. Martinsville, Ill., Feb. 26, 1926; s. Roy V. and Dorothy Irene (Downey) S.; m. Earla Long, Aug. 16, 1960. BS, Ind. State U., 1950. With Ill. Savs. and Loan Commn., Springfield, Ill., 1950-77, chief dept. commr., 1971-77; exec. v.p. Bank for Savs. & Loan Assn., Chgo., 1977-81, pres., 1981-90, dir. Dir., treas. Country Fair White Elephant, Green Valley, Ariz. With USNR, 1944-63. Mem. VFW (life), Nat. Assn. State Savs. and Loan Suprs. (pres. 1972-73), Am. Legion (life), Green Valley C. of C., Kiwanis (pres. Crete, Ill. 1977-78, treas. Green Valley, Ariz. 1994, 95), Elks (treas.).

SWOPE, JEFFREY PEYTON, lawyer; b. Evanston, Ill., June 11, 1945; s. Oliver P. and Elspeth E. (Cahill) S.; m. Linda Lee, Aug. 26, 1967; children: Matthew, Gregory, Timothy. AB, Harvard U., 1967, JD, 1970. Bar: Mass. 1970, U.S. Dist. Ct. Mass. 1971, U.S. Ct. Appeals (1st cir.) 1973, U.S. Ct. Claims 1974, U.S. Supreme Ct. 1979. Assoc. Palmer & Dodge, Boston, 1970-76, ptnr., 1977—; treas. Social Law Libr., Boston, 1984—. Treas. Ella Lyman Cabot Trust, Holliston, Mass., 1979—. Mem. Mass. Audubon Soc. (bd. dirs. 1985—). Home: 54 Hyde St Newton Highlands MA 02161-1206 Office: Palmer & Dodge 1 Beacon St Boston MA 02108-3106

SWOPE, JOHN FRANKLIN, lawyer, retired insurance executive; b. Mt. Kisco, N.Y., June 21, 1938; s. Gerard and Marjorie (Park) S.; m. Marjory Mason, June 9, 1962; children: Kristin, Kevin, John. BA, Amherst Coll., 1960; LLB, Yale U., 1963. Bar: N.H. 1963; CLU. Atty. United Life and Accident Ins. Co., Concord, N.H., 1963-67; asst. counsel United Life and Accident Ins. Co., 1967-69, corp. sec., counsel, 1969-70, v.p., 1970-74, sr. v.p., 1974-77, pres., dir., 1977-91; pres. Chubb Life Ins. Co. Am., 1981-94; pres., dir. Colonial Life Ins. Co. Am., N.J., 1981-94; of counsel Sheehan, Phinney, Bass & Green, N.H., 1995—; pres., dir. Vol. State Life Ins. Co., Tenn., 1984-91; exec. v.p. Chubb Corp., N.Y.C., 1988-94; pres., dir. Chubb Sovereign Life Ins. Co., Calif., 1993-94; chmn. Chubb Securities Corp., 1988-94; bd. dirs. Pub. Broadcasting Sys., 1992—; mem. bd. govs. Sta. WNHP-TV, 1985—, pres., 1985-92; trustee N.E. Utilities, 1992—; mem. Loma Edn. Com., 1992-95; interim gen. mgr. N.H. Pub. TV, 1995. Trustee N.H. Higher Edn. Assistance Found., 1969-80, Shaker Village, Inc., 1981-86, Currier Gallery Art, 1986—, Tabor Acad., 1987—; mem. nom. com. PBS, 1990-91; vice-chmn. New Eng. Found. for Arts, 1988-94; mem. Concord Zoning Bd., 1973-82, Concord Planning Bd., 1995—; bd. dirs. Concord Regional Devel. Corp., 1975-82, N.H. Bus. Com. for the Arts, chmn., 1986-95; N.H. adv. com. to U.S. Commn. on Civil Rights, 1982-85; pres., bd. dirs. N.H. Pub. TV, 1988-92; incorporator N.H. Charitable Fund, 1984-90; mem. N.H. State Coun. on Arts, 1985-92; pres. Greater Concord C. of C., 1975-76. Mem. ABA, N.H. Bar Assn., Merrimack County Bar Assn., Assn. Life Ins. Counsel. Home: 21 Long Pond Rd Concord NH 03301

SWORD, CHRISTOPHER PATRICK, microbiologist, university dean; b. San Fernando, Calif., Sept. 9, 1928; s. Christopher Patrick and Mary (Ross) S.; m. Mary Rose Gerhardt, June 18, 1959; children—Mary Anne, Carolyn, Jacqueline, Christopher. B.S. in Biology, Loyola U., Los Angeles, 1951; Ph.D. in Microbiology, UCLA, 1959. Research asso. in microbiology U. Kans., 1958-59, from asst. prof. to prof., 1959-70; research asso. Argonne (Ill.) Nat. Lab., 1961; prof. life scis., chmn. dept. Ind. State U., Terre Haute, 1970-76; prof. microbiology Center Med. Edn., 1971-76; prof. microbiology, dir. research, grad. dean S.D. State U., Brookings, 1976—; cons., evaluator for N. Cen. Assn. Colls. and Schs. Author numerous articles in field. Grantee USPHS, grantee Am. Heart Assn. Mem. Am. Soc. Microbiology,

N.Y. Acad. Scis., AAAS, AAUP, Nat. Council U. Research Adminstrs., Council Grad. Schs., Midwestern Assn. Grad. Schs., Sigma Xi, Phi Kappa Phi. Home: 1500 Buffalo Trl Brookings SD 57006-3608 Office: SD State U Grad Sch Brookings SD 57007

SWORT, ARLOWAYNE, retired nursing educator and administrator; b. Bartlesville, Okla., Dec. 9, 1922; d. Arlington L. and Clara E. (Church) S. Diploma, St. Luke's Hosp. Sch. Nursing, Kansas City, Mo., 1944; BSN, U. Colo., 1958; MS in Nursing, Cath. U. Am., 1961; EdD, Columbia U., 1973. Dean, prof. Sch. Nursing U. Tex. Health Scis. Ctr., Houston, 1977-83, prof. nursing, 1983-85; prof., assoc. in adminstrn. Johns Hopkins U. Sch. Nursing, Balt., 1985-87; prof., assoc. dean for adminstrn. and grad. acad. affairs Johns Hopkins U. Sch. Nursing, Balt., 1987-89, sr. assoc. dean, 1990-91. Recipient numerous rsrch. grants. Mem. ANA, NLN, APHA, AAUW, Am. Assn. for History of Nursing Soc., Am. Assn. Univ. Adminstrs., Am. Assn. for Higher Edn., Am. Nurses Found.-Century Club, Am. Assn. Nurse Execs., Nat. Gerontol. Nurses Assn., Found. for Nursing of Md., Inc., Sigma Theta Tau, Kappa Delta Pi. Home: 1105 Timber Trail Rd Baltimore MD 21286-1602

SWYGERT, H. PATRICK, law educator, university president; b. Phila., Mar. 17, 1943; s. LeRoy and Gustina (Rodgers) Huzzy; m. Sonja Branson, Aug. 22, 1969; children: Haywood Patrick, Michael Branson. AB in History, Howard U., 1965, JD cum laude, 1968. Bar: D.C. 1968, Pa. 1970, N.Y. 1970. Law clk. to chief judge U.S. Ct. Appeals (3d cir.), Phila., 1968-69; assoc. Debevoise, Plimpton, Lyons & Gates, N.Y.C., 1969-70; adminstrv. asst. to Congressman Charles B. Rangel, N.Y., 1971-72; spl. asst. dist. atty., Phila., 1973; from asst. prof. to prof. law Temple U., 1972-90, v.p. adminstrn., 1982-88, exec. v.p., 1988-90; pres. SUNY, Albany, 1990-95, pres. Howard U., Washington, D.C., 1995—. Bd. dirs. New Community Devel. Corp., HUD, 1980-82; gov.'s rep. Southeastern Pa. Transp. Authority, 1987-91, also bd. dirs. Vice-chmn. Phila. Pub. Service Com., 1974-77, Sta. WHYY-TV, 1987-90; bd. trustees Inst. Pub. Adminstrn., 1992—; mem. exec. com. Pub. Law Ctr. Phila., 1980-88, N.Y. State Coun. on Humanities, 1991—; bd. dirs. Albany area chpt. ARC, 1991—, Nat. Pub. Radio, 1995—; chmn. N.Y. State Spl. Commn. on ednl. structure, policies and practices, 1993—; co-chair joint task force grad. edn. Nat. Assn. State Univs. and Land Grant Colls., Am. Assn. State Colls. and Univs., 1993—. Mem. ABA, Amnivs. Coun. Edn. Commn. Women in Higher Edn., Middle States Assn Colls. and Schs. (commn. on higher edn. 1992-95), The Victory Funds (bd. trustees). Home: 3119 Arizona Ave NW Washington DC 20016 Office: Howard U Office of Pres 2400 6th St NW Ste 402 Washington DC 20059-0001

SWYMER, STEPHEN, principal. Prin. Gen. Wayne Mid. Sch., Malvern, Pa. Recipient Blue Ribbon award U.S. Dept. Edn., 1990-91. Office: Gen Wayne Mid Sch 20 Devon Rd Malvern PA 19355-3071

SYDNOR, EDGAR STARKE, lawyer; b. Lynchburg, Va., Nov. 30, 1943; s. Charles Raine and Louise Allen (Starke) S.; m. Rita Frances Johnson, Dec. 28, 1965; children: Edgar Starke Jr., Elizabeth Sydnor Norris, Carlton Allen. BA in English, Washington & Lee, 1966, JD, 1973. Bar: Va. 1973. Assoc. Edmunds, Williams, Robertson, Sackett, Baldwin & Graves, Lynchburg, 1973-75, ptnr., 1975-81; atty. Vulcan Materials Co., Birmingham, Ala., 1981-84; gen. atty. Vulcan Materials Co., Birmingham, 1984-88, asst. gen. counsel, dir. pub. affairs, 1988-95, elected officer of co., 1992—, asst. gen. counsel chems. and environ., 1995—. Mem., bd. dirs. Pub. Affairs Rsch. Coun. of Ala., Birmingham, 1988—, Birmingham Summerfest, 1988—, Cornerstone Schs. Ala., Birmingham, 1995—; trustee Birmingham Hist. Soc., 1992—. Capt. USAF, 1966-71. Mem. ABA, Va. Bar Assn., Am. Corp. Counsel Assn. Presbyterian. Avocations: reading, walking, computers. Office: Vulcan Materials Co 1 Metroplex Dr Birmingham AL 35209

SYDNOR, ROBERT HADLEY, state government geologist; b. Whittier, Calif., July 1, 1947; s. Thurston Edward and Mary Edith (Thompson) S.; divorced; 1 child, Christopher. BA, Whittier Coll., 1969; MS, U. Calif.-Riverside, 1975. Registered geologist, Calif., Alaska, Ariz.; cert. engring. geologist, Calif.; cert. hydrogeologist, Calif. Asst. petroleum geologist Mobil Oil Corp., Anchorage, 1970-71; staff engring. geologist Leighton & Assocs., Irvine, Calif., 1973-77; assoc. engring. geologist Orange County, Laguna Niguel, Calif., 1977-79; sr. engring. geologist VTN Corp., Irvine, 1979; chief engring. geologist R&M Cons., Inc., Irvine, 1979-82; supervising geologist Calif. Div. Mines and Geology, San Francisco, 1982-90, sr. engr. geologist, Sacramento, 1990—; mem. exam. com. Calif. State Bd. of Registration for Geologists and Geophysicists, Sacramento, 1977—, chmn., 1978. Co-editor CDMG spl. publ. on the 1989 Loma Prieta earthquake, 1992 Cape Mendocino earthquake, 1992 Landers earthquake, 1994 Northridge earthquake; contbr. many cons. reports on landslides and seismicity. Mem. alumni scholarship com. U. Calif.-Riverside, 1978-86; mem. City of Los Angeles Grading Appeals Bd., 1979-84; alt. mem. County of Orange Grading Appeals Bd., 1980-84. Donnel Foster Hewett fellow U. Calif., 1972. Mem. Calif. Acad. Sci. (life), Assn. Engring. Geologists (assoc. editor Bull. 1979-86, chmn. So. Calif. sect. 1979-80), Geol. Soc. Am., Seismol. Soc. Am. (life), Am. Assn. Petroleum Geologists, Am. Inst. Profl. Geologists, Nat. Assn. Geology Tchrs., Am. Quarternary Assn., Arctic Inst. N.Am. (life), ASTM, Am. Geophys. Union (life), Sigma Gamma Epsilon (life). Republican. Presbyterian. Home: 4930 Huntridge Ln Fair Oaks CA 95628-4823 Office: Calif Divsn Mines and Geology 801 K St MS 12-31 Sacramento CA 95814-3531

SYKES, ALSTON LEROY, analytical chemist, musician; b. Chgo., Sept. 1, 1948; s. Leslie McKoy and Perline Alphonsine (Holden) S.; m. Elizabeth White, Feb. 10, 1973; children: Brian A., Kevin M. BS in Chemistry, Campbell U., 1972. Cert. profl. chemist. Intern in chemistry N.C. State Bur. of Invest, Raleigh, 1970-72; chemist N.C. Dept. Natural Resources, Raleigh, 1972-77, Rsch. Triangle Inst., Research Triangle Park, N.C., 1977-80; sr. scientist TRW/Radian Corp., Research Triangle Park, N.C., 1980-88; corp. quality assurance mgr., lab. dir. Acurex Environ., Research Triangle Park, N.C., 1988-93; prin. scientist, mgr. Quanterra Environ. Svcs., Raleigh, 1994—; pres. Rsch. Triangle Environ. Tech., 1993—. Author (computer database) NIOSH Analytical Methods, 1986; contbr. articles to profl. jours. Mem. Am. Chem. Soc., Air and Waste Mgmt. Assn. Achievements include research in air sampling and analysis methods; developed new methods for testing indoor air, ambient air, recycling, and pollutant sources; contractor U.S. EPA rsch. labs, 1977—. Home: 8905 Jeanew Ct Raleigh NC 27613 Office: Quanterra Environ Svcs 8100A Brownleigh Dr Raleigh NC 27612

SYKES, BRIAN DOUGLAS, biochemistry educator, researcher; b. Montreal, Que., Aug. 30, 1943; s. Douglas Lehman and Mary (Anber) S.; m. Nancy Lynne Sengelaub, May 25, 1968; children: David, Michael. B.Sc., U. Alta., 1965; Ph.D., Stanford U., 1969. Asst. prof. chemistry Harvard U., Cambridge, Mass., 1969-74; assoc. prof. Harvard U., 1974-75; assoc. prof. biochemistry U. Alta. (Can.), Edmonton, 1975-80, prof., 1980—, McCalla rsch. prof., 1994-95. Assoc. editor Biochemistry and Cell Biology, 1983-93; mem. editl. bd. Bull. Magnetic Resonance, 1983—, Magnetic Resonance in Chemistry, 1983-95; assoc. editor Jour. Biomolecular NMR 1991—. Recipient Steacie prize Nat. Sci. Engring. Rsch. Coun., 1982, Kaplan Rsch. award, 1992; Woodrow Wilson fellow, 1965, Alfred P. Sloan fellow, 1971. Fellow Royal Soc. of Can.; mem. Can. Biochem. Soc. (pres., Ayerst award 1982), Biophys. Soc. (councillor 1989-92), Am. Chem. Soc., Protein Soc. Home: 11312 37th Ave, Edmonton, AB Canada T6J 0H5

SYKES, GRESHAM M'CREADY, sociologist, educator, artist; b. Plainfield, N.J., May 26, 1922; s. M'Cready and Beatrice (Evans) S.; m. Carla Adelt, July 13, 1946. A.B. summa cum laude, Princeton U., 1950; Ph.D. (Woodrow Wilson fellow 1950-51, Univ. fellow 1951-52), Northwestern U., 1953; M.A. (hon.), Dartmouth Coll., 1961. Instr. sociology Princeton U., 1952-54, asst. prof., bicentennial preceptor, 1954-58; assoc. prof. Northwestern U., Evanston, Ill., 1958-60; prof. sociology Dartmouth Coll., Hanover, N.H., 1960-63; chmn. dept. Dartmouth Coll., 1961-63; exec. officer Am. Sociol. Assn., 1963-65; research prof. law and sociology, dir. adminstrn. of justice program U. Denver, 1965-72; chmn. dept. sociology U. Houston, 1973; prof. sociology U. Va., Charlottesville, 1974-88, chmn. dept., 1978-81, emeritus prof., 1988—; chmn. Salzburg (Austria) Seminar in Am. Studies, summer 1965; working as artist, with frequent group and one-man exhbns., 1988—. Author: Crime and Society, rev. edit., 1967, The Society of Captives, 1958, Law and the Lawless, 1969, Social Problems in America, 1971, Criminology, 1978, rev. edit., 1992, The Future of Crime, 1980; criminology editor Jour. Criminal Law, Criminology and Police Sci., 1959-64; assoc. editor Rev. Am. Sociol. Assn., 1960-62, Contemporary Sociology, 1977-80, Criminology, 1980-84; contbr. articles and revs. to Ency. Britannica, profl. jours. Served to capt., C.E. AUS, 1942-46, ETO. Recipient Edwin H. Sutherland award Am. Soc. Criminology, 1980. Home: 311 2nd St NW # B Charlottesville VA 22902-5011

SYKES, LYNN RAY, geologist, educator; b. Pitts., Apr. 16, 1937; s. Lloyd Ascutney and Margaret (Woodburn) S. BS, MS, MIT, 1960; PhD in Geology, Columbia U., 1964. Phys. sci. aide geophys. lab. U.S. Geol. Survey, Silver Spring, Md., summer 1956; participant summer coop. program Geophys. Svc. Inc., Dallas, 1958; Summer Rsch. fellow Woods Hole (Mass.) Oceanographic Inst., 1959; rsch. asst. Lamont-Doherty Earth Obs. Columbia U., 1961-64; rsch. assoc. in seismology Lamont-Doherty Geol. Observatory Columbia U., 1964-66, adj. asst. prof. geology, 1966-68, asst. prof., 1968-69, assoc. prof., 1969-73, prof., 1973-78, Higgins prof. geology, 1978—, mem. univ. com. on acad. priorities, 1977-79; research geophysicist earth scis. labs. U.S. Dept. Commerce, 1966-68; Mem. panel polar geophysics Nat. Acad. Scis., 1968; adv. com. to ESSA Rsch. Labs., 1968-69; mem. subcom. geodesy and cartography applications steering com. NASA, 1968-70; mem. com. on world-wide standardized network Nat. Acad. Scis./NRC, 1969, com. seismology, 1972-73, panel earthquake prediction, 1973-75; organizing sec. Internat. Symposium Mech. Properties and Processes of Mantle of Internat. Upper Mantle Com., 1970; mem. panel on deep crustal drilling in marine areas JOIDES, 1970-71; advisor N.Y. State Geol. Survey and N.Y. State Environ. Protection Agy., 1970-80; mem. U.S. Geodynamics Panel on Mid-Atlantic Ridge, 1971-72; mem. working group U.S./USSR Joint Program for Earthquake Prediction, 1973-77; mem. U.S. Del. on Earthquake Prediction to USSR, fall, 1973; mem. adv. com. on proposals for earthquake prediction U.S. Geol. Survey, 1974, adv. panel earthquake hazards program, 1977-82; mem. U.S. Tech. Del. for talks on treaty on Threshold Limitations Underground Nuclear Explosions, Moscow, USSR, summer, 1974; mem. rev. panel earth scis. NSF, 1974-77; mem. study groups on plate interiors and Cocos and Caribbean plates U.S. Geodynamics Com.; mem. U.S. Seismology Group to People's Republic of China, fall, 1974; vis. prof. Earthquake Rsch. Inst. of Tokyo (Japan) U., fall 1974; Fairchild vis. scholar Calif. Inst. Tech., 1981; vis. fellow Clare Hall, Cambridge U., 1982; chmn. nat. earthquake prediction evaluation coun., U.S. Geol. Survey, 1984-88; mem. com. acad. priorities Columbia U., 1977-78, Columbia U. Arms Control Seminar, 1984-93, mem. external rev. com. Nat. Earthquake Hazards Reduction Program, 1987-88; mem. com. on verification of nuclear testing, treaties, Office Tech. Assessment, U.S. Congress, 1986-87; participant Belmont (Md.) Conf. on Nuclear Test Ban Policy, 1988; U.S. com. for decade of natural hazards reduction NRC, 1989-90; participant on TV show NOVA. Contbg. author: History of the Earth's Crust, 1968, Geodynamics of Iceland and the North Atlantic Area, 1974, Encounter with the Earth, 1975; Assoc. editor: Jour. Geophys. Research, 1968-70; Contbr. numerous articles to profl. jours. Pres. Far West 77th St. Block Assn., N.Y.C., 1973-74. Recipient H. O. Wood award in seismology Carnegie Instn. of Washington, 1967-70, Edward John Noble Leadership award during first three years grad. study, Pub. Service award Fedn. Am. Scientists, 1986, John Wesley Powell award U.S. Geol. Survey, 1991; Sloan fellow, 1969-71; grantee NSF, AEC, Air Force Office Sci. Rsch., NASA, N.Y. State Sci. and Tech. Found., N.Y. State Atomic and Space Devel. Authority, U.S. Geol. Survey, Sloan Found., John D. and Catherine T. MacArthur Found., Carnegie Corp., 1988-89; Guggenheim fellow, 1988-89; Proctor & Gamble scholar. Fellow Am. Geophys. Union (Macelwave award to Outstanding Young Geophysicist for 1970, Walter H. Bucher medal for original contbns. to basic knowledge of Earth's crust 1975, pres. sect. tectonophysics 1972-74, pres. sect. on seismology 1982-84), Seismol. Soc. Am., Geol. Soc. Am., Geol. Soc. London; mem. Nat. Acad. Scis., Am. Acad. Arts. and Scis., Royal Astron. Soc., N.Y. Acad. Scis. (pres. geol. sect. 1970-71). Research includes maj. contbns. on plate tectonics, earthquake prediction and dicrimination of underground nuclear explosions from earthquakes, arms control. Home: 100 Washington Springs Rd Palisades NY 10964-1624 Office: Columbia U Lamont-Doherty Earth Obs Palisades NY 10964

SYKES, MELVIN JULIUS, lawyer; b. Balt., Jan. 9, 1924; s. Philip Louis and Sara (Klein) S.; m. Judith Janet Konowitz, Sept.24, 1950; children: David K., Rachel A., Daniel E., Israel J. Grad., Balt. City Coll., 1940, Balt. Hebrew Coll., 1941; AB with honors, Johns Hopkins U., 1943; LLB magna cum laude, Harvard U., 1948. Bar. Md. 1949, U.S. Ct. Appeals (4th cir.) 1949, U.S. Dist. Ct. Md. 1950, U.S. Supreme Ct. 1955. Law clk. to Judge Morris A. Soper U.S. Ct. Appeals (4th cir.), 1948-49; pvt. practice Balt., 1949—; draftsman Md. Dept. Legis. Reference, 1949-50; rsch. cons. Md. Commn. Adminstrv. Orgn., 1951-52; reporter Md. commns. to study judiciary, 1953, to revise laws relating to pub. svc. commn., 1953-55; mem. standing com. on rules of practice, procedure Md. Ct. Appeals, 1954-72, 78—; mem. legis. coun. Commn. on Revision Condemnation Laws, 1961-63, Balt. Charter Revision Commn., 1962-63; pres. Bar Libr. of Balt., 1962-63; mem. Md. Constl. Conv. Commn., 1966-67; cons. Gov. Md. Commn. to Revise Testamentary Laws, 1967-69; mem. Gov. Md. commns. to study state aid to nonpub. edn., 1969-71, on annotated code Md., 1970-78. Co-author: West's Maryland Procedural Forms, 1964; co-translator Elon, Jewish Law—History, Principles, Sources, 1994. Mem. governing coun. Am. Assn. Jewish Edn., 1968-81; v.p. Balt. Jewish Coun., 1970-72; bd. dirs. Balt. chpt. Am. Jewish Com., Balt. Neighborhoods, Inc.; mem., former chmn. bd. trustees Balt. Hebrew Coll. With USAF, 1943-45. Fellow Am. Coll. Trial Lawyers, Am. Coll. Trust and Estate Counsel, Am. Bar Found., Md. Bar Found. (chmn. 1981-83); mem. ABA, Am. Law Inst., Md. Bar Assn., Balt. City Bar Assn. (lectr. continuing edn. programs), Am. Jewish Congress, Zionist Orgn. Am., B'nai B'rith, Phi Beta Kappa Fellows. Democrat. Home: 3811 fords Ln Baltimore MD 21215 Office: 310 Maryland Bar Ctr 520 W Fayette St Baltimore MD 21201-1781

SYKES, ROBERT REED, lawyer, former U.S. magistrate; b. Dallas, May 21, 1952; s. Bobby Reed and Patsy Ruth (West) S.; m. Lisa Jolley, Oct. 10, 1981; children: Reed, Nathan, Grant. BBA, Tex. A&M U., 1974; JD, So. Meth. U., 1977. Bar: Tex. 1977, U.S. Dist. Ct. (no. dist.) Tex. 1980, U.S. Dist. Ct. (we. dist.) Tex. 1986, U.S. Ct. Appeals (5th cir.) 1994, U.S. Supreme Ct. 1995. Asst. county atty. Tom Green County Atty.'s Office, San Angelo, Tex., 1978-81; trust landman First Nat. Bank Midlan, Midland, Tex., 1978-81, RepublicBank First Nat., Midland, 1981-85; pvt. practice atty. Midland, 1985—; U.S. fed. magistrate judge U.S. Dist. Ct. (we. dist.) Tex., Midland, 1988-92. 1st lt. USAR, 1974-88. Mem. State Bar Tex., Midland County Bar Assn., Midland A&M Club. Baptist. Office: 203 W Wall St Ste 606 Midland TX 79701-4516

SYKES, STEPHANIE LYNN, library director, archivist, museum director; b. Hamilton, Ont., Can., Sept. 14, 1948; d. Harold Joseph John and Ida Fern (Merritt) S. BA with honors, U. Western Ont., London, Ont., 1971; MA in History, U. Western Ont., 1978, MLS, 1984; cert. edn., Althouse Coll., Ont., 1972. Archival asst. D.B. Weldon Libr., London, Ont., Can., 1974-77; govt. pubs. libr. D.B. Weldon Libr., London, Ont., 1977-80; tech. svcs. libr. Bell Canada Hist. Svcs., Montréal, Québec, Can., 1980-81, sect. mgr. archives, 1981-83, dir. archives, libraries, and museum, 1983—. Editor: (catalogue) Regional Collection D.B. Weldon Library, 1977. Mem. Soc. Quebec Mus., Assn. Can. Archivists, Soc. Am. Archivists. Office: Bell Canada Hist Svcs, 1050 Beaver Hall Hill Rm 820, Montreal, PQ Canada H2Z 1S4

SYKES, SUSAN WILKINS, computer services company executive. V.p., sec. Sykes Enterprises Inc., Tampa, Fla.; v.p. community relations Sykes Enterprises Inc., 1995—. Office: Sykes Enterprises Inc 100 N Tampa St Ste 3900 Tampa FL 33602-5809*

SYKES, TRACY ALLAN, lawyer; b. Waukesha, Wis., Apr. 27, 1961; s. George and Florence May (Fowler) S. BA in Econs. magna cum laude, U. Wis., Eau Claire, 1983; JD, Boston U., 1986. Bar: Mass. 1986, U.S. Ct. Appeals (1st cir.) 1986, U.S. Dist. Ct. Mass. 1986, Minn. 1988, U.S. Ct. Appeals (8th cir.) 1988, U.S. Dist. Ct. (ea. dist.) Wis. 1989, U.S. Dist. Ct. Minn. 1990, D.C. 1992. Assoc. Rubin & Rudman, Boston, 1986-88, Doherty, Rumble & Butler, Mpls., 1988-90, Robins, Kaplan, Miller & Ciresi, Mpla., 1990-92; ptnr. Robins, Kaplan, Miller & Ciresi, Mpls. and Boston, 1992—; mediator Crime and Justice Found., Boston, 1987-88. Author: Hiring, Firing and Managing, 1992, ADA...Employers' Perspective, 1993. Mem. ABA, ATLA, Minn. Bar Assn., Boston Bar Assn., D.C. Bar Assn. Avocations: golf, scuba diving, photography. Office: Robins Kaplan Miller Ciresi 222 Berkeley St Boston MA 02116

SYKORA, DONALD D., utility company excutive; b. Stamford, Tex., Aug. 23, 1930; s. John E. and Lillie A. S.; m. Beverly J. Dawson, Feb. 7, 1952; 1 child, Sandra Lynn. BBA, U. Houston, 1957; JD, South Tex. Coll. Law, 1969. Bar: Tex. 1969. With Houston Lighting & Power Co., 1956—, power cons. residential mktg., 1956-63, supr. residential devel., 1963-68, gen. supr. residential mktg., 1968-70, asst. mgr. comml. sales, 1970-72, mgr. comml. sales, 1972-74, mgr. orgnl. devel., 1974, gen. mktg. mgr., 1974-77, v.p. mktg., 1977-78, v.p. customer relations, 1978-80, v.p. customer and pub. relations, 1980-81, exec. v.p., 1981-93, pres., chief operating officer, 1993—, also bd. dirs.; also v.p., bd. dirs. parent co. Houston Industries Inc.; bd. dirs. Primary Fuels, Inc., Utility Fuels, Inc. Chmn. exec. adv. bd. customer service and mktg. com. Edison Electric Inst., Washington, 1974—; mem. exec. bd. Electrification Council, 1974—, Salvation Army, Houston, 1980—. Mem. Tex. Bar Assn., Houston C. of C. Club: Houston. Home: 9614 Briar Forest Dr Houston TX 77063-1007 Office: Houston Industries Inc 11 Louisana PO Box 1700 Houston TX 77251-1700*

SYKORA, HAROLD JAMES, military officer; b. Tripp, S.D., Mar. 10, 1939; s. James J. and Mary (Tucek) S.; m. Patricia Ann Friedrich, Dec. 26, 1962; children: Montgomery James, Gina Marie. BS, U. S.D., 1961, MA in Math., 1965; postgrad., U. Wis., 1971-72, Indsl. Coll. Armed Forces, Ft. McNair, Washington, 1987-88. Math. tchr. Mitchell (S.D.) Sr. High Sch., 1961-64, 65-71, 72-74; commd. U.S. Army; advanced through grades to maj. gen.; with U.S. Army Command and Gen. Staff Coll., Ft. Leavenworth, Kans., 1974-75; exec. officer hdqs. 147th F.A. S.D. N.G., Pierre, 1975-80; tng. officer hdqrs. S.D. N.G., Rapid City, 1980-83, chief of staff, 1983-87, adj. gen., 1988—. Mem. N.G. Assn. U.S., N.G. Assn. U.S. (pres. 1979-80), Am. Legion, Assn. U.S. Army, Adjutant's Gen. Assn. U.S. (sec. 1991—, Army res. forces policy com. 1992—, chmn. Army res. forces policy com. 1995—), Kiwanis. Republican. Roman Catholic. Home: 5204 Pinedale Hts Rapid City SD 57702-2010 Office: SD NG 2823 W Main St Rapid City SD 57702-8170

SYLBERT, PAUL, production designer, art director; b. N.Y.C., Apr. 16, 1928. Art dir.: (films) The Wrong Man, 1956, (with Rolland M. Brooks and Howard Hollander) Teenage Millionaire, 1961; prodn. designer: (films) (with Richard Sylbert) Baby Doll, 1956, (with R. Sylbert) A Face in the Crowd, 1957, The Tiger Makes Out, 1967, The Drowning Pool, 1975, One Flew Over the Cuckoo's Nest, 1975, Mikey and Nicky, 1976, Hardcore, 1979, Kramer vs. Kramer, 1979, Wolfen, 1979, Resurrection, 1980, Blow Out, 1981, Gorky Park, 1983, Without a Trace, 1983, Firstborn, 1984, The Pope of Greenwich Village, 1984, The Journey of Natty Gann, 1985, Ishtar, 1987, Nadine, 1987, The Pick-Up Artist, 1987, Biloxi Blues, 1988, Fresh Horses, 1988, Career Opportunities, 1991, (with W. Steven Graham) The Prince of Tides, 1991 (Academy award nomination best art direction 1991), Rush, 1992, Sliver, 1993, Milk Money, 1994; prodn. designer, art dir.: (films) Riot, 1969, (with Edwin O'Donovan) Heaven Can Wait, 1978 (Academy award best art direction 1978); screenwriter: The Steagle, 1971, (with David Shaber) Night Hawks, 1981. Address: 52 E 64th St Ste 3 New York NY 10021-7356 Office: IATSE Local 876 11365 Ventura Blvd Ste 315 Studio City CA 91604-3148

SYLBERT, RICHARD, production designer, art director; b. N.Y.C., Apr. 16, 1928. V.p. prodn. Paramount Pictures, 1975-78. Art dir.: (films) Patterns, 1956, Wind Across the Everglades, 1958, The Fugitive Kind, 1960, Mad Dog Coll, 1961, Splendor in the Grass, 1961, Walk on the Wild Side, 1962, Lilith, 1964, The Pawnbroker, 1965, The Heartbreak Kid, 1972, (TV series) Inner Sanctum, 1951-53; prodn. designer: (films) Crowded Paradise, 1956, (with Paul Sylbert) Baby Doll, 1956, Edge of the City, 1957, (with P. Sylbert) A Face in the Crowd, 1957, Murder, Inc., 1960, The Young Doctors, 1961, The Connection, 1962, How to Murder Your Wife, 1965, Who's Afraid of Virginia Woolf?, 1966 (Academy award best art direction 1966), Grand Prix, 1966, The Graduate, 1967, Rosemary's Baby, 1968, The April Fools, 1969, Catch-22, 1970, Carnal Knowledge, 1971, Fat City, 1972, The Day of the Dolphin, 1973, Chinatown, 1974 (Academy award nomination best art direction 1974), The Fortune, 1975, Shampoo, 1975 (Academy award nomination best art direction 1975), Players, 1979, Reds, 1981 (Academy award nomination best art direction 1981), Frances, 1982, Partners, 1982, Breathless, 1983, The Cotton Club, 1984 (Academy award nomination best art direction 1984), Under the Cherry Moon, 1986, Shoot to Kill, 1988, Tequila Sunrise, 1988, Bonfire of the Vanities, 1990, Mobsters, 1991, Carlito's Way, 1993; prodn. designer, art dir.: (films) Long Day's Journey into Night, 1962, (with Phil Jeffries) The Manchurian Candidate, 1962, All the Way Home, 1963, Dick Tracy, 1990 (Academy award best art direction 1990), (TV movie) Last Hours Before Midnight, 1975; assoc. prodr.: (films) What's New Pussycat?, 1965; visual arts cons.: (films) The Illustrated Man, 1969; set designer: (theatre) The Prisoner of Second Avenue, 1971-74.

SYLK, LEONARD ALLEN, housing company executive, real estate developer; b. Phila., Feb. 25, 1941; s. Harry S. and Gertrude (Bardy) S.; m. Barbara Ann Lovenduski, Dec. 1, 1975; children: Tristan, Tyler, Galen. BS in Econs., U. Pa., 1963; MBA, Columbia U., 1965. Cert. comml. property builder. Founder, chmn. bd., chief exec. officer Shelter Systems Corp., Hainesport, N.J., 1965—; bd. dirs. Home Owners Warranty Corp., N.J., v.p., 1988—; bd. dirs. Am. Arbitration Assn., Internat. Housing Com., Nat. Comml. Builders Coun., 1986—; vice chmn. USA Bancshares, Inc.; chmn., bd. govs. Mid. East Forum; trustee Nat. Bldg. Sys. Coun., 1986—; pressdl. advisor on housing trade with Soviet Union, 1990. Contbr. articles to industry publs. Chmn. ann. awards dinner Jewish Nat. Fund, Phila., 1987, v.p., bd. dirs.; bd. dirs. Phila. Orch. Assn., 1990—, Pa. Ballet, 1994—, Resources for Childrens' Health, 1993—, Acad. Music, Phila., 1990—, Jewish Nat. Fund, 1987—, Rock Sch. of Pa. Ballet, 1995—; N.J. chmn. Builders for Bush, 1988; trustee Hahnemann U. and Hosp., 1991—, St. Christopher's Hosp. for Children, Phila., 1994—, St. Peter's Sch., Phila., 1995—. Named Man of Yr., 1988; recipient Tree of Life award presented by Rt. Hon. Margaret Thatcher, 1995. Mem. Nat. Assn. Homebuilders (com. chmn., nat. bd. dirs. 1984—, mem. exec. com. 1990—, fundraising chmn. 1991, Man of Yr. in Industrialized Housing 1990), Wood Truss Coun. Am. (bd. dirs. 1983—, pres. 1987, named to Hall of Fame 1990), Builders League South Jersey (v.p., bd. dirs. 1984—), N.J. Builders Assn. (bd. dirs., com. chmn., exec. com. 1990—), Le Club (N.Y.C.), Atlantic City Country Club, Vesper Club, Union League, Capitol Club (Washington), Masons. Republican. Home: 500 Delancey St Philadelphia PA 19106-4106 Office: Shelter Systems Corp Park Ave Hainesport NJ 08036

SYLKE, LORETTA CLARA, artist; b. Parkston, S.D., Nov. 4, 1926; d. Jacob and Maria Magdelin (Frey) Sprecher; m. Arthur C. Sylke, Apr. 26, 1961; children: Michael Arthur, Patricia, Constance, Sharon, Catherine, Charles (dec.). Grad. H.S., Chgo. Represented by Becca Gallery Berlin, Wis. Works have appeared at N.Mex. Art League, Albuquerque, 1991, El Dorado Gallery, Colorado Springs, Mont. Miniature Show, Billings, The New Eng. Fine Art Inst., The N.E. Trade Ctr., Woburn, Mass., 1993, El Dorado Gallery, Colorado Springs, 1993, 20th Annual Am. Nat. Miniature Show, Laramie, Wyo., Art in the Park, Lenexa, Kans., Gov.'s office, Madison, Wis., Custer County Art Ctr., Miles City, Mont., 1995, Laramie (Wyo.) Miniature Show, 1995; juried exhibns., Beloit, Wis., Minature Show: Custer County Art Ctr., Miles City, Mont., 1995. Recipient Masco award Madison Art Supply, 1982. Mem. Nat. Mus. Women in the Arts, Soc. Exptl. Artists, Wis. Women in the Arts, Catherine Lorillard Wolfe Art Club. Avocations: sewing, gardening. Home: N4392 Wicks Lndg Princeton WI 54968-8508 Office: 1714 Studio Princeton WI 54968

SYLLA, RICHARD EUGENE, economics educator; b. Harvey, Ill., Jan. 16, 1940; s. Benedict Andrew and Mary Gladys (Curran) S.; m. Edith Anne Dudley, June 22, 1963; children: Anne Curran, Margaret Dudley. BA, Harvard U., 1962, MA, 1965, PhD, 1969. Prof. econs. and bus. N.C. State U., Raleigh, 1968-90; Henry Kaufman prof. history fin. insts. and markets NYU, N.Y.C., 1990—, prof. econs., 1990—; cons. Citibank NA, N.Y.C., 1979-82, Chase Manhattan Bank, N.Y.C., 1983-85; vis. prof. U. Pa., Phila., 1983, U. N.C., Chapel Hill, 1988. Author: The American Capital Market, 1975; co-author: Evolution of the American Economy, 1980, 2d edit., 1993,

A History of Interest Rates, 1991, rev. edit., 1996; co-editor: Patterns of European Industrialization, 1991, Anglo-American Financial Systems, 1995; editor Jour. Econ. History, 1978-84. Study fellow NEH, 2975-76; Rsch. grantee NSF, 1985-94, Rsch. grantee Sloan Found., 1995—. Mem. Am. Econs. Assn., Econ. History Assn. (v.p. 1987-88, trustee 1977-88, Arthur H. Cole prize 1970), Bus. History Conf. (trustee 1991-94), So. Econ. Assn. (v.p. 1981-82). Avocations: golf, hiking, fishing, stamp collecting, arts. Home: 110 Bleecker St Apt 23D New York NY 10012-2106 Office: NYU 44 W 4th St New York NY 10012-1126

SYLVESTER, GEORGE HOWARD, retired air force officer; b. Riverside, N.J., Aug. 10, 1927; s. Ralph Davis and Dorothy Clarisse (Mealley) S.; m. Elaine Ruth Winderling, June 7, 1949; children—Wendy, Susan, David. B.S., U.S. Mil. Acad., 1949; M.A., Georgetown U., 1956. Commd. 2d lt. U.S. Air Force, 1949, advanced through grades to lt. gen., 1976; pilot, 1949-54; asst. prof. social scis. U.S. Mil. Acad., 1956-60; long-range planner Hdqrs. U.S. Air Force, 1961-64; mil. asst. to sec. def., 1964-66; squadron comdr. F-4 squadron Vietnam, 1966; comdr. Danang Air Base, Vietnam, 1967; dir. test Eglin AFB, Fla., 1968-70; asst. dir. tactical systems test and evaluation Office Sec. Def., 1970-73; dep. for systems ASD, Wright-Patterson AFB, Ohio, 1973-74; vice comdr. ASD, 1974-76, comdr., 1976-79; vice comdr. AF Systems Command, Andrews AFB, Md., 1979-81; ret., 1981, ind. aerospace cons., 1981—. Decorated D.S.M. with 1 oak leaf cluster, Legion of Merit with 2 oak leaf clusters, D.F.C., Air medal with 7 oak leaf clusters, Air Force Commendation medal with 2 oak leaf clusters. Lutheran. Home: 4839 Conicville Rd Mount Jackson VA 22842-2800

SYLVESTER, MICHAEL LANE, vocalist; b. Noblesville, Ind., Aug. 21, 1951; s. Charles Jr. and Judith Ann (Pickett) S.; m. Sandra Michele Weed, Aug. 3, 1973 (div. Oct. 1979); 1 child, Steven David; m. Michele Ann Kidd, May 15, 1981; 1 child, Griffin Parker. MB, Westminster Choir Coll., 1974; MusM, Ind. U., 1978. Assoc. prof. voice Ind. U., Bloomington, 1974-78; asst. prof. voice Ind. Ctrl. U., Indpls., 1976-78; prof. voice Cameron U., Lawton, Okla., 1978-79. Appeared in maj. opera houses throughout world; leading roles at The Met. Opera, N.Y., The Royal Opera at Covent Garden, London, The Vienna State Opera, Milan's Teatro alla Scala, San Francisco Opera, The Chgo. Lyric, Berlin State Opera, Paris' Opera Bastille. Recipient Alumni Merit award Westminster Choir Coll., 1993, 1st place Met. Opera Auditions, Met. Opera Nat. Coun., N.Y.C., 1986, MacAllister Voice Competition, Indpls., 1986, San Francisco Opera Merola, 1982. Mem. Am. Guild Musical Artists. Republican. Avocations: writing, computer programming.

SYLVESTER, RONALD CHARLES, newspaper writer; b. Springfield, Mo., Feb. 10, 1959; s. Edgar Donald and Barbara Jean (Hedgecock) S.; 1 child, Christian Alexander. Sports writer Springfield (Mo.) News-Leader, 1976-88, entertainment writer, 1988—; mem. media panel Leadership Music, Nashville, 1993. Author: Branson: On Stage in the Ozarks, 1994; contbr. articles to New Country Music, Gannett News Svc., Colliers Ency. Bd. dirs. Entertainers Guild of Branson, Mo., 1993-94. Mem. Country Music Assn. Mem. Christian Ch. (Disciples of Christ). Avocations: music, reading, outdoor recreation. Office: Springfield News-Leader 651 N Boonville Ave Springfield MO 65806-1005

SYLVESTRE, JEAN GUY, former national librarian; b. Sorel, Que., Can., May 17, 1918; s. Maxime Arthur and Yvonne Marie (Lapierre) S.; m. Francoise Poitevin, Feb. 27, 1943; children: Marie, Jean, Paul. B.A., U. Ottawa, 1939, B.Ph., 1940, M.A., 1942, D.L.S. (hon.), 1969, D.Litt. (hon.), 1970, LL.D. (hon.), 1974, 75, 82. Translator Dept. Can. Sec. of State, 1942-44; editor Wartime Info. Bd., 1944-45; asst. pvt. sec. to minister of justice, 1945-47, pvt. sec. to sec. of state for external affairs, 1947-48, pvt. sec. to prime minister, 1948-50; adminstrv. officer Dept. Resources and Devel., 1950-53; asst. librarian Library of Parliament, Ottawa, Ont., 1953-56; asso. parliamentary librarian Library of Parliament, 1956-68, nat. librarian, 1968-83; pres., chmn. bd. Can. Inst. for Hist. Microprodns., 1983-86; chmn. Ottawa Valley Book Festival, 1988-92; hon. chmn., 1993—. Author: Louis Francoeur, journaliste, 1941, Situation de la poésie canadienne, 1941, Anthologie de la poésie canadienne-française, 1943, 58, 64, 66, 68, 74, Poètes catholiques de la France contemporaine, 1944, Sondages, 1945, Impressions de théâtre, 1950, Amours, délices et orgues, 1953, Panorama des lettres canadiennes-francaises, 1964, Canadian Writers, 1964, Literature in French Canada, 1967, A Century of Canadian Literature, 1967, The Future of the National Library of Canada, 1980, Guidelines for National Libraries, 1987 French, Spanish and Arabic edits., 1988; also articles in profl. jours., encys.; editor: A Canadian Errant (J.P. Manion), 1960; editor: Canadian Universities Today, 1961, Structures sociales du Canada francais, 1967. Chmn. Gov. Gen.'s Lit. Awards, 1960-62; organizer, chmn. World Poetry Conf., Expo 1967; chmn. Can. Council Com. on Aid-to-Publs., 1960-68; lectr. U. Ottawa Library Sch., 1954-71; v.p. Can. Library Week Council, 1965-67; Bd. dirs. Can. Writers Found., pres., 1960-61. Decorated comdr. Ordre International du Bien Public, officer Order of Can.; comdr. Order of Merit of Poland; recipient Centennial medal., Outstanding Pub. Service award, Internat. Fedn. Libr. Assn. medal. Fellow Royal Soc. Can. (hon. sec. 1959-62, pres. sect. I 1963-64, hon. libr. 1969-91, pres. 1973-74); mem. Soc. Ecrivains Canadiens, Can. Libr. Assn. (life), Ont. Libr. Assn. (hon. life), Can. Assn. Info. Sci. (pres. 1971-72), Assn. Scis. et Techniques (life). Home: 2286 Bowman Rd, Ottawa, ON Canada K1H 6V6

SYMANSKI, ROBERT ANTHONY, treasurer; b. Mineola, N.Y., June 17, 1946; s. Anthony John and Mary (Jozef) S.; m. Eileen Margaret Eardley; children: Susan, Robert, Patti. AAS, SUNY, Delhi, 1966; BBA, Pace U., 1972; MBA, Fairleigh Dickinson U., 1984. Sr. credit rep. Union Carbide Corp., N.Y.C., 1967-71; credit mgr. GAF Corp., N.Y.C., 1971-73; dir. cash mgmt. GAF Corp., Wayne, N.J., 1973-77; mgr. corp. cash Coca-Cola Bottling Co. N.Y., Hackensack, N.J., 1977-81; asst. treas. The BOC Group Inc., Montvale, N.J., 1981-86; treas. The BOC Group Inc., Murray Hill, N.J., 1986—. Sgt. USAF, 1967-69. Mem. Nat. Assn. Corp. Treas., Treasury Mgmt. Assn., Fin. Execs. Insts. Roman Catholic. Home: 16 Susan Dr Chatham NJ 07928-1049 Office: The BOC Group Inc 575 Mountain Ave New Providence NJ 07974-2097

SYMCHYCH, JANICE M., lawyer; b. St. Boniface, Man., Can., 1951. BA magna cum laude, U. Minn., 1973; JD magna cum laude, William Mitchell Coll. Law, 1977. Bar: Minn. 1977, U.S. Dist. Ct. (Minn. dist.) 1977, U.S. Ct. Appeals (8th cir.) 1981. Asst. atty. Hennepin County, Minn., 1977-80; asst. U.S. atty. U.S. Attys. Office, Minn., 1980-85; U.S. magistrate judge Dist. Minn., 1985-89; ptnr. Dorsey & Whitney, Mpls.; mem. task force on gender fairness in cts. Minn. Supreme Ct., 1987-90. Mem. Minn. State Bar Assn. (mem. task force on complex litigation 1991—, mem. civil litigation gov. coun. 1986—, chair Minn. CLE bd. dirs. 1990—). Office: Dorsey & Whitney 220 S 6th St Minneapolis MN 55402*

SYME, SHERMAN LEONARD, epidemiology educator; b. Dauphin, Man., Can., July 4, 1932; came to U.S., 1950; s. Robert and Rose (Bay) S.; m. Marilyn Elaine Egenes, July 28, 1932; children: Karen, David, Janet. BA, UCLA, 1953, MA, 1955; PhD, Yale U., 1957. Commd. USPHS, Washington, 1957-68; advanced through grades to chief Tng. Sta. USPHS, San Francisco, 1962-68; sociologist USPHS, Washington, 1957-60; exec. sec. NIH, Bethesda, Md., 1960-62; prof. emeritus epidemiology U. Calif., Berkeley, 1968—; chmn. Dept. Epidemiology, U. Calif., 1975-80; vis. prof. Teikyo U., Tokyo, 1977, York (Eng.) U., 1975, St. Thomas Sch. Medicine, London, 1980, U. London, 1989; expert adv. panels WHO, Geneva, 1975—. Co-editor Social Stress and Heart Disease, 1967, Social Support and Health, 1985; contbr. 115 articles to profl. jours. Fellow Am. Heart Assn., Soc. Epidemiol. Research; mem. Inst. Medicine, Am. Epidemiol. Soc. Office: U Calif Haviland Hall Berkeley CA 94720

SYMENS, MAXINE TANNER, restaurant owner; b. Primghar, Iowa, June 12, 1930; d. George Herman and Irene Marie (Dahnke) Brinkert; m. Jack Frederiksen Tanner, Dec. 28, 1950 (dec. Oct. 1976); m. Delbert Glenn Symens, Sept. 26, 1981. BS magna cum laude, Westmar Coll., 1970. Cert. tchr., Iowa. Elem. tchr. Rural Sch. O'Brien Co., Primghar, 1949-54, Gaza (Iowa) Com. Sch., 1954-60; secondary tchr. Primghar Com. Sch., 1960-81; fitness salon owner Slim 'N' Trim, George, Rock Rapids, Iowa, 1982-87; restaurant owner George Cafe, 1985-90, Pizza Ranch, 1988-96; with network mktg. divsn. Espial and STS, 1996—. Pres. Primghar Edn. Assn., 1970-71. Mem. George C. of C., George Kiwanis Club (sec. 1991-95), Delta Kappa Gamma. Lutheran. Home: 307 Dell St NE George IA 51237-1030

SYMINGTON, J. FIFE, III, governor; b. N.Y.C., Aug. 12, 1945; s. John Fife Jr. and Martha (Frick) S.; m. Leslie Marion Barker, June 1, 1968 (div. Jan. 1973); childen: Fife IV, Scott; m. Ann Pritzlaff, Feb. 7, 1976; children: Whitney, Richard, Tom. Student, Harvard U., 1968. Ptnr. Lincoln Property Co., Phoenix, 1972-76; chmn. of the bd. The Symington Co., Phoenix, 1976-89; gov. State of Ariz., 1991—. Precinct committeeman Ariz.'s Legis. Dist. 24, Paradise Valley; fin. chmn. State Republican Party, Phoenix, 1982-84; campaign advisor Rep. John Rhodes, Sen. John McCain, Ariz.; chmn. Phoenix Citizens Police Protection Bond Com., 1988; v.p. bd. trustees Heard Mus.; mem. Men's Art Coun., Environ. Quality Commn., 1971-73, Ariz. Children's Found.; dep. sheriff Maricopa County Air Posse; exec. bd. Phoenix Community Alliance. Capt. USAF, 1968-71. Mem. Western Govs.' Assn. (chmn. 1992—). Episcopalian. Office: Govs Office 1700 W Washington St Phoenix AZ 85007-2812

SYMMERS, WILLIAM GARTH, international maritime lawyer; b. Bronxville, N.Y., Nov. 30, 1910; s. James Keith and Agnes Louise (Shuey) S.; m. Marina Baruch, Apr. 25, 1936; children: Benjamin Keith, Ann St. Clair (Mrs. Edward L. Reed); m. Anne H. Ellis, Mar. 20, 1946; children: Barbara (Mrs. Thomas M. Bancroft, Jr.), Susan (Mrs. Peter Amory Bradford), Deborah. Grad., Lawrenceville (N.J.) Sch., 1929; AB, U. Va., 1933, JD, 1935. Bar: N.Y. 1937, U.S. Supreme Ct. 1940, D.C. 1953. Assoc. Bigham, Englar, Jones & Houston, N.Y.C., 1935-37; mem. Dow and Symmers, N.Y.C., 1940-56; founding ptnr. Symmers, Fish & Warner, N.Y.C., 1956-91; ret.; admiralty counsel U.S. Maritime Commn., 1937-41; spl. counsel to naval affairs com. U.S. Ho. of Reps.; active investigation loss of SS Normandie, 1942; spl. counsel War Shipping Adminstrn, 1942-45, admiralty and shipping litigation; U.S. del., v.p. Antwerp Conf., Comité Maritime Internat., 1947; also del. Maritime Law Assn. U.S. to succeeding confs., Amsterdam, 1949, Brighton, 1952, Madrid, 1955, N.Y.C., 1966, Tokyo, 1968, Rio de Janeiro, 1977, Montreal, 1981; titular mem. Comité Maritime Internat., 1955—; mem. U.S. Supreme Ct. adv. com. on admiralty rules, 1960-72. Contbr. articles to maritime publs. Mem. ABA, Assn. Bar City of N.Y. (chmn. admiralty com. 1953-56), Am. Soc. Internat. Law, Maritime Law Assn. U.S. (chmn. com. revision U.S. Supreme Ct. admiralty rules 1952-56, mem. exec. com. 1958-61, 1st v.p. 1964-66), Internat. Maritime Arbitration Orgn. (U.S. rep. 1978-81), Internat. C. of C., St. Andrew's Soc. N.Y., English-Speaking Union U.S., Down Town Assn., N.Y. Yacht Club, Indian Harbor Yacht Club (Greenwich, Conn.), Phi Delta Phi, Phi Delta Theta. Address: 444 E 52nd St New York NY 10022-6446

SYMMES, WILLIAM DANIEL, lawyer; b. Spokane, Wash., Sept. 10, 1938; s. William John and Sheila (Deacon) S.; m. Jayne Peters, June 20, 1959; children: Ashley, William. AB cum laude, Georgetown U., 1960; MBA, Columbia U., 1962; LLB, Stanford U., 1965. Bar: Calif. 1966, U.S. Ct. Appeals (9th cir.) 1966, Wash., 1968, U.S. Supreme Ct. 1982. Assoc. Burris & Lagerlof, L.A., 1965-68, Witherspoon, Kelley, Davenport & Toole, Spokane, 1968—; adj. prof. Gonzaga U., Spokane, 1971-77; part owner, officer, dir. Pacific Coast League AAA Spokane Indians, 1978-82, Las Vegas Stars, 1983-85. Bd. dirs. Greater Spokane Sports Assn., 1984—, Spokane Youth Sports Assn., 1985—, also others. Named Outstanding Young Man Yr. Spokane Jr. C. of C., 1969. Fellow Am. Coll. Trial Lawyers; mem. ABA, Am. Bd. Trial Advocates, Wash. State Bar Assn., Calif. Bar Assn., Spokane County Bar Assn. (chmn. jud. liaison com. 1982-84), Def. Rsch. Inst., Wash. Def. Lawyers Assn., Spokane C. of C., Empire Club, Spokane Club, Manito Golf and Country Club. Home: 3606 S Eastgate Ct Spokane WA 99203-1411 Office: Witherspoon Kelley Davenport & Toole 1100 Nat Bank Bldg Spokane WA 99201

SYMMONDS, RICHARD EARL, gynecologist; b. Greensburg, Mo., Mar. 19, 1922; s. Emmett E. S. A.B., Central Coll., Fayette, Mo., 1943; M.D., Duke U., 1946; M.S. in Ob-Gyn, U. Minn., 1953. Intern Los Angeles County Hosp., 1946, resident in Ob-Gyn, 1950-53, resident in gen. surgery, 1954-56; practice medicine specializing in gen. surgery Rochester, Minn., 1958—; mem. faculty Mayo Clinic, Rochester, 1953—; emeritus prof. gynecologic surgery Mayo Clinic, 1960—, chmn. dept., 1970-92, chmn. emeritus, 1992—. Contbr. articles to profl. jours. Served with USN, 1947-49. Fellow A.C.S.; mem. Am. Gynecol. Soc., Am. Assn. Obstetricians and Gynecologists, Soc. Pelvic Surgeons, Soc. Gynecologic Oncologists, Am. Coll. Obstetricians and Gynecologists. Office: 200 1st St SW Rochester MN 55905-0001

SYMON, LINDSAY, retired neurological educator; b. Aberdeen, Scotland, Nov. 4, 1929; s. William Lindsay and Isabel (Shaw) S.; m. Pauline Barbara Rowland, Aug. 14, 1953; children: Lindsay Fraser, Barbara Rosemary, Fiona Margaret. MB, ChB with honors, Aberdeen U., Scotland, 1951; Diplomate, Royal Coll. Surgeons, 1957. Jr. specialist, house surgeon Royal Infirmary, Aberdeen, Scotland, 1952-3; surgical registrar Royal Infirmary, Aberdeen, 1956-58; clin. rsch. fellow med. rsch. coun. neurosurgical registrar Middlesex & Maida Vale Hosp., London, 1958-61, sr. registrar in Neurosurgery, 1962-65; Rockefeller travelling fellow in medicine Wayne U., Detroit, 1961-62; cons. neurosurgeon Nat. Hosp. for Nervous Diseases, London, 1965-78; cons. St. Thomas Hosp., London, 1970-78; prof. Neurol. Surgery Inst. Neurology U. London Nat. Hosp. Queens Sq., London, 1978-95; cons. (hon.) Hammersmith Hosp., London, Royal Ear, Nose and Throat Hosp., London; civilian advisor in Neurol. Surgery, The Royal Navy. Contbr. articles to profl. jours.; mem. many editorial bds. med. jours. Vol. Mobile Neurosurg. Unit, Territorial Army, Keogh Barracks, Mytchett, 1975-81. Maj. Royal Army Med. Corps, 1953-55. Decorated with Territorial decoration, The Queen, 1968, Comdr. of British Empire, Queen's Birthday, 1994. Fellow ACS (hon.), Royal Coll. Surgeons (Edinborough), Royal Coll. Surgeons (London), Royal Soc. Medicine; mem. Soc. Brit. Neurol. Surgeons, World Fedn. Neurosurg. Socs. (pres. 1989-93), Caledonian Slub, St. andrews Royal and Ancient Golf Club, others. Avocations: golf, medieval history. Home: Maple Lodge Rivar Rd, Shalbourne/Marlborough, EN5 4 DS Wiltshire SN8 3QE, England

SYMONDS, PAUL SOUTHWORTH, mechanical engineering educator, researcher; b. Manila, Aug. 20, 1916; came to U.S., 1917; s. George R.B. and Claire Louise (Southworth) S.; m. Ilese Powell, Jan. 23, 1943; children: Alan Powell, Robin Peter. BS, Rensselaer Poly. Inst., 1938; MS, Cornell U., 1941, PhD, 1943; Docteur en Sciences Appliquées (hon.), Faculté Polytechnique de Mons, Belgium, 1988. Instr. mechanics Cornell U., Ithaca, N.Y., 1941-43; physicist Naval Research Lab., Washington, 1943-47; asst. prof. engring. Brown U., Providence, 1947-51, assoc. prof., 1951-54, prof., 1954-83, prof. engring. rsch. emeritus, 1983—, chmn. div. engring., 1959-62. Editl. bd. Quar. Applied Math., 1965—; mem. adv. bd. Internat. Jour. Mech. Sci., 1978—; mem. editl. adv. bd. Internat. Jour. Impact Engring., 1983—, Computer Methods in Applied Mechanics and Engring., 1983—; also numerous papers in tech. jours. Recipient Fulbright award 1949-50, 57-58; fellow Imperial Chem. Industries, Cambridge, U.K., 1950-51; Guggenheim fellow Swansea, Wales, 1957-58; NSF sr. postdoctoral fellow Oxford, Eng., 1964-65. Fellow ASME, ASCE, Am. Acad. Mechanics; mem. Internat. Assn. Bridge and Structual Engring. Home: 229 Medway St Apt 110 Providence RI 02906-5300 Office: Brown U Divsn Enging Providence RI 02912

SYMONS, EDWARD LEONARD, JR., lawyer, educator, investment advisor; b. Pitts., Dec. 21, 1941; s. Edward Leonard and Lillian Mae (Daniel) S.; m. Louise Quinn, July 18, 1970; children: Amy, Colin. B.A., Cornell U., 1963; J.D. summa cum laude, U. Pitts., 1969. Assoc., ptnr. Reding, Blackstone, Rea & Sell, Pitts., 1969-72; asst. atty. gen., chief counsel Pa. Dept. Banking, Harrisburg, 1972-74; prof. law U. Pitts. Sch. Law, 1974—; tax cons., Wash. State, 1987, Del., 1995; pres. Dollins Symons Mgmt., Inc., 1983—; mem. adv. coun. Conflict Resolution Ctr. Internat., 1994—; mem. bd. internat. scholars Ctr. for Comml. Law Studies, Queen Mary and Westfield Coll., U. London, 1993—. Co-author, Pennsylvania Professional Corporations, 1974, Banking Law Teaching Materials, 2d edit., 1984, 3d edit., 1991; contbr. articles to profl. jours. Commr. Mt. Lebanon, Pa., 1976-80; bd. dirs. Performing Arts for Children, Pitts., 1980-84, Mt. Lebanon Hosp. Authority, 1993—, St. Clair Hosp. Found., Pitts., 1994—, St. Clair Hosp Bd., 1995—. 1st lt. arty. AUS, 1964-66, Korea. Mem. ABA (banking law com., consumer fin. svcs. com., devel. in investment svcs. com.), Order of Coif. Office: U Pitts Sch Law 3900 Forbes Ave Pittsburgh PA 15213

SYMONS, J. KEITH, bishop; b. Champion, Mich., Oct. 14, 1932. Student, St. Thomas Sem., Bloomfield, Conn., St. Mary Sem., Balt. Ordained priest Roman Catholic Ch., 1958, consecrated bishop, 1981. Titular bishop of Siguritanus and aux. bishop of St. Petersburg Fla., 1981-83, bishop of Pensacola-Tallahassee, 1983-90, bishop of Palm Beach, 1990—. Office: 9995 N Military Trl Palm Beach Gardens FL 33410*

SYMONS, JAMES MARTIN, theater and dance educator; b. Jacksonville, Ill., May 7, 1937; s. James and Pauline (Barton) S.; m. Judith White, Nov. 14, 1959; children: Tracy, Kelly, Carrie. BA, Ill. Coll., 1959; MA, So. Ill. U., 1964; PhD, Cornell U., 1970. Asst. prof. Yankton (S.D.) Coll., 1964-67; assoc. prof. Coll. St. Catherine, St. Paul, 1970-74, SUNY, Albany, 1974-77; prof., chair Trinity U., San Antonio, 1977-84; prof., chair theatre and dance dept. U. Colo., Boulder, 1984—; actor Off-Broadway, N.Y.C., 1959, Mo. Repertory Theatre, Kansas City, 1984; dir., actor Colo. Shakespeare Festival, Boulder, 1985—, producing artistic dir., 1994-95; leader People-to-People Del. of Theater Educators, USSR and Czechoslovakia, 1991. Author: Meyerhold's Theatre of the Grotesque, 1971 (Freedley Meml. award Theatre Libr. Assn. 1971); contbr. articles to scholarly jours. Lt. (j.g.) USN, 1960-63. Mem. Assn. for Theatre in Higher Edn. (pres. 1989-91), Assn. for Communication Adminstrn. (pres. 1990). Democrat. Methodist. Office: U of Colorado Dept Theatre And Dance Boulder CO 80309

SYMONS, JAMES MARTIN, environmental engineer, educator; b. Champaign, Ill., Nov. 24, 1931; s. George Edgar and Virginia (Thompson) S.; m. Joan Mildred Kinsman, June 29, 1958; children: Andrew James, Linda Joan, Julie Ann. BCE, Cornell U., 1954; SM in San. Engring., MIT, 1955, ScD in San. Engring., 1957. Registered engr., Tex.; diplomate Am. Acad. Environ. Engrs. Asst. prof. san. engring. MIT, 1957-62; rsch. engr. USPHS, Cin., 1962-1970; supr. rsch. engr. U.S. EPA, Cin., 1970-82; prof. civil engring. U Houston, 1982-95; Cullen disting. prof. civil engring. U. Houston, 1995—. Contbr. articles to profl. jours. Fellow ASCE; mem. Am. Water Works Assn. (hon., life, chmn. water quality div. 1980-81), Water Environment Fedn., Nat. Acad. Engring. Methodist. Avocations: photography, golf. Office: U of Houston Dept Civil Environ Eng Houston TX 77204-4791

SYMONS, ROBERT SPENCER, electronic engineer; b. San Francisco, July 3, 1925; s. Spencer W. and Avesia (Atkins) S.; m. Alice Faye Smith, Dec. 21, 1960; children: Julia Ann, Robert Spencer Jr. BS, Stanford U., 1946, MS, 1948. Engr. Eitel-McCullough, Inc., San Bruno, Calif., 1947, Heinz & Kaufman, South San Francisco, 1948, Pacific Electronics Co., Los Gatos, Calif., 1949; sr. engring. mgr. Varian Assocs., Palo Alto, Calif., 1950-83; tech. dir. Litton Industries, San Carlos, Calif., 1983—. Recipient Charles B. Thornton award for Advanced Technology Achievement, 1991. Patentee in field. Served to 1st lt. AUS, 1950-53. Fellow IEEE (assoc. editor Transactions on Electron Devices jour. 1980-83); mem. Phi Beta Kappa, Tau Beta Pi. Club: Commonwealth of Calif. Home: 290 Surrey Pl Los Altos CA 94022-2146 Office: Litton Industries 960 Industrial Rd San Carlos CA 94070-4116

SYMONS, TIMOTHY JAMES MCNEIL, physicist; b. Southborough, Kent, Eng., Aug. 4, 1951; came to U.S., 1977; s. Henry McNeil and Catherine Muriel (Rees) S.; m. S.B. Master, Mar. 1, 1987; children: Henry Benjamin, Daniel Robert. BA, Oxford (Eng.) U., 1972, MA, DPhil, 1976. Rsch. fellow Sci. Rsch. Coun., Eng., 1976-77; postdoctoral fellow Lawrence Berkeley (Calif.) Lab., 1977-79, div. fellow, 1979-84, sr. physicist, 1984—, dir. nuclear sci. div., 1985-95; vis. scientist Max-Planck Inst., Heidelberg, Germany, 1980-81; mem. U.S. nuclear physics del. to USSR, 1986; mem. program adv. coms. Gesellschaft fur schwerionen forschung, 1987-88, Continuous Electron Beam Accelerator Facility, 1989-92, Brookhaven Nat. Lab., 1991-92; mem. policy com. Relativstic Heavy Ion Collider, 1988—. Contbr. over 70 articles to sci. jours. Fellow Am. Phys. Soc. (chmn. Bonner prize com. 1990). Avocations: music, gardening, travel. Office: Lawrence Berkeley Lab Nuclear Sci Divsn 1 Cyclotron Rd 70A-3307 Berkeley CA 94720

SYMOSEK, PETER FRANK, research scientist; b. Lawrence, Mass., Sept. 22, 1953; s. Frank John and Theresa Alice (McTiernan) S. BS, Merrimack Coll., North Andover, Mass., 1978; ScM, Brown U., 1980, PhD, 1985. Sr. prin. rsch. scientist Honeywell, Inc., Mpls., 1985—. Contbr. articles to IEEE Jour., Computer Graphics Image Processing. Mem. IEEE, Soc. Photo-optical Instrumentation Engrs., Toastmasters. Avocations: golfing, scuba diving, swimming, bicycling, reading. Office: Honeywell Tech Ctr MN65-2500 3660 Technology Dr Minneapolis MN 55418

SYNAN, EDWARD ALOYSIUS, JR., clergyman, former institute president; b. Fall River, Mass., Apr. 13, 1918; s. Edward Aloysius and Mary F. (McDermott) S. AB, Seton Hall Coll., 1938; student, U. Louvain, Belgium, 1938-40, Immaculate Conception Sem., Darlington, N.J., 1940-41; STL, Cath. U. Am., 1942; LMS, Pontifical Inst. Medieval Studies, Toronto, 1951; MA, PhD, U. Toronto, 1952. Ordained priest Roman Cath. Ch., 1942. Curate Immaculate Conception Ch., Montclair, N.J., 1942-44; prof. philosophy, chmn. dept. Seton Hall U., South Orange, N.J., 1952-59; prof. history of mediaeval philosophy Pontifical Inst. Mediaeval Studies, U. Toronto, 1959, pres., 1973-79, acting pres., 1989-90. Author: The Popes and The Jews in the Middle Ages, 1965, The Works of Richard of Campsall, Vol. I, 1968, Vol. II, 1982; assoc. editor, contbr.: The Bridge, Yearbook of Judaeo-Christian Studies, 1955-62; adv. bd.: Speculum, 1971-74; contbr. chpts. to books, articles and revs. to publs. Served as capt. (chaplain) USAAF/.USAF, 1944-48. Fellow Royal Soc. Can.; mem. Am. Cath. Philos. Assn. (Aquinas medal 1991), Mediaeval Acad. Am., Renaissance Soc. Am., Am. Soc. Polit. and Legal Philosophy. Address: 59 Queen's Park, Toronto, ON Canada M5S 2C4

SYNNOTT, MARCIA GRAHAM, history educator; b. Camden, N.J., July 4, 1939; d. Thomas Whitney and Beatrice Adelaide (Colby) S.; m. William Edwin Sharp, June 16, 1979; children: Willard William Sharp, Laurel Beth Sharp. AB, Radcliffe Coll., 1961; MA, Brown U., 1964; PhD, U. Mass., 1974. History tchr. MacDuffie Sch., Springfield, Mass., 1963-68; instr. U. S.C., Columbia, 1972-74, asst. prof., 1974-79, assoc. prof. history, 1979—, dir. grad. studies history dept., 1990-92. Author: The Half-Opened Door, 1979; mem. editl. bd. History of Edn. Quar., 1996—; contbr. essays to books. Fulbright scholar, 1988; Am. Coun. Learned Socs. grantee, 1981. Mem. Am. Hist. Assn., So. Hist. Assn., Orgn. Am. Historians (membership com. 1990-93), S.C. Hist. Assn. (pres. 1994-95). Avocations: historic sites and museums, snow skiing, walking. Office: U SC Dept History Columbia SC 29208

SYNNOTT, WILLIAM RAYMOND, retired management consultant; b. Fall River, Mass., Dec. 29, 1929; s. William Joseph and Marie Aurore (Labrie) S.; m. Suzanne Pauline Moseley, Oct. 21, 1967; children—Dianne, Mark, Amy. Grad. cert., Rutgers U. Stonier Grad. Sch. Banking, 1958; B.S. summa cum laude, Boston U., 1973; grad. advanced mgmt. program, Harvard U., 1973. Sr. v.p. Bank of Boston, 1967-87; sr. dir. The Yankee Group, Boston, 1987-88; dir. Nolan Norton & Co., Lexington, Mass., 1988-91; pres. W.R. Synnott Assocs., Wellesley Hills, Mass., 1990-94; lectr., seminar leader on info. technology worldwide. Author: The Information Weapon, 1987; co-author: Information Resource Management, 1981. Served as sgt. U.S. Army, 1951-53, Korea. Avocations: skiing; tennis; golf. Home: Green Hill Rd Jackson NH 03846

SYNODINOS, JOHN ANTHONY, academic administrator; b. Balt., Sept. 6, 1934; s. Anthony John and Jean (Asimakes) S.; m. Glenda J. Davis, Sept. 5, 1959; children: Jean Louise Ganias, Victoria Lynn Gertenbach. BS, Loyola Coll., Balt., 1959; EdM, Temple U., 1977. Control buyer Montgomery Ward, Balt., 1959-60; asst. dir. admissions Johns Hopkins U., Balt., 1960-63, dir. spl. events, 1963-65, assoc. dir. pub. rels., 1965-67, asst. dir. Ctr. for Study Social Orgn. Schs., 1960-68; assoc. dir. devel. Franklin & Marshall Coll., Lancaster, Pa., 1968-70, asst. to pres., 1970-71, v.p. advancement, 1971-84; ptnr. John A. Synodinos & Assocs., Lancaster, 1984-88; pres. Lebanon Valley Coll., Annville, Pa., 1988—; bd. dirs. Econ. Devel. Corp. Lebanon County, Pa. Bd. dirs. United Way Lebanon County, 1989-93. Cpl. U.S. Army, 1952-55. Mem. Coun. Advancement & Support of Edn., Fortnightly Club (Lancaster) (pres. 1980). Democrat. Greek Orthodox. Avocation: acting. Home: 25 Cart Way Lebanon PA 17042-9469 Office: Lebanon Valley Coll Office of Pres Annville PA 17003-0501

SYPERT, GEORGE WALTER, neurosurgery educator, clinical neurosurgeon, research neurophysiologist; b. Marlin, Tex., Sept. 25, 1941; s. Claude Carl and Ruth Helen (Brown) S.; children: Kirsten Dianne, Shannon Ruth; m. Elaine Joy Arpin, Oct. 3, 1987. BA, U. Wash., 1963, MD with highest honors, 1967. Intern, Barnes Hosp., St. Louis, 1967-68; asst. resident in neurol. surgery U. Wash. Sch. Medicine, Seattle, 1968, 1970-72, chief resident, 1973-74, instr., 1973-74; asst. prof. neurol. surgery and neurosci. grad. faculty U. Fla. Coll. Medicine, Gainesville, 1974-77, assoc. prof., 1977-80, prof., 1980-84; C.M. and K.E. Overstreet Family prof. and eminent scholar, 1984-89; mem. staff Shands Hosp. U. Fla., 1974-89, Southwest Fla. Med. Ctr, 1989—, Cape Coral Hosp., 1989—; neurobiology reviewer NSF, NIH, USPHS, 1979—; mem. merit rev. bd. neurobiology VA, 1979-82; examiner Am. Bd. Neurol. Surgery, 1984. Served to capt. U.S. Army, 1968-70. Fellow Internat. Coll. Surgeons; mem. Soc. Neurol. Surgeons, Am. Physiol. Soc., AAAS, Congress Neurol. Surgeons (exec. com. 1980-83), Am. Assn. Neurol. Surgeons (mem. exec. com. sect. spinal disorders 1982-85, pres. 1985-87), Soc. Neurosci., Am. Soc. Stereotactic and Functional Neurosurgery (pres. 1983-85; mem. exec. com. 1985-89), Internat. Congress Physiol. Sci., Brain Surgery Soc., Neurosurgery Forum, AMA, Alachua Inst. Union Physiol. Sci., Internat. Neurosurgery Forum (pres. 1984-85), S.W. Fla. Neurosurg. Assn., (pres. 1989—), S.W. Fla. Neurol. Inst. (chmn. 1989—), Fiddlesticks Country Club, Sigma Xi, Alpha Omega Alpha, Phi Sigma. Home: 15548 Fiddlesticks Blvd Fort Myers FL 33912-4037 Office: SW Fla Neuro Surgical Assocs 12700 Creek Side Lane Ste 101 Fort Myers FL 33919*

SYPHERD, PAUL STARR, microbiologist; b. Akron, Ohio, Nov. 16, 1936; s. Pearle Clinton and Mary Mildred (Flanick) S.; m. Linda J. Burden, Mar. 19, 1983; children: David Paul, Mary Denise, Gregory Dean, Cynthia Jean, Sean Michael Watkins, Scott Christopher Watkins. BS, Ariz. State U., 1959; MS, U. Ariz., 1960; PhD, Yale U., 1963. NIH postdoctoral fellow U. Calif., San Diego, 1962-64; asst. prof. U. Ill., Urbana, 1964-68, assoc. prof., 1968-70; assoc. prof. microbiology U. Calif. Coll. Medicine, Irvine, 1970-72, prof., 1972-93, chmn. dept., 1974-87, vice chancellor rsch., 1989-93, dean grad. studies, 1989-93; sr. v.p., provost U. Ariz, Tucson, 1993—; mem. NIH study sect., 1977-80, 87-91, chmn., 1990-91; mem. microbiology test com. Nat. Bd. Med. Examiners, 1980-84; mem. panel on basic biomed. scis. Nat. Rsch. Coun., 1981-86. Editor Jour. Bacteriology, 1979-83, mem. editorial bd., 1969-74; editor Molecular and Cellular Biology, 1980-87; contbr. articles to profl. jours. Sr. fellow NSF, 1970. Mem. AAAS, Am. Soc. Microbiology, Am. Soc. for Biochemistry and Molecular Biology, Am. Acad. for Microbiology. Office: U Ariz 512 Administration Tucson AZ 85721

SYRON, RICHARD FRANCIS, financial services executive, economist; b. Boston, Oct. 25, 1943; s. Dominick Richard and Elizabeth (McQuire) S.; m. Margaret Mary Garatoni, Oct. 21, 1972; children: Erin Elizabeth, Brendan Paul. BS in Econs.-Acctg. with high honors, Boston Coll., 1966; MA in Econs., Tufts U., 1969, PhD in Econs., 1971. Dep. dir. budget Commonwealth of Mass., 1973-74; v.p., economist Fed. Res. Bank of Boston, 1974-82, sr. v.p., econ. advisor, 1982-85; exec. asst. to sec. U.S. Treasury, Washington, 1979-80; dep. sec. for econ. policy U.S. Treasury, 1980-81; asst. to Chmn. Volcker Fed. Res. Bd., Washington, 1981-82; pres., CEO Fed. Home Loan Bank of Boston, 1986-88; pres., chief exec. officer Fed. Res. Bank of Boston, 1989-94; chmn. Am. Stock Exch., N.Y.C., 1994—; vice chmn. Boston Coll.; past chmn. Boston Pvt. Industry Coun.; bd. dirs. John Hancock Mut. Life Ins. Co., Boston. Author: Urban Fire Insurance, 1972; contbr. articles to profl. jours. Teaching fellow Tufts U., 1966-69. Mem. Boston Econ. Club (past pres.), Comml. Club Boston, Clover Club (Boston), Wianno Yacht Club, N.Y. Athletic Club, N.Y. Athletic Club Yacht Club, Siwanoy Country Club. Office: Am Stock Exch 86 Trinity Pl New York NY 10006-1872

SYROPOULOS, MIKE, school system director; b. Kato Hora, Navpactos, Greece, Jan. 18, 1934; came to U.S., 1951; s. Polykarpos Dimitri and Constantoula P. (Konstantinopoulos) S.; m. Sandra Francis Flick, Jan. 3, 1942; children: Pericles, Connie, Tina. BS, Wayne State U., 1960, MEd, 1965, EdD, 1971. Cert. secondary tchr., Mich. Tchr. Detroit Pub. Schs., 1960-66, dept. head, 1966-67, acting supr., 1967-69, rsch. asst., 1969-74, program assoc., 1976—; asst. dir. Wayne (Mich.) County Intermediate Dist., 1974-76. Contbr. articles to reports. V.p. St. John Greek Orthodox Ch., Sterling Heights, Mich., 1987, pres., 1988. With U.S. Army, 1956-58. Mem. ASCD, Am. Edn. Rsch. Assn., Am. Hellenic Edn. Progressive Assn. (athletic dir. 1992, treas. 1994, sec. 1995), Mich. Assn. Supervision Curriculum (bd. dirs. 1994-95, 95-96), Mich. Edn. Rsch. Assn. Greek Orthodox. Avocation: golfing. Home: 46602 Red River Rd Macomb MI 48044 Office: Detroit Pub Schs 5035 Woodward Ave Detroit MI 48202-4015

SYTSMA, FREDRIC A., lawyer; b. Grand Rapids, Mich., Jan. 12, 1944. BA, Mich. State U., 1964; JD, U. Mich., 1968. Bar: Mich. 1968. Mem. Varnum, Riddering, Schmidt & Howlett, Grand Rapids. Fellow Am. Coll. Trust and Estate Counsel; mem. ABA, State Bar Mich. (mem. coun. probate and estate planning sect. 1977—, chmn. 1986-87), Grand Rapids Bar Assn. Office: Varnum Riddering Schmidt & Howlett PO Box 352 333 Bridge St NW Grand Rapids MI 49501-0352

SYVERTSON, CLARENCE ALFRED, engineering and research management consultant; b. Mpls., Jan. 12, 1926; s. Alfred and Esther Louise (Goertemiller) S.; m. Helen Hammond Gonnella, May 4, 1953 (dec. May 1981); 1 child, Marguerite Louise.; m. JoAnn Mary Caruso, May 8, 1982. B. Aero. Engring., U. Minn., 1946, M.S., 1948; postgrad., Stanford U., 1950-57; grad., Advanced Mgmt. Program, Harvard U., 1977. Research scientist Ames Aero. Lab., NACA, Moffett Field, Calif., 1948-58; exec. dir. Joint Dept. Transp./NASA Civil Aviation Research and Devel. Policy Study, 1970-71; with Ames Research Center, NASA, Moffett Field, 1958-84; dep. dir. Ames Research Center, NASA, 1969-78, dir., 1978-84; mem. adv. bd. Coll. Engring., U. Calif., Berkeley, 1980-85; cons. prof. Stanford U., 1985-88. Served with U.S. Army, 1946-47. Recipient invention and contbn. award NASA, 1964, Exceptional Service medal, 1971, Disting. Service medal, 1984, Outstanding Achievement award U. Minn., 1982, Commanders award for civilian service U.S. Army, 1984. Fellow AIAA (Lawrence Sperry award 1957), Am. Astronautical Soc.; mem. Nat. Acad. Engring. Home: 15725 Apollo Heights Ct Saratoga CA 95070-6361

SZABAD, GEORGE MICHAEL, lawyer, former mayor; b. Nizhni Novgorod, Russia, Feb. 21, 1917; s. Michael and Nita (Szereszewski) S.; m. Shirley Meyers, Nov. 8, 1938 (dec. Dec. 1992); children: Peter James, Ellen Jo Szabad Ljung; m. Janet Fulton, Dec. 16, 1995. B.S., Columbia U., 1937, LL.B., 1939. Bar: N.Y. 1940. Participated reorgn. Asso. Gas & Electric System, 1940-42; with Dept. Labor, 1942-47, chief appellate sect., 1944-47; with Dept. State, 1945-46; with firm Blum, Haimoff, Gersen, Lipson, Slavin & Szabad, N.Y.C., 1947—, ptnr., 1949-80; former mayor Village of Scarsdale, N.Y.; v.p. Burndy Corp., 1956-76, sr. v.p., 1976-82. Served with USCG, 1943; Served with OSS, U.S. Army, 1945. Mem. Am. Arbitration Assn. (panel), Assn. Bar City N.Y., Am., Fed. bar assns. Club: Scarsdale Town. Home: 3300 Darby Rd Haverford PA 19041-1061 *Apart from personal relationships and professional and corporate career, my greatest fulfillment comes from the work in the field of human and intergroup relations to preserve and strengthen the American pluralist miracle, based on the balance of unity and diversity.*

SZABLYA, HELEN MARY, author, language professional, lecturer; b. Budapest, Hungary, Sept. 6, 1934; came to U.S., 1963; d. Louis and Helen (Bartha) Kovacs; m. John Francis Szablya, June 12, 1951; children: Helen, Janos, Louis, Stephen, Alexandra, Rita, Dominique-Mary. Diploma in Sales, Mktg., U.B.C., 1962; BA in Fgn. Lang., Lit., Wash. State U., 1976. Freelance writer, translator, 1967—; columnist Cath. News, Trinidad, W.I., 1980-91; adult educator TELOS Bellevue (Wash.) Community Coll., 1987-89; adult educator Pullman-Spokane (Wash.) Community Coll., 1976-80; faculty Christian Writers' Conf., Seattle, 1983-88, Pacific Northwest Writers' Conf., Seattle, Tacoma, 1987—; hon. consul for Wash., Oreg., Idaho Republic of Hungary, 1993—; lectr. Washington Commn. for Humanities, 1987-89. Author: (with others) Hungary Remembered, 1986 (Guardian of Liberty award, 1986, George Washington Honor medal, Freedoms Found. award 1988), 56-os Cserkészcsapat, 1986, (with others) The Fall of the Red Star, 1996 (1st prize Wash. Press Assn.); pub., editor Hungary Internat. newsletter, 1990-93; columnist Hungarian Bus. Weekly, 1994—; translator: Emlèkezünk, 1986, Mind Twisters, 1987. Recipient Nat. 1st place editorial Nat. Fedn. Press Women, 1987, Senator Tom Martin Meml. award Pacific N.W. Writers Conf., 1979; grantee Hungarian Am. Assn. Wash., 1986, Wash. Com. for Humanities, 1986; named Community Woman of Yr., Am. Bus. Women Assn., 1990. Mem. AAUW, Wash. Press Assn. (pres. 1987-88, 1st and 2d place awards, several editorial and profile awards 1983, 87, 89, 90, 91, 92, Communicator of Achievement award 1987), Nat. Fedn. Press Women (Affiliate Pres.' award 1988, bd. dirs. edn. fund northwest quadrant, mem. 21st century planning com.), Authors Guild, Am. Translators Assn., Arpad Acad. (Gold medal 1987), Nat. Writers Club, Internat. P.E.N. Club, Sigma Delta Chi (editorial award 1989). Avocations: children, reading, dancing, swimming, traveling. Home and Office: 4416 134th Pl SE Bellevue WA 98006-2104

SZABLYA, JOHN FRANCIS, electrical engineer, consultant; b. Budapest, Hungary, June 25, 1924; arrived in Can., 1957, naturalized, 1962; came to U.S., 1963, naturalized, 1979; s. John and Alexandra (Huszar) S.; m. Helen M. Bartha-Kovacs, June 12, 1951; children—Helen A., Janos L., Louis J., Stephen J.P., Alexandra H.R., Rita H.C., Dominique-Mary H. Diploma edn., Jozsef Nador U., Budapest, 1948, diploma engring., 1947, Dr. Econs., 1948. Registered profl. engr., Wash., Mont., Alaska, Wyo., Oreg., Colo., Idaho, B.C. and Ont., Can. Design engr. Ganz Elec. Works, Budapest, 1947-56; assoc. prof. Tech. U. Budapest, 1951-56; assoc. prof. U. B.C., Vancouver, 1957-63; prof. elec. engring. Wash. State U., 1963-82, now prof. emeritus; vis. prof. Technische Universitat Braunschweig, 1973-74, U. W.I., 1983—, U. Wash., 1985—, Seattle U., 1987; mgr. electrical, instrumentation and control engring. EBASCO Services Inc., 1981-90; ret., 1990; cons. engr., v.p. Szablya Cons., Inc., 1990—. Contbr. numerous articles to profl. jours., publ. over 150 articles. Recipient Zipernowszky medal Hungarian Inst. Elec. Engrs., 1954, Academia Gold medal ARPAD, 1991. Fellow IEEE, Instn. Elec. Engrs. (London); mem. Osterreichischer Verband der Elekrotechnik, European Register Higher Tech. Professions, Sigma Xi. Roman Catholic. Home: 4416 134th Pl SE Bellevue WA 98006-2104

SZABO, ALBERT, architect, educator; b. N.Y.C., Nov. 7, 1925; s. Benjamin and Jane (Margolies) S.; m. Brenda Dyer, Dec. 26, 1951; children: Ellen Szabo Laughlin, Stephen, Rebecca Szabo Salvadori, Jeannette. Student, Bklyn. Coll., 1942-47, Inst. Design, Chgo., 1947-48; MArch, Harvard U., 1952. Apprentice Marcel Breuer Architect, 1947-48; instr. Inst. Design, Chgo., 1951-53; prof. architecture Grad. Sch. Design Harvard U., Cambridge, Mass., 1954-96; prof. emeritus, 1996—; chmn. dept. archtl. scis. Harvard U., Cambridge, Mass., 1964-68, assoc. chmn., head tutor dept. visual and environ. studies, 1968-70, prof. visual and environ. studies, chmn. dept. visual and environ. studies, 1970-72, sec. faculty design, 1964-74, prof. visual and environ. studies, 1970-91; archtl. design practice with Brenda Dyer Szabo, Chgo. and Cambridge, 1953—; ptnr. Soltan/Szabo Assocs., Inc., Cambridge, 1967-71; vis. prof. Rensselaer Poly. Inst., 1967-68; Fulbright cons. to municipality of Tehran, Iran; Fulbright Hayes lectr. in architecture, Tehran, 1972, Kabul U. Afghanistan, 1974-76; cons. U.S. AID, Afghanistan, 1974-76, Govt. Afghanistan, 1974-76; acting curator Loeb Fellowship in Advanced Environ. Studies, 1974, cons. King Faisal U. Coll. Architecture and Planning, 1983; mem. edn. com. Boston Archtl. Ctr. Sch. Architecture, 1981-90; Osgood Hooker prof. visual art Faculty of Arts and Scis., 1991-96, prof. emeritus, 1996—. Author: (with others) The Shape of Our Cities, 1957; editor: (with others) Housing generated by User Needs, 1972, (with B.D. Szabo) Preliminary Notes on Indigenous Architecture of Afghanistan, 1978, (with T.J. Barfield) Afghanistan: An Atlas of Indigenous Domestic Architecture, 1991 (Outstanding Acad. Book award ALA 1992). Served with USAAF, 1944-45. Recipient Alpha Rho Chi medal Harvard U., 1952; Wheelwright travelling fellow Harvard U., 1963, Nat. Endowment for Arts fellow, 1980; Tozier Fund rsch. grantee Harvard U., 1963, Milton Fund rsch. grantee, 1966, 72, 77, 84, 87, Faculty rsch. grantee, 1978, The Aga Khan Program Islamic Architecture grantee, 1988. Mem. Boston Soc. Architects (assoc.), AIA, Assn. Collegiate Schs. Architecture (N.E. regional dir. 1969-70), Mass. Assn. Architects. Office: Harvard U Carpenter Ctr 19 Prescott St Cambridge MA 02138-3902

SZABO, BARNA ALADAR, mechanical engineering educator, mining engineer; b. Martonvasar, Hungary, Sept. 21, 1935; came to U.S., 1967, naturalized, 1974; s. Jozsef and Gizella (Ivanyi) S.; m. Magdalin Gerstmayer, July 23, 1960; children: Mark, Nicholas. B.A.Sc., U. Toronto, Ont., Can., 1962; M.S., SUNY, Buffalo, 1966, Ph.D., 1969. Registered profl. engr., Mo. Mining engr. Internat. Nickel Co. Can., 1960-62; engr. Acres Cons. Services Ltd., Niagara Falls, Can., 1962-66; instr. SUNY, Buffalo, 1966-68; mem. faculty Washington U., St. Louis, 1968—, prof. mech. engring., 1974—, Albert P. and Blanche Y. Greensfelder prof., 1975—, dir. Ctr. Computational Mechanics, 1977-92; chmn. engring. software Rsch. and Devel., Inc., St. Louis, 1989—. Author: (with Ivo Babuska) Finite Element Analysis, 1991; contbr. articles to profl. jours. Mem. ASME, Hungarian Acad. Sci., Soc. Engring. Sci., Internat. Assn. Computational Mechanics. Club: St. Louis Soaring Assn. Home: 48 Crestwood Dr Clayton MO 63105-3033 Office: Washington U Campus Box 1129 Saint Louis MO 63130-4899

SZABO, DANIEL, government official; b. Budapest, Hungary, Mar. 23, 1933; came to U.S., 1950, naturalized, 1954; s. Alexander and Maria (Berger) S.; m. Corinne Holiber, July 3, 1955; children—Nancy Beth, Peter Stuart. B.A., CCNY, 1957; M.A., Johns Hopkins U., 1959. Internat. economist U.S. Tariff Commn., 1959-60; desk officer for Vietnam, Cambodia and Laos U.S. Dept. Commerce, 1960-63; spl. asst. to U.S. Senator Jacob K. Javits, 1963-69; dep. asst. sec. state for Inter-Am. Affairs, Washington, 1969-74; sr. adviser Inter-Am. Devel. Bank, Washington, 1974-95; cons Rockville, Md., 1995—; mem. nat. adv. coun. Am. Jewish Com. Mem. World Affairs Coun. of Washington. Served with U.S. Army, 1954-56. Home: 11600 Danville Dr Rockville MD 20852-3716 *In approaching life I want my work to represent a service to our society. I am attracted to new ideas and new ways of solving old problems.*

SZABO, DENIS, criminologist, educator; b. Budapest, Hungary, June 4, 1929; s. Jenö and Catherine (Zsiga) S.; m. Sylvie Grotard; children—Catherine, Marianne. Doctorate in Social and Polit. Scis., U. Louvain, Belgium, 1956; diploma in criminology, Sorbonne U., Paris, 1958; hon. doctorate, U. Sienna, Italy, 1984, U. Budapest, Hungary, 1985, U. Aix-Marseille, 1992. Asst. in sociology U. Louvain, 1951-56; lectr. sociology Cath. Univs., Paris, Lyon, 1956-58; mem. research group Centre Nat. de la Recherche Scientifique, Paris, 1954-58; asst. prof. sociology U. Montreal, 1958, assoc. prof., 1959-66, founder, dir. dept. criminology, 1960-70, prof., 1966—; founder, dir. Internat. Center for Comparative Criminology, 1969-84; prof. emeritus, 1995—; emeritus prof. law U. Ecuador, Quito, 1984. Author, editor: Canadian Criminal Justice System, 1977, Criminologie et Politique Criminelle, 1978, La Criminologie Empirique au Quebec, 1985, Science et Crime, 1986, De L'Anthropologie a la criminologie comparee, 1993, Le Traite di criminologie Empirique, 1993. Decorated officer Order Can.; recipient Beccaria award German Society Criminology, 1970; named prof. emeritus Law Faculty, Central U. Ecuador, Quito, 1984. Fellow Royal Soc. Can., Am. Sociol. Soc., Am. Soc. Criminology (exec. coun., Sutherland award 1968); mem. Internat. Soc. Criminology (pres. 1978-85, hon. pres.), Can. Soc. Criminology (v.p. 1962-64), Soc. de Criminology (v.p. 1962-64), Soc. de Criminologie du Que. (sec.-gen. 1960-70), Internat. Assn. Sociology, Nat. Order of Merit (comdr. Ivory coast 1987), Hungarian Acad. Scis. (elected). Roman Catholic. Home: PO Box 26, Georgeville, PQ Canada J0B 1T0 Office: 3150 Jean Brillant, Montreal, PQ Canada H3C 3J7

SZABO, PETER JOHN, investment company executive, financial planner, mining engineer, lawyer; b. Bklyn., Nov. 22, 1946; s. Paul Simon and Marita Ellen (Coughlin) S.; m. Dorothy Anne Steward, Nov. 14, 1970; children: Peter, David, John Paul Steward. BS in Mining Engring., Columbia U., 1968; LLB, LaSalle Law Sch., 1975; MS in Fin. Planning, Coll. Fin. PLanning, 1994. registered profl. engr., CFP. Mining engr. Halecrest Co., Mt. Hope, N.J., 1973-74; mgr. solid fuels & minerals Ford, Bacon & Davis, N.Y.C., 1974-75; asst. v.p. Mfrs. Hanover Trust Co., N.Y.C., 1975-77, Irving Trust Co., N.Y.C., 1977; v.p. Republic Nat. Bank of Dallas, 1977-80; mgr. bus. devel. AMOCO Minerals, Denver, 1980-84; investment broker B.J. Leonard, Denver, 1984-85; investment exec. Wedbush Nobel Cook, Denver, 1985; regional sr. v.p. Alliance Fund Distbrs., N.Y.C., 1985-92, sr. v.p., 1992—; mining engr. U.S. Bur. Mines, Dallas, 1971-72, IRS, Washington, 1972-73. Treas. Columbia Sch. Engring., 1968—. Lt. USMC, 1969-71, Vietnam, capt. Res. Mem. VFW (post sr. vice comdr. 1993-94, post comdr. 1994-95, all state team post comdrs. 1995, 16th dist. jr. vice comdr. 1995—, 16th dist. sr. vice comdr. 1996—, nat. aide-de-camp 1995-96), Mil. Order of the Cootie (sr. vice comdr. 1994-95). Republican. Roman Catholic. Avocations: sailing, golf, tennis, jogging, scripophily. Home and Office: Alliance Fund Distbrs 810 Oxford Way Benicia CA 94510-3646

SZABO, ZOLTAN, medical science educator, medical institute director; b. Szeged, Hungary, Oct. 5, 1943; came to U.S., 1967; s. Imre and Maria (Szikora) S.; m. Wanda Toy, Dec. 5, 1976; children: Eva, Maria. Student, U. Med. Sch., Szeged, 1962-65; PhD, Columbia Pacific U., 1983. Tech. dir. microsurgery lab. R.K. Davies Med. Ctr., San Francisco, 1972-80; dir. Microsurgery and Operative Endoscopy Tng. (MOET) Inst., San Francisco, 1980—; assoc. dir. advanced laparoscopic surgery tng. ctr. Sch. Medicine U. Calif., San Francisco, 1992—; rsch. assoc. oral and maxillofacial surgery U. of Pacific, San Francisco, 1980-83, adj. asst. prof., 1983—. Author: Microsurgery Techniques, vol. 1, 1974, vol. 2, 1984 (1st Place award for excellence in med. writing 1982); co-author: Tissue Approximation in Endoscopic Surgery, 1995; editor-in-chief Surgical Technology Internationa, Vol. 3, 1994, Vol. 4, 1995; contbr. chpt. books, articles to profl. jours. With U.S. Army, 1969-71. Recipient cert. of Merit, AMA, 1978, commendation Accreditation Coun. for Continuing Med. Edn., 1984, 90, 94, Spl. Recognition award Sch. Medicine Cen. U. Venezuela, 1988, Sci. Poste Sessions Hon. Mention award Am. Urol. Assn., 1992, 1st prize Roundtable for New Techs. and Innovations we. sect., 1992, James Barrett Brown award Am. Assn. Plastic Surgeons, 1993. Fellow Internat. Coll. Surgeons (Disting. Svc. award 1994); mem. Hungarian Gynecol. Soc. (hon.), Medico-Dental Study Guild Calif., Internat. Microsurg. Soc., Soc. Am. Gastrointestinal Endoscopic Surgeons (hon., 1st prize Residents and Fellows Rsch. and Sci. Presentation 1992), Am. Fertility Soc., Am. Soc. Reconstructive Microsurgery (assoc.), Am. Soc. for Peripheral Nerve. Avocations: gardening, landscaping, oil painting, travel, competitive air pistol target shooting. Office: Microsurgery Operative Endoscopy Tng Inst 153 States St San Francisco CA 94114-1403

SZALA, SCOTT J., lawyer; b. Chgo., May 30, 1953. BA, Knox Coll., 1975; JD, Northwestern U., 1978. Bar: Ill. 1978, U.S. Dist. Ct. (no. dist.) Ill. 1978, U.S. Ct. Appeals (7th cir.) 1979. Law clk. to Hon. Dom J. Rizzi Ill. Appellate Ct., 1979-80; ptnr. Winston & Strawn, Chgo. Capt. USAR (JACG), 1985—. Mem. ABA (mem. litigation, jud. adminstrn. divsn., econs. of practice, antitrust and taxation sects., mem. young lawyers divsn., trial editor Barrister Mag. 1982-88, speaker conv. Sydney, Australia 1980), Ill. State Bar Assn., Chgo. Bar Assn. (mem. young lawyers sect., co-chmn. law explorers 1982-83, moot ct. 1983-84, chmn. bench/bar com. 1984-85, mem. exec. coun. 1982-85, mem. sr. bar tort litigation 1978-84), Assn. Trial Lawyers Am. Office: Winston & Strawn 35 W Wacker Dr Chicago IL 60601-1614*

SZALKOWSKI, CHARLES CONRAD, lawyer; b. Amarillo, Tex., Apr. 14, 1948; s. Chester Casimer and Virginia Lee (Hess) S.; m. Jane Howe, Dec. 28, 1971; children: Jennifer Lee, Stephen Claude. BA, BS in Acctg., Rice U., 1971; MBA, JD, Harvard U., 1975. Bar: Tex. 1975. Assoc. Baker & Botts, L.L.P., Houston, 1975-82, ptnr., 1983—; speaker in field. Chmn. ann. fund campaign Rice U., Houston, 1991-93, chmn. fund coun., 1995-96; chmn. adminstrv. bd. St. Luke's United Meth. Ch., Houston, 1994; bd. dirs., DePalchia Children's Ctr., Houston, 1996—; adv. bd. Meth. Home, Waco, MIT Enterprise Forum of Tex., Houston, The Entrepreneurship Inst., Houston Chamber Orch. Mem. ABA (fed. regulation of securities com.), Am. Law Inst., State Bar Tex. (chmn., vice chmn. bus. law sect. 1990-92), Houston Bar Assn. (chmn., vice chmn., corp. counsel sect. 1988-90), Harvard Law Sch. Assn. Tex. (pres. 1983-84), Tex. Bus. Law Found. (bd. dirs., exec. com. 1988—, vice chmn. 1995—), Assn. Rice U. Alumni (chmn. various coms. 1981-86), Assn. for Corp. Growth (adv. bd. Houston chpt.), Lincoln's Inn Soc., Houston Philos. Soc. Office: Baker & Botts LLP 1 Shell Plz 910 Louisiana St Houston TX 77002

SZAMEK, PIERRE ERVIN, research anthropologist; b. Budapest, Hungary; s. Eugene Jeno and Olga S. Grad., The Pingry Sch., Elizabeth, N.J.; B.A., Upsala Coll., 1942; M.A., Columbia U., 1944; A.M., fellow, Princeton U., 1946, Ph.D., 1947. Corr. Cen. European Press Service, 1939; etymol. asst. in linguistic anthropology to Dr. Harold H. Bender, etymol. editor The Webster Dictionary, 1947-48; vis. post-doctoral research fellow Princeton U., 1947-48; ednl. broadcasting CBS, N.Y.C., 1948-65; research anthropologist Newark, 1950—; exec. dir. Internat. Ctr. Ednl. Advancement, 1984—, chancellor, 1989; vis. prof. anthropology Drew U., 1966-67, N.J. State Coll., 1968-71; Disting. vis. prof. Seton Hall U., 1980; lectr. New Sch. for Social Research, 1980; dir. Am. Sci. Research and Mktg.; mem. radio program Invitation to Learning, CBS Network, 1948-63; permanent chmn., moderator Invitation to Ideas, Nat. Pub. Broadcasting Series, 1981—; anthrop. cons. CBS-TV, 1950-65; chmn. bd. The Logos Scientific Rsch. Ctr., 1989; special anthrop. cons. Nat. Com. for Habitat in affiliation with UNCHS, sr. vice chmn. for Hungarian devel., the Hungarian Nat. Com. for Habitat; sr. rsch. scientist, anthrop. cons. XEL Advanced Techs. Internat. Ltd. (XELAT); chancellor Gen. Conv. Planetary Preservation; founder (with Eugene Paul Wigner and Daniel J.G. Peabody-Smidt) Millennium Three SuperProject. Author, contbg. critic: Invitation to Learning, 1966; contbg. editor Green Earth; contbr. numerous articles, broadcasts in Am. jours. and fgn. press; inventor multi-gyro ball-bearing, dual stage radio communications synthesizer; patentee. Served with USCGR, 1942-43. Decorated victory medal, knight Order of Star (Italy); knight officer Gold Cross of Royal Order of Phoenix (Greece); Order of St. Agatha (San Marino); chevalier de l'Ordre des Palmes Académiques, chevalier de la Legion d'Honneur (France); officer Order St. John (Eng.); N.J. Com. for Humanities fellow; NEH Match Fund grantee, 1947. Fellow Royal Anthrop. Inst. Gt. Britain and Ireland; mem. AAUP, Am. Oriental Soc., Am. Acad. Polit. Sci., N.J. Acad. Sci. Office: c/o Law Offices PO Box 255 Glen Ridge NJ 07028-0255

SZAREK, STANISLAW JERZY, mathematics educator; b. Ladek Zdroj, Poland, Nov. 13, 1953; came to U.S., 1980; s. Mieczyslaw and Bronislawa (Brzezinska) S.; m. Malgorzata Chwascinska, June 22, 1980; children: Martina, Natalia; 1 stepchild, Olga. M in Math., Warsaw (Poland) U., 1976; PhD in Math. Scis., Polish Acad. Scis., Warsaw, 1979. Rsch. asst. Math. Inst. Polish Acad. Scis., Warsaw, 1976-79, rsch. fellow, 1979-83; asst. prof. Case Western Res. U., Cleve., 1983-87, prof., 1987—, chair math. dept., 1994-96; vis. positions U. Ill., Urbana, 1980, Ohio State U., Columbus, 1981, U. Tex., Austin, 1981-83, Inst. des Hautes Etudes Scientifiques, Bures-Sur-Yvette, France, 1986-89, U. Paris, 1990, 92, 95, Math. Scis. Rsch. Inst., Berkeley, Calif., 1996. Contbr. articles to profl. jours. Recipient Prize of Sci. Sec., Polish Acad. Scis., 1979; rsch. grantee NSF, 1983—, U.S.-Israel Binat. Sci. Found., 1993—; Sloan fellow Alfred P. Sloan Found., 1986-88. Mem. Am. Math. Soc. Avocations: skiing, sailing, diving, bridge. Office: Case Western Res U Dept of Math Cleveland OH 44106

SZAREK, WALTER ANTHONY, chemist, educator; b. St. Catharines, Ont., Can., Apr. 19, 1938; s. Anthony and Sophia (Kania) S. BSc, McMaster U., 1960, MSc, 1962; PhD, Queen's U., 1964. Postdoctoral fellow in chemistry Ohio State U., Columbus, 1964-65; asst. prof. biochemistry Rutgers U., New Brunswick, N.J., 1965-67; asst. prof. chemistry Queen's U., Kingston, Ont., 1967-71, assoc. prof., 1971-76, prof., 1976—, dir. Carbohydrate Research Inst., 1976-85; founding mem., prin. investigator Neurochem, Inc., 1993—; cons. to govt. and industry; mem. Premier's Coun. Tech. Fund. Mem. editorial adv. bd. Carbohydrate Rsch. jour., 1973—, Jour. of Carbohydrate Chemistry, 1994—; contbr. articles on chemistry of carbohydrates to profl. jours. Recipient Teaching Excellence award Queen's U. Arts and Sci. Undergrad. Soc., 1988-89. Fellow Chem. Inst. Can.; mem. AAAS, Am. Chem. Soc. (chmn. divsn. carbohydrate chemistry 1982-83, Claude S. Hudson award in carbohydrate chemistry 1989, Melville L. Wolfrom award 1992), Inst. Theol. encounter with Sci. and Tech., Royal Soc. Chemistry, N.Y. Acad. Scis., Soc. Glycobiology. Roman Catholic. Office: Queen's U, Dept Chemistry, Kingston, ON Canada K7L 3N6

SZARWARK, ERNEST JOHN, lawyer; b. South Bend, Ind., May 11, 1951; s. Stanley I. and Genevieve (Zalejski) S.; m. Mary Christy Smith, June 3, 1978; children: Mary Crespa, Catherine Case. BS with highest honors, U. Notre Dame, 1973, JD with highest honors, 1976. Bar: Ind. 1976, U.S. Claims Ct. 1977, U.S. Tax Ct. 1977, U.S. Ct. Appeals (7th cir.) 1980, Fla. 1982, U.S. Ct. Appeals (6th cir.) 1986. Atty. advisor to Hon. Richard C.

Wilbur U.S. Tax Ct., Washington, 1976-78; assoc. Barnes & Thornburg, South Bend, 1978-85, ptnr., 1985—. Bd. dirs. South Bend Art Ctr., 1985-88; mem. fin. com. Stanley Clark Sch. Fellow Ind. Bar Found.; mem. Ind. Bar Assn. (bd. dirs. taxation sect. 1985-93, chmn. taxation sect. 1992-93), Ind. Soc. of Chgo., Polish Nat. Alliance, Michiana Arts and Scis. Counsel, South Bend Country Club. Roman Catholic. Avocations: golf, cross country skiing, numismatics, reading. Home: 1140 E Woodside St South Bend IN 46614-1482 Office: Barnes & Thornburg 600 1st Source Ctr 100 N Michigan St South Bend IN 46601-1630

SZASZ, THOMAS STEPHEN, psychiatrist, educator, writer; b. Budapest, Hungary, Apr. 15, 1920; came to U.S., 1938, naturalized, 1944; s. Julius and Lily (Wellisch) S.; m. Rosine Loshkajian, Oct. 19, 1951 (div. 1970); children: Margot Szasz Peters, Susan Marie Szasz Palmer. AB, U. Cin., 1941, MD, 1944; DSc (hon.), Allegheny Coll., 1975, U. Francisco Marroquin, Guatemala, 1979. Diplomate: Nat. Bd. Med. Examiners, Am. Bd. Psychiatry and Neurology. Intern 4th Med. Service Harvard, Boston City Hosp., 1944-45; asst. resident medicine Cin. Gen. Hosp., 1945-46, asst. clinician internal medicine div. out-patient dispensary, 1946; asst. resident psychiatry U. Chgo. Clinics, 1946-47; tng. research fellow Inst. Psychoanalysis, Chgo., 1947-48; rsch. asst. Inst. Psychoanalysis, 1949-50, staff mem., 1951-56; practice medicine, specializing in psychiatry, psychoanalysis Chgo., 1949-54, Bethesda, Md., 1954-56, Syracuse, N.Y., 1956—; prof. psychiatry SUNY Health Sci. Ctr., Syracuse, 1956-90, prof. psychiatry emeritus, 1990—; vis. prof. dept. psychiatry U. Wis., Madison, 1962, Marquette U. Sch. Medicine, Milw., 1968, U. N.Mex., 1981; holder numerous lectureships, including C.P. Snow lectr. Ithaca Coll., 1970; E.S. Meyer Meml. lectr. U. Queensland Med. Sch.; Lambie-Dew orator Sydney U., 1977; Mem. nat. adv. com. bd. Tort and Med. Yearbook; cons. com. mental hygiene N.Y. State Bar Assn.; mem. research adv. panel Inst. Study Drug Addiction; adv. bd. Corp. Econ. Edn., 1977—. Author: Pain and Pleasure, 1957, The Myth of Mental Illness, 1961, Law, Liberty and Psychiatry, 1963, Psychiatric Justice, 1965, The Ethics of Psychoanalysis, 1965, Ideology and Insanity, 1970, The Manufacture of Madness, 1970, The Second Sin, 1973, Ceremonial Chemistry, 1974, Heresies, 1976, Karl Kraus and the Soul-Doctors, 1976, Schizophrenia: The Sacred Symbol of Psychiatry, 1976, Psychiatric Slavery, 1977, The Theology of Medicine, 1977, The Myth of Psychotherapy, 1978, Sex by Prescription, 1980, The Therapeutic State, 1984, Insanity: The Idea and its Consequences, 1987, The Untamed Tongue: A Dissenting Dictionary, 1990, Our Right to Drugs: The Case for a Free Market, 1992, A Lexicon of Lunacy, 1993, Cruel Compassion, 1994, The Meaning of Mind, 1996; editor: The Age of Madness, 1973; cons. editor of psychiatry and psychology: Stedman's Medical Dictionary, 22d edit, 1973; contbg. editor: Reason, 1974—, Libertarian Rev., 1986—; mem. editorial bd. Psychoanalytic Rev, 1965—, Jour. Contemporary Psychotherapy, 1968—, Law and Human Behavior, 1977—, Jour. Libertarian Studies, 1977—, Children and Youth Services Rev, 1978—, Am. Jour. Forensic Psychiatry, 1980—, Free Inquiry, 1980—. Comdr. M.C., USNR, 1954-56. Recipient Stella Feiss Hofheimer award U. Cin., 1944, Holmes-Munsterberg award Internat. Acad. Forensic Psychology, 1969; Wisdom award honor, 1970; Acad. prize Institutum atque Academia Auctorum Internationalis, Andorra, 1972; Distinguished Service award Am. Inst. Pub. Service, 1974; Martin Buber award Midway Counseling Center, 1974, Thomas S. Szasz award Ctr. Ind. Thought , 1990, Alfred R. Lindesmith award for achievement in field of scholarship and writing Drug Policy Found., 1991; others; named Humanist of Year Am. Humanist Assn., 1973; Hon. fellow Postgrad. Center for Mental Health, 1961, Mencken award, 1981, Humanist Laureate, 1984, Statue of Liberty-Ellis Island Found. Archives Roster, 1986. Fellow Am. Psychiat. Assn. (life), Am. Psychoanalytic Assn., Internat. Psychoanalytic Soc., Western N.Y. Psychoanalytic Soc. Home: 4739 Limberlost Ln Manlius NY 13104-1405 Office: 750 E Adams St Syracuse NY 13210-2306

SZATHMÁRY, LOUIS ISTVÁN, II, former restaurateur, writer; b. Rakospalota, Hungary, June 2, 1919; came to U.S., 1951, naturalized, 1963; s. Louis Istvan and Irene (Strauss) S.; m. Sadako Tanino, May 9, 1960; 1 dau., Magda. Ph.D., U. Budapest, 1944. Chef New Eng. Province Jesuits, Manresa Island, Conn., 1952-55; exec. chef Mut. Broadcasting System, N.Y.C., 1955-58; plant supt. Reddi Fox, Inc., Darien, Conn., 1958-59; exec. chef Armour & Co., Chgo., 1959-64; chef, owner Bakery Restaurant, Chgo., 1962-89; owner Louis Szathmáry Assocs.; chef laureate Johnson and Wales U., Providence. Author: The Bakery Restaurant Cookbook; author-editor: Cookery Americana, 16 vols. Mem. AFTRA, Chgo. Acad. Scis. (trustee emeritus), Internat. Food, Wine and Traveel Writers Assn., Soc. Profl. Mgmt. Cons., Coun. on Hotel, Restaurant and Instnl. Edn., SAG, Acad. Chefs U.S.A., Nat. Space Soc. (bd. govs.), Grolier Club (N.Y.C.), Caxton Club, Cliff Dwellers Club. *I always enjoyed my work so much that it was embarrassing to receive payment for what I did with gusto and zest. I love to live - so I hope, that when I die, the world will be a little bit better than it was, when I was born - and my life and work contributed - if not more, then a teeny weeny little bit - to this improvement.*

SZCZARBA, ROBERT HENRY, mathematics educator, mathematician; b. Dearborn, Mich., Nov. 27, 1932; s. Michael and Julie (Hanas) S.; m. Arlene Lee Roschild, June 18, 1955; children: Garrett Lee, Cheryl Anne. BS, U. Mich., 1955; MA, U. Chgo., 1957, PhD, 1960. Instr. DePaul U., 1959-60; ONR rsch. assoc. Yale U., New Haven, 1960-61, asst. prof. math., 1961-65, assoc. prof., 1965-74, prof., 1974—; chmn. dept. Yale U., 1980-83; acting chmn. dept. Yale U., New Haven, fall 1995, dep. provost phys. scis. and engring., 1989-95; vis. mem. Inst. Advanced Study, Princeton, N.J., 1964-65, 72. Author: Calculus in Vector Spaces, 1979, Multivariable Calculus, 1982. Mem. Bethany Bd. Fin., Conn., 1971-77; treas. Bethany Democratic Com., 1980-83. NSF postdoctoral fellow, 1964-65. Mem. Am. Math. Soc., Conn. Acad. Arts and Scis. Office: Yale U Dept Math PO Box 208283 New Haven CT 06520-8283

SZCZEPANSKI, SLAWOMIR ZBIGNIEW STEVEN, lawyer; b. Lodz, Poland, Mar. 9, 1948; s. Wladyslaw and Janina Szczepanski; m. Cynthia Ellen Weagley, Sept. 30, 1972; children: Christine, Diana. BS in Chem. Engring., Rensselaer Poly. Inst., 1971; MS in Chem. Engring., Rennselaer Poly. Inst., 1972; JD, Union U., Albany, N.Y., 1975. Bar: N.Y. 1976, D.C. 1976, Ill. 1977, U.S. Dist. Ct. (no. dist.) Ill. 1977, U.S. Ct. Appeals (fed. cir.) 1988. Atty. Philips Petroleum Co., Washington, 1975-77; from assoc. to ptnr. Willian, Brinks, Hofer, Gilson & Lione, Chgo., 1977—. Author: Licensing in Foreign and Domestic Operations, 1985—; editor (legal periodical) Licensing Law and Business Report, 1986—; contbr. articles to profl. jours. Mem. ABA, Am. Intellectual Property Law Assn., Internat. Assn. Protection Indsl. Property, Assn. Trial Lawyers of Am., Nat. Advocates Soc., Licensing Execs. Soc., Intellectual Property Law Assn. of Chgo., Univ. Club. Avocations: tennis, sailing. Home: 641 W Willow St Apt 107 Chicago IL 60614-5176 Office: Arnold White & Durkee 800 Quaker Tower 321 N Clark St Chicago IL 60610

SZCZESNY, RONALD WILLIAM, lawyer; b. Detroit, Nov. 26, 1940; s. Raymond Joseph and Sophie (Welc) S.; children: Timothy, Laurie, Kristen; m. Susan Joy Feragne, May 25, 1985. BA in Chemistry, Wayne State U., 1963, JD, 1972. Bar: Mich. 1975, U.S. Dist. Ct. (ea. dist.) Mich. 1975, U.S. Tax Ct. 1975, U.S. Supreme Ct. 1983, U.S. Ct. Appeals 1985. Rsch. chemist Wyandotte Chems., Mich., 1961-64; exptl. chemist Cadillac Motor Car Co., Detroit, 1964-66, gen. supr. material lab., 1966-69; materials engr., 1969-72, staff analysis engr. Gen. Motors Co., Warren, Mich., 1972-77; assoc. firm Zeff and Zeff & Materna, Detroit, 1977-89; assoc. Stern Cohan and Stern, Southfield, Mich., 1989—. Mem. ABA, ATLA, Mich. Trial Lawyers Assn., Detroit Bar Assn., Oakland County Bar Assn., Macomb County Bar Assn., Soc. Automotive Engrs., Advocates Bar Assn., Am. Acad. Forensic Scis., Am. Welding Soc., Am. Boat & Yacgt Coun., Internat. Assn. Arson Investigators, Mich. Assn. Arson Investigators, U. Mich. Pres.'s Club, Am. Soc. Safety Engrs., Nat. Assn. Fire Investigators, Nat. Fire Protection Assn. Republican. Roman Catholic. Home: 27300 Spring Arbor Dr Southfield MI 48076-3543 Office: PO Box 440 Southfield MI 48037-0440

SZE, ANDY HOK-FAN, transportation executive; b. Hong Kong, Feb. 21, 1951; s. Wing-Cheung and Soo-Feng (Chan) S.; m. Lola Kong, Aug. 2, 1955; children: Stephanie Ping-Ping, Andrew Dunway. BS in Indsl. Engring., Ill. Inst. Tech., 1973; MS, Northwestern U., 1976; MBA, U. Chgo., 1982. Dir. research and devel. Clipper Exxpress Co., Chgo., 1976-78, asst. v.p. movement control, 1979-80, v.p. ops., 1980-82, exec. v.p., 1982-83, pres., chief exec. officer, 1983—; mem. bus. adv. com. Transp. Ctr. Northwestern U.; bd. dirs. Agile Freight System, Lemont, Ill., Agrl. Express Am., Lemont. Bus. adv. council Coll. Bus. Adminstrn. U. Ill., Chgo., 1984—; examiner Malcolm Baldridge Nat. Quality award, 1991, 92. Recipient Dwight D. Gardener award Am. Inst. Ind. Engrs., 1972; Murphy fellow Northwestern, 1973. Mem. Am. Soc. Transp. and Logistics. Clubs: Chgo. Yacht, Econ. Chgo. Avocation: fishing.

SZE, HELEN WANG YEE, lawyer; b. Shanghai, Sept. 21, 1953; d. Shiu Chuen and Fung Sin (Yu) S. BA, U. Hawaii, 1975; MBA, Cornell U., 1978, JD, 1979. Bar: N.Y. 1980, Calif. 1982. Assoc. Whitman, Breed, Abbott & Morgan, N.Y.C., 1979-82, Graham & James, Singapore, 1982-83, Orrick, Herrington & Sutcliffe, San Francisco, 1984-86, AirTouch Comm. (formerly Pactel Corp.), San Francisco, 1986—. Office: AirTouch Comm 1 California St San Francisco CA 94111

SZE, SIMON M., engineer; b. Nanking, China, Mar. 21, 1930. BS, Nat. Taiwan U., 1957; MS, U. Wash., 1960; PhD, Stanford U., 1963. Prof. engring. Nat. Chiao Tung U. Fellow IEEE; mem. Nat. Acad. Engring. Office: Inst Electronics, Nat Chiao Tung U/1001 Ta Hsueh Rd, Hsin-chu Taiwan*

SZEBEHELY, VICTOR G., aeronautical engineer; b. Budapest, Hungary, Aug. 10, 1921; s. Victor and Vilma (Stockl) S.; m. Jo Betsy Lewallen, May 21, 1970; 1 dau., Julia. M.E., U. Budapest, 1943, Ph.D. in Engring, 1945; Dr. (hon.), Eotvos U. Budapest, 1991. Asst. prof. U. Budapest, 1945-47; research asso. State U. Pa., 1947-48; asso. prof. Va. Poly. Inst., 1948-53; research asso. Model Basin, U.S. Navy, 1953-57; research mgr. Gen. Electric Co., 1957-62; asso. prof. astronomy Yale U., 1962-68; prof. aerospace engring. U. Tex., Austin, 1968—; chmn. dept. U. Tex., 1977-81, R.B. Curran Centennial chair in engring., 1983—; cons. NASA-Johnson Space Center, U.S. Air Force Space Command, Lawrence Berkeley Lab., U. Calif. Author 18 books; contbr. over 200 articles on space research, celestial mechanics and ship dynamics to profl. jours. Knighted by Queen Juliana of Netherlands, 1956. Fellow AIAA, AAAS; mem. Am. Astron. Soc. (Brouwer award div. dynamical astronomy 1977), Internat. Astron. Union (pres. commn. on celestial mechanics), NAE, European Acad. Arts, Scis., Lit. Home: 2501 Jarratt Ave Austin TX 78703 Office: U Tex Dept Aerospace Engring & Engring Mechs Austin TX 78712

SZEGO, CLARA MARIAN, cell biologist, educator; b. Budapest, Hungary, Mar. 23, 1916; came to U.S., 1921, naturalized, 1927; d. Paul S. and Helen (Elek) S.; m. Sidney Roberts, Sept. 14, 1943. A.B., Hunter Coll., 1937; M.S. (Garvan fellow), U. Minn., 1939, Ph.D., 1942. Instr. physiology U. Minn., 1942-43; Minn. Cancer Research Inst. fellow, 1943-44; rsch. assoc. OSRD, Nat. Bur. Standards, 1944-45, Worcester Found. Exptl. Biology, 1945-47; rsch. instr. physiol. chemistry Yale U. Sch. Medicine, 1947-48; mem. faculty UCLA, 1948—, prof. biology, 1960—. Named Woman of Year in Sci. Los Angeles Times, 1957-58; Guggenheim fellow, 1956; named to Hunter Coll. Hall of Fame, 1987. Fellow AAAS; mem. Am. Physiol. Soc., Am. Soc. Cell Biology, Endocrine Soc. (CIBA award 1953), Soc. for Endocrinology (Gt. Britain), Biochem. Soc. (Gt. Britain), Internat. Soc. Rsch. Reprodn., Phi Beta Kappa (pres. UCLA chpt. 1973-74), Sigma Xi (pres. UCLA chpt. 1976-77). Achievements include rsch. and numerous publs. on steroid protein interactions, mechanisms of hormone action and lysosome participation in normal cell function. Home: 1371 Marinette Rd Pacific Palisades CA 90272-2627 Office: U Calif Dept Molecular Cell and Devel Biology Los Angeles CA 90095-1606

SZELENYI, IVAN, educator; b. Budapest, Apr. 17, 1938; came to the U.S., 1981; s. Gusztav and Julianna (Csapo) S.; m. Kataline Varady, Jan. 31, 1960; children: Szonja, Lilla, Balazs. PhD, Hungarian Acad. Scis., Budapest, 1973, DSc, 1990; hon. doctorate, Budapest U. Econs., 1992. Rsch. fellow Hungarian Acad. Scis., Budapest, 1963-75; found. prof. Flinders U., Adelaide, Australia, 1975-80; prof. U. Wis., Madison, 1981-86; disting. prof. CUNY Grad. Ctr., 1986-88; prof. UCLA, L.A., 1988—. Author: Urban Inequalities under State Socialism, 1983, Socialist Entrepreneurs, 1988 (C. Wright Mills award 1989); co-author: Intellectuals on the Road to Class Power, 1979. Mem. Hungarian Acad. Scis.

SZENASY, SUSAN SELMA, magazine editor; b. Vecsés, Hungary, Jan. 5, 1944; came to U.S., 1956; d. James and Ethel (Giczy) S. BA, Rutgers U., 1969, MA, 1971. Asst. editor Modern Photography, 1971-76; sr. editor Interiors, N.Y.C., 1976-78; editor-in-chief Residential Interiors, N.Y.C., 1978-81; freelance writer, 1981-86; editor-in-chief Metropolis, Bellerophon Publs., N.Y.C., 1986—; instr. design history Parsons Sch. Design, N.Y.C., 1991—; spkr., moderator design and architecture topics. Author: The Home, 1984, Light, 1986. Office: Bellerophon Publs 177 E 87th St New York NY 10128

SZENBERG, MICHAEL, economics educator, editor, consultant; b. Sosnowiec, Poland, Apr. 8, 1934; came to U.S., 1961, naturalized, 1966; s. Henry and Sara (Rosensaft) S.; m. Miriam Silverstein, Sept. 2, 1962; children: Naomi, Avi. Student, Bar Ilan U., Israel, 1959-61; BA summa cum laude, L.I. U., 1963; PhD, CUNY, 1970. Faculty L.I. U., Bklyn. Center, 1965—, prof. econs., 1974-83; prof. econs. Lubin Grad. Sch. Bus. Pace U., 1983—; dir. Ctr. Applied Rsch., 1994—; adj. prof. Hunter Coll., 1970-76, Pace U., 1975-83; founder, dir. Lecture Bur. Econs., 1973; chmn. 1st Met. Grad. Conf. Econs., 1973; assoc. mem. Ctr. Tech. Assessment, Newark Coll. Engring., 1973; vis. prof. econs. NYU, summers 1977, 78, 79; cons. in field. Author: Economics of the Israeli Diamond Industry, 1973, The Welfare Effects of Trade Restrictions: A Case Study of the Untied States Footwear Industry, 1977, The Economics of the American Footwear Industry, 2d edit., 1984; editor: Essays in Economics, The John Commons Memorial Lectures, 1986, Eminent Economists: Their Life Philosophies, 1992; assoc. editor: Am. Economist, 1973-75, editor-in-chief, 1975—; econs. co-editor: Cambridge Univ. Press Encyclopedia; contbr. articles to profl. jours. and chpts. to books. Served with Israeli Air Force, 1956-59. Recipient Dean Hudson award L.I. U., 1962, Am. Coll. Abroad award, 1962, Dean Abelson award CUNY, 1963; fellow econs. CUNY, 1963; grantee Israel Diamond Inst., 1970; recipient Irving Fisher Monograph award, 1971; fellow Internat. Honor Soc. in Econs., 1972; grantee Dept. Labor, 1975; recipient Kenan award for teaching excellence Pace U., 1983, Schalkenbach Found. Research award, 1987, First Prize Recognition award for scholarly productivity, 1989, Tchr. of the Year Pace U., 1992, Teaching Excellence award Acad. Bus. Admin., 1993, Achievement award CUNY, 1993, Outstanding Publication award Pace U., 1993, 94, 95. Mem. Atlantic Econ. Soc., Internat. Trade and Fin. Assn., Internat. Fedn. Sci. Editors, Ea. Econ. Assn., Am. Econ. Assn., Assn. Cultural Econs., Internat. Honor Soc. Econs. (exec. bd. 1975—, regional dir. 1971-74), Optimates Soc. (pres. 1972-80). Home: 1442 E 9th St Brooklyn NY 11230-6405

SZEP, PAUL MICHAEL, editorial cartoonist; b. Hamilton, Ont., Can., July 29, 1941; came to U.S., 1966; s. Paul Joseph and Helen (Langhorne) S.; m. Angela Diane Garton, Feb. 27, 1965 (div. 1976); children: Amy, Jason. A.O.C.A., Ont. Coll. Art, 1964; A.O.C.A. hon. degree, 1975, Framingham State Coll., 1975, Worcester State Coll., 1980, William Penn Coll., 1981. Sports cartoonist Hamilton Spectator, 1958-61; graphics designer Financial Post, Toronto, Ont., 1965-66; editorial cartoonist Boston Globe, 1966—; vis. fellow Harvard U., 1981; lectr. various univs. Author: In Search of Sacred Cows, 1967, Keep Your Left Hand High, 1969, At This Point in Time, 1973, The Harder They Fall, 1975, Unvote for a New America, 1976, Them Damned Pictures, 1977, Warts and All, 1979, To a Different Drummer, 1983, The Gang of Eight, 1985, The Next Szep Book, 1985, Often in Error, Never in Doubt, 1987, And Then Jack Said to Arnie, 1991, And Then Arnie Told Chi Chi And Then Chi Chi Said to Fuzzy, 1993; editl. cartoonist Sta. WNEV-TV, Boston; contbr. Golf Digest. Served with F.A. Royal Canadian Army, 1957-58. Recipient Pulitzer prize, 1974, 77, award Sigma Delta Chi, 1974, 77, Toyl award Boston Jaycees, 1976, Headliners award, 1977, Reuben award for best editorial cartoonist Nat. Cartoonist Soc., 1979, Thomas Nast award; Internat. Cartoonist award, Best Sports Cartoonist award Nat. Cartoonists Soc., 1988. Mem. Soc. Illustrators, Kittansett Club, Harvard Club, Weston Golf Club, Sterling Country Club. Home: 7 Stetson St Brookline MA 02146-3406 Office: Boston Globe Boston MA 02107

SZER, WLODZIMIERZ, biochemist, educator; b. Warsaw, Poland, June 3, 1924; came to U.S., 1968; s. Max and Chaia (Szapiro) S.; m. Felicja Kirsz, Oct. 1, 1946; children: Caroline, Ilona. M.S. in Chemistry, U. Lodz (Poland), 1950; Ph.D. in Biochemistry, Inst. Biochemistry and Biophysics, Polish Acad. Scis., 1959. Dozent Inst. Biochemistry and Biophysics, Warsaw, 1963-68; asst. prof., then assoc. prof. biochemistry Sch. Medicine, NYU, N.Y.C., 1968-73, prof., 1973—. Contbr. articles and revs. to profl. jours. Recipient Jacob K. Parnas Polish Biochem. Soc., 1964; recipient Faculty Am. Cancer Soc., 1973; USPHS grantee, 1971—. Mem. Am. Soc. Biol. Chemists, Harvey Soc. Office: NYU Sch Medicine Dept Biochemistry 550 1st Ave New York NY 10016-6481

SZERI, ANDRAS Z., engineering educator; b. Nagyvarad, Hungary, June 6, 1934; came to U.S., 1967; s. Andras F. and Julie (Farkas) S.; m. Mary J. Parkinson, Apr. 25, 1962; children: Andrew J., Elizabeth C., Maria J. B.S. with 1st class honors, U. Leeds, Eng., 1959, Ph.D., 1962. Research engr. English Electric Co., Stafford, Eng., 1962-64; prof. Universidad Santa Maria, Valparaiso, Chile, 1964-66; asst. prof. U. Pitts., 1967-70, assoc. prof., 1970-76, prof. math., 1977-93, prof. mech. engring., 1977-94, chmn. dept. mech. engring., 1984-87, William Kepler Whiteford prof. engring., 1990-94; Robert Lyle Spencer prof. mech. engring., chmn. U. Del., Newark, 1994—; cons. Westinghouse Electric Co., Pitts., 1967-82; external examiner U. W.I., 1989—. Editor: Tribology, 1980. Fellow ASME (assoc. editor Jour. Tribology 1978-87, tech. editor 1987-93); mem. Am. Acad. Mechanics, The Soc. Rheology, Soc. Engring. Sci., Soc. Natural Philosophy. Office: U Del Dept Mech Engring Newark DE 19716

SZEWCZYK, ALBIN ANTHONY, engineering educator; b. Chgo., Feb. 26, 1935; s. Andrew Aloysius and Jean Cecelia (Wojcik) S.; m. Barbara Valerie Gale, June 16, 1956; children: Karen Marie Knop, Lisa Anne, Andrea Jean Simpson, Terese Helen Sinka. BS, U. Notre Dame, 1956, MS, 1958; PhD, U. Md., 1961. Staff engr. Northrop Aircraft Corp., Hawthorne, Calif., 1956-57; grad. asst. U. Notre Dame, Ind., 1957-58, asst. prof. engring., 1962-65, assoc. prof., 1965-67, prof., 1967—, chmn. dept., 1978-88; research asst. U. Md., College Park, 1958-61, postdoctoral researcher, 1961-62; mem. tech. staff Aerospace Corp., El Segundo, Calif., 1962; cons. Argonne (Ill.) Nat. Lab., 1968-80, Miles Lab., Elkhart, Ind., 1983-88, Chung Shan Inst. Sci. and Tech., Taiwan, 1987-89; vis. prof. Imperial Coll., London, 1989, Kernforschungzentrum, Karlsruhe, Germany, 1990. Editor: Development in Mechanics, 1971. Fellow AIAA (assoc.), ASME; mem. AAAS, Am. Phys. Soc., Am. Soc. Engring. Edn., N.Y. Acad. Sci., Sigma Xi, Pi Tau Sigma, Sigma Gamma Tau. Roman Catholic. Club: South Bend Country (bd. dirs. 1982-89, pres. 1986-88). Avocations: golfing, model railroading. Home: 17331 Willowbrook Dr South Bend IN 46635-1750 Office: Dept Aero & Mech Engring U Notre Dame Notre Dame IN 46556

SZIGETHY, NANCY SUE, accountant; b. Dallas, May 7, 1968; d. John William and Judy Ann (Jones) Smith; m. Stephen Michael Szigethy, May 18, 1991. AA, North Harris Coll., 1992; student, U. Houston, 1990-91, 92-93. Tax acct. Stewart & Stevenson, Houston, 1987-93; clk. cash receipts Reiss Media Enterprises, Englewood, Colo., 1994—. Mem. Inst. Mgmt. Accts. (dir. attendence 1988-93, award for 100% attendence 1988, 90, 92). Home: 11458 N Settlers Dr Parker CO 80134-8033

SZILAGYI, D(ESIDERIUS) EMERICK, surgeon, researcher, educator; b. Nagykaroly, Hungary, June 20, 1910; came to U.S.,, naturalized, 1931; m. Martha Evelyn Fowlkes Harper (dec.); children: Martha, Christine; m. Sally Bolton, 1989. Diploma, Calvinist Coll., Klausenburg, Hungary, 1928; exam., U. Paris-Sorbonne; student, U. Debrecen; MD, U. Mich., 1935, MS, 1940; MD (hon.), Semmelweis Med. U., Budapest, Hungary, 1988. Diplomate Am. Bd. Surgery. Intern U. Mich. Hosp., Ann Arbor, 1935-36, asst. resident in surgery, 1936-37, instr. pathology, 1937-39; asst. resident in surgery Henry Ford Hosp., Detroit, 1939-42, chief resident, 1945, asst. surgeon, 1945-46, assoc. surgeon, 1946-49, chief div. II gen. surgery, 1949-66, chmn. dept. surgery, 1966-75, cons. vascular surgery, 1975—, chief of staff, 1968-71; emeritus clin. prof. surgery U. Mich. Med. Sch., Ann Arbor; dir. med. dept. Ford Rubber Plantations, Para, Brazil, 1942-45; Edwin A. Jarecki Meml. lectr. Albert Einstein Med. Ctr., Phila., 1964; David W. Yandell lectr. U. Louisville Med. Sch., 1973; William Mayo lectr. U. Mich., 1978; Matas Meml. lectr. XV Internat. Congress of Internat. Cardiovascular Soc., Athens, Greece, 1981. Editor Jour. Vascular Surgery, 1983—; contbr. articles to profl. jours. Mem. ACS, AMA, Am. Fedn. Clin. Rsch., Am. Surg. Assns., Am. Thyroid Assn., Ctrl. Surg. Assn. (past pres.), Internat. Soc. Cardiovascular Surgery (past chpt. pres.), Internat. Soc. Surgery, Midwestern Vascular Surg. Soc., (past pres.), Soc. Vascular Surgery (past pres.), Western Surg. Assn. (past v.p., pres.), Detroit Acad. Surgery, Detroit Surg. Assn., Mich. Med. Soc., Wayne County Med. Soc.; hon. mem. Sociedad Argentina de Angiologia, Sociedad Columbiana de Angiologia, Royal Australasian Coll. Surgeons, Deutsche Gesellschaft für Gefässchirurgie, Hungarian Soc. of Angiology. Home: 1008 Stratford Pl Bloomfield Hills MI 48304-2934 Office: Henry Ford Hosp 2799 W Grand Blvd Detroit MI 48202-2608 *I regard it as an accidental stroke of good fortune that the beginning of my career as a surgeon coincided with the birth of a new branch of the surgical art: the surgery of the arterial system. Thus, I had the rare opportunity of making and publishing observations that were original and useful not because of their brilliance but because of their newness. The contribution for which I may perhaps take personal credit was a firm determination to describe my observations objectively and draw my conclusions honestly.*

SZIRMAI, ENDRE ANREAS FRANZ, physician, writer; b. Budapest, Hungary, Aug. 21, 1922; s. Károly Péter and Erzsébet R. (Schwartz) S.; Dr.med., MD, Med. U. Szeged, Hungary, 1947; D in Sci. Medicine, PhD, Kobe U., Tokyo, 1961; Dr. med. lic., Innenministerium, Stuttgart, Germany, 1962; numerous hon. degrees from France, Hungary, Germany, Netherlands, Spain, U.S., Chile, Japan, Brazil, Ceylon, Mex., India, Italy, Can., Poland, Australia, USSR, New Zealand, Eng., others; m. Ilona Mikes, Feb. 13, 1945; children: Marta, Andrea. Specialist in lab. internal medicine, clin. pathology, biochemistry, nuclear and gen. hematology, ob-gyn, oncology, myology, hon. prof., 1954—; chmn. dept. nuclear hematology Inst. Nuclear Engring. and assoc. univs., London, 1960, Stuttgart, 1966—; prof. Univ. O.M.H. Sci , Des Moines, Iowa, 1965—, U. Louisville, 1975—, U. San Diego, 1985—, U.S. Internat. U.; dir. Inst. Stress Mgmt.; elected cons. Min. Sci. Zagreb, Croatia; founder Szirmai Archives; pres. bd. advisors Nobel Sci. Found., 1992. Proposed for Nobel Prize, 1969; recipient Letter of Appreciation Min. Sci. Croatia; Commemorative plaque Okayama U., Japan, others. Fellow Inst. Nuclear Engring. and Coll. Angiology of N.Y., Royal Soc. Medicine, Royal Soc. Chemists; mem. Internat. Nomenclature Com. (pres.), Germ. Ph. Acad. Sci., Hungarian Acad. Scis., Italian Acad. Scis., N.Y. Acad. Scis., Mex. Acad. Gerontology (hon.), also numerous med., nuclear, and lit. assns. Author books, poetry and novels transl. into 35 langs., numerous abstracts in 49 langs., publs. on med. atomic energy, linguistic arts; editorial bd. several jours.; research biochem. methods, drugs; developer myotonometer, angiomyograph, myograph, utero-embryo cardiotonograph, electrocoagulometer; developer theories in medicine, philosophy, music and art; established Rutherford Szirmai prize Szirmai Univ. Found.; Szirmai archives established libraries worldwide. Address: Adolf-Kroener Str 11, D-70184 Stuttgart Germany

SZKODY, PAULA, astronomy educator, researcher; b. Detroit, July 17, 1948; d. Julian and Pauline (Wolski) S.; m. Donald E. Brownlee, Mar. 19, 1976; children: Allison, Carson. BS in Astrophysics, Mich. State U., 1970; MS in Astronomy, U. Wash., 1972, PhD in Astronomy, 1975. Rsch. asst. Observatoire de Geneve, 1969, Kitt Peak Nat. Obs., 1970; rsch., teaching asst. U. Wash., Seattle, 1970-75, rsch. assoc., lectr., 1975-82, sr. rsch. assoc., 1982-83, rsch. assoc. prof., 1983-91, rsch. prof., 1991-93, prof., 1993—; part-time mem. faculty Seattle U., 1974-75, 82, Bellevue Coll., 1975-77; vis. scientist Kitt Peak Nat. Obs., 1976; vis. instr. UCLA, 1977, adj. asst. prof., 1980, 81; vis. asst. prof. U. Hawaii, 1978; vis. assoc. prof. Calif. Inst. Tech., 1978-79, 80; mem. users com. Internat. Ultraviolet Explorer, 1983-85, 93—; mem. A.J. Cannon adv. com. AAUW, 1986-91, chmn. 1988-90; mem. ops. working group on Ultraviolet/Visual/Relativity, NASA, 1988-91. Contbr. numerous articles to profl. jours. Recipient Annie J. Cannon award, 1978. Fellow AAAS (mem. nominating com. 1990-93, chairperson 1993, mem.-at-large 1995—); mem. Am. Assn. Variable Star Observers, Am. Astron. Soc. (councilor 1996—), Internat. Astron. Union (mem. commn. 42 organizing com. 1991—), Astron. Soc. Pacific (bd. dirs. 1988-92), Phi Beta Kappa. Office: U Wash Dept Astronomy Seattle WA 98195

SZMIT, FREDERICK ANDREW, paper manufacturing company executive; b. Lowell, Mass., May 26, 1938; s. Andrew and Jane (Dziekiewicz) S.; m. Frances Slavin, May 20, 1960; children: Kathleen Anne, Andrew Michael. BS, Lowell U., 1959; postgrad. program for mgmt. devel., Harvard U., 1981. Chemist Geigy Chem. Co., Ardsley, N.Y., 1960-61; mill mgr. Spaulding Fibre Co., North Rochester, N.H., 1961-71; mill mgr. Boise-Cascade Splty. Div., Brattleboro, Vt., 1971-78, mfg. mgr., 1978-83, gen. mgr., 1983-85; dir. Old Forge Pulp & Paper, Lyons Falls, N.Y., 1986—; pres., chief exec. officer, bd. dirs. Lyons Falls (N.Y.) Pulp & Paper, Inc., 1985—, Lyons Falls Hydroelectric, Inc., 1986—; bd. dirs. Am. Paper Inst., N.Y.C., 1976-85, Associated Industries of Vt., Montpelier, 1977-85, Bank of Vt. Adv. Bd., Brattleboro, 1980-85; del. Vt. Gov.'s Conf. Forest Industries, Montpelier, 1985. Pres. Southern Vt. Health Services Corp., Brattleboro, 1984-87; pres. Brattleboro Meml. Hosp., 1981-84; chmn. United Fund of Brattleboro, 1979. Mem. Am. Paper Inst. (bd. dirs.), Paper Industry Mgmt. Assn., Associated Industries of N.Y., Tech. Assn. Pulp and Paper. Home: 54 S Shore Rd Spofford NH 03462-4016

SZOKA, EDMUND CASIMIR CARDINAL, archbishop; b. Grand Rapids, Mich., Sept. 14, 1927; s. Casimir and Mary (Wolgat) S. B.A., Sacred Heart Sem., 1950; J.C.B., Pontifical Lateran U., 1958, J.C.L., 1959. Ordained priest Roman Catholic Ch., 1954; asst. pastor St. Francis Parish, Manistique, Mich., 1954-55; sec. to bishop Marquette, Mich., 1955-57, 59-62; chaplain St. Mary's Hosp., Marquette, 1955-57; tribunal, notary, defender of bond Marquette, 1960-71; asst. chancellor Diocese of Marquette, 1962-69, chancellor, 1970-71; pastor St. Pius X Ch., Ishpeming, Mich., 1962-63, St. Christopher Ch., Marquette, 1963-71; bishop Diocese of Gaylord, Mich., 1971-81; archbishop of Detroit, 1981-90; elevated to cardinal, 1988; sec.-treas. Mich. Cath. Conf., Lansing, 1972-77; chmn. region VI Nat. Conf. Cath. Bishops, 1972-77; treas., mem. adminstrv. bd. and adminstrv. com., budget and fin. com. Nat. Conf. Cath. Bishops/U.S. Cath. Conf., 1981-84; trustee, mem. exec. com., chmn. com. for univ. relations Cath. U. Am., 1981-90; trustee Nat. Shrine of the Immaculate Conception, Washington, 1981-90; chmn. bd. trustees Cath. Telecommunications Network Am., 1984-90; pres. Prefecture for Econ. Affairs of the Holy See, 1990; mem. Secretariat of State, 2d sect. Coun. for Rels. with States. Mem. Congregation for Insts. Consecrated Life and Socs. Apostolic Life, Congregation for Causes of Saints, Congregation for Bishops, Congregation for Evangelization of Peoples, Congregation for Clergy. Address: Prefecture for Econ Affairs, 00120 Vatican City Vatican City

SZOVERFFY, JOSEPH, educator, medieval scholar; b. Clausenbourgh, Transylvania, June 19, 1920. MA, State Coll. H.S. Tchrs., Budapest, 1944; PhD, Budapest U., 1943; PhD, U. Fribourg, 1950. Prof. fgn. lang. Glenstall Coll. (Ireland), 1950-52; archivist Irish Folklore Commn., Dublin, 1952-57; spl. prof. classics and medieval Latin U. Ottawa, 1957-58, asst. prof., 1958-59; from asst. prof. to assoc. prof. German philology U. Alta., 1959-62; assoc. prof. mediaeval German lit. Yale U., 1962-65; prof. German, medieval lit. Boston Coll., 1965-70, acting chmn. German studies, dir. grad. studies, 1968-70; prof. comparative lit. SUNY-Albany, 1970-77, chmn. dept., 1972-75; vis. prof. Byzantine studies Dumbarton Oaks Ctr. Byzantine Studies, Washington, 1977-78; prof. medieval lit. Sch. Hist. Studies, Inst. Advanced Study, 1978-79; Richard Merton vis. prof. Inst. Medieval Studies Freie U., Berlin (W.Ger.), 1980—; hon. rsch. assoc. Harvard Ukrainian Research Inst., Harvard U., 1975—; with Inst. Advanced Studies, Berlin, 1983-84; vis. prof. Medieval Studies U. Vienna, Austria, 1984-85, 87-88. Author: Der hl Christophorus und sein Kult, 1942; Irisches Erzahlgut im Abendland, 1957; Annalen der lateinischen Hymnendichtung I-II, 1964-65; Weltliche Dichtungen des lateinischen Mittelaters, 1970; Peter Abelard's Hymnarius Paraclitensis Vol I-II, 1975; Bermanistische Abhandlugen, 1977; A Guide to Byzantine Hymnography, Vol I-II, 1979-80; Repertorium Novum Hymnorum Medii Aevi, Vol I-IV, 1982, Religious Lyrics of the Middle Ages, 1983, A Concise History of the Medieval Latin Hymnody, 1985, Typology of Latin Hymns, 1988, Turnhout Across the Centuries...Harvard Lectures, 1988, Secular Latin Lyrics, Vol. I-IV, 1992-95, Memoirs, 1996. Recipient Chgo. Folklore prize U. Chgo., 1954; fellow Guggenheim Found. 1961, 69-70, Am. Philos. Soc., 1965, 72, Ctr. Medieval and Early Renaissance Studies, SUNY, 1973—, NEH, 1978-79; grantee Guggenheim Found. 1963, 71, 75. Mem. Mediaeval Acad. Am., MLA, Am. Comparative Lit. Assn., Conn. Acad., West Berlin Acad.

SZUCH, CLYDE ANDREW, lawyer; b. Bluefield, W.Va., Nov. 22, 1930; s. Nicholas and Aranka (Rubin) S.; m. Rosalie Hirschman Wulfson, Sept. 5, 1954; children: Peter Alan, Richard Coleman. BA, Rutgers, 1952; LLB, Harvard U., 1955. Bar: N.J. 1955, U.S. Dist. Ct. N.J. 1955, U.S. Ct. Appeals (3rd cir.) 1958, U.S. Supreme Ct. 1962. Law clk. to assoc. justice William J. Brennan Jr. U.S. Supreme Ct., Washington, 1956-57; asst. U.S. atty. U.S. Attys. Office, Newark, 1957-58; assoc. Pitney, Hardin & Kipp, Newark, 1958-62; ptnr. Pitney, Hardin, Kipp & Szuch, Morristown, N.J., 1962—; mem. panel Ctr. for Pub. Resources, N.J.; bd. dirs. Vt. Rlwy. Inc., Clarendon & Pittsford R.R. Co., Burlington, Vt., Brennan Ctr. for Justice; panelist AAA Large Complex Cases. Trustee Morris Mus., Morristown; gov. N.J. region Nat. Conf. Christians & Jews. Fellow Am. Bar Found.; mem. ABA, Am. Law Inst., N.J. State Bar Assn., Morris County Bar Assn., Essex County Bar Assn., Fed. Bar Assn. (N.J. chpt.), Ctr. Pub. Resources Panel, Nat. Legal Aid Defender Assn., Hist. Soc. U.S. Ct. Appeals for 3d Cir., Park Ave. Club. Office: Pitney Hardin Kipp & Szuch PO Box 1945 Morristown NJ 07962-1945

SZUCS, ZOLTAN DANIEL, religious organization executive, minister, psychologist, educator; b. Pastovce, Sloviakia, Oct. 29, 1935; came to U.S., 1958; m. Barbara Cecil Kizer; children: Ildiko, Aniko. Grad. summa cum laude, Reformed Kollegium, Papa, Hungary, 1954; postgrad., Reformed Theol. Seminary, Budapest, Hungary, 1955, U. Vienna, 1957-58, U. Del., 1959; grad., Princeton (N.J.) Theol. Seminary, 1962; MEd, Temple U.; PhD in Counseling Psychology, Tex. A&M U. Ordained to ministry Hungarian Reformed Ch. Am., 1960, Presbyn. Ch., 1963. With Brethren Svc. Commn., Linz; youth counselor World Coun. Chs., Steinbach Am Attersee; pastor St. George and Delaware City Presbyn. Chs., Del., 1963-73; dir. campus ministry Tex. A&M, College Station, 1973-78; pastor First Presbyn. Ch., Sealy, Tex., 1977-80, South Side Presbyn. Ch., Niles, Ohio, 1977-80; sr. pastor Hungarian Reform Ch., United Ch. Christ, Lorain, Ohio, 1980—; gen. sec. Calvin synod United Ch. Christ, 1989-93, bishop, 1993—, exec. coun., 1993—; chaplain Del. State Senate, 1965-66; adj. prof. psychology Wilmington Coll., New Castle, Del., 1970-73; instr. Tex. A&M Univ., College Station, 1973-77; del. Interdenominational Ch. Com. to Palestinians, Beirut, 1980; U.S. rep. Internat. Com. World Alliance of Reformed Chs. Soviet Union, 1989. Office: United Ch of Christ 3036 Globe Ave Lorain OH 44055-1727

SZUHAJ, BERNARD FRANCIS, food research director; b. Lilly, Pa., Nov. 27, 1942; s. Theodore and Rose Dorothy (Karmen) S.; m. Carole Ann Brady, Dec. 26, 1964; children: Matthew, Timothy, Bernard. BS, Pa. State U., 1964, MS, 1966, PhD, 1969. Grad. asst. Pa. State U., Univ. Park, Pa., 1964-66; research asst. Pa. State U., Univ. Park, 1966-68; scientist Cen. Soya Co., Inc., Fort Wayne, Ind., 1968-73; research dir. Cen. Soya Co., Inc., Fort Wayne, 1973-84, dir. food research, 1984—; v.p. Am. Oil Chemists'Soc. Found., Ill., 1988—; bd. dirs. POS Pilot Plant Corp., Saskatoon, Canada, 1987—. Patentee in field; co-editor Lecithins, 1985; editor: (lecithins) Sources Manufacture & Uses, 1989. Mem. Am. Oil Chemists' Soc. (bd. dirs. 1989—), Am. Chem. Soc., Inst. Food Technologists, Inst. Shortening & Edible Oils, Sigma Xi. Democrat. Roman Catholic. Office: Cen Soya Co Inc PO Box 1400 Fort Wayne IN 46801-1400

SZULC, TAD, journalist, commentator; b. Warsaw, Poland, July 25, 1926; came to U.S., 1947, naturalized, 1954; s. Seweryn and Janina (Baruch) S.; m. Marianne Carr, July 8, 1948; children: Nicole, Anthony. Student, U. Brazil, 1943-45; LHD (hon.), Am. Coll. Switzerland, 1987. Reporter AP, Rio de Janeiro, 1945-46; corr. at UN for UPI, 1949-53; mem. staff N.Y. Times, after 1953; corr. N.Y. Times, Latin Am., 1955-61; with Washington bur. N.Y. Times, 1961-65, 69-72, corr. to Spain and Portugal, 1965-68, corr. to Eastern Europe, 1968-69, commentator fgn. policy, 1972—. Author: Twilight of the Tyrants, 1959, The Cuban Invasion, 1962, The Winds of Revolution, 1963, Dominican Diary, 1965, Latin America, 1966, Bombs of Palomares, 1967, United States and the Caribbean, 1971, Czechoslovakia since World War II, 1971, Portrait of Spain, 1972, Compulsive Spy: The Strnage Career of E. Howard Hunt, 1974, The Energy Crisis, 1974, Innocents at Home, 1974, The Illusion of Peace, 1978, Diplomatic Immunity, 1981, Fidel: A Critical Portrait, 1986, Then and Now: The World Since WW II, 1990, The Secret Alliance, 1991, Pope John Paul II: The Biography, 1995. Decorated Cross of Chevalier of Legion d'Honneur France, Order of Duarte, Sánchez, Meliá Dominican Republic; recipient Maria Moors Cabot gold medal Columbia U., Medal of Honor, World Bus. Coun., 1987. Mem. Overseas Press Club (award for best mag. interpretation fgn. affairs 1976, citations 1966, 74-75, 77-78, award for best book on fgn. affairs 1979, 86, 91), Cosmos Club. Address: 4515 29th St NW Washington DC 20008-2144

SZWARC, MICHAEL, polymer scientist; b. Poland, June 9, 1909; came to U.S., 1952; s. Maier and Regina (Prager) S.; m. Marja Frenkel, Aug. 6, 1933; children: Raphael, Myra, Rina. Ch.E., Warsaw Poly. Inst., Poland, 1932; PhD in Organic Chemistry, Hebrew U., Jerusalem, 1945; PhD in Phys. Chemistry, Manchester (Eng.) U., 1947, DSc (hon.), 1949; D (hon.), U. Leuven, Belgium, 1974; D.Sc. (hon), Uppsala U., Sweden, 1975, Louis Pasteur U., Strasbourg, France, 1978. Researcher Hebrew U., Jerusalem, 1935-45; researcher Manchester U., Eng., 1946-52, univ. fellow, lectr. phys. chemistry, 1949-52; mem. faculty SUNY-Syracuse Coll. Environ. Scis., 1952-79; disting. prof. chemistry SUNY-Syracuse Coll. Forestry, 1964-80, dir. polymer ctr., 1966-80, prof. emeritus, 1980—. Author: Carbanions, Living Polymers and Electron Transfer Processes, 1968, Ionic Polymerization and Living Polymers, 1993; editor: Ions and Ion Pairs in Organic Chemistry, Vol. I, 1972, Vol. II, 1974. Recipient Polymer Chemistry award Am. Chem. Soc., 1970, Herman Mark award, 1989; Gold medal Internat. Soc. Plastics Engrs., 1972, Benjamin Franklin Soc., 1978, Kyoto prize for advanced tech., 1991. Fellow Royal Soc. (London); mem. Polish Acad. Scis. (fgn.), Soc. Polymer Sci. (Japan). Office: Univ So Calif Hydrocarbon Rsch Insti Los Angeles CA 90089

SZYBALSKI, WACLAW, molecular geneticist, educator; b. Lwów, Poland, Sept. 9, 1921; came to U.S., 1950, naturalized, 1957; s. Stefan and Michalina (Rakowska) S.; m. Elizabeth Hunter, Feb. 5, 1955; children: Barbara A. Szybalski Sandor, Stefan H. BSChemE, Poly. Inst. Lwów, 1943; DSc, Poly Inst. Gdańsk, Poland, 1949; Ph.D. (hon.), U. Marie Curie, Lublin, Poland, 1980, U. Gdańsk, Poland, 1989. Asst. prof. Poly. Inst., Gdańsk, 1946-50; mem. staff Cold Spring Harbor (N.Y.) Biol. Labs., 1951-55; asst. prof. Inst. Microbiology, Rutgers U., New Brunswick, N.J., 1955-60; prof. oncology McArdle Lab., U. Wis.-Madison, 1960—; mem. recombinant DNA adv. com. (RAC) NIH, 1974-78; Wendel H. Griffith meml. lectr. St. Louis U., 1975. Author numerous papers, revs., abstracts and books in field; editor-in-chief: Gene, 1976-96, hon. and founding editor-in-chief, 1996—; mem. editorial bd. other jours. Recipient Karl A. Forster lecture award U. Mainz, 1970, A. Jurzykowski Found. award in biology, 1988, Hilldale award in biology U. Wis., 1994, Gold G.J. Mendel Hon. medal for merit in biol. scis. Acad. Scis. of Czech Republic, 1995; Cogene lectr. Internat. Union Biochem., Nairobi, 1987, Cairo, 1988, Harare, Zimbabwe, 1989. Mem. AAAS, Am. Soc. Biochemists, Genetic Soc. Am., Am. Soc. Microbiologists (chmn. virology divsn. 1972-74, chmn. divsn. IV 1974-75), European Molecular Biology Orgns. (lectr. 1971, 76), Polish Soc. Microbiologists (hon.), Italian Soc. Exptl. Biology (hon.), Polish Med. Alliance (hon.), Polish Acad. Scis. (fgn. mem.). Home: 1124 Merrill Springs Rd Madison WI 53705-1317 Office: U Wis McArdle Lab Madison WI 53706 *The profession should also be the hobby and a constant source of enjoyment and satisfaction.*

SZYGENDA, STEPHEN A., electrical and computer engineering educator, researcher; b. McKeesport, Pa., Oct. 5, 1938; s. Stephen A. Sr. and Elizabeth B. (Zolczer) S.; m. Marie A. Deli, Apr. 2, 1960; children: Stepahnie Livingston, Diana, Mark. BS, Fairleigh Dickinson U., 1965; MS, Northwestern U., 1967, PhD, 1968. Registered profl. engr., Tex. Engr. Comprehensive Design, N.J., 1959-62; mem. tech. staff Bell Telephone Labs., N.J., Ill., 1962-68; assoc. prof. elec. engring. and computer engring. U. Mo., Rolla, 1968-70; prof. elec. engring. and computer engring. So. Meth. U., Dallas, 1970-73; prof. elec. engring. and computer engring. U. Tex., Austin, 1973-86, dir. Ctr. for Tech. Tran., 1986-89, Clint Murchison Sr. Chair of Free Enterprise prof., 1986—, chmn. elec. and computer engring. dept., 1993—; pres. CCSS, Austin, 1972-81, Comsat Gen. Int. Sys., Austin, 1981-83, SBI, Inc., Austin, 1985—; pres., CEO Rubicon Group, Austin. 1983-85; active Tex. Gov. Coun. for Sci. and Tech., 1984-87. Contbr. articles to profl. jours. Dir. Laguna Gloria Mus., Austin, 1981-83; pres. bd. Austin Ballet, 1983. With USN, 1956-59. Fellow IEEE (bd. dirs. 1973-75); mem. Assn. Computing Machinery (Svc. award 1975, 79, 87, 88, Disting. lectr. 1991-95). Roman Catholic. Achievements include pioneering in CAD, simulation, fault tolerant computing, telecommunications, entrepreneurship, and software engineering. Home: 4506 Cat Mt Dr Austin TX 78731 Office: U Tex Dept Elec and Computer Engring Austin TX 78712-1084

SZYMANSKI, EDNA MORA, rehabilitation psychology and special education educator; b. Caracas, Venezuela, Mar. 19, 1952; came to U.S., 1952; d. José Angel and Helen Adele (McHugh) Mora; m. Michael Bernard, Mar. 30, 1973. BS, Rensselaer Poly. Inst., 1972; MS, U. Scranton, 1974; PhD, U. Tex., 1988. Cert. rehab. counselor. Vocat. evaluator Mohawk Valley Workshop, Utica, N.Y., 1974-75; vocat. rehab. counselor N.Y. State Office Vocat. Rehab., Utica, N.Y., 1975-80; sr. vocat. rehab. counselor N.Y. State Office Vocat. Rehab., Utica, 1980-87; rsch. assoc. U. Tex., Austin, 1988-89; asst. prof. U. Wis., Madison, 1989-91, assoc. prof., 1991-93, assoc. dean sch. edn., 1993—, dir. rehab. rsch. and tng. ctr., 1993-96, prof. rehab. psychology and spl. edn., 1993—; cons. Rsch. Assocs. Syracuse, N.Y., 1988-90. Co-author various book chpts.; co-editor: Rehabilitation Counseling Basics and Beyond, 1992; co-editor Work and Disability, 1996, Rehabilitation Counseling Bull., 1994—; contbr. articles to profl. jours. Mem. Pres.'s Com. on Employment of People with Disabilities, Washington, 1987—. Recipient Rsch. award Am. Assn. Counselor Edn. and Supr., 1991. Mem. ACA (chair rsch. com. 1992-94, Rsch. awards 1990, 93, 95), Am. Rehab. Counseling Assn. (pres. 1985-86, Rsch. award 1989, 94), Coun. Rehab. Edn. (chair rsch. com. 1990-95, v.p. 1993-95), Nat. Coun. Rehab. Edn. (chair rsch. com. 1992—, Rehab. Edn. Rschr. of Yr. 1993, New Career in Rehab. Edn. award 1990). Office: U Wis Dept Rehab Psychology and Spl Edn 432 N Murray St Madison WI 53706-1407

SZYMCZAK, EDWARD JOSEPH, mechanical engineer; b. Anderson, Tex., Sept. 28, 1938; s. Harold and Verna (Walkoviak) S.; m. Lorena Jane Sharp, Sept. 26, 1964; children: Denise, Lisa, Brian. Student, U. St. Thomas, 1958; BSME, Tex. A&M, 1961; MBA, U. Houston, 1970. Registered profl. engr., Tex. Engr. trainee to engring. mgr. Cameron Iron Works, Houston, 1961-90; dir. engring. ea. hemisphere Cooper Oil Tool Div./Cooper Industries, London, 1990-91; dir. engring. Cooper Oil Tool Div./Cooper Industries, Houston, 1991-95, Cameron div. Cooper Cameron Corp., Houston, 1995—; chmn. indsl. adv. bd. U. Southwestern La., Lafayette; councilor Tex. A&M U. Rsch. Found., College Station, 1994—. Patentee (6) on oil tool equipment. Mem. ASME, Tex. A&M Former Students Assn., Tex. A&M 12th Man Found., Soc. Petroleum Engrs., Nat. Assn. Corrosion Engrs. Republican. Roman Catholic. Avocations: ranching, farming, mechanic, investing, tech. and personnel recruiting. Home: 4002 Cypress Hill Spring TX 77388

SZYMONIAK, ELAINE EISFELDER, state senator; b. Boscobel, Wis., May 24, 1920; d. Hugo Adolph and Pauline (Vig) Eisfelder; Casimir Donald Szymoniak, Dec. 7, 1943; children: Kathryn, Peter, John, Mary, Thomas. BS, U. Wis., 1941; MS, Iowa State U., 1977. Speech clinician Waukesha (Wis.) Pub. Sch., 1941-43, Rochester (N.Y.) Pub. Sch., 1943-44; rehab. aide U.S. Army, Chickasha, Okla., 1944-46; audiologist U. Wis., Madison, 1946-48; speech clinician Buffalo Pub. Sch., 1948-49, Sch. for Handicapped, Salina, Kans., 1951-52; speech pathologist, audiologist, counselor, resource mgr. Vocat. Rehab. State Iowa, Des Moines, 1956-85; mem. Iowa Senate, Des Moines, 1989—. Mem. Des Moines City coun., 1978-88; bd. dirs. Nat. League Cities, Wahsington, 1982-84, Girl Scouts U.S., Civic Ctr., House of Mercy, Westminster House, Iowa Leadership Consortium, Coun. on Internat. Understanding, Iowa Commn. on Status of Women, Young Christian Assn.; chairperson Greater Des Moines Coun. for Internat. Understanding, United Way, 1987-88, Urban Dreams, Iowa Maternal and Child Health com. Named Woman of Achievement YWCA, 1982, Visionary Woman, Young Women's Resource Ctr. Mem. Am. Speech Lang. and Hearing Assn., Iowa Speech Lang. and Hearing Assn. (pres. 1977-78), Nat. Coun. State Legislators (fed. state com. on health, adv. com. on child protection), Women's Polit. Caucus, Nexus (pres. 1981-82). Avocations: reading, traveling, swimming. Home: 2116 44th St Des Moines IA 50310-3011 Office: State Senate State Capitol Des Moines IA 50319

TAAFFE, EDWARD JAMES, geography educator; b. Chgo., Dec. 11, 1921; s. Edward James and Julia Loretta (Murphy) T.; m. Marialyce Dunne, Sept. 7, 1948; children: Maura Joan, Edward James Jr., Michael Robert, Julianne, Susan Deirdre, Brian Thomas, Karen Elizabeth, David Matthew. BS in Meteorology, NYU, 1944; BS in Journalism, U. Ill., 1945; SM in Geography, U. Chgo., 1949, PhD in Geography, 1952. Istr. U. Ill., Chgo., 1948-51; from instr. to asst. prof. econs. dept. Loyola U., Chgo., 1951-56; from asst. to assoc. prof. geography dept. Northwestern U., Evanston, Ill., 1956-63; prof. Geography dept. Ohio State U., Columbus, 1963—, chmn. geography dept., 1963-75; mem. editorial bd. cons. World Book Atlas, Chgo., 1963-69; cons. editor McGraw-Hill Pub. Co., 1969-79; adv. bd. geography coun. Ontario U., Toronto, Can., 1972-73. Author: (books) Air Pass Hinterland of Chicago, 1952, The Peripheral Journey-To-Work, 1963, Geography of Transportation, 1996; editor: (book) Geography, 1973. 1st lt. USAAF, 1943-46, West Europe. Mem. Assn. Am. Geographers (counselor 1966-69, v.p. 1970-71, pres. 1971-72, Honors award 1982, Edward Ullman award 1990), Nat. Coun. Geog. Edn. (Master Tchr. award 1983), Soc. Sci. Rsch. Coun. (dir.-at-large 1970-74). Roman Catholic. Home: 4314 Olentangy Blvd Columbus OH 43214-3036 Office: Ohio State U Dept Geography 154 N Oval Mall Columbus OH 43210-1330

TAAFFE, JAMES GRIFFITH, university administrator, educator; b. Cin., Sept. 15, 1932; s. Griffith C. and Mary (Ropp) T.; m. Donna Click, June 8, 1955 (dec. 1986); children: Lauren Kathleen, Patrick Michael; m. Allison S. Blair, Nov. 7, 1987; 1 child, Michael Sean. AB, Columbia U., 1954; MA, Ind. U., 1956, PhD, 1960. Instr. English Williams Coll., Williamstown, Mass., 1959-62; asst. prof. English Vassar Coll., 1962-64; from asst. prof. to prof. English Case Western Res. U., Cleve., 1964—, chmn. advanced placement in English, 1968-73, chmn. dept., 1969-72, asst. to pres., 1971-72, dean grad. studies, 1972-74, v.p. undergrad. and grad. studies, 1974-81, univ. v.p. acad. affairs, 1981-86, acting chair dept. theatre arts, 1989-90; v.p. for acad. affairs U. Ala., Tuscaloosa, 1990-91, provost, v.p. for acad. affairs, 1991—; mem. Joint Council, East Cleve. Sch. Dist., 1970. Co-author: A Milton Handbook, 1970; editor: Abraham Cowley, 1970; co-editor: Poems on Poetry, 1965, Reading English Poetry, 1971. Newberry Libr. fellow, 1964; Am. Philos. Soc. fellow, 1967, 69; NEH fellow, 1971. Mem. MLA, Milton Soc., Dante Soc. Home: 9201 Enterprise Ave NE Tuscaloosa AL 35406-1005

TAAM, RONALD EVERETT, physics and astronomy educator; b. N.Y.C., Apr. 24, 1948; s. Lawrence and Julia (Louie) T.; m. Rosa Wen Mei Yang, Oct. 19, 1974; children: Jonathan, Alexander. BS, Poly. Inst., N.Y.C., 1969; MA, Columbia U., 1971, PhD, 1973. Postdoctoral fellow U. Calif., Santa Cruz, 1973-76; vis. faculty U. Calif., Berkeley, 1976-78; asst. prof. Northwestern U., Evanston, Ill., 1978-83, assoc. prof., 1984-86, prof. physics and astronomy, 1986—, chmn. physics and astronomy, 1995—. Fellow Am. Phys. Soc.; mem. Am. Astron. Soc., Royal Astron. Soc., Internat. Astron. Union. Office: Dept Physics and Astronomy Northwestern U 633 Clark St Evanston IL 60208-0001

TABAK, RONALD JEROME, lawyer; b. Bklyn., July 23, 1949; s. Abraham S. and Frieda C. Tabak. BA, Yale U., 1971; JD, Harvard U., 1974. Bar: N.Y. 1975, U.S. Dist. Ct. (ea. and so. dists.) N.Y. 1975, U.S. Ct. Appeals (2nd cir.) 1975, U.S. Ct. Appeals (11th cir.) 1983, U.S. Ct. Appeals (5th cir.) 1984, U.S. Supreme Ct. 1984, U.S. Dist. Ct. (no. dist.) Calif. 1985, U.S. Ct. Appeals (9th cir.) 1985, Alaska 1988. Law clk. to hon. judge John F. Dooling Jr. U.S. Dist. Ct. (ea. dist.) N.Y., Bklyn., 1974-75; assoc. Hughes Hubbard & Reed, N.Y.C., 1975-83, spl. counsel, 1983-85; spl. counsel Skadden, Arps, Slate, Meagher & Flom, N.Y.C., 1985—; mem. exec. com. Lawyers for Legal Aid, N.Y.C., 1989—. Contbr. articles to profl. jours. Pres. N.Y. Lawyers Against the Death Penalty, N.Y.C., 1988—; vice chairperson Justice-PAC, N.Y.C., 1990—; bd. dirs. Appleseed Found., 1995—, N.Y. Civil Liberties Union, 1995—. Recipient Outstanding Vol. Svc. award Legal Aid Soc., 1984, Thurgood Marshall award N.Y. State Assn. Criminal Def. Lawyers, 1996. Mem. ABA (chairperson death penalty com. sect. individual rights and responsibilities 1988—, mem. sect. policy coun. 1994—), N.Y. State Bar Assn. (Pres.'s Pro Bono Svc. award 1985, Outstanding Contbn. to Def. Svcs. award 1990), Alaska Bar Assn., Coun. N.Y. Law Assocs. (bd. dirs. 1987-91), Assn. of Bar of City of N.Y. (mem. civil rights com. 1994—, mem. com. on capital representation 1994—). Avocations: jogging, baseball. Office: Skadden Arps Slate Meagher & Flom 919 3rd Ave New York NY 10022-3897

TABASCIO, STEFANO ANTONINO, chemical lubricant company executive; b. Toronto, Ont. Can., Sept. 26, 1965; s. Josef Antonino and Helena Ana (Neuhort) T.; m. Linda Ann Wade (div. 1994). Degree in Engring., Karlova U., Prague, Czechoslovakia, 1984; degree in Bus. Adminstrn., Calif. State U., L.A., 1989; degree in Chemistry, U. Nev., Las Vegas, 1991. Automotive engr. Zavodi Crevena Zastava, Knagujevac, Yugoslavia, 1984-85, Yugo Cars, Sun Valley, Calif., 1985; cons. Yugo Am., N.J., 1985-86; automobile dealer Mik Auto Inc./Bertone, North Hollywood, Calif., 1986-89; automotive designer Moretti, Torino, Italy, 1989-90; v.p. engring. Skocar, Markham, Ont., 1990-91; CEO Synlube, Inc. (formerly Pentagram Products), Las Vegas, 1991—. Author: All About Oil, 1989, What You Don't Know About Oil...Will Hurt Your Car", 1993, Q & A of Lubrication, 1994. Mem. Soc. Automotive Engrs., Soc. Tribologists and Lubrication Engrs., Sports Car Club Am. Avocation: automobile racing. Office: Synlube Inc 2961 Industrial Rd #300 Las Vegas NV 89109-1188

TABATZNIK, BERNARD, physician, educator; b. Mir, Poland, Jan. 8, 1927; came to U.S., 1959, naturalized, 1966; s. Max and Fay (Ginsberg) T.; m. Marjorie Turner, Jan. 8, 1956; children: Darron Mark, Keith Donald, Ilana Wendy; m. Charline Edwards Harmon, Aug. 7, 1992. B.Sc., U. Witwatersrand, South Africa, 1945; M.B., B.Ch., 1949. Intern Baragwanath Hosp., Johannesburg, South Africa, 1950-51, Hillingdon Hosp., Ashford Hosp., also research unit Canadian Red Cross Meml. Hosp., Taplow, Eng., 1951-54; med. registrar Ashford Hosp., 1954-56, Johannesburg Gen. Hosp., 1956-58; physician Baragwanath Hosp., 1958-59; fellow medicine Johns Hopkins Sch. Medicine, 1959-60, fellow cardiology, 1960-61, asst. prof. medicine, 1966—; head cardiopulmonary div. Sinai Hosp., Balt., 1961-72; asso. chief medicine Sinai Hosp., 1964-72; chief cardiology dept. North Charles Gen. Hosp., Balt., 1972; also dir. med. edn., dir. Postgrad. Inst., coordinator ambulatory services; med. dir. Nurse Practitioner-Physician Asst. Program, Ch. Hosp., Balt., 1987-90. Contbr. articles to profl. jours. Recipient Save-A-Heart Humanitarian award, 1977, Maimonides award, 1983, Shaarei Zion Humanitarian award, 1987. Fellow Royal Coll. Physicians (London); mem. South African Cardiac Soc., Am. Heart Assn., Md. Heart Assn. (chmn. health careers 1964-66), Laennec Cardiovascular Sound Group. Home: HC 3 Box 180 Monterey VA 24465-9313 Office: 8417 Bellona Ln Baltimore MD 21204-2014

TABBERNEE, WILLIAM, academic administrator, theology educator; b. Rotterdam, The Netherlands, Apr. 21, 1944; came to U.S., 1991; s. Adrianus and Neeltje Jannetje (Koonings) T.; m. Sandra Violet Parker, Jan. 15, 1966; children: Nicole, Jason, Michelle. Primary tchr. cert., Coburg Tchr. Coll., 1965; diploma in religious edn., Melbourne Coll. Divinity, 1968, lic. in theology, 1968; diploma with honors, Churches of Christ Theol. Coll, 1970; BA with honors, U. Melbourne, 1972; STM, Yale U., 1973; PhD, U. Melbourne, 1979. Ordained to ministry Churches of Christ in Australia, 1970. Headmaster Swan Reach Primary Sch., Victoria, Australia, 1966; tchr. Newlands H.S., Melbourne, Australia, 1967-68; min. The Patch Church of Christ, Victoria, Australia, 1971-72; lectr. Coll. of the Bible, Melbourne, 1973-76; lectr. Coll. of the Bible, 1977-80, chair dept. Christian thought and systematic theology, 1977-80; dean Evang. Theol. Assn., Melbourne, 1979-80; prin. Coll. of the Bible, 1981-91; pres., prof. Christian thought and history Phillips Theol. Sem., Enid and Tulsa, Okla., 1991—; part-time lectr. Coll. of the Bible, 1971-72. Editor, author (with others): Marriage in Australian Churches, 1982, Initiation in Australian Churches, 1984, Australian Churches' Response to Baptism, Eucharist and Ministry, 1986, Ministry in

Australian Churches, 1987, Montanist Inscriptions and Testimonia, 1996; contbr. numerous articles to profl. jours. Mem. Am. Acad. Religion, Assn. Disciples Theol. Discussion, N. Am. Patristics Soc., Australian and New Zealand Soc. Theol. Studies, Internat. Bilateral Commn. Dialogue Between Disciples Ecumenical Consultative Counc. and Pontifical Counc. Promotion Christian Unity, Internat. Bilateral Commn. Dialogue Between Disciples Ecumenical Counc. and World Alliance Reformed Chs. Office: Phillips Theological Sem PO Box 2335 Enid OK 73702

TABELL, ANTHONY, financial analyst; b. Bklyn., Aug. 5, 1931; s. Edmund Weber and Margaret (Suydam) T.; m. Ellen Margaret Molwitz, May 23, 1953; children—Margaret Ellen, Roberta Jane, Sarah Elizabeth. Grad., St. Luke's Sch., New Canaan, Conn., 1948; A.B., Colgate U., 1952; student, N.Y. U., 1957-65. With Walston & Co. Inc., N.Y.C., 1954-70, v.p., 1961-65, sr. v.p., dir., 1965-70; asso. Delafield, Harvey, Tabell div. Janney, Montgomery Scott, Inc., Princeton, N.J., 1970-83, v.p. parent co., 1971-83; mng. dir. Delafield, Harvey, Tabell Inc., Princeton, 1983-92; sr. v.p. U.S. Trust Co. of N.J., Princeton, 1992-93. Served with AUS, 1952-54. Mem. N.Y. Soc. Security Analysts, Market Technicians Assn. (pres. 1975-76), Nassau Club. Episcopalian. Home: 76 Crooked Tree Ln Princeton NJ 08540-2950

TABER, CAROL A., magazine publisher. AA, Green Mountain Coll., 1965. Network mgr. Media Networks, Inc., 1970-74; N.Y. advt. mgr. Ladies' Home Jour., 1974-79; assoc. pub., advt. dir. Working Woman, N.Y.C., 1979-83, pub., 1984-94; pub. Working Mother, N.Y.C., 1994—; exec. v.p., group pub. Working Woman and Working Mother mags., 1989. Office: Working Mother 230 Park Ave Fl 7 New York NY 10169-0799*

TABER, EDWARD ALBERT, III, investment executive; b. Jacksonville, Fla., Aug. 25, 1943; s. Edward Albert, Jr. and Janet Gladys (Bickford) T.; m. Teresa Marie Scheidle, Nov. 13, 1982; children: Linley Marie, Laura Elizabeth, Lisa Kimberly. AB, Dartmouth Coll., 1965; MBA, Harvard Coll., 1971. V.p., treas. Fed. Home Loan Bank, Boston, 1971-73; v.p. T. Rowe Price Assocs., Inc., Balt., 1975-92, also bd. dirs.; sr. exec. v.p. Legg Mason, Inc., 1992—. Capt. USMC, 1965-69, Vietnam. Decorated Silver Star, Purple Heart. Republican. Episcopalian.

TABER, MARGARET RUTH, electrical engineering technology educator, electrical engineer; b. St. Louis, Apr. 29, 1935; d. Wynn Orr and Margaret Ruth (Feldman) Gould Stevens; m. William James Taber, Sept. 6, 1958. B.Engring. Sci., Cleve. State U., 1958, B.E.E., 1958; M.S. in Engring., U. Akron, 1967; Ed.D., Nova U., 1976; postgrad., Western Res. U., 1959-64. Registered profl. engr., Ohio; cert. engring. technologist. Engring. trainee Ohio Crankshaft Co., Cleve., 1954-57, devel. engr., 1958-64, tng. dir., 1963-64; instr. elec.-electronic engring. tech. Cuyahoga Community Coll., Cleve., 1964-67, asst. prof., 1967-69, assoc. prof., 1969-72, prof., 1972-79, chmn. engring. tech., 1977-79; assoc. prof. elec. engring. tech. Purdue U., West Lafayette, Ind., 1979-83, prof., 1983—; lectr. Cleve. State U., 1963-64; mem. acad. adv. bd. Cleve. Inst. Electronics, 1981—, ednl. cons., author, 1979—. Author: (with Frank P. Tedeschi) Solid State Electronics, 1976, (with Eugene M. Silgalis) Electric Circuit Analysis, 1980, (with Jerry L. Casebeer) Registers, (with Kenneth Rosenow) Arithmetic Logic Units, Timing and Control, Memory Units, 1980, 6809 Architecture and Operation, 1984, Programming I: Straight Line, 1984; contbr. articles to profl. jours. Bd. dirs. West Blvd. Christian Ch., deaconess, 1974-77, elder, 1977-79; deacon Federated Ch., 1981-84, 86-89, Stephen Leader, 1988—; mem. Cancer Support Group; co-chair svc. and rehab. com. Am. Cancer Soc., 1992—; vol. CanSurmount, 1993—; vol. Lafayette Reading Acad., 1992—; ednl. resource vol., vol. tchr. Sunburst Farm Rainbow Acres, Inc., Ariz., 1988—. Recipient Helen B. Schleman Gold Medallion award Purdue U., 1991, The Greater Lafayette Community Survivorship award, 1994, Outstanding Alumni award U. Akron Coll. Engring., 1994; Margaret R. Taber Microcomputer Lab. named in her honor Purdue U., 1991; NSF grantee, 1970-73, 78. Fellow Soc. Women Engrs. (counselor Purdue chpt. 1983—, Disting. Engring. Educator award 1987); mem. IEEE (sr.), Am. Bus. Women's Assn. (ednl. chmn. 1964-66), Am. Soc. Engring. Edn., Am. Tech. Edn. Assn., Tau Beta Pi (hon.), Phi Kappa Phi. Avocations: robotics; camping; housekeeping. Home: 3036 State Rd 26 W West Lafayette IN 47906-4743 Office: Purdue U Elec Engring Tech Dept Knoy Hall Tech West Lafayette IN 47907

TABER, PATRICK E., computer programmer; b. Lawrence, Kans., June 4, 1972; s. Patrick E. and Shirley M. (Pruske) T. BS, Trinity U., San Antnonio, Tex., 1994. Tech. support/programmer Southwest Software, Austin, 1995—. Home: 7201 Hart Lne # 2071 Austin TX 78731

TABER, ROBERT CLINTON, retired army officer; b. Ithaca, N.Y., Oct. 11, 1917; s. Laurence Sebring and Ethel (Lanning) T.; m. Jane Feeter, July 20, 1940 (dec. 1982); 1 child, John Robert; m. Lynn Parker, June 12, 1992. B.S., Cornell U., 1938; grad., Army War Coll., 1958. Commd. 2d lt. U.S. Army, 1940; advanced through grades to lt. gen.; comdg. gen. Joint U.S. Mil. Adv. Group Cambodia, 1963; asst. div. comdr. 82d Airborne Div., 1964-65; asst. comdt. U.S. Army Command and Gen. Staff Coll. Leavenworth, Kans., 1965-66; chief of staff U.S. Army Vietnam, 1967-68; dir. doctrine and systems Dept. Army, 1968-69; comdg. gen. 3d Inf. Div. Germany, 1970-71; prin. dep. asst sec. def. manpower and res. affairs, 1971-74. Decorated DSM with 2 oak leaf clusters, Legion of Merit with 3 oak leaf clusters, Bronze Star, Purple Heart, Joint Commendation medal, Army Commendation medal with 2 oak leaf clusters, Air medal with 2 oak leaf clusters. Mem. U.S. Naval Acad. Sailing Sqdn. Clubs: Cruising of Am, Ocean Cruising, Internat. Aerobatic. Home: 2109 Fox Ridge Rd Tuscaloosa AL 35406

TABIN, JULIUS, patent lawyer, physicist; b. Chgo., Nov. 8, 1919; s. Sol and Lillian (Klingman) T.; m. Johanna Krout, Sept. 7, 1952; children: Clifford James, Geoffrey Craig. B.S., U. Chgo., 1940, Ph.D. in Physics, 1946; LL.B., Harvard U., 1949. Bar: Calif., D.C. 1949, Ill. 1950. Jr. physicist metall. lab. U. Chgo., 1943-44; physicist Los Alamos Sci. Lab. (U. Calif.), N.Mex., 1944-45, Argonne Nat. Lab., AEC, Chgo., 1946; staff mem., group supr. Inst. Nuclear Studies, Mass. Inst. Tech., 1946-49; patent examiner U.S. Patent Office, Washington, 1949-50; asso. firm Fitch, Even, Tabin & Flannery, Chgo., 1950-52; mem. firm Fich, Even, Tabin & Flannery, 1952—; lectr. U. Chgo., 1959. Mem. Am., D.C., Calif., Ill., Chgo. bar assns., Sigma Xi. Home: 162 Park Ave Glencoe IL 60022-1352 Office: 135 S La Salle St Chicago IL 60603-4105

TABLER, BRYAN G., lawyer; b. Louisville, Jan. 12, 1943; s. Norman Gardner and Sarah Marie (Grant) T.; m. Susan Y. Beidler, Dec. 28, 1968 (div. June 1987); children: Justin Elizabeth, Gillian Gardner; m. Karen Sue Strome, July 24, 1987. AB, Princeton U., 1969; JD, Yale U., 1972. Bar: Ind. 1972, U.S. Dist. Ct. (so. dist.) Ind. 1972, U.S. Dist. Ct. (no. dist.) Ind. 1976, U.S. Ct. Appeals (7th cir.) 1976, U.S. Supreme Ct. 1976. Assoc. Barnes & Thornburg, Indpls., 1972-79, ptnr., chmn. environ. law dept., 1979-94; sr. v.p., gen. counsel, sec. IPALCO Enterprises, Inc., 1996—; sr. v.p., gen. coun., sec. Indpls. Power & Light Co., 1994—; mem. exec. com. Environ. Quality Control, Inc., Indpls., 1985—. Mem. Indpls. Mus. of Art, 1972—; bd. dirs. Indpls. Symphony Orch. 1st lt. U.S. Army, 1964-68, Vietnam. Mem. Ind. C. of C. (chmn. air com.), Indpls. C. of C. (govt. affairs coun. 1986-94), ABA, Ind. Bar Assn., Bar Assn. of the 7th Cir., Indpls. Bar Assn. Avocations: trap and skeet shooting, reading, golf. Home: 8932 Wickham Rd Indianapolis IN 46260-1644 Office: Indpls Power & Light Co One Monument PO Box 1595 Indianapolis IN 46206

TABLER, NORMAN GARDNER, JR., lawyer; b. Louisville, Oct. 15, 1944; s. Norman Gardner and Marie (Grant) T.; m. Dawn Carla Martin, May 6, 1989; 1 child, Rachel Ann Ayres. BA, Princeton U., 1966; MA, Yale U., 1968; JD, Columbia U., 1971. Bar: Ind. 1971, U.S. Dist. Ct. (so. dist.) Ind. 1971. Assoc. Baker & Daniels, Indpls., 1971-77, ptnr., 1978—; adj. prof. Ind. U. Law Sch., Indpls., 1984-88; mem. adv. com. Ctr. for Law and Health, Ind. U., Indpls., 1987-91; mem. antitrust task force Ind. Dept. Health, 1993-94; lectr. Ind. U. Ctr. on Philanthropy. Bd. dirs. Ind. Repertory Theatre, Inc., Indpls., 1984—, Indpls. Art Ctr., 1988-93, Indpls. Pub. Broadcasting, 1992—, Indpls. 500 Festival, 1992—, Brickyard 400 Festival, 1993—, Found. of Indy Festivals, 1995—, Indy Festivals, 1995—; mem. Ind. Sec. of State's Com. on Revision of Ind. Nonprofit Corp. Act, 1989-92; mem. Ind. Ednl. Fin. Authority, 1989-93; mem. Ind. Recreational Devel. Commn., 1993—; mem. Medicaid Task Force Ind. Commn. Health Policy, 1990-92. Mem. ABA (health care com. sect. antitrust law forum health com., health com. of sect. bus. law), Ind. Bar Assn. (health law sect.), Indpls. Bar Assn. (health law sect.), Am. Acad. Healthcare Attys. (com. on managed care and integrated delivery sys., com. on environ. law and OSHA com. on antitrust), Nat. Health Lawyers Assn. (vice chmn.), U.S. Squash Racquets Assn., Princeton Alumni Assn. Ind. (pres. 1988—), Indpls. Athletic Club (bd. dirs. 1994—), Skyline Club (bd. govs. 1992—), Princeton Club N.Y., Indpls. Press Club. Avocations: reading biographies, squash. Office: Baker & Daniels 300 N Meridian St Ste 2700 Indianapolis IN 46204-1755

TABLER, WILLIAM BENJAMIN, architect; b. Momence, Ill., Oct. 28, 1914; s. Clyde Lyeth and Frances Beatrice (Ridley) T.; m. Phyllis May Baker, June 12, 1937; children: William, Judith. B.S. cum laude, Harvard U., 1936, B.Arch., 1939, M.Arch., 1939. Architect specializing in hotels; prin. works include Hilton hotels in N.Y.C., Bklyn., Dallas, Pitts., San Francisco, Toronto, Rye Town, N.Y., Long Branch and Woodcliff Lake, N.J., Washington and Izmir, Turkey; Conrad Internat. Istanbul, Turkey; Intercontinental hotels in Lahore, Rawapindi, Jamaica, Ras Al Khaimah, Jeddah, Nairobi, Lusaka, Dacca, Amman, Karachi and Jerusalem; Marriott Phila., Sheraton Universal City, New Orleans, Brussels and Sheraton Centre, Toronto; Meridien hotels in Colombo, Sri Lanka, Cairo and Heliopolis, Egypt and Jakarta, Indonesia, Othon Palace in Rio and Bahia; Registry in Bloomington and Scottsdale; Grand Kempinski, Dallas; Hosts of Houston and Tampa; Sonesta Bermuda; Radisson Duluth, Lough Key, Ireland; New Otani L.A., Chosen, Korea; Stouffers, Chgo. and St. Louis; Bonaventure Montreal; Hanover, Woodstock and Princeton Inns; 15 Hospitality Motor Inns; also Harper and Stony Brook Coll. Dormitories; many others; mem. bldg. constrn. adv. council N.Y.C. Bldg. Dept., 1967—. Bd. dirs. Manhattan Eye, Ear and Throat Hosp., Community Hosp., Glen Cove. Served as lt. USNR, 1943-46, PTO. Recipient Horatio Alger award Am. Schs. and Colls. Assn., 1958; 1st prize for excellence in design Internat. Hotel, Queens C. of C., N.Y., 1958; Producers Council award, 1967. Fellow AIA (nat. chmn. bldg. codes com., pres. N.Y. chpt. 1967-68), ASCE; mem. Royal Inst. Brit. Architects, Bldg. Research Inst., N.Y. Bldg. Congress, NYU Hotel and Restaurant Soc., Am. Nat. Standards Inst. (exec. com. constrn. standards bd.), Nat. Fire Protection Assn. (chmn. sect. com. on residential occupancies, com. on safety to life), Ave. of Americas Assn. (bd. dirs.). Club: Harvard (bd. mgrs., exec. com., chmn. house com. N.Y.C.). Home: 44 Wolver Hollow Rd Glen Head NY 11545-2808 Office: 333 7th Ave New York NY 10001-5004

TABOR, CURTIS HAROLD, JR., library director; b. Atlanta, July 3, 1936; s. Curtis Harold and Gertrude Olive (Casey) T.; m. Dorothy May Corbin, June 30, 1957; children: Timothy M., John M. AA, Fla. Coll., Temple Terrace, 1957; BA, Harding Coll., 1960; MA, Butler U., 1967; MDiv, Bapt. Missionary Assn. Theol. Sem., Jacksonville, Tex., 1974; MLS, Tex. Woman's U., 1977. Min. Ch. of Christ, Bowling Green, Ky., 1960-61, Hamilton, Ont., Can., 1961-64, Indpls., 1964-67, Nacogdoches, Tex., 1967-75, Dallas, 1976-77, Columbus, Miss., 1977-79, Tampa, Fla., 1993—; tchr. Gt. Lakes Christian Coll., Beamville, Ont., Can., 1961-64; bible chair Stephen F. Austin State U., Nacogdoches, 1967-75; prof., libr. Fla. Coll., Temple Terrace, 1979-85, libr. dir., 1985—; participated archaeol. excavations, Tell Gezer, Israel, 1969, Tell Lachish, Israel, 1980. Author: (with others) Resurrection, 1973, Biblical Authority, 1974, The Lord of Glory, 1980. Cub master Cub Scouts Am., Nacogdoches, 1970-75; pres. Nacogdoches Baseball Assn., 1974-75. Recipient scouters key Cub Scouts Am., 1975. Mem. ALA, Fla. Libr. Assn., Tampa Bay Libr. Consortium (treas. 1986-89), Eta Beta Rho, Beta Phi Mu. Republican. Mem. Ch. of Christ. Avocation: Am. radio operator-KC4XS-Locksmith. Home: 12316 Kelly Ln Thonotosassa FL 33592-2754 Office: Fla Coll Libr 119 N Glen Arven Ave Tampa FL 33617-5527

TABOR, EDWARD, physician, researcher; b. Washington, Apr. 30, 1947; married; 4 children. BA, Harvard U., 1969; MD, Columbia U., 1973. Intern and resident Columbia-Presbyn. Med. Ctr., N.Y.C., 1973-75; rsch. investigator Bur. Biologics, Bethesda, Md., 1975-83; dir. divsn. anti-infective drug products FDA, Rockville, Md., 1983-88; assoc. dir. for biol. carcinogenesis Nat. Cancer Inst./NIH, Bethesda, 1988-95; dir. divsn. transfusion transmitted diseases FDA, Bethesda and Rockville, Md., 1995—. Contbr. articles to more than 200 publs. Capt. USPHS, 1975—. Achievements include research in hepatitis viruses, hepatocellular carcinoma. Office: FDA/CBER HFM-310 1401 Rockville Pike Rockville MD 20852-1448

TABOR, HERBERT, biochemist; b. N.Y.C., Nov. 28, 1918; s. Edward and Henrietta (Tally) T.; m. Celia White, Apr. 8, 1946; children: Edward, Marilyn, Richard, Stanley. AB, Harvard U., 1937, MD, 1941. Intern Yale U. and New Haven Hosp., 1942; chief Lab. Biochem. Pharmacology Nat. Inst. Diabetes, Digestive and Kidney Disease, Bethesda, Md., 1943. Editor in chief Jour. Biol. Chemistry; contbr. articles to profl. jours. Mem. NAS, Am. Soc. Pharm. and Exptl. Therapeutics, Am. Chem. Soc., Am. Soc. for Biochemistry and Molecular Biology, Am. Acad. Arts and Scis. Office: NIH Bldg 8 Rm 225 8 Center Dr Bethesda MD 20892-0830

TABOR, JOHN KAYE, retired lawyer; b. Uniontown, Pa., Apr. 19, 1921; s. Edward Otto and Marguerite B. (Kaye) T.; m. Kate Hill Williams, Dec. 13, 1952; children: John Kaye, William H. BA, Yale U., 1943; BA (Henry fellow), Corpus Christi Coll., Cambridge, Eng., 1947, MA, 1950; LLB, Harvard U., 1950; DHL, Alliance Coll., 1974. Bar: N.Y. 1950, Pa. 1953, D.C. 1976. Assoc. Winthrop, Stimpson, Putnam & Roberts, N.Y.C., 1950-53; assoc. Kirkpatrick, Pomeroy, Lockhart & Johnson, Pitts., 1953-58, ptnr., 1958-63; ptnr. Kirkpatrick, Lockhart, Johnson & Hutchison, Pitts., 1970-73, Purcell & Nelson, Washington, 1976-80, Reavis & McGrath, Washington, 1980-85; adj. prof. law George Mason U., Arlington, Va., 1986-87; pvt. practice Washington, 1985-90; sec. commerce State of Pa., 1963-67, sec. internal affairs, 1967-68, sec. labor and industry, 1968-69; chmn. Pa. Indsl. Devel. Authority, 1963-67; sec. Pa. Gen. State Authority, 1967-69; under sec. U.S. Dept. Commerce, Washington, 1973-75; chmn. housing task force and housing strike force Allegheny County Health and Welfare Assn., 1970-73. Trustee Masaryk Publs. Trust; bd. dirs. Citizens Assn. of Georgetown, 1985-89, 91; vestryman St. John's Ch., Georgetown. Lt. USNR, 1943-46, PTO. Mem. ABA (ad hoc criminal code and civil RICO coms.), Met. Club (Washington), Phi Beta Kappa. Home: 1616 34th St NW Washington DC 20007-2710

TABOR, THEODORE EMMETT, chemical company research manager; b. Great Falls, Mont., Dec. 28, 1940; s. John Edward and Alviva Lillian (Thorson) T.; m. Jacqueline Lou Hart, Aug. 5, 1959; children: Lori, John, Lexi. BA, U. Mont., 1962; PhD, Kansas State U., 1967. Various research and devel. positions Dow Chem. Co., Midland, Mich., 1967-81, mgr. coop. research, 1981—; co. rep. to Coun. for Chem. Rsch., 1982—; co. rep. to Indsl. Rsch. Inst., External Rsch. Dirs. Network, 1991—; co. rep. to Am. Chem. Soc., Co. Corp. Assocs., 1993—; program mgr. The Dow Chem. Co. Found., 1989-94. Mem. AAAS, Am. Chem. Soc., Soc. Rsch. Adminstrn., Nat. Coun. Univ. Rsch. Adminstrn. (assoc.), Assn. Univ. Tech. Mgrs. (affiliate), Tech. Transfer Soc. Mem. United Ch. Home: 2712 Mount Vernon Dr Midland MI 48642 Office: Dow Chem Co 1801 Building Midland MI 48674

TABORN, JEANNETTE ANN, real estate investor; b. Cleve., June 9, 1926; d. Ralph Mason and Catherine MArie (Mitchell) Tyler; m. Albert Lorenzo Taborn, Oct. 4, 1947 (dec. 1994); children: Wesley Orren, Annette Loren, KAren Faye, Albert Lorenzo II, Thomas Tyler. Student, Ohio State U., 1944-47. Real estate agt. and investor Cleve., 1947-61; tech. proofreader Sass-Widder Tech Writers, Port Hueneme, Calif., 1961-66, Upjohn Co., Kalamazoo, Mich., 1966-84; mktg. rep. pvt. practice, Kalamazoo, Mich., 1984—; regional mgr. Primerica, 1994; co-facilitator Healing Racism Series. Pres. Kalamazoo County Parent Tchr. Student Assn., 1975; active YWCA, 1981, NAACP, 1983; Kalamazoo Pub. Sch. bd., 1978; Greater Kalamazoo Arts Coun., 1979, Mich. sch. bd. vocat./Edn., Liberty com. C. of Com.; pres. Loy Norrix Trustee Fund, 1983; trustee Kalamazoo Intermediate Sch.; regional mgr. Al Williams. Recipient Cmty. Medal of Arts. Mem. So. West Mich. Alzheimer's Assn. (bd. mem.), Delta Sigma Theta (Mary McLeod Bethune award). Mem. Bahai Faith. Office: PO Box 50853 Kalamazoo MI 49005

TACAL, JOSE VEGA, JR., public health official, veterinarian; b. Ilocos Sur, Philippines, Sept. 5, 1933; came to U.S., 1969; s. Jose Sr. and Cristina (Vega) T.; m. Lilia Caccam, 1959; children: Joyce, Jasmin, Jose III. DVM, U. Philippines, Quezon City, 1956; diploma, U. Toronto, 1964. Diplomate Am. Coll. Vet. Preventive Medicine; lic. vet., Calif. Provincial veterinarian Philippine Bur. Animal Industry, Manila, 1956-57; instr. vet. medicine U. Philippines, Quezon City, 1957-64, asst. prof., chmn. dept. vet. microbiology, pathology and pub. health, 1965-69; pub. health veterinarian San Bernardino (Calif.) County Dept. Pub. Health, 1970-83, sr. pub. health veterinarian, program mgr., sect. chief, 1984—; zoonotic diseases lectr. Calif. State U., San Bernardino, spring 1984; lectr. U. Calif. Extension, Riverside, spring, 1985; vis. prof. vet. pub. health U. Philippines at Los Banos, Laguna, 1988. Columnist L.A. Free Press, 1991, Pilipinas Times, 1993, Mabuhay Times, 1994-95; contbr. more than 50 articles to profl. jours. Pres. Filipino Assn. of San Bernardino County, Highland, Calif., 1979; charter mem. Greater Inland Empire Filipino Assn., Highland, 1986—; del. First Filipino Media Conf. N.Am., L.A., 1993. Recipient Donald T. Fraser Meml. medal U. Toronto, 1964, Cert. of Merit, Philippine Vet. Med. Assn., 1965, Cert. of Appreciation Calif. State Bd. Examiners in Vet. Medicine, 1979, 84, Cert. of Recognition, Congressman George E. Brown Jr., 42d Congl. Dist. Calif., 1994, Assemblyman Joe Baca, 62d Assembly Dist., Calif. State Legis., 1994, Colombo Plan Study fellow Can./Philippine Govts., 1963-64. Mem. AAAS, AVMA, Orange Belt Vet. Med. Assn., Western Poultry Disease Conf., Soc. for the Advancement of Rsch., Phi Kappa Phi, Phi Sigma. Office: San Bernardino County Dept Pub Health 351 N Mountain View Ave San Bernardino CA 92415-0010

TACHA, ATHENA, sculptor, educator; b. Larissa, Greece, Apr. 23, 1936; came to U.S., 1963; MA, Nat. Acad. Fine Arts, Athens, Greece, 1959; MA in Art History, Oberlin Coll., 1961; PHD, U. Paris, 1963. Curator modern art Allen Art Mus., Oberlin, Ohio, 1963-73; prof. art Oberlin Coll., 1973—. One-woman shows include Zabriskie Gallery, N.Y., 1979, 81, Max Hutchinson Gallery, N.Y., 1984, High Mus. Art, Atlanta, 1989, Franklin Furnace, N.Y., 1994, and many other exhibits throughout the world, 1966—; prin. pub. commns. include sculptures at Dept. Environ. Protection, Trenton, N.J., Case-Western Res. U., Cleve., U. South Fla., Ft. Myers, Low Water Dam Riverfront Pk., Tulsa, Dept. of Transp., Hartford, Conn., City of Sarasota, Fla.; collections include Hirshhorn Mus., Washington, Mus. Fine Arts, Houston, Nat. Coll. Fine Arts, Washington, Cleve. Mus. Art, Allen Art Mus., Oberlin; author: (as A. T. Spear) Rodin Sculpture in the Cleveland Museum of Art, 1967, Brancusi's Birds, 1969; contbr. articles to profl. jours. Recipient 1st prize May Show, Cleve. Mus. Art, 1968, 71, 79; NEA grantee, 1975. Home: 291 Forest St Oberlin OH 44074-1509

TACHA, DEANELL REECE, federal judge; b. Jan. 26, 1946. BA, U. Kans., 1968; JD, U. Mich., 1971. Spl. asst. to U.S. Sec. of Labor, Washington, 1971-72; assoc. Hogan & Hartson, Washington, 1973, Thomas J. Pitner, Concordia, Kans., 1973-74; dir. Douglas County Legal Aid Clinic, Lawrence, Kans., 1974-77; assoc. prof. law U. Kans., Lawrence, 1974-77, prof., 1977-85, assoc. dean, 1977-79, assoc. vice chancellor, 1979-81, vice chancellor, 1981-85; judge U.S. Ct. Appeals (10th cir.), Denver, 1985—. Office: US Ct Appeals 10th Cir 4830 W 15th St Ste 100 Lawrence KS 66049-3846

TACHIWAKI, TOKUMATSU, chemistry educator; b. Kyoto, Japan, Oct. 27, 1938; s. Sensuke and Yasu (Kishimoto) T.; m. Teruko Otsubo, May 25, 1965; children: Kenji, Yasushi, Yuuko. B. Tech., Doshisha U., Kyoto, 1961, M. Tech., 1963; D Tech., Osaka (Japan) U., 1992. Asst. prof. dept. chem. engring. Doshisha U., Kyoto, 1963-83, lectr. prof. dept. chem. engring., 1983-88, assoc. prof. dept. chem. engring., 1988-94, prof., 1994—. Contbr. articles to profl. jours. Mem. Am. Inst. Chem. Engrs. Avocations: golf, gardening, fishing. Home: 11-41 Tenjinyama Miyamaki, Tanabe-cho, Kyoto 610-03, Japan Office: Doshisha U Dept Chem Engring & Material Sci, 1-3 Miyakotani Tatara Tanabe-cho, 610-03 Kyoto Japan

TACHMINDJI, ALEXANDER JOHN, systems engineering consultant; b. Athens, Greece, Feb. 16, 1928; came to U.S., 1950, naturalized, 1958; s. John and Athina (Andreades) T.; m. Diane E. Primeau, Dec. 4, 1965. B.Sc. with distinction, King's Coll., U. Durham, England, 1949; B.Sc. with honors, King's Coll., U. Durham, 1950; M.S., MIT, 1951; postgrad., U. Md., 1951-54. Head research and propeller br. David Taylor Model Basin, Washington, 1951-59; head tactical warfare group Inst. for Def. Analyses, Washington, 1959-64; asst. dir., dept. dir. sci. and tech. div. Inst. for Def. Analyses, 1964-69, dir. systems evaluation div., 1969-72; dir. tactical tech. office Def. Advanced Research Projects Agy., Washington,, 1972-73; dep. dir. Def. Advanced Research Projects Agy., 1973-75; chief scientist The MITRE Corp., McLean, Va., 1975-76, v.p., 1976-79, v.p. and gen. mgr. Washington ops., 1979-84; sr. v.p. and gen. mgr. C3I divsn. The MITRE Corp., Bedford, Mass., 1984-85, sr. v.p., 1985-89; cons., 1989—. Editor: Jour. Def. Rsch., 1969-91; patentee in field. Recipient Meritorious Civilian Svc. award USN, 1956, Sec. of Def. Meritorious Civilian Svc. medal, 1975. Fellow AAAS, AIAA (pubs. com. 1976-91, fin. com. 1990—), Royal Inst. Naval Architects; mem. Ops. Rsch. Soc. Am., N.E. Coast Inst. Engrs. and Shipbuilders, Soc. Naval Architects and Marine Engrs. (chmn. hydroelasticity panel, 1967-73, hydrodynamics com. 1967-86), Sigma Xi. Club: Cosmos (Washington).

TACKER, WILLIS ARNOLD, JR., academic administrator, medical educator, researcher; b. Tyler, Tex., May 24, 1942; s. Willis Arnold and Willie Mae (Massey) T.; m. Martha J. McClelland, Mar. 18, 1967; children: Sarah Mae, Betsy Jane, Katherine Ann. BS, Baylor U., 1964, MD, PhD, 1970. Lic. physician, Ind., Alaska, Tex. Intern Mayo Grad. Sch. Medicine Mayo Clinic, Rochester, Minn., 1970-71; pvt. practice Prudhoe Bay, Alaska, 1971; instr. dept. physiology Baylor Coll. Medicine, Houston, 1971-73, asst. prof. dept. physiology, 1973-74; clin. prof. family medicine Ind. U. Sch. Medicine, West Lafayette, Ind., 1981—; vis. asst. prof. Biomed. Engring. Ctr., Purdue U., West Lafayette, 1974-76, assoc. prof. Sch. Vet. Medicine, 1976-79; assoc. dir. William A. Hillenbrand Biomed. Engring. Ctr., Purdue U., West Lafayette, 1980-93, prof. Sch. Vet. Medicine, 1979—, acting dir., 1991-93; exec. dir. Hillenbrand Biomed. Engring. Ctr., 1993-95; vis. rsch. fellow Sch. Aerospace Medicine, Brooks AFB, San Antonio, 1982; with Corp. Sci. and Tech., State of Ind., 1985-88; presenter, cons. in field. Author: Some Advice on Getting Grants, 1991; co-author: Electrical Defibrillation, 1980; author: (with others) Handbook of Engineering and Medicine and Biology, 1980, Implantable Sensors for Closed-Loop Prosthetic Systems, 1985, Encyclopedia of Medical Devices and Instrumentation, 1988; contbr. numerous articles to profl. jours. Chmn. bd. dirs. Assn. Advancemnt Med. Instrumentation Found., Arlington, Va., 1987-95. Mem. Am. Heart Assn. (bd. dirs. Ind. affiliate 1975-81, med. edn. com. 1975-81, pub. health edn. com. 1975-81, chmn. ad hoc com. CPR tng. for physicians 1976-77, rsch. review com. 1988-90), Am. Physiol. Soc., Ind. State Med. Assn., Tippecanoe County Med. Soc., Assn. Advancement Med. Instrumentation (chmn. various coms., bd. dirs. 1981-84, pres. 1985-86), Am. Men and Women Sci., Alpha Epsilon Delta, Beta Beta Beta, Soc. Sigma Xi. Achievements include research in biomedical engineering, cardiovascular physiology, medical education, emergency cardiovascular care, motor evoked potentials, skeletal muscle ventricle; patents for an apparatus and method for measurement and control of blood pressure, electrode system and method for implantable defibrillators, pressure mapping system with capacitive measuring pad. Office: Purdue U 1293 A A Potter Bldg 204 West Lafayette IN 47907

TACKETT, STEPHEN DOUGLAS, education services specialist; b. Waverly, Ohio, Apr. 27, 1939; s. James Elbert and Zelma Iola (Manahan) T.; m. Magdalena Schneider, Jan. 4, 1958; children: Doris, Janice, Jerry, Suzanne. AA, El Paso C.C., 1974; BS, SUNY, Albany, 1976; MA, Ball State U., 1979. Nat. cert. counselor; lic. profl. clin. counselor. Enlisted U.S. Army, 1955, advanced through grades to Command Sgt. Maj., 1973, retired, 1982; instr. Mt. Wachusett C.C., Gardner, Mass., 1979-81; asst. dir. Evaluation U.S. Army Sgts. Maj. Acad., Ft. Bliss, Tex., 1981-82; dir. substance abuse treatment Sun Valley Hosp., El Paso, Tex., 1982-84; from guidance counselor to ednl. svcs. officer U.S. Army, Germany, 1984-86, 88-90; edn. advisor U.S. Army Sgts. Maj. Acad., Fort Bliss, 1990-92; edn. svcs. specialist Mil. Entrance Processing Sta., El Paso, 1992—; mem. adv. bd. for Counselor Edn. U. Tex., El Paso, 1983. Cubmaster Boy Scouts Am., Ft. Leonard Wood, Mo., 1970-71, com. mem., Frankfurt, Germany, 1972-73, asst. scoutmaster, Kaiserslautern, Germany, 1976-79. Mem. ACA, Am. Vocat. Assn., Nat.

Assn. Secondary Sch. Prins., N.Mex. Sch. Counselors Assn., Tex. Assn. Secondary Sch. Prins., Tex. Counseling Assn., Internat. Platform Assn. Office: Mil Entrance Processing Sta 700 E San Antonio Ave Fl 5 El Paso TX 79901-7020

TACKI, BERNADETTE SUSAN, principal; b. Kenosha, Wis., Oct. 21, 1913; d. Peter Frank and Anna (Rathke) T. BS in Edn., Dominican Coll., 1952; MA in Edn., Northwestern U., 1958. Tchr. Whitley Sch., Brighton Twp., Wis., 1932-33, Highland Sch., Pleasant Prairie, Wis., 1933-41, Victory Sch., Pleasant Prairie, 1941-47, Paris (Wis.) Consol. Sch., 1947-53, Southport Sch., Kenosha, 1953-61; prin. Harvey Sch., Kenosha, 1961-80; tchr. St. Casimir, Kenosha, 1983-93, vol. tchr. part-time, 1983—. Pres. Kenosha County Hist. Soc., 1985-89, St. James Parish Coun., Kenosha, 1975-89. Recipient Disting. Svc. award Wis. State Dept., 1980. Mem. AAUW, PTA, Ret. Tchrs. Assn., Kenosha County Tchrs. Assn. (past pres.), Kenosha Edn. Assn. (past pres.), Schubert Club, Quota Club, Delta Kappa Gamma (past pres.). Republican. Roman Catholic. Avocations: reading, traveling. Home: 7527 37th Ave Kenosha WI 53142-7217

TACKMAN, ARTHUR LESTER, newspaper publisher, management consultant; b. Chgo., July 28, 1916; s. Arthur Lester and Lucy Louise (Gutekunst) T.; m. Mary Lillian Connor, Mar. 31, 1939; children: Arthur Lester III, Laurence Connor, Alan Rhead. BA, Ohio State U., 1938, MPA, 1939. With various depts. U.S. Govt., Washington, 1938-49; staff asst., mem. pers. policy bd. Dept. Def., Washington, 1949; asst. mgr. Savannah river plant AEC, Aiken, S.C., 1950-55; asst. dir. inspection AEC, Washington, 1955-59, dir. pers., 1959-65; dir. pers. HUD, Washington, 1965-70; mgmt. cons. Glenwood, N.Mex., 1970-78; owner, operator Deep Creek Ranch, Inc., Glenwood, 1972—; publisher Catron Co. Pub. Co., Inc., Reserve, N.Mex., 1986-91. Pres. Gila Nat. Forest Permittees, Reserve, 1978-86; mem., treas. N.Mex. Pub. Lands Coun., Albuquerque, 1967-87; coun. mem. Boy Scouts Am., S.C., Washington, 1950-65. Lt. USN, 1943-46. Recipient Man Yr. Award Aiken County C. of C., 1953, Citation for Meritorious Svc. United Def. Fund, 1957. Mem. N.Mex. Press Assn. Democrat. Unitarian. Home: Deep Creek Ranch Glenwood NM 88039

TACKOWIAK, BRUCE JOSEPH, lawyer; b. Milw., July 10, 1956; s. Eugene Charles and Bernadine (Van Engle) T.; m. Deborah A. Moore, Dec. 11, 1994. BA in History and Polit. Sci., U. Wis., 1979; cert. emergency med. technician, Madison Area Tech. Coll., 1981; Diploma in Internat. and Comparative Law, Magdalen Coll., U. Oxford, Eng., 1986; JD, U. San Diego, 1988. Bar: Calif. 1990, Ill. 1991, U.S. Dist. Ct. (ctrl. and so. dists.) Calif. 1990, U.S. Ct. Appeals (4th cir.) 1990. Atty. LaFollette, Johnson, De Haas, Fesler & Ames, L.A., 1990-92, Hillsinger & Costanzo, L.A., 1992-93, Roxborough, Pomerance & Gallegos, LLP, L.A., 1993—; assoc. Am. Inns of Ct., 1992—. Sr./mng. editor U. San Diego Jour. Contemporary Legal Issues, 1987-88. Mem. ABA, Calif. Bar Assn., Los Angeles County Bar Assn., Ill. Bar Assn., Chgo. Bar Assn., World Futurist Soc. (profl.). Avocations: team sports, running, tennis. Office: Roxborough, Pomerance & Gallegos LLP Ste 1200 10866 Wilshire Blvd Los Angeles CA 90024

TACKWELL, ELIZABETH MILLER, social worker; b. Caney, Kans., Mar. 14, 1923; d. Jesse Winfield and Mattie (Shuler) Miller; m. Joseph J. Tackwell, Dec. 13, 1946 (dec. Mar. 1988); children: Steven, Tiana Tackwell David, Christy Tackwell Reyner. BA, U. Okla., 1953, MSW, 1962. Bd. cert. diplomate Am. Bd. Examiners in Clin. Social Work; lic. social worker, Okla. Social worker Dept. Pub. Welfare, Tulsa/Cleve./Okla. County, Okla., 1958-59; med. social analyst Dept. Pub. Welfare, Okla., 1960-61; assoc. John Massey M.D. Clinic, Oklahoma City, 1964-69; clin. asst. prof. Okla. U. Sch. Social Work, Oklahoma City, 1964—; asst. prof., clin. instr. dept. psychiatry/behavioral scis. Okla. U. Health Scis. Ctr., Oklahoma City, 1963—; psychiat. social worker VA Med. Ctr., Oklahoma City, 1961—, chief mental health sect., 1976—, adminstrv. dir. day treatment ctr., 1993—; pvt. practice Oklahoma City, 1971—; VA Med. Ctr.; psychiat. surveyor Health Care Fin. Adminstrn., Dept. Human Svcs., Washington, 1985—. Recipient Svc. Commendation award DAV, 1980, Chi Omega Scholastic award, Awards Am. Ex-Prisoners of War, 1994, 95, 96. Mem. NASW (diplomate in clin. social work, pres. Okla. chpt. 1971-73, Social Worker of the Yr. Western Okla. chpt. 1975), Acad. Cert. Social Workers, Okla. Health and Welfare Assn. (conf. chmn. 1975—), Pi Gamma Mu. Home: 1328 Tarman Cir Norman OK 73071-4846 Office: Vets Affairs Med Ctr 921 NE 13th St Oklahoma City OK 73104-5007

TADDEI, GIUSEPPE, baritone; b. Genova, Italy. Appeared as Figaro in The Marriage of Figaro, Salzburg, 1948; N.Y. Met. debut as Falstaff in Falstaff, 1985; performances include Vienna Staatsoper, 1946—; numerous recs. including La Bohème, Ernani, Un Ballo in Maschera, Guillaume Tell, Rigoletto, Falstaff, Don Giovanni, Cosi Fan Tutte, others. Also: c/o Stattstheater Stuttgart, Oberer Schlossgarten 6, D-7000 Stuttgart 1, Germany

TADE, GEORGE THOMAS, university dean; b. Casey, Ill., Dec. 17, 1923; s. Thomas Clement and Lena (Myers) T.; m. Wilma Jean Daily, July 7, 1946; children—Mitzi Jean Tade Mills, Terry Nan Tade Helmick. B.S., Ind. State U., 1945, M.S., 1946; Ph.D., U. Ill., 1955. Ordained to ministry Disciples of Christ Ch., 1946. Asst. prof., then assoc. prof. speech Greenville (Ill.) Coll., 1946-53, dean coll., prof. speech, 1953-59; dean Chapman (Calif.) U., 1959-62; prof. speech, chmn. dept., chmn. div. humanities Tex. Christian U., Ft. Worth, 1962-72, acting dean Sch. Fine Arts, 1972-73, dean Sch. Fine Arts, 1973-87, dean Coll. Fine Arts and Communication, 1987-89, emeritus dean, 1989—; interim headmaster Ft. Worth Acad., 1989-90; cons. communication to pvt. and govt. agy.; coord. liberal arts study N. Central Assn. Colls., 1959. Contbr. numerous articles to profl. jours. Councilman-at-large, Greenville, Ill., 1956-59; bd. dirs. Ft. Worth Acad., Van Cliburn Internat. Piano Competition; mem. exec. bd. Arts Council, Ft. Worth and Tarrant County. Mem. Speech Communication Assn., So. Speech Assn. (exec. council 1972-75), Western Coll. Deans Assn. (sec. 1960-62), Internat. Council Fine Arts Deans, Nat. Conf. Acad. Deans (vice chmn. 1984, chmn. 1985), Tex. Council on Arts in Edn. (v.p. 1975-77, pres. 1978-80), Tex. Speech Communication Assn. (pres. 1973-74), Pi Kappa Delta, Gamma Theta Upsilon, Sigma Alpha Eta. Mem. Univ. Christian Ch. (chmn. gen. bd., trustee 1973-75). Home: 3705 Arborlawn Dr Fort Worth TX 76109-3304

TAESCHLER, DEBRA ANN, advertising executive; b. Jersey City, Jan. 7, 1953; d. Edward George and Marion Madeline (Naas) Miller; m. John Paul Taeschler, June 24, 1978. BA summa cum laude, Rutgers U., 1975. With mech. arts dept. Vornado, Inc., Garfield, N.J., 1975-76; asst. account exec. Clifton (N.J.) Graphix Assn., 1976-77; advt. mgr. Davis Printing Corp., Carlstadt, N.J., 1977-80; v.p. account mgr. Landmark Assocs., Whippany, N.J., 1980-85; account mgr. R.Z.A. Advt., Inc., Park Ridge, N.J., 1985-86; pres. Grafica, Inc., Chester, N.J., 1986—. Mem. Phi Beta Kappa. Roman Catholic. Avocations: art, theater, dancing. Office: Grafica Inc 50 Main St Chester NJ 07930-2535

TAEUBER, CONRAD, demography educator, former government statistician; b. Hosmer, S.D., June 15, 1906; s. Richard Ernst and Emmy (Mussgang) T.; m. Irene Barnes, July 26, 1929 (dec. Feb. 24, 1974); children: Richard Conrad, Karl Ernst; m. Dorothy Harris, Sept. 10, 1979. A.B., U. Minn., 1927, M.A., 1929, Ph.D., 1931; student, U. Heidelberg (1929-30), Germany, U. Wis., 1930-31. Instr. U. Wis., 1930-31; asst. prof. Mt. Holyoke Coll., 1931-33; assoc. econ. analyst Fed. Emergency Relief Adminstrn., 1934-35; agrl. economist Bur. Agrl. Econ., Dept. Agr., 1935-40, sr. social scientist, 1940-42, prin. social sci., acting head div. of farm population and rural welfare, 1942-43; head agrl. economist Bur. Agrl. Econ., 1943-46; statistician Food and Agrl. Orgn. of UN, 1946-51; asst. dir. Bur of Census, 1951-68, assoc. dir., 1968-73; Joseph F. Kennedy Sr. prof. demography Kennedy Inst., Georgetown U., Washington, 1973-85. Contbr. articles to social science jours.; Author: (with C.E. Lively) Rural Migration in the United States, 1939, (with Irene B. Taeuber) The Changing Population of the United States, 1958, People of the United States in the 20th Century, 1972. Recipient U. Minn. award, 1951, Exceptional Service award Dept. Commerce, 1963. Fellow Am. Statis. Assn., AAAS, Am. Sociol. Assn. (Disting. Career award for Practice of Sociology 1986); mem. Population Assn. Am. (former pres.), Inter-Am. Statis Inst. (past pres.), Rural Sociol. Soc., Internat. Statis. Inst., Sociol. Research Assn. Club: Cosmos (Washington). Home: 10 Allds St Nashua NH 03060-4716

TAFEL, EDGAR, architect; b. N.Y.C., Mar. 4, 1912; s. Samuel and Rose (Chary) T. Student, NYU, 1930-32. Sr. fellow Frank Lloyd Wright's Taliesin Fellowship, Spring Green, Wis., 1932-41; practice architecture N.Y.C., 1946—; lectr. USIS, Eng., Israel, India, Netherlands, 1972-73, New Sch. for Social Rsch., N.Y.C., 1974; faculty Smithsonian Instn., 1978; co-producer, actor (video) The Frank Lloyd Wright Way. Author: Years with Frank Lloyd Wright, About Wright, 1993; contbr. articles to profl. jours.; Prin. works include: Protestant Chapel at Kennedy Airport, 1964, First Presbyn. Ch. Addition, 1959, De Witt Ch., all N.Y.C., Fine Arts Bldg., State U. N.Y. at Geneseo, 1967, Fulton-Montgomery Community Coll, Johnstown, N.Y., 1969, Grace Ch, White Plains, 1970, Allentown (Pa.) Art Mus. addition, 1975, Columbia-Greene Community Coll, Hudson, N.Y., 1974, Salvation Army Corps Community Centers; master plans for: State Coll. at Geneseo, York Coll., N.Y.C., Cadet Corps Hdqrs., Bronx, N.Y.; designed over 100 residences. Bd. dirs. N.Y.C. Mission Soc. Served with AUS, World War II, CBI. Recipient award of merit for Presbyn. Ch. Fifth Ave. Assn., N.Y.C., service citation State U. N.Y. Coll. at Geneseo, 1970. Fellow AIA; mem. Nat. Acad. Arts (assoc.), Taliesin Fellowship (coun.), Fallingwater (adv. com.). Home and Office: 14 E 11th St New York NY 10003-4402

TAFELSKI, MICHAEL DENNIS, psychologist; b. Wyandotte, Mich., Apr. 12, 1949; s. Chester John and Veronica (Machcinski) T. BA in Sociology and Psychology, Wayne State U., 1973, MSW, 1975, MEd, 1976. Lic. med. social worker, Mich. Caseworker home attendent div. N.Y.C. Dept. Human Resouces, 1976-78; intake case mgr. Phoenix House Found., Inc., N.Y.C., 1978-81; ptnr. GR Social Svcs., Grand Rapids, Mich., 1982-84; founding ptnr. Tafelski, Tafelski & Gatz and predecessor firm Tafelski, Tafelski, Gatz & Robaskewicz, P.C., Grand Rapids, 1984—. Contbr. to Profl. Jour. of Social Work, 1984-86, DNC, 1992—. State of Mich. Higher Edn. grantee, Lansing, 1969. Mem. Polish Falcons Soc., KC (Grand Knight). Democrat. Roman Catholic. Avocations: photography, psychopathology, lit. Office: Tafelski Tafelski Gatz 4254 Lamdale Ct SE Ste 9B Grand Rapids MI 49546-2403

TAFLOVE, ALLEN, electrical engineer, educator, researcher, consultant; b. Chgo., June 14, 1949; s. Harry and Leah (Natovich) T.; m. Sylvia Hinda Friedman, Nov. 6, 1977; children: Michael Lee, Nathan Brent. BS with highest distinction, Northwestern U., 1971, MS, 1972, PhD, 1975. Assoc. engr. IIT Rsch. Inst., Chgo., 1975-78, rsch. engr., 1978-81, sr. engr., 1981-84; assoc. prof. Northwestern U., Evanston, Ill., 1984-88, prof., 1988—; originator 6-yr. BS/PhD degree program in engring. Northwestern U., 1988—; cons. Electric Power Rsch. Inst., Palo Alto, Calif., 1985-86, Lawrence Livermore Nat. Lab., 1985-87, Lockheed Missiles and Space Co., Sunnyvale, Calif., 1985-88, MRJ Inc., Oakton, Va., 1987-90, U.S. Naval Rsch. Lab., Washington, 1988-95, Cray Rsch., Inc., Eagan, Minn., 1991—, Village of Wilmette, Ill., 1991-93, City of Wheaton, Ill., 1991-92, B.C. Hydro, Vancouver, Can., 1991-92, Commonwealth Edison, Chgo., 1992—, MIT Lincoln Lab., 1992-93, The Intec Group, 1995—. Co-author: Computational Electromagnetics: Integral Equation Approach, 1993; author: Computational Electrodynamics: The Finite-Difference Time-Domain Method, 1995; contbr. 9 book chpts. and over 60 articles to profl. jours.; patentee in field. Keynote spkr. Salishan Conf. on High-Performance Computing, 1994, Instn. Elec. Engrs. Internat. Conf. on Antennas and Propagation, 1995. Recipient Adviser of Yr. award Northwestern U., 1991; Cabell fellow, 1975; rsch. grantee USAF, Electric Power Rsch. Inst., Lawrence Livermore Nat. Lab., NSF, Office Naval Rsch., Gen. Dynamics Corp., Northrop Corp., Lockheed Corp., Sci. Applications, Inc., Cray Rsch., Inc., Northwestern Meml. Hosp., NASA Ames Ctr., NASA Lewis Ctr., 1977—. Fellow IEEE (Best Paper award 1983); mem. AAAS, IEEE Antennas and Propagation Soc. (Disting. nat. lectr. 1990-91, chmn. tech. program com. Internat. Symposium 1992), Electromagnetics Acad., Internat. Union Radio Sci. (commn. B, D and K), N.Y. Acad. Scis., Sigma Xi, Eta Kappa Nu, Tau Beta Pi. Achievements include pioneer of finite-difference time-domain method in computational electromagnetics. Office: Northwestern U Dept Elec Engring Comp Sci 2145 Sheridan Rd Evanston IL 60208-0834

TAFOYA, ARTHUR N., bishop; b. Alameda, N.Mex., Mar. 2, 1933; s. Nicholas and Rosita Tafoya. Ed., St. Thomas Sem., Denver, Conception (Mo.) Sem. Ordained priest Roman Cath. Ch., 1962. Asst. pastor Holy Rosary Parish, Albuquerque, 1962-65; pastor Northern N.Mex., from 1965, San Jose Parish, Albuquerque; rector Immaculate Heart of Mary Sem., Santa Fe; ordained bishop of Pueblo Colo., 1980—. Office: 1001 N Grand Ave Pueblo CO 81003-2915*

TAFT, BOB, state official; b. Jan. 8, 1942; m. Hope Taft; 1 child, Anna. BA, Yale U., 1963; MA, Princeton U., 1967; JD, U. Cin., 1976. Pvt. practice; rep. Ohio Ho. Reps., 1976-80; commr. Hamilton County, Ohio, 1981-90; sec. of state Ohio, 1990—. Office: 30 E Broad St Fl 14 Columbus OH 43266-0418

TAFT, ROBERT ANTHONY, government official, educator; b. N.Y.C., Apr. 13, 1946; s. Robert Davis and Margaret (Neracher) T.; m. Pamela Heller; children: Kristine, Mary Shea. BA in English, St. Michael's Coll., 1968; cert. in mgmt., U. Va., 1973; MBA, U. Conn., 1975. Vol. Peace Corps, The Philippines, 1968-70; policy analyst Dept. Commerce, Washington, 1976-80, mgr. export promotion svcs., 1980-86; comml. min. Dept. Commerce, Australia, 1986-90, Venezuela, 1990-92; dir. western hemisphere Dept. Commerce, Washington, 1993-94, dep. asst. sec., 1994—. Internat. Bus. fellow Dept. Commerce, 1974. Office: Dept Commerce 14th & Constitution Ave NW Washington DC 20230

TAFT, SETH CHASE, retired lawyer; b. Cin., Dec. 31, 1922; s. Charles Phelps and Eleanor K. (Chase) T.; m. Frances Prindle, June 19, 1943; children: Frederick, Thomas, Cynthia, Tucker. B.A., Yale U., 1943, LL.B., 1948. Bar: Ohio 1948. Assoc. Jones, Day, Reavis & Pogue, Cleve., 1948-59, ptnr., 1959-88. Mem. Cuyahoga County (Ohio) Bd. Commrs., 1971-78, pres., 1977-78; mem. Cuyahoga County Charter Commn., 1958-59; Rep. candidate for mayor of Cleve., 1967, for gov. of Ohio, 1982; pres. Fedn. for Community Planning, Cleve., 1986-89, Cleve. Internat. Program, 1990-94; chmn. Substance Abuse Initiative Greater Cleve., 1989—. With USNR, 1943-46. Home: 6 Pepper Ridge Rd Cleveland OH 44124-4904 Office: Jones Day Reavis & Pogue 901 Lakeside Ave E Cleveland OH 44114-1190

TAFT, SHELDON ASHLEY, lawyer; b. Cleve., Mar. 2, 1937; s. Kingsley Arter and Louise Parsons (Dakin) T.; m. Rebecca Sue Rinehart, Dec. 26, 1962; children: Mariner R., Ashley A., Curtis N. BA, Amherst Coll., 1959; LLB, Harvard U., 1962. Bar: Ohio 1962. Assoc. Vorys, Sater, Seymour & Pease, Columbus, Ohio, 1965-69, 71-73, ptnr., 1974—; chief legal counsel Pub. Utilities Commn. Ohio, Columbus, 1969-71; Ohio bd. advisors Chgo. Title Ins. Co., 1967—. Rep. candidate for justice Ohio Supreme Ct., 1974; bd. advisors Coun. on Econ. Regulation, 1986—; trustee Opera Columbus, 1989—, pres., 1991-93, life trustee, 1995—. 1st lt. USAF, 1963-65. Mem. ABA (mem. pub. utilities sect.), Ohio State Bar Assn. (pres. pub. utilities com. 1984-87), Columbus Bar Assn., Ohio Camera Collectors Soc. (pres. 1985-87), Rocky Fork Hunt and Country Club, Univ. Club (Columbus), Capital Club, 41 Club. Congregationalist. Avocations: camera collecting, sailing. Home: 317 Stanbery Ave Columbus OH 43209-1468 Office: Vorys Sater Seymour & Pease PO Box 1008 52 E Gay St Columbus OH 43216-1008

TAFT, WILLIAM HOWARD, journalism educator; b. Mexico, Mo., Oct. 24, 1915; s. Raymond E. and Ferrie (Dains) T.; m. Myrtle Marie Adams, Jan. 18, 1941; children: Marie, William Howard, Alice. AB, Westminster Coll., 1937; B in Journalism, U. Mo., 1938, MA, 1939; PhD, Western Res. U., 1951. Dir. pub. rels. Hiram (Ohio) Coll., 1939-40, 47-48; asst. prof. journalism Youngstown (Ohio) Coll., 1946-48; prof. Defiance (Ohio) Coll., 1948-50; assoc. prof. Memphis State Coll., 1950-56; prof. U. Mo., Columbia, 1956-81, assoc. dean grad. programs, 1980-81; yearbook cons., 1957—. Author: Let's Publish That Top-Rated Yearbook, 1961, (with others) Modern Journalism, 1962, Missouri Newspapers, 1964, Missouri Newspapers, When and Where, 1808-1962, 1964, American Journalism History, 1968, rev. edit., 1977, Newspapers as Tools for Historians, 1970, (with others) Mass Media and the National Experience, 1971, Donrey Media; A Low Profile Group, 1976, Magazines for the Eighties, 1981, Encyclopedia of 20th Century Journalists, 1986, Missouri Newspapers and the Missouri Press Association, 125 Years of Service, 1867-1992, 1992, Wit and Wisdom of Country Editors, 1996; contbr. articles to profl. jours. and encys. With USAAF, 1941-45. Recipient Faculty-Alumni citation U. Mo., 1979, Alumni Achievement award Westminster Coll., 1987; rsch. fellow Washington Journalism Ctr., 1967. Mem. Assn. Edn. Journalism and Mass. Comm. (Presdl. award 1991), Boone County Hist. Soc. (past pres.), Kiwanis (past pres., Churchman of Yr. 1987, Kiwanian of Yr. 1993), Delta Tau Delta (life), Pi Delta Epsilon, Kappa Tau Alpha (nat. treas., exec. dir. 1962-91). Republican. Methodist. Home: 107 Sondra Ave Columbia MO 65202-1416

TAGATZ, GEORGE ELMO, obstetrician, gynecologist, educator; b. Milw., Sept. 21, 1935; s. George Herman and Beth Elinore (Blain) T.; m. Susan Trunnell, Oct. 28, 1967; children: Jennifer Lynn, Kirsten Susan, Kathryn Elizabeth. A.B., Oberlin Coll., 1957; M.D., U. Chgo., 1961. Diplomate Am. Bd. Obstetricians and Gynecologists, Am. Bd. Reproductive Endocrinology (examiner, bd. reproductive endocrinology 1976-79). Rotating intern Univ. Hosps. of Cleve., 1961-62, resident in internal medicine, 1962-63; resident in ob-gyn U. Iowa, 1965-68; sr. research fellow in endocrinology U. Wash. dept. obstetrics and gynecology, 1968-70; asst. prof. ob-gyn U. Minn. Med. Sch., 1970-73, asso. prof., 1973-76, prof., 1976—, asst. prof. internal medicine, 1970-73, dir. div. reproductive endocrinology, 1974-92; mem. fertility and maternal health adv. com. FDA, USPHS, HHS, 1982-86; cons. in field, 1986-87. Ad hoc editor: Am. Jour. Ob-Gyn, Fertility and Sterility; contbr. articles to profl. publs. Served with M.C. U.S. Army, 1963-65. Mem. AMA, Minn., Hennepin County med. socs., Minn. Obstet. and Gynecol. Soc., Am. Coll. Ob-Gyn (subcom. on reproductive endocrinology 1979-82), Endocrine Soc., Am. Fertility Soc., Central Assn. Obstetricians and Gynecologists, U. Iowa Ob-Gyn Alumni Soc. Home: 5828 Long Brake Trl Minneapolis MN 55439-2622 Office: U Minn Hosps & Clinic PO Box 395 Minneapolis MN 55455

TAGER, JACK, historian, educator; b. Bklyn., Oct. 18, 1936; s. Alexander and Mildred T.; children: David, Miriam. B.A., Bklyn. Coll., 1958; M.A., U. Calif.-Berkeley, 1959; Ph.D., U. Rochester, N.Y., 1965. Asst. prof. Ohio State U., Columbus, 1964-67; prof. history U. Mass., Amherst, 1967—; dir. univ. honors program U. Mass., 1978-82. Author: The Intellectual as Urban Reformer: Brand Whitlock and the Progressive Movement, 1968, The Historical Atlas of Massachusetts, 1991, also articles; editor: Urban Vision, 1970, Massachusetts in the Gilded Age, 1985. Served with U.S. Army, 1959, 61-62. Mem. Orgn. Am. Historians, Am. Hist. Assn. Home: PO Box 2417 Amherst MA 01004-2417 Office: U Mass History Dept Amherst MA 01003

TAGGART, G. BRUCE, government program executive; b. Phila., Apr. 8, 1942; s. Robert Henry Taggart and Rachael Elizabeth Burtt. BS in Physics, Coll. William and Mary, 1964; postgrad. in engineering mechanics, U. Pa., 1964-65; PhD in Physics, Temple U., 1971. Instr. dept. physics Drexel U., Phila., 1970; asst. prof. dept. physics Va. Commonwealth U., Richmond, 1971-77, assoc. prof., 1977-82, prof., 1982-83; from mgr. materials sci. tech. to prin. staff mem., phys. scis. tech. divsn. BDM Internat., McLean, Va., 1983-90; program dir. materials theory, divsn. materials rsch. NSF, Washington, 1990—; vis. asst. prof. dept. physics Temple U., Phila., 1970-71; rsch. assoc. with theory group Oak Ridge (Tenn.) Nat. Lab., 1974; vis. prof. dept. theoretical physics Oxford (Eng.) U., 1978, Fed. U. Pernambuco, Recife, Brazil, 1980; vis. assoc. prof. dept. physics U. Ill., Urbana, 1978-79; guest worker with statis. physics group thermophysics divsn. Nat. Inst. Standards and Tech., Gaithersburg, Md., 1978-88; lectr. dept. physics and astronomy U. Md., College Park, 1989-90; vis. scientist divsn. materials rsch. on leave from BDM Internat., NSF, 1989-90; presenter in field. Referee: Phys. Rev., Physics Letters, Jour. of the Physics and Chemistry of Solids, Acad. Press, DARPA, NSF; contbr. numerous articles to profl. jours. Scholar Coll. William and Mary, 1964; Ford fellow U. Pa., 1964-65; NSF summer fellow and Univ. fellow Temple U., 1971. Mem. AAAS, Am. Phys. Soc. (condensed matter physics divsn., materials physics divsn., high polymer physics divsn.), Materials Rsch. Soc., Sigma Pi Sigma. Achievements include research in condensed matter physics, materials science and statistical mechanics. Office: Nat Sci Found 4201 Wilson Blvd Arlington VA 22230-0001

TAGGART, GANSON POWERS, management consultant; b. Albany, N.Y., Aug. 16, 1918; s. Ralph Cone and Ruth Harriett (Townsend) T.; m. Paulett Long, June 30, 1945; children: H.Tee, Paulett Long, Cornelia V.C. B.S. in Chem. Engring., U. Mich., 1940, M.S. in Chem. Engring., 1941; postgrad., Northeastern Sch. Advanced Mgmt., 1964. Registered engr., Mass. Mng. dir. Badger N.V., The Hague, Netherlands, 1965-70; v.p. world sales Badger Co., Cambridge, Mass., 1970-71; sr. v.p., dir. Badger Co. Inc., Cambridge, 1978-82; mgmt. cons. Devel. Scis. Inc., Sandwich, Mass., 1972-77; chmn. bd. Serapis Energy Inc., Boston, 1982-85, dir.; pres. Mgmt. Systems Inc., 1984—; chmn. bd. William K. Stout Pub. Co., 1995—. Contbr. articles to mags. Oil mem. Energy Facilities Siting Coun. Mass., Boston, 1979-82; mem. Winchester (Mass.) Planning Bd., 1971-77, Winchester Town Meeting, 1960-64; mem. exec. com. Internat. Sch. The Hague, 1965-70; trustee Ledges Condominium Assn., USS Constn. Mus., 1989-95, treas. 1991-92; moderator Winchester Unitarian Soc., 1983-93; active Mus. Sci., Boston, Found. Global Cmty. Lt. (j.g.) USNR, 1944-48. Mem. AIChE (chmn. Boston sect. 1955, Order of Xiphias), Soc. Chem. Industry (London), Conservation Law Found., Am. Chem. Soc., World Bus. Acad., Inst. Noetic Scis., Chemists Club (N.Y.C.), Annisquam Yacht Club (Gloucester, Mass.), Downtown Club (Boston). Office: PO Box 516 7 Church St Winchester MA 01890-0716 *Hard work and flexibility in doing and thinking pays big dividends, as long as you are honest with yourself and others. I have always tried to see things from the other person's point of view, to give them the benefit of the doubt. I strive always to do the best I can and I do not spend a lot of time analyzing or criticizing what is wrong with others. And most important is a wonderful wife who accepts constructively life as it is dealt to you.*

TAGGART, THOMAS MICHAEL, lawyer; b. Sioux City, Iowa, Feb. 22, 1937; s. Palmer Robert and Lois Allette (Sedgwick) T.; m. Dolores Cecilia Baroway Renfro, Jan. 4, 1963; children: Thomas Michael Jr., Theodore Christopher; m. Mary Ann Gribben, Feb. 7, 1976. BA, Dartmouth Coll., 1959; JD, Harvard U., 1965. Bar: Ohio 1965, U.S. Dist. Ct. (so. dist.) Ohio 1967, U.S. Dist. Ct. (no. dist.) Ohio 1981. Ptnr. Vorys, Sater, Seymour & Pease, Columbus, Ohio, 1965—; lectr. Ohio Legal Ctr. Inst., Ohio Mfrs. Assn., Capital U. Ctr. for Spl. and Continuing Legal Edn. Served to capt. USMC, 1959-63. Mem. ABA, Ohio State Bar Assn. (bd. govs. 1991-96), Columbus Bar Assn. (bd. govs., pres. 1989-90), Ohio Assn. Civil Trial Attys., Am. Arbitration Assn., Columbus Area C. of C., Univ. Columbus Club. Methodist. Home: 145 Stanbery Ave Columbus OH 43209-1465 Office: Vorys Sater Seymour & Pease 52 E Gay St Columbus OH 43215-3108

TAGGE, ANNE KATHERINE, not-for-profit organization administrator; b. Waltham, Mass., Oct. 20, 1954; d. Raymond Carl and Anne (Weller) T. BA, Wellesley Coll., 1977. Pres., founder Susan Lee Campbell Inst., Wellesley, Mass., 1986—; Spkr. in field. Contbr. to newspapers, mags., jours. and books. Pres. Mass. chpt. Fulbright Assn.; adv. bd. Ctr. Am. Studies. Recipient US/UNEP Achievement award, Enterprise award Rolex; East European Rsch. Ctr. fellow; Town of wellesley scholar, Fulbright scholar. Mem. Explorers Club. Avocations: athletics. Home: Moshup Trail Martha's Vineyard MA 02535 Office: 37 Avon Rd Wellesley MA 02181-4618

TAGIURI, CONSUELO KELLER, child psychiatrist, educator; b. San Francisco; d. Cornelius H. and Adela (Rios) Keller; m. Renato Tagiuri; children: Robert, Peter, John. BA, U. Calif.-Berkeley; MD, U. Calif.-San Francisco. Diplomate Am. Bd. Psychiatry and Neurology. Resident psychiatry Mass. Gen. Hosp., Boston; staff psychiatrist Children's Hosp., Boston, 1951-59; med. dir. Gifford Sch., Weston, Mass., 1965-85; chief psychiatrist Cambridge (Mass.) Guidance Ctr., 1961-84; mem. faculty dept. psychiatry Harvard Med. Sch., Cambridge, 1965—; cons. early childhood program Children's Hosp., 1985—. Contbr. articles in field to books. Fellow Am. Orth. psychiat. Assn., Mass. Med. Soc., New Eng. Council Child Psychiatry.

TAGLIABUE, PAUL JOHN, national football league commissioner; b. Jersey City, Nov. 24, 1940; s. Charles and Mary T.; m. Chandler M. Minter, Aug. 28, 1965; children: Drew, Emily. BA, Georgetown U., 1962; JD, NYU, 1965. Bar: N.J 1965, D.C. 1969. Atty. to sec. def. Dept. Def., Washington, 1966-69; assoc. Covington & Burling, Washington, 1969-74, ptnr., 1969-89; commissioner NFL, N.Y.C., 1989—. Contbr. articles to profl. jours. Mem. ABA (chmn. sports and entertainment industry com. antitrust sect. 1986), D.C. Bar Assn. Office: NFL Commr's Office 410 Park Ave New York NY 10022-4407

TAGLIAFERRI, LEE GENE, investment banker; b. Mahanoy City, Pa., Aug. 14, 1931; s. Charles and Adele (Cirilli) T.; B.S., U. Pa., 1957; M.B.A., U. Chgo., 1958; m. Maryellen Stanton, Apr. 29, 1962; children—Mark, John, Maryann. Div. comptroller Campbell Soup Co., Camden, N.J., 1958-60; securities analyst Merrill, Lynch, Pierce, Fenner & Smith, Inc., N.Y.C., 1960-62; asst. v.p. U.S. Trust Co. of N.Y., 1962-71; v.p. corporate finance div. Laidlaw & Co., Inc., N.Y.C., 1972-73; pres. Everest Corp., N.Y.C., 1973—; dir. Fairfield Communities Inc., UEC, Inc., LRA, Inc., Industrialized Bldg. Systems, Inc. Past pres. West Windsor Community Assn. Trustee Schuyler Hall, Columbia, Madison Sq. Boys Club. Served with AUS, 1953-55. K.C. Clubs: University of Pa., Princeton (N.Y.C.). Home: 77 Lillie St Princeton Junction NJ 08550-1307 Office: 1 Penn Plz New York NY 10119-0002

TAGLIATTINI, MAURIZIO, construction executive, research historian, writer; b. Messina, Italy, June 2, 1933; came to U.S., 1959, naturalized, 1970; s. Giovanni and Vittoria (Federighi) T.; m. Marsha Croce, Nov. 4, 1973 (div. 1979). Diploma of Geometra, Inst. Tech. per Geometri, Modena, Italy. Founder, past pres. Tagliattini Marble Co., N.Y.C. Author: The Discovery of North America by European Navigators (with a critical study on the origin of Christopher Columbus), 1992. With NATO Air Force, 1957-58. Roman Catholic.

TAGUCHI, YOSHITAKA, architect; b. Urawa, Japan, Feb. 12, 1933; s. Washio and Masa Taguchi; m. Yukiko Misuda, Apr. 21, 1968; children: Naeko, Morihiko. B in Architecture, Tokyo Inst. Tech., 1955. Dir. design div. Ministry Posts and Telecom., Tokyo, 1979-84; dir. gen. bldg. dept. Ministry Post and Telecommunication, Tokyo, 1984-87; prin. Taguchi Yoshitaka Architect Office, Tokyo, 1987-89; pres. Marunouchi Architects & Engrs., Tokyo, 1989—. Prin. works include Mielbarque Matsuyama, Mielbarque Okayama, Casa de Kampo Urayasu, Fukuoka Ctrl. Post Office, Nagoya Sorting Office, Sapparo Ctrl. Post Office, Miyazaki Ctrl. Post Office., KDD Kobe, Kampo Hotel Ohme, Internat. Telecom Japan. Mem. Japan Inst. Architects. Home: Naruse 5092-3-803, Machidashi, Tokyo 194, Japan Office: Yurakucho 1-8-1-419, Chiyodaku, Tokyo 100, Japan

TAGUE, CHARLES FRANCIS, retired engineering, construction and real estate development company executive; b. N.Y.C., Aug. 16, 1924; s. Charles and Isabelle (Carey) T.; m. Alicia Patricia Murtha, Aug. 6, 1949; children: Patrick, Charles, Thomas, Mary Alicia Haberman, James, Beth Anne Giuliano. B.S., Fordham U., 1952. Auditor Scovell, Wellington & Co., N.Y.C., 1951-57; comptroller Chem. Constrn. Corp., N.Y.C., 1957-75; controller Burns and Roe, Inc., Oradell, N.J., 1975-81; fin. dir. Alfred Sanzari Enterprises, Hasbrouck Heights, N.J., 1981-84; v.p. fin. Alexander Summer Co., 1984-93; ret., 1993; domestic and fgn. tax cons. Mem. Colts Neck (N.J.) Sports Found.; active Boy scouts Am.; mem. Lacawac Sanctuary Steering Com.; pres. parish coun. Ch. of Presentation; mem. pastoral coun. St. Thomas More Cath. Ch. Served with USNR, 1943-46, PTO, ETO, NATOUSA. Mem. Controllers Inst., Nat. Contract Mgmt. Assn., Assn. Govt. Accountants. Democrat. Roman Catholic. Address: PO Box 401 Lake Ariel PA 18436-0401

TAHARA, EIICHI, pathologist, educator; b. Yokohama, Japan, July 19, 1936; s. Yoshinori and Sadako T.; m. Yoshie Shimamoto, Mar. 28, 1963; children: Hidetoshi, Makoto, Eiji. MD, Hiroshima U., 1963, PhD, 1968; dipolma nat. exam. dor med. practitioners. Asst. dept. pathology Hiroshima U. Sch. Medicine, 1968-72, asst. prof., 1972-77, assoc. prof., 1977-78, prof., chmn., 1978—; chief rsch. facilities for lab. animal sci. Hiroshima U., 1994—; councilor Hiroshima U., 1985-87; chief div. anatomical pathology Hiroshima U. Hosp., 1986-92; rep. Cancer Rsch. Project of Cancer Stromal Interaction, 1993—, Project of Gastric Intestinal Metaplasia, 1994—; chief rsch, fac, for lab. Animal Sci. of Hiroshima U., 1994—; mem. cancer Rsch. Project of genetic Instability in Human Cancer, 1994—. Author, editor: Gastric Cancer, 1993, Gann Monograph on Cancer Research, 1994; editor Differentiation, Jour. Cancer Rsch. and Clin. Oncology, Jour. Exptl. Therapeutics and Oncology, Jour. Pathology, Exptl. and Toxicologic Pathology, others; contbr. articles to profl. jours. Grantee Found. for Promotion Cancer Rsch., 1991, Princess Takamatsu Cancer Rsch. Fund, 1990, Ministry Health and Welfare, 1989-91, Ministry of Edn. Sci. and Cult., Japan, 1990-93, 94—; recipient award Hiroshima aMed. Assn., 1972. Mem. Interant. Soc. Differentiation (pres. elect 1994—, organizer 8th internat. conf. 1994), Japanese Soc. Pathology (bd. dirs. 1991-93, 95—), Japanese Cancer Assn. (dir., assoc. editor 1995—), Japanese Soc. for Gastric Cancer (sec.), Japan Soc. for Cancer Therapy (councilor), Hiroshima Soc. for Cancer Therapy (pres.), Japanisch-Deutsche Gesellschaft Hiroshima (v.p. 1990—), Hiroshima Humboldt Club (chmn.). Buddhist. Office: Hiroshima U Sch Medicine, 1-2-3 Kasumi Minami-ku, Hiroshima 734, Japan

TAI, CHEN-TO, electrical engineering educator; b. Soochow, China, Dec. 30, 1915; came to U.S., 1943; m. Chia Ming Shen, Apr. 28, 1941; children: Arthur, Bing, Julie, David, James. BSc, Tsing Hua U., Beijing, 1937; DSc, Harvard U., 1947. Rsch. fellow Harvard U., Cambridge, Mass., 1947-49; sr. rsch. scientist Stanford Rsch. Inst., Palo Alto, Calif., 1949-54; assoc. prof. Ohio State U., Columbus, 1954-56, prof., 1960-64; prof. Tech. Inst. Electronics, Brazil, 1956-60; prof. U. Mich., Ann Arbor, 1964-86, prof. emeritus, 1986—. Author: Dyadic Green's Functions, 1971, 2d edit., 1994, Generalized Vector and Dyadic Analysis, 1991; contbr. numerous articles to profl. jours. Fellow IEEE (life, Centennial award 1985); mem. U.S. Nat. Acad. Engring. Home: 1155 Arlington Blvd Ann Arbor MI 48104-4023 Office: Univ of Mich Dept EECS Ann Arbor MI 48109

TAICHMAN, NORTON STANLEY, pathology educator; b. Can., May 27, 1936; s. Louis and Frances (Kline) T.; m. Louise Sheffer, June 1, 1958; children: Russell, Susan, Darren, Leslie, Audrey. DDS, U. Toronto, 1961; Diploma in Periodontics, Harvard U., 1964; PhD, U. Toronto, 1967; MSc (hon.), U. Pa., 1972. Asst. prof. U. Toronto, 1967-69, assoc. prof., 1969-72; prof. pathology dept. sch. dental medicine U. Pa., Phila., 1972—, chmn. dept. pathology, 1972-95; assoc. dean acad. affairs, 1990-95. Recipient Birnberg award Columbia U., 1987, Disting. Alumnus award Harvard U., 1988. Mem. Internat. Assn. Dental Rsch. (Rsch. Basic Sci. award 1985), Am. Soc. Microbiology, Soc. for Leukocyte Biology. Office: U Pa Dept Dental Pathology 4010 Locust St Philadelphia PA 19104-6002

TAIFA, NKECHI, law school administrator; b. Washington, Dec. 29, 1954; d. Elmo and Josephine (McIntosh) Caldwell; m. Kwasi Seitu, Aug. 14, 1993; 1 child, Sermeska Mariama Seitu. BA, Howard U., 1977; JD, George Washington U., 1984. Bar: D.C. 1985, U.S. Dist. Ct. (D.C. cir.) 1987, U.S. Supreme Ct. 1993. Elem. sch. tchr. Watoto Sch., Washington, 1977-79; network organizer Washington Office on Africa, 1980-83; staff atty. Nat. Prison Project, Washington, 1984-87; pvt. practice Washington, 1987-89; pub. policy counsel Womens' Legal Def. Fund, Washington, 1989-91; legis. counsel ACLU, Washington, 1991-95; dir. pub. svc. program Sch. Law Howard U., Washington, 1995—; bd. dirs. Nat. Conf. Black Lawyers, Washington, D.C. Prisoner Legal Svcs. Author: Shining Legacy, 1983, The Adventures of Kojo & Ama, 1992; contbg. author: Reparations, Yes, 1987. D.C. statehood coord. Leadership Conf. Civil Rights, 1992-94; organizer Citywide Coalition Against Death Penalty, Washington, 1992; convenor Coalition for Equitable Sentencing, Washington, 1992-95. Recipient Mega Mensch award Motor Voter Coalition, Washington, 1993, Hobson, King, Parks, Douglas, Heutte award Statehood Edn. Found., Washington, 1993; individual artist fellowship D.C. Commn. Arts & Humanities, 1983. Mem. Nat. Conf. Black Lawyers (co-chmn. section criminal justice, spl. recognition award 1988), Nat. Assn. Criminal Def. Lawyers. Avocations: writing children's books, performance poetry, reading. Office: Howard U Sch Law 2900 Van Ness St NW Washington DC 20008

TAIMUTY, SAMUEL ISAAC, physicist; b. West Newton, Pa., Dec. 20, 1917; s. Elias and Samia (Hawatt) T.; BS, Carnegie Inst. Tech., 1940; PhD, U. So. Calif., 1951; m. Betty Jo Travis, Sept. 12, 1953 (dec.); children: Matthew, Martha; m. Rosalie Richards, Apr. 3, 1976. Physicist, U.S. Naval Shipyard, Phila. and Long Beach, Calif., 1942-46; rsch. asst. U. So. Calif., 1947-51; sr. physicist U.S. Naval Radiol. Def. Lab., 1950-52, SRI Internat., Menlo Park, Calif., 1952-72; sr. staff engr. Lockheed Missiles & Space Co., Sunnyvale, Calif., 1972-89; cons. physicist, 1971—. Mem. Am. Phys. Soc., Sigma Xi. Episcopalian. Contbr. articles to sci. publs. Patentee in field. Home: 3346 Kenneth Dr Palo Alto CA 94303-4217

TAISHOFF, LAWRENCE BRUCE, publishing company executive; b. Washington, Aug. 30, 1933; s. Sol Joseph and Betty (Tash) T.; m. Nancy Lee Stuckey, Sept. 17, 1962 (div. 1979); children: Robert Paul, Randall Lawrence, Jonathan Bradford. AB, Duke U., 1955. Asst. dir. Sta. WTOP-TV, Washington, 1955-56; with Broadcasting Publs., Inc., Washington, 1958—, pres., pub., 1971-91, chmn., 1991—, also dir.; adviser Cahners Consumer/Entertainment Pub. div. Cahners Pub. Co., 1991—; v.p. Jolar Corp., Washington, 1952-72, dir., 1958-72; gen. ptnr. Jolar Assocs., Washington, 1972—; chmn. bd., pres. Graphictype, Inc., 1976-86, also dir.; chmn., pres. Solar Corp., 1982-86; chmn. Broadcasting-Taishoff Found., 1982—; chmn., CEO Chuckie Broadcasting, Ardmore, Okla., 1993—, Trustco, Washington, 1988—; trustee Washington Journalism Ctr., 1982-93, Nat. Press. Found., 1993—, mem. adv. bd., 1993—; bd. dirs. Nat. Press Found., 1982—, mem. exec. com., 1990-94; mem. journalism and communications exec. com. Capital Campaign for Arts and Sci., Duke U., 1984—; bd. advisors Am. Journalism Ctr., Budapest, 1991-95; bd. dir. Ardissone, Naples, Fla., 1994—; mem. White House Press Corps, 1983—; mem. Met. Washington Bd. Trade, 1970—. Co-author radio and TV segment Britannica Book of the Year, 1983—. Team capt. pubs. div. United Givers Fund drive, 1965; mem. admissions adv. com. Duke Alumni Assn., 1968-70; mem. U.S. Senate and Ho. of Reps. Periodical Press Gallery, 1958—; trustee Broadcast Pioneers Ednl. Fund Inc., 1985; judge VFW Voice of Democracy contest, 1978—; mem. bd. judges Peabody awards, 1985-91; mem. Am. U. Sch. Communications Disting. Adv. Commn., 1985—; mem. Founders Soc. Duke U., 1985—, The Mus. of TV and Radio Roundtable, 1988-89; bd. dirs. Ardissone, Naples, Fla., 1994—; chmn., trustee Taishoff Family Found.; cons. High Point Contracting Corp., Naples, Fla.; ptnr. L & D Ventures, LLC, Naples, Fla. With AUS, 1956-58. Mem. IEEE (sr.), Internat. Radio & TV Soc., Broadcast Pioneers (life, bd. dirs., exec. com. Broadcast Pioneers Library), Am. Sportscasters Assn. (exec. com. 1990—), White House Corrs. Assn., Nat. Press Club, Woodmont Country Club (Rockville, Md.), Bryce Resort Club (Basye, Va.), Cosmos Club (Washington), Sigma Delta Chi, Zeta Beta Tau. Jewish. Office: 1705 Desales St NW Washington DC 20036-4405

TAIT, ELAINE, restaurant critic. Restaurant critic The Phila. Inquirer, Phila., Pa. Office: The Philadelphia Inquirer 400 N Broad St Philadelphia PA 19130-4015

TAIT, JOHN CHARLES, Canadian government official; b. Montreal, Que., Can., Dec. 4, 1945; s. John Watterson and Eleanor (Raymond) T.; m. Sonia Plourde. BA, Princeton U., 1967, Oxford (Eng.) U., Eng., 1969; MA, Oxford (Eng.) U., 1995; BCL, McGill U., Montreal, 1972. Bar: Que. 1974. Asst. sec. Cabinet Privy Coun. Office, Can., 1978-81; asst. dep. minister Can. Dept. Indian Affairs, 1981-83; asst. dep. minister Can. Dept. Justice, 1983-86, dep. solicitor gen., 1986-88; dep. minister of justice Can. Dept. Justice, Ottawa, Ont., Can., 1988-94; sr. advisor Privy Coun. Office, Ottawa, 1994—; Skelton-Clark fellow Queen's U. Sr. fellow Can. Ctr. for Mgmt. Devel., 1994—; Rhodes scholar, Eng., 1967. Mem. Can. Bar Assn. Avocation: sports. Office: Privy Council Office, 80 Wellington St, Ottawa, ON Canada K1A 0A3

TAIT, JOHN EDWIN, insurance company executive; b. Moline, Ill., July 8, 1932; s. Edwin Marshall and Hazel Marie (Dodson) T.; m. Erlane Dorothy Dauffenbauch, July 20, 1953; children: Michael, Robert, Kathryn. LLB, U. Ill., 1961. V.p. mortgages Penn Mut. Life Ins. Co., Phila., 1975-79, v.p. investments, 1979-80, fin v.p., 1980-82, v.p., 1981-82, pres., COO, 1982-88, 91-94, COO, 1982-86; pres., CEO Penn. Mut. Life Ins. Co., Phila., 1987-88, chmn., CEO, 1988-94, chmn., 1995—; bd. dirs. Janney, Montgomery, Scott Inc., Phila., Penn. Mut. Life Ins. Co., Phila., Mut. Life Ins. Co., Phila., Mut. Life Ins. Tax Com.; chmn., bd. dirs. Indepro Group, Phila Airport Adv. Com., 1988-93; mem. task force Phila. Police, 1987, tax com. Mut. Life Ins., 1988-95. Civ. Bd. dirs. Drama Guild, 1982-90, Phila. Ranger Corps, Phila Orch., 1991—, Penjerdel, 1991-95, Women's Way, 1991—; elder Bryn Mawr (Pa.) Presbyn. Ch., 1978, trustee, 1986; bd. visitors U. Ill. Coll. Law, 1979-88; trustee Penn Mut. Charitable Trust, 1982-95; active Mayor's Mgmt. And Productivity Task Force, 1992—; vice chmn. Mayor's Mgmt. Implementation Partnership, 1993—, mem. Exec. Svc. Corps., 1996—. With USAF, 1952, Korea, Maj. Air Nat. Guard. Mem. Am. Coun. Life Ins. (bd. dirs.), Ins. Fedn. Pa., Greater Phila. C. of C. (bd. dirs., chmn. bd. dirs. 1995-96), Greater Phila. First (bd. dirs.), Phila. Country Club, Blue Bell Country Club, Union League Phila. Republican. Avocations: flying, tennis, golf, boating, scuba diving. Office: Penn Mut Life Ins Co Independence Sq Philadelphia PA 19106

TAIT, JOHN REID, lawyer; b. Toledo, Ohio, Apr. 7, 1946; s. Paul Reid and Lucy Richardson (Rudderow) T.; m. Christina Ruth Bjornstad, Mar. 12, 1972; children: Gretchen, Mary. BA, Columbia Coll., 1968; JD, Vanderbilt U., 1974. Bar: Idaho 1974, U.S. Dist. Ct. Idaho 1974. Assoc. Keeton & Tait, Lewiston, Idaho, 1974-76, ptnr., 1976-86, 89—, Keeton, Tait & Petrie, 1986-88, Keeton & Tait, 1989—. Chmn. bd. No. Rockies Action Group, Helena, Mont., 1985-86, bd. dirs. 1981-88, Lewiston Hist. Preservation Commn., Idaho, 1975-94, chmn., 1988-94; bd. dirs. Idaho Legal Aid Svcs., Boise, 1975—, Idaho Housing Agy., Boise, 1984-91, St. Joseph Regional Med. Ctr. Found., Inc., 1989-94; Dem. precinct committeeman, 1976-86, state committeeman, 1977-94; co-chmn. Idaho state re-election com. John V. Evans, 1978; Idaho del. Nat. Dem. Conv., N.Y., 1980, standing com. on credentials, N.Y., 1980, San Francisco, 1984; treas. Larry LaRocco for Congress, 1990, 92. Served with U.S. Army, 1968-71. Recipient Pro Bono Svc. award Idaho State Bar 1988, Community Recognition award Lewiston Intergovtl. Coun., 1992, Spl. Recognition award Idaho Legal Aid Svcs., Inc., 1993. Mem. ABA, Assn. Trial Lawyers Am., Idaho Trial Lawyers Assn. (regional dir. 1976-77, 86-88), Clearwater Bar Assn. (sec. 1974-76, pres. 1984-86). Democrat. Office: Keeton & Tait 312 Miller St # E Lewiston ID 83501-1944

TAIT, PATRICIA ANN, secondary education educator; b. Sacramento, Calif., Nov. 26, 1942; d. Frank Scott and Anna Mae (Chubbey) Smith; m. Arthur Fitzwilliam Tait, Jr., Dec. 27, 1968; children: Arthur Fitzwilliam III, Lauryn Kristine. BS in Edn., Tex. Western Coll., 1965; BA in English, U. Tex., El Paso, 1966, MA in English, 1974. Cert. secondary educator, English, ESOL, Fla., Tex. Tchr. English Cheyenne Mountain High Sch., Colorado Springs, 1966-69; tchr. English, dept. chairperson Christ the King Internat. Sch., Okinawa, Japan, 1970-71; pres. Accurate Secretarial and Typing Svc., 1971—; tchr. English Forest High Sch., Ocala, Fla., 1979—, co-chair Eng. dept., 1990—; cons. Fla. Writing Project, Gainesville, 1984—; presenter Marion County Tchrs. English, Ocala, 1985—. Author: Joseph Conrad: The Development of Character in the Jungle, 1974. Named Master Tchr., State of Fla., 1983-84, 84-85. Mem. NEA, Nat. Coun. Tchrs. English, Fla. Coun. Tchrs. English, Marion County Tchrs. English, Marion County Edn. Assn., Fla. Tchrs. Profl. Edn. Assn. Democrat. Episcopalian. Avocations: equine activities. Home: 5109 SE 4th St Ocala FL 34471-3304 Office: Forest High Sch 1614 SE Fort King St Ocala FL 34471-2535

TAIT, ROBERT E., lawyer; b. Lima, Ohio, Sept. 3, 1946; s. Robert and Helen (Smith) T.; m. Donna G. Dome, June 22, 1968; children: Heather, Jennifer, Robert. BA, Kenyon Coll., 1968; JD, U. Mich., 1973. Bar: Ohio 1973, U.S. Dist. Ct. (so. dist.) Ohio. 1976, U.S. Dist. Ct. (no. dist.) Ohio 1976, U.S. Dist. Ct. Md. 1980, U.S. Ct. Appeals (6th cir.) 1981, U.S. Supreme Ct. 1982. Ptnr. Vorys, Sater, Seymour & Pease, Columbus, Ohio, 1973—. Staff counsel Govs. Select Com. on Prevention Indsl. Accidents, Columbus, 1977-78. Served with U.S. Army, 1969-70. Fellow Columbus Bar Found.; mem. ABA (litigation sect., products liability com.), Ohio Bar Assn. (worker's compensation com.), Columbus Bar Assn. (workers compensation and professionalism coms.), Def. Rsch. Inst. (workers compensation com.), Columbus Def. Assn., Assn. Def. Trial Attys. (exec. com. 1991-94). Clubs: Capital, Columbus Country. Home: 2045 Wickford Rd Columbus OH 43221-4223 Office: Vorys Sater Seymour & Pease PO Box 1008 52 E Gay St Columbus OH 43215-3161

TAJON, ENCARNACION FONTECHA (CONNIE TAJON), retired educator, association executive; b. San Narciso, Zambales, Philippines, Mar. 25, 1920; came to U.S., 1948; d. Espiridion Maggay and Gregoria (Labrador) Fontecha; m. Felix B. Tajon, Nov. 17, 1948; children: Ruth F., Edward F. Teacher's cert., Philippine Normal Coll., 1941; BEd, Far Eastern U., Manila, 1947; MEd, Seattle Pacific U., 1976. Cert. tchr., Philippines. Tchr. pub. schs. San Narciso and Manila, 1941-47; coll. educator Union Coll. Manila, 1947-48; tchr. Auburn (Wash.) Sch. Dist., 1956-58, Renton (Wash.) Sch. Dist., 1958-78; owner, operator Manila-Zambales Internat. Grill, Seattle, 1980-81, Connie's Lumpia House Internat. Restaurant, Seattle, 1981-84; founder, pres. Tajon-Fontecha, Inc., Renton, 1980—, United Friends of Filipinos in Am. Found., Renton, 1985—; founder Labrador Fontecha and Baldovi-Tajon Permanent Scholarship Fund of The Philippine Normal U., 1990; co-founder The United Filipino-Am. Coll. Fund for the USA and the Philippines, 1995; bd. mem. World Div. of the Gen. Bd. of Global Ministries of the United Meth. Ch., 1982-84, Ch. Women United Seattle Chapt.; mem. advisory bd Univ. Wash. Burke Mus., 1991—; mem. King TV Asian Am. Adv. Forum, 1993. Editor bull. Renton 1st United Meth. Ch., 1994. Bd. dirs. women's divsn. Gen. Bd. Global Ministries United Meth. Ch., 1982-84, Renton Area Youth Svcs., 1980-85, Girl's Club Puget Sound, Ethnic Heritage Coun. Pacific N.W., 1989—; mem. Mcpl. Arts Commn., Renton, 1980—; chairperson fundraising steering com. Washington State Women's Polit. Caucus, 1985-89; governing mem. nat. steering com. state coun. Nat. Women's Polit. Caucus, 1990—; mem. vol. action, 1990 Goodwill Games, Seattle; vol. worker Native Am. Urban Ministries, 1990—; mem. adv. bd. Renton Cmty. Housing Devel.; mem. cmty. adv. bd. U. Wash. Thomas Burke Meml. Mus., 1990—; mem. program com. UN, 1992—; mem. Asian Pacific task force Ch. Coun. Greater Seattle, 1993—; mem. Renton-Rainier area planning com. 1996 World Day of Prayer; coord. establishment and devel. Seattle-Renton area United Filipino-Am. Coll. Fund, 1995, coord. internat. buffet dinner United Filipino-Am. Coll. Fund for U. Wash., Filipino Youth Empowerment Project and Mentor's Child Sponsoring Program; emeritus bd. mem. Ethnic Heritage Coun. Pacific N.W., 1993—; co-chmn. Ann. Filipino and Filipino Am. youth Activities Pres.'s Day Spelling Bee Greater Seattle and Vicinity, 1990-96; coord. Ecumenical World Cmty. Day celebration luncheon Greater Seattle unit Ch. Women United, 1994. Recipient spl. cert. of award Project Hope, 1976, U.S. Bicentennial Commn., 1976, UNICEF, 1977, Spirit of Liberty award Ethnic Heritage Coun. Pacific Northwest, 1991; named Parent of Yr. Filipino Community of Seattle, Inc., 1984, One of 500 Seattle Pacific U. Centennial "Alumni of a Growing Vision", 1991. Mem. NEA, Wash. State Edn. Assn. (bd. dirs. 1990-92), Am. Assn. Ret. Persons, Nat. Ret. Tchrs. Assn., Renton Ret. Tchrs. Assn., U. Wash. Alumni Assn. (life), U. Wash. Filipino Alumni Assn. (pres. Wash. state chpt. 1985-87), Renton Hist. Mus. (life), Internat. Platform Assn., United Meth. Women, Pres.'s Forum, Alpha Sigma, Delta Kappa Gamma. Democrat. Avocations: reading, bowling, crocheting, cooking, walking. Home and Office: 2033 Harrington Pl NE Renton WA 98056-2303 *The values learned in school and taught by my beloved parents such as hard steady work, optimism, enthusiasm, individualism, creativity, getting along with people, listenability, trusting, flexibility, integrity, respectability, faithfulness, thankfulness, givingfulness, forgivingfulness, lovingfulness, prayerfulness, and selfhelpfulness helped me to live a full rounded well balanced life even at retirement.*

TAKAHASHI, JOSEPH S., neuroscientist; b. Tokyo, Dec. 16, 1951; s. Shigeharu and Hiroko (Hara) T.; m. Barbara Pillsbury Snook, June 28, 1985; children: Erika S., Matthew N. BA, Swarthmore (Pa.) Coll., 1974; PhD, U. Oreg., 1981. Pharmacology rsch. assoc. NIMH, NIGMS, Bethesda, Md., 1981-83; asst. prof. Northwestern U., Evanston, Ill., 1983-87; assoc. chmn. Neurobiology and Physiology Northwestern U., Evanston, Ill., 1988—, assoc. prof., 1987-91, prof., 1991-96; Walter and Mary Elizabeth Glass prof. life scis. Northwestern U., Evanston, Ill., 1996—; acting assoc. dir. Inst. for Neuroscience Northwestern U., Evanston, 1988-95; active NIMH Psychobiology and Behavior Rev. Com., 1988-92. Assoc. editor Neuron; mem. adv. bd. Jour. Biol. Rhythms, 1984—; contbr. over 90 articles to profl. jours. Grantee Bristol-Myers Squibb, 1995—; recipient Alfred P. Sloan award A.P. Sloan Found., 1983-85, Searl Scholars award Chgo. Cmty. Trust, 1985-88, Merit award NIMH, 1987, Honma prize in Biol. Rhythms Honma Found., 1986, Presdl. Young Investigator award NSF, 1985-90, 6th C.U. Ariens Kappers award Netherlands Soc. for Advancement Nat. Scis., Medicine and Surgery, 1995. Mem. AAAS, Soc. Neurosci., Assn. for Rsch. in Vision and Ophthalmology, Soc. for Rsch. on Biol. Rhythms (mem. adv. bd. 1986—), Mammalian Genome Soc. Achievements include discovery of the expression of circadian oscillations in cells from vertebrates; and isolation of first circadian clock mutant in mice. Office: Northwestern U Neurobiology 2153 North Campus Dr Evanston IL 60208-3520

TAKAHASHI, KEIICHI, zoology educator; b. Yokkaichi, Japan, May 31, 1931; s. Shozo and Toshi (Imamura) T.; m. Mihoko Terada, Sept. 26, 1957; children: Michiko, Yoshiki. BSc, U. Tokyo, 1953, MSc, 1955, PhD, 1960. Instr. U. Tokyo, 1956-68, assoc. prof., 1968-73, prof., 1973-92, emeritus prof., 1992—; prof. Internat. Christian U., Tokyo, 1992—; rsch. fellow Bedford Coll., U. London, 1960-62; dir. Misaki Marine Biol. Sta., U. Tokyo, 1988-92. Contbr. numerous articles to profl. jours. Mem. Japanese Soc. for Comparative Physiology and Biochemistry (pres. 1990-93), Japan Soc. for Biol. Scis. in Space (v.p. 1987-92), Japan Soc. for Biol. Scis. Edn. (v.p. 1984-95), Japan Soc. for Cell Biology (councillor 1983), Zool. Soc. Japan (councillor), Japan Soc. for Sci. Edn. (bd. dirs.), Inst. of Biology of U.K., Sci. Coun. of Japan. Mem. Christian Ch. Avocations: music, arts. Home: 14-31 Yochomachi, Shinjuku-Ku, Tokyo 162, Japan Office: Internat Christian U Dept Biology, 3-10-2 Osawa, Mitaka, Tokyo 181, Japan

TAKAHASHI, LOREY K., psychiatry educator, scientist; b. Honolulu, July 25, 1953; s. George H. and Margie Y. (Yamashita) T.; m. Chintana Yongnorasethkul, Aug. 22, 1982; children: Edwin A., Cyrus G. BA in Psychology, U. Hawaii, 1975, MA in Psychology, 1978; PhD in Psychology, Rutgers U., 1982. Rsch. asst. dept. psychology U. Hawaii, Honolulu, 1976-78; teaching asst. dept. psychology Rutgers U., New Brunswick, 1978-82; asst. scientist dept. psychiatry Med. Sch. U. Wis., Madison, 1986-90, clin. asst. prof., 1989-90, asst. prof. psychiatry, 1990—. Contbr. articles to profl. jours. Japanese Nat. Student Exch. Rsch. fellow Tokyo U. of Edn., 1977; postdoctoral fellow dept. biology Princeton (N.J.) U., 1982-86. Mem. AAAS, APA, Animal Behavior Soc., Internat. Brain Rsch. Orgn., Internat. Soc. for Rsch. on Aggression, Soc. Neurosci., Soc. Study of Reproduction, Sigma Xi (Madison chpt.). Home: 6406 Olympic Dr Madison WI 53705 Office: U Wis Dept Psychiatry Med Sch 600 Highland Ave Madison WI 53792

TAKANO, MASAHARU, physical chemist; b. Tainan, Taiwan, Jan. 20, 1935; s. Shuzo and Misao (Rengakuji) T.; m. Hiroko Takenoshita, Aug. 28, 1965; children: Kentaro, Jojiro, Miwako. B.S., Hokkaido U., 1957; M.S., U. Tokyo, 1959, D.Sc., 1963. Postdoctoral fellow McGill U, Montreal, 1963-67; with Monsanto Co., St. Louis, 1967-90; pres. Takano Internat., St. Louis, 1991—; cons. on bus., travel, tech. Sr. contbr. articles on phys. chemistry to profl. jours. Fellow Am. Inst. Chemists; mem. AAAS, Am. Chem. Soc., Am. Phys. Soc., Japan Am. Soc., Japanese Am. Citizens League, Nat. Geog. Soc., World Affairs Coun., Japan Soc., Mo. Sheriffs Assn. (hon.). Buddhist. Home: 13146 Roundstone Ct Saint Louis MO 63146-3642 Office: 425 N New Ballas Rd Ste 280 Saint Louis MO 63141-6848 *This country has everything which other countries envy: a vast land, rich environment, natural resources and opportunities. We can work for all human beings if we want, and there are a million things to do.*

TAKASAKI, ETSUJI, urology educator; b. Tokyo, Apr. 24, 1929; s. Kuranosuke and Fumi Takasaki; m. Sachiko Shinkai, Nov. 1, 1960; children: Satoshi, Masumi, Hiromi. MD, U. Tokyo, 1955, D. Med. Sci., 1960. Instr. urology U. Tokyo, 1960-62, asst. prof., 1962-67; chief. urol. svc. Musashino Red Cross Hosp., Tokyo, 1967-69, Komagome Met. Hosp., Tokyo, 1969-74; prof. urology Dokkyo U. Sch. Medicine, Tochigi, Japan, 1974-95, emeritus prof., 1995—; lectr. U. Tokyo, 1969-74. Author: Urolithiasis, 1978; contbr. articles to Japanese Jour. Urology, 1960, Jour. Urology, 1986, Urologia Internat., 1989, 95, British Jour. Urology, 1994. Mem. Japanese Urol. Assn. (bd. dirs. 1963—), Japanese Soc. Andrology (bd. dirs. 1982—), Japanese Soc. Endourology and ESWL (bd. dirs. 1988—), Internat. Soc. Urology (Paris). Avocation: Kendo (Japanese fencing).

TAKASHIMA, HIDEO, lawyer, accountant; b. Kobe, Hyogo-Ken, Japan, Mar. 2, 1919; came to U.S., 1956; s. Yoshimitsu and Yoshie (Akagi) T.; m.

Adrianna Elizabeth Selch Coe, Oct. 31, 1961 (div. Apr. 1984); children: James, George K., Oliver Sachio Hydon; m. Chizu Kojima, Mar. 14, 1986. Chartered acct., Kanagawa U., Yokohama, Japan, 1941; LLM in Criminal Law, Taihoku Imperial U., Japan, 1943; LLM in Bus. Law, Yale U., 1957; SJD in Antitrust Laws, N.Y. Law Sch., 1959; postgrad., Yale U., 1961-62. Bar: D.C. 1973, N.Y. 1990, U.S. Tax Ct. 1973, U.S. Ct. Appeals (D.C. cir.) 1973, N.J. 1974, U.S. Dist. Ct. N.J. 1974, U.S. Ct. Claims 1974, U.S. Ct. Appeals (3d cir.) 1977, U.S. Supreme Ct. 1977, U.S. Ct. Appeals (2d cir.) 1993. Lectr. criminology Yen Ping Coll., Taipei, Taiwan, 1946-47; mgr. Taiwan br. Warner Bros. F.N. Pix, Inc., Taipei, 1947-52; with labor union activities dept. FOA MSM/C, Am. Embassy, Taipei, 1953-54; tax editor Prentice-Hall, Inc., Englewood Cliffs, N.J., 1961-66; editor-in-chief Washington Publs., Inc., N.Y.C., 1966-69; tax atty., editor Am. Inst. CPAs, N.Y.C., 1971-72; pres., Charles Hideo Coe, P.A., Park Ridge, N.J., 1973—; corp. coun. DNP Am., Inc., 1973-90; dir. Coe & Coe, Inc., Park Ridge, N.J., 1973—; pvt. practice acctg., 1980—; gen. counsel Rissho Kosei Kai N.Y. Buddhist Ctr., Inc., 1990—. U.S. del. U.S./Japan Bilateral Session: A New Era in Legal and Econ. Relations, Tokyo, Aug.-Sept., 1988. People to People legal del. to European countries to assist U.S. immigration law legislation, 1979; People's Republic China and USSR, 1989; gen. coun. Rissho Kosei Kai N.Y. Buddhist Ctr., Inc., 1990—. Author: My Unsuspecting Formosa, 1944; editor-in-chief The Tax Barometer, 1966-69. Instr. Judo-Kendo New Milford (N.J.) Recreation Commn., 1963-69, Park Ridge Recreation Com., 1969-72, Pascack Valley Kendo Club, Park Ridge, 1969-71. Served as capt. Chinese Kuo-Min-Tang, Taipei, 1945. Yale Law Sch. fellow, 1956-57; N.Y. Law Sch. scholar, 1958, Prentice-Hall, Inc. scholar grad. div. NYU Sch. Law, 1961-63. Mem. Am. Immigration Lawyers Assn. (sec. N.J. chpt. 1978-83), Assn. Trial Lawyers Am., N.Y. State Bar Assn., Japanese Am. Assn. N.Y., Yale U. Law Sch. Alumni Assn., NYU Law Alumni Assn., Taihoku Imperial U. Law Sch. Alumin Assn., Kanagawa U. O.B. Judo Club. Republican. Club: Yale. Office: 3 Park Ave Park Ridge NJ 07656-1231

TAKASUGI, NAO, state official, business developer; b. Oxnard, Calif., Apr. 5, 1922; s. Shingoro and Yasuye (Hayashi) T.; m. Judith Shigeko Mayeda, Mar. 23, 1952; children—Scott, Russell, Ronald, Tricia, Lea. B.S., Temple U., 1945; M.B.A., U. Pa. Wharton Sch., 1946. Mem. city council City of Oxnard, Calif., 1976-82, mayor, 1982-92; mem. Calif. State Assembly, 1992—, chmn. revenue and taxation com.; bus. developer, cons. Mem. Oxnard Planning Commn., 1974-76; pres. World Trade Ctr. Assn., Oxnard; apptd. (by Calif. gov.) chmn. UN Anniversary; assemblyman Calif. State Assembly 37th Dist. Decorated Order of Sacred Treasure with Gold Rayette medal Japanese Gov., 1992. Mem. Ventura County Japanese Am. Citizens League, World Trade Ctr. Assn. (pres. Oxnard chpt.), U.S. Conf. Mayors (mem. nat. adv. bd.), Nat. League of Cities (nat. bd. dirs.), Ventura County Transp. Com., League Calif. Cities (bd. dirs.), South Coast Area Bd. Dirs. (chmn. transp. com.), Assn. Ventura County Cities, Oxnard Housing Authoritry (chmn.), Oxnard Redevel. Agy. (chmn.), Optimists Club (Oxnard). Republican. Methodist. Home: 1221 El Portal Way Oxnard CA 93035-2511 Office: Rm 5158 State Capitol Sacramento CA 95814 also: 221 Daily Dr Ste 7 Camarillo CA 93010-5833

TAKASUGI, ROBERT MITSUHIRO, federal judge; b. Tacoma, Sept. 12, 1930; s. Hidesaburo and Kayo (Otsuki) T.; m. Dorothy O. Takasugi; children: Jon Robert, Lesli Mari. BS, UCLA, Los Angeles, 1953; LLB, JD, U. So. Calif., 1959. Bar: Calif. bar 1960. Practiced law Los Angeles, 1960-73; judge East Los Angeles Municipal Ct., 1973-75, adminstrv. judge, 1974, presiding judge, 1975; judge Superior Ct., County of Los Angeles, 1975-76; U.S. dist. judge U.S. Dist. Ct. (cen. dist.) Calif., 1976—; nat. legal counsel Japanese Am. Citizens League; guest lectr. law seminars Harvard U. Law Sch. Careers Symposium; commencement spkr.; mem. Legion Lex U. So. Calif. Law Ctr.; chmn. Pub. Defs. Indigent Def. & Psychiat. Panel Com.; mem. Affirmative Action Com., Habeas Corpus-Death Penalty Com., Exec. Com., Jury Com., Settlement Rule Com., Adv. Com. on Codes of Conduct of the Jud. Conf. of the U.S., 1988-92, Code of Conduct of Judges. Mem. editorial bd. U. So. Calif. Law Rev., 1959; contbr. articles to profl. jours. Mem. Calif. adv. com. Western Regional Office, U.S. Commn. on Civil Rights; chmn. blue ribbon com. for selection of chancellor L.A. C.C. With U.S. Army, 1953-55. Harry J. Bauer scholar, 1959; recipient U.S. Mil. Man of Yr. award for Far East Theater U.S. Army, 1954, Jud. Excellence award Criminal Cts. Bar Assn., cert. of merit Japanese-Am. Bar Assn., Disting. Svc. award Asian Pacific Ctr. and Pacific Clinics, 1994, Freedom award Sertoma, 1995, Pub. Svc. award Asian Pacific Am. Legal Ctr. So. Calif., 1995, Trailblazer award So. Calif. region NAPABA, 1995, Spl. award Mex. Am. Bar Assn., 1996; named Judge of Yr. Century City Bar Assn., 1995. Mem. U. So. Calif. Law Alumni Assn. (dir.). Office: US Dist Ct 312 N Spring St Los Angeles CA 90012-4701

TAKAYAMA, AKIRA, economics educator; b. Yokohama, Japan; came to U.S., 1957; s. Tsunaki and Shoko (Takeuchi) T.; m. Machiko Onabe, Jan. 31, 1970 (dec. Jan. 1996). B.A., Internat. Christian U., Tokyo, 1957; M.A., U. Rochester, 1960, Ph.D., 1962; Ph.D., Hitotsubashi U., Tokyo, 1964. Instr., then asst. prof. econs. Internat. Christian U., Tokyo, Japan, 1962-64; fellow in econ. stats. U. Manchester, Eng., 1964-65; vis. assoc. prof. econs. U. Minn.-Mpls., 1965-66; assoc. prof. econs. Purdue U.-West Lafayette, 1967-68, prof. econs., 1968-80; prof. econs. Tex. A&M U., College Station, 1978-82, Kyoto U., Japan, 1982-85; Vandeveer prof. econs. So. Ill. U., Carbondale, 1983—; vis. prof. econs. U. Rochester, 1969-70, Australian Nat. U., 1968, 77, U. Hawaii, 1971-72, U. Tokyo, 1974-75, Doshisha U., Japan, 1989, Tulane U., New Orleans, 1991, Internat. Christian U., Japan, 1993, 94; J. Fish Smith profl. Brigham Young U., Provo, Utah, 1976. Author: Mathematical Economics, 1974, 2d edit. 1985, International Trade, 1972, Analytical Methods in Economics, 1994; co-editor: Economic Development in East and Southeast Asia, 1990, Trade, Policy and International Adjustments, 1991; contbr. articles to profl. jours. Mem. Am. Econs. Assn., Econometric Soc., Econ. Rsch. Ctr. Japan, Japan Assn. Econs. and Econometrics.

TAKETOMI, SUSAMU, physicist, researcher; b. Chiba City, Japan, Sept. 25, 1950; s. Manjiro and Kimie (Kida) T. B of Enging., U. Tokyo, 1975; DSc, Keio U., Yokohama, Japan, 1989. Rschr. Ctrl. Rsch. Lab. Fuji Elec. Co. Ltd., Yokosuka City, Japan, 1975-85; rschr. Matsumotoyushi Seiyaku Co. Ltd., Yao City, Japan, 1985—; vis. rschr. Keio U., Yokohama, Japan, 1985-89, Seikei U., Tokyo, 1990-95, U. Ctrl. Fla., 1995—; lectr. in field. Author: (book) Magnetic Fluids: Principle and Application, 1988, Magnetic Fluid Handbook, 1995. Mem. Japan Phys. Soc., Japan Applied Phys. Soc., Japan Soc. Mech. Engrs., Japan Magnetic Soc. Avocation: playing violin. Home: 10600 Bloomfield Dr #621 Orlando FL 32825 Office: U Central Fla Dept Physics Orlando FL 32816

TAKEUCHI, KUMIKO, synthetic, organic and medicinal chemist; b. Nihama, Ehima, Japan; came to U.S., 1973; d. Hajime and Fujiko (Miyazaki) T. Diploma, Niihama Tech. Coll., 1967; MA, Coll. of William and Mary, 1976, Columbia Bible Coll., 1978; PhD, U. S.C., 1987. Postdoctoral rsch. fellow U. Mich., Ann Arbor, 1987-89; sr. organic chemist Eli Lilly and Co., Indpls., 1989-94, rsch. scientist, 1995—. Mem. Am. Chem. Soc., Internat. Soc. of Heterocyclic Chemistry, Sigma Xi. Office: Lilly Rsch Labs Drop 0528 Lilly Corporate Ctr Indianapolis IN 46285

TAKUMI, ROY MITSUO, state representative; b. Honolulu, Oct. 13, 1952; m. Wanda A. Kutaka; children: Aisha, Jaron. BA, Friends World Coll., 1991; MPA, U. Hawaii, 1993. Cmty. organizer Osaka, Japan, 1977-83; program dir. Am. Friends Svc. Com., Honolulu, 1984-90; polit. coord. Hawaii State AFL-CIO, Honolulu, 1990-92; rep. Ho. of Reps., Honolulu, 1992—. Office: State Ho of Reps State Capitol Honolulu HI 96813

TALALAY, PAUL, pharmacologist, physician; b. Berlin, Mar. 31, 1923; came to U.S., 1940, naturalized, 1946; s. Joseph Anton and Sophie (Brosterman) T.; m. Pamela Judith Samuels, Jan. 11, 1953; children—Antony, Susan, Rachel, Sarah. S.B., Mass. Inst. Tech., 1944; student, U. Chgo. Sch. Medicine, 1944-46; M.D., Yale U., 1948; D.Sc. (hon.), Acadia U., 1974. House officer, asst. resident surg. services Mass. Gen. Hosp., Boston, 1948-50; asst. prof. surgery U. Chgo., 1950-51, asst. prof. biochemistry, 1955-57, asso. prof., then prof., 1957-63; asst. prof. Ben May Lab. Cancer Research, 1951-57, asso. prof., then prof., 1957-63; John Jacob Abel prof., dir. dept., pharmacology and exptl. therapeutics Johns Hopkins Sch. Medicine, 1963-75, John Jacob Abel Distinguished Service prof., 1975—, Am. Cancer Soc. prof., 1958-63, 77—; sr. asst. surgeon USPHS, 1951-53; vis. prof. Guy's Hosp. Med. Sch., London, 1970, 74-76; nat. adv. cancer council USPHS, 1967-71; vis. com. dept. biology Mass. Inst. Tech., 1964-67; bd. sci. advisers Jane Coffin Childs Meml. Fund for Cancer Research, 1971-80; bd. sci. consultants Sloan-Kettering Inst. Cancer Research, 1971-81. Hon. editorial adv. bd.: Biochem. Pharmacology, 1963-68; editorial bd.: Jour. Biol. Chemistry, 1961-66, Molecular Pharmacology, 1965-68, 71-80; editor-in-chief, 1968-71. Recipient Premio Internationale La Madonnina Milan, 1978; Med. Alumni Disting. Service award U. Chgo., 1978; Am. Cancer Soc. scholar, 1954-58; Guggenheim Meml. fellow, 1973-74. Fellow Am. Acad. Arts and Scis.; mem. AAAS (Theobald Smith award med. scis. 1957), Nat. Acad. Scis., Am. Philosophical Soc., Am. Soc. Biol. Chemists, Am. Soc. Clin. Investigation, Biochem. Soc., Am. Chem. Soc., Am. Soc. Pharm. and Exptl. Therapeutics, Phi Beta Kappa, Sigma Xi, Alpha Omega Alpha. Home: 5512 Boxhill Ln Baltimore MD 21210-2039 Office: Johns Hopkins U Sch Medicine Baltimore MD 21205

TALAN, JAMIE LYNN, science journalist; b. N.Y.C, June 25, 1956; d. Jack Robert Talan and Suzanne Lois (Robinson) Habib; m. Richard Carl Firstman, Mar. 25, 1990; children: Amanda, Allison, Jordan. BA in Psychology, SUNY, Stony Brook, 1978. Freelance sci. writer, 1978-85; sci. reporter Newsday, Melville, N.Y., 1985—. Recipient Harvey Hypertension award Am. Med. Writers Assn., 1986, Journalism award Epilepsy Found., 1986, APA, 1988, Nat. Alliance for Mentally Ill, 1990. Mem. Mat. Assn. Sci. Writers, Am. Psychol. Assn., Am. Psychiat. Assoc. Office: Newsday 235 Pinelawn Rd Melville NY 11747-4226

TALBERT, BOB, newspaper columnist. Columnist Detroit Free Press. Office: Detroit Free Press Inc 321 W Lafayette Blvd Detroit MI 48226-2705

TALBERT, JAMES LEWIS, pediatric surgeon, educator; b. Cassville, Mo., Sept. 26, 1931; s. William David and Frances (Lewis) T.; m. Alice Quintavell, July 25, 1958; children: William David, Alison Whitney. B.A., Vanderbilt U., 1953, M.D., 1956. Diplomate: Am. Bd. Surgery (with cert. of spl. competence in pediatric surgery), Am. Bd. Thoracic Surgery. Intern, then resident in surgery Johns Hopkins Hosp., 1956-64, resident in pediatric surgery, 1964-65, Harvey Cushing fellow, 1958-59; instr. surgery, Garrett scholar pediatric surgery Johns Hopkins U. Med. Sch., 1965-66, asst. prof., 1966-67; mem. faculty U. Fla. Med. Sch., Gainesville, 1967—; prof. pediatric surgery, chmn. div., chief children's surgery U. Fla. Med. Sch., 1970—; mem. affiliated faculty VA Hosp., Gainesville; med. dir. Fla. Regional Med. Program for Diagnosis and Treatment Cancer in Children, 1970-73, N. Referral Center Children's Med. Service Program Fla., 1970-80; chmn. Alachua County Emergency Med. Services Adv. Council, 1973-75; chmn. emergency med. services com. N. Central Fla. Health Planning Council, 1972-73; mem. Fla. Emergency Med. Services Adv. Council, 1973-75, 76-79. Author numerous articles in field; contbr. 16 chpts. to books. Served with USPHS, 1960-62. Recipient Founders medal, Roche award Vanderbilt U. Med. Sch., 1956. Fellow ACS (chmn. Fla. trauma com. 1969-77, gov.-at-large 1979-85, sec. bd. govs. 1982-85, rep. to Coun. of Med. Spl. Socs. 1988-89), Am. Acad. Pediatrics (exec. com. sect. oncology and hematology 1978-85); mem. AMA, Am. Pediatric Surg. Assn. (founding mem., chmn. trauma com. 1976-79), Pediatric Oncology Group (chmn. group retreat 1980), Am. Fedn. Clin. Rsch., Assn. Acad. Surgery, Soc. U. Surgeons, Soc. Pediatric Rsch., Am. Coll. Emergency Physicians, Am. Surg. Assn., Halsted Soc., Am. Assn. Surgery Trauma, Am. Burn Assn., Am. Pediatric Soc., Brit. Assn. Pediatric Surgeons, Soc. Internat. Chirurgie, So. Soc. Pediatric Rsch., So. Surg. Assn., Fla. Med. Assn., Fla. Heart Assn. (chmn. cardio-pulmonary resuscitation com. 1972-76), Fla. Assn. Pediatric Surgeons (pres. 1976-78), Fla. Assn. Pediatric Tumor Programs (pres. 1973—), Alachua County Med. Soc. (chmn. emergency med. svcs. adv. com. 1973-75), Phi Beta Kappa, Alpha Omega Alpha, Phi Eta Sigma. Office: J Hillis Miller Health Ctr PO Box 100286 Gainesville FL 32610-0286

TALBERT, LUTHER MARCUS, physician; b. Abington, Va., Dec. 30, 1926; s. Marcus Aurelius and Mary Elizabeth (Thompson) T.; m. Annie Brown Edmondson, Dec. 24, 1949; children: John T., Luther E., Martha C. B.A., Emory and Henry Coll., 1949, D.Sc. (hon.), 1980; M.D., U. Va., 1953. Med. intern U. Va., 1953-54, resident in Ob-Gyn, 1954-58, fellow in reproductive physiology, 1956-57; mem. faculty U. N.C. Med. Sch., Chapel Hill, 1958-92; prof. Ob-Gyn. U. N.C. Med. Sch., 1975-92, dir. div. reproductive endocrinology, 1975-84; dir. clin. svcs. N.C. Ctr. for Reproductive Medicine, Cary, N.C. Served with USN, 1944-46. Mem. Assn. Profs. Ob-Gyn (pres. 1979-80), Soc. Gynecologic Investigation, Am. Gynecol. and Obstet. Soc., AAAS. Republican. Baptist. Home: 101 Stoneridge Dr Chapel Hill NC 27514-9733 Office: NC Ctr for Reproductive Medicine 204/60 Asheville Dr Cary NC 27514-4216

TALBERT, MELVIN GEORGE, bishop; b. Clinton, La., June 14, 1934; s. Nettles and Florence (George) T.; m. Ethlelou Douglas, June 3, 1961; 1 child, Evangeline. BA, So. U., 1959; MDiv, Interdenominational Theol. Ctr., Gammon Theol. Sem., Atlanta, 1962; DD hon., Huston Tillotson Coll., Austin, 1972; LLD (hon.), U. Puget Sound, Tacoma, 1987. Ordained deacon, Meth. Ch., 1960 , elder, 1962, elected to episcopacy, United Meth. Ch., 1980. Pastor Boyd Chapel, Jefferson City, Tenn., 1960-61, Rising Sun, Sunrise, Tenn., 1960-61, St. John's Ch., L.A., 1961-62, Wesley Ch., L.A., 1962-64, Hamilton Ch., L.A., 1964-67; mem. staff So. Calif.-Ariz. Conf. United Meth. Ch., L.A., 1967-68; dist. supr. Long Beach dist. So. Calif.-Ariz. Conf. United Meth. Ch., 1968-73; gen. sec. Gen. Bd. Discipleship, Nashville, 1973-80; resident bishop Seattle area Pacific N.W. conf. United Meth. Ch., 1980-88, resident bishop San Francisco area Calif.-Nev. Conf., 1988—, sec. coun. bishops, 1988—; mem. exec. com. World Meth. Coun., 1976-81, 84—; mem. governing bd. Nat. Coun. Chs., 1980—; v.p., chmn. funding com. Gen. Commn. on Religion and Race, 1980-84, pres., 1984-88; chmn. Missional Priority Coordinating com. Gen. Coun. Ministries, 1980-84; mem. Gen. Commn. on Christian Unity and Interreligious Concerns, 1984—, African Ch. Growth and Devel. Com., 1981-84; now pres. elect Nat. Coun. Ch. Christ in the U.S.A. Mem. steering com. Student Non-Violent Coordinating com. Atlanta U. Ctr., 1960-61; trustee Gammon Theol. Sem., Atlanta, 1976—, U. Puget Sound, Tacoma, 1980-88 , Sch. Theology at Claremont, Calif., 1981-88, Pacific Sch. Religion, 1988—; bd. dirs. Glide Found., 1988—. Recipient award of merit for outstanding svc. in Christian edn. Gen. Bd. Edn., 1971; recipient Spl. achievement award Nat. Assn. Black Bus. Women, 1971; Nat. Meth. scholar, 1960; Crusade scholar, 1961. Mem. Theta Phi. Democrat. Home: 8735 W Camden Dr Elk Grove CA 95624-3037*

TALBERT, ROY, JR., history educator; b. Cheraw, S.C., Aug. 1, 1943; s. Roy and Betty Jean (Harper) T.; BA (Furman Scholar), Furman U., 1965; MA (NDEA fellow), Vanderbilt U., 1967, PhD, 1971; grad. Inst. Ednl. Mgmt., Harvard U., 1981; grad. Computer Literacy Inst., Pepperdine U., 1983; Jane Boyd Holbert, Oct. 24, 1986; children: Matthew, Rebecca Anne, Drew, Elizabeth. Sr. teaching fellow Vanderbilt U., Nashville, 1967-70; asst. prof. history Ferrum (Va.) Coll., 1974-76, dir. curriculum and programs, 1976-79; vice chancellor for acad. affairs Coastal Carolina U., Conway, 1979-84, assoc. prof. history, 1979-89, prof., 1989—, chmn. 1991—; producer, host The Public Eye, TV show, 1978-79; host Waccamaw Mag., TV show, 1983; project dir. numerous film, TV and pub. programming projects for community and civic groups, 1975-79. Served to capt. U.S. Army, 1970-72. Mem. So. Hist. Assn., Orgn. Am. Historians. Methodist. Author: FDR's Utopian: Arthur Morgan of the TVA, 1987, Negative Intelligence: The Army and the American Left, 1917-41, 1991, No Greater Legacy: The Centennial History of Willcox, McLeod, Buyck and Williams, 1995. Home: 106 Wofford Ln Conway SC 29526-8823 Office: Coastal Carolina Univ History Dept Conway SC 29526

TALBOT, ARDITH ANN, editor; b. Superior, Nebr., Mar. 11, 1933; d. Charles Howard and Dollie Eunice (Ryan) Snell; m. Richard Charles Talbot, Oct. 17, 1954; children: Richard Daryl, Robert Charles. BA in Edn., U. Nebr., 1956. Recorded Friends min., 1993. Tchr. high sch. Pub. Schs., Juniata, Nebr., 1957-59, Hudson, Iowa, 1962-68, New Providence, Iowa, 1968-71; owner Retail Bookstore, Sutherland, Iowa, 1971-72, Marshalltown, Iowa, 1972-74, Mason City, Iowa, 1974-89; mgr. book store Friends United Mktg., Richmond, Ind., 1986-89; mgr., editor Friends United Press, Richmond, Ind., 1989—. Republican. Avocations: antiques, public speaking. Home: Box 343 Lynn IN 47355 Office: Friends United Meeting 101 Quaker Hill Dr Richmond IN 47374-1926

TALBOT, BERNARD, government medical research facility official, physician; b. N.Y.C., Oct. 6, 1937; s. Harry and Gertrude (Salkin) T.; m. Ane Katrine Larsen, June 2, 1963; children: Akia, Kamilla. B.A., Columbia U., 1958, M.D., 1962; Ph.D, MIT, 1967. NIH postdoctoral fellow MIT, 1962-69; NSF postdoctoral fellow U. Rome, 1969-70; commd. USPHS, 1975—, advanced through grades to med. dir.; med. officer Nat. Cancer Inst., Bethesda, Md., 1971-75; spl. asst. intramural affairs NIH, Bethesda, 1975-78; spl. asst. to dir. NIH, 1978-81; dep. dir. Nat. Inst. Allergy and Infectious Diseases, Bethesda, 1981-87, med. officer nat. ctr. for rsch. resources, 1987—. Contbr. articles on protein chemistry to profl. jours., chpts. on recombinant DNA guidelines to books. Recipient Commendation medal USPHS, 1977, Meritorious Service medal, 1984. Mem. Phi Beta Kappa. Office: NIH 9000 Rockville Pike Bethesda MD 20892-0001

TALBOT, CARMEN V., county official; b. Highland Park, Mich., July 18; d. Albert Kennedy and Verda Muriel Bowers Carter; children: Jeffery Thomas, Cheryl Lynn Ellis. Newspaper reporter Southfield (Mich.) Sun Newspaper, 1970-73; adminstrv. asst. Charter Twsp. of Highland, Mich., 1980-84; legal sec. Willis C. Bullard, Jr., Milford, Mich., 1987-89; exec. sec. mktg. and pub. rels. Jervis B. Webb Co., Farmington Hills, Mich., 1985-88, prodn. coord. mktg. dept., 1988-89; exec. sec. Barbier & Tolleson, P.C., Troy, Mich., 1989-90, Patterson, Potter, Carniak & Anderson, Auburn Hills, Mich., 1990-92; transition team dir. L. Brooks Patterson, Oakland County Exec.-Elect, Pontiac, Mich., 1992; state govt. liaison County of Oakland, Pontiac, 1993—. Campaign coord. Willis C. Bullard Jr., 1982-86; Rep. precinct del. for Highland Twsp., 1982-92; Rep. conv. del. Highland Twsp. to Mich. State Rep. Convs., 1985-92; sec. 6th dist. Mich. 6th Congl. Dist. Exec. Bd., 1986-88; mem. exec. com. Oakland County Rep. Exec. Com., 1984-92, sec., 1989-92; regional coord. Oakland County 6th Dist. George Bush for Pres., 1986-88; polit. advisor David Galloway for State Rep., 1992, 94; scheduler L. Brooks Patterson for Oakland County Exec., 1992; trustee Highland Twsp., Mich., 1984-92. Lutheran. Office: County of Oakland Dept 409 1200 N Telegraph Rd Dept 409 Pontiac MI 48341-1032

TALBOT, DONALD ROY, consulting services executive; b. Bridgeport, Conn., Jan. 23, 1931; s. Grant Edward and Elvera (Gilbert) T.; m. Beverly Rinebold, Aug. 15, 1953; children: Donna, Randall, Theodore, Timothy, Thomas. B in Marine Enging., N.Y. State Maritime Coll. Project engr. atomic power equipment div. GE, San Jose, Calif., 1952-58; mgr. nuclear labs., nuclear div. Martin Marietta Corp., Balt., 1958-62, project dir. nuclear div., 1962-67; dir. spl. studies Martin Marietta Corp., Friendship, Md., 1967-71; project dir. environ. programs Martin Marietta Corp., Balt., 1971-74; dir. environ. tech. ctr. Martin Marietta Corp., Relay, Md., 1974-83; gen. mgr. environ. systems div. Martin Marietta Corp., Columbia, Md., 1984-87; corp. v.p. Versar, Inc., Springfield, Va., 1987-89; pres. R.E. Mgmt. Svc., Inc., Towson, Md., 1989—. Recipient Antarctica Svc. medal Civil Engrs. Corps USN, 1965, Cert. of Appreciation Sec. Dept. Commerce, 1975. Avocation: outdoor activities. Home: 712 Hickory Lot Rd Baltimore MD 21286-1427 Office: R E Mgmt Svcs Inc PO Box 10614 Baltimore MD 21285-0614

TALBOT, EMILE JOSEPH, French language educator; b. Brunswick, Maine, Apr. 12, 1941; s. Joseph Emile and Flora (Schinck) T.; m. Elizabeth Mullen, Aug. 6, 1966; children: Marc, Paul. BA, St. Francis Coll., Biddeford, Maine, 1963; MA, Brown U., 1965, PhD, 1968. Instr. French U. Ill., Urbana, 1967-68, asst. prof., 1968-73, assoc. prof., 1973-86, prof., 1986—, head dept. French, 1988-94. Author: Stendhal and Romantic Esthetics, 1985, Stendhal Revisited, 1993; editor: La Critique stendhalienne, 1979; assoc. editor: Quebec Studies, 1993-96; rev. editor: The French Review, 1979-82, Quebec Studies, 1988-93; mem. editl. bd.: Nineteenth-Century French Studies, 1986—, La Revue Francophone, 1990—. Fellow Ctr. for Advanced Study U. Ill., 1973, assoc., 1988; NEH fellow, 1973-74; Camargo Found. fellow, France, 1976. Mem. MLA, Am. Comparative Lit. Assn., Am. Assn. Tchrs. French, Assn. for Can. Studies in U.S., Am. Coun. for Quebec Studies (v.p. 1995—). Roman Catholic. Office: U Illinois Dept French 707 S Matthews Ave Urbana IL 61801-3625

TALBOT, HOWARD CHASE, JR., retired museum administrator; b. New Berlin, N.Y., Oct. 6, 1925; s. Howard Chase and Gladys (Jacobs) T.; m. Alice Caroline Losee, Sept. 11, 1948; children—Julia Anna, Judith Ann, James Clayton. Student, Utica (N.Y.) Sch. Commerce, 1946-47. Acct. Leatherstocking Corp., Cooperstown, N.Y., 1947-51; asst. dir., then asst. treas. Nat. Baseball Hall of Fame and Mus., Cooperstown, 1951-78; dir. Nat. Baseball Hall of Fame and Mus., 1978-93; ret., 1993; dir. N.Y. Central Mut. Fire Ins. Co., Edmeston. Trustee Village of Cooperstown, 1957-62, mayor, 1962-63; bd. dirs. Little League Mus., Williamsport, Pa. Served with AUS, 1942-46. Mem. Am. Legion. Republican. Clubs: Cooperstown Rotary (past pres.), Masons.

TALBOT, LEE MERRIAM, ecologist, educator, association executive; b. New Bedford, Mass., Aug. 2, 1930; s. Murrell Williams and Zenaida (Merriam) T.; m. Martha Walcott Hayne, May 16, 1959; children: Lawrence Hayne, Russell Merriam. B.A., U. Calif., Berkeley, 1953, M.A., 1963, Ph.D., 1963. Biologist Arctic Research Lab., Point Barrow, Alaska, 1951; staff ecologist Internat. Union for Conservation, Brussels, 1954-56; ecologist, dir. East African ecol. research project Nat. Acad. Scis., Govts. of Kenya and Tanzania, 1959-63; wildlife advisor UN Spl. Fund, Africa, 1963-64; dir. S.E. Asia project Internat. Union for Conservation, 1964-65; resident ecologist, field rep. for internat. affairs Smithsonian Instn., Washington, 1966-70; sr. scientist, dir. internat. activities Pres.'s Council on Environ. Quality, Washington, 1970-78; sr. sci. advisor Internat. Council Sci. Unions, Paris, 1978-83; dir. conservation, spl. sci. advisor World Wildlife Fund Internat., Switzerland, 1978-80; dir. gen. Internat. Union for Conservation of Nature and Natural Resources, Gland, Switzerland, 1980-83; research fellow Environ. and Policy Inst., East West Ctr., 1983-87; vis. fellow World Resources Inst., Washington, 1984-89; sr. environ. advisor World Bank, 1984—; pres. Lee Talbot Assocs. Internat., 1991—; sr. prof. environ. scis., internat. affairs and pub. policy George Mason U., Va., 1994—; cons. UNESCO, World Bank, Asian Devel. Bank, Nat. Geog. Soc., Inter-Am. Devel. Bank, The Nature Conservancy, U.S. Govt., U. Calif., UN Spl. Fund, WHO, UN Environment Program, UN Univ.; conservation coord. Internat. Biol. Program, 1965-70; v.p. Fauna and Flora Internat., London; bd. dirs. Ecologically Sustainable Devel., Inc., Inst. Ecosys. Studies. Author 13 books and monographs; contbr. articles to profl. jours. Active Boy Scouts Am., Geneva, 1980-82, Washington, 1987—. With USMC, 1953-54. Decorated officer Order of Lion (Senegal); recipient Fgn. Field Rsch. award Nat. Acad. Scis., 1959, CINE Golden Eagle award, 1969, Albert Schweitzer medal, 1975, Regents Lectureship award U. Calif.-Santa Barbara, 1986, Pierre Chaleur prize for lit. French Acad. Scis., 1993. Fellow Royal Geog. Soc., Royal Soc. Arts, AAAS, N.Y. Zool. Soc.; mem. Am. Inst. Biol. Scis. (Disting. Svc. award 1979), Acad. Medicine, World Conservation Union (hon.), Am. Assn. for Club of Rome, Am. Soc. Mammalogists, Ecol. Soc., Wildlife Soc. (Outstanding Publ. award 1963), Soc. for Conservation Biology, Internat. Soc. for Ecol. Econs., Boone and Crockett Club (N.Y.C.), Explorers Club (N.Y.C.), Cosmos Club (Washington), Sigma Xi, Phi Kappa Sigma. Achievements include incorporation of ecological principles in international development; development of new principles for management of wild resources; biodiversity conservation; definition of ecosystem dynamics of tropical savannahs including role of fire, feeding habits and migrations of wild herbivores; development and negotiation of international agreements for environmental protection. Home: 6656 Chilton Ct Mc Lean VA 22101-4422 *My career is based on two premises: first, that our most important challenges are environmental issues which determine the earth's carrying capacity for human life and, equally important, the quality of that life; and second, that it is important to obtain direct experience in as much of the world as possible (over 125 countries so far) to understand the human ecological setting as a basis for action to improve it.*

TALBOT, MATTHEW J., oil company executive, rancher; b. Sept. 4, 1937; s. Matthew J. and Margaret A. (Green) T.; m. Maureen Donlan, June 3, 1958; children: Maureen A., Matthew J., Kathleen M. BBA in Acctg., Iona Coll., 1963. Acct. S.D. Leidesdorf (now Ernst & Young), N.Y.C., 1961-67; sr. analyst Gen. Foods Corp., White Plains, N.Y., 1967-68; asst. to comptroller Tosco Corp., Los Angeles, 1968-70, comptroller, 1970-83, v.p., 1972-

76, sr. v.p., 1976-78, exec. v.p., 1978-83; pres. Tosco Corp., Santa Monica, Calif., 1983-87, Talbot Ranch, 1987—; s.r. consultant Edward White & Co., Woodland Hills, 1987—. Treas., bd. dirs. Ctr. Theatre Group, Los Angeles; trustee Craft and Folk Art Mus., Los Angeles. Mem. Am. Inst. CPA's, Fin. Execs. Inst., Sunkist Growers. Roman Catholic. Office: Edward White & Co 21700 Oxnard StSte 400 Woodland Hills CA 91367-3642

TALBOT, PAMELA, public relations executive; b. Chgo., Aug. 10, 1946. BA in English, Vassar Coll., 1968. Reporter Worcester, Mass. Telegram and Gazette, 1970-72; account exec. Daniel J. Edelman, Inc., Chgo., 1972-74, account supr., 1974-76, v.p., 1976-78, sr. v.p., 1978-84, exec. v.p., gen. mgr., 1984-90; pres. Edelman West, Chgo., 1990—; Consumer Worldwide, 1995.

TALBOT, PHILLIPS, Asian affairs specialist; b. Pitts., June 7, 1915; s. Kenneth Hammet and Gertrude (Phillips) T.; m. Mildred Aleen Fisher, Aug. 18, 1943; children: Susan Talbot Jacox, Nancy, Bruce Kenneth. BA, U. Ill., 1936, BS in Journalism, 1936; student, London Sch. Oriental Studies, 1938-39, Aligarh Muslim U., India, 1939-40; Ph.D., U. Chgo., 1954; LL.D. (hon.), Mills Coll., 1963. Reporter, Chgo. Daily News, 1936-38; corr. Chgo. Daily News, India and Pakistan, 1946-48, 49-50; assoc. Inst. Current World Affairs, Eng. and India, 1938-41; part-time Inst. Current World Affairs, 1946-51; instr. U. Chgo., 1948-50; instr. Columbia U., N.Y.C., 1951; exec. dir. Am. Univs. Field Staff, 1951-61; asst. sec. Near Eastern and S. Asian affairs Dept. State, 1961-65; U.S. ambassador to Greece, 1965-69; pres. Asia Soc., N.Y.C., 1970-81; emeritus Asia Soc., 1981—; Phi Beta Kappa vis. scholar, 1973-74. Author: (with S.L. Poplai) India and America, 1958, India in the 1980s, 1983; editor: South Asia in the World Today, 1950. Trustee emeritus Aspen Inst., U.S.-Japan Found.; counselor United Bd. for Christian Higher Edn. in Asia; elder Presbyn. Ch. 2d lt. cav. Officers Res. Corps, 1936; 1st lt. N.G., 1937-38; lt. comdr. USNR, 1941-46. Mem. Am. Acad. Diplomacy, Coun. Am. Ambs., Assn. Asian Studies, Coun. Fgn. Rels., Century Assn., Cosmos Club. Address: 200 E 66th St New York NY 10021-6728

TALBOT, PRUE, biology educator. BA, Wilson Coll., 1966; MA, Wellesley Coll., 1968; PhD, U. Houston, 1972. Postdoctoral fellow U. Houston; from asst. prof. to assoc. prof. U. Calif., Riverside, 1977-85, prof., 1986—. Assoc. editor several profl. jours.; contbr. articles to profl. jours. Mem. Am. Soc. Cell Biology, AAAS, Crustacean Soc., Sigma Xi. Office: U Calif Riverside Dept Biology Riverside CA 92521

TALBOT, RICHARD JOSEPH, library administrator; b. Lynn, Mass., Dec. 18, 1932; s. Joseph Anthony and Mary Kathleen (Connolly) T.; m. Joanne Frances Hines, Sept. 2, 1961; children: Mary Frances, Jean Ann. A.B., Manhattan Coll., 1954; M.S. in Library Sci., Simmons Coll., 1961; M.B.A., Syracuse U., 1980. Reference librarian N.Y. Pub. Library, N.Y.C., 1961-62; cataloger, acquisitions librarian, library systems analyst NASA, Cambridge, Mass., Dept. Air Force, Bedford, Mass., 1962-70; asso. dir. U. Mass. Library, Amherst, 1970-73; dir. libraries U. Mass. Library, 1973—; bd. dirs. Nelinet. Contbr. articles to profl. jours. Served to 1st lt. USAF, 1954-57. Mem. ALA, Assn. Coll. and Research Libraries (dir., exec. com., chmn. fin. com. 1980-83), Assn. Research Libraries (dir. 1982-86, pres. 1984-85). Roman Catholic. Home: 40 High Point Dr Amherst MA 01002-1224 Office: U Mass U Libr Amherst MA 01003

TALBOT-KOEHL, LINDA ANN, dancer, ballet studio owner; b. Fremont, Ohio, July 22, 1956; d. Donald Ray and Doris Ann (Opperman) Talbot; m. James G. Koehl, July 30, 1983. Student, U. Akron, 1974-76; BA in Psychology, Heidelberg Coll., 1984. Owner, instr. BalleTiffin, Inc., Tiffin, Ohio, 1987—; choreographer Heidelberg Summer Theater, Tiffin, 1986, Singing Collegians, 1993; choreographer Calvert H.S. Theater, Tiffin, 1986-88, Swing Choir, 1987-89, 91-92. Appeared (ednl. film) Rights on the Job, State of Ohio Dept. Edn., 1986. Mem. Dance Masters Am., Nat. Multiple Sclerosis Soc., The Ritz Players (choreographer 1985, 88-89, 96, make-up designer, advisor 1989-92, sound booth operator 1993—). Avocations: reading, photography, music, community theater, travel. Home and Office: BalleTiffin Inc 449 Melmore St Tiffin OH 44883-3628

TALBOTT, BEN JOHNSON, JR., lawyer; b. Louisville, May 2, 1940; s. Ben Johnson and Elizabeth (Farnsley) T.; m. Sandra Riehl, Oct. 19, 1963; children: Elizabeth, Betty, John, Ben, Sandra. AB magna cum laude, Xavier U., Cin., 1961; LLB, Harvard U., 1964. Bar: Ky. 1965, U.S. Ct. Appeals (6th cir.) 1967. Law clk. to presiding justice U.S. Dist. Ct. Ky., Louisville, 1964-65; assoc. Middleton, Reutlinger & Baird, Louisville, 1965-68, ptnr., 1968-80; ptnr. Westfall, Talbott & Woods, Louisville, 1980—; atty. Stitzel-Weller Distillery, 1970-72, Louisville Gen. Hosp., 1974-83, Louisville and Jefferson County Bd. Health, 1974-80, U. Louisville, Louisville, 1980—. Mem. adv. bd. Louisville 15, Sta. WKPC-TV, Bd. dirs., 1972-74, pres. 1974; past bd. dirs. U. Louisville Found., U. Louisville Med. Sch. Fund Orgn.; bd. dirs. Louisville Theatrical Assn., 1971—, pres., 1975-76, chmn., 1977-78; bd. dirs. Def. Enterprise Fund, 1994—; bd. dirs. Macauley Theatre, 1975, TARC Adv. Com., 1971, Jefferson County Capital Constrn. Com., 1971, Louisville Orch., 1976-86, pres., 1979-81; bd. trustees, trustee U. Louisville, 1970-79, sec., 1974, vice chmn., 1975, chmn. fin. com., 1976; bd. dirs. Ky. Ctr. for the Arts, 1983—, Louisville Lung Assn., 1974-75, treas., 1975; bd. dirs. Historic Homes Found., 1972-78, v.p. 1978, advisor, atty. 1978—. Named Outstanding Young Man of Louisville, Louisville Jaycees, 1976. Mem. ABA, Ky. Bar Assn. (chmn. 1989, Gen. Practice Session of the CLE), Louisville Bar Assn. (past mem. exec. com.), Nat. Assn. Coll. and Univ. Attys., The Def. Rsch. and Trial Lawyers Assn., Am. Ins. Attys., Harvard Law Sch. Assn. of Ky. (sec. 1965, pres. 1989—), Phi Kappa Phi. Avocations: golf, tennis, skiing. Home: 566 Blankenbaker Ln Louisville KY 40207-1167 Office: Westfall Talbott & Woods 501 S 2nd St Louisville KY 40202-1864

TALBOTT, FRANK, III, lawyer; b. Danville, Va., Mar. 26, 1929; s. Frank and Margaret (Jordan) T.; m. Mary Beverley Chewning, July 11, 1952; children: Beverley, Frank IV. BA, U. Va., 1951, LLB, 1953. Bar: Va. 1952. Gen. practice law Danville, 1956-66; with Dan River Inc., 1966-76, v.p., gen. counsel, 1968-76; partner firm Clement, Wheatley, Winston, Talbott & Majors, Danville, 1977-78; individual practice law Danville, 1979-92; gen. counsel Va. Mfrs. Assn. Inc., 1983-92; of counsel Woods, Rogers & Hazlegrove, Danville, Va., 1992—; chmn. adv. bd. NationsBank, Danville, 1984-94. Vice-chmn. Danville Sch. Bd., 1964-70; trustee Va. Student Aid Found., 1963-68; bd. dirs. United Fund Danville, 1959-63, Meml. Hosp., Danville, 1977-90. Served with AUS, 1953-56. Decorated Commendation medal. Fellow Am. Bar Found. (life); mem. Va. Bar Assn. (v.p. 1965-66, exec. com. 1967-70), Danville Bar Assn. (pres. 1965-66), Am. Judicature Soc., Newcomen Soc., U. Va. Alumni Assn. (bd. mgrs.), Danville Golf Club, German Club, Farmington Country Club, Country Club Va., Delta Psi, Phi Alpha Delta. Methodist. Home: 420 Maple Ln Danville VA 24541-3532 Office: PO Box 560 Danville VA 24543-0560

TALBOTT, MARY ANN BRITT, secondary education educator; b. Augusta, Ga., Nov. 29, 1945; d. Charles Hubert and Mary Ann (Day) Britt; m. Lonnie Loyd Talbott, Oct. 20, 1978. AB, U. Ga., 1967, EdS, 1981, Cert. in Adminstrn./Supervision, 1989; MEd, Augusta Coll., 1975. Cert. tchr. support specialist. Tchr. English Hilsman Jr. H.S., Athens, Ga., 1967-68; tchr. English, chmn. dept. Tubman Jr. H.S., Augusta, Ga., 1969-73, Aquinas H.S., Augusta, 1973-79; tchr. English Winder (Ga.)-Barrow H.S., 1979-82; tchr. remedial writing/reading/math, career planning, Latin Morrow (Ga.) H.S., 1982-91, tchr. English, 1982-93; tchr. English Brunswick (Ga.) H.S., 1993—, mem. discipline task force, 1995—; instr. English Clayton State Coll., Morrow, 1991-92, Ga. Mil. Coll., Ft. Gordon, 1975-77; instr. staff devel. Clayton County Bd. Edn., Jonesboro, Ga., 1985-91. Elder Stockbridge (Ga.) Presbyn. Ch., 1989-92; active Am. Cancer Soc., Augusta Choral Soc., Athens Choral Soc.; mem. Evangel. Luth. Ch. Resurrection, Augusta, Ga., 1995—. Mem. Delta Kappa Gamma (pres. 1978-80, chmn. music com. 1985-87, 89-91, chair Psi State Achievement Award Com. 1979-81, dist. dir. 1981-83, scholar 1980, 87, golden Gift award 1984), Alpha Lambda Delta, Kappa Delta Sigma, Phi Delta Kappa (Tchr. of Yr. 1989). Lutheran. Avocations: reading, travel, fine arts, computers. Home: PO Box 13163 Jekyll Island GA 31527-3163 Office: Brunswick High Sch Habersham St Brunswick GA 31520

TALBOTT, RICHARD DAVID, physician; b. Jackson, Mich., Dec. 31, 1930; s. James Ernest and Ellen (McGowan) T.; m. Katherine Marie Bonney, June 18, 1983; children: James M., William J., Judith M. AB, Yale U., 1952; MD, Northwestern U., 1956. Diplomate Am. Bd. Orthopaedic Surgery. Intern Denver Gen. Hosp., 1956-57; resident St. Luke's Hosp., Denver, 1957-58, Lahey Clinic, Boston, 1958-59, Shriners Hosp. for Crippled Children, Springfield, Mass., 1959-60, Boston City Hosp., 1960-61; pvt. practice Orthopaedic Assocs., P.C., Denver, 1961-86; dir. dept. orthopaedic surgery Denver Gen. Hosp., 1987-95; ptnr. InMed Evaluations, Denver, 1995—. Avocations: boating, fishing, tennis, golf. Home: Four Polo Field Ln Denver CO 80209 Office: InMed Evaluations 135 W 10th Ave Denver CO 80204

TALBOTT, STROBE, journalist; b. Dayton, Ohio, Apr. 25, 1946; s. Nelson S. and Josephine (Large) T.; m. Brooke Lloyd Shearer, Nov. 14, 1971; children: Devin Lloyd, Adrian Nelson. BA, Yale U., 1968, MA (hon.), 1976; MLitt, Oxford U., Eng., 1971. East european corr. Time Mag., 1971-73, U.S. state dept. corr., 1973-75, white house corr., 1975-77, diplomatic corr., 1977-84, chief Washington bur., 1984-89; editor at large, 1989—. editor, translator: Khrushchev Remembers, 1970, Khrushchev Remembers: Last Testament, 1974; author: Endgame: Inside Story of SALT II, 1979, Deadly Gambits: Reagan Administration & Arms Controls, 1984, The Russians and Reagan, 1984, Reagan and Gorbachev, 1987, Master of the Game, 1988. Trustee Yale U. 1976-82, Hotchkiss Sch., 1982-87; bd. dirs. Carnegie Endowment Internat. Peace; Council on Fgn. Relations. Recipient Edward Weintal Prize for Disting. Diplomatic Reporting Georgetown U., Overseas Press Club award, Stanley Hillman award. Office: Time Magazine 1050 Connecticut Ave NW Washington DC 20036-5303

TALENT, JAMES M., congressman, lawyer; b. St. Louis, Mo., Oct. 18, 1956; m. Brenda Lyons, 1984; children: Michael, Kathleen Marie. BA in Polit. Sci., Washington U., 1978; JD, U. Chgo. Law Sch., 1981. Law clk. 7th Ct. Appeals, 1981-82; adj. prof. law, 1982-84; mem. Mo. State Ho. Reps., 1984-93; minority leader, 1989-93; mem. 103rd-104th Congresses from 2nd Mo. Dist., 1993—, mem. econ. & ednl. opportunity com., nat. security com., chmn. small bus. subcom. on regulation and paperwork. Legislative Achievement award Mo. Hosp. Assn., 1989. Mem. Mo. Bar Assn. (Award for significant contbns. to adminstrv. justice 1989), Mo. C. of C. (Spirit of Enterprise award 1990), Order of the Coif. Republican. Office: US Ho Reps 1022 Longworth Office House Members Washington DC 20515-2502

TALESE, GAY, writer; b. Ocean City, N.J., Feb. 7, 1932; s. Joseph Francis and Catherine (DiPaola) T.; m. Nan Ahearn, June 10, 1959; children—Pamela, Catherine. B.A. in Journalism, U. Ala., 1953. Staff writer N.Y. Times, N.Y.C., 1955-65; writer Esquire mag., N.Y.C., 1960. Author: New York - A Serendipiter's Journey, 1961, The Bridge, 1964, The Overreachers, 1965, The Kingdom and the Power, 1969, Fame and Obscurity, 1970, Honor Thy Father, 1971, Thy Neighbor's Wife, 1980, Unto the Sons, 1992; co-author: (with Barbara Lounsberry) The Literature of Reality, 1995; contbr. articles to Esquire mag., others. Served to 1st lt. AUS, 1954-56. Mem. P.E.N. (v.p. 1984-87, bd. dirs. 1980—), Phi Sigma Kappa. Home: 109 E 61st St New York NY 10021-8101 also: 154 E Atlantic Blvd Ocean City NJ 08226-4511

TALESE, NAN AHEARN, publishing company executive; b. N.Y.C., Dec. 19, 1933; d. Thomas James and Suzanne Sherman (Russell) Ahearn; m. Gay Talese, June 10, 1959; children: Pamela Frances, Catherine Gay. B.A., Manhattanville Coll. of Sacred Heart, 1955. Fgn. exchange student 1st Nat. City Bank, London and Paris, 1956; editorial asst. Am. Eugenics Soc., N.Y.C., 1957-58, Vogue mag., N.Y.C., 1958-59; copy editor Random House Pub., N.Y.C., 1959-64; assoc. editor Random House Pub., 1964-67, sr. editor, 1967-73; sr. editor Simon & Schuster Pubs., N.Y.C., 1974-81; v.p. Simon & Schuster Pubs., 1979-81; exec. editor, v.p. Houghton Mifflin Co., N.Y.C., 1981-83, v.p., editor-in-chief, 1984-86, v.p., pub., editor-in-chief, 1986-88; sr. v.p. Doubleday & Co., N.Y.C., 1988-90; pres., pub., editorial dir. Nan A. Talese Books, 1990—. Home: 109 E 61st St New York NY 10021-8101

TALIAFERRO, NANCY ELLEN TAYLOR, artist; b. Richmond, Va., Feb. 16, 1937; d. Samuel Beryl and Nancy Loomis (Brinton) Taylor; m. Charles Mitchell Taliaferro, July 3, 1958; children: Chester Parsons, Nancy Brinton. BFA, Va. Commonwealth U., 1959. Comml. artist, illustrator, 1959-63, drawings, pastel portraits, 1963—, oil paintings, 1978—. Exhbns. include Nat. Assn. Women Artists Traveling Exhbn. USA, 1996-98, Chrysler Mus., Norfolk, Va., 1994, Du Pont Art Gallery, Washington and Lee U., Lexington, Va., 1993, Uptown Gallery, Richmond, 1992-96, Art Gallery, Ashland, Va., 1992-96, Va. Gen. Assembly Bldg. and State Capitol, 1989, 91, 93, Jacob Javits Fed. Bldg., N.Y.C., 1986, Women's Resource Ctr., U. Richmond, 1985. Recipient award The Artists Mag., 1992. Mem. Nat. Assn. Women Artists (medal of honor, Audrey Hope Shirk Meml. award 1995), Uptown Gallery (charter mem.), James River Art League, U. Painters. Republican. Methodist. Home: 6724 Forest Hill Ave Richmond VA 23225-1802 Studio: 8413 Forest Hill Ave Richmond VA 23235-3125

TALINGDAN, ARSENIO PREZA, health science administrator; b. Dolores, Abra, The Philippines, Mar. 30, 1930; came to U.S., 1973; s. Mariano T. and Candida (Tordil) Preza; m. Josefa Fernandez Biason. Apr. 21, 1954; children: Melda, Arsenio Jr., Jocelyn Almerick, Mario, Abe. AA, U. Philippines, 1951, AB, MPA, 1955; MAPA, The Am. U., 1956; BS, La Salle Extention U., Chgo., 1977; MBA, Century U., 1983, PhD, 1985. Cert. nursing home adminstr., life, health and securities underwriter. Job analyst, orgn. analyst, budget examiner Kroeger & Assocs. Project, Philippine Budget Commn., Manila, 1954-55; scholar, tech. asst., participant USA-ICA-NEC Program, 1955-56; supr. mgmt. analyst Philippine Budget Commn., Manila, 1957-59; asst. budget dir., IBM coordinator U. Philippines, Quezon City, 1959-65, mgmt. specialist, chief of studies, 1969-70; asst. v.p. for budget and mgmt. Sarmiento Enterprises, Inc., Makati, Rizal, Philippines, 1965-69; adminstr. Philippine Gen. Hosp., Manila, 1970-73; budget and facilities mgr. Hunter Coll., CUNY, N.Y.C., 1973-76; acctg. systems editor J.C. Penney Co., N.Y.C., 1977; regional med. care adminstr. N.Y. State Dept. Health, Office Health Systems Mgmt., N.Y.C., 1977-78; assoc. med. care adminstr., Medicaid mgmt. info. systems Dept. Health State of N.Y., N.Y.C., 1978—; with dental Medicaid program Dept. Health State of N.Y., 1978-82, with med. ops. br., 1982-84, with dental ops. br., 1984-91, with patient care investigations, long term care program, 1991—; asst. prof., chmn. social scis. dept. U.P. Coll., Manila, 1969-73; 1st Philippine tech. assistance fellow on orgn. and mgmt. U.S. Agy. for Internat. Devel., Washington, 1955-56; professorial lectr. U. Philippines, Manila, 1960-69. Co-author: Accounting, Auditing and Internal Auditing, 1964; author: Public Administration and Management, 1966, Management and Supervision, 1966, Work Simplification Handbook, 1957 and others; contbr. articles to profl. jours. Pres. Abra Varsitarians, Quezon City, 1949-53; founder, Dolores Young Men and Women's Assn., Manila, Abra, 1949-71; founder, pres. Philippine Execs. and Profls. Golf Assn., Quezon City, 1965-69, others. Maj. Res. Officer, Philippine Army, 1960-73. Recipient Hall of Nations award Am. U., 1956, Pub. Health Sci. award Del. Valley Assn. Philippines, 1980, Profl. award in Pub. Adminstrn. U. Philippines Alumni Assn. Am., 1991. Mem. Pub. Employees Fedn., U. of the Philippines Alumni Assn. in N.J. (founder, 1st pres. 1979-83), U. of the Philippines Alumni Assn. in Am. (founder, 1st pres. 1980-83), Filipino Am. Soc. of Teaneck (pres. 1983-84). Republican. Avocation: writing.

TALKINGTON, ROBERT VAN, state senator; b. near Patrick, Tex., Aug. 23, 1929; s. William Henry and Nannie J. (Patrick) T.; m. Donna Jill Schmaus, Mar. 25, 1951; children—Jill Talkington McCaskill, Jacki Talkington Chase, James, Thomas, Lisa. A.A., Tyler Jr. Coll., 1949; B.S., U. Kans., 1951, LL.B., 1954, J.D., 1971. Bar: Kans. 1954. County atty. Allen County, Kans., 1957-63; city atty. Moran, Kans., 1968—; mem. Kans. Ho. of Reps. from 10th Dist., 1969-73; mem. Kans. Senate from 12th Dist., 1973-89, v.p., 1977-81, majority leader, 1981-85, pres., 1985-89; mem. State Bd. of Regents, 1995—; chmn. Republican Party, Allen County, 1964-68, state treas., 1964-66. Trustee Iola Pub. Libr., 1962-70; mem. adv. bd. Greater Univ. Fund, U. Kans., 1967-72. With U.S. Army Counter Intelligence Corp, 1954-56. Mem. Am. Legion, Sigma Alpha Epsilon, Phi Delta Phi. Clubs: Masons, Shriners, Elks. Home: 20 W Buchanan St Iola KS 66749-1823 Office: 20 N Washington St Iola KS 66749-2836

TALKINGTON, WILLIAM ALE, publishing company executive; b. Seymour, Ind., Apr. 14, 1948; s. Robert James and Margaret (Ale) T.; m. Marilyn Kay Huffman, Aug. 30, 1969; children—Matthew A., Bradley. A.B. in English, Ind. U., 1970. Mktg. mgr. McGraw-Hill, N.Y.C., 1974-75, dist. mgr., 1975-78, editor, 1978-80, regional mgr., 1980-82, editorial dir., 1982-84, dir. mktg. services, 1984-92; v.p. sales and mktg. Merrill Pub., 1984-92; pres. Holt, Rinehart & Winston, Austin, 1992—. Mem. Am. Mgmt. Assn., Assn. Am. Pubs. *

TALL, FRANKLIN DAVID, mathematics educator; b. N.Y.C., Apr. 21, 1944; s. Martin and Faye T. AB, Harvard U., 1964; PhD, U. Wis., 1969. Asst. prof U. Toronto, Ont., Can., 1969-74; assoc. prof. U. Toronto, 1974-80, prof. math., 1980—. Author: (monograph) Set Theoretic Consistency Results and Topological Theorems Concerning the Normal Moore Space Conjecture and Related Problems, 1977, The Work of Mary Ellen Rudin, 1993. Nat. Scis. and Engring. Research Council Can. grantee, 1973—. Mem. Am. Math. Soc. (mem. editl. bd. Proc.), Can. Math. Soc., Assn. Symbolic Logic, Japan-Can. Soc., Internat. Assn. Neurolinguistic Programming. Office: U Toronto, Dept Math, Toronto, ON Canada M5S 1A1

TALLACKSON, HARVEY DEAN, real estate and insurance salesman; b. Grafton, N.D., May 15, 1925; s. Arthur J. and Mabel R. (McDougald) T.; m. Glenna M. Walstad, Aug. 4, 1946; children: Lynda, Thomas, Debra, Amy, Laura. Grad. h.s., Park River, N.D. Grain and potato farmer Grafton, 1946-68; ins. agt. Tallackson Ins., Grafton, 1968—; mem. N.D. Senate, Grafton, 1976—; real estate salesman Johnson Real Estate, Grafton, 1982—; chmn. appropriation com. N.D. Senate, 1987-93. Bd. dirs. Nodak Rural Electric Coop., Grand Forks, N.D., 1965—; bd. dirs. Minnkota Power Coop., Grand Forks, 1979—, pres., 1990—. Recipient Pub. Svc. award N.D. Lignite Coun., 1989; named Outstanding Young Farmer by Area Chamber of Walsh & Pembina Counties, 1951-52. Mem. Nat. Coun. Ins. Legislatures (mem. exec. com. 1985—, pres. 1996-97), Lions (pres. 1977-79), Masons. Democrat. Lutheran. Avocations: golf, curling, travel, reading. Office: Tallackson Ins & Real Estate 53 W 5th St Grafton ND 58237-1468

TALLCHIEF, MARIA, ballerina; b. Fairfax, Okla., Jan. 24, 1925; d. Alexander Joseph and Ruth Mary (Porter) T.; m. Henry Paschen, Jr., June 3, 1956; 1 child, Elise. DFA (hon.), Lake Forest (Ill.) Coll., Colby Coll., Waterville, Maine, 1968, Ripon Coll., 1973, Boston Coll., Smith Coll., 1981, Northwestern U., Evanston, Ill., 1982, Yale U., 1984, St. Mary-of-the-Woods (Ind.) Coll., 1984, Dartmouth Coll., 1985, St. Xavier Coll., 1989. Ballerina Ballet Russe de Monte Carlo, 1942-47; with N.Y.C. Ballet Co., 1947-65, prima ballerina, 1947-60; founder Chgo. City Ballet, 1979; now artistic dir. Lyric Opera Ballet; prima ballerina Am. Ballet Theatre, 1960; founder Sch. Chgo. Ballet. Guest star, Paris Opera, 1947, Royal Danish Ballet, 1961; created roles in Danses Concertantes, 1944, Night Shadow, 1946, Four Temperaments, 1946, Orpheus, 1948, The Firebird, 1949, Bourée Fantastique, 1949, Capriccio Brillante, 1951, Á la Françaix, 1951, Swan Lake, 1951, Caracole, 1952, Scotch Symphony, 1952, The Nutcracker, 1954, Allegro Brillante, 1956, The Gounod Symphony, 1958; appeared in films Presenting Lily Mais, 1943, Million Dollar Mermaid, 1953. Named Hon. Princess Osage Indian Tribe, 1953; recipient Disting. Service award U. Okla., 1972, award Dance mag., 1960, Jane Addams Humanitarian award Rockford Coll., 1973, Bravo award Rosary Coll., 1983, award Dance Educators Am., 1956, Achievement award Women's Nat. Press Club, 1953, Capezio award, 1965, Leadership for Freedom award Roosevelt U. Scholarship Assn., 1986. Mem. Nat. Soc. Arts and Letters.

TALLENT, STEPHEN EDISON, lawyer; b. Columbus, Nebr., Aug. 10, 1937; s. William E. and Helen T.; m. Martha Sutcliffe, Apr. 6, 1971; 1 child, Jennifer Diane. BA, Stanford U.; JD, U. Chgo., LLD (hon.), Lincoln U. Bar: Calif. 1963, U.S. Dist. Ct. (so. and cen. dists.) Calif. 1965, U.S. Dist. Ct. (so. and ea. dists.) N.Y., 1989, U.S. Ct. Appeals (D.C. cir.) 1981, U.S. Ct. Appeals (2d cir.) 1987, U.S. Ct. Appeals (3d cir.) 1980, U.S. Ct. Appeals (4th cir.) 1982, U.S. Ct. Appeals (6th cir.) 1986, U.S. Ct. Appeals (9th cir.) 1968, U.S. Ct. Mil. Appeals 1965, U.S. Supreme Ct. 1973. Ptnr. Gibson, Dunn & Crutcher, L.A., 1962—; former adj. prof. Loyola Law Sch., L.A.; mem. vis. com. U. Chgo. Law Sch. Former mem. Calif. Atty. Gen.'s adv. com. for Evaluation of Anti-Organized Crime Programs; mem. L.A. Town Hall, L.A. World Affairs Council; mem. bd. vis. Stanford Law Sch.; founding dir. Am. EMployment Law Coun., 1993—. Mem. ABA (coun. of labor and employment law sect.), Calif. Bar Assn., D.C. Bar Assn., N.Y. Bar, L.A. County Bar Assn., Indsl. Rels. Rsch. Assn. Home: 7020 Glenbrook Rd Bethesda MD 20814-1223 Office: Gibson Dunn & Crutcher 1050 Connecticut Ave NW Ste 900 Washington DC 20036-5303 also: 333 S Grand Ave Los Angeles CA 90071-1504

TALLENT, WILLIAM HUGH, chemist, research administrator; b. Akron, Ohio, May 28, 1928; s. Charles Othar and Agnes Annette (Johnson) T.; m. Joy Anne Redfield, Aug.23, 1952; children: Elizabeth Ann, Cinda Marie, Raymond Charles. BS, U. Tenn., 1949, MS, 1950; PhD, U. Ill., 1953. Chemist Nat. Heart Inst., Bethesda, Md., 1953-57, G.D. Searle & Co., Skokie, Ill., 1957-64; head new crops evaluation investigations Agr. Rsch. Svc., USDA, Peoria, Ill., 1964-69, chief indsl. crops lab., 1969-74, asst. dir., 1974-75, ctr. dir. No. Regional Rsch. Ctr., 1975-83, regional adminstr. N.E. region, 1983-84; asst. adminstr. Agr. Rsch. Svc., USDA, Washington, 1984-94; tech. transfer advisor Agr. Rsch. Svc., USDA, Beltsville, Md., 1994—. Recipient Merit award Gamma Sigma Delta, 1979, Presdl. Rank award for Sr. Execs., 1988, NASA Tech. 2002 award for lifetime achievement in tech. transfer, 1992. Mem. AAAS, Am. Chem. Soc., Soc. Econ. Botany. Home: Apt 4L 6100 Westchester Park Dr College Park MD 20740-2844 Office: USDA Agr Rsch Svc Bldg 005 BARC-W Beltsville MD 20705-2350

TALLETT, ELIZABETH EDITH, biopharmaceutical company executive; b. London, Apr. 2, 1949; d. Edward and Edith May (Vickers) Symons; m. James Edward Wavle Jr.; children: James Edward Tallett, Alexander Martin Tallett, Christopher Andrew Wavle. BS with honors, U. Nottingham (Eng.), 1970. Ops. rsch. analyst So. Gas Bd., 1970-73; mgmt. svcs. mgr. Warner-Lamber (UK), Eastleigh, Eng., 1973-77, strategic planning mgr., 1977-81; internat. dir. strategic planning Warner-Lambert, Morris Plains, N.J., 1981-82, corp. dir. strategic planning, 1982-84; dir. mktg. ops. Parke-Davis, Morris Plains, 1984-87; exec. v.p. therapeutic products Centocor, Malvern, Pa., 1987-89, pres. pharms. div., 1989-92; pres., CEO Transcell Techs., Inc., Monmouth Junction, N.J., 1992-96, Dioscor, Inc., Stockton, N.J.; bd. dirs. Prin. Mut. Life Ins. Co., Varian Assoc., Inc.; dir. Biotech. Coun. N.J., Prosperity N.J., Inc. Contbr. articles to profl. jours. Apptd. by Gov. Christine Todd Whitman to Prosperity N.J. Commn., 1995—. Mem. Ch. of Eng. Avocations: acting, badminton, travel, skiing.

TALLEY, CAROL LEE, newspaper editor; b. Bklyn., Sept. 10, 1937; d. George Joseph and Viola (Kovash) T.; children—Sherry, Jill, Scott. Student, U. Ky., 1955-57, Ohio U., 1957-58. Reporter Easton (Pa.) Daily Express, 1958-60; reporter N.J. Herald, 1962-64, edn. editor, 1964-66; reporter Daily Advance, Dover, N.J., 1966-68, polit. editor, investigative reporter, from 1969, mng. editor, 1974-81; editor Evening Sentinel, Carlisle, Pa., 1982—; Mem. A.P. Task Force N.J., 1970, Pa. Associated Press Mng. Editor's Bd. Dirs. Past bd. dirs. Helen Stevens Cmty. Mental Health Ctr. (chair), Carlisle; past pres. bd. dirs. Stevens Mental Health Ctr., Carlisle. Recipient pub. service awards Nat. Headliners, 1971, Sigma Delta Chi, 1971, George Polk Meml. award for local reporting, 1974, Dew Meml. award Pa. Newspaper Pub.'s Assn., 1985. Mem. Pa. Newspaper Editors Soc., Kiwanis Club. Office: 457 E North St Carlisle PA 17013-2620

TALLEY, CHARLES RICHMOND, commercial banking executive; b. Richmond, Va., Dec. 23, 1925; s. Charles Edward and Marie (Throckmorton) T.; m. Anne Marie Smith, June 4, 1948; children: Laurie Anne, Charles Richmond. B.A. in Econs, U. Richmond, 1949; postgrad., Sch. Banking Rutgers U., 1959-61, Sch. Fin. Pub. Relations, Northwestern U., 1954-55; grad. exec. program, U. Va., 1974. Asst. cashier 1st & Mchts. Nat. Bank, Richmond, 1955-57; asst. v.p. 1st & Mchts. Nat. Bank, 1957-63, v.p., 1963-69, sr. v.p., 1969-73, exec. v.p., 1973-84; corp. exec. officer Sovran Bank N.A., 1984-86, ret., 1986; bd. dirs. Security Atlantic Life Ins. Co., Richmond; v.p., bd. dirs. Security Atlantic Ins. Agy., Richmond; bd. dirs. Sovran Properties, Inc.; vice chmn. bd. dirs. Va. Edn. Loan Authority, 1983-87, chmn., 1988-91. Pres. Richmond Jr. C. of C., 1960-61; pres. Bapt. Extension Bd. Va., 1973-75, bd. dirs., 1985-95; treas. Richmond chpt. Nat.

Found., 1956—; v.p., mem. exec. com. Richmond Eye and Ear Hosp., pres. 1988-91; bd. dirs. Commonwealth Eye and Ear Inst., 1986-89; bd. dirs. Richmond Symphony Orch., Richmond Better Bus. Bur. With USNR, 1944-46. Mem. Richmond Met. C. of C. (bd. dirs. 1979-89), Richmond Clearing House Assn. (pres. 1977), Willow Oaks Country Club (pres. 1971), Bull and Bear Club, Farmington Country Club, Rotary (bd. dirs. Richmond 1981-83). Home: 4301 Stratford Rd Richmond VA 23225-1060

TALLEY, DARRYL VICTOR, professional football player; b. Cleveland, July 10, 1960. Degree in Physical Edn., U. W.Va., 1983. Linebacker Buffalo Bills, 1983—. Named linebacker The Sporting News Coll. All-Am. Team, 1982, outside linebacker The Sporting News NFL All-Pro Team, 1990, 93. Played in Pro Bowl, 1990, 91. Office: Buffalo Bills 1 Bills Dr Orchard Park NY 14127-2237

TALLEY, GEORGE TYLER, lawyer; b. Valdosta, Ga., Mar. 6, 1944; s. William Giles and Mary (McGlamry) T.; m. Polly Jane Tyson, June 2, 1963; children: George Tyler Jr., Gregory Tyson, Debra Lynn, Charles Scott. BS, U. S.C., 1965, JD, 1968. Bar: S.C. 1968, Ga. 1968, U.S. Dist. Ct. (mid. dist.) Ga. 1969, U.S. Ct. Appeals (11th cir.) 1994. Solicitor State Ct. Ga., Lowndes County, 1972-76; atty. City of Valdosta, 1976—. Mem. State Bar Ga. (chmn. workers compensation sect. 1993-94), Ga. Mcpl. Assn. Republican. Methodist. Avocations: golf, hunting, fishing. Office: Tillman McTier ColemanTalley et al 910 N Patterson St Valdosta GA 31601

TALLEY, LINDA JEAN, food scientist, dietitian; b. Hearne, Tex., July 15, 1948; d. Roy Wesley and Dorothy Louise (Allen) Dugger; m. Thomas James Talley, May 15, 1970; children: John Paul, Jo Ann. BS in Food Tech., Tex. A & M U., 1969, MS in Food Sci. and Tech., 1979, PhD in Food Sci. and Tech., 1981. Registered dietitian Am. Dietetic Assn.; registered sanitarian; lic. dietitian, Tex. Technician I soil and crop scis. dept. Tex. A & M U., College Station, 1969-72; technician I in horticulture scis. Tex. A&M U., College Station, 1977-78, grad. asst., 1978-81; quality assurance mgr. food products divsn. Southland Corp., Ft. Worth, 1972-73; pub. health inspector Ft. Worth Pub. Health Dept., 1973-74; dir. quality assurance plant sanitation and product devel. Kimbell Foods, Inc., Mfg. Divsn., Ft. Worth, 1974-75; profl. cons. Ft. Worth, 1975-76; v.p., cons. TALCO, Dallas, 1981-91; sr. food scientist Enersyst Devel. Ctr., Inc., Dallas, 1990—; presenter in field. Contbr. articles to profl. jours. Mem. Inst. Food Techs., Sigma Xi, Phi Tau Sigma. Avocations: gardening, reading, needlework. Home: 3706 Oak Ridge Dr Bryan TX 77802-3426 Office: Enersyst Devel Ctr 2051 Valley View Ln Dallas TX 75234-8920

TALLEY, ROBERT BOYD, physician; b. Scottsbluff, Nebr., Jan. 21, 1931; s. Richard Bedelle and Eloise Earline (Taylor) T.; m. Louise Carroll Settle, Dec. 28, 1954; children—Robert Boyd, Edwin T. Student, Northwestern U., 1949-52; M.D., U. Colo., 1956. Diplomate Am. Bd. Internal Medicine. Intern Wayne County Gen. Hosp., Eloise, Mich., 1956-57; resident State U. Iowa, Iowa City, 1959-62, instr. dept. internal medicine, 1962-63, postdoctoral fellow dept. internal medicine, 1962-63; practice medicine specializing in internal medicine and gastroenterology Stockton, Calif.; clin. instr. medicine U. Calif.-San Francisco, 1965-70; chief staff St. Joseph's Hosp., chief of medicine, 1975-77, trustee, 1984—; cons. Calif. HCSA Data Com.; mem. adv. com. on nat. health ins. Ways and Means Com., U.S. Congress, 1978-80 dir. Delta IPA, 1980—; v.p. statewide Calif. PPO, United Preferred Provider Orgn., 1982; mem. exec. com., sec. United Founds. for Med. Care, 1978-79, treas., 1980-82, v.p. 1982-84, pres., 1984—; pres. San Joaquin Found. for Med. Care, 1973-79. Served with USN, 1957-59. Packard undergrad. scholar in surgery, 1956. Fellow ACP (community service com. 1971-81, trustee Commn. on Profl. and Hosp. Activities 1973-82, pres., chmn. bd. 1979-81); mem. HMO's Group Health Assn. of Am. (tech. adv. com. 1982-84), Inst. Medicine of Nat. Acad. Scis., AMCRA (bd. dirs. 1984—), Calif. Acad. Medicine, San Joaquin Med. Soc., Calif. Med. Assn., Sigma Nu. Office: 1617 N California St Ste 2E Stockton CA 95204-6117

TALLEY, ROBERT MORRELL, aerospace company executive; b. Erwin, Tenn., Mar. 13, 1924; s. Robert Taylor and Anna Laura (Morrell) T.; m. Mary Sue Williams, June 5, 1948; children: David, Carol. Student, East Tenn. State Coll., 1942-43, U. Va., 1943-44; B.S. U. S.C., 1945; M.S., U. Tenn., 1948, Ph.D., 1950. Chief infrared br., chief solid state div. U.S. Naval Ordnance Lab., White Oak, Md., 1951-58; mgr. lab. Santa Barbara Rsch. Ctr. subs. Hughes Aircraft, Calif., 1958-69, v.p., 1969-76, pres., 1976-89, ret.; chair engring. com. U. Calif.-Santa Barbara Found. Contbr. articles to profl. jours.; patentee in field. Trustee U. Calif.-Santa Barbara Found.; bd. dirs. Industry Edn. Coun., Santa Barbara; commr. econ. devel. Santa Barbara County. With USN, 1943-46. Fellow Am. Phys. Soc.; mem. Optical Soc. Am., LaCumbre Club, Sigma Xi.

TALLEY, TRUMAN MACDONALD, publisher; b. N.Y.C., Feb. 3, 1925; s. Truman Hughes and Helen Nicholson (Macdonald) T.; m. Madelon DeVoe, Oct. 17, 1953; children: Melanie, Macdonald, Marina. Student, Buckley Sch., Deerfield Acad., Sorbonne, 1945-46; grad. cum laude, Princeton U., 1949. Assoc. editor New Am. Library of World Lit., N.Y.C., 1949-59; editorial v.p. New Am. Library of World Lit., 1959-64; pres., editorial dir. Weybright & Talley, N.Y.C., 1966-78; pub. Truman Talley Books with Times Books, 1978-82; with E.P. Dutton, 1983—; mem. grad. bd. Princeton Tiger, 1950—. Trustee Clinton Hall Assn. Mercantile Library, N.Y.C. Served with AUS, 1943-46, ETO. Decorated Purple Heart. Mem. P.E.N. Clubs: Anglers, Brook, Maidstone, Southampton Beach. Office: Dutton/Signet Penguin USA 375 Hudson St New York NY 10014-3658

TALLEY, WILLIAM GILES, JR., container manufacturing company executive; b. Adel, Ga., Sept. 25, 1939; s. William Giles and Mary (McGlamry) T.; BSBA, U. S.C., 1961; m. Jacqueline Vickery, Apr. 14, 1962; children: William Giles, John Lindsey, Bronwyn Ashley. Mgmt. trainee Talley Veneer & Crate Co., Inc., Adel, 1961-62, plant mgr., salesman, Waynesboro, Ga., 1965-67; with Talley's Box Co., Leesburg, Fla., 1962-69, plant mgr., partner, 1967-69; gen. mgr. Growers Container Coop., Inc., Leesburg, 1969—; pres. Talley Acres, Inc., 1979—, pres. Talley Classic Woods, Inc., 1992—; bd. dirs. Sun Trust Bank, Ctrl. Fla., N.A., Orlando, Fla. Past chmn. and bd. dirs. Leesburg Hosp. Assn. Served with USAAF, 1961. Mem. Leesburg C. of C. (dir.), Fla. Forestry Assn. (dir. 1977—), Elks, Kiwanis, Sigma Alpha Epsilon. Democrat. Methodist. Home: 2206 Talley Court Rd Leesburg FL 34748-3177 Office: PO Box 490817 Leesburg FL 34749-0817

TALLICHET, LEON EDGAR, retired publishing executive, financial administrator; b. Tupelo, Miss., Jan. 10, 1925; s. Leon Edgar and Irene Elizabeth (Reid) T.; m. Betty Jean Baumann, May 31, 1947; children: Judie Elizabeth, Kathryn Louise. B.M.E., U. Louisville, 1946; M.B.A., Harvard U., 1949. Office mgr. Brown-Forman Distillers Corp., Louisville, 1949-58; from asst. sec. and asst. treas. to sr. v.p. and treas. Courier-Jour. and Louisville Times Co., Standard Gravure Corp., WHAS Inc., Louisville, 1958-86; dir. Courier-Jour. and Louisville Times Co., Standard Gravure Corp., WHAS Inc., 1975-86; fin. adminstr. Barry Bingham, Sr., Louisville, 1987-88, Mary C. Bingham, 1987-95; pres. chpt. Fin. Exec. Inst., 1969-70. Bd. dirs. Met. United Way Louisville, 1972-74; chmn. investment com. Ky. Ctr. for Arts Endowment Fund, 1991—; mem. fin. com. Louisville Community Found., 1988—; commr., treas. City of Ten Broeck, Ky., 1988—. With USNR, 1943-46, lt. USNR, 1950-52.

TALLMAN, CLIFFORD WAYNE, school system administrator, consultant; b. Columbus, Ohio, June 13, 1932; s. Frank Albert and Ella Louise (Ott) T.; m. Ruth Anne Fletcher, Apr. 6, 1958; children: Martin, David, Kathryn Haines. BS in Edn., Capital U., 1954; MA, Ohio State U., 1960; EdS, Bowling Green U., 1965. Cert. supt., Ohio, Ill., Mich., Ky., Pa., N.Y. Tchr. Southwestern City Schs., Grove City, Ohio, 1954-60; supt. Republic (Ohio) Local Schs., 1960-63, Columbus Grove Schs., Grove City, 1963-65, Jackson Local Schs., Massillon, Ohio, 1965-73, Brecksville (Ohio) City Schs., 1973-78, Kent County Schs., Independence, Ky., 1978-80, Otsego Local Schs., Tontogany, Ohio, 1980-86; prof. Bowling Green (Ohio) U., 1980-86; supt. Coloma (Mich.) Community Schs., 1986-93; pres. Tallman Ednl. Cons., 1993—; prof. Southwestern C.C., 1996—; ednl. cons. AMA, Chgo., 1963; commr. Right to Read, Washington, 1973; cons. Am. Arbitratioin Assn., Tech. Adv. Svcs. for Attys.; speaker at local, state and nat. edn. profl. orgns. Contbr. articles to profl. jours. Active Berrien County Hist. Assn., Coloma, Selective Svc. Bd., Washington; newsletter editor Rotary Club, Coloma, 1986-90. With USNR, 1951-54, USA, 1954-56. I/D/E/A scholar, 1969; Found. for Econ. Edn. scholar, 1971; named to Honorable Order Ky. Cols. Mem. Ohio Edn. Assn., Mich. Assn. Sch. Bds., Berrien Assn. Sch. Adminstrs., Am. Assn. Sch. Adminstrs., Mich. Assn. Sch. Adminstrs., Buckeye Assn. Sch. Adminstrs., Coloma C. of C., Bowling Green U. Alumni Assn., Lions Club, Phi Delta Kappa. Lutheran. Avocations: gardening, computers, organ music, chess, traveling. Home: 5540 Red Arrow Hwy Coloma MI 49038-9730 Office: PO Box 550 Coloma MI 49038-0550

TALLMAN, RICHARD C., lawyer; b. Oakland, Calif., Mar. 3, 1953; s. Kenneth A. and Jean M. (Kemppe) T.; m. Cynthia Ostolaza, Nov. 14, 1981. BSC, U. Santa Clara, 1975; JD, Northwestern U., 1978. Bar: Calif. 1978, Wash. 1979, U.S. Dist. Ct. (no. dist.) Calif. 1979, U.S. Dist. Ct. (we. dist.) Wash. 1979, U.S. Ct. Appeals (9th cir.) 1979, U.S. Dist. Ct. Hawaii 1986. Law clk to Hon. Morrell E. Sharp U.S. Dist. Ct. (we. dist.) Wash., Seattle, 1978-79; trial atty. U.S. Dept. Justice, Washington, 1979-80; asst. U.S. atty. U.S. Dist. Ct. (we. dist.) Wash., Seattle, 1980-83; ptnr. Schweppe, Krug & Tausend, PS, Seattle, 1983-89, Bogle & Gates, Seattle, 1990—; chmn. western region Wash. Lawyer Reps. to Ninth Cir. Jud. Conf., 1996-97. Instr. Nat. Park Svc. Seasonal Ranger Acad., Everett and Mt. Vernon, Wash., 1983-93; chmn. Edmonds C.C. Found., Lynnwood, Wash., 1990-92; gen. counsel Seattle-King County Crime Stoppers, 1991—. Mem. ABA, FBA (trustee 1992-93, v.p. 1994, pres. 1995), Seattle-King County Bar Assn., Rainier Club, Wash. Athletic Club. Avocations: hunting, hiking, fishing. Office: Bogle & Gates Two Union Sq 601 Union St Seattle WA 98101-2346

TALLMAN, ROBERT HALL, investment company executive; b. Creston, Iowa, Aug. 10, 1915; s. Ralph H. and Hazel Verne (Hall) T.; m. Elizabeth Childs, Sept. 19, 1938; children: Susan, Mary, Timothy. BS, U. Nebr., 1937. Trainee to dist. mgr. Firestone Tire & Rubber Co., Akron, Ohio, 1937-50; pres. Tallman Oil Co., Fargo, N.D., 1950-80; chmn. bd. State Bank of Hawley, Minn., 1966-70, 1st Nat. Bank of Barnesville, Minn., 1965-88; pres. Tallman Investment Ent., Fargo, 1980—; pres., dir. Dak Tech. Inc.; dir. Bell Farms. Past pres. Fargo Bd. Edn., N.D. Petroleum Coun.; past pres. St. Lukes Hosp. Assn.; past chmn. trustees 1st Congl. Ch. of Fargo. Mem. Fargo C. of C. (past pres.), Am. Assn. Ret. Persons, Nat. Rifle Assn., N.D. State U. Teammakers Club (past pres.), Fargo Country Club, Kiwanis (past pres.), Masons, Shriners, Elks. Republican. Congregationalist. Avocations: golf, hunting, fishing, travel, photography. Home: 3201 16th Ave S Fargo ND 58103-8421 Office: Box 9723 2108 S University Dr Fargo ND 58103-5348

TALLMER, MARGOT SALLOP, psychologist, psychoanalyst, gerontologist; b. N.Y.C., Sept. 8, 1925; d. Harry and Mildred (Schifrin) Sallop; m. Jonathan Tallmer, Apr. 12, 1949 (dec.); children—Mary, Megan, Jill, Andrew. M.S., N.Y. U., 1948; M.A., Yeshiva U., 1962, Ph.D., 1967. Mem. faculty dept. ednl. founds. Hunter Coll., N.Y.C., 1969—; assoc. prof. Hunter Coll., 1976-79, prof., 1979—; staff psychologist Mt. Sinai Hosp., 1967-68; postgrad. Center for Mental Health, 1968-69; pvt. practice psychoanalysis N.Y.C., 1967—; faculty, trustee, bd. dirs. Nat. Psychol. Assn. for Psychoanalysis; faculty N.Y. Ctr. for Psychoanalytic Tng. Editor: Sex and Life Threatening Illness, HIV Testing Positive, The Child and Death, also books on aging and loss; editorial bd. Current Issues in Psychoanalysis, Psychoanalytic Rev.; contbr. chpts. to textbooks, articles to profl jours. Mem. APA, Boston Soc. Gerontologic Psychiatry, N.Y. State Psychol. Assn. (pres. divsn. adult devel. and aging). Address: 26 E 81st St New York NY 10028-0246

TALLY, LURA SELF, state legislator; b. Statesville, N.C., Dec. 9, 1921; d. Robert Ottis and Sara (Cowles) Self; A.B., Duke U., 1942; M.A., N.C. State U., Raleigh, 1970; m. J.O. Tally, Jr., Jan. 30, 1943 (div. 1970); children: Robert Taylor, John Cowles. Tchr., former guidance counselor Fayetteville (N.C.) city schs.; mem. N.C. Ho. of Reps. from 20th Dist., 1971-83, chmn. com. higher edn., from 1975, also 1980-83, vice chmn. com. appropriations for edn., 1973-86; state senator from 12th Dist. N.C., 1983-95; chmn. N.C. Senate Com. of Natural Resources, Community Devel. and Wildlife, 1987, Environment and Natural Resources, 1989-94. Past pres. Cumberland County Mental Health Assn., N.C. Historic Preservation Soc.; trustee Fayetteville Tech. Inst., 1981-94; mem. Legis. Research com. Mem. Am. Personnel and Guidance Assn., Fayetteville Bus. and Profl. Women's Club, Kappa Delta, Delta Kappa Gamma. Methodist. Club: Fayetteville Woman's (past pres.). Office: W Jones St Raleigh NC 27601

TALLY, TED, screenwriter; b. Winston-Salem, N.C., Apr. 9, 1952; s. David K. and Dorothy E. (Spears) T.; m. Melinda Kahn, Dec. 11, 1977. BA, Yale U., 1974, MFA, 1977. Scripts include (plays) Terra Nova, 1977 (Kazan award Yale U. 1977, Theron Rockwell Field prize Yale U. 1977, Obie award 1984), Hooters, 1978, Coming Attractions, 1980 (John Gassner Playwriting award N.Y. Outer Critics Cir. 1981), Silver Linings, 1983, Little Footsteps, 1986, (with others) Urban Blight, 1988, The Gettysburg Sound Bite, 1989, (screenplays) White Palace, 1990, The Silence of the Lambs, 1991 (Acad. award best adapted screenplay 1991, Writers Guild award), Before and After, 1995, The Juror, 1995, (TV) Hooters, 1983, Terra Nova, 1984, The Father Clements Story, 1987 (Christopher award 1988). Columbia Broadcasting Sys. Found. Playwriting fellow Yale U., 1977, Guggenheim fellow, 1985-86; N.Y. State Creative Artists Pub. Svc. grantee, 1980, NEA Playwriting grantee, 1983-84. Office: ICM 8899 Beverly Blvd Los Angeles CA 90048-2412

TALMA, LOUISE J., composer, educator; b. Arcachon, France, Oct. 31, 1906. Student, Inst. Mus. Art, N.Y.C., 1922-30; pupil, Isidore Philipp and Nadia Boulanger, Fontainebleau Sch. Music, 1926-39; B.Mus., NYU, 1931; M.A. in Music, Columbia U., 1933; L.H.D. (hon.), Hunter Coll, CUNY, 1983; D.Arts (hon.), Bard Coll., 1984. Tchr. Manhattan Sch. Music, 1926-28, Fontainebleau Sch. Music, summers 1936-39, 78, 81-83, 87; mem. faculty Hunter Coll., 1928-79, prof. music, 1952-76, prof. emeritus, 1976—; Clark fellow Scripps Coll., 1975; Sanford fellow Yale, 1976; mem. Pres.'s Circle, Hunter Coll., 1977; Bd. dirs. League-ISCM. Compositions include: (with Thornton Wilder as librettist) opera The Alcestiad, premiered Frankfurt, West Germany (Marjorie Peabody Waite award Nat. Inst. Arts and Letters 1960); 2 piano sonatas, 6 études for piano, 1 string quartet, 1 sonata for violin and piano, Toccata for orch., Dialogues for piano and orch., Clarinet Quintet; chamber opera Have you heard? Do you know?, Diadem; Flute Quartet; Full Circle for Chamber Orch. Recipient Koussevitzky Music Found. commn., 1959, Nat. Fedn. Music Clubs award, 1963, Nat. Assn. Am. Composers and Condrs. award, 1963, Sibelius medal, 1963, numerous others; Guggenheim fellow, 1946, 47; sr. Fulbright research grantee, 1955-56; Nat. Endowment of the Arts grantee, 1966, 75. Fellow Am. Guild Organists; mem. League of Composers (dir. 1950—), Fontainebleau Fine Arts and Music Assn. (trustee 1950, v.p. 1982-86), Edward MacDowell Assn. (corporate mem.), ASCAP, Am. Inst. Arts and Letters, Phi Beta Kappa, Sigma Alpha Iota (hon.). *I believe order is better than disorder, and clarity better than obscurity. I endeavor to put this into practice in my work. Three people have especially influenced my life: my mother who was my first teacher; Nadia Boulanger, who was the first to see in me a talent for composition, and Thorton Wilder who gave me, the only composer ever, the opportunity to work with him on a full length opera.*

TALMADGE, JOHN BARNES, science foundation administrator; b. Needham, Mass., Mar. 30, 1936; s. Nelson Alcorn and Mildred Francis (Barnes) T.; m. Elinor Beth Dunsmore, Nov. 27, 1965 (div. Nov. 1976); children: Leslie Jean, Alison Elinor; m. Patricia Russell, Apr. 24, 1993. BA, Williams Coll., 1958. Pub. info. officer NASA Ames Rsch. Ctr., Moffett Field, Calif., 1962-64; adminstrv. asst. to pres. Reed Coll., Portland, Oreg., 1964-66; adminstrv. asst. to Congressman John Dellenback, U.S. Ho. of Reps., Washington, 1967; fed. rels. assoc. Assn. Am. Colls., Washington, 1968-70; various positions NSF, Washington, 1970, now head Polar coordination, 1986—. Staff asst. Lodge for Senate, Mass., 1962, McCall for Sec. State, Oreg., 1964; campaign mgr. Dellenback for Congress, Eugene, Oreg., 1966. Capt. USMCR, 1958-61. Episcopalian. Avocations: hiking, canoeing, ecotourism. Home: 4433 Westover Pl NW Washington DC 20016-5556 Office: Geosciences 4201 Wilson Blvd Arlington VA 22203-1803

TALMAGE, DAVID WILSON, microbiology and medical educator, physician, former university administrator; b. Kwangju, Korea, Sept. 15, 1919; s. John Van Neste and Eliza (Emerson) T.; m. LaVeryn Marie Hunicke, June 23, 1944; children: Janet, Marilyn, David, Mark, Carol. Student, Maryville (Tenn.) Coll., 1937-38; BS, Davidson (N.C.) Coll., 1941; MD, Washington U., St. Louis, 1944. Intern Ga. Baptist Hosp., 1944-45; resident medicine Barnes Hosp., St. Louis, 1948-50; fellow medicine Barnes Hosp., 1950-51; asst. prof. pathology U. Pitts., 1951-52; asst. prof., then assoc. prof. medicine U. Chgo., 1952-59; prof. medicine U. Colo., 1959—, prof. microbiology, 1960-86, disting. prof., 1986—, chmn. dept., 1963-65, assoc. dean, 1966-68, dean, 1969-71; dir. Webb-Waring Lung Inst., 1973-83, assoc. dean for research, 1983-86; mem. nat. council Nat. Inst. Allergy and Infectious Diseases, NIH, 1963-66, 73-77. Author: (with John Cann) Chemistry of Immunity in Health and Disease; editor: Jour. Allergy, 1963-67, (with M. Samter) Immunological Diseases. Served with M.C. AUS, 1945-48. Markle scholar, 1955-60. Mem. NAS, Inst. Medicine, Am. Acad. Allergy (pres.), Am. Assn. Immunologists (pres.), Phi Beta Kappa, Alpha Omega Alpha. Office: U Colo Sch Med Box C321 Denver CO 80262

TALMAGE, LISA BIRNSTEIN, music educator; b. Riverhead, N.Y., Feb. 8, 1966; d. Alfred Rudolf and Edith Laviny (Bunke) Birnstein; m. Douglas Nathaniel Talmage, July 22, 1989; 1 child, David Nathaniel. MusB in Flute Performance, New England Conservatory, 1988; MS in Edn., C.W. Post Coll./L.I. U., 1991. Cert. tchr. music K-12. Flute instr. Foxborough (Mass.) H.S., 1987-88; chamber music instr. N.E. Conservatory Prep. Div., Boston, 1987-88; flute instr. The Music Box, Riverhead, 1988-89, Ea. Suffolk Sch. Music, Riverhead, 1988-89; choral instr. Riverhead Mid. Sch., 1991—; choir dir. Our Redeemer Luth. Ch., Aquebogue, N.Y., 1990-91, First Congl. Ch., Riverhead, 1992-93. Sunday sch. tchr. Baiting Hollow (N.Y.) Congregational Ch., 1991—. Named winner club competition N.Y. Flute Club, 1987, C.W. Post Concerto Competition, 1990. Mem. Am. Choral Dirs. Assn., Music Educators Nat. Conf., N.Y. State Sch. Music Assn., Suffolk County Music Educators Assn. (exec. bd. dirs. 1992-94, choral festival chair 1992-94), Mu Phi Epsilon (N.Y.C. alumni chpt.). Lutheran. Avocations: playing in pit orchestras, boating, science fiction, family. Home: 2850 Sound Ave Riverhead NY 11901-1113 Office: Riverhead Mid Sch 600 Harrison Ave Riverhead NY 11901-2741

TALMI, YOAV, conductor, composer; b. Kibbutz Merhavia, Israel, Apr. 28, 1943; diploma Rubin Acad. Music, Tel Aviv; postgrad. diploma Juilliard Sch. Music; m. Erella Gottesmann; 2 children. Assoc. condr. Louisville Orch., 1968-70; co-condr. Israel Chamber Orch., 1970-72; artistic dir., condr. Gelders Symphony Orch., Arnhem, 1974-80; prin. guest condr. Munich Philharm. Orch., 1979-80; artistic dir., condr. Israel Chamber Orch., 1984-88; music dir. New Israeli Opera, 1985-89, San Diego Symphony Orch., 1990—, Waterloo Festival, N.J., 1994-95; guest condr. Berlin Philharm., Munich Philharm., London Philharm., Philharmonia, Royal Philharm., Concertgebouw, Rotterdam Philharm., Israel Philharm., Tokyo Symphony, New Japan Philharm., Vienna Symphony, St. Petersburg Philharm., Pitts. Symphony, Detroit Symphony, St. Louis Symphony, Houston Symphony, Dallas Symphony, N.Y. Chamber Symphony, L.A. Chamber Orch., Oslo Philharm., Tonhalle Orch. Zurich, others. Composer: Dreams for choir a capella, Music for Flute and Strings; Overture on Mexican Themes (recorded), 3 Monologues for Flute Solo (pub.), Inauguration Fanfare; recs. include: Bruckner 9th Symphony (Oslo Philharm.), Gliére 3rd Symphony, Brahms Sextet/4 Serious Songs, Rachmaninov's Isle of the Dead, Berlioz Overtures, Berlioz Romeo et Juliette (San Diego Symphony), Tchaikowsky/Scoenberg, Bloch/Barber/Grieg/Puccini (Israel Chamber Orch.); (with Erella Talmi) works for flute and piano. Recipient Boskovitch prize for composition, Israel, 1965; Koussevitzky Meml. Conducting prize, Tanglewood, 1969; award Ruppert Found. Condr. competition, London, 1973. Home: PO Box 1384, Kfar Saba 44113, Israel Office: ICM Artists 40 W 57th St New York NY 10019 also: San Diego Symphony Orch 1245 7th Ave San Diego CA 92101-4302

TALTON, CHESTER LOVELLE, bishop; b. El Dorado, Ark., Sept. 22, 1941; s. Chester Talton and Mae Ola (Shells) Henry; m. Karen Louise Warren, Aug. 25, 1963; children: Kathy Louise, Linda Karen, Frederick Douglass, Benjamin Albert. BS, Calif. State U., Hayward, 1967; MDiv, Ch. Divinity Sch. of Pacific, 1970. Ordained to ministry Episcopal Ch., as deacon, 1970, as priest, 1971, as bishop, 1991. Vicar Good Shepherd Episc. Ch., Berkeley, Calif., 1970-71, St. Mathias Mission, Seaside, Calif., 1971-73, Ch. of the Holy Cross, Chgo., 1973-76; curate All Sts. Episc. Ch., Carmel, Calif., 1971-73; rector St. Philips Episc. Ch., St. Paul, 1976-81, St. Philips Ch., N.Y.C., 1985-90; mission officer Parish of Trinity Ch., N.Y.C., 1981-85; suffragan bishop Diocese of L.A., Episc. Ch., 1990—. Pres. Community Svc. Coun. Greater Harlem, N.Y.C., 1985-90, Upper Manhattan Child Devel. Ctr., N.Y.C., 1985-90, Peter Williams Jr. Housing Corp., N.Y.C., 1988-90. Mem. Union of Black Episcopalians. Office: Episc Diocese LA PO Box 2164 1220 W 4th St Los Angeles CA 90017-1412*

TALUCCI, SAMUEL JAMES, retired chemical company executive; b. Newark, Del., Feb. 13, 1929; s. Anthony and Josephine (Valocchi) T.; m. Charlotte Sisofo, Sept. 22, 1951 (dec. Oct. 1985); children: Samuel J., Charlene, Anthony, Catherine, Christina, Louisa; m. Louise Coulter, Oct. 1987. BS, U. Del., 1951. Resident mgr. Italian Subs. Rohm & Haas Co., Milan, 1956-58; gen. mgr. Italian Subs. Rohm & Haas Co., 1958-66; mng. dir. Brit. Subs. Rohm & Haas Co., London, 1966-68; dir. European ops. Rohm & Haas Co., Phila., 1968; asst. gen. mgr. Internat. div. Rohm & Haas Co., 1971, v.p. gen. mgr. Plastics div., 1974, v.p. corporate bus., group dir. agrl. and indsl. chems. Plastics div., 1975-83, regional dir. N.Am. region, 1983-89, ret., 1989. Bd. dirs. Rosemont Coll. Mem. Nat. Agrl. Chems. Assn. (bd. dirs.), Pa. Chamber Bus. & Industry (bd dirs.), Middle States Assn. Colls. and Secondary Schs. (mem. commn. on secondary schs.). Address: 140 Golf House Rd Haverford PA 19041-1060

TALVI, ILKKA ILARI, violinist; b. Kuusankoski, Finland, Oct. 22, 1948; came to U.S., 1977; s. Veikko Tuomo and Irja Margareta (Saajos) T.; m. Judith Frances Aller, Sept. 4, 1969 (div. Aug. 1982); children: Silja Joanna, Sonja Louisa; m. Marjorie Jill Kransberg, Aug. 29, 1984; children: Anna Mirjam, Sarah Lilian. Diploma in violin, Sibelius Acad., Helsinki, Finland, 1966; student Heifetz master class, U. So. Calif., 1967-68; student, Curtis Inst., Phila., 1968-69; pvt. studies, Bouillon, Odnoposoff, Paris, Vienna, 1965-67. Lectr. Sibelius Acad., Helsinki, 1969-75, Porin Musiikkiopisto, Pori, Finland, 1970-76; concertmaster Malmö (Sweden) Symphony, 1976-77; prin. Los Angeles Chamber Orch., Pasadena, Calif., 1979-85; concertmaster Seattle Symphony, 1985—, Seattle Opera, 1985—, Waterloo Festival, N.J., 1988—; guest concertmaster Seattle Symphony, 1983-85; freelance violinist, film, TV, and recording industries, Los Angeles, 1977-85. Performed as soloist and in recital in Europe, U.S., 1965—; appeared in Finland, U.S., 1972—; played Klami Violin Concerto, Albert "In Concordian," Diamond 2, violin concerto and numerous other recordings. Recipient Kuusankoski (Finland) award, 1967, numerous grants, Finland, 1965-75. Lutheran. Avocations: dogs, computers, science. Home: 3456 10th Ave W Seattle WA 98119-1413 Office: Seattle Symphony Seattle Center House 305 Harrison St Fl 4 Seattle WA 98109-4623

TALWANI, MANIK, geophysicist, educator; b. Patiala, India, Aug. 22, 1933; came to U.S., 1954; s. Bir Sain and Saraswati (Khosla) T.; m. Anni Fittler, Apr. 3, 1958; children: Rajeev Manik, Indira, Sanjay. BSc with honors, Delhi U., India, 1951, MSc, 1953; PhD, Columbia U., 1959; PhD (hon.), Oslo U., 1981. From rsch. scientist to assoc. prof. Lamont-Doherty Geol. Obs., Columbia U., N.Y.C., 1959-70, dir. obs., 1972-81; prof. Columbia U., N.Y.C., 1970-82; dir. Ctr. for Crustal Studies Gulf R & D Co., Pitts., 1981-83; chief scientist exploration div. Gulf R & D Co., Houston, 1983-85; Schlumberger prof. geophysics Rice U., Houston, 1985—; cons. Govt. of Iceland, 1982—; dir. Geotech. Rsch. Inst., Houston Advanced Rsch. Ctr., Woodlands, 1985—; co-chmn. exec. com. Energy Rsch. Clearing House; Sackler disting. lectr. U. Tel Aviv, 1987; mem. adv. coun. Indian Oil and Gas Corp. Co-author: Geophysical Atlas of the Norwegian Sea; editor 7 books on earth sci., Maurice Ewing Meml. Symposium; co-editor: Geophysical Atlases of Indian, Atlantic and Pacific Oceans; contbr. over 100 papers to profl. jours. Recipient Krishnan award Indian Geophys. Union, 1964, Exceptional Sci. Achievement award NASA, 1973, Guggenheim award, 1974, Alfred Wegener medal European Union Geoscis., 1993; Fulbright-Hays fellow, 1974. Fellow AAAS, Am. Geophys. Union (James B. Macelwane award 1964, Maurice Ewing award 1981), Geol. Soc. Am. (George P. Woollard award 1984); mem. Soc. Exptl. Geophysicists, Am. Assn.

Petroleum Geologists, Norwegian Acad. Scis., Petroleum Club, Acad. Nat. Scis. Russian Fedn., Houston Geophys. Soc. (hon. mem. 1993), Houston Philos. Soc, Sigma Xi. Home: 1111 Hermann Dr Apt 10 D Houston TX 77004-6929 Office: Rice U PO Box 1892 Houston TX 77251-1892

TAM, WILLIAM, retired secondary school principal. Prin. Kalaheo High Sch., Kailua, Hawaii. Recipient Blue Ribbon award U.S. Dept. Edn., 1990-91. Office: Kalaheo High Sch 730 Iliaina St Kailua HI 96734-1815

TAMAN, LARRY, Canadian provincial official. Law clk. to Mr. Justice Laskin Supreme Ct. Can., 1971; tchr. law, assoc. dean Osgoode Hall Law Sch., 1971-80; with firm McMillan, Binch, Toronto, 1980-89; litigation ptnr. Tory Tory DesLauriers & Binnington, 1989-94; dep. atty. gen. Province of Ont., Toronto, 1994—; asst. atty. gen. for constl. law and policy, 1987-89. Office: Office of Dep Atty Gen, 720 Bay St, Toronto, ON Canada M5G 2K1*

TAMARELLI, ALAN WAYNE, chemical company executive; b. Wilkinsburg, Pa., Aug. 13, 1941; s. John Adam Tammarelli and Florence Eleanor (Heacock) T.; m. Carol Ann Crawford, Aug. 3, 1963; children: Robin Carol, Alan Wayne. BS, Carnegie Mellon U., 1963, MS, 1965, PhD, 1966; MBA, NYU, 1972. Engr. Exxon Corp., Linden, N.J., 1966, project leader, 1968-70; corp. planner Engelhard Minerals & Chem. Corp., Newark, 1970-71, asst. to exec. v.p., 1971-74, gen. mgr., 1974-77, v.p., 1977-79, group v.p., 1979-81; sr. v.p. Engelhard Corp., Iselin, N.J., 1981-83; chmn., chief exec. officer Dock Resins Corp, Linden, NJ, 1983—. Mem. exec. com. nat. adv. coun. for environ. policy and tech. U.S. Dept. Environment Protection, Gov's. Econ. Task Force, N.J.; mem. exec. com. Alliance for Union County. Capt. U.S. Army, 1966-68. NSF fellow, 1963-66. Mem. Synthetic Organic Chems. Mfrs. Assn. (chmn., vice chmn., bd. govs.), Am. Chem. Soc., N.Y. Paint and Coatings Assn. (chmn., pres., v.p., sec., treas., bd. dirs.), Chem. Industry Coun. (chmn., bd. dirs., exec. com.), N.J. Energy Rsch. Inst. (founding trustee), Am. Mgmt. Assn., N.Y. Acad. Scis., Scabbard and Blade, Rotary (pres., v.p., sec. Linden Club), Linden Indsl. Assn. (pres.), Sigma Xi, Tau Beta Pi, Phi Kappa Phi, Omicron Delta Kappa. Home: 49 Wexford Way Basking Ridge NJ 07920-2432 Office: Dock Resins Corp 1512 W Elizabeth Ave Linden NJ 07036-6323

TAMAREN, MICHELE CAROL, special education educator; b. Hartford, Conn., Aug. 2, 1947; d. Herman Harold and Betty (Leavitt) Liss; m. David Stephen Tamaren, June 8, 1968; 1 child, Scott. BS in Elem. Edn., U. Conn., 1969; MA in Spl. Edn., St. Joseph Coll., West Hartford, Conn., 1976. Cert. elem. and spl. edn. tchr., Conn., Mass. Tchr. N.Y. Inst. for Spl. Edn., Bronx, 1971-74; ednl. cons. Renbrook Sch., West Hartford, 1975-78; grad. instr. St. Joseph Coll., 1978; elem. tchr. Acton (Mass.) Pub. Schs., 1969-70, tchr. spl. edn., 1978-94; learning specialist and writer Educators Pub. Svc., Cambridge, Mass., 1994-96; inclusion and behavioral specialist Acton (Mass.) Pub. Schs., 1996—; ednl. cons. to schs., parents, orgns., pubs., 1980—; internat. and nat. lectr. on bldg. self-esteem in classroom, 1988—. Author: I Make a Difference!, 1992; also articles. Bd. dirs. United Way of Acton-Boxborough. Horace Mann grantee Mass. Dept. Edn., 1987, 88, Mass. Gov.'s Alliance Against Drugs, 1992. Mem. Coun. for Exceptional Children, Learning Disabilities Assn., Orton Dyslexia Soc., Nat. Ctr. Learning Disabilities, Nat. Coun. for Self-Esteem, Internat. Platform Assn., Phi Kappa Phi, Kappa Delta Pi. Avocations: travel, writing, reading, distance walking. Home: 15 Willis Holden Dr Acton MA 01720-3208

TAMARO, GEORGE JOHN, consulting engineer; b. Weehawken, N.J., Mar. 16, 1937; s. Giorgio Angelo and Giacomina (Chiesa) T.; m. Rosemary Ann Volta, June 24, 1961; children: Peter Louis, Jean Marie, Paul Anthony, Mark Joseph. B of Civil Engring., Manhattan Coll., 1959; M of Civil Engring., Lehigh U., 1961; M of Archtl. Tech., Columbia U., 1969. Profl. engr., N.Y., N.J., D.C., Md., Pa., Calif., Ill., Tex., La., Wis., Wash., R.I., Ark., Mo., Miss.; structural engr., Ill., Mass.; geotech. engr., Calif.; chartered engr., U.K.; registered European engr. Staff engr. Port Authority of N.Y. & N.J., N.Y.C., 1961-71; v.p., chief engr. ICOS Corp. Am., N.Y.C., 1971-80; ptnr. Mueser Rutledge Cons. Engrs., N.Y.C., 1980—. Patentee in field; author tech. papers. Chmn. Bergen County Planning Bd., N.J., 1978-82; vice-chair Leonia (N.J.) Plannig Bd., 1971-89; mem. Bd. Adjustment, Leonia, 1974-76; councilman Borough Governing Body, Leonia, 1972. Fellow ASCE (Martin S. Kapp Found. Engr. award 1987), Instn. Civil Engrs. U.K., Instn. Structural Engrs. U.K.; mem. Nat. Acad. Engring., Internat. Soc. Soil Mechs. and Found. Engrs., Post-Tensioning Inst. (com. on rock and coil anchors), Deep Found. Inst. (slurry wall com.), The Moles (trustee), Coun. on Tall Bldgs. and Urban Habitat, Am. Inst. Steel Constrn., Chi Epsilon (hon. mem. award 1990), TAu Beta Pi. Avocations: sailing, photography.

TAMBARO, MARIE GRACE, health specialist, nursing educator; b. N.Y.C., June 28, 1946; d. Louis Vincent and Jeanette (Motto) Nunziato; m. Arthur Michael Tambaro, Sept. 20, 1964; children: Celeste, Joseph, Arthur Michael Jr., Louis Derek. BSN with honors, CUNY, 1981; postgrad., Seton Hall U., 1985. CCRN, ACLS. Critical care staff nurse Richmond Meml. Hosp., S.I., N.Y., 1980-83; nursing insgr. Brookdale C.C., Lincroft, N.J., 1983—; health specialist Holmdel (N.J.) Bd. Edn., 1990—. Apptd. to Holmdel Twp. Bd. of Health, 1989—, Holmdel Bd. of Edn. Dist. Instrnl. Coun., 1994; chair Holmdel Drug and Alcohol Commn., 1986-88; rep. to N.J. State Drug and Alcohol Commn., 1987. Mem. AAUW. Republican. Roman Catholic. Avocations: reading, gourmet cooking, fitness. Home: 15 Seven Oaks Dr Holmdel NJ 07733-1924 Office: Holmdel Twp Bd Edn 4 Crawfords Corner Rd Holmdel NJ 07733-1908

TAMBOLI, AKBAR RASUL, consulting engineer; b. Babhulgon, India, July 20, 1942; s. Rasul M. and Chandbi T.; m. Rounkbi A. Tamboli, June 1, 1969; children: Tahira, Ajim, Alamgir. BS, U. Poona, India, 1965; MS, Stanford U., 1967. Sr. engr. Miller Assocs., Pottsville, Pa., 1967-69; assoc. Edwards & Hjorth, N.Y.C., 1970-76; sr. project engr. Engrs. Inc., East Orange, N.J., 1977-80; v.p. Office of Irwin G. Cantor PC, N.Y.C., 1981-91; consulting engr. CUH2A Inc., Princeton, N.J., 1992—. Editor: Steel Design LFRD Method Handbook, 1996. Vol. Cancer Fund Drive, N.J., 1986. Fellow ASCE; mem. Am. Steel Constrn., Am. Soc. Welding. Avocations: golf, boating. Home: 10 Davenport Dr Cranbury NJ 08512-1801 Office: CUH2A Inc 211 Carnegie Ctr Princeton NJ 08540

TAMBOR, JEFFREY, actor, theatre director, educator; b. San Francisco, July 8, 1944. BA, San Francisco State; MFA, Wayne State U. acting tchr. Milton Katselas' Acting Workshops, Beverly Hills, Calif. Appearences include (theatre) Sly Fox, 1976 (Broadway and L.A.), Measure for Measure, The Hands of the Enemy, Flea in Her Ear, American Mosaic, (films) ...And Justice For All, 1979, Saturday the 14th, 1981, The Man Who Wasn't There, 1983, Mr. Mom, 1983, No Small Affair, 1984, Desert Hearts, 1985, Three O'Clock High, 1987, Lisa, 1990, City Slickers, 1991, Life Stinks, 1991, Pastime, 1991, Article 99, 1992, Brenda Star, 1992, Crossing the Bridge, 1992, Radioland Murders, 1994, Heavyweights, 1994, (TV series) The Ropers, 1979-80, Hill Street, 1981-87, 9 to 5, 1982, Mr. Sunshine, 1986, Max Headroom, 1987-88, Studio 5B, 1989, American Dreamer, 1990, The Larry Sanders Show, 1992— (Emmy award nominee 1993), (TV episodes) M*A*S*H, Barney Miller, L.A. Law, The Golden Girls, Empty Nest, Who's The Boss, Doogie Houser, M.D., Equal Justice, Murder She Wrote, Tales From The Crypt (Dead Right), (TV movies) Eddie and Herbert, 1977, Alcatraz: The Whole Shocking Story, 1980, A Gun in the House, 1981, The Star Maker, 1981, Take Your Best Shot, 1982, The Zertigo Diamond Caper, 1982, The Awakening of Candra, 1983, Cocaine: One Man's Seduction, 1983, Sadat, 1983, The Three Wishes of Billy Grier, 1984, Robert Kennedy and His Times, 1985, Wildfire, 1986, The Burden of Proof, 1992, (TV spls.) Living and Working in Space: The Countdown Has Begun; dir. for numerous theatre companies including Seattle Repertory Theatre, Actors Theatre of Louisville, Milw. Repertory Theatre, Acad. Festival Theatre, Chgo., San Diego Shakespeare Festival, South Coast Repertory Theatre, Loeb Drama Ctr., Cambridge, Mass., Sky Light Theatre, L.A. Office: Care The Gersh Agency 232 N Canon Dr Beverly Hills CA 90210-5302*

TAMBORLANE, WILLIAM V., JR., physician, biomedical researcher, pediatrics educator; b. N.Y.C., Aug. 25, 1946; s. William and Eleanor (Bernabo) T.; m. Kathleen Mary Blinn, Dec. 27, 1969; children: Melissa, Amy, James. BS, Georgetown U., 1968, MD, 1972. Diplomate Am. Bd. Pediatrics, Am. Bd. Pediatric Endocrinology. Attending physician Yale New Haven Hosp., 1977—; asst. prof. pediatrics Yale U., New Haven, 1977-81, dir. Children's Diabetes Ctr., 1977—; assoc. prof. pediatrics Sch. Medicine, New Haven, 1981-86; acting chief Pediatric Endocrinology, New Haven, 1982-83; chief pediatric endocrinology and diabetes Yale Sch. Medicine, 1985—, prof. prdiatrics, 1986—; program dir. Yale Children's Clin. Rsch. Ctr., N.H., Conn., 1986—; chmn. Lawson Wilkens Diabetes Com., 1988-89. Recipient Jonathan May award, Charles Best award Am. Diabetes Assn., 1979, Clin. Investigator award NIH, 1979-82. Mem. Am. Fedn. Clin. Rsch., Am. Soc. Clin. Investigation, Endocrine Soc., Soc. Pediatric Rsch., Phi Beta Kappa. Office: Yale U Sch Med Children's Clin Rsch Ctr 333 Cedar St New Haven CT 06510-3206

TAMBS, LEWIS ARTHUR, diplomat, historian, educator; b. San Diego, July 7, 1927; s. Fred B. and Marguerite Johanna (Tambs) Jones; m. Phyllis Ann Greer, 1982; children: Kari, Kristin, Jennifer, Heidi, Greer, Michael, Alexa. B.S., U. Calif.-Berkeley, Berkeley, 1953; M.A., U. Calif.-Santa Barbara, 1962, Ph.D., 1967. Plant engr. Standard Brands, San Francisco, 1953-54; pipeline engr. Creole Petroleum Co., Caracas, Maracaibo, Venezuela, 1954-57; gen. mgr. Cacyp, Maracaibo, 1957-59; instr. Creighton U., 1965-67, asst. prof., 1967-69; prof. history Ariz. State U., Tempe, 1969-82, 87—, dir. Center Latin Am. Studies, 1972-76; cons. Nat. Security Council, 1982-83; U.S. ambassador to Colombia, 1983-85, U.S. ambassador to Costa Rica, 1985-87. Author: East European and Soviet Economic Affairs, 1975, Historiography, Method and History Teaching, 1975, (with others) Hitler's Spanish Legion, 1979; editor: United States Policy Toward Latin America, 1976, Inter-American Policy for the 80's; co-author periodical guides; contbr. articles to profl. jours. Bd. dirs. Ariz.-Mex. Commn., 1974-82, Coun. Inter-Am. Security, 1979-90. With U.S. Army, 1945-47, 50-51. Faculty grantee Ariz. State U., 1970, 71, 74, 78, 79. Roman Catholic. Office: Ariz State U Dept History Tempe AZ 85287-2501

TAMBURRO, PETER JAMES, JR., social studies secondary school educator; b. Hoboken, N.J., Jan. 20, 1947; s. Peter James and Rose Catherine (Verta) T.; m. Andrea Everitt Huber, Aug. 21, 1976; children: Peter James III, Christopher Harding, Matthew Everitt. BA in Polit. Sci, Dickinson Coll., 1969; MAT in Social Studies, Trenton State Coll., 1973. Cert. secondary sch. tchr., social studies, N.J. Tchr. Morris Sch. Dist., Morristown, N.J., 1973-76, Hanover Park Regional High Sch. Dist., East Hanover, 1976—; cross country, volleyball coach Hanover Park H.S., East Hanover, 1990—; judge Bicentennial Com., N.J.; asst. basketball coach Caldwell (N.J.) Coll., 1989-93; cons. Hist. Commn., East Hanover, N.J., 1989-92; cons. for developing AP history programs; asst. basketball coach Hanover Park H.S., 1994-95. Author: Gateway to Morris, 1993; editor: (with Dale Brandreth) The Chess Diary of Rudolph Spielmann, 1995; editor Atlantic Chess News, 1973-76; contbr. articles to chess mags.; nationally syndicated columnist for U.S. Chess Fedn., 1994-95 (National Chmn., Historical Committee, U.S. Chess Fedn. 1995-96). Rep. County Committeeman, Hanover Twp., N.J., 1984-88; legis. aide to Assemblyman Robert Martin, Trenton, N.J., 1985-89; mem. Hist. Commn., Washington Twp., N.J., 1994-96; scoutmaster Boy Scouts Am., 1994-95. With U.S. Army, 1969-71. Recipient Taft fellowship Taft Inst. on Two Party Govt., Fairleigh Dickinson U., 1984, Woodrow Wilson fellowship Woodrow Wilson Found., 1991, National fellowship Coun. for Basic Edn., Washington, 1993, Chess Journalists of Am. award, 1995; named N.J.'s Outstanding Tchr. of History, DAR, 1990 ; grantee NSF, 1978, Dodge Found., Madison, N.J., 1987. Mem. Nat. Coun. for Social Studies, Morris County Hist. Soc., Hanover Park Regional Ednl. Assn. (v.p. 1994-95, pres. 1995—). Avocations: rare books, chess. Home: 3 Powder Mill Rd Long Valley NJ 07853-3034 Office: Hanover Park High Sch 63 Mount Pleasant Ave East Hanover NJ 07936-2601

TAMHANE, AJIT C., statistician, engineer, educator; b. Bhiwandi, India, Nov. 12, 1946; came to U.S., 1970; s. Chintaman M. and Sarla C. (Durve) T.; m. Meenal A. Dikshit, June 18, 1975; children: Shalaka, Salil. B Tech. in Mech. Engring., Indian Inst. Tech., Bombay, 1968; MS, Cornell U., 1973, PhD, 1975. Design engr. Larsen & Toubro Ltd., Bombay, 1968-70; prof. Northwestern U., 1975—; cons. in field. Co-authored: Multiple Comparison Procedures, 1987. W-J-Youden award Chem. Proceedings Divns. Am. Soc. Quality Controll, 1985. Fellow Am. Stats. Assn. (pres. N.E. Ill. chpt. 1993). Office: Northwestern U 2006 Sheridan Rd Evanston IL 60208

TAMI, MARY E., visiting nurse; b. St. Marys, Pa., July 7, 1959; d. Robert Sr. and Elizabeth (Lanzel) Cotter; children: Justin, Amanda. AS magna cum laude, U. Pitts., St. Marys, 1990. RN, Pa. Formerly oper. rm. nurse Bradford (Pa.) Regional Med. Ctr., St. Marys; now vis. nurse Community Nurses of Elk and Cameron Counties, St. Marys. Home: PO Box 1027 Saint Marys PA 15857-5027

TAMIR, THEODOR, electrophysics researcher, educator; b. Bucharest, Roumania, Sept. 17, 1927; came to U.S., 1958, naturalized, 1968; s. Martin and Helena (Hart) Berman; m. Hadassah Cohen, Oct. 5, 1949; children: Jonathan, Yael. B.S. Technion, Israel Inst. Tech., 1953, Dipl. Ingenieur, 1954, M.S., 1958; Ph.D., Poly. Inst. Bklyn., 1962. Instr. Technion Israel Inst. Tech., Haifa, 1956-58; mem. rsch. staff Poly. Inst., Bklyn., 1958-62; mem. faculty Poly. Univ., Bklyn., N.Y., 1962—; prof. electrophysics Poly. Inst. N.Y., 1969-92, Univ. prof., 1992—, head dept. elec. engring., 1974-79; sci. and engring. cons. to indsl. and govtl. labs. Editor, author: Integrated Optics, 1975 (transl. into Russian and Chinese), Guided Wave Optoelectronics, 1988 (transl. into Russian); co-editor: Springer Series in Optical Sciences, 1979—; contbr. chpts. to books, articles to profl. jours. Served with Israeli Army, 1947-49. Awarded Instn. Premium, 1964, Electronics Premium, 1967, Instn. Elec. Engrs., London; citation for disting. research Polytechnic chpt. Sigma Xi, 1978. Fellow IEEE, Instn. Elec. Engrs. (London), Optical Soc. Am.; mem. Internat. Union Radio Sci., Sigma Xi. Home: 981 E Lawn Dr Teaneck NJ 07666-6604 Office: 100 Tech Pl Brooklyn NY 11201-2923

TAMKIN, S. JEROME, business executive, consultant; b. L.A., Apr. 19, 1926; s. William W. and Thelma (Brandel) T.; m. Judith Deborah, Mar. 23, 1963; children: Wendy Lynn, Gary William, Sherry Dawn. B.S., U. So. Calif., 1950; M.A., Fremont Coll., 1951, Ph.D., 1952; LL.D., St. Andrews U., London, 1954. Mem. rsch. staff chemistry dept. U. Calif. at Los Angeles, 1943; rsch. chemist, analyst supr. synthetic rubber div. U.S. Rubber Co., 1943-44; pres., gen. mgr. Majicolor, Inc., Los Angeles, 1947-49; rsch. engr. Coll. Engring., U. So. Calif., 1946-48; gen. mgr. Pan Pacific Oil Co., Long Beach, Calif., 1948-55; plant mgr. indsl. sales and mfg., 1953-55; v.p., sales mgr. Wilco Co., Los Angeles, 1948-55; v.p. charge indsl. sales and mfg. Wilco Co., 1953-55; v.p., sales mgr. Unit Chem. Corp., Los Angeles, 1955-56; pres. Phillips Mfg. Co. (merger Instl. Food Equipment Corp.), Los Angeles, 1957-62, Waste King Corp. (subs. Instl. Food Equipment Corp.), 1962-67; also dir.; v.p., dir. Dyna Mfg. Co., Los Angeles, 1962-68; pres., dir. Profl. Rsch. Inc., Los Angeles, 1965-73; exec. v.p. Am. Med. Internat., Inc., Beverly Hills, Calif., 1966-71; dir. Am. Med. Internat., Inc., 1966-89; sec., dir. Rodger Young, Inc., L.A., 1971-77; pres., chmn. bd. TGT Petroleum Corp., Wichita, 1972—; pres., dir. Tamkin Cons. Corp., 1978—; owner, operator Tamkin Securities Co., 1979-86; vice chair bd., dir. Integrated Voice Solutions Inc., Chattanooga, 1991—; bd. dirs. CAPP Care Inc., Newport Beach, Calif., 1991—; tech. cons. Daylin Inc., Beverly Hills, 1973-75; founder First Beverly Bank, Beverly Hills. Contbr. articles to profl. jours. Cmty. warden W. Adams-Baldwin Hills Cmty. CD, 1950-52; bd. govs. We. Los Angeles County coun. Boy Scouts Am.; dep. sheriff Los Angeles County, 1949; bd. dirs. Sunair Home Asthmatic Children; city commr. L.A. Bd. Environ. Quality, 1972-73; bd. dirs. Recovery Found., Fund for Higher Edn.; mem. exec. com. adv. coun. crime prevention L.A. Police, 1985—; U. Calif. at Irvine trustee Calif. Coll. Medicine, 1989-94; bd. visitors UCLA Sch. Medicine, 1990—; trustee Morehouse Sch. Medicine, 1995—. Served as officer USNR, 1944-46. Mem. AIM, Am. Mgmt. Assn., Inst. Aero. Scis., Am. Soc. Naval Engrs., Soc. Am. Mil. Engrs., Am. Chem. Soc., IEEE, Soc. Motion Picture and TV Engrs., Am. Inst. Chem. Engrs., Soc. Advancement Mgmt., U.S. Naval Inst., Calif. Scholarship Fedn. (life), Nat. Eagle Scout Assn., Sunrise Country Club, The Springs Country Club, Malibu Riding and Tennis Club, Alpha Eta Rho. Patentee electronic gas detector, circuits for automatic control hazardous vapors. Home: Pacific Palisades CA Office: 2100 Sawtelle Blvd Ste 201 Los Angeles CA 90025

TAMMEUS, WILLIAM DAVID, journalist, columnist; b. Woodstock, Ill., Jan. 18, 1945; s. W. H. and Bertha H. (Helander) T.; children: Lisen, Kate. BJ, U. Mo., Columbia, 1967; postgrad., U. Rochester, 1967-69. Reporter Rochester (N.Y.) Times-Union, 1967-70; reporter Kansas City (Mo.) Star, 1970-77, Starbeams columnist, 1977—; syndicated columnist N.Y. Times News Svc., 1989—. Editor-at-large Presbyn. Outlook, 1993; contbg. editor Mo. Life mag., 1980-81; commentator Sta. KCPT-TV, 1979-90. Co-recipient Pulitzer prize for gen. local reporting of Hyatt Regency Hotel disaster, 1982, recipient 1st pl. opinion-editl. divsn. Heart of Am. award Kansas City Press Club, 1991, 1st pl. opinion-analysis divsn. Heart of Am. award Kansas City Press Club, 1993, 1st pl. column divsn., 1994. Mem. Nat. Soc. Newspaper Columnists (v.p. 1990-92, pres. 1992-94, 1st pl. items divsn. Writing award 1992), Soc. Profl. Journalists. Presbyterian. Office: 1729 Grand Blvd Kansas City MO 64108-1413

TAMRES, MILTON, chemistry educator; b. Warsaw, Poland, Mar. 12, 1922; s. Morris and Lillian (Solberg) T.; m. Francoise Raymonde Lucot, Aug. 16, 1960; children—Louise R., Marc P. B.A. in Sci., Bklyn. Coll., 1943; Ph.D., Northwestern U., 1949. Control chemist Celanese Corp., Cumberland, Md., 1943-44; research and teaching fellow Northwestern U., Evanston, Ill., 1944-48; instr. chemistry U. Ill., Champaign-Urbana, 1948-51, asst. prof., 1951-53; asst. prof. chemistry U. Mich., Ann Arbor, 1953-57, assoc. prof., 1957-63, prof., 1963-87, prof. emeritus, 1987—; vis. scholar U. Tokyo, 1974. Contbr. articles to profl. jours. Guggenheim fellow, 1959-60; Am. Chem. Soc.-Petroleum Research Fund internat. fellow, 1966-67. Fellow AAAS, Am. Inst. Chemists; mem. Am. Chem. Soc., Sigma Xi, Phi Lambda Upsilon (past nat. pres.), Alpha Chi Sigma. Home: 1307 Brooks St Ann Arbor MI 48103-3171 Office: Univ Mich 3533 Chemistry Ann Arbor MI 48109

TAMURA, CARY KAORU, fundraiser; b. Honolulu, Jan. 9, 1944; s. Akira and Harue (Otake) T.; m. Denise Jeanne Mitts, Oct. 17, 1987; children from previous marriage: Jennifer Joy, Matthew D. Student, U. Hawaii, 1961-63; BA in Philosophy, Nyack Coll., 1966; MA in Theology, Fuller Sem., 1986. Cert. fund-raising exec. Dir. svc. tng. ops. Fin. Adv. Clinic of Hawaii, Honolulu, 1972-76; dir. planned giving The Salvation Army, Honolulu, 1976-78; planned giving cons. InterVarsity Christian Fellowship, Portland, Oreg., 1978-80; account exec. Am. Income Life, Portland, Oreg., 1980-81; dir. planned giving The Salvation Army, Portland, Oreg., 1981-84, L.A., 1984-85; dir. devel., planned giving U. So. Calif., 1985-90; dir. gift planning UniHealth America, Burbank, Calif., 1990-94; pvt. gift planning cons. Brea, Calif., 1995—; bd. dirs. Nat. Com. on Planned Giving, Indpls., 1991-93, sec. exec. com., 1993; mem. adv. com., adj. faculty UCLA Extension; lectr. in field. Bd. dirs. Japanese Evang. Missionary Soc., 1990-95, v.p., 1993; bd. deacons Evang. Free Ch., 1992-95. With U.S. Army, 1969-72. Mem. Planned Giving Round Table So. Calif. (pres. 1989-91, Pres.'s award 1992), Nat. Soc. Fund Raising Execs., (Greater L.A. chpt. bd. dirs. 1990—, v.p. 1993, 95, chair Fund Raising Day 1994, Profl. Fund Raiser of Yr. 1995), So. Calif. Assn. Hosp. Developers, Asis Pacific Legal Soc. (exec. adv. bd. 1995—). Republican. Avocations: photography, golf, travel. Home and Office: 1413 N Robert Ct Brea CA 92821-2165

TAN, AMY RUTH, writer; b. Oakland, Calif., Feb. 19, 1952; d. John Yuehhan and Daisy Ching (Tu) T.; m. Louis M. DeMattei, Apr. 6, 1974. BA in Linguistics and English, San Jose (Calif.) State U., 1973, MA in Linguistics, 1974; LHD (hon.), Dominican Coll. San Rafael, 1991. Specialist lang. devel. Alameda County Assn. for Mentally Retarded, Oakland, 1976-80; project dir. M.O.R.E. Project, San Francisco, 1980-81; free-lance writer, 1981-88. Author: The Joy Luck Club, 1989 (Nat. Book Critics Circle award for best novel nomination 1989, L.A. Times Book award nomination 1989, Gold award for fiction Commonwealth Club 1990, Bay Area Book Reviewers award for best fiction 1990), The Kitchen God's Wife, 1991, The Moon Lady, 1992, The Chinese Siamese Cat, 1994, The Hundred Secret Senses, 1995; also numerous short stories and essays; screenwriter, prodr.: (film) The Joy Luck Club, 1993. Recipient Best Am. Essays award, 1991. *

TAN, COLLEEN WOO, communications educator; b. San Francisco, May 6, 1923; d. Mr. and Mrs. S.H. Nq Quinn; m. Lawrence K.J. Tan; children: Lawrence L., Lance C. BA in English/Am. Lit., Ind. U., 1950, MA in English, 1952; MA in Speech Arts, Whittier Coll., 1972; postgrad., U. Calif. Berkeley, 1952-53. Cert. secondary edn. tchr., K-12, community coll., Calif. Tchng. aide English U. Calif., Berkeley, 1952-53; tchr. English and Social Studies Whittier (Calif.) High Sch., 1957-60; prof. speech comms. Mt. San Antonio Coll., Walnut, Calif., 1960-94; dir. forensics, 1969-80; sen. acad. senate Mt. San Antonio Coll., Walnut, Calif., 1982-90, faculty rep., 1990—; mem. numerous collegiate coms., campus advisor to Chinese Club and Asian Students Assn. Recipient Woman of Achievement Edn. award San Gabriel Valley, Calif. YWCA, 1995; named Outstanding Prof. Emeritus, Mt. San Antonio Coll. Found., 1994. Mem. AAUW (pres. Whittier Br. 1982, cultural interests chair Calif. state divsn. 1985-87, Fellowship award 1973-74, Las Distinguidas award 1992), Calif. Asian-Am. Faculty Assn., Delta Kappa Gamma, Phi Beta Kappa (Outstanding Educator of Am. award 1972). Roman Catholic. Avocations: creative writing, reading fiction, attending theater, music, dance. Home: 13724 Sunrise Dr Whittier CA 90602-2547 Office: Mt San Antonio 1100 N Grand Ave Walnut CA 91789-1341

TAN, ENG MENG, immunologist, biomedical scientist; b. Seremban, Malaysia, Aug. 26, 1926; came to U.S., 1950; s. Ming Kee and Chooi Eng (Ang) T.; m. Liselotte Filippi, June 30, 1962; children: Philip, Peter. B.A., Johns Hopkins U., 1952, M.D., 1956. Rsch. assoc. Rockefeller U., N.Y.C., 1962-65; asst. prof. Washington U. Sch. Medicine, St. Louis, 1965-67; assoc. mem. Scripps Rsch. Inst., LaJolla, Calif., 1967-70, mem., 1970-77, dir. Autoimmune Disease Ctr., 1982—; prof. U. Colo. Sch. Medicine, Denver, 1977-82; chmn. allergy and immunology rsch. com. NIH, Bethesda, Md., 1982-84; mem. nat. arthritis adv. bd. HHS, Washington, 1981-85. Contbr. chpts. to books, articles to profl. jours. Named to Nat. Lupus Hall Fame, 1984; recepient U.S. Sr. Scientist award Humboldt Found., Fed. Republic Germany, 1986, award Ciba-Geigy-Internat. League Against Rheumatism, 1989, Carol Nachman award Wiesbaden, Fed. Republic Germany, 1989, Paul Klemperer award and medal N.Y. Acad. Medicine, 1993. Fellow AAAS; mem. Arthritis Found. (Lee Howley Sr. award 1989), Am. Coll. Rheumatology (pres. 1984-85, Disting. Investigator award 1991), Assn. Am. Physicians, Am. Soc. Clin. Investigation, Western Assn. Physicians (v.p. 1980-81), Am. Assn. Immunologists, Brazilian Soc. Rheumatology (hon.), Australian Rheumatism Assn. (hon.), Brit. Soc. Rheumatology (hon.). Rsch. on characterization of autoantibodies in autoimmune diseases, systemic lupus erythematosus, scleroderma, Sjogren's syndrome, myositis and mixed connective tissue disease; relationship of autoantibodies to pathogenesis. Home: 8303 Sugarman Dr La Jolla CA 92037-2224 Office: Scripps Rsch Inst 10666 N Torrey Pines Rd La Jolla CA 92037-1027

TAN, HUI QIAN, computer science and civil engineering educator; b. Tsingtao, China, June 12, 1948; s. Dumen Tan and Ruifan Rao; m. Ren Zhong, June 16, 1994; children: William W., Danny D. BA, Oberlin Coll., 1982; MS, Kent State U., 1984, PhD, 1986. Asst. prof. computer sci. and civil engring. U. Akron, Ohio, 1986-89, assoc., 1990—; rsch. prof. Kent (Ohio) State U., 1987. Contbr. articles to profl. jours. Grantee NASA, 1987—, 91—, NSF, 1988-92. Mem. IEEE Computer Soc., Assn. for Computing Machinery, SIGSAM Assn. for Computing Machinery, Phi Beta Kappa. Avocations: classical music, history, literature, swimming, cycling.

TAN, SENG C., research scientist, materials research executive; b. Kluang, Johore, Malaysia, June 4, 1955; came to U.S., 1980; s. Kim L. and Chen (Lee) T.; m. Ming Yung Chen, Aug. 3, 1985; children: Anthony Wenwei, Max Bowen. BS in Mech. Engring., Nat. Taiwan U., 1978; PhD, U. Utah, 1983. Teaching asst. Nat. Taiwan U., Taipei, 1978-79; rsch. asst. U. Utah, Salt Lake City, 1980-83; rsch. assoc. NRC, Washington, 1984-86; sr. rsch. scientist AdTech Sys. Rsch. Inc., Dayton, Ohio, 1986-90; rsch. fellow, rsch. assoc. prof. Northwestern U., Evanston, Ill., 1991-92; pres., CEO Wright Materials Rsch. Co., Beavercreek, Ohio, 1990—. Author: Stress Concentration in Laminated Composites, 1994; contbr. more than 40 articles to profl. jours. Recipient fellowships, contracts, and grants. Mem. ASTM, ASME, Am. Soc. for Composites (founder-mem.), SAMPE, Soc. Mfg. Engrs. Avocations: jogging, ballroom dancing, music, badminton. Home and Office: 3591 Apple Grove Dr Beavercreek OH 45430-1480 also: Lab 1948 Woodman Ctr Dr Dayton OH 45420

TAN, TJIAUW-LING, psychiatrist, educator; b. Pemalang, Java, Indonesia, June 2, 1935; came to U.S., 1967; naturalized, 1972; s. Ping-Hoey and Liep-Nio (Liem) T.; m. Esther Joyce Kho, June 2, 1961; children: Paul Budiman, Robert Yuling, Alice Ayling. BS, U. Indonesia Faculty Medicine, 1957, MD, 1961; postgrad. U. Indonesia, Jakarta, 1961-65, U. Calif. at L.A., 1967-71, Pa. State U., 1971-72. Diplomate Am. Bd. Psychiatry and Neurology, Am. Bd. Gen. Psychiatry, Am. Bd. Geriatric Psychiatry. Lectr. psychiatry U. Indonesia, Jakarta, 1965-67; psychiat. cons. Central Gen. Hosp., Jakarta, 1965-67; postdoctoral fellow U. Calif. at L.A. Brain Rsch. Inst., 1967-69; asst. rsch. psychiatrist, dept. psychiatry Neuropsychiat. Inst. U. Calif., L.A., 1969-70; asst. prof. psychiatry Pa. State U., 1972-87; assoc. prof. psychiatry Pa. State U., 1987—; chief inpatient psychiatry Univ. Hosp. Milton S. Hershey Med. Ctr., 1972—, dir. Behavioral Medicine Clinic, co-dir. Biofeedback Lab., 1975—; cons. psychiatry Family and Children's Svc. Lebanon County, Lebanon, Pa., 1971-79. Bd. dirs. Retarded Children's Assn. Dauphin County, Inc., 1971-73. Fellow Am. Psychiat. Assn.; mem. Pa. Psychiat. Soc., Central Pa. Psychiat. Soc., Assn. Advancement Behavior Therapy, Assn. Applied Psychophysiology and Biofeedback, Soc. Behavioral Medicine, Assn. Psychophysiol. Study of Sleep, Am. Acad. Sleep Disorder Medicine, Am. Assn. for Geriatric Psychiatry, Am. Geriatric Soc. Contbr. articles to profl. jours. Home: 1478 Bradley Ave Hummelstown PA 17036-9143 Office: Pa State U Coll Medicine Dept Psychiatry 500 University Dr Hershey PA 17033-2360

TAN, VERONICA Y., psychiatrist; b. Manila, The Philippines, Oct. 8, 1944; came to U.S., 1970; children: Terrence, Kristine. MD, U. St. Thomas, Manila, 1969. Diplomate Am. Bd. Psychiatry and Neurology. Intern U. Ill. Hosp., Chgo., 1970-71; resident Lafayette Clinic and Children's Hosp., Detroit, 1971-775; child and adolescent psychiatrist Bon Secours Hosp., Grosse Pointe, Mich., 1993—. Author: The Gifted Child, 1970.

TAN, WILLIAM LEW, lawyer; b. West Hollywood, Calif., July 25, 1949; s. James Tan Lew and Choon Guey Louie; m. Shelly Mieko Ushio. BA, U. Pa., 1971; JD, U. Calif. Hastings Coll. Law, San Francisco, 1974. Bar: Calif. 1975, U.S. Dist. Ct. (cen. dist.) Calif. 1975, U.S. Ct. Appeals (9th cir.) 1975, U.S. Supreme Ct. 1979. Assoc. Hiram W. Kwan, Los Angeles, 1974-79; ptnr. Mock & Tan, Los Angeles, 1979-80; sole practice Los Angeles, 1980-81; ptnr. Tan & Sakiyama, L.A., 1981-86, 88—, Tan & Sakiyama, P.C., L.A., 1986-88; bd. dirs. Am. Bus. Network, L.A.; pres., bd. dirs. Asian Rsch. Cons., L.A., 1983-85; mem. adv. bd. Cathay Bank, 1990-91. Co-founder Asian Pacific Am. Roundtable, L.A., 1981; chmn. bd. dirs. Leadership Edn. for Asian-Pacifics, L.A., 1984-87; alt. del. Dem. Nat. Conv., San Francisco, 1984; mem. Calif. State Bd. Pharmacy, Sacramento, 1984-92, v.p., 1988-91, pres., 1991-92; mem. L.A. City and County Crime Crisis Task Force, 1981, L.A. Asian Pacific Heritage Week Com., 1980-85, Asian Pacific Women's Network, L.A., 1981, L.A. City Atty.'s Blue Ribbon Com. of Advisors, 1981, cmty. adv. bd. to Mayor of L.A., 1984, allocations vol. liaison team health and therapy divsn. United Way, L.A., 1986, mem. nominating com. bd. dirs. 1994-95; bd. dirs. Chinatown Svc. Ctr., L.A., 1983; conf. advisor U.S.-Asia, L.A., 1981-83; atty. L.A. City Housing Adv. Com.; mem. Pacific Bell Consumer Product Adv. Panel; vice chair cmty. adv. bd. Sta. KCET-TV, PBA, 1993-94; mem. adv. commn. State of Calif. Com. on State Procurement Practices, 1989-90; mem. L.A. City Attys. Citizens' Task Force on Pvt. Club Discrimination, 1989-90; mem. Calif. Med. Summit, 1993; mem. Mayor's Commn. Children, Youth and Families, 1993-96; mem. pub. access subcom. Mayor's Spl. adv. Com. on Tech. Implementation, 1994—. Named one of Outstanding Young Men of Am., 1979. Mem. ABA (mem. numerous coms.), ATLA, Calif. State Bar Assn. (vice chmn. com. ethnic minority rels. 1983-85, chmn. pub. affairs com. 1981-82, mem. others), L.A. County Bar Assn. (trustee 1984-86, vice chair human rights com. 1980-82, mem. numerous coms.), So. Calif. Chinese Lawyers Assn. (pres. 1980-81, chmn. 1987-88, mem. various coms.), Minority Bar Assn. (chmn. 1981-82, sec. 1980-81, chmn. adv. bd. 1982-83), Asian Pacific Bar of Calif., Nat. Asian Pacific Am. Bar, Japanese Am. Bar Assn., Bench and Bar Media Coun., Consumer Attys. of Calif., Soc. Intercultural Edn. (conf. coord., advisor panelist tng. and rsch. com. 1983). Avocations: gourmet cooking, bicycling, swimming, tennis, water color painting. Office: 300 S Grand Ave Ste 2750 Los Angeles CA 90071-3137

TANAKA, HARUMI, linguist, educator; b. Tokyo, Kanto, Sept. 16, 1930; s. Suehiro and Aiko (Sugiura) T. BA in English, Rikkyo U., Tokyo, 1952; BA in Linguistics, Tokyo U. Edn., 1954, MA in Linguistics, 1956; PhD in Linguistics, Brown U., 1971. Lic. English tchr. Instr. Rikkyo U., Tokyo, 1960-63, assoc. prof., 1963-68; assoc. prof. Tokyo U. Edn., 1968-76; prof. Nanzan U., Nagoya, Japan, 1976—; vis. rschr. East-West Ctr., Honolulu, 1974-76. Author: An Introduction to Linguistics, 1975, Invitation to Linguistics, 1978, Seminar in Linguistics, 1982, Seibido's Dictionary of Linguistics, 1988. Pianist Ensemble Eucalyptus, Nagoya, 1980—. Mem. Japan Assn. Coll. English Tchrs. (trustee 1973-94), Inst. for Rsch. in Lang. Tchg. (trustee 1971—), English Linguistic Soc. Japan (trustee 1988-95). Avocations: playing piano, listening to music, collecting stamps, traveling. Office: Nanzan U, 18 Yamazato-cho Showa-ku, Nagoya 466, Japan

TANAKA, KAY, genetics educator; b. Osaka, Japan, Mar. 2, 1929; came to U.S., 1969; d. Kumaji and Fusa (Nakamae) T.; m. Tomoko Hasegawa, Nov. 5, 1954; children: Atau, Elly Margaret. MD, U. Tokyo, 1956, Dr. Med. Sci., 1961; MA (hon.) Yale U., 1983. Asst. prof. medicine Harvard Med. Sch., Boston, 1969-73; sr. research scientist Yale U., New Haven, Conn., 1973-82, prof. genetics, 1983-94, prof. emeritus, 1995—; mem. biochemistry study sect. NIH, Bethesda, Md., 1983-84. Contbr. numerous articles to sci. jours., chpts. to books. Grantee NIH, 1971-95, March of Dimes, 1974-92. Mem. Am. Soc. Biol. Chemistry, Am. Soc. Human Genetics, Soc. Inborn Metabolic Disorders. Office: Yale U Dept Genetics 333 Cedar St New Haven CT 06510-3206

TANAKA, KOUICHI ROBERT, physician, educator; b. Fresno, Calif., Dec. 15, 1926; s. Kenjiro and Teru (Arai) T.; m. Grace Mutsuko Sakaguchi, Oct. 23, 1965; children—Anne M., Nancy K., David K. B.S., Wayne State U., 1949, M.D., 1952. Intern Los Angeles County Gen. Hosp., 1952-53; resident, fellow Detroit Receiving Hosp., 1953-57; instr. Sch. Medicine, UCLA, 1957-59, asst. prof. medicine, 1959-61, assoc. prof. medicine, 1961-68, prof., 1968—; asso. chmn., chief hematology, dept. medicine Harbor-UCLA Med. Center, Torrance, Calif., 1961—. Served with AUS, 1946-48. Fellow ACP (gov. so. Calif. region I 1993—); mem. Am. Fedn. Clin. Rsch., Western Soc. Clin. Investigation, L.A. Soc. Internal Medicine (pres. 1971), Am. Soc. Hematology, Internat. Soc. Hematology, Western Assn. Physicians, Am. Soc. Clin. Investigation, Assn. Am. Physicians, Sigma Xi, Alpha Omega Alpha. Research red cell metabolism. Home: 4 Cayuse Ln Rancho Palos Verdes CA 90275-5172 Office: Harbor UCLA Med Ctr PO Box 2910 Torrance CA 90509-2910

TANAKA, RICHARD I., computer products company executive; b. Sacramento, Dec. 17, 1928; s. G. and Kei Tanaka; m. Edith M. Arita, Aug. 18, 1951; children: Steven Richard, Jean Elizabeth, John Richard, Anne Mariko. BS with highest honors, U. Calif., Berkeley, 1950, MS, 1951; PhD, Calif. Inst. Tech., 1958. Sr. rsch. engr. N.Am. Aviation, Inc., 1951-54; mem. tech. staff Hughes Aircraft Co., 1954-57; dept. mgr., sr. mem. comuter rsch. Lockheed Missiles & Space Co., Palo Alto, Calif., 1957-65; sr. v.p. Cal Comp (Calif. Computer Products, Inc.), Anaheim, 1966-77; pres. Internat. Tech. Resources Co., Tustin, Calif., 1977-80; pres., CEO Systonetics, Inc., Fullerton, Calif., 1980-86; pres. Lundy Electroincs & Sys., Inc., Glen Head, N.Y., 1986-89; chmn., CEO, pres. Scan-Optics, Inc., East Hartford, Conn., 1989—; vis. prof. U. Calif., Berkeley, 1962. Author: Residue Arithmetic and Its Applications to Computer Technology, 1967. Hughes fellow Calif. Inst. Tech., 1955-57. Fellow IEEE (nat. chmn. computer soc. 1965-66, centennial medal); mem. Internat. Fedn. Info. Processing (pres. 1974-77, hon. life mem., U.S. del.), Am. Fedn. Info. Processing Socs. (pres. 1969-71, disting. service award 1983), Phi Beta Kappa, Tau Beta Pi, Eta Kappa Nu. Home: 19 Stratford Park Bloomfield CT 06002-2143 Office: Scan-Optics Inc 22 Prestige Park Cir East Hartford CT 06108-1917

TANAKA, RICHARD KOICHI, JR., architect, planner; b. San Jose, Calif., Oct. 16, 1931; s. Richard Inoru and Mae Yoshiko (Koga) T.; m. Barbara Hisako Kumagai, Oct. 7, 1961; children: Craig, Todd, Sandra, Trent. BArch, U. Mich., 1954; M in Urban Planning, Calif. State U., San Jose, 1978. Exec. v.p. Steinberg Group, San Jose, L.A., 1954—. Author: American on Trial, 1988. Dir. Human Rels. Com., San Jose, 1969-73; dir., pres. Bicentennial Com., San Jose, 1974-77; bd. dirs. Santa Clara County Sch. Bd. Assn., 1980—; pres. Internment of Local Japanese Ams., San Jose, 1984—; past pres., trustee East Side H.S. Dist., San Jose, 1971-92, Japanese Am. Citizens League, San Jose; mem. bd. govs. Boy Scouts Am., San Jose, 1978—, NCCJ, San Jose, 1976—; past pres. Tapestry and Talent, 1976-80; trustee San Jose/Evergreen C.C., 1992—, pres., 1993-94; bd. dirs., first v.p. Calif. C.C. Trustees. Mem. AIA, Am. Planning Inst., Constrn. Specification Inst., Rotary. Avocations: golf, painting. Home: 14811 Whipple Ct San Jose CA 95127-2570 Office: 60 Pierce Ave San Jose CA 95110-2819

TANAKA, TOGO W(ILLIAM), real estate and financial executive; b. Portland, Oreg., Jan. 7, 1916; s. Masaharu and Katsu (Iwatate) T.; m. Jean Miho Wada, Nov. 14, 1940; children: Jeannie, Christine, Wesley. AB cum laude, UCLA, 1936. Editor Calif. Daily News, 1935-36, L.A. Japanese Daily News, 1936-42; documentary historian War Relocation Authority, Manzanar, Calif., 1942; staff mem. Am. Friends Service Com., Chgo., 1943-45; editor to head publs. div. Am. Tech. Soc., 1945-52; pub. Chgo. Pub. Corp., 1952-56; pub. School-Indsl. Press, Inc., L.A., 1956-60; chmn. Gramercy Enterprises, L.A.; dir. T.W. Tanaka Co., Inc.; city commr. Community Redevel. Agy., L.A., 1973-74; dir. L.A. Wholesale Produce Market Devel. Corp., 1979-89, Fed. Res. Bank, San Francisco, 1979-89; mem. adv. bd. Calif. First Bank, L.A., 1976-78, bd. dirs. Meth. Hosp., So. Calif., 1978-93. Author: (with Frank K. Levin) English Composition and Rhetoric, 1948; (with Dr. Jean Bordeaux) How to Talk More Effectively, 1948; (with Alma Meland) Easy Pathways in English, 1949. Mem. citizens mgmt. rev. com. L.A. Unified Sch. Dist., 1976-77; adv. coun. to assessor L.A. County, 1981-84; bd. dirs. Goodwill Industries of So. Calif.; trustee Wilshire United Meth. Ch., 1976-78, Calif. Acad. Decathlon, 1978-81; adv. bd. Visitors and Conv. Bur., 1984-88, Am. Heart Assn., 1984-88, New Bus. Achievement, Inc., YMCA Met. L.A., 1977-91, Boy Scouts Am. Coun., 1980-86; mem. adv. council Calif. World Trade Commn., 1986-87; active Nat. Strategy Info. Ctr. N.Y., Nat. Wellness Community, Western Justice Ctr. Found.; trustee Whittier Coll.; chmn. L.A. chpt. Nat. Safety Coun.; Recipient merit award Soc. Advancement Mgmt., 1950, mag. award Inst. Graphic Arts, 1953, 1st award Internat. Council Indsl. Editors, 1955, UNESCO Literacy award, 1974, L.A. Archbishop's Ecumenical award, 1986, Frances Larkin award ARC, 1993, Spirit of Wellness award, 1995. Mem. L.A. Area C. of C. (dir. 1975-77), Japan-Am. Soc. So. Calif. (coun. 1960-78), L.A. Athletic Club, Lincoln Club, Masons, Shriners, Rotary (dir., pres. L.A. club 1983-84), Phi Beta Kappa, Pi Sigma Alpha, Pi Gamma Mu. Home: 949 Malcolm Ave Los Angeles CA 90024-3113 Office: 626 Wilshire Blvd Los Angeles CA 90017-3209

TANAKA-YAMAWAKI, MIEKO, computer science educator, physicist; b. Ikeda, Osaka, Japan, Aug. 4, 1950; d. Eizo and Mitsuko (Shibata) Tanaka; m. Koichi Yamawaki, Apr. 15, 1976 (div. 1986). BS in Physics, Kyoto (Japan) U., 1974; MS in Physics, Nagoya (Japan) U., 1976; PhD in Physics, U. Rochester (N.Y.), 1983. Rsch. assoc. CUNY, 1983-85; asst. prof. physics SUNY, Fredonia, 1985-86, North Adams (Mass.) State Coll., 1986-90; assoc. prof. Computer Sci. Sugiyama Jogakuen U., Nagoya, Japan, 1991—. Mem. IEEE, N.Y. Acad. Scis., Am. Phys. Soc., Japan Phys. Soc., Japan Soc. of Artificial Intelligence, Japan Soc. for Indsl. and Applied Math. Avocations: opera, classical music. Home: 1-22-1 Uesonocho Meitoku Rm 503, Aichi Nagoya 465, Japan Office: Sugiyama Jogakuen U, 3-17 Hoshigaoka-motomachi, Chikusaku Nagoya 464, Japan

TANCREDI, LAURENCE RICHARD, law and psychiatry educator, administrator; b. Hershey, Pa., Oct. 15, 1940; s. Samuel N. and Alvesta (Pera) T. A.B. in English, Franklin and Marshall Coll., 1962; M.D., U. Pa., 1966; J.D., Yale U., 1972. Diplomate Am. Bd. Neurology and Psychiatry. Bar: N.Y. 1982. Sr. profl. assoc. Inst. of Medicine, Nat. Acad. Scis., Washington, 1972-74; fellow dept. psychiatry Columbia U. Coll. Physicians and Surgeons, N.Y.C., 1974-75; postdoctoral fellow in psychiatry Yale Med. Sch., New Haven, 1975-77; assoc. prof. psychiatry and law NYU Med. Sch., 1977-84, adj. prof. law Sch. of Law, 1977-84; Kraft Eidman prof. medicine and law U. Tex. Health Sci. Ctr., Houston, 1984-92, dir. Health Law Program, U. Tex. Health Sci. Ctr., Houston, 1984-92; prof. clin. psychiatry med. sch., NYU, 1992—; med. dir. The Regent Hosp., N.Y.C., 1992-93; clin. prof. healthcare scis. U. Calif., San Diego Med. Sch., 1993—. v.p. Internat. Acad. of Law and Mental Health, 1987-95; pvt. practice, N.Y.C.; mem. tech. bd. dirs. Milbank Meml. Fund, N.Y.C., 1981-84; mem. adv. com. on transplantations Health Care Fin. Adminstrn., Dept. Health and Human Svcs., 1981-84; nat. adv. bd. NIMH Ctr. for the Study of Pub. Mental Health N.Y. State Office Mental Health, 1994—; mem. cmty. svcs. bd. Dept. Mental Health, Mental Retardation and Alcohol Svcs., City of N.Y., 1995—; mem. sci. adv. com. Am. Suicide Found., 1995—; cons. Commn. on Med. Profl. Liability, co-prin. investigator study ABA, 1978-80; cons. in field. Co-author 7 books. Editor and contbg. author 4 books. Contbr. articles to profl. jours. Mem. editorial bd. Ann. Bibliography on Bioethics, Kennedy Inst. Bioethics, 1979—. Mem. Am. Psychiat. Assn. (chmn. council on govt. policy and the law 1979-81), Am. Soc. Law and Medicine, Soc. Med. Jurisprudence (trustee 1983-85), Am. Coll. Psychiat., Group for the Advancement of Psychiatry. Office: 129B E 71st St New York NY 10021-4201

TANDLER, BERNARD, cell biology educator; b. Bklyn., Feb. 18, 1933; s. Arthur and Pauline (Solomon) T.; m. Helen Weisman, Dec. 25, 1955 (dec. Aug. 14, 1986); children: Janice Dena, Evan Charles. B.S., Bklyn. Coll., 1955; A.M., Columbia U., 1957; Ph.D., Cornell U., 1961. Instr. anatomy NYU, N.Y.C., 1962-63; assoc. Sloan Kettering Inst., 1963-67; asst. prof. cell biology Cornell U., N.Y.C., 1965-67; assoc. prof. Case Western Res. U., Cleve., 1967-72, prof. oral biology, 1972-91, acting chmn. dept. oral biology, 1987-89; affiliate prof. oral biology U. Wash., Seattle, 1993—; vis. prof. U. Copenhagen, 1973, U. Cagliari, 1983, Kyushu Dental Coll., 1994—; cons. NIH, NSF, VA. Author: (with C.L. Hoppel) Mitochondria, 1972; assoc. editor: Anatomical Record, 1974—; guest editor: Microscopy Rsch. and Technique, 1993-94, European Jour. Morphology, 1995-96; contbr. chpts. to books, articles to profl. jours. Recipient Disting. Alumnus award Bklyn. Coll., 1981, Robert E. Kennedy award for Acad. Freedom, Ohio chpt. AAUP, 1992; USPHS fellow, 1957-62. Mem. Am. Assn. Anatomists, Am. Soc. Cell Biology, Electron Microscopy Soc. Am., Japanese Soc. Oral Biology, Japanese Assn. Anatomists, Internat. Assn. Dental Research, Am. Soc. Mammalogists, Italian Soc. Anatomy (hon.), Sigma Xi.

TANDON, RAJIV, psychiatrist, educator; b. Kanpur, India, Aug. 3, 1956; came to U.S., 1984; s. Bhagwan Sarup and Usha (Mehrotra) T.; m. Chanchal Nammi Vohra; children: Neeraj, Anisha, Gitanjali. Student, St. Xavier's Coll., Bombay, India, 1974; BS, All India Inst., New Delhi, 1980; MD, Nat. Inst. of MH, India, 1983. Sr. resident Mental Health and Neuro-Scis., India, 1983-84; resident U. Mich. Hosps., Ann Arbor, 1984-87, attending psychiatrist, 1987—; dir. schizophrenia program U. Mich., Ann Arbor, 1987—, assoc. prof., 1993—; cons. Lenawee County Community Mental Health, Adrian, Mich., 1985—. Author: Biochemical Parameters of Mixed Affective States; Negative Schizophrenic Symptoms: Pathophysiology and Clinical Implications; contbr. more than 120 articles to profl. jours. Recipient Young Scientist's award Biennial Winter workshop on Schizophrenia, 1990, 92, Travel award Am. Coll. Neuropsychopharmacology/Mead, 1990, Rsch. Excellence award Am. Assn. Psychiatrists from India, 1993, Sci. award, Best Drs. in Am. award, 1994-95, Gerald Klerman award for outstanding rsch. by a Nat. Alliance for Rsch. in Schizophrenia and Depression young investigator, 1995. Mem. Am. Psychiat. Assn. (Wisniewski Young Psychiatrist Rschr. award 1993), World Fedn. Mental Health, Soc. for Neurosci., N.Y. Acad. Scis., Soc. Biol. Psychiatry, Mich. Psychiat. Soc. Democrat. Hindu. Office: U Mich Med Ctr Dept Psychiatry 1500 E Medical Center Dr # 8D Ann Arbor MI 48109-0999

TANDY, JEAN CONKEY, art educator; b. Reese, Mich., May 17, 1931; d. Samuel Hall and Christine Margaret (Walker) Conkey; m. Norman Edward Tandy, Jan. 25, 1952; children: Michelle Tandy Ryan, Kristen, Peter Spence. BA, Mich. State U., 1962, MA in Fine Arts, 1965. Instr. French French Bath (Mich.) Cmty. Schs., 1961-62, designer program art curriculum, instr., 1962-65; instr. art Mahar Regional Schs., Orange, Mass., 1966-67, Athol (Mass.)-Royalston Regional Schs., 1967-68; invited designer, developer art curriculum Mt. Wachusett C.C., Gardner, Mass., 1968, chair art dept., 1968—, prof. art, 1968—. Watercolors and clay exhibited on regular basis, 1950—. Mt. Wachusett C.C. grantee, 1970-94, Fed. Govt. grantee, 1968. Mem. Am. Crafts Coun., Mass. C.C. Coun., Women in Arts, Teaching Faculty Assn. (v.p. 1979-80, pres. 1980-81, grievance officer 1981-82). Independent. Avocations: gardening, writing and telling children's stories, reading, travel. Home: 539 Whipple Hill Rd PO Box 2 Winchester NH 03470

TANE, SUSAN JAFFE, retired manufacturing company executive; b. N.Y.C.; d. Irving and Beatrice (Albert) J.; m. Irwin R. Tane; children by previous marriage: Robert Wayne, Stephen Mark. BS, Boston U., 1964; postgrad., Hofstra U., C.W. Post U. Elem. sch. tchr. Long Beach, N.Y., 1964-67; pres. Fashions by Appointment, Glen Cove, N.Y., 1967-71; adminstrv. asst. Peerless Sales Corp., Elmont, N.Y., 1967-71; sales mgr., then mktg. dir. United Utensils Co., Inc., Port Washington, N.Y., 1973-78; v.p. ops. and control United Molded Products div. United Utensils Co., Inc., Port Washington, 1978-80; v.p. mktg. Utensco, Port Washington, 1980-88; bd. dirs. Peerless Aerospace Corp. Co-inventor plastic container and handling assembly. Trustee, sr. v.p. Am. Jewish Congress; mem. Dirs. Circle, Folger Shakespeare Libr.; life mem. Hadassah, Ronald McDonald House; mem. Friends of the Arts-L.I. U., Inner Circle-Nassau County Mus. Art; friend N.Y. Pub. Libr. Mem. Boston U. Alumni Assn. Home: 249 12th Ave Sea Cliff NY 11579-1021 Office: PO Box 735 Glenwood Landing NY 11547-0735

TANEN, NED STONE, motion picture company executive; b. Los Angeles, 1931. Grad., UCLA, 1954. With MCA Inc. (and subsidiaries); v.p. MCATTV, 1964-67; founder UNI Records, later MCA Records, 1967; exec. v.p. Universal City Records, Calif., 1967-69; v.p. MCA Inc., Universal City, 1967—; pres. Universal Theatrical Motion Pictures div., 1976; pres. Universal Picture div., 1979-82, also dir.; pres. motion picture group Paramount Pictures, 1985—; ind. producer, 1982—. Served with USAF, 1950-52. Office: Paramount Pictures Motion Picture Group 5555 Melrose Ave Los Angeles CA 90038-3149

TANENBAUM, BASIL SAMUEL, engineering educator; b. Providence, R.I., Dec. 1, 1934; s. Harry Milton and Rena Ada (Herr) T.; m. Carol Binder, Aug. 26, 1956; children: Laurie, Stephen, David. B.S. summa cum laude, Brown U., 1956; M.S. (NSF fellow, 1956-60), Yale U., 1957, Ph.D. in Physics, 1960. Staff physicist Raytheon Co., Waltham, Mass., 1960-63; prof. engrng. Case Western Res. U., Cleve., 1963-75; dean of faculty Harvey Mudd Coll., Claremont, Calif., 1975-93, prof. engrng., 1975—; Norman F. Sprague, Jr. prof. of life scis. Harvey Mudd Coll., Claremont, 1996—; vis. scientist Cornell U., Arecibo (P.R.) Obs., 1968-69; vis. assoc. prof. Northwestern U., Evanston, Ill., 1970; vis. scholar U. Calif. Irvine Beckman Laser Inst., 1993-94; mem. sci. adv. com. Nat. Astronomy and Ionosphere Ctr., 1972-77, Calif. Poly. Inst., Pomona, 1976-87; mem. engrng. and sci. adv. com. Calif. State U., Fullerton, 1976-87; mem. nat. adv. com. Rowan Coll., Glassboro, N.J., 1993—, chmn. curriculum subcom.; mem. Eisenhower adv. com. Calif. Postsecondary Edn. Com., 1993—; dir. Minority Engrs. Indsl. Opportunity Program, 1973-75; dir. summer sci. program Thacher Sch., Ojai, Calif., 1977-82; cons. various corps., univ. labs., govt. agys. Author: Plasma Physics, 1967. Woods Hole Oceanog. Inst. fellow, 1959; sr. Sterling fellow, 1959; recipient Wittke teaching award, 1974. Mem. AAAS, Am. Phys. Soc., Am. Soc. for Engrng. Edn., IEEE, AAUP, Sigma Xi (research award 1969). Home: 611 W Delaware Dr Claremont CA 91711-3458 Office: Harvey Mudd Coll 301 E 12th St Claremont CA 91711-5901

TANENBAUM, BERNARD JEROME, JR., corporate executive; b. Little Rock, Nov. 26, 1934; s. Bernard Jerome and Naomi (Dante) T.; m. Patricia Wise, June 9, 1955; children: Bernard Jerome III, Albert Wise. B.B.A., Tulane U., 1956; D.Pub. Service, Ark. Bapt. Coll., 1974. Salesman Dantan Co., Dumas, Ark., 1955; buyer Dantes Stores, Dumas, 1956-61; exec. v.p. Dante and Tanenbaum, Dumas, 1961; pres. UDS Inc. (formerly United Dollar Stores, Inc.), Dumas, 1967—; pres. Pudata Inc.; chmn. JAT II, Inc., vice chmn. Ark. Tax Revision Commn. County chmn. ARC, 1957-60; v.p., dir. Desota coun. Boy Scouts Am.; pres. Henry S. Jacobs Camp, S.W. region Union Am. Hebrew Congregations, also vice chmn. bd. trustees, mem. exec. com., mem. nat. com. camps and instns., rep. S.W. region to long-range planning com.; chmn. N.Am. bd. World Union Progressive Judaism, 1995, mem. exec. governing body, 1989; pres., dir. Camp Assn. So. Temples; mem. bd. govs. Hebrew Union Coll.-Jewish Inst. of Religion; trustee adv. bd. Tulane U.; trustee Leo N. Levi Hosp., 1994; bd. dirs. Dante & Tanenbaum Found., Ark. dept. NCCJ, Ark. chpt. Arthritis Found., Hot Spring Documentary Film Festival, 1994, Hot Springs Music Festival, 1995, "50 for the Future", Hot Springs, 1995. Recipient Ark. Ten Outstanding Young Men award, 1971, Outstanding Service award Sickle Cell Anemia Found., 1973, Distinguished Arkansan award, 1974. Mem. Ark. Retail Mchts. Assn. (dir.), Dumas Mchts. Assn. (past chmn.), Dumas Jr. C. of C. (past pres.), Ark. Jr. C. of C. (past internat. dir.), Dumas C. of C., Zeta Beta Tau.; mem. B'nai B'rith (past dir.). Jewish religion (past pres., trustee temple). Club: Mason (32). Home: 130 S Lakeland Pt Hot Springs National Park AR 71913-7608 Office: 1401 Malvern Ave Ste 160 Hot Springs National Park AR 71901-6370

TANENBAUM, JAY HARVEY, lawyer; b. N.Y.C., Nov. 17, 1933; s. Leo Aaron and Regina (Stein) T.; m. Linda Goldman, May 28, 1961; children: Susan Hillary, Steven Eric. BA, Hobart and William Smith Colls., 1954; LLB, Union U., 1957, JD, 1961. Bar: N.Y. 1957, U.S. Dist. Ct. (so. dist.) N.Y. 1961, U.S. Supreme Ct. 1967. Internat. trader Associated Metals and Minerals Corp., N.Y.C., 1960-64; pvt. practice, N.Y.C., 1964—; corp. counsel Internat. Gate Corp., Gen. Gate Corp. Mem. N.Y. State Bar Assn., N.Y. Trial Lawyers Assn., Bronx County Bar Assn. Jewish. Club: St. James (London), Le Club (N.Y.).

TANEY, J. CHARLES, advertising agency executive. Formerly sr. exec. v.p. FCB/Leber Katz Ptnrs., N.Y.C., pres., chief operating officer. Office: FCB Leber Katz Partners 150 E 42nd St New York NY 10017*

TANG, CYRUS, investment company executive. CEO Tang Industries, Mt. Prospect, Ill. Office: 1650 W Jefferson Ave Trenton MI 48183-2136 also: Tang Industries Inc 1699 Wall St Ste 720 Mount Prospect IL 60056*

TANG, DEBBY TSENG, counselor; b. Taichung, Taiwan, Aug. 20, 1956; came to U.S., 1979;. MS, Purdue U., 1980, PhD, 1984. Nat. cert. counselor and career counselor; lic. profl. counselor, Mich.; lic. clin. profl. counselor, Ill. Counselor Purdue U., West Lafayette, Ind., 1981-84; oranizational cons. U. Mich., Ann Arbor, 1984-86; counselor Wayne State U., Detroit, 1987-95, pvt. practice, 1996—; mem. faculty Ea. Mich. U., Ysilanti, 1989—. Named Counselor of Yr., Mich. Minority Women's Network, 1989. Mem. ACCA (exec. coun. 1995-97), ACA, AAUP (Wayne State chpt. chair acad. staff steering com. 1989-90), Mich. Coll. Pers. Assn. (pres. 1993-94, editor newsletter 1989-91), Phi Kappa Phi. Home: 1337 Green Trails Dr Naperville IL 60540

TANG, IRVING CHE-HONG, mathematician, educator; b. Macau, China, Dec. 29, 1931; came to U.S., 1948; s. Man-yan and Susie Wei-chun (Chung) T. BS, U. Calif., Berkeley, 1952; MS, U. Ill., 1953; DS, Washington U., St. Louis, 1965. Chartered engr., Brit. Engring. Coun. Design engr. Friden Calculators, San Leandro, Calif., 1955-56; staff engr. IBM Corp., San Jose, Calif., 1956-66; postdoctoral fellow U. Oslo, 1966-68; head math. dept. NSW Inst. Tech., Sydney, Australia, 1969-76, Hong Kong Poly., 1977-89; prof. math. Phillips U., Enid, Okla., 1989-91, Oklahoma City C.C., Rose State Coll., 1991-94, Okla. State U., Oklahoma City, 1994—. Contbr. articles to profl. jours. Fellow Brit. Computer Soc.; mem. Math. Assn. Am., Hong Kong Math. Soc. (pres. 1977-81), Sigma Xi, Tau Beta Pi, Eta Kappa Nu. Office: Okla State U 900 N Portland Oklahoma City OK 73107

TANG, PAUL CHI LUNG, philosophy educator; b. Vancouver, B.C., Can., Jan. 23, 1944; came to U.S., 1971; s. Pei-Sung and Violet (Wong) T. BSc with high distinction, U. B.C., 1966; MA in Edn., Simon Fraser U., Vancouver, 1971; MA, Washington U., St. Louis, 1975, PhD, 1982; cert. in ethics, Kennedy Inst. Ethics, 1983; diploma in piano, U. Toronto, 1962. Teaching asst. philosophy of edn. Simon Fraser U., 1969-71; instr. philosophy St. Louis C.C. at Meramec, Kirkwood, Mo., 1975-82; instr., lectr. philosophy Washington U., 1972-76; adj. asst. prof. Harris-Stowe State Coll., St. Louis, 1980-82; asst. prof. philosophy Grinnell (Iowa) Coll., 1982-85;

asst. prof. to assoc. prof. to prof. dept. philosophy Calif. State U., Long Beach, 1985—, chmn. dept. philosophy, 1988-94. Contbr. numerous articles and revs. to profl. publs.; editor Philosophy of Sci. Assn. Newsletter, 1985-90; asst. editor Philosophy of Sci. acad. jour., 1972-75. Senator Internat. Parliament for Safety and Peace, Palermo, Italy. Decorated knight Templar Order of Jerusalem, knight Order Holy Cross of Jerusalem, knight comdr. Lofsenic Ursinius Orer, chevalier Grand Crois de Milice du St. Sepulcre; recipient cert. of merit Student Philosophy Assn., 1988-90, 93-94, spl. award, 1992; named faculty advisor of yr. Assoc. Students, 1987, 90, 91, 95, Highland Lord of Carnster, Scotland, 1995; Paul Tang prize in philosophy named in his honor, 1996—; fellow Washington U., 1971, summer rsch. fellow Calif. State U., 1988, NEH fellow Harvard U., 1988, NEH Summer Seminar fellow, 1968; internat. scholar Phi Beta Delta, interdisciplinary scholar Phi Kappa Phi, 1993; grantee vis. philosophers program Coun. for Philos. Studies, 1987, 91, 92; Disting. Vis. Scholars and Artists Fund, Calif. State U., 1988, 89, rsch. grantee, summer 1996. Fellow World Lit. Acad.; mem. Am. Philos. Soc. (Excellence in Tchg. award 1995), Philosophy of Sci. Assn., History of Sci. Soc., Kennedy Inst. Ethics, Hastings Ctr., Iowa Philos. Soc. (pres. 1985-86), Internat. Platform Assn., Brit. Soc. Philosophy of Sci., Soc. Philosophy and Psychology, Internat. House Intellectuals of Acad. Francaise, Internat. Order Merit (Eng.), Golden Key (hon.), numerous others. Avocations: hiking, tennis, chess, music, travel. Home: 5050 E Garford St Apt 228 Long Beach CA 90815-2859 Office: Calif State U Dept Philosophy 1250 N Bellflower Blvd Long Beach CA 90840-0006

TANG, WILSON HON-CHUNG, engineering educator; b. Hong Kong, Aug. 16, 1943; came to U.S., 1962, naturalized, 1979; s. Shu-Chun and Shui-Kuen Chan T.; m. Bernadette Yim, July 29, 1969; children: Tze-John, Joyce Wing-Yi. BS, MIT, 1966, MS, 1967; CE, PhD, Stanford U., 1969. Asst. prof. civil engring. U. Ill., Urbana-Champaign, 1969-74, assoc. prof., 1974-79, prof., 1979—, assoc. head dept. civil engring., 1989-91; prof. Hong Kong U. Sci. and Tech., 1996—; Guggenheim fellow Norwegian Geotech. Inst., Oslo, Imperial Coll., London, 1976-77; vis. prof. Nat. U. Singapore, U. Hong Kong, 1983, prin. Wilson Tang and Assocs., 1986—; cons. to indsl. firms and govtl. agys. on reliability evaluation of structure and geotech. performances; mem. rev. panel Fulbright awards. Author: (with A. H-S. Ang.) Probability Concepts in Engineering Planning and Design, Vol. I, 1975, Vol. II, 1984; mem. editorial bd. Internat. Jour. Structural Safety, 1989—. Guggenheim fellow, 1976; NSF research grantee, 1972—; recipient Campus teaching award, 1991. Fellow ASCE (scholar 1965, Outstanding Tchr. award 1980, chmn. com. on reliability of offshore structures 1984-87, State of the Art Paper award 1990, co-chmn. com. on geotechnical safety and reliability, 1993—); mem. Geotech. Bd. of Nat. Rsch. Coun. (chmn. com. on workshop on Reliability Methods for Risk Mitigation in Geotech. Engring.), Am. Soc. Engring. Edn., Internat. Geostatis. Assn., Internat. Assn. for Structural Safety and Reliability, Internat. Assn. for Civil Engring. Reliability and Risk Analysis, Internat. Soc. Soil Mechanics and Found. Engring., Chinese-Am. Assn. Natural Disaster Mitigation Rsch. (bd. dirs. 1989-91). Home: 310 E Willard St Urbana IL 61801-6653 Office: 205 N Mathews Ave Urbana IL 61801-2350

TANG, YINGCHAN EDWIN, marketing educator; b. Taipei, Taiwan, Apr. 1, 1953; came to U.S., 1981; s. Shiu-Yuan Shih; m. Chih-Ping Wang; children: James Devon, Deborah Charlotte. BA, BS, Nat. Chengchi U., Taiwan, 1976; MS in Bus. Adminstrn., Tex. Tech. U., 1984; PhD in Mgmt. Sci., U. Tex., Dallas, 1989. Rsch. asst. Nat. Chengchi U., Taiwan, 1974-76; rsch. asst. U. Tex., Dallas, 1984-88, teaching fellow, 1987-88; vis. asst. prof. N. C. State U., 1988-91; asst. prof. mktg. N.C. State U., Raleigh, 1992-94; vis. lectr. Chinese U. of Hong Kong, 1994-96. Adv. bd. N.C. Taiwanese Found., 1990—; chair N.C. chpt. Taiwanese Am. Assn., 1994. With Chinese Marine Corps, 1976-78. Recipient Grad. Student scholarship U. Tex., Dallas, 1984-88, Best Rsch. Paper award Sixth Ann. Southwestern Doctoral Symposium on Doctoral Rsch. in Mktg., U. Houston, 1987, Southwestern Doctoral Consortium fellow, 1987. Mem. Am. Mktg. Assn., Am. Statis. Assn., Acad. Mgmt., The Inst. of Mgmt. Sci., TIMS Mktg. Coll. Avocations: fishing, biking. Home: Flat F 27/F Capilano Ct, Pictorial Garden, Sha Tin Hong Kong Office: Marketing Dept, Chinese Univ of Hong Kong, Sha Tin Hong Kong

TANGOREN, GULEN F., anesthesiologist, pain management specialist; b. Istanbul, Turkey, July 7, 1934; came to U.S., 1959; d. Ahmet Hamdi Iyigun and Hasene Kant; married; 5 children. MD, U. Istanbul, 1957. Diplomate Am. Bd. Pain Mgmt. Pvt. practice; sec., treas. dept. anesthesia Sibley Meml. Hosp. Founding mem. Muslim Community Ctr.; active Simon Viescutul Ctr. Fellow Am. Coll. Anesthesiologists; mem. AMA, Am. Soc. Anesthesiologists, Md., D.C. Soc. Anesthesia, Internat. Anesthesia Soc. Republican. Muslim. Home: 6456 Windermere Cir Rockville MD 20852-3539

TANGUAY, PETER EUGENE, child and adolescent psychiatry educator; b. Quebec City, Que., Can., Nov. 6, 1935; came to U.S., 1960, naturalized, 1971; s. Oscar E. and Marion L. (Grady) T.; m. Margaret Fife, Dec. 22, 1960; children: Heather Louise, Gretchen Marie. BA, U. Ottawa, Ont., Can., 1956, MD, 1960. Diplomate Am. Bd. Psychiatry and Neurology (com. for cert. in child and adolescent psychiatry 1981-87, written exam. com. for child and adolescent psychiatry 1981-87, chmn. 1985-87, dir. 1990—). Intern Harper Hosp., Detroit, 1960-61; resident in psychiatry UCLA Med. Ctr.-Harbor Gen. Hosp., 1961-64; registrar in psychiatry Kingsway Hosp., Derby, Eng., 1966-68; fellow in child psychiatry UCLA Ctr. for Health Scis., 1968-70, from asst. prof. to assoc. prof., 1970-8076, prof., 1980-94, dir. child psychiatry clin. rsch. ctr., 1977-87, assoc. chief div., 1984-91, acting chief, 1992-94; Ackerly prof. child psychiatry U. Louisville Sch. Medicine, 1994—; tech. advisor Rainman, 1988; vis. prof. U. Tours, France, 1982, U. Hawaii, 1987, 90; Roy Grinker vis. prof. Michael Reese Hosp., Chgo., 1984; mem. gen. assembly Am. Bd. Med. Specialists, 1990—, rep. to Accreditation Coun. on Continuing Med. Edn., 1993—, mem. exec. com., 1994-96; bd. advisors Rieger Found., Santa Barbara, Calif., 1992—; mem. psychol. scis. rev. com. NIMH, 1976-80; lectr., presenter in field; editl. cons. EEG and Clin. Neurophysiology, 1979-85; numerous others. Author: (with Margaret Tanguay) Travel Adventure in Europe with Tent, Van or Motorhome, 1970; contbr. over 60 articles, abstracts and book revs. to sci. jours., over 20 chpts. to books. Mem. Clinton-Gore Nat. Leadership Coun., 1991-93. Recipient career sci. devel. award NIMH, 1970-75; grantee USPHS, 1977-87, 84-89, NIMH, 1980-95, MacArthur Found., 1983-88. Fellow Am. Psychiat. Assn. (coun. on rsch. 1980-95, vice chmn. 1981-94, mem. com. on chronically ill-emotionally handicapped child 1990-94), Am. Acad. Child and Adolescent Psychiatry (assoc. editor Jour. 1988—, co-chmn. task force on universal access to health care 1991—), Am. Coll. Psychiatry; mem. AMA, AAAS, Group for Advancement Psychiatry (chmn. child com. 1988—), Soc. for Rsch. in Child and Adolescent Psychopathology, Royal Coll. Psychiatry (Gt. Britain, affiliate). Democrat. Avocations: microcomputers, vegetable gardening, travel. Home: 1129 Cardinal Dr Louisville KY 40213-1363 Office: U Louisville Bingham Child Guidance Ctr 200 E Chestnut St Louisville KY 40202-1822

TANGUY, CHARLES REED, foundation administrator, consultant, former foreign service officer; b. Phila., Dec. 24, 1921; s. Edward Earley and Dorothy (Reed) T.; m. Irene Jane McDaniel, Sept. 4, 1943; children: Charles Reed, Sarah Beauchamp, Peter Sackville. Student (scholar), Swarthmore Coll., 1939-41; A.B., Pa. State Coll., 1947; postgrad., George Washington U., summer 1946, Johns Hopkins U., 1947. Joined U.S. Fgn. Service, 1947; 3d sec. Athens, Greece, 1947-49; vice consul Rabat, Morocco, 1949-52; assigned State Dept., 1952; 2d sec. Rome, 1953-54, Bern, Switzerland, 1954-55; consul, prin. officer Penang, Malaya, 1955-56; assigned State Dept., 1957, internat. relations officer, 1957-59, officer charge Malayan affairs, 1959-61; 2d sec., later 1st sec., dep. chief polit. sect. Ankara, Turkey, 1961-65; 1st sec. dep. chief polit. sect. Paris, 1965-68; country dir. France and Benelux, Dept. State, 1968-72; minister-counselor Am. embassy, The Hague, Netherlands, 1972-75; mem., pres. 18th sr. seminar in fgn. policy Dept. State, Washington, 1975-76; sr. fgn. service insp., 1976-78; dep. dir. Office of Equal Employment Opportunity, 1978-80; ret., 1980; exec. dir. Netherlands-Am. Amity Trust, Inc., Washington, 1980—; program dir. Com. for a Community of Democracies-U.S.A., Washington, 1984-90. Mem. original bldg. com., warden St. Nicolas Anglican Episc. Ch., Ankara, 1962; mem. Companions in World Mission. Served to 1st lt. AUS, 1942-46. Decorated officer Order of Orange Nassau (The Netherlands); recipient John Jacob Rogers award Dept. State. Mem. Sigma Alpha Epsilon. Home: 2235 Q St NW Washington DC 20008-2825 Office: 1725 Desales St NW Ste 300 Washington DC 20036-4406

TANHAM, GEORGE KILPATRICK, retired research company executive; b. Englewood, N.J., Feb. 23, 1922; s. Francis Thomas and Irene (Kilpatrick) T.; m. Mary Finch, 1958 (div. 1962); m. Barbara Hunt, May 27, 1966 (div. 1989); children: George K., Gerald Francis, Helen Tanham Woods, Barbara Tanham Stampora, Maedi Carney, Ruth Tanham Marshall, Ramsey; m. Kathleen Van Wyck, Oct. 27, 1989. BA, Princeton U., 1943; MA, Stanford U., 1947, PhD, 1951. Assoc. prof., master student houses Calif. Inst. Tech., Pasadena, 1947-55; research staff Rand Corp., Santa Monica, Calif., 1955-58; dep. to v.p. Rand Corp., Washington, 1958-64, 65-68, v.p., trustee, 1971-82, sr. researcher, 1982-87, cons., 1987—; assoc. dir. AID, Saigon, Vietnam, 1964-65; minister counsellor U.S. Embassy, Bangkok, Thailand, 1968-70; cons. ESL, Sunnyvale, Calif.; lectr. in field. Author: Communist Revolutionary Warfare: The Vietminh in Indochina, 1961, 67, 85, War Without Guns: American Civilians in Rural Vietnam, 1966, Contribution a l'Histoire de la Resistance Belge, 1971, Trial in Thailand, 1974; co-author: (with Douglas S. Blaufarb) Who Will Win a Key: An Answer to the Puzzle of Revolutionary War, 1989, (with Marcy Agmon) The Indian Air Force: Trends and Prospects, 1996, (with K. Bhapal and A. Mattoo) Securing Indian Strategic Thought of an Emerging Power; contbr. chpts. to books, articles to profl. jours. Bd. visitors Patterson Sch. of Diplomacy and Internat. Commerce, U. Ky., 1985—, U. Pitts., 1982-92; bd. dirs. Ethics and Pub. Policy Ctr., 1988—; adv. trustee Rand Corp., 1988—. Served with U.S. Army, World War II. Decorated Purple Heart, Silver Star with oak leaf cluster, Air medal; Croix de Guerre avec etoile d'argent (Republic of France); Most Exalted Order of White Elephant (Thailand); Belgian-Am. Edn. Found. grantee, 1950; Ford Found. fellow, 1952-53; Social Scis. Research Council grantee, 1955-57; grantee U.S. Inst. Peace and Rockefeller Found., 1989-91; Rajiv Gandhi Found. vis. fellow, New Delhi, 1995. Mem. Coun. Fgn. Rels., Internat. Inst. Strategic Studies, Cosmos Club, Spl. Forces Club (London), India Internat. Ctr. (New Delhi). Avocations: music, travel, gardening, sports. Home: PO Box 373 Strasburg VA 22657-0373 Office: Rand 2100 M St NW Ste 800 Washington DC 20037-1270

TANI, SHOHEI, pharmacy educator; b. Komi, Ngano, Japan, Mar. 5, 1942; s. Seitetsu and Kazuko (Tani) T.; m. Masako Onzawa, July 23, 1980; 1 child, Shoko. BS, Sizuoka (Japan) U. Pharmacy, 1965; MS, Chiba (Japan) U., 1967; PHD, Kyoto (Japan) U., 1972. Pharm. diplomate. Rsch. fellow U. Hawaii, Honolulu, 1972-73; rsch. asst. Kobe (Japan) Gakuin U., 1974-75, asst. prof., 1975-76, assoc. prof., 1976-85, prof., 1985—; vis. fellow U. N.C., Chapel Hill, 1984-86. Contbr. articles to profl. jours. Mem. Pharm. Soc. Japan, Mass Spectroscopy Soc. Japan, Am. Chem. Soc., Am. Soc. Phamacognosy, N.Y. Acad. Scis. Home: 6-23-17 Hontamon, Tarumi Ku, Kobe 655, Japan Office: Kobe Gakuin U 518 Arise, Ikawadani Nishi Ku, Kobe 651-21, Japan

TANICK, MARSHALL HOWARD, lawyer, law educator; b. Mpls., May 9, 1947; s. Jack and Esther (Kohn) T.; m. Cathy E. Gorlin, Feb. 20, 1982; children: Lauren, Ross. BA, U. Minn., 1969; JD, Stanford U., 1973. Bar: Calif. 1973, Minn. 1974. Law clk. to presiding justice U.S. Dist. Ct., Mpls., 1973-74; assoc. Robins, Davis & Lyons, Mpls., 1974-76; ptnr. Tanick & Heins, P.A., Mpls., 1976-89, Mansfield & Tanick, Mpls., 1989—; prof. constrn., real estate and media law U. Minn., Mpls., 1983—, Hamline U., St. Paul, 1982—; prof. constl. law William Mitchell Coll. Law, 1994. Editor: Hennepin Lawyer, Bench, Bar and Litigation mag.; contbr. articles to mags. Avocation: writing. Home: 1230 Angelo Dr Minneapolis MN 55422-4710 Office: Ste 1560 Internat Ctr Minneapolis MN 55402

TANIGUCHI, TOKUSO, surgeon; b. Eleele, Kauai, Hawaii, June 26, 1915; s. Tokuichi and Sana (Omaye) T.; BA, U. Hawaii, 1941; MD, Tulane U., 1946; 1 son, Jan Tokuichi. Intern Knoxville (Tenn.) Gen. Hosp., 1946-47; resident in surgery St. Joseph Hosp., also Marquette Med. Sch., Milw., 1947-52; practice medicine, specializing in surgery, Hilo, Hawaii, 1955—; chief surgery Hilo Hosp.; teaching fellow Marquette Med. Sch., 1947-49; v.p., dir. Hawaii Hardware Co., Ltd. Capt. M.C., AUS, 1952-55. Diplomate Am. Bd. Surgery. Fellow Internat., Am. colls. surgeons; mem. Am., Hawaii med. assns., Hawaii County Med. Soc., Pan-Pacific Surg. Assn., Phi Kappa Phi. Contbr. articles in field to profl. jours. Patentee automated catheter. Home: 277 Kaiulani St Hilo HI 96720-2530

TANIS, JAMES ROBERT, library director, history educator, clergyman; b. Phillipsburg, N.J., June 26, 1928; s. John Christian and Bertha Marie (Tobiasson) T.; m. Florence Borgmann, June 26, 1963; children—Marjorie Martha, James Tobiasson. B.A., Yale, 1951; B.D., Union Theol. Sem., N.Y.C., 1954; Dr. Theol., U. Utrecht, Netherlands, 1967; LittD (hon.), Dickinson Coll., Carlisle, Pa., 1994. Ordained to ministry Presbyn. Ch., 1954. Co-pastor Greystone Presbyn. Ch., Elizabeth, N.J., 1954-55; librarian, mem. faculty Harvard Div. Sch., 1956-65; univ. librarian Yale U., 1965-68; mem. faculty Yale Div. Sch., 1968-69; dir. libraries, prof. history Bryn Mawr (Pa.) Coll., 1969—. Author: Calvinistic Pietism in the Middle Colonies, 1967; co-author: Bookbinding in America, 1983, Images of Discord/De Tweedracht Verbeeld, 1993. Knighted as Officer in Order of Orange-Nassau, The Netherlands, 1993. Home: 105 Burnside Rd Villanova PA 19085-1315 Office: Bryn Mawr Coll Canaday Libr 101 N Merion Ave Bryn Mawr PA 19010-2899

TANIS, NORMAN EARL, retired university dean, library expert; b. Grand Rapids, Mich., Aug. 15, 1929; s. Aaron Orrie and Gertrude (Medendorp) T.; m. Terese R. Tiernan; children: Kathryn, Laura. AB, Calvin Coll., 1951; AM in Libr. Sci., U. Mich., 1952, MA in History, 1956, MA in Edn., 1961; DHL (hon.), U. San Fernando, 1973; LLD (hon.), Mid-Valley Coll. Law, 1976. Cataloger Strauss Meml. Libr., U. Mich., 1951-52; statis. clk. polio vaccine evaluation ctr. U. Mich., Ann Arbor, 1955; libr. Henry Ford Community Coll., Dearborn, Mich., 1956-63, head libr., 1963-66; dir. librs. Kans. State U., Pittsburg, 1966-69; dean librs. Calif. State U., Northridge, 1969-91, ret., 1991, librarian emeritus; team mgr./planner robotically controlled book storage unit Leviathian II, Calif. State U., 1986-91, chmn. editl. adv. bd. for univ. history, 1988-91; trustee San Fernando Valley Coll. Law, 1977-79; mem. adv. coun. Libr. Sch., UCLA, 1970-77; mem. adv. com. Libr. Sch., U. So. Calif., 1971-74; disting. alumnus-in-residence Sch. Info. and Libr. Svc., U. Mich., 1989; part-time libr. Our Lady Queen of the Angels Sem., 1993-94; assoc. Libr. Congress. Co-author: Three Hundred Million Books, 1974, Problems in Developing Academic Library Collections, 1974, Native Americans of North America, 1975, Lynton R. Kistler: Printer-Lithographer, 1976, Cost Analysis of Library Functions: A Total System Approach, 1978, China in Books, 1979, India and its People, A Bibliography, 1980, The Twilight of Orthodoxy in New England, 1987; contbr. articles to profl. publs.; editor: Northridge Facsimilie Series, 1974-91; exec. editor Santa Susana Press, 1975-91. Mem., lectr., extraordinary eucharistic min. and catechist for prison ministries St. John Eudes Roman Cath. Ch., Chatsworth, Calif.; postulant Oblates of Monastery of Risen Christ, San Luis Obispo, Calif., 1991—; with Knights of the Imaculata Militia. With USMCR, 1948-50; with U.S. Army, 1952-54. Named knight comdr. Supreme Order and Mil. of Temple of Jerusalem, 1990—, knight of Order of St. Constantine, 1991—, mil. and hospitaller knight of Order of St. Lazarus of Jerusalem, 1992—. Mem. ALA, Nat. Librs. Assn. (pres. 1980), Bibliog. Soc. Calif. State U.-Northridge, Acad. and Rsch. Librs. (pres. 1983-84), ALA divsn. Cath. Libr. Assn., Order of St. Lawrence-Malta (duke), Marine Meml. Club (San Francisco), Rounce and Coffin Club, Phi Beta Phi, Phi Beta Mu. Home: 10009 Jovita Ave Chatsworth CA 91311-3938 Office: Calif State U Libr Rm 202 1811 Nordhoff St Northridge CA 91324

TANIUCHI, KIYOSHI, retired mechanical engineering educator; b. Kahoku-choo, Kami-gun, Kōchi-ken, Japan, Aug. 8, 1926; s. Takeshi and Toshi (Yoshimoto) T.; m. Teiko Wakamatsu, Jan. 7, 1960; 1 child, Satoshi. Student, Kanto Gakuin Tech. Coll., Yokohama, Japan, 1946; BEng, Meiji U., Tokyo, 1952, DEng (hon.), 1980. Asst. Meiji U. Sch. Sci. and Tech., Kawasaki-shi, Japan, 1957-81, lectr. mech. engring., 1981-91, assoc. prof., 1991-95; ret. Meiji U. Sch. Sci. and Tech., 1995; instr. engring. Shibaura Inst. Tech., Ohmiya-shi, Saitama-ken, Japan, 1974-90. Co-author 3 books on mech. engring.; also papers. Mem. ASTM, Internat. Soc. Optical Engring., Soc. Exptl. Mechanics, Japanese Soc. Mech. Engrs. Avocations: photography, art appreciation. Home: 5-10-12 Wakamatsu, Sagamihara 229, Japan

TANKIN, RICHARD SAMUEL, fluid dynamics engineer, educator; b. Balt., July 14, 1924; s. Harry Jacob and Bertha (Haberer) T.; m. Anne Raudelunas, Dec. 2, 1956; children: Roberta, David, John. B.A., Johns Hopkins U., 1948, B.S., 1950; M.S., Mass. Inst. Tech., 1954; Ph.D., Harvard U., 1960. Asst. prof. U. Del., 1960-61; mem. faculty Northwestern U., 1961—, prof. fluid dynamics, 1968—, chmn. dept. mech. engring. and astronautical scis., 1973-78. Served with AUS, 1943-44; Served with USNR, 1944-45. Mem. ASME, Am. Inst. Aeros. and Astronautics, Am. Geophys. Union, Tau Beta Pi. Home: 820 Ridge Ter Evanston IL 60201-2430

TANNEHILL, DARCY ANITA, academic administrator; b. Pitts., May 14, 1958; d. Joseph Paul Bartins and Ileane Anita (Roy) Bartins Yerman; m. Gary Edward Mack, Oct. 28, 1979 (div. Apr. 1989); 1 child, Courtney Anita; m. Norman Bruce Tannehill Jr., Feb. 14, 1991; children: Andrea, Bruce. BA, Duquesne U., 1978, MSEd, 1986. Rsch. asst. U. Pitts., 1979-81; adult edn. tchr. Allegheny Intermediate Unit, Pitts., 1985-86, counselor, statistician, 1986-90; coord. evening programs Robert Morris Coll., Coraopolis, Pa., 1990-92; asst. dir. academic svcs. Robert Morris Coll., Coraopolis, Pa., 1992-93; assoc. dir. academic svcs. Robert Morris Coll., Corapolis, Pa., 1993-94, assoc. dean admissions, 1994—. Mem. Pa. Am. coun. on Edn., Nat. Identification Program. Republican. Presbyterian. Avocations: reading, music. Home: 4482 Battleridge Rd McDonald PA 15057 Office: Robert Morris Coll Narrows Run Rd Coraopolis PA 15108

TANNEHILL, JOHN C., aerospace engineer, educator; b. Salem, Ill., Oct. 14, 1943; s. John Bell and Pearl Hanna (Trulin) T.; m. Marcia Kay George, Jan. 28, 1967; children: Michelle, Johnny. BS, Iowa State U., 1965, MS, 1967, PhD, 1969. Aerospace engr. NASA Flight Rsch. Ctr., Edwards, Calif., 1965; mem. tech. staff Aerospace Cor., El Segundo, Calif., 1967; NASA-ASEE fellow NASA Ames Rsch. Ctr., Moffett Field, Calif., 1970-71; asst. prof. aerospace engring. Iowa State U., Ames, 1969-74, assoc. prof., 1974-79, prof., 1979—, mgr. Computational Fluid Dynamics Ctr., 1984—; chmn. bd. Engring. Analysis, Inc., Ames, 1976—. Co-author: Computational Fluid Mechanics and Heat Transfer, 1984, Handbook of Numerical Heat Transfer, 1988; contbr. articles to profl. jours. NSF trainee, 1965-68; Iowa State U. Rsch. Found. fellow, 1968-69; NASA fellow, 1970-71. Fellow AIAA (chmn. Iowa sect. 1989-91); mem. Am. Soc. Engring. Edn., Sigma Xi, Sigma Gamma Tau, Tau Beta Pi. Home: 3214 Greenwood Cir Ames IA 50014-4570 Office: Aerospace Engring & Engring Mechanics Dept Aerospace & Mechs Engring Ames IA 50011

TANNEN, DEBORAH FRANCES, writer, linguist; b. Bklyn., June 7, 1945; d. Eli S. and Dorothy (Rosen) T. BA, SUNY, Binghamton, 1966; MA, Wayne State U., 1970, U. Calif., Berkeley, 1976; PhD, U. Calif., 1979. Instr. Greek-Am. Cultural Inst., Herakleion, Greece, 1966-67; instr. in English as fgn. lang. Hellenic Am. Union, Athens, Greece, 1967-68; English instr. Detroit Inst. Tech., 1969, Mercer County C.C., Trenton, N.J., 1970-71; lectr. in acad. skills CUNY, Bronx, N.Y., 1971-74; asst. prof. Georgetown U., Washington, 1979-85, assoc. prof. linguistics, 1985-90, prof. linguistics, 1989-91, univ. prof., 1991—; McGraw disting. lectr. in writing Coun. for Humanities and dept. anthropology Princeton U., fall 1991; visitor Inst. for Advanced Study, Princeton, spring 1992; fellow Ctr. for Advanced Study in Behavioral Scis., Stanford, Calif., 1992-93. Author: Lilika Nakos, 1983, Conversational Style: Analyzing Talk Among Friends, 1984, That's Not What I Meant!: How Conversational Style Makes or Breaks Your Relations With Others, 1984, Talking Voices: Repetition, Dialogue and Imagery in Conversational Discourse, 1989, You Just Don't Understand: Women and Men in Conversation, 1990, Gender and Discourse, 1994, Talking From 9 to 5: How Women's and Men's Conversational Styles Affect Who Gets Heard, Who Gets Credit, and What Gets Done at Work, 1994; editor: Analyzing Discourse: Text and Talk, 1982, Spoken and Written Language: Exploring Orality and Literacy, 1982, Coherence in Spoken and Written Discourse, 1984, Perspectives on Silence, 1985, Linguistics in Context, 1986, Linguistics in Context: Connecting Observation and Understanding, 1988, Gender and Conversational Interaction, 1993, Framing In Discourse, 1993. Rockefeller Humanities fellow, 1982-83; grantee NEH, 1980, 85, 86; recipient Elizabeth Mills Crothers prize U. Calif., 1976, Dorothy Rosenberg Meml. prize U. Calif., 1977, Joan Lee Yang Meml. Poetry prize U. Calif., 1977, Shrout Short Story prize, 1978, Emily Chamberlain Cook prize, 1978. Office: Georgetown U Linguistics Dept Washington DC 20057

TANNENBAUM, BERNICE SALPETER, association executive; b. N.Y.C.; d. Isidore and May Franklin; BA, Bklyn. Coll.; 1 child, Richard Salpeter. chmn. Commn. on the Status of Women of the World Jewish Congress; mem. exec. bd. Am. sect. World Jewish Congress, chmn. internat. affairs com.; mem. Zionist Gen. Council; active Exec. World Zionist Orgn.; bd. govs., mem. gen. assembly Jewish Agy.; bd. dirs., v.p. United Israel Appeal; mem. exec. com. Am. Zionist Mvmt.; mem. Conf. of Pres. of Maj. Jewish Orgns.; nat. pres. Hadassah, N.Y.C., 1976-80; nat. chmn. Hadassah International, 1984-95; v.p. Jewish Telegraphic Agy.; bd. govs. Hebrew U. Office: Hadassah 50 W 58th St New York NY 10019-2500

TANNENBAUM, RICHARD NEIL, lawyer; b. Jersey City, July 10, 1951; s. Paul H. and Sonia (Pearson) T.; children: Brette Morgan, Joshua Daniel. BA, George Washington U., 1973; JD, Ohio No. U., 1976. Bar: N.Y. 1977, U.S. Dist. Ct. (ea. dist.) N.Y. 1979, U.S. Dist. Ct. (so. dist.) N.Y. 1981, U.S. Ct. Appeals (2d cir.) 1987, U.S. Supreme Ct. 1983. Ptnr. Tannenbaum & Tannenbaum, Great Neck, N.Y., 1976-83, Tannenbaum & Reisman, Great Neck, 1983-86; staff atty. Laborers Local 1298 Legal Svcs., Hempstead, N.Y., 1984-85; of counsel Slotnick & Baker, P.C., N.Y.C., 1986-89; ptnr. Richard N. Tannenbaum, N.Y.C., 1986—; arbitrator Civil Ct. Queens County, Kew Gardens, N.Y., 1983-86, 95—; law guardian Nassau County Family Ct., Westbury, N.Y., 1978-82; vis. lectr. Law Sch., U. Iceland, Reykjavik, 1976-77. Author, composer 3 ballads, other musical compositions. Candidate for N.Y. State Senate, 7th S.D., 1980; vol. N.Y.C. Parks and Recreation, 1994. Named Outstanding Defender of Victims, Crime Victims Polit. Platform, N.Y.C., 1989. Mem. N.Y. Trial Lawyers Assn., Greak Neck Lawyers Assn. (chmn. bd. 1985, pres. 1984), N.Y. County Lawyers Assn., Songwriters Guild of Am. Avocations: piano, basketball, swimming, tennis, songwriting. Office: 225 Broadway Rm 2700 New York NY 10007-3001

TANNENBAUM, STEVEN ROBERT, toxicologist, chemist; b. N.Y.C., Feb. 23, 1937; m. Carol Eigen, Sept. 6, 1959; children: Lisa, Mark. B.S. in Food Tech, MIT, 1958, Ph.D. in Food Sci. and Tech, 1962. Asst. prof. MIT, Cambridge, Mass., 1964-69; assoc. prof. MIT, 1969-74, prof. food chemistry, 1974-81, prof. chemistry and toxicology divsn. toxicology, registration and admissions officer, 1981-95; vis. prof. Hebrew U. of Jerusalem, 1973-74; BASF vis. prof. U. Kaiserslautern, 1994; mem. com. on food stds. and fortification policy NAS-NCR, 1970-73; mem. adv. com. on biochemistry and chem. carcinogenesis Am. Cancer Soc., 1977-81; bd. sci. advisors divsn. cancer etiology, NCI, 1994-95, Frederick Cancer Sch. Facility, 1995—, Nat. Cancer Inst., 1989-93; mem. cancer spl. program adv. com., 1979-82; mem. peer rev. com. Nat. Toxicology Program, 1983-85; founder, bd. dirs. Vicam, Ltd., Partnership; mem. sci. adv. bd. Xenometrix, Inc., Transcend Pharmaceutics. Editor: (with R.I. Mateles) Single-Cell Protein, 1968, (with D.I.C. Wang) Single-Cell Protein II, 1975, (with others) The Economics, Marketing and Technology of Fish Protein Concentrate, 1974, (with J.R. Whitaker) Food Proteins, 1977, Nutritional Safety Aspects of Food Processing, 1979, (with others) Gastrointestinal Cancer: Endogenous Factors, 1981, (with R.A. Scanlan) N-Nitroso Compounds, 1981; mem. editl. bd. Japanese Jour. Cancer Rsch., 1986—, Chem. Rsch. Toxicology, 1988-91, 95—, Cancer Epidemiology, Prevention and Biomarkers, 1990—, Cancer Rsch., 1993—; contbr. over 300 articles to profl. jours. Mem. AAAS, Am. Chem. Soc., Inst. Food Technologists (sect. councillor N.E. chpt. 1966-69, Samuel Cate Prescott Rsch. award 1970, Babcock Hart award 1980), editorial bd. sci. jour. 1970-73, Am. Inst. Nutrition, Am. Assn. Cancer Rsch., Sigma Xi. Achievements include 7 U.S. patents. Office: MIT Dept Chemistry Toxicology Bldg 16 Rm 822a 77 Massachusetts Ave Cambridge MA 02139-4301 *Motto: Crisis equals danger plus opportunity.*

TANNENBERG, DIETER E. A., manufacturing company executive; b. Chevy Chase, Md., Nov. 24, 1932; s. E.A. Wilhelm and Margarete Elizabeth (Mundhenk) T.; m. Ruth Hansen, Feb. 6, 1956; 1 child, Diana Tannenberg Collingsworth Cann Marlinski. BSME, Northwestern U., 1959. Registered profl. engr., N.Y., Conn., Ohio, Ill., Ind., Wis., N.J. Supervising engr. Flexonics div. Calumet & Hecla, Inc., Chgo., 1959-61, chief engr., 1961-63, program mgr. advanced space systems, 1963-65, dir. mfg. services, 1965-67;

dir. mfg. engring. SCM Corp., Cortland, N.Y., 1967-69; tech. dir. internat. Singer Co., N.Y.C., 1969-71; v.p. ops. internat. div. Addressograph-Multigraph Corp., Cleve., 1971-74; mng. dir. Addressograph Multigraph GmbH, Frankfurt/Main, W. Ger., 1974-78; v.p., gen. mgr. Europe, Middle East, Africa AM Internat. Inc., Chgo., 1978-79; pres. AM Bruning div., 1979-82, AM Multigraphics Div., Mt. Prospect, Ill., 1982-86; corp. v.p. AM Internat., Inc., 1981-83, corp. sr. v.p., 1983-86; chmn. bd. dirs., pres., chief exec. officer Sargent-Welch Sci. Co., Skokie, Ill., 1986-89; pres., CEO ExhibitGroup, Inc., Elk Grove Village, Ill., 1990-91, Bell & Howell Document Mgmt. Products Co., Chgo., 1991-94, Bell & Howell Postal Sys. Inc., Chgo., 1994—; corp. v.p. Bell & Howell Co., Skokie, Ill., 1991—; chmn. AM Internat. GmbH, Frankfurt, 1977-86; bd. dirs. Gerard Daniel & Co., GDC Internat., Inc. Contbr. chpts. to handbooks, articles to tech., trade mags.; patentee in machinery field. Served with M.I., U.S. Army, 1953-56. Named Man of Yr. Quick Print Mag., 1985. Mem. NSPE, ASME, ASCE, Assn. Reprodn. Materials Mfrs. (bd. dirs. 1979-82, v.p. 1980-82), Nat. Assn. Quick Printers (bd. dirs. 1982-84), Nat. Printing Equipment and Supplies Mfg. Assn. (bd. dirs. 1983-86, chmn. govt. affairs com. 1985-86), Computer and Bus. Equipment Mfg. Assn. (bd. dirs. 1983-86, 91-93), Soc. Am. Value Engrs. (hon. v.p. 1985—), Value Found. (trustee 1985—), Chgo. Coun. Fgn. Rels., German-Am. C. of C. (Chgo.), Barrington Hills Country Club, Execs. Club of Chgo., Econ. Club, Pi Tau Sigma. Office: Bell & Howell Co 6800 N Mccormick Blvd Chicago IL 60645-2785

TANNENWALD, PETER, lawyer; b. Washington, Apr. 8, 1943; s. Judge Theodore and Selma (Peterfreund) T.; m. Carol B. Baum, May 25, 1969; 1 child, Jonathan Mark. AB, Brown U., 1964; LLB, Harvard Coll., 1967. Bar: U.S. Dist. Ct. D.C. 1968, U.S. Ct. Appeals (D.C. cir.) 1968, U.S. Supreme Ct. 1972. Assoc. Arent, Fox, Kintner, Plotkin & Kahn, Washington, 1967-74, ptnr., 1975-94; ptnr. Irwin, Campbell & Tannenwald, P.C., Washington, 1994—. Columnist The LPTV Report, 1988-92. Mem. cmty. coun. Sta. WAMU-FM, Washington, 1986-93, 94—; dir. Brown Broadcasting Svc., Inc., Providence, 1970—; chmn. maj. law firms divsn. Nat. Capital Area affiliate United Way, 1977-79. Mem. Harvard Law Sch. Assn. D.C. (pres. 1979-80), Harvard Law Sch. Assn. (sec. 1982-84). Avocations: electronics, photography. Office: Irwin Campbell Tannenwald Ste 200 1730 Rhode Island Ave NW Washington DC 20036-3101

TANNENWALD, THEODORE, JR., federal judge; b. Valatie, N.Y., July 28, 1916; s. Theodore and Myra (Barnet) T.; m. Selma Peterfreund, Aug. 3, 1940; children: Peter, Robert. A.B. summa cum laude, Brown U., 1936; LL.B. magna cum laude, Harvard U., 1939; D.L.L., U. Cin., 1976; D.H.L., Hebrew Union Coll., 1976. Bar: N.Y. 1939, D.C. 1946. Assoc. Weil, Gotshal & Manges, N.Y.C., 1939-42; ptnr. Weil, Gotshal & Manges, 1947-65; judge U.S. Tax Ct., Washington, 1965-81; chief judge U.S. Tax Ct., 1981-83, sr. judge, 1983—; prin. legal cons. Lend Lease Adminstrn., 1942; acting asst. chief, fgn. funds control divsn. Dept. State, 1942-43; spl. cons. sec. war, 1943-45, cons. sec. def., 1947-49, coun. to spl. asst. to pres., 1950-51; asst. dir., chief of staff to dir. for mut. security Exec. Office pres., 1951-53; spl. counsel to Moreland Commn., 1955-58; N.Y. mem. Tri-State Tax Commn., 1958-59; mem. Pres.'s Task Force on Fgn. Aid, spl. asst. to sec. state, 1961; professorial lectr. George Washington U. Sch. Law, 1968-76; lectr. Sch. Law U. Miami, 1976-85; disting. adj. prof. Sch. Law U. San Diego, 1985-90; adj. prof. Sch. Law U. Minn., 1996—. Hon. chmn., hon. mem. bd. govs. Hebrew Union Coll.-Jewish Inst. Religion; mem. nat. exec. coun. Am. Jewish Com. Mem. ABA, Fed. Bar Assn., D.C. Bar Assn., Am. Law Inst., Coun. Fgn. Rels., Cosmos Club (D.C.), Phi Beta Kappa. Office: US Tax Ct 400 2nd St NW Washington DC 20217-0001

TANNER, DANIEL, curriculum theory educator; b. N.Y.C., Sept. 22, 1926; s. Jack and Lillian (Jupiter) T.; m. Laurel Nan Jacobson, July 11, 1948 (div. 1988). BS with honors, Mich. State U., 1949, MS, 1952; Ph.D. (Univ. Scholar), Ohio State U., 1955. Asst. prof. edn. San Francisco State Coll., 1955-60; assoc. prof. edn., coord. Midwest program on airborne TV instrn. Purdue U., 1960-62; assoc. prof. edn., assoc. dir. internat. program for edn. leaders Northwestern U., 1962-64; assoc. prof. rsch. divsn. tchr. edn. City U. N.Y., 1964-66; prof. edn., dir. Ctr. for Urban Edn., U. Wis.-Milw. Sch. Edn., 1966-67; prof. edn., dir. grad. programs in curriculum theory and devel. Grad. Sch. Edn., Rutgers U., New Brunswick, N.J., 1967—; chmn. dept. curriculum and instrn. Grad. Sch. Edn., Rutgers U., 1969-71, faculty rsch. fellow, 1974-75, 88-89; vis. lectr. U. Kansas City, summer 1956, Tchrs. Coll. Columbia, summer 1966; vis. prof. Emory U., summer 1968, SUNY, Binghamton, winter 1968, U. London, 1975, King Abdulaziz U., Saudi Arabia, winter 1992; disting. lectr. ASCD, 1985, 86, Dewey Meml. lectr., 1984, Raths Meml. lectr., SUNY, 1984; Leadership Inst. lectr. U. Del., summer 1990; vis. scholar U. London Inst. Edn., 1974-75; mem. rev. bd. coll. work-study program U.S. Office Edn., 1965; mem. symposium on comparative curriculum history Inst. Sci. Edn. Kiel U., Fed. Republic Germany, 1989; cons. U. Tex. Med. Ctr., 1961-62, Chgo. Sch. Survey, 1964-65, ctr. Urban Edn., N.Y.C., 1964-65, West Chgo. Sch. Survey, 1963-64, Nat. Ednl. TV Ctr., N.Y.C., 1963, Campbell County (Va.) Sch. Survey, 1970, Memphis Schs., 1977-78, ASCD Commn. on Gen. Edn., 1980-81, West Orange, N.J., Curriculum Study, 1984, ASCD Commn. on Secondary Sch. Practices, 1985, ASCD Ednl. Policy Task Force, 1985, NASSP Curric Coun., 1985-95; SUNY Buffalo External Evaluation, 1988; dir. Nat. Curriculum Inst., 1987; delivered founder's day address Delaware Valley Coll., 1985. Author: Schools for Youth: Change and Challenge in Secondary Education, 1965, Secondary Curriculum: Theory and Development, 1971, Secondary Education: Perspectives and Prospects, 1972, Using Behavioral Objectives in the Classroom, 1972, Curriculum Development: Theory into Practice, 3rd edit., 1995, Supervision in Education, 1987, History of the School Curriculum, 1990, Crusade for Democracy: Progressive Educaiton at the Crossroads, 1991; contbg. author: Ann. Review of Rsch. for Sch. Leaders, 1996, Curriculum Issues, 187th Yearkbook NSSE, 1988, Ency. of Ednl. Rsch., 5th edit., 1982, Readings in Educaiton Psychology, 1965, Yearbook of the Association for Student Teaching, 1962, The Great Debate, Our Schools in Crisis, 1959, Educational Issues in a Changing Society, 1964, Programs, Teachers and Machines, 1964, View on American Schooling, 1964, The Training of America's Teachers, 1975, Curriculum and Instruction, 1981, Annual Review of Research for School Leaders, 1996; co-author: Teen Talk: Curriculum Materials in Communications, 1971; co-editor: Improving the School Curriculum, 1988, Restructuring for an Interdisciplinary Curriculum, 1992, Curriculum Issues and the New Century, 1995; contbg. editor: Ednl. Leadership, 1969-74; mem. editorial bd.: Tex. Tech. Jour. Edn., 1984-89, Teaching Edn., 1986-90, Jour. Curriculum Supervision; editorial cons.: Ency. of Ednl. Rsch., 5th edit., Jour. Ednl. Psychology; contbr. Atlantic Monthly Bull. of Atomic Scientists and other nat. mags., ednl. jours. Trustee Delaware Valley Coll., Doylestown, Pa., 1981-95; bd. dirs. Ohio State Alumni Assn. N.J., 1990—. Recipient Excellence award Edn. Press Am., 1989, Distinguished Educator award Rider U., 1996. Fellow AAAS, John Dewey Soc. (bd. dirs. 1985-88, archivist 1989—); mem. AAUP, Am. Ednl. Rsch. Assn., N.Y. Acad. Sci., Am. Polit. Sci. Assn., Am. Ednl. Studies Assn., Nat. Soc. Study Edn., Phi Kappa Phi, Phi Delta Kappa (Svc. award 1957). Home: Highwood Rd Somerset NJ 08873 Office: Grad Sch Edn Rutgers U New Brunswick NJ 08903 *The essential quality of education and life is growth. Hence problems must be seen as opportunities and not as limitations if solutions are to be found and progress is to be made.*

TANNER, DOUGLAS ALAN, lawyer; b. Palo Alto, Calif., Aug. 30, 1953; s. Bernard R. and Caroline (Orris) T.; m. Carol Scilacci, May 28, 1977; children: Lauren Elizabeth, Wynn Ann, Leigh Caroline. AB in History, Stanford U., 1974, MBA, 1978, JD, 1978. Bar: Calif. 1978, U.S. Dist. Ct. (no. dist.) Calif. 1978, U.S. Ct. Appeals (9th cir.) 1979, N.Y. 1987. Law clk. to judge U.S. Ct. Appeals (9th cir.), San Francisco, 1978-79; assoc. Orrick, Herrington & Sutcliffe, San Francisco, 1979-83; ptnr. Orrick, Herrington & Sutcliffe, San Jose, Calif., 1984-86, N.Y.C., 1986-89; ptnr. Milbank, Tweed, Hadley & McCloy, L.A., 1989-92, Hong Kong, 1992—. Mem. San Francisco Barristers (chmn. corps. com. 1981-82), Order of Coif, Phi Beta Kappa. Republican. Episcopalian. Home: Grenville House Apt G5, 1 Magazine Gap Rd, Hong Kong Hong Kong Office: Milbank Tweed Hadley & McCloy, 3007 Alexandra Hs/16 Chater Rd, Hong Kong Hong Kong

TANNER, HAROLD, investment banker; b. N.Y.C., May 7, 1932; s. Irving and Pauline (Steinlauf) T.; m. Estelle Newman, July 6, 1957; children: David, James, Karen. B.S., Cornell U., 1952; M.B.A., Harvard U., 1956. V.p., dir. Blyth & Co. Inc., N.Y.C., 1956-69; exec. v.p. New Court Securities Corp., N.Y.C., 1969-76, Blyth Eastman Dillon & Co., Inc., N.Y.C., 1977-80; ptnr. Salomon Bros. Inc., 1980-81, mng. dir., 1981-87; pres. Tanner & Co., Inc., N.Y.C., 1987—; co-founder Vol. Urban Cons. Group; dir. TIG Holdings, Inc. Vice-chmn. bd. trustees Cornell U., Russell Sage Found.; chmn. bd. trustees Am. Jewish Com. Lt. (j.g.) USNR, 1952-54. Mem. Coun. on Fgn. Rels., Century Country Club, Harmonie Club. Home: 18 Kensington Rd Scarsdale NY 10583-2217 Office: 650 Madison Ave New York NY 10022-1029

TANNER, HELEN HORNBECK, historian; b. Northfield, Minn., July 5, 1916; d. John Wesley and Frances Cornelia (Wolfe) Hornbeck; m. Wilson P. Tanner, Jr., Nov. 22, 1940 (dec. 1977); children: Frances, Margaret Tanner Tewson, Wilson P., Robert (dec. 1983). AB with honors, Swarthmore Coll., 1937; MA, U. Fla., 1949; PhD, U. Mich., 1961. Asst. to dir. pub. rels. Kalamazoo Pub. Schs., 1937-39; with sales dept. Am. Airlines Inc., N.Y.C., 1940-43; teaching fellow, then teaching asst. U. Mich., Ann Arbor, 1949-53, 57-60, lectr. extension svc., 1961-74, asst. dir. Ctr. Continuing Edn. for Women, 1964-68; project dir. Newberry Libr., Chgo., 1976-81, rsch. assoc., 1981-95, sr. rsch. fellow, 1995—; dir. D'Arcy McNickle Ctr. for Indian History, 1984-85; cons., expert witness Indian treaties; mem. Mich. Commn. Indian Affairs, 1966-70. Author: Zespedes in East Florida 1784-1790, 1963, 89, General Green Visits St. Augustine, 1964, The Greenevelle Treaty, 1974, The Territory of the Caddo Tribe of Oklahoma, 1974, The Ojibwas, 1992; editor: Atlas of Great Lakes Indian History, 1987, The Settling of North America: An Atlas, 1995. NEH grantee, 1976, fellow, 1989; ACLS grantee, 1990. Mem. Am. Soc. Ethnohistory (pres. 1982-83), Am. Hist. Assn., Conf. Latin Am. History, Soc. History Discoveries, Orgn. Am. Historians, Chgo. Map Soc., Fla. Hist. Soc. Home: 5178 Crystal Dr Beulah MI 49617-9618 Office: The Newberry Libr 60 W Walton St Chicago IL 60610-3305

TANNER, JACK EDWARD, federal judge; b. 1919; m. Glenda M. Martin; children: Maryetta J. Greaves, Donnetta M. Gillum. Sole practice Tacoma, 1955-78; judge U.S. Dist. Ct. (we. dist.) Wash., Tacoma, 1978—, now sr. judge. Mem. Nat. Bar Assn. Office: US Dist Ct 1102 A St Tacoma WA 98402

TANNER, JIMMIE EUGENE, college dean; b. Hartford, Ark., Sept. 27, 1933; s. Alford C. and Hazel Ame (Anthony) T.; m. Carole Joy Yant, Aug. 28, 1958; children—Leslie Allison, Kevin Don. BA, Okla. Baptist U., 1955; MA, U. Okla., 1957, PhD, 1964. Assoc. prof. English, Franklin Coll., Ind., 1964-65; prof. English, Okla. Bapt. U., Shawnee, 1958-64, 65-72; v.p. acad. affairs Hardin-Simmons U., Abilene, Tex., 1972-78, La. Coll., Pineville, 1978-80; dean William Jewell Coll., Liberty, Mo., 1980—, interim pres., 1993-94. Contbr.: The Annotated Bibliography of D.H. Lawrence, Vol. 1, 1982, Vol. 2, 1985. Mem. Shawnee Sch. Bd., 1966-72; mem. edn. commn. So. Bapt. Conv., 1967-72. So. Fellowships Fund fellow, 1960-61; Danforth fellow, 1962-63. Mem. AAUP, Am. Assn. for Higher Edn. Democrat. Baptist. Avocations: tennis; photography. Home: 609 Lancelot Dr Liberty MO 64068-1023 Office: William Jewell Coll Office Provost Liberty MO 64068 *As I reflect on my life, the thought that presses on me is my incredible luck at having been born in America in the 20th century, my good fortune in having the opportunity for education, for a satisfying career, for supportive family, friends, mentors at every stage of my life. I must recognize any accomplishment as communal as well as individual.*

TANNER, JOHN D., real estate developer, contractor; b. Calgary, Alta., Can., Feb. 2, 1939; came to U.S., 1956; s. Earl Pingree and Betty (Bridge) T.; m. Barbara Steed, Dec. 27, 1965; children: Jeffrey, Scott, Daniel, David, William, Joanna, Trisha. BS, Brigham Young U., 1965. Constrn. engr. Tide Water Oil Co., Sacramento, Calif., 1965-67; regional constrn. engr. Phillips Petroleum Co., Inc., San Francisco, 1967-69; mgr., v.p. Staiger Constrn. Co., Inc., Sacramento, 1969-71, owner, pres., 1971-76; owner, pres. Tanner Industries, Inc., Roseville, Calif., 1972—, Western Single Ply. Nev., Inc., Las Vegas, 1987—, Western Single Ply. Calif. Inc., Loomis, 1981—. Pres. sch. bd. dirs. Eureka Sch. Dist., Granite Bay, Calif., 1987—. Mem. Granite Bay Golf Club (founding mem.). Republican. Mem. LDS Ch. Home: 7150 J Bar B Dr Granite Bay CA 95746-9453

TANNER, JOHN S., congressman, lawyer; b. Dyersburg, Tenn., Sept. 22, 1944; s. E.B. and Edith (Summers) T.; m. Betty Ann Portis, Sept. 2, 1967; children: Elizabeth Tanner Atkins, John Portis. BS, U. Tenn., 1966, JD, 1968. Bar: Tenn., 1968. Mem. Tenn. Ho. of Reps., 1976-88, 101st-104th Congresses from 8th Tenn. dist., Washington, 1988—; mem. Nat. Security Commn., Sci. Commn. Active Obion County Cancer Soc.; bd. visitors USAF Acad.; founding mem. The Coalition; former chmn. bd. visitors U.S. Mil. Acad. Lt. USN, 1968-72; col. Tenn. Army N.G., 1974—. Mem. Obion County C. of C., Obion County Bar Assn., Rotary. Democrat. Disciples of Christ. Avocations: golf, hunting. Office: US House of Reps 1127 Longworth House Washington DC 20515

TANNER, LAUREL NAN, education educator; b. Detroit, Feb. 16, 1929; d. Howard Nicholas and Celia (Solvich) Jacobson; m. Daniel Tanner, July 11, 1948; m. Kenneth J. Rehage, Nov. 25, 1989. BS in Social Sci, Mich. State U., 1949, MA in Edn., 1953; EdD, Columbia U., 1967. Pub. sch. tchr., 1950-64; instr. tchr. edn. Hunter Coll., 1964-66, asst. prof., 1967-69; supr. Milw. Pub. Schs., 1966-67; mem. faculty Temple U., Phila., 1969—; prof. edn. Temple U., 1974-89, U. Houston, 1989—; vis. professorial scholar U. London Inst. Edn., 1974-75; vis. scholar Stanford U., 1984-85, U. Chgo., 1988-89; curriculum cons., 1969—; disting. vis. prof. San Francisco State U., 1987. Author: Classroom Discipline for Effective Teaching and Learning, 1978, La Disciplina en la enseñanza y el Aprendizaje, 1980; co-author: Classroom Teaching and Learning, 1971, Curriculum Development: Theory into Practice, 1975, 3d edit., 1995, Supervision in Education: Problems and Practices, 1987, (with Daniel Tanner) History of the School Curriculum, 1990; editor Nat. Soc. Study Edn. Critical Issues in Curriculum, 87th yearbook, part 1, 1988. Faculty rsch. fellow Temple U., 1970, 80, 81; recipient John Dewey Rsch. award, 1981-82, Rsch. Excellence award U. Houston, 1992; Spencer Found. rsch. grantee, 1992. Mem. ASCD (dir. 1982-84), Soc. Study Curriculum History (founder, 1st pres. 1978-79), Am. Edn. Rsch. Assn. (com. on role and status of women in ednl. R & D 1994—), Profs. Curriculum Assn. (Factotum 1983-84, chair membership com. 1994-95), Am. Ednl. Studies Assn., John Dewey Soc. (bd. dirs. 1989-91), Alumni Coun. Tchrs. Coll. Columbia U. *In my view, America has progressed over the years, and the best days are still to come. We have the single necessary resource to solve our most urgent problems and achieve our deepest moral values —human intelligence.*

TANNER, PATRICIA RUTH, gerontology nurse; b. Trego, Mont., July 30, 1935; d. Elmer E. and Jennie M. (Dukeshire) Pomeroy; children: Michael F. Ehart, Crystal Y. Blair, Karen Alexander. AS, Walla Walla (Wash.) County Coll., 1973. Dir. nursing edn. Desert Palms Convalescent Hosp., Indio, Calif.; dir. nursing svc. Leisure Lodge, Mountain Home, Ark.; day charge nurse Hill Brook Nursing Home, Clancy, Mont.; charge and staff relief nurse Nursing Profls. Inc. Nursing Agy., Yakima, Wash., 1989-92; charge nurse Selah (Wash.) Convalescent Facility, 1991-92; med. and treatment on-call nurse Yakima Convalescent, 1993-94, med. and treatment nurse, 1995—; part-time and on-call nurse, resident care coord. Chinook Convalescent Ctr., 1994—, p.m. charge nurse, 1995—; resident care coord., staff devel., infection control nurse Selah Convalescent, 1995; p.m. medication nurse Yakima (Wash.) Convalescent, 1995—. Mem. Wash. State Nurse's Assn., Nightingale Soc. (pres.). Home: 1411 Naches Heights Rd Yakima WA 98908-8849 Office: Yakima Convalescent Ctr 818 W Yakima Ave Yakima WA 98902

TANNER, R. MARSHALL, lawyer; b. Santa Monica, Calif., Dec. 4, 1946; s. Stanley Robert and Kathryn (Lau) Tanner; m. Colleen Bonner, Sept. 3, 1969; children: David, Brent, Julie, Glenn, Scott, Holly. BA, Brigham Young U., 1970; JD, UCLA, 1977. Ptnr. Lawler, Felix & Hall, L.A., 1977-86, Pettit & Martin, Newport Beach, Calif., 1986-95, Sheppard, Mullin, Richter & Hampton, 1995—. Lt. USNR, 1970-74. Mem. Calif. State Bar Assn., Orange County Bar Assn. Mem. LDS Ch. Office: Sheppard Mullin Richter & Hampton 4695 Macarthur Ct # 7 Newport Beach CA 92660-1882

TANNER, ROBERT HUGH, engineer, consultant; b. London, July 22, 1915; s. George John and Evelyn (Stratton) T.; m. Joan Margaret Garnham, July 6, 1940; children: Christopher John, Rosemary June, Peter Pinckney, David Stephen. BS in Engring., U. London, 1936, MS in Engring., 1962; LLD, Concordia U., 1989. Registered profl. engr., Eng., Can., Fla. From TV to rsch. engr. BBC, London, 1936-47; from engr. to dir. info. No. Electric Co., Ltd., Ottawa, Can., Ont., 1947-70; dir. info. Bell-No. Rsch., Ottawa, Can., Ont., 1970-72; pres. IEEE, N.Y.C., 1972; dir. indsl. rsch. Can. Dept. Comm., Ottawa, 1973-75; pvt. practice cons. engr. Naples, Fla., 1975—; cons. in field. Inventor various patents. Maj. Brit. Army, 1939-45, ETO. Fellow IEEE (pres. 1972, McNaughton Gold medal 1974, Pratt award 1981, Award for Engring Professionalism, 1993), Acoustical Soc. Am., Engring. Inst. Can., Instn. of Elec. Engrs.; mem. Nat. Coun. Acoustical Cons. (bd. dirs. 1982-88). Episcopalian. Office: PO Box 655 Naples FL 33939-0655

TANNER, TRAVIS, travel company executive; b. 1951. With So. Airlines, Inc., Ft. Lauderdale, Fla., 1972-79, Republic Airlines Inc., Mpls., 1984-90, Walt Disney Travel Co. Inc., Orlando, Fla.; pres. Carlson Travel Group, Inc., Mpls., 1990—; pres., CEO Carlson Wagonlit Travel, Mpls., 1990—. Office: Carlson Travel Group Inc Carlson Pkwy 701 Tower Minneapolis MN 55459

TANNER, W(ALTER) RHETT, lawyer; b. Athens, Ga., May 16, 1938; s. John Bryson and Walterette (Arwood) T.; m. Carolyn Laverne Watson, Nov. 11, 1967; 1 child, Walter Rhett (dec. 1989). A.B. cum laude, U. Ga., 1960, J.D. cum laude, 1962. Bar: Ga. 1961. Assoc. firm Hansell, Post, Bandon & Dorsey, Atlanta, 1963-66; ptnr. Hansell, Post, Bandon & Dorsey, 1966-89; ptnr. Jones, Day, Reavis & Pogue, Atlanta, 1989-95, of counsel, 1995—. Bd. dirs. Atlanta Symphony Orch., 1975—, mem. exec. com., 1977-86, v.p., 1978, chmn. maj. gifts campaign, 1980; mem. Leadership Atlanta, 1980, Leadership Ga., 1982; bd. visitors Grady Meml. Hosp., 1983—; bd. dirs. Econ. Opportunity Atlanta, 1986-87; trustee Ga. Legal History Found., 1986—. Lt. comdr. USNR, 1964-72. Mem. ABA, Atlanta Bar Assn. (bd. dirs. 1982-87, exec. com. 1983-87), State Bar Ga. (vice chmn. bar and media com. 1979-82), Atlanta Bar Found. (trustee 1985-91), U. Ga. Alumni (pres. chpt. 1973-74, chmn. Atlanta/Met. coun. 1975, mem. state bd. mgrs., v.p. 1976-78), Atlanta Lawyers Club, Gridiron, Phi Beta Kappa, Omicron Delta Kappa, Phi Kappa Phi, Phi Delta Phi, Delta Tau Delta. Club: Capital City. Office: Jones Day Reavis & Pogue 3500 One Peachtree Ctr 303 Peachtree St NE Atlanta GA 30308-3242

TANNIAN, FRANCIS XAVIER, economist, educator; b. Boston, Dec. 5, 1933; s. John Joseph and Marie (Killian) T.; m. Beatrix Laube, May 19, 1962; children—Monica, Margaret Joyce, Mark, Michele. B.A., Boston Coll., 1955, M.A., 1959; Ph.D., U. Va., 1965. Bus trainee Gen. Electric Co., Schenectady, 1955-56; asst. prof. econs. Duquesne U., Pitts., 1962-66; assoc. prof. econs. U. Del., Newark, 1967-72, prof. urban econs., 1972—, assoc. dean, 1978-79; vis. prof. U. Stuttgart, Fed. Republic Germany, 1972-73, U. Karlsruhe, Fed. Republic Germany, 1982, San Diego State U., 1989, U. Nitra, Czechoslovakia, 1990; cons. Fed. Water Pollution and Control Adminstrn., 1965-68, Deutsche Gesellschaft, Frankfurt, Fed. Republic Germany, 1982-83; lectr. urban studies U.S. Dept. State, Budapest, Bucharest, Belgrade, 1975; guest lectr. Czechoslovakian Acad. Scis., 1975. Editor: Externalities, 1972; contbr. articles to profl. jours. Mem. Del. Gov.'s Econ. Adv. Council, 1969-72; bd. dirs. Del. OIC, Wilmington, 1970-78; bd. dirs. Parity Econ. Devel. Corp., Wilmington, 1978-84; mem. Wilmington Mayor's Econ. Devel. Com., 1976-82. Served with U.S. Army, 1957-58. Mem. Am. Econ. Assn., So. Econs. Assn., Am. Real Estate and Urban Econs. Assn. Democrat. Roman Catholic. Home: 910 Baylor Dr Newark DE 19711-3128 Office: U Del Coll Urban Affairs Newark DE 19711

TANOUS, PETER JOSEPH, banker; b. N.Y.C., May 21, 1938; s. Joseph Carrington and Rose Marie (Mokarzel) T.; BA in Econs., Georgetown U., 1960; m. Barbara Ann MacConnell, Aug. 18, 1962; children: Christopher, Helene, William. With Smith, Barney & Co., Inc. (now Smith Barney, Inc.), N.Y.C., 1963-78, 2d v.p., mgr. Paris office, 1967, v.p., 1968-78, resident European sales mgr., Paris, 1969-71, internat. sales mgr., N.Y.C., 1971-78, 1st v.p., 1975-78; chmn. bd. Petra Capital Corp., N.Y.C., 1978-81, dir.; pres. Lynx Investment Advisory Inc., Washington, 1992—; exec. v.p., Bank Audi (USA), N.Y.C., 1984-92; del. U.S.-Saudi Arabian Joint Econ. Commn. Bus. Dialogue; trustee Browning Sch., N.Y.C., 1987-93; bd. dirs. Cedars Bank, L.A., Interstate Resources, Inc., Rosslyn, Va. Chmn. Am. Task Force for Lebanon, Washington, 1988-91; bd. advisors Coll. Arts and Scis. Georgetown U. 1st lt. AUS, 1961-63. Recipient Medal of Honor Ellis Island, 1994. Mem. Am. Geographical Soc. (councillor), Georgetown U. Alumni Assn. (gov. 1968-71), Georgetown Club France (pres. 1968-71). Roman Catholic. Clubs: Met. (N.Y.C.), University (Washington); Automobile de France (Paris). Author: The Earhart Mission, 1979; co-author: The Petrodollar Takeover, 1975, The Wheat Killing, 1979. Earhart Mission, 1979. Office: 1100 Connecticut Ave NW Washington DC 20036-4101

TANPHAICHITR, KONGSAK, rheumatologist, allergist, immunologist, internist; b. Bangkok, Feb. 22, 1946; came to U.S., 1971; s. Boonchoo and Hong (Nayakovit) T.; m. Sirirat Tareesung, June 17, 1973; children: Saksiri Marc, Marisa. Student, Mahidol U., Bangkok, Thailand, 1964-66, MD cum laude, 1970. Diplomate Am. Bd. Internal Medicine, Am. Bd. Rheumatology, Am. Bd. Allergy and Immunology; cert. Rheumatologist Royal Coll. Physicians Can. Straight med. intern Detroit Gen. Hosp.-Wayne State U., 1971-72; resident Barnes Hosp.-Washington U., St. Louis, 1972-74, fellow in rheumatology and immunology, 1974-76; instr. in medicine Washington U., St. Louis, 1976-77, asst. prof. medicine, 1977—; attending physician Barnes Hosp., St. Louis, 1976—, Jewish Hosp. of St. Louis, 1981—; dir. Allergy, Rheumatology & Immunology Specialists, St. Louis; cons. rheumatology Washington U., St. Louis, 1976—. Author: Amyloid Fibrils in Joint Fluid, 1976, Studies of Tolerance in NZB/NZW Mice, 1977, Vasculitis and Multiple Sclerosis, 1980, Buddhism and Science, 1987, Buddhism: Answers to Common Questions, 1990, Buddhism Answers Life, 1995. Dharma tchr., bd. dirs., sec. Wat Phrasriratanaram Buddhist Temple, St. Louis, 1983—; co-dir. Buddhist Coun., St. Louis, 1985-90. Fellow ACP, Am. Acad. Allergy and Immunology, Am. Coll. Rheumatology, Royal Coll. Physicians Can.; mem. Thai Physicians Assn. Am. (treas. Midwest chpt. 1994), Thai Assn. Greater St. Louis (pres.), Thai Temple Karate Shorinryu Club (Black Belt). Avocations: karate, karaoke, insight meditation, swimming. Home: 12413 Ladue Rd Saint Louis MO 63141-8100 Office: Allergy Rheum & Immun Specs 11115 New Halls Ferry Rd Saint Louis MO 63033-7613

TANSELLE, GEORGE THOMAS, English language educator, foundation executive; b. Lebanon, Ind., Jan. 29, 1934; s. K. Edwin and Madge R. (Miller) T. BA magna cum laude, Yale U., 1955; MA, Northwestern U., 1956, PhD, 1959. Instr. Chgo. City Jr. Coll., 1958-60; instr. U. Wis., Madison, 1960-61, asst. prof., 1961-63, assoc. prof., 1963-68, prof. English, 1968-78; v.p. John Simon Guggenheim Meml. Found., 1978—; adj. prof. English and comparative lit. Columbia U., 1980—; mem. Planning Inst. Commn. on English, 1961; mem. exec. com. Ctr. for Edits. Am. Authors, 1970-73; mem. adv. com. for drama for bicentennial Kennedy Ctr., 1974-76; mem. Soviet-Am. symposium on editing Ind. U., 1976; mem. adv. com. Howells Meml., Kittery Point, 1976-78; exec. com. Ctr. for Scholarly Edits., 1976-81; mem. nat. adv. bd. Ctr. for Book, Libr. of Congress, 1978—; mem. adv. bd. Burton's Anatomy of Melancholy, 1978—, Pub. and Printing History, A Guide to Manuscript Resources in the U.S., 1980—; bd. dirs. Lit. Classics of U.S., Inc., 1979—, chmn. editl. standards com., 1979—, corp. sec., 1989—; mem. adv. com. N.Am. imprints program, 1980-92; Hanes lectr. U. N.C., 1981; mem. adv. coun. Rosenbach Mus. and Libr., 1980—; mem. adv. coun. Ind. U. Inst. Adv. Study, 1983—; mem. faculty Summer Rare Book Sch., Columbia U., 1984—; mem. adv. bd. Ctr. for Am. Culture Studies, Columbia U., 1985-94; mem. adv. coun. Am. Trust for the Brit. Libr., 1987—; Rosenbach lectr. U. Pa., 1987; mem. adv. coun. Am. Literary Manuscripts project, 1988—; bd. dirs. 18th Century Short-Title Catalogue/N.Am., Inc., 1988—, chmn., 1994—, Mark Twain Edition Project, 1991—; mem. vis. com. Lilly Libr., 1988-92; mem. adv. bd. Ctr. for Renaissance and Baroque Studies, U. Md., 1990—; mem. adv. com. Writings of J.F. Cooper, 1990—. Author: Royall Tyler, 1967, Guide to the Study of United States Imprints, 1971, A Checklist of Editions of Moby-Dick, 1976, Selected Studies in Bibliography, 1979, The History of Books as a Field of Study, 1981, Textual Criticism since Greg, 1987, A Rationale of Textual Criticism, 1989, Parkman Dexter Howe Library, Hawthorne and Melville, 1989, Textual Criticism and Scholarly Editing, 1990, Libraries, Museums, and Reading, 1991, A Description of Descriptive Bibliography, 1992, The Life and Work of Fredson Bowers, 1993; co-editor: The Writings of Herman Melville, 1968—, Samuel Johnson's Translation of Sallust, 1993; editor: Library of Am. Melville, 1982-83, Books as a Way of Life: Essays by Gordon N. Ray, 1988; mem. editorial bd. Contemporary Literature, 1962-91, Abstracts of English Studies, 1964-78, Papers of Bibliog. Soc. Am, 1968-80, Resources for American Literary Study, 1971—, Analytical and Enumerative Bibliography, 1977—, Review, 1978—, Am. Literature, 1979-82, Literary Research, 1986-90, Common Knowledge, 1991—; contbr. articles to books and profl. jours. Mem. coun. Friends of Columbia U. Librs., 1990-94; bd. dirs. Friends of Lilly Libr., 1990-92. Recipient Kiekhofer Teaching award U. Wis., 1963, Jenkins award for bibliography, 1973; Guggenheim fellow, 1969-70; Am. Council Learned Socs. fellow, 1973-74; Nat. Endowment for the Humanities fellow, 1977-78, Laureate award Am. Printing History Assn., 1987. Mem. MLA (mem. exec. com. bibliog. evidence group 1974-75, methods of lit. rsch. div. 1979-83, chmn. 1982, mem. Hubbell award Com. Am. lit. sect. 1978-82, chmn. 1982, mem. com. on prize for ind. scholars 1983-87, chmn. 1985-87, chmn. ad hoc com. on future of print record 1993-95), Modern Humanities Rsch. Assn., Bibliog. Soc. London (pres. Am. Friends 1992—), Bibliog. Soc. Australia, Bibliog. Soc. Am. (mem. council 1970-94, vice chmn. publs. com. 1974-76, chmn. 1981-84, sec. 1976-78, chmn. com. on regional groups, 1978-80, 2d v.p. 1978-80, 1st v.p. 1980-82, pres. 1984-88), Bibliog. Soc. U. Va. (pres. 1992—), Oxford, Cambridge, Edinburgh, Birmingham, No. Ill., Can. bibliog. socs., Soc. for Bibliography of Natural History, Printing Hist. Soc. (Am. corr. 1970-84), Am. Prstee N.Y. chpt. 1979-85), Pvt. Librs. Assn., Ind. Research Libraries Assn. (com. on standards for rare book cataloging in machine-readable form 1978-79), Fellows Morgan Libr., Manuscript Soc. (bd. dirs. 1974-79), Am. Pub. Libr. Film Project (bd. advisors 1993—), Am. Antiquarian Soc. (mem. publs. com. 1972-81, chmn. com. 1978-81, mem. council 1974-92, hon. councillor, 1992—, del. to Am. Coun. Learned Socs. 1978-93, exec. com. dels., 1987-89, chmn. exec. com. program on book in Am. culture 1983-89, com. on edn., 1982-85, chmn., 1983-85, chmn. com. on libr. 1988-91), Soc. Textual Scholarship (adv. bd. 1979—, pres. 1981-83), The Johnsonians (chmn. 1993), Melville Soc. (pres. 1982), Book Club Calif., Typophiles, Guild Book Workers, Wis. Acad. Scis., Arts and Letters, Renaissance Soc. Am., Am. Soc. 18th-Century Studies, Renaissance English Text Soc., Assn. Documentary Editing (chmn. Julian Boyd award com. 1986, Boydston award com. 1995), Soc. Scholarly Pub., Assn. internationale de bibliophilie, Soc. History of Authorship, Reading and Publishing (bd. dirs. 1993—), Phi Beta Kappa. Clubs: Century, Yale, Caxton, Grolier (publs. com. 1979-82, 83-87, council 1980—, small exhbns. com. 1979-87, chmn. 1980-82, sec. 1982-86, chmn. library com. 1985-86, pres. 1986-90), Odd Volumes. Office: John Simon Guggenheim Meml Found 90 Park Ave New York NY 10016

TANSILL, FREDERICK JOSEPH, lawyer; b. Washington, Feb. 27, 1948; s. Frederick Riker and Mary Eileen (Loftus) T.; m. Joan Louise Trefsgar, July 10, 1971; children: Brendan Frederick, Brooke Charlotte, Charlotte Trefsgar. BA with honors, Brown U., 1970; JD, Georgetown U., 1974, LLM in Taxation, 1982. Bar: D.C. 1974, U.S. Tax Ct. 1976, Va. 1983. Assoc. Cross, Murphy & Smith, Washington, 1974-77; ptnr. Bird & Tansill, Washington, 1977-79; assoc. Ober, Grimes & Shriver, Washington, 1979-81; ptnr. Lewis, Mitchell & Moore, Vienna, Va., 1981-86; counsel Boothe, Prichard & Dudley, McLean, Va., 1986-87; ptnr. McGuire, Woods, Battle & Boothe, McLean, 1987-90; shareholder Verner, Liipfert, Bernhard, McPherson & Hand, Chartered, McLean, 1990—; bd. dirs. Atlantic Trust Co. Fellow Am. Coll. Trust and Estate Counsel; mem. ABA, Va. Bar Assn. (coun. taxation sect. 1989-92, coun. and legis. com. wills sect. 1993—, trusts and estates sect. 1983—, bd. govs. 1988—, chmn. bd. govs. 1991-92, co-chmn. spl. task force lawyers as fiduciaries 1993-95), D.C. Bar Assn. (steering com. estates, trusts and probate law sects. 1995—), Fairfax County Bar Assn. (chmn. will sect. 1986, chmn. tax sect. 1987-88, CLE com. 1988-89), No. Va. Estate Planning Coun. (exec. com. 1987-92, pres. 1990-91), Tower Club (bd. dirs. 1988—). Office: Verner Liipfert Bernhard McPherson & Hand 8280 Greensboro Dr Fl 6 Mc Lean VA 22102-3807

TANSILL, FREDERICK RIKER, retired judge; b. Washington, July 12, 1914; s. Frederick Guida and Elizabeth Estele (Riker) T.; m. Mary Eileen Loftus, Dec. 31, 1940; children: Claire Tansill Hermann, Constance Tansill Gelfuso, Fred, Celine Tansill Kramer, Eileen Tansill Suddath. BSS, Georgetown U., 1936, JD, 1941; postgrad., Benjamin Franklin U., 1951-53. Bar: D.C. 1940. Credit reporter Dun & Bradstreet, Washington, 1938; instr. R.O.T.C., Georgetown U., 1940-42; spl. atty. IRS, N.Y.C., 1945-48; ptnr. Goodwin, Rosenbaum & Meacham, Washington, 1948-68, Cox, Langford & Brown, Washington, 1968-69, McInnis, Wilson, Munson & Woods, Washington, 1969-72, Bird & Tansill, Washington, 1972-79, Ober, Grimes & Shriver, Balt. and Washington, 1979-80; spl. trial judge U.S. Tax Ct., 1980-86; sole practice Washington, 1986—; instr. tax Ben Franklin U., 1956-57, instr. econs., 1967; appointed hearing examiner of two cases Legal Svcs. Corp., 1987, 89. Acting gen. counsel Children to Children, Inc., Washington, 1975-79; bd. dirs. Woodley Park Community Assn., Washington, 1968-76, v.p., 1975-76; pres. parish council Roman Cath. ch., 1973-76, 78-79. Served with AUS, 1940-45. Mem. ABA, Fed. Bar Assn., D.C. Bar Assn., Bar Assn. D.C., Delta Theta Phi. Republican. Home: 3001 Veazey Ter NW Apt 516 Washington DC 20008-5401

TANSOR, ROBERT HENRY, investor; b. Chgo., Apr. 1, 1935; s. John S. and Leora Caroline (Buhmann) T.; m. Stephanie Trainor, Sept. 10, 1977; children: John Frederick, Adam Robert. BS, Northwestern U., 1957. CPA, Ill., N.J. Sr. acct. Arthur Young & Co., Chgo., 1961-65; mem. corp. staff Litton Industries, 1965-67; v.p. fin., controller Royal Typewriter Co., Conn., 1968-72, Sweda Internat. div. Litton Industries, Pinebrook, N.J., 1973-75; v.p. fin., adminstrn. Paramount Pictures Corp., N.Y.C., 1975-77, Otis Elevator Corp., Farmington, Conn., 1977-83; v.p. fin., chief fin. officer Gulton Industries Inc., Princeton, N.J., 1983-86; sr. v.p., treas., chief fin. officer The Polymer Corp., Reading, Pa., 1986-89; pvt. investor, 1989—. Served to lt. (j.g.) USN, 1957-61; ret. comdr. USNR, 1980. Mem. AICPA, Ill. CPA Soc., Fin. Execs. Inst., Navy League U.S. Republican. Roman Catholic. Avocations: golf, swimming, theater, music.

TANUR, JUDITH MARK, sociologist, educator; b. Jersey City, Aug. 12, 1935; d. Edward Mark and Libbie (Berman) Mark; m. Michael Isaac Tanur, June 2, 1957; children: Rachel Dorothy, Marcia Valerie. BS, Columbia U., 1957, MA, 1963; PhD, SUNY, Stony Brook, 1972. Analyst Biometrics Rsch., N.Y.C., 1955-67; lectr. SUNY, Stony Brook, 1967-71, from asst. prof. to prof. sociology, 1971-94, disting. teaching prof., 1994—; cons. NBC, N.Y.C., 1976-89, Lang. of Data Project, Los Altos, Calif., 1980-89, Inst. for Rsch. on Learning, 1994-95; mem. Com. on Nat. Stats. of NAS, 1980-87; trustee NORC, U. Chgo., 1987—. Editor: Statistics: A Guide to the Unknown, 1972, Internat. Encyclopedia of Statistics, 1978, Cognitive Aspects of Survey Methodology, 1984, Questions About Questions, 1991; editor Internat. Ency. of Social Scis., N.Y.C., 1963-67; contbr. articles to sci., statis. and social sci. jours. Bd. dirs. Vis. Nurse Svc., Great Neck, N.Y., 1970—; bd. govs. Gen. Soc. Survey, Chgo., 1989-92. Sr. rsch. fellow, Am. Statis. Assn./NSF/Bur. Labor Statistics, 1988-89. Fellow, AAAS, Am. Statis. Assn.; mem. Internat. Statis. Inst., Phi Beta Kappa. Home: 17 Longview Pl Great Neck NY 11021-2508 Office: SUNY Dept Sociology Stony Brook NY 11794

TANZER, LESTER, editor; b. N.Y.C., Aug. 3, 1929; s. Charles and Clara (Ente) T.; m. Marlene June Luckton, June 29, 1949; children—Stephen Drew, Jeffrey Marc, Andrew Wayne, M. David. A.B., Columbia U., 1951, M.S., Sch. Journalism, 1952. Reporter, Washington bur. Wall St. Jour., 1952-59; assoc. editor Changing Times mag., Washington, 1959-64; assoc. editor U.S. News & World Report, Washington, 1964-76, mng. editor, 1976-85; editor Cosmos Jour., 1990-93. Author: (with Stefan Ilok) Brotherhood of Silence, 1962; editor: The Kennedy Circle, 1961. Mem. Nat. Symphony Assn. Club: Cosmos. Home: 4859 30th St N Arlington VA 22207-2715

TANZI, CAROL ANNE, interior designer; b. San Francisco, Apr. 9, 1942; d. Raymond Edward and Anne Marie Giorgi. BA, U. San Jose, Calif., 1966. Teaching credential, Calif.; cert. interior designer, Calif. Home furnishings coord. R.H. Macy's, San Francisco, 1966-72; owner, pres. Carol A. Tanzi & Assocs., Burlingame, Calif., 1972—; instr. interior design Recreational Ctrs., Burlingame/Foster City, Calif., 1972-85; design cons. Am. Cancer Soc., San Mateo, Calif., 1994-95; mem. adv. com. for interior design students Coll. San Mateo, 1984-87; head designer San Mateo Battered Women's Shelter Pro Bono, 1993. Interior designer mags. Sunset, 1982, House Beautiful, 1992, 1001 Home Ideas, 1983; monthly cable TV program Interior Deesign by Tanzi, 1994—. Pres. Aux. to Mission Hospice, Burlingame, 1988-89, Hist. Soc. Burlingame, 1992-93; v.p. Cmty. for Edn., Burlingame, 1993-94; mem. adv. com. Breast Ctr./Mills Peninsula Hosp., 1994-95; mem. Oaks His. Adv. Bd., 1993—; commr., pres. San Mateo County Commn. on Status of Women, 1990-95. Recipient Recogniton of Outstanding Performance Rotary Club of Burlingame, 1988—, Congl. Recognition U.S.A., Burlingame, 1994, Commendation Bd. Suprs., County of San Mateo, 1994, Recognition Calif. Legis. Assembly, Burlingame, 1994; named Superior Interior Designer Bay Area San Francisco Examiner, 1991, Woman of Distinction Soroptimist Internat., Burlingame/San Mateo, 1994. Mem. Am. Soc. Interior Designers (v.p. 1988, Presdl. Citation for disting. svc. 1986, 87, 88, Calif. Peninsula Chpt. Design award 1995), Burlingame C. of C. Women's Forum (chair 1986-95), Rotary Club of Burlingame (sec. 1988—). Avocations: miniatures, reading, exercising, basketball. Home: 1528 Columbus Ave Burlingame CA 94010-5512 Office: Carol A Tanzi & Assocs PO Box 117281 Burlingame CA 94011-7281

TANZMANN, VIRGINIA WARD, architect; b. Tuxedo, N.Y., July 6, 1945; d. John A. Ward and Helen Pfund. BA in Architecture, Syracuse U., 1968, BArch, 1969. Registered architect, Calif., Nev., NCARB. Intern architect Burke Kober Nicolais Archuleta, Los Angeles, 1969-72; project architect Daniel L. Dworsky & Assocs., Los Angeles, 1972-74, SUA, Inc., Los Angeles, 1974-75; staff architect So. Calif. Rapid Transit Dist., L.A., 1975-78; prin. The Tanzmann Assocs., L.A., 1978—. Prin. works, clients, include transp. facilities, retail stores, comml. and office facilities 8 railroad stations, L.A. MTA Red and Blue Lines, L.A. Metro North Hollywood Sta., Conv. Ctr. Expansion Team, Renovation of Hollywood Bowl, Petroleum Lab. Chevron USA, Inc., El Segundo, Calif., Hyperion Treatment Plant, UCLA Med. Ctr., L.A. Unified Sch. Dist., L.A. Mission, So. Calif. Gas Co. Valencia, Gas Co. Computer Ctr., L.A. Dept. Water and Power, Oxnard Housing Authority, L.A. Housing Authority. Work exhibited: Monterey Design Conf., Calif., 1981, 87, 100/100 Exhibit, PDC, 1995. Pres. YWCA of L.A., 1984-87. founder, Kay Bixby Libr. on Volunteerism, 1992; mem. exec. com. United Way of L.A., 1992-93, bd. dirs. 1992-93; pres. Vol. Ctr. L.A., 1990-91, mem., 1973-94; exec. com. Dorland Mountain Arts Colony, 1990-91; mem. Mus. Contemporary Art, L.A. Conservancy; founder Women's Transp. Coalition, 1993, pres. 1993, 94, 95; bd. dirs. Info Line, 1995. Recipient Vesta award, 1991, Architect of Yr. award Women Construction Owners and Execs., 1994. Fellow AIA (CCAIA bd., 1989-91, 92-94, L.A. pres. 1994); mem. Assn. Women in Architecture (pres. 1977-78, 87-88), Archtl. Guild (treas. 1987-88, v.p. 1988-89, pres. 1990), Calif. Women in Environ. Design (founder), Architects Designers and Planners for Social Responsibility, L'Union Internationale des Femmes Architectes. Office: The Tanzmann Assocs 820 E 3rd St Los Angeles CA 90013-1820

TAO, CHIA-LIN PAO, humanities educator; b. Soochow, Kiangsu, China, July 7, 1939; came to U.S., 1961; d. Tsung-han and Hoi-chin Pao; m. Jing-shen Tao, Aug. 22, 1964; children: Rosalind, Jeanne, Sandy. BA, Nat. Taiwan U., Taipei, 1961; MA, Ind. U., 1963, PhD, 1971. Assoc. prof. Nat. Taiwan U., Taipei, 1969-76, 78-79; vis. assoc. prof. U. Ariz., Tucson, 1976-79-85, assoc. prof., 1989—; v.p. Hist. Soc. for 20th Century China in N.Am., 1992-93, pres., 1993-94. Editor, author: Studies in Chinese Women's History 4 vols., 1979—. Mem. Tucson-Taichung Sister-City Com., Tucson, 1984—; sec. Ariz. Asian Am. Assn., 1989, dir., 1989-93. Rsch. grantee Nat. Sci. Coun., Taipei, 1971-72, 73-74, Harvard-Yenching Inst., Cambridge, Mass., 1972-74, Pacific Cultural Found., Taipei, 1984-85. Mem. Assn. for Asian Studies (pres. Western conf. 1994), Am. Assn. for Chinese Studies, Hist. Soc. for Gender Studies, Tucson Chinese Am. Profl. Soc. (pres. 1996), Tucson Chinese Assn. (bd. dirs.). Democrat. Office: Dept East Asian Studies Univ Ariz Tucson AZ 85721

TAPE, GERALD FREDERICK, former association executive; b. Ann Arbor, Mich., May 29, 1915; s. Henry A. and Flora (Simmons) T.; m. Josephine Waffen, June 18, 1939; children: Walter Richard, James William, Thomas Gerald. A.B., Eastern Mich. U., 1935, Sc.D. (hon.), 1964; M.S., U. Mich., 1936, Ph.D., 1940. Asst. physics Eastern Mich. U., 1933-35, U. Mich., 1936-39; instr. physics Cornell U., 1939-42; staff mem. radiation lab. Mass. Inst. Tech., 1942-46; asst., then assoc. prof. physics U. Ill., 1946-50; asst. to dir., then dep. dir. Brookhaven Nat. Lab., 1950-62; v.p., then pres. Associated Univs., Inc., 1962-63, pres., 1969-80, spl. asst. to pres., 1980-82; commr. AEC, 1963-69; U.S. rep. to IAEA with rank of amb., 1973-77; former pres., cons. Associated Univs., Inc.; dir. Sci. Service Inc., 1971—, Atomic Indsl. Forum, 1970-73; mem. Pres.'s Sci. Adv. Com., 1969-73, Def. Sci. Bd., 1970-73, chmn., 1970-72; mem. sci. adv. com. IAEA, 1972-73; mem. gen. adv. com. ERDA, 1975-77; mem. adv. council Electric Power Research Inst., 1978-85; mem. U. Chgo. bd. govs. for Argonne Nat. Lab., 1982-85. Author: (with L.J. Haworth) Relay Radar Chapter of MIT Radiation Laboratory Technical Series, 1947; also papers, reports. Recipient Army-Navy Certificate of Appreciation, 1947, Meritorious Civilian Service medal Sec. Def., 1969, Dept. State Tribute Appreciation, 1969, Dept. Def. medal for pub. service, 1973; Henry DeWolf Smyth Nuclear Statesman award Atomic Indsl. Forum/Am. Nuclear Soc., 1978; Disting. Pub. Service award NSF, 1980; Disting. Assoc. award Dept. Energy, 1980; Enrico Fermi award U.S. Energy Dept., 1987; decorated comdr. Order Leopold II, Belgium. Fellow Am. Phys. Soc., Am. Nuclear Soc., AAAS; mem. Nat. Acad. Engring., Am. Astron. Soc., Phi Beta Kappa, Sigma Xi, Phi Kappa Phi, Kappa Delta Pi. Home: 4970 Sentinel Dr Apt 502 Bethesda MD 20816-3569 Office: Associated Univs Inc 1400 16th St NW Ste 730 Washington DC 20036-2217

TAPELLA, GARY LOUIS, manufacturing company executive; b. Antioch, Calif., Sept. 1, 1943; s. Anthony M. and Mary (Lopez) T.; m. Karen Kent, June 24, 1967; children: Robert, Michael. BA in Internat. Rels., San Francisco State U., 1969. Staff asst. Rheem Mfg. Co., N.Y.C., 1969-71; plant mgr. Rheem Can., Vancouver, 1971-73; mktg. mgr. Rheem Can., Toronto, 1973-79; regional sales mgr. Rheem Mfg. Co., New Orleans, 1979-80; mng. dir. Rheem Far East, Singapore, 1980-85; gen. mgr. Rheem Can., Toronto, 1985-89; corp. v.p. internat. Rheem Mfg. Co., N.Y.C., 1989-90, chief oper. officer, 1990-91, pres., chief exec. officer, 1991—; dir. various Rheem Cos. With USN, 1961-63. Avocation: scuba diving. Office: Rheem Mfg Co 405 Lexington Ave 22 Fl New York NY 10174*

TAPIA, RICHARD ALFRED, mathematics educator; b. Santa Monica, Calif., Mar. 25, 1939; s. Amado and Magda Tapia; m. Jean Rodriguez, July 25, 1959; children: Circee (dec.), Richard, Rebecca. BA, UCLA, 1961, MA, 1966, PhD, 1967. Asst. prof. math. rsch. ctr. U. Wis., Madison, 1968-70; asst. prof. math. scis. Rice U., Houston, 1970-72, assoc. prof., 1972-76, prof. math. scis., 1976—, chair dept. math. scis., 1978-83, assoc. dir. minority affairs Office Grad. Studies, 1989—; vis. assoc. prof. ops. rsch. Stanford (Calif.) U., 1976-77. Author: Nonparametric Density Estimation; contbr. articles to profl. publs. Named to 20 Most Influential in Minority Math. Edn., NSF, 1990; recipient Nat. Achievement award for Edn. Hispanic Engring. Mag., 1990, A. Nico Habermann award Computer Rsch. Assn., 1994; named Prof. of Yr., Assn. Hispanic Sch. Adminstrs., 1994. Mem. NAE, Am. Math. Soc. (mem. com. on edn.), Soc. for Indsl. and Applied Math. (trustee, lectr. 1988), Math. Assn. Am., Math. Programming Soc., Soc. for Advancement of Chicanos and Native Ams. in Sci. Home: 5723 Portal Dr Houston TX 77096-6010 Office: Rice U Dept Math Scis PO Box 1892 Houston TX 77251-1892

TÀPIES, ANTONI, painter, sculptor; b. Barcelona, Spain, Dec. 13, 1923. Attended, Royal Coll. Art, London; ArtsD (hon.), U. Barcelona, 1988, U. Glasgow, Scotland, 1990. One man shows include Palacio Mudejar, Seville, Spain, 1992, Mus. Modern Art, N.Y.C., 1992-93, Detroit Inst. Arts, 1992-93, Mus. de Arte Contemporaneo, Caracas, Venezuela, 1993, Galerie Adriana Schmidt, Stuttgart, Germany, 1993, Galerie Lelong, Paris, 1994, Lunds Konsthall, Lund, Sweden, 1994, Galerie Nat. du Jeu de Paume, Paris, 1994, Guggenheim Mus., N.Y.C., 1995; sculpture include Waddington Galleries, London, 1992, Antoni Tàpies & Eduardo Chillida, Schirn Kunsthalle, Frankfurt, Germany, 1993, Magic Blue, Galerie Beyeler, Basel, Switzerland, 1994, Nitsch, Baselitz, Poliakoff, Kirkeby; commn. Monument to Picasso, City of Barcelona, 1983, large mosaic, Plaza Cataluña, Santa Boi, Barcelona, 1983, sculpture Núvol i Cadira, Fundació Antoni Tàpies, Barcelona, 1990, mural, Catalan pavilion, 1992, mural, Internat. Olympics pavilion, 1992; author: Memoria Personal, 1978. Recipient Guggenheim Found. award, 1964, Peace prize Spanish Assn. for UN, 1984, Picasso medal UNESCO, 1993. Mem. Royal Acad. Arts (Stockholm), Gesellschaft Bildener Kustler Österreichs (hon.), Kunstlerhaus (hon.), Royal Acad. Arts London (hon.), Am. Acad. Arts and Scis. (hon.). Home: Saragossa 57, Barcelona 6 Spain Office: Pace Gallery 142 Greene St New York NY 10012

TAPLETT, LLOYD MELVIN, human resources management consultant; b. Tyndall, S.D., July 25, 1924; s. Herman Leopold and Emiley (Nedvidek) T.; B.A., Augustana Coll., 1949; M.A., U. Nebr., 1958; postgrad. S.D. State U., U. S.D., U. Iowa, Colo. State U.; m. Patricia Ann Sweeney, Aug. 21, 1958; children: Virginia Ann, Sharon Lorraine, Carla Jo, Carolyn Patricia, Catherine Marie, Colleen Elizabeth. Accredited pers. mgr. Profl. Human Resources. Tchr., Sioux Falls (S.D.) public schs., 1952-69; with All-Am. Transport Co., Sioux Falls, 1969-78, Am. Freight System, Inc., Overland Park, Kans., 1978-79; dir. human resources and public relations, corp. affirmative action compliance ofcl. Chippewa Motor Freight Inc., Sioux Falls, 1979-80; human resource and mgmt. cons., 1980-81; mgr. Sioux Falls Job Svcs. 1981-85, Pioneer Enterprises, Inc., 1985-86; ops. mgr. ATE Environ., Inc., 1986-88, cons. Royal River Casino, 1988-90; acad. dean Huron U., Sioux Falls, 1990-92, instr. econs. Coll. Bus., 1992—; chmn. Chippewa Credit Union; mem. adv. bd. dirs. Nelson Labs., Sioux Falls 1981-82; evening mgmt. instr Nat. Coll., Sioux Falls, 1981-90, chmn. adv. com., 1984—, Huron U., 1990—, S.F. Washington High Sch. Sports Heritage 1899-1989. Past bd. dirs. Jr. Achievement, United Way, Sioux Vocat. Sch. for Handicapped; past mem. Gov.'s Adv. Bd. for Community Adult Manpower Planning; chmn. bus. edn. adv. com. Sioux Falls Public Schs., 1982-85; chmn. adv. com. South East Area Vocat. Sch., 1982-85 ; mem. alumnae bd. Augustana Coll., 1985-88. Capt. USMC, 1943-46, 50-52, Korea. Recipient V.F.W. Commendation award, 1990, Liberty Bell award S.D. Bar Assn., 1967; Sch. Bd. award NEA/Thom McAn Shoe Corp., 1966, S.D. Unsung Heroes Edn. Recognition award 1992; named Boss of Yr., Sioux Falls, 1977; cert. tchr. and counselor, S.D. Mem. Am. Soc. for Personnel Adminstrn. (accredited personnel mgr. life, S.D. dist. dir. 1980-84), Am. Trucking Assn. (mem. pub. rels. coun.), NEA (life mem., Pacemaker award), S.D. Edn. Assn. (life), Sioux Falls Personnel Assn. (past pres.), Sales and Mktg. Club Sioux Falls, Sioux Falls Traffic Club, VFW (life, Nat. Polit. Action Recognition award 1990), Am. Legion. Republican. Roman Catholic. Clubs: Toastmasters (past gov. dist. 41, Disting. Toastmaster award, Outstanding Toastmaster award dist. 41, Hall of Fame 1977), Elks. Contbr. articles to nat. mags. Office: Huron U PO Box 90003 Sioux Falls SD 57105-9060

TAPLEY, BYRON DEAN, aerospace engineer, educator; b. Charleston, Miss., Jan. 16, 1933; s. Ebbie Byron and Myrtle (Myers) T.; m. Sophia Philen, Aug. 28, 1959; children: Mark Byron, Craig Philen. B.S., U. Tex., 1956, M.S., 1958, Ph.D., 1960. Registered profl. engr., Tex. Engr. Structural Mechanics Research Lab. U. Tex., Austin, 1954-58, instr. mech. engring., 1958, prof. aerospace engring. and engring. mechanics, 1960—, chmn. dept. aerospace engring. and engring. mechanics, 1966-77, Woolrich prof. engring., 1974-80, dir. Ctr. Space Research, 1983—; dir. Tex. Space Grant Consortium, 1990—; Clare Cockrell Williams chair in aerospace engring. U. Tex., Austin, 1984—; mem. adv. com. on guidance control and nav. NASA, 1966-67, com. on space rsch., panel I, 1974-76, chmn. region IV, engring. coun. on profl. devel., 1974-76; chmn. geodesy com. NRC, 1981-84, mem. aeros. and space engring. bd., 1984-86, mem. space sci. bd., chmn. com. on earth studies, 1988-91; bd. dirs. Tex. Space Grant Consortium. Editor: Celestial Mech. Jour, 1976-79; assoc. editor: Jour. Guidance and Control, 1978-79; assoc. editor: Geophys. Revs, 1979-81. Dir. Tex. Space Grant Consortium, 1990—. Recipient NASA Exceptional Sci. Achievement medal, 1983, NASA Pub. Svc. medal, 1994. Fellow AAAS (pres. engring. sect.), AIAA (chmn. com. on astrodynamics 1976-78, mech. and control of flight award 1989), Am. Geophys. Union (pres. geodesy sect. 1984-86); mem. ASME, IEEE, NAE, Am. Acad. Mechanics, Am. Astronautical Soc. (pres. divsn. dynamic astronomy 1988-89, Dirk Brouwer award 1995), Soc. Engring. Sci., Internat. Astron. Union, Sigma Xi, Pi Tau Sigma, Sigma Gamma Tau, Phi Kappa Phi, Tau Beta Pi. Home: 3100 Perry Ln Austin TX 78731-5327

TAPLEY, DONALD FRASER, university official, physician, educator; b. Woodstock, N.B., Can., May 19, 1927; s. Roy Donald and Velma (Fraser) T.; m. Caroline Southall, Sept. 14, 1957; children—Katherine, Elizabeth, Sarah Tapley Bangs. B.S., Acadia U., 1948; M.D., U. Chgo., 1952. Intern Presbyn. Hosp., N.Y.C., 1952-53; asst. resident, 1953-54, asst. attending physician, 1957-64, assoc. attending physician, 1964-72, attending physician, 1972—; Life Ins. Research fund fellow dept. physiol. chemistry Johns Hopkins U., Balt., 1954-56; Jane Coffin Childs fellow dept. physiol. chemistry Oxford U., Eng., 1956-57; asst. prof. medicine Columbia U., 1956-64, assoc. prof., 1964-72, prof., 1972—, assoc. dean for faculty affairs Coll. Physicians and Surgeons, 1970-73, acting dean, 1973-74, dean, 1974-84, alumni prof., sr. dep. v.p., 1984—. Trustee Morris Jumel Mansion, The Riverkeeper, The Mary Imogene Bassett Hosp., Cooperstown, N.Y. Contbr. numerous articles to profl. publs. Assoc. editor Endocrinology Mag., 1963-68. Mem. Am. Soc. Clin. Investigation, Endocrine Soc., Am. Thyroid Assn., Harvey Soc., N.Y. Med. and Surg. Soc. Office: Columbia U Coll Physicians & Surgeons 630 W 168th St New York NY 10032-3702

TAPLEY, JAMES LEROY, retired lawyer, railway corporation executive; b. Greenville, Miss., July 10, 1923; s. Lester Leroy and Lillian (Clark) T.; m. Priscilla Moore, Sept. 9, 1950. AB, U. N.C., 1947, JD with hons., 1950. Bar: N.C. 1951, D.C. 1962. With So. Ry. Co., Washington, 1953-83; gen. solicitor So. Ry. Co., 1967-74, asst. v.p. law, 1974-75, v.p. law, 1975-83; v.p. Washington counsel Norfolk So. Corp., Washington, 1983-87. Mem. Phi Beta Kappa, Kappa Sigma. Clubs: Chevy Chase.

TAPLEY, PHILIP ALLEN, English language and literature educator; b. Blackwell, Okla., June 11, 1938; s. Robert G. Sr. and Valena M. (Simmons) T.; m. Mary Stringer, Aug. 10, 1974; children: Mary Margaret, Laura Katherine. BA, U. North Tex., 1960, MA, 1962; PhD, La. State U., 1974. Cert. secondary tchr., Tex. Teaching asst. U. North Tex., Denton, 1960-61; teaching asst. La. State U., Baton Rouge, 1961-65, 68-69, instr., 1965-68; asst. prof. La. Coll., Pineville, 1969-74, assoc. prof., 1974-80, acting chmn. dept. English, journalism and langs., 1980, prof. dept. English, journalism and langs., 1980—; maj. scholar, presenter La. Endowment for the Humanities, Alexandria, 1977—; vis. cons. Ctrl. La. Electric Co., Pineville, 1989-95. Author: A History of First United Methodist, 1976, 2d edit., 1989, (with others) Procs. of the Red River Symposium, 1987, 2d edit., 1991; contbr. articles to profl. jours. Pres., Friends of Rapides Libr., Alexandria,1985-86, bd. dirs., 1996. Mellon Found. fellow, 1982, 88, Ford Found. fellow, 1989. Mem. AAUP, South Ctrl. MLA (program chair so. lit. 1979), La. Folklore Soc. (pres. 1978-79), Hist. Assn. Ctrl. La. (pres. 1978-80, bd. dirs. 1978—), Phi Kappa Phi, Alpha Chi, Sigma Tau Delta, Omicron Delta Kappa. Democrat. Episcopalian. Avocations: reading, music, historic preservation, folklore collecting. Home: 1721 Polk St Alexandria LA 71301-6334 Office: La Coll English Dept 1140 College Dr Pineville LA 71359-0001

TAPLIN, FRANK E., JR., trustee education and arts institutions and associations; b. Cleve., June 22, 1915; s. Frank Elijah and Edith R. (Smith) T.; m. Ngaio I. Thornton, Sept. 3, 1943 (div. Mar. 1951); children: Caroline I. Taplin Ruschell, Jennifer Taplin Jerome, David F.; m. Margaret A. Eaton, Apr. 27, 1953; stepchildren: Jennifer A. Sichel Dickerman, Martha D. Sichel Kelly, Susan Sichel Panella. BA in History, Princeton U., 1937; MA in Jurisprudence (Rhodes scholar), Oxford U., 1939; JD, Yale U., 1941; MusD (hon.), Cleve. Inst. Music, 1981; DHL (hon.), Fordham U., 1984; Dr. Mus. Arts (hon.), Manhattan Sch. Music, 1984; LLD (hon.), Rider Coll., 1988. Bar: Ohio 1946. With firm Jones, Day Cockley & Reavis, Cleve., 1946-50; asst. to Sen. Taft in Ohio senatorial campaign, 1950; pvt. bus. investments Cleve., 1951-57; asst. to pres. Princeton U., 1957-59; chmn. bd. Scurry-Rainbow Oil, Ltd., 1954-74; trustee Inst. for Advanced Study, Princeton U., 1972-88, trustee emeritus, 1988—; dir. NACCO Industries, Inc., trustee Environ. Def. Fund., 1990—; pres. Cleve. Inst. Music, 1952-56; trustee Cleve. Orch., 1946-57, pres., 1955-57; pres. Nat. Council Met. Opera, 1961-64; dir. Met. Opera Assn., 1961-91, hon. dir., 1991—, pres., chief exec. officer, 1977-84; hon. trustee Bradford (Mass.) Coll.; trustee Princeton (N.J.) Day Sch., 1966-72, Princeton Area United Community Fund, 1963-76; mem. Princeton U. Music Dept. Adv. Council, 1960-85, hon. mem., 1987—, chmn., 1965-71; trustee Sarah Lawrence Coll., 1969-77, chmn., 1973-77, hon. trustee, 1977—;

trustee Lincoln Center for Performing Arts, 1972-88, trustee emeritus, 1988—, vice chmn., 1981-84; trustee, founding pres. Lincoln Center Chamber Music Soc., 1969-73; fellow Morgan Library; mem. council Friends Princeton Library; chmn. bd. Marlboro Sch. Music, 1964-70; now trustee; trustee Woodrow Wilson Nat. Fellowship Found., 1972—, Am. Schs. Oriental Research, 1970-75, Western Res. Hist. Soc., Cleve.; internat. bd. dirs. United World Colls., London, 1973-76; also chmn. United World Colls. (U.S. com.), 1973-75; bd. dirs. Am. Friends of Covent Garden and Royal Ballet, Friends of Aldeburgh Festival.; mem. vestry Trinity Ch., Princeton, 1984-87. Vice chmn. council of fellows Morgan Library, 1987-90. Served from ensign to lt. comdr. USNR, 1941-46. Decorated hon. mem. (mil. div.) Order Brit. Empire.; recipient Gold Medal award Nat. Inst. Social Scis., 1983, Disting. Service award Third St. Music Sch. Settlement, 1983. Mem. ABA, Assn. Am. Rhodes Scholars, Am. Philos. Soc., Am.-Scandinavian Found. (exec. trustee), Univ. Club (N.Y.C.), Century Assn. (N.Y.C., bd.mgmt. 1981-84), Springdale Golf Club, Nassau Club (Princeton), Pretty Brook Club (Princeton), Tavern Club (Cleve.).

TAPLIN, WINN LOWELL, historian, retired senior intelligence operations officer; b. Saint Albans, Vt., Oct. 3, 1925; s. Winn Lowell and Elinor (Cunningham) T.; m. Ellajean Allard, July 16, 1949; children: Leslie Taplin Baumann, Mark Allard. BSCE, U. Mich., 1946, AB, 1948, AM, 1950, PhD, 1956. Oper. officer CIA, Washington, 1955-81; cons. Stowe, Vt., 1981-94, Sarasota, Fla., 1994—. Author: Secret New England: Spies of the American Revolution, 1991, We Vermonters, 1992. Pres. Vt. Hist. Soc., 1989-93, trustee; pres. Mansfield View Water Corp., Stowe, 1989-92. 1st lt. USMC, 1943-46, U.S., 1950-52, Korea. Decorated Bronze Star, Intelligence Medal of Merit. Mem. Central Intelligence Retirees Assn., Assn. Former Intelligence Officers (dir. New England chpt.), First Day Cover Soc., Am. Philatelic Assn., Am. Legion, Disabled Am. Vets., U. Mich. Club Sarasota (dir. 1994—), Sigma Chi. Avocations: historical research, genealogy, classical music, stamp collecting. Home (summer): 903 Worcester Loop Stowe VT 05672-4326 Home: 7641 Sandalwood Way Sarasota FL 34231

TAPPÉ, ALBERT ANTHONY, architect; b. Pitts., Aug. 12, 1928; s. Albert Anthony and Martha Ann (McKee) T.; m. Jean Bates, June 27, 1963; children: Eliza Bruce, Albert Anthony III. Student, William and Mary Coll., 1947-48, Fontainebleau Fine Art and Music Sch., 1951; B.S., U. Va., 1952; M.Arch., MIT, 1958, M.City Planning. Designer, McLeod & Ferrara (Architects), Washington, 1954-55; planner Boston City Planning Bd., 1957-58; architect and planner Architects Collaborative, Cambridge, Mass., 1958-61; partner Huygens & Tappé, Inc. (architects and planners), Boston, 1962-80; pres. A. Anthony Tappé & Assocs., Inc., Boston, 1980—; instr. dept. city planning MIT, 1959-60; cons. architect Mass. Bur. Library Extension, 1965-76; chmn. bldg. commn., Brookline, Mass., 1977, mem. bd. examiners, Brookline; v.p. Guild Religious Architecture; mem. Back Bay Archtl. Commn.; bd. dirs. Boston Archtl. Center, 1980. Author: Guide to Planning a Library Building, 1967; important works include: Longy Concert Hall, Cambridge, Mass., Campus N.H. Coll., Franklin Park Zoo, Boston, Lynn Inst. for Savs., Interfaith Religious Ctr., Columbia, Md., student housing W.Va. Wesleyan Coll., Hotel, Costa Smeralda, Sardinia, Newton Pub. Libr., Beverly Pub. Libr., Am. Coll., Athens, Greece; also residences in U.S., France, Switzerland, housing projects in New Eng. Served with AUS, 1946-47, 52-54. Recipient Progressive Architecture Design award, 1966, 1st place single family category Plywood Design Awards Program, 1973, award of Merit, 1974. Fellow AIA (mem. nat. urban planning and design com. 1975, citation, hon. mentions 1969, 1st honor award 1970, honor award New Eng. Regional Council 1976); mem. Mass. Assn. Architects (exec. com.), Boston Soc. Architects (dir., v.p. 1981-82, pres. 1982-83), Am. Inst. Planners, Am. Planning Assn., Am. Inst. Cons. Planners. Clubs: Union Boat (Boston); Eastern Point Yacht (Gloucester, Mass.). Home: 58 Lincoln St Brookline MA 02146-4045 Office: 132 Lincoln St Boston MA 02111-2522

TAPPER, JOAN JUDITH, magazine editor; b. Chgo., June 12, 1947; d. Samuel Jack and Anna (Swoiskin) T.; m. Steven Richard Siegel, Oct. 15, 1971. BA, U. Chgo., 1968; MA, Harvard U., 1969. Editor manuscripts Chelsea House, N.Y.C., 1969-71, Scribners, N.Y.C., 1971; editor books Nat. Acad. Scis., Washington, 1972-73; assoc. editor Praeger Pubs., Washington, 1973-74; editor New Rep. Books, Washington, 1974-79; mng. editor spl. pubs. Nat. Geog. Soc., Washington, 1979-83; editor Nat. Geog. Traveler, Washington, 1984-88; editor-in-chief Islands (internat. mag.), Santa Barbara, Calif., 1989—. Recipient Pacific Asia Travel Assn. Journalist of the Yr. award, 1995. Mem. Am. Soc. Mag. Editors, Soc. Am. Travel Writers (editors' coun.), Channel City Club. Democrat. Jewish. Avocations: travel, reading, tennis. Home: 603 Island View Dr Santa Barbara CA 93109-1508 Office: Islands Mag 3886 State St Santa Barbara CA 93105-3112

TAQQU, MURAD SALMAN, mathematics educator; b. Mar. 21, 1942. Diploma in physics, Inst. Tech., Lausanne, Switzerland, 1965; licence in math., U. Lausanne, 1966; MA, Columbia U., 1969, PhD, 1972. Lectr. math. Hebrew U., Jerusalem, 1972-73; postdoctorate rsch. fellow Weizmann Inst., Rehovot, Israel, 1973-74; asst. prof. Cornell U., Ithaca, N.Y., 1974-81, assoc. prof., 1981-85, prof., 1985-86; prof. Boston U., 1985—; vis. assoc. prof. Stanford (Calif.) U., 1981-82; vis. rsch. scientist Courant Inst., NYU, N.Y.C., 1985; vis. scholar Harvard Coll., Cambridge, Mass., 1987-88; organizer profl. confs.; cons. sci. reviewer. Author: Stable Non-Gaussian Random Processes: Stochastic Models with Infinite Variance, 1994; editor: Dependence in Probability and Statistics, 1986; assoc. editor Stochastic Processes and their Applications, 1989—; contbr. articles to profl. publs. Recipient William J. Bennett award IEEE Comms. Soc., 1995, W.R.G. Baker prize award IEEE, 1996; John Simon Guggenheim fellow, 1987. Fellow Inst. Math. Stats., Am. Math. Soc., Internat. Statis. Inst., Ops. Rsch. Soc. Am., Bernoulli Soc. Office: Boston U Dept Math 111 Cummington St Boston MA 02215-2411

TAQUEY, CHARLES HENRI, writer, consultant; b. Paris; came to U.S., 1937, naturalized, 1942; s. Henri and Marguerite (Normand) T.; m. Ruth McVitty, Feb. 1, 1947 (dec. May 1994); children: Antony, Chantal Sanders. B.S., U. Paris, 1929; Lauréat, Ecole Libre des Sciences Politiques, 1933; Licencié and Lauréat, D.E.S, Paris Law Sch., 1934. French Treasury rep. Paris, London, Berlin, N.Y.C., 1934-39; local currencies mgr. ECA, 1948-51; staff officer Exec. Office of Pres., 1952-57; fgn. service econ. officer Am. embassies Phnom-Penh, Cambodia, Tunis, Tunisia, Kingston, Jamaica; also detailed to Dept. Commerce as dep. dir. fgn. activities mgmt., 1957-70; mgmt. cons., ecol. economist (internat. trade and resources recovery), 1970—; expert witness Internat. Trade Commn., Ways and Means Com. U.S. Ho. of Reps., GAO, fgn. govts. Author: German Financial Crisis, 1931, Richard Cobden, 1938, Trusts and Patents, 1946, Obstacles to Development in Indonesia, 1952, Fisheries in Cambodia, 1959, Against Full Employment, 1973, Democracy and Socialism, 1976, Transnational Corporations and the State, 1979, Beyond Free Trade, 1983, Free Trade, Morality of Nations, 1987. Served as lt., arty. French Army, 1940; lt., arty. AUS, 1942-46; capt. 1952. Mem. Consumers for World Trade. Address: 1681 31st St NW Washington DC 20007-2968 also: Les Quatre Vents, 84580 Oppède France

TARAN, LEONARDO, classicist, educator; b. Galarza, Argentina, Feb. 22, 1933; came to U.S., 1958, naturalized, 1976; s. Miguel and Liuba (Etlis) T.; m. Judit Sofia Lida, Dec. 10, 1971; 1 child, Gabriel Andrew. Legal degree, U. Buenos Aires, 1958; Ph.D. in Classics, Princeton U., 1962. Jr. fellow Inst. Research in Humanities, U. Wis., 1962-63, Center Hellenic Studies, Washington, 1963-64; asst. prof. classics U. Calif., Los Angeles, 1964-67; mem. faculty Columbia U., 1967—, prof. Greek and Latin, 1971—, Jay prof. Greek and Latin, 1987—, chmn. dept., 1976-79; mem. Inst. Advanced Study, Princeton, N.J., 1966-67, 78-79; trustee Assn. Mems. Inst. Advanced Study, 1974-79; mem. mng. com. Am. Sch. Classical Studies, 1976—. Author: Parmenides, 1965, Asclepius of Tralles, Commentary to Nicomachus' Introduction to Arithmetic, 1969, Plato, Philip of Opus and the Pseudo-Platonic Epinomis, 1975, Anonymous Commentary on Aristotle's De Interpretatione, 1978, Speusippus of Athens, 1981; co-author: Eraclito: Testimonianze e imitazioni, 1972; Editorial bd.: Columbia Studies in the Classical Tradition, 1976-80. Am. Coun. Learned Socs. fellow, 1966-67, 71-72, Guggenheim Found. fellow, 1975, NEH fellow, 1986-87; grantee Am. Philos. Soc., 1963, 71, 75, Am. Coun. Learned Socs., 1968, 72, NEH, 1985-87, 88-89. Mem. Am. Philol. Assn., Classical Assn. Atlantic States, Soc. Ancient Greek Philosophy, Assn. Guillaume Bude. Home: 39 Claremont Ave New York NY 10027-6824 Office: Columbia U 615 Hamilton Hall New York NY 10027

TARANIK, JAMES VLADIMIR, geologist, educator; b. Los Angeles, Apr. 23, 1940; s. Vladimir James and Jeanette Downing (Smith) T.; m. Colleen Sue Glessner, Dec. 4, 1971; children: Debra Lynn, Danny Lee. B.Sc. in Geology, Stanford U., 1964; Ph.D., Colo. Sch. Mines, 1974. Chief remote sensing Iowa Geol. Survey, Iowa City, 1971-74; prin. remote sensing scientist Earth Resources Observation Systems Data Ctr., U.S. Geol. Survey, Sioux Falls, S.D., 1975-79; chief non-renewable resources br., resource observation div. Office of Space and Terrestrial Applications, NASA Hdqrs., Washington, 1979-82; dean mines Mackay Sch. Mines U. Nev., Reno, 1982-87, prof. of geology and geophysics, 1982—, Arthur Brant chair of geology and geophysics, 1996—; pres. Desert Research Inst., Univ. and Community Coll. System Nev., 1987—; adj. prof. geology U. Iowa, 1971-79; vis. prof. civil engring. Iowa State U., 1972-74; adj. prof. earth sci. U. S.D., 1976-79; program scientist for space shuttle large format camera expt. for heat capacity mapping mission, liaison Geol. Scis. Bd., Nat. Acad. Scis., 1981-82; dir. NOAA Coop. Inst. Aerospace Sci. & Terrestrial Applications, 1986-94; program dir. NASA Space Grant consortium Univ. and Community Coll. System Nev., Reno, 1991—; team mem. Shuttle Imaging Radar-B Sci. Team NASA, 1983-88, mem. space applications adv. com., 1986-88; chmn. remote sensing subcom. SAAC, 1986-88; chmn. working group on civil space commercialization Dept. Commerce, 1982-84, mem. civil operational remote sensing satellite com., 1983-84; bd. dirs. Newmont Gold Co., 1986—; mem. adv. com. NASA Space Sci. and Applications, 1988-90, Nat. Def. Exec. Rsch., 1986—, AF studies bd., com. on strategic relocatable targets, 1989-91; mem. pre-launch rev. bd., NASA, Space Radar Lab., 1993-94; mem. fed. lab. rev. task force, NASA, 1994—; prin. investigator Japanese Earth Resources Satellite, 1991-94; mem. environ. task force MEDEA, Mitre Corp., McLean, Va., 1993—; cons. Jet Propulsion Lab. Calif., Hughes Aircraft Corp., Lockheed-Marietta Corp., Mitre Corp., TRW; developer remote sensing program and remote sensing lab. for State of Iowa, ednl. program in remote sensing for Iowa univs. and U. Nev., Reno; program scientist for 2d space shuttle flight Office Space and Terrestrial Applications Program; mem. terrestrial geol. applications program NASA, 1981—; co-investigator Can. Radarsat Program, 1995—. Contbr. to profl. jours. Served with C.E. U.S. Army, 1965-67; mil. intellegence officer Res. Decorated Bronze Star medal; recipient Spl. Achievement award U.S. Geol. Survey, 1978, Exceptional Sci. Achievement medal NASA, 1982, NASA Group Achievement award Shuttle imaging radar, 1990, NASA Johnson Space Ctr. Group Achievement award for large format camera, 1985; NASA prin. investigator, 1973, 83-88, prin. investigator French Spot-1 Program to Evaluate Spot 1986-88; NDEA fellow, 1968-71. Home: PO Box 7175 Reno NV 89510-7175 also: 2108 Calle De Espana Las Vegas NV 89102-4013 Office: Univ & Community Coll Sys Desert Rsch Inst Pres Reno NV 89512 *I have always been in awe of the universe in which we live and the little time we have on earth to perceive and understand it.*

TARANTINO, DOMINIC A., accounting firm executive; b. San Francisco, Aug. 1, 1932; m. Leona Lazzareschi, July 24, 1954; children: John Robert, Stephen, Leanne. BS, U. San Francisco, 1954. With Price Waterhouse, 1957—, mem. policy bd. and mgmt. com., 1979-93, vice chmn. tax svcs., 1982-88, co-chmn. bd., mng. ptnr., 1988-93; chmn. Price Waterhouse World Firm, 1995—; mem. IRS Commr.'s Adv. Group, 1978. Mem. AICPA (mem. bd. dirs. 1988-95, vice chair 1992-3, chmn. 1993-94, Dixon Meml. award 1990). Office: Price Waterhouse 1251 Ave Of The Americas New York NY 10020-1104*

TARANTINO, QUENTIN, film director, screenwriter; b. Knoxville, Tenn., 1963; s. Tony and Connie T. Screenwriter, dir., actor: Reservoir Dogs, 1992, Pulp Fiction, 1994 (Palme d'Or,Cannes Internat. Film Festival, 1994, Academy award best original screenplay 1994); screenwriter: True Romance, 1993; story: Natural Born Killers, 1994; producer: Killing Zoe, 1994; film appearances include Sleep With Me, 1994, Destiny Turns On the Radio, 1995; TV appearances include The Golden Girls, All-American Girl; actor: Desperado, 1995, Girl 6, 1996, From Dusk Till Dawn, 1996; producer: Red Rain, 1995, Four Rooms, 1995, From Dusk Till Dawn, 1996, Curdled, 1996. Office: A Band Apart Production Capra Bldg 112 10202 Washington Blvd Culver City CA 90232-3119 also: 6201 Sunset Blvd Ste 35 Los Angeles CA 90028*

TARAR, AFZAL MUHAMMAD, management consultant; b. Gujranwala, Punjab, Pakistan, Apr. 1, 1962; came to the U.S., 1989; s. Abdul Wahid and Ghulam Sugra Tarar; m. Saiko Mori, Sept. 8, 1988. BE in Computer Engring., Tsinghua U., 1988; MS in Computer Sci., Case Western Res. U., 1991. Systems specialist EG&G, Inc., Beijing, 1986-89; mgr. Deloitte & Touche Consulting Group, Cleve., 1990-91; officer, project mgr. KeyCorp./Key Svcs. Corp., Cleve., 1991-95; mgr. Deloitte & Touche Consulting Group, N.Y.C., 1995—. Mem. Internat. Assn. Knowledge Engrs., Soc. for Mgmt. Applied Intelligent and Relevant Techs. in Fin. Svcs., Japan Soc. Cleve. (trustee 1992-94), Rotary, Strategic Leadership Forum.

TARAS, PAUL, physicist, educator; b. Tunis, Tunisia, May 12, 1941; emigrated to Can., 1957, naturalized, 1962; s. Wladimir and Benita (Koort) T.; m. Marja-Leena Malinen, Aug. 3, 1963; children—Lisa Helene, Michele Anne. B.A.Sc., U. Toronto, 1962, M.A., 1963, Ph.D., 1965. Asst. prof. physics U. Montreal, Que., Can., 1965-70; assoc. prof. U. Montreal, 1970-76, prof., 1976—; spokesman U. Montreal in rsch. projects. Helios, SDC, Pep-II. Rsch. on nuclear and particle physics; co-managed conception and constrn. of 8pi Spectrometer, Chalk River Nuclear Labs, 1984-86; contbr. articles to profl. jours.; presenter papers to profl. confs. U. Toronto, Province of Ont., U.K. Atomic Energy Authority fellowships; France-Que., NRC, Natural Scis. and Engring. Research Council Can. grantee. Mem. Am. Phys. Soc., Can. Assn. Physicists. Home: 1639 Norway Rd, Montreal, PQ Canada H4P 1Y3 Office: Univ de Montreal, Lab Physique Nucleaire, Montreal, PQ Canada H3C 3J7

TARASI, LOUIS MICHAEL, JR., lawyer; b. Cheswick, Pa., Sept. 9, 1931; s. Louis Michael and Ruth Elizabeth (Records) T.; m. Patricia Ruth Finley, June 19, 1954; children: Susan, Louis Michael III, Elizabeth, Brian, Patricia, Matthew. BA, Miami U., Ohio, 1954; JD, U. Pa., 1959. Bar: Pa. 1960, U.S. Dist. Ct. (we. dist.) Pa. 1960, U.S. Ct. Appeals (3d cir.) 1964, U.S. Supreme Ct. 1969, U.S. Dist. Ct. (we. dist.) Tex. 1988, U.S. Ct. appeals (4th cir.) 1994. Assoc., owner Burgwin, Ruffin, Perry & Pohl, Pitts., 1960-68; ptnr. Conte, Courtney & Tarasi, Beaver County, Pa., 1968-78, Tarasi & Tighe, Pitts., 1978-82, Tarasi & Johnson, P.C., Pitts., 1982-95, Tarasi & Assocs. P.C., Pitts., 1995—. Mem. parish coun. St. James Ch., Sewickley, Pa.; mem. Sewickley Borough Allegheny Coun. With U.S. Army, 1954-56. Fellow Internat. Soc. Barristers; mem. Assn. Trial Lawyers Am. (gov., rep.), Pa. Trial Lawyers Assn. (pres. 1979-80), Acad. Trial Lawyers Allegheny County, Allegheny County Bar Assn., Pa. Bar Assn., West Pa. Trial Lawyers Assn. (pres. 1975), St. Thomas More Soc. (award 1991), Melvin Belli Soc. Democrat. Roman Catholic. Avocations: reading, golf, lecturing. Home: 1 Way Hollow Rd Sewickley PA 15143-1192 Office: Tarasi & Assocs PC 510 3d Ave Pittsburgh PA 15219

TARAZI, FAHMY ISSAM, neuroscientist, researcher; b. Cairo, June 6, 1963; came to U.S., 1988; s. Issam F. and Eva A. (Baramki) T. BS, Ain Shams U., Cairo, 1984; MS, U. Md., Balt., 1990; PhD, Rutgers U., Newark, 1995. Clin. biochemist Ain Shams U., 1984-87; grad. rsch. asst. U. Md., Balt., 1988-90, faculty rsch. asst., 1990-91; grad. rsch. asst. Rutgers U., 1991-95; instr. psychiatry and neurosci. Harvard Med. Sch., Belmont, Mass., 1995—. Co-author: Principles of Medical Biology, 1995; contbr. articles to Nature, European Jour. Pharmacology, Harvard Rev. Psychiatry. Recipient Young Investigator award Am. Soc. Neurochemistry, 1994, Am. Soc. Pharmacology and Exptl. Therapeutics, 1994; Sigma Xi Rsch. Soc. rsch. grantee, 1994, 95. Mem. Am. Soc. Neurosci., Internat. Brain Rsch. Orgn., Internat. Soc. for Neurochemistry (Young Scientist award, 1995); N.Y. Acad. Scis. Avocations: tennis, soccer, volleyball. Office: Harvard U Med Sch 115 Mill St Belmont MA 02178

TARBELL, DAVID S., federal agency administrator; married. BS in Mgmt., Rensselaer Poly. Inst.; M in Pub. Policy Analysis, U. Pa. Presdl. mgmt. intern U.S. Govt., 1979-81; asst. for energy security policy Office of Under Sec. Def. for Policy, U.S. Dept. Def., 1981-83, dep. dir. internat. econ. and energy affairs, 1983-85, dir., 1985-94, dir. Def. Tech. Security Adminstrn., 1994—; mgr. responsibility-sharing effort during Desert Shield/Desert Storm; past mem. staff NSC, dir. internat. econ. affairs, 1987. Office: Dept of Defense/Internat Security Policy/Internat Economic & Energy Affairs/The Pentagon Washington DC 20301*

TARBELL, DEAN STANLEY, chemistry educator; b. Hancock, N.H., Oct. 19, 1913; s. Sanford and Ethel (Millikan) T.; m. Ann Hoar Tracy, Aug. 15, 1942; children: William Sanford, Linda Tracy, Theodore Dean. A.B., Harvard U., 1934, M.A., 1935, Ph.D., 1937. Postdoctoral fellow U. Ill., 1937; mem. faculty U. Rochester, 1938—, successively instr., asst. prof., asso. prof., 1938-48, prof. chemistry, 1948-62, Charles Frederick Houghton prof. chemistry, 1960—, chmn. dept., 1964—; Disting. prof. chemistry Vanderbilt U., 1967—, Branscom disting. prof., 1975-76, disting. prof. emeritus, 1981—; Guggenheim fellow and vis. lectr. chemistry Stanford U., 1961-62; Fuson lectr., 1972; cons. USPHS, Army Q.M.C.; mem. various sci. adv. bds. to govt. agencies. Author: (with Ann T. Tarbell) Roger Adams, Scientist and Statesman, 1981, Essays on the History of Organic Chemistry in the United States, 1875-1955, 1986 , also papers on history of chemistry. Recipient Herty award Ga. Sect. Am. Chem. Soc., 1973 Dexter award Div. History of Chemistry Am. Chem. Soc., 1989; Guggenheim fellow, 1946-47. Mem. Nat. Acad. Sci., Am. Chem. Soc. (chmn. div. history of chemistry 1980-81), Chem. Soc. London, Am. Acad. Arts and Scis., History of Sci. Soc. Home: 6033 Sherwood Dr Nashville TN 37215-5734

TARBOX, FRANK KOLBE, retired insurance company executive; b. Mineola, N.Y., Feb. 27, 1923; s. John Preston and Mary (Kolbe) T.; m. Eleanor Borden, May 1, 1948; children: John Borden, Kathryn Ann. Student, Swarthmore Coll., 1940-42; A.B., U. Pa., 1947, LL.B., 1950. Pvt. practice law, 1950-53, 55-60; asst. U.S. atty. Eastern Dist. Pa., 1953-55; v.p. adminstrn. Penn Mut. Life Ins. Co., Phila., 1960-71; pres. Penn Mut. Life Ins. Co., 1971-78, chief exec. officer, 1973-86, chmn. bd. dirs., 1979-87; ret., 1995; bd. dirs. Penn Mut. Life Ins. Co. With USNR, 1942-46. Office: Penn Mut Life Ins Co Independence Sq Philadelphia PA 19172*

TARBOX, GURDON LUCIUS, JR., retired museum executive; b. Plainfield, N.J., Dec. 25, 1927; s. Gurdon Lucius and Lillie (Hodgson) T.; B.S., Mich. State U., 1952; M.S., Purdue U., 1954, D Pub. Svc. U. S.C., 1993; m. Milver Ann Johnson, Sept. 25, 1952; children—Janet Ellen LeGrand, Joyce Elaine Schumacher, Paul Edward, Lucia Ann. Asst. dir. Brookgreen Gardens, Murrells Inlet, S.C., 1954-59, trustee, 1959—, dir., 1963-94, pres., 1990—. Chmn. Georgetown County Mental Health Commn., 1964-66; mem. exec. council Confedn. S.C. Local Hist. Socs., 1976—; trustee S.C. Hall Fame, 1976—, S.C. Heritage Trust, 1981-86, S.C. Mansion Commn., 1986—. Served with AUS, 1946-48. Recipient Francis K. Hutchinson medal for svc. to conservation TGarden Club of Am., 1994. Mem. Soc. Am. Foresters, Am. Assn. Bot. Gardens and Arboreta (dir. 1971-74, sec.-treas. 1982, v.p. 1983, pres. 1985-86), Georgetown County Hist. Soc. (pres. 1970-74), Am., Royal hort. socs., Am. Assn. Mus. (council 1983), Southeastern Mus. Conf. (dir. 1977-80), S.C. Fedn. Museums (pres. 1974-76), Am. Assn. State and Local History, S.C. Confedn. Local Hist. Socs. Episcopalian. Lodge: Rotary (pres. 1979-80). Home: 641 Crooked Oak Dr Pawleys Island SC 29585

TARBUTTON, LLOYD TILGHMAN, motel executive, franchise consultant; b. Easton, Md., Jan. 3, 1932; s. William Lloyd and Ethel Ford T.; m. Virginia Rachael Johnson, Nov. 1, 1952 (div. 1977); children: Gregory Alan, Kenton Lyle.; m. Layne E. Johnson, Apr. 15, 1981; 1 stepchild, C. Todd Woolston. Dr Comml. Sci. in Mktg., Pacific Western U., 1993. Grad. Realtors Inst.; cert. franchise exec., La. State U., cert. hotel adminstr. Divsn. sales mgr. Reuben H. Donnelley Corp. (advt. agy.), Norfolk, Va., 1953-58; owner, operator Tie Centre Stores, Norfolk, 1958-60; gen. mgr. Hembree Realty Co., Norfolk, 1960-62; chmn. bd., dir. Tarbutton Assocs., Inc., comml. real estate, real estate tax assessment Contesting, hotel-motel mgmt., and franchise cons., Norfolk, 1962—; co-founder, dir., pres., chmn. bd. Econo Lodges of Am. (formerly Econ-Travel Motor Hotel Corp.), Norfolk, 1967-83, chmn. bd. emeritus, 1983—; co-founder, chief judge Franchising Hall of Fame, Washington, 1979-82; co-founder, chmn. Coun. Franchise Suppliers, Washington, 1986-88. Author: Franchising--The How To Book, 1986. Trustee Edn. Found. Old Dominion U., 1979-86, chmn. bd. trustees Ctr. Econ. Edn., Old Dominion U., 1983-84. Hon. editor Hotel and Motel Mgmt. Mag., 1974-83; hon. mem. Motel Day's Com. Internat. Hotel and Motel Ednl. Exposition, 1974-83; recipient Hon. Tchr. award Maury High Sch., Norfolk, 1959. Mem. Internat. Franchise Assn. (hon. life, chmn. bd. dirs., chmn. 1st Asian Symposium on Franchising, Tokyo 1978, 1st European Symposium on Franchising, Amsterdam 1978, 1st Indonesian Symposium on Franchising, Jakarta 1991), Internat. Council Hotel/Motel Mgmt., Va. Hotel and Motel Assn., Realtor's Inst. Norfolk (chmn. 1965), Nat. Assn. Realtors, Nat. Assn. Real Estate Brokers, Norfolk Bd. Realtors (dir., v.p.), Internat. Sales Execs. Club (dir., v.p., Distinguished Sales award 1957), Norfolk C. of C., Internat. Platform Assn., Airplane Owners and Pilots Assn. Presbyterian. Clubs: Cove Point Yacht (commodore), Cavalier Golf and Yacht, Town Point, Registry Resort Tennis. Office: Birdneck Pla Bldg 1072 Laskin Rd Ste 202 Virginia Beach VA 23451-6364 *I believe the greatest assist to my progress in business and personal life came when I became more aware of the "value of self" and thus others.*

TARDE, GERARD, magazine editor. Editor Golf Digest, Trumbull, Conn. Office: Golf Digest 5520 Park Ave Trumbull CT 06611-3426

TARDIO, THOMAS A., public relations executive; b. Pa., Jan. 26, 1952. V.p. strategic planning and other positions Columbia Pictures Industries, 1979-88; CFO, v.p. adminstrn. Rogers & Cowan, Inc., L.A., 1988-89, exec. v.p. entertainment sect., 1989-91, pres., CEO, 1991-95; co-chmn. mng. dir., 1996—. Mem. So. Calif. chmn. U.S. Olympic Com. Mem. Pub. Rels. Soc. Am., Nat. Acad. Recording Arts and Scis., Acad. Motion Picture Arts and Scis. Office: Rogers & Cowan Inc 1888 Century Park East Los Angeles CA 90067-1709

TARDY, MEDNEY EUGENE, JR., otolaryngologist, facial plastic surgeon; b. Scottsburg, Ind., Dec. 3, 1934. MD, Ind. U., 1960. Diplomate Am. Bd. Otolaryngology (v.p. 1993, pres. 1994). Intern Tampa Gen. Hosp., 1960-61; resident in otolaryngology U. Ill. Hosp., 1963-67, fellow head, neck and plastic surgery, 1967-68; otolaryngologist St. Joseph Hosp., Chgo.; prof. clin. otolaryngology U. Ill.; pvt. practice Chgo.; dir. divsn. facial plastic and reconstructive surgery U. Ill.; prof. clin. otolaryngology Ind. U. Med. Ctr. Pres. Am. Bd. Otolaryngology; bd. govs., Chgo. Symphony Orch., Hubbard St. Dance Co. Mem. ACS, Am. Acad. Facial Plastic and Reconstructive Surgery, Am. Acad. Otolaryngology, Am. Laryngological Soc., Am. Rhinological Soc. Office: 2913 N Commonwealth Ave Ste 430 Chicago IL 60657-6224

TAREN, JAMES ARTHUR, neurosurgeon, educator; b. Toledo, Nov. 10, 1924; s. Joseph Clarence and Mary Frances (Walker) T. BS, U. Toledo, 1948; MD, U. Mich., 1952. Diplomate Am. Bd. Neurosurgery. Intern U. Mich. Hosp., Ann Arbor, 1952-53, resident in surgery, 1953-54, resident neurosurgery, 1955-57; clin. instr. U. Mich. Med. Sch., Ann Arbor, 1955-57, instr. neurosurgery, 1957-58, asst. prof., 1958-63, assoc. prof., 1963-67, prof. neurosurgery, 1967—, dir. neurobehavioral sci. program, 1975-78, assoc. dean acad. programs, 1978-87, dir. Brain Tumor Lab., 1985-88; dir. Integrated Acad. Info. Mgmt., 1988-89; dir. neuromodulation program U. Mich. Med. Sch., Ann Arbor, 1994—; neurosurgeon Wayne County Gen. Hosp., Eloise, Mich., 1957-71, VA Hosp., Ann Arbor, 1957-73, U.S.S. Hope (Project Hope), Peru, 1962, Ecuador, 1963, Guinea, 1965; vis. prof. Hosp. Foch, Paris, 1966-67, St. Anne Hosp., Paris, 1981, Karolinski Inst., Stockholm, 1981, Haukland Sykehus, Bergen, Norway, 1984, Gumma U., Japan, 1989, Nihon U. Sch. Medicine, Tokyo, 1990. Author, co-editor: Correlative Neurosurgery, 1969, 3rd edit., 1982; contbr. articles to profl. jours. Dep. med. examiner Washtenaw County Dept. Health, Ann Arbor, 1962—. Served with USMC, 1943-46, PTO. Fellow NIH, 1953; rsch. fellow in neurosurgery Boston Children's Hosp., Peter Bent Brigham Hosp., Boston, 1955. Fellow ACS; mem. AMA, Congress of Neuro. Surgeons, Am. Assn. Neuro. Surgery, Am. Assn. Med. Colls., Am. Soc. for Stereotactic and Functional Neurosurgery, Am. Neuromodulation Soc. (treas. 1994—), Royal Soc. Medicine (affiliate), Brit. Med. Soc., Internat. Assn. Study of Pain,

Ferrari Club Am. Office: U Mich Hosps Sect Neurosurgery Box 0338 2124 Taubman Ann Arbor MI 48109

TARGAN, DONALD GILMORE, lawyer; b. Apr. 7, 1933; s. Solomon and Mollie (Simons) T.; m. Pamela Targan. BA, Juanita Coll.; JD, Am. U., 1961. Bar: N.J. 1961. Assoc. Arcus & Cooper, Atlantic City, N.J., 1961-65; atty. U.S. Atty.'s Office, Camden, N.J., 1966-69; ptnr. Targan & Kievit, Atlantic City, 1969—. Book rev. editor Am. U. Law Jour., 1960, editor-in-chief, 1961; contbr. articles to legal jours. With U.S. Army, 1954-56. Burton Smith scholar, 1961. Mem. ATLA, Assn. Trial Lawyers N.J. (bd. dirs. 1983), Am. Bd. Trial Advocates (cert. civil trial atty.), N.J. State Bar Assn. Home: 1706 Shore Rd Northfield NJ 08225 Office: Targan & Kievit 1 S New York Ave Atlantic City NJ 08401

TARJAN, ROBERT WEGG, information services executive; b. Evanston, Ill., July 28, 1943; s. Robert David and Constance Rita (Wegg) T.; m. Elizabeth Lindner; children: Robert J., Anne Marie, Katie, Michael, Eileen. BS in Math., Loyola U., Chgo., 1965. Programmer Kemper Nat. Ins. Cos., Long Grove, Ill., 1965-67, supr., 1967-79, teleprocessing mgr., 1969-78, tech. systems mgr., 1978-81, ops. and system support mgr., 1981-85, asst. mgr. info. svcs., 1985-86, v.p. info. svcs., 1986—; bd. dirs. Acord, Pearl River, N.Y. Roman Catholic. Avocation: golf. Office: Kemper Nat Ins Cos 1 Kemper Dr Long Grove IL 60047-9108

TARKOFF, MICHAEL HARRIS, lawyer; b. Phila., Oct. 3, 1946. BA, U. Miami, 1968, JD, 1971. Bar: Fla. 1973, U.S. Supreme Ct. 1976, N.Y. 1983, U.S. Tax Ct. 1984. Asst. pub. defender Miami Pub. Defender's Office, Fla., 1973-77; guest lectr. U. Miami Sch. Law, 1977; ptnr. Flynn, Rubio & Tarkoff, Miami, 1977-83; ptnr. Flynn and Tarkoff, Miami, 1983-90; pvt. practice, 1990—; mem. substantial asst. in trafficking cases com. criminal law sect. Fla. Bar. Mem. Dade County Dem. Exec. Com., 1970-72, Tiger Bay; legal counsel Dade County Dem. Com., 1978. Sponsor, South Fla. coun. Boy Scouts Am.; USTA sectional umpire; active FTA Jr. Tournament Com., FTA Dist. Dir. Officials. Mem. ABA, Fla. Bar Assn. (narcotics practice, legis. com. criminal law sect., crim. law sect., fed. practice com., criminal procedure rules subcom. 1989-95), Nat. Inst. Trial Advocacy (mem. faculty), Nat. Assn. Criminal Def. Lawyers (membership com., NORML legal com.), Fla. Criminal Def. Lawyers Assn. Office: 100 SE Second St Ste 3500 Miami FL 33131-2130

TARLETON, LARRY WILSON, newspaper editor; b. Wadesboro, N.C., July 19, 1943; s. Harold Wilson and Martha (Roberson) T.; m. Judith Elaine Huntley, Sept. 8, 1963; children: Laurie Leigh, Larry Huntley. BA in Journalism, U. N.C., 1965. Reporter The Charlotte (N.C.) Observer, 1965-73; sporte writer The Miami (Fla.) Herold, 1973-74; sports editor The Charlotte Observer, 1974-76; exec. sports editor, mng. editor, exec. editor The Dallas Times Herald, 1976-88; exec. editor The Post and Courier, Charleston, S.C., 1988—. Mem. Am. Soc. Newspaper Editors, S.C. Press Assn., Dallas Press Club (pres. 1988). AP Mng. editors, AP Sports Editors. Avocations: golf, travel. Home: 27 New St Charleston SC 29401-2405 Office: The Post and Courier 134 Columbus St Charleston SC 29403-4809

TARLETON, ROBERT STEPHEN, producer and distributor fine arts videos; b. N.Y.C., Feb. 27, 1946; s. Rollin and Helen (Boyle) Tarleton. BA, Wesleyan U., Middletown, Conn, 1968; postgrad. studies, U. Pa., Columbia, N.Y.U. V.p., exec. dir. Intercollegiate Broadcasting System, Vails Gate, N.Y., 1973-74; adjudicator U.S. VA, N.Y.C., 1974-88; prin. Applause Prodns., Inc., Port Washington, N.Y., 1989&. Author: (book) The Spirit of Kappa Alpha, 1994; (booklet) Always...Everywhere. Mem. operating com. John Philip Sousa Band Shell, Port Washington, 1985—. Sgt. U.S. Air Force, 1969-73. Recipient several svc.-wide awards for journalism while in air force. Mem. Broadcast Found. of Coll., Univ. Students (bd. dirs. 1977), Omega Gamma Delta (nat. pres. 1970-82, nat. sec. stats. 1989—), Kappa Alpha Soc. (internat. sec. 1993—). Avocations: amateur radio, philately. Home and Office: 89 Longview Rd Port Washington NY 11050

TARLOV, ALVIN RICHARD, former philanthropic foundation administrator, physician, educator, researcher; b. Norwalk, Conn., July 11, 1929; s. Charles and Mae (Shelinsky) T.; m. Joan Hylton, June 12, 1956 (div. 1976); children: Richard, Elizabeth, Jane, Suzanne, David. BA, Dartmouth Coll., 1951; MD, U. Chgo., 1956. Intern Phila. Gen. Hosp., 1956-57; resident in medicine U. Chgo. Hosps., 1957-58, 62-63, research assoc., 1958-61; asst. prof. medicine U. Chgo., 1963-68, assoc. prof., 1968-70, prof., 1970-84, chmn. dept. medicine, 1969-81; chmn. grad. med. edn. nat. adv. com. HHS, Washington, 1980; pres. Henry J. Kaiser Family Found., Menlo Park, Calif., 1984-90; sr. scientist New Eng. Med. Ctr., Boston, 1990—, exec. dir. The Health Inst., 1995—; prof. of Pub. Health Harvard U., Boston, 1990—; prof. of medicine Tufts U., 1990—. Pres. Med. Outcomes Trust, Inc., 1993—; chmn. bd., pres. Mass. Health Data Consortium, 1994—. Served to capt. U.S. Army, 1958-61. Recipient Research Career Devel. award NIH, 1962-67; John and Mary Markle Found. scholar, 1966-71. Mem. ACP (master), Inst. Medicine of Nat. Acad. Scis. Office: The Health Inst New Eng Med Ctr 750 Washington St # 345 Boston MA 02111-1533

TARN, NATHANIEL, poet, translator, educator; b. Paris, June 30, 1928; s. Marcel and Yvonne (Suchar) T.; children : Andrea, Marc. BA with honors, Cambridge (Eng.) U., 1948, MA, 1952; postgrad., U. Sorbonne, U. Paris, 1949-51; MA, U. Chgo., 1952, PhD, 1957; postgrad., London Sch. Econs., 1953-58. Anthropologist Guatemala, Burma, Alaska, and other locations, 1952—; prof. comparative lit. Rutgers U., 1970-85; vis. prof. SUNY, Buffalo and Princeton, 1969-70. Author: Old Savage/Young City, 1964, Where Babylon Ends, 1968, The Beautiful Contradictions, 1969, October, 1969, A Nowhere for Vallejo, 1971, Lyrics for the Bride of God: Section: The Artemision, 1972, The Persephones, 1974, Lyrics for the Bride of God, 1975, The House of Leaves, 1976, Birdscapes, with Seaside, 1978, The Desert Mothers, 1985, At the Western Gates, 1985, Palenque, 1986, Seeing America First, 1989, Flying the Body, 1993, Multitude of One, 1995, Views from the Weaving Mountain: Selected Essays in Poetics and Anthropology, 1991; co-author: (with Janet Rodney) The Forest, 1978, Atitlan/Alashka, 1979, The Ground of Our Great Admiration of Nature, 1978; contbg. author: Penguin Modern Poets No. Seven: Richard Murphy, Jon Silkin, Nathaniel Tarn, 1965, A.P.E.N. Anthology of Contemporary Poetry, 1966, The Penguin Book of Modern Verse Translation, 1966, Poems Addressed to Hugh MacDiarmid, 1967, Music and Sweet Poetry: A Verse Anthology, 1968, Frontier of Going: Anthology of Space Poetry, 1969, Shaking the Pumpkin, 1972, America: A Prophecy, 1973, Open Poetry, 1973, Active Anthology, 1974, Symposium of the Whole, 1983, Random House Book of Twentieth Century French Poetry, 1983, Beneath a Single Moon: Buddhism in American Poetry, 1991, American Poetry since 1950: Innovators and Outsiders, 1993; translator: The Heights of Macchu Picchu (Pablo Neruda), 1966, Stelae (Victor Segalen), 1969, Zapotec Struggles, 1993; editor, co-translator: Con Cuba: An Anthology of Cuban Poetry of the Last Sixty Years, 1969, Selected Poems (Pablo Neruda), 1970; editor Cape Edits. and founder-dir. Cape Goliard Press, J. Cape Ltd., 1967-69. Recipient Guinness prize for poetry, 1963. Office: PO Box 8187 Santa Fe NM 87504-8187

TARNOFF, PETER, governmental official; b. N.Y.C., Apr. 19, 1937; s. Norman Tarnoff and Henrietta (Goldfarb) Laing; m. Daniele Oudinot, Jan. 13, 1962 (div. Oct. 1981); children: Nicholas, Alexander; m. Mathea Falco, Dec. 24, 1981; 1 child, Benjamin. Student, U. Paris, 1956-57, postgrad., 60-61; BA, Colgate U., 1958; postgrad., U. Chgo., 1958-60. Joined Fgn. Svc., Dept. State, 1961; spl. asst. to amb. Am. Embassy, Bonn, Fed. Republic Germany, 1969; trainee Nat. Sch. Adminstrn., Paris, 1970; prin. officer Am. Consulate Gen., Lyon, France, 1971-73; dep. chief of mission Am. Embassy, Luxembourg, 1973-75; dir. Office Rsch. and Analysis for Western Europe Dept. State, Washington, 1975-76, exec. sec. Dept. State, 1977-81; fgn. affairs fellow Dept. State, San Francisco, 1981-82; exec. dir. World Affairs Coun. No. Calif., San Francisco, 1983-86; pres., dir. Coun. on Fgn. Rels., N.Y.C., 1986-93; under sec. state for polit. affairs Dept. State, Washington, 1993—. Office: Dept State 2201 C St NW Washington DC 20520-0001

TARNOPOL, MICHAEL LAZAR, bank executive; b. 1936; s. Irving and Charlotte (Weber) T.; m. Lynne Lichtenstein, June 29, 1958; children: Lisa Silverman, Lori Moore. Gen. ptrn., sr. mng. dir., also bd. dirs. Lehman Bros. Inc., 1959-75; with Bear Stearns Cos. Inc., 1975—, exec. v.p., dir.; mem. exec. com., chmn. investment banking divsn./bd. dirs. Bear Stearns Internat.; bd. dirs. Leslie Fay Cos. Bd. dirs. U.S. Equestrian Team, Cap Care Found., U.S. Polo Assn., U.S. Polo Tng. Found., Robert Steel Found., Inc.; mem. pres.'s coun. Solomon R. Guggenheim Found.; trustee U. Pa., mem. bd. overseers Wharton Sch. Mem. Palm Beach Polo Club, Palm Beach Country Club, Harmonie Club, East Hampton Tennis Club, Greenwich Polo Club (bd. dirs.). Office: 245 Park Ave New York NY 10167-0002

TARONJI, JAIME, JR., lawyer; b. N.Y.C., Nov. 20, 1944; s. Jaime and Ruth (Vazquez) T.; m. Mary Pineda, May 16, 1970; children: Ian A., Mark N., Nicole V. BA, George Washington U., 1972; JD, Georgetown U., 1976. Bar: Va. 1977, U.S. Ct. Appeals (4th and D.C. cirs.) 1977, D.C. 1978, U.S. Dist. Ct. D.C. 1978. Congl. intern U.S. Ho. of Reps., Washington, 1971; asst. to dep. staff dir. U.S. Commn. on Civil Rights, Washington, 1972-76; trial atty. FTC, Washington, 1976-79; antitrust counsel Westinghouse Electric Corp., Pitts., 1979-81; group legal counsel Dana Corp., Toledo, 1982-88; v.p., gen. counsel, asst. sec. Packaging Corp. Am. subs. Tenneco, Evanston, Ill., 1988-95; corp. law cons., 1995—. Author: The 1970 Census Undercount of Spanish Speaking Persons, 1974. Editor: Puerto Ricans in the U.S., 1976. Bd. dirs. Puerto Rican Legal Def. and Edn. Fund. Served to capt. M.I., U.S. Army, 1965-70, Vietnam. Recipient spl. achievement award U.S. Commn. on Civil Rights, 1976; award for meritorious service FTC, 1979. Mem. ABA (antitrust and litigation sects.), Am. Corp. Counsel Assn., Fibre Box Assn. (chmn. legal adv. com.), Am. Forest and Paper Assn. (paper industry gen. counsel group). Democrat. Roman Catholic. Home: 1146 Furlong Dr Libertyville IL 60048-3701 Office: Packaging Corp of America 1603 Orrington Ave Evanston IL 60201-3841

TARPLEY, BRENDA MAE See LEE, BRENDA

TARPLEY, JAMES DOUGLAS, journalism educator, magazine editor; b. Los Angeles, May 2, 1946; Cert. tchr., Mo. BS in Edn., SW Mo. U., 1968, MA in English, 1972; MA in Mass Comm., Cen. Mo. U., 1976; PhD in Journalism, So. Ill. U., 1983. Prof. journalism Evangel Coll., Springfield, Mo., 1976-87; chmn. Sch. of Journalism Regent U. (formerly Christian Broadcasting Network U.), Virginia Beach, Va., 1987—; guest lectr. Cen. Mo. U., S.W. Mo. U., So. Ill. U., U. Ohio summer journalism workshops, 1976—. Youth page editor Eldon Advertiser, 1972-76, mng. editor Home Free, 1988-90, High Adventure, 1983-87, Criminal Justice Management, 1978-81, editor Ranger News, 1979-81, design and layout editor Vision Mag., 1984-87; free-lance writer, contbr. biog. entries to profl. publs.; free-lance photographer; graphic artist, copywriter Disco-Fair advt. dept., 1964-68. Exec. com. Eldon PTA, 1971-74; youth dir. Eldon Assembly of God, 1968-75; Sunday sch. supt. Cen. Assembly of God, Springfield, Mo., 1978-82; mem. Sch. Effectiveness Evaluation Team Springfield Pub. Schs., 1985-86, 86-87. Recipient Mo. Journalism Tchr. Yr. award, 1976, Cert. of Merit Columbia U., 1984, Gold Medal of Merit Columbia U. Scholastic Press Assn., 1984; named Outstanding Grad., Dept. Mass Communication Cen. Mo. U. 1976; fellow U. Pa. and Freedom Found. project on press freedom, 1984, Nat. Newspaper Fund Fellow Dow Jones and U. Mo., 1975; named fellow of Scripps-Howard CCCU Washington D.C. Copstone proj., 1995. Mem. Assn. Christian Collegiate Media (nat. exec. dir. 1995—), Coll. Media Advisers (bd. dirs., chmn. various coms., pres. citation 1981, 84-89), Soc. Coll. Journalists (pres. 1992—, exec. dir. 1983-92, pres. citation 1981, 85, 87, 90), Assn. Christian Collegiate Media (exec. dir. 1995—), Assn. Edn. in Journalism and Mass Comm., Nat. Conf. Editl. Writers (com. scholarly rsch. 1985), Soc. Newspaper Design (edn. com. 1986-88), Broadcast Edn. Assn. (intern. com. 1984), Assn. Journalism Historials, Inst. Cert. Photographers, Mo. Tchrs. Assn., Evang. Press Assn., Pi Delta Kappa. Republican. Lodge: Kiwanis. Avocations: writing, photography, painting.

TARPY, THOMAS MICHAEL, lawyer; b. Columbus, Ohio, Jan. 4, 1945; s. Thomas Michael and Catherine G. (Sharshal) T.; m. Mary Patricia Canna, Sept. 9, 1967; children: Joshua Michael, Megan Patricia, Thomas Canna, John Patrick. A.B., John Carroll U., 1966; J.D., Ohio State U., 1969. Bar: Ohio 1969, U.S. Dist. Ct. (so. dist.) Ohio 1972, U.S. Dist. Ct. (no. dist.) Ohio 1974, U.S. Ct. Appeals (6th cir.) 1982. Assoc. Vorys, Sater, Seymour & Pease, Columbus, 1969-76, ptnr., 1977-85; v.p., chief adminstrv. officer Liebert Corp, Columbus, 1985-87; ptnr. Vorys, Sater, Seymour & Pease, Columbus, 1987—. Chmn. Columbus Graphics Commn., 1980; mem. Columbus Area Leadership Program, 1975. Served with U.S. Army, 1969-75. Mem. ABA, Ohio State Bar Assn., Columbus Bar Assn. Office: Vorys Sater Seymour & Pease PO Box 1008 52 E Gay St Columbus OH 43215-3161

TARQUINIO, ANTOINETTE CAMILLE, special education educator; b. Pitts., June 13, 1956; d. Edythe Marie Tarquinio. BS in Edn., Calif. U. Pa., 1993. Merchandising asst. Wetterau Inc., Belle Vernon, Pa., 1979-91; pvt. tutor Monessen, Pa., 1991-93; devel. specialist Early Intervention, Monessen, 1994—, Diversified Human Svcs., Monessen, 1994—; residential program worker community living arrangements Diversified Human Svcs., Monessen, 1991-93. Choir dir. Epiphany of Our Lord Ch., Monessen, 1990—. Named All Am. Scholar, 1993; recipient Nat. Collegiate award U.S. Achievement Acad., 1991, 93. Mem. Coun. for Exceptional Children, Sigma Pi Epsilon Delta, Kappa Delta Pi. Democrat. Roman Catholic. Avocations: camping, hiking, reading, Wildlife preservation, animal protection, music, sports. Home and Office: 144 Meadowview Dr Canonsburg PA 15317-2309

TARR, CHARLES EDWIN, physicist, educator; b. Johnstown, Pa., Jan. 14, 1940; s. Charles Larned and Mary Katherine (Wright) T.; m. Bex Suzanne Harrell, Sept. 4, 1964 (div. Feb. 1977); m. Gudrun Kiefer, Nov. 18, 1977. B.S. in Physics (Morehead scholar 1957-61), U. N.C., Chapel Hill, 1961, Ph.D., 1966. Research assoc. U. N.C., Chapel Hill, 1966, U. Pitts., 1966-68; mem. faculty U. Maine, Orono, 1968—; assoc. prof. physics U. Maine, 1973-78, prof., 1978—, chmn. dept., 1977-79, assoc. dean Coll. Arts and Scis., 1979-81, acting dean Grad. Sch., 1981-87, acting v.p. research, 1984-87, dean Grad. Sch., 1987—; past docent U. Groningen, Netherlands, 1975-76; dir. Maine Toxicology Inst., 1992—, co-chair, 1993, chair, 1994; mem. exec. com. Coun. Rsch. Policy and Grad. Edn. of Nat. Assn. State Colls. and Land Grant Univs., 1993—; cons. in field. Contbr. articles to profl. jours. NASA grantee, 1970-72; NSF grantee, 1972—. Mem. IEEE, Am. Phys. Soc., Assn. Computing Machinery, Northeastern Assn. Grad. Schs. (mem. at large 1988—, pres. elect 1990-91, pres. 1991—), Sigma Xi. Quaker. Home: 519 College Ave Orono ME 04473-1211 Office: Univ Maine Off Dean Grad Sch Orono ME 04469

TARR, CURTIS W., business executive; b. Stockton, Calif., Sept. 18, 1924; s. F.W. and Esther (Reed) T.; m. Elizabeth May Myers, 1955 (div. 1978); children: Pamela Elizabeth, Cynthia Leigh; m. Marilyn Van Stralen, 1979 (div. 1991); m. Mary Katherine Stegmiller, 1992. B.A., Stanford U., 1948, Ph.D., 1962; M.B.A., Harvard U., 1950; L.H.D., Ripon Coll., 1965, Grinnell Coll., 1969, Lincoln Coll., 1980; LL.D., Lawrence U., 1974, Ill. Wesleyan U., 1980. Rsch. asst., instr. Harvard U., 1950-52; v.p. Sierra Tractor & Equipment Co., Chico, Calif., 1952-58; staff mem. 2d Hoover Commn., 1954-55; asst. dir. summer session Stanford U., 1961-62, dir., 1962-63, asst. dean humanities and scis., 1962-63, lectr. bus. sch., 1962-63; pres. Lawrence U., Appleton, Wis., 1963-69; asst. sec. for manpower and res. affairs Air Force, 1969-70; dir. SSS, Washington, 1970-72; under sec. state for security assistance, 1972-73, acting dep. under sec. state for mgmt., 1973; v.p. overseas devel. Deere & Co., Moline, Ill., 1973; v.p. parts distbn. and materials mgmt. Deere & Co., 1973-81, v.p. mgmt. devel., 1981-83; dean and prof. Johnson Sch. Mgmt., Cornell U., 1984-89, prof. mgmt., 1989-90, dean emeritus, 1990—; vice chmn. Intermet Corp., 1992-95; trustee Inst. Paper Chemistry, 1963-69; bd. dirs. Intermet Corp., Atlanta, State Farm Mut. Ins. Co., Bloomington, Ill., Phyton Corp., Ithaca, N.Y., State Farm Ins. Co.; mem. Internat. Rsch. Coun. Ctr. for Strategic and Internat. Studies, Washington, 1989-92; adj. prof. mgmt. Emory U., 1991-93. Author: Private Soldier, 1976, By the Numbers, 1981, Youth, 1994. Chmn. Task Force on Govt. Orgn., Fin. and Tax Distbn. for State Wis., 1967-69; chmn. Def. Manpower Commn., 1974-76, Ill. State Scholarship Commn., 1978-79, Quad Cities Grad. Study Ctr., 1982-84, Rep. candidate for Congress 2d Dist., Calif., 1958; trustee Am. Coll., Bryn Mawr, Pa., 1989-92. Served with AUS, 1943-46, ETO. Recipient Exceptional Civilian Service medal Air Force Dept., 1970; Distinguished Service award SSS, 1975. Mem. University Club (Chgo., N.Y.C.), Cosmos (Washington). Methodist.

TARR, DAVID WILLIAM, political scientist, educator; b. Melrose, Mass., July 25, 1931; s. Charles Howard and Pauline (Bryant) T.; children: Susan, Bryant. B.A., U. Mass., 1953; M.A., U. Chgo., 1956, Ph.D., 1961. Instr. Amherst and Mt. Holyoke colls., 1958-59; nat. def. analyst Legis. Reference Service, Library of Congress, 1959-62; research assoc. Washington Center Fgn. Policy, 1962-63; mem. faculty U. Wis.-Madison, 1963—, prof. polit. sci., 1969—, dir. nat. security studies group, 1966-69, chmn. dept., 1972-75, fellow Inter-univ. Seminar on armed Forces and Soc., 1975—, dir. Ctr. for Internat. Cooperation and Security Studies, 1988—; rsch. assoc. Ctr. Sci. and Internat. Affairs Harvard U., 1977. Author: American Strategy in the Nuclear Age, 1966, Nuclear Deterrence and International Security: Alternative Nuclear Regimes, 1991; co-editor: Modules in Security Studies, 1974; contbr. articles to profl. jours. Chmn. U. Wis. Athletic Bd., 1979-86. Served to 1st lt. AUS, 1953-55. Rockefeller grantee, 1962-63; fellow, 1977. Mem. Internat. Studies Assn., Am. Polit. Sci. Assn. Unitarian.

TARR, DELBERT HOWARD, JR., seminary president, clergyman; b. Aitkin, Minn., June 14, 1934; s. Delbert Howard and Catherine Elizabeth (Boomer) T.; m. Dorothy D. Hill, June 12, 1954; children: Cindy Sharon, Terry Mark, Randel Ray. B.A. in Bible, North Central Bible Coll., 1956; postgrad. Ecole Lemania, Switzerland, 1959-60; M.A. in Comm., U. Minn., 1969; Ph.D. in Comm., 1979. Ordained to ministry Assemblies of God Ch., 1957; pastor Assemblies of God Ch., Hopkins, Minn., 1956-58; apptd. fgn. missionary Burkina Faso (formerly Upper Volta), West Africa, 1960-63; dir. Mossiland Bible Sch., 1964-67; co-founder, dean West African Advanced Sch. Theology, Lome, Togo, 1970-73; prof., coordinator cross-cultural comm. studies Assemblies of God Theol. Sem. (formerly Assemblies of God Grad. Sch.), Springfield, Mo., 1973-77, dean missions div., 1977-80, chmn. missions dept., 1980-82; pres. Calif. Theol. Sem., Fresno, 1983-90, Assemblies of God Theol. Sem., 1990—; guest lectr. Far East Advanced Sch. Theology, Manila, Philippines, 1983. Author: Double Image, 1994. Research grantee African speech mannerisms, 1976-77. Mem. Am. Soc. Missiology, Acad. Evangelism, Soc. Pentecostal Studies, Greenleaf Servant Leadership. Office: Assemblies of God Theol Sem 1445 N Boonville Ave Springfield MO 65802-1894

TARR, JOEL ARTHUR, history and public policy educator; b. Jersey City, May 8, 1934; s. Max Alfred and Florence (Levin) Tartalsky; m. Arlene Green, Sept. 2, 1956 (dec. June 1969); children: Michael Jay, Joanna Sue; m. Tova Brafman, Aug. 11, 1978; children: Maya Leah, Ilana Ariel. BS, Rutgers U., 1956, MA, 1957; PhD, Northwestern U., 1963. Asst. prof. Calif. State U., Long Beach, 1961-66; vis. prof. U. Calif., Santa Barbara, 1966-67; asst. prof. Carnegie Mellon U., Pitts., 1967-70, assoc. prof., 1969-72, prof. history and pub. policy, 1973-90, Richard S. Caliguiri prof. urban and environ. history and policy, 1990—, dir. program in tech. and soc., 1975-87, co-dir. program in applied history and social sci., 1978-86, acting dean Sch. Urban and Pub. Affairs, 1986, assoc. dean Coll. Humanities and Social Sci., 1988-91, acting dean Coll. Humanities and Social Sci., 1991-92, acting head dept. history, 1992-93. Author: A Study in Boss Politics, 1971; editor: Patterns of City Growth, 1974, Retrospective Technology Assessment, 1977, Transportation Innovation and Spatial Change in Pittsburgh, 1850-1934, 1978, Pittsburgh-Sheffield: Sister Cities, 1986, Technology and the Rise of the Networked City in Europe and America, 1988. Bd. dirs. Action Housing, Pitts., 1983; trustee Hist. Soc. Western Pa., 1993—. NEH fellow, 1969-70; grantee NSF, 1975-79, 78-80, 83-85, NOAA, 1982-84; recipient Robert Doherty Prize for contbns. to excellence in edn., 1992. Mem. AAAS, Pub. Works Hist. Soc. (pres. 1982-83, Abel Wolman prize 1989), Orgn. Am. Historians, Pub. History Assn. (nat. council), Am. Soc. Environ. History, Soc. for the History of Tech. Democrat. Jewish. Home: 5418 Normlee Pl Pittsburgh PA 15217-1116 Office: Carnegie-Mellon U Schenley Pk Pittsburgh PA 15213

TARR, RALPH WILLIAM, lawyer, former federal government official; b. Bakersfield, Calif., Sept. 29, 1948. BA, Dartmouth Coll., 1970; MPA, Calif. State U., 1973; JD, U. Calif., Hastings, 1976. Extern to assoc. justice Calif. Supreme Ct., 1976; rsch. atty. to presiding justice Ct. Appeal (5th dist.) Calif., 1976-77; assoc. Baker, Manock & Jensen, Fresno, Calif., 1977-81, dir., mem. exec. com., 1981-82; mem. adminstrv. com. Fed. Register, Washington, 1982-85; dep. asst. atty. gen. U.S. Dept. Justice, Washington, 1982-84, acting asst. atty. gen., 1984-85; solicitor U.S. Dept. Interior, Washington, 1985-89, counselor to the solicitor, 1989-90; pvt. practice L.A., 1990—. Home: 24011 Alder Pl Calabasas CA 91302-2394 Office: Andrews & Kurth LLP 601 S Figueroa St Fl 4200 Los Angeles CA 90017-5747

TARR, ROBERT JOSEPH, JR., publishing executive, retail executive; b. Freeport, N.Y., Dec. 7, 1943; s. Robert Joseph and Janet Christman (Laughton) T.; m. Molly Worthington Upton, Feb. 28, 1970; children: William Upton, Robert Joseph, III, David Worthington. BS, U.S. Naval Acad., 1966; MBA, Harvard U., 1973; MA, Fletcher Sch. Law & Diplomacy, 1976. Asst. v.p. corp. fin. Paine Webber Jackson Curtis, Boston, 1973-75; dir. corp. planning, then v.p., treas. Gen. Cinema Corp., Chestnut Hill, Mass., 1976-78, sr. v.p., 1978-83, exec. v.p., COO, 1983-85, pres., COO, 1985-91; pres., CEO, COO Harcourt Gen., Inc. (Gen. Cinema Corp., 1993), Chestnut Hill, Mass., 1991—; pres., COO The Neiman marcus Group, Inc., 1987-91, pres., bd. dirs., CEO, COO, 1991—; bd. dirs. Nat. Retail Fedn., Open Market, Inc. Trustee Tenacre Country Day Sch., Belmont Hill Sch. Lt. USN, 1966-71. Mem. Univ. Club (Boston), Comml. Club Boston, Quissett Yacht Club, Brae Burn Country Club. Home: 40 White Oak Rd Wellesley MA 02181-1435 Office: Harcourt Gen Inc 27 Boylston St Chestnut Hill MA 02167-1719

TARRANCE, VERNON LANCE, JR., public opinion research executive; b. Harlingen, Tex., Dec. 4, 1940; s. Vernon Lance Sr. and Mary Gilmore (Rea) T.; m. Eugenia Aline McCuistion, July 2, 1966; children: Vernon Lance III, Haloway McCuistion, Kyle Rea. BA, Washington & Lee U., 1962; postgrad., U. Mich., 1971; MA, Am. U., 1973; postgrad., Harvard U., 1973-74. Dir. research Tex. Rep. Party, Austin, 1964-67, Rep. Nat. Com., Washington, 1969-70; spl. asst. to dir. U.S. Census Bur., Washington, 1970-73; v.p. Decision Making Info. Inc., Santa Ana, Calif., 1974-77; pres., founder Tarrance, Hill, Newport & Ryan, Houston, 1977-92; bd. dirs. Gallup Orgn.; pres., mng. dir. Gallup China Ltd., Beijing, 1993-95; vis. prof. polit. sci. Tex. A&M U., 1995—; cons. Gallup Internat. Rsch. Ctr., Lincoln, Nebr.; co-chmn. adv. adjustment panel U.S. Census. Co-author: A New Force in American Politics, 1972, The Ticket Splitter, 1990; editor: Texas Precinct Votes '66, '68, '70, '71. Fellow John F. Kennedy Inst. Politics Harvard U., 1973-74; named one of 150 People Who Influence Fed. Govt. Nat. Jour. Mag., 1986. Mem. Asia Soc., Houston World Affairs Coun., Coun. on Fgn. Rels. (Houston com.), Kappa Sigma. Avocations: mountain trekking, golf, aviculture, travel.

TARRANT, R(ICHARD) J(OHN), classicist, educator; b. Bklyn., Apr. 4, 1945; s. John Joseph and Bertha (Slaney) T.; m. Jacqueline Brown, Sept. 14, 1968. B.A., Fordham U., 1966; D.Phil., Oxford U., 1972; A.M. hon., Harvard U., 1982. P.S. Allen jr. research fellow Corpus Christi Coll., Oxford, Eng., 1968-70; lectr. Univ. Coll., Toronto, Ont., Can., 1970-71, asst. prof., 1971-74, assoc. prof., 1974-79; prof. U. Toronto, 1979-82; prof. Greek and Latin Harvard U., Cambridge, Mass., 1982-87, Carl A. Pescosolido prof. Roman civilization, 1987-93, Pope prof. Latin language and Literature, 1993—, chmn. dept., 1988-94; acting dean Grad. Sch. Arts and Scis., 1995-96; vis. Mellon prof. Inst. for Advanced Study, Princeton, 1991-92; vis. fellow Corpus Christi Coll. U. Oxford, 1992. Author: Greek and Latin Lyric Poetry in Translation: A Bibliographical Survey, 1972, Seneca, Agamemnon, 1976, (with others) Texts and Transmission: A Survey of the Latin Classics, 1983, Seneca's Thyestes, 1985; editor Phoenix: Jour. Classical Assn. Can., 1978-82, Harvard Studies in Classical Philology, 1985-88, 93-94; editorial bd. Toronto Medieval Latin Texts, 1977—, Cambridge Classical Texts and Commentaries, 1992—; advisory bd. Text: Transactions of the Soc. for Textual Scholarship, 1994—; contbr. articles to profl. jours. Cabot fellow, 1993-94; Marshall scholar, 1966-69. Mem. Am. Philol. Assn. (bd. dirs. 1987-89, v.p. publs. 1992-95), Cambridge Philol. Assn., Classical Assn. Can., Classical Assn. New Eng., Phi Beta Kappa. Office: Harvard U Dept. Classics 319 Boylston Hall Cambridge MA 02138

TARRANT, ROBERT FRANK, soil science educator, researcher; b. Portland, Oreg., Mar. 11, 1918; s. Frank A. and Vera Leona (Tibbils) T.; m. Jean Inez Horton, Sept. 20, 1941; children: Christopher R., Susan J., Brian H., Stephanie A. Tarrant Martin. BS, Oreg. State U., 1941. Soil scientist

USDA Pacific N.W. Forest Research Sta., Portland, 1946-71, asst. dir., 1971-74, dep. dir., 1975, dir., 1975-79; prof. forest scis. Oreg. State U., Corvallis, 1979—. Co-editor: The Biology of Alder, 1968, From the Forest to the Sea, 1988, Biology and Management of Red Alder, 1994; contbr. articles, reports to profl. jours. Bd. dirs. Oreg. Easter Seal Soc., Portland, 1969-75, pres., 1971-73. Served to lt. comdr. USN, 1942-45, ETO, PTO, also 1950-52. Recipient Superior Svc. award USDA, Washington, 1971, Tarrant Rsch. fellowship Oreg. State U., 1993—. Mem. N.W. Sci. Assn. (hon. life), Oreg. Hardwoods Commn., Sigma Xi Rsch. Soc. Episcopalian. Home: 2660 SW Fairmont Dr Corvallis OR 97333-1424

TARRANTS, WILLIAM EUGENE, government official; b. Liberty, Mo., Dec. 9, 1927; s. Joseph Eugene and Mildred Jane (Wright) T.; m. Mary Jo Edman, Jan. 19, 1952 (div. 1981); children: James Timothy, Jennifer Lynn; m. Lorna D. Lundberg, Sept. 24, 1988; stepchildren: David Murphy, Christine Walls, Janelle McCrea. B in Indsl. Engring., Ohio State U., 1951; MS in Indsl. Engring., 1959; PhD, NYU, 1963. Registered profl. engr., Calif., Ohio, N.Mex. Instr. indsl. engring. Ohio State U., Columbus, 1958-59; asst. prof., research asso. N.Y. U., 1959-64; chief accident research div. Bur. Labor Stats., Dept. Labor, Washington, 1964-67; dir. manpower devel. div. Nat. Hwy. Traffic Safety Adminstrn., Dept. Transp., 1967-80; chief scientist Office of Program and Demonstration Evaluation, 1980-84; program analyst Office of Occupant Protection, 1984-87, program analyst evaluation staff, 1987-90, also chmn. sci. and tech. info. adv. bd., 1984-91; instr. Johns Hopkins U., 1984-91, U. Md., 1991-92; planning and adminstrn. transp. safety mem. Transp. Rsch. Bd., NAS; cons. on safety program evaluation Indsl. Commn. Ohio, 1959; exec. com. Related Accreditation Commn., 1994—; accreditation bd. Engring. and Tech., Inc., 1994—. Contbr.: chpt. to Selected Readings in Safety, 1973, Readings in Industrial Accident Prevention, 1980; Author: chpt. to A Selected Bibliography of Reference Materials in Safety Engineering and Related Fields, 1967, Dictionary of Terms Used in the Safety Profession, 1971, Measurement of Safety Performance, 1980, Handbook of Occupational Safety and Health, 1987, also manuals and articles in field; mem. editorial bd.: Jour. Safety Research, Accident Analysis and Prevention, An Internat. Jour.; editor-in-chief: Traffic Safety Evaluation Research Rev. Trustee, ch. chmn. Evang. Covent Ch., 1976-80, 84-88, region 8 rep. to bd. trustees East Coast Conf., 1986-92. Capt. USAF, 1951-57. Recipient Founder's Day award NYU, 1963, 1st pl. Nat. Tech. Paper awards, 1961, 63, 67, cert. for outstanding performance Nat. Hwy. Traffic Safety Adminstrn., 1973, 86, Disting. Svc. to Safety award Nat. Safety Coun., 1989, Disting. Career Svc. award U.S. Dept. Transp., 1990; inducted into Safety and Health Hall of Fame Internat., 1990. Fellow Am. Soc. Safety Engrs. (dir., v.p. rsch. and tech. devel., pres. 1977-78, chmn. acad. accreditation coun. 1978—, fellow rev. bd. 1980-88); mem. AAAS, Am. Soc. Safety Rsch. (trustee), Am. Inst. Indsl. Engrs., Human Factors Soc., System Safety Soc., Evaluation Rsch. Soc., Vets. of Safety, Am. Nat. Stds. Inst. (stds. com.), Soc. for Risk Analysis, Nat. Safety Coun. (chmn. rsch. projects com. 1973-78, exec. com. indsl. conf. 1977-78, Disting. Svc. award 1989), Alpha Pi Mu, Kappa Delta Pi. Mem. Evangelical Covent Ch. (trustee, ch. chmn. 1976-80, 84-88). Home: 606 Woodsmans Way Crownsville MD 21032-2317 Office: 400 7th St SW Washington DC 20590-0001 *We often look with awe at the successful person, much as we admire a well designed structure or a beautiful painting. Behind the finished product usually lies exhaustive effort, frustration, disappointment, and even failure which is obscured by the glow of accomplishment. Success is achieved by some ability, lots of hard work, perserverance, courage of convictions, help and support from others, a desire to reach a goal, self-discipline, and considerable personal sacrifice as we make choices concerning the use of our limited resources. The ability to bounce back from adversity is crucial. Most important of all is the strength and insight gained through prayer and the willingness to permit your life to be guided by Christian faith.*

TARRO, GIULIO, virologist; b. Messina, Italy, July 9, 1938; s. Emanuele and Emanuela (Iannello) T. MD, U. Naples, 1962, postgrad. in nervous diseases, 1968, PhD in Virology, 1971; postgrad. in med. and biol. scis., Roman Acad., 1979; hon. degree, U. Pro Deo, Albany, N.Y., 1989, St. Theodora Acad., N.Y., 1991. Asst. in med. pathology Naples U., Italy, 1964-66; rsch. assoc. divsn. virology and cancer rsch. Children's Hosp., Cin., 1965-68; asst. prof. rsch. pediat. U. Cin. Coll. Medicine, 1968-69; rsch. fellow Nat. Rsch. Coun., Naples, 1966-74, rsch. chief, 1974; prof. oncologic virology Coll. Medicine U. Naples, 1971-85, prof. microbiology adn immunology Sch. Specialization, 1972—; chief divsn. virology D. Cotugno Hosp. for Infectious Diseases, Naples, 1973—; dean faculty natural and phys. scis. Nobile Accademia di Santa Teodora Imperatrice, Capua, Italy, 1993—; sr. scientist Nat. Cancer Inst. Frederick (Md.) Ctr., 1973; project dir. Nat. cancer Inst., Bethesda, Md., 1971-75; edn. min. rep. Zool. Sta., Naples, 1975-79; cons. Italian Pharmacotherpic Inst., Rome, 1980—; pres. De Beaumont Bonelli Found. for Cancer Rsch., Naples, 1978—, nat. com. on bioethics, 1995—. Author: Virologia Oncologica, 1979 (award 1985), Patologia dell'AIDS, 1991, Con in Cancro si Può Vivere, 1992, AIDS COsa Possiamo Fare Cosa Dobbiamo Sapere, 1994; contbr. over 300 sci. papers to profl. publs.; patentee in field. Pres. Sci. Cultural Com., Torre Annunziata, Italy, 1984, Tumor Prevention Assn., Rome, 1984; mem. acad. senate Constantinian U., Providence, 1990, U. Pro Deo, N.Y., 1994. Maj. Italian Navy, 1982-84, lt. col., 1993-95. Decorated Comdr. Nat. Order of Merit, 1991, Star of Europe, 1980; recipient Internat. Lenghi award Lincei Acad., 1969, Gold Microscope award Italian Health Min., 1973, Knights of Humanity award Internat. Register of Chivalry, Malta, 1978, gold medal of Culture, Pres. of Italian Republic, 1975, Culture award, 1985, 1st prize in Biomed. Rsch., Italian Acad. Arts and Scis., 1987, Castello di Pietrarossa award, Italy, 1991, gold Cesare award Padova, 1991, 20th Century award in Medicine, 1994, Knight of Grand Cross Sovereign Constantinian order of St George, 1993 Gold Little Horse , Transnat., European Federation, Rome 1996. Fellow AAAS; mem. Am. Soc. Microbiology, Internat. Assn. for Leukemias, Internat. League Drs. for Abolition of Vivisection (pres. 1992—), Italian Soc. Immuno-Oncology (v.p. 1975—, pres. 1990—), Italian Assn. for Viral Study and Rsch. (pres. 1995—), Assn. Res. Prevention of Cancer (mem. sci. com. 1995), N.Y. Acad. Scis., Lions (pres. Pompei chpt. 1987-89, vice gov. dist. 108y 1991-92, pres. to fight cancer 1992-94, pres. com. sci. and life 1994-95, pres. com. to fight drug addiction and AIDS 1995-96, Melvin Jones fellow 1993). Roman Catholic. Achievements include discovery of RSV virus in infant deaths in Naples. Home: 286 Posillipo, 80123 Naples Italy Office: D Cotugno Hosp USL 41, 54 Quagliariello, 80131 Naples Italy

TARR-WHELAN, LINDA, policy center executive; b. Springfield, Mass., May 24, 1940; d. Albert and Jane Zack; m. Keith Tarr-Whelan; children: Scott, Melinda. BSN, Johns Hopkins U., 1963; MS, U. Md., 1967. Program dir. AFSCME AFL-CIO, Washington, 1968-74, union area dir., 1974-76; adminstrn. dir. N.Y. State Labor Dept., Albany, N.Y., 1976-79; dep. asst. to pres. Carter White House, Washington, 1979-80; dir. govt. rels. NEA, Washington, 1980-86; CEO, pres. Ctr. for Policy Alternatives, Washington, 1986—, bd. dirs., 1985—; apptd. rep. UN Commn. on Status of Women, 1996—. Bd. dirs. Benton Found., Adv. Inst., Ind. Sector, Voters for Choice, State Issues Forum. Recipient Disting. Grad. award Johns Hopkins U., 1981, Breaking the Glass Ceiling award, 1996; leadership fellow Japan Soc., 1987-88. Democrat. Avocations: walking, travel. Home: 3466 Roberts Ln Arlington VA 22207-5335 Office: Ctr for Policy Alternatives 1875 Connecticut Ave NW Washington DC 20009-5728

TARSKY, EUGENE STANLEY, accountant, management and systems consultant; b. Meriden, Conn., Mar. 10, 1935; s. Joseph and Fannie (Apkin) T.; m. Irene M. Goldstein, Sept. 22, 1957; children: Julie B., Jeffrey A. Grad., U. Mass., 1957; M of Sci. in Taxation, Bentley Coll., 1978. CPA, Mass. Salesman, mgr. Margene Supply Co., Springfield, Mass., 1951-57; entry level acct. Coopers & Lybrand, Boston, 1957-58, auditor, system designer, 1961-64; CPA Martin Braver & Co., Chestnut Hill, Mass., 1964-65; pvt. practice Boston, 1965-70; ptnr. Orlando C. Moyer & Co. CPAs, Boston, 1970-72; pvt. practice Newton, Mass., 1972-82; pres. Eugene S. Tarsky CPA, Inc., Needham, Mass., 1982—; guest lectr. Continuing Edn. Program, Northeastern U., Boston, 1980, Boston U., 1982. Bd. dirs., asst. treas. Hospice of the Good Shepherd, Newton, 1982-85; bd. dirs., treas. Newton Boys and Girls Club, 1988—. With USAF, 1958-61. Recipient Benefactor of Youth award West Suburban YMCA, 1986, 89. Mem. AICPA, Mass. Soc. CPA's (speaker's bur. 1976—, discussion leader continuing edn. program 1983-90, mgmt. of acctg. practice com. 1984-89, Disting. Speaker award 1985), Route 128 Practitioners Forum (guest lectr. 1990, 93), Newton-Needham C. of C. (bd. dirs. 1975-76, 81-90, treas. 1986-87, pres. 1987-88, Outstanding Leadership award 1989, 10-Yr. Loyal Svc. award 1990), Kiwanis (bd. dirs. Newton 1989-94). Avocations: swimming, golf, bridge, travel, family. Home: 280 Boylston St Chestnut Hill MA 02167 Office: 56 Pickering St Needham MA 02192-3156

TARSON, HERBERT HARVEY, university administrator emeritus; b. N.Y.C., Aug. 28, 1910; s. Harry and Elizabeth (Miller) T.; m. Lynne Barnett, June 27, 1941; 1 son, Stephen. Grad., Army Command Gen. Staff Coll., 1942, Armed Forces Staff Coll., 1951, Adavnced Mgmt. Sch. Sr. Air Force Comdrs., George Washington U., 1954; B.A., U. Calif., Los Angeles, 1949; Ph.D., U.S. Internat. U., 1972. Entered U.S. Army as pvt., 1933, advanced through grades to maj., 1942; transfered to U.S. Air Force, 1947, advanced through grades to lt. col., 1949; adj. exec. officer Ft. Snelling, Minn., 1940-42; asst. adj. gen. 91st Inf. Div., 1942-43; chief of personnel, advance sec. Comd. Zone, ETO, 1944-45; dir. personnel services 8th Air Force, 1946-47; dep. dir. dept. info. and edn. Armed Forces Info. Sch., 1949-51; dir. personnel services Japan Air Def. Force, 1951-53, Continental Air Command, 1953-62; dir. adminstrv. services, spl. asst. to Comdr. 6th Air Force Res. Region, 1962-64; ret., 1964; asst. to chancellor L.I. U., Brookville, 1964-69; dean admissions Tex. State Tech. Inst., San Diego Indsl. Center, 1970-72; v.p. acad. affairs Nat. U., San Diego, 1972-75, sr. v.p., 1975-88, founding sr. v.p. emeritus, 1988—. Decorated Bronze Star medal with oak leaf cluster, Air Force Commendation medal with 2 oak leaf clusters. Fellow Bio-Med Research Inst.; mem. Doctoral Soc. U.S. Internat. U., Am. Soc. Tng., Devel., World Affairs Council, Air Force Assn., Navy League U.S., Pres.'s Assos. of Nat. U. (presidential life). Home: 4611 Denwood Rd La Mesa CA 91941-4803 *The greatest motivating force in my life is to explore the challenging frontiers of the future. Nothing can be compared to it.*

TARTER, CURTIS BRUCE, physicist, science administrator; b. Louisville, Sept. 26, 1939; s. Curtis B. and Marian Turner (Cundiff) T.; m. Jill Cornell, June 6, 1964 (div. 1975); 1 child, Shana Lee; m. Marcia Cyrog Linn, Sept. 6, 1987. BS, MIT, 1961; PhD, Cornell U., 1967. Teaching asst. Cornell U., Ithaca, N.Y., 1961-63, rsch. asst., 1964-67; physicist Lawrence Radiation Lab., Livermore, Calif., summers 1962, 63; staff mem. Theoretical Physics div. U. Calif., Lawrence Livermore Nat. Lab., 1967-69, group leader macroscopic properties of matter, 1969-71, assoc. div. leader, 1971-74, group leader opacities, 1972-78, div. leader, 1974-84; dep. assoc. dir. for physics Lawrence Livermore Nat. Lab., 1984-88, assoc. dir. for physics, 1988-94, dep. dir., 1994; dir., 1994—; sr. scientist Applied Rsch. Labs. Aeronutronic Div. Philco-Ford Corp., 1967; lectr., grad. student advisor dept. applied sci., U. Calif., Davis/Livermore, 1970—; cons. Hertz Found., 1970—, field com. study on astronomy in the 80's, NRC, 1980; mem. Army Sci. Bd., Washington, 1989—. Contbr. numerous articles to profl. jours. Mem. Am. Phys. Soc., Am. Astron. Soc., Internat. Astron. Union. Republican. Avocations: golf, squash, bridge. Home: 676 Old Jonas Hill Rd Lafayette CA 94549-5214 Office: Lawrence Livermore Nat Lab PO Box 808 Livermore CA 94551-0808

TARTER, FRED BARRY, advertising executive; b. Bklyn., Aug. 16, 1943; s. Irving and Edna (Kupferberg) T.; children: Scott Andrew, Heather, Megan. BS, CCNY, 1966. Pres. Jamie Publs. Hootenanny Enterprises, Inc., 1962-65; mdse. dir. Longines Symphonette Soc., 1965-67; with Universal Communications, Inc., N.Y.C., 1967—, pres., chief exec. officer, 1969-74; exec. v.p. Deerfield Communications, Inc., N.Y.C., 1974-87, pres., chief exec. officer, 1977-88; pres. Deerfield Books, Inc., N.Y.C., 1988-89; pub. S.E.W. mag., N.Y.C., 1977-88; pres. The Rainbow Group Ltd., N.Y.C., 1988—; bd. dirs. Caribbean Internat. News Corp., Screenvision, Inc., Lakeside Group, Inc., Boardwalk Entertainment, Ltd.; chmn. Pharmacy Fund, Inc.; vice chmn. Affinity Comm., Inc.; exec. prodr. Joanne Carson's VIP's Miss Am. Teenager Pageant, 1972-73; pres. The Programme Exch., U.K. Ltd.; prodr. Spenser Judas Goat, Ceremony, Wounded Heart, Lover's Leap, Hearts Adrift, 1995, Marriage Counselor, 1994. Mem. Friars Club, The Reform Club (London). Home: 9 Davis Dr Armonk NY 10504-3006 Office: The Pharmacy Fund Inc 680 Fifth Ave New York NY 10019 *An integral part of success is the capacity for failure. Persistence, combined with responsibility, has proven to be the winning combination time and again.*

TARTER, MICHAEL ERNEST, biostatistician, educator; b. Bronx, N.Y., Dec. 20, 1938; s. William Tarter and Frieda Browdy; m. Orna Benzenburg, Aug. 30, 1975; children: Douglas, Robin. BA in Math., UCLA, 1959, MA in Math., 1961, PhD in Biostats., 1963. Asst. prof. U. Mich., Ann Arbor, 1964-66, assoc. prof., 1967; assoc. prof. U. Calif., Irvine, 1968-70; assoc. prof. U. Calif., Berkeley, 1970-76, prof., 1977—. Author books and articles; editor: Jour. Am. Statis. Assn. (screening editor for applications 1971-80). Fellow Am. Statis. Assn. (chmn. com. resources biometrics sect. 1981—, editorial bds. computational stats. and data analysis 1983-86, biometrics 1976-84, communications in stats. 1977—). Office: U Calif Sch Pub Health Dept Biomed Environ Health Scis 140 Warren Hall Berkeley CA 94720

TARTIKOFF, BRANDON, broadcast executive; b. L.I., N.Y., Jan. 13, 1949; m. Lilly Samuels, 1982; children: Calla Lianne, Elizabeth Justine. B.A. with honors, Yale U., 1970. With promotion dept. ABC TV, New Haven, Conn., 1971-73; program exec. dramatic programming Sta. WLS-TV (ABC), Chgo., 1973-76; mgr. dramatic devel. ABC TV, N.Y.C., 1976-77; writer, producer Graffiti; dir. comedy programs NBC Entertainment, Burbank, Calif., 1977-78, v.p. programs, 1978-80, pres., 1980-90; chmn. NBC Entertainment Group, 1989-91, Paramount Pictures, 1991-92, New World Entertainment, Ltd., 1994—. Co-author: The Last Great Ride, 1992. Named 1 of 10 Outstanding Young Men Am. U.S. Jaycees, 1981; recipient Tree of Life award Jewish Nat. Found., 1986. Office: New World Entertainment Ltd 1440 S Sepulveda Blvd Los Angeles CA 90025-3492

TARUN, ROBERT WALTER, lawyer; b. Lake Forest, Ill., Sept. 1, 1949; s. Donald Walter and Bonnie Jean (Cruickshank) T.; m. Helen J. McSweeney, May 1, 1987; children: Abigail Esch, Tyler Vincent, Parker Donald, Aimée Dakota. AB, Stanford U., 1971; JD, DePaul U., 1974; MBA, U. Chgo., 1982. Bar: Ill. 1974, Calif. 1975, U.S. Dist. Ct. (no. dist.) Ill. 1974, U.S. Dist. Ct. (we. dist.) Ark. 1986, U.S. Dist. Ct. (so. dist.) Ind. 1995, U.S. Dist. Ct. (no. dist.) Calif. 1995, U.S. Dist. Ct. (ea. dist.) Mich. 1996, U.S. Ct. Appeals (7th cir.) 1975, U.S. Ct. Appeals (5th cir.) 1992, U.S. Ct. Appeals (3d cir.) 1993, U.S. Ct. Appeals (Fed. cir.) 1995, U.S. Ct. Appeals (9th and 11th cirs.) 1996, U.S. Supreme Ct. 1978. Asst. atty. gen. State of Ill., Chgo., 1974-76; asst. atty. U.S. Dept. Justice, Chgo., 1976-79, dep. chief criminal div., 1979-82, exec. asst. U.S. atty. no. dist. Ill., 1982-85; ptnr. Reuben & Proctor, Chgo., 1985-86, Isham, Lincoln & Beale, Chgo., 1986-88, Winston & Strawn, Chgo., 1988—; lectr. criminal law practice Northwestern U. Sch. Law, 1986; instr. Atty. Gen.'s Advocacy Inst., Washington, 1980-85, Nat. Inst. Trial Adv., 1990. Author: (with Dan K. Webb) Corporate Internal Investigations, 1993. Bd. dirs. Chgo. Ctrl. Area Com., 1994—. Fellow Am. Coll. Trial Lawyers (mem. fed. criminal procedure com. 1993—); mem. ABA, Bar Assn. San Francisco, Chgo. Bar Assn., Nat. Assn. Criminal Def. Lawyers, U. Chgo. Grad. Sch. Bus. Alumni Assn. (bd. dirs. 1986), Racquet Club, Wong Sun Soc. (San Francisco), Kenilworth Club, Chgo. Stanford Assn. Presbyterian. Avocations: screenplays, architecture, 20th Century Louisiana politics, forensic science. Office: Winston & Strawn 35 W Wacker Dr Ste 4700 Chicago IL 60601-1614

TARVER, JACKSON WILLIAMS, newspaper executive; b. Savannah, Ga., Mar. 2, 1917; s. Otis Merritt and DeLuth (Williams) T.; m. Margaret Birch Taylor, Mar. 24, 1940; children: Jack Williams, Margaret (Mrs. Peter Jason). Student, U. Ga., 1936; A.B., Mercer U., 1938, LL.D., 1965. Reporter Vidalia (Ga.) Advance, 1938; editor Toombs County (Ga.) Democrat, 1939-40, Macon (Ga.) News, 1940-43; asso. editor Atlanta Constn., 1943-49; asst. to pres. Atlanta Newspapers, Inc. (pub. Atlanta Jour., Atlanta Constn.), 1950-53, gen. mgr., 1953-58, v.p., 1956-58, pub., 1958—, also dir.; chmn. Fed. Res. Bank of Atlanta, 1962-68; chmn., dir. Theaters Service Co.; vice chmn. Cox Enterprises, Inc.; dir. So. Bell Telephone Co., Am. Motors Corp., Maccabees Mut. Ins. Co.; chmn. A.P., 1977-82. Mem. Ga. Bd. Edn., 1942-43; trustee Mercer U. Reid Found. fellow to S.A., 1949; recipient Humanitarian of Yr. award Inst. Human Relations, 1979. Mem. Am. Newspaper Pubs. Assn. (chmn. bur. advt. 1962-64), So. Newspaper Pubs. Assn. (pres. 1976-77), Am. Soc. Newspaper Editors, Sigma Delta Chi, Sigma Alpha Epsilon. Clubs: Capital City (Atlanta), Piedmont Driving (Atlanta), Commerce (Atlanta), Stadium (Atlanta). Office: 72 Marietta St NW Atlanta GA 30303-2804

TARVER, MICHAEL KEITH, lawyer; b. Monroe, La., Oct. 12, 1941; s. Mike Davis and Bernadine (Kilcrease) T. Student, U. Paris Inst. Polit. Studies, 1962; BA, Tulane U., 1963, LLB, 1966; LLM, NYU, 1967. Bar: La. 1966, N.Y. 1987. Assoc. Jones, Walker, Waechter, Poitevent, Carrere & Denegre, New Orleans, 1967-72, ptnr., 1972-95, ret., 1995. Asst. editor Tulane Law Rev., 1961-63. Mem. Am. Coll. Real Estate Lawyers, Phi Beta Kappa. Roman Catholic. Home: 828 Burgundy St New Orleans LA 70116-3062

TASAKA, SHUJI, engineering educator; b. Imabari, Japan, Mar. 6, 1949; s. Masaaki and Atsuko (Tasaka) T.; m. Mari Tamura, Oct. 8, 1977; children: Misato, Keisuke. BE, Nagoya (Japan) Inst. Tech., 1971; ME, U. Tokyo, 1973, PhD in Electronic Engring., 1976. Rsch. assoc. Nagoya Inst. Tech., 1976, lectr., 1976-78, assoc. prof., 1978-92, prof. dept. elec. and computer engring., 1992—. Author: Performance Analysis of Multiple Access Protocols, 1986. Mem. IEEE, Inst. Electronics, Info. and Comm. Engrs. (sec. tech. com. on info. networks 1987-89, assoc. editor IEICE Transactions on Comm.), Info. Processing Soc. Japan, Assn. for Computing Machinery. Avocations: reading, music, movies. Home: Hanami-dori 1-94-4 Showa-ku, Nagoya 466, Japan Office: Nagoya Inst Tech/Elec & Comp Eng, Gokiso-cho Showa-ku, Nagoya 466, Japan

TASCO, FRANK JOHN, insurance brokering company executive; b. N.Y.C., Aug. 18, 1927; s. Frank and Jean (Pisapia) T.; m. Edwardine Dordoni, Oct. 30, 1954; children—Jill, Lisbeth, Diana. B.A., NYU, 1949. Vice pres. Guy Carpenter & Co., N.Y.C., 1962-76; dir. Guy Carpenter & Co., 1971—, pres., chief exec. officer, 1976-84; pres., chief operating officer Marsh & McLennan Cos., N.Y.C., 1984-85, chmn., chief exec. officer, 1986-92, also bd. dirs.; now retired chmn. & cons.; chmn. bd. dirs. Borden, Inc.; bd. dirs. Faugere & Jutheau, Paris, Terra Nova Ins. Co., London, N.Y. Telephone Co.; mem. industries adv. com. Advt. Coun., publishers' adv. panel Fortune mag.; chmn. Listed Cos. adv. com. to N.Y. Stock Exch. Mem. Pres.'s Drug Adv. Coun.; Corp. Fund Leadership com. Lincoln Ctr., N.Y.C.; bd. Inner-City scholarship fund; bd. dirs., chmn. St. Francis Hosp., Roslyn, N.Y., 1981, Phoenix Ho. Found. Inc., N.Y.C. Partnership; bd. dirs. Nat. Multple Sclerosis Soc.; trustee Nat. Commn. Against Drunk Driving; patron Project 100 for Mentally Handicapped of Bermuda; bd. govs. Met. N.Y. U.S. Olympic Com. With USN, 1945-46. Mem. Fgn. Policy Assn., Bus. Coun. of UN, Life Saving Benevolent Assn., City Midday Drug and Chem. (bd. dirs. 1972-77), Econ. Club, Links (N.Y.C.), Meadow Brook Club (Jericho, N.Y.). Clubs: Economic, Links (N.Y.C.); Meadow Brook (Jericho, N.Y.). *

TASH, MARTIN ELIAS, publishing company executive; b. N.Y.C., Jan. 24, 1941; s. David and Esther (Milch) T.; m. Arlene Sue Klein, June 23, 1962; children: Nathan, Faye, Jill. B.B.A., Baruch Sch. City Coll. N.Y., 1962. C.P.A. Staff accountant S.D. Leidesdorf & Co. (C.P.A.'s), N.Y.C., 1962-66; v.p. fin., dir. LMC Data Inc., N.Y.C., 1966-71; with Plenum Pub. Corp., N.Y.C., 1971—, chmn. bd., pres., 1977—; chmn. bd. Gradco Systems, Inc., 1990—. Office: Plenum Pub Corp 233 Spring St New York NY 10013-1522

TASH, PAUL C., editor-in-chief; b. South Bend, Ind., July 17, 1954; s. Robert N. and Barbara R. (Eller) T.; m. Karyn E. Krayer, Aug. 19, 1983; children: Kaley Marie, Kendyl Barbara. BA, Ind. U., 1976; LLB, Edinburgh (Scotland) U., 1978. Reporter Times Pub. Co., 1978-83, city editor, 1983-86, metro editor, 1986-90, editor, pub. Fla. Trend Mag., 1990-91, Washington Bur. chief, 1991-92; exec. editor, v.p. St. Petersburg Times, 1992—; Bd. dirs. Times Pub. Co., Fla. Trend Mag. Bd. dirs. Leadership Fla., Tallahassee, 1994. Scholar Marshall Aid Commemoration Commn., 1976-78. Mem. Phi Beta Kappa. Home: 111 Bay Point Dr NE Saint Petersburg FL 33704-3805 Office: St Petersburg Times 490 1st Ave S Saint Petersburg FL 33701-4204

TASHIMA, ATSUSHI WALLACE, federal judge; b. Santa Maria, Calif., June 24, 1934; s. Yasutaro and Aya (Sasaki) T.; m. Nora Kiyo Inadomi, Jan. 27, 1957; children: Catherine Y., Christopher I., Jonathan I. AB in Polit. Sci., UCLA, 1958; LLB, Harvard U., 1961. Bar: Calif. 1962. Dep. atty. gen. State of Calif., 1962-67; atty. Spreckels Sugar divsn. Amstar Corp., 1968-72, v.p., gen. atty., 1972-77; ptnr. Morrison & Foerster, L.A., 1977-80; judge U.S. Dist. Ct. (ctrl. dist.) Calif., L.A., 1980-96, U.S. Ct. Appeals (9th cir.), Pasadena, Calif., 1996—; mem. Calif. Com. Bar Examiners, 1978-80. With USMC, 1953-55. Mem. ABA, State Bar Calif., Los Angeles County Bar Assn. Democrat. Office: US Ct Appeals 125 S Grand Ave Pasadena CA 91105-1652

TASKER, JOHN BAKER, veterinary medical educator, college dean; b. Concord, N.H., Aug. 28, 1933; s. John Baker and Catherine Mabel (Baker) T.; m. Grace Ellen Elliott, June 17, 1961; children—Sybil Alice, Sarah Catherine, Sophia Ethel. DVM, Cornell U., 1957, PhD, 1963. Instr. Cornell U., Ithaca, N.Y., 1960-61; from assoc. prof. to prof. Cornell U., 1967-78; from asst. prof. to assoc. prof. Colo. State U., Fort Collins, 1963-67; prof. vet. clinical pathology, assoc. dean La. State U., 1978-84; prof. vet. pathology Coll. Vet. Medicine Mich. State U., East Lansing, 1984-95; prof. vet. pathology Coll. Vet. Medicine/Mich. State U., East Lansing, 1984-95; dean, prof. emeritus Mich. State U., East Lansing, 1995; cons. Ralston-Purina Co., St. Louis, 1978, Universidad Nacional P. Urena, Dominican Republic, 1980, U. Nebr., Lincoln, 1982-83. Editor: Veterinary Clinics of North America, 1976. Served to lst lt. U.S. Army, 1958-60. Recipient Outstanding Instr. award Colo. State U. Vet. Coll., 1967; Norden Teaching award Cornell U. Vet. Coll., 1977. Mem. AVMA, Mich. Vet. Med. Assn., Am. Coll. Vet. Pathologists (diplomate; examiner 1972-74), Am. Soc. Vet. Clin. Pathology (pres. 1971-72), Assn. Am. Vet. Med. Colls. (exec. com. 1986-91, pres. 1989-90). Avocations: reading; traveling. Home: RR 2 box 238C Delmar DE 19940

TASKER, STEVEN JAY, professional football player; b. Leoti, Kans., May 19, 1962. Student, Dodge City C.C.; B in Communication Studies, Northwestern, 1985. With Houston Oilers, 1985-86; wide receiver Buffalo Bills, 1986—. Played in Pro Bowl 1987, 90-93. Office: Buffalo Bills 1 Bills Dr Orchard Park NY 14127-2237

TASMAN, ALLAN, psychiatry educator; b. Louisville, Ky., Feb. 8, 1947; s. Goodman and Zelda (Shalinsky) T.; m. Cathy Faye Goldstein, May 24, 1970. BA in Chemistry, Franklin and Marshall Coll., 1969; MD, U. Ky., 1973. Diplomate Am. Bd. Psychiatry and Neurology. Resident in psychiatry U. Ky. Med. Sch., Lexington, 1973-74, U. Cin. Med. Ctr., 1974-76; asst. prof. psychiatry U. Conn. Med. Sch., Farmington, 1976-82, assoc. prof. psychiatry, 1982-88, prof. psychiatry, 1988-91; prof. psychiatry and behavioral scis., tenure and chmn. U. Louisville Sch. Medicine, 1991—; pres.-elect Am. Assn. Chmn. Depts. Psychiatry, 1995-96. Editor: Annual Review of Psychiatry, Vol. II, 1992, Clinical Challenges in Psychiatry, 1993, Less Time to Do More, 1993. Fellow Am. Psychiat. Assn. (pres. 1996—, Nancy Roeske award for excellence in med. student edn. 1991); mem. Am. Assn. Dirs. of Psychiat. Residency Tng. (pres. 1993-94), Assn. Acad. Psychiatry (pres. 1993-94). Office: U Louisville Sch Medicine Dept Psychiatry & Behavioral Scis Louisville KY 40292

TASMAN, WILLIAM SAMUEL, ophthalmologist, medical association executive; b. Phila., 1929. MD, Temple U., 1955. Intern Phila. Gen. Hosp., 1955-56; resident in ophthalmology Wills Eye Hosp., Phila., 1959-61; fellow Mass. Eye and Ear Infirmary, Boston, 1961-62; prof., chmn. dept. ophthalmology Jefferson Med. Coll., Phila., 1985—; attending surgeon Wills Eye Hosp., Phila., 1974—, ophthalmologist-in-chief, 1985—. Mem. AMA, Am. Acad. Ophthalmologists (sec. ann. meeting 1992—), Pa. Acad. Ophthalmologists, Am. Ophthal. Soc. Office: Wills Eye Hosp 900 Walnut St Philadelphia PA 19107-5509

TASSÉ, ROGER, lawyer, former Canadian government official; b. Montreal, Que., Can., 1931. BA, Coll. St. Marie, Montreal, 1952; Lic. in Law, U. Montreal, 1955; diploma d'Etudes Superieures, U. Ottawa, Ont., Can., 1957. Bar: Que. 1956, Ont. 1986; called to Queens Counsel 1971. Joined Dept. Justice, 1956, civil law counsel for Can. govt., from 1957, supt. bankruptcy,

1965-68, asst. dep. min. consumer and corp. affairs, 1968-72; dep. min. Dept. of Solicitor Gen., 1972-77; dep. min. of justice, atty. gen. of Can., 1977-85; ptnr. Land Michener Lash Johnston, Toronto and Ottawa, Noel Décary Aubry & Assocs., Hull, Que., 1985-88; exec. v.p. legal and environ. affairs Bell Can., 1988-91; of counsel Fraser & Beatty, Toronto, 1992-95, Gowling, Strathy & Henderson, Ottawa, 1995—; prin. constl. advisor to Spl. Joint Com. of the Senate and the House of Commons on a Renewed Can., 1991-92. Mem. Citizens' Forum on Canada's Future, 1990; co-chair task force Can. Mags., 1993; mem. DTH Panel, 1995. Decorated officer Order of Can. Avocations: skiing, tennis. Office: Gowling Strathy & Henderson, 160 Elgin St Ste 2600, Ottawa, ON Canada K1P 1C3

TASSINARI, MELISSA SHERMAN, toxicologist; b. Lawrence, Mass., Sept. 26, 1953; m. R. Peter Tassinari; children: Michael, Emily, Sara. AB, Mt. Holyoke Coll., 1975; postgrad., U. St. Andrews, Scotland, 1973-74; PhD, Med. Coll. Wis., 1979. Diplomate Am. Bd. Toxicology. Rsch. asst. in orthopedic surgery., Lab. Human Biochemistry Children's Hosp. Med. Ctr., Boston, 1981-83; rsch. affiliate in toxicology Toxicology Dept. Forsyth Dental Ctr., Boston, 1983-86, staff assoc., 1986-89; asst. prof. cell biology U. Mass. Med. Ctr., Worcester, 1989-91; mgr. reproductive toxicology Pfizer Ctrl. Rsch., Groton, Conn., 1991—; rsch. fellow oral biology Harvard Sch. Dental Medicine, Boston, 1978-81, instr. oral biology and pathophysiology, 1981-83; asst. prof. biol. scis. Wellesley Coll., Mass., 1983-86, cons. teratology Arthur D. Little, Inc., Cambridge, Mass., 1985-91; asst. prof. biology Simmons Coll., Boston, 1986-87. Contbr. abstracts, articles to profl. jours. Mem. Teratology Soc., Neurobehavioral Teratology Soc., Mid Atlantic Reproduction and Teratology Assn. (steering com. 1994), Soc. Toxicology. Office: Pfizer Central Research Eastern Point Rd Groton CT 06340

TASSINARY, LOUIS GEORGE, psychology educator, director laboratory; b. Bridgeport, Conn., Dec. 27, 1954; s. Louis Evangelist and June Theresa (Davis) T.; m. Melanie Marie Ihrig, July 15, 1990; children: Damien David, Alexas Marie. BA in Psychology, Eckerd Coll., 1976; PhD in Psychology, Dartmouth Coll., 1985. Rsch. asst. U. Conn. Mental Health Ctr., Farmington, 1976-77; grad. rsch. asst. Dartmouth Coll., Hanover, N.H., 1978-84; postdoctoral fellow U. Iowa, Iowa City, 1985-86, asst. rsch. scientist, 1986-89, vis. asst. prof., 1989-90; asst. prof., dir. psychophysiology lab. Tex. A&M U., College Station, 1990—. Co-editor: Principles of Psychophysiology: Physical, Social and Inferential Elemtns, 1990; contbr. articles to profl. jours. USDA Forest Svc. Rsch. grantee, 1991-94, U.S. Golf Assn. grantee, 1991-94; Presidl. Faculty fellow, 1993-98. Mem. APA, N.Y. Acad. Scis., Internat. Soc. Ecol. Psychology, Soc. for Psychophysiol. Rsch., Sci. Rsch. Assn., Sigma Xi. Democrat. Achievements include discovery that electrocortical potentials can signify whether a facial action is spontaneous or intended; documentation of important boundary conditions on the sensitivity & specificity of facial electromyograpphy as a tool. Home: 304 W Dexter Dr College Station TX 77840-2921 Office: Tex A&M U Environ Psychophysiol Lab Coll Architecture College Station TX 77843-3137

TASTO, COLLEEN MARIE, Spanish language educator; b. Mpls., Oct. 5, 1950; d. Richard Stafford and Shirley Margurite (Gorman) Cassady; m. Jerome Jenry Tasto, Nov. 18, 1972; children: Joseph, David, Thomas, Michael, John. BA in Spanish Philosophy, Theology, Loretto Hts. Coll., 1972; MA in Liberal Studies, Hamline U., 1995. Tchr. religion Sacred Heart Sch., Robbinsdale, Minn., 1972—; dir. religious edn. St. Michael's Parish, Madison, Minn., 1975-76; farmer Tasto Farm, Madison, Minn., 1975-85; tchr. Spanish New Ulm (Minn.) Pub. Schs., 1985—. AAUW grantee; named Borwn County Hist. Soc. Woman of Yr., 1991, Tchr. of Yr., New Ulm Edn. Assn., 1991. Mem. NEA, Minn. Edn. Assn., Am. Assn. Tchrs. Spanish, MCTFL.

TASWELL, HOWARD FILMORE, pathologist, blood bank specialist, educator; b. Paterson, N.J., July 21, 1928; s. Herman Albert and Pauline Ruth (Abels) T.; children: Amy, Carl, Eric, Steven, Laura, Ruth; m. Beryl Byman, May 7, 1989. A.B., Harvard U., 1949; M.D., NYU, 1953; M.S. in Pathology, U. Minn. Mayo Grad. Sch. Medicine, 1961. Diplomate Am. Bd. Pathology; subcert. in clin. and anatomic pathology, blood banking/transfusion medicine. Intern St. Albans Naval Hosp., N.Y., 1953-54; resident in internal medicine Mayo Clinic, Rochester, Minn., 1956-57; resident in anatomical and clin. pathology Mayo Clinic, 1957-61; assoc. pathologist Harrisburg Hosp., Pa.; asst. prof. pathology Hahneman Coll. Medicine, Phila., 1961-63; head sect. blood bank and transfusion services Mayo Clinic; prof. lab. medicine Mayo Med. Sch., Rochester, Minn., 1963-88, Vernon F. and Earlene D. Dale prof. lab. medicine, 1985-93, prof. emeritus, 1993—; fellow Bush Found. of Minn., dept. psychiatry U. Chgo. Hosps., 1993-95; cons. Nat. Heart, Lung, Blood Inst., FDA Bur. Biologics; mem. assoc. faculty Chgo. Ctr. for Family Health, 1995—. Contbr. over 200 articles to med. jours. and textbooks. Served to lt. comdr. USNR, 1953-56. Mem. AMA, Minn. Med. Assn., Ill. State Med. Soc., Am. Assn. Blood Banks (pres. 1978-79), Minn. Assn. Blood Banks (pres. 1969-70), Minn. Soc. Clin. Pathologists (pres. 1972-73), Am. Soc. Clin. Pathology, Am. Soc. Hematology, Coll. Am. Pathologists, Internat. Soc. Blood Transfusion, Am. Family Therapy Acad., Sigma Xi. Home: 2500 N Lakeview Ave Apt 3204 Chicago IL 60614-1829

TATA, GIOVANNI, publishing executive; b. Taranto, Italy, Apr. 26, 1954; came to U.S., 1974, naturalized, 1982; s. Vito and Angela (Colucci) T.; m. Brenda Susan Smith, Feb. 14, 1978; children: Elizabeth Ariana, Katherine Allison, Margaret Anne, Michael Anthony. BS cum laude (scholar), Brigham Young U., 1977, MA, 1980; grad. cert. area studies U. Utah, 1980; PhD, 1986; postgrad. U. Turin (Italy), 1980-81. Archaeologist, Utah State Hist. Soc., Salt Lake City, 1979; instr. dept. langs. U. Utah, Salt Lake City, 1983-85; Mediterranean specialist Soc. Early Hist. Archaeology, Provo, Utah, 1978-91; mus. curator Pioneer Trail State Park, Salt Lake City, 1982-83; instr. dept. art Brigham Young U., Provo, 1982-84; research fellow Direzione Generale per la Cooperazione Scientifica Culturale e Technica, Rome, 1980-81; research curator Utah Mus. Fine Arts, Salt Lake City, 1985-87; chmn. 35th Ann. Symposium on the Archaeology of the Scriptures, 1986; pres. Transoft Internat., Inc., 1988—, Mus. Info. Systems, 1987-93; chmn. Taras Devel. Corp., 1994—. Chmn. MuseuMedia, Inc., 1995—. Republican. Mem. Ch. Jesus Christ of Latter-day Saints. Mem. Am. Assn. Museums, Internat. Coun. Museums, Utah State Hist. Soc. Home: PO Box 2194 Provo UT 84603-2194 Office: Taras Devel Corp 117 #250 W Center St Provo UT 84603

TATARSKII, VALERIAN IL'ICH, physics researcher; b. Kharkov, USSR, Oct. 13, 1929; s. Il'ya A. and Elizabeth A. (Lapis) T.; m. Maia S. Granovskaia, Dec. 22, 1955; 1 child, Viatcheslav V. MS, Moscow State U., 1952; PhD, Acoustical Inst. Acad. Scis., 1957; DSc, Gorky State U., 1962. Scientific rschr. Geophys. Inst. Acad. Sci. USSR, Moscow, 1953-56; scientific rschr. Inst. Atmospheric Physics, Acad. Sci. USSR, Moscow, 1956-59, sr. scientific rschr., 1959-78, head lab., 1978-90; head dept. Lebedev. Phys. Inst. Acad. Sci., Moscow, 1990-91; sr. rsch. assoc. U. Colo. Coop. Inst. for Rsch. in Environ. Sci., Boulder, 1991—, NOAA/ERL. Environ. Tech. Lab., Boulder. Author: Wave Propagation in a Turbulent Medium, 1961, 67, The Effect of the Turbulent Atmosphere on Wave Propagation, 1971, Principles of Statistical Radiophysics, 1989; contbr. articles to profl. jours. Recipient of Max Born award, 1994, Optical Soc. of Am., USSR State prize, 1990. Fellow Optical Soc. Am. (Max Born award 1994); mem. Russian Acad. Sci., U.S.A. Nat. Acad. Engring. (fgn. assoc.), N.Y. Acad. Sci. Avocations: classical music, kayaking. Office: NOAA ERL ETL 325 Broadway St Boulder CO 80303-3328

TATE, BARBARA MARIE, art director; b. Canton, Ohio, Jan. 13, 1958; d. John Lawrence and Dolores Magaret (Hill) T.; m. Charles Allan Kerecz, May 25, 1985. Student, Kent State U., 1975-79, Sch. Visual Arts, N.Y.C., 1979-80. Assoc. art dir. All in Style Mag., N.Y.C., 1975-81; art dir. Macy's, N.Y.C., 1981-83, Direct Mktg. Group, N.Y.C., 1983, Avon, N.Y.C., 1983-84; design dir. Tateworks, N.Y.C., 1984—. Avocations: interior design, art photography, Alpine skiing, golf, filmmaking. Office: 24 W 30th St Fl 6 New York NY 10001-4410

TATE, CURTIS E., management educator; b. Trezvant, Tenn., July 5, 1920; s. Curtis E. and Mary Kathryn (Haskins) T.; m. Evelyn Ruth Mann, Apr. 12, 1945 (div. May, 1969); m. Mary Jim Combs, Aug. 28, 1977; children: Curtis Emory, Milton Oglesby. Student, N. Ga. Coll., 1943-44, U. Ga., 1945-46; AB, Bethel Coll., 1946; MS, U. Tenn., 1952. Clk. Family Gen. Grocery, Trezevant, Tenn., 1938-42; clk. purchasing dept. P&G Defense Corp., Milan, Twnn., 1942; plant mgr. Keathley Pie Co., Memphis, 1946-50; instr. Furman U., Greenville, S.C., 1952-53; bus. mgr. Lander Coll., Greenwood, S.C., 1953-56; from asst. to assoc. prof. Coll. of Bus. Adminstrn. U. Ga., Athens, 1956-92; prof. emeritus Terry Coll. of Bus. U. Ga., Athens, 1991—; bd. dirs. Flexible Products, Inc., Marietta, Ga., 1968-76, Case Pub. Corp.; asst. dean fund raising, 1991—. Co-author: Successful Small Business Management, 1975, latest rev. edit., 1985, Complete Guide to Your Own Business, 1977, Dow-Jones-Irwin Business Papers, 1977, Bus. Policy: Administrative, Strategic and Constitigency Issues, 1983, 92, Managing for Profits, 1984, Small Business Management and Entrepreneurship, 1992; mem. adv. bd. Am. Jour. Case Rsch. With U.S. Army, 1942-45, ETO. Fellow N. Am. Case Rsch. Assn. (sec., v.p., bd. dirs., pres. so. casewriters, Outstandinc Case Contbr. 1992), Acad. Mgmt., Kiwanis, Sigma Iota Epsilon, Beta Gamma Sigma. Home and Office: 1640 Broadlands Dr Watkinsville GA 30677-2148

TATE, DANIEL CLYDE, JR., legislative aide; b. Athens, Ga., Dec. 14, 1966; s. Danny Clyde and Ruth (McGaughey) T. BA, Amherst Coll., 1988. With spl. events CNN, Washington, 1989; legis. dir. Congressman W.J. Tanzin, Washington, 1989-93; dep. asst. sec. for House liaison U.S. Dept. Energy, Washington, 1993-95; spl. asst. to Pres. for legis. affairs The White House, Washington, 1995—. Field worker Mondale for Pres., Maine, 1984; issues aide Robb for Senate, Fairfax, Va., 1988; vol. Clinton-Gore Campaign, Washington and Pa., 1992. Avocations: lacrosse, golf, skiing. Home: 1276 N Wayne St Apt 1225 Arlington VA 22201-5857 Office: The White House East Wing 1600 Pennsylvania Ave Washington DC 20585

TATE, HAROLD SIMMONS, JR., lawyer; b. Taylors, S.C., Sept. 19, 1930; s. Harold Simmons and Cleone (Clayton) T.; m. Elizabeth Anne Coker, Dec. 22, 1952; children—Mary Elizabeth Anne, Martha Coker, Virginia Clayton. A.B. cum laude, Harvard U., 1951, J.D., 1956, postgrad., 1954. Bar: S.C. 1956. Ptnr. firm Sinkler and Boyd, P.A. (formerly Boyd, Knowlton, Tate & Finlay), Columbia, S.C., 1962—; chmn. U.S. Dist. Ct. (S.C.) Adv. Com., 1984—; lectr. Am. Law Inst.-ABA seminars; mem. adv. com. on rules and procedures U.S. Ct. Appeals (4th cir.), 1990-95. Co-author: South Carolina Appellate Practice, 1985; bd. editors Federal Litigation Guide Reporter, 1985—; contbr. articles and book revs. to profl. jours. Chmn. Richland County Mental Health Ctr., 1965-66; co-chmn. Columbia Hearing and Speech Ctr., 1962-64; mem. admission and scholarship com. Harvard U., 1961—; chmn. subcom. on legislation, legislation and fin. study commn. Gov.'s Adv. Group on Mental Health Planning, 1963-65; chmn. Columbia Bd. Supervisory of Registration, 1961-70; pres. Columbia Philharm. Orch., 1966-67, Town Theatre, 1967-70; trustee Richland County Pub. Libr., 1973-78, Hist. Columbia Found., 1971-75, Caroliniana soc., 1978—, Bostick Charitable Trust, 1968—; bd. mgrs. S.C. Hist. Soc., 1993—; commr. S.C. Commn. of Archives and History, 1995—. Capt. U.S. Army, 1951-53. Mem. ABA, Am. Law Inst., Am. Judicature Soc., S.C. Bar Assn., Assn. Bar City N.Y., Richland County Bar Assn., S.C. Hist. Soc. (bd. mgrs. 1993—), Harvard Law Sch. Assn. S.C. (sec.-treas. 1968-70, pres. 1988—), Forest Lake Country Club, Columbia Drama Club (pres. 1963-64), Palmetto Club (sec. 1963-70, pres. 1973-76), The Forum Club, Harvard Club (N.Y.C.), Harvard Club S.C. Episcopalian. Home: 15 Gibbes Ct Columbia SC 29201-3923 Office: Sinkler & Boyd 1426 Main St Columbia SC 29201-2834

TATE, JAMES VINCENT, poet, English educator; b. Kansas City, Mo., Dec. 8, 1943; s. Samuel Vincent Appleby and Betty Jean Whitsitt. BA, Kans. State Coll., 1965; MFA, U. Iowa, 1967. Instr. U. Iowa, Iowa City, 1966-67; vis. lectr. U. Calif., Berkeley, 1967-68; asst. prof. English Columbia U., N.Y.C., 1969-71; assoc. prof., now prof. English U. Mass., Amherst, 1971—; poet-in-residence Emerson Coll., 1970-71; cons. Coord. Coun. Literary Mags., 1971-74, Ky. Arts Commn., 1979; mem. Bollingen Prize Com., 1974-75; poetry editor Dickinson Rev., 1967-76; trustee, assoc. editor Pym-Randall Pr., 1968-80; assoc. editor Barn Dream Pr. Author: (poems) Cages, 1966, The Destination, 1967, The Lost Pilot, 1967 (Yale Younger Poets award 1966), Notes of Woe, 1968, Camping in the Valley, 1968, Mystics in Chicago, 1968, The Torches, 1968, Row with Your Hair, 1969, Is There Anything?, 1969, Shepherds of the Mist, 1969, Amnesia People, 1970, Are You Ready Mary Baker Eddy, 1970, Deaf Girl Playing, 1970, The Oblivion Ha-Ha, 1970, Wrong Songs, 1970, Hints to Pilgrims, 1971, Nobody Goes to Visit the Insane Anymore, 1971, Absences, 1972, Apology for Eating Geoffrey Movius' Hyacinth, 1972, A Dime Found in the Snow, 1973, Hottentot Ossuary, 1974, Marfa, 1974, Suffering Bastards, 1975, Who Gets the Bitterroot?, 1976, Viper Jazz, 1976, Riven Doggeries, 1979, The Rustling of Foliage, the Memory of Caresses, 1979, If It Would All Please Hurray, 1980, Land of Little Sticks, 1981, Constant Defender, 1983, Just Shades, 1985, Reckoner, 1986, Distance from Loved Ones, 1990, Selected Poems, 1991 (Pulitzer Prize for poetry 1992), Worshipful Company of Fletchers, 1993 (Nat. Book Award for Poetry 1994); (novel) Lucky Darryl, 1977. Named Poet of Yr. by Phi Beta Kappa, 1972; recipient Nat. Inst. Arts and Letters award for poetry, 1974; Mass. Arts and Humanities fellow, 1975, Guggenheim fellow, 1976, Nat. Endowment for the Arts fellow, 1980. Office: U Mass Dept English Amherst MA 01003*

TATE, KAREN GRIFFIN, quality assurance professional, consultant; b. Springfield, Ohio, Sept. 8, 1951; d. Juddy Wayne and Betty Jean (Springer) Griffin; m. Andrew Lee Tate, May 20, 1978; children: James, Jordan. Student of Engring., Vanderbilt U., 1969-71; student of Bus., U. Louisville, 1971-74; BS in Fin., Bloomsburg U., 1985; postgrad. in Bus. Adminstrn., Xavier U., 1991-94. Registered engr. in tng., Ky. Designer GE, Louisville, Gainesville, Ky., Fla., 1969-71; systems designer Hueblein, Ky. Fried Chicken, Louisville, 1976-77; engr. Bechtel Petroleum, Louisville, 1977-82; sr. constrn. engr. Bechtel Power, Berwick, Pa., 1982-85, Huntsville, Ala., 1985-86; project mgr. Belcan Engring. Group, Inc., Cin., 1986-91, mgr. corp. quality, 1991—; cons. Xavier U., Ctr. for Mgmt. and Profl. Devel., Cin., 1991. Mem. planning comm. Sycamore Community Schs., Cin., 1987-91, Am. Lung Assn. S.W. Ohio Camp Superkids; cons. Jr. Achievement Project. Mem. Soc. Womens Engrs., Project Mgmt. Inst. (cert. project mgmt. profl.), Assn. for Quality and Productivity, Ohio Quality and Productivity Forum, GOAL/QPC (cert. instr.). Avocations: skiing, hiking, biking, tennis. Home: 11830 Loganfield Ct Cincinnati OH 45249-1771 Office: Belcan Engring Group BGP Svcs 650 Northland Blvd Cincinnati OH 45240-3214

TATE, MANFORD BEN, guided missile scientist, investor; b. Okolona, Ark., Aug. 3, 1916; s. Ernest and Mabel (Burley) T.; m. Marjorie Belle Stone, Sept. 9, 1942; children: Howard Ernest, Virginia Louise (Gina) Tate Smythe, Barbara Anne. Student, Cen. Coll. Liberal Arts, 1935-37; BSCE, U. Mo., 1940, MSCE, 1942; PhD in Theoretical and Applied Mechanics, Iowa State U., 1949. Grad. fellow, instr., asst. prof., assoc. prof. U. Mo., Columbia, 1940-51; lectr, engring. mechanics U. Va., Hampton, 1944-45; grad. fellow, instr. Iowa State U., Ames, 1946-47; engr. U.S. Naval Ordnance Lab., White Oak, Md., 1950-56; lectr., advisor U. Md., White Oak, 1950-56; guided missile rsch. scientist Johns Hopkins U. Applied Physics Lab., Laurel, Md., 1956-78, prof. missile structures, 1958-64; pres., gen. ptnr. Tate Ptnrs., Silver Spring, Md., 1968—; concrete inspector Mo. Hwy. Dept., 1940; vis. prof. Cath. U. Am., Washington, 1956-58; aeronautical rsch. Nat. Adv. Com. Aeronautics, Langley Field, Va., 1944-45; cons. in field. Bridge designer Bur. of Bridges, 1941; Crane designer Dravo Corp. Pitts.; co-inventor Tomahawk Cruise Missile (patentee 1971); derived theoretical solution for shock strength of the Fat Man Atom Bomb; author: (with others) Selected Problems in Materials Testing, 1943; contbr. more than 400 articles to profl. jours./publs. Cub scouts chmn., cubmaster Boy Scouts Am., 1956-61, chmn. rev. bd., 1962-65; ciCD chmn. PTA, 1961-63; hon. coun. mem. Lakota Sioux Indian Tribe, Chamberlain, S.D., Ogalala Sioux Indian Tribe, Rapid City, S.D. Recipient Disting. Svc. in Engring. award U. Mo., 1995. Mem. ASCE, ASTM, ASME, Am. Soc. Engring Edn., Am. Soc. Ordnance Engrs., Soc. Exptl. Stress Analysis, Sigma Xi, Phi Kappa Phi, Chi Epsilon. Democrat. Methodist. Achievements include patents on the Tomahawk Cruise Missile; first investigator in world to derive theoretical solution for air oscillations in ducted missiles/derived theoretical solution for shock strength of the Fat Man atom bomb.

TATE, RANDALL J. (RANDY TATE), congressman; b. Puyallup, Wash., Nov. 23, 1965; m. Julie; 1 child. AA, Tacoma C. C., Wash.; BA in Econs. and Polit. Sci., We. Wash. U. Mem. Wash. Ho. of Reps., 1988-94, 104th Congress from 9th Wash. dist., 1994—; former mem. com. rules, com. fin. instns. and ins., judiciary com., Wash. Ho. Reps.; mem. Congrl. com. transp. and infrastructure, com. govt. reform. Home: 13011 Meridian E # 301 Puyallup WA 98373 Office: US House Reps House Office Bldg 1118 Longworth Washington DC 20515-4709

TATE, SHARON SUE, special events and catering executive; b. Gainesville, Tex., Sept. 21, 1949; d. Lucien Harvey and Ollie Pauline (Insel) T. AA, Cooke County Coll., 1972; postgrad., U. North Tex., 1973-74, So. Meth. U., 1984. Credit collections cons. J.C. Penney, Dallas, 1978-80; exec. v.p. Orville McDonald Assocs., Dallas, 1980-86; conf. coord. Plaza Ams. Hotel, Dallas, 1986-92; spl. events and catering mgr. dani' Foods at the Dallas Mus. Art, 1992-95; pres. Orville McDonald Assocs., Dallas, 1995—. Republican. Avocations: tennis, Renaissance art, ancient history. Home: 8780 Park Ln Apt 1017 Dallas TX 75231-5504 Office: Orville McDonald Assocs PO Box 823185 Dallas TX 75382-3185

TATE, SHEILA BURKE, public relations executive; b. Washington, Mar. 3, 1942; d. Eugene L. and Mary J. (Doherty) Burke; m. William J. Tate, May 2, 1981; children: Hager Burke Patton, Courtney Paige Patton. BA in Journalism, Duquesne U., 1964; postgrad. in mass communications, U. Denver, 1975-76. former chairperson bd. dirs. Corp. for Pub. Broadcasting. Rsch. asst. Westinghouse Air Brake Co.; asst. account exec. Falhgren and Assos.; copywriter Ketchum, MacLeod and Grove, 1964-66; account exec. Burson-Marsteller Assocs., Pitts., 1967; sr. v.p. Burson-Marsteller Assocs., Washington, 1985-87; public rels. mgr. Colo. Nat. Bank, Denver, 1967-70; account exec. Hill and Knowlton, Inc., Houston, 1977-78; v.p. Hill and Knowlton, Inc., Washington, 1978-81; dep. to the chmn. Hill and Knowlton Inc., Washington, 1987-88; press sec. to First Lady White House, Washington, 1981-85; press sec. George Bush for Pres. Campaign, 1988; press sec. to Pres.-elect George Bush, 1988-89; vice chmn. Cassidy and Assocs. Pub. Affairs, Washington, 1989-91; pres. Powell Tate, Washington, 1991—; bd. dirs. Corp. for Pub. Broadcasting, vice chmn., 1990-92, chmn., 1992-94. Mem. civilian pub. affairs adv. bd. U.S. Mil. Acad.; mem. adv. bd. Ronald Reagan Inst. Emergency Medicine, George Washington U. Hosp., Washington. Mem. Nat. Press Club, Nat. Press Found. (bd. dirs.). Clubs: Duquesne U. Century, F Street, Washington Golf and Country, Farmington Country Club. Office: Powell Tate 700 13th St NW Ste 1000 Washington DC 20005-3960

TATE, STONEWALL SHEPHERD, lawyer; b. Memphis, Dec. 19, 1917; m. Janet Graf; children: Adele Shepherd, Shepherd Davis, Janet Reid Walker. BA, Southwestern at Memphis (now Rhodes Coll.), 1939; JD, U. Va., 1942; LLD (hon.), Samford U., 1979, Suffolk U., 1982, Capital U., 1989, Rhodes Coll., 1993. Bar: Va. 1941, Tenn. 1942. Mem. Martin, Tate, Morrow & Marston, P.C. (and predecessor firms), Memphis, 1947—; chmn. pres.'s coun. Rhodes Coll., 1995-96. Sec. bd. trustees Rhodes Coll., 1968-77, 1979-84; pres. Episcopal Churchmen of Tenn., 1961-62; sec. standing com. Episcopal Diocese of Tenn., 1969-71; pres. Chickasaw Coun. Boy Scouts Am., 1967-78. With USNR, 1942-46; comdr. USNR; ret. Decorated Order of Cloud Banner (China); recipient Silver Beaver award Boy Scouts Am., 1963, Disting. Eagle Scout award, 1980, Disting. Svc. medal Rhodes Coll., 1978, Disting. Alumni award, 1991, Lawyers' Lawyer award Memphis Bar Assn., 1990; Memphis Rotary Club Civic Recognition award, 1983; Paul Harris fellow, 1985. Fellow Am. Bar Found., Am. Coll. Trust and Estate Counsel, Internat. Acad. Estate and Trust Law, Coll. Law Practice Mgmt. (hon.), Tenn. Bar Found., Memphis and Shelby County Bar Found.; mem. ABA (chmn. standing com. on profl. discipline 1973-76, chmn. standing com. on scope and correlation of work 1977, chmn. task force on lawyer advt. 1977, pres. ABA 1978-79, chmn. standing com. on lawyer competence 1982-92), Am. Judicature Soc. (past bd. dirs.), Am. Law Inst., Am. Arbitration Assn. (large complex case panel 1993—), Lawyer-Pilots Bar Assn., Tenn. Bar Assn. (pres. 1963-64), Memphis and Shelby County Bar Assn. (pres. 1959-60), Nat. Conf. Bar Pres. (pres. 1972-73), U.S. 6th Cir. Jud. Conf. (life), U. Va. Law Sch. Alumni Assn. (mem. exec. coun. 1974-77), Rhodes Coll. Alumni Assn. (pres. 1951-53), Order of Coif, Raven Soc., Rotary (pres. 1982-83, bd. dirs. 1974, 80-84, 89-90), Phi Beta Kappa, Omicron Delta Kappa, Phi Delta Phi, Sigma Alpha Epsilon (highest effort award N.Y.C. Alumni Assn. 1979). Office: Martin Tate Morrow & Marston PC Falls Bldg 22 N Front St Ste 1100 Memphis TN 38103-1182

TATE, THADDEUS W(ILBUR), JR. (THAD TATE), history educator, historical institute executive, historian; b. Winston-Salem, N.C., May 27, 1924; s. Thaddeus Wilbur and Elizabeth Kent (Llewellyn) T. A.B., U. N.C., 1947, M.A., 1948; Ph.D., Brown U., 1960. Historian U.S. Nat. Park Service, 1948-54; research assoc. Colonial Williamsburg Found., (Va.), 1954-57, asst. dir. research, 1957-61; book rev. editor William and Mary Quar., Williamsburg, 1961-66, editor, 1966-72; asst. prof. history Coll. William and Mary, 1961-64, assoc. prof., 1964-69; prof. Coll. William and Mary, 1969-90; Murden prof. humanities Coll. William and Mary, 1990-92, emeritus, 1992—; dir. Inst. Early Am. History and Culture, Williamsburg, 1972-89, Commonwealth Ctr. for Study of Am. Culture, Williamsburg, 1988-92. Author: Negro in Eighteenth-Century Williamsburg, 1966; co-author: Colonial Virginia: A History, 1986, The College of William and Mary: A History, 1993; co-editor, contbg. author: Chesapeake in the Seventeenth Century, 1979; co-editor: Saints and Revolutionaries, 1984, An Uncivil War: The Southern Backcountry in the American Revolution, 1985; mem. adv. bd.: Environ. Rev., 1976-85; chair editorial adv. bd.: Papers of John Marshall. Mem. Williamsburg Wetlands Bd., 1980-93; chair bd. dirs. Va. Found. for Humanities and Pub. Policy, 1990-92; mem. tercentary commn. Coll. William and Mary, 1988-93. With USNR, 1943-46. Recipient Grad. Alumni citation Brown U., 1985; Thomas Jefferson award Coll. William and Mary, 1986; Brown U. fellow, 1949-51; NEH fellow, 1982-83; fellow Am. Council Learned Socs., 1970-71. Mem. Orgn. Am. Historians, Am. Hist. Assn., So. Hist. Assn., Va. Hist. Soc. (hon.), Am Soc. Legal History, Mass. Hist. Soc., Am. Soc. Environ. History, Assocs. John Carter Brown Library, Am. Antiquarian Soc., Library Co. Phila., Phi Beta Kappa, Phi Alpha Theta. Democrat. Episcopalian. Home: 313 Half Burns Lane Williamsburg VA 23185-3908

TATEL, DAVID STEPHEN, federal judge; b. Washington, Mar. 16, 1942; s. Howard Edwin and Molly (Abramowitz) T.; m. Edith Sara Bassichis, Aug. 29, 1965; children: Rebecca, Stephanie, Joshua, Emily. BA, U. Mich., 1963; JD, U. Chgo., 1966. Bar: Ill. 1966, U.S. Dist. Ct. (no. dist.) Ill. 1966, U.S. Dist. Ct. D.C. 1970, U.S. Ct. Appeals (7th and D.C. cirs.) 1970, U.S. Supreme Ct. 1971, U.S. Ct. Appeals (5th cir.) 1976, U.S. Ct. Appeals (11th and 4th cirs.) 1986. Instr. U. Mich., Ann Arbor, 1966-67; assoc. Sidley & Austin, Chgo. and Washington, 1967-69, 70-72; dir. Chgo. Lawyer's Com., 1969-70, Nat. Lawyers Commn. for Civil Rights Under Law, Washington, 1972-74; dir. Office for Civil Rights HEW, Washington, 1977-79; ptnr. Hogan & Hartson, Washington, 1979-94; circuit judge D.C. Circuit, Washington, D.C., 1994—; lectr. Stanford U. Law Sch., 1991-92; co-chmn. Nat. Lawyers Com. for Civil Rights Under Law, Washington, 1989-91; bd. dirs. Washington Lawyers Com. for Civil Rights Under Law; chmn., bd. dirs. Spencer Found., Chgo., 1990—. Mem. editorial adv. com. West's Edn. Law Reporter, Mpls., 1983-89; mem. vis. com. to law sch. U. Chgo., 1986-89; spl. master U.S. Dist. Ct. D.C., Washington, 1988-89; mem. Montgomery County Bd. Edn. Com. on Excellence in Teaching, Rockville, Md., 1985-87; mem. adv. com. on the goverance of edn. Carnegie Found. for Advancement in Teaching, Princeton, N.J., 1980-82; gen. counsel Legal Svcs. Corp., Washington, 1975-76; bd. dirs. Refugee Policy Group, Washington, 1985-90, Mental Health Law Project; active Pew Forum on Edn. Reform, 1992—. Mem. D.C. Bar Assn. (bd. govs. Washington chpt. 1980-81), Chgo. Coun. Lawyers (bd. govs. Chgo. chpt. 1969-70). Office: 333 Constitution AveRm 5423 Washington DC 20001*

TATGENHORST, (CHARLES) ROBERT, lawyer; b. Cin., Apr. 21, 1918; s. Charles and Clara (Strebel) T.; m. Louise Thompson, Sept. 6, 1951; children: David, John, James, Richard. A.B., Dartmouth Coll., 1940; LL.B., U. Cin., 1947. Bar: Ohio 1947. Asst. atty. gen. State of Ohio, 1947-49; assoc. firm Taft, Stettinius & Hollister, Cin., 1951-58; ptnr. firm Tatgenhorst & Tatgenhorst, Cin., 1958-61; prin. firm Robert Tatgenhorst & Assocs., Cin., 1961-85; ptnr. Tatgenhorst & Bruestle, Cin., 1986—, 1986-95; adj. prof. law Chase Coll. Law, No. Ky. U., 1962-86. Pres. Westwood Civic Assn., Cin., 1959, Meth. Union, 1960; chmn. dist. Boy Scouts Am., 1970; trustee Twin

Towers Retirement Ctr., 1968-93, Westwood United Meth. Ch., bd. trustees 1985-88, pres., 1990-92, trustee, 1992. With CIC U.S. Army, 1942-46. Mem. Ohio State Bar Assn., Cin. Bar Assn. (sec. 1973-75), Ryland Lakes Country Club, Optimists (pres. Cin. club 1962), Dartmouth of Cin. Club (pres. 1965), Masons (33 deg.), Sigma Alpha Epsilon, Phi Alpha Delta (pres. 1946). Republican.

TATHAM, DAVID FREDERIC, art historian, educator; b. Wellesley, Mass., Nov. 29, 1932; s. Richard Merton and Florence Elizabeth (Mallette) T.; m. Cleota Reed, Dec. 12, 1979. A.B., U. Mass., 1954; M.A., Syracuse U., 1960, Ph.D., 1970. Dean students Syracuse (N.Y.) U., 1966-71, assoc. prof. fine arts, 1972-78, prof., 1978—, chmn. dept. fine arts, 1980-86. Author: The Lure of the Striped Pig, 1973, Prints and Printmakers of New York State, 1986, Winslow Homer and the Art of the Book, 1990, Winslow Homer and the Illustrated Book, 1992, Winslow Homer in the Adirondacks, 1996, (exhbn. catalogs) Winslow Homer Drawings, 1979, Art, Artists and Museums, 1980, Bolton Brown, 1981, Abraham Tuthill, 1983; contbr. articles to profl. jours. Served with U.S. Army, 1956. Daniels research fellow, 1974; Am. Philos. Soc. grantee, 1980, 86; Am. Art Jour. award for outstanding scholarship, 1984; NEH grantee, 1987-88. Mem. Am. Antiquarian Soc. (rec. sec. 1988-93), Coll. Art Assn., Fellow Athenaeum of Phila. Home: 329 Westcott St Syracuse NY 13210-2107 Office: Syracuse U Dept Fine Arts Bowne Hall Syracuse NY 13244

TATHAM, JULIE CAMPBELL, writer; b. N.Y.C., June 1, 1908; d. Archibald and Julia deFres (Sample) Campbell; student pvt. schs., N.Y.C.; m. Charles Tatham, Mar. 30, 1933; children—Charles III, Campbell. Author more than 30 juvenile books including: The Mongrel of Merryway Farm, 1952; The World Book of Dogs, 1953; To Nick from Jan, 1957; author Trixie Belden series, 1946—, Ginny Gordon series, 1946—; co-author Cherry Ames and Vicki Barr series, 1947—; author: The Old Testament Made Easy, 1985; many series books transl. into fgn. langs.; contbr. numerous mag. stories and articles to popular publs., 1935—; free-lance writer, 1935—; contbr. numerous articles to Christian Sci. publs., including Christian Sci. Monitor, 1960—. Address: 1202 S Washington St Apt 814 Alexandria VA 22314-4446

TATIBOUET, ANDRE STEPHAN, condominium and resort management firm executive; b. Honolulu, Mar. 10, 1941; s. Joseph J. F. and Annalie (Knaack) T.; m. Jane Inez Barrows, Apr. 19, 1968; children: Cartier, Cecily. BA in Russian and Am. History, U. Hawaii, 1964. Cert. Hotel Adminstr. Owner, developer Pacific Beach Hotel, Honolulu, 1968-69; founder, pres. Aston Hotels & Resorts (formerly Hotel Corp. of Pacific), Honolulu, 1969—; chmn., CEO Aston Hotels & Resorts. Life mem. founders circle Punahou Sch., 1981—; mem. Honolulu chpt. Am. Friends of Hebrew U., 1982—; emeritus mem. U. Hawaii Pres. Club, 1983—; state chmn. U.S. Commn. on Civil Rights, 1985—; 2d v.p. Waikiki Improvement Assn., 1985—; mem. travel industry mgmt. adv. com. U. Hawaii, 1986—; mem. Honolulu Symphony Soc., 1986—, vice chmn. bd. dirs., 1988-89; mem. travel industry mgmt. adv. coun. Hawaii Pacific Coll., 1988—; mem. Hawaii Coun. Econ. Edn., 1988—; trustee Honolulu Chamber Music Soc., 1975-85, Jewish Fedn. Hawaii, 1982-86; bd. dirs. Hawaii Performing Arts Co., 1982-87; regent Chaminade U., 1986—. Recipient Gov.'s award for svc. as mem. of Commn. on Yr. 2000, 1978, Man of Yr. award Temple Emanu-El, 1986, Beautification award Hawaii Outdoor Circle, 1987, Judah L. Magnes Gold Medal award Am. Friends Hebrew U., 1988, Exec. of Yr. award Hawaii chpt. Profl. Secs. Internat., 1988. Mem. Hawaii Execs. Coun., Hawaii Hotel Assn. (pres. 1987-88, treas. polit. action com. 1985—), Am. Hotel and Motel Assn. (nat. bd. dirs. 1985-87), Waikiki Beach Operators Assn. (founding charter mem., exec. dir. 1984—), Soc. of Family Hoteliers of Am. Hotel and Motel Assn., Hawaii ParkConv. Coun. (founding dir., sustaining mem.), Young Pres.' Orgn., Skal Club Hawaii, Plaza Club, Beverly Hills Country Club, Honolulu Club, Oahu Country Club, Outrigger Canoe Club. Congregationalist. Avocations: tennis, music, history, literature. Office: Aston Hotels & Resorts 2155 Kala Kau Ave Ste 500 Honolulu HI 96815-2658*

TATLOCK, ANNE M., trust company executive; b. White Plains, N.Y., July 1, 1939; d. John and Kathleen (McGrath) McNiff; m. William Tatlock, Apr. 29, 1967; children: Julina, Kerry, Christopher. BA, Vassar Coll., 1961; MA in Econs., NYU, 1968. 1st v.p. Smith Barney Harris Upham, N.Y.C., 1962-84; exec. v.p. Fiduciary Trust Internat., N.Y.C., 1984-94, pres., 1994—; pres.; bd. dirs. Franklin United LIfe Inst. Co., Garden City, N.Y., Am. Gen. Corp., Houston, PHH Corp., Hunt Valley, Md. Treas., bd. dirs. West Side Day Nursery, N.Y.C., 1977-94, Stanley Isaacs Neighborhood Ctr., N.Y.C., 1988-90; trustee, chair fin. com. Am. Ballet Theatre, N.Y.C., 1994—; trustee Vassar Coll., 1994—, The Teagle Found., Inc., N.Y.C., 1995—; chmn. Cultural Instns. Retirement Sys., N.Y.C., 1989—, Andrew W. Mellon Found., 1995—. Elected to Acad. Women Achievers, YWCA, N.Y.C., 1983.

TATTERSALL, HARGREAVES VICTOR, III, lawyer; b. Bronx, Jan. 18, 1943; s. Hargreaves Victor Tattersall Jr. and Florence (Mary) Stephens; m. Bonnie Lee Opielowski (div. 1976); children: Hargreaves Victor IV, Sanderson Cole; m. Cynthia Louise Wood (div. 1995); 1 child, Jennifer Elizabeth. BSBA, U. New Haven, 1969; JD, U. Conn., 1972. Bar: Conn. 1972, Ohio 1994, U.S. Dist. Ct. Conn. 1975, U.S. Dist. Ct. (no. dist.) Ohio 1994, U.S. Supreme Ct. 1994. Assoc. gen. counsel Tilo, Inc. subs. Reynolds Metals Co., Stratford, Conn., 1973-75; ptnr. Rakosky & Smith, P.C., New London, Conn., 1975-80; sec., gen. counsel Dunham-Bush, Inc. subs. Signal Cos., Inc, West Hartford, Conn., 1980-84; v.p., sec., gen. counsel Stanadyne, Inc., Windsor, Conn., 1984-90; with Tattersall Enterprises, 1991—; ptnr. O'Rourke & Assocs., 1994-96. Chmn. Rep. Town Com., New London, 1979. Served with USN, 1960-64. Mem. ABA, Conn. Bar Assn. (exec. com. corp. counsel sect.), Ohio State Bar Assn., Cleve. Bar Assn., Am. Soc. Corp. Secs. (pres. Hartford chpt. 1987-88), Am. Corp. Counsel Assn., Am. Arbitration Assn. (nat. panel arbitrators and mediators). Roman Catholic.

TATUM, JOAN GLENNALYN JOHN, secondary school educator; b. Scottsbluff, Nebr., Jan. 5, 1934; d. Glenn Edwin and Blanche Constance (Dundon) John; m. William Earl Tatum, Apr. 6, 1954 (div. Apr. 1988); children: Cherie Elizabeth Tatum Love, Michele Tatum Brackett, John William, Amy Denise Tatum Stanton. AA, U. Fla., 1954; BA, U. South Fla., 1969, MA, 1971. Cert. tchr., Fla. Substitute tchr. Pub. Sch. Dist., Sarasota, Fla., 1966-67; bus., vocat. edn. tchr. Riverview High Sch., Sarasota, 1969—, Sarasota Tech. Inst., 1969—; curriculum coord. bus.-vocat. edn. dept. Riverview H.S., 1990—; adj. prof. St. Francis Coll., Joliet, Ill., 1988, 91, 93, 94; state and dist. textbook evaluation teams Fla. Dept. Edn., Sarasota, sch. to dist. tech. rep., 1985—; chmn., tech. coord. Riverview Tech. Com., 1987—; assoc. master tchr. State Fla. Bd. Edn., 1984-87; coun. chair Dist. Sch. Based Mgmt., Sarasota, 1991-93; chmn. Riverview Sch. Based Mgmt., 1991-93; project coord. Riverview Sr. Acad. Integrated Studies, 1991-95; dance tchr. various studios, Sarasota, 1949-67; sec. and office staff various govtl., cmty. and dance studios, Sarasota, 1951-59. Supervisory com. Sarasota Coastal Credit Union, 1985—. Senate Edn. scholar Sarasota High/Fla. Legislature, 1951; named Tchr. of Yr. Riverview High Sch., 1991-92. Mem. Internat. Soc. Bus. Educators, Nat. Bus. Edn. Assn., Am. Vocat. Assn., So. Bus. Edn. Assn., Fla. Bus. Edn. Assn., Fla. Vocat. Assn., Sarasota County Vocat. Adult Assn. (pres. 1989-90), Order of Rainbow (mem. adv. bd. 1977—, Grand Cross Color award 1949), Order Ea. Star, Kappa Delta Pi, Delta Pi Epsilon, Alpha Delta Kappa (chpt. treas. 1982-86, chpt. pres. 1986-88, chmn. state ad hoc com. 1989-90, chmn. state candidate qualifications com. 1994-96, dist. treas. 1987-92, dist. chmn. 1992-94, State Honoris Causa award 1992). Presbyterian. Avocations: theatre, choreography, dance, family, walking. Home: 4561 Ashton Rd Sarasota FL 34233-3405 Office: Riverview HS One Ram Way Sarasota FL 34231

TATUM, RONALD WINSTON, physician, endocrinologist; b. Joplin, Mo., Apr. 29, 1935; s. Dorothy Elizabeth (Messick) T.; m. Phyllis Wainman, June 25 (div. May 1974); children: Jeffrey, Stacey; m. Yvonne Marie Laug, Oct. 8, 1994; children: Christina, Candice. AB, Harvard U., 1957; MD, U. Rochester, 1961. Intern Strong Meml. Hosp., Rochester, N.Y., 1961-62; resident U. Rochester, 1962-64, fellow, 1964-66; clin. endocrinologist in pvt. practice Albuquerque, 1966—; active staff Presbyn. Hosp. and St. Joseph Hosp., Albuquerque, 1966—; med. dir. Cottonwood Treatment Ctr., Albuquerque, 1985-90, N.Mex. Monitored Treatment Program, Albuquerque, 1990—; clin. endocrine cons. Charter Hosp. and Heights Psychiat. Hosp., Albuquerque, 1985—. Contbr. articles to profl. jours. Mem. med. adv. com. Hospice Home Health Care, Albuquerque, 1991—. Mem. Am. Assn. Clin. Endocrinologists (charter), Am. Assn. Internal Medicine, Am. Diabetes Assn. (pres. N.Mex. chpt. 1970, 74), Am. Soc. Addiction Medicine, Assn. for Med. Rsch. in Substance Abuse. Avocations: photography, computer investing. Home: 408 Poinsettia Pl SE Albuquerque NM 87123 Office: 8008 Constitution Pl NE Albuquerque NM 87110-7628

TATUM, WILBERT ARNOLD, editor, publisher; b. Durham, N.C., Jan. 23, 1933; s. Eugene Malcolm Tatum and Mittie Novesta (Spell) Tatum-Smith; m. Susan Kohn, June 17, 1966; 1 child, Elinor Ruth. BS, Lincoln U., 1972; MS, Occidental Coll., 1972; DHL (hon.), Coll. Human Svcs., N.Y.C., 1988. Dep. pres. Borough of Manhattan, N.Y.C., 1970-71; dir. planning and devel. City of N.Y., 1971-77; sr. v.p. Health Ins. Plan of Greater N.Y., N.Y.C., 1978-86; editor, pub., CEO N.Y. Amsterdam News, N.Y.C., 1983—; vice chmn. Inner City Broadcasting, N.Y.C., 1970-73; chmn. bd. Tatum-Kohn Assn., N.Y.C., 1980—, Amnews Corp., N.Y.C., 1983—, Palisades Amsterdam Comm., N.Y.C., 1988—. Cpl. USMC, 1951-54, Far East. Fellow Nat. Urban Fellows, 1971-72. Mem. Nat. Newspaper Pubs. Assn. (bd. dirs.), N.Y. Urban League (Bldg. brick 1993), Wallenberg Com. of U.S. (v.p.). Democrat. Baptist. Home: 34 E 3d St New York NY 10003 Office: Amnews Corp 2340 Frederick Douglas Blvd New York NY 10027

TATYREK, ALFRED FRANK, consultant, materials/environmental engineer, analytical/research chemist; b. Hillside, N.J., Jan. 23, 1930; s. Frank Peter and Frances (Luxa) T. BS, Seton Hall U., 1954; postgrad., Rutgers U., 1956-57. Rsch. chemist Bakelite div. Union Carbide, Bloomfield, N.J., 1953-58, U.S. Radium Corp., Morristown, N.J., 1959-62; analytical chemist insp. Chem. Procurement Dist. U.S. Army, N.Y.C., 1962-64; rsch. chemist Picatinny Arsenal U.S. Army, Dover, N.J., 1964-73; chem. materials engr. U.S. Army Armament Rsch., Devel. and Engrng. Ctr., N.J., 1973-95; cons. polymer materials, environ. chemistry. Patentee pyrotechnic compositions, chemiluminescent compounds and processes, crank case oil vacuum purification sys. for internal combustion engines; lectr., contbr. articles on mountaineering expdns. and adventures in the great mountain ranges of N.Am., S.Am., Europe and Africa to mags.; contbr. more than 50 sci. and tech. reports. 1st aid instr. ARC, Essex County, N.J., 1969-82; chief 1st aid Maplewood (N.J.) CD, 1971-91; patrol dir. Nat. Ski Patrol, Phoenicia, N.Y., 1978-84, sr. lifetime Nat. Ski patroller So. N.Y. region, 1979—. Mem. Nat. Soc. Inventors, Nat. Assn. Underwater Instrs. (cert. advanced diver and underwater photographer 1971—), Magician's Roundtable, Internat. Magician's Soc., Alpine Club of Can., Appalachian Mountain Club, Sierra Club, The Scientific Rsch. Soc., Sigma Xi (pres. Picatinny chpt. 1974-75, 79-80, 85-86). Roman Catholic. Achievments include 6 patents in field. Also climbed 15,771 feet on Mt. Blanc, highest mountain peak in Europe; climbed to highest summit of 19,730 feet on Mt. Kilimanjaro, highest mountian peak in Africa, 1972; leader of climb on Matterhorn and Monte Rosa, Switzerland's highest peak; participant in numerous mountain expdns. in U.S. and Can., including 3 first ascents in No. Cascades of Wash. (S.E. ridge of Mt. Goode, Aug. 1963, Peak 7732 via the Snow Chute, Aug. 1964, East ridge of Bear Mountain Aug. 1964). Home: 27 Orchard Rd Maplewood NJ 07040-1919 *"God has given us a world rich in physical and intellectual beauty as well as intriguing scientific discovery. To earn these rewards we must seek out and meet the challanges of life, not as distastful burdens, but as true opportunities upon which to build where others have failed or left off, using all the infinite resources that God has given to all of us".*

TAUB, ELI IRWIN, lawyer, arbitrator; b. N.Y.C., July 6, 1938; s. Max and Belle (Slutsky) T.; m. Nancy Denise Bell, May 15, 1983. 1 child, Jennifer. BA, Bklyn. Coll., 1960; JD, NYU, 1963. Bar: N.Y. 1964, U.S. Dist. Ct. (no. dist.) N.Y. 1979. Ptnr. Silverman, Silverman & Taub, Schenectady, 1971-77; pres. Eli I. Taub, P.C., Schenectady, 1978—; chmn. Bd. Assessment Review, Schenectady, 1972-81; arbitrator Am. Arbitration Assn., Pa., N.Y. Employment Rels. Bd., 1966—; N.Y. State Pub. Employer's Rels. Bd.; hearing officer articles 72 and 75 proceedings N.Y. State/CSEA Arbitration Panel; mem. paralegal adv. com. Schenectady County C.C.; counsel Alcoholism Coun. Schenectay County. Chmn. trustees Joseph Egan Supreme Ct. Library, Schenectady, 1980, 81, 84; pres. Schenectady County Republican Club, 1985-86; v.p. Jewish Fedn. Schenectady, 1983-86; mem. surrogate decision making com. N.Y. State Commn. on Quality of Care for the Mentally Disabled; bd. dirs. Jewish Community Ctr., NE Parent and Child Soc., United Jewish Fedn. of N.E. N.Y.; advocate Nat. Coll. of Advocay. Mem. Assn. Trial Lawyers Am., Am. Arbitration Assn., Nat. Orgn. of Social Security Claimant Reps., Indsl. Rels. Research Assn., N.Y. State Bar Assn., N.Y. State Trial Lawyers Assn., Schenectady County Bar Assn., Capital Dist. Trial Lawyers Assn., B'nai B'rith (pres. 1976-77, spl. award 1982, youth services award 1985). Jewish. Home: 105 N Ferry St Schenectady NY 12305-1610 Office: 705 Union St Schenectady NY 12305-1504

TAUB, HENRY, retired computer services company executive; b. Paterson, N.J., Sept. 20, 1927; s. Morris and Sylvia (Sievitz) T.; m. Marilyn Adler, Sept. 13, 1958; children: Judith, Steven, Ira. B.S., N.Y. U., 1947. Pres. Automatic Data Processing, Inc., Roseland, N.J., 1949-69; chmn. bd. Automatic Data Processing, Inc., 1970-77, 82-86, chmn. exec. com., 1977—, hon. chmn. bd., 1986—; dir. Leumi Bank & Trust Co., N.Y.C., Rite Aid Corp., Hasbro, Inc.; past pres., hon. chmn. Joint Distbn. Com. Chmn., hon. pres. N.Y. chpt. Hemophilia Found., 1970-76; past vice chmn. Nat. Hemophilia Found.; bd. dirs. Am. Friends Hebrew U., Interfaith Hunger Appeal, 1979—, N.Y. Shakespeare Festival, 1981—, Ch. United Israel Appeal, 1986-90; trustee NYU, Avi Chai Found.; mem. bd. govs. Jewish Agy., 1981-90; pres. Jewish Community Ctr. of Palisades, 1980-84; chmn. Bus. Employment Found., Inc., 1980-90. Mem. Am. Technion Soc. (chmn., internat. bd. govs. 1990—), Paterson Alumni Assn. (chmn. 1987-94). Office: ADP Inc 1 A D P Blvd Roseland NJ 07068-1728 also: NJ Nets Meadowlands Arena East Rutherford NJ 07073

TAUB, JESSE J., electrical engineering researcher; b. N.Y.C., Apr. 27, 1927; s. Julius and Ida (Orlansky) T.; m. Eva Pollack, Dec. 24, 1955 (dec. Nov. 1973); children: Richard Lawrence, Jocelyn Cara, Suzanne Mara; m. Naomi Etta Trachtenberg, June 30, 1974. BEE, CCNY, 1948; MEE, Poly. U., 1949. Group leader microwave electronics, Material Lab. USN, Bklyn., 1949-55; engr. Airborne Instruments Lab., Mineola, N.Y., 1955-58, sect. leader, 1958-61, engrng. cons., 1961-75; chief scientist AIL Systems Inc., Melville, N.Y., 1975-93; cons., 1993—. Author: (with others) Microwave Measurements, 1963; contbr. numerous papers to profl. publs.; patentee microwave techniques. With USN, 1945-46. Fellow IEEE (centennial medal 1984, C.A. Fowler award 1993, adminstrv. com. 1972-74, program chmn. microwave symposium, steering com., chmn. L.I. sect.); mem. Archaeology Inst. Am. Democrat. Jewish. Avocations: classical musician, contract bridge, archaeology. Home: 115 Northgate Cir Melville NY 11747-3045 Office: AIL Systems Inc Commack Rd Deer Park NY 11729

TAUB, RICHARD PAUL, social sciences educator; b. Bklyn., Apr. 16, 1937; s. Martin Glynn and Frances (Israel) T.; m. Doris Susan Leventhal, Aug. 14, 1961 (dec. Feb. 1996); children: Neela Robin, Zachariah Jacob. BA, U. Mich., 1959; MA, Harvard U., 1962, PhD in Social Relations, 1966. Asst. prof. sociology Brown U., Providence, 1965-69; from asst. prof. to Paul Klapper prof. of social scis. U. Chgo., 1969—, assoc. dean Coll. of Univ., 1982-86; adv. bd. Neighborhood Preservation Initiative, 1993—; chair adv. bd. Nat. Comty. Devel. Initiative, 1991-95; dir. South Ark. Rural Devel. Study, 1988—. Author: Community Capitalism, Bureaucrats Under Stress, (with D. Garth Taylor and Jan Dunham) Paths of Neighborhood Change, (with Doris L. Taub) Entrepreneurship in India's Small Scale Industries; editor: (with Doris L. Taub) American Society in Tocqueville's Time and Today; co-editor Studies of Urban Soc., 1978—; contbr. articles to profl. jours. Chmn. bd. St. Thomas the Apostle Sch., Chgo., 1983-86; bd. dirs. Hyde Park Kenwood Cmty. Conf., Chgo., 1972-75; bd. seminary Coop Bookstore, Chgo., 1994—. Angell scholar U. Mich., 1956; Woodrow Wilson fellow Harvard U., 1959-60; grantee Am. Inst. Indian Studies, Ford Found., MacArthur Found., NSF, Wieboldt Found., Nat. Inst. Justice. Mem. Am. Sociol. Assn., Midwest Sociol. Soc., Assn. for Asian Studies. Avocations: bicycling, music. Office: Univ Chgo 5845 S Ellis Ave Rm 223 Chicago IL 60637-1404

TAUB, ROBERT ALLAN, lawyer; b. Denver, Nov. 25, 1923; s. Clarence Arthur and Mary Frances (Jones) T.; m. Doris Irene Schroeder, Dec. 22, 1945; children: Amanda, Jonathan, Barbara. BA, U. Chgo., 1944, JD, 1947. Bar: Ill. 1947. Legal staff Marshall Field & Co., Chgo., 1947-50; mgr. exec. compensation Ford Motor Co., Dearborn, Mich., 1950-63; asst. sect. Ford Motor Co., Dearborn, 1963-74, dir. corp. affairs planning, 1974—. Pres. Dearborn Community Arts Council, 1971-72; trustee Internat. Mus. Photography, George Eastman House, Rochester, N.Y., 1976—, chmn., 1979-82; mem. adv. bd. U. Mich. Dearborn, 1980—, Met. Mus. Art, N.Y.C., 1987—; trustee Henry Ford Hosp., Detroit, 1983—; chmn. Dearborn Pub. Libr., 1986—; bd. dirs., mem. exec. com., chmn. fin. com., Health Alliance Plan, 1992—. Mem. ABA, Ill. Bar Assn. Presbyterian. Home: 1824 Hawthorne St Dearborn MI 48128-1448 Office: Ford Motor Co The American Rd Rm #950 Dearborn MI 48126

TAUBE, HENRY, chemistry educator; b. Sask., Can., Nov. 30, 1915; came to U.S., 1937, naturalized, 1942; s. Samuel and Albertina (Tiledetski) T.; m. Mary Alice Wesche, Nov. 27, 1952; children: Linda, Marianna, Heinrich, Karl. BS, U. Sask., 1935, MS, 1937, LLD, 1973; PhD, U. Calif., 1940; PhD (hon.), Hebrew U. of Jerusalem, 1979; DSc (hon.), U. Chgo., 1983, Poly. Inst., N.Y., 1984, SUNY, 1985, U. Guelph, 1987; DSc honoris causa, Seton Hall U., 1988; Lajos Kossuth U. of Debrecen, Hungary, 1988; DSc, Northwestern U., 1990; hon. degree, U. Athens, 1993. Instr. U. Calif., 1940-41; instr., asst. prof. Cornell U., 1941-46; faculty U. Chgo., 1946-62, prof., 1952-62, chmn. dept. chemistry, 1955-59; prof. chemistry Stanford U., 1962-90; prof. emeritus chemistry Stanford U, 1990—; Marguerite Blake Wilbur prof. Stanford U., 1976, chmn. dept., 1971-74; Baker lectr. Cornell U., 1965. Hon. mem. Hungarian Acad., Scis., 1988. Guggenheim fellow, 1949, 55; recipient Harrison Howe award, 1961, Chandler medal Columbia U., 1964, F. P. Dwyer medal U. NSW, Australia, 1973, Nat. medal of Sci., 1976, 77, Allied Chem. award for Excellence in Grad. Tchg. and Innovative Sci., 1979, Nobel prize in Chemistry, 1983, Bailar medal U. Ill., 1983, Robert A. Welch Found. award in Chemistry, 1983, Disting. Achievement award Internat. Precious Metals Inst., 1986, Brazilian Order of Sci. Merit award, 1994. Fellow Royal Soc. Chemistry (hon.), Indian Chem. Soc. (hon.); mem. NAS (award in chem. scis. 1983), Am. Acad. Arts and Scis., Am. Chem. Soc. (Kirkwood award New Haven sect. 1965, award for nuclear applications in chemistry 1955, Nichols medal N.Y. sect. 1971, Willard Gibbs medal Chgo. sect. 1971, Disting. Svc. in Advancement Inorganic Chemistry award 1967, T.W. Richards medal NE sect. 1980, Monsanto Co. award in inorganic chemistry 1981, Linus Pauling award Puget Sound sect. 1981, Priestley medal 1985, Oesper award Cin. sect. 1986, G.M. Kosolapoff award Auburn sect. 1990), Royal Physiographical Soc. of Lund (fgn. mem.), Am. Philos. Soc., Finnish Acad. Sci. and Letters, Royal Danish Acad. Scis. and Letters, Coll. Chemists of Catalonia and Beleares (hon.), Can. Soc. Chemistry (hon.), Hungarian Acad. Scis. (hon. mem.), Royal Soc. (fgn. mem.), Brazilian Acad. Scis. (corr.), Engrng. Acad. Japan (fgn. assoc.), Australian Acad. Scis. (corr.), Chem. Soc. Japan (hon. mem. 1993), Phi Beta Kappa, Sigma Xi, Phi Lambda Upsilon (hon.). Office: Stanford U Dept Chemistry Stanford CA 94305-5080

TAUBER, ALFRED IMRE, hematologist, immunologist, philosopher of science; b. Washington, June 24, 1947; s. Laszlo Nandor Tauber and Lilly Katherine (Manovill) Endrei; m. Susan Alice Swerdlow, Dec. 22, 1966; children: Joel, Dylan, Benjamin, Hannah. BS, Tufts U., 1969, MD, 1973. Intern, resident in internal medicine U. Wash., Seattle, 1973-75; clin. and research fellow in hematology Tufts-N.Eng. Med. Ctr., Boston, 1975-77; instr. in medicine Harvard Med. Sch., Boston, 1978-80; jr. assoc. in medicine Brigham and Women's Hosp., Boston, 1979-82; research assoc. Robert B. Brigham Hosp., Boston, 1979-82; asst. prof. medicine Harvard Med. Sch., Boston, 1980-82; assoc. prof. medicine, assoc. rsch. prof. biochemistry Boston U. Sch. Medicine, 1982-86, prof. medicine, 1986—, assoc. prof. pathology, 1985-87, prof. pathology, 1987—; prof. philosophy Boston U., 1992—, dir. Ctr. for Philosophy and History of Sci., 1993—; assoc. vis. physician Boston City Hosp., 1982-87, vis. physician, 1988—, chief hematology and oncology, 1982-91. Author: The Immune Self: Theory or Metaphor?, 1994; co-author: Metchnikoff and the Origins of Immunology, 1991; editor: Organism and the Origins of Self, 1991, The Elusive Synthesis: Aesthetics and Science, 1996; contbr. more than 150 articles on neutrophil biochemistry and history/philosophy of biology to profl. jours. Fellow Brandeis U. Waltham, Mass., 1978. Fellow ACP; mem. Am. Soc. Hematology, Reticuloendothelial Soc., Am. Assn. Immunology, Am. Soc. Cell Biology, Am. Assn. Biol. Chemistry and Molecular Biology, Am. Soc. Clin. Investigation, Assn. Am. Physicians, History of Sci. Soc., Am. Assn. History of Medicine, Am. Philos. Assn., Philosophy of Sci. Assn. Jewish. Office: Boston Univ 745 Commonwealth Ave Boston MA 02215-1401

TAUBER, JOEL DAVID, manufacturing company executive; b. Detroit, June 28, 1935; s. Benjamin and Anne (Merliss) T.; m. Shelley Tauber; children: Julie, Ellen, Benjamin Brian, Melissa, Juliana. B.B.A., U. Mich., 1956, J.D., 1959, M.B.A., 1963. Bar: Mich. 1959. Pres. Key Internat. Mfg. Inc., Southfield, Mich., 1969-86; pres. Tauber Enterprises, 1986—; trustee Nat. Indsl. Group Pension Plan, 1980; bd. dirs. Fed. Home Loan Bank, 1986-91, Reid Plastics Inc., 1989-93; chmn. bd. Key Mfg. Group, Inc., Key Plastics, Inc., Keywell Corp., 1986—; chmn. bd. dirs. Complex Tooling & Molding; established Tauber Mfg. Inst., U. Mich., 1995. Pres. Jewish Welfare Fedn., Detroit, 1983-86, Jewish Cmty. Ctr., 1978-80; nat. chmn. United Jewish Appeal, 1992-94, pres., 1994-96; bd. dirs. United Found., 1980—, v.p., 1986—; co-chmn. Detroit Round Table-Nat. Coun. Christians, Jews and Muslims, 1989-91; trustee Sinai Hosp., Detroit, 1980-91; mem. Fed. Judges Selection Panel Ea. Dist. Mich., 1978; mem. U. Mich. Devel. Adv. Bd., 1986-96, vis. com., 1996—; trustee Growth Fund, 1988—. Recipient Frank A. Wetsman Meml. Leadership award Jewish Welfare Fedn., 1970, Butzel award, 1990; named Entrepreneur of Yr., 1990. Mem. Mich. Bar Assn., World Bus. Council, Franklin Hills Country Club, Detroit Athletic Club, U. Mich. Alumni Club, U. Mich. Victors Club, Masons. Office: Tauber Enterprises 27777 Franklin Rd Ste 1850 Southfield MI 48034 *To give life meaning and fulfillment one must live life to its fullest everyday and do one's best each of these days.*

TAUBER, MARK J., lawyer; b. Detroit, Mar. 25, 1949; s. Max M. and Beatrice R. (Roth) T.; m. Anita L. Tilben, June 23, 1970; children: Melissa A., Benjamin M., Allison B. BA, U. Mich., 1970; JD, George Washington U., 1973. Bar: D.C. 1973, Md. 1974, U.S. Supreme Ct. 1980. Assoc. Pierson, Ball & Dowd, Washington, 1973-79, ptnr., 1980-82; ptnr. Piper & Marbury, Washington, 1982—. Home: 11515 Big Piney Way Potomac MD 20854-1365 Office: Piper & Marbury 1200 19th St NW Washington DC 20036-2412

TAUBER, ORNER J., SR., petrochemical company executive; b. 1914; married. Grad., Tex. Christian U. With MKT R.R., 1932-35, So. Steamship Line, 1937-39; asst. to pres. Eastern States Petroleum Co., Inc., 1942-50; with Gabriel Oil Co., 1950-53; with Tauber Oil Co., Houston, 1953—, chmn., 1977—, also bd. dirs. Office: Tauber Oil Co 55 Waugh Dr Ste 700 Houston TX 77007-5837*

TAUBER, RONALD STEVEN, investment banker; b. N.Y.C., Jan. 24, 1944; s. William and Lillian (Slanger) T.; m. Adele Sharon Lieberman, June 21, 1966; children: Daniel, Miriam, Michael, Elizabeth. BA, Bklyn. Coll., 1965; LLB, Harvard U., 1968. Bar: N.Y. 1969. Law clk. presiding justice U.S. Dist. Ct., Bklyn, 1968-70; assoc. Stroock & Stroock & Lavan, N.Y.C., 1970-76, ptnr., 1976-79; sr. v.p. J. Aron & Co., Inc., N.Y.C., 1979-81; gen. ptnr. Goldman, Sachs & Co., N.Y.C., 1981-86, limited ptnr., 1987-88; mng. officer Brook Street Assocs. L.P., N.Y.C., 1987-88; pres., chief exec. officer Rayner & Stonington, L.P., 1988-91; pres. Tricon Fin. Svcs., Co., N.Y.C., 1991-93, Blenheim Investments, Inc., Somerset, N.J., 1993—. Trustee Maimonides Hosp., Bklyn., 1978-88. Mem. Comex Clearing Assn. (gov. 1984-87), Futures Industry Assn. (bd. dirs. 1985-87), Nat. Futures Assn. Home: 885 Park Ave New York NY 10021-0325 Office: Blenheim Investments Inc C/O R&S Mgmt Group 126 E 56th St Rm 1500 New York NY 10022-3613

TAUBMAN, A. ALFRED, real estate developer; b. Pontiac, Mich., Jan. 31, 1925; s. Philip and Fannie Ester (Blustin) T.; m. Reva Kolodney, Dec. 1, 1949 (div. July 1977); children: Gayle Kalisman, Robert S., William S.; m. Judith Mazor, June 17, 1982. Student, U. Mich., 1945-48, LLD (hon.), 1991; student, Lawrence Inst. Tech., 1948-49, DArch (hon.), 1985; D in Bus. (hon.), Eastern Mich. U., 1984; D in Edn. (hon.), Mich. State U., 1993; HHD (hon.), No. Mich. U., 1995. Chmn. The Taubman Co., Bloomfield Hills, Mich., 1950—, Taubman Ctrs., Inc., Bloomfield Hills, Mich., 1992—;

chmn. Sotheby's Holdings, Inc., N.Y.C., 1983—; bd. dirs. Live Entertainment of Can., Inc. Trustee Ctr. for Creative Studies, Detroit, Harper-Grace Hosps., Detroit; chmn. emeritus Archives Am. Art Smithsonian Inst., Washington, U. Pa. Wharton Real Estate Ctr., Phila.; pres. Arts Commn. of Detroit; mem. nat. bd. Smithsonian Assocs.; established Taubman Ctr. for State and Local Govt. Harvard U., Cambridge, Mass., chmn. Mich. Partnership for New Edn., Program in Am. Instns., U. Mich., Brown U.'s Pub. Policy and Am. Instns. Program; prin. benefactor A. Alfred Taubman Health Care Ctr. and A. Alfred Taubman Med. Libr., U. Mich.; bd. dirs. Detroit Renaissance, Inc., Friends of Art and Preservation in Embassies, Washington; active State of Mich. Gaming Commn. Recipient Bus. Statesman award Harvard Bus. Sch. Club of Detroit, 1983, Sportsman of Yr. award United Found. Detroit, SE Mich. Chpt. March of Dimes Birth Defects, 1983; named Michiganian of Yr. The Detroit News, 1983. Mem. Urban Land Inst. (trustee), Nat. Realty Com. (bd. dirs.).

TAUBMAN, MARTIN ARNOLD, immunologist; b. N.Y.C., July 10, 1940; s. Herman and Betty (Berger) T.; m. Joan Petra Mikelbank, May 30, 1965; children: Benjamin Abby, Joel David. B.S., Bklyn. Coll., 1961; D.D.S., Columbia U., 1965; Ph.D., SUNY, Buffalo, 1970. Asst. mem. staff Forsyth Dental Center, Boston, 1970—; head immunology dept. Forsyth Dental Center, 1972—, assoc. mem. staff, 1974-80, sr. staff mem., 1980—; asst. clin. prof. oral biology and pathophysiology Harvard U. Sch. Dental Medicine, 1976-79, assoc. clin. prof., 1979—; mem. oral biology and medicine study sect. NIH, 1980-84. Editor: (with J. Siots) Contemporary Microbiology and Immunology; contbr. articles to profl. jours, chpts. to books. Recipient Rsch. Career Devel. award, 1971-76, Fred Birnberg Alumni award for disting. dental rsch. Columbia U. Assn. Dental Alumni, Disting. Faculty award Harvard Sch. Dental Medicine, 1990, MERIT award NIH, 1991; USPHS fellow, 1962-63; postdoctoral fellow, 1966-70. Mem. Am. Soc. Microbiology, , Soc. Mucosal Immunology, Internat. Assn. Dental Research (Oral Biology award 1991), Am. Assn. Immunologists, Am. Assn. Dental Research (v.p. 1987—, pres. elect 1988, pres. 1989). Office: Forsyth Dental Ctr 140 Fenway Boston MA 02115-3782

TAUBMAN, WILLIAM CHASE, political science educator; b. N.Y.C., Nov. 13, 1941; s. Howard and Nora (Stern) T.; m. Jane Dea Andelman, May 18, 1969; children—Alexander, Phoebe. A.B., Harvard U., 1962; M.A., Columbia U., 1965, cert. of Russian Inst., 1965, Ph.D., 1969; M.A. (hon.), Amherst Coll., 1978. Instr. Amherst Coll., Mass., 1967-69; asst. prof. Amherst Coll., 1969-73, assoc. prof., 1973-78, prof. dept. polit. sci., 1978-83, Bertrand Snell prof., 1983—; mem. planning staff U.S. Dept. State, Washington, 1970-71; mem. bd. Internat. Rsch. and Exch. Bd., N.Y.C., 1971-74, mem. selection com., 1984-85; vis. assoc. prof. Yale U., New Haven, spring 1975; chmn. adv. com. Cold War Internat. History Project, Woodrow Wilson Ctr., Washington, 1993—; mem. Internat. Acad. Adv. Group, Russian Fgn. Ministry Archives, 1992—. Author: The View from Lenin Hills, 1967; Governing Soviet Cities, 1973; Stalin's American Policy, 1982; co-author: (with Jane Taubman) Moscow Spring, 1989; editor, translator: Khrushchev on Khrushchev (Sergei N. Khrushchev), 1990; editor: Globalism and Its Critics, 1973. Woodrow Wilson Nat. Found. fellow, 1962; Ford Found. fellow, 1963-67; Council Fgn. Relations fellow, 1970-71; Rockefeller Found. fellow, 1983; Columbia U. Harriman Inst. sr. fellow, 1987; grantee Nat. Council Soviet and East European Research, 1984; Fulbright-Hays Faculty Rsch. fellow, 1988, NEH fellow, 1992. Fellow Russian Research Ctr. Harvard U.; mem. Council Fgn. Relations, Authors Guild. Home: 43 Hitchcock Rd Amherst MA 01002-2500 Office: Amherst Coll Dept Polit Sci Box 2259 Amherst MA 01002-5000

TAUC, JAN, physics educator; b. Pardubice, Czechoslovakia, Apr. 15, 1922; came to U.S., 1969, naturalized, 1978; s. Jan and Josefa (Semonska) T.; m. Vera Koubelova, Oct. 18, 1947; children: Elena (Mrs. Milan Kokta), Jan. Ing.Dr. in Elec. Engring., Tech. U. Prague, 1949; RNDr., Charles U., 1956; Dr.Sc. in Physics, Czechoslovak Acad. Scis., 1956. Scientist microwave research Sci. and Tech. Research Inst., Tanvald and Prague, 1949-52; head semiconductor dept. Inst. Solid State Physics, Czechoslovak Acad. Scis., 1953-69; prof. exptl. physics Charles U., 1964-69, dir. Inst. Physics,, 1968-69; mem. tech. staff Bell Telephone Labs., Murray Hill, N.J., 1969-70; prof. engring. and physics Brown U., 1970-83, L. Herbert Ballou prof. engring. and physics, 1983-92, L. Herbert Ballou prof. emeritus, 1992—, dir. material research lab., 1983-88; dir. E. Fermi Summer Sch., Varenna, Italy, 1965; vis. prof. U. Paris, 1969, Stanford U., 1977, Max Planck Inst. Solid State Research, Stuttgart, Germany, 1982; UNESCO fellow, Harvard, 1961-62. Author: Photo and Thermoelectric Effects in Semiconductors, 1962, also numerous articles; editor: The Optical Properties of Solids, 1966, Amorphous and Liquid Semiconductors, 1974; co-editor: Solid State Communications, 1963-92. Recipient Nat. prize Czechoslovak Govt., 1955, 69; Sr. U.S. Scientist award Humboldt Found., 1981, Silver medal Union of Czechoslovak Mathematicians and Physicists, 1992. Fellow AAAS, Am. Phys. Soc. (Frank Isakson prize 1982, David Adler award 1988); mem. NAS, European Phys. Soc. (founding), Czechoslovak Acad. Scis. (corr. 1963-71, 90-91, fgn. 1991-92, Hlavka medal 1992). Office: Brown U Divsn Engring Providence RI 02912

TAUCHERT, THEODORE RICHMOND, mechanical engineer, educator; s. Elwyn Harding and Eleanor (Richmond) T.; m. Ann Dudley Bradlee, May 10, 1958; children: Amy T. Teicher, Sarah T. Rushing, Rebecca T. McGowan, Charles W., Macy G. B.S.E., Princeton U., 1957; M.Eng., Yale U., 1960, D.Eng., 1964. Structural engr. Sikorsky Aircraft, Stratford, Conn., 1957-61; research asoc., lectr. Princeton U., N.J., 1964-65, asst. prof., 1965-70; assoc. prof. U. Ky., Lexington, 1970-76, prof. engring. mechanics, 1976—, chmn. dept., 1980-84, 88-94. Editorial bd.: Acta Mechanica, 1976—, Jour. Thermal Stresses, 1981—; author: Energy Principles in Structural Mechanics, 1974; contbr. articles to profl. jours. Served to 2d lt. U.S. Army, 1957-58. Mem. ASCE, ASME, Am. Soc. Engring. Edn., Soc. Engring. Sci., Sigma Xi. Home: 1620 Richmond Rd Lexington KY 40502-1620

TAUREL, SIDNEY, pharmaceutical executive; b. Casablanca, Morocco, Feb. 9, 1949; came to U.S., 1986; s. Jose and Marjorie (Afriat) T.; m. Kathryn H. Fleischmann, Mar. 22, 1977; children: Alexis, Patrick, Olivia. BSBA, Ecole des Hautes Etudes Commerciales, Paris, 1969; MBA, Columbia U., 1971. Mktg. assoc. Eli Lilly Internat. Corp., Indpls., 1971-72; mktg. planning mgr. Eli Lilly Do Brasil Limitada, Sao Paulo, Brazil, 1972-75, gen. mgr., 1982-83; mgr. pharm. ops. Eastern Europe Eli Lilly und Elanco Gesmbh, Vienna, Austria, 1976; sales mgr. pharm. Eli Lilly France SA, Paris, 1977-79, mktg. dir. pharm., 1980-81; v.p. Europe Lilly European ops., London, 1984-85; exec. v.p. Eli Lilly Internat. Corp., Indpls., 1986, pres., 1986-91, exec. v.p. pharm. divsn., 1991-93; exec. v.p. Eli Lilly and Co., 1993—, pres. pharm. divsn., 1993—, bd. dirs., 1993—; now pres., COO Eli Lilly & Co.; bd. overseers Columbia Bus. Sch. Mem. Indpls. Symphony Orch.; bd. dirs. RCA Tennis Championships. Mem. Pharm. Rsch. and Mfrs. Assn. (chmn. internat. com. 1994—, chmn. membership com. 1994—, bd. dirs., treas. 1995—), Indpls. Racquet Club. Avocations: tennis, music. Home: 6160 Sunset Ln Indianapolis IN 46208-1456*

TAURO, JOSEPH LOUIS, federal judge; b. Winchester, Mass., Sept. 26, 1931; s. G. Joseph and Helen Maria (Petrossi) T.; m. Elizabeth Mary Quinlan, Feb. 7, 1959 (dec. 1978); children—Joseph L., Elizabeth H., Christopher M.; m. Ann Lefavour Jones, July 12, 1980. AB, Brown U., 1953; LLB, Cornell U., 1956; JD (hon.), U. Mass., 1985, Suffolk U., 1986, Northeastern U., 1990, New Eng. Sch. Law, 1992. Bar: Mass. 1956, D.C. 1960. Assoc. Tauro & Tauro, Lynn, Mass., 1958-59; asst. U.S. atty. Dept. Justice, Boston, 1959-60; ptnr. Jaffee & Tauro, Boston and Lynn, Mass., 1960-71; chief legal counsel Gov. of Mass., Boston, 1965-68; U.S. atty. Dept. Justice, Boston, 1972; judge U.S. Dist. Ct., Boston, 1972—; chief judge U.S. Dist. Ct., Mass., 1992—; mem. exec. com. Cornell Law Sch., Ithaca, N.Y., 1968-71; mem. adv. coun. Cornell Law Sch., Ithaca, 1975-80; adj. prof. law Boston U. Law Sch., 1977—; mem. Jud. Conf. U.S., 1994—, mem. com. on operation of jury sys., 1979-86, mem. adv. com. on codes of conduct, 1988-94. Trustee Brown U., 1978—, Mass. Gen. Hosp., Boston, 1968-72, Children's Hosp. Med. Ctr., Boston, 1979-94. 1st lt. U.S. Army, 1956-58. Recipient Disting. Alumnus award Cornell U. Law Sch., 1992, Brown Bear award Brown U., 1993; named one of 10 Outstanding Young Men, Greater Boston Jaycees, 1966. Fellow Am. Bar Found.; mem. ABA, Mass. Bar Assn., Boston Bar Assn. (coun. 1968-71), D.C. Bar Assn., Boston Yacht Club (Marblehead, Mass.). Republican. Roman Catholic. Avocations: sports; reading; music; films; theater. Office: US Dist Ct Mccormack PO Courthous Rm 1 Boston MA 02109

TAUSCHER, JOHN WALTER, retired pediatrician, emeritus educator; b. LaSalle, Ill., Feb. 3, 1929; s. John Robert and Ella (Danz) T.; m. Mary Claire Cline, June 19, 1954 (dec. 1989); children—Michael, John, Claire, Mark, Matthew. B.S., U. Ill., 1952, M.D., 1954. Diplomate Am. Bd. Pediatrics. Intern Cook County Hosp., Chgo., 1954-55; resident in pediatrics Hurley Hosp., Flint, Mich., 1958-60; practice medicine specializing in pediatrics Flint, 1960-75; assoc. prof. human devel. Coll. Human Medicine, Mich. State U., East Lansing, 1975-80, prof. pediatrics and human devel., 1980-94, prof. emeritus, 1994; ret., 1994; v.p. After Hours Pediatric Care, P.C., Flint, 1972-87; chmn. pediatrics Hurley Med. Ctr., 1980-90, dir. pediatric edn., dir. primary care pediatrics, 1991-94; dir. clin. svcs. Mott Children's Health Ctr., 1981-85, v.p. health affairs, 1985-91. Served with USAF, 1955-58. Recipient Outstanding Teaching award Coll. Human Medicine, Mich. State U., 1977, 84, 85, Clin. Instr. of Yr. award St. Joseph Hosp., 1977, Disting. Community Faculty award Mich. State U., 1989. Mem. AMA, Genesee County Med. Soc. (pres. 1990), Mich. State Med. Soc., Northeastern Mich. Pediatric Soc., Am. Acad. Pediatrics. Roman Catholic. Home: 1069 Rayna Dr Davison MI 48423-2845 Office: Dept Pediatric Edn One Hurley Plaza Flint MI 48503-5905

TAUSSIG, JOSEPH KNEFLER, JR., retired government official, lawyer; b. Newport, R.I., May 28, 1920; s. Joseph Knefler and Lulie Augusta (Johnston) T.; m. Betty Carney, Dec. 2, 1943; children: Joseph Knefler III, Susan Taussig Graves (dec.). B.S., U.S. Naval Acad., 1941; J.D. with honors, George Washington U., 1949. Bar: U.S. Supreme Ct., 1975. Commd. U.S. Navy, 1937, advanced through grades to capt., 1954, ret., 1954; exec. sec. U.S. Naval Inst., Annapolis, Md., 1954-56; also pub. books, mags. U.S. Naval Inst., 1952-56; in various positions Westinghouse, Joy Mfg., Raytheon, Washington, 1956-62; pres. Taussig-Tomb & Assocs., Washington, 1962-81, 93—; dep. asst. sec. Dept. Navy, Washington, 1981-85; asst. dep. undersec. for safety and survivability Dept. Navy, Arlington, Va., 1985-93. Contbr. numerous articles to various publs., 1942—. Candidate for U.S. Congress from Md., 1956; pres. Md. Easter Seal Soc., 1968-74; pres. Internat. Assn. Pollution Control, Washington, 1970-74. Decorated Navy Cross, 2 Navy Disting. Pub. Svc. medals; recipient commendation U.s. Atty. Gen., 1994, Pres.'s award Ret. Officers Assn., 1966, 68. Mem. Naval Hist. Found. (trustee 1980—), U.S. Naval Inst. (sec.-treas. 1952-56), U.S. Naval Acad. Alumni Assn. (trustee 1956-60), Navy League (local bd. dirs. 1962-64). Republican. Episcopalian. Club: Army-Navy (treas. 1974-80) (Washington). Lodge: Rotary (bd. dirs. local club 1954-58). Avocations: philately; boating; piano playing. Home: 400 Ridgely Ave Annapolis MD 21401-1306

TAUSSIG, LYNN MAX, healthcare administrator, pulmonologist, pediatrician, educator; b. Milw., July 19, 1942; m. Lisa Peter; children: Heather, Jennifer. AB cum laude, Harvard U., 1964; MD, Washington U., St. Louis, 1968. Diplomate Am. Bd. Pediats., Nat. Bd. Med. Examiners, Am. Bd. Pediat. Pulmonary. Rsch. asst. dept. neuroanatomy Marquette U., Milw., 1965; intern in pediats. St. Louis Children's Hosp., 1968-69; resident in pediats. U. Colo. Med. Ctr., Denver, 1969-70; clin. assoc. pediat. metabolism br. Nat. Inst. Arthritis, Metabolism, and Digestive Diseases, NIH, Bethesda, Md., 1970-72; pulmonary fellow Montreal (Que., Can.) Children's Hosp., 1972-74; asst. prof. pediats. Ariz. Health Scis. Ctr., Tucson, 1974-77, cystic fibrosis ctr. dir., 1974-85, assoc. chief pulmonary function labs., 1974-85, dir. pulmonary sect., 1974-85, asst. dir. divsn. respiratory scis., 1976-92, assoc. prof. pediats., 1977-81, assoc. head dept. pediats., 1979-84, prof. pediats., 1981-93, head dept. pediats., 1985-93, dir. Steele Meml. Children's Rsch. Ctr., 1986-93; prof. pediats. U. Colo. Health Scis. Ctr., Denver, 1993—; pres., CEO Nat. Jewish Ctr. for Immunology and Respiratory Medicine, Denver, 1993—; Frank Stevenson vis. prof. U. Con., 1977, 82; Robert Chinnock Meml. lectr. Loma Linda U., Calif., 1983; Jour. Pediats. vis. prof. U. Chgo., 1984; Brennenman lectr. L.A. Pediat. Soc., 1988, 94; Danis Meml. lectr. St. Louis U., 1989; Talamo Meml. lectr. Johns Hopkins U., Balt., 1989; Anna Zager vis. lectr. in pediats. Technion U., Haifa, Israel, 1990; Sir Clavering Fison vis. prof. Inst. Child Health, U. London, 1992; Benjamin Meaker vis. prof. U. Bristol, Eng., 1992; Ben Kagan vis. lectr. Cedars-Sinai Hosp., L.A., 1993. Mem. editl. bd. Chest, 1983-88, Am. Rev. Respiratory Diseases, 1983-89; contbr. articles to profl. jours. Trustee Congregation Anshei Israel, 1978-80; bd. dirs. Jerwish Cmty. Ctr., 1982-90, sec., 1984-86, v.p., 1987-89; mem. allocations com. Jewish Fedn. So. Ariz., 1985, 88; bd. dirs. Colo. Biomed. Venture Ctr., 1994—; active Martin Luther King Jr. Minority Scholarship Program, 1994—, Colo. Concern, 1995—. Cystic Fibrosis Found. Clin. fellow, 1972-74, Sr. Internat. fellow Fogarty Internat. Ctr., 1980-81; Young Investigator Pulmonary Rsch. grantee Nat. Heart and Lung Inst., 1974-76, and numerous other med. grants; Pfizer Labs. Med. scholar, 1966; recipient Lang Med. Book award, 1966. Mem. Am. Acad. Pediats. (mem. exec. com. sect. on diseases of chest 1978-80, ad hoc com. for pediat. pulmonary bds., sect. on diseases of chest 1978-85), Am. Pediat. Soc., Am. Thoracic Soc. (mem. com. to advise pres. 1975-76, sec. sci. assembly for pediats. 1975-77, mem. respiratory care com. 1976-78, mem. nominating com. 1977, 84-85, chmn. prograom com. 1979-81, mem. ann. meeting com. 1979-81, mem. rsch. rev. com. 1981-82, chmn. publs. policy com. 1988-89, 90-92, exec. com. 1989-90, sec.-treas. 1989-90, and many other coms.), Am. Coll. Chest Physicians (mem. steering group for com. on cardiopulmonary diseases in children 1977-79), Ariz. Pediat. Soc., Ariz. Lung Assn., Pima County Pediat. Soc., Soc. Pediat. Rsch. (founder Lung Club 1985), Western Soc. Pediat. Rsch. (mem. nominating com. 1979-80, elected to coun. 1994—), Harvard Club of So. Ariz. (schs. com. 1982-93, sec.-treas. 1989-93), Alpha Omega Alpha. Office: Nat Jewish Ctr for Immunology and Respiratory Medicine 1400 N Jackson St Denver CO 80206

TAUZIN, W. J. BILLY, II (WILBERT J. TAUZIN), congressman; b. Chackbay, LA, June 14, 1943; s. Wilbert Joseph and Enola (Martinez) T.; m. Cecile Bergeron, May 29, 1993; children: Kristie René, Wilbert J. III, John Ashton, Thomas Nicholas, Michael James. BA, Nicholls State U., 1964; JD, La. State U., 1967. Bar: La. 1967. Practice Houma and Thibodaux, La., 1967-80; mem. firm Marcel Fanguy & Tauzin, 1967-72, Tauzin-Sonnier, 1972-80; mem. La. Ho. of Reps., 1971-80, house floor leader, 1974-79, chmn. Teche Clearinghouse Rev. Bd., 1975-78, chmn. house natural resources com., 1975-80; mem. 96th-104th Congresses from 3d La. Dist., 1980—; mem. energy, commerce, merchant marine, fisheries coms., subcoms. energy, power, telecom., coast guard, navigation, wildlife conservation, environment. Mem. Thibodaux Playhouse, 1967-75; mem. Criminal Justice Inst. Recipient Thibodaux Outstanding Young Man award, 1971. Mem. ABA, La. State Bar Assn., Lafourche Parish Bar Assn. (past pres.), Chackbay-Choupic Jr. C. of C. (past pres.), Nicholls Alumni Council (v.p.). Lodges: Kiwanis; K.C. Home: Rienzi B-5 PO Box 1407 Thibodaux LA 70302-1407 Office: 2183 Rayburn US Ho Reps Washington DC 20515-1803*

TAVALLALI, JALAL CHAICAR, lawyer; b. Madrid, Apr. 13, 1964; came to U.S., 1975; s. Djamchid and Nini (Chaicar) T. BA in Internat. Rels., Georgetown U., 1985, JD, 1988. Bar: N.Y. 1990, D.C. 1990, U.S. Supreme Ct. 1995. Rsch. asst. Wilkes, Artis, Hedrick & Lane, Washington, summer 1984; assoc. Goodwin & Soble, Washington, summer 1987, Wald, Harkrader & Ross, Washington, summer 1987, Milbank, Tweed, Hadley & McCloy, N.Y.C., 1988-90; mng. dir. Persico, Inc., Washington, 1986—; mng. atty. Chaikar Tavallali & Ptnrs., Washington and Baku, Azerbaijan, 1990—, Ashgabat, Turkmenistan and Tehran, Iran, 1990—; sr. assoc. New Europe Assocs., Washington and Europe, 1991-93; rschr. UN Devel. Program, N.Y.C., summer 1984. Rschr. U.S. Senator John Glenn for U.S. Pres. campaign, Washington, 1983. Mem. ABA, Am. Soc. Internat. Law, D.C. Bar Assn., Epicurean Soc. (founder 1979—), Old Stoic Soc., Phi Alpha Delta. Avocations: international affairs, travel, antiques, the arts, poetry. Office: Chaikar Tavallali & Ptnrs 4729 Yuma St NW Washington DC 20016-2047

TAVARES, TONY, professional hockey team executive; b. Fall River, Mass., Oct. 17, 1949; m. Elizabeth Tavares; children: Sheila, Kristen, Mark. BS in Acctg., Roger Williams Coll. Comptroller, acting dir. Providence Civic Ctr.; with Centrum, Worcester, Mass., New Haven Vets. Meml. Coliseum, Nassau Vets. Meml. Coliseum, Uniondale, N.Y.; with Spectacor Mgmt. Group, pres., CEO; cons. Walt Disney Co.; pres. Disney Sports Enterprises, Inc., Anaheim, Calif., 1993—; pres., alt. gov. Mighty ducks of Anaheim, 1993—. Mem. Internat. Assn. Auditorium Mgrs. Office: Mighty Ducks of Anaheim PO Box 61077 2695 E Katella Ave Anaheim CA 92803-6177

TAVEGGIA, THOMAS CHARLES, management educator, management consultant; b. Oak Lawn, Ill., June 15, 1943; s. Thomas Angelo and Eunice Louise (Harriss) T.; m. Brigitte I. Adams, Jan. 23, 1965; children: Michaela, Francesca. BS, Ill. Inst. Tech., 1965; MA, U. Oreg., 1968, PhD, 1971. Prof., U. Oreg., Eugene, 1970, U. B.C. (Can.), Vancouver, 1970-73, U. Calif.-Irvine, 1973-74, Ill. Inst. Tech., Chgo., 1974-77; mgmt. cons. Towers, Perrin, Forster & Crosby, Chgo., 1977-80; ptnr. Manplan Cons., Chgo., 1980-81; ptnr. Coopers & Lybrand, San Francisco, 1981-86; ptnr. Touche Ross, San Francisco, 1986-88; prof. Calif. Sch. Profl. Psychology, Berkeley, 1988—. NDEA Title IV fellow, 1967-71; U. B.C. faculty rsch. grantee, 1970, 71, 73. Faculty Rsch. grantee Calif. Sch. Profl. Psychology, 1993-96. Mem. Acad. Mgmt. Soc., Am. Sociol. Assn., Nat. Bur. Profl. Mgmt. Cons., Human Resource Mgmt. Soc., Inst. Mgmt. Cons. Presbyterian. Author: (with R. Dubin and R. Arends) From Family and School To Work, 1967; (with Dubin) The Teaching-Learning Paradox: A Comparative Analysis of College Teaching Methods, 1968; (with Dubin and R.A. Hedley) The Medium May Be Related to the Message: College Instruction by TV, 1969; contbr. numerous articles to books and profl. jours. Home: 2188 Lariat Ln Walnut Creek CA 94596-6515 Office: Calif Sch Profl Psychology 1005 Atlantic Ave Alameda CA 94501-1148

TAVEL, MARK KIVEY, money management company executive, economist; b. Cambridge, Mass., May 9, 1945; s. Bernard Benjamin and Elizabeth (Rogers) T.; m. Susana Sara Doño, Dec. 14, 1980; children: Sarah Emily, Rachel Florence, Amanda Victoria, Nathaniel Benjamin, Roberto Aaron Doño. BA cum laude, Harvard U., 1967; MBA, Columbia U., 1968. Pres. Rothschild Asset Mgmt., Inc., N.Y.C.; also bd. dirs. Rothschild N.Am., N.Y.C.; bd. dirs. N. M. Rothschild Internat. Asset Mgmt., London. Trustee The Day Sch. of the Ch. of the Heavenly Rest, N.Y.C. Mem. Harvard Club (N.Y.C.). Home: 110 Riverside Dr New York NY 10024-3715 Office: Rothschild Inc 1251 Avenue Of The Americas New York NY 10020-1104

TAVEL, MORTON ALLEN, physics educator, researcher; b. Bklyn., June 14, 1939; s. Irving and Sylvia (Cutler) T.; m. Judith Carol Fibkins, June 29, 1969; 1 child, Phillip Alden. B.S., CCNY, 1960; M.S., Stevens Inst., 1962; Ph.D., Yeshiva U., 1964. Asst. scientist Brookhaven Nat. Lab., Upton, N.Y., 1964-67; asst. prof. Vassar Coll., Poughkeepsie, N.Y., 1967-69, assoc. prof., 1970-75, prof. physics, 1975—; vis. prof. Va. Poly., Blacksburg, Va., 1971-72, SUNY-Stony Brook, 1976-77; mem. summer faculty IBM, Poughkeepsie, N.Y., 1978-80, engring. cons., 1980—. Author: Introduction to Electricity and Magnetism I and II, 1971, Information Theory, 1989. NSF fellow, 1962-64. Mem. IEEE (sr.), Am. Phys. Soc., Soc. Wine Educators, Sigma Xi. Avocation: oenology. Home and Office: Vassar Coll PO Box 471 Poughkeepsie NY 12602-0471

TAVENAS, FRANÇOIS, civil engineer, educator; b. Bourg de Péage, Drôme, France, Sept. 12, 1942; arrived in Can., 1966; s. Adrien and Marie Thérèse (Bazin) T.; m. Gundula Schlichting, Apr. 27, 1963; children: Anne Catherine, Philippe, Sophie. BCE, Inst. Nat. des Scis. Appliquées, Lyon, France, 1963; PhD, U. Grenoble, France, 1965. Registered profl. engr., Que. Engr. Piette & Assocs., Que., Can., 1966-70; asst. prof. civil engring. Laval U., Que., 1970-73, assoc. prof., 1973-79, prof., 1979-85, dean, 1985-89; vice prin. planning and resources McGill U., Montreal, Que., 1989—; cons. Golder & Assocs., Toronto, Ont. Can., 1973-75, Terratech, Montreal, 1975-85, Soc. d'Energie de la Baie James, Montreal, 1980-84; mem. coun. Natural Scis. and Engring. Rsch. Coun. Can., 1989—. Author: (with others) Embankments On Soft Soils, 1985; contbr. articles to profl. jours. Mem. ASCE, Can. Geotech. Soc. (v.p. 1982-85, pres.-elect 1990, pres. 1991-92), Internat. Soc. Soil Mechanics and Found. Engring. Avocations: tennis, travel. Office: McGill U, 845 Sherbrooke St W # 536, Montreal, PQ Canada H3A 2T5

TAVERAS, JUAN MANUEL, physician, educator; b. Dominican Republic, Sept. 27, 1919; came to U.S., 1944, naturalized, 1950; s. Marcos M. and Ana L. (Rodriguez) T.; m. Bernice Helen McGonigle, June 12, 1947 (dec. 1990); children: Angela Taveras Summers, Louisa Helen Taveras Koranda, Jeffrey Lawrence; m. Mariana Margarita Bucher, Mar. 18, 1991. BS, Normal Sch. Santiago, Dominican Republic, 1937; MD, U. Santo Domingo, Dominican Republic, 1943, U. Pa., 1949; MS honoris causa, Harvard Med. Sch., 1971; Dr. honoris causa, Univ. Nacional Pedro Henriquez Ureña, Dominican Republic, 1987; Doctor Honoris Causa, U. Catolica Madre Y Maestra, Santiago, Dominican Republic, 1992. Diplomate: Am. Bd. Radiology. Instr. anatomy U. Santo Domingo, 1943-44; fellow radiology Grad. Hosp. U. Pa., 1945-48; rotating intern Misericordia Hosp., Phila., 1949-50; asst. radiologist Presbyn. Hosp., N.Y.C., 1950-52; asst. attending radiologist Presbyn. Hosp., 1953-56, assoc. attending radiologist, 1956-60, attending radiologist, 1960-65; dir. radiology Neurol. Inst., N.Y.C., 1952-65; cons. USPHS Hosp., S.I., N.Y., 1952-65, Morristown (N.J.) Meml. Hosp., 1957-65, St. Barnabas Hosp., N.Y.C., 1959-65, VA Hosp., Bronx, N.Y., 1960-65; asst. instr. radiology U. Pa. Sch. Medicine, 1947-48; faculty Columbia Coll. Phys. and Surg., 1950-65, prof. radiology, 1959-65; prof. radiology, chmn. dept., dir. Mallinckrodt Inst. Radiology, Washington U. Sch. Medicine, St. Louis, 1965-71; radiologist-in-chief Barnes and Allied Hosps., St. Louis, 1965-71; cons. neuroradiology service Unit 1 St. Louis City Hosp., 1966-71; cons. radiology Jewish Hosp., St. Louis, 1966-71; prof. radiology Harvard Med. Sch., 1971-89, prof. radiology emeritus, 1989—; radiologist-in-chief Mass. Gen. Hosp., Boston, 1971-88; pres. VII Symposium Neuroradiologieum, 1964. Author: Neuroradiology, 1996; (with Ross Golden) Roentgenology of the Abdomen, 1961, (with Ernest H. Wood) Diagnostic Neuroradiology, 1964, 2d edit., 1976, (with Norman Leeds) Dynamic Factors in Diagnosis of Supratentorial Brain Tumors by Cerebral Angiography, 1969, (with F. Morello) Normal Neuroradiology, 1979, (with James Provenzale) Clinical Cases in Neuroradiology, 1994, (with Laszlo Szlavy) Noncoronary Angioplasty, 1994; editor: (with others) Recent Advances in the Study of Cerebral Circulation, 1970, Cysticercosis of the Central Nervous System, 1983, Radiology: Diagnosis, Imaging, Intervention, 1986; chief editor: Am. Jour. Neuroradiology, 1980-89; contbr. numerous articles to profl. jours. Bd. dirs. Edward Mallinckrodt, Jr. Found., 1980—. Decorated knight Order of Duarte Sanchez y Mella (Dominican Republic) 1972; Juan M. Taveras professorship established in his honor Harvard Med. Sch., 1988. Fellow Am. Coll. Radiology (gold medal 1985); mem. AMA, Am. Neurol. Assn., Am. Roentgen Ray Soc. (gold medal 1988), Radiol. Soc. N.Am. (gold medal 1981), Mass. Med. Soc., Inter-Am. Coll. Radiology, World Fedn. Neurology, Am. Soc. Neuroradiology (pres. 1962-64, gold medal, 1995), N.Y. Acad. Scis., Am. Assn. Neurol. Surgeons (assoc.), Assn. U. Radiologists (gold medal 1985), Mass. Radiol. Soc., New Eng. Roentgen Ray Soc.; pres. Iberian Latin Am. Soc. of Neurol. 1988-91, pres. IV Congress of Iberian Latin Am. Soc. of Neurol. 1992, hon. mem. Phila. Roentgen Ray Soc., Radiol. Soc. Venezuela, Rocky Mountain Radiol. Soc., Tex. Radiol. Soc., Radiol. Assn. Ctrl. Am. and Panama, Hungarian Radiologic Soc., European Soc. Neuroradiology (hon.), Alpha Omega Alpha. Republican. Home: 122 Glen Rd Wellesley MA 02181-1551 Office: Mass Gen Hosp Boston MA 02114

TAVLIN, MICHAEL JOHN, telecommunications company executive; b. Lincoln, Nebr., Dec. 16, 1946. BEd, Oklahoma City U., 1970; JD, U. Nebr., 1973; LLM in Taxation, Washington U., St. Louis, 1977. Bar: Nebr. 1973, Mo. 1974. Ptnr. Nelson & Harding, Lincoln, 1973-77; sr. tax. mgr. Touche Ross & Co., Lincoln and Tulsa, 1979-84, Coopers & Lybrand, Tulsa, 1984-86; v.p., treas., sec. Lincoln Telecomms. Co. and subs., 1986—. Office: Lincoln Telecommunications Co 1440 M St Lincoln NE 68508-2513

TAVON, MARY E., public relations, marketing and communications executive; b. Montreal, Apr. 4, 1958. Student, Marianopolis Coll. Lit. and Langs., 1977; BA in English, Theatre and Film, McGill U., 1980. Mktg. analyst Korea Trade Promotion Assn., 1980-82; advt., pub. rels. asst. Ann Taylor, 1983-84; acct. exec. Michael Klepper Assocs., N.Y.C., 1984-86, acct. supr., 1986-88, v.p., 1988-89, pres., exec. prodr., 1989. Recipient cert. merit Chgo. Internat. Film Festival, 1990. Office: Michael Klepper Assoc Inc 805 3rd Ave New York NY 10022-7513

TAVOULARIS, DEAN, motion picture production designer; b. Lowell, Mass., May 18, 1932; s. Nicholas John and Pota (Georges) T.; m. Barbara

Joan Wiess; children: Alison, Gina; m. Aurore Clement, Sept. 7, 1980. Student, Otis Art Inst., L.A., El Camino City Coll., L.A., L.A. City Coll. Prodn. designer various films, 1968—. Prodn. designs include Bonnie and Clyde, 1968, The Conversation, 1974, The Godfather, 1972, Godfather II, 1974, Godfather III, 1990, The Brink's Job, 1978, Apocalypse Now, 1979, Zabriskie Point, 1970, Little Big Man, 1970, One From the Heart, 1981, Hammett, 1982, Peggy Sue Got Married, 1986, Final Analysis, 1992, Rising Sun, 1993, I Love Trouble, 1994, others. Recipient Acad. award Acad. Motion Picture Arts and Scis., 1974, nominations, 1978, 79, 88, 90; Brit. Acad. award Brit. Acad. Film and TV Arts, 1988. Office: care Art Directors Guild 11365 Ventura Blvd Ste 315 Studio City CA 91604-3148*

TAW, DUDLEY JOSEPH, sales executive; b. Cleve., Mar. 11, 1916; s. William C. and Ella (Gedeon) T.; m. Louise E. Forshey, Sept. 10, 1938; children: Judith (Mrs. William W. Beck, Jr.), Dudley Joseph. Student, Hiram Coll., 1938. With McKesson & Robbins, Inc. (pharm. co.), after 1937; sales mgr. McKesson & Robbins, Inc. (pharm. co.), Boston, 1947; v.p. sales McKesson & Robbins, Inc. (pharm. co.), N.Y.C., 1953-60; v.p. Revlon, Inc., N.Y.C., 1960-64; v.p. mktg. East Ohio Gas Co., Cleve., 1964-74, pres., 1975-81, chmn., 1981-82; chmn. Middtaw, Ltd., Inc., 1982; bd. dirs. No. New England Gas Corp., First Union Mgmt. Co., Biskind Devel. Co., Vt. Gas Systems Inc. Mem. Better Bus. Bur., Cleve., chmn., 1973; trustee Lakewood Hosp.; treas. Salvation Army, Cleve. With USNR, 1946-47. Named Sales Exec. of Year Sales and Mktg. Execs. Cleve., 1966, Man of Year, 1977. Mem. Sales and Mktg. Execs. Cleve. (pres. 1969-70), Westwood Country Club, Union Club, Pepper Pike Club, Rotary (pres. Cleve. 1972-73). Methodist. Home (summer): 20975 Avalon Dr Cleveland OH 44116-1303 Home (winter): 6050 Bahia Del Mar Cir Bldg 3 Saint Petersburg FL 33715-3304 Office: 806 Statler Office Tower Cleveland OH 44115

TAWADROS, AZMI MILAD, oral surgeon; b. Cairo, Egypt, Mar. 14, 1957; came to U.S., 1962; s. Milad A. and Sabah T.; m. Deborah Ann Hulderman, Apr. 16, 1988; children: Brianna, Alyssa. BS in Pharmacy, Purdue U., 1979; DDS, Indiana U., 1983; MD, Hahnemann U., 1990. Diplomate Am. Bd. Oral and Maxillofacial Surgery. Pharmacist Indpls., 1979-84; resident Emory U., Atlanta, 1984-85, Henry Ford Hosp., Detroit, 1985-88; pharmacist Phila., 1988-90; resident Ga. Baptist Med. Ctr., Atlanta, 1990-91; pvt. practice Acworth, Ga., 1991—. Mem. ADA, AMA, Northwest Dist. Dental Soc., Ga. Dental Assn. Avocations: outdoor sports, family, reading. Home: 726 Creek Trl Kennesaw GA 30144-2132 Office: 5471 Bells Ferry Rd Ste 104 Acworth GA 30102-7520

TAYAR, MEMDUH ALI, architect; b. Istanbul, Turkey, Nov. 16, 1959; came to U.S., 1983; s. Omer Tayyar and Ilhan (Cekmegil) T. Diploma in engring., U. Stuttgart, Germany, 1983; MS in Architecture Studies, MIT, 1986. Registered architect, N.Y. Mem. project team Lev Zetlin Assocs., N.Y.C., 1986-88; project architect FTL Assocs., N.Y.C., 1988-91; prin. Parallel Design Partnership Ltd., N.Y.C., 1991—; lectr. MIT, Cambridge, 1985, Ill. Inst. Tech., Chgo., 1992, CUNY, 1993; guest critic Columbia U., N.Y.C., N.J. Inst. Tech., Newark, U. Pa., N.J. Exhibited in group shows at Jacob Javits Ctr., N.Y.C., 1993, 94, Gallery Neotu, Paris, 1994, Mus. Modern Art, N.Y., 1995; featured in N.Y. Times, 1990, Elle Decor, 1994, Internat. Design Yearbook, 1994, Elle Deco Japan, 1995, etc. Achievements include design patent for aluminum parallel ruler, design patent for aluminum shelving system. Office: Parallel Design Partnership Ltd 430 W 14th St Rm 408 New York NY 10014-1020

TAYLER, EDWARD WILLIAM, English language educator; b. Berlin, Germany, Mar. 13, 1931; came to U.S.,; s. William Robert and Violetta Jesse (Klavin-Zeiden) T.; m. Irene B. Smith, June 3, 1961; m. 2d Christina Lee Moustakis, Mar. 3, 1978; children: William E., David S., Letta M., Edward W., Jesse W. B.A., Amherst Coll., 1954; Ph.D., Stanford U., 1960. Prof. English Columbia U., N.Y.C., 1960—. Author: Nature and Art in the Renaissance, 1964, Milton's Poetry, 1979, Donne's Idea of a Woman, 1991; editor: (anthology) Literary Criticism of 17th Century England, 1967. Office: Columbia Univ 116th St and Broadway New York NY 10027

TAYLER, IRENE, English literature educator; b. Abilene, Tex., July 13, 1934; d. B. Brown and Madeline (Bowron); m. Edward W. Tayler, June 3, 1961 (div. 1971); children: Edward Jr., Jesse; m. Saul Touster, Jan. 14, 1978. BA in Philosophy, Stanford U., 1956, MA in Am. Lit., 1961, PhD in English Lit., 1968. Tchr. Breadloaf Sch. of Eng., Middlebury, Vt., 1970, 71, 75, 76; teaching asst. Stanford U., Calif., 1958-60; lectr. Columbia U., N.Y., 1961-71; asst. prof. CUNY, 1971-73, assoc. prof., 1973-76; assoc. prof. MIT, Cambridge, 1976-82, prof., 1982—, sec. of the faculty, 1993-95; chair gov. com. The English Inst., 1981. Author: (book) Blake's Illustrations to the Poems of Gray, 1971, Holy Ghosts: The Male Muses of Emily and Charlotte Bronte, 1990; contbr. numerous articles to profl. jours. Faculty Rsch. Found. grantee CUNY, 1972-73, Study grantee ACLS, 1968-69; Mac Vicar Faculty fellow MIT, 1993—, Sr. Scholar fellow NEH, 1980, Wilson fellow Stanford U., 1961-62, Internat. Inst. fellow U. Munich, 1957-58. Office: M I T 14 N 412 Cambridge MA 02139

TAYLOR, ALFRED HENDRICKS, JR., former foundation executive; b. Evanston, Ill., May 16, 1930; s. Alfred Hendricks and Joy (Scheidenhelm) T.; m. Elizabeth Ann Turner, Sept. 29, 1953; children: John, Elizabeth, Jeffrey, Ann. BA, Williams Coll., 1952; LLD (hon.), Albion Coll., 1986, Monmouth Coll., 1991, Western New England Coll., 1994; LHD (hon.), Ill. Coll., 1988. Group v.p. Harris Bank, Chgo., 1955-69; asst. dir. OEO, Washington, 1970-72; chmn. Kresge Found., Troy, Mich., 1972-94, trustee, 1972—; bd. dirs. Comerica Bank, Detroit. Chmn., trustee Am. Farmland Trust, 1989—; trustee emeritus Nat. Trust for Hist. Preservation, 1990—; bd. dirs. The Conservation Fund, Washington, 1990—. Lt. USNR, 1952-55. Recipient g. Mennen Williams humanitarian award, 1988, Michiganian of Yr. award, 1991, award for exemplary leadership in philanthropy Nat. Soc. Fund Raising Execs., 1993. Mem. Williams Coll. Alumni Assn. (pres. Chgo. chpt. 1969-70, chmn. 25th Reunion Class '52, class agt. 1992—). Home: 1165 Main St Williamstown MA 01267-2621 office: The Kresge Foundation PO Box 3151 3215 W Big Beaver Road Troy MI 48007

TAYLOR, ALFRED RALEIGH, geologist; b. Eure, Gates County, N.C., July 7, 1928; s. Raleigh Jackson and Annie B. Taylor; m. Eugenia Dare Eure, Nov. 9, 1946; children: Patricia Dare, Teri Ann. BS in Geology, U. N.C., 1955. Cert. geologist Va. Geologist U.S. Geol. Survey, Worldwide, 1955-81, Minerals Mgmt. Svc., Reston, 1981-82, Bur. Land Mgmt., Reston and Washington, 1982-83; geol. cons. Somerset, Ky., 1984-87; sr. geologist Va. Divsn. of Mineral Resources, Cedar Bluff, Va., 1988-89; geol. cons. Cedar Bluff, 1989; supr. geologist Va. Divsn. Min. Resources, Dept. Mines, Minerals & Energy, Abingdon, Va., 1990—; adj. faculty in geology and geography Somerset C.C. of U. Ky., Somerset, 1968-77, 86-88. Contbr. over 50 articles and chpts. to books and profl. jours. S/sgt. USMC, PTO, ATO; lt. USNR. Recipient Antarctic Svc. medal, commendation U.S. Dept. Interior, 1961, citations U.S. Geol. Survey; Alfred Taylor Mountain in Antarctica named for him; named Ky. Col. Mem. Am. Assn. Petroleum Geologists, Am. Inst. Profl. Geologists (cert. prof. geologist), Geol. Soc. Washington, Geol. Soc. Ky., Fleet Res. Assn., VFW (life), Am. Legion, Naval Res. Assn., Sigma Gamma Epsilon. Office: Va Divsn Mineral Resources PO Box 144 Abingdon VA 24212-0144

TAYLOR, ALLAN BERT, lawyer; b. Cin., June 28, 1948; s. H. Ralph and Henrietta Irene (Medalia) T.; m. Sally Ann Silverstein, June 6, 1971; children: Rachel Elizabeth, Karen Ruth. AB, Harvard U., 1970, M in Pub. Policy, 1975, JD, 1975. Bar: Conn. 1975, U.S. Ct. Appeals (D.C. cir.) 1977, U.S. Dist. Ct. Conn. 1978, U.S. Dist. Ct. (so. dist.) N.Y. 1979, U.S. Ct. Appeals (2d cir.) 1979, U.S. Supreme Ct. 1979, U.S. Ct. Appeals (1st and 10th cirs.) 1991. Law clk. to J. Skelly Wright D.C. Cir., Washington, 1975-76; law clk. to Thurgood Marshall U.S. Supreme Ct., Washington, 1976-77; assoc. Day, Berry & Howard, Hartford, Conn., 1977-83, ptnr., 1983—; overseer Bushnell Meml. Hall Corp., Hartford, 1992—. Elected mem. Hartford City Coun., 1981-87, Hartford Bd. Edn., 1989-93, v.p., 1991-93, pres., 1992-93; mem. Conn. State Bd. Edn., 1994—; bd. dirs. Conn. Assn. Bds. Edn., Hartford, 1989-93, Hartford Infant Action Project, 1990—. Mem. ABA, Conn. Bar Assn., Hartford County Bar Assn., Phi Beta Kappa. Democrat. Jewish. Avocations: astronomy, reading. Home: 238 Whitney St Hartford CT 06105-2270 Office: Day Berry & Howard City Place Hartford CT 06103

TAYLOR, ALLAN RICHARD, retired banker; b. Prince Albert, Sask., Can., Sept. 14, 1932; s. Norman and Anna Lydia (Norbeck) T.; m. Shirley Irene Ruston, Oct. 5, 1957; children: Rodney Allan, Leslie Ann. LLD (hon.), U. Regina, Sask., 1987, Concordia U., Montreal, Can., 1988; DBA (hon.), Laval U., Quebec City, Can., 1990; LLD (hon.), Queen's U., Kingston, Ont., 1991; Doctorate of Univ. (hon.), U. Ottawa, 1992. With Royal Bank of Can., Toronto, Ont., Can., 1949-95; pres., COO, dir. Royal Bank of Can., Toronto, 1983-86, chmn., CEO, dir., 1986-94, chmn., 1994-95, ret., 1995; d. dirs. Royal Bank of Can., TransCan. Pipelines Ltd., Toronto, Can.-Pacific Ltd., GM Can. Ltd., Oshawa, Ont.; mem. adv. coun. Can. Exec. Svc. Overseas; former chmn. Can. Bankers Assn.; past pres. Internat. Monetary Conf. Mem. adv. com. Sch. Bus. Adminstrn., U. We. Ont., London; hon. mem. Corp.-Higher Edn. Forum; chmn. Coun. Patrons, Outward Bound of Can.; past chmn., bd. dirs. Jr. Achievement Can.; gov. Olympic Trust, Can.; former chmn. corp. program IMAGINE; mem. adv.bd. Can. Found. AIDS Rsch. Decorated officer Order of Can. Address: 200 Bay St 18th Fl North Tower, Toronto, ON Canada M5J 2J5

TAYLOR, ALLAN ROSS, linguist, educator; b. Palisade, Colo., Dec. 24, 1931; s. Athel Ross and Marjorie Verle (Walters) T.; m. Mary Callas, Sept. 8, 1958; children: Artemisia, Anthony, Peter, Anna, Yoana. AB, U. Colo., Boulder, 1953; PhD (Woodrow Wilson fellow, Fulbright fellow, NDEA fellow), U. Calif., Berkeley, 1969. Teaching asst., lectr. U. Calif., Berkeley, 1958-63; instr. U. Colo., 1964-65, asst. prof., 1965-70, assoc. prof., 1970-77, prof., 1977-93, prof. emeritus, 1993—, also past chmn. dept. linguistics, dept. French and Italian; cons. bilingual edn. for Native Ams. Active Dem. Party and in environ. issues. With U.S. Army, 1954-57. NEH grantee, 1972-76, 80-82, 87-90, 89-93. Mem. Linguistic Soc. Am., Am. Anthrop. Assn. Home: 787 17th St Boulder CO 80302-7601 Office: U Colo Dept Linguistics PO Box 295 Boulder CO 80309-0295 *Reading in physical anthropology and genetics, and many years of an advocacy role in environmental issues, have convinced me that man's highest calling is custodial: to protect, preserve, and pass on inviolate the world and all of its inhabitants, even when it may appear to be against our own short-term interest to do this. For the grand plan, if there is any, is to allow diversity to make the choices which prove ultimately to be the only viable ones.*

TAYLOR, ANDREW C., rental leasing company executive; b. 1947. Degree, Denver U., 1970. With Enterprise Rent-A-Car, St. Louis, 1972—, now CEO. Office: Enterprise Rent-A-Car 600 Corporate Park Dr Saint Louis MO 63130*

TAYLOR, ANN LOUISE, marketing executive; b. Fairmont, Minn., Aug. 8, 1937; d. Eugene and Celia Ethel (Fulton) Lundahl; m. James Harold Taylor, May 23, 1959; children: Kimberly Taylor Locey, Jayme K. BA in Edn., U. Minn., 1959; postgrad., Am. Inst. Banking, 1985-87. Tchr. Nokomis Jr. High Sch., Mpls., 1959-61, Helen Keller Mid. Sch., Easton, Conn., 1973-75; photojournalist Suburban & Wayne Times, Berwyn, Pa., 1975-80; cons. pub. relations Fla. Internat. Bank, Miami, Fla., 1981-84; v.p. Fla. Internat. Bank, Miami, 1984-94; employee rels. mgr. Am. Bankers Ins. Group, Miami, 1994-96; freelance writer, pub. rels. cons., 1996—. Contbr. articles to profl. jours. Mem. women's adv. coun. Bapt. Hosp. of Miami, 1991—. Mem. Women in Comms. (pres. Greater Miami chpt. 1987-88, v.p. so. region 1989-92, v.p. fin. 1993-94, nat. pres. elect 1994-95, nat. pres. 1995-96), Greater South Dade-South Miami C. of C. (bd. dirs. 1987-94, pres.-elect 1989—, chmn. 1991-92), Founders of South Dade (pres. 1987-88). Republican. Lutheran. Avocations: tennis, boating, music, dancing.

TAYLOR, ANNA DIGGS, federal judge; b. Washington, Dec. 9, 1932; d. Virginius Douglass and Hazel (Bramlette) Johnston; m. S. Martin Taylor, May 22, 1976; children: Douglass Johnston Diggs, Carla Cecile Diggs. BA, Barnard Coll., 1954; LLB, Yale U., 1957. Bar: D.C. 1957, Mich. 1961. Atty. Office Solicitor, Dept. Labor, W, 1957-60; asst. prosecutor Wayne County, Mich., 1961-62; asst. U.S. atty. Eastern Dist. of Mich., 1966; ptnr. Zwerdling, Maurer, Diggs & Papp, Detroit, 1970-75; asst. corp. counsel City of Detroit, 1975-79; U.S. dist. judge Eastern Dist. Mich. Detroit, 1979—. Hon. chair, United Way Cmty. Found., S.E. Mich. Found. Soc., Detroit Inst. Arts, Greater Detroit Health Coun., Eastern Region Henry Ford Health Sys.; co-chair, vol. Leadership Coun. for S.E. Mich. Mem. Fed. Bar Assn., State Bar Mich., Wolverine Bar Assn. (v.p.), Yale Law Assn. Episcopalian. Office: US Dist Ct 740 US Courthouse 231 W Lafayette Blvd Detroit MI 48226-2719

TAYLOR, ARTHUR ROBERT, college president, business executive; b. Elizabeth, N.J., July 6, 1935; s. Arthur Earl and Marion Hilda (Scott) T.; m. Kathryn Pelgrift; 3 daus. by previous marriage. B.A. magna cum laude, Brown U., 1957, M.A. in Am. Econ. History, 1961; H.H.D. (hon.), Bucknell U., 1975, Allentown Coll. of St. Francis de Sales; L.H.D. (hon.), Rensselaer Poly. Inst., 1975, Simmons Coll., 1975; LL.D. (hon.), Mt. Scenario Coll., 1975. Asst. dir. admissions Brown U., Providence, 1957-61; with First Boston Corp., N.Y.C., 1961-70, asst. v.p., 1964-66, v.p., 1966-70, also dir.; v.p. fin. Internat. Paper Co., N.Y.C., 1970-71, exec. v.p., dir., 1971-72; pres. CBS Inc., N.Y.C., 1972-76, also dir.; pres. Muhlenberg Coll., Allentown, Pa., 1992—; chmn. Arthur Taylor & Co., Inc., 1977—; chmn. The Enterntainment Channel, 1980-83; dean faculty of bus. Fordham U., 1985-92; bd. dirs. Nomura Pacific Basin Fund, Pitney Bowes, La. Land & Exploration Co., Jakarta Growth Fund, Japan OTC Equity Fund; mem. adv. com. Toshiba Internat. Mem. Population Resource Ctr.; trustee Brown U. Mem. Coun. Fgn. Rels., Trilateral Commn., Phi Beta Kappa. Congregationalist. Clubs: Brook, Century (N.Y.C.); Met. (Washington); California (Los Angeles). Office: Muhlenberg Coll Office of Pres 2400 W Chew St Allentown PA 18104-5564

TAYLOR, AUBREY ELMO, physiologist, educator; b. El Paso, Tex., June 4, 1933; s. Virgil T. and Mildred (Maher) T.; m. Mary Jane Davis, Apr. 4, 1953; children: Audrey Jane Hildebrand, Lenda Sue Brown, Mary Ann Smith. BA in Math. and Psychology, Tex. Christian U., 1960; PhD in Physiology, U. Miss., 1964; Postdoctoral fellow biophysics lab. Harvard U. Med. Sch., Boston, 1965-67; from asst. prof. to prof. dept. physiology U. Miss. Coll. Medicine, Jackson, 1967-77; prof., chmn. dept. physiology U. South Ala. Coll. Medicine, Mobile, 1977—; mem. pulmonary score com. Nat. Heart, Lung and Blood Inst., 1976; with Surgery and Manpower Com., 1979-82; chmn. RAP, 1983. Author 5 books; contbr. chpts. to books, 680 articles to profl. jours; assoc. editor Jour. Applied Physiology, 1984-94, Critical Care medicine, 1987—; mem. editorial bd. Circulation Rsch. Am. Jour. Physiology, Microvascular Rsch., Internat. Pathophysiology, Microcirculatory and Lymphatic Rsch., Microcirculation, Chinese Jour. of Physiology Jour. Biomed. Science, Jour. Biomed. Rsch. Served with U.S. Army, 1953-55. NIH grantee, 1967—; recipient Lederle Faculty award, 1967-70, Philip Dow award U. Ga., 1984, NIH Merit award, 1988—, Lucian award McGill U., 1988, John Whitney award U. Ark., 1990, Gelen award Intestinal Shock Soc., 1991; named Disting. Physiologist Am. Coll. Chest Physicians, 1994. Fellow AAAS, Am. Heart Assn. (circulation, coun., cardiopulmonary and critical care coun. 1977—, chmn. 1993—, chmn. So. regional rev. com. 1977-81, EIA Review Com. 1986-95, mem. pulmonary and devel. rev. com. 1987-95, chmn. grant/review com., 1994-95, chmn. med. student rsch. award com. 1992-94, nat. rsch. com. 1990-95, Dickson Richards award 1988, Bronze award miss. AHA, 1976, Outstanding Alabaman AHA program 1993, sci. coun. achievement award, 1995, ACDP Svc. award, 1995), Royal Soc. Medicine, NAS (mem. com. for Internat. Union Physiol. Sci.); mem. Am. Physiol. Soc. (coun. 1984-87, chmn. membership com. 1985-87, pres. 1987-90, Wiggers award 1987, chmn. Perkins fellow com., 1996—), Microcirculatory Soc. (coun. 1977-81, pres. 1981-83, Landis award 1985), Ala. Acad. Scis. (Rsch. award 1988), Internat. Lymphology Soc., N.Am. Soc. Lymphology (pres. 1988-90, recipient First Cecil Drinker award 1988), Internat. Pathophysiology Soc. (v.p. 1991—), N.Y. Acad. Scis., Biophys. Soc., Fedn. Am. Socs. for Exptl. Biology (bd. dirs. 1988-90), Alpha Omega Alpha, Sigma Xi. Democrat. Presbyterian. Current work: Cardio-pulmonary physiology; fluid balance, edema, microcirculation and capillary exchange of solute and water. Subspecialties: Physiology (medicine); Pulmonary medicine. Home: 11 Audubon Pl Mobile AL 36606-1907

TAYLOR, BARBARA ANN, educational consultant; b. St. Louis, Feb. 8, 1933; d. Spencer Truman and Ann Amelia (Whitney) Olin; m. F. Morgan Taylor Jr., Apr. 5, 1954; children: Frederick M. III, Spencer O., James W., John F. AB, Smith Coll., 1954; M of Mgmt., Northwestern U., 1978, PhD, 1984; LHD, U. New Haven, 1995. Mem. faculty Hamden (Conn.) Hall Country Day Sch., 1972-74; cons. Booz, Allen & Hamilton, Inc., Chgo., 1979; program assoc. Northwestern U., Evanston, Ill., 1982; co-founder, exec. dir. Nat. Ctr. Effective Schs. Rsch. & Devel., Okemos, Mich., 1986-89, rsch. assoc., 1987; cons. on effective schs. rsch. and reform Nat. Ctr. Effective Schs. R&D, U. Wis., Madison, 1990-96; pres. Excelsior! Found., Chgo., 1994—; mem. exec. com. Hudson Inst., New Am. Schs. Devel. Corp. Design Team, 1990—; Danforth Disting. lectr. U. Nebr., Omaha, 1993. Co-author: Making School Reform Happen, 1993, Keepers of the Dream, 1994, The Revolution Revisited: Effective Schools and Systemic Reform, 1995; editor: Case Studies in Effective Schools Research, 1990; contbr. articles to profl. jours. Pres. Jr. League of New Haven, 1967-69; pres. NCCJ, New Haven, 1971-73; co-chair Coalition Housing and Human Resources, Hartford-New Haven, 1970-73; co-chair steering com. Day Care Conn., Hartford, 1971-73; bd. dirs. U. New Haven, 1961-71, Smith Coll., Northampton, Mass., 1984-90. Recipient Humanitarian award Mt. Calvary Bapt. Ch., 1988, Outstanding Alumna award John Burroughs Sch., 1994. Mem. ASCD, Nat. Commn. Citizens Edn. (bd. dirs. 1980-86), Nat. Staff Devel. Coun., Phi Delta Kappa. Episcopalian. Office: Nat Ctr Effective Schs Rsch & Devel 222 E Wisconsin Ave Ste 301 Lake Forest IL 60045-1723

TAYLOR, BARBARA CRIST, newspaper editor; b. Columbus, Ohio, Oct. 7, 1935; d. Chester Milton and Ada Leona (Harvey) Crist; m. Stanley Keith Douglass, June 20, 1954 (div. Feb. 1959); 1 child, Scott Keith Douglass Taylor; m. Loren Ray Taylor, July 9, 1960 (dec. Feb. 1970); children: Michael Ray and Leigh Cristine Taylor Veshosky. BSJ, Ohio U., 1957. Wire editor The Athens (Ohio) Messenger, 1957-59; society editor, photographer Gallup (N.Mex.) Daily Independent, 1959-60; reporter, life editor, columnist Albuquerque Tribune, 1960-67; copy editor, asst. news editor The Washington Star, 1967-74; asst. news editor, chief make-up editor, metro copy chief The Washington Post, 1974-84; asst. mng. editor, copy desk chief, late news editor The Washington Times, 1985—; adj. prof. Am. U., Washington, 1967-70; vis. prof. U. Md., College Park, 1974-75, George Washington U., Washington, 1976-78. Mem. parish coun. Christ Ch., Washington, 1967-68, register St. Columba's Episc. Ch., Washington, 1970-72. Recipient numerous awards from Nat. Fedn. Press Women and N.Mex. Press Women. Mem. Am. Quarter Horse Assn, 1974—, Internat. Blugrass Music Assn, 1985—. Avocations: promoting bluegrass music, travel. Home: 6000 Little Falls Rd Arlington VA 22207 Office: The Washington Times 3600 New York Ave NE Washington DC 20002

TAYLOR, BARBARA JO ANNE HARRIS, government official, librarian, educator, civic and political worker; b. Providence, Sept. 9, 1936; d. Ross Cameron and Anita (Coia) Harris; m. Richard Powell Taylor, Dec. 19, 1959; 1 child, Douglas Howard. Student, Tex. Christian U., 1952, Salve Regina Coll., 1952-53; Student, Our Lady of the Lake Coll. and Convent, 1953-54, St. Mary's U., 1954, Incarnate Word Coll., 1954-55, Georgetown U., 1956-59, 62-63; BS cum laude, Georgetown U., 1963. Adminstrv. asst. prof. devel. and welfare NEA, Washington, 1956-59; asst. to dir. Georgetown U., Washington, 1956-59; exec. asst. All Am. Conf. to Combat Communism, Washington, 1960; spl. legis. asst. mil. affairs to chmn. mil. R & D subcom. U.S. Senate Armed Svcs. Com., 1971-72; U.S. nat. commr. UNESCO, 1982—, mem. exec. com. U.S. nat. commn., 1983—, sr. advisor 22d gen. conf., 1983; speaker in field. Contbr. articles to profl. jours. Del. numerous internat. confs.; U.S. commr. Nat. Commn. Librs. and Info. Sci., 1985-96, mem. various coms.; gen. chmn. George Bush for Pres. Md. State Steering Com., 1987-88; co-chmn. Md. del. Rep. Nat. Conv., 1988, 92; dep. chmn. Md. Victory '88, Bush-Quayle Campaign; mem. Nat. Fin. Com. Reagan for Pres., 1980, Reagan-Bush, 1984; state fin. chmn. Md. Rep. Party, 1980; mem. Nat. Rep. Club; mem. exec. bd. Salvation Army Aux., Washington, 1967-75, chmn. membership com., 1969-70, chmn. fund-raising com., 1968-69, mem. exec. com. of exec. bd., 1970-75, treas., mem. fin. com., 1970-71, v.p., 1971-72, historian, 1972-73, editor newsletter, 1968-69, chmn. nominating com., 1974-75, spl. awards. for exceptional vol. svc., 1969, 72; mem. exec. bd. Welcome to Washington Internat., 1969-74, bd. advisers, 1969-74, dir. workshop, 1969-74; exec. bd. Am. Opera Sch. Soc., Washington, 1970—, v.p., 1974—; mem. Episc. Ch. Home for Aged Women's Aux., 1970-75, Episc. Ctr. for Emotionally Disturbed Children Women's Aux., 1970-75; exec. bd. St. David's Episc. Ch. Aux., 1970-72, 73-74; bd. dirs., treas. Spanish-Portuguese Study Group, 1970-72; mem. exec. bd. League Rep. Women D.C., 1964-67, 75-77, treas., 1964-67; mem. nat. coun. Women's Nat. Rep. Club, N.Y.C., 1969—, chmn. Washington-Md.-Va. legis. com., 1970-75; mem. Nat. Fedn. Rep. Women, 1964—; mem. nat. fin. com. Reagan for Pres., 1979-80; mem. governing bd. Capital Speakers Club, 1973-75, chmn. by-laws com., 1973-74; mem. exec. bd. Nat. Vols. in Action, 1975-77; mem. adv. com. Rock Creek Found. Mental Health, 1982-87; mem. 50th anniversary com. Save the Children; mem. fund-raising com. Washington Choral Arts Soc., 1982-84; state fin. chmn. Reagan-Bush campaign Md. Rep. Com., 1980; Md. coord. Nat. Inaugural Com., 1981, 85; trustee Crossnore Sch., Inc., N.C., 1983—, vice chmn. bd; trustee Kate Duncan Smith DAR Sch., Grant, Ala., 1983-86, Tamassee (S.C.) DAR Sch., 1983-86; adviser Bacone Am. Indian Coll., Inc., Muscogee, Okla., 1983-88. Mem. ALA, Spl. Librs. Assn., Coun. on Libr. Resources (commn. on preservation and access), Am. Libr. Trustees Assn., Libr. Adminstrn. and Mgmt. Assn., Assn. Coll. and Rsch. Librs., Am. Antiquarian Soc., Internat. Platform Assn., Spanish-Portuguese Study Group, Nat. Lawyers' Wives, Nat. Capital Law League, Nat. Soc. DAR (chmn. nat. resolutions com. 1980-83, chmn. nat. Nat. Soc. DAR sch. com. 1983-86; state historian 1978-80, mem. state bd. mgmt. 1973—, Nat. Soc. DAR libr. gen., mem. exec. com. and nat. corp. bd. mgmt. 1986-89, chmn. nat. commemorative events com. 1992-95, chmn. nat. Nat. Soc. DAR libr. centennial com. 1995—), Nat. Soc. Children Am. Revolution (sr. nat. asst. registrar 1978-80, mem. sr. nat. bd. mgmt. 1978-80, sr. nat. exec. com. 1978-80), Nat. Assn. Parliamentarians, World Affairs Coun., League of Rep. Women, Md. Fedn. Rep. Women, Women's Nat. Republican Club, Nat. Fed. Rep. Women, Commn. on Preservation and Access, Lit. Vols. Am. (Washington Met. area affiliate), Exec. Women in Govt., Am. News Women's Club, Internat. Club, Capital Hill Club, Univ. Club Washington, W Club, Congl. Country Club (Potomac, Md.).

TAYLOR, BARRY LLEWELLYN, microbiologist, educator; b. Sydney, Australia, May 7, 1937; came to U.S., 1967; s. Fredrick Llewelyn and Vera Lavina (Clarke) T.; m. Desmyrna Ruth Tolhurst, Jan. 4, 1961; children: Lyndon, Nerida, Darrin. BA, Avondale Coll., Cooranbong, New South Wales, 1959; BSc with honors, U. New South Wales, Sydney, 1966; PhD, Case Western Res. U., 1973; postgrad., U. Calif., Berkeley, 1973-75. Vis. postdoctoral fellow Australian Nat. U., Canberra, 1975-76; asst. prof. biochemistry Loma Linda (Calif.) U., 1976-78, assoc. prof. biochemistry, 1978-83, prof. biochemistry, 1983—, prof., chmn. dept. microbiology and molecular genetics, 1988—, interim dir. Ctr. for Molecular Biology, 1989-94. Contbr. articles to profl. publs. Rsch. grantee Am. Heart Assn., 1978-85, NIH, 1981—. Mem. Am. Soc. Microbiology, Am. Soc. Biochemistry and Molecular Biology. Office: Loma Linda U Dept Microbiology and Molecular Genetics Loma Linda CA 92350

TAYLOR, BARRY NORMAN, physicist; b. Phila., Mar. 27, 1936; s. Morris and Sarah (Weiss) T.; m. Sheila Anne Cohen, Dec. 28, 1958; children: Deborah Susan, David Joel, Denise Beth. AB, Temple U., Phila., 1957; MS, U. Pa., 1960, PhD, 1963. Instr., then asst. prof. physics U. Pa., 1963-66; mem. tech. staff RCA Rsch. Labs., 1966-70; chief absolute elec. measurements sect. Nat. Bur. Standards (name changed to Nat. Inst. of Standards and Tech. 1988), Gaithersburg, Md., 1970-74, adminstr. NIST Precision Measurement Grants Program, 1974—, chief electricity divsn., 1974-89; mgr. Fundamental Cons. Data Ctr., 1989—; instr. Rider Coll., Trenton, N.J., 1969-70; mem., chairperson nat. and internat. tech. coms. Co-author: Fundamental Constants and Quantum Electrodynamics, 1969; co-editor: Precision Measurement and Fundamental Constants, 1971; Co-editor: Precision Measurement and Fundamental Constants II, 1984; contbr. articles to sci. jours. Recipient Silver medal U.S. Dept. Commerce, 1975, Gold medal, 1989, John Price Wetherill medal Franklin Inst., 1975. Fellow IEEE, Am. Phys. Soc. (chair topical group on fundamental constants and precise tests of phys. laws 1990-92), Washington Acad. Scis.; mem. Sigma Xi. Office: Nat Inst of Stds and Tech Bldg 245 Rm C229 Gaithersburg MD 20899-0001

TAYLOR, BENJAMIN B., newspaper publishing executive; b. 1947; s. John I. T.; m. Katherine Taylor; children: Abigail, Samuel, William. Grad., Harvard U. Various positions including asst. mng. editor/local news, consumer affairs reporter, polit. reporter Boston Globe, 1972-88, exec. editor, 1988; v.p. Globe Newspaper Co., 1991, exec. v.p., 1992, pres., 1993—, COO, 1994—. Trustee Radcliffe Coll., Park Sch., Brookline, Mass. Office: Globe Newspapers Co 135 Morrissey Blvd Boston MA 02107*

TAYLOR, BERNARD J., II, banker; b. Phila., Nov. 10, 1925; s. Bernard and Marie (Pearce) T.; m. Barbara Silverstein; children: Dorothy Taylor Tomlinson, Lawrence Dean, David Stewart. B.S., U. Pa., 1949. Asst. mgr. McCrory Stores Corp., Phila., 1949-51; fin. analyst Fidelity Bank, Phila., 1951-57; asst. to v.p. investments Fidelity Bank, 1957-59, asst. to pres., 1959-60, corp. sec., 1960-63, v.p., sec., 1963-66, sr. v.p. in charge adminstrn. dept., 1966-72, exec. v.p., 1972-74; v.p. Fidelcor, Inc. (parent co. Fidelity Bank), 1969-72, exec. v.p., 1973-76; sr. exec. v.p., 1976-79; pres., dir. Fidelity Bldg. Corp., 1970-79; pres., CEO Wilmington (Del.) Trust Co., Del., 1979-92; dir. Wilmington (Del.) Trust Co., 1979—, chmn., 1980-92; ptnr. Golf Ptnrs. (Hartefield Nat. Golf Course), 1993—. Pres. Savoy Opera Co., Phila., 1961-63, prodn. mgr., dir., 1970-75; pres., bd. dirs. Pa. Opera Theatre, 1975-80, treas., bd. dirs., 1980-93; mem. adv. bd. mgrs. Inglis House Phila., 1967-70; mem. Del. Round Table, 1980-92; bd. dirs. Greater Wilmington Devel. Coun., 1980-84, Sta. WHYY, PBS-TV, Phila., 1980-92; bd. dirs., 1986-91; bd. dirs. Del. Theatre Co., 1987-91. With AUS, 1944-46, PTO. Clubs: Orpheus (Phila); Wilmington Country. Home: 6 Hillspur Rd Kennett Square PA 19348-2702

TAYLOR, BEVERLY LACY, stringed instrument restorer, classical guitarist; b. Denver, Mar. 1, 1928; d. Frederick Thurlow and Ruth (Rogers) Lacy; m. Arthur D. Taylor, Mar. 18, 1967. BA, Wheaton Coll., Norton, Mass., 1949; postgrad., U. Denver, 1951-53, U. Colo., 1953. Scene designer, tech. dir. Piper Players, Idaho Springs, Colo., 1949-51; art instr. Denver Art Mus., 1952; craft and speech instr. Wallace Sch., Denver, 1953; illustrator dept. native art Denver Art Mus., 1954-56; designer, owner The Art Studio, Santa Fe, 1956-58; instr., owner Classic Guitar Studio, Santa Fe, 1959—; instr. classical guitar Santa Fe Conservatory of Music, 1966-67, Coll. Sante Fe, 1971-72; stringed instrument restorer Lacy Taylor Studio, Santa Fe, 1967—. One-woman shows of mosaic panels include Mus. N.Mex., Santa Fe, 1959; exhibited in group shows at Mus. New Mex., 1962, 63; executed mosaic panels Denver Art Mus. Recipient Miriam Carpenter Art prize Wheaton Coll., 1949, prize N.Mex. State Fair, 1959, 61. Mem. Guild Am. Luthiers, Assn. String Instrument Artisans. Avocations: drawing, gardening, dog training. Home: 1210 Canyon Rd Santa Fe NM 87501-6128

TAYLOR, BILLIE WESLEY, retired secondary education educator; b. Charleston, W.Va, Aug. 14, 1940; s. Billie W and Effie (Adams) T.; m. Elisabeth Julia Coler, Jan. 27, 1960; 1 child, Rose Letitia Taylor Allen. BA, Wilmington Coll., 1961; MA, Ohio State U., 1963; PhD, Columbia Pacific U., 1993. Cert. secondary tchr., prin., Ohio. Tchr. Columbus Pub. Schs., Ohio, 1961-64; records, forms, mgnt. officer VI U.S. Army Corps, Battle Creek, Mich., 1964-65; production planner Hoover Ball & Bearing Co., Ann Arbor, Mich., 1965-66; dist. exec. Boy Scouts of Am., Detroit, 1966-72; sales tng. Standard Register Co., Dayton, Ohio, 1972-74; tchr. Dayton Pub. Schs., Dayton, Ohio, 1974—, curriculum specialist for computer tech., 1989-93. Author: History of the D-MC Park District, 1988, Classroom Discipline, 1987. Pres., Johnson Sch. Parent Tchrs. Assoc., Taylor, Mich., 1966-67; dist. chmn., Boy Scouts of Am., Dayton, 1974-79; bd. mem., Southeast Dayton Priority Bd., Dayton, 1976-77. Recipient Pres. trophy Boy's Scouts of Am., 1970; Jenning's scholar Martha Holden Jennings Found., 1980-81. Mem. Nat. Geographic Soc. (life), Nat. Audubon Soc., Smithsonian Nat. Assocs. (charter mem.), Libr. of Congress Assocs. (charter), Nat. Mus. of the Am. Indian (charter), Western Ohio Edn. Assn. (del.), Am. Birding Assn., The Nature Conservancy (life), Am. Assn. Individual Investors (life), Masons. Avocations: birding, motorhoming, foreign travel, reading, investing. Home: 131 Snow Hill Ave Kettering OH 45429-1705

TAYLOR, BILLY (WILLIAM EDWARD TAYLOR), jazz musician; b. Greenville, N.C., July 24, 1921; s. William Edward and Antoinette (Bacon) T.; m. Theodora Castion, June 22, 1946; children: Duane, Kim. B.S. in Music, Va., State Coll., 1942; D. Mus. Edn., U. Mass.; L.H.D., Fairfield U.; D. Mus., Va. State Coll.; Ph.D., Clark Coll.; Mus.D. (hon.), Berklee Coll. Mus., 1981. lectr. Music Educators Nat. Conf., 1957, New Eng. Music Tchrs. Assn., 1958, New Jazz Soc., Phila., 1967; owner Sta. WSOK, Savannah, Ga., Sta. WLIB, also WBLS-FM, N.Y.C.; pres. Billy Taylor Productions, Duane Music Co., both N.Y.C.; spl. cons. to chmn. Nat. Endowment Arts; chmn. bd. Creative Arts Public Service. Jazz pianist, 1937—; producer, staff: weekly jazz TV program Billy Taylor Show, 1965; performer, narrator: TV prodns. The Pop Explosion, 1966, Dial M for Music, 1965; pres., founder: TV prodns. Jazz Mobile, 1967; host, narrator, performer: TV prodns. Black, White and Blue, 1966; music dir., cons., leader orch. TV prodn. The Subject was Jazz, 1957; program dir. WLIB-FM, 1965-69; mus. dir. David Frost Show, N.Y.C., from 1969; mus. cons. TV prodns., 1964—; host: Jazz Alive, Nat. Public Radio; guest soloist numerous symphonies; composer music ballet Your Arms Too Short to Box with God; Suite for Jazz Piano and Orch., Make a Joyful Noise, Peaceful Warrior, For Rachel; numerous other works; mus. dir. PBS variety show. Black Jour. Tonight; recs. include: Jazz Alive, 1977, Where've You Been, 1980, Dr. T, 1993, Custom Taylored, 1994, It's A Matter of Pride, 1994; author: Jazz Piano. Bd. dirs. Harlem Cultural Council; trustee Rockefeller Found., 1978—; mem. Nat. Council Arts, 1972-78. Recipient Mayor's award for arts and culture, 1981; Edward E. Elson Disting. Service award Nat. Public Radio, 1981; named to Nat. Assn. Jazz Educators Hall of Fame, 1979; George Foster Peabody award, 1981; Emmy award; Lifetime Achievement award Down Beat mag., 1984. Mem. Arts and Bus. Council N.Y. (pres.), Nat. Acad. Rec. Arts and Scis. (v.p. 1964—), ASCAP (dir. 1976-78), Acad. TV Arts and Scis.

TAYLOR, BILLY D., principal. Prin. Dyersburg (Tenn.) High Sch. Recipient Blue Ribbon award U.S. Dept. Edn., 1990-91. Office: Dyersburg High Sch 125 Us Highway 51 Byp N Dyersburg TN 38024-3660

TAYLOR, CALVIN LEE, public administrator; b. Marietta, Ohio, Dec. 27, 1946; s. Fred O. and Wilma B. Taylor; m. Nancy Downs, Mar. 29, 1969; children: Christina, Matthew. BSc in Natural Resources, Ohio State U., 1969, PhD in Environ. Scis., 1977; MPA, Golden Gate U., 1973. Project officer Corps of Engrs. Sacramento (Calif.) Dist., 1970-73; asst. planning chief Ohio EPA, Columbus, 1973-74; acad. advisor Ohio State U. Sch. of Natural Resources, Columbus, 1974-75; asst. to dir. Ohio Water Resources Ctr., Columbus, 1975-76; adminstr. Ohio Dept. Natural Resources, Columbus, 1976-82; chief of pub. rels. Ohio Adj. Gen.'s Dept., 1982-88; chief ops. and tng. Ohio Emergency Mgmt. Agy., Columbus, 1988-94; chief of emergency planning State of Ohio, Columbus, 1994—; lectr. in field. Contbr. articles to profl. jours. Chmn., mem. Worthington Devel. Commn./ Archl. Rev. Bd., 1976-82, active coms. Worthington United Meth. Ch., 1980—. Lt. col. U.S. Army Res., 1970—. Named Outstanding Young Man of Am. U.S. Bd. Jaycees, 1981. Mem. Ohi Acad. Sci., Assn. U.S. Army, Ohio State U. Alumni Assn. (pres. natural resources 1979-80), Ohio State U. Army ROTC Alumni Assn. (v.p., pres.), Columbus Acad. Fathers' Assn. Avocations: snow skiing, water skiing, jogging. Home: 701 Morning St Worthington OH 43085-3772 Office: Ohio Emergency Mgmt Agy 2855 W Granville Rd Columbus OH 43235

TAYLOR, CARL ERNEST, physician, educator; b. Landour, Mussoorie, India, July 26, 1916; s. John C. and Elizabeth (Siehl) T.; m. Mary Daniels, Feb. 14, 1943; children—Daniel, Elizabeth, Henry. B.S., Muskingum Coll., 1937, D.Sc., 1962; M.D., Harvard, 1941, M.P.H., 1951, D.P.H., 1953; L.H.D. (hon.), Towson U., 1974. Diplomate: Am. Bd. Preventive Medicine. Intern, resident pathology, surg. staff, tropical disease research Gorgas Hosp., Panama C.Z., 1941-44; charge med. service Marine Hosp., Pitts., 1944-46; supt. Meml. Hosp., Fategarh, India, 1947-50; research assoc. Harvard Sch. Pub. Health, Boston, 1950-52; asst. prof. epidemiology Harvard Sch. Pub. Health, 1957-59, assoc. prof., 1959-61; prof. preventive and social medicine Christian Med. Coll., Ludhiana, Punjab, India, 1953-56; prof. internat. health Johns Hopkins Sch. Hygiene and Pub. Health, Balt., 1961-83; prof. emeritus Johns Hopkins Sch. Hygiene and Pub. Health, 1984—, chmn. dept. internat. health, 1961-83; Cons. AID, 1959—; UNICEF country rep. in China, 1984-87; mem. expert com. WHO, 1963, 66, 67, 70, 71, 72, 73, 75; mem. Inst. Medicine, Nat. Acad. Medicine, Nat. Adv. Commn. Health Manpower; chmn. Nat. Council for Internat. Health. Contbr. numerous articles to profl. jours. Fellow Royal Coll. Physicians (Can.), Royal Soc. Tropical Medicine and Hygiene, Am. Pub. Health Assn.; mem. Assn. Tchrs. Preventive Medicine, Am. Soc. Tropical Medicine and Hygiene, Indian Assn. for Advancement Med. Edn. Research on rural health, population dynamics, nutrition, epidemiology of leprosy. Home: Bittersweet Acres 1201 Hollins Ln Baltimore MD 21209-2209 *The growing complexity of human relationships around this increasingly crowded world presents new challenges to concerned scientists. Solutions to our problems must come from new collaborative styles of work bridging the usual boundaries between people, since the problems we face are mutual.*

TAYLOR, CAROLYN L., principal. Prin. James Madison High Sch., Madison, Wis. Recipient Blue Ribbon award U.S. Dept. Edn., 1990-91. Office: James Madison Meml High Sch 201 S Gammon Rd Madison WI 53717-1404

TAYLOR, CARSON WILLIAM, electrical engineer; b. Superior, Wis., May 24, 1942; s. William Stanley and Elizabeth Marie (Christophersen) T.; m. Gudrun Renate Leistner, Dec. 28, 1966; 1 child, Natasha Marie. BSEE, U. Wis., 1965; M in Engring., Rensselaer Poly. Inst., 1969. Elec. engr. U.S. Bur. Reclamation, Billings, Mont., 1967-68; elec. engr. Bonneville Power Adminstrn., Portland, Oreg., 1969-89, prin. engr., 1989—; prin. Carson Taylor Seminars, Portland, 1986—. Author: Power System Voltage Stability, 1994; contbr. papers to profl. publs.; patentee in field. Lt. U.S. Army, 1965-67. Lt. U.S. Army, 1965-67. Fellow IEEE (chmn. working group 1982—); mem. Conférence Internationale des Grands Réseaux Électrigues a Haute Tension (CIGRE), Eta Kappa Nu. Lutheran. Avocations: fishing, hunting, woodworking, reading, computers. Office: Bonneville Power Adminstrn PO Box 3621 Portland OR 97208-3621

TAYLOR, CECIL PERCIVAL, pianist, composer, educator; b. N.Y.C., Mar. 15, 1933; s. Percy Clinton and Almeida (Maitie) Ragland. Studied music privately; studied music, N.Y. Coll. Music, New Eng. Conservatory. Music intructor U. of WI, 1970-71, Antioch Coll., Yellow Springs, OH, 1972-74, Glassboro State College; instr. U. Wis., 1970-72, Antioch Coll., 1972-74, Glassboro State Coll. Played with Hot Lips Page, Lawrence Brown; formed own quartet in late 1950's; performed with Archie Shepp and Jimmy Lyons, 1961; recorded and performed as solo pianist and with quartet including Jimmy Lyons, Andrew Cycille, Sam Rivers; compositions include Indent; albums include: Jazz Advance, 1956, Nefertiti, the Beautiful One Has Come, 1962, Unit Structures, 1966, Conquistador!, 1966, Silent Tongues, 1974, Air Above Mountains, 1976, Cicil Taylor, 1978, 3 Phasis, 1978, One Too Many Salty Swift and Not Goodbye, 1986, For Olim, 1986, Garden, 1986, The Eight, 1987, Cecil Taylor in Berlin '88, 1988, Looking, 1989, In Florescence, 1990, Dark to Themselves, 1990, Looking Ahead, 1990. Recipient Record of Year Downbeat Critics Poll, 1975; winner Down Beat Critics Poll for best acoustic piano, 1984; recipient Piano Player of Year award, 1972, 79; named to Downbeat Hall of Fame, 1975; Guggenheim fellow, 1973.

TAYLOR, CELIANNA ISLEY, information systems specialist; b. Youngstown, Ohio; d. Paul Thornton and Florence (Jacobs) Isley; divorced; children: Polly, Jerry, Jim. BA in Philosophy, Denison U., 1939; MLS, Western Res. U., 1942. Worked in several pub. librs. and univ. librs., 1939-50; head Libr. Cataloging Dept. Battelle Mem. Inst., Columbus, Ohio, 1951-53; head pers. office, assoc. prof. libr. adminstrn. Ohio State U. Librs., Columbus, 1954-65; coord. info. svcs. and assoc. prof. libr. adminstrn. Nat. Ctr. for Rsch. in Vocat. Edn., Ohio State U., Columbus, 1966-70; sr. rsch. assoc., adminstrv. assoc. and assoc. prof. libr. adminstrn. dept. computer and info. sci. Ohio State U., Columbus, 1970-86, assoc. prof. emeritus Univ. Librs., 1986—; mem. Task Force on a Spl. Collections Database, Ohio State U. Librs., Columbus, 1988-89, comm. systems and recs. coord. Ohio State U. Retirees Assn., Columbus, 1992-93; cons. for several profl. orgns. including Ernst & Ernst CPA's and Oreg. State Sys. of Higher Edn., 1961-82. Author: (with J. Magisos) book, Guide for State Voc-Tech Edn. Dissemination Systems 1971, (with A.E. Petrarca, and R.S. Kohn) book, Info. Interaction 1982; several articles for profl. jours.; designer: info. systems, CALL System, 1977-82, Channel 2000 Proj. Home Info. Svc., 1980-81, Continuing Education Info. Ctr., 1989-90, Human Resources (HUR) System, 1976-77,1979-82, DECOS, 1975-86, Computer-asst. libr. System, Optical Scan System, 1972-73, ERIC Clearinghouse for vocat. edn., 1966-70. Bd. dirs. Columbus Reg. Info. Svc., 1974-78, Cmty. Info. Referral Svc., Inc. 1975-81; chmn. subcom. on design, info. and ref. com. Columbus United Cmty. Coun., 1972-73; dir. Computer Utility for Pub. Info. Columbus, 1975-81; acct. coord. Greater Columbus Free-net, 1994—. Mem. ALA, Assn. Computing Machinery (Ctrl. Ohio chpt.), Am. Soc. Info. Sci.,Assn. Faculty and Profl. Women Ohio State U., Columbus Metro Club, Coun. for Ethics in Econs., Olympic Indoor Tennis Club. Avocations: bicycling, bird watching, folk dancing, gourmet cooking, tennis. Home and Office: 3471 Greenbank Ct Columbus OH 43221-4724

TAYLOR, CHARLES H., congressman; b. Brevard, N.C., Jan. 3, 1941; m. Elizabeth Owen; 3 children. BA, Wake Forest U., 1963, JD, 1966. Mem. N.C. Ho. of Reps., Raleigh, 1967-73, minority leader, 1969-73; mem. N.C. Senate, Raleigh, 1973-75, minority leader, 1973-75; mem. 102nd-104th Congresses from 11th N.C. dist., Washington, 1991—; mem. appropriations subcoms. commerce, justice, state jud. and related agys., legis. com., subcom. on interior; tree farmer N.C. Baptist. Office: U S Ho of Reps 231 Cannon HOB Washington DC 20515 also: 22 S Pack Sq Ste 330 Asheville NC 28801-3524

TAYLOR, CHARLES HENRY, psychoanalyst, educator; b. Boston, Oct. 2, 1928; s. Charles Henry and Rosamond (Stewardson) T.; m. Diana Burgess, 1950; children: Stephen, Diana Beth, Charles S., Eleanor; m. Patricia Finley, 1988. B.A., Yale U., 1950, M.A., 1952, Ph.D., 1955; postgrad., Cambridge (Eng.) U., 1950-51. Instr., then asst. prof. English Ind. U., 1955-61; asst. dean, then assoc. dean, also assoc. prof. English Yale U., 1961-63, acting provost, 1963-64, provost, prof. English,, 1964-72, pres. rep., 1972-76; grad. C.G. Jung Inst., N.Y., 1979; pvt. practice psychoanalysis, 1976—; bd. dirs. Globe Newspaper Co. Inc., Meridian Audio, Ltd. Author: The Early Collected Editions of Shelley's Poems, 1958; editor: Essays on the Odyssey, 1963; contbr. articles to profl. jours. Mem. com. on libr. Yale U. Coun., 1990-95; trustee Hampshire Coll., 1988-93. Mem. Internat. Assn. Analytical Psychology Archive for Rsch. in Archetypal Symbolism (pres. 1987-93, treas. 1993—), N.Y. Assn. Analytical Psychology, Nat. Assn. for Advancement Psychoanalysis, Phi Beta Kappa. Home: 40 Rogers Ave Milford CT 06460-6435

TAYLOR, CHARLOTTE, fraternal organization administrator. Dir. Alpha Delta Pi. Office: Alpha Delta Pi 1386 Ponce De Leon Ave NE Atlanta GA 30306-4604

TAYLOR, CLAUDE J., sales executive, consultant; b. Winston-Salem, N.C., Apr. 29, 1943; s. Claude V. and Jessie K. T.; m. Frances T. Denty, Dec. 22, 1962; children: Joseph Vinston, Jeffrey Alan, Marc David, Michael Edward. Student, U.S. Army Schs., 1961-62; AS in Aircraft Comms., Nat. Inst., 1966-68, AS in Indsl. Electronics, 1968-71; student, Palm Beach Jr. Coll., 1971-73. Inside salesman and office ops. Graybar Electric Co., West Palm Beach, Fla., 1964-66; mgr. Lewisville (N.C.) Shell Svc., 1966-67; salesman Joyce Foods, Inc., Lewisville, 1967-69; instrument tech. Pratt-Whitney Aircraft, West Palm Beach, 1969-73; tech. resp., instr., tech. mgr. Siemens Med. Systems, Iselin, N.J., 1973-87; salesman, mfr. rep. Ohmeda div. BOC, LIttleton, Colo., 1987-88; dist. sales mgr. Planmeca, Inc. and Planmed, Wood Dale, 1988-93; owner, pres. dental and medical sales Tech. Splty. Mktg., Jupiter, Fla., 1993—; cons. Instrumentarium Imaging, Inc., Milw., 1993—. With U.S. Army, 1961-64. Home: PO Box 1443 Jupiter FL 33468-1443 Office: Tech Splty 16220 128th Trl N Jupiter FL 33478-6527

TAYLOR, CLAYBORNE DUDLEY, engineering educator; b. Kokomo, Miss., July 15, 1938; s. Dudley Clayborne and Winnie Lee (Holmes) T.; m. Mary Jean Blue, June 23, 1963; children: Clayborne Dudley Jr., David Edward, Rebecca Lynn Taylor Burg. BS in Physics, Miss. State U., 1961; MS in Physics, N.Mex. State U., 1964, PhD in Physics, 1965. Registered profl. engr., Miss. Tech. staff mem. Sandia Labs., Albuquerque, 1965-67; assoc. prof. Miss. State U., Starkville, 1967-69, 1969-71, prof. elec. engring., 1972-86, 88-91, assoc. dean. engring., 1991—; prof. elec. engring. U. Miss., Oxford, 1971-72; vis. Stocker prof. Ohio U., Athens, 1986-88; cons. Phillips Lab., Albuquerque, 1972—. Author: High-Power Microwave Systems and Effects, 1994; contbr. articles to tech. jours. Recipient Cert. of Recognition, NASA, 1986; Electromagnetic Pulse Tech. fellow Summa Found., 1988. Mem. IEEE (sr.), Internat. Union of Radio Scientists, Am. Soc. Engring. Edn. Presbyterian. Home: 517 Greensboro St Starkville MS 39759 Office: Miss State U Coll Engring 106 McCain Bldg PO Box 9544 Mississippi State MS 39762

TAYLOR, CLYDE CALVIN, JR., literary agent; b. Anderson, S.C., July 27, 1936; s. Clyde Calvin and Ellen Letitia (Hamilton) T.; m. children: Katie Taylor Legnini, Emily Taylor Bradley, Andrew Hamilton. A.B., Wofford Coll., 1958. Tchr. Westminster Schs., Atlanta, 1958; advt. copywriter Harper and Row, 1960, Macmillan & Co., 1961; advt. mgr. Collier-Macmillan Library Div., 1962; asst. bus. mgr. book div. Am. Heritage Pub. Co., 1963-65; dir. subs. rights G.P. Putnam's Sons, 1965-69; v.p. World Pub. Co., 1970; v.p., gen. mgr. G.P. Putnam's Sons, N.Y.C., 1972-74; v.p., pub. G.P. Putnam's Sons, 1974-77, exec. v.p., pub., 1977; pres. Clyde Taylor Lit. Agy., Inc., 1978-79; v.p. Curtis Brown Ltd., 1980-94; lit. agt. affiliated with Knox Burger Assocs., Ltd., 1994-96; v.p. Curtis Brown Ltd., 1996—. Home: 216 E 6th St New York NY 10003-8212

TAYLOR, CYNTHIA RENA, real estate credit and collections director; b. Bklyn., Sept. 6, 1951; d. Raymond Ward and Hazel McDonald Lovett; m. Charles D. Taylor, Aug. 31, 1974 (div.); children: Charles, Chanay, Candejah. BBA, Bernard M. Baruch Coll., N.Y.C., 1983. Lic. real estate salesperson. Mortgage modification corr. Met. Life Ins. Co., N.Y.C., 1972-79, examiner and approver mortgages, 1979-81, leasing adminstr., 1981-83; lease compliance auditor Helmsley-Spear Inc., N.Y.C., 1983-85; dir. lease compliance Helmsley-Spear Nat. Inc., N.Y.C., 1985-89; br. commn. credit mgr. Helmsley-Spear, Inc., N.Y.C., 1990-91, credit/collection mgr., 1991—; office mgr., personnel liaison dir. Empire State Bldg, N.Y.C., 1993—; spl. project coord. Helmsley-Spear Inc., 1990—. Mem. Sigma Alpha Delta. Democrat. Roman Catholic. Avocations: aerobics, reading, volleyball.

TAYLOR, D. LANSING, cell biology educator; b. Balt., Dec. 26, 1946. BS, U. Md., 1968; PhD in Biology, SUNY, Albany, 1973. Fellow biophysics Marine Biol. Labs., 1973-74; asst. prof. biology Harvard U., 1974-78, assoc. prof., 1978-82; prof. biology Carnegie-Mellon U., Pitts., 1982—. Editor Jour. Cell Biology, 1981—, Jour. Cell Motility, 1981—. Mem. Am. Soc. Cell Biology, Biophys. Soc., N.Y. Acad. Sci. Achievements include research in molecular basis of amoeboid movements, utilizing biochemical, cell biological and biophysical approaches and fluorescence spectroscopy. Office: Carnegie Mellon U Dept Biomed Engring Program 4400 5th Ave Pittsburgh PA 15213-2617*

TAYLOR, D(ARL) CODER, architect, engineer; b. Ft. Wayne, Ind., July 18, 1913; s. Frank A. and Edith (Zook) T.; m. Audrey Helen Larkin, June 5, 1944; children: Barbara Helen Taylor Reddy, Thomas Coder, Julie Marie Taylor Hitchins; m. Harriett Pribble Sinding, July 27, 1985. BArch, Carnegie Inst. Tech., 1935; spl. student, U. Wash., 1933. Draftsman Chgo., 1935; partner Zook & Taylor, architects, Chgo., 1939-42, Holsman, Holsman, Klekamp & Taylor, architects, Chgo., 1948-52, Yost & Taylor, architects and engrs., Kenilworth, Ill., 1952-60; chmn. Coder Taylor Assos., Inc., architects-engrs.-planners, Kenilworth, 1960-78; chmn. bd. Coder Taylor Assos., Inc., 1978-81, spl. cons., 1981—; cons. in field, 1935—. Prin. works include Mcpl. Bldg., St. Charles, Ill., 1940, listed Nat. Register Hist. Places, 1990, Prize Home No. 1, 1946 (Chgo. Tribune prize home competition), Sherman Garden Apts., 1951 (Chgo. chpt. AIA honor award), Kincheloe AFB, Mich., 1962 (Best Family Housing Project No. Area), Chanute AFB, Ill., 1959 (Best Family Housing Project Cen. Area), U.S. Naval Tng. Ctr., Great Lakes, Ill., 1964 (Merit award FHA), Swimming Pool House, Northfield, Ill., 1967 (Chgo. chpt. AIA-Chgo. Assn. Commerce and Industry Disting. Bldg. award), 510 Green Bay Rd. Bldg., Kenilworth, Ill. (AIA-Chgo. Assn. Commerce and Industry award 1967), Roberts Residence, Lake Forest, Ill., 1968 (AIA-Chgo. Assn. Commerce and Industry Disting. Bldg. award), Glenview Pub. Libr., 1970 (Chgo. chpt. AIA-Chgo. Assn. Commerce and Industry Disting. Bldg. award), Kroch's & Brentano's stores, Chgo., 1961-77, Des Plaines Pub. Libr., 1974 (Des Plaines C. of C. Outstanding Achievement award), Wilmette (Ill.) Park Dist. Recreation Ctr., 1974, Wilmette Village Adminstrn. Bldg., 1975, Glenview Cen. Fire Sta., 1976 (Glenview Appearance Commn. Outstanding Bldg. and Landscape award), Internat. Hdqrs. Alpha Phi Frat., Evanston, Ill., 1975, Barrington Area Pub. Libr., 1977; represented in spl. exhbns. and permanent collections Art Inst. Chgo., Chgo. Hist. Soc., Wilmette Hist. Soc., Evanston Hist. Soc., Graham Found.; author: Oral History of D. Coder Taylor, 1989; contbr. articles to profl. jours. Mem. Glenview (Ill.) Planning Commn., 1962-65; chmn. Glenview Appearance Commn., 1968-72, Picasso Day Com., Chgo., 1967; mem. fine arts com. Ill. Sesquicentennial Commn., 1967-68; exec. com., treas. Fedn. Open Lakefront, 1966-68; mem. tech. studies adv. com. NAS-NRC, 1962—; mem. tech. panel, adv. com. HUD, NAS, NAE, 1969; nat. panel arbitrators Am. Arbitrators Assn., 1952—. Lt. comdr. Civil Engr. Corps USNR, 1942-45. Recipient merit award for archtl. accomplishments Carnegie-Mellon U. Alumni Assn., 1982. Fellow AIA (dir. Chgo. chpt. 1965-66, pres. 1967, v.p. Ill. council 1968); mem. Ill. Assn. Professions (dir. 1968), Mich. Soc. Architects, Nat. Assn. Redevel. Ofcls., Tau Sigma Delta (pres. 1934- 35), Sigma Phi Epsilon (pres. 1934-35), Scarab (1934-35). Methodist. Club: North Shore Country (Glenview, Ill.). Home and Office: 727 Redwood Ln Glenview IL 60025-4460 *"Early in my professional career, I decided that quality of work created was more important than quantity. To have the largest practice was not to be the goal, but rather to have personal involvement in the work produced, which would result in less work, but work of high class and character.". Architecture has been the focus of my life from childhood to the present day! Its interesting history dates to the earliest of times, with design appearances reflecting society, religion, geography, economy, and materials. My lifelong practice has given me a wonderful, rewarding and pleasurable existence, and it has been most gratifying to be able to make some contribution.*

TAYLOR, DAVID, clergy member, religious administrator. Dir. World Witness Dept. of the Pentecostal Free Will Baptist Ch., Dunn, N.C. Office: The Pentecostal Baptist Ch PO Box 1568 Dunn NC 28335-1568

TAYLOR, DAVID BROOKE, lawyer, banker; b. Salt Lake City, Oct. 14, 1942; s. Lee Neff and June Taylor; m. Carolyn Kaufholz, May 29, 1965; children: Stewart, Allison. BA, U. Utah, 1964; JD, Columbia U., 1967. Bar: N.Y. 1967, N.C. 1995. Ptnr. Wickes, Riddell, Bloomer, Jacobi & McGuire, N.Y.C., 1967-79, Morgan, Lewis & Bockius, N.Y.C., 1979-89; banker, lawyer Chase Manhattan Bank, N.A., N.Y.C., 1989-92; pres. Geoenertec Corp., N.Y.C., 1992-93; ptnr. Fennebresque, Clark, Swindall & Hay, Charlotte, N.C., 1994—. Mem. ABA, N.Y. State Bar Assn., Internat. Bar Assn. Home: 3815 Beresford Rd Charlotte NC 28211 Office: Fennebresque Clark Swindell & Hay 100 N Tryon St Ste 2900 Charlotte NC 28202-4000

TAYLOR, DAVID GEORGE, retired banker; b. Charlevoix, Mich., July 29, 1929; s. Frank Flagg and Bessie (Strayer) T.; m. Robyne T. McCarthy, July 28, 1990; children from previous marriage: David, Amy, Jeanine. BS, Denison U., 1951; MBA, Northwestern U., 1953. With Continental Ill. Nat. Bank and Trust Co. Chicago, 1958-86, asst. cashier, 1961-64, 2d v.p., 1964-66, v.p., 1966-72, sr. v.p., 1972-74, exec. v.p., 1974-80, exec. v.p., treas., 1980-83, vice chmn., 1983-84, chmn., chief exec. officer, 1984; vice chmn. Irving Trust Co., N.Y.C., 1986-89; group exec. Chem. Bank, N.Y.C., 1989-94, ret., 1994. Mem. Dealer Bank Assn. Com. on Glass-Steagall Reform, 1985-86. Bd. dirs. Evanston Hosp., Glenbrook Hosp.; trustee Art Inst. Chgo., 1981-86; advisor J.L. Kellogg Grad. Sch. Mgmt., Northwestern U., 1984—; bd. dirs. CNA Income Shares. Served to lt. USN, 1953-56. Mem. Pub. Securities Assn. (bd. dirs. 1977-78, chmn. 1977, treas. 1978), Govt. and Fed. Agys. Securities Com. (chmn. bd. dirs. 1982-83), Assn. Res. City Bankers (asset/liability com/govt. relations com. 1983—). Republican. Presbyterian.

TAYLOR, DAVID KERR, international business educator, consultant; b. Oxford, N.C., Oct. 11, 1928; s. David Kerr and Myrtle Norman (Shamburger) T.; m. Isabel de Sousa Botelho de Albuquerque, Apr. 23, 1960; children: Anne de Albuquerque Taylor Grave, Katherine Rowena Taylor. BA, Duke U., 1947, JD, 1949. Bar: N.Y., N.C. Atty. Ins. Co.

N.Am., N.Y.C., 1949-51, Milbank, Tweed, Hadley & McCloy, N.Y.C., 1954-55; internat. exec. Mobil Corp., N.Y.C., Washington, Can., Portugal, Nigeria, France, others, 1955-86; rsch. prof. internat. affairs, sr. fellow intrnat. bus. Georgetown U. Sch. Fgn. Svc., Washington, 1987—; pres. Luso-Am. Bus. Coun., 1987-89; bd. visitors Duke U. Law Sch. 1st lt. U.S. Army, 1951-54, Germany. Mem. Am. Portuguese Soc. (bd. dirs., pres. 1968-70, 76-80), Washington Export Coun., Textile Mus. Adv. Coun., Washington Inst. Fgn. Affairs, Cosmos Club, Phi Beta Kappa. Avocations: piano playing, singing. Home: 2737 Devonshire Pl NW Washington DC 20008-3479 Office: Georgetown U Sch Fgn Svc Washington DC 20057

TAYLOR, DAVID WYATT AIKEN, retired clergyman; b. Tsingkiangpu, Kiangsu, China, Dec. 13, 1925; s. Hugh Kerr and Fanny Bland (Graham) T.; m. Lillian Ross McCulloch, Aug. 25, 1951; children: Frances Bland, David Wyatt. B.A., Vanderbilt U., 1949; B.D. cum laude, Union Theol. Sem. Va., 1952; Th.M., Princeton Theol. Sem., 1953; D.D. (hon.), King Coll., Bristol, Tenn., 1959. Ordained to ministry Presbyn. Ch. U.S., 1952. Pastor chs. Elkton, Va., 1953-55, Bristol, Va., 1955-62; ednl. sec. bd. world missions Presbyn. Ch. U.S., 1962-68, program div. dir., 1968-73; ecumenical officer gen. assembly mission bd. Presbyn. Ch. U.S., Atlanta, 1973-82; pastor Orange Park Presbyn. Ch., Orange Park, Fla., 1982-86; gen. sec. for strategy and interpretation Consultation on Ch. Union, Princeton, N.J., 1986-88, gen. sec., 1988-93; ret., 1993; instr. Bible Presbyn. Jr. Coll., Maxton, N.C., 1951; mem. program bd., div. Christian edn. Nat. Council Chs., 1965-69, bd. mgrs., dept. edn. for mission, 1962-68, mem. program bd., div. overseas ministries, 1968-78, mem. governing bd., 1976-80, chmn. governing bd. credentials com., 1978; chmn. Church World Service, Inc., 1973-75; mem. adminstrn. and fin. com. Nat. Council Chs., 1973-75, mem. commn. on faith and order, 1978-93; mem. commn. on interchurch aid World Council Chs., 1973-75; mem. 5th Assembly, 1975; rep. Presbyn. Ch. U.S. to World Alliance Ref. Chs., 1976-82; bd. dirs. Presbyn. Survey mag., 1963-68; mem. Consultation on Ch. Union, 1974-93; chmn. Nat. Ecumenical Officers Assn., 1978-81. Bd. dirs. Abingdon Presbytery's Children's Home, Wytheville, Va., 1958-62. Served with AUS, 1944-46, PTO. Mem. Sigma Chi. Home: PO Box 1909 Elizabethtown NC 28337-1909

TAYLOR, DERMOT BROWNRIGG, pharmacology researcher; b. Ireland, Mar. 30, 1915; came to U.S., 1950, naturalized, 1955; s. Roland L. and Sarah J. (White) T.; m. Charlotte C. Taylor, 1965; 1 child, Tina. B.A., Trinity Coll., Dublin, 1937, M.B., B.Ch., 1938, M.A., M.D. Asst. to prof. physiology Trinity Coll., 1938-39; lectr. physiology King's Coll., U. London, 1939-45, lectr. pharmacology, 1945-50; assoc. prof. pharmacology U. Calif., San Francisco, 1950-53; prof. pharmacology UCLA, 1953-85, chmn. dept., 1953-68; prof., biomed. researcher U. Calif., Santa Barbara, 1985—. Contbr. to: Essentials of Pharmacology, 1968, A Guide to Molecular Pharmacology-Toxicology, 1973, Green Medicine. Travelling fellow U. London, 1948; fellow Yale, 1948. Mem. Faraday Soc., Biochem. Soc., Physiol. Soc., Brit. Pharmacol. Soc., Soc. Pharmacology and Exptl. Therapeutics, Soc. Exptl. Biology and Medicine. Home: 4325 Via Presada Santa Barbara CA 93110-2225 Office: U Calif Dept Pharmacology Santa Barbara CA 93106

TAYLOR, DONALD, retired manufacturing company executive; b. Worcester, Mass., June 2, 1927; s. John A. B. and Alice M. (Weaver) T.; m. Ruth L. Partridge, June 24, 1950; children: Linda Taylor Robertson, Donald, Mark, John. BSME, Worcester Poly. Inst., 1949; grad., Northeastern U. Mgmt. Devel. Program, 1962, Harvard Bus. Sch. Advanced Mgmt. Program, 1979. Registered profl. engr., Mass. With George J. Meyer Mfg. Co., Milw., 1954-69; pres. mfg. div. A-T-O, Inc., 1969; exec. v.p. Nordberg div. Rex Chainbelt, Inc., Milw., 1969-73; v.p. ops. Rexnord Inc., Brookfield, Wis., pres., chief operating officer, 1978-85, chief exec. officer, from 1985, chmn., 1985-88; pres. Nordberg Machinery Group, Milw., 1973-78; dir. Harnischfeger Corp., Johnson Controls, Inc., Banta Corp. Bd. dirs. Blood Ctr. Southeastern Wis., Greater Milw. Com., Met. Milw. YMCA; bd. dirs. Milw. Symphony Orch. Served with USNR, 1951-54. Mem. ASME. Clubs: Milw. Country, Milw. Athletic, Town, Univ., Masons. Office: 7850 N Club Cir Milwaukee WI 53217-2939

TAYLOR, DONALD ARTHUR, marketing educator; b. Windsor, Ont., Can., Sept. 27, 1923; came to U.S., 1947, naturalized, 1955; s. David Cameron and Eva (Perry) T.; m. Shirley Marion Jenner, 1949; children: John Cameron, Stephen Bruce, Michael James. B.A., U. Western Ont., 1947; M.B.A., U. Mich., 1949, Ph.D. (Horace H. Rackham fellow), 1955. Asst. prof. marketing Mich. State U. at, East Lansing, 1955-58; asso. prof. Mich. State U. at, 1958-62, prof., 1962—, chmn. dept. marketing and transportation adminstrn., 1969-81, prof., 1981-84, chmn. dept. mktg. and transp. adminstrn., 1984-86, chmn., prof. emeritus, 1986—; adviser, chief of party to mission at various univs., Brazil, 1956-58, 62-64; dir. Latin Am. Studies Center, 1968-69; also co-dir. Latin-Am. Market Planning Center, sr. cons. food distbn. studies, N.E. Brazil, Colombia; cons. Geigy Agrl. Chems., Johnson & Johnson Domestic Operating Co., Ford Motor Co., Westinghouse Electric Corp., Whirlpool Corp., Burroughs Corp.; dir. Clark-Graveley Corp., 1972-77. Author: (with D.J. Luck, D.A. Taylor, H. Wales, R. Rubin) Marketing Research, 6th edit, 1982, (with T.A. Staudt, D.A. Taylor and D.J. Bowersox) A Managerial Introduction to Marketing, 3d edit, 1976, (with D.A. Taylor) Institution Building in Business Administration: The Brazilian Experience, 1968, (with Bowersox, Cooper, Lambert and Taylor) Management in Marketing Channels, 1980. Mem. bd. edn. Holt Sch. Dist., 1960-62. Recipient Homenagen Especial award 1st graduating class Escola de Administracao de Empresas, Sao Paulo, Brazil, 1958; named hon. prof., 1964. Mem. Am. Marketing Assn. (bd. dirs. 1969). Home: 3724 Harolds Rd Traverse City MI 49686-9435

TAYLOR, DONNA LYNNE, adult education coordinator; b. Balt., July 1, 1944; d. Noel Leroy and Dorothy Anna (Henry) Welsh; 1 child, Tom A., Jr. BS, Okla. State U., 1965, EdD, 1992; MS, Phillips U., 1984. Cert. vocat. bus. and trade and indsl. edn. tchr., prin., supt., vocat. adminstr., Okla. Retail sales Tulsa, 1961-62; secretary Okla. State U. Coop. Extension Svc., Stillwater, 1965-67; secondary instr. social studies Waller Jr. High, Enid, Okla., 1967-69; substitute instr. Autry Tech. Ctr., Enid, 1971-78, instr. vocat. bus. part-time, 1978-84, instr. vocat. bus. full time, 1984-94, coord. adult edn., 1994—; small bus. owner Lynne's Country Crafts, Enid, 1975-85; coord. adult edn. Autry Tech. Ctr., Enid, 1994—; adult educator Sch. Continuing Edn., Enid, 1981-85; mem. strategic planning com. and policy and procedures com. Staff Devel. Affirmative Action, Enid, 1989—; presenter ann. confs. and meetings Okla. State Dept. Vocat. Tech., Stillwater, 1991-92; coord., chair Articulation Agreement Com., Enid, 1991—; advisor FBLA/Phi Beta Lambda, Enid, 1990-94; mem. North Ctrl. Accreditation Steering Com., 1992-93, staff devel. chair, 1993-94. Bd. dirs. Sch. Continuing Edn., Enid, 1975-85; mem. vol. YWCA, March of Dimes, Am. Heart Assn., MS Soc., Am. Diabetes Assn., Enid Art Assn., 1985—; deacon Christian Ch., Enid, 1986-88, elder, 1988-92, 95—; active Leadership Greater Enid. Recipient Women of Achievement award March of Dimes, 1992; named Okla. Bus. Tchr. of Yr., 1994. Mem. ASCD, Am. Vocat. Assn., Okla Vocat. Assn., Mountain Plains Bus. Edn. Assn., Okla. Bus. Edn. Assn., Nat. Bus. Edn. Assn., Nat. Assn. Classroom Bus. Educators, Vocat. Bus. and Office Edn., Enid C. of C. (edn. com. 1991-92), Phi Delta Kappa (sec. 1992—), PEO. Republican. Avocations: art, volunteering, reading. Home: 2110 Appomattox Enid OK 73703-2008 Office: Autry Tech Ctr 1201 W Willow Rd Enid OK 73703-2506

TAYLOR, DORIS DENICE, physician, entrepreneur; b. Indpls., Sept. 19, 1955; d. Eugene and Mary Catherine (Ryder) T. BA, U. Minn., 1976, cert. behavior analyst, 1977, MD, 1983; BS, Purdue U., 1979. Diplomate Nat. Bd. Med. Examiners. Pvt. practice Locumtenens, 1989—; mng. dir. Sebree-Watkins-Ovbokhan Meml. Cancer Fund, Indpls.; pres., CEO Taylors of Indy Corp., Indpls.; oncologic svcs. cons. and developer. Lange scholar, U. Minn., 1980, Joseph Collins Found. scholar, 1980-81, Nat. Med. Fellowship scholar, 1980-81. Mem. AMA, Am. Soc. for Therapeutic Radiology and Oncology, Am. Soc. Clin. Oncologists. Office: Taylors of Indy Corp 55 Monument Cir Ste 814 Indianapolis IN 46204

TAYLOR, EDWARD CURTIS, chemistry educator; b. Springfield, Mass., Aug. 3, 1923; s. Edward Curtis and Margaret Louise (Anderson) T.; m. Virginia Dion Crouse, June 29, 1946; children: Edward Newton, Susan Raines. Student, Hamilton Coll., 1942-44, DSc (hon.), 1969; AB, Cornell U., 1946, PhD, 1949. Postdoctoral fellow Nat. Acad. Scis., Zurich, Switzerland, 1949-50; DuPont postdoctoral fellow chemistry U. Ill., 1950-51, faculty, 1951-54, asst. prof. organic chemistry, 1952-54; faculty Princeton U., 1954—, prof. chemistry, 1964—, A. Barton Hepburn prof. organic chemistry, 1966—, chmn. dept. chemistry, 1974-79; vis. prof. Technische Hochschule, Stuttgart, Fed. Republic Germany, 1960, U. East Anglia, 1969, 71; Disting. vis. prof. U. Buffalo, 1968, U. Wyo., 1977; Backer lectr. U. Groningen, Holland, 1969; mem. chemistry adv. com. Office Sci. Research, USAF, 1962-73, Cancer Chemotherapy Nat. Service Ctr., 1958-62; mem. internat. adv. bd. Ctr. Medicinal Chemistry, Bar-Ilan U., Israel, 1994—; cons. rsch. divs. Procter & Gamble, 1953-80, Eastman Kodak Co., 1965-83, Tenn. Eastman Co., 1968-83, Eli Lilly & Co., 1970—, Burroughs Wellcome Co., 1983-95, E.I. duPont de Nemours & Co., 1986-90, Polaroid Corp., 1986—, Dow Elanco Co., 1989—, DuPont Merck Pharm. Co., 1990—. Author: (with McKillop) Chemistry of Cyclic Enaminonitriles and o-Aminonitriles, 1970, Principles of Heterocyclic Chemistry: film and audio courses, 1974; editor (with Raphael and Wynberg) Advances in Organic Chemistry, vols I-V, 1960-65, (with Wynberg) Vol VI, 1969, vols. VII-IX, 1970-79 (with W. Pfleiderer) Pteridine Chemistry, 1964, The Chemistry of Heterocyclic Compounds, 1968—, General Heterocyclic Chemistry, 1968—; organic chemistry editl. advisor John Wiley & Sons, Inc., 1968—; mem. editl. adv. bd. Jour. Medicinal Chemistry, 1962-66, Jour. Organic Chemistry, 1971-75, Synthetic Communications, 1971—, Heterocycles, 1973—, Chm. Substructure Index, 1971—, Advances in Heterocyclic Chemistry, 1983—, Pteridines, 1989—. Recipient rsch. awards SmithKline and French Found., 1955, Hoffmann-LaRoche Foun., 1964-65, Ciba Found., 1971, Disting. Hamilton award, 1977, U.S. Sr. Scientist prize Alexander von Humboldt Found., 1983, Disting. Alumni medal Hamilton Coll., 1990, F. Gowland Hopkins medal, 1993; sr. faculty fellow Harvard U., 1959; Guggenheim fellow, 1979-80. Fellow N.Y. Acad. Scis., Am. Inst. Chemists; mem. Am. Chem. Soc. (award for creative work in synthetic organic chemistry, 1974, chmn. organic chemistry div. 1976-77, Arthur C. Cope scholar award 1994), German Chem. Soc., Chem. Soc. London, Internat. Soc. Heterocyclic Chemistry (5th Internat. award 1989), Phi Beta Kappa, Sigma Xi, Phi Kappa Phi. Home: 288 Western Way Princeton NJ 08540-5337

TAYLOR, EDWARD STEWART, physician, educator; b. Hecla, S.D., Aug. 20, 1911; s. Robert Stewart and Sylvia Frances (Dewey) T.; m. Ruth Fatherson, June 15, 1940; children: Edward Stewart, Elizabeth Dewey Taylor Bryant, Catherine Wells Taylor Lynn. B.A., U. Iowa, 1933, M.D., 1936. Diplomate Am. Bd. Ob-Gyn (dir. 1962-69). Intern, Hurley Hosp., Flint, Mich., 1936-37; splty. tng. ob-gyn L.I. Coll. Hosp., 1937-41; prof. ob-gyn, chmn. dept. Sch. Medicine, U. Colo., 1947-76, clin. prof., 1976-81, prof., chmn. emeritus, 1981—; cons. ob-gyn Fitzsimons Gen. Hosp.; attending obstetrician and gynecologist St. Joseph's Hosp., Rose Hosp. Med. Center, both Denver; nat. cons. ob-gyn to surg. gen. USAF, 1958-62. Author: Manual of Gynecology, 1952, Essentials of Gynecology, 4th edit.; editor: Beck's Obstetrical Practice, 10th edit.; editor-in-chief for obstetrics: Obstetrical and Gynecol. Survey, 1967-92. Trustee Denver Symphony Orch., 1979-85. Served to lt. col. AUS, 1942-45; surgeon 107th Evacuation Hosp., ETO. Fellow ACS, Am. Coll. Obstetricians and Gynecologists (Disting. Svc. award 1984); mem. AMA, Am. Gynecol. Soc. (v.p. 1974-75), Am. Assn. Obstetricians and Gynecologists (pres. 1970-71), Ctrl. Assn. Obstetricians and Gynecologists, S.W. Obstet. and Gynecol. Soc. (hon.), Am. Gynecol. and Obstet. Soc., Assn. Profs. Ob-Gyn (pres. 1974-75), Western Surg. Soc., Finnish Gynecol. Soc. (hon.), University Club (Denver), Alpha Omega Alpha. Congregationalist. Club: University (Denver). Home: 80 S Dexter St Denver CO 80222-1051

TAYLOR, ELDON, psychologist researcher; b. Anchorage, Utah, Jan. 27, 1945; s. Blaine Eldon and Helen Gertrude (George) T.; m. Ravinder Kaur Sadana, June 17, 1990; children: Roy, Angela, Eric, Cassandra, Hillarie, Preston. Student, Weber State Coll., Ogden, Utah, 1971-74; BS, MS, DD, U. Metaphysics, L.A., PhD in Pastoral Psychology, 1986; PhD in Clin. Psychology, St. John's U., Springfield, La., 1990; HHD (hon.), Sem. Coll., 1987; PhD in Pastoral Psychology (hon.), World U. Roundtable, Benson, Ariz., 1988. Sales mgr. Sears, Roebuck & Co., Salt Lake City, 1964-76; v.p. mktg. Dictograph Security, Salt Lake City, 1976-77; dir. Bulwark, Salt Lake City, 1977-84; pres., dir. Progressive Awareness Rsch., Spokane, Wash., 1984—; bd. dirs. World U. Roundtable, Benson, Ariz.; co-founder Creative Living Inst., 1993; mem. adj. faculty St. John's U., 1989—. Author: Thinking Without Thinking, 1995, Subliminal Communication, 1986, Subliminal Learning, 1988, Simple Things and Simple Thoughts, 1989, Wellness: Just a State of Mind, 1993, others; contbr. numerous articles and poetry to various publs.; author numerous audiocassettes on self-improvement; patentee whole brain info. audio processor. Spiritual advisor Intermountain Hospice Ctr., Salt Lake City, 1987-88; counselor Utah State Prison, Draper, 1986-88; sports motivation trainer U.S. Judo Team, Colorado Springs, Colo., 1989—. Named Ky. Col., State of Ky., 1984; recipient Golden Poet award Am. Poetry Soc., 1985-87. Fellow Nat. Assn. Clergy Hypnotherapists; mem. Am. Psychol. Practitioners Assn., Am. Law Enforcement Officers Assn., Internat. Assn. for Forensic Hypnosis, Am. Counselors Soc., Internat. Soc. Stress Analysts, Am. Assn. Religious Counselors. Avocations: physics, horses. Home: PO Box 13249 Spokane WA 99213 Office: Progressive Awareness Rsch 21203 W Beechwood Medical Lake WA 99002

TAYLOR, ELDON DONIVAN, government official; b. Holdenville, Okla., July 29, 1929; s. Rome B. and Alma (Collins) T.; m. Hypatia Ethel Roberts, Feb. 7, 1953; 1 child, Teresa Lynn. Student, Murry State A. and M. Coll., 1948-49, George Washington U., 1949-50; B.S. cum laude, Am. U., 1959, M.A., 1966, postgrad., 1966-68. Research budget analyst, budgetary adminstrn. Office Naval Research, Navy Dept., Washington, 1949-51, 55-56; chief research and devel. budget sect., research and devel. planning adminstrn. Bur. Ordnance, 1956-60; dir. program rev. and resources, mgmt. div. research, devel. planning and adminstrn. Office Space Scis., NASA, Washington, 1960-70; dep. asst. adminstr. for resources mgmt. EPA, 1970-73; asst. dir. adminstrn. NSF, 1973-79; insp. gen. NASA, 1979-80; dir. adminstrn. Va. Ctr. Innovative Tech., 1984-85; v.p. Assn. Univs. for Research in Astronomy, 1985-86; pres. Taylor Mgmt. Assistance Inc., 1987—. Served with USAF, 1951-55. Recipient Commendation award for outstanding performance Dept. Navy, 1958; William A. Jump Meritorious award for achievement in pub. adminstrn., 1964; Exceptional Service award NASA, 1969; Disting. Service award NSF, 1978. Mem. Am. Soc. Pub. Adminstrn. (past sec. com. research pub. adminstrn.), Assn. Univs. for Research in Astronomy, Pi Sigma Alpha, Phi Theta Kappa. Home and Office: 7931 Wolf Run Hills Rd Fairfax Station VA 22039-2101

TAYLOR, ELISABETH COLER, secondary school educator; b. N.Y.C., Jan. 24, 1942; d. Gerhard Helmut and Judith (Horowitz) C.; m. Billie Wesley Taylor II, Jan. 27, 1960; children: Letitia Rose, Billie Albert. Student, Wilmington Coll., 1959-60; BS, Wayne State U., Detroit, 1969; MS, The Ohio State U., 1980; postgrad., Wright State U., Dayton, Ohio, 1989—. Cert. home economist. H.s. tchr. home econs., computer sci., lang. arts Dayton (Ohio) City Schs., 1972—. Bd. mem. Camp Fire Girls, 1970-71, vol. Detroit Mus. of Art, 1970-71, group leader Camp Fire Girls, Boy Scouts, Detroit, 1968-74. Mem. AAUW (life), NEA, Ohio Edn. Assn., Dayton Edn. Assn. Avocations: birding, travelling, needlework. Home: 131 Snow Hill Ave Dayton OH 45429-1705

TAYLOR, ELIZABETH ROSEMOND, actress; b. London, Feb. 27, 1932; d. Francis and Sara (Sothern) T. Student, Byron House, Hawthorne Sch., Metro-Goldwyn-Mayer Sch. Motion pictures include There's One Born Every Minute, 1942, Lassie Come Home, 1943, The White Cliffs of Dover, 1944, Jane Eyre, 1944, National Velvet, 1944, Courage of Lassie, 1946, Cynthia, 1947, Life with Father, 1947, A Date with Judy, 1948, Julia Misbehaves, 1948, Little Women, 1950, Conspirator, 1950, The Big Hangover, 1950, Father of the Bride, 1950, Father's Little Dividend, 1951, A Place in the Sun, 1951, Callaway Went Thataway, 1951, Love Is Better Than Ever, 1952, Ivanhoe, 1952, The Girl Who Had Everything, 1953, Elephant Walk, 1954, Rhapsody, 1954, Beau Brummel, 1954, The Last Time I Saw Paris, 1954, Giant, 1956, Raintree County, 1957, Cat on a Hot Tin Roof, 1958, Suddenly Last Summer, 1959, Scent of Mystery, 1960, Butterfield 8, 1960 (Acad. award best actress), Cleopatra, 1963, The V.I.P.'s, 1963, The Sandpiper, 1965, Who's Afraid of Virginia Woolf?, 1966 (Acad. award best actress), The Taming of the Shrew, 1967, The Comedians, 1967, Reflections in a Golden Eye, 1967, Dr. Faustus, 1967, Boom!, 1968, Secret Ceremony, 1968, The Only Game in Town, 1970, Under Milkwood, 1971, X, Y and Zee, 1972, Hammersmith Is Out, 1972, Night Watch, 1973, Ash Wednesday, 1973, That's Entertainment, 1974 (guest star), The Driver's Seat, 1974, Blue Bird, 1975, Winter Kills, 1977, A Little Night Music, 1977, The Mirror Crack'd, 1980, Young Toscanini, 1988, The Flintstones, 1994; TV appearances include Divorce His/Divorce Hers, 1973, Victory at Entebbe, 1977, Return Engagement, 1979, Between Friends, 1982, Hotel (series), 1984, Malice in Wonderland, 1986, North and South (miniseries), 1986, There Must Be a Pony, 1986, Poker Alice, 1987, Sweet Bird of Youth, 1989; theatre appearances in The Little Foxes, 1981 (Broadway debut), Private Lives, 1983; narrator film documentary Genocide, 1981; author: (with Richard Burton) World Enough and Time, poetry reading, 1964, Elizabeth Taylor, 1965, Elizabeth Taylor Takes Off: On Weight Gain, Weight Loss, Self Esteem and Self Image, 1988; lics. (fragrances) Elizabeth Taylor's Passion, Passion for Men, White Diamonds/Elizabeth Taylor, Elizabeth Taylor's Diamonds & Emeralds, Diamonds & Rubies, Diamonds & Sapphires, (jewelry) The Elizabeth Taylor Fashion Jewelry Collection for Avon. Active philanthropic, relief, charitable causes internationally, including Israeli War Victims Fund for the Chaim Sheba Hosp., 1976, UNICEF, Variety Children's Hosps., med. clinics in Botswana; initiated Ben Gurion U.-Elizabeth Taylor Fund for Children of the Negev, 1982; supporter AIDS Project L.A., 1985; founder, nat. chmn. Am. Found. for AIDS Rsch. (AmFAR), 1985—, internat. fund, 1985—; founder Elizabeth Taylor AIDS Found., 1991—. Named Comdr. Arts Letters (France), 1985; recipient Legion of Honor (France), 1987 (for work with AmFAR), Aristotle S. Onassis Found. award, 1988, Jean Hersholt Humanitarian Academy award, 1993 (for work as AIDS advocate), Life Achievement award Am. Film Inst., 1993; honored with dedication of Elizabeth Taylor Med. Ctr. Whitman-Walker Clinic, Washington, 1993. Address: care Chen Sam & Assocs Inc 506 E 74th St Ste 3E New York NY 10021-3486

TAYLOR, ELLEN BORDEN BROADHURST, civic worker; b. Goldsboro, N.C., Jan. 18, 1913; d. Jack Johnson and Mabel Moran (Borden) Broadhurst; student Converse Coll., 1930-32; m. Marvin Edward Taylor, June 13, 1936; children: Marvin Edward, Jack Borden, William Lambert. Bd. govs. Elizabethan Garden, Manteo, N.C., 1964-74; mem. Gov. Robert Scott's Adv. Com. on Beautification, N.C., 1971-73; mem. ACE nat. action com. for environ. Nat. Coun. State Garden Clubs, 1973-75; bd. dirs. Keep N.C. Beautiful, 1973-85; mem. steering com., charter mem. bd. dirs. Keep Johnston County (N.C.) Beautiful, 1977-92; life judge roses Am. Rose Soc.; chmn. local com. that published jointly with N.C. Dept. Cultural Resources: An Inventory of Historic Architecture, Smithfield, N.C., 1977; co-chmn. local com. to survey and publish jointly with N.C. Div. Archives and History: Historical Resources of Johnston County, 1980-91; charter life mem. N.C. Mus. History Assocs., 1994; charter mem. founder's circle New Mus. History Bldg., Raleigh, 1994. Mem. Nat. Coun. State Garden Clubs (life; master judge flower shows), Johnston County Hist. Soc. (charter), Johnston County Arts Coun. (Spl. award for 1987 projects of Pub. Libr. Johnston County & Smithfield 1965-87), N.C. Geneal. Soc. (charter), Johnston County Geneal. Soc. (charter), Hist. Preservation Soc. N.C. (life), N.C. Art Soc. (life). Democrat. Episcopalian. Clubs: Smithfield (N.C.) Garden (charter; pres. 1969-71), Smithfield Woman's (v.p. 1976), DAR (organizing vice-regent chpt. 1976), Gen. Soc. Mayflower Descs. (life), Descs. of Richard Warren, Nat. Soc. New Eng. Women (charter mem. Carolina Capital chpt.), Colonial Dames Am. (life), Magna Charta Dames, Nat. Soc. Daus. of Founders and Patriots Am. Home: 616 Hancock St Smithfield NC 27577-4008

TAYLOR, ELOUISE CHRISTINE, artist; b. Berkeley, Calif., Sept. 17, 1923; d. Charles Vincent and Lola Lucile (Felder) T.; m. P.S. Carnohan, Sept. 8, 1947 (div. 1982); children: Marcus Jay, Max Todd, Cecilia Ann. Student, Chgo. Opera Ballet Sch., Hollywood, Calif., 1941, San Francisco Opera Ballet Sc. Featured skater Sonja Henie Hollywood Ice Revue, 1941-51, Ctr. Theater, N.Y.; artist Reno, Nev.; instr. figure skating and painting. Oil paintings featured in numerous group and one-woman shows; portrait of Sonja Henie and several others in permanent collection at World Figure Skating Hall of Fame and Mus., Colorado Springs, Colo.; paintings exhibited local shows Los Altos, Calif., 1970-74, Santa Rosa, 1974-79, also Half Moon Bay-Shoreline Sta. Gallery & art shows, 1981, 82, Parklane Mall, Reno, Nev., 1993; numerous commd. paintings. Mem. Family Fitness Ctr. Avocations: designing and hand knitting, designing/hand-carving rubber stamps, swimming, dancing, writing poetry. Home: 122 Asbury St San Jose CA 95110

TAYLOR, ESTELLE WORMLEY, English educator, college dean; b. Washington, Jan. 12, 1924; d. Luther Charles and Wilhelmina Wormley; m. Ivan Earle Taylor, Dec. 26, 1953. BS magna cum laude, Miner Tchrs. Coll., 1945; MA, Howard U., 1947; PhD, Cath. U. Am., 1969. Instr. English Howard U., 1947-52; tchr. Langley Jr. High Sch., Washington, 1952-55, Eastern Sr. High Sch., Washington, 1955-63; instr. D.C. Tchrs. Coll., 1963-66, asst. prof., 1966-69, assoc. prof., 1969-71, prof., 1971-91, prof. English emerita, 1991—, acad. dean, 1975-76; assoc. provost Fed. City Coll., Washington, 1974-75; prof. Howard U., 1976-91, chmn. dept. English, 1976-85, assoc. dean Coll. Liberal Arts, 1985-86; dir. expository writing program Grad. Sch. Arts and Scis., 1988-91; mem., sec. Edn. Licensure Commn. of D.C., 1993—; mem. Commn. on Higher Edn., Mid. States Assn. Colls. and Schs., 1984-87, 88-90, co-chair steering com. to revise Characteristics of Excellence, 1992-93; mem. ctrl. exec. com. Folger Inst. Renaissance and 18th Century Studies, 1982-91. 1st v.p. Order Daus. of King Episc. Ch. Diocese, Washington, 1994—; commr. Edn. Licensure Com. of D.C., 1993—, also sec., vice chmn., 1995—; trustee U. D.C., 1979-83, vice chmn., 1983; mem. D.C. Cmty. Humanities Coun., 1990-91; co-chmn. planning com. Centennial Celebration of the Andrew Rankin Chapel Howard U., 1994. Named Disting. Alumni, Howard U., 1995; So. fellow, 1968-69; Rockefeller/Aspen Inst. fellow, 1978-79. Mem. MLA (del. assembly 1994—), Nat. Assn. for Equal Opportunity in Higher Edn., Coll. Lang. Assn., Shakespeare Assn. Am., Pub. Mems. Assn. Fgn. Svc. Dept. of State, Links (v.p. Capital City chpt. 1979-81, corr. sec. 1989, rec. sec. 1991-93, 95—). Democrat. Home: 3221 20th St NE Washington DC 20018-2421 *Throughout my career I have been climbing a giant ladder, invisible to all but me. The challenging but humbling feature of this ladder is that whenever I get the feeling that I have almost reached the top, several additional rungs attach themselves to my Jacob's Ladder. Thus, that thing called success is for me forever a goal to be reached. As long as I continue to feel a restlessness and a yearning to climb another rung, I shall know that I am alive.*

TAYLOR, FOSTER JAY, retired university president; b. Gibsland, La., Aug. 9, 1923; s. Lawrence Foster and Marcia Aline (Jay) T.; m. Lou Kavanaugh; 1 son, Terry Jay. Student, La. Poly. Inst., 1940-42; BA, U. Calif., Santa Barbara, 1948; MA, Claremont (Calif.) Grad. Sch., 1949; PhD, Tulane U., 1952. Assoc. prof. history, dean men. La. Coll., Pineville, 1952-56; prof. La. Coll., 1956-62, dean coll., 1960-62; pres. La. Tech. U., Ruston, 1962-87, pres. emeritus, 1987—; past chmn. La. Labor Mediation Bd.; arbitrator Am. Arbitration Assn., Fed. Mediation and Conciliation Svc.; former mem. La. Adv. Coun. on Vocat.-Tech. Edn.; mem. Air Force ROTC Adv. Coun.; bd. dirs. Michael;s Stores, Pizza Inn, Inc., Ill. Ctrl. R.R. Author: The United States and the Spanish Civil War, 1936-39, 1956, Reluctant Rebel, The Secret Diary of Robert Patrick, 1861-1865, 1959. Bd. dirs. Ruston Civic Symphony; trustee Falcon Found. Served to lt. comdr., aviator USNR, 1942-46. Mem. Am. Hist. Assn., Miss. Valley Hist. Assn., So. Hist. Assn., Nat. Acad. Arbitrators., Phi Alpha Theta. Club: Rotary. Home: 2502 Tanglewood Dr Ruston LA 71270-2244

TAYLOR, FRED M., school system administrator. Supt. Gadsden (Ala.) City Schs. State finalist Nat. Supt. Yr. award, 1993. Office: Gadsden City Schs 1026 Chestnut St Gadsden AL 35901-3918

TAYLOR, FREDERICK WILLIAM, JR. (FRITZ TAYLOR), lawyer; b. Cleve., Oct. 21, 1933; s. Frederick William Sr. and Marguerite Elizabeth (Kistler) T.; m Mary Phyllis Osborne, June 1, 1985. BA in History, U. Fla., 1957; MA in Near East Studies, U. Mich., 1959; JD cum laude, NYU, 1967. Bar: N.Y. 1968, Calif. 1969, U.S. Dist. Ct. (cen. dist.) Calif. 1969. Govt. rels. rep. Arabian Am. Oil Co., Dhahran, Saudi Arabia, 1959-63; oil supply coord. Arabian Am. Oil Co., N.Y.C., 1963-68; sr. counsel Arabian Am. Oil Co., Dhahran, 1969-71, gen. mgr. govt. rels. orgn., 1971-74, v.p. indsl. rels., 1974-78; assoc. O'Melveny & Myers, L.A., 1968-69; ptnr. Burt & Taylor, Marblehead, Mass., 1978-80; pres., chief exec. officer nat. med. enterprises Internat. Group, L.A., 1980-82; counsel Chadbourne, Parke & Afridi, United Arab Emirates, 1982-84; ptnr. Sidley & Austin, Cairo, 1984-87, Singapore,

1987-93; spl. counsel Heller Ehrman White & McAuliffe, L.A. and Singapore, 1993-95; sr. counsel law divsn. Lucent Techs. Internat. Inc., Riyadh, Saudi Arabia, 1995—. Contbr. articles to profl. jours. Mem. ABA, Calif. Bar Assn., Order of Coif, Singapore Cricket Club, Tanglin Club, Chanqi Sailing Club, Singapore Am. Club, Dirab Golf Club. Home: Box 6942 Taos NM 87571 Office: AT&T Internat, PO Box 4945 al Mutlaq Bldg Sitteen St, Riyadh 11412, Saudi Arabia

TAYLOR, G. JEFFREY, geologist, geophysics educator; b. Port Jefferson, N.Y., June 27, 1944; married, 1965; 5 children. AB, Colgate U., 1966; MA, Rice U., 1968, PhD in Geology, 1970. Rsch. fellow lunar mineral & petroleum Smithsonian Rsch. Found., 1970-72, rsch. assoc., 1972-73; asst. prof. Washington U., 1973-76; sr. rsch. assoc. Inst. Meteoritics U. N.Mex., 1976-90; prof. geology Hawaii Inst. Geophysics & Planetology U. Hawaii, Menoa, 1990—; assoc. prof. Harvard U., 1970—; vis. scientist Lunar Sci. Inst., 1974-76. Mem. AAAS, Am. Geophysics Union, Geochem. Soc., Meteoritical Soc. Office: U Hawaii Manoa Inst Geophysics & Planetology 2525 Correa Rd Honolulu HI 96822*

TAYLOR, GARY L., federal judge; b. 1938. AB, UCLA, 1960, JD, 1963. Assoc. Wenke, Taylor, Evans & Ikola, 1965-86; judge Orange County Superior Ct., 1986-90, U.S. Dist. Ct. (ctrl. dist.) Calif., Santa Ana, 1990—. With U.S. Army, 1964-66. Mem. Am. Coll. Trial Lawyers, State Bar Calif., Orange County Bar Assn. (bd. dirs. 1980-82, founder, chmn. bus. litigation com., Disting. Svc. award 1983). *

TAYLOR, GARY LEE, marketing executive; b. Akron, Ohio, Mar. 28, 1953; s. Robert Eugene and Betty Jayne (Mayles) T.; m. Karen Sue Bates, Oct. 7, 1978; children: Lindsay Rose, Craig Scott. BBA in Mktg., U. Akron, 1975, MBA in Mktg., 1977. Media coordinator Rex Humbard Found., Akron, 1977-79, gen. mgr. advt., 1979-80, dir. mktg., 1980-82; pres., chief exec. officer InfoCision Mgmt. Corp., Akron, 1982—. Publisher newsletters TeleResponse and TeleFunding, 1992—; contbr. articles to Religious Broadcasting mag., Fundraising Mgmt. mag. Speaker, lectr. Nat. Religious Broadcasters Conv., TBT Convention, Am. Telemarketing Assn.; chmn. bd. Profl. Transp. Svcs., Inc., 1988—; bd. dirs. Sports Scis., Inc., 1992—; chmn. bd. dirs. Soltis Tangeman & Ptnrs., 1992—; mem. Rep. House Majority Trust, 1995—; mem. Christian Coalition Inner Circle, 1990—. Republican. Methodist. Avocations: golf, fishing. Office: InfoCision Mgmt Corp 325 Springside Dr Akron OH 44333-4505

TAYLOR, GENE, congressman; b. New Orleans, La., Sept. 17, 1953; m. Margaret Gordon; children: Sarah, Emily, Gary. BA, Tulane U.; grad., U. So. Miss. Sales rep. Stone Container Corp.; U.S. senator from Miss., dist. 46, 1984-89; mem. 101st-104th Congresses from 5th Miss. dist., 1989—; mem. govt. reform & oversight com., ranking minority mem. merchant marine. With USCGR. Mem. Lions, Rotary, Kappa Sigma. Roman Catholic. Office: US House of Reps 2447 Rayburn Washington DC 20002-1025*

TAYLOR, GEORGE ALLEN, advertising agency executive; b. Lake City, Iowa, Oct. 26, 1906; s. Bertrand Franklin and Mabel (Minard) T.; m. Regina Helen Wickland, July 3, 1938 (div. 1956). PhB in Fine Arts, Northwestern U., 1947, MEd, 1951, postgrad., 1951-54; art edn. diploma, U. No. Iowa, 1926. Art supr. pub. schs. Indianola, Iowa, 1926-29; instr. art Simpson Coll., Indianola, 1926-29; designer Modern Art Studios, Chgo., 1929-30; display designer W.J. Rankin Corp., Chgo., 1930-35; creative dir. Arthur Meyerhoff Assocs., Inc., Milw., 1935-38; br. mgr. Arthur Meyerhoff Assocs., Inc., L.A., 1938-42; account exec. Arthur Meyerhoff Assocs., Inc., Chgo., 1942-59, account supr., 1959-61, v.p. adminstrn., 1961-65, vice chmn., 1965-80; pres. GATA Ltd.; lectr. semantics Ill. Inst. Tech., Chgo., 1947-50, Northwestern U. Sch. Commerce, 1948. Lyricist popular songs. Reader Recs. for Blind, Inc., 1956-94, CRIS Radio, 1981-85; mem. Chgo. Architecture Found., Landmarks Preservation Coun. Ill. Recipient 1st place awards in copy and layout L.A. Advt. Club, 1940. Mem. AAAS, Friends of Downtown, Art Inst. Chgo. Home (summer): 1212 N Lake Shore Dr Apt 29a-s Chicago IL 60610-2371 Home (winter): 4767 Ocean Blvd Apt 201 San Diego CA 92109-2475

TAYLOR, GEORGE FREDERICK, newspaper publisher, editor; b. Portland, Oreg., Feb. 28, 1928; s. George Noble and Ida Louise (Dixon) T.; m. Georga Bray, Oct. 6, 1951; children—Amelia Ruth, Ross Noble. B.S., U. Oreg., 1950. Reporter Astoria (Oreg.) Budget, 1950-52, Portland Oregonian, 1952-54; copy reader Wall St. Jour., 1955-57, reporter, 1957-59, Detroit Bur. chief, 1959-64, Washington corr., 1964-68; asst. mng. editor Wall St. Jour., San Francisco, 1966-69; mng. editor Wall St. Jour., N.Y.C., 1970-77, exec. editor, 1977-86; pub. North Bend (Oreg.) News, 1986—, Prime Time, 1987—, Coquille Valley Sentinel, 1989—. Served to lt. USAF, 1955-57. Office: 1 Bartons Aly Coquille OR 97423-1270

TAYLOR, GEORGE KIMBROUGH, JR., lawyer; b. Atlanta, Aug. 28, 1939; s. George Kimbrough and Helen Whiteside (Shepard) T.; m. Carol Ann McKinney, July 1, 1961 (div. 1976); children: George Kimbrough III, Thomas Haynes; m. Triska Ashley Drake, Oct. 2, 1981. BA, Emory U., 1961; LLB, U. Va., 1964. Bar: Ga. 1964, U.S. Dist. Ct. (no. dist.) Ga. 1964, U.S. Ct. Appeals (11th cir.) 1964. Assoc. Kilpatrick & Cody, Atlanta, 1964-70, ptnr., 1970—; bd. dirs. Ont. Reins. Co. Ltd., Cayman Islands; pres., bd. dirs. Rugby Holdings, Inc., Atlanta, 1984-94, Norcros U.S.A., Inc., Atlanta, U.S. Properties, Inc., Atlanta, 1983-92. Chmn. bd. dirs. Spl. Audiences, Inc., Atlanta, 1985-87; bd. dirs. Atlanta Symphony Orch., 1986—, treas., 1995—; bd. dirs. Atlanta Opera, 1995—, Ga. Humanities Coun., Atlanta, 1986-93, Ga. Conservancy, 1979-85; bd. dirs. Ga. Coun. Internat. Visitors, Atlanta, 1987-94, pres., 1993; bd. dirs. Brit.-Am. Bus. Group, 1989—, pres., 1994; bd. visitors Emory U., Atlanta, 1993—; mem. exec. com. Brit.-Am. Bus. Coun., 1995—; mem. alumni coun. U. Va. Law Sch.; active Leadership Atlanta. Woodrow Wilson fellow, 1961. Mem. ABA, Internat. Bar Assn., Atlanta Bar Assn., Order of Coif, Soc. Internat. Bus. Fellows, Phi Beta Kappa, Omicron Delta Kappa. Democrat. Clubs: Capital City, World Trade (Atlanta). Avocations: sailing, skiing. Office: Kilpatrick & Cody 1100 Peachtree St NE Ste 2800 Atlanta GA 30309-4528

TAYLOR, GERALD H., communications company executive; b. 1941; married. BS in Physics, San Francisco State U. With MCI Telecom. Corp., 1969—, past pres. Mid-Atlantic and West divsns., MCI Airsignal, MCI Consumer Markets, now pres., COO; also pres., COO MCI Comm. Corp., 1994—, also bd. dirs. Office: MCI Telecommunications Corp 1133 19th St NW Washington DC 20036-3604 also: MCI Comm Corp 1801 Pennsylvania Ave NW Washington DC 20006*

TAYLOR, GLEN, professional sports team executive, printing and graphics company executive. State senator Minnesota Senate, 1980-90; pres. Taylor Corp., Mankato, Minn.; owner Minnesota Timberwolves, Minneapolis, Minn., 1994—. Office: Taylor Corp 1725 Roe Crest Dr Mankato MN 56003 Office: Minnesota Timberwolves Target Ctr 600 1st Ave N Minneapolis MN 55403-1400*

TAYLOR, GUY WATSON, symphonic conductor; b. Anniston, Ala., Dec. 25, 1919; s. Stokely Brackston and Ola Mae (Shaw) T.; m. Renee Lifton, Oct. 19, 1947; children: Eric Anthony, Ellen Jane. Diploma, Birmingham Conservatory of Music, 1941, Juilliard Sch. Music, 1948; pvt. studies and workshops with, Dimitri Mitropoulos, 1941-42, L'Ecole Monteux, 1949, Eugene Ormandy, 1953, George Szell, 1956. Conductor Springfield (Ohio) Symphony Orch., 1948-51, Nashville Symphony Orch., 1951-59, Phoenix Symphony Orch., 1959-69, Fresno Philharmonic Orch., 1969-84; guest conductor, U.S., Gt. Britain, Philippines, P.R., Can. and Mexico City; musical commentator Springfield News & Sun, 1948-51, Ariz. Republic, 1959-61, Fresno Bee, 1970-76. Has appeared on, BBC Radio, CBS-TV. Served with AUS, 1942-45. Recipient Conductor Recognition award Am. Symphony Orch. League, 1960, Alice M. Ditson Orch. award, 1961, citation for adventuresome programming of contemporary music ASCAP, 1977. Mem. Am. Symphony Orch. League, Phi Mu Alpha Sinfonia.

TAYLOR, HAROLD ALLEN, JR., industrial mineral marketing consultant; b. San Jose, Calif., June 27, 1936; s. Harold Allen and Marie Anna (Briody) T.; B.A., Brown U., 1958; M.A., U. Minn., 1968; m. Theresa Josephine Kustritz, Aug. 29, 1963; children: Harold A., III, Ruth F. Cook, Jonathan L.E. Project leader office Mineral Supply, U.S. Bur. Mines, Mpls., 1968-70, commodity specialist div. ferrous metals, Washington, 1970-74; commodity analyst U.S. Internat. Trade Commn., Washington, 1974-80; sr. commodity specialist br. indsl. minerals U.S. Bur. Mines, Washington, 1980-95; pres. Basic/Mines, Summit Point, W.Va., 1995—. Pres. Arlington (Va.) Interfaith Coun., 1994, 95. Mem. AIME (sec. 1983-84, first vice chmn. 1984-85, chmn. 1985-86, exec. adv. bd. mineral econs. subsect. 1981-83, 87-91), Am. Soc. Testing and Materials (chair subcom. nomenclature of com. on dimension stone 1987—, sec. com. dimension stone 1990-95), Soc. Govt. Economists (chmn. materials policy panels 1979-84), Toastmasters (pres. 1978, 81, 87, 91, asst. area gov. 1978-79, area gov. 1979-80, dep. div. lt. gov. 1989-90), Capitol Metals Forum (steering com. 1979-85), Sigma Gamma Epsilon. Contbr. articles to profl. jours. and encys. Address: PO Box 185 Summit Point WV 25446-0185

TAYLOR, HELEN LAVON HOLLINGSHED, association executive, early childhood consultant; b. Fort Valley, Ga., July 27, 1942; d. Earl Herman Hollingshed and Helen (Flowers) Southall; m. Robert Joseph Taylor, Sept. 11, 1965. BA, Howard U., 1964; MA, Cath. U., 1973; cert. mgmt., Tex. Tech. U., 1985, UCLA, 1991. Grad. asst. Howard U., Washington, 1964-65; social worker Nat. Child Day Care Assn., Washington, 1966-68, head start program dir., 1968-70, preschool project dir., 1971-78, exec. dir., chief exec. officer, 1979-83; mem. early childhood cons. various orgns., 1970—; founder, bd. dirs. Washington Child Devel. Coun., 1975—; mem. child care adv. com. Nat. Black Child Devel. Inst., Washington, 1988—; assoc. commr. Head Start Bur., DHHS, 1994—. Chairperson D.C. Coun. Adv. Com. on Child Care Facilities, Washington, 1974-78, Mayor's Adv. Com. for Early Childhood Devel., Washington, 1986—; chair pers. com. Bright Beginnings, Inc., Washington, 1991-92. Recipient Svc. award Adminstrn. for Children, Youth and Families, Washington, 1986, Svc. award Nat. Head Start Assn., Alexandria, Va., 1988, Cmty. Svc. award D.C. Dept. Consumer and Regulatory Affairs, Washington, 1990, Guardian award Nat. Black Child Devel. Inst., 1994, Martin Luther King Cmty. Svc. award, United Planning Orgn., 1994. Mem. Nat. Assn. for Edn. Young Children (conf. chairperson 1982, bd. mem. 1991—), Assn. for Childhood Edn. Internat. (publ. com. 1983-85), Washington (D.C.) Assn. for Edn. Young Children (co-chairperson 1978-80, Svc. award 1991), Delta Sigma Theta, Inc. (chair arts and letters com. 1984-86), Coalition of 100 Black Women). African Methodist Episcopal. Office: Nat Child Day Care Assn 1501 Benning Rd NE Washington DC 20002-4532

TAYLOR, HENRY ROTH, sales and marketing executive; b. Phila., Sept. 25, 1940; s. Henry and Helen Jacquelyn (Roth) T.; B.S., Millersville State Coll., 1962; postgrad., Pa. State U., 1963-65; MS, Temple U., 1966; postgrad., Queens Coll., Oxford U., summer 1973; m. Cynthia Mary DeMarco, Aug. 17, 1968; children: Christopher, Peter, Brett, Melissa. Mng. editor Montgomery Newspapers, Ft. Washington, Pa., 1962-66; news bur. dir. Drexel U., Phila., 1966-68, ann. fund dir., 1971-72; dir. pub. relations Ursinus Coll., Collegeville, Pa., 1968-71, Widener U., Chester, Pa., 1972-74; asst. v.p., dir. athletics Spring Garden Coll., Phila., 1974-87, lectr. mass media, 1979-87; exec. dir. Phila. sect. Profl. Golfers Assn., 1987-89; dir. Athletics, chmn. physical edn. Phila. Coll. Textiles and Sci., 1989-92; v.p. sales and pub. rels. Fleer/Sky Box Internat. Corp., Mt. Laurel, N.J., 1992—; mem. exec. com. Eastern Pa. Athletic Conf., 1982-86; pres. Eastern States Athletic Conf., 1985-87; part-time sportscaster, talk show host, announcer Sta. WIFI, Phila., 1965-70; with Ted Taylor Assocs., Abington, Pa., part-time 1965-74; part-time sportscaster and announcer WIBF Radio, Jenkintown, Pa., 1970-74, Sta. WNPV, Lansdale, Pa., 1983-88; host collectibles syndicated radio show, Sports By-Line USA, 1992—. Founding pres. Glenside Boys Athletic Club, 1958-63; commr. Keystone State Football Conf., 1959-62; dir. Pop Warner Found., 1963-65; pres. Warminster Youth 963-65; pres. Warminster Youth Activities Orgn., 1965-71; mem. Abington Twp. Spl. Police, 1974-81, sec., 1977-78; exec. com. Highland Sch. PTA, 1974-81; mem. Abington Twp. Police Rev. Bd., 1977-81; co-chmn. Phila. Baseball Card and Sports Memorabilia Shows, 1975-82, Ocean City (N.J.) Shows, 1981-84, North Penn. Shows, 1991-92. Named Man of Yr., Hatboro Jr. C. of C., 1962, Suburban Bucks Jr. C. of C., 1967, Citizen of Yr., Southampton Kiwanis, 1972, One of 100 Outstanding Grads. in 100 Yrs., Cheltenham (Pa.) High Sch., 1984; recipient Ursinus Coll. Varsity Club award, 1970; Piece of the Walk civic award Ocean City, N.J., 1981. Mem. Council for Advancement and Support of Edn., Pa. Assn. Colls. and Univs., Phila. Pub. Relations Assn., Pub. Relations Soc. Am., Suburban Pub. Relations Club, Phila. Sportswriters Assn., Coll. Sports Info. Dirs. Am., Eastern Pa. Sports Collectors Club (pres. 1978-82). Republican. Presbyterian. Lodge: Rotary. Author: (with Robert E. Schmierer) Phillies Cheklist Book, 1979, World Series Baseball Cards, 1987, The Rookie Book, 1988, 300 All-Time Baseball Stars, 1988, Encyclopedia of Baseball Cards, 1988, Sports Card Explosion, 1993; assoc. editor Sports Collectors Bible, 1978; columnist Sports Collectors Digest, 1980-92, Phila. Daily News, 1991—; contbr. articles to profl. jours. Home: 1527 Edgehill Rd Abington PA 19001-2609 Office: Fleer/Sky Box Internat Exec Plz 1120 Route 73 Mount Laurel NJ 08054-5112

TAYLOR, HENRY SPLAWN, literature educator, poet, writer; b. Loudoun County, Va., June 21, 1942; s. Thomas Edward and Mary Marshall (Splawn) T.; m. Sarah Spencer Bean, June 12, 1965 (div. 1967); m. Frances Ferguson Carney, June 29, 1968 (div. 1995); children: Thomas Edward, Richard Carney; m. Sarah Spencer, June 11, 1995. BA, U. Va., 1965; MA, Hollins (Va.) Coll., 1966. Instr. English Roanoke (Va.) Coll., 1966-68; asst. prof. U. Utah, 1968-71; mem. faculty Am. U., Washington, 1971—, prof. lit., 1976—, co-dir. M.F.A. program in creative writing, 1982—, dir. Am. studies program, 1983-84; dir. U. Utah Writers' Conf., 1970-72; writer-in-residence Hollins Coll., spring 1978; poet-in-residence Wichita State U., 1994. Author: (poems) The Horse Show at Midnight, 1966, Breakings, 1971, An Afternoon of Pocket Billiards, 1975, Desperado, 1979, The Flying Change, 1985 (Pulitzer prize 1986), (essays) Compulsory Figures: Essays on Recent American Poets, 1992, (textbooks) Poetry: Points of Departure, 1974, The Water of Light: A Miscellany in Honor of Brewster Ghiselin, 1976, (cassette album) Landscape with Tractor, 1985, co-translator: The Children of Herakles, 1981, (poems) Understanding Fiction: Poems 1986-96, 1996; contbg. editor: Hollins Critic, 1971-78; editorial cons.: Magill's Literary Ann, 1972-90; cons. editor: Poet Lore, 1977-84; translator: The Weevil, 1995. Fellow creative writing Nat. Endowment Arts, 1978, 86; grantee Nat. Endowment Humanities, 1980-81. Mem. Agrl. History Soc., Am. Lit. Translators Assn. Democrat. Quaker. Home: PO Box 23 Lincoln VA 22078-0023 Office: Am U Dept Lit Washington DC 20016

TAYLOR, HOWARD FRANCIS, sociology educator, researcher, consultant; b. Cleveland, Ohio, July 7, 1939; s. Arthur Leo and Murtis (Howard) T.; m. Patricia Epps, Aug. 10, 1963; 1 dau., Carla Yvonne. A.B., Hiram Coll., 1961; M.A., Yale U., 1964, Ph.D., 1966. Asst. prof., research assoc. Ill. Inst. Tech., 1965-68; assoc. prof. Syracuse U., 1968-73; prof. sociology Princeton U., 1973—; cons. in field. Author: Balance in Small Groups, 1970, The IQ Game, 1980; also numerous articles, chpts. in profl. publs.; adv. editor Am. Social Rev., 1975-84, Social Psychology Quar., 1980—, Sociol. Methods and Rsch., 1980—, Nat. Jour. Sociology, 1985—. Trustee Hiram Coll., 1981—, Princeton Day Sch., 1987—; bd. dirs. Nat. Civil Rights Mus. Hall of Fame, 1985—. Grantee Maurice Falk Med. Fund, 1979, Cornerhouse Fund, 1981—, NIMH, 1982, GRE Bd., 1985—, Ford Found., 1989—. Fellow Sociol. Research Assn.; mem. Am. Sociol. Assn., Eastern Sociol. Assn. (v.p. 1986-87), AAUP, Garfield Soc. of Hiram Coll., Assn. Black Sociologists, NAACP Legal Def. Fund, Phi Beta Kappa. Democrat. Episcopalian. Office: Princeton U Dept Sociology Green Hall Princeton NJ 08544

TAYLOR, HUGH PETTINGILL, JR., geologist, educator; b. Holbrook, Ariz., Dec. 27, 1932; s. Hugh Pettingill and Genevieve (Fillerup) T.; m. Candis E. Hoffman, 1982. B.S., Calif. Inst. Tech., 1954; A.M., Harvard U., 1955; Ph.D., Calif. Inst. Tech., 1959. Asst. prof. geochemistry Pa. State U., 1960-62; mem. faculty div. geol. and planetary scis. Calif. Inst. Tech., 1962—, now prof. geology, Robert P. Sharp prof., 1981; Crosby vis. prof. M.I.T., 1978; vis. prof. Stanford U., 1981; William Smith lectr. Geol. Soc. London, 1976; Hofmann lectr. Harvard U., 1980; Cloos lectr. Johns Hopkins U., 1986; with U.S. Geol. Survey, Saudi Arabia, 1980-81. Author: The Oxygen Isotope Geochemistry of Igneous Rocks, 1968, Stable Isotopes in High Temperature Geological Processes, 1986, Stable Isotope Geochemistry, 1991; assoc. editor Bull. Geol. Soc. Am, 1969-71, Geochimica Cosmochimica Acta, 1971-76; editor Chem. Geology, 1985-91. Recipient Day medal Geol. Soc. Am., Urey medal European Assn. Geochem., 1995. Fellow NAS, Soc. Econ. Geol., Geol. Soc. Am., Am. Geophys. Union, Mineral. Soc. Am. (councillor), Am. Acad. Arts and Scis.; mem. Geochem. Soc. (councillor). Republican.

TAYLOR, HUMPHREY JOHN FAUSITT, information services executive; b. Meshed, Iran, Sept. 6, 1934; came to U.S., 1976; s. Geoffrey Fausitt and Frances Margaret (Kenyon) T.; m. Penelope Helen Taylor, Dec. 19, 1970; children: Zanthe, Helena. BA with honors, Cambridge (Eng.) U., 1958. Dist. officer Govt. of Tanganyika, 1959-62; mktg. and opinion researcher Nat. Opinion Poll, Eng., 1963-66; mng. dir. Opinion Rsch. Ctr., Eng., 1966-76; with Louis Harris and Assocs., N.Y.C., 1976-81; pres. Harris and Assocs., N.Y.C., 1981—, CEO, 1992—. Trustee U.S. com. UNICEF, N.Y.C., 1981-87, Overseas Devel. Coun., Washington, 1987—, Am. Health Found., 1988-91, chmn.; trustee Royal Soc. Medicine Found., 1992—. 2d lt. Brit. Army, 1953-55. Avocations: history, biographies, skiing, tennis, traveling. Address: Louis Harris & Assoc 111 5th Ave FL 8 New York NY 10003-1005

TAYLOR, JACK C., rental, leasing company executive; b. 1922. With Lindburg Cadillac, St. Louis, 1944-50, Forrest Cadillac, St. Louis, 1951-56; chmn. bd. Enterprise Rent-A-Car, St. Louis, 1980—. With USN, ret. Office: Enterprise Rent-A-Car 600 Corporate Park Dr Saint Louis MO 63105*

TAYLOR, JACK G., JR., art director. Art dir.: (films) Nine to Five, 1980, Looker, 1981, Uncommon Valor, 1983, Nightmares, 1983, Star 80, 1983, Real Genius, 1985, Gung Ho, 1986, Cape Fear, 1992, A Perfect World, 1993; prodn. designer: (films) Million Dollar Mystery, 1987. Office: care Art Directors Guild 11365 Ventura Blvd Ste 315 Studio City CA 91604-3148

TAYLOR, JACQUELINE SELF, state legislator; b. Thomas, Okla., Feb. 16, 1935; d. MArtin Richard and Bertha Inez (Murray) Self; m. Nelson Edwin Taylor, May 17, 1952; children: Lucinda Susan Shannon, Robin Melinda. BA in Social Work, Boise State U., 1971. Lic. social worker Idaho. Dir. vol. svcs. Idaho Dept. of Health & Welfare, Caldwell, 1971-77; dir. Clatsop County Assn. REtarded Citizens, Astoria, Oreg., 1980-81; ptnr., owner Johnson Drug Store, Warrenton, Oreg., 1984-92; state rep. Legis. Assembly State of Oreg., 1991-93. Bd. dirs. Pioneer House, Warrenton, 1992, Astoria C. of C., 1988-91, treas., 1988-91; civil svc. com. City of Astoria, 1988-91; mem. North Coast Women's Polit. Caucus, 1988 (named Outstanding Woman 1988), Oreg. Women's Polit. Caucus. Democrat. Avocations: gardening, history, tribal work. Home: 1324 Miller Ln Astoria OR 97103-3947 Office: Oreg State Legis State Capitol Salem OR 97310

TAYLOR, JAMES, JR., lawyer; b. Florence, S.C., Dec. 6, 1942; s. James and Thelma (Baker) T.; m. Jayne S.C. Bridge, May 19, 1974; children: James Robson, Ashley Baker. BA cum laude, U. of the South, 1965; JD, Georgetown U., 1973. Bar: D.C. 1973, U.S. Ct. Internat. Trade 1977, U.S. Ct. Appeals (fed. cir.) 1982, U.S. Supreme Ct. 1978. Assoc. Busby Rivkin Sherman Levy and Rehm, Washington, 1973-76, Busby and Rehm, Washington, 1977-78; ptnr. Busby Rehm and Leonard, Washington, 1979-87, Dorsey & Whitney, Washington, 1988-92, Stroock & Stroock & Lavan, Washington, 1992-95, Abondi, Foster, Sobin & Davidow, P.C., Washington, 1996—. Lt. USN, 1967-70; Vietnam. Mem. ABA, D.C. Bar Assn., Club Interallié (Paris). Episcopalian. Avocations: skiing, fishing, languages. Home: 3319 Cleveland Ave NW Washington DC 20008-3456 Office: Abondi Foster Sobin Davidow Ste 500 1130 Connecticut Ave NW Washington DC 20036

TAYLOR, JAMES BLACKSTONE, aviation company executive; b. N.Y.C., Dec. 14, 1921; s. James Blackstone Taylor, Jr. and Aileen (Sedgwick) Taylor Lippincott; m. Margaret Krout, May 3, 1947; children—James Blackstone IV, Ray K., Jane A., W. Thorne. Grad., Taft sch., Watertown, Conn. Pres. Upressitmetal Cap Corp., N.Y.C., 1948-59; v.p. Am. Flange, N.Y.C., 1959-62, Pan Am. World Airways, N.Y.C., 1962-69, Cessna Aircraft, Wichita, Kans., 1969-76; pres., CEO Canadair, Inc., Westport, Conn., 1976-85; pres., chief exec. officer, dir. Gates Learjet Corp., Tucson, 1985-88; pres. James B. Taylor Assoc., Westport, Conn., 1988—. Served to lt. naval aviator USNR, 1942-46. Named Runner Up World Skeet Shooting Championship, 1962, 83; recipient Meritorious Svc. to Aviator award NBAA, 1992, Elder Statesman of Aviation award, 1992; named Man of Yr. Gathering of Eagles, 1984. Mem. Nat. Aviation Club, Wings Club (v.p., bd. dirs. 1965-67, 83-87), Country Club of Fairfield, Weston Gun Club, Nat. Aviation Assn. (bd. dirs.), Assn Naval Aviation, USS Yorktown Assn. and Found. Republican. Episcopalian. Home: 32 Regents Park Westport CT 06880-5533

TAYLOR, JAMES DAVID, health care executive; b. Pitts., Oct. 3, 1947; s. Howard Alvin and Florence Elizabeth (Dale) T.; m. Helen Blair, Apr. 14, 1973; children: Megan, Brian. BA, Westminster Coll., 1969; MBA, Duquesne U., 1972; MPH, U. Pitts., 1974. Fin. trainee Gen. Electric Co., Erie, Pa., 1969-70; adminstrv. trainee Presbyn. U. Hosp., Pitts., 1972; adminstrv. resident Montefiore Hosp., Pitts., 1973-74; mgr. Geisinger Med. Ctr., Danville, Pa., 1974-76, adminstrv. officer, 1976-78; asst. adminstr. Scott & White, Temple, Tex., 1978-81; dir. Scott & White co., Temple, Tex., 1982-91; prin. Inova, Temple, Tex., 1991-93; exec. dir. Christie Clinic Assn., Champaign, Ill., 1993—; chmn. of bd. Personal Care Health Mgmt. Inc., 1993—; fellowship preceptor Scott & White, Temple, Tex., 1985—; chmn. Joint Am. Coll. of Health Care Execs. and Med. Group Mgmt. Nat. Com., Chgo. and Denver, 1986-87; bd. dirs. Personal Care HMO and Covenant Med. Ctr. Contbr. articles to profl. jours. Bd. dirs. Columbia-Montour Home Health, Bloomburg, Pa., 1976-78; chmn. Grace Sch., Temple, 1980-86; elder Grace Presbyn. Ch., Temple, 1985-87. Recipient Third Place Nat. award Health Industry Mfg. Assn., 1975. Fellow Am. Coll. Healthcare Execs., Am. Coll. Med. Group Adminstrs.; mem. Med. Group Mgmt. Assn. (chmn. joint Am. Coll. Healthcare Execs. nat. com. 1986-87), Beta Gamma Sigma, Omicron Delta Epsilon. Republican. Avocations: golfing, running, coin collecting. Home: 2003 O Donnell Dr Champaign IL 61821-6466 Office: Christie Clinic Assos 101 W University Ave Champaign IL 61820-3909

TAYLOR, J(AMES) HERBERT, cell biology educator; b. Corsicana, Tex., Jan. 14, 1916; s. Charles Aaron and Delia May (McCain) T.; m. Shirley Catherine Hoover, May 1, 1946; children: Lynne Sue, Lucy Delia, Michael Wesley. B.S., So. Okla. State U., 1939; M.S., U. Okla., 1941; Ph.D., U. Va., 1944. Asst. prof. bacteriology and botany U. Okla., Norman, 1946-47; assoc. prof. botany U. Tenn., Knoxville, 1948-51; asst. prof. botany Columbia U., N.Y.C., 1951-54; assoc. prof. Columbia U., 1954-58, prof. cell biology, 1958-64; prof. biol. sci. Fla. State U., Tallahassee, 1964-83, Robert O. Lawton disting. prof. biol. sci., 1983-90, prof. emeritus, 1990—; assoc. dir. Inst. Molecular Biophysics, Fla. State U., 1970-79; dir. Inst. Molecular Biophysics, 1980-85; cons. Oak Ridge Nat. Lab., 1949-51; research collaborator Brookhaven Nat. Lab., 1951-58; nat. lectr. Sigma Xi Research Soc. Author: Molecular Genetics, Vol. 1, 1963, Vol. 2, 1965, Vol. 3, 1979; DNA Methylation and Cellular Differentiation, 1983; also papers on molecular genetics; contbr. over 100 articles in field to profl. jours. Pres. Unitarian Ch. Tallahassee, 1968-70. Served with M.C. U.S. Army, 1944-46, PTO. Recipient Meritorious Research award Mich. State U., 1960; Guggenheim fellow Calif. Inst. Tech., 1958-59. Mem. Nat. Acad. Scis., AAAS, Am. Inst. Biol. Sci., Am. Soc. Cell Biologists (pres. 1969-70), Biophysics Soc., Genetics Soc. Am. Democrat. Office: Fla State U Inst Molecular Biophysics Tallahassee FL 32306

TAYLOR, JAMES JOHN, academic adminstrator; b. Mpls., July 26, 1940; s. James John and Mary Elizabeth (Mason) T.; m. Margaret Claire Zacha, Dec. 28, 1976; children: Jerry William, John Allen. BA, Oblate Coll. of S.W., 1966; MEd, St. Louis U., 1969, MBA in Fin., 1972; cert. of advanced studies, Harvard U., 1977. Dept. head, tchr. Althoff High Sch., Belleville, Ill., 1966-71; asst. to controller U. of South Fla., Tampa, 1972-79; project mgr. W.Va. Bd. of Regents, Morgantown, 1979-83; prin., project dir. Am. Mgmt. Systems, Arlington, Va., 1983-90; mng. cons. Taylor Mgmt. Group, Arlington, 1990-91; v.p. bus. and finance Guam Community Coll., 1991—; founder, treas. Guam Eldl. Radio Found., KPRG-FM. Member adv. com. on spl. edn. Arlington Sch. Bd., 1981-83; founder, producer St. Louis High

Sch. Film Makers Festival, 1968-72; contbr. articles to profl. jours. Founding mem. Harvard Club at Nat. Press Club; mem. Phi Delta Kappa. Avocations: photography, duplicate bridge, scuba diving. Home: Cruz Heights #29 Talofofo GU 96930

TAYLOR, JAMES VERNON, musician; b. Boston, Mar. 12, 1948; s. Isaac M. and Gertrude (Woodard) T.; children: Sarah Maria, Benjamin Simon. Student, Milton Acad., Mass., 1962-66, Arlington Sch., Belmont, Mass., 1966-67. Recorded for Apple Records, 1968, Warner Bros. Records, 1970-77, CBS Records, 1977; numerous concert appearances; composer, performer: (albums) Sweet Baby James, 1970, Mud Slide Slim and The Blue Horizon, 1971, One Man Dog, 1972, Walking Man, 1974, Gorilla, 1975, In the Pocket, 1976, James Taylor's Greatest Hits, 1977, J.T., 1977, Flag, 1979, Dad Loves His Work, 1981, That's Why I'm Here, 1985, Never Die Young, 1986, New Moon Shine, 1991, James Taylor (Live), 1993. Recipient 13 Gold Album awards, 4 Platinum Album awards, 3 Gold Single awards, Grammay award; named Best Pop Vocal Male, 1971, 77. Office: care Peter Asher Mgmt 644 N Doheny Dr West Hollywood CA 90069-5526

TAYLOR, JAMES WALTER, marketing educator; b. St. Cloud, Minn., Feb. 15, 1933; s. James T. and Nina C. Taylor; m. Joanne Syktte, Feb. 3, 1956; children: Theodore James, Samuel Bennett, Christopher John. BBA, U. Minn., 1957; MBA, NYU, 1960; DBA, U. So. Calif., 1975. Mgr. research div. Atlantic Refining, Phila., 1960-65; dir. new product devel. Hunt-Wesson Foods, Fullerton, Calif., 1965-72; prof. mktg. Calif. State U., Fullerton, 1972-95; mng. dir. Innovative Mgmt. Devel. Co., Laguna Beach, Calif., 1995—; cons. Smithkline Beecham Corp., Tokyo, Govt. of Portugal, Lisbon, Austrade, Govt. of Australia, Hagenfeldt-Affarerna AB, Stockholm. Author: Profitable New Product Strategies, 1984, How to Create a Winning Business Plan, 1986, Competitive Marketing Strategies, 1986, The 101 Best Performing Companies in America, 1987, The Complete Manual for Developing Winning Strategic Plans, 1988, Every Manager's Survival Guide, 1989, Developing Winning Strategic Plans, 1990, How to Develop Successful Advertising Plans, 1993, The Complete Manual for Marketing Strategy & Planning, 1996. Fulbright scholar Ministry of Industry, Lisbon, Portugal, 1986-87, U. We. Sydney, Australia, 1989-90; recipient Merit award Calif. State U., 1986-90. Mem. The Planning Forum, Am. Mktg. Assn., Strategic Mgmt. Assn., Assn. for Consumer Rsch., Acad. Mktg. Sci. Home: 3190 Mountain View Dr Laguna Beach CA 92651-2056

TAYLOR, JANELLE DIANE WILLIAMS, writer; b. Athens, Ga., June 28, 1944; d. Alton L. and Frances (Davis) Williams; m. Michael H. Taylor, Apr. 8, 1965; children: Angela Michelle, Alisha Melanie. Student, Augusta Coll., 1980-81. Orthodontic nurse Dr. W.H. Williams, Athens, 1962-65, Dr. James Metts, Augusta, Ga., 1969-72, Dr. Jack Carter, Augusta, 1973; med. research technologist Med. Coll. Ga., Augusta, 1975-77; writer Ga., 1977—; bd. dirs. Jo Beth Williams Romance Screenplay Award; lectr. writing Augusta Coll., other schs. and workshops, 1982—. Author: Savage Ecstasy, 1981, Valley of Fire, 1984, First Love, Wild Love, 1984 (Maggie awd. 1984), Golden Torment, 1984 (Reviewer's Choic awd. Romantic Times 1984), Savage Conquest, 1985, Stolen Ecstasy, 1985, Moondust and Madness, 1986, Sweet, Savage Heart, 1986 (Golden Pen cert. 1986), Destiny's Temptress, Defiant Ecstasy, 1982, Forbidden Ecstasy, 1982, Brazen Ecstasy, 1983, Tender Ecstasy, 1983, Love Me With Fury, 1983, Bittersweet Ectasy, 1987, Wild Is My Love, 1987, Fortune's Flames, 1988, Passions Wild and Free, 1988, Wild Sweet Promise, 1989, Kiss of the Night Wind, 1989, Whispered Kisses, 1990, Follow the Wind, 1990 (Romantic Times Revievers Choice award 1990-91), Forever Ecstacy, 1991, Promise Me Forever, 1991, Christmas Rendezvous, 1991, Sharing Christmas, 1991, Stardust and Shadows, 1992, Midnight Secrets, 1992, Taking Chances, 1993, Janelle Taylor Three Complete Novels, 1993, The Last Viking Queen, 1994, Chase The Wind, 1994, Starlight And Splendor, 1994, The New Janelle Taylor Three Novel Collection, 1994, Destiny Mine, 1995, Anything for Love, 1995, Moonbeams and Magic, 1995; contbr. How to Write a Romance and Get It Published, 1983, 2d edit., 1984, Candlelight, Romance and You, 1983, My First Real Romance, 1985, Booksellers' Cookbook, 1988. Recipient trophy award for Indian series Romantic Times, 1985, Sioux Sacred Medicine Wheel and Cheyenne Red-tail Hawk Feather Coup hon. Gray Eagle Siouc Indian series, 1983-84; cert. Vocat. Indsl. Clubs Am., 1986, cert. of merit AAUW, 1986, Bronze Pen award, 1988, Silver Pen award, 1989; named to Writers' Hall of Fame, Romantic Times, 1988, Cowboy Hall of Fame; named hon. flying col. Delta Airlines, 1987. Mem. Romance Writers Am., Novelists Inc., Western Writers Am., Ga. Romance Writers Am., Aughors League/ Authors Guild, Ga. Writers Coalition for Literacy, Augusta Author's Club. Republican. Baptist. Avocations: collecting spoons and coins, swimming, fishing, genealogy, English, Indian and American history. Office: PO Box 211646 Augusta GA 30917-1646

TAYLOR, JANET WINONA MILLS, secondary school educator; b. Shelby, N.C., Aug. 3, 1948; d. Robert Lee Sr. and Janet Elizabeth (Plair) Mills; m. Bernard D. Taylor, Dec. 31, 1983; 1 child, Adam Jason. BS in Health Edn., Morgan State Coll., 1974; MS in Ednl. Leadership, Morgan State U., 1986, EdD in Ednl. Adminstrn., 1994. Md. State Dept. Edn. Advanced Profl. cert. for supt., supr., secondary prin., health and gen. sci. tchr. grades 5-12. Tchr. Baltimore (Md.) City Pub. Schs., 1973-78; health educator Morgan State Coll., Balt., 1978-79; tchr. Montgomery County Pub. Schs., Rockville, 1979—; tech. writer, cons. The Assignment Group, Rockville, Md., 1990—; rsch. cons., rsch. assoc. Inst. for Urban Rsch., Morgan State U., 1992-93; libr. adv. bd. mem. Morgan State U., Balt., 1993—; grant cons. United Missionary Bapt., Inc., Balt., 1993—; GED test adminstr. Md. State Dept. Edn., Balt., 1993-94; co-dir. for grants and proposals United Missionary Bapt. Devel. Corp. Md., Balt., 1993—; mem. selection and evaluation adv. com. Montgomery County Pub. Schs., Rockville, 1993—. Editor (monthly jour.) The Doorkeeper, 1987-88. Dir. youth ministry Mt. Hebron Bapt. Ch., Balt., 1990-94; co-dir. children's ministry Bapt. Congress Christian Edn., Balt., 1992-94; corr. sec. Bapt. Congress Christian Edn., Balt., 1993—. Sgt. USAR, 1975-80. Mem. AERA, Zeta Phi Beta. Baptist. Avocations: reading, traveling, playing computer games and chess. Home: 1822 Wadsworth Way Baltimore MD 21239-3109

TAYLOR, JANICE LARUE, elementary education educator; b. Salina, Utah, Nov. 15, 1946; d. Wallace Gustave and Arnelda (Murphy) Poulson; m. Roger Eldon Elkins, Aug. 26, 1967 (wid. Feb. 1990); children: Bobbi Jan, Becki LaRue, Brendi Mae, Wesly Eldon; m. Richard Don Taylor, Jan. 2, 1992; stepchildren: Jared, Renerah. BS, Brigham Young U., 1990; MA, U. Phoenix, 1993. ESL aide Plano (Tex.) Ind. Sch. Dist., 1983-87; tchr. second grade Alpine Sch. dist., Orem, Utah, 1989-90; tchr. sixth grade Provo (Utah) Sch. Dist., 1990—; arts specialist Maeser Elem., Provo, 1992—; profl. devel. com. Bonniville Uniserve, Provo, 1994; K-12 curriculum com. Provo Sch. Dist., 1994; P.E.A. rep. Provo Edn. Assn., 1994—. Co-author: Student Organizer, 1993-94. Artists-in-residence grantee Utah Arts Coun., Provo, 1994-95; career edn. grantee Provo Sch. dist., 1994-95. Mem. NEA, Utah Edn. Assn., Provo C. of C. (mem. bus. and edn. partnership com. 1994). Avocations: running, bicycling, cross country skiing, collecting children's lit. Home: 1928 N 230 E Orem UT 84057-2255 Office: Maeser Elem 1505 500 E Provo UT 84606

TAYLOR, JIMMIE WILKES, naval officer; b. Nashville, Apr. 16, 1934; s. James Wilkie and Mary Elizabeth (Steagall) T.; m. Annette Lee, June 20, 1958; children: Jimmie W. II, Todd L. (dec.), Tracey E. Taylor. Student, U. Tenn., 1952-54, Mid. Tenn. State U., 1954-56; BA in Geography, San Diego State U., 1979. Commd. ensign USNR, 1958; augmented in USN, 1965, advanced through grades to rear adm., 1987, various assignments, 1958-65; air launch missile officer USS Constellation, 1965-67; asst. ops. officer Fighter Squadron 124, 1967-68; ops. officer Fighter Squadron 51, 1968-70; squadron ops. officer Fighter Squadron 124, 1970-74; exec. officer Fighter Squadron 2, 1974-75, comdg. officer, 1975-76; officer in charge, comdr. Navy Blue Force Air Test and Evaluation Squadron 4, 1976-77; detailed to Naval Adminstrv. Command, Naval Tng. Ctr., San Diego, 1977-79; ops. officer USS Coral Sea, 1979-81; chief of staff Comdr. Fighter Airborne Early Warning Wing, Pacific, 1981-82; comdr. Tng. Air Wing 2, 1982-84; head aviation plans and program div. Office of Chief of Naval Ops., 1984-85; vice chief naval edn. and tng., 1985-88, chief naval air tng., 1988-91; v.p. armed svcs. Pensacola (Fla.) Area C. of C. Contbr. articles to profl. jours. Bd. dirs. USO, Corpus Christi, Tex., 1988-91; pres. Tex. aux. Navy-Marine Corps Relief Soc., Corpus Christi, 1988-91. Decorated Legion of Merit with two gold star, Meritorious Svc. Medal, Air medal with7, Navy Expeditionary Medal, Nat. Def. Svc. Medal, Armed Forces Expeditionary Medal, Vietnam Svc. Medal with Silver Star; Gallantry Cross Color (Republic of Vietnam); recipient Topcat award USN/Grumman Aerospace Corp., 1973. Mem. Assn. Naval Aviation Inc. (life), Naval Aviation Mus. Found. (life), Navy Tailhook Assn. (life), Corpus Christi C. of C. (bd. dirs. 1989-91), Corpus Christi Yacht Club, Kappa Sigma, Pensacola Sports Assn. Avocations: racquetball, golf, skiing, hunting, fishing. Home: 6064 Forest Green Rd Pensacola FL 32505-1850 Office: Burdeshaw Assocs Ltd 4701 Sangamore Rd Bethesda MD 20816-2508 also: 117 W Garden St PO Box 550 Pensacola FL 32505

TAYLOR, JOB, III, lawyer; b. N.Y.C., Feb. 18, 1942; s. Job II and Anne Harrison (Flinchbaugh) T.; m. Mary C. August, Oct. 24, 1964 (div. 1978); children: Whitney August, Job IV; m. Sally Lawson, May 31, 1980; 1 child, Alexandra Anne. BA, Washington & Jefferson Coll., 1964; JD, Coll. William and Mary, 1971. Bar: N.Y. 1972, U.S. Dist. Ct. (ea. and no. dists.) N.Y. 1973, U.S. Ct. Appeals (2d cir.) 1973, U.S. Ct. Claims 1974, U.S. Tax Ct. 1974, U.S. Supreme Ct. 1975, U.S. Ct. Appeals (9th cir.) 1976, U.S. Ct. Mil. Appeals 1977, U.S. Ct. Appeals (D.C. and 10th cirs.) 1977, D.C. 1981, U.S. Ct. Internat. Trade 1981, U.S. Ct. Appeals (fed. cir.) 1982, U.S. Dist. Ct. (no. dist.) Calif. 1983, U.S. Ct. Appeals (6th cir.) 1987, U.S. Ct. Appeals (3d cir.) 1990. Ptnr. Olwine, Connelly, Chase, O'Donnell & Weyher, N.Y.C., 1971-85, Latham & Watkins, N.Y.C., 1985—. Served to lt. USN, 1964-68. Mem. ABA, Assn. Bar City N.Y., La Confrerie des Chevaliers du Tastevin, Racquet and Tennis Club, Wee Burn Country Club (Darien, Conn.), New Canaan Country Club.. Republican. Episcopalian. Avocations: squash, tennis, golf, reading. Office: Latham & Watkins 885 3rd Ave New York NY 10022-4834

TAYLOR, J(OCELYN) MARY, museum administrator, zoologist, educator; b. Portland, Oreg., May 30, 1931; d. Arnold Llewellyn and Kathleen Mary (Yorke) T.; m. Joseph William Kamp, Mar. 18, 1972 (dec.). B.A., Smith Coll., 1952; M.A., U. Calif., Berkeley, 1953, Ph.D., 1959. Instr. zoology Wellesley Coll., 1959-61, asst. prof. zoology, 1961-65; assoc. prof. zoology U. B.C., 1965-74; dir. Cowan Vertebrate Mus., 1965-82, prof. dept. zoology, 1974-82; collaborative scientist Oreg. Regional Primate Research Ctr., 1983-87; prof. (courtesy) dept. fisheries and wildlife Oreg. State U., 1984—; dir. Cleve. Mus. Nat. History, 1987—; adj. prof. dept. biology Case Western Res. U., 1987—. Assoc. editor Jour. Mammalogy, 1981-82. Contbr. numerous articles to sci. jours. Trustee Benjamin Rose Inst., 1988-93, Western Res. Acad., 1989-94, U. Circle, Inc., 1987—, The Cleve. Aquarium, 1990-93, Cleve. Access to the Arts, 1992—; corp. bd. Holden Arboretum, 1988—. Fulbright scholar, 1954-55; Lalor Found. grantee, 1962-63; NSF grantee, 1963-71; NRC Can. grantee, 1966-84; Killam Sr. Research fellow, 1978-79. Mem. Soc. Women Geographers, Am. Soc. Mammalogists (1st v.p. 1978-82, pres. 1982-84, Hartley T. Jackson award 1993, Lake County environ. award 1996), Australian Mammal Soc., Cooper Ornithol., Assn. Sci. Mus. Dirs. (v.p. 1990-93), Rodent Specialist Group of Species Survival Commn. (chmn. 1989-93), Sigma Xi. Episcopalian. Office: Cleve Mus Natural History 1 Wade Oval Dr Cleveland OH 44106-1701

TAYLOR, JOE CLINTON, judge; b. Durant, Okla., Mar. 28, 1942; s. Luther Clinton and Virena (Parker) T.; m. Margaret Pearl Byers, June 8, 1963; children: Marna Joanne, Leah Alison, Jocelyn Camille. Student, Southeastern State Coll., 1960-62; B.A., Okla. State U., 1965; J.D., U. Okla., 1968. Bar: Okla. 1968. Practice law Norman, Okla., 1968-69; apptd. spl. dist. judge Durant, 1969-72; asso. dist. judge Bryan County, Okla., 1972-76; dist. judge, chief judge 19th Dist. Ct., 1976-93; presiding judge Southeastern Okla. Jud. Adminstrv. Dist., 1984-92, Choctaw Tribal Ct., 1979-83; pres. Okla. Jud. Conf., 1987-88; chmn. Assembly Presiding Judges, 1989-90; presiding judge trial div. Okla. Ct. on the Judiciary, 1991-93; Okla. Ct. of Tax Rev., 1992—; judge Okla. Ct. of Appeals, Tulsa, 1993—. Chmn. bd. dirs. Durant Youth Svcs., 1976-93; bd. dirs. Bryan County Youth Svcs., Inc., 1971-93. Mem. Phi Sigma Epsilon, Delta Theta Phi. Mem. Ch. of Christ. Club: Lion. Home: PO Box 329 Durant OK 74702-0329 Office: Ct Appeals 601 State Bldg 440 S Houston Ave Tulsa OK 74127-8916

TAYLOR, JOEL SANFORD, lawyer; b. Hazleton, Pa., Oct. 8, 1942; s. Robert Joseph and Alice Josephine (Sanford) T.; m. Donna Rae Caron, Mar. 26, 1967; children: Jason, Adam, Jeremy. BA, Swarthmore Coll., 1965; LLB, Columbia U., 1968. Bar: N.Y. 1969, U.S. Dist. Ct. (so. and ea. dists.) N.Y. 1970, U.S. Ct. Appeals (2d cir.) 1970, Ohio 1973, U.S. Dist. Ct. (no. dist.) Ohio 1974, U.S. Supreme Ct. 1974, U.S. Dist. Ct. (so. dist.) Ohio 1975, U.S. Ct. Appeals (6th cir.) 1975, U.S. Dist. Ct. (ea. dist.) Ky. 1979. Law clk. hon. Constance B. Motley U.S. Dist. Ct., N.Y.C., 1968-69; assoc. Paul, Weiss, Rifkind, Wharton & Garrison, N.Y.C., 1969-72; exec. asst. Ohio Office of Budget & Mgmt., Columbus, Ohio, 1972-74; asst. atty. gen. Ohio Atty. Gen., Columbus, 1974-83, chief counsel, 1983-91; ptnr. Dinsmore & Shohl, Columbus, 1991—; pres. Ohio Sundry Claims Bd., Columbus, 1972-74, Ohio State Controlling Bd., Columbus, 1973-74; mem., bd. trustees Ohio State Tchrs. Retirement System, Columbus, 1986-91. Mem. ABA, Ohio State Bar Assn., Columbus Bar Assn., Environ. Law Inst., Columbia Law Alumni Assn., Ohio Sierra Club. Office: Dinsmore & Shohl 175 S 3d St Ste 1000 Columbus OH 43215-5134

TAYLOR, JOHN BRIAN, economist, educator; b. Yonkers, N.Y., Dec. 8, 1946; s. John Joseph and Lorraine (Crowley) T.; m. Raye Allyn Price, Dec. 30, 1972; children: Jennifer Lynn, John Andrew. AB in Econs. summa cum laude, Princeton U., 1968; PhD, Stanford U., 1973. Asst. prof. econs. Columbia U., N.Y.C., 1973-77, assoc. prof., 1977-79, prof., 1979-80; prof. econs. and pub. affairs Princeton U., 1980-84; prof. econs. Stanford U., 1984—, dir. ctr. for Econ. Policy Rsch., 1994—; vis. prof. econs. Yale U., 1980; sr. staff economist Pres.'s Coun. Econ. Advisers, 1976-77, mem., 1989-91; econometric cons. Townsend-Greenspan and Co., N.Y., 1978-81; rsch. advisor Fed. Res. Bank Phila., 1981-84; rsch. assoc. Nat. Bur. Econ. Rsch., 1980—; exec. com. Am. Econ. Assn., 1991-94; rsch. economist Bank Of Japan, Tokyo, 1987; hon. adviser, 1994—; panel of econ. advisers Congl. Budget Office, 1995—. Author: Macroeconomics, 1986; Macroeconomic Policy in the World Economy, 1993, Economics, 1995; co-editor Am. Econ. Rev., 1985-89; assoc. editor Econometrica, 1981-85, Jour. Econ. Dynamics and Control, 1978-85, Jour. Monetary Econs., 1978-83; contbr. articles to profl. jours. NSF grantee, 1979-81, 81-83, 83-86, 86-89, 92-95; Guggenheim Found. fellow, 1983-84; sr. fellow Hoover Instn., 1996. Fellow Econometric Soc., Am. Acad. of Arts and Sci. Office: Stanford U Dept Econs Stanford CA 94305

TAYLOR, JOHN CHESTNUT, III, lawyer; b. N.Y.C., Jan. 7, 1928; s. John Chestnut and Jean Elizabeth (Willis) T.; m. Dolores Yvonne Sunstrom, Nov. 17, 1950; children: Jane Willis Taylor Salem, John Sunstrom, Anne Holliday Taylor Bambino. B.A., Princeton U., 1947; LL.B., Yale U., 1950. Bar: N.Y. 1950, D.C. 1972. Assoc. Paul, Weiss, Rifkind, Wharton & Garrison, N.Y.C., 1950, 52-60, ptnr., 1961-85, 87-91, of counsel, 1986-87, 92—; exec. v.p., dir. AEA Investors Inc., N.Y.C., 1985-86, pres., 1986-87. Bd. dirs. AFS Intercultural Programs, Inc., N.Y.C., 1972-80, trustee, 1973-79, chmn., 1975-79; trustee Carnegie Corp. N.Y., N.Y.C., 1975-84, chmn., 1979-84; bd. dirs. Vocat. Tng. Ctr., Inc., 1986-88, N.Am. Tng. Svcs. Inc., 1988-92; trustee, mem. exec. com. Devereux Found., 1992—, vice chmn., 1994—. Served to capt. JAGC, AUS, 1950-52. Mem. Assn. of Bar of City of N.Y., Order of Coif, Phi Beta Kappa, Phi Delta Phi. Democrat. Home: 1 Hammock View Ln Savannah GA 31411-2603 Office: Paul Weiss Rifkind Wharton & Garrison 1285 Avenue Of The Americas New York NY 10019-6028

TAYLOR, JOHN JACKSON (JAY), writer, international consultant, retired foreign service officer; b. Little Rock, Dec. 4, 1931; s. Alfred Wesley and Annie Laurie (Cain) T.; m. Elizabeth Rose, July 9, 1954; children: John Jr., Laurie, Amy, Cynthia. BA, Vanderbilt U., 1952; MA, U. Mich., 1968. 3d sec. U.S. Fgn. Service, Accra, Ghana, 1957-59; 2d sec. U.S. Fgn. Service, Taichung and Taipei, Republic of China, 1960-65; Chinese affairs analyst Dept. State, Washington, 1966-67; staff assoc. Ctr. for Chinese Studies, U. Mich., Ann Arbor, 1967-68; U.S. consul Kuching, Malaysia, 1968-70; chief external reporting U.S. Consulate Gen., Hong Kong, 1970-74; officer-in-charge Chinese affairs Dept. State, Washington, 1974-75; staff mem. Asian affairs Nat. Security Council, Washington, 1975-77; polit. counselor U.S. Embassy, Pretoria/Capetown, 1977-80; polit. cons. U.S. Embassy, Peking, 1980-82; research fellow Fairbanks Ctr. for Chinese Studies, Harvard U., Cambridge, Mass., 1982-83; dir. East Asian analysis Dept. State, Washington, 1983-85; dep. asst. sec. state Bur. Intelligence and Research, Dept. State, Washington, 1986-87; chief of mission U.S. Interests Sect., Havana, Cuba, 1987-90; diplomat in residence Carter Presdl. Ctr., Emory U., 1990-92; sr. mem. State Task Force 2000, 1992-93; vice pres. Global Bus. Access; assoc. in rsch. Fairbank Ctr. for East Asian Studies, Harvard U.; guest faculty Emory U. and Spelman Coll. Author: China and Southeast Asia, 1974, 76, The Dragon and the Wild Goose, 1987, 90, The Rise and Fall of Totalitarianism, 1993; contbr.: China and National Security, 1985. Served as Naval Aviator with USMC, 1953-57. Mem. Fgn. Svc. Assn., Asian Soc., Royal Asian Soc., Acad. of Polit. Sci. Unitarian.

TAYLOR, JOHN JOSEPH, nuclear engineer; b. Hackensack, N.J., Feb. 27, 1922; s. John J.D. and Johanna F. (Thibideau) T.; m. Lorraine Crowley, Feb. 5, 1943; children: John B., Nancy M., Susan M. BA, St. John's U., Jamaica, N.Y., 1942, DSc (hon.), 1975; MS, U. Notre Dame, 1947. Mathematician Bendix Aviation Corp., Teterburo, N.J., 1946-47; engr. Kellex Corp., N.Y.C., 1947-50; v.p. water reactor div. Westinghouse Electric Corp., Pitts., 1950-81; v.p. nuclear power Electric Power Rsch. Inst., Palo Alto, Calif., 1981-95; energy cons., 1985—; mem. adv. com. Oak Ridge (Tenn.) Nat. Lab., 1973-83, Brookhaven Nat. Lab., Upton, N.Y., 1986-92, Inst. for Nuclear Power Ops., 1988-95; mem. adv. com. Argonne (Ill.), Nat. Lab., 1980-86, bd. dirs.; cons. Office Tech. Assessment, Washington, 1975-93; mem. internat. adv. group IAEA, Vienna, Austria, 1992-95; mem. nuclear rsch. rev. com. NRC, 1995—. Co-author: Reactor Shielding Manual, 1953, Naval Reactor Physics Manual, 1956, Nuclear Power, Policy and Prospects, 1987, Management and Disposition of Excess Weapons Plutonium; contbr. articles to profl. jours. Bd. regents St. Mary's Coll., Moraga, Calif. Lt. (j.g.) USN, 1942-45. Recipient Order of Merit, Westinghouse Electric Corp., 1957, George Westinghouse Gold medal ASME, 1990. Fellow Am. Nuclear Soc. (bd. dirs. Walter Zinn award 1993); mem. NAE, Am. Phys. Soc., Cosmos Club (Washington). Republican. Roman Catholic. Home: 15 Oliver Ct Menlo Park CA 94025-6685 Office: Electric Power Research Inst PO Box 10412 3412 Hillview Ave Palo Alto CA 94304-1395

TAYLOR, JOHN L., communications executive; b. 1951. BS, U. N.C., Charlotte, 1976. With Deloitte Haskins & Sells, Charlotte, 1976-84, Video Vision, Inc., Charlotte, 1986; various positions, now pres., CEO Ingram Entertainment Inc., La Vergne, Tenn.; now owner, pres. Moovies Inc., Greenville, SC. Office: Moovies Inc 201 Brookfield Pkwy Ste 200 Greenville SC 29607*

TAYLOR, JOHN LOCKHART, city official; b. N.Y.C., Nov. 4, 1927; s. Floyd and Marian (Lockhart) T.; m. Barbara Becker, July 19, 1952; children: Catherine Fair, Robert, William, Susan. A.B., Middlebury Coll., 1952; M.Govtl. Adminstrn., U. Pa., 1956. Reporter Providence Jour.-Bull., 1952-54; adminstrv. intern City of Xenia, Ohio, 1955-56; mcpl. mgr. Borough of Narberth, Pa., 1956-60, Twp. of Lakewood, N.J., 1960-64; asst. city mgr. Fresno, Calif., 1964-65; city mgr., 1965-68, Kansas City, Mo., 1968-74, Berkeley, Calif., 1974-76; lectr. U. Pa., 1957-58, Golden Gate U., 1977; sr. urban mgmt. specialist Stanford Research Inst., 1977-80; dir. Internat. Devel. Center, 1980-82; clk. of bd. suprs. City of San Francisco, 1982—; pres. Calif. Clks. Bd. Suprs. Assn., 1988-89. Served with USN, 1945-48. Mem. Internat. City Mgrs. Assn., Am. Soc. Pub. Adminstrn., Mcpl. Execs. Assn. (pres. 1991-93). Office: City Hall 401 Van Ness Ave San Francisco CA 94102-4522

TAYLOR, JOHN WILKINSON, education educator; b. Covington, Ky., Sept. 26, 1906; s. John Wesley and Ethel (Wilkinson) T.; m. Katherine Willis Wright; 1 child, Walter Bradford; m. Helen Hutchinson Greene (dec. Jan. 1966); stepdau., Patricia (Mrs. H.E. Thornber, Jr.); m. June Cornell Fairbank (dec. Oct. 1986); step-children: Margaret, (Mrs. Terrill K. Jory) (dec. Aug. 1985), Laura (Mrs. Louis C. Sudler, Jr.), Kellogg III, Susan (Mrs. Walter B. Taylor), Elizabeth (Mrs. John W. Cameron), David. A.B., Columbia, 1929, A.M., 1930, Ph.D., 1936; H.D., St. Joseph Coll., 1970. Asst. curriculum research Tchrs. Coll., Columbia, 1927; asst. elementary edn. Tchrs. Coll., 1928, asst. curriculum, 1929, asst. secondary edn., 1929-30, instr. comparative edn., 1930; tchr. English Kaiser Friederich Realgymnasium, Berlin-Neukoeln, Germany, 1930-31; ednl. adviser to pres. John Day Co., 1932-33; asso. in edn., dir. fgn. study Columbia, 1934-35; also asst. to chmn. Columbia (New Coll.), 1935-37; chmn. admissions, scholarship, loan, curriculum and personnel guidance coms., 1937-38; assoc. prof. comparative edn. and sec. instnl. survey com., adminstrv. asst. to pres. La. State U., 1938-40, dir. bur. ednl. research, 1941-43; pres. U. Louisville, 1947-50; dep. dir.-gen. UNESCO, 1951-54, acting dir.-gen., 1952-53; exec. dir. Chgo. Ednl. TV Assn., 1954-71, bd. mem., 1969-73; acting pres. Learning Resources Inst., N.Y.C., 1960-63; pres. Learning Resources Inst., Chgo., 1963-70; dir. Midwestern Ednl. Television Network, Inc., 1966-70; bd. dirs. Fed. Res. br. Bank Louisville, 1948-50; spl. cons. on ednl. TV N.Y. U., 1958; Dir. Adult Edn. Council Greater Chgo., 1956-62, vice chmn., 1959-60; mem. Chgo. Council on Fgn. Relations, 1954-72, bd. mem., 1970-72; citizens bd. U. Chgo., 1956-80; adv. com. Midwest Office Inst. Internat. Edn., 1954-58; S.E. Chgo. Commn., 1955-63; mem. Midwest Council on Airborne TV Instrn., 1959-62; Exec. sec. to Am. Council on Edn. Commn., survey U. Ill., 1942; on leave from La. State U.; mem. Round Table Meeting on Peace UNESCO, Paris, 1966; Bd. dirs. Chgo. Area Sch. TV, 1964-70, Sight Systems Inst., 1974-78; mem. Mass. Edn. Study, 1963-64; Mem. bus. adv. council Chgo. City Jr., 1964-66; chmn. bd. Chgo. City Coll., 1966-84; bd. dirs. North River Commn., 1967-70; Bd. dirs. Internat. Inst. Adminstrv. Scis., 1951-55; council advisors U.S. Commr. Edn., 1950-52; adv. panel Comptroller Army, 1950-53. Author: Youth Welfare in Germany, 1936, also survey reports.; contbr. articles to edn. profl. jours. Mem. Supts. Roundtable No. Ill., 1954-71, Tri-county Ednl. TV Coun., 1955-63, Citizens Com. U. Ill., 1959-73, Chgo. Civic Com. World Refugees, 1960-69. Commd. capt. O.R.C. AUS; div. mil govt. occupied countries, 1943; maj., 1944; lt. col., 1945, promoted to brig. gen. (assimilated rank), 1946, NATOUSA; North Africa asst. dir., then dir. studies Mil. Govt. Sch. and Holding Ctr., 1943-44; chief edn. and religious affairs br. U.S. Mil. Govt. for Germany (planning unit in Eng., 1944-45, operational unit in Berlin, 1945-47); U.S. rep. on Quadripartite Edn. Com. for Germany 1945-47, Berlin. Decorated Legion of Merit; chevalier French Legion of Honor; officer French Legion of Honor; named Man of Year Louisville, 1950, Chicagoan of Yr. in Edn. Jr. C. of C., 1962; recipient Chgo. medal for merit, 1972, Disting. Alumnus award Peabody Demonstration Sch.-Univ. Sch. Nashville, 1990. Mem. NEA, Am. Acad. Polit. and Social Sci., Am. Legion, Chgo. Assn. Commerce and Industry (chmn. edn. com. 1959-69), Internat. Platform Assn., Acad. TV Arts and Scis. (gov. Chgo. 1958-71), Omicron Delta Kappa, Phi Delta Kappa, Kappa Delta Pi, Phi Kappa Phi. Presbyn. Clubs: Executives (Louisville), Filson (Louisville), Arts (Louisville), Rotary (Louisville), Salmagundi (Louisville), Pendennis (Louisville); Allied Circle (London); Union League (Chgo.), Wayfarers (Chgo.), Casino (Chgo.), Commercial. (Chgo.). Home and Office: 2960 N Lake Shore Dr Apt 2706 Chicago IL 60657-5662

TAYLOR, JONATHAN FRANCIS, agribusiness executive; b. Kampala, Uganda, Aug. 12, 1935; came to U.S., 1980; s. Reginald William and Ruth (Tyson) T.; m. Anthea Gail Proctor, May 1965; children: Luke Augustus James, Matthew Justinian Robert, James Maximillian Rex. B.A., Oxford U. (Eng.), 1957, M.A., 1959. Adminstrv. sec. Booker Agribusiness Ltd., London, 1960-64; mgr. projects Booker Agribusiness Ltd., Nigeria, Kenya, Indonesia & others, 1964-76; chmn. Booker Agribusiness Ltd., 1976-84; chief exec. Booker PLC, London, 1984-93, chmn., 1993—; bd. dirs. Arbor Acres Farm Inc., Glastonbury, Conn., Tate & Lyle PLC, London, MEPC PLC, London, Equitable Life Assurance Soc.; chmn. Ellis & Everard PLC, Bradford. Chmn. Bodleian Libr. campaign; gov. Sch. Oriental and African Studies London U; chmn. Found. Devel. of Polish Agriculture; dir. Internat. Agribus. Mgmt. Assn., Winrock Internat. Inst. Agrl. Devel.; gov. Royal Agrl. Soc. Clubs: Knickerbocker (N.Y.C.); Travellers (London). Office: Booker PLC, Portland Ho / Stag Pl, London SW1E 5AY, England

TAYLOR, JOSEPH HOOTON, JR., radio astronomer, physicist; b. Phila., Mar. 29, 1941; s. Joseph Hooton and Sylvia Hathaway (Evans) T.; m. Marietta Bisson, Jan. 3, 1976; children: Jeffrey, Rebecca, Anne-Marie. BA in Physics, Haverford Coll., 1963; PhD in Astronomy, Harvard U., 1968; DSc (hon., U. Chgo., 1985, U. Mass., 1994. Research fellow, lectr. Harvard

U., 1968-69; asst. prof. astronomy U. Mass., Amherst, 1969-72; assoc. prof. U. Mass., 1973-77, prof., 1977-81; prof. physics Princeton U., 1980—, James McDonnell Disting. prof. physics, 1986—. Author: Pulsars, 1977. Recipient Dannie Heineman prize in astrophysics Am. Inst. Physics/Am. Astron. Soc., 1980, Tomalla Found. prize in gravitation and cosmology, 1985, Magellanic Premium award Am. Philos. Soc., 1990, Einstein prize laureate Albert Einstein Soc., 1991, Wolf Prize in Physics, Wolf Found., 1992, Nobel Prize in Physics, Nobel Foundation, 1993; MacArthur fellow, 1981. Fellow Am. Acad. Arts and Scis., Am. Phys. Soc.; mem. NAS (Henry Draper medal 1985, John J. Carty medal Advancement Sci. 1991), Am. Philos. Soc., Am. Astron. Soc., Internat. Sci. Radio Union, Internat. Astron. Union. Mem. Soc. of Friends. Home: 272 Hartley Ave Princeton NJ 08540-5656 Office: Princeton U Dept Physics PO Box 708 Princeton NJ 08544*

TAYLOR, JOYCE, religious organization executive. Pres. Youth Dept. of Ch. of God in Christ Internat. Office: 137-17 135th Ave Jamaica NY 11436-2146

TAYLOR, JUDITH ANN, sales executive; b. Sheridan, Wyo., July 9, 1944; d. Milo G. and Eleanor M. (Wood) Rinker; m. George I. Taylor, Sept. 15, 1962; children: Monte G., Bret A. Fashion dept. mgr. Montgomery Ward, Sheridan, 1968-73; pers. mgr., asst. mgr. Dan's Ranchwear, Sheridan, 1973-80; sales/prodn. coord. KWYO Radio, Sheridan, 1981-83; sales mgr., promotions coord. KROE Radio, Sheridan, 1984—; mng. editor BOUNTY Publ., 1993—; notary pub. State of Wyo., 1985—; lectr., instr. BSA Merit U.; lectr. acad. achievement LVA Adv. Bd., 1993—, instr. Tongue River Middle Sch. Academic Enrichmen t Program, 1994-95; S.C. Ambs., 1980—, pres., 1995—. mng. editor BOUNTY Publ., 1993—. Sec.-treas. Sheridan County Centennial Com., 1986-89; local sec.-treas. Wyo. Centennial Com., Sheridan, 1986-90; exec. dir. Sheridan-Wyo. Rodeo Bd., 1983—; bd. dirs. Sheridan County Fair Bd., 1991—, treas., 1995—; bd. dirs. "Christmas in April" Sheridan County, 1992—; mem. WJTP Coun., Cheyenne, 1990-92; mem. adv. coun. Tutor-Literacy Vols. of Am., 1993—; Mrs. Santa Claus for local groups; vol. coord. AIDS Quilt. Mem. Wyo. Assn. Broadcasters, S.C. C. of C. (dir. 1988—, pres. 1989-91), UMWA Aux. (pres. 1982-89), Kiwanis (v.p. 1992—, pres.-elect 1993, pres. 1994), S.C. Ambassadors (pres. 1995—), Ft. Phil Kearney/Bozeman Trail (bd. dirs. 1995—). Democrat. Christian Ch. Home: 98 Decker Rd Sheridan WY 82801-9612 Office: KROE AM PO Box 5086 Sheridan WY 82801-1386

TAYLOR, JUDITH CAROLINE, entrepreneur; b. Quincy, Ill., June 23, 1948; d. Earl George and Caroline Clara (Knuffman) Schenk; m. Richard Odell Taylor, Nov. 28, 1970; children: Alexander James and Nicholas James (twins). BA, Quincy (Ill.) U., 1985. Resident mgr. Landing Heights Apts., Brighton, N.Y., 1973-75; facilitator adult student program Quincy U., 1983-85; dist. mgr. Creative Expressions, 1981-85; mgr. mem. svcs. Quincy Conv. and Visitors Bur., 1985; sales dir. Motor Inn Hotel, Quincy, 1986; entrepreneur Taylor Enterprises, Quincy, 1985—; exec. dir. The Kensington, Quincy, 1987-90; mgr., salesperson, cons. Taylor's Fine Furniture & Gifts, Quincy, 1990—; cons., freelance designer. Designed, marketed series I and II Quincy Postcards, 1987, 90; photo show John Wood C.C., 1993. House tour chairperson Quincy Perserves Bd., 1989; pres. Quincy Newcomers Club, 1980; pres. Great Rivers Mothers of Twins, Quincy, 1979. Recipient Americanism award VFW, Quincy, 1966. Mem. AAUW, Older Womens League (pres. 1988), The Atlantis Study Group, Quincy Conv. and Visitors Bur., Altrusa Club. Mem. Unity Ch. Avocations: photography, poetry writing, spirituality. Home: 1461 Maine St Quincy IL 62301-4260 Office: Taylors Fine Furniture & Gifts 123 N 4th St Quincy IL 62301-2913

TAYLOR, JULIA W., bank executive; b. 1936. Student, N.C. Cen. U., Stonier Graduate Sch. of Banking. With Mechanics and Farmers Bank, Raleigh, 1955-60, asst. cashier, 1966-77, v.p., mgr., 1967-78, sr. v.p., city exec. officer, 1978-83, pres., chief exec. officer, 1983-87, chmn., pres. and chief exec. officer, 1987—; With Bank of Am., L.A., 1960, Broadway Fed. Savs. and Loan Assn., L.A., 1961-63; bd. dirs., exec. com. Mechanics and Farmers Bank, Durham; bd. dirs. Am. Inst. of Banking, Triangle Better Bus. Bur., Downtown Raleigh Devel. Corp., Wheeler Flying Svc., Inc.; mem. N.C. Assembly on Women and Economy; bd. trustees U. N.C., Wilmington. Trustee bd. St. Joseph's African Meth. Episcopal Ch., Durham; vice chmn. N.C. State Ednl. Assistance Authority; bd. dirs. Jr. Achievement of Raleigh and Wake Co., N.C. Bus. Adv. Bd. Fuqua Sch. of Bus. Duke U., N.C. 4-H Devel. Fund, Inc.; mem. Raleigh Civic Ctr. Authority; bd. assocs. N.C. Child Advocacy Inst.; mem. N.C. Bus. COns. Adv. Bd. Fuqua Sch. Bus. Duke U. Named Women of Achievement award Silver Medallion in Bus. and Industry YWCA, 1985, The Tarhell of the Week News and Observer, 1986, Atlanta Regional Minority Bus. Advocate of Yr. award U.S. Dept. of Commerce Minority Bus. Devel. Agy., 1987, Nat. Minority Bus. Advocate of Yr. award U.S. Dept. Commerce, 1987; recipient Citizen award Ind. Weekly 1988, 1989. Mem. N.C. Ctrl. U. Sch. Law (bd. vis.), N.C. Citizens for Bus. & Industry, Conf. State Bank Suprs. (regional rep.), Forest at Duke (bd. dirs.), Africa News (bd. dirs.), N.C. Bankers Assn. (bd. dirs.), Cmty. Bankers Assn. N.C. (scholarship com.), Nat. Assn. Women Bus. Owners (N.C. chpt.). Office: Mechanics & Farmers Bank PO Box 1932 Durham NC 27702-1932

TAYLOR, JUNE RUTH, minister; b. Annapolis, Md., June 27, 1932; d. Benjamin and Naomi Medora (Dill) Michaelson; m. Thomas Wayne Taylor, Mar. 20, 1954; children: Rebecca Susan Taylor DeLameter, Michael Steven. AB, Goucher Coll., 1952; MRE, Presbyn. Sch. of Christian Edn., Richmond, Va., 1954; MDiv., McCormick Theol. Sem., 1978. Ordained to ministry Presbyn. Ch. (U.S.A.), 1976. Min. Christian Edn. Congl. United Ch. of Christ, Arlington Heights, Ill., 1974-79; dir. pastoral svcs. Presbyn. U. Hosp., Pitts., 1979-89; dir. chaplaincy svcs. Ephrata (Pa.) Community Hosp., 1991—; chaplain Rush-Presbyn. St. Luke's Med. Ctr., Chgo., 1976-78; chair exec. com. Presbyn. Assn. Specialized Pastoral Ministries, Louisville, 1987-89; bd. dirs. Cocalico Place. Book reviewer in field. Fellow Coll. Chaplains (sec. exec. com. 1985-87); mem. Soc. Chaplains, Hosp. Assn. Pa. (pres. 1983), Assn. Mental Health Clergy, Assn. for Clin. Pastoral Edn. (clin.), Rotary (liaison to Boys and Girls Club S.W. Pitts. chpt. 1990-91), Gamma Phi Beta Alumnae Club (pres. 1990-91).

TAYLOR, KAREN ANNETTE, mental health nurse; b. Kinston, N.C., Oct. 7, 1952; d. Emmett Green and Polly Ann (Taylor) Tyndall; m. Paul Othell Taylor Jr., June 24, 1979; 1 child, Clarissa Anne. AA, Lenoir C.C., Kinston, 1972; Diploma, Lenoir Meml. Hosp. Sch. of, Nursing, 1984; student, St. Joseph's Coll., Windham, Maine, 1993-94. RN, N.C. Staff nurse Lenoir Meml. Hosp., 1984-86; staff nurse, relief patient care dir. Brynn Marr Hosp., Jacksonville, N.C., 1987-90; staff nurse, quality assurance Naval Hosp., Camp Lejeune, N.C., 1990-92. Recipient Meritorious Unit Commendation Am. Fedn. of Govt. Employees, 1992. Baptist. Avocations: reading, crochet.

TAYLOR, KENDRICK JAY, microbiologist; b. Manhattan, Mont., Mar. 17, 1914; s. William Henry and Rose (Carney) T.; BS, Mont. State U., 1938; postgrad. (fellow) U. Wash., 1938-41, U. Calif. at Berkeley, 1952, Drama Studio of London, 1985; m. Hazel Marguerite Griffith, July 28, 1945; children: Stanley, Paul, Richard. Rsch. microbiologist Cutter Labs., Berkeley, Calif., 1945-74; microbiologist Berkeley Biologicals, 1975-86. Committeeman Mount Diablo coun. Boy Scouts Am., 1955, dist. vice-chmn., 1960-61, dist. chmn., 1962-65, cubmaster, 1957, scoutmaster, 1966; active Contact Ministries, 1977-80; bd. dirs. Santa Clara Community Players, 1980-84; vol. instr. English as a Second Lang., 1979-80; vol. ARC Blood Ctr., VA Hosp., San Jose; life mem. PTA; census taker, 1980; mem. Berkely Jr. C. of C., 1946-49. Served with AUS, 1941-46, lt. col. Res., ret. Recipient Scout's Wood badge Boy Scouts Am., 1962; recipient Golden Diploma Mont. State U., 1988. Mem. Am. Soc. Microbiology (chmn. local com. 1953, v.p. No. Calif. br. 1963-65, pres. 1965-67), Sons and Daus. Mont. Pioneers, Mont. State Univ. Alumni Assn., Mont. Hist. Soc., Gallatin County Hist. Soc., Headwaters-Heritage Hist. Soc., Am. Legion Post 89, Parent-Tchrs. Assn. Calif. (life). Presbyterian (trustee 1951-53, elder 1954—). Home: 550 S 13th St San Jose CA 95112-2361

TAYLOR, KENNETH BYRON, JR., librarian, minister, religion educator; b. Russellville, Ala., Dec. 25, 1953; s. Kenneth Byron Sr. and Willene Martha (Sudduth) T.; m. Sheila Carol Mashburn, May 24, 1975; children: Justin, Jonathan, Jordan, Jessica. BS, U. North Ala., 1975; JD, U. Ala., 1978; MDiv, New Orleans Bapt. Theol. Sem., 1986, PhD, 1993; MLIS, La. State U., 1994. Bar: Ala. 1979; ordained to ministry Bapt. Ch., 1987. Staff atty. Legal Svcs. Corp. Ala., Florence, 1979-83; assoc. pastor Elysian Fields Ave. Bapt. Ch., New Orleans, 1984-87, pastor, 1987—; dir. libr. New Orleans (La.) Bapt. Theol. Sem., John T. Christian Libr., 1991—, asst. prof. Evangelism, 1993—. Avocations: hiking, gardening. Office: New Orleans Bapt Theol Sem John T Christian Libr 4110 Seminary Pl New Orleans LA 70126-4619

TAYLOR, KENNETH DOUGLAS, stockbroker, finance and computer consultant, educator; b. Topeka, Nov. 21, 1942; s. Olin Orlando and Lola Louise (Conley) T.; AB, George Washington U., 1964, MS in Stats., 1966; MS in Computer Sci. SUNY, 1990, PhD in Math. Eurotech, 1992, (univ. fellow); student of Peter Hilton; postgrad., McGill U., 1974, Bowdoin Coll., U. Montreal; m. Joy Ellen Rice, May 25, 1973 (div. Nov. 1981); m. Elizabeth Flanagan Brunner, May 6, 1995. Registered rep./stockbroker. Sr. programmer C-E-I-R, Inc., 1963, 69; instr. Army Map Svc., 1964-65; student instr. McGill U., 1966-71; rsch. assoc. U. Va. Med. Sch., 1972; fin. and computer cons., Plymouth, N.Y., 1973-87; computer scientist USAF, 1989-90; broker Russell Hawkes Assoc./Linsco/Pvt. Ledger, 1993-94, LESKO Fin Svcs, 1994—; sec. Richmond (Va.) Computer Club, 1977. Summer grantee NSF, Can. Research Council. Mem. ASTM, Am. Math. Soc. Author papers in field. Home: PO Box 288 Montrose PA 18801-0288 Office: LESKO Fin Svcs 135 Front St Binghamton NY 13905-3114

TAYLOR, KENNETH GRANT, chemistry educator; b. Paterson, N.J., May 12, 1936; s. Ulysses Grant and Susan (De Haan) T.; m. Carla May Rydell, June 17, 1961; children: Koren Lynn, Kevin Grant, Kaylyn Jo. BA, Calvin Coll., 1957; PhD, Wayne State U., 1963. Rsch. assoc. MIT, Cambridge, 1963-64; sr. rsch. assoc. Wayne State U., Detroit, 1964-66; from asst. to assoc. prof. chemistry U. Louisville, 1966-73, prof., 1974—, acting chmn., 1973-74, vice chmn., 1976-78, chmn., 1978-87, assoc. dean. Rsch., Arts and Scis., 1991—; prof. associé Univ. de Nancy I, Nancy Cedex, France, 1974-75, 82-83; vis. prof. U. Lund, Sweden, 1991. Contbr. numerous articles to profl. jours.; co-author, presentor numerous papers at sci. meetings. Rsch. and teaching grantee NIH, NSF, Am. Cancer Soc., Am. Chem. Soc., Dept. Interior, U. Louisville, 1966—. Fellow AAAS; mem. Am. Chem. Soc., Ky. Acad. Sci. Democrat. Presbyterian. Home: 1838 Yale Dr Louisville KY 40205-2031 Office: U Louisville Dept Chemistry Louisville KY 40292

TAYLOR, KENNETH J., diagnostic sonologist; b. Rochford, Essex, Eng., Mar. 8, 1939; s. William Albert and Florence (Soulsby) T.; m. Anne Bowen Simpkins, Apr. 8, 1964 (div. Nov. 1968); 1 child, Sally-Anne; m. Caroline Rix, May 17, 1975; children: Andrew, Ian. BSc, London U., 1961; MBBS, London U./Guys Hosp., Eng., 1964, PhD, 1972; MD, U. London, 1975; MA, Yale U., 1979, FACP, 1979. House surgeon Royal Surrey Hosp., Guildford, U.K., 1964-66; sr. house surgeon Guys Maudsley Hosp., London, 1966-67; jr. lectr. Guys Hosp. Med. Sch., London, 1967-70, lectr., 1970-72; sr. fellow Royal Marsden Hosp., Sutton, Surrey, U.K., 1973-75; assoc. prof. radiology Yale U., New Haven, Conn., 1975-77, tenured assoc. prof., 1977-79, tenured prof., 1979—; co-dir. Yale Ctr. for Ultrasonics and Sonics, New Haven, 1992—; dir. Exptl. Lab. Yale Radiology, 1991—, Yale Vascular Lab., 1992—; ad hoc adv. bd. NIH, Washington. Chmn. editl. bd. Clinics in Diagnostic Ultrasound, 1978—; co-editor: Doppler in Clinic Diagnosis, 1988, 2d edit., 1995; assoc. editor Radiology Jour., 1992—; author: Atlas of Ultrasound, 1978, 2d edit., 1984. Bd. dirs. Friends of Hospice, New Haven, 1980. Lt. Royal Navy Res., 1962-65. Rsch. grantee Am. Cancer Soc., N.Y., 1976, 82, NIH Cancer Inst., Washington, 1988-89, 88-91. Fellow Am. Inst. Ultrasound Med. (bd. gov. 1978-82), Am. Coll. Physicians; mem. Radiol. Soc. N.Am. Achievements include pioneering applications for grey scale ultrasound, applications of Doppler ultrasound. Home: 1611 Great Hill Rd Guilford CT 06437-3647 Office: 333 Cedar St New Haven CT 06510-3206

TAYLOR, KENNETH NATHANIEL, publishing executive, author; b. Portland, Oreg., May 8, 1917; s. George Nathaniel and Charlotte Bodwell (Huff) T.; m. Margaret Louise West, Sept. 13, 1940; children: Becky, John, Martha, Peter, Janet, Mark, Cynthia, Gretchen, Mary Lee, Alison. BA Wheaton Coll., 1938, DLitt (hon.), 1965; student, Dallas Theol. Sem., 1940-43; ThM, No. Bapt. Theol. Sem., 1944; DLitt (hon.), Trinity Evang. Div. Sch., 1972; LHD (hon.), Huntington Coll., 1974, Taylor U., 1989. With Moody Press (pub. protestant religious lit.), Chgo., 1947-63; dir. Moody Press (pub. protestant religious lit.), 1948-62, Moody Lit. Mission (prodn. and distbn. lit.), 1948-62; pres. Tyndale House Publishers, 1963-84, chmn. bd., 1984—; chmn. bd. Coverdale House Pubs., London, Eng., 1969-79; pres. Tyndale House Found., 1964-79, bd. dirs., 1964—; dir. Inter-Varsity Christian Fellowship, 1956-59, Evang. Lit. Overseas, 1951-70, Short Terms Abroad, 1963-77; pres. Living Bibles Internat., Wheaton, Ill., 1968-77, internat. pres., 1977-90, internat. chmn. emeritus, 1990-92; chmn. Unilit., Inc., Portland, 1972-73. Author: Is Christianity Credible, 1946, Living Letters: The Paraphrased Epistles, 1962; juveniles Stories for the Children's Hour, 1953, Devotions for the Children's Hour, 1954, I See, 1958 (reprinted as Small Talks About God, 1995), Bible in Pictures for Little Eyes, 1956, Lost on the Trail, 1959, Romans for the Children's Hour, 1959; Living Prophecies - The Minor Prophets Paraphrased, 1965, Living Gospels, 1966, Living Psalms and Proverbs With the Major Prophets Paraphrased, 1967, The Living New Testament, 1967, Living Lessons of Life and Love, 1968, Living Books of Moses, 1969, Living History of Israel, 1970, The Living Bible, 1971, Taylor's Bible Story Book, 1970; juveniles What High School Students Should Know About Creation, 1983, What High School Students Should Know About Evolution, 1983, Big Thoughts for Little People, 1983, Giant Steps for Little People, 1985, Wise Words for Little People, 1987, Next Steps for New Christians (originally How To Grow), 1989, My First Bible in Pictures, 1989 (ann. Angel award 1990, Platinum Book award 1990), The Good Samaritan, 1989, Jesus Feeds A Crowd, 1989, The Lost Sheep, 1989, The Prodigal Son, 1989; Good News for Little People, 1991 (ann. Angel award 1992), My Life, A Guided Tour, 1991, Daniel and the Lions' Den, 1992, Noah's Ark, 1992, Family-Time Bible in Pictures, 1992, A Boy Helps Jesus, 1994, The Good Neighbor, 1994, Noah Builds a Boat, 1994, A Very Special Baby, 1994, The Story of Noah's Ark, 1994, Small Talks About God, 1995; co-editor: The Bible for Children, 1990 (ann. Angel award 1991); pub. The Christian Reader, 1964-92, Have a Good Day, 68—. Bd. dirs. Christian Libr. Svc., 1972-75, InterSkrift forlage Aktiebolag, Sweden, Internat. Bible Soc., 1992-94; trustee Living Bible Found., Fuller Theol. Sem.; mem. adv. bd. Internat. Bible Reading Assn. Recipient citation Layman's Nat. Bible Com., 1971; award Religious Heritage Am., 1972; disting. svc. citation Internat. Soc. Christian Endeavor, 1973; Nelson Bible award, 1973; Better World award VFW Aux., 1974; disting. pub. svc. award 1974; Recognition award Urban Ministries, Inc., 1977; Svc. award Wheaton Coll. Alumni Assn., 1977; Crusader award Wheaton Coll., 1979; Gutenberg award Chgo. Bible Soc., 1981; Internat. Christian Edn. Assn. award, 1983; Inducted into DuPage County Heritage Gallery, 1983; named Man of Yr. Com. Internat. Goodwill, 1983; recipient 1st Ann. Lit. award Evang. Lit. Overseas, 1983; Svc. award YFC/USA, 1984; Gold Medallion Achievement award Evang. Pubs. Assn., 1984; named to Christian Booksellers Hall of Fame, 1989; recipient Ann. James DeForest Murch award Nat. Assn. Evangelicals, 1995. Mem. Wheaton Coll. Scholastic Honor Soc. Home: 1515 E Forest Ave Wheaton IL 60187-4469 Office: 351 Executive Dr Carol Stream IL 60188-2420 *Who but God could make an unending universe, sized by billions of light years? And who could dream of knowing such a God personally? I am one who believes this, and have based my life on the Bible as God's message to mankind, and to you and me. But how to manage Bible reading when it is in such an ancient language? How to crack the shell of the coconut and find the milk and meat? That is why I spent 16 years translating the Bible into living English, with 37 million copies now in print.*

TAYLOR, KRISTIN CLARK, media specialist; b. Detroit, Mar. 26, 1959; d. James W. and Mary Elizabeth (Moore) Clark; m. Lonnie Paul Taylor; children: Lonnie Paul II, Mary Elizabeth. BA in Classical Lit., Mich. State U., 1982. Editor, writer USA Today, Washington, 1982-86; corp. writer Gannett Co., Inc., Washington, 1986; bus. corr. Gannett News Svc., Washington, 1987; asst. press sec. to Vice President Bush White House, Washington, 1987-88, spl. asst. to Vice President Bush for press rels., 1988-89; dir. White House media rels., 1989-90; dir. comm. BellSouth Corp., Washington, 1990-94; v.p. external affairs Student Loan Mktg. Assn. (Sallie Mae), Washington, 1994—. Author: The First To Speak, A Woman of Color Inside the White House, 1993. Republican.

TAYLOR, LANCE JEROME, economics educator; b. Montpelier, Idaho, May 25, 1940; s. Walter Jerome and Ruth (Robinson) T.; m. Yvonne S.M. Johnsson, May 31, 1963; children: Ian Lance, Signe Marguerite. BS with honors, Calif. Inst. Tech., 1962; PhD, Harvard U., 1968. Instr. econs. Harvard U., Cambridge, Mass., 1967-68; asst. prof., assoc. prof. Harvard U., 1970-74; research assoc. MIT, Cambridge, 1968-70; prof. econs. MIT, 1974-93, New Sch. for Social Rsch., N.Y.C., 1993—; vis. prof. U. Brasilia, 1974, Pontifical Cath. U. Rio de Janeiro, 1981, U. Delhi, 1987-88, Stockholm Sch. Econs., 1990; Marshall lectr. Cambridge U., 1986-87; cons. World Bank, UN, various fgn. govts. Author: Macro Models for Developing Countries, 1979, Models of Growth and Distribution for Brazil, 1980, Structuralist Macroeconomics, 1983, Varieties of Stabilization Experience, 1988, Income Distribution, Inflation, and Growth, 1991, The Market Meets its Match: Restructuring the Economies of Eastern Europe, 1994. Fulbright fellow, 1962-63. Mem. Am. Econ. Assn., Royal Econ. Soc. Home: PO Box 378 Washington ME 04574-0378 Office: New School for Social Rsch Grad Faculty 65 5th Ave New York NY 10003-3003

TAYLOR, LAWRENCE, sports commentator, former professional football player; b. Williamsburg, Va., Feb. 4, 1959; s. Clarence and Iris Taylor; m. Linda Taylor; children: T.J., Tanisha, Paula. Student, U. N.C. With N.Y. Giants, 1981-93; sports commentator The Stadium Show TNT, 1994—; owner All-Pro Products, 1993—; mem. Superbowl Championship Team, 1986, 90. Author: Living on the Edge, 1987. Recipient Bert Bell award, Humanitarian award Nat. Black United Fund; NFL Rookie of the Year, 1981, named Most Valuable Player NFL, 1986, NFL Player of Yr. AP, Def. Player of Yr. AP, Player of Yr. Sporting News mag., Schick Co., Washington Touchdown Club, Seagrams Corp., Gillette Co., Tums Co.; named to All-NFL team, All-NFC team, All-Star game NFL Pro Bowl, 1981-90; elected Top Linebacker NFL Players' Assn. Led NFL in sacks, 1986. Office: NY Giants Giants Stadium East Rutherford NJ 07073

TAYLOR, LAWRENCE PALMER, diplomat; b. Cleve., Apr. 18, 1940; s. Sheldon A. and Juanita (Springer) T.; m. Lynda Ellen Gorham; children: Lori, Tracey, Scott. AB, Ohio U., 1963; MA, Am. U., 1969; MPA, Harvard U., 1977. Consular officer Zagreb, Yugoslavia, 1972-73; econ. officer U.S. Embassy, Belgrade, Yugoslavia, 1973-76; petroleum attache U.S. Embassy, Jakarta, Indonesia, 1976-79; energy officer U.S. Embassy, Ottawa, Can., 1980-84; econ. minister U.S. Embassy, Ottawa, Ont., Can., 1989-92; econ. counselor U.S. Embassy, London, 1985-89; dir. Fgn. Svc. Inst., Washington, 1992-95; amb. to Estonia, 1995—. Avocation: collecting polit., military ephemera, maps. Home: 2025 Mummasburg Rd Gettysburg PA 17325-7465 Office: Am Embassy Tallinn Dept of State Washington DC 20521-4530

TAYLOR, LEIGH HERBERT, college dean; b. Chgo., Oct. 23, 1941; s. Herbert and Leona Taylor; m. Nancy E. Young; children: Jennifer, Jeremiah. BA, U. Tulsa, 1964, JD, 1966; LLM, NYU, 1969. Bar: Okla. 1966, Ill. 1976. Trial atty. Civil Rights div. Dept. Justice, Washington, 1966-68; prof. DePaul U. Coll. Law, Chgo., 1969-77; asst. dean DePaul U. Coll. Law, 1972-73, assoc. dean, 1973-77; dean Coll. Law, Ohio No. U., Ada, 1977-78, Sch. Law Southwestern U., L.A., 1978—; mem. adv. bd. 1st Woman's Bank of L.A., 1981-85; dir. Law Sch. Admissions Svcs., Inc., 1982-86; chmn. audit com. Law Sch. Admissions Coun., 1989-91, trustee, 1991-98, chair-elect, 1994-95, chair, 1995-97; mem. bd. trustees Coun. on Legal Edn. Opportunity, 1993-96. Editor-in-chief Tulsa Law Jour., 1966; author: Strategies for Law-Focused Education, 1977; (with others) Law in a New Land, 1972; mem. editorial bd. Family Law Quarterly, 1977-78. Bd. dirs. Criminal Def. Consortium Cook County (Ill.), Inc., 1975-77, L.A. Press Club Found. With AUS, 1959. Fellow Am. Bar Found.; mem. ABA (accreditation com. 1991-95), Law in Am. Soc. Found., Ill. Bar Assn., Chgo. Bar Assn. (rec. sec.), L.A. County Bar Assn., Okla. Bar Assn. Office: Southwestern U Sch Law Office of Dean 675 S Westmoreland Ave Los Angeles CA 90005-3905

TAYLOR, LEONARD STUART, engineering educator, consultant; b. N.Y.C., Dec. 28, 1928; m. Lillian Rachel Schlang, Apr. 12, 1954; children: Robin Jolie, Allyn Lise. AB, Harvard Coll., 1951; MSc, N.Mex. State U., 1955, PhD, 1960. Microwave engr. Raytheon Mfg. Co., Bedford, Mass., 1950-55; research physicist Gen. Electric Co., Phila., 1960-63; assoc. prof. Case Western Res. U., Cleve., 1964-67; prof. U. Md., College Park, Md., 1967-96; prof. emeritus U. Md., College Park, 1996—; cons. USN, Silver Spring, Md., 1967-96. Contbr. articles to profl. jours; inventor Microwave Scalpel, Implantable Microwave Hyperthermia Applicator and numerous others. Recipient Disting. Alumni N.Mex. State U. 1975. Fellow IEEE (life), Am. Soc. for Laser Medicine and Surgery; mem. Am. Phys. Soc., Optical Soc. of Am., Bioelectromagnetics Soc. Avocations: tennis, music. Office: U Md EE Dept College Park MD 20742

TAYLOR, LINDA RATHBUN, bd. dirs. Fluid Mgmt., Inc., 1987-93; trustee Montgomery County Md. Employees' Retirement Sys., 1987-93; com. mem. Vassar Coll. Endowment Fund, 1992—; elder Bradley Hills Presbyn. Ch., 1992—; dir. Washington Internat. Horse Show.

TAYLOR, LYLE DEWEY, economic development company executive; b. Traer, Iowa, Sept. 26, 1934; s. John Dewey and Lorriane (Burrows) T.; m. Margaret Conn, Dec. 29, 1955; children: Lylette, Robin, Carla, Pennie. Student, LaJunta Jr. Coll., 1951-52. Plant worker Rath Packing co., Waterloo, Iowa, 1952-61; rec. sec. local 46 United Food & Comml. Workers Union, 1961-69, pres. local 46, 1969-82, exec. v.p., 1982-83; pres., chief exec. officer Rath Packing Co., 1983-85; v.p. Blackhawk Holding Co., Waterloo, 1985-88; pres. Black Hawk Econ. Devel. Co., Waterloo, 1988—; pres. Ray Price Cherokee Farms, 1986-89; dir. Am. Meat Inst., Washington, 1983. Sec. Cedar Valley Partnership, 1989-95; past mem. Gov.'s Adv. Com. on OSHA, Iowa U. Alumni Adv. Bd., Ames; past bd. dirs. Goodwill, Inc., Waterloo, Adult's Care, Exceptional Persons. With USAR, 1956-64. Democrat. Baptist. Home: 826 Skyview Rd Waterloo IA 50703-9301 Office: Black Hawk Econ Devel Co 403 Jefferson St PO Box 330 Waterloo IA 50704-0330

TAYLOR, MARIA CENTOFANTI, marketing professional; b. Youngstown, Ohio, Sept. 5, 1963; d. Louis Frances and Elaine Marie (Haus) Centofanti; m. Steven Scott Taylor, Oct. 8, 1988. ABJ, U. Ga., 1985. Spl. events dir. Cystic Fibrosis Found., Atlanta, 1985-86, Stone Mountain Pk., Atlanta, 1986-87; account exec. A. Brown-Olmstead Assocs., Atlanta, 1987-88; mktg. mgr. Sta. WSB, Atlanta, 1988-94, ABC Sch. Supply, Duluth, Ga., 1994—. Mem. pub. rels. com. Boys Club of Atlanta, 1988-93, Nat. Kidney Found. of Ga., Atlanta, 1988; mem. assoc. bd. Cystic Fibrosis Found., Atlanta, 1987—. Recipient Am. Women in Radio and TV-TARA award, 1989. Mem. Pub. Rels. Soc. Am. (chmn. banquet com. Atlanta chpt. 1987, chmn. hosp. com. 1989—, Pres.'s award, 1986, 87, 88, 89). Office: ABC Sch Supply 3312 North Berkeley Lake Rd Duluth GA 30136*

TAYLOR, MARK DOUGLAS, publishing executive; b. Geneva, Ill., Jan. 16, 1951; s. Kenneth Nathaniel and Margaret Louise (West) T.; m. Carol E. Rogers, May 28, 1973; children: Jeremy Peter, Kristen Elizabeth, Margaret Louise, Rebecca Cynthia, Stephen Rogers. BA, Duke U., 1973. Exec. dir. Tyndale House Found., Wheaton, Ill., 1973-78; v.p. Tyndale House Pubs., Wheaton, Ill., 1978-84; pres., chief exec. officer Tyndale House Pubs., 1984—; dir. Living Bibles Internat. U.S., Naperville, Ill., 1972-92. Author The Complete Book of Bible Literacy, 1992. Mem. Wheaton Liquor Control Commn., 1986—, chmn., 1994—; chmn. bd. dirs. Outreach Cmty. Ctr., 1986-93. Mem. Internat. Bible Soc. (bd. dirs. 1992—). Office: Tyndale House Publishers Inc 351 Executive Dr Box 80 Wheaton IL 60189 *What we accomplish in life is soon forgotten. Our best legacy is to pass on to our children and grandchildren our positive values.*

TAYLOR, MELDRICK, professional boxer, Olympic athlete. Jr. welterweight champion Internat. Boxing Fedn., 1988-90; welterweight champion World Boxing Assn., 1991-92. Recipient Gold medal boxing featherweight divsn. Olympics, 1984.

TAYLOR, MESHACH, actor; b. Boston, Apr. 11; m. Bianca Taylor; 4 children. Student, Fla. A&M U. With Organic Theatre Group, Chgo. Leading role in the touring co. of Hair, Chgo., (play) Sizwe Banzi is Dead (Joseph Jefferson award) Goodman Theatre, Chgo., 1976, Huckleberry Finn (Emmy award) PBS Prodn., Chgo.; actor: (film) Damien - Omen II, Buffalo

Bill, (motion picture for TV) How to Murder a Millionaire; co-star: Mannequin, House of Games.; guest star (TV series) Barney Miller, Lou Grant, The White Shadow, M*A*S*H; host: (TV show) WMAQ-TV Black Life; with TV series Designing Women, 1986-93, Dave's World, 1993—. Avocations: travel, studying fgn. langs. Office: care Innovative Artists 1999 Ave of the Stars Ste 2850 Los Angeles CA 90067*

TAYLOR, MICHAEL ALAN, psychiatrist; b. N.Y.C., Mar. 6, 1940; s. Edward D. and Clara D. T.; m. Ellen Schoenfield, June 28, 1963; children—Christopher, Andrew. B.A., Cornell U., 1961; M.D., N.Y. Med. Coll., 1965. Intern Lenox Hill Hosp., N.Y.C., 1965-66; resident N.Y. Med. Coll., 1966-69, asst. prof. psychiatry, 1971-73; asso. prof. SUNY Med. Sch., Stony Brook, 1973-76; prof. psychiatry Univ. Health Scis., Chgo. Med. Sch., 1976—, dept., 1976-94. Author: The Neuropsychiatric Mental Status Examination, 1981; sr. author: General Hospital Psychiatry, 1985, The Neuropsychiatric Guide to Modern Everyday Psychiatry, 1993; editor-in-chief Neuropsychiat., Neuropsychology and Behavioral Neurology Jour.; also numerous articles. Served to lt. comdr. M.C. USNR, 1969-71. Grantee NIMH, 1971-73; Grantee Ill. Dept. Mental Health, 1976-81; VA grantee, 1985-93. Fellow Am. Psychiat. Assn.; mem. AAAS, Am. Psychopath. Assn., Soc. Biol. Psychiatry, Ill. Psychiat. Assn. Office: FUHS Chgo Med Sch 3333 Green Bay Rd North Chicago IL 60064-3037

TAYLOR, MICHAEL R., federal agency administrator, lawyer. BA in Political Science, Davidson (N.C.) Coll.; JD, U. Va. Atty. Office of the Gen. Counsel FDA, 1976-80, exec. asst. to commr., 1980-81; assoc. King & Spalding, Washington, 1981-84, ptnr., 1984-91; dep. commr. for policy FDA; acting undersecretary for food safety U.S. Dept. Agr., 1994—; mem. Nat. Acad. Scis. Com. on Scientific and Regulatory Issues Underlying Pesticide Use Patterns and Agrl. Innovation. mem. editl. bd. Food Drug Cosmetic Law Jour., 1988-91. With U.S. Army, 1971-73. Office: Dept Agr/Food Safety & Inspect Svc/J Whitten Bldg Rm 331 E 14th & Independence Washington DC 20250*

TAYLOR, MILLARD BENJAMIN, concertmaster, educator; b. Crete, Nebr., Aug. 9, 1913; s. Joseph Elbert and Anna Blodgett (Bennett) T.; m. Marie Jeanne Capasso, Jan. 2, 1939; children: Virginia Ann (Mrs. James Edward Smith), Jeanne Taylor Hernandez. MusB, Eastman Sch. Music, 1935; MusD, Doane Coll., 1967; DLitt, Nebr. Wesleyan U., 1975. Prof. violin Eastman Sch. Music, Rochester, N.Y., 1944-79; prof. emeritus Eastman Sch. Music, 1979—, chmn. string dept., 1950-76; Edward F. Arnold vis. prof. music Whitman Coll., 1979-80; head string dept. Chautauqua Summer Music Schs. Concertmaster Nat. Symphony Orch., 1938-44, Rochester Philharm. Orch., 1944-67, Pro-Musica Chamber Orch. of Columbus, 1980-89, Naples (Fla.) Philharm., 1983-92; concertmaster Dallas Symphony Orch., N.J. Symphony Orch.; violinist Eastman Piano Quartet, 1967-79, Eastman String Trio, New Eng. Piano Quartet, 1992-96; 1st violinist, leader Chautauqua String Quartet; contbr. articles to Instrumentalist mag. Bd. dirs. Rochester Civic Music Assn., 1969-72. Named Musician of Year Rochester chpt. Mu Phi Epsilon, 1966. Mem. Pi Kappa Lambda, Phi Mu Alpha Sinfonia.

TAYLOR, MORRIS ANTHONY, chemistry educator; b. St. Louis, July 10, 1922; s. Henry Clay Nathaniel and Georgia Lee Anna (Kenner) T.; m. Millie Betty Fudge, July 17, 1948 (dec. Jan. 1969); children: Carla Maria, Morris Jr.; m. Veonnia Joyce McDonald, Aug. 4, 1973; children: Dorcas Lynnea, Demetrius Sirrom. BS in Chemistry, St. Louis U., 1952. Rsch. chemist Universal Match Corp., Ferguson, Mo., 1952-54; mfg. chemist Sigma Chem., St. Louis, 1954; clin. chemist 5th Army Area Med. Lab., St. Louis, 1955-56; analytical chemist U.S. Dept. Agr.-Agrl. Rsch. Svc. Meat & Poultry Inspection, St. Louis, 1956-67; supervisory chemist U.S. Dept. Agr.-Food Safety and Quality Svc., St. Louis, 1967-76, chemist in charge, 1976-79; adj. prof. chemistry St. Louis Community Coll., 1981—; rating panel mem. Bd. CSC, St. Louis, 1969-79; reviewer Assn. Ofcl. Analytical Chemists, St. Louis, 1969-79; collaborator FDA Labs. on Analytical Methods, St. Louis, 1969-79. Bd. mem. Draft Bd. III, St. Louis, 1970-76. With U.S. Army, 1942-46. Fellow Am. Inst. Chemists; mem. Am. Chem. Soc., Internat. Union Pure and Applied Chemistry, St. Louis U. Alumni Chemists. Roman Catholic. Home: 10410 Monarch Dr Saint Louis MO 63136-5612 Office: Saint Louis CC 5600 Oakland Ave Saint Louis MO 63110-1316

TAYLOR, NICOLE RENÉE, model; b. Miami, Fla.; d. Ken and Barbara T. With Irene Marie, Miami, 1989; contracts with L'Oreal, 1990-92, Cover Girl Makeup; appeared in Seventeen (cover girl) 1989, Vogue, Elle, Mademoiselle, Harper's Bazaar; modeled for Yves Saint Laurent, Karl Lagerfeld. Office: IMG Models 170 Fifth Ave 10th Fl New York NY 10010

TAYLOR, NORMAN FLOYD, band director, computer educator, administrator; b. Dover, Ohio, Oct. 29, 1932; s. James Benton and Lela Augusta (Sinden) T.; m. Peggy Ann Cox, Sept. 7, 1952; children: Norman Dudley, Steven Dexter, Gregory Dennis. BS, U. Houston, 1954; MEd, Kent State U., 1963, EdS, 1977. Band dir. Ashtabula (Ohio) Area City Schs., 1958-70, prin., 1970-74; prin. Shaker Heights (Ohio) City Schs., 1974-81, Perry (Ohio) Local Schs., 1981-85; treas. Jos. Badger Local Schs., Kinsman, Ohio, 1987-89; supr. computer instrn. support svcs. Ashtabula (Ohio) Area City Schs., 1989-93, computer instr., 1993—; asst. prof. Computer Sci. Kent State U., Burton, Ohio, 1982-86, Ashtabula, 1987-88. Contbr. articles to profl. jours. Dir. Ashtabula Ch. Choir, 1958-78; mem. Ludlow Community Assn., Shaker Heights, 1974-81. Mem. NEA, Ohio Edn. Assn., Ohio Asn. Elem. Sch. Adminstrs., Shaker Heights Elem. Prins. Assn. (pres. 1980-81), Ashtabula Mid. Mgmt. Assn. (pres. 1973-74), Kiwanis Club, Phi Delta Kappa. Presbyterian. Avocations: music, golf, skiing. Home: 2501 Southwood Dr Painesville OH 44077-4956 Office: Ashtabula Area City Schs 401 W 44th St Ashtabula OH 44004-6807

TAYLOR, NORMAN WILLIAM, economics educator; b. Wigan, Eng., Jan. 9, 1923; s. Albert and Jessie (Slonker) T.; m. Eleanor Dorothy Harper, July 18, 1953; children—David Gordon, Laurie Elizabeth. B.Sc., U. London, 1950; M.A., Yale, 1954, Ph.D., 1958; LLD (hon.), Tohoku Gakuin U., Japan, 1988. Clk. London, Midland & Scottish Ry. Co., Preston, Eng., 1939-40; clk. City Treas. Office, Wigan, 1940-42, 47-48; exec. officer War Office, U.K., 1948-49; asst. instr. econs. Yale, 1955-57, instr. econs., 1957-59; asst. prof. econs. Lawrence U., 1959-62; vis. asst. prof. econs. U. Wis., 1961-62; assoc. prof. econs. Franklin and Marshall Coll., Lancaster, Pa., 1962-69; prof. econs. Franklin and Marshall Coll., 1969-80, Charles A. Dana prof. econs., 1980-88, emeritus, 1988—, chmn. dept., 1964-79, 81-84; vis. prof. Tunghai U., Taiwan, 1967-68. Contbr. articles profl. jours. Served to capt. Brit. Army, 1942-47. Recipient Lindback award for disting. teaching, 1981. Mem. Am. Econ. Assn.

TAYLOR, PATRICIA, theater company managing director. BA in English and Econs., Vassar Coll.; MFA in Theater Mgmt., Columbia U. With mgmt. svcs. dept. Theatre Comms. Group; gen. mgr. Williamstown Theatre Festival; mng. dir. Classic Stage Co., N.Y.C., 1990—; mgmt. assoc. for Broadway prodrs. and gen. mgrs. McCann and Nugent for prodns. including Crimes of the Heart, Amadeus, Mass Appeal, Good, Pacific Overtures; various theater mgmt. positions Manhattan Theatre Club, Shubert Orgn., The Lucille Lortel Theatre, Vivian Beaumont Theatre. Contbr. articles on mgmt. issues Am. Theatre, Mgr.'s Bull., Trustee Newsletter. Office: Classic Stage Co 136 E 13th St New York NY 10003-5306

TAYLOR, PATRICIA LEE, special education educator; b. Cadillac, Mich., Dec. 2, 1946; d. Leo Arthur and Betty Jean (Norden) Dunbar; m. Thomas Taylor, Dec. 26, 1974 (div. Oct. 1985); children: David, Christopher, Taryn. BA, Mich. State U., 1971, MA, 1973; MEd, U. Ctrl. Fla., 1993. Cert. elem. tchr., spl. edn. tchr., tchr. mentally handicapped and emotionally impaired. Tchr. primary emotionally handicapped Ctr. for Adjustive Edn., Sarasota, Fla., 1971-72, Roosevelt Jr. High Sch., Cocoa Beach, Fla., 1973-76, Edgewood Jr. High Sch., Merritt Island, Fla., 1973-76; tchr. varying exceptionalities Cadillac Sr. High Sch., 1976-77, tchr., 1982-89; tchr. pre-sch. Tom Thumb Coop. Nursery, Cadillac, 1979-81; tchr. devel. kindergarten Kenwood Elem. Sch., Cadillac, 1981-82; tchr. exceptional edn. on-the-job tng. Maynard Evans High Sch., Orlando, Fla., 1989-94; asst. prin. Magnolia Sch., Orlando, Fla., 1994—; faculty rep., exec. bd. Classroom Tchrs. Assn., Cadillac, 1985-87; coach disabled sports team, Orlando, 1989-90; mem. com. Standards for Student Support Svcs. Mich. State Bd. Edn., Lansing, 1987-88; mentor gifted/talented Cadillac H.S., 1988-89; mem. Hospitality, Health and Industry Tng. Adv. Coun.; Cmty. Based Instrn. Com., Orlando, 1990-91; participant Four Seasons project Nat. Center for Restructuring Edn., Schs., Tchg., 1993. Author: Students Do the Job, 1991; editor: Feelings, Reflections, 1988, The Writer's Grip, 1989; editor yearbook, 1977. Mem. Mercy Hosp. Aux. Guild, Cadillac, 1976-81; troop leader Girl Scouts U.S., Cadillac, 1986-87; den mother Boy Scouts Am., Cadillac, 1986-87. Recipient Innovative Classroom Practices award Found. for Orange County Pub. Schs./Walt Disney World, 1991, Teacheriffic award Found. for Orange County Pub. Schs./Walt Disney World, 1992. Mem. NEA, ASCD, Nat. Assn. Realtors Coun. for Exceptional Children (mini-grantee 1991), Mich. Assn. Children with Learning Disabilities, Fla. Edn. Assn., Mich. Edn. Assn., Nat. Urban Alliance/Foxfire, Coun. for Exceptional Children (chpt. 155 pres. 1995—), Assn. Univ. Women, Coun. Adminstrs. Exceptional Children, Phi Delta Kappa, Kappa Delta Phi. Democrat. Presbyterian. Avocations: painting, creative writing, scuba diving, flying, tennis. Home: 7112 Caloosa Ct Orlando FL 32819 Office: Magnolia Sch 1900 Matterhorne Rd Orlando FL 32818

TAYLOR, PAUL, choreographer; b. Allegheny County, Pa., July 29, 1930; s. Paul B. and Elizabeth (Rust) T. Student, Syracuse U., 1949-52, Juilliard Sch. Music, 1952-53; hon. doctoral degrees include, Duke U., 1983, Conn. Coll., 1983, Syracuse U., Juilliard, SUNY at Purchase; doctorate (hon.), Skidmore U., 1995. Artistic dir. Paul Taylor Dance Co., 1957—; dancer Merce Cunningham Co., 1954, Martha Graham, 1955-60. Paul Taylor Dance Co. has performed in over 300 U.S. cities and made 34 overseas tours; participated numerous arts festivals in 36 nations; PBS TV appearances include Dance in America, Live From the American Dance Festival, Two Landmark Dances, Three Modern Classics, The Taylor Company: Recent Dances; choreographer over 100 works including Aureole, 1962, Private Domain, 1969, Esplanade, 1975, Cloven Kingdom, 1976, Airs, 1978, Le Sacre du Printemps (the Rehearsal), 1980, Arden Court, 1981, Mercuric Tidings, 1982, Sunset, 1983, Roses, 1985, Last Look, 1985, Musical Offering, 1986, Ab Ovo Usque ad Mala, 1986, Syzygy, 1987, Kith and Kin, 1987, Minikin Fair, 1989, Speaking in Tongues, 1989, Company B, 1991, Spindri Ft., 1993, A Field of Grass, 1993, Oz, 1993, Moonbine, 1994, Aureole, 1994; author: (autobiography) Private Domain, 1987 (Nat. Book Critics Circle award for biography 1987). Decorated Chevalier des Arts et Lettres, France, elevated to officier, 1984; Guggenheim fellow, 1961, 66, 83, MacArthur Found. fellow, 1985; recipient Internat. Circle of Criticism for Artistic Rsch. and Cultural Exch. award Festival Nations, Paris, 1962, Best Fgn. Attraction prize Critics of Chile, 1966, Capezio Dance award, 1967, Creative Arts award Brandeis U., 1978, Dance Mag. award, 1980, Samuel H. Scripps Am. Dance Festival award. 1983, Arts award State N.Y., 1987, Lions of Performing Arts award N.Y. Pub. Libr., 1989, Emmy award Speaking in Tongues, 1992,Kennedy Ctr. Honors award, 1992, Am. Soc. Graphic Artists award, 1992,Nat. Medal Arts, 1993, Meadows award So. Meth. U., 1995; named Dancer of Yr. London's Dance and Dancers, 1965, Nat.Mus. Dance Hall of Fame, 1995. Office: Paul Taylor Dance Co 552 Broadway New York NY 10012-3922

TAYLOR, PAUL ALBERT, banker; b. St. John, N.B., Can., June 17, 1943; s. Albert and Mary Kathleen (McCullough) T.; children—Beth E., Brian P., Stephen C. B.A. in Econs., U. Western Ont., 1966; M.B.A. in Fin., U. Windsor, 1971. Area exec. Orion Bank Ltd., London, 1974-76, exec. dir., 1977-78; sr. mgr. Global fin. Royal Bank of Can., Montreal, Que., 1978-80, asst. gen. mgr. Global Fin., 1980; asst. gen. mgr. national accts. Royal Bank of Can., Toronto, Ont., 1980-82, sr. v.p. national accts., 1982-83, sr. v.p. world corp. banking, 1983-86; sr. v.p. investment banking, internat. and dep. chmn. Orion Royal Bank, London, 1986-88; exec. v.p. investment banking head office Royal Bank Can., Toronto, Ont., 1988-90, exec. v.p. treasury and investment banking head office, 1990-95, exec. v.p. trading head office, 1995—; bd. dirs. RBC Dominion Securities Ltd.; co-chmn. fin. sector Can. Japan Bus. Com. Mem. Halton Prog. Conservative Assn., Founders Club, Zeta Psi. Roman Catholic. Office: Royal Bank of Can, 200 Bay St Royal Bank Plaza, Toronto, ON Canada M5J 2J5

TAYLOR, PAUL B., dancer. Attended, Syracuse U. soloist Martha Graham Dance Co., 1955-62; guest artist George Balanchine's Episodes N.Y.C. Ballet, 1959; author: (autobiography) Private Domain, 1987. elected to knighthood as "Chevalier de l'Ordre des Arts et des Lettres" French Gov't., 1969, officier, 1984, commdr., 1990. Recipient more than forty awards including 3 Guggenheim fellowships and six hon. Doctor of Fine Arts degrees, and lifetime achievement awards; Emmy award for outstanding individual achievement in choreography Speaking in Tongues, 1991; Nat. Medal of Arts award by Pres. Clinton The White House and numerous others. Office: Paul Taylor Dance Co 552 Broadway New York NY 10012-3922

TAYLOR, PETER VAN VOORHEES, advertising and public relations consultant; b. Montclair, N.J., Aug. 25, 1934; s. John Coard and Mildred (McLaughlin) T.; m. Janet Kristine Kirkebo, Nov. 4, 1978; 1 son, John Coard III. BA in English, Duke U., 1956. Announcer Sta. WQAM, Miami, 1956; announcer, program dir. Sta. KHVH, Honolulu, 1959-61; promotion mgr. Sta. KPEN, San Francisco, 1962; with Kaiser Broadcasting, 1962-74, GE Broadcasting Co., 1974-78; program/ops. mgr. Sta. KFOG, San Francisco, 1962-66; mgr. Sta. WXHR AM/FM, Cambridge, Mass., 1966-67; gen. mgr. Sta. WJIB, Boston, 1967-70; v.p., mgr. FM div. Kaiser Broadcasting, 1969-72; v.p., gen. mgr. Sta. KFOG, San Francisco, 1970-78; pres. Taylor Communications, 1978-90, Baggott & Taylor, Inc., 1990-91, Taylor Advt. & Pub. Rels., 1991—, Broadcast Skills Bank, 1975-76, Roast Host, 1993—. Trustee, WDBS, Inc., Duke U., 1974-80; bd. dirs. San Francisco BBB, 1976-78, 89-94, San Francisco Boys & Girls Club, 1991-93, Coast Guard Found., 1991—, Leukemia Soc., San Francisco, 1992-93, San Francisco Found., 1994—, Duke Devel. Coun., 1992—. Mem. No. Calif. Broadcasters Assn. (pres. 1975-77, bd. dirs. 1984-86), Nat., Internat. Radio Clubs, Mus. Assn., San Francisco Symphony, Bay Area Publicity Club, Worldwide TV/FM Dx Assn., Advt. Tennis Assn. (pres. 1975-77), Olympic Club, Golden Gate Breakfast Club (v.p. 1995—), The Family Club, Rotary (San Francisco - bd. dirs. 1988-93, 1st v.p. 1990-91, pres. 1991-92, dist. 5150 - pub. rels. chmn. 1986-89, conf. chmn. 1990, area rep. 1992-93, bd. dirs. 1994-95, dist. governor nom., 1995—). Lt. USCGR, 1957-63. Home and Office: 2614 Jackson St San Francisco CA 94115-1123

TAYLOR, PEYTON TROY, JR., gynecologic oncologist, educator; b. Tuscaloosa, Ala., July 21, 1941; s. Peyton Troy Sr. and Frances (Sutter) T.; m. Helena Ström, Sept. 23, 1967; children: Annika, Karin, Sarah. BS, U. Ala., 1963; MD, Med. Coll. Ala., 1968. Intern U. Va. Hosp., Charlottesville, 1968-69, resident, 1969-70, 72-75; asst. prof. ob-gyn U. Va., Charlottesville, 1976-79, assoc. prof., dir. divsn. ob-gyn., 1981-87, Richard N. and Louise R. Crockett prof., 1987—; prof. ob-gyn., dir. divsn. ob-gyn. U. Va. Health Scis. Ctr., Charlottesville, 1987—; assoc. dir. U. Va. Cancer Ctr., 1995—; clin. assoc. surgery Nat. Cancer Inst., Bethesda, Md., 1970-72; assoc. prof. U. Ala., Birmingham, 1979-81. Contbr. articles to profl. jours. Served with USPHS, 1970-72. Fellow ACS, Am. Coll. Obstetricians and Gynecologists; mem. Assn. Acad. Surgeons, Soc. Gynecol. Oncologists, Soc. Surg. Oncology, Am. Soc. of Clin. Oncology, Am. Assn. for Cancer Rsch., Internat. Gynecol. Cancer Soc. Episcopalian. Office: U Va PO Box 387 Charlottesville VA 22902-0387

TAYLOR, PRESTON M., JR., federal agency administrator; m. Audrey Taylor; children: Christopher, Cinthia. BA, Pepperdine U.; MA, Ctrl. Mich. U.; grad., Indsl. Coll. of Armed Forces, Air Command and Staff Coll., Air Force Squadron Officer's Sch. Commd. USAF, advanced through grades to brig. gen.; with Air Nat. Guard; supr. naval aircraft engine and avionics logistics sect. Naval Air Warfare Ctr., Lakehurst, N.J.; dep. adj. gen. of N.J., ret., 1993, asst. sec. of Labor for Vets.' Employment and Tng., 1993—. Decorated Legion of Merit, Air Force Commendation medal, Air Force Orgnl. Excellence award, Armed Forces Res. medal, N.J. Medal of Honor, N.J. Merit award. Office: Vet Employment & Training Svcs 200 Constitution Ave NW Washington DC 20210-0001

TAYLOR, R. WILLIAM, trade association executive. Master's degree, Ohio U. Cert. assn. exec. Chief staff exec. AIME, N.Y.C., 1963-68, Soc. Mfg. Engrs., Dearborn, Mich.; pres. Am. Soc. Assn. Execs., Washington, 1981—. Hon. co-chmn. Clinton/Gore Inaugural. With USAF. Inductee Hall of Leaders, Conv. Liaison Coun. Office: Am Soc Assn Execs The ASAE Bldg 1575 Eye St NW Washington DC 20005-1168

TAYLOR, RALPH ARTHUR, JR., lawyer; b. Washington, Jan. 19, 1948; s. Ralph Arthur Sr. and Mary Florence (Aylor) T.; m. Joanna Lamb Moorhead, Jan. 30, 1988; children: Alison M., John Duncan. BS in Engring. with honors, Princeton, 1970; JD, U. Va., 1975. Bar: Va. 1975, D.C. 1976, Md. 1989, U.S. Dist. Ct. D.C. 1977, U.S. Dist. Cts. (ea. and we. dists.) Va. 1986, U.S. Dist. Ct. Md. 1988, U.S. Ct. Appeals (4th cir.) 1991, U.S. Ct. Appeals (D.C. cir.) 1977, U.S. Ct. Appeals (6th cir.) 1991, U.S. Ct. Claims 1985, U.S. Supreme Ct. 1980. Program advisor U.S. EPA, Boston, 1970-72; assoc. Steptoe & Johnson, Washington, 1975-84; assoc. Shaw, Pittman, Potts, & Trowbridge, Washington, 1984-86, ptnr., 1986—. Assoc. editor Litigation News, 1985—; notes editor Va. Law Rev., 1974-75; contbg. author: International Technology Transfers, 1995. Pres. Cloisters West Homeowners Assn., Washington, 1989, 90; pres. 1625 Q St. Condominium Assn., Washington, 1982-86. Lt. USPHS, 1970-72. Mem. Order of the Coif, Met. Club (Washington), Kenwood Golf and Country Club, Barristers, Princeton Club (Washington). Protestant. Avocations: sailing, skiing, tennis, squash, amateur radio. Office: Shaw Pittman Potts & Trowbridge 2300 N St NW Washington DC 20037-1122

TAYLOR, RAMONA GARRETT, executive assistant; b. Dallas, 1930. Student So. Meth. U. Sec. to pres. Universal Fin. Co., Dallas, 1957-61; corp. sec., exec. asst. to chmn. bd. dirs., CEO Lomas Fin. Corp., Dallas, 1965-90, sr. v.p., sec., 1990—. Office: Lomas Fin Corp Tex Commerce Tower 2200 Ross Ave Ste 4300 E Dallas TX 75201

TAYLOR, RAY, state senator; b. Steamboat Rock, Iowa, June 4, 1923; s. Leonard Allen and Mary Delilah (Huffman) T.; student U. No. Iowa, 1940-41, Baylor U., 1948-49; m. Mary Allen, Aug. 29, 1924; children—Gordon, Laura Rae Taylor Hansmann, Karol Ann Taylor Rogers, Jean Lorraine Taylor Mahl. Farmer, Steamboat Rock, Iowa, 1943—; mem. Iowa Senate, 1973-95; bd. dirs., sec. Am. Legis. Exchange Council, 1979—. Sec., Hardin County Farm Bur., 1970-72; mem. Iowa div. bds. Am. Cancer Soc.; chmn. Am. Revolution Bicentennial Com. Mem. Steamboat Rock Community Sch. Bd., 1955-70; coordinator Republican youth, 1968-72. Chmn. bd. Faith Bapt. Bible Coll.; pres. Am. Council Christian Chs.; chmn. Iowans for Responsible Govt. Named Guardian of Small Bus., NFIB/Iowa, 1989-90, for outstanding support for good govt. and accessible, affordable health care in Iowa, Iowa Physician Assistant Soc., 1991, Ind. Bapt. fellow of the Midwest, Christian Patriots, 1994, Hon. alumnus Faith Bapt. Bible Coll. & Theol. Sem., 1995; recipient Contenders award Am. Coun. Christian Chs., 1991, Legislator of Yr. award Iowa Soc. of Friends, 1991-92. Mem. Wildlife Club. Baptist. Home: 31363 185th St Steamboat Rock IA 50672-8107

TAYLOR, RAYMOND ELLORY, mechanical engineering researcher; b. Ames, Iowa, Oct. 19, 1929; s. Alva A. and Maude Marguerite (Crowe) T.; m. Elfa M. Shaffer, Apr. 22, 1952; children, Wayne, David. BS in Chem. Tech., Iowa State U., 1951; MS in Phys. Chemistry, U. Idaho, 1956; PhD in Solid State Tech., Pa. State U., 1967. Chemist, supr. GE, Richland, Wash., 1951-56; sr. rsch. engr. Atomics Internat., Canoga Park, Calif., 1957-64; assoc. sr. rschr. Thermophysical Properties Rsch. Lab/Purdue U., West Lafayette, Ind., 1967-75, dir., 1975-95; cons. Ordinance Enrging. Assocs., GE, Sandia Nat. Labs., Lockheed Missle and Space Co., Atomic Energy Commn. Can., Bendix Brake Divsn., Theta Industries, Technometrics, Air Force Materials Lab., Combustion Engring. Co., Supertemp Co., Argonne Nat. Lab., GM, Office Naval Rsch., Pennwalt Corp., Vesuvius Crucible Co., Gibson Electric Co., Proctor and Gamble, ALCOA, Corning Glass Co., Dept. Energy, Naval Surface Weapons Ctr., Bethlehem Steel, Cohart Refractories Co., Corp., Roll Mfrs. Inst., Carborundum Co., Areospace Corp., Sandvik Corp., Cummings Engine Corp., Travenol Labs., Sloan Kettering, Dana Perfect Circle, Teledyne Energy Systems, Pfizer Inc., Hughes Aircraft, Allegheny Ludlum Steel Co., CMW Inc., We. Electric Co., Reliance Universal Inc., AMP Inc., Kock Rsch. and Tech. Ctr., Ctrl. Inst. Indsl. Rsch., Semi-Alloys, Gen. Scis. Inc., Carpenter Techs., Hercules Aerospace Co., Bush-Wellman, Brunswick Corp., North Am. Refractories, Zicar Corp., Hayes Internat., E. I. DuPont, Ferro Corp., Storgae Techs., CTS, IBM Inc., Sci. Applications, Outboard Marine Corp.; presenter in field. Editor Review Sci. Instruments; contbr. numerous articles and reports to sci. jours.; co-inventor direct heating flash diffusivity apparatus, device and techniques to measure thermal diffusivity/conductivity of thin films; research in transport properties at high tempuratures, diffusivity of composite materials, transport properites, multiproperty measurements, thermophotovoltaic energy conservation work, computer applications in the laboratory, high tempurature thermal conductivity reference standards, sonic measurements of insulations; inventor automatic non-destructive aircraft brake discs. Mem. ASTM (governing bd.), North Am. Thermal Analysis Soc., Internat. Thermal Expansion Symposium (governing bd., by-laws com.), Sigma Xi, Phi Lambda Upsilon, Phi Eta Sigma, Phi Kappa Phi. Home: 618 Essex St Lafayette IN 47906-1531 Office: Purdue U Thermophysical Properties Rsch Lab 2595 Yeager Rd West Lafayette IN 47906-1335

TAYLOR, REESE HALE, JR., lawyer, former government administrator; b. Los Angeles, May 6, 1928; s. Reese Hale and Kathryn (Emery) T.; m. Lucille Langdon, Dec. 29, 1948 (div. 1959); children: Reese Hale (dec.), Stuart Langdon, Anne Kathryn, Lucille Emery; m. Jolene Yerby, June 30, 1972. B.A. with distinction, Stanford U., 1949; LL.B., Cornell U., 1952. Bar: Calif. 1954, Nev. 1966. Assoc. Gibson, Dunn & Crutcher, Los Angeles, 1952-58; pvt. practice Los Angeles, 1958-65; assoc. Wiener, Goldwater & Galatz, Las Vegas, Nev., 1966-67; chmn. Nev. Pub. Service Commn., Carson City, 1967-71; ptnr. Laxalt, Berry & Allison, Carson City, 1971-78, Allison, Brunetti, MacKenzie & Taylor, Carson City, 1978-81; chmn. ICC, Washington, 1981-85; ptnr. Heron, Burchette, Ruckert & Rothwell, Washington, 1986-90, Taylor & Morell, Washington and Long Beach, Calif., 1990-91, Taylor, Morell & Gitomer, Washington and Long Beach, 1992-94; of counsel Keesal, Young & Logan, Long Beach, 1994—; vice chmn. Nev. Tax Commn., Carson City, 1967-69; mem. Nev. Gov.'s Cabinet, Carson City, 1967-70, Carson City Bd. Equalization, 1979-81, chmn., 1979-80; bd. dirs. U.S. Rail Assn., Washington, 1981-85. Del. Republican Nat. Conv., Kansas City, Mo., 1976, mem. platform com., 1976, alt. del., Detroit, 1980; mem. Rep. Nat. Com., 1980-81. Mem. ABA, Am. Judicature Soc., Capitol Hill Club, Cornell Club (N.Y.), Order of Coif, Phi Gamma Delta, Phi Delta Phi. Episcopalian. Office: Keesal Young & Logan Union Bank Bldg 400 Oceangate PO Box 1730 Long Beach CA 90801-1730

TAYLOR, REGINA, actress; b. Dallas; d. Nell Taylor. Student, So. Meth. U. TV appearances include (movies) Crisis at Central High, 1981, Howard Beach: Making the Case for Murder, 1989, (mini-series) Children of the Dust, 1995, (series) I'll Fly Away, 1991-93 (Emmy award nominee best actress in a drama 1993, Golden Glove award), Law and Order, 1990, 94; films include Lean on Me, 1989, Losing Isaiah, 1995, Clockers, 1995; stage appearances include Romeo and Juliet, 1986, King Lear, 1987, The Tempest, 1988, one-woman show Escape From Paradise, 1994. Office: c/o William Morris Agency 1350 Avenue Of The Americas New York NY 10019-4702*

TAYLOR, RICHARD, philosopher, educator; b. Charlotte, Mich., Nov. 5, 1919; s. Floyd Clyde and Marie Louise (Milbourn) T.; m. Thelma Maxine Elworthy, Jan. 14, 1944 (div. 1961); children: Christopher, Randall; m. Hylda Carpenter Higginson, Dec. 26, 1961 (div. 1985); 1 step dau., Molly; m. Kim Fontana, Oct. 8, 1985; children: Aristotle, Xeno. A.B., U. Ill., 1941; A.M., Oberlin Coll., 1947; Ph.D., Brown U., 1951. Faculty Brown U., 1951-52, 53-63, prof. philosophy, 1958-63, chmn. dept., 1959-60, William Herbert Perry Faunce prof. philosophy, 1959-63; prof. philosophy grad. faculty Columbia, 1963-66; prof. philosophy U. Rochester, N.Y., 1966—; chmn. dept. U. Rochester, 1966-69; Faculty Swarthmore Coll., 1953, Ohio State U., summer 1959, Cornell U., summer 1961; vis. prof. philosophy Columbia, 1962, Ohio State U., 1963; vis. Robert D. Campbell prof. philosophy Wells Coll., 1967-68; vis. Robert H. Truax prof. philosophy Hamilton Coll., 1971; vis. Melvin Hill prof. humanities Hobart-William Smith Colls., 1974; Leavitt-Spencer adj. prof. philosophy Union Coll., 1981-89; Disting. resident philosopher Hartwick Coll., 1989—. Author: Metaphysics (Spanish, Dutch, Japanese, Portugese, Korean transl.), 1963, rev. edit., 1974, 83, 91, Action and Purpose, 1965, Good and Evil, 1970, Freedom, Anarchy and the Law, 1973, With Heart and Mind, 1973, Having Love Affairs, 1982, 2d edit., 1990, Ethics, Faith and Reason, 1985; editor:

Theism (J.S. Mill), 1957, Selected Essays (Schopenhauer), 1963; assoc. editor: Am. Philos. Quar. 1972-81; Contbr. articles to publs., U.S., Eng., Australia. Served to lt. USNR, 1943-47. Mem. Am. Philos. Assn., Phi Beta Kappa. Home: 9374 State Route 89 Trumansburg NY 14886-9227

TAYLOR, RICHARD EDWARD, physicist, educator; b. Medicine Hat, Alta., Can., Nov. 2, 1929; came to U.S., 1952; s. Clarence Richard and Delia Alena (Brunsdale) T.; m. Rita Jean Bonneau, Aug. 25, 1951; 1 child, Norman Edward. B.S., U. Alta., 1950, M.S., 1952; Ph.D., Stanford U., 1962; Docteur honoris causa, U. Paris-Sud, 1980; DSc, U. Alta., 1991; LLD (hon.), U. Calgary, Alta., 1993; DSc (hon.), U. Lethbridge, Alta., 1993, U. Victoria, B.C., Can., 1994. Boursier Lab. de l'Accelerateur Lineaire, Orsay, France, 1958-61; physicist Lawrence Berkeley Lab., Berkeley, Calif., 1961-62; staff mem. Stanford (Calif.) Linear Accelerator Ctr., 1962-68, assoc. dir., 1982-86, prof., 1968—. Fellow Guggenheim Found., 1971-72, von Humboldt Found., 1982; recipient Nobel prize in physics, 1990. Fellow AAAS, Am. Acad. Arts and Scis., Am. Phys. Soc. (W.K.H. Panofsky prize div. particles and fields 1989), Royal Soc. Can.; mem. Can. Assn. Physicists, Nat. Acad. Scis. (fgn. assoc.). Office: Stanford Linear Accelerator Ctr PO Box 4349, M/S 96 Stanford CA 94309

TAYLOR, RICHARD JAMES, lawyer; b. Merrill, Wis., Jan. 19, 1939; s. M.N. and Billie (Mead) T.; m. Nancy Hildebrand, Nov. 25, 1966. BA, U. Wis., 1962; DEF, U. Orleans, France, 1963; JD, U. Mich., 1966; postgrad., U. Paris II, 1971-72. Bar: N.Y. 1968. Assoc. Langner Parry Card & Langer, N.Y.C., 1966-68, Conboy Hewitt O'Brien & Boardman, N.Y.C., 1968-71; asst. prof. U. Paris I Law Sch., 1973-78; trademark and copyright counsel Colgate-Palmolive Co., N.Y.C., 1978—; seminar leader Am. Law and Lang., N.Y.C., 1987—; pro bono counsel Hearts and Voices, N.Y.C., 1992—; mem. com. of experts World Intellectual Property Orgn. Trademark Law Treaty, Geneva, 1993, 94; lectr. intellectual property symposia. Co-author: Doing Business in France, 1973, Worldwide Trademark Transfers, 1992; contbr. chpt. to book, articles to Nat. Law Jour., Trademark Reporter, Jour. Japan Trademark Assn., Bus. Latin Am., others. Mem. ABA (chair com. on internat. trademark treaties and laws 1990-91, del. to World Trademark Symposium 1992), Internat. Trademark Assn. (chair internat. com. 1987-89, mem. internat. task force 1989-90, bd. dirs. 1992-95, mem. task force on trademark law treaty 1991—).

TAYLOR, RICHARD POWELL, lawyer; b. Phila., Sept. 13, 1928; s. Earl Howard and Helen Moore (Martin) T.; m. Barbara Jo Anne Harris, Dec. 19, 1959; 1 child, Douglas Howard. BA, U. Va., 1950, JD, 1952. Bar: Va. 1952, D.C. 1956. Law clk. U.S. Ct. Appeals for 4th Circuit, 1951-52; assoc. Steptoe & Johnson, Washington, 1956-61, ptnr., 1962—, chmn. transp. dept., 1978—; sec., corp. counsel Slick Corp., 1963-69, asst. sec., 1969-72, also bd. dirs., 1965-68; sec., corp. counsel Slick Indsl. Co., 1963-72; sec., bd. dirs. Slick Indsl. Co. Can. Ltd. 1966-72; bd. dirs. Intercontinental Forwarders, Inc., 1969-72. Mem. Save the Children 50th Anniversary Com., 1982; gen. counsel Am. Opera Scholarship Soc., 1974—; mem. lawyer's com. Washington Performing Arts Soc., 1982—; mem. adv. com. Rock Creek Found. Mental Health, 1982—; mem. nat. adv. bd. DAR, 1980-83, chmn., 1983—; mem. men's com. Project Hope Ball, 1980—; nat. vice chmn. for fin. Reagan for Pres., 1979-80; mem. exec. fin. com. 1981 Presdl. Inauguration; mem. President's Adv. Com. for Arts, 1982—, Rep. Nat. Com., 1983—; Md. fin. chmn. Reagan-Bush '84, Bush-Quayle '88. Served to lt (j.g.), Air Intelligence USNR, 1952-56. Mem. ABA (co-chmn. aviation com. 1964-76, chmn. 1976-77), Fed. Bar Assn., D.C. Bar Assn., Va. Bar Assn., Fed. Energy Bar Assn., Am. Judicature Soc., Assn. Transp. Practitioners, Internat. Platform Assn., Raven Soc., Order of Coif. Episcopalian. Clubs: Univ., Capitol Hill, Nat. Aviation, Aero, Congl. Country (Washington), Potomac (Md.) Polo. Home: 14914 Spring Meadows Dr Germantown MD 20874-3444 Office: Steptoe & Johnson 1330 Connecticut Ave NW Washington DC 20036-1704 *Everyone should devote a portion of his or her life to efforts which help ensure that our country remains free and strong and that its concept of government under law is maintained and expanded throughout the world.*

TAYLOR, RICHARD TRELORE, retired lawyer; b. Kewanee, Ill., Aug. 5, 1917; s. Earl G. and Lucile (Cully) T.; m. Maureen Hoey, Feb. 9, 1946. B.S., U. Ill., 1939, J.D., 1946; LL.M., Columbia U., 1947. Bar: Ill. 1946, N.Y. 1947. Assoc. Cadwalader, Wickersham & Taft, N.Y.C., 1947-57, ptnr., 1957-87, presiding ptnr., 1977-87, of counsel, 1988-89. Trustee Marlboro Coll., Vt. Served with U.S. Army, 1941-45. Decorated Bronze Star. Mem. ABA. Clubs: University (N.Y.C.), The Pilgrims (N.Y.C.). Home: 870 United Nations Plz New York NY 10017

TAYLOR, RICHARD WILLIAM, investment banker, securities broker; b. Toledo, Sept. 16, 1926; s. Everett Ellsworth and Hazel (Broer) T.; m. Lyn Westerlund, Sept. 11, 1954; children: Julie Everett, Richard William, Alison Nichols, Jennifer Broer, Liane Westerlund. BS, U.S. Naval Acad., 1949; postgrad., U. Calif., 1952. Mem. Ohio Ho. of Reps. (100th gen. assembly from 9th Dist.); asst. mgr. Navy sales Martin Aircraft, Balt., 1953-56; with McKinsey & Co. (mgmt. cons.), N.Y.C., 1956-60; asst. to v.p. Cerro Corp., N.Y.C., 1960-62, spl. asst. to pres., 1965; pres. Cerro Aluminum Co., N.Y.C., 1962-65; successively v.p., exec. v.p., pres. and CEO Carter, Walker & Co., Inc., 1967-69; pres., CEO Burton, Dana, Westerlund, Inc., N.Y.C., 1969—; v.p. Sterling, Grace & Co., Inc., 1971-74, sr. v.p. corp. fin., 1980-81; v.p. corp. fin. Moseley, Hallgarten, Estabrook & Weeden Inc., 1975-80; v.p. Kidder, Peabody & Co. Inc., 1981-93, Oppenheimer & Co., Inc., 1993—. Bd. dirs., v.p. YWCA Retirement Fund, Inc. With USN, 1944-52. Decorated Air medal, Navy Commendation medal. Mem. U.S. Naval Acad. Alumni Assn., Downtown Athletic Club (bd. govs.). Home: Elmwood Orange VA 22960 Office: Oppenheimer & Co Inc Oppenheimer Tower World Financial Ctr New York NY 10281

TAYLOR, RICHARD WIRTH, political science educator; b. Cleve., Jan. 15, 1923; s. Robert and Irmgard (Wirth) T.; m. Sadie White, Sept. 19, 1946; children: Peter, Karla, Mark, Stephen. B.A., U. Ill., 1947, M.A., 1948, Ph.D., 1950. Instr. polit. sci. U. Minn., Mpls., 1950-52; asst. prof. polit. sci. Lehigh U., Bethlehem, Pa., 1952-55, Wis. State U., Stevens Point, 1955-56; vis. asst. prof. Northwestern U., Evanston, Ill., 1956-57; assoc. prof. Coe Coll., Cedar Rapids, Iowa, 1957-60, chmn., prof., 1960-67; prof. polit. sci. Kent State U., Ohio, 1967-92, prof. emeritus, 1992—, chmn., 1974-82; vis. prof. Karl-Marx-Universität, Leipzig, Fed. Republic Germany, 1990. Co-exec. editor Peace and Change, 1986-87. Mem. policy com. Friends Com. Nat. Legis., Washington, 1964-85, exec. com., 1986-87; mem. acad. adv. com., ombudsman com. Internat. Bar Assn., Edmonton Alta., Can., 1980—.

TAYLOR, ROBERT BROWN, medical educator; b. Elmira, N.Y., May 31, 1936; s. Olaf C. Taylor and Elizabeth (Place) Brown; m. Anita Dopico; children: Diana Marie, Sharon Jean. Student, Bucknell U., 1954-57; MD, Temple U., 1961. Diplomate Am. Bd. Family Practice. Gen. practice medicine New Paltz, N.Y., 1964-78; faculty physician Bowman Gray Sch. Medicine Wake Forest U., Winston-Salem, N.C., 1978-84; prof., chmn. dept. family medicine Oreg. Health Scis. U. Sch. Medicine, Portland, 1984—; mem. comprehensive part II com. Nat. Bd. Med. Examiners, Phila., 1986-91. Author: Common Problems in Office Practice, 1972, The Practical Art of Medicine, 1974; editor: Family Medicine: Principles and Practice, 1978, 4th edit., 1994, Helath Promotion: Principles and Clinical Applications, 1982, Difficult Diagnosis, 1985, Difficult Medical Management, 1991, Difficult Diagnosis II, 1992, Fundamentals of Family Medicine, 1996; contbg. editor Physicians Mgmt. Mag., 1972—; editl. bd. The Family Practice Rsch. Jour., 1980-90, The Female Patient, 1984—, Frontiers of Primary Medicine, 1983—, Am. Family Physician, 1990—, Jour. of Family Practice, 1990-93, Me. Tribune, 1993—. Served as surgeon USPHS, 1961-64. Fellow Am. Acad. Family Physicians (sci. program com.), Am. Coll. Preventive Medicine; mem. Soc. Tchrs. Family Medicine (bd. dirs. cert. of excellence), Assn. Am. Med. Colls., Am. Assn. for Study Headache, City Club, Multnomah Athletic Club, Phi Beta Kappa, Alpha Omega Alpha.. Home: 680 SW Regency Ter Portland OR 97225-6070 Office: Oreg Health Scis U Sch Medicine Mail Code FP 3181 SW Sam Jackson Park Rd Portland OR 97201-3011

TAYLOR, ROBERT HOMER, quality assurance professional, pilot; b. Rochester, N.Y., Mar. 18, 1922; s. C. Gilbert and Josephine Mary (Woodward) T.; m. Mignon Jane Beight, Aug. 1945; children: Robert Jr., Douglas Beight, Scott Woodward, Sondra Lee. BSME, Case Western Res. U., 1947. Commd. 2d lt. USAF, 1944, advanced through grades to lt. col., 1975; v.p., gen. mgr. Taylor Corp., 1947-53; mgr. quality assurance Spectra Physics Laserplane, Dayton, Ohio, 1976-89; pres., gen. mgr. CON-AV Corp., Tipp City, Ohio, 1989—; chief quality assurance staff on NASA Mercury Booster for USAF, Cape Canaveral, Fla., 1961-63; mgr. nuc. tng. weapons devel. USAF Weapons Lab., 1964-67; CAT I test mgr. F-111, 1967-68; instr. pilot C-7, tng. officer, Vietnam, 1969; project element monitor T-43, attache, A-37, C-130 aircraft, Pentagon, 1970-74; br. chief WPAFB, 1974-75. Advisor Aero Scis. Alternatives, Tipp City, 1990—. Lt. col. CAP. Decorated Air medal with three oak leaf clusters, DFC; named to Aviation Hall of Fame, 1986. Mem. VFW, Exptl. Aircraft Assn., Flying Angels, Inc. (pres. 1991), Masons, Beta Theta Pi (Case chpt. pres. 1942), Theta Tau, Early Birds. Episcopalian. Avocations: boating, flying, fishing, refurbishing antique aircraft. Home: 5855 Us Route 40 Tipp City OH 45371-9419 Office: CON-AV Corp 5855 Us Route 40 Tipp City OH 45371-9419

TAYLOR, ROBERT LEE, financial services and sales executive, information systems account executive, educator; b. Adrian, Mich., Jan. 9, 1944; s. Jack Raleigh and Virginia Dixon (Oakes) T.; m. Janice Grace George, Dec. 9, 1961; children—Robin, Lynne, David. A.A., Siena Heights Coll., 1974, B.A., 1976. With computer operation Gen. Parts div. Ford Motor Co., Rawsonville, Mich., 1965-66, prodn. monitoring supr., Saline Plant, Mich., 1966-75, methods and systems analyst, Ypsilanti Plant, Mich., 1975-77, data processing supr. Milan Plant, Mich., 1977-82, sr. systems analyst, Plastics, Paint and Vinyl div., Wixom, Mich., 1982-85; systems engr. Electronic Data Systems, Warren, Mich., 1985-86, systems engr. mgr. Romulus (Mich.) Parts Distbn. Ctr. Plant, 1986-87, customer service mgr., Toledo, 1987-88; project mgr. Computer Task Group, Southfield, Mich., 1988-89; tech. svcs. mgr., 1989-92, spl. agent Prudential, Tecumseh, Mich., 1992-94; ret. plan specialist Variable Annuity Life Ins. Co., Tecumseh, Mich., 1994—; instr. data processing Siena Heights Coll., Adrian, 1985-86; bd. dirs. Lenawee Area Life Underwriters, 1993—, pub. chmn., 1993, nat. committeeman, 1994, pres-elect 1995—. Commr. Tecumseh Planning Commn., 1976-80, vice-chmn., 1981-82; trustee Tecumseh Bd. Edn., 1981-82, sec., 1983-84, chmn. citizens adv. com., 1983, chmn. computer adv. com., 1984, chmn. policy com., 1983-84; chmn. Tecumseh Area Laymen's Assn., 1983; mem. exec. com. Lenawee County Republican party, 1982-88, precinct del., 1982-88, chmn. computer com., 1984-86; state del. State of Mich., 1983-85, 87; founding advisor Evang. Free Ch. Adrian-Tecumseh, 1984-85, elder, 1986-88, 90-92, 94—, Sunday Sch. supt., 1984-87, 89-90, chmn. Christian edn., 1986-89, 90-91, chmn. planning-bldg. com., 1987-93; asst. Sunday Sch. supt. Berean Baptist Ch., Adrian, 1980-83; tchr. mentally impaired, 1977-83; deacon, Sunday Sch. supt., Grace Bible Ch., Tecumseh, 1973-76; chmn. bd. deacons First Bapt. Ch., Tecumseh, 1970-71, youth advisor, 1968-71, Layman of Yr., 1970; vice chmn. Tecumseh Area Crusade for Christ, 1973, facilities chmn. Lenawee County Crusade for Christ, 1986; chmn. Life Action Crusade, 1987; mem. div. chmn. Lenawee Area Celebration, 1996. Served with USAF, 1961-65. Mem. Computer & Automated Systems Assn. (sr.) Mfg. Automation Protocol, Lenawee Assn. Life Underwriter, Nat. Assn. Life Underwriters, Mich. Assn. Life Underwriters, Soc. Mfg. Engrs. Avocations: golf, genealogy. Home: 603 Outer Dr Tecumseh MI 49286-1446 Office: VALIC 603 Outer Dr Tecumseh MI 49286-1446

TAYLOR, ROBERT LEWIS, academic administrator; b. Pitts., Dec. 10, 1939; s. Robert William and Elinor (Miller) T.; m. Linda Taylor Shapiro, Oct. 28, 1988; 1 child, Kara; children by previous marriage: Rob, Mike. AB in Am. Studies, cum laude, Allegheny Coll., 1961; MBA, Ohio State U., 1966; D in Bus. Adminstrn., Mgmt., Ind. U., 1972. Asst. prof., dir. rsch. USAF Acad., Colorado Springs, Colo., 1971-77, assoc. prof., dir. instrn. dept. econ., geography, mgmt., 1977-79, prof. mgmt., head dept. econs., geography, mgmt., 1980-81; assoc. dean Coll. Letters and Sci., head div. Bus. and Econs., Carl N. Jacobs Prof. of Bus. U. Wis., Stevens Point, 1981-84; dean Coll. Bus. Pub. Adminstrn. U. Louisville, 1984—; chmn. bd. dirs. Ky. Wood Floors, Louisville; bd. dirs. Pvt. Industry Coun., Louisville, Banc One Ky. Corp., Louisville; cons., advisor Kellogg Nat. Fellowship program Kellogg Found., Battle Creek Mich., 1985-89. Co-author, editor: Contemporary Issues in Leadership: In Pursuit of Excellence, 1984, 3d edit., 1996, Leadership Challenges for Today's Manager, 1988; contbr. articles to profl. jours. Chmn. Mayor's Strategic Planning Group, Louisville, 1986—; mem. Gov.'s Econ. Devel. Com., Frankfort, Ky., 1987-89, exec. com. Bus. Advs., 1988-92, task force on econ. devel. Ky. Legis. Rsch. Coun., 1991, Leadership Louisville, 1986, Leadership Ky., 1987. Mem. Acad. Mgmt. (proceedings editor 1976-77, newsletter editor 1983-86), Louisville C. of C. (bd. dirs., exec. com 1990—), Sigma Xi, Beta Gamma Sigma, Pi Gamma Mu. Mem. Eastern Orthodox Ch. Avocations: travel, walking, stamp collecting, reading. Home: 1516 Sylvan Way Louisville KY 40205-2408 Office: U Louisville Coll Bus & Pub Adminstrn Louisville KY 40292

TAYLOR, ROBERT P., lawyer; b. Douglas, Ariz., May 6, 1939; s. Paul Burton and Mary Ruth (Hart) T.; m. Sybil Ann Cappelletti, May 30, 1963 (div. Apr. 1974); children: David Scott, Nicole; m. Anne Dale Kaiser, Sept. 21, 1991. BSEE, U. Ariz., 1961; JD, Georgetown U., 1969. Bar: U.S. Ct. Appeals (9th circ.) 1969, U.S. Ct. Appeals (1st, 2d, 3d, 6th, and Fed. circs.), U.S. Supreme Ct., 1975. Elec. engr. Motorola Corp., Phoenix, 1961, Bell & Howell, Pasadena, Calif., 1964-65; examiner U.S. Patent Office, Washington, 1966-69; atty. Pillsbury Madison & Sutro, San Francisco, 1969-96, Howrey & Simon, Palo Alto, Calif., 1996—; mem. adv. commn. Patent Law Reform, Washington, 1990-92; mem. adv. bd. Litigation Risk Analysis, Palo Alto, Calif., 1985—. Contbr. articles to profl. jours. Dir. Ind. Colls. of No. Calif., San Francisco, 1982—, officer, 1988-96. Fellow Am. Coll. Trial Lawyers; mem. ABA (chair sect. antitrust 1991-92), Am. Law Inst. Avocations: Bicycling, cooking, hiking. Office: Howrey & Simon 2300 Geng Rd Palo Alto CA 94303

TAYLOR, ROBERT SUNDLING, English educator, art critic; b. Newton, Mass., Jan. 19, 1925; s. Frank Millikan and Elsie (Sundling) T.; m. Brenda K. Slattery, June 20, 1964; children: Gillian, Douglas. A.B., Colgate U., 1947; postgrad., Brown U. Art, music, film and theatre critic Boston Herald, 1948-67; editor publs. Inst. Contemporary Art, Boston, 1967; art critic Boston Globe, 1967-90, arts editor, 1973-76, book columnist, 1978—; prof. English, Wheaton Coll., Norton, Mass., 1961-96; fiction coord. Ea. States Writers Conf., Salem (Mass.) State Coll., 1979-80. Author: (novel) In Red Weather, 1961, Saranac: America's Magic Mountain, 1986, Fred Allen: His Life and Wit, 1989, New England: The Home Front, WWII, 1991; co-author: Treasures of New England, 1976. Trustee, Abbot Public Library, Marblehead, Mass., 1980-83. Served with USN, 1943-46. Mem. Mass. Hist. Soc. Club: St. Botolph (Boston). Home: 1 Thomas Cir Marblehead MA 01945-1203 Office: Wheaton Coll Norton MA 02766

TAYLOR, ROBERT WILLIAM, professional society administrator; b. Brownsville, Tenn., July 28, 1929; s. Charles William and Annie Laura (Taliaferro) T.; m. Jeanette Henshaw, Jan. 4, 1953; children: Robert William, Teresa, Mark Thomas. B.S. in Chemistry, Murray (Ky.) State U., 1949; M.S. in Journalism, Ohio U., 1950. Asst. editor Jour. Petroleum Tech., 1953, editor, 1954-63; exec. dir., sec. AIME, 1963-68; exec. v.p., gen. mgr. Soc. Mfg. Engrs., 1968-81; publishing dir. Mfg. Engring., 1968-81; pres. Am. Soc. Assn. Execs., Washington, 1981—, ASAE Found., Washington, 1981—, ASAE Service Corps., Washington, 1981—, ASAE Ins. Co., 1993—; bd. dirs. Inst. Orgn. Mgmt., Points of Light Fedn. Assoc. editor: Petroleum Prodn. Handbook, 1961. Past bd. dirs. One to One Found., Mfg. Engring. Edn. Found.; hon. co-chmn. Clinton/Gore Inaugural. Served to 2d lt. USAF, 1951-53. Fellow Soc. Mfg. Engrs., Jr. Engring. Tech. Soc. (past dir.), Am. Soc. Engring. Edn. (past dir.), Council Engring. and Sci. Soc. Execs. (past pres.), Am. Assn. Engring. Socs. (past dir.). Club: City of Washington (dir.). Home: 1401 N Oak St Apt 605 Arlington VA 22209-3648 Office: Am Soc of Assoc Executives 1575 I St NW Washington DC 20005-1105

TAYLOR, ROBIN LYNN, anchorperson, reporter; b. Pittsfield, Mass., May 11, 1964; d. Orley R. and Toni Taylor. BA, U. Wis., 1986. Anchor, reporter Sta. KAAL-TV, Austin, Minn., 1987-88, Sta. WROC-TV, Rochester, N.Y., 1988-94, Sta. WITI-TV, Milw., 1994—. Participant Day of Caring, United Way, Rochester, 1994; fundraiser Cystic Fibrosis, Milw., 1995; telethon vol. Muscular Dystrophy Assn., Milw., 1995. Recipient hon. mention for best newscast AP, 1992, Excellence in Journalism award Radio TV News Dirs.' Found., 1994, Emmy nomination, 1994. Office: Sta WITI-TV 9001 N Green Bay Rd Milwaukee WI 53217

TAYLOR, ROGER CONANT, writer; b. Newport, R.I., Nov. 18, 1931; s. Conant and Marjorie Perry (Buffum) T.; m. Priscilla Greene, June 12, 1953; children: Roger Conant, John Dean, Rebecca Buffum, Stephen Greene; m. 2d, Kathleen Elizabeth Carney, Aug. 17, 1991. AB, Harvard U., 1953; MS, Boston U., 1966. Commd. ensign U.S. Navy, 1953, advanced through grades to comdr. Res., 1967, ret., 1975; served in destroyers and submarines; editorial dir. U.S. Naval Inst., Annapolis, Md., 1960-69; pres. Internat. Marine Pub. Co., Camden, Maine, 1969-86. Author: Good Boats, 1977, More Good Boats, 1979, Still More Good Boats, 1981, The Elements of Seamanship, 1982, The Fourth Book of Good Boats, 1984, Knowing the Ropes, 1989, Thirty Classic Boat Designs, 1992. Mem. U.S. Naval Inst. (life). Home: 59 Summer St Westerly RI 02891

TAYLOR, RONALD LEE, school administrator; b. Urbana, Ill., Nov. 11, 1943; s. Lee R. and Katherine L. (Becker) T.; m. Patricia D. Fitzsimmons, Mar. 10, 1973; children: Jamie, Lara, Meredith, Dana. AB, Harvard U., 1966; MBA, Stanford U., 1971. Asst. contr. Bell & Howell, Chgo., 1971-73; pres. DeVry Inc./Keller Grad. Sch., Chgo., 1973—; bd. dirs. Precision Plastic, Columbia City, Ind., L. Karp & Sons, Elk Grove Village, Ill., Chernin's Shoes, Inc., Chgo. Pres. Hinsdale (Ill.) Sch. Bd., 1983-91; com. chmn. Ill. Bd. Higher Edn., Springfield, 1985—; state chmn. Employer Support of Guard and Res. Mem. Ill. State C. of C. (mem. edn. com. 1987—). Office: DeVry Inc 1 Tower Ln Villa Park IL 60181

TAYLOR, ROWAN SHAW, music educator, composer, conductor; b. Ogden, Utah, June 1, 1927; s. Hugh Taylor and Lucille (Olsen) Gaenger; m. Dorothy Foulger, June 26, 1946 (div. 1953); children: Kathleen, Scott; m. Priscilla Pulliam, Aug. 29, 1957; children: Mark, Dianne, Paul, Eric, Brent, Charlotte. BA, Brigham Young U., 1952, MA, 1957. Tchr. San Juan Sch. Dist., Blanding, Utah, 1948-50; with C.F. Braun Engring. Firm, 1950-58; tchr. L.A. Unified Dist., 1958-64; from instr. to prof. L.A. C.C., Woodland Hills, Calif., 1964—; condr., composer numerous symphonies and mus. works. Condr., composer 166 symphonies and numerous musical works, 1994—. With U.S. Army, 1955-56, Korea. Republican. Mem. Ch. Jesus Christ of LDS. Avocation: collecting cologne bottles. Home: 22544 Tiara St Woodland Hills CA 91367-3335

TAYLOR, ROY LEWIS, botanist, educator; b. Olds, Alta., Can., Apr. 12, 1932; s. Martin Gilbert and Crystal (Thomas) T. B.Sc., Sir George Williams U., Montreal, Que., Can., 1957; Ph.D., U. Calif. at Berkeley, 1962. Pub. sch. tchr. Olds Sch. Div., 1949-52; jr. high sch. tchr. Calgary Sch. Bd., Alta., 1953-55; chief taxonomy sect., research br. Can. Agrl. Dept., Ottawa, Ont., 1962-68; dir. Bot. Garden, prof. botany, prof. plant scis. U. B.C., Vancouver, 1968-85; pres., CEO Chgo. Horticultural Soc., 1985-94; dir. Chgo. Bot. Garden, Glencoe, Ill., 1985-94; exec. dir. Rancho Santa Ana Bot. Garden, Claremont, Calif., 1994—; prof. botany, chmn. botany program Claremont Grad. Sch., 1994—; pres. Western Bot. Svcs. Ltd. Author: The Evolution of Canada's Flora, 1966, Flora of the Queen Charlotte Islands, Vols. I and II, 1968, Vascular Plants of British Columbia: A Descriptive Resource Inventory, 1977; The Rare Plants of British Columbia, 1985. Mem. State of Ill. Bd. Natural Resources and Conservation, 1987-94; trustee Nature Ill. Found., 1990-94. Fellow Linnean Soc. London; mem. Can. Bot. Assn. (pres. 1967-68), Biol. Coun. Can. (pres. 1973-74), Am. Assn. Mus. (accreditation com. 1980-85, chmn. 1985-91, chmn. ethics commn. 1991-93), Am. Assn. Bot. Gardens and Arboreta (pres. 1976, 77, award of merit 1987), Chicago C. of C. (bd. dirs. 1995-98), Ottawa Valley Curling Assn. (pres. 1968-69), B.C. Soc. Landscape Archs. (hon.), U. B.C. Bot. Garden (hon.), Chgo. Hort Soc. (life, medal 1994), Gov. Gen.'s Curling Club Can. (life), Univ. Club Claremont, Men's Garden Club L.A. Office: Rancho Santa Ana Bot Garden Claremont CA 91711-3157

TAYLOR, SAMUEL ALBERT, playwright; b. San Francisco, June 13, 1912; m. Suzanne Combes, June 4, 1940; children: Ellinor, Michael, David. Student, U. Calif., Berkeley. Ind. playwright, 1950—; chmn. emeritus Dramatists Play Svc., Inc., N.Y.C. Playwright: The Happy Time, 1950, Sabrina Fair, 1953, The Pleasure of His Company, 1958, First Love, 1961, No Strings (mus. with Richard Rodgers), 1962, Beekman Place, 1964, Avanti!, 1968, A Touch of Spring, 1975, Legend, 1976, Perfect Pitch, 1978, Flying Colours, 1985, Three by Three, 1988. Mem. Dramatists Guild, Authors Guild, Writers Guild Am., Acad. Motion Picture Arts and Scis. Club: Century Assn. (N.Y.C.). Home: Meadow Rue East Blue Hill ME 04629

TAYLOR, SAMUEL E., health facility administrator; b. Sekondi, Ghana, Nov. 26, 1944; s. Kurankyi and Beatrice (Oware) T.; m. Shirley Taylor, Sept. 24, 1975; children: Eszylfie, Swazi. Diploma, Pasadena City Coll., 1980; BA in Econs., Gordon Coll., 1972; MTS, Gordon-Conwell Theol. Sem., 1973; MA, Pepperdine U., 1988; PhD in Leadership and Human Behavior, U.S. Internat. U., San Diego, 1994. RN, Calif. Staff devel. Congress Convalescent Hosp., Pasadena, Calif., dir. staff devel.; asst. nurse mgr. Los Angeles County-U. So. Calif. Med. Ctr., L.A.; staff developer, educator High Desert Hosp., Lancaster, Calif. Mem. Calif. Assn. Marriage and Family Therapists. Home: PO Box 6192 Altadena CA 91003

TAYLOR, SAMUEL JAMES, mathematics educator; b. Carrickfergus, Northern Ireland, Dec. 13, 1929; came to U.S., 1984; s. Robert James and Janie (Catherwood) T.; married; children—Richard, Charles, Jonathan, Helen. B.Sc., Queen's U., Belfast, No. Ireland, 1950; Ph.D., Cambridge U., 1954. Bye fellow Peterhouse, Cambridge U., Eng., 1953-55; lectr. Birmingham U., Eng., 1955-62; prof. London U., 1962-75, Liverpool U., Eng., 1975-83; vis. prof. U. B.C., Vancouver, Can., 1983-84; Whyburn prof. math. U. Va., Charlottesville, 1984—, chmn. dept., 1986-89. Author: Introduction to Measure and Probability, 1966, Exploring Mathematical Thought, 1970, Introduction to Measure and Integration, 1973; editor: Decomposition of Probability Distributions, 1964. Procter vis. fellow Princeton U., N.J. 1952. Fellow Cambridge Philos. Soc., Inst. Math. Stats.; mem. London Math. Soc. (sec. 1962-65, 68-71, editor 1980-83), Am. Math. Soc. Presbyterian. Office: U Va Dept Math Kirchoff Hall Charlottesville VA 22903-3145

TAYLOR, SHERRIL WIGHTMAN, broadcasting company executive; b. Salt Lake City, Jan. 4, 1924; s. Kenneth E. and Florence May (Wightman) T.; m. Josephine Vermillion, May 2, 1970; 1 child by previous marriage, Sarah. Student, U. Utah, 1943-46; BJ, U. Mo., 1947; postgrad., Yale U. Promotion mgr. KSL Radio, Salt Lake City, 1947-51; sales promotion mgr. CBS, Hollywood, Calif., 1951-53; CBS radio sales CBS, N.Y.C., 1953-56; dir. sales promotion and advt. CBS Radio, N.Y.C.; also v.p. Radio Advt. Bur., N.Y.C., 1956-58; sr. group head J. Walter Thompson, Chgo., 1958-61; ind. TV producer Kukla, Fran, and Ollie Show, N.Y.C., 1961-64; v.p. Nat. Assn. Broadcasters, Washington, 1964-67; dir. Nat. Assn. Broadcasters, 1969-78; v.p. affiliate relations CBS, 1967-79; cons. Bonneville Internat. Corp., 1979-85; pres. Taylor Co., 1985-91; vice chmn. Coltrin & Assoc., 1991—; pvt. sector coordinator USIA, Washington, 1982, cons., 1982—; chmn. adv. com. Voice of Am., Washington, 1989—; vis. lectr. Brigham Young U., Provo, Utah, 1980—, Emerson Coll., Boston, Mich. Central U., Southern Vt. Coll.; adv. faculty-industry seminar, 1980, 81; bd. dirs. Am. Communications Inc., Utica-Rome TV Svcs. Inc., 1988—. Author: Radio Programming in Action, 1967. Mem. Carnegie Hall com. for Utah Symphony, Park Avenue Preservation Com.; chmn. Freedom of Info. Fund, U. Mo.; past trustee The Helene Toolen Inst. Med. Rsch., Bennington, Vt., 1985—; mem. futures com. Bennington Mus., 1985—; bd. dirs. Nautical Ventures Inc., N.Y.C., 1987—. Mem. So. Calif. Broadcasters Assn. (dir.), Internat. Radio and TV Soc. (v.p., bd. dirs., pres., chmn., bd. dirs. found.), Broadcasters' Found. (dir.), Food and Wine Soc. (N.Y. chpt.), Am. Values Inc. (officer, bd. dirs.), Belleair (Fla.) Country Club, Sigma Chi. Episcopalian. Home: 430 E 86th St New York NY 10028-6441

TAYLOR, STEPHEN EMLYN, publishing executive; b. Cambridge, Eng., Apr. 28, 1951; s. Charles Henry and Diana (Burgess) T.; m. M. E. Malone, May 24, 1987; children: Maxwell, Conrad. BA in Psychology, Yale U., 1973. U.S. sales mgr., tech. advisor Snapir Ltd., Conn., 1973-74; mgr., sail designer North Sails, Boston, 1974-80; mgmt. trainee Boston Globe, 1980-82, asst. to bus. mgr., 1980-82, dir. info. svcs., 1982-86, asst. bus. mgr., 1986-88, bus. mgr., 1988-91, v.p., 1991-93, exec. v.p., 1993—. Bd. dirs. Greater Boston Food Bank, 1991—; mem. corp. Woods Hole (Mass.) Oceanographic Inst., 1993—; mem. U.S. Olympic Yachting Com., 1980-84. Mem. New

Eng. Newspaper Assn. (bd. dirs.), Yale Sailing Assocs. (treas., trustee), Cruising Club Am., N.Y. Yacht Club, New Bedford Yacht Club. Home: 18 Webster Rd Milton MA 02186-5318 Office: Globe Newspaper Co PO Box 2378 Boston MA 02107-2378

TAYLOR, STEPHEN LLOYD, food toxicologist, educator, food scientist; b. Portland, Oreg., July 19, 1946; s. Lloyd Emerson and Frances Hattie (Hanson) T.; m. Susan Annette Kerns, June 23, 1973; children: Amanda, Andrew. BS in Food Sci. Tech., Oreg. State U., 1968, MS in Food Sci. Tech., 1969; PhD in Biochemistry, U. Calif., Davis, 1973. Research assoc. U. Calif., Davis, 1973-74, research fellow, 1974-75; chief food toxicology Letterman Army Inst., San Francisco, 1975-78; asst. prof. food toxicology U. Wis., Madison, 1978-83, assoc. prof., 1983-87; head dept. food sci. technology, dir. Food Processing Ctr. U. Nebr., Lincoln, 1987—; cons. in field, 1978—. Contbr. articles to profl. jours. Fellow Nat. Inst. Environ. Health Sci., Nat. Acad. Scis. (chair food chems. codex com., bd. food and nutrition), Inst. Food Technologists (divsn. chmn. 198182, sect. chmn. 1984-85, exec. com. 1988-91); mem. Am. Acad. Asthma, Allergy and Immunology, Am. Chem. Soc. Democrat. Presbyterian. Home: 941 Evergreen Dr Lincoln NE 68510-4131 Office: U Nebr Dept Food Sci Tech Lincoln NE 68583-0919

TAYLOR, STEVE HENRY, zoologist; b. Inglewood, Calif., Mar. 18, 1947; s. Raymond Marten and Ardath (Metz) T.; 1 child, Michael Travis; m. Sarah Margaret Young, May 14, 1993. BA in Biology, U. Calif.-Irvine, 1969. Animal keeper Los Angeles Zoo, 1972-75, assoc. curator, 1975-76; children's zoo mgr. San Francisco Zoo, 1976-81; zoo dir. Sacramento Zoo, 1981-88; dir. Cleve. Met. Zoo, 1989—. Bd. dirs. Sacramento Soc. Prevention Cruelty to Animals, 1983-87, Sacramento Red Cross, 1988-89, Conv. and Visitor Bur. of Greater Cleve., 1995—. Fellow Am. Assn. Zool. Parks and Aquariums (infant care diet advisor 1979, 85, bd. dirs. 1987-93, pres. 1991-92, chmn. pub. edn. com. 1987-89, bd. regents, mgmt. sch., Outstanding Svc. award); mem. Captive Breeding Specialist Group, Internat. Union of Dirs. Zool. Gardens, The Wilds (bd. dirs. Ohio club), Sierra Club, Audubon Soc. Democrat. Home: 1265 Elmwood Rd Rocky River OH 44116-2236 Office: Cleveland Metroparks Zoo 3900 Brookside Park Dr Cleveland OH 44109-3132

TAYLOR, STEVEN BRUCE, agriculture company executive; b. Salinas, Calif., Dec. 29, 1954; s. Edward Horton and Joanne (Church) T.; m. Kathryn Hagler, Dec. 17, 1978; children: Meghan Jean, Kyle Hagler, Christian Steven. BA, U. Calif., Berkeley, 1978; MBA, Harvard U., 1985. Pres. Fresh Concepts, San Marino, Calif., 1985-87; mktg. staff Bruce Church, Inc., Salinas, Calif., 1987-91; pres. Fresh Express Retail Mktg., Salinas, 1991—, Fresh Internat., Salinas, 1991—; v.p. Salinas Valley Lettuce Co-op, Salinas, 1990—; bd. dirs. Produce for Better Health, Del., 1991—. Bd. Elders First Presbyn. Ch., Salinas, 1989-92, personnel com. 1989-94, bldg. com. 1990—; founding mem. Lincoln Club of Monterey County, Salinas, 1990. Avocations: basketball, skiing, soccer coach, bible study, board games. Home: 515 Santa Paula Dr Salinas CA 93901 Office: Fresh Internat 1020 Merrill St Salinas CA 93901-4409*

TAYLOR, STRATTON, state senator, lawyer; b. Sallisaw, Okla., Jan. 25, 1956; s. Owen and Velma T. AA, Claremore (Okla.) Jr. Coll., 1976; BSE with hons., U. Tulsa, 1978, JD, 1983. Bar: Okla. 1983. State rep. State of Okla., 1978-82, state senator, 1982—; ptnr. Carle, Higgins, Mosier & Taylor, Claremore, 1985—; commr. Uniform Commrs. on State Laws, 1985—; pres. pro tempore of Okla.Sen., 1994—. Chmn. Okla. Senate Jud. com., 1985-88, appropriations chmn., 1988-94; bd. dirs. Energy & Jobs, Oklahoma City, 1988—, Acypl Tour of Japan, Claremore Regional Med. Ctr. Mem. Okla. Bar Assn., Okla. Trial Lawyers Assn. Democrat. Baptist. Home: PO Box 1267 Claremore OK 74018-1267 Office: Oklahoma State Senate 522 State Capital Bldg Oklahoma City OK 73105

TAYLOR, STUART ROSS, geochemist, author; b. Ashburton, New Zealand, Nov. 26, 1925; s. Thomas Stuart and Anne Grace (Lloyd) T.; m. Noel Elvie White, May 21, 1958; chidlren: Susanna, Judith, Helen. BSc, U. New Zealand, 1948, MSc, 1951; PhD, Ind. U., 1954; DSc, Oxford U., 1978. Lectr. U. Oxford, Eng., 1954-58; sr. lectr. U. Cape Town, South Africa, 1958-60; professorial fellow Australian Nat. U., Canberra, 1961-90, vis. fellow, 1990—; prof. U. Vienna, 1992; vis. scientist Lunar and Planetary Inst., Houston, 1969-90. Author: Lunar Science: Post-Apollo View, 1975, Planetary Science, 1982, Solar System Evolution, 1992, (with others) Continental Crust, 1985; contbr. more than 200 articles to profl. jours. Recipinet Goldschmidt medal Geochem. Soc., 1993, Gilbert award Geol. Soc. Am., 1994. Fellow Royal Soc. New Zealand (hon.), Australian Acad. Sci., Geol. Soc. London (hon.), Geol. Soc. India (hon.); mem. NAS (fgn. assoc.), Meteoritical Soc. (pres. 1989-90). Office: Australian Nat U, Dept Nuclear Physics, Canberra 2601, Australia

TAYLOR, TELFORD, lawyer, educator; b. Schenectady, Feb. 24, 1908; s. John Bellamy and Marcia Estabrook (Jones) T.; m. Mary Eleanor Walker, July 2, 1937 (dec.); children: Joan, Ellen, John Bellamy II, Ursula Taylor Rechnegal; m. Toby Barbara Golick, Aug. 9, 1974; children: Benjamin Waite, Samuel Bourne. AB, Williams Coll., 1928, AM, 1932, LLD, 1949; LLB, Harvard U., 1932; LHD (hon.), Yeshiva U., 1987; D in Civil Law (hon.), Union U., 1987; LLD (hon.), Brandeis U., 1988. Instr. history and polit. sci. Williams Coll., 1928-29; law clk. to U.S. circuit judge N.Y.C., 1932-33; asst. solicitor U.S. Dept. Interior, Washington, 1933-34; sr. atty. A.A.A., 1934-35; assoc. counsel U.S. Senate com. on inter-state commerce, 1935-39; spl. asst. to atty. gen. U.S., 1939-40; gen. counsel FCC, 1940-42; practiced with Taylor, Scoll, Ferencz & Simon; vis. lectr. Yale U. Law Sch., 1957-76; vis. lectr. Columbia U. Law Sch., 1958-63, prof. law, 1963-74, Nash prof., 1974-76, emeritus, 1976—; prof. Cardozo Law Sch., 1976-77, 78—; vis. prof. Harvard U. Law Sch., 1977-78; Fed. Spl. master U.S. Dist. Ct. for So. Dist. N.Y., 1977-82; Adminstr. Small Def. Plants Adminstrn., 1951-52; counsel Joint Council for Edn. TV, 1951-61; chmn. N.Y.C. Adv. Bd. Pub. Welfare, 1960-63, mem., 1963-66. Author: Sword and Swastika, 1952, Grand Inquest, 1954, The March of Conquest, 1958, The Breaking Wave, 1967, Two Studies in Constitutional Interpretation, 1969, Nuremberg and Vietnam, 1970, Courts of Terror, 1976, Munich: The Price of Peace, 1979 (Nat. Book Critic's Circle award 1980), The Anatomy of the Nuremberg Trials; also articles on polit., legal, mil. subjects. Commd. maj. M.I. service U.S. Army, 1942; lt. col. Gen. Staff Corps, 1943; col. (assigned as mil. intelligence officer ETO, 1943-45) assoc. counsel, U.S. rep. for prosecution of war criminals, brig. gen. 1946; U.S. chief of counsel for war crimes Office Mil. Govt., 1946-49, U.S. Decorated DSM; Order Brit. Empire; French Legion of Honor; Polonia Restituta Poland; comdr. Order of Orange-Nassau, Netherlands, 1950; Lateran Cross, 3d class Vatican); recipient Nat. critics prize for non-fiction, 1979; Overseas fellow Churchill Coll., Cambridge, 1969. Fellow Am. Acad. Arts and Scis.; mem. Assn. of Bar of City of N.Y., Am. Law Inst., ASCAP, Res. Officer's Assn., Author's Guild, Mil. Order World Wars, Theta Delta Chi. Democrat. Club: Harvard. Home: 54 Morningside Dr New York NY 10025-1740

TAYLOR, TERRY R., editor, educator; b. Valley Forge, Pa., Oct. 4, 1952; d. Thomas R. and Anna P. (Bystrek) T. BA in Journalism, Temple U., 1974. Reporter gen. assignments, sch. news Charlotte (N.C.) News, 1974-77; supr., writer AP, Phila., 1977-81; supr., writer sports desk AP, N.Y.C., 1981-85, asst. editor sports, 1985-87, dep. editor sports, 1987-91, asst. chief bur., 1991-92, editor sports, 1992—; asst. editor sports N.Y. Times, 1991; assoc. in journalism Columbia U., N.Y.C., 1991-95; adv. bd. Honda Awards, 1996—. Recipient John A. Domino Meml. award St. Bonaventure U., 1996. Roman Catholic. Office: AP Sports 50 Rockefeller Plz New York NY 10020-1605

TAYLOR, THEODORE BREWSTER, physicist, business executive; b. Mexico City, July 11, 1925; s. Walter Clyde and Barbara (Howl) T.; m. Caro Dwight Arnim, June 13, 1948; children: Clare E. Taylor Hastings, Katherine W. Taylor Robertson, Christopher H., Robert P., Jeffrey J. B.S., Calif. Inst. Tech., 1945; Ph.D., Cornell U., 1954. Theoretical physicist U. Calif. Radiation Lab., Berkeley, 1946-49, Los Alamos Sci. Lab., 1949-56; sr. research adviser Gen. Atomic div. Gen. Dynamics Corp., San Diego, 1956-64; dep. dir. (sci.) Def. Atomic Support Agy., Dept. Def., 1964-67; chmn. bd. Internat. Research & Tech. Corp., 1967-76; vis. lectr. Princeton U., 1976-80; pres. Appropriate Solar Tech. Inst., 1980-87, Nova, Inc., 1980—; also bd. dirs.; pres. So. Tier Environ. Protection Soc., 1990—; mem. Pres.'s Commn. on Accident at Three-Mile Island, 1979; cons. Los Alamos Sci. Lab., 1956-64, Aerospace Corp., 1960-61, Air Force Sci. Adv. Bd., 1955-58, AEC, 1966-70, Def. Atomic Support Agy., 1966-69, U.S. Army Sci. Adv. Panel, 1967-71, Office of Tech. Assessment, 1976—, Rockefeller Found., 1977-80, Princeton U., 1980—, Fedn. Am. Scientists, 1986—; chmn. Los Alamos Study Group, Air Force Space Study Com., 1961; mem. panel outer space ACDA, 1961; mem. adv. bd. Solar Energy Research Inst., 1980-81. Served to ensign USNR, 1942-46. Recipient Ernest Orlando Lawrence award, 1965. Home and Office: PO Box 662 Wellsville NY 14895-0662

TAYLOR, THEODORE LANGHANS, author; b. Statesville, N.C., June 23, 1921; s. Edward Riley and Elnora Alma (Langhans) T.; m. Gweneth Ann Goodwin, Oct. 25, 1946; children: Mark, Wendy, Michael; m. Flora Gray Schoenleber, Apr. 18, 1981. Student, Fork Union Mil. Acad., 1939-40, U.S. Mcht. Marine Acad., 1942-44. Reporter Portsmouth (Va.) Star, 1941-42, Bluefield (W.Va.) News, 1946-47; sportswriter NBC-Radio, N.Y.C., 1942; asst. dir. pub. relations N.Y. U., 1947-48; dir. pub. relations YMCA Schs. and Colls., N.Y.C., 1948-50; publicist Paramount Pictures, Hollywood, Calif., 1955-56; assoc. producer Perlberg-Seaton Prodns., Hollywood, 1956-61. Free lance writer 1961—; author: The Magnificent Mitscher, 1954, Fire on the Beaches, 1957, People Who Make Movies, 1968, The Cay, 1969 (Jane Addam's Children's Book award 1970), The Children's War, 1971, Air Raid: Pearl Harbor, 1971, The Maldonado Miracle, 1973, Rebellion Town, 1973, Showdown, 1973, Teetoncey, 1974, Teetoncey and Ben O'Neal, 1975, Battle in the Arctic Seas, 1976, The Odyssey of Ben O'Neal, 1977, A Shepherd Watches, A Shepherd Sings, 1977, Jule, 1979, Battle of Midway Island, 1981, The Trouble with Tuck, 1981, Sweet Friday Island, 1981, HMS Hood vs Bismarck, 1982, Battle in the English Channel, 1983, The Cats of Shambala, Rocket Island, 1985, Walking Up a Rainbow, 1986, The Stalker, 1987, The Hostage, 1988, Monocolo, 1989, Sniper, 1989, Tuck Triumphant, 1991, The Wierdo, 1991, Maria, 1992, To Kill the Leopard, 1993, Timothy of the Cay, 1993, The Bomb, 1995, Rogue Wave, 1996. Served with USNR, 1945-46, 50-55. Recipient Lewis Carroll Shelf award, 1970, Silver medal Commonwealth Club, 1970, Best Book award So. Calif. Coun. on Children's Lit., 1970, Best Book award U. Calif. at Irvine, 1970, 74, Best Non-Fiction award Western Writers Am., 1977, Young Reader's medal Calif. Reading Assn., 1984, 92, Edgar Allan Poe award, 1992, Utah Young Adult Book award, 1993, Md. Children's Book award, 1994, Scott O'Dell Best Hist. Fiction award, 1995. Mem. Calif. Writers Guild, Acad. Motion Picture Arts and Scis., Screen Writers Guild. Republican. Lutheran. Address: 1856 Catalina Laguna Beach CA 92651-3340

TAYLOR, THERESA EVERETH, registered nurse, artist; b. Carthage, N.Y., Aug. 9, 1938; d. Michael Patrick and Angelina (Cerroni) Evereth; m. James Edgar Taylor II, Mar. 12, 1966; children: Britt, Priscilla, Blackwell. Diploma in nursing, House of Good Samaritan Sch. Nursing, Watertown, N.Y., 1959; BFA summa cum laude, Ursuline Coll., 1992, post-grad., 1996—. RN, N.Y., Ohio. Home health nurse DON WillCare, Cleve., 1994—. Exhbns. in group shows. Pres. Wasmer Gallery Coun., Pepper Pike, Ohio, 1992-96; clk. vestry St. Christopher's by the River, Gates Mills, 1979-81; treas. Welcome Wagon, Chesterland, Ohio, 1984-85; vol. artist Cleve. Ctr. Contemporary Art, 1993—. Avocations: art, political activism, medical AIDS activities. Home: 12060 Caves Rd Chesterland OH 44026-2104 Office: 615 Wilson Mills Highland Heights OH 44143

TAYLOR, THOMAS ALEXANDER, III, retired newspaper editor; b. Mobile, Ala., Apr. 9, 1930; s. Thomas Alexander and Mary Helen (McKee) T.; m. Nadine Cecelia Lose, Dec. 5, 1956 (div.); children—Sean Edwin, Julia Marie Taylor Lolley, Stephen Alexander; m. Sandra Joy Johnson McCarter, Jan. 17, 1976; 1 child, Thomas Alexander IV; stepchildren—Steven, Samantha Baxley. B.A., U. Ala.-Tuscaloosa, 1952. Reporter Biloxi Daily Herald, Miss., 1949-50, 52; reporter Columbus Dispatch, Ohio, 1956-57; reporter Mobile Press Register, Ala., 1954-56, 57-60, asst. news editor, then news editor, 1960-83, exec. editor, 1983-94. Served to 1st lt. USAF, 1952-54, col. Res., 1954-79. Mem. Soc. Profl. Journalists (pres. Mobile chpt. 1963), Ala. AP Assn. (pres. 1973-74, treas. 1979-85), Mobile United (treas. 1991-94), Press Club of Mobile (pres. 1981, 93, Career Achievement award 1980). Episcopalian.

TAYLOR, THOMAS WILLIAM, lawyer; b. Columbus, Ind., Feb. 11, 1943; s. Virgil W. and Margaret Emma (Voiles) T.; m. Linda Kay Followell, Jan. 1, 1964; children: Pamela Kay, William Lansing. AB with honors, Ind. U., 1965; LLB cum laude, Harvard U., 1968. Bar: Mass. 1968, U.S. Dist. Ct. Mass. 1969. Assoc. Ropes & Gray, Boston, 1968-78, ptnr., 1978—; lectr. Pres.'s urban policy program seminars U.S. Coun. of Mayors, 1982; chmn. tax panel nat. workshop Coun. of Infrastructure Financing Authorities, 1993. Mem. Nat. Assn. Bond Lawyers (opinions com., chmn. securities law panel Washington workshop 1992, lectr. atty.'s workshop Chgo. 1983—), Am. Coll. Bond Counsel (founding fellow). Avocations: rock climbing, snowboarding, orienteering, trumpet playing. Office: Ropes & Gray 1 International Pl Boston MA 02110-2600

TAYLOR, TIMOTHY LEON, college dean; b. Danville, Ill., May 7, 1963; s. Howard L. and A. Jane (Pate) T.; m. Melisa Sue Swenny, May 25, 1991. AAS in Electronics Tech., Danville Area C.C., 1985, AAS in Indsl. Maintenance, 1986; BS in Electronics Mgmt., So. Ill. U., 1989, MS Ed. in Vocat. Edn., 1991. Store mgr. Marty K Restaurant, Danville, 1979-86; owner, operator Tayco Sys., Pekin, Ill., 1986-87; mgr. Gatsby's Bar & Billiards, Carbondale, Ill., 1988-91; machine operator Ambrosia Chocolate Co., Milw., 1991-92; dir. electronics MBTI Bus. Tng. Inst., Milw., 1992-94; assoc. dean indsl. occupations, agr. and apprenticeship Blackhawk Tech. Coll., Janesville, Wis., 1994—; cons., owner Taylor Info. Mgmt. Sys., Stoughton, Wis., 1991—. Recipient Curriculum Devel. award Accrediting Coun. Indpendent Colls. and Schs., 1993. Mem. ASCD. Baptist. Avocations: music performance, basketball, baseball, football. Office: Blackhawk Tech Coll 6004 Prairie Ave Janesville WI 53547

TAYLOR, TONY S., research scientist. Head stability physics group Gen. Atomics, San Diego. Recipient Excellence in Plasma Physics Rsch. award Am. Phys. Soc., 1994. Office: General Atomics PO Box 85608 San Diego CA 92186-9784

TAYLOR, VESTA FISK, real estate broker, educator; b. Ottawa County, Okla., July 15, 1917; d. Ira Sylvester and Judie Maude (Garman) Fisk; m. George E. Taylor, Aug. 17, 1957 (dec. Oct. 1963); stepchildren: Joyce, Jean, Luther. AA, Northeastern Okla. A&M, 1931; BA, N.E. State U., Tahlequah, Okla., 1937; MA, Okla. State U., 1942. Life cert. Spanish, English, history, elem. Tchr. rural sch. grades 1-4 Ottawa County, Okla., 1931-33; tchr. rural sch. grades 1-8 Ottawa County, 1933-38; tchr. H.S. Spanish, English Wyandotte, Okla., 1938-42; tchr. H.S. Spanish, English, math. Miami, Okla., 1942-57; tchr. H.S. Spanish Jacksonville, Ill., 1960-65; tchr. H.S. Spanish, English Miami, 1965-79; owner, broker First Lady Realty, Miami, 1979—; tchr. real estate for licensing N.E. Okla. Vocat.-Tech., Afton, 1980—; radio spellmaster weekly-county groups Coleman Theater Stage, 1954-57, radio program weekly 4-H, Miami, 1953-57. Author: (poem) The Country School, 1994. Sec. Ottawa County Senior's Ctr., 1993—; restoration com. Friends of Theater, 1993—. Named Outstanding Coach Ottawa County 4-H Clubs, Miami, 1955, 67, Outstanding Alumnus All Yrs. H.S. Reunion, Wyandotte, Okla., 1992, Champion Speller N.E. Okla. Retirees, Oklahoma City, 1991. Mem. AAUW (pres. 1978-80, treas. 1994—), Ottawa County Retired Educators (treas. 1990—), Spanish Study Club (pres., instr. 1962-63), Miami Classroom Tchrs. (v.p. 1973-77, sec. 1994—), Tri-State Travel Club (purser 1989—), Kappa Kappa Iota. Democrat. Baptist. Avocations: gardening, reading, travel, volunteering. Home: 821 Jefferson St Miami OK 74354-4910 Office: First Lady Realty 206 A St NW Miami OK 74354

TAYLOR, VOLNEY, marketing company executive; b. Portsmouth, Ohio, Dec. 6, 1939; s. Lafayette and Martha Louise (Frederick) T.; m. Kathleen Ann MacMahon, May 17, 1969; children—Lafayette, Lloyd MacMahon, Kerry Erin, Frederick Daly. B.S. in Indsl. Engring, Ohio State U., 1962; M.B.A., Harvard U., 1966. Asso. mem. McKinsey & Co., Inc. (mgmt. cons.), N.Y.C., 1966-72; exec. v.p., dir. Funk & Wagnalls, Inc., N.Y.C., 1972-74; v.p. fin. Reuben H. Donnelley Co., N.Y.C., 1974-76; dir. corp. planning Dunn & Bradstreet Corp., N.Y.C., 1976-77, v.p. corp. planning, 1977-78, corp. v.p., 1979-80, sr. v.p., 1980-82, exec. v.p., 1982—, also bd. dirs.; gen. mgr. Official Airline Guides, Oak Brook, Ill., 1978-79, also bd. dirs.; chmn. bd. dirs. Dun & Bradstreet Info. Svcs., Murray Hill, N.J., 1991—; bd. dirs. Dun & Bradstreet, Inc., Dun & Bradstreet Europe, Dun & Bradstreet Internat., Dun's Mktg. Svcs., Inc., Moody's Investors Svc.; pres. The Reuben H. Donnelley Corp., 1988-90. Served to lt. (j.g.) USNR, 1962-64. Mem. Harvard Bus. Sch. (N.Y.C.) Club, Beta Theta Pi. Office: Dunn & Bradstreet Info Svcs 1 Diamond Hill Rd New Providence NJ 07974*

TAYLOR, W. O. (BILL TAYLOR), state legislator, business consultant; b. Zanesville, Ohio, July 29, 1932; s. Henry Ray and Lorena Louise (Winkler) T.; m. Shirley Ann Jacobs, Mar. 11, 1951; children: Bill, Larry, Sallie, Charles, Richard, Julie. AA in Bus. Adminstrn., Jacksonville (Fla.) U., 1957; B of Sci. Edn., Midwestern State U., Wichita Falls, Tex., 1968, MEd, 1972. Advanced secondary cert., Idaho. Acct. Swift & Co., Jacksonville, 1951-58; v.p. Taylor Bros. Inc., Baton Rouge, 1958-60; pres. Carter Paint Co., Inc., Wichita Falls, 1960-68; tchr. econs. Wichita Falls Pub. Sch., 1968-78; pres. Taylor Enterprises, Inc., Nampa, Idaho, 1978—; mem. Ho. of Reps, State of Idaho, Boise, 1986—, chmn. bus. com., 1994. Bishop Ch. of Jesus Christ of Latterday Saints, Wichita Falls, 1964-69. Served to sgt. USMC, 1950-53, Korea. Named Republican of Yr., Canyon County Rep. Ctrl. Com., 1987. Mem. DAV, Sertoma (life, pres. 1965, Sertoman of Yr. award 1964). Republican. Avocations: history, geneaology. Home: 8367 Track Rd Nampa ID 83686-9424 Office: Idaho Ho of Reps State Capitol Boise ID 83720

TAYLOR, WALTER WALLACE, lawyer; b. Newton, Iowa, Sept. 18, 1925; s. Carroll W. and Eva (Greenly) T.; A.A., Yuba Coll., 1948, A.B., 1950; M.A., U. Calif., 1955, J.D., McGeorge Coll. Law, 1962; m. Mavis A. Harvey, Oct. 9, 1948; children—Joshua Michael (dec. 1980), Kevin Eileen, Kristin Lisa, Jeremy Walter, Margaret Jane, Melissa E., Amy M. Adminstrv. analyst USAF, Sacramento, 1951-53; personnel, research analyst Calif. Personnel Bd., Sacramento, 1954-56; civil service, personnel analyst, chief counsel, gen. mgr. Calif. Employees Assn., Sacramento, 1956-75; staff counsel, chief profl. standards Calif. Commn. Tchr. Credentialing, 1975-88, ret. 1988; staff counsel State Office Real Estate appraiser Licensing and Certification, 1992-94, ret.; tchr. discipline civil service, personnel cons. Served USCGR, 1943-46. Mem. Calif. State Bar, Am., Sacramento County bar assns. Democrat. Author: Know Your Rights, 1963-64. Home: 4572 Fair Oaks Blvd Sacramento CA 95864-5336

TAYLOR, WELFORD DUNAWAY, English language educator; b. Caroline County, Va., Jan. 3, 1938; s. George Welford and Minnie (Durrette) T.; m. Carole Virginia Wickham, Jan. 19, 1942; 1 child, Virginia Welford. BA, U. Richmond, 1959, MA, 1961; PhD, U. Md., 1966. Tchr. Randolph-Macom Acad., Front Royal, Va., 1959-60, St. Christopher's Sch., Richmond, Va., 1960-61; instr. English Va. Commonwealth U., Richmond, 1961-63; prof. English U. Richmond (Va.), 1964—; chmn. English dept. U. Richmond, 1978-86, James H. Bostwick chair English, 1991—; book reviewer Richmond Times-Dispatch, 1986—. Author: Amélie Rives (Princess Troubetzkoy), 1973, Sherwood Anderson, 1977, Robert Frost and J. J. Lankes: Riders on Pegasus, 1996, The Woodcut Art of J. J. Lankes, 1996; editor: The Buck Fever Papers, 1971, The Newsprint Mask, 1990, Our American Cousin/The Play That Changed History, 1990. Mem. Poe Found. (1st v.p.-sec. 1994), Sherwood Anderson Soc. (founder 1976), Va. Writers Club, English-Speaking Union, Country Club Va. (Richmond). Republican. Episcopalian. Avocations: book collecting, art collecting. Home: 5 Calycanthus Rd Richmond VA 23221-3101 Office: U Richmond Dept English Richmond VA 23173

TAYLOR, WESLEY BAYARD, JR., retired army officer; b. Covington, Ky., June 5, 1944; s. Wesley B. Sr. and Varina Martha (Morgan) T.; m. Linda L. Taylor, June 2, 1967; children: Kathleen C., Clint C. BS, U.S. Mil. Acad., 1965; MA in Internat. Rels., U. Calif., Santa Barbara, 1973; student, U.S. Army War Coll., 1985-86. Commd. 2d lt. U.S. Army, 1965, advanced through grades to brig. gen., 1990; asst. bn. advisor, sr. bn. advisor Airborne Divsn. Adv. Detachment, U.S. Mil. Assitance Command, Vietnam, 1967-68; staff officer Dept. of Army, Washington, 1980-81; bn. comdr. 3rd Bn., 5th Inf. U.S. Army, Republic of Panama, 1981-83; bn. comdr. 1st Ranger Bn. U.S. Army, Hunter Army Airfield, Ga., 1983-85; strategic fellow U.S. Army War Coll., Carlisle Barracks, Pa., 1986-87; regimental comdr. 75th Ranger Regiment, Ft. Benning, Ga., 1987-89; asst. divsn. comdr. 1st Armored Divsn., Germany, 1989-91; dep. dir. ops, readiness and mobilization Dept. of Army, Washington, 1991-92; dep. asst. sec. of def. for policy and missions Office Sec. of Def. for Spl. Ops. and Low Intensity Conflict, Washington, 1992-94; pres., CEO Cal Farley's Boys Ranch & Girlstown, U.S.A., Amarillo, Tex., 1995—. Dist. commr. Boy Scouts Am., Germany, 1989-91. Decorated DSM, Def. Superior Svc. medal, Silver Star, Legion of Merit, Def. Meritorious Svc. medal, Bronze Star medal with oak leaf cluster, Air medals. Mem. Assn. U.S. Army, U.S. Army Ranger Assn., 75th Ranger Regiment Assn., Soc. Vietnamese Airborne Advisors, Soc. 173rd Airborne Brigade. Methodist. Avocations: fishing, hunting. Office: Cal Farleys Boys Ranch & Girlstown USA PO Box 1890 Amarillo TX 79174-0601

TAYLOR, WILLIAM AL, church administrator; b. Danville, Va., Sept. 26, 1938; s. Preston Floyd and Helen Elizabeth (Doss) T.; m. Brenda Flo Owen, June 4, 1961; children: Fawnia Rae Ricks, Albert Todd, Athena Dawn Jarman. AA, Lee Coll., 1957; postgrad., U. Calif., Santa Barbara, 1980. Br. mgr. Ency. Britannica, Greensboro, N.C., 1960-62; divsn. trainer Ency. Britannica, Mpls., 1963; dist. mgr. Ency. Britannica, Omaha, 1964-72; adminstrv. asst. Forward in Faith Internat. Broadcast, Cleveland, Tenn., 1972-80; gen. mgr. Sta. WQNE-FM, Cleveland, 1980—; dir. stewardship Ch. of God Internat. Offices, Cleveland, 1980—; pres. Pathway Credit Union, Cleveland, 1985—, Vision Found., Cleveland, 1985—, exec. dir., 1979-80; chmn. Internat. Commn. on Prayer, Cleveland, 1986—. Author: Proving God, 1991, Days of Heaven on Earth, 1993, Stewardship Masterplanning, 1993. Pres. Clean Water Soc., Gastonia, N.C., 1974-75; speaker Citizens Against Legalized Liquor, Bradley County, Tenn., 1973, 75; advisor Mothers on March, Cleveland, 1976; active Nat. Conf. on Drug Abuse, Washington, 1978; master of ceremonies Nat. Religious Leaders Conf. on Alcohol and Drug Abuse, Indpls., 1979. Recipient Mass Communications award Ch. of God Media Ministries, 1980, Stephen award Ch. of God Lay Ministries, 1990. Mem. Nat. Assn. Evangelicals (bd. adminstrs. 1985—, chmn. stewardship commn. 1985-89), Christian Stewardship Assn. (bd. dirs. 1990-94). Avocations: flying, travel, racquetball. Office: Ch of God Dept Stewardship 2490 Keith St NW Cleveland TN 37311-1309 *We are all spending the precious gift of life, and we have been given the privilege to decide upon what we shall spend it. I have found the most worthy and fulfilling investment of life is God's stated purpose, "that we be conformed to the image of His son Jesus Christ."*

TAYLOR, WILLIAM BERLEY, history educator; b. L.A., Mar. 23, 1943; s. James Chapman and Alma (Berley) T.; m. Barbara E. Tresch, June 17, 1964; children: Karin Elise, Jill Linda. BA, Occidental Coll., L.A., 1964; MA, U. of Ams., Mexico City, 1965; PhD, U. Mich., 1969. Asst. prof. history U. Colo., Denver/Boulder, 1969-72; assoc. prof. history U. Colo., Boulder, 1972-77; prof. history U. Colo., 1977-82; Edward F. Arnold Disting. prof. Whitman Coll., Walla Walla, Wash., 1980; vis. prof. history Harvard U., Cambridge, Mass., 1981; prof. history U. Va., Charlottesville, 1982-93; Edmund and Louise Kahn prof. history So. Meth. U., Dallas, 1993—; nat. adv. com. John Carter Brown Libr., Providence, 1986-89; internat. adv. bd. The Mesoamerican Archive, U. Colo., 1989—; cons., expert witness Cochiti Queblo, 1979-85, U.S. Dept. Justice, 1974-82. Author: Magistrates of the Sacred..., 1995, Drinking, Homicide and Rebellion..., 1979, Landlord and Peasant in Colonial Oaxaca, 1972. Nat. Humanities Ctr. fellow, 1990-91, Inst. for Advanced Study fellow, 1987, Guggenheim fellow, 1979-80, NEH fellow, 1974-75, U. Colo. tchg. awardee, 1974. Mem. Am. Hist. Assn., Conf. on Latin Am. History, Phi Beta Kappa. Office: So Meth Univ Dallas TX 75275

TAYLOR, WILLIAM D., biophysics educator, university dean; b. Cardiff, Wales, May 23, 1934; came to U.S., 1959; m. Andrea M. Mastro; children: Maria, Daniel, Timothy. BSc in Chemistry with honours, Manchester (Eng.) U., 1956, PhD in Phys. Chemistry, 1959. Postdoctoral fellow physics dept. Pa. State U., University Park, 1959-61, asst. prof. biophysics, 1963-68, assoc. prof., 1968-71, prof., 1971—, head dept., 1971-75, assoc. chmn. dept. microbiology and cell biology, 1975-83, mem. Environ. Resources Rsch.

Inst., 1987-90, assoc. dean for rsch. and grad. edn., 1989-91, acting dir. Biotech. Inst., 1990-92, dir. intercoll. rsch. program, 1991—, acting dir. Intercoll. Materials Rsch. Inst., 1993—, acting dean Grad. Sch., 1995—, chmn. faculty senate, 1972-73; vis. lectr. Donner Lab., Berkeley, Calif., summer 1967; vis. scientist Imperial Cancer Rsch. Fund Lab., London, 1973-74, Biochemistry Inst., German Cancer Rsch. Ctr., Heidelberg, 1985-86. Contbr. articles to sci. jours., chpts. to books. Scholar Glamorganshire County, 1953-57; Courtaulds rsch. fellow, 1957-59, NIH postdoctoral fellow Pa. State U., 1959-61; grantee Pa. State U., 1969-70, Nat. Inst. Gen. Med. Scis., 1972-77, Nat. Cancer Inst., 1976-81, NASA, 1982-87, USPHS, 1988-92, also others. Mem. AAAS, Radiation Rsch. Soc., Biophys. Soc., Am. Soc. for Photobiology, Am. Soc. Biol. Chemists, Am. Soc. for Microbiology. Office: Pa State U Intercollege Materials Rsch Lab 202 MRL University Park PA 16802-5807

TAYLOR, WILLIAM JAMES (ZAK TAYLOR), lawyer; b. Milw., Jan. 26, 1948; s. William Elmer and Elizabeth Emily (Lupinski) T.; m. Marlou Belyea, Sept. 20, 1975; children: Danielle Belyea, James Zachary Belyea. BA in Econs., Yale U., 1970; JD, Harvard U., 1976. Bar: Calif. 1976, U.S. Dist. Ct. (cen. dist.) Calif. 1976, U.S. Dist. Ct. (no. dist.) Calif. 1977, U.S. Ct. Appeals (9th cir.) 1977, U.S. Dist. Ct. (ea. dist.) Calif. 1980, U.S. Supreme Ct. 1980, U.S. Tax Ct. 1988. Law clk. to presiding judge U.S. Ct. Appeals (9th cir.), L.A., 1976-77; assoc. Broebeck, Phleger & Harrison, San Francisco, 1977-83; ptnr. Broebeck, Phleger and Harrison, San Francisco, 1983-95; shareholder Taylor & Jenkins, P.C., Oakland, Calif., 1995—; bd. dirs. Berkeley (Calif.) Law Found., 1988-91, Legal Svcs. for Children (recipient Jean Waldman Child Advocacy award, San Francisco 1988), 1983-89; co-chmn. Attys. Task Force for Children, San Francisco, 1983-89. Editor-in-chief Harvard Civil Rights, Civil Liberties Law Rev., 1976; bd. editors No. Dist. Calif. Digest, 1978-83; co-author: California Antitrust Law, 1991; contbg. editor: Calif. Bus. Law Reporter, 1995—. With U.S. Army, 1970-73. Mem. ABA, Bar Assn. San Francisco (bd. dirs. 1986-87, chair antitrust sect. 1987, chair fed. cts. sect. 1995), Am. Bus. Trial Lawyers Assn., Barristers of San Francisco (bd. dirs. 1980-82, v.p. 1982-83. Democrat. Office: Taylor & Jenkins PC 2030 Franklin St 5th Fl Oakland CA 94612-9999

TAYLOR, WILLIAM JAMES, III, federal official; b. Petersburg, Va., Feb. 12, 1954; s. William James Jr. and Erma Glenn (Brown) T.; m. Elneita Sylvia Hutchins, Dec. 11, 1982; children: Royce Alan, Christian Alexander, Kellye Audrey. BA in Mass Comm., Howard U., 1977; JD, U. Tex. Sch. Law, 1981. Bar: Tex., 1981. Adminstrv. asst. Office Hon. William P. Hobby, Lt. Gov., Tex., 1980-81; staff atty. II Tex. Edn. Agy., 1981-82; campaign coord. Bill Hobby Campaign, 1982; exec. asst. county atty. Office Harris County Atty. Mike Driscoll, 1983; coun. coord. Office former Houston Councilman Rodney Ellis, 1984; divsn. chief Office Harris County Atty. Mike Driscoll, 1983; adminstrv. asst., legal coun. Office late congressman Mickey Leland, 1985-88; atty. Hutcheson & Grundy L.L.P., 1989-93; asst. sec. congl. and intergovernmental affairs Dept. Energy, Washington, 1993-95; counsellor to the Sec. of Commerce Dept. of Commerce, Washington, 1995—. mem. bd. regents East Tex. State U., 1991-93; v.p. Houston Housing Fin. Corp., 1992-93; pres. Tex. Black Leadership Congress, 1988-93; mem. bd. dirs. Juvenile Ct. Vols. Harris County, 1989-92, Tex. Lyceum Assn., Inc., 1989, NAACP, 1991-93, Ctr. for the Retarded, 1991-93, Houston Prep. Acad., 1991-93; com. cons., chmn. legis. com. Houston Mus. Fine Arts, 1989-93; lectr. CLE programs U. Houston Law Ctr., 1990-91; mem. citizens adv. com. Tex. Lottery Startup, 1991; mem. adv. bd. The Chinquapin Sch., 1992-93. Mem. Thurgood Marshall Legal Soc. (pres. 1980). Avocations: basketball, skiing. Office: Counselor to the Sec Dept of Commerce 14th & Constitution Ave NW Washington DC 20230

TAYLOR, WILLIAM JAPE, physician; b. Booneville, Miss., Sept. 5, 1924; s. William Melton and Cora Leona (Smith) T.; m. Audrey Y. Dennison, Jan. 31, 1948; children—J. Holley, Andrew D., Richard M., D. Lee. B.S., Yale U., 1944; M.D., Harvard U., 1947. Intern in internal medicine Boston City Hosp., 1947-48; resident in internal medicine Duke U. Hosp., 1948-50, fellow in cardiology, 1950-52, 54-55; instr. Duke U. Med. Sch., 1954-55, U. Pitts. Med. Sch., 1955-58; mem. faculty U. Fla. Coll. Medicine, Gainesville, 1958—; prof. medicine U. Fla. Coll. Medicine, 1964—, chief cardiology, 1958-74, disting. service prof. medicine, 1974-95; emeritus, 1995—; vis. prof. U. Ife (Nigeria) Med. Sch., 1974-75; bd. dirs. PSRO, Fla. Area II, 1977-81. Author papers in field, chpts. in books. Mem. human rights advocacy committee mentally retarded Fla. Dist. III, 1977-81; bd. dirs. Gainesville-Natagalpa Sister City, 1988—. Fellow ACP (rsch. fellow 1950-51), Am. Coll. Cardiology; mem. Assn. U. Cardiologists, Am. Heart Assn. (fellow coun. clin. cardiology), Am. Fedn. Clin. Rsch., So. Soc. Clin. Investigation (pres. 1972-73), Fla. Heart Assn. (Disting. Svc. award 1975), Am. Soc. Tropical Medicine and Hygiene, Physicians for Social Responsibility (ho. of dels. 1985-90). Democrat. Home: 500 NW 80th Blvd Gainesville FL 32607-1531 Office: U Fla Med Sch Dept Medicine Gainesville FL 32610

TAYLOR, WILLIAM MALCOLM, educator; b. South Hiram, Maine, June 18, 1933; s. William Myers and Gladys Marie (Weldy) T.; stepson Edna (Tyson) Taylor; m. Carrie Mae Fiedler, Aug. 31, 1957 (div. Sept. 1980); children: William Stephan, Alyson Marie, Eric Fiedler; m. Elizabeth Van Horn, June 18, 1983. Student, George Sch., 1948-50; BA in Liberal Arts, Pa. State U., 1956. Instr. ESL Anatolia Coll., Am. Lang. Ctr., Salonica, Greece, 1956-58; tchr. biology-chemistry Coral Shores H.S., Tavernier, Fla., 1961-62; pk. naturalist Everglades Nat. Pk., Fla., 1962-65; tech. editor Nat. Pk. Svc., Washington, 1965-67; chief naturalist Canyonlands Nat. Pk., Utah, 1967-71; environ. edn. specialist western regional office Nat. Pk. Svc., Calif., 1971-77; dir. program devel. Living History Ctr., Novato, Calif., 1981-83; exec. recruiter, ptnr. Van Horn, Taylor & Assocs., Santa Cruz, Calif., 1983-95; mem. 2d World Conf. on Nat. Parks and Equivalent Reserves, 10th Internat. Seminar on Nat. Parks, U.S., Can., Mex. Author: The Strands Walk, Exercises in Guided Inquiry for Children; founder, developer (ednl. program) Environ. Living Program, 1973 (Calif. Bicentennial Commn. award 1974, Don Perryman award Calif. Social Studies Coun., 1975, Nat. Bicentennial Adminstrn. sponsorship 1976). Bd. dirs. Internat. Sonoran Desert Alliance, 1996, Novato Environ. Quality Com., 1973-76; mem. Calif. Conservation Com., 1973-76; mem. Utah Environ. Com., 1968-71. Mem. Friends of Pronatura, Am. Bonanza Soc., Lighthawk, Internat. Sonoran Desert Alliance (treas.), Flying Samaritans, Mensa, Oreg. Pilots Assn. Avocations: flying, birding, natural history, theater. Home: P O Box 972 Corvallis OR 97339

TAYLOR, WILLIAM OSGOOD, newspaper executive; b. Boston, July 19, 1932; s. William Davis and Mary (Hammond) T.; m. Sally Coxe, June 20, 1959; children: William Davis II, Edmund C., Augustus R. B.A., Harvard U., 1954. With Globe Newspaper Co., Boston, 1956—, treas., 1963—, bus. mgr., 1965-69, gen. mgr., 1969—; now chmn. bd., pub. Boston Globe. Trustee Boston Pub. Libr.; bd. dirs. United Way New Eng., Boston Adult Literacy Fund; trustee Mus. of Fine Arts. With U.S. Army, 1954-56. Mem. Newspaper Assn. Am. (bd. dirs.). Office: Globe Newspaper Co 135 Morrissey Blvd Boston MA 02107*

TAYLOR, WILSON H., diversified financial company executive. Grad., Trinity Coll. With Conn. Gen., 1954-82, sr. v.p., chief fin. officer, 1980-82; v.p. Aetna Ins. Co., 1975; exec. v.p. Cigna Corp., Phila., 1982-88, pres. property casualty group, 1983-88, corp. vice-chmn., chief operating officer, from 1988, chief operating officer, 1988, pres., chief exec. officer, 1988—, then chmn., pres., chief exec. officer, now chmn., chief exec. officer. Phi Beta Kappa. Office: Cigna Corp 1 Liberty Plz Philadelphia PA 19192-2078*

TAYLOR CLAUD, ANDREA, educational consultant; b. Warrenton, Va., Nov. 5, 1952; d. Andrew Earl and Catherine (Dennis) Taylor; m. Maurice J. Claud. BS, Norfolk State U., 1974, MA, 1983; postgrad., Old Dominion U., 1975-76, 89. Profl. collegiate cert. in learning disabilities, mentally handicapped and emotionally handicapped. Classrm. tchr. Facquier County Sch. System, Warrenton, 1974-75; child devel. specialist, team leader Norfolk Pub. Schs., Norfolk, Va., 1976-82; ednl. diagnostician Norfolk Pub. Schs., 1982-87; ednl. cons. Va. State Dept. Edn., Norfolk, 1987—; v.p. DECAA Enterprises, Norfolk, 1983—. Mem. Lindenwood Civic League, Norfolk, Urban League of Hampton Roads, Bute St. 1st Bapt. Ch., Norfolk; troop leader Girl Scouts U.S.A., Norfolk, 1977-79. Named Debutante, Norfolk Med. Soc. Aux., 1969, Outstanding Young Women of Am., 1983. Mem. NAFE, NEA, Va. Edn. Assn., Norfolk Edn. Assn., Coun. Exceptional Children, Assn. Supervision and Curriculum Devel., Delta Sigma Theta. Democrat. Avocations: traveling, reading, listening to music. Office: Children's Hosp of King's Daus Hosp Edn Program 601 Childrens Ln Norfolk VA 23507-1910

TAYLOR-GRIGSBY, QUEENIE DELORES, minister, consultant; b. Oklahoma City, Aug. 21, 1948; d. Barnett C., Sr. and Bedell (Boles) Taylor; m. Walter Thomas White II, Nov. 26, 1966 (div. June 1976); children: Walter Thomas III, Robin Orlando; m. James O. Grigsby, Oct. 19, 1976 (dec. Dec. 1976); 1 child, James Jumaané. BS, Howard U., 1970. Ordained to ministry Ray Deliverance Found., 1989. Assoc. cons. Trust Inc., Richmond, Va., 1974-80, Orgnl. Devel. Cons., Richmond, 1980-82; cons., pres. Taylor & Co., Phoenix, 1974—; min. Man Child Ministries, Phoenix, 1988—; cons. MARTA Atlanta, 1980-82, Fredrick County, Md., 1974, Richmond Pub. Sch. System, 1977, Black Police Officers, Tulsa, 1986. Author poetess. Advocate child welfare Dept. of Corrections, Phoenix, 1990, advocate tchr. rights, 1991; active tchr. rights Phoenix Pub. Sch. System, 1992; supr. elections County Election Bd., Maricopa County, Ariz., 1987. Lucille McMahn scholar, 1965, Nellie Green scholar, 1965; recipient Danforth Leadership award, 1965, Golden Poet award, 1991. Mem. Soc. Tng. and Devel. (cert. housing specialist), Housing Specialist Inst. Avocations: reading, swimming, hunting, fishing, camping. Office: Taylor & Co PO Box 9605 Phoenix AZ 85068-9605

TAYLOR-PICKELL, LAVONNE TROY, editor; b. Riverside, Calif., May 20, 1941; d. Troy Virgil Bradstreet and R. Victoria (Freeman) Chambers; m. Robert Martin Taylor, May 15, 1958 (div. 1975); children: Dana Freeman, Timothy Rene; m. Herman Pickell, Feb. 14, 1985; children: Marianne, Barry, David. Reporter Thousand Oaks (Calif.) Chronicle; with prodn. News Chronicle, Thousand Oaks, prodn. supr., 1979-81; with prodn. Ind. Jour., Thousand Oaks, Herald Examiner, L.A., L.A. Times; asst. mgr. Publ. Typography, Agoura, Calif., 1981-85; owner Excellence Enterprises, L.A., 1982—; sr. editor arts Glencoe/McGraw-Hill Sch. Pub., Mission Hills, Calif., 1987-96; speaker various writers clubs. Editor, pub. L.A. My Way, 1991, On the Wings of Song, 1994; mng. editor The BookWoman, 1991-93. Mem. pub. rels. com. Conejo Players Theatre, Thousand Oaks, 1970-75, Betty Mann for 38th Assembly Dist., Agoura, 1975-76. Mem. NAFE, Nat. Writers Club (pres. 1990-91, Merit Svc. award 1991), Women's Nat. Book Assn. (L.A. chpt. pres. 1992-93, newsletter editor, bd. dirs.). Avocations: reading, writing, gardening, music, art.

TAYON, JEFFREY EARL, engineering and design executive; b. St. Louis, June 19, 1963; s. James Edward and Frances Kay (Brooks) T.; m. Janna Lynn Burrell, Nov. 2, 1985; children: Jenna Lea, James Earl, Joel Edward. Student, Moberly Area C.C., 1981-92. Apprentice plumber Tayon Plumbers, Inc., St. Louis, 1979-81; tool crib attendant Orbco Mfg. Co., Moberly, Mo., 1981; with Orscheln Co., Moberly, 1981-83, draftsman, 1983-86, R&D engr., 1986, design engr., 1986-88, lead design engr., 1988-90, mgr. lever design, 1990-94; mgr. advanced cable devel. Dura Automotive Systems, Moberly, 1994—. Patentee brake apparatus with controlled flyback, electromechanical park brake, in-line adjuster, non-jamming self-adj pawl and ratchet mech., method and apparatus for terminating wire or other elongated generally rigid elements. Chmn. youth coun. 1st Assembly of God, Moberly, 1982-83; trustee Grace Bapt. Ch., Moberly, 1986—. Republican. Avocations: scuba diving, photography, remodeling, fishing, woodworking. Home: RR 2 Box 73A Moberly MO 65270-9605 Office: Dura Automotive Systems Inc 1600A N Morley Moberly MO 65270

TAYS, GLENNY MAE, secondary education educator; b. Presho, S.D., Mar. 12, 1933; d. Glen Harold and Grayce Agnes (LaVelle) Trimble; m. Richard Ray Tays, May 29, 1954; children: Robert Glen, Thomas Gene. BA, Dakota Wesleyan U., 1956; MEd, U. Mont., 1961. Cert. secondary sch. tchr. and prin. Bus. tchr. Kimball (S.D.) H.S., 1956-58; English/bus. tchr. Burke (S.D.) H.S., 1962-65; Bus. Inst. dept. head DesMoines Area C.C., Boone, Iowa, 1966-78; English/journalism tchr. St. Martin's Acad., Rapid City, S.D., 1979-82; English tchr., dept. head Todd County H.S., Mission, S.D., 1982—; pres. Des Moines Area C.C. Faculty Assn., Boone, 1968, 69, 70; pres.-elect Iowa Bus. Edn. Assn., State of Iowa, 1972-73, pres., 1973-74; editor North Ctrl. Bus. Edn. Conv. Bull., Des Moines, 1972; part time tchr. Bus. Inst., Black Hills State U. Br. Campus, Rapid City, S.D., 1981-82, Sinte Gleska U., Mission, S.D., 1983-84. Pres. Burke (S.D.) Women's Club, 1961-63; vol. ARC, Easter Seals, United Fund, Boone, 1965; coord. Country Club Jr. Program, Boone, 1968-74; golf mother Booster Club, Boone (Iowa) H.S., 1972-73; spl. projects chmn. Soroptimist Club Internat., Boone, 1973. Named Outstanding Young Women in Am., 1970. Mem. ASCD, NEA, Nat. Coun. Tchrs. English, Cath. Daus. Am., Delta Kappa Gamma (com.). Democrat. Roman Catholic. Avocations: reading, writing, antiquing, collecting pre-1900 books, golfing. Home: Box 991 Mission SD 57555 Office: Todd County HS Box 726 Mission SD 57555

TCHAIKOVSKY, LESLIE J., judge; b. 1943. BA, Calif. State Univ., Hayward, 1967; JD, Univ. of Calif., Berkeley, 1976. Law clk. to Hon. John Mowbray Nev. Supreme Ct., 1976-77; with Dinkelspiel, Steefel, Leavitt & Weiss, 1977-80, Gordon, Peitzman & Lopes, 1981, Dinkelspiel, Donovan & Reder, 1981-88; bankruptcy judge U.S. Bankruptcy Ct. (Calif. no. dist.), 9th circuit, Oakland, 1988—. Office: US Courthouse 1300 Clay St Oakland CA 94612-1425

TCHERKASSKY, MARIANNA ALEXSAVENA, ballerina; b. Glen Cove, N.Y., Oct. 28, 1952; d. Alexis and Lillian (Oka) T.; m. Terrence S. Orr. Student, Washington Sch. Ballet (scholar), 1965-67, Sch. Am. Ballet and Profl. Children's Sch., 1967-70; pupil of Edward Caton. Appeared with Bolshoi Ballet in Ballet Sch., 1961, 62, N.Y.C. Ballet in A Midsummer Night's Dream, 1963; profl. debut with Andre Eglevsky Ballet Co., 1968; mem., Am. Ballet Theatre, 1970—, soloist, 1972-76, prin. dancer, 1976—, guest appearances throughout U.S. and in Europe, also on TV; roles include The Nutcracker, La Bayadere, Bruch Violin Concerto No. 1, Coppelia, Giselle, Etudes, Les Liaisons Dangereuses, Romeo and Juliet, The Sleeping Beauty, La Sylphide, Les Sylphides, The Leaves are Fading. Winner Nat. Soc. Arts and Letters competition, 1967; Ford Found. scholar, 1967-70. Office: care Am Ballet Theatre 890 Broadway New York NY 10003-1211

TCHOBANOGLOUS, GEORGE, civil engineering educator; b. Patterson, Calif., May 24, 1935; s. Christo and Penelope (Megdani) T.; m. Rosemary Ash, June 16, 1957; children—Kathryn, Lynn, Julianne. B.C.E., U. Pacific, 1958; M.C.E., U. Calif., Berkley, 1960; Ph.D., Stanford U., 1969. Registered profl. engr., Calif., Mont. Research engr. U. Calif.-Berkeley, 1960-62; cons. Metcalf & Eddy Engrs., Palo Alto, Calif., 1963-81, Nolte & Assocs., Sacramento, 1981—, Calif. Water Resources Control Bd., 1972-80; assoc. prof. U. Calif.-Davis, 1970-76, prof. engring., 1976—. Prin. author: Wastewater Engineering: Collection, Treatment, Disposal, 1972; author: (with R. Smith and R. Crites) Wastewater Management: A Guide to Information Sources, 1976, (with H. Theisen and R. Eliassen) Solid Wastes: Engineering Principles and Management Issues, 1977, (with Schroeder) Water Quality: Characteristics, Modeling, Modification, 1985, (with Peavy and Rowe) Environmental Engineering, 1985, (with H. Theisen, S.A. Vigil) Integrated Solid Waste Management: Engineering Principles and Management Issues, 1993; co-author: Wastewater Engineering: Treatment, Disposal, Reuse, 1991; author, editor: Wastewater Engineering: Collection and Pumping of Wastewater, 1981; co-editor: Pumping Station Design, 1989; contbr. numerous articles to profl. jours. Mem. bd. Calif. Integrated Waste Mgmt.; lectr. T.R. Camp, 1990. Mem. AAAS, ASCE, Assn. Environ. Engring. Profs. (bd. dirs., past pres.), Am. Acad. Environ. Engrs., Water Environ. Fedn. (Gordon Masken Fair medal 1985), Am. Water Works Assn. (Thomas R. Camp lectr. 1991), World Mariculture Soc., Sigma Xi. Home: 662 Diego Pl Davis CA 95616-0123

TEACHOUT, NOREEN RUTH, writer; b. Oak Park, Ill., July 12, 1939; d. Anselm Uriel and R. Lydia (Bagne) Asp; m. Willem Heyneker, Nov. 20, 1958 (dec. 1968); children: Carolyn Heyneker Fors, Diana Heyneker Olds; m. Richard Kenneth Teachout, Jan. 21, 1966 (div. 1982); children: Jill, Janelle. BS, U. Minn., 1965; postgrad., Am. Inst. Holistic Theology, 1996—. Tchr. Bloomington (Minn.) Pub. Schs., 1965-85; writer, pubr., CEO The Peace Curriculum, Mpls., 1986—; educator Stockton & Franks Chiropractors, Burnsville, Minn., 1986-92; edn. svcs. dept. coord. Dame Comms., Plymouth, Minn., 1990—; cons., workshop leader Dame Comms.; writer U. Calif., Berkeley, 1967, Environ. Sci. Ctr., Mpls., 1968-69; educator, presenter Women's World Peace Conf., Dallas, 1988, World Peace Conf., San Jose, Costa Rica, 1989, 92; sponsor Therapeutic Humor Inst. Minn., Colo., 1996; dir. Wellness NOW, A Learning Place, Colo., 1996. Author curriculum programs, health and revitalization programs. Avocations: ballroom dancing, reading, gardening, horsepersonship.

TEAGAN, JOHN GERARD, newspaper executive; b. Detroit, Sept. 23, 1947; s. Stanley John and Margaret Suzanne (Sullivan) T.; m. Carla Kay Eurich, Sept. 13, 1975; 1 child, Elizabeth Margaret. B.B.A., U. Notre Dame, 1969. C.P.A., Mich. Audit supr. Ernst & Whinney (C.P.A.s), Detroit, 1969-73; acctg. mgr. Detroit Free Press, 1973-77, treas., controller, 1977-83, v.p. fin., treas., 1983-89, v.p., bus. mgr., 1989—. Adv. bd. Providence Hosp., Southfield, Mich., 1984—, sec., 1989, vice chmn. 1990, chmn., 1991. Mem. AICPA, Internat. Newspaper Fin. Execs., Mich. Assn. CPAs, Detroit Club, Notre Dame Club (Detroit dir. 1970-76, 92—, treas. 1993-94, sec. 1994-95, pres.-elect 1995-96). Roman Catholic. Office: Detroit Free Press Inc 321 W Lafayette Blvd Detroit MI 48226-2705

TEAGUE, HYMAN FARIS, former publishing company executive; b. San Angelo, Jan. 14, 1916; s. John Henry and Minnie Adele (Gauldin) T.; m. Sophia Golda Harvey, Dec. 26, 1944; children: Carl Robin, Alan Cole. B.A., McMurry Coll., 1935, postgrad., 1940; postgrad, Hardin Simmons U., 1935-36. Tchr., public schs. Tex., 1935-43; prodn. mgr. Steck Vaughn Co. (and predecessor co.), Austin, 1946-57; editor in chief Steck Vaughn Co. (and predecessor co.), 1957-65, v.p., 1964-65, pres., 1965-80, chmn., 1981-82, dir., 1965-82; v.p. Intext Inc., Scranton, Pa., 1975-80. Served with USNR, 1943-46. Democrat. Baptist. Clubs: Austin, Rotary. Home: 4906 Rollingwood Dr Austin TX 78746-5527

TEAGUE, LARRY GENE, editor; b. Victoria, Tex., May 13, 1954; s. Edward Marvin and Nettie Naomi (Welch) T. BJ, U. Houston, 1980. Outdoor correspondent Houston Post, 1977-80; editor Gulf Tide mag. Gulf Coast Conservation Assn., Houston, 1980-85; editor Southern Outdoors mag. Bass Anglers Sportsmans Soc., Montgomery, Ala., 1985—; cons. editor So. Outdoor Saltwater mag., 1986-87. Served with U.S. Army, 1972-75. Recipient writing, photography awards. Avocations: fishing, hunting, gardening, photography. Home: 5832 Red Barn Rd Montgomery AL 36116-1034 Office: Southern Outdoors 5845 Carmichael Rd Montgomery AL 36117-2329

TEAGUE, MARY KAY, realtor; b. Troy, Ohio, May 15, 1925; d. Carl Joseph and Laura Mae (Jones) Wack; m. Roger A. Teague, Apr. 29, 1944 (dec. Nov. 1980); children: Margaret Colleen, Barbara Lynn, Roger A. Jr., Mary P., Betty A., Howard J. Realtor Teague Real Estate, Hitchcock, Tex., 1962—. Chmn. Hitchcock Planning Bd., 1987-93; dir. Hitchcock Indsl. Devel. Bd., 1983—. Mem. Nat. Assoc. Realtors, Tex. Assn. Realtors, Texas City-LaMarque Bd. Realtors (dir. 1974-78, 81-87, sec. 1979, pres. 1980, 88, Realtor of Yr. award 1986), Women's Coun. Realtors (sec. 1988, pres. 1991, Golden Rule award 1983), Hitchcock C. of C. (bd. dirs. 1984-91). Republican. Roman Catholic. Avocation: duplicate bridge. Home: 301 Greenwood Dr Hitchcock TX 77563-1413 Office: Teague Real Estate PO Box 21 Hitchcock TX 77563-0021

TEAGUE, PEYTON CLARK, chemist, educator; b. Montgomery, Ala., June 26, 1915; s. Robert S. and Sara McGehee (Clark) T.; m. Patricia Cussons Lamb, June 12, 1937; 1 dau., Norah Teague Grimball. Student, Huntingdon Coll., 1932-34; B.S., Auburn U., 1936; M.S., Pa. State U., 1937; Ph.D., U. Tex., 1942. Research chemist Am. Agrl. Chem. Co., Newark, 1937-39; instr. dept. chemistry Auburn U., Ala., 1941-42, asst. prof., 1943-45; research chemist U.S. Naval Research Lab, 1942-45; asst. prof. U. Ga., Athens, 1945-48, U. Ky., Lexington, 1948-50; assoc. prof. dept. chemistry U. S.C., Columbia, 1950-56, prof., 1956-82, disting. prof. emeritus, 1982—, assoc. dean grad. sch., 1966-68, chmn. grad. council, 1980-81, dept. dir. grad. studies, 1971-82; sec. grad. admission com. U. S.C., 1982—; vis. prof. Univ. Coll., Dublin, Ireland, 1963-64, 77; dir. Teague Hardware Co., Montgomery, Ala., 1955-74. Contbr. articles to sci. jours. Vestryman Trinity Episcopal Cathedral, 1968-71, lay reader, 1963—; bd. dirs. S.C. chpt. Arthritis Found., 1983-86; bd. dirs. Columbia Town Theatre, 1984-91. Recipient Outstanding Tchr. award U. S.C., 1976. Mem. Am. Chem. Soc. (chmn. S.C. sect. 1958-59), Phytochem. Soc. N.Am. (pres. 1969-70), S.C. Acad. Sci., Blue Key, Sigma Xi (pres. U. S.C. chpt. 1962-63), Phi Kappa Phi, Phi Lambda Upsilon, Phi Delta Theta. Club: Forest Lake Country. Lodge: Kiwanis. Home: 1550 Adger Rd Columbia SC 29205-1408 Office: U SC Dept Chemistry Columbia SC 29208

TEAGUE, RANDAL CORNELL, SR., lawyer; b. Durham, N.C., May 19, 1944; s. Roy M. Sr. and Lottie (Rhew) T.; children: R. Cornell, R. Townsend, Mary Robb Durham, James K.B. BA, Am. U., 1967; JD, George Washington U., 1971, LLM with highest honors, 1972; LLD (hon.), Allen U., 1973. Bar: Fla. 1972, D.C. 1972, U.S. Dist. Ct. D.C. 1972, U.S. Tax Ct. 1972, U.S. Ct. Mil. Appeals 1972, U.S. Ct. Appeals (D.C. and fed. cirs.) 1972, U.S. Ct. Appeals (5th cir.) 1973, U.S. Supreme Ct. 1975, Mass. 1979, U.S. Ct. Appeals (1st cir.) 1979, U.S. Dist. Ct. Mass. 1979, U.S. Ct. Internat. Trade. Coordinator policy devel. OEO, Washington, 1971-73; adminstrv. asst., legis. counsel to Rep. Jack F. Kemp Ho. of Reps., Washington, 1973-79; div. counsel Cabot Corp., 1979-81; counsel Vorys, Sater, Seymour & Pease, Washington, 1981-83, ptnr., 1984—. Pres. Internat. Exch. Coun., 1984—; trustee Fund Am. Studies, Washington, 1976—, Air Force Acad. Found., Colorado Springs, Colo., 1983—; chmn. adv. com. voluntary aid U.S. AID, 1987-91; trustee Agrl. Coll. Humid Tropics, Costa Rica, 1987—; ccouncillor Atlantic Coun. of U.S., 1990—; co-founder Am. Inst. on Polit. and Econ. Sys., Charles U., Prague, 1993—. Named one of Outstanding Young Men Am., 1973; recipient George Washington medal Freedoms Found., 1978. Mem. ABA, Fed. Bar Assn., Fla. Bar Assn. Republican. Episcopalian. Club: University (Washington). Office: Vorys Sater Seymour & Pease 1828 L St NW Ste 11 Washington DC 20036-5109

TEAGUE, SAM FULLER, association executive, educator,; b. Birmingham, Ala., Aug. 2, 1918; s. Sam Fuller and Virginia (White) T.; m. Frances Middleton, July 2, 1939; children: John Russell, Melanie Olivia. B.S., Auburn U., 1939. Chemist Sloss-Sheffield Steel & Iron Co., Birmingham, 1939-40; asst. dir. sales Monsanto Chem. Co., St. Louis, 1945-60; gen. mgr. sales ITT Rayonier, Inc., N.Y.C., 1960-67; v.p. planning and devel. ITT Rayonier, Inc., 1967-68, sr. v.p., 1968-72, v.p., product mgr., paper and splty. pulp sales, 1972-78, v.p., dir. pulp sales, 1978-80, v.p. prodn./mktg. devel., 1981-83, ret., 1983, also dir.; exec. dir. Rayon/Acetate Council, Inc., Auburn, Ala., 1983-93; adj. prof. textile engring. Auburn U., 1983—; dir., mem. exec. com. Rayonier Can. Pres. Auburn Heritage Assn., 1985-86; v.p. Auburn Beautification Council, 1985-86; councilman, mayor pro tem City of Auburn, 1986—; vestryman and sr. warden Holy Trinity Episcopal Ch., 1985-86. Served to lt. col. AUS, 1940-45. Decorated Bronze Star with oak leaf cluster. Mem. Am. Chem. Soc., Salesmen's Assn. Am. Chem. Industry (past dir.), Auburn C. of C. (treas. and bd. dirs. 1986, pres. 1989, bd. dirs. 1994). Clubs: Town (Newcastle) (past sec., dir.); Whippoorwill (Armonk, N.Y.) (pres. 1968-69, gov.); Chemists (N.Y.C.) (trustee 1970, pres. 1976-77). Home: 1349 Burke Ln Auburn AL 36830-5140 Office: Auburn U Textile Bldg Auburn AL 36849 *My career is based on honesty, fairness, consideration for my fellow man, trust in God, and always trying to follow the principles set forth by Jesus Christ. I've always felt that people are the most important element of any organization. Whereas bricks and mortar can be bought, people must be considered as individuals.*

TEAGUE, WAYNE, state education official; b. Cullman, Ala., Nov. 19, 1927; s. Levi Wade and Floy Irene (McKelvey) T.; m. Eleanor Josephine Jones, June 5, 1949; children—Karen Jo, Dewey Wayne. B.S., Auburn U., 1950, M.S., 1953, Ed.D., 1962; LL.D., Troy State U., 1978. Tchr., coach, asst. prin. Heard High Sch., Franklin, Ga., 1950-55; prin. Marion County Elem. and High Sch., Buena Vista, Ga., 1955-56, Jonesboro (Ga.) Sr. High Sch., 1956-58, S.W. DeKalb High Sch., Decatur, Ga., 1958-63; coordinator field services Sch. Edn., dir. correspondence study, asso. prof. edl. adminstrn. Auburn (Ala.) U., 1963-69; supt. Auburn City Schs., 1969-75; state supt. edn. Ala. Dept. Edn., 1975-95; ret. Served with USAAC, 1946. Methodist. Club: Masons.

TEAL, GORDON KIDD, physical scientist; b. Dallas, Jan. 10, 1907; s. Olin Allison and Azelia Clyde (Kidd) T.; m. Lyda Louise Smith, Mar. 7, 1931; children: Robert Carroll, Donald Fraser, Stephen O'Banion Teal. AB in Math. and Chemistry with spl. honors, Baylor U., 1927, LLD (hon.), 1969; ScM (Marston scholar), Brown U., 1928, PhD (Univ. fellow, Metcalf fellow), 1931, ScD (hon.), 1969. Mem. research staff Bell Telephone Labs., N.Y.C., Murray Hill, N.J., 1930-53; postdoctoral researcher with Nobel Laureate Harold C. Urey Columbia U., 1932-35; asst. v.p., dir. materials and components research Tex. Instruments, Dallas, 1952-55; asst. v.p., dir. research, dir. Central Research Labs. Tex. Instruments, 1955-61, asst. v.p. research and engring., 1961-62; asst. v.p., internat. tech. dir. Tex. Instruments, London, Paris and Rome, 1962-65; asst. v.p. in charge tech. devel., equipment group Tex. Instruments, 1967-68, v.p., chief scientist, 1968-72; cons. to industry and govt., 1972—; 1st dir. Inst. Materials Research, Nat. Bur. Standards, Washington, 1964-67; cons. Dept. Def., 1956-64, 70-72, NASA, 1970-72, Nat. Bur. Standards, 1972-73, Tex. Instruments, Inc., 1972-77; chmn. exec. tech. devel. bd. Poly. Inst. Bklyn., 1963-72; mem. materials adv. bd. NAS-NRC, 1960-64; mem. NAS panel to India, chmn. NAS panel to Ceylon to hold indsl. rsch. workshops in India and Ceylon, 1970; mem. ad hoc com. on materials and processes for electron devices NAS-NAE-NRC, 1970-72; mem. NAS-NAE-NRC adv. panel Inst. Applied Tech., Nat. Bur. Standards, 1969-75; chmn. NAS-NRC adv. panel to Nat. Bur. Standards electronics technology div., 1972-75; chmn. panel for study research facilities and sci. opportunities in use of low and medium energy neutrons NAS-NRC adv. panel electronics technology div., 1977-78; mem. NAS panel to Republic of China and Am. Workshop on Indsl. Innovation and Product Devel. in Taiwan, 1975. Contbr.: Transistor Technology, 1952, 58, Mikroelektronik, 1965, Washington Colloquium on Science and Society, 1967; chmn., co-editor: Technology Forecast for 1980, 1971; contbr. Bicentennial issue IEEE Transactions on Electron Devices, 1976; editorial adv. bd.: Internat. Jour. Solid State Electronics, 1960-68; contbr. chpts. to books, articles to profl. jours.; co-developer first junction transistor; inventor grown junction method making single crystal junction transistor structures; patentee in field. Mem. pres.'s coun. Calif. Inst. Tech., 1969-71; trustee Brown U., 1969-74, trustee emeritus, 1974—; trustee Baylor U., Baylor U. Med. Center, Dallas, 1970-79; mem. vis. com. elec. engring. dept. U. Tex., Austin, 1969-73; mem. U. Tex. at Austin Sch. Arts and Scis. Found. adv. coun., 1972-78, Coll. Natural Scis. Found. adv. coun., 1978—, Coll. Edn. Found. adv. coun., 1977—; hon. life mem. Coll. Natural Scis., 1985. Recipient Disting. Alumni award Baylor U., 1965; Inventor of Yr. award Patent, Trademark and Copyright Research Inst., George Washington U., 1966; Golden Plate award Am. Acad. Achievement, 1967; 50th Anniversary Grad. Sch. citation Brown U., 1978; Omicron Delta Kappa Outstanding Alumnus award Baylor U., 1978; 25th anniversary first comml. silicon transistor citation by Tex. Instruments Inc., 1980; Semmy award Semicondr. Equipment and Materials Inst., 1984. Fellow IEEE (past bd. dirs., editorial bd., awards bd., Medal of Honor 1968, Centennial medal 1984), Am. Phys. Soc., Am. Chem. Soc. (Creative Invention award 1970, Doherty award Dallas-Ft. Worth chpt. 1974), Am. Inst. Chemists (50th ann. meeting honor scroll, fellows lectr. 1973), AAAS (v.p., chmn. indsl. sect. 1969-70, mem. coun. 1968-71, chmn. com. coun. affairs 1969-71, chmn. com. on industry, tech. and soc. 1972-74), Tex. Acad. Sci. (pres., hon. life fellow 1960), Wash. Acad. Sci., Instn. Elec. Engrs. U.K. (chartered elec. engr.), NAE (aeros. and space adv. bd. 1970-73), Coun. Sci. Socs., Dallas-Ft. Worth (co-founder, past dir., chmn. exec. com.), Dirs. Indsl. Rsch., Indsl. Rsch. Inst., Athenaeum Club (Loon), Cosmos Club (Washington), Sigma Xi, Sigma Pi Sigma (hon.), Kappa Epsilon Alpha. Address: 5515 Glen Lakes Dr # 514 Dallas TX 75231-4338

TEARE, BERNICE ADELINE, elementary school educator, reading specialist; b. Camden, N.J., May 31, 1942; d. Harry Kenneth and Lorraine P. (Blazer) Schwab; m. Paul A. Teare, Aug. 19, 1967; 1 child, Paul Brian. BA, Glassboro State Coll., 1964, MA, 1967; cert. prin./supr., Trenton State Coll., 1977, MEd, 1979, cert. reading specialist, 1979. Cert. tchr., N.J.; cert. reading specialist, N.J. Elem. tchr. Cherry Hill (N.J.) Pub. Schs., 1964-86, reading specialist, 1986—; conf. presenter West Jersey Reading Coun., Marlton, 1992-94, Reading Coun. South Jersey, Marlton, 1992-94, ASCD, 1993, Internat. Reading Assn., Toronto, 1994, Anaheim, Calif., 1995; staff devel. trainer Cherry Hill Sch. Dist., 1991-95. Author: Update '93 Resource Book, 1992, First Grade Resource Book, 1993, Second Grade Resource Book, 1994, Primary '94 Resource Book, 1994; contbr. articles to profl. jours. Mem. Internat. Reading Assn., N.J. Reading Assn., Reading Coun. South Jersey, West Jersey Reading Coun., Kappa Delta Pi. Avocations: reading, travel, teddy bear collecting, children's literature, computers. Office: Kingston Sch Kingston Rd Cherry Hill NJ 08034

TEARE, IWAN DALE, retired research scientist; b. Moscow, Idaho, July 24, 1931; s. Mylrea Henry and Crystal Ann (Atkinson) T.; m. Claudia Joy Patterson, Sept. 14, 1952; children: Steven, Bradley, Kurtis, Kelly. BS in Agronomy, U. Idaho, 1953; MS in Agronomy, Wash. State U., 1959; PhD, Purdue U., 1963. Instr. agronomy Purdue U., West Lafayette, Ind., 1961-63; asst. prof. agronomy Wash. State U., Pullman, 1963-69; prof. agronomy Kans. State U., Manhattan, 1969-79; dir. Agrl. Rsch. and Edn. Ctr., U. Fla., Quincy, 1979-82; rsch. scientist U. Fla., Quincy, 1982-96; ret., 1996. Active Boy Scouts Am. Served to 1st lt. U.S. Army, 1954-56. Recipient Disting. Grad. Faculty award Kans. State U., 1974; U. Fla. scholar. Fellow Am. Soc. Agronomy; mem. Am. Soc. Crop Sci., Sigma Xi, Phi Kappa Phi, Gamma Sigma Delta. Mem. Ch. Jesus Christ of Latter-Day Saints. Assoc. editor Agronomy Jour., 1979-85, tech. editor, 1986-92; co-editor: Crop-Water Relations, 1983; assoc. editor Contemporary Issues, Jour. Prodn. Agr., 1996—; editor symposium, conf. proceedings; contbr. numerous articles to profl. jours. Home: 420 Maxwell Dr Cairo GA 31728-3554 Office: N Fla Rsch & Edn Ctr Univ of Fla RR 3 Box 4370 Quincy FL 32351-9500

TEARE, JOHN RICHARD, JR., lawyer; b. Phila., Sept. 23, 1954; divorced; 1 child, John III; m. Gale Angela Waters, June 5, 1982; children: Angela, Stephanie. BS in Criminal Justice summa cum laude, Wilmington Coll., 1987; JD cum laude, U. Richmond, 1990. Bar: W.Va. 1990, U.S. Dist. Ct. (so. dist.) W. Va. 1990, U.S. Ct. Appeals (4th cir.) 1991. Sec. guard U. Del., Newark, 1973-76; police officer City of Dover (Del.), 1976-85; summer assoc. Hirschler Fleischer Weinberg Cox & Allen, Richmond, 1989; assoc. Bowles Rice McDavid Graff & Love, Charleston, W.Va., 1990—; counsel Charleston Police Civil Svc. Commn. Cub scout leader Boy Scouts Am., Felton, Del., 1984-88, asst. scoutmaster, Richmond, 1988-89, Charleston, 1991—; chmn. pub. safety commn. Greater Charleston C. of C., 1991; sec. United Meth. Men, 1993; dir. Charleston Leadership Coun. on Pub. Safety, 1993—, chmn. police dept. resource task force, 1994—. Mem. ABA, W.Va. Bar Assn., Kanawha County Bar Assn., Def. Rsch. Inst., Def. Trial Counsel W.Va., Fraternal Order of Police, Nat. Eagle Scout Assn., McNeill Law Assn., Greater Charleston C. of C., Delta Epsilon Rho. United Methodist. Avocations: camping, stamp collecting. Home: 1565 Virginia St E Charleston WV 25311-2416 Office: Bowles Rice McDavid Graff & Love PO Box 1386 Charleston WV 25325-1386

TEARE, RICHARD WALLACE, ambassador; b. Cleve., Feb. 21, 1937; m. Jeanie Walter; 3 children. BA, Harvard U., 1958; student, Naval War Coll., 1977-78. Joined Fgn. Svc., 1959; vice consul U.S. Consulate, Bridgetown, Barbados, 1960-62; consular officer U.S. Embassy, Manila, The Philippines, 1962-64; polit. officer U.S. Embassy, Saigon, Vietnam, 1965-67, Mexico City, 1971-74; counselor for polit. affairs U.S. Embassy, Vientiane, Laos, 1974-76; dep. chief mission U.S. Embassy, Wellington, New Zealand, 1983-86, Canberra, Australia, 1986-89; dep. and acting prin. officer U.S. Consulate Gen., Nha Trang, Vietnam, 1973; intelligence and rsch. specialist Vietnam Working Group Dept. State, 1967-69, desk officer, 1969-71, spl. asst. to asst. sec. for East Asian and Pacific Affairs, 1976-77, dep. dir. Office Philippine Affairs, 1978-80, dep. and acting U.S. rep. for Micronesian Status Negotiations, 1980-83, dir. Office of Indonesia, Malaysia, Brunei and Singapore Affairs, 1989-92, spl. projects officer Office of Dir. Gen., 1992-93, U.S. amb. to Papua New Guinea, Solomon Islands and Vanuatu, 1993—. Mem. Am. Fgn. Assn., Sr. Fgn. Svc. Assn., Asia Soc., Malaysia-Am. Soc., Indonesian-Am. Soc., Nat. Trust Hist. Preservation. Office: Port Moresby Dept of State Washington DC 20521-4240

TEASDALE, KENNETH FULBRIGHT, lawyer; b. St. Louis, Nov. 8, 1934; s. Kenneth and Ann (Fulbright) T.; m. Elizabeth Driscol Langdon, June 13, 1964; children: Caroline, Doug, Cindy. AB, Amherst Coll., 1956; LLB, Washington U., St. Louis, 1961. Bar: Mo. 1961. Atty. antitrust div. U.S. Dept. Justice, Washington, 1961-62; asst. counsel Dem. Policy Com. U.S. Senate, Washington, 1962-63, gen. counsel Dem. Policy Com., asst. to majority leader, 1963-64; assoc. Armstrong, Teasdale, Kramer & Vaughan, St. Louis, 1964-67, ptnr., 1967-86; mng. ptnr. Armstrong, Teasdale, Schlafly & Davis, St. Louis, 1986-93, chmn. of firm, 1993—; bd. dirs. Magna Bank Mo., St. Louis, GTE S.W. Corp. Trustee United Way Greater St. Louis, Sci. Ctr. St. Louis; trustee, chmn. bd. regents St. Louis U.; mem. nat. coun. Washington U. Law Sch., 1988—. Mem. ABA, Bar Assn. Mo., Bar Assn. St. Louis, Racquet Club, Noonday Club, Old Warson Country Club. Presbyterian. Office: Armstrong Teasdale Schlafly & Davis Metropolitan Sq Saint Louis MO 63106

TEASE, JAMES EDWARD, judge; b. Sheffield, Ala., Dec. 28, 1939; s. James Albert and Hattie Wayne (Counts) T.; m. Anne Elizabeth Gilley, Sept. 2, 1972. B.S., Florence State U., 1961; LL.B., U. Ala., 1964; grad., Nat. Coll. State Judiciary, 1971. Bar: Ala. 1964. Gen. practice law Florence, 1965-67, city prosecutor, 1966-67; dep. dist. atty. Lauderdale County, Ala., 1967-71; circuit judge 11th Jud. Cir. Ala., Florence, 1971-89; extra judge Ala. Ct. Civil Appeals, 1989; U.S. adminstrv. law judge Social Security Adminstrn., Office Hearings & Appeals, Florence, Ala., 1989—; Mem. Ala. Constl. Commn.; chmn. Ala. Citizens Adv. Com. on Election Reform; mem. Ala. Ct. of Judiciary, 1981-89. Bd. dirs. Regional Library System. Served with AUS, 1964-65. Named Florence Outstanding Young Man Jaycees, 1974, Alumnus of Year U. N. Ala., 1975. Mem. Am. Judicature Soc., Nat. Conf. State Trial Judges, Ala. Assn. Circuit Judges (pres. 1986), Lauderdale County Bar Assn. (pres.), Am. Legion, Sigma Delta Kappa. Baptist. Home: 1926 Monticello Rd Florence AL 35630-2740 Office: Walnut St Exec Ctr 205 S Walnut St Ste D Florence AL 35630-5721

TEATER, DOROTHY SEATH, county official; b. Manhattan, Kans., Feb. 11, 1931; d. Dwight Moody and Martha (Stahnke) Seath; m. Robert Woodson Teater, May 24, 1952; children: David Dwight, James Stanley, Donald Robert, Andrew Scott. BS, U. Ky., 1951; MS, Ohio State U., 1954. Home econs. tchr. Georgetown (Ky.) City Schs., 1951-53; extension specialist Ohio Coop. Extension, Columbus, 1967-73; consumer affairs adminstr. City of Columbus, 1974-79, Bank One Columbus NA, 1980-85; councilmember Columbus City Coun., 1980-85; commr. Franklin County, Columbus, Ohio, 1985—; active Ohio Cmty. Corrections Adv. Bd., Columbus, Columbus Met. Area Cmty. Action Orgn., Land Policy & Boom Bust Real Estate Markets, 1994, Lincoln Inst. Land Policy. Bd. dirs. BBB; mem. hon. adv. bd. Girl Scouts. Recipient Outstanding Alumnus award U. Ky., 1989, Women of Achievement award YWCA, 1995; named Disting. Alumni, Ohio State U., 1977. Mem. County Commrs. Assn. Ohio (pres. 1994), Columbus Met. Club. Republican. Methodist. Avocations: gardening, sewing. Office: Franklin County Commrs 373 S High St Columbus OH 43215-4591

TEATES, CHARLES DAVID, radiologist, educator; b. Luray, Va., July 1, 1936; s. Gilbert Grove and Mae Frankie (Pierce) T.; m. Mary Bruce Bucher, June 6, 1958; children—Elizabeth Susan, David Bruce, Mary Catherine. B.S., Lebanon Valley Coll., Annville, Pa., 1958; M.S., U. Va., Charlottesville, 1963, M.D., 1963. Diplomate Am. Bd. Radiology, Am. Bd. Nuclear Medicine. Intern U. Kans. Med. Ctr., 1963-64; resident in radiology U. Va. Med. Ctr., 1964-67; Asst. prof. radiology U. Va., Charlottesville, 1969-73, assoc. prof., 1973-79, prof., 1979—. Contbg. author books on radiology and nuclear medicine. Served to maj. M.C., U.S. Army, 1967-69, Vietnam. Mem. Am. Coll. Radiology (pres. Va. chpt. 1984-85), Soc. Nuclear Medicine (pres. Mid-Eastern chpt. 1984-86), AMA, Alpha Omega Alpha. Home: 4635 Watts Passage Charlottesville VA 22911 Office: U Va Med Ctr PO Box 170 Charlottesville VA 22908

TEBALDI, RENATA, opera singer; b. Pesaro, Italy, Feb. 1, 1922; d. Teobaldo and Giuseppina (Barbieri) T. Student, Arrigo Boito Conservatory, Parma, Gioacchino Rossini Conservatory, Pesaro; Pupil, Carmen Melis, Giuseppe Pais. Lyric soprano, profl. debut in Mefistofele, Rovigo, 1944; debut at LaScala, 1946; singer opera houses of Naples, Rome, Venice, Bologna, Florence, Modena, Cesana, Turin, Venice, Pompeii; Am. debut in Aida, San Francisco Opera Co., 1950; debut in Otello, Met. Opera House, N.Y.C., 1955; singer operatic roles in La Boheme, Madama Butterfly, Tosca, Die Meistersinger. Toured U.S.S.R., 1975, 76; ret. 1976. Named Commander for Arts and Letters, France, 1987. Roman Catholic.

TEBBEL, JOHN, writer, educator; b. Boyne City, Mich., Nov. 16, 1912; s. William and Edna (Johnston) T.; m. Kathryn Carl, Apr. 29, 1939; 1 child, Judith. A.B., Central Mich Coll. Edn., 1935; M.S., Columbia U., 1937. City editor Isabella Co. Times-News, Mt. Pleasant, Mich., 1935-36; writer Newsweek mag., 1937; reporter Detroit Free Press, 1937-39; feature writer, roto news editor Providence Jour., 1939-41; mng. editor Am. Mercury, 1941-43; Sunday staff writer N.Y. Times, 1943; assoc. editor E.P. Dutton & Co., 1943-47; asst. in journalism Sch. Journalism Columbia U., 1943-45; chmn. dept. journalism N.Y. U., 1954-65, prof. journalism, 1965—; Cons. Ford Found., 1966—. Author: An American Dynasty, 1947, The Marshall Fields, 1947, George Horace Lorimer and the Saturday Evening Post, 1948, Battle for North America, 1948, Your Body, 1951, The Conqueror, 1951, Touched With Fire, 1952, The Life and Good Times of William Randolph Hearst, 1952, George Washington's America, 1954, A Voice in the Street, 1954, The Magic of Balanced Living, 1956, The American Indian Wars, 1960, The Inheritors, 1962, The Epicure's Companion, 1962, David Sarnoff, 1963, Compact History of the American Newspaper, 1964, From Rags to Riches, 1964, Open Letter to Newspaper Readers, 1968, Compact History of American Magazines, 1969, A History of Book Publishing in the United States, 4 vols, 1972, 75, 78, 81, The Battle of Fallen Timbers, 1972, The Media in America, 1975, The Press and the Presidency, 1985, Between Covers, 1987, A Certain Club, 1989, The Magazine in America, 1991, Turning the World Upside Down, 1993; contbr. to Sat. Rev., other mags. Named to Pub. Hall of Fame. Home: 4033 The Forest at Duke 2701 Pickett Rd Durham NC 27705-5654 *From the time my writing career began, at 14, I have tried to write as well and clearly and accurately as I can, so that I could best inform the people who read my books and articles about the world they live in. To me it is the obligation of every writer to recognize the responsibility his talent imposes on him, and understand that he is one of the transmitters of knowledge upon whom the world depends for advancement and the betterment of human society.*

TECCO, ROMUALD GILBERT LOUIS JOSEPH, violinist, concertmaster; b. Toulon, Var, France, May 1, 1941; came to U.S., 1960; s. Raymond Charles and Angele (Cornille) T. Student, Paris Conservatoire, 1954-60; diploma, postgrad. diploma, Juilliard Sch. Music, 1967-68. Mem. N.Y. String Quartet, 1969-72; concertmaster Juilliard Ensemble, N.Y.C., 1969-72, St. Paul Chamber Orch., 1972—; soloist Chgo. Symphony, Bavarian Radio Orch., Orch. of Mex., Orchestre Colonne, Paris, Rotterdam Philharm.; performer numerous festivals, Sweden, Finland, France, Italy, U.S. Recs. with Aaron Copland and Lou Harrison Chamber Music. Served with French Navy, 1964-65, NATO hdqrs. Recipient first prize in violin Conservatoire Paris; recipient first prize chamber music Conservatoire Paris. Mem. St. Paul Univ. Club. Office: St Paul Chamber Orch 408 St Peter St Saint Paul MN 55102-1497

TECKLENBURG, HARRY, pharmaceutical products executive; b. Seattle, Nov. 3, 1927; s. Harry and Frieda (Rasche) T.; m. Mary Louise Beaty, Sept. 1, 1951; children: Don, Bruce. B.S. in Chem. Engring., MIT, 1950; M.S. in Chem. Engring., U. Wash., 1952. With Procter & Gamble Co., Cin., 1952—; chem. engr., group leader, sect. leader. dir., mgr. research and devel. dept., v.p. research and devel. Procter & Gamble Co., 1952-76; sr. v.p., 1976—; gen. mgr. Norwich Div. N.Y., 1984—; rep. to Indsl. Research Inst., 1973-76. Mem. corp. devel. com. MIT, 1977-82; trustee Ohio Valley Goodwill Industries Rehab. Center, 1969-84, pres., 1974-82; bd. dirs. Goodwill Industries Am., 1978-84, vice chmn. bd., 1980-82, chmn. bd., 1982-84, dir. emeritus, 1984-87; mem. vis. com. dept. chem. engring. U. Wash., 1983; chmn. Goodwill Industries Internat. Fund, 1986. Served with AUS, 1946-48. Mem. Engring. Soc. Cin., Am. Inst. Chem. Engrs., Am. Chem. Soc., Pharms. Mfrs. Assn. (dir. 1984—), TAPPI, AAAS. Office: Norwich Eaton Pharms Inc Norwich NY 13815

TECLAFF, LUDWIK ANDRZEJ, law educator, consultant, author, lawyer; b. Czestochowa, Poland, Nov. 14, 1918; came to U.S., 1952, naturalized, 1958; s. Emil and Helena (Tarnowska) T.; m. Eileen Johnson, May 30, 1952. Mag Iuris, Oxford (Eng.) U., 1944; MS, Columbia U., 1955; LLM, NYU, 1961, JSD, 1965. Attaché Polish Fgn. Ministry, London, 1943-46; consul in Ireland, Polish Govt. in London, 1946-52; student libr. Columbia U. Sch. Libr. Sci., 1953-54; libr. Bklyn. Pub. Libr., 1954-59; rsch. librar. Fordham U. Sch. Law, 1959-62, asst. prof. law, 1962-65, assoc. prof. law, 1965-68, prof. 1968-89, prof. emeritus, 1989—, bd. dirs. law libr., 1962-86; cons. in field. Trustee Pilsudski Inst., N.Y.C. With Polish Army, 1940-43, France, Eng. Recipient Clyde Eagleton award in internat. law NYU, 1965. Mem. Am. Soc. Internat. Law, Internat. Law Assn., Am. Law Librs. Assn., Internat. Coun. Environ. Law, Internat. Water Law Assn. Roman Catholic. Author: The River Basin in History and Law, 1967; Abstraction and Use of Water, 1972; Legal and Institutional Responses to Growing Water Demand, 1978; Economic Roots of Oppression, 1984, Water Law in Historical Perspective, 1985; editor: (with Albert E Utton) International Environmental Law, 1974, Water in a Developing World, 1978, International Groundwater Law, 1981, Transboundary Resources Law, 1987; contbr. articles on water law, law of the sea and environ. law to law jours. Office: Fordham U Sch Law 140 W 62nd St New York NY 10023-7407

TEDDER, DANIEL WILLIAM, chemical engineering educator; b. Orlando, Fla., Apr. 13, 1946; s. Daniel Webster and Adelaide Katheryn (Bruechert) T.; m. Wendy Elizabeth Widhelm, Aug. 3, 1968; children: Lisa Christine, Rachel Marie. Student, Kenyon Coll., 1964-67; B Chem. Engring. with highest honors, Ga. Inst. Tech., 1972; MS, U. Wis., 1973, PhD, 1975. Registered profl. engr., Tenn., Ga. Lab. technician Agrico Chem. Co., Pierce, Fla., 1965-67, Puritan Chem. Co., Atlanta, 1967-68; engr. Humble Oil and Refining Co., Baytown, Tex., summer 1972; staff engr. Oak Ridge (Tenn.) Nat. Lab., 1975-79; asst. prof. chem. engring. Ga. Inst. Tech., Atlanta, 1979-84, assoc. prof., 1984—; organizer symposia Emerging Techs. for Hazardous Waste Mgmt.; conf. presenter in field, 1977—; engring. cons. BCM Techs., Inc., Amherstberg, Ont., Can., 1985, Nat. Bur. Standards, U.S. Dept. Commerce, 1986—, Thermax Inc., Atlanta, 1987-88, Exxon R & D Lab., Baton Rouge, 1989—, Waste Policy Inst., Blacksburg, Va., 1992—, Geotech ChemNuclear, Golden, Colo., 1992—, Martin Marietta, Oak Ridge, 1992—, Resource Preservation Corp., Union City, Ga., 1992—; reviewer Jour. Phys. Chemistry, 1993—; others. Sr. series editor: Radioactive Waste Management Handbook; exec. editor Toxic and Hazardous Substance Control; assoc. editor Solvent Extraction and Ion Exchange; editor: (with F.G. Pohland) Emerging Technologies in Hazardous Waste Management, 1989, I, 1990, II, 1991, III, 1993, IV, 1994, V, 1995; contbr. numerous articles to profl. jours., chpts. to books. Mem. AIChE (pub. awareness com. Knoxville 1978-79), Am. Chem. Soc. (symposium chmn. I&EC divsn. 1989—), Am. Nuclear Soc., Water Pollution Control Fedn. Achievements include patents in process producing absolute ethanol by solvent extraction and vacuum distillation, fractional distillation of C2/C3 hydrocarbon at optimum pressures, others. Office: Ga Inst Tech Sch Chem Engring 778 Atlantic Dr Atlanta GA 30332-0100

TEDDER, THOMAS FLETCHER, immunology educator, researcher; b. Chateauroux, France, May 14, 1956; came to U.S. 1959; s. Raymond Percy and Barbara (Hagemann) T. AA, Okaloosa-Walton Community Coll, Niceville, Fla., 1976; BS with honors, U. Fla., 1978, MS, 1980; PhD, U. Ala., Birmingham, 1984. Rsch. fellow in pathology Harvard Med. Sch., Boston, 1984-85, instr. pathology, 1987-88, asst. prof. pathology, 1988-93; assoc. prof. pathology Harvard U. Med. Sch., Boston, 1993; prof. immunology Duke U. Med. Ctr., Durham, N.C., 1993—, chmn. dept., 1993—; lectr. in immunology, Harvard Med. Sch., 1988—, prof. tumor immunology grad. course, 1990—. Assoc. editor Jour. Immunology, 1989-93, sect. editor, 1993—; contbr. numerous articles to med. jours., including Jour. Immunology, Cell Immunology, Jour. Gen. Virology. Recipient LeRoy Collins Disting. Alumnus award Fla. Assn. C.C.'s; named 25th Anniversary Disting. Alumnus, Okaloosa-Walton C.C., 1989; Damon Runyon-Walter Winchell rsch. fellow, 1985-87; scholar Leukemia Soc. Am., 1991-96, Stohlman scholar, 1995-96. Mem. Am. Soc. for Microbiology (Pres. Fellow 1982), Am. Assn. Immunologists, Sigma Xi, Phi Kappa Phi. Achievements include identification and determination of structure and function of many human B lymphocyte cell-surface molecules. Office: Duke U Med Ctr Dept Immunology PO Box 3010 Durham NC 27710

TEDESCHI, ERNEST FRANCIS, JR., naval officer; b. New Britain, Conn., Mar. 28, 1942; s. Ernest and Rose (Malucci) T.; m. Christine Ann DiEleuterio, Apr. 15, 1972; children: Gina, Ernest. BS in Marine Engring., U.S. Naval Acad., 1965; MS in Mgmt., Salve Regina U., 1987. Commd. ensign USN, advanced through grades to rear adm., 1992; weapons officer USS Gridley (CG 21), San Diego, 1974-76; operational test & evaluation force Pacific USS John Paul Jones (DDG 32), 1978-81; commdg. officer USS Duncan (FFG 10), Long Beach, Calif., 1982-85; instr. Surface Warfare Officers Sch., Newport, R.I., 1985-87; sponsor, chief of naval ops. Aegis Program, Washington, 1987-89; commdg. officer USS Valley Forge (CG 50), San Diego, 1990-91; dir. plans and policy Supreme Allied Commdr. Atlantic NATO, Norfolk, Va., 1991-93; commdr. naval base, combat logistics group 1 USN, San Francisco, 1993—; weapons officer USS Brownson (DD 868), Newport, R.I., 1970-72; exec. com. Fed. Exec. Bd., Oakland, Calif., 1993-94. Bd. dirs. ARC, San Francisco, 1993-94; regional chmn. Navy/Marine Corps Relief Soc., No. Calif., 1993-94. Decorated Disting. Svc. medal, Meritorious Svc. medal with gold star, Bronze Star with combat "V", Legion of Merit with gold star, Def. Superior Svc. medal. Mem. Ret. Officer's Assn., Surface Navy Assn., San Francisco C. of C. (exec. bd. 1993-95). Roman Catholic. Avocations: tennis, basketball, jogging, baseball. Home: 5 Whiting Way San Francisco CA 94130-1512 Office: Commdr Naval Base SF Treasure Island 410 Palm Ave San Francisco CA 94130

TEDESCHI, JOHN ALFRED, historian, librarian; b. Modena, Italy, July 17, 1931; came to U.S., 1939, naturalized, 1944; s. Caesar George and Piera (Forti) T.; m. Anne Wood Christian, Sept. 8, 1956; children: Martha, Philip, Sara. BA, Harvard U., 1954, MA, 1960, PhD, 1966. Bibliographer European history and lit. Newberry Library, Chgo., 1965-84, curator rare books and manuscripts, head dept. spl. collections, 1970-82, dir. Ctr. Renaissance Studies, 1979-84; curator rare books and spl. collections Meml. Library U. Wis.-Madison, 1984-96; lectr. history U. Chgo., 1969-71; vis. prof. U. Ill.-Chgo., 1972-73, adj. prof., 1979-84. Co-editor: (series) Corpus Reformatorum Italicorum, 1968—; editor-in-chief: Bibliographie Internat. de L'Humanisme et de la Renaissance, 1977-82; editor: Italian Reformation Studies in Honor of Laelius Socinus, 1965, (with Anthony Molho) Renaissance Studies in Honor of Hans Baron, 1971, (with Gustav Henningsen) The Inquisition in Early Modern Europe: Studies on Sources and Methods, 1986, The Prosecution of Heresy: Collection Studies on the Inquisition in Early Modern Italy, 1991, Tomasso Sassetti, Il Massacro di San Bartolomeo, 1995; translator: (with Anne Tedeschi) The Cheese and the Worms. The Cosmos of a Sixteenth-Century Miller (Carlo Ginzburg), 1980 (named an Outstanding Acad. Book by Choice mag.), The Night Battles. Witchcraft and Agrarian Cults in the Sixteenth and Seventeenth Centuries (Carlo Ginzburg), 1983, Clues, Myths, and the Historical Method (Carlo Ginzburg), 1989, Hans Urs von Balthasar: A Theological Style (Angelo Scola), 1995, Domenico Scandella Known as Menocchio: His Trials Before the Inquisition (1583-1599) (Andrea Del Col), 1996; mem. editl. com.: Index des Livres Interdits (Sherbrooke), Collected Works of Erasmus (Toronto); mem. editl. bd.: Studi e Testi per la Storia Religiosa Italiana del '500 (Florence); contbr. articles to profl. jours. Served with U.S. Army, 1954-56. Grantee Am. Philos. Soc., 1961; grantee NEH, 1967; Old Dominion fellow Harvard U. Ctr. Renaissance Studies, Florence, Italy, 1967-68; fellow Inst. Research in Humanities, U. Wis.-Madison, 1976-77; Huntington Library fellow, 1984. Mem. Am. Soc. Reformation Research (pres. 1972), Renaissance Soc. Am. (exec. bd. 1971—), 16th Century Studies Conf. (pres. 1987), Am. Hist. Assn. Home: RR1 Box 169 Ferryville WI 54628

TEDESCO, FRANCIS JOSEPH, university administrator; b. Derby, Conn., Mar. 8, 1944; s. Lena (Tufano) Tedesco; m. Luann Lee Ekern, Aug. 1, 1970; 1 child, Jennifer Nicole. BS cum laude, Fairfield U., 1965; MD cum laude, St. Louis U., 1969. Asst. instr. Hosp. of U. Pa., Phila., 1971-72; asst. prof. Washington U. Sch. Medicine, St. Louis, 1974-75; asst. prof. U. Miami (Fla.) Sch. Medicine, 1975-77, co-dir. clin. research, 1976-78, assoc. prof., 1977-78; assoc. prof. Med. Coll. Ga., Augusta, 1978-81, chief of gastroenterology dept., 1978-88, prof., 1981—, acting v.p. clin. activities, 1984, v.p. for clin. activities, 1984-88, Interim dean Sch. of Medicine, 1986-88, pres., 1988—; cons. Med.-Letter/AMA div. drugs, Dwight D. Eisenhower Army Med. Ctr., Ft. Gordon, Ga., VA Med. Ctr., Augusta, Walter Reed

Army Med. Ctr., Washington; mem. gastroenterology spl. study sect. NIH, Washington, 1982—, mem. nat. digestive disease adv. bd., 1985-88, vice chmn., 1986-87, chmn., 1987-88. Contbr. numerous articles to profl. jours. Bd. dirs. Augusta Country Day Sch., 1981-83, Am. Cancer Soc., Augusta, 1985—, v.p., 1986—; bd. dirs., exec. com. Ga. Coalition for Health, 1995—; chmn. Gov.'s Health Strategies Coun., 1992—. Capt. N.G., 1970-72. Recipient Eddie Palmer award for gastrointestinal endoscopy, 1983, cert. of appreciation Am. Cancer Soc., 1986, Outstanding Faculty award Med. Coll. Ga. Sch. Medicine, 1988, Profl. Achievement award Fairfield U., 1993; Avalon Found. scholar St. Louis U., 1968-69, Paul Harris fellow Rotary, 1990. Fellow ACP, Am. Fedn. Clin. Investigation, Am. Gastroent. Assn., Am. Soc. Gastrointestinal Endoscopy (treas. 1981-84, pres.-elect 1984-85, pres. 1985-86, Rudolph Schindler award 1993); mem. Am. Coll. Gastroenterology, So. Soc. Clin. Investigation, Richmond County Med. Soc., Med. Assn. Ga. Roman Catholic. Avocations: reading, swimming. Home: 920 Milledge Rd Augusta GA 30912-7600 Office: Med Coll Ga Office Pres 1120 15th St Augusta GA 30912

TEDESCO, PAUL HERBERT, humanities educator; b. Nashua, N.H., Dec. 28, 1928; s. Steven R. and Ruth (Weaver) T.; m. Eleanor Martha Hollis, Jan. 24, 1953; children: Steven Anthony, Sara Adams Taggett, James Beattie. AB in History, Harvard Coll., 1952; AM in History, Boston U., 1955, PhD in History, 1970; CAGS in Adminstrn., Northeastern U., Boston, 1974. Instr. humanities Mich. State U., East Lansing, 1955-60; tchr. history Great Neck (N.Y.) North H.S., 1960-62; chair dept. social studies Canton (Mass.) H.S., 1962-65; prof./chair edn. Northeastern U., Boston, 1965-87; Fulbright prof. history Peking U., Beijing, China, 1988-89; historian-in-residence City of Haverhill, Mass., 1989-90; lectr. bus., history, govt. edn. Asian divsn. U. Md., Korea, Japan, Guam, 1990-94; team leader/lectr. Joint Siberian-Am. Faculty, Irkutsk State U., Siberia, 1994-95; edn. coord. Asian divsn. U. Md., 1995—; nat. dir. BHelp (Bus., History and Econ. Life Program), Boston, 1968—; cons. in field. Author: Teaching with Case Studies, 1978, A New England City: Haverhill Massachusetts, 1987, Attleboro, Massachusetts: The Hub of the Jewelry Industry, 1979, Protection, Patriotism and Prosperity: James M. Swank, the AISA, and the Tariff, 1872-1913, 1985; author, editor: The Creative Social Science Teacher, 1970, The Thunder of the Mills, 1981. Mem. Town Fin. Com., Canton, Mass., 1966-68. With U.S. Army, 1952-54. Recipient FEI Nat. collegiate award, 1985, Freedoms Found. George Washington medal for econ. edn., 1984. Mem. New Eng. History Tchrs. Assn. (past pres., Kidger award 1975). Home: PO Box 204 Dover MA 02030-0204

TEDFORD, CHARLES FRANKLIN, biophysicist; b. Lawton, Okla., June 26, 1928; s. Charles E. and Loula B. (Waters) T.; m. Julie Reme Sauret, Sept. 15, 1951; children: Gary Franklin, Mark Charles, Philip John. BS with distinction in Chemistry, S.W. Tex. State U., 1950, MS, 1954; postgrad. in radiobiology Reed Coll., 1957, in biophysics U. Calif., Berkeley, 1961-63. Enlisted USN, 1945-47, commd. ensign, 1950, advanced through grades to capt., 1968; biochemist U.S. Naval Hosp., San Diego, 1953-54, U.S. Naval Biol. Lab., Oakland, Calif., 1954-56; sr. instr., radiation safety officer Nuclear, Biol. and Chem. Warfare Def. Sch., Treasure Island, Calif., 1956-61; asst. chief nuclear medicine div. Navy Med. Sch., Bethesda, Md., 1963-66; adminstrv. program mgr. radiation safety br. Bur. Medicine and Surgery, Washington, 1966-72; dir. radiation safety and health physics program Navy Regional Med. Center, San Diego, 1972-74; mgr. Navy Regional Med. Clinic, Seattle, 1974-78, ret., 1978; dir. radiation health unit Ga. Dept. Human Resources, Atlanta, 1978-79; dir. Ariz. Radiation Regulatory Agy., Tempe, 1979-91; chief, Radiological Health Prog., Juneau, Alaska, 1991-93, ret. 1993; cons. 1993—. elected chmn. Conf. Radiation Program Dirs., 1987; named Ariz. Southwestern Low Level Radioactive Waste Compact Commr., 1990. Recipient Ariz. Adminstr. of Yr. award Ariz. Adminstrs. Assn., 1988; decorated Legion of Merit, Meritorious Service medal. Mem. Health Physics Soc., Am. Nuclear Soc. Contbr. articles on radiation safety to profl. publs.

TEDLOCK, BARBARA HELEN, anthropologist, educator; b. Battle Creek, Mich., Sept. 9, 1942; d. Byron Taylor and Mona Gerteresse (O'Connor) McGrath; m. Dennis E. Tedlock, July 19, 1968. BA in Rhetoric, U. Calif., 1967; MA in Anthropology, Wesleyan U., 1973; PhD in Anthropology, SUNY, Albany, 1978. Lectr. in music Tufts U., Medford, Mass., 1977-78, asst. prof. anthropology, 1978-82, assoc. prof., 1982-87; assoc. prof. anthropology SUNY, Buffalo, 1987-89, prof. anthropology, 1989—. Author: Time and the Highland Maya, 1982, The Beautiful and the Dangerous Encounters with Zuni Indians, 1992; editor: Dreaming: Anthropological and Psychological Interpretations, 1987; co-editor: Teaching From the American Earth, 1975; assoc. editor Jour. of Anthropol. Rsch., 1987-93; sr. editor Dreaming, 1990-95. Adv. bd. Mus. of Indian Arts, Santa Fe, 1991; mem. Roycrofters-at-large East Aurura, N.Y., 1989—; mem. humanities panel WGBH, Boston, 1983-84; judge pottery Southwestern Assn. on Indian Affaris, Santa Fe, 1981-83. Fellowships NEH, 1986, 93, sr. fellowship Am. Coun. of Learned Socs., 1994, Weatherhead fellowship Sch. of Am. Rsch., 1980; recipient Charles Bordon, Geoffrey Bushnell Juan Cosmos Prize in linguistics Internat. Congress of Americanists, 1979. Fellow Am. Anthropol. Assn. (bd. dirs. 1991-93, editor-in-chief Am. Anthropologist 1994—), Soc. for Cultural Anthropology; mem. Soc. for Humanistic Anthropology (pres. 1991-93, Writing prize 1986), Soc. for Psychol. Anthropology (bd. dirs. 1993—), Assn. for Study of Dreams (bd. dirs. 1990—), Soc. for Ethnohistory (exec. bd. 1980-82), Am. Studies Assn. (exec. bd. 1983-85). Avocations: skiing, running, swimming, dancing, videoing. Office: SUNY Buffalo Dept Anthropology Buffalo NY 14261

TEDLOCK, DENNIS, anthropology and literature educator; b. St. Joseph, Mo., June 19, 1939. BA, U. N.Mex., 1961; PhD in Anthropology, Tulane U., 1968. Asst. prof. anthropology Iowa State U., 1966-67; asst. prof. rhetoric U. Calif., Berkeley, 1967-69; research assoc. Sch. Am. Research, 1969-70; asst. prof. anthropology Bklyn. Coll., 1970-71; asst. prof. Yale U., 1972-73; assoc. Univ. prof., anthropology and religion Boston U., 1973-82, Univ. prof., anthropology and religion, 1982-87; James H. McNulty prof. dept. English SUNY, Buffalo, 1987—, rsch. prof. dept. anthropology, 1987—; vis. asst. prof. Wesleyan U., 1971-72; adj. prof. U. N.Mex., 1980-81; mem. Inst. for Advanced Study, 1986-87. Author: Finding the Center: Narrative Poetry of the Zuni Indians, 1972, The Spoken Word and the Work of Interpretation, 1983, Days from a Dream Almanac, 1990 (Victor Turner prize 1991), Breath on the Mirror: Mythic Voices and Visions of the Living Maya, 1993; co-editor: Teachings from the American Earth, 1975, The Dialogic Emergence of Culture, 1996; co-editor-in-chief Am. Anthropologist, 1994—; contbr. articles to profl. jours. Dumbarton Oaks fellow in pre-Columbian Studies, 1993-94, Guggenheim fellow, 1986; recipient PEN transl. prize for Popol Vuh: The Mayan Book of the Dawn of Life, 1986. Office: SUNY Buffalo Dept English Buffalo NY 14260

TEDROW, JOHN CHARLES FREMONT, soils educator; b. Rockwood, Pa., Apr. 21, 1917; s. John Wesley and Emma Grace (Younkin) T.; m. Mary Jane Lough, Mar. 20, 1943 (dec. Mar. 1991); children: John Charles Fremont, Thomas Lough. BS, Pa. State U., 1939; MS, Mich. State U., 1940; PhD, Rutgers U., 1950. Jr. soil technologist Dept. Agr., 1941-42, soil scientist, 1946-47; instr. Rutgers U., New Brunswick, N.J., 1947-50, asst. prof., 1950-53, assoc. prof., 1953-57, prof. soils, 1957-84, prof. emeritus, 1984—; cons. N.S. Research Found., 1949—; sr. pedologist Boston U., 1953—; prin. investigator Arctic Inst. N.Am., Washington, 1955-68, NSF, 1961-62, Atomic Energy Commn., Washington, 1961-63; cons. to govt. and industry. Author: (with R.C. Murray) Forensic Geology: Earth Sciences and Criminal Investigation, 1974, Soils of the Polar Landscapes, 1977, (with K.A. Linell) Soil and Permafrost Surveys in the Arctic, 1981, Soils of New Jersey, 1986, (with R.C. Murray) Forensic Geology, 1991; editor in chief Soil Science, 1968-79; editor: Antarctic Soils and Soil Forming Processes, 1966. Served to lt. USNR, 1942-46. Recipient Lindback Research award Rutgers U., 1978, Antarctic Service medal. Fellow Am. Soc. Agronomy, Soil Sci. Soc. Am., Arctic Inst. N.Am.; mem. Internat. Soc. Soil Sci., Am. Geophys. Union, Am. Arbitration Assn., Sigma Xi, Alpha Zeta (hon.), Phi Mu Delta. Investigator polar soils in Alaska, Can., Greenland, Scandinavia, Siberia and Antarctica. Home: 5 Bluebird Ct Edison NJ 08820-3677 Office: Rutgers U Environ Resources PO Box 231 New Brunswick NJ 08903-0231

TEEGARDEN, KENNETH LEROY, clergyman; b. Cushing, Okla., Dec. 22, 1921; s. Roy Albert and Eva B. (Swiggart) T.; m. Wanda Jean Strong, May 28, 1944; children: David Kent, Marshall Kirk. Student, Okla. State U., 1938-40; A.B., Phillips U., 1942, M.A., 1945, D.D., 1963; B.D., Tex. Christian U., 1949, D.D., 1976; D.D., Bethany Coll., 1974; LL.D., Lynchburg Coll., 1975; L.H.D., Culver-Stockton Coll., 1975. Ordained to ministry Christian Ch. (Disciples of Christ), 1940; pastor in Chandler, Okla., 1944-47, Texas City, Tex., 1947-48, Healdton, Okla., 1948-49, Vernon, Tex., 1949-55, Fort Smith, Ark., 1955-58; exec. minister Christian Ch. in Ark., 1958-65; asst. to pres. Christian Ch. in U.S. and Can., Indpls., 1965-69; exec. minister Christian Ch. in Tex., 1969-73; gen. minister, pres. Christian Ch. in U.S. and Can., 1973-85; faculty Brite Div. Sch., Tex. Christian U., 1985-89; mem. governing bd. Nat. Council Chs., 1973-85; del. 5th Assembly of World Council Chs., Nairobi, Kenya, 1975, 6th Assembly, Vancouver, B.C., Can, 1983; rep. Nat. Council Chs. in Exchange of Ch. Leadership with Soviet Union, 1974. Author: We Call Ourselves Disciples, 1975. Named Disting. Alumnus Tex. Christian U., 1973, Phillips U., 1975; Outstanding Citizen Vernon, Tex., 1954. Home: 7013 Serrano Dr Fort Worth TX 76126-2317

TEEGUARDEN, DENNIS EARL, forest economist; b. Gary, Ind., Aug. 21, 1931; s. Gary Leon and Mary Dessa (Pursifull) T.; m. Sally Annette Gleason, Dec. 23, 1954; children—Jason Earl, Julie Annette, Justin Gary. B.S. in Forestry with honors, Mich. Tech. U., Houghton, 1953; M.Forestry, U. Calif., Berkeley, 1958, Ph.D. in Agrl. Econs. (Bidwell research fellow 1962-63), 1964. Rsch. aid U.S. Forest Service, 1957; asst. rsch. specialist U. Calif., Berkeley, 1958-64, mem. faculty, 1964-91, prof. forestry econs. Sch. Forestry, 1964-91, S.J. Hall prof. forest econs., 1989-91, prof. emeritus, 1991—, chmn. dept. forestry and resource mgmt., 1978-86, acting dir. forest products lab., 1987-88, assoc. dean for acad. affairs, 1990-92, assoc. dean rsch. and extension, 1992-93; mem. Calif. Commn. on Agr. and Higher Edn., 1993-95; mem. com. scientists Dept. Agr., 1977-80; cons. in field; mem. adv. bd. U. Calid. Forest Products Lab., 1994—. Co-author: Forest Resource Management: Decision-Making Principles and Cases, 1979; contbr. articles to profl. jours. Trustee Mich. Tech. Fund, Mich. Tech. U., Houghton, 1994—. Lt. USNR, 1953-57, Korea. Recipient Outstanding Alumnus award Mich. Tech. U., 1993, Berkeley citation U. Calif., Berkeley, 1994; grantee U.S. Forest Svc., Bur. Land Mgmt.; named to Honor Acad. Sch. Forestry and Wood Products, Mich. Tech. U., 1995. Fellow Am. Foresters; mem. Western Forest Economists, Calif. Water Fowl Assn. Home: 4732 Westwood Ct Richmond CA 94803-2441 Office: U Calif Coll Natural Resources Berkeley CA 94720

TEEL, JAMES E., supermarket and drug store retail executive; b. 1930. V.p. Raley's, West Sacramento, 1950-1991; co-chmn., dir., 1991—. Office: Raleys 500 W Capitol Ave Broderick CA 95605*

TEEL, JOYCE, supermarket and drugstore retail executive; b. 1930. Dir. Raley's, West Sacramento, 1950—; co-chmn., 1991—. Office: Raley's 500 W Capitol Ave Broderick CA 95605*

TEELE, THURSTON FERDINAND, economist; b. New Rochelle, N.Y., Mar. 27, 1934; s. Stanley Ferdinand and Dorothy Thurston (Newman) T.; m. Shari May Barton, June 15, 1957 (div. 1965); children: Edward B., Stacia L.; m. Dorothy Locy, Aug. 1967 (div. 1980); children: Kristy A., Allen F.; m. Barbara Mangrum Carmichael. BA, Amherst Coll., 1956; MA, Tufts U., 1962; PhD, Georgetown U., 1964. Fgn. svc. officer U.S. Dept. State, Washington and Athens, Greece, 1956-64; cons. economist, chief party Checchi. Co., Washington and overseas, 1964-75; pres., CEO Chemonics Internat., Washington, 1975—; vice chmn. Profl. Svc. Coun. AID Task Force, Washington, 1992. With U.S. Army, 1957-58. Democrat. Mem. United Ch. of Christ. Avocations: travel, reading, working out. Home: 2231 Q St NW Washington DC 20008-2825 Office: Chemonics Internat 1133 20th St NW Washington DC 20036-3307

TEEM, JOHN MCCORKLE, retired association executive; b. Springfield, Mo., July 23, 1925; s. Lon Vester and Judith (McCorkle) T.; m. Sylvia Victoria Konvicka; children—Judith Majka Teem Donald, Paul Norman. A.B., Harvard U., 1949, M.A., 1951, Ph.D., 1954. Sr. research fellow Calif. Inst. Tech., Pasadena, 1954-60; v.p., chief scientist Electro Optical Systems, Pasadena, 1960-67; dir. tech. staff, research and devel. Xerox Corp., Stamford, Conn., 1967-72; asst. gen. mgr., dir. phys. research AEC, Washington, 1973-75; asst. adminstr. ERDA, Washington, 1975-76; pres. Assn. Univs. for Research in Astronomy, Washington, 1977-86. Served with U.S. Army, 1943-46. Recipient Disting. Service medal AEC, 1975; named Fairchild Disting. scholar Calif. Inst. Tech., 1976-77. Fellow AAAS; mem. Am. Astron. Soc. Democrat. Roman Catholic. Home: 3800 Fairfax Dr Apt 1710 Arlington VA 22203-1706

TEEM, PAUL LLOYD, JR., savings and loan executive; b. Gastonia, N.C., Mar. 10, 1948; s. Paul Lloyd Sr. and Ruth Elaine (Bennett) T. BA, U. N.C., 1970; Cert., Inst. Fin. Edn., Chgo., 1984, Diploma, 1985, Degree of Distinction, 1989. Cert. tchr. N.C., consumer credit exec.; licensed real estate broker. Exec. v.p., sec. Gaston Fed. Savs. and Loan Assn., Gastonia, N.C., 1983—; exec. v.p., sec., bd. dirs. Gaston Fin. Svcs., Inc., Gastonia, 1988—. Bd. dirs. Gastonia Mchts. Assn., Inc., 1981-83; lay reader Episcopal Ch. Decorated Order Purple Cross, Legion of Honor; named Ky. Col., 1995. Fellow Soc. Cert. Credit Execs.; mem. SAR, CCV, Mil. Order of Stars and Bars, Masons (32d degree, bd. dirs. 1981—, Disting. Svc. award 1987, Gold Honor award 1988, Active Legion of Honor 1989, Order of the Purple Cross of York 1990), Shriners, KT, Royal Order of Scotland, Hon. Order Ky. Cols., Phi Alpha Theta. Democrat. Avocation: genealogy. Home: 1208 Poston Cir Gastonia NC 28054-4634 Office: Gaston Fed Savs and Loan Assn 245 W Main Ave PO Box 2249 Gastonia NC 28053-2249

TEEPEN, THOMAS HENRY, newspaper editor, journalist; b. Nashville, Jan. 19, 1935; s. Albert George and Elizabeth Blanche (Winfree) T.; m. Nancy Irene Roux, Feb. 2, 1957 (div. 1974); children—Kristina Lynn, Jeremy Roux; m. Sandra Jean Richards, May 14, 1975; 1 stepchild, Jennifer Koerlin. B.S. in Journalism, Ohio U., 1957. Reporter Urbana (Ohio) Daily Citizen, 1957-58; asst. editor Kettering-Oakwood Times, Dayton, Ohio, 1958-59; from reporter to editorial writer Dayton Daily News, 1959-68, editorial page editor, 1968-82; editorial page editor Atlanta Constitution, 1982-92; nat. corr. Cox Newspapers, Atlanta, 1992—. Contbg. columnist Liberal Opinion Week. Former pres. Joel Chandler Harris Assn., Atlanta; mem. Atlanta Opera, 1985—, Joint Internat. Observer Group, Ethiopian Elections, 1992; mem. internat. adv. com. The African-Am. Inst., N.Y.C., 1985—; mem. Capital Area Mosaic; bd. dirs. Genesis Shelter. Profl. journalism fellow Stanford Univ., 1967. Home: 900 Charles Allen Dr NE Atlanta GA 30308-1722 Office: Cox Newspapers care The Atlanta Constn Box 4689 Atlanta GA 30302

TEEPLE, FIONA DIANE, librarian, lawyer; b. St. Thomas, Ont., Can., Jan. 9, 1943; d. William Lloyd and Grace (Hathaway) T. BA, U. Western Ont., London, 1964; BLS, U. B.C., Vancouver, 1965; MLS, U. Toronto, Ont., 1976; LLB, York U., Toronto, 1980. Bar: Ont., 1985. Asst. law librarian U. Western Ont., London, 1965-70; reference librarian York U. Law Library, Toronto, 1971-77; adminstrv. asst. Ont. Legis. Library, Toronto, 1980, exec. asst., 1981-83; chief librarian Supreme Ct. of Can., Ottawa, 1983-90, dir. libr., 1990—. Editor: Practitioner's Desk Book, 1976-80; mng. editor CALL Newsletter, 1973-75; contbr. articles, revs., book chpts. in field. Mem. Can. Assn. Law Librs., Law Soc. Upper Can. Mem. United Ch. Can.

TEER, KAY STOLTZ, museum director; b. Southern Pines, N.C., July 30, 1947; d. John Wesley and Ellen Kathrine (Wheeless) Stoltz; m. William Stewart Teer, June 2, 1968; children: John Stewart, Marguerite Kathrine. BS, East Carolina U., 1969; postgrad., U. S.C., 1971-89, U. N.C., 1983. Tchr. English Sch. Dist. 17, Sumter, S.C., 1969-73; exec. dir. Sumter Gallery of Art, 1982-88; grants writer S.C. Arts Commn., Columbia, 1988-89; advocacy coord. S.C. Arts Alliance, Columbia, 1988-89; exec. dir. Sumter County Mus., 1989—. Bd. dirs. Sumter Sch. Dist. 17, 1978-94, S.C. Arts Alliance, 1985-88, Fine Arts Coun., Sumter, 1986-93. Mem. Am. Assn. Mus., S.C. Fedn. Mus. (sec. 1994—), Southwestern Mus. Conf., Sumter C. of C. (bd. dirs. 1979-81, 90-92), Rotary. Mem. Am. Assn. Mus., S.C. Fedn. Mus. (sec. 1994—), Southeastern Mus. Conf., Sumter C. of C. (bd. dirs. 1979-81, 90-92). Methodist. Avocations: reading, travel, family, singing. Home: 11 Snowden St Sumter SC 29150-3224 Office: Sumter County Mus PO Box 1456 Sumter SC 29151-1456

TEES, RICHARD CHISHOLM, psychology educator, researcher; b. Montreal, Que., Can., Oct. 31, 1940; s. Ralph Charles and Helen Winnifred (Chisholm) T.; m. Kathleen F. Coleman, Sept. 1, 1962; children: Susan M., Carolyn V. B.A., McGill U., 1961; Ph.D., U. Chgo., 1965. Asst. prof. U. B.C., Vancouver, 1965-67, assoc. prof., 1969-75, prof. psychology, 1975—; head dept. psychology U. B.C., 1984-94; rsch. prof. U. Sussex, Brighton, Eng., 1972-73, 77-78; chmn. grant selection panel Nat. Scis. and Engring. Rsch. Coun. Can., Ottawa, 1993—, B.C. Health Care Rsch. Found., Vancouver, 1984-87; chmn. studentship com. Med. Rsch. Coun., Ottawa, 1985-92. Author: (with Kolb) Cerebral Cortex of the Rat, 1990; mem. editorial bd. Can. Jour. Exptl. Psychology, 1975-84, 87—; contbr. articles to profl. jours., chpts. to books. Research fellow Killam Found., 1972-73, 77-78; research fellow Can. Council, 1972-73. Fellow APA, Am. Psychol. Soc., Can. Psychol. Assn.; mem. Soc. for Neurosci., Psychonomic Soc., U. B.C. Senate, Faculty Club. Home: 1856 Acadia Rd, Vancouver, BC Canada V6T 1R3 Office: U BC, Dept Psychology, Vancouver, BC Canada V6T 1Z4

TEETER, DWIGHT LELAND, JR., journalism educator; b. L.A., Jan. 6, 1935; s. Dwight Leland and Ruth Elizabeth (Sauer) T.; m. Letitia Ruth Thoreson, July 7, 1956; children: Susan Letitia Hall, John Thoreson, William Weston. A.B. in Journalism, U. Calif.-Berkeley, 1956, M.J., 1959; Ph.D. in Mass Communications, U. Wis., 1966. Reporter Waterloo Daily Courier, Iowa, 1957-60; asst. prof. Iowa State U., Ames, 1964-66; asst. to assoc. prof. U. Wis., Madison, 1966-72; assoc.prof. to prof. U. Ky., Lexington, 1972-77, dir. journalism dept., 1975-77; prof. journalism, chmn. dept. journalism U. Tex., Austin, 1977-84, William P. Hobby Centennial prof. communication, 1983-87; prof., dept. mass communications U. Wis., Milw., 1987-91; dean, prof. Coll. Communications U. Tenn., Knoxville, 1991—; vis. assoc. prof. U. Wash., Seattle, 1969-70; treas. Journalism Council, Inc., N.Y.C., 1972-81. Author: (with Don R. Le Duc) Law of Mass Communications, 8th edit., 1995, (with Jean L. Folkerts) Voices of a Nation: A History of Media in the United States, 2d edit., 1994; contbr. articles to legal, hist., comm. jours. Chair Headliners Club of Tex. Media Contest, 1979-83; judge Tex. Bar Assn. Media Contest, 1981-85; mem. pub. affairs com. Tex. State Bar, 1985-87. Recipient Tex. Excellence in Teaching award Tex. Ex-Students' Assn., 1983, Harold L. Nelson award U. Wis., 1985. Mem. Assn. for Edn. in Journalism and Mass Comm. (chmn. prof. freedom and responsibility com. 1971-73, pres. 1985-86), Soc. Profl. Journalists (Disting. Tchr. award 1991), Phi Kappa Phi, Kappa Tau Alpha. Office: U Tenn Coll Comm Knoxville TN 37996

TEETER, KARL VAN DUYN, retired linguistic scientist, educator; b. Berkeley, Calif., Mar. 2, 1929; s. Charles Edwin and Lura May (Shaffner) T.; m. Anita Maria Bonacorsi, Aug. 25, 1951; children—Katharine Emilie, Judith Ann, Teresa Maria, Martha Elisabeth. AB in Oriental Langs. with highest honors, U. Calif., Berkeley, 1959, PhD Linguistics, 1962; AM (hon.), Harvard U., 1966. From instr. to prof. linguistics Harvard U., 1962-89, prof. emeritus, 1989—, chmn. dept. linguistics, 1966-69, 70-71, 77-78; assoc. Kirkland Ho., Harvard U., 1977-82, fellow, 1983-89, hon. assoc., 1989—; guest rsch. fellow Rsch. Inst. Logopedics and Phoniatrics, Faculty of Medicine, Tokyo U., 1969-70; mem. summer faculty U. Mich., 1962, UCLA, 1966, U. N.C., 1972. Author: Maliseet Texts, 1963, The Wiyot Language, 1964, Wiyot Handbook, I and II, 1993; editor: In Memoriam Peter Lewis Paul, 1902-89, 1993. Bd. dirs. Mass. Found. for Humanities and Pub. Policy, 1984-90, exec. com., 1985-89; bd. dirs. New Eng. Found. for Humanities, 1986-93; active New Eng. Native Am. Inst., 1992—. Served with AUS, 1946, 51-54. Fulbright rsch. fellow Japan, 1969-70; NSF grantee, 1990—. Mem. Linguistic Soc. Am. (life, long range planning com. 1969-73, lang. rev. com. 1980-82), Soc. Study Indigenous Langs. of the Ams., Phi Beta Kappa, Sigma Xi. Home: 14 Half Woodbridge St Cambridge MA 02140-1220 Office: Harvard Univ Widener T Cambridge MA 02138

TEETERS, NANCY HAYS, economist; b. Marion, Ind., July 29, 1930; d. S. Edgar and Mabel (Drake) Hays; m. Robert Duane Teeters, June 7, 1952; children: Ann, James, John. A.B. in Econs., Oberlin Coll., 1952, LL.D. (hon.), 1979; M.A. in Econs., U. Mich., 1954, postgrad., 1956-57, LL.D. (hon.), 1983; LL.D. (hon.), Bates Coll., 1981, Mt. Holyoke Coll., 1983. Tchg. fellow U. Mich., 1954-55, instr., 1956-57; instr. U. Md. Overseas, Germany, 1955-56; staff economist govt. fin. sect. Bd. Govs. of FRS, Washington, 1957-66; mem. bd. Bd. Govs. of FRS, 1978-84; economist (on loan) Coun. Econ. Advs., 1962-63; economist Bur. Budget, 1966-70; sr. fellow Brookings Instn., 1970-73; sr. specialist Congl. Rsch. Svc., Library of Congress, Washington, 1973-74; asst. dir., chief economist Ho. of Reps. Com. on the Budget, 1974-78; v.p., chief economist IBM, Armonk, N.Y., 1984-90; bd. dirs., trustee Prudential Mut. Funds, 1985—; bd. dirs. Inland Steel Industries; mem. Coun. on Fgn. Rels., Forum for World Affairs, Women in Mgmt. Author: (with others) Setting National Priorities: The 1972 Budget, 1971, Setting National Priorities: The 1973 Budget, 1972, Setting National Priorities: The 1974 Budget, 1973; contbr. articles to profl. publs. Recipient Comfort Starr award in econs. Oberlin Coll., 1952; Disting. Alumnus award U. Mich., 1980. Mem. Nat. Economists Club (v.p. 1973-74, pres. 1974-75, chmn. bd. 1975-76, gov. 1976-79), Am. Econ. Assn. (com. on status of women 1975-78), Am. Fin. Assn. (dir. 1969-71). Democrat. Home: 243 Willowbrook Ave Stamford CT 06902-7020

TEETS, JOHN WILLIAM, diversifed company executive; b. Elgin, Ill., Sept. 15, 1933; s. John William and Maudie Teets; m. Nancy Kerchenfaut, June 25, 1965; children: Jerri, Valerie Sue, Heide Jane, Suzanne. Student, U. Ill.; LLD (hon.), Trinity Coll., 1982; DBA in Foodsvc. Mgmt. (hon.), Johnson and Wales U., 1991; D in Comml. Sci. (hon.), Western Internat. U., 1992. Pres., ptnr. Winter Garden Restaurant, Inc., Carpenterville, Ill., 1957-63; v.p. Greyhound Food Mgmt. Co.; pres. Post Houses, Inc., and Horne's Enterprises, Chgo., 1964-68; pres., chief operating officer John R. Thompson Co., Chgo., 1968-71; pres., corp. v.p. pub. restaurant divsn. Canteen Corp., Chgo., 1971-75; divsn. pres. Jacques Restaurant Group, 1975; exec. v.p., CEO Bonanza Internat. Co., Dallas, 1975; group v.p. food svcs., pres. Greyhound Food Mgmt., Inc. (now named Restaura), Phoenix, 1975; vice chmn. The Greyhound Corp., Phoenix, 1980; chmn., CEO Greyhound Corp. (now The Dial Corp), Phoenix, 1981—; now chmn., pres., CEO The Dial Corp, Phoenix; vice chmn. Pres.' Conf. on Foodservice Industry. Recipient Silver Plate award, Golden Plate award Internat. Foodsvc. Mgrs. Assn., 1980, Bus. Leadership award Harvard Bus. Sch. Club Ariz., 1985, Order of the Crown, Kingdom of Belgium, 1990, Ellis Island medal of honor Nat. Ethnic Coalition of Orgns. Found., 1995; named Top Bus. Spkr. of Yr., Forbes Mag., 1990, Capt. of Achievement, Acad. of Achievement, 1992, CEO of Yr., Leaders Mag., 1986. Mem. Nat. Inst. Foodsvc. Industry (trustee), Am. Mgmt. Assn., Christian Businessmen's Assn. (chmn. steering com. 1977). Office: The Dial Corp 1850 N Central Ave Phoenix AZ 85077-0001

TEETS, PETER B., aerospace executive; b. 1942. BS, U. Colo., MS, 1978. V.p. Denver Aerospace subs. Martin Marietta Corp., Colo., 1980-85, corp. v.p., pres., 1985-87, sr. v.p., 1987—; pres., COO, Info. & Tech. Svcs. Sector Lockheed Martin Corp., Bethesda, M.D.; sr. v.p., group pres., Martin Marietta Corp. Office: Martin Marietta Astronautics PO Box 179 Denver CO 80201-0179 Office: Lockheed Martin Corp 6801 Rockledge Dr Bethesda MD 20817*

TEEVAN, RICHARD COLLIER, psychology educator; b. Shelton, Conn., June 12, 1919; s. Daniel Joseph and Elizabeth (Halliwell) T.; m. Virginia Agnes Stehle, July 28, 1945; children—Jan Elizabeth, Kim Ellen, Clay Collier, Allison Tracy. B.A., Wesleyan U., Middletown, Conn., 1951; M.A., U. Mich., 1952, Ph.D., 1955. Rubber buffer Sponge Rubber Product Co., Derby, Conn., 1939-41; with U. Mich., 1951-57, teaching fellow, 1951-53, instr., 1953-57; asst. prof. Smith Coll., 1957-60; assoc. prof. Bucknell U., 1960-64, prof., 1964-69; chmn. psychology, prof. SUNY-Albany, 1969—; pres. Teevan Assocs., Cons., 1991—; cons. on coll. teaching, 1989—. Author: Reinforcement, 1961, Instinct, 1961, Color Vision, 1961, Measuring Human Motivation, 1962, Theories of Motivation in Learning, 1964, Theories of Motivation in Personality and Social Psychology, 1964, Motivation, 1967, Fear of Failure, 1969, Readings in Elementary Psychology, 1973; contbr. articles to sci. jours. Served to capt. AUS, 1941-47; prisoner of war 1943-45, Ger. Office Naval Research grantee, 1958-72; recipient Lindbach award Bucknell U., 1966. Mem. AAAS, AAUP, Am. Psychol. Assn. (Disting. visitor 1981-85), Eastern Psychol. Assn., Phi Beta Kappa, Sigma Xi.

Home: 45 Pine St Delmar NY 12054-3413 Office: SUNY Dept Psychology 1400 Washington Ave Albany NY 12222-0100

TEGGE, FRANK ALLEN, stock brokerage company executive; b. Dearborn, Mich., Oct. 29, 1942; s. Frank Alfred and Marjorie Mildred (Allen) T.; 1 child from previous marriage, Kurt Eric; m. Sophia Branoff. BA, Albion Coll., 1964; postgrad., Garrett Theol. Sem., Evanston, Ill., 1965-66, Loyola U., Chgo., 1966-67, Wayne State U., 1967-68; cert. investment mgmt. analyst, U. Pa., 1992. Registered investment advisor. Stock broker Manley, Bennett, McDonald & Co., Lansing, Mich., 1970-73, ltd. ptnr., 1973-75, ptnr., 1975-82, sr. v.p., 1982-84; v.p. Thomson McKinnon Securities, Inc., Lansing, 1984-89; 1st v.p. McDonald and Co. Securities, Inc., East Lansing, Mich., 1989-94, sr. v.p., 1994—; bd. dirs. Manley, Bennett, McDonald, Detroit. Bd. trustees Cen. United Meth. Ch., Lansing, 1985-88, Woldumar Nature Ctr., Lansing, 1986-92, R.E. Olds Mus., Lansing, 1984-86, Chief Okemos Coun., Boy Scouts Am.Trust Fund, Lansing, 1988—, coun. exec. com., 1989—, dist. com., asst. scoutmaster, Wharton Ctr. for Arts, Mich. State U., 1993—; mem. investment com. YMCA, Lansing, 1987-93; bd. dirs. Mid-Mich. chpt. ARC, 1993—; mem. long range planning com. Capital area United Way, 1994—; mem. deans com. coun. Coll. Arts and Letters Mich. State U., 1995—. Decorated Bronze star, Purple Heart, Army Commendation medal with oak leaf cluster; named One of 100 Best New-Style Brokers of 1994, Fin. Planning on Wall St. mag., 1994. Mem. Internat. Assn. Fin. Planners, Investment Mgmt. Cons. Assn., Comdrs. Club of Mich. (pres. 1984), Rotary (bd. dirs. 1989-92, pres. 1992-93). Republican. Avocations: fishing, hunting, camping. Home: 1400 Dennison Rd East Lansing MI 48823-2180 Office: McDonald and Co Securities 4660 S Hagadorn Rd Ste 190 East Lansing MI 48823-5353

TEGTMEYER, RENE DESLOGE, lawyer; b. St. Louis, Jan. 5, 1934; s. Adolph Henry and Elise (Desloge) T.; m. Joan Lynch, Aug. 2, 1969; children: Stephen W., Jean M. BSME, Wash. U., 1956; JD, George Washington U., 1963. Bar: Va., D.C., U.S. Ct. Appeals (Fed. cir.). Patent examiner U.S. Patent and Trademark Office, Washington, 1959-64; specialist legis. and internat. affairs U.S. Patent and Trademark Office, 1964, dir. legis. and internat. affairs, 1964-71, asst. commr. for appeals legis. and trademarks, 1971-73, asst. commr. for trademarks, 1973-75, asst. commr. for patents, 1975-89; ptnr. Fish & Richardson, Washington, 1989—. Contbr. articles to profl. jours. Lt. USAF, 1956-59; with Res. 1960-68. Congl. fellowship Am. Polit. Sci. Assn., 1967-68. Mem. ABA, Am. Intellectual Property Law Assn., Fed. Bar Assn., N.J. Patent Law Assn. (Jefferson medal 1985), Pi Tau Sigma, Tau Beta Pi. Republican. Roman Catholic. Avocations: reading, skiing. Home: 1332 Timberly Ln Mc Lean VA 22102-2504 Office: Fish & Richardson 601 13th St NW Washington DC 20005-3807

TEHAN, JOHN BASHIR, lawyer; b. Utica, N.Y., May 13, 1948; s. Louis Bashir and Frances Mary (Argenzia) T.; m. Regina Anne Callahan, Aug. 1, 1970; children—Aaron J., Lauren R., Eileen L. B.A., LeMoyne Coll., 1970; J.D., Catholic U., Washington, 1973. Bar: N.Y. 1974, U.S. Dist. Ct. (so. and ea. dists.) N.Y. 1975, U.S. Ct. Appeals (2d cir.) 1975. Assoc. Sullivan & Cromwell, N.Y.C., 1973-81; ptnr. Simpson Thacher & Bartlett, N.Y.C., 1981—. Roman Catholic. Home: 10 Warwick Rd Rockville Centre NY 11570-1337 Office: Simpson Thacher & Bartlett 425 Lexington Ave New York NY 10017-3903*

TEHRANI, FLEUR TAHER, electrical engineer, educator, researcher; b. Tehran, Feb. 16, 1956; came to U.S., 1984; d. Hassan and Pourandokht (Monfared) T. BS in Elec. Engring., Sharif U. of Tech., Tehran, 1975; DIC in Comm. Engring., Imperial Coll. Sci. and Tech., London, 1977; MSc in Comm. Engring., U. London, 1977, PhD in Elec. Engring., 1981. Registered profl. engr., Calif. Comm. engr. Planning Orgn. of Iran, Tehran, 1977-78; lectr. A elec. engring. Robert Gordon's Inst. Tech., Aberdeen, U.K., 1982-83; lectr. II elec. engring. South Bank U., London, 1984; asst. prof. elec. engring. Calif. State U., Fullerton, 1985-91, assoc. prof. elec. engring., 1991-94, prof. elec. engring., 1994—; vis. assoc. prof. elec. engring. Drexel U., Phila., 1987-88; sys. cons. Telebit Corp., Cupertino, Calif., 1985; engring. cons. PRD, Inc., Dresher, Pa., 1989-92; mem. NASA/Am. Soc. Engring. Edn. summer faculty Jet Propulsion Lab., Calif. Inst. Tech., Pasadena, 1995. Contbr. articles to profl. jours.; patentee in field. Recipient Best Ann. Rsch. Manuscript award Assn. for the Advancement of Med. Instrumentation, 1993, Outstanding Excellence in Rsch. Faculty award Calif. State U., 1993. Mem. IEEE, Women in Sci. and Engring. (chair Calif. State U. chpt. 1990-91), Assn. Profs. and Scholars of Iranian Heritage (pres. 1991-92), Sigma Delta Epsilon. Avocations: music, literature, poetry, stamp collecting. Office: Calif State U Dept Elec Engring 800 N State College Blvd Fullerton CA 92631-3547

TEI, TAKURI, accountant; b. Korea, Feb. 25, 1924; s. Gangen and Isun (Song) T.; came to U.S., 1952, naturalized, 1972; diploma Concordia Theol. Sem., 1959; B.D., Eden Theol. Sem., 1965; M.Ed., U. Mo., 1972; m. Maria M. Ottwaska, Dec. 1, 1969; 1 dau., Sun Kyung Lee. Partner, Madeleine Ottwaska & Assos., St. Louis, 1968—; pres. TMS Tei Enterprises Inc., Webster Groves, Mo., 1969—; instr. Forest Park Community Coll. Mem. Am. Coll. Enrolled Agts. (pres. 1976—), Am. Accounting Assn., Am. Taxation Assn., Assn. Asian Studies, NAACP. Republican. Lutheran. Home and Office: 7529 Big Bend Blvd Saint Louis MO 63119-2103

TEICH, MALVIN CARL, electrical engineering educator; b. N.Y.C., May 4, 1939; s. Sidney R. and Loretta K. Teich. S.B. in Physics, MIT, 1961; M.S.E.E., Stanford U., 1962; Ph.D. in Quantum Electronics, Cornell U., 1966. Research scientist MIT Lincoln Lab., Lexington, Mass., 1966-67; prof. engring. sci. Columbia U., N.Y.C., 1967-96; prof. emeritus Columbia U., N.Y.C, 1996—; chmn. dept. elec. engring. Columbia U., N.Y.C., 1978-80, mem. Columbia Radiation Lab./faculty applied physics dept.; prof. elec. and computer engring., prof. bioengring. Boston U., 1995—; mem. Ctr. Photonics Rsch., Hearing Rsch. Ctr.; mem. sci. bd. Inst. Physics, Czech Acad. Scis., Prague. Author: (with B.E.A. Saleh) Fundamentals of Photonics, 1991; dep. editor Quantum Optics, 1988-92; bd. editors Jour. Visual Comm. and Image Representation, 1989-92, Jemná Mechanika a Optika, 1994—; contbr. articles to profl. jours.; patentee in field. Recipient Citation Classic award Inst. for Sci. Info., 1981, Meml. Gold medal of Palacky U., Czech Republic, 1992; Guggenheim Meml. Found. fellow, 1973. Fellow AAAS, IEEE (Browder J. Thompson Meml. prize 1969), Optical Soc. Am. (editl. adv. panel Optics Letters 1977-79), Am. Phys. Soc., Acoustical Soc. Am.; mem. Assn. Rsch. in Otolaryngology, N.Y. Acad. Scis., Sigma Xi, Tau Beta Pi. Office: Boston U Dept Elec and Computer Engr 44 Cummington St Boston MA 02215

TEICHER, MORTON IRVING, social worker, anthropologist, educator; b. N.Y.C., Mar. 10, 1920; s. Sam and Celia (Roth) T.; m. Mildred Adler, Oct. 4, 1941; children: Phyllis Margaret, Oren Jonathan. B.S. in Social Sci., CCNY, 1940; M.S.W., U. Pa., 1942; Ph.D., U. Toronto, 1956. Chief social worker in New Eng. VA, 1946-48; asst. prof., clin. tchr. U. Toronto, 1948-56; cons. Oppenheimer Coll., No. Rhodesia (Zambia), 1962-63; dean Sch. Social Work, Yeshiva U., 1956-72, prof., 1956-72; prof. Sch. Social Work, U. N.C., Chapel Hill, 1972-81, 83-85; dean Sch. Social Work, U. N.C., 1972-81; adjutant prof. dept. anthropology, 1972-85; dean emeritus Sch. Social Work, U. N.C., 1985—; prof. sociology and psychiatry, dir. Center on Aging, U. Miami, Coral Gables, 1981-83; instr. Elders Inst. Fla. Internat. U., 1987-88; faculty advisor Walden U., 1993—; seminar assoc. creativity in sci. NYU, 1959-73; cons. Bar Ilan U., Israel, 1965-69, VA, 1965-69; cons., vis. prof. Henrietta Szold Inst., Jerusalem, 1975; preceptor Ctrl. Inst. Mgmt., Sr. Civil Svc., Israel, 1975; external examiner U. Zambia, 1968-69; cons. in field, 1950—; cons. U. W.I., 1982; chmn. U.S. com. Internat. Coun. Social Welfare, 1978-79; mem. adminstrv. bd. Sch. Pub. Health, U. N.C., 1974-79. Author: Windigo Psychosis, 1960, Looking Homeward: A Thomas Wolfe Photo Album, 1993; co-author Distant Partners, 1990; sr. editor Inside Books, 1988-89; co-editor: Reaching the Aged, Data-Based Planning in the Field of Aging, 1982; book rev. editor: Jour. Jewish Communal Service, 1961-68, Jewish Floridian, 1982-86; mem. editorial bd. Human Orgn., 1963-66, Jour. Am. Soc. Cybernetics, 1970-72, Ednl. Gerontology, 1978-84; book reviewer South Fla. Jewish Jour., Phila. Jewish Exponent, Metrowest Jewish News, Jerusalem Post; also contbr. numerous articles to profl. jours., books. Rsch. chmn. Westchester Dem. Com., 1958-62; bd. dirs. Lake Success Capital Corp., 1967-71; trustee Wurzweiler Found., 1966-90, Coler Found., 1970-72; participant Fla. Gov.'s Challenge Program, 1981; exec. sec. Nat. Conf. Jewish Communal Svc., 1968-70; mem. exec. com. Miami chpt. Am. Jewish Com., 1981-83, mem.-at-large nat. exec. coun., 1980-82; bd. dirs. N.Y. Social Work Recruiting Ctr., 1960-70; mem. policy bd. Carolina Population Ctr., 1973-77; bd. dirs. Internat. Conf. Jewish Communal Svc., 1965-85, Hillel, U. Miami, 1981-83, Beth David Synagogue, Miami, 1991—; pres. Durham-Chapel Hill Jewish Fedn., 1980; mem. planning and budgeting com. Project Renewal Commn., Miami Jewish Fedn., 1981—; adv. coun. Sch. Social Work Barry U., 1986—. 1st lt. AUS, 1942-46, CBI. Recipient Disting. Alumnus cert. U. Pa., 1979; Louis Round Wilson Libr. fellow U. N.C., 1995—. Fellow Am. Anthropol. Assn.; mem. AAUP, Am. Assn. Ret. Persons (v.p. South Miami Beach chpt. 1992), Acad. Cert. Social Workers, Nat. Assn. Social Workers (chmn. Westchester chpt. 1960-62, mem. commn. ethics 1964-67, mem. exec. com. Ea. N.C. chpt. 1972-74, chmn. profl. advancement travel com. 1980-83), Thomas Wolfe Soc. (dir. 1981—, v.p. 1985-87, pres. 1987-91, Citation of Merit 1992). Anthrop. field work among the Eskimo and Iroquois; tour leader to internat. social welfare confs. in Athens, Helsinki, Nairobi, The Hague, San Juan, Jerusalem, Hong Kong, and Brighton, Eng. Home: 4275 Nautilus Dr Miami FL 33140-2821

TEICHERT, CURT, geologist, educator; b. Koenigsberg, Germany, May 8, 1905; came to U.S., 1952, naturalized, 1959; s. Richard and Luise (Zander) T.; m. Gertrud Margarete Kaufmann, Dec. 28, 1928. Student, U. Munich, Germany, 1923-25, U. Freiburg, Germany, 1925, U. Koenigsberg, 1925-28; Ph.D., Albertus U., 1928; D.Sc., U. Western Australia, Perth, 1944. Rockefeller fellow U.S., 1930; privatdozent Tech. U., Berlin, 1931-35; research paleontologist U. Copenhagen, Denmark, 1933-37; research lectr. U. Western Australia, 1937-45; asst. chief govt. geologist Dept. Mines, Melbourne, Australia, 1946-47; sr. lectr. U. Melbourne, 1947-53; Fulbright scholar U. Kans., Lawrence, 1951-52; prof. geology N.Mex. Sch. Mines, 1953-54; geologist U.S. Geol. Survey, 1954-64; chief Petroleum Geology Lab., 1954-58, research geologist, 1958-61; AID adviser Geol. Survey, Pakistan, 1961-64; Regents Distinguished prof. geology, dir. Paleontol. Inst. U. Kans., Lawrence, 1964-75; prof. emeritus U. Kans., 1975—; adj. prof. geol. scis. U. Rochester, N.Y., 1977—; geologist Danish N.E. Greenland Expdn., 1931-32; guest prof. U. Bonn, Germany, U. Goettingen, U. Freiburg, 1958, U. Tex., 1960, Free U. Berlin, 1974; U.S. coordinator AID-CENTO Stratigraphic Working Group, 1965-76; Cons. to oil cos., 1940-53, Australian Bur. Mineral Resources, 1948-52. Author: Ordovician and Silurian Faunas from Arctic Canada, 1937, (with Clarke, Prider) Elements of Geology, 1944, 4th edit., 1967, Elementary Practical Geology, 1946, 4th edit., 1968, (with others) Treatise on Invertebrate Paleontology, Park K, 1964; several book size monographs; editor: (with others) Treatise on Invertebrate Paleontology, 1964-80; also miscellaneous symposia; contbr. articles to profl. jours. Recipient David Syme Prize sci. research U. Melbourne, 1950, R.C. Moore medal for excellence in paleontology Soc. Econ. Paleontologists and Mineralogists, 1982. Fellow Geol. Soc. Am., Geol. Soc. London (hon.), AAAS; mem. Internat. Geol. Congress (past sec. internat. com. Gondwana sys.), Soc. Geol. France (fgn. assoc.), Paleontol. Soc. (past corr., pres. 1971-72, medal 1984), Palaeont. Gesellschaft (hon.), Soc. Geol. Belgique (hon.), Royal Soc. Western Australia (hon.), Paleontol. Soc. India (fgn. corr.), Geol. Soc. Australia (hon.), Senckenberg. Naturforsch. Gesellschaft (corr. mem., Curt Teichert Festschrift 1989), Internat. Paleontol. Union (1st v.p. 1968-72), Internat. Paleontol. Assn. (pres. 1976-80). Office: 5505 10th St N Arlington VA 22205-2416

TEICHNER, LESTER, management consulting executive; b. Chgo., Apr. 21, 1944; s. Ben Bernard and Eva Bertha (Weinberg) T.; m. Barbara Rae Bush, Jan. 30, 1966 (div. Aug. 1969); m. Doris Jean Ayres, Jan. 31, 1980; children: Lauren Ayres, Caroline Ayres. BSEE, U. Ill., 1965; MBA in Mktg. and Fin., U. Chgo., 1969. Sales engr. Westinghouse Electric Corp., Chgo., 1965-69; v.p. ops. Intec Inc., Chgo., 1969-74; pres., CEO The Chgo. Group Inc., 1974—, also bd. dirs.; bd. dirs. Strategic Processing Inc., N.Y.C., Dees Communications Ltd., Vancouver, B.C., Maxcor Mfg. Co., Colorado Springs; CEO, bd. dirs. Axcess Worldwide Ltd., Coal Gasification, Inc., Chgo.; guest lectr. U. Chgo. Grad. Sch. Bus., 1982-92. Co-inventor U.S. patent electronic marketplace; contbr. articles to profl. publs. Mem. The Chgo. Forum, 1976—; bd. dirs. Am. Israeli C. of C. Mem. Am. Mgmt. Assn., Am. Mktg. Assn., Midwest Planning Assn. (bd. dirs. 1981). Republican. Jewish. Avocations: comml. renovation, astronomy, skiing, venture capital investment. Home: 2230 N Seminary Ave Chicago IL 60614-3507 Office: Chgo Group Inc 744 N Wells St Chicago IL 60610*

TEICHROB, CAROL, Canadian provincial official; b. Sask., Can., Aug. 27, 1939; d. J. Delbert and Elizabeth (Spenst) Sproxton; m. Donald P. Teichrob, Mar. 1, 1958; children: Lori, Sharon, James. Sr. matriculation, Notre Dame Convent, Morinville, Alta., Can. Cert. profl. ct. reporter, exec. mem. Can. and Saskatchewan Fedns. Agriculture, 1976-81; chmn. Can. Turkey Mktg. Agy., 1980-81, Plains Poultry Wynyard, Sask., 1981-88; founding ptnr. Primrose Books, Saskatoon, Sask., 1988—. Reeve, Rural Muncipality of Corman Park, Saskatoon, Sask., 1981-91; active U. Sask. Senate, 1981-86; mem. legis. assembly N.D.P. Caucus, 1991-96; appointed to cabinet as Min. of Edn., 1991-93, Min. of Mcpl. Govt., 1995—. Recipient Golden Wheel award Sask. Rotary, 1990; named Woman of Yr. in Bus., Sask. YWCA, 1981, Woman of Yr., 1992. Mem. Saskatoon C. of C. Office: Min Mcpl Govt, Legis Bldg, Rm 307, Regina, SK Canada S4S 0B3

TEIGER, DAVID, management consultant; b. Newark, June 13, 1929; s. Samuel and Fannie (Ginsburg) T.; children: Lauren, Douglas. B.S., Cornell U., 1951. Ptnr. Samuel Teiger & Co., Newark, 1953-59, Ira Haupt & Co., N.Y.C., 1959-64, Bache & Co., N.Y.C., 1964-65; exec. v.p. Shearson, Hammill & Co., Inc., N.Y.C., 1965-73; chmn., chief exec. officer United Rsch. Co., Morristown, N.J., 1973-90; chmn. Gemini Consulting, Morristown, N.J., 1990-95. Served to lt. U.S. Army, 1951-53. Clubs: Meadowood; Mountain Ridge. Office: Teiger Inc 51 Peachcroft Dr Bernardsville NJ 07924

TEIMAN, RICHARD B., lawyer; b. Bklyn., May 19, 1938. AB, Princeton U., 1959; LLB, Harvard U., 1962. Bar: N.Y. 1963. Ptnr. Winston & Strawn and predecessor Cole and Deitz, N.Y.C., 1968—. Trustee Citizens Budget Commn., 1993—. Mem. Assn. Bar City N.Y. (com. Admiralty 1975-78, 87, chair 1988-91), Maritime Law Assn. (com. Maritime Financing 1980—, chmn. subcom. Recodification U.S. Ship Mortgage Act 1986-91, chmn. subcom. U.S. Coastguard, Citizenship and Related Matters 1988-94), Phi Beta Kappa. Home: 5 Pryer Ln Larchmont NY 10538-4012 Office: Winston & Strawn 200 Park Ave New York NY 10166-4193

TEIRSTEIN, PAUL SHEPHERD, physician, health facility administrator; b. N.Y.C., July 5, 1955; s. Alvin Stanley and Alice Teirstein. BA in Biology, Vassar Coll., 1976; MD, CUNY, 1980. Diplomate Am. Bd. Internal Medicine and Cardiovascular Diseases. With Lab. of Vision Rsch. NIH, Bethesda, Md., 1977-79; intern and resident Brigham & Women's Hosp., Boston, 1980-83; fellow in cardiology Stanford (Calif.) U., 1983-86; fellow in advanced coronary angioplasty Mid-Am. Heart Inst., Kansas City, Mo., 1986-87; fellow in stents, artherectomy and lasers NIH, Bethesda, 1987; dir. interventional cardiology Scripps Clinic and Rsch. Found., La Jolla, Calif., 1987—; presenter at Am. Coll. Cardiology, 1987-94, Am. Heart Assn., 1990-93, The French Hosp., San Luis Obispo, Calif., 1989, St. Luke's Med. Ctr., Phoenix, 1989, Cardiology for the Cons., Rancho Santa Fe, 1989, U. Calif., Irvine, 1989, ACP, Scottsdale, Ariz., 1989, Presbyn. Hosp., Whittier, Calif, 1989, St. Jude Med. Ctr., Fullerton, Calif., 1990, Oscala Med. Ctr., Osaka, Japan, 1992, Cedars-Sinai Med. Ctr., L.A., 1993, European Congress of Cardiology, Nice, France, 1993, Tokyo U., 1993, Lenox Hill Hosp., N.Y., 1993, Japanese Soc. Internat. Cardiology, 1994, Nat. Hindu Hosp., Bombay, 1994, G.B. Pant Hosp., Delhi, India, 1994, Escort's Hosp., 1994, B.M. Birla Hosp., Calcutta, 1994, Shaare Zedek Med. Ctr., Jerusalem, 1994, XV Congresso da Sociedad de Cardiology de Sao Paulo, Ribeirao Preto, Brazil, 1994, and others. Grantee NSF, 1975. Fellow Am. Coll. Cardiology, Assn. for Rsch. in Vision and Ophthalmology, Beta Beta Beta, Alpha Omega Alpha. Office: Scripps Clinic & Rsch Found 10666 N Torrey Pines Rd La Jolla CA 92037-1027

TEITEL, SIMON, economist; b. Buenos Aires, Dec. 5, 1928; came to U.S., 1961; s. Gregorio and Regina (Tarnorudzka) T.; m. Raquel Schenkolewski, June 20, 1954; children: Rut Gabriela, Ariel Dan. BS in Indsl. Engring., U. Buenos Aires, 1956, MS in Indsl. Engring., 1963; PhD in Econs., Columbia U., 1969. Econ. affairs officer Ctr. for Indsl. Devel., UN, N.Y.C., 1963-67; sr. indsl. devel. officer policies and programming div. UN Indsl. Devel. Orgn., Vienna, Austria, 1967-68; sr. cons. Office Program Advisor to Pres., Inter-Am. Devel. Bank, Washington, 1968-76, sr. econ. advisor econ. and social devel. dept., 1976-89; sr. rsch. adv., 1989-92; rsch. cons. World Bank, Washington, 1992-94; econ. cons. UN, 1994—; adj. assoc. prof. econs. Cath. U. Am., Washington, 1971-77, adj. prof., 1977-81, prof., 1981-88; adj. prof. Am. U., 1992; profl. lectr. Georgetown U., Washington, 1996; vis. lectr. internat. econs. Yale U., New Haven, 1977-78; lectr. to numerous profl. assns. and univs.; occasional referee Econ. Devel. and Cultural Change, Jour. Devel. Econs., World Devel., Latin Am. Rsch. Rev.; mem. spl. internat. panel on appropriate techs. for developing countries Bd. on Sci. and Tech. for Internat. Devel., NAS-Nat. Acad. Engring., 1974-77. Author: Politica Económica en Centro y Periferia, 1976, Integracion Economica, 1977, Trade, Stability, Technology and Equity in Latin America, 1982, Symposium on Technological Change and Industrial Development, 1984, Growth, Reform and Adjustment: Latin America's Trade and Macroeconomic Policies in the 1970s and 1980s, 1986, Handbook of Latin American Studies, Library of Congress, Economics: Argentina, 1989, Towards a New Development Strategy for Latin America, 1992, Industrial and Technological Development, 1993, Technology and Enterprise Development, 1994, From Anarchy to Competition-Technology and Skills in Zimbabwe's Manufacturing, 1996; contbr. articles to profl. jours. Mem. Am. Econ. Assn. Jewish. Home: 5610 Wisconsin Ave Apt 606 Chevy Chase MD 20815-4417

TEITELBAUM, IRVING, retail executive; b. Montreal, Que., Apr. 12, 1939; s. Nathan and Esther T.; m. Maida Shier, June 19, 1960; children: Carole, Joel. B of Commerce, Concordia U., Montreal, 1960. V.p., gen. mgr. Shier Ltee, Que., 1960-66, also bd. dirs., 1960—; chmn. Suzy Shier Ltd. and Suzy Shier Inc., Montreal, 1966—; bd. dirs. Tanurb Devels., Toronto, St. Regis Real Estate Montreal; chmn. Wet Seal Inc., Irvine, Calif., 1984—, La Senza Lingerie Inc., La Senza PLC, London, 1994—; pres. 1st Can. Mgmt. Cons. Ltd., Montreal, 1976—. Avocations: tennis, cycling, mountain hiking.

TEITELBAUM, MARILYN LEAH, special education educator; b. Bklyn., June 12, 1930; d. Abraham and Fay (Ingis) Nober; m. Harry Teitelbaum, Nov. 7, 1953; children: Mark, David, Deborah. BA, Bklyn. Coll., 1953; MS, Queens Coll., 1968, L.I. U., 1982. Cert. tchr., N.Y. Elem. and spl. edn. tchr. Franklin Square, Franklin's Square, N.Y., 1955-57; elem. tchr. Manetto Hill Sch., Plainview, N.Y., 1968-70; elem. tchr. Northport (N.Y.) Sch. Dist., 1970-78, spl. edn. tchr., 1978-87; pvt. spl. edn. tchr Laguana Niguel, Calif., 1988—. Author: Teachers as Consumers-What They Should Know About the Hearing Impaired Child, 1981. V.p. Friends of Libr., Laguna Niguel Pub. Libr., 1988—. Recipient award Northport PTA, 1987. Mem. NEA, Coun. Exceptional Children, United Tchrs. Northport, Orange County Dyslexic Soc. Avocations: reading, travel, painting, piano. Home: 29562 Avante Laguna Niguel CA 92677-7949

TEITELBAUM, PHILIP, psychologist; b. Bklyn., Oct. 9, 1928; s. Bernard and Betty (Schechter) T.; m. Osnat Boné; children: Benjamin, Daniel, David, Jonathan, Gideon. B.S., CCNY, 1950; M.A., Johns Hopkins U., 1952, Ph.D., 1954. Instr., asst. prof. physiol. psychology Harvard U., 1954-59; assoc. prof. psychology U. Pa., Phila., 1959-63; prof. U. Pa., 1963-73; prof. psychology U. Ill.-Urbana-Champaign, 1973-85, emeritus prof., 1985—, Disting. prof. Ctr. Advanced Studies, 1980-85; grad. research prof. U. Fla., Gainesville, 1984—. Author: Fundamental Principles of Physiological Psychology, 1967; editor: (with E. Satinoff) Motivation: Handbook Behavioral Neurobiology, 1983. Contbr. chpts. to books, articles to profl. jours. Fellow Ctr. for Advanced Study in Behavioral Scis., Stanford U., 1975-76, Fulbright fellow Tel Aviv U., 1978-79, Guggenheim fellow, 1984-85, Carnegie Found. fellow Inst. Neurol. Scis., U. Pa. Med. Sch., 1958-59. Fellow APA (pres. div. physiol. psychology, disting. sci. contbn. award 1978), Am. Psychol. Soc. (William James fellow); mem. NAS, AAAS, Am. Physiol. Soc., Soc. for Neurosci., Soc. Exptl. Psychology. Home: 2239 NW 17th Ave Gainesville FL 32605-3909 Office: U Fla Dept Psychology Gainesville FL 32611

TEITELBAUM, STEVEN LAZARUS, pathology educator; b. Bklyn., June 29, 1938; s. Hyman and Rose Leah (Harnick) T.; m. Marilyn Ruth Schaffner; children: Caren Beth, Aaron Michael, Rebecca Lee. BA, Columbia U., 1960; MD, Washington U., St. Louis, 1964. Intern Washington U. Sch. Medicine, St. Louis, 1964-65, 3d. yr. asst. resident, ACS clin. fellow, 1967-68; intern NYU, 1965-66, 2d yr. resident, 1966-67; assoc. pathologist Jewish Hosp. at Washington U. Med. Ctr., St. Louis, 1969-89, pathologist-in-chief, 1987—; asst. pathologist Barnes Hosp., St. Louis, 1986—; pathologist St. Louis Shriners Hosp. for Crippled Children, 1986—; Wilma and Roswell Messing prof. pathology Washington U. Sch. Medicine, St. Louis, 1987—; mem. Othopedics and Musculoskeletal Study Sect. NIH, 1983-87. Author 210 published sci. articles in med. jours., 1965—, 12 chpts. in med. books and texts, 1976—; mem. editorial bd. Calcified Tissue Internat., 1980-85, 89-91, Human Pathology; mem. bd. assoc. editors Jour. Orthopaedic Rsch., Jour. Cellular Biochemistry. Mem. Am. Soc. Clin. Investigation, Assn. Am. Physicians, Am. Acad. Orthopaedic Surgeons (Ann Doner Vaughan Kappa Delta award 1988), Paget's Disease Found. (adv. panel), Am. Soc. for Bone and Mineral Rsch. (pres.). Office: Washington U Med Ctr Jewish Hosp 216 S Kingshighway Blvd Saint Louis MO 63110-1026

TEITELBAUM, STEVEN USHER, lawyer; b. Chgo., Nov. 29, 1945; s. Jerome H. and Marion Judith (Berlin) T.; m. Cathy Ann Rosenblatt, Mar. 11, 1984. A.B., Boston U., 1967; J.D., Union U., 1975. Bar: N.Y. 1976, U.S. Dist. Ct. (no. dist.) N.Y. 1976, U.S. Supreme Ct. 1980, U.S. Ct. Appeals (2d cir.) 1993; cert. arbitrator. Sr. atty. N.Y. State Dept. Health, Albany, 1976-79; counsel N.Y. State Office Bus. Permits, Albany, 1979-83; sole practice, Albany, 1983-95; dep. commr., gen. counsel N.Y. State Dept. Taxation and Fin., 1995—; staff judge advocate U.S. Army Res. Watervliet Arsenal, N.Y., 1978-84. Author: Streamlining the Regulatory Procedures of the Department of Agriculture, 1982. Active Found. Bd. Ctr. for Disabled, Empire State Performing Arts Ctr., Nat. Alumni Coun. Albany Law Sch.; bd. dirs. Nat. Kidney Found. Northeastern N.Y. Served with U.S. Army, 1968-69. Mem. Am. Arbitration Assn. (arbitrator 1979—), N.Y. State Bar Assn. (com. on pub. health 1976-80, faculty on adminstrv. law 1980, com. on adminstrv. law 1980-84, 93—, labor and employment sect., taxation sect. 1985—). Clubs: Fort Orange (Albany), Country Club Troy (N.Y.). Home: 17 Carstead Dr Slingerlands NY 12159-9266 Office: WA Harriman Office Campus Bldg 9 Rm 205 Albany NY 12227

TEITELL, CONRAD LAURENCE, lawyer, author; b. N.Y.C., Nov. 8, 1932; s. Benson and Belle (Altman) T.; m. Adele Mary Crummins, May 26, 1957; children: Beth Mary, Mark Lewis. A.B., U. Mich., 1954; LL.B., Columbia U., 1957; LL.M., N.Y. U., 1968. Bar: N.Y. 1958, D.C., 1968. Mem. Prerau & Teitell, White Plains, N.Y., 1964-96, Cummings & Lockwood, Stamford, Conn., 1996—; dir. Philanthropy Tax Inst., Old Greenwich, Conn., 1964—. Author: Philanthropy and Taxation, 5 vols., 1993-96; editor, pub. Taxwise Giving, 1964—; contbr. articles to legal jours. Served with U.S. Army, 1957. Recipient Disting. Svc. to Higher Edn. award Am. Coll. Pub. Relations Assn., 1970, Disting. Svc. award Nat. Com. on Planned Giving, 1990, Harrison Tweed Spl. Merit award Am. Law Inst./ABA, 1992. Fellow Am. Coll. Trust and Estate Counsel; mem. ABA (former co-chmn. com. charitable giving, trusts, founds.), Assn. of Bar of City of N.Y., Nat. Assn. Coll. Univ. Attys., Am. Soc. Hosp. Attys. Home: 16 Marlow Ct Riverside CT 06878-2614 Office: Cummings & Lockwood Four Stamford Plaza PO Box 120 Stamford CT 06904-0120 also: 13 Arcadia Rd Old Greenwich CT 06870-1701

TEIXEIRA, ARTHUR ALVES, food engineer, consultant; b. Fall River, Mass., Jan. 30, 1944; s. Arthur Araujo and Emelia (Alves) T.; m. Jean E. Lamb, Dec. 26, 1966 (dec. Dec. 1983); children: A. Allan, Scott C.; m. Marjorie St. John, June 28, 1986; 1 stepchild, Craig St. John. PhD, U. Mass., 1971. Profl. engr., Fla., Mass. Rsch. engr. Ross Labs., Columbus, Ohio, 1971-73, R&D group leader, 1973-77; sr. cons. Arthur D. Little, Inc., Cambridge, Mass., 1977-82; assoc. prof. U. Fla., Gainesville, 1982-89, prof., 1989—; sci. advisor Escola Superior de Biotecnologia, Porto, Portugal, 1991—, FMC Corp., Santa Clara, Calif., 1989-92; internat. cons. Brazil, Cuba, Hungary, Poland, Portugal, Romania and Bulgaria. Author: Computerized Food Processing Operations, 1989; contbr. 8 chpts. to books, 30 articles to profl. jours. Judge Internat. Sci. Fair, Orlando, Fla., 1991; reviewer USDA, Washington, 1991-94. Sr. Guest fellow NATO, 1988, 89; Fulbright grantee U.S. Info. Agy., 1990-91. Fellow Am. Soc. Agrl. Engrs. (dir. 1988-90, Paper awards 1988-89, assoc. editor Transactions of ASAE 1985—); mem. AICE, Inst. Food Technologists (mem. editl. bd. 1980-83), Am. Soc. Engring. Edn., Inst. Thermal Process Specialists, Coun. on Agrl. Sci. and Tech., R & D Assocs. Republican. Roman Catholic. Achievements include design of on-line process control system to assure safety of sterilized canned foods; tech. and econ. feasiblity for radiation sterilization of disposable feeding devices; research in computer optimization and control of food sterilization processes. Office: U Fla Rogers Hall Gainesville FL 32611-0570

TEIXEIRA, JOSEPH, advertising executive; b. Azores, Portugal, Aug. 11, 1949; came to U.S., 1961, naturalized, 1968; s. Fernando J. and Luisa M. (Mendonca) T.; m. Angelica Maria Cabral, Oct. 12, 1974; children: Christine, Debora. B.S. Bently Coll., 1975. Vice pres. Arnold & Co., Boston, 1978-80, sr. v.p., 1980-82, exec. v.p., 1982-95, exec. v.p., CFO, 1995—. Served with U.S. Army, 1969-71. Roman Catholic. Office: Arnold & Co Inc 101 Arch St Boston MA 02110-1103

TEJA, AMYN SADRUDIN, chemical engineering educator, consultant; b. Zanzibar, Tanzania, May 11, 1946; came to U.S., 1980; s. Sadrudin N. and Amina (Dharsi) T.; m. Carole Rosina Thurlow, July 3, 1971; children: Kerima Amy, Adam Riaz. BSc in Engring., U. London, London, 1968; PhD, U. London, 1972. Intern Warren Springs Lab., Stevenage, Eng., summer 1966, Brit. Gas Corp., London, summer 1968; rsch. fellow in chem. engring. Loughborough (U.K.) U. Tech., 1971-74; chem. engring. lectr. Loughborough (Eng.) U. Tech., 1974-80; assoc. prof. chem. engring. Ga. Inst. Tech., Atlanta, 1980-83, prof., 1984-90, regents prof. Woodruff Sch. Mech. Engring., 1991—, regents prof. Sch. Chem. Engring., 1990—, dir. Fluid Properties Rsch. Inst., 1985—, co-dir. Specialty Separations Ctr., 1992—, assoc. dir. grad. studies, 1994—; vis. assoc. prof. chem. engring. U. Del., Newark, 1978-79, Ohio State U., 1980; cons. Laporte Chems., Eng., 1971, Mobil Rsch. and Devel. Co., N.J., 1979, Conoco Ltd., Humberside Refinery, Eng., 1980, Milliken Chem. Co., Spartanburg, S.C., 1981-83, Hoechst Celanese Corp., Corpus Christi, Tex., 1984, Charlotte, 1992. Philip Morris U.S.A., Richmond, Va., 1984-87, DuPont Co., 1988, Union Carbide Corp., South Charleston, W.Va., 1989—, Shell Oil Co., 1989-93; presenter in field, reviewer various jours. Editor: Chemical Engineering and the Environment, 1981; mem. editl. bd. Reports on the Progress of Applied Chemistry, 1972-76, Critical Reports on Applied Chemistry, 1976-80, Jour. Chem. and Engring. Data, 1991—, Chem. Engring. Rsch. Compendium, 1990—, Jour. Supercritical Fluids, 1990—; assoc. editor The Chem. Engring. Jour., 1973—; contbr. more than 170 articles to profl. jours. Recipient Hinchley medal Instn. Chem. Engrs., 1968, IBM Rsch. scholarship, 1968-71, Gas Coun. Rsch. scholarship, 1968-71, Brit. Coun. Younger Rsch. Workers award, 1977, Outstanding Tchr. award Omega Chi Epsilon, 1990. Mem. AIChE (pub. com. 1992—, jour. rev.), Am. Soc. Engring. Edn., Am. Chem. Soc., Sigma Xi (v.p. Ga. Tech. chpt. 1991-92. pres. 1992-93, Supr. Outstanding MS Thesis in Engring. 1984, 90, Supr. Outstanding PhD Thesis 1993, Sustained Rsch. award 1987). Avocations: tennis, science fiction. Home: 1953 Huntington Hall Ct Atlanta GA 30338-5712 Office: Ga Inst Tech Dept Chem Engring Atlanta GA 30332-0100

TEJADA, FRANCISCO, physician, educator; b. Moyobamba, San Martin, Peru, July 25, 1942; s. Francisco Tejada and Semiramis Reatequi; m. Barbara Ann Kotowski, Feb. 1, 1970; children: Anamaria, Semiramis, Barbara Lee, Francisco, James. BS, U. Nacional Mayor de San Marcos, Lima, Peru, 1961; MD, U. Peruana Cayetano Heredia, Lima, 1967. Diplomate Am. Bd. Internal Medicine, Am. Bd. Oncology. Resident in medicine Johns Hopkins U., Balt., 1969-72; sr. cancer researcher Nat. Cancer Inst., NIH, Bethesda, Md., 1972-75; asst. clin. dir. Comprehensive Cancer Ctr. Fla., Miami, Fla., 1975-80; asst. prof. U. Miami, 1975-79, assoc. prof., 1979-85, prof., 1985—; vis. prof. U. Peruana Cayetano Heredia, Lima, 1994—; sr. ptnr. Oncology Assocs., Miami, 1980-85; chief cancer control Papanicolaou Cancer Ctr., Miami, 1984-86; assoc. dir. AMC Cancer Rsch. Ctr., Denver, 1986-87; pres. Am. Oncology Ctrs., Miami, 1985—; prof. U. San Agustin, Arequipa, Peru, 1992—, U. Peruana Cayetano Heredia, Lima, Peru, 1994—; oncology expert Pan Am. Health Orgn., Washington, 1975-85, Nat. Cancer Inst., Bethesda, Md., 1984-86; dir. Miami Cancer Inst., 1980—; dir. Peruvian-Am. Endowment Inc., 1993—, v.p., 1995—. Editor Miami Med. Letter, 1986—; inventor cancer risk assessment. Mem. Beacon Coun., Miami, 1984, Latin Am. Cancer Info., Washington, 1976, Hispanic Cancer Rsch. Network, Washington, 1990; chpt. pres. Peruvian Am. Med. Soc., Miami, 1986. Lt. Peruvian Army, 1966-67. Recipient Gold Medal Merit award Ministry of Edn., Lima, 1959, Hipolito Unanue award Hipolito Unanue Inst., Lima, 1968. Fellow ACP, Johns Hopkins U., Nat. Cancer Inst.; mem. Colegio Medico del Perú, Am. Assn. Cancer Rsch., Am. Soc. Clin. Oncology, Am. Soc. Hematology, Bolivian Cancer Soc. (hon. mem.), Peruvian Cancer Soc. (hon. mem.), Chilean Soc. Cancer (hon. mem.), Argentinian Soc. Head and Neck Pathology (hon. mem.). Roman Catholic. Avocations: hiking, photography, reading. Office: 1321 NW 14th St Ste 401 Miami FL 33125-1653

TEJADA, SUSAN MONDSHEIN, magazine editor; b. Providence, Dec. 16, 1945; d. Jacob Meyer and M. Gertrude (Shindler) Mondshein; 1 child, Justin. BA, Barnard Coll., 1967. Apprentice Le Progres newspaper, Lyon, France, 1966; project editor, filmstrips Harcourt, Brace, Jovanovich, Pleasantville, N.Y., 1967-68; vol. U.S. Peace Corps, Manila, 1968-70; editor Action, Washington, 1971-74, Office Pers. Mgmt., Washington, 1974-80, U.S. EPA, Washington, 1980-88; editor-in-chief Nat. Geographic Soc., Nat. Geog. World, Washington, 1988—; instr. Highlights Found. Writers' Workshop, Chautauqua, N.Y., 1994. Author: Geo-Whiz!, 1988; co-author: Small Inventions, 1984, Why in the World?, 1985; contbr. articles to mags. and jours. Judge Parents' Choice Found. Awards, Waban, Mass., 1994-96; mem. publs. com. Jewish Hist. Soc. of Greater Washington, 1993-96. Mem. Ednl. Press Assn. Am. (Excellence in Ednl. Journalism award 1987), Am. Soc. Mag. Editors. Avocation: ice hockey. Office: Nat Geog Soc 1145 17th St NW Washington DC 20036

TEJEDA, FRANK, congressman; b. San Antonio, Tex., Oct. 2, 1945; 3 children. BA in Government, St. Mary's U., 1970; JD, U. Calif., Berkeley, 1974; MPA, Harvard U., 1980; LLM, Yale U., 1989. Lawyer; mem. Tex. Ho. of Reps., 1977-87, Tex. State Senate from Dist. 19, 1987-93; mem. house armed svcs. com., mem. house vets. affairs com. 103rd-104th Congress from 28th Tex. dist., Washington, D.C., 1993—; chmn. com. judicial affairs Tex. Ho. Reps., 1983; chmn. sub-com. Urban Affairs Tex. Senate, 1991; mem. senate fin. com. Tex. Senate, 1991; mem. nat. security com., vets affairs com.; chmn. intergovernmental rels. com. urban affairs Tex. Senate, 1991. Maj. USMCR, Vietnam. Decorated Bronze Star, Purple Heart. Mem. Cath. War Vets., Marine Corps. League. Democrat. Roman Catholic. Office: US Ho of Reps 323 Cannon Washington DC 20515-4328

TE KANAWA, KIRI, opera and concert singer; b. Gisborne, N.Z., Mar. 6, 1944; d. Thomas and Elanor Te Kanawa; m. Desmond Park, Aug. 30, 1967; children—Antonia Aroha, Thomas Desmond. Student, St. Mary's Coll., Auckland, N.Z., 1957-60, London Opera Centre, 1966-69; DMus (hon.), Oxford U., 1983; DLitt (hon.), U. Warwick, Coventry, England, 1989. Joined Royal Opera House, London, 1971; appeared in role of Countess in Le Nozze di Figaro, 1973; U.S. debut in Santa Fe Festival, 1971; Met. Opera debut as Desdemona in Otello, 1974; appears regularly with all major European and Am. opera houses, including Australian opera cos., Royal Opera House, Covent Garden, London, Paris Opera, Houston Opera, Munich Opera, La Scala, others; opera appearences include Boris Gudonov, Carmen, Don Giovanni, the Magic Flute, Eugene Onegin, La Boheme, Manon Lescant, many others; appeared in film Don Giovanni as Elvira, 1979; recs. include Blue Skies, 1986, Kiri Sings Gershwin, 1987, Kiri Te Kanawa: Italian Opera Arias, 1991, Kiri Her Greatest Hits, Ave Maria (Sacred and Devotional Music By Handel, Gounod, et. al., Kiri on Broadway, The Kiri Selection, Kiri Side Tracks, My Fair Lady (with Jeremy Irons, Warren Mitchell, John Gielgud, et. al.; PBS appearance: Great Performances: West Side Story, 1985; author: Land of the Long White Cloud, 1989. Decorated comdr. Order Brit. Empire, 1973, Dame Comdr. Brit. Empire, 1983. also:: c/o Nick Grace Mgmt Ltd. 500 Chiswick High Rd, London W4 5RG, England also: London Records/Philips c/o PGD World Wide Plz 825 8th Ave New York NY 10019 also: c/o IMG Artists (N Am) 420 W 45th St New York NY 10036

TEKBALI, ALI OMAR, geology consultant, educator; b. Tripoli, Libya, Dec. 15, 1952; came to the U.S., 1981; s. Omar Ghasim and Hawa Ahmed (Musrati) T.; m. Karima Fitouri Zummit, July 20, 1978; children: Sara, Dunia, Salam, Yusra. BS, U. Tripoli, Libya, 1976; MS, U. Calif., Davis, 1987; PhD, U. Tex., El Paso, 1994. Geologist Amoseas Oil Co., Tripoli, 1972-76; asst. instr. U. Tripoli, Libya, 1976-82; cons. Dept. Soil and Water Rsch., Tripoli, 1985-94, Indsl. Rsch. Ctr., Tripoli, 1985-94; asst. prof. geology U. Tripoli, Libya, 1994—; cons. Gulf Petro, Dallas, 1992—; asst. instr. geology U. Tex., El Paso, 1989-94. Contbr. articles to profl. jours. Corr. Beirout Times Newspaper, L.A., 1990-93; active YMCA, El Paso, 1992; coach West Tex. League, El Paso, 1992-93. Merit scholar U. Tripoli, Libya, 1982-94. Mem. Am. Assn. Strategic Planning, Geol. Soc. Am. Earth Scis. Soc. Libya (Recognition award 1976). Achievements include establishment of the first palynological zonations in western Libya; first accurate dating for the continental nubian deposits in western Libya; first thorough investigation of silurian land plants spores; others. Home: 6016 Alcalde St El Paso TX 79912-5204

TELANG, NITIN T., cancer biologist, educator; b. Bombay, India, July 3, 1943; came to U.S., 1976; s. Trimbak Pandharinath and Madhumalati (Kanitkar) T. BSc, U. Poona, India, 1963, MSc, 1966, PhD, 1974. Assoc. rsch. scientist Tata Meml. Hosp. Cancer Rsch., Bombay, 1974-76; rsch. assoc. U. Nebr., Lincoln, 1976-78; staff fellow Am. Health Found., Valhalla, N.Y., 1978-81; rsch. assoc. Sloan-Kettering Inst., N.Y.C., 1981-85; asst. attending biochemist Meml. Sloan-Ketering Cancer Ctr., N.Y.C., 1985-91; assoc. prof. Cornell U. Med. Coll., N.Y.C., 1991—; dir. divsn. carcinogenesis & prevention Strang-Cornell Cancer Rsch. Lab., N.Y.C., 1991-95, dir. carcinogenesis and nutrition core lab., 1991—; dir. divsn. carcinogenesis prevention Strang Cancer Rsch. Lab., Rockefeller U., 1995—; vis. investigator The Rockefeller U., N.Y.C., 1985-89. Contbr. numerous articles to profl. jours. Mem. Am. Assn. Cancer Rsch., Am. Soc. Cell Biology, Am. Inst. Nutrition, European Assn. Cancer Rsch. Office: Strang Cancer Rsch Lab Rockefeller Univ 1230 York Ave New York NY 10021

TELBERG, RURICK RICK, journalist; b. N.Y.C., Feb. 12, 1956; s. Val George and Lelia (Katine) T.; m. Doranne Phillips, Nov. 17, 1979; children: Devon Phillips, Katerina Elizabeth. AB in Journalism, NYU, 1978. Reporter Long Island Traveler-Watchman, Riverhead, N.Y., 1978-79; copy editor Beaumont (Tex.) Enterprise, 1979-81; fin. editor Nation's Restaurant News, N.Y.C., 1981-86, exec. editor, 1987—. Mem. Soc. Profl. Journalists, Deadline Club N.Y., N.Y. Fin Writers Assn. Home: 3 Cedar St Dobbs Ferry NY 10522-1711

TELENCIO, GLORIA JEAN, elementary education educator; b. Trenton, N.J., Sept. 3, 1955; d. John and Anne (Tymoch) T. BA cum laude, Georgian Ct. Coll., 1977. Cert. elem. edn. Math and sci. tchr. grade 8 St. Anthony's Grammar Sch., Trenton, 1977-78; elem. tchr. grade 7 St. Mary's Assumption Sch., Trenton, 1978-79; elem. tchr. grade 2 Hamilton Twp. Bd. Edn., Trenton, 1979-85, elem. tchr. grade 1, 1985—; sch. coord. Regional Curriculum Svc. Unit, Learning Resource Ctr.-Ctrl., 1990-95. Recipient State of N.J. Gov.'s Tchr. Recognition award State of N.J., 1991, Resolution of Commendation, Town Coun. of the Twp. of Hamilton, 1991; mini-grantee Bd. Edn., 1987-88. Mem. NEA, N.J. Edn. Assn., Hamilton Edn. Assn., Sunnybrae PTA (tchr. rep. exec. bd. 1981-91, co-chair PTA 25th Anniversary com. 1990-91), Kappa Delta Pi, Sigma Tau Delta, Pi Delta Phi, Delta Tau Kappa. Republican. Byzantine Catholic. Avocations: reading, theatre, music. Home: 31 Newkirk Ave Trenton NJ 08629 Office: Sunnybrae Elem Sch 166 Elton Ave Yardville NJ 08620

TELESCA, FRANCIS EUGENE, architect; b. Dunmore, Pa., Oct. 22, 1921; s. Joseph J. and Bernetta (Bocchiccio) T.; children: Celeste Ann Sullivan, Anthony, Francis Eugene II (Gino), Tina Le; m. Alyce G. Wuenstel, July 28, 1992. B.Arch. summa cum laude, Catholic U. Am., 1953. Designer-draftsman, architect various archtl. and engring. firms Washington and Miami, Fla., 1951-59; pvt. practice architecture Miami, 1959-63; pres. Greenleaf/Telesca, engrs., planners and architects, Miami, 1964-85; exec. v.p. Genesis III, Miami Lakes, Fla., 1985-87; chief programming Miami Internat. Airport, 1987—; dir. Greenleaf Enterprises, Inc., Bonefish Towers, Inc.; mem. Nat. Com. Architecture for Commerce and Industry, 1965-66, Fla. Planning and Zoning Assn., 1960—, Met. Dade County Uniform Code Enforcement Com., 1963-64; bd. dirs. South Fla. Inter-Profl. Council, 1965; planning com. U. Miami Inst. Urban Affairs, 1965; adv. com. City Miami Coconut Grove Zoning, 1965; adv. com. dept. architecture and bldg. constrn. Miami Dade Jr. Coll., 1966. (award of merit Fla. chpt. AIA for Miami Lakes Sr. High Sch., award of excellence for 20th St. Transfer Sta., Dade County 1980, Archtl. award of excellence for Hangar 2, Miami Internat. Airport, Am. Inst. Steel Constrn. 1974, also Grand Conceptor award Am. Cons. Engrs. Council 1974, award of excellence for Primera Casa, Fla. Internat. U., Fla. Concrete and Products Assn. 1973, award for outstanding concrete structure for Acad. One Bldg., Fla. Internat. U. 1980). Past pres., dir. Coconut Grove Assn. (arts festival), Grove House (sch. and marketplace for Fla. craftsmen). Served with AUS, 1940-45, 50-51. Decorated Bronze Star; recipient Grand Nat. award Nat. Community Fallout Shelter competition (shopping center), 1964. Mem. AIA (pres. Fla. South chpt. 1965, dir. Fla. 1966-69), Coconut Grove C. of C. (past pres., dir.), Greater Miami C. of C. (mem. aviation com.), Phi Eta Sigma. Roman Catholic. Home: 3509 Estepona Ave Miami FL 33178-2952 Office: Miami Internat Airport Aviation Dept PO Box 592075 Miami FL 33159

TELESCA, MICHAEL ANTHONY, federal judge; b. Rochester, N.Y., Nov. 25, 1929; s. Michael Angelo and Agatha (Locurcio) T.; m. Ethel E. Hibbard, June 5, 1953; children: Michele, Stephen. A.B., U. Rochester, 1952; J.D., U. Buffalo, 1955. Bar: N.Y. 1957, U.S. Dist. Ct. (we. dist.) N.Y. 1958, U.S. Ct. Appeals (2d cir.) 1960, U.S. Supreme Ct. 1967. Ptnr. Lamb, Webster, Walz, Telesca, Rochester, N.Y., 1957-73; surrogate ct. judge Monroe County, N.Y., 1973-82; judge U.S. Dist. Ct. (we. dist.) N.Y., Rochester, 1982—, chief judge, 1989-95; bd. dirs. Fed. Jud. Ctr. Bd. govs. Genesee Hosp., Rochester; mem. adv. bd. Assn. for Retarded Citizens, Al Sigl Ctr., Rochester. Served to 1st lt. USMC, 1955-57. Recipient Civic medal Rochester C. of C., 1983, Hutchinson medal U. Rochester, 1990. Mem. ABA, Am. Judicature Soc., Am. Inns. of Ct. (founder, pres. Rochester chpt.), Justinian Soc. Jurists, N.Y. State Bar Assn., Monroe County Bar Assn. Republican. Roman Catholic. Office: US Dist Ct 272 US Courthouse 100 State St Rochester NY 14614-1309

TELESETSKY, WALTER, government official; b. Boston, Jan. 22, 1938; s. Keril and Nellie (Krelka) T.; m. Sharron-Dawn Lamp, July 15, 1961; children: Stephanie Ann, Anastasia Marie. BS in Mech. Engring., Northeastern U., 1960; MBA, U. Chgo., 1961; postgrad., Harvard U., 1977. Engr. trainee Chrysler Corp., Detroit, 1956-59; rsch. asst. Microtech Rsch. Co., Cambridge, Mass., 1959-60; engr. Allis Chalmers Mfg. Co., Milw., 1960-61; mem. tech. staff The Mitre Corp., Bedford, Mass., 1962-68; sr. mem. tech. staff Data Dynamics, Inc., Washington, 1969; phys. scientist NOAA, Rockville, Md., 1970-71, U.S. Gate Project coord., 1972-74, dir. U.S. Global Weather Experiment Project Office, 1974, dir. Program Integration Office, 1975-77, dir. Programs and Tech. Devel. Office, 1977-79, dir. Programs and Internat. Activities Office, 1979-81; dep. assoc. dir. for tech. svcs., chief AFOS ops. div. Nat. Weather Svc., Silver Spring, Md., 1981-86, dir. Office of Systems Ops., 1986—; liaison to NAS coms. on atmospheric scis., geophysics studies and internat. environ. programs, 1975-81; U.S. coord. U.S./Japan Coop. Program in Natural Resources, 1980-88; chmn. U.S.-Japan Marine Resources and Engring. Coordination Com., 1980-88; U.S. del. governing coun. UN Environ. Program and World Meteorol. Orgn.; mem. commn. for Basic Systems World Meteorol. Orgn., 1988—; speaker in field. Contbr. articles to profl. publs. Recipient Silver medal Dept. Commerce, 1975. Mem. AAAS, Am. Geophys. Union, Am. Meteorol. Soc., Am. Soc. Mech. Engrs., Marine Tech. Soc. Home: 16 Eton Overlook Rockville MD 20850-3003 Office: 1325 E West Hwy Silver Spring MD 20910-3280

TELFORD, IRA ROCKWOOD, anatomist, educator; b. Lincoln, Idaho, May 6, 1907; s. John Witt and Martha Starr (Rockwood) T.; m. Thelma Challis Shrives, June 13, 1933; children—Ira Ralph, John Larry, Kent Matthews, Martha Ann. Student, Ricks Coll., 1924-26; A.B., U. Utah, 1931, A.M., 1933; student, U. Calif. at Berkeley, 1937-40; Ph.D., George Washington U., 1942. High sch. adminstr., 1933-37; instr., asst. prof. anatomy George Washington U., 1940-47, prof., exec. officer dept. anatomy, 1946-47, prof., chmn. dept., 1953-72; prof., chmn. dept. anatomy U. Tex. Dental Br., 1947-53; cons. anatomy (Univ. Hosp.), 1953-72; prof. anatomy Georgetown U., Washington, 1972-78; vis. prof. anatomy Uniformed Services U., Bethesda, Md., 1978-93; ret., Jan. 1995. Contbr. articles to biol., med. jours. Fulbright scholar Gt. Britain, 1960. Fellow AAAS (council 1958-60); mem. Am. Assn. Anatomists, Soc. Exptl. Biology and Medicine, Am. Acad. Neurology, Tex. Acads. Sci., Internat. Soc. Dental Research, AMA (asso.), Sigma Xi (chpt. pres. 1958-59), Phi Sigma (chpt. pres. 1932-33). Mem. Ch. of Jesus Christ of Latter-day Saints. Home: 3424 Garrison St NW Washington DC 20008-2037

TELL, A. CHARLES, lawyer; b. Chgo., May 9, 1937; s. William K and Virginia S (Snook) T.; m. Wendy Thomsen, June 16, 1962; children—Tracey, Melissa, A. Charles, Jr. A.B., Dartmouth Coll., 1961; J.D., Ohio State U., 1963. Ptnr. George, Greek, King & McMahon, Columbus, Ohio, 1964-78, Baker & Hostetler, Columbus, 1978—; dir. Kaplan Trucking Co., Cleve.; trustee Ohio Trucking Assn., 1989—. Editor Your Letter of the Law, 1984. Contbr. articles to profl. jours. Served with U.S. Army, 1958-60. Mem. ABA, Am. Judicature Soc., Ohio State Bar Assn., Columbus Bar Assn., Transp. Lawyers Assn. (pres. 1986-87). Republican. Presbyterian. Clubs: City (pres. 1985), Columbus Country (pres. 1989-90), University. Office: Baker & Hostetler 65 E State St Columbus OH 43215-4213

TELL, WILLIAM KIRN, JR., oil company executive, lawyer; b. Evanston, Ill., Feb. 27, 1934; s. William Kirn and Virginia (Snook) T.; m. Karen Nelson, July 16, 1960; children—Catherine, Caroline, William F. B.A. in Govt., Dartmouth Coll., 1956; J.D., U. Mich., 1959. Bar: Ohio, 1960, D.C., 1979. Atty. Texaco Inc., N.Y.C., 1968-70, asst. to v.p., gen. counsel, 1970, assoc. gen. counsel, 1970-73, asst. to chmn., 1973; v.p. Texaco Inc., Washington and N.Y.C., 1973-79, sr. v.p., 1979—; pres. Texaco Corp. Communications Div., 1989—. Mem. adv. bd. dirs. Met. Opera, N.Y.C., 1983—. Mem. Am. Petroleum Inst. (bd. dirs. 1980—), Greenwich Country Club, Congressional Club, Metropolitan Club, Everglades Club. Home: 320 Old Church Rd Greenwich CT 06830-4824 Office: Texaco Inc 2000 Westchester Ave White Plains NY 10650-0001

TELLEEN, JOHN MARTIN, retired judge; b. Cambridge, Ill., Dec. 16, 1922; s. Leonard E. and Vina (Elm) T.; m. Nell Joanne Larson, June 17, 1950 (dec. 1987); children—Jane, Mary, John D., Thomas; m. Kari Arentzen Larson, May 29, 1988. A.B., Augustana Coll., 1947; LL.B., U. Ill., 1950. Bar: Ill. 1950. Practice in Moline, 1950-53, Rock Island, 1953-81; partner firm Katz, McAndrews, Durkee & Telleen, Rock Island, 1953-81; judge 14th Judicial Circuit, 1981-94; ret., 1994; mem. exec. com. Ill. Jud. Conf., 1986-92; former counsel Luth. Hosp., Moline. Bd. dirs. Augustana Coll., Rock Island, 1968-76, sec., 1968-70, vice chmn., 1970, chmn., 1971-76; bd. dirs. Luth. Hosp., 1957-68. Served with USNR, 1943-46. Mem. ABA, Ill. Bar Assn., Rock Island County Bar Assn. (pres. 1970). Home: 4 Windy Pt Rock Island IL 61201-9219

TELLEFSEN, GERALD, management consultant; b. Jersey City, Sept. 19, 1938; s. James and Anna (Freudenberg) T.; children: Eric, Jill, Lynn. BA, Columbia U., 1960. Programmer System Devel. Corp., Paramus, N.J., 1961-63; analyst Internat. Electric Co., Paramus, 1963-64, IBM, Poughkeepsie, N.Y., 1964-65; mgr. Western Union, Mahwah, N.J., 1965-67; sr. scientist Control Data Corp., N.Y.C., 1967-68; sr. v.p. Booz Allen & Hamilton, N.Y.C., 1968-84, Tellefsen Cons. Group, N.Y.C., 1984—; bd. dirs. Nat. Consumer Products Co., Atlanta, Delphi Ptnrs., Atlanta. Contbr. articles to profl. jours. Mem. Futures Industry Assn. Avocations: golf, fishing. Office: Tellefsen Cons Group 19 Rector St Rm 1708 New York NY 10006-2301*

TELLEM, SUSAN MARY, public relations executive; b. N.Y.C, May 23, 1945; d. John F. and Rita C. (Lietz) Cain; m. Marshall R.B.. Thompson; children: Tori, John, Daniel. BS, Mt. St. Mary's Coll., L.A., 1967. Cert. pub. health nurse; RN. Pres. Tellem Pub. Rels. Agy., Marina del Rey, Calif., 1977-80, Rowland Grody Tellem, L.A., 1980-90; chmn. The Rowland Co., L.A., 1990—; pres., CEO Tellem, Inc., L.A., 1992-93; instr. UCLA Extension, 1983—; speaker numerous seminars and confs. on pub. rels. Editor: Sports Medicine for the '80's, Sports Medicine Digest, 1982-84. Bd. dirs. Marymount High Sch., 1984-87, pres., 1984-86; bd. dirs. L.A. Police Dept. Booster Assn., 1984-87; mem. Cath. Press Coun.; mem. pres.'s coun. Mus. Sci. and Industry. Mem. Am. Soc. Hosp. Mktg. and Pub. Rels., Healthcare Mktg. and Pub. Rels. Assn., Pub. Rels. Soc. Am. (bd. dirs. 1994—), L.A. Counselors, PETA, Am. Lung Assn. (chair comm. com. L.A. chpt.) Soc. for Prevention of Cruelty to Animals (chair PetSet), Sports Club (L.A.). Roman Catholic. Avocations: reading, tennis, aerobic dance. Office: Tellem Inc Museum Sq 5757 Wilshire Blvd Ste 655 Los Angeles CA 90036-3686

TELLEP, DANIEL MICHAEL, aerospace executive, mechanical engineer; b. Forest City, Pa., Nov. 20, 1931; m. Pat. Tellep; 6 children. B.S. in Mech. Engring. with highest honors, U. Calif., Berkeley, 1954, M.S., 1955; grad. Advanced Mgmt. Program, Harvard U., 1971. Prin. scientist Lockheed Missiles & Space Co., 1955-69, chief engr. missile systems div., 1969-75, v.p., asst. gen. mgr. advanced systems div., 1975-83, exec. v.p., 1983-84, pres., 1984—; pres. Lockheed Missiles & Space Systems Group, 1986—; chmn., chief exec. officer Lockheed Corp., 1989-95; chmn. bd. Lockheed Martin Corp., Bethesda, Md., 1996—, chmn., 1996—; cons. in field; bd. dirs. Wells Fargo, SCE Corp. Contbr. article to profl. jours. Bd. govs. Music Ctr. L.A. County, 1991-95; mem. adv. bd. U. Calif. Berkeley Sch. Engring.; mem. Calif. Bus. Roundtable, 1992—; nat. chmn. vol. com. U.S. Savs. Bond Campaign, 1993. Recipient Tower award San Jose Stte U., 1985, Aeronautics and Propulsion Laurels award Aviation Week and Space Tech., 1993, John R. Alison award, 1993; named Exec. of Yr., NMA, 1993, James V. Forrestal award, 1995, award Calif. Mfrs., 1996, Nat. Engring. award Am. Assn. Engring. Socs., 1996. Fellow AIAA (hon., Lawrence Sperry award 1964, Missile Sys. award, 1986), Am. Astronautical Soc. (Indsl. Leadership award 1992); mem. NAE, Nat. Aero. Assn., Soc. Mfg. Engrs., Sigma Xi, Pi Tau Sigma. Office: Lockheed Martin Corp 6801 Rockledge Dr Bethesda MD 20817

TELLER, EDWARD, physicist; b. Budapest, Hungary, Jan. 15, 1908; naturalized, 1941; s. Max and Ilona (Deutch) T.; m. Augusta Harkanyi, Feb. 26, 1934; children: Paul, Susan Wendy. Student, Inst. Tech., Karlsruhe, Germany, 1926-28, U. Munich, 1928; Ph.D., U. Leipzig, Germany, 1930; D.Sc. (hon.), Yale U., 1954, U. Alaska, 1959, Fordham U., 1960, George Washington U., 1960, U. So. Calif., 1960, St. Louis U., 1960, Rochester Inst. Tech., 1962, PMC Colls., 1963, U. Detroit, 1964, Clemson U., 1966, Clarkson Coll., 1969; LL.D., Boston Coll., 1961, Seattle U., 1961, U. Cin., 1962, U. Pitts., 1963, Pepperdine U., 1974, U. Md. at Heidelberg, 1977; D.Sc., L.H.D., Mt. Mary Coll., 1964; Ph.D., Tel Aviv U., 1972; D.Natural Sci., DeLaSalle U., Manila, 1981; D. Med. Sci. (n.c.), Med. U. S.C., 1983. Research assoc. Leipzig, 1929-31, Goettingen, Germany, 1931-33; Rockefeller fellow Copenhagen, 1934; lectr. U. London, 1934-35; prof. physics George Washington U., Washington, 1935-41, Columbia, 1941-42; physicist U. Chgo., 1942-43, Manhattan Engr. Dist., 1942-46, Los Alamos Sci. Lab., 1943-46; prof. physics U. Chgo., 1946-52; prof. physics U. Calif., 1953-60, prof. physics-at-large, 1960-70, Univ. prof., 1970-75; Univ. prof. emeritus, chmn. dept. applied sci. U. Calif., Davis and Livermore, 1963-66; asst. dir. Los Alamos Sci. Lab., 1949-52; cons. Livermore br. U. Calif. Radiation Lab., 1952-53; assoc. dir. Lawrence Livermore Lab., U. Calif., 1954-58, 60-75; dir. Lawrence Livermore Radiation Lab., U. Calif., 1958-60; now dir. emeritus, cons. Lawrence Livermore Nat. Lab., U. Calif., Manhattan Dist. of Columbia, 1942-46; also Metall. and Lab. of Argonne Nat. Lab., U. Chgo., 1942-43, 46-52, and Los Alamos, N.Mex., 1943-46; also Radiation Lab., Livermore, Calif., 1952-75; sr. research fellow Hoover Instn. War, Revolution and Peace, Stanford U., 1975—; mem. sci. adv. bd. USAF; bd. dirs. Assn. to Unite the Democracies; past mem. gen. adv. com. AEC; former mem. Pres.'s Fgn. Intelligence Adv. Nat. Space Coun. Bd. Author: (with Francis Owen Rice) The Structure of Matter, 1949, (with A.L. Latter) Our Nuclear Future, 1958, (with Allen Brown) The Legacy of Hiroshima, 1962, The Reluctant Revolutionary, 1964, (with G.W. Johnson, W.K. Talley, G.H. Higgins) The Constructive Uses of Nuclear Explosives, 1968, (with Segre, Kaplan and Schiff) Great Men of Physics, 1969, The

Miracle of Freedom, 1972, Energy: A Plan for Action, 1975, Nuclear Energy in the Developing World, 1977, Energy from Heaven and The Earth, 1979, The Pursuit of Simplicity, 1980, Better a Shield than a Sword, 1987, Conversations on the Dark Secrets of Physics, 1991. Past bd. dirs. Def. Intelligence Sch., Naval War Coll.; bd. dirs. Fed. Union, Hertz Found., Am. Friends of Tel Aviv U.; sponsor Atlantic Union, Atlantic Council U.S., Univ. Ctrs. for Rational Alternatives; mem. Com. to Unite Am., Inc.; bd. govs. Am. Acad. Achievement. Recipient Joseph Priestley Meml. award Dickinson Coll., 1957, Harrison medal Am. Ordnance Assn., 1955; Albert Einstein award, 1958; Gen. Donovan Meml. award, 1959; Midwest Research Inst. award, 1960; Research Inst. Am. Living History award, 1960; Golden Plate award Am. Acad. Achievement, 1961; Gold medal Am. Acad. Achievement, 1982; Thomas E. White and Enrico Fermi awards, 1962; Robins award of Am., 1963; Leslie R. Groves Gold medal, 1974; Harvey prize in sci. and tech. Technion Inst., 1975; Semmelweis medal, 1977; Albert Einstein award Technion Inst., 1977; Henry T. Heald award Ill. Inst. Tech., 1978; Gold medal Am. Coll. Nuclear Medicine, 1980; A.C. Eringen award, 1980; named ARCS Man of Yr., 1980, Disting. Scientist, Nat. Sci. Devel. Bd., 1981; Paul Harris award Rotary Found., 1980; Disting. Scientist Phil-Am. Acad. Sci. and Engring., 1981; Lloyd Freeman Hunt Citizenship award, 1982; Nat. medal of Sci., 1983; Joseph Handleman prize, 1983, Sylvanus Thayer Medal, 1986; Shelby Cullom Davis award Ethics & Pub. Policy Assn., 1988; Presdl. Citizen medal Pres. Reagan, 1989; Ettore Majorana Erice Scienza Per La Pace award, 1990; Order of Banner with Rubies of the Republic of Hungary, 1990. Fellow Am. Nuclear Soc., Am. Phys. Soc., Am. Acad. Arts and Scis., Hungarian Acad. Scis. (hon.); mem. Nat. Acad. Scis., Am. Geophys. Union, Soc. Engring. Scis., Internat. Platform Assn. Research on chem., molecular and nuclear physics, quantum mechanics, thermonuclear reactions, applications of nuclear energy, astrophysics, spectroscopy of polyatomic molecules, theory of atomic nuclei. Office: Stanford U Hoover Inst Stanford CA 94305 also: PO Box 808 Livermore CA 94551-0808

TELLER, MARC JOEL, computer systems engineer, consulting researcher; b. Bklyn., Dec. 2, 1951; s. Philip and Lillian (Greenberg) T.; m. Mette Hansen, Aug. 24 1980. BS in Biology, Columbia U., 1972. Systems mgr., head systems devel. Brain Rsch. Labs., NYU Med. Ctr., N.Y.C., 1974-76; mem. programming staff Bell Labs., AT&T Long Lines, Holmdel, N.J., 1977-82; various positions, then sr. market specialist UNIX, Perkin-Elmer Data Systems, Tinton Falls, N.J., 1983-85, sr. tech. specialist, then strategic product plannerr, 1985, 87; sr. systems engr. UNIX, AT&T Bell Labs., Holmdel, N.J., 1985-86; mgr. operating systems engring. Unisoft Corp., Cambridge, Mass., 1987-89; cons. operating systems engr. Phoenix Techs., Norwood, Mass., 1989-90; prin. cons. engr., program mgr. operating systems rsch. Encore Computer Corp., Marlborough, Mass., 1990-91; leader operating systems rsch., prin. tech. rsch. cons. Worcester Poly. Inst. Ctr. High Performance Computing, Marlborough, Mass., 1991-93; ind. sys. cons. M.J. Teller Cons., Mansfield, Mass., 1993—; mgr. HSM devel. EMASS, Inc., Eng., 1994—. Contbr. articles to profl. jours. Mem. IEEE (Posix stds. group 1984-89, 88open binary compatibility stds. com. 1987-89, cert. of apprecition 1988), IEEE Computer Soc., NRA (instr. 1992—), Lionel Collectors Club Am., Colo. Symphony Assn., Mass. Hort. Soc., Boston Symphony Orch. Avocations: O-gauge model rai.roading, target pistol competition, music, conservation. Home and Office: 3694 Deer Creek Dr Parker CO 80134-4568

TELLIER, HENRI, retired Canadian military officer; b. Montreal, Que., Can., Sept. 1, 1918; s. Henry Joseph and Jeanne (St. Cyr) T.; m. Virginia Wright, July 23, 1945; children: Pierre, Michele, Suzanne, John, Nicole. Student, U. Montreal, 1935-40, U. Ottawa, 1946-47, Canadian Army Staff Coll., 1942-43, Imperial Def. Coll., London, Eng., 1966, Dept. Def. Computer Inst., Washington, 1968. With Robert Howard & Co. (ins. brokers), Montreal, 1937-40; commd. 2d lt. Canadian Army, 1940, advanced through grades to lt. gen., 1973; asst. sec. to minister (Nat. Def.), 1945-48; comdg. officer (Royal 22d Regt.), 1948-51; instr. (Canadian Army Staff Coll.), 1951-54; army mem. (Joint Intelligence Staff), 1954-57; mil. adviser Vietnam, 1957-58; chief of staff (Que. Mil. Dist.), 1958-60; mil attache Rome, Italy, 1960- 63; dir. mil. ops. and plans Army, 1963-64, dir. internat. plans, 1964-65; comdr. (Canadian Contingent), Cyprus, 1965-66; dir. gen. plans (Forces Hdqrs.), Ottawa, Ont., 1967-70; dep. chief plans (Forces Hdqrs.), 1970-71; Canadian mil. rep. to mil. com. (NATO Hdqrs.), Brussels, Belgium, 1971-73; ret., 1973; assoc. nat. commr. Canadian Red Cross Soc., Toronto, Ont., 1973-75, nat. commr., 1975, sec.-gen., 1981-83, hon. v.p.; pvt. mem. Refugee Status Adversary Com., 1984-89; chmn. Canadian sect. Mil. Coop. Com. Can.-U.S., Joint Permanent Bd. Def. Can.-U.S.; commr. Commn. for Strategic and Internat. Studies; mem. adv. council Can. Exec. Services Orgn. Decorated Disting. Service Order (Canada); Queens medal Netherlands; comdr. Order of Merit (Italy), officer Order of Red Cross; named to Order of Can. Mem. Canadian Inst. Internat. Affairs., Can. Exec. Svc. Orgn., Inst. Assn. Execs., The Empire Club of Can., Royal 22 Regiment Assn., UN Assn. Office: 19 Bay Hill Ridge, Stittsville, ON Canada K2S 1B9

TELLIER, PAUL M., Canadian railway transportation executive; b. Joliette, Que., Can., May 8, 1939; s. Maurice J. and Eva M. (Bouvier) T.; m. Andree Poirier, June 6, 1959; children: Claude, Marc. BA, U. Ottawa, 1959, LLL, 1962; BLitt, Oxford U., 1966; LLD (hon.), U. Alta., Can., 1996. Bar: Que. bar 1963. Sr. gov. official Can., 1967-92; dep. minister Indian affairs and no. devel., 1979-82, dep. minister energy, mines and resources, 1982-85; chmn. governing bd. Internat. Energy Agy., 1985-92; clk. of Privy Council and sec. to Cabinet Govt. of Can., Ottawa, 1985-92; dir. Petro Can., 1985-92; pres., CEO Canadian Nat. Railways Co., 1992—; bd. dirs. Manulife Fin., Toronto, Grand Trunk Corp., Detroit, Bell Can., Montreal, Can., SNC-Lavalin Group Onc., Montreal, McCain Foods Ltd., Florenceville, Can.; bd. dirs. Conf. Bd. Canada. Decorated companion Order of Can.; recipient Pub. Svc. Outstanding Achievement award, 1989, Pub. Policy Forum Achievement award, 1989; named to Queen's Privy Coun., Her Majesty Queen Elizabeth, 1992; Queen's counsel, 1981. Mem. Que. Bar, Railway Assn. Can. (dir.), Assn. Am. Railroads (dir.). Roman Catholic. Office: Can Nat Railway Co, 935 De La Gauchetiere St West, Montreal, PQ Canada H3B 2M9 also: PO Box 8100, Montreal, PQ Canada H3C 3N4

TELLIER, RICHARD DAVIS, management educator; b. Darby, Pa., Feb. 18, 1942; s. Joseph Campbell and Jane Grace (Davis) T.; m. Susan Gammon, June 10, 1974; children: John-Jo and Tiekka (twins). BSEE, Drexel U., 1967; MBA, Fla. State U., 1971, DBA, 1973. Elec. engr. Philco-Ford Corp., Phila., 1960-67; aerospace sys. engr. GE, Cape Canaveral, Fla., 1967-70; lectr. Fla. State U., Tallahassee, 1970-73; prof. mgmt. Calif. State U., Fresno, 1973—, chmn. dept. mgmt. and mktg., 1979-84, assoc. dean Sch. Bus., 1984-85, asst. dean, 1990-92, assoc. provost acad. resources, 1995—; cons. ops. mgmt., market rsch. orgnl. behavior. Author: Operations Management: Fundamental Concepts and Methods, 1978, Production and Operations Management Test Bank, 1990 ; contbr. articles to profl. jours. Grantee 1975; recipient Meritorious Performance award, 1987, 88, 90. Mem. Ops. Research Soc. Am., Phi Kappa Phi. Home: 8294 N Academy Ave Clovis CA 93611-9454 Office: Calif State U Shaw and Maple Aves Fresno CA 93740-0007

TELLING, EDWARD RIGGS, former retail, insurance, real estate and financial services executive; b. Danville, Ill., Apr. 1, 1919; s. Edward Riggs and Margaret Katherine (Matthews) T.; m. Nancy Hawkins, Dec. 29, 1942; children: Edward R. III, Pamela Telling Grimes, Kathryn Telling Bentley, Nancy Telling O'Shaughnessy, Thomas Cole. PhB, Ill. Wesleyan U., 1942, LLD, 1978; LLD, St. Norbert Coll., 1985. With Sears, Roebuck & Co., 1946-85, store mgr., 1954-59, zone mgr., 1960-64, mgr. mdse. N.Y.C. area ops., 1965-67; adminstrv. asst. to v.p. Ea. ter. Sears, Roebuck & Co., Phila., 1968, v.p. Ea. ter., 1969-74; exec. v.p. Midwestern ter. Sears, Roebuck & Co., Chgo., 1974-75, sr. exec. v.p. field, 1976-77, chmn., CEO, 1978-85. Lt. USNR, 1941-45. Mem. Bus. Coun., Chgo. Club, Old Elm Club, Seminole Club, Lost Tree Club (Fla.). Office: Sears Tower PO Box 06619 Sears Tower 9800 Chicago IL 60606

TELLINGTON, WENTWORTH JORDAN, engineer; b. Gorham, N.H., Oct. 11, 1916; s. Jesse James and Myrtle Meneleh (Jordan) T.; m. Elizabeth Haman-Ashley, Apr. 29, 1939 (div. 1956); children: Wentworth J. Jr., Joan Elizabeth Gabert. AB, Columbia U., 1940. Instr. U.S. Mil. Acad., West Point, N.Y., 1941-45; field supr. Century Geophys. Corp., Tulsa, 1946-48; chief geophysicist Pacific Petroleums Ltd., Calgary, Alberta, Can., 1949-51; exec. v.p. Overland Inds. Ltd., Edmonton, Alberta, Can., 1952-55; head math. dept. Chadwick Sch., Rolling Hills, Calif., 1956-60; proprietor Pacific Coast Equestrian Rsch. Farm, Badger, Calif., 1961-70, Whitehurst Products Co., San Francisco, 1970-75, Deep Moon Gold Mine, Downieville, 1982-92; chmn. Airdock Enterprise Inc., Phoenix, 1994; adj. prof. Prescott (Ariz.) Coll., 1972-75. Author: (books) Military Maps and Air Photos, 1979, Endurance and Competitive Trail Riding, 1979, Gold and a Hideaway of Your Own, 1993, Crazy in America, 1994; inventor: vehicle tracker, device for tracking and recording locations, 1944, floating airport, 1995. Engr. ethics com. Soc. Profl. Engrs., Can., 1953-54; bd. govs. Western States Trail Assn., Auburn, Calif., 1962-80. Recipient Creative Citizenship in Calif. award Gov. Ronald Reagan, 1968. Mem. Am. Assn. Petroleum Geologists. Republican. Congregationalist. Achievements include patents for Vehicle Tracker, device for tracking and recording locations, 1944, Floating Airport, 1995. Avocations: tennis, riding, aerobatic flying. Office: Airdock Enterprise PO Box 68291 Tucson AZ 85737

TELLO MACAIS, MANUEL, diplomat; s. Manuel Tello and Guadalupe Macías Viadero. Amb. to Gt. Britain Govt. of Mexico, London, 1977-79, under-sec. fgn. affairs, 1979-82; permanent rep. internat. orgns. Govt. of Mexico, Geneva, 1983-89; amb. to France Govt. of Mexico, 1989-92; sec. fgn. rels. Govt. of Mexico, Mexico City, 1994-95; now permanent rep. of Mexico to UN N.Y.C. Office: Permanent Mission of Mexico 2 United Nations Plaza 28th Fl New York NY 10017

TELMER, FREDERICK HAROLD, steel products manufacturing executive; b. Edmonton, Alta., Can., Dec. 28, 1937; Ingar and Gertrude Bernice (Floen) T.; m. Margaret Goddard Hutchings, Oct. 30, 1959; children: Christopher, Kevin, Colin. BA in Econs., U. Alberta, 1961, MA in Econs., 1964. With Stelco, Inc., Hamilton, Ont., Can., 1963—, gen. mgr. corp. affairs and strategic planning, 1984-85, v.p. corp. affairs and strategic planning, 1985-87, pres. Stelco Steel, 1988-90, dir., 1989, chmn., chief exec. officer, 1991—; dir. Inco Ltd., CT Fin. Svcs., Inc., Internat. Iron and Steel Inst., Am. Iron and Steel Inst., chmn. N.Am. steel coun.; dir., chmn. Can. Steel Prodrs. Assn.; founding dir. Japan Soc.; vice chmn. Inst. for Work & Health, Can.-Japan Bus. Com. Mem. Toronto Club, Hamilton Club, Burlington Golf and Country Club, Hamilton Golf and Country Club, Delta Kappa Epsilon. Avocations: golf, woodworking, tennis, skiing, piano. Office: Stelco Inc, PO Box 2030, Hamilton, ON Canada L8N 3T1

TELTSER, MICHAEL, chemical engineer; b. Orange, N.J., Jan. 28, 1958; s. Milton and Belle Teltser. BSChemE, Rutgers U., Piscataway, 1995. Cert. in phlebotomy Am. Soc. Clin. Pathologists; cert. emergency med. technician N.J. Cons. Breakers Realty, Springfield, N.J., 1990—; phlebotomy cons. Robert Wood Johnson Trauma Ctr., New Brunswick, N.J., 1992-94; validation engr. Merck & Co., Inc., West Point, Pa., 1995—. Mem. AIChE, Internat. Soc. Pharm. Engrs., Am. Soc. Law Enforcement Trainers. Avocations: martial arts, skiing, weightlifting. Home: 115 Redwood Rd Springfield NJ 07081 Office: Merck & Co Inc P O Box 4 WP42T-1 West Point PA 19486

TEMA-LYN, LAURIE, management consultant; b. Bklyn., Mar. 25, 1951; d. Morton and Jeanne (Lite) Carlin. BA, Bklyn. Coll., 1972. Mgmt. supr. Rapp & Collins, Inc., N.Y.C., 1972-78, v.p., 1978-80; assoc. Synectics, Cambridge, Mass., 1980-83; founder, gen. ptnr. IdeaScope Assocs., Cambridge, Mass., 1983-95; prin. Practical Imagination Enterprises, Carlisle, Mass., 1995—; presenter European Conf. on Innovation and Creativity, 1987, 94. Contbr. articles to bus. publs. Bd. dirs. Arica Inst., N.Y.C., 1979-80; v.p. bd. dirs. Savoyand Light Opera Co. Mem. Creative Problem Solving Inst. (presenter, leader), Am. Mktg. Assn., Direct Mktg. Assn. (presenter), Product Devel. Mgmt. Assn., Creative Edn. Found., New Eng. Bus. Assn. for Social Responsibility, Mgmt. Roundtable, Sharing a New Song. Office: Practical Imagination Enterprises PO Box 693 Carlisle MA 01741-0693

TEMAM, ROGER M., mathematician; b. Tunis, Tunisia, May 19, 1940; s. Ange M. and Elise (Ganem) T.; m. Claudette Cukorja, Aug. 21, 1962; children: David, Olivier, Emmanuel. M in Math., U. Paris, 1962, DSc, 1967. Asst. prof. math. U. Paris, 1960-67, prof., 1967—; prof. Ecole Polytechnique, Paris, 1968-85. Author: Numerical Analysis, 1969, Navier-Stokes Equations, 1977, Mathematical Problems in Plasticity, 1983, Infinite Dimensional Dynamical Systems in Mechanics and Physics, 1988; contbr. over 200 articles to sci. jours.; editor Math. Model. and Num. Analysis, Physica D, assoc. editor other profl. jours. Recipient Grand Prix Joannidès, Acad. Sci. Paris, 1993. Mem. AAAS, Am. Math. Soc., Am. Physical Soc., N.Y. Acad. Scis., Soc. Indsl. and Applied Math., Soc. Math. Applications of Industry (founding pres. 1983-87).

TEMERLIN, LIENER, advertising agency executive; b. Ardmore, Okla., Mar. 27, 1928; s. Pincus and Julie (Kahn) T.; m. Karla Samuelsohn, July 23, 1950; children: Dana Temerlin Crawford, Lisa Temerlin Gottesman, Hayden Crawford, Sandy Gottesman. BFA, U. Okla., 1950. Assoc. editor Sponsor Mag., N.Y.C., 1950-51; copywriter Glenn Advt. Inc., Dallas, 1952-54, creative dir., 1954-70, chief oper. officer, 1970-74; pres. Glenn, Bozell & Jacobs, Inc., 1974-79; chmn. bd. dirs. Bozell & Jacobs Inc., 1979-86, Bozell, Jacobs, Kenyon & Eckhardt, Dallas, 1986-89; chmn. Bozell, 1989-92, Temerlin McClain, 1992—. Chmn. Winston Churchill Found. award dinner, 1986; chmn. Dallas Symphony Assn., 1986-88, pres., 1984-86, mem. bd. govs., 1982-84, pres. coun., 1989—; mem. Blair House Restoration Com., 1987-88; vice chmn. Am. Film Inst., 1992-93, bd. trustees, 1992—; bd. dirs. United Way of Met. Dallas Exec. Com., 1986-89, Dallas Bus. Com. for Arts, 1989, Dallas Citizen's Coun., 1984-86, 92; trustee Southwestern Med. Found., 1988—, bd. trustees, 1992—, So. Meth. U., trustee com. Univ. devel., 1988, exec. bd., 1990-91; trustee and chmn. of devel. com. Dallas Mus. Art, 1993-96; mem. steering com. Susan G. Komen Found., 1989-91, art acquisition com. Meyerson Symphony Ctr., 1989-92, exec. coun. Daytop/Dallas, 1989—; chmn. grand opening fortnight Morton H. Meyerson Symphony Ctr., 1989; mem. Madison Coun. Libr. Congress, Washington, 1991—. Recipient Bill D. Kerss award Dallas Advt. League, 1983, Brotherhood award NCCJ, 1984, Susan G. Komen Found. for Breast Cancer Rsch. Community award, 1989, James K. Wilson Silver Cup award, 1990, Linz award 1990, Silver Medal award Dallas Advt. League, 1991, Vol. Fundraiser of Yr. award Nat. Soc. Fundraising Execs., 1991, Best Man in Advt. award McCall's Mag., 1992; named Dallas Father of Yr., 1991. Office: 201 E Carpenter Fwy Irving TX 75062

TEMES, GABOR CHARLES, electrical engineering educator; b. Budapest, Hungary, Oct. 14, 1929; s. Erno and Rozsa (Angyal) Wohl-Temes; m. Ibi Kutasi-Temes, Feb. 6, 1954; children: Roy Thomas, Carla Andrea. Dipl.Ing., Tech. U. Budapest, 1952, DSc (hon.), 1991; Dipl. Phys., Eotvos U., Budapest, 1954; Ph.D., U. Ottawa, Ont., Can., 1961. Asst. prof. Tech. U. Budapest, 1952-56; project engr. Measurement Engring. Ltd., 1956-59; dept. head No. Electric Co. Ltd., 1959-64; group leader Stanford Linear Accelerator Center, 1964-66; corp. cons. Ampex Corp., 1966-69; prof. elec. engring. UCLA, 1969-90, chmn. dept., 1975-80; dept. head Oreg. State U., Corvallis, 1990—; cons. Xerox Corp., ANT GmbH. Author: (with others) Introduction to Circuit Synthesis and Design, 1977, Analog MOS Integrated Circuits for Signal Processing, 1986; assoc. editor: (with others) Jour. Franklin Inst, 1971-82; co-editor, contbg. author: (with others) Modern Filter Theory and Design, 1973, Oversampling Delta-Sigma Data Converters, 1991. Recipient Western Electric Fund award Am. Soc. Engring. Edn., 1982, Humboldt Sr. Rsch. award, 1991; NSF grantee, 1970—. Fellow IEEE (editor Transactions on Circuit Theory 1969-71 Best Paper award 1969, 81, 85, Centennial medal 1984, Edn. award 1987, Tech. Achievement award 1989). Home: 7100 NW Grandview Dr Corvallis OR 97330-2708 Office: Oreg State U Dept Elec Engring Corvallis OR 97330

TEMIN, MICHAEL LEHMAN, lawyer; b. Phila., July 18, 1933; s. Henry and Annette (Lehman) T.; divorced; children—Aaron Lehman, Seth Lehman. B.A. magna cum laude, Yale U., 1954; LL.B. cum laude, U. Pa., 1957. Bar: Pa. 1958, U.S. Ct. Appeals (3d cir.) 1958, U.S. Supreme Ct. 1969, U.S. Ct. Appeals (2d cir.) 1986, U.S. Ct. Appeals (9th cir.) 1992. Asst. U.S. atty. U.S. Atty.'s Office, Phila., 1958-59; assoc. Wolf, Block, Schorr and Solis-Cohen, Phila., 1959-66, ptnr., 1966—; lectr. Law Sch., U. Pa., Phila., 1982-90, adj. prof., 1990-93, 94-95; Thomas A. O'Boyle vis. disting. practitioner, 1985, I. Grant Irey lectr., 1988. Editor U. Pa. Law Rev., 1955-57. Vice chmn. Ednl. Nominating Panel, Phila., 1981-83; bd. dirs. Citizens Com. in Pub. Edn., Phila., 1970—, pres. 1980-82. Fellow Am. Coll. Bankruptcy; mem. Phila. Bar Assn. (chmn. bankruptcy com., sect. corp., banking and bus. law 1979-86, chmn. profl. guidance com. 1985, sec. sect. corp. banking and bus. law 1985, treas. sect. corp. banking and bus. law 1986, vice chmn. sect. corp. banking and bus. law 1987, chmn. sect. corp. banking and bus. law 1988), Pa. Bar Assn. (ho. of dels. 1985-89, 90—), ABA (bus. bankruptcy com. of sect. corp. banking and bus. law chmn. rules subcom., 1985-92, vice chmn. chpt. 11 subcom. 1992—, vice chmn. ea. dist. Pa. bankruptcy conf. 1994-95, chmn. ea. dist. Pa. bankruptcy conf., 1995-96), Order of Coif. Jewish. Office: Wolf Block Schorr & Solis-Cohen 12th Fl Packard Bldg Philadelphia PA 19102

TEMIN, PETER, economics educator; b. Phila., Dec. 17, 1937; s. Henry and Annette T.; m. Charlotte Brucar Fox, Aug. 21, 1966; children: Elizabeth Sara, Melanie Wynn. B.A., Swarthmore (Pa.) Coll., 1959; Ph.D., Mass. Inst. Tech., 1964. Mem. faculty MIT, 1965—, prof. econs., 1970—. Author: Iron and Steel in Nineteenth Century America, 1964, The Jacksonian Economy, 1969, Casual Factors in American Economic Growth in the 19th Century, 1975, Did Monetary Forces Cause the Great Depression?, 1976, Taking Your Medicine: Drug Regulation in the United States, 1980, The Fall of the Bell System, 1987, Lessons from the Great Depression, 1989, Inside the Business Enterprise, 1991. Mem. Am. Econ. Assn., Econ. History Assn., Econ. History Soc., Phi Beta Kappa. Home: 15 Channing St Cambridge MA 02138-4713 Office: MIT Dept Econs Cambridge MA 02139

TEMKIN, HARVEY L., lawyer; b. Madison, Wis., Jan. 1, 1952; s. Joe L. and Sylvia (Libanoff) T.; m. Barbara Jean Myers, June 13, 1976; children: James, Daniel, Eli. BA, U. Wis., 1974; JD, U. Ill., 1978. Bar: Wis. 1978. Assoc. Foley & Lardner, Madison, 1978-83; prof. Tulane Law Sch., New Orleans, 1983-87; ptnr. Foley & Lardner, Madison, 1987—; lectr. U. Wis. Law Sch.; mem. U.S. Senator Feingold's Bus. Adv. Group. 1st v.p. Hillel Found., Madison, 1982-83, bd. dirs., 1987—; chmn. edn. com. Beth Israel Synagogue, Madison, 1980-82; chmn. Downtown Madison, Inc., 1989-91; chmn. Jewish edn. panel Madison Jewish Community Coun., 1993—. Fellow Am. Coll. Real Estate Lawyers; mem. ABA (real property probate and trust sect., reporter significant legis. panel 1983-85, significant lit. panel 1985-87). Home: 6609 Inner Dr Madison WI 53705-4218 Office: Foley & Lardner PO Box 1497 150 E. Gilman St Madison WI 53701-1497

TEMKIN, LARRY SCOTT, philosopher, educator; b. Milw., May 29, 1954; s. Blair Huntly and Leah Dahlia (Sigman) T.; m. Margaret Ellen Grimm, May 26, 1975; children: Daniel Eric, Andrea Beth, Rebecca Leigh. BA-Honors degree in Philosophy, U. Wis., 1975; student, Oxford U., Eng., 1978-79; PhD, Princeton U., 1983. Instr. philosophy Rice U., Houston, 1980-83, asst. prof., 1983-89, assoc. prof., 1989-95, prof., 1995—; vis. appointment U. Pitts., 1986; speaker in field. Author: Inequality; contbr. articles to profl. jours. Recipient Phi Beta Kappa Outstanding Tchr. award, George R. Brown awards for superior teaching, George R. Brown awards for excellence in teaching; Danforth fellow, Nat. Humanities Ctr. fellow, Weiner fellow, Harvard fellow for Program in Ethics and the Professions. Mem. Am. Philos. Assn., Phi Beta Kappa. Avocations: camping, sports. Home: 4924 Valerie St Bellaire TX 77401-5708 Office: Rice U Dept Philosophy 6100 S Main Houston TX 77005-1892

TEMKIN, ROBERT HARVEY, accountant; b. Boston, Oct. 21, 1943; s. Max and Lillian (Giller) T.; m. Ellen Phyllis Band, Sept. 25, 1966; children: Aron, Rachel, Joshua. BBA, U. Mass., 1964. CPA, Mass., N.Y. With Ernst & Young, 1964-72, 73—, ptnr., 1976—; nat. dir. auditing standards Arthur Young & Co., CPAs, 1980-88; assoc. prof. NYU, 1982. Bd. dirs. Jewish Home for Elderly of Fairfield County, 1979-94, pres., 1985-87; mem. Bd. Edn., Weston, Conn., 1983-87; dir. United Synagogue Am.; mem. bus. adv. coun. U. Mass., chmn. acctg. alumni advisory coun.; bd. dirs. Jewish Cmty. Ctrs. of Greater Boston, Combined Jewish Philanthropies of Greater Boston; mem. exec. bd. N.E. region Anti-Defamation League; treas. Synagogue Coun., Mass., 1988-93; bd. dirs. Temple Reyim, Newton, Mass., 1995—, asst. treas., 1995-96. Recipient Acctg. Alumni award U. Mass., 1978, Alumnus Award Sch. Mgmt. U. Mass., 1986. Mem. AICPA (staff dir. commn. on auditors responsibilities 1976-78, mem. task force on auditor's report 1978-81, peer rev. com. 1982-84, auditing stds. bd. 1984-88, chmn. internat. auditing task force 1988-90), Mass. Soc. CPAs (Silver medal 1964), N.Y. State Soc. CPAs, Mass. Bd. Pub. Accountancy (sec. 1996), Greater Boston C. of C. (bd. dirs.), N.E.-Israel C. of C. (bd. dirs.), Bostonian Club (adv. bd.). Home: 1611 Commonwealth Ave Newton MA 02165-2800 Office: Ernst & Young 200 Clarendon St Boston MA 02116-5021

TEMKO, ALLAN BERNARD, writer; b. N.Y.C., Feb. 4, 1924; s. Emanuel and Betty (Alderman) T.; m. Elizabeth Ostroff, July 1, 1950; children: Susannah, Alexander. AB, Columbia U., 1947; postgrad, U. Calif., Berkeley, 1949-51, Sorbonne, 1948-49, 51-52. Lectr. Sorbonne, 1953-54, Ecole des Arts et Metiers, Paris, 1954-55; asst. prof. journalism U. Calif., Berkeley, 1956-62, lectr. in city planning and social scis., 1966-70, lectr. Grad. Sch. Journalism, 1991; prof. art Calif. State U., Hayward, 1971-80; lectr. art Stanford U., 1981, 82; architecture critic San Francisco Chronicle, 1961-93, art editor, 1979-82; archtl. planning cons.; chmn. Yosemite Falls Design Workshop, 1992; Pulitzer Prize juror, 1991-92. Author: Notre Dame of Paris, 1955, Eero Saarinen, 1962, No Way To Build a Ballpark and Other Irreverent Essays on Architecture, 1993; contbr. articles to U.S. and fgn. mags. and newspapers; West Coast editor, Archtl. Forum, 1959-62. Served with USNR, 1943-46. Recipient Gold medal Commonwealth Club Calif., 1956, Silver medal, 1994, Journalism award AIA, 1961, Silver Spur award San Francisco Planning and Urban Renewal Assn., 1985, AIA Inst. Honor award, 1991, Nathaniel A. Owings award AIA Calif. Coun., 1995, 1st prize in archtl. criticism Mfrs. Hanover/Art World, 1986, Critic's award Mfrs. Hanover/Art World, 1987, Profl. Achievement award Soc. Profl. Journalists, 1988, Pulitzer Prize for criticism, 1990; grantee Rockefeller Found., 1962-63, 20th Century Fund, 1963-66, NEA, 1988, Graham Found., 1990; Guggenheim fellow, 1956-57. Home: 1015 Fresno Ave Berkeley CA 94707-2517 *My chief intellectual and professional goal has always been to create excellence in a democratic America and, where possible, in the world at large. This Jeffersonian aim, which came to me directly from Lewis Mumford, naturally includes architecture, environmental planning, the fine arts, and literature. Through education, in which history, criticism, and serious journalism play important roles, I think it is still possible to attain such excellence despite the complex problems of technological civilization.*

TEMKO, STANLEY LEONARD, lawyer; b. N.Y.C., Jan. 4, 1920; s. Emanuel and Betty (Alderman) T.; m. Francine Marie Salzman, Mar. 4, 1944; children: Richard J., Edward J., William D. AB, Columbia U., 1940, LLB, 1943. Bar: N.Y. 1943, D.C. 1951. Practice in N.Y.C., 1943, 46-47; law clk. Mr. Justice Wiley Rutledge, U.S. Supreme Ct., Washington, 1947-48; asso. firm Covington & Burling, Washington, 1949-55; ptnr. Covington & Burling, 1955-90, sr. counsel, 1990—. Editor-in-chief: Columbia Law Rev, 1942-43. Trustee Beauvoir Sch., 1963-69; trustee Columbia U., 1980-91, trustee emeritus, 1991—, mem. bd. visitors Sch. Law, 1961—; mem. bd. govs. St. Albans Sch., 1967-73, chmn., 1971-73. 2nd lt. U.S. Army, 1943-46. Decorated Bronze Star; recipient medal for conspicuous alumni svc. Columbia U., 1979. Fellow Am. Bar Found. (chmn. rsch. com. 1970-72); mem. ABA, Am. Law Inst., D.C. Bar Assn., Columbia U. Sch. Law Alumni Assn. (pres. 1982-84), Met. Club, Nat. Press Club, City Tavern Club, Phi Beta Kappa. Home: 4811 Dexter Ter NW Washington DC 20007-1020 Office: Covington & Burling 1201 Pennsylvania Ave NW PO Box 7566 Washington DC 20044

TEMMER, GEORGES MAXIME, physicist; b. Vienna, Austria, Apr. 10, 1922; came to U.S., 1939; s. Frederic M. and Margaret D. (Jeiteles) T.; m. Odette Fluchere (div. 1978); m. Sylvia Bjornberg, Feb. 25, 1979. BS in Physics, Queens Coll., 1943; MA in Physics, U. Calif., Berkeley, 1944, PhD in Physics, 1949; ScD (hons.), Queens Coll., 1994. Rsch. assoc. U. Rochester, N.Y., 1949-51; physicist Nat. Bur. Standards, Washington, 1951-53; staff mem. Carnegie Instn. of Washington, 1953-63; prof., dir. Nuclear Physics Lab., Fla. State U., Tallahassee, Fla., 1960-63; dir. Nuclear Physics Lab., Rutgers U., New Brunswick, N.J., 1963-85; prof. of physics Rutgers U., New Brunswick, 1963-85, univ. prof., 1985-91, prof. emeritus, 1991—; mem. adv. bd. Nat. SANE/freeze campaign for global security, 1990—, physics panel NSF; vis. prof., scholar, Denmark, France, Switzerland, Germany, Austria, China, Mexico, Italy. Translator (from Italian) Fundamentals of Atomic Mech., E. Persico; (from French) Quantum Mechanics, AML Messiah, 1960, Atomic Rivals, B. Goldschmidt, 1990; editor Chinese Physics Am. Inst. of Physics, 1985-92; contbr. more than 100 articles on nuclear and atomic physics to profl. jours. Vice chmn. Coalition for Nuclear Disarmament, Princeton, N.J., 1988—; With U.S. Navy, 1944-46. Recipient John S. Guggenheim Meml. fellowship, 1956-57, Lindback award Rutgers Univ., 1975, Alexander von Humboldt prize, Humboldt Found., Bonn, Germany, 1984; named Sr. Exchange Fellow, Nat. Acad. of Sci., People's Republic of China, 1980. Fellow Am. Physical Soc.; mem. Cosmos Club. Achievements include discoveries in basic experimental nuclear physics. Home: 42 Skillman Rd Skillman NJ 08558-1616 Office: Rutgers U Dept Physics New Brunswick NJ 08903

TEMPEL, JEAN CURTIN, venture capitalist; b. Hartford, Conn., Mar. 23, 1943; d. John J. and Sally (Miller) Curtin Jr.; m. Louis J. Tempel, Nov. 23, 1968 (div. 1978); m. Peter A. Wilson, May 10, 1980. BA, Conn. Coll., 1965; MS, Rensselaer Poly. Inst., 1972; advanced mgmt. program cert., Harvard U., 1979. Sr. v.p., mgr. of custody The Boston Co., 1983, pres. Boston Safe Clearing Corp., 1984-90, exec. v.p., chief ops., info. officer, 1985, exec. v.p., COO, 1988-90; prin. Tempel Ptnrs. Inc., Boston, 1991; pres., COO Safeguard Scientifics Inc., Wayne, 1992-93, mem. bd. dirs.; gen. ptnr. TL Ventures LP, Boston, 1994—; bd. dirs. Cambridge (Mass.) Tech. Ptnrs., Dallas, Centocor, Malvern, Pa.; trustee Scudder Funds, Boston; overseer Northeastern U.; trustee Conn. Coll. Mem. Internat. Women's Forum (dir.). Avocations: skiing, bicycling, sailing. Office: Safeguard Scientifics Inc Ste 1325 10 Post Office Sq Boston MA 02109

TEMPEL, THOMAS ROBERT, army officer, periodontist; b. Denver, Mar. 12, 1939; s. Carl W. and Ruth (Rochow) T.; m. Elaine Gardner, 1963; children: T. Robert, Carl G., Kimberly Lynn. AA, Kemper Mil. Coll., 1959; DDS, U. Pa., 1963; MS in Edn., U. Kans., 1976. Diplomate Am. Bd. Periodontology. Commd. 2d lt. U.S. Army, 1959, advanced through grades to maj. gen., 1990; dental intern Madigan Army Med. Ctr., Ft. Lewis, Wash., 1963-64; with 8th Med. Bn., 8th Inf. Div., 1964-66; clinic chief Coleman Army Dental Clinic, 768th Med. Detachment, Mannheim, Fed. Republic Germany, 1966-67; guest scientist Nat. Inst. Dental Rsch., NIH, Washington, 1968-70; periodontal resident Walter Reed Army Med. Ctr., Washington, 1970-71; chief periodontist Letterman Army Inst. Rsch., San Francisco, 1971-74; student Command and Gen. Staff Coll., Ft. Leavenworth, Kans., 1974-75; dep. comdr. U.S. Army Inst. Dental Rsch., Walter Reed Army Med. Ctr., Washington, 1976-77; chief periodontics Hosp. Dental Clinic, then chief of clinic and chief periodontics svc., Walter Reed Army Med. Ctr. Washington, 1977-79; dir. grad. dental edn. Army Edn. and Tng. Div., USAMEDDPERSA, Washington, 1979-81; student Army War Coll., Carlisle, Pa., 1981-82; comdr. U.S. Army Dental and 123d Med. Det., Wuerzburg, Fed. Republic Germany, 1982-83; dep. to chief Army Dental Corps, Washington, 1983-87; dep. comdr. 7th Med. Command, Heidelberg, Fed. Republic Germany, 1987-90; asst. surgeon gen., chief Army Dental Corps; dir. med. info. mgmt. systems Office of Army Surgeon Gen., Falls Church, Va., 1990-94; dep. surgeon gen., 1994-96, health care mgmt. cons., 1996—. Cons. Jour. Periodontology, 1984-85; contbr. articles to profl. jours. Pres. Am.-German Friendship Club, Heidelberg, 1987-90, Girl Scout Fund Coun., Heidelberg, 1987-90; chmn. Boy Scout Activities, Hdqrs. U.S. Army Europe, Heidelberg, 1987-90. Decorated D.S.M., Legion of Merit, Meritorious Svc. medal; recipient 'A' Designator in Periodontics award Army Surgeon Gen., 1981, German Army sports badge in gold, 1990. Mem. ADA, Am. Acad. Periodontology, Am. Assn. Dental Schs., Assn. Mil. Surgeons, Am. Coll. Dentists, Omicron Kappa Upsilon. Republican. Lutheran. Avocations: swimming, wood carving, fishing, cycling. Home: PO Box 3046 Atlantic Beach NC 28512 Office: Office Army Surgeon Gen 5109 Leesburg Pike Falls Church VA 22041-3208

TEMPELIS, CONSTANTINE HARRY, immunologist, educator; b. Superior, Wis., Aug. 27, 1927; s. Harry and Thelma Marie (Hoff) T.; m. Nancy Louise Foster, Aug. 27, 1955; children: William H., Daniel S. BS, U. Wis.-Superior, 1950; MS, U. Wis.-Madison, 1953, PhD, 1955. Project assoc. immunology U. Wis., Madison, 1955-57; instr. immunology U. W.Va., Morgantown, 1957-58; asst. rsch. immunologist U. Calif., Berkeley, 1958-66, assoc. prof. immunology, 1966-72, prof., 1972-95, prof. emeritus, 1995—; vis. scientist Wellcome Rsch. Labs., Beckenham, Kent, Eng., 1977-78, U. Innsbruck, Austria, 1985, 90, 91; cons. in field. Contbr. articles to profl. jours. Served with USNR, 1945-46. Recipient Rsch. Career Devel. award, 1965-70; Fogarty sr. internat. fellow NIH, 1977-78. Mem. AAAS, N.Y. Acad. Scis., Am. Assn. Immunologists, Fedn. Am. Soc. Exptl. Biology, Sigma Xi. Office: U Calif Sch Pub Health Berkeley CA 94720

TEMPEST, HARRISON F., bank executive. Pres. LaSalle Nat. Bank, Chgo.; dir. LaSalle Bank, Lakeview; chmn., pres. ABN Amro (formerly European Am. Bank), N.Y.C., N.Y., 1990—. Office: ABN Amro 500 Park Ave New York NY 10022*

TEMPESTI, EZIO UGONE, chemistry educator; b. Cairo, Oct. 26, 1943; arrived in Italy, 1961; s. Ugo and Albina (Perricone) T.; m. Maria Antonia Capizzi, July 30, 1979; children: Lucilla, Francesca. MS, Italian Salesian Inst., 1961; PhD, U. Pavia, 1968. Asst. Politecnico di Milano, Italy, 1968-69, asst. prof., 1969-82, assoc. prof., 1982-86; prof. U. L'Aquila, Italy, 1986-90, U. Brescia, Italy, 1990—; vis. prof. U. Calabria, Cosenza, Italy, 1976-83; rschr. SNIA, Montedison, SISAS, Snamprogetti, Mira Lanza, ICI, Euratom, De Nora, Elk Atochem; project leader Italian Ministry Scientific Rsch., Centro Nazionale delle Ricerche, Ente Nazionale Energie Alternative, European Cmty. Author numerous articles in profl. jours.; patentee in field. Active Comune di Milano, 1991, Comune di Castiglione, Mantova, Italy, 1992. Mem. Soc. Chimica Italiana, Associazione Italiana di Ingegneria Chimica, N.Y. Acad. Scis. Avocation: tennis. Home: Via Carnia 33, 20132 Milan Italy Office: Dip to Chimica Fisica Mater, Via Branze 38, 25133 Brescia Italy

TEMPLE, ARTHUR E., health facility administrator; married; 2 children. BA in Chemistry, Colo. Coll., 1967; BSChemE, Bucknell U., 1969; MBA in Mgmt., NYU, 1974. Project mgr. project mgmt. staff N.Y.C. Bur. Budget, 1972-73; sr. project mgr. housing and devel. adminstrn. project City of N.Y., 1973-74; mem. project mgmt. staf N.Y.C. Bd. Edn., Bklyn., 1974-76; dir. Bur. Pupil Transp. N.Y.C. Bd. Edn., Long Island City, 1976-78; sr. asst. N.Y.C. Health and Hosp. Corp., 1978-80, dir. hosp. billing svcs. dept., 1981; CFO, Queens Hosp. Ctr., Jamaica, N.Y., 1982-85, assoc. exec. dir., 1985-86; CFO, Bellevue Hosp. Ctr., N.Y.C., 1986-91, COO, 1991—; adj. prof. Queens Coll., CUNY, 1986. Sr. policy fellow and mgmt. fellow Nat. Assn. Pub. Hosps. Mem. Am. Coll. Healthcare Execs., Hosp. Fin. Mgmt. Assn. Office: Bellevue Hosp Ctr 462 1st Ave New York NY 10016

TEMPLE, DONALD, allergist, dermatologist; b. Chgo., May 21, 1933; s. Samuel Leonard and Matilda Eve (Riff) T.; m. Sarah Rachel Katz, Sept. 29, 1957; children: Michael A., Matthew D., Madeline B. AB in Biology cum laude, Harvard U., 1954; MD, U. Chgo., 1958. Am. Bd. Allergy and Immunology, Am. Bd. Dermatology, Nat. Bd. Med. Examiners; lic. Intern Michael Reese Hosp., Chgo., 1958-59; resident in dermatology U. Chgo. Hosps., 1959-62; clin. asst., dept. dermatology Boston U. Sch. Medicine, 1963-64; clin. instr. dermatology Stanford U. Sch. Medicine, 1965; preceptee in allergy Offices of Leon Unger, M.D., and Donald Unger, M.D., Chgo., 1965-69; practice medicine specializing in allergy and dermatology Des Plaines, Ill., 1969-76; mem. allergy dept. Glen Ellyn (Ill.) Clinic, 1972—; mem. dermatology and allergy staff, Louis A. Weiss Hosp., Chgo., 1965-73, allergy sect. Loyola U. Med. Ctr., Maywood, Ill., 1977-80, exec. and contract medicine coms. Glen Ellyn; clin. asst. prof. dermatology Abraham Lincoln Sch. Medicine, U. Ill., 1972-75; clin. asst. prof. medicine sect. allergy and dermatology, Loyola U., 1977-85; mem. staff Cen. DuPage Hosp., Winfield, Ill., 1973—, Glen Oaks Med. Ctr., Glendale Heights, Ill., Glendale Heights Community Hosp., 1980-92. Contbr. articles to profl. jours. Bd. dirs. Am. Lung Assn., DuPage, McHenry counties, 1980—; chmn. Contract Medicine, HMO Com., Glen Ellyn Clinic, 1985, mem. exec. com., 1988-92. Fellow Am. Coll. Chest Physicians, Am. Assn. Cert. Allergists, Am. Coll. Allergists, Am. Acad. Allergy, Ill. Soc. Allergy and Clin. Immunology, Chgo. Dermatol. Soc.; mem. AMA, Ill. State Med. Soc., DuPage County Med. Soc., Chgo. Med. Soc. Jewish. Avocations: sailing, investing. Home: 110 E Delaware Pl Apt 2004 Chicago IL 60611-1440 Office: Glen Ellyn Clinic 454 Pennsylvania Ave Glen Ellyn IL 60137-4402

TEMPLE, JOSEPH GEORGE, JR., retired pharmaceutical company executive; b. Bklyn., Aug. 29, 1929; s. Joseph George and Helen Frances (Beney) T.; m. Ann Elizabeth McFerran, June 21, 1952; children: Linda Jo, James, John. BSChemE, Purdue U., 1951, DEng (hon.), 1988. With Dow Chem. Co., Midland, Mich., 1951-89, v.p. mktg., 1976-78, dir., 1979-94; pres. Dow Chem. Latin Am., Coral Gables, Fla., 1978-80; group v.p. human health Dow Chem. Co., Cin., 1980-83; chief exec. officer, pres. Merrell Dow Pharms. Inc., Cin., 1983-87; exec. v.p. Dow Chem. Co., 1983-89; chief exec. officer, chmn. bd. dirs. Merrell Dow Pharms. Inc., Cin., 1988-89; chmn., chief exec. officer Marion Merrell Dow, Inc., Kansas City, Mo., 1989-92, also bd. dirs.; chmn. Marion Merrell Dow Pharms. Inc., 1992-94; vice chmn., 1994-95, ret., 1995; former trustee Com. for Economic Devel. Mem. pres.'s coun. Purdue U., 1978—; bd. fellows Saginaw Valley State U., 1987-89. Recipient Disting. Engr. Alumni award Purdue U., 1978, Outstanding Chem. Engr. award Purdue U., 1993. Mem. Am. Inst. Chem. Engrs., Soc. Plastics Industry (bd. dirs. 1980-82), Pharm. Mfrs. Assn. (bd. dirs. 1981-83), Mgmt. Assn. (Silver Knight award 1976, Gold Knight award 1982). Episcopalian.

TEMPLE, LARRY EUGENE, lawyer; b. Plainview, Tex., Dec. 26, 1935; s. Herman Edward and Grace Eileen (Ivey) T.; m. Laura Louann Atkins, Feb. 23, 1963; children: Laura Allison, John Lawrence. BBA, U. Tex., 1957, LLB with honors, 1959; LLD (hon.), Lamar U., 1985. Bar: Tex., U.S. Dist. Ct. (we. dist.) Tex., U.S. Ct. Appeals (5th cir.), U.S. Supreme Ct. Law clk. to justice Tom Clark U.S. Supreme Ct., Washington, 1959-60; assoc. Powell, Rauhut, McGinnis, Reavley & Lochridge, Austin, Tex., 1960-63; legal adminstrn. asst., exec. asst. Tex. Gov. John B. Connally, Austin, 1963-67; spl. counsel to pres. Lyndon Baines Johnson, Washington, 1967-69; pvt. practice Austin, 1969—; bd. dirs. Temple-Inland, Inc., Guaranty Fed. Bank. Mem. U. Tex. Cancer Found., Houston, 1978-84, U. Tex. Devel. Bd., Austin, 1980-85, 90—, chmn., 1993-95; mem. Tex. Higher Edn. Coordinating Bd., Austin, 1983-89, chmn., 1983-87; chmn. Select Com. for Higher Edn., Austin, 1985-87; bd. dirs. Lyndon B. Johnson Found., 1986—, vice chmn., 1989—; trustee U. Tex. Law Sch. Found., 1989—. Recipient Faculty award U. Tex. Law Sch., 1987, Humanitarian award Austin region NCCJ, 1988, Santa Rita award U. Tex. System, 1989, Disting. Alumnus award U. Tex., Austin, 1990. Fellow Tex. Bar Found.; mem. ABA, Tex. Bar Assn. (chmn. legis. com. 1980, 83-86), Tex. Jr. Bar Assn. (chmn. bd. dirs. 1967), Austin Jr. Bar Assn. (pres. 1962-63). Democrat. Episcopalian. Home: 2606 Escondido Cv Austin TX 78703-1610 Office: 400 W 15th St Ste 1510 Austin TX 78701-1648

TEMPLE, LEE BRETT, architect; b. Balt., June 7, 1956. BArch, Cornell U., 1979. Cert. Nat. Coun. Archtl. Registration Bds. Gen. ptnr. Temple Gebelein Partnership, Ithaca, N.Y., 1981-91; prin. and sole propr. Lee Temple Architect AIA, Ithaca and Crestone, Colo., 1985—; vis. critic dept. architecture Cornell U., Ithaca, 1981; vis. prof. architecture Hobart Coll., 1981-82, prof., 1992-93; asst. prof. architecture Syracuse (N.Y.) U., 1982-87. Prin. works include Athena Residence, Chapelle Frontenac; author: Medieval Town Study, 1981. Chmn. social justice com. Cornell Cath. Cmty., Ithaca, 1989-92, trustee parish coun., 1989-90; mem. founding bd. dirs. Eco Village at Ithaca, 1991-93; mem. steering com. Tibetan Resettlement Project at Ithaca, 1991-92; founder Sustainable Resource Ctr., Crestone, 1993. Recipient 1st prize Storey Com. Compact House Competition, 1983; Eidlitz fellow dept. arch. Cornell U., 1979, 81. Mem. AIA (design excellence award 1987, residential design award 1987, Ctrl. N.Y. chpt.), AIA Colo., N.Y. State Assn. Architects, Cousteau Soc. Home and Office: PO Box 220 Crestone CO 81131

TEMPLE, RILEY KEENE, lawyer; b. Richmond, Va., July 9, 1949; s. David L. Sr. and Helen B. (Jones) T. AB, Lafayette Coll., 1971; JD, Georgetown U., 1974. Bar: Va. 1975, D.C. 1978. Asst. gen. coun. Corp. Pub. Broadcasting, Washington, 1974-77; legis. asst. U.S. Senator Charles Mathias, Washington, 1977-78; sr. counsel RCA Global Comms., N.Y.C., 1978-80; comm. counsel U.S. Senate Com. on Commerce, Sci. & Transp., Washington, 1980-83; asst. v.p. comm. policy Bell Comm. Rsch., Inc., Livingston, N.J., 1983-85; ptnr. Halprin, Temple, Goodman & Sugrue, Washington, 1993—; Oliver Cromwell Cox lectr. Harvard U., Cambridge, Mass., 1983. Pres. bd. dirs. Arena Stage, Whiteman-Walker Clinic, Washington; trustee WETA Pub. TV & Radio, Lafayette Coll., Easton, Pa., Frederick B. Abramson Meml. Found.; mem. cmty. bd. The John F. Kennedy Ctr. for Performing Arts, The Ellington Fund of Duke Ellington Sch. Performing Arts. Mem. Fed. Comm. Bar Assn. Republican. Episcopalian. Office: Halprin Temple & Goodman 1100 New York Ave NW Ste 650 E Washington DC 20005-3934 also: Arena Stage 6th & Maine Ave SW Washington DC 20024

TEMPLE, WAYNE CALHOUN, historian; b. nr. Richwood, Ohio, Feb. 5, 1924; s. Howard M. and Ruby March (Calhoun) T.; m. Lois Marjorie Bridges, Sept. 22, 1956 (dec. Apr. 1978); m. Sunderine Wilson, Apr. 9, 1979; 2 stepsons, James C. Mohn, Randy E. Mohn. A.B. cum laude, U. Ill., 1949, A.M., 1951, Ph.D., 1956; Lincoln Diploma Honor, Lincoln Meml. U., Harrogate, Tenn., 1963. Rsch. asst. history U. Ill., 1949-53, teaching asst., 1953-54; curator ethnohistory Ill. State Mus., 1954-58; editor-in-chief Lincoln Herald, Lincoln Meml. U., 1958-73, assoc. editor, 1973—, also dir. dept. Lincolniana, dir. univ. press, John Wingate Weeks prof. history, 1958-64; with Ill. State Archives, 1964—, now chief dep. dir.; lectr. U.S. Mil. Acad., 1975; Sec.-treas. Nat. Lincoln-Civil War Council, 1958-64; mem. bibliography com. Lincoln Lore, 1958—; hon. mem. Lincoln Sesquicentennial Commn., 1959-60; advisory council U.S. Civil War Centennial Commn., 1960-66; maj. Civil War Press Corps, 1962—. Author: Indian Villages of the Illinois Country: Historic Tribes, 1958, rev. edits., 1966, 77, 87, Lincoln the Railsplitter, 1961, Abraham Lincoln and Others at the St. Nicholas, 1968, Alexander Williamson-Tutor to the Lincoln Boys, 1971, (with others) First Steps to Victory: Grant's March to Naples, 1977, Lincoln and Grant: Illinois Militiamen, 1981, Stephen A. Douglas: Freemason, 1982, Lincoln as a Lecturer, 1982, By Square and Compasses: The Building of Lincoln's Home and Its Saga, 1984, Lincoln's Connections with the Illinois and Michigan Canal, 1986, Dr. Anson G. Henry: Personal Physician to the Lincolns, 1988, Abraham Lincoln: From Skeptic to Prophet, 1995; co-author: Illinois's Fifth Capitol: The House that Lincoln Built, 1988; contbg. author: Capitol Centennial Papers, 1988; editor: Campaigning with Grant, 1961, 72, The Civil War Letters of Henry C. Bear, 1961; 71 radio scripts A. Lincoln 1809-1959, Indian Villages of the Illinois Country: Atlas Supplement, 1975; editorial advisory bd. Am. Biog. Inst., 1971—, Ency. Indians of Ams., 1973—; contbr. to profl. jours., encys. Sponsor Abraham Lincoln Bay, Washington Nat. Cathedral; mem. Ill. State Flag Comm., 1969—; bd. dirs. Vachel Lindsay House; trustee, regent Lincoln Acad. Ill., 1970-82; bd. govs. St. Louis unit Shriners Hosps. for Crippled Children, 1975-81; mem. commissioning com., hon. crew mem. and plank owner USS Springfield submarine, 1990—; hon. crew mem. USS Abraham Lincoln aircraft carrier, 1989—. With U.S. Army, 1943-46, gen. Res. (ret.). Decorated Bronze Star Medal, Silver Citizenship medal SAR, 1993, Literary Merit Gold medal Ill. Lodge of Rsch., 1993; recipient Order of Arrow Boy Scouts Am., 1957, Scouters award, 1960, Scouter's Key, also medallion, 1967, Lincoln medallion Lincoln Sesquicentennial Commn., 1960, award of Achievement U.S. Civil War Centennial Commn., 1965, Algernon Sydney Sullivan medallion, 1969, Distinguished Service award Ill. State Hist. Library, 1969, 77, I.H. Duval Distinguished Service award, 1971, legion of honor Internat. Supreme Council, Order of De Molay, 1972, Disting. Service award Civil War Round Table of Chgo., 1983, 91, Cert. Excellence Ill. State Hist. Soc., 1985; named Hon. Ky. Col., Marshall of Okla. Territory. Fellow Royal Soc. Arts (life); mem. Lincoln Group D.C. (hon.), U. Ill. Alumni Assn., Ill. State Hist. Soc., Board of Advisor, The Lincoln Forum, Ill. Profl. Land Surveyors Assn., Ill. State Dental Soc. (citation plague 1966), Res. Officers Assn., Lincoln Fellowship of Wis., NRA (life), Iron Brigade Assn. (hon. life), Mil. Order Loyal Legion U.S. (hon. companion), Masons (33 degree, meritorious svc. award, Red Cross of Constantine, grand rep. to Grand Lodge of Colo.), Shriners, K.T., Kappa Delta Pi, Phi Alpha, Phi Alpha Theta (Scholarship Key award), Chi Gamma Iota, Tau Kappa Alpha, Alpha Psi Omega, Sigma Pi Beta (Headmaster), Sigma Tau Delta (Gold Honor Key award for editorial writing). Presbyterian (elder). Home: 1121 S 4th Street Ct Springfield IL 62703-2200 Office: Ill State Archives Springfield IL 62756 *Only in America could a poor farm boy from Ohio work his way through a great university, like the University of Illinois, and receive a doctor's degree. Life has been kind to me, and I have tried hard and worked hard. I am proud to be an American.*

TEMPLE, WICK, journalist; b. Little Rock, Oct. 24, 1937; s. Robert Wickliffe and Lorene (Bullard) T.; m. Margaret A. McCay, May 27, 1989; children by previous marriage: Wick III, Ellen Wallace, Carol Halter, Shawn Temple. A.A., Texarkana Coll., 1957; postgrad., U. Tex., 1958-59. Reporter, sports editor Texarkana (Tex.) Gazette-News, 1954-58; reporter Austin (Tex.) American-Statesman, 1958-59; reporter, news editor AP, Little Rock, 1959-65; corr. AP, St. Louis, 1965-66; bur. chief AP, Helena, Mont., 1966-68, Seattle, 1968-73; sports editor AP, N.Y.C., 1973-80, mng. editor, 1980-85, dir. human resources, 1985-88, v.p., 1988, dir. newspaper membership, 1988—. Home: 10 Berkeley Rd Millburn NJ 07041-2012 Office: AP 50 Rockefeller Plz New York NY 10020-1605

TEMPLETON, ALAN ROBERT, biology educator; b. Litchfield, Ill., Feb. 28, 1947; s. John Smith and Lois Arlene (McCormick) T.; m. Bonnie A. Altman, Dec. 20, 1969; children: Jeremy Alan, Jeffrey Alan. BA, Washington U., 1969; MS in Stats., U. Mich., 1972, PhD in Genetics, 1972. Jr. fellow Mich. Soc. Fellows, Ann Arbor, 1972-74; asst. prof. U. Tex., Austin, 1974-77; assoc. prof. Washington U., St. Louis, 1977-81, prof., 1981—; cons. St. Louis Zool. Park, 1979—; founding mem., dir. Soc. for Conservation Biology, 1985—. Editor: Theoretical Population Biology, 1981-91; mem. editorial bd. Molecular Phylogenetics & Evolution, 1991—, Brazilian Jour. of Genetics, 1991—; contbr. numerous article to profl. jours. Grantee NSF, 1974-80, 90—, NIH, 1980—, Nixon Griffis Fund for Zool. Rsch., 1986-87. Mem. Soc. for Study Evolution (v.p. 1982, pres. 1995-96), Genetics Soc. Am., Soc. Conservation Biology (bd. dirs. 1985-88), Nature Conservancy (trustee Mo. chpt. 1988—). Avocations: hiking, caving, music, ethnomusicology, scuba diving. Office: Washington U Dept Biology Saint Louis MO 63130-4899

TEMPLETON, CARSON HOWARD, engineer, policy analyst; b. Wainwright, Alta., Can., Sept. 9, 1917; s. Samuel Howard and Ellen Florence T.; m. Laurie Jean MacLachlan, May 29, 1948; children—Colleen, Neil. B.S., U. Alta., 1943. L.L.D. (hon.), U. Man., 1982; D.E.S. (hon.), U. Waterloo, 1983. Registered profl. engr., B.C., Alta., Man. Chief engr. Greater Winnipeg Dyking Bd., Can., 1948-50; sr. ptnr. Templeton Engring. Co., Winnipeg, 1955-81; pres. Templeton Facilities Ltd., Winnipeg, 1958—; v.p. Teshmont Cons., Inc., Winnipeg, 1970-81; cons. Pub. Utilities Bd. Man., 1962-70. Bd. dirs. Childrens Hosp. Winnipeg, 1958-70; vice chmn. bd. govs. U. Man. Recipient Gzowski medal Engring. Inst. Can., 1951, fellow, 1978; named Officer of the Order of Can. Gov. Gen. of Can., 1978. Mem. Assn. Profl. Engrs. Man. (recipient merit award, named for outstanding service), Assn. Cons. Engrs. Can. (pres. 1968-69).

TEMPLETON, IAN MALCOLM, retired physicist; b. Rugby, Eng., July 31, 1929; emigrated to Can., 1957, naturalized, 1967; s. William and Eleanor Clayton (Butcher) T.; m. Elsa Wood, Aug. 11, 1956; children—Nicola Jean, Jennifer Jane. M.A., Univ. Coll., Oxford, Eng., 1950, D.Phil., 1953. Fellow NRC Can., Ottawa, Ont., 1953-54; asst. rsch. officer NRC Can., 1957-60, assoc. rsch. officer, 1960-64, sr. rsch. officer, 1964-71, prin. rsch. officer, 1971-94, joint head metal physics group, 1969-76, head electronic structure and calorimetry group, 1976-87; mem. staff rsch. lab. Associated Elec. Industries, Rugby, Eng., 1955-57. Contbr. articles to profl. jours. Fellow Inst. Physics, Royal Soc. Can. Home: 17 Dunvegan Rd, Ottawa, ON Canada K1K 3E8

TEMPLETON, JOHN ALEXANDER, II, coal company executive; b. Chgo., Mar. 31, 1927; s. Philip Henry and Florence (Moore) T.; B.S., Ind. U., 1950; m. Norma Frazier, Aug. 10, 1949; children—Lori, Linda, Leslie, Sally. Agt., Conn. Mut. Life Ins. Co., Terre Haute, Ind., 1949-51; ptnr. Miller, Templeton, Scott Ins. Agy., Terre Haute, 1951-64; exec. v.p. Templeton Coal Co., Inc., Terre Haute, 1964-72, pres., 1972-94, elected chmn. 1994, also dir.; pres. Sherwood Templeton Coal Co., Inc., Indpls., 1968—, also dir.; bd. dirs. Plumb Supply Co., Des Moines, 1965—, Dicksons, Inc., Seymour, Ind., 1986—, Franklin (Ind.) Plastic Products Co., 1986; dir. Mchts. Nat. Bank of Terre Haute. Chmn., Vigo County Goldwater for Pres. Com., 1964; trustee Union Hosp., 1968—, v.p., 1975—, chmn. bd. dirs., 1986—; bd. dirs. Ind. State U. Found., 1970—; trustee U. Evansville, 1974-77; bd. of assocs. Rose-Hulman Inst. Tech., 1977; v.p., trustee Ind. Asbury Towers, Greencastle, Ind., 1980-83. Served with U.S. Army, 1946-48. Mem. Ind. Assn. Ins. Agts. (pres. 1959-60), Ind. Coal Assn. (dir.), Lynch Coal Ops. Reciprocal Assn., Interstate Coal Conf., Ind. State C. of C. (bd. dirs. 1981—), Ind. U. Alumni Assn. (exec. council 1983-86). Republican. Methodist. Clubs: Masons, Elks, Scottish Rite.

TEMPLETON, JOHN MARKS, JR., pediatric surgeon, foundation executive; b. N.Y.C. Feb. 19, 1940; s. John Marks and Judith Dudley (Folk) T.; BA, Yale Coll., 1962; MD, Harvard U., 1968; m. Josephine J. Gargiulo, Aug. 2, 1970; children: Heather Erin, Jennifer Ann. Intern, Med. Coll. Va., Richmond, 1968-69, resident, 1969-73; prof. pediatric surgery U. Pa. and Children's Hosp. of Pa., 1995, dir. trauma program, 1989-95; chmn. bd. Templeton Growth Fund, Ltd. Assoc. editor: Textbook of Pediatric Emergencies, 1993. Chmn. health and safety, exec. bd. Cradle of Liberty Coun. Boy Scouts Am.; Ea. Coll., Nat. Recreation Found., Melmark Charitable Found.; nat. bd. dirs., pres. Pa. div. Am. Trauma Soc.; bd. dirs. Layman's Nat. Bible Assn.; pres. John Templeton Found. Served with M.C., USNR, 1975-77. Barclay fellow Templeton Coll. Oxford U. Mem. ACS, AMA, Am. Pediatric Surg. Assn., Am. Acad. Pediatrics, Am. Assn. Surgery of Trauma, Ea. Assn. Surgery of Trauma, Phila. Coll. Physicians, Union League, Nat. Layman's Bible Assn. (bd. dirs.), Merion Cricket Club. Republican. Evangelical. Office: 4 King St West, Toronto, ON Canada M5W 1M3

TEMPLETON, ROBERT EARL, engineering and construction company executive; b. Pitts., June 21, 1931; s. Robert James and Alice Wilma (Scheppele) T.; m. Barbara Ann McDonald, June 9, 1956; children: Shirley Anne (dec.), Susan Elaine, Sally Irene. BSCE, Carnegie Mellon U., 1953, MSCE, 1954; MBA in Mgmt., NYU, 1960. Registered profl. engr., N.Y. With M.W. Kellogg Co., Houston, 1954-93, project engr., 1963-66, mgr. contract status, 1966-68, mgr. sales forecasting, 1968-72, mgr. market forecasting, 1972-73; mgr. Venture Analysis, Houston, 1973-74, mgr. analysis and methods div., 1974-76, mgr. Project Cost Services div., 1976-81, mgr. Cost Mgmt. Services div., 1981-85, project control mgr., 1985-93; pres. Templeton Enterprises, Houston, 1993—; cons. project mgmt. profl., total cost mgmt., work process improvement, reengring., benchmarking, electronic data interchange, Internat. Stds. Orgn., 9000 Quality Sys. Stds., Houston, 1993—. Mem. editl. bd. Engring. and Process Econs., 1976-85. Area chmn. United Campaign, Summit, N.J., 1969-70; v.p. Jefferson Sch. PTA, Summit, 1965-67, pres., 1967-69; security chmn. Fonn Villas Civic Assn., Houston, 1973, chmn. archtl. stds. com., 1974, v.p., 1975, pres., 1976; mem. exec. com., bd. dirs. Houston Advs. for Mentally Ill Children; active Can Care of Houston Inc., For-By-To Cancer Survivors (ch. ministry), Income Tax Assistance (VITA), Tax Counseling for the Elderly (TCE), AARP, Houston. J. Waldo Smith Hydraulic fellow ASCE, 1953-54. Fellow Am. Assn. Cost Engrs. (award of merit 1977, award of recognition 1980, cert. cost engr.; nat. pres. 1971-72, nat. adminstrv. v.p. 1970-71, nat. adv. staff 1973—, spl. projects chmn. 1974-75, cert. bd. chmn. 1976-79, chmn. assn. standards and recommended practices com. 1985-89, chmn. quality mgmt. com. 1988—, chmn. inter-orgnl. liaison com. 1995—); mem. N.Am. Soc. Corporate Planners (program dir. 1974, chmn. ad hoc cert. com. 1986—), Am. Assn. Engring. Socs., Project Mgmt. Inst. (cert. project mgmt. profl., v.p. certification Houston chpt. 1993-94, v.p. edn. 1985-86, 87-88, 91-92, pres. 1988-89, chmn. advisor 1989-90), Sigma XI (Sec. M.W. Kellogg br. 1973-74), Sigma Xi (2d v.p. 1976-77, 84-85, 1st v.p. 1985-86), Houston Comml. Bridge League (v.p. 1973-75), Houston C. of C. (life mem., dir. engring. and constrn. internat. bus. network exec. com.), Am. Mktg. Assn., Acad. for Health Services Mktg. (profl. mem.), Health Services Mktg. Soc. (bd. dirs.), Tau Beta Pi, Beta Theta Pi. Republican. Presbyterian (deacon 1956-59, elder 1980-82). Club: M.W. Kellogg Quarter Century (pres. 1986-87). Home and Office: 12718 Old Oaks Dr Houston TX 77024-4016

TEMPLIN, JOHN LEON, JR., healthcare consulting executive; b. New Brunswick, N.Y., Aug. 5, 1940; s. John Leon and Theresa Veronica (Revolinski) T.; m. Barbara Maria Ribley, Sept. 12, 1970; children: John, Joseph, Kevin, Nan, Danielle, Christopher. BS in Mgmt. Engring., Rensselaer Poly. Inst., 1962, MS in Mgmt., 1969. Cert. healthcare cons. Am. Assn. Healthcare Cons. Mgr. customer svc. Norton Abrasives, Troy, N.Y., 1968-70; cons., sr. cons. Hosp. Assn. N.Y. State, Albany, 1970-79, dir. mgmt. svcs., 1979-80, sr. dir. mgmt. svc., 1981-83; dir. productivity improvement Applied Leadership Technologies, Inc., Greenfield Center, N.Y., 1983-84, v.p., productivity improvement div., 1984-85, pres., 1985-86; pres. Templin Mgmt. Assocs., Inc., Greenfield Center, 1987—, The Northeastern Cons. Alliance, Greenfield Center, 1995—. Editor quar. jour. Healthcare Supr., 1983—; mem. editorial com. ann. Manual for Workload Recording, 1978-91. Mem. budget com. Greater Saratoga Sch. Dist., Saratoga Springs, N.Y., 1978-79; mem. energy com. Blue Cross Assn., Chgo., 1978-81; mem. Gov.'s Task Force on Nursing, Albany, 1980; mem. parish coun. St. Joseph's Ch., Greenfield Center, 1981-87. Capt. U.S. Army, 1962-64. Fellow Am. Coll. Healthcare Execs., Healthcare Info. and Mgmt. Sys. Soc. (liaison Coll. Am. Pathologists 1978-91); mem. Am. Hosp. Assn. (seminar spkr. 1980-93), Clin. Lab. Mgmt. Assn. (bd. dirs. 1980-84), KC. Republican. Roman Catholic. Avocations: karate, golf, computers, gardening, fishing. Home and Office: Templin Mgmt Assocs Inc 265 Locust Grove Rd Greenfield Center NY 12833-1501

TEMPLIN, KENNETH ELWOOD, paper company executive; b. Mason City, Nebr., Jan. 26, 1927; s. Otto Rudolph and Marianna (Graf) T.; m. Harriet Elaine Ressel, Aug. 24, 1951; children: Steven, David, Daniel, Benjamin, Elizabeth. B.S. in Bus. Adminstrn, U. Nebr., 1950; M.B.A., Wayne State U., 1961. Fin. analyst Ford Motor Co., 1950-54; fin. analyst, corp. staff Chrysler Corp., 1955-60, div. controller marine engine div., 1961-63, gen. sales mgr., 1964-65; v.p. Marsh and Templin, N.Y.C., 1966-69; v.p., gen. mgr. operating group Saxon Industries, N.Y.C., 1970-79; group v.p. Saxon Industries, 1979-82, sr. v.p., 1982-85; v.p.-converting Paper Corp. Am., Wayne, Pa., 1985-86; exec. v.p. Quality Park Products Inc., St. Paul, 1986-88, 1986-88, pres., 1988—; mem. exec. com. Single Service Inst., 1971-79. Regional chmn. Minn. devel. com. Nat. Multiple Sclerosis Soc., 1970-71; co-pres. Home and Sch. Assn., Bernardsville, N.J., 1975-76. Served with U.S. Army, 1945-47, 50-51. Mem. Envelope Mfrs. Assn. Am. (postal affairs com. 1989—, fin. com. chmn. 1994-95, bd. dirs. 1990-91, 93-95). Presbyterian. Home: 3993 County Rd 42 NE Alexandria MN 56308

TENAGLIA, JOHN FRANC, broadcasting executive; b. Clairton, Pa., Jan. 17, 1935; s. Fileno Albert and Gina (Zucconi) T.; m. Judith Ann Droder, June 30, 1962; children: Christine Mary, Lisa Ann. BBA, U. Pitts., 1958. Gen. mgr. local affiliate ABC, Pitts., 1959-69; exec. v.p. GCC Communications Inc., Boston, 1970-80; prin. owner, pres., chief exec. officer TK Communications Inc., Bala Cynwyd, Pa., 1980—; bd. dirs. WK Cable, Junction City, Kans. Served with U.S. Army, 1954-56. Mem. Nat. Assn. Broadcasters. Republican. Roman Catholic. Avocations: skiing, golf, boating. Office: Sta WSRF-AM 3000 SW 60th Ave Fort Lauderdale FL 33314-1783

TENAZAS, LUCILLE LOZADA, graphic designer; b. Aklan, The Philippines, Dec. 17, 1953; came to U.S., 1979; d. Audines Torrefiel and Lamberta (Lozada) T.; m. Richard David Barnes, July 3, 1990; 1 child, Maximilian. BFA, Coll. of Holy Spirit, The Philippines, 1975; postgrad., Calif. Coll. Arts & Crafts, 1979; MFA, Cranbrook Acad. Art, 1982. Owner, prin. Tenazas Design, San Francisco, 1986—; adj. prof. Calif. Coll. Arts and Crafts, San Francisco, 1985—; lectr. Icograda Conf. Lisbon, 1995, Soc. Graphic Designers Can., Vancouver, Edmonton, 1995; vis. faculty Yale U., R.I. Sch. Design, Calif. Inst. of Arts. Art dir. (book) The Body: Photographs of the Human Form, 1994, Witness: Endangered Species of North America, 1994; juror design and architecture competitions. Mem. Champion Internat. Design Coun., Stamford, Conn., 1995—; panelist design arts Nat. Endowment for Arts, Washington, 1991-94; bd.dirs. Am. Inst. Graphic Arts, N.Y.C., 1992-95. Mem. Headlands Ctr. for Arts (bd. dirs.). Avocations: travel, reading, cultural activities. Office: Lucille Tenazas Design 605 3rd St Ste 208 San Francisco CA 94107-1911

TEN CATE, ARNOLD RICHARD, dentistry educator; b. Accrington, Lancashire, Eng., Oct. 21, 1933; s. Gys Johan and Lien (Dalenoord) Ten C.; m. Alice Mitchell, Apr. 7, 1956 (dec.); children: Pauline Ann, Jill Elaine, Ian Richard. B.Sc., U. London, 1955, Ph.D. in Anatomy, 1957, B.D.S., 1960; DSc (hon.), McGill U., 1989, U. Western Ont., 1989; DDS (hon.), Nihon U., 1995. Leverhulme fellow in dental sci. Royal Coll. Surgeons, Eng., 1961-63; sr. lectr. in anatomy in relation to dentistry Guy's Hosp. Med. Sch., U. London, 1963-68; prof. dentistry Faculty Dentistry, U. Toronto, Ont., Can., 1968-77; chmn. div. biol. scis. Faculty Dentistry, U. Toronto, 1971-77, dean, 1977-89, vice provost health scis., 1989-94; Chmn. bd. dirs. Aboutface, Oralife Group. Author: Advanced Dental Histology, 4th edit., 1983, Oral Histology, Development, Structure and Function, 1980, 4th edit., 1994; others, also articles. Recipient Colyer prize Royal Soc. Medicine, 1962; Mil. Hellman award Am. Assn. Orthodontists, 1975. Mem. Internat. Assn. Dental Research (pres. 1984, Isaac Schour Meml. award 1978). Conservative. Mem. Christian Ch. Home: 50 Squire Baker's Ln, Markham, ON Canada L3P 3G9 Office: Faculty of Dentistry, 123 Edward St, Toronto, ON Canada M5G 1G6

TENDLER, DAVID, international trade company executive; b. N.Y.C., Jan. 15, 1938; s. Philip and Pearl (Berman) T.; m. Beatrice Weisberg, Oct. 11, 1958; children: Pearl, Karen. BBA in Internat. Econs., CCNY, 1959. With Philipp Bros. Co., 1960—, mgr. Far Eastern ops., 1968-75; pres. Philipp Bros. Co., N.Y.C., 1975—; dir. parent corp. Engelhard Minerals & Chems. Corp. (name changed to Phibro Corp. 1981), N.Y.C., 1975-85; vice chmn. bd. Engelhard Minerals & Chems. Corp. (name changed to Phibro Corp. 1981), 1979-81, chmn. bd., chief exec. officer, 1981—; co-chmn., co-chief exec. officer Phibro-Salomon Inc., 1983-84; founder Tendler Beretz Assocs. Ltd., 1985—; chmn. subcom. trade U.S.-German Dem. Rep. Trade and Econ. Coun., 1978-84; bd. dirs., mem. exec. com. U.S./USSR Trade and Econ. Coun., 1979-85, U.S.-China Bus. Coun., 1983-94; bd. dirs. Biotech. Gen. Corp., Iselin, N.J.; chmn. bd. dirs. Melville Biologics Inc., L.I., N.Y. Mem. bd. overseers NYU Grad. Sch. Bus., 1981-85; trustee Lenox Hill Hosp., 1981-94; mem. exec. com. N.Y. Blood Ctr., 1987—; bd. dirs., mem. exec. com. Fgn. Policy Assn., 1983-96. Recipient Torch of Liberty award metals and metal products div. Anti-Defamation League, 1976, Edith and Herbert Lehman award Henry St. Settlement, 1982; named Man of Yr., Fgn. Trade Soc., Baruch Coll., CUNY, 1985. Office: Tendler Beretz Assocs 101 E 52nd St New York NY 10022-6018

TENDLER, PAUL MARC, lawyer; b. N.Y.C., Oct. 22, 1943; s. Leonard and Gladys (Steisel) T.; m. Elaine Lynn Isaacson, Mar. 28, 1971; children: Jamie Meredith, Seth Evan. B.A., Queens Coll., N.Y.C., 1965; M.S., So. Ill. U., Carbondale, 1966; J.D., Howard U., 1969; postgrad. U. Pitts., 1969-70. Bar: D.C. 1980. Press asst to Congressman Begich, Washington, 1971; legis. asst. to Congressman Halpern, Washington, 1972, Congressman Rinaldo, 1973; dir. legis. rsch. Cost of Living Council, Washington, 1973-74; asst. dir. govt. affairs Am. Nurses Assn., Washington, 1974-75; pres. Paul Tendler Assocs., Washington, 1975—; mng. ptnr. Tendler & Biggins, 1982-89; ptnr. Tendler, Goldberg, Biggins & Geltzer, 1989—; adj. prof. Georgetown U., 1980-83, asst. prof., 1975-80; dir. bus. program Trinity Coll., Washington, 1983-86. Author: The Federal Government at Work, 1976; An LPNs Guide to the Federal Government, 1978, 84. Ford Found. scholar, 1967-69. Mem. D.C. Bar Assn., Am. Arbitration Assn., ABA, Assn. Trial Lawyers Am., Delta Sigma Rho, Tau Kappa Alpha. Democrat. Jewish. Home and Office: 1090 Vermont Ave NW Washington DC 20005-4905

TENENBAUM, IRVING, lawyer, judge; b. Woodbourne, N.Y., Oct. 24, 1908; s. Joseph and Anna (Friedman) T.; m. Gertrude Lyman, Mar. 31, 1935 (dec. Feb. 1973); m. Hannah Cohn, Nov. 22, 1977; 1 child, Kenneth Jay. Student, CCNY, 1925-26, Fordham U., 1926-28; LLB, Fordham U., 1931. Bar: N.Y. 1934, U.S. Dist. Ct. (so. dist.) N.Y. 1937, U.S. Treasury Dept. 1938, Immigration & Naturalization 1940, U.S. Dist. Ct. (ea. dist.) N.Y. 1953, U.S. Supreme Ct. 1967, U.S. Ct. Appeals (2d cir.) 1970. Revision clk. state senate State of N.Y., Albany, 1933-38; ptnr. Lyman & Tenenbaum, P.C., Garden City, N.Y., 1934—; acting village justice Roslyn (N.Y.) Village Ct., 1967—, Great Neck (N.Y.) Village Ct., 1986-88; village justice Great Neck Plaza Ct., 1983—; acting city judge Long Beach (N.Y.) City Ct., 1987, Glen Cove (N.Y.) City Ct., 1988; jud. hearing officer Supreme and County Cts., Mineola, N.Y., 1987-90; of counsel Great Neck Sewer Dist., 1968-75; lectr., adminstr., cons. Office of Ct. Adminstrn., Albany, 1984—; referee all cts. State of N.Y., 1934—; cons. numerous law firms, N.Y.C., 1950—. Contbr. numerous articles to law jours. Recipient Frank A. Gulotta Criminal Justice award Asst. Dist. Atty's Office State of N.Y. 1988. Mem. N.Y. State Bar Assn. (jud. sect.), Bronx Bar Assn. (50th yr. award 1984), Nassau Bar Assn. (50th yr. award 1984, svc. award 1975), Nassau Magistrates Assn. (magistrate of yr. 1986), N.Y. State Magistrates Assn. (disting. jurist and dean 1983, magistrate of yr. 1986), Kiwanis (pres. Great Neck club 1954-55, lt. gov. internat. club 1955-56), Temple Israel. Jewish. Avocations: reading, writing, lecturing, fishing, enjoying outdoors. Home: 22 Park Pl Great Neck NY 11021-5012 Office: Lyman & Tenenbaum PC 350 Old Country Rd Garden City NY 11530-1701

TENENBAUM, MICHAEL, steel company executive; b. St. Paul, July 23, 1913; s. Harry and Ida Vivian (Kolohoski) T.; m. Helen Zlatovski, Aug. 16, 1941 (div. 1981); children: Susan Rose Tenenbaum Uyama, Anne Louise Benjamin; m. Martha Smith Berner, July 30, 1982. Met.E., U. Minn., 1936, M.S., 1937, Ph.D., 1940; D.Sc. hon., Northwestern U., 1976. Metallurgist Inland Steel Co., East Chicago, Ind., 1940-50, mgr., 1950-65; v.p. Inland Steel Co., Chgo., 1965-71, pres., 1971-78, dir., 1971-84; cons., 1984—. Fellow AIME (hon., Hunt and Raymond award 1949), Am. Soc. Metals (disting. mem.); mem. The Metall. Soc. (pres.), Western Soc. Engrs. (Washington award 1976), Brit. Metals Soc. (Bessemer Gold medal 1980), Assn. Iron and Steel Engrs., Am. Iron and Steel Inst., Nat. Acad. Engring. Home: 4049 220th Pl SE Issaquah WA 98029-7212

TENER, CAROL JOAN, retired secondary education educator; b. Cleve., Feb. 10, 1935; d. Peter Paul and Mamie Christine (Dombrowski) Manusack; m. Dale Keith Tener, Feb. 13, 1958 (div. Aug. 1991); children: Dean Robert, Susan Dawn. Student, Cleve. Mus. Art, 1949-53, Cleve. Art Inst., 1953-54; BS in Edn. cum laude, Kent State U., 1957; MS in Supervision, Akron U., 1974; postgrad., Kent State U., 1964, 81, 88-90, Akron U., 1975, 79, John Carroll U., 1982, 83, 85-86, Ohio U., 1987, Baldwin Wallace Coll., 1989. Cert. permanent K-12 tchr., Ohio. Stenographer Equitable Life Iowa, Cleve., 1953-54; tchr. elem. art Cuyahoga Falls (Ohio) Bd. Edn., 1957-58, 62-63, 1965-68, tchr. jr. h.s., 1968-69; tchr. h.s. Brecksville (Ohio)-Broadview Heights Sch. Dist., 1969-94; chmn. dept. art Brecksville-Broadview Heights (Ohio) H.S., 1979-94; ret., chmn. curriculum devel., 1982, 89; instr. for children Kent State U., 1956; advisor, prodr. cmty. svc. in art Brecksville Broadview Heights Bd. of Edn., 1969-94; former tchr. recreation and adult art edn. 1967-68, City of Cuyahoga Falls, 1967-68; com. mem. North Ctrl. Evaluation Com., Nordonia City, Ohio, 1978, Solon City, Ohio, 1989; chmn. north ctrl. evaluation com. Garfield Heights H.S., 1991; chair pilot program curriculum devel. com. in art/econs. Brecksville-Broadview Heights H.S., 1985, 86. Contbr. articles to newspapers, brochures, mags.; commd. artist for mural Brecksville City's Kids Quarters, 1994, Christopher Columbus/John Glen portraits in relief commemorating Columbus Day, 1961, Wooster (Ohio) Products Co. Chmn. Artmart Invitational Exhibit PTA, 1982—; active Meals on Wheels, Brecksville Broadview, Cancer, Leukemia, Heart Disease collection, Stow-Glen Assisted Living Visitations, NCR Assisted Living transp. provision to hosps. and dr. in neighboring county; trustee Gettysburg Devel. Block Group Parma, Kids Quarters, 1994. Recipient Ohio Coun. on Econ. Edn. award, 1985-86, award for significant svc. to cmty. Retired and Sr. Vol. Program of USA, 1996; Pres.'s scholar Kent State U., 1954-57. Mem. ASCD, Nat. Art Edn. Assn., Ohio Ret. Tchrs. Assn., Internat. Platform Assn., Brecksville Edn. Assn., Acad. Econ. Edn., Cleve. Mus. Art, NAFE, Nat. Mus. Women in Arts, S.W. Area Retired Educators (program chair 1996—), Phi Delta Kappa Pi. Roman Catholic. Avocations: European and American museum tours, photography, collecting books on architecture, painting. Home: 7301 Sagamore Rd Parma OH 44134-5732

TENG, JULIET, artist; d. Teng Lenten and Ho Wai Yu; children: Brendan, Trish, Jamie, Stacy, Phaeleau. B Commerce, U. Rangoon. Programmer First Boston Corp., N.Y.C.; systems programmer Chase Manhattan, N.Y.C., Merrill Lynch, Pierce, Fenner & Smith, Inc., N.Y.C.; artist/painter, 1976—. Exhbns. include Nat. Arts Club, N.Y.C., Pastel Soc. Am., N.Y.C., Audubon Artists Soc., N.Y.C., Catherine Lorrilard Wolf Art Club, N.Y.C., Painters and Sculptors Soc. N.J., N.Y.C., Knickerbocker Artists Am. Soc., N.Y.C., Keene-Mason Galleries, N.Y.C., Nat. Art Ctr., N.Y.C., Hudson Valley Art Assn., Westchester, N.Y., Manchester Art Ctr., Vt., Five Point Gallery, East Chatham, N.Y., Connoisseur Gallery, Rhinebeck, N.Y., Ridgewood Art Inst., N.J., The New England Fine Art Inst., Boston, numerous others. Mem. Nat. Arts Club, Art Students League. Avocations: Flamenco dance, ballroom dance, fashion designing, gardening, carpentry. Home: 34 Sesame St Old Chatham NY 12136

TENGI, FRANK R., lawyer, insurance company executive; b. Garfield, N.J., Aug. 11, 1920; s. John and Mary (Fedush) T.; m. Shirley H. Mitchell, May 17, 1952; children: Christopher, Nancy. BS, Georgetown U., 1946; LLD, Fordham U., 1951. CPA, N.J. Bar: N.Y. 1955, U.S. Supreme Ct. 1967, U.S. Ct. Claims 1967, U.S. Dist. Ct. (so. dist.) N.Y. 1967, U.S. Dist. Ct. (ea. dist.) N.Y., 1967, U.S. Tax Ct. 1968. Asst. sec. Am. Internat. Aviation Agy., Inc., N.Y.C., 1961-69; assoc. Lee Mulderig & Celentano, N.Y.C., 1965-70; asst. sec. Am. Internat. Underwriting Corp., N.Y.C., 1965—, Am. Internat. Underwriters Assn., 1965—, Starr Tech. Risks Agy., Inc., 1967-78; asst. comptroller taxation A.I.G., Inc., N.Y.C., 1971-75; asst. sec. C.V. Starr & Co., Inc., N.Y.C., 1965—; pres. Estate Maintenance Co., Inc., N.Y.C., 1969-71; mgr. reinsurance security World-wide, Am. Internat. Group, Inc., N.Y.C., 1978—. Mem. Mayor's Budget Adv. Com. Plainfield, 1980-81. Treas., Starr Found., 1970—. Served with U.S. Army, 1941-46; ETO. Mem. N.Y. State Bar Assn., Tax Execs. Inst. Home: 17 Madison Ave Apt 58 Madison NJ 07940-1466 Office: 70 Pine St New York NY 10270-0002

TENHOEVE, THOMAS, academic administrator; b. Bklyn., Oct. 1, 1935; s. Thomas and Adeline Ruth (Vander Hill) T.; m. Suzanne Underwood, June 7, 1957; children: Thomas III, Carol, Timothy. AB, Hope Coll., 1956; MA, U. Mich., 1957; PhD, U. Toledo, 1965; postgrad., U. Western Mich. Biology tchr. South Haven. Mich. Pub. Schs., 1957-58; biology instr. Northwestern Coll., Orange City, Iowa, 1958-63; supr. biology students U. Toledo, Ohio, 1963-65; acad. dean, acting pres. Northwestern Coll., Orange City, 1965-70; pres. Butler (Pa.) County Community Coll., 1970-84, Oakton Community Coll., Des Plaines, Ill., 1984-95. Bd. dirs. Sister Cities, 1986-95; trustee Northwestern Coll., 1988-95; mem. Ill. C.C. State Found. Bd., 1993-95, Ill. Math. and Sci. Acad. Selection Bd., 1986, 87, Cook County Sheriff's Scholarship Panel; exec. com. Golden Corridor, 1986-92. Recipient Pacesetter award Nat. Coun. for Community Rels., 1986, Orchard Village award. Mem. Am. Coun. on Internat. Intercultural Edn. (chmn. 1992-95), Coun. North Ctrl. Two-Yr. Colls. (state rep. 1988-92, exec. bd. 1989-95, 2d v.p. 1990-91, 1st v.p. 1991-92, pres. 1992-93).

TENNANT, JOHN RANDALL, management advisory company executive; b. North Bend, Wash., Aug. 23, 1940; s. Maurice Andrew and Jane Downing (Vinnedge) T.; m. Nikki Mae Priem, July 17, 1965 (div.); children: Ann Elizabeth, Randall Warren; m. Deborah Ann Francis, Oct. 25, 1986 (div.); 1 child, Alyssa Jane. B.S. in Indsl. Engring., Stanford U., 1962; M.B.A., U. Wash., 1966. Registered profl. engr., Wash. Sr. research engr. Boeing Co., Seattle, 1962-68; mgr. Price Waterhouse, Seattle, 1968-73; ptnr. Price Waterhouse, Tokyo, 1973-79, Los Angeles, 1979-89; founder, chief exec. officer Manex, Inc., Newport Beach, Calif., 1989—; dir. subs. Price Waterhouse Assocs., Pacific region, 1975-79. Mem. John Tracy Clinic Men's Com., Santa Catalina Island Conservancy, pres., 1985-87. Mem. NSPE, Japan Computer Assn. (founder, pres. 1976-77), Japan Modapts Assn. (founder), Japan Am. Soc., Inst. Mgmt. Cons., Am. Inst. Indsl. Engrs. (pres. Seattle chpt. 1970-71), Data Processing Mgmt. Assn., Tokyo Lawn and Tennis Club, L.A. Country Club, Jonathan Club, Empty Saddle Club, Los Rancheros Visitadores Club, Los Caballeros Club. Home: 13928 Tahiti Way Apt 111 Marina Del Rey CA 90292

TENNANT, THOMAS MICHAEL, lawyer; b. Anniston, Ala., July 23, 1948; s. Thomas Edward and Mary Eugenia (Warren) T.; m. Sharon Leigh Ebert, Mar. 21, 1970; children: Sharon Michelle, Michael Ebert. BS, Auburn U., 1970; JD, Walter F. George Sch. Law, 1973. Assoc. Webb, Fowler & Tanner, Lawrenceville, Ga., 1973-76, ptnr., 1976-77; mng. ptnr. Tennant, Andersen & Davidson, P.C., Lawrenceville, 1978-81, Tennant, Andersen, Davidson & Edmondson, P.C., Lawrenceville, 1982-85, Tennant, Davidson & Edmondson, P.C., Lawrenceville, 1985-86, Tennant, Davidson & Thompson, P.C., Lawrenceville, 1986-87, Tennant, Davidson, Thompson & Sweeny, Lawrenceville, 1987-89, Tennant, Thompson & Sweeny, 1990, Alston & Bird, Atlanta, 1991—; judge Recorder's Ct., Lawrenceville, 1979-80; mem. State Disciplinary Bd., 1988-91. Bd. dirs. Gwinnett Found., Inc., Lawrenceville, 1984—. Served to 1st lt. U.S. Army, 1970-78. Mem. State Bar Ga. (chmn. lawyer ethics com. young lawyers sect. 1979-80, bd. govs. 1986-92), Gwinnett County Bar Assn. (pres. 1978), Ga. Trial Lawyers Assn., Atlanta Lawyers Club, Gwinnett County C. of C. (pres. 1986). Presbyterian. Home: 4069 Nobleman Pt Duluth GA 30136-2363 Office: Alston & Bird One Atlantic Ctr 1201 W Peachtree St Atlanta GA 30309-3424

TENNE, DONALD PAUL, financial planner; b. Bronx, N.Y., Nov. 28, 1954; s. Gerard Lawrence and Rita Rose (Delli Bovi) T.; m. Marybeth Rose Taylor, Oct. 12, 1985. Grad., Adirondack C.C., 1973-75. Account rep. Met. Ins. Co., Glens Falls, N.Y., 1982-87; fin. planner MetLife, Glens Falls, N.Y., 1987—; fin. editor Sta. WCKM Radio, Lake George, N.Y., 1994—; instr. Skidmore Coll., Saratoga, N.Y., 1989—, Boces, Hudson Falls, N.Y., 1989—; Metlife Leader's Conf. qualifier, 1994-96. Guest columnist Glens Falls Bus. Jour., 1990. Fund raising com. Literacy Vols. of Glens Falls, 1990-93. Mem. Glens Falls Masons (master), Fort Edward/Hudson Falls Elks, Nat. Assn. of Life Underwriters, Nat. Assn. of Securities Dealers. Avocations: softball, tennis. Office: MetLife Securities Inc 420 Glen St Glens Falls NY 12801-2929

TENNENBAUM, MICHAEL ERNEST, investment banker; b. St. Petersburg, Fla., Sept. 17, 1935; s. Reubin and Frieda (Miller) T.; m. Suzanne Stockfisch; children by previous marriage—Mark Stephen, Andrew Richard. B.S., Ga. Inst. Tech., 1958; M.B.A. with honors, Harvard U., 1962. Assoc. Burnham & Co., N.Y.C., 1962-64; assoc. Bear, Stearns & Co., N.Y.C., 1964-69, sr. mng. dir., 1969—, vice chmn. investment banking div., 1988-93; chmn. bd. dirs. Tech. Park, Atlanta, 1978-81, Ariz. City Devel. Co., 1978—. Bd. govs., nat. bd. trustees Boys and Girls Clubs Am.; mem. nat. adv. bd. Ga. Inst. Tech., 1971-77; mem. vis. com./Harvard U. Sch. Bus., Cambridge, Mass., 1986-92, bd. assocs., 1992—; bd. trustees Ga. Inst. Tech. Found., Inc., Atlanta, 1988—; bd. dirs. Joffrey Ballet, 1990-92, chmn. exec. com., 1991-92; bd. dirs. Music Ctr. L.A. County Unified Fund Cabinet, 1990-91; chmn. L.A. Mayor's Spl. Adv. Com. on Fiscal Adminstrn., 1993-94; commr. Calif. Intercity HighSpeed Ground Transp. Commn. Mem. Malibu Racquet Club. Home: 118 Malibu Colony Rd Malibu CA 90265-4642 Office: 32d Fl 1999 Avenue Of The Stars Fl 32 Los Angeles CA 90067-6022 *The older I get, the luckier I feel.*

TENNENT, VALENTINE LESLIE, accountant; b. Apia, Western Samoa, Apr. 5, 1919; came to U.S., 1922; s. Hugh Cowper and Madge Grace (Cook) T.; m. Jeanne Marie Elder, Dec. 10, 1941; children: Madeline Jeanne Walls, Hugh Cowper II, Michael Waller, Val Leslie, Paul Anthony. Student, U. Calif., Berkeley, 1938-40. CPA, Hawaii, La. Mgr. Tennent & Greaney, CPAs, Hilo, Hawaii, 1945-50; ptnr. Cameron, Tennent & Dunn, CPAs, Honolulu, 1950-56; ptnr. KPMG Peat Marwick LLP, Honolulu, 1956-79, cons., 1979-84; ind. rschr. pub. fin. and banking, politico-econ. sci., moral philosophy, San Diego, 1984—. Founding trustee, pres., treas. Tennent Art Found., Honolulu, 1955-77; trustee, treas. Watumull Found., Honolulu, 1963-90; bd. dirs. Iolani Sch., Inst. for Human Svcs., Honolulu, Lyman Mus., Hilo. Capt. USAF, 1941-45. Recipient Bishop's Cross for disting. svc. Protestant Episcopal Ch., Dist. Hawaii, 1965. Mem. AICPA (governing coun. 1961-64), Hawaii Soc. CPAs (pres. 1960). Episcopalian. Avocations: swimming, fine arts, music, literature. Home and Office: 700 Front St Unit 1607 San Diego CA 92101-6011 *Joy in life comes from knowing the things you want to accomplish within God's overall purpose, pursuing them to the end regardless of difficulties, and accepting full responsibility for inevitable failures.*

TENNEY, DUDLEY BRADSTREET, lawyer; b. N.Y.C., July 13, 1918; s. Parker Gillespie and Josephine (Keeler) T.; m. Margaret Carter, June 13, 1941 (div. Oct. 1977); children: Ann, Janet Greene; m. Dorothy Walsh, Jan. 7, 1978 (dec. Sept. 1982); m. Joyce McPherson, Jan. 4, 1986. A.B. summa cum laude, Oberlin Coll., 1939; J.D. magna cum laude, Harvard U., 1942. Bar: N.Y. 1948. Assoc. firm Cahill, Gordon & Reindel, N.Y.C., 1946-54, ptnr., 1955-86. Pres.: Harvard U. Law Rev., 1941-42. Served to maj. AUS, 1942-46, CBI. Mem. ABA, Assn. Bar City of N.Y., World Trade Ctr. Club (N.Y.C.), Manhasset Bay Yacht Club (Port Washington, N.Y.). Home: Wood Rd Harbor Acr Port Washington NY 11050 Office: Cahill Gordon & Reindel 80 Pine St New York NY 10005-1702

TENNEY, STEPHEN MARSH, physiologist, educator; b. Bloomington, Ill., Oct. 22, 1922; s. Harry Houser and Caroline (Marsh) T.; m. Carolyn Cartwright, Oct. 18, 1947; children: Joyce B., Karen M., Stephen M. AB, Dartmouth; MD, Cornell U.; ScD (hon.), U. Rochester. From instr. to assoc. prof. of medicine and physiology U. Rochester Sch. Medicine, 1951-56; prof. physiology Dartmouth Med. Sch., Hanover, N.H., 1956-74; dean Dartmouth Med. Sch., 1960-62, acting dean, 1966, 73, dir. med. scis., 1957-59, chmn. dept. physiology, 1956-77, Nathan Smith prof. physiology, 1974-88, Nathan Smith prof. emeritus, 1988—; med. dir. Parker B. Francis Found., 1975-83, exec. v.p., 1984-89; Chmn. physiology study sect. NIH, 1962-65; tng. com. Nat. Heart Inst., 1968-71; mem. exec. com. NRC; mem. physiology panel NIH study Office Sci. and Tech.; mem. regulatory biology panel NSF, 1971-75; chmn. bd. sci. counselors Nat. Heart and Lung Inst., 1974-78; chmn. Commn. Respiratory Physiology Internat. Union Physiol. Scis. Asso. editor: Jour. Applied Physiology, 1976—, Handbook of Physiology; notes editor: News in Physiol. Sci., 1989—; editorial bd.: Am. Jour. Physiology, Circulation Research, Physiol. Revs; Contbr. articles to sci. jours. Served with USNR, 1947-49; sr. med. officer Shanghai. Markle scholar in med. sci., 1954-59; recipient Disting. Achievement award Dartmouth, 1994. Fellow Am. Acad. Arts and Scis., AAAS; mem. Inst. Medicine of Nat. Acad. Scis., Am. Physiol. Soc., Am. Soc. Clin. Investigation, N.Y. Acad. Scis., Gerontol. Soc., Am. Heart Assn., Assn. Am. Med. Colls., , Alpha Omega Alpha, Sigma Xi.

TENNEY, TOM FRED, bishop; b. DeRidder, La., Dec. 6, 1933; s. Fred and Jenny Veve (Nichols) T.; m. Thetus Pearl Caughron, Dec. 27, 1952; children: Tom Gregory, Teri Denise Tenney Spears. Student, Apostolic Bible Inst., St. Paul, 1952; DD (hon.), 1992. Ordained to ministry United Pentecostal Ch., 1954. Pastor United Pentecostal Ch., Monroe, La., 1953-56, DeRidder, 1976-78; youth pres. La. dist. United Pentecostal Ch., 1953-60; dist. supt. for La. United Pentecostal Ch., Tioga, 1978—; youth pres. United Pentecostal Ch., Internat., St. Louis, 1960-69, dir. fgn. missions, mem. exec. bd., 1969-76, mem. gen. bd., 1978—; internat. radio speaker Harvestime, St. Louis, 1976-78. Author: Pentecost: What's That?, 1975, The Flame Still Burns, 1989, The Main Thing, 1993, Advice to Pastors and Other Saints, 1995. Trustee Tupelo (Miss.) Children's Mansion, Spirit of Freedom, Metairie, La., Lighthouse Ranch for Boys, Hammond, La. Democrat. Home and Office: PO Box 248 Tioga LA 71477-0248

TENNIES, ROBERT HUNTER, headmaster; b. Bogotá, Colombia, Aug. 19, 1952; s. Leo C. and Ruth (Winston) T.; m. Ruth Ellen Fischer, June 14, 1975; children: Debbie, Julie. BS, Wheaton (Ill.) Coll., 1973; MA, U. South Fla., 1975; EdS, Fla. Atlantic U., 1978, EdD, 1982. Sci. tchr. Cypress Lake Middle Sch., Ft. Myers, Fla., 1973-77; sci. tchr. Boca Raton (Fla.) Christian Sch., 1977-78, asst. adminstr., 1978-84, headmaster, 1984—, min. of children, 1984-90; interim. min. of edn., 1991-93; Spkr. Internat. Conf. Religious Edn., Petrozavodsk, Russia. Recipient Excellence in Edn. award Nat. Assn. Elem. Prins., 1990. Mem. Nat. Sci. Tchrs. Assn., Assn. of Christian Schs. Internat. (accreditation commn.), Nat. Assn. Elem. Sch. Prins. Avocation: camping. Home: 2415 NW 30th Rd Boca Raton FL 33431-6214 Office: Boca Raton Christian Sch 600 NW 4th Ave Boca Raton FL 33432-3670

TENNIS, CALVIN CABELL, bishop. Bishop Episcopal Ch., Wilmington, Del., 1986—. Office: Diocesan Office 2020 N Tatnall St Wilmington DE 19802-4821

TENNSTEDT, KLAUS, conductor; b. Merseburg, Germany, June 6, 1926. Formerly gen. music dir. Dresden Opera, and dir., State Orch. and Theatre in Schwerin, Ger.; gen. music dir. and resident condr. Buehnen der Landeshauptstadt Kiel, Ger., N.Am. debut, Toronto Symphony, U.S. debut, Boston Symphony, 1974; named prin. guest condr. Minn. Orch., 1978, has since conducted all major orchs. of world including Cleve. Symphony, Phila. Orch., N.Y. Philharm., Chgo. Symphony, Berlin Philharm., Israel Philharm., Swedish Radio Orchestra,, Metropolitan Opera; prin. guest condr. The London Philharm., music dir. 1983-87, condr. laureate, 1987—; chief condr. Norddeutscher Rundfunk Orchestra, 1979; recordings include Complete Symphonies of Mahler. Home: Roesoll 13, Heikendorf 2305 Kiel Germany Office: The London Philharm, 35 Doughty St, London WC1N 2AA, England

TENNYSON, G(EORG) B(ERNHARD), English educator; b. Washington, July 13, 1930; s. Georg B. and Emily (Zimmerli) T.; m. Elizabeth Caroline Johnstone, July 13, 1953; children: Cameron, Holly. BA, George Wash. U., 1953, MA, 1959; MA, Princeton U., 1959, PhD, 1963. Instr. English U. N.C., Chapel Hill, 1962-64; asst. prof. to prof. English UCLA, 1964—. Author: Sartor Called Resartus, 1965, An Introduction to Drama, 1969, Victorian Devotional Poetry, 1981, Owen Barfield on C.S. Lewis, 1990, Literary Language, 1991, A Carlyle Reader, 1984, Nature and the Victorian Imagination, 1977, An Index to Nineteenth-Century Fiction, 1977, Religion and Modern Literature, 1975, Victorian Literature: Prose and Poetry (2 vols.), 1976; author, prodr. video film Owen Barfield: Man and Meaning, 1995; contbr. articles to profl. jours.; editor: Nineteenth Century Fiction, 1971-73, Nineteenth Century Literature, 1983—. With U.S. Army, 1954-56. Fullbright fellow, Freiburg, Germany, 1953-54, Guggenheim fellow, Guggenheim Found., London, 1970-71. Mem. MLA (chmn. Victorian sect. 1973), Philological Assn. of Pacific Coast (chmn. English 2 1969), Carlyle Soc. (Edinburgh). Republican. Anglican. Office: UCLA Dept of English Los Angeles CA 90095-1530

TENNYSON, PETER JOSEPH, lawyer; b. Winona, Minn., Mar. 18, 1946; s. Richard Harvey and Sylvia Josephine (Jadrich) T.; m. Mary Eileen Fay, Jan. 3, 1970; children: Mark Christian, Rachel Christine, Matthew Patrick, Erica Ruth/. BA, Purdue U., 1968; JD, U. Va., 1975. Bar: Calif. Assoc. atty. O'Melveny & Myers, L.A., 1975-82; v.p., gen. counsel Cannon Mills Co., Kannapolis, N.C., 1982-84; ptnr. Stradling, Yocca, Newport Beach, Calif., 1984-89, Jones, Day, Reavis & Pogue, Irvine, Calif., 1990-95, Paul, Hastings, Janofsky & Walker, Costa Mesa, Calif., 1995—; mem. Calif. Commn. on Future of Legal Profession and State Bar, 1994; lectr. in field. Mem. St. Joseph Hosp. Benefit, Orange, Calif., 1987-93; bd. dirs. Lincoln Club Orange County, 1991-93, South Coast Symphony, 1989-92. Capt. U.S. Army, 1968-72. Mem. Orange County Bar Assn., Performing Arts Fraternity. Roman Catholic. Avocations: down hill skiing, swimming. Home: 2621 Circle Dr Newport Beach CA 92663-5616 Office: Paul, Hastings, Janofsky & Walker 695 Pound Center Dr 17th Fl Costa Mesa CA 92626*

TENNYSON, RODERICK C., aerospace scientist; b. Toronto, Ont., Can., June 7, 1937; m. Judith Grace Williams, June 17, 1961; children: Shân, Marc, Kristin. BA, U. Toronto, Ont., 1960, MA, 1961, PhD, 1965. Prof. inst. aerospace studies U. Toronto, 1974—, dir., 1985—, chmn. dept. engring. sci., 1982-85; selected as Can. experimimenter on space shuttle flights; dir. ctr. excellence for Inst. Space & Terrestrial Sci.; chmn. Can. Found. for Internat. Space U.; cons. in field. Contbr. numerous articles to profl. jours., chpts. to books. Fellow Can. Aeronautic and Space Inst. Avocations: sailing, writing, recreations. Home: 104 McClure Dr, King City, ON Canada M3H 5T6 Office: Inst Aerospace Studies, 4925 Dufferin St, Downsview, ON Canada M3H 5T6

TENOPYR, MARY LOUISE WELSH (MRS. JOSEPH TENOPYR), psychologist; b. Youngstown, Ohio, Oct. 18, 1929; d. Roy Henry and Olive (Donegan) Welsh; AB, Ohio U., 1951, MA, 1951; PhD, U. So. Calif., 1966; m. Joseph Tenopyr, Oct. 30, 1955. Psychometrist, Ohio U., Athens, 1951-52, also housemother Sigma Kappa; personnel technician to research psychologist USAF, 1953-55, Dayton, Ohio, 1952-53, Hempstead, N.Y.; indsl. research analyst to mgr. employee evaluation N.Am. Rockwell Corp., El Segundo, Calif., 1956-70; asso. prof. Calif. State Coll.-Los Angeles, 1966-70; assoc. research educationist UCLA, 1970-71; program dir. U.S. CSC, 1971-72; dir. selection and testing AT&T, N.Y.C., 1972—; lectr. U. So. Calif., Los Angeles, 1967-70; vice chmn. research com. Tech. Adv. Com. on Testing, Fair Employment Practice Commn. Calif., 1966-70; adviser on testing Office Fed. Contract Compliance, U.S. Dept. Labor, Washington, 1967-73. Pres. ASPA Found., 1985-87; mem. Army Sci. Bd.; trustee N.J. Psychol. Found., 1995—. Fellow Am. Psychol. Assn. (bd. profl. affairs, edn. and training bd., mem. council reps., pres. divsn. indsl. organizational psychology, pres. divsn. evaluation, measurement and stats. 1994—); mem. Eastern Psychol. Assn., Am. Soc. Personnel Adminstrn. (bd. dirs. 1984-87), Nat. Acad. Sci. (coms. on ability testing, math. and sci. edn., panel on secondary edn.), Soc. Indsl. and Organizational Psychology (pres. 1979-80, Profl. Practices award 1984), Nat. Council Measurement in Edn., Psychometric Soc., Met. N.Y. Assn. Applied Psychology, N.J. Psychol. Assn. (bd. trustees 1995—), Am. Ednl. Research Assn., Sigma Xi, Sigma Kappa, Psi Chi, Alpha Lambda Delta, Kappa Phi. Editorial bd. Jour. Applied Psychology, 1972-87, Jour. Vocat. Behavior; assoc. editor Jour. Applied Psychology; contbr. chpts. to books and articles to profl. jours. Office: 100 Southgate Pky Morristown NJ 07960-6441

TENUTA, JEAN LOUISE, sports reporter, medical technologist; b. Kenosha, Wis., Apr. 12, 1958; d. Fred and Lucy Ann (Taylor) Tenuta; m. Robert Louis Bennett, Nov. 22, 1989. BS in Biology, U.Wis., 1979; BA in Journalism, Marquette U., 1983; MS in Print Journalism, Northwestern U., 1989. Sports reporter Kenosha News, 1978-84, Washington Post, 1984-86, Jour. Messenger, Manassas, Va., 1986, Jour. Times, Racine, Wis., 1988-89; med. technologist St. Therese Med. Ctr., Waukegan, Ill., 1980-83, 86-87, Suburban Hosp., Bethesda, Md., 1985-86, Group Health Assn., Washington, 1985-86, St. Francis Hosp., Milw., 1988-89; sports reporter Jour.-Gazette, Ft. Wayne, Ind., 1989-90; med. technologist Columbia Hosp., Milw., 1991; tech. assoc. Coll. Am. Pathologists, 1991—. Recipient 1st place in sports writing Capital Press Women, 1986, 87, Women's Press Club of Ind., 1990, 91, Nat. Fedn. Press Women, 1986, 91. Mem. Assn. Women in Sports Media (Midwest region coord. 1990-95, v.p. adminstrn. 1995—), Nat. Fedn. Press Women (treas. Capital area 1985-87, 1st pl. in sports writing 1986, 91), Soc. Profl. Journalists, Women in Comms. (v.p., sec. Milw. chpt.), Nat. Writers Club, Midwest Assn. for Toxicology & Therapeutic Drug Monitoring (sec., treas. 1995—, newsletters editor 1995—), Italian Geneaol. Soc. of Am., DAR (publicity chmn. mag. chmn. Kenosha chpt. 1994—), Friends of Kenosha Pub. Libr. (life). Democrat. Avocations: computers, reading, baseball. Home: 9110 32nd Ave Kenosha WI 53142-5426 Office: Coll Am Pathologists 325 Waukegan Rd Northfield IL 60093-2719

TEPEDINO, FRANCIS JOSEPH, business management company executive; b. Bklyn., Mar. 3, 1937; s. Frank and Maria (Panza) T.; children: Scott, Robert, Michael. BS in Marine Engring., Maine Maritime Acad., 1958; BS in Indsl. Mgmt., Fairleigh Dickinson U., 1963; MBA, Pacific Luth. U., 1968; JD, U. San Diego, 1974. Bar: Calif. 1975, Oreg. 1978, U.S. Supreme Ct. 1980; lic. marine engr. Naval officer USN, USS DeSoto County, 1958-60; design engr. Worthington Corp., Harrison, N.J., 1960-63; indsl. engr. Gen. Dynamics Corp., New London, Conn., 1963-66; mgr. fin. analysis Boeing Corp., Seattle, 1966-68; mgr. contracts Nat. Steel & Shipbuilding Co., San Diego, 1968-71; mgr. purchasing Gen. Atomic Corp., San Diego, 1971-75; corp. atty. FMC Corp., Portland, Oreg., 1975-77; corp. mgr. contracts Pacific Power & Light, Portland, 1977-82; pres., CEO The Condor Group, San Diego, 1982—. Author: Contract Claims and Litigation Avoidance, 1988. Pres. Planning Commn., Tigard, Oreg., 1977-83; atty., referee Calif. State Bar Atty./Client Dispute Panel, San Diego, 1991—. Lt. USN, 1958-60. Mem. State Bar of Calif., State Bar of Oreg., U.S. Supreme Ct. Bar, Am. Arbitration Assn. (arbitrator 1991—), Nat. Assn. Contract Mgmt., Nat. Mgmt. Cons. Orgns. Avocations: model A club, H.O. train model club, col. in confederate airforce. Office: The Condor Group 3638 Camino Del Rio N Ste 100 San Diego CA 92108-1769*

TEPHLY, THOMAS ROBERT, pharmacologist, toxicologist, educator; b. Norwich, Conn., Feb. 1, 1936; s. Samuel M. and Anna (Pieniadz) T.; m. Joan Bernice Clifcorn, Dec. 17, 1960; children: Susan Lynn, Linda Ann, Annette Michele. B.S., U. Conn., 1957; Ph.D., U. Wis., 1962; M.D., U. Minn., 1965. Research asst. U. Wis., Madison, 1957-62, instr., 1962; asst. prof. U. Mich., Ann Arbor, 1965-69, assoc. prof., 1969-71; prof. pharmacology U. Iowa, Iowa City, 1971—. Contbr. articles to profl. jours. Rsch. scholar Am. Cancer Soc., 1962-65; recipient John Jacob Abel award, 1971, Kenneth P. Dubois award, 1992; Fogarty sr. internat. fellow NIH, 1978; rsch. grantee NIH, 1966. Mem. Am. Soc. Pharmacology and Exptl. Therapeutics, Soc. Toxicology, AAAS, Am. Soc. Biol. Chemists, Research Soc. on Alcholism. Home: 6 Lakeview Dr NE Iowa City IA 52240-9142 Office: U Iowa Dept Pharmacology Iowa City IA 52242

TEPLOW, THEODORE HERZL, valve company executive; b. Brockton, Mass., Apr. 14, 1928; s. Edward Abraham and Evelyn (Stone) T.; m. Charlotte Leah Savitz, June 14, 1953; children: Rachel P., David I., Deborah R., Evan S., Jonathan P. BS, U.S. Mcht. Marine Acd., 1950; MBA, Harvard U., 1953. Mgmt. trainee to pres. Crosby Valve Inc. an FMC Corp. subs., Wrentham, Mass., 1953-82, cons., 1982—; dir. Emerson Investment Mgmt., Inc., Boston, 1985—; cons. Firesafe Products Corp., N.Y.C., 1982—. Trustee Am. Mcht. Marine Mus. Found., Kings Point, N.Y., 1988—, Roten Internat., Boston, 1990—, Hebrew Coll., Brookline, Mass., 1971—, chmn., 1992—; v.p., bd. dirs. Internat. Catacomb Soc., Boston, 1982—, Cong. Beth El-Atereth Israel, Newton Center, Mass., 1975-85, Beth El Cmty. Hebrew Sch., Newton Center, 1965-85, USMMA Found., Kings Point, 1988—; asst. treas., dir. Am. Com. for Weizmann Inst. Sci., N.Y., 1987—; gov. Weizmann Inst. Sci., Rehovoth, Israel, 1991—; bd. dirs. Wilstein Inst. Jewish Policy Studies, L.A., Stone Charitable Found.; dir. Archives for Hist. Documentation, Boston, 1994—. Comdr. USNR. Recipient Outstanding Profl. Achievement award U.S. Mcht. Marine Acad. Alumni Assn., 1970, Meritorious Alumni Svc. award, 1990, Disting. Svc. award, 1995. Democrat. Office: Crosby Valve Inc 43 Kendrick St Wrentham MA 02093-1553

TEPPER, LLOYD BARTON, physician; b. L.A., Dec. 21, 1931; m. Lamonte Leverage; children: Jeffrey Hamilton, Evan Clothier. AB, Dartmouth Coll., 1954; MD, Harvard U., 1957, MIH, 1960, ScD in Hygiene, 1962. Diplomate in occupational medicine Am. Bd. Preventive Medicine. Rsch. fellow Harvard Med. Sch., Boston, 1958-59; clin. fellow Mass. Gen. Hosp., Boston, 1958-60; rsch. assoc. MIT, Cambridge, 1959-61; physician U.S. AEC, Washington, 1962-65; prof. environ. health U. Cin., 1965-72; assoc. dir. Kettering Lab., Cin., 1965-72; assoc. commr. U.S. FDA, Washington, 1972-76; corp. med. dir. Air Products and Chems., Inc., Allentown, Pa., 1976—; dir. Chem. Industry Inst. Toxicology, Research Triangle Park, N.C., 1982-89; trustee Am. Bd. Preventive Medicine, vice chair, 1986-94. Editor Jour. Occupational Medicine, 1979-91. Fellow Am. Coll. Occupational and Environ. Medicine, Am. Acad. Occupational Medicine (pres. 1980-81). Office: Air Products and Chems Inc 7201 Hamilton Blvd Allentown PA 18195-1501

TEPPER, LYNN MARSHA, gerontology educator; b. N.Y.C., Mar. 16, 1946; d. Jack Mortimer and Ida (Golembe) Drukatz; m. William Chester Tepper, Aug. 27, 1967; children: Sharon Joy, Michelle Dawn. BS, SUNY, Buffalo, 1967; MA, Wayne State U., 1971; MS, Columbia U., 1977, EdM, 1978, EdD, 1980. Instr. John F. Kennedy Sch., Berlin, 1967-68, ednl. counselor, 1968-69; ednl. coordinator Army Edn. Ctr., Berlin, 1969-71; psychologist U.S. Dept. Def., Berlin, 1971-73; prof. Gerontology L.I. U., Dobbs Ferry, N.Y., 1979—, Columbia U., N.Y.C., 1982—; cons. NATO, Belgium, Naples, Italy, 1969-71, numerous nursing homes, N.Y.C., 1978—, Found. for Long Term Care, 1992—; prof. gerontology Mercy Coll., Dobbs Ferry, 1979—; dir. Gerontology Resource Ctr., Ctr. for Geriatrics and Gerontology, Columbia U., N.Y.C., 1980-85, dir. divsn. behavioral sci., 1982—; del. White House Conf. on Aging, 1980. Author: (textbooks) Long Term Care, 1993, Respite Care, 1993; contbr. articles to profl. jours. and textbooks. Advisor Office on Aging, State of N.Y., Albany, 1980—; dir. Mercy Coll., Inst. Gerontology, 1990—; trustee St. Cabrini Nursing Home, 1991—. Brookdale Inst. on Aging fellow, 1983. Fellow Gerontol. Soc. Am.; mem. Northeastern Gerontol. Soc., N.Y. Assn. Gerontol. Edn., Am. Psychol. Assn. Avocations: physical fitness. Home: 50 Burnside Dr Hastings Hdsn NY 10706-3013 Office: Columbia U Med Campus Box 20 630 W 168th St New York NY 10032

TEPPER, MICHAEL HOWARD, publishing company executive; b. Balt., Sept. 4, 1941; s. Jack and Betty Lee (Chodak) T,; m. Veronica Ann Schofield, Nov. 15, 1972; children: Alex, Megan, Sarah. B.A., U. Md., 1963; M.A., NYU, 1965, Ph.D., 1970. Pres., mng. editor Geneal. Pub. Co., Inc., Balt., 1971—. Author: American Passenger Arrival Records, 1988; editor: The Famine Immigrants (7 vols.), 1983-86, Passenger Arrivals at the Port of Philadelphia 1800-1819, 1986, Passenger Arrivals at the Port of Baltimore 1820-1834, 1982, New World Immigrants (2 vols.), 1979, Immigrants to the Middle Colonies, 1978, Passengers to America, 1977, Emigrants to Pennsylvania, 1975. Recipient Founders' Day award NYU, 1970. Office: Geneal Pub Co Inc 1001 N Calvert St Baltimore MD 21202-3809

TERAN, TIMOTHY ERIC ALBA, marketing professional; b. N.Y.C., Apr. 11, 1956; s. Eric Henry Alba and Patricia (Wheel) T. BA in Market Psychology, Oberlin Coll., 1978. Rsch. intern Needham Harper & Steers, Chgo., 1977; rsch. exec. Grey Advt., N.Y.C., 1979-80, sr. rsch. exec., 1981, asst. rsch. dir., 1982-83, assoc. rsch. dir., 1984, v.p. assoc. rsch. dir., 1985-88, v.p. sr. assoc. dir. strategic svcs., 1989-92, sr. v.p., deputy dir. strategic svcs., 1992—. Home: 13 Gramercy Park S New York NY 10003-1755 Office: Grey Advt 777 3rd Ave New York NY 10017

TERAO, TOSHIO, physician, educator; b. Shimizu, Japan, Jan. 18, 1930; s. Eiji and Mitsuko (Katagiri) T.; m. Setsuko Nishigaki, Nov. 13, 1961; children: Toshiya, Yasuo, Yoshio. Diploma U. Tokyo, 1953, M.D., 1960. Intern, Tokyo U. Hosp., 1953-54; sr. scientist Nat. Inst. Radiol. Sci., Chiba, Japan, 1963-67; research assoc. Mayo Clinic, Rochester, Minn., 1970-72; asst. U. Tokyo, 1972-77, lectr. in medicine 1977-79; prof. medicine Teikyo U., 1980-91, prof. neurology, 1991—; pres. Teikyo U. Med. Hosp., 1987-93, dean, 1993—. Author, editor in field. Mem. Am. Acad. Neurology, Japanese Soc. Internal Medicine, Japanese Soc. Neurology, Japanese Soc. Neuropathology, Japanese Soc. EEG and Electromyography, Japanese Soc. Psychiatry and Neurology, Japanese Soc. Cerebrovascular Disease, Sigma Xi. Office: Teikyo U, 2-11-1 Kaga Itabashiku, Tokyo 173, Japan

TERASMAE, JAAN, geology educator; b. Estonia, May 28, 1926; s. Enn and Virge (Lepik) T.; m. Vaike Jurima, July 31, 1954. Phil. Cand., U. Uppsala, Swden, 1951; Ph.D., McMaster U., Can., 1955. Head palynology lab. Geol. Survey of Can., 1955-67, head paleoecology and geochronology sect., 1968; prof. dept. geology Brock U., St. Catharines, Ont., Can., 1968-91; prof. emeritus Brock U., St. Catharines, Ont., 1991—; chmn. dept. geology Brock U., St. Catharines, Ont., Can., 1969-73, 75-76. Contbr. numerous articles to profl. jours. Fellow Geol. Assn. Can., Geol. Soc. Am., Royal Soc. Can.; mem. Am. Assn. Stratigraphic Palynologists, Am. Quaternary Assn., Arctic Inst. N.Am., Can. Assn. Palynologists (pres. 1984-85), Can. Quaternary Assn. (William A. Johnston medal 1990), Internat. Assn. Gt. Lakes Rsch., Internat. Glaciological Soc., Internat. Limnological Soc., Internat. Orgn. Palaeobotany, Internat. Peat Soc., Tree-Ring Sooc., Royal Can. Geog. Soc. Lutheran. Avocation: photography. Home: 196 Woodside Dr, Saint Catharines, ON Canada L2T 1X6 Office: Brock U, Dept Geol Sciences, Saint Catharines, ON Canada L2S 3A1

TERBORG-PENN, ROSALYN MARIAN, historian, educator; b. Bklyn., Oct. 22, 1941; d. Jacques Arnold Sr. and Jeanne (Van Horn) Terborg; 1 dau., Jeanna Carolyn Terborg Penn. B.A. in History, Queens Coll., CUNY, 1963; M.A. in History, George Washington U., 1967; Ph.D. in Afro-Am. History, Howard U., 1978. Day care tchr. Friendship House Assn., Washington, 1964-66; program dir. Southwest House Assn., Washington, 1966-69; adj. prof. U. Md.-Balt. County, Catonsville, 1977-78, Howard Community Coll., Columbia, Md., 1970-74; prof. history Morgan State U., Balt., 1969—, project dir. oral history project, 1978-79, coord. grad. programs in history, 1986—; project dir. Assn. Black Women Hist. Research Conf., Washington, 1982-83. Author: (with Thomas Holt and Cassandra Smith-Parker) A Special Mission: the Story of Freedmen's Hospital, 1862-1962, 1975. Editor (with Sharon Harley) The Afro-American Woman: Struggles and Images, 1978, 81; (with Sharon Harley and Andrea Benton Rushing) Women in Africa and The African Diaspora, 1987. History editor Feminist Studies, 1984-89; mem. editl. bd. Md. Hist. Mag., 1988-94. Founding mem. Howard County Commn. for Women. Ford Found. fellow, 1980-81, Smithsonian Instn. fellow, 1982, 94-95; Howard U. grad. fellow in history, 1973-74, recipient Rayford W. Logan Grad. Essay award Howard U., 1973. Mem. Assn. Black Women Historians (co-founder, 1st nat. dir. 1980-82, nat. treas. 1982-84, cert. outstanding achievement 1981), Am. Hist. Assn. (mem. com. on women historians 1978-81, Joan Kelly Prize com. 1984-86, chair com. on women historians 1991-94), Orgn. Am. Historians (mem. black women's history project adv. com. 1980-81), Alpha Kappa Alpha. Office: Morgan State U 1700 E Cold Spring Baltimore MD 21239

TERENZIO, PETER BERNARD, hospital administrator; b. N.Y.C., Mar. 6, 1916; s. Vincent and Marianna (Piantino) T.; m. Eileen Alma Mosher, May 29, 1941; children—Mary Ellen Alecci, Vincent, Nancy Britton, Peter Bernard. Student, Yale U., 1934-37; J.D., U. Conn., 1940; M. Hosp. Adminstrn., Northwestern U., 1950. Bar: Conn. bar 1941. Practice in New Haven, 1945-48; with standardization div. A.C.S., Chgo., 1948-49; adminstrv. resident Evanston (Ill.) Hosp., 1949-50; asst. dir. Roosevelt Hosp., N.Y.C., 1950-52; exec. v.p., dir. Roosevelt Hosp., 1953-76, cons., 1976-81; pres. Hosp. Bur. Inc., Pleasantville, N.Y., 1977-81; dir. Greenville (S.C.) Gen. Hosp., 1952-53; cons. to surgeon gen. USPHS, 1960-65, 66-69; to commr. Dept. Hosps., N.Y.C., 1961-68; prof. clin. dentistry community Sch. Dental and Oral Surgery, Columbia U., 1963-84; univ. lectr. pub. health and adminstrv. medicine; adj. prof. Pace U., 1978-82, New Sch. Social Research 1977-85; Mem. facilities planning com. Hosp. Rev. and Planning Council of So. N.Y., 1963-69; mem. vol. adv. staff N.Y. State Health and Mental Retardation, 1966-69. Adv. editorial bd., Hosp. and Health Services Adminstrn. Bd. dirs., exec. com. Asso. Hosp. Service N.Y., 1970-74, N.Y. Coll. Podiatry, 1971-73; bd. dirs. Blue Cross-Blue Shield Greater N.Y., 1974-78, Abacus, 1965-86, Dominican Sisters Home Health Agy., 1977-82, Health Services Improvement Fund, 1978-85; mem. exec. adv. bd. Hosp. Home Care Santa Ana, Calif., 1984-86; vol., assoc., Sr. Friendship Health Ctr., Naples, Fla., 1986—, mem. adv. bd., 1992—. Capt., Med. Adminstrn. Corps AUS, 1941-45. Fellow Am. Coll. Hosp. Execs. (gov. 1964-65, regent 2d dist. 1960-64, pres. 1966-67, chmn. bd. dirs.), Am. Pub. Health Assn.; mem. Am. Hosp. Assn. (ho. of dels. 1969-76, rep. Am. Blood Commn., trustee liaison com. podiatry), Hosp. Research and Devel. Inst., N.Y. Acad. Medicine, Pub. Health Assn. N.Y.C. (dir., v.p. 1973-74, pres. 1976-77), Roosevelt Hosp. Alumni Assn. (asso.), Hosp. Assn. N.Y. (pres. 1970-71), Middle Atlantic Hosp. Assembly (bd. govs.), Hosp. Adminstrs. Study Soc., Am. Bar Assn., Greater N.Y. Hosp. Assn. (pres. 1960), Hosp. Adminstrs. Club (pres. 1959), Hosp. Soc. (pres. 1965), Coquina Club of Naples, Inc. (sec., treas. 1984-86, pres. 1987-90). Roman Catholic. Home and Office: 122 Moorings Park Dr Apt G608 Naples FL 33942-2124 Home (summer): 85 Hartford Ave Madison CT 06443

TERESI, JOSEPH, publishing executive; b. Mpls., Mar. 13, 1941; s. Cliff I.A. and Helen Ione (Leslie) T.; divorced; 1 child, Nicholas. Chief exec. officer Jammer Cycle Products Inc., Burbank, Calif., 1968-80, Paisano Pubs. Inc., Agoura Hills, Calif., 1970—. Pub. (mags.) Easyriders, 1971—, In the Wind, 1974—, Biker Lifestyle, 1986—, Tatto, 1986—, Am. Rodder, 1987, Womens Enterprise, 1987-89, Eagles Eye, 1989—, Tattoo Flash, 1993—, Tattoo Savage, 1993—, VQ, 1994—, Early-Riders, 1994—, Quick Throttle, 1995—, Roadware, 1995—. Holds world speed record for motorcycles set at 322 miles per hour, 1990. Avocations: motorcycles, race cars, boats, marlin fishing, skiing. Office: Paisano Pubs Inc PO Box 3000 Agoura Hills CA 91376-3000

TERHAR, LOUIS F., waste management administrator; b. 1949. BS in Enging., U.S. Naval Acad., 1972; MBA, Syracuse U., 1978; degree in Liberal Arts, Harvard U., 1982. With W. R. Grace & Co., N.Y.C., 1978-83, Emhart Corp., Balt., 1983-89; with SHV N.Am. Corp., Cin., 1989—, now pres., COO. With USN, 1972-78. Office: SHV North Am Corp 300 Pike St Cincinnati OH 45202-4222*

TERHORST, CHERYL ANN, journalist; b. Buffalo, Aug. 3, 1960; d. Paul Bernard and Mary Jean (McNab) terH.; m. Burt W. Constable, Mar. 26, 1988. BS in Journalism, U. Ill., 1982. Editorial asst. Woman;s Day mag., N.Y.C., 1982-84; city reporter Daily Herald, Arlington Heights, Ill., 1984-85, edn. reporter, 1985-86, feature writer, 1987—. Vol. Community Response, Oak Park, Ill., 1992-94. Recipient Peter Lisagor award Soc. Profl. Journalists, 1991, 94. Avocations: flying, travel. Office: Daily Herald PO Box 280 Arlington Heights IL 60006

TERHORST, JERALD FRANKLIN, public affairs counsel; b. Grand Rapids, Mich., July 11, 1922; s. John Henry and Maude (Van Strien) ter H.; m. Louise Jeffers Roth, Jan. 20, 1945; children: Karen Bayens Morris, Margaret Fulton Robinson, Peter Roth, Martha Morgan Lubin. Student, Mich. State U., 1941-42; A.B., U. Mich., 1947. Reporter Grand Rapids Press, 1946-51; mem. staff Detroit News, 1953-74, city and state polit. writer, 1953-57, Washington corr., 1958-60; chief Detroit News (Washington bur.), 1961-74; White House press sec. to Pres., 1974; columnist Detroit News/Universal Press Syndicate, 1974-81; nat. dir. public affairs Ford Motor Co., 1981-91; fgn. assignments include Berlin crisis Geneva Fgn. Ministers Conf., Yugoslavia, 1959, 70, Israel, 1960, Eng., Ireland, Germany, Italy and France, 1963, 69, Vietnam, India and Pakistan, 1966, 70, China, 1972, Moscow, 1974, Africa, 1978; writer N.Am. Newspaper Alliance, 1958-74. Author: Gerald Ford and Future of the Presidency, 1974, The Flying White House: The Story of Air Force One, 1979; contbr. to mags. and TV documentaries. Bd. dirs. Nat. Press Found., Gridiron Found., Grad. Sch. Polit. Mgmt., George Washington U., Washington, Handgun Control, Inc. Officer USMCR, 1943-46, 51-52. Mem. Pub. Rels. Soc. Am., Soc. Profl. Journalists, Psi Upsilon. Presbyterian (elder). Clubs: Gridiron, Nat. Press. Overseas Writers.

TERHUNE, ROBERT WILLIAM, optics scientist; b. Detroit, Feb. 8, 1926; married; 2 children. BS, U. Mich., 1947, PhD in Physics, 1957; MA, Dartmouth Coll., 1948. Supr. digital computation and logic design sect. Willow Run Labs. U. Mich., 1951-54, rsch. physicist, 1954-59, mgr. Solid State Physics Lab., 1959-60; rsch. physicist Sci. Lab. Ford Motor Co., Dearborn, Mich., 1960-65, mgr. physics electronics dept., 1965-75, sr. staff scientist engring. and rsch. staff, 1976-87; sr. mem. tech. staff JPL Calif. Tech., 1988-94, cons., 1995—; vis. scholar Stanford U., 1975-76. Editor Optics Let. Jour., 1977-83. Recipient Sci. and Engring. award Drexel Inst. Tech., 1964, Frederic Ives Medal, 1992, Optical Soc. Am. Mem. IEEE, Optical Soc. Am. (editor jour. 1984-87, Frederic Ives medal 1992), Am. Phys. Soc. Achievements include research in quantum electronics, nonlinear optics, optical properties of solids and surfaces, molecular spectroscopy, advanced instrumentation. Office: 1460 Pegfair Estates Dr Pasadena CA 91103-1929

TERILLI, JOSEPH ANTHONY, secondary education educator; b. Winthrop, Mass., June 14, 1948; s. Joseph Anthony and Mary Grace (Colontuoni) T.; m. Carol Ann Saccardo, Oct. 8, 1971; 1 child, Joseph Anthony III. BS, Boston Coll., 1970, MEd, 1973. Tchr., adminstr. Boston Pub. Schs., 1972-77; tchr. Coolidge Jr. H.S., Reading, Mass., 1977-84; tchr. Reading Meml. H.S., 1984—, mentor tchr., 1988—; pres., CEO Terilli Enterprises Devel. Corp., Aruba, 1986—; mem. Profl. Devel. Com., Reading, 1988-92. Author: Blood on the Chalkboard, How Children Succeed, also newspaper articles, booklets, monographs and mock trial; pub. (newsletter) Political Action Network (PAN). Mem. exec. bd., Mass. state chair Dem. Party (New Dems.). Mem. C. of C., Kiwanis (past sec.). Roman Catholic. Avocations: politics, travel, writing, collecing comic books. Home: 27 Lawndale Rd Stoneham MA 02180-1014 Office: Reading Meml HS 62 Oakland Rd Reading MA 01867-1613

TERILLI, SAMUEL A., JR., newspaper publishing executive. Gen. Coun. The Miami Herald, Fla. Office: The Miami Herald 1 Herald Plz Miami FL 33132-1609

TERKEL, STUDS (LOUIS TERKEL), author, interviewer; b. N.Y.C., May 16, 1912; s. Samuel and Anna (Finkel) T.; m. Ida Goldberg, July 2, 1939; 1 son, Dan. PhB, U. Chgo., 1932, JD, 1934. Stage appearances include Detective Story, 1950, A View From the Bridge, 1958, Light Up the Sky, 1959, The Cave Dwellers, 1960; moderator: (TV program) Studs Place, 1950-53, (radio programs) Wax Museum, 1945— (Ohio State Univ. award 1959, UNESCO Prix Italia award 1962), Studs Terkel Almanac, 1952—, Studs Terkel Show, Sta. WFMT-FM, Chgo.; master of ceremonies Newport Folk Festival, 1959, 60, Ravinia Music Festival, 1959, U. Chgo. Folk Festival, 1961, others; panel moderator, lectr., narrator films; author: (books) Giants of Jazz, 1957, Division Street: America, 1967, Hard Times: An Oral History of the Great Depression, 1970, Working: People Talk about What They Do All Day and How They Feel about What They Do, 1974 (Nat. Book award nomination 1975), Talking to Myself: A Memoir of My Times, 1977, American Dreams: Lost and Found, 1980, The Good War: An Oral History of World War II (Pulitzer prize in nonfiction 1985), Chicago, 1986, The Great Divide: Second Thoughts On The American Dream, 1988, Race: How Blacks and Whites Think and Feel About the American Obsession, 1992, Coming of Age, 1995; (play) Amazing Grace, 1959; also short stories. Named Communicator of Yr. U. Chgo. Alumni Assn., 1969. Office: WFMT Radio 5400 N St Louis Ave Chicago IL 60625

TERKEL, SUSAN NEIBURG, author; b. Lansdale, Pa., Apr. 7, 1948; d. Sidney Aaron and Deborah (Burstein) Neiburg; m. Lawrence Arthur Terkel, Oct. 25, 1970; children: Ari Garth, Marni Anne, David Samuel. BS, Cornell U., 1970. Freelance writer, 1978—. Author: Ethics, 1992, Finding Your Way, 1995, People Power, 1996. Co-founder, bd. dirs. Spiritual Life Soc., Hudson, Ohio, 1978—, Ohio State Freeze Campaign, Columbus, 1987, Soviet-Am. Youth Ambs., 1988. Charles Rieley Armington Found. grantee Case Western Res. U., 1988. Mem. P.E.N., Author's Guild, Soc. Children's Writers. Democrat. Jewish. Avocation: painting.

TER KEURS, HENK E. D. J., cardiologist, educator; b. Delft, The Netherlands, Aug. 27, 1942; married; 3 children. Degree, Huygens Lyceum, Voorburg, The Netherlands, 1960; MD, State Univ. Leiden, The Netherlands, 1966, PhD cum laude, 1970, Splty. Cert. Med. Physiology, 1980, Splty. Cert. Cardiology, 1983. Cert. cardiology specialist, Can., 1988. Rsch. asst. dept. physiology State Univ. Leiden, 1963-66, docent dept. physiology, 1966-73, sr. rsch. assoc dept. cardiology, 1973-84; med. scientist Alta. (Can.) Heritage Found., 1984—; prof. medicine and med. physiology U. Calgary, Alta., 1984—; Merck Frosst chair in cardiovascular rsch. U. Calgary, Alta., 1994—; established investigator dept. cardiology Netherlands Heart Found., State U. Leiden, 1976-81; rsch. fellow Midhurst Med. Rsch. Inst., U.K., 1979-85; chmn. sci. rev. com. Heart and Stroke Found. Can., 1992—; mem. cardiovascular A com. Med. Rsch. Coun. Can., 1990—; mem. cardiovascular study sect. NIH, 1991—; vis. scholar dept. anesthesiology U. Wash., 1976-77; guest lectr. dept. physiology U. Surinam, 1972-75. Assoc. editor: Can. Jour. Physiology and Pharmacology, 1989—, editorial referee, 1984—; editorial referee Pflugers Archive Jour. Gen. Physiology, 1977—, Jour. Gen. Physiology, 1977—, Jour. Cellular Molecular Cardiology, 1984—, Jour. Neurosci. Methodology, 1984—, Biophys. Jour., 1985—, Circulatory Rsch., 1989—; contbr. articles, abstracts to Cardiovascular Rsch., Brain Rsch., Jour. Physiology, Circulation, Biophysics Jour., others. Sec./treas. Einthoven Found., 1983-84, adv. coun., 1989—; fellow Coun. Circulation Am. Heart Assn., 1986. Recipient AKZO Medicine prize Dutch Sci. Soc., 1980. Fellow Royal Coll. Physicians and Surgeons Can.; mem. Am. Biophys. Soc., Dutch Fedn. Physiology, Can. Cardiovascular Soc., Physiolog. Soc. U.K. (fgn.). Office: U Calgary-Cardiovascular Rsch, 3330 Hospital Dr NW, Calgary, AB Canada T2N 4N1

TERKLA, LOUIS GABRIEL, retired university dean; b. Anaconda, Mont., Mar. 24, 1925; s. George G. and Blanche (Wareham) T.; m. Phyllis Jean Cohn, Aug. 21, 1949; children—David G., Linda J. Student, U. Mont., 1946-48; D.M.D., U. Oreg., 1952. Mem. faculty U. Oreg. Dental Sch., 1952—, prof., asst. to dean acad. affairs, 1961-67, dean, 1967-84, rsch. prof. and dean emeritus, 1984—. Author: (with others) Partial Dentures, 3d edit, 1963; also articles, chpts. in books. Served with inf. AUS, World War II. Fellow AAAS, Am. Coll. Dentists (pres. 1973-74), Acad. Gen. Dentistry (hon.); mem. Am. Dental Assn., Oreg. Dental Assn., Am. Assn. Dental Schs. (pres. 1975-76), Western Conf. Dental Examiners and Dental Sch. Deans (pres. 1975-76), Omicron Kappa Upsilon. Home: 1215 SW Kari Ln Portland OR 97219-6446 *Much of my success as a school of dentistry administrator can be attributed to a willingness to listen patiently to the problems borne by faculty, students and staff and to make a sincere effort toward their resolution. This requires an absolutely open-door administrative style, integrity and dedication to being a service agent to the people who make the school live.*

TERMAN, LEWIS MADISON, electrical engineer, researcher; b. San Francisco, Aug. 26, 1935; s. Frederick Emmons and Sibyl (Walcott) T.; m. Barbara Chertok, Aug. 28, 1958. BS in Physics, Stanford U., 1956, MSEE, 1958, PhD, 1961. Mem. rsch. staff T.J. Watson Rsch. Ctr., IBM, Yorktown Heights, N.Y., 1961-89, sr. mgr., 1989-91, sr. mem. tech. planning staff, 1991-93; mgr. VLSI processor design IBM, Yorktown Heights, N.Y., 1993-94; program mgr., 1994—; co-chmn. Symposium on Very Large Scale Integrated Technology, Systems and Application, Taiwan, 1989, 91, 93, 95, tech. program co-chmn., 1985, 87, tech. program chmn. Internat. Solid State Cirs. Conf., N.Y.C., 1983; chmn. Symposium on Very Large-Scale Integrated Tech., Kobe, Japan, 1985, San Diego, 1986, Symposium on Very Large-Scale Integrated Cirs., Karuizawa, Japan, 1988, Kyoto, Japan, 1989, Symposium on Low Power Electronics, San Diego, 1994. Contbr. articles to profl. jours.; holder 24 patents. Pres. Twin Lakes Water Works Corp., S. Salem, N.Y., 1980—. Recipient IEEE Solid-State Cirs. Tech. Field award, 1995. Fellow AAAS; mem. IBM Acad. Tech. (chair components and processes com., tech. coun, 1996—, co-chair of tech. program com. 19965), Electron Devices Soc. of IEEE (v.p. 1988-89, pres. 1990-91, Disting. Svc. award 1995), Solid State Circuits Coun. of IEEE (treas. 1988-89, editor jour. 1974-77, v.p. 1996—), IEEE Tech. Activities Bd. (chmn. tech. mtgs. coun. 1993-94, treas. 1995-96), Circuits and Sys. Soc. of IEEE (adminstrv. com. 1981-83); Nat. Academy of Engrin., 1996. Avocations: music, theatre, opera, hiking. Home: 61 Twin Lakes Rd South Salem NY 10590-1012 Office: IBM TJ Watson Rsch Ctr PO Box 218 Yorktown Heights NY 10598-0218

TERMEER, HENRICUS ADRIANUS, biotechnology company executive; b. Tilburg, Holland, Feb. 28, 1946; s. Jacques and Mary (Van Gorp) T.; came to U.S., 1971. Student, Ekonomisch Hogeschool, Rotterdam, Netherlands, 1969; M.B.A., U. Va., 1973. Mgr. mgmt. services Norvic Co., Norwich, England, 1969-71; mgr. internat. product planning Baxter Travenol, Inc., Deerfield, Ill., 1973-74, internat. mktg. mgr., 1975-76; gen. mgr. Travenol GMBH, Munich, W.Ger., 1976-79, v.p. Hyland Therapeutics div. Baxter Travenol, Glendale, Calif., 1979-81, exec. v.p., 1981-83 ; pres. Genzyme Corp., Inc., Boston, 1983—, chief ops. officer, 1983-85, chief exec. officer, 1986—, chmn., 1988—; dir. Geltex Corp., Xenova Ltd, Autoimmune Corp. Abiomed, Xenova Ltd., Mass. Cystic Fibrosis Found., Neozyme Corp., Genzyme Transgenetics Corp.; chmn. Biotech. Industry Orgn., Mass. High Tech. Coun. Trustee Hambrecht & Quist Healthcare Investors Fund, Mus. of Sci., Boston, Darden Bus. School U. of Virginia. Served to 1st lt. Netherlands Royal Air Force, 1966-67. Office: Genzyme Corp 1 Kendall Sq Cambridge MA 02139-1562

TERMINI, DEANNE LANOIX, research company executive; b. New Orleans, May 2, 1943; d. Albert Oliver and Freida (Fisher) Lanoix; m. Raymond Joseph Termini, Sept. 4, 1965; 1 dau., Andrea. BA, Tulane U., 1964; MA, U. Tex., Austin, 1968. Research analyst Belden Assocs., Dallas, 1968-70, research assoc., 1970-75, v.p., 1975-79, sr. v.p., 1979-87, exec. v.p., 1987-89, pres., 1989—; discussion leader Am. Press Inst., Reston, Va., 1983—. Author research reports. Speaker European and Latin confs., 1986—. Mem. Am. Mktg. Assn., Newspaper Assn. Am., Internat. Newspaper Mktg. Assn., Coun. Am. Survey Rsch. Orgns. Home: 13641 Far Hills Ln Dallas TX 75240-5533 Office: Belden Assocs 3102 Oak Lawn Ave Ste 500 Dallas TX 75219-4260

TERMINI, ROSEANN BRIDGET, lawyer; b. Phila., Feb. 2, 1953; d. Vincent James and Bridget (Marano) T. BS magna cum laude, Drexel U., 1975; MEd, Temple U., 1979, JD, 1985. Bar: Pa. 1985, U.S. Dist. Ct. (ea. dist.) Pa. 1985, D.C. 1986. Jud. clk. Superior Ct. of Pa., Allentown, 1985-86; atty. Pa. Power & Light Co., Allentown, 1986-87; corp. counsel food and drug law Lemmon Co., Sellersville, Pa., 1987-88; sr. dep. atty. bur. consumer protection plain lang. law Office of Atty. Gen., Harrisburg, Pa., 1988—; Contbr. articles to profl. jours., law revs.; spkr. continuing legal edn.-plain lang. laws, environ. conf.; adj. prof. Widener U. Sch. Law, 1993—. Contbr. articles to profl. jours, law revs.; speaker environ. conf. Active in Sr. Citizens Project Outreach, Hospice, 1986—; mem. St. Thomas More Law Bd. Named Outstanding Young Women of Yr., Dauphin County Bar Assn., 1987; Edn. fellow Temple U., 1978-79. Mem. ABA (various coms.), Bar Assn. D.C., Pa. Bar Assn. (ethics, exceptional children and environ. sects.), Temple U. Law Alumni Assn., Drexel U. Alumni Assn., Omicron Nu, Phi Alpha Delta. Avocations: tap dancing, hiking, cross-country skiing. Home: 5511 Blakeslee Dr Harrisburg PA 17111 Office: Office Atty Gen Harrisburg PA 17120 *Notable cases include: Waste Conversion case, 1990, violation of Pa. Solid Waste Mgmt. Act.*

TERMUENDE, EDWIN ARTHUR, chemistry educator; b. Joliet, Ill., Oct. 16, 1941; s. Gustav John Jr. and Alice Emily (Stienfatt) T.; m. Eileen Rose Grages, Aug. 5, 1967; children: Dawn Lynn Fokken, Amy Leigh. BS, So. Ill. U., 1965; MEd in Adminstn. and Supervision, Loyola U., 1972; MA, Govs. State U., 1976. Sci. tchr. Dwight D. Eisenhower H.S., 1966-68, Harold L. Richards H.S., 1968-75, Alan B. Shepard H.S., 1975-93; chemistry tchr. Polaris Sch. for Individual Edn., 1993—; mem. sch. improvement com. Polaris Sch. for Individual Edn., 1993—, mem. dirs. coun., 1994-95; mem. NCA sch. and community evaluation com. Alan B. Shepard H.S., 1991-92, co-chair NCA evaluation com., 1976-77; advisor CHSD 218 spl. edn. tchrs. for 2 yr. spl. edn. sci. curriculum, 1991-92; reviewer textbooks Delmar Pubs., 1991-94; presenter in field. Asst. leader Peotone Pep Pushers 4-H Club, 1982-94; bd. dirs. Ill. 4-H Found., 1990—; mem. state 4-H conf. com., Ill., 1989; chaperone for Ill. del. Nat. 4-H Congress, 1990, vol. coord., 1990, 91; mem. authoring com. Ill. 4-H Awards Application, 1992-93. Recipient Ill. 4-H Alumni award U. Ill., 1990. Mem. AAAS, ASCD, Nat. Sci. Tchrs. Assn., Ill. Sci. Tchrs. Assn., Ill. Assn. of Chemistry Tchrs., Am. Chem. Soc. Avocations: photography, 4-H leader. Home: 630 Catalpa Box 1283 Beecher IL 60401 Office: Polaris Sch for Ind Edn 4625 W 107th St Oak Lawn IL 60453-5293

TERNBERG, JESSIE LAMOIN, pediatric surgeon; b. Corning, Calif., May 28, 1924; d. Eric G. and Alta M. (Jones) T. A.B., Grinnell Coll., 1946, Sc.D. (hon.), 1972; Ph.D., U. Tex., 1950; M.D., Washington U., St. Louis, 1953; Sc.D. (hon.), U. Mo., St. Louis, 1981. Diplomate: Am. Bd. Surgery. Intern Boston City Hosp., 1953-54; asst. resident in surgery Barnes Hosp., St. Louis, 1954-57; resident in surgery Barnes Hosp., 1958-59; research fellow Washington U. (Sch. Medicine), 1957-58; practice medicine specializing in pediatric surgery St. Louis, 1966—; instr., trainee in surgery Washington U., 1959-62, asst. prof. surgery, 1962-65, assoc. prof., 1965-71, prof. surgery in pediatrics, 1975—, prof. surgery, 1971—, chief div. pediatric surgery, 1972-90; mem. staff Barnes Hosp., 1974-90, pediatric surgeon in chief, 1974-90, mem. operating room com., 1971—, mem. med. adv. com., 1975—; mem. staff Children's Hosp., dir. pediatric surgery, 1972-90. Contbr. numerous articles on pediatric surgery to profl. jours. Trustee Grinnell Coll., 1984—. Recipient Alumni award Grinnell Coll., 1966, Faculty/Alumni award Washington U. Sch. Medicine, 1991, 1st Aphrodite Jannopaulo Hofsommer award, 1993. Fellow ACS; mem. AAAS, SIOP, Am. Pediatric Surg. Assn., We. Surg. Assn. (2d v.p. 1984-85), St. Louis Med. Soc., Soc. Surgery of the Alimentary Tract, Am. Acad. Pediatrics, Soc. Pelvic Surgeons (v.p. 1991-92), Brit. Assn. Paediatric Surgeons, Mo. State Surg. Soc., St. Louis Surg. Soc. (pres. 1980-81), St. Louis Pediatric Soc., Soc. Surg. Oncology, Pediatric Oncology Group (chmn. surg. discipline 1983—), St. Louis Childrens Hosp. Soc. (pres. 1979-80), St. Louis Soc. for Med. Sci. Edn. (councilor, trustee), Barnes Hosp. Soc., Phi Beta Kappa, Sigma Xi, Iota Sigma Pi, Alpha Omega Alpha. Office: St Louis Childrens Hosp 1 Childrens Pl Saint Louis MO 63110

TERP, DANA GEORGE, architect; b. Chgo., Nov. 5, 1953; s. George and June (Hansen) T.; m. Lynn Meyers, May 17, 1975; children: Sophia, Rachel. BA in Architecture, Washington U., St. Louis, 1974; postgrad., Yale U., 1975-76; MArch, Washington U., 1977. Registered architect, Ill., Calif., Fla. Architect Skidmore Owings & Merrill, Chgo., 1976, 1978-84, Terp Meyers Architects, Chgo., 1984—; prin. Arquitectonica Chgo. Inc., 1986—. Exhibited in group shows at Moming Gallery, Chgo., 1980, Printers Row Exhibit, 1980, Frumkin Struve Gallery, Chgo., 1981, Chgo. Art Inst., 1983; pub. in profl jours. including Progressive Architecture, Los Angeles Architect; work featured in various archtl books; exhibited 150 Yrs. of Chgo. Architecture. Bd. dirs. Architecture Soc. Art Inst. Chgo. Recipient hon. mention Chgo. Townhouse Competition, 1978, award Progressive Architecture mag., 1980, Archtl. Record Houses, 1989, GLOBAL Architecture Ga. Houses/26, 1989, Casa Vogue, 1989, 2d place award Burnham Prize Competition, 1991. Office: Terp Meyers Architects 919 N Michigan Ave Ste 2402 Chicago IL 60611-1601

TERP, THOMAS THOMSEN, lawyer; b. Fountain Hill, Pa., Aug. 12, 1947; s. Norman T. and Josephine (Uhran) T.; m. Pamela Robinson; children: Stephanie, Brian, Adam; step-children: Taylor Mefford, Grace Mefford. BA, Albion (Mich.) Coll., 1969; JD, Coll. of William and Mary, 1973. Bar: Ohio 1973, U.S. Dist. Ct. (so. dist.) Ohio 1973, U.S. Ct. Appeals (6th cir.) 1973, U.S. Supreme Ct. 1979. Assoc. Taft, Stettinius & Hollister, Cin., 1973-80, ptnr., 1981—; bd. dirs. Starflo Corp., Orangeburg, S.C., Attorney's Liability Assurance Soc., Ltd., Hamilton, Bermuda, 1995—, ALAS, Inc., Chgo., 1995—. Editor-in-chief Coll. of William & Mary Law Rev., 1972-73; mem. bd. editors Jour. of Environ. Hazards, 1988—, Environ. Law Jour. of Ohio, 1989—. Mem. Cin. Athletic Club, Coldstream Country Club, Epworth Assembly (Ludington, Mich.), Lincoln Hills Golf Club (Ludington). Avocations: tennis, golf, racquetball, travel. Office: 1800 Star Bank Ctr 425 Walnut St Cincinnati OH 45202-3904

TERPSTRA, VERN, marketing educator; b. Wayland, Mich., Aug. 20, 1927; s. Benjamin and Lucy (Jonker) T.; m. Bonnie Lou Fuller; children: Benjamin Mark, Kathryn Ann, James Richard. BA, U. Mich., 1950, MBA, 1951, PhD, 1965. Dir. normal sch. Grace Mission, Zaire, 1952-61; rsch. asst. Mktg. Sci. Inst., Phila., 1963-66; asst. prof. mktg. Wharton Sch. U. Penn., Phila., 1964-66; prof. Sch. Bus. U. Mich., Ann Arbor, 1967-92, prof. emeritus, 1992—; cons. govt., bus. and acad. orgns., 1972—. Author: The Cultural Environment of International Business, 1978, 3d edit., 1991, International Marketing, 1972, 6th edit., 1994. Fellow Ford Found., Mktg. Sci. Inst., Acad. Internat. Bus.; mem. Am. Mktg. Assn., Acad. Internat. Bus. Presbyterian. Avocations: tennis, travel, theatre, reading. Office: U Mich Bus Sch Ann Arbor MI 48109-1234

TERR, ABBA ISRAEL, allergist, immunologist; b. Cleve., 1930. MD, Case Western Res. U., 1956. Cert. in allergy and immunology; cert. internal medicine. Intern U. Wis. Hosps., Madison, 1956-57; resident in internal medicine U. Mich. Med. Ctr., Ann Arbor, 1957-60, fellow in allergy, 1960-62; physician Stanford (Calif.) U. Med. Ctr.; clin. prof. medicine Stanford U. Fellow ACP, Am. Acad. Allergy, Asthma, and Immunology; mem. Am. Thoracic Soc. Address: 450 Sutter St Ste 2534 San Francisco CA 94108-4204

TERR, LENORE CAGEN, psychiatrist, writer; b. N.Y.C., Mar. 27, 1936; d. Samuel Lawrence Cagen and Esther (Hirsh) Cagen Raiken; m. Abba I. Terr; children: David, Julia. AB magna cum laude, Case Western Res. U., 1957; MD with honors, U. Mich., 1961. Diplomate Am. Bd. Psychiatry and Neurology. Intern Med. Ctr. U. Mich., Ann Arbor, 1961-62, resident Neuropsychiat. Inst., 1962-64, fellow Children's Psychiat. Hosp., 1964-66; from instr. to asst. prof. Med. Sch. Case Western Res. U., Cleve., 1966-71; pvt. practice Terr Med. Corp., San Francisco, 1971—; from asst. clin. prof. to clin. prof. psychiatry Sch. Medicine U. Calif., San Francisco, 1971—; lectr. law, psychiatry U. Calif., Berkeley, 1971—, U. Calif., Davis, 1974; bd. dirs. Am. Bd. Psychiatry and Neurology, Deerfield, Ill., 1988-96. Author: Too Scared to Cry, 1990, Unchained Memories, 1994; contbr. articles to profl. jours. Rockefeller Found. scholar-in-residence, Italy, 1981, 88; project grantee Rosenberg Found., 1977, 80-81, William T. Grant Found., 1986-87; recipient Career Tchr. award NIMH, 1967-69, Child Advocacy award, APA, 1994. Fellow Am. Psychiat. Assn. (Child Psychiatry Rsch. award 1984, Clin. Rsch. award 1987), Am. Coll. Psychiatrists (program chair 1991-92, Bowis award 1993), Am. Acad. Child and Adolescent Psychiatry (coun. 1984-87); mem. Group for Advancement Psychiatry (bd. dir. 1986-88), Phi Beta Kappa, Alpha Omega Alpha. Avocations: piano, walking, travel. Office: Terr Med Corp 450 Sutter St Rm 2534 San Francisco CA 94108-4204

TERRACCIANO, ANTHONY PATRICK, banker; b. Bayonne, N.J., Oct. 27, 1938; s. Patrick and Grace Terracciano; m. Rita Cuddy, Apr. 20, 1963; children: Laura, Karen, Kenneth. BS in Econs. St. Peter's Coll., Jersey City, N.J., 1960; MA in Philosophy, Fordham U., 1962. with Chase Manhattan Bank, N.Y.C., 1964—, exec. v.p. internat., 1974-76, 84-85, exec. v.p., treas., 1976-80, exec. v.p. ops. trusts and systems dept., 1980-83, exec. v.p., chief fin. officer, 1983-84, vice chmn. global banking, 1985-87, pres., chief operating officer, Mellon Bank Corp., Pitts., 1987-90, chmn., pres., chief exec. officer, First Fidelity Bancorp., Newark, N.J., 1990—; dir. N.J. Bell Tel. Co., Pitcairn Co.. Dir. N.J. Performing Arts Ctr. Copr, N.Y. Philharm., Metro Newark C. of C.; mem. exec. coun. Better Bus. Bur., Newark; trustee Renaissance Newark, Inc.; mem. Coun. on Fgn. Rels. 1st lt. U.S. Army, 1962-64. Mem. N.J. Banker's Assn. (exec. com.). Avocations: music, reading. Office: First Fidelity Bancorp 550 Broad St Newark NJ 07102*

TERRACE, HERBERT S(YDNEY), psychologist, educator; b. Bklyn., Nov. 29, 1936; s. Morris Abraham and Esther (Marsh) T.; m. Kathleen A. Frederick, July 26, 1986; children: Gillian Frederick, Jonathan Frederick. A.B., Cornell U., 1957, M.A., 1958; Ph.D., Harvard U., 1961. Instr. psychology Columbia U., 1961-63, asst. prof. psychology, 1963-66, assoc. prof., 1966-68, prof., 1968—; vis. prof. Harvard U., 1972-73. Author: Introduction to Statistics, 1971, (with Scott Parker) Individual Learning Systems, 1971, Nim, 1979; editor: (with T.G. Bever) Human Behavior: Prediction and Control in Modern Society, 1973, (with H.L. Roitblat and T.G. Bever) Animal Cognition, 1983, (with C. Locurto and J. Gibbon) Autoshaping and Conditioning Theory, 1981, (with P. Marler) Biology of Learning, 1984; editor Jour. Exptl. Analysis Behavior, 1966-74; assoc. editor Animal Learning and Behavior, 1971-75, 83-86, Learning and Motivation, 1970-72, Behaviorism, 1972-84, Jour. Exptl. Psychology: Animal Learning Processes, 1986—. John Simon Guggenheim fellow, 1969-70; Harry Frank Guggenheim fellow, 1976-77; NIMH grantee, 1962—; NSF grantee, 1963-81; Fulbright sr. research scholar, 1983-84; W.T. Grant Found. grantee, 1975-76; fellow All Souls Coll., Oxford U., 1983-84; Whitehall Found. grantee, 1986-91. Fellow Am. Psychol. Assn., AAAS, Soc. Exptl. Analysis Behavior (pres. 1972-73), Soc. Exptl. Psychologists; mem. Eastern Psychol. Assn. (bd. dirs. 1986-96). Home: 460 Riverside Dr Apt 91 New York NY 10027-6820 Office: 418 Schermerhorn Hall Columbia U New York NY 10027

TERRACINA, ROY DAVID, food executive; b. Chgo., Aug. 24, 1946; s. Angelo R. and Josephine T.; m. Dana Wheeler, July 6, 1984; children: Joseph, Vincent, Angela, Peter, Paul. BS in Fin., Marquette U., 1968, MBA, 1972. Officer First Wis. Nat. Bank, Milw., 1968-71; account exec. Robert W. Baird Co., Milw., 1971-74; v.p. mktg. Midwest Retail Group, Milw., 1974-76; mgmt. cons. Anderson-Roethle, Milw., 1976-77; v.p., treas. Farm House Foods Corp., Milw., 1977-84; pres. Sterling Foods, Inc., San Antonio, 1984-93, pvt. investor, 1994—; instr. personal fin. Marquette U.; instr. fin. Trinity U.; bd. dirs. Tex. Commerce Bank, Security Trust; entrepreneur in residence St. Mary's U. Bd. dirs. YMCA, San Antonio; chmn. Tex. Spl. Olympics. Mem. Young Pres.'s Orgn., Marquette U. Alumni Assn. (pres. 1977-78), Lions Internat. (pres. 1975-76). Roman Catholic. Office: 7900 Callahan San Antonio TX 78225

TERRAGNO, PAUL JAMES, information industry executive; b. Ogden, Utah, May 17, 1938; s. Charles L. and Florence E. (Gabardi) T.; m. Nancy Robinson, Aug. 26, 1961; children—Thomas C., Paul A., Teresa A. B.A., U. Utah, 1960; M.S., U. Wyo., 1962. Vice pres. Westat, Inc., Rockville, Md., 1962-70; vice pres. Remac Information, Gaithersburg, Md., 1970-76; dir. U.S. Patent Office, Washington, 1976-80; v.p. Pergamon Internat., McLean, Va., 1980-84; pres. Pergamon InfoLine, McLean, Va., 1984-87, Pergamon ORBIT InfoLine, McLean, 1987-89, Maxwell Online, Inc., 1989-92; pres. Pergamon Orbit InfoLine, Ltd., London, 1984-89, Pergabase, Inc., Gainesville, Fla., 1985-92, pres. Topate Information Svcs. Inc., 1992—. Contbr. articles to various publs. Mem. Am. Soc. Info. Sci. Roman Catholic. Home: 10607 Vantage Ct Rockville MD 20854-4244 Office: Topate Info Svcs 10607 Vantage Ct Potomac MD 20854-4244

TERRAS, AUDREY ANNE, mathematics educator; b. Washington, Sept. 10, 1942; d. Stephen Decatur and Maude Mae (Murphy) Bowdoin. BS with high honors in Math., U. Md., 1964; MA, Yale U, 1966, PhD, 1970. Instr. U. Ill., Urbana, 1968-70; asst. prof. U. P.R., Mayaguez, 1970-71; asst. prof. Bklyn. Coll., CUNY, 1971-72; asst. prof. math. U. Calif.-San Diego, La Jolla, 1972-76, assoc. prof., 1976-83, prof., 1983—, vis. positions MIT, fall 1977, 83, U. Bonn (W.Ger.), spring 1977, Inst. Mittag-Leffler, Stockholm, winter, 1978, Inst. Advanced Study, spring 1984, Math. Scis. Rsch. Inst., Berkeley, Calif., winter 1992, spring 1995; dir. West Coast Number Theory Conf., U. Calif.-San Diego, 1976, AMS joint summer rsch. conf., 1984; lectr. in field. Author: Harmonic Analysis on Symmetric Spaces and Applications, Vol. I, 1985, Vol. II, 1988. Contbr. articles and chpts. to profl. publs. Woodrow Wilson fellow, 1964; NSF fellow, 1964-68; NSF grantee Summer Inst. in Number Theory, Ann Arbor, Mich., 1973; prin. investigator NSF, 1974-88. Fellow AAAS; mem. AAAS (nominating com. math. sect. project 2061), Am. Math. Soc. (com. employment and ednl. policy com. on coms., council, transactions editor, com. for the yr. 2000), Math. Assn. Am. (program com. for nat. meeting 1988-90, chair joint com. Am. Math. Soc. and Math. Assn. Am. 1991), Soc. Indsl. and Applied Math., Assn. for Women in Math., Assn. for Women in Sci. Research in harmonic analysis on symmetric spaces and number theory. Office: U Calif San Diego Dept Math La Jolla CA 92093-0112

TERRAS, VICTOR, Slavic languages and comparative literature educator; b. Poltsamaa, Estonia, Jan. 21, 1921; came to U.S., 1952, naturalized, 1956; s. Evald and Elena (Rosenberger) T.; m. Rita Schubert, 1951; 1 child, Alexander. Mag. Phil., U. Tartu, Estonia, 1942; Ph.D., U. Chgo., 1963. Lectr. U. Tartu, 1943-44; instr. to assoc. prof. U. Ill., Urbana, 1959-64, prof. Slavic langs., 1965-66; prof. U. Wis., Madison, 1966-70; prof. Slavic langs. and comparative lit. Brown U., Providence, 1970-88, prof. emeritus, 1988—. Author: The Young Dostoevsky: A Critical Study, 1969, Belinskij and Russian Literary Criticism, 1974, A Karamazov Companion, 1981, Vladimir Mayakovsky, 1983; editor: Handbook of Russian Literature, 1984, The Idiot: An Interpretation, 1990, A History of Russian Literature, 1991. Mem. Am. Assn. Advancement Slavic and East European Studies, Am. Assn. Tchrs. Slavic and East European Langs. (pres. 1981-82), Internat. Dostoevsky Soc. (v.p. 1983—). Home: 128 Maple Ave Little Compton RI 02837-1714 Office: Brown U Box E Providence RI 02912

TERREAULT, R. CHARLES, engineer, management educator, researcher; b. Montreal, Que., Can., Mar. 21, 1935; s. Charles Terreault and Antonia Clark; m. Marie Rolland, Sept. 10, 1960; children: Genevieve, François, Patrick, Olivier-Hugues. BA, Coll. Stanislas, Montreal, 1954; BA in Sci., Ecole Poly., Montreal, 1959; hon. doctorate, U. Que., 1986. Engr. Bell Can., Montreal, 1959-65, staff engr., 1967-69, chief engr., 1971-73, asst. v.p. rsch., 1978-91; researcher Bell Telephone Labs., Holmdel, N.J., 1965-67; dir. planning Bell No. Rsch., Ottawa, Ont., Can., 1969-71; v.p. systems engring. Bell No. Rsch., Montreal, 1973-78; Jvr Cyr prof. mgmt. tech. Ecole Poly., Montreal, 1991—; bd. dirs. Visiocom Inc.; bd. dirs. Natural Scis. and Engring. Rsch. Coun. Can., Ottawa, 1989—. Contbr. articles to profl. jours. Fellow IEEE (Armstrong award 1984); mem. Canadian Acad. Engring., Ordre Ingénieurs de Que., Inst. Mgmt. Sci., Que. Assn. Indsl. Rsch. (Annual award 1992). Avocations: computers, classical music, skiing. Home: 1665 Victoria # 804, Saint Lambert, PQ Canada J4R 2T6 Office: Ecole Polytechnique, PO Box 6079 Br Centre-ville, Montreal, PQ Canada H3C 3A7

TERREL, RONALD LEE, civil engineer, business executive, educator; b. Klamath Falls, Oreg., Sept. 2, 1936; s. Theodore Thomas and Ruth Margaret (Fausset) T.; m. Susan Laura Harrower, Feb. 28, 1959 (div. July 1981); children: Douglas Scott, Nancy Dawn, Janet Lynn; m. 2d Alice Marie Blanchard, July 23, 1981. B.S.C.E., Purdue U., 1960, M.S., 1961; Ph.D., U. Calif.-Berkeley, 1967. Estimator J.H. Pomeroy & Co., San Francisco, 1955; lab. asst. Purdue U., 1956-60; asst. field geologist Bear Creek Mining Co., Mpls., 1957-58; materials engr. U.S. Bur. Reclamation, Denver, 1960-64; project engr. J.H. Pomeroy & Co., Antigua, B.W.I. and, Calif., 1964-65; research asst. U. Calif.-Berkeley, 1965-67; asst. prof. civil engr. U. Wash., Seattle, 1967-70, assoc. prof., 1970-75, prof., 1975-85, prof. emeritus, 1985—, head Transp. Constrn. and Geometronics divsn., 1976-79; prof., sr. researcher Oreg. State U., 1989-94; pres. Pavement Systems Inc., 1970-82; exec. v.p. Seattle Engring. Internat., Inc., 1979-81; pres. Terrel Assocs., Inc., 1981-85; owner Terrel Research, 1986—; v.p. Pavement Technologies Inc., 1985-86; bd. dirs., v.p. Hydrogenesis, Inc.; cons. in field. Patentee in field. Co-founder, dir. Wash. State Transp. Ctr., 1981-84. Nominated Constrn. Man of Yr. Engring. News-Record, 1972; Purdue Alumni scholar, 1959-60; Ford fellow, 1965-67. Mem. ASTM, ASCE, Transp. Rsch. Bd., Assn. Asphalt Paving Technologists (bd. dirs. 1979-83, Emmons award 1983, 95, award of merit 1990), Triaxial Inst. (chmn. 1971-73), Can. Tech. Asphalt Assn., Internat. Soc. for Asphalt Pavements (founding mem. 1987), Sigma Xi, Tau Beta Pi, Chi Epsilon, Sigma Gamma Epsilon. Office: 9703 241st Pl SW Edmonds WA 98020-6512

TERRELL, DOMINIQUE LARA, dramatic soprano, actress, real estate and marketing executive; b. South Bend, Ind., Apr. 26; d. Harold J. Metzler and Margaret Terrell (Whiteman) Metzler Fogarty. BA, Ithaca Coll., 1960; diploma, Brown's Bus. Coll., Decatur, Ill., 1960; postgrad. in real estate sales, NYU, 1984. Lic. securities dealer, real estate salesperson. Exec. legal asst. Carb Luria Glassner Cook & Kufeld, N.Y.C., 1962-64; Exec. legal asst.

Graubard Moskovitz McGoldrick Dannett & Horowitz, N.Y.C., 1964-79; opera and concert singer N.Y.C.; real estate salesperson Rosemary Edwards Realty, N.Y.C., 1985, Kenneth D. Laub & Co., Inc., N.Y.C., 1987-89, GSW Realty, Inc., N.Y.C., 1990-91, Kuzmuk Realty, Inc., 1992-94, Gala 72 Realty, Inc., 1994—; bd. dirs., singer Broadway-Grand Opera, 1992—; pres. Mystique of Dominique, Whiteman and Stewart Prodns., DharMacduff Publs.; corr. sec., bd. dirs. Community Opera, Inc., N.Y.C., 1984—. Mem. internat. affairs com. and other coms. Women's Nat. Rep. Club, N.Y.C., 1968-82; active Rep. County Vols., N.Y.C., 1976-82; mem. nominating com. Ivy Rep. Club, N.Y.C., 1983-87; bd. dirs. Am. Landmark Festivals, 1986—. Named Female Singer of Yr., Internat. Beaux Arts, Inc., 1978-79, Princess Nightingale, Allied Indian Tribes N.Am. Continent-Cherokee Nation, 1985. Mem. Wagner Internat. Instn. (dir. pub. rels. 1982-84), Navy League U.S. (life, mem. N.Y. coun.), Assn. Former Intelligence Officers (assoc.), Friends of Spanish Opera (bd. dirs. 1982—), Finlandia Found., Inc. (life), The Bohemians, Nat. Arts Club (music com. 1983-87), N.Y. Opera Club. Avocations: tennis, swimming, dancing, travel, antiques.

TERRELL, G. IRVIN, lawyer; b. Houston, Sept. 28, 1946; s. George I. and Adella (Weichert) T.; m. Karen Steenberg, Jan. 8, 1984; 1 child, Katharine. BA, U. Tex., 1968, JD, 1972. Bar: Tex., U.S. Supreme Ct., U.S. Ct. Appeals (5th cir.), U.S. Dist. Ct. (so. dist.) Tex. Assoc. Baker & Botts, Houston, 1972-79; ptnr. Baker & Botts, 1980—. Mem. ABA, Houston Bar Assn., Internat. Soc. Barristers. Office: Baker & Botts 3000 One Shell Pla 910 Louisiana St Houston TX 77002

TERRELL, J. ANTHONY, lawyer; b. N.Y.C., Sept. 20, 1943; s. Claude M. and Kathleen L. (Prevost) T.; m. Karen E. Terrell, Aug. 8, 1969; 1 child, Elizabeth S. BA, NYU, 1965, LLM in Taxation, 1975; JD, Villanova U., 1968. Bar: N.Y. With Frueauff, Farrell, Sullivan & Bryan, N.Y.C., 1970-74, ptnr., 1974; assoc. Reid & Priest, N.Y.C., 1974-76, ptnr., 1977—. Mem. ABA (sect. bus. law, sect. taxation, sect. pub. utility, comm. and transp. law, vice chmn. corp. finance com., Nat. Assn. Bond Lawyers, Belle Haven Club, Met. Club, Coral Beach and Tennis Club. Home: Indian Harbor Greenwich CT 06830 Office: Reid & Priest 40 W 57th St New York NY 10019-4097

TERRELL, (NELSON) JAMES, physicist; b. Houston, Aug. 15, 1923; s. Nelson James Sr. and Gladys Delphine (Stevens) T.; m. Elizabeth Anne Pearson, June 9, 1945; children—Anne (dec.), Barbara, Jean. B.A., Rice U., 1944, M.A., 1947, Ph.D., 1950. Research asst. Rice U., Houston, 1950; asst. prof. physics Western Res. U., Cleve., 1950-51; mem. staff Los Alamos Nat. Lab., U. Calif., 1951-89, assoc., 1989-94; affiliate, 1994—. Producer (computer generated movie) The X-Ray Sky, 1969-76; contbr. articles to profl. jours. and encys. Served to 1st lt. AUS, 1944-46. Graham Baker scholar, 1943-44; fellow Rice U., 1946-48, AEC, 1948-50. Fellow Am. Phys. Soc., AAAS; mem. Am. Astron. Soc., Internat. Astron. Union, Phi Beta Kappa, Sigma Xi. Research in relativity, quasars, x-ray and gamma ray astronomy, nuclear physics, lasers. Home: 85 Obsidian Loop Los Alamos NM 87544-2528 Office: Los Alamos Nat Lab Mail Stop D436 Los Alamos NM 87545

TERRELL, JAMES DANIEL, lawyer; b. Kansas City, Oct. 22, 1956; s. D. Ronald and Bobbie L. (Graham) T.; m. Lori J. McAlister, May 31, 1980; children: Justin Daniel, Christopher James, Alexander Graham. BS, Ctrl. Mo. State U., 1979; JD, U. Mo., 1982. Bar: Mo. 1982, U.S. Dist. Ct. (we. dist.) 1982, U.S. Dist. Ct. (ea. dist.) Mo. 1984. Assoc. Wasinger, Parham & Morthland, Hannibal, Mo., 1982-87; ptnr. Wasinger, Parham, Morthland Terrell & Wasinger, Hannibal, 1987—. Bd. dirs. Marion County Svcs. for the Developmentally Disabled, Hannibal, 1989—. Mem. Mo. Bar Assn. (family law sect.), 10th Jud. Cir. Bar Assn., U. Mo. Alumni Assn. (life), Phi Delta Phi. Office: Wasinger Parham Morthland Terrell & Wasinger 2801 Saint Marys Ave Hannibal MO 63401-3775

TERRELL, W(ILLIAM) GLENN, university president emeritus; b. Tallahassee, May 24, 1920; s. William Glenn and Esther (Collins) T.; m. Gail Strandberg Terrell; children by previous marriage: Francine Elizabeth, William Glenn III. BA, Davidson Coll., 1942, LLD (hon.), 1969; MS, Fla. State U., 1948; PhD, State U. Iowa, 1952; LLD (hon.), Gonzaga U., 1984, Seattle U., 1985. Instr., then asst. prof. Fla. State U., Tallahassee, 1948-55; asst. prof., then assoc. prof., chmn. dept. psychology U. Colo., Boulder, 1955-59, assoc., acting dean Coll Arts and Scis., 1959-63; prof. psychology, dean Coll. Liberal Arts and Scis., U. Ill. at Chgo. Circle, 1963-65, dean faculties, 1965-67; pres. Wash. State U., Pullman, 1967-85, pres. emeritus, 1985—; Pres. Nat. Assn. State Univs. and Land-Grant Colls., 1977-78; cons. The Pacific Inst., Seattle, 1987—. Contbr. articles to profl. jours. Served to capt. inf. U.S. Army, 1942-46, ETO. Recipient Disting. Alumnus award U. Iowa, 1985. Fellow APA, Soc. Rsch. in Child Devel.; mem. AAAS, Sigma Xi, Phi Kappa Phi. Avocations: golf, reading, traveling. Home: 2438 36th Ave W Seattle WA 98199-3704 Office: The Pacific Inst 1011 Western Ave Seattle WA 98104-1040

TERRILL, CLAIR ELMAN, animal scientist, geneticist, consultant; b. Rippey, Iowa, Oct. 27, 1910; s. Otis Wallace and Mary Irene (Grow) T.; m. Zola Mae Alexander, June 9, 1932; children: Ronald Lee (dec.), Richard Eugene. BS, Iowa State U., 1932; PhD, U. Mo., 1936. Rsch. asst. U. Mo., 1932-36; asst. animal husbandman Ga. Expt. Sta. USDA, 1936; animal husbandman Agrl. Rsch. Svc. USDA, Dubois, Idaho, 1936-53, dir. U.S. Sheep Expt. Sta., 1953-55; chief sheep and fur animal rsch. br. USDA, Beltsville, Md., 1955-72, staff scientist nat. program staff Agrl. Rsch. Svc., 1972-81, collaborator nat. program staff, 1981—; Mem. sub-panel Pres.'s Sci. Adv. Com. World Food Supply, 1966; adj. prof. Utah State U., Logan, 1986-87; cons. FAO, 1984. Contbr. chpts. to several books. Recipient Silver Ram award Am. Sheep Industry, 1975, Saddle and Sirloin Portrait award, 1989; inductee Internat. Stockmen's Hall of Fame, 1987, Agrl. Rsch. Svc. Hall of Fame, 1993; Fulbright grantee U NSW, Kensington, Australia, 1969. Fellow AAAS, Am. Soc. Animal Sci. (pres. Western sect. 1951, chmn. com. rsch. 1950-52, com. monographs 1955-60, editorial bd. 1954-57, sec.-treas. 1960-62, v.p. 1963, pres. 1964, bd. dirs.); mem. World Assn. Animal Prodn. (coun. 1965-68), Am. Forage and Grasslands Coun. (bd. dirs. 1963-68), Am. Registry Profl. Animal Scientists, Internat. Goat Assn. (bd. dirs.), Genetic Soc. Am., Am. Genetic Assn. (coun. 1965-68, v.p., pres. 1970), Am. Meat Sci. Assn., Am. Assn. Anatomists, Am. Inst. Biol. Scis., Soc. Study Reprodn., Sigma Xi, Alpha Zeta, Gamma Sigma Delta. Home: 318 Apple Grove Rd Silver Spring MD 20904-2745 Office: USDA Nat Program Staff Agrl Rsch Svc Barc W # 005 Beltsville MD 20705

TERRILL, JAMES E., computer manufacturing company executive. Pres., CEO Jefferson Smurfit Corp., Clayton, Mo. Office: Smurfit Newsprint Corp PO Box 70 Newberg OR 97132-0070 also: Jefferson Smurfit Corp 8182 Maryland Ave Clayton MO 63105*

TERRILL, JULIA ANN, elementary education educator; b. St. Joseph, Mo., Nov. 24, 1954; d. Jule Holmes and Beverly Jean (Brown) T. BS in Elem. Edn., N.W. Mo. State U., 1976, MEd, 1980. Tchr. learning disabilities Nodaway-Holt, Maitland, Mo., 1976-79; tchr. learning disabilities Lexington (Mo.) R-V, 1979-84, classroom tchr., 1984—. Mem. Young Citizens for Jerry Litton, Chillicothe, Mo., 1972, 76; mem., historian PTO, 1993-94, 94-95. Mem. ASCD, Mo. State Tchrs. Assn., Comty. Tchrs. Assn. (sec. 1992-93), Order Ea. Star, Delta Kappa Gamma. Baptist. Avocations: reading, playing piano and giving lessons, swimming, walking, traveling.

TERRILL, ROBERT CARL, hospital administrator; b. Oklahoma City, Dec. 10, 1927; s. D. Willard and Velma (Mitchell) T.; m. Jessica Doe, Dec. 14, 1957; children—Thane Bennett, Sarah Haven. BA, U. Okla., 1948, MA in History, 1961; MA in Hosp. Adminstrn., State U. Iowa, 1954; EdD in Ednl. Adminstrn., Ind. U., 1978. Adminstrv. resident Mary Fletcher Hosp., Burlington, Vt., 1953-55; asst. adminstr., personnel dir. Mary Fletcher Hosp., 1955-61, assoc. adminstr., 1961-65; adminstr. Hosps. of U. Okla., Oklahoma City, 1965-72; dir. Ind. Univ. Hosps., Indpls., 1972-76; instr. health adminstrn. Ind. U., 1976-77; assoc. prof. Coll. Mgmt. U. Mass., Boston, 1977-87; preceptor in hosp. adminstrn. Washington U., St. Louis, Trinity U., San Antonio; asst. prof. U. Okla. Health Scis. Center.; pub. edn. planning svcs. corp., 1987—. Fellow Am. Coll. Hosp. Adminstrs.; mem. Mass. Hosp. Assn., Am. Hosp. Assn., Assn. Programs in Hosp. Adminstrn., Pub. Health Assn., New Eng. Hosp. Assembly, Nat. League for Nursing, State U. Iowa. Alumni Assn., Ind. U. Alumni Assn. Club: Rotarian. Home: 26 Grove St Sandwich MA 02563-2125 Office: 93 Old Kings Hwy Sandwich MA 02563-1877

TERRILL, ROSS GLADWIN, author, educator; b. Melbourne, Australia; Came to U.S., 1965, naturalized, 1979; s. Frank and Miriel (Lloyd) T. B.A. with 1st class honors, U. Melbourne; Ph.D., Harvard U., 1970. Tutor in polit. sci. U. Melbourne, 1962-63; staff sec. Australian Student Christian Movement, 1964-65; teaching fellow Harvard, 1968-70, lectr. govt., 1970-73, asso. prof., 1974-78, research fellow East Asian studies, 1970—; dir. student programs Harvard (Center Internat. Affairs), 1974-78; contbg. editor Atlantic Monthly, 1970-84; research fellow Asia Soc., 1977-79. Author: China Profile, 1969, China and Ourselves, 1971, 800,000,000: The Real China, 1972, R.H. Tawney and His Times, 1973, Flowers on an Iron Tree, 1975, The Future of China, 1978, The China Difference, 1979, Mao: A Biography, 1980, revised 1993, White-Boned Demon, 1984, The Australians, 1987, Madam Mao, 1992, China in Our Time, 1992; contbr. numerous articles to profl. jours. Recipient Nat. Mag. award, 1972; George Polk Meml. award outstanding mag. reporting, 1972; Sumner prize, 1970. Mem. Authors Guild, PEN. Club: Harvard of N.Y.C. Home: 200 Saint Botolph St Boston MA 02115-4911

TERRILL, THOMAS EDWARD, health facility administrator; b. Mpls., Oct. 4, 1939; married. BS, U. Minn., 1961; M Health Care Adminstrn., U. Pitts., 1963, DS, 1970. Adminstrv. resicent Homestead (Pa.) Hosp., 1962-63; adminstrv. asst. Truman Med. Ctr.-West, Kanasas City, Mo., 1963-65, asst. adminstr., 1965-67; asst. prof. U. Pitts., 1967-73, assoc. prof., 1973-74; dir. mktg. and planning Mountain States Regional Med. Program, Boise, Idaho, 1974-76, divsn. dir., 1976-77; v.p. Hollywood Presbyn. Med. Ctr., L.A., 1977; assoc. dir. Akron (Ohio) City Hosp., 1978-81, v.p. med. affairs, 1981-83; sr. mgr. Peat Marwick Mitchell, Phila., 1983-87; v.p. Network Inc., Randolph, N.J., 1987-90; exec. v.p. Univ. Health Sys., New Brunswick, N.J., 1990—. Contbr. articles to profl. publs. Home: Univ Health System Plaza 11 6009 Hunters Glen Dr Plainsboro NJ 08536 Office: Univ Health Sys 317 George St New Brunswick NJ 08901*

TERRIS, ALBERT, metal sculptor; b. N.Y.C., Nov. 10, 1916; s. Aaron and Fania (Rosenthal) Teraspulsky; children: Susan, Abby, David, Enoch. BSS, CCNY, 1939; postgrad., NYU Inst. Fine Arts, 1939-42. lectr. Met. Mus. Art, 1941-42; tchr. fine arts N.Y.C. High Sch. System, 1947-54; prof. emeritus Bklyn. Coll., 1947-86. Steel sculptures include Non-Fixed Relationship, 1948, Anti-Gravity, 1950, Giraffes, 1953, Short Art, 1953, Pro-Gravity Chains, 1956, Tools, 1956, Crushed Sculpture, 1956, Words, 1957, Discursive-Illegible-Boustrophedon, 1975, Plates of Charlemagne, 1975, Fireharps, 1975, Cycle of Life, 1977; one-man shows: Saidenberg, 1955, Duveen-Graham, 1958, Carnagie Internats., 1958, 62, Bklyn. Mus. Biennale (awarded first prize), 1960, Allan Stone, 1962, Critics Choice, 1972, Artists Space, 1975, Gloria Cortella, 1977, (retrospective) The Artist in the Civil Service Bklyn. Coll. Gallery, 1985; exhibited in group shows at Tanager Gallery, 1952-61, Stable anns., 1952-60, Mus. Modern Art, N.Y.C., 1962, others; represented in permanent collections: Stephen Paine, Boston, Arnold Maremont, Evanston, G. David Thompson Estate, NBC-TV, others. Served with 1st Allied Airborne, 1942-45. Home: 280 S Ocean Ave Freeport NY 11520-4939

TERRIS, MILTON, physician, educator; b. N.Y.C., Apr. 22, 1915; s. Harry and Gussie (Dokshitski) T.; m. Rema Lapouse, Nov. 23, 1941 (dec. Aug. 1970); children—Andrew David, Eugene Charles (dec.); m. Lillian Long, Feb. 6, 1971. A.B., Columbia, 1935; M.D., N.Y.U., 1939; M.P.H., Johns Hopkins, 1944. Intern Harlem Hosp., N.Y.C., 1939-41; resident Bellevue Hosp., N.Y.C., 1941-42; practice medicine specializing in preventive medicine Buffalo, 1951-58, N.Y.C., 1960-80, South Burlington, Vt., 1980—; asst. dean post-grad. edn. Sch. Medicine, U. Buffalo, 1951-58, assoc., 1952-54, asst. prof., 1954-55, assoc. prof. preventive medicine, 1955-58; prof. epidemiology Sch. Medicine, Tulane U., 1958-60; head chronic disease unit dept. epidemiology Pub. Health Research Inst., N.Y.C., 1960-64; prof. preventive medicine N.Y. Med. Coll., 1964-80, chmn. dept. community and preventive medicine, 1968-80; vis. prof. U. Toronto, 1984-93, U. Montreal, 1985—. Author: Goldberger on Pellagra, 1964, La Revolución Epidemiológica y la Medicina Social, 1980; Editor: Jour. Public Health Policy, 1980—. Recipient Abraham M. Lilienfeld award Am. Coll. Epidemiology. Fellow N.Y. Acad. Medicine, Am. Pub. Health Assn. (past pres.; Sedgwick Meml. award 1984); mem. Assn. Tchrs. Preventive Medicine (Duncan Clark award 1984; past pres.), Soc. Epidemiologic Research (past pres.), Nat. Assn. Pub. Health Policy (past pres.), Phi Beta Kappa, Alpha Omega Alpha, Delta Omega. Home and Office: 208 Meadowood Dr South Burlington VT 05403

TERRIS, SUSAN, physician, cardiologist; b. Morristown, N.J., Sept. 5, 1944; d. Albert and Virginia (Rinaldy) T. BA in History, U. Chgo., 1967, PhD in Biochemistry, 1975, MD, 1976. Diplomate Am. Bd. Internal Medicine, Am. Bd. Endocrinology and Metabolism, Am. Bd. Cardiovascular Disease. Resident in internal medicine Washington U., Barnes Hosp., St. Louis, 1976-78; fellow in endocrinology and metabolism U. Chgo., 1978-80, fellow cardiology, 1980-83; fellow cardiology U. Mich., Ann Arbor, 1983-85, instr. cardiology, 1985-86; head cardiac catheterization lab., head cardiology Westland (Mich.) Med. Ctr., 1985. Contbr. articles to Jour. Biol. Chemistry, Am. Jour. Physiology, Am. Jour. Cardiology, Jour. Clin. Investigation, other profl. publs. Grantee Juvenile Diabetes Found., 1978-80, NIH, 1978-79. Mem. AAAS, Am. Heart Assn., N.Y. Acad. Sci., Am. Women in Sci. Achievements include rsch. demonstrating dependence of intracellular degradation of insulin upon its prior receptor-mediated uptake by liver; studies of effects of various drugs on human circulatory system.

TERRITO, MARY C., health facility administrator, oncologist. BS in Biology, Wayne State U., 1965, MD, 1968. Intern/resident in internal medicine Parkland Hosp., Dallas, 1971-73; fellow in hematology/oncology Harbor-U. Calif., L.A., 1973-74, UCLA, 1974-75; rsch. assoc. Wadsworth VA Hosp., L.A., 1975-81; asst. prof. dept. medicine UCLA, 1975-81, assoc. prof., 1981—, dir. bone marrow transplant program Ctr. Health Scis., 1981—. Contbr. articles to profl. jours. Office: UCLA Bone Marrow Transplantation Program Center for Health Sciences Los Angeles CA 90024

TERRY, CLARK, musician; b. St. Louis, Dec. 14, 1920; m. Pauline Reddon; 2 children. Privately educated. Pres. Etoile Music Prodns., 1955—, Pastel Music, 1958—; v.p. Creative Jazz Composers, Inc., 1972—; itinerant jazz clinician and educator; exec. dir. Internat. of Jazz. Leader, Clark Terry Big Bad Band, 1966—; albums include: The World of Duke Ellington, Vol. 2, Duke Ellington Such Sweet Thunder, The Terry-Brookmeyer Quintet, Cruisin', Cool Blues, Oscar Peterson Trio with Clark Terry, Clark Terry's Big Bad Band Live on 57th Street, The Happy Horns of Clark Terry, Yes, The Blues, 1981, Paris 1960, 1985, Live at the Village Gate, 1991, (with Red Mitchell) Jive at Five, 1993. Author: Let's Talk Trumpet, 1973, Interpretation of the Jazz Language, 1976, Circular Breathing, 1977. Served with USN, 1942-45. Recipient numerous awards, including Grammy nominations, Pote Distinguished Jazz Artist, Phil., 1989. Office: care Pablo Records 451 N Canon Dr Beverly Hills CA 90210-4819

TERRY, CLIFFORD LEWIS, journalist; b. Highland Park, Ill., Jan. 19, 1937; s. Clifford Lewis and Isabelle (Marlow) T.; m. Patricia West Dickelman, Sept. 1, 1966; children: Christopher West, Scott Marlow. Student, Carleton Coll., Northfield, Minn., 1954-55; BA, Trinity Coll., Hartford, Conn., 1958; postgrad., Columbia U., 1962-63. Tchr., English and history Mt. Hermon (Mass.) Sch., 1958-59; police reporter City News Bur. Chgo., 1959-60; mem. staff Chgo. Tribune, 1960-94, movie critic, 1965-70; assoc. editor Chgo. Tribune (Sunday mag.), 1970-82, feature writer, 1982-85, TV critic, 1985-89, arts feature writer, 1989-94; ind. writer, 1994—. Served with AUS, 1960. Nieman fellow Harvard U., 1969-70. Mem. Phi Beta Kappa.

TERRY, F. DAVIS, JR., investment company executive; b. Atlanta, Apr. 30, 1954; s. Frederick Davis and Jane Frances (Hargrave) T.; m. Tai Chang, June 23, 1979. BA, Yale U., 1976; MBA, U. Pa., 1979. Assoc. Dillon, Read & Co. Inc., N.Y.C., 1979-82, v.p., 1983-85, sr. v.p., 1986-89, mng. dir., 1989—. Office: Dillon Read & Co Inc 535 Madison Ave New York NY 10022-4212

TERRY, FRANK JEFFREY, bishop. Bishop Diocese of Spokane, Wash., 1991—. Office: Diocese of Spokane 245 E 13th Ave Spokane WA 99202-1114

TERRY, FREDERICK ARTHUR, JR., lawyer; b. Buffalo, May 24, 1932; s. Frederick Arthur and Agnes Elizabeth (Tranter) T. BA, Williams Coll., 1953; LLB, Columbia U., 1956. Bar: N.Y. 1957, U.S. Dist. Ct. (so., no. and ea. dists.) N.Y., U.S. Ct. Appeals (2d cir.), U.S. Tax Ct., U.S. Supreme Ct. Law clk. U.S. Ct. Appeals (2nd cir.), 1956-57; assoc. Sullivan & Cromwell, N.Y.C., 1957-65, ptnr., 1965—. Bd. dirs. Eisenhower Exch. Fellowships, Grand Ctrl. Partnership, Inc., Natural Resources Def. Coun., Am. Fedn. for Aging Rsch., Inc., Weinman Found.; sec., mem. bd. McIntosh Found.; trustee, chmn. com. on trust and estate gift plans Rockefeller U.; trustee Harold K. Hochschild Found., Guild Hall, East Hampton; chmn. Flagler Found. Mem. ABA, N.Y. State Bar Assn., Assn. Bar City N.Y., Maidstone Club (East Hampton, N.Y.), Century Assn., River Club, Union Club (N.Y.C.), Lyford Cay Club (Bahamas). Office: Sullivan & Cromwell 125 Broad St New York NY 10004-2400

TERRY, GARY A., lawyer, former trade association executive; b. Ogden, Utah, Apr. 2, 1935; s. Hyrum Aceal and Viola (Sorenson) T.; m. Carole Ann Eitel, June 23, 1962; children—Stephanie Ann, Brendan Gary. B.A. in Polit. Sci., UCLA, 1964; J.D., George Washington U., 1968. Bars: Va. 1969 D.C. 1969. Mem. staff U.S. Ho. of Reps., Washington, 1964-65; Washington staff Bethlehem Steel Corp., 1965-69; atty. HUD, Washington, 1969; exec. v.p. Am. Land Devel. Assn. (now Am. Resort Devel. Assn.), Washington, 1969-82, pres., 1982-91; also dir. Am. Land Devel. Assn. (now Am. Resort Devel. Assn.); with Jones, Waldo, Holbrook & McDonough, Washington, 1991—, St. George, 1995—; dir. Internat. Found. for Timesharing, Washington, 1981-91, mem. consultative council Nat. Inst. Bldg. Scis., Washington, 1982-85; U.S. rep. land use and town planning com. Internat. Real Estate Fedn., Brussels, 1984-91; mem. Found. for Internat. Meetings, Washington, 1984—; del. Lincoln Inst. Land Policy, Harvard U., 1984, 85. Contbr. articles to profl. jours. Asst. to exec. dir. Presdl. Inaugural Com., 1969-70; mem. adv. bd. NOAA, Washington, 1972; bd. dirs. Zacchaeus Free Med. and Legal Clinics, Washington, 1991-95, co-chair lawyers com., 1992-95. Seved with USN, 1953-56. Decorated Am. Spirit of Honor medal. Mem. Va. Bar Assn., D.C. Bar Assn., Am. Soc. Assn. Execs. Mem. LDS Ch. Avocations: music; literature; architectural design; art; travel. Home: 952 E Lizzie Lane St. George UT 84790 Office: Jones Waldo Holbrook & McDonough 2300 M St NW Ste 900 Washington DC 20037-1434 Office: 249 E Tabernacle Ste 200 St. George UT 84770-2978

TERRY, GEORGE MARSHALL, vocational studies educator; b. Aulander, N.C., Jan. 19, 1944; s. Godfrey Jackson and Virginia Elizabeth (Burden) T.; m. Judith Elaine Bland, June 12, 1964; children: Randy, Jeffrey, Michelle, Cynthia. AS, Mt. Olive Coll., 1982. Cert. tchr., N.C. Vocat. tchr. Bertie Jr. H.S., Windsor, N.C., 1970-72; home builder various locations, 1967—; tchr. carpentry Lakewood H.S., Roseboro, N.C., 1984-93; vocat. testing coord. Sampson County Schs., 1993-95; tchr. constrn. tech. Midway H.S., Dunn, N.C., 1995—; curriculum carpentry team leader N.C. Trade and Indsl. Dept. Edn., Raleigh, 1989-93; trade and industry adv. bd. N.C. Dept. Pub. Edn., Raleigh, 1989-93. Pastor Weldon (N.C.) Pentecostal Holiness Ch., Mt. Olive, N.C., 1979-82, Sharon Pentecostal Holiness Ch., Clinton, N.C., 1982-94. Mem. NEA, ASCD, Am. Vocat. Assn., Nat. Assn. Trade and Indsl. Educators, N.C. Vocat. Assn., Associated Gen. Contractors Am. (cert. master residential carpenter), Millenium/Aulander Lions Club (pres. 1970-71). Republican. Home: PO Box 603 Salemburg NC 28385 Office: Sampson County Schs PO Box 439 Clinton NC 28328-0439

TERRY, GLENN A., retired nuclear chemist; b. St. Paul, Aug. 26, 1922; s. Claude Alexander and Loretta (Glenn) T.; m. Evelyn Jean Lehmann, Aug. 16, 1947; 1 child, Stephen Allan. BS, So. Ill. U., 1947; PhD, U. Wis., 1951. Rsch. chemist Mallinckrodt Chem. Works, St. Louis, 1951-56; process improvement head Mallinckodt Chem. Works, St. Louis, 1956-59; sect. leader Spencer/Gulf, Kansas City, Mo., 1959-68; tech. dir. Nuclear Fuel Svcs., Erwin, Tenn., 1968-73; nuclear process engr. U.S. Nulcear Regulatory Com., Washington, 1973-81, sect. leader, 1981-88, ret., 1988. Contbr. articles to profl. jours.; patentee in field. Lt. (j.g.) USN, 1942-46, PTO. Mem. Am. Chem. Soc. (emeritus), Am. Nuclear Soc. (emeritus), Am. Legion, VFW, Elks. Republican. Achievements include patents in field. Home: 3824 Brooke Meadow Ln Olney MD 20832

TERRY, JAMES JOSEPH, JR., lawyer; b. Yonkers, N.Y., July 2, 1952; s. James Joseph Sr. and Marie Catherine (O'Boyle) T.; m. Marguerite Mary O'Connor, Sept. 29, 1985; 1 child, James Daniel. BA, NYU, 1974; JD, Columbia U., 1977. Bar: N.Y. 1978, U.S. Dist. Ct. (so. and ea. dists.) N.Y. 1978, U.S. Ct. Appeals (2d cir.) 1981, U.S. Ct. Appeals (3d cir.) 1989. Assoc. Cole & Deitz, N.Y.C., 1977-86; ptnr. Winston & Strawn (formerly Cole & Deitz), N.Y.C., 1986—. Mem. ABA, N.Y. State Bar Assn., Def. Rsch. Inst. Democrat. Roman Catholic. Avocations: fishing, reading. Home: 190 Kneeland Ave Yonkers NY 10705-2713 Office: Winston & Strawn 200 Park Ave New York NY 10166-4193

TERRY, JOHN ALFRED, judge; b. Utica, N.Y., May 6, 1933; s. Robert Samuel and Julia Berenice (Collins) T. B.A. magna cum laude, Yale U., 1954; J.D., Georgetown U., 1960. Bar: D.C. 1960. Asst. U.S. atty. for D.C., 1962-67; staff atty. Nat. Commn. Reform of Fed. Criminal Laws, Washington, 1967-68; pvt. practice law Washington, 1968-69; chief appellate div. U.S. Atty.'s Office for D.C., 1969-82; judge D.C. Ct. Appeals, 1982—. Mem. D.C. Bar (bd. govs. 1977-82), ABA, Phi Beta Kappa. Office: DC Ct Appeals 500 Indiana Ave NW Washington DC 20001-2131

TERRY, JOHN HART, lawyer, former utility company executive, former congressman; b. Syracuse, N.Y., Nov. 14, 1924; s. Frank and Saydee (Hart) T.; m. Catherine Jean Taylor Phelan, Apr. 15, 1950; children: Catherine Jean (Mrs. Richard Thompson), Lynn Marie (Mrs. Robert Tacher), Susan Louise (Mrs. Stanley Germain), Mary Carole (Mrs. Stephen Brady). B.A., U. Notre Dame, 1945; J.D., Syracuse U., 1948. Bar: N.Y. bar 1950, D.C. bar 1972. Asst. to partner Smith & Sovik, 1948-59; asst. sec. to Gov. State of N.Y., 1959-61; sr. partner firm Smith, Sovik, Terry, Kendrick, McAuliffe & Schwarzer, 1961-73; sr. v.p., gen. counsel, sec. Niagara Mohawk Power Corp., Syracuse, 1973-87; counsel Hiscock & Barclay, Syracuse, 1987-94; atty. in pvt. practice, 1994—; mem. N.Y. State Assembly, 1962-70, 92d Congress from 34th N.Y. Dist., 1971-73; presdl. elector, 1972. State chmn. United Services Orgn., 1964-73; past pres. John Timothy Smith Found.; Founder, dir. Bishop Foery Found., Inc.; dir. St. Joseph's Hosp. Council; past pres. Lourdes Camp; bd. dirs. N.Y. State Traffic Council; past nat. bd. dirs. Am. Cancer Soc.; mem. adv. council Syracuse U. Sch. Mgmt.; past pres. Cath. Youth Orgn.; bd. dirs. Syracuse Community Baseball Club. Served to 1st lt. AUS, 1943-46. Decorated Purple Heart, Bronze Star; named Man of Year Syracuse Jr. C. of C., 1958, Man of Yr. N.Y. State Jr. C. of C., 1959, Young Man of Yr. U. Notre Dame Club Cen. N.Y., 1959. Mem. ABA (utility law sect.), N.Y. State Bar Assn. (chmn. com. on public utility law), Onondaga County Bar Assn. (chmn. membership and legis. coms.), D.C. Bar Assn., County Officers Assn., Citizens Found., U. Notre Dame, Syracuse U. law assns., Am. Legion, VFW, DAV, 40 and 8, Mil. Order of Purple Heart. Roman Catholic. Clubs: Century, Bellevue Country, Capitol Hill (Washington), Vero Beach Country.

TERRY, JOHN JOSEPH, transportation investor; b. Chgo., July 29, 1937; s. Michael Parnell and Honore (Ryan) T.; m. Terese Rose Mulkern, Dec. 31, 1960; children—Michael P., Gregory, Deirdre. B.S., Loyola U., Chgo., 1959; postgrad., U. So. Fla., 1967. C.P.A., Ill. With Touche, Ross & Co., 1959-65; v.p. Nat. City Lines, Denver, 1965-71; v.p. fin. Pepsico Transp., Inc., Tulsa, 1971-74; v.p. U.S. Rwy. Assn., Washington, 1974-76; chmn. P.I.E. Transport Europe, 1976-79; exec. v.p. IU Internat. Corp., Wilmington, Del., 1976-85; pres. Transp. Mgmt. Investment Group, Inc.,, Phila., 1985—; v.p.-at-large Am. Trucking Assn., Washington, 1984-85, chmn., internat. competitiveness task force, 1991, tax policy com., 1987—; bd. dirs. Caldwell Freight Lines, Lenoir, N.C., Basin Western, Inc., Roosevelt, Utah, Ampace Corp.; cons. freight transp. World Bank and European Bank for Reconstrn. and Devel., 1986—. Served with U.S. Army, 1960-63. Recipient Best Motor Carrier Rsch. award Transp. Rsch. Forum, 1991. Office: Transp Mgmt Investment Group Inc 103 Eton Rd Yardley PA 19067-7311

TERRY, LEON CASS, neurologist, educator; b. Northville, Mich., Dec. 22, 1940; s. Leon Herbert and Zella Irene (Boyd) T.; m. Suzanne Martinson, June 27, 1964; children: Kristin, Sean. Pharm. D., U. Mich., 1964; MD, Marquette U., 1969; PhD, McGill U., 1982, MBA, U. S. Fla., 1994. Dipolmate Am. Bd. Psychiatry and Neurology, Am. Bd. Med. Mgmt. Intern, U. Rochester, N.Y., 1969-70; staff assoc. NIH, 1970-72; resident in neurology McGill U., Montreal, Que., Can., 1972-75, MRC fellow, 1975-78; assoc. prof. U. Tenn., Memphis, 1978-81; prof. neurology U. Mich., Ann Arbor, 1981-89, assoc prof. physiology, 1982-89; asst. chief neurology VA Med. Ctr., Ann Arbor, 1982-89; prof. neurology and physiology, chmn. dept. neurology Med. Coll of Wis., Milw., 1989—; dir. clin. neurosci. ctr. and multiple sclerosis clinic, Med. Coll. Wis.; vice chief of staff Froedtert Hosp., 1994—. Contbr. articles to profl. jours., chpts. to books. Served to lt. comdr. USPHS, 1970-72. NIH grantee, 1981-92; VA grantee, 1980-92; VA Clin. Investigator award, 1980-81. Mem. AMA, Am. Soc. Clin. Investigation, Cen. Soc. Clin. Investigation, So. Soc. Clin. Investigation, Am. Neurol. Assn., Am. Coll. Physician Execs. (vice chmn. academic health ctr. soc. 1994-95, chair, 1995—, leader forum health care delivery 1995—), Am. Coll. Healthcare Execs., Endocrine Soc., Am. Acad. Neurology, Internat. Soc. Neuroendocrinology, Internat. Soc. Psychoneuroendocrinology, Soc. Neurosci, Soc. Rsch. Biol. Rhythms, Milw. Acad. Physicians, Wis. Neurol. Assn., Wis. State Med. Soc., Med. Soc. Milw. County, Milw. Neuropsychiatric Soc. (pres.-elect). Avocations: pilot, skiing, scuba diving, computers. Office: Med Coll Wis Dept Neurology Froedtert Hosp 9200 W Watertown Plank Rd Milwaukee WI 53226-3557

TERRY, MARGARET SMOOT, special education educator; b. Elkin, N.C., July 5, 1945; d. Claude Dennis and Eula (Powell) Smoot; div.; 1 child, Susan Leigh. BEd, Fla. Atlantic U., 1966, MEd, 1969; Edn. Specialist, U. South Fla., 1985. Cert. tchr., Fla. Tchr. Wynnebrook Elem. Sch., West Palm Beach, Fla., 1967-73; tchr. spl. edn. Boca Raton (Fla.) Elem. Sch., 1973-75, J.C. Mitchell Elem. Sch., Boca Raton, 1975-83, Loggers Run Mid. Sch., Boca Raton, 1983-84; computer specialist Palm Beach County Schs., West Palm Beach, 1984-89; coord. exceptional student edn. Addison Mizner Elem. Sch., Boca Raton, 1989-92, Del Prado Elem. Sch., Boca Raton, 1992—; adj. prof. Fla. Atlantic U., Boca Raton, 1987-89; computer trainer Palm Beach County Schs., 1984-89, tech. trainer, 1991-92; cons. Weiss Sch. for Gifted, West Palm Beach, 1988-89; presenter program at computer conf., Palvia, Bulgaria, 1984. Mem. Fla. Assn. Sci. Tchrs., Fla. Assn. Gifted, Phi Beta Kappa, Delta Kappa Gamma (pres. Alpha Omega chpt. 1988-90). Democrat. Home: 735 Heron Dr Delray Beach FL 33444-1923 Office: Del Prado Elem Sch Del Prado Cir Delray Beach FL 33483

TERRY, MARSHALL NORTHWAY, JR., English language educator, author; b. Cleve., Feb. 7, 1931; s. Marshall Northway and Margaret Louise (Carpenter) T.; m. Antoinette Barksdale, Sept. 5, 1953; children: Antoinette, Terry Bryant, Mary Marshall. Student, Amherst Coll., 1949-50, Kenyon Coll., 1950-51; B.A., So. Meth. U., 1953, M.A., 1954. Teaching fellow English So. Meth. U., Dallas, 1954; dir. pub. relations, lectr. English So. Meth. U., 1957-64, instr. English, 1956, 65-67, asst. dir., 1968, assoc. prof., 1969-71, prof. English, 1972—, chmn. dept., 1971-75, 79-82, dir. creative writing program; book critic Dallas News, 1970-75; pres. faculty senate So. Meth. U., 1993-94, assoc. provost, 1994—. Author: Old Liberty, 1961, Tom Northway, 1968, Dallas Stories, 1986, Ringer, 1987, My Father's Hands, 1993, Land of Hope and Glory, 1996; contbr. short stories to various jours. and mags.; editor Prize Stories, 1986. Past trustee Incarnate Word Coll., San Antonio; sec. bd. trustees Fort Burgwin Research Ctr., Ranchos de Taos, N.Mex. Recipient Jesse H. Jones fiction award Tex. Inst. Letters, 1968, Best Short Story award S.W. Rev., 1973, S.W. Writer of Yr. award, 1988, Willis M. Tate award So. Meth. U., 1990, 94, Lon Tinkle award for continuing excellence in Letters, Tex. Inst. Letters, 1991. Mem. AAUP (chpt. pres. 1971), Coll. Conf. Tchrs. English, South Central MLA, Tex. Inst. Letters (pres. 1977-79, councilor 1980—). Democrat. Methodist. Home: 2717 Lovers Ln Dallas TX 75225-7905 Office: So Meth Univ Dept English Dallas TX 75275

TERRY, MEGAN, playwright, performer , photographer; b. Seattle, July 22, 1932; d. Harold Joseph and Marguerite Cecelia (Henry) Duffy. Student, Banff Sch. Fine Arts, summers, 1950-52, 56, U. Alta., Edmondton, Can., 1952-53; B.Ed., U. Wash., 1956. Founding mem. Open Theater, N.Y.C., 1963; ABC fellow Yale U., 1966-67; founding mem., v.p. N.Y. Theatre Strategy, 1971; adj. prof. theatre U. Nebr., Omaha, until 1977; Hill prof. fine arts U. Minn.-Duluth, spring 1983; Bingham prof. humanities U. Louisville, 1981; mem. theatre panel, mem. overview panel Nat. Endowment Arts, 1976-86, mem. opera/music theatre panel, 1985, mem. advancement panel, 1987; mem. theatre panel Rockefeller Found., 1977-85; mem. performing arts panel Nebr. State Council for Arts, 1977; mem. Nebr. Com. for Humanities, 1983-86; mem. Gov.'s Com. on Film and Telecommunications, 1985-86; founding mem. N.Y. Open Theatre, 1963-73; judge playwriting competition Mass., Wis., Ohio, Oreg. states, So. Playwrights Competition; Nat. Endowment Arts vis. artist in residence U. Iowa, 1992. Dir. Cornish Players, Cornish Sch. Allied Arts, Seattle, 1954-56, founding dir. playwrights workshop, Open Theatre, N.Y.C., 1963-68, playwright-in-residence, literary mgr. Omaha Magic Theatre, 1974—; author plays including: Kegger, Comings and Goings, The Magic Realists, Sanibel & Captiva, The People vs. Ranchman, Kepp Tightly Closed in a Cool Dry Place, The Gloaming Oh My Darling, Approaching Simone, Viet Rock, Massachussetts Trust, The Tommy Allen Show, Calm Down Mother, Sleazing Toward Athens, Babes in the Big House, Ex Miss Copper Queen, Mollie Bailey's Traveling Family Circus, Goona-Goona, Retro, Hothouse, Dinner's in the Blender, Objective Love, Katmandu, Fifteen Million Fifteen Year Olds, Fireworks, The Trees Blew Down, Choose a Spot on the Floor, Future Soap, Brazil Fado, Pro Game., Amtrak, Headlights, Breakfast Serial, Do You See What I'm Saying?, The Snow Queen, India Plays, I Forgot How Much I Like You; editor, writer: plays including Sea of Forms, Nightwalk, 1001 Horror Stories of The Plains, Running Gag, Couplings and Groupings, Walking Through Walls, Babes Unchained, Cancel That Last Thought; or See The 270 Foot Woman in Spandex, X-Raydiate: E-Motion in Action, Body Leaks, Sound Fields, Belches on Couches, Star Path Moonstop; photographer/editor: Right Brain Vacation Photos: Production Photographs of Omaha Magic Theatre Productions, 1972-92; mem. performance ensemble Omaha Magic Theatre nat. and internat. performance tours Body Leaks, 1991, Body Leaks, 1992, Sound Fields, 1993, 94, Belches on Couches, 1993, 94; contbr. articles in field to profl. jours. Mem. Nebr. Artist-in-the Schs., 1987—. Recipient Stanley Drama award, 1965, Office of Advanced Drama Rsch. award, 1965, Obie award, 1970, Disting. Contbrn. To and Svc. in Am. Theatre Silver medal Amoco Oil Co., 1977; Dramatists Guild Com. of Women Ann. award, 1983, Nebr. Artist of Yr. 1992; Gov. award Nebr., 1992; Rockefeller grantee, 1968, 87; NEA Lit. fellow, 1973; Guggenheim fellow, 1978; NEA playwriting fellow, 1989, Lifetime Am. Theatre fellow, 1994. Mem. NEA (reporter and panelist for theatre program, 1975-85), Women's Theatre Coun. (founding 1971), Women's Forum (charter), Am. Theatre Assn. (co-chmn. playwriting program 1977, chmn. playwrights project com. 1978-79, C. Crawford playwriting judge of 1987), Theatre Comm. Group (bd. dirs. 1988-92), New Dramatists (alumni, judge nat. playwriting competition 1987-88), ASSISTEJ-USA (bd. dirs. 1986-91). Home: 2309 Hanscom Blvd Omaha NE 68105-3143 Office: E Marton Agy Rm 612 One Union Sq New York NY 10003-3303

TERRY, MIRIAM JANICE, minister; b. Aliceville, Ala., May 4, 1956; d. Ernest Lee Jr. and Nolie (Lee) T. Student, U. Tex., Arlington, 1974-75, Am. Banking Sch., Tampa, Fla., 1978; BA in Bibl. Studies, Living Word Coll. and Sem., St. Louis, 1991, MRE, 1993, postgrad., 1993—. Ordained to ministry Life Anew Missionary Fellowship, 1987. Children's pastor Brandonville (Fla.) Christian Ch., 1975, Oxford (Ala.) Ch. of God, 1980-81; dir. children's ministries Newark Heights Ch. of God, Newark, Ohio, 1982-83, Life Christian Ctr., Madisonville, Ky., 1984—; dir. promotions Life Anew Ministries, Inc./Sta. WLCN-TV, Madisonville, 1984—; dir. edn. Life Christian Acad., Madisonville, 1990—; dir. day care Life Ctr. Day Care Plus, Madisonville, 1991—. Dir., producer seasonal dramas and musicals, 1989—; contbr. articles to religious jours. Vol. Regional Med. Ctr., Madisonville, 1984—, mem. laughter therapy com., 1990-91; vol. St. Jude's Children's Hosp., 1991—; vol. pediatric chaplain to various hosps.; dir ann. Summer Camp for children, 1988—. Recipient Outstanding Svc. award Regional Med. Ctr., 1986. Republican. Office: Life Anew Ministries Inc 721 Princeton Pike PO Box 1087 Madisonville KY 42431-1087 *The teaching of Jesus declares that life does not consist in the abundance of things which one possesses. This I have experienced to be true. The essence of life is not in things of material value but in the ideals and aspirations of the human spirit being in harmony with all of mankind and the world.*

TERRY, MORTON, academic administrator, physician; b. Utica, N.Y., Mar. 23, 1921; s. Isadore and Fanny (Brooks) T.; m. Geraldine Marie Rafferty, Oct. 31, 1948; children: Matthew, Jeffrey, Sheryl, Pamela. BA, Bklyn. Coll., 1942; DO, Phila. Coll. Osteo. Medicine, 1945, MS, 1950; postgrad., Am. Coll. Osteo. Internists, 1961. Diplomate Am. Osteo. Bd. Internal Medicine, Am. Osteo. Bd. Nuclear Medicine. Intern Osteo. Hosp. Phila., 1945-46, resident in internal medicine, 1946-48; internist, chmn. dept. internal medicine, exec. com. staff Biscayne (Fla.) Osteo. Hosp., 1953-60, chief staff, 1956-57; internist, chmn. dept. internal medicine Osteo. Gen. Hosp., 1960-75, chief staff, 1962-76; pres., founder Coll. Ostheopathic Medicine Southeastern U. Health Scis., North Miami Beach, Fla., 1979—; cons. internal medicine, 1949—; bd. dirs. County Nat. Bank. Chmn. osteo. div. United Way Dade County, 1966-75; bd. dirs. Am. Heart Assn. Gereater Miami, 1971—, del. state of Fla., 1975-77; bd. dirs. Comprehensive Health Planning Coun. Dade County, 1969-73, Health Systems Agy. South Fla., 1976-79, Dade County unit Am. Cancer Soc., 1974-76, Am. Osteo. Bd. Internal Medicine, 1971-73, South Fla. Scholarship and Awards Found, 1973-81, Boys Town Fla., 1958-71, Biscayne Osteo. Found., 1979-82, Southeastern Coll. Osteo. Medicine, 1979—. Recipient Recognition and Appreciation cert. City North Miami Beach, 1973, Outstanding Svc. award, Osteo. Profession and Community, 1973, Recognition and Appreciation cert. State of Fla., 1982, Leadership award Fla. chpt. Bklyn. Coll. Pharmacy, 1989, O. J. Snyder medal Disting. Alumnus Phila. Coll. Osteo. Medicine, 1990. Mem. Am. Coll. Osteo. Internists (bd. dirs. 1975—, Disting. Svc. award 1981), Am. Assn. Colls. Osteo. Medicine (bd. dirs. 1979—), Am. Osteo. Assn. (life), Fla. Osteo. Med. Assn. (pres. 1961-62, hon. life), Dade County Osteo. Med. Assn. (pres. 1952-53), Sigma Sigma Phi (hon.). Office: Southeastern U Health Sci 1750 NE 168th St North Miami Beach FL 33162-3021

TERRY, PANDORA ELAINE, lawyer; b. East Point, Ga., Dec. 12, 1965; d. Perry Monroe and Doreen (Murphy) Dykes; m. Wilbur Ray Terry, Aug. 14, 1989; 1 child, Tiffany Nicole. BA in Criminal Justice, U. Ga., 1988; JD, Ga. State U., 1994. Bar: Ga. 1994, U.S. Ct. Appeals (11th cir.) 1994, U.S. Dist. Ct. (no. dist.) Ga. 1995. Rsch. asst. Capital Jury Project, 1992-93; legal extern Fed. Pub. Defender, Atlanta, 1993; rsch. asst. Ga. Justice Project, Atlanta, 1993-94; attu. pvt. practice, Jonesboro, Ga., 1994—. Mem. ABA, Assn. Trial Lawyers Am., Nat. Assn. Criminal Defense Lawyers, Am. Bus. Women's Assn., Ga. Trial Lawyers Assn., Ga. Assn. Criminal Defense Lawyers, Clayton County Bar Assn., Fayette County Bar Assn. Republican. Baptist. Home: 345 Plantation Cir Riverdale GA 30296 Office: 216 N McDonough St Jonesboro GA 30236

TERRY, RICHARD ALLAN, consulting psychologist, former college president; b. Lincoln, Nebr., June 4, 1920; s. Lester C. and Dorothy (Weeden) T.; m. Z. Inci Incikaya, June 3, 1959; 1 child, Deniz. A.B., U. Notre Dame, 1944; M.S., Catholic U. Am., 1950, Ph.D., 1954. Instr., asst. prof., chmn. psychol. dept. U. Portland, Oreg., 1953-59; prin. scientist, chief advanced research, life scis. North Am. Aviation, Downey, Calif., 1959-63; assoc. prof. indsl. engring., dir. systems research center U. Okla., Norman, 1963-69; prof., head dept. psychology U. Tulsa, 1970-73; prof. psychology SUNY Coll. at Oswego, 1973-75, dean grad. studies and research, 1973-75, acting v.p. acad. affairs, 1973-74; v.p. for instrn. and curriculum SUNY Coll. at Brockport, 1975-78; pres. Quinnipiac Coll., Hamden, Conn., 1978-86; sr. ptnr. Richard Allan Terry Assocs., Cons., Hamden, 1986-91; vis. prof. Hacettepe U., Ankara, Turkey, 1969-70; v.p. Found. for Study of Behavioral Scis., Downey, 1965-68; assoc. fellow Timothy Dwight Coll., Yale U., 1982—; v.p. Conn. Council Higher Edn., 1983-84, pres., 1984-85. Trustee Chamber Orch. of New Eng., 1979-82, chmn. bd., 1982-83; vice chmn. Mgmt. Study Group, Town of Hamden, 1982-83; bd. dirs. Urban League Greater New Haven, 1983-90, sec. 1988-90; chmn. oversight com. Study of Police-Media Rels., 1983-84; mem. steering com. New Haven Initiative for Excellence in Edn., 1986-90, steering com. Town of Hamden Plan for the Future, 1988-91, adv. bd. Conn. Small Bus. Devel. Ctr., 1989-91; mem. Town of Hamden Planning and Zoning Commn., 1991-93. Mem. Am. Psychol. Assn., Conn. Conf. Ind. Colls. (sec.-treas. 1983-86), Greater New Haven C. of C. (bd. dirs. 1982-86, chmn. jobs compact planning com., 1984-85, steering com. 1985-86) Sigma Xi. Democrat. Roman Catholic. Home: 24 Talon Dr Schenectady NY 12309-1839

TERRY, RICHARD EDWARD, public utility holding company executive; b. Green Bay, Wis., July 7, 1937; s. Joseph Edward and Arleen (Agamet) T.; m. Catherine Lombardo, Nov. 19, 1966; children—Angela, Edward. BA, St. Norbert's Coll., West DePere, Wis., 1959; LLB, U. Wis., 1964; postgrad., Harvard U., 1986. Assoc. Ross & Hardies, Chgo., 1964-72; atty. Peoples Energy Corp., Chgo., 1972-79, asst. gen. counsel, 1979-81, v.p., gen. counsel, 1981-84; exec. v.p. People's Energy Corp., Peoples Gas Light & Coke Co. and North Shore Gas Co., 1984-87, pres., COO, 1987-90; chair, CEO People's Energy Corp., Peoples Gas Light & Coke Co. and North Shore Gas Co., Chgo., 1990—; bd. dirs. Peoples Energy Corp., Peoples Gas Light, North Shore Gas Co., Harris Bankcorp, Harris Trust & Savs., Amsted Industries. Bd. dirs. Mus. Sci. & Ind., 1991—, Inst. Gas Tech., 1987—, Ill. Coun. on Econ. Edn., 1987—, Big Shoulders, 1991—; mem. Chgo. Area Ctrl. Com., 1991—; mem. bus. adv. coun. Chgo. Urban League, 1991—; prin. Chgo. United, 1991—; trustee St. Xavier U., 1989—, St. Norbert Coll., 1982—, DePaul U., 1992—. 1st lt. U.S. Army, 1959-61. Mem. Am. Gas Assn. (bd. dirs. 1991—), Nat. Petroleum Coun., Chgo. C. of C. (bd. dirs. 1988—), Univ. Club, Mid-Am. Club, Chgo. Club, Econ. Club, Comml. Club Chgo. (mem. civic com. 1991—). Avocations: golf, fishing, reading. Office: Peoples Energy Corp 130 E Randolph St Chicago IL 60601

TERRY, ROBERT DAVIS, neuropathologist, educator; b. Hartford, Conn., Jan. 13, 1924; m. Patricia Ann Blech, June 27, 1952; 1 son, Nicolas Saul. AB, Williams Coll., 1946, DSc (hon.), 1991; MD, Albany (N.Y.) Med. Coll., 1950. Diplomate: Am. Bd. Pathology, Am. Bd. Neuropathology. Postdoctoral tng. St. Francis Hosp., Hartford, 1950, Bellevue Hosp., N.Y.C., 1951, Montefiore Hosp., N.Y.C., 1952-53, 54-55, Inst. Recherches sur le Cancer, Paris, France, 1953-54; sr. postdoctoral fellow Inst. Recherches sur le Cancer, 1965-66; asst. pathologist Montefiore Hosp., 1955-59; assoc. prof. dept. pathology Einstein Coll. Medicine, Bronx, N.Y., 1959-64; prof. Einstein Coll. Medicine, 1964-84, acting chmn. dept. pathology, 1969-70, chmn., 1970-84; prof. depts. neuroscis. and pathology U. Calif.-San Diego, 1984-94, prof. emeritus, 1994—; mem. study sect. pathology NIH, 1964-68; study sects. Nat. Multiple Sclerosis Soc., 1964-72, 74-78; mem. bd. sci. counselors Nat. Inst. Neurol. and Communicative Disorders and Stroke, NIH, 1976-80, chmn., 1977-80; mem. nat. sci. coun. Huntington's Disease Assn., 1978-81; mem. med. and sci. adv. bd. Alzheimer Assn., 1978-88; mem. sci. adv. bd. Max Planck Inst., Martinsried, 1990—. Mem. editorial adv. bd. Jour. Neuropathology and Exptl. Neurology, 1963-83, 85-88, Lab. Investigation, 1967-77, Revue Neurologique, 1977-87, Annals of Neurology, 1978-82, Ultrastructural Pathology, 1978-86, Am. Jour. Pathology, 1985-89. Served with AUS, 1943-46. Recipient Potamkin prize for Alzheimer Rsch., 1988, Met. Life Found. award, 1991. Fellow AAAS, Am. Acad. Arts and Sci.; mem. Am. Assn. Neuropathologists (pres. 1969-70, Meritorious Contbn. award 1989), N.Y. Path. Soc. (v.p. 1969-70, pres. 1971-73), Am. Assn. Pathologists, Am. Neurol. Assn., Am. Acad. Neurologists. Achievements include research and publications on Alzheimer's disease and Tay Sachs disease. Office: U Calif San Diego Dept Neuroscis La Jolla CA 92093

TERRY, ROBERT MEREDITH, foreign language educator; b. Danville, Va., Dec. 16, 1939; s. Willard Terry and Martha Willeford; m. Anne Reynolds Beggarly, Jan. 30, 1965; children: Michael Reynolds, Christopher Robert, Meredith Anne. BA in French, Randolph-Macon Coll., Ashland, Va., 1962; PhD in Romance Langs., Duke U., Durham. N.C., 1966. Asst. prof. French U. Fla., Gainesville, Fla., 1966-68; assoc. prof. U. Richmond, Richmond, Va., 1968-83, prof., 1983—; pres. Am. Coun. on Tchg. Fgn. Langs., 1994. Co-author: Accent: Conversational French I, 1980, Vous Y Etes!, 1990, Intersections, 1991; editor Dimension, So. Conf. on Lang. Tchg., 1991—; assoc. editor ACTFT Foreign Language Education Series, 1994, 96; contbr. articles to profl. jours. Recipient Stephen A. Freeman award N.E. Conf. on Teaching Fgn. Lang., 1990, Robert J. Ludwig Nat. Fgn. Lang. Leadership award, 1995. Mem. Am. Coun. on Tchg. Fgn. Langs., Fgn. Lang. Assn. Va., Am. Assn. Tchrs. French, So. Conf. on Lang. Tchg., Pacific N.W. Coun. for Langs., Wis. Assn. Fgn. Lang. Tchrs. Home: 1504 Cloister Dr Richmond VA 23233 Office: Univ Richmond PO Box 25 28 Westhampton Way University Of Richmond VA 23173

TERRY, RONALD ANDERSON, bank holding company executive; b. Memphis, Dec. 5, 1930; s. John Burnett and Vernon (Lucas) T.; m. Wynoka W. Evans, May 21, 1989; children by previous marriage: Natalie Carol, Cynthia Leigh. B.S., Memphis State U., 1952; postgrad., So. Meth. U., 1961, Harvard U., 1970. Mgmt. trainee First Tenn. Bank, Memphis, 1957; pres. First Tenn. Nat. Corp., Memphis, 1971, chmn., 1973—; chmn. First Tenn. Bank N.A., Memphis, 1979-95, also bd. dirs.; bd. dirs. BellSouth Corp., AutoZone Inc., Delta Life Corp., Promus Hotel Corp., St. Jude Hosp. Past pres. Boys Clubs Memphis, Future Memphis, Memphis Job Conf.; chmn. adv. com. Bapt. Meml. Hosp.; past Tenn. state chmn. Com. for Econ. Devel.; mem. adv. bd. Memphis Arts Coun. Lt. USN, 1953-57. Mem. Am. Bankers Assn. (treasury adv. com., bd. dirs., past chmn. govt. relations council), Assn. Res. City Bankers (dir., past chmn. govt. relations com. and pub. affairs com.), Assn. Bank Holding Cos. (legis. policy com., past pres. fed. adv. council), Econ. Club of Memphis (past pres.). Office: Ste 375 6410 Poplar Ave Memphis TN 38119

TERRY, STEPHEN, gynecologist/obstetrician; b. N.Y.C., Jan. 3, 1936; s. James Hendrick and Theodosia Ruggels Hatch T.; m. Barbara Anne Brown, Sept. 3, 1960; children: Stephen Wilson, Andrew Brock, Sarah Elizabeth. BA in Chemistry cum laude, U. Ariz., 1957, BA in Zoology cum laude, 1957; MD, Columbia U., 1961. Diplomate Am. Bd. Ob/Gyn. Intern in medicine, surgery Bellevue Hosp., N.Y.C., 1961-62; resident in ob-gyn N.Y. Lying-In Hosp., 1962-65; ob-gyn U.S. Army Med. Corps, Nuremberg, Germany, 1965-68, Okla. City Clinic, 1968-69; fellow in gynecology/oncology M.D. Anderson Hosp., Houston, 1969-70; pvt. practice ob/gyn Tucson, 1970—; clin. asst. Cornell Med. Sch., N.Y.C., 1963-65, U. Okla. Med. Sch., Oklahoma City, 1968-69; co-chief ob-gyn Pima County Hosp., Tucson, 1970; bd. dirs. Gaslight Enterprises, Tuscon; lect. U. Ariz. Med. Sch., Tuscon, 1992—; rsch. cons., investigator Argus Rsch., Tucson, 1993—. Recipient commendation medal U.S. Army, 1968, certificate of achievement, 1967. Fellow Am. Coll. Ob-Gyn., Am. Fertility Soc., Am. Urogynecol. Soc.; mem. S.W. Obstet.-Gynecol. Soc. (coun. 1989, pres. 1994), Med. Soc. U.S. and Mex., Am. Soc. Colposcopy, Am. Assn. Gynecol. Laparascopists, Am. Gynecol. Laser Soc., Tucson Obstet. and Gynecol. Soc. (pres. 1982), Social Register Assn., Knights of the Vine, Phi Beta Kappa, Delta Sigma Phi (social chmn., scholarship chmn.), Phi Lambda Upsilon, Beta Beta Beta. Avocations: genealogy, philately, oenology. Home: 6121 E San Marino Tucson AZ 85715-3017 Office: 5295 E Knight Dr Tucson AZ 85712-2147

TERRY, WARD EDGAR, JR., lawyer; b. Denver, Aug. 1, 1943; s. Ward E. and Peggy Helen Louise (Smith) T.; m. Juliann Dire, Apr. 8, 1967; children: Seth S., Nicole E. BA, U. Colo., 1965, JD, 1968; LLM in Taxation, U. Denver, 1976. Bar: Colo. 1968, U.S. Dist. Ct. Colo. 1968, U.S. Tax Ct. 1980. Assoc. McMartin & Burk, Englewood, Colo., 1968-70, Modesitt & Shaw, Denver, 1970-71, Gorsuch, Kirgis, Campbell, Walker & Grover, Denver, 1971-72, Hopper and Kanouff, Denver, 1976-78; sec., dir. Ward Terry and Co., Denver, 1972-76; ptnr. Hopper, Kanouff, Smith, Peryam & Terry, Denver, 1979-91; shareholder Hopper and Kanouff, P.C., Denver, 1991—, also bd. dirs.; gen. ptnr. PSW Investments Ltd., Denver, 1984—. Trustee Denver Country Day Sch., Englewood, 1969-70; campaign chair Roseanne Ball Election Com., Denver, 1974. Mem. ABA (bus. law sect., real estate and probate sect., taxation sect., antitrust sect.), Colo. Bar Assn. (bus. law and taxation sect.), Denver Bar Assn., Denver Gyro Club (pres. 1994-95, v.p. 1993-94, membership chmn. 1991-92), Phi Alpha Delta. Republican. Presbyterian. Avocations: long-distance running, golf, skiing, bicycling. Office: Hopper and Kanouff PC 1610 Wynkoop St Ste 200 Denver CO 80202-1196

TERRY, WAYNE GILBERT, healthcare executive, hospital administrator; b. Plymouth, Mass., Oct. 2, 1932; s. Lawrence Arthur Terry and Betty Frances (Boutemain) McClellan; m. Barbara Bromwell, Sept. 20, 1980; children: Karleton Wayne, Dale Duane, Kendrick Shane, Kristen Alayne, Tammye Van Clief, Wade Bromwell Delk. AA, Allan Hancock Jr. Coll., Santa Maria, Calif., 1960; BBA, U. Hawaii, 1966; M. Hosp. Adminstrn., Med. Coll. Va., 1973. Commd. maj. USAF Med. Svc. Corps, 1987; asst. adminstr. for registrar activities USAF Hosp., Orlando AFB, Fla., 1966-67; assoc. adminstr. aeromed. evacuation activities USAF, Hickam AFB, Hawaii, 1967-71; adminstrv. resident USAF Regional Hosp., Langley AFB, Va., 1972-73; CEO USAF Hosp., Columbus AFB, Miss., 1973-75; nat. health edn. and tng. program advisor Office of Surgeon Gen., Dept. of Air Force, Washington, 1975-78; dir. health professions pers. planning and policy divsn. Office of Asst. Sec. Def. for Health Affairs, The Pentagon, Washington, 1978-80; dep. project mgr./adminstrv. dir. King Faisal U. Teaching Hosp., Al-Khobar, Saudi Arabia, 1980-82; dep. project mgr., hosp. dir. North Yemen Healthcare Project, As-Salem Hosp., Sadah, Yemen Arab Republic, 1982-83; hosp. dir., CEO Armed Forces Hosps., Khamis Mushayt, Saudi Arabia, 1983-84; chief adminstr./commissioning team chief Orbit Summit Health, Ltd., Riyadh, Saudi Arabia, 1984-85; hosp. dir., adminstrv. dir. Truk State Dept. Health Svcs., Moen, Federated States of Micronesia, 1985-87; assoc. adminstr. support svcs. King Fahad Hosp., Saudi Arabian N.G., Riyadh, 1987-90; project mgr., CEO N.W. Armed Forces Hosps. Program, Tabuk, Saudi Arabia, 1990—; lectr. in field; cons. in field; mem. supervisory bd. Royal Coll. Surgeons in Ireland/Witikar Saudi Arabia Ltd., 1990-96; active various symposium organizing coms. Contbr. articles to profl. jours. Warden to Am. Cmty. N.W. Region of Yemen Arab Republic to Am. Embassy in Sanaa, 1982-83, warden to Am. Cmty. N.W. Region of Saudi Arabia to Am. Embassy in Riyadh, 1990-96; mem. Internat. Sch. Sys. Coord. Com., Tabuk, 1990-96; bd. dirs. Taif Sch. Dist. Sys., Saudi Arabia, 1981-82. Major USAF Med. Svc. Corps, 1987. Decorated Air medal with 2 oak leaf clusters, Air Force Commendation medal with 2 oak leaf clusters; recipient Citation of Appreciation Nat. Coun. Social Welfare, Seoul, Republic of Korea, 1963, Suchan Province Govt., Choong Nam, Republic of Korea, 1963, Outstanding Rsch. award Med. Coll. Va., 1973, Men of Achievement award, Cambridge, Eng., 1982, Citation of Appreciation Gov. Truk State, Federated States of Micronesia, 1987, Citation of Merit Internat. Red Cross Commn., 1991, N.W. Armed Forces Hosps., Ministry of Def. and Aviation, Tabuk, 1991, Citation of Appreciation Presidency of Gen. Staff Hdqs., 1992, 93, 95, 96. Fellow Am. Coll. Healthcare Execs., Royal Soc. Health; mem. Am. Hosp. Assn., Am. Mgmt. Assn., Air Force Med. Svc. Corps Assn., Air Force Assn., Assn. Mil. Surgeons of U.S. Republican. Baptist. Avocations: tennis, numismatics, travel. Office: NW Armed Forces Hosp Program USMTM Unit 62007 APO AE 09810-2007

TERTZAKIAN, HOVHANNES, bishop; b. Aleppo, Syria, Jan. 3, 1924. Philosophy & Theology, Pontifical Gregorian U., Rome, Italy, 1949. ordained priest Sept. 8, 1948. Teacher, then Dean Mekhitarist Sch., Alexandria, Egypt, 1949-56; dean of studies & admin. Mekhitarist Sch., Aleppo, Syria, 1956-60; headmaster Mekhitarist Sch., Aleppo, 1960-70; rector Moorat-Raphael Coll., Venice, Italy, 1970-79, Samuel-Moorat Coll., Sevres, France, 1980-82, St. Anne's Armenian Catholic Cathedral, New York, N.Y., 1986-89; Pro Exarch, 1989-90, Exarchate Chancellor, 1990-95; Apostolic Exarch for Armenian Catholics 1995—; mem. Mekhitarist Order of Venice (superior 1960-70, gen. council mem. 1970-76, gen. admin. 1976-79, provincial supr. 1979-80, Abbot Gen. 1982-84). Office: Chancery Office 110 E 12th New York NY 10003*

TERWILLEGAR, LINDA S., administrative assistant; b. West Fork, Ind., Aug. 26, 1956; adopted d. Paul Arthur and Leona (Andres) Lawson; m. Kent Wilson Dodge, Aug. 31, 1974 (div. Aug. 1987); children: Beverly Lynn Dodge Bewley, Mark Wilson Dodge (dec.); m. LeRoy J. Terwillegar, Feb. 6, 1988. Grad. high sch., New Albany, Ind. Asst. to pres. Jer-L-Lee, Inc. dba Papeno's Pizza, Restaurant, Video, Tanning Salon, Greenville, Ind., 1984—. Home: PO Box 337 8969 Hwy 150 Greenville IN 47124 Office: Jer-L-Lee Inc PO Box 337 Greenville IN 47124-0337

TERWILLIGER, GEORGE JAMES, III, lawyer; b. New Brunswick, N.J., June 5, 1950; s. George James Jr. and Ruth Nancy (Mellilo) T.; m. Carol Anne Hitchings, Dec. 18, 1976; children: Sarah Katherine, George Zachary Grant, Virginia. BA in Communications, Seton Hall U., 1973; JD, Antioch Law Sch., 1978. Bar: D.C. 1978, U.S. Dist. Ct. D.C., 1979, U.S. Ct. Appeals

(D.C. cir.) 1979, U.S. Dist. Ct. (so. dist.) Fla. 1980, U.S. Dist. Ct. Vt. 1981, U.S. Ct. Appeals (2d cir.) 1982, Vt. 1983, U.S. Supreme Ct. 1992, U.S. Ct. Appeals (4th cir.) 1993. Asst. U.S. atty. Office of U.S. Atty., Washington, 1978-81; asst. U.S. atty. Dist. of Vt., Burlington, 1981-86, U.S. atty., 1986-91; dep. atty. gen. Washington, 1992-93; ptnr.-in-charge McGuire, Woods, Battle & Boothe, Washington, 1993—. Mem. ABA, Vt. Bar Assn., D.C. Bar Assn., Rep. Nat. Lawyers Assn. (pres. 1994-95). Republican. Congregationalist. Avocations: skiing, tennis, fishing. Office: McGuire, Woods, Battle & Boothe Army and Navy Club Building 1627 I St NW Washington DC 20006-4007

TERZIAN, GRACE PAINE, publisher; b. Boston, Oct. 19, 1952; d. Thomas Fite and Grace Hillman (Benedict) Paine; m. Philip Henry Terzian, Oct. 20, 1979; children: William Thomas, Grace Benedict. BA in Art History, Williams Coll., 1974. Art dir. The New Republic, Washington, 1976-78; asst. editor The Chronicle of Higher Edn., Washington, 1978-79; rsch. editor Archtl. Digest, L.A., 1982-85; pub. The Women's Quar., Arlington, Va., 1994—. Mem. Soc. Colonial Dames in Am., Phi Beta Kappa. Episcopalian. Home: 10505 Adel Rd Oakton VA 22124 Office: The Womens Quarterly 2111 Wilson Blvd Ste 550 Arlington VA 22201

TERZIAN, PHILIP HENRY, journalist; b. Kensington, Md., July 5, 1950; s. L.A. and Louise (Anderson) T.; m. Grace Barrett Paine, Oct. 20, 1979; children: William Thomas Hillman, Grace Benedict Paine. BA, Villanova U., 1973; DTS, Episcopal Theol. Sem., Va., 1995; postgrad., Oxford (Eng.) U., 1976. Desk editor Reuters, Washington, 1973, U.S. News & World Report, Washington, 1973-74; asst. editor The New Republic, Washington, 1974-78; mem. policy planning staff Dept. State, Washington, 1978-79; asst. editor Anniston (Ala.) Star, 1979-80; assoc. editor Lexington (Ky.) Herald, 1980-82; asst. editor of editorial pages L.A. Times, 1982-86; editor of editorial pages Providence Jour., 1986-92, assoc. editor, syndicated columnist, 1992—; panelist Washington Week in Review, C-SPAN, etc.; mem. bd. of advisors, Inst. of Am. Values, Nichols Coll. Contbr. articles to newspapers and jours. Pres. Providence Com. Fgn. Rels., 1989-92. Recipient Edn. Writers award Edn. Writers Assn., 1981, Ida Lee Willis Svc. to Preservation award Ida Lee Willis Found., 1982; named finalist Pulitzer prize Disting. Commentary, 1991, Pulitzer Prize juror, 1994-95. Mem. Am. Coun. on Germany, Va. Hist. Soc., St. Andrew's Soc. Washingtonm Theodore Roosevelt Assn., Soc. King Charles the Martyr, Wolver Beagles, Nat. Press Club, Hope Club. Republican. Episcopalian. Avocations: reading, book collecting, riding, music. Home: 10505 Adel Rd Oakton VA 22124-1605 Office: Providence Jour 400 N Capitol St NW Washington DC 20001-1511

TERZIAN, YERVANT, astronomy and astrophysics educator; b. Alexandria, Egypt, Feb. 9, 1939; came to U.S., 1960, naturalized, 1971; s. Bedros and Maria (Kiriakaki) T.; m. Araxy M. Hovsepian, Apr. 16, 1966; children: Sevan, Tamar. BS, Am. U., Cairo, 1960; MS, Ind. U., 1963, PhD, 1965, DSc (hon.), 1989; DSc (hon.) Yerevan State U., 1994. Rsch. assoc. Arecibo Obs., P.R., 1965-67; asst. prof. astronomy and astrophysics Cornell U., Ithaca, N.Y., 1967-72, assoc. prof., 1972-77, prof., 1977—, chmn. dept. astronomy, 1979—, dir. Program in Sci. Edn., 1988—, James A. Weeks prof. in phys. scis., 1990. Editor: Interstellar Ionized Hydrogen, 1968; Planetary Nebulae, 1978; co-editor: Cosmology and Astrophysics, 1982; assoc. editor The Astrophysical Jour., 1989—; contbr. over 180 articles to tech. jours. Recipient Clark Disting. Teaching award Cornell U., 1984. Mem. Internat. Astron. Union, Soc. Sci. Exploration, Internat. Sci. Radio Union, Am. Astron. Soc., Armenian Acad. Sci. (fgn. mem.). Home: 109 Brandywine Dr Ithaca NY 14850-1747 Office: Cornell U Astronomy Dept Space Scis Bldg Ithaca NY 14853

TESAR, DELBERT, machine systems and robotics educator, researcher, manufacturing consultant; b. Beaver Crossing, Nebr., Sept. 2, 1935; s. Louis and Clara (Capek) T.; m. Rogene Kresak, Feb. 1, 1957; children: Vim Lee, Aleta Anne, Landon Grady, Allison Jeanne. B.Sc. in Mech. Engring., U. Nebr., 1958, M.Sc., 1959; Ph.D., Ga. Tech. U., 1964. Assoc. prof. U. Fla., Gainesville, 1965-71, prof., 1972-83, grad. research prof., 1983-84, dir., founder Ctr. Intelligent Machines and Robotics, 1978-84; Curran chair in engring. U. Tex., Austin, 1985—; lectr. in field; mem. rev. panel Nat. Bur. Stds., Gaithersburg, Md., 1982-88; mem. sci. adv. bd. to Air Force, 1982-86; mem. standing com. NRC for Space Sta. (ISSA), 1992-95; interactor with Russian Acad. Sci. on sci. and tech. Author: (with others) Cam System Design, 1975. Patentee in field; contbr. articles to profl. jours.; assoc. editor 3 computer and mfg. jours. Expert witness house sci. and tech. com. U.S. Ho. of Reps., 1978-84. Fellow AAAS; mem. Fla. Engring. Soc. (Outstanding Tech. Achievement award 1982), ASME (machine design award 1987). Avocations: antiques, art, travel. Home: 8005 Two Cove Dr Austin TX 78730-3125 Office: U Tex Dept Mechanical Engineering Austin TX 78712-1063

TESAR, MILO BENJAMIN, agricultural researcher, educator, and administrator; b. Tobias, Nebr., Apr. 7, 1920; s. Frank and Frances (Cihal) T.; m. Marian Olive Hunt, Sept. 3, 1944; children: Robert, Ann, Joyce, Janet. BS with distinction, U. Nebr., 1941; MS, U. Wis., 1947, PhD, 1949; DSc (hon.), U. Nebr., 1989. Asst. prof. crop-soil sci. Mich. State U., East Lansing, 1949-53, assoc. prof., 1953-58, prof., 1958-88, prof. emeritus, 1988—, chmn. dept. crop and soli sci., 1964-66; agrl. advisor China (Inner Mongolia), Australia, New Zealand, Scotland, USSR, Okinawa, Japan, Eng., Brazil, Somalia, Egypt, Finland. Author: Forage Management, 1982, 2d edit., 1984, 3d edit., 1986; editor: Physiological Basis of Crop Growth and Development, 1988; author: (with others), assoc. editor: Alfalfa Science and Technology, 1972, Alfalfa and Alfalfa Improvement, 1988; contbr. articles to profl. jours.; patentee alfalfa cultivar "Webfoot." Chmn. bd. elders People's Ch., East Lansing, 1966; mem. East Lansing Sch. Bd., 1966-70. Maj. U.S. Army, 1942-46, PTO, Hiroshima, Japan. Decorated Silver Star, Bronze Star; named NATO fellow NSF, Hurley, Eng., 1959-60; recipient King Charles Educator award Nebr Czechs, 1987, Disting. Rsch. award Mich. State U. Coll. Agr., 1985, hon. extension svc. award, 1984, Alumni Achievement award U. Nebr., 1991. Fellow AAAS, Am. Soc. Agronomy (cert. agronomist, crop scientist, Agronomic Achievement award 1984), Crop Sci. Soc. Am. (DeKalb-Prizer Disting. Crop Sci. Career award 1988); mem. Mich. State U. Pres.'s Club, Sigma Xi, Gamma Sigma Delta. Republican. Home: 2379 Emerald Forest Cir East Lansing MI 48823-7214 Office: Mich State U Dept Crop Soil Sci East Lansing MI 48824

TESAREK, WILLIAM PAUL, business process re-engineering consultant, writer, financial executive; b. Albuquerque, May 6, 1958; s. Dennis George and Caroline Arrena (Myers) T.; m. Nancy Anne Pence, May 12, 1984 (div. Feb. 1991); children: Michelle Marie, Allison Elaine. BS in Econs., U. Houston, 1986, MA in Econs., 1988, MBA in Fin., 1993, PhD, 1994. Instr. econs. U. Houston, 1987-88; sr. sales tax analyst Tex. State Comptroller, Austin, 1988-89; adj. prof. fin. U. Houston, 1989-93; sr. economist Asset Analysis & Mgmt., Houston, 1993; sr. fin. economist Asset Dynamics, Houston, 1993-94; owner The Tesarek Group, Houston, 1994—; cons. in strategic planning and process reengring. mgmt. Author: Housing Price and Regional Real Estate Cycles: Market Adjustments in Houston, 1991; Beyond Counting the Beans: How Chief Financial Executives Use Knowledge to Advance the Corporation, 1995. With USN, 1976-80. Econ. Honors. Soc. Achievement award, 1986. Mem. Am. Econs. Assn., Am. Fin. Assn., Western Econ. Assn., Tex. Econ. & Demographic Assn., Allied Soc. Sci. Assn., Houston Bus. Process Reengring. Share Group. Republican. Mem. Ch. of Christ. Avocations: wood working, photography. Home and Office: The Tesarek Grp 16011 Silver Valley Dr Houston TX 77084-2960

TESCHNER, DOUGLASS PAUL, state legislator; b. Cambridge, Mass., Oct. 29, 1949; s. Douglass P. Teschner and Mary Elizabeth (Bernt) Teschner Zeller; m. Martha Weaver, Sept. 26, 1981. BS in Forestry, U. Mass., 1971, EdD in Adminstrn., 1985; MS in Botany, U. Vt., 1978. Land surveyor Lincoln Engring. and Burnell Land Surveying, 1974, 78; tchr. White Mountain Sch., 1976; dir. Inst. Exptl. Studies, various locations, 1981-84, 86-88; fin. officer Becket Acad., East Haddam, Conn., 1984-86; devel. dir. Riverbend Comty. Mental Health, Concord, 1988—; state rep. N.H. Ho. Reps., Concord, 1988—. Co-editor: Wilderness Challenge: Outdoor Education Alternatives for Youth in Need, 1984; contbr. articles to profl. jours. Mem. Haverhill Hist. Soc.; vol. Peace Corps, 1971-73; trustee Mt. Washington Obs. Mem. Congregational Ch. Avocations: mountaineering, hiking, rock and ice climbing, skiing. Home: RR 2 Box 173 Pike NH 03780-9706 Office: Riverbend Comty Mental Hlth PO Box 2032 Concord NH 03302-2032

TESCHNER, RICHARD REWA, retired lawyer; b. Milw., Feb. 5, 1908; s. Bruno A. and Thekla (Rewa) T.; m. D. Joy Griesbach, Sept. 24, 1932; 1 son, Richard Vincent. B.A., U. Wis., 1931, LL.B., 1934; L.H.D. (hon.), Carroll Coll., 1976. Bar: Wis. 1934, U.S. Supreme Ct. 1944. Tax counsel Wis. Dept. Taxation, 1938-45; ptnr. Quarles & Brady, 1945-87. Mem. Milwaukee County War Meml. Devel. Com., chmn., 1960-70; mem. Greater Milw. Com.; past mem. Wis. Arts Bd.; chmn. Milw. Performing Arts Center, 1969-74; co-chmn. United Performing Arts Fund drive, 1977; pres. Will Ross Meml. Found.; chmn. Milw. Found., 1978-79; bd. dirs. Second Harvesters of Wis., Inc., 1980-91, Ice Age Park and Trail of Wis. Found., 1980-89. Mem. ABA, Wis. Bar Assn., Milw. Bar Assn. (pres. 1964-65), Pi Kappa Alpha, Phi Delta Phi. Presbyterian. Lodge: Rotary. Home: 1840 N Prospect Ave Milwaukee WI 53202-1975

TESFARMARIAM, BERNICE JEFFERSON, school administrator, counselor; b. Pitts., Nov. 29, 1940; q. Felix A. and Geraldine (Conner) Bell. MS in Edn., Duquesne U., 1991; postgrad., John Jay Coll., Duquesne U., 1993—. Libr. tech. asst. N.Y. Pub. Libr., N.Y.C., 1968-79; law clk. U.S. Steel, Pitts., 1979-86; resident advisor Transitional Svcs., Pitts., 1987-89; primary case mgr. adolescent impatient unit, prevention specialist Mercy Ctr., Pitts., 1989-92; project coord. Bd. of Edn., Pitts., 1993—; pvt. practice counselor Bernice Tesfarmariam & Assocs., Pitts., 1991—; com. mem. Youth Employment Alliance, Pitts., 1994—; v.p. Ciloets USX, Pitts., 1985-86; presenter, cons. and group facilitator on motivation, empowerment, addiction, prevention, intervention and self esteem. Author brochures, tng. manuals in field. Bd. dirs. Beltzhoover Neighborhood Cmty., Pitts., 1994; adv. bd. Literacy Coun., Pitts., 1984, McGovern Ctr., Pitts., 1992; v.p. Local 1930 Newspaper Guild, N.Y.C., 1977-79. Recipient Cert. of Appreciation, Dist. Wide chpt. 1, 1994, MA/MR/D&A Allegheny County, 1992, Am. Heart Assn., 1986; Literacy Coun. grantee USS Corp., 1986. Mem. Phi Delta Kappa, Chi Sigma Iota (life). Democrat. Baptist. Avocations: collecting African art, opera, theatre, museum, writing. Home: 400 Chalfont St Pittsburgh PA 15210-1421 Office: Pitts Pub Schs Office Pupil Affairs 341 S Bellefield Ave Pittsburgh PA 15213-3552

TESH, JOHN, television talk show host; b. Garden City, N.Y., 1953; s. John and Mildred Tesh; m. Connie Sellecca, Apr. 4, 1992; children: Gib, Prima. Co-host Entertainment Tonight, 1986—; host One-On-One with John Tesh, 1991; co-host John and Leeza from Hollywood, 1993. Television appearances include: The U.S. Open Tennis Championship, 1985, Macy's Thanksgiving Day Parade, 1987, Wimbledon, 1991; film appearances include Shocker, 1989, Soapdish, 1991; albums include Tour de France, 1988, The Early Years, 1990, Ironman, 1992, The Games, 1992, Monterey Nights, 1993, A Romantic Christmas, 1993; composers theme music Bobby's World, 1990, The Knife and Gun Club, 1990, One on One, 1991, NFL Live. Recipient 4 Emmy awards for composing, 2 Emmy awards for reporting. Office: Paramount TV 5555 Melrose Ave Los Angeles CA 90038-3149

TESKE, RICHARD HENRY, veterinarian; b. Christiansburg, Va., July 22, 1939; s. August Frank and Peggy Marie (Macomber) T.; m. Mary Helen Webb, June 11, 1961; children: Helen Desiree, Mary Michele. BS, Va. Tech. U., 1962; DVM, U. Ga., 1965; MS, U. Fla., 1966. Diplomate Am. Bd. Vet. Toxicology. Asst. prof. U. Fla., Gainesville, 1967; dir. toxicology Hill Top Rsch., Inc., Miamiville, Ohio, 1967-70; chief pharmacology/toxicology br. Ctr. for Vet. Medicine FDA, Beltsville, Md., 1971-77, dep. dir. div. med. rsch. Ctr. for Vet. Medicine, 1977-78, dir. div. vet. med. rsch. Ctr. for Vet. Medicine, 1978-82; assoc. dir. for sci. Ctr. for Vet. Medicine FDA, Rockville, Md., 1982-85, dep. dir. Ctr. for Vet. Medicine, 1985-95, assoc. dir. for policy, 1995—; mem. vet. med. adv. bd. panel U.S. Pharmacopeial Conv., Rockville, 1984—. Fellow Am. Acad. Vet. Pharms. and Therapeutics, Am. Acad. Vet. and Comparative Toxicology. Office: FDA Ctr for Vet Medicine 7500 Standish Pl Rockville MD 20855-2773

TESLER, LAWRENCE GORDON, computer company executive; b. N.Y.C., Apr. 24, 1945; s. Isidore and Muriel (Krechmer) T.; m. Shelagh Elisabeth Leuterio, Oct 4, 1964 (div. 1970); 1 child, Lisa Traci; m. Colleen Ann Barton, Feb. 17, 1987. BS in Math., Stanford U., 1965. Pres. Info. Processing Corp., Palo Alto, Calif., 1963-68; rsch. asst. Stanford U. Artificial Intelligence Lab., 1968-73; mem. rsch. staff Xerox Corp., Palo Alto, 1973-80; sect. mgr. Lisa div. Apple Computer, Inc., Cupertino, Calif., 1980-82, cons. engr., 1983-86, v.p. advanced tech., 1986-90, v.p. advanced products, 1990-92, v.p. engring., 1992-93, chief scientist, 1993-96, v.p. internat. platforms, 1996—; bd. dirs. Advanced RISC Machines Ltd.; mem. Computer Sci. and Telecom. Bd., 1991-94. Contbr. articles to profl. jours., various computer software. Bd. dirs. Peninsula Sch., Menlo Park, Calif., 1974-78. Mem. Assn. Computing Machinery (conf. co-chmn. 1987-88). Office: Apple Computer Inc 1 Infinite Loop Cupertino CA 95014-2083

TESSER, ABRAHAM, social psychologist; b. N.Y.C., May 24, 1941; s. Louis and Ruth (Buchholz) T.; m. Marsha Richman Rosenthal, June 4, 1967 (div. Feb. 22, 1983); children: Louis J., Rachel A.; m. Carmen Chaves, Dec. 15, 1990. BA, L.I. U., 1962; MS, Purdue U., 1965, PhD, 1967. Rsch. assoc. Inst. for Behavioral Rsch., U. Ga., 1971-78, assoc. dir., 1978-84, acting dir. Ctr. for Rsch. on Deviance, 1984-86, dir., 1984-94; from asst. prof. to assoc. prof. social psychology U. Ga., 1967-74, prof., 1974-89, rsch. prof. psychology, 1989—; vis. fellow Yale U., 1976-77, Princeton U., spring 1983; fellow Ctr. for Advanced Studies in the Behavioral Scis., Stanford, Calif., 1992-93. Editor Jour. Personality and Social Cognition, 1991-94; contbr. numerous articles to profl. jours. Mem. AAUP, APA, Am. Psychol. Soc., Soc. for Personality and Social Psychology, Soc. Exptl. Social Psychology, So. Soc. for Social Psychology. Office: Univ Ga Dept Psychology Athens GA 30602

TESSLER, ALLAN R., trucking company executive; b. 1936. AB, Cornell U., 1958, LLB, 1963. Bar: N.Y. 1963. Atty., mem. exec. com. Shea & Gould, 1976-88; chmn. bd. dirs. Internat. Controls Corp., Kalamazoo, Mich., 1989—, Great Dane Holdings Inc.; pres. Internat. Financial Group, N.Y.C.; chmn. bd. dirs. Internat. Fin. Group, Inc., N.Y.C., Enhance Fin. Svcs., Ameriscribe Corp. Lt. USN, 1958-61. Office: Great Dane Holdings Inc 2016 N Pitcher St Kalamazoo MI 49007-1869 Office: Intl Financial Group 25 E 78th St 3rd Fl New York NY 10021*

TESSMANN, CARY ANNETTE, controller; b. Wausau, Wis., Oct. 30, 1956; d. Orin Sidney Olson and Phyllis Olga (Radtke) O. AS, U. Wis., Waukesha, 1986; BBA in Acctg., U. Wis., Whitewater, 1989; MBA in Acctg., U. Wis., 1995. Cert. mgmt. acct.; CPA 1995. Clk.-typist I, II, III Waukesha County Dept. Social Svc., 1974-83; acct. clk. I Northview Nursing Home, Waukesha, 1984; from acct. clk. II, adminstrv. asst.-fiscal mgmt. I, budget technician, sr. fin. analyst to bus. mgr. Waukesha County Health & Human Svcs. Dept., 1984-94; contr. Waukesha County Tech. Coll., Pewaukee, 1994—; mem. acctg. curriculum adv. com. Waukesha County Tech. Coll., 1993—; cons., Sussex, Wis., 1990-93. Vol. Wis. Lutheran Child & Family Svc., Milw., 1989—, Bargain Ctr.-WELS Synod, Milw., 1970-83, Milw. Women's Ctr., 1989-92; vol. tax preparer IRS, Pewaukee, 1989-93; mem. bd. Waukesha County Cmty. Housing Initiatives, 1995—. Recipient Certificate of Spl. Recognition from Christoph Meml. YWCA Women of Distinction Award Program, 1986. Mem. Inst. Mgmt. Accts. (del. Mid-Am. coun. 1992—, chair corp. & acad. devel. 1994-95, co-dir. mem. attendance 1989-90, v.p. comm. 1990-92, v.p. fin. & adminstrn. 1991-92, pres. 1992-93), Southeastern Wis. Fin. Mgrs. Assn. (planning com. 1987-94), Govt. Fin. Officers Assn. (budget reviewer 1994—). Avocations: sports, dancing, reading, handicrafts, exercise. Office: Waukesha County Tech Coll 800 Main St Pewaukee WI 53072-4601

TESTA, DOUGLAS, biotechnology company executive; b. Concord, Mass., May 22, 1944; s. Morris and Alice (Crawford) T.; m. Rosemary Adorno, Aug. 20, 1966; children: Jonathan Douglas, Jaymes Andrew. AA, Queensborough Community Coll., 1965; BS, CCNY, 1967, MS in Edn., 1971, PhD, 1976. Cert. tchr. N.Y. Chmn. dept. biology N.Y.C. Pub. Schs., 1967-70; lect. Hunter Coll. CCNY, 1970-76; project leader Ortho Diagnostics, Inc., Raritan, N.J., 1979-80; asst. dir. biologics Hydron Labs., Inc., New Brunswick, N.J., 1980-84; exec. dir. R & D, Interferon Scis., Inc., New Brunswick, 1981-84, v.p. rsch., 1984-87, v.p. R&D, 1987-93, v.p. rsch., devel. and clin. affairs, 1993-95; pres. AAG Inc., Phillipsburg, N.J., 1995—; adj. asst. prof. Hunter Coll. of CCNY, 1978-81; adj. assoc. prof. Rutgers U., New Brunswick, 1985-89; advisor to molecular biology hons. prog. L.I. U., Bklyn., Middlesex Community Coll., N.J., 1984-87. Contbr. articles to profl. jours.; patentee in field. V.p. Glen Eagles Homeowners Assn., Branchburg, N.J., 1984. Mem. Am. Soc. Biol. Chem., Am. Soc. Microbiology, Internat. Soc. for Hematology, Internat. Soc. for Interferon Research, N.Y. Acad. Scis., Sigma Xi, Phi Sigma. Office: AAG Inc PO Box 6 Phillipsburg NJ 08865

TESTA, MICHAEL HAROLD, lawyer; b. N.Y.C., Sept. 4, 1939; m. Carol Waldenberg, June 16, 1962; 2 children. BS summa cum laude, NYU, 1958, LLB cum laude, 1961, LLM in Taxation, 1967. Bar: N.Y. 1961. Assoc. White & Case, N.Y.C., 1962-71; assoc. Skadden, Arps, Slate, Meagher & Flom, N.Y.C., 1971-72, ptnr., 1972-91; spl. counsel Living Oceans Program, Nat. Audubon Soc., 1993—; advisor U.S. Delegation to UN Conf. on Straddling Fish Stocks and Highly Migratory Fish Stocks, 1994-95; advisor U.S. Delegation to Kyoto Internat. Conf. on Sustainable Contribution of Fisheries to Food Security, 1995; adj. assoc. prof. law NYU Law Sch., 1986; lectr. in field. Assoc. editor, contbr.: NYU Law Rev., 1960-61; contbr. articles to legal jours. Mem. planning bd. Town of Tuxedo (N.Y.), 1971-76. Served to capt. USAFR, 1961-72. Root-Tilden scholar, 1959-61. Mem. ABA, N.Y. State Bar Assn. (mem. exec. com. tax sect. 1978-82), Assn. Bar of City of N.Y. (mem. environ. law com. 1993-95), Order of Coif. Home: 32 Wildwood Dr Great Neck NY 11024-1246 Office: 919 3rd Ave New York NY 10022

TESTA, STEPHEN MICHAEL, geologist, consultant; b. Fitchburg, Mass., July 17, 1951; s. Guiseppe Alfredo and Angelina Mary (Pettito) T.; m. Lydia Mae Payne, July 26, 1986; 1 child, Brant Ethan Gage. AA, Los Angeles Valley Jr. Coll., Van Nuys, 1971; BS in Geology, Calif. State U., Northridge, 1976, MS in Geology, 1978. Registered geologist, Calif., Oreg.; cert. profl. geol. scientist., Idaho, Alaska; cert. engring. geologist, Calif.; registered environ. asessor, Calif. Engring. geologist R.T. Frankian & Assocs., Burbank, Calif., 1976-78, Bechtel, Norwalk, Calif., 1978-80, Converse Cons., Seattle, 1980-82; sr. hydrogeologist Ecology Environment, Seattle, 1982-83; sr. geologist Dames & Moore, Seattle, 1983-86; v.p. Engring. Enterprises, Long Beach, Calif., 1986-89; CEO Applied Environ. Svcs., San Juan Capistrano, Calif., 1990-94; pres. Testa Environ. Corp., San Juan Capistrano, Calif., 1994—. Author: Restoration of Petroleum Contaminated Aquifers, 1990, Principles of Technical Consulting and Project Management, 1991, Geological Aspects of Hazardous Waste Management, 1994, Reuse and Recycling of Contaminated Soil, 1996; editor Geologic Field Guide to the Salton Basin, 1988, Environmental Concerns in the Petroleum Industry, 1989; contbr. more than 60 articles to profl. jours., a preface and chpts. to books. Mem. AAAS, Am. Inst. Profl. Geologists (profl. devel. com. 1986, continuing edn. com. program chmn., 1988—, Presidential Cert. of Merit, 1987 and 1994, Nat screening bd. mem. 1992-94, chmn. 1995—, exec. bd. del. 1993, nat. v.p. 1994, bd. trustees 1995—), L.A. Basin Geol. Soc. (pres. 1991-92), Geol. Soc. Am., Am. Assn. Petroleum Geologists (Pacific sect. environ. com., co-chmn. 1993—), Am. Mineralogical Soc., South Coast Geol. Soc., Assn. Ground Water Scientists and Engrs., Assn. Engring. Geologists, Assn. Mil. Engrs., Environ. Assessment Assn., Mineral Soc. Can., Hazardous Materials Rsch. Inst., Calif. Water Pollution Control Assn., Sigma Xi. Roman Catholic. Achievements include research ingenous and metamorphic petrology, asphalt chemistry; development of methods for subsurface hydrogeologic characterization and remediation, proprietary processes for incorporation of contaminated soil and other materials considered toxic and hazardous via recycling into a variety of cold-mix asphaltic products. Home: 31232 Belford Dr San Juan Capistrano CA 92675-1833 Office: Testa Environ Corp 31831 Camino Capistrano Ste 100 San Juan Capistrano CA 92675

TESTANI, ROSA ANNA, lawyer; b. N.Y.C., Oct. 1, 1963; d. Ernesto and Antonietta (Sanita) T. BS, Fordham U., 1985; JD, Yale U., 1988. Bar: Conn. 1988, N.Y. 1989, U.S. Dist. Ct. (so. dist.) N.Y. 1990. Assoc. Skadden, Arps, Slate, Meagher & Flom, N.Y.C., 1988—. Contbr. articles to profl. jours. (Israel Peres award 1988). Fordham Presdl. Merit scholar, 1981; Phi Kappa Phi fellow, 1985. Mem. ABA, Bar Assn. of City of N.Y. Avocations: traveling, photography, cooking. Home: 196 27 Pompeii Ave Hollis NY 11423

TETELMAN, ALICE FRAN, city government official; b. N.Y.C., Apr. 15, 1941; d. Harry and Leah (Markovitz) T.; m. Martin A. Wenick, Dec. 7, 1980. BA, Mt. Holyoke Coll., South Hadley, Mass., 1962. Rsch. and info. asst. Edn. and World Affairs, N.Y.C., 1963-67; legis. asst. U.S. Sen. Charles Goodell, Washington, 1968-70; land use and energy specialist Citizens Adv. Com. on Environ. Quality, Washington, 1973-74; sr. assoc. prog. mgr. Linton & Co., Washington, 1971-73, 75-76; pub policy cons. Washington, 1977-78; adminstrv. asst. U.S. Congressman Bill Green (N.Y.), Washington, 1978-81; cons. The Precious Legacy Project, Prague, Czechoslovakia, 1982-83; Rep. staff dir. Select Com. on Hunger, U.S. Ho. of Reps., Washington, 1984-85; dir. State of N.J. Washington Office, 1986-90; exec. dir. Coun. of Gov/'s Policy Advisors, Washington, 1991-94; dir. Washington Office The City of N.Y., 1994—. Bd. mem. Republican Women's Task Force, Nat. Women's Polit. Caucus, 1976-80. European Community grantee, 1975. Mem. Ripon Soc. (nat. exec. com. 1971-73). Republican. Office: City of NY Washington Office 555 New Jersey Ave NW Washington DC 20001-2029

TETER, GORDON F., fast food chain company executive. Past exec. v.p. Wendy's Internat. Inc., Dublin, Ohio, pres., CEO, COO. Office: Wendy's Internat Inc 4288 W Dublin Granville Rd Dublin OH 43017*

TETHER, ANTHONY JOHN, aerospace executive; b. Middletown, N.Y., Nov. 28, 1941; s. John Arthur and Antoinette Rose (Gesualdo) T.; m. Nancy Engle Pierson, Dec. 27, 1963 (div. July 1971); 1 child, Jennifer; m. Carol Suzanne Dunbar, Mar. 3, 1973; 1 child, Michael. AAS, Orange County C.C., N.Y., 1961; BS, Rensselaer Poly Inst., 1963; MSEE, Stanford (Calif.) U., 1965, PhD, 1969. V.p., gen. mgr. Sys. Control Inc., Palo Alto, Calif., 1968-78; dir. nat. intelligence Office Sec. of Def., Washington, 1978-82; dir. strategic tech. DARPA, Washington, 1982-86; corp. v.p. Ford Aerospace, Newport Beach, Calif., 1986-90, LORAL, Newport Beach, 1990-92; corp. v.p., gen. mgr. Sci. Application Internat., Inc., San Diego, 1992-94; CEO Dynamics Tech. Inc., Torrance, Calif., 1994—; chmn., bd. dirs. Condyne Tech., Inc., Orlando, Fla., 1990-92; dir. Orincon, La Jolla, Calif. Contbr. articles to profl. jours. Recipient Nat. Intelligence medal DCI, 1986, Civilian Meritorious medal U.S. Sec. Def., 1986. Mem. IEEE, Cosmos Club, Sigma Xi, Eta Kappa Nu, Tau Beta Pi. Avocations: ham radio, skiing. Home: 4518 Roxbury Rd Corona Del Mar CA 92625-3125

TETLEY, GLEN, choreographer; b. Cleve., Feb. 3, 1926; s. Glenford and Eleanor (Byrne) T. Student, Franklin and Marshall Coll., 1944-46; BS, NYU, 1948; student contemporary dance with, Hanya Holm, Martha Graham, 1946; student classical ballet with, Margaret Craske, Anthony Tudor at Met. Opera Ballet Sch., 1949. guest instr. Yale Dramatic Workshop, 1947-48, Colo. Coll., 1946-49, Hanya Holm Sch. Contemporary Dance, 1946-52, Ballet Rambert, 1966-68, Netherlands Dance Theatre, 1962-65, B. De Rothschild Found., Israel, 1965-67. Featured dancer in Broadway musical Kiss Me Kate, 1949, Out of This World, 1950, Juno, 1958; premiered in Broadway musical Menotti's Amahl and the Night Visitors, NBC Opera, 1951; soloist with Broadway musical, N.Y.C. Opera, 1951-54, John Butler's Am. Dance Theatre, 1951-55, Robert Joffrey Ballet, 1955-56, Martha Graham Dance Co., 1957-59, Am. Ballet Theatre, 1959-61, Jerome Robbins: Ballets USA, 1961-62, Netherlands Dance Theater, 1962-65, own co., 1962-69; made govt.-sponsored tour of Europe, 1969, appearances at Spoleto Festival, all maj. Am. dance festivals; guest choreographer, Netherlands Dance Theatre; artistic dir.: Netherlands Dance Theatre, 1969; guest choreographer, Am. Ballet Theatre, Ballet Rambert, Batsheva Co. Israel, Robert Joffrey Ballet, Alvin Alley Co., U. Utah Repertory Dance Theatre, Vancouver Festival, Royal Danish Ballet, 1969, Royal Ballet Covent Garden, Royal Swedish Ballet, Den Norske Opera, Hamburg State Opera, Stuttgart Ballet; former artistic dir., Stuttgart Ballet Co.; artistic assoc., Nat. Ballet of Canada, Toronto, 1987-89; ballets include Pierrot Lunaire, 1962, Birds of Sorrow, 1962, The Anatomy Lesson, 1964, Sargasso, 1964, Field Mass, 1965, Mythical Hunters, 1965, Ricercare, 1966, Chronochromie, 1966, Tehilim,

1966, Freefall, 1967, The Seven Deadly Sins, 1967, Dithyramb, 1967, Ziggurat, 1967, Circles, 1968, Embrace Tiger and Return to Mountain, 1968, Arena, 1968, Imaginary Film, 1970, Mutations, 1970, Field Figures, 1971, Rag Dances, 1971, Small Parades, 1971, Threshold, 1972, Laborintus, 1972, Strophe-Antistrophe, 1972, The Moveable Garden, 1973, Gemini, 1973, Voluntaries, 1973, Sacre du Printemps, 1974, Tristan, 1974, Strender, 1974, Daphnis and Chloe, 1975, Greening, 1975, Alegrias, 1975, Poeme Nocturne, 1977, Sphinx, 1978, Praeludium, 1979, The Tempest, 1979, Contredances, 1979, Summer's End, 1980, Dances of Albion-Dark Night: Glad Day, 1980, Firebird, 1981, Murderer Hope of Women, 1983, Revelation and Fall, 1984, Pulcinella, 1984, Dream Walk of the Shaman, 1985, Alice, 1986, Orpheus, 1987, La Ronde, 1987, Tagore, 1989, Dialogues, 1991, Oracle, 1994; off-Broadway choreographer-dir. ballets including Fortuna, 1961, Ballet Ballads, 1961. Patron Benesh Inst. Choreology; bd. dirs. Tag Found., N.Y.C. Served with USNR, 1944-46. Recipient German critics award for Die Feder; Queen Elizabeth II Coronation award Royal Acad. Dancing, 1981; recipient Prix Italia Rai prize, 1982, Tennant Caledonia award Edinburgh Festival, 1983, Ohioana Career Medal, 1986, achievement award N.Y.U., 1988. Address: 15 W 9th St New York NY 10011-8918

TETLIE, HAROLD, priest; b. Madison, Minn., Aug. 24, 1926; s. H. Ben and Anna (Mauland) T. BA cum laude, St. Olaf Coll., Northfield, Minn., 1951; MBA, U. Denver, 1956; postgrad., Cornell U., 1959-60; MDiv, Luther Sem., St. Paul, 1965. Ordained to ministry Am. Luth. Ch., 1965. Pastor Christ the King Chs. (Evang. Cath. Ch.), Alice, Tex., 1965—, congregation supr., 1969—; cir. parish priest, Nuevo Leon, Tamaulipas, Hidalgo, San Luis Potosi, Mex. Author numerous poems. Coord. Joint Action in Cmty. Svc., Inc., Alice, 1970—. Sgt. U.S. Army, 1945-46, PTO. Recipient Svc. to Manking award Sertoma Club, Corpus Christi, Regional Vol. of Yr. award Joint Action in Cmty. Svc., 1991, Michael Madhusudan award for poem, Calcutta, 1996; Ky. Col., 1992. Mem. NEA (life), VFW, Am. Legion, 40 et 8, Family Motor Coach Assn., Sons of Norway, Order of Ky. Col., Internat. Platform Assn., Thousand Trails. Home and Office: Christ the King Chs PO Box 1607 Alice TX 78333-1607 *It is by the Power of Jesus Christ: He tells us in John 13:34: "Love one another, even as I loved you."*

TETLOW, EDWIN, author; b. Altrincham, Eng., May 19, 1905; s. William Chadwick and Mary (Entwistle) T.; m. Kathleen Whitworth Brown, Sept. 14, 1932; children: Susan Edwina, Timothy Chadwick. Student, Manchester (Eng.) U., 1924. Trainee journalist Daily Dispatch, Manchester, 1924-30; mem. staff Eve. News, London, 1930-33, Daily Mail, London, 1933-45; naval war corr. Daily Mail, 1940-42, army War corr., 1942-45; Berlin corr. Daily Telegraph, 1945-50, N.Y. corr., 1950-65; freelance author Esopus, N.Y., 1965—. Author: Eye on Cuba, 1966, The United Nations, 1971, The Enigma of Hastings, 1974, 2d edit., 1993, As It Happened, 1990; book reviewer: Christian Sci. Monitor; contbr.: Economist newspaper, Director Mag., London, Telegraph Sunday Mag., London, N.Y. Times, New Republic. Life mem. Fgn. Press Assn. (pres. 1964-65, mem. exec. bd. 1965—). Home: Druids' Dell PO Box 140 Esopus NY 12429-0140

TETTEGAH, SHARON YVONNE, education educator; b. Wichita Falls, Tex., Jan. 14, 1956; d. Lawrence Guice and Doris Jean (Leak) Oliver; 1 child, Tandra Ainsworth; m. Joseph Miller Zangai, Dec. 22, 1978 (div. 1983); 1 child, Tonia Monjay Zangai; m. George Tettegah, Apr. 28, 1989; 1 child, Nicole Jennifer Tettegah. AA, Coll. Alameda, 1985; BA, U. Calif., Davis, 1988, teaching cert., 1989, MA, 1991; postgrad., U. Calif., Santa Barbara. Cert. elem. tchr., Calif. Clk. II Alameda County Mcpl. Ct., Oakland, Calif., 1976-77; acct. clk. Alameda County Social Svcs., Oakland, 1977-78, eligibility technician, 1978-82; supervising clk. Alameda County Health Care Svcs., Oakland, 1982-84; tchr. Davis (Calif.) Joint Unified Sch. Dist., 1988-89, L.A. Unified Schs., L.A., 1990-92; tchr. Oakland Unified Sch. Dist., Oakland, 1992—, tchr. sci. mentor, 1993—; teaching asst. U. Calif., Santa Barbara, 1993-94; adminstrv. intern Oxnard Unified Sch. Dist., 1994, U. Calif. Cultural Awareness Program, Santa Barbara, 1994—; rsch. cons. to vice chancellor students affairs, cons. tchr. edn. program, facilitor registrar's office U. Calif., Santa Barbara, 1995-96, rsch. asst. Grad. Sch. Edn., 1996—; cons. U. Calif. , Davis, 1988-89, Montessori Ctr. Sch., Santa Barbara, Calif., 1996; multicultural cons. Davis Unified Sch. Dist., 1988-89; edn. cons. Ednl. Testing Svc., Emeryville, Calif., 1994; chair diversity com. of Santa Barbara Village Charter Sch.; mem. academic senate com. undergrad enrollment and admissions U. Calif. Santa Barbara, 1995, tchr. cross-cultural interactions course, summer, 1995; mem. academic affairs affirmative action com. U. Calif. Santa Barbara, 1995-96, grad. sch. of edn., grad. affairs and affirmative action comms. U. Calif. Santa Barbara, 1995-96. Mem. U. Calif. Santa Barbara Acad. Senate Bd. Undergraduate Admissions and Records; co-chair Diversity Com. Montecito-Santa Barbara Charter Sch.; pres. African-Am. Grad. and Profl. Students Orgn., Davis, 1988-89. Recipient Charlene Richardson Acad. Honors award Coll. Alameda, 1985; Calif. State Acad. fellow, 1989-91, Grad. Opportunity Acad. Excellence fellow, 1994-95, Vice Chancellors Acad. Achievement fellowship U. Calif. Santa Barbara, 1995-96, Vice Chancellors Acad. Fellowship Grad. Divsn., 1995-96. Mem. Am. Ednl. Researchers Assn., Calif. Sci. Tchrs. Assn., Calif. Advocacy for Math and Sci., Calif. Tchrs. Assn., Calif. Media Libr. Educators Assn., PTA, Multicultural Curriculum Assn., Supervision and Curriculum Leadership Assn., Bay Area Sci. and Tech. Educators Corsortium, Pan-African Students Assn., Kappa Delta Pi. Avocations: travelling, reading, preparing gourmet foods, tennis. Address: PO Box 1782 Santa Barbara CA 93116-1782 Office: U Calif Santa Barbara Sch Edn/Ednl Psychology Santa Barbara CA 93106

TETTLEBAUM, HARVEY M., lawyer; m. Ann Safier; children: Marianne, Benjamin. AB, Dartmouth Coll., 1964; JD, Washington U. Sch. Law, 1968, AM in History, 1968. Asst. dean Washington U. Sch. Law, 1969-77; asst. atty. gne., chief counsel Consumer Protection and Anti-Trust Div., 1970-77; pvt. practice Jefferson City, Mo., 1977-90; ptnr., chmn. health care, adminstrv. and govtl. law dept. Husch & Eppenberger, Jefferson City, Mo., 1990—; vice-chmn. Nat. Health Lawyers Long Term Care and the Law Programs, mem., bd. dirs., 1993—; legal subcom. Am. Health Care Assn., 1994—. Contbr. articles to profl. jours. Treas. Mo. Rep. com., 1976—; v.p. Moniteau County R-1 Sch. Dist. Bd., 1991-95, pres., 1995-96; mem. Calif. R-1 Sch. Bd., 1990-96, v.p., 1993-95, pres., 1995—. Mem. Nat. Health Lawyers Assn. (bd. dirs.), Mo. Bar Assn. (health and hosp. law com., chmn. adminstrv. law com.), Am. Health Care Assn. (legal subcom. 1994—0, Rep. Nat. Health Lawyers Assn. (bd. dirs.). Home: Rte # 2 Box 2726 California MO 65018 Office: Husch & Eppenberger Monroe House Ste 300 235 E High St PO Box 1251 Jefferson City MO 65101-3236

TETZELI, FREDERICK EDWARD, banker; b. Chomutove, Czech Rep., Sept. 12, 1930; came to U.S., 1961; s. Louis and Sophie (Deym) T.; m. Margaret Lee Weld, Sept. 6, 1958; chilren: Frederick John, William George, Christopher Weld. BS, Georgetown U., 1952. Assoc. Merrill Lynch, Havana, Cuba, 1952-54; treas. Cuban Trading Co., Havana, 1954-61; exec. adminstr. Waterman S.S. Corp., Mobile, Ala., 1962-64; mng. dir. J.P. Morgan, N.Y.C., 1964—; Bd. dirs., chmn. investment com. Luso Am. Bus. Council. Chmn., mem. exec. com. Am. Portuguese Soc., 1980—, bd. dirs., past chmn. Spain-U.S. C. of C., 1979—, past pres., bd. dirs. Belgian-Am. C. of C., 1973—; councillor French C. of C., 1973—; bd. dirs., past pres. Am.-Italy Soc., 1973—; bd. dirs. U.S.-Netherlands C. of C., 1980—; bd. dirs., mem. exec. com. France Am. Soc. Decorated grand officer Order of Italian Republic, knight Order of Royal House for Civilian Merit, Spain; mem. Legion of Comdrs. (Italy). Mem. U.S.-Italy C. of C. (bd. dirs.), Am. C. of C. Cuba (bd. dirs., vice chmn.), Bankers Assn. for Fgn. Trade (vice chmn. membership com.). Republican. Roman Catholic. Clubs: Downtown Assn., Met. (N.Y.C.); Sloane (London). Home: 336 Rosedale Rd Princeton NJ 08540-6708 Office: JP Morgan 60 Wall St New York NY 10005-2807

TETZLAFF, KAREN MARIE, state official; b. Florence, Oreg., Mar. 9, 1950; d. Chester Arthur and Martha Jane (Howell) Mitchell; m. Sterling Franklin Tetzlaff, July 16, 1988; children: Michelle René Reece, André Scott Matney, Derrick Anthony. Diploma, Chemeketa C.C., Salem, Oreg., 1981. Notary pub., Oreg. Sec. Oreg. Corrections div., Madras, 1977-78; intake-release data clk. community corrections Oreg. Corrections div., Salem, 1979-80, correctional officer, 1980-83, records mgr., 1983—, instr., 1990—; master facilitator trainer breaking barriers Oreg. Corrections div., 1995—; facilitator, trainer breaking barriers Gordon Graham & Co., Salem, 1992—, developing capable people, Salem, 1993—; instr., law enforcement data system rep. Oreg. Women's Correctional Ctr., Salem, 1984—, facilitator, 1993—. Head usher John Jacobs Evangelistic Assn., Salem, Medford, Redmond, Oreg., 1990-92; youth worship leader South Salem Foursquare Ch., Salem, 1990—; vol. Driving Under Influence Tng. Task Force, Salem, 1992—; v.p. Marion County chpt. Mothers Against Drunk Driving, 1994-95. Recipient 5-yr. outstanding svc. award Law Enforcement Data System, 1990, Investing in People, Svc. to State Tng. award Exec. Dept., 1992, traffic safety award Oreg. Dept. Transp., 1993, Employee of Quarter award Oreg. Women's Correctionala Ctr., 1993. Mem. Am. Correctional Assn., Oreg. Corrections Assn., Nat. Notary Assn., Cognitive Restructuring Network (letter of appreciation 1993). Republican. Avocations: paralegal studies, reading, singing. Office: Oreg Women's Correctional Ctr 2809 State St Salem OR 97310-1307

TETZLAFF, THEODORE R., lawyer; b. Saukville, Wis., Feb. 27, 1944. AB magna cum laude, Princeton U., 1966; LLB, Yale U., 1969. Bar: Ind. 1969, D.C. 1969, Ill. 1974. Legis. asst. to Congressman John Brademas, 1970; exec. dir. Nat. Conf. Police Community Rels., 1970-71; acting dir. U.S. Office Legal Svcs., Office Econ. Opportunity, Washington, 1972-73; counsel, Com. Judiciary U.S. Ho. of Reps., Washington, 1974; v.p., legal and external affairs Cummins Engine Co., 1980-82; gen. coun. Tenneco, Inc., Houston, 1992—, Greenwich, C.T.; ptnr. Jenner & Block, Chgo., 1976-80, 80—. Pres. Chgo. area Found. Legal Svcs., 1983—; commr. Pub. Bldg. Commn. Chgo., 1990—. Reginald Heber Smith fellow, 1969-70. Mem. ABA (chair sect. litigation 1991-92), Ill. State Bar Assn., Ind. State Bar Assn., D.C. Bar. Office: Tenneco Inc 1275 King St Greenwich CT 06831-2946 also: Jenner & Block 1 E Ibm Plz Fl 4200 Chicago IL 60611*

TEUBNER, FERDINAND CARY, JR., retired publishing company executive; b. Phila., Sept. 22, 1921; s. Ferdinand Cary Teubner and Esther Roslyn (Test) Alperstein; m. Ruth May Hazen, Nov. 1, 1953; 1 child, Janell Caron Teubner Crispyn. Student, U. Pa., 1940-41; grad., Charles Morris Price Sch. Advt. and Journalism, 1949. Rep. W.H. Hoedt Studios, Inc., Phila., 1945-52; account exec. Patterson Prodns., Inc., Phila., 1955-56, v.p., 1956-57; staff exec. Am. Assn. Advt. Agys., N.Y.C., 1957-59; rep. W.H. Martin & Co., Inc., N.Y.C., 1959-62; advt. salesman Editor & Pub. Co., Inc., N.Y.C., 1962-65, advt. mgr., 1965-76, gen. mgr., treas., 1976-78, treas., pub., 1978-95, dir., 1969-95; sec.-treas., dir. E & P Research, Inc., N.Y.C., 1985-95, ret., 1995. Served with USAAF, 1942-45, ETO; served to maj. U.S. Army, 1952-55, Korea. Decorated Purple Heart; recipient Silver Shovel award Internat. Newspaper Mktg. Assn., 1993. Mem. Sales Execs. Club N.Y.C., Res. Officer Assn. Episcopalian. Clubs: Union League, Lake Valhalla Country. Home: 18 Lenape Dr Montville NJ 07045-9795

TEUSCHER, GEORGE WILLIAM, dental educator; b. Chgo., Jan. 11, 1908; s. Albert Christian and Elizabeth (Klesch) T.; m. Eleanor C. Oeler, Sept. 29, 1934 (div.); children: Carol Ann, John William; m. Eleanor E. Wilson, May, 1968. D.D.S., Northwestern U., 1929, M.S.D., 1936, A.M., 1940, Ph.D., 1942; Sc.D. (hon.), N.Y. U., 1965. Charter mem. Am. Acad. Pedodontics (pres. 1960-61), Am. Bd. Pedodontics. Engaged in gen. practice of dentistry, 1929-34, in pedodontics, 1934-69; instr. pedodontics Northwestern U., 1933-38, asst. prof., 1938-41, assoc. prof., 1941; lectr. surgery Northwestern U. Med. Sch., 1945—, prof. pedodontics, 1946—; dean Northwestern U. Med. Sch. (Dental Sch.), 1953-71; mem. staff Wesley Meml. Hosp., 1946-69, chief dental sect. dept. otolaryngology, 1961-69; mem. adv. com. dentistry Smithsonian Instn., 1967—; lectr. on pedodontics and edn. in, U.S. and Can.; cons. Naval Dental Research Inst., Gt. Lakes. Editor: Dental Progress, 1959-63, Jour. Dentistry for Children, 1967—, Jour. Dental Edn, 1970-73; contbr. articles to dental jours. Bd. dirs. Tb Inst. Chgo. and Cook County, 1964-70; regent Nat. Library Medicine, 1968-72; bd. govs. Chgo. Heart Assn., 1967-74; Pres. Gen. Alumni Assn., Northwestern U., 1948-51. Served with Res. Officers Corps, 1929-42. Fellow Am. Coll. Dentists, Inst. Medicine Chgo.; mem. Internat. Assn. Dental Research, Am. Assn. Dental Schs. (pres. 1962-63), Am. Dental Assn. (council dental edn. 1964-70), Ill. Dental Soc., Chgo. Dental Soc. (pres. 1958-59), Odontographic Soc. (pres. 1952-53), Am. Soc. Dentistry for Children (pres. 1952-53, exec. officer 1982—), Am. Dental Soc. Europe (hon.), Xi Psi Phi, Omicron Kappa Upsilon. Clubs: Tavern (Chgo.), Chicago Literary (Chgo.). Home: 730 Blaney Dr Dyer IN 46311-2306

TEVRIZIAN, DICKRAN M., JR., federal judge; b. Los Angeles, Aug. 4, 1940; s. Dickran and Rose Tevrizian; m. Geraldine Tevrizian, Aug. 22, 1964; children: Allyson Tracy, Leslie Sara. BS, U. So. Calif., 1962, JD, 1965. Tax acct. Arthur Andersen and Co., Los Angeles, 1965-66; atty., ptnr. Kirtland and Packard, Los Angeles, 1966-72; judge Los Angeles Mcpl. Ct., Los Angeles, 1972-78, State of Calif. Superior Ct., Los Angeles, 1978-82; ptnr. Manatt, Phelps, Rothenberg & Tunney, Los Angeles, 1982-85, Lewis, D'Amato, Brisbois & Bisgaard, Los Angeles, 1985-86; judge U.S. Dist. Ct., Los Angeles, 1986—. Mem. Calif. Trial Lawyer's Assn. (trial judge of yr. 1987), L.A. County Bar Assn. (trial judge of yr. 1994-95). Office: US Dist Ct Royal Federal Bldg 255 E Temple St Los Angeles CA 90012-3334

TEWELL, JOSEPH ROBERT, JR., electrical engineer; b. Albany, N.Y., May 19, 1934; s. Joseph Robert and Florence Edna (MacKinnon) T.; m. Barbara Ann Johnson, Nov. 20, 1960; children—Patricia Ann, Donna Lynn, Joseph Robert, III. B.E.E., Rensselaer Poly. Inst., 1955, M.E.E., 1958. Research engr. N.Am. Aviation, Inc., Downey, Calif., 1955; assoc. research engr. Lockheed Aircraft Corp., Burbank, Calif., 1956; instr. Rensselaer Poly. Inst., 1957-64; sr. research scientist Martin Marietta Corp., Denver, 1964-79; mgr. advanced programs Martin Marietta Corp., Michoud, La., 1979-87, mgr. shuttle-C project, 1988-90, mgr. computer-aided productivity, 1991—; founding sponsor Challenger Ctr.; cons. Redford Corp., Scotia, N.Y., 1961. Contbr. articles to profl. jours.; inventor dual action single drive actuator, spacecraft docking and retrieval mechanism. Founding sponsor Challenger Ctr. Served with Army Security Agy., 1957. Recipient NASA Manned Awareness citation, 1970, NASA Skylab Achievement award, 1974, NASA New Tech. award, 1976, Tech. Achievement award Martin Marietta Corp., 1977, Sustained Performance award Martin Marietta Corp., 1981, NASA cert. of recognition, 1977, Author of Yr. award, 1986, also 38 publ. awards, 1965—. Fellow Explorers Club; mem. AIAA, Smithsonian Assocs., Air and Space Mus., Unmanned Vehicle Sys., Nat. Audubon Soc., Sigma Xi, Eta Kappa Nu, Tau Beta Pi, Theta Chi. Home: 619 Legendre Dr Slidell LA 70460-3427 Office: Mail No 4220 PO Box 29304 New Orleans LA 70189

TEWI, THEA, sculptor; b. Berlin, Germany; came to U.S., 1938, naturalized, 1943; d. Jules and Claire (Kochmann) Wittner; m. Charles K. Schlachet; 1 son, Peter. Grad., Nat. Acad. Fine Arts, Berlin; student New Sch., Art Students League, N.Y.C., 1956-57. Pres. League of Present Day Artists, 1964-70; pres. Sculptors League, 1970-88. Exhibited in one-man shows at, Village Art Center, N.Y.C., 1961, La Boetie Gallery, N.Y.C., 1966, 68, 70, Sala Michelangelo, Carrara, Italy, 1969, Lehigh U., Bethlehem, Pa., 1970, U. Notre Dame, 1970, Hallway Gallery, Washington, 1976, 80, Randall Gallery, N.Y.C., 1977, 79, 81, 83, Vorpal Gallery, N.Y.C., 1985, 87, Bklyn. Bot. Garden, 1989, N.Y. Acad. Scis., 1992, 93, others; exhibited in numerous group shows; represented in permanent collections at, Smithsonian Instn., Washington, Cin. Art Mus., Norfolk (Va.) Mus. Arts and Scis., U. Notre Dame, Norton Simon Collection, Citicorp, N.Y., Fort Worth Nat. Bank, Parks Dept. City of N.Y., N.Y. Acad. Scis., Govt. Ecuador; also represented in pvt. collections U.S., France, Italy, Spain, Switzerland, Japan. Recipient numerous awards and purchase awards, including 1st prize Am. Soc. Contemporary Artists, 1971, 75, 76, 78, medal of merit Nat. Arts Club, 1974, Nawa Peabody award Nat. Acad., 1975, medal of merit Knickerbocker Artists, 1975. Mem. Nat. Assn. Women Artists (1st prize, medal of honor 1969), Am. Soc. Contemporary Artists, Sculptors League (founder, pres. 1971-88). Home: 10030 67th Dr Forest Hills NY 11375-3147

TEWKESBURY, JOAN F., film director, writer; b. Redlands, Calif., Apr. 8, 1936; d. Walter S. and Frances M. (Stevenson) T.; m. Robert F. Maguire, III, Nov. 30, 1960 (div.); children: Robin Tewkesbury, Peter Harlan. Student, Am. Sch. Dance, 1947-54, Mt. San Antonio Jr. Coll., Walnut, Calif., 1956-58; drama scholar, U. So. Calif., 1958-60. Dancer in: film Unfinished Dance, 1946; dancer, flying understudy Peter Pan, LosAngeles and N.Y.C., 1954-55; choreographer film, Los Angeles, 1958-70, tchr. dance and drama, U. So. Calif., 1966-69, Immaculate Heart Coll., Los Angeles, 1960-63, Am. Sch. Dance, Los Angeles, 1959-69; tchr. film writing UCLA, 1986; choreographer, dir., actress, U. So. Calif. Repetory Co., 1965-68, London and Edinburgh (Scotland) Festival, 1965-68; scriptgirl: film McCabe and Mrs. Miller, 1970; author: screenplays Thieves Like Us, 1974, Nashville, 1975 (Los Angeles Critics Best Screenplay award), A Night in Heaven, 1983; playwright, dir. Cowboy Jack Street, 1978; dir. film Old Boyfriends, 1979; film writer, dir. TV 10th Month, 1979, The Acorn People, 1981; dir. film documentary Anna Freud, 1976; writer, dir. (TV show) Alfred Hitchcock Presents, from 1986, (TV movie for TNT) Cold Sassy Tree, 1989; screenwriter, dir., scriptwriter, co-exec. producer TV pilot Elysian Fields, 1988; dir. (Time-Life cable TV film) Sudie and Simpson; scriptwriter, dir.(TV) Shannon's Deal; dir. (TV movie) Wild Texas Wind, 1991, The Stranger (HBO), 1992; dir. (TV episodes) Northern Exposure, 1992, Picket Fences, 1992, Doogie Hauser, 1992; dir.(theater) Chippy, 1993; dir. (TV movie Disney Cable) On Promised Land, 1993. Mem. Literacy Vols. Am. Mem. Writers Guild Am., Dirs. Guild Am., ACLU, Nat. Abortion Rights Action League, Calif. Abortion Rights Action League.

TEWKSBURY, ROBERT ALAN, professional baseball player; b. Concord, N.H., Nov. 30, 1960. Student, Rutgers U., St. Leo Coll. With N.Y. Yankees, 1981-87, Chgo. Cubs, 1987-88; pitcher St. Louis Cardinals, 1989-94, Tex. Rangers, 1994—; player Nat. League All-Star Game, 1992. Ranked 2d in Nat. League for earned run average, 1992, 3d in Nat. League for wins. *

TEWSLEY, ROBERT WILLIAM, dancer; b. Leicester, Eng., Apr. 13, 1972; came to Can., 1990; s. Eric William and June (Sainsbury) T. Grad., Royal Ballet Sch., London, 1990. Soloist Nat. Ballet Can., Toronto, 1992-93, 1st soloist, 1993-94, prin., 1994—. Prin. roles include the Nutcracker, 1991, Swan Lake, 1994, Giselle, 1992, Onegin, 1994, Tghe Sleeping Beauty, 1994, La Sylphide, Romeo and Juliet, The Merry Widow, Divertimento No. 15, The Four Temperaments, The Taming of the Shrew, The Actress, Frames of Mind, Interrogating Slam, Now and Then, The Rite of Spring, Voluntaries; guest credits include Larry Long's Nutcracker, Chicago, 1993, The Nijunsky Gala, Hamburg, 1994, Onesin with Nice Operaballet, 1996; TV credits include The Inaugural De Maurier World Stage Gala, Vancouver, 1995, Dancing Romeo and Juliet Balcony Pasdedeux. Avocations: hiking, camping, playing piano. Office: Nat Ballet of Can, 157 King St E, Toronto, ON Canada M5C 1G9

TEXTOR, ROBERT BAYARD, cultural anthropology writer, consultant, educator; b. Cloquet, Minn., Mar. 13, 1923; s. Clinton Kenney and Lillian (Nickles) T.; divorced; children: Alexander Robertson, Marisa Elizabeth. Student, Lafayette Coll., 1940-41, Antioch Coll., 1941-43; B.A. in Asian Studies, U. Mich., 1945; Ph.D. in Cultural Anthropology, Cornell U., 1960. Civil info. and edn. officer Mil. Govt., Kyoto-Wakayama, Japan, 1946-48; rsch. fellow anthropology and S.E. Asia studies Yale U., 1959-60, assoc., 1960-61; rsch. fellow in stats. Harvard U., 1962-64; assoc. prof. edn. and anthropology Stanford U., 1964-68, prof. edn. and anthropology, 1968-86, prof. anthropology, 1986-90, prof. anthropology emeritus, 1990—; vis. prof. U. Saar, Saarbrücken, Germany, 1984-85; cons. Motorola U., 1991—; mem. S.E. Asia Coun., 1974-77; cons. cultural anthropology to govt. agys., 1957-58, 61-62. Author: (most recent) Roster of the Gods: An Ethnography of The Supernatural in a Thai Village, 6 vols., 1973, Austria 2005: Projected Sociocultural Effects of the Microelectronic Revolution, 1983, Anticipatory Anthropology, 1985, (with Sippanondha Ketudat) The Middle Path for the Future of Thailand, 1990; assoc. editor Jour. Conflict Resolution, 1965-70; mem. editorial bd. Human orgn., 1966-71, Jour. Cultural Futures, 1979-87; adv. editor Behavior Sci. Rsch., 1974-86. Bd. dirs. Vols. in Asia, Stanford, Calif., 1968-73; mem. Metro Portland Future Vision Commn., 1993-95. Served with U.S. Army, 1943-46. Fellow Rockefeller Found., 1951-52, fgn. area tng. fellow Ford Found., Thailand 1955-58, Carnegie fellow, 1958-59, Fulbright West Europe rsch. fellow, 1984-85, East-West Ctr. fellow, 1988-90; NSF grantee, Thailand, U.S., 1969-73, Volkswagen Found. grantee, Thailand and Germany, 1984. Fellow Am. Anthrop. Assn. (life mem.); mem. Siam Soc. (life mem.), Assn. Asian Studies (life mem.), Council on Anthropology and Edn. (pres. 1974-75), AAUP (pres. Stanford chpt. 1975-76), Phi Kappa Phi.

TEZAK, EDWARD GEORGE, dean; b. Steelton, Pa., Oct. 16, 1940; s. John Frank and Mary Cecilia (Shiprak) T.; m. Martha Katherine Leyko, Sept. 10, 1966; children: Christine Louise, Edward Scott. BS, U.S. Mil. Acad., 1963; MS in Astrodynamics, UCLA, 1967; PhD in Engring. Mechanics, Va. Poly. Inst. and State U., 1979. Commd. 2d lt. U.S. Army, 1963, advanced through grades to col., 1985; co. comdr., XO B Co. 13th Engr. Battalion, Camp Casey, Korea, 1964-65; engr. battalion advisor 6th ARVN Engr. Group, QuiNhon and DaNang, Vietnam, 1967-68; instr., then asst. prof. dept. mechanics U.S. Mil. Acad., West Point, N.Y., 1969-72; plans officer U.S. Army Engr. Group, Saigon, Vietnam, 1972-73; USMA fellow Army War Coll., Carlisle, Pa., 1982-83; group dir. dept. mechanics U.S. Mil. Acad., 1976-88, dep. head dept. mechanics, 1988, assoc. dean, 1989-93; ret. U.S. Army, 1993; dean Sch. Info. Sys. and Engring. Tech. SUNY, Utica, 1993—; mem. adv. bd. dept. math. U.S. Mil. Acad., 1993—. Mem. Cmty. Counsel, Utica, 1994—. Decorated Legion of Merit. Mem. ASME, Am. Soc. Engring. Edn. (bd. dirs. 1993-95, chair PIC III, mem. exec. com. mech. divsn., program chair 1989-93), Phi Kappa Phi. Roman Catholic. Avocations: bowling, golf, skiing. Home: 6 Crown Ln Whitesboro NY 13492 Office: SUNY Inst Tech PO Box 3050 Utica NY 13504

THACHER, CARTER POMEROY, diversified manufacturing company executive; b. 1926. With Wilbur-Ellis Co., San Francisco, 1960—, v.p., 1963-67, pres., from 1967, chmn. bd., 1989—, also bd. dirs. Office: Wilbur-Ellis Co 320 California St 2nd Fl San Francisco CA 94104*

THACKER, STEPHEN BRADY, medical association administrator, epidemiologist; b. Independence, Mo., Dec. 30, 1947; m. 1976; 2 children. AB, Princeton U., 1969; MD, Mt. Sinai Sch. Medicine, 1973; MSc, London Sch. Hygiene and Tropical Medicine, 1984. Chief consolidated surveillance and cmty. activity epidemiol. progress office Ctr. Disease Control, 1978-83, dir. surveillance and epidemiol. studies, 1983-86; asst. dir. sci. Ctr. Environ. Health and Injury Control, 1986-89; dir. epidemiol. progress office Ctr. Disease Control, 1989—; acting dir. Nat. Ctr. Environ. Health, 1993—; mem. steering com. Assn. Behavioral Sci. Med. Edn., 1971-74; assoc. Dept. Cmty. Medicine, Med. Ctr. Duke U., Durham, N.C., 1975-76; lectr. Cmty. Ctr. Mt. Sinai Sch. Medicine, N.Y.C., 1978—, Sch. Medicine Emory U., Atlanta, 1985-86; cons. epidemiology Arab Republic Egypt, 1979-91; clin. asst. prof. cmty. health Sch. Medicine Emory U., 1986—. Editor: Am. Jour. Epidemiology, 1990—. Clin. scholar Robert Wood Johnson Found., 1974-75; recipient Mosby Bood award for excellence, 1973, Saul Horowitz Jr. Meml. award, 1990, Supervisory award for contbr. advantage of women, 1991. Rsch. public health surveillance, infectious disease, environ. health, alcohol abuse, health care delivery, meta-analysis, technology assessment. Office: Ctr for Disease Control & Prevent MS F29 4770 Buford Hwy NE Atlanta GA 30341-3724

THACKERAY, JONATHAN E., lawyer; b. Athens, Ohio, July 30, 1936; s. Joseph Eugene and Betty Rutherford (Boright) T.; m. Sandra Ann McMahon, 1979; children: Jennifer, Sara, Amy, Jonathan. A.B. cum laude, Harvard U., 1958, J.D., 1961. Bar: Ohio 1961, U.S. Dist. Ct. (no. dist.) Ohio 1961, U.S. Supreme Ct. 1972, U.S. Ct. Appeals (6th cir.) 1973, U.S. Ct. Appeals (9th cir.) 1982, N.Y. 1993. Assoc. Vorys, Sater, Seymour & Pease, Columbus, Ohio, 1961; assoc. Baker & Hostetler, Cleve., 1965-72, ptnr., 1973-93; v.p., gen. counsel The Hearst Corp., N.Y.C., 1993—. Served to lt. USNR, 1961-65. Mem. ABA, Ohio Bar Assn., Cleve. Bar Assn., Am. Law Inst. Office: The Hearst Corp 959 8th Ave New York NY 10019-3767 *Notable cases include: administrative proceedings leading to approval of joint newspaper operating agreements in Cincinnati, Seattle and Las Vegas; litigation of newspaper antitrust cases in Cin., Seattle, Memphis, Trenton and Dallas.*

THACKRAY, ARNOLD WILFRID, historian, foundation executive; b. Eng., July 30, 1939; came to U.S., 1967, naturalized, 1982; s. Wilfrid Cecil and Mary (Clarke) T.; m. Barbara Hughes, 1965 (div. 1990); children: Helen Mary, Gillian Winifrid, Timothy Arnold; m. Diana Schueller, 1994. B.Sc., Bristol (Eng.) U., 1960; M.A., Cambridge (Eng.) U., 1965, Ph.D., 1966. Research chemist Robert Dempster and Co., Yorkshire, Eng., 1960-61; research fellow Churchill Coll., Cambridge U., 1965-68; prof. history and sociology of sci. U. Pa., Phila., 1968-96, Joseph Priestley prof. emeritus history/sociology of sci., 1996—, chmn. dept., 1970-77, dir. Beckman Ctr.

for History of Chemistry, 1982—; prof. history, prof. chemistry, dean grad. studies and research U. Md., 1985-86; exec. dir., libr. Chem. Heritage Found., 1987—; vis. lectr. Harvard U., 1967-68; vis. fellow All Souls Coll., Oxford, Eng., 1977-78; mem. Inst. Advanced Study, 1980. Editor: Isis, an Internat. Rev. of History of Science and its Cultural Influences, 1978-85, Osiris, 1985-94, Science After '40, 1992, Constructing Knowledge in the History of Science, 1995, Private Science, 1996, (with others) Science and Values, 1974, Toward a Metric of Science, 1978; author: Atoms and Powers, 1970, John Dalton, 1972, (with others) Gentlemen of Science, 1981-82, Chemistry in America, 1985; mem. editorial bd. Minerva, History of Science, The Scientist; contbr. articles to profl. jours. Recipient Gladstone Essay prize, also pub. speaking prize Churchill Coll., Cambridge U.; Guggenheim fellow, 1971-72, 85-86; Ctr. for Advanced Study in Behavioral Scis. fellow, 1973-74, 83-84. Fellow AAAS, Am. Acad. Arts and Scis., Royal Hist. Soc., Royal Chem. Soc.; mem. Am. Chem. Soc. (Dexter award 1983), Am. Hist. Assn., Manchester LIt. and Philos. Soc. (corr.), History of Sci. Soc., Am. Coun. Learned Socs. (bd. dirs., treas. 1985—), Soc. for Social Studies of Sci. (pres. 1981-83), Am. Coun. on Edn. (bd. dirs. 1987), Chemists Club (N.Y.C.), Cosmos Club (Washington). Episcopalian.

THACKRAY, RICHARD IRVING, psychologist; b. Wausau, Wis., Jan. 27, 1927; s. Irving Brownsell and Virginia (Weaver) T.; m. Marilyn Ann Patterson, June 20, 1953; children: Rick, Susette. B.A., Lawrence U., 1950; M.A., U. Mo., 1952; Ph.D., Purdue U., 1956. Instr. psychology U. Wis., 1952-54; asst. prof. psychology Allegheny Coll., Meadville, Pa., 1956-59; research psychologist Wright-Patterson AFB, Dayton, Ohio, 1959-65; psychophysiologist Inst. Pa. Hosp., 1965-67; instr. U. Pa. Med. Sch.; supr. stress behavior research Civil Aeromed. Inst., FAA, Oklahoma City, 1967-90; pvt. cons. in aviation human factors, 1991—; prin. scientist Galaxy Sci. Corp., 1993-95. Contbr. articles to profl. jours. Fellow Am. Psychol. Assn., Aerospace Med. Assn. (Raymond F. Longacre award 1988); mem. Human Factors Soc., Sigma Xi, Psi Chi.

THACKSTON, EDWARD LEE, engineer, educator; b. Nashville, Apr. 29, 1937; s. Guy Carleton and Sydney Virginia (Adams) T.; m. Betty Tucker, Mar. 19, 1961; children: Carol Elizabeth Thackston Nixon, Leah Virginia Thackston Hawkins. BE summa cum laude, Vanderbilt U., 1961; MS, U. Ill., 1963; PhD, Vanderbilt U., 1966. Registered profl. engr., Tenn. City engr. City of Lebanon, Tenn., 1959; design engr. City of Nashville, 1961-62; instr. Vanderbilt U., Nashville, 1965-66, asst. prof., 1966-69, assoc. prof., 1969-75, prof. engring., 1975—, chmn. dept. civil and environ. engring., 1980—; asst. to gov. for environ. affairs, State of Tenn., 1972-74; cons. in field. Author book, tech. reports; contbr. to profl. publs. Bd. dirs. Tenn. Environ. Coun., Nashville, 1971-76; bd. dirs. Tenn. Conservation League, Nashville, 1974—, v.p., 1977, pres., 1978-80; trustee Cumberland Mus., Nashville, 1986-92. Named Tenn. Conservationist of Yr., 1974. Fellow ASCE; mem. Am. Water Works Assn. (life), Water Environ. Fedn., Assn. Environ. Engring. Profs., Tenn. Hist. Soc., Tau Beta Pi, Chi Epsilon. Republican. Episcopalian. Avocations: genealogy, history, hiking, photography, basketball. Office: Vanderbilt U PO Box 133 Nashville TN 37235-0133

THADDEUS, PATRICK, physicist, educator; b. Wilmington, Del., June 6, 1932; s. Victor and Elizabeth (Ross) T.; m. Janice Petherbridge Farrar, Apr. 6, 1963; children: Eva, Michael. B.Sc., U. Del., 1953; M.A., Oxford (Eng.) U., 1955; Ph.D., Columbia U., 1960. Research assoc. Columbia Radiation Lab., 1960-61; research assoc. Goddard Inst. Space Studies, N.Y.C., 1961-63; mem. sci. staff Goddard Inst. Space Studies, 1963-86; mem. faculty Columbia U., 1965-86, adj. prof. physics, 1971-86; prof. astronomy and applied physics Harvard U., 1986—; mem. sci. staff Smithsonian Astrophys. Obs., 1986—; vis. com. Nat. Radio Astronomy Obs., 1973-76, 91-94; mem. Astronomy Survey Com., 1978-80, 89-90; Fairchild Disting. Scholar Calif. Inst. Tech., 1994; Russell Marker lectr. Pa. State U., 1989; vis. fellow Inst. Astronomy, Cambridge, Eng., 1983. Author papers on microwave spectroscopy, optical and radio astronomy. Recipient Exceptional Sci. Achievement medal NASA, 1970, 85; John C. Lindsay Meml. award Goddard Space Flight Center, 1976; Alexander von Humboldt award, 1983; Fulbright fellow, 1953-55. Fellow Am. Phys. Soc.; mem. Am. Astron. Soc., Am. Acad. Arts and Scis., Nat. Acad. Scis., Internat. Astronomical Union, Sigma Xi. Address: 58 Garfield St Cambridge MA 02138-1802

THADEN, EDWARD CARL, history educator; b. Seattle, Apr. 24, 1922; s. Edward Carl and Astrid (Engvik) T.; m. Marianna Theresia Forster, Aug. 7, 1952. B.A., U. Wash., 1944; student, U. Zurich, Switzerland, 1948; Ph.D., U. Paris, 1950. Instr. Russian history Pa. State U., 1952-55, asst. prof., 1955-58, asso. prof., 1958-64, prof., 1964-68; vis. prof. Ind. U., 1957, U. Marburg, 1965, U. Ill., Urbana, 1980, U. Halle, German Dem. Republic, 1988, U. Helsinki, Finland, 1990; prof. U. Ill., Chgo., 1968—, chmn. dept. history, 1971-73; editorial cons. Can. Rev. Studies in Nationalism, 1973-78; vis. rsch. scholar USSR Acad. Scis., 1975, 88, 90; Ford Found. project prin. researcher, 1975-78; U.S. rep. to Internat. Congress of Hist. Scis., 1980; project dir. NEH grant, 1980-82. Author: Conservative Nationalism in Nineteenth-Century Russia, 1964, Russia and the Balken Alliance of 1912, 1965, Russia Since 1801: The Making of a New Society, 1971, Russia's Western Borderlands, 1710-1870, 1984, Interpreting History: collected Essays on Russia's Relations with Europe, 1990, Essays in Russian and East European History: Festschrift in Honor of Edward C. Thaden, 1995; co-author, editor: Russification in the Baltic Provinces and Finland, 1955-1914, 1981; co-author, co-editor: Finland and the Baltic Provinces in the Russian Empire, 1984; mem. editorial bd. Jour Baltic Studies, 1984-93, assoc. editor, 1987-93. Served to lt. (j.g.) USNR, 1943-46. Carnegie Inter-Univ. Com. travel grantee to USSR, 1956; Fulbright research grantee Finland, 1957-58; Fulbright research grantee Germany, 1965; Fulbright research grantee Poland and Finland, 1968; Soc. Sci. Research Council grantee, 1957; Am. Council Learned Socs. grantee, 1963, 65-66; fellow Woodrow Wilson Internat. Center for Scholars, 1980. Mem. Am. Assn. for Advancement Slavic Studies (pres. Midwest br. 1975-76, exec. sec. 1980-82), Chgo. Consortium for Slavic and Ea. European Studies (pres. 1982-84), Baltische Historische Kommission, Göttingen (corr. mem. 1985—), Commn. Internat. des Etudes Historiques Slaves (v.p. 1985-95, pres. 1995-2000). Office: U Ill Dept History 913 UH (M/C 198) 601 S Morgan St Chicago IL 60607-7109

THAGARD, NORMAN E., astronaut, physician, engineer; b. Marianna, Fla., July 3, 1943; s. James E. Thagard and Mary F. Nicholson; m. Rex Kirby Johnson; children: Norman Gordon, James Robert, Daniel Cary. BS, Florida State U., 1965, MS, 1966; M.D., U. Texas Southwest Med. Sch., 1977. Intern, internal medicine Medical U. South Carolina, 1977-78; astronaut NASA, 1978—; mission specialist NASA Space Shuttle Challenger Flight STS-7, deployed satellites (ANIK C-2, PALAPA B-1), operated Remote Manipulator Sys., conducted experiments, 1983, NASA Spacelab-3 Mission STS-51 B, 1985, NASA Space Shuttle Atlantis Flight STS-30, deployed Magellan Venus exploration spacecraft, 1989; payload commander NASA Space Shuttle Discovery Flight STS-42, International Microgravity Lab.-1 module experiments, 1992; crew mem. Space Station MIR-18, 1995. Contbr. articles to profl. jours. With USMC, 1966-70, Capt. 1967-70, in Vietnam flew 163 combat missions. Decorated 11 Air medals, Navy Commednation medal with Combat V, Marine Corps E award, Vietnam Svc. medal, Vietnamese Cross of Gallantry with Palm. Mem. AIAA, Phi Kappa Phi. Avocations: classical music, electronic design; broke U.S. space endurance record of 84 continuous days aboard the Russian space station Mir. Office: Lyndon B Johnson Space Ctr NASA 2101 Nasa Rd 1 Houston TX 77058-3607

THAHANE, TIMOTHY, federal government official. V.p., sec. Internat. Bank for Reconstruction and Devel., 1980. Office: IBRD Secretary 701 18th St NW Washington DC 20433*

THAKOR, HAREN BHASKERRAO, manufacturing company executive; b. Ahmedabad, Gujarat, India, Dec. 12, 1938; came to U.S., 1960; s. Bhaskerrao Balvantrai and Kumud T.; m. Barbara Ann Martin, July 26, 1969; children: Manisha Ann, Sunil Haren. B.Civil Engring., Gujarat U., 1960; M.S. in Structural Engring., U. Ill., 1961; M.B.A., U. Calif.-Berkeley, 1965. Acct. Friden, Inc., San Leandro, Calif., 1965-67; sr. acct. bus. product group Xerox, Rochester, N.Y., 1967-69; mgr. budget and planning Xerox, Chgo., 1969-70; sr. policy analyst Xerox, Stamford, Conn., 1970-72, mgr. intercompany pricing, 1972-74; dir. bus. planning, automotive div. Arvin Industries, Inc., Columbus, Ind., 1974-77, v.p. fin. automotive div., 1977-81, treas., 1981-82, chief fin. officer, dir., 1982-90, pvt. investor, cons. Mem. AICPA, N.C. Assn. CPAs. Club: Chapel Hill Country. Home and Office: The Oaks 1023 Cleland Dr Chapel Hill NC 27514-5619

THAL, HERBERT LUDWIG, JR., electrical engineer, engineering consultant; b. Mt. Vernon, N.Y., Feb. 15, 1932; s. Herbert Ludwig and Mildred (Martinson) T.; m. Joan Madeline Ragsdale, Jan. 30, 1954; children: Herbert Ludwig III, Wayne, Carolyn, David, Eric. BEE, Rensselaer Poly. Inst., 1953, MEE, 1955, PhDEE, 1962. Rsch. assoc. Rensselaer Poly. Inst., Troy, N.Y., 1953-56; project engr. GE, Schenectady, 1956-67; staff engr. GE, King of Prussia, Pa., 1967-77, mgr. electromagnetics, 1977-89; v.p. Microlab/FXR, Livingston, N.J., 1989-92; adj. prof. Drexel U., Phila., 1983-90; adj. assoc. prof. U. Pa., Phila., 1986-87. 2d lt. U.S. Army, 1957. Fellow IEEE, Sigma Xi, Tau Beta Pi, Eta Kappa Nu. Presbyterian.

THAL, LEON JOEL, neuroscientist; b. N.Y.C., June 17, 1944; s. Bernard and Esther (Beller) T.; m. Donna Jean Norbo, June 25, 1967. MD, Downstate Med. Ctr., N.Y.C., 1969. Diplomate Am. Bd. Psychiatry and Neurology. Instr., asst. prof., assoc. prof. neurology Albert Einstein Coll. Medicine, Bronx, N.Y., 1975-85; assoc. prof. neurosci. U. Calif. San Diego, 1985-89, prof. neurosci., 1989—. Editor: Cognitive Disorders, 1992; contbr. chpts. in books and articles to profl. jours. Lt. comdr. USPHS, 1970-72. Home: 402 Brighton Ave Cardiff CA 92007 Office: Univ Calif Dept Neuroscience 9500 Gilman Dr La Jolla CA 92093-0624

THALACKER, ARBIE ROBERT, lawyer; b. Marquette, Mich., Apr. 17, 1935; s. Arbie Otto and Jeanne (Emmett) T.; m. Rita Annette Skaaren, Sept. 11, 1956 (div. July 1992); children: Marc Emmett, Christopher Paul, Robert Skaaren. AB, Princeton U., 1957; JD, U. Mich., 1960. Bar: N.Y. 1961, U.S. Ct. Appeals (2d cir.) 1962. Assoc. Shearman & Sterling, N.Y.C., 1960-68, ptnr., 1968—; dir. Detrex Corp., Detroit, 1981—, chmn. bd., 1993-96. Leader Rep. Dist. Com., 1966-68; v.p., trustee Greenwich Village Soc. for Hist. Preservation; trustee The Naropa Inst.; bd. dirs. Meredith Monk House Found., Shambhala Internat. Mem. ABA, N.Y. Bar Assn., Assn. Bar City N.Y. (securities regulatory commn. 1975-78), Wine and Food Soc. (bd. dirs. 1976-78, 85-93, 94—), Chevaliers du Tastevin, Commanderie de Bordeaux, Siwanoy Country Club (bd. govs. 1976-79), Derby Club, Links Club, Verbank Hunting and Fishing Club. Home: 17 Commerce St New York NY 10014-3763 Office: Shearman & Sterling 599 Lexington Ave New York NY 10022-6030

THALDEN, BARRY R., architect; b. Chgo., July 5, 1942; s. Joseph and Sibyl (Goodwin) Hechtenthal; m. Irene L. Mittleman, June 23, 1966 (div. 1989); 1 child, Stacey. BArch, U. Ill., 1965; M in Land Architecture, U. Mich., 1969. Landscape architect Hellmuth, Obata, Kassebaum, St. Louis, 1969-70; dir. landscape architecture PGAV Architects, St. Louis, 1970-71; pres. Thalden Corp (formerly Saunders-Thalden & Assocs. Inc.), St. Louis, 1971—. Prin. works include Rock Hill Park, 1975 (AIA award 1977), Wilson Residence, 1983 (AIA award), Nat. Bowling Hall of Fame, 1983 (St. Louis RCGA award 1984), Village Bogey Hills (Home Builders award 1985, St. L. ASLA award 1994), St. Louis U. Campus Mall (St. L. ASLA award 1989), Horizon Casino Resort, Lake Tahoe, Nev., St. Louis Airport's Radisson Hotel, Lady Luck, Treasure Bay, Palace Casinos, Biloxi, Miss., Boomtown Casino, New Orleans, Pres. Casino on the Admiral, St. Louis, Plaza of Champions, Busch Stadium, St. Louis. Bd. dirs. St. Louis Open Space Coun., 1973-83; apptd. Mo. Lands Architect Coun., 1990. Named Architect of Yr. Builder Architect mag., 1986. Fellow Am. Soc. Landscape Architects (nat. v.p. 1979-81, pres. St. Louis chpt. 1975, trustee 1976-79, nat. conv. chair 1991); mem. AIA, World Future Soc. (pres. St. Louis chpt. 1984-94, keynote conf. spkr. 1995). Avocations: painting, gardening, tennis, guitar. Home: 8 Edgewater Is Saint Louis MO 63105 Office: Thalden Corp 7777 Bonhomme Ave Ste 2200 Saint Louis MO 63105-1911

THALER, PAUL SANDERS, lawyer, mediator; b. Washington, May 4, 1961; s. Martin S. Thaler and Barbara (Friedman) Mishkin; m. Melinda Ann Frostic, Oct. 12, 1991; children: Rachel Leigh, Daniel Martin. AB, Vassar Coll., 1983; JD, Georgetown U., 1987. Bar: Md. 1987, D.C. 1988, U.S. Ct. Appeals (D.C. and 4th cirs.) 1988, U.S. Dist. Ct. Md. 1988, U.S. Ct. Appeals (fed. cir.) 1989, U.S. Dist. Ct. D.C. 1989, U.S. Ct. Internat. Trade 1990. Assoc. Cooter & Gell, Washington, 1987-93; pres. The Thaler Group, Bethesda, Md., 1993—; ptnr. The Robinson Law Firm, Washington, 1993-96, Thaler & Liebeler, 1996—. Treas. Montgomery Highlands Estates Homeowners Assn., Silver Spring, Md., 1990—; mediator Superior Ct. of D.C., 1991—. Mem. ABA (sect. dispute resolution, vice chmn. ethics 1994-96), D.C. Bar Assn., Md. Bar Assn., Soc. Profls. in Dispute Resolution, Acad. Family Mediators. Home: 3329 Sea Port Way Silver Spring MD 20902-2200 Office: Thaler & Liebeler Ste 400 1775 Pennsylvania Ave NW Washington DC 20006

THALER, RICHARD H., economics educator; b. East Orange, N.J., Sept. 12, 1945; s. Alan M. and Roslyn (Melnikoff) T.; children: Gregory Scott, Maggie Rose, Jessica Lynn. BA, Case Western Res. U., 1967; MA, U. Rochester, 1970, PhD, 1974. Asst. prof. U. Rochester (N.Y.), 1974-78; assoc. prof. Cornell U., Ithaca, N.Y., 1978-86, prof., 1986—, H.J. Louis prof., 1988—; vis. scholar Nat. Bur. Econ. Rsch., Stanford, Calif., 1977-78, Russell Sage Found., N.Y.C., 1991-92; vis. prof. U. B.C., Vancouver, 1984-85. Author: The Winner's Curse, 1992; contbr. articles on psychology and econs. Mem. Am. Econs. Assn.

THALER, RICHARD WINSTON, JR., investment banker; b. Boston, Apr. 9, 1951; s. Richard Winston and Victoria Louise (Sears) T.; m. Mary Alice Gast, June 28, 1980; children: Julia Davis, Sarah Sears, Hannah Warren. BA in Am. Polit. History cum laude, Princeton U., 1973; MBA, Harvard U., 1978. Salesman Media Networks, N.Y.C., 1973-74; banker Bank of Boston, Rio De Janeiro, Brazil, 1975-77, Boston, 1978-80; mng. dir. investment banking Lehman Bros., N.Y.C., 1980—. Spl. gifts solicitor Princeton U. Ann. Giving, N.Y.C., 1987-88, class agt., 1988-93; trustee Daily Princetonian, 1989—, Episc. Divinity Sch., Cambridge, Mass., 1995—; mem. vestry Chapel of St. James the Fisherman, Wellfleet, Mass.; trustee at large Plymouth Plantation, Plymouth, Mass., 1995—. Mem. Mass. Soc. Mayflower Descendants, Princeton Club, Siwanoy Country Club, University Cottage Club, Bond Club of N.Y. Democrat. Episcopalian. Avocations: gardening, sailing, Am. polit. hist., exotic travel. Office: Lehman Bros Am Express World Fin Ctr Am Express Tower New York NY 10285

THALL, BURNETT MURRAY, newspaper executive; b. Toronto, Ont., Can., Sept. 27, 1922; s. Henry and Selina (Harris) Rosenthal; m. Eleanor Langbord, Sept. 23, 1945; children: Nelson Spencer, Martin Evan. B.A.Sc., U. Toronto, 1945, M.A.Sc., 1947, Ph.D., 1949. Registered profl. engr., Ont. Spl. lectr. applied sci. and engring. U. Toronto, 1947; cons. engr., then prodn. engr. Toronto Star, 1947-50, v.p., 1958-68, sr. v.p., 1968—, also dir.; chmn. Toronto Star Newspapers Ltd. Author articles in field. Trustee Atkinson Charitable Found.; bd. govs., hon. treas. Women's Coll. Hosp., 1963—; bd. dirs. Princess Margaret Hosp., Ont. Cancer Treatment and Research Found.; bd. govs. U. Toronto. Urgent Care Centre named in his honour Women's Coll. Hosp., 1989; named to Hall of Distinction Engring. Alumni U. Toronto, 1990. Mem. Am. Newspaper Pubs. Assn., Assn. Profl. Engrs. Ont. (Citizenship medal 1991), Can. Daily Newspaper Pubs. Assn. Home: 15 Rosemary Ln, Toronto, ON Canada M5P 3E7 Office: The Toronto Star, 1 Yonge ST, Toronto, ON Canada M5E 1E6

THALL, RICHARD VINCENT, education program director; b. San Francisco, Sept. 12, 1940; s. Albert Vincent and Alice Stella (O'Brien) T.; m. Ellyn Marie Wisherop, June 15, 1963; children: Kristen Ellyn, Richard Vincent Jr. AA, City Coll. San Francisco, 1961; BA, San Francisco State Coll., 1964; MA, San Francisco State U., 1971. Cert. elem. tchr., Calif.; cert. secondary tchr., Calif.; cert. community coll. tchr., Calif. Tchr. biology San Francisco Unified Sch. Dist., 1965-66; tchr. biology Mt. Diablo Unified Sch. Dist., Concord, Calif., 1966-79, program dir. water environ. studies program, 1979—; ranger/naturalist State of Calif., Branna Island, 1973-78; naturalist Adventure Internat., Oakland, Calif., 1979-81; lectr. Princess Cruise Lines, 1982-84, Sea Goddess, 1986—, Sun Lines, 1987, Sitmar Lines, 1989, RCCL, 1991-95; spkr. commencements U. Calif., Berkeley, 1989. Author: Ecological Sampling of the Sacramento-San Joaquin Delta, 1976; Water Environment Studies Program, 1986; co-author: Project MER Laboratory Manual, 1982. Mem. Contra Costa County (Calif.) Natural Resources Commn., 1975-78, vice-chmn., 1977-78; active Save Mt. Diablo, Concord, 1969-76, v.p., 1974-75; mem. citizens com. Assn. Bay Area Govt. Water Quality, 1979-82, vice-chmn., 1980-82; active John Marsh Home Restoration Com., Martinez, Calif., 1977-78; mem. edn. adv. com. Marine World/Africa USAd, Vallejo, Calif., 1988—; troop com. chmn. Boy Scouts Am., Concord, 1984-86, asst. scoutmaster, 1985-87. Recipient Recognition and Excellence cert. Assn. Calif. Sch. Adminstrs., 1984, Wood Badge award Boy Scouts Am., 1986; grantee State Calif., 1982, 84, San Francisco Estuary Project, 1992, EPA, 1992, Shell Oil Co., 1993. Mem. AAAS, Nat. Assn. Biology Tchrs., Nat., Audubon Soc., Am. Mus. Natural Hist., Nat. Geog. Soc., Smithsonian Instn. (assoc.). Republican. Roman Catholic. Avocations: skiing, jogging, reading, hiking, photography. Home: 1712 Lindenwood Dr Concord CA 94521-1109 Office: Mt Diablo Unified Sch Dist 1936 Carlotta Dr Concord CA 94519-1358

THAMES, REBECCA EDWARDS, advertising executive; b. Canton, Ga., June 25, 1946; d. James Alfred and Myrtle Mae (Little) E.; m. Michael Bruce Thames, Dec. 31, 1966. AA, Reinhardt Coll., 1966; BA, U. Ga., 1968. Pub. relations writer Piedmont So. Life Ins., Atlanta, 1966-69; prodn. asst. Liller, Neal, Battle and Lindsey Advt., Atlanta, 1968-69; media planner/buyer William Cook Advt., Jacksonville, Fla., 1969; media supr. William Cook Advt., Jacksonville, 1979-87, assoc. media dir., 1987-91, v.p., 1991—; spkr. Nat. Cable Advt. Bur. Conv., 1992. Contbg. writer feature stories Atlanta Jour. Constn., 1960, So. Bus.and Realty, 1968-69, North Ga. Tribune, 1960-65, Westside Story, 1975. Mem. Jacksonville Advt. Fedn. Episcopalian. Avocations: music, decorating, sewing, writing. Home: 4137 Churchwell Rd Jacksonville FL 32210-5802 Office: William Cook Advt 225 Water St Ste 1600 Jacksonville FL 32202-5149

THAR, FERDINAND AUGUST (BUD THAR), trade company executive; b. Paw Paw, Mich., Oct. 26, 1940; s. James Ferdinand and Louise Olga (Schmidt) T.; m. Siri Ashelman, Jan. 28, 1967; Jonathan Justin, Christina Sheri, Amanda Hope. BA, Mich. State U., 1964; postgrad., Boston U., 1964-65, Am. U., 1968-72, U. Ga. Sch. Internat. Law, 1978. Program officer Govtl. Affairs Inst., Washington, 1964-73; led Govs.' Trade Mission to Taiwan, 1979; exec. dir. Ctr. Internat. Transp. for Nat. Govs.' Assn., 1980-82; assoc. dir. Battle Creek (Mich.) Unltd., 1982-84; mem. mfg. trade mission to France, 1983; pres. Eagle Trade, Battle Creek, 1983—; exec. dir. Great Lakes World Trade Ctr., Detroit, 1986; instr. MBA Internat. Trade Ednl. Svcs. Exch. with Peoples Republic of China, 1987-88, with Hungary, 1992; U.S. del. 1st World Agrl. Fair, New Delhi, 1959-60, Internat. Farm Youth Exch., Israel, 1962; mem. White House Conf. on Internat. Cooperation, 1972, White House Conf. on Balanced Growth, 1978; mem. intergovtl. rels. com. Transp. Rsch. Bd., NSF, 1985—; guest govts. of France, Jamaica, Taiwan, Yogoslavia, Germany and Brit. Rail, Eng.; cons. Gt. Lake Regional Commn., Ann Arbor, Mich., 1984-85, others. Author: Influence of International Travel on Teens Vocational Choice, 1963, Rural Youth in Michigan, 1964. Leader youth vol. group, Costa Rica, 1963; chief elder Battle Creek Bible Ch., 1991-92. Mem. Gideons Internat. Home: 3439 Maple Dr Ypsilanti MI 48197 Office: Charles Reinhart Co Realtor Ann Arbor MI

THARNEY, LAURA CHRISTINE, lawyer; b. New Brunswick, N.J., June 19, 1965; d. Thaddeus Raphael and Madeline Kay (Baumann) T. AA in Liberal Arts, Union County Coll., 1984; BA in History, Rutgers U., 1986, JD, 1991. Bar: N.J. 1991, U.S. Dist. Ct. N.J. 1991, N.Y. 1992. With Specialized Legal Svcs., N.Y. and N.J., 1991-94; dep. county counsel Office of Middlesex County Counsel, New Brunswick, 1992-94; assoc. Law Offices of Edward J. Buzak, Montville, N.J., 1994-95, Heine Assocs., P.A., Cherry Hill, N.J., 1995-96. Mem. ABA, N.J. State Bar Assn. (mentor 1994—), N.Y. Bar Assn., Morris County Bar Assn. (mentor, mediator 1994—), Camden County Bar Assn., Phi Alpha Theta. Avocations: running, rock climbing, scuba diving. Office: Heine Assocs PA Ste 2 161 S Main St Milltown NJ 08850

THARNEY, LEONARD JOHN, education educator, consultant; b. New Haven, Nov. 6, 1929; s. Lillian A. Batey; m. Denise A. Gauvin, June 20, 1981; children: Karen L., Linda L. BS, Trenton (N.J.) State Coll., 1954; MEd, Rutgers U., 1959; postgrad., Lehigh U., Bethlehem, Pa., Columbia U.; grad., Command & Gen. Staff Coll., Ft. Leavenworth, Kans., 1972. Cert. secondary math. and sci. tchr., elem. tchr. Tchr. (elem. demonstration) Trenton State Coll., 1954-60; tchr. (Jr. High demonstration) Ewing Twp. (N.J.) Schs., 1960-63; cons.-evaluator Am. Coun. on Edn., Washington, 1975-95, field coord., 1995—; cons., evaluator Mid. States Assn., Phila., 1987—; prof. Trenton (N.J.) State Coll., 1963-92, prof. emeritus, 1993—, dept. chmn., 1988-92; cons. to internat. schs. for curriculum or sci. edn., Monrovia, Accra, Athens, Mogadishu, Cairo, Alexandria, Aleppo, Damascus, 1975—; tchr. grad. courses in curriculum and ednl. rsch. at overseas sites, Spain, Cyprus, Saudi Arabia, Syria, 1981—; exch. prof. Worcester Coll. Higher Edn., Eng., 1984-85; presenter sci. edn. workshops, AISA Internat. Conf., Nairobi, 1987; rep. from Coll. to Prins. Tng. Ctr., London, 1994; bd. dirs. People to People Internat., Trenton, v.p. chpt. 1995. Co-author 7 manuals for uniform constrn. codes. Col. AUS, 1947-81. Recipient ACE award for outstanding svc. in mil. evaluations, 1987, cert. of appreciation, presdl. citation, 1989, spl. plaque award, others; decorated meritorious svc. medal U.S. Army, 1981, army commendation medal, 1976. Mem. ASCD, Assn. Tchr. Educators, Assn. for Edn. Tchrs. in Sci, Nat. Coun. Social Studies. Home: 20 Lawrenceville Penning Rd Lawrenceville NJ 08648-1648

THARP, BENJAMIN CARROLL, JR., architect; b. Austin, Tex., Sept. 3, 1919; s. Benjamin Carroll Tharp and Norris (Ophelia) Wallis; m. Mae Sibley; children: Ronald Emery, Carolyn Jeanine Tharp Love. BArch, U. Tex., 1943. Registered architect, Tex. Draftsman Wurdeman & Beckett, L.A., 1944, Richard Neutra, L.A., 1945, Merrill Baird, L.A., 1946, Golemon & Rolfe, Houston, 1947, Milton Foy Martin, Houston, 1948; prin. Koetter & Tharp, Houston, 1949-64, Koetter, Tharp & Cowell, Houston, 1964-78; architect Koetter, Tharp, Cowell and Lockwood, Andrews, Newman, Houston, 1978-81; ret. Lockwood, Andrews, Newman, 1981. Bd. dirs. Harris County Soil and Water Conservation Dist., Houston, 1972-82; pres. Constrn. Industry Coun., Houston, 1970. Recipient 1st Restoration award Red Cedar Shingle and Handsplit Shake Bur./AIA, Seattle, 1975. Fellow AIA, Tex. Soc. Architects (chmn. hist. resources com. 1986); mem. Montgomery (Tex.) Hist. Soc., Optimist Club (pres. Houston chpt. 1970). Republican. Baptist. Home: RR 3 Box 51A Montgomery TX 77356-2323

THARP, ROLAND GEORGE, psychology, education educator; b. Galveston, Tex., June 6, 1930; s. Oswald Roland and Berma Lucille (Keefer) T.; m. Stephanie Dalton; children: Donald Martin, Thomas Roland, David Michael, Julie. Student, Middlebury Coll., 1956, 60; BA cum laude, U. Houston, 1957; MA, U. Mich., 1958, PhD, 1961. Cert. Am. Bd. Examiners in Profl. Psychology. Reporter Tex. City Sun, 1946-47; mgr. Tharp Lumber Co., LaMarque, Tex., 1949-54; intern VA Hosp., Menlo Park, Calif., 1960; asst. prof. U. Ariz., Tucson, 1961-65, assoc. prof., 1965-68; prof., dir. clin. studies, dir. multicultural ctr. for higher edn. U. Hawaii, Honolulu, 1968-87; provost and v.p. for acad. affairs U.S. Internat. U., San Diego, 1987-89; prof. edn., psychology U. Calif., Santa Cruz, 1990—; dir. Nat. Rsch. Ctr. for Diversity, 1995—; dir. Ctr. for Rsch. on Edn., Diversity and Excellence, 1996—; prin. investigator Kamehameha Early Edn. Program, Honolulu, 1969-89; field selection officer Peace Corps, Washington, 1965-67. Author: (poetry) Highland Station, 1978; co-author: (book) Behavior Modification in the Natural Environment, 1969, Self-Directed Behavior, 1980, Rousing Minds to Life, 1988; writer, producer, dir. film Scenes from the Life, 1981 (Purchase prize The Contemporary Mus. 1981). Mem. Bd. Psychologist Examiners, Ariz., 1964-67; pres. Hawaii Literary Arts Coun., Honolulu, 1982. Robert Frost fellow Middlebury Coll., 1960; recipient Am. Film Mag. award for filmmaking Hawaii Internat. Film Festival, 1990, Grawemeyer award edn., 1993. Mem. Am. Ednl. Rsch. Assn., Am. Anthropol. Assn. Episcopalian. Avocation: tennis. Office: University of California Crown College Santa Cruz CA 95064

THARP, TWYLA, dancer, choreographer; b. Portland, Ind., July 1, 1941; m. Peter Young (div.); m. Robert Huot (div.); 1 child, Jesse. Student, Pomona Coll.; BA in Art History, Barnard Coll., 1963; D of Performing Arts (hon.), Calif. Inst. Arts, 1978, Brown U., 1981, Bard Coll., 1981; LHD, Ind. U., 1987; DFA, Pomona Coll., 1987; studied with Richard Thomas,

Merce Cunningham, Igor Schwezoff, Louis Mattox, Paul Taylor, Margaet Craske, Erick Hawkins. Dancer Paul Taylor Dance Co., 1963-65; freelance choreographer with own modern dance troupe and various other cos. including Joffrey Ballet and Am. Ballet Theatre, 1965-87; founder, choreographer Twyla Tharp Dance Found., N.Y.C., 1965-87; artistic assoc., resident choreographer Am. Ballet Theatre, N.Y.C., 1987-91; teaching residencies various colls. and univs. including U. Mass., Oberlin Coll., Walker Art Ctr., Boston U.; choreographer White Oak Dance Project. Choreographer: Tank Dive, 1965, Re-Moves, 1966, One Two Three, 1966, Forevermore, 1967, Generation, 1968, Medley, 1969, After Suite, 1969, Dancing in the Streets of London and Paris, 1969, The One Hundreds, 1970, The Fugue, 1970, The Big Pieces, 1971, Eight Jelly Rolls, 1971, The Raggedy Dances, 1972, Deuce Coupe, 1973, As Time Goes By, 1974, Sue's Leg, 1975, Ocean's Motion, 1975, Push Comes to Shove, 1976, Once More Frank, 1976, Mud, 1977, Baker's Dozen, 1979, When We Were Very Young, 1980, Nine Sinatra Songs, 1982, The Catherine Wheel, 1982, Bach Partita, 1984, The Little Ballet, 1984, (with Jerome Robbins) Brahms/Handel, 1984, At the Supermarket, 1984, In the Upper Room, 1987, Ballare, 1987, Stations of the Crossed, 1988, Everlast, 1989, Quartet, 1989, Bum's Rush, 1989, The Rules of the Game, 1990, Brief Fling, 1990, Grand Pas: Rhythm of the Saints, 1991, Deuce Coupe II, 1992, The Men's Piece, 1992, (with Mikhail Baryshnikov) Cutting Up, 1992-93, Demeter and Persephone, 1993, Waterbaby Bagatelles, 1994, Demeter and Persephone, 1994, Red, White & Blues, 1995, How Near Heaven, 1995, I Remember Clifford, 1995, Jump Start, 1995, Americans We, 1995; (film) Hair, 1979, Ragtime, 1981, Amadeus, 1984, White Nights, 1985, Valmont, 1989, I'll Do Anything, 1994; (video spls.) Making Television Dance, 1977, CBS Cable Confessions of a Corner Maker, 1980; (Broadway shows) Sorrow Floats, 1985, Singin' In The Rain, 1985; (TV) Baryshnikov by Tharp (Emmy award Outstanding Choreography 1985, Emmy award Outstanding Writing of Classical Music/Dance Programming 1985, Emmy award Outstanding Directing of Classical Music/Dance Programming 1985), The Catherine Wheel, 1982 (Emmy award nom. Outstanding Choreography 1982); author (autobiography): When Push Comes to Shove, 1992. MacArthur Found. Chgo. fellow, 1992; recipient Creative Arts award Brandeis U., 1972, Dance mag. award, 1981, Univ. Excellence medal Columbia U., 1987, Lions of the Performing Arts award N.Y. Pub. Libr., 1989, Samuel M. Scripps award Am. Dance Festival, 1990. *

THARPE, FRAZIER EUGENE, journalist; b. Panama City, Fla., Jan. 10, 1941; s. Henry Clayton and Margaret Jane (Jenkins) T.; m. Barbara Ann Hembree, Oct. 30, 1971. B.A. in Polit. Sci. and History, Vanderbilt U., Nashville, 1963. Reporter Miami (Fla.) News, 1963; reporter U.P.I., Atlanta and Columbia, S.C., 1964; pub. relations exec. Atlanta, 1965-69; fin. editor Atlanta Constn., 1969-73. Editorial assoc., columnist, 1974-83, columnist Helpline, 1983—, Free-lance writer. Office: 72 Marietta St NW Atlanta GA 30303-2804

THATCHER, GEORGE ROBERT, banker; b. Austin, Pa., Sept. 18, 1922; S. Walter Robert and Roberta Estelle (Bernard) T.; widowed; children: Georgia Anne Thatcher Faneca, Janie Estelle Thatcher Holmes, Walter Wimberly. BA in English, U. Miss., 1948; grad. diploma in bus., Ind. U., 1973; degree of distinction, Inst. Fin. Edn., Chgo. Enlisted U.S. Army, 1942, advanced through grades to maj., 1948, stationed in Pacific, Korea, ret., 1952; ptnr. Rand-Thatcher Advt. Agy., Gulfport, Miss., 1948-69; COO Coast Fed. Savings, Gulfport, 1969-81; pres. coast divsn. Magnolia Fed. Bank, Gulfport, 1981-92; also bd. dirs Magnolia Fed. Bank, Hattiesburg, Miss.; councilman City of Gulfport, 1989; bd. dirs. Miss. Econ. Coun., Jackson, 1991-94. Author: Misrepresentation in Mississippi, 1954. Commr. Miss. Arts Commn., Jackson, 1991—; past chmn. United Way, Harrison County, Gulfport Carnegie Libr., Harrison County Libr.; past trustee Gulfport Meml. Hosp. Found.; past pres. Episcopal Laymen of Miss.; past sr. warden, layreader St. Peter's Episcopal Ch., Gulfport; mem., co-chmn. planned giving com. Episcopal Diocese Miss.; past dir. Miss. Hist. Assn. Decorated Bronze Star; named Outstanding Citizen, Gulfport Jaycees. Mem. Gulfport Rotary Club (pres. 1995—, named Citizen of Yr. 1993, Paul Harris fellow), Century Club (pres.), Gulfport Yacht Club (chmn. Olympic Sailing Commn.), Bayou Bluff Tennis Club, Great So. Club., Newcomen Soc. of U.S., Miss. Gulf Coast C. of C. Republican. Avocations: tennis, chess, reading, classical music. Home: 1302 2nd St Gulfport MS 39501-2219 Office: Magnolia Fed Bank 2200 14th St Gulfport MS 39501-2005

THATCHER, REX HOWARD, newspaper publisher; b. Williamston, Mich., Feb. 22, 1932; s. Howard Alden and Emma (Rappuhn) T.; m. Yvonne Lee Taft, Mar. 22, 1954; children: Thomas D., Richard M., Karen L., Dana L. BJ, Mich. State U., 1954. Advt. salesman The Jackson (Mich.) Citizen Patriot, 1964-69, promotion mgr., 1970, mktg. dir., 1971, asst. gen. mgr., 1972; pub. The Saginaw News, 1990—. Bd. dirs. Bay Medical Ctr., 1983—; mem., officer Bay Area C. of C., 1974-83, Bay Area Community Found., 1982-88. Mem. Mich. Press Assn., Inland Daily Press Assn., Am. Newspaper Pubs. Assn., Rotary. Presbyterian. Avocations: fly fishing, hunting, competitive and postal chess. Office: The Saginaw News 203 S Washington Ave Saginaw MI 48607-1283

THATCHER, SANFORD GRAY, publishing executive; b. Washington, Aug. 4, 1943; s. Harold Wesley and Genevieve (Harnett) T.; m. Barbara Boal, June 1966 (div.); m. Catherine Dammeyer, May 27, 1980; children: Corinne, Christopher. BA summa cum laude, Princeton U., 1965, postgrad., 1966-67; postgrad., Columbia U., 1965-66. Editor manuscript div. Princeton (N.J.) U. Press, 1967-69, editor social sci. divsn., 1969-78, asst. dir., 1978-85, editor in chief, 1985-89; dir. Pa. State U. Press, University Park, 1989—. Author: AAUP Guide to 1976 Copyright Law, 1977; contbr. articles to profl. jours. Mem. Ch. and Soc. Commn., St. Paul's United Meth. Ch., 1990-92; bd. dirs. The Daily Collegian newspaper, Pa. State U., 1991—. Mem. Am. Philos. Assn., L.Am. Studies Assn., Assn. Am. Pubs. (copyright com. 1972—, freedom to read com. 1982-86), Assn. Am. Univ. Presses (chmn. copyright com. 1972, bd. dirs. 1995—), Assn. for Copyright Enforcement (bd. dirs. 1988-93), Copyright Clearance Ctr. (bd. dirs. 1992—). Democrat. Methodist. Avocations: swimming, sailing, tennis, rare book collecting, music. Home: 2239 Concord Dr State College PA 16801-2461 Office: Pa State U Press 820 N University Dr University Park PA 16802-1012

THATCHER, SHARON LOUISE, medical educator; b. Seattle, Feb. 17, 1942; d. Ralph McDonald and Audra Joy (Clauson) Thatcher. AB, Ga. State Coll., Milledgeville, 1964; degree in med. tech., Spartanburg Gen. Hosp., 1965; MEd, Ga. State U., 1981, EdS, 1987. Technologist chemistry dept. Greenville (S.C.) Gen. Hosp., 1965-66, Emory U. Hosp., Atlanta, 1966; hematology and bone marrow technologist Office of Dr. Spencer Brewer Jr., Atlanta, 1966-67; asst. lab. supr. chemistry dept. Grady Hosp., Atlanta, 1967-69; lab. technologist Ga. Mental Health Inst., Atlanta, 1969-70; chief lab. technologist Habersham County Hosp., Clarksville, Ga., 1970-72; survey officer Ga. Dept. Human Resources, 1972-74; part owner, gen. mgr. Nolan Biology Labs., Stone Mountain, Ga., 1974-75; bacteriology dept. technologist Northside Hosp., Atlanta, 1975-76; sales rep. Curtin Mathison Sci. Products, Atlanta, 1976-78; night supr. labs. Decatur (Ga.) Hosp., 1978; dir., ednl. coord. med. lab. tech. and phlebotomy tech. programs DeKalb Tech. Inst., Clarkston, Ga., 1978—, chairperson dept. allied health, 1980-86; cons. Med. Lab. Cons., Atlanta, 1987—; mem. site survey team Nat. Accrediting Agy. for Clin. Lab. Scis., Chgo., 1980, 85, 91, site survey team coord., 1993, 94, 95, 96; speaker and presenter in field. Named Outstanding Speaker Am. Soc. for Phlebotomy Technicians, 1986. Mem. Am Soc. for Clin. Lab. Scientists (exhibit chair region III 1971-72), Am. Microbiology Soc., Ga. Soc. for Clin. Lab. Scientists (chair membership 1970-71, exhibit chair 1971-72, pres.-elect 1974-75, pres. 1975-76, bd. dirs. 1976-77, convention chair ann. state meeting 1989-90, Omicron Sigma award 1990, Gloria F. Gilbert achievement award 1993), Kappa Delta Pi. Avocations: ceramics, cross-stitch, 5K walks, gardening. Office: DeKalb Tech Inst 495 N Indian Creek Dr Clarkston GA 30021-2359

THAU, WILLIAM ALBERT, JR., lawyer; b. St. Louis, June 22, 1940; s. William Albert and Irene Elizabeth (Mundy) T.; m. Jane Hancock, Sept. 7, 1961; children: William Albert, Caroline Jane, Jennifer Elizabeth. BS in Indsl. Mgmt., Georgia Inst. Tech., 1962; JD, U. Tex., 1965. Bar: Tex. 1965. Ptnr., head of real estate sect. Jenkens & Gilchrist, Dallas, 1965—; chmn. real estate developer/builder symposium S.W. Legal Found, 1975-79; bd. dirs. Southwestern Film Archives, So. Meth. U.; lectr. Practicing Law Inst. Bd. dirs. St. Philips Sch., Tex., Dallas, 1988, So. Meth. U.; trustee Dallas Can. Acad., 1987-88. Mem. ABA, Tex. State Bar Assn. (chmn real estate, probate, trust law sect.), Am. Coll. Real Estate Lawyers, Brook Hollow Golf Club. Republican. Episcopalian. Author: Negotiating the Purchase and Sale of Real Estate, 1975; editor Tex. State Bar Assn. Newsletter on Real Estate, Probate & Trust Law, 1978-81, Best Lawyers in Am., 1983—; contbr. articles to Real Estate Rev., 1983—. Office: Jenkens & Gilchrist 1445 Ross Ave Ste 3200 Dallas TX 75202-2770

THAXTON, MARVIN DELL, lawyer, farmer; b. Electra, Tex., June 1, 1925; s. Montgomery Dell and Ida (Scheuer) T.; m. Carolyn Moore Alexander, Aug. 30, 1949; children: Rebecca Thaxton Henderson, Gail Thaxton Fogleman, Marvin D. Jr. JD, U. Ark., 1949. Bar: Ark. 1949, U.S. Dist. Ct. (ea. dist.) Ark. 1952, U.S. Dist. Ct. (we. dist.) Ark. 1978, U.S. Dist. Ct. (we. dist.) Okla., U.S. Supreme Ct. 1987. Prin. Thaxton Furniture Co., Newport, Ark., 1949-50; ptnr. Thaxton, Hout & Howard, Attys., Newport, 1950—; spl. assoc. justice Ark. Supreme Ct., 1978, 84; examiner Ark. State Bd. Law Examiners, 1968-73, chmn. 1973. Pres. Newport C. of C., 1956, Newport Sch. Dist. Bd. Edn., 1964; past pres. Ea. Ark. Young Men's Clubs; adult leader Newport area Boy Scouts Am., 1949-94. Officer U.S. Mcht. Marine, 1945-46, PTO. Fellow Ark. Bar Found.; mem. Ark. Bar Assn. (honor cert. 1973), Ark. Trial Lawyers Assn., Newport Rotary Club (past pres., Paul Harris fellow 1990), Sigma Chi. Democrat. Methodist. Avocations: hunting, fishing, boating. Home: 12 Lakeside Ln Newport AR 72112-3914 Office: Thaxton Hout & Howard 600 3rd St Newport AR 72112

THAYER, CHARLES J., investment banker; b. Abilene, Kans., Feb. 28, 1944; s. Bruce V. and Neoma (Obermeyer) T.; 1 child, Travis J. Grad., U. Kans., 1967. Exec. v.p., CFO Citizens Fidelity Bank, Louisville, 1977-87; exec. v.p. fin. PNC Bank Corp., Pitts., 1987-89; chmn., mng. dir. Chartwell Capital Ltd., Ft. Lauderdale, Fla., 1989—; interim chmn. Sunbeam-Oster, Providence, 1993; bd. dirs. Sunbeam-Oster, Providence, 1993; bd. dirs. Sunbeam Corp., Ft. Lauderdale, 1990—, vice chmn., 1996—; adv. dir. Keefe Mgrs., Inc., N.Y.C., 1990—; bd. dirs. NRG Generating (U.S.) Mpls., 1996—, Digital Wireless Corp., LA., 1995—. Trustee Cystic Fibrosis Found., Washington, 1980—; chmn. Cystic Fibrosis Svcs., Washington, 1994—. Avocation: sailing. Office: Chartwell Capital Ltd 56 Fiesta Way Fort Lauderdale FL 33301-1415

THAYER, EDWIN CABOT, musician; b. Weymouth, Mass., May 16, 1935; s. Elliot Pierce and Barbara (Senior) T.; m. Joan Peregoy, June 24, 1961; children: Bruce, Laura, Richard, William. MusB cum laude, U. Ill., 1957, MusM with performing honors, 1958. Instr. horn Brevard (N.C.) Music Center, summers 1957, 58, 62; grad. asst. U. Ill., 1957-58; prin. horn Washington Brass Choir, 1958-61, Norfolk (Va.) Symphony, 1961-65, Richmond (Va.) Symphony, 1960-72; assoc. prof. music Va. Commonwealth U. (formerly Richmond Profl. Inst.), Richmond, 1963-72; head piano dept. Va. Commonwealth U., 1965-69, head brass and winds dept., 1969-72, music librarian, 1965-72; prin. horn Washington Nat. Symphony, 1972—; hornist Nat. Symphony Wind Soloists, 1978—, Euterpe Chamber Players, 1981-89, Chamber Soloists Washington, 1986—, Tanglewood (Mass.) Berkshire Music Festival Orch., summers 1955-56; hornist Brass Prins. and Woodwind Prins. Quintets Nat. Symphony Orch., 1988—; solo recitalist, chamber ensemble recitalist, horn soloist; guest artist Internat. Horn Workshops, Hartford, Ct., 1977, Potsdam, N.Y., 1981, Towson, Md., 1985; mem. World Philharm. Orch., Rio de Janeiro, 1986. Served with AUS, 1958-61. Disting. tchr. White House Commn. on Presdl. Scholars, 1995. Mem. Internat. Horn Soc., Musicians Union, Pi Kappa Lambda, Phi Mu Alpha Sinfonia. Home: 11902 Triple Crown Rd Reston VA 22091-3016 Office: Nat Symphony Orch Kennedy Ctr for Performing Arts Washington DC 20566

THAYER, GERALD CAMPBELL, beer company executive; b. Rockville Centre, N.Y., July 19, 1943; s. Gerald Earl and Celia Storrs (Campbell) T.; m. Candace Wheatley, June 29, 1968; children—Jonathan, Matthew. B.A., Middlebury Coll., 1965; M.B.A., Columbia U., 1970. Sr. planning analyst Anheuser-Busch Co., St. Louis, 1970-73, asst. to v.p. fin., 1973-75, asst. treas., 1975-81, treas., 1981-85; v.p., treas. Anheuser-Busch Co., 1985-93, v.p., contr., 1994—. Served to capt. U.S. Army, 1966-68, Vietnam. Home: 12749 Topping Acres Saint Louis MO 63131-1435 Office: Anheuser-Busch Cos Inc 1 Busch Pl Saint Louis MO 63118-1849

THAYER, JANE See WOOLLEY, CATHERINE

THAYER, LEE, educator, author, consultant; b. Grenola, Kans., Dec. 18, 1927; s. Garrett Osborne and Ruth (Ray) T.; m. Suzanne Katherine Schwan, Apr. 27, 1986: children: Joshua Lee, Jessica Sam. B.A. cum laude, U. Wichita, 1953, M.A., 1956; Ph.D., U. Okla., 1963. Instr. U. Okla., 1956-58; with Pratt & Whitney Co., Inc., 1958-59; assoc. prof. adminstrn. and psychology U. Wichita, 1959-64; prof., dir. Center Advanced Study Communication, U. Mo. at Kansas City, 1964-68; George H. Gallup prof. communication research U. Iowa, Iowa City, 1968-73; prof. communication studies Simon Fraser U., Burnaby, B.C., Can., 1973-76; vis. prof. U. Mass., 1976-77; Fulbright prof. U. Helsinki, Finland, 1977; Disting. vis. prof. U. Houston, 1978-80; prof. and past chmn. communication U. Wis.-Parkside, 1978-93, founding dir. Parkside Honors Program, 1983-87; disting. vis. prof. Kuring-gai Coll. Advanced Edn., Sydney, Australia, 1986, Queensland (Australia) U. Tech., 1994; cons. to govt. and industry, 1956—. Author: Administrative Communication, 1961, Communication and Communication Systems, 1968, On Communication: Essays in Understanding, 1988, Pieces: Toward a Revisioning of Communication/Life, 1996, Making High-Performance Organizations: The Logic of Virtuosity, 1996; editor: Communication: Theory and Research, 1967, Communication: Concepts and Perspectives, 1967, Communication: General Semantics Perspectives, 1969, Communication: Ethical and Moral Issues, 1974, Ethics, Morality, and the Media, 1980, Organization-Communication: Emerging Perspectives I, 1985, vol. II, 1987, vol. III, 1995, vol. IV, 1994, editor book series: The Human Context, 1985—; founding editor Communication, 1970-80. Served to lt. USNR, 1953-55. Danforth Found. tchr., 1961-63; Found. Econ. Edn. fellow, 1963-64; Ford Found. fellow, 1963-64, 65, Fulbright fellow U. Helsinki, 1977-78. Home: 908 Melrose Avenue Ext Tryon NC 28782-3223

THAYER, MARTHA ANN, small business owner; b. Santa Fe, N.Mex., May 8, 1936; d. Duren Howard and Lena Odessa (Fox) Shields; m. Norman S. Thayer Jr., Jan. 30, 1960; children: Murray Norman, Tanya Noelle. BS, U. N.Mex., 1960. Child welfare worker State of N.Mex., Farmington and Santa Fe, 1961-63; owner Baskets by Thayer, Albuquerque, 1975-83, Noelle's, Albuquerque, 1985-89; ptnr., co-owner Indian Originals, Albuquerque, 1989-94, Native Design, 1995—; treas. DHS Properties, Inc., 1994—; agent for Elizabeth Akeyta, Adrian Quintana, Alexandria Rohschieb Albuquerque, 1995—; crafts instr. Village Wool, Continuing Edn., Albuquerque, 1975-78; trustee Shields Trust, 1994—. Contbr. articles, revs. to craft publs.; juried show, Mus. of Internat. Folk Arts, 1975; baskets exhibited in group shows at N.Mex. State Fair, 1980 (1st place award), Women's Show, 1983 (1st place award). Campaign mgr. Dem. Candidate for State Supreme Ct., Bernalillo County, N.Mex., 1970; founding mem. Women's Polit. Caucus, Bernalillo County; chmn. Mother's March of Dimes, Bernalilto County, 1974. Mem. AAUW, Hist. Preservation Soc., Petroleum Club, Genealogy Club of Albuquerque Pub. Libr., Mus. Albuquerque (assoc.). Avocations: genealogy, gardening, anthropology, politics, antiques, Native American art collector. Office: Native Design 1516 Plaza Encantada NW Albuquerque NM 87107

THAYER, RUSSELL, III, airlines executive; b. Phila., Dec. 5, 1922; s. Russell and Shelby Wentworth (Johnson) T.; m. Elizabeth Wright Mifflin, June 12, 1947; children: Elizabeth, Dixon, Shelby, Samuel, David. Student, St. George's Sch., 1937-42; A.B., Princeton U., 1949. Mgmt. trainee Eastern Air Lines, 1949-52; mgr. cargo sales and service Am. Airlines, Los Angeles, 1952-63; v.p. mktg. Seaboard World Airlines, N.Y.C., 1963-70; sr. v.p. Braniff Airways, Inc., Dallas, 1970-72; exec. v.p. Braniff Airways, Inc., 1972-77, pres., chief oper. officer, 1977-80, vice chmn., 1981-82; dir. (Braniff Airways, Inc.), 1971-82; v.p. Pan Am. World Airways, Inc., N.Y.C., 1982-84, sr. v.p., 1984-88; sr. v.p. Airline Econs., Inc., Washington, 1988—, also bd. dirs., 1988—; dir. Ft. Worth Nat. Bank, 1977-82; vice chmn. Airline Capital Assn; bd. dirs. Kiwi Internat. Airlines, Inc., World Aux. Power Corp. Mem. Trinity Ch. Ushers Guild, Princeton, N.J., 1968—; Trustee Aviation Hall of Fame N.J. Served with USAAF, 1942-45, ETO. Decorated D.F.C., Air medal with 11 oak leaf clusters. Mem. Am. Aviation Hist. Assn., Air Force Assn., Exptl. Aircraft Assn., Nat. Aeros. Assn., Ivy Club (Princeton), Pretty Brook Tennis Club (Princeton), Bay Head (N.J.) Yacht Club, Nassau Club (Princeton), Princeton Club (N.Y.C.), Phila. Club, Delta Psi. Home: 21 Lilac Ln Princeton NJ 08540-3021 Office: Airline Econs Inc 1130 Connecticut Ave NW # 675 Washington DC 20036-3904

THAYER, W(ALTER) STEPHEN, III, state supreme court justice; b. N.Y.C., Jan. 13, 1946; s. Walter S. and Dorothy (Pflum) T.; m. Judith O. O'Brien, Dec. 27, 1982. B.A. in Polit. Sci., Belmont Abbey Coll., 1968; J.D., John Marshall Law Sch., Chgo., 1974. Bar: N.H. 1975, U.S. Dist. Ct. N.H. 1975, U.S. Ct. Appeals (1st cir.) 1981. Sole practice Law Offices W. Stephen Thayer, III, Manchester, N.H., 1975-81; U.S. atty. Dist. N.H., Concord, 1981-84; assoc. justice N.H. Superior Ct., 1984-86, N.H. Supreme Ct., 1986—; legal counsel N.H. State Senate, 1978-80, N.H. Rep. State Com., 1977-80; cons. GSA, Washington, 1981. Alt. del. Rep. nat. conv., 1980; presdl. elector electoral coll., 1980. Served to 1st lt. U.S. Army, 1968-71. Decorated Bronze Star. Mem. N.H. Bar Assn., N.H. Trial Lawyers Assn. Roman Catholic. Home: 1943 Elm St Manchester NH 03104-2528 Office: NH Supreme Ct Noble Dr Concord NH 03301*

THÊ, HOANG-DINH, middle school educator; b. Thua-Thien, Vietnam, Mar. 12, 1943. BS, Lincoln U., 1966, MA, 1973; cert. in edn., U. San Francisco, 1979; MA, San Diego State U., 1980; D Naturopathy, Internat. U., 1993. Cert. tchr., Calif. Instr. Def. Lang. Inst., Monterey, Calif., 1966-71; social worker Internat. Inst. of San Francisco, 1975-78; spl. asst. to the dean Lincoln U., San Francisco, 1971-73; tchr. social studies, math. and scis. Francisco Mid. Sch., San Francisco, 1980—; cons. Ctr. for Internat. Communication and Devel., Long Beach, Calif., 1988—. Mem. Nat. Geographic Soc., Internat. Phonetic Assn., Internat. Soc. of Naturopathy. Avocations: reading, writing, stamp collector, Tai-Chi. Home: PO Box 42-5386 San Francisco CA 94142-5386

THEALL, DONALD FRANCIS, retired university president; b. Mt. Vernon, N.Y., Oct. 13, 1928; s. Harold A. and Helen (Donaldson) T.; m. Joan Ada Benedict, June 14, 1950; children: Thomas, Margaret, John, Harold, Lawrence, Michael. BA with honors, Yale U., 1950; MA with 1st class honors, U. Toronto, 1951, PhD with 1st class honors, 1954. Teaching fellow U. Toronto, 1950-52, mem. faculty, 1952-65, prof. English, chmn. joint depts. English, 1964-65; dir. communication studies York U., also prof. English and communications, 1965-66; dir. English Atkinson Coll., 1965-66; mem. faculty McGill U., Montreal, Que., Can., 1966-79; prof. English McGill U., 1966-79, chmn. dept., 1966-74, Molson prof., 1972-79, dir. grad. program in communications, 1976-79; adj. prof. grad. comm. McGill U., Montreal, Que., Can., 1989-91; pres., vice chancellor, prof. English and cultural studies Trent U., Peterborough, Ont., 1980-87, univ. prof., 1987-94, univ. prof. emeritus, 1994—; cultural exch. prof. Govt. of Can. and China, 1974; mem. adv. bd. Semiotic Inquiry, 1982—; cons. in field. Author: (with Robinson and Wevers) Let's Speak English, 4 vols., 1960-61, The Medium Is the Rear View Mirror: Understanding McLuhan, 1971, (with G.J. Robinson) Studies in Canadian Communications, 1975; Beyond the Word: Reconstructing Sense in the Joyce Era of Technology, Culture, and Communication, 1995; mem. editl. bd. Sci. Fiction Studies, 1976—, Can. Jour. Comm., 1979—, Jour. Can. Studies, 1980-87. Mem. Greater Peterborough Econ. Council, 1982-87; mem. fed. adv. council to minister employment and immigration for Peterborough area, 1986-87. Recipient awards Social Sci. and Humanities Rsch. Coun., 1991-94, 94—, Can. Fedn. Humanities-Aid to Scholarly Publs., 1994; grantee Humanities Rsch. Coun. Can., 1954-56, 73-76, Ont. Dept. Edn., 1956-59, 91, Atkinson Found., 1960, CBC, 1961, Can. Coun., 1966-68, 73-76, Eastman Kodak Corp., Nat. Film Bd. Can., Can. Dept. Industry, Can. Dept. Trade and Commerce, Can. Ctrl. Mortgage and Housing, 1967-69, Que. Ministry Comm., 1977; sr. leave fellow Can. Coun., 1975. Corr. fellow Acad. Medicine (Toronto); mem. Internat. Communications Assn. (dir. 1978-81), Can. Communications Assn. (chmn. com. to investigate formation 1978, pres. 1979-80), MLA, Philol. Soc. Gt. Britain, Can. Assn. Chmn. English (founding chmn. 1971-74), Assn. Can. Univ. Tchrs. English, Internat. Inst. Communications, Soc. Arts Publs. (v.p. 1967-68), Sci. Fiction Research Assn., University Club of Toronto, Yale Club (Toronto), McGill Faculty Club, Elizabethan Club (Yale). Office: Trent Univ, Dept English, Peterborough, ON Canada K9J 7B8

THEE, CHRISTIAN, artist, designer; b. Long Branch, N.J., Sept. 27, 1934; s. Walter Christian and Edith Draper (Steinmetz) T. Degree in arch. and design, U. S.C., 1964; degree in stage/lighting/costume design, Columbia U., 1966; student, Lester Polakov Forum Stage Des, 1968-71; design asst. to Joe Mielziner, Ben Edwards and Howard Bay. Illustrator: Behind the Curtain, 1994; commissions include portrait of Prince Andrew of Eng., 1981, mural for Taj Mahal Casino Hotel, Atlantic City, lobby decor of Empire Hotel, N.Y.C., sky ceiling for lobby of LINPRO Corp., Wilmington, Del., Lincoln Post-Hotel, Houston, St. Paul Hotel, New Belvue Stratford, Phila., Clarion Hotel, New Orleans, Belk Dept. Store, Columbia, S.C., Willard Hotel, Washington, Stouffer's Riverview Plaza Hotel, Mobile, Ala., Trompe L'Oeil elevator for Inn at Nat. Hall, Wesport, Conn., mural for Southeastern Frieght, West Columbia, S.C.; designed numerous theatrical prodns. including Rashmon, The Robber Bridegroom, Irma La Douce, Pal Joey, Brigadoon, View from a Bridge, Dracula, The Countess Dracula, You Can't Take it With You, Sweet Bird of Youth, The Prime of Miss Jean Brodie, Monique, The Last of the Red Hot Lovers, Finian's Rainbow, Pajama Game, Old Herbaceous, Cabaret, Teh Importance of Being Earnest, The Ballad of the Sad Cafe, Richard III, The Miraculous Mandarin, Charlie's Aunt, The Physicists, Androcles and the Lion, Drat, Flight into Egypt, Carnival, Under the Yum Yum Tree, Amican Buffalo, Something's Afoot, A Christmas Carol, The Marriage Go-Around, The Vinegar Tree, Cat on a Hot Tin Roof, The Time of the Coo-Coo, The Visit, and numerous others; theatrical designs for regional and stock cos. including Am. Place Theatre, N.Y.C., Olney (Md.) Theatre, Avondale Playhouse, Indpls., Cafe La Mama, N.Y.C., Equity Libr. Theatre, N.Y.C., Spoleto Festival, Charlestown, S.C., Scott Repertory Theatre, Ft. Worth, and many books and mags. Avocation: performing magic. Office: Christian Thee & Assoc 6196 Eastshore Rd Columbia SC 29206-4310

THEEN, ROLF HEINZ-WILHELM, political science educator; b. Stadthagen, Germany, Feb. 20, 1937; came to U.S., 1956, naturalized, 1962; s. Walter and Gertrud (Tysper) T.; m. Norma Lee Plunkett, June 14, 1959; children: Tanya Sue, Terrell René. B.A. magna cum laude, Manchester Coll., 1959; M.A., Ind. U., 1962, cert. with high distinction Russian and East European Inst., 1962, Ph.D., 1964. Asst. prof. Iowa State U., 1964-67, assoc. prof., 1968-70; assoc. prof. polit. sci. Purdue U., West Lafayette, Ind., 1971-73, prof., 1974—; dir. Purdue U.-Ind. U. study program U. Hamburg, 1980-81; translator, editor U.S. Joint Publs. Research Service. Author: Lenin: Genesis and Development of a Revolutionary, 1973, 74, 79; co-author: Comparative Politics: An Introduction to Seven Countries, 1992, 96; editor, translator: The Early Years of Lenin (N. Valentinov), 1969; editor: The USSR First Congress of People's Deputies: Complete Documents and Records, 4 vols., 1991; contbr. articles to profl. jours., chpts. to books. Recipient Wilton Park award Iowa State U., 1971; Fgn. Area Tng. fellow Russian and East European Inst., 1962-64; grantee Am. Philos. Soc., Inter Univ. Com., Joint Com. Slavic Studies, Fulbright grantee, 1995; NEH sr. fellow, 1974-75, rsch. fellow Kennan Inst. Advanced Russian Studies, Woodrow Wilson Internat. Ctr. for Scholars, 1976, Ctr. Humanistic Studies fellow Purdue U., 1982, 88, 91. Mem. Am. Polit. Sci. Assn., Am. Assn. Advancement Slavic Studies, Am. Acad. Social and Polit. Sci. Mem. Ch. of Brethren. Home: 717 Orchard Dr Lafayette IN 47905-4435 Office: Purdue U Dept Polit Sci Liberal Arts/Edn Bldg 2221 West Lafayette IN 47907-1363

THEEUWES, FELIX, physical chemist; b. Duffel, Belgium, May 25, 1937. Licentiate physics, Cath. U. Louvain, 1961, DSc in Physics, 1966. Tchr. St. Vincent Sch., Westerlo, Belgium, 1961-64; rsch. fellow CERN, Geneva, 1964-66; rsch. assoc. chemistry U. Kans., 1966-68, asst. prof., 1968-70; rsch. scientist pharm. chemistry Alza Corp., Palo Alto, Calif., 1970-74, prin. scientist, 1974—, v.p. product R & D, 1980-82, v.p.rsch., chief scientist, 1982-94, pres. Tech. Inst., chief scientist, 1994-95, pres. R&D, chief scientist, 1995—; Louis Busse lectr. dept. pharmacology U. Wis., 1981. Named Inventor of Yr., Peninsula Patent Law Assn., 1980. Fellow Am. Assn. Pharm. Scientists (award for advancement of indsl. pharmacy 1983); mem. AAAS, Controlled Release Soc., Internat. Soc. for Chronobiology, Am. Chem. Soc.,

Acad. Pharm. Sci., N.Y. Acad. Scis. Achievements include research in osmosis, diffusion, solid state physics, cryogenics, high pressure, thermodynamics, pharmacology, pharmacokinetics, calorimetry. Office: Alza Corp PO Box 10950 950 Page Mill Rd Palo Alto CA 94303-0802

THEIL, HENRI, economist, educator; b. Amsterdam, Netherlands, Oct. 31, 1924; s. Hendrik and Hermina (Siegmann) T.; m. Eleonore A.I. Goldschmidt, June 15, 1951. Ph.D. in Econs, U. Amsterdam, 1951; LL.D. (hon.), U. Chgo., 1964; D. honoris causa, Free U., Brussels, 1974, Erasmus U., Rotterdam, 1983; LL.D. (hon.) Hope Coll. 1985. Mem. staff Central Planning Bur. (The Hague), 1952-55; prof. econometrics Netherlands Sch. Econs., Rotterdam, 1953-66; vis. prof. econs. U. Chgo., 1955-56, 64, Stanford U., 1956, 59, Harvard U., 1960, U. So. Calif., 1979, 80, 81, U. Western Australia, 1982; dir. Econometric Inst. (Netherlands Sch. Econs.), 1956-66; prof. U. Chgo., 1965-81, dir. Center Math. Studies in Bus. and Econs., 1965-81; McKethan-Matherly prof. econometrics and decision scis. U. Fla., 1981—. Author: Linear Aggregation of Economic Relations, 1954, Economic Forecasts and Policy, 2d edit., 1961, Optimal Decision Rules for Government and Industry, 1964, Operations Research and Quantitative Economics, 1965, Applied Economic Forecasting, 1977, Economics and Information Theory, 1967, Principles of Econometrics, 1971, Statistical Decomposition Analysis with Applications in the Social and Administrative Sciences, 1972, Theory and Measurement of Consumer Demand, Vol. 1 1975, Vol. 2 1976, Introduction to Econometrics, 1978, The System-Wide Approach to Microeconomics, 1980, System-Wide Explorations in International Economics, Input-Output Analysis, and Marketing Research, 1980, International Consumption Comparisons, 1981, Exploiting Continuity, 1984, Applied Demand Analysis, 1987, International Evidence on Consumption Patterns, 1989, Contributions to Consumer Demand and Econometrics: Essays in Honour of Henri Theil, 1992, Henri Theil's Contributions to Economics and Econometrics, 1992, Studies in Global Econometrics, 1996; editor Mathematical and Managerial Economics, 1964—; co-editor Series on Econometrics and Management Sciences, 1984—. Fellow Am. Acad. Arts and Scis., Royal Netherlands Acad. Scis., Am. Statis. Assn.; mem. Internat. Statis. Inst., Am. Econ. Assn., Ops. Research Soc. Am., Econometric Soc. (pres. 1961), Inst. Mgmt. Scis. (council 1961-64). Home: PO Box 518 Saint Augustine FL 32085-0518

THEILEN, GORDON HENRY, veterinary surgery educator; b. Montevideo, Minn., May 29, 1928; s. Lou Ernst and Ema Kathryn (Schaller) T.; m. Carolyn June Simon, Mar. 6, 1953; children—Kyle, John, Ann. B.S., U. Calif.-Davis, 1953, D.V.M., 1955. Pvt. practice, Tillamook, Oreg., 1955-56; specialist, lectr. U. Calif.-Davis, 1956-57, instr., 1957-58, asst. prof., 1958-64, assoc. prof., 1964-70, prof., chief clin. oncology, 1970—. Co-author: Veterinary Cancer Medicine, 1979, 2nd edit., 1987; co-discoverer Feline sarcoma virus and simian sarcoma virus, 1968, 70; patentee Bovine leukemia virus, 1980; feline leukemia virus vaccine, 1977; contbr. articles to profl. jours. Served with U.S. Army, 1946-48. NIH fellow, 1964-66; N.Y. Cancer Immunology fellow, 1972-73; Alexander von Humboldt Sr. Scientist award, 1979-80; Fleishmann Found. award, 1980-85; Ralston Purina award in Small Animal Medicine, 1982, Alumni Achievement award U. Calif.-Davis, 1987. Mem. AVMA, Am. Coll. Vet. Internal Medicine, Assn. Vet. Clinicians, Am. Assn. Cancer Rsch., Vet. Cancer Soc., Internat. Assn. for Comparative Rsch. on Leukemia and Related Diseases (mem. world com. 1990—), Am. Brittany Club (bd. dirs. 1992—), Phi Zeta, Sigma Xi. Democrat. Lutheran. Office: U Calif Surg & Radiol Scis Vet Med Davis CA 95616

THEIS, FRANCIS WILLIAM, business executive; b. Joliet, Ill., July 10, 1920. Student, Joliet Jr. Coll., 1937-39; B.S., Purdue U., 1941. Dir. devel. PPG Industries, Barberton, Ohio, 1951-56; mgr. planning chem. div. PPG Industries, Pitts., 1956-60; pres., chief exec. officer PPG Internat., Pitts., 1960-63, v.p. internat., 1963-65; pres., chief exec. officer Devoe & Raynaolds Co., Louisville, 1965-67; pres. Celanese Chem. Co., N.Y.C., 1967-71; group v.p. Celanese Corp., N.Y.C., 1971-72; exec. v.p. Internat. Paper Corp., N.Y.C., 1972-73; pres., chief exec. officer Hooker Chem. Corp., Stamford, Conn., 1973; dir. Occidental Petroleum Corp., Stamford, 1973; pres., chief exec. officer, dir. Am. Ship Bldg. Co., Cleve., 1975-79; dir., pres., chief operating officer GATX Corp., Chgo., 1979-86. Named Disting. Alumnus Purdue U., 1965. Mem. Shipbuilders Council Am. (dir.), Nat. Maritime Council (bd. govs.). Clubs: Cleve. Athletic (Cleve.), Union (Cleve.); Shaker Heights (Ohio) Country); Clifton (Lakewood, Ohio); Landmark (Stamford); Sky (N.Y.C.); Chicago. Office: 9 Middleton Rd Savannah GA 31411-1420

THEIS, FRANK GORDON, federal judge; b. Yale, Kans., June 26, 1911; s. Peter F. and Maude (Cook) T.; m. Marjorie Riddle, Feb. 1, 1939 (dec. 1970); children: Franklin, Roger. A.B. cum laude, U. Kans., 1933; J.D., U. Mich., 1936. Bar: Kans. 1937. Since practiced in Arkansas City; sr. mem. firm Frank G. Theis, 1939—; atty. Kans. Tax Commn., 1937-39; chief counsel OPS for Kans., 1951-52; U.S. dist. judge Dist. Kans., 1967—; chief judge, 1977-81, active sr. status, 1981—; Pres. Young Democrats Kan., 1942-46, Kans. Dem. Club, 1944-46; chmn. Kans. Dem. Com., 1955-60; mem. nat. adv. com. polit. orgn. Dem. Nat. Com., 1956-58, nat. committeeman from Kans., 1957-67; chmn. Dem. Midwest Conf., 1959-60; Dem. nominee for Kans., Supreme Ct., 1950, U.S. Senate, 1960. Mem. ABA, Kans. Bar Assn., Kans. Jr. Bar Conf. (pres. 1942), Phi Beta Kappa., Phi Delta Phi, Sachem. Presbyterian. Club: Mason. Office: US Dist Ct 414 US Courthouse 401 N Market St Wichita KS 67202-2000

THEIS, PETER FRANK, engineering executive, inventor; b. Chgo., Mar. 21, 1937; s. Frank Victor and Hazel (Ericsson) T.; m. Jill Anne Pendexter, May 9, 1970; children: Juliana, Ethan. B.E. in Elec. Engring., Yale U., 1958; MBA in Fin., U. Chgo., 1966; JD, Ill. Inst. Tech.-Kent Coll Law, Chgo., 1974; postgrad., U. Stockholm. Bar: Ill. 1975. Engr. ASEA, Ludvika, Sweden, 1959, Signode Corp., Glenview, Ill., 1959-61; importer Internat. Idea, Inc., Chgo., 1961-62; systems analyst Continental Ill. Nat. Bank and Trust, Chgo., 1963-64; sales rep. Honeywell, Inc., Chgo., 1964-68; exec. Morgan Industries, Inc., Chgo., 1968-87; pres. Conversational Voice Technologies Corp., Chgo., Gurnee, Ill., 1973-91, Theis Rsch., Inc., Gurnee, 1991—; cons. Ill. Tech. Transfer LLC, 1994—; cons., mng. mem. Theis Rsch. & Engring. LLC, 1994—. Patentee in field. With Air N.G., 1961-66. Mem. Tech. Exec. Roundtable (bd. dirs. 1992—), Licensing Execs. Soc., Execs. Club of Chgo. (bd. dirs. 1972-74), Intellectual Property Creators (bd. dirs. 1993—). Avocations: canoeing, hiking, sailing. Office: Theis Rsch Inc 4223 Grove Ave Gurnee IL 60031-2134

THEIS, WILLIAM HAROLD, lawyer, educator; b. Chgo., Nov. 8, 1945; s. Clarence M. and Marion K. (McLendon) T.; m. Maria Luisa Belfiore, Dec. 5, 1973; children: Catherine, Elizabeth. AB, Loyola U. Chgo., 1967; JD, Northwestern U., 1970; LLM, Columbia U., 1977, JSD, 1982. Bar: Ill. 1970, D.C. 1971, U.S. Ct. Appeals (7th cir.) 1971, U.S. Supreme Ct. 1974. Assoc. prof. La. State U. Law Ctr., 1972-78; assoc. prof. Loyola U. Law Sch., Chgo., 1978-81; sole practice, Chgo., 1981—; part-time lectr. admiralty Northwestern Sch. Law, Chgo. Served to lt. USNR, 1970-72. Mem. Am. Law Inst. Contbr. articles to legal jours. Office: 53 W Jackson Blvd Ste 1460 Chicago IL 60604

THEISEN, EDWIN MATHEW, utility company executive; b. 1930. BA, St. Johns U., 1952. With No. States Power Co., Mpls., 1954—, v.p., 1970-80, pres., chief oper. officer, from 1980, also dir. 1st. lt. USMC, 1952-54. Office: Northern States Power Co-Minn 414 Nicollet Mall Minneapolis MN 55401

THEISEN, RUSSELL EUGENE, electrical engineer; b. Norfolk, Va., Aug. 3, 1937; s. Richard Roudolph and Pansie Mae (Garnette) T.; m. Mary Ann Asbury, May 30, 1962; children: Timothy Mark, Yvette Marie. BSEE, Old Dominion, 1962; MBA, Rollins Coll., 1973. Registered profl. engr., N.Y., Fla. Svc. mgr. Mastercraft Elect., Norfolk, 1955-62; design engr. IBM Corp., Endicott, N.Y., 1962-64; plant mgr. Compton Industries, Vestal, N.Y., 1964-66; sr. engr. Martin Marietta Aerospace, Orlando, Fla., 1966-74; sr. project engr. General Dynamics Corp., Longwood, Fla., 1974-76; sr. mem. profl. staff Martin Marietta Aerospace, Orlando, 1976-92; sr. system software analyst SCI Systems Inc., Huntsville, Ala., 1992—; nat. dir. Halbert Genealogy, Bath, Ohio, 1987—; pres., 1996—, cert. mgr., 1996, Nat. Mgmt. Assn.; Ala. Dir. Am. Enterprise Inst., High Teck Valley Coun., 1996-97. Contbng. author: Reliability And Maintainibility, 1967; contbr. articles to profl. jours. Dir. Theisen Clan Theisen Genealogy Group, 1988-95; dir. Fla. Libr. Adv. Bd., 1967-79; bd. dirs. Am. Fedn. Info. Processing Soc., 1983-85. With USMC, 1953-65. Mem. IEEE (v.p. 1983-85, Fla. Coun. pres. 1987-89, sr.), Nat. Mgmt. Assn. (v.p. 1992-95, sr.), ACM (area chmn. 1987-89, sr.). Achievements include developed data bus standard S-100, HPIB, IEEE-488; helped launch IEEE Computer Soc. Mag, Computer PAMI design and test, microsystems software. Avocations: computer software development, fishing, golf, biking. Home: 3106 Heatherhill Dr Huntsville AL 35802-1140 Office: SCI Systems Inc 8600 Meml Pkwy Huntsville AL 35807-4001

THEISMANN, JOSEPH ROBERT, former professional football player, announcer; b. New Brunswick, N.J., Sept. 9, 1949; s. Joseph James and Olga (Tobias) T.; m. Chery Lynn Brown, Dec. 5, 1970 (div.); children: Joseph Winton, Amy Lynn, Patrick James. B.A. in Sociology, U. Notre Dame, 1971. With Toronto Argonauts, CFL, 1971-74; with Washington Redskins, 1974-86, punt returner, 1974-79, starting quarterback, 1979-86; analyst CBS Nat. Football League broadcasts, 1987-88, ESPN Nat. Football League broadcasts, 1988—; tchr. Offense-Def. Football Camp; Superstar participant, 1979-80, played in Pro-Bowl, 1983-84; mem. Pres.'s Athletic Adv. Com., 1975; active Pres. Nat. Svc. Adv. Com., 1993. Author: Quarter Backing. Mem. corp. bd. Children's Hosp. Nat. Med. Center, Washington; participant benefits for Multiple Sclerosis children's hosps., Armed Forces Christmas benefits. High sch. All-Am. Football, 1967; All-Am. Coll., 1971; Acad.-All-Am.; All-Pro UPI; recipient Brian Picollo award; played in Pro Bowl, 1982, 83; mem. Super Bowl XVII Championship Team, 1982; cable Ace award, Best Sports Commentator-Analyst, 1994. Mem. Nat. Football Players Assn. Republican. Methodist. Office: JRT Assocs 5912 Leesburg Pike Falls Church VA 22041-2202

THELEN, BRUCE CYRIL, lawyer; b. St. Johns, Mich., Nov. 24, 1951. BA, Mich. State U., 1973; JD, U. Mich., 1977. Bar: N.Y. 1978, Mich. 1980, Ill. 1992. Assoc. Dewey, Ballantine, Bushby, Palmer & Wood, N.Y.C., 1977-80; assoc. Dickinson, Wright, Moon, Van Dusen & Freeman, Detroit, 1981-83, ptnr., 1984—; mem. U.S. Dept. Commerce-Mich. Dist. Export Coun., 1995—. Contbr. articles to profl. publs. Mem. allocation panel, mem. spkrs. bur., vice chmn. rsch. and tech. com. United Way of Detroit, 1987—; mem. State of Mich. Task Force on Internat. Trade, Lansing, 1990; mem. Detroit Com. on Fgn. Rels., Greater Detroit-Windsor Japan Am. Soc. Mem. N.Y. Bar Assn. (mem. internat. law sect.), Mich. Bar Assn., State Bar Mich. (chmn. internat. law sect. 1990-91), Internat. Bar Assn., Am. Soc. Internat. Law, Ill. Bar Assn. (internat. law sect.), Internat. Law Assn., French-Am. C. of C. of Detroit, German Am. C. of C. of Midwest (bd. dirs. 1992—, pres. Mich. chpt. 1994—), Greater Detroit C. of C. (chmn. European mission com. 1991-92, 95, export com. 1992-95, Leadership Detroit VIII program 1986-87), World Trade Club (exec. com. 1992—). Office: Dickinson Wright Moon Van Dusen & Freeman One Detroit Center 500 Woodward Ave Ste 4000 Detroit MI 48226-3423

THELEN, GIL, newspaper editor; b. Chgo.; s. Gilbert Carl and Violet (Okonn) T.; m. Carol Abernathy, July 1966 (div. Apr. 1978); children: Deborah Brooke, Todd Foster; m. Cynthia Jane Struby, Sept. 2, 1979; children: Matthew David, Jonathan Whitfield. BA, Duke U., 1960. Reporter Milw. Jour., 1960-61, AP, Washington, 1965-72; writer Consumer Reports, Mt. Vernon, N.Y., 1972-77; reporter Chgo. Daily News, 1977-78; asst. met. editor Charlotte (N.C.) Observer, 1978-82, met. editor, 1982-83, asst. mng. editor, 1983-87; editor The Sun News, Myrtle Beach, S.C., 1987-90; exec. editor The State, 1990—; adj. prof. U. S.C., Aiken, 1989—. Pres. Montgomery County Big Brothers, Bethesda, Md., 1967-69; co-founder Alpha Group, Myrtle Beach, S.C., 1989. Mem. Am. Soc. Newspaper Editors, S.C. Press Assn., Columbia Rotary Club, Leadership S.C., Leadership Columbia, Phi Beta Kappa, Omicron Delta Kappa. Methodist. Avocations: golf, tennis, reading, classical music. Home: 128 Alexander Cir Columbia SC 29206-4956 Office: The State Newspaper 1401 Shop Rd Columbia SC 29201-4843

THELEN, MAX, JR., lawyer, foundation executive; b. Berkeley, Calif., Aug. 18, 1919; s. Max and Ora Emily (Muir) T.; m. Phyllis J. Barnhill, Mar. 8, 1952; children—Nancy B. Thelen Rehkopf, Jane M. Thelen Greene, Max, III, William B. A.B. with highest honors, U. Calif., Berkeley, 1940; J.D. cum laude, Harvard U., 1946. Bar: Calif. 1946. Ptnr. Thelen, Marrin, Johnson & Bridges, San Francisco, 1946-87; v.p., dir. S.H. Cowell Found., 1970—. Trustee World Affairs Council. Served to lt. USNR, 1942-46. Mem. State Bar Calif., Am. Coll. Trial Lawyers, Commonwealth Club, World Trade Club, Marines Meml. Club. Home: 199 Mountain View Ave San Rafael CA 94901-1347 Office: 2 Embarcadero Ctr Ste 2100 San Francisco CA 94111

THELIN, JOHN ROBERT, academic administrator, education educator, historian; b. West Newton, Mass., Oct. 15, 1947; s. George Willard and Rozalija Katherine (Komarec) T.; m. Anna Sharon Blackburn, June 24, 1978. AB, Brown U., 1969; MA, U. Calif., Berkeley, 1972, PhD, 1973. Rsch. asst. Brown U., Providence, 1968-69; researcher, lectr. U. Calif., Berkeley, 1972-74; asst. prof. U. Ky., Lexington, 1974-77; asst. dean Pomona Coll., Claremont, Calif., 1977-79; from asst. dir. to rsch. dir. Assn. Ind. Calif. Colls. and Univs., Santa Ana, 1979-81; chancellor prof. Coll. William and Mary, Williamsburg, Va., 1981-93, pres. faculty assembly, 1990-91; prof. higher edn. & philanthropy Ind. U., Bloomington, 1993-96; prof. ednl. policy and history U. Ky., Lexington, 1996—; vis. prof. grad. sch. Claremont U., 1978-81; vis. scholar U. Calif., Berkeley, 1995; curator Marquandia Soc., 1971-96; essay rev. editor Rev. of Higher Edn., 1979-91; rsch. cons. NSF, Washington, 1991. Author: Higher Education and Its Useful Past, 1982, The Cultivation of Ivy, 1976, (with others) The Old College Try, 1989, Higher Education and Public Policy, 1991, Games Colleges Plays, 1994; assoc. editor: (jour.) Higher Education: Theory and Research, 1983-91. Pres., bd. dirs. United Way, Williamsburg, 1987-89; pres. Friends of Williamsburg Libr., 1989. Rsch. grantee Spencer Found., 1989-91; Regents fellow U. Calif., 1972. Mem. Assn. for Study of Higher Edn. (bd. dirs. 1988-90, keynote spkr. 1994), History of Edn. Soc. (editl. bd. 1988-91), Phi Beta Kappa. Avocations: long-distance running, history of Los Angeles and California, sports history. Home: 324 Chinoe Rd Lexington KY 40502 Office: U Ky Edn Policy Studies Lexington KY 40503

THEMELIS, NICKOLAS JOHN, metallurgical and chemical engineering educator; b. Athens, Greece. B in Engring., McGill U., Montreal, Que., Can., 1956, PhD, 1961. Registered profl. engr., Conn. Mgr. engring. divsn. Noranda Tech. Ctr., Pointe Claire, Que., 1962-72; v.p. tech. Kennecott Corp., N.Y.C., 1972-80; Stanley-Thompson prof. chem. metallurgy Columbia U., N.Y.C., 1980—. Author 4 books; contbr. articles to profl. jours. Fellow Minerals, Metals and Materials Soc.; mem. NAE, Metallurgical Soc. AIME (3 gold medals). Democrat. Mem. Christian Orthodox Ch. Avocations: sailing, music. Office: Columbia Univ Earth Engring Ctr 500 W 120th St #1047 New York NY 10027

THEOBALD, EDWARD ROBERT, lawyer; b. Chgo., Feb. 10, 1947; s. Edward Robert Theobald Jr. and Marie (Turner) Logan; m. Bonnie J. Singer, July 18, 1970; children: Debra Marie, Kimberly Ann. BA, So. Ill. U., 1969; JD, Ill. Inst. Tech., 1974. Bar: Ill. 1974, U.S. Dist. Ct. (no. dist.) Ill. 1974. Asst. state's atty. Cook County, Chgo., 1974-79, supr. felony trial div., 1980-81; assoc. Conklin, Leahy & Eisenberg, Chgo., 1977; ptnr. Boharic & Theobald, Chgo., 1981-83, owner, ptnr., 1983—; legal adv. Sheriff of Cook County, Ill., 1986-89; spl. state's atty. U.S. Dist. Ct. no. dist. Ill., 1989-91; apptd. spl. corp. counsel City of Chgo., 1994. Mem. Parent adv. bd. Downers Grove (Ill.) South H.S., 1992-94. Named Number One Trial Atty. in Felony Trial Div. of Office of Cook County State's Atty., Felony Trial Div. Suprs., 1979. Mem. ABA (sect. on tort and ins. law, sect. on labor and employment law, chmn. com. on sentencing alternatives young lawyers sect. 1982-83, tort and ins. practice sect., labor and employment law sect.), Chgo. Bar Assn. (bd. mgrs. 1985-87, labor and employment law com. 1983—, com. on coms. 1990-94, membership com. 1990-95), Ill. Bar Assn., Assn. Trial Lawyers Am., Christian Legal Soc. (bd. dirs. Ill. chpt. 1993—), Civil War Roundtable (Chgo. chpt.). Roman Catholic. Home: 7104 Grand Ave Downers Grove IL 60516-3915 Office: 135 S La Salle St Ste 2148 Chicago IL 60603-4204

THEOBALD, H RUPERT, retired political scientist; b. Berlin, Mar. 12, 1930; came to U.S., 1950; s. Hans Herman and Marlene (Rackow) T.; m. Elizabeth Joanna Frisella, Nov. 3, 1951 (dec. Mar. 1996); children: H. Michael, Marlies J., Peter J. MA, U. Wis., 1960, PhD, 1971. Rschr. Wis. Legis. Reference Bur., Madison, 1957-60, coord., 1960-63, acting chief, 1963-64, chief, 1964-94; ret., 1994; lay mem. bd. govs. State Bar Wis., 1994-96. Editor: Laws of Wisconsin, 1991-94; contbr. articles to profl. jours. Mem. Coun of State Governments, 1963-94 (Charles McCarthy award 1986), Com. on Suggested State Legis., 1964-94.

THEOBALD, THOMAS CHARLES, banker; b. Cin., May 5, 1937; m. Gigi Mahon, Jan. 1987. AB in Econs., Coll. Holy Cross, 1958; MBA in Fin. with high distinction, Harvard U., 1960. With Citibank, N.A. div. Citicorp, 1960-87; vice-chmn. Citicorp, N.Y.C., 1982-87; CEO, chmn. Continental Bank Corp., Chgo., 1987-94; chmn. bd. dirs. Continental Bank N.A., Chgo., 1987-94; ptnr. Blair Capital Ptnrs, LLC (formally Blair Capital Mgmt), Chgo., 1994—; bd. dirs. Xerox Corp., Enron Global Power and Pipelines. Trustee Nat. Lekotek Ctr., Mut. of N.Y., Northwestern U.; bd. dirs. Assocs. of Harvard Bus. Sch., Chgo. Coun. on Fgn. Rels.; mem. com. on arch. Art Inst. of Chgo. Mem. Ill. Bus. Roundtable, Comml. Club (civic com.), Chgo. United Inc., Econ. Club (Chgo.). Office: Blair Capital Partners, LLC 222 W Adams St Ste 3300 Chicago IL 60606*

THEODORE, EUSTACE D., alumni association executive, management consultant; b. Marietta, Ohio, Aug. 4, 1941; s. Demetrios E. and Nicoletta D. T.; m. Carol Nagy, June 13, 1964; children: Kyle James, Graham Clark. B.A., Yale U., 1963; M.A., Cornell U., 1965, Ph.D., 1967. Mem. faculty Hollins Coll., Roanoke, Va., 1967-71, Mt. Holyoke Coll., South Hadley, Mass., 1971-72; dean Calhoun Coll., Yale U., New Haven, 1972-81; exec. dir. Assn. Yale Alumni, 1981—; mgmt. cons., 1965—. Contbr. articles to jours. Recipient NSF-COSIP award, 1966. Mem. Coun. Alumni Assn. Execs. (bd. dirs. 1991—, pres. 1995-96), Coun. for Advancement and Support Edn. (trustee 1993—, chair internat. task force 1994—), Commn. on Alumni Rels. (chair 1992-96). Office: Yale U Alumni Assn PO Box 209010 New Haven CT 06520-9010

THEODORE, NICK ANDREW, lieutenant governor; b. Greenville, S.C., Sept. 16, 1928; s. Andrew John and Lula (Meros) T.; m. Emilie Demosthenes, Apr. 25, 1955; children: Drew, Angela, Stephanie. BA, Furman U., 1952. Mem. S.C. Ho. of Reps., Columbia, 1963-66, 69-78, chmn. house edn. and pub. works commn., 1977-78; mem. S.C. Senate, Columbia, 1967-68, 81-86, co-chmn. S.C. edn. fin. act. task force com., chmn. joint legis. study com. on alcohol and drugs, chmn. state employees com., mem. textile commn.; lt. gov. State of S.C., Columbia, 1986-90, 90-94; pres. William Goldsmith Agy. Past co-dir. ARC; past co- chmn. March of Dimes Campaign; sec. St. George Greek Orthodox Ch., 1955-57; chmn. Commn. on the Future of S.C., 1987-89, Hazardous Waste Task Force, 1987-88. Named Outstanding Young Man Greenville County, 1962, Outstanding Young Man S.C., 1962, Outstanding Rep., S.C. Sch. Bd. Assn., 1976-77, Outstanding Legislator, S.C. Alcohol and Drug Abuse Assn., 1978, Citizen of Yr. S.C. Hosp. Assn.; recipient Friend of Edn. award Phi Kappa Delta, 1987. Mem. Greenville Jaycees (pres. 1957-58). Office: PO Box 1827 Greenville SC 29602-1827

THEODORESCU, RADU AMZA SERBAN, mathematician, educator; b. Bucharest, Romania, Apr. 12, 1933; emigrated to Can., 1968, naturalized, 1975; s. Dan and Ortensia Maria (Butoianu) T.; children: Dan, Paul, Anne. BSc, U. Bucharest, 1954, DSc, 1967; PhD, Acad. Romania, 1958. Asst. prof. Inst. Math. of Acad., Romania, Bucharest, 1954-57; sr. asst. prof. Inst. Math. of Acad., 1957-60, assoc. prof., sci. sec., 1960-64; prof., head dept. Center Math. Statistics, 1964-68; prof. U. Bucharest, 1968-69, Laval U., Quebec, Que., Can., 1969—; guest prof., lectr. univs. in Europe, N.Am. and Australia. Author: (with G. Ciucu) Processes with Complete Connections, 1960, (with S. Guiasu) Mathematical Information Theory, 1968, Uncertainty and Information, 1971, (with M. Iosifescu) Random Processes and Learning, 1969, (with W. Hengartner) Concentration Functions, 1973, 2d edit., 1980, Monte-Carlo Methods, 1978; mem. editorial bd. Annales des Sciences Mathématiques du Québec, Optimization, Statistics and Decisions; contbr. articles to profl. jours. Mem. bd. European Orgn. Quality Control, 1966-69. Recipient prize Acad. Romania, 1960. Fellow Inst. Math. Stats., Am. Soc. Quality Control; mem. Can. Math. Soc., Statis. Soc. Can., Am. Math. Soc., Internat. Statis. Inst. Home: Apt 1603, 9 Jardins MÉrici, Quebec, PQ Canada G1S 4S8 Office: Laval U, Dept Math and Stats, Quebec, PQ Canada G1K 7P4

THEODORIDIS, GEORGE CONSTANTIN, biomedical engineering educator, researcher; b. Braila, Romania, Dec. 3, 1935; came to U.S., 1959; s. Constantin George and Anastasia (Haritopoulos) T.; m. Lilly Kate Hyman, Sept. 20, 1975; 1 child, Alexander. BS in Mechanical and Elec. Engring., Nat. Tech. U. Athens, 1959; DSc, MIT, Cambridge, Mass., 1964. Rsch. assoc. MIT, Cambridge, Mass., 1964; sr. scientist Am. Sci. Engring., Cambridge, Mass., 1964-68; assoc. prof. in residence U. Calif., Berkeley, 1968-70; biomedical engring. U. Va., Charlottesville, 1970—; prof. elec. engring. U. Patras, Greece, 1976-83; cons. Food and Drug Adminstrn., Washington, 1975-76, Applied Physics Lab, Columbia, Md., 1978-79. Author: Applied Math, 1983; contbr. articles to profl. jours. Den leader Boy Scouts Am., Charlottesville, Va., 1984-85. Fulbright fellow U.S. Govt., MIT, 1959-60; Nato fellow NATO, MIT, 1961-64; Spl. fellow NIH, U. Calif., 1968-70; recipient teaching award GE, MIT, 1963. Mem. Inst. Elec. and Electronics Engrs., Sigma Xi. Greek Orthodox. Avocations: history, travel. Home: 1817 Fendall Ave Charlottesville VA 22903-1613 Office: U Va Dept Biomed Engring Box 377 Medical Ctr Charlottesville VA 22908

THEODOSIUS, HIS BEATITUDE METROPOLITAN See LAZOR, THEODOSIUS

THEOHARIDES, THEOHARIS CONSTANTIN, pharmacologist, physician, educator; b. Thessaloniki, Macedonia, Greece, Feb. 11, 1950; s. Constantin A. and Marika (Krava) T.; m. Efthalia I. Triarchou, July 10, 1981; children: Niove, Konstantinos. Diploma with honors, Anatolia Coll., 1968, BA in Biology and History of Sci. and Medicine, Yale U., 1972, MS in Immunology, 1975, MPhil. in Endocrinology, 1975, PhD in Pharmacology Yale U., 1978, MD Yale U., 1983. Asst. in rsch. biology Yale U., 1968-71, asst. in rsch. pharmacology, 1973-78, exec. sec. univ. senate, 1976-78, rsch. assoc. faculty clin. immunology, 1978-83; spl. instr. modern Greek Yale U., 1974, 77; vis. faculty Aristotelian U. Sch. Medicine, Thessaloniki, 1979; asst. prof. biochemistry and pharmacology Tufts U., 1983-88, co-dir. med. pharmacology curriculum, 1983-85, dir. med. pharmacology, 1985-93, assoc. prof. pharmacology, biochemistry and psychiatry, 1989-94, prof. pharmacology and internal medicine, 1995—, dir. grad. pharmacology, 1994—; clin. pharmocologist Commonwealth Mass. Drug Formulary Commn., 1985—; co-chmn. neuro-immunology 2d and 3d World Conf. on Inflammation, Monte Carlo, 1986, 89; mem. internat. adv. bd. 4th, 5th and 6th World Conf. on Inflammation, Geneva, 1991, 93, 95, 97; spl. cons. Min. of Health, Greece, 1993—; chmn. Internat. Com. to Upgrade Med. Edn. in Greece, 1994; bd. dirs., spl. cons. Inst. Pharm. Rsch. & Tech., Athens, 1994—. Trustee Anatolia Coll. 1984-85. Author books on pharmacology; mem. editorial bd. numerous jours.; contbr. articles to profl. jours.; patentee in field. Bd. dirs., v.p. for rels. with Greece, Krikos, 1978-79; sec. Assn. Greeks to Yale, 1974-79, pres., 1982-83. Recipient Theodore Cuyler award Yale U., 1972; George Papanicoalou Grad. award, 1977; Med. award Hellenic Med. Soc. N.Y., 1979, 83; M.C. Winternitz prize in pathology Yale U., 1980; Disting. Service award Tufts U. Alumni Assn., 1986, Spl. Faculty Recognition award Tufts U. Med. Sch., 1987, 88. Mem. Hellenic Biochem. and Biophys. Soc., AMA, AAUP, N.Y. Acad. Scis., Am. Inst. History Pharmacy, AAAS, Soc. Health and Human Values, Am. Assn. History Medicine, Am. Soc. Cell Biology, Soc. Neurosci., Am. Fedn. Clin. Research, Conn. Acad. Arts and Scis., Am. Soc. Pharmacology and Exptl. Therapeutics, Hellenic Soc. Cancer Research, Hellenic Soc. Med. Chemistry, Internat. Soc. Immunopharmacology, Am. Soc. Microbiology, Am. Assn. Immunologists, Internat. Soc. History of Medicine, Mass. Med. Soc., N.E. Hellenic Med. Soc. (sec. 1984-85, v.p. 1985-86, 94—, pres. 1986-87), Hellenic Sci. Assn. Boston (bd. dirs. 1985), Internat. Anatolia Alumni Assn. (sec. 1984-85). Alpha Omega Alpha (citation for excellence in teaching 1989, 90, 91, 92, 93, 94, 96), Sigma Xi. Research on mechanisms of release of secretory products; hormonal induction of ornithine decarboxylase and membrane functions of polyamines; pathophysiology of mast cells in neuroimmunoendocrine diseases such as irritable bowel syndrome, interstitial cystitis, migraines and multiple sclerosis. Home: 14 Parkman St Apt 2

Brookline MA 02146-3802 Office: Tufts U Sch Med Dept Pharmacology & Exptl Therapeutics 136 Harrison Ave Boston MA 02111-1800

THEON, JOHN SPERIDON, meteorologist; b. Washington, Dec. 12, 1934; s. Lewis and Merope (Xydias) T.; m. Joanne Edens, July 31, 1965; children—Christopher James, Catherine. B.S. in Aero. Engring. U. Md., 1957; B.S. in Meteorology, Pa. State U., 1959, M.S., 1962; Ph.D. in Engring. Sci. and Mechanics, U. Tenn., 1985. Aero. engr. Douglas Aircraft Co., Santa Monica, Calif., 1957-58; engr. U.S. Naval Ordnance Lab., White Oak, Md., 1962; rsch. meterologist, 1962-74; head meterology br. NASA Goddard Space Flight Center, Greenbelt, Md., 1974-77; asst. chief Lab. for Atmospheric Scis., 1977-78, Nimbus project scientist, 1972-78, Landsat discipline leader meteorol. investigations, 1974-78; mgr. global weather research program NASA Hdqrs., Washington, 1978-82, chief Atmospheric Dynamics and Radiation br., 1982-89; Spacelab 3 program scientist NASA Hdqrs., 1979-86, chmn. space shuttle weather adv. panel, 1985-87; chief atmospheric, dynamics, radiation and hydrol. processes, 1989-93, climate br., 1993-94, divsn. program scientist, 1994-95, exec. sec. task force on observations and data mgmt., 1994-95; cons. Inst. for Global Environ. Strategies, Orbital Scis. Corp., 1995—. Contbr. articles to profl. jours. Served with USAF, 1958-60. Recipient Nimbus F Instrument Team award NASA-Goddard, 1976, Goddard Exceptional Performance award, 1978, NASA Exceptional Performance award, 1986, Radio Wave award Ministry of Posts & Telecomm. of Japan, 1995; name Disting. Alumnus U. Tenn., 1989. Fellow Am. Meteorol. Soc., AIAA (assoc. fellow, chmn. atmospheric environment tech. com. 1986-89, Losey Atmos. Sci. award 1986); mem. Am. Geophys. Union, Sigma Xi. Presbyterian. Home: 6801 Lupine Ln Mc Lean VA 22101 Office: 6801 Lupine Ln Mc Lean VA 22101

THERNSTROM, STEPHAN ALBERT, historian, educator; b. Port Huron, Mich., Nov. 5, 1934; s. Albert George and Bernadene (Robbins) T.; m. Abigail Mann, Jan. 3, 1959; children—Melanie Rachel, Samuel Altgeld. B.S., Northwestern U., 1956; A.M., Harvard, 1958, Ph.D., 1962. Instr. history Harvard U., Cambridge, Mass., 1962-66, asst. prof., 1966-67, prof., 1973-81, Winthrop prof., 1981—, chmn. com. on higher degrees in history of Am. civilization, 1985-92; prof. Brandeis U., 1967-69, UCLA, 1969-73; Pitt. prof. Am. history and instns. Cambridge U., 1978-79; dir. Charles Warren Ctr. for Research in Am. History, 1980-83. Author: Poverty and Progress, 1964, Poverty, Planning and Politics in the New Boston, 1969, The Other Bostonians, 1973, History of the American People, 1984, 88; editor: Harvard Ency. Am. Ethnic Groups; co-editor: Harvard Studies in Urban History; Cambridge Interdisciplinary Perspectives on Modern History Series. Recipient Bancroft prize, R.R. Hawkins award, Faculty prize Harvard U. Press, Waldo G. Leland prize; Guggenheim fellow; John M. Olin fellow; ACLS fellow. Office: Harvard U Robinson Hall Cambridge MA 02138

THEROUX, PAUL EDWARD, author; b. Medford, Mass., Apr. 10, 1941; s. Albert Eugene and Anne (Dittami) T.; m. Anne Castle, Dec. 4, 1967 (div. 1993); children: Marcel, Louis; m. Sheila Donnelly, Nov. 18, 1995. BA, U. Mass., Amherst, DLitt, 1988; DLitt, Trinity Coll., Washington, 1980, Tufts U., 1980. Lectr. U. Urbino, Italy, 1963, Soche Hill Coll., Malawi, 1963-65; mem. faculty English dept. Makerere U., Uganda, 1965-68, U. Singapore, 1968-71; vis. lectr. U. Va., 1972-73. Author: (fiction) Waldo, 1967, Fong and the Indians, 1968, Girls at Play, 1969, Murder in Mt. Holly, 1969, Jungle Lovers, 1971, Sinning with Annie, 1972, Saint Jack, 1973, The Black House, 1974, The Family Arsenal, 1976, The Consul's File, 1977, Picture Palace, 1978 (Whitebread prize for fiction), A Christmas Card, 1978, London Snow, 1980, World's End, 1980, The Mosquito Coast, 1981, The London Embassy, 1982, Half Moon Street, 1984, O-Zone, 1986, My Secret History, 1988, Chicago Loop, 1990, Millroy the Magician, 1993, My Other Life, 1996, (nonfiction) V.S. Naipaul, 1973, The Great Railway Bazaar, 1975, The Old Patagonian Express, 1979, The Kingdom by the Sea, 1983, Sailing Through China, 1983, Sunrise with Sea Monsters, 1985, The White Man's Burden, 1987, Riding the Iron Rooster, 1988, The Happy Isles of Oceania, 1992, The Pillars of Hercules, 1995, (film script) Saint Jack, 1979. Recipient Editorial award Playboy mag., 1972, 76, 77, 79, Lit. award AAAL, 1977, James Tait Black award, 1982, Yorkshire Post Best Novel award, 1982, Thomas Cook Travel Book prize, 1989. Fellow Royal Soc. Lit., Royal Geog. Soc.; mem. AAAL.

THESEN, ARNE, industrial engineering educator; b. Oslo, May 6, 1943; came to U.S., 1963; s. Gudbrand and Astrid (Siggerud) T.; m. Maria Tan, Jan. 25, 1969 (div. Dec. 1987); children: Anita Mei-Ling, Britt Wei-Ling; m. Sharon W. Foster, June 21, 1991 (div. Mar. 1994). Student, Schous Tekniske Inst., Oslo, 1961-63; B.S., U. Ill., 1965, M.S., 1968, Ph.D., 1972. Systems analyst Bell Telephone Labs., Piscataway, N.J., 1970-72; prof. dept. indsl. engring. U. Wis.-Madison, 1972—; chmn. dept. indsl. engring., 1978-81, 91-95, prof. dept. computer sci., 1981-93; ptnr. Troll Assocs., Madison, 1976-84; prin. Troll Software, Madison, 1984—. Author: Computer Methods in O.R., 1976; co-author: Systems Tools for Planning, 1976, Simulation for Decision Making, 1992; contbr. articles to profl. jours. With Royal Norwegian Air Force, 1965-66. Mem. INFORMS, Assn. Computer Machinery, Inst. for Indsl. Engring. Home: 4310 Fawn Ct Cross Plains WI 53528-9780 Office: Univ Wis Dept Indsl Engring 1513 University Ave Madison WI 53706-1539

THEUNER, DOUGLAS EDWIN, bishop; b. N.Y.C., Nov. 15, 1938; s. Alfred Edwin Kipp and Grace Elizabeth (MacKean) T.; m. Jane Lois Szuhany, May 16, 1959; children: Elizabeth Susan, Nicholas Frederick Kipp. BA, Coll. of Wooster, 1960; BD, Kenyon Coll., 1962; MA, U. Conn., 1968. Ordained to ministry Episcopal Ch. as deacon, then priest, 1962. Curate St. Peter's Episcopal Ch., Ashtabula, Ohio, 1962-65; vicar St. George's Episcopal Ch., Bolton, Conn., 1965-68; rector St. Paul's Episcopal Ch., Wllimantic, Conn., 1968-74, St. John's Episcopal Ch., Stamford, Conn., 1974-86; bishop Diocese of N.H., Concord, 1986—. Chmn. Community Housing Coalition, Stamford, Conn., 1975-86, Instituto Pastoral Hispano, N.Y.C., 1979-86; pres. Holderness (N.H.) Sch., 1987—, White Mountain Sch., Littleton, N.H., 1987—. Mem. N.H. Coun. Chs. (v.p.). Avocations: photography, cooking, hiking, skiing. Office: Concord Diocese Diocesan Office 63 Green St Concord NH 03301-4243

THEURER, BYRON W., aerospace engineer, business owner; b. Glendale, Calif., July 1, 1939; s. William Louis and Roberta Cecelia (Sturgiss) T.; m. Sue Ann McKay, Sept. 15, 1962 (div. 1980); children: Karen Marie, William Thomas, Alison Lee. BS in Engring. Sci., USAF Acad., 1961; MS in Aero. Sci., U. Calif., Berkeley, 1965; MBA, U. Redlands, 1991. Commd. USAF, 1961, advanced through grades to lt. col., ret. 1978; project officer Space Shuttle Devel. Prog., Houston, 1971-76; chief of test F-15 Systems Prog. Office Wright Patterson AFB, Ohio, 1976-78; sr. engr. Veda, Inc., Dayton, 1979-81, Logicon Inc., Dayton, 1981-83; project mgr. Support Systems Assocs., Inc., Dayton, 1983-84, CTA Inc., Ridgecrest, Calif., 1985-89; owner, operator The Princeton Rev. of Ctrl. Calif., Ridgecrest, 1989-92, San Luis Obispo, 1993—; cons. in field. Decorated Silver Star, D.F.C., Air Medals (16); named Officer of the Yr., Air Force Flight Test Ctr., Edwards AFB, 1970. Mem. Air Force Assn., Assn. Old Crows, USAF Acad. Assn. Grads. (nat. bd. dirs. 1972-75, chpt. pres. 1981-83). Republican. Episcopalian. Avocations: long distance running. Home: PO Box 697 Cayucos CA 93430-0697

THEUT, C. PETER, lawyer; b. Center Line, Mich., July 24, 1938; s. Clarence William and Anna Marie (Martens) T.; m. Judith Fern Trombley, Aug. 4, 1962; children: Elizabeth Anne, Kristin Claire, Peter Christopher, Sarah Nicole. BA, U. Mich., 1960, LLB, 1963. Bar: Calif. 1964, Mich. 1964, U.S. Dist. Ct. (no. dist.) Ohio 1968, U.S. Dist. Ct. (ea. dist.) Mich. 1968. Assoc. Overton, Lyman & Prince, L.A., 1963-67; ptnr. Foster, Meadows and Ballard, Detroit, 1968-72; ptnr. Theut & Schellig, Mt. Clemens, Mich., 1972-80; ptnr. Hill, Lewis, Mt. Clemens, 1980-88, Butzel, Long, Detroit, 1988—, stockholder; gen. counsel Nat. Marine Bankers Assn., Mich. Boating Industries Assn. Mem. ABA (TIPS admiralty com.), Detroit Bar Assn., Calif. State Bar Assn., Mich. State Bar Assn., Macomb County Bar Assn., Maritime Law Assn. (chmn. com. recreational boating, immediate past chmn.), Nat. Marine Bankers Assn. (gen. counsel), Mich. Boating Industry Assn. (gen. counsel), North Star Sail Club. Republican. Home: 38554 Hidden Ln Clinton Township MI 48036-1826 Office: Butzel Long 150 W Jefferson Ave Ste 900 Detroit MI 48226-4415

THEVENET, PATRICIA CONFREY, social studies educator; b. Norwich, Conn., Apr. 16, 1924; d. John George and Gertrude Pauline (Doolittle) Confrey; m. Rubén Thevenet, Dec. 15, 1945 (dec. Mar. 1983); children: Susanne, Gregory, Richard, R. James. BS, U. Conn., 1944; AM, U. Chgo., 1945; EdM, Columbia U., 1992, EdD, 1994. Cert. elem. tchr., N.J. Counselor testing and guidance U. Chgo., 1945; home economist Western Mass. Electric Co., Pittsfield, 1946; tchr. Unquowa Sch., Fairfield, Conn., 1950-53, Alpine (N.J.) Sch., 1968-86; program asst. soc. studies Tchrs. Coll. Columbia U., N.Y.C., 1987-93; ret., 1993; historian Borough Northvale, N.J., 1987-94; participant summer seminar Smithsonian Instn., Washington, 1984. Del 2d dist. rep. Town Mtg., Trumbull, Conn., 1954-56; pres., trustee Northvale Pub. Libr. Assn., 1957-63; trustee Northvale Bd. Edn., 1963-72, pres. Northvale Bd. Edn., 1969-70; exec. bd. dirs. Bergen County (N.J.) County Bds. Edn., 1965-72; mem. Evening Sch. Comm. No. Valley Regional Dist., Bergen County, 1976-83. Mem. Am. Hist. Assn., Nat. Coun. Social Studies, Alumni Coun. Tchrs. Coll., Columbia U., Conn. Hist. Soc., Voluntown Hist. Soc., Friends of Slater Mus. (bd. dirs.). Avocations: sailing, swimming, reading. Home: 88 N Shore Rd # B Voluntown CT 06384-1719

THIBADEAU, EUGENE FRANCIS, education educator, consultant; b. N.Y.C., May 18, 1933; s. Eugene Servanis and Lillian (Archer) T.; 1 child, Christine; m. Patricia M. Batchelder, March 16, 1993. BA, NYU, 1959, MA, 1967; MA, NYU, 1968, PhD, 1973. Instr. NYU, N.Y.C., 1968; lectr. in philosophy Dowling Coll., Oakdale, N.Y., 1968-70; prof. edn. Indiana U. of Pa., Indiana, Pa., 1970—; vis. assoc. prof. Adelphi U., Garden City, N.Y., 1974-75; vis. scholar NYU, N.Y.C., 1984-85; vis. prof. Hofstra U., Hempstead, N.Y., 1974, 75, 84, 86; cons. Central Bur. of Ednl. Visits, London, 1980-81, Commonwealth Speakers Bur., Harrisburg, Pa., 1983-85, U.S. Dept. Edn., Washington, 1983-85, Pa. Dept. Edn., Harrisburg, 1988—. Author: Opening Up Education-In Theory and Practice, 1976, Curriculum Theory, 1988, Existentialism in the Classroom, 1994; rev. editor: Focus on Learning, 1973-77, editor, 1977-84; contbg. editor: International Encyclopedia of Education, 2d edit., International Encyclopedia of Teaching and Teacher Education, 2nd edit.; contbr. articles to profl. jours. Active in United Way, Indiana, Pa., 1980—, NAACP, Indiana, 1985—, Red Cross, Indiana, 1985—. Fulbright sr. lectr. Thames Polytechnic, London, 1978-79, Janus Pannonius U., Peces, Hungary, 1990-91; foreign expert Shanghai (China) Tchrs. U., 1988; designated faculty rsch. assoc. Inst. for Applied Rsch. and Pub. Policy, Indiana U. of Pa., 1989; named Commonwealth Teaching fellow, Pa. State Colls. and Univ. Disting. Faculty Awards Com., 1976; recipient Founder's Day award, NYU, 1973. Fellow Am. Philosophy Edn. Soc.; mem. Am. Ednl. Studies Assn., AAUP, The S.W. Philosophy Edn. Soc., ASCD. Avocations: traveling, skiing, tennis, reading, chess. Home: RR 1 Box 103 Penn Run PA 15765-9733 Office: Indiana Univ of Pa 133 Stouffer Hall Indiana PA 15701

THIBAULT, J(OSEPH) LAURENT, service company executive; b. Sturgeon Falls, Ont., Can., Dec. 31, 1944; s. J. Rene and Leone (Doucet) T.; m. Paulette Patricia Lalonde, June 4, 1966; children—Alain, Andre. B.A. in Econs., Laurentian U., Sudbury, 1966; M.A. in Econs., U. Toronto, Ont., 1968. Cons. Kates, Peat & Marwick Co., Toronto, 1968-72; dir. econs. and communications Can. Mfrs. Assn., Toronto, 1972-76; v.p. Can. Mfrs. Assn., 1976-81, sr. exec. v.p., 1981-84, pres., exec. dir., 1985-91; co-chair Can. Labour Force Devel. Bd., Ottawa, Ont., Can., 1991-95; fin. advisor Equion Group, Mississauga, Ont., 1995—. Club: National. Home: 24 Cindebarke Terr, Georgetown, ON Canada L7G 4S5 Office: City Ctr Plz, 1 City Centre Dr Ste 1520, Mississauga, ON Canada L5B 1M2

THIBEAULT, GEORGE WALTER, lawyer; b. Cambridge, Mass., Sept. 21, 1941; s. George Walter and Josephine (Maraggia) T.; m. Antoinette Miller, June 30, 1963; children—Robin M., Holly Ann. B.S., Northeastern U., 1964; M.B.A., Boston Coll., 1966, J.D., 1969. Bar: Mass. 1969. Assoc. Gaston & Snow, Boston, 1969-73; ptnr. Testa, Hurwitz & Thibeault, Boston, 1973—. Mem. ABA, Mass. Bar Assn., Am. Arbitration Assn. Home: 181 Caterina Hts Concord MA 01742-4773 Office: Testa Hurwitz & Thibeault High St Tower 125 High St Boston MA 02110

THIBERT, ROGER JOSEPH, clinical chemist, educator; b. Tecumseh, Ont., Can., Aug. 29, 1929; s. Charles and Violet (Hebert) T.; m. Audrey M. Wissler, July 10, 1954; children: Mark Roger, Robert Francis. BA, U. Western Ont., 1951; MS, U. Detroit, 1954; PhD, Wayne State U., 1958. Diplomate: Am. Bd. Clin. Chemistry, also past bd. dirs. Mem. faculty U. Windsor, Ont., Can., 1953—; prof. chemistry U. Windsor, 1967-94, dir. clin. chemistry, 1972-94, prof. emeritus, 1994—; prof. pathology Med. Sch. Wayne State U., Detroit, 1972-94; asso. div. head, clin. chemistry Detroit Receiving Hosp., Univ. Health Center, 1972-94; mem. med. staff Detroit Receiving Hosp.-Univ. Health Center, 1973—; cons. med. biochemistry Med. Labs. Windsor, Ont., Can. Contbr. articles on chemistry, biochemistry, analytical chemistry, clin. chemistry to profl. jours. Recipient Smith Kline award Am. Assn. Clin. Chemistry, 1980, Alumni Teaching award U. Windsor, 1988, Alumni Award of Merit, 1994, Teaching award Ont. Confedn. U. Faculty Assns., 1990, Beckman Edn. Excellence award Canadian Soc. Clin. Chemists, 1992; Chem. Inst. Can. fellow, 1968—; Nat. Acad. Clin. Biochemistry fellow, 1978—; recipient grants Natural Scis. and Engring. Rsch. Coun., Can., award Union Carbide, Chem. Inst., Can., 1978. Fellow AAAS, Can. Acad. Clin. Biochemistry; mem. Am. Chem. Soc., Chem. Inst. Can., Assn. Chem. Profession Ont., Am. Assn. Clin. Chemistry, Nat. Acad. Clin. Biochemistry, Can. Soc. Clin. Chemists (Ames award 1988), Ont. Soc. Clin. Chemists, Am. Soc. for Biochemistry and Molecular Biology, Fedn. Am. Socs. Exptl. Biology, Can. Soc. Biochemistry and Molecular Biology, Can. Fedn. Biol. Scis., Can. Assn. Univ. Tchrs., Can. Soc. for Chemistry, Sigma Xi. Roman Catholic. Home: 4612 Dali Ct, Windsor, ON Canada N9G 2M8 Office: U Windsor, Dept Chemistry/Biochemistry, Windsor, ON Canada N9B 3P4

THIBODEAU, GARY A., academic administrator; b. Sioux City, Iowa, Sept. 26, 1938; m. Emogene J. McCarville, Aug. 1, 1964; children: Douglas James, Beth Ann. BS, Creighton U., 1962; MS, S.D. State U., 1967, S.D. State U., 1970; PhD, S.D. State U., 1971. Profl. service rep. Baxter Lab., Inc., Deerfield, Ill., 1963-65; tchr., researcher dept. biology S.D. State U., Brookings, 1965-76, asst. to v.p. for acad. affairs, 1976-80, v.p. for adminstrn., 1980-85; chancellor U. Wis., River Falls, 1985—; mem. investment com. U. Wis., River Falls Found.; trustee W. Cen. Wis. Consortium U. Wis. System; bd. dirs. U. Wis. at River Falls Found.; mem. Phi Kappa Phi nat. budget rev. and adv. comm., Phi Kappa Phi Found. investment comm., comm. on Agrl. and Rural Devel., steering commn. Coun. of Rural Colls. and Univs., Joint Coun. on Food and Agrl. Scis., USDA. Author: Basic Concepts in Anatomy and Physiology, 1983, Athletic Injury Assessment, 1994, Structure and Function of the Body, 1996, The Human Body in Health and Disease, 1996, Textbook of Anatomy and Physiology, 1996. Mem. AAAS, Sigma Xi, Phi Kappa Phi, Gamma Sigma Delta, Gamma Alpha. Office: U Wis 116 N Hall River Falls WI 54022

THIBODEAU, ROBIN ANN, mail carrier, union official; b. Southington, Conn., Oct. 27, 1956; d. Robert Edward and Irene Josephine (Bendott) Dunbar; m. Roland Leo Thibodeau, Feb. 25, 1978 (div. Aug. 1983); children: Christina Ann Thibodeau, Desilyn Joanne Nelson. Grad. high sch., Southington; grad., Porter & Chesters Auto. Inst. Sec. Bd. of Edn., Southington, 1974-75; cashier, clk. Cumberland Farms, Plantsville, Conn., 1974; acctg. clk. to contbr. Waterbury Farrel, Mfg., Cheshire, Conn., 1975-76; machinist Supreme Lake Mfg., Plantsville, 1976-77; auto transmission re-builder Transmission Works, Hartford, Conn., 1978-79; rural carrier substitute Southington Post Office, 1979-81, Terryville (Conn.) Post Office, 1980; regular rural carrier Plainville (Conn.) Post Office, 1981-84, Farmington (Conn.) Post Office, 1984—; local union steward Plainville Post Office, 1981-84; local/area steward Farmington Post Office, 1985-94. Democrat. Avocations: computer bulletin board, RV travel, crafting, gardening. Home: 17 Spruce St Plainville CT 06062-2327 Office: Conn Rural Letter Carrier Assn 210 Main St Farmington CT 06032-2959

THIEDE, RICHARD WESLEY, communications educator; b. Detroit, Mar. 30, 1936; s. Harold Victor and Blanche May (Gross) T. BS, Ea. Mich. U., 1961; MA, U. Ill., 1963; PhD, U. Mo., 1977. Teaching asst. U. Ill., Urbana, 1961-62; tchr. Cen. High Sch., Battle Creek, Mich., 1962-63, Shafer High Sch., Southgate, Mich., 1963-64, Chadsey High Sch., Detroit, 1964-68, Stevenson High Sch., Livonia, Mich., 1968-71; part-time instr. Schoolcraft Coll., Livonia, 1969-71; teaching/tech. asst. U. Mo., Columbia, 1971-74; instr. Ottumwa Hts. Coll., Iowa, 1975-76, Midland Luth. Coll., Fremont, Nebr., 1976-77; prof. dept. communication arts The Defiance (Ohio) Coll., 1978—; tchr. summer sch. Southwestern High Sch., Detroit, 1966, Cody High Sch., Detroit, 1967, 68; tchr. evening sch. Chadsey High Sch., 1965-67, Stevenson High Sch., 1969-70. Mem. AAUP, Assn. for Theatre in Higher Edn., Ohio Theatre Alliance, Alpha Psi Omega, Kappa Delta Pi. Democrat. Home: PO Box 1101 Defiance OH 43512-1101 Office: The Defiance Coll 701 N Clinton St Defiance OH 43512-1610

THIEL, ARTHUR WARREN, journalist; b. Hot Springs, Mont., Nov. 27, 1952; s. Robert Harry and Mary (Previs) T.; m. Julia Claire Akoury, July 16, 1988. BA, Pacific Luth. U., 1975. Reporter News Tribune, Tacoma, 1972-76; reporter, asst. sports editor Jour. Am., Bellevue, Wash., 1976-80; reporter, columnist Post-Intelligencer, Seattle, 1980—; commentator, talk-show host Sta. KIRO, Seattle, 1989—; commentator Sta. KZOK-FM, Seattle, 1991—. Bd. dirs. Alzheimers Assn. Western and Ctrl Wash., Seattle, 1990—. Named State Sportswriter of Yr., Nat. Sportswriter & Sportscasters Assn., 1990, 92, 96, Disting. Alumnus Pacific Luth. U., 1991. Avocations: sea kayaking, gardening, adventure travel. Office: Seattle Post-Intelligencer 101 Elliott Ave W Seattle WA 98119-4220

THIEL, PHILIP, design educator; b. Bklyn., Dec. 20, 1920; s. Philip and Alma Theone (Meyer) T.; m. Midori Kono, 1955; children: Philip Kenji, Nancy Tamiko, Susan Akiko, Peter Akira (dec.). BSc, Webb Inst. Naval Architecture, 1943; MSc, U. Mich., 1948; BArch, MIT, 1952. Instr. naval architecture MIT, Cambridge, 1949-50; instr. U. Calif., Berkeley, 1954-56, asst. prof., 1956-60; assoc. prof. U. Wash., Seattle, 1961-66; prof. visual design and experiential notation U. Wash., 1966-91; guest prof. Tokyo Inst. Tech., 1976-78; prof. Sapporo (Japan) Sch. of Arts, 1992—; lectr., U.S., Can. Japan, Norway, Denmark, Sweden, Eng., Austria, Switzerland, Peru, Bolivia; cons. FAO, Rome, 1952; co-founder Environment and Behavior, 1969; founder Ctr. for Experiential Notation, Seattle, 1981. Author: Freehand Drawing, 1965, Visual Awareness and Design, 1981, People, Paths and Purposes, 1996; patentee in field. Soc. Naval Architects and Marine Engrs. scholar, 1947; Rehmann scholar AIA, 1960; NIMH grantee, 1967, Nat. Endowment for Arts, 1969, Graham Found., 1995.

THIEL, THELMA KING, foundation executive; b. East Orange, N.J., Feb. 12, 1926; d. Thaddeus and Elizabeth Clara (Fickert) King; m. Charles T. Thiel, Mar. 25, 1954 (div. 1976); children: Mark Douglas, Donna Kalani, Dean Alan (dec.). B.A. in Health Edn. and Sch. Nursing, Jersey City State Coll., 1973. Cert. health educator, N.J. Exec. dir. Am. Council for Healthful Living, East Orange, 1973-79; commr. Nat. Com. of Digestive Diseases, Bethesda, Md., 1977-79; founder, chair Dean Thiel Found., Cedar Grove, N.J., 1971—; vice chmn, exec. dir. Am. Liver Found., Cedar Grove, N.J., 1979-84, pres., COO, 1984-94; founder, chair, CEO Hepatitis Found. Internat., 1994—. active Nat. Digestive Diseases Adv. Bd.; advisor Nat. Digestive Diseases Edn. and Info. Clearinghouse; charter mem. Rutgers U. Sch. Communication, Info. and Library Studies Bd. of Adv. Assocs. Author: Foundation for Decision Making, 1978. Mem. AAUW, Digestive Diseases Nat. Coalition (chmn. 1985-90, chmn. Nat. Health Coun., nom. com. 1989-91), Am. Nursing Assn., Soroptimist Internat., Am. Assn. Occupational Health Nurses. Presbyterian (elder). Office: 30 Sunrise Ter Cedar Grove NJ 07009-1423

THIELE, GLORIA DAY, retired librarian, small business owner; b. Los Angeles, Sept. 4, 1931; d. Russell Day Plummer and Dorothy Ruby (Day) Plummer Thi.; m. Donald Edward Cools, June 13, 1953 (div.); children: Michael, Ramona, Naomi, Lawrence, Nancy, Rebecca, Eugene, Maria, Charles. MusB, Mt. St. Mary's Coll., L.A., 1953. Libr. asst. Anaheim (Calif.) Pub. Libr., 1970-73, head Biblioteca de la Comunidad, 1973-74, children's libr. asst., 1974-76, children's br. specialist, 1976-78, children's libr., 1978-81; head children's svcs. Santa Maria (Calif.) Pub. Libr., 1981-85; cons. Literature Continuum, Santa Maria Sch. Dist., 1981-85; cons. Organizational Ch.-Sch. Libr., L.A., 1980; guest lectr. children's lit. Allan Hancock Coll., Santa Maria, 1981-85; owner, founder Discovery Garden, Grass Valley, Calif., 1989-93. Libr. liaison Casa Amistad Community Svc. Group, Anaheim, 1973-74; mem. outreach com. Santiago Libr. System, Orange County, 1973-74, mem. children's svcs. com., 1971-81; mem. Community Svcs. Coordinating Council, Santa Maria, 1982-85; chairperson children's svcs. com. Black Gold Libr. System, 1983-84; cons. children's libr. programs, 1986—; profl. storyteller, 1989—; Allegro Alliance vol. for music in the mountains, 1994—. Contbr. poems to Amherst Soc.'s Am. Poetry Ann., 1988. Mem. So. Calif. Council Lit. for Children and Young People, Kiwanis (sec., publicity chair 1996—), Delta Epsilon Sigma. Republican. Roman Catholic.

THIELE, HOWARD NELLIS, JR., lawyer; b. Dayton, Ohio, June 22, 1930; s. Howard Nellis and Irma Laura (Scheibe) T.; m. Alma Kuhn, Oct. 14, 1995; children: Leslie, Howard III, Craig. AB, Miami U., Oxford, Ohio, 1952; JD with distinction, U. Mich., 1955. Bar: Ohio 1955. Assoc., ptnr. Smith & Schnacke, LPA, Dayton, Ohio, 1957-89; ptnr. Thompson, Hine & Flory, Dayton, 1989-95; ret., 1995. Pres. Dayton Art Inst., 1981-85; v.p., gen. counsel Jr. Achievement; bd. dirs. Dayton Area chpt. ARC, 1983—, 1st vice chmn., 1990-91, chmn., 1992-94. Capt. USAF, 1955-57. Mem. ABA, Ohio State Bar Assn., Dayton Bar Assn., Order of the Coif, Engrs. Club, Phi Beta Kappa. Republican. Episcopalian.

THIELE, PAUL FREDERICK, mining company executive; b. Appleton, Wis., Aug. 5, 1914; s. William Frederick and Villa (Crawford) T.; m. Bernice Hoppe, Aug. 21, 1936 (dec.); 1 child, Lessie Elaine; m. Loretha Akins, Jan. 1995. BSEE, U. Wis., 1936. Test engr. GE, 1936-38; with dept. sales quotations GE, Schenectady, N.Y., 1938; elec. engr. Combined Locks (Wis.) Paper Co., 1938-41; engr. Inst. Paper Chemistry, Appleton, 1946; mgr., treas.-sec. Thiele Kaolin Co., Sandersville, Ga., 1947-60, CEO, pres., chmn. bd., 1960-87, CEO, chmn. bd., 1987—. Mem. adv. coun. Office State Supt. Schs., Atlanta, 1978-79; exec. bd. Cen. Ga. coun. Boy Scouts Am., Macon; chmn. Hosp. Authority Washington County, Sandersville; bd. dirs., mem. Community Concert Assn., Sandersville. With USNR, 1942-45. Recipient Silver Beaver award Boy Scouts Am., Hon. Alumni award Brewton-Parker Coll., 1991. Mem. Am. Mgmt. Assn., Tech. Assn. Pulp and Paper Industry, Ga. Mining Assn. (past pres., bd. dirs.), China Clay Producers Assn., Clay Minerals Soc., Ga. Bus. and Industry Assn. (v.p., bd. dirs., Entrepreneur of Yr. award 1979), Ga. Found. for Ind. Colls. (chmn., bd. dirs. 1979-81), Washington County Hist. Soc. (chmn. fin. com. 1979-80). Office: Thiele Kaolin Co PO Box 1056 Sandersville GA 31082-1056

THIELSCH, HELMUT JOHN, engineering company executive; b. Berlin, Nov. 16, 1922; came to U.S., 1939, naturalized, 1954; s. Kurt and Anna-Sibylle T.; m. Margaret E. McKenna, Aug. 16, 1952; children: Barbara Anne, Donald Kurt, Deborah Lee, Helmut John. BS, Auburn U., 1943; postgrad., U. Mich., 1943-45, Lehigh U., 1948. Registered profl. engr., R.I., Mass., Maine, N.J., Ga., Calif. Research engr. Allis Chalmers Co., Milw., 1945-46; metall. engr. Black, Sivalls & Bryson, Inc., Kansas City, Mo., 1946-47; research engr. Lukens Steel Co., Coatsville, Pa., 1948-49; engr. Welding Research Council, N.Y.C., 1949-52; dir. research Eutectic Welding Alloys Co., N.Y.C., 1952-53; v.p., dir. research, devel. and engring. ITT Grinnell Corp., Providence, 1954-84; pres. Thielsch Engring., Inc., Providence, 1984—; pres. HiTech Realty Assocs. Inc.; cons. on failure analysis to industry, public utilities, equipment builders, 1954—; lectr. at confs. on failures and failure prevention; mem. component tech. com. Argonne (Ill.) Nat. Lab.; bd. dirs. Ind. Energy, Inc. Author: Defects and Failures in Pressure Vessels and Piping, 1965; contbr. numerous articles to profl. publs.; patentee in field. Recipient Nat. Safety award Nat. Bd. Boiler and Pessure Vessel Insps., 1990. Fellow ASME, Am. Soc. Metals, Am. Soc. Nondestructive Testing, Am. Welding Soc. (Adams Lecture award 1982); mem. TAPPI, Am. Soc. Quality Control, Am. Nuclear Soc., Nat. Assn. Corrosion Engrs., Am. Chem. Soc., Am. Mgmt. Assn., Am. Soc. Profl. Engrs. (Freeman award 1985), Am. Bd. Forensic Examiners. Office: 195 Frances Ave Cranston RI 02910-2211

THIEMANN, CHARLES LEE, banker; b. Louisville, Nov. 21, 1937; s. Paul and Helen (Kern) T.; m. Donna Timperman, June 18, 1960; children: Laura Gerette, Charles Lee, Rodney Gerard, Jeffrey Michael, Matthew Joseph. BA in Chemistry, Bellarmine Coll., 1959; MBA, Ind. U., 1961, DBA, 1963. Mem. faculty Grad. Sch. Bus. and Grad. Sch. Savs. and Loan,

Ind. U., Bloomington, 1959-61; mgmt. cons., 1961-63; mem. rsch. dept. Fed. Res. Bank, St. Louis, 1963-64; with Fed. Home Loan Bank, Cin., 1964—, sr. v.p., then exec. v.p., 1974, pres., 1975—; adj. prof. Grad. Sch. Bus., Xavier U., Cin., mem. bus. adv. coun. Coll. Bus. Adminstrn., chmn. bd. dirs. Office Fin.; trustee Fin. Instns. Retirement Fund, Leadership Group Social Compact; mem. First Step Home; past chmn. bd. Resolution Funding Corp. Directorate. Past mem. Mayor of Cin. Housing Com.; past chmn. real estate exec. adv. coun. U. Cin. Mem. Cin. C. of C., Queen City Club, Rotary. Roman Catholic. Office: Fed Home Loan Bank 221 E 4th St Cincinnati OH 45202-4124

THIEMANN, RONALD FRANK, dean, religion educator; b. St. Louis, Oct. 4, 1946; s. Frank Joseph and Marie Magdalene (Graeser) T.; m. Beth Arlene Barkow, June 15, 1968; children: Sarah Elizabeth, Laura Kristen. B.A. magna cum laude, Concordia Sr. Coll., Fort Wayne, Ind., 1968; M.Div., Concordia Sem., St. Louis, 1972; M.A., Yale U., 1973, M.Philosophy, 1974, Ph.D., 1976; postgrad., Eberhard-Karls Universitat, Tubingen, W.Ger., 1974-75. Asst. prof. dept. religion Haverford Coll., Pa., 1976-82, assoc. prof. dept. religion, 1982-85, prof. dept. religion, 1985-86, acting provost, 1985, acting pres., 1986; dean Div. Sch. Harvard U., Cambridge, Mass., 1986—; John Lord O'Brian prof. divinity Harvard U., Cambridge, 1986—; vis. prof. honors program Villanova U., 1981; vis. asst. prof. Luth. Theol. Sem., Phila., 1977; mem. Ctr. Theol. Inquiry, Princeton, N.J., 1982-83; mem. consultation on Christianity and Marxism, U.S.A. nat. com. Luth. World Fedn., 1979-83, mem. consultation on civil religion, 1983-86, mem. consultation on problem of common good, 1985-88; bd. dirs. Trinity Press Internat.; mem. exec. com. Assn. Theol. Schs., 1994—. Author: Revelation and Theology, 1985, Constructing a Public Theology: The Church in a Pluralistic Culture, 1991, Religion in American Public Life: A Dilemma for Democracy, 1995; editor: The Legacy of H. Richard Niebuhr, 1991; mem. editl. bd. Dialog, 1987—; contbr. numerous articles to profl. jours. Mem. bd. trustees Buckingham Browne & Nichols Schs., 1988-90; mem. task force on theol. education, Evang. Luth. Ch. in Am., 1989-91, task force on Luth.-Reformed Conversations, Evang. Luth. Ch. Am., 1988-92. Recipient Disting. Teaching award Lindback Found., 1982; Mellon Found. fellow, 1982-83; Deutscher Akademischer Austauschdienst fellow, 1974-75. Mem. Am. Acad. Religion, (chmn. narrative interpretation and theology group 1982-86). Avocations: tennis; squash; piano. Home: 44 Francis Ave Cambridge MA 02138-1912 Office: Harvard Div Sch 45 Francis Ave Cambridge MA 02138-1911

THIEME, GEORGIA LEE, special education educator; b. Urbana, Ohio, Feb. 12, 1952; d. Howard Carrol and Marion Irene (Teague) Odum; m. Leslie Ralph Thieme, Apr. 10, 1970; children: Jacquelene, Tracy, Frank, Jennifer, Bryan, Benjamin. AA, Glen Oaks Community Coll., Centreville, Mich., 1988; BS, Western Mich. U., 1990; MA, 1993. Tchr. spl. edn. White Pigeon (Mich.) Comty. Schs., 1990—; part-time instr. Western Mich. U., 1994—; mem. St. Joe County (Mich.) Intermediate Sch. Dist. Past bd. dirs. St. Joe County Domestic Assault Shelter, Three Rivers, Mich.; mem. Three Rivers Community Players, Adoption and Foster Parents Mich. Assn., Lansing; family St. Joe County Foster Parents, Centreville, Mich., 1984-91. Zora Ellsworth scholar Western Mich. Edn. Dept., Kalamazoo, 1989-90, presdl. scholar Spl. Edn. Dept., 1990. Mem. AAUW, Student Coun. for Exceptional Children (bd. govs. 1989-90), Mich. Edn. Assn., Golden Key Honor Soc., Phi Kappa Phi, Beta Sigma Phi. Avocations: community theatre, reading sci. fiction, needle work, gardening. Home: 22660 Williams Landing Rd Sturgis MI 49091-9218

THIER, SAMUEL OSIAH, physician, educator; b. Bklyn., June 23, 1937; s. Sidney and May Henrietta (Kanner) T.; m. Paula Dell Finkelstein, June 28, 1958; children: Audrey Lauren, Stephanie Ellen, Sara Leslie. Student, Cornell U., 1953-56; MD, SUNY, Syracuse, 1960, DSc (hon.), 1987; DSc (hon.), Tufts U., 1988, Mt. Sinai Sch. Medicine, CUNY, 1988, George Washington U., 1989, Hahnemann U., 1989, U. Pa., 1994; LHD (hon.), Rush U., 1988, Va. Commonwealth U., 1992, Med. Coll. Pa., 1992, Brandeis U., 1994. Diplomate: Am. Bd. Internal Medicine (dir. 1977-85, exec. com. 1981-85, chmn. 1984-85). Intern Mass. Gen. Hosp., Boston, 1960-61; asst. resident Mass. Gen. Hosp., 1961-62, sr. resident, 1964-65, clin. and research fellow, 1965, chief resident, 1966; clin. asso. Nat. Inst. Arthritis and Metabolic Diseases, 1962-64; from instr. to asst. prof. medicine Harvard U. Med. Sch., 1967-69; prof. medicine, health care policy Harvard Med. Sch., 1994—; asst. in medicine, chief renal unit Mass. Gen. Hosp., Boston, 1967-69; asso. prof., then prof. medicine U. Pa. Med. Sch., 1969-72, vice chmn. dept., 1971-74; assoc. dir. med. svcs. Hosp. U. Pa., 1969-71; David Paige Smith prof. medicine Yale U. Sch. Medicine, 1978-81, Sterling prof. medicine, 1981-85, chmn. dept., 1975-85; pres. Inst. Medicine NAS, Washington, 1985-91; Univ. prof. Brandeis U., Waltham, Mass., 1991-94; pres. Mass. Gen. Hosp., Boston, 1994—, Ptnrs. HealthCare Sys., Inc., Boston, 1994—; chief medicine Yale-New Haven Hosp., 1975-85, trustee, 1978-85; bd. dirs. Conn. Hospice, Inc., 1976-82. Mem. editorial bd.: New Eng. Jour. Medicine, 1978-81; Contbr. articles to med. jours. Mem. adv. com. to the dir. NIH, 1980-85. Served with USPHS, 1962-64. Recipient Christian R. and Mary F. Lindback Found. Distinguished Teaching award, 1971. Fellow ACP (bd. regents 1982-85); mem. Assn. Am. Med. Colls. (adminstrv. bd. coun. acad. socs.), John Morgan Soc., Am. Fedn. Clin. Rsch. (pres. 1976-77), Am. Soc. Nephrology, Am. Physiol. Soc., Internat. Soc. Nephrology, Assn. Profs. Medicine, Assn. Am. Physicians, Interurban Clin. Club, Alpha Omega Alpha. Home: 99-20 Florence St Apt 4B Chestnut Hill MA 02167-1927

THIEROLF, RICHARD BURTON, JR., lawyer; b. Medford, Oreg., Oct. 27, 1948; s. Richard Burton Sr. and Helen Dorothy (Rivolta) T. BA, Columbia U., N.Y.C., 1970; JD, U. Oreg., 1976. Bar: Oreg. 1976, U.S. Dist. Ct. Oreg. 1976, U.S. Ct. Appeals (9th cir.) 1977, U.S. Dist. Ct. (no. dist.) Calif. 1980, U.S. Supreme Ct. 1993, U.S. Ct. Fed. Claims 1993. Staff atty. Orgn. of the Forgotten Am., Inc., Klamath Falls, Oreg., 1976-77, exec. dir., 1977-79; ptnr. Jacobson, Jewett & Thierolf, P.C., Medford, 1980—. Mem. City of Medford Planning Commn., 1990-92; mem. Medford Sch. Dist. 549-C Budget Com., 1991-92, chmn., 1991. Mem. ABA, Fed. Bar Assn., Oreg. State Bar (local profl. responsibility com. 1987-89, mem. fed. practice and procedure com. 1994—, sec. 1995—), Jackson County Bar Assn. (sec. 1988). Episcopalian. Avocation: violin. Home: 234 Ridge Rd Ashland OR 97520-2829 Office: Jacobson Jewett & Thierolf PC Two N Oakdale Ave Medford OR 97501

THIERRY, JOHN ADAMS, heavy machinery manufacturing company executive, lawyer; b. Watertown, Mass., May 8, 1913; s. Louis Sidney and Adelaide (Hamlin) T.; m. Mary Mills Hatch, June 6, 1953 (div.); 1 child, Charles Adams; m. Silvie Marie Frère, Dec. 1977. A.B. summa cum laude, Harvard U., 1935, A.M., 1936, J.D., 1940; postgrad. (Sheldon traveling fellow Harvard), U. Cambridge, Eng., 1936-37. Bar: Wis. 1941. With Bucyrus-Erie Co., South Milwaukee, Wis., 1940-82; sec. Bucyrus-Erie Co., 1958-77, gen. atty., 1958-76, v.p., 1960-77, sr. v.p., 1977-78, dir., 1961-79, mem. exec. com., 1967-78; v.p., dir. Bucyrus Erie Co. Can., Ltd., 1959-78; dir. Ruston-Bucyrus, Ltd., Lincoln, Eng., 1964-79, Komatsu-Bucyrus K.K., Japan, 1971-81; former dir. Bucyrus (Australia) Pty. Ltd., Bucyrus Internat., Inc., Brad Foot Gear Works, Inc., Pitts. Gear Co., South Milw. Marine Bank, Atlas Chain & Precision. Dir. Wis. Pub. Expenditure Survey, 1954-78; v.p., bd. dirs. Bucyrus-Erie Found., 1963-78; bd. dirs. Pub. Expenditure Research Found., 1964-78, YMCA, Milw., 1973-78, Milw. Symphony Orch., 1974-78; trustee Wis. Conservatory Music, 1969-78, S.E. Asia Art Found., 1977—; pres. United Performing Arts Fund, Milw., 1969; mem. adv. council Coll. Engring. U. Wis.-Milw., 1975-78, mem. adv. council Sch. Bus., 1975-78; mem. council Med. Coll. Wis., 1975-78; pres. Milw. Patent Law Assn., 1961-62. Served to capt., C.E. AUS, 1942-46. Recipient Granite State award U. N.H., 1986. Mem. Mass., Wis. patent office bars, Cambridge Union Soc., Phi Beta Kappa. Episcopalian. Club: Harvard (Boston and N.Y.C.). Home: Murray Hill Rd Hill NH 03243-9711

THIERYUNG, KAREN JEAN, accountant; b. Bklyn., Dec. 18, 1967; d. Nikolaus and Ruth (Denzer) T. AA with honors, Pasco-Hernando C.C., 1991; BS in Acctg. summa cum laude, Tampa Coll., 1993. Gen. office clk. Marsha's Dept. Store, Huntington, N.Y., 1984; bookkeeper Hernando Egg Producers, Masaryktown, Fla., 1985-88; acct. U. Med. Svc. Assn. Dept. Psychiatry U. South Fla., Tampa, Fla., 1993—. Mem. Inst. Mgmt. Accts., Phi Theta Kappa. Avocations: embroidery, computers, coin collecting, reading. Office: U South Fla Dept Psychiatry 3515 E Fletcher Ave Tampa FL 33613-4706

THIES, AUSTIN COLE, retired utility company executive; b. Charlotte, N.C., July 18, 1921; s. Oscar Julius and Blanche (Austin) T.; m. Marilyn Joy Walker, June 26, 1945 (dec. Dec. 1992); children: Austin Cole, Robert Melvin, Marilyn Leone; m. Fay Best Britt, May 7, 1993; stepchildren: Jeff Britt, Mike Britt. BSME, Ga. Inst. Tech., 1943. With Duke Power Co., Charlotte, 1946-86; mgr. steam prodn. Duke Power Co., 1963-65, asst. v.p., 1965-67, v.p. prodn. and operation, 1967-71, sr. v.p., 1971-82, exec. v.p., 1982-86, also dir.; past chmn. prodn. com., engring. and operating div. Southeastern Electric Exchange; chmn. tech. advisory com. Carolinas Va. Nuclear Power Assos.; chmn. N.C. Air Control Advisory Council. Mem. nat. adv. bd. Ga. Inst. Tech.; pres. Arts and Scis. Council; chmn. bd. dirs. Mercy Hosp.; trustee Alexander Childrens Center; bd. visitors Boy's Town.; 1st v.p. Sci. Museums of Charlotte; bd. dirs. Sci. Mus. Served with USNR, 1943-46. Decorated Purple Heart; named to Ga. Tech. Hall of Fame, 1994. Mem. Edison Electric Inst. (past chmn. engring. and operating div. exec. com.), IEEE, Charlotte C. of C., ASME (past chmn. Piedmont Carolina sect.), Am. Nuclear Soc., Air Pollution Control Assn., N.C. Soc. Engrs. (past pres., Engr. of Yr. 1985), Charlotte Engrs. Club (Disting. Service award 1984), Nat. Rifle Assn. (life), Kappa Sigma. Presbyterian (elder). Clubs: Rotary (past pres., dir. N. Charlotte), Cowans Ford Country (bd. dirs.), Quail Hollow Country (bd. dirs.), Charlotte City (bd. dirs.), Charlotte Ga. Inst. Tech. (past pres.), Charlotte Rifle and Pistol (past pres.). Home: 2429 Red Fox Trl Charlotte NC 28211-3766 Office: 422 S Church St Charlotte NC 28242-0001

THIES, RICHARD BRIAN, lawyer; b. Chgo., Dec. 14, 1943; s. Fred W. and Loraine C. (Mannix) T.; m. Anita Marie Rees, Aug. 5, 1972; children: Emily Marie, Richard Clarke. BA, Miami U., 1966; JD, Loyola U., 1974. Bar: Ill. 1974, U.S. Tax Ct. 1989. Assoc. Wilson & McIlvaine, Chgo., 1974-78; assoc.-ptnr. Isham, Lincoln & Beale, Chgo., 1978-88; ptnr. Wildman, Harrold, Allen & Dixon, Chgo., 1988—. Bd. govs. Chgo. HEart Assn., 1980-87, exec. com., 1982-87; bd. dirs. Juvenile Protective Assn., Chgo., 1984—; v.p. Samaritan Counseling Ctr., Evanston, 1989-94, pres., 1994. Mem. ABA, Chgo. Bar Assn., Chgo. Estate Planning Coun. Avocations: coaching children's sports, photography, music. Home: 305 Driftwood Ln Wilmette IL 60091-3441 Office: Wildman Harrold Allen & Dixon 225 W Wacker Dr Chicago IL 60606-1224

THIESEN, GREGORY ALAN, accountant; b. Denver, Apr. 24, 1958; s. Gene Duane and Virginia Ruth (Haas) T.; m. Karen Elise McGrew, Aug. 17, 1984; children: Jeffrey Richard, Jeremy Eugene. BS in Bus., U. Colo., 1980. CPA, Colo. Sr. mgr. Ernst & Whinney, Denver, 1980-89; chief fin. officer, chief info. officer Monfort, Inc., Greeley, 1989-95, CFO, CIO ConAgra Refrigerated Products, 1995—. Mem. student adv. coun. U. No. Colo.; mem. exec. com. Pvt. Industry Coun. Weld County; active Weld County Retirement Bd. Mem. MIT Enterprise Forum Colo. (mem. exec. com. 1987-89), Greeley Country Club, St. Charles Country Club. Office: 2000 S Batavia Geneva IL 60134

THIESENHUSEN, WILLIAM CHARLES, agricultural economist; b. Waukesha, Wis., Feb. 12, 1936; s. Arthur Henry and Myrtle O. (Honeyager) T.; children—James Waring, Kathryn Hague, Gail Ann. BS, U. Wis., 1958, MS, 1960, PhD, 1965; M.P.A. (Danforth Found. fellow), Harvard U., 1962, postgrad., 1968-69. Instr. agrl. extension U. Wis., Madison, 1959-61; exec. asst. Land Tenure Center and Instituto de Economia Universidad de Chile research team in, Santiago, 1963-65; asst. prof. agrl. econs. Land Tenure Center and Instituto de Economia Universidad de Chile research team in, 1965-68, asso. prof. agrl. econs., 1971-72, asso. prof. agrl. journalism, 1968-72, prof. agrl. journalism and agrl. econs., 1972—; dir. Land Tenure Ctr., 1971-75, 94—; asst. prof. econs. U. Wis., Milw., 1966-67; prof. agrl. econs. Escuela Nacional de Agricultura, Chapingo, Mex.; under AID contract, summer 1965; vis. prof. Universidad Autonoma de Madrid, Fulbright Program, 1977; cons., condr. seminars in field; Fulbright-Hays lectr., 1965, 72. Author: Chile's Experiments in Agrarian Reform, 1966, Reforma Agraria en Chile: Experimentos en Cuatro Fundos de la Iglesia, 1968, Broken Promises: Agrarian Reform and the Latin American Campesino, 1995; editor: Searching for Agrarian Reform in Latin America, 1989; mem. editl. bd. Latin Am. Rsch. Rev., Pakistan Devel. Rev.; contbr. articles to profl. jours. Served with USAR, 1960. Recipient award for best article Am. Jour. Agrl. Econs., 1969; Alpha Zeta nat. fellow, 1957; U. Wis. fellow, 1956; Harvard U. Adminstrn. fellow, 1962. Mem. Am. Agrl. Econs. Assn., Am. Econ. Assn., Latin Am. Studies Assn., Council Internat. Exchange Scholars (chmn. com. econs. selection 1979-80), Inter-Am. Found. (selection bd.), Wis. Acad. Scis., Arts and Letters, Phi Kappa Phi, Alpha Zeta, Sigma Delta Chi. Unitarian. Office: U Wis Land Tenure Ctr 1300 University Ave Madison WI 53706-1510

THIESSEN, DELBERT DUANE, psychologist; b. Julesberg, Colo., Aug. 13, 1932; s. David and Eva Peters (Wetherby) T.; children—Trevor, Theron, Kendell Courtney. B.A. in Psychology with great distinction, San Jose (Calif.) State Coll., 1958; Ph.D., U. Calif., Berkeley, 1963. Extension instr. U. Calif., La Jolla, fall 1964; asst. sect. med. psychology, div. psychiatry and neurology Scripps Clinic and Research Found., La Jolla, 1962-65; mem. faculty U. Tex., Austin, 1965—; prof. psychology U. Tex., 1971—; research cons. NIMH. Author: Gene Organization and Behavior, 1972, The Evolution and Biochemistry of Aggression, 1976, Bitter-Sweet Destiny: The Stormy Evolution of Human Behavior, 1996; contbr. articles and chpts. to books. Served with AUS, 1952-54, Korea. Fellow USPHS, 1960-61; recipient Career Devel. award NIMH, 1967-72, grantee, 1967-78; grantee Russel Sage Found.; grantee NSF; grantee U. Tex. Research Inst. Mem. AAAS, Alumni Assn. Roscoe B. Jackson Meml. Lab., Am. Psychol. Assn., Am. Genetic Assn., Psychonomic Soc., Animal Behavior Soc., Southwestern Psychol. Assn., Behavior Genetics Assn., Sigma Xi, Phi Kappa Phi, Psi Chi. Home: 7300 Barcelona Dr Austin TX 78752-2003 Office: Univ Tex Dept Psychology Mezes 330 Austin TX 78712

THIESSEN, GORDON GEORGE, banker; b. South Porcupine, Ont., Can., Aug. 14, 1938; m. Annette Margaret Hillyar, Oct. 3, 1964; 2 children. BA with honours, U. Sask., 1960, MA, 1961; PhD in Econs., London Sch. Econs., 1972. Lectr. U. Sask., Saskatoon, Can., 1961-62; Economist Bank of Can., Ottawa, Ont., 1963-73; chief monetary and fin. analysis dept. Bank of Can., Ottawa, 1975-79, adviser, 1979-84, dep. gov., 1984-87, sr. dep. gov., 1987-94; gov. Bank of Can., Ottawa, Ont., 1994—; also chmn. bd. dirs. Bank of Can., Ottawa; vis. economist Res. Bank Australia, Sydney, 1973-75. Avocations: sailing; skiing.

THIGPEN, ALTON HILL, motor transportation company executive; b. Kinston, N.C., Feb. 3, 1927; s. Kirby Alton and Alice (Hill) T.; m. Rebecca Ann Braswell, May 16, 1953; children: David Alton, Jennifer Ann, Steven Roy. B.S. in Indsl. Engring, N.C. State U., 1950. With Asso. Transport, Inc., Burlington, N.C., 1950-71; engr. Asso. Transport, Inc., 1950-57; asst. terminal mgr. Asso. Transport, Inc., Phila., 1957-58; terminal mgr. Asso. Transport, Inc., Knoxville, Tenn., 1959; regional mgr. Asso. Transport, Inc., Valley region, 1960-62, South region, 1962-68; v.p.-dir. So. div. Asso. Transport, Inc., 1968-71; v.p. R.S. Braswell Co. Inc., Kannapolis, 1971-80; pres. R.S. Braswell Co. Inc., 1980—, Hartford Motor Inn Inc., North Myrtle Beach, S.C., 1982—, A.T. Developers, Inc., North Myrtle Beach, S.C., 1983—; pres. Cherokee 2 Inc., Shelby, N.C., 1986—, bd. dirs.; bd. dirs. First Union Nat. Bank, Earl Ownsby Studios Inc., Shelby. Bd. regents Berkshire Christian Coll., Lenox, Mass., 1975—; mem. adv. bd. Salvation Army. Served with USNR, 1945-46. Mem. Motor Carriers Va. (pres. 1967-68), N.C. Motor Carriers Assn. (dir. 1968—), Sigma Chi, Tau Beta Pi. Mem. Advent Christian Ch. Club: Mason (32 deg.), Lions. Home: 5395 Mooresville Rd Kannapolis NC 28081-8726 Office: PO Box 1197 Kannapolis NC 28082-1197

THIGPEN, LEWIS, engineering educator; b. Quincy, Fla., Aug. 29, 1938; s. Alonzo and Emma (Ray) T. BS magna cum laude in Mech. Engring., Howard U., 1964; MS, Ill. Inst. Tech., 1967, PhD, 1970. Profl. engr., Washington, D.C. Tech. staff mem. Sandia Nat. Labs., Albuquerque, 1969-73; asst. prof. Lowell (Mass.) Technol. Inst., 1973-75; from physicist to task leader containment program Lawrence Livermore Lab., Livermore, Calif., 1975-88; chmn. mech. engring. Howard U., Washington, 1988—; adv. com. mechanics NSF, Washington, 1990-91; program evaluator Mass. Higher Edn. Coord. Coun., Boston, 1991. Asst. leader Boy Scouts Am., Chgo., 1967-69. Served in U.S. Army, 1955-58, Germany. NASA fellow, 1964-67. Mem. ASME (accreditation bd. engring. and tech. evaluator 1991—), AIAA, Am. Soc. Engring. Edn. (fellowship rev. panel 1990—), Sigma Xi, N.Y. Acad. Scis. Achievements include patent in field and research in earth penetrating projectiles, constitutive modelling of geologic materials and theoretical seismology. Avocations: fishing, painting. Office: Howard U Dept Mech Engring 2300 6th St NW Washington DC 20001-2323

THIGPEN, RICHARD ELTON, JR., lawyer; b. Washington, Dec. 29, 1930; s. Richard Elton and Dorathy (Dotger) T.; m. Nancy H. Shand, Dec. 15, 1951; children: Susan B., Richard M. AB, Duke U., 1951; LLB, U. N.C., 1956. Bar: N.C., 1956, U.S. Ct. Appeals (4th cir.) 1960, U.S. Ct. Appeals (5th cir.) 1960, U.S. Ct. Appeals (10th cir.) 1974, U.S. Tax Ct. 1958, U.S. Ct. Claims 1978. Lawyer FTC, Washington, 1956-58, Thigpen & Hines, Charlotte, N.C., 1958-84, Moore & Van Allen, Charlotte, N.C., 1984-88; counsel Poyner & Spruill, Charlotte, N.C., 1988-93; gen. counsel Richardson Sports, 1994—. Dir. Charlotte-Mecklenburg YMCA, 1964-88, Heineman Med. Rsch. Ctr., Charlotte, 1970—, Charlotte C. of C., 1982-85. Lt. USNR, 1951-53. Fellow Am. Bar Found., Am. Coll. Tax Counsel (regent 1989-95, vice chmn. 1992, chmn. 1993-94); mem. ABA, N.C. State Bar, N.C. Bar Assn. (pres. 1988-89, chmn. tax sect. 1976-80), Sports Lawyers Assn. (bd. dirs. 1995—). Avocation: golf, travel. Home: 2518 Forest Dr Charlotte NC 28211-2110 Office: Richardson Sports 227 W Trade St Ste 1650 Charlotte NC 28202-1675

THIMANN, KENNETH VIVIAN, biology educator; b. Ashford, Eng., Aug. 5, 1904; came to U.S., 1930, naturalized Am. citizen; s. Israel Phoebus and Muriel Kate (Harding) T.; m. Ann Mary Bateman, Mar. 20, 1929; children—Vivianne Thimann Nachmias, Karen Thimann Romer, Linda Thimann Dewing. Student, Caterham Sch., Eng., 1915-21; B.Sc., Imperial Coll. Sci and Tech. London Royal Coll. Sci., 1924, A.R.C.S., 1924, Ph.D., 1928; A.M. (hon.), Harvard U., 1938; Ph.D. (hon.), U. Basel, Switzerland, 1960, U. Clermont-Ferrand, France, 1961; DSc (hon.), Brown U., 1989. Demonstrator bacteriology Kings Coll., London, 1927-29; instr. biochemistry and bacteriology Calif. Inst. Tech., Pasadena, 1930-35; lectr. botany Harvard U., 1935-36, asst. prof. plant physiology, 1936-39, assoc. prof., 1939-46, prof., 1946-62, Higgins prof. biology, 1962-65, prof. emeritus, 1965—; dir. Biol. Labs., Harvard U., 1946-50, tutor in biology Eliot House, 1936-52, assoc., 1952-65; master East House, Radcliffe Coll., 1962-65; exch. prof. U. Paris, 1954-55; prof. biology U. Calif., Santa Cruz, 1965-84, prof. emeritus, 1984—; provost Crown Coll., 1965-72; vis. prof. U. Mass., 1974, U. Tex., 1976; pres. XI Internat. Bot. Congress, 1969; pres. 2d Nat. Biol. Congress, Miami, 1970, Internat. Plant Growth Substance Assn. Triennial Meeting, Tokyo, 1973. Author: (with F. W. Went) Phytohormones, 1937, L'Origine et les Fonctions des Auxines, 1956, The Life of Bacteria, 2d edit., 1963, The Natural Plant Hormones, 1972, Hormones in the Whole Life of Plants, 1977, (with J.H. Langenheim) Botany: Plants and Human Affairs, 1982; author (with others) and editor Senescence in Plants, 1981; editor (with R.S. Harris) Vitamins and Hormones (ann.) Vol. 1, 1943, to Vol. 20, 1962, (with G. Pincus) The Hormones, 5 vols., 1948, 55, 63; mem. editorial bd. Archives of Biochemistry and Biophysics, 1949-70, Canadian Jour. Botany, 1966-73, Plant Physiology, 1974-85; contbr.over 300 articles to tech. jours. Bd. dirs. Found. Microbiology, Biol. Scis. Info. Services. Served as civilian scientist, USN, 1942-45. Recipient Stephen Hales prize research Am. Soc. Plant Physiologists, 1936; Guggenheim fellow, Eng., 1950-51, Italy, 1958; medallist Internat. Plant Growth Substance Assn., 1976, Balzan prize, 1982. Fgn. mem. Royal Soc. (London), Soc. Nazionale dei Lincei (Rome), Akad. Leopoldina (Halle), Acad. Nat. de Roumanie (Bucharest), Acad. des Sci. (Paris), Acad. d' Agr. de France, Bot. Soc. Netherlands, Bot. Soc. Japan, Indian Soc. Plant Physiology; mem. Am. Soc. Biol. Chemists, Am. Philos. Soc. (council 1973-76), Am. Acad. Arts and Scis., Nat. Acad. Scis. (chmn. botany sect. 1962-65, mem. council 1967-71, exec. com. assembly life scis. 1972-76), Bot. Soc. Am. (pres. 1960), AAAS (dir. 1968-72), Am. Soc. Plant Physiologists (pres. 1950-51), Soc. Gen. Physiologists (pres. 1949-50), Biochem. Soc., Am. Soc. Naturalists (pres. 1954-55), Am. Inst. Biol. Scis. (pres. 1965), Soc. Study Devel. and Growth (pres. 1955-56). Home: 3300 Darby Rd Apt 3314 Haverford PA 19041-1070

THIMOTHEOSE, KADAKAMPALLIL GEORGE, psychologist; b. Karipuza, India, Feb. 11, 1938; came to the U.S., 1976; s. K.G. and Mariamma Varghese; m. Mariamma Thimotheose, May 20, 1968 (div.); children: Geebee, Sonia. MA in Psychology, Kerala U., India, 1967, B in Edn., 1960, MA in Sociology, 1969; MA in History, Kerala U., 1975, PhD in Psychology, 1975; D Therapeutic Philosophy (hon.), World U., 1989. Lic. psychologist, marriage and family therapist, Mich.; diplomate Am. Bd. Med. Psychotherapists, Am. Bd. Psychotherapy, Am. Bd. Sexology, Am. Bd. Forensic Examiners. Lectr., head dept. ednl. psychology S.N. Tchrs. Coll., Trivandrum, India; clin./adminstrv. dir. Alexandrine House, Inc., Detroit, 1976-81; chief exec. officer Cen. Therapeutic Svcs., Inc., Southfield, Mich., 1981—; adv. bd. Trivandrum Med. Coll. Hosps., 1969-75; edn. faculty mem. U. Calicut, Kerala, India, 1969-75; v.p. forum ednl. rsch. and studies Kerala U., 1969-73. Author: Educational Psychology for B.Ed. Students, 1970; editor: Kerala University Journal of Education, 1969-73. Fellow Am. Bd. Med. Psychotherapists, Am. Acad. Clin. Sexologists; mem. APA, Am. Coll. Sexologists (sexologist), Am. Coll. Forensic Examiners, Am. Bd. Sexology (clin. supr.), World U. Round Table (hon. cultural doctorate in therapeutic philosophy). Republican. Avocations: photography, travel, reading, sightseeing. Home: 3048 Brewster Ct West Bloomfield MI 48322-2421 Office: Cen Therapeutic Svcs Inc 17600 W 8 Mile Rd Ste 7 Southfield MI 48075-4316

THISSELL, JAMES DENNIS, physicist; b. Lincoln County, S.D., June 1, 1935; s. Oscar H. and Bernice G.J. (Olbertson) T. BA cum laude, Augustana Coll., 1957; MS, U. Iowa, 1963. Rsch. physicist U. Iowa, Iowa City, 1958-64; engr. McDonnell Douglas, St. Louis, 1965-66; scientist E.G. & G., Inc., Las Vegas, Nev., 1967-68; engr. Bendix Field Engring. Corp. Ames Rsch. Ctr., Moffett Field, Calif., 1970-77, Lockheed Missiles & Space Co., Sunnyvale, Calif., 1978—. Mem. AIAA, IEEE, Am. Phys. Soc., Am. Geophys. Soc., Sigma Xi. Republican. Lutheran. Home: 38475 Jacaranda Dr Newark CA 94560-4727 Office: Lockheed Corp 0/23-20 B-100 FAC 1 PO Box 61687 Sunnyvale CA 94088-1687

THISTLETHWAITE, DAVID RICHARD, architect; b. Burlington, Iowa, Aug. 24, 1947; s. Robert and Nona (Binder) T.; m. Carol Anne Armstrong, Aug. 22, 1970. BArch, Iowa State U., 1971. Registered arch., Calif., Minn.; registered Nat. Coun. Archtl. Registration Bds. Designer Morrison Architects, St. Paul, 1971-73, Times Architects, Mpls., 1973-74; project architect Bentz/Thompson Assocs., Mpls., 1974-77; project mgr. Setter Leach Lindstrom, Mpls., 1977-78; project architect Wurster Bernardi Emmons, San Francisco, 1978-79, Strotz & Assocs., Tiburon, Calif., 1979-81, Hood Miller Assoc., San Francisco, 1981-84; prin., ptnr. R S T Architects, San Francisco, 1984-88; prin. Thistlethwaite Archtl. Group, San Francisco, 1988—. Contbr. articles to profl. jours. Mem. AIA (nat. profl. devel. com. 1983-86, treas. San Francisco chpt. 1985-86, chmn. Calif. coun. health facilities com. 1994-96, chmn. design com. Acad. Architecture for Health, 1994-96, mem. Calif. coun. ins. bd. trustees 1988—, mem. Calif. coun. legis. com. 1996—), Am. Soc. Hosp. Engrs., Design Profls. Safety Assn. (bd. dirs.). Office: 250 Sutter St San Francisco CA 94108-4403

THODE, EDWARD FREDERICK, chemical engineer, educator; b. N.Y.C., May 31, 1921; s. E. Frederick and Kathleen V. (McGowan) T.; m. Isobel Zoeller, May 27, 1944; children: Karen (Mrs. Paul M. O'Neil), Stephen Frederick, Jonathan Edward. S.B., M.I.T., 1942, S.M., 1943, Sc.D., 1947. Registered profl. engr., Maine, N.Mex. Chem. engr. Boston Woven Hose & Rubber Co., Cambridge, Mass.; asst. prof. chem. engring. U. Maine, Orono, 1947-49; asso. prof. U. Maine, 1949-54; sr. research engr. 3M Co., St. Paul, 1954-55; research asso., faculty mem. Inst. Paper Chemistry, Appleton, Wis., 1955-63; mgr. dept. engring. computer and computer ctr. Inst. Paper Chemistry, 1959-63; prof. chem. engring. N.Mex. State U., Las Cruces, 1963-74; head dept. chem. engring. N.Mex. State U., 1963-74, prof. mgmt., 1974-86, prof. emertus chem. engring. and mgmt., 1986—; cons. Am. Cyanamid Co., IBM, Gen. Elec. Co., Bell Telephone Labs.; affiliate staff mem. Los Alamos Sci. Lab., 1965-90; propr. EIT Cons., 1972-91. Contbr. numerous articles to profl. jours. Mem. exec. bd. Yucca council Boy Scouts Am., 1968-

72; dir. Mesilla Park Heritage Assn., 1988-93, sec., 1988-89, v.p., 1990, pres. 1991; treas. Mesilla Valley Conf. Chs., 1989; vestryman, lay reader, lay eucharistic minister, warden, 1970, 71, 87, 93, 94. Recipient Disting. faculty award N. Mex. State U., 1981, 83. Mem. Am. Inst. Chem. Engrs. (chmn. Rio Grande sect. 1990), Am. Soc. Engring. Edn., Sigma Xi, Tau Beta Pi, Beta Gamma Sigma, Phi Kappa Phi. Republican. Episcopalian. Home: 905 Conway Ave Apt 45 Las Cruces NM 88005-3775 *To discover God's will for our lives is difficult; the search is worth the effort.*

THOEN, JOHN EUGEN, psychiatric nurse; b. Homestead, Fla., Jan. 17, 1959; s. Victor Isidor and Eugenia (Franco) T. LPN, South Miami Hosp., 1983; BSN, U. Miami, 1983. Diplomate Am. Bd. Quality Assurance and Utilization Rev. Charge nurse Cmty. Health, Inc., Miami, Fla., 1982-84; dir. nursing N.W. Dade Ctr., Inc., Hialeah, Fla., 1984-94, dir. quality improvement, 1990-92, utilization rev. cons., 1994—; evening supr. START program Bayview Ctr., Hollywood, Fla., 1988-93; team leader mobile crisis Harborview Hosp., Miami, 1992-93; v.p. clin. ops. and quality asurance St. Thomas Health Svcs., Inc., Coral Gables, Fla., 1994-95; dir. rehab. svcs. N.W. Dade Ctr., Inc., Hialeah, Fla., 1995—; infection control cons. Harbor View Hosp., Miami, 1993—; bilingual nurse cons. Am. Day Treatment Ctr., Miami, 1993; infection control chmn. N.W. Dade Ctr., Inc., Hialeah, 1987-89, 90, 92, profl. exec. staff sec., 1987, 88, safety com. chmn., 1987, 88; mem. bd., pres. Total Nursing Care, 1988, 89, 90; bd. mem. St. Thomas Managed Health Svcs., Inc., 1994. Vol. Reagan campaign Rep. party, Miami, 1980, Hurricane Response Team, Health and Rehab. Svcs., Miami, 1992-93, Friendship Games, Dade County Mental Health Alliance, Miami, 1986-88. Mem. Am. Bd. Quality Assurance (affiliate mem.), South Fla. Mental Health Nurses Assn. (treas. 1989, 90). Republican. Baptist. Avocations: antique collecting, aquatic sports, gardening, voice, guitar. Home: 9205 SW 149th St Miami FL 33176-7920 Office: NW Dade Ctr Inc 4175 W 20th Ave Hialeah FL 33012

THOLE, MARY ELIZABETH, insurance sales representative; b. Salt Lake City, July 29, 1950; d. John Bernard and Emily Josephine T.; 1 child, William Lance Ulich. BA, U. Hawaii, Hilo, 1984, paralegal cert. cum laude, 1989; postgrad.in bus. administrn., U. Hawaii, Manoa, 1985-86. Lic. ins. agt. Hawaii. Regional rep. Lightolier, Inc., Salt Lake City, 1978-80; group sales rep. FHP/Utah, Salt Lake City, 1980-81; health net rep. Blue Cross Corp., L.A., 1981-82; v.p. fin. Bus. Support Systems, Hilo, 1983-89; rep. Prudential Ins. and Fin. Svcs., Honolulu, 1989—; registered rep. Pruco Securities Corp. subs. The Prudential, 1989—. Docent Lyman House, 1984-85, L.A. County Mus. of Art, 1980-81, S.L.C. Art Mus., 1970-80; bd. dirs. YWCA, Hawaii Island, 1980-91, 1st v.p., 1988. Recipient Nat. Quality award 1991, 92, 93, 94, Nat. Sales Achievement award 1992, 93; named YWCA Vol. of Yr., 1991. Fellow Life Underwriters Tng. Coun.; mem. AAUW (fundraiser chair Kona chpt. 1992, bd. dirs. Hilo chpt. 1987-89, comty. area rep. 1989), Am. Bus. Women's Assn. (pres. Nani O Hilo chpt. 1995—, cmty. svc. chair 1993-95, audit com. chair Kanoelani chpt. 1992, program chair Hilo chpt. 1985, expansion com. Hilo Lehua chpt. 1985, Steven Bufton grantee 1985, ways and means com. 1984, memberships chair Lehua chpt. 1983), Nat. Assn. Life Underwriters (legis. rep. West Hawaii 1989—), Million Dollar Round Table (qualifying mem. 1992, 93, 94, 95). Roman Catholic.

THOM, DOUGLAS ANDREW, paper company executive; b. San Mateo, Calif., Nov. 1, 1939; s. Andrew Phillip and Mary Agnes (Bailey) T.; m. Lisbeth Jane Steinhauer, Mar. 17, 1962; children: Cathryn, Mark, Kristen. BS in Graphic Communications, Calif. Poly. State U., 1962. Supr. Container Corp. Am., Oakland, Calif., 1962-68; supr. Ga. Pacific, San Francisco, 1968-70, plant mgr., 1970-73; gen. mgr. Ga. Pacific, Sheboygan, Wis., 1973-79, regional mgr., 1979-85; regional mgr. Ga. Pacific, Atlanta, 1985, v.p. package div., 1985-88; v.p. Containerboard Mfg., Atlanta, 1989-90, v.p. packaging div., 1990—. Bd. dirs. YMCA, Sheboygan, 1979-85. Mem. Fiber Box Assn. (chmn. 1988-89, bd. dirs.), Internat. Corrugated Packaging Found. (bd. dirs.), Internat. Corrugated Case Assn. (bd. dirs.), Pine Hills Country Club (pres. 1983-84), Cherokee Town and Country Club. Republican. Roman Catholic. Avocation: golf.

THOM, JOSEPH M., librarian; b. Bronx, N.Y., Oct. 22, 1919; s. Harry and Jennie T.; m. Lillian Rosenstein, Sept. 1, 1945; children—Janice Eleanor, Eric Frederick. B.A., N.Y.U., 1948, M.A., 1949; M.S. in L.S, Columbia, 1950; postgrad., Washington U., St. Louis, 1951-53, Ohio U., 1958-59. Library asst. N.Y.U., 1940-42, 46-49; library fellow Bklyn. Coll., 1949-50; chief reference dept. Washington U., 1950-53, instr. librarianship, 1950-54; dir. Research Information Service of St. Louis, 1954-55; supr. records and library Goodyear Atomic Corp., 1955-60; dir. libraries Yeshiva U., 1960; librarian Port Jefferson (N.Y.) Schs.; library and multi-media cons. on design and services. Editor: Reference Sources in Education, 1953, Personnel Notes and News; Compiler: Reference Sources in Politcal Science, 1953; Contbr. articles to profl. jours. Served with AUS, 1942-45. Home: PO Box 2514 East Setauket NY 11733-0755

THOM, RICHARD DAVID, aerospace executive; b. St. Louis, Oct. 4, 1944; s. Reginald James and Vlasta (Koukl) T.; m. Linda Marie Hunt, Sept. 9, 1967; children: Elizabeth Marie, Robert James. BS in Physics, U. Mo., Rolla, 1967; MSEE, UCLA, 1971. Co-op engr. McDonnell Aircraft Corp., St. Louis, 1962-67; head advanced tech. group IR systems dept., aerospace group Hughes Aircraft Co., Culver City, Calif., 1967-72; mem. tech. staff Santa Barbara Rsch. Ctr., Hughes Aircraft Co., Goleta, Calif., 1972-76, asst. mgr. R&D Lab., 1976-80, mgr. advanced applications, 1980-83, chief engr., 1984-86, chief scientist, 1986-90, dir. tech., 1990-95; tech. program exec. Hughes Aircraft Co., Goleta, Calif., 1995—. Contbr. articles to profl. jours.; patentee in field. Recipient Hughes Group Patent award for pioneering contbns. in infrared detector tech., 1990. Mem. IEEE, Tau Beta Pi, Sigma Pi Sigma, Delta Sigma Phi. Republican. Avocation: freelance travel writing and photography, specializing in railway travel around the world. Home: 1236 Camino Palomera Santa Barbara CA 93111-1013 Office: Santa Barbara Rsch Ctr 75 Coromar Dr Goleta CA 93117-3088

THOMAJAN, ROBERT, lawyer, management and financial consultant; b. N.Y.C., May 4, 1941; s. Leon and Fay T. BS, NYU, 1962; JD, St. John's U., 1965. Bar: N.Y. 1965, U.S. Ct. Appeals (2nd cir.) 1966, U.S. Dist. Ct. (ea. and so. dists.) N.Y. 1967, U.S. Ct. Internat. Trade 1975, U.S. Supreme Ct. 1975, U.S. Ct. Appeals (9th cir.) 1976, U.S. Dist. Ct. (we. dist.) Tex. 1979, Tex. 1987. Atty. Nixon, Mudge, Rose, Guthrie, Alexander & Mitchell, N.Y.C., 1964-68; ptnr. Milgrim, Thomajan & Lee, N.Y.C., 1968-91; mng. dir. Caribbean Capital Ltd., 1994—; pres. Eterna Benefits, Austin, Tex., 1995—. Arbitrator Civil Ct., N.Y., 1981-86; mem. adv. bd. Ronald McDonald House, 1988-90; bd. dirs., counsel Big Bros./Big Sisters, 1988-90; mem. World Econ. Forum, 1990-93. Mem. Am. Soc. Internat. Law, Asia-Pacific Layers Assn., Internat. Law Assn. Office: 7800 MoPac Expy N Ste 105 Austin TX 78759

THOMAN, G. RICHARD, computer company executive; b. Tuscaloosa, Ala., June 25, 1944; s. Richard S. and Evelyn (Zumwalt) T.; m. Wenke Helina Brier, Aug. 25, 1966 (div. Dec. 1987); children: Camille, Alexis; m. Lynn Susan Bendheim, Sept. 24, 1989; children: Arielle, Max. BA with honors, McGill U., 1966; diploma, Grad. Inst. Internat. Studies, Geneva, 1968; MA in Internat. Econs., Tufts U., 1971, PhD Fletcher Sch. Law & Diplomacy, 1971. Exec. trainee Citicorp, N.Y.C., 1968-69; sr. fin. analyst Exxon Corp., N.Y.C., 1968-72; sr. assoc. McKinsey and Co., N.Y.C and Paris, 1972-79; exec. v.p., CFO Am. Express Travel Related Svcs., N.Y.C., 1979-85, pres., Travel Related Svcs. Internat., 1985-89, chmn., CEO, 1989-92; pres., CEO Nabisco Internat. RJR Nabisco, Inc., N.Y.C., 1992-94; sr. v.p., group exec. IBM Corp., Somers, N.Y., 1994—; now sr. v.p., cfo IBM Corp., Armok, NY; bd. dirs. Union Banque Prive, Geneva, Club Med, Paris. Author: Foreign Investment and Regional Development, 1972. Bd. dirs. Ams. Soc., N.Y.C., 1990—; bd. advisors Fletcher Sch. of Law and Diplomacy, Tufts U., Medford, Mass., 1990—. Recipient Legion of Honors, Govt. of France, 1992. Mem. Coun. on Fgn. Rels. Avocations: tennis, reading, jogging, travel. Office: IBM Corp Old Orchard Rd Armonk NY 10504*

THOMAN, HENRY NIXON, lawyer; b. Cin., May 5, 1957; s. Richard B. and Barbara (Lutz) T.; m. Kathleen Brewer Thoman, Aug. 14, 1982; children: Victoria E., Nicholas B. BA, Duke U., 1979; JD, U. Chgo., 1982. Bar: Ohio 1982, U.S. Dist. Ct. (so. dist.) Ohio, 1982. With Taft, Stettinius & Hollister, Cin., 1982-88; sr. atty. John Morrell & Co., Cin., 1988-90; sr. counsel Chiquita Brands Internat. Inc., Cin., 1990-91, corp. planner, 1991-92; sr. dir. CTP ops. Chiquita Brands, Inc., Cin., 1993-94, chief adminstrv. officer Armuelles divsn., 1994-95; corp. counsel The Loewen Group, Covington, Ky., 1995—. Mem. counselors com. U.S. Swimming, Colo., 1983-89; bd. dirs. Friends of Cin. Parks, 1990-93, 96—, Mariemont Aquatic Club, v.p., 1992-93; pres. Club Atletico Y Socialde Chiriqui, 1994-95. Mem. Ohio State Bar, Cin. Bar Assn. Office: The Loewen Group 50 E River Center Blvd Covington KY 41011

THOMAN, MARK, lawyer; b. Cin., Apr. 28, 1935; s. Henry Augustus and Valeska (Wurlitzer) T.; child by previous marriage, George; m. Nancy Flaun Karlins, Oct. 1, 1981. B.A., Yale U., 1956; LL.B., Harvard U., 1959. Bar: N.Y. 1960. Assoc. Lord Day & Lord, Barrett Smith and predecessor firm, N.Y.C., 1960-66, ptnr., 1966-94; ptnr. McDermott, Will & Emery, N.Y.C., 1994—. Mem. N.Y. Athletic Club. Home: 100 Ridgewood Ave Glen Ridge NJ 07028-1016 Office: McDermott Will & Emery 1211 6th Ave New York NY 10036

THOMAN, MARK EDWARD, pediatrician; b. Chgo., Feb. 15, 1936; s. John Charles and Tasula Mark (Petrakis) T.; AA, Graceland Coll., 1956; BA, U. Mo., 1958, MD, 1962; m. Theresa Thompson, 1984; children: Marlisa Rae, Susan Kay, Edward Kim, Nancy Lynn, Janet Lea, David Mark. Intern, U. Mo. at Columbia, 1962-63; resident in pediatrics Blank Meml. Children's Hosp., Des Moines, 1963-65, chief resident, 1964-65; cons. in toxicology, 1966-67; chief dept. pediatrics Shiprock (N.Mex.) Navajo Indian Hosp., dir. N.D. Poison Info. Center, also practice medicine, specializing in pediatrics Quain & Ramstad Clinic, Bismarck, N.D., 1967-69; dir. Iowa Poison Info. Center, Des Moines, 1969—; pvt. solo practice pediatrics, Des Moines, 1969—; sr. aviation med. examiner, accident investigator FAA, 1976—, cons., lectr., 1977—; faculty Iowa State U., U. Iowa, U. Osteo. Sci. and Health; dir. Cystic Fibrosis Clinic, 1973-82; dir. Mid-Iowa Drug Abuse Program, 1972-76; mem. med. adv. bd. La Leche League Internat., 1965—; pres. Medic-Air Ltd., 1976—; aviation seminars lectr. Editor-in-chief AACTION, 1975-90. Bd. dirs. Polk County Pub. Health Nurses Assn., 1969-77, Des Moines Speech and Hearing Center, 1974-79, Ecumenical Coun. of Iowa, 1990—; bd. govs. Mo. U. Sch. Medicine Alumni, 1988—, pres.- elect, 1995. Served with USMCR, 1954-59; lt. comdr. USPHS, 1965-66; capt. USNR, 1993—; dir. Dept. Health Svcs. USNR. Recipient N.D. Gov.'s award of merit, 1969; Cystic Fibrosis Rsch. Found. award, 1975, Am. Psychiat. Assn. Thesis award, Diplomate Am. Bd. Pediatrics, Am. Bd. Med. Toxicology (examiner). 1962. Mem. AMA (del. 1970-88), NRA (life), Assn. Am. Physicians & Surgeons, Polk County Med. Soc., Iowa State Med. Assn., Aerospace Med. Assn., Res. Officers Assn., Civil Aviation Med. Assn., Am. Public Health Assn., 1986—, Soc. Adolescent Medicine, Inst. Clin. Toxicology, Internat. Soc. Pediatrics, Am. Acad. Pediatrics (chmn. accident prevention com. Iowa chpt. 1975—), Cystic Fibrosis Club, Am. Acad. Clin. Toxicology (trustee 1969-90, pres. 1982-84), Am. Assn. Poison Control Centers, U.S. Naval Inst. Republican. Elder mem. Reorganized Latter-Day Saints Ch. Clubs: Flying Physicians, Aircraft Owners and Pilots Assn., Nat. Pilots Assn. (Safe Pilot award), Hyperion Field and Country. Editor in chief AACTION, 1976-90. Home: 6896 Trail Ridge Dr Johnston IA 50131-1322 Office: 1426 Woodland Ave Des Moines IA 50309-3204

THOMAS, ADRIAN WESLEY, laboratory director; b. Edgefield, S.C., June 23, 1939; s. Hasting Adrian and Nancy Azalena (Bridges) T.; m. Martha Elizabeth McAllister, July 12, 1964; children: Wesley Adrian, Andrea Elizabeth. BS in Agrl. Engring., Clemson U., 1962, MS in Agrl. Engring., 1965; PhD, Colo. State U., 1972. Rsch. scientist USDA-Agrl. Rsch. Svc., Tifton, Ga., 1965-69, Fort Collins, Colo., 1969-72; rsch. leader USDA-Agrl. Rsch. Svc., Walkinsville, Ga., 1972-89; lab. dir. USDA-Agrl. Rsch. Svc., Tifton, 1989—; mem. acad. faculty Colo. State U. Ft. Collins, 1969-72; acad. faculty U. Ga., Athens, 1973—, grad. faculty, 1988—. Contbr. agrl. rsch. articles to profl. jours. With U.S. Army, 1962-63. Mem. Am. Soc. Agrl. Engrs., Am. Soc. Agronomy, Soil and Water Conservation Soc. Am., Soil Sci. Soc. Am., Sigma Xi, Alpha Epsilon, Gamma Sigma Delta, Phi Kappa Phi. Lutheran. Avocations: reading, gardening, yard care, remodeling home, sports. Office: USDA Agrl Rsch Svc PO Box 946 Tifton GA 31793-0946

THOMAS, ALAN RICHARD, natural resources products executive; b. Toronto, Ont., Can., Dec. 14, 1942; s. Ronald H. Thomas and Edna M. Green; m. Jill H.E. Parkinson; children: Kimberley Anne, Michael. B in Commerce, U. Toronto, 1964. Chartered acct., Ont. Ptnr. Enrst & Young, Toronto, 1964-87; CFO, treas. Noranda Inc., Toronto, 1987—. Recipient Bronze medal Can. Inst. Chartered Accts., 1967. Mem. Ont. Inst. Chartered Accts., Donalda Club, Toronto Cricket Club, Cambridge Club, Royal Ottawa Golf Club. Mem. United Ch. Can. Office: Noranda Inc, 181 Bay St Ste 4100 PO Box 755, Toronto, ON Canada M5J 2T3

THOMAS, ALLEN LLOYD, lawyer, private investor; b. Orange, N.J., Sept. 15, 1939; s. Richard Lloyd and Dorothy (Carr) T.; m. Virginia Dehnert, June 24, 1961 (div. 1974); children: Sarah Ann, Anne Marjorie; m. Barbara Singer, Mar. 12, 1978; 1 child, Allen Lloyd Jr. BA, Wesleyan U., 1961; LLB, Yale U., 1964. Bar: N.Y. 1965, U.S. Ct. Appeals (D.C. cir.) 1981. Ptnr. Paul Weiss Rifkind Wharton & Garrison, N.Y.C., 1964-92; resident ptnr. Hong Kong, 1983-87; dir., gen. counsel Gerard Atkins & Co. Ltd., 1992-94; gen. counsel Gen. Atlantic Group Ltd, 1992-94; chmn. Ockham Holdings PLC; bd. dirs. Penna PLC. Chmn. Urban Bus. Assis. Corp., N.Y.C., 1971-82; chmn. Hong Kong Ballet, 1985-87; co-chmn. Internat. Com., N.Y.C. Ballet, 1986-91; pres. Internat. Salzburg Assn. Am., 1987-92; dir., mem. exec. com., gen. counsel Child Care Action Campaign, 1990-92. Fellow Am. Coll. Investment Counsel, Hartford, Conn. Mem. River Club, N.Y. Met. Club of Washington, Hong Kong Club, Royal Hong Kong Jockey Club, Coral Beach and Tennis Club, Lenox Club, Buck's Club. Home: 3 Chester St, London SW1X 7BB, England

THOMAS, ALTA PARKER, secondary school educator; b. Butte, Mont., Sept. 18, 1940; d. Charles Clayton and Sarah Elizabeth (Bennett) Parker Hopkins; m. Vivian William Thomas Jr., Aug. 19, 1962; children: Christine Michelle, Thomas Walters, Tracy Ann, Thomas, Lisa Janine Thomas Julson. BS, Mont. State U., 1962; MEd, Walla Walla Coll., 1991. Cert. tchr., Wash. Rsch. chemist Dow Chem. Co., Midland, Mich., 1962-64; tchr. Granite Sch. Dist., Salt Lake City, 1964-65; home and hosp. tchr. Richland (Wash.) Schs., 1975-77; sci. tchr. Kennewick (Wash.) Sch. Dist., 1977-84, high sch. biology tchr., 1984—, sci. dept. chair, 1992-94; coord. Internat. Baccalaureate Kennewick Sch. Dist., 1994—, chmn. sci. curriculum com., 1987-89, rep. dist. circle com., 1991—; coach sci. olympiad team Kennewick H.S., 1988-94, mem. staff devel. com., 1985-91, site coun., 1995. Patented oven cleaner formula; editor: Curnutt Family Cookbook, 1986. Founder acad. booster club Kennewick High Sch., 1985. REST fellow Battelle Pacific N.W. Lab., 1988. Mem. Nat. Assn. Biology Tchrs., NEA, Wash. Edn. Assn., Kennewick Edn. Assn. (rep., negotiator 1977—), Wash. Sci. Tchr. Assn., Delta Kappa Gamma (membership chair, polit. affairs chair 1984—). Presbyterian. Avocations: birding, hiking, cross stitch, quilting, reading. Home: 4029 S Cascade St Kennewick WA 99337-5185 Office: Kennewick High Sch 500 S Dayton St Kennewick WA 99336-5640

THOMAS, ANN VAN WYNEN, lawyer, educator; b. The Netherlands, May 27, 1919; came to U.S., 1921, naturalized, 1926; d. Cornelius and Cora Jacoba (Daansen) Van Wynen; m. A.J. Thomas Jr., Sept. 10, 1948. AB with distinction, U. Rochester, 1940; JD, U. Tex., 1943; post doctoral degree, So. Meth. U., 1952. U.S. fgn. svc. officer Johannesburg, South Africa, London, The Hague, The Netherlands, 1943-47; rsch. atty. Southwestern Legal Found., Sch. Law So. Meth. U., Dallas, 1952-67; asst. prof. polit. sci. Sch. Law So. Meth. U., 1968-73, assoc. prof., 1973-76, prof., 1976-85; prof. emeritus So. Meth. U. Sch. Law, 1985—. Author: Communism versus International Law, 1953, (with A.J. Thomas Jr.) International Treaties, 1950, Non-Intervention—The Law and its Import in the Americas, 1956, OAS: The Organization of American States, 1962, International Legal Aspects of Civil War in Spain, 1936-1939, 1967, Legal Limitations on Chemical and Biological Weapons, 1970, The Concept of Aggression, 1972, Presidential War Making Power: Constitutional and International Law Aspects, 1981, An International Rule of Law—Problems and Prospects, 1974. Chmn. time capsule com. Grayson County Commn. on Tex. Sesquicentennial, 1986-88; co-chmn. Grayson County Commn. on Bicentennial U.S. Constn., 1988-93; co-chmn. com. Grayson County Sesquicentennial, 1994—. Recipient Am. medal Nat. DAR Soc., 1992. Mem. Tex. Bar Assn., Am. Soc. Internat. Law, Grayson County Bar Assn. Home: Spaniel Hall RR 2, Box 444T Pottsboro TX 75076

THOMAS, BARBARA ANN, record company executive; b. Bklyn., Feb. 5, 1948; d. Wilfred Godfrey and Violet Rose (Howell) Swaby; m. Ronald L. Hannah (div.). Adminstrv. asst. Million Dollar Record Poll, College Park, Ga., 1985-86, Points East Records, College Park, 1986-87, Greer Booking Agy., Atlanta, 1986-87; pres. Gunsmoke Records, College Park, 1988—; v.p. Toroy Mercedes Records, 1994—; mgr. Jesse James, 1983—. Mem. NAFE, Blues Found., Atlanta Top Star Awards, Nat. Young Black Programmers (bd. dirs.), Nat. Club Owners, Promoters and Entertainment Assn. (bd. dirs.). Democrat. Roman Catholic. Office: Gunsmoke Records 2523 Roosevelt Hwy Ste 3D Atlanta GA 30337-6243

THOMAS, BERTHA SOPHIA, office manager, paralegal; b. Chgo., May 18, 1959; d. James Winston, Jr. and Juanita (Smith) T.; 1 child, Kamarya Lynell. Cert., Am. Inst. Paralegal Studies, 1988; student, Nat. Coll. Edn., 1988—. Supr. filing systems Susan E. Loggans & Assocs., Chgo., 1979-81; legal sec. Harth, Stroger, Boarman & Blue, Chgo., 1982-83, Lidov & Block, Chgo., 1984-86; paralegal, office mgr. Law Office Mary L. Sfasciotti, Chgo., 1987-89; paralegal, personal injury specialist Neal B. Strom and Assocs., Ltd., Chgo., 1988-90; office mgr., paralegal Spencer W. Schwartz & Assocs., P.C., Chgo., 1990-93; co-owner B&B Paralegal Svc., Chgo., 1994—. Mem. NAFE, PHA, Ill. Notary Assn., Order Eastern Star, Heroines of Jericho, Daughters of Isis, Omega Pearl, Omega Psi Phi. Democrat. Roman Catholic. Avocations: literature, chess, sports. Home: 11329 S Peoria St Chicago IL 60643-4611 Office: B&B Paralegal Svc 11329 S Peoria St Chicago IL 60643-4611

THOMAS, BESSIE, primary education educator; b. Shreveport, La., Nov. 30, 1943; d. Fleen and Tommie Lee (Anderson) Myles; m. Jesse Thomas, May 11, 1968 (dec. 1995). BS, Grambling Coll., 1966; MS, Grambling State U., 1976; postgrad., various colls. and univs., 1967-79. Cert. primary and elem. tchr., La. 1st grade tchr. Pine St. Sch., Hamburg, Ark., 1966-67, Pine Grove Elem. Sch., Shreveport, 1967-70, Mooringsport (La.) Sch., 1970-81; early childhood edn. tchr. Fairfield Elem. Sch., Shreveport, 1981—. Active Word of Faith Christian Ctr. Grantee Caddo Pub. Edn. Found., 1995—. Mem. NEA, Nat. Assn. for Edn. Young Children, ASCD, Reading Tchr., Assn. for Childhood Edn. Internat., PTA. Democrat. Avocations: inspirational reading, painting T-shirts, travel, interacting with children, viewing works of art. Home: 2831 Abbie St Shreveport LA 71103-2130

THOMAS, BETTY, actress; b. St. Louis. BFA, Ohio U. Former sch. tchr.; co-star Hill St. Blues, from 1981; Joined Second City Workshop, Chgo.; appeared on Second City TV, 1984; appeared in after sch. spl. The Gift of Love, 1985, Prison of Children, 1986. Appeared in The Fun Factory game show, 1976; film: Troop Beverly Hills, 1989; in TV film Outside Chance, 1978, Nashville Grab, 1981, When Your Lover Leaves, 1983; star TV series Hill Street Blues, 1981-87 (Emmy nominations 1981, 82, 83); dir.: (TV) Dream On: "For Peter's Sake" (Emmy award, Outstanding Individual Achievement in Directing in a Comedy Series, 1993), 1993, (film) The Brady Bunch Movie, 1995. Emmy Best Supporting Actress, 1985. Office: care ICM c/o Richard Feldman 8942 Wilshire Blvd Beverly Hills CA 90211*

THOMAS, BEVERLY IRENE, special education educator; b. Del Rio, Tex., Nov. 12, 1939; d. Clyde Louis and Eve Naomi (Avant) Whistler; m. James Henry Thomas, Jan. 28, 1972; children: Kenneth (dec.), Wade, Robert, Darcy, Betty Kay, James III, Debra, Brenda, Michael. BM summa cum laude, Sul Ross State U., 1972, MMEd, 1976, MEd in Counseling, 1992. Cert. music, elem. edn., music edn., learning disabilities, spl. edn. generic, ednl. diagnosis, ednl. counseling, spl. edn. counseling and mid. mgmt. Spliedn Supr. Edn. diagnostician West Tex. State Sch., Tex. Youth Commn. Mem. AAUW, ASCD, NEA, MENSA, Assn. for Children with Learning Disabilities (local sec. 1974), Tex. State Tchrs. Assn. (treas. 1991-94), Tex. Ednl. Diagnosticians Assn., Tex. Profl. Ednl. Diagnosticians, Reeves County Assn. of Children with Learning Disabilities, Nat. Coun. Tchrs. of Maths., Nat. Coun. Tchrs. English, Learning Disabilities Assn., Learning Disabilities Assoc., Tex., Coun. for Exceptional Children, Tex. Counseling Assn., Alpha Chi, Kappa Delta Pi. Home: 2410 S Eddy St Pecos TX 79772-7514

THOMAS, BILLY MARSHALL, retired army officer; b. Crystal City, Tex., Aug. 14, 1940; s. Harold Dennis and Ivy Marie (Moore) T.; m. Judith Kathryn McConnell, Jan. 31, 1981; children: Jonathon Scott, Kimberly Michelle, Jeanette Kirsten, David Eldon. BS, Tex. Christian U., 1962; MS, George Washington U., 1974; postgrad., Army War Coll., Carlisle, Pa., 1980, Harvard U., 1986. Commd. 2d lt. U.S. Army, 1962, advanced through grades to lt. gen., 1990; co. comdr. U.S. Army, Vietnam, 1968; pers. staff officer U.S. Army Mil. Pers. Ctr., Alexandria, Va., 1974-77; bn. comdr. 5th signal bn. 5th Div., Ft. Polk, La., 1977-79; brigade comdr. 93d signal brigade VII U.S. Corps, Stuttgart, Germany, 1981-83; dep. comdg. gen. U.S. Army Signal Ctr. and Sch., Ft. Gordon, Ga., 1983-85; mem. staff for rsch., devel. and acquisition Dept. Army, Washington, 1985-87; comdg. gen. Communications and Electronics Command, Ft. Monmouth, N.J., 1987-90; dep. comdg. gen. for rsch., devel. and acquisition Army Materiel Command, Alexandria, 1990-92; founder, chmn. Engring. and Mgmt. Execs. Inc., Alexandria, Va., 1992-95; v.p. bus. devel. ITT Def. and Electronics, McLean, Va., 1995—; spkr. regional and nat. forums on quality mgmt., 1988-92. Contbr. articles to mil. publs. Host, chmn. Ft. Monmouth Mayor's Roundtable, 1987-90; host CEO's Round Table, Ft. Monmouth, 1987-90. Decorated Legion of Merit with two oak leaf clusters, Bronze Star medal with oak leaf cluster, D.S.M. with oak leaf cluster; named Vol. of Yr., Big Bros. and Big Sisters, N.J., 1990. Mem. Armed Forces Communications and Electronics Assn. (internat. bd. dirs. 1986-92, chmn. scholarship com. Edn. Found. 1986-90), Am. Def. Preparedness Assn., Assn. U.S. Army, Nat. Mil. Family Assn., DAV. Methodist. Avocations: golf, skiing, reading, jazz. Home: 8249 Clifton Farm Ct Alexandria VA 22306 Office: ITT Def and Electronics 1650 Tysons Blvd Ste 1700 Mc Lean VA 22102

THOMAS, BRENDA C., county official; b. Russell, Ky., Mar. 16, 1948; d. Charles X. and Jeannette Frances (Thompson) Calia; m. Evan Thomas, July 11, 1972; children: Alexandra Logan, Jessica Theon, Erin Elizabeth. Dir. Am. Lang. Ctr., Fez, Morocco, 1968-70; proprietor The Bookshop, St. Paul, 1981-90. Commr. human rights Roseville, Minn., 1979-88, chmn., 1986-88; mem. Roseville City Coun., 1990-92; commr. Ramsey County, 1993—. Office: Office Bd County Commrs Courthouse RM 220 15 Kellogg Blvd W Saint Paul MN 55102-1635

THOMAS, BRIAN CHESTER, state legislator, engineer; b. Tacoma, Wash., May 19, 1939; s. Ralph R. and Katheryne (Chester) T.; m. Judith Lynn Adams, Feb. 20, 1965; children: Jeffrey, Kyle, Cheryl. BS in Indsl. Engring., Oreg. State U., 1961; postgrad., U. Wash., 1968-70; MBA, Pacific Luth. U., 1979. Civil engr. U.S. Coast Guard, Seattle, 1962-63; ops. officer U.S. Coast Guard, Astoria, Oreg., 1964-65; sr. sales engr. Puget Sound Power & Light Co., Bellevue, Wash., 1965-70, mgr. market rsch., 1971-80, rsch. adminstr., 1981-89, prin. engr., 1989—; mem. Wash. Ho. of Reps., Olympia, 1993—, with joint select com. on edn. restructuring, 1991—; chmn. joint adminstrn. rules rev. com., 1995—; chmn. fin., edn., natural resources coms. Wash. Ho. of Reps., Olympia, 1991—; chair EEI Rsch. Mgmt. Com., Washington, 1988-89, EPRI Renewable Com., Palo Alto, Calif., 1989-90; adv. bd. Nat. Renewable Energy Lab., Golden, Colo., 1990-92; mem. adv. bd. sch. elec. engring. Oreg. State U., Corvallis, 1991-95; dep. dir. region 10 U.S. Dept. Transp. Emergency Orgn., Seattle, 1989-93. Bd. dirs. Issaquah (Wash.), Sch. Dist., 1989-93. Capt. USCGR, 1961-84. Mem. Issaquah Rotary (pres. 1982-83), Rainier Club. Republican. Avocation: restoring Studebakers. Home: 14715 182nd Pl SE Renton WA 98059-8028 Office: Wash Ho Reps PO Box 40610 Olympia WA 98504-0610 Office: Puget Sound Power & Light PO Box 97034 Bellevue WA 98009-9734

THOMAS, BROOKS, publishing company executive; b. Phila., Nov. 28, 1931; s. Walter Horstman and Ruth Sterling (Boomer) T.; m. Galen Pinckard Clark, Apr. 15, 1969 (div. 1973). B.A., Yale U., 1953, LL.B., 1956; grad., Advanced Mgmt. Program, Harvard, 1973. Bar: Pa. 1957, N.Y.

1960. With law firm Winthrop, Stimson, Putnam & Roberts, N.Y.C., 1960-68; sec., gen. counsel Harper & Row, Pubs., Inc., N.Y.C., 1968-69; v.p., gen. counsel Harper & Row, Pubs., Inc., 1969-73, exec. v.p., 1973-79, chief operating officer, 1977-81, pres., 1979-87, chief exec. officer, 1981-87, chmn. bd., 1986-87; chmn. bd. Harper & Row, Ltd., London, 1973-87; dir. Harper & Row, Pty. Ltd., Australia, Harla S.A. de C.V., Mex., Harper & Row Pubs. Asia, Pte. Ltd., Singapore. Pres., bd. dirs. Butterfield House, 1968-72, 90-93; trustee, dir. RADG, Inc., 1987-89; dir. Thompson Island Outward Bound Edn. Ctr., 1987—, Colo. Outward Bound Sch., 1990—; bd. dirs. Young Audiences, Inc., 1977—, chmn., 1985—; trustee Outward Bound USA, 1980—, vice chmn., 1983-84, chmn., 1984-87; chmn. Am. Book Awards, 1984-85, dir., 1985-87; mem. devel. bd. Yale U., 1985-89; adv. bd. Yale Sch. Orgn. and Mgmt., 1987—; chmn. Vail Valley Inst., 1989—. Lt. (j.g.) USNR, 1956-59. Mem. Am. Bar Assn., Assn. Bar City of N.Y., Assn. Am. Pubs. (bd. dirs. 1980-85, chmn. 1983-85), Council Fgn. Relations, Yale U. Alumni Assn. (law sch. rep. 1980-83). Clubs: Merion Cricket (Phila.); Century (N.Y.C.), Yale (N.Y.C.), University (N.Y.C.), N.Y. Yacht (N.Y.C.); Essex Yacht (Conn.). Home: 37 W 12th St New York NY 10011-8502 also: 141 Saybrook Rd Essex CT 06426-1412 also: 63 Willow Pl Vail CO 81657-5304

THOMAS, CALVERT, lawyer; b. Balt., Nov. 1, 1916; s. William Douglas Nelson and Elizabeth Steuart (Calvert) T.; m. Margaret Somervell Berry, Sept. 1, 1943; children—Calvert Bowie, Carolyn Brooke Dold. Douglas Mackubin. B.S., Washington and Lee U., 1938; LL.B., U. Md., 1940. Bar: Md. bar 1940, D.C. bar 1972, Mich. bar 1947, N.Y. State bar 1974, Conn. bar 1979. Asso. atty. Legal Aid Bur., Balt., 1940-41; atty. Lehmeyer & Moser, Balt., 1941-42, Solicitor's Office, Dept. Labor, Washington, 1942-43, Tax Ct. of U.S., Washington, 1943-44, Chief Counsel's Office, Bur. Internal Revenue, Washington, 1944-46; atty. legal staff Gen. Motors Corp., Detroit, 1946-72; asst. gen. counsel Gen. Motors Corp., 1972-78; sec., asst. gen. counsel in charge N.Y. legal staff, N.Y.C., 1973-78; chmn. Thomas Cadillac, Inc., 1978—. Councilman, Franklin Village, Mich., 1958-60, pres., 1960-64; Bd. dirs. Franklin Community Assn., 1956-58; vice chmn. Kingswood Sch., Cranbrook, 1968-69, chmn., 1969-71; trustee Cranbrook Schs., 1971-73, Washington and Lee U., 1975—; chmn. Old Guard West Hartford, 1992-93. Mem. Am., Fed., Detroit, Md., D.C., N.Y. bar assns., State Bar Mich. (chmn. tax sect. 1971-72), Am. Soc. Corp. Secs., So. Md. Soc., Soc. Colonial Wars, Lords of Md. Manors, Descendants of the Signers of the Declaration of Independence, Sons of the Am. Revolution, Soc. of the Ark and Dove, Soc. of Founders and Patriots of Am., Beta Theta Pi, Phi Delta Phi, Omicron Delta Kappa. Republican. Episcopalian. Clubs: Orchard Lake (Mich.) Country; Recess (Detroit); Princeton (N.Y.C.); Country of Farmington (Conn.); Hartford, Hartford Golf. Home: 138 Stoner Dr West Hartford CT 06107-1306 Office: 170 Weston St Box 1778 Hartford CT 06144-9999

THOMAS, CAROL TAYLOR, general services coordinator; b. Carthage, N.C., Jan. 13, 1952; d. Elbert Watson and Lela Frances (Reynolds) Taylor; m. Michael Conley Thomas, Sept. 8, 1973; children: Kelli R. Thomas, Melvin Conley Thomas. Student, Sandhills Community Coll., 1970-72. Asst. purchasing officer County of Moore, Carthage, N.C., 1978-83, purchasing officer, 1983—, purchasing officer, airport mgr., 1988—. Mem. Moore County Airport Adv. Com., N.C. Airport Assn., Nat. Purchasing Mgmt. Assn., Purchasing Mgmt. Assn. of Carolinas-Va. Inc. (triangle chpt. 1988—). Presbyterian. Avocations: gardening, exercising, bicycling, go kart racing, family. Office: Moore County Airport Moore County Courthouse PO Box 905 Carthage NC 28327

THOMAS, CHARLES ALLEN, JR., molecular biologist, educator; b. Dayton, Ohio, July 7, 1927; s. Charles Allen and Margaret Stoddard (Talbott) T.; m. Margaret M. Gay, July 7, 1951; children: Linda Carrick, Stephen Gay. AB, Princeton (N.J.) U., 1950; PhD, Harvard U., 1954. Rsch. scientist Eli Lilly Co., Indpls., 1954-55; NCR fellow U. Mich., Ann Arbor, 1955-56, prof. biophysics, 1956-57; prof. biophysics Johns Hopkins U., Balt., 1957-67; prof. biol. chemistry Med. Sch. Harvard U., Boston, 1967-78; chmn. dept. cellular biology Scripps Clinic & Rsch. Found., La Jolla, Calif., 1978-81; pres., dir. Helicon Found., San Diego, 1981—; founder, CEO The Syntro Corp., San Diego, 1981-82; founder, CEO, now dir. of R&D Pantox Corp., San Diego, 1989—; mem. genetics study sect. NIH, 1968-72; mem. rsch. grants com. Am. Cancer Soc., 1972-76, 79-85. Mem. editorial bd. Virology, 1967-73, Jour. Molecular Biology, 1968-72, BiOphysics Jour., 1965-68, Chromosoma, 1969-79, Analytic Biochemistry, 1970-79, Biochim Biophys. ACTA, 1973-79, Plasmid, 1977—. With USNR, 1945-46. NRC fellow, 1965-66. Mem. AAAS, Am. Acad. Arts and Scis., Am. Fedn. Biol. Chemists, Genetics Soc. Am., Am. Chem. Soc. Achievements include rsch. in genetic and structural orgn. of chromosomes and devel. of a practical assessment of ind. antioxidant def. system by analytical biochemistry. Home: 1640 El Paso Real La Jolla CA 92037-6304 Office: Helicon Foundation 4622 Santa Fe St San Diego CA 92109-1601

THOMAS, CHARLES HOWARD, II, federal official; b. Buffalo, June 23, 1934; s. John Charles Thomas and Helen (Wright) Cogswell; m. Lourana Swift, Dec. 28, 1956; children: John, Stuart, Jennifer Thomas McGrath, Andrew. AB, Harvard U., 1956; student, Nat. War Coll., 1977-78. Fgn. service officer U.S. Consulate, Cuidad Juarez, Mex., 1960-62, U.S. Embassy, La Paz, Bolivia, 1962-64, Dept. State, Washington, 1964-66; dep. dir. Peace Corps, Tegucigalpa, Honduras, 1966-67; dir. Peace Corps, Montevideo, Uruguay, 1967-69; polit. counselor U.S. Embassy, Lisbon, Portugal, 1974-77; dep. chief of mission U.S. Embassy, Brussels, 1982-85; dir. ops. ctr. Dept. State, Washington, 1970-74, dir. NATO affairs, 1978-82, dep. asst. sec. of state for European and Can. Affairs, 1985-89; amb. to Hungary Dept. State, Budapest, 1990-94; spl. envoy for Burdensharing Bur. Politico-Mil. Affairs Dept. State, Washington, 1994; exec. dir. Spl. Group. on Ea. Europe, 1994; spl. envoy for former Yugoslavia, U.S. rep. on contact group, 1994-95, spl. envoy for Bosnian Fedn., 1995. Served to lt., USN, 1956-59. Recipient Heroism award, Dept. State, 1965. Mem. Am. Fgn. Service Assn. Episcopalian. Avocation: skiing.

THOMAS, CHRISTOPHER YANCEY, III, surgeon, educator; b. Kansas City, Mo., Oct. 27, 1923; s. Christopher Yancey and Dorothea Louise (Engel) T.; m. Barbara Ann Barcroft, June 27, 1946; children—Christopher, Gregg, Jeffrey, Anne. Student, U. Colo., 1942-44; M.D., U. Kans., 1948. Diplomate Am. Bd. Surgery. Intern U. Utah Hosp., Salt Lake City, 1948-49; resident in surgery Cleve. Clinic Found., 1949-52; pvt. practice specializing in surgery Kansas City, Mo., 1954-89; mem. staff St. Luke's Hosp., chief surgery, 1969-70; mem. staff Children's Mercy Hosp.; prof. surgery U. Mo., Kansas City Med. Sch.; pres. St. Luke's Hosp. Edn. Found., 1977-83, Med. Plaza Corp., 1977-79; pres. Midwest Organ Bank, 1977-82. Editor IMTRAC investment adv. letter, 1978—. Served to capt. M.C., U.S. Army, 1952-54. Fellow ACS; mem. AMA, Southwestern Surg. Congress, Central Surg. Assn., Mo. State Med. Soc., Kansas City Surg. Soc. (pres. 1968), Jackson County Med. Soc. (pres. 1971). Republican. Methodist. Club: Kansas City Country. Home: 5830 Mission Dr Shawnee Mission KS 66208-1139 Office: 4210 Shawnee Mission Pky Mission KS 66205-2506

THOMAS, CLARA MCCANDLESS, retired English language educator, biographer; b. Strathroy, Ont., Can., May 22, 1919; d. Basil and Mabel (Sullivan) McCandless; m. Morley Keith Thomas, May 23, 1942; children: Stephen, John. B.A., U. Western Ont., London, 1941, M.A., 1944; Ph.D., U. Toronto, 1962; DLitt (hon.), York U., 1986, Trent U., 1991; LLD (hon.), Brock U., 1992. Instr. English U. Western Ont., London, 1947-61, U. Toronto, 1958-61; asst. prof. English York U., Toronto, 1961-68; prof. York U., 1969-84, prof. emeritus, 1984—; acad. adv. panel Social Scis. and Humanities Research Council, 1981-84; mem. Killam Awards Selection Bd., 1978-81. Author biography of Anna Jameson, 1967, of Egerton Ryerson, 1969, of Margaret Laurence, 1969, 75, of William Arthur Deacon, 1982; Literary criticism (Can.), 1946, 72, 94; mem. editl. bd. Literary History of Can., 1980—, Collected Works of Northrop Frye, 1993—. Recipient Internat. Coun. of Can. Studies prize No. Telecom, 1989; grantee Can. Coun., 1967, 73, Social Sci. and Humanities Rsch. Coun. Can., 1978-80. Fellow Royal Soc. Can.; mem. Assn. Can. Univs., Tchrs. English (pres. 1971-72), Assn. Can. and Que. Lit., Bus. and Profl. Women's Club, Assn. for Can. Studies. New Democratic. Office: York U 305 Scott Libr, 4700 Keele St, Downsview, ON Canada M3J 1P3

THOMAS, CLARENCE, United States supreme court justice; b. Savannah, Ga., June 23, 1948. BA, Holy Cross Coll., 1971; JD, Yale U., 1974. Bar: Mo. Asst. atty. gen. State of Mo., Jefferson City, 1974-77; atty. Monsanto Co., St. Louis, 1977-79; legis. asst. to Sen. John C. Danforth, Washington, 1979-81; asst. sec. for civil rights Dept. Edn., Washington, 1981-82; chmn. U.S. EEOC, Washington, 1982-90; judge U.S. Ct. Appeals, Washington, 1990-91; assoc. justice U.S. Supreme Ct., Washington, 1991—. Office: US Supreme Court Supreme Ct Bldg 1 First St NE Washington DC 20543*

THOMAS, CLAUDEWELL SIDNEY, psychiatry educator; b. N.Y.C., Oct. 5, 1932; s. Humphrey Sidney and Frances Elizabeth (Collins) T.; m. Carolyn Pauline Rozansky, Sept. 6, 1958; children: Jeffrey Evan, Julie-Anne Elizabeth, Jessica Edith. BA, Columbia U., 1952; MD, SUNY, Downstate Med. Ctr., 1956; MPH, Yale U., 1964. Diplomate Nat. Bd. Med. Examiners, Am. Bd. Psychiatry. From instr. to assoc. prof. Yale U., New Haven, 1963-68, dir. Yale tng. program in social community psychiatry, 1967-70; dir. div. mental health service programs NIMH, Washington, 1970-73; chmn. dept. psychiatry U.M.D.N.J., Newark, 1973-83; prof. dept. psychiatry Drew Med. Sch., 1983—, chmn. dept. psychiatry, 1983-93; prof. dept. psychiatry UCLA, 1983-94, vice chmn. dept. psychiatry, 1983-93, prof. emeritus dept. psychiatry, 1994—; cons. A.K. Rice Inst., Washington, 1978-80, SAMSA/PHS Cons., 1991—; mem. L.A. County Superior Ct. Psych. Panel, 1991—. Author: (with B. Bergen) Issues and Problems in Contemporary Society, 1966; editor (with R. Bryce LaPorte) Alienation in Contemporary Society, 1976, (with J. Lindenthal) Psychiatry and Mental Health Science Handbook; mem. editorial bd. Internat. Jour. Mental Health, Adminstrn. In Mental Health. Served to capt. USAF, 1959-61. Fellow APHA, Am. Psychoanalytic Assn. (hon.), Am. Psychiat. Assn. (life), Royal Soc. Health, N.Y. Acad. Sci., N.Y. Acad. Medicine; mem. Am. Sociol. Assn. Avocations: tennis, racquetball, violin, piano. Home and Office: 30676 Palos Verdes Dr W Palos Verdes Peninsula CA 90274 *Personal philosophy: Integrity sooner or later calls upon courage. If courage is not home integrity goes away.*

THOMAS, CLAYTON ALLEN, JR., telecommunications executive; b. Lynchburg, Va., May 18, 1962; s. Clayton Allen T. and Alice Thomas (Knight) McLaughlin. BA, U. Va., 1985. Mktg. asst. IBM, Charlottesville, Va., 1983-84; mgr. info. systems Commonwealth of Va., Richmond, 1985-86; account exec. Bell Atlantic, Roanoke, Va., 1986-90; regional account mgr. Bell Atlantic, Washington, 1990-92, mgr. corp. accounts, 1992-93; pres. Net2000 Group, Inc., McLean, Va., 1993—. Event organizer, fundraiser local chpt. Cystic Fibrosis, Washington, 1991-92. Mem. Telecommunications Mgrs. Capitol Area, U. Va. Alumni Assn., Pi Kappa Alpha. Republican. Avocations: triathlons, golf, tennis, skiing, travel. Office: Net2000 Group Inc 1430 Spring Hill Rd Ste 401 Mc Lean VA 22102-3000

THOMAS, CLAYTON JAMES, air force executive; b. St. Joseph, Mo., Oct. 29, 1920; s. Gustave Bernard and Edith May (Eason) T.; m. Jerene Elizabeth Snuffer, Sept. 6, 1942; children: Sherry Kapfer, Theresa D'Alessandro, Ann Russell, Bruce, Julie Canavan. BS in Math., U. Chgo., 1942, MS in Math., 1947. Sr. mathematician, chief evaluation divsn. Inst. Air Weapons, U. Chgo., 1947-55; instr. U. Chgo., Roosevelt Coll., 1947-50; ops. rsch. analyst, chief rsch. group Office Ops. Analysis Hdqrs. USAF, Washington, 1955-71, sci. tech. advisor, chief scientist Studies & Analysis Agy., 1971—. Assoc. editor Mil. Ops. Rsch., 1993—. Mem. PTA, Park Forest, Ill., 1949-55, pres. 1954; mem. PTA, Arlington, Va., 1955-58, Annadale, Va., 1958-67, Great Falls, Va., 1967-83; com. mem., chair local coun. Girl Scouts Am., Cook County, Ill., Arlington, Va., 1953-57; hostparent, asst. to area chair Am. Field Svc. Student Exch. Program, Annandale, Great Falls, 1959—. Capt. U.S. Army, 1942-45. Recipient Exceptional Civilian Svc. award USAF, 1975, Citation of Honor Air Force Assn., 1980, Meritorious Exec. award Pres. of U.S., 1991, Lanchester prize Ops. Rsch. Soc. Am., 1958. Fellow AAAS, Mil. Ops. Rsch. Soc. (pres. 1973-74, Wanner award 1988, INFORMS Mil. App. sect., Stinhardt award 1994); mem. AIAA, Am. Math. Soc., Washington Soc. Engring., N.Y. Acad. Sci., Washington Ops. Rsch. and Mgmt. Sci. Coun., Phi Beta Kappa. Avocations: music (piano), reading (science, math, fiction), Foreign students and languages. Home: PO Box 932 Great Falls VA 22066-0932 Office: Hdqrs USAF AFSAA/SAN 1570 Air Force Pentagon Washington DC 20330-1570

THOMAS, COLIN GORDON, JR., surgeon, medical educator; b. Iowa City, July 25, 1918; s. Colin Gordon and Eloise Kinzer (Brainerd) T.; m. Shirley Forbes, Sept. 14, 1946; children: Karen, Barbara, James G., John F. B.S., U. Chgo., 1940, M.D., 1943. Diplomate Am. Bd. Surgery. Intern U. Iowa Hosp., 1943-44, resident surgery, 1944-45, 47-50; assoc. in surgery U. Iowa Med. Sch., 1950-51, asst. prof., 1951-52; mem. faculty U. N.C. Med. Sch., Chapel Hill, 1952—, prof. surgery, 1961—, Byah Thomason Doxey-Sanford Doxey prof. surgery, 1982—, chmn. dept., 1966-84, chief div. gen. surg., 1984-89, part-time prof., 1991—. Contbr. surg. texts, numerous articles to med. jours. Served to capt., M.C. AUS, 1945-47. Recipient Prof. award U. N.C. Sch. Medicine, 1964, Disting. Svc. award U. Chgo., 1982, Med. Alumni Disting. faculty award U. N.C., 1984; Berryhill lectr. U. N.C., 1989; recipient Fleming Fuller award U. N.C. Hosps., 1994. Mem. AMA, ACS (Disting. Leadership award N.C. chpt. 1990), AAUP, Am. Thyroid Assn., Am. Assn. Cancer Research, Am. Assn. Endocrine Surgeons (pres. 1989-90), Soc. Univ. Surgeons, So. Surg. Assn. (v.p. 1989-90), N.Y. Acad. Scis., Halsted Soc., Ga. Surg. Soc., Soc. Exptl. Biology and Medicine, Am. Surg. Assn., Womack Surg. Soc. (pres. 1981-83), Soc. Internationale de Chirurgie, Soc. Surgery Alimentary Tract, N.C. Surg. Assn., Internat. Assn. Endocrine Surgeons, Alpha Omega Alpha. Episcopalian (warden 1961-62). Home: 408 Morgan Creek Rd Chapel Hill NC 27514-4934

THOMAS, CRAIG, senator; b. Cody, Wyo., Feb. 17, 1933; s. Craig E. and Marge Oweta (Lynn) T.; m. Susan Roberts; children: Peter, Paul, Patrick, Alexis. BS, U. Wyo., 1955. V.p. Wyo. Farm Bur., Laramie, 1959-66; with Am. Farm Bur., 1966-75; gen. mgr. Wyo. Rural Elec. Assn., 1975-89; mem. Wyo. Ho. of Reps., 1984-89, 101st-103rd Congresses from Wyo., Washington, 1989-94; U.S. senator from Wyoming, 1995—. Former chmn. Natrona County (Wyo.) Rep. Com.; state rep. Natrona County Dist.; del. Rep. Nat. Conv., 1980. Capt. USMC. Mem. Am. Soc. Trade Execs., Masons. Methodist. Office: 302 Hart Senate Office Bldg Washington DC 20510

THOMAS, CYNTHIA ELIZABETH, advanced practice nurse; b. Highland, Ind., Sept. 3, 1958; d. James William and Naomi Elizabeth (Rice) T. BS in Animal Sci., Purdue U., 1980; ADN, Purdue U. Calumet, 1986, BSN, 1988, MSN, 1990. RN, Ind.; cert. adult nurse practitioner, family nurse practitioner, clin. specialist in med.-surg. nursing. Med.-surg. open heart ICU/CCU staff nurse, charge nurse Porter Meml. Hosp., Valparaiso, Ind., 1986-94; med.-surg. clin. instr. Purdue U. North Ctrl., Westville, Ind., 1993-94, Purdue U.-North Ctrl., Westville, Ind., 1993-94; advanced practice nurse Cmty. Health Ctrs.-Koontz Lake, LaCrosse, North Judson, Ind., 1994-95, Starke Meml. Hosp., Knox, Ind.; nurse practitioner/office coord. Hanna Family Med. Ctr., LaPorte Hosp./Lakeland Area Health Svcs., 1995-96; nursing instr. LaPorte (Ind.) Hosp., Mishawaka, Ind., 1995-96; adult medicine/pulmonary nurse practitioner Arnett Clinic, Lafayette, Ind., 1996—. Mem. AACN, Am. Acad. Nurse Practitioners, Ceres, Alpha Zeta.

THOMAS, DALE E., lawyer; b. New Rochelle, N.Y., Jan. 25, 1947. AB summa cum laude, Princeton U., 1969; MDiv, Yale Divinity Sch., 1973; JD, Yale U., 1974. Bar: Ill. 1975. Law clerk U.S. Ct. Appeals 2d cir., 1974-75; ptnr. Sidley & Austin, Chgo. Mem. ABA, Ill. State Bar Assn., Chgo. Bar Assn., Phi Beta Kappa. Office: Sidley & Austin 1 First Nat Plz Chicago IL 60603*

THOMAS, DANIEL FOLEY, telecommunications company executive; b. Washington, Aug. 24, 1950; s. Richard Kenneth and Margaret (Foley) T.; m. Barbara Jane Clark, June 30, 1973; 1 child, Alison Clark. BS in Acctg., Mt. St. Mary's Coll., 1972. CPA, Va. Auditor Deloitte, Haskins and Sells, Washington, 1972-74; various fin. positions Communications Satellite Corp., Washington, 1974-78, asst. treas., 1984-85, treas., 1986-87, controller, 1987-89; controller Comsat Telesystems, Washington, 1978-79; mgr. acctg. and taxes Satellite Bus. Systems, McLean, Va., 1979-81, treas., 1981-84; v.p. fin. Comsat Tech. Products, Inc., Washington, 1985-86, Comsat Video Enterprises, Inc., Washington, 1989-90; v.p. Leasetec Corp., Boulder, Colo., 1990—. Named One of Outstanding Young Men Am., 1981. Mem. AICPA, Va. Jaycees (life), Great Falls Jaycees (pres. 1978). Roman Catholic. Avocations: running, raquetball. Home: 1299 S Teal Ct Boulder CO 80303-1480 Office: Leasetec Corp 1401 Pearl St Boulder CO 80302-5319

THOMAS, DANIEL FRENCH, lawyer; b. Balt., Sept. 9, 1937; s. William Daniel and Lillian Hanway (Thompson) T.; m. Patricia Ann Thomas Truffer, Apr. 20, 1963 (div. Aug. 1989). BA, Loyola Coll., Balt., 1959; JD, U. Md., 1962. Bar: Md. 1962, U.S. Dist. Ct. Md. 1963. Law clk. to Hon. William M. Horney Ct. of Appeals of Md., Annapolis, 1962-63; atty. Bregel & Bregel, Balt., 1963-70, Thomas & Kalichman, Balt., 1971—; lectr. Md. Inst. for Continuing Profl. Edn. of Lawyers, Balt., 1980—. Editor: Maryland Divorce and Separation Law, 1987, 92, 96; contbr. articles to profl. jours. Home: 1101 Saint Paul St Apt 2104 Baltimore MD 21202-2673 Office: Thomas & Kalichman 7 Saint Paul St Ste 950 Baltimore MD 21202-1626

THOMAS, DANIEL HOLCOMBE, federal judge; b. Prattville, Ala., Aug. 25, 1906; s. Columbus Eugene and Augusta (Pratt) T.; m. Dorothy Quina, Sept. 26, 1936 (dec. 1977); children: Daniel H., Jr., Merrill Pratt; m. Catharine J. Miller, Oct. 25, 1979. LL.B., U. Ala., 1928. Bar: bar. Pvt. practice Mobile, Ala., 1929; asst. solicitor Mobile County; mem. firm Lyons, Chamberlain & Courtney, Mobile County, 1932-37, Lyons & Thomas, Mobile County, 1937-43, Lyons, Thomas & Pipes, Mobile County, 1946-51; judge U.S. Dist. Ct., Mobile, 1951—, now sr. judge. Mem. exec. bd. Mobile Area council Boy Scouts Am., 1963—, v.p., 1967-69, pres., 1973—, mem. nat. council, 1973—, Trustee dept. archieves and history, State of Ala. Served with USNR, 1943-45. Recipient Silver Beaver award Boy Scouts Am., 1970, Silver Antelope award, 1975. Methodist. Club: Mobile Country. Home: 13 Dogwood Cir Mobile AL 36608-2308 Office: US Dist Ct 459 US Courthouse Mobile AL 36602

THOMAS, DAVID ANSELL, retired university dean; b. Holliday, Tex., July 5, 1917; s. John Calvin Mitchell and Alice (Willet) T.; m. Mary Elizabeth Smith, May 18, 1946; 1 dau., Ann Elizabeth. B.A., Tex. Tech. Coll., 1937; M.B.A., Tex. Christian U., 1948; Ph.D., U. Mich., 1956. C.P.A., Tex. Accountant Texaco, Inc., 1937-42; asso. prof. Tex. Christian U., 1946-49; lectr. U. Mich., 1949-53; prof. accounting Cornell U., Ithaca, N.Y., 1953-84; assoc. dean Cornell U. Grad. Sch. Mgmt., 1962-79; acting dean Cornell U. Grad. Sch. Bus. and Pub. Adminstrn., 1979-81; dean Samuel Curtis Johnson Grad. Sch. Mgmt. Cornell U., 1981-84. Author: Accelerated Amortization of Defense Facilities, 1958, Accounting for Home Builders, 1952; Contbr. numerous articles to publs.; Editor: Fed. Accountant, 1956-58. Pres. Exec. Investors, Inc.; exec. dir. Charles E. Merrill Family Found., 1954-57, Robert A. Magowan Found., 1957-60; adminstr. Charles E. Merrill Trust, 1957-81, Ithaca Growth Fund.; Bd. dirs. Ithaca Opera Assn., Cornell Student Agys. Served to capt. USAAF, 1942-46, PTO. Mem. Tex. Soc. C.P.A.'s, Nat. Assn. Accountants, Am. Accounting Assn., Phi Beta Kappa, Beta Alpha Psi. Clubs: Cornell of N.Y., University, Statler (pres., dir.). Home: Devenshire Park 1560 Jasper Ct Venice FL 34292-4336

THOMAS, DAVID HURST, archaeologist; b. Oakland, Calif., May 27, 1945; s. David Hurst and Barbara (Longwell) T.; m. Lorann S.A. Pendleton, Aug. 25, 1985; 1 child, David Hurst III. BA, U. Calif., Davis, 1967, MA, 1968, PhD in Anthropology, 1971. Asst. prof. anthropology CCNY, 1971-72; asst. curator Am. Mus. Natural History, 1972-77, assoc. curator, 1977-82, curator, 1982—, chmn. dept. anthropology, 1976-84; adj. curator Fla. State Mus.; overseers com. to visit the Peabody Mus. Harvard U., 1983-89; founding trustee Nat. Mus. of the Am. Indian, 1990—, vice chmn., 1992-96; panelist in behavioral sci. NSF, 1988-91; exec. com. Soc. Am. Archeology, 1986-88. Author: Predicting the Past, 1974, Figuring Anthropology, 1976, Archaeology, 1979, 89, Refiguring Anthropology, 1986, St. Catherines: An Island in Time, 1988, The Native Americans, 1993, Exploring Ancient Native America, 1994; gen. editor: The North American Indian, 1986, Columbian Consequences: vol. 1, 1989, vol. 2, 1990, vol. 3, 1991, The Archaeology and History of the Spanish Borderlands (25 vol.), 1991; editor American Anthropologist, 1990—, Illustrated History of Humankind, 5 vols., 1993, Native Am. 1995; mem. editorial bd. Geoarchaeology; adv. bd. N.Am. Archaeologist, Advances in Archaeol. Method and Theory, Jour. Quantative Anthropology, New Directions in Archaeology. Recipient Presidential recognition award Soc. Am. Archeology, 1991, Franciscan Inst. medal, 1992; NSF grantee, 1977-78; Edward John Noble Found. grantee, 1974—; Nat. Geographic Soc. grantee, 1975-76, 81. Mem. NAS, Soc. Am. Archaeology (exec. com. 1986-88), Am. Anthrop. Assn. (arch. section editor), Internat. Union Pre-and Proto-Sci., Writers Guild of Am. Research on Desert West and Am. S.E. Home: 200 Piermont Ave Nyack NY 10960-4507 Office: Am Mus Natural History Dept of Anthropology New York NY 10024

THOMAS, DAVID PHILLIP, forestry educator, college administrator; b. Wasco, Oreg., July 7, 1918; s. William Phillip and Mabel Josephine (Hulery) T.; m. Geraldine Alaire Culross, Oct. 15, 1943; children: Larry K., Jeffrey A., Glenn R. B.S., U. Wash., 1941, M.F., 1947; postgrad., N.Y. State Coll. Forestry, Syracuse U., 1947-50. Research asso. Engring. Expt. Sta., U. Wash., Seattle, 1946-47; instr. wood tech. N.Y. State Coll. Forestry, 1947-50; mem. faculty U. Wash., Seattle, 1950—; prof. forest resources U. Wash., 1966-84, prof. emeritus, 1984—, spl. asst. to v.p. acad. affairs, 1964-72, dir. Inst. Forest Products, 1966-72, asso. dean Coll. Forest Resources, 1973-75; chmn. mgmt. and social scis. div. U. Wash. (Coll. Forest Resources), 1975-80; Instl. rep. Assn. Naval ROTC Colls., 1966-72; curriculum cons. U.S. Army ROTC program, 1969; program dir. Peace Corps, U. Wash., 1968-72; mem. Chile Forestry Vol. Tech. Support Program, 1968-72; del. Internat. Union Forestry Research Orgns., 1967, 76, World Forestry Congress, 1978. Trustee Nellie Martin Carmen Coll. Scholarship, 1992—; mem. King County Environ. Devel. Commn., Seattle, 1972-79; mem. exec. bd., chief Seattle coun. Boy Scouts Am., 1957-80, coun. commr., 1965-67; mem. Wash. State Forest Practices Adv. Com., 1974-79, Wash. State Forest Practices Appeals Bd., 1981-85; trustee Keep Wash. Green Assn., 1975-86, adv. com., 1986-90, Wash. State Forestry Conf., 1985-90; bd. dirs. U. Lions Found., 1986—, chmn., 1991—. Lt. comdr. USNR, 1941-45. Recipient Silver Beaver award Boy Scouts Am., 1961; Outstanding Service award Wash. State Forestry Conf., 1984; Stewart H. Holbrook Disting. Service award for wild fire prevention Keep Wash. Green Assn., 1987. Fellow Soc. Am. Foresters (chmn. S. Puget Sound chpt. 1977-78, chmn.-elect state soc. 1979-80, chmn. 1980-81 Forester of Yr. award Wash. Soc. 1982); mem. Forest Products Rsch. Soc., Forest History Soc., Soc. Wood Sci. and Tech., Western Forestry and Conservation Assn., U. Wash. Foresters Alumni Assn. (pres. 1978-79, Honored Alumnus award 1985), Am. Forestry Assn. (life), Lions Internat. Svcs. Club, Sigma Xi, Xi Sigma Pi, Phi Sigma. Mem. United Ch. of Christ. Home: 3607 NE 100th St Seattle WA 98125-7818

THOMAS, (CHARLES) DAVIS, editor; b. Detroit, Dec. 20, 1928; s. Charles Richard and Nellie Clare (Davis) T.; m. Karin Ronnefeldt, Apr. 21, 1956; 1 child, Cord Alexander. B.A., U. Mich., 1950. Reporter Detroit News, 1950; reporter Life Mag., N.Y.C., 1954-57; staff corr. Life Mag., Los Angeles, 1957-60; photography editor Saturday Evening Post, Phila., 1961; asst. mng. editor Saturday Evening Post, 1962, mng. editor, 1962-63; editor in chief Ladies' Home Jour., N.Y.C., 1964-65; pub. cons. N.Y.C., Toronto, Geneva, Switzerland, 1965-70; exec. editor Holiday Mag., N.Y.C., 1970, Travel & Leisure Mag., N.Y.C., 1971-75; editor in chief Down East Mag., Camden, Maine, 1976-93, v.p., assoc. pub., 1984-93; editor at large Down East Mag., 1994—. Editor: Moon, Man's Greatest Adventure, 1970 (Annual award Aviation Space Writers' Assn. 1971), (with Karin Ronnefeldt) People of the First Man: Life Among the Plains Indians in their Final Days of Glory, 1976. Served with AUS, 1951-54. Home and Office: 57 Meguntikook St Camden ME 04843-1643

THOMAS, DEBI (DEBRA J. THOMAS), ice skater; b. Poughkeepsie, N.Y., Mar. 25, 1967; d. McKinley and Janice T.; m. Brian Vanden Hogen. Student, Stanford U. Competitive figure skater, 1976-88. Winner U.S. figure Skating Championship, 1986, 88, Women's World Figure Skating Championship, 1986, World Profl. Figure Skating Championship, 1988, 89. Recipient Am. Black Achievement Award, Ebony mag., named Women Athlete of Yr., 1986; winner Bronze medal Olympic Games, 1988. Address: care IMG 22 E 71st St New York NY 10021-4911

THOMAS, DEBORAH ALLEN, English educator; b. Biddeford, Maine, Sept. 1, 1943; d. Donald Paine and Marjorie (Thompson) Allen; m. Gordon Albert Thomas, Sept. 10, 1966; 1 child, Allen Mansfield. AB magna cum laude, Brown U., 1965; MA, Duke U., 1966; PhD, U. Rochester, 1972.

Assoc. in humanities Eastman Sch. Music U. Rochester, N.Y., 1969-72; adj. asst. prof. English Fairleigh Dickinson U., Madison, N.J., 1973-76; co-adj. asst. prof. English Rutgers U., New Brunswick and Newark, N.J., 1976-80; asst. prof. English Villanova (Pa.) U., 1980-84, assoc. prof. English, 1984-91, prof. English, 1991—; visiting scholar Harvard U., Cambridge, Mass., 1985-86. Author: Dickens and the Short Story, 1982, Thackeray and Slavery, 1993; editor: Dickens, Selected Short Fiction, 1976; contbr. articles to profl. jours. Scholar Duke U., 1965-66; fellow U. Rochester, 1966-67, NEH fellow, 1985-86; faculty rsch. grantee Villanova U., summer 1984, 87, 92. Mem. MLA, N.E. Victorian Studies Assn., Dickens Soc. (sec., treas. 1979-81), Phi Beta Kappa. Avocations: swimming, hiking, aerobics. Office: Villanova U English Dept Villanova PA 19085

THOMAS, DERRICK VINCENT, professional football player; b. Miami, Fla., Nov. 1, 1967. Student, U. Ala. Linebacker Kansas City Chiefs, 1989—. Named to Sporting News Coll. All-Am. 2d team, 1987, 1st team, 1988, named to Sporting News NFL-All Pro Team, 1990-92; selected to Pro Bowl, 1989-94; recipient Butkus award for outstanding coll. linebacker, 1988. Office: Kansas City Chiefs 1 Arrowhead Dr Kansas City MO 64129

THOMAS, DUDLEY BRECKINRIDGE, newspaper pubisher; b. Caldwell, N.J., Oct. 29, 1933; s. Calvin Lewis and Margaret M. (Mosier) T.; m. Elisabeth Platt, Jan. 27, 1957; children: Gregory Calvin, Thomas Laurence. BA in History, Washington and Lee U., 1955; LLB, George Washington U., 1960. Advt. sales, mgmt. Washington Post, 1958-70; bus. mgr. Star-Exponent, Culpeper, Va., 1970; editor, bus. mgr. Daily Record, Long Branch, N.J., 1971-74; pub. Lake County News-Herald, Willoughby, Ohio, 1974-88, Bridgeport (Conn.) Post and Bridgeport Telegram, 1988-92, Conn. Post, Bridgeport, 1992—. With USMC, 1956-58. Republican. Episcopalian. Avocations: walking, boating, Civil War History. Office: Conn Post 410 State St Bridgeport CT 06604-4501

THOMAS, DUKE WINSTON, lawyer; b. Scuddy, Ky., Jan. 25, 1937; s. William E. and Grace T.; m. Jill Staples, Oct. 24, 1964; children: Deborah L., William E. II, Judith A. BSBA, Ohio State U., 1959, JD, 1964. Bar: Ohio 1964, U.S. Dist. Ct. Ohio 1966, U.S. Ct. Appeals (3d cir.) 1971, U.S. Ct. Appeals (6th cir.) 1972, U.S. Supreme Ct. 1973, U.S. Ct. Appeals (7th cir.) 1979. Ptnr. Vorys, Sater, Seymour and Pease, Columbus, Ohio, 1964—; bd. dirs. Clinton Gas System, Columbus, Ohio Bar Liability Ins. Co., Columbus, Symix Inc., Columbus. Fellow Am. Coll. Trial Lawyers (chmn. Ohio ho. and senate joint select com. on jud. compensation 1987), Am. Bar Found., Ohio Bar Found., Columbus Bar Found.; mem. ABA (ho. of dels. 1985—, state del. 1989-95, bd. govs. 1995—), Ohio Bar Assn. (pres. 1985), Columbus Bar Assn. (pres. 1978), Pres.'s Club Ohio State U., Golf Club, Worthington Hills Country Club, Columbus Athletic Club. Home: 2090 Sheringham Rd Columbus OH 43220-4358 Office: Vorys Sater Seymour & Pease PO Box 1008 52 E Gay St Columbus OH 43216-1008

THOMAS, DWIGHT REMBERT, writer; b. Savannah, Ga., Dec. 8, 1944; s. Huguenin and Alma (Sanders) T. BA in English with honors, Emory U., 1967; PhD in Am. Lit., U. Pa., 1978. Fellow English dept. U. Pa., Phila., 1971-78; writer Savannah, 1979—; cons. Film Odyssey, Washington, 1988-89. Author: The Poe Log: A Documentary Life of Edgar Allan Poe, 1987. Dir. Edgar Allan Poe Mus., Richmond, Va., 1988—. With U.S. Army, 1969-71. Mem. MLA, Am. Med. Writers Assn., Mensa (treas. Savannah area 1985-88, local sec. 1989-90), Phi Beta Kappa. Roman Catholic. Avocations: German lang., current cinema, bicycling. Home: 7 E Gordon St Savannah GA 31401-4925

THOMAS, EDWARD DONNALL, physician, researcher; b. Mart, Tex., Mar. 15, 1920; married; 3 children. BA, U. Tex., 1941, MA, 1943; MD, Harvard U., 1946; MD (hon.), U. Cagliari, Sardinia, 1981, U. Verona, Italy, 1991, U. Parma, Italy, 1992, U. Barcelona, Spain, 1994. Lic. physician Mass., N.Y., Wash.; diplomate Am. Bd. Internal Medicine. Intern in medicine Peter Bent Brigham Hosp., Boston, 1946-47, rsch. fellow hematology, 1947-48; NRC postdoctoral fellow in medicine dept. biology MIT, Cambridge, 1950-51; chief med. resident, sr. asst. resident Peter Bent Brigham Hosp., 1951-53, hematologist, 1953-55; instr. medicine Harvard Med. Sch., Boston, 1953-55; rsch. assoc. Cancer Rsch. Found. Children's Med. Ctr., Boston, 1953-55; physician-in-chief Mary Imogene Bassett Hosp., Cooperstown, N.Y., 1955-63; assoc. clin. prof. medicine Coll. Physicians and Surgeons Columbia U., N.Y.C., 1955-63; attending physician U. Wash. Hosp., Seattle, 1963-90; prof. medicine Sch. Medicine U. Wash., Seattle, 1963-90, head divsn. oncology Sch. Medicine, 1963-85, prof. emeritus medicine Sch. Medicine, 1990—; dir. med. oncology Fred Hutchinson Cancer Rsch. Ctr., Seattle, 1974-89, assoc. dir. clin. rsch. programs, 1982-89, mem., 1974—; mem. hematology study sect. NIH, 1965-69; mem. bd. trustees and med. sci. adv. com. Leukemia Soc. Am., Inc., 1969-73; mem. clin. cancer investigation review com. Nat. Cancer Inst., 1970-74; 1st ann. Eugene C. Eppinger lectr. Peter Bent Brigham Hosp. and Harvard Med. Sch., 1974; Lilly lectr. Royal Coll. Physicians, London, 1977; Stratton lectr. Internation Soc. Hematology, 1982; Paul Aggeler lectr. U. Calif., San Francisco, 1982; 65th Mellon lectr. U. Pitts. Sch. Medicine, 1984; Stanley Wright Meml. lectr. Western Soc. Pediatric Rsch., 1985; Adolfo Ferrata lectr. Italian Soc. Hematology, Verona, Italy, 1991. Mem. editl. bd. Blood, 1962-75, 77-82, Transplantation, 1970-76, Proc. of Soc. for Exptl. Biology and Medicine, 1974-81, Leukemia Rsch., 1977-87, Hematological Oncology, 1982-87, Jour. Clin. Immunology, 1982-87, Am. Jour. Hematology, 1985—, Bone Marrow Transplantation, 1986—. With U.S. Army, 1948-50. Recipient A. Ross McIntyre award U. Nebr. Med. Ctr., 1975, Philip Levine award Am. Soc. Clin. Pathologists, 1979, Disting. Svc. in Basic Rsch. award Am. Cancer Soc., 1980, Kettering prize Gen. Motors Cancer Rsch. Found., 1981, Spl. Keynote Address award Am. Soc. Therapeutic Radiologists, 1981, Robert Roesler de Villiers award Leukemia Soc. Am., 1983, Karl Landsteiner Meml. award Am. Assn. Blood Banks, 1987, Terry Fox award Can., 1990, Internat. award Gairdner Found., 1990, N.Am. Med. Assn. Hong Kong prize, 1990, Nobel prize in medicine, 1990, Presdl. medal of sci. NSF, 1990,. Mem. NAS, Am. Assn. Cancer Rsch., Am. Assn. Physicians (Kober medal 1992), Am. Fedn. Clin. Rsch., Am. Soc. Clin. Oncology (David A. Karnoksky Meml. lectr. 1983), Am. Soc. Clin. Investigation, Am. Soc. Hematology (pres. 1987-88, Henry M. Stratton lectr. 1975), Internat. Soc. Exptl. Hematology, Internat. Soc. Hematology, Academie Royale de Medicine de Belgique (corresponding mem.), Swedish Soc. Hematology (hon.), Swiss Soc. Hematology, Royal Coll. Physicians and Surgeons Can. (hon.), Western Assn. Physicians, Soc. Exptl. Biology and Medicine, Transplantation Soc., Nat. Acad. Medicine (hon.). Office: Fred Hutchinson Cancer Ctr 1124 Columbia St Seattle WA 98104-2015

THOMAS, EDWARD FRANCIS, JR., synthetic fuel executive; b. N.Y.C., Feb. 19, 1937; s. Edward Francis and Helen Kathryn (Baker) T.; m. Barbara Joyce Mahler, Mar. 23, 1975 (div. 1980); children: Edward, Diana, Eric, Tanya Ann. BA, Va. Mil. Inst., 1959; MBA, NYU, 1970. Asst. v.p. Citibank, N.A., N.Y.C., 1962-70; sr. fin. analyst Atlantic Richfield Co., N.Y.C., 1970-73; nat. sales mgr. Easton-Mahler Corp., N.Y.C., 1973-80; exec. v.p. Superfuel Inc., Phoenix, 1980-83; asst. v.p. The Ariz. Bank, Yuma, 1983-85; sr. v.p. Lumber Country, Inc., Tucson, 1985-87; exec. v.p. Synergistic Energy Systems, Inc., Phoenix, 1987—; cons. in field; instr. S.W. Acad. Tech., Am. Coll., North Am. Coll., Marywood Coll., Ariz. Western Coll., Webster U. Past bd. dirs. Boys and Girls Club, Yuma, Cocopah Indian Tribe Econ. Devel. Com., Somerton, Ariz., Wesley Community Ctr., Phoenix, 1990, Cath. Community Svcs., Tucson, Episc. Community Svcs., Tucson, Sahuaro coun. Girl Scouts U.S., Interfaith Coun. for Homeless, Tucson, Mayor's Community Partnership for Homeless, Tucson; past mem. exec. com. Yuma Econ. Devel. Com. 1st lt. U.S. Army. Mem. Yuma Leadership, Ariz. Assn. Indsl. Developers, Rotary, Masons. Avocations: church youth leadership activities, sports. Office: Synergistic Energy Systems 3850 E Friess Dr Phoenix AZ 85032-5725

THOMAS, EDWARD ST. CLAIR, hospital administrator; b. Montgomery, Ala., Nov. 11, 1934; married. BS, Xavier U., 1956; MHA, U. Mich., 1970. Adminstrv. resident Harper Hosp., Detroit, 1968-69, adminstrv. asst., 1969-70, asst. adminstr., 1970-77, assoc. adminstr., 1977-79; dir. corp. adminstrn. Harper-Grace Hosps., Detroit, 1979-81, v.p. corp. adminstrv. affairs, 1981; pres., ceo Detroit Receiving Hosp., 1991—; now sr. v.p. Detroit Med. Cntr. Mem. Mich. Hosp. Assn. (mem. various coms.). Office: Detroit Medical Center 4201 Saint Antoine St Detroit MI 48201-2153*

THOMAS, ELLA COOPER, lawyer; b. Ft. Totten, N.Y.; d. Avery John and Ona Caroline (Gibson) C.; m. Robert Edward Lee Thomas, Nov. 22, 1938 (dec. Jan. 1985); 1 child, Robert Edward Lee Jr. Student, Vassar Coll., 1932-34, U. Hawaii, 1934-35, George Washington U., 1935-36; JD, George Washington U., 1940. Bar: U.S. Dist. Ct. D.C. 1942, U.S. Ct. Appeals (D.C. cir.) 1943, U.S. Supreme Ct. 1947, U.S. Tax Ct. 1973. Secret maps custodian U.S. Dist. Engrs., Honolulu, 1941-42; contbg. editor Labor Rels. Reporter, Washington, 1942; assoc. Smith, Ristig & Smith, Washington, 1942-45; law libr. George Washington Law Sch., Washington, 1946-53; reporter of decisions U.S. Tax Ct., Washington, 1953-75. Author: Law of Libel and Slander, 1949. Mem. Inter-Am. Bar Assn. (coun. mem. 1973—), D.C. Bar Assn. Avocations: physical fitness, crostics, mote marine lab. vol. computer.

THOMAS, ELLIOTT G., bishop; b. Pittsburgh, PA, July 15, 1926. ordained priest June 6, 1986. Bishop Diocese of St. Thomas in the Virgin Islands, 1993—. Office: Bishop's Residence PO Box 1825 68 Kronprind Gade Charlotte Amalie VI 00803*

THOMAS, ESTHER MERLENE, elementary education educator; b. San Diego, Oct. 16, 1945; d. Merton Alfred and Nellie Lida (Von Pilz) T. AA with honors, Grossmont Coll., 1966; BA with honors, San Diego State U., 1969; MA, U. Redlands, 1977. Cert. elem. and adult edn. tchr. Tchr. Cajon Valley Union Sch. Dist., El Cajon, 1969—; sci. fair coord. Flying Hills Sch.; tchr. Hopi and Navajo Native Americans, Ariz, Utah, 1964-74, Goose and Gander Nursery School, Lakeside, Calif., 1964-66; dir., supt. Bible and Sunday schs. various chs., Lakeside, 1961-87; mem. sci. com., math coun. Cajon Valley Union Sch. Dist., 1990-91. Author: Individualized Curriculum in the Affective Domain; contbg. author: Campbell County, The Treasured Years, 1990, Legends of the Lakeside; songwriter for Hilltop Records, Hollywood, Calif; songs released Never Trouble Trouble, Old Glory, Born to Win, Daniel's Prayer; contbr. articles to profl. jours. and newspapers. Tem. U.S. Senatorial Club, Washington, 1984—, Conservative Caucus, Inc., Washington, 1988—, Ronald Reagan Presdl. Found., Ronald Reagan Rep. Ctr., 1988, Rep. Presdl. Citizen's Adv. Commn., 1989—, Rep. Platform Planning Com., Calif., 1992, at-large del. representing dist. #45, Lakeside, Calif., 1992, 1995—, Am. Security Coun., Washington, 1994, Congressman Hunter's Off Road Adv. Coun., El Cajon, Calif., 1994, Century Club, San Diego Rep. Century Club, 1995; mem. health articulation com. project AIDS, Cajon Valley Union Sch. Dist., 1988—, Concerned Women Am., Washington, Recruit Depot Hist. Mus., San Diego, 1989, Citizen's Drug Free Am., Calif., 1989—, The Heritage Found., 1988—; charter mem. Marine Corps Mus.; mem. Lakeside Centennial Com., 1985-86; hon. mem. Rep. Presdl. Task Force, Washington, 1986; del. Calif. Rep. Senatorial Mid-Term Conv., Washington, 1994; mus. curator Lakeside Hist. Soc., 1992-93. Recipient Outstanding Svc. award PTA, 1972-74; recognized for various contbns. Commdg. Post Gen., San Diego Bd. Edn., 1989. Mem. Tchrs. Assn., Calif. Tchrs. Assn., Nat. Trust for Hist. Preservation, Cajon Valley Educators Assn. (faculty advisor, rep. 1980-82, 84-86, 87-88), Christian Bus. and Profl. Women, Capitol Hill Women's Club, Am. Ctr. for Law and Justice, Internat. Christian Women's Club (Christian amb. to Taiwan, Korea, 1974). Republican. Avocations: world traveling, Christian teaching, vocal music, piano, guitar. Home: 13594 Highway 8 Business Apt 3 Lakeside CA 92040-5235 Office: Flying Hills Elem Sch 1251 Finch St El Cajon CA 92020-1433

THOMAS, FRANK EDWARD, professional baseball player; b. Columbus, Ga., May 27, 1968. Student, Auburn U. With Chgo. White Sox, 1990—. Named to Sporting News All-Star Coll. All Am. team, 1989; Sporting News All-Star team, 1991, 93-94; recipient Silver Slugger award, 1991, 93, 94; mem. Am. League All-Star Team, 1993-95; recipient Am. League MVP award, 1994; named Major League Player of Yr., Sporting News, 1993. Office: Chgo White Sox Comiskey Park 333 W 35th St Chicago IL 60616-3621*

THOMAS, FRANK M., JR., lawyer; b. Feb. 20, 1947. BA, Amherst Coll., 1969; M in City Planning, Harvard U., 1973; JD, U. Pa., 1977. Bar: Pa. 1977, U.S. Supreme Ct. 1983. Ptnr. Morgan, Lewis & Bockius, Phila. Office: Morgan Lewis & Bockius 2000 One Logan Sq Philadelphia PA 19103*

THOMAS, FRANKLIN AUGUSTINE, foundation executive; b. Bklyn., May 27, 1934; s. James and Viola (Atherley) T.; divorced; children: Keith, Hillary, Kerrie, Kyle. B.A., Columbia U., 1956, LL.B., 1963; LL.D. (hon.), Yale U., 1970, Fordham U., 1972, Pratt Inst., 1974, Pace U., 1977, Columbia U., 1979. Bar: N.Y. 1964. Atty. Fed. Housing and Home Finance Agy., N.Y.C., 1963-64; asst. U.S. atty. for So. Dist. N.Y., 1964-65; dep. police commr. charge legal matters N.Y.C., 1965-67; pres., chief exec. officer Bedford Stuyvesant Restoration Corp., Bklyn., 1967-77; pres. The Ford Found., 1979-96; bd. dirs. Citicorp/Citibank, ALCOA, Cummins Engine Co., AT&T Lucent Techs. Trustee Ford Found., Columbia U., 1969-75. Served with USAF, 1956-60. Recipient LBJ Found. award for contbn. to betterment of urban life, 1974, medal of excellence Columbia U., 1976, Alexander Hamilton award Columbia U., 1983.

THOMAS, FREDERICK BRADLEY, lawyer; b. Evanston, Ill., Aug. 13, 1949; s. Frederick Bradley and Katherine Kidder (Bingham) T.; m. Elizabeth Maxwell, Oct. 25, 1975; children: Bradley Bingham, Stephens Maxwell, Rosa Macaulay. AB, Dartmouth Coll., 1971; JD, U. Chgo., 1974. Bar: Ill. 1974. Law clk. to hon. judge John C. Godbold U.S. Ct. Appeals (5th cir.), Montgomery, Ala., 1974-75; assoc. Mayer, Brown & Platt, Chgo., 1975-80, ptnr., 1981—. Bd. dirs. St. Gregory Episcopal Sch., 1989—; bd. trustees La Rabida Children's Hosp., 1990—. Mem. ABA, Chgo. Council Lawyers. Republican. Episcopalian. Office: Mayer Brown & Platt 190 S La Salle St Chicago IL 60603-3410

THOMAS, GARETH, metallurgy educator; b. Maesteg, U.K., Aug. 9, 1932; came to U.S., 1960, naturalized, 1977; s. David Bassett and Edith May (Gregory) T.; 1 child, Julian Guy David. B.Sc., U. Wales, 1952; Ph.D., Cambridge U., 1955, Sc.D., 1969. I.C.I. fellow Cambridge U., 1956-59; asst. prof. U. Calif., Berkeley, 1960-63; asso. prof. U. Calif., 1963-67, prof. metallurgy, 1967—, assoc. dean grad. div., 1968-69, asst. chancellor, acting vice chancellor for acad. affairs, 1969-72; founder, sci. dir. Nat. Ctr. Electron Microscopy, 1982-93; cons. to industry. Author: Transmission Electron Microscopy of Metals, 1962, Electron Microscopy and Strength of Crystals, 1963, (with O. Johari) Stereographic Projection and Applications, 1969, Transmission Electron Microscopy of Materials, 1980; editor-in-chief: Acta and Scripta Mat., 1995—; contbr. articles to profl. jours. Recipient Curtis McGraw Rsch. award Am. Soc. Engring. Edn., 1966, E.O. Lawrence award Dept. Energy, 1978, I-R 100 award R & D mag., 1987, Henry Clifton Sorby award Internat. Metallographic Soc., 1987, Albert Sauveur Achievement award, 1991; Guggenheim fellow, 1972. Fellow Am. Soc. Metals (Bradley Stoughton Young Tchrs. award 1965, Grossman Publ. award 1966), Am. Inst. Mining, Metall. and Petroleum Engrs.; mem. Electron Microscopy Soc. Am. (prize 1965, pres. 1976), Am. Phys. Soc., Nat. Acad. Scis., Nat. Acad. Engring., Brit. Inst. Metals (Rosenheim medal 1977), Internat. Fedn. Electron Microscopy Socs. (pres. 1986-90), Brit. Iron and Steel Inst. Club: Marylebone Cricket (Eng.). Patentee in field. Office: U Calif Dept Materials Sci/Engring 561 Evans Hall Berkeley CA 94720-1760

THOMAS, GARTH JOHNSON, psychology educator emeritus; b. Pittsburg, Kans., Sept. 8, 1916; s. Leslie Homer and Lou Opal (Johnson) T.; m. Mary Mona Gee, Sept. 21, 1945; children—Gregory Allen, Barbara Elizabeth. A.B., Kans. State Tchrs. Coll. at Pittsburg, 1938; M.A., U. Kans., 1941, Harvard, 1943; Ph.D., Harvard, 1948. Instr., asst. prof. U. Chgo., 1948-54; asso. prof. U. Ill. Med. Sch., 1954-57; research prof. physiology and elec. engring. U. Ill., Urbana, 1957-66; prof. U. Rochester, N.Y., 1966-82, dir. Ctr. for Brain Rsch., 1970-77, prof. emeritus, 1982—; mem. rev. com. Exptl. Psychology Fellowship panel NIMH, 1965-70, chmn., 1970; mem. psychobiology panel NSF; cons. editor Sinauer Press, Inc. Cons. editor: Jour. Comparative and Physiol. Psychology, 1969-75, 82-91, editor, 1975-81; cons. editor: McGraw Hill Ency. of Sci. and Tech.; contbr. articles to profl. jours. Served to 1st lt. AUS, 1944-47. Recipient research grants NSF, research grants NIMH, research grants U.S. Army, 1951—; Alumni Meritorious Achievement award Kans. State Coll. at Pittsburg, 1976. Mem. Am. Psychol. Assn., Animal Behavior Soc., AAAS, Psychonomic Soc., Soc. Exptl. Psychology, Soc. for Neurosci. Home: 186 Buckland Ave Rochester NY 14618-2139

THOMAS, GARY EDWARD, science educator, researcher; b. Lookout, W.V., Oct. 25, 1934; s. Garland Eugene Thomas and Dorothy Mae (Fish) Johnson; m. Susan Jude Cherup, Jan. 20, 1963; children: Curtis Andrew, Jennifer Ann. BS, N.Mex. State U., 1957; PhD, U. Pitts., 1963. Rsch. assoc. Svc. d'Aeronomie du CNRS, Paris, France, 1962-63; staff scientist Aerospace Corp., El Segundo, Calif., 1965-67; prof. U. Colo., Boulder, 1967—; sec. Internat. Comm. on Meteorology of the Upper Atmosphere, 1988-95. Assoc. editor Jour. Geophys. Rsch., 1992&; contbr. more than 100 articles to profl. jours. 1st lt. Signal Corps U.S. Army, 1963-65. Recipient Award Rsch. Excellence U. Colo., 1994; fellowship U. Colo., 1974-75. Mem. Am. Geophysical Union (assoc. editor 1992). Office: U Colo CB 392 Boulder CO 80309-0392

THOMAS, GARY LYNN, financial executive; b. Port Vue, Pa., May 15, 1942; s. Willis L. and Luella M. (Rorabaugh) T.; m. Sharen A. Gibbons, May 13, 1967; children—Gregory Scott, Tara Elizabeth. B.S. in Bus. Adminstrn, Pa. State U., 1964; grad., Sch. Bank Adminstrn., U. Wis., 1973. CPA, Pa. Sr. auditor Arthur Andersen & Co., Los Angeles and Pitts., 1964-69; v.p. and dep. comptroller Pitts. Nat. Bank, 1969-77; v.p. and treas. Md. Nat. Corp., Balt., 1977-80; v.p., mgr. corp. fin. div. Md. Nat. Bank, Balt.; exec. v.p. adminstrn. Peterson, Howell & Heather, Hunt Valley, Md., 1980-82; v.p. fin. Am. TeleServices, Inc, a Metromedia co., Balt., 1983-85; chief fin. officer First Cellular Group, Inc., Balt., 1985-88, Schelle, Warner, Murray & Thomas, Inc., Balt., 1988—; mng. dir. Schelle Cellular Group, Inc., 1989—; pres. Ruxton Capital Group, Inc., 1989—; chief fin. officer Am. Personal Communications, Inc., Balt. and D.C., 1990—; adj. instr. Sch. Bank Adminstrn., U. Wis., 1975-80; speaker 14th ann. Bank Tax Inst., 1978. Mem. adv. bd., fin. com. St. Joseph Hosp., Balt.; bd. dirs. industry luncheon club Towson State U. Served with USAR, 1968. Inducted into McKeesport H.S. Hall of Fame, 1994. Mem. AICPA, Pa. Inst. CPAs, Md. Assn. CPAs (prior chmn. mems. in industry com.). Republican. Methodist. Home: 2211 Spring Lake Dr Lutherville Timonium MD 21093-3352

THOMAS, GLADYS ROBERTS, foundation executive. BA, Bryn Mawr Coll. Pub. relations mgr. Am. Internat. Group, N.Y., 1978-80, dir. corp. communications, 1980-90; v.p. The Starr Found., N.Y.C., 1990—. Mem. India House (gov.). Republican. Office: Starr Found 70 Pine St New York NY 10270-0002

THOMAS, HAROLD ALLEN, JR., civil engineer, educator; b. Terre Haute, Ind., Aug. 14, 1913; s. Harold A. and Katherine (Sass) T.; m. Gertrude A. Grim, July 2, 1935; children—Harold Allen III, Stephen C., Calvin R. B.S. in Civil Engring, Carnegie Inst. Tech., 1935; S.D., Harvard, 1938. Faculty mem. Harvard, 1939—, successively instr., asst. prof., asso. prof., 1939-56, Gordon McKay prof. civil and san. engring., 1956-84, prof. emeritus, 1984—; profl. cons. HEW, 1949—; div. med. scis. NRC-Nat. Acad. Scis., 1943-63, also Dept. Def., AEC; cons. Exec. Office Pres., also Dept. Interior, 1961—; Mem. sci. bd. for Middle East and Southeast Asia, Nat. Acad. Scis., 1964-66, exec. com. social consequences of population changes, 1968—. Co-author: Design Water Resource Systems, 1961, Models for Managing Regional Water Quality, 1973. Fellow Am. Acad. of Arts and Scis.; mem. Am. Geophys. Union (RE Horton medal 1978), ASCE, Nat. Acad. Engring., Boston Soc. C.E. Home: 61 Cotuit Rd Sandwich MA 02563-2654 Office: Harvard U Dept Civil Engring Cambridge MA 02138

THOMAS, HAROLD WILLIAM, avionics systems engineer, flight instructor; b. Cle Elum, Wash., Sept. 29, 1941; s. Albert John and Margaret Jenny (Micheletto) T.; children: Gregg Wallace, Lisa Michele. BS, U. Wash., 1964; M of Engring., U. Fla., 1968. Sci. programmer Aerojet Gen. Corp., Sacramento, Calif., 1964-65; systems analyst GE Co., Daytona Beach, Fla., 1965-69; systems engr. GE Co., Phoenix, 1969-70; sr. software engr. Sperry Flight Systems, Phoenix, 1970-77; sr. systems engr. Honeywell, Inc., Phoenix, 1977-80; engr. section head Sperry Flight Systems, Phoenix, 1980-87; free lance flight instr., 1981—; tech. staff Honeywell, Inc., Phoenix, 1987—; designated engring. rep. Fed. Aviation Adminstrn., Long Beach, 1987—. Mem. AIAA, SAE Internat. Internat. Soc. Air Safety Investigators, Am. Mensa Ltd. Achievements include patent for rotating round dial aircraft engine instruments, patent for dynamic approach display format with plan and profile views. Home: 2514 W Pershing Ave Phoenix AZ 85029-1445 Office: Honeywell INc 21111 N 19th Ave Phoenix AZ 85027-2708

THOMAS, HAZEL BEATRICE, state official; b. Franklin, Tenn.; d. William Henry Fuller and Mattie Betty (Covington) Fuller Young; m. Charles B. Thomas (dec. 1969); children; Charles Bradford Jr., Deborah Carlotta (dec.). BA, Fisk U., 1946; MA, Tenn. State U., 1972. Cert. elem. and secondary tchr., Tenn. Tchr. elem. Met.-Nashville Schs., 1954-87; rsch. assoc. Johns Hopkins U., Balt., 1978-79, Marquette U., Milw., 1979-86; exec. asst. to commr. edn. Tenn. Dept. Edn., Nashville, 1987—; cons. Peer Mediated Learning System, Nashville, 1980-82; instr. Met. Schs. Tchr. Ctr., Nasvhville, 1985-87. Author training modules Substitute Teaching, Tchr. Aides. Pres. Davidson County Dem. Women, Nashville, 1985-87; v.p. Tenn. Fedn. Dem. Women, 1989-91; pres.-elect Nashville Women's Polit. Caucus, 1991—; pres. Tenn. Women's Polit. Caucus, 1994-95; mem. adminstrv. com. of bd. Nat. Women's Polit. Caucus, 1993-95; mem. Tenn. Leadership, Inc., 1992—. Recipient Svc. to Edn. and Teaching Profession award Nat. Coun. Negro Women, 1988; Nat. Def. Edn. Act scholar, 1965, 67. Mem. Am. Bus. Womens Assn. (charter), Tenn. Edn. Assn. (pres. dept. classroom tchrs. 1974-75, state dept. affiliate, pres. 1988-90), Bellevue C. of C. (bd. govs. 1990-91), Assn. Classroom Tchrs. (pres. S.E. region 1975-76), Met. Nashville Edn. Assn. (exec. bd. 1971-77), Bellevue Sertoma Club (life, pres. 1990-91), Nat. Women's Polit. Caucus (v.p. 1995—). Democrat. Baptist. Avocations: reading, bridge. Office: Tenn Dept Edn Gateway Plz 710 James Robertson Pkwy Nashville TN 37243

THOMAS, HELEN A. (MRS. DOUGLAS B. CORNELL), newspaper bureau executive; b. Winchester, Ky., Aug. 4, 1920; d. George and Mary (Thomas) T.; m. Douglas B. Cornell. BA, Wayne U., 1942; LLD, Eastern Mich. State U., 1972, Ferris State Coll., 1978, Brown U., 1986; LHD, Wayne State U., 1974, U. Detroit, 1979; LLD, St. Bonaventure U., 1988, Franklin Marshall U., 1989, No. Michigan U., 1989, Skidmore Coll., 1992; Susquehanna U., 1993, Sage Coll., 1994, U. Mo., 1994; LLD, Northwestern U., 1995, Franklin Coll., 1995; Hon. degree, Mich. State U., 1996. With UPI, 1943—; wire svc. reporter UPI, Washington, 1943-74; White House bur. chief UPI, 1974—. Author: Dateline White House. Recipient Woman of Yr. in Comm. award Ladies Home Jour., 1975, 4th Estate award Nat. press Club, 1984; Journalism award U. Mo., Dean of Sch. Journalism award, Al Newharth award, 1990, Ralph McGill award, 1995. Mem. Women's Nat. Press Club (pres. 1959-60, William Allen White Journalism award), Am. Newspaper Women's Club (past v.p.), White House Corrs. Assn. (pres. 1976), Gridiron Club (pres. 1993), Sigma Delta Chi (fellow, Hall of Fame), Delta Sigma Phi (hon.). Home: 2501 Calvert St NW Washington DC 20008-2620 Office: UPI World Hdqrs 1400 I St NW Washington DC 20005-2208

THOMAS, HENRY LEE, JR., professional football player; b. Houston, Jan. 12, 1965. Student, La. State U. Defensive tackle Minnesota Vikings, 1987—. Played in Pro Bowl, 1991, 92. Office: Minnesota Vikings 9520 Viking Dr Eden Prairie MN 55344-3825

THOMAS, HERMAN L., school system administrator. Asst. supt. Arkadelphia (Ark.) Sch. Dist. Recipient Blue Ribbon Sch. Award, 1990-91. Office: Arkadelphia Sch Dist 235N 11th St Arkadelphia AR 71923

THOMAS, HOWARD PAUL, civil engineer, consultant; b. Cambridge, Mass., Aug. 20, 1942; s. Charles Calvin and Helen Elizabeth (Hook) T.; m. Ingrid Nybo, Jan. 4, 1969; children: Kent Michael, Lisa Karen, Karina Michelle. BS in Engring., U. Mich., 1965, MS in Engring., 1966. Registered profl. engr., Alaska, Calif. Engr. Ove Arup & Ptnrs., London, 1966-67; project engr. Woodward-Clyde Cons., San Francisco, 1967-73; assoc. Woodward-Clyde Cons., Anchorage, 1975-89; spl. cons. Cowiconsult Cons., Copenhagen, 1973-75; prin. engr. Harding-Lawson Assocs., Anchorage, 1989-90; v.p., chief engr. EMCON Alaska, Inc., Anchorage, 1991-94; gen. mgr. Internat. Tech. Corp., Anchorage, 1994—; chmn. Nat. Tech. Coun.

Cold Regions Engring., 1988-89, chmn. com. program and publs., 1982-84; chmn. 4th Internat. Conf. Cold Regions Engring., Anchorage, 1986; liaison NAS/Nat. Rsch. Coun. Polar Commn., 1989-93. Contbr. articles to profl. jours. Named Alaskan Engr. Yr., 1986. Fellow ASCE (pres. Anchorage chpt. 1985-86, mem. mgmt. group A. 1994—); mem. Internat. Soc. Soil Mechs. and Found. Engring., Soc. Am. Mil. Engrs., Cons. Engrs. Coun. Alaska (pres. 1989-90), Am. Cons. Engrs. Coun. (nat. dir. 1990-91), Project Mgmt. Inst. (v.p. Alaska chpt. 1991-95), Toastmasters (pres. Anchorage club 1984), Sons of Norway. Lutheran. Avocations: music, travel, skiing, sailing. Home: 2611 Brittany Dr Anchorage AK 99504-3332

THOMAS, IAN LESLIE MAURICE, publisher; b. Bearsden, Scotland, May 10, 1937; came to U.S., 1989; s. Maurice and Fanny Olive (White) T.; m. Margaret June Thomas, Aug. 13, 1960; children: Fiona, Diana, Ian. BSc with honours, U. Glasgow, Scotland, 1960; ARCST with honors, U. Strathclyde, Scotland, 1960. Chartered engr., U.K. Indentured apprentice Brit. Polar Engines, Scotland, 1955-60; installation engr. Free Piston Engine Co., Singapore, 1960-62; prodn. mgr. Imperial Chem. Industries, Eng., 1962-73; gen. mgr. wall coverings Reed Internat., 1973-78; mng. dir. Odhams (Watford) Ltd., 1979-82; CEO Reed Travel Group, Eng., 1983-92, Reed Telepublishing, Secaucus, N.J., 1983—; bd. dirs. Reed Internat. PLC, Reed Elsevier PLC. Mem. Instn. Mech. Engrs. Avocations: sailing, rugby. Office: Reed Travel Group 500 Plaza Dr Secaucus NJ 07094-3619

THOMAS, ISIAH LORD, III, former professional basketball player, basketball team executive; b. Chgo., Apr. 30, 1961. Grad. in Criminal Justice, Ind. U., 1987. With Detroit Pistons, 1981-94; v.p. Toronto Raptors, 1994—, now v.p.; mem. U.S. Olympic Basketball Team, 1980, NBA Championship Teams, 1989-90. Named to All-Star team, 1982-93, All NBA First Team, 1984, 85, 86; recipient All-Star team MVP award, 1984, 86, NBA Playoff MVP award, 1990, NBA Finals MVP, 1990. Named to NBA All-Rookie team 1982. Office: Toronto Raptors, Water Park Pl 20 Bay St Ste 1702, Toronto, ON Canada M5J 2N8*

THOMAS, J. EARL, physicist; b. Seattle, Sept. 7, 1918; s. Jacob Earl and Ursula May (Johnson) T.; m. Margaret Louise Johnston, June 15, 1977; children—Richard Bruce, Jacob Earl, John Calvin, James Hayden, Denise May, Stillman Jefferson. A.B., Johns Hopkins U., 1939; Ph.D., Calif. Inst. Tech., 1943. Group leader rocket devel. Calif. Inst. Tech., Pasadena, 1942-45; group leader Manhattan Project, U. Calif., Los Alamos, 1945-46; asst. prof. elec. engring. M.I.T., Cambridge, 1946-51; mem. tech. staff Bell Telephone Labs., Murray Hill, N.J., 1951-52; group leader M.I.T. Lincoln Labs., Lexington, 1952-55; prof., chmn. dept. physics Wayne State U., Detroit, 1955-59; dir. research Sylvania Electric, Woburn, Mass., 1959-62; mgr. solid state devel. IBM, Poughkeepsie, N.Y., 1962-64; mgr. new product devel. Gen. Instrument Co., Newark, 1964-67; v.p. Carman Sapphire Co., Reseda, Calif., 1967-70; cons. Warnecke Electron Tubes, Des Plaines, Ill., 1970-71; dir. components research Victor Comptometer Co., Des Plaines, 1971-75; mgr. advanced devel. NCR Corp., Ithaca, N.Y., 1975-84; cons. pvt. cos. and govt. agys. Contbr. articles to sci. jours. Active S.E. Asian refugee resettlement program. Recipient Service award U.S. Office Sci. Research and Devel., 1946. Fellow IEEE, Am. Phys. Soc.; mem. Sigma Xi, Phi Beta Kappa, Tau Beta Pi. Democrat. Presbyterian. Patentee in field. Home: 323 Savage Farm Dr Ithaca NY 14850

THOMAS, JACK WARD, wildlife biologist; b. Ft. Worth, Sept. 7, 1934; s. Scranton Boulware and Lillian Louise (List) T.; m. Farrar Margaret Schindler, June 29, 1957 (dec. Feb. 1944); children: Britt Ward, Scranton Gregory. BS, Tex. A&M U., 1957; MS, W.Va. U., 1969; PhD, U. Mass., 1972. Biologist Tex. Game & Fish Commn., Sonora, 1957-60; rsch. biologist Tex. Parks & Wildlife Dept., Plano, 1962-67; wildlife rsch. biologist, forestry sci. lab., Northeastern Forest Exptl. Sta. U.S. Forest Svc., Morgantown, W.Va., 1967-71; project dir. environ. forestry rsch. Pinchot Inst. Environ. Forestry, 1971-73; project leader range & wildlife habitat rsch. Pacific Northwest Forest Exptl. Sta. U.S. Forest Svc., LaGrande, Oreg., 1973-93; chief U.S. Dept. Agr.- Forest Svc., Washington, 1993—. Author, editor: Wildlife Habitats in Managed Forests, 1979 (award The Wildlife Soc. 1980), Elk of North America, 1984 (award The Wildlife Soc. 1985); contbr. numerous articles to profl. jours. Served to lt. USAF, 1957. Recipient Conservation award Gulf Oil Corp., 1983, Earle A. Childs award Childs Found., 1984, Disting. Svc. award USDA, Disting. Citizen's award, E. Oreg. State Coll., Nat Wildlife Fedn. award for Sci., 1990, Disting. Achievement award Soc. for Cons. Biology, 1990, Giraffe award The Giraffe Project, 1990, Scientist of Yr. award Oreg. Acad. Sci., 1990, Disting. Svc. award Soc. Conservation Biology, 1991, Sci. Conservation award Nat. Wildlife Fedn., 1991, Chuck Yeager award Nat. Fish and Wildlife Found., 1992, Conservationist of Yr. award Oreg. Rivers Coun., 1992, Chief's Tech. Transfer award USDA, 1992, Tech. Transfer award Fed. Lab. Consortium, 1993. Fellow Soc. Am. Foresters; mem. The Wildlife Soc. (cert., hon., pres. 1977-78, Oreg. chpt. award 1980, Arthur Einarsen award 1981, spl. svcs. award 1984, Aldo Leopold Meml. medal 1991, group achievement award 1990), Am. Ornithologists Union, Am. Soc. Mammalogists, W.Va. U. Alumni Assn., U. Mass.-Amherst Alumni Assn., Lions, Elks. Avocations: hunting, fishing, white-water rafting, shooting, carpentry. Office: US Forest Svc PO Box 96090 14th & Independence Washington DC 20090

THOMAS, JACQUELINE MARIE, journalist, editor; b. Nashville, Aug. 31, 1952; d. John James and Dorothy Jacqueline (Phillips) T. B.A., Briarcliff Coll., 1972; M.Internat. Affairs, Columbia U., 1974. Reporter Chgo Sun-Times, 1974-85; assoc. editor Courier-Jour. and Louisville Times, 1985-86, Detroit Free Press, 1986-93; deputy bureau chief, news editor Detroit News, Washington Bureau, 1993-94, bureau chief, 1994—; instr. Roosevelt U., Chgo., 1983. Nieman fellow Harvard U., 1983. Mem. Chgo. Assn. Black Journalists (Print Journalist of Yr. 1982), Nat. Assn. Black Journalists, Am. Soc. Newspaper Editors. Office: Detroit News Washington Bur 1148 National Press Building Washington DC 20045-2101

THOMAS, JACQUELYN MAY, librarian; b. Mechanicsburg, Pa., Jan. 26, 1932; d. William John and Gladys Elizabeth (Warren) Harvey; m. David Edward Thomas, Aug. 28, 1954; children: Lesley J., Courtenay J., Hilary A. BA summa cum laude, Gettysburg Coll., 1954; student U. N.C., 1969; MEd, U. N.H., 1971. Libr. Phillips Exeter Acad., Exeter, N.H., 1971-77, acad. libr., 1977—, chair governing bd. Child Care Ctr., 1987-91; chair Com. to Enhance Status of Women, Exeter, 1981-84; chair Loewenstein Com., Exeter, 1982—; pres. Cum Laude Soc., Exeter, 1984-86; James H. Ottaway Jr. prof., 1990—. Editor: The Design of the Libr.: A Guide to Sources of Information, 1981, Rarities of Our Time: The Special Collections of the Phillips Exeter Academy Libr. Trustee, treas. Exeter Day Sch., 1965-69; mem. bd. Exeter Hosp. Vols., 1954-59; mem. Exeter Hosp. Corp., 1978—; mem. bldg. com. Exeter Pub. Libr., 1986-88; chair No. New Eng., Coun. for Women in Ind. Schs., 1985-87; chmn. Lamont Poetry Program, Exeter, 1984-86; dir. Greater Portsmouth Community Found, 1990—; active AAC&U, On Campus with Women, Wellesley Coll. Ctr. for Rsch. on Women. N.H. Coun. for Humanities grantee, 1981-82; NEH grantee, 1982; recipient Lillian Radford Trust award, 1989. Mem. ALA, Internat. Assn. Sch. Librs., New Eng. Libr. Assn., N.H. Ednl. Media Assn., New Eng. Assn. Ind. Sch. Librs., Am. Assn. Sch. Librs. (chmn. non-pub. sch. sect.), Phi Beta Kappa. Home: 16 Elm St Exeter NH 03833-2704 Office: Acad Libr Phillips Exeter Acad 20 Main St Exeter NH 03833-2438

THOMAS, JAMES BERT, JR., government official; b. Tallahassee, Mar. 16, 1935; s. James Bert and Stella E. (Lewis) T.; m. Sharon Mae Kelly, June 16, 1962; children: James Bert III, Mary Elizabeth, John Christopher. B.S., Fla. State U., 1957. C.P.A., Fla. Spl. auditor Office State Comptroller, Jacksonville, Fla., 1958; jr. auditor J.D.A. Holley & Co., C.P.A.'s, Tallahassee, 1959; sr. auditor Office of the State Auditor, Tallahassee, 1959-60; trainee, audit dir. HUD audit div., Washington, 1960-71; asst. dir. Bur. Accounts ICC, Washington, 1972-75, dir. Bur. Accounts, 1977-80; inspector gen. U.S. Dept. HUD, Washington, 1975-77, U.S. Dept. Edn., Washington, 1980-95; dir. auditing Office of the Gov., State of Fla., Tallahassee, 1995—; mem. Pres.'s Coun. Integrity and Efficiency, chmn. audit stds. subcom., 1984-95, chmn. audit com., 1989-90. Mem. AICPA (strategic planning com. 1987-90, chmn. govt. auditing standards adv. coun. 1991—), Inst. Internal Auditors (trustee Rsch. Found. 1991-92), Assn. Govt. Accts. (chmn. fin. mgmt. standards bd. 1985-86), Accts. Roundtable. Roman Catholic. Home: Unit 601 4737 Tory Sound Ln Tallahassee FL 32308 Office: Exec Office of Governor Rm 2107 The Capitol Tallahassee FL 32399-0001

THOMAS, JAMES EDWARD, accountant; b. Darlington, S.C., Oct. 18, 1944; s. Willie Thomas and Cleola (Sawyer) T.; m. Joan Yvette Grant, Mar. 15, 1945; 1 child, James E. II. BS in Acctg., Johnson C. Smith Coll., Charlotte, N.C., 1966; MA in Fin., C.W. Post Coll., Greenvale, N.Y., 1980; diploma, Fordham U., 1995. Asst. mgr. Mfrs. Hanover Trust, N.Y.C., 1970-78, Met. Savs. Bank, N.Y.C., 1978-81; auditor N.Y. State Dept. Social Svcs., N.Y.C., 1981-83; acct. N.Y.C. Bd. Edn., 1983-86; acct., agt. IRS, N.Y.C., 1987—; instr. Katherine L. Gibbs, Inc., N.Y.C., 1987-89. Mem. Assn. MBA Execs., Am. Mgmt. Assn., Internat. Platform Assn., Sigma Rho Sigma. Avocations: woodworking, basketball, basebell, track, reading. Home: 37-06 104th St Apt 4C Flushing NY 11368-1901

THOMAS, JAMES LEWIS, biomedical research scientist; b. Atlanta, May 18, 1949; s. Ruble Anderson and Mary Jo (Bass) T.; m. Kathleen Lee Hunter, Aug. 18, 1979; children: Jack, Mary Kate. BA, Emory U., 1971; PhD, U. Ala., Birmingham, 1981. Rsch. assoc. Washington U. Med. Sch., St. Louis, 1981-85, rsch. instr., 1985-91, rsch. asst. prof., 1991—. Contbr. articles to profl. jours. Mem. AAAS, Endocrine Soc., Soc. for Study of Reprodn., Pi Alpha, Delta Tau Delta. Achievements include research on structure/function relationships of enzyme catalytic amino acids; how changes in enzyme conformation participate in reaction mechanisms. Home: 7210 Stanford Ave Saint Louis MO 63130-3029 Office: Washington U Sch Medicine Dept Ob-Gyn 4911 Barnes Plz Saint Louis MO 63110

THOMAS, JAMES PATRICK, special education educator; b. Chgo., Sept. 24, 1946; s. Jacque Anthony and Dorothy Lucille (Brown) T.; m. Cathy E. Hanks, Sept. 29, 1979 (div. Aug. 1990); 1 child, Nicholas Jacque. BA in History and Polit. Sci., Drake U., 1973; MS in Pub. Adminstrn., Troy State U., 1983; MS in Spl. Edn., Johns Hopkins U., 1994, Cert. advanced grad. studies, 1994. cert. spl. educator. Commd. 2nd lt. USAF, 1973, advanced through grades to maj., 1985; missile launch officer, instr., crew comdr., contr. 91st Strategic Missile Wing, Minot, N.D., 1974-78; exec. officer, asst. ops. officer, resource advisor 6916th Electronic Security Squadron, Hellenikon Air Base, Greece, 1978-81; chief programs br. 6940th Electronic Security Wing, Ft. Meade, Md., 1981-82; program mgr. USAF Ops. Security Hq USAF/XOEO Directorate of Electronic Combat, Washington, 1982-85; intelligence collection activities mgr./chief Hdqrs. U.S. European Command, Stuttgart, Germany, 1986-88; signals intelligence planning staff officer Nat. Security Agy., Ft. Meade, 1988-90; cons. spl. edn. Balt., 1991—; adj. faculty mem. Catonsville (Md.) C.C., 1991—; spl. educator Howard County Sch. System, Columbia, 1992-94, Boonsborro (Md.) Middle Sch., 1994—. Author: (pamphlet) Your Rights to Legal Advice, 1994. Pres. Cath. Men Parish Athens, Greece, 1979-81, Minot AFB, N.D., 1975-78; asst. den leader, vice dean leader Cub Scouts, Boy Scouts Am., Ellicott City, Md., 1987-90. With USN, 1964-73. Decorated Purple Heart, 2 Def. Meritorious Svc. medals, Meritorious Svc. medals, Air Force Commendation medal. Mem. Phoenix Soc., Mil. Order Purple Heart (life), Am. Legion China Post 1, Ret. Officers Assn. (life), Vets. Vietnam War, Soaring Assn. Am., Swiftboat Sailors Assn. Inc. (pres. 1995—), Phi Delta Gamma (v.p. Gamma chpt.). Roman Catholic. Avocations: pilot of sailplanes, sailing, snorkeling, golf, running, photography. Address: 513 Bentley Ct Hagerstown MD 21740

THOMAS, JANEY SUE, elementary school principal; b. Clarksville, Tenn., Feb. 10, 1949; d. James Ernest and Ethel Mae (Evans) Kirkland; m. Tony Lee Thomas, Oct. 9, 1965; children: Jeff, Kelli. BS in Elem. Edn., Austin Peay State U., 1979, MA in Elem. Edn. Adminstrn., 1982, postgrad., 1987-89. Tchr. Charlotte (Tenn.) Jr. High Sch., 1979-86; prin. Vanleer (Tenn.) Elem. Sch., 1986-91, Oakmont Elem. Sch., Dickson, Tenn., 1991—. Ednl. rep. Concerned Citizens for Edn., Dickson County, 1988; mem. com. United Way Med. Tenn., Dickson County, 1990-91, bd. dirs., 1992-93. Recipient Nat. Sch. of Recognition award U.S. Dept. Edn., 1990. Mem. NAESP (Excellence in Edn. award 1989-90), Tenn. Assn. Elem. Sch. Prins. (Nat. Exemplary Sch. award 1989-90), Dickson County Edn. Assn. (pres. 1989-90). Baptist. Avocations: reading, traveling, shopping. Home: 226 Druid Hills Dr Dickson TN 37055-3331 Office: Oakmont Elem Sch 630 Highway 46 S Dickson TN 37055-2552

THOMAS, JAY, actor; b. New Orleans; s. Harry and Kathy Thomas; m. Sally Michelson, Dec. 1986. Morning disk jockey KPWR, L.A., 1986—. Performances include: (TV) Mork and Mindy, 1979-81, Cheers, 1987-90, Married People, 1990, Murphy Brown, 1990-92, Love and War, 1992-95 (Emmy award nominee for lead actor in comedy series 1994); (films) C.H.U.D., 1984, The Gig, 1992, Straight Talk, 1992. Office: Don Buchwald and Assocs 9229 Sunset Blvd Ste 710 Los Angeles CA 90069*

THOMAS, JEAN-JACQUES ROBERT, Romance languages educator; b. Mirecourt, Vosges, France, Jan. 20, 1948; s. Jean-Robert and Yvonne Marie-Rose (Ladner) T.; m. Mary Lorene Hammial, Aug. 21, 1976; children: Dominick, Robert. Lic., U. Lille, France, 1968, M, 1969; diplome in lang. Orientales, U. Paris, France, 1972, PhD, 1972. Teaching asst. U. Paris, 1969-71, asst. researcher, 1971-72; lectr. U. Mich., 1972-75; asst. prof. Columbia U., N.Y.C., 1975-81; assoc. prof. Duke U., Durham, N.C., 1981-87, prof., 1989—, chmn. romance studies, 1989-94; pres. Educo, Paris, 1988-89, 95-96; dir. Institute French Studies U. Calif., Santa Barbara, 1991—; bd. dirs. Studies in Twenty-Century Lit., Lincoln, Nebr., Palmes Académiques, 1994. Author: Lire Leiris, 1972, La Langue la Poésie, 1987, La Langue Volée, 1988; co-author: Poétique Générative, 1978, Poética Generativa, 1983, 89; translator:Sémiotique de la Poésie, 1983; assoc. editor: Sub-Stance, 1975—, Poetics Today, 1980—. Grantee Rackham Found., 1973, IBM, 1984, Sloan Found., 1985. Mem. MLA (chmn. divsn. 1980-81, 86-87, 93-95), N.E. MLA (chmn. sect. 1982-83), Semiotic Soc. Am. Home: 26 Porchlight Ct Durham NC 27707-2442 Office: Duke U Dept Romance Studies Durham NC 27706

THOMAS, JERRY, pharmacist; b. Milan, Ga., Oct. 2, 1942; s. Robert Guy and Myrtice (Hinson) T.; m. Marianne Norris, Nov. 14, 1964; children: Angela, Tammy, Melanie, Jamey, Jason. BS in Pharmacy, Auburn (Ala.) U., 1966. Lic. pharmacist, Ala. Pharmacist Harco Drug Inc., Tuscaloosa, 1966-75, v.p., 1975-79, exec. v.p., 1979-93, pres., 1993—. Bd. dirs. West Ala. Easter Seal Rehab., 1994-95, Salvation Army, 1993-95, fin. chmn. Mem. Am. Pharm. Assn. (legis. affairs com.), Ala. Pharm. Assn. (A.A. Ribbon Bowl of Hygiene 1989), Lions (pres. 1987). Baptist. Avocations: jogging, reading. Home: 4929 Emerald Bay Dr Northport AL 35476 Office: Harco Drug Inc 3925 Rice Mine Rd NE Tuscaloosa AL 35406-1523*

THOMAS, JIM, professional basketball team executive. Mng. gen. ptnr. Sacramento Kings. Office: Sacramento Kings 1 Sports Pky Sacramento CA 95834-2300*

THOMAS, JIMMY LYNN, financial executive; b. Mayfield, Ky., Aug. 3, 1941; s. Alben Stanley and Emma Laura (Alexander) T.; m. Kristin H. Kent, Oct. 1986; children: James Nelson, Carter Danforth. BS, U. Ky., 1963; MBA, Columbia U., 1964. Fin. analyst Ford Motor Co., Detroit, 1964-66; asst. treas. Joel Dean Assocs., N.Y.C., 1966-67; asst. contr. Trans World Airlines, N.Y.C., 1967-73; sr. v.p. fin. svcs., treas. Gannett Co., Inc., Arlington, Va., 1973—; bd. dirs. Marine Midland Bank, Rochester, Arkwright Boston Mut. Ins. Co-Atlantic Region, Tremont Ptnrs., Brown Devel. Co., Newspaper Printing Corp., Pacific Media, Inc., Guam Publs., Gannett Supply Corp., Gannett Fla. Corp., Gannett Pacific Corp. With U.S. Army, 1966-72. Ashland Oil Co. scholar, 1959-63, McKinsey scholar 1964; Samuel Bronfman fellow, 1963-64. Mem. U. Ky. Alumni Assn., Columbia U. Alumni Assn., Fin. Execs. Inst., Inst. Newspaper Contrs. and Fin. Officers, Country Club of Rochester, Genessee Valley Club, Georgetown Club, Washington Golf and Country Club, Beta Gamma Sigma, Omicron Delta Kappa, Sigma Alpha Epsilon. Democrat. Mem. Christian Ch. (Disciples of Christ). Home: 100 Gibbon St Alexandria VA 22314-3836 Office: Gannett Co Inc 1100 Wilson Blvd Arlington VA 22234

THOMAS, JOAB LANGSTON, academic administrator, biology educator; b. Holt, Ala., Feb. 14, 1933; s. Ralph Cage and Chamintney Elizabeth (Stovall) T.; m. Marly A. Dukes, Dec. 22, 1954; children: Catherine, David, Jennifer, Frances. AB, Harvard U., 1955, MA, 1957, PhD, 1959; DSc (hon.), U. Ala., 1981; LLD (hon.), Stillman Coll., 1987; LHD (hon.), Tri-State U., 1994. Cytotaxonomist Arnold Aboretum, Harvard, 1959-61; faculty U. Ala., University, 1961-76, prof. biology, 1966-76, 88-91, asst. dean Coll. Arts and Scis., 1964-65, 69, dean for student devel. Coll., 1969-74, v.p., 1974-76, dir. Herbarium, 1961-76, dir. Arboretum, 1964-65, 66-69; pres. U. Ala., Tuscaloosa, 1981-88; chancellor N.C. State U., Raleigh, 1976-81; pres. Pa. State U., University Park, 1990-95, pres. emeritus, 1995—; bd. dirs. Blount, Inc., Lukens, Inc., Mellon Corp.; intern acad. adminstrn. Am. Coun. on Edn., 1971. Author: A Monographic Study of the Cyrillaceae, 1960, Wildflowers of Alabama and Adjoining States, 1973, The Rising South, 1976, Poisonous Plants and Venomous Animals of Alabama and Adjoining States, 1990. Bd. dirs. Internat. Potato Ctr., 1977-83, chmn. 1982-83; bd. dirs. Internat. Svc. for Nat. Agrl. Rsch., 1985-91. Named Ala. Acad. Honor, 1983, Citizen of Yr., Tuscaloosa, 1987; recipient Palmer Mus. Art medal. Mem. Golden Key, Phi Beta Kappa, Sigma Xi, Omicron Delta Kappa, Phi Kappa Phi. Office: Pa State U 201 Old Main University Park PA 16802-1503

THOMAS, JOE CARROLL, human resources director; b. Belmont, N.C., Nov. 2, 1931; m. Ruth Stone, June 17, 1951; children: Joe, Jerry, Angela. BA, Belmont Abbey Coll., 1954; MS, Cornell U., 1961. Mgr. terr. sales Gen. Foods Corp., San Antonio, 1954-62; asst. dir. personnel textiles divsn. Kendall Co., Charlotte, N.C., 1962-64; dir. personnel S.E. region Gifford Hill & Co., Charlotte, 1964-71; dir. mgmt. svcs. Ervin Industries, Charlotte, 1971-75; v.p. indsl. rels. Crompton & Knowles, Charlotte, 1975-76; exec. v.p., dir. human resources Barclays Group Inc. (USA), Charlotte, 1976—; mem. adv. coun. Sch. Bus., Western Carolina U., Cullowhee, N.C., 1980-84. Vice chmn. bd. trustees Belmont Abbey Coll., 1982-88; chmn. fundraising campaign Charlotte chpt. Am. Heart Assn., 1984; mem. bd. visitors Mercy Hosp., Charlotte, 1984-87; bd. dirs. Mercy Health Svcs., Charlotte, 1988—; bd. dirs. Jr. Achievement Charlotte, 1985-88; chmn. bd. dirs. INROADS div. Charlotte, Inc., 1987-88; bd. visitors Johnson C. Smith Univ., 1989-92. Mem. Soc. for Human Resource Mgmt., The Employers Assn. (bd. dirs. 1993—, exec. com. 1995), Charlotte Athletic Club (pres. 1982-83), Charlotte Rotary, Tower Club, Charlotte C. of C. (bd. advisors 1992—). Democrat. Methodist. Avocations: golf, reading. Office: Barclays Group Inc (USA) 201 N Tryon St Charlotte NC 28202-2136

THOMAS, JOHN BOWMAN, educator, electrical engineer; b. New Kensington, Pa., July 14, 1925; s. John Bowman and Lenna Iva (Sturms) T.; m. Eleanor W. Graefe, June 3, 1944; children—Sharon Lenore (Mrs. Guy G. Miller), Bronwyn Lee (Mrs. Robert Knight), John Andrew, Gwendolyn Elizabeth, Randall Stuart, Gailyn Brooke. A.B., Gettysburg Coll., 1944; B.S., Johns Hopkins, 1952; M.S., Stanford, 1953, Ph.D., 1955. Elec. engr., then asst. chief engr. Koppers Co., Inc., 1946-52; faculty Princeton, 1955—, prof. elec. engring., 1962—; Indsl. cons., 1955—. Author tech. papers, books. Served with AUS, 1944-46. NSF sr. postdoctoral fellow Berkeley, Stanford, 1967-68. Fellow I.E.E.E. (exec. com. Princeton sect. 1955-63), IEEE (officer 1960-63); mem. Sigma Xi, Tau Beta Pi. Home: 3651 Las Pilitas Rd Santa Margarita CA 93453-9637

THOMAS, JOHN CHARLES, lawyer, former state supreme court justice; b. Norfolk, Va., Sept. 18, 1950; s. John and Floretta V. (Sears) T.; m. Pearl Walden, Oct. 9, 1982; children: John Charles Jr., Ruby Virginia, Lewis LeGrant. B.A. in Am. Govt. with distinction, U. Va., 1972, J.D., 1975. Bar: Va. 1975, U.S. Dist. Ct. (ea. and we. dists.) 1976, U.S. Ct. Appeals (4th cir.) 1976, U.S. Supreme Ct. 1979, U.S. Ct. Appeals (D.C. cir.) 1980, U.S. Ct. Appeals (10th cir.) 1991, U.S. Ct. Appeals (11th cir.) 1992. Assoc. Hunton & Williams, Richmond, Va., 1975-82, ptnr., 1982-83, 89—; justice Supreme Ct. of Va., Richmond, 1983-89; mem. adv. con. on appellate rules U.S. Jud. Conf. Bd. dirs. U. Va. Law Sch. Found., Thomas Jefferson Meml. Foun. Master John Marshall Inn of Ct. (exec. com.); fellow Am. Bar Found., Va. Bar Found.; mem. Am. Arbitration Assn. (bd. dirs., exec. com.), Am. Acad. Appellate Lawyers, Va. State Bar, Va. Bar Assn., Bar Assn. City of Richmond, Old Dominion Bar Assn., Omega Psi Phi. Office: Hunton & Williams Riverfront Plz East Tower 951 E Byrd St Richmond VA 23219-4040

THOMAS, JOHN COX, JR., publisher; b. Port Chester, N.Y., July 27, 1927; s. John Cox and Henrietta Edna (Cook) T.; widowed; children: Mark Gregory, Pamela Cook, Suzanne Elizabeth. BA, Columbia U., 1948, MBA, 1950. Advt. salesman McCall's mag., N.Y.C., 1953-58; advt. salesman Time mag., N.Y.C., 1959-62, mgr. Los Angeles, 1962-67, dir. N.Y. sales, 1967-71, U.S. sales dir., 1971-73; pub. N.Y. mag., N.Y.C., 1973-76, New West mag., Los Angeles, 1975-76; pres. A/S/M Communications, N.Y.C., 1978-89; chmn. ADWEEK Mags, N.Y.C., 1989—. Sr. Warden St. John's of Lattingtown, Locust Valley, N.Y., 1986. Mem. Mag. Pubs. Assn. Clubs: The Creek (Locust Valley), The Links (N.Y.C.). Avocations: golf, travel. Home: 305 Bayville Rd Locust Valley NY 11560-1401 Office: ADWEEK Mags 1515 Broadway New York NY 10036*

THOMAS, JOHN DAVID, musician, composer, arranger, photographer, recording engineer, producer; b. Muncie, Ind., Mar. 30, 1951; s. John Charles and Phyllis Lorraine (Wear) T.; m. Rosalie Faith Baldwin, July 27, 1974 (div. 1991); children: Bethany Carol, Mark David. Student, Purdue U., 1969-71, Jordan Coll. of Music, Indpls., 1961-65; BS in Music Theory and Composition, Ball State U., 1976. Musician, composer, 1955—; cellist The Howe String Quartet (with Ann Pinney, Mary Ann Tilford, Anne Wuster), Indpls., 1967-68; keyboardist, vocalist, cellist Fire and The Rebel Kind rock bands, Indpls., 1967-69, Good Conduct rock band, Muncie, Ind., 1972-73; pianist The Pavillion at Olde Towne, Los Gatos, Calif., 1969; radio announcer John David's Late Night Rock Show WCCR-AM, West Lafayette, Ind., 1969-70; photographer Indpls., 1964-84, 91—; budget analyst Office of Comptr. USAFAC, Indpls., 1976-84; co-leader, keyboardist, composer, arranger, vocalist, sound technician JETSTREAM Band, Indpls., Kokomo, Columbus, Bloomington, Ind., 1979-83; co-leader, keyboardist, vocalist, sound technician The Thomas Bros., King's Crown Inn, Kokomo, 1979; sound/audio visual technician Valley Cathedral Ch., Phoenix, 1987; solo pianist Cascade Club, Everett, Wash., 1990; pianist, synthesist Paul Thomas and Night and Day, The Tim Barnett Band, Indpls. Mus. Art, 1992, Radisson Hotel and Broadmoor Country Club, Indpls., 1991, Highland Country Club, Indpls., The Ritz Charles Hotel and Summertrace, Carmel, Ind., Stonehenge Resort, Bedford, Ind., 1991; solo pianist Terranova Mansion, Paradise Valley, Ariz., 1987, Wrigley Mansion, Phoenix, 1988, Boulders Resort, Carefree, Ariz., 1987, Clarion Inn/McCormick's Ranch Resort, Scottsdale, Ariz., 1986, The Terranova mansion, Paradise Valley, Ariz., 1987, China Gate, Phoenix, 1988, Victor's, Phoenix, 1988; keyboardist, synthesist, key bassist, The Guich Gang, Pinnacle Peak Patio, Scottsdale, 1984, Dee Dee Ryan, The Longhorn Saloon, Apache Junction, Ariz., 1984-86, The Last Straw Band, Country City saloon, Mesa, Ariz., 1986; keyboardist, pianist, vocalist with Peter, Paul and John, Anderson Coll., Anderson, Ind., 1977; CEO, composer, arranger, prodr., musician, engr. John David Thomas Prodns., Indpls., 1993—. Composer, lyricist of over 200 classical, religious, comml., rock, jazz, popular and avante garde/futuristic compositions, including Infinity, 1970-71, Death of Rock and Roll, 1970, Night Visions, 1972, First Things First, 1972, Two Nudes and a Fire Hydrant, 1972-73, Zeitgeist: The Spirit of the Time, 1974, The Little Prince, 1973, When We Dead Awaken, 1973, Pray, 1972, Apogee, 1974, Chinese Baby, 1973, Alabama DA (Top Forty recording), 1973, Angel, 1974, Music for French Horn, Cello, and Piano, 1976, Cruising Beyond, 1979, Jetstream Theme, 1979, Chrissy, 1979, In Your Heart, 1983, Future Music, 1987, The Recurrent New Millenium Orchestral Olympic Disco Festival Dance, 1989, Jubilee in F, 1989, Praise Him, The King Liveth, 1989, Love Flowers: Reflections and Meditations on Beauty and Truth, 1990, Sheena's Theme, 1992, I Want You Forever You're My Miracle, 1992, My Pseudo-Erotic, Sensual, Exotic Musical Fantasy and Romance for Our Heavenly Nocturnal Starry-Skied Carpet Ride to Paradise in Istanbul and Constantinople, 1992, I'm in Love with Someone Beautiful, 1992, Improvisations for Sheena, 1992, Music for Baritone Vocal and String Orch., 1995; (albums) The Journey of Life, Destiny's Calling: Improvisations, 1994, Musical Essences, 1995, Pathway to Love, 1996, (broadcast) Hometown Hour, Sta. WFBQ-FM, Indpls., 1979-80; performed orginal composition, Someday, WFBM-TV, Indpls., 1969; designer automotive concepts and popular fashions; recordings of over 45 original songs and compositions, Ind., Ariz., Wash., 1970—; author (poetry with others) Mind, 1993, 96. Musician, vocalist, composer Downey Ave. Christian Ch., Indpls., 1961-69, Univ. Presbyn. Ch., West Lafayette, Ind., 1969-71, Castleview Bapt. Ch., Indpls., 1974-84, Valley Cathedral CPhoenix,

1986-87, Edmonds (Wash.) Christian Ch., 1988-90, Edmonds United Meth. Ch., 1989-90; page to speaker Ho. of Reps. Ind. State Legislature, 1963; active All Souls Unitarian Ch., Indpls. GM scholar Purdue U., 1969-70, Hoosier scholar, 1969, Palmer Meml. Music scholar Ball State U., 1971-74; named to Ind. All-State Orch. (cellist), 1968; recipient 1st place award (cellist) Ind. State Music Contest, 1968, God and Country award, 1965, Outstanding Musician award Irvington Music Club, Indpls., 1969, Purdue U. Symphonette, 1970, Hometown Hour award WFBQ-FM Radio Sta., Indpls., 1979. Mem. ASCAP, AAAS, Am. Contract Bridge League, Am. Mus. Natural History, U.S. Chess Fedn., Nat. Geographic Soc., World Futurist Soc., World Wildlife Fund, Audio Engring. Soc., Met. Opera Guild (N.Y.C.), Mus. Modern Art (N.Y.C.), The Guggenheim Mus. (N.Y.C.), Inst. of Noetic Scis., Planetary Soc., Audubon Soc., Mus. Sci. Industry, Met. Mus. Art, La. Societé des Amis du Louvre (Paris), Mensa, Sierra Club, Internat. Amnesty Internat. Avocations: concerts, hi-fi, cd's, listening to music, travel. Home and Office: 2704 Central Ct Indianapolis IN 46280-1930

THOMAS, JOHN EDWIN, retired academic administrator; b. Fort Worth, Tex., Apr. 23, 1931; s. John L. and Dorothy F. T.; m. Janice Paula Winzinek, Jan. 29, 1967; children—John L., Christa T., Scott A., Brandon F. BSEE, U. Kans., 1953; JD, U. Mo., Kansas City, 1961; MS, Fla. State U., 1965, DBA, 1970. With Wagner Electric Corp., St. Louis, 1955-63; mgr. elec. apparatus div. Wagner Electric Corp., Atlanta, 1961-63; with NASA, Cape Kennedy, Fla., 1963-70; chief requirements and resources office, dir. tech. support NASA, 1966-70; prof., head gen. bus. dept. East Tex. State U., 1970-72; dean (Coll. Scis. and Tech.), 1972-74; vice chancellor for acad. affairs Appalachian State U., Boone, N.C., 1974-79; chancellor Appalachian State U., 1979-93; ret. N.C. Utilities Commn., Raleigh, 1993; spl. advisor for sci., tech. & higher edn. Gov. State of N.C., Raleigh, 1994, ret., 1994; chair N.C. Utilities Commn., 1993-94; spl. advisor to Gov. of State of N.C. on sci./tech. and higher edn., 1994. Mem. N.C. Agy. for Pub. Telecommunications. Served with USN, 1949-50, USMC, 1953-55. NDEA fellow, 1968. Mem. Fed. Bar Assn., Soc. Advancement Mgmt., Sc. Mgmt. Assn., Phi Delta Kappa, Pi Sigma Epsilon, Delta Gamma Sigma., Phi Kappa Phi. Methodist. Club: Kiwanis. Home: Rt 4 Box 26 Daisy Ridge Banner Elk NC 28604

THOMAS, JOHN HOWARD, astrophysicist, engineer, educator; b. Chgo., Apr. 9, 1941; s. William Whitney and Dorothy Loretta (Derris) T.; m. Lois Ruth Moffit, Aug. 11, 1962; children: Jeffrey, Laura. B.S. in Engring. Sci., Purdue U., 1962, M.S. in Engring. Sci., 1964, Ph.D. in Engring. Sci., 1966. Lic. profl. engr., N.Y. NATO postdoctoral fellow U. Cambridge, Eng., 1966-67; asst. prof. mech. and aerospace sci. U. Rochester, 1967-73, assoc. prof., 1973-81, prof., 1981—, prof. astronomy, 1986—, assoc. dean for grad. studies Coll. Engring. and Applied Sci., 1981-83, univ. dean grad. studies, 1983-91; vis. astronomer Nat. Solar Obs., Sunspot, N.Mex.; vis. scientist Max-Planck Inst. for Physics and Astrophysics, Munich, 1973-74, High Altitude Obs., Boulder, Colo., 1985; vis. fellow Worcester Coll, vis. prof. dept. theoretical physics Oxford (Eng.) U., 1987-88; affiliate scientist Nat. Ctr. for Atmospheric Rsch., Boulder, 1989—; vis. prof. Rsch. Ctr. for Theoretical Astrophysics, U. Sydney, Australia, 1991, Sch. Math. and Stats., 1993; prin. investigator NASA, NSF, USAF, Office Naval Rsch. Editor: Physics of Sunspots, 1981, Sunspots: Theory and Observations, 1992; assoc. editor Astrophys. Jour., 1993-96, sci. editor, 1996—; author articles on astrophysics, solar physics and fluid dynamics. NSF fellow, 1963-66; Guggenheim fellow, 1993-94. Mem. AAAS, Am. Astron. Soc. (chair solar physics divsn. 1995—), Internat. Astron. Union, Am. Phys. Soc., Am. Geophys. Union, Sigma Xi, Tau Beta Pi, Sigma Delta Chi. Office: U Rochester 223 Hopeman Bldg Rochester NY 14627

THOMAS, JOHN LOVELL, history educator; b. Portland, Maine, Oct. 28, 1926; d. John White and Ruth Arlene (Lovell) T.; m. Patricia Ann Blake, Sept. 30, 1951; children: John Blake, Jayn. B.A., Bowdoin Coll., 1947; M.A., Columbia U., 1950; Ph.D., Brown U., 1960. Instr. Barnard Coll., N.Y.C., 1950-52; instr. Brown U., Providence, 1955-59, asst. prof., 1959-60, assoc. prof., prof. history, 1964—, George L. Littlefield Prof. Am. History; asst. prof. history Harvard U., Cambridge, Mass., 1960-64. Author: The Liberator, 1963 (recipient Bancroft prize 1963), Alternative America, 1983; editor: Slavery Attacked, 1966, John C. Calhoun, 1965. Recipient Allan Nevins prize Soc. Am. Historians, 1960; fellow Guggenheim Found., 1970; Charles Warren fellow Harvard U., 1967; fellow Woodrow Wilson Found., 1982. Mem. Am. Hist. Assn. Office: Brown U Dept History 142 Angell St Providence RI 02912-9040

THOMAS, JOHN MELVIN, retired surgeon; b. Carmarthen, U.K., Apr. 26, 1933; came to U.S., 1958; s. Morgan and Margaret (Morgan) T.; m. Betty Ann Mayo, Nov. 3, 1958; children: James, Hugh, Pamela. MB, BChir, U. Coll. Wales, U. Edinburgh, 1958. Intern Robert Packer Hosp., Sayre, Pa., 1958-59, chief surg. resident, 1963, pres. med. staff, 1968; assoc. surgeon Guthrie Clinic Ltd., Sayre, 1963-69, chmn. dept. surgery, 1969-91; pres. bd. dirs. Guthrie Clinic Ltd., 1972-89; trustee Robert Packer Hosp.; chmn. exec. com. Guthrie Healthcare Sys., 1990-92, dir., 1994—; guest examiner Am. Bd. Surgery, 1979, 81, 85; bd. dirs. Measurement Innovations Corp., Citizen Fin. Bank, Mansfield, Pa., Trianalytics Corp.; cons. The Hunter Group, 1995—. Bd. dirs. Donald Guthrie Found. for Rsch., pres., 1983—; bd. dirs. Pa. Trauma Sys. Found., 1984-90, pres., 1988, 89; chmn. licensure and accountability Gov.'s Conf., 1974; bd. dirs. Vol. Hosps. Am., 1993-95; trustee Mansfield (Pa.) U. Found., 1991—; trustee Mansfield Univ. Found., 1991-95. Mem. ACS (gov. 1985-91), AMA, Am. Group Practice Assn., Soc. for Surgery Alimentary Tract, Pa. Med. Soc., Bradford County Med. Soc., Cen. N.Y. Surg. Soc., Internat. Soc. Surgery, Soc. Surgery Alimentary Tract, Ea. Vascular Soc., Ithaca Country Club, Moselem Springs Golf Club. Presbyterian. Home: 383 Lansing Station Rd Lansing NY 14882-8606

THOMAS, JOHN RICHARD, chemist; b. Anchorage, Ky., Aug. 26, 1921; s. John R. and Mildred (Woods) T.; m. Beatrice Ann Davidson, Dec. 7, 1944; children: Jonnie Sue Jacobs, Richard G. B.S., U. Calif., Berkeley, 1943, Ph.D., 1947. With U.S. AEC, 1949-51; rsch. chemist Chevron Rsch. Co., Richmond, Calif., 1948-49; sr. rsch. assoc. Chevron Rsch. Co., 1951-60, sr. rsch. scientist, 1961-67, pres., also bd. dirs., 1970-86; v.p. petroleum rsch. Chevron Corp., 1984-86, ret., 1986; mgr. R&D Ortho div. Chevron Chem. Co., Richmond, 1967-68; asst. sec. Standard Oil Co., Calif., 1968-70. Contbr. articles to profl. jours. Mem. Am. Chem. Soc. Republican. Patentee in field. Home: 847 McEllen Way Lafayette CA 94549-5134 Office: Chevron Research Co 576 Standard Ave Richmond CA 94801-2016

THOMAS, JOHN THIEME, management consultant; b. Detroit, Aug. 21, 1935; s. John Shepherd and Florence Leona (Thieme) T.; m. Ellen Linden Taylor, June 27, 1959; children: Johnson Taylor, Evan Thurston. BBA, U. Mich., 1957, MBA, 1958. Mfg. dept. mgr. Procter & Gamble Co., Cin., 1958-60, brand mgr., 1960-63; sr. cons. Glendinning Cos. Inc., Westport, Conn., 1964-66; v.p. Glendinning Cos. Inc., London, 1967-69; exec. v.p. Glendinning Cos. Inc., Westport, 1970-74; also bd. dirs.; exec. v.p., chief operating officer Ero Industries, Chgo., 1974-76; v.p. Lamalie Assocs. Inc., Chgo., 1977-81; pres. Wilkins & Thomas Inc., Chgo., 1981-87; ptnr. Ward Howell Internat., Chgo., 1987—, mng. dir., cons. practice, 1992—, chief of staff, 1995—; also bd. dirs.; exec. com. Procter & Gamble Alumni Assn., Chgo., 1981—. Pub. Proctor & Gamble Mfg. Alumni directory, 1981—; author articles in profl. jours. Chmn. bd. dirs. Winnetka (Ill.) Youth Orgn., 1986—; selector Winnetka Town Coun., 1978, 80, 84. Mem. Nat. Assn. Corp. & Profl. Recruiters, Assn. Exec. Search Cons., Am. Soc. Personnel Adminstrn. Club: Fairfield (Conn.) Hunt (treas. 1971-74). Avocations: gardening, music, playing tuba. Home: 525 Ash St Winnetka IL 60093-2601 Office: Ward Howell Internat 300 W Wacker Dr Chicago IL 60606

THOMAS, JOSEPH ALLAN, lawyer; b. L.A., Aug. 12, 1929; s. Joseph Smith and Blanche Aileen (Henry) T.; m. Jacquelynne Beverly Jones, June 13, 1954; children: Douglas, Scott, Kevin, Matthew. B.S., U. So. Calif., 1954, J.D., 1957. Bar: Calif. 1958, U.S. Supreme Ct. 1990. Pvt. practice law Downey, Calif., 1958-60; with law dept. Pacific Mut. Life Ins. Co., Newport Beach, Calif., 1960-92; sr. v.p., gen counsel Pacific Mut. Life Ins. Co., 1978-92; of counsel Barger and Wolen, Irvine, Calif., 1992—; treas. Assn. for Calif. Tort Reform, 1981-92. Mem. bd. advisors Fairview State Hosp., 1985-93. Fellow Life Office Mgmt. Inst.; mem. Calif. Bar Assn., Assn. Life Ins. Counsel (bd. govs. 1990-94), Inst. Corp. Counsel (bd. govs. 1985-92). Office: Barger & Wolen 19800 Macarthur Blvd Ste 800 Irvine CA 92715-2437

THOMAS, JOSEPH ERUMAPPETTICAL, psychologist; b. Piravom, Kerala, India, Feb. 11, 1937; came to U.S., 1971; s. Iype Erumappettiyil and Kunjamma M. (Padiyil) T.; m. Chinnamma Kavatt, Nov. 23, 1964; children: Joseph Jr., Kurian, Elizabeth. BA, Kerala U., India, 1957, MA, 1960, PhD, 1969. Diplomate Internat. Acad. Behavioral Medicine, Counseling, and Psychotherapy; lic. psychologist. Lectr. psychology U. Kerala, Trivandrum, India, 1967-70; postdoctoral fellow in psychology Northwestern U. Med. Sch., Chgo., 1971-72; psychologist U. Chgo., 1972-74; instr. psychiatry Northwestern U. Med. Sch., Chgo., 1972-76, asst. prof. dept. psychiatry, 1977—; psychologist Northwestern Meml. Hosp., Chgo., 1974-80; pvt. practice psychology Chgo., 1980—; cons. Michael Reese Hosp., Chgo., 1980-86; founding mem. Inst. Psychiatry, Northwestern U., Chgo. Contbr. articles to profl. jours. Mem. Dupage County Health Planning Com., Wheaton, Ill., 1984; founding mem., trustee St. Thomas Ch. Chgo., St. Gregorios Orthodox Ch., Oak Park, Ill. Commonwealth fellow Govt. U.K., U. Glasgow, 1970. Mem. Am. Psychological Assn., Mental Health Assn. DuPage County (bd. dirs. 1982-84), Biofeedback Soc. Ill. (pres. 1984-85). Home: 16 W 731 89th Pl Hinsdale IL 60521 Office: Ste B 103 1776 S Naperville Rd Wheaton IL 60187

THOMAS, JOSEPH FLESHMAN, architect; b. Oak Hill, W.Va., Mar. 23, 1915; s. Robert Russel and Effie (Fleshman) T.; m. Margaret Ruth Lively, Feb. 28, 1939 (dec.); children: Anita Carol, Joseph Stephen; m. Dorothy Francene Root, Apr. 29, 1967 (div.); m. Bonnie Abbott Buckley, June 15, 1991. Student, Duke, 1931-32; B.Arch., Carnegie-Mellon U., 1938. Practice architecture various firms W. Va., Va., Tenn., Calif., 1938-49; staff architect Calif. Div. Architecture, Los Angeles, 1949-52; prin. Joseph F. Thomas, architect, Pasadena, Calif., 1952-53; pres. Neptune & Thomas (architects-engrs.), Pasadena and San Diego, 1953-78; Mem. Pasadena Planning Commn., 1956-64, chmn., 1963-64; pres. Citizens Coun. for Planning, Pasadena, 1966-67; mem. steering com. Pasadena NOW, 1970-74; mem. Pasadena Design Com., 1979-86; mem. adv. bd. Calif. Office Architecture and Constrn., 1970-72; mem. archtl. adv. com. Calif. State U. System, 1981-84; mem. adv. coun. Sch. Environ. Design Calif. Poly. Inst., 1983—; mem. outreach for architecture com. Carnegie Mellon U., 1989—, pres.'s devel. com., 1991—. Prin. works include Meth. Hosp., Arcadia, Calif., Foothill Presbyn. Hosp., Glendora, Calif., master plans and bldgs., Citrus Coll., Azusa, Calif., Riverside (Calif.) Coll., Westmont Coll., Monticeto, Calif., Northrop Inst. Tech., Inglewood, Calif, Indian Valley Coll., Marin County, Calif., Pepperdine U., Malibu, Calif., UCLA, U. Calif., San Diego, Long Beach (Calif.) State U., Calif. Inst. Tech., Pasadena, Calif., other coll. bldgs. Pacific Telephone Co., Pasadena, L.A. County Superior Ct. Bldg., U.S. Naval Hosp., San Diego. Trustee Almansor Edn. Ctr., 1986-92; bd. dirs., co-founder Syncor Internat., 1973-83; founding dir. Bank of Pasadena, 1962-65. Lt. (j.g.) USNR, 1943-46. Recipient Service award City of Pasadena, 1964; Disting. Service award Calif. Dept. Gen. Services, 1972; Gold Crown award Pasadena Arts Council, 1981. Fellow AIA (4 awards honor, 13 awards merit 1957-78, dir. Calif. coun. 1966-68, exec. com. 1974-77, pres. Pasadena chpt. 1967, chmn. Calif. sch. facilities com. 1970-72, mem. nat. jud. bd. 1973-74, nat. dir. 1974-77, treas. 1977-79, exec. com., planning com., chmn. finance com.); mem. Breakfast Forum (chmn. 1983), Annandale Golf Club, Pi Kappa Alpha. Republican. Methodist. Home: 330 San Miguel Rd Pasadena CA 91105-1446

THOMAS, JOYCE CAROL, author, educator; b. Ponca City, Okla., May 25, 1938; children—Monica, Gregory, Michael, Roy. BA, San Jose (Calif.) State U., 1966; MA, Stanford U., 1967. Former asst. prof., later prof. San Jose State U.; prof. English U. Tenn, 1989—; vis. prof. English, Purdue U., 1984. Author: (poetry) Bittersweet, 1973, Black Child, 1981, Inside the Rainbow, 1982, Brown Honey in Broomwhea Tea, 1993, Gingerbread Days, 1995; (novels) Marked by Fire (Nat. Book award), 1982, Bright Shadow, 1983, Water Girl, 1986, The Golden Pasture, 1986, Journey, 1988, When the Nightengale Sings, 1992; editor: A Gathering of Flowers, 1990, (short story) Young Reverend Zelma Lee Moses. Office: care Internat Creative Mgmt Inc 40 W 57th St New York NY 10019-4001

THOMAS, KAREN P., composer, conductor; b. Seattle, Sept. 17, 1957. BA in Composition, Cornish Inst., 1979; MusM in Composition, Conducting, U. Wash., 1985. Condr. The Contemporary Group, 1981-85; condr., music dir. Wash. Composers Forum, 1984-86; artistic dir., condr. Seattle Pro Musica, 1987—. Conducting debut Seattle, 1987; composer: Four Delineations of Curtmantle for Trombone or Cello, 1982, Metamorphoses on a Machaut Kyrie for Strong Orch. or Quartet, 1983, Cowboy Songs for Voice and Piano, 1985, There Must Be a Lone Range for Soprano and Chamber Ensemble, 1987, Brass Quintet, 1987, Four Lewis Carroll Songs for Choir, 1989, (music/dance/theater) Boxiana, 1990, Elementi for Clarinet and Percussion, 1991, (one-act children's opera) Coyote's Tail, 1991, Clarion Dances for Brass Ensemble, 1993, Roundup for Sax Quartet, 1993, Three Medieval Lyrics for Choir, 1992, Sopravvento for Wind Quartet and Percussion, 1994, When Night Came for Clarinet and Chamber Orch.. or Clarinet and Piano, 1994, also numerous others. Recipient Composers Forum award N.W. Chamber Orch., 1984, King County Arts Commn., 1987, 90, Artist Trust, 1988, 93, Seattle Arts Commn., 1988, 91, 93, New Langton Arts, 1988, Delius Festival, 1993, Melodious Accord award 1993; fellow Wash. State Arts Commn., 1991; Charles E. Ives scholar AAAL. Mem. Broadcast Music, Am. Music Ctr., Internat. Alliance for Women in Music, Soc. Composers, Chorus Am.

THOMAS, KATHERINE JANE, newspaper business columnist; b. Bryan, Tex., Mar. 22, 1942; d. William Holt Jr. and Mary Anne (McCasland) Oliver; m. Robert Wayne Thomas, June 1, 1968; children: Jennifer Ann, Michael Frederick. BA, U. Tex., 1964. News reporter Abilene Reporter, Tex., 1964-67; with Ralston Purina Co., 1967-68; journalist The Eagle, Bryan, Tex., 1969-72, Wall St. Jour., Houston Bus. Jour., 1976-80; bus. columnist Houston Post, 1980-95; freelance bus. columnist Daily Ct. Rev., West U. Jour. Judge Houston Women on the Move Sect. Com., 1989-90, 91; judge Houston Area Inc. Mag. Entrepreneur of Yr., 1995; vol. judge out-of-state journalism competitions. Recipient Writing awards Tex. Press Assn., 1978-79, AP, 1966, 88, 91, Dallas Press Club Katie Finalist, 1990, 94, Matrix, 1989-90, Press Club of Houston, 1987, 89, 90, 91, 95, Sierra Club of Houston, 1989, St. Louis United Fund, 1968, Abilene C. of C., 1965. Mem. Press Club of Houston (bd. dirs., sec. 1991), Press Club of Houston Ednl. Found. (treas. 1991, bd. dirs.). Episcopalian. Avocations: sailing, entertaining, walking, reading.

THOMAS, KENNETH EASTMAN, cardiothoracic surgeon; b. Evanston, Ill., Mar. 3, 1934; s. Kenneth Henry and Eloise (Eastman) T.; m. Sara Anne Stephens, Aug. 14, 1971; children: Diana, Allison, Michael. BA, Dartmouth Coll., 1956; MD, Stanford U., 1959. Med. diplomate, Ga. Med. intern dept. medicine U. Minn. Hosp., Mlps., 1959-60; med. resident dept. medicine U. Minn. Med. Sch., Mlps., 1960-61; surg. resident dept. surgery W.Va. U. Sch. Medicine, Morgantown, 1961-66, cancer rsch. fellow dept. surgery, 1966; clin. instr. thoracic surgery Med. Coll. Va., Richmond, 1969-71, fellow thoracic and cardiovascular surgery, 1969-71; ptnr., officer Peachtree Cardiovascular and Thoracic Surgeons, Atlanta, 1972—; bd. trustees St. Joseph's Hosp., Atlanta, 1990—, chmn. and dir. cardiothoracic surgery, 1992-94; active staff St. Joseph's Hosp., Piedmont Hosp., Ga. Bapt. Hosp; courtesy hosp. staff Northside Hosp., Dunwoody Med. Ctr. Contbr. articles to profl. jours. Participant Talented and Gifted Program of Fulton County Schs., Atlanta, 1985—; mem. adv. bd. Atlanta (Ga.) Heart Ball, 1993—. Capt. USAF-Med. Corp., 1966-69, Vietnam. Decorated Bronze star USAF, Vietnam, 1969. Mem. ACS, AMA, Med. Assn. Ga., Med. Assn. Atlanta, Am. Heart Assn., Ga. Heart Assn., Soc. Thoracic Surgeons, Ga. Thoracic Soc., Am. Coll. Cardiology, So. Thoracic Surg. Assn., Am. Coll. Chest Physicians, N.Am. Soc. of Pacing and Electrophysiology. Republican. Episcopalian. Avocations: golf, travel, investments. Office: Peachtree Cardiovascular 5669 Peachtree Dunwoody Rd NE Atlanta GA 30342-1786

THOMAS, KENNETH GLYNDWR, mining executive; b. Llanelli, Wales, June 25, 1944; arrived in Can., 1980; m. Elizabeth June Hickman, Sept. 25, 1976; children: Louise June, Kelly Jane. BSc in Metallurgy, U. Wales, Cardiff, 1970; MSc in Mgmt. Sci., U. London, 1971; PhD in Tech. Sci., U. of Delft, The Netherlands, 1994. Chartered engr., U.K.; registered profl. engr., Ont., Can. Metallurgist Brit. Steel Corp., Wales, 1959-67, Anglo Am. Corp., Kitwe, Zambia, 1971-75; plant supt. Anglo Am. Corp., Klerksdorp, South Africa, 1975-80; design metallurgist Kilborn Engring., Toronto, Ont., 1980-85; mill supt. Giant Yellowknife (Can.) Mines Ltd., N.W.T., 1985-87; sr. v.p. metallurgy and constrn. Barrick Gold Corp., Toronto, 1987-95, sr. v.p. tech. svcs., 1995—. Contbr. articles to tech. jours.; co-patentee in field. Mem. Inst. Materials (U.K.), Can. Inst. Mining, Metallurgy and Petroleum (Mill Man of Yr. award 1990). Office: Barrick Gold Corp, Royal Bank Pla S Twr 200 Bay St, Toronto, ON Canada M5J 2J3

THOMAS, LAVON BULLOCK, interior designer; b. San Angelo, Tex., Oct. 6, 1929; d. J. T. and Ina (Malone) Bullock; m. W. Grant Thomas, June 9, 1956; children: Lorin Gwen Thomas Tavel, Lance Kevin. BS, Sam Houston State U., 1950; MEd, U. Houston, 1961. Tchr. Houston Ind. Sch., 1950-58; youth dir. St. Paul's Meth. Ch., Houston, 1958-60; designer Grant Thomas, Inc., Houston, 1960—, builder, 1994—; real estate broker Houston, 1975—. Unit pres. LWV, Houston, 1990, 91; v.p. Houston Assembly Delphian Chpts., Houston, 1992-93; bd. dirs. Panhellenic, Houston, 1993-94; active Houston UN Assn., 1994; Harris County Forest Landowners Assn. Recipient Cachet award for community svc. Women Helping Women, 1993. Mem. Nat. Assn. Realtors, Tex. Assn. Interior Designers, Tex. Assn. Realtors, Tex. Forestry Assn., Houston Assn. Realtors, Alph Chi Omega (pres. Beta Zeta Beta Chpt. 1994-96). Democrat. Methodist. Avocations: art, music, drama. Home: 15422 Mauna Loa Ln Houston TX 77040-1345

THOMAS, LAWRENCE B., food products executive; b. St. Joseph, Mo., Mar. 3, 1936; m. Jann Walker, Aug. 23, 1958; 3 children. BS in Bus. Adminstrn., Kans. U., 1958; MBA in Fin., Ind. U., 1959. Asst. to treas. ConAgra, Inc., Omaha, 1960-66, asst. treas., 1966-69, v.p. fin., 1969-74, v.p. fin., treas., 1974-91, v.p. fin., treas., sec., 1991—, sr. v.p. fin., sec., 1993—; bd. dirs. Exch. Bank, Mound City, Mo., Exch. Holding Co.; mem. mgmt. exec. com., capital com., employee benefits com. ConAgra, Inc.; officer, dir. subsidiaries,ConAgra, Inc., Omaha. Chmn. adv. bd., Christmas appeal, mem. trust fund bd., treas. Salvation Army; bd. dirs., pres. bd. trustees, mem. exec. com., found. bd., chmn. fin. com., corp. fund drive Omaha Cmty. Playhouse; mem. exec. bd. Mid-Am. coun., fin. com., dir. leadership divsn., co-chmn. sustaining membership enrollment drive Boy Scouts Am.; bd. dirs., v.p. exec. com., treas., sec., chmn. fund dirve, past pres., mem. nat. corp. bd. Jr. Achievement Omaha; past sec. bd. dirs., mem. program, planning and budget com., nominating com., finance com., exec. com., chmn. major firm sect. United Way drive United Way Midlands; past mem. bd. mgmt. Downtown branch, new YMCA planning com., fund drives, mem. metro. fin. com. Omaha YMCA.; trustee Bishop Clarkson Meml. Hosp.; trustee, mem. audit com. Bridges Investment Fund, Inc., Kiewit Mutual Fund; bd. trustees, treas. bd., mem. fin. com., joint com. Methodist Hosp.; treas. bd., mem. human resources com. Nebr. Methodist Health Syss.; mem. adv. coun. Omaha Coll. Fine Arts, Coll. Bus. Adminstrn., U. Nebr.; bd. dirs. PTA Dundee Sch., Lewis and Clark Jr. H.S.; adv. bd. Joslyn Art Mus.; mem. adv. com. Omaha Human Rels. Bd., Omaha Pub. Schs. Acad. Fin.; governing bd. Omaha Safety Coun.; mem. merger com. Omaha/Council Bluffs United Way; bd. dirs., v.p. Dan Cary Youth Founds.; dir. Omaha Cmty. Found.; chmn. coordinating com. Leadership Omaha. Recipient leadership award Boy Scouts Am., Silver Leadership award Nat. Jr. Achievement Leadership Jr. Achievement Omaha. Mem. Christian Home Assn./Children's Square (treas. exec. bd., mem. exec. com., found. bd., chmn. fin. com.), Big Brothers/Big Sisters Assn. Omaha and Council Bluffs (bd. trustees, past pres., v.p., sec., treas., chmn. fund drive, chmn. fin. com., bd. dirs.), The Omaha Club (pres. bd. dirs., past sec., past chmn. athletic com., past treas., past v.p., squash champion), Omaha Exec. Inst. (past chmn.), Sister City Assn. (bd. dirs.), Omaha Jr. C. of C. (bd. dirs., Silver Key holder, nominated Outstanding Young Man), Fin. Execs. Inst. (charter mem. Ak-Sar-Ben chpt., mem. nat. govt. liaison com.), The Conf. Bd. (mem. sr. fin. execs. panel), Omaha Symphony Assn. (bd. dirs.), Am. Soc. Corp. Secs., Inc. Office: Conagra Inc 1 Conagra Dr Omaha NE 68102-5001

THOMAS, LAWRENCE ELDON, mathematics educator; b. Columbus, Ohio, Mar. 15, 1942; s. Bertram D. and Glorian (Butler) T.; m. Rebecca Nolan, June 13, 1970; children: David Nolan, Kathleen Rebecca. BS, U. Mich., 1964; PhD, Yale U., 1970. Rsch. asst. math. dept. Swiss Fed. Inst. Tech., Zurich, 1970-72; rsch. asst. physics dept. U. Geneva, 1972-74; asst. prof. math. U. Va., Charlottesville, 1974-76, assoc. prof., 1976-82, prof., 1982—, chmn. dept., 1989-93. Contbr. articles on theory of Schrodinger operators, statis. mechanics and stochastic processes to profl. jours. Mem. Am. Math. Soc., Am. Physics Soc., Internat. Nat. Math. Physics, Phi Beta Kappa. Avocations: sailing, tennis. Home: 2308 Glenn Ct Charlottesville VA 22901-2913 Office: U Va Dept Math Cabell Dr Charlottesville VA 22903

THOMAS, LEO J., imaging company executive; b. St. Paul, Oct. 30, 1936; s. Leo John and Christal (Dietrich) T.; m. Joanne Juliani, Dec. 27, 1958; children: Christopher, Gregory, Cynthia, Jeffrey. Student, Coll. St. Thomas, 1954-56; BS, U. Minn., 1958; MS, U. Ill., 1960, PhD, 1961. Rsch. chemist Eastman Kodak Co., Rochester, N.Y., 1961-67, lab. head, 1967-70, asst. div. head color photography div., 1970-72, tech. asst. to dir., 1972-75, asst. dir., 1975-77, v.p., dir., 1977-78, sr. v.p., dir., 1978-84; sr. v.p., gen. mgr. Life Scis., Rochester, N.Y., 1985-88; vice-chmn., chmn. Sterling Drug Inc., N.Y.C., 1988-89; group v.p., gen. mgr. Health Eastman Kodak Co., Rochester, 1989-91, group v.p., pres. imaging, 1991-94; exec. v.p. Eastman Kodak Co., Rochester, N.Y., 1994—; bd. dirs. Frontier Corp., John Wiley and Sons, Inc., N.Y.C., Eastman Kodak Co. Mem. AIChE, AAAS, Am. Acad. Arts and Scis., Am. Inst. for Med. and Bioengring, Nat. Acad. Engring., Rochester C. of C. Office: Eastman Kodak Co 343 State St Rochester NY 14650-0234

THOMAS, LEONA MARLENE, health information educator; b. Rock Springs, Wyo., Jan. 15, 1933; d. Leonard H. and Opal (Wright) Francis; m. Craig L. Thomas, Feb. 22, 1955; (div. Sept. 1978); children: Peter, Paul, Patrick, Alexis. BA, Govs. State U., 1982, MHS, 1986; cert. med. records adminstrn., U. Colo., 1954. Dir. med. records dept. Meml. Hosp. Sweetwater County, Rock Springs, Wyo., 1954-57; staff assoc. Am. Med. Records Assn., Chgo., 1972-77, asst. editor, 1979-81; statistician Westlake Hosp., Melrose Park, Ill., 1982-84; asst. prof. Chgo. State U., 1984—, acting dir. health info. adminstrn. program, 1991-92; acting dir. health info. Internat. Coll., Naples, Fla., 1994; dir. health info. adminstrn. program Chgo. State U., 1994—; chairperson Coll. Allied Health Pers., 1986-88; mem. rev. bd. network Newsletter of Assembly on Edn. Co-pres. Ill. Dist. 60 PTA, Westmont; liaison Ill. Trauma Registry, 1991; mem. adv. com. Health Info. Tech. Program Morraine Valley Cmty. Coll., Palos Hills, Ill., 1995—, Health Info. Tech. Program Robert Morris Coll., Orland Pk., Ill., 1995—, Wellness Ctr., Chgo. State U. Mem. Assembly on Edn., Am. Health Info. Mgmt. Assn., Am. Pub. Health Assn., Ill. Pub. Health Assn., Chgo. and Vicinity Med. Records Assn. (publicity com. 1989-90), Ill. Assn. Allied Health Profls., Gov.'s State Alumni Assn. Democrat. Methodist. Home: 6340 Americana Dr Apt 1101 Clarendon Hills IL 60514-2249 Office: Chgo State U Coll Nursin & Allied Health 95th at King Dr Chicago IL 60628

THOMAS, LEWIS JONES, JR., anesthesiology educator, biomedical researcher; b. Phila., Dec. 13, 1930; s. Lewis Jones and Margaretta Eleanore (Schmid) T.; m. Jane E. Priem, June 18, 1955; children: Lewis Jones III., Sarah Jane Thomas Snell. BS in Biology, Haverford Coll., 1953; MD cum laude, Washington U., St. Louis, 1957. Diplomate Am. Bd. Anesthesiology. Assoc. dir. Biomed. Computer Lab., Washington U. Sch. Med., St. Louis, 1972-75, dir., 1975—, assoc. prof. physiology and biophysics, 1974-85, assoc. prof. elec. engring., 1978—, assoc. prof. anesthesiology, biomed. engring., 1974—, assoc. prof. physiology, dept. cell biology and physiology, 1985—; assoc. prof. Inst. Biomed. Computing, Washington U., 1984-89, prof., 1989—, assoc. dir. Inst. for Biomed. Computing, 1984-91, 92—, acting dir., 1991-92; cons. Health Resources Admin., Rockville, Md., 1974-75, Nat. Ctr. Health Svc. Rsch., Washington, 1978-82; mem. biomed. rsch. tech. rev. com., div. rsch. resources NIH, 1988-92; cons. Diagnostic Radiology Coordinating Com. NIH Planning Subcom., 1990; Nat. Task Force NIH Stategic Plan, 1992; NIH Reviewers Reserve NCRR, 1992—. Contbr. articles to profl. jours. and books. Bd. dirs. Bd. Edn., University City, Mo., 1970, 72-73; v.p. Symphony Orch., University City, 1969-78, pres. 1978-91. Sr. asst. surg. USPHS, 1962-64. Recipient USPHS Rsch. Career Devel. award, 1966. Mem. Am. Physiol. Soc., AAAS, N.Y. Acad. Scis. Avocations: music performance, recreational computing. Office: Washington U Biomed Computer Lab 700 S Euclid Ave Saint Louis MO 63110-1012

THOMAS, LINDA JOYCE, English composition and literature educator; b. Glasgow, Ky., Mar. 13, 1944; d. Dennis Cloyd and Mary Dorothy (Cary) T. BA in English, French and Secondary Edn., Western Ky. U., 1966, MA in English, 1968; postgrad., Beaver Coll., 1982-83, U. Ky. Cert. tchr., Ky. Grad. asst. to dean women Western Ky. U., Bowling Green, 1966-68, asst. to dean students, 1968-69; instr. English Butler High Sch., Louisville, 1969-70; tchr. writing and lit. Pinkerton High Sch., Midway, Ky., 1970-73; prof. writing and lit. Midway Coll., 1970—; dir. Writing Across the Curriculum, Midway Coll., 1982-84, 90—, chairperson arts and humanities divsn., 1983-86, apptd. faculty rep. to pres.'s instl. planning com., 1992—, strategic planning; mem. Internat. Book Project, Lexington, 1988-90; mem. Nat. English Lang. Standards Project Task Force, 1992—. Mem. adv. com. Writer's Voice YMCA Ctrl. Ky., Lexington, 1992—, co-chair, 1994—; mem. Writer's Voice YMCA of Am.; friend Ky. Ednl. TV; supporter Ky. Humanities Coun. Grantee NEH, 1982, 93, 94, Ky. Humanities Coun., 1985-86. Mem. NEA, MLA, Nat. Coun. Tchrs. English, Nat. Mus. Women Artists (charter), Conf. on Coll. Composition and Comm., Ky. Coun. Tchrs. English/Lang. Arts (sec. exec. bd. 1992-94, 94—), Ky. Edn. Assn. (faculty advisor student programs 1975-93, Outstanding Svc. award 1992, 93, 94), Smithsonian Assocs., Western Ky. Alumni Assn., Chi Omega, Phi Theta Kappa (hon., faculty advisor, Horizon Svc. award 1992). Democrat. Mem. Ch. Christ. Avocations: photography, fast walking/jogging, water and snow skiing, drawing, theater. Home: 3708 Cottage Cir Lexington KY 40513-1108 Office: Midway Coll 512 E Stephens St Midway KY 40347-1112

THOMAS, LINDSEY KAY, JR., research biologist, educator, consultant; b. Salt Lake City, Apr. 16, 1931; s. Lindsey Kay and Naomi Lurie (Biesinger) T.; m. Nancy Ruth Van Dyke, Aug. 24, 1956; children: Elizabeth Nan Thomas Cardinale, David Lindsey, Wayne Hal, Dorothy Ann Thomas Brown. BS, Utah State Agrl. Coll., 1953; MS, Brigham Young U., 1958; PhD, Duke U., 1974. Park naturalist Nat. Capital Parks, Nat. Park Svc., Washington, 1957-62, rsch. park naturalist Region 6, Washington, 1962-63, rsch. park naturalist Nat. Capital Region, Washington, 1963-66, rsch. biologist S.E. Temperate Forest Park Areas, Washington, 1966, Durham, N.C., 1966-67, Great Falls, Md., 1967-71, rsch. biologist Nat. Capital Parks, Great Falls, 1971-74, rsch. biologist Nat. Capital Region, Triangle, Va., 1974-93, Washington, 1985-93, Nat. Biol. Svc., Washington and Triangle, 1993-96; resource mgmt. specialist Balt.-Washington Pky., Greenbelt, Md., 1996—; adj. prof. George Mason U., Fairfax, Va., 1988—, George Washington U., Washington, 1992—; instr. Dept. Agr. Grad. Sch., 1964-66; aquatic ecol. cons. Fairfax Count (Va.) Fedn. Citizens Assns., 1970-71; guest lectr. U. D.C., 1976. Wildlife mgmt. cons. Girl Scouts Am., Loudoun County, Va., 1958; asst. scoutmaster and scoutmaster, merit badges counselor Boy Scouts Am., 1958—, Scouters Tng. award, 1961. Recipient incentive awards Nat. Park Service, 1962; research grantee Washington Biologists' Field Club, 1977, 82. Mem. AAAS, Bot. Soc. Washington, Ecol. Soc. Am., George Wright Soc., Nature Conservancy, Soc. Early Hist. Archaeology, So. Appalachian Bot. Soc., Washington Biologists Field Club, Sigma Xi. Mormon. Contbr. articles profl. jours. Home: 13854 Delaney Rd Woodbridge VA 22193-4654 Office: Balt-Washingtn Pky 6565 Greenbelt Rd Greenbelt MD 20770-3207 also: Prince William Forest Park PO Box 209 Triangle VA 22172

THOMAS, LLOYD BREWSTER, economics educator; b. Columbia, Mo., Oct. 22, 1941; s. Lloyd B. and Marianne (Moon) T.; m. Sally Leach, Aug. 11, 1963; 1 child, Elizabeth. AB, U. Mo., 1963, AM, 1964; PhD, Northwestern U., 1970. Instr. Northwestern U., Evanston, Ill., 1966-68; asst. prof. econs. Kan. State U., Manhattan, 1968-72, assoc. prof., 1974-81, prof., 1983—; asst. prof. Fla. State U., Tallahassee, 1973-74; vis. prof. U. Calif., Berkeley, 1981-82, U. Del., 1993; prof., chair dept. econs. U. Idaho, 1989. Author: Money, Banking and Economic Activity, 3d edit., 1986, Principles of Economics, 2d edit, 1993, Principles of Macroeconomics, 2d edit,, 1993, Principles of Microeconomics, 2d edit, 1993, Money, Banking and Monetary Policy, 1996; contbr. articles to profl. jours. Mem. Am. Econs. Assn., Midwest Econs. Assn., So. Econs. Assn., Western Econs. Assn., Phi Kappa Phi. Avocations: tennis, classical music. Home: 1501 N 10th Ct Manhattan KS 66502

THOMAS, LOWELL, JR., author, lecturer, former lieutenant governor, former state senator; b. London, Oct. 6, 1923; s. Lowell Jackson and Frances (Ryan) T.; m. Mary Taylor Pryor, May 20, 1950; children: Anne Frazier, David Lowell. Student, Taft Sch., 1942; B.A., Dartmouth Coll., 1948; postgrad., Princeton Sch. Pub. and Internat. Affairs, 1952. Asst. cameraman Fox Movietone News, S.Am., 1939, Bradford Washburn Alaskan mountaineering expdn., 1940; illustrated lecturer, 1946—; asst. economist, photographer with Max Weston Thornburg, Turkey, 1947, Iran, 1948; film prodn. Iran, 1949; Tibet expdn. with Lowell Thomas, Sr., 1949; field work Cinerama, S.Am., Africa, Asia, 1951-52; travels by small airplane with wife, writing and filming Europe, Africa, Middle East, 1954-55; mem. Rockwell Polar Flight, first flight around the world over both poles, Nov., 1965; mem. Alaska State Senate, 1967-74; lt. gov. State of Alaska, 1974-79; owner Talkeetna Air Taxi, Inc., air contract carrier, Anchorage, Alaska, 1980-94. Producer series of films Flight to Adventure, NBC-TV, 1956; producer, writer TV series High Adventure, 1957-59; producer documentary film Adaq, King of Alaskan Seas, 1960; producer two films on Alaska, 1962, 63, film on U. Alaska, 1964, South Pacific travel documentary, 1965, film on Arctic oil exploration, Atlantic-Richfield Co., 1969. Author: Out of this World, A Journey to Tibet, 1950, (with Mrs. Lowell Thomas, Jr.) Our Flight to Adventure, 1956, The Silent War in Tibet, 1959, The Dalai Lama, 1961, The Trail of Ninety-Eight, 1962, (with Lowell Thomas Sr.) More Great True Adventures, 1963, Famous First Flights that Changed History, 1968. past pres. Western Alaska coun. Boys Scouts Am.; bd. dirs. Anchorage unit Salvation Army, Alaska Conservation Found. 1st lt. USAAF, 1943-45. Mem. Nat. Parks and Conservation Assn. (bd. dirs.), Alaska C. of C., Aircraft Owners and Pilots Assn. Clubs: Explorers, Marco Polo, Dutch Treat (N.Y.C.); Rotary, (Anchorage), Press (Anchorage); Dartmouth Outing; American Alpine. Address: 10800 Hideaway Lake Dr Anchorage AK 99516-1145

THOMAS, LYDIA WATERS, research and development executive; b. Norfolk, Va., Oct. 13, 1944; d. William Emerson and Lillie Ruth (Roberts) Waters; m. James Carter Thomas (div. 1970); 1 child, Denee Marrielle. BS in Zoology, Howard U., 1965, PhD in Cytology, 1973; MS in Microbiology, Am. U., 1971. Sr. v.p., gen. mgr. The MITRE Corp., McLean, Va., 1973-96, Mitretek Sys., McLean, Va., 1996—; affiliate Ctr. Sci. and Internat. Affairs, Harvard U., Cambridge, Mass., 1990—; bd. dirs. Cabot Corp.; mem. Draper Labs., Inc. Author: Automation Impacts on Industry, 1983. Mem. Environ. Adv. Bd., U.S. C.E., 1980-82; expert witness, Senate, U.S. govt. pub. hearings, Washington, 1985; mem. adv. bd. INFORM, N.Y.C., George Wash. U. Va. Campus; mem. Supt.'s Bus./Industry Adv. Coun. Fairfax County Pub. Schs. Recipient Tribute to Women in Internat. Industry YMCA, 1986, EBONE Image award Coalition of 100 Black Women, 1990, Dean's award Black Engineer of the Year, 1991. Mem. AAAS, AIAA, Am. Def. Preparedness Assn., Am. Mgmt. Assn., Am. Soc. Toxicology, Am. Astronautical Soc., Nat. Energy Resources Orgn., Nat. Security Indsl. Assn., Teratology Soc., U.S. Energy Assn., Women in Aerospace, Nat. Space Club, Conf. Bd./Townley Global Mgmt. Ctr., Sigma Xi (steering com.), Alpha Kappa Alpha. Office: Mitretek Systems 7525 Colshire Dr Mc Lean VA 22101-7492

THOMAS, MABLE, communications company executive, former state legislator; b. Atlanta, Nov. 8, 1957; d. Bernard and Madie Thomas. BS in Pub. Adminstrn., Ga. State U., 1982, postgrad., 1983—. With acctg. dept. Trust Co. Bank, Atlanta, 1977; recreation supr. Sutton Cmty. Sch., Atlanta, 1977-78; data transcriber Ga. Dept. Natural Resources, Atlanta, 1978-79; clk. U.S. Census Bur., Atlanta, 1980; laborer City of Atlanta Parks and Recreation, 1980-81; student asst. Ga. State U., Atlanta, 1981-82; mem. Ga. Ho. Reps., Atlanta, 1984-94; pres. Master Comms. Inc., Atlanta, 1994—; mem. exec. com. Ga. Legis. Black Census, Atlanta, 1985—. Mem. adv. youth coun. Salvation Army Bellwood Club, 1975; founder, pres. Greater Vine City Opportunities Program Inc., 1996; founder Vine City Cmty. improvement Assn., Atlanta, 1985; mem. neighborhood planning unit adv. bd. of comprehensive youth svcs. Ga. State U., 1988—; mem. Nat. Black Woman's Health Project, Ga. Housing Coalition; bd. dirs. Ga. Coalition Black Women, 1996, Am. Cancer Soc., 1988—. Recipient Bronze Jubilee award City of Atlanta Cultural Affairs, 1984, Disting Svc. award Grady Hosp., 1985, Human Svc. award for cmty. and polit. leadership for disadvantaged, 1986, Exceptional Svc. award Young Cmty. Leaders, 1986, Citizenship award Salvation Army Club, Leadership and Achievement award Ga. Breast Cancer Prevention Coalition, 1994, Adopt a Sch. Appreciation award Atlanta Pub. Schs., 1996; named Outstanding Freshman Legislator, 1986, one of Outstanding Young People of Atlanta, 1987. Mem. Nat. Polit. Congress Black Women (bd. dirs., Fannie Lou Hamer award Phila. chpt. 1995), Conf. Minority Pub. Adminstrn. (Outstanding Svc. award), Ga. Assn. Black Elected Ofcls. (mem. housing and econ. devel. com.). Democrat. Methodist. Home: PO Box 573 Atlanta GA 30301-0573

THOMAS, MARGARET JEAN, clergywoman, religious research consultant; b. Detroit, Dec. 24, 1943; d. Robert Elcana and Purcella Margaret (Hartness) T. BS, Mich. State U., 1964; MDiv, Union Theol. Sem., Va., 1971; DMin, San Francisco Theol. Sem., 1991. Ordained to ministry United Presbyn. Ch., 1971. Dir. rsch. bd. Christian edn. Presbyn. Ch. U.S., Richmond, Va., 1965-71; dir. rsch. gen. coun. Presbyn. Ch. U.S., Atlanta, 1972-73; mng. dir. rsch. div. support agy. United Presbyn. Ch. U.S.A., N.Y.C., 1974-76; dep. exec. dir. gen. assembly mission coun. United Presbyn. Ch. U.S.A., 1977-83; dir. N.Y. coordination Presbyn. Ch. (U.S.A.), 1983-85; exec. dir. Minn. Coun. Chs., Mpls., 1985-95; synod exec. Synod of Lakes and Prairies Presbyn. Ch. (U.S.A.), Bloomington, Minn., 1995—; mem. Permanent Jud. Commn., Presbyn. Ch. (U.S.A.), 1985-91, moderator, 1989-91, mem. adv. com. on constn., 1992—, moderator, 1996—; sec. com. on ministry Twin Cities Area Presbytery, Mpls., 1985-91, vice moderator, 1991-92, moderator, 1992-93; mem. joint religious legis. coalition, 1985-95; mem. Commn. on Regional and Local Ecumenism Nat. Coun. Chs., 1988-91, officer Ecumenical Networks, 1992-95, mem. Unity and Rels. unit, 1992-93; treas. Nat. Coun. of Chs., 1996—; mem. nat. planning com. Nat. Workshop on Christian Unity, 1992-95; bd. dirs. Franklin Nat. Bank, Mpls., 1987—. Contbr. articles to profl. jours. Mem. adv. panel crime victims svcs. Hennepin County Atty.'s Office, 1985-86, Police and Cmty. Rels. Task Force, St. Paul, 1986; mem. adv. panel Hennepin County Crime Victim Coun., 1990-93, chmn., 1990-93; bd. dirs. Minn. Foodshare, 1985-95, Minn. Coalition on Health, 1986-92, Minn. Black-on-Black Crime Task Force, 1988, Twin Cities Coalition Affordable Health Care, 1986-87, Presbyn. Homes of Minn., 1995—, Clearwater Forest, Deerwood, Minn., 1995—; co-chmn. Minn. Interreligious Com., 1988-95; bd. dirs. Abbott Northwestern Pastoral Counseling Ctr., 1988-91, chmn., 1990-91. Recipient Human Rels. award Jewish Community Rels. Coun./Anti-Defamation League, 1989, Gov.'s Cert. of Commendation for Women's Leadership, 1993. Mem. N.Am. Acad. Ecumenists, NOW (Outstanding Woman of Minn. 1986). Mem. Democrat-Farm-Labor Party. Office: Synod of Lakes and Prairies Presbyn Ch USA 8012 Cedar Ave S Bloomington MN 55425-1204

THOMAS, MARIANNE GREGORY, school psychologist; b. N.Y.C., Dec. 10, 1945. BS, U. Conn., 1985; MS, So. Conn. State U., 1987. Cert. sch. psychologist, Conn., N.Y. Sch. psychology intern Greenwich (Conn.) Pub. Schs., 1986-87; sch. psychologist Hawthorne (N.Y.)-Cedar Knolls, U.F.S.D., 1987-88, Darien (Conn.) Pub. Schs., 1988—. Mem. AAUW, NASP (cert.), Conn. Assn. Sch. Psychologists. Home: 154 Indian Rock Rd New Canaan CT 06840-3117

THOMAS, MARLIN ULUESS, industrial engineering educator, academic administrator; b. Middlesboro, Ky., June 28, 1942; s. Elmer Vernon and Helen Lavada (Banks) T.; m. Susan Kay Stoner, Jan. 18, 1963; children: Pamela Claire Thomas Davis, Martin Phillip. BSE, U. Mich., Dearborn, 1967; MSE, U. Mich., Ann Arbor, 1968, PhD, 1971. Registered profl. engr., Mich. Asst. and assoc. prof. dept. ops. rsch. Naval Postgrad. Sch., Monterey, Calif., 1971-76; assoc. prof. systems design dept. U. Wis., Milw., 1976-78; mgr. tech. planning and analysis vehicle quality-reliability Chrysler Corp., Detroit, 1978-79; prof. dept. indsl. engring. U. Mo., Columbia, 1979-82; prof. indsl. engring., chmn. dept. Cleve State U., 1982-88, acting dir. Advanced Mfg. Ctr., 1984-85; prof., chmn. indsl. engring. Lehigh U., Bethlehem, Pa., 1988-93; prof., head Sch. Indsl. Engring. Purdue U., West Lafayette, Ind., 1993—; program dir. NSF, Washington, 1987-88. Contbr. numerous articles on indsl. engring. and ops. rsch. to profl. jours. With USN, 1958-62; capt. USNR, 1971—. Named Outstanding Tchr., U. Mo. Coll. Engring., 1980, Coll. Man of Yr, Cleve. State U. Coll. Engring., 1985. Fellow Inst. Indsl. Engrs; mem. Ops. Rsch. Soc. Am., Am. Soc. for Engring. Edn., Am. Soc. Quality Control, Am. Statis. Assn., Soc. Am. Mil. Engrs., VFW. Office: Purdue U Sch Indsl Engring 1287 Grissom Hall West Lafayette IN 47907-1287

THOMAS, MARLO (MARGARET JULIA THOMAS), actress; b. Detroit, Nov. 21, 1943; d. Danny and Rose Marie (Cassanti) T.; m. Phil Donahue, May 21, 1980. Ed., U. So. Calif. Theatrical appearances in Thieves, Broadway, 1974, Barefoot in the Park, London, Social Security, Broadway, 1986, The Shadow Box, Broadway, 1994; star: TV series That Girl, 1966-71 (Golden Globe award Best TV actress, 1967); appeared in TV films: The Body Human: Facts for Girls (Emmy award Best Performer Children's Program), 1981, The Last Honor of Kathryn Beck, 1984 (also exec. prodr.), Consenting Adults, 1985, Nobody's Child, 1986 (Emmy Best Dramatic Actress), Held Hostage: The Sis and Jerry Levin Story, 1991, Ultimate Betrayal, 1994, Reunion, 1994; conceived book and record, starred in TV spl. Free to Be. . . You and Me, 1974 (Emmy for best children's show); films include Thieves, 1977, In the Spirit, 1991, Jenny, 1963; conceived book, record and TV spl. Free to Be A Family (Emmy Best Children's Show). Recipient 4 Emmys, Golden Globe award, George Foster Peabody award, Tom Paine award Nat. Emergency Civil Liberties Com. Mem. Ms. Found., Nat. Women's Polit. Caucus. Office: CAA 9830 Wilshire Blvd Beverly Hills CA 90212-1804*

THOMAS, NATHANIEL CHARLES, clergyman; b. Jonesboro, Ark., June 24, 1929; s. Willie James and Linnie (Elias) T.; B.A., Miss. Indsl. Coll., Holly Springs, 1951; B.D., Lincoln U., 1954, M.Div., 1974; student Lancaster (Pa.) Theol. Sem., 1952-53; D.Div., Tex. Coll., Tyler, 1981; m. Juanita Fanny Jefferson, May 20, 1961 (dec. 1970); children—Gina Charlise, Nathaniel Charles, Keith Antony; m. 2d, Mary Elizabeth Partee, June 8, 1971. Ordained to ministry Christian Meth. Episcopal Ch., 1954; dir. Christian edn. 8th dist. Christian Meth. Episc. Ch., 1954-58; pastor in Waterford, Miss., 1949-51, Wrightville, Ark., 1955-57, Hot Springs, Ark., 1957-60, Little Rock, 1960-62, Mt. Pisgah Christian Meth. Episc. Ch., Memphis, 1966-67, Greenwood Christian Meth. Episc. Ch., Memphis, 1980-81; dir. Christian edn., adminstrv. asst. to Bishop B. Julian Smith, Christian Meth. Episc. Ch., Memphis, 1954-74, presiding elder South Memphis dist., 1971-74, sec. gen. conf. of ch., 1970-82, gen. sec. gen. bd. personnel services, 1978—, also mem. gen. connectional bd., program adminstr. ministerial salary supplement program, 1974-90, asst. to sec. gen. Gen. Bd. Pensions, 1974-78; program dir. CME Ch. Group Fire & Casualty Ins. Plan, 1978—, Annual CME Convocation and CME Reader Resource Series, 1990—; sec. Ministerial Assn. Little Rock, 1960-62; v.p. youth work sect., div. Christian edn. Nat. Council Chs., del. World Council Chs. Conf., Upsalla Sweden, 1968. Dir. Haygood-Neal Garden Apts., Inc., Eldorado, Ark., 1969—, Smith-Keys Village Apts., Inc., Texarkana, Ark., 1968—, East Gate Village Apts., Inc., Union City, Tenn., 1971—; trustee Collins Chapel Health Care Center, Memphis, 1974—, Tex. Coll., 1981—; bd. dirs. Family Service Memphis, 1972-73, Newsday Coop., Inc., exec. trustee; chmn. bd. dirs. Memphis Opportunities Indsl. Ctr., 1976-78. Mem. NAACP, Urban League, Community on Move for Equality, Memphis Interdenomminational Ministers Alliance, Memphis Ministers Assn., Tenn. Assn. Chs., Ark. Council Chs., Ark. Council Human Relations, Tenn. Council Human Relations, Family Service Memphis, A.B. Hill PTA. Author: Christian Youth Fellow Guide, 8th Episcopal District, 1959; Living Up to My Obligations to the Christian Methodist Episcopal Church, 1956; Steps Toward Developing an Effective Program of Christian Education, 1972; co-author: Worship in the Local Church, 1966; co-author, editor: Coming to Grips with the Teaching Work of the Church, 1966, Discipleship: Creation, Covenant, Community, 1994—. Co-editor: Developing Black Families, 1975; compiling editor: Dedicated . . . Committed-Autobiography of Bishop B. Julian Smith, 1978—. Home: PO Box 9 Memphis TN 38101-0009 Office: PO Box 74 Memphis TN 38101-0074

THOMAS, NED ALBERT, insurance agent; b. Columbus, Ohio, July 15, 1943; s. Hiram Albert and Leona Mary (Hart) T.; m. Marilyn Jane Fredrick, Dec. 2, 1967; children: Amy, Joy, Barrett. BA, Ohio State U., 1968. CLU, ChFC; registered security rep. Ins. agent Mut. Benefit Life, Columbus, Ohio, 1968-74; supr. Mut. Benefit Life, Columbus, 1974-75; pension adminstr. Compensation Underwriting Svcs., Columbus, 1975-79; dir. employee benefits Kientz & Co., Columbus, 1979-82; wholesaler Robert Fulton & Assocs., Columbus, 1982-84; pvt. practice fin. planning Columbus, 1984-86; pres. Compensation Underwriting Svcs., Columbus, 1986-91; estate planning specialist Merrill Lynch, Columbus, 1991—; bd. dirs. Harvest Life Ins. Co., Orlando, Fla.; pres. Ohio Preneed Mktg. Cons., Columbus, 1986; pension cons., pre-retirement planning cons. Blue Cross Cen. Ohio, Columbus; mktg. cons. Harvest Ins. Agy., Cleve.; pre-retirement planning cons. GE Superabrasives, Worthington, Ohio; lectr. pensions and extended life expectancy, 1977. Cubmaster Westerville area Boy Scouts Am., 1989-91; mem. German Village Soc. 1st lt. Air N.G., 1967-73. Mem. Nat. Assn. Securities Dealers, Columbus Life Underwriters Assn. (past pres.), Ohio State Pres. Club, Westerville C. of C., Internat. Soc. Retirement Planners (trustee 1989-90), Am. Soc. CLU and ChFC, Capitol Club. Republican. Office: Merrill Lynch 65 E State St Columbus OH 43215-4213

THOMAS, ORVILLE C., physician; b. Haynesville, La., Aug. 23, 1915; children—David, Diane, Cody. Pre-med. Student, Marian Mil. Inst., 1932-33, Tulane U., 1933; M.D., Tulane U., 1939. Diplomate Am. Bd. Pediatrics. Diplomate Am. Bd. Allergy and Immunology. Intern Shreveport Charity Hosp., La., 1939-40; asst. resident in pediatrics Children's Meml. Hosp., Chgo., 1946-47, resident in pediatrics, 1947, chief resident in pediatrics, 1948; active staff Tex. Children's Hosp., Houston, 1962—, fellow pediatric allergy, 1963-65, chief allergy sect., 1973-78; fellow in pediatric allergy Baylor Coll. Medicine, Houston, 1963-65; chief pediatrics Schumpert Meml. Hosp., Shreveport, La, 1958-61, chief of staff, 1958; sr. staff pediatrics Confederate Meml. Hosp., Shreveport, La, 1948-61; active staff Highland Hosp., Shreveport, La, 1948-61, North La. Hosp., Shreveport, La, 1948-61, Physicians and Surgeons Hosp., Shreveport, La, 1948-61, Ben Taub Gen. Hosp., Houston, 1962—, Hermann Hosp., Houston, 1966-69; hon. staff St. Luke's Hosp., Houston, 1962—; cons. staff Meth. Hosp., Houston, 1962—, St. Joseph Hosp., Houston, 1966—, Bellaire (Tex.) Gen. Hosp., 1966-86, Rosewood Gen. Hosp., Houston, 1967—, Meml. Bapt. Hosp., Houston, 1968—, Pasadena Bayshore Hosp., Pasadena, Tex., 1970—; instr. pediatrics Northwestern U. Sch. Medicine, Chgo., 1948; assoc. prof. pediatrics La. State U. Postgrad. Sch. Medicine, 1956-61; clin. instr. pediatrics Baylor Coll. Medicine, Houston, 1961-66, asst. clin. prof. pediatrics, 1966-76, assoc. clin. prof. pediatrics, 1977—; assoc. clin. prof. allergy and immunology U. Tex. Grad. Sch. Biomed. Scis., Houston, 1970—. Book reviewer: Venom Diseases; Aspects of Allergy and Applied Immunology. Contbr. articles to profl. jours. Served to maj. USMC AUS, 1942-46. Fellow Am. Coll. Allergy and Immunology (pediatrics com. 1964—, pres. 1978), Am. Acad. Allergy and Immunology, Am. Assn. Cert. Allergists (bd. govs. 1974, pres. 1979); mem. AMA, Am. Acad. Pediatrics, So. Med. Assn. (chmn. allergy sect. 1970-71), Tex. Allergy Research Found. Houston(research and edn. com. 1966-86, chmn. sci. adv. council 1973—), Tex. Pediatric Soc., Harris County Med. Soc., Tex. Med. Assn. (chmn. allergy sect. 1976-77), Am. Assn. for Inhalation Therapy (awards com. 1969-72, spl. edn. com. 1969-72), Greater Houston Allergy Soc. (pres. 1977), Joint Council of Allergy and Immunology, Internat. Assn. of Allergology and Clin. Immunology (U.S. rep. 1981-85). Home: 1111 Bering Dr Apt 704 Houston TX 77057-2320 Office: 6969 Brompton St Houston TX 77025-1611

THOMAS, OWEN CLARK, clergyman, educator; b. N.Y.C., Oct. 11, 1922; s. Harrison Cook and Frances (Arnold) T.; m. Margaret Ruth Miles, June 6, 1981; children: Aaron Beecher, Addison Lippitt, Owen Clark Jr. A.B., Hamilton Coll., 1944, D.D., 1970; grad. student physics, Cornell U., 1943-44; B.D., Episcopal Theol. Sch., Cambridge, Mass., 1949; Ph.D., Columbia U., 1956. Ordained to ministry Episcopal Ch., 1949. Dir. coll. work Episcopal Diocese, N.Y., 1951-52; chaplain to Episcopal students Sarah Lawrence Coll., 1950-52; mem. faculty Episcopal Div. Sch. (formerly Episcopal Theol. Sch.), Cambridge, Mass., 1952—, prof. theology, 1965-93, prof. emeritus, 1993—; chmn. dept. coll. work Episcopal Diocese Mass., 1956-59; vis. prof. Pontifical Gregorian U., 1973-74, N. Am. Coll., Rome, 1982-83. Author: William Temple's Philosophy of Religion, 1961, Science Challenges Faith, 1967, Attitudes Toward Other Religions, 1969, rev. edit., 1986, Introduction To Theology, 1973, rev. edit., 1983, God's Activity in the World, 1983, Theological Questions: Analysis and Argument, 1983; contbr. chpts. to books. Mem. Cambridge Democratic City Com., 1966-80, 88—. Served to ensign USNR, 1944-45. Elihu Root fellow Hamilton Coll., 1943; Univ. fellow Columbia U., 1949-50; scholar in residence Rockefeller Found. Study and Conf. Ctr., Bellagio, Italy, 1991. Fellow Soc. Values in Higher Edn.; mem. Am. Theol. Soc., Phi Beta Kappa. Home: 243 Concord Ave Apt 12 Cambridge MA 02138-1362

THOMAS, PAMELLA DELORES, medical director, physician, educator; b. Wetmoreland, Jamaica, May 11, 1947; came to U.S., 1976; d. Wellesley Johnston and Hyacinth Ida Muir; m. Earl A. Thomas, Apr. 9, 1977; children: Ramogi O., Monifa J. MD, U. W.I., 1974; MPH, Med. Coll. Wis., 1990. Diplomate Am. Bd. Preventive Medicine in Occupational Medicine. Intern in surgery Brookdale Hosp., Bklyn., 1976-77, attending physician, 1979-83; resident in surgery Cath. Med. Ctr., Queens, N.Y., 1978-79; staff physician N.Y.C. Transit, Bklyn., 1983-86, asst. med. dir., 1986-89; med. dir. Lockheed Aeronautics, Marietta, Ga., 1989—; asst. adj. prof. Emory Sch. Pub. Health, 1992, chairperson residency adv. com. occupl. medicine program, 1995—. Bd. dirs. Am. Cancer Soc., Cobb County, Ga., 1989—; mem. Promina N.W. Hosp. Found., 1993—; dir. pub. rels. Cobb Med. Soc., 1992—; v.p. bd. govs. Atlanta Wellness Alliance, 1993—. Fellow Am. Coll. Preventive Medicine, Am. Coll. Occupational and Environ. Medicine (pres. Ga. chpt. 1996—); mem. AMA, APHA, Am. Occupational Medicine Assn., Tchrs. Pub. Health Med. Assn. Ga., Am. Aerospace Med. Assn. Avocations: reading, baking, gardening, music. Office: Lockheed Aeronautics 86 S Cobb Dr # 0454 Marietta GA 30063-1000

THOMAS, PATRICIA ANNE, retired law librarian; b. Cleve., Aug. 21, 1927; d. Richard Joseph and Marietta Bernadette (Teevans) T.; BA, Case Western Res. U., 1949, JD, 1951. Admitted to Ohio bar, 1951, U.S. Supreme Ct. bar, 1980; libr. Arter & Hadden, Cleve., 1951-62; asst. libr., then libr. IRS, Washington, 1962-78; libr. dir. Adminstrv. Office, U.S. Cts., 1978-93; ret. 1993. Mem. Am. Assn. Law Libraries, Law Librs. Soc. D.C. (pres. 1967-69), Soc. Benchers (Case We. Res. Law Sch.).

THOMAS, PATRICIA GRAFTON, secondary school educator; b. Michigan City, Ind., Sept. 30, 1921; d. Robert Wadsworth and Elinda (Oppermann) Grafton; student Stephens Coll., 1936-39, Purdue U., summer 1938; BEd magna cum laude, U. Toledo, 1966; postgrad. (fellow) Bowling Green U., 1968; m. Lewis Edward Thomas, Dec. 21, 1939; children: Linda T., Stephanie A. (Mrs. Andrew M. Pawuk), I. Kathryn (Mrs. James N. Ramsey), Deborah (Mrs. Edward Preissler). Lang. art and art tchr. Toledo Bd. Edn., 1959-81, tchr. lang. arts Byrnedale Sch., 1976-81; pres. Jr. High Coun., 1963. Dist. capt. Planned Parenthood, 1952-53, ARC, 1954-55; mem. lang. arts curriculum com. Toledo Bd. Edn., 1969, 73, mem. grammar curriculum com., 1974, pres. Jr. High Coun. Toledo Pub. Schs.; bd. dirs. Anthony Wayne Nursery Sch., 1983—; bd. dirs. Toledo Women's Symphony Orch. League, 1983—, sec., 1985—; co-chmn. Showcase of the Arts, 1990-92. Adolf Dehn fellow, 1939. Mem. AAUW, Toledo Soc. Profl. Engrs. Aux., Helen Kreps Guild, Toledo Artists' Club, Spectrum, Friends of Arts (bd. dirs. 1989—), Phi Kappa Phi, Phi Delta Kappa, Kappa Delta Pi, Pi Lambda Theta (chpt. pres. 1978-80), Delta Kappa Gamma (chpt. pres. 1976-78, area membership chmn. 1978-80, 1st place award for exhbn. 1985). Republican. Episcopalian. Home: 4148 Deepwood Ln Toledo OH 43614-5512

THOMAS, PATRICK HERBERT, information services company executive; b. Atlanta, Aug. 29, 1942; s. Joseph Murray and Ruby Lois (Davis) T.; m. Nell McLaurin, Aug. 28, 1965; children—Laurin Nicole, William Patrick. B.S., Ga. State U., 1971. Ops. officer First Nat. Bank, Atlanta, 1968-71; treas. First Fin. Mgmt., Atlanta, 1971-72, exec. v.p., 1972-74, chmn. bd., pres., chief exec. officer, 1974—; v.p. First Ga. Bank, Atlanta, 1973-75; sr. v.p. First R.R. and Banking, Augusta, Ga., 1977—; dir. First Fin. Mgmt., T.A. Communications, Atlanta, Ga. Interchange Network, Atlanta. Served to 1st lt. U.S. Army, 1962-66. Republican. Methodist. Clubs: Atlanta Athletic, Sporting (Atlanta). Home: 7485 Brigham Dr Atlanta GA 30350-5613 Office: 1st Fin Mgmt Corp 3 Corporate Sq NE Atlanta GA 30329-2013*

THOMAS, PATRICK ROBERT MAXWELL, oncology educator, academic administrator; b. Exmouth, Devon, Eng., Feb. 23, 1943; came to

U.S., 1976; s. Christopher Codrington and Aileen Daphne (Gordon) T.; m. Linda Sharon Rich, June 23, 1976 (dec. 1977), m. Geraldine M. Jacobson, Mar. 2, 1986. Diploma in biochemistry, London U., 1965, MB, BS, 1968. Lectr. Inst. Cancer Rsch., London, 1974-76; assoc. chief clinician Roswell Park Meml. Inst., Buffalo, 1976-79; asst. prof. Washington U., St. Louis, 1979-83, assoc. prof., 1983-89, prof., 1989-90; prof., chmn. Temple U., Phila., 1991—; extramural bd. PDQ, Bethesda, Md., 1989—; mem. in-svc. exam. com. Am. Coll. Radiology, Reston, Va., 1990—; examiner Am. Bd. Radiology, Louisville, 1990—. Fellow Am. Coll. Radiologists, Royal Coll. Physicians of London. Home: 106 Pier Five 7 N Columbus Blvd Philadelphia PA 19106-1422 Office: Temple U 3401 N Broad St Philadelphia PA 19140-5103

THOMAS, PAUL EMERY, mathematics educator; b. Phoenix, Feb. 15, 1927; m. Chi-Yuen Chan, 1958; children: Jenny, Valerie. BA, Oberlin Coll., 1950, Oxford U., Eng., 1952; PhD in Math, Princeton U., 1955. Rsch. instr. Columbia U., 1955-56; asst. prof. math. U. Calif., Berkeley, 1956-60, assoc. prof., 1960-63, prof., 1963-91, prof. emeritus, 1991—; prof. Miller Inst. Basic Rsch. in Sci., 1966-67, mem. exec. com., 1983-89; exec. dir. Miller Inst. Basic Research in Sci., 1987-89; dep. dir. Math. Scis. Rsch. Inst., 1987-90; vis. prof. Princeton U., fall 1971, mem. adv. coun. dept. math., 1987—. Served with USNR, 1945-46. NSF fellow Princeton U., 1955, U. Calif., 1958-59; Guggenheim Meml. Found. fellow, 1961; Rhodes scholar Oxford U., 1950-53. Mem. Am. Math. Soc. (trustee 1980-84, chmn. bd. trustees 1983). Office: Evans Hall Mathematics Dept U Calif Berkeley CA 94720

THOMAS, PAUL S., principal. Prin. Passel-Cokato (Minn.) Sr. High Sch. Recipient Blue Ribbon award U.S. Dept. Edn., 1990-91. Office: Dassel-Cokato Sr High Sch Hwy # 12 and Wright County Rd # 100 Cokato MN 55321

THOMAS, PAYNE EDWARD LLOYD, publisher; b. Balt., May 11, 1919; s. Charles C. and Nanette (Payne) T.; m. Sally Claire Gunther; children: John Fuller, Michael Payne, Peter Charles, LeAnne Marie, Jennifer Nanette. Founder, dir. Thomas Found. and its memorials: Edward Waldron Payne Library, Harvey Cushing Hall, Chapel of Margaret and Charles Crankshaw; exec. v.p. Charles C Thomas, Pub., Springfield, Ill., 1942-48; editor- in-chief sci., tech., med. depts. Charles C Thomas, Pub., 1948-55, pres., 1955—. Mem. Tavern Club Chgo., Coral Reef Yacht Club (Miami, Fla.), Riviera Country Club (Miami). Presbyterian. Home and Office: 600 Biltmore Way #1104 Coral Gables FL 33134-7534

THOMAS, PHILIP STANLEY, economics educator; b. Hinsdale, Ill., Oct. 23, 1928; s. Roy Kehl and Pauline (Grafton) T.; m. Carol Morris, Dec. 27, 1950; children: Lindsey Carol, Daniel Kyle, Lauren Louise, Gay Richardson. B.A., Oberlin Coll., 1950; M.A., U. Mich., 1951, Ph.D., 1961; post-grad., Delhi U., 1953-54. Instr. U. Mich., 1956-57; asst. prof. Grinnell (Ia.) Coll., 1957-63, assoc. prof., 1963-65; assoc. prof. econs. Kalamazoo Coll., 1965-68, prof. econs., 1968-94, prof. emeritus, 1994—; econ. advisor Pakistan Inst. Devel. Econs., 1963-64, USAID, 1965, 66, 67, 68, 71, Planning Commn., Pakistan, 1969-70, Ctrl. Bank of Swaziland, 1974-75, Ministry of Planning, Kenya, 1980-81, 83, 84, 85, 86-88, Ministry of Fin., Swaziland, 1990, Kenya, 1991, 92. Contbr. articles to profl. jours. Mem. alumni coun. Oberlin Coll., 1961-63, 74-76, 83-86, 95—. Served with AUS, 1954-56. Fulbright scholar; Ford Found. overseas fellow India, 1953-54. Mem. Am. Econs. Assn., Phi Beta Kappa. Home: 313A S Shabwasung St Northport MI 49670-9604 Office: Kalamazoo Coll Dept Econ Kalamazoo MI 49006

THOMAS, R. DAVID, food services company executive; b. Atlantic City, July 2, 1932; s. R. and Olivia (Sinclair) T.; m. I. Lorraine Buskirk, May 21, 1954; 5 children. Student pub. schs. Past owner, mgr. Ky. Fried Chicken Franchise; founder, chmn. bd. Wendy's Internat., Inc. (parent co. Wendy's Old Fashioned Hamburgers restaurants), Columbus, Ohio, from 1969, also Dublin, Ohio.; now sr. chmn. bd., founder Wendy's Internat., Inc. (parent co. Wendy's Old Fashioned Hamburgers restaurants), also Dublin, 1981—. Bd. dirs. Children's Hosp., Columbus, Ohio, St. Jude Children's Research Hosp., Memphis. Served with U.S. Army. Recipient Horatio Alger award, 1979. Mem. Ohio Restaurant Assn., Nat. Restaurant Assn. (dir.). Club: Ohio Commodores. Office: Wendy's Internat Inc PO Box 256 4288 W Dublin Granville Rd Dublin OH 43017-2093*

THOMAS, RALPH CHARLES, III, federal official; b. Roanoke, Va., Apr. 10, 1949; s. Ralph C. Jr. and Dorothy (Easley) T. BA, U. Calif., Berkeley, 1975; JD, Harvard U., 1978. Assoc. Bergson, Borkland, Margolis & Adler, Washington, 1978-80; sr. ptnr. Thomas, John & Everett, Washington, 1980-85; clin. instr. in Law Sch. George Washington U., Washington, 1982-83; exec. dir. Nat. Assn. Minority Contractors, Washington, 1985-92; assoc. adminstr. for small/disadvantaged bus. utilization NASA, Washington, 1992—; bd. dirs. Am. Coun. on Constrn. Edn., 1991-92; adj. instr. U. Va., Charlottesville, 1989-91; mem. Small Bus. Procurement Adv. Com., 1994—; co-chmn. Fed. Small Bus. Dirs. Interagy. Coun., 1994—. Contbr. articles to profl. jours. Mem. Pres.'s Interagy. Working Group on Minority Bus. Devel., 1995. Staff sgt. USAF, 1967-71, Vietnam. Recipient Fed. Adv. award, 1994, Exceptional Svc. medal NASA, 1994. Office: NASA Small & Disadvantaged Bus Utilization 300 E St SW Washington DC 20546-0001

THOMAS, REGINALD HARRY, SR., minister; b. Wilkes-Barre, Pa., Aug. 1, 1954; s. Warren Leroy and Nancy Carol (Roche) T.; m. Linda Lee Fine, May 31, 1975; children: Reginald H., Jamie Lynn. BA, Messiah Coll., Grantham, Pa., 1976. Ordained to ministry Primitive Meth. Ch. in the USA, 1981. Minister Boone (Iowa) Primitive Meth. Ch., 1976-77, Shamokin (Pa.) Primitive Meth. Ch., 1977-78, 2nd Primitive Meth. Ch., Pitts., 1978-80, Maitland Meml. Primitive Meth. Ch., New Castle, Pa., 1980-82, Messiah Primitive Meth. Ch., Wilkes-Barre, Pa., 1982—; sec. bd. trustees Primitive Meth. Ch. Conf., 1982-89, pres., 1992-94, conf. gen. sec., 1989—; mem. world relief commn. Nat. Assn. Evangelicals. Track and Field ofcl. Pa. Interscholastic Athletic Assn.; bd. dirs. Wyo. Valley Striders Running Assn. Republican. Home: 110 Pittston Blvd Wilkes Barre PA 18702-9620 Office: Messiah Primitive Meth Ch 100 Pittston Blvd Wilkes Barre PA 18702-9620

THOMAS, RHONDA CHURCHILL, lawyer; b. 1947; m. J. Regan Thomas; children: Ryan, Aaron, Evan. BA, Drury Coll., 1969; JD, U. Mo., 1972, Yale U., 1973. Bar: Mo. 1973. Newswoman Sta. KFRU Radio, Columbia, Mo., 1969-70; law clk. to Hon. Robert E. Seiler Supreme Ct. of Mo., Jefferson City, 1973-74; asst. city counselor City of Columbia, 1974-76, city counselor, chief legal advisor to city coun., dept. heads, 1976-79; assoc. prof. law U. Mo., 1979-82; ptnr. Thompson Coburn, St. Louis, 1985—; past chmn. franchise com. Nat. Inst. Mcpl. Law Officers. Contbr. articles to profl. jours. Past chmn. Boone County Home Rule Charter Commn.; past pres. Boone County Indsl. Devel. Authority. Mem. ABA (local govt. law sect., taxation sect.), Mo. Bar Assn. (mem. edn. law com., mem. local govt. law com., mem. med.-legal rels. com., past mem. spl. com. on quality and methods of practice), St. Louis Bar Assn., Nat. Assn. Bond Lawyers, Mo. Mcpl. Attys. Assn. (past pres.). Office: Thompson Coburn 1 Mercantile Ctr Ste 3400 Saint Louis MO 63101-1623

THOMAS, RICHARD, actor; b. N.Y.C., June 13, 1951; s. Richard and Barbara (Fallis) T.; m. Alma Gonzalez, Feb. 14, 1975 (div.); children: Richard F., Barbara, Gwyneth and Pilar (triplets); m. Georgiana Bischoff, Nov. 20, 1995; children: Brooke, Kendra. Student, Columbia U. Owner, prin. Melpomene Prodns. Made Broadway debut at age 7 in Sunrise at Campobello, 1958; regular on children's series One, Two, Three - Go!, 1961-62, regular on TV series The Waltons, 1972-77 (Emmy award 1973); films include Winning, 1969, Last Summer, 1969, You Can't Have Everything, 1970, Red Sky at Morning, 1971, The Todd Killings, 1971, Cactus in the Snow, 1971, You'll Like My Mother, 1972, 9/30/55, 1977, Battle Beyond the Stars, 1980; stage appearances include Sunrise at Campobello, 1958, Whose Life Is It Anyway?, 1980, The Fifth of July, 1981, The Sea Gull, 1984, The Count of Monte Cristo, 1985, Citizen Tom Paine, 1986, The Front Page, 1986, Hamlet, 1987, Peer Gynt, 1989, Love Letters, 1989-90, Square One, 1990, Lisbon Traviata, 1990, Danton's Death, 1992, Richard II, 1993, Richard III, 1994; author: Poems by Richard Thomas, Vols. I and 2, 1974; TV dramatic spl. and movies The Homecoming— A Christmas Story, 1971, The Red Badge of Courage, 1974, The Silence, 1975, All Quiet on the Western Front, 1979, The Hank Williams Jr. Story, 1983, Hobson's Choice, 1984, The Master of Ballantrae, 1984, Glory!, Glory!, 1990, Andre's Mother, 1990, It, 1990, Mission of the Shark, 1991, Yes, Virginia, There Really Is a Santa Claus, 1991, I Can Make You Love Me: The Stalking of Laura Black, 1993, A Walton's Thanksgiving Reunion, 1993, Death in Small Doses, 1993, Linda, 1993, A Walton Wedding, 1995; host children's spl. H.M.S. Pinafore, 1973. Nat. chmn. Better Hearing Inst., 1987—. Office: care Springer Assoc 1501 Broadway Ste 1314 A New York NY 10036-5601

THOMAS, RICHARD, civilian military employee; b. Boise, Idaho, May 29, 1941; s. Ormond and Mary Lacey T.; m. Linda Hill, Oct. 5, 1963; children: Lauren, Sharon, Steven. BS Aeronautical Engring., Rensselaer Polytech. Inst., 1963; MS Ops. Rsch., George Washington U., 1973; postgrad. program for sr. execs., MIT, 1986. Rschr. David Taylor Rsch. Ctr., Carderock, Md., 1963-68; head support forces, logistic sect. Office Naval Ops., 1969-75; mgr. Am. Mgmt. Systems Inc., 1976-77; dir. Office Policy and Plans Maritime Adminstrn. (U.S. Dept. Commerce, now U.S. Dept. Transp.), Washington, 1978-82; dir. resources and policy evaluation Office Asst. Sec. Navy U.S. Dept. Navy, 1983-90, dep. asst. sec. Shore Resources, 1991—. Office: Installations & Environment 1000 Navy Pentagon Washington DC 20350-1000

THOMAS, RICHARD DALE, newspaper editor; b. Hogansville, Ga., Oct. 8, 1949; s. Benjamin J. Thomas and Marie (Phillips) Cook; m. Martha Yates, June 25, 1971; children: Richard J., Elizabeth L. BA, Mercer U., 1975. Pub. affairs coord. Sta. WMAZ-TV-AM, Macon, Ga., 1971-72; mng. editor Boca Raton (Fla.) News, 1977-81, editor, 1981-83; reporter The Macon Telegraph, 1973, city editor, 1973-76, asst. mng. editor, 1976-77, v.p., editor, 1983—. Pres. Goodwill Industries, Macon, 1988-89, Macon (Ga.) Arts Alliance, 1994-95; chmn. Kids Voting/Ga., Macon, 1992-94. Profl. Journalism fellow Stanford (Calif.) U., 1979-80. Mem. Am. Soc. Newspaper Editors, Ga. Press Assn. (bd. dirs. 1991-93, treas. 1995—). Roman Catholic. Home: 1132 Saint Andrews Dr Macon GA 31210-4776 Office: The Macon Telegraph 120 Broadway Macon GA 31201-3444

THOMAS, RICHARD LEE, banker; b. Marion, Ohio, Jan. 11, 1931; s. Marvin C. and Irene (Harruff) T.; m. Helen Moore, June 17, 1953; children: Richard L., David Paul, Laura Sue. BA, Kenyon Coll., 1953; postgrad. (Fulbright scholar), U. Copenhagen, Denmark, 1954; MBA (George F. Baker scholar), Harvard U., 1958. With First Nat. Bank Chgo., 1958—, asst. v.p., 1962-63, v.p., 1963-65; v.p., gen. mgr. First Nat. Bank Chgo. (London (Eng.) br.), 1965-66; v.p. term loan divsn. First Nat. Bank, Chgo., 1968; sr. v.p., gen. mgr. First Chgo. Corp., 1969-72, exec. v.p., 1972-73, vice chmn. bd., 1973-75, pres., 1975-92, chmn., pres., CEO, 1992-94; chmn. First Chgo. NBD, Chgo., 1994-96,, 1973—; chmn. First Chgo. NBD Corp., 1995—; dir. CNA Fin. Corp., Sara Lee Corp. Trustee, past chmn. bd. trustees Kenyon Coll., Orchestral Assn.; trustee Rush-Presbyn.-St. Luke's Med. Ctr.; trustee Northwestern U. With AUS, 1954-56. Mem. Chgo. Coun. Fgn. Rels., Sunningdale Golf Club (London), Econ. Club (past pres.), Comml. Club (past pres.), Chgo. Club, Casino Club, Mid-Am. Club, Indian Hill Club (Winnetka, Ill.), Old Elm Club (Highland Park, Ill.), Phi Beta Kappa, Beta Theta Pi. Office: First Chgo NBD Corp 1 First Nat Plz Chicago IL 60670

THOMAS, RICHARD VAN, state supreme court justice; b. Superior, Wyo., Oct. 11, 1932; s. John W. and Gertrude (McCloskey) T.; m. Lesley Arlene Ekman, June 23, 1956; children: Tara Lynn, Richard Ross, Laura Lee, Sidney Marie. B.S. in Bus. Adminstrn. with honors, U. Wyo., 1954, LL.B. with honors, 1956; LL.M., NYU, 1961. Bar: Wyo. 1956, U.S. Ct. Appeals (10th cir.) 1960, U.S. Ct. Mil. Appeals 1960, U.S. Supreme Ct. 1960. Law clk. to judge U.S. Ct. Appeals (10th Circuit), Cheyenne, 1960-63; asso. firm Hirst & Applegate, Cheyenne, 1963-64; partner firm Hirst, Applegate & Thomas, Cheyenne, 1964-69; U.S. atty. Dist. Wyo., Cheyenne, 1969-74; justice Wyo. Supreme Ct., Cheyenne, 1974—, chief justice, 1985-86. Pres. Laramie County United Way, 1972, trustee, 1973-74, chmn. admissions and allocations com., 1968-69, chmn. exec. com., 1973, chmn. combined fed. campaign, 1974; bd. dirs. Goodwill Industries Wyo., Inc., 1974-77; exec. com. Cheyenne Crusade for Christ, 1974; v.p., exec. com. Wyo. Billy Graham Crusade, 1987; bd. dirs. Cheyenne Youth for Christ, 1978-81; chancellor Episcopal Diocese of Wyo., 1972—, lay dep. gen. conv., 1973—, chmn. search evaluation nomination com., 1976-77, lay reader, 1969—; bd. dirs. Community Action of Laramie County, 1977-82; chmn. Cheyenne dist. Boy Scouts Am., 1977-78, mem. nat. council, 1982-84, mem. Longs Peak council, 1977—, v.p. dist. ops., v.p. membership relationships, 1979-81, pres., 1981-83; mem. North Cen. Region Exec. Bd., 1986—, pres. Old West Trails Area, 1988—; chmn. Laramie County Health Planning Com., 1980-84. Served with JAGC USAF, 1957-60. Named Boss of Year, Indian Paintbrush chpt. Nat. Secs. Assn., 1974; Civil Servant of Year, Cheyenne Assn. Govt. Employees, 1973; Vol. of Yr., Cheyenne Office, Youth Alternatives, 1979; recipient St. George Episcopal award, 1982, Silver Beaver award Boy Scouts Am., 1985. Mem. Am., Laramie County bar assns., Wyo. State Bar, Phi Kappa Phi, Phi Alpha Delta, Omicron Delta Kappa, Sigma Nu. Clubs: Kiwanis (Cheyenne) (program com. 1969-70, dir. 1970-72, chmn. key club com. 1973-76, disting. pres. 1980-81), Masons (Cheyenne) (33 deg., past master); Shriners; Nat. Sojourners (Cheyenne). Office: Wyo Supreme Ct Supreme Ct Bldg Cheyenne WY 82002*

THOMAS, RITCHIE TUCKER, lawyer; b. Cleve., Aug. 12, 1936; s. Myron F. and Marjorie (Ritchie) T.; m. Elizabeth Blackwell Haynes Main, Jan. 1, 1994. BA, Cornell U., 1959; JD, Case-Western Res. U., 1964. Bar: Ohio 1964, U.S. Dist. Ct. (no. dist.) Ohio 1964, U.S. Ct. Appeals (D.C. cir.) 1971, U.S. Ct. Appeals (fed. cir.) 1973, U.S. Ct. Internat. Trade 1976, U.S. Ct. Appeals (9th cir.) 1985. Assoc. office of gen. counsel U.S. Tariff Commn., Washington, 1964-67; assoc. Squire, Sanders & Dempsey, Cleve., 1967-69, Cox, Langford & Brown, Washington, 1969-74; ptnr. Squire, Sanders & Dempsey, Washington, 1974—; mem. exec. com. Meridian House Internat., Washington, 1977-94; Washington rep. Am. C. of C. in Germany, 1984—; v.p. bd. dirs. Belgian Am. Assn., 1989—. Assoc. editor Western Res. U. Law Rev., 1964; contbr. articles to profl. jours. Recipient various book award West Pub. Co., 1964. Mem. Fed. Bar Assn., Ohio Bar Assn., D.C. Bar Assn., Order of Coif. Home: 6700 Bradley Blvd Bethesda MD 20817-3045 Office: Squire Sanders & Dempsey 1201 Pennsylvania Ave NW PO Box 407 Washington DC 20044

THOMAS, ROBERT ALLEN, environmental policy administrator, educator; b. Luling, Tex., Apr. 10, 1946; s. Julian H. and Katie (Schneider) T.; m. Paulette M. Jung, Aug. 17, 1968; children: Jennifer Leigh, Aimee Kathryn, Patrick Julian. BS, U. Southwest La., 1970; MS, Tex. A&M U., 1974, PhD, 1976. Lectr. Tex. A&M U., College Station, 1976-77; instr. La. State U. Med. Ctr., New Orleans, 1977-78; exec. dir. La. Nature and Sci. Ctr., New Orleans, 1978-94; v.p. environ. policy The Audubon Inst., 1994; adj. prof. biol. sci. U. New Orleans, 1979—; cons. for environ. issues, New Orleans. Contbr. articles to profl. jours.; columnist. Recipient Elsie Naumburg award Nat. Sci. for Youth Found., 1983; Margaret Stone medal The Garden Club Am., 1994. Mem. Soc. for Study of Amphibians and Reptiles, Herpetologists League, Am. Soc. Ichthyologists and Herpetologists, La. Assn. Mus. (pres. 1986-88), Am. Assn. Mus. (accreditation commn.), Southwestern Assn. Naturalists (bd. govs. 1982-85), East New Orleans C. of C. (exec. com.). Roman Catholic. Lodge: Rotary (pres. 1984-85, 94-96). Avocations: tennis; writing. Office: The Audubon Inst PO Box 4327 New Orleans LA 70178-4327

THOMAS, ROBERT DEAN, publisher; b. Elkhart, Ind., Mar. 28, 1933; s. Floyd D. and Ottie (Silvers) T.; m. Beverly I. Neuhaus, Apr. 21, 1956; children: Mary Beth, Matthew, Susanna. Grad., Bradley U., 1956. Staff asst. to gen. mgr. Reuben H. Donnelley Co., 1958; dist. mgr., Western mgr. Conde Nast, 1964; account mgr. Mademoiselle Mag.; Western mgr. Ladies Home Jour., N.Y.C., 1966; account mgr., pub. Ladies Home Jour.; pub. Bon Appetit mag., 1990-91. Served with U.S. Army, 1956-58. Mem. Silver Spring Country Club (Ridgefield, Conn.). Home: 223 Mariomi Rd New Canaan CT 06840-3315

THOMAS, ROBERT EGGLESTON, former corporate executive; b. Cuyahoga Falls, Ohio, July 28, 1914; s. Talbott E. and Jane S. (Eggleston) T.; children: Robert Eggleston, Barbara Ann. B.S. in Econs, U. Pa., 1936. Asst. to gen. mgr., sec., mgr. r.r. investments Keystone Custodian Funds, Boston, 1936-53; v.p. Pennroad Corp., N.Y.C., 1953-59; chmn. exec. com., dir. M.-K.- T. R.R., 1956-65; mem. exec. com. MAPCO Inc., 1960-84, dir., chief exec. officer, 1960-80, pres., 1960-76, chmn. bd., 1973-84; adv. bd. BancOkla. Corp. Mem. Am. Petroleum Inst. (hon. dir.), Nat. Mining Assn. (hon. dir.), Newcomen Soc., Chgo. Club, So. Hills Country Club (Tulsa), San Diego Yacht Club, Desert Horizons Country Club (Indian Wells, Calif.), Wianno (Mass.) Club, Teton Pines Country Club (Jackson Hole, Wyo.). Episcopalian. Office: MAPCO Inc PO Box 645 Tulsa OK 74101-0645

THOMAS, ROBERT JOSEPH, columnist, author; b. San Diego, Jan. 26, 1922; s. George H. and Marguerite (Creelman) T.; m. Patricia Thompson, Sept. 6, 1947; children: Nancy Katherine, Janet Elizabeth, Caroline Brooke. Student, UCLA, 1943. With AP, 1943—, Hollywood columnist, 1944—; radio, TV, lecture appearances; editor Action Mag., 1968-74. Author: The Art of Animation, 1958; (novel) Flesh Merchants, 1959; The Massie Case, 1966, King Cohn, 1967, Walt Disney: Magician of the Movies, 1967, Will Penny, Star, 1968, Thalberg, 1969, Selznick, 1970, The Heart of Hollywood, The Secret Boss of California, Winchell, 1971; (novel) Weekend '33, 1972; Marlon, 1974, Walt Disney, An American Original, 1976, Bud and Lou, The Abbott and Costello Story, 1977, The Road to Hollywood (with Bob Hope), 1977, The One and Only Bing, 1977, Joan Crawford, 1978, Golden Boy, the Untold Story of William Holden, 1983, Astaire, 1984, I Got Rhythm, The Ethel Merman Story, 1985; also numerous mag. articles. Mem. Beta Theta Pi. Office: Associated Press 221 S Figueroa St Ste 300 Los Angeles CA 90012

THOMAS, ROBERT LEE, financial services company executive, consultant; b. San Antonio, Dec. 29, 1938; s. Lawrence Grant and Mabel Louise (Carlson) T.; m. Terry Eileen Morgan, Dec. 14, 1972; 1 child, Evan Grant. Cert., Am. Coll., 1984, 85, cert. in fin. planning, 1990, cert. in health underwriting, 1991; postgrad., Northeastern U., 1991—. Cert. fin. planner, investment specialist; designated registered employee benefit cons. Various middle mgmt. positions Gen. Fin. Corp., Dallas, 1962-65; full charge mgmt. positions TransAm. Fin. Corp., Dallas, 1965-74; sr. agt. Am. Security Life, San Antonio, 1974-81; chmn., pres. Thomas Fin. Svcs., Inc., Dallas, 1981—; bd. dirs. Cherokee Children's Home; mem. adv. bd. Am. Security Life, 1977—; frequent guest on internat. and nat. radio and TV talk shows; host radio program, 1986—; nat. and internat. spkr. in field; initiator/tchr. fin. planning course for H.S. students. Mem. fin. profl. adv. panel Digest of Financial Planning Ideas mag., 1984; designer, creator Mortgage Pre-Payment System, 1990, Mortgage Management Software, 1990; author: Cost Cutter Mortgage Management Manual, 1990; creator Commercial Debt Expense Reduction System and Debt Cash Flow Analysis Software, 1991; columnist Jour. Shepherding group leader Meadowview Ch. Christ, Mesquite, Tex., 1983—, Bible class tchr., 1978—, deacon, 1987—; regular spokesman pub. svc. and promotional messages various civic orgns.; chmn. charity telethon Million Dollar Round Table; leader internat. missions ministry, Papau, New Guinea, 1989, S.E. Asia, 1990; team mem. for tribal contact, New Guinea, 1991-94, 95, 96; dir. Sr. Info. Svcs. of Ameritech, 1994—; bd. dirs. Cherokee Home for Children, 1994—. Recipient Lone Star Leader award Tex. Assn. Life Underwriters, 1982—, Nat. Sales Achievement award, Nat. Quality award Nat. Assn. Life Underwriters, 1976—. Fellow Life Underwriting Tng. Coun.; mem. Dallas Estate Planning Coun., Dallas Assn. Life Underwriters (chmn. health com. 1979-80, president's cabinet 1989—, pub. rels. com. 1992—), Internat. Assn. Registered Fin. Planners, Internat. Assn. Fin Planning, Am. Soc. CLUs, Am. Inst. Cert. Fin. Planners, Am. Assn. Fin. Profls., Am. Health Ins. Assn., Investment Rsch. Inst., Million Dollar Round Table (life), Dallas Assn. Life Underwriters (mem. steering com. 1992—), Tex. Assn. Life Underwriters (nat. sales achievement award 1976—, nat. quality award 1976—), Am. Arbitration Assn (nat. arbitration panel, securities arbitrator 1989—), Better Bus. Bur. (sr. arbitrator nat. panel), Gen. Agts. and Mgmt. Assn. (yearling achievement 1975), Internat. Platform Assn., Internat. Assn. Registered Fin. Planners, Tex. Investment Mgmt. Coun., Aircraft Owners and Pilots Assn. Avocations: diving, travel, exploration, flying. Office: Thomas Fin Svcs Inc Ste 360 9330 Lyndon B Johnson Fwy Dallas TX 75243-3443

THOMAS, ROBERT MORTON, JR., lawyer; b. Kansas City, Kans., Jan. 1, 1941; s. Robert Morton Sr. and Arlowyne Edith (Arganbright) T.; m. Rebecca Ann Myers, Aug. 21, 1965; children: Brooke J., Austin B. BA, U. Kans., 1962; LLB, Harvard U., 1966. Bar: N.Y., U.S. Dist. Ct. (so. dist.) N.Y., U.S. Ct. Appeals (2nd cir.). Local govt. advisor Republic of Botswana, Gaborone, 1966; dist. officer Republic of Botswana, Serowe, 1967; dist. commr. Republic of Botswana, Maun, 1968; assoc. Sullivan & Cromwell, N.Y.C., 1969-75, ptnr., 1975—; ptnr.-in-charge Sullivan & Cromwell, London, 1979-82; mng. ptnr. gen. practice group Sullivan & Cromwell, N.Y.C., 1986-91. Mem. ABA, N.Y. State Bar Assn., Assn. of Bar of City of N.Y., Internat. Bar Assn., India House, Buck's Club, Harvard Club, Mill Reef Club, Verbank Hunting and Fishing Club (dir., sec.). Republican. Presbyterian. Office: Sullivan & Cromwell 125 Broad St New York NY 10004-2400

THOMAS, ROBERT MURRAY, educational psychology educator; b. Cheyenne, Wyo., July 28, 1921; s. Robert MacDonald and Elizabeth (Carson) T.; m. Shirley Louise Moore, July 3, 1948; children: Robert Gilmour, Kathryn Elizabeth. A.B., Colo. State Coll., 1943, M.A., 1944; Ph.D., Stanford U., 1950. Tchr. Kamehameha Schs., Honolulu, 1944-45; Tchr. Mid-Pacific Inst., Honolulu, 1945-47; instr. San Francisco State Coll., 1949-50; prof. State U. Coll., Brockport, N.Y., 1950-58, Padjadjaran (Indonesia) U., 1958-61, 64-65; prof. ednl. psychology U. Calif. at Santa Barbara, 1961-64, 69-91, prof. emeritus ednl. psychology, 1992—; dean U. Calif. at Santa Barbara (Grad. Sch.), 1965-69. Author: Judging Student Progress, 2d edit, 1960, Ways of Teaching, 1955, Integrated Teaching Materials, 2d edit, 1963, Individual Differences in the Classroom, 1965, Social Differences in the Classroom, 1965, Aiding the Maladjusted Pupil, 1967, A Chronicle of Indonesian Higher Education, 1973, Comparing Theories of Child Development, 1979, 4th edit., 1996, Japanese edit., 1985, Education in American Samoa-1700 to 1980, 1987, The Puzzle of Learning Difficulties-Applying a Diagnostic and Treatment Model, 1989, Counseling and Life-span Development, 1990, Classifying Reactions to Wrongdoing, 1995, and numerous others. editor: Strategies for Curriculum Change: Cases from 13 Nations, 1968, Politics and Education: Cases from 11 Nations, 1983, Ency. of Human Development and Education, 1990, International Comparative Education, 1990, Education's Role in National Development Plans, 1992; co-author: Decisions in Teaching Elementary Social Studies, 1971, Curriculum Patterns in Elementary Social Studies, 1971, Penggunaan Statistik Dalam Ilmu Pengetahuan Sosial, 1971, Teaching Elementary Social Studies: Readings, 1972, Indonesian Education: An Annotated Bibliography, 1973, Social Strata in Indonesia, 1975, Political Style and Education Law in Indonesia, 1980, Schooling in the ASEAN Region, 1980, Schooling in East Asia, 1983, Schooling in the Pacific Islands, 1984, Die Entwicklung des Kindes, 1986, Educational Technology, 1987, Oriental Theories of Human Development, 1988, What Wrongdoers Deserve, 1993, Etude Comparée des Théories du Dévelopment de l'Enfant, 1994, Prevent, Repent, Reform, Revenge, 1995. Home: 1436 Los Encinas Dr Los Osos CA 93402-4520

THOMAS, ROBERT WILBURN, broadcasting and advertising executive; b. Athens, Ga., Nov. 20, 1937; s. Ernest Wilburn and Bobbie (Morton) T.; m. Betsey Ruth Thorne, Sept. 6, 1958; children: Richard Gregory, Coleen Suzanne. BS in Speech, Northwestern U., 1960, MA, 1961. Producer radio, TV broadcasts Northwestern U., Evanston, Ill., 1961-68, instr., 1967-68; exec. producer Sta. WCNY-TV, Syracuse, N.Y., 1968-70; gen. mgr., v.p. Sta. WEKT-FM, Hammondsport, N.Y., 1970-71; gen. mgr. Sta. KWMU-FM, St. Louis, 1971-76; dir. broadcasting Sta. KWIT, Sioux City, Iowa, 1976-79; sta. expansion mgr. Corp. for Pub. Broadcasting, Washington, 1979-82; exec. dir. Cable Comm. Prince Georges County (Md.), 1982-83; cable adminstr. City of Raleigh (N.C.), 1983-86; pres. B&B Media, Inc. (advt. and pub. rels. agy.), 1986—; co-owner, gen. mgr. Sta. WBLB, Pulaski, Va., 1986-89; co-innkeeper Claytor Lake Homestead Inn, Draper, Va., 1990-91; news, pub. affair dir. Sta. WRAD-WRIQ, Radford, Va., 1993-94; bd. dirs. S.W. Devel. Financing, Inc.; mem. Emmy awards com. Chgo. chpt. Nat. Acad. TV Arts and Scis., 1962-65; mem. radio adv. com. Ill. Telecommunications Commn., 1968; chmn. radio divsn. Midwest Telecommunications Conf., Nat. Assn. Ednl. Broadcasters, 1972; mem. Va. News Network adv. bd., 1987—; co-founder, bd. dirs. Pulaski County HOSTS, pres. 1991; bd. dirs. New River Valley HOSTS tourism project, 1992-93. mem. pack com. Cub Scouts Am., Florissant, Mo., 1971-72; chmn. Mo. Jr. Miss Pagent, 1971-72, co-chmn., 1972-73, exec. dir., 1973-76; past bd. dirs. Sioux City Youth Orch. Assn., Siouxland Arts Coun., Sioux City Chamber Music Assn.; founding mem.

Pub. Radio in Mid. Am., program chmn., 1976-77; bd. dirs. Pulaski County United Way, 1987-92, pub. rels. chmn., 1987-89; bd. dirs. Salvation Army, 1987-90, pub. rels. chmn., 1987, v.p., 1988; bd. dirs. Count Pulaskifest, 1987-90; prodr., dir. Ms. Va. Sr. Citizen Pageant, 1993—; bd. dirs. Pulaski County Emergency Needs Task Force, 1989-92, Radford Heritage Found., pub. rels. chmn., 1993—; chmn. Environ. Commn. City of Radford, 1995—. Recipient award Freedoms Found., 1963, 65, Outstanding Program award Ill. Med. Soc., 1965; named Outstanding State chmn. in Nation America's Jr. Miss Pageant, 1974. Mem. Mo. Pub. Radio Assn. (pres. 1975-76), Nat. Assn. Telecom. Officers and Advisors (bd. dirs. 1982-86, sec. 1983-85, v.p. 1985-86), Pulaski County C. of C. (bd. dirs. 1987-89), Pulaski Mchts. Assn. (chmn. promotions com. 1986-89, bd. dirs. 1987-89, 4th of July com. 1987, 91, town hist. com. 1987-89), Pulaski Main St. (chmn. corp. rels. com. 1988-89), Rotary (v.p. Radford 1993-94, pres.-elect 1994-95, pres. 1995-96, Paul Harris fellow 1990). Home and Office: 1006 3rd St Radford VA 24141-1306 *Without belief in and enthusiasm for the undertakings of life, achievement is slowed, if not actually blocked.*

THOMAS, ROBERTA WILL, home care agency administrator; b. Knoxville, Tenn., July 13, 1950; d. Robert Spicer Thomas and Naoma Kathleen (Burchell) Winningham; 1 child, Lindsey Kelly. BS in Edn., U. Tenn., 1974, ADN, 1979; MS in Health Svcs. Adminstrn., Coll. of St. Francis, Joliet, Ill., 1991. Staff nurse clin. rsch. Vanderbilt U. Med. Ctr., Nashville, 1979-80; charge nurse surg. gynecology Owensboro (Ky.)-Daviess County Hosp., 1980-81; nurse mgr. med./surg. Nashville Meml. Hosp., 1981-84; dir. nursing edn. Clover Bottom Devel. Ctr., 1984-92; edn. coord. Physician's Home Health Care, 1992-93; dir. infusion svcs. Home Tech. Healthcare-Mid South, 1993—; adminstr. Home Tech. Healthcare-Tenn., 1994—; CPR instr. AHA and ARC, Nashville, 1981—; guest lecr. Tenn. Assn. Home Care, 1991—; ind. trainer various mental retardation facilities, Tenn., 1992—. Author, implementor tng. program Medication Administration Training for Medicaid Waiver Group Homes, 1985. Mem. Mid. Tenn. Assn. Healthcare Quality, Mid. Tenn. Orgn. Nurse Execs. Office: Home Tech Health Care 112 Louise Ave Nashville TN 37203-1730

THOMAS, ROGER MERIWETHER, lawyer; b. Hartford, Conn., Feb. 28, 1930; s. Frederick Metcalf and Helen Meriwether (Lewis) T.; m. Mary Dorothea Wyman, Dec. 4, 1965; children—Donald Wyman, Helen Dorothea. A.B., Princeton U., 1952; LL.B., Va. U., 1957; LL.M., Boston U., 1964. Bar: N.Y. 1958, Mass. 1960, U.S. Dist. Ct. (Mass) 1965, U.S. Tax Ct. 1965, U.S. Supreme Ct. 1967. Assoc. Angulo, Cooney, Marsh & Ouchterloney, N.Y.C., 1957-60; assoc., then ptnr. Gaston & Snow, Boston, 1960-91; counsel Condit & Assocs., P.C., Boston, 1992-94; outline author and lectr. Mass. Continuing Legal Edn., Inc., Boston; past panelist New Eng. Law Inst. Estate Planning Forums, Boston. Trustee Buckingham Browne & Nichols Sch., Cambridge, Mass., 1967-69. Served to 1st lt. U.S. Army, 1952-54, Korea. Mem. Am. Coll. Trust and Estate Counsel, Boston Bar Assn., Mass. Bar Assn. Avocations: reading; sports; old movies. Home: 40 Byron Rd Weston MA 02193-2229

THOMAS, ROGER WARREN, lawyer; b. South Weymouth, Mass., Sept. 17, 1937; s. Clement Rogers and Beatrice (Merritt) T.; m. Maria Sava Brenner, July 5, 1968; children: Caroline, Andrew, Phillip. BA, U. N.H., 1959; postgrad. (Rotary Internat. fellow), Free U. Berlin, 1960; LLB (Root-Tilden scholar), NYU, 1963, LLM (Ford Found. grantee), 1965; postgrad., U. Chile, Santiago, 1965. Bar: N.Y. 1964. Assoc. Cleary, Gottlieb, Steen and Hamilton, N.Y.C., 1965-66, 69-74; partner Cleary, Gottlieb, Steen and Hamilton, 1974—; mem. Harvard-Chile Tax Reform Project, 1966-68, head project in Chile, 1968-69; cons. to UN, Santiago, 1969; adj. prof. taxation NYU, 1974-96. Co-author: El Impuesto a la Renta, 1969. Bd. dirs. Spanish Repertory Theatre. Mem. ABA, Am. Fgn. Lawyers Assn. (dir.), N.Y. State Bar Assn., N.Am.-Chilean C. of C. (pres. 1984—), Am. Soc., Coun. of Am., Down Town Assn. N.Y.C., Knickerbocker Club. Home: 1165 Fifth Ave New York NY 10029-6931 Office: 1 Liberty Plz New York NY 10006-1404

THOMAS, ROY LEE, minister; b. Greeley, Colo., Sept. 14, 1930; s. Rue and Mary (Malone) T.; m. Patricia A. King, July 19, 1954; children: Patsy Lee, Mark Randall. BA, Free Will Bapt. Bible Coll., 1960; MDiv, Luther Rice Sem., 1978; postgrad., Calif. Ch. Coll., 1970; DD, Bethany Bible Coll. & Sem., 1989. Farmer Castleford, Idaho, 1948-49; pastor 1st Free Will Bapt. Ch., Artesia, N.Mex., 1954-56, Springfield, Tenn., 1956-57; pastor Shady Grove Free Will Ch., Clarksville, Tenn., 1957-60; missionary 1st Free Will Bapt. Ch., Denver, 1960-70; assoc. dir. Home Missions Dept., Nashville, 1970-78, dir., 1978—. Author: Planting & Growing A Fundamental Church, 1978, Studies on the Church Covenant, 1993; editor: Benjamin Randall Journal, 1993. With USAF, 1951-55. Office: Free Will Baptists Nat Assn PO Box 5002 Antioch TN 37011-5002

THOMAS, RUSSELL ALVIN, hardware company executive; b. Butler, Pa., Aug. 7, 1939; s. Lawrence Rosco and Helen (Hemphill) T.; m. Joan Macefe, Feb. 18, 1961; children: Mark Russell, Jo Alison, Lara, Joclyn. BA, Grove City Coll., 1961; postgrad., George Washington U., 1965-66, St. Francis U., Loretto, Pa., 1975-79. Contract negotiator Spang & Co., Butler, 1969-70; dir. indsl. relations Wolverine Toy Co., Booneville, Ark., 1971-74; mgr. employee relations Am. Hardware Supply Co., Butler, 1974-78, asst. v.p. personnel, 1978-80, v.p. personnel, 1980-91, sr. v.p. human rels., 1991—; pers. cons. Speer Hardware Co., Ft. Smith, Ark., 1976—, bd. dirs. 1991; v.p. pers. Advocate Svcs., Inc., Butler, 1982—, Tech Expn. Concepts, Inc., Harrisburg, Pa., 1985—; bd. dirs. C. of C. Svc. Corp., 1993—. Author: People Part of Retail, 1988, The People Part of Rental, 1990, The Services of Servistar, 1992. Bd. dirs. Easter Seal Soc., Butler, 1982-85, United Way Butler County, 1995—, Butler County Meml. Hosp., 1995—; mem. adv. bd. Slippery Rock (Pa.) Coll., Butler, 1987—. Lt. USN, 1961-69. Named Outstanding Bus. Leader Booneville Bus. and Profl. Women, 1973. Mem. VFW, Am. Soc. Personnel Adminstrs., Butler County Human Relations Assn. (bd. dirs. 1984—, pres. 1986-87), Butler Personnel Assn., Pitts. Personnel Assn., C. of C. Svc. Corp. (bd. dirs. 1994—). Lodge: Elks. Avocations: skiing, swimming, fishing, flying. Home: 5 Oakhurst Dr Butler PA 16001-3870 Office: Servistar Corp PO Box 1510 Marie St Butler PA 16003-1510

THOMAS, S. BERNARD, history educator; b. N.Y.C., Oct. 17, 1921; s. Hyman and Rose (Samilow) T.; m. Evelyn Green Hechtlinger, Dec. 28, 1955; 1 child, Ruth Thomas; stepchildren: Ira, John. BS in Social Sci., CCNY, 1942; MA, Columbia U., 1947, cert. East Asian Inst., 1951, PhD, 1964. Rsch. assoc. internat. secretariat Inst. Pacific Rels., 1950-55; chmn. social studies Colby Acad., N.Y.C., 1955-58; tchr. social studies Forest Hills (N.Y.) High Sch., 1958-65; asst. prof. history Oakland U., Rochester, Mich., 1965-67, assoc. prof., 1967-71, prof., 1971-89, prof. emeritus, 1989—, chmn. area studies programs, 1967-71, chmn. dept. history, 1984-87. Author: Government and Administration in Communist China, 1953, reprinted 1972, Labor and the Chinese Revolution, 1983, Season of High Adventure: Edgar Snow in China, 1996; contbr. numerous articles and revs. to profl. jours. With Signal Corps, AUS, 1942-46. East Asian Inst. fellow, 1962, Fulbright fellow, 1969-70. Mem. Assn. Asian Studies, Fulbright Assn. Home: 926 Norwich Rd Troy MI 48084-2671 Office: Oakland U Dept History Rochester MI 48309-4401

THOMAS, SCOTT E., federal government executive, lawyer; b. Buffalo, Wyo., Mar. 5, 1953; s. Ralph E. and Bonnie E. (Kaan) T.; m. Elena W. King, Apr. 28, 1984. BA, Stanford U., 1974; JD, Georgetown U., 1977. Bar: D.C., U.S. Ct. Appeals (9th cir.) 1980, U.S. Supreme Ct. 1981. Atty. Office of Gen. Counsel, Fed. Election Commn., Washington, 1977-80, asst. gen. counsel, 1980-83; exec. asst. to commr. Fed. Election Commn., Washington, 1983-86, commr., 1986—. Mem. D.C. Bar Assn. Office: Fed Election Commn 999 E St NW Washington DC 20463-0001

THOMAS, SHARYN LEE, elementary education educator; b. Springfield, Mass., Nov. 6, 1948; d. John H. and Meta L. (Postell) T. BFA, U. Mass. at Amherst, 1974; MEd, Springfield Coll., 1980; postgrad. in Spanish, Worcester State Coll., Am. Internat. Coll.; postgrad., Our Lady of Elms Coll., Anna Maria Coll., 1990, Fitchburg State Coll., 1994. Cert. elem. educator K-8, Mass., art educator K-12, Mass. Classroom tchr. Springfield (Mass.) Pub. Schs., 1980-83, tchr. K-4 FLES/Spanish, art and art appreciation, 1983-88, tchr. grades 5 and 6, 1988-91, tchr. 3rd grade, 1991—; tchr. tng. task force Springfield Coll., 1993. Recipient Dept. Edn. Bd. Edn. Citation Merit for Exemplary Ednl. Program, 1986, Springfield Edn. Fund Mini-Grant, 1986. Mem. Mass. Fgn. Lang. Assn., Am. Assn. Tchrs. Spanish and Portuguese, Mass. Tchrs. Assn., Springfield Edn. Assn. Home: PO Box 90598 Springfield MA 01139-0598

THOMAS, SHIRLEY, author, educator, business executive; b. Glendale, Calif.; d. Oscar Miller and Ruby (Thomas) Annis; m. W. White, Feb. 22, 1949 (div. June 1952); m. William C. Perkins, Oct. 24, 1969. BA in Modern Lit., U. Sussex, Eng., 1960, PhD in Comm., 1967; diploma, Russian Fedn. Cosmonautics, 1995. Actress, writer, producer, dir. numerous radio and TV stas., 1942-46; v.p. Commodore Prodns., Hollywood, Calif., 1946-52; pres. Annis & Thomas, Inc., Hollywood, 1952—; prof. technical writing U. So. Calif., L.A., 1975—; Hollywood corr. NBC, 1952-56; editor motion pictures CBS, Hollywood, 1956-58; corr. Voice of Am., 1958-59; now free lance writer; cons. biol. scis. communication project George Washington U., 1965-66; cons. Stanford Rsch. Inst., 1967-68, Jet Propulsion Lab., 1969-70. Author: Men of Space vols. 1-8, 1960-68, Spanish trans., 1961, Italian, 1962; Space Tracking Facilities, 1963, Computers: Their History, Present Applications and Future, 1965; The Book of Diets, 1974. Organizer, chmn. City of L.A. Space Adv. Com., 1964-73, Women's Space Symposia, 1962-73; foudner, chmn. aerospace hist. com. Calif. Mus. Sci. and Industry; chmn. Theodore von Karman Postage Stamp Com., 1965—, stamp issued 1992. Recipient Aerospace Excellence award Calif. Mus. Found. 1991, Nat. Medal Honor DAR, 1992, Yuri Gagarin Medal Honor, 1995. Fellow Brit. Interplanetary Soc.; mem. AIAA, AAAS, Internat. Soc. Aviation Writers, Air Force Assn. (Airpower Arts and Letters award 1961), Internat. Acad. Astronautics, Nat. Aero. Assn., Nat. Asn. Sci. Writers, Soc. for Tech. Communications, Am. Astronautical Soc., Nat. Geog. Soc., Am. Soc. Pub. Adminstrn. (sci. and tech. in govt. com. 1972—), Achievement Awards for Coll. Scientists, Muses of Calif., Theta Sigma Phi, Phi Beta. Home: 8027 Hollywood Blvd Los Angeles CA 90046-2510 Office: U So Calif Profl Writing Program University Park Waite-Phillips Hall 404 Los Angeles CA 90089-4034

THOMAS, SIDNEY, fine arts educator, researcher; b. N.Y.C., Dec. 21, 1915; s. Hyman and Rose (Samilowitz) T.; m. Rae Dinkowitz, May 26, 1940; children: David Phillip, Deborah Rose. B.A., CCNY, 1935; M.A., Columbia U., 1938, Ph.D., 1943. Tutor in English CCNY, N.Y.C., 1939-43; instr. English Queens Coll., N.Y.C., 1946-54; self-employed as editor, 1954-58; asst. editor Merriam-Webster, Springfield, Mass., 1958-61; assoc. prof. fine arts Syracuse U. (N.Y.), 1961-66, prof., 1966-85, prof. emeritus, 1985—, dir. humanities doctoral program, 1964-72, chmn. dept. fine arts, 1969-73; bibliographer Shakespeare Assn., N.Y.C., 1949-54. Author: The Antic Hamlet, 1943; co-editor: The Nature of Art, 1964; editor: Images of Man, 1972. Served to sgt., inf. U.S. Army, 1943-45, ETO. Research fellow Folger Shakespeare Library, Washington, 1947-48. Fellow Royal Soc. Arts (London); mem. MLA (life), Shakespeare Assn. Am., Internat. Shakespeare Assn., AAUP (pres. Syracuse U. chpt. 1974), ACLU, Phi Beta Kappa. Office: Syracuse U Dept Fine Arts Syracuse NY 13210

THOMAS, STEPHEN J., anesthesiologist; b. Washington, 1943. Intern San Francisco Gen. Hosp., 1968-69; resident in anesthesiology Mesa Gen. Hosp., Boston, 1971-73, fellow, 1973-74; assoc. prof. NYU Med. Ctr. Office: NYU Med Ctr 560 1st Ave New York NY 10016-6402*

THOMAS, STEPHEN PAUL, lawyer; b. Bloomington, Ill., July 30, 1938; s. Owen Wilson and Mary Katherine (Paulsen) T.; m. Marieanne Sauer, Dec. 7, 1963 (dec. June 1984); 1 child, Catherine Marie; m. Marcia Aldrich Toomey, May 28, 1988; 1 child, Ellen Antonia. BA, U. Ill., 1959; LLB, Harvard U., 1962. Bar: Ill. 1962. Vol. Peace Corps, Malawi, Africa, 1963-65; assoc. Sidley & Austin and predecessor firms, Chgo., 1965-70, ptnr., 1970—; lectr. on law Malawi Inst. Pub. Adminstrn., 1963-65. Pres. Hyde Park-Kenwood Cmty. Conf., Chgo., 1988-90; trustee Chgo. Acad. for Arts, 1991—, chmn., 1992—; bd. dirs. Ctr. for Ethics Garrett-Evang. Theol. Sem., Evanston, Ill., 1995—. Recipient Paul Cornell award Hyde Park Hist. Soc., 1981. Mem. ABA, Chgo. Bar Assn., Chgo. Fedn. of Musicians, Legal and Law Clubs Chgo., Union League Club Chgo. Democrat. Roman Catholic. Avocation: jazz piano playing. Home: 5740 S Harper Ave Chicago IL 60637-1841 Office: Sidley & Austin 1 First National Plz Chicago IL 60603

THOMAS, TED, SR., minister; b. Raeford, N.C., Oct. 19, 1935; s. Simuel and Nancy Anna (McPhatter) T.; m. Charletta Virginia Clifton, May 30, 1957; children: Ted, Christopher, Marc, Charles, Jonathan, Reuben. BS, Norfolk State Coll., 1959; MA in Math., Edn. and Secondary Edn., Hampton Inst., 1972. Ordained to ministry Ch. of God in Christ Inc., 1957. Pastor New Community Ch. of God in Christ, Churchland, Portsmouth, Va., 1967—; State project dir. Chs. of God in Christ, Va. Jurisdiction 1, 1965—; supt. cen. dist. Chs. of God in Christ, Va., 1964—; asst. prin. Ruffner Jr. High Sch., Norfolk, Va., 1983-84; past pres. young people Willing Works, 1962-66; Sunday sch. supt., 1970-73; asst. bishop 1st jurisdiction Chs. of God in Christ Inc. of Va., 1977-84, State Bishop, 1984—. Mem. NEA, Va. Edn. Assn., Edn. Assn. Norfolk. Home: 4145 Sunkist Rd Chesapeake VA 23321-3131 Office: Ch of God in Christ 3615 Tyre Neck Rd Portsmouth VA 23703-3125

THOMAS, THOMAS DARRAH, chemistry educator; b. Glen Ridge, N.J., Apr. 8, 1932; s. Woodlief and Jean (Darrah) T.; m. Barbara Joan Rassweiler, Sept. 8, 1956; children: David, Steven, Kathleen, Susan. BS, Haverford Coll., 1954; PhD, U. Calif., Berkeley, 1957. Instr. chemistry U. Calif., Berkeley, 1957-58, asst. prof., 1958-59; research assoc. Brookhaven Nat. Lab., Upton, N.Y., 1959-61; asst. prof. Princeton (N.J.) U., 1961-66, assoc. prof., 1966-71; prof. Oreg. State U., Corvallis, 1971-89, disting. prof., 1989—, chmn. dept. chemistry, 1981-84, dir. Ctr. Advanced Materials Research, 1986-91; cons. Los Alamos (N.Mex.) Sci. Lab., 1965. Contbr. articles to profl. jours. Fellow Alfred P. Sloan Found., 1966-68, Guggenheim Found., 1969, U. Liverpool, Eng., 1984-85. Fellow AAAS, Am. Phys. Soc.; mem. Am. Chem. Soc., Sigma Xi, Phi Beta Kappa. Home: 1470 NW Greenwood Pl Corvallis OR 97330-1827 Office: Oreg State U Dept Chemistry Gilbert Hall # 153 Corvallis OR 97331-4003

THOMAS, THURMAN, professional football player; b. Houston, May 16, 1966. Student, Okla. State U. With Buffalo Bills, 1988—. Named to Pro-Bowl team, 1989-93, Sporting News All-Pro team, 1990, 91; named MVP, NFL, 1991, Player of Yr., Sporting News, 1991. Office: care Buffalo Bills 1 Bills Dr Orchard Park NY 14127-2237

THOMAS, TOM, retired plastics company executive; b. Malang, Java, Indonesia, Feb. 15, 1932; arrived in Can., 1954; s. Ferdinand and Elfrieda Emma (Macht) T.; m. Jannie Chine Sneep, Jan. 19, 1956; children: Gregory John, Renée Sonja Elfrieda, Michael Grant, Thomas. Grad. high sch., The Hague, Holland. Jr. mgr. Lever Bros. Ltd., Toronto, Ont., Can., 1954-60; sr. mgr. Impac & Somerville Plastics, Toronto, Ont., Can., 1960-64; founder, C.E.O. Can. Cup Inc., Toronto, Ont., Can., 1964—, also bd. dirs., 1964-93; ret., 1993; Inventor in field. Trustee Frazer Inst., Vancouver, B.C., Can., 1977-93; gov. Massey and Roy Thomson Hall, Toronto, 1991-92; bd. dirs. Toronto Symphony, 1986-92, mem. Maestro's Club, 1984, mem. pres.'s coun. Can. Opera Co., 1980, adv. coun. Toronto Symphony, 1995, pres. Coun. Can. Opera, 1980-95. Avocations: sailing, history, classical music, chess.

THOMAS, VINCENT COX, editor; b. Louisville, July 5, 1920; s. Vincent Cox and Mary Tuley Thomas; m. Violette McLaughlin, Aug. 26, 1945; children: Dian Speed, Sheilah Nehan, Vincent Cox III, Jeanne-Marie Stuart. BA, Centre Coll., Danville, Ky., 1941; postgrad., U. Louisville, 1946-47. With Louisville Courier-Jour., 1946-50; commd. ensign USN, 1942, advanced through grades to capt., 1962, commdg. officer ops., pub. affairs officer, 1950-70, spl. asst. pub. affairs to chief of naval ops., 1961-64, dir. pub. affairs U.S. European Command, 1964-66, fleet pub. affairs officer U.S. Pacific Fleet, 1966-69; dir. community rels. Office Sec. Def., 1969-70; dir. pub. affairs, exec. dir. Navy League U.S., 1970-82; editor Almanac of Seapower, Summerland Key, Fla., 1983—. U.S. Editor Jane's fighting Ships, 1985—; contbg. editor Sea Power mag., 1983—. Decorated Legion of Merit (3), others. Republican. Episcopalian. Avocations: swimming, canoeing, sports. Home and Office: 919 Bay Dr Summerland Key FL 33042-4837

THOMAS, VIOLETA DE LOS ANGELES, real estate broker; b. Buenos Aires, Dec. 21, 1949; came to U.S., 1962; d. Angel and Lola (Andino) de Rios; m. Jess Thomas, Dec. 23, 1974; 1 child, Victor Justin. Student, Harvard U. and U. Buenos Aires, 1967-73. Mgr. book div. Time-Life, N.Y.C., 1967-73; real estate broker First Marin Realty, Inc., Mill Valley, Calif., 1985-95; assoc. broker Trump Corp., N.Y.C., 1995—. Bd. dirs. Alliance Francaise, St. Louis, 1995-96, City of Tuburon, Calif., 1987-93, Art and Heritage Commn., Tiburon. Named Woman of Yr., City of Buenos Aires, 1977, Agt. of Yr., Marin County and San Francisco, 1987-92. Office: Trump Corp 725 Fifth Ave 15th Fl New York NY 10022

THOMAS, W. DENNIS, paper company executive, former government official; b. Balt., Dec. 8, 1943; s. George Crosby and Justa Mae (Witherspoon) T.; m. Dawn Frances Haines, 1965; 1 son, William David. B.S., Frostburg State Coll., 1965; M.S.W., U. Md., 1967. Asst. to Hon. J. Glenn Beall, Jr., Washington, 1969-71, spl. asst., 1971-73, adminstrv. asst., 1973-77; adminstrv. asst. to Hon. William V. Roth, Jr., Washington, 1977-81; asst. sec. legis. affairs Dept. Treasury, Washington, 1981-83; dep. asst. to Pres. legis. affairs White House, 1983-85; ptnr. Touche Ross and Co., Inc., 1985; asst. to Pres., The White House, 1985-87; v.p. govt. rels. Internat. Paper Co., Washington, 1987—. Republican. Office: Internat Paper 1101 Pennsylvania Ave NW Washington DC 20004-2514

THOMAS, WALTER DILL, JR., forest pathologist, consultant; b. St. Louis, July 3, 1918; s. Walter D. and Helen (Gardner) T.; m. Dolores B. Thomas, Dec. 31, 1939 (div. May 1984); children: Sandra Thomas Bosworth, Arthur D; m. Nancy McCarthy, Feb. 15, 1985. BS, Colo. State U., 1939; MS, U. Minn., 1943, PhD, 1947. Diplomate Am. Bd. Forensics Examiners. Prof. plant pathology Colo. State U., Ft. Collins, 1947-55; supr. biol. research Chevron Chem. Co., Richmond, Calif., 1955-70; v.p. rsch. Nat. Resource Mgmt., Eureka, Calif., 1970-72; pres. Forest Ag Corp., Lafayette, Calif., 1972-86; coord. bd. forest stewardship Calif. Dept. Forestry and Fire Control, 1990-94; cons. in field, 1986—. Author: Field Manual of Forest and Shade Tree Diseases, 1947, Not Long Apart, 1965, Mauget Field Manual: Insects and Diseases of Shade Trees, 1995. commr. Park and Recreation Com., Ft. Collins, 1949-54, Concord, Calif., 1959-65; city forester, Ft. Collins, 1950-55. Comdr. USNR, 1944-80. Fellow AAAS (life); mem. Am. Phytopathol. Soc., Soc. Am. Foresters, Foresters Assn. (Calif. lic.), Pesticide Applicators Profl. Assn., Internat. Soc. Arboriculture, Nat. Forensic Soc., Bd. Forensics Examiners, Assn. Cons. Foresters, Am. Soc. Cons. Arborists, Soc. Tech. Comms. (sr. mem.), VFW, Elks, Lions. Republican. Avocations: swimming, writing, music. Home and Office: 2435 Heatherleaf Ln Martinez CA 94553-4337 *It is better to fail humbly while trying to succeed than to never even try.*

THOMAS, WAYNE LEE, lawyer; b. Tampa, Sept. 22, 1945; s. Willard McSwain and June Frances (Jones) T.; m. Patricia H., Mar. 16, 1968; children: Brigitte Elisabeth, Kate Adelaide. BA, U. Fla., 1967, JD cum laude, 1971. Bar: Fla., 1971, U.S. Supreme Ct., 1975, U.S. Ct. Appeals (5th cir.), 1975, U.S. Ct. Appeals (11th cir.), 1981, U.S. Ct. Claims 1976, U.S. Dist. Ct. (mid. dist.) Fla., 1973, U.S. Dist. Ct. (so. dist. trial bar) Fla., 1975; cert. mediator. Law clk. U.S. Dist. Ct. (mid. dist.) Fla., 1971-73; assoc. Trenam, Simmons, Kemker, Scharf, Barkin, Frye & O'Neill, P.A., Tampa, 1973-77, ptnr., 1978-81; founder, pres. McKay & Thomas, P.A., Tampa, 1981-89; ptnr. Carlton, Fields, Ward, Emmanuel, Smith & Cutler, P.A., 1989-95; pvt. practice, Tampa, 1995—. Mem. Fla. Bar (chmn. sect. gen. practice, 1981-83, mem. ethics com., vice chmn. unauthorized practice law com. 1994—, vice chmn. fed. practice com. 1995-96, chmn. 1996—, mem. bd. bar examiners 1986-91, chmn. 1990-91), ABA, Hillsborough County Bar Assn. (chmn. grievance com. 1985-86), Order of Coif, Fla. Blue Key, Phi Kappa Phi, Omicron Delta Kappa. Democrat. Office: 707 N Franklin St 10th Fl Tampa FL 33602

THOMAS, W(ILLIAM) BRUCE, retired steel, oil, gas company executive; b. Ripley, Mich., Oct. 25, 1926; s. William and Ethel (Collins) T.; m. Phyllis Jeanne Smith, June 25, 1950; 1 son, Robert William. BA magna cum laude, Western Mich. U., 1950; JD with distinction, U. Mich., 1952; postgrad., Law Sch., NYU, 1953. Bar: Mich. 1952. With USX Corp. (formerly U.S. Steel) and subs., various locations, 1952-91; tax atty. Oliver Iron Mining Div., Duluth, Minn., 1952-53; tax atty., tax supr., comptroller Orinoco Mining Co., N.Y.C. and Venezuela, 1953-64, dir., v.p. taxes, 1967-70, v.p., asst. treas., 1970-71, v.p., treas., 1971-75; exec. v.p., CFO, dir. USX Corp., Pitts., 1975-82, vice chmn., CFO, dir., 1982-91; bd. dirs. Chase Manhattan Corp. and Chase Manhattan Bank. Bd. dirs. Duquesne U., Allegheny Gen. Hosp.; trustee Kenyon Coll. With USAAF, 1943-45. Mem. ABA, Mich. Bar Assn., Fin. Execs. Inst., Order of Coif, Duquesne Club, Pitts. Club, Laurel Valley Golf Club, Rolling Rock Club, Allegheny Country Club, Sky Club, Links, Belleair Country Club, Phi Alpha Delta. Methodist. Home: Blackburn Rd Sewickley PA 15143 Office: USX Corp 600 Grant St Ste 6200 Pittsburgh PA 15219

THOMAS, WILLIAM GERAINT, museum administrator; b. Columbo, Sri Lanka, June 27, 1931; came to U.S., 1941; s. Cecil James and Iris Katharine (Evans) T.; m. Maria Alcalde, Jan. 2, 1976; 1 child, Laura. BA, U. Calif., Berkeley, 1952. Reporter, editor San Francisco Chronicle, 1952-64; asst. to mayor City of San Francisco, 1964-66; chief cons. majority caucus Calif. State Assembly, Sacramento, 1966-68; adminstrv. asst. U.S. Congressman Phillip Burson, Washington, 1968-70; cons. interior com. U.S. Ho. of Reps., Washington, 1970-72; ptnr. Thomas & Iovino, San Francisco, 1972-78; asst. regional dir. Nat. Park Svc., San Francisco, 1978-89; supt. San Francisco Maritime NHP, 1989—. Mem. Nat. Dem. Club; bd. dirs. Nat. Libery Ship Meml., 1978-80. Sgt. U.S. Army, 1952-54, Korea. Mem. Nat. Maritime Mus. Assn., Nat. Maritime Hist. Soc., Press Club of San Francisco (pres. 1973-74, Best News Story 1963). Episcopalian. Avocation: sailing. Office: San Francisco Maritime Bldg 201 Ft Mason San Francisco CA 94123

THOMAS, WILLIAM GRIFFITH, lawyer; b. Washington, Nov. 1, 1939; s. Henry Phineas and Margaret Wilson (Carr) T.; m. Suzanne Campbell Foster, June 7, 1960. Student Williams Coll., 1957-59, Richmond Coll., 1960; J.D., U. Richmond, 1963. Bar: Va. 1963. Mem., pres. Hazel & Thomas, P.C., Alexandria, Va., 1987—; Va. Electric and Power Co., Richmond. Sec., Va. Dem. Com., 1968-70, chmn., 1970-72. Mem. ABA, Va. State Bar Assn., Alexandria Bar Assn., Am. Law Inst., Am. Coll. Real Estate Lawyers. Home: 200 S Fairfax St # 14 Alexandria VA 22314-3331 Office: Hazel & Thomas 510 King St Ste 200 Alexandria VA 22314-3132

THOMAS, WILLIAM HARRISON, professional football player; b. Amarillo, Tex., Aug. 13, 1968. Student, Tex. A&M U., 1987-91. Linebacker Phila. Eagles, 1991—. Selected to Pro Bowl, 1995. Office: Philadelphia Eagles 3501 S Broad St Philadelphia PA 19148

THOMAS, WILLIAM KERNAHAN, federal judge; b. Columbus, Ohio, Feb. 15, 1911; m. Dorothy Good, 1936 (dec.); children: John R., Richard G., Stephen G., Cynthia G. B.A., Ohio State U., 1932, LLB, JD, 1935. Bar: Ohio 1935. Practiced in Cleve., until 1950; judge Ct. Common Pleas, Geauga County, Ohio, 1950-53, Ct. of Common Pleas, Cuyahoga County, Cleve., 1953-66; now judge U.S. Dist. Ct., No. Dist. Ohio, Eastern div., Cleve., sr. judge, 1981—. Served with USNR, 1944-46. Mem. Common Pleas Judges Assn. (pres. 1959-60), Nat. Conf. State Trial Judges (chmn. sociopathic offender com. 1963-66), 6th Circuit Dist. Judges Assn. (pres. 1981-82), Jud. Conf. U.S. (com. on adminstrn. bankruptcy system 1968-71, com. on operation of jury system in U.S. 1971-77, subcom. on fair trial free press 1977—), Ohio State Bar Assn. (Ohio Bar medal 1994). Office: US Dist Ct 223 US Courthouse Cleveland OH 44114-1201

THOMAS, WILLIAM LEROY, geography educator, cruise lecturer; b. Long Beach, Calif., Mar. 18, 1920; s. William LeRoy and Margaret Lucile (Young) T.; m. Mildred Phyllis Smith, Apr. 10, 1942 (div.); children: Barbara Jean, Lawrence Charles, Virginia Jane, Margaret Joan, Pamela June; m. Loida Ayson Aquino, Aug. 29, 1964 (dec.); children: William John Aquino, Lloyd Aquino; m. Rosalinda Zuñiga Valencia, July 4, 1986; 1 adopted child, Don Valencia. A.B., UCLA, 1941, M.A., 1948; Ph.D., Yale U., 1955. Instr. geography Rutgers U., 1947-50; research asst. S.E. Asia studies Yale U., 1949-50; asst. dir. research Wenner-Gren Found. Anthrop. Research, N.Y.C., 1950-57; assoc. to assoc. prof. geography U. Calif., Riverside, 1957-63; prof. anthropology and geography Calif. State U., Hayward,

1963-71, chmn. dept. anthropology and geography, 1963-66, prof. geography and Southeast Asian studies, 1971-91, prof. emeritus, 1983—, chmn. dept. geography, 1971-74; assoc. dir. Ctr. for Filipino Studies Calif. State U., 1990-91; v.p. rsch. and devel. Heritage Tours, Ltd., Oakland, Calif., 1981-83; v.p. rsch. and devel., chmn. bd. Geo-Expdns. Internat., Inc., 1981-83; pres. Thomas Opportunity Program Services, 1983-90; vis. prof. La. State U., spring 1966, U. Hawaii, summer 1966, U. Wis., fall 1966, U. Toronto, Canada, fall 1968, 69, Georgetown U., 1992; vis. research assoc. Inst. Philippine Culture, Ateneo de Manila U., Quezon City, 1970, 76-77; Fulbright lectr. Centre for Asian Studies, U. Western Australia, Nedlands, 1974; Fulbright sr. research scholar Mariano Marcos State U., Batac, Ilocos Norte, Philippines, 1984-85; organizer internat. symposium Man's Role in Changing the Face of the Earth, Princeton, N.J., 1955; cons. Nat. Acad. Scis.-NRC, in orgn. of sect. 6th Nat. Conf. UNESCO, 1957; mem. tech. cons. group Calif. Pub. Outdoor Recreation Plan Com., 1958-60; geog. cons. Pacific Missile Range, Pt. Mugu, Calif., 1958-60; organizer geography sect. 10th Pacific Sci. Congress, 1961; foreign field research, Philippines, 1961-62, Philippines, Thailand, Burma, 1970, Australia, Indonesia, 1974, Philippines, 1976-77, 84-85, 86, French Polynesia, 1992, 93, Thailand, Malaysia, Indonesia, Singapore, 1993, Indonesia, 1994, 95 Northern Australia, 1995; mem. ad hoc com. on geography Nat. Acad. Scis.-NRC, 1963-65, cons. effects of herbicides in, Vietnam, 1972-74; chmn. Asian studies council Calif. State Colls., 1971-72; mem. com. internat. symposium earth as transformed by human action Clark U., Worcester, Mass., 1987; invited speaker V.I. Vernadsky anniversary symposium USSR Acad. Scis., Leningrad, Kiev, Moscow, 1988; guest lectr. Cunard Line 'Vistafjord' cruise, Feb. 1992, Royal Viking Line 'Sun' Cruise, 1992, Paquet Cruise Company 'Ocean Pearl' cruise, 1993, Cunard Line 'Sagafjord' cruise, 1993, Seven Seas Cruise Line 'Song of Flower' cruise, 1993-94, Cunard Line 'Vistafjord' Cruise, 1994, Crystal Cruises 'Crystal Harmony' Cruise, 1994, Regency Cruises 'Regent Sea' Cruise, 1994, Orient Line 'Marco Polo' Cruise, 1994, Holland-Am. Line 'Rotterdam' Grand World Voyage Cruise, 1995, Orient Line 'Marco Polo' Cruise, 1995, Royal Caribbean Cruises on Sun Viking, Far East, 1996. Author: (with J. F. Embree) Ethnic Groups of Northern Southeast Asia, 1950, Land, Man and Culture in Mainland Southeast Asia, 1957, (with J.E. Spencer) Cultural Geography, 1969, Asia, East by South, 2d edit, 1971, Introducing Cultural Geography, 1973, 2d edit., 1978; Editor: (with Anna M. Pikells) International Directory of Anthropological Institutions, 1953, Yearbook of Anthropology, 1955, Current Anthropology, 1956, Man's Role in Changing the Face of the Earth, 1956, Am. Anthrop. Assn. Bull, 1958-60, Man, Time, and Space in Southern California, 1959;paperback series Man-Environment System in The Late 20th Century, 1969-75. Moderator United Ch. Hayward, 1988-90. 1st lt. C.E., AUS, 1942-45. Mem. Assn. Asian Studies, Asian Studies on Pacific Coast (chmn. standing com. 1979-80, conf. chmn. 1980), Pacific Sci. Assn. (U.S. mem. sci. com. on geography), Assn. Am. Geographers (Pacific Coast regional councilor 1971-74, citation for meritorious contbn. to geography 1961), Assn. Pacific Coast Geographers (v.p. 1976-77, pres. 1977-78, Disting. Svc. award 1988), Calif. Geog. Soc. (pres. 1967-68, Outstanding Educator award 1986). Democrat. Address: 307 Shalako Dr Oakdale CA 95361-9683

THOMAS, WILLIAM MARSHALL, congressman; b. Wallace, Idaho, Dec. 6, 1941; s. Virgil and Gertrude Thomas; m. Sharon Lynn Hamilton, Jan. 1968; children: Christopher, Amelia. B.A., San Francisco State U., 1963, M.A., 1965. Mem. faculty dept. Am. govt. Bakersfield (Calif.) Coll., 1965-74, prof., 1965-74; mem. Calif. State Assembly, 1974-78, 96th-104th Congress from 18th, now 21st Calif. Dist., 1979—; vice chmn. of House Task Force on Campaign Fin. Reform; mem. Ho. of Reps. Ways and Means Com.; chmn. Com. on House Oversight, Ways & Means Health Subcom.; mem. Ways & Means subcom on Trade; mem. del. to Soviet Union, by Am. Council Young Polit. Leaders, 1977; chmn. Kern County Republican Central Com., 1972-74; mem. Calif. Rep. Com., 1972-80; del. Republican Party Nat. Conv., 1980, 84, 88; mem. Rep. Leader's Task Force on Health Care Reform. Office: Ho of Reps 2208 Rayburn Ho Office Bldg Washington DC 20515

THOMAS, WILLIAM SCOTT, lawyer; b. Joliet, Ill., Aug. 16, 1949. AB, Stanford U., 1971; JD, U. Calif., Hastings, 1974; LLM in Taxation, Golden Gate U., 1981. Bar: Calif. 1975, U.S. Dist. Ct. (no. dist.) Calif. 1975, U.S. Tax Ct. 1982. Tax editor Internat. Bur. Fiscal Documentation, Amsterdam, Holland, 1974-75; tax atty. Chevron Corp., San Francisco, 1975-77; from assoc. to ptnr. Brobeck, Phleger & Harrison, San Francisco, 1978—; bd. dirs. Value Line Inc., N.Y.C. Mem. ABA (taxation sect.), Calif. Bar Assn. (exec. com. taxation sect. 1984-89, chmn. 1987-88). Office: Brobeck Phleger & Harrison 1 Market Plz San Francisco CA 94105

THOMAS, WYNN P., art director, production designer. Art dir.: (films) Beat Street, 1984, She's Gotta Have It, 1986; prodn. designer: (films) Eddie Murphy Raw, 1987, School Daze, 1988, Do the Right Thing, 1989, Mo' Better Blues, 1990, The Five Heartbeats, 1991, Jungle Fever, 1991, Malcolm X, 1992, A Bronx Tale, 1993, Crooklyn, 1994. Office: care Art Directors Guild 11365 Ventura Blvd Ste 315 Studio City CA 91604-3148

THOMASCH, ROGER PAUL, lawyer; b. N.Y.C., Nov. 7, 1942; s. Gordon J. and Margaret (Molloy) T.; children: Laura Leigh, Paul Butler. BA, Coll. William and Mary, 1964; LLB, Duke U., 1967. Bar: Conn. 1967, Colo. 1974. Assoc. atty. Cummings & Lockwood, Stamford, Conn., 1967-70; trial atty. U.S. Dept. Justice, Washington, 1970-73; ptnr. Roath & Brega, Denver, 1975-87; mng. ptnr. Ballard, Spahr, Andrews & Ingersoll, Denver, 1987—; vis. assoc. prof. of law Drake U. Sch. Law, Des Moines, 1973-74; frequent lectr. in field, U.S. and Can.; co-dean comml. litigation program of Nat. Advanced Coll. of Advocacy, 1982-86; adj. faculty mem. U. Denver Coll. Law, 1976-80. Recipient Leland Forrest Outstanding Prof. award, Drake U. Sch. Law, 1973. Mem. ABA, Colo. Bar Assn., Denver Country Club, Univ. Club, Denver Athletic Club. Office: Ballard Spahr Andrews & Ingersoll 1225 17th St Denver CO 80202-5534

THOMASON, FRANK W., superintendent. Supt. Dalton City Schs., Dalton, Ga. Recipient State Finalist for Nat. Supt. of Yr. award, 1993. Office: Dalton City Schs PO Box 1408 100 S Hamilton St Dalton GA 30720-4216

THOMASON, SCOTT, automobile executive; b. 1953. Prin. Thomason Toyota, Gladstone; pres. Dee A. Thomason Ford Co., Gladstone, 1974—, Thomason Nissan Inc., Gladstone, 1990—, Heritage Auto Ctr. Inc., Kirkland, Wash., 1991—. Office: 19405 SE McLoughlin Gladstone OR 97027

THOMASSEN, PAULINE F., medical, surgical nurse; b. Cleve., Jan. 19, 1939; d. Henry Clifford and Mabel Pauline (Hill) Nichols; m. Ruben Thomassen, Nov. 10, 1979; children: Rhonda, Terry, Diana, Philipp, Jody, Barbara. AA in Nursing, So. Colo. State Coll., 1974, BA in Psychology with distinction, 1975; BSN magna cum laude, Seattle Pacific U., 1986. RN, Wash. Staff nurse III orthopedic unit, preceptor orientation RNs and student RNs Swedish Hosp. Med. Ctr., Seattle, 1975—; mem. planning task force and faculty National Nurses Conference, The Nurse and Spinal Surgery, Cleve. Author: Spinal Disease and Surgical Interventions. Mem. Nat. Assn. Orthop. Nurses.

THOMASSON, PATSY, federal official. BA, Henderson State U.; MA, U. Mo. Staff asst. to congressman Wilbur D. Mills U.S. House Reps., Washington, Ark., 1969-71, 72-74; exec. dir. Dem. Party Ark.; assoc. adminstr. Doctors Hosp., Little Rock; pres. So. Mgmt. Assn.; exec. v.p., pres. Phoenix Group; spl. asst. to pres., dir. Office adminstrn. Mgmt. and Adminstrn., Washington, 1993—; dep. asst. to the pres., dep. dir. Washington. Overseer Coord. Campaign Ark. Mem. Am. Assn. State Highway and Transp. Officials. Office: The White House Office of Presidential Personnel 1600 Pennsylvania Ave NW Washington DC 20500-0001*

THOMLINSON, RALPH, demographer, educator; b. St. Louis, Feb. 12, 1925; s. Ralph and Ora Lee (Barr) T.; m. Margaret Mary Willits, Dec. 21, 1946; children: Elizabeth Barr, William Lockwood. BA, Oberlin Coll., 1948; postgrad., U. Pitts., 1943-44, Harvard U., 1948; MA, Yale U., 1949; PhD, Columbia U., 1960. Asst. town planner Montclair, N.J., 1949-50; asst. city planner Paterson, N.J., 1950; research asst. Bur. Applied Social Research, N.Y.C., 1952; med. statistics asst. actuarial dept. Met. Life Ins. Co., N.Y.C., 1952-53; instr. statistics and population U. Wis., 1953-56; instr. sociology and anthropology Denison U., Granville, Ohio, 1956-59; asst. prof. sociology Calif. State U., L.A., 1959-62; assoc. prof. Calif. State U., 1962-65, prof., 1965-88, prof. emeritus, 1988—, chmn. dept. sociology, 1967-69; vis. prof. sociology U. Alta., Can., 1966; vis. prof. biostatistics U. N.C., Chapel Hill, 1972-73; demographic adviser Inst. Population Studies, Chulalongkorn U., Bangkok, Thailand, 1969-71; cons. Nat. Family Planning Program, Thailand, Census of Thailand, 1970-71, Population/Food Fund, 1977-79, also various research centers abroad, 1969-73; cons. to fourteen book pubs., 1965—; field assoc. Population Coun., N.Y.C., 1969-71; rsch. adviser Ctr. for Rsch. and Demographic Studies, Rabat, Morocco, 1972-73; acad. visitor Population Investigation Com., London Sch. Econs., 1973; vis. scholar Nat. Inst. Demographic Studies, Paris, 1973-74. Author: A Mathematical Model for Migration, 1960, Population Dynamics, 2d edit, 1976, Sociological Concepts and Research, 1965, Demographic Problems, 2d edit, 1975, Urban Structure, 1969, Thailand's Population, 1971, (with others) The Methodology of the Longitudinal Study of Social, Economic and Demographic Change, 1971; editor: (with Visid Prachuabmoh) The Potharam Study, 1971; adv. editor: Sociol. Abstracts, 1963-67, Sociology Quar, 1978-84; cons. editor: As-Soukan, 1972-73; assoc. editor: Pacific Sociol. Rev, 1976-83; Sociol. Perspective, 1983-85; chmn. editorial bd. Calif. Sociologist, 1981-84; cons.: Dictionary of Modern Sociology, 1969; contbr. to: Dictionary of Demography, 5 vols., 1985-86; books, profl. jours. Served with AUS, 1943-45, ETO. Mem. Population Assn. Am., Internat. Union for Sci. Study Population, Am. Sociol. Assn., Internat. Assn. Survey Statisticians, Assn. Asian Studies. Home: 712 Coronado Ln Foster City CA 94404-2925

THOMLISON, RAY J., university dean, educator; b. Edmonton, Alta., Can., Jan. 22, 1943; s. Herbert MacLeod and Margaret Patricia (Hagen) T.; m. Barbara Buckler, Aug. 22, 1964; children: Lynn, Breanne. BSc, U. Alta., 1963; B in Social Work, U. B.C., 1964, MSW, 1965; PhD, U. Toronto, 1972. Social worker Dept. Pub. Welfare, Edmonton, 1964-65; psychiat. social worker Mental Health Ctr., Burnaby, B.C., Can., 1965-67; mental health cons. Lower Mainland & North B.C., 1967-68; assoc. prof. Wilfrid Laurier U., Waterloo, Ont., Can., 1971-73; prof. U. Toronto, Ont., 1973-83; prof., dean U. Calgary, Alta., 1983—; vis. prof. U. B.C., Vancouver, 1980-81, U. Regina, Sask., Can., 1977; sessional faculty Atkinson Coll., York U., Downsview, Ont., 1978-83, Wilfrid Laurier U., 1974-83; mem. adv. com., chair Com. Native Social Work Edn., Alta, 1986-90; mem. adv. com. Profl. Exam. Bd. Social Work, Alta., 1983-87; mem. bd. accreditation Can. Assn. Schs. Social Work, 1978; mem. Univ. Coord. Coun., Alta., 1984-86; content advisor Nat. Film Bd.; employee assistance cons. Esso Can., Bank of Montreal. Editor: Perspectives on Industrial Social Work Practice, 1983, (with J.S. Ismael) Perspectives on Social Services and Social Issues, 1987, (with C.R. Bagley) Child Sexual Abuse: Critical Perspectives on Prevention, Intervention, and Treatment, 1991, (with J. Hudson and J. Mayne) Action-Oriented Evaluation in Organizations: Canadian Practices, 1992; contbr. articles to profl. jours., book chpts., reports, and papers to confs. U. Toronto Faculty teaching fellow, 1974. Mem. Coun. Social Work. Edn., Assn. Advancement Behaviour Therapy, Assn. Behavioral Social Work, Rsch. Inst. Social Work (People's Rep. of China), Assn. Social Workers of Russia, Alberta Assn. Social Workers, Met. Toronto Children's Aid (bd. dirs. 1979-83), Family Service Assn. Met. Toronto Employee Assistance Program (adv. bd. 1977-83). Home: 142 Schiller Crescent NW, Calgary, AB Canada T3L 1W9 Office: U of Calgary Faculty Soc Work, 2500 Univ Dr NW, Calgary, AB Canada T2N 1N4

THOMOPULOS, GREGS G., consulting engineering company executive; b. Benin City, Nigeria, May 16, 1942; s. Aristoteles and Christiana E. (Ogiamien) T.; m. Patricia Walker, Sept. 4, 1966 (div. 1974); 1 child, Lisa; m. Mettie L. Williams, May 28, 1976; children: Nicole, Euphemia. BSCE with highest distinction, U. Kans., 1965; MS in Structural Engring., U. Calif., Berkeley, 1966; PhD (hon.), Teikyo Marycrest U., 1996. Sr. v.p. internat. div. Stanley Cons., Inc., Muscatine, Iowa, 1978-84, sr. v.p. project divsn., 1984-87; pres. Stanley Consultants, Inc., Muscatine, Iowa, 1987—; exec. v.p. SC Co., Inc., Muscatine, 1992—, also bd. dirs.; chmn., CEO Stanley Cons. Environ., Inc., Chgo., 1991—, also bd. dirs.; chmn., CEO SC Power Devel., Inc., 1992—; CEO Stanley Design-Build, Inc., Muscatine, 1995—; chmn., CEO Stanley Design-Build, Inc., 1995—; bd. dirs. Stanley Cons., Inc., Muscatine. Bd. dirs. Goodwill Industries Ea. Iowa, 1987—, pres., 1992-94; mem. adv. bd. U. Iowa Coll. Engring., Ctrl. State U. Water Resources Ctr. Fellow ASCE, Am. Cons. Engring. Coun.; mem. NSPE, 33 Club (pres. 1987), Rotary. Presbyterian. Avocations: tennis, computers, music. Home: 1002 Estron St Iowa City IA 52246-4602 Office: Stanley Cons Inc 225 Iowa Ave Muscatine IA 52761-3730

THOMPSON, ADAM MARK, lawyer; b. Bklyn., July 20, 1964; s. Margie Joan (Lichtenberg) T. BA, CUNY, 1985; JD, Temple U., 1988. Bar: N.Y. 1989, N.J. 1991, U.S. Dist. Ct. (ea. and so. dists.) N.Y., U.S. Ct. Appeals (2d cir.) 1992. Assoc. Legal Aid Soc., N.Y.C., 1988-91; pvt. practice N.Y.C., 1991—; atty., mem. indigent panel Assigned Counsel Plan, N.Y.C., 1991—; spkr., mem. spkr.'s bur. N.Y. State Trial Lawyers Assn., N.Y.C., 1991-92. Mem. ABA, ATLA, N.Y. State Trial Lawyers Assn., N.Y. State Bar Assn. Democrat. Avocations: saxophone, writing, sports, baseball, basketball, dog training. Office: Law Office of Adam Thompson 15 Park Row Ste 1111 New York NY 10038

THOMPSON, ALDEN LLOYD, biblical studies educator, author; b. Loma Linda, Calif., Sept. 9, 1943; s. George Alden and Lola Elizabeth (Lukens) T.; m. Wanda Diane Hoffman, June 8, 1965; children: Karin, Krista. BA, Walla Walla Coll., 1965; MA, Andrews U., 1966, BD, 1967; PhD, U. Edinburgh, Scotland, 1975. Ordained to ministry, Seventh-day Adventist Ch., 1971. Assoc. pastor local ch. Redlands, Calif., 1967-68; pastor local ch. Fontana, Calif., 1968-70; mem. staff Sch. Theology Walla Walla (Wash.) Coll., 1970—, prof. bibl. studies, 1990—, provost, 1986-90; exch. tchr. Marienhoehe Sem., Darmstadt, Germany, 1980-81. Author: Responsibility for Evil in the Theodicy of IV Ezra, 1977, Who's Afraid of the Old Testament God?, 1988, Inspiration: Hard Questions, Honest Answers, 1991, Bible Amplifier: 1 and 2 Samuel, 1995; columnist: Signs of the Times, 1985-94, Gleaner, 1987-90, 92—. Office: Walla Walla Coll 204 S College Ave College Place WA 99324-1139

THOMPSON, ALICE M. BROUSSARD, special education administrator; b. Opelousas, La., May 15, 1950; d. Melvin and Roseanna (Joseph) Broussard; m. Samuel Joe Thompson; 1 child, Tameka Rose Thompson. BS in Vocat. Home Econs., McNeese State U., 1973; MEd in Spl. Edn., U. Mo., St. Louis, 1993; cert. in mid-mgmt., Tex. So. U., 1993; completed studies, Harvard U., 1995. Food svc. supr. Parkland Meml. Hosp., Dallas, 1982-83; tchr. home econs. Milw. pub. Schs., 1984-85; tchr. career lab. Ft. Bend Ind. Sch., Sugarland, Tex., 1985-87; tchr. home econs. Epworth Pvt. Sch., Webster Grove, Mo., 1988-91; tchr. resource math. Ft. Bend Ind. Sch. Dist., Sugarland, 1991-92, coord. spl. edn., 1993—; cons. Inclusion, Tex., 1993; coord. Inclusion Adv. Bd., Sugarland, 1993—; mem. Inclusion Works Adv. Bd., Austin, 1994—. Mem. NAFE, ASCD, Coun. for Exceptional Children, Nat. Assn. Black Educators, Alpha Kappa Alpha (dean of pledges 1973). Avocations: reading, tennis, traveling. Home: 2811 Plantation Wood Ln Missouri City TX 77459-4253 Office: Ft Bend Ind Sch Dist PO Box 1004 Sugar Land TX 77487-1004

THOMPSON, ALVIN J., internist; b. Washington, 1924; m. Faye Thompson; children—Michael, Donna, Kevin, Susan, Gail. MD, Howard U., 1946. Diplomate Am. Bd. Internal Medicine. Intern St. Louis City Hosp. (Phillips), 1946-47, resident, 1947-51; pvt. practice medicine specializing in internal medicine, gastroenterology, 1957—; mem. attending staff Providence Hosp., Swedish Hosp. Med. Ctr.; attending physician VA Hosp., Univ. Hosp., Harborview Med. Ctr.; founder, dir. Gastroenterology Lab. Providence Hosp., Seattle, 1963-77, chief of medicine, 1972-74, pres. med. staff, 1970-71, hosp. trustee, 1974-75; clin. prof. U. Wash. Sch. of Medicine, Seattle, 1972—; physician, gastroenterologist VA, Seattle, 1953-57; bd. dirs. Puget Sound Health Planning Bd., 1974-76, Puget Sound Health Systems Agy., 1974; v.p., acting pres. King County Comprehensive Health Planning Council, 1973; mem. Nat. Commn. Correctional Health Care, 1987—; trustee King County Blue Shield, 1972-74, Northwest Kidney Ctr., 1981—, Hospice of Seattle, 1987—; mem. Wash. State Profl. Services Rev. Orgn. and PRO/W, 1982—; mem. community medicine study group for health care needs of the poor U. Wash. Sch. of Pub. Health and Community Medicine, 1982—; mem. Wash. State Health Coordinating Council, 1979—, Gov.'s Task Force on Health Planning, 1982—, Gov.'s Task Force on the Costs of Med. Care, 1983—, Nat. Commn. on Correctional Health Care, 1987—; mem. vis. com. Schs. of Nursing and Social Work U. Wash. Editorial bd. Jour. Jail and Prison Health; contbr. articles to Archives of Internal Medicine, Northwest Medicine, other profl. jours. Pres. bd. dirs. East Madison YMCA, 1956; trustee Seattle Urban League, 1958-59, Seattle Goodwill Industries, 1986—, Providence Med. Ctr. Found., Travelers Aid Soc., 1960-64, Civic Unity Com., 1960-64, Anti-Tb League, 1961-62, Hospice of Seattle, 1987—; mem. vestry Christ Ch., Seattle, 1958-60; mem. Emmanuel Ch., Mercer Island, 1963—; treas. Boy Scout Troop 451, Mercer Island, 1965-68; mem. Fair Housing Com. City of Mercer Island, 1961—; mem. and cast Gilbert and Sullivan Soc., 1954-57; trustee Seattle Ballet Assn., 1968-69; mem. adv. com., chmn. human services com. Salvation Army, 1979-82, also mem. lay bd.; co-chmn. King County Medic I Com., 1979; mem., trustee Pacific Sci. Ctr. Found., 1980—; vis. com. U. Wash. Sch. Social Work, 1985—. Apptd. U.S. Naval Acad., 1940; chief med. service U.S. Air Force, Ramey AFB Hosp., 1951-53; served to maj. USAFR, 1953-59. Recipient Kappa Cup for Superior Scholarship Howard U., 1941; Robert H. Williams Superior Leadership award Seattle Acad. Internal Medicine, 1979; award Seattle C. of C., 1983; award for Outstanding Contbns. in Health Nat. Assn. Med. Minority Educators, 1983; named Philanthropist of Yr. Washington Gives, 1989. Mem. AMA (del. 1980—), NAS, ACP (Wash. and Alaska ,gov. 1974-78), Wash. State Med. Assn. (trustee 1969-70, pres. 1977-78, past. pres., chmn. exec. com. 1978-79), Wash. State Soc. Internal Medicine (ASIM del. 1969-70, pres. 1970-71), King County Med. Soc. (del. 1969-71, trustee 1969-71, pres. 1974), Seattle Acad. Internal Medicine (sec.-treas. 1970-71, pres. 1972-73), ACP, Am. Gastroenterologic Assn., Am. Soc. for Gastrointestinal Endoscopy, North Pacific Soc. Internal Medicine, Am. Soc. Internal Medicine, Nat. Med. Assn., Inst. of Medicine, Wash. State Assn. Biomed. Rsch. (pres. 1988—), , Wash. State Assn. Black Profls. in Health Care (chmn. 1980—), Seattle C. of C. (mem. health care policy com. 1976-79), NAACP (life). Lodge: Rotary (Seattle).

THOMPSON, ANGELA COLEMAN, nurse, educator; b. Miami, Fla., July 14, 1949; d. William Carl Sr. and Roberta (Demmons) Coleman; m. Rodney David Thompson Sr., Sept. 13, 1969; children: Rodney David, Catrece Dionne. AA in Nursing, Miami Dade Med. Ctr., 1975; BA, Fla. A&M U., 1970. RN, Fla. Charge nurse Humana Hosp. Biscayne, Miami, 1975-91; supr. nursing Pines Rehab. Ctr., Miami, 1990-91; dir. edn. Concorde Career Inst., Miami, 1991—. Mem. AMA, Black Nurses Assn. Democrat. Methodist. Home: 17330 NW 16th Ave Miami FL 33169-5115

THOMPSON, ANNA BLANCHE, retired educator; b. Ft. Worth, Oct. 8, 1914; d. George Lewis and Gula Gertrude (Cook) Turnbow; m. Jess Lee, May 27, 1939; children: Jess Lee II, Mary Ann Thompson Archbold. BA in Edn., Ariz. State U., Tempe, 1935; postgrad., U. Ariz., 1940, U. Hawaii, 1964, Pepperdine U., 1967. Tchr. Parke (Ariz.) Elem. Sch., 1935-40; tchr. music Parker High Sch., 1940-42; tchr. Scottsdale (Ariz.) Elem. Sch., 1948-71; tchr. U. Hawaii, Laie, 1971-72; tchr. U. Hawaii, 1972-79, ret., 1979. Mem. edn. bd. Phoenix Women's Club, 1983-84; pres. Ariz. Res. Officers Ladies, Phoenix, 1982-84, state pres., 1986-87; pres. Ladies of the Ribbon, Phoenix, 1987-90, Tempe Garden Club, 1987-88. Recipient Mus. plaque Phoenix Symphony Symphonette, 1982-83, Cert. of Appreciation, St. Luke's Hosp. Aux., 1985, Cert. of Appreciation, Mil. Order of World Wars, 1989. Mem. Ariz. Res. Officers Ladies (state sec. 1990—), Tri-City Angels of Ariz. (pres. 1984—), Collectors Club Am. (nat. pres. 1987—), Ikebana Internat., AAUW (historian Tempe chpt. 1987-90), Delta Kappa Gamma (pres. Phoenix chpt. 1974-76, 88-90, parliamentarian 1990—). Avocations: needlepoint, travel. Home: 533 E Fairmont Dr Tempe AZ 85282-3722

THOMPSON, ANNE ELISE, federal judge; b. Phila., July 8, 1934; d. Leroy Henry and Mary Elise (Jackson) Jenkins; m. William H. Thompson, June 19, 1965; children: William H., Sharon A. BA, Howard U., 1955, LLB, 1964; MA, Temple U., 1957. Bar: D.C. bar 1964, N.J. bar 1966. Staff atty. Office of Solicitor, Dept. Labor, Chgo., 1964-65; asst. dep. public defender Trenton, N.J., 1967-70; mcpl. prosecutor Lawrence Twp., Lawrenceville, N.J., 1970-72; mcpl. ct. judge Trenton, 1972-75; prosecutor Mercer County, Mercer County, Trenton, 1975-79; judge U.S. Dist. Ct. N.J., Trenton, 1979—, now chief judge; vice chmn. Mercer County Criminal Justice Planning Com., 1972; mem. com. criminal practice N.J. Supreme Ct., 1975-79, mem. com. mcpl. cts., 1972-75; v.p. N.J. County Prosecutors Assn., 1978-79; chmn. juvenile justice com. Nat. Dist. Attys. Assn., 1978-79. Del. Democratic Nat. Conv., 1972. Recipient Assn. Black Women Lawyers award, 1976, Disting. Service award Nat. Dist. Attys. Assn., 1979, Gene Carte Meml. award Am. Criminal Justice Assn., 1980, Outstanding Leadership award N.J. County Prosecutors Assn., 1980, John Mercer Langston Outstanding Alumnus award Howard U. Law Sch., 1981; also various service awards; certs. of appreciation. Mem. Am. Bar Assn., Fed. Bar Assn., N.J. Bar Assn., Mercer County Bar Assn. Democrat. Office: US Dist Ct US Courthouse 402 E State St Trenton NJ 08608-1507

THOMPSON, ANNIE FIGUEROA, academic director, educator; b. Río Piedras, P.R., June 7, 1941; d. Antonio Figueroa-Colón and Ana Isabel Laugier; m. Donald P. Thompson, Jan. 23, 1972; 1 child, John Anthony. BA, Baylor U., 1962; MSLS, U. So. Calif., 1965; AMD, Fla. State U., 1978, PhD, 1980. Educator Mayan Sch., Guatemala City, Guatemala, 1962-63; cataloger libr. system U. P.R., Río Piedras, 1965-67, head music libr., 1967-81, assoc. prof. librarianship, 1981-85; dir. grad. sch. libr. info. sci. U. P.R., Rio Piedras, 1986-93; prof. U. P.R., Río Piedras, 1986—. Author: An Annotated Bibliography About Music in Puerto Rico, 1975; co-author: Music and Dance in Puerto Rico from the Age of Columbus to Modern Times, An Annotated Bibliography, 1991; contbr. articles to profl. jours.; performed song recitals Inst. of P.R. Culture and U. P.R. Artist Series, 1974-78; soloist with P.R. Symphony Orch., San Juan, 1978; performed in opera, on radio and TV, San Juan, 1968-81;. Sec. P.R. Symphony Orch League, San Juan, 1982-84; mem. pub. libr. adv. com. Adminstrn. for Devel. of Arts and Culture, P.R., 1982-84, Pub. Libr. Adv. Bd., 1989-94. Recipient Lauro a la Instrucción Bibliotecaria Sociedad de Bibliotecarios de P.R., 1985, Lauro a la Bibliografía Puertorriqueña, 1993. Mem. ALA, Assn. Libr. and Info. Sci., San Juan Rotary, Sociedad de Bibliotecarios de P.R. (pres. 1994-96), Music Libr. Assn., Sigma Delta Kappa, Mu Phi Epsilon, Beta Phi Mu. Episcopalian. Home: N-64 Acadia St Park Gardens Rio Piedras San Juan PR 00926 Office: Grad Sch Library & Info Sci U of PR PO Box 21906 Rio Piedras San Juan PR 00931-1906

THOMPSON, ANNIE LAURA, foreign language educator; b. Henderson, Tenn., July 8, 1937; d. Wesley Sylvester and Letha Irene (Jones) T.; m. Edward L. Patterson, June 7, 1980. BA, U. Ala., 1959; MA, Duke U., 1961; PhD, Tulane U., 1973. Instr. Spanish lang. U. Miss., Oxford, 1960-64; instr. Auburn (Ala.) U., 1964-66; teaching asst. Tulane U., New Orleans, 1966-70; prof. Spanish lang. Delgado C.C., New Orleans, 1970—; instr. Spanish for Physicians and Med. Persons Tulane U., La. State U. Med. Eye Ctr., Ochsner Clinic and Hosp. Author: Religious Elements in the Quijote, 1960, The Attempt of Spanish Intellectuals to Create a New Spain, 1930-36, 1973, The Generation of 1898: Intellectual Politicians; asst. editor The Crusader, 1961-64. Rep. candidate for gov. State of La., 1991, 95, for 1st Dist. U.S. Congress, 1992; alt. mem. La. Coastal Commn., 1984—; del. Women's State Rep. Conv., 1987, La. State Rep. Conv., 1990, 93; active Women for Better La., 1986-89, La. Coastal Adv. Coun., 1988, Pan Am. Commn., 1992-95; v.p. pub. rels. Alliance for Good Govt., 1990. Recipient Outstanding Tchr. award Delgado Coll. Student Govt. Assn., 1974; Woodoow Wilson fellow, 1959-60; NDEA fellow, 1968-69. Mem. AAUP, MLA (South Cen. and South Atlantic), Pachyderm Club, Women's Rep. Club, Phi Beta Kappa, Phi Alpha Theta, Sigma Delta Pi. Republican. Mem. Ch. of Christ. Home: PO Box 24399 New Orleans LA 70184-4399 Office: Delgado Coll Isaac Delgado Hall 113W-1 615 City Park Ave New Orleans LA 70119

THOMPSON, A(NSEL) FREDERICK, JR., environmental engineering and consulting company executive; b. Birmingham, Ala., Oct. 19, 1941; s. Ansel Frederick Sr. and Irene (Turner) T.; m. Susan Elizabeth Weston, Dec. 28, 1963; children: Ansel Frederick III, Jennifer Katherine, Melissa Susan. BSE, Pa. State U., 1963; MSCE, Calif. Inst. Tech., 1965, PhDCE, 1968; postgrad., U. Pa., 1989. Lic. profl. engr. Pa., 1970. Project engr. Roy F. Weston, Inc., West Chester, Pa., 1967-70, prin. engr., 1970-73, dept. mgr., 1973-75, v.p. engring. design, 1975-79, v.p. design and constrn. mgmt., 1979-80, v.p. quality assurance and fin., 1980-87, exec. v.p., 1987-90, vice-chmn., 1990-91, chmn., 1991—; bd. dirs. PSG, Inc. Bd. dirs. S.E. chpt. ARC; bd. trustees University City Sci. Ctr.; bd. govs. Pa. Econ. League, Phila.; mem. Pa. State Great Valley Adv. Bd. Mem. ASCE (mem. corp. adv. bd. Civil Engring. Rsch. Found. 1989—), Newcomer Soc., Am. Acad. Environ. Engrs. (diplomate), Water Environ. Fedn., Am. Water Works Assn., Profl. Svcs. Mgmt. Assn., Sigma Xi. Avocations: tennis, photography, music, travel, reading. Office: Roy F Weston Inc Weston Way West Chester PA 19380

THOMPSON, ANTHONY RICHARD, electrical engineer, astronomer; b. Hull, Yorkshire, Eng., Apr. 7, 1931; came to U.S., 1957; s. George and Ada Mary (Laybourn) T.; m. Sheila Margaret Press, Oct. 12, 1963; 1 child, Sarah Louise. BSc in Physics with honors, U. Manchester, Eng., 1952, PhD, 1955. Engr. E.M.I. Electronics Ltd., Feltham, Eng., 1956-57; rsch. fellow Coll. Obs. Harvard U., Cambridge, Mass., 1957-62; sr. rsch. assoc. Radio Astronomy Inst. Stanford (Calif.) U., 1962-72; head electronics divsn., VLA and VLBA projects Nat. Radio Astronomy Obs., Charlottesville, Va., 1973-92, dep. head Ctrl. Electronics Lab., 1993—; vis. sr. rsch. fellow Owens Valley Radio Obs., Calif. Inst. Tech., Pasadena, 1966-72; mem. Com. on Radio Frequencies NAS, Washington, 1980-91; sec. Interunion Commn. on Frequency Allocations for Radio Astronomy and Space Sci., 1982-88, mem., 1991—; guest lectr. in radio astronomy Ukrainian Acad. Sci., 1988. Prin. author: (monograph) Interferometry and Synthesis in Radio Astronomy, 1986; contbr. articles to Astrophys. Jour., Astron. Jour., Proceedings of IEEE, Sci., Radiosci. Fellow IEEE; mem. Internat. Telecom. Union (radiocommunication sector, chmn. working group on radio astronomy U.S. Study group 7 1978—), Am. Astron. Soc., Internat. Astron. Union. Achievements include research in astronomy and contributions to system design of the VLA and VLB array; design of instruments: frequency coordination for radio astronomy. Office: Nat Radio Astronomy Obs 520 Edgemont Rd Charlottesville VA 22903-2454

THOMPSON, ANTHONY WAYNE, metallurgist, educator, consultant; b. Burbank, Calif., Mar. 6, 1940; s. William Lyman and Mary Adelaide (Nisbet) T.; m. Mary Ruth Cummings, Aug. 24, 1963; children: Campbell Lyman, Michael Anthony. BS, Stanford U., 1962; MS, U. Wash., 1965; PhD, MIT, 1970. Research engr. Jet Propulsion Lab., Pasadena, Calif., 1962-63; mem. tech. staff Sandia Labs., Livermore, Calif., 1970-73, Rockwell Sci. Ctr., Thousand Oaks, Calif., 1973-77; assoc. prof. Carnegie Mellon U., Pitts., 1977-79, prof., 1980-94, dept. head, 1987-90; staff scientist Lawrence Berkeley Lab., Berkeley, Calif., 1994—; vis. scientist U. Cambridge, Eng., 1983, Risø, Denmark, 1987, U. Calif., 1991; cons. Sandia Labs., 1977—, GE, 1988—. Editor: Work Hardening, 1976, Metall. Transactions, 1983-88; co-editor: Hydrogen in Metals, 1974, Hydrogen Conf. Proc., 1976, 81, 89, 94; mem. editl. bd. Internat. Metals Revs., 1980-88; contbr. articles to profl. jours. Overseas fellow Churchill Coll. Cambridge U., 1982. Fellow Am. Soc. Metals; mem. AAAS, AIME, Sigma Xi. Democrat. Clubs: Sierra, Nat. Model R.R. Assn. Home: 2942 Linden Ave Berkeley CA 94705-2328 Office: Lawrence Berkeley Lab Material Sci Divsn Berkeley CA 94720

THOMPSON, BARBARA STORCK, state official; b. McFarland, Wis., Oct. 15, 1924; d. John Casper and Marie Ann (Kassabaum) Storck; m. Glenn T. Thompson, July 1, 1944; children—David C., James T. B.S., Wis. State U., 1956; M.S., U. Wis., 1959, Ph.D., 1969; L.H.D. (hon.), Carroll Coll., 1974. Tchr. pub. schs. West Dane County, Mt. Horeb, Wis., 1944-56; instr. Green County Tchrs. Coll., Monroe, Wis., 1956-57; coordinator curriculum Monroe Pub. Schs., 1957-60; instr. U. Wis., Platteville, 1960; supr. schs. Waukesha County Schs., Wis., 1960-63; supt. schs. Waukesha County Schs., 1963-65; prin. Fairview Elem. Schs., Brookfield, Wis., 1962-64; adminstrv. cons. Wis. Dept. Pub. Instrn., Madison, 1964-72; state coordinator Wis. Dept. Pub. Instrn., 1971-72; instr. U. Wis., Madison and Green Bay, 1972; supt. pub. instrn. Madison, State of Wis., 1973-81; mem. Wis. State Bd. Vocat. Edn., 1973-81, Wis. Edn. Comm. Bd., 1973-81. Author: A Candid Discussion of Critical Issues, 1975; Mem. editorial bd.: The Education Digest, 1975—; Contbr. articles to profl. jours. Mem. White House Conf. Children, 1970, Gov.'s Com. State Conf. Children and Youth, 1969-70, Manpower Council, 1973-81; bd. dirs. Vocational, Tech. and Adult Edn., 1973-81, Ednl. Communications, 1973-81, Higher Edn. Aids, 1973-81, Agy. Instructional TV, 1975-81; mem. nat. panel on SAT score decline; bd. regents U. Wis., 1973-81. Recipient State Conservation award Madison Lions CLub, 1956; Waukesha Freeman award, 1961. Mem. Nat. Council Adminstrv. Women in Edn. (named Woman of Year 1974), Nat. Council State Cons. in Elementary Edn. (pres. 1974-75), Wis. Assn. Sch. Dist. Adminstrs., Assn. Supervision and Curriculum Devel., Wis. Assn. Supervision and Curriculum Devel., Southwestern Wis. Assn. Supervision and Curriculum Devel., Southeastern Wis. Assn. Supervision and Curriculum Devel. (mem. exec. council 1972-73), Dept. Elementary Sch. Prins., Wis. Elementary Sch. Prins. Assn., NEA, Wis. Edn. Assn. (pres. local chpt. 1970-71); life mem. So. Wis. Edn. Assn., Wis. Ednl. Research Assn., Dept. Elementary-Kindergarten-Nursery Edn., Assn. Childhood Edn. Internat., Assn. Childhood Edn., Council Chief State Sch. Officers, Edn. Commn. of States, Nat. Council State Cons. in Elementary Edn. (pres. 1974-75), Am. Assn. Sch. Dist. Adminstrs. (chmn. policy com. 1963-81), Delta Kappa Gamma. Office: 204 3rd St W Bradenton FL 34205-8856

THOMPSON, BASIL F., ballet master; b. Newcastle-on-Tyne, Eng., 1937; came to U.S., 1958; Grad., Royal Acad. Dance; studies with, David Lichine, Tania Riabouchinska; student, Sch. Classical. Ballet, 1958-60. Dancer Covent Garden Opera Co., Sadler Wells Opera Co., London, 1954-55, Royal Ballet Eng., London, 1955-58; instr. ballet and character Eugene Loring Sch. Ballet, L.A., 1958-60, Al Gilber Sch. Ballet, L.A., 1958-60; instr. ballet Michael Panaieff Sch. Ballet, L.A., 1958-60; soloist Am. Ballet Theatre, N.Y.C., 1960-67; ballet master Joffrey Ballet Co., N.Y.C., 1967-79; ballet master, choreographer N.J. Ballet Co., West Orange, 1979-80; mem. faculty ballet and character N.J. Ballet Sch., Morristown/West Orange, 1979-80; ballet master Milw. Ballet, 1981-86, also artistic head; currently ballet master Pa. and Milw. Ballet; apptd. artistic dir. Milw. Ballet, spring 1995; guest ballet instr. Internat. Ballet Inst., Aix-en-Provence, France, 1980; guest instr. character Am. Ballet Co. Sch., 1981. Roles include (prin.) Billy the Kid, Sleeping Beauty, Graduation Ball, La Sylphide, Moon Reindeer, Peter and The Wolf, Three Cornered Hat, others, (soloist) Rodeo, Fall River Legend, Fire Bird, Coppelia, Swan Lake, Cinderella, La Boutique Fantastic, Undertow, others (opera) Aida; guest appearances include for Dame Margo Fontayne Royal Acad. Gala, Pres. John F. Kennedy, Pres. Lyndon B. Johnson, L.A. Civic Light Opera, Michael Panaieff Ballet Theatre; TV appearances include Bell Telephone Hour Spectacular prodn. Graduation Ball, NBC prodn. Sleeping Beauty and Cinderella; Broadway prodns. On a Clear Day You Can See Forever, Tavarich, Happiest Girl in the World; choreographer La Traviata. Office: Milw Ballet 504 W National Ave Milwaukee WI 53204-1746

THOMPSON, BENNIE, professional football player. Student, Grambling State. Safety Kansas City Chiefs, Mo., 1989-94; with Cleveland Browns, 1994—. Played in Pro Bowl, 1991. Office: Cleveland Browns 80 First Ave Berea OH 44017-0679

THOMPSON, BENNIE G., congressman; b. Bolton, Miss.. BA Polit. Sci., Tougaloo Coll.; MS Ednl. Adminstrn., Jackson State U., Miss.; grad., U. So. Miss. Alderman Bolton, Miss., 1970-74, mayor, 1974-80; supr. dist. 2 Hinds County Bd., Miss., 1980-93; mem. 103d-104th U.S. Congress from 2d dist. Miss., 1993—; mem. agr. com., 1993—, mem. Small Bus. Com.; Presdl. appointee Nat. Coun. Health Planning and Devel. Bd. trustees Tougaloo Coll.; bd. dirs. So. Regional Coun., Housing Assistance Coun. Mem. Miss. Assn. Black Mayors (founder), Miss. Assn. Black Suprs. Democrat. Original plaintiff in 1975 Ayers case. Office: 1408 Longworth House Office Bl Washington DC 20515*

THOMPSON, BERT ALLEN, retired librarian; b. Bloomington, Ind., Dec. 13, 1930; s. James Albert and Dorothy Fern (Myers) T.; m. Martha Ellen Palmer; children—John Carter II, Anne Palmer, Paul Julian. B.S., Ball State Tchrs. Coll., 1953; A.M., Ind. U., 1960; certificate in archival adm., U. Denver, 1967. Tchr., librarian Ind. pub. schs., 1953-55; reference asst. Indpls. Pub. Library, 1956-59; head reference service Mankato (Minn.) State Coll., 1959-61; instr. Grad. Library Sch., No. Ill. U., Dekalb, 1961-63; dir. libraries, asst. prof. ednl. media Kearney (Nebr.) State Coll., 1963-69; dir. library service Ill. Benedictine Coll., Lisle, Ill., 1969-90, spl. collections librarian, 1990-92. Mem. exec. bd. Ill. regional Library Council, 1976-79. Recipient 1st Melvin R. George LIBRAS award for Outstanding Svc. to Libr. Cooperation, 1993. Mem. Ill. (de Lafayette Reid Research scholar 1976), Catholic Library Assn. (treas. Ill. chpt. 1973-75, nat. sec.-treas. coll./univ. sect. 1981-85, nat. bd. dirs. 1987-93), Nebr. Library Assn. chmn. coll. and univ. sect. 1963-64). Episcopalian. Home: 1011 N Cross St Wheaton IL 60187-3587

THOMPSON, BERTHA BOYA, retired education educator, antique dealer and appraiser; b. New Castle, Pa., Jan. 31, 1917; d. Frank L. and Kathryn Belle (Park) Boya; m. John L. Thompson, Mar. 27, 1942; children: Kay Lynn Thompson Koolage, Scott McClain. BS in Elem. & Secondary Edn., Slippery Rock State Coll., 1940; MA in Geography and History, Miami U., 1954; EdD, Ind. U., 1961. Cert. elem. and secondary edn. tchr. Elem. tchr., reading specialist New Castle (Pa.) Sch. System, 1940-45; tchr., chmn. social studies Talawanda Sch. System, Oxford, Ohio, 1954-63; assoc. prof. psychology and geography, chair edn. dept. Western Coll. for Women, Oxford, 1963-74; assoc. prof. edn., reading clinic Miami U., Oxford, 1974-78, prof. emeritus, 1978—; pvt. antique dealer, appraiser Oxford, 1978—. Contbr. articles to profl. jours. Mem. folk art com. Miami U. Art Mus., Oxford, 1974-76; mem. adv. com. Smith libr., Oxford Pub. Libr., 1978-81. Mem. AAUP, Nat. Coun. Geographic Edn. (exec. bd. dirs. 1966-69), Nat. Soc. for Study Edn., Assn. Am. Geographers, Soc. Women Geographers, Nat. Coun. for the Social Studies, Pi Lambda Theta, Zeta Tau Alpha, Pi Gamma Mu, Gamma Theta Upsilon, Kappa Delta Pi. Avocations: antique collecting, reading, travel, tennis. Home: 6073 Contreras Rd Oxford OH 45056-9708

THOMPSON, BRIAN JOHN, university administrator, optics educator; b. Glossop, Eng., June 10, 1932; came to U.S., 1962; s. Alexander William and Edna May (Gould) T.; m. Joyce Emily Cheshire, Mar. 31, 1956; children: Karen Joyce, Andrew Derrick. B of Sci. Tech., U. Manchester, Eng., 1955, PhD, 1959. Demonstrator in physics Dept. Tech., U. Manchester, 1955-56, asst. lectr., 1957-59; lectr. physics U. Leeds, Eng., 1959-62; sr. physicist Tech. Optics, Inc., Burlington, Mass., 1963-65, dir. dept. optics, 1966-67, mgr. tech. ops. west, tech. dir., 1967-68; prof. Inst. Optics U. Rochester, N.Y., 1968-94, dir. Inst. Optics, 1968-75, dean Coll. Engring. and Applied Scis., 1975-84, Wm. F. May prof. engring., 1982-85, provost, 1984-94, provost emeritus, Disting. univ. prof., 1994—. Internat. editor; Optics and Laser Tech., 1969—; assoc. editor: Optical Engring., 1972-76, Optics Comm., 1978-86; Am. editor: Optica Acta, 1981-85; editor: Optical Engineering Series, vol. 1-42, 1980—; mem. editl. adv. bd. Laser Focus, 1970—, Particle Characterization, 1984-95, Optics and Lasers in Engring., 1985, Milestone Series of Selected Papers Vols. 1-114, 1984—, Optical Engring., 1991—; chmn. adv. bd. Marquis Who's Who Directory Optical Scientists and Engrs., 1983-86; contbr. articles to profl. jours. Served with Brit. Army, 1950-52. Fellow Optical Soc. Am. (bd. dirs. 1969-72, exec. com. 1970-73, assoc. editor jour. 1966-77), Inst. Physics and Phys. Soc. (Gt. Britain 1955), Soc. Photo-Optical Instrumentation Engrs. (life, pres. 1974, 75-76, gen. editor series of selected papers 1983—, editor Optical Engring. Jour., 1991—, Pres.'s award 1967, Pezzuto award 1978, Kingslake medal 1978, Gold medal 1986); mem. AAAS, Am. Phys. Soc. Home and Office: 692 Mount Hope Ave Rochester NY 14620-2731

THOMPSON, BRUCE EDWARD, JR., brokerage house executive, former government official; b. Cleve., June 5, 1949; s. Bruce Edward and Mary Ruth (Miller) T.; m. Kathleen Ann Vaughn, May 27, 1972; children: Lesley, Bret. B.S.B.A. in Fin., Georgetown U., 1971. Sr. analyst Govt. Research Corp., Washington, 1971-74; legis. asst. U.S. Sen. William V. Roth Jr., 1974-81; dep. asst. sec. legis. affairs U.S. Treasury Dept., 1981-83, asst. sec. bus. and consumer affairs, 1983-84, asst. sec. legis. affairs, 1984-86; v.p., dir. govt. rels. Merrill Lynch & Co., Inc., 1986—. Staff dir. fiscal and monetary affairs subcom. Republican Platform Com., 1980; adviser Pres. Reagan's Tax Policy Task Force; asst. Pres. Reagan's Transition Hqrs., 1980. Recipient Alexander Hamilton award, 1986. Roman Catholic. Office: Merrill Lynch & Co Inc 3000 K St NW Ste 620 Washington DC 20007-5109

THOMPSON, CAROL FETTERLY, manufacturing executive; b. Columbia, S.C., Apr. 14, 1948; d. Orville Dale and Gwendolyn Elizabeth (Spratlin) Fetterly; children: Robert Julian, Michael Dale. BA in Anthropology, U. S.C., 1974; MA in Sociology, U. Tenn., 1982. Case worker Dept. Social Svcs., Lexington, S.C., 1973-75; rsch. assoc. Oak Ridge (Tenn.) Associated Univs., 1980-82; coord. maintenance tng. Goodyear Atomic, Piketon, Ohio, 1982-84; designer tng. program Goodyear Tire & Rubber Co., Akron, Ohio, 1984-86; mgr. mfg. & support tng. Goodyear Tire & Rubber Co., Akron, 1991-93; mgr. EEO and govtl. pers. rels. Goodyear Tire & Rubber Co., Lawton, Okla., 1986-88; mgr. prodn. bus. ctr. Goodyear Tire & Rubber Co., Lawton, 1988-90, Danville, Va., 1990-91; plant mgr. Goodyear Tire & Rubber Co., Spartanburg, S.C., 1993—. Bd. dirs. United Way of Spartanburg, 1994; active exec. selection com. Girl Scouts, Spartanburg, 1994. Office: Goodyear Tire & Rubber Co 1095 Simuel Rd Spartanburg SC 29301-4340

THOMPSON, CAROL LEWIS, editor; b. N.Y.C., Dec. 26, 1918; d. Jasper Robert and Freda (Rafalsky) Lewis; m. Elbert Paul Thompson, July 4, 1942; children: Timothy Lewis, Ellen, John, Abigail. A.B., Wellesley Coll., 1940; M.A., Mt. Holyoke Coll., 1942. Asst. editor Current History, 1943, asso. editor, 1943-55, editor, 1955-91, editorial cons., 1991—; editor Ency. of Developing Nations; asso. editor Forum mag., 1945-49; contbr. to Ency. Brit., World Book Ency. Mem. Am. Hist. Assn., Nat. Council Social Studies, Phi Beta Kappa. Mem. Soc. of Friends. Home and Office: Apt J112 Pennswood Village Newtown PA 18940

THOMPSON, CAROLINE WARNER, film director, screenwriter; b. Washington, Apr. 23, 1956; d. Thomas Carlton Jr. and Bettie Marshall (Warner) T.; m. Alfred Henry Bromell, Aug. 28, 1982 (div. 1985). BA summa cum laude, Amherst Coll., 1978. Author: First Born, 1983; screenwriter: (films) Edward Scissorhands, 1990, The Addams Family, 1991, Homeward Bound: The Incredible Journey, 1993, The Secret Garden, 1993, Tim Burton's The Nightmare Before Christmas, 1993; screenwriter, dir.: Black Beauty, 1994. Mem. Phi Beta Kappa. Avocation: horseback riding. Office: William Morris Agency Inc 151 S El Camino Dr Beverly Hills CA 90212-2704

THOMPSON, CARSON R., retail, manufacturing company executive; b. Wilson, Okla., Feb. 10, 1939; s. Silas and Della (Woods) T.; m. Charlotte Arwine, Dec. 26, 1959; children—Shelley Elaine, Susan Denise. B.S., Tex. Wesleyan U., 1962, D Bus. and Fin. (hon.). Leather buyer, mdse. mgr. Tandy Leather Co., Ft. Worth, 1970-74, 74-77; pres. Tex Tan Welhausen Co., Yoakum, Tex., 1978; v.p. Tandy Brands Corp., Fort Worth, 1981—, chmn., CEO, 1982—; chmn. bd. Bombay Co., Inc. (formerly Tandy Brands, Inc.); chmn. bd., pres., CEO CRT Group, Inc., 1991—. Home: 1801 Sanguinet St Fort Worth TX 76107-3765 Office: 2501 Avenue J Ste 110 Arlington TX 76006-6182

THOMPSON, CHARLES MURRAY, lawyer; b. Childress, Tex., Oct. 13, 1942; s. Walter Lee and Lois S. (Sheehan) T.; m. Charlotte Ann McKay, June 13, 1970; children: Murray McKay, McLean Ann. BS with honors, Colo. State U., 1965; JD cum laude, U. S.D., 1969, LLD (hon.), 1995. Bar: S.D. 1969, U.S. Dist. Ct. S.D. 1969, U.S. Ct. Claims 1989, U.S. Ct. Appeals (8th cir.) 1972, U.S. Supreme Ct. 1973. Ptnr. May, Adam, Gerdes & Thompson, Pierre, S.D., 1969—; speaker at trial lawyer and state bar seminars; bd. dirs. Bank West, Pierre, S.D. Editor S.D. Law Rev., 1969. Pres. S.D. Council Sch. Attys., 1984-86. Fellow Am. Bar Found. (chmn. 1991-92, bd. dirs. 1989-92), Coll. Law Practice Mgmt., Internat. Acad. Trial Lawyers, Am. Coll. Trial Lawyers; mem. ABA (ho. of dels. 1978—, bd. govs. 1983-86), State Bar S.D. (pres. young lawyers sect. 1974-75, pres. 1986-87), S.D. Bar Found. (pres. 1991), Assn. Trial Lawyers Am., Am. Bd. Trial Advs., Am. Counsel Assn., S.D. Trial Lawyers Assn. (pres. 1980-81), Jackrabbit Bar Assn. (chancellor 1981-82), Am. Judicature Soc. (bd. dirs. 1981-85), Nat. Conf. Bar Pres.'s (exec. coun. 1986-94, pres. 1992-93), Am. Bar Endowment (bd. dirs. 1991—), Kiwanis (pres. local club 1977). Democrat. Avocations: flying, ranching. Home and Office: PO Box 160 Pierre SD 57501-0160

THOMPSON, CHESTER FRANKLIN, graphic arts and advertising executive; b. Washington, June 2, 1931; m. Ann L. Butler, Feb. 3, 1955; children—Stephen, Glenn. Pres. C.F. Thompson Group, Inc., Windsor, Conn., 1955—; pres. Thompson Assocs., Inc., Frank Thompson Assocs., Inc., both graphic arts cos.

THOMPSON, CLAIRE LOUISA, nurse, educator, administrator; b. Columbus, Ohio, Sept. 29, 1938; d. Harry Edgar and Clara Etta (Brackenbusch) McKeever; m. Roger Lee Thompson, Dec. 20, 1958 (div. 1988); children: Jeffrey, Michael. Diploma, Bethesda Hosp. Sch. Nursing, Cin., 1959; student, Ball State, 1970, Ind. U., 1981, Purdue U., 1982-83. RN, Ohio, Ind., Calif.; cert. ins. rehab. specialist, 1985, CCM case mgr., 1993. Oper. rm./emergency rm. nurse Greene Meml. Hosp., Xenia, Ohio, 1959-60; med.-surg. nurse, charge nurse Bethesda Hosp., 1960-64; med.-surg. nurse Porter Meml. Hosp., Valparaiso, Ind., 1965-66; staff and charge nurse Mercy Hosp., Elwood, Ind., 1968-74; gen. practice nurse W. A. Scea, MD, Elwood, 1970-74; exec. dir. Vis. Nurse Assn., Elwood, 1974-78; analyst Blue Cross/Blue Shield of Indpls., 1978; supr. Meth. Hosp. Clinic, Indpls., 1979-80; dir. nursing Upjohn Health Care, Indpls., 1980; staff nurse Americana Health Care Ctr., Indpls., 1981; instr. health occups. Washington Twp. Schs., Indpls., 1981-84; br. mgr. health & rehab. Crawford & Co., Indpls., 1984-88; regional med. svcs. advisor western region Crawford & Co., San Francisco, 1988-92; br. mgr. Crawford & Co., Health Care Mgmt., Modesto, Calif., 1992-94; ret., 1994; developer in case mgmt. nursing svcs., 1984-94. Founder Meals on Wheels, Elwood, 1975, Vis. Nurses Assn., Elwood, 1976. Mem. NLN, Assn. Rehab. Nurses (pres. Ind. chpt. 1987-88), Nat. Ins. Womens Assn., Case Mgmt. Soc. Am., San Francisco Ins. Womens Assn., Rehab. Ins. Nurses Group. Roman Catholic. Avocations: walking, photography, rose gardening, cats, family. Home: 1232 Whitney Ln Westerville OH 43081

THOMPSON, CLEON F., JR., university administrator. BS in Biology, N.C. Cen. U., 1956, MS in Biology, 1958; PhD in Edn. Adminstrn., Duke U., 1977. Vice-pres. student services and spl. programs U. N.C., to 1985; chancellor Winston-Salem State U., N.C., 1985—. Office: Winston Salem State U Office of Chancellor Winston Salem NC 27110

THOMPSON, CLIFF F., lawyer, educator; b. Kansas City, Mo., Aug. 15, 1934; s. James Frederick and Grace Caroline (Wiese) T.; m. Judith Anne Phillips, June 23, 1957; children: James Frederick, Laura Marie, John Phillips, Hannah Caroline. AB magna cum laude, Harvard U., 1956, JD, 1960; MA (Rhodes scholar), Oxford (Eng.) U., 1962. Bar: Kans. 1960, U.S. Dist. Ct. (we. dist.) Wis. 1984. Asst. program officer Near East and Africa program Ford Found., N.Y.C., 1960-61; law lectr., dir. Sudan Law Project, U. Khartoum, Sudan, 1961-65; assoc. dir., co-founder Africa Law Ctr., Columbia U., 1965-66; co-founder, sr. lectr. law sch. U. Zambia, 1966-68; dean, prof. law Haile Selassie I U., Ethiopia, 1969-73; prof. law So. Meth. U., Dallas, 1973-77; prof. law, dean Law Sch., U. Hawaii, 1977-78, Coll. Law, U. Idaho, 1978-83; dean U. Wis. Law Sch., Madison, 1983-90, prof. law, 1983—; dir. African studies program U. Wis., 1992-93; legal edn. adv. Govt. of Indonesia, 1993—; cons. legal edn., Ethiopia, Sudan, Uganda, Tanzania, Kenya, Zambia, Zimbabwe. Author: Land Law of the Sudan, 3 vols., 2d edit, 1979; founder Zambia Law Reports, 1969, African Law Digest, 1965; contbr. articles to law jours. Bd. dirs. Hawaii Legal Aid, 1977-78, Idaho Law Found., 1978-83, Four Lakes Coun. Boy Scouts Am., 1984-93; chmn. screening com. Fulbright Law Award, Washington, 1988-90, 92. Fulbright Disting.Prof. award to Africa, 1983; hon. vis. scholar Inst. Advanced Legal Studies and Sch. Oriental and African Studies, U. London, 1990-91. Fellow, Explorers Club; mem. ABA, Rotary, Signet Soc., Phi Beta Kappa, Phi Kappa Phi. Democrat. Methodist. Avocations: reading, tennis, walking. Home: 4133 Nakoma Rd Madison WI 53711-3018 Office: U Wis Law Sch 975 Bascom Mall Madison WI 53706-1301

THOMPSON, CLIFTON C., chemistry educator, university administrator; b. Franklin, Tenn., Aug. 16, 1939; s. Clifton C. and Ruby M. (Moore) T.; m. Sarah Ellen Gaunt, Dec. 1, 1978; children: Brenda Kay, Victoria Lea. B.S., Middle Tenn. State U., 1961; Ph.D., U. Miss., 1964. Asst. prof. Rutgers U., New Brunswick, N.J., 1965, Marshall U., Huntington, W.Va., 1965-66; assoc. prof. Middle Tenn. State U., Murfreesboro, 1966-68, Memphis State U., 1968-74; prof. chemistry, dept. head, dean Coll. Sci. and Math., dir. Ctr. for Sci. Rsch., assoc. v.p. for grad. studies and rsch. S.W. Mo. State U., Springfield, 1974—; research assoc. U. Tex., Austin, 1964-65; research Oak Ridge Nat. Lab., 1968; cons. Mid-South Research Assocs., Memphis, 1969-71; mem. med. tech. rev. com. Nat. Accrediting Agy. for Clin. Lab. Sci., Chgo., 1974-80. Author: Ultraviolet-Visible Absorption Spectroscopy, 1974. Mem. health care com. Springfield C. of C., 1978-79, mem. econ. devel. com., 1983-89; bd. dirs. United Hebrew Congregation, Springfield, 1983-86, United Hebrew Found., Inc., 1994—. NSF fellow, 1961-64; Sigma Xi grantee-in-aide, 1970; NSF sr. fgn. scientist grantee, 1971; NSF coop-coll. sch. sci. grantee, 1972; Higher Edn. Applied Projects grantee, 1987-90. Mem. Am. Chem. Soc., Royal Soc. Chemistry, AAAS, Sigma Xi, Phi Kappa Phi. Jewish. Office: SW Mo State U 901 S National Ave Springfield MO 65804-0027

THOMPSON, CRAIG SNOVER, corporate communications executive; b. Bklyn., May 24, 1932; s. Craig F. and Edith (Williams) T.; m. Masae Sugizaki, Feb. 21, 1957; children: Lee Anne, Jane Laura. Grad., Valley Forge Mil. Acad., 1951; B.A., Johns Hopkins U., 1954. Newspaper and radio reporter Easton (Pa.) Express, 1954-55, 57-59, Wall St. Jour., 1959-60; account exec. Moore, Meldrum & Assocs., 1960; mgr. pub. relations Cen. Nat. Bank of Cleve., 1961-62; account exec. Edward Howard & Co., Cleve., 1962-67; v.p. Edward Howard & Co., 1967-69, sr. v.p., 1969-71; dir. pub. relations White Motor Corp., Cleve., 1971-76; v.p. pub. relations No. Telecom Inc., Nashville, 1976-77, White Motor Corp., Farmington Hills, Mich., 1977-80; v.p. corp. communications White Motor Corp., 1980-81; dir. exec. communications Rockwell Internat. Corp., Pitts., 1981-86, El Segundo, Calif., 1986-91, Seal Beach, Calif., 1992—. Bd. dirs. Shaker Lakes Regional Nature Center, 1970-73. Served to 1st lt., inf. U.S. Army, 1955-57. Mem. Pub. Rels. Soc. Am. (accredited), Alumni Assn. Valley Forge Mil. Acad. (bd. dirs. 1988-94). Office: Rockwell Internat Corp 2201 Seal Beach Blvd Seal Beach CA 90740-8250

THOMPSON, DALE WILLARD, JR., career officer; b. Oklahoma City, Feb. 2, 1938; s. Dale William and Virginia Lee (Crosby) T.; m. Cheryl Lea Stokes, June 8, 1960; children: Dale Willard III, Stacey Ann Grosvenor. BS, USAF Acad., 1960; MPA, Auburn U., 1976. Commd. 2d lt. USAF, 1960, advanced through grades to lt. gen., 1993; F-111 pilot 20th Tactical Fighter Wing, Upper Heyford Air Base, Eng., 1971-75, dep. comdr. ops., 1979-80, comdr., vice comdr., 1981-86; student Air War Coll., Maxwell AFB, Ala., 1975-76; chief support div. J-3, Joint Chiefs of Staff, Pentagon, Washington, 1976-79; dir. fighter ops. Hdqrs. U.S. Air Forces in Europe, Ramstein Air Base, Fed. Republic Germany, 1980-81; vice comdr. Ogden Air Logistics Ctr., Hill AFB, Utah, 1986-87, comdr., 1990-93; vice comdr. Air Force Materiel Command, 1993-95; chief of staff Hdqrs. Air Force Logistics Command, Wright-Patterson AFB, Ohio, 1987-90. Decorated D.S.M., Legion of Merit, D.F.C with three oak leaf clusters, Def. D.S.M. Mem. Air Force Assn., Rotary (Ogden club). Avocations: skiing, golf. Home: 30 Camwood Trl Austin TX 78738-1423

THOMPSON, DAVID ALFRED, industrial engineer; b. Chgo., Sept. 9, 1929; s. Clifford James and Christobel Eliza (Sawin) T.; children: Nancy, Brooke, Lynda, Diane, Kristy. B.M.E., U. Va., 1951; B.S. in Indsl. Engring, U. Fla., 1955, M.S. in Engring, 1956; Ph.D., Stanford U., 1961. Registered profl. engr., Calif; cert. profl. ergonomist. Research asst. U. Fla. Engring. and Industries Exptl. Sta., Gainesville, 1955-56; instr. indsl. engring. Stanford U., 1956-58, acting asst. prof., 1958-61, asst. prof., 1961-64, asso. prof., 1964-72, prof., 1972-83, prof., asso. chmn. dept. indsl. engring., 1972-73, prof. emeritus, 1983—; mem. clin. faculty occupational medicine U. Calif. Med. Sch., San Francisco, 1985—; pres., chief scientist Portola Assocs., Palo Alto, Calif., 1965—; prin. investigator NASA Ames Research Center, Moffatt Field, Calif., 1974-77; cons. Dept. State, Fed. EEO Commn., maj. U.S. and fgn. cos.; cons. emergency commn. ctr. design Santa Clara County Criminal Justice Bd., 1974, Bay Area Rapid Transit Control Ctr., 1977, Govt. of Mex., 1978, Amadahl Corp., 1978-79, Kerr-McGee Corp., 1979, Chase Manhattan Bank, 1980, St. Regis Paper Co., 1980-82, Pacific Gas & Electric, 1983-85, Pacific Bell, 1984-86, 89-93, IBM, 1988-91, Hewlett-Packard, 1990-91, Reuter's News Svc., 1990-92, Safeway Corp., 1992—, New United Motors Mfg., 1993-95, Sun Microsys., 1993-94, Microsoft, 1995—; mem. com. for office computers Calif. OSHA. Dir., editor: documentary film

Rapid Answers for Rapid Transit, Dept. Transp., 1974; mem. editorial adv. bd. Computers and Graphics, 1970-85; reviewer Indsl. Engring. and IEEE Transactions, 1972-86; contbr. articles to profl. jours. Served to lt. USNR, 1951-54. HEW grantee, 1967-70. Mem. IEEE,. Home: 121 Peter Coutts Cir Stanford CA 94305-2519 Office: Portola Assocs 2600 El Camino Real Ste 414 Palo Alto CA 94306-1705

THOMPSON, DAVID B., bishop. Ordained priest, 1950; consecrated bishop, 1989. Coadjutor bishop Diocese of Charleston, S.C., 1989-90, bishop, 1990—. Office: Bishop of Charleston 119 Broad St Charleston SC 29401

THOMPSON, DAVID JEROME, chemical company executive, biochemist, nutritionist; b. Sand Creek, Wis., July 21, 1937; s. Marshall and Bernice (Severson) T.; m. Virginia Ruth Williams, Aug. 11, 1962; children—Keith D., Craig M. B.S., U. Wis., 1960, M.S., 1961, Ph.D., 1963; M.B.A., U. Chgo., 1975. Research biochemist Internat. Minerals and Chem. Corp., Libertyville, Ill., 1964-68, supr. animal research, 1968-69, dir. tech. service, Mundelein, Ill., 1969-79, sales mgr., 1979-81, v.p. sci. and tech., Northbrook, Ill., 1981-84, 85-87, v.p. and gen. mgr. Sterwin div., 1984-85; v.p. planning and devel., Pitman-Moore, Inc., Mundelein, Ill., 1987-92; ret., 1992; cons. Am. Assn. Feed Control Ofcls., 1974-85; com. mem. NRC, NAS, 1976-80. Co-author: Mineral Tolerance of Domestic Animals, 1980; contbr. articles to profl. jours. Chmn. bd. dirs. United Way of Lake County, Ill., 1995—. Mem. Am. Inst. Nutrition, AAAS, Poultry Sci. Assn., Am. Dairy Sci. Assn., Am. Soc. Animal Sci., Am. Chem. Soc., N.Y. Acad. Scis., Am. Feed Mfrs. Assn. (chmn. nutrition council 1980), Sigma Xi, Gamma Alpha, Phi Lambda Upsilon, Theta Delta Chi. Club: Liberty Road and Track. Avocations: competitive running, jazz and classical music, art, landscape gardening.

THOMPSON, DAVID RENWICK, federal judge; b. 1930. BS in Bus., U. So. Calif., 1952, LLB, 1955. Pvt. practice law with Thompson & Thompson (and predecessor firms), 1957-85; judge U.S. Ct. Appeals (9th cir.), 1985—. Served with USN, 1955-57. Mem. ABA, San Diego County Bar Assn., Am. Bd. Trial Lawyers (sec. San Diego chpt. 1983, v.p. 1984, pres. 1985). Office: US Ct Appeals 940 Front St San Diego CA 92189

THOMPSON, DAVID RUSSELL, engineering educator, academic dean; b. Cleve., Apr. 4, 1944; s. Dwight L. and Ella Caroline (Wolff) T.; m. Janet Ann Schall, Aug. 27, 1966; children: Devin Mathew, Colleen Michelle, Darin Michael. BS in Agrl. Engring., Purdue U., 1966, MS in Agrl. Engring., 1967; PhD in Agrl. Engring., Mich. State U., 1970. Asst. prof. agrl. engring., food sci. and nutrition depts. U. Minn., St. Paul, 1970-75, assoc. prof., 1975-81, prof., 1981-85; prof. agrl. engring., head dept. Okla. State U., Stillwater, 1985-91, assoc. dean Coll. Engring., Architecture and Tech., 1991—; engr. ops. dept. Green Giant Co., La Sueur, Minn., 1978-79; reviewer Colo. State U., CRS, USDA, Ft. Collins, 1989, foods, feeds and prodn. cluster U. Mo., Columbia, 1989, 93, dept. agrl. engring. Pa. State U., University Park, 1990, Tex. A&M U., College Station, 1992, Utah State U., Logan, 1993, Washington State U., Pullman, 1995, others; reviewer USDA, 1983; vis. scholar Va. Poly. Inst. and State U., Blacksburg. Author: The Influence of Materials Properties on the Freezing of Sweet Corn , 1984, Mathematical Model for Predicting Lysine and Methionine Losses During Thermal Processing of Fortified Foods; contbr. over 50 articles to sci. jours., including Jour. Food Sci. Fellow Am. Soc. Agrl. Engrs. (div. chmn. 1976-77, bd. dirs. 1981-84, 87-89, v.p. 1994—, FIEI Young Rschr. award 1983, Pres.'s citation 1989); mem. ASHRAE, NSPE (chair Okla. mid-north sect. 1994-95), Inst. Food Technologists (program com. 1982-85, state officer 1987-89), Am. Soc. Engring. Edn. (chair Midwest sect. 1994-95), Sigma Xi Phi Kappa Phi, Tau Beta Pi, Alpha Epsilon, Phi Eta Sigma, Gamma Sigma Delta. Office: Okla State U Coll Engring Arch & Tech 111 Engineering N Stillwater OK 74078-0522

THOMPSON, DAVID WALKER, astronautics company executive; b. Phila., Mar. 21, 1954; s. Robert H. and Nancy S. (Walker) T.; m. Catherine K. Ahulii, April 16, 1983. BS in Aeronautics and Astronautics, MIT, 1976; MS, Calif. Inst. Tech., 1977; MBA, Harvard U., 1981. Project engr. Jet Propulsion Lab., Pasadena, Calif., 1976; aerospace engr. NASA, Houston, 1977; project mgr. NASA, Huntsville, Ala., 1977-79; spl. asst. to pres. Hughes Aircraft Co., Los Angeles, 1981-82; pres., chief exec. officer Orbital Scis. Corp., Dulles, Va., 1982—; cons. Rockwell Internat., Thousand Oaks, Calif., 1980-81, Rand Corp., Santa Monica, Calif., 1982. Recipient Nat. award Space Found., Houston, 1981, Nat. Medal Tech. U.S Dept. Commerce Tech. Adminstrn., 1991; Nat. Air and Space Mus. Trophy, 1990; fellow Hertz Found., 1976, NSF fellow, 1976, Rockwell Internat. fellow, Harvard U. fellow, 1979; named Va. Industrial of Yr., 1991, Satellite Exec. of Yr., 1990, George M. Low Space Transportation award, Am. Inst. of Aeronautics and Astronautics, 1994. Fellow AIAA (assoc., Young Engr./Scientist Yr. award 1984, George M. Low Space Trans. award 1994), mem. Nat. Space Club. Office: Orbital Sciences Corp 21700 Atlantic Blvd Dulles VA 20166-6801*

THOMPSON, DAVID WILLIAM, business educator; b. Ft. Wayne, Ind., Sept. 3, 1914; s. William Byron and Georgia Louise (Davis) T.; m. M. Miriam Vollmer, Dec. 21, 1956 (dec.). B.S., Ind. U., 1938, M.S., 1940. C.P.A., N.Y., Ill., Ind., Va., N.C., N. Mex., La. Prof. Samford U., Birmingham, Butler U., Indpls., 1941-42, Ind. U., Bloomington, 1942-54; cons. Gen. Electric Co., N.Y.C., 1954-56; ptnr. Peat, Marwick, Mitchell & Co., N.Y.C., 1956-76; Frank S. Kaulback Jr. prof. commerce McIntire Sch. Commerce U. Va., Charlottesville, 1976—; chmn. State Bd. Examiners C.P.A.s, N.Y.C., 1966-70, State Bd. Pub. Accountancy, N.Y.C., 1974-76. Dir. Univ. of the Ams., Mexico City, U. of the Ams. Found., San Antonio. Mem. AICPA, Ind. U. Acad. Alumni Fellows, Indpls. Athletic Club, India House Club N.Y.C., Univ. Club N.Y.C., Farmington Country Club Charlottesville Va. Home: Ednam Forest 425 Wellington Dr Charlottesville VA 22903-4746 Office: U Va Monroe Hall McIntire Sch Commerce Charlottesville VA 22903

THOMPSON, DAYLE ANN, aerospace company executive; b. Grand Forks, N.D., Jan. 6, 1954; d. Duane Theodore and anna Mae (Desautel) T.; m. Michael Gary Sciulla, Aug. 6, 1977 (div. Sept. 1980); m. Manfred Hans von Ehrenfried II, June 11, 1982. Secretarial degree, Aaker's Bus. Coll., Grand Forks, 1973; cert. of completion mgmt., George Washington U., 1979, Masters Cert. in Project Mgmt., 1995. Receptionist U.S. Rep. Norman F. Lent U.S. Ho. of Reps., Washington, 1973-74; office mgr., personal sec. U.S. Rep. Les AuCoin, U.S. Ho. of Reps., Washington, 1975-78; bus. mgr., bookkeeper Virgin Islands POST, St.Thomas, USVI, 1978; office and pers. mgr. Internat. Energy Assocs. Ltd., Washington, 1978-82; program support mgr. MSI Svcs. Inc., Washington, 1982-84; pres., treas., chief exec. officer Tech. and Adminstrv. Svcs. Corp., Washington, 1984—; Hosp. vol. ARC, Arlington, Va., 1987. Recipient Group Achievement award NASA, 1984, 93, Commendation Letter, NASA, 1985, 87, 88, 91, 93, 94, Small Bus. Prime Contractor of Yr. award Small Bus. Adminstrn. Region 3, 1994. Mem. Washington Space Bus. Roundtable (sponsor-benefactor 1990-92), Women in Aerospace. Republican. Roman Catholic. Avocations: boating, fishing, reading. Home: 4250 42nd Ave S Saint Petersburg FL 33711-4231 Office: TADCORPS 400 Virginia Ave SW Ste 730 Washington DC 20024-2511

THOMPSON, DENISSE R., mathematics educator; b. Keesler AFB, Miss., Aug. 26, 1954. BA, BS, U. South Fla., 1976, MA, 1980; PhD, U. Chgo., 1992. Cert. tchr., Fla. Tchr. Hernando County Schs., Brooksville, Fla., 1977-82; instr. maths. Manatee C.C., Bradenton, Fla., 1982-87; asst. prof. U. South Fla., Tampa, 1991—; cons. in field. Author: Fundamental Skills of Mathematics, 1987, Advanced Algebra, 1990, 2nd edit., 1995, (with others) Precalculus and Discrete Mathematics, 1992; (with others) Nat. Coun. Tchrs. of Math. Yearbook, 1991, 93, 94, 95. Recipient Carolyn Hoefer Meml. award Pi Lambda Theta, 1988. Mem. ASCD, Math. Assn. Am., Nat. Coun. Tchrs. Math., Nat. Coun. Suprs. Math., Assn. Women in Maths., Phi Delta Kappa, Phi Kappa Phi. Office: U South Fla College of Edn EDU208B Tampa FL 33620

THOMPSON, DENNIS FRANK, political science and ethics educator, consultant; b. Hamilton, Ohio, May 12, 1940; s. Frank and Florence (Downs) T.; m. Carol Thompson, June 22, 1963; children: Eric, David. BA, Coll. of William and Mary, 1962, Oxford U., 1964; MA, Oxford U., 1968; PhD, Harvard U., 1968; LHD (hon.), Coll. of William and Mary, 1990. Instr. govt. Harvard U., Cambridge, Mass., 1967-68; Alfred North Whitehead prof. Harvard U., 1986—, dir. univ. program in ethics and professions, 1986—; asst. prof. politics Princeton U., N.J., 1968-72, assoc. prof., 1972-75, dept. chmn., 1972-73, 76-79, 82-83, prof., 1975-86; cons. to spl. counsel U.S. Senate Select Com. on Ethics, 1990-91, U.S. Dept. HHS, 1980, FDA, 1993. Author: The Democratic Citizen, 1970, John Stuart Mill and Representative Government, 1976, Political Ethics and Public Office, 1987, Ethics in Congress, 1995, (with A. Gutmann) Democracy and Disagreement, 1996; mem. editl. bd. Polit. Theory, 1974—, Philosophy and Pub. Affairs, 1971—, Am. Polit. Sci. Rev., 1985-88. Trustee Smith Coll., 1994—. Fellow Am. Acad. Arts and Scis.; mem. Am. Soc. Legal and Polit. Philosophy (v.p. 1977-80, pres. 1986-89). Home: 9 Shady Hill Sq Cambridge MA 02138-2035 Office: Harvard Univ 406 Taubman 79 JFK St Cambridge MA 02138-5801

THOMPSON, DENNIS PETERS, plastic surgeon; b. Chgo., Mar. 18, 1937; s. David John and Ruth Dorothy (Peters) T.; m. Virginia Louise Williams, June 17, 1961; children: Laura Faye, Victoria Ruth, Elizabeth Jan. BS, U. Ill., 1957, BS in Medicine, 1959, MS in Physiology, MD, 1961. Diplomate Am. Bd. Surgery, Am. Bd. Plastic Surgery. Intern Presbyn.-St. Lukes Hosp., Chgo., 1961-62; resident in gen. surgery Mayo Clinic, Rochester, Minn., 1964-66, fellow in gen. surgery, 1964-66; resident in gen. surgery Harbor Gen. Hosp., Los Angeles, 1968-70; resident in plastic surgery UCLA, 1971-73, clin. instr. plastic surgery, 1975-82, asst. clin. prof. surgery, 1982—; practice medicine specializing in plastic and reconstructive surgery, Los Angeles, 1974-78, Santa Monica, Calif., 1978—; chmn. plastic surgery sect. St. John's Hosp., 1986-91; mem. staff Santa Monica Hosp., UCLA Ctr. Health Scis.; chmn. dept. surgery Beverly Glen Hosp., 1978-79; pres. Coop. of Am. Physicians Credit Union, 1978-80, bd. dirs., 1980—, chmn. membership devel. com., 1983—, treas., 1985—. Contbr. articles to med. jours. Moderator Congl. Ch. of Northridge (Calif.), 1975-76, chmn. bd. trustees, 1973-74, 80-82; bd. dirs. L.A. Bus. Coun., 1987-90. Am. Tobacco Inst. research grantee, 1959-60. Fellow ACS; mem. AMA (Physicians Recognition award 1971, 74, 77, 81, 84, 87, 90, 93), Calif. Med. Assn., L.A. County Med. Assn. (chmn. bylaws com. 1979-80, chmn. ethics com. 1980-81, sec.-treas. dist. 5 1982-83, program chmn. 1983-84, pres. 1985-86, councilor 1988-96), Pan-Pacific Surgical Assn., Am. Soc. Plastic and Reconstructive Surgeons, Calif. Soc. Plastic Surgeons (chmn. bylaws com. 1982-83, chmn. liability com. 1983-85, councilor 1988-91, sec. 1993-95, v.p. 1995—), Los Angeles Soc. Plastic Surgeons (sec. 1980-82, pres. 1982—), Lipoplasty Soc. N.Am. (chmn. bylaws com. 1995—), UCLA Plastic Surgery Soc. (treas. 1983-84), Am. Soc. Aesthetic Plastic Surgery, Am. Assn. Accreditation of Ambulatory Surg. Facilities (bd. dirs. 1995—), Western Los Angeles Regional C. of C. (bd. dirs. 1981-84, 86-89, chmn. legis. action com. 1978-80), Phi Beta Kappa, Alpha Omega Alpha, Nu Sigma Nu, Phi Kappa Phi, Delta Sigma Delta, Omega Beta Pi, Phi Eta Sigma. Republican. Office: 2001 Santa Monica Blvd Santa Monica CA 90404-2102

THOMPSON, DONALD CHARLES, electronics company executive, former coast guard officer; b. Hollis, N.Y., Nov. 9, 1930; s. Arthur I. and Gertrude M. (Hauck) T.; m. Jeannie Germaine Kline, Oct. 4, 1952; children: Dennis C., Mitchell L., Sandra J., Janice M., Theresa A., Patrick J. B.S., U.S. Coast Guard Acad., 1952; M.S. (Krannert scholar), Krannert Grad. Sch., Purdue U., 1966. Commd. ensign USCG, 1952, advanced through grades to vice adm., 1986; shipboard navigator and engr., 1952-54, naval flight tng., 1954-55; search and rescue aviator and aircraft maintenance officer Calif., Ill., Alaska and Fla., 1955-65; chief computer-based mgmt. info. div. Elizabeth City, N.C., 1966-70; chief aero. engring. div. USCG Hdqrs., 1970-74; capt. of the port, group comdr., air sta. comdr. San Diego, 1974-76; chief ops. 11th USCG Dist., Long Beach, Calif., 1976-78; chief of staff 11th USCG Dist., 1979; chief office of engring. USCG Hdqrs., Washington, 1979-81; chief office of ops. USCG Hdqrs., 1981-82, chief staff, 1984-86, comdr. Atlantic area, 1986-88; comdr. 7th Coast Guard Dist., Miami, Fla., 1982-84; math. instr. Coll. Albermarle, N.C., 1967-70, Nat. U., San Diego, 1975-76; chmn. Interagy. Com. Search and Rescue, 1981-82; ret. USCG, 1988; v.p. strategic devel. R&E Electronics, Inc., Wilmington, N.C., 1990-93; pres., consulting firm, 1994—; v.p.'s coordinator for S.E. region Nat. Narcotics Border Interdiction System, 1983-84. Contbr. articles to profl. jours. Coordinator White House South Fla. Task Force on Crime, 1983-84. Decorated DSM with two gold stars, Coast Guard Meritorious Service medal, Def. Superior Service medal, Commendation medal with three gold stars, Legion of Merit with gold star. Mem. Soc. Am. Mil. Engrs. (dir. 1979-81), Am. Soc. Naval Engrs., Am. Helicopter Soc. (dir. 1981-82), Air Force Assn., Naval Inst. Roman Catholic. Clubs: Propeller, Nat. Aviation. Home: 1903 Market St Wilmington NC 28403-1015

THOMPSON, DOROTHY BARNARD, elementary school educator; b. Flushing, N.Y., Aug. 14, 1933; d. Henry Clay and Cecilia Minnie Theresa (La Pardo) Barnard; m. Norman Earl Thompson, Aug. 12, 1956; children: Greg, Scot, Henry, Marc, Matthew. BSEd, SUNY, New Paltz, 1953; MS, Hofstra U., 1984. Cert. elem. tchr. K-6th grades, reading specialist K-12th grades, N.Y. Adjunct prof. Suffolk Community Coll., Brentwood, N.Y., 1987—, Nassau Community Coll., Uniondale, N.Y., 1986—; adjunct prof., instr. Ctr. for Acad. Achievement Long Island U., Greenvale, N.Y., 1984-92; tchr. reading, K-5th grades Long Beach (N.Y.) Pub. Schs., 1988—; mem. founding group Parent/Tchr., The Learning Tree, Garden City, N.Y., 1971; founder parent coop. Happy Day Nursery Sch., Bellmore, N.Y., 1975; parent-tchr. Commonwealth Sch., Bay Shore, Oakdale, 1976-82. Mem. NEA, Nassau Reading Coun., N.Y. State Tchrs. Assn., Assn. for Supervision and Curriculum Devel. Home: 2385 Warren Ave Bellmore NY 11710-2545 Office: 456 Neptune Blvd Long Beach NY 11561-2425

THOMPSON, DUNCAN MCLEAN, SR., military security and intelligence officer; b. Paris, Tex., Sept. 6, 1945; s. Duncan Maxine and Joan (Branch) T.; m. Mary Susan Smith, Sept. 27, 1969; stepchildren: Gehrig Lewis Riley, Karen L. Miller; 1 child, Duncan McLean. Student, Baylor U., 1968; BS and MS in Criminal Justice, Troy State U., 1980. Cert. in computer security, pers. security mgmt. Staff tng. officer USAR, Tulsa, 1974-77; police officer Consol. Govt., Columbus, Ga., 1977-80; parole officer State of Ga., Columbus, 1980; inf. co. comdr. U.S. Army, Schofield Barracks, Hawaii, 1980-82; post comdr. Ft. DeRussy, Honolulu, 1982-84; comdt. Hawaii Mil. Acad., Ft. Ruger, 1984-87; staff tng. officer 83d Army Res. Command, Columbus, Ohio, 1987-90; dir. of security Def. Constrn. Supply Ctrl., Columbus, 1990-93; security and intelligence officer Army Software Devel. Ctr., Ft. Lee, Va., 1993-95; ground opers. officer U.S. Atlantic Command, Norfolk, Va., 1995—. Re-enactor 12th Va. Inf., Civil War-Confederate States Am., Richmond, 1993—. Col. USAR, 1969—. Decorated Purple Heart, Bronze Star. Presbyterian. Avocations: military history, re-enacting Civil War, fresh water fishing. Office: US Atlantic Command Bldg NH95 Norfolk VA 22222

THOMPSON, EARL ALBERT, economics educator; b. Los Angeles, Oct. 15, 1938; s. Hyman Harry and Sue (Field) T.; m. Velma Montoya, June 9, 1961; 1 son, Bret. B.A., UCLA, 1959; M.A. (fellow), Harvard U., 1961, Ph.D., 1961. Asst. prof. econs. Stanford (Calif.) U., 1962-65; asst. prof. econs. UCLA, 1965-68, assoc. prof., 1968-70, prof., 1970—. Grantee NSF; Grantee Lily Found.; Grantee Found. Research Econs. and Edn. Mem. Am. Econ. Assn. Home: 6970 Los Tilos Rd Los Angeles CA 90068-3107

THOMPSON, EDWARD FRANCIS, corporate executive; b. Waukegan, Ill., June 23, 1938; s. Francis Edward and Elsie (Birtic) T.; m. Gail Jean Walulis, Dec. 26, 1964; children—Michele Lisa, Melinda Joy, Holly Beth. B.S. in Aerospace Engring., U. Ill., 1961; M.B.A. in Fin., Santa Clara U., 1968. Assoc. engr. Lockheed Missiles, Sunnyvale, Calif., 1963-65; mgr. mktg. IBM, Palo Alto, Calif., 1965-68; dist. mgr. Computer Scis. Corp., Los Altos, Calif., 1968-72; v.p. equity devel. U.S. Leasing Internat., San Francisco, 1972-76; v.p. fin. Amdahl Corp., Sunnyvale, Calif., 1976—, also dir.; sr. advisor Fujitsu America Inc., San Jose, CA; dir. Digital Network Engring. SPA, Rome, Amdahl Corp., Sunnyvale; chmn. Amdahl Ireland Ltd., Dublin. Bd. dirs. Jr. Achievement, 1981-85; deacon Presbyn. Ch. Mem. Fin. Execs. Inst., Beta Gamma Sigma. Republican. Avocations: golf; tennis; skiing. Home: 1517 Edgewood Dr Palo Alto CA 94303-2818 Office: Fujitsu America Inc 3055 Orchard Dr San Jose CA 95134*

THOMPSON, EDWARD IVINS BRAD, biological chemistry and genetics educator, molecular endocrinologist, department chairman; b. Burlington, Iowa, Dec. 20, 1933; s. Edward Bills and Lois Elizabeth (Bradbridge) T.; m. Lynn Taylor Parsons; children: Elizabeth Lynn, Edward Ernest Bradbridge. BA with distinction, Rice U., 1955; postgrad., Cambridge U., 1957-58; MD, Harvard U., 1960. Intern The Presbyn. Hosp., N.Y.C., 1960-61, asst. resident internal medicine, 1961-62; rsch. assoc. Nat. Inst. Mental Health, NIH, Bethesda, Md., 1962-64; rsch. scientist Nat. Inst. Arthritis and Metabolic Diseases, NIH, Bethesda, Md., 1964-68; rsch. scientist Lab of Biochemistry, Nat. Cancer Inst., NIH, Bethesda, Md., 1968-73, sect. chief, 1973-84; I.H. Kempner prof. U. Tex. Med. Br., Galveston, 1984, prof., chmn. dept. human biol. chemistry and genetics, 1984—, prof. internal medicine, 1984—; attending physician Nat. Naval Med. Ctr., Bethesda, 1978-80; chmn. hormones and cancer task force NIH, Bethesda, 1978-80; co-chmn. Gordon Research Conf., 1980; mem. adv. com. on Biochem. & Chem. Carcinogenesis, Am. Cancer Soc., 1982-86; mem. revision com. Endocrinology adv. panel U.S. Pharmacopoeial Conv., Inc., 1980-85; mem. council for clin. investigation and research awds., Am. Cancer Soc., 1989-93; bd. scientific overseers Pennington Nutrition Rsch. Ctr. La. State U., 1991—; Fulbright prof., Marburg, Germany. 1992-93. Co-editor Gene Exoression and Carcinogenesis in Cultured Liver, 1975, Steroid Receptors and the Management of Cancer, 1979, DNA: Protein Interactions and Gene Regulation, other vols. in field; assoc. editor Cancer Rsch. jour., 1976-86; corr. editor Jour. Steroid Biochemistry, 1977-85; founding editor-in-chief Molecular Endocrinology Jour., 1985-92; contbr. over 200 sci. articles to profl. jours. Mem. troop com. Girl Scouts U.S., Rockville, Md., 1970-76; mem. PTA, Rockville, 1967-77, Wilderness Soc., Washington, 1964-75; initiator sci. edn. liaison program Galveston Pub. Schs., 1991; mem. pres.'s cabinet U. Tex. Med. Br. Served as med. dir. USPHS, 1962-84. Grantee NIH, Walls Rsch., Nat. Inst. Diabetes and Digestive and Kidney Diseases, Nat. Cancer Inst.; Am. Cancer Soc. scholar, 1992-93; Fulbright scholar. Mem. Am. Soc. Cell Biology, Am. Assn. Cancer Rsch., Am. Soc. Biol. Chemists, Endocrine Soc., Am. Soc. Microbiology, Am. Coll. Med. Genetics (affiliate), Tissue Culture Assn., S.W. Environ. Mutagen Soc., Rotary Internat., The Yacht Club, Racquet Club, Harvard Club, Pres.'s Clubs of Rice U. and U. Tex. Med. Br., Phi Beta Kappa, Alpha Omega Alpha. Achievements include patent on anti-tumor activity of a modified fragment of glucocorticoid receptor. Office: U Tex Med Br Dept Human Biol Gene Galveston TX 77555

THOMPSON, EDWARD KRAMER, editor, publisher; b. Mpls., Sept. 17, 1907; s. Edward T. and Bertha E. (Kramer) T.; m. Marguerite M. Maxam, May 14, 1927 (div.); children—Edward T. Colin R.; m. Lee Eitingon, Apr. 1, 1963. A.B., U. N.D., 1927, H.H.D., 1958. Editor Foster County Independent, Carrington, N.D., 1927; city editor Fargo (N.D.) Morning Forum, 1927; picture editor, asst. news editor Milw. Jour., 1927-37; asso. editor Life, 1937-42, asst. mng. editor, 1945-49, mng. editor, 1949, editor, 1961-68; spl. asst. to sec. state, 1968; editor, pub. Smithsonian mag., 1969-81, cons. to sec., 1981-83, cons. to editor, pub., 1983—. Author: A Love Affair with Life and Smithsonian, 1995. Served to lt. col. USAAF, 1942-45. Decorated Legion of Merit Order Brit. Empire; named to N.D. Hall of Fame, 1968; named Editor of Yr. Nat. Press Photographers Assn., 1968; recipient Joseph Henry medal Smithsonian Instn., 1973, Lifetime Achievement award Internat. Ctr. of Photography, 1986, Sioux Achievement award U. N.D., 1987, Dumke award for achievement in visual comm. Wis. News Photographers Assn., 1988; named to Pub. Hall of Fame, 1987, U. N.D. Mil. Hall of Fame, 1988. Mem. Phi Beta Kappa, Sigma Delta Chi, Phi Delta Theta. Office: Smithsonian Instn Smithsonian Mag Washington DC 20560

THOMPSON, EDWARD THORWALD, magazine editor; b. Milw., Feb. 13, 1928; s. Edward Kramer and Marguerite Minerva (Maxam) T.; m. Margaret Kessler, 1949; children: Edward T. III, Anne B., Evan K., David S.; m. Nancy Cale, May 28, 1966; 1 child, Julie.; m. Susan L. Jacobson, Nov. 28, 1981. Grad., Lawrenceville Sch., 1945; SB, MIT, 1949. Engr. Mobil Oil Co., Beaumont, Tex., 1949-52; assoc. editor Chem. Engr. mag., N.Y.C., 1952-55; mng. editor Chem. Week mag., N.Y.C., 1955-56; assoc. editor Fortune mag., 1956-60; with Reader's Digest., Pleasantville, N.Y., 1960-84; asst. mng. editor, then mng. editor Reader's Digest., 1973-76, editor-in-chief, mem. exec. com., 1976-84; cons. in pub. Waccabuc, N.Y., 1984—; pres. Thompson Assocs.; bd. dirs. The Quarton Group, Tech. Rev. Mag. Pres. Lewisboro Vol. Ambulance Corps. Recipient Golden Plate award Am. Acad. Achievement, 1977. Mem. Am. Soc. Mag. Editors, Waccabuc Country Club. Home: 3 Hunt Farm Waccabuc NY 10597-1100

THOMPSON, EMMA, actress; b. London, Apr. 15, 1959; d. Eric Thompson and Phyllida Law; m. Kenneth Branagh, Aug. 1989. Student of English, Cambridge U., Eng. Performances include: (films) Henry V, 1989, The Tall Guy, 1989, Dead Again, 1991, Impromptu, 1991, Howard's End, 1992 (Acad. award for best actress 1993), Peter's Friends, 1992, Much Ado About Nothing, 1993, The Remains of the Day, 1993 (Acad. award nominee for best actress 1993), In the Name of the Father, 1993 (Acad. award nominee for best supporting actress 1993), My Father, the Hero, 1994, Junior, 1994, Carrington, 1995 (Best Actress award Nat. Bd. Rev. 1995), Sense and Sensibility, 1995 (Golden Globe award nominee for best actress in film 1996, Acad. award nominee for best actress 1996); (TV in Eng.) Al Fresco, Up For Grabs (a.k.a. Sexually Transmitted), Tutti Frutti, (miniseries) Fortunes of War, Thompson; (TV in Am.) Fortunes of War, Cheers, 1991; (London stage) Me and My Girl, Look Back in Anger; also writer screen adaptation: Sense and Sensibility (Jane Austin), 1995 (Best Screenplay award N.Y. Film Critics 1995, L.A. Film Critics 1995, Boston Film Critics 1995, Golden Globe award for best adapted screenplay 1996, Acad. award for best adapted screenplay 1996, BAFTA Best Actress award 1996). Active in Footlights Theatrical Group, Cambridge, Eng. Office: William Morris Agy 151 El Camino Beverly Hills CA 90212

THOMPSON, EUGENE MAYNE, minister; b. Oxford, N.S., Can., Jan. 5, 1931; s. Curry Allison and Hortense Elsie (Mayne) T.; m. Rhoda Mitchell, May 21, 1955; children: Adrian Calvin, Nancy Lynn, Howard Allison. BA, Acadia U., 1954; MDiv, Acadia Divinity Coll., 1976; D of Ministry, So. Bapt. Theol. Sem., 1979. Pastor South End United Bapt. Ch., Dartmouth, N.S., 1954-58; assoc. sec. of Christian Edn. United Bapt. Conv. of Atlantic Provinces, St. John, N.B., 1958-61, exec. min., 1984-96; area min. for West N.S. United Bapt. Conv. of Atlantic Provinces, Middleton, N.S., 1974-84; pastor Immanuel Bapt. Ch., Truro, N.S., 1961-65, Hillcrest Bapt. Ch., St. John, N.B., 1965-68; area min. for Man. Bapt. Union of Western Can., 1968-74; ret., 1996; coun., exec. mem. Can. Bapt. Ministries, Mississauga, Ont.; bd. dirs. Atlantic Bapt. Sr. Citizen Homes, Inc., Moncton, N.B.; bd. govs Atlantic Bapt. Coll., Moncton; trustee Acadia Div. Coll.; mem. Bapt. Found. Author: Baptist Youth Fellowship Handbook, 1958, New Design for a Dynamic Church, 1973. Avocations: music, gardening, cross country skiing.

THOMPSON, EWA M., foreign language educator; b. Kaunas, Lithuania; came to U.S., 1963; d. Jozef and Maria (Adamowicz) Majewski; m. James R. Thompson. BA in English and Russian, U. Warsaw, Poland, 1963; MFA in Piano, Sopot Conservatory Music, 1963; MA in English, Ohio U., 1964; PhD in Comparative Lit., Vanderbilt U., 1967. Instr. Vanderbilt U., Nashville, Tenn., 1964-67; asst. prof. Ind. State U., Terre Haute, 1967-68, Ind. U., 1968-70; asst. prof. Rice U., Houston, 1967-73, assoc. prof., 1974-79, prof., 1979—, chair, 1987-90; assoc. prof. U. Va., Charlottesville, 1973-74; cons. NEH, 1973—, The John D. and Catherine T. MacArthur Found., The John Simon Guggenheim Found., U.S. Dept. Edn.; vis. cons. Tex. A&M U.; seminar dir. NEH Summer Inst., Southeastern La. U., 1990; chair Russian lit. conf. Rice U., 1989; lectr. various colls. and univs. Author: Russian Formalism and Anglo-American New Criticism: A Comparative Study, 1971, Witold Gombrowicz, 1979, Understanding Russia: The Holy Fool in Russian Culture, 1987 (Chinese translation 1995), The Search for Self-Definition in Russian Literature, 1991; contbr. articles to profl. jours., chpts. to books. Mellon grant, 1990, Rice U. grant 1990, Internat. Rsch. and Excahnges Sr. Scholar grant, 1991; Hoover Inst. fellow, 1988; scholar Vanderbilt U., 1964-67; recipient Silver Thistle award Houston's Scottish Heritage Found., 1988. Roman Catholic. Office: Rice University PO Box 1892 6100 South Main Houston TX 77251

THOMPSON, FRANK JOSEPH, political science educator; b. New Ulm, Minn., Mar. 21, 1944; s. Joseph Mariem and Alice Louise (Lindquist) T.; m. Benna Miriam, June 15, 1944; children: Samuel, Aliza, Elizabeth. BA in Polit. Sci., U. Chgo., 1966; MA in Polit. Sci., U. Calif., Berkeley, 1967, PhD in Polit. Sci., 1973. Asst. prof. polit. sci. Calif. State U., Long Beach, 1971-

72; asst. prof. U. Ga., Athens, 1972-78, assoc. prof., 1978-83, prof., 1983-88, head dept., 1982-87; prof. pub. adminstrn., policy, polit. sci. and pub. health SUNY, Albany, 1987—, acting dean Grad. Sch. of Pub. Affairs, 1988, dean, 1988—, acting provost Rockefeller Coll., 1989, assoc. provost, 1990—; analyst HEW, Washington, 1968, part-time with City Govt. Oakland, Calif., 1968-71; cons. USPHS, 1976-79, 82, U.S. Pres.'s Commn. for Nat. Agenda for 80's, 1980, Am. Pub. Welfare Assn., 1981-83; publ. cons. U.S. Adv. Commn. on Intergovtl. Rels., 1983; mem. task force on exec. and mgmt. devel. U.S. Office Pers. Mgmt., 1990; exec. dir. Nat. Commn. on the State and Local Pub. Svc., 1991—. Author: Personnel Policy in the City, 1975, Health Policy and the Bureaucracy, 1981, Public Administration: Challenges, Choices, Consequences, 1990; editor: Classics of Public Personnel Policy, 1979, 2d edit., 1991, Revitalizing State and Local Public Service, 1993; contbr. articles to profl. jours. Mem. Ga. PTA, Athens, 1980-86, N.Y. PTA, 1989—; bd. dirs. Upper Hudson Planned Parenthood, 1990—. Pub. adminstrn. fellow U.S. Pub. Health Service, 1975-76, NSF fellow, 1970-71; recipient Simon award Internat. Jour. Pub. Adminstrn., 1981. Fellow Nat. Acad. Pub. Adminstrn.; mem. Am. Pub. Health Assn., Assn. for Pub. Policy Analysis and Mgmt., Am. Soc. for Pub. Adminstrn. (publs. com. 1982-84, William E. Mosher award 1983), Am. Polit. Sci. Assn. (chmn. departmental services com. 1985-87, exec. com. sect. pub. adminstrn. 1985-87, 89—, chair sect. pub. adminstrn. 1990-91, chair Gaus award com. 1991-92), Nat. Assn. Schs. Pub. Affairs and Adminstrn. (peer rev. com. 1984-86, 1st chmn. commn. on peer rev. and accreditation 1986-87, chmn. task force on revitalizing the pub. svc., v.p. 1990-91, pres. 1991-92), N.Y. State Acad. Pub. Adminstrn. (bd. dirs. 1994—). Home: 9 Harvard Ave Albany NY 12208-2019 Office: SUNY Grad Sch Pub Affairs Albany NY 12222

THOMPSON, FRED, senator; b. Sheffield, Ala., Aug. 19, 1942. BS, Memphis State U., 1964; JD, Vanderbilt U., 1967. Asst. U.S. atty. Mid. Tenn., 1969-72; min. counsel Senate Watergate Com., 1973-74; pvt. practice, 1975-94; spl. counsel U.S. Intelligence and Fgn. Rels. Coms., 1980-81, Senate Intelligence Com., 1982; atty. Arent, Fox, Kintner, Plotkin & Kahn, 1991-94; U.S. senator from Tenn., 1994—. Appeared in 18 films including The Hunt for Red October, In the Line of Fire, Cape Fear, 1985-94. Office: US Senate 523 Dirksen Senate Bldg Washington DC 20510-4203

THOMPSON, FRED CLAYTON, engineering executive, consultant; b. Snow Shoe, Pa., Feb. 26, 1928; s. Clayton Alfred and Edna (Pearl) T.; m. M. Joanne Bender; children: Marjorie Ann, Richard Clayton, Scott David, Carol Ann. BSEE, Pa. State U., 1950, MSEE, 1958. Electronics engr. Martin Corp., Balt., 1965-54; tech. dir. HRB System S, State Coll., Pa., 1954-68; v.p. engring. Locus, Inc., State Coll., 1958-78, pres., chmn., 1978-88, cons., 1989—. Patentee in microwave circuitry. Past pres. and dir. Private Industry Coun. With U.S. Army, 1950-52. Named Hon. Alumni Pa. State U., 1987, Disting. Toastmaster, Toastmaster Internat., 1976. Avocation: barbershop quartet singing. Office: care Locus Inc PO Box 740 State College PA 16804-0740

THOMPSON, GARY W., public relations executive; b. Berkeley, Calif., July 15, 1947. BA, Northwestern U., England, 1969—. Acct. exec. Allen & Doward Advt., 1971-74; acct. exec. Hoefer-Amedei Assocs., 1978-81, acct. supr., 1978, v.p., 1978-81; v.p., assoc. dir. Ketchum, 1981-82, sr. v.p., dir., 1982-84, exec. v.p., 1984-87, exec. v.p., dir. we. region, 1987-89, exec. v.p., dir. U.S.A., 1989-90; pres., CEO Hi-Tech Comm., 1990—. Mem. Pub. Rels. Soc. Am. (counselors acad., membership chmn. San Francisco chpt. 1983, placement, newsletter chmn. 1985), Internat. Assn. Bus. Communicators,. Office: Hi-Tech Comm 101 Howard St San Francisco CA 94105-1629*

THOMPSON, GEORGE ALBERT, geophysics educator; b. Swissvale, Pa., June 5, 1919; s. George Albert Sr. and Maude Alice (Harkness) T.; m. Anita Kimmell, July 20, 1944; children: Albert J., Dan A., David C. BS, Pa. State U., 1941; MS, MIT, 1942; PhD, Stanford U., 1949. Geologist, geophysicist U.S. Geol. Survey, Menlo Park, Calif., 1942-76; asst. prof. Stanford (Calif.) U., 1949-55, assoc. prof., 1955-60, prof. geophysics, 1960—, chmn. geophysics dept., 1967-86, chmn. geology dept., 1979-82, Otto N. Miller prof. earth scis., 1980-89, dean sch. earth scis., 1987-89; cons. adv. com. on reactor safeguards Nuclear Regulation Commn., Washington, 1974-94; mem. bd. earth sci. NRC, 1986-88, vice chmn. Yucca Mountain Hydrology-tectonics panel NRC, 1990-92; mem. exec. com. Inc. Rsch. Inst. for Seismology, Washington, 1990-92; mem. sr. external events rev. com. Lawrence Livermore Nat. Lab., 1989-93; mem. Coun. on Continental Sci. Drilling, 1990-94; cons. Los Alamos Nat. Lab. on volcano-tectonic processes, 1993-96, S.W. Rsch. Inst., 1993; chair com. to review sci. issues NRC, Ward Valley, Calif., 1994-95; mem. panel on probabalistic volcanic hazard analysis Geomatrix Cons., Inc., 1995-96. Author over 100 research papers. With USNR, 1944-46. Recipient G.K. Gilbert award in seismic geology, 1964; NSF postdoctoral fellow, 1956-57; Guggenheim Found. fellow, 1963-64. Fellow AAAS, Geol. Soc. Am. (coun. mem. 1983-86, George P. Woollard award 1983, v.p. 1995), Am. Geophys. Union; mem. NAS, Seismol. Soc. Am., Soc. Exploration Geophysicists. Avocation: forestry. Home: 421 Adobe Pl Palo Alto CA 94306 Office: Stanford U Geophysics Dept Stanford CA 94305-2215

THOMPSON, GEORGE LEE, consulting company executive; b. Denver, June 12, 1933; s. George H. and Frances M. (Murphy) T.; m. Patricia M. MacKenzie, Sept. 25, 1993; children: Shannon, Tracy, Bradley. BS in Bus., U. Colo., 1957; postgrad. in advanced mgmt., NYU, 1969. With GTE Sylvania, Denvers, Mass., 1957-65, nat. sales mgr., 1965-67, mktg. mgr., 1967-68; v.p. sales entertainment products Batavia, N.Y., 1968-73; dir. corp. mktg. Stamford, Conn., 1973-74; v.p. mktg. Servomation Corp., N.Y.C., 1974-76, exec. v.p., 1976-78; exec. v.p. Singer Co., Edison, N.J., 1978-81, pres., 1981-83; pres. consumer products SCM Corp., N.Y.C., 1983-86; pres., CEO Smith-Corona Corp., New Canaan, Conn., 1986-89, chmn., CEO, 1989-95; chmn. Mackenzie-Thompson Assocs., Palm City, Fla., 1995—; bd. dirs. Vol. Products, Inc. Bd. dirs. Internat. Tennis Hall of Fame, Am. Jr. Golf Found., United Way of New Canaan, 1989-93; chmn. EC-92 Standards Com. U.S. Dept. Commerce; mem. bus. alumni adv. coun. U. Colo., 1989-94; mem. bd. overseers Sch. Bus. U. Conn.; mem. Pres.'s Export Coun., 1991-93; mem. bd. advisors Jr. league. Recipient Disting. Bus. Alumni award U. Colo., 1990. Mem. Computer and Bus. Equipment Mfg. Assn. (bd. dirs. 1992-94), Sales and Mktg. Execs. Internat. (trustee), Am. Mgmt. Assn. (bd. trustees, exec. com. chmn., gen. mgmt. coun.), St. John Assn. (bd. dirs., pres. 1983-93), New Canaan Field Club, Woodway Country Club, Club at Seabrook Island, Wilton Riding Club (bd. govs. 1980-83), Navesink Country Club (bd. govs. 1981-83), Harbour Ridge Yacht and Country Club, Chi Psi. Episcopalian. Home: 13507 Wax Myrtle Tr Palm City FL 34990 Office: Mackenzie Thompson Assocs 13507 Wax Myrtle Tr Palm City FL 34990

THOMPSON, GEORGE RALPH, church denomination administrator; b. Barbados, Mar. 20, 1929; s. George Gilbert and Edna (Griffith) T.; m. Imogene Clotilde Barker, July 19, 1959; children: Carol Jean, Linda Mae, Gerald Randolph. BA, Atlantic Union Coll., 1956; MA, Andrews U., 1958, BD, 1962, DD (hon.), 1983. Ordained to ministry Seventh-day Adventists, 1959. Evangelist South Caribbean conf. Seventh-day Adventists, Trinidad and Tobago, 1950-53; tchr., ch. pastor, chmn. dept. theology Caribbean Union Coll., Trinidad and Tobago, 1953-54, 59-64; pres. East Caribbean conf. Seventh-day Adventists, Barbados, 1964-70; pres. Caribbean Union conf. Seventh-day Adventists, Trinidad and Tobago, 1970-75; v.p. Gen. Conf. Seventh-day Adventists, Washington, 1975-80; sec. Gen. Conf. Seventh-day Adventists, Silver Spring, Md., 1980—; host radio shows, Barbados. Office: Gen Conf Seventh-day Adventist Ch 12501 Old Columbia Pike Silver Spring MD 20904-6601

THOMPSON, GERALD E., historian, educator; b. Oakland, Calif., Nov. 27, 1947; s. Norman J. and Margaret L. (Daniels) T.; m. Margaret H. Hood, June 6, 1970. BA, U. Ariz., 1969, MA, 1972, PhD, 1978. Editorial asst. Ariz. and the West, Tucson, 1975-77; asst. editor Ariz. and the West, 1977-78; asst. prof. history U. Toledo, 1978-83, assoc. prof., 1983-88, prof., 1988—; editor The Historian, Toledo, 1983-90; hist. cons. Mescalero Apache Tribe, various pubs.; humanities lectr. U. Toledo, 1993-94; vis. assoc. prof. dept. history U. Ariz., summer 1984; instr. Pima Coll., fall 1977. Author: Army and the Navajo, 1976, Edward F. Beale and the American West, 1983; compiler: A Guide to History-Related Microform Holdings, 1986; contbr. articles to profl. jours., chpts. to books. Counselor Ariz. Dept. Corrections, 1970-71. Served with Ariz. N.G., 1969-75. Recipient Ariz. Hist. Found. award, Exceptional Faculty Mem. award U. Toledo, 1985, 91; Edwin Turville fellow U. Ariz., 1975. Mem. Am. Hist. Assn., Western Hist. Assn., Nat. Assn. Scholars, Soc. Calif. Pioneers, Orgn. Am. Historians, Ariz. Hist. Soc., Ohio Acad. History (publs. awards com. 1982-83), Phi Beta Kappa, Phi Kappa Phi, Phi Alpha Theta (historian 1983-90, merit achievement award 1989). Office: U Toledo Dept History 2801 W Bancroft St Toledo OH 43606-3328

THOMPSON, GERALD LUTHER, operations research and applied mathematics educator; b. Rolfe, Iowa, Nov. 25, 1923; s. Luther and Sylva Carlotta (Larson) T.; m. Dorothea Vivian Mosley, Aug. 25, 1954; children: Allison M., Emily A., Abigail E. B.S. in Elec. Engring, Iowa State U., 1944; M.S. in Math, Mass. Inst. Tech., 1948; Ph.D., U. Mich., 1953. Instr. math. Princeton, 1951-53; asst. prof. math. Dartmouth, 1953-58; prof. math. Ohio Wesleyan U., Delaware, 1958-59; assoc. prof. applied math. and indsl. adminstrn. Carnegie-Mellon U., Pitts., 1959-63; prof. Carnegie-Mellon U., 1963—, IBM prof. systems and operations research, 1980—; E.D. Walker Centennial fellow IC2 Inst. U. Tex., 1985—; cons. Econometric Research Program, Princeton, IBM, Bethlehem Steel Co., Port Authority of Allegheny County, McKinsey & Co., Applied Devices Corp., PPG Industries, Westinghouse Electric Corp., Timken Co., J & L Steel, GM; prin. investigator Mgmt. Scis. Research Group, Carnegie-Mellon U. Co-author, author: Introduction to Finite Mathematics, 1957, Finite Mathematical Structures, 1959, Finite Mathematics with Business Applications, 1962, Industrial Scheduling, 1963, Programming and Probability Models in Operations Research, 1973, Mathematical Theory of Expanding and Contracting Economies, 1976, Optimal Control Theory: Management Science Applications, 1981, Computational Economics: Economic Modeling with Optimization Software, 1992; assoc. editor: Inst. Mgmt. Scis. Jour, 1966-69; Contbr. articles to profl. jours. Rep. of Inst. Mgmt. Scis. to NRC. Served with USNR, 1943-46. Ford Found. research fellow, 1963-64. Mem. AAAS, Math. Assn. Am., Inst. Mgmt. Scis., Operations Research Soc. Am., Phi Beta Kappa, Phi Kappa Phi, Tau Beta Phi, Eta Kappa Nu, Phi Mu Alpha. Home: 15 Wedgewood Ln Pittsburgh PA 15215-1560

THOMPSON, GLENN JUDEAN, library science educator; b. Sioux Falls, S.D., Oct. 16, 1936; s. Carl Melvin and Emma Bertina (Johnson) T.; m. Agnes Myrleen Nord, Aug. 23, 1958; children—Christine Faye, Nathan Glenn. B.S., Augustana Coll., Sioux Falls, S.D., 1958; M.A., U. Minn., 1966; Ed.D., U. S.D., 1969. Cert. music tchr., English tchr., librarian, audiovisual dir., Minn. Music tchr. Wayzata Pub. Schs. (Minn.), 1958-63; librarian, audiovisual dir. Perham Pub. Schs. (Minn.), 1963-66; mem. faculty St. Cloud State Coll., (Minn.), 1966-70; mem. faculty U. Wis.-Eau Claire, 1970—, chmn. dept. library sci. and media edn., 1972-90, prof., 1988—. Mem. ALA, Wis. Library Assn., Wis. Ednl. Media Assn., NEA. Home: N7191 540th St Menomonie WI 54751-5588 Office: U Wis Eau Claire Found & Libr Sci Dept Garfield Ave Eau Claire WI 54702-4004

THOMPSON, GORDON, JR., federal judge; b. San Diego, Dec. 28, 1929; s. Gordon and Garnet (Meese) T.; m. Jean Peters, Mar. 17, 1951; children—John M., Peter Renwick, Gordon III. Grad., U. So. Calif., 1951, Southwestern U. Sch. Law, Los Angeles, 1956. Bar: Calif. 1956. With Dist. Atty.'s Office, County of San Diego, 1957-60; partner firm Thompson & Thompson, San Diego, 1960-70; U.S. dist. judge So. Dist. Calif., San Diego, 1970—, chief judge, 1984-91, sr. judge, 1994—. Bd. dirs. Sharp Meml. Hosp. Mem. Am. Bd. Trial Advocates, ABA, San Diego County Bar Assn. (v.p. 1970), Delta Chi. Club: San Diego Yacht. Office: US Dist Ct 940 Front St San Diego CA 92101-8994

THOMPSON, GORDON WILLIAM, dentist, educator, administrator; b. Vancouver, B.C., Can., Dec. 22, 1940; s. Clarence and Emma Jean T.; m. Marilyn Jean Lust, May 23, 1964; children: Janice Lynne, Phillip Glen, Andrew James. Student, U. B.C., Vancouver, 1958-61; D.D.S., U. Alta., Edmonton, Can., 1965; M.Sc.D., U. Toronto, Ont., Can., 1967, Ph.D., 1971. Practice dentistry Wetaskiwin, Alta., 1965; asst. prof. dentistry U. Toronto, 1969-72, asso. prof., 1972-77, prof., 1977-78; prof., dean Faculty of Dentistry, U. Alta., 1978-89, chmn. dept. dental health care, 1989-94; exec. dir. Alta. Dental Assn., Edmonton, 1994—; condr. rsch. programs in Scotland, Portugal, Ecuador. Editor Ont. Dental Assn. Jour., 1977-78; contbr. over 100 articles and 60 abstracts to profl. jours. Fellow Royal Coll. Dentists (Can.), Internat. Coll. Dentists, Acad. Dentistry Internat.; mem. Alta. Dental Assn., Can. Dental Assn., Internat. Assn. Dental Rsch., Assn. Can. Faculties of Dentistry (pres. 1982-84), Can. Fund. for Dental Edn. (chmn. 1991-93), Dentistry Can. Fund (chmn. 1993-95), Can. Soc. Pub. Health Dentists (pres. 1995—). Conservative. Mem. United Ch. Canada. Home: 12429 28th Ave, Edmonton, AB Canada T6J 4G4 0ffice: Alta Dental Assn, 8230 105th St, Edmonton, AB Canada T6E 5H9

THOMPSON, GRANVILLE BERRY, animal science researcher; b. Sedalia, Mo., June 18, 1929; s. Granville Samples and Hazel (Berry) T.; m. Gertrude Stokley Alexander, July 20, 1958; children: Mark, Matt, Dan. BS in Agriculture, U. Mo., 1951, MS in Animal Sci., 1955, PhD in Animal Nutrition, 1958. Registered profl. animal scientist. Asst. county extension agt. U. Mo., Columbia, 1951, 53-55, grad. asst., 1953-55, instr., 1955-58, asst. prof., 1958-63, assoc. prof., 1963-69, prof., 1969-76; resident dir. rsch. Tex. A&M U., Amarillo, 1976—; rsch. assoc. U. Calif., Davis, 1965-66; cons. in field. Author, co-editor: The Feedlot, 1983, Cattle Feeding: A Guide to Management, 1991; patentee in field of beef cattle nutrition. Chmn. adminstrv. bd. Meth. Ch., Amarillo, 1983; coach Little League, Amarillo, 1970-74. Maj. USAFR, 1951-64. Named Hon. State Farmer, Mo. Future Farmers Am., 1970; recipient Citation of Merit, U. Mo. Alumni Assn., 1986. Mem. Am. Soc. Animal Sci. (program com.), Am. Registry Profl. Animal Scientists, Plains Nutrition Coun. (pres. 1980), Acad. Vet. Cons., Coun. Agriculture and Tech., Am. Forage and Grassland Coun., Am. Med. Ctr. Occupants Assn. (chmn. 1984-86), Rotary (pres. local chpt. 1984-85). Avocations: fishing, hunting, fly tieing. Office: Tex A&M U Ctr 6500 W Amarillo Blvd Amarillo TX 79106-1706*

THOMPSON, GUY BRYAN, investment company executive; b. N.Y.C., Mar. 10, 1940; s. Frederick Roeck and Carolyn Laura (Bryan) T.; m. Sallie Ann Mullins, Apr. 22, 1972 (div. Feb. 1982); 1 child, Kathryn Clarke. BA, U. Tex., 1962; postgrad., Baylor Law Sch., 1962-63; MBA, Columbia U., 1970. Adminstrv. asst. Alaska Barge & Transport, Inc., Southeast Asia, 1967; asst. mgr. corp. trading First Boston Corp.,, N.Y.C., 1970-72; sr. assoc. corp. fin. dept. Reynolds Securities, Inc., N.Y.C., 1972-73; portfolio mgr./fin. analyst Continental Ins. Cos.,, N.Y.C., 1973-74; asst. v.p. domestic banking 1st City Nat. Bank, Houston, 1974-77; dir. corp. relations, v.p. Credit Suisse, Houston, 1977-82; sr. v.p., prin. fin. officer Seneca Oil Co., Okla. City, 1982-83; chief fin. ops. exec. Seneca Exploration Co., Okla. City, 1982-83; pres., sec., dir. Seneca Fin. Svcs., Inc., Oklahoma City, 1983; exec. v.p. MPetroleum Corp, Dallas, 1984-86; pres. Austin Investment Co., 1987—; mng. dir. Houston Investment Co., 1989—; pres., CEO Thompson Oil Co., Houston, 1990—; sr. ptnr. Nagel-Thompson Enterprises, Austin, Tex., 1960—, gen. ptnr. Gibraltar Ltd., Houston, 1976-89, San Jacinto Investment Co., Houston, 1979-92. Mem. principal's cir. St. Francis Episcopal Day Sch., Houston, 1983; patron Houston Ballet, 1981—, Stephen F. Austin Coll., 1983, Kinkaid Sch., Houston, 1987-93; mem. Cultural Arts Council Houston, 1984; charter mem. Rep. Presdl. Task Force, Washington, 1984; sponsor Rep. Presdl. Fund Nat. Com., 1980—, mem. Associated Reps. Tex., Austin, 1990—; patron Houston Lyric Theater Found., 1985; benefactor Worthan Ctr., Houston, 1983; mem. Mus. Fine Arts, Houston. Capt. USNR, 1963—; Vietnam. Recipient medal of merit Pres. of U.S., 1988, Rep. Presdl. Legion of Merit, 1992; named hon. adm. Tex. Navy, 1975, commd. adm., 1992; also various mil. decorations, commendations and svc. awards from U.S. and fgn. govt., 1964-86. Mem. SAR, SCV, Houston C. of C. (ports and waterways com. 1978-83), Dallas C. of C. (natural resources com. 1984-86, internat. com. 1985), Dallas Geol. Soc. (assoc. 1985-86), English Speaking Union U.S., Naval Order U.S., Navy League U.S., Naval Res. Assn., Res. Officers Assn. U.S., Heritage Soc., Mil. Order Stars and Bars, Sons Republic Tex., Tex. Corinthian Yacht Club, Houston Club, Camp Fire Am. Club, Houstonians Club, Cadre Club (chmn. bd., pres. 1993-94, bd. dirs. 1989-90), Forum Club. Avocations: tennis, sailing, hunting, golf, antique collecting. Home: 5828 Valley Forge Dr Houston TX 77057-2241

THOMPSON, GUY THOMAS, safety engineer; b. Chattanooga, Dec. 29, 1942; s. Thomas Nelson and Dorothy Leona (Dobbs) T.; m. Joy Ann Gray, July 22, 1966 (div. 1978); children: Jeffrey Leighton, Lydia Ann; m. Vicki Lynn Brogdon, Dec. 6, 1979; 1 child, Laura Lynn. BA in Engring. Electronic, Park Coll., Parkville, Mo., 1976; MS in Indsl. Safety, Middle Tenn. State U., 1989. Factory rep. Modern Maid Appliances, Chattanooga, 1966-68; biomed. tech. USAF, 1968-77, commd. 2d. lt., 1977, advanced through grades to capt., 1981, ret., 1987; tng. and safety coord. Murfreesboro (Tenn.) Area Vocat. Tech. Sch., 1987—; cons. Tenn. Elec. Coop. Assn., Nashville, 1987—, Tenn. Mcpl. Elec. Power Assn., Brentwood, 1987-92; dir. safety and loss control Okla. Assn. Electric Coops., 1992—. Author: Tech/Logistic Development Plans, 1978, Comprehensive Safety, 1988; copyright: Root Causes of Electric Contact Accidents and Electric Utility Safety Policy; inventor hyperbaric breathing apparatus. Coach Little League, Charleston, S.C., 1962-64, Girl's Softball League, Warner Robins, Ga., 1978-80, Girl's Softball, Tullahoma, Tenn., 1984-86. Mem. Am. Soc. Safety Engrs., Nat. Utility Tng. and Safety Edn. Assn. (coord. conf. 1989), Nat. Safety Coun., Tenn. Safety Congress (exec. com.), Am. Tech. Edn. Assn., Tri-County Bowling Assn. (pres. 1982-88), Arnold Engring. & Devel. Ctr. Golf Club (coun. 1984-88), Am. Legion, Phi Kappa Phi. Republican. Methodist. Avocations: golf, boating, Indian artifacts, bowling. Home: 15089 N Oak Dr Choctaw OK 73020-7009 Office: Okla Assn Electric Coops PO Box 54309 Oklahoma City OK 73154-1309

THOMPSON, HAROLD LEE, lawyer; b. Dayton, Ohio, Feb. 17, 1945; s. Harold Edward Thompson and Johnita Dorothy (Cox) Metcalf; children: Aishah T., Aliya S. BS in Acctg., Cen. State U., Wilberforce, Ohio, 1967; JD, U. Conn., 1972. Bar: Ohio 1975, U.S. Dist. Ct. (so. dist.) Ohio 1975, D.C. 1976, U.S. Ct. Appeals (4th cir.) 1990. Acct. Communication Satellite Corp., 1968-69; atty. Ohio State Legal Service, Columbus, Ohio, 1972-74; of counsel Ohio Indsl. Commn., Columbus, 1974-76; sole practice Columbus, 1976—; ptnr. Jones & Thompson, Columbus, 1984-88; prin. H. Lee Thompson Co. L.P.A., Columbus, 1988—; pres. toys and clothing H. Lee Toy Co., Columbus, 1988—; adj. prof. law Columbus State Coll., 1989; instr. Acad. Ct. Reporting, 1989; adj. prof. tax and prins. of acctg. Bliss Coll., 1990-91; mem. Am. Bd. Forensic Examiners. Reginald Heber Smith fellow U.S. Fed. Ct., 1972. Mem. ATLA (exec. mem. birth trauma litigation group), Ohio Bar Assn., Am. Coll. Legal Medicine, Ohio Acad. Trial Lawyers, Franklin County Trial Lawyers Assn., Univ. Club, Columbus Met. Club. Roman Catholic. Avocations: reading, music, jogging. Office: 85 E Gay St Ste 810 Columbus OH 43215-3118

THOMPSON, HENRY NAINOA, hospital administrator; b. Honolulu, July 15, 1921; s. Henry Nainoa Sr. and Irmgard Luukia (Harbottle) T.; m. Pearl Elvina Mary Barbel, Nov. 16, 1946; children: Scott Henry Nainoa, Noni Nora Glynnis Bridget Skeffington, Kirk Leopold Kumulani, Jonah Henry Nainoa, Allegra Luukia, Lois Wise, Isaiah Kumulani, Jacob Kepookalani. Student, U. Wash., 1940-42, Columbia U., 1942-44; BA in Phys. Therapy, Columbia U., 1946, MA in Corrective Phys. Edn. & Rehab., 1950; cert. poliomyelitis, U. So. Calif., L.A., 1950; cert. adminstr. phys. therapy, Stanford U., 1950; cert. adminstrn. rehab., Inst. Phys. Medicine & Rehab., 1953; cert. adminstrn. pers., U. Hawaii, 1956; cert. job sampling testing, Ins. for Crippled and Disabled, 1958; cert. analysis fin. statements, U. Hawaii, 1960. Phys. therapist VA Regional Office, N.Y.C., 1946; chief phys. therapy Nat. Soc. for Crippled Children and Adults, Honolulu, 1948-49, Kauikeolani Children's Hosp., Honolulu, 1950-53; asst. dir. Rehab. Ctr. Hawaii, Honolulu, 1953-68; adminstr. Wahiawa (Hawaii) Gen. Hosp., 1968-71; hosp. adminstr. The Queen's Med. Ctr., Honolulu, 1971-74; dir. arthritis ctr. U. Hawaii Sch. Medicine, Honolulu, 1974-75; dep. dir. county state hosps. Dept. of Health, State of Hawaii, Honolulu, 1975-82; adminstr. Hawaii State Health Planning and Devel. Agy. State of Hawaii, Honolulu, 1982-86; past dir. Family Medicine, Inc., Honolulu. Past pres. Hawaii Kai Comty. Assn.; past pres., dir. Abilities Unltd. With AUS, 1946-48. Named one of 12 Nat. Phys. Fitness Leaders of Am., Pres.'s Johnson's Program for Phys. Fitness, 1965. Fellow Am. Coll. Hosp. Adminstrs.; mem. APHA, Am. Health Planning Assn., Hosp. Assn. Hawaii (assoc.), Am. Hosp. Assn. (assoc.), Koko Head Athletic Club (past pres.), Hawaii State Health Coun. (past pres.), Nat. Rehab. Assn. (past dir. Hawaii chpt.), Am. Assn. Phys. Therapy (past pres. Hawaii chpt.), Elks. Home and Office: 6815 Niumalu Loop Honolulu HI 96825

THOMPSON, HERBERT, JR., bishop; b. N.Y.C.; m. Ruselle Cross, 1968; children: Herbert, Owen, Kyrie. Grad. cum laude, Lincoln U., 1962; MDiv, Gen. Theol. Sem., N.Y.C., 1965; postgrad., Stony Brook U., Ch. Divinity Sch. of Pacific; D of Ministry, United Theol. Sem., Dayton, Ohio, 1992. Ordained to ministry Episcopal Ch. as deacon, 1965, then as priest. Chaplain Chester County, Pa.; vicar St. Gabriel's Ch., Bklyn.; rector Christ Ch., Bellport, N.Y., 1971-77, Grace Ch., Jamaica, 1977-88; bishop coadjutor Diocese of So. Ohio, 1988-91, bishop, 1992—; exec. dir. Interfaith Svcs., Bklyn.; colloquium moderator Gen. Theol. Sem.; instr., lectr. Mercer Sch. Theology; bd. dirs. Jamaica Devel. Corp. Reader Gen. Ordination Exams.; mem. Presiding Bishop's Commn. on Black Ministries, Coalition for Human Needs; mem. joint standing com. on planning for Gen. Conv., coun. of advice to pres. of Ho. of Deps.; bd. dirs. Cen. Queens YMCA, Queens Fedn. Chs., St. Christopher-Ottilie Home; chmn. Mayor's Commn. on Children, Cin. Served with USAF. Named Hon. Canon Cathedral of the Incarnation Diocese of Long Island, 1985. Mem. Jamaica C. of C. (bd. dirs). Address: 412 Sycamore St Cincinnati OH 45202-4166

THOMPSON, HERBERT ERNEST, tool and die company executive; b. Jamaica, N.Y., Sept. 8, 1923; s. Walter and Louise (Joly) T.; student Stevens Inst. Tech., 1949-51; m. Patricia Elaine Osborn, Aug. 2, 1968; children: Robert Steven, Debra Lynn. Foreman, Conner Tool Co., 1961-62, Eason & Waller Grinding Corp., 1962-63; owner Endco Machined Products, 1966-67, Thompson Enterprises, 1974—; pres. Method Machined Products, Phoenix, 1967; pres., owner Quality Tool, Inc., 1967—. Served to capt. USAAF, 1942-46. Decorated D.F.C., Air medal with cluster. Home: 14009 N 42nd Ave Phoenix AZ 85023-5306 Office: 4223 W Clarendon Ave Phoenix AZ 85019-3618

THOMPSON, HERBERT STANLEY, neuro-ophthalmologist; b. Shansi, China, June 12, 1932; came to U.S., 1949, naturalized, 1955; s. Robert Ernest and Ellen (Mulligan) T.; m. Delores Lucille Johnson, June 27, 1953; children: Geoffrey, Peter, Kenneth, Philip, Susan. Student, Methodist Coll., Belfast, No. Ireland, 1947-49; B.A., U. Minn., 1953, M.D., 1961; M.S., U. Iowa, 1966. Diplomate Am. Bd. Ophthalmology (assoc. examiner 1972-88, bd. dirs. 1989-96, chmn. ABO 1996). Intern U. Iowa, Iowa City, 1961-62; resident in ophthalmology U. Iowa, 1962-66; fellow in pupillography Columbia Coll. Physicians and Surgeons, 1962; fellow in clin. neuro-ophthalmology U. Calif., San Francisco, 1966-67; prof. ophthalmology U. Iowa, Iowa City, 1976—; dir. neuro-ophthalmology unit U. Iowa, 1967—; practice medicine specializing in neuro-ophthalmology Iowa City, 1967—. Editor: Topics in Neuro-opthalmology, 1979; assoc. editor Am. Jour. Ophthalmology, 1981-84, book rev. editor, 1984-91; cons. Stedman's Med. Dictionary, 26th edit. Served with AUS, 1954-55. NIH spl. fellow, 1966-67; research career devel. awardee, 1968-72. Fellow Am. Acad. Ophthalmoogy, N.Am. Neuro-ophthalmol. Soc.; mem. Am. Ophthalmol. Soc., Cogan Ophthalmic History Soc. (Charles Snyder lectr. 1995). Primary research interest: movements of the pupil of human eye. Office: U Iowa Dept Ophthalmology Iowa City IA 52242

THOMPSON, HOWARD ELLIOTT, business educator; b. West Allis, Wis., July 30, 1934; s. Leonard Adolph and Hulda Axelina (Granstrom) T.; m. Judith M. Gram, June 30, 1956; children: Linda Kay, Karen Marie, James Howard, John Leonard, Ann Elizabeth. BS, U. Wis., 1956, MS, 1958, PhD, 1964. Mathematician, ops. rsch. analyst A.O. Smith Corp., Milw., 1957-61; asst. prof. Sch. Bus. U. Wis., Madison, 1964-67, assoc. prof., 1967-69, prof., 1969—, Mary Rennebohm prof., 1975-85, Kuechenmeister-Bascom prof., 1985—; vis. prof. Ohio State U., 1970-71; cons. various utilities and utility commns., 1968—; cons. World Bank, 1981-83; Wis. atty. gen., 1973-74; cons. U.S. Energy Info. Adminstrn., 1990—. Author: Applications of Calculus in Business and Economics, 1973, A Brief Calculus with Applications to Business and Economics, 1976, Management Science, 1981, Regulatory Finance, 1991; contbr. articles to profl. jours. Mem. Am. Fin. Assn., Am. Econs. Assn., Ops. Rsch. Soc., Am. Inst. Mgmt. Scis., Am. Inst. Decision Scis., Math. Assn. Am., Pi Mu Epsilon, Beta Gamma Sigma, Alpha Iota Delta, Phi Kappa Phi. Home: 7529 Fox Point Cir Madison WI 53717-

1058 Office: Univ Wis Sch Business Grainger Hall 975 University Ave Madison WI 53706-1324

THOMPSON, HUGH LEE, academic administrator; b. Martinsburg, W.Va., Mar. 25, 1934; s. Frank Leslie and Althea T.; m. Patricia Smith; children: Cheri, Linda, Tempe, Vicki. B.S., B.A. in English and Secondary Edn, Shepherd Coll., Shepherdstown, W.Va., 1956; MS, Pa. State U., 1958; Ph.D. in Higher Edn. Adminstrn, Case Western Res. U., 1969. Mem. faculty Pa. State U., 1957-60, Akron (Ohio) U., 1960-62; mem. faculty Baldwin-Wallace Coll., Berea, Ohio, 1962-70, asst. to pres., 1966-69, dir. instl. planning, asst. to pres., 1969-70; coordinator Associated Colls., Cleve., 1970-71; pres. Siena Heights Coll., Adrian, Mich., 1971-77, Detroit Inst. Tech., 1977-80; chancellor Ind. U., Kokomo, 1980-90; pres. Washburn U., Topeka, 1990—; mem. president's adv. coun. Assn. Governing Bds. Univs. and Colls. Mem. Am. Assn. State Colls. and Univs. (coun. of state reps., steering com. urban and met. univs. coun.), North Ctrl. Assn. (evaluator, cons.). Home: 3130 SW Shadow Ln Topeka KS 66604-2541 Office: Washburn U Office of Pres Topeka KS 66621 *I have found that to be successful in any field of endeavor an individual must work very diligently at finding solutions to problems, should be highly goal oriented, honest and forthright, and adhere to the teachings of Christ.*

THOMPSON, HUNTER STOCKTON, author, political analyst, journalist; b. Louisville, July 18, 1937; s. Jack R. and Virginia (Ray) T.; 1 child, Juan. Carribean corr. Time mag., 1959, N.Y. Herald Tribune, 1959-60; South Am. corr. Nat. Observer, 1961-63; West Coast corr. The Nation, 1964-66; columnist Ramparts, 1967-68, Scanlan's, 1969-70; nat. affairs editor Rolling Stone, 1970—; global affairs corr. High Times, 1977-82; political columnist San Francisco Examiner, 1985—; editor at large Smart, 1988—; polit. analyst European mags. London Observer, Tempo, Time Out, Das Magazine, Nieuwe Revu, Die Woche, 1988—; judge Nat. Book Awards, 1975. Author: Prince Jellyfish, 1960, Hell's Angels, 1966, The Rum Diary, 1967, Fear and Loathing in Las Vegas, 1972, Fear and Loathing On the Campaign Trail '72, 1973, The Great Shark Hunt, 1979, (with Ralph Steadman) The Curse of Lono, 1983, Generation of Swine, 1988, Songs of the Doomed, 1990, Screwjack, 1991, Better Than Sex, 1993; creator Gonzo journalism. Mem. Pitkin County (Colo.) Sheriff's Adv. Com., 1976-81; mem. president's task force ACLU; mem. nat. adv. bd. NORML, 1976—; founder 4th Amendment Found. Mem. NRA (exec. dir.), U.S. Naval Inst. (exec. dir.), Air Force Assn. (exec. dir.), Hong Kong Fgn. Corrs., Kona Coast Marlin Fisherman's Assn., Vincent Black Shadow Soc., Woody Creek Rod and Gun Club (exec. dir.), Overseas Press Club (exec. dir.), Nat. Press Club. Clubs: Key West Mako, Nat. Press, Hong Kong Fgn. Corrs. Office: Janklow & Nesbit 598 Madison Ave New York NY 10022-1614

THOMPSON, J. ANDY, bank executive; b. Ft. Worth, Sept. 21, 1943; s. Fredrick Dickson and Mary Alice (Rhea) T.; m. Nancy Sealy, Jan. 15, 1966; children: J. Andrew Jr., Christopher Sealy. BBA, U. Tex., 1965. Exec. v.p. Internat. Svc. Ins. Co., Ft. Worth, 1968-83; exec. v.p. Ctrl. Bancorp. Inc., Ft. Worth, 1984-86, pres., 1986-88, chmn., chief exec. officer, 1988—; chmn., chief exec. officer Cen. Bank & Trust, Ft. Worth, 1988—, North Ft. Worth Bank, 1988—; adv. bd. Policy Mgmt. Systems, Columbia, S.C., 1975-83; bd. dirs. Ft. Worth C. of C., 1989—. Mem. adminstrv. bd. First Meth. Ch.; trustee, chmn. Harris Meth. Hosp., Ft. Worth; vice chmn., trustee Harris Meth. Health System; mem. exec. com., bd. dirs. Lena Pope Home for Children: bd. dirs. James L. West Presbyn. Spl. Care Ctr. Capt. U.S. Army, 1966-68, Vietnam. Mem. Tex. Banker's Assn., Am. Banker's Assn., Ft. Worth Club (pres. 1993—, mem. bd. govs.), Rotary Internat. Republican. Methodist. Avocations: tennis, sailing, golf.

THOMPSON, J. KEN, gas, oil industry executive. Mgr., v.p. Arco Exploration Prodn. Tech., Plano, Tex. Office: ARCO Alaska Inc PO Box 100360 Anchorage AK 99510-0360*

THOMPSON, JACK EDWARD, mining company executive; b. Central City, Nebr., Nov. 17, 1924; s. Ray Elbert and Bessie Fay (Davis) T.; m. Maria del Carmen Larrea, May 8, 1948; children: Jack Edward, Ray Anthony, Robert Davis. Student, Northwestern U., 1942-43, Colo. Sch. Mines, 1943-45; D of Engring. (hon.), Colo. Sch. Mines, 1993. V.p. Cía. Química Comercial de Cuba S.A., 1946-60, Cía. de Fomento Químico S.A., 1946-60; with Newmont Mining Corp., N.Y.C., 1960-86; asst. to pres. Newmont Mining Corp., 1964-67, v.p., 1967-71, dir., 1969-86, exec. v.p., 1971-74, pres., 1974-85, vice chmn., 1985-86, cons., 1986-90. Chmn. bd. trustees Minerals Industry Ednl. Found.; mem. Pres.'s Coun. Colo. Sch. Mines. Recipient Distinguished Achievement medal Colo. Sch. Mines, 1974. Mem. AIME, Mining and Metall. Soc. Am., Mining Found. of S.W. (pres., bd. govs.), Tucson Country Club.

THOMPSON, JAMES BURLEIGH, JR., geologist, educator; b. Calais, Maine, Nov. 20, 1921; s. James Burleigh and Edith (Peabody) T.; m. Eleanora Mairs, Aug. 3, 1957; 1 son, Michael A. A.B., Dartmouth, 1942, D.Sc. (hon.), 1975; Ph.D., Mass. Inst. Tech., 1950. Instr. geology Dartmouth, 1942; research asst. Mass. Inst. Tech., 1946-47, instr., 1947-49; instr. petrology Harvard, 1949-50, asst. prof., 1950-55, asso. prof. mineralogy, 1955-60, prof., 1960-77, Sturgis Hooper prof. geology, 1977-92, Sturgis Hooper prof. geology emeritus, 1992—; guest prof. Swiss Fed. Inst. Tech., 1977-78; adj. prof. geology Dartmouth Coll., 1992—. Served to 1st lt. USAAF, 1942-46. Guggenheim fellow, 1963; Sherman Fairchild distinguished scholar Calif. Inst. Tech., 1976. Fellow Mineral. Soc. Am. (pres. 1967-68, recipient Roebling medal 1978), Geol. Soc. Am. (A.L. Day medal 1964), Am. Acad. Arts and Scis.; mem. NAS, AAAS, Am. Geophys. Union, Geochem. Soc. (pres. 1968-69, Goldschmidt medal 1985), Mineral. Soc. of Gt. Britain and Ireland (hon.), Sigma Xi. Office: Harvard U Dept of Ed Cambridge MA 02138

THOMPSON, JAMES CLARK, utilities executive; b. St. Louis, Sept. 24, 1939; s. Leonard Andrew and Virginia Evelyn (Clark) T.; m. Gerry Marie Rush, Oct. 2, 1965; children: Ren James, David James. BSBA, Washington U., St. Louis, 1968. Various positions then corp. sec. Union Electric Co., St. Louis, 1982—; sec. Union Electric Devel. Corp., 1982—, also dir. Trustee Laumeier Sculpture Park. Petty officer 2d class USN, 1957-60. Mem. Am. Soc. Corp. Secs. (pres. St. Louis chpt. 1989-90), U.S. Naval Cryptologic Vets. Assn., 1904 World's Fair Soc. (sec. 1987—). Republican. Avocation: collecting 1904 World's Fair memorabilia. Office: Union Electric Co PO Box 149 Saint Louis MO 63166-0149

THOMPSON, JAMES DAVID, financial services company executive, lawyer; b. Gulfport, Miss., Oct. 22, 1945; s. James David and Dorothy (O'Dom) T.; m. Carol Vail, Aug. 23, 1969; children: Meredith, Adrienne, James. BA in Econs., Millsaps Coll., Jackson, Miss., 1967; JD, U. Miss., 1970. Bar: Miss. 1970, U.S. Dist. Ct. (no. dist.) Miss. 1970, U.S. Ct. Mil. Appeals 1971. Asst. gen. counsel ITT Fin. Corp., St. Louis, 1974-77, sr. v.p., gen. counsel, 1977-90, exec. v.p., 1990-93, dir. ins. ops., 1981-93, also bd. dirs.; pres., CEO ITT Diversified Fin. Corp., St. Louis, 1990-93; chmn. ITT Fed. Bank, 1990-93; chmn., pres., CEO Lyndon Ins. Group, 1984-93; exec. v.p., CFO ING Am. Life, Atlanta, 1993-95; pres. Columbine Life Ins. Co.; pres., chief oper. officer Southland Life Ins. Co., 1995—; bd. dirs. Security Life Ins. Co. of Denver, Life Ins. Co. of Ga., Southland Life Ins. Co. Served to capt. USAF, 1970-74. Mem. ABA, Miss. Bar Assn., Bar Assn. Met. St. Louis, Ga. Life and Health Ins. Guarantee Assn. (bd. dirs.). Methodist. Office: ING Am Life 5780 Powers Ferry Rd NW Atlanta GA 30327-4349

THOMPSON, JAMES HOWARD, historian, library administrator; b. Memphis, Aug. 20, 1934; s. Curtis Barnabas and Clara (Terry) T.; m. Margareta Ortenblad, Nov. 24, 1961; children—Ralph, Anna, Howard. B.A. in History, Rhodes Coll., Memphis, 1955; M.A., U. N.C., Chapel Hill, 1957, Ph.D. in History, 1961; M.S. in Library Sci, U. Ill., 1963. Teaching fellow U. N.C., Chapel Hill, 1955-56; departmental asst. U. N.C., 1956-57, reference asst., 1959-61, dir. undergrad. library, lectr. in history, 1968-70; circulation asst. U. Ill., 1961-63; asst. Center for Russian Area and Lang. Studies, 1962-63; cataloger Duke U., 1963-65; asst. prof. history U. S.W. La., 1965-66; asst. prof. U. Colo., 1966-68; dir. libraries, prof. history U. N.C., Greensboro, 1970-94; ret., 1994; bd. dirs. Southeastern Library Network, 1979-82, treas., 1981-82. Contbr. articles, revs. to profl. jours. Ford Found. research fellow, 1957-58; U. Colo. grantee, 1967; U. N.C. at Greensboro grantee, 1977-78, 89. Mem. Phi Beta Kappa (chpt. pres. 1979-80), Beta Phi Mu, Phi Alpha Theta, Chi Beta Phi. Episcopalian. Home: 3006 New Hanover Dr Greensboro NC 27408-6710

THOMPSON, JAMES ROBERT, JR., lawyer, former governor; b. Chgo., May 8, 1936; s. James Robert and Agnes Josephine (Swanson) T.; m. Jayne Carr, 1976; 1 dau., Samantha Jayne. Student, U. Ill., Chgo., 1953-55, Washington U., St. Louis, 1955-56; J.D., Northwestern U., 1959. Bar: Ill. 1959, U.S. Supreme Ct. 1964. Asst. state's atty. Cook County, Ill., 1959-64; assoc. prof. law Northwestern U. Law Sch., 1964-69; asst. atty. gen. State of Ill., 1969-70; chief criminal div., 1969, chief dept. law enforcement and pub. protection, 1969-70; 1st asst. U.S. atty. No. Dist. Ill., 1970-71, U.S. atty., 1971-75; counsel firm Winston & Strawn, Chgo., 1975-77, ptnr., chmn. exec. com., 1991—; gov. Ill., 1977-91; mem. joint com. to revise Ill. criminal code, mem. drafting subcom. Chgo.-Ill. Bar Assns., 1959-63, chmn. joint com. to draft indigent def. legis., 1966-68; mem. com. to draft handbooks for petit jurors in civil and criminal cases and for grand jurors Jud. Conf. Ill., 1959; mem. com. to draft uniform instrn. in criminal cases Ill. Supreme Ct.; co-dir. criminal law course for Chgo. Police and Indsl. Security Pers., 1962-64; mem. Chgo. Mayor's Com. to Draft Legis. to Combat Organized Crime, 1964-67; adviser Pres.' Commn. Law Enforcement and Adminstrn. Justice, 1966; mem. Pres.' Task Force on Crime, 1967; lectr. Northwestern U. Law Sch., U. Calif.-Davis, Mich. State U., Nat., Ill., Ohio, N.D., Va., N.J., Ala., Md. and Ga. Prosecutors' Assns.; former bd. dirs. Chgo. Crime Commn.; v.p. Ams. for Effective Law Enforcement, 1967-69; chmn. Pres.' Intelligence Oversight Bd., 1989-93, adv. bd. Fed. Emergency Mgmt. Agy., 1991-93, Ill. Acad. Fine Arts; bd. govs. Chgo. Bd. Trade; trustee FMC Corp., Jefferson Smurfit Corp., Prime Retail Inc., Pechiney, Internat., Wackenhut Corrections Corp., Hollinger Internat., Inc., Union Pacific Resources, Inc., Chgo. Mus. Contemporary Art, Chgo. Hist. Soc., Lyric Opera Chgo., Econ. Club Chgo., Civic Com., Comml. Club Chgo., Execs. Club Chgo. Co-author: Cases and Comments on Criminal Justice, 2 vols, 1968, 74, Criminal Law and Its Adminstration, 1970, 74; asst. editor-in-chief: Jour. Criminal Law, Criminology and Police Sci., 1965-69; bd. editors: Criminal Law Bull. Pres. Ill. Math. and Sci. Acad. Found.; co-chmn. U.S. Atty. Gen's. Task Force on Violent Crime, 1981; chmn. Rep. Gov's. Assn., 1982, Coun. Gt. Lakes Gov's., 1985, NGA Task Force on Teen Pregnancy, 1987, NGA Task Force on Transp. Infrastructure, 1988, NGA Task Force on Global Climate Change, 1989; mem. Nat. Commn. to Prevent Infant Mortality, 1986. Mem. ABA, Ill. Bar Assn. (past chmn. criminal law sect.), Fed. Bar Assn., Chgo. Bar Assn., Nat. Gov's. Assn. (chmn. 1983). Republican. Office: Winston & Strawn 35 W Wacker Dr Chicago IL 60601-1614

THOMPSON, JAMES WILLIAM, lawyer; b. Dallas, Oct. 22, 1936; s. John Charles and Frances (Van Slyke) T.; BS, U. Mont., 1958, JD, 1962; m. Marie Hertz, June 26, 1965 (dec. 1995); children: Elizabeth, Margaret, John. Acct., Arthur Young & Co., N.Y.C., summer 1959; instr. bus. adminstrn. Eastern Mont. Coll., Billings, 1959-60, U. Mont., Missoula, 1960-61; admitted to Mont. bar, 1962; assoc. Cooke, Moulton, Bellingham & Longo, Billings, 1962-64, James R. Felt, Billings, 1964-65; asst. atty. City of Billings, 1963-64, atty., 1964-66; ptnr. Felt, Speare & Thompson, Billings, 1966-72, McNamer, Thompson & Cashmore, 1973-86, McNamer & Thompson Law Firm PC, 1986-89, McNamer, Thompson, Werner & Stanley, P.C., 1990-93, McNamer Thompson Law Firm PC, 1993—; bd. dirs. Associated Employers of Mont., Inc., 1989—. Mem. Billings Zoning Commn., 1966-69; v.p. Billings Community Action Program (now Dist. 7 Human Resources Devel. Council), 1968-70, pres., 1970-75, trustee, 1975—; mem. Yellowstone County Legal Services Bd., 1969-70; City-County Air Pollution Control Bd., 1969-70; pres. Billings Symphony Soc., 1970-71; bd. dirs. Billings Studio Theatre, 1967-73, Mont. Inst. of Arts Found., 1986-89, Downtown Billings Assn., 1986-90, Billings Area Bus. Incubator, Inc., 1991-94, Found. of Mont. State U., Billings, 1992—; mem. Diocesan exec. council, 1972-75; mem. Billings Transit Commn., 1971-73; mem. City Devel. Agy., 1972-73; bd. dirs. United Way, Billings, 1973-81. CPA, Mont. Mem. ABA, Am. Acad. Estate Planning Attys., Nat. Acad. Elder Law Attys., State Bar Mont., Yellowstone County Bar Assn. (bd. dirs. 1983-87, pres. 1985-86), C. of C., Elks, Kiwanis (pres. Yellowstone chpt. 1974-75), Sigma Chi (pres. Billings alumni assn. 1963-65). Episcopalian. Home: 123 Lewis Ave Billings MT 59101-6034 Office: 300 First Bank Bldg Billings MT 59101

THOMPSON, JAMES WILLIAM, banker; b. Dunn, N.C., June 18, 1939; s. William J. and Lucy (Pope) T.; m. Meredith Cromartie, June 10, 1961; children—Ann, Lucy, Bill. BSBA, U. N.C., 1961. Credit analyst NCNB Corp., Charlotte, N.C., 1963-68; v.p., bond dept. mgr. NCNB Corp., 1968-71, investment portfolio mgr., 1971-74, sr. v.p., funds mgmt. exec., 1974-77, exec. v.p., 1977-83, corp. exec. v.p., 1983-85, vice chmn. bd., 1985-96; chmn. Southeastern Banking, Charlotte, 1988-91. Past pres. Mint Mus. of Charlotte; mem. bd. visitors U. N.C.; bd. dirs. Found. of U. N.C., Charlotte, Univ. Rsch. Pk., N.C. Performing Arts Ctr., pres., 1993—; trustee U. N.C., Charlotte; mem. Gov.'s Bus. Coun. of Arts and Humanities; past pres. N.C. Edn. Coun. Mem. Bankers Roundtable, Charlotte City Club (past pres.). Democrat. Methodist. Office: NationsBank Corp NC1-007-56-25 NationsBank Corp Ctr Charlotte NC 28255

THOMPSON, JEAN TANNER, retired librarian; b. San Luis Obispo, Calif., June 15, 1929; d. Chester Corey and Mildred (Orr) T.; 1 child, Anne Marie Miller. Student, Whitworth Coll., Spokane, Wash., 1946-49; A.B., Boston U., 1951; postgrad., U. Wis., Eau Claire, 1964-67; M.S.L.S., Columbia U., 1973; Ed.M., U. Va., Charlottesville, 1978. Asst. social sci. librarian Univ. Libraries Va. Polytechnic Inst. and State U., Blacksburg, 1973-77, head social sci. dept. Univ. Libraries, 1977-83; head reference dept. Meml. Library U. Wis., Madison, 1983-86, asst. dir. reference and info. svcs., 1986-91, ret. Contbg. editor: ALA Guide to Information Access, 1994; mem. editorial bd. RQ, 1984-89. Mem. ALA, Assn. Coll. and Research Libraries (edn. and behavioral sci. sect. vice chmn. 1985-86, chmn. 1986-87), Wis. Library Assn., Wis. Assn. of Acad. Librarians. Methodist. Home: 103 S Hunter Ln Troy AL 36081-8206

THOMPSON, JERE WILLIAM, retail food company executive; b. Dallas, Jan. 18, 1932; s. Joe C. and Margaret (Philp) T.; m. Peggy Dunlap, June 5, 1954; children: Michael, Jere W., Patrick, Deborah, Kimberly, Christopher, David. Grad. high sch., 1950; B.B.A., U. Tex., 1954. With Southland Corp., Dallas, 1954—; v.p. stores Southland Corp. (merged with Thompson Co. 1988), Dallas, 1962-73, exec. v.p., 1973-74, pres., 1974-91, dir., 1962—, chief exec. officer, 1986-91, co-vice chmn., 1991—; pres. The Williamsburg Corp., Dallas, TX, 1995—; bd. dirs. MCorp. Bd. dirs. St. Paul Hosp. Found. Served to lt. (j.g.) USNR, 1954-56. Office: The Williamsburg Corp. 3838 Oak Lawn Ave Ste 1850 Dallas TX 75219-4519*

THOMPSON, JEREMIAH BEISEKER, international medical business executive; b. Harvey, N.D., July 20, 1927; s. Linden Brown and Ferne Althea (Beiseker) T.; m. Paula Maria Ketchum, Feb. 5, 1960; children: Cole, Per, Gover, Susannah. BS, U. Minn., 1949, MD, 1953. Rsch. assoc. U. Colo. Med. Sch., Denver, 1955-56, U. Calif. Med. Sch., San Francisco, 1956-57; assoc. Stanford U., 1957-59; applications rsch. scientist Beckman/Spinco Co., Palo Alto, Calif., 1959-61; mgr. Asia and Africa Hewlett Packard Co., Palo Alto, 1965-71; med. cons. Alyeska Pipeline Co., Anchorage, 1973-76; mgr. Asia, Africa, Australasia Corometrics Med. Systems, Wallingford, Conn., 1976-82; dir. internat. ops. Oximetrix (Abbott), Mountain View, Calif., 1982-84, Novametrix Med. Systems, Wallingford, 1984-88; ptnr. TMC Internat., Tokyo and Concord, Calif., 1988—; advisor, cons. Yokogawa-Hewlett Packard, Tokyo, 1966-70; cons. Kupat Holim, Tel Aviv, Israel, 1967-87, Itochu, Tokyo, 1984-90, Nat. Heart-Lung Inst., Beijing, China, 1984-94. Project dir. Comparative Study of Western and Japanese Medicine in Taisho and Showa Eras, 1991—. With USN, 1945-46; PTO. Founding fellow Brit. Interplanetary Soc.; assoc. Japan Found., Assn. Asian Studies; mem. Kokusai Bunka Kaikan, Tokyo, World Affairs Coun., Mechanics Inst. Achievements include cancer research, joint Japan/U.S. project screening and evaluation for anti-cancer activity of halogenated methane derivatives, augmentation of irradiation effects by chemotherapy. Home and Office: TMC Internat 3718 Barrington Dr Concord CA 94518-1614

THOMPSON, JESSE ELDON, vascular surgeon; b. Laredo, Tex., Apr. 7, 1919; s. Jesse Eathel and Sara Gail (Bolton) T.; m. Madeleine Jane Curtis, Sept. 18, 1944; children: Sally C., Jesse E., Janet E., Diane B. BA, U. Tex., 1939; MD, Harvard U., 1943; Rhodes scholar, Oxford U., 1949-50. Intern Mass. Gen. Hosp., Boston, 1943; resident in surgery Mass. Gen. Hosp., 1944-48; practice medicine specializing in surgery, tchr. surgery Boston U., 1949-54; practice medicine specializing in surgery, tchr. vascular surgery Baylor Hosp., Dallas, 1954—; chief vascular surgery Baylor Hosp., 1980-86; clin. prof. surgery U. Tex. Southwestern Med. Sch., Dallas; attending surgeon Baylor Hosp., 1954—; chief surgery Baylor Hosp., Dallas, 1982-86; Mem Tex. and Dist. Rhodes Scholar Selection Coms. Author: Surgery for Cerebrovascular Insufficiency, 1968; editorial bd.: Surgery, 1975-89, Jour. Cardiovascular Surgery, 1975—; sr. editor Jour. Vascular Surgery, 1984-86; contbr. numerous articles to profl. jours. Served to capt. M.C. AUS, 1945-47. Fulbright sr. fellow, 1949-50. Fellow ACS (treas.); mem. Am. Surg. Assn., So. Surg. Assn., Tex. Surg. Soc., Soc. Vascular Surgery, Internat. Cardiovascular Soc., Internat. Soc. Surgery, So. Assn. for Vascular Surgery, Dallas Petroleum Club, Dallas Country Club, Masons. Methodist. Home: 3705 Stanford Ave Dallas TX 75225-7204 Office: 712 N Washington Ave Ste 509 Dallas TX 75246-1635

THOMPSON, JOANNE GUIMOND, pediatric nurse, educator; b. North Attleboro, Mass., June 10, 1945; d. Joseph R. and Peggy Lillian (Vest) G.; m. William Clark Thompson, Sept. 15, 1962; children: William Clark, Jeffrey Mark, Theresa Dawn. ASN, Fla. Jr. Coll., Jacksonville, 1981; BSN, Fla. Atlantic U., Boca Raton, 1993; postgrad., PFS U., Boynton Beach, Fla., 1995. RN, Fla.; cert. pediatric and adolescent nurse; lic. life ins. and variable annuities agt. Staff nurse pediatrics St. Vincent's Med. Ctr., Jacksonville, Fla., 1981; charge nurse adult Humana Hosp. of Palm Beaches, West Palm Beach, Fla., 1981-82; charge nurse pediatrics Boca Raton (Fla.) Cmty. Hosp., 1982-86; charge nurse pediatrics Wellington Regional Med. Ctr., West Palm Beach, 1986-88, pediatric and adult nurse mgr., 1988-89; sch. nurse and health instr. Jewish Cmty. Day Sch., West Palm Beach, 1991-93; nursing supr. Palms West Hosp., Loxahatchee, Fla., 1991-93, charge nurse pediatrics, 1989-96; owner A Legal-Med. Nurse Cons., 1995—; life ins., variable annuities agt. Primerica Fin. Svcs.; vol. child immunizer HRS, West Palm Beach, 1992-96; mem. Am. Cancer Nurse Bd., West Palm Beach, 1988-89; mem. health educator adv. bd. Palm Beach County Sch. Bd., West Palm Beach, 1991-93; owner A Legal-Med. Nurse Cons., 1995.Financial svs. Atlanta, Ga., 1995—. Author numerous ednl. leaflets; contbr. articles to profl. jours. Mem. ANA (polit. action com. 1993-95), Fla. Nurses Assn. (2d v.p. Area 9 1995—). Democrat. Roman Catholic. Avocations: sewing, fishing, writing, reading, painting. Home and Office: 3332 Mission Ridge Rd Atlanta GA 30339

THOMPSON, JOE FLOYD, aerospace engineer, educator; b. Grenada, Miss., Apr. 13, 1939; s. Joe Floyd and Bernice Thompson; m. Emilie Kay Wilson, June 1, 1974; children: Mardi, Douglass. BS, Miss. State U., 1961, MS, 1963; PhD, Ga. Tech., 1971. Aerospace engr. NASA Marshall, Huntsville, Ala., 1963-64; prof. Miss. State U., Starkville, 1964—, Disting. prof. aerospace engring., 1995—; mem. tech. rev. bd. Army Rsch. Lab., Adelphi, Md., 1993-95; dir. computer code Nat. Grid Project 1993—; dir. NSF Engring. Rsch. Ctr. for Computational Field Simulation, 1990-95. Author: Numerical Grid Generation, 1985, (computer code) Eagle Grid System, 1987; sr. assoc. editor Applied Math. and Computation, 1985-94; assoc. editor Numerical Heat Transfer, 1989—; mem. edit. bd. Computational Fluid Dynamics Jour., 1993—, Jour. Computational Physics, 1995—. Recipient Commdr.'s award Army Waterways Exp. Sta., Vicksburg, Miss., 1992. Mem. IEEE, IEEE Computer Soc., AIAA (Aerodynamics award 1992), SIAM. Presbyterian. Achievements include establishment of NSF Engineering Research Center; pioneering work in field of numerical grid generation. Home: Miss State U Box 255 Mississippi State MS 39762 Office: Miss State U PO Box 6176 Mississippi State MS 39762-6176

THOMPSON, JOHN, college basketball coach; b. Washington, Sept. 2, 1941. Student, Providence Coll., 1960-64; M in Counseling and Guidance, U. D.C., 1971; LHD (hon.), St. Peter's Coll., 1982; H.H.D., Wheeling Coll., 1982. Player Boston Celtics, Nat. Basketball Assn., 1964-66; basketball coach St. Anthony High Sch., Washington, 1966-72; basketball coach Georgetown U., Washington, 1972—, presdl. asst. on urban affairs, 1977; founder Summer Basketball Sch. Georgetown U.; mem. Nat. Invitation Tournament Championship Team, 1963, Nat. Basketball Assn. Championship Team, 1965, 66; won NCAA championship, 1984, 2nd place NCAA championship, 1982, 85. Inducted Providence Coll. Hall of Fame, 1974; U.S. asst. coach Olympic Games Montreal, Que., Can., 1976; recipient Pres.'s award, Patrick Healy award Georgetown U., 1982; named U.S. Basketball Writers Assn. Coach of Yr., 1982; recipient other awards; named Coach of Yr., United Press Internat., 1987; Coach U.S. Olympic Games, Seoul, Korea, 1988; recipient bronze medal Olympic Games, 1988. Mem. Nat. Assn. Basketball Coaches (bd. dirs. 1976—, chmn. selection com. for east team, NABC Coach of Yr. 1984-85). Office: Georgetown U Basketball Office Washington DC 20057*

THOMPSON, JOHN DOUGLAS, financier; b. Montreal, Que., Can., Sept. 28, 1934; s. William Douglas and Anne F. (Whebby) T.; children: Jacqueline, Catherine, Peter, Anne Marie, Francois. B.Eng., McGill U., 1957; M.B.A., U. Western Ont., 1960. Dep. chmn. bd. Montreal Trustco Inc.; past chmn. bd. dirs. Trust Cos. Assn. of Can.; vice chmn. Domtar, Inc.; bd. dirs. Société Générale de financement de Que., J.S. Redpath Holdings Inc., BCE Mobile, Montrusco Assocs. Inc., Boréal Assurances Inc., Sedgwick, Air Transat, Capital d'Amérique CDPQ Inc., Benvest Capital Inc. Bd. dirs. MacDonald Stewart Found., Windsor Found., Salvation Army, chmn. Montreal adv. bd.; chmn. Montreal YMCA Found.; mem. audit com. McGill U.; past pres. St. Mary's Hosp. Found.; gov., past pres. St. Mary's Hosp. Ctr. Mem. Assn. Profl. Engrs., Que. and Ont., Mt. Royal Club (Montreal), Royal Montreal Golf Club, Montreal Amateur Athletic Club, Mt. Bruno Country Club Inc., The Forest and Stream Club. Roman Catholic. Office: 12th Fl, 1800 McGill College Ave, Montreal, PQ Canada H3A 3K9

THOMPSON, JOHN E., principal. Prin. Ardmore (Okla.) Middle Sch. Recipient Blue Ribbon Sch. award U.S. Dept. Edn., 1990-91. Office: Ardmore Mid Sch PO Box 1709 Ardmore OK 73402-1709

THOMPSON, JOHN HENRY, consulting executive; b. Ute, Iowa, May 15, 1933; s. Frederick Stephen and Georgia (Wilkins) T.; m. Beverly Diane Price, Aug. 25, 1956; 1 child, Jennifer. BA in Psychology, Calif. State U., Fresno, 1960; PhD in Psychology, U. Ill., 1964. Lic. psychologist, Ill., Wash., Calif. Asst. prof. psychology Gonzaga U., Spokane, Wash., 1964-65, chmn. psychology dept., 1965-67; staff psychologist Rohrer, Hibler & Replogle, Portland, Oreg., 1967-69; mng. ptnr. Rohrer, Hibler & Replogle, Seattle, 1969-72; mgr. Rohrer, Hibler & Replogle, L.A., 1972-75; v.p. Rohrer, Hibler & Replogle, 1975-83; exec. v.p. Rohrer, Hibler & Replogle, 1984-85; pres., COO Rohrer, Hibler & Replogle, Chgo., 1985-87; pres., CEO RHR Internat. Co., Wood Dale, Ill., 1987-96, chmn., CEO, 1991-96; chmn., 1996—; bd. dirs. Target Sales, Fresno, Calif., 1978-84. Contbr. articles to profl. jours. and chpts. to books. Mem. State Bd. Med. Quality Assurance, Calif., 1974-77. Sgt. USMC, 1952-55, Korea. Roman Catholic. Avocations: hunting, fishing, target shooting, hiking, music. Office: RHR Internat Co 220 Gerry Dr Wood Dale IL 60191-1139

THOMPSON, JOHN HERD, history educator; b. Winnipeg, Man., Can., Sept. 18, 1946; came to U.S. 1989; s. Joseph Whyte and Gladys Kate (Campain) T.; m. Katrin Ann Partelpoeg, Jan. 15, 1977; children: Anne Marie, Mark Thomas. BA with honors, U. Winnipeg, 1968; MA, U. Man., 1969; PhD, Queens U., Kingston, Ont., 1975. Faculty Duke U., Durham, N.C., 1989—. Author: Harvests of War, 1978, Decades of Discord: Canada 1922-1939, 1985, Canada and the United States: Ambivalent Allies, 1994. Mem. Am. Hist. Assn., Can. Hist. Assn., Soc. for Am. Baseball Rsch., Assn. for Can. Studies in the U.S. Avocation: baseball. Home: Duke Univ Dept History Durham NC 27708

THOMPSON, JOHN KENTON, energy company executive, natural gas engineer; b. McAllen, Tex., Sept. 25, 1947; s. Forrest Arnold and Virginia Lee (Womeldorf) T.; m. Mary Elizabeth White, June 18, 1971; children: Kathleen Ann, John Allen. BS in Natural Gas Engring., Tex. A&M U., Kingsville, 1971. Registered profl. engr., Tex. Gas engr. Sun Oil Co., Oklahoma City, 1972-75; dist. gas engr. Sun E&P Co., McAllen, 1975-78; OBO plant engr./gas mktg. rep. Sun Gas Co., Dallas, 1978-86; mgr. OBO plants Oryx Energy Co., Dallas, 1986-92; mgr. joint venture plants/pipelines Mitchell Energy & Devel. Corp., The Woodlands, Tex., 1992—; class instr.

Petroleum Ext. Svc.- U. Tex., 1995; net coord. USN/USMC Radio Svc. Net, Oklahoma City, 1974-75; session chmn. regional mtg. Gas Processors Assn., 1975; corp. ops. rep. to Spl. Revenue Project Phase III, 1989-91; class instr. Petroleum Extension Svc. U. Tex., 1995. Sect. leader Custer Rd. United Meth. Ch., Plano, Tex., 1990; mem. com. Boy Scouts Am., Plano, 1989; co-chmn. edn. and family life com. St. Mark United Meth. Ch., McAllen, 1976; mem. adminstrv. bd. Woodlands (Tex.) Meth. Ch., 1994-96; event co-supr. Tri-Regional Games-Tex. Spl. Olympics, 1995-96. Mem. Am. Inst. Chem. Engrs., Woodlands Kiwanis (dir. 1993-94, v.p. 94-96, chmn. Key Club/Kiwanis Spl. Fund Event 1995). Republican. Avocations: golf, bicycle riding, chess. Home: 10 Gate Hill Dr The Woodlands TX 77381 Office: PO Box 4000 The Woodlands TX 77380

THOMPSON, JOHN MORE, management consultant; b. Leicester, Eng., Nov. 26, 1938; came to U.S., 1963; s. John Kenneth and Jenny (More) T.; m. Carol Jane Valpy,, Sept. 28, 1963; children: Rupert, Juliet, Jessica. BA, Cambridge U., Eng., 1962, MA, 1962. Tech. specialist Shell Chem., 1962-63; mktg. mgr. Celanese Corp., 1963-68; v.p. Interactive Data Corp., Waltham, Mass., 1968-73; vice chmn. Index Group, Cambridge, Mass., 1973-89; chmn., CEO CSC Europe, London, 1989-93. Chmn. bd. trustees Charles River Sch., Dover, Mass., 1974-78; pres. Ind. Schs. Chairmens Assn., N.Y.C., 1978. Lt. Royal Signals, Brit. Army, 1957-59. Named One of Top Ten Mgmt. Cons. in U.S., Info. Week, 1988. Mem. Royal Overseas Club.

THOMPSON, JOHN TILYNN, ophthalmologist, educator; b. Ann Arbor, Mich., June 8, 1956; s. John Morgan and Dorothy Georgene (Kinne) T.; m. Mary Ann Serpi; children: Lauren Alexis, John Michael. Student, Oberlin Coll., 1973-75; BA cum laude, Johns Hopkins U., 1977, MD, 1980. Diplomate Am. Bd. Ophthalmology, 1985. Intern Cedars-Sinai Med. Ctr., L.A., 1980-81; resident Wilmer Ophthalmologic Inst., Balt., 1981-84, asst. chief svc., 1986; asst. prof. Yale U., New Haven, Conn., 1986-90, assoc. prof., 1990-91; assoc. clin. prof. U. Md., Balt., 1993—; ptnr. The Retina Inst. Md., Balt., 1991—; dir. retina sect. Yale U., 1986-91. Contbr. articles to profl. jours. Grantee Conn. Lions Eye Found., 1986-91, The Hearst Found., 1989-90; Wilmer Ophthalmologic Inst. fellow, 1984-85, Heed Found. fellow, 1984; recipient Lamport award Biomed. Rsch. Johns Hopkins U., 1978. Fellow Am. Acad. Ophthalmology (honor award 1988); mem. AMA, Assn. Rsch. in Vision & Ophthalmology, The Retina Soc., The Macula Soc., The Vitreous Soc., Phi Beta Kappa. Avocations: tennis, classical piano, computer programming. Office: The Retina Inst Md 7505 Osler Dr Ste 103 Baltimore MD 21204-7737

THOMPSON, JOHN WILLIAM, international management consultant; b. Hurricane, Utah, Oct. 14, 1945; s. Thomas Thurman and Lula (Brinkerhoff) T.; m. Pamela Ruth Williams, Sept. 14, 1991. BSEE, Utah State U., 1969, MBA, 1972; PhD, U. Oreg., 1978. Rsch. asst. Utah State U., Logan, Utah, 1967-69, tching. asst., 1971-72; elec. engr. Collins Radio, Newport Beach, Calif., 1969-72; tching. fellow U. Oreg., Eugene, 1972-78; tng. dir. Lifespring Inc., San Rafael, Calif., 1978-80; pres., CEO Human Factors Inc., San Rafael, Calif., 1980—; chmn. bd. Acumen Internat., San Rafael, Calif., 1985—. Author: The Human Factor: An Inquiry into Communication and Consciousness, 1983, Leadership in the 21st Century in New Traditions in Business, 1992, The Renaissance of Learning in Learning Organizations: Developing Cultures for Tomorrow's Workplace, 1994; author of software based management assessment programs, system theory based management development courses, 1980-92. Rockefeller Found. grantee, 1971. Avocations: sailing, raising Koi, gardening, bicycling, scuba diving. Office: Human Factors Inc 4000 Civic Center Dr Ste 500 San Rafael CA 94903

THOMPSON, JONATHAN SIMS, army officer; b. Ft. Benning, Ga., Nov. 19, 1947; s. Donald Frederick and Gene Elizabeth (Pierce) T.; m. Dinetha Lynn Richards, Aug. 26, 1979; children: Jonathan S. II, Tiffany A. BSME, Tex. A&M U., 1970, M Indsl. Engring., 1978; M Bus. Mgmt., Ctrl. Mich. U., 1980; diploma in program mgmt., Def. Sys. Mgmt. Coll., 1987. Registered profl. engr., Tex. Commd. 2d. lt. U.S Army, 1971, advanced through grades to col.; engr. platoon leader 27th Engr. Battalion U.S Army, Ft. Bragg, N.C., 1971-72, staff engr. 5th Spl. Forces Group, 1973-74; engr. instr. Spl. Forces Sch. U.S Army, Ft. Bragg, 1974-75; co. comdr. 2d Engr. Battalion U.S Army, Camp Castle, Korea, 1976-77; project dir. Engr. Strategic Studies Ctr. U.S Army, Rockville, Md., 1978-81; plans and ops. officer 317th Engr. Battalion U.S Army, Eschborn, Germany, 1982-84; engr. staff officer Office of Chief of Staff U.S Army, Washington, 1985-87, ops. rsch. analyst Office of Sec. of Army, 1987-88; battalion comdr. 2d Engr. Battalion U.S Army, Camp Castle, 1989-90; dep. chief of staff Corps. of Engrs. U.S Army, Washington, 1991-92, exec. dir. Office of Chief of Engrs., 1992-93, fellow Ctr. Stratetic/Internat. Studies U.S. Army War Coll., 1993-94; brigade comdr. 20th Engr. Brigade U.S Army, Ft. Bragg, N.C., 1994—; sr. fellow U.S. Dept. State, 1996—. Editor: Peacetime Defensive Preparations in Europe, 1981 (deMarche award 1985); author govt. study, article in field. Adult leader, asst. scoutmaster Boy Scouts Am., Dale City, Va., 1990-92, chmn. troop advancement com., Ft. Bragg, 1994—; coun. rep. Recreation Ctr. Bd., Dale City, 1985-89. Decorated Legion of Merit with 2 oak leaf clusters; fellow in govt. affairs Coun. for Excellence in Govt., 1991-92. Fellow Soc. Am. Mil. Engrs. (nat. bd. dirs. 1990-92, post pres. 1994—); mem. NSPE, Army Navy Club, Shriners (life mem., Noble), Masons (Companion, Sir Knight). Presbyterian. Achievements include leading the world's largest military engineering task force into Haiti during Operation Uphold Democracy to restore the government and rebuild the infrastructure; principal deputy to engineer commander of 24th infantry "Hail Mary" task force during Operation Desert Storm and the liberation of Kuwait. Avocations: skiing, golf, parachuting. Home: 20 Adams St Fort Bragg NC 28307-2049 Office: Hdqrs 20th Engr Brigade Airborne Fort Bragg NC 28307-5000

THOMPSON, JOSIE, nursing administrator; b. Ark., Apr. 16, 1949; d. James Andrew and Oneda Fay (Watson) Rhoads; m. Mark O. Thompson, Feb. 14, 1980. Diploma, Lake View Sch. Nursing, 1970; student, Danville C.C., 1974-75, St. Petersburg Jr. Coll., 1979. RN, Ill., Wyo. Staff nurse St. Elizabeth Hosp., Danville, Ill., 1970-78, Osteopathetic Hosp., St. Petersburg, Fla., 1980-81, Wyo. State Hosp., Evanston, 1981-83; staff nurse Wyo. Home Health Care, Rock Springs, 1984—, adminstr., 1986-95; pres. Home Health Care Alliance Wyo., 1991-92. Mem. nursing program adv. bd. Western Wyo. Community Coll.; mem. Coalition for the Elderly, Spl. Needs Com. Sweetwater County, 1992-93. Home: 1207 McCabe PO Box 1154 Rock Springs WY 82902

THOMPSON, JOYCE ELIZABETH, arts management educator; b. Pasadena, Tex., Aug. 15, 1951; d. James Little and Ruth Lake (Skinner) Wilkison; divorced; children: Christine Joy, Cassidy Jane. BA in Psychology, David Lipscomb Coll., 1974; MA in Speech, Theater, Murray State U., 1976; postgrad., U. Tex., 1978; MA in Arts Adminstrn., Ind. U., 1981. Asst. prof. speech Vincennes (Ind.) U., 1976-79; asst. dir. mktg. Hartford (Conn.) Ballet, 1981-82; touring dir. Hartford Ballet/Conn. Opera, 1982-84; exec. dir. Wyo. Arts Coun., Cheyenne, 1984-91, South Snohomish County Arts Coun., Lynwood, Wash., 1991-92; asst. prof. arts mgmt. U. Ill., Springfield, Ill., 1992—; adj. instr., Manchester (Conn.) Cmty. Coll., 1982-84, Chapman Coll., 1990—, Edmonds Cmty. Coll., 1992—; mem. selection com. Coca-Cola Coll., 1992—; mem. selection com. Coca-Cola Scholars Found., 1989, 90, 91, 95. Mem. adv. bd. Cheyenne Little Theatre Players, 1986, Cheyenne Civic Ctr., 1987-88; bd. dirs. Assembly of Ill. Cmty. Arts. Orgns., 1995—. Mem. Assn. Arts Adminstrn. Educators (sec.), Assn. Performing Arts Producers, Speech Comm. Assn., Western States Arts Fedn. (bd. dirs. 1984-91, chair performing arts com. 1985-87), Assn. Arts Adminstrn. Educators (bd. dirs. 1994—). Democrat. Avocations: singing, theater, reading. Home: 854 S Glenwood Ave Springfield IL 62704-2453 Office: U Ill PAC 370 Springfield IL 62794-9243

THOMPSON, JULIA ANN, physicist, educator; b. Little Rock, Mar. 13, 1943; d. Erwin Arthur and Ruth Evelyn (Johnston) T.; m. Patrick A. Thompson, Mar. 22, 1964 (div. 1974); 1 child, Diane E.; m. David E. Kraus, Jr., June 22, 1976; children: Vincent Szewczyk, Larry Lynch. BA, Cornell Coll., Mt. Vernon, Iowa, 1964; MA, Yale U., 1966, PhD, 1969. Research assoc. Brookhaven Lab., Upton, N.Y., 1969-71; research assoc./assoc. instr. U. Utah, Salt Lake City, 1971-72; asst. prof. physics U. Pitts., 1972-78, assoc. prof., 1978-85, prof., 1986—, dir. undergrad. rsch. program, 1992—; mem. users coms. Brookhaven Nat. Lab., 1983-86; condr. expts. Inst. Nuclear Physics, Novosibirsk, USSR, Ctr. Europeene Recherche Nucleaire, Switzerland, Brookhaven Natl. Lab., L.I.; spokesperson hyperon decay expt BNL, 1972-80. Contbr. articles to profl. jours. Bd. dirs. 1st Unitarian Ch., Pitts., 1980-83; zone councillor Soc. Physics Students, 1986-88; with Nat. Acad. Sci. Exch. to USSR, 1989-90. Woodrow Wilson fellow, 1964-65. Mem. Am. Phys. Soc. (com. on status of women in physics 1983-86, exec. com. forum on physics and soc. 1990—). Democrat. Unitarian. Avocations: promoting effective science education, hiking, reading, music. Achievements include research with W.E. Cleland and D.E. Kraus in optical triggering; with the collaboration with AFS and HELIOS expt. in direct photon and lepton production, leading to modified understanding of the gluon function, and limits on anomalous electron production; studies of rare and semi-rare kaon decays.

THOMPSON, KENNETH W(INFRED), educational director, author, editor, administrator, social science educator; b. Des Moines, Aug. 29, 1921; s. Thor Carlyle and Agnes (Rorbeck) T.; m. Beverly Bourret; children: Kenneth Caryle, Paul Andrew, James David, Carolyn A. A.B., Augustana Coll., 19[illegible], L.H.D. (hon.), 1986, LLD, 1986; M.A., U. Chgo., 1948, Ph.D., 1950; LL.D., U. Notre Dame, 1964, Bowdoin Coll., 1972, St. Michael's Coll., 1973, St. Olaf Coll., 1974, U. Denver, 1983; L.H.D., W.Va. Wesleyan U., 1970, Nebr. Wesleyan Coll., 1971. Lectr. social scis. U. Chgo., 1948, asst. prof. polit. sci., 1951-53; asst. prof. polit. sci. Northwestern U., 1949-55, chmn. internat. relations com., 1951-55; cons. internat. relations Rockefeller Found., 1953-55, asst. dir. social scis, 1955-57, assoc. dir. social scis., 1957-60, dir. social scis., 1960-61, v.p., 1961-73; dir. higher edn. for devel. Internat. Council for Ednl. Devel., 1974-76; Commonwealth prof. govt. and fgn. affairs U. Va., 1975-78, White Burkett Miller prof. govt. and fgn. affairs, 1979-86; J. Wilson Newman prof. govt. and fgn. affairs, 1986—, dir. White Burkett Miller Ctr. of Public Affairs, 1978—; Riverside Meml. lectr. Riverside Ch., N.Y.C., 1958; Lilly lectr. Duke, 1959; James Stokes lectr. N.Y.U., 1962; Rockwell lectr. Rice U., 1965; Ernest Griffith lectr. Am. U.; Andrew Cecil lectr. U. Tex., 1983; Stuber lectr. U. Rochester, 1984; Morgenthau Meml. lectr., N.Y.C., Mike Mansfield Ctr. lectr., U. Mont.; dir. Inst. Study World Politics, N.Y.C., 1975—. Author, editor: Principles and Problems of International Politics, 1951, 82, Man and Modern Society, 1953, Christian Ethics and the Dilemmas of Foreign Policy, 1959, 81, Conflict and Cooperation Among Nations, 1960, Political Realism and the Crisis of World Politics, 1960, 82, American Diplomacy and Emergent Patterns, 1962, 82, Foreign Policies in a World of Change, 1964, The Moral Issue in Statecraft, 1966, Reconstituting the Human Community, 1972, Foreign Assistance: A View From Private Sector, 1972, 82, Higher Education for National Development, 1972, Understanding World Politics, 1975, Higher Edn. and Social Change, 1976, World Politics, 1976, Truth and Tragedy, 1977, Ethics and Foreign Policy, 1978, Interpreters and Critics of the Cold War, 1978, Foreign Policy and the Democratic Process, 1978, Ethics, Functionalism and Power, 1979, Morality and Foreign Policy, 1980, Masters of International Thought, 1980, The Virginia Papers, vols. 1-29, 1979-95, The President and the Public Philosophy, 1981, Cold War Theories: World Polarization, 1944-53, Vol. I, 1981,91. Winston S. Churchill's World View, 1983, 89, Toynbees's World Politics and History, 1985, Moralism and Morality, 1985, Theory and Practice of International Relations, 1987, Arms Control and Foreign Policy, 1990, Traditions and Values in Politics and Diplomacy, 1992, Fathers of International Thought, 1994; editor: Am. Values Series, Vols. I-XX, Presdl. Nominating Process, Vols. I-IV, Portraits of American Presidents, Vols. I-XI, Herbert Butterfield: The Ethics of History; The American Presidency, Vols. I-III, 1982-83, Ethics and International Relations, 1985, Moral Dimensions of American Foreign Policy, 1985, 94, The Credibility of Leadership and Institutions, Vols. I-XX, 1983-86, Rhetoric and Political Discourse, Vols.I-XX, Governance, Vols. I-VI, 1990-95, Constitutionalism, Vols. I-VII, 1989-91, Presidency and Science Advising, Vols. I-VIII, 1986-90, Political Transitions and Foreign Policy, Vols. I-IX, 1985-91; bd. editors Va. Quar. Rev., Society, Ethics and International Affairs, Interpretation, The Rev. of Politics; contbr. articles to profl. jours. Pres. Dist. of Scarsdale and Mamaroneck (N.Y.) Bd. Edn., 1965-68; trustee Union Theol. Sem., 1967-71, Dillard U., 1975—, Social Sci. Found., U. Denver, 1974-94, Compton Found., 1975—. 1st lt. AUS, 1943-46. Named Va. laureate, 1981; recipient Phi Beta Kappa and Va. Coll. Stores prizes, Va. Social Sci. Assn. ann. award, English Speaking Union award, medal U. Chgo., 1968. Fellow Soc. Religion Higher Edn., Am. Acad. Arts and Scis.; mem. Century Club, Scarsdale Town Club, Raven Soc. (ann. award U. Va.), Phi Beta Kappa (pres.), Omicron Delta Phi. Office: Univ Va Miller Ctr PO Box 5106 Charlottesville VA 22905-5106

THOMPSON, LARRY A., principal. Prin. Lake Region Mid. Sch., Bridgton, Maine. Recipient Elem. Sch. Recognition award U.S. Dept. Edn., 1989-90. Office: Lake Region Middle Sch Kansas Rd Bridgton ME 04009

THOMPSON, LARRY ANGELO, producer, lawyer, personal manager; b. Clarksdale, Miss., Aug. 1, 1944; s. Angelo and Anne (Tuminello) T.; BBA, U. Miss., 1966, JD, 1968. Bar: Miss. 1968, Calif. 1970. In-house counsel Capitol Records, Hollywood, Calif., 1969-71; sr. ptnr. in entertainment law Thompson, Shankman and Bond, Beverly Hills, Calif., 1971-77; pres. Larry A. Thompson Orgn., Inc., 1977—; co-owner New World Pictures, 1983-85; lectr. entertainment bus. UCLA, U. So. Calif., Southwestern U. Law Sch. Co-chmn. Rep. Nat. Entertainment Com.; apptd. by Gov. of Calif. to Calif. Entertainment Commn. Recipient Show Bus. Atty. of Yr. award Capitol Records, 1971. Mem. Inauguration of Thompson Ctr. for Fine Arts in Clarksdale, Miss., 1986. Served with JAGC, U.S. Army, 1966-72. Mem. ABA, Miss. Bar Assn., Calif. Bar Assn., Inter-Am. Bar Assn., Hon. Order Ky. Colonels, Am. Film Inst., Nat. Acad. Recording Arts and Scis., Acad. TV Arts and Scis. Republican. Roman Catholic. Author: How to Make a Record Deal & Have Your Songs Recorded, 1975, Prime Time Crime, 1982; producer: (TV) Jim Nabors Show, 1977 (Emmy nominee), Mickey Spillane's Margin for Murder, 1981, Bring 'Em Back Alive, 1982, Mickey Spillane's Murder Me, Murder You, 1982, The Other Lover, 1985, Convicted, 1986, Intimate Encounters, 1986, The Woman He Loved, 1988, Original Sin, 1989, Class Cruise, 1989, Little White Lies, 1989, Lucy and Desi: Before The Laughter, 1990, Broken Promises, 1993, Separated By Murder, 1994, Face of Evil, 1996; (motion pictures) Crimes of Passion, 1984, Quiet Cool, 1987, My Demon Lover, 1987, Breaking the Rules, 1992. Recipient Vision award, 1993. Home: 9451 Hidden Valley Pl Beverly Hills CA 90210-1310 Office: Larry A Thompson Orgn 335 N Maple Dr Ste 361 Beverly Hills CA 90210-3857

THOMPSON, LARRY DEAN, lawyer; b. Hannibal, Mo., Nov. 15, 1945; s. Ezra W. and Ruth L. (Robinson) T.; m. Brenda Anne Taggart, June 26, 1970; children: Larry Dean, Gary E. BA cum laude, Culver-Stockton Coll., Canton, Mo., 1967; MA, Mich. State U., 1969; JD, U. Mich., 1974. Bar: Mo. 1974, Ga. 1978. Indsl. rels. rep. Ford Motor Co., Birmingham, Mich., 1969-71; atty. Monsanto Co., St. Louis, 1974-77, King & Spalding, Atlanta, 1977-82; U.S. atty. U.S. Dist. Ct. (no. dist.) Ga., 1982-86; ptnr. King & Spalding, Atlanta, 1986—; mem. lawyer's adv. com. U.S. Ct. Appeals for 11th Cir.; ind. counsel HUD investigation, 1995; mem. Ga. Bd. Bar Examiners. Editor: Jury Instructions in Criminal Antitrust Cases 1976-80, 1982. Chmn. Atlanta Urban League; mem. bd. trustees Met. Atlanta Crime Commn.; bd. dirs. Ga. Rep. Found. Recipient Outstanding Achievement award FBA, 1992. Mem. ABA, Nat. Bar Assn. Presbyterian. Home: 2015 Wallace Rd SW Atlanta GA 30331-7756 Office: King & Spalding 191 Peachtree St NE Atlanta GA 30303-1740

THOMPSON, LARRY FLACK, semiconducrtor equipment company executive; b. Union City, Tenn., Aug. 31, 1944; s. Rufus Russell and Polly (Flack) T.; m. Joan Bondurant, Aug. 30, 1964; children: Anthony Scott, Russell Allen. BS, Tenn. Tech. U., Cookeville, 1966; MS, Tenn. Tech. U., 1968; PhD, U. Mo., Rolla, 1970. Mem. tech. staff Bell Labs., Murray Hill, N.J., 1971-80; dept. head AT&T Bell Labs., Murray Hill, N.J., 1981-94; v.p. product devel. Integrated Solutions, Inc., Austin, Tex., 1994—. Author: Introduction to Microlithography, 1993; patentee in field. Mem. NAE, Am. Chem. Soc. (bd. dirs. 1993—, Indsl. Chemistry award 1993, Roy W. Tess award 1993), Am. Inst. Chem. Engring. Avocations: gardening, hunting. Home: 309 Comet St Austin TX 78734 Home: 309 Comet St Austin TX 78734

THOMPSON, LAWRENCE FRANKLIN, JR., computer corporation executive; b. Winchester, Tenn., Feb. 12, 1941; s. Lawrence Franklin and Mildred C. T.; m. Carol Lee Lufkin, Oct. 9, 1965; children: Jeffrey, Maureen. BS in Internat. Affairs, U.S. Air Force Acad., 1963. Enlisted USAF, 1958; cadet USAF Acad., 1959-63, commd. 2d lt., 1963, advanced through grades to capt., 1966, pilot, 1963-69, resigned, 1969; pres. Collectors Showcase, Orange, Calif., 1973-76; owner Lufkins (Limited Edition Collectibles), Mission Viejo, Calif., 1971—; CEO Computer City, Inc., Austin, Tex., 1979-91; pres., CEO Productivity Unltd., Inc., Austin, 1991—; v.p. ABC Computers, Inc., Austin, Tex., 1981-83; pres. Computer Craft of Austin, 1983-84. Decorated D.F.C., Silver Star. Office: Process Dynamics Internat Ste 202 9442 Capital Of Tex Hwy Austin TX 78759

THOMPSON, LAWRENCE HYDE, federal agency official; b. Hamilton, Ohio, Oct. 6, 1943; s. William Hayton and Evelyn (Covault) T.; m. Catherine Crosby, Feb. 3, 1973; children: Bradford Stephen, Sarah Catherine. BS, Iowa State U., 1964; MBA, U. Pa., 1966; PhD, U. Mich., 1971. Economist Office Sec. Health, Edn. and Welfare, Washington, 1974-77, dir. Soc. Security Planning, 1977-79; assoc. commr. Social Security Adminstrn., Washington, 1979-81, dir. rsch., 1981-83; chief economist Gen. Acctg. Office, Washington, 1983-89, asst. comptroller gen., 1989-93; prin. dep. commr. Social Security Admnistrn., 1993-95; sr. fellow The Urban Inst., Washington, 1996—. Contbr. articles to pubs., books. Mem. Am. Economic Assn., Nat. Acad. Social Ins. (dir. 1985-93). Avocations: racquetball, choral singing. Office: The Urban Inst 2100 M St NW Washington DC 20037

THOMPSON, LAWRENCE LEONARD, federal agency administrator; b. St. Paul, Jan. 11, 1937; s. Theodore Spencer and Louise Catherine (Leonard) T.; m. Gretchen Converse Laun, June 25, 1960 (div. June 1980); children: Heidi Louise, Erik Converse, Mark Laun, Holly Anne; m. Anna Sophia Zaremba, Oct. 23, 1982. BA, Harvard Coll., 1958; MPA, Princeton U., 1963. Microwave tube engr. Raytheon Co., Burlington, Mass., 1958-61; budget examiner U.S. Office Mgmt. and Budget, Washington, 1963-67; sr. rsch. assoc. Rep. Nat. Com., Washington, 1967-69; spl. asst. to under sec. U.S. Dept. Housing and Urban Devel., Washington, 1969-70; area dir. U.S. Dept. Housing and Urban Devel., Hartford, Conn., 1970-78; assoc. prof. pub. adminstrn. U. Hartford, West Hartford, 1979-82; exec. dir. Hartford (Conn.) Redevel. Agy., 1982-89; exec. asst. to asst. sec. U.S. Dept. Housing and Urban Devl., Washington, 1989-91, gen. dep. asst. sec. for policy devel. and rsch., 1991—. Mem. ASPA, Harvard Club Washington, Capitol Hill Choral Soc. Republican. Roman Catholic. Avocations: choral music, baseball, history, travel. Home: 1018 E Capitol St NE Washington DC 20003-3916 Office: US Dept Housing Urban Devel 451 7th St SW Washington DC 20410-0001

THOMPSON, LEONARD ALLEN, insurance sales and marketing specialist, consultant; b. Freeport, Ill., Apr. 1, 1927; s. Allen Marvin and Anna (Baughman) T.; m. Esther Gertrude Johnson, Nov. 4, 1949; children: Daniel J., David C., Deborah D. BTh, No. Bapt. Sem., Chgo., 1949; postgrad., U. Iowa, 1950-53. Salesman Bankers Trust Life, Phoenix, Ariz., 1957-64; nat. sales mgr. Sons of Norway, Mpls., 1964-80, salesman, 1980-87, CEO, 1987-89; cons., 1990—. Mem. Nat. Assn. Life Underwriters, Chartered Life Underwriters, Million Dollar Round Table (life), Fraternal Gield Mgrs. Assn. (bd. dirs., pres. 1965-71), Nat. Assn. Fraternal Ins. Counselors (bd. dirs. 1984—, pres. 1994-95). Republican. Home: 5565 Zachary Ln N Minneapolis MN 55442-3903

THOMPSON, LESLIE MELVIN, college dean, educator; b. Trinidad, Colo., May 19, 1936; s. J. Roy Thompson and E. Irene (Lance) Campbell; m. Margaret Sue Coward, June 14, 1959; children: Stephen Gregory, Michael Christopher. BA, Wayland Bapt. U., 1959; MA, Tex. Tech U., 1963, PhD, 1965. Cert. health edn. specialist. Instr. Tex. Tech U., Lubbock, 1965; asst. prof., dir. grad. studies in English So. Ill. U., Edwardsville, 1965-68; prof., dir. grad. studies in English Stephen F. Austin State U., Nacogdoches, Tex., 1968-79; dean grad. sch., dir. rsch. Ga. So. Coll., Statesboro, 1979-84; assoc. v.p. for rsch., dean grad. sch. Tex. Woman's U., Denton, 1984—. Mem. editorial bd. Papers on Lang. and Lit., 1967-71, Loss Grief and Care (jour.), 1986—; assoc. editor essays Illness, Crises and Loss; contbr. articles to profl. jours., chpts. to books. Cons. Ga. Endowment for Humanities, 1982-84; mem. budget com. United Way, Nacogdoches, 1975-76; mem. Ptnrs. of Ams., Statesboro, 1981-84; bd. dirs. Home Bound Services, Statesboro, 1982-84. Served with U.S. Army, 1959-61. Named Danforth Assoc. Stephen F. Austin State U., 1969-79; Nat. Def. Edn. Act fellow Office Edn., 1961-65. Mem. Coun. Soc. Grad. Schs. (pres. 1985-86), Coun. Grad. Schs. (bd. dirs.), Humanities and Tech. Assn. (v.p. 1984-87), Tex. Folklore Soc., Conf. Christianity and Lit., Hastings Ctr., Denton C. of C., Assn. for Advancement of Health Edn., Phi Kappa Phi (pres. Statesboro chpt. 1981-83, chmn. nat. investment com. 1983-89). Democrat. Presbyterian. Avocations: numismatics, antiques. Office: Tex Woman's U Grad Sch PO Box 22479 Denton TX 76204-0479

THOMPSON, LOHREN MATTHEW, oil company executive; b. Sutherland, Nebr., Jan. 21, 1926; s. John M. and Anna (Ecklund) T.; children: Terence M., Sheila M., Clark M. Ed., U. Denver. Spl. rep. Standard Oil Co., Omaha, 1948-56; sales mgr. Frontier REF. Co., 1956-67, v.p. mktg., 1967-68; mgr. mktg. U.S. region Husky Oil Co., Denver, 1968-72; v.p. Westar Stas., Inc., Denver, 1967-70; chmn. bd. Colo. Petroleum, Denver, 1971—. Served with USAAF, 1944-46. Mem. Colo. Petroleum Council, Am. Petroleum Inst., Am. Legion. Lutheran. Clubs: Denver Petroleum, Denver Oilman's, Lodge: Lions. Home: 2410 Spruce Ave Estes Park CO 80517-7146 Office: Colo Petroleum 4080 Globeville Rd Denver CO 80216-4906

THOMPSON, LOIS JEAN HEIDKE ORE, psychologist; b. Chgo., Feb. 22, 1933; d. Harold William and Ethel Rose (Neumann) Heidke; m. Henry Thomas Ore, Aug. 28, 1954 (div. May 1972); children: Christopher, Douglas; m. Joseph Lippard Thompson, Aug. 3, 1972; children: Scott, Les, Melanie. BA, Cornell Coll., Mt. Vernon, Iowa, 1955; MA, Idaho State U., 1964, EdD, 1981. Lic. psychologist, N.Mex. Tchr. pub. schs. various locations, 1956-67; tchr., instr. Idaho State U., Pocatello, 1967-72; employee/orgn. devel. specialist Los Alamos (N.Mex.) Nat. Lab., 1981-84, tng. specialist, 1984-89, sect. leader, 1989-93; pvt. practice indsl. psychology and healthcare, Los Alamos, 1988—; sec. Cornell Coll. Alumni Office, 1954-55, also other orgns.; bd. dirs. Parent Edn. Ctr., Idaho State U., 1980; counselor, Los Alamos, 1981-88. Editor newsletter LWV, Laramie, Wyo., 1957; contbr. articles to profl. jours. Pres. Newcomers Club, Pocatello, 1967, Faculty Womens Club, Pocatello, 1968; chmn. edn. com. AAUW, Pocatello, 1969. Mem. APA, ACA, N.Mex. Psychol. Assn. (bd. dirs. divsn. II 1990, sec. 1988-90, chmn. 1990), N.Mex. Soc. Adlerian Psychology (pres. 1990, treas. 1991-95, bd. dirs. 1996—), Soc. Indsl. and Orgn. Psychology, Assn. for Adult Devel. and Aging. Mem. LDS Ch. Avocations: racewalking, backpacking, skiing, tennis, biking. Home and Office: 340 Aragon Ave Los Alamos NM 87544-3505 *Honesty, dependability, spiritual imagination, and always doing our best are ingredients that lead to a successful and happy life.*

THOMPSON, LORING MOORE, retired college administrator, writer; b. Newton, Mass., Feb. 17, 1918; s. Henry E. and Ella (Gould) T.; m. Pearl E. Judiesch, Dec. 30, 1949; children—Bruce C., Douglas P. (dec.). B.S. in Indsl. Engring, Northeastern U., 1940; M.S., U. R.I., 1947; Ph.D., U. Chgo., 1956. Instr. U. R.I., 1946; asst. to pres. Assn. Colls. Upper N.Y., 1947-49; assoc. prof. U. Toledo, 1952-59, asst. dean acad. adminstrn., 1958-59; dir. univ. planning Northeastern U., Boston, 1959-63; dean adult programs Northeastern U., 1964-66, v.p. planning, 1967-80, emeritus, 1980—; faculty assoc. continuing edn. Ariz. State U., 1982-84; cons. in field. Author: (with others) Business Communication, 1949; contbr. (with others) articles to profl. publs. Bd. dirs. Back Bay Assn., Boston, 1961-63, v.p., 1963; trustee Huntington Gen. Hosp., Boston, 1970-80; mem. Fenway Project Area Com., 1973-76; mem. Mass. conf. ch. and edn. com. United Ch. of Christ, 1972-78, chairperson, 1973-74, mem. task force on ch. growth, 1978-80; mem. Chandler Area Coun., 1988-89; sec. Interfaith Coun. Greater Sun Lakes, 1993—. Lt. USNR, 1942-45. Mem. Spiritual Frontiers Fellowship, Tau Beta Pi. Home: 25408 S Sedona Dr Sun Lakes AZ 85248-6636

THOMPSON, LOUIS MILTON, agronomy educator, scientist; b. Throckmorton, Tex., May 15, 1914; s. Aubrey Lafayette and Lola Terry (Frazier) T.; m. Margaret Stromberg, July 10, 1937 (dec. Nov. 1972); children: Louis Milton, Margaret Ann, Glenda Ray (dec.), Carolyn Terry, Jerome Lafayette; m. Ruth Hiatt Phipps, July 7, 1990. BS, Tex. A&M U., 1935; MS, Iowa State U., 1947, PhD, 1950. Soil surveyor Tex., 1935-36, 39-

40; instr. Tex. A&M U., 1936-39, 40-42; asst. prof. soils Iowa State U., Ames, 1947-50; prof. soils, head farm operation curriculum Iowa State U., 1950-58, assoc. dean agr. charge resident instrn., 1958-83, emeritus prof. agronomy, 1983—, assoc. dean emeritus, 1984—. Author: Soils and Soil Fertility, rev. edit., 1957, co-author rev. edit., 1978, 83, 93, Russian edit., 1983; contbr. articles on weather-crop yield models and climate change to profl. jours. Elder Presbyn. Ch. With AUS, 1942-46; col. Res. (ret.). Recipient Henry A. Wallace award for Disting. Svc. to Agr., 1982, Faculty citation Iowa State U. Alumni Assn., 1990, Disting. Achievement citation, 1993, Alumni Recognition medal, 1996, Disting. Iowa Scientist award Iowa Acad. Sci., 1991, Agr. Innovator award Iowa State U. Agr. Alumni Soc., 1992, Friends of Agrl. award Iowa Dept. Agr. and Nat. Agrl. Mktg. Assn., 1993, Disting. Svc. to Iowa Agr. award Iowa Farm Bur., 1995. Fellow AAAS, Am. Soc. Agronomy, Soil Sci. Soc. Am., Soil and Water Conservation Soc. (pres.'s citation); mem. Am. Meterol. Soc., Farm House (hon.), Rotary (past local pres., Paul Harris fellow), Sigma Xi, Alpha Zeta (Tall Corn award 1957), Gamma Sigma Delta (nat. pres. 1956-58), Phi Kappa Phi (chpt. pres. 1961). Home: 414 Lynn Ave Ames IA 50014-7318 *To succeed in an academic community one must become an authority on a subject and be able to communicate it.*

THOMPSON, LYNN KATHRYN SINGER, educational director; b. Ames, Iowa, Nov. 30, 1947; d. William Andrew and Virginia Preston (Russell) Singer. BA, Cornell Coll., Mt. Vernon, Iowa, 1970; MA in Edn., Ariz. State U., 1980; EdD, No. Ariz. U., 1990. Cert. tchr. and adminstr., Ariz. Tchr. Crane Elem. Dist., Yuma, Ariz., 1970-81, 86-90; coord. fed. programs Crane Elem Dist., Yuma, Azri., 1981-83, asst. prin., 1983-85, dir. lang. acquisition and fed. programs, 1990—. Bd. dirs. Zonta Internat., Yuma, 1991, Yuma Fine Arts Assn., 1982-84; mem. Ariz. State Com. Practitioners, Phoenix, 1994—. Recipient Golden Bell award Ariz. Sch. Bds. Assn., 1992; Delta Kappa Gamma scholar, 1987, 89. Mem. PEO Internat., Delta Kappa Gamma (pres. 1988-90), Phi Delta Kappa (bd. dirs., rsch. chair 1991-95). Avocations: home restoration, camping, antiques, reading. Office: Crane Elem Dist 4250 W 16th St Yuma AZ 85364-4031

THOMPSON, MACK EUGENE, history educator; b. Burley, Idaho, Feb. 24, 1921; s. Eugene and Nora (McFate) T.; m. Helen Goldhamer, Oct. 30, 1945. A.B., Queen's Coll., CUNY, 1948; M.A., Brown U., 1951, Ph.D., 1955. Instr. history Brown U., 1954-55; asst. prof. Calif. Inst. Tech., 1955-56; asst. prof. U. Calif. at Riverside, 1956-62, asso. prof., 1962-66, prof., 1966-77; emeritus prof., 1977—; chmn. div. humanities U. Calif. at Riverside, 1961-63, asso. univ. dean acad. planning, 1965-66, dean, div. undergrad. studies, 1971-74; exec dir. Am. Hist. Assn., Washington, 1974-81; Chmn. editorial bd. Experiment and Innovation: New Directions in Edn., U. Calif., 1966-68. Author: The Ward-Hopkins Controversy and the American Revolution in Rhode Island: An Interpretation, 1959, Moses Brown, Reluctant Reformer, 1962, Causes and Circumstances of the Du Pont Family's Emigration, 1969. Bd. dirs. Harry S. Truman Libr. Inst., 1974-81. With AUS, 1942-45. Home: 1378 River Oaks Ct Oldsmar FL 34677

THOMPSON, MARCIA SLONE, choral director, educator; b. Ary, Ky., June 30, 1959; d. Ray and Wevena (Hall) Slone; m. Randall C. Thompson, Sept. 22, 1979; children: Tiffany, Ashley, Brittany, Alicia, Jessica, Matthew. B in Music Edn., Pikeville Coll., 1981; M in Secondary Edn., Morehead State U., 1985. Cert. Rank I supervision, music edn. tchr. with endorsement, grades K-12. Guitarist Slone Family Band, 1970-77; pvt. practice Hindman, Ky., 1977-93; band, choral dir. Pike County Bd. Edn., Pikeville, Ky., 1981-82, Floyd County Bd. Edn., Eastern, Ky., 1982-87; choral dir. Knott County Bd. Edn., Hindman, 1987—, Knott County Central High, Hindman, Ky, 1987—; piano instr. guitar instr., Upward Bound program Pikeville Coll., Hindman, 1977. Albums include Appalachian Bluegrass, 1972, Ramblin' Round with Slone Family, 1977; appeared on the Grand Ole Opry, 1976. Band conductor jr. high divsn. Pike County All-County Festival, Pikeville, 1981; music chair Red White Blue Festival, Martin, Ky., 1982; music judge Floyd County All-County Band, Prestonsburg, Ky., 1982-87; band dir. Ky. Derby Festival Parade, Louisville, 1985; piano accompanist choir 1st Bapt. Ch., Hindman, 1990-91, nursery asst., 1990-93, dir. youth choir, 1992, choral dir. music makers (children's music), 1994, Bapt. young women's hospitality officer, 1995, mem. sch. com.; performer Senator Benny Bailey Salute, Prestonsburg, 1991, Gingerbread Festival, Hindman, 1992-95; active Bapt. Young Women, 1993-95; co-founder Knott County Fine Arts Day Celebration, 1992—, hospitality officer Hindman Baptist Ch. Young Women's Group, 1995. Mem. Nat. Educators Assn., Am. Choral Dirs. Assn., Ky. Educators Assn., Ky. Music Educators. Democrat. Avocations: arranging music, playing piano, guitar, skating, reading. Home: PO Box 15 Hindman KY 41822-0015 Office: Knott County Ctrl High Sch Hindman KY 41822

THOMPSON, MARGARET M., physical education educator; b. nr. Falls Church, Va., Aug. 1, 1921; d. Lesley L. and Madeline (Shawen) T. B.S., Mary Washington Coll., 1941; M.A., George Washington U., 1947; Ph.D., U. Iowa, 1961. Tchr., supr. phys. edn. Staunton (Va.) City Schs., 1941-44; tchr. jr. high sch. phys. edn. Arlington County, Va., 1944-47; instr. women's phys. edn. Fla. State U., Tallahassee, 1947-51; instr., asst. prof., assoc. prof. phys. edn. Purdue U., Lafayette, Ind., 1951-65; dir. gross motor therapy lab. Purdue U., 1963-65; assoc. prof. phys. edn. U. Mo., Columbia, 1965-68; prof. U. Mo., 1968-71, dir. Cinematography and Motor Learning Lab. Dept. Health and Phys. Edn., 1965-71; prof. phys. edn. U. Ill., Champaign-Urbana, 1971-87, prof. emeritus, 1987—. Author: (with Barbara B. Godfrey) Movement Pattern Checklists, 1966, (with Chappelle Arnett) Perceptual Motor and Motor Test Battery for Children, 1968, (with Barbara Mann) An Holistic Approach to Physical Education Curriculum: Objectives Classification System for Elementary Schools, 1977, Gross Motor Inventory, 1976, revised edit., 1980, Developing the Curriculum, 1980, Setting the Learning Environment, 1980, Sex Stereotyping and Human Development, 1980; also film strips, articles. Mem. AAHPER, Internat. Assn. Phys. Edn. and Sports for Coll. Girls and Women. Home: 1311 Wildwood Ln Mahomet IL 61853-9770 Office: U Ill Freer Gymnasium Dept Kinesiology 906 S Goodwin Ave Urbana IL 61801-3816

THOMPSON, MARK LEE, art educator, sculptor; b. Ft. Sill, Okla., 1950; s. James B. and Beverly J. T. Student, Va. Polytech Inst., 1968-70; BA in Art, U. Calif., Berkeley, 1972, MA in Sculpture, 1973. Lectr. conceptual design San Francisco State U., 1988-89, lectr. sculpture, 1991-93; adj. prof. sculpture Calif. Coll. Arts and Crafts, 1993—; vis. lectr. U. Coll. London, 1990; grad. workshop San Francisco State U., 1992, U. Colo., Boulder, 1994, Chgo. Sch. Art Inst. Chgo., 1995, Stanford U., 1995, So. Ill. U., Carbondale, 1995; presenter in field. Exhibits include Va. Polytech. Inst., blacksburg, 1969, U. Calif., Berkeley, 1973, San Francisco Civic Ctr. Plz., 1975, Headlands Ctr. for Arts, Fort Barry, Calif., 1987, Palo Alto (Calif.) Cultural Ctr., 1990, Whitechapel Art Gallery, London, 1990, Hartnell Coll., Salinas, Calif., 1993, M.H. de Young Meml. Mus., San Francisco, 1995, others; contbr. articles to profl. jours. Office: Calif Coll Arts & Crafts 5212 Broadway Oakland CA 94618-1487

THOMPSON, MARTIN CHRISTIAN, news service executive; b. Council Bluffs, Iowa, Oct. 25, 1938; s. Ross Kenneth and Mary Ellen (Pierce) T.; m. Janet Ann Morrow, Aug. 4, 1962; children: Chris Michael, Sean Martin. B.A. in Communications, U. Wash., 1960. Newsman Sta. KEDO, Longview, Wash., 1960-61; news dir. Sta. KREW, Sunnyside, Wash., 1961-66; newsman AP, Seattle, 1966-68; corr. AP, Reno, Nev., 1968-70; newsman AP, San Francisco, 1970-72; news editor AP, 1972-75; chief of bur. AP, San Francisco, 1975-86, Los Angeles, 1986-88; mng. editor AP, N.Y.C., 1989-92, dir. state news, 1992—. Mem. Beta Rho Tau, Sigma Delta Chi. Methodist. Office: 50 Rockefeller Plz New York NY 10020-1605

THOMPSON, MARY KOLETA, sculptor, non-profit organization director; b. Portsmouth, Va., Dec. 27, 1938; m. James Burton Thompson, May 5, 1957; children: Burt, Suzan, Kate, Jon. BFA, U. Tex., 1982; postgrad., Boston U. Cert. fund raising exec. Pres. The Planning Resource People, Austin, Tex., 1990—; Tex. fin. devel. specialist ARC Tex., 1994—; devel. dir. Very Spl. Arts Tex., 1991-92; dir. devel. ARC, Austin, 1992-94; dir. Tex. Children's Mus., Fredericksburg, 1987-88, Internat. Hdqrs. SHAPE Command Arts and Crafts Ctr., 1985-86; com. chmn. Symposium for Encouragement Women in Math. and Natural Sci., U. Tex., Austin, 1990. Sculptor portrait busts. Bd. dirs. Teenage Parent Coun., Austin, 1990-92. Named U.S. Vol. of Yr., Belgium, 1986; grantee NEA, 1988. Mem. AAUW (life, pres. 1990-92), Women in Comm. (co-chmn. S.W. regional conf.), U. Tex. Ex-Student Assn. (life), Tex. Hist. Found. (life), Leadership Tex. (life), Leadership Tex. Alumnae Assn. (bd. dirs.), Raleigh Tavern Soc. (founder), Austin Antiques Forum (founder). Avocations: writing, lecturing, meeting and strategic planning. Office: San Antonio Area Chpt ARC 3642 E Houston St San Antonio TX 78219-3818

THOMPSON, MICHAEL F., food service executive; b. 1948. Grad., John Carroll U., 1970. Ski instr. N.Y., Calif., 1970-75; ops. control mgr. racetrack divsn. Del. North Cos. Inc., 1975-78; pvt. cons., 1978-80; with Sportservice Corp., Buffalo, 1980—, pres., 1984—. Office: Sportservice Corp 438 Main St Buffalo NY 14202-3207*

THOMPSON, MORLEY PUNSHON, textile company executive; b. San Francisco, Jan. 2, 1927; s. Morley Punshon and Ruth (Wetmore) T.; m. Patricia Ann Smith, Jan. 31, 1953 (dec.); children: Page Elizabeth Tredennick, Morley Punshon. A.B., Stanford U., 1948; M.B.A., Harvard U., 1950; J.D., Chase Law Sch., 1969; LL.D., Xavier U., 1981. CPA, Ohio. Chmn. Stearns Tech. Textiles Co., Cin., 1985—, Stearns Can., Inc., Cin., 1985—. Bd. dirs. Cin. Inst. Fine Arts. Lt. Supply Corps USNR, 1952-54. Mem. Beta Theta Pi. Office: 100 Williams St Cincinnati OH 45215-4602

THOMPSON, M(ORRIS) LEE, lawyer; b. Hutchinson, Kans., Nov. 29, 1946; s. Morris J. and Ruth W. (Smith) T.; m. M. Susan Morgan, May 26, 1974; children: Deborah, Erin, Andrew, Christopher. BA, Wichita State U., 1968; MA, Emporia State U., 1970; JD, George Washington U., 1974. Bar: Kans., 1974, U.S. Dist. Ct. Kans., 1974, U.S. Ct. Appeals (10th cir.) 1976, U.S. Supreme Ct., 1978. Instr., lectr. Emporia (Kans.) State U., 1969-70; lctr. in speech George Washington U., Washington, 1970-71; asst. to Senator James Pearson Washington, 1971-75; assoc. Martin, Pringle, et al., Wichita, Kans., 1976-78, ptnr., 1979-89; U.S. atty. for dist. of Kans., Dept. Justice, Wichita, 1990-93; mng. ptnr. Triplett, Woolf & Garretson, Wichita, 1993—. Treas. Kansans for Kassebaum, Wichita, 1978-88; mem. Kans. State Rep. Cen. Com., Topeka, 1978-79, 88-90; candidate U.S. Ho. of Reps., Kans., 1988; chmn. civil issues subcom. Atty. Gen.'s Adv. Com. of U.S. Attys., 1992-93. Mem. Kans. Bar Assn. (pres. criminal law sect. 1994-95). Methodist. Office: Triplett Woolf & Garretson 151 N Main St Ste 800 Wichita KS 67202-1409

THOMPSON, MOZELLE WILLMONT, lawyer, federal agency administrator; b. Pitts., Dec. 11, 1954; s. Charles and Eiko (Suzaki) T. AB, Columbia U., 1976; M in Pub. Affairs, Princeton U., 1980; JD, Columbia U., 1981. Bar: N.Y. 1984, D.C. 1984, U.S. Dist. Ct. (ea. dist.) Mich. 1984, U.S. Dist. Ct. (so. and ea. dists.) N.Y. 1985, U.S. Ct. Appeals (11th cir.) 1986. Clk. to presiding judge U.S. Dist. Ct. (so. dist.) Fla., Miami, 1981-82; assoc. Skadden, Arps, Slate, Meagher & Flom, N.Y.C., 1982-90; spl. counsel to supr. Town of Babylon, N.Y., 1988-90; counsel and sec. N.Y. State Housing Fin. Agy., N.Y.C.; counsel, sec. N.Y. State Med. Care Facilities Fin. Agy., N.Y. State Affordable Housing Corp., N.Y. State Mcpl. Bond Bank Agy., N.Y. State Project Fin. Agy., N.Y.C., 1990-93; sr. v.p., gen. coun. N.Y. State Mortgage Agy., N.Y.C., 1993; dep. asst. sec. for govt. fin. policy Dept. of Treasury, Washington, 1993-96; prin. dep. asst. sec. for govt. fin. policy Dept. Treasury, Washington, 1996—; gen. counsel North Amityville Cmty. Econ. Coun., Inc., 1989-90; pres. Greenwich Corp., 1987-93; adj. assoc. prof. Bklyn. Law Sch., 1986-91, Fordham U. Law Sch., 1992—; mem. adv. bd. Udall Ctr., U. Ariz., Tucson, 1994—. Mem. exec. bd. Practicing Attys. for Law Students, N.Y.C., 1986-93. Mem. ABA (coms. litigation, tort and ins. practice 1984—), Nat. Coun. State Housing Agys. (co-chair legal affairs com., disclosure task force, 1991-93), Nat. Coun. Health Care Facilities Fin. Authorities (co-chair advocacy and strategic planning coms., 1991-93) N.Y. State Bar Assn., N.Y. County Lawyers Assn. (com. on fed. cts. 1984-86), D.C. Bar Assn., Assn. of Bar of City of N.Y., Assn. Princeton Grad. Alumni, Assn. Black Princeton Alumni, Columbia Law Sch. Alumni Assn., Columbia Coll. Alumni Assn., Columbia Black and Latino Alumni Assn., Columbia Coll. Class 1976 (pres. 1986—). Avocations: music, theater arts, architecture. Home: 107 6th St NE Washington DC 20002-6243 Office: Dept of Treasury 1500 Pennsylvania Ave NW Washington DC 20005-1007

THOMPSON, MYRON H., federal judge; b. 1947. BA, Yale U., 1969, JD, 1972. Asst. atty. gen. State of Ala., 1972-74; sole practice Montgomery, Ala., 1974-79; ptnr. Thompson & Faulk, Montgomery, 1979-80; judge U.S. Dist. Ct. (mid. dist.) Ala., Montgomery, 1980—, chief judge, 1991—. Mem. ABA, Ala. Bar Assn., Nat. Bar Assn., Ala. Lawyers Assn. Office: US Dist Ct PO Box 235 Montgomery AL 36101-0235*

THOMPSON, NANCY JO, special education educator, elementary education educator, consultant; b. Crawfordsville, Ind., Apr. 17, 1950. BE, Manchester Coll., 1971; MEd, Ind. U., South Bend, 1978. Cert. elem. tchr., tchr. emotionally disturbed K-12, Ind. Tchr. 6th grade Boone County Sch. Corp., Dover, Ind., 1971-72; lead tchr. N. Manchester (Ind.) Day Care Ctr., 1972-73; processor H & R Block, Elkhart, Ind., 1973; dept. head, sales Grinnell's Music Store, Elkhart, Ind., 1974-75; administrv. asst. Oaklawn Psychiat. Ctr., Elkhart, 1975-76; tchr. emotionally handicapped Treehouse-Day Treatment Program Oaklawn Psychiat., Elkhart, 1976-78; tchr. emotionally handicapped Elkhart Community Schs., 1978-85, resource team cons., 1985-94; tchr. diagnostic class EH Diagnostic Day Sch., Elkhart, 1994—; state trainer Ind. Dept. Edn., Indpls., 1987-89; bd. dirs. Loveway, Inc., Therapeutic Horseback Riding. Treas. Hively Ave. Nursery Sch., Elkhart, 1974; band mem. Elkhart Mcpl. Band, 1974-77; youth adv. Hively Ave. Mennonite Ch., Elkhart, 1980-84. Mem. NEA, Coun. Exceptional Children (cert. excellence profl. standards, practices Tri-County Coun. 1984), Coun. Children with Behavioral Disorders, Nat. Coun. Autistic Citizens, Ind. State Tchrs. Assn. Avocations: traveling, music, theater, handi-crafts, cross-country skiing. Office: Elkhart Community Schools Eastwood Elem Sch Dept Diagnostic 53215 (R5) CR 15 N Elkhart IN 46514

THOMPSON, NEAL PHILIP, food science and nutrition educator; b. Bklyn., July 18, 1936; s. Thomas I. and Ellenor (Backie) T.; m. Beverly Ethel Godshall, Oct. 4, 1958; children: Erick, Victor, Clifford, Karen, Stuart. BS, Wheaton Coll., 1957; MA, Miami U., 1962; PhD, Princeton U., 1965. From asst. to assoc. prof. U. Fla., Gainesville, 1965-76, prof., 1976, asst. dean, 1980-86, assoc. dean, 1986-93. Capt. USNR, ret. Home: 727 SW 27th St Gainesville FL 32607-3137 Office: U Fla Inst Food & Agrl Scis Food & Environ Toxicology Gainesville FL 32611-0720

THOMPSON, N(ORMAN) DAVID, insurance company executive; b. Rockville Centre, N.Y., July 30, 1934; s. Norman J. and Laurel H. (Johnson) T.; m. Joyce L. Angeletti, June 7, 1958; children: John L., Jennifer L., Sarah S. BA with distinction, Wesleyan U., 1956; LLB, Columbia U., 1959; postgrad., Harvard U., 1973. Bar: N.Y. Pvt. practice law N.Y.C., 1961-62; corp. sec. Gen. Reins. Corp., N.Y.C., 1964-69; v.p. Gen. Reins. Corp., Greenwich, Conn., 1969; v.p., gen. counsel, sec. Gen. Reins. Corp., 1976-77; exec. v.p. N.Am. Reins. Corp., N.Y.C., 1977-78; pres. N.Am. Reins. Corp., 1978-92; chmn., CEO Swiss Reins. Am. Corp. (formerly N.Am. Reins.), 1992-95, Swiss Re Am. Holding Corp. (formerly SwissRe Holding Co.), 1992—; chmn. SwissRe Group Cos. (U.S.), 1992-95. Dir. Nat. Legal Ctr. for Pub. Interest, chmn., 1992-95; trustee Coll. Ins., 1992. With U.S. Army, 1959-60. Mem. Reins Assn. Am. (chmn. 1982-83), Nat. Assn. Casualty and Surety Execs. (pres. 1986-87), Am. Arbitration Assn. (bd. dirs., chmn. fin. com. 1992-93), Am. Inst. Property and Casualty Underwriters (trustee), Univ. Club (N.Y.C.), Saugatuck Harbor Yacht Club (Westport, Conn.). Home: 47 Kettle Creek Rd Weston CT 06883-2208

THOMPSON, NORMAN WINSLOW, surgeon, educator; b. Boston, July 12, 1932; s. Herman Chandler and Evelyn Millicent (Palmer) T.; m. Marcia Ann Veldman, June 12, 1956; children: Robert, Karen, Susan, Jennifer. BA, Hope Coll., 1953; MD, U. Mich., 1957; MD (hon.), U. Linköping, Sweden, 1995. Diplomate Am. Bd. Surgery. Intern U. Mich., Ann Arbor, 1957-58, resident in surgery, 1959-62, instr., 1962-64, asst. prof., 1964-66, assoc. prof., 1966-71, prof. surgery, 1971-79, Henry King Ranson prof. surgery, 1979—, chief endocrine surg. svc., 1979—. Contbr. articles to profl. jours. Trustee Hope Coll., Holland, Mich., 1973-88. Mem. ACS (gov. 1979-85), Ctrl. Surg. Assn., Western Surg. Assn. (1st v.p. 1992-93, pres. 1994-95), F.A. Coller Surg. Soc. (pres. 1986), Am. Surg. Assn., Am. Thyroid Assn., Soc. Surg. Alimentary Tract, Internat. Assn. Endocrine Surgeons (pres. 1989-91), Internat. Soc. Surgeons (v.p. 1995—), Am. Assn. Endocrine Surgeons (pres. 1980-81, 81-82), Royal Soc. Medicine, Brit. Assn. Endocrine Surgeons, Assn. French Endocrine Surgeons, Scandanvian Surg. Soc., Alpha Omega Alpha. Home: 465 Hillspur Rd Ann Arbor MI 48105-1048 Office: U Mich Med Ctr 2920 Taubman Bldg Ann Arbor MI 48109

THOMPSON, OTIS NATHANIEL, JR., professional society executive; b. Balt., Aug. 28, 1923; s. Otis Nathaniel and Mary Willie (Holman) T.; m. Lorraine Cornelia Jones, Mar. 14, 1959; children: Bruce Campbell, Kimberly Ann. B of Journalism, Lincoln U., 1950. Asst. city editor St. Louis Argus Newspaper, 1950-55; pub. rels. assoc. Moss H. Kendrix Orgn., Washington, 1955-61; reporter Assoc. Corr. News Svc., Washington, 1961-63; info. specialist USDA, Washington, 1963-74, chief, 1974-87; exec. dir. Orgn. Profl. Employment USDA, Washington, 1989—. Pres. D.C. chpt. Lincoln U. Alumni Assn., Washington. 1989-92, Whitfield Civic Assn., Lanham, Md., 1966-72. Sgt. U.S. Army Corps Engrs., 1943-46. Methodist. Avocation: collecting historical data on African Am. achievements. Office: OPEDA PO Box 381 Washington DC 20044-0381

THOMPSON, PAUL HAROLD, university president; b. Ogden, Utah, Nov. 28, 1938; s. Harold Merwin and Elda (Skeen) T.; m. Carolyn Lee Nelson, Mar. 9, 1961; children: Loralyn, Kristyn, Shannyn, Robbyn, Daylyn, Nathan. BS, U. Utah, 1964; MBA, Harvard U., 1966, D Bus. Adminstrn., 1969. Rsch. assoc. Harvard U., Cambridge, Mass., 1966-69; asst. prof. Harvard U., Cambridge, 1969-73; assoc. prof. bus. Brigham Young U., Provo, Utah, 1973-78, prof., 1978-84, asst. dean, 1978-81, dean, 1984-89, v.p., 1989-90; pres. Weber State U., Ogden, Utah, 1990—; cons. Goodyear, Hughes Aircraft, Portland GE, Esso Resources Ltd., GE. Co-author: Organization and People: Readings, Cases, and Exercises in Organizational Behavior, 1976, Novations: Strategies for Career Management, 1986; also articles. Named Outstanding Prof. of Yr., Brigham Young U., 1981; Baker scholar Harvard U., 1966. Mem. Am. Assn. State Colls. and Univs. (com. 1991—), Ogden C. of C. (exec. com. 1990—), Rotary (prograam com. Ogden 1991—, Harris fellow 1992—), Phi Beta Kappa. Office: Weber State U 3750 Harrison Blvd Ogden UT 84408-0001

THOMPSON, PAUL MICHAEL, lawyer; b. Dubuque, Iowa, Aug. 30, 1935; s. Frank W. and Genevieve (Cassutt) T.; m. Mary Jacqueline McManus, Jan. 30, 1960; children—Anne, Tricia, Paul, Tim, Jim. B.A. magna cum laude, Loras Coll., 1957; LL.B., Georgetown U., 1959. Bar: Iowa 1959, D.C. 1959, Va. 1966. Atty. appellate ct. br. NLRB, Washington, 1962-66; assoc. Hunton & Williams, Richmond, Va., 1966-71, ptnr., 1971—; adj. prof. The T.C. Williams Sch. Law, U. Richmond. Served with JAGC, USAF, 1960-62. Mem. ABA, Va. State Bar, Va. Bar Assn., Internat. Bar Assn. Roman Catholic. Club: Downtown (Richmond). Office: Hunton & Williams 951 E Byrd St Riverfront Pla E Tower Richmond VA 23219-4074

THOMPSON, PETER L. H., golf course architect; b. Modesto, Calif., Apr. 26, 1939. BS in East Asian Studies, U. Oreg., 1962, B in Landscape Architecture, 1971, M in Urban Planning, 1971; postgrad., U. Calif., Berkeley, 1975, Nat. U. Registered landscape arch., Calif., Oreg., Wash., Nev. With Oreg. Planning Commn., Lane County, 1965-70; commr. Oreg. Planning Commn., Eugene, 1981-83; sr. assoc. Ruff, Cameron, Lacoss, Eugene, Oreg., 1971-75; prin. Peter L. H. Thompson & Assocs., Eugene, 1975-83, John H. Midby & Assocs., Las Vegas, 1983-86, Thompson-Wihlborg, Ltd., Corte Madera, Calif., 1982-89, Thompson Planning Group, Ltd., San Rafael, Calif., 1989—; with Oreg. Planning Commn., commr., 1981-83, Novato, Calif. Planning Commn., commr. 1989-93, pres. 1989-93; spkr. Oreg. Home Builders Conf., 1980, Pacific Coast Builders Conf., 1984, Tacoma Country Club Pro-Pres. Tournament, 1991, Madrona Links Men's Golf Club, 1991, Twin Lakes Country Club Pro-Pres. Tournament, 1992, Golf Expo, Palm Springs, Calif., 1993, 95, Golf Expo, Nashville, 1993, Golf Expo, Monterey, Calif., 1994, others. Contbr. articles to mags. Mem. citizen's adv. bd. City of Eugene, Oreg., City of Las Vegas. Mem. USGA, Am. Soc. Landscape Archs., Am. Assn. Planners, Nat. Golf Found., Urban Land Inst., Rotary Internat. Office: Thompson Planning Gp Ltd 2175 Francisco Blvd E Ste A San Rafael CA 94901-5524

THOMPSON, RALPH GORDON, federal judge; b. Oklahoma City, Dec. 15, 1934; s. Lee Bennett and Elaine (Bizzell) T.; m. Barbara Irene Hencke, Sept. 5, 1964; children: Lisa, Elaine, Maria. BBA, U. Okla., 1956, JD, 1961. Bar: Okla. 1961. Ptnr. Thompson, Thompson, Harbour & Selph (and predecessors), Oklahoma City, 1961-75; judge U.S. Dist. Ct. for Western Dist. Okla., Oklahoma City, 1975—; chief judge U.S. Dist. Ct. (we. dist.) Okla., 1986-93; mem. Okla. Ho. of Reps., 1966-70, asst. minority floor leader, 1969-70; spl. justice Supreme Ct. Okla., 1970-71; tchr. Harvard Law Sch. Trial Advocacy Workshop, 1981—; apptd. by chief justice of U.S. to U.S. Fgn. Intelligence Surveillance Ct., 1990—. Rep. nominee for lt. gov., Okla., 1970; chmn. bd. ARC, Oklahoma City, 1970-72; chmn., pres. Okla. Young Lawyers Conf., 1965; mem. bd. visitors U. Okla., 1975-78; pres. bd. dirs. St. John's Episcopal Sch., Oklahoma City. Lt. USAF, 1957-60, col. Res., ret. Decorated Legion of Merit; named Oklahoma City's Outstanding Young Man, Oklahoma City Jaycees, 1967, Outstanding Fed. Trial Judge, Okla Trial Lawyers Assn., 1980; recipient Regents Alumni award U. Okla., 1990, Disting. Svc. award, 1993; inducted Okla. Hall of Fame, 1995. Fellow Am. Bar Found.; mem. ABA, Fed. Bar Assn., Okla. Bar Assn. (chmn. sect. internat. law and gen. practice 1974-75), Oklahoma County Bar Assn. (Jud. Svc. award 1988), Jud. Conf. U.S. (com. on ct. adminstrn. 1981-89, com. on fed.-state jurisdiction 1988-91), U.S. Dist. Judges Assn. 105h Cir. (pres. 1992-94), Rotary (hon.), Order of Coif, Am. Inns of Ct. (pres. XXIII 1995-96, Pres. 1990-96), Phi Beta Kappa (pres. chpt. 1985-86, Phi Beta Kappa of Yr. 1991), Beta Theta Pi, Phi Alpha Delta. Episcopalian. Office: US Dist Ct 200 NW 4th St Oklahoma City OK 73102-3003

THOMPSON, RALPH NEWELL, former chemical corporation executive; b. Boston, Mar. 4, 1918; s. Ralph and Lillian May (Davenport) T.; m. Virginia Kenniston, Jan. 31, 1942; children: Pamela, Nicholas, Diana. B.S., MIT, 1940. Research engr. Middlesex Products Co., Cambridge, Mass., 1940-42; tech. dir. Falulah Paper Co., Fitchburg, Mass., 1945-48; staff engr. to v.p., div. gen. mgr. Calgon Corp., Pitts., 1948-70; v.p. mktg., corp. devel. Pa. Indsl. Chem. Corp., Clairton, 1970-74; gen. mgr. chem. div. Thiokol Corp., Trenton, N.J., 1974-76; group v.p.-chem. Thiokol Corp., Newtown, Pa., 1976-82; marine artist, specializing in lighthouses and historic sailing vessels, 1982—; dir. Mulford Co. Inc., Mass., 1956-82, Thiokol Can. Ltd., 1975-82, Thiokol Chems., Ltd., Eng., 1976-82, Toray Thiokol Co. Ltd., Japan, 1976-82, Nisso-Ventron K.K., Japan, 1977-82, S.W. Chem. Services Inc., Tex., 1978-82, S.W. Plastics Europe (S.A.), Belgium, 1978-82, Dynachem. Corp., Calif., 1979-82, Carstab Corp., Ohio, 1980-82. Patentee in field. Mem. Mt. Lebanon (Pa.) Civic League, 1950-74. Served with USNR, 1942-45. Recipient Goodreau Meml. Fund medal in chemistry, 1936. Fellow Am. Inst. Chemists; mem. TAPPI (contributor monograph series 1950-65), N.Y. Acad. Scis., Soc. Chem. Industry, Nat. Maritime Soc., Am. Soc. Marine Artists, Mil. Order World Wars, Pa. Soc., Soc. Descs. Colonial Clergy. Republican. Presbyterian.

THOMPSON, RAYMOND HARRIS, anthropologist, educator; b. Portland, Me., May 10, 1924; s. Raymond and Eloise (MacIntyre) T.; m. Molly Kendall, Sept. 9, 1948; children: Margaret Kelsey Luchetta, Mary Frances. B.S., Tufts U., 1947, A.M., Harvard U., 1950, Ph.D., 1955. Fellow div. hist. research Carnegie Instn., Washington, 1950-52; asst. prof. anthropology, curator Mus. Anthropology, U. Ky., 1952-56; faculty U. Ariz., 1956—, prof. anthropology, 1964—, Riecker Disting. prof., 1980—, head dept., 1964-80; dir. Ariz. State Mus., from 1964; mem. adv. panel program in anthropology NSF, 1963-64, mem. mus. collections program, 1983-85; mem. NSF grad. fellowship panel Nat. Acad. Scis.-NRC, 1964-66; mem. research in nursing in patient care rev. com. USPHS, 1967-69; com. on social sci. commn. edn. in agr. and natural resources Nat. Acad. Scis., 1968-69; mem. anthropology com. examiners Grad. Record Exam., 1967-70, chmn., 1969-70; mem. com. recovery archaeol. remains, 1972-77, chmn., 1973-77; collaborator Nat. Park Service, 1972-76; mem. Ariz. Hist. Adv. Commn., 1966—, chmn., 1971-74, chmn. hist. sites rev. com., 1971-83; chmn. Ariz. Humanities Council, 1973-77, mem., 1979-85; adv. bd. Ariz. Hist. Recors, 1976-84; mem. research review panel for archaeology NEH, 1976-77, mem. rev. panel for museums, 1978, Ariz. Archaeology Adv. Commn., 1985—; cons. task force on archaeology Adv. Council on Historic Preservation, 1978. Author: Modern Yucatecan Maya Pottery Making,

1958; editor: Migrations in New World Culture History, 1958, When is a Kiva, 1990; mem. editl. bd. Science, 1972-77. Trustee Mus. No. Ariz., 1969—; bd. dirs. Tucson Art Mus., 1974-77; cons. Nat. Mus. Act Coun., 1984-86. Served with USNR, 1944-45, PTO. Recipient Pub. Svc. award Dept. Interior, 1990. Fellow AAAS (chmn. sect. H 1977-78), Tree-Ring Soc., Am. Anthrop. Assn. (Disting. Svc. award 1980); mem. Soc. Am. Archaeology (editor 1958-62, exec. com. 1963-64, pres. 1976-77), Am. Soc. Conservation Archaeology (Conservation award 1980), Seminario de Cultura Maya, Am. Assn. Museums (accreditation vis. com. 1972, 82-90, cons. mus. assessment program 1983-89, repatriation task force 1987, steering com. mus. data collection program 1988-93), Internat. Coun. Museums (assoc.), Coun. Mus. Anthropology (dir. 1978-79, pres. 1980-83), Assn. Sci. Mus. Dirs. (sec.-treas. 1978—), Ariz. Acad. Sci., Ariz. Archaeol. and Hist. Soc. (Byron Cummings award 1993), Mus. Assn. Ariz. (pres. 1983, 84), Phi Beta Kappa, Sigma Xi. Office: Univ Ariz Ariz State Museum Tucson AZ 85721

THOMPSON, RENOLD DURANT, mining and shipping executive; b. Cleve., July 28, 1926; s. James Renold and Gertrude Goldie (Meyers) T.; m. Shirley Ann Sprague, June 24, 1949; children: Renold Durant, Jr., Bradley Sprague, Patricia Sprague Hickey. B.A., Dartmouth Coll., 1946; B.S., Case Inst. Tech., 1948. Metallurgist, U.S. Steel Corp., Cleve. and Duluth, Minn., 1948-52; with Oglebay Norton Co., Cleve., 1952—; sr. v.p. Oglebay Norton Co., 1972-73, exec. v.p. ops., 1973-81, exec. v.p., 1981-82, pres., chief exec. officer, 1982-92, vice chmn., 1992—, also dir.; bd. dirs. 1st Union Mgmt., Inc.; chmn., CEO Work in N.E. Ohio Coun. Mem. Pepper Pike Club, Chagrin Valley Hunt Club, Union Club. Office: Oglebay Norton Co 1100 Superior Ave E Ste 2000 Cleveland OH 44114-2518

THOMPSON, RICHARD FREDERICK, psychologist, neuroscientist, educator; b. Portland, Oreg., 1930; s. Frederick Albert and Margaret St. Clair (Marr) T.; m. Judith K. Pedersen, May 22, 1960; children: Kathryn M., Elizabeth K., Virginia St. C. B.A., Reed Coll., 1952; M.S., U. Wis., 1953, Ph.D., 1956. Asst. prof. med. psychology Med. Sch. U. Oreg., Portland, 1959-63, assoc. prof., 1963-65, prof., 1965-67; prof. psychobiology U. Calif., Irvine, 1967-73, 75-80; prof. psychology Harvard U., Cambridge, Mass., 1973-74; Lashley chair prof. Harvard U., Cambridge, 1973; prof. psychology, Bing prof. human biology Stanford U., Palo Alto, Calif., 1980-87; Keck prof. psychology and biol. scis. U. So. Calif., L.A., 1987—, dir. neuroscience program, 1989—. Author: Foundations of Physiological Psychology, 1967, (with others) Psychology, 1971, Introduction to Physiological Psychology, 1975; Psychology editor (with others), W.H. Freeman & Co. publs., chief editor, Behavioral Neurosci., 1983—; editor: Jour. Comparative and Physiol. Psychology, 1981-83; regional editor: (with others) Physiology and Behavior; contbr. (with others) articles to profl. jours. Fellow AAAS, APA (Disting. Sci. Contbn. award 1974, governing coun. 1974—), Soc. Neurosci. (councilor 1972-76); mem. NAS, Am. Acad. Arts and Scis., Internat. Brain Rsch. Orgn., Psychonomic Soc. (gov. 1972-77, chmn. 1976), Am. Psychol. Soc. (pres. 1994-96), Western Psychol. Assn. (pres. 1994-95), Soc. Exptl. Psychology (Warren medal). Office: Univ of So Calif Neuroscis Program HNB 122 Univ Park Los Angeles CA 90007

THOMPSON, RICHARD LEON, pharmaceutical company executive, lawyer; b. Rochester, N.Y., Dec. 5, 1944; s. Leslie L. and Marion (Cosad) T.; m. Catherine Jean Terry, July 6, 1974; children: Kristin Anne, Catherine Elizabeth. AB cum laude, SUNY, Albany, 1966; MA, Syracuse U., 1967; JD, Cath. U., 1975. Staff dir., counsel U.S. Ho. of Reps., Washington, 1973-78; dir. Abbott Labs., Washington, 1978-83; v.p. Squibb Corp., Washington, 1983-89, Bristol-Myers Squibb Corp., Washington, 1989—; chmn. legis. adv. com. Proprietary Assn., Washington, 1984; bd. dirs. Bus. Govt. Rels. Coun. Mem. com. on changing enrollments Fairfax (Va.) County Pub. Sch., 1983-84, supts. adv. com., 1984-85, mem., 1988—; mem. Fed. City Coun., 1992; chmn. legis. com. P.R.-U.S.A. Found., 1985—; co-chair edn. in 2010; bd. dirs. D.C. Hospice, Bryce Harlow Found., 1990-95. 1st lt. U.S. Army, 1968-69, Vietnam. Named one of Outstanding Young Men of Am., Jaycees, 1976. Mem. ABA, D.C. Bar Assn., Pharm. Mfrs. Assn. (chmn. Washington reps. com.1988), Congl. Country Club, Georgetown Club, City Club. Home: 1005 Woburn Ct Mc Lean VA 22102-2133 Office: Bristol-Myers Squibb Corp 655 15th St NW Ste 410 Washington DC 20005-5701

THOMPSON, RICHARD LLOYD, pastor; b. Lansing, Mich., May 8, 1939; s. Lloyd Walter and Gladys V. (Gates) T.; m. Dianne Lee Tuttle, Nov. 14, 1958; children: Matthew, Beth Ann, Douglas. BA, Azusa Pacific U., 1969; MDiv, Concordia Theol. Sem., 1973. Aerospace industry test engr. Hycon Mfg. Co., Monrovia, Calif., 1961-69; pastor Trinity Luth. Ch., Cedar Rapids, Iowa, 1973-84, Billings, Mont., 1984-94; pastor Good Shepherd Luth. Ch., Watertown, Wis., 1994—; chmn. mission com. Iowa E. dist. Luth. Ch. Mo. Synod, 1979-81, 2nd v.p. Iowa dist. E., Cedar Rapids, 1981-84, bd. mgr. Concordia plans, St. Louis, 1983-86, bd. dirs., St. Louis, 1986—, chmn. bd. dirs., 1992—; served on various task forces and coms. dealing with structure and vision setting for chs. at local, dist. and nat. level, 1975—. Mem. Nat. Exch. Club, Cedar Rapids, 1982-84, Billings, 1986. With USN, 1957-61. Avocations: attending auctions, yard work, travel, exercise activity. Office: Good Shepherd Luth Ch 1611 E Main Watertown WI 53094

THOMPSON, RICHARD STEPHEN, management consultant; b. Des Moines, Oct. 14, 1931; s. Richard Stephen and Mary Ellen (Dailey) T.; m. Nancy Ann Jensen, Apr. 17, 1954; children—Traci Nan, Gregory Christian, Jonathan Richard. B.S.C., State U. Iowa, 1953; M.B.A., Ind. U., 1960. Regional dir. Bristol Meyers Co., N.Y.C., 1969-75; regional dir. Warner Lambert Co., Morris Plains, N.J., 1975-78; exec. v.p. Milton Bradley Co., Milton Bradley Internat., Inc., Springfield, Mass., 1979-83, pres., 1983-84; sr. v.p. internat., dir. Hasbro, Inc., Pawtucket, R.I., 1984-89; pres. Richard Thompson Assocs., London, 1989—. Served to 1st lt. USAF, 1954-55. Republican. Clubs: Chatham Beach Tennis (Mass.); Pilgrims (London and N.Y.); American (London); Roehampton (London). Avocations: tennis; skiing; hiking; reading.

THOMPSON, ROBERT CHARLES, lawyer; b. Council, Idaho, Apr. 20, 1942; s. Ernest Lavelle and Evangeline Montgomery (Carlson) T.; m. Marilyn Ann Wilcox, Jan. 17, 1960 (dec. Mar. 1962); m. Patricia Joan Price, June 1, 1963 (div. 1969); m. Jan Nesbitt, June 29, 1973; 1 child, Tanya. AB, Harvard U., 1963, LLB, 1967. Bar: Mass. 1967, Calif. 1983, U.S. Dist. Ct. (ea. dist.) Mass. 1975, U.S. Ct. Appeals (1st cir.) 1976, U.S. Ct. Appeals (9th cir.) 1984, U.S. Dist. Ct. (no. dist.) Calif. 1983, U.S. Dist. Ct. (ea. dist.) Calif., 1996. Assoc. Choate, Hall & Stewart, Boston, 1967-73; asst. regional counsel EPA, Boston, 1973-75, regional counsel, 1975-82, assoc. gen. counsel, 1979-82; regional counsel EPA, San Francisco, 1982-84; ptnr. Graham & James, San Francisco, 1984-91, LeBoeuf, Lamb, Greene & MacRae, San Francisco, 1992—. Contbr. articles to profl. jours. Bd. dirs. Peninsula Indsl. and Bus. Assn., Palo Alto, Calif., 1986—; chmn. Cambridge (Mass.) Conservation Commn., 1972-74; co-chmn. The Clift Confs. on Environ. Law, 1983-96. John Russell Shaw traveling fellow Harvard Coll., 1963-64; recipient Regional Administrs. Bronze medal EPA, 1976, 84. Mem. ABA (natural resources sect., com. on native Am. natural resources law, spl. com. on mktg.), Natural Resources Def. Coun., Sierra Club, Commonwealth Club, Phi Beta Kappa. Democrat. Episcopalian. Avocations: personal computers, yoga, antiques, wines, cooking. Office: LeBoeuf Lamb Greene & MacRae One Embarcadero Ctr San Francisco CA 94111

THOMPSON, ROBERT ELLIOTT, columnist, writer; b. Los Angeles, June 28, 1921; s. Robert W. and Sadie (Berry) T.; m. Mary C. Mattern, Feb. 27, 1954; children: Robert Elliott, Monica Louise. A.B., Ind. U., 1949. Reporter Ft. Wayne (Ind.) Jour.-Gazette, 1949-51, INS, 1951-58; press sec. John F. Kennedy's re-election campaign in, Mass., 1958; reporter N.Y. Daily News, 1959-62; White House corr. Los Angeles Times, 1962-66; chief Washington bur. Hearst Newspapers, 1966-68, nat. editor, 1968-74, columnist, 1978—; pub. Seattle Post-Intelligencer, 1974-78, chief Washington bur., 1978-89. Author: (with Hortense Myers) Robert Kennedy: the Brother Within, 1962. Mem. standing com. Corrs. House and Senate, 1960-62, chmn., 1961. Served with USNR, 1942-45. Mem. White House Corr. Assn. (pres. 1966-67), Seattle C. of C. (past trustee). Episcopalian. Clubs: Nat. Press, Cosmos, Gridiron (Washington).

THOMPSON, ROBERT L., JR., lawyer; b. St. Paul, Aug. 9, 1944; s. Robert L. and Dorothy R. (Bergstrom) T.; m. Carolyn H. Foss, Aug. 4, 1973; children: Sarah, Kathryn, Jill. BA, Macalester Coll., St. Paul, 1967; JD, U. Oreg., 1973; LLM, NYU, 1988. Bar: Minn. 1973, U.S. Dist. Ct. Minn. 1978, N.Y. 1984. Corp. counsel Northrup King Co., Mpls., 1974-84; assoc. gen. counsel Sandoz Corp., N.Y.C., 1984-88, v.p., gen. counsel, sec., 1989—; mem. adv. bd. Allendale Ins. Co., N.Y.C., 1990—; dir. Orgn. for Internat. Investment, Washington, 1993—; mem. bd. visitors U. Oreg. Law Sch., 1995—. Trustee Sandoz Found., 1993—. 1st lt. U.S. Army, 1968-70. Mem. ABA, Am. Corp. Counsel Assn., European-Am. Gen. Counsels Assn., Assn. Bar City N.Y. Republican. Congregationalist. Office: Sandoz Corp 608 Fifth Ave New York NY 10020-2303

THOMPSON, ROBERT LEE, agricultural economist, nonprofit executive; b. Canton, N.Y., Apr. 25, 1945; s. Robert M. and Esther Louise (Weatherup) T.; m. Karen Hansen, Aug. 9, 1968; children—Kristina Marie, Eric Robert. B.S., Cornell U., Ithaca, N.Y., 1967; M.S., Purdue U., West Lafayette, Ind., 1969, Ph.D., 1974. Vol. agriculturalist Internat. Vol. Service, Pakse and Vientiane, Laos, 1968-70; vis. prof. Fed. Univ. Vicosa, Brazil, 1972-73; prof. Purdue U., West Lafayette, Ind., 1974-93, dean of agriculture, 1987-93; rsch. scholar Internat. Inst. for Applied Systems Analysis, Laxenburg, Austria, 1983; sr. staff economist Council Econ. Advisers, Washington, 1983-85; asst. sec. econs. U.S. Dept. Agr., Washington, 1985-87; pres., CEO Winrock Internat. Inst. Agrl. Devel., 1993—; vis. prof. Econ. Rsch. Svc., USDA, 1979-80; bd. dirs. Vigoro Corp., Nat. Coop. Bank, Washington, Commodity Credit Corp., Washington, 1985-87, PSI Resources and P.S.I. Energy, 1987-94; chmn. adv. coun. Nat. Ctr. for Food and Agrl. Policy, Washington, 1987-92; mem. Ind. Commn. on Agr. and Rural Devel., 1989-93, Nat. Commn. on Agrl. Trade and Export Policy, 1985-86; bd. agr. NRC, 1987-92, Internat. Policy Coun. on Agr. and Trade, USDA Joint Coun. on Food and Agrl. Scis.; cons. USAID, Agr. Can., Ford Found., Brazilian Agr. Ministry, FAO, World Bank, Internat. Food Policy Rsch. Inst., Internat. Maize and Wheat Improvement Ctr., U.S. Feed Grains Coun., Nat. Planning Assn., USIA, Centre for Internat. Econs., Canberra, Club d'Experts en Economie Agricole Internat., Paris, Danish Coun. Rsch. Policy, FAO, Rome. Contbr. numerous articles to profl. publs. Author monographs, book chpts. Bd. dirs. Ind. 4-H Found., Ind. Inst. Agr. Food and Nutrition, 1987-93, Inst. for Sci. in Soc., 1991-93, USDA Grad. Sch., Washington, 1985-87; mem. nat. adv. coun. Minorities in Agr., Natural Resources and Related Sci.; bd. dirs. Farm Found., 1987-92, chmn. 1991-92. Recipient Agrl. Rsch. award Purdue U., 1983, Outstanding Alumni award Cornell U., 1988, Superior Svc. award USDA, 1989, Justin Smith Morrill award, 1995, Nat. 4-H Alumni award, 1992, Chgo. Farmers Agriculturalist of Yr. award, 1992. Fellow AAAS, Am. Agrl. Econs. Assn. (editorial coun. 1983-85, quality com. award 1979, 91, 93); mem. Internat. Agribus Mgmt. Assn. (bd. dirs.), Am. Econ. Assn., Internat. Assn. Agrl. Economists (pres.), Coun. on Fgn. Rels. (Bretton Woods com.), Royal Swedish Acad. Agr. and Forestry (fgn.), Ukrainian Acad. Agrl. Scis., Cosmos Club (Washington), Sigma Xi, Alpha Gamma Rho, AlphaZeta, Gamma Sigma Delta. Republican. Avocation: foreign language study. Office: Winrock Internat Inst Agr Devel 38 Winrock Dr Morrilton AR 72110-9537

THOMPSON, ROBERT MCBROOM, publishing executive; b. Evanston, Ill., Nov. 15, 1928; s. William M. and Ethel L. (McBroom) T.; m. Barbara J. Roepke, June 8, 1957; children: Janet, Sandra, Steven, Michael, Linda. BS, U. Ill., 1950. CPA, Ill. Sr. acct. Walton, Joplin, Langer & Co., Chgo., 1952-57; contr. Modern Hosp. Pub. Co., Chgo., 1957-64; asst. contr. McGraw-Hill, Inc., N.Y.C., 1964-65, contr., 1966-93, v.p., 1969-93; retired, 1993. With U.S. Army, 1950-52, Korea. Mem. AICPA, Fin. Execs. Inst. Home: 21 Gulf Rd East Brunswick NJ 08816-1362

THOMPSON, ROBERT RANDALL (ROBBY THOMPSON), professional baseball player; b. West Palm Beach, Fla., May 10, 1962. Student, Palm Beach Jr. Coll., Fla. State U. With San Francisco Giants, 1983—; mem. Nat. League All-Star Team, 1988, 93. Named Sporting News Rookie Player of Yr., 1986, Nat. League Leader in Triples, 1989, Nat. League Gold Glove 1993, Silver Slugger Team 1993; named to Sporting News All-Star Team, 1988, 93. Office: San Francisco Giants Candlestick Park San Francisco CA 94124*

THOMPSON, ROBERT REX, lawyer; b. Toledo, Aug. 29, 1930; s. Burdette Chauncey and Edna Louise (Ziefle) T.; m. Patricia Anne Baur, Aug. 12, 1950; children: Gerald Robert, Debra Lynn Thompson Stone. BS in Mathematics, U. Toledo, 1958; postgrad. in physics, U. Detroit, 1960-62; JD, Detroit Coll. Law, 1966. Bar: Mich., 1966, U.S. Supreme Ct., 1970, U.S. Tax Ct., 1977. Head electron multiplier group Bendix Corp., 1958-64; chief physicist Rockwell Standard Corp., Troy, Mich., 1964-67; sr. ptnr. Krandle, Thompson & Mier, P.C., Livonia, Mich., 1967-84; ptnr. Thompson & Donaldson, P.C., Livonia, 1984-86; sec, gen. counsel Campus Crusade for Christ, Inc., San Bernardino, Calif., 1986-91; v.p., gen. counsel Internat. Sch. Theology, San Bernardino, 1987-92; sr. ptnr. Thompson & Thompson, P.C., Novi, Mich., 1994—. Author: How to Start Your Own Business and Make Money, 1977, Organizing for Accountability, 1991, The 5 Marks of an Accountable Nonprofit Organization, 1995; patentee (with others) laminated articles and methods of bonding and debonding, electron multiplier, spatial discriminator for particle beams, others. Bd. dirs. Mfr. Bank-Livonia, 1976-84. Mem. ABA (past chairperson religious orgn. subcom. 1991-94), Mich. Bar Assn. Republican. Presbyterian. Avocations: rare coin collecting, Remington Bronze collecting, walking. Home: 16832 Bell Creek Ln Livonia MI 48154-2939

THOMPSON, ROBERT THOMAS, lawyer; b. Pontiac, Ill., Feb. 15, 1930; s. McDuffie and Ivy (Slaughter) T.; m. Elaine Cheshire, Oct. 1, 1950; children: Robert Thomas, Randall C., David L. A.B., Emory U., 1950, J.D. with honors, 1952. Bar: Ga. 1951, S.C. 1964, D.C. 1973. Assoc., ptnr. Wilson, Branch, Barwick & Vandiver, Atlanta, 1952-64; sr. ptnr. Thompson & Hutson, Greenville, S.C., 1964—, Washington, S.C., 1970—; lectr. Law Sch. Emory U.; mgmt. adv. U.S. Del. to Internat. Labor Orgn., 1970; mem., chmn. task force NLRB, 1974-77; mem. pub. Adminstrv. conf. U.S. Bd. vistors Emory U.; chmn. bd. advisors Furman U.; past trustee Buncombe St. United Meth. Ch. Contr. articles to profl. jours. Bd. dirs., v.p. Greenville Symphony Assn. Recipient medal Emory U., 1989. Fellow Am. Bar Found. (life); mem. State Bar Ga. (past pres. young lawyers sect., past bd. govs.), S.C. Bar Assn., Atlanta Bar Assn. (past sec.-treas.), U.S. C. of C. (past chmn. bd. dirs., past chmn. labor rels. and bylaws coms.), S.C. C. of C. (spl. counsel labor rels., adv. com. on labor rels.), Poinsett Club, Commerce Club, Met. Club (Washington and N.Y.C.). Office: Thompson & Hutson Nations Bank Plz Greenville SC 29601 also: 1317 F St NW Ste 900 Washington DC 20004-1105

THOMPSON, ROBERT W., surgeon; b. Grand Rapids, Mich., Aug. 12, 1957. MD, U. Mich., 1983. Diplomate Am. Bd. Surgery, Am. Bd. Gen. Vascular Surgery. Intern Brigham & Women's Hosp., Boston, 1983-84, resident in gen. surgery, 1984-91; fellow in gen. vascular surgery U. Calif., San Francisco, 1991-92; vascular surgeon Barnes Hosp., St. Louis, 1992—; asst. prof. Washington U., St. Louis, 1992—. Faculty fellow ACS, 1994. Office: Queeny Tower Ste 5103 1 Barnes Hosp Plz Saint Louis MO 63110

THOMPSON, ROBY CALVIN, JR., orthopedic surgeon, educator; b. Winchester, Ky., May 1, 1934; s. Roby Calvin and Mary Davis (Guerrant) T.; m. Jane Elizabeth Searcy, May 2, 1959; children: Searcy Lee, Roby Calvin, III, Mary Alexandria. BA, Va. Mil. Inst., 1955; MD, U. Va., 1959. Diplomate Am. Bd. Orthopaedic Surgery (mem. bd. 1983). Intern Columbia Presbyn. Med. Center, N.Y.C., 1959-60; asst. resident, then resident in orthopedic surgery Columbia Presbyn. Med. Center, 1963-67; instr. orthopaedic surgery Coll. Phys. and Surg. Columbia U., 1967-68; mem. faculty Med. Sch. U. Va., 1968-74, prof. orthopaedic surgery, vice chmn. dept. Med. Sch., 1973-74; prof., chmn. dept. Med. Sch. U. Minn., 1974-95; chief med. officer U. Minn. Health Sys., 1995—; mem. merit rev. bd. VA, 1977-80; mem. study sect. on applied physiology and orthopedics NIH, 1980-83; adv. council mem. NIH, Nat. Inst. Arthritis, Musculoskeletal Disease and Skin, 1987—. Trustee Jour. Bone and Joint Surgery, 1988—, chmn. bd. trustees, 1991—; contbr. articles to med. jours. Capt. M.C. USAR, 1960-61. Grantee John Hartford Found., NIH. Mem. ACS, Orthopaedic Rsch. and Edn. Found. (bd. trustees 1990-96), Am. Acad. Orthopaedic Surgeons (bd. dirs. 1975-76, 83-90, pres. 1986), Orthopaedic Rsch. Soc. (pres. 1978), Am. Orthopaedic Assn., Musculoskeletal Tumor Soc. (pres. 1988-89), U. Va. Med. Alumni Assn. (bd. dirs. 1979-84), Woodhill Club (Wayzata). Republican. Presbyterian. Club: Woodhill Wayzata, Minn. Office: U Minn Hosps & Clinic Haward St at E River Rd Minneapolis MN 55455

THOMPSON, RONALD EDWARD, lawyer; b. Bremerton, Wash., May 24, 1931; s. Melville Herbert and Clara Mildred (Griggs) T.; m. Marilyn Christine Woods, Dec. 15, 1956; children—Donald Jeffery, Karen, Susan, Nancy, Sally, Claire. B.A., U. Wash., 1953, J.D., 1958. Bar: Wash. 1959. Asst. city atty. City of Tacoma, 1960-61; pres. firm Thompson, Krilich, LaPorte, Tucci & West, P.S., Tacoma, 1961—; judge pro tem Mcpl. Ct., City of Tacoma, Pierce County Dist., 1972—, Pierce County Superior Ct., 1972—. Chmn. housing and social welfare com. City of Tacoma, 1965-69; mem. Tacoma Bd. Adjustment, 1967-71, chmn., 1968; mem. Tacoma Com. Future Devel., 1961-64, Tacoma Planning Commn., 1971-72; bd. dirs., pres. Mcpl. League Tacoma; bd. dirs. Pres. Tacoma Rescue Mission, Tacoma Pierce County Cancer Soc., Tacoma-Pierce County Heart Assn., Tacoma-Pierce County Council for Arts, Econ. Devel. Council Puget Sound, Tacoma Youth Symphony, Kleiner Group Home, Tacoma Community Coll. Found., Pierce County Econ. Devel. Corp., Wash. Transp. Policy Inst.; Coalition to Keep Wash. Moving, precinct committeeman Republican party, 1969-73. Served with AUS, 1953-55; col. Res. Recipient Internat. Community Service award Optimist Club, 1970, Patriotism award Am. Fedn. Police, 1974, citation for community service HUD, 1974, Disting. Citizen award Mcpl. League Tacoma-Pierce County, 1985; named Lawyer of the Yr. Pierce County Legal Secs. Assn., 1992. Mem. Am. Arbitration Assn. (panel of arbitrators), ABA, Wash. State Bar Assn., Tacoma-Pierce County Bar Assn. (sec. 1964, pres. 1979, mem. cts. and judiciary com. 1981-82), Assn. Trial Lawyers Am., Wash. State Trial Lawyers Assn., Tacoma-Pierce County C. of C. (bd. dirs., exec. com., v.p., chmn.), Downtown Tacoma Assn. (com. chmn., bd. dirs. exec. com., chmn.), Phi Delta Phi, Sigma Nu. Roman Catholic. Clubs: Variety (Seattle); Lawn Tennis, Tacoma, Optimist (Tacoma, Internat. Pres. 1973-74). Home: 3101 E Bay Dr NW Gig Harbor WA 98335-7610 Office: 524 Tacoma Ave S Tacoma WA 98402-5416

THOMPSON, RONALD MACKINNON, family physician, artist, writer; b. N.Y.C., Oct. 19, 1916; s. George Harold and Pearl Anita (Hatfield) T.; m. Ethel Joyce Chastant, June 30, 1950; children: Phyllis Anita, Walter MacKinnon, Charles Chastant, Richard Douglas. BS, U. Chgo., 1947, MS, 1948, MD, 1949. Diplomate Am. Bd. Family Practice. Intern U. Mich., Ann Arbor, 1950-51; resident in psychiatry U. Tex., Galveston, 1951-52; pvt. practice, family and internal medicine South Dixie Med. Ctr., West Palm Beach, Fla., 1952-85; instr. Anatomy, U. Chgo., 1946-47, Pharmacology, 1948-49. Contbr. articles to profl. jours.; exhibited in 7 one-man shows (over 30 awards for painting in regional and nat. shows); represented in permanent collections at 5 mus. Mem. Civitan Club W. Palm Beach, Fla., 1951; former bd. dirs. Norton Gallery Mus. of Art, West Palm Beach. Mem. Fla. Nat. Guard, 1936-40; cadet Army Air Force, 1943-44. Over thirty awards for painting in juried regional and nat. shows. Fellow Am. Acad. Family Physicians; mem. AMA, Fla. Med. Assn., Fla. Acad. of Family Physicians, Palm Beach County Med. Soc., Nat. Watercolor Soc., Ariz. Watercolor Soc. Republican. Episcopalian. Avocations: chess, tennis, writing, square and round dancing. Home: 308 Leisure World Mesa AZ 85206-3142

THOMPSON, RONELLE KAY HILDEBRANDT, library director; b. Brookings, S.D., Apr. 21, 1954; d. Earl E. and Maxine R. (Taplin) Hildebrandt; m. Harry Floyd Thompson II, Dec. 24, 1976; children: Clarissa, Harry III. BA in Humanities magna cum laude, Houghton Coll., 1976; MLS, Syracuse U., 1976; postgrad., U. Rochester, 1980, 81; cert., Miami U., 1990. Libr. asst. Norwalk (Conn.) Pub. Libr., 1977; elem. libr. Moriah Cen. Schs., Port Henry, N.Y., 1977-78; div. coord. pediatric gastroenterology and nutrition U. Rochester (N.Y.) Med. Ctr., 1978-81, cons., mem. pediatric housestaff libr. com., 1980-81; dir. Medford Libr. U. S.C., Lancaster, 1981-83; dir. Mikkelsen Libr., Libr. Assocs., Ctr. for Western Studies, mem. acad. computing com., libr. com. Augustana Coll., Sioux Falls, S.D., 1983—, mem. adminstrv. pers. coun., 1989-94; presenter in field. Contbr. articles to profl. jours. Mem. adv. com. S.D. Libr. Network, 1986—, chair, 1989-91, 94—; mem. Sioux Falls Community Playhouse, S.D. Symphony, Sioux Falls Civic Fine Arts Assn.; advisor Minnehaha County Libr., pers. dept. City of Sioux Falls. Named one of Outstanding Young Women Am., 1983; Syracuse U. Gaylord Co. scholar, 1976; recipient YWCA leader award, 1991. Mem. ALA, AAUW, Assn. Coll. and Rsch. Librs. (nat. adv. coun. coll. librs. sect. 1987—), Mountain Plains Libr. Assn. (chair acad. sect., nominating com. 1988, pres. 1993-94), S.D. Libr. Assn. (chair interlibr. coop. task force 1986-87, pres. 1987-88, chair recommended minimum salary task force 1988, chair local arrangements com. 1989-90), S.D. Libr. Network (adv. coun. 1986—, exec. com. 1992—, chair adv. coun. 1994—). Office: Augustana Coll Mikkelsen Libr 29th & Summit Sioux Falls SD 57197

THOMPSON, RUFUS E., lawyer; b. Lubbock, Tex., Aug. 15, 1943; s. Glenn Wesley and Naomi Elvina T.; m. Sandra Jean Lemons, Aug. 8, 1965; children—Michael Glenn, Mark Gregory, Matthew Wesley. B.B.A., U. Tex., Austin, 1965, J.D., 1968. Bar: Tex. bar 1968, N.Mex. bar 1969. Assoc. firm Atwood & Malone, Roswell, N.Mex., 1968-71; ptnr. firm Atwood, Malone, Mann & Cooter, Roswell, 1971-78; U.S. Atty. Dist. N.Mex., Albuquerque, 1978-81; now ptnr. firm Modrall, Sperling, Roehl, Harris & Sisk, Albuquerque; mem. Nat. Conf. Commrs. on Uniform State Laws, 1975-79; chmn. N.Mex. Supreme Ct. Com. on Rules of Evidence, 1972-94; U.S. Atty. for N.Mex. Com., 1978-82; mem. U.S. Atty. Gen.'s Adv. Com., 1980—, chmn., 1981. Mem. N.Mex. Democratic Party Central Com., 1972-78; mem. N.Mex. State Senate, 1973-78; mem. Gov's. Commn. on Prevention of Organized Crime, 1985-89. Mem. Am. Bar Assn. (exec. council young lawyers sect. 1972), N.Mex. Bar Assn. (chmn. young lawyers sect. 1970). Baptist. Office: PO Box 607 Albuquerque NM 87103-0607

THOMPSON, SALLY ENGSTROM, state official; b. Spokane, Wash., Feb. 17, 1940; d. Logan C. and Ava Leigh (Phillips) Engstrom; m. Donald Edward Colcun, 1981; children: Lauri Thompson, Tom Thompson, Tami Thompson, Sheri Colcun Trumpfheller. BS magna cum laude, U. Colo., 1975. CPA, Colo. 1976, Kans. 1986. Audit mgr. and mgmt. cons. Touche Ross & Co., Denver, 1975-82; v.p., mgr. planning and fin. analysis United Bank, Denver, 1982-85; pres., chief oper. officer Shawnee Fed. Svgs., Topeka, 1985-90; treas. State of Kans., 1990—. Past editorial advisor New Accountant mag. Bd. dirs. Everywoman's Resource Ctr., Topeka, 1988-92, Community Svc. Found. Kans., Kids Voting Kans. (hon.); v.p., bd. dirs. Downtown Topeka Inc., YWCA, Topeka, 1986-93, Woman of Achievement award, 1984; mem. fin. com. Girl Scouts U.S., Kaw Valley, various coms., United Way of Greater Topeka; chmn. art auction com. KTWU-TV, summer concert, Topeka Civic Theatre. Recipient Disting. Community Leadership award Topeka Pub. Schs., 1989, Disting. Leadership award Nat. Assn. Community Leadership, 1991, 1991 Class Leadership Kans. Mem. AICPAs, Am. Soc. Women Accts., Kans. Soc. CPAs, Kansas C. of C. and Industry, Greater Topeka C. of C. (bd. dirs. 1989-92), Emporia State U. Bus. Sch. Adv. Bd., Nat. Assn. State Auditors, Controllers and Treas., Nat. Assn. State Treas. (v.p., Midwest regional chair), Women Execs. in Govt., Beta Alpha Psi. Democrat. Offices: Office State Treasurer Landon State Office Bldg 900 SW Jackson St Ste 201N Topeka KS 66612-1220*

THOMPSON, SHELDON LEE, refining company executive; b. Mpls., Oct. 7, 1938; s. Wallace E. and Madeline A. (King) T.; m. Karen Beatrice Gallison, Aug. 25, 1962; children: Jeffrey, Paul, Daniel. BS, U. Minn., 1960, MS, 1962; grad. advanced mgmt. program, Harvard U., 1983. Registered profl. chem. engr., Pa. Rsch. engr. Sun Refining & Mktg. Co., Marcus Hook, Pa., 1962-69, assoc. engr., 1969-70, chief engring. rsch., 1970-72, rsch. program mgr. corp. R & D, 1972-74, mgr. venture engring., 1974-77, mgr. R & D chems., 1977-80, dir. R & D, 1980-88; v.p. chems., lubricants and tech. Sun Refining & Mktg. Co., Phila., 1988-91; sr. v.p., chief adminstrv. officer Sun Co., Inc., Phila., 1992—. Inventor 11 patents chems., fuels and lubes processing. Mem. exec. edn. adv. bd. Wharton sch. Bus., U. Pa.; bd. trustees Acad. Nat. Scis., Phila. Orch. Mem. AIChE, Am. Petroleum Inst., Greater Phila. C. of C. (exec. com.). Republican. Presbyterian. Avocation: music. Office: Sun Co Inc 1801 Market St Philadelphia PA 19103-1628

THOMPSON, STANLEY B., church administrator. Pres., CEO, dir. The Free Meth. Found., Spring Arbor, Mich. Office: The Free Meth Found PO Box 580 Spring Arbor MI 49283-0580

THOMPSON, STEPHEN ARTHUR, publishing executive; b. Englewood, N.J., Jan. 24, 1934; s. Stephen Gerard and Doris Lillian (Evans) T.; m. Joan Frances O'Connor, May 12, 1955 (div. 1978); children: Stephen Andrew, Craig Allen, David John; m. Sandra Rene Fingernut, May 27, 1979. BS, Ohio State U., 1961. Physicist Rocketdyne div. North Am. Aviation, Canoga Park, Calif., 1961-62, Marquardt Corp., Van Nuys, Calif., 1962-63; mem. tech. staff Hughes Rsch. Labs., Malibu, Calif., 1963-69; editor Electronic Engr. mag. Chilton Co., L.A., 1969-72, in advt. sales Instruments and Controls Sys., mag., 1972-77; regional advt. sales Design News mag. Cahners Pub. Co., L.A., 1977-84; sales mgr. Design News mag. Cahners Pub. Co., Newton, Mass., 1984-87, pub. Design News mag., 1987—, group. pub. mfg. group, 1989—, sr. v.p. integrated mktg., 1993-94, gen. mgr. Boston divsn., 1995—; founder Design News Engring. Edn. Found., Newton, 1991—; pub. Design News Mag., 1993—; group pub. Mfg. Group. Author: Basketball for Boys, 1970; contbr. articles to Jour. Spacecraft/Rockets, 1966. Club leader YMCA, Canoga Park, 1963-78; active PTA, Canoga Park, 1961-80; bd. dirs. Chatsworth (Calif.) High Booster Club, 1972-80. 1st lt., jet fighter pilot USAF, 1952-58. Mem. Bus. Profl. Advt. Assn. (Golden Spike award 1980, 81, 82, 83), L.A. Mag. Reps. Assn. (life), Nat. Fluid Power Assn., BPA Internat. (bd. dirs.). Achievements include patents for ion source, system and method for ion implantation of semiconductors. Office: Cahners Pub Co 275 Washington St Newton MA 02158-1646

THOMPSON, STEVE ALLAN, writer; b. Mpls., Sept. 10, 1951; s. John Thomas and Charlotte Joan (Ellis) T.; m. Michele Rae Jones, July 16, 1983; 1 child, Kent Lloyd. Student, U. Minn., 1969-73. Dept. supr. Hennpin County Libr., Edina, Minn., 1973-87; writer, 1987—; cons. Okefenokee Glee & Perloo Inc., Manassa, Va., 1988—. Author: Walt Kelly Collector's Guide; co-author: Pogo Files for Phophiles, 1992; editor The Fort Mudge Most 1988—; contbr. articles to profl. jours. Mem. Walt Kelly Soc. (pres. 1987—), Lewis Carroll Soc., Bakr Street Irregulars. Achievements include international recognized on life and career of Walt Kelly. Home: 6908 Wentworth Ave S Richfield MN 55423

THOMPSON, SUE WANDA, small business owner; b. Azle, Tex., Nov. 26, 1935; d. Weldon W. Beasley and Eula Mae Hardee; m. William Henry Clark, Feb. 20, 1952 (div. 1959); children: Gloria, Russ, Bonnie; m. Robert L. Thompson Jr., Sept. 20, 1963; stepchildren: Christene, Lee. Nurse Harris Hosp., Ft. Worth, 1960-62, Denton State Sch., 1962-63; owner, v.p. Dalworth Med. Labs., Ft. Worth, 1963-68; sales leader, trainer Home Interior and Gifts, Dallas, 1970-80; owner, pres. Thompson Enterprises, 1980—; mgr., trainer Jafra Cosmetics, West Lake Village, Calif., 1981-84, Jewels by Park Lane, Chgo., 1984-89, Just Am., Rutlerfordton, N.C., 1989-91; with sales Dyna Tech Nutritionals, Willston Park, N.Y., 1993-94. Dir. parks and recreation City Forest Hills, Tex., 1970. Mem. Beta Sigma Phi (treas. Eta Lambda chpt. 1971-72, pres. 1972-73, Girl of Yr. 1974). Republican. Mem. Ch. Nazarene. Avocations: sports collecting, Gospel singing, crafts. Home: 4717 Applewood Rd Fort Worth TX 76133-7435

THOMPSON, SUSAN A., mayor; b. Winnipeg, Man., Can.. Grad., U. Winnipeg. With Eatons; group dept. mgr. Eatons, Calgary; nat. buyer The Bay, Montreal, Que, 1979-80; mayor City of Winnipeg. Mem. Econ. Coun. of Can., Man. Econ. Adv. Coun., Winnipeg Found., Downtown Winnipeg Assn., Urban Idea Centre, BIZ Task Force, Winnipeg 2000 Interfaith Pastoral Inst.; bd. dirs. Can. West Found., U. Man. Faculty of Mgmt., Winnipeg Symphony Orch. Mem. Rotary. Office: Council Bldg, Civic Ctr 510 Main St, Winnipeg, MB Canada R3B 1B9

THOMPSON, SUSANNAH ELIZABETH, lawyer; b. Fullerton, Calif., May 20, 1953; d. Harry Lowell and Susannah Elizabeth (Glover) Rupp; m. James Avery Thompson, Jr., May 16, 1987; 1 child, Sarah Mary Elizabeth Thompson. BA, Calif. State U., Fullerton, 1980; JD with hons., Am. Coll. of Law, 1989. Bar: Calif. 1989, U.S. Dist. Ct. (cen. dist.) 1989, U.S. Dist. Ct. (so. dist.) 1991. Legal asst. Minyard & Minyard, Orange, Calif., 1987-89; assoc. Simon & Simon, San Bernardino, Calif., 1989-91; pvt. practice Temecula, Calif., 1991—. Asst. editor Law Rev./Am. Coll. Law, Brea, Calif., 1989. Sec. student bar assn. Am. Coll. Law, 1987-88. Mem. ABA, Riverside County Bar Assn., Calif. Women Lawyers Assn., Inland Empire Bankruptcy Forum, Women Lawyers Assn. (chmn. mem. 1994—), Temecula C. of C. Republican. Avocations: bowling, Disneyana, reading, skating, tennis. Office: Ste 201 41593 Winchester Rd Temecula CA 92590

THOMPSON, THEODORE J., financial services executive. Nat. dir., fund adminstr. Thornton Grant, Chgo. Office: Fl 8 1 Presidential Plz Chicago IL 60601

THOMPSON, THEODORE ROBERT, pediatric educator; b. Dayton, Ohio, July 18, 1943; s. Theodore Roosevelt and Helen (Casey) J.;m. Lynette Joanne Shenk; 1 child, S. Beth. BS, Wittenberg U., 1965; MD, U. Pa., 1969. Diplomate Am. Bd. Pediatrics (Neonatal, Perinatal Medicine). Resident in pediatrics U. Minn. Hosp., Mpls., 1969-72, chief resident in pediatrics, 1971-72, fellow neonatal, perinatal, 1974-75, asst. prof., 1975-80, dir. div. of neonatology and newborn intensive care unit, 1977-80, assoc. prof., 1980-85, prof., 1985—, co-dir. Med. Outreach, 1988-91, dir. med. outreach, 1991—, assoc. chief of pediatrics, 1988—; med. dir. U. Minn. Clin. Assocs., 1992—. Editor: Newborn Intensive Care: A Practical Manual, 1983. Bd. dirs. Life Link III, St. Paul, 1987—; cons. Maternal and Child Health, Minn. Bd. Health, 1975—. With USPHS. 1972-74. Fellow Am. Acad. Pediatrics (chmn. perinatal newborn com. Minn. chpt. 1985-92); Gt. Plains Orgn. for Perinatal Health Care (Sioux Falls, S.D., Kunshe award 1989). Lutheran. Office: U Minn Hosp and Clinic 420 Delaware St SE # 39 Minneapolis MN 55455-0374

THOMPSON, THOMAS HENRY, philosophy educator; b. Sioux City, Iowa, Jan. 10, 1924; s. Elmer Edwin and Ruth Alma (Baker) T.; m. Diane Sargent, Nov. 23, 1955; children: Brenda, Alicia, Mark, Rosemary. B.A., U. Iowa, 1948, M.A., 1950, Ph.D., 1952. Asst., instr. U. Iowa, Iowa City, 1948-52; mem. faculty U. No. Iowa, Cedar Falls, 1952—; prof. philosophy U. No. Iowa, 1969—, head dept., 1969-81, acting dean Coll. Humanities and Fine Arts, 1981-82, dean Coll. Humanities and Fine Arts, 1982-90; prof. emeritus, 1994—. Mem. Sigmund Freud Gesellschaft (Vienna), Am. Philosophy Assn. Home: 2122 California St Cedar Falls IA 50613-4721 Office: Baker 35 1222 W 27th St Cedar Falls IA 50613-4800

THOMPSON, THOMAS MARTIN, lawyer; b. Albion, Pa., Jan. 7, 1943; s. Donald C. and Mabel Louise (Martin) T.; m. Judith E. Daucher; children: Reid, Chad, Matthew, Molly. AB, Grove City Coll., 1965; JD cum laude, Harvard U., 1968. Bar: Pa. 1968. Ptnr. Buchanan Ingersoll, Pitts., 1968—, chair corp. fin. group; adj. prof. law U. Pitts.; dir., past chairperson Pa. Lawyer Trust Acct. Bd. Past pres. Neighborhood Legal Svcs. Assn.; bd. dirs., past pres. Pitts. chpt. Assn. for Corp. Growth; bd. dirs. Pitts. Pub. Theater. Mem. ABA, Pa. Bar Assn. (Pro Bono award 1989, mem. corp., bus. and banking coun.), Allegheny County Bar Assn. (past chairperson pub. svc. com., chair corp., banking and bus. coun.). Democrat. Home: 1142 Dartmouth Rd Pittsburgh PA 15205-1705 Office: Buchanan Ingersoll One Oxford Ctr 301 Grant St 20th Fl Pittsburgh PA 15219-1410

THOMPSON, THOMAS SANFORD, former college president; b. Lewistown, Mont., Apr. 9, 1916; s. Thomas Swing and Sadie (Mixer) T.; m. Margaret Ann Wiese, June 1, 1941; children—Roger John, Thomas Warren, Pamela Ann, Mary Ann. B.S., Pacific U., 1938, L.H.D., 1966; postgrad., U. Wash., 1939, U. Oreg., 1941; M.Ed., Oreg. State U., 1949. Tchr.-coach Siuslaw Union High Sch., Florence, Oreg., 1938; prin. Siuslaw Union High Sch., 1939-42; coordinator tng. within industry War Manpower Commn., Portland, Oreg., 1942-43; employee utilization dir. North Pacific div. U.S. Army C.E., 1946-47; acting prin. Portland Apprentice Sch., 1947-48; partner Davis Sales Cons., Portland, 1948-51; dir. devel. Lewis and Clark Coll., Portland, 1952-57; dir. sustaining assos. program Washington U., St. Louis, 1957-60; dir. devel. Knox Coll., Galesburg, Ill., 1960-63; v.p. for devel. U. Pacific, Stockton, Calif., 1963-69; pres. Morningside Coll., Sioux City, Iowa, 1969-78; lectr. coll.-univ. devel. adminstrn. Cons. Council on Christian Philanthropy, 1970, Council for Financial Aid to Edn., 1963. Bd. dirs. United Fund, Sioux City, 1969-78, Pacific Med. Center, San Francisco, 1966-68, Marian Health Center, Sioux City, 1977-78, St. Joseph's Hosp., Stockton, 1979-85. Served to lt. col USAAF, 1943-46; Served to lt. col USAF, 1951-52. Mem. Greater Stockton C. of C. (dir. 1967-69), Galesburg C. of C. (dir. 1961-63), Sioux City (dir. 1971-78), Oreg. Mental Health Assn. (pres. 1956-57), Assn. Am. Colls., Am. Colls. Pub. Relations Assn., Royal Rosarians, Phi Delta Kappa. Democrat. Roman Catholic. Club: Rotary (Sioux City) (past pres.). Home: 6879 Atlanta Cir Stockton CA 95219-3233

THOMPSON, TIMOTHY CHARLES, research scientist; b. Indpls., Apr. 9, 1951; s. Charles Avery and Gladys Kathryn T.; m. Sang Hee Park, Feb. 9, 1988; 1 child, Benjamin Paul. AB, Ind. U., 1974; PhD, Colo. U., 1985; postdoctoral fellow, Imperial Cancer Rsch. Fund, London, 1988. Asst. prof. Dept. of Urology and Cell Biology Baylor Coll. of Medicine, Houston, 1988-92, dir. rsch. Scott Dept. of Urology, 1992—, assoc. prof. Dept. of Urology, Cell Biology and Radiology, 1992—; cons. reviewer for acad. jours. Cancer Rsch., 1991—; mem. pathology B study sect. NIH, Bethesda, Md., 1993—; cons. Oncor, Inc., Gaithersburg, Md., 1994—, UroCor, Inc., Oklahoma City, 1995—. Contbr. numerous articles to profl. jours. and chpts. to books. Adult class Sun. sch. tchr. Rice Temple Bapt. Ch., Houston, 1992—. Grantee NIH, 1989—. Mem. Soc. of Basic Urological Rsch. (program com. 1989—), CaP CURE (bd. sci. dir. 1993—), Metastasis Rsch. Soc., Keystone Symposia (co-organizer 1996 Symposium). Democrat. Achievements include devel. of in vivo mouse model for prostate cancer; genetic completmentation in prostate cancer; rsch. on molecular and cellular determinants of prostate cancer metastasis; patent for seminal vesicle specific markers of invasive prostatic neoplasia. Office: Baylor Coll of Medicine One Baylor Plz Houston TX 77030

THOMPSON, TINA LEWIS CHRYAR, publisher; b. Houston, Dec. 31, 1929; d. Joshua and Mary Christine (Brown) Thompson; m. Joseph Chryar, May 25, 1943; 1 child, Joseph Jr. Cosmotologist, Franklin Coll., Houston, 1950; student, Crenshaw Coll., L.A., 1961. Pubr., composer, author B.M.I., N.Y.C., 1964-74; pubr. ASCAP, N.Y.C., 1974-86, The Fox Agy., N.Y.C., 1986—, Tech. World, L.A., 1990—; v.p. music Asset Records, L.A., 1978—; music dir., v.p. Roach Records, L.A., 1968; music dir. Rendezvous Records, Hollywood, 1950; v.p. Assoc. Internat., L.A., 1973; bd. govs. ABI, Inc., 1994; pres. Cling Music Pub., Soprano Music; pub. processor music catalogs Broadcast Music Inc. Author: Soprano Poems, 1985; creator/designer Baby Napin brand form-fitting, no-leak, no pins baby diaper, 1967, Saver Belt, 1993; patentee/pub. Letter's Tech in Word, used by TV stas. to advertise, 1972. Recipient recognition award IBC, Cambridge, Eng., 1991, cert. of proclamation Internat. Woman of Yr., 1991-92, Merit award Pres. Ronald Reagan, 1986; named Most Admired Woman of Decade, ABI, 1993. Mem. AAUW, NARAS, NOW, ABI (bd. govs. 1994), Am. Soc. Authors and Composers, Nat. Mus. Pubs. Assn., Songwriters Guild Am. (Cert. of Ranks of Composers and Lyracists 1991), Am. Fedn. Label Co. Unions, Am. Theatre Assn. Broadcast Music Inc. (pres. Soprano Music Publ. 1968), Rec. Acad. Country Music Acad., Internat. Platform Assn., L.A. Women in Music. Home: PO Box 7731 Beverly Hills CA 90212-7731

THOMPSON, TOMMY GEORGE, governor; b. Elroy, Wis., Nov. 19, 1941; s. Allan and Julia (Dutton) T.; m. Sue Ann Mashak, 1969; children: Kelli Sue, Tommi, Jason. BS in Polit. Sci. and History, U. Wis., 1963, JD, 1966. Polit. intern U.S. Rep. Thomson, 1963; legis. messenger Wis. State Senate, 1964-66; sole practice Elroy and Mauston, Wis., 1966-87; mem. Dist. 87 Wis. State Assembly, 1966-87, asst. minority leader, 1972-81, floor leader, 1981-87; self-employed real estate broker Mauston, 1970—; gov. State of Wis., 1987—; alt. del. Rep. Nat. Conv., 1976; chmn. Intergovtl. Policy Adv. Commn. to U.S. Trade Rep.; mem. nat. govs. assn. exec. com.; bd. dirs. AMTRAK. Served with USAR. Recipient med. award for Legis. Wis. Acad. Gen. Practice, Thomas Jefferson Freedon award Am. Legis. Exchange Coun., 1991, Most Valuable Pub. Official award City and State Mag., 1991, Governance award Free Congress Found., 1992. Mem. ABA, Wis. Bar Assn., Rep. Govs. Assn., Phi Delta Phi. Roman Catholic. Office: Office of Gov PO Box 7863 Madison WI 53707-7863*

THOMPSON, TRAVIS, psychology educator, administrator, researcher; b. Mpls., July 20, 1937; s. William Raymond and Loretta (Travis) T.; m. Anna Leyens, June 12, 1970; children: Rebecca Lynn, Jennifer Eva, Andrea Laura, Peter Erich. BA, U. Minn., 1958, MA, PhD, 1961. Lic. psychologist. NSF postdoctoral fellow U. Md., College Park, 1961-63; asst. prof. U. Minn., Mpls., 1963-66, assoc. prof., 1966-69, prof., 1969-91, dir. inst. disabilities studies, 1987-91; prof., dir. John F. Kennedy Ctr. Vanderbilt U., Nashville, 1991—; vis. fellow Cambridge (U.K.) U., 1968-69; vis. scientist Nat. Inst. Drug Abuse, Rockville, Md., 1979-80; mem. rsch. review com. Nat. Inst. Child Health, Bethesda, Md. Hastings Ctr., Rights of Retarded, Hastings-on-Hudson, 1977-78; mem. instl. review bd. Minn. Dept. Human Svcs., 1986-89; mem. exec. com. 1990 planning com. Gatlinburg Conf. on Rsch. in Mental Retardation, 1988—, exec. com., 1992; mem. Human Devel. 3 Rsch. Review com. NIH, 1988-91; mem. adv. com. Inst. on Community Intergration, U. Minn., 1988-91, Rehab. Rsch. and Tng. Ctr in Adolescent Health, 1989-91; mem. local adv. com. Geriatric Rsch., Edn. and Clin. Ctr., VA Med. Ctr., Mpls., 1989-91; cons. in field, including North Star Rsch. and Devel. Inst., Mpls., 1963-65, Honeywell, Inc., Mpls., 1964-67, Faribault (Minn.) State Hosp., 1968-75, 87—, Cambridge (Minn.) State Hosp., 1972-74, Ctr. for Behavioral Therapy, Mpls., 1973-80, Clara Doerr Residence, Inc., Mpls., 1975-77, Ill. Sci. Adv. Com. on Mental Health and Devel. Disabilities, 1975-77, Minn. Dept. Pub. Welfare, 1978-80, Psychol. and Behavioral Cons., St. Paul., 1981-85, People, Inc., Mpls., 1985., NIH, 1986, Emerson Sch., 1986-87, U. Tex. Mental Scis. Inst., 1991—, Livonia (Mich.) Pub. Schs., 1992; invited speaker in field including Oxford (U.K.) U., 1968, Mario Negri Inst., Milan, Italy, 1969, York U., Toronto, Can., 1971, Uppsala U., Sweden, 1972, U. Auckland, New Zealand, 1974, European Behaviour Therapy Assn. Meeting, Uppsala, 1977, Bermuda Coll., 1983, Maudsley Hosp., U. London, 1985, European Behavioral Pharmacology Soc. Meeting, Antwerp, Belgium, 1986, Amsterdan, The Netherlands, 1990, Rehab. Inst., Dalhouise U., Halifax, Nova Scotia, Can., 1989, U. Otago, New Zealand, 1992. Author: (with C.R. Schuster) Behavioral Pharmacology, 1968, (with J.G. Grabowski) Reinforcement Schedules and Multi-operant Analysis, 1972; editor: Behavioral Modification of Mental Retardation, 1972, 2d edit., 1977, (with S.C. Hupp) Saving Therapy (mem.-at-large 1971-72, pres. Minn. chpt. 1972-73, chair profl. affairs ethics com. 1973-81), Am. Coll. Neuropsychopharmacology (sci. assoc. 1979-81), Am. Assn. for Behavioral Analysis (sustaining, program chair for behavioral pharmacology and toxicology 1984, 85, editl. adv. com. 1986-90), Am. Acad. Pediatrics (com. on DSM IV PC), Nat. Assn. for Dual Diagnosis, Behavioral Pharmacology Soc. (pres. 1972-73), European Behavioral Pharmacology Soc., Twin Cities Soc. for Children and Adults with Autism (hon., bd. profl. advisors 1982-91). Predoctoral fellow USPHS, 1959-61. Fellow APA (divsns. exptl. analysis behavior, history psychology, pres. divsn. psychopharmacology 1974, divsn. mental retardation, 1990, com. ethics in protection of human participants in rsch. bd. sci. affairs 1988-91, congl. testifier 1988, 89, 90, 92, Don Hake award 1990), Coll. on Problems Drug Abuse (charter); mem. Am. Acad. Mental Retardation (state chpt. award 1981), Am. Assn. Univ. Affilited Programs (exec. bd. 1989—), Assn. for Advancement Behavior Therapy (mem.-at-large 1971-72, pres. Minn. chpt. 1972-73, chair profl. affairs ethics com. 1973-81), Am. Coll. Neuropsychopharmacology (sci. assoc. 1979-81), Am. Assn. for Behavioral Analysis (sustaining, program chair for behavioral pharmacology and toxicology 1984, 85, editorial adv. com. 1986-90), Am. Acad. Pediatrics (com. on DSM IV PC), Nat. Assn. for Dual Diagnosis, Behavioral Pharmacology Soc. (pres. 1972-73), European Behavioral Pharmacology Soc., Twin CiSoc. for Children and Adults with Autism (hon., bd. profl. advisors 1982-91). Achievements include co-discovery of technique for screening abuse liability of new drugs. Office: Vanderbilt U John F Kennedy Ctr Box 40 GPC Nashville TN 37203

THOMPSON, TRINA LYNN, lawyer; b. Oakland, Calif., June 3, 1961; d. Woodrow Thompson and Dorothy Mae (Martin) McCullough; foster parents: Michael and Hazel Wilson; 1 child, Daniel Jackson Jr. AB, U. Calif., Berkeley, 1983; JD, U. Calif., 1986. Bar: Calif. 1987, U.S. Dist. Ct. (no. dist.) Calif. 1990. Tchg. asst. coun. on legal edn. opportunities U. Calif., 1984; law clk. Nat. Ctr. for Youth Law, San Francisco, 1984; clin. law clk. Alameda County Dist. Atty.'s Office, Oakland, 1985; law clk. to Hon. Henry Ramsey Alameda County Superior Ct., Oakland, 1986; sr. legal asst. Alameda County Pub. Defender's Office, 1986-87; asst. pub. defender III, Alameda County Pub. Defender's Office, Oakland, 1987-91; pvt. practice, Oakland, 1991—. Editing mem. Black Law Jour., 1983-85. Bd. dirs. Oakland Ensemble Theatre, 1991-93, Family Law and Violence Ctr., Berkeley, 1990-92; vol. Boys and Girls Clubs of Oakland, 1993—. Fellow Coun. on Legal Edn. Opportunities, 1983-85, grad. minority fellow, 1983-85; Yee scholar, 1985-86. Mem. ABA, Nat. Bar Assn., Calif. Pub. Defenders Assn., Alameda County Bar Assn., Calif. Attys. for Criminal Justice (bd. dirs. 1994—, President's award 1994), Alpha Kappa Alpha. Democrat. Baptist. Avocation: collecting African American historical memorabilia. Office: Ste 82C 1970 Broadway Oakland CA 94612

THOMPSON, VIRIGINA A., elementary education educator; b. Logan, Ohio, May 4, 1940; d. Charles Frederick and Margaret Frances (Shelton) Wilcoxen; m. Paul Calvin Reed, Sept. 24, 1958 (div. Jan. 1974); children: P. Bradley, John C., Thomas G.; m. James Willard Thompson, Jr., June 11, 1976. BS in Elem. Edn., Ohio State U., 1977; MS in Sch. Counseling, U. Dayton, Ohio, 1990. Cert. in elem. edn. 1-8, elem. guidance and counseling, Ohio. Classroom tchr. Anna (Ohio) Local Schs., 1977—; chair Old Trails Uniserv Coun., Piqua, Ohio, 1982-86. Chair bd. trustees Shelby County Mental Health, Sidney, Ohio, 1989-94; mem. Dem. Ctr. Com. of Shelby County, Sidney, 1992—; mem. com. Black Achievers Scholarship, Sidney, 1988—; treas. Botkins (Ohio) Hist. Soc., 1987—. Recipient Bus. Adv. Coun. Tchr. Yr. award C. of C., Sidney, 1992, Pres.'s Award univ. scholar Ohio State Univ., 1976. Mem. Ohio Edn. Assn. (voting del.), Anna Local Tchrs. Assn. (pres. 1978, 85, 91-94), Ohio State Alumni Assn., Phi Kappa Phi. Democrat. Methodist. Avocations: travel, antiques, theatre. Home: 106 W State St Botkins OH 45306 Office: Anna Local Sch Dist 204 N 2d St Anna OH 45302

THOMPSON, WADE FRANCIS BRUCE, manufacturing company executive; b. Wellington, New Zealand, July 23, 1940; came to U.S., 1961, naturalized, 1990.; m. Angela Ellen Barry, Jan. 20, 1967; children: Amanda and Charles (twins). B in Commerce, Cert. Acctg., Victoria U., Wellington, 1961; MSc, NYU, 1963. Dir. diversification Sperry & Hutchinson, N.Y.C., 1967-72; v.p. Texstar Corp., N.Y.C., 1972-77; chmn. Hi-Lo Trailer Co., Butler, Ohio, 1977—; chmn., pres., chief exec. officer Thor Industries Inc., Jackson Center, Ohio, 1980—. Trustee Mystic Seaport Mus., Conn., 1984—; trustee Wade F.B. Thompson Charitable Found. Inc., 1985—, N.Y. Studio Sch., 1993—, Mcpl. Art Soc., N.Y.C., 1993—. Mem. Union Club, N.Y. Yacht Club (N.Y.C.). Avocations: tennis, collecting contemporary art. Office: Thor Industries Inc 419 W Pike St Jackson Center OH 45334-9728

THOMPSON, WARREN A., mental health services educator, director; b. Bristow, Okla., June 27, 1927; married; 3 children. BS in Acctg., U. Okla., 1950; MBA, Okla. State U., 1962; PhD in Mgmt., U. Mo., 1966. Auditor Traders & Gen. Ins. Co., Dallas, 1950-51; acct., roughneck Unit Drilling Co., Bristow, 1951-53; self-employed gasoline and oil products wholesaler Woodward, Okla., 1954-58; bus. administr. Western State Hosp., Ft. Supply, Okla., 1958-61; instr. bus. mgmt. Coll. Bus. & Pub. Adminstrn. U. Mo., Columbia, 1963-65; exec. dir. Psychiat. Rsch. Found. Mo., St. Louis, 1966-75; prof. grad. program health adminstrn. and planning Sch. Medicine Washington U., St. Louis, 1975-80; adminstrv. dir. Mo. Inst. Psychiatry, St. Louis, 1965-80; prof. dept. psychiat. Sch. Medicine U. Mo., Columbia, 1965-80; prof. Health Svcs. Mgmt. Sch. Medicine U. Mo., 1980—, dir. grad. studies Health Svcs. Mgmt., 1993—; chair psychiat. adv. com. hosp. adminstrv. svcs. Am. Hosp. Assn., Chgo., 1966-69; mem. adv. com. Community Mental Health Ctrs., Fin. Adminstrn. and Mental Health Svcs., NIMH, 1968, Am. Hosp. Assn., 1968-69; mem. program com. Am. Psychiat. Assn., 1974; cons., evaluator, project dir. Farmington (Mo.) State Hosp., 1970;mem. adv. com., conf. participant to establish nat. commn. adminstrv. standards in mental health; expert witness, participant Commn. Edn. for Health Adminstrn., 1974; commr. Accrediting Commn. Edn. on Health Svcs. Adminstrn., 1976-79; many other coms. in field; lectr. Sch. Nursing, St. Louis U., 1980. Numerous civic, ch. activities 1954-61. Recipient Appreciation award Mental Health Assn. St. Louis; NIMH grantee. Fellow Am. Coll. Healthcare Execs, Assn. Mental Health Adminstrs. (pres. 1973-74, gov. at large 1974-75, exec. com. 1972-075, chair adminstrv. rsch. and practices com. 1968-72, credentials com. 1984-87, cert. merit 1978, cert. appreciation 1975, Harold C. Pepenbrink award 1984, founder & editor Jour. Mental Health Adminstrn. 1972-78); mem. AAUP, Assn. Human Resource Mgmt. and Orgnl. Behavior, Orgnl. Behavior Teaching Soc., Mo. Assn. Mental Health Adminstrs. (founder, meeting coord.), Mental Health Assn. Mo. (pres. 1977-78, v.p. 1973-76, bd. dirs., exec. com. Appreciation award 1980, cons. 1983-87), Alpha Kappa Psi (life). Office: Univ of Mo 324 Clark Hall Columbia MO 65211

THOMPSON, WAYNE WRAY, historian; b. Wichita, Jan. 30, 1945; s. Clarence William and Elaine Maxine (Wray) T. m. Lillian Evelyn Hurlburt, June 28, 1969. BA, Union Coll., Schenectady, 1967; student, U. St. Andrews, Scotland, 1965-66; PhD, U. Calif., San Diego, 1975. Historian USAF, 1975—, Checkmate Air Campaign Planning Group, 1990-91; sr. hist. advisor Gulf War Air Power Survey, 1991-93. Contbr. Congress Investigates (Arthur M. Schlesinger Jr. and Roger Bruns, editors), 1975; editor Air Leadership, 1986; contbr. War in the Pacific (Bernard Nalty, editor), 1991. Served with AUS, 1971-72. Mem. Am. Hist. Assn., Orgn. Am. Historians, Air Force Hist. Found., Air Force Assn., Soc. Historians Am. Fgn. Rels., Soc. for Mil. History, U.S. Commn. on Mil. History, Inter-Univ. Seminar on Armed Forces, Assn. Asian Studies, Asia Soc., World History Assn., Phi Beta Kappa. Home: 9203 Saint Marks Pl Fairfax VA 22031-3045 Office: Hdqrs USAF History Washington DC 20332

THOMPSON, WESLEY DUNCAN, grain merchant; b. Blenheim, Ont., Can., Oct. 18, 1926; s. Wesley Gairdner and Anna Corneil (McCallum) T.; m. Patricia Florence Coatsworth, June 6, 1957; children—Wesley, Jennifer, Frank. B.A., U. Western Ont., London, Can., 1950. Pres., chmn. bd. dirs. W.G. Thompson & Sons Ltd, Blenheim, Can., 1950—; v.p. Hyland Farms Ltd., Ridgetown, Ont. Office: W G Thompson & Sons Ltd, 122 George St, Blenheim, ON Canada N0P 1A0

THOMPSON, WILLIAM, JR., engineering educator; b. Hyannis, Mass., Dec. 4, 1936; s. William and Dinella Helen (Szeliga) T.; m. Martha Marion Cate, July 4, 1959; children: Melanie A., Sharon E., Jennifer L., Keith W. SB, MIT, 1958; MS, Northeastern U., 1963; PhD, Pa. State U., 1971. Staff engr. Raytheon Co., Wayland, Mass., 1958-60; sr. engr. Cambridge (Mass.) Acoustical Assocs., 1960-66; research asst. Applied Research Lab., State College, Pa., 1966-72; asst. prof. engring. sci. Pa. State U., University Park, 1972-78, assoc. prof., 1978-85, prof., 1985—; head transducer group Applied Rsch. Lab., State College, 1971-80; sabbatic leave Naval Rsch. Lab., Orlando, Fla., 1988-89. Contbr. articles to profl. jours.; patentee in field. Bd. dirs., treas., past pres. Nittany Mountain chpt. Am. Diabetes Assn., State College, 1979-92; bd. dirs., asst. treas., treas. Mid-Pa. affiliate, Bethlehem, Pa., 1980-90. Recipient Disting. Svc. citation Mid-Pa. Affiliate Am. Diabetes Assn., 1981, and Affiliate Svc. award, 1988. Fellow Acoustical Soc. Am. (patent reviewer of soc. jour. 1990—); mem. IEEE (sr.), Soc. Engring. Sci., Lions (pres. State College 1981-82, 89-90, sec.-treas. 1984-88, 90-92, treas. 1992—, dist. diabetes chmn. 1983-88, 94—, chmn. Ctr. Lions Foresight Commn. 1992—, Melvin Jones fellow 1991). Republican. Avocations: sports, reading, photography. Home: 601 Glenn Rd State College PA 16803-3475 Office: Pa State U Dept of Engring Sci and Mechanics 230B Hammond Bldg University Park PA 16802

THOMPSON, WILLIAM BENBOW, JR., obstetrician, gynecologist, educator; b. Detroit, July 26, 1923; s. William Benbow and Ruth Wood (Locke) T.; m. Constance Carter, July 30, 1947 (div. Feb. 1958); 1 child, William Benbow IV; m. Jane Gilliland, Mar. 12, 1958; children: Reese Ellison, Belinda Day. AB, U. So. Calif., 1947, MD, 1951. Diplomate Am. Bd. Ob-Gyn. Resident Gallinger Mun. Hosp., Washington, 1952-53; resident George Washington U. Hosp., Washington, 1953-55; asst. ob-gyn. La. State U., 1955-56; asst. clinical prof. UCLA, 1957-64; assoc. prof. U. Calif.-Irvine Sch. Med., Orange, Calif., 1964-92; dir. gynecology U. Calif.-Irvine Sch. Med., 1977-92; prof. emeritus U. Calif.-Irvine Sch. Med., Orange, 1993—; vice chmn. ob-gyn. U. Calif.-Irvine Sch. Med., 1978-89; assoc. dean U. Calif.-Irvine Coll. Med., Irvine, 1969-73. Inventor: Thompson Retractor, 1976; Thompson Manipulator, 1977. Bd. dirs. Monarch Bay Assn. Laguna Niguel, Calif. 1969-77, Monarch Summitt II A ssn. 1981-83. With U.S. Army, 1942-44, PTO. Fellow ACS, Am. Coll. Ob-Gyn. (life), L.A. Ob-Gyn. Soc. (life); mem. Orange County Gynecology and Obstetrics Soc. (hon.), Am. Soc. Law and Medicine, Capistrano Bay Yacht Club (commodore 1975), Internat. Order Blue Gavel. Avocation: boating. Office: UCI Med Ctr OB/GYN 101 City Blvd W Orange CA 92668-2901

THOMPSON, WILLIAM DAVID, investment banking executive; b. Pitts., Nov. 30, 1921; s. Ross Ephraim and Blanche (Watson) T.; m. Mimi Wainwright Coleman, June 12, 1992; B.S., Yale U., 1944. Asst. advt. mgr. Scovill Mfg. Co., Waterbury, Conn., 1945-48; acctg. supr. James Thomas Chirurg, N.Y.C., 1948-52; mgr. mktg. dept. McCann-Erickson, N.Y.C., 1951-52; exec. v.p. Young & Rubicam, N.Y.C., 1952-89; chmn. Ctr. Devel. Investments, Inc., Greenwich, Conn., 1990; bd. dirs. Recovery Engring., Inc., Mpls. Lt. U.S. Army, 1943-44. Mem. Union League (N.Y.C.), Wee Burn Country Club, John's Island Club. Republican. Presbyterian. Avocations: golf, tennis. Home and Office: John's Island Ste 345 650 Beach Rd Vero Beach FL 32963-3394

THOMPSON, WILLIAM DAVID, minister, homiletics educator; b. Chgo., Jan. 11, 1929; s. Robert Ayre and Mary Elizabeth (McDowell) T.; m. Linda Brady Stevenson, Nov. 2, 1968; children—Tammy, Kirk, Lisa, Rebecca, Gwyneth. A.B., Wheaton Coll., Ill., 1950; B.D., No. Baptist Sem., 1954; M.A., Northwestern U., 1955, Ph.D., 1960. Ordained to ministry Am. Baptist Ch., 1954. Instr. speech Wheaton Coll., 1952-55; pastor Raymond Baptist Ch., Chgo., 1956-58; assoc. prof. homiletics No. Bapt. Sem., Chgo., 1958-62; mem. faculty Eastern Bapt. Sem., Phila., 1962-87, prof. preaching, 1969-87; minister 1st Bapt. Ch., Phila., 1983-90; pres. Thompson Comm., 1988—. Author: A Listener's Guide to Preaching, 1966, Recent Homiletical Thought, 1967, Dialogue Preaching, 1969, Preaching Biblically, 1981, Listening on Sunday for Sharing on Monday, 1983, Philadelphia's First Baptists, 1989. Mem. Phila. Hist. Commn., 1984-92. Vis. fellow Cambridge U., 1968-69. Mem. Nat. Speakers Assn., Acad. Homiletics (pres. 1973), Religious Speech Communication Assn. (v.p. 1983, pres. 1984), Union League Club. Republican. Home: 765 Ormond Ave Drexel Hill PA 19026-2417

THOMPSON, WILLIAM IRWIN, humanities educator, author; b. Chgo., July 16, 1938; s. Chester Andrew and Lillian Margaret (Fahey) T.; m. Gail Joan Gordon, Feb. 3, 1960 (div. Jan. 1979); children: Evan Timothy, Hilary Joan, Andrew Rhys; m. Beatrice Madeleine Rudin, Mar. 1, 1979. B.A. with honors in Philosophy, Pomona Coll., 1962; M.A. (Woodrow Wilson fellow), Cornell U., 1964, Ph.D. (Woodrow Wilson dissertation fellow), 1966. Instr. humanities MIT, Cambridge, 1965-66; asst. prof. MIT, 1966-67, Old Dominion fellow, 1967, assoc. prof. humanities, 1968; assoc. prof. humanities York U., Toronto, Ont., Can., 1968-72; prof. York U., 1973; vis. prof. religion Syracuse (N.Y.) U., 1973; vis. scholar in polit. sci. U. Hawaii, 1981, vis. prof., 1985; vis. prof. Celtic studies U. Toronto, 1984; founding dir. Lindisfarne Assocs., 1972—. Author: Imagination of an Insurrection: Dublin, Easter 1916, 1967, At the Edge of History, 1971, Passages about Earth, 1974, Evil and World Order, 1976, Darkness and Scattered Light, 1978, The Time Falling Bodies Take to Light, 1981, From Nation to Emanation, 1981, Blue Jade from the Morning Star, 1983, Islands Out of Time, 1985, Pacific Shift, 1986, GAIA: A Way of Knowing, 1987, Imaginary Landscape, 1989, Selected Poems 1959-89; GAIA TWO: Emergence, the New Science of Becoming, 1991, Reimagination of the World, 1991, The American Replacement of Nature, 1991, Coming into Being, 1996, Worlds Interpenetrating and Apart, 1996. Hon. colleague and Lindis Farne Scholar of the Cathedral of St. John the Divine, N.Y.C. Recipient Obstfelder prize Oslo Internat. Poetry Festival, 1986; Rockefeller scholar Calif. Inst. Integral Studies, 1993-95; Laurance S. Rockefeller fellow, 1992-96. Address: Cathedral St John the Divine 1047 Amsterdam Ave New York NY 10025

THOMPSON, WILLIAM JOSEPH, secondary school educator, coach; b. Sedalia, Mo., Jan. 4, 1953; s. Robert Clark and Maxine Flavia (Pettyjohn) T.; m. Deborah Ann St. Germaine, Dec. 21, 1992; children: Bleys Kueck, Jordan Kueck, Seth Thompson. BA in History, Okla. State U., 1975; MA in History, U. Mo., 1981. Cert. tchr.Colo., Mo. Grad. tchg. asst. history U. Mo., Columbia, 1975-79; social studies tchr. Rampart H.S., Colorado Springs, Colo., 1983—, sch. writing assessment com., 1991-93, mem. sch. accountability com., 1993-94. Named Coach of Yr., Gazette Telegraph, 1986. Mem. Nat. Coun. for the Social Studies, Colo. H.S. Activities Assn., Nat. Soccer Coaches Assn. Am., Phi Delta Kappa. Office: Rampart HS 8250 Lexington Dr Colorado Springs CO 80920-4301

THOMPSON, WILLIAM MOREAU, radiologist, educator; b. Phila., Oct. 20, 1943; s. Charles Moreau and Aileen (Haddon) T.; m. Judy Ann Seel, July 27, 1968; children—Christopher Moreau, Thayer Haddon. B.A., Colgate U., 1965; M.D., U. Pa., 1969. Diplomate Am. Bd. Radiology. Intern, Case Western Res. U., Cleve., 1969-70; resident in radiology Duke U., Durham, N.C., 1972-75, asst. prof. Duke U. Med. Center, 1976-77, assoc. prof., 1977-82, prof. radiology, 1982-86; prof., chmn. dept. radiology, Vilhelmina and Eugene Gedgared chair in Radiology, U. Minn. Hosp. and Clinic, Mpls., 1986—. Served with USPHS, 1970-72. Recipient James Picker Found. Scholar in Acad. Medicine award, 1975-79; research and devel. grantee VA, 1977-86. Fellow Am. Coll. Radiology; mem. AMA, Radiology Soc. N.Am. (program chmn. 1994—), Minn. Med. Soc., Am. Roentgen Ray Soc., Assn. Univ. Radiologists (pres. 1989-90), Soc. Gastrointestinal Radiology (pres. 1995), Sigma Xi. Republican. Presbyterian. Contbr. chpts. to books, articles to profl. jours. Home: 18700 Woolman Dr Minnetonka MN 55345-3164 Office: U Minn Med Sch UMHC Box 292 Harvard Street Rd Minneapolis MN 55455-0361

THOMPSON, WILLIAM REID, public utility executive, lawyer; b. Durham, N.C., Aug. 13, 1924; s. William Reid and Myrtle (Siler) T.; m. Mary Louise Milliken, Aug. 16, 1952; children: Mary Elizabeth, William Reid III, John Milliken, Susan Siler. BS, U. N.C., 1945; LLB, Harvard U., 1949. Bar: N.C. 1949. Ptnr. Barber and Thompson, Pittsboro, N.C., 1949-58; judge Superior Cts. N.C., 1958-60; assoc. gen. counsel Carolina Power & Light Co., 1960-63, v.p., gen. counsel, 1963-67, exec. v.p., 1967-71; chmn. bd., chief exec. officer Potomac Electric Power Co., Washington, 1971-89, chmn. bd., 1989-92; bd. dirs. Potomac Elec. Power Co. Bd. dirs. Nat. Symphony Orch. Assn.; mem. Fed. City Coun., N.C. Gen. Assembly from Chatham County, 1955-57. Served to lt. (j.g.) USNR, 1943-45, PTO. Mem. ABA, Edison Electric Inst. (bd. dirs., past chmn.), Southeastern Electric Exchange (past pres.), Assn. Edison Illuminating Cos. (past pres.), Bus. Council, Bus. Roundtable, Phi Beta Kappa, Delta Kappa Epsilon. Democrat. Methodist. Clubs: Met., Burning Tree, Chevy Chase, 1925 F St (Washington). Lodge: Rotary. Office: Potomac Electric Power Co 1900 Pennsylvania Ave NW Washington DC 20068-0001

THOMPSON, WILLIAM SCOTT, lawyer; b. Grand Rapids, Mich., Feb. 6, 1930; s. William Scott Thompson and Mary Louise (Chatel) Kruse; m. Margaret Jane Favier, June 16, 1951; children: William, Michelle, Marta, Rebecca. BSME, U. Mich., 1952; JD, U. Notre Dame, 1959. Bar: Ind. 1959, U.S. Dist. Ct. (so. dist.) Ind. 1959, U.S. Ct. Appeals (Fed. cir.) 1963. Engr. Bendix Corp., South Bend, Ind., 1954-57, patent agt., 1957-59, patent atty., 1959-64, regional patent counsel, Utica, N.Y. and Detroit, 1964-74; patent dept. mgr. Caterpillar Inc., Peoria, Ill., 1974-94; with Internat. Intellectual Property Cons., Ft. Myers, Fla., 1994—. 1st lt. USAF, 1952-54. Mem. Am. Intellectual Property Law Assn. (past pres.), Internat. Patent and Trademark Assn. (v.p.), Assn. Corp. Patent Counsel, ABA (internat. activities coord.).

THOMPSON, WILLIAM TALIAFERRO, JR., internist, educator; b. Petersburg, Va., May 26, 1913; s. William Taliaferro and Anne C. (McIlwaine) T.; m. Jessie G. Baker, June 21, 1941; children—William Taliaferro III, Addison Baker, Jessie Ball. A.B., Davidson Coll., 1934, Sc.D. (hon.), 1975; M.D., Med. Coll. Va., 1938. Diplomate Am. Bd. Internal Medicine. Intern 4th med. service Boston City Hosp., 1938-40; asst. resident Mass. Gen. Hosp., 1940-41; resident Med. Coll. Va., Richmond, 1941, mem. faculty, 1946—, William Branch Porter prof., chmn. dept. medicine, also chief med. services hosps., 1959-73, prof., 1959-75, emeritus prof., 1975—, W.T. Thompson Jr. prof., 1978; mem. staff McGuire Clinic-St. Luke's Hosp., 1946-54; chief medicine service McGuire VA Hosp., 1954-59; med. dir. Westminister-Canterbury House, Richmond, 1975-87. Editor Va. Med. Monthly, 1976-82; contbr. to med. jours. Chmn. bd. mgrs., mem. med. adv. bd. Alfred I. DuPont Inst. and Nemours Found., 1962-78; med. adv. bd. Greenbrier Clinic; pres. Va. Assn. Mental Health, 1955-57, Richmond Bd. Housing and Hygiene, 1952-59; bd. dirs. Meml. Guidance Clinic, 1950-59, Maymont Found., Richmond, 1975-78; bd. dirs. Med. Coll. Va. Found., 1981—; trustee Collegiate Sch., 1952-69, pres., 1965-67; trustee Davidson Coll., 1965-73, 78-80, bd. visitors, 1981—; bd. visitors Longwood Coll., 1982-84; trustee, Union Theol. Sem., Richmond, 1960-70, 78—, Crippled Childrens' Hosp., 1975—, Westminster Canterbury House, 1982-86, St. Luke's Hosp., 1981-85, Westminster Canterbury Found., 1987—. Served to maj. M.C. AUS, 1941-46. Recipient cert. of disting. svc. Med. Soc. Va., 1982, Outstanding Tchr. award Med. Coll. Va., 1985, Outstanding Med. Alumnus award, 1986, Disting. Svc. to Medicine award Med. Coll. Va., 1986, Lettie Pate Evans/Whitehead Evans award Westminster Canterbury House. Mem. ACP (master, chmn. Va. sect. 1961, gov. for Va. 1971-75, Laureate award Va. chpt. 1986), Am. Clin. and Climatological Assn., N.Y. Acad. Scis., Am. Fedn. Clin. Research, So. Soc. Clin. Investigation, Richmond Acad. Medicine (pres. 1972), Davidson Coll. Nat. Alumni Assn. (pres. 1979-80), Phi Beta Kappa, Alpha Omega Alpha, Omicron Delta Kappa, Kappa Sigma. Presbyterian (deacon, elder). Clubs: Country of Va. (Richmond), Commonwealth (Richmond). Home: PO Box 29709 Richmond VA 23242-0709

THOMPSON, W(ILMER) LEIGH, pharmaceutical company executive, physician, pharmacologist; b. Shreveport, La., June 25, 1938; s. Wilmer Leigh and Mary Bissell (McIver) T.; m. Maurice Eugenie Horne, Mar. 29, 1957; 1 child, Mary Linton Bounetheau. BS, Coll. Charleston, 1958; MS in Pharmacology, Med. U. S.C., 1960, PhD, 1963; MD, John Hopkins U., 1965; ScD (hon.) Med. U. S.C., 1994. Diplomate Am. Bd. Internal Medicine. Intern, Johns Hopkins Hosp., 1965-66, resident, 1966-67, 69-70; staff assoc. NIH, Bethesda, Md., 1967-69; asst. prof. medicine and pharmacology Johns Hopkins U., Balt., 1970-74, dir. critical care medicine and emergency medicine, 1970-74; prof. medicine, assoc. prof. pharmacology Case Western Res. U., Cleve., 1974-82, head critical care and clin. pharmacology, 1974-82; prof. medicine Ind. U., 1985—; dir. Lilly Rsch. Labs., Eli Lilly & Co., Indpls., 1982, exec. dir., 1982-86, v.p., 1986-88, group v.p., 1988-91, exec. v.p., 1992-93, chief sci. officer, 1993-94; chmn., CEO Profound Quality Resources Consulting, Charleston, 1995—; mem. bd. dirs. Corvas Internat., DNX Inc., Guilford Pharmaceuticals, Genemedicine, Houghton, Inspire, Ontogeny, Orphan Medical,, Medarex, Roper Found., Pharmaceutical Development, Inc. Editor: Textbook of Critical Care Medicine, 1984, 89, State of the Art: Critical Care, 1980-83. Served to surgeon USPHS, 1967-69. Burroughs Wellcome Fund scholar 1975-80; recipient Faculty Devel. award Pharm. Mfrs. Assn. Found. Fellow ACP, Am. Coll. Critical Care Medicine; mem. Soc. Critical Care Medicine (pres. 1981-82, hon. life mem. 1987), Cen. Soc. Clin. Rsch., Am. Soc. Pharmacology and Exptl. Therapeutics. Episcopalian and Huguenot. Office: Profound Quality Resources Consulting 54 King St Charleston SC 29401-2731

THOMPSON, WINFRED LEE, university president, lawyer; b. Little Rock, July 28, 1945; s. Vester Lee and Willow Mae (Mills) T.; m. Carmen Angeles Tiongson; children: Emily, Michael. BA, U. Ark., 1967; MA, U. Chgo., 1970, PhD, 1987; JD, George Washington U., 1978. Congl. aide U.S. Ho. of Reps., Washington, 1973-77; exec. asst. to asst. sec. labor U.S. Dept. Labor, Washington, 1977-78; atty. Hatfield and Thompson, Searcy, Ark., 1978-81; dir. devel. Ark. State U., Jonesboro, 1981-82, v.p. for planning and devel., 1982-84; v.p. for fin. and adminstrn. U. Ark. System, Fayetteville, 1984-85; vice chancellor for fin. and adminstrn. U. Ark, Fayetteville, 1985-87; pres. U. Cen. Ark., Conway, 1988—; bd. dirs. Ark. Sci. and Tech. Authority, Little Rock, 1984-89. Bd. dirs. Ark. Symphony Orch., 1991-94. 2d lt. USAR. Woodrow Wilson fellow U. Chgo., 1969-70. Mem. Phi Beta Kappa. Home: 140 Donaghey Ave Conway AR 72032-6252 Office: U Ctrl Ark Office of the President 201 Donaghey Ave Conway AR 72035

THOMPSON, WYNELLE DOGGETT, chemistry educator; b. Birmingham, Ala., May 25, 1914; d. William Edward and Dollie Odessa (Ferguson) Doggett; m. Davis Hunt Thompson, Sept. 17, 1938; children: Carolyn Wynelle, Helen Hunt, Cynthia Carle, Davis Hunt, jr. BS summa cum laude, Birmingham Southern, 1934, MS, 1935; MS, U. Ala., 1956, PhD, 1960. From grad. lab. asst. to instr. chemistry Birmingham (Ala.) Southern Coll., 1934-36,39-44; tchr. Bd. Edn., Sheffield, Ala., 1936-37; jr. chemist Bur. Home Econs. USDA, Washington, 1937-38; instr. chemistry U. Ala. extension ctr., Birmingham, 1950-54; grad. asst. biochemistry U. Ala. Med. Coll., Birmingham, 1954-55; from asst. prof. chemistry to prof. emerita Birmingham (Ala.) Southern Coll., 1955-76; rsch. assoc. U. Ala. Dept. Biochemistry, Birmingham, 1965, 1968, 1969, Dept. Biophysics, 1976-78; adj. prof. chemistry New Coll. Tuscaloosa, Ala., 1980—. Contbr. articles to profl. jours. Bd. dirs. Cahaba Coun. Girl Scouts U.S. (vol. chmn. troop orgn., camping.). Grantee NSF, Appleton, Wis., Emory U., Atlanta; recipient disting. alumna award Birmingham So. Coll., 1976, medal of svc. award, 1994. Fellow Am. Inst. Chemists; mem. AAUW (bd. dirs., treas.), Am. Chem. Soc. (sec. 1942-44, 72-73, chmn.-elect 1966-67, chmn. 1967-68, 50-Yr. Mem. award 1992), Ala. Acad. Sci. (chmn. edn. sect. 1960-62), Phi Beta Kappa, Sigma Xi (sec. 1970-72), Theta Chi Delta, Delta Phi Alpha, Theta Sigma Lambda, Kappa Delta Epsilon, Delta Kappa Gamma, Kappa Mu Epsilon. Republican. Methodist. Avocations: music, camping, travel, needlework. Home: 1237 Berwick Rd Birmingham AL 35242

THOMS, JEANNINE AUMOND, lawyer; b. Chgo.; d. Emmett Patrick and Margaret (Gallet) Aumond; m. Richard W. Thoms; children: Catherine Thoms, Alison Thoms. AA, McHenry County Coll., 1979; BA, No. Ill. U., 1981; JD, Ill. Inst. Tech., 1984. Bar: Ill. 1984, U.S. Dist. Ct. (no. dist.) Ill. 1984, U.S. Ct. Appeals (7th cir.) 1985. Assoc. Foss Schuman Drake & Barnard, Chgo., 1984-86; assoc. Zukowski Rogers Flood & McArdle, Crystal Lake and Chgo., 1986-92, ptnr., 1992—; bd. dirs. McHenry County Mental Health Bd., 1991—, pres., 1995—; arbitrator 19th Jud. Ct. Ill., 1991—; cert. mediator Acad. Family Mediators, Ill., 1992—. Mem. women's adv. coun. to Gov., State of Ill. Mem. ABA, LWV, Ill. State Bar Assn., Chgo. Bar Assn., McHenry County Bar Assn., Am. Trial Lawyers Assn., Acad. Family Mediators, Women's Network, Phi Alpha Delta. Office: Zukowski Rogers Flood & McArdle 50 N Virginia Crystal Lake IL 60014 also: 100 S Wacker Dr Chicago IL 60600

THOMSEN, DONALD LAURENCE, JR., institute executive, mathematician; b. Stamford, Conn., Apr. 21, 1921; s. Donald Laurence and Linda (Comstock) T.; m. Linda Rollins Leach, June 14, 1958; children: Melinda Rollins, Katherine Thomsen Love, Donald Laurence III. Grad., Phillips Exeter Acad., 1938; BA in Math. magna cum laude, Amherst Coll., 1942; PhD, MIT, 1947. Tchg. fellow MIT, 1942, instr., 1943-47; instr., then asst. prof. Haverford (Pa.) Coll., 1947-50; rsch. fellow, then rsch. engr. Jet Propulsion Lab., Calif. Inst. Tech., 1950-52; asst. prof. Pa. State U., 1952-54; with IBM Corp., 1954-72, spl. asst. to dir. edn., 1961-62, dir. profl. activities, 1963-66, corp. dir. engring. edn., 1967-72; pres. Societal Inst. of Math. Scis., New Canaan, Conn., 1973—, also bd. dirs.; mem. vis. com. Coll. Sci., Drexel Inst. Tech., 1969-71; mem. adv. com. for Individualized sci. instrnl. sys. Coll. Edn., Fla. State U., 1973-75; prin. investigator rsch. studies in environ. pollution and human exposure, 1973—; AIDS rschr., 1988—. Author: Higher Transcendental Functions, 3 vols; contbr. articles to profl. jours. Recipient Spl. cert. Milw. Sch. Engring., 1969. Mem. AAAS, Am. Math. Soc., Am. Statis. Assn., Math. Assn. Am. (chmn. com. insts.), Soc. Indsl. and Applied Math. (pres. 1959, chmn. trustees 1960-72, Merit cert. Inst. Math. and Soc. 1972), Am. Fedn. Info. Processing Socs. (chmn. edn. com. 1965-66, chmn. U.S. com. IFIP Congress 1968, 66-69, bd. dirs. 1969-77, exec. com. 1975-77), Assn. Computing Machinery, Am. Ordnance Assn. (chmn. rsch. divsn.), Internat. Fedn. Info. Processing (chmn. exhibits com. N.Y.C. Congress 1965), Conf. Bd. Math. Scis. (chmn. budget and fin. com.), Internat. AIDS Soc., Internat. Soc. Exposure Analysis, Conn. Acad. Arts and Scis., Cosmos Club (Washington), The Princeton Club (N.Y.C.), Woodway Country Club (Darien, Conn.), Phi Beta Kappa, Sigma Xi, Delta Tau Delta. Presbyterian. Home and Office: Societal Inst Math Scis 97 Parish Rd S New Canaan CT 06840

THOMSEN, MARCIA ROZEN, marketing executive; b. St. Louis, Sept. 23, 1958; d. Saul and Ruth (Burstein) Rozen; m. Timothy Lars Thomsen, Sept. 3, 1984; 1 child, David Rozen. B in Journalism, U. Mo., 1980. Media planner, buyer Leo Burnett Co., Chgo., 1980-82, asst. acct. exec., 1982-83; acct. exec. D'Arcy Masius, Benton & Bowles, St. Louis, 1983-85, acct. supr., 1985-86, v.p., 1986-89; dir. mktg. Pizza Hut, Inc. subs. PepsiCo Inc., St. Louis, 1989-90; dir. of delivery mktg. Pizza Hut, Inc. subs. PepsiCo Inc., Wichita, Kans., 1990-91, sr. dir. nat. segment mktg., 1991-92, v.p. nat. mtkg., 1992—; chmn. com. DMB&B Account Mgmt., St. Louis, 1988—. Mem. Chgo. Advt. Club. Office: Pizza Hut Inc 6600 LBJ Freeway Ste 100 Dallas TX 75240*

THOMSEN, MARK WILLIAM, religious organization administrator; b. Owatonna, Minn., Feb. 24, 1931; s. Jens Harry and Helena Rogna (Hansen) T.; m. Mary Lou Kafer, Nov. 29, 1952; children: Mark Lawrence, Derek James, Sandra Kay, Sheryl Louise. BA, Dana Coll., 1953; BDiv, Trinity Theol. Sem., 1956; ThM, Princeton Theol. Sem., 1957; PhD, Northwestern U., 1971; DD, Dana Coll., 1982. Vice prin. acad. affairs, mem. faculty Theol. Coll. No. Nigeria, Bukuru, 1957-66; Luth. campus pastor U. No. Iowa, Cedar Falls, 1966-67; assoc. prof. philosophy and religion Dana Coll., Blair, Nebr., 1967-72; pastor St. Peter Luth. Ch., Dubuque, 1972-80; assoc. prof. mission and world religions Luth. Northwestern Theol. Sem., St. Paul, 1980-81; dir. Divsn. for World Mission and Interch. Coop. Am. Luth. Ch., Mpls., 1981-87; exec. dir. Divsn. for Global Mission Evang. Luth. Ch. in Am., Chgo., 1987—; guest lectr. mgmt. of ministry Wartburg Theol. Sem., Dubuque, 1979; bd. dirs. Luth. World Relief, N.Y.C.; project com. Dept. for Mission and Devel., Luth. World Fedn., Geneva, 1990—; mem. gen. bd. Nat. Coun. of the Chs. of Christ in USA, N.Y.C., 1988—; advisor Ch. Coun., Evang. Luth. Ch. in Am., Chgo., 1988—. Author: Introducing New Testament Theology, 1964, The Word and the Way of the Cross: Christian Witness Among Muslim and Buddhist People, 1993, (booklet) Together in Witness: A Study of the Acts of the Apostles, 1983. Recipient Disting. Alumnus award Dana Coll., 1988. Mem. Am. Soc. Missiology. Lutheran. Avocations: jogging, golf.

THOMSEN, THOMAS RICHARD, communications company executive; b. Avoca, Iowa, July 29, 1935; s. Howard August and Edna Mary (Walker) T.; m. Raylene Alice Tomes, Sept. 1, 1956; children: Jeffrey, Cathy. BSME, U. Nebr., 1958; MS, MIT, 1973. Engr. Western Electric Co., Omaha, 1957-64; mgr. Western Electric Co., Columbus, Ohio, 1964-72; v.p. Bell Sales West Western Electric Co., Morristown, N.J., 1979-80; asst. v.p. ops. staff AT&T, Basking Ridge, N.J., 1980-81; exec. v.p. Western Electric Corp., N.Y.C., 1981-82; pres. AT&T Tech. Systems, Berkeley Heights, N.J., 1982-90, ret., 1990; chmn. bd. Lithium Tech Corp, Plymouth Meeting, Pa., 1994—; bd. dirs. AT&T Credit Corp., Sandia Corp., Albuquerque, Olivetti Corp., Western Electric Corp. Trustee Rensselaer Poly. Inst. Mem. Telephone Pioneers Am. (former pres.), Pi Tau Sigma, Sigma Tau. Republican. Presbyterian. Avocations: golf, tennis. Home: 26 Bellinghamshire Pl New Hope PA 18938-5657 Office: Lithium Tech Corp 5115 Campus Dr Plymouth Meeting PA 19462-1129

THOMSON, ALEX, cinematographer. Cinematographer: (films) Fear Is the Key, 1973, The Cat and the Canary, 1978, The Class of Miss MacMichael, 1978, Excalibur, 1981 (Academy award nomination best cinematography 1981), The Keep, 1983, Blueshot, 1983, Eureka, 1984, Electric Dreams, 1984, Labyrinth, 1985, Year of the Dragon, 1985, Legend, 1986, Raw Deal, 1986, The Sicilian, 1987, Date with an Angel, 1987, Duet for One, 1987, High Spirits, 1988, Track 29, 1988, Leviathan, 1989, The Rachel Papers, 1989, Mr. Destiny, 1990, Alien 3, 1992, Cliffhanger, 1993, Demolition Man, 1993, Black Beauty, 1994. Office: Treetops 11 Croft Rd, Chalfront St Peter Gerrards Crossing, Buckinghamshire England

THOMSON, BASIL HENRY, JR., lawyer, university general counsel; b. Amarillo, Tex., Jan. 17, 1945; m. Margaret Shepard, May 4, 1985; children: Christopher, Matthew, Robert. BBA, Baylor U., 1968, JD, 1973. Bar: Tex. 1974, U.S. Ct. Mil. Appeals 1974, U.S. Supreme Ct. 1977, U.S. Dist. Ct. (we. dist.) Tex. 1988, U.S. Ct. Appeals (fed. cir.) 1990. Oil title analyst Hunt Oil Co., Dallas, 1971-73; atty., advisor Regulations and Adminstrv. Law div. Office of Chief Counsel USCG, Washington, 1973-77; dir. estate planning devel. dept. Baylor U., Waco, Tex., 1977-80, gen. counsel, 1980—; adj. prof. law Baylor U.; lobbyist legis. Ind. Higher Edn., 71st Session of Tex. Legislature; mem. legis. com. Gov.'s Task Force on Drug Abuse; dir. govtl. relations Baylor U.; speaker at meetings of coll. and univ. adminstrs.; assisted in drafting legis. for Texan's War on Drugs Tex. Legislature. Active Heart O'Tex. coun. Boy Scouts Am., Heart of Tex. Coun. on Alcoholism and Drug Abuse, bd. dirs., 1987-91. Recipient Pres.'s award Ind. Colls. and Univs. of Tex., 1994, Dist. award of merit Boy Scouts Am. Fellow Coll. State Bar Tex.; mem. ABA, FBA, Nat. Assn. Coll. and Univ. Attys. (fin., nominations and elections coms. 1994-95, bd. dirs. 1988-91), Tex. Bar Assn., Waco Bar Assn., McLennan County Bar Assn., Owners Assn. of Sugar Creek, Inc. (dir. 1995—). Baptist. Avocations: backpacking, running, environ. concerns. Home: 100 Sugar Creek Pl Waco TX 76712-3410 Office: Baylor U PO Box 97034 Waco TX 76798-7034

THOMSON, GEORGE RONALD, lawyer, educator; b. Wadsworth, Ohio, Aug. 25, 1959; s. John Alan and Elizabeth (Galbraith) T. BA summa cum laude, Miami U., Oxford, Ohio, 1982, MA summa cum laude, 1983; JD with honors, Ohio State U., 1986. Bar: Ill. 1986, U.S. Dist. Ct. (no. dist.) Ill. 1986. Teaching fellow Miami U., 1982-83; dir. speech activities Ohio State U., Columbus, 1983-86; assoc. Peterson, Ross, Schloerb & Seidel, Chgo., 1986-87, Lord, Bissell & Brook, Chgo., 1987-94; asst. corp. counsel City of Chgo., 1994—; adj. prof. dept. comm. De Paul U., Chgo., 1988-90; presenter in field. Contbr. articles to profl. jours. Fundraiser Chgo. Hist. Soc., Steppenwolf Theater Co., AIDS Legal Counsel Chgo., Smithsonian Instn., Washington, 1988—, U.S. Tennis Assn., 1990—; bd. dirs. Metro Sports Assn., 1992-94, Gerber-Hart Libr. and Archives, 1993-95, Gay and Lesbian Tennis Alliance Am., 1993-95, Team Chgo., 1994-96; mem. coord. coun. Nat. Gay and Lesbian History Month; mem. Lawyer's Com. for Ill Human Rights; dir. Chgo. Internat. Charity Tennis Classic, 1993, 94, 95. Recipient Spl. Commendation Ohio Ho. of Reps., 1984, 85, Nat. Forensics Assn. award, 1982. Mem. ABA, Chgo. Bar Assn., Lesbian and Gay Bar Assn., Speech Comm. Assn. Am., Mortar Bd., Phi Beta Kappa, Phi Kappa Phi, Omicron Delta Kappa, Delta Sigma Rho-Tau Kappa Alpha, Phi Alpha Delta. Presbyterian. Avocations: tennis, flute, antiques, folk arts and crafts, reading, travel. Home: 2835 N Pine Grove Ave Unit 2S Chicago IL 60657-6109 Office: City of Chgo Dept of Law 30 N LaSalle Ste 700 Chicago IL 60602

THOMSON, GERALD EDMUND, physician, educator; b. N.Y.C., 1932; s. Lloyd and Sybil (Gilbourne) T.; m. Carolyn Webber; children: Gregory, Karen. M.D., Howard U., 1959. Diplomate Am. Bd. Internal Medicine (bd. govs. 1985-92, exec. com. 1988-92, chmn. elect 1990-91, chmn. 1991-92). Intern SUNY-Kings County Hosp. Center, Bklyn., 1959-60; resident in medicine SUNY-Kings County Hosp. Center, 1960-62, chief resident, 1962-63, N.Y. Heart Assn. fellow in nephrology, 1964-65, asst. vis. physician, 1963-70, clin. dir. dialysis unit, 1965-67; practice medicine specializing in internal medicine N.Y.C., 1963—; attending physician SUNY Med. Bklyn. Hosp., 1966-70; instr. in medicine SUNY, Bklyn., 1963-68; clin. asst. prof. medicine SUNY, 1968-70; asso. chief med. services Coney Island Hosp., Bklyn., 1967-70; attending physician Presbyn. Hosp., 1970—; dir. nephrology Harlem Hosp. Center, N.Y.C., 1970-71; dir. med. services Harlem Hosp. Center, 1971-85, pres. med. bd., 1976-78; assoc. prof. medicine Columbia Coll. Physicians and Surgeons, 1970-72, prof., 1972—, Samuel Lambert prof. medicine, 1980—; exec. v.p. for profl. affairs, chief of staff Columbia-Presbyn. Med. Ctr., 1985-90; assoc. dean Coll. Physicians and Surgeons, Columbia U., N.Y.C., 1990—; Mem. Health Rsch. Coun. City N.Y., 1972-75; mem. med. adv. bd. N.Y. Kidney Found., 1971-82; mem. Health Rsch. Coun., State N.Y., 1975-81; mem. hypertension info. and edn. adv. com. NIH, 1973-74, N.Y. State Adv. Com. on Hypertension, 1977-80; com. on non-pharm. treatment of hypertension Inst. of Medicine, Nat. Acad. Scis., 1980; mem. med. adv. bd. Nat. Assn. Patients on Hemodialysis and Transplantation, 1973-83; mem. adv. bd. Sch. Biomed. Edn., CUNY, 1979-83, Med. News Network, 1993-95; mem. com. on mild hypertension Nat. Heart and Lung Inst., 1976, mem. clin. trials rev. com., 1980-85, mem. rev. panel, 1979; bd. dirs. N.Y. Heart Assn., 1973-81, chmn. com. high blood pressure, 1976-81, Primary Care Devel. Corp.; chmn. com. hypertension N.Y. Met. Regional Med. Program, 1974-76; mem. adv. com. Heart and Hypertension Inst. of N.Y. State, 1984; mem. N.Y. Gov.'s Health Adv. Council, 1981-84, pub. Health Coun., N.Y., 1983-95, Joint Nat. Com. High Blood Pressure NIH, 1983-84, 87-88, mem. rev. panel hypertension detection and follow-up program, 1980; mem. policy monitoring bd. study cardiovascular risk factors in young Nat. Heart, Lung and Blood Inst., 1984-90; mem. panel on receiving and withholding med. treatment ACLU, 1984-88; mem. Grad. Med. Edn. Commn., State of N.Y., 1984-86, mem. Commn. on End-State Renal Disease, 1985, 89-90; pres. Washington Heights-Inwood Ambulatory Care Network Corp., 1986-91; bd. dirs. Primary Care Devel. Corp., 1993—. Mem. adv. bd. Jour. Urban Health, 1974-80, Med. News Network, 1993-94. Chmn. ad hoc com. on access to nursing homes Pub. Health Council State of N.Y.; pres. Washington Heights-Inwood Ambulatory Care

Network Corp., 1986-91; chmn. Federated Coun. Internal Medicine, 1991-92; mem. Mayor's Commn. Health and Hosps. Corp.; dir. Harlem Ctr. for Health Promotion and Disease Prevention; bd. dirs. Primary Care Devel. Corp. Recipient Nat. Med. award Nat. Kidney Found. N.Y., 1984, Outstanding Alumnus award Howard U., 1987, Dean's Outstanding Tchg. award Coll. Physicians and Surgeons Columbia U., 1986. Fellow ACP (Gov.'s coun. downstate region 1982-89, chmn. com. health pub. policy N.Y. chpt. 1982-89, health care professions com. 1987-90, bd. regents 1990—, chmn. nat. health and pub. policy com. 1993-94, pres.-elect 1994-95, pres. 1995-96), N.Y. Acad. Medicine (mem. com. medicine in soc. 1974-76); mem. AAAS, N.Y. Soc. Nephrology (pres. 1973-74), Am. Fedn. Clin. Research, Federated Coun. for Internal Medicine (chmn. 1991-92, 95-96), Soc. Urban Physicians (pres. 1972-73), Am. Soc. Artificial Internal Organs, Assn. Prog. Dirs. in Internal Medicine, Pub. Health Assn. N.Y.C. (dir. 1983-86), Physicians for Social Responsibility of N.Y. (dir. 1983-85), Assn. Acad. Minority Physicians (pres. 1988-90). Home: Premium Pt New Rochelle NY 10801-5327 Office: Coll Physicians & Surgeons Columbia U New York NY 10032

THOMSON, GRACE MARIE, nurse, minister; b. Pecos, Tex., Mar. 30, 1932; d. William McKinley and Elzora (Wilson) Olliff; m. Radford Chaplin, Nov. 3, 1952; children: Deborah C., William Earnest. Assoc. Applied Sci., Odessa Coll., 1965; extension student U. Pa. Sch. Nursing, U. Calif., Irvine, Golden West Coll. RN, Calif., Okla., Ariz., Md., Tex. Dir. nursing Grays Nursing Home, Odessa, Tex., 1965; supr. nursing Med. Hill, Oakland, Calif.; charge nurse pediatrics Med. Ctr., Odessa; dir. nursing Elmwood Extended Care, Berkeley, Calif.; surg. nurse Childrens Hosp., Berkeley; med./surg. charge nurse Merritt Hosp., Oakland, Calif.; adminstr. Grace and Assocs.; advocate for emotionally abused children; active Watchtower and Bible Tract Soc.; evangelist for Jehovah's Witnesses, 1954—.

THOMSON, H. BAILEY, editor; b. Aliceville, Ala., Feb. 4, 1949; s. William Joshua and Attie (Kimbrell) T.; m. Reba Kristi Garrison, Nov. 19, 1977; 1 child, Sarah Rachel. BA, U. Ala., 1972, MA, 1974, PhD, 1995. Copy editor Huntsville (Ala.) Times, 1971-72, staff writer, 1975-77; reporter, copy editor Tuscaloosa (Ala.) News, 1972-75; editorial page editor Shreveport (La.) Jour., 1977-86; chief editorial writer Orlando (Fla.) Sentinel, 1986-91; assoc. editor Mobile (Ala.) Press Register, 1992—. Author: Shreveport, 1986. vice chmn. La. Endowment Humanities, 1984-85. Profl. journalism fellow Stanford U., 1981-82; finalist Pulitzer prizes for editl. writing, 1995, Green Eyeshade awards, 1988, 1996. Mem. Nat. Conf. Editl. Writers (bd. dirs. 1991-92). Methodist. Avocations: historical writing, reading. Home: 706 Oak Bluff Dr Daphne AL 36526-7534 Office: The Mobile Press Register Inc PO Box 2488 304 Government St Mobile AL 36630-0001

THOMSON, JAMES ALAN, research company executive; b. Boston, Jan. 21, 1945; s. James Alan and Mary Elizabeth (Pluff) T.; m. Darlene Thomson; children: Kristen Ann, David Alan. BS, U. N.H., 1967; MS, Purdue U., 1970, PhD, 1972. Research fellow U. Wis., Madison, 1972-74; systems analyst Office Sec. Def., U.S. Dept. Def., Washington, 1974-77; staff mem. Nat. Security Council, White House, Washington, 1977-81; v.p. RAND, Santa Monica, Calif., 1981-89, pres., chief exec. officer, 1989—. Contbr. articles to profl. jours. and chpts. to books. Mem. Internat. Inst. for Strategic Studies (council 1985—), Coun. Fgn. Rels. Office: Rand 1700 Main St Santa Monica CA 90407-2138

THOMSON, JOHN ALAN, graphic designer, editor; b. Elkins, W.Va., Jan. 14, 1950; s. John Russell and Marilynn Jane (Bird) T. BA, U. South Fla., 1974. Reporter Orlando (Fla.) Sentinel, 1970-72; freelance editor, writer, designer San Francisco, Tampa, Fla., 1972-80; asst. graphics dir. Tampa Tribune, 1980-87; asst. mng. editor Gannett Westchester Newspapers, White Plains, N.Y., 1987-89; graphics dir., dep. mng. editor Dayton (Ohio) Newspapers, Inc., 1989—; mem. U. Fla. Coll. Journalism Adv. Coun., 1995—. Active Working Assets Group, San Francisco, 1988—, Am. Forests, Washington, 1994—, Walden Woods Project, Boston, 1989—. Mem. Soc. Newspaper Design, Soc. Profl. Journalists. Avocations: wine collecting, hiking. Office: Dayton Daily News 45 S Ludlow St Dayton OH 45402-1810

THOMSON, JOHN U., veterinarian, university official. BS in Animal Sci., Iowa State U., 1965, DVM, 1967; MS in Sci., N.W. Mo. State U., 1987. Pvt. practice, Clearfield, Iowa, 1967-87; ext. veterinarian S.D. State U., Brookings, 1987-90, acting head vet. sci. dept., 1990-93, head, 1993—, acting dir. S.D. Animal Disease Rsch. and Diagnostic Lab., 1990-93, dir., 1993—; pvt. vet. medicine cons., 1987-90. Contbr. articles to sci. jours. Grantee USDA, S.D. Agrl. Expt. Sta. Office: SD State U Dept Vet Sci PO Box 2175 Brookings SD 57007-1396

THOMSON, KEITH STEWART, science museum administrator, writer; b. Heanor, Eng., July 29, 1938; s. Ronald William and Marian Adelaide (Coster) T.; m. Linda Gailbreath Price, Sept. 27, 1963; children: Jessica Adelaide, Elizabeth Rose. B.Sc. with honors, U. Birmingham, Eng., 1960; A.M., Harvard U., 1961, Ph.D. (NATO fellow), 1963. NATO postdoctoral fellow Univ. Coll., London U., 1963-65; asst. prof. to prof. biology Yale U., 1965-87, dean Grad. Sch., 1979-87; dir. Peabody Mus. Natural History, 1976-79; pres. Acad. Natural Scis., Phila., 1987-95; dir. Sears Found. Marine Rsch. and Oceanographic History; hon. rsch. fellow Australian Nat. U., 1967; trustee, mem. corp. Woods Hole Oceanographic Inst.; bd. dirs. Wistar Inst., Ctrl. Phila. Devel. Corp., Wetlands Inst., Phila. Cultural Alliance; rschr. in vertebrate evolution. Mem. editl. bd. Paleobiology, Jour. Morphology, 1988, Aspects of Lower Vertebrate Evolution, 1968, Origin of Terrestrial Vertebrates, 1968, Saltwater Fishes of Conn., 1971, 88, Priorities and Needs in Systematic Biology, 1981, Morphogenesis and Evolution, 1988, Living Fossil, 1991, The Common But Less Frequent Loon and Other Essays, 1993, HMS Beagle, 1995. Fellow Linnean Soc. London, Zool. Soc. London; mem. Soc. Vertebrate Palaeontology, Sigma Xi. Office: Acad Natural Scis 1900 Benjamin Franklin Pky Philadelphia PA 19103-1101

THOMSON, KENNETH R. (LORD THOMSON OF FLEET), publishing executive; b. Toronto, Ont., Can., Sept. 1, 1923; s. Lord Thomson of Fleet; m. Nora Marilyn Lavis, June 1956; children: David Kenneth Roy, Peter John, Lesley Lynne. Student, Upper Can. Coll., Toronto; BA, MA, U. Cambridge, Eng., 1947. With editorial dept. Timmins Daily Press, Eng., 1947; with advt. dept. Cambridge (Galt) Reporter, 1948-50, gen. mgr., 1950-53; owner Thomson Newspapers, Toronto, 1953—; chmn., bd. dirs. Thomson Corp., Thomson Corp. Plc, Thomson U.S. Inc., The Woodbridge Co. Ltd.; pres., bd. dirs. Thomson Works of Art Ltd.; bd. dirs. Hudson's Bay Co., Markborough Properties Inc. With RCAF, World War II. Mem. Granite Club, Hunt Club, National Club, Toronto Club, York Club, York Downs Club. Baptist. Avocations: collecting paintings and works of art, walking. Home: 8 Castle Frank Rd, Toronto, ON Canada M4W 2Z4 Office: Thomson Corp, 65 Queen St W Ste 2500, Toronto, ON Canada M5H 2M8

THOMSON, MABEL AMELIA, retired elementary school educator; b. Lancaster, Minn., Oct. 28, 1910; d. Ernest R. and Sophie Olinda (Rotert) Poore; m. Robert John Thomson, June 20, 1936; children: James Robert, William John. BS, U. Ill., 1933; MEd, Steven F. Austin Coll., Nacogdoches, Tex., 1959. Tchr. La Harpe (Ill.) Sch. Dist., 1930, Scotland (Ill.) Sch. Dist., 1934, Washburn (Ill.) Sch. Dist., 1935-36, Tyler (Tex.) Ind. Sch. Dist., 1959-76; ret., 1976; substitute tchr. Tyler (Tex.) Ind. Sch. Dist., 1976-86. Past pres. Woman's Soc. Christian Svc. of local Meth. Ch. Mem. AAUW (pres. Tyler chpt. 1947-48), Am. Childhood Edn. (pres. 1960-61), Alpha Delta Kappa (charter Tyler br.), Phi Mu (life). Republican. Methodist. Avocations: reading, gardening, bridge.

THOMSON, MARJORIE BELLE, sociology educator, consultant; b. Topeka, Dec. 4, 1921; d. Roy John and Bessie Margaret (Knarr) Anderson; m. John Whitner Thomson, Jan. 4, 1952 (div. June 9, 1963); 1 child, John Coe. Diploma hostess, Trans World Airlines, 1945; diploma, U.Saltillo, Mex., 1945; BS, Butler U., 1957; MS, Ft. Hays Kans. State U., 1966; postgrad., U. Calif., Santa Barbara, 1968, Kans. State U., 1972-73, Kans. U., 1973. Cert. elem. tchr., Calif., Colo., Ind., Kans., jr. coll. tchr. Tech. libr. N.Am. Aviation, Dallas, 1944-45; flight attendant TWA, Kansas City, Mo., 1945-50; recreation dir. U.S. Govt., Ft. Carson, Colo., 1951-52; elem. tchr. Indpls. Pub. Schs., 1954-57; jr. high tchr. Cheyenne County Schs., Cheyenne Wells, Colo., 1958-59; elem. tchr. Sherman County Schs., Goodland, Kans., 1961-62; lectr. Calif. Luth. U., Thousand Oaks, 1967-69; instr. Ft. Hays Kans. State U., 1969-71; dir. HeadStart Kans. Coun. of Agrl. Workers and Low Income Families, Inc., Goodland, 1971-72; supr. U.S. Govt. Manpower Devel. Programs, Plainville, Kans., 1972-74; bilingual counselor Kans. Dept. Human Resources, Goodland, 1975-82; leader trainee Expt. in Internat. Living, Brattleboro, Vt., 1967-71; cons. M. Anderson & Co., Lakewood, Colo., 1982—; participant Internat. Peace Walk, Moscow to Archangel, Russia, 1991, N.Am. Conf. on Ecology and the Soviet Save Peace and Nature Ecol. Collective, Russia, 1992; amb. internat. Friendship Force, Tiblisi, Republic of Georgia, 1991, Republic South Africa, 1995; presenter State Conv. AAUW, Aurora, Colo., 1992, nat. conv. Am. Acad. Audiology, Denver, 1992; cons. Gov.'s Conf. in Libr. and Info. Svc., Vail, Colo., 1992—. Docent Colo. Gallery of the Arts, Littleton, 1989; spkr., state resource chairperson Internat. Self Help for Hard of Hearing, Inc., Denver, 1990—; mem. Denver Deaf and Hard of Hearing Access Com., 1991—; spkr. Ret. Sr. Vol. Program, Denver, 1992—; dir. Holiday Project, Denver, 1992; mem. Lakewood Access Com., 1994—, Arvada Ctr.'s Women's Voices com., 1995—; participant women readers com. Rocky Mountain News, Denver, 1995; trustee Internat. Self Help Hard of Hearing People, Inc., Bethesda, Md., 1995—; program chairperson Lakewood Woman's Club, 1996. Grantee NSF, 1970, 71; recipient Svc. award Mayor of Lakewood, 1995, Honorable Mention Four Who Dare, Colo. Bus. and Profl. Women and KCNC Channel 4, 1995, J.C. Penney Nat. Golden Rule award for cmty. vol. svc., 1996. Mem. AAUW (life, v.p., program chairperson Lakewood br. 1996), AARP (pres. Denver-Grandview chpt. 1994), VFW Aux. (life), Sociologists for Women in Soc., Bus. and Profl. Woman's Club, Internat. Peace Walkers, Spellbinders, Denver Press Club, Lakewood Woman's Club, TWA Internat. Clipped Wings (cert.), Mile High Wings, Order Ea. Star (life), Sons of Norway (life), UNESCO, Pi Gamma Mu, Alpha Sigma Alpha (life). Democrat. Presbyterian. Avocations: photography, traveling, whitewater rafting, storytelling, writing. Home: 12313 W Louisiana Ave Lakewood CO 80228-3829 Office: M Anderson & Co # G 6941 W 13th Ave Apt # G Lakewood CO 80215-5259

THOMSON, RICHARD MURRAY, banker; b. Winnipeg, Man., Can., Aug. 14, 1933; s. H.W. and Mary T. BASC in Engring., U. Toronto, 1955; MBA, Harvard U., 1957; fellow course in banking, Queen's U., 1958. With Toronto Dominion Bank, Ont., Can., 1957—, asst. to pres. head office, 1963-68, chief gen. mgr., 1968-71, v.p., chief gen. mgr., dir., 1971-72, pres., 1972-77, pres. and CEO, 1977-78, chmn., CEO, 1978—; also bd. dirs. Toronto Dominion Bank; bd. dirs. C.G.C. Inc., Eatons of Can., S.C. Johnson & Son Inc., The Prudential Ins. Co. Am., The Thomson Corp., Inco Ltd., The Hosp. for Sick Children Found. Office: Toronto-Dominion Bank, 55 King St PO Box 1, Toronto, ON Canada M5K 1A2

THOMSON, ROBERT JAMES, natural gas distribution company executive; b. Detroit, Dec. 16, 1927; s. Harold E.J. and Irene L. (Silsbee) T.; m. Doris L. Mullen, Sept. 19, 1953; children—Gregory R., Susan C., Jeffrey S., Arthur J. AB, Mich. State U., 1951, MBA, 1967. CPA, Mich. Mgr. Arthur Andersen & Co., Detroit, 1951-58; v.p. Southeastern Mich. Gas Co., Port Huron, 1961-71, pres., 1971-84, pres., chief exec. officer, 1984-86; pres., CEO Southeastern Mich. Gas Enterprise, Inc., Pt. Huron, 1977-93; chmn. Southeastern Mich. Gas Enterprise, Inc., Port Huron, 1987-95; bd. dirs. Mich. Nat. Bank-Port Huron, 1972—. Trustee Cmty. Found. St. Clair County, 1972—, pres., 1981-83; bd. dirs. Indsl. Devel. Corp., Port Huron, 1972-86, pres. 1976-78; trustee Port Huron Hosp., 1981-90, vice chmn., 1985-90; bd. dirs. Blue Water Health Svcs. Corp., 1981—, vice chmn., 1981-93, chmn., 1993—; trustee Marwood Manor Nursing Home., 1987—, chmn. 1996—; vestryman Grace Episcopal Ch., Port Huron, 1990-93. With USN, 1946-47. Mem. Mich. C. of C. (bd. dirs. 1982-88), Mich. Utilities Assn. (bd. dirs., treas. 1983-85), Renaissance Club, Port Huron Golf Club, Port Huron Yacht Club, Mich. State U. Advanced Mgmt. Program Club, Port Huron/Marysville C. of C. (bd. dirs. 1973-75). Home: 3355 Lomar Dr Fort Gratiot MI 48059-4207 Office: Mich Nat Bank Bldg 800 Military St Rm 302 Port Huron MI 48060-5461

THOMSON, SHIRLEY LAVINIA, museum director; b. Walkerville, Ont., Can., Feb. 19, 1930; d. Walter Cull. BA in History with honors, U. West Ont., 1952; MA in Art History, U. Md., 1974; PhD in Art History, McGill U., 1981; PhD (hon.), Ottawa U., 1988; D (hon.), Mt. Allison U., 1990, U. West Ont., 1990. Editor conf. NATO, Paris, 1956-60; asst. sec.-gen. World Univ. Svc. WUSC, Toronto, 1960-63; asst. sec. gen. Can. Commn. for UNESCO, Ottawa, 1964-67; sec.-gen. Can. Commn. for UNESCO, Montreal, 1985-87; rsch. coord., writer Memoirs of Sen. Thérèse Casgrain, 1968-70; spl. coord. Largillière Exhbn., Mus. Fine Arts, Montreal, 1981; dir. McCord Mus., 1982-85, Nat. Gallery Can., Ottawa, 1987—. Officer Order of Can., 1994. Decorated Chevalier des Arts et Letters, France, 1977-78. Mem. Can. Soc. Decorative Arts (coun.), Assn. Art Mus. Dirs. Office: Nat Gallery Can, 380 Sussex Dr, Ottawa, ON Canada K1N 9N4

THOMSON, THYRA GODFREY, former state official; b. Florence, Colo., July 30, 1916; d. John and Rosalie (Altman) Godfrey; m. Keith Thomson, Aug. 6, 1939 (dec. Dec. 1960); children—William John, Bruce Godfrey, Keith Coffey. B.A. cum laude, U. Wyo., 1939. With dept. agronomy and agrl. econs. U. Wyo., 1938-39; writer weekly column Watching Washington pub. in 14 papers, Wyo., 1955-60; planning chmn. Nat. Fedn. Republican Women, Washington, 1961; sec. state Wyo. Cheyenne, 1962-86; mem. Marshall Scholarships Com. for Pacific region, 1964-68; del. 72d Wilton Park Conf., Eng., 1965; mem. youth commn. UNESCO, 1970-71, Allied Health Professions Council HEW, 1971-72; del. U.S.-Republic of China Trade Conf., Taipei, Taiwan, 1983; mem. lt. gov.'s trade and fact-finding mission to Saudi Arabia, Jordan, and Egypt, 1985. Bd. dirs. Buffalo Bill Mus., Cody, Wyo., 1987—; adv. bd. Coll. Arts and Scis., U. Wyo., 1989, Cheyenne Symphony Orch. Found., 1990—. Recipient Disting. Alumni award U. Wyo., 1969, Disting. U. Wyo. Arts and Scis. Alumna award, 1987; named Internat. Woman of Distinction, Alpha Delta Kappa; recipient citation Omicron Delta Epsilon, 1965, citation Beta Gamma Sigma, 1968, citation Delta Kappa Gamma, 1973, citation Wyo. Commn. Women, 1986. Mem. N.Am. Securities Adminstrs. (pres. 1973-74), Nat. Assn. Secs. of State, Council State Govts. (chmn. natural resources com. Western states 1966-68), Nat. Conf. Lt. Govs. (exec. com. 1976-79). Home: 3102 Sunrise Rd Cheyenne WY 82001-6136

THOMSON, WILLIAM BARRY, retail company executive; b. Morristown, N.J., Dec. 3, 1952; s. James Bruce and Ruth Janet (Hill) T. BA, Drew U., 1974. Dir. spl. projects F.W. Woolworth Co., N.Y.C., 1979-82, asst. sec., 1982-86, sec., 1986-90; v.p. pub. affairs Woolworth Corp. (formerly F.W. Woolworth Co.), N.Y.C., 1990-91, sr. v.p. adminstrn., 1991-93; sr. v.p., chief adminstrv. officer Woolworth Corp., N.Y.C., 1993-96.

THON, PATRICIA FRANCES, pediatrics nurse, medical/surgical nurse; b. Portland, Oreg., Sept. 25, 1959; d. Anthony William and Catherine Mary (Scully) Brenneis; m. Eric Phillip Thon, Apr. 30, 1988. AS, Johnson County C.C., 1980; BSN, U. Kans., Kans. City, 1982; MA, Webster U., 1992; postgrad., Portland State U., 1977; grad., St. Louis U., 1994. Staff nurse in pediatrics and oncology St. Luke's Hosp., Kansas City, Mo., 1982-84; commd. nurse officer USAF, 1984, advanced through grades to maj., 1988; staff nurse USAF, Scott AFB, Ill., 1984-88; flight nurse USAF, Scott AFB, 1988-91, sr. staff nurse in pediatrics and orthopedics, 1992; head nurse, flight chief maternal/child health Pediatric Clinic, Altus AFB, Okla., 1994—. Avocations: running, biking, sewing, reading. Office: 97 MDG/SGOB 301 N 1st St Altus AFB OK 73523-5005

THON, WILLIAM, artist; b. N.Y.C., Aug. 8, 1906; s. Felix Leo and Jane (Upham) T.; m. Helen Elizabeth Walters, June 3, 1929. Student, Art Students League, 1924-25; A.F.D., Bates Coll., 1957. Represented in nat. art exhibits at Corcoran Gallery Art, Washington, Art Inst. Chgo., Pa. Acad., Va. Mus., Toldeo Mus., Met. Mus., Nat. Acad., Carnegie Inst.; one-man show Farnsworth Mus., Rockland, Me.; included in permanent collections Swope Art Gallery, Terre Haute, Ind., Farnsworth Mus., Bloomington Art Assn., Ency. Brit., Toledo Mus., Am. Acad. Arts and Letters, Mus. of Ann Arbor, Mich., Met. Mus. Art, N.Y.C., Portland Mus. Art, U. Hawaii, Honolulu, Johnson's Wax Collection, Bklyn. Mus., Whitney Mus., Portland Mus., Oquenquet Mus., others.; artist-in-residence Am. Acad., Rome, 1956. Served with USNR, 1942-46. Recipient prize Salmagundi Club, 1941, Dana watercolor medal Pa. Acad., 1950, prize Bklyn. Mus., 1945, Prix de Rome, 1947, Maine State award, 1970, Florence and H. Samuel Slater Meml. award Adirondacks Nat. Exhibit, Arts Guild Old Forge, Inc., 1992, Pulsifer award, 1993, Hardware prize, 1995. Mem. NAD (2d Altman prize for landscape 1951, 1st 1954, 67, Palmer Meml. prize 1944, Samuel F.B. Morse medal 1956, Altman prize for landscape 1961, Adolph and Clara Obrig prize 1965, Ranger Fund purchase award 1976, Ogden Pliessner Meml. prize 1988, William A. Patton prize 1991, Adolph and Clara Obrig award 1992), Nat. Inst. Arts and Letters (grantee 1951), Am. Watercolor Soc. (silver medal 1957, 67, Gordon Grant Meml. award 1963, gold medal of honor 1970, 79, Lena Newcastle Meml. award 1976, Caroline Stern award 1986), Audubon Artists (silver medal 1986, Lillian Judith Newman award 1992), Friendship Sloop Soc. Home: Port Clyde ME 04855

THONG, TRAN, biomedical company executive; b. Saigon, Vietnam, Dec. 8, 1951; came to U.S., 1969, naturalized, 1980; s. Vy and Vinh-Thi (Nguyen) T.; m. Thuy Thi-Bich Nguyen, Jan. 12, 1978. BSEE, Ill. Inst. Tech., 1972; MS in Engring., Princeton U., 1974, MA, 1974, PhD, 1975. Rsch. scientist Western Geophys. Houston, 1975-76; computer devel. engr. GE Co., Syracuse, N.Y., 1976-79; dir. electronic system lab. Tektronix, Inc., Beaverton, Oreg., 1980-90, v.p. enging., and digital signal processing gen. mgr., Tektronix Fed. Systems Inc., Beaverton, Oreg., 1990-93, v.p. systems design and devel. Micro Systems Engring., Inc., Lake Oswego, Oreg., 1993—; adj. asst. prof. Syracuse U., 1979-81, Oreg. State U., Corvallis, 1980-83, U. Portland, Oreg., 1981-83; adj. assoc. prof. Oreg. Grad. Ctr., Beaverton, 1984—; founding mem. Pacific Advanced Comm. Consortium, Eugene, Oreg. Founding mem., chmn. Vietnamese Assn. for Computing, Engring. Tech. and Sci., 1994-95, past pres., 1995—. Author numerous sci. papers and U.S. patents. Princeton U. fellow, 1974. Fellow IEEE (com. chmn. 1982-88, assoc. editor transaction 1979-81, gen. chmn. 1989, exec. v.p. circuits and sys. 1989); mem. Eta Kappa Nu, Tau Beta Pi, Sigma Xi. Republican. Office: Micro Sys Engring 6024 Jean Rd Lake Oswego OR 97035-5369

THOPPIL, CECIL KOSHEY, pediatrician, educator; b. Trivandrum, India, Aug. 4, 1961; s. T.K. and M. (Koshey) T.; m. Jennifer Carrol Gallego, Apr. 25, 1992; children: Cecilia, Ruth. Pre-degree, Mar Ivanios Coll., Trivandrum, Kerala, India, 1979; MB, BS, Med. Coll. Hosp., Trivandrum, 1984. Diplomate Am. Bd. Pediatrics; cert. in neonatal advanced life support, pediatric advanced life support, BLS; instr. NALS, PALS. Compulsory rotating internship Med. Coll. Hosp., Trivandrum, Kerala, India, 1985-86; postgrad. tng. pediatric medicine dept. child health S.A.T. Hosp., Trivandrum, Kerala, India, 1986-87; postdoctoral rsch. assoc. dept. perinatal pediatrics U. Tex. Med. Br., Galveston, 1987-89; pediatric internship Univ. Hosps. Cleve. Rainbow Babies and Children's Hosp., 1989-90; pediatric residency dept. pediatrics Scott & White Meml. Hosp./Tex. A&M U. Coll. Medicine, Temple, 1990-92; pediatrician Surry County Health Dept., Dobson, N.C., 1992-94, Med. Assocs. of Surry, Carolina Medicorp Inc., Mt. Airy, N.C., 1994—; physician cons. Surry County Sch. Health Adv. Coun., Surry Presch. Interagy. Coun., Surry County Day Care Assn.; pediat. cons. Surry Smart Start Task Force. Contbr. articles to profl. jours. Provider for "Caring" Program; mem. Haymore Bapt. Ch. Recipient Father Kuncheria Goldmedal for First Rank in Loyola Sch. for Matriculation. Fellow Am. Acad. Pediat.; mem. AMA, N.C. Med. Soc., N.C., Pediatric Soc., Surry-Yadkin Med. Soc. Home: 860 Cross Creek Dr Mount Airy NC 27030-9229 Office: Med Assocs of Surry 865 W Lake Dr Mount Airy NC 27030

THOR, LINDA MARIA, college president; b. L.A., Feb. 21, 1950; d. Karl Gustav and Mildred Dorrine (Hofius) T.; m. Robert Paul Huntsinger, Nov. 22, 1974; children: Erik, Marie. BA, Pepperdine U., 1971, EdD, 1986; MPA, Calif. State U., Los Angeles, 1980. Dir. pub. info. Pepperdine U., Los Angeles, 1971-73; pub. info. officer L.A. C.C. Dist., 1974-75, dir. comm., 1975-81, dir. edn. svcs., 1981-82, dir. high tech., 1982-83, sr. dir. occupl. and tech. edn., 1983-86; pres. West Los Angeles Coll., Culver City, Calif., 1986-90, Rio Salado C.C., Phoenix, 1990—; bd. dirs. Coun. for Adult and Experiential Learning, 1990—, Tech. Exch. Ctr., 1986—, Greater Phoenix Econ. Coun., 1994—. Editor: Curriculum Design and Development for Effective Learning, 1973; author: (with others) Effective Media Relations, 1982, Performance Contracting, 1987; contbr. articles to profl. jours. Active Am. Assn. Cmty. Coll. Commn. Acad. and Student Devel., 1995—, Continuous Quality Improvement Network for Cmty. Colls., 1991—, Am. Coun. Edn. Commn. on Leadership Devel., 1995—; mem. Ariz. Gov.'s Adv. Coun. on Quality, 1992; pres. Ariz. Cmty. Coll. Pres.'s Coun., 1995-96. Recipient Delores award Pepperdine U., 1986, Alumni Medal of Honor, 1987, Outstanding Achievement award Women's Bus. Network, 1989; named Woman of the Yr., Culver City Bus. and Profl. Women, 1988. Office: 2323 W 14th St Tempe AZ 85281

THOR, PAUL VIETS, computer science educator, software engineer, consultant; b. Schenectady, N.Y., Mar. 10, 1946; s. Donald D. and Eleanor B. (Viets) T.; m. Barbara K. Nelson, Mar. 27, 1982 (div. Dec. 1993). BSME, U. Denver, 1968; MS in Engring. Mgmt., UCLA, 1976; MS in Computer Sci., George Mason U., 1993. Engr. Martin Marietta Corp., Denver, 1968-69; commd. 2d lt. USAF, 1969, advanced through grades to maj., 1982; pilot trainee USAF-Williams AFB, Phoenix, Ariz., 1970-71; pilot C141A 15 MAS-Norton AFB, San Bernardino, Calif., 1971-75, pilot C141B, 1981-84; communications and computer officer 2044 CG-Pentagon, Washington, 1977-81; air field mgr. 18TFW-Kadena AB, Okinawa, Japan, 1984-86; pilot C12 1402 MAS-Andrews AFB, Washington, 1986-87; communications and computer officer 7 Communications Group-Pentagon, Washington, 1987-89; cons. George Mason U., Fairfax, Va., 1990-93; ind. cons. Colorado Springs, Colo., 1993—; wing flight examiner 63 MAW-Norton AFB, San Bernardino, 1981-84; acquisitions officer 7th Comms. Group-Pentagon, 1987-89; assoc. prof. computer sci. Colo. Tech. U., Colorado Springs, 1993—. Mem. Computer Soc. of IEEE, Assn. Computer Machinery, Air Force Assn. (life), Ret. Officers Assn. Avocations: personal computers, woodworking, crafts, photography, book collector. Home: 5330 Slickrock Dr Colorado Springs CO 80918-7646 Office: Colo Tech U 4435 N Chestnut St Colorado Springs CO 80907

THORBECKE, ERIK, economics educator; b. Berlin, Feb. 17, 1929; s. William and Madelaine (Salisbury) T.; m. Charla J. Westerberg, Oct. 17, 1954; children: Erik Charles, Willem, Jon. Student, Netherlands Sch. Econs., Rotterdam, 1948-51; PhD, U. Calif., 1957; hon. doctorate, U. Ghent, 1981. Asst. prof. econs. Iowa State U., 1957-60, assoc. prof., 1960-63, prof., 1963-73; prof. Cornell U., 1974—, chmn. dept. econs., 1975-78, H.E. Babcock prof. econs. and food econs., 1978—; econ. adviser Nat. Planning Inst., Lima, Peru, 1963-64; asso. asst. adminstr. for program policy AID, Washington, 1966-68, mem. research advisory com., 1976-81; sr. economist world employment program Internat. Labor Office, Geneva, 1972-73; vis. prof. Erasmus U., Rotterdam, 1980-81; mem. com. on internat. nutritional programs NRC-NAS, 1979-81; dir. program on comparative econ. devel., Cornell U., 1988—; sr. rsch. fellow USAID Inst. Policy Reform, 1990—. Author: The Tendency Towards Regionalization in International Trade, 1960, (with Irma Adelman) Theory and Design of Economic Development, 1966, (with K. Fox, J. Sengupta) Theory of Quantitative Economic Policy, 1968, Role of Agriculture in Economic Development, 1968, (with G. Pyatt) Planning Techniques for a Better Future, 1976; (with J. Defourny) Structural Path Analysis and Multiplier Decomposition within a Social Matrix, 1984, (with J. Foster, J. Greer) A Class of Decomposable Poverty Measures, 1984, (with J. Lecaillon, C. Morrisson) Economic Policies and Agricultural Performance of Low Income Countries, 1987, Planning Techniques for Social Justice In: The Balance between Industry and Agriculture in Economic Development, vol. 4, 1989, (with I. Adelman) The Role of Institutions in Economic Development, Special Issue of World Development, 1989, (with others) Adjustment and Equity in Indonesia, 1992, (with T. van der Pluijm) Rural Indonesia: Socio-economic Development in a Changing Environment, 1993. Mem. Am. Econ. Assn., Am. Assn. Agrl. Econs. (Nat. award for best pub. research 1970). Home: 108 N Sunset Dr Ithaca NY 14850-1460 Office: Cornell U Dept Econs Ithaca NY 14853

THORBURN, DAVID, literature educator; b. N.Y.C., Aug. 14, 1940; s. Frank and Claire (Feller) T.; m. Barbara Ellen Levitan, June 30, 1963; children: Daniel, Adam, Rachel. AB, Princeton U., 1962; MA, Stanford U., 1966, PhD, 1968. With dept. English Yale U., New Haven, 1966-76, successively instr., asst. prof., then assoc. prof.; prof. lit., dir. film and media studies, cultural studies project MIT, Cambridge, 1976—; vis. appointments include U. Calif., Santa Barbara, U. Ill. Author: Conrad's Romanticism,

1974; contbr. articles to profl. jours.; editor scholarly collections; gen. editor Media and Popular Culture, 1986—. Fulbright fellow, Morse fellow, Woodrow Wilson fellow and Rockefeller fellow, 1966-77. Mem. MLA, Popular Culture Assn., Am. Studies Assn., Soc. for Cinema Studies. Democrat. Avocation: basketball. Office: MIT 14N-335 Lit Faculty Cambridge MA 02139

THORBURN, JAMES ALEXANDER, humanities educator; b. Martins Ferry, Ohio, Aug. 24, 1923; s. Charles David and Mary Edna (Ruble) T.; m. Lois McElroy, July 3, 1954; children: Alexander Maurice, Melissa Rachel; m. 2d, June Yingling O'Leary, Apr. 18, 1981. BA, Ohio State U., 1949, MA, 1951; postgrad., U. Mo., 1954-55; PhD, La. State U., 1977. Head English dept. high sch., Sheridan, Mich., 1951-52; instr. English, U. Mo., Columbia, 1952-55, Monmouth (Ill.) Coll., 1955-56, U. Tex., El Paso, 1956-60, U. Mo., St. Louis, 1960-61, La. State U., Baton Rouge, 1961-70; prof. Southeastern La. U., Hammond, 1970-89, ret., named prof. emeritus English and linguistics; testing and cert. examiner English Lang. Inst., U. Mich., 1969—; participant Southeastern Conf. on Linguistics; mem. Conf. Christianity and Lit. Contbg. author: Exercises in English, 1955, also poetry, short stories; book rev. editor: Experiment, 1958-87; editor: Innisfree, 1984-89. With F.A., AUS, 1943-46. Mem. MLA, Linguistic Assn. S.W., Avalon World Arts Acad., Linguistic Soc. Am., Am. Dialect Soc., La. Assn. for Coll. Composition, La. Retired Tchrs. Assn., Internat. Poetry Soc., Internat. Acad. Poets, Sociedad Nacional Hispánica, Sigma Delta Pi, Phi Kappa Phi (named emeritus life), Phi Mu Alpha Sinfonia. Republican. Presbyterian. Home: 602 Susan Dr Hammond LA 70403-3444 Office: Southeastern La U # 739 Hammond LA 70402 *I have always felt that no experience is wasted, if it is not selfish or vicious. Every such experience adds something, I believe, to that inner fund on which one draws, consciously or unconsciously, throughout one's life.*

THORE, STEN ANDERS, economics and aerospace engineering educator; b. Stockholm, Apr. 22, 1930; came to U.S., 1978, naturalized, 1985; s. Eric and Elsa (Ostberg) T.; m. Margrethe Munck; children: Susanne, Alexander, Clementine. M. Commerce, U. Birmingham, Eng., 1954; Filosofie Doktor, U. Stockholm, 1961. Prof. econs. Norwegian Sch. Econs. and Bus. Adminstrn., Bergen, Norway, 1964-78; Gregory A. Kozmetsky Centennial fellow IC2 Inst., U. Tex., Austin, 1984—; instr. U. Tex., Austin, Washington, 1996—; vis. prof. Northwestern U., Carnegie-Mellon U., U. Va. Author: Economic Logistics, 1992, The Diversity, Complexity and Evolution of High Tech Capitalism, 1995; (with G.L. Thompson) Computational Economics, 1991; contbr. articles to profl. jours. Named Hon. Citizen, State of Tex., 1981. Mem. Inst. Mgmt. Scis. Econometric Soc. Home: 809 Electra St Austin TX 78734-4213 Office: U Tex Austin IC2 Inst 2815 San Gabriel St Austin TX 78705-3596

THORFINNSON, A. RODNEY, hospital administrator; b. Kandahar, Sask., Can., Nov. 30, 1934; married. BA, U. Sask., Can., 1958; MA, U. Toronto, 1960. Adminstrv. resident Humber Meml. Hosp., Toronto, 1959-60; cons. Dept. Pub. Health, Regina, Sask., 1960-61; asst. dir. Sask. Hosp. Assn., Regina, 1961-62, exec. dir., 1962-64; asst. dir. Univ. Hosp., Saskatoon, Sask., 1964-65; adminstr. Victoria Hosp., London, Ont., 1966-69; v.p. Comtron Systems, Inc., London, Ont., 1969-70; exec. dir. Victoria Hosp. Corp., London, Ont., 1970-78, pres., 1978-85; pres. Health Scis. Ctr., Winnipeg, Man., 1985—. Office: Health Scis Ctr, 820 Sherbrook St Rm GB127B, Winnipeg, MB Canada R3A 1R9

THORIN, DONALD E., cinematographer. Cinematographer Thief, 1981, An Officer and a Gentleman, 1982, (with Bruce Surtees) Bad Boys, 1983, Against All Odds, 1984, Purple Rain, 1984, Mischief, 1985, Wildcats, 1986, The Golden Child, 1986, American Anthem, 1986, Midnight Run, 1988, Collision Course, 1988, The Couch Trip, 1988, Tango & Cash, 1989, Troop Beverly Hills, 1989, Lock Up, 1989, The Marrying Man, 1991, Out On A Limb, 1992, Scent of a Woman, 1992, Cloak and Diaper, 1992, Undercover Blues, 1993, Little Big League, 1994, Boys on the Side, 1995, Ace Ventura II, 1995, First Wives Club, 1996, Nothing To Lose, 1996. Office: Broder Kurland Webb Uffner Agy 9242 Beverly Blvd Ste 200 Beverly Hills CA 90210-3710

THORN, ANDREA PAPP, lawyer; b. Greenwich, Conn., May 22, 1960; d. Laszlo G. and Judith (Liptak) Papp; m. Craig Thorn IV, Aug. 27, 1982; children: C. Alexander, Kelsey Amanda. BA, Dartmouth Coll., Hanover, N.H., 1982; JD, Harvard U., 1987. Bar: Mass. 1987, N.H. 1993. Assoc. Bingham Dana & Gould, Boston, 1987-89, Gaffin & Krattenmaker PC, Boston, 1989-90, Phillips, Gerstein & Holber, Haverhill, Mass., 1993-84; spl. asst. to sec. of N.Mex. Dept. of Environment, 1991-92. Mem. ABA, Mass. Bar Assn., N.H. Bar Assn. Home: Phillips Academy Andover MA 01810-4161

THORN, GEORGE WIDMER, physician, educator; b. Buffalo, Jan. 15, 1906; s. George W. and Fanny R. (Widmer) T.; m. Doris Weston, June 30, 1931 (dec. Jan. 1984); 1 son, Weston Widmer; m. Claire Steinert, Dec. 28, 1985 (dec. Mar. 1990). Student, Coll. of Wooster, 1923-25; MD, U. Buffalo, 1929; MA (hon.), Harvard U., 1942, DSc (hon.), 1987; DSc (hon.), Temple U., 1951, Suffolk U., 1961, Coll. Wooster, 1963, N.Y. Med. Coll., 1972, Boston U., 1983; LLD (hon.), Dalhousie U., 1950; LLD, Queen's U., Can., 1954; DMed, Cath. U., Louvain, 1960; MD (hon.), U. Geneva, 1965; DSc (hon.), Med. Coll. of Ohio, Toledo, Rockefeller U., 1993; U. Buffalo, 1995. Diplomate Am. Bd. Internal Medicine. House officer Millard Fillmore Hosp., Buffalo, 1929-30; researcher dept. physiology U. Buffalo, 1930-31, asst. researcher dept. physiology and medicine, 1931-34; asst. prof. physiology Ohio State U., Columbus, 1935-36; asst. physician Johns Hopkins Hosp., Balt., 1937-39, assoc. prof. medicine, 1938-42, assoc. physician, 1939-42; mem. med. adv. bd. Howard Hughes Med. Inst., 1955-85, dir., res., 1956-78, chmn. med. adv. bd., 1975-85, mem. exec. com., 1977-84, pres., 1981-84, chmn. bd. trustees, 1984-90; physician-in-chief Peter Bent Brigham Hosp., Boston, 1942-72, physician-in-chief emeritus, 1972—; Samuel A. Levine prof. medicine Harvard U., Cambridge, 1967-72, Samuel A. Levine prof. emeritus, 1972—, Hersey prof. theory and practice physic emeritus, 1972—; Hugh J. Morgan vis. prof. Vanderbilt U., 1967; vis. prof. medicine Columbia Coll. Physicians and Surgeons, 1968, Cornell U. Med. Sch. and N.Y. Hosp., 1970; Wingate Johnson vis. prof. Bowman Gray Sch. Medicine Wake Forest U., 1972; cons. internist Boston Psychopathic Hosp., 1943—; mem. research and devel. adv. bd. Smith, Kline and French Labs., 1953-69; cons. Children's Med. Ctr., USPHA, U.S. Army Med. Services Grad. Sch.; mem. com. stress NRC; mem. Nat. Com. on Radiation, 1958—; mem. drug research bd. NRC-Nat. Acad. Scis., 1972; lectr.U. London, 1957; Jacobaeus lectr., Oslo, 1957; Maurice C. Pincoff lectr. U. Md. Sch. Medicine, 1958; Mellon lectr. U. Pitts., 1959; Banting Meml. lectr. Am. Diabetes Assn., 1959; 1st Lilly lectr. Royal Coll. Physicians, 1966, Soc. Mexicana de Nutricion y Endocrologia, Mexico, 1969; Thayer lectr. Johns Hopkins U., 1967; Billings lectr. AMA, 1968; John C. Leonard Med. lectr. Hartford Med. Soc., 1969; mem. corp. MIT, 1965—, Mus. Sci., 1979—; v.p. Whitaker Health Scis. Fund, Inc., 1974-92; bd. visitors Boston u. Sch. Medicine, 1979—; chmn. sci. adv. bd. Whitaker Found., 1979-93. Editor-in-chief Principles of Internal Medicine, 8th edit., 1974. Pres. Howard Hughes Med. Inst., Boston, 1981-84, chmn. bd. dirs. and trustee, 1984—. Rockefeller fellow in medicine, Harvard U., 1936-37, Johns Hopkins U. Sch. Medicine, 1938, Read Ellsworth fellow in medicine John Hopkins U. Sch. Medicine, 1938; recipient Chancellor's medal U. Buffalo, 1943, Osler oration Can. Med. Assn., 1949, U.S. Pharm. Mfrs. Assn. award 1950, Alvarenga award, 1951, Dr. Charles V. Chapin Meml. award 1956, Ann. Meml. award Buffalo Urol. Soc., 1958, Modern Medicine award, 1961, Oscar B. Hunter Meml. award Am. Therapeutic Soc., 1967, Robert H. Williams award Assn. Profs. of Medicine, 1972, George M. Kober medal Assn. Am. Physicians, 1976, Gold-Headed Can. Soc. award, 1976, Medical Times Physician of Excellence award, 1980, Hubert H. Humphrey Research Ctr. award Boston U., 1980, Gold medal Phi Lambda Kappa, 1981. Fellow Royal Coll. Physicians (London), ACP (master, John Phillips Meml. award 1955); mem. Am. Soc. Clin. Investigation (emeritus), AMA (gold medalist 1932, 39, George Minot award 1963), Assn. Am. Physicians (pres. 1970), Am. Physiol. Soc., Royal Soc. of Medicine (hon. mem. endocronology sect.), Endocrine Soc. (pres. 1962), Am. Clin. and Climatol. Assn. (pres.), Am. Acad. Arts and Scis., Royal Soc. Medicine (hon.), Royal Acad. of Medicine of Belgium, Interurban Clin. Club, John Hopkins Soc. Scholars, Aesculapian Club, Orpolito of Peru (comdr. 1960), Sigma Xi, Nu Sigma Nu, Alpha Omega Alpha. Clubs: Harvard, Harvard Faculty; Country (Brookline); Essex County, St. Botolph, Tavern, Badminton & Tennis, Singing Beach (Manchester). Office: Howard Hughes Med Inst 320 Longwood Ave Enders 661 Boston MA 02115

THORN, JAMES DOUGLAS, safety engineer; b. Tyler, Tex., May 20, 1959; s. Douglas Howard and Patricia Ann (Kolb) T. Student, U. of Mary, Manama, Bahrain, 1982, S.W. Tex. State U., 1984-86, La. State U., 1989, W.Va. Tech., 1991-92, Berlitz Sch. Langs., 1993. Cert. EMT, BTLS, ACLS, CPR instr., hazardous materials ops., hazardous waste ops., hazardous and indsl. waste mgmt. 3d officer Jackson Marine S.A., Manama, 1981; constrn. foreman Brown & Root S.A., Manama, 1982-83; barge officer Rezayat/Brown & Root E.C., Manama, 1983-84; safety insp. Brown & Root U.S.A., Carson, Calif., 1987-88; sr. safety insp. Brown & Root U.S.A., Taft, La., 1988-89; project safety mgr. Brown & Root Braun, Institute, W.Va., 1989-93; mgr. safety and health Brown & Root Braun, Phila., 1993-94; safety supt. Brown & Root, Carson, Calif., 1994; safety/security mgr. L.A. Export Terminal, 1995—; safety cons. Assn. Builders and Contractors, Charleston, W.Va., 1990-93, chmn. safety seminar, 1991-93; drill monitor Kanawha Valley Emergency Preparedness Coun., South Charleston, W.Va., 1990-93; v.p. Arco Contractors Safety Coun., Carson, 1995-96. Youth counsellor Neon League, St. Albans, W.Va., 1991; den leader cub scouts Boy Scouts Am., 1991-93; bd. dirs. NFL Booster Club Orange County, 1995—; v.p. Area Contractors Safety Coun., 1995—. Mem. Am. Soc. Safety Engrs., Nat. Assn. EMTs, Team 911, Great Wall of Tex. Soc., Angels Booster Club (bd. dirs. 1995—), Rams Booster Club (bd. dirs. 1995). Avocations: golf, snow skiing, scuba diving. Office: Brown & Root PO Box 320 Long Beach CA 90801

THORN, TERENCE HASTINGS, gas industry executive; b. Takoma, Md., July 6, 1946; s. John Hastings and Norine R. (Freytag) T.; m. Judith Carol Bailey, Aug. 15, 1970; children: Kristin Lynn, Matthew Hastings. BA, U. Md., 1969, MA, 1973. Dir. congl. rels. Am. Gas Assn., Arlington, Va., 1975-79; dir. govt. rels. J. Walter Thompson Co., Washington, 1979-81; v.p. govt. rels. Houston Natural Gas Co., Washington, 1981-85; exec. v.p. Mojave Pipeline Co., Houston, 1986-89; pres., CEO Transwestern Pipeline Co., Houston, 1993—; sr. v.p., exec. mgmt. com. bd. ENRON Corp., 1993—; chmn. Pacific Coast Gas Assn., 1994—. Bd. dirs. Houston Pops, 1989-90, Pin Oak Charities, Houston, 1991—; city alderman, 1992-93; mem. Hermann Soc., 1993—, Energy Industry Sector Adv. Com. U.S. Dept. Commerce; prin. liason Pres.'s Coun. Sustainable Devel. Democrat. Avocation: tennis. Office: ENRON Corp PO Box 1188 Houston TX 77251-1188

THORNBERRY, TERENCE PATRICK, criminologist, educator; b. N.Y.C., Jan. 28, 1945; s. Patrick and Rose (Small) T.; children: Donna Ann, Patrick. BA, Fordham U., 1966; MA, U. Pa., 1971, PhD, 1971. Asst. dir. Ctr. for Studies in Criminology and Criminal Law, U. Pa., Phila., 1971-79; dir. Research Ctr. in Crime and Delinquency, U. Ga., Athens, 1979-84; dean Sch. Criminal Justice, SUNY, Albany, 1984-89; prof. 1984—; dir. Rochester Youth Devel. Study, 1986—; cons. Commn. on Obscenity and Pornography, 1970, Nat. Commn. on Marijuana and Drug Abuse, 1973, Commn. on Rev. of Nat. Policy Toward Gambling, 1975-76; chmn. criminal and violent behavior rev. com. NIMH, 1988-90. Author: Evaluating Criminology, 1978, The Criminology Index, 1978, The Criminally Insane: A Community Followup of Mentally Ill Offenders, 1979 (ABA Gavel award, cert of merit 1980), From Boy to Man: From Delinquency to Crime, 1987; editor: Images of Crime: Offenders and Victims, 1974, Crime and Delinquency: Dimensions of Deviance, 1974; mem. editorial bd.: Jour. Criminal Law and Criminology, Social Forces, Jour. Quantitative Criminology, Criminology: An Interdisciplinary Jour.; contbr. articles to profl. jours. Recipient Appreciation certificate Nat. Inst. Mental Health, 1990. Mem. Am. Soc. Criminology (v.p. 1974-75, exec. counsellor 1974-77, 82, 85—, Presdl. Citation 1975), Am. Sociol. Assn. Home: 188 Jay St Albany NY 12210 Office: SUNY Sch Criminal Justice 135 Western Ave Albany NY 12203-1011

THORNBERRY, WILLIAM M. (MAC THORNBERRY), congressman; b. Clarendon, Tex., July 15, 1958; m. Sally Thornberry; 2 children. BA in History summa cum laude, Tex. Tech U., 1980; JD, U. Tex., 1983. Legis. coun. Rep. Tom Loeffler, 1983-85; chief of staff Rep. Larry Combest, 1985-88; dep. asst. sec. legis. affairs U.S. State Dept., 1988-89; def. atty. Peterson, Farris, Doores & Jones, Amarillo, Tex., 1989—; mem. 104th Congress from 13th Tex. dist., 1995—; family rancher. Mem. Tex. and Southwestern Cattle Raisers Assn. Republican. Office: US House Reps 1535 Longworth House Office Bldg Washington DC 20515-4313*

THORNBURG, FREDERICK FLETCHER, diversified business executive, lawyer; b. South Bend, Ind., Feb. 10, 1940; s. James F. and Margaret R. (Major) T.; children: James Brian, Charles Kevin, Christian Sean, Christopher Herndon; m. Patricia J. Malloy, Dec. 4, 1981. AB, DePauw U., 1963; postgrad., U. Notre Dame, 1965; JD magna cum laude, Ind. U., 1968. Bar: Ind. 1968, U.S. Tax Ct. 1970, U.S. Ct. Appeals (7th cir.) 1970, U.S. Supreme Ct. 1971. Tchr., coach U.S. Peace Corps, Colombia, 1963-65; law clk. to chief judge U.S. Ct. Appeals (7th cir.), 1968-69; assoc. Thornburg, McGill, Deahl, Harman, Carey & Murray, South Bend, 1969-75, ptnr., 1975-80; v.p. systems and svcs. group The Wackenhut Corp., Coral Gables, Fla., 1981-82, sr. v.p. adminstrn., 1982-86, exec. v.p. 1986-88, also bd. dirs.; pres. Wackenhut Internat. Corp. and Wackenhut Svcs., Inc.; v.p. and legal counsel St. Thomas U., 1988-90, adj. prof. law, 1989-90; pres., CEO PropServ, Inc., 1991-94; pres. EPS Ltd., 1995—; cons. Ideas N Motion, Inc., Musselman Steel Corp., Private Freezer Corp., Am. Tel Corp.; legal & mgmt. cons., mem. bd. advisors, Publix Supermarkets, Inc., 1994—, St. Thomas U.; bd. dirs. Doral Oaks Inc. Assocs., 1993-94; trustee U. Cmty. Hosp. Found., 1991-94; adj. prof. bus. St. Mary's Coll., 1975-78; vis. prof. CTA, 1985—; vice-chmn., pvt. sec. adv. coun. Fla. Sec. of State, 1985-90. Assoc. editor in chief: Ind. Law Jour., 1967-68; contbr. articles to legal and bus. jours. Bd. dirs. YMCA, Channel 34, Symphony Orch. Assn. Fulbright selectee, Halleck scholar. Mem. ABA, Ind. Bar Assn., Greater Miami C. of C. (former corp. rep. trustee), Elks Club, Doral Park Country Club, Order of Coif, Phi Delta Phi, Alpha Delta Sigma. Office: 10005 NW 52 Terrace Miami FL 33178

THORNBURG, LEE ELLIS, film executive, director; b. Houston, Feb. 16, 1942; s. Richard Ellis and Lucyle (Comstock) T.; m. Jane Kaiser (div. 1981); children: Janette Mattas, Deanne Waddell; m. Patricia Ann Kirkham, June 16, 1987. Tech. svc. engr. Dresser Industries, Houston, 1970-76; pres. Lone Star Pictures Internat., Inc., Dallas, 1976—. Dir. films including Hollywood High Part II, 1981, 6-Pack, 1991; producer films including Kings of the Hill, 1976, Mr. Mean, 1978. Mem. Am. Film Market Assn. Republican. Methodist. Office: Lonestar Pictures Internat 8831 Sunset Blvd Ste 204 Los Angeles CA 90069

THORNBURGH, DICK (RICHARD L. THORNBURGH), lawyer, former United Nations official, former United States attorney general, former governor; b. Pitts., July 16, 1932; s. Charles Garland and Alice (Sanborn) T.; m. Virginia Walton Judson, Oct. 12, 1963; children: John, David, Peter, William. B in Engring., Yale, 1954; LLB, U. Pitts., 1957; hon. degrees, from 30 colls. and univs. Bar: Pa. 1958, U.S. Supreme Ct. 1965. Atty. Kirkpatrick & Lockhart, Pitts., 1959-69, 77-79, 87-88, 91-92, 94—; U.S. atty. for Western Pa. Pitts., 1969-75; U.S. asst. atty. gen. Dept. Justice, Washington, 1975-77; gov. State of Pa., Harrisburg, 1979-87; U.S. atty. gen. Washington, 1988-91; under-sec.-gen. for adminstrn. and mgmt. UN, N.Y.C., 1992-93; del. Pa. Constl. Conv., 1967-68. Mem. Coun. Fgn. Rels.; trustee Urban Inst., Henry L. Stimson Ctr., Dole Found. for Employment of People with Disabilities. Fellow Am. Bar Found.; mem. Am. Judicature Soc., Nat. Acad. Pub. Adminstrn. Republican. Office: Kirkpatrick & Lockhart 1800 Massachusetts Ave NW Washington DC 20036-1800

THORNBURGH, RON, state official; b. Burlingame, Kans., Dec. 31, 1962; m. Annette Thornburgh. Student, Washburn U., 1985. Dep. asst. sec. of state, then asst. sec. of state State of Kans., Topeka, 1985-87, sec. of state, 1995—; asst. sec. of state Sec. of State's Office, Topeka, 1991-95, sec. of state, 1995—; vice chairperson blue ribbon panel on ethical conduct State of Kans., 1989. Mem. Kids Voting Kans. Exec. Com.; mem. adv. com. United Way. Toll fellow Henry Toll Fellowship Program, 1995. Mem. Washburn U. Alumni Bd., 20/30 Club Internat. Methodist. Office: Sec of State 2d Fl Statehouse 300 SW st Topeka KS 66612*

THORNBURY, JOHN ROUSSEAU, radiologist, physician; b. Cleve., Mar. 16, 1929; s. Purla Lee and Gertrude (Glidden) T.; m. Julia Lee McGregor, Mar. 20, 1955; children: Lee Allison, John McGregor. A.B. cum laude, Miami U., Oxford, Ohio, 1950; M.D., Ohio State U., 1955. Diplomate: Am. Bd. Radiology. Intern Hurley Hosp., Flint, Mich., 1955-56; resident U. Iowa Hosps., Iowa City, 1958-61; instr., asst. prof. radiology U. Colo. Med. Center, Denver, 1962-63; practice medicine specializing in radiology Denver, 1962-63, Iowa City, 1963-66, Seattle, 1966-68, Ann Arbor, Mich., 1968-79, Albuquerque, 1979-84, Rochester, N.Y., 1984-89, Madison, Wis., 1989-94; mem. staff U. Wisconsin Hosp., Madison, prof. radiology, chief sect. of body imaging, Med. Sch., 1989-94, prof. emeritus, 1994—; asst. prof. radiology U. Iowa Hosps., 1963-66, U. Wash. Hosp., Seattle, 1966-68; assoc. prof. radiology U. Mich. Med. Ctr., 1968-71, prof. radiology, 1971-79; prof. radiology, chief divsn. diagnostic radiology dept. radiology Sch. Medicine, U. N.Mex., 1979-84; prof. radiology U. Rochester Sch. Medicine, 1984-89, acting chmn., 1985-87; chmn. sci. com. on efficacy studies Nat. Coun. on Radiation Protection, 1980-95; rapporteur/mem. sci. group on indications/limitations of x-ray diagnostic procedures WHO, 1983; cons. com. on efficacy of magnetic resonance nat. health tech. adv. panel Australian Inst. Health, 1986; invited U.S. cons. MRI program, Nijmegen, The Netherlands, 1992; lectr. in field; cons. tech. assessment and outcome rsch., 1994—; cons. to Am. Soc. of Neuroradiology, 1995-97. Co-author/cons. Clin. Efficacy Assessment Project, Am. Coll. Physicians, 1986-89; assoc. editor: Yearbook of Radiology, 1971-82; editorial bd.: Contemporary Diagnostic Radiology, 1977-84, Urologic Radiology, 1977-84. Served to capt., M.C. USAF, 1956-58. Grantee Agy. Health Care Policy and Rsch., 1986-91, U. Rochester, 1986-89, U. Wis., Madison, 1989-91. Fellow Am. Coll. Radiology; mem. Soc. Uroradiology (pres. 1976-77, dir. 1977-79), Assn. Univ. Radiologists (pres. 1980-81), Radiol. Soc. N.Am., Am. Roentgen Ray Soc. (Caldwell medal 1993), Colo. Radiol. Soc., Phi Beta Kappa, Delta Tau Delta, Omicron Delta Kappa, Phi Chi. Republican. Lutheran. Address: 185 Morgan Pl Castle Rock CO 80104-9061 Home: Castle Pines Village 185 Morgan Pl Castle Rock CO 80104-9061 *"Mooring Post" relationships and sharing have been essential to success and achievements in my multi-disciplinary research. "Mooring Post" persons range from expert mentors and stellar colleagues, to the bedrock of a loving and supportive family. Further, to me, Rule One in medicine has always been, "The patient comes first."*

THORNDIKE, EDWARD HARMON, physicist; b. Pasadena, Calif., Aug. 2, 1934; s. Edward Moulton and Louise (Harmon) T.; m. Elizabeth H. Wenger, Sept. 8, 1955; children—Susan Lee, Patricia Lynn, Edward Harmon Jr. A.B., Wesleyan U., Middletown, Conn., 1956; M.S., Stanford U., 1957; Ph.D., Harvard U., 1960. Research fellow Harvard U., Cambridge, Mass., 1960-61; mem. faculty U. Rochester, N.Y., 1961—; asso. prof. physics U. Rochester, 1965-72, prof., 1972—; vis. prof. U. Geneva, 1969-70; vis. scientist CERN, Geneva, 1969-70; mem. adv. coun. Ctr. Environ. Info., Rochester, 1974-93; mem. adv. com. Stanford Linear Accelerator Ctr. Exptl. Program, 1987-89; mem. vis. com. for Fermilab, Univs. Rsch. Assn., 1993-95. Author: Energy and Environment, a Primer for Scientists and Engineers, 1976; contbr. articles to profl. jours. NSF fellow, 1970, Guggenheim fellow, 1987-88. Fellow Am. Phys. Soc. Office: U Rochester Dept Physics/Astronomy Rochester NY 14627

THORNDIKE, JOHN LOWELL, investment executive; b. Boston, Oct. 17, 1926; s. Augustus and Olivia (Lowell) T.; m. Dorothy Wood Dudley, Sept. 16, 1950; 1 child, John Amory. BS, Harvard U., 1949. Registered rep Tucker Anthony & Co., Boston, 1950-57; v.p. Putnam Mgmt. Co., Boston, 1957-62; asst. to treas. Harvard U., Cambridge, Mass., 1962-66; v.p. Fiduciary Trust Co., Boston, 1966-92, also bd. dirs.; dir. Fiduciary Co. Inc., 1984—; trustee Provident Instn. for Savs., Boston, 1965-85; trustee, ptnr. Eaton Vance Mut. Funds, Boston, 1977—. Trustee Boston Symphony Orch., 1960-80, treas., 1965-77, v.p., 1977-80; trustee Brigham and Women's Hosp., 1982-87, Cotting Sch., treas., 1982—; mem. warrant com. Town of Dover, Mass., 1966-69, chmn., 1968-69, town moderator, 1971-75; mem. Mass. Health and Ednl. Facilities Authority, Boston, 1970-88, sec., 1972-84, chmn., 1984-87; mem. cemetery commn. Town of Dover, 1992—; bd. dirs. Mass. Audubon Soc., 1971-89, chmn., 1984-89. With Army Air Corps, 1945. Recipient 1st prize Assn. Town Fin. Coms., 1969. Mem. Boston Security Analyst Soc., Boston Econ. Club, Union Club of Boston (pres. 1978-79), Harvard Club of Boston (pres. 1980-83), Harvard Mus. Assn. (pres. 1988-91). Republican. Episcopalian. Avocations: tennis, bird watching. Home: 10 Main St Dover MA 02030-2022 Office: Fiduciary Trust Co 175 Federal St Boston MA 02110-2210

THORNDIKE, JOSEPH JACOBS, JR., editor; b. Peabody, Mass., July 29, 1913; s. Joseph Jacobs and Susan Ellison (Farnham) T.; m. Virginia Lemont, Sept. 7, 1940; children—John, Alan; m. Margery Darrell, Oct. 3, 1963; 1 son, Joseph Jacobs III. A.B., Harvard, 1934. Asst. editor Time Mag., 1934-36; assoc. editor Life Mag., 1936-46; mng. editor Life, 1946-49; pres. Thorndike, Jensen & Parton, Inc.; co-founder, contbg. editor Am. Heritage Pub. Co. Author: The Very Rich, 1976, The Magnificent Builders, 1978, The Coast, 1993; editor: Seafaring America, 1974, Mysteries of the Past, 1977, Discovery of Lost Worlds, 1979, Mysteries of the Deep, 1980, Three Centuries of American Architects, 1981. Unitarian. Club: Harvard (N.Y.C.). Home: 34 Oak St Harwich MA 02645-2703

THORNDIKE, RICHARD KING, former brokerage company executive; b. Millis, Mass., 1913; s. Richard King and Florence A. (Macy) T.; m. Lucy Saltonstall Rantoul, Sept. 21, 1935 (dec. May 1958); children: Richard III, Rose, Sylvia; m. Mercy Bours Archibald, Oct. 1, 1960. Grad., Harvard, 1935. With F.S. Moseley & Co., Boston, 1935—; asst. analyst F.S. Moseley & Co., 1937-46, partner, 1947-73; v.p. Moseley, Hallgarten, Estabrook & Weeden Inc., 1973-83. Republican. Episcopalian. Clubs: Myopia (Hamilton, Mass.); Ponte Ve dra Inn and Club; Phoenix-SK (Harvard), Lenox (Lenox, Mass.). Home: Apt F-206 1000 Vicars Landing Way Ponte Vedra Beach FL 32082-3127

THORNE, BARBARA LOCKWOOD, guidance counselor, secondary education educator; b. Rochester, N.Y., Nov. 12, 1938; d. Harvey J. and Clara (Lee) Lockwood; m. Marc E. Thorne, July 21, 1962; children: John, Andrew. BA, Westminster Coll., 1960; MEd, Cornell U., 1961; MS, U. Bridgeport, 1987, 6th Yr. Cert., 1991. Cert. tchr., N.Y., counselor, Conn. Tchr. social studies Greece Olympia High Sch., Rochester, N.Y., 1961-63, East High Sch., Rochester, 1963-64; tchr. recreation Fairfield (Conn.) YMCA, 1965-70; tutor, substitute tchr. Needham (Mass.) Alternate High Sch., 1970-78; tchr. social studies Alternate Learning Program Darien (Conn.) High Sch., 1978-88, team leader, 1982-88, guidance counselor, 1988—, coord. student assistance team, 1991—; locat advisor A Better Chance, Darien, 1989—. Chmn. Youth Commn., Darien, 1982-85, Park and Recreation Commn., Darien, 1985—, chmn., 1991-96; vol. soup kitchen Salvation Army, Stamford, Conn., 1988-90. Recipient Vol. Svc. award Community Coun., Darien, 1977. Mem. ASCD, AAUW, NEA, LWV (pres., bd. dirs. 1975-85, Sears Found. award 1963, Vol. in govt. award 1993), Assn. Secondary Sch. Adminstrn., Am. Assn. Counseling and Devel., Nat. Coun. Social Studies, Jr. League Stamford/Norwalk. Democrat. Congregationalist. Avocations: reading, tennis, cross-country skiing.

THORNE, FRANCIS, composer; b. Bay Shore, N.Y., June 23, 1922; s. Francis Burritt and Hildegarde (Kobbé) T.; m. Ann Cobb, Dec. 9, 1942; children: Ann Boughton (Mrs. William F. Niles), Wendy Oakleigh (Mrs. William H. Forsyth, Jr.), Candace Kobbé (Mrs. Anthony M. Canton). B.A. in Music Theory, Yale, 1942. Founder, pres. Thorne Music Fund, Inc., 1965-75; pub. Edward B. Marks Music Corp., 1963—, Gen. Music Pub. Co., 1971—, G. Schirmer/AMP, 1985—, Theodore Presser Co., 1989—; exec. dir. Lenox Arts Center, 1972-76, Am. Composers Alliance, 1975-85; co-founder, pres. Am. Composers Orch., 1976—. Composer: Elegy for Orch., 1964, Burlesque Overture, 1966, Lyric Variations for Orch., 1967, Symphony No. 1, 1963, No. II, 1966, No. III, 1970, No. IV, 1977, Fortuna, 1961-62, Liebesrock, 1969, Sonar Plexus, 1969, Six Set-Pieces, 1969, Contra Band Music, 1970, Antiphonies, 1970, Simultaneities, 1971, Quartessence, 1971, Fanfare, Fugue and Funk, 1972, Lyric Variations II, 1972, Piano Sonata, 1972, Lyric Variations III, 1973, Cantata Sauce, 1973, Evensongs, 1973, Cello Concerto, 1974, Piano Concerto, 1974, Violin Concerto, 1975, String Quartet 1, 1960, 2, 1967, 3, 1976, 4, 1983, Spoon River Overture, 1976, Grand Duo, 1976, Five Set Pieces, 1976, Love's Variations, 1976, Pop Partita, 1978, The Eternal Light for Soprano and Orchestra, 1979, Divertimento for Flute, Strings and Percussion, 1979, Lyric Variations IV for Solo Violin, 1980, Divertimento 2 for Bassoon and Stringed Instruments, 1980, Eine Kleine Meyermusik, 1980, Gems From Spoon River, 1980, Lyric Variations No. 6 for solo clarinet, 1981, Divertimento No. 3, 1982, Praise and Thanksgiving, 1983, Lyric Variations No. 5 for Orch., 1980-81, Symphony No. 5, 1984, Concerto Concertante, 1985, Rhapsodic Variations, No. 2, 1985, Humoresque for Orch., 1985, Rhapsodic Variations No. 3 for Oboe and Strings, 1986, The Affirming Flame for Soprano and Chamber Ensemble, 1987; seven simple syncopations for Piano solo, 1987, Rhapsodic Variations No. 4 For Viol Solo, 1987, Rhapsodic Variations No. 5 for Violins and Piano, 1988, Money Matters for Tenor and Chamber Ensemble, 1988, Piano Concerto No. 3, 1989, Remembering Dizzy for Brass Quintet, 1990, Pop Partita No. 2 for woodwinds and strings, 1991, Mario and The Magician, opera after Thomas Mann, in Prologue and 1 Act, 1991, Symphony No. 6 for Strings, 1992, Symphony No. 7 Along the Hudson for chorus and orch., 1994, Cello Concerto No. 2, 1995, Echo for Soprano and Mixed Chorus, 1995; recs. on Composers' Recs., Inc., Serenus, Owl, Louisville Opus One and New World; founder, pres. Am. Composers Orch., 1976. Trustee Am. Symphony Orchestra League, Manhattan Sch. Music, Am. Music Center, MacDowell Colony, Walter W. Naumburg Found., Contemporary Music Soc., Theater Devel. Fund, Group for Contemporary Music., Am. Brass Quintet. Served to lt. USNR, 1942-45. Nat. Endowment Arts grantee, 1966, 73; fellow, 1976, 79; Nat. Inst. Arts and Letters grantee, 1968; N.Y. State Arts Council ballet commn., 1973. Mem. AAAL, BMI, Contemporary Music Soc. (bd. dirs.), Am. Composers Alliance, League Composers, Century Assn. Club: Century Assn. (N.Y.C.). Home: 116 E 66th St New York NY 10021-6547 *Having spent ten years as a businessman, I have been privileged to serve my composer colleagues as an administrator for musical organizations. The practical experience has also served me well as a creative artist in having instilled the virtues of discipline. Serving music as composer and administrator gives the highest sense of satisfaction, from participating in this life-giving world in a total comprehensive way.*

THORNE, FRANK LEADLEY, plastic surgeon; b. Rochester, N.Y., 1933. MD, U. Pa., 1957. Diplomate Am. Bd. Plastic and Reconstructive Surgery. Intern U. Mich., Ann Arbor, 1957-58; resident surgery U. Wash., Seattle, 1962-65; resident plastic surgery Duke U., Durham, N.C., 1965-68; surgeon Swedish Hosp., Seattle; clin. prof. plastic surgery U. Wash., Seattle; pres. Am. Assn. Hand Surgery, 1977-78, Plastic Surgery Ednl. Found., 1988-89; gov. ACS, 1990-96; dir. Am. Bd. Plastic Surgery, 1990-96, vice chmn., 1995-96. Fellow Am. Coll. Surgeons; mem. AMA, Am. Assn. Hand Surgeons, Am. Soc. Plastic and Reconstructive Surgery. Office: 1229 Madison St Ste 790 Seattle WA 98104-1381

THORNE, JOHN REINECKE, business educator, venture capitalist; b. Pitts., Mar. 25, 1926; s. John Mueller and Louise (Reinecke) T.; m. Barbara Siebert, Aug. 31, 1951 (dec. Feb. 1995); children: John S., Barbara L., Richard W. BS, Brown U., 1947; MSEE, U. Pitts., 1949; MS in Indsl. Adminstrn., Carnegie Mellon U., 1952. Devel. engr. Westinghouse Elec. Corp., Pitts., 1947-50; mgr. fin. analysis Hughes Aircraft Co., L.A., 1952-54; dir. computer systems lab. Litton Industries, L.A., 1954-61; chmn., pres. The Scionics Corp., L.A., 1961-69; cons., L.A., 1969-72; prof. bus. Carnegie-Mellon U., Pitts., 1972—, Morgenthaler prof. entrepreneurship, 1987—, dir. Donald H. Jones Ctr. for Entrepreneurship, 1990—; founder, chmn. Enterprise Corp. Pitts., 1983—; gen. ptnr. Pitts. Seed Fund, 1985—; bd. dirs. Orion Capital Corp., other pvt. corps. Contbr. numerous articles on entrepreneurship to profl. jours. Named Fin. Svcs. Adv. of Yr. by SBA, 1988. Mem. Duquesne Club, Rolling Rock Club, University Club. Unitarian. Home: Furnace Run Laughlintown PA 15655 Office: Carnegie-Mellon U Dept of Bus Schenley Park Pittsburgh PA 15213

THORNE, JOHN WATSON, III, advertising and marketing executive; b. Washington, Jan. 16, 1934; s. John Watson, Jr. and Mary Washington (Tucker) T.; m. Joan Kramer Vail, Mar. 2, 1957; children: Vail Tucker, Tracy Tucker, John Watson, IV. BA in Polit. Sci., George Washington U., 1955; MA in Sociology, New Sch. Social Research, 1974. Asst. account exec. Young & Rubicam, Inc., N.Y.C., 1957-59; advt. mgr. Gen. Electric Co., Decatur, Ill., 1959-63; dir. advt. promotion Brand Names Found., N.Y.C., 1963-66; account exec. Tatham-Laird & Kudner (advt.), N.Y.C., 1966-67; v.p., mgmt. supr. Wells, Rich, Greene, Inc., N.Y.C., 1973-76; v.p., account supr. Batten, Barton, Durstine & Osborn, Inc., N.Y.C., 1967-73, sr. v.p., mgmt. supr., 1976-81, exec. v.p., 1981-87, also dir., mem. operating com.; chmn., CEO Thorne & Assocs., N.Y.C., 1987—; pres. Telerx Mktg., Spring House, Pa., 1991-95; chmn. Alliance Telemanagement, Inc., Doylestown, Pa., 1995—; mem. bus. program com. Proprietary Assn., Washington, 1984-85; adj. prof. advt. Syracuse (N.Y.) U. Pres. Hastings-on-Hudson (N.Y.) Bd. Edn.; bd. dirs. Young Concert Artists, N.Y.C.; mem. communications coms. Nat. Urban League, Carnegie Hall. Served as 1st lt. USMCR, 1955-57. Mem. Buckingham Racquet Club. Republican. Roman Catholic. Home: 100 Stoneybrook Rd Newtown PA 18940-2506 Office: Alliance Telemgmt Inc Ste 119 350 S Main Doylestown PA 18901

THORNE, OAKLEIGH BLAKEMAN, publishing company executive; b. Santa Barbara, Calif., 1932. BA, Harvard U., 1954. With First Nat. City Bank N.Y., 1954-62; chmn., dir. Ct Corp. Systems; with Commerce Clearing House, Inc., Deerfield, Ill., 1959—; chmn., pres. legal info. Commerce Clearing House, Inc., Deerfield, 1975—. Office: Commerce Clearing House Inc 2700 Lake Cook Rd Deerfield IL 60015-3867 Office: CCH Computax Inc 21250 Hawthorne Blvd Torrance CA 90503-5506*

THORNE, RICHARD MANSERGH, physicist; b. Birmingham, Eng., July 25, 1942; s. Robert George and Dorothy Lena (Goodchild) T.; children: Peter Baring, Michael Thomas. B.Sc., Birmingham U., 1963; Ph.D., M.I.T., 1968. Grad. asst. M.I.T., 1963-68; asst. prof. dept. atmospheric scis. UCLA, 1968-71, asso. prof., 1971-75, prof., 1975—, chmn. dept., 1976-79; vis. fellow St. Edmunds Coll., Cambridge (Eng.) U., 1986-87, 92; cons. Jet Propulsion Lab., Aerospace Corp. Contbr. articles to profl. jours. Recipient numerous grants NSF, NASA, NATO, Jet Propulsion Lab. Mem. Am. Geophys. Union. Home: 10390 Caribou Ln Los Angeles CA 90077-2809 Office: UCLA Dept Atmospheric Scis Los Angeles CA 90024

THORNELL, JACK RANDOLPH, photographer; b. Vicksburg, Miss., Aug. 29, 1939; s. Benjamin O. and Myrtice (Jones) T.; divorced; children—Candice, Jay Randolph. Ed. pub. schs. Photographer Jackson (Miss.) Daily News, 1960-64; with A.P., 1964—; assigned A.P., Dominican Republic, 1965, Selma, Ala., 1965; assigned Democratic Nat. Conv., 1968. Served with AUS, 1958-60. Recipient Pulitzer prize for news photography of shooting of James Meredith, 1967; Headliners Photography award, 1967. Home: 5236 Utica St Metairie LA 70006-6446 Office: 3800 Howard Ave New Orleans LA 70140-1002

THORNER, MICHAEL OLIVER, medical educator, research center administrator; b. Beaconsfield, Eng., Jan. 14, 1945; came to U.S., 1977; s. Hans and Ilse T.; m. Prudence Maria Ross, July 7, 1966; children—Benjamin Bruno, Anna Rosa. M.B.B.S., Middlesex Hosp., U. London, 1970. Intern, resident Middlesex Hosp., St. Bartholomeo Hosp.,, London; lectr. in chem. pathology St. Bartholomews Hosp., London, 1974, research fellow, 1974-75, lectr. in medicine, 1975-77; assoc. prof. medicine U. Va., Charlottesville, 1977-82, prof. medicine, 1982—, head div. endocrinology and metabolism, 1986—, dir. Clin. Research Ctr., 1984—, assoc. dir. CRC, 1981-84, Kenneth R. Crispell prof. in internal medicine, 1990—; mem. FDA Endocrinologic and metabolic drugs adv. com., 1984-88, NIH biochem. endocrinology study sect., 1985-89. Contbr. articles to profl. jours. Recipient Albion O. Bernstein award, 1984, Virginia Scientist of Yr. award, 1985, Gen. Clin. Rsch. Ctrs. program award, 1995, The Pituitary Soc. Annual award for contbns. to understanding pituitary disease, 1995. Fellow Royal Coll. Physicians, ACP; mem. Soc. Endocrinology, Endocrine Soc. (Edwin B. Astwood award 1992), Assn. Am. Physicians, Am. Soc. Clin. Investigations. Home: Mount Ammonett RR 1 Box 487 North Garden VA 22959-9639 Office: U Va Hosps Dept Internal Medicine PO Box 511-66 Charlottesville VA 22908-0001

THORNER, PETER, retail executive; b. Bklyn., Oct. 7, 1943; s. Alice Cecilly (Blei) Horelick; children: Brian Reid, Sarah Jill. BS in Econs., CUNY, Bklyn., 1965. Ptnr. Deloitte, Haskins & Sells, N.Y.C., 1978-82; sr. v.p., chief fin. officer Ogden Corp., N.Y.C., 1982-85; CFO, exec. v.p. Rapid-Am. Corp., N.Y.C., 1985-87, also bd. dirs.; mng. dir. Wheelabrator Techs., Inc., Hampton, N.H., 1987-90; CFO, exec. v.p. Ames Dept. Stores, Rocky Hill, Conn., 1990-92, acting CEO, pres., COO, 1992-94; pres. New Eng. Strategies, Weston, Conn., 1994-95; vice chmn., pres., COO Bradlees, Inc., Braintree, Mass., 1995—. Chmn. Vitam Youth Treatment Ctr. Mem. AICPA, N.Y. State Soc. CPAs, N.Y. Econs. Club, Fin. Execs. Inst., Fairfield County Fish and Game Protecting Assn., Bristol Gun Club. Office: Bradlees Inc Bradlees Cir Braintree MA 02184

THORNE-THOMSEN, THOMAS, lawyer; b. El Dorado, Kans., Oct. 22, 1949; s. Fletcher and Barbara (Macoubrey) T.-T. BA, Vanderbilt U., 1972; JD, U. Colo., 1976; LLM in Taxation, NYU, 1983. Bar: Colo. 1976, Ga. 1977, Ill. 1983. Law clk. to Chief Judge Alfred A. Arraj U.S. Dist. Ct. Colo., Boulder, 1976-77; assoc. Alston & Bird, Atlanta, 1977-82; assoc., ptnr. Keck, Mahin & Cate, Chgo., 1983-95; ptnr. Schiff, Harden & Waite, Chgo., 1995—. Bd. dirs. Century Place Devel. Corp., Chgo., 1989—, Sutherland Neighborhood Devel. Corp., Chgo., 1989—, South Shore Neighborhood Devel. Crop. Chgo. 1990—, Argyle Neighborhood Devel. Corp., Chgo., 1991—, Heartland Alliance for Human Rights and Human Need, 1995—, Howard Brown Health Ctr., Chgo., 1991-94; com. mem. Chgo.'s Comprehensive Housing Affordability Strategy, Chgo., 1992—; mem. bond leverage trust fund task force Ill. Housing Authority, 1993. Mem. ABA, Colo. State Bar Assn., Ill. State Bar Assn., Ga. State Bar Assn. Avocations: jogging, biking, swimming, boating. Home: 680 N Lake Shore Dr Apt 1110 Chicago IL 60611-4407 Office: Schiff Harden & Waite 7200 Sears Tower Chicago IL 60606-6473

THORNHILL, ARTHUR HORACE, JR., retired book publisher; b. Boston, Jan. 1, 1924; s. Arthur Horace and Mary Josephine (Peterson) T.; m. Dorothy M. Matheis, Oct. 28, 1944; children: Sandra Susanne Thornhill Brushart, Arthur Horace. AB magna cum laude, Princeton U., 1948. With Little, Brown & Co., Inc., Boston, 1948-88; v.p. Little, Brown & Co., Inc., 1955-58, gen. mgr., 1960-87, chief exec. officer, pres., 1962-87, chmn. bd., 1970-87; chmn., pres., dir. Little, Brown & Co. (Can.), Ltd., 1955-84; v.p. Time, Inc., 1968-87; vice chmn. Time-Life Books, Inc., 1976-86; dir. Conrac Corp., 1971-87; mem. adv. council history dept. Princeton U., 1964-85; trustee, treas. Princeton U. Press, 1972-85; dir. Am. Textbook Pubs. Inst., 1965-68, Grosett & Dunlop, 1965-67, Bantam Books, Inc., 1965-67. Trustee Bennington Coll., 1969-76; fellow emeritus Ctr. for Creative Photography U. Ariz.; bd. dirs. Am. Book Pubs. Council, 1964-67. Served to 1st lt. USAAF, World War II. Decorated Air medal; recipient Princeton U. Press medal, 1985. Mem. Assn. Am. Pubs. (dir. 1978-81), Edgartown Yacht Club, Edgartown Reading Room (pres. 1990-92), Union Club (N.Y.C.), Princeton Club (N.Y.C.), Century Club (N.Y.C.), Publs. Lunch Club (N.Y.C.), PEN, Union Club (Boston), St. Botolph (Boston). Home: 50 S School St Portsmouth NH 03801-5258

THORNHILL, BARBARA COLE, marketing executive; b. Rahway, N.J., Sept. 4, 1960; d. Clayton Eugene and Margaret (Fitzgerald) Cole; m. Matthew Thomas Thornhill, Oct. 15, 1983 (div. 1996); children: Allison, Clark. BBA in Mktg., Coll. of William and Mary, 1982. Asst. account exec. March Direct/McCann Direct, N.Y.C., 1983-84, account exec., 1984-86, account supr., 1986-87; dir. comml. client divsn. Huntsinger & Jeffer Direct, Richmond, Va., 1987-89; v.p., account supr. The Stenrich Group, Richmond, 1989-90, sr. v.p., dir. account mgmt., 1990-92, exec. v.p., dir. account mgmt., bd. dirs., 1992-95; exec. v.p. for integrated mktg. comm., mem. exec. com. The Martin Agy., Richmond, 1995—; mem. profit sharing com. The Martin Agy., Richmond, 1993—. Exec. com. bd. trustees Richmond Children's Mus., 1992—, dir. bd. trustees, 1991-92; area coord. William and Mary Alum Admissions Network, Richmond, 1988—. Recipient Silver Echo award Direct Mktg. Assn., 1991, 94, Richmond Area Marketeer of Yr. award Am. Mktg. Assn., 1992, 93, 94, Gold Effie award, 1992. Avocations: travel, family, reading, golf. Office: The Martin Agy 500 N Allen Ave Richmond VA 23220

THORNLEY, SHIRLEY BLUMBERG, architect; b. Cape Town, South Africa, Feb. 4, 1952; d. Alec and Anne (Minkowitz) Katz; m. Scott; 1 child, Charles R. Attended, U. Cape Town; BArch (with honors), U. Toronto, 1976. Assoc. Barton Myers Assoc., 1977-87; architect Kuwabara Payne McKenna Blumberg Architects; selected projects incl. Hazelton Townhouses Toronto, 1983, Unionville Libr. Markham, 1984, Hasbro Corp. H.Q. Phase One R.I., 1986; selected projects with present firm include Hasbro Corp. H.Q. Phase Two R.I., 1994, King James Place Toronto, 1991, The Design Exch., Toronto, 1994, Minn. Culture, Tourism & Recreation Niagara Falls, 1995, Ammirati & Puris/Lintas Offices, N.Y.C., 1995; adj. asst. prof. U. Toronto, 1987, 90; guest critic Carleton U., U. Waterloo; Hyde chair for excellence Coll. of Architecture U. Nebr., Lincoln, 1994; mem. bd. dirs. Royal Arch. Inst. can., 1990-93, mem. bd. trustees Ont. Sci. Ctr., 1988-91. Recipient Toronto Arts award for Architecture & Design, 1993, Gov. Gen's. award of Merit King James Place, 1992, Gov. Gen's. award for Architecture Royal Archtl. Inst. Can., 1992. Mem. Ont. Assn. Architects, Royal Arch. Inst. Can. Office: Kuwarbara Payne McKenna Blumberg, 322 King St W 3rd Fl, Toronto, ON Canada M5V 1J2

THORNLOW, CAROLYN, law firm administrator, consultant; b. Kew Gardens, N.Y., May 25, 1954. B.B.A. magna cum laude, Bernard M. Baruch Coll., 1982. Gen. mgr. Richard A. Ramm Assocs., Levittown, N.Y., 1972-78; adminstr. Tunstead Schechter & Torre, N.Y.C., 1978-82, Cowan Liebowitz & Latman, P.C., N.Y.C., 1982-84, Rosenberg & Estis, P.C., N.Y.C., 1984-85; controller Finkelstein, Borah, Schwartz, Altschuler & Goldstein, P.C., N.Y.C., 1986-92; pres. Concinnity Services, Hastings, N.Y., 1984—; instr. introduction to law office mgmt. seminars Assn. Legal Adminstrs., N.Y.C., 1984. Editor: The ABA Guide to Profl. Mgrs. in the Law Office; contbr. numerous articles to profl. jours. Mem. N.Y. Assn. Legal Adminstrs. (v.p. 1982-83), Internat. Assn. Legal Adminstrs. (asst. regional v.p. 1983-84, regional v.p. 1984-85), Nat. Soc. Tax Profls. (cert. tax profl.), Am. Mgmt. Assn., Adminstrv. Mgmt. Soc. (cert.), ABA, Inst. Cert. Mgmt. Accts., Mensa, Beta Gamma Sigma, Sigma Iota Epsilon. Home and Office: 445 Broadway Hastings On Hudson NY 10706

THORNSBERRY, CLYDE, microbiologist; b. Pippa Passes, Ky., June 20, 1930; s. Columbus B. and Ollie Mae (Sparkman) T.; m. Glenda L. Martin, May 13, 1952; children: Teresa, David, Robert. BS, U. Ky., 1958, PhD, 1966. Supr. rsch. micrbiology, chief antimicrobial investigations br. Ctrs. for Disease Control, Atlanta, Ga., 1966-89; dir. Inst. for Microbiol. Rsch., Franklin, Tenn., 1989-93, MRL Pharm. Svcs., Franklin, 1993—; lectr. in field; chmn., vice-chmn. Intersci. Conf. Anti-Agts., Washington, 1989-94; adv. bd. several pharm. cos., 1980—. Contbr. articles to profl. jours. Recipient awards USPHS, Washington, 1982, 87. Fellow Infectious Disease Soc. of Am.; mem. Am. Soc. Microbiology, Am. Acad. Microbiology, N.Y. Acad. Scis., WHO Coms. on Antibiotics, Nat. Com. Clin. Lab. Studys. Democrat. Achievements include patent-use of antimicrobial agts. to sterilize tissue for implanting; study of antimicrobials, antimicrobial resistance, and in vitro testing of antimicrobial activity; lab. was designated a WHO lab. for antimicrobial agts. Home: 5182 Waddell Hollow Rd Franklin TN 37064 Office: MRL Pharm Svcs 357 Riverside Dr Franklin TN 37064

THORNSBERRY, WILLIS LEE, JR., chemist; b. Sturgis, Ky., Aug. 10, 1940; s. Willis Lee and Jane (Hall) T.; m. Mary Elizabeth Gaswint, June 19, 1965; children: Brian, Michele. BS, Murray State U., 1963; MS, U. Ark., 1967; PhD, Tulane U., 1974. Rsch. chemist Freeport-McMoran Inc., Belle Chasse, La., 1967-74, sr. rsch. chemist, 1974-92; pres. Tech. Devel. Svcs. Inc., Harvey, La., 1992—. Contbr. articles to profl. jours. Coach, leader for youth groups Jefferson Parish Playgrounds, Gretna, La., 1970-84, Boy Scouts Am., Gretna, 1975-82. 1st lt. U.S. Army, 1963-65. Mem. Am. Chem. Soc. (sect. chmn. 1969—), Sigma Xi (nominating com. 1967—). Democrat. Achievements include numerous patents for process for uranium recovery from phosphoric acid, recovery of silica from hydrofluorosilicic acid, stabilization of gypsum for construction purposes, preparation and use of fertilizer additives. Office: Tech Devel Svcs Inc 1024 Main St Sturgis KY 42459

THORNTON, ANNA VREE, pediatrics and medical-surgical nurse; b. Chgo., June 10, 1936; d. Edward and Elizabeth Vree; m. George Q. Thornton, June 19, 1982. BA in Edn. Psych., Barrington Coll., 1960; postgrad., NYU, 1960-62; ADN., Dutchess C.C., Poughkeepsie, N.Y., 1986. Tchr. Saugerties (N.Y.) Cen. Schs., 1960-64, Kingston (N.Y.) Consolidated Schs., 1964-66, 68-70; owner BeeVer House, Saugerties, 1970-76; ins. agt. Combined Life Ins. Co., Poughkeepsie, N.Y., 1976-82; staff nurse Putnam County Community Hosp., Carmel, N.Y., 1983-86; charge nurse Calloway County Community Hosp., Murray, Ky., 1986—; tchr. U.S. Peace Corps, Nigeria, 1966-68. Pres. Saugerties Busnessmen's Orgn., 1977. Baha'i'. Avocations: travel, reading, gardening. Home: RR 1 Box 183 Kirksey KY 42054-9728 Office: Calloway County Comm Hosp Calloway County Comm Hosp 800 Poplar St Murray KY 42071-2566

THORNTON, CAMERON MITCHELL, financial planner; b. L.A., Sept. 30, 1954; s. H. Walter and Naomi L. (Brown) T.; m. Jane Kubasak, June 18, 1978; children: Mitchell, Kathryn, Andrew. BA, U. So. Calif., L.A., 1976; MBA, U. La Verne, 1983. CFP. Planner Lockheed Calif. Co., Burbank, 1980-84; adv. assoc. Fin. Network Adv. Corp., Burbank, 1983—; fin. cons. Fin. Network Investment Corp., Burbank, 1983—; prin. Cameron Thornton Assocs., Burbank, 1982—; lic. charitable gift planner Renaissance Inc., 1992—. Author: (manual) Computer Aided Planning System, 1982-83. Mem., vice chair St. Joseph Med. Ctr. Found., 1988-92, chmn. planned giving dept., 1991-92; mem., chair Burbank Police Commn., 1981-85, Burbank Planning Commn., 1989-93; with ARC, Burbank, 1984-88, chmn. 1985-87. Lt. comdr. USN/USNR, 1976-88. Named Friend of Campfire, Camp Fire Coun., Pasadena, Calif., 1989, 92. Mem. Nat. Assn. Renaissance Advisors, Inst. CFP's, Internat. Assn. for Fin. Planning, Cert. Fin. Planner Bd. Standards, Burbank C. of C. Republican. Roman Catholic. Avocations: fishing, reading, snow skiing, water skiing. Office: Cameron Thornton Assocs 290 E Verdugo Ave Ste 205 Burbank CA 91502-1342

THORNTON, CHARLES VICTOR, metals executive; b. Salt Lake City, Feb. 8, 1915; s. Charles Victor and Winnie May (Fitts) T.; m. Margaret Louise Wiggins, Apr. 17, 1937; children: Charles Victor III, Carolyn Louise (Mrs. John J. Moorhouse), David Frank. BS in Civil Engring., U. Utah, 1935; HHD, Ind. Inst. Tech., 1972. Registered profl. engr., Ohio, Tex. Engr. Truscon Steel Co., Youngstown, Ohio, 1935-37; dist. engr. Truscon Steel Co., Washington, 1937-40; chief engr. So. Iron Works, Inc., Alexandria, Va., 1940-45; pres. Thornton Industries, Inc., Ft. Worth, 1945-75; chmn. bd. Thornton Industries, Inc., 1975-88; ptnr. TRANSOL Transp. Cons., 1993—; bd. dirs. Bank Commerce and Comml. Fin. Corp. Author: American Association of Private Railroad Car Owners Roster of Private R.R. Cars, 1991, Autobiography, 1993, Charlie, 1994, Winnie, 1994. Chmn. bd. Southview Corp., 1980—, chmn. emeritus Shriners Hosps. for Crippled Children; mem. nat. adv. coun. U. Utah, 1985—; chmn. investment com. Longhorn coun. Boy Scouts Am., 1985-88; v.p. campaign chmn. Ft. Worth Arts United, 1989; v.p. Tarrant County Arts Coun., 1989; pres. Tarrant County Water Bd., 1984-88; mem. policy com. Dallas-Ft. Worth Railtran, 1991—; pres. Ft. Worth chpt. Internat. Good Neighbor Coun., 1991-92. Recipient Salesman of Yr. award Ft. Worth Sales and Mktg. Execs., 1984, Good Neighbor of Yr. award Internat. Good Neighbor Coun., 1984, Merit of Honor award U. Utah, 1986; holder airplane speed record Dallas to Wichita, Kans., 1969. Mem. ASCE (life) (Tex. sect. Svc. to People award 1995), Tex. Assn. Bus. (life), Ft. Forth C. of C. (pres. 1960), Am. Assn. Pvt. R.R. Car Owners (pres. 1982-83), Fort Worth Club, City Club, Exch. Club of Fort Worth (past pres.), La Cima Club, Oxford Club, Grand Coun. (Fort Worth chpt. Confrerie Saint Etienne), Masons (33 degree s.r.), Shriners (past imperial potentate), Kiwanis (past pres.), Elks, Tau Beta Pi. Office: PO Box 136397 Fort Worth TX 76136-0397

THORNTON, CLARENCE GOULD, electronics engineering executive; b. Detroit, Aug. 3, 1925; s. Lorenzo C. and Violet (Gould) T.; m. Gloria Fuchs, June 18, 1949; children: Susan Carol, Richard Scott. BS, U. Mich., 1949, MS, 1950, PhD, 1952. Project engr. Sylvania Electric Co., Woburn, Mass., 1951-52; sect. head to dir. Semiconductor div. Philco Corp., Lansdale, Pa., 1952-60; dir. R&D Philco Corp., Blue Bell, Pa., 1960-72; dir. Electronics Technology and Devices Lab., U.S. Army, Fort Monmouth, N.J., 1972-92; directorate exec. Army Rsch. Lab., 1992-95; mem. Commn. on Engring. and Tech. Sys. Bd. on Army Sci. and Tech., Nat. Rsch. Coun., 1995—; sci., tech., bus. cons. 1995—. Contbr. articles to profl. jours. Mem. Colts Neck Bd. Health, 1974-79. Served with USN, 1944-46. Recipient Local Svc. award Boy Scouts Am., 1963, Sci. Conf. award Dept. Army, 1976, Rsch. and Devel. Achievement award, 1976, Lab. of Yr. award, 1980, 83, 88, Lab. Excellence award, 1981, 85, 86, Sr. Exec. award, 1980-93, Gold medal Armed Forces Comms. and Electronics Assn., 1983, Handicapped Adv. Coun. award of achievement, 1985, Exceptional Civilian Svc. medal Dept. Army, 1985, Presdl. Rank award of Meritorious Svc., 1986, Presdl. Rank award of Disting. Sr. Exec., 1987, Crozier award, 1990, Superior Civilian Svc. medal, 1995, Exceptional Civilian Svc. medal, 1995. Fellow IEEE (Centennial medal 1994, Engring. Leadership Recognition award 1994, Joint Logistics Comdrs. award 1994); mem. AAAS, Electrochemical Soc., Am. Chem. Soc., Armed Forces Electronics Assn., Sr. Execs. Assn. (Exec. Achievement award 1994), Am. Defense Preparedness Assn., Alpha Chi Sigma, Phi Kappa Phi, Phi Lambda Upsilon. Mem. Reformed Ch. Patentee in field of electronics. Home: 28 Glenwood Rd Colts Neck NJ 07722-1015 Office: AMSRL-EP Fort Monmouth NJ 07703

THORNTON, D. WHITNEY, II, lawyer; b. Miami, Fla., Oct. 17, 1946; s. Dade Whitney and Hilda (Bryan) T.; m. Jane Collis, Nov. 27, 1971; children: Bryan Whitney, Elizabeth Jane, Virginia Anne. B.A., Washington and Lee U., 1968, J.D., 1970. Bar: Va. 1970, D.C. 1976, Calif. 1987, U.S. Ct. Appeals (4th cir.) 1978, U.S. Ct. Appeals (9th cir.) 1987, U.S. Sup. Ct. 1980, Calif. 1987, U.S. Ct. Appeals (9th cir.) 1987. Atty., Naval Air Systems Command, Dept. Navy, Washington, 1970-73; asst. counsel to comptroller Dept. Navy, 1973-74, asst. to gen. counsel, 1974-76; assoc. Sullivan & Beauregard, Washington, 1976-77, ptnr., 1977-81; ptnr. Bowman, Conner, Touhey & Thornton, Washington, 1981-83; pres. Continental Maritime Industries, Inc., San Francisco, 1983-87; ptnr. Dempsey, Bastianelli, Brown & Touhey, San Francisco, 1987-91; ptnr. Seyfarth, Shaw, Fairweather & Geraldson, San Francisco, 1992—. Mem. ABA (public contract law sect.; chmn. suspension and debarment com. 1977), Fed. Bar Assn. (vice chmn. govt. contracts council; Disting. Service award 1981). Republican. Methodist. Club: Washington Golf and Country (Arlington, Va.). Contbr. articles to profl. jours. Office: Seyfarth Shaw Fairweather 101 California St Ste 2900 San Francisco CA 94111

THORNTON, DEAN DICKSON, retired airplane company executive; b. Yakima, Wash., Jan. 5, 1929; s. Dean Stoker and Elva Maud (Dickson) T.; m. Joan Madison, Aug. 25, 1956 (div. Apr. 1978); children—Steven, Jane Thornton; m. Mary Shultz, Nov. 25, 1981; children—Volney, Scott, Peter, Todd Richmond. B.S. in Bus., U. Idaho, 1952. C.P.A., Wash. Acct. Touche, Ross & Co., Seattle, 1954-63; treas., controller Boeing Co., Seattle, 1963-70; various exec. positions Boeing Co., 1974-85; pres. Boeing Comml. Airplane Co., 1985-94, retired, 1994; sr. v.p. Wyly Co., Dallas, 1970-74; bd. dirs. Seafirst Corp., Prin. Fin. Group, Flow Internat. Bd. dirs. YMCA, Seattle, 1966-68, Jr. Achievement, Seattle, 1966-68; chmn. Wash. Council on Internat. Trade, Seattle, 1984-87. Served to 1st lt. USAF, 1952-54. Named to U. Idaho Alumni Hall of Fame. Mem. Phi Gamma Delta. Republican. Presbyterian. Clubs: Rainier, Seattle Tennis, Seattle Yacht, Conquistadores de Cielo. Avocations: skiing; sailing; fishing. Home: 1602 34th Ct W Seattle WA 98199-3906 Office: Boeing Co 7755 E Marginal Way PO Box 3707 Seattle WA 98124-2207

THORNTON, DOROTHY HABERLACH, artist, photographer; b. Tillamook, Oreg., May 20, 1913; d. Carl Emil and Amanda (Tinnerstet) Haberlach; m. Robert Y. Thornton, Mar. 13, 1937; 1 child, Thomas Wells. BA, U. Oreg., 1934; postgrad., George Washington U., 1936-37, Willamette U., 1940-60, U. Mich., 1943. Draftsman USN, Tillamook, 1942-43; pvt. practice Salem, Oreg., 1952—. Editor Jour. Watermark, 1988-91; photographer (books) Images of Oreg. Women, 1983, N.W. Originals, 1987; photographer for 5 TV documentaries on Japan; rsch. photographer Preventing Crime in America & Japan: A Comparative Study, 1992; exhibited in group show Oreg. Women Artists, 1993. Docent, bd. dirs. Fortland Art Mus., 1987—, mentor, 1991—; campaign chmn. Robert Thornton for State Atty. Gen., Oreg., 1952-67, Robert Thornton for Ct. Appeals Judge, Oreg., 1968-80; founder, mem. Mid Valley Art Commn., Salem Art Assn. Guides, Salem Assistance League; active Oreg. Commn. for Humanities; pres. Friends of Libr. Willamett U., town and gown, 1996. Named Art Citizen of Yr., Oreg. Art Commn., 1991. Mem. AAUW (state pres., nat. bd. dirs., v.p. North Pacific Region States, nat. arts com. chmn. 1970-80, Nat.

Endowment Rsch. grantee (hon.)), Photog. Soc. Am. (nat. chmn., pub. rels. com. 1985, hon. Assoc. Photo. Soc. of Am. degree), Arts Oreg. Coun. (bd. dirs., past state chmn.), Watercolor Soc. Oreg. (bd. dirs. 1991—), Oreg. UN Assn. (bd. dirs. 1980—, past state pres.), Ikebana Internat., Alpha Phi. Democrat. Episcopalian. Avocations: civic activities, art consulting, tour docent, photography, artist. Home: 2895 Alvarado Ter S Salem OR 97302-5433

THORNTON, EARLENE HAIRSTON, newspaper editor. BA in Edn., Winston-Salem U.; MA in Reading and Spl. Edn., Va. State U.; student, U. Va., 1966-67, Syracuse U., 1969-71; EdD, George Washington U., 1989. Cert. Md. Advanced Profl., N.Y. Permanent Advanced Profl. Elem. and Mid. Sch. supr., elem. and mid. sch. prin., spl. edn., reading specialist, English tchr., counselor. Asst. dir. Coll. Reading Clinic Va. Union U., Richmond, 1966-67; lang. arts chairperson, reading specialist Elmira, N.Y., 1967-72; reading specialist Montgomery County Sch. System, Md., 1975-88, guidance counselor, 1988—; counselor county schs., Md., 1975-94; exec. editor The County Globe, Frederick, Md., 1990—; adj. coll. prof.; v.p. G.E.D. Corp.; title I evaluator N.Y. State Dept. Edn., 1971; instr. English Frederick C.C., 1976-81. Chmn. Frederick County Ethnic Festival, 1977-86; v.p. Patuxent Women, 1990-94; bd. dirs. Cmty. Living, Inc. Mem. NEA (edn. com. Frederick's Human Rels. Coun.), AAUW (past v.p.), Internat. Reading Assn. (past pres.), Md. Coun. Edn. Assn., Frederick Negro Bus. and Profl. Women, Frederick County's Human Rels. Coun. (chmn.), Delta Kappa Gamma (chmn. profl. affairs com., pres. Gamma chpt.), Phi Delta Kappa. Home: 5503 Hines Rd Frederick MD 21701-6885

THORNTON, GEORGE WHITELEY, investment company executive; b. York, Pa., Aug. 11, 1936; s. Henry Moser and Virginia (Whiteley) T.; m. Dianne Fay George, Sept. 9, 1961; children: Sandra Whiteley, William Foster. B.A., U. Va., 1958. Asst. to pres. mfg. Dentsply Internat., York, Pa., 1963-69, v.p. mfg., 1969-79, sr. v.p., 1979-85; pres., bd. dirs. Thornton Group Ltd., 1985—; chmn., chief exec. officer Thornton-White Inc., Charleston, S.C., 1986-92; bd. dirs. Dentsply Internat., York, Commonwealth Nat. Bank (York region). Bd. dirs. United Way, York County, 1974-76; exec. com. Nat. Alliance Businessman, York, 1972-73, chmn., York metro, 1974-75; bd. dirs. Pennsylvanians for Right to Work, 1979-81; bd. trustees Right to Work Def. and Edn. Found., 1979-81. Recipient Dirksen Meml. award Pennsylvanians for Right to Work, 1979, Employer of Yr. award. Mem. Country Club of York (Pa.), Delta Phi. Republican. Presbyterian. Home: 1040 Box Hill Ln York PA 17403-4436

THORNTON, IVAL CRANDALL, interior architect; b. American Falls, Idaho, Apr. 28, 1932; s. Crandall Dunn and Enid Rosalie (Walker) T.; m. Bonnie Jean Larson, June 10, 1951 (div. May 1961); children: Blake, Brek; m. Cheryl Lynn Bader, July 13, 1974; 1 child, Anne Bader. Student, Weber State Coll., 1956-58, Colo. Inst. Art, 1959-60, Art Ctr. Sch. of Design, L.A., 1963-64. Artist Richard Daly Art Studio, Salt Lake City; illustrator Victor Gruen & Assocs., L.A., Carlos Diniz Assocs., L.A.; sr. assoc. Arthur Gensler Assocs., San Francisco, 1972-75. Prin. works include Investment Mortgage Internat., San Francisco (design award 1984), Mountain Bell Tng. Ctr., Denver (design award), Denver Sporting House Interior (1st pl.), Caesar's Palace Forum Shops and Gateway, Internat. Cruise Ships and Corp. Aircraft Interiors, including SS U.S. Cruise Vessel, Elitch's Amusement Pk., Denver, Princess Cruises Grand Princess 97, Prince Fahd's Summer Palace interior, Saudi Arabia, Hall of Fame Colo. Inst. Art, 1995, painted murals in Salt Lake Temple, 1962. With USMC. Republican. Mem. LDS Ch. Avocations: skiing, sailing, painting, golf, music.

THORNTON, J. EDWARD, lawyer; b. Starkville, Miss., Nov. 25, 1907; s. Marmaduke Kimbrough and Annie (Knox) T.; m. Mary Belle Quinn. A.B., Miss. Coll., 1928; LL.B., Harvard, U., 1933. Bar: Ala. bar 1934, Mass. bar 1936. Asst. prosecutor Jefferson County, 1936-39; asst. gen. counsel Ala. Dept. Revenue, 1939-42; mem. firm Thornton & McGowin, Mobile.; Mem. Spl. Supreme Ct. Ala., 1967-68, Ala. Ct. of Judiciary, 1984, 87, Jud. Conf. 5th Cir. U.S., 1951-78; mem. adv. com. on proposed new appellate rules Ala. Supreme Ct., 1972-74, mem. standing com. on appellate rules, 1974-80; chmn. sect. on practice and procedure Ala. State Bar, 1969-72, 73-75. Contbr. articles to prof. publs. Pres. Mobile Chamber Music Soc., 1972-73; adv. coun. home health svcs. Mobile County Bd. Health, 1969-74; Mem. Ala. Democratic Com., 1950-54. Lt. comdr. USNR, 1942-45. Fellow Am. Bar Found.; mem. ABA (ho. dels., state del. for Ala. 1958-59), Ala. Bar Assn. (chmn. com. on jurisprudence and law reform 1951-63, pres. 1963-64), Mobile Bar Assn. (pres. 1955, founder, editor Mobile Bar Bull. 1966-91), Selden Soc., Am. Law Inst., Ala. Law Inst., Mobile Arts Coun. (pres. 1956), English Speaking Union (pres. Mobile 1960-61), Mobile Opera Guild (pres. 1963-65), Mobile C. of C., Scribes. Baptist. Clubs: Athelstan, Bienville (dir.), International Trade. Address: PO Box 23 Mobile AL 36601-0023

THORNTON, J. RONALD, technology center director; b. Fayetteville, Tenn., Aug. 19, 1939; s. James Alanda and Thelma White (McGee) T.; m. Mary Beth Packard, June 14, 1964 (div. Apr. 1975); 1 child, Nancy Carole; m. Martha Klemann, Jan. 23, 1976 (div. Apr. 1982); 1 child, Trey; m. Bernice McKinney, Feb. 14, 1986; 1 child, Paul Leon. BS in Physics & Math., Berry Coll., 1961; MA in Physics, Wake Forest Coll., 1964; postgrad., U. Ala., 1965-66, Rollins Coll., 1970. Research physicist Brown Engrng. Co., Huntsville, Ala., 1963-66; sr. staff engr. Martin Marietta Corp., Orlando, Fla., 1966-75; dep. dir. NASA, Washington, 1976-77; exec. asst. Congressman Louis Frey, Jr., Orlando, 1978; pres. Tens Tec, Inc., Orlando, 1978-79; dir. So. Tech. Applications Ctr. U. Fla., Gainesville, 1979—; mem. light wave tech. com. Fla. High Tech. and Indsl. Coun., Tallahassee, 1986-93, NASA Tech. Transfer Exec. Com., Washington, 1987—, Javits Fellowship Bd., Washington, 1986-91, Gov.'s New Product Award Com., Tallahassee, 1988—, Fla. K-12 Math., Sci. and Computer Sci. Edn. Quality Improvement Adv. Coun., 1989-92, Fla. Sci. Edn. Improvement Adv. Com., 1991-92. Pres. Orange County Young Rep. Club, Orlando, 1970-71; treas. Fla. Fedn. Young Reps., Orlando, 1971-72; chmn. Fla. Fedn. Young Reps., Orlando, 1972-74; pres. Gainesville Area Innovation Network, 1988-89. Named Engr. Exhibiting Tech. Excellence and Accomplishment cen. Fla. chpt. Fla. Engrng. Soc., 1975, Achievement award NASA, 1977. Mem. IEEE, SME, Tech. Transfer Soc., Nat. Assn. Mgmt. and Tech. Assistance Ctrs. (bd. dirs. 1988, pres. 1992), Gainesville Area C. of C. Republican. Avocations: music, travel, reading. Home: 17829 NW 20th Ave Newberry FL 32669-2143 Office: U Fla So Tech Applications Ctr 1 Progress Blvd Ste 24 Alachua FL 32615-9536

THORNTON, JOHN IRVIN, forensic scientist, educator; b. Sacramento, Jan. 11, 1941; s. Lewis T. and Zilpha G. (Bowman) T.; m. Kim Stanchfield Wildman, May 22, 1976; children: Edward Lewis, Christian John, Chad Wildman, Reed Wildman. BS in Criminology, U. Calif., Berkeley, 1962; MS in Criminology, U. Calif., 1968, D of Criminology, 1974. Criminalist Contra Costa County (Calif.) Sheriff's Dept., Martinez, 1963-72, supervising criminalist, 1970-72, lab. dir., 1969-70; prof. forensic sci. U. Calif., Berkeley, 1982-94, prof. emeritus, 1994—; cons. Law Enforcement Assistance Adminstrn. U.S. Dept. Justice, 1974, 75, 78, Calif. Coun. on Criminal Justice, 1970-71, Am. Coun. on Edn., 1978, Internal Rev. Bur. Dept. Transp. and Pub. Facilities, State of Alaska, 1978; various police agys., pub. defender's offices and attys., 1972—; mem. project adv. com. Nationwide Crime Lab. Proficiency Testing Project, Forensic Sci. Found., 1979. Contr. numerous articles to jours. in forensic sci. Mem. Am. Acad. Forensic Scis. (chmn. criminalistics sect. 1979, mem. coun. 1979-80, award criminalistics sect. 1979), Am. Chem. Soc., Calif. Assn. Criminalists (pres. 1974-75, editl. sec. 1967-70, Disting. Mem. award 1989), Sigma Xi. Mem. Soc. of Friends. Home: 1093 Lokoya Rd Napa CA 94558-9565 Office: U Calif Sch Pub Health Berkeley CA 94720

THORNTON, JOHN S., IV, bishop. Bishop Diocese of Idaho, Boise, 1990—. Office: Diocese of Idaho Box 936 510 W Washington St Boise ID 83702-5953*

THORNTON, JOHN VINCENT, lawyer, educator; b. N.Y.C., Jan. 13, 1924; s. Thomas Francis and Elizabeth Rose (McCullough) T.; m. Edna Grace Lawson, June 28, 1952; children: John, Nancy, Sarah, Amy, Laura. BS, St. John's U., 1944; JD, Yale U., 1948; LLD (hon.), N.Y. Law Sch., 1969. Bar: N.Y. 1948. Assoc. in law Columbia U., 1948-49; assoc. Skadden Arps, 1949; law clk. to assoc. judge N.Y. Ct. of Appeals, 1950-52; ptnr. Whitman & Ransom, N.Y.C., 1952-69, of counsel, 1989-93; asst. gen. counsel Consol. Edison Co. N.Y. Inc., 1969, v.p., 1970-73, v.p., treas., 1973-76, sr. v.p. fin., 1976-79, exec. v.p. fin., 1979-80, sr. exec. v.p., 1980-84, vice chmn., 1984-89; exec. v.p. Columbia U., N.Y.C., 1989-92; of counsel Whitman & Ransom, N.Y.C., 1989-93, Whitman, Breed, Abbott & Morgan, N.Y.C., 1993-95, Noumairz Riad, N.Y.C., 1996—; asst. sec., counsel N.Y. World's Fair Corp., 1960-67; mem. bd. mgrs. Arden Conf. Ctr., 1989-92; treas. Empire State Electric Energy Rsch. Corp., 1975-78; bd. dirs. Nuclear Electric Ins. Ltd., 1981-89, chmn., 1986-89; bd. dirs. Pub. Utilities Reports, Inc., 1980-89, chmn., 1986-89; adj. prof. law NYU Sch. Law, 1949-66; Lubin lectr. Pace U., 1982; adj. prof. law, assoc. dean N.Y. Law Sch., 1964-69, v.p., 1969-73, chmn., 1973-85, hon. chmn., 1985—; asst. in econs. Yale U., 1946-48; instr. econs. Albertus Magnus Coll., 1946-48; assoc. dir. study on heart disease and the law USPHS, 1958-61; counsel judiciary com. N.Y. State Constl. Conv., 1967; mem. Bronxville (N.Y.) Bd. Edn., 1970-76, pres. bd., 1972-74. Contbg. editor: Ann. Survey of Am. Law, 1950-60, Ann. Survey of N.Y. Law, 1950-60, Jour. Occupational Medicine, 1964-67, Pub. Utilities Fortnightly, 1969-89. Bd. dirs., sec. Hall of Sci. N.Y.C., 1968-76; trustee Pace U., N.Y. Bot. Garden; vice chmn. Lawrence Hosp., 1990-93, trustee, 1990-95, mem. fin. com., 1990—; trustee Arden Conf. Ctr.; mem. com. and fund for modern cts. N.Y.C. Citizens Budget Commn., 1983-88; mem. bd. advisers Dickinson Coll., chmn., 1979-81, trustee, 1979-89; mem. pres.'s adv. coun. NYU Sch. Social Work, 1969-75; mem. Can.-Am. Com., 1980-85; trustee Lawrence Park Assn., 1966-70, pres. bd., 1968-70. Mem. Order of Coif, Phi Delta Phi. Home: John's Island 181 Silver Moss Dr Vero Beach FL 32963 Office: Noumairz Riad 200 Park Ave New York NY 10166-0005

THORNTON, JOSEPH CRAIG, hydrogeologist; b. Louisville, Apr. 2, 1955; s. Joseph L. and Thelma L. (Schardein) T. BS in Geology, Western Ky. U., 1977. Registered geologist, Ind., Ky., Wyo. Geologist U.S. Corps of Engrs., Nashville, 1977-79, Ky. Divsn. of Water, Frankfort, 1979-81; hydrogeologist U.S. Ecology, Inc., Louisville, 1981-86, Riedel Environ. Svc., Chesterfield, Mo., 1986-87; environ. engr. Cummins Engine Co., Columbus, Ind., 1987-91; environ. scientist Greenbaum Assocs., Louisville, 1991-92; hydrogeologist McCoy & McCoy Environ., Lexington, Ky., 1992-93, sr. project scientist, 1993—. Nat. Groundwater Assn., Am. Inst. Profl. Geologists. Avocations: computers, biking. Office: McCoy and McCoy Environ 2285 Executive Dr Ste 200 Lexington KY 40505-4810

THORNTON, JOSEPH SCOTT, research institute executive, materials scientist; b. Sewickley, Pa., Feb. 6, 1936; s. Joseph Scott and Evelyn (Miller) T.; divorced; children: Joseph Scott III, Chris P. BSME, U. Tex., 1957, PhD, 1969; MSMetE, Carnegie Mellon U., 1962. Engr. Walworth Valve Co., Boston, 1958; metall. engr. Westinghouse Astronuclear Lab., Large, Pa., 1962-64; instr., teaching assoc. U. Tex., Austin, 1964-67; group leader Tracor Inc., Austin, 1967-69, dept. dir., 1973-75; dept. mgr. Horizons Rsch., Inc., Cleve., 1969-73; chmn., chief exec. officer Tex. Rsch. Internat., Inc. (formerly Tex. Rsch. Inst., Inc.), Austin, 1975—. Contbr. numerous tech. papers to profl. publs.; editor: WANL Materials Manual, 2 vols., 1964; patentee in field. Fellow Alcoa, Austin, 1964, RC Baker Found., 1967. Mem. ASME, ASTM, Am. Soc. Metals Internat. (exec. com. 1965-66), Adhesion Soc. Office: Tex Rsch Internat Inc 9063 Bee Caves Rd Austin TX 78733-6201

THORNTON, LARRY LEE, psychotherapist, author, educator; b. Lake, Miss., Nov. 9, 1937; s. Harvey L. and Onzell (Goodson) T.; children: Matt Alan, Leigh Ann. BA, Miss. Coll., 1959; MDiv, New Orleans Bapt. Theol. Sem., 1963, MRE, 1964; MS, U. So. Miss., 1966, PhD, 1969; postgrad., Harvard U., 1985. Dir. admissions Miss. Coll., Clinton, 1961; sr. prof. psychology Delta State U., Cleveland, Miss., 1968—; founder, dir. Lic. Profl. Counseling, Assocs., Cleveland, 1988—; chmn. Miss. Bd. Lic. Profl. Counselors, 1992-93. Author: Insights into Human Development, 1978. Charter mem. Internat. Devel. Coun., Bapt. Theol. Sem., Rûschlikon, Zurich, Switzerland, 1992. Recipient Panhellenic Outstanding Faculty award, 1996, S.E. Rossman Outstanding Tchr. award, 1991. Mem. APA, ACA. Avocations: golf, tennis, jogging. Home: PO Box 11 104 S 4th Ave Cleveland MS 38732

THORNTON, RAY, congressman; b. Conway, AR, July 16, 1928; s. R.H. and Wilma (Stephens) T.; m. Betty Jo Mann, Jan. 27, 1956; children: Nancy, Mary Jo, Stephanie. B.A., Yale, 1950; J.D., U. Ark., 1956. Bar: Ark. 1956, U.S. Supreme Ct 1956. Pvt. practice in Sheridan and Little Rock, 1956-70; atty. gen. Ark., 1971-73; mem. 93d-95th Congresses from 4th Ark. dist.; exec. dir. Quachita Bapt. U./Henderson State U. Joint Ednl. Consortium, Arkadelphia, Ark., 1979-80; pres. Ark. State U., Jonesboro and Beebe, 1980-84, U. Ark. System, Fayetteville, Little Rock, Pine Bluff, Monticello, 1984-89; mem. 102nd-103rd Congresses from 2d Ark. dist., 1991—; chmn. Ark. Bd. Law Examiners, 1967-70; Del. 7th Ark. Constl. Conv., 1969-70. Chmn. pres.'s devel. council Harding Coll., Searcy, Ark., 1971-73. Served with USN, 1951-54, Korea. Mem. AAAS (chmn. com. on sci., engrng. and public policy 1980). Office: US Ho of Reps 1214 Longworth Bldg Washington DC 20515-0004*

THORNTON, SPENCER P., ophthalmologist, educator; b. West Palm Beach, Fla., Sept. 16, 1929; s. Ray Spencer and Mae (Phillips) T.; m. Annie Glenn Cooper, Oct. 6, 1956; children: Steven Pitts, David Spencer, Ray Cooper, Beth Ellen. BS, Wake Forest Coll., 1951, MD, 1954. Diplomate: Am. Bd. Ophthalmology. Intern Ga. Bapt. Hosp., Atlanta, 1954-55; resident gen. surgery U. Ala. Med. Center, 1955-56; resident ophthalmology Vanderbilt U. Sch. Medicine, 1960-63; practice medicine specializing in ophthalmic surgery Nashville, 1960—; med. dir. Thornton Eye Ctr., 1995—; mem. staff Bapt. Hosp., chief ophthalmology svc., 1982-87; guest prof., vis. lectr. U. Toronto, 1990, 91, 92, U. Paris, 1989, Rothchilds Inst., Paris, 1992, 94, U. Pretoria, 1991, 93, others; instr. Moscow Inst. Eye Microsurgery, 1981; instr. ophthalmic surgery Am. Acad. Ophthalmology Ann. Courses; lectr. lens implant symposiums Eng., Spain, Australia, Switzerland, Can., Sweden, Greece, Germany, France, Republic of South Africa, Japan; Berzelius lectr. U. Lund, Sweden, 1992; P.J. Hay Gold medal lectr., North of Eng. Ophthal. Soc., Scarborough, 1992. King Features syndicated newspaper columnist, 1959-60, feature writer, NBC radio and TV, 1958-60; author, coauthor textbooks on cataract and refractive surgery; mem. editl. bd. Jour. Refractive and Corneal Surgery, Jour. Cataract and Refractive Surgery, Video Jour. Ophthalmology, Ocular Surgery News (Ophthalmologist of Yr. 1996), Ophthalmic Practice (Can.), Eye Care Tech. Mag. (Lifetime Achievement award 1996); contbr. articles to profl. jours.; inventor instruments and devices for refractive and lens implant surgery. Named among Outstanding Young Men of Yr., U.S. Jaycees, 1965; recipient Honor award Can. Implant Assn., 1993, Outstanding Achievement award Bowman Gray Sch. Medicine, 1995. Fellow ACS, Am. Acad. Ophthalmology (Honor award 1995); mem. Am. Soc. Cataract and Refractive Surgery (pres.-elect 1995, chmn. internat. com. stds. and quality control for ophthalmic instruments and devices), Am. Med. Soc. Vienna (life), South African Intraocular Implant Soc. (life), Can. Implant Soc. (life), Tenn. Soc. Medicine, Nashville Acad. Medicine, Internat. Refractive Surgery Club (v.p. 1994), Phi Rho Sigma, Delta Kappa Alpha. Baptist. Home: 5070 Villa Crest Dr Nashville TN 37220-1425 Office: 2010 Church St Nashville TN 37203-2012

THORNTON, THEODORE KEAN, investment advisor; b. St. Louis, June 4, 1949; s. Leonard Frend and Maxine Belle (McKinley) T.; m. Colleen Bridget Purdy, June 23, 1974; children, Theodore McKinley, Alastair Griffin. BA, MBA, Harvard U. Asst. treas. Chase Manhattan Bank, N.Y.C., 1975-79; asst. treas. Colgate-Palmolive Co., N.Y.C., 1979-84, Sperry Corp., N.Y.C., 1984-85; v.p., treas. Household Internat., Prospect Heights, Ill., 1985-87, v.p. investments, 1987-91, pres., 1991—; pres. Marble Corp., 1991-94. Mem. Am. Fin. Assn. Clubs: Harvard (N.Y.C.). Home: 885 Maplewood Rd Lake Forest IL 60045-2415 Office: 225 W Washington St Ste 1650 Chicago IL 60606-3418

THORNTON, THOMAS NOEL, publishing executive; b. Marceline, Mo., Apr. 23, 1950; s. Bernard F. and Helen F. (Kelley) T.; m. Cynthia L. Murray, Nov. 26, 1971; children: T. Zachary, Timothy. B.J., U. Mo., 1972. Asst. to editor Universal Press Syndicate, Kansas City, Mo., 1972; v.p. Universal Press Syndicate, 1974, dir. mktg., 1976; v.p., dir. mktg. Universal Press Syndicate and Andrews & McMeel, Kansas City, 1976-87; pres. Andrews & McMeel, 1987—. Office: Universal Press Syndicate 4900 Main St Kansas City MO 64112-2630

THORNTON, WILLIAM E., mayor, oral surgeon; b. Abilene, Tex., 1945; m. Carolyn Cleveland Giles; children: Kate, Ted. BS in Biology, Trinity U., 1966; DDS, Baylor Coll. Dentistry, 1969; MSD, Baylor U., 1972. Diplomate Am. Bd. Oral and Maxillofacial Surgeons. Clin. prof. U. Tex. Health Sci. Ctr.; chmn. Bexar County Hosp. Dist., 1981-91; mayor San Antonio, 1995—; chmn. bd. dirs. Greater San Antonio C. of C., 1989. Active San Antonio Symphony Soc., Trinity Baptist Ch., Am. Red Cross, United Way, Am. Cancer Soc., Nat. Conf. Christians and Jews. Office: Office of the Mayor PO Box 839966 San Antonio TX 78283

THORNTON, WILLIAM JAMES, JR., composer, music educator; b. Birmingham, Ala., July 31, 1919; s. William James and Ada Blanche (Gray) T.; m. Vivian Quine Dyer, Nov. 11, 1939 (dec. 1981); m. Alice Marilyn Dutcher, Mar. 3, 1984 (dec. 1993); m. Katherine Cornell, Nov. 26, 1993. B.Mus., La. State U., 1941, Mus.M., 1948; B.A., Birmingham-So. Coll., 1949; Ph.D., U. So. Calif., 1953. Instr. music U. Minn., 1955-56; prof., chmn. div. fine arts Parsons Coll., Fairfield, Iowa, 1956-60; prof., chmn. music dept. Trinity U., San Antonio, 1960-80, prof. music theory and composition, 1980-88, prof. emeritus, 1988—; tchr. music Pointe Coupee Parish, La., 1939-40; tchr. music St. James Parish, La., 1942, San Juan Capistrano, Calif., 1952-54, Pleasanton, Calif., 1954-55; prof. emeritus Trinity U. San Antonio, 1988; lectr. music composition U. Tex., San Antonio, 1991-93. Performer double bass, 1939-54; composer: major mus. works including String Quartet 1, 1949, Sonata for Cello and Piano, 1950, Serenade for Winds, 1950, Symphony 1, 1953, Sonata for Piano, 1955, Festive Music for Orchestra, 1962, Ceremony of Psalms for Soloists, Choir, Percussion, Organ, 1969, Sinfonia Bejar, Bicentennial commn. San Antonio Symphony, 1976, Sonata for piano, 4 hands, 1982, Solomon Songs, 1983, Sonata for Saxophone and Piano, 1985, Sonata for Harp, 1986, Spirit Divine for chorus and organ, 1986, Fanfare for brass, 1986, Homage for Chamber Orch. commd. Tex. Fedn. Music Clubs Manuscript Archives Com., 1987, Fanfare for Band commd. Trinity U. Wind Symphony and Tex. Composers Forum, 1987, The Grasshopper for chorus, 1987, Psalm No. 1 for mezzo-soprano, harp and flute, 1988, Then in Thy Mercy for mezzo-soprano and organ, 1988, Elegy for Trumpet and Piano, 1989, Woodwind Quintet commd. The King William Winds, 1991, Elegy for Trumpet and Strings to the Memory of Halsey Stevens, 1992, Jambalaya for Four Guitars, 1992, Te Deum Laudamus for organ, 1993, also others. Served with USAAF, 1942-46, PTO. Recipient composition commns. from San Antonio Symphony, Parsons Coll., La. State U., Trinity U., Manuscript Archives Commn., Manor Baptist Ch. (San Antonio) for dedication of new organ: Festive Music for Organ, 1995. Mem. Phi Mu Alpha Sinfonia, Phi Kappa Phi, Phi Sigma Iota, Sigma Nu. Home: 15927 Alsace San Antonio TX 78232-2791

THORNTON, WINFRED LAMOTTE, railroad executive; b. Winston-Salem, N.C., July 9, 1923; s. Winfred Lewis and Mildred (Cain) T.; m. Mary Ann Hege, Aug. 18, 1951; children: Winfred LaMotte, Mary Ann. B.S., Va. Mil. Inst., 1950. With So. Ry. System, 1950-59; chief operating officer Fla. East Coast Ry. Co. (now Fla. East Coast Industries Inc.), St. Augustine, 1960, v.p., chief operating officer, 1961-64, pres., CEO, 1964—, also chmn., dir., 1983—; pres., chief operating officer St. Joe Paper Co., Jacksonville, Fla.; pres., dir. Fla. Sugar Refinery, Inc., Talisman Sugar Corp.; dir. Charter Co., Fruit Growers Express Co.; pres. St. Joe Industries Inc.; pres., chief exec. officer Atlantic East Coast Terminal, Dade County Land Holding Co.; chmn., chief exec. officer Gran Cen. Corp. Bd. dirs. U.S. Indsl. Council; bd. dirs. Nat. Right to Work Com.; v.p., bd. dirs. Nemours Children's Hosp., Inc.; bd. dirs. Nemours Health Clinic, Inc.; mem. Fla. Council 100; co-trustee Alfred I. duPont Estate. Mem. Am. Ry. Engring. Assn., Am. Assn. R.R. Supts. Baptist (deacon). Office: St Joe Paper Co 1650 Prudential Ctr Jacksonville FL 32207-8147 also: Fla E Coast Industries Inc 1 Malaga St Saint Augustine FL 32084-3580*

THORP, BENJAMIN A., III, paper manufacturing company executive; b. Albany, N.Y., May 31, 1938; s. Benjamin A. Jr. and Anna C. (Head) T.; m. Barbara Sue Telloch, Aug. 1, 1964 (div. Mar. 1986); 1 child, Benjamin A. IV; m. Laurie Diane Murdock, Oct. 25, 1987. Student in elec. engring., Rensselaer Poly. Inst., 1956-61, postgrad. in mgmt., 1967-68; BS in Physics, U. Md., 1964; postgrad. in engring., U. Bridgeport, 1966; postgrad. in mktg., U. Tenn., 1970. Product devel. mgr. Huyck Formex div. Huyck, Greenville, Tenn., 1969-71, mktg. mgr., 1971-73, v.p., gen. mgr., 1973-75; v.p., gen. mgr. Huytech Systems div., Wake Forest, N.C., 1975-78; v.p., dir. research Huyck Corp., Rensselaer, N.Y., 1978-80; pres. Benjamin A. Thorp Inc., Albany, 1980-82, POYRY-BEK Inc., Raleigh, N.C., 1982-84; v.p. engring. BE&K Inc., Birmingham, Ala., 1984-85, James River Corp., Richmond, Va., 1984-95; v.p. mfg. tech. Chesapeake Corp., richmond, Va., 1996—; mem. exec. com. Pulp and Paper Found. Bd., Ga. Inst. Tech., 1991-95, pres., 1993-95. Tech. editor Paper Machine Operations, Vol. 7, 3d edit., 1991; contbr. over 50 articles to profl. jours.; patentee in field. Bd. dirs. Richmond Math. and Sci. Ctr., 1987-93, Sic. Mus. of Va. Found., 1989—; chmn. papermaking project adv. com. Inst. Paper Sci. and Tech., 1990-94. Fellow TAPPI (chmn. appermakers com. 1984-86, vice chmn. paper and bd. divsn. 1988-90, chmn. 1990-92, bd. dirs. Leadership award 1994); mem. Paper Industry Mgmt. Assn. (1st v.p.), Exptl. Aircraft Assn. Presbyterian. Office: Chesapeake Corp PO Box 2350 Richmond VA 23218-2350

THORP, JAMES SHELBY, electrical engineering educator; b. Kansas City, Mo., Feb. 7, 1937; s. Joseph Chester and Ruth Vefe (McNamara) T.; m. Barbara Anne Curit, June 27, 1959 (div. July 1976); children: Jeffrey Barton, Elizabeth Anne; m. Christine Annette Moore, Aug. 10, 1980 (div. 1995); children: Gregory, William. BEE, Cornell U., 1959, MS, 1961, PhD, 1962. Asst. prof. Cornell U., Ithaca, N.Y., 1962-66, assoc. prof., 1966-75, prof., 1975—, assoc. dir. Sch. Elec. Engring., 1991-94, dir. Sch. Elec. Engring., 1994—; faculty intern Am. Electric Power Svc. Corp., N.Y.C., 1976-77; Charles H. Mellowes prof. engring., 1994—; fellow Churchill Coll., U. Cambridge, Eng., 1988—; cons. Am. Electric Power Svc. Corp., 1977-83, Dowty Control Techs., Boonton, N.J., 1988—. Author: Computer Relaying for Power Systems, 1988; contbr. chpts. to books, articles to profl. jours. Fellow IEEE, Nat. Acad. Engring. Avocation: golf. Office: Cornell Univ Phillips Hall Ithaca NY 14853

THORPE, JAMES, humanities scholar; b. Aiken, S.C., Aug. 17, 1915; s. J. Ernest and Ruby (Holloway) T.; m. Elizabeth McLean Daniells, July 19, 1941; children: John D., Sally Jans-Thorpe. A.B., The Citadel, 1936, LL.D., 1971; M.A., U. N.C., 1937; Ph.D., Harvard U., 1941; Litt.D., Occidental Coll., 1968; L.H.D., Claremont Grad. Sch., 1968; H.H.D., U. Toledo, 1977. Instr. to prof. English Princeton, 1946-66; dir. Huntington Libr., Art Gallery and Bot. Gardens, San Marino, Calif., 1966-83; sr. research assoc. Huntington Libr., San Marino, Calif., 1966—. Author: Bibliography of the Writings of George Lyman Kittredge, 1948, Milton Criticism, 1950, Rochester's Poems on Several Occasions, 1950, Poems of Sir George Etherege, 1963, Aims and Methods of Scholarship, 1963, 70, Literary Scholarship, 1964, Relations of Literary Study, 1967, Bunyan's Grace Abounding and Pilgrim's Progress, 1969, Principles of Textual Criticism, 1972, 2d edit., 1979, Use of Manuscripts in Literary Research, 1974, 2d edit., 1979, Gifts of Genius, 1980, A Word to the Wise, 1982, John Milton: The Inner Life, 1983, The Sense of Style: Reading English Prose, 1987, Henry Edwards Huntington: A Biography, 1994, H.E. Huntington: A Short Biography, 1996. Served to col. USAAF, 1941-46. Decorated Bronze Star medal.; Guggenheim fellow, 1949-50, 65-66. Fellow Am. Acad. Arts and Scis., Am. Philos. Soc.; mem. MLA, Am. Antiquarian Soc., Soc. for Textual Scholarship. Democrat. Episcopalian. Clubs: Zamorano, Twilight. Home: 1199 Arden Rd Pasadena CA 91106-4143 Office: Huntington Libr San Marino CA 91108

THORPE, JANET CLAIRE, lawyer; b. Bklyn., Dec. 8, 1953; d. Burton Walter and Phyllis Claire (Read) T.; m. David Frank Palmer, Aug. 26, 1978 (div. Aug. 1988); children—Katherine Elaine, Jennifer Claire; m. James Francis Box, June 29, 1991; children: Melissa Richelle, Maergrethe Cashel. Student, Boston U., 1972-74; A.B. in Polit. Sci. and History with honors, Union Coll., 1975; postgrad. Western New Eng. Sch. Law, 1975-76; J.D., Emory U., 1978. Bar: Ga. 1978, U.S. Dist. Ct. (no. dist.) Ga. 1978, U.S. Ct. Appeals (5th and 11th cirs.) 1978, 80, Fla. 1987, U.S. Dist. Ct. (mid. dist.) Fla. 1987. Comptroller's asst. Boston U., 1974-75; law librarian Western New Eng. Coll., Springfield, Mass., 1976; law clk. to judge U.S. Dist. Ct., Atlanta, 1978; regional atty. Comptroller of Currency, Atlanta, 1978-80; assoc. corp. counsel Trust Co. Ga., Atlanta, 1980-86; dir. Trusco Properties, Inc., Atlanta 1981-86; gen. counsel, corp. sec. SunTrust Banks of Fla., Inc.,

1986—, sr. v.p., 1986; bd. mem., corp. sec. SunTrust Bank Card N.A.; gen. counsel SunTrust Bank, Ctrl. Fla., N.A., 1986—; group v.p. SunTrust Banks, Inc., 1995—. Mem. Council on Battered Women, Atlanta, 1983-86, bd. dirs., 1986; bd. visitors Cornell Mus. Fine Art, Rollins Coll., 1995—. Mem. Ga. Bar Assn., Fla. Bar Assn., Assn. Bank Holding Cos. (lawyers com. 1983-90), Am. Corp. Counsel Assn. (bd. dirs. ctrl. Fla. chpt. 1991-94), Am. Diabetes Assn. (bd. dirs. Fla. chpt. 1989—), Atlanta Arts Alliance, 1985, Leadership Orlando. Democrat. Episcopalian. Avocations: gardening; child rearing; house renovation; photography. Office: SunTrust Banks Inc 200 S Orange Ave Orlando FL 32801-3410

THORPE, LEON FERBER, real estate investment company executive; b. Pitts., May 29, 1940; s. Benjamin and Freda (Ferber) T.; m. Suzanne Rosenthal (div. 1972); children: Joshua Ferber, David Lewis. AB, Harvard U., 1961, LLB, 1964. V.p. B. Thorpe & Co., Pitts., 1966-69; pres. Leon Thorpe Realty Co., Pitts., 1969—, Thor Parking Corp., Pitts., 1992—. Mem. com. univ. resources Harvard U., Cambridge, 1983-85; bd. dirs. Chatham Coll., Pitts., 1985-88, investment com. United Jewish Fedn. Western Pa., 1992—; mem. vis. com. Coll. of Harvard U., 1987-92. Mem. Nat. Parking Assn. (bd. dirs. 1978-82, 91-92). Avocations: exercise, travel, piano, reading. Office: Leon Thorpe Realty Co 818 Liberty Ave Pittsburgh PA 15222-3707

THORPE, OTIS HENRY, professional basketball player; b. Boynton Beach, Fla., Aug. 5, 1962. Student, U. Providence. Basketball player Kansas City Kings, 1984-85, Sacramento Kings (formerly Kansas City), 1985-88, Houston Rockets, 1988-94, Portland Trail Blazers, 1994—, now with Detroit Pistons. Mem. NBA championship team 1994. NBA All-Star, 1992. Address: Detroit Pistons Two Championship Dr Auburn Hills MI 48362*

THORPE, RICHARD L., medical association administrator. CEO Am. Coll. Health Care Adminstrs., 1987. Office: Am Coll Health Care Adminstrs 325 S Patrick St Alexandria VA 22314*

THORSEN, JAMES HUGH, aviation director, airport manager; b. Evanston, Ill., Feb. 5, 1943; s. Chester A. and Mary Jane (Currie) T.; m. Nancy Dain, May 30, 1980. BA, Ripon Coll., 1965. FAA cert. comml. pilot, flight instr. airplanes and instruments. Asst. dean of admissions Ripon (Wis.) Coll., 1965-69; adminstrv. asst. Greater Rockford (Ill.) Airport Authority, 1969-70; airport mgr. Bowman Field, Louisville, 1970-71; asst. dir. St. Louis Met. Airport Authority, 1971-80; dir. aviation, airport mgr. City of Idaho Falls (Idaho), 1980—. Named Hon. Citizen, State of Ill. Legislature, 1976, Ky. Col., Flying Col. Delta Airlines; recipient Contbns. to Aviation Safety award FAA, 1994, Aviator Wings and Red Flag award Sky Warriors Aviation Challenge, 1996. Mem. Am. Assn. Airport Execs. (accredited airport exec., pres. N.W. chpt., 1995-96, conv. spkr. 1996), Idaho Airport Mgmt. Assn. (pres. 1991—), Internat. NW Aviation Council, Greater Idaho Falls C. of C. (bd. dir. 1986-89), (charter) Westside Rotary Club of Idaho Falls, Mensa, Quiet Birdmen Club, Sigma Alpha Epsilon. Home: 334 Westmoreland Dr Idaho Falls ID 83402 Office: Mcpl Airport Idaho Falls ID 83402

THORSEN, NANCY DAIN, real estate broker; b. Edwardsville, Ill., June 23, 1944; d. Clifford Earl and Suzanne Eleanor (Kribs) Dain; m. David Massie, 1968 (div. 1975); 1 child, Suzanne Dain Massie; m. James Hugh Thorsen, May 30, 1980. BSc in Mktg., So. Ill. U., 1968, MSc in Bus. Edn., 1975; grad. Realtor Inst., Idaho, 1983. Cert. resdl. and investment specialist, fin. instr.; Designated Real Estate Instr. State of Idaho; accredited buyer rep. Personnel officer J.H. Little & Co. Ltd., London, 1969-72; instr. in bus. edn. Spl. Sch. Dist. St. Louis, 1974-77; mgr. mktg./ops. Isis Foods, Inc., St. Louis, 1978-80; asst. mgr. store Stix, Baer & Fuller, St. Louis, 1980; assoc. broker Century 21 Sayer Realty, Inc., Idaho Falls, Idaho, 1981-88, RE/MAX Homestead Realty, 1989—; speaker RE/MAX Internat. Conv., 1990, 94, RE/MAX Stars Cruise, 1993, RE/MAX Pacific N.W. Conv., 1994, Century 21 Austral-Asia, 1995, women's seminar Clemson U., 1996; real estate fin. instr. State of Idaho Real Estate Commn., 1994; founder Nancy Thorsen Seminars, 1995. Bd. dirs. Idaho Vol., Boise, 1981-84, Idaho Falls Symphony, 1982; pres. Friends of Idaho Falls Libr., 1981-83; chmn. Idaho Falls Mayor's Com. for Vol. Coordination, 1981-84; power leader Power Program, 1995. Recipient Idaho Gov.'s award, 1982, cert. appreciation City of Idaho Falls/Mayor Campbell, 1982, 87, Civitan Disting. Pres. award, 1990; named to Two Million Dollar Club, Three Million Dollar Club, 1987, 88, Four Million Dollar Club, 1989, 90, Top Investment Sales Person for Eastern Idaho, 1985, Realtor of Yr. Idaho Falls Bd. Realtors, 1990, Outstanding Realtors Active in Politics, Mem. of Yr. Idaho Assn. Realtors, 1991, Women of Yr. Am. Biog. Inst., 1991, Profiles of Top Producers award Real Estate Edn. Assn.; named Western Region Power Leader, Darryl Davis Seminars. Mem. Nat. Spkrs. Assn., Idaho Falls Bd. Realtors (chmn. orientation 1982-83, chmn. edn. 1983, chmn. legis. com. 1989, 95—, chmn. program com. 1990, 91), Idaho Assn. Realtors (pres. Million Dollar Club 1988—, edn. com. 1990-93), So. Ill. U. Alumni Assn., Idaho Falls C. of C., Newcomers Club, Civitan (pres. Idaho Falls chpt. 1988-89, Civitan of Yr. 1986, 87, outstanding pres. award 1990), Real Estate Educators Assn. Office: RE/MAX Homestead Inc 1301 E 17th St Ste 1 Idaho Falls ID 83404-6273

THORSON, CONNIE CAPERS, library educator; b. Dallas, July 25, 1940; d. Ewing Ashby and Constance (Romberg) Capers; m. James Llewellyn, June 6, 1970. BA, U. Ark., 1962, MA, 1964; PhD, U. N.Mex., 1970; MS in Library Sci., U. Ill., 1977. Instr. English S.E. Mo. State U., Cape Girardeau, 1963-67; with U. N.Mex., Albuquerque, 1970-71, 79—, acquistitions libr., 1980-94, head reference, 1994-95, assoc. prof. libr., 1984-90, prof., 1990-95; prof., libr. dir. Allegheny Coll., Meadville, Pa., 1995—. Editor: A Million Stars, 1981, Pocket Companion for Oxford, 1989. Mem. South Cen. Soc. for 18th Century Studies (pres. elect 1988-89, pres. 1989-90), Modern Lang. Assn. Am., Am. Soc. for 18th Century Studies, ALA. Avocations: traveling, reading, walking. Office: Allegheny Coll Pelletier Libr Meadville PA 16335

THORSON, JOHN MARTIN, JR., electrical engineer, consultant; b. Armstrong, Iowa, Dec. 16, 1929; s. John Martin and Hazel Marguerite (Martin) T.; m. Geraldine Carol Moran, Apr. 21, 1956 (dec. 1975); children—John Robert, James Michael; m. Lee Houk, Sept. 24, 1977. B.S.E.E., Iowa State U., 1951. Transmission engr. No. States Power Co., Mpls., 1953-58, system operation relay engr., 1962-74; telephone engr. No. States Power Co., Minot, N.D., 1958-62; utility industry mktg. mgr. Control Data Corp., Mpls., 1974-77, product/program mgr. utilities, 1977-84, sr. cons. energy mgmt. systems, 1984-90; pres. Thorson Engrs., Inc., Chanhassen, Minn., 1991—; inductive coordination cons. SNC Corp., Oshkosh, Wis., 1985—; tech. cons. Power Technologies, Inc., Schenectady, N.Y., 1991—, Control Corp., Osseo, Minn., 1992-93, Control Data, Plymouth, Minn., 1991-92, Hathaway, Denver, 1992-93, Scottish Hydro-Electric, PLC, Perth, Scotland, 1992—, NRG Energy Inc., Mpls., 1993—, Stanford Rsch. Inst., 1995—, Univ. Online, Inc., 1995—. Contbr. tech. papers to profl. jours. Dist. commr. Boy Scouts Am., Minn., 1954-58, 64-65, coun. commr. N.D., Mont., 1959-62; mem. coun. St. Philip Luth. Ch., Wayzata, Minn., 1968-69; county del. Rep. Com., Chanhassen, Minn., 1980-82. 1st lt. USAF, 1951-53. Recipient Alumni Service award Iowa State U., 1972. Fellow IEEE (life mem., bd. dirs. 1981-82, dir. region 4, 1981-82, mem. U.S. activities bd. 1981-82, regional activities bd. 1981-82, Centennial medal 1984); mem. Internat. Conf. on Large High Voltage Electric Sys., Iowa State U. Alumni Assn. (v.p., pres. 1963-66). Republican. Avocations: canoeing; back packing; mountain climbing. Home and Office: 7320 Longview Cir Chanhassen MN 55317-7905

THORSON, LEE A., lawyer; b. Seattle, Nov. 10, 1949; s. Theodore Arthur and Irene Mary (Dakers) T.; m. Elizabeth Clayton Hay, June 7, 1975; children: Kirk Hunter, Alex Peter. BA, U. Wash., 1971; JD, U. Pacific, Sacramento, 1975; LLM Taxation, Boston U., 1976. Atty. Dahlgren & Dauenhauer P.S., Seattle, 1976-79, Lane Powell Spears Lubersky, Seattle, 1980-93; shareholder Birmingham Thorson & Barnett, P.C., 1993—; lectr. U. Wash. Grad. Program in Taxation, 1995—. Mem. ABA (health law forum), Internat. Found. Employee Benefits, Employee Benefits and Health Law coms., Wash. State Bar Assn. Avocations: bicycling, skiing. Office: Birmingham Thorson Barnett 601 Union St Ste 3315 Seattle WA 98101-2327

THORSON, OSWALD HAGEN, architect; b. Forest City, Iowa, Dec. 19, 1912; s. Thorwald and Josephine (Hagen) T.; m. Maxine Rustad, Dec. 27, 1941; children: Sigrin, Thorwald. BArch, U. Minn., 1937. Registered architect, Iowa. Ptnr. Thorson & Thorson, Forest City, 1939-52, Thorson & Brom, Forest City, 1952-65, Thorson Brom Broshar Snyder, Waterloo, Iowa, 1965-79, ret. Fellow AIA (nat. sec. 1965-67, Lifetime Achievemnt award Iowa chpt. 1982). Democrat. Home: 919 N Barfield Dr Marco Island FL 34145-2348

THORSON-HOUCK, JANICE HARGREAVES, speech, language pathologist; b. Birmingham, Ala., Oct. 22, 1943; d. Harold Trevelyn and Johnnie Lou (Phillips) Hargreaves; m. William Gerald Thorson, July 4, 1974 (dec. 1984); children: Alice, William, Laura, Elizabeth, Ronald, John; m. Lawrence Clifton Houck, June 25, 1994. BA in Speech/Lang. Pathology, U. Ala., 1969, MA, 1974. Cert. speech/lang. pathologist. Speech/lang. pathologist S.E. Ala. Rehab. Ctr., Dothan, 1969-71, Birmingham City Schs., 1974-90, Midfield (Ala.) City Schs., 1990—. Cub scout den leader Boy Scouts Am., Birmingham, 1978-79; trustee Nat. Reye's Syndrome Found., Bryan, Ohio, 1985—, nat. sec., 1983-84, pres. Ala. region, 1981-85. Recipient John Dieckman Disting. Svc. award Nat. Reye's Syndrome Found., 1986. Mem. Am. Speech-Lang.-Hearing Assn., Speech and Hearing Assn. Ala. (chair sch. affaris com. 1991-95, Cert. of Appreciation 1986, 90), Pub. Sch. Caucus (sec. 1993-94), Phi Beta Kappa, Delta Kappa Gamma (2d v.p. 1994-96). Presbyterian. Avocations: handcrafts, water sports, boating. Home: 3905 Rock Creek Dr Birmingham AL 35223 Office: Birmingham Pub Schs 417 29th St S Birmingham AL 35233

THORSTAD, DALE J., manufacturing company executive; b. St. Paul, Oct. 30, 1950; s. Joseph H. and Ardell C. (Johnson) T.; m. Andrea L. Peterson, June 22, 1971; children: Jeffrey A., Janelle L., Jocelyn M., Jolana J. Student, Mpls. Vocat. Tech. Sch., 1970. Quality control mgr. Starkey Labs., Inc., Mpls., 1971-75, service mgr., 1975-79, service mgr., quality control mgr., 1978-79, plant mgr., 1979-81, v.p. ops., 1981—. Mem. Internat. Soc. Hybrid Microelectronics. Jehovah's Witness. Home: 2941 Hampshire Ave N Minneapolis MN 55427-3031 Office: Starkey Labs Inc 6700 Washington Ave S Eden Prairie MN 55344-3405*

THORSTEINSSON, RAYMOND, geology research scientist; b. Wynyard, Sask., Can., Jan. 21, 1921; m. Jean Kristjansson, Dec. 23, 1944; children: Eirikur, Anna Ingrid. BA, U. Sask., 1944; MA, U. Toronto, Can., 1950; PhD, U. Kans., 1955. Rsch. scientist Geol. Survey of Can., Calgary, 1952-92, emeritus rsch. sci., 1992—. Contbr. articles, bulletins and papers to various jours. Decorated officer Order of Can.; recipient Founders medal Royal Geog. Soc., London, 1968, Outstanding Achievement in Sci. award Govt. Province of Alta., 1973, Massey medal Royal Can. Geog. Soc., 1981, Commemorative medal 125th Anniversary Can. Confedn., 1992, Massey medal, 1981, R.J.W. Douglas medal Can. Soc. Petroleum Geologists, 1982, Gold medal Sci. Profl. Inst. Pub. Svc. Can., 1987. Fellow Arctic Inst. N.Am., The Royal Soc. Can. (Willet G. Miller medal 1973), Geol. Assn. Can. (Logan medal 1979). Office: Geol Survey Can, 3303 33 St NW, Calgary, AB Canada T2L 2A7

THORSTENBERG, (JOHN) LAURENCE, oboe and English horn player; b. Salt Lake City, Dec. 6, 1925; s. Laurence Nathaniel and Alys Josephine (Blomquist) T. MusB, Curtis Inst. Music, Phila., 1951. Instrumental tchr., 1975—, New Eng. Conservatory, Boston U., 1980—; mem. Symphony Orch. Balt., 1951-52, Dallas Symphony Orch., 1952-54, Chgo. Symphony Orch., 1954-63, Boston Symphony Orch., 1964-93; appeared summers, Marlboro (Vt.) Music Festival, 1952-54. Served with U.S. Army, 1944-46, ETO. Mem. Internat. Conf. Symphony and Opera Musicians.

THOULESS, DAVID JAMES, physicist, educator; b. Bearsden, Scotland, Sept. 21, 1934; came to U.S., 1979; U.S. citizen, 1994; s. Robert Henry and Priscilla (Gorton) T.; m. Margaret Elizabeth Scrase, July 26, 1958; children: Michael, Christopher, Helen. BA, U. Cambridge, Eng., 1955, ScD, 1986; PhD, Cornell U., 1958. Physicist Lawrence Berkeley Lab., Calif., 1958-59; rsch. fellow U. Birmingham, Eng., 1959-61, prof. math. physics, 1965-78; lectr., fellow Churchill Coll. U. Cambridge, Eng., 1961-65; prof. physics Queen's U., Kingston, Ont., Can., 1978; prof. applied sci. Yale U., New Haven, 1979-80; prof. physics U. Wash., Seattle, 1980—. Author: Quantum Mechanics of Many Body Systems, 2d edit., 1972. Recipient Maxwell medal Inst. Physics, 1973, Holweck prize Soc. Francaise de Physique-Inst. Physics, 1980, Fritz London award for Low temperature physics, Fritz London Meml. Fund, 1984, Wolf prize in physics, 1990, Paul Dirac medal Inst. Physics, 1993; Edwin Uehling disting. scholar U. Wash., 1988—. Fellow Royal Soc., Am. Acad. Arts and Scis., Nat. Acad. Sci. Office: U Wash Dept Physics Box 351560 Seattle WA 98195

THOW, GEORGE BRUCE, surgeon; b. Toronto, Mar. 24, 1930; came to U.S., 1965; s. George and Helen Bruce (Smith) T.; m. Marion Bernice Perry, Sept. 7, 1956; children—Deborah, George, Helen, Catherine. M.D., U. Toronto, 1954. Diplomate Am. Bd. Gen. Surgery, Am. Bd. Colon and Rectal Surgery (pres. 1983-84, adv. coun. 1989—, sr. examiner 1989—). Intern Toronto East Gen. Hosp., 1954-55; gen. practice medicine Toronto, 1955-56; instr. anatomy U. Toronto; resident in gen. and colon and rectal surgery Mayo Postgrad. Sch. Medicine, Rochester, Minn., 1957-63; gen., colon and rectal surgeon Lockwood Clinic, Toronto, 1963-65; founder and dir. colon and rectal residency program U. Ill. Med. Sch. and Carle Found. Hosp., Urbana, 1974-85; dir. dept. colon and rectal surgery Carle Clinic Assocs., Urbana, Ill., 1974-85; clin. assoc. Sch. Basic Med. Scis., U. Ill., Urbana, 1973-77; clin. asst. prof. Coll. Medicine, U. Ill., Urbana-Champaign, 1975-78; clin. assoc. prof. Coll. Medicine, U. Ill., 1978-85; prof. clin. nutrition, dept. food sci. U. Ill., Urbana, 1981-85; practice medicine specializing in colon and rectal surgery Chattanooga, 1985—; vice chmn. Residency Rev. Bd. in Colon and Rectal Surgery, 1980-82; active Am. Bd. Med. Specialties, 1979-84; mem. interspecialty bd. AMA, Chgo., 1974-80. Assoc. editor Diseases of the Colon and Rectum Jour., 1978—; contbr. chpt. to book, numerous articles to profl. publs.; inventor Thow tube, Colovage operative irrigation tube. Cmty. coord. Urbana conv. Inter-Varsity Christian Fellowship, Ill., 1967-84. Recipient Med. Edn. award Carle Found., 1982. Fellow Royal Coll Surgeons (Can.) (cert. 1963), ACS (credentials com. 1980-82); mem. Priestley Surg. Soc., Mid-West Colon and Rectal Surg. Soc. (pres. 1985-86), Can. Assn. Gen. Surgeons, Am. Bd. of Colon and Rectal Surgery (chmn. exam. com.1980-83, pres. 1983-84, adv. coun. 1989), Soc. Surgery Alimentary Tract, Am. Cancer Soc. (pres. Champaign County unit 1975-77, Ill. Top Ten award 1973-74), United Ostomy Assn. (founding mem. Champaign-Urbana chpt.). Presbyterian. Home: 7142 Revere Cir Concord Highlands Chattanooga TN 37421-1205 Office: Univ Surg Assocs Inc Med Ctr Plz North 979 E 3d St Ste 300 Chattanooga TN 37403-2186

THOW, JOHN H., music educator, composer; b. L.A., Oct. 6, 1949; s. George H. and Marie (Dykes) T.; m. Margaret Wait, June 24, 1971; children: Diana Corinna, Caroline Miranda. BMus in Composition magna cum laude, U. So. Calif., 1971; MA in Music Composition, Harvard U., 1973, PhD in Music Composition, 1977; diploma d'onore (Composition), Accademia Musicale Chigiana, Siena, Italy, 1974. Asst. prof. music theory and composition Boston U. Sch. for the Arts, 1978-80; asst. prof. in music composition U. Calif. Dept. Music, Berkeley, 1981-86, assoc. prof., 1986-90, prof., 1990—. Composer: Madrone (Bklyn. Philharm. commn. 1987), Image Double & Envoi, All Hallows, 1982 (NEA rec. grant 1983, Breath of the Sun 1993, Boston Musica Viva/New Eng. Found. for the Arts Commn. 1981), Seven Charms for a New Day, Canto del Quetzal, Chinese Poems, Divergences, Trombone Concerto, Songs for the Earth, 1994 (Am. Acad. award 1994), Into the Twilight, 1988 (San Francisco Symphony commn. 1988), Trigon, 1974 (Debut Orchestra award 1976), Live Oak (Musical Elements N.Y. commn. 1983). Guggenheim fellowship Guggenheim Fdn., 1986, Djerassi Fdn. fellowships, 1986, 87, Regents Jr. Faculty fellowship U. Calif., 1983, Goddard Lieberson fellowship Am. Acad. and Inst. of Arts and Letters, 1983, Dorland Mountain Colony fellow, 1981, Yaddo fellowships, 1976, 1980, John Knowles Paine Travelling fellowship (Harvard), 1976-77, Fulbright Grad. fellowship to Italy, 1973-74; Margaret Jory Fairbanks Copying Assistance grants (The Am. Music Ctr.), 1978, 92, Meet the Composer grants, 1980, 82, 86, 87, 92, 95; Acad. award in Music Composition AAAL, 1994. Fellow Am. Academy in Rome (Rome Prize fellowship 1977); mem. BMI, Am. Music Ctr., Am. Composers Forum. Home: 1045 Ordway St Albany CA 94706 Office: Univ of Calif-Berkeley Dept Music 104 Morrison Hall Berkeley CA 94720

THOYER, JUDITH REINHARDT, lawyer; b. Mt. Vernon, N.Y., July 29, 1940; d. Edgar Allen and Florence (Mayer) Reinhardt; m. Michael E. Thoyer, June 30, 1963; children: Erinn, Michael John. AB with honors, U. Mich., 1961; LLB summa cum laude, Columbia U., 1965. Bar: N.Y. 1966, D.C. 1984. Law libr. U. Ghana, Accra, Africa, 1963-64; assoc. Paul, Weiss, Rifkind, Wharton & Garrison, N.Y.C., 1966-75, ptnr., 1975—; mem. TriBar Opinion Com., 1995—. Mem. bd. visitors Law Sch. Columbia U., N.Y.C., 1991—; bd. dirs. Women's Action Alliance, N.Y.C., 1975-89, pro bono counsel, 1975—; mem. Women's Coun. Dem. Senatorial, mem. campaign com., 1993—. Mem. N.Y. County Lawyers Assn. (mem. securities and exchs. com.), Assn. of Bar of City of N.Y. (mem. securities regulation com. 1976-79, mem. recruitment of lawyers com. 1980-82). Home: 1115 5th Ave Apt 3B New York NY 10128-0100 Office: Paul Weiss Rifkind Wharton & Garrison 1285 Avenue Of The Americas New York NY 10019-6028

THRALL, ARTHUR ALVIN, artist; b. Milw., Mar. 18, 1926; s. Irving and Helen (Fabich) T.; m. Winifred Rogers, 1960; children: Grant, Wade, Sara, Jay. BS, Milw. State Tchrs. Coll., 1950; MS, U. Wis., Milw., 1954; postgrad. (fellow), U. Ill., 1954-55. Tchr. art Lincoln Jr. High Sch., Kenosha, Wis., 1951-54; asst. prof. SUNY, Geneseo, 1955-56; assoc. prof. Milw.-Downer Coll., 1956-64; prof., Farrar-Marrs prof. fine arts Lawrence U., Appleton, Wis., 1964-90; prof. emeritus Lawrence U., Appleton, 1990—. One-man shows include Smithsonian Instn., 1960, U. Dubuque, Iowa, 1993, Mt. Mary Coll., Milw., 1994, St. Norbert Coll, De Pere, Wis., 1995, also others; group shows include Corcoran bienials, Washington, 1951, 53, 55, 57, 62, Bklyn. Mus. annuals, Mus. Modern Art, N.Y.C., NAD, N,Y,C, Audubon Artists, N.Y.C., 1985, S.A.G.A., N.Y.C., 1985; represented in permanent collections Tate Gallery, Victoria and Alberta Mus., Brit. Mus., all London, Phila. Mus., Seattle Mus., Art Inst. Chgo., Bklyn. Mus., others. Served with U.S. Army, 1944-46, ETO. Recipient Bklyn. Mus. print awards 1952, 64; Pa. Acad. Arts award 1960; NAD awards 1956, 68); Louis Comfort Tiffany fellow, 1963. Mem. AAUP, Boston Printmakers (awards 1963, 65), Soc. Am. Graphic Artists (awards 1951, 52, 60, 78), Audubon Artists Inc. (award 1977). Home: 4225 N Woodburn St Milwaukee WI 53211-1504

THRALL, DONALD STUART, artist; b. Detroit, Mar. 29, 1918; s. Ernest Lawrence and Gertrude Marie (Aikenhead) T. B.A., Mich. State U., 1940; M.A., Columbia U. Tchrs. Coll., 1946; summer student, Skowhegan (Maine) Sch. Painting and Sculpture, 1947, Black Mountain (N.C.) Coll., 1948. Instr. painting and design Cass Tech. Sch., Detroit, 1949-55; edn1. coordinator Guggenheim Mus., N.Y.C., 1961-73; Bd. dirs. Mich. Watercolor Soc., 1950-55, Detroit Met. Art Assn., 1948-54; exhibiting mem. Detroit Inst. Arts, 1947-53. One-man exhbn., Contemporary Arts Gallery, N.Y.C., 1961, group exhbns. include, Met. Mus. Art, 1950, Detroit Inst. Arts, 1947-55 (award 1950, 53, 55), Mich. Artists invited survey show, 1951, Butler Inst. Am. Art, Youngstown, Ohio, 1950-52 (1st prize 1951), Whitney Mus., N.Y.C., 1953, Bklyn. Mus., 1961, others, group exhbns. include, Wildenstein Galleries, N.Y.C., 1952 (Hallmark Art prize), Downtown Gallery, N.Y.C., 1950-53, Detroit Artists Market, 1948-54, Scarab Gallery, Detroit, 1948-53 (award 1948, 51, 53, 54), Mich. Watercolor Soc., 1949-55 (award 1950, 52, 53, 55), Mich. State Fair, 1952 (1st prize 1952), Detroit Art Instr. Exhbn., 1946-53 (1st award 1946, 48, 50, 51, 53), 16th Serigraph Internat., N.Y.C., 1955, others; represented in permanent collections, Detroit Inst. Arts, Butler Inst. Am. Art, U. Mich. Mus. Art, Mus. Wayne State U., Cranbrook Acad. Art Mus., Bloomfield Hills, Mich., numerous pvt. collections, U.S. and abroad. Served with AUS, 1941-45. Guggenheim fellow, 1955. Mem. Mich. Acad. Sci., Arts and Letters, Beta Alpha Sigma (pres. 1940). Address: 945 W End Ave New York NY 10025-3566

THRALL, JAMES HUNTER, radiology educator; b. Ann Arbor, Mich., 1943. BA, U. Mich., 1964, MD, 1968. Intern Walter Reed Army Med. Ctr., Washington, 1968-69, resident in radiology, 1969-72, fellow in nuclear medicine, 1972-73, asst. chief nuclear med. svc. dept. radiology, 1973-75; asst. prof. radiology and nuclear medicine U. Mich., Ann Arbor, 1975-78, assoc. prof., 1978-81, prof., 1981-83; now Juan M. Taveras prof. radiology Harvard U., Cambridge, Mass.; cons. nuclear medicine Ann Arbor VA Hosp.; chmn. radiology dept. Henry Ford Hosp., Detroit, 1983; radiologist in chief, Mass. Gen. Hosp., Boston, 1983—. Maj. M.C., U.S. Army, 1968-75. Office: Mass General Hosp Fruit St Boston MA 02114

THRASH, EDSEL E., educational administrator; b. Lake, Miss., Aug. 28, 1925; m. Jessie McLendon, Apr. 16, 1949; children—Jane, Catherine, George. B.S. in Bus. Adminstrn, La. State U., 1950, M.B.A., 1951, Ph.D., 1963. Acct. Esso Standard Oil Co., 1951-55; dir. alumni affairs La. State U., 1957-68, mem. dept. econs., 1966-68; exec. sec., dir. bd. trustees State Instns. Higher Learning in Miss., Jackson, 1968-87; Disting. prof. health care econs. U. Miss. Med. Ctr., Jackson, 1987—. Bd. dirs. Miss. Heart Assn., 1970-76; mem. exec. council Andrew Jackson council Boy Scouts Am.; mem. council on ministries United Meth. Ch., Raymond, Miss., 1973—. Recipient Silver Beaver award Boy Scouts Am., 1977, Gold Heart award Miss. Heart Assn., 1976; elected to La. State U. Alumni Hall of Distinction, 1993. Mem. State Higher Edn. Exec. Officers (nat. pres. 1984-85), Omicron Delta Kappa, Alpha Kappa Psi. Office: U Miss Health Care Ctr PO Box 13872 Jackson MS 39236-3872

THRASH, PATRICIA ANN, educational association administrator; b. Grenada, Miss., May 4, 1929; d. Lewis Edgar and Weaver (Betts) T. BS, Delta State Coll., 1950; MA, Northwestern U., 1953, PhD, 1959; cert. Inst. Edn. Mgmt., Harvard U., 1983. Tchr. high sch. English Clarksdale, Miss., 1950-52; head resident Northwestern U., 1953-55, asst. to dean women, 1955-58, asst. dean women, 1958-60, lectr. edn., 1959-65, dean women, 1960-69, assoc. prof. edn., 1965-72, assoc. dean students, 1969-71; asst. exec. sec. Commn. on Instns. Higher Edn., North Central Assn. Colls. and Schs., 1972-73, assoc. exec. dir., 1973-76, assoc. dir., 1976-87, exec. dir., 1988—; mem. adv. panel ACE/MIVER program evaluation mil. base program, 1991-94; mem. nat. adv. panel Nat. Ctr. Postsecondary Tchg., Learning & Assessment, 1991-95. Author (with others): Handbook of College and University Administration, 1970; contbr. articles to ednl. jours. Mem. Nat. Assn. Women Deans and Counselors (v.p. 1967-69, pres. 1972-73), Ill. Assn. Women Deans and Counselors (sec. 1961-63, pres. 1964-66), Am. Coll. Pers. Assn. (editl. bd. jour. 1971-74), Coun. Student Pers. Assns. in Higher Edn. (program nominations com. 1974-75, adv. panel Am. Coll. Testing Coll. Outcome Measures project 1977-78, staff COPA project for evalution nontraditional edn. 1977-78, mem. editl. bd. Jour. Higher Edn. 1975-80, guest editor Mar.-Apr. 1979, co-editor NCA Quar. 1988—, vice-chair regional accrediting dirs. group 1993, exec. com. Nat. Policy Bd. for Higher Edn. Inst. 1993-95), Mortar Bd. (hon.), Phi Delta Theta, Pi Lambda Theta, Alpha Psi Omega, Alpha Lambda Delta. Methodist. Home: 2337 Hartrey Ave Evanston IL 60201-2552

THRASHER, DIANNE ELIZABETH, mathematics educator, computer consultant; b. Brockton, Mass., July 11, 1945; m. George Thomas Thrasher, Jan. 28, 1967; children: Kimberly Elizabeth, Noelle Elizabeth. BA in Math., Bridgewater State Coll., 1967, postgrad. in computer sci., 1984-87. owner New Eng. Regional Kumon Ednl. Franchise, 1991-95; approved profl. point devel. provider for tchr. cert. State of Mass., 1996. Tchr. math. Plymouth/Carver Regional Schs., Plymouth, Mass., 1976-78, Alden Sch., Duxbury, Mass., 1980-82, Marshfield (Mass.) High Sch., 1982-84; computer cons. TC2I-Thrasher Computer Cons. and Instrn., Duxbury, Mass., 1988—; dir., owner Internat. Ednl. Franchise, 1991-95; owner Duxbury Math. Ctr. K-Adult, 1995—; owner New Eng. Regional Kumon Ednl. Franchise, 1991-95; Mass. State approved profl. point devel. provider for tchr. cert., 1996. Active U.S. Figure Skating Assn., Colorado Springs, 1978-85; 2d reader First Ch. Christ Scientist, Plymouth, 1971-73; bd. govs. Skating Club of Hingham, Mass., 1978-85, pres., 1983-85, dir. Learn to Skate program, 1983-85; mem. First Ch. Christ Scientist, Boston, 1964—; with New Eng. Regional Kumon Franchise Owners, 1991-95; charter mem. Nat. Adv. Coun. of the U.S. Navy Meml. Found., 1992. Recipient Ed Taylor Meml. Vol. Svc. award Skating Club Hagham, 1995. Mem. NAFE, AAUW, Nat. Coun. Tchrs. Math., Boston Computer Soc., Duxbury Bus. Assn. Avocations: antiques, bicycling, skating, sailing. Home: 140 Toby Garden St Duxbury MA 02332-4945

THRASHER, JAMES PARKER, writer; b. Waltham, Mass., Jan. 15, 1932; s. Linus James and Doris Melissa (Parker) T.; B.S. in Indsl. Adminstrn., Yale U., 1953; children: Deborah Anne, Linda Carol, Anne Elizabeth. With U.S. Steel Corp., Cleve., 1953-60; cons. Booz, Allen & Hamilton Internat.,

London, 1960-65; mgmt. cons. McKinsey & Co., Inc., London, 1965-67; v.p. for Europe, Integrated Container Service, Inc., London, 1967-69, pres., chief exec. officer, N.Y.C., 1970-75; v.p., dir. Interway Corp., N.Y.C., 1969-75, pres., chief exec. officer, dir., 1975-79, Transam. Interway, Inc. subs. Transam. Corp., San Francisco, 1979-81. Author: A Crisis of Values, 1985. Home: 365 Lynn Cove Rd Asheville NC 28804-1914

THRASHER, JERRY ARTHUR, library director; b. Fairfield, Ala., Oct. 3, 1942; s. Arthur E. and Elizabeth M. Thrasher; m. Alice Wilson, Dec. 1, 1967; children: Alexander, Andrew. BA, U. Ala., 1969; MSLS, Fla. State U., 1970. Circulation libr. R.W. Woodruff Libr., Emory U., Atlanta, 1970-72; libr. City Island Libr., Daytona Beach, Fla., 1972-74; dir. Haywood County Pub. Libr., Waynesville, N.C., 1975-77; assoc. dir. Forsyth County Pub. Libr., Winston Salem, N.C., 1977-79; dir. Cumberland County Pub. Libr. and Info. Ctr., Fayetteville, N.C., 1980—; dir. N.C. Libr. Assn., 1984-85; mem. Gov.'s Confs. on Libr. and Info. Svcs. for N.C., 1990-91; mem. pub. libr. adv. com. Online Computer Libr. Ctr., 1991-93. Editor: Haywood County Public Library: An Analysis of Its Community Resources, Services and Plans for Development, 1977, The People and Their Public Library, 1983, Meeting the Challenge - The Public Library in the 21st Century, 1995; contbr. articles to profl. jours. Adv. bd. cape Fear Bot. Gradens, 1990-92; chmn. WFSS-FM, PBS, Fayetteville (N.C.) State U., 1990-91; dir.-at-large Pub. Libr. Assn. Bd., 1995—; v.p. United Way Cumberland County, 1991; pres. Terry Sanford H.S. PTA, 1991-93. With U.S. Army, 1961-64. Recipient Roll of Honor award Freedom to Read Found., New Orleans, 1993. Mem. ALA, N.C. Pub. Libr. Dirs. Assn. (Libr. Dir. of Yr. 1989, pres. 1984), N.C. State Libr. Comm., N.C. Info. Hwy. Libr. Com., Info. Futures Inst., Fayetteville (N.C.) Kiwanis Club (pres. 1993-94). Office: Cumberland County Pub Libr 300 Maiden Ln Fayetteville NC 28301-5032

THRASHER, ROSE MARIE, critical care and community health nurse; b. Urbana, Ohio, Jan. 19, 1948; d. Jesse and Anna Frances (Clark) T. Student, Mercy Med. Ctr. Sch. Med. Tech., 1966-67, Wittenberg U., 1969-70; BSN, Ohio State U., 1974, BA in Anthropology, 1994, postgrad., 1994—. RN, Ohio; cert. cmty. health nurse ANA; cert. provider BCLS and ACLS, Am. Heart Assn. Pub. health nurse Columbus (Ohio) Health Dept., 1977-78; critical care nurse VA Med. Ctr., San Francisco, 1981, Staff Builders Health Care Svc., Oakland, Calif., 1975-76, 81-85; supr., case mgr. home health nurse passport program and intermittent care program Interim Health Care (formerly Med. Pers. Pool), Columbus, 1976-77, 85—. Recipient numerous acad. scholarships Wittenberg U. and Ohio State U.; mem. Nat. Women's Hall of Fame. Mem. AACN, ANA (coun. cmty. health nursing), AAUW, Ohio Nurses Assn., Intravenous Nurses Soc., Ohio State U. Alumni Assn., Am. Anthropol. Assn., Ohio Acad. Sci.

THREEFOOT, SAM ABRAHAM, physician, educator; b. Meridian, Miss., Apr. 10, 1921; s. Sam Abraham and Ruth Frances (Lilienthal) T.; m. Virginia Rush, Feb. 6, 1954; children: Barbara Jane Stockton Mattingly, Ginny Ruth Threefoot Lindberg, Tracyann Threefoot Esenstad, Shelley Ann Threefoot Cowan. B.S., Tulane U., 1943, M.D., 1945. Diplomate: Am. Bd. Internal Medicine. Intern Michael Reese Hosp., Chgo., 1945-47; asst. vis. physician Charity Hosp. New Orleans, 1947-50, vis. physician, 1950-57, sr. vis. physician, 1957-69, cons., 1969-70, 76—; clin. asst. dept. medicine Touro Infirmary, New Orleans, 1953-56; jr. asst. Touro Infirmary, 1956-60, sr. asst., 1960-63, dir. med. edn., 1953-63, dir. research, 1953-70, sr. dept. medicine, 1963-70; fellow dept. medicine Tulane U., 1947-49, instr., 1948-53, asst. prof., 1953-59, asso. prof., 1959-63, prof., 1963-70, 76-91, prof. emeritus, 1991—, asst. dean, 1979-91, adj. prof. emeritus Sch. Pub. Health & Tropical Medicine, 1993—; chief of staff VA Hosp. (Forest Hills div.), Augusta, Ga., 1970-76; asso. chief staff VA Hosp., New Orleans, 1976-79; chief of staff VA Hosp., 1979-91, cons., 1991—; asst. dean Med. Coll. Ga., 1970-76, prof. medicine, 1970-76; Cons. physician Lallie Kemp Charity Hosp., Independence, La., 1951-53. Editor: Lymphology, 1967-70; Contbr. articles profl. jours. Served with AUS, 1943-45. La. Heart Assn. grantee, 1953-55; John A. Hartford Found. grantee, 1956-74; Am. Heart Assn. grantee, 1959-61; USPHS grantee, 1953-66. Fellow A.C.P., Am. Coll. Cardiology, N.Y. Acad. Sci.; mem. Am. Heart Assn. (v.p. 1970, fellow council on circulation), Central Soc. Clin. Research, So. Soc. Clin. Investigation (pres. 1967), AAAS, Internat. Soc. Lymphology, Soc. Exptl. Biology and Medicine, Soc. Nuclear Medicine, Microcirculatory Conf., Inc., Am. Fedn. Clin. Research, La. Heart Assn. (pres. 1967), Nat. Assn. VA Chiefs of Staff (pres. 1987-88), Phi Beta Kappa, Sigma Xi. Jewish. *I am one of those fortunate individuals who has been able to approach goals set early in life. Although my achievements are far short of my aspirations, at least I have had the opportunity. In dealing with both people and things, I have always felt that no detail was too small to receive attention.*

THREET, JACK CURTIS, oil company executive; b. Dundas, Ill., Aug. 16, 1928; s. Ivy Clemon and Daryl (Curtis) T.; m. Catherine Irene Hall, Mar. 24, 1951; children—Linda Sue, Judith Ann. B.A. in Geology, U. Ill., 1951. Geologist, dist. geologist, div. exploration mgr., area exploration mgr. Shell Oil Co., various locations including Oklahoma City, Amarillo, Tex., Denver, Pitts., Lafayette, La., Billings, Mont., N.Y.C., L.A., 1951-69; gen. mgr. exploration and prodn. Shell Australia Ltd., Melbourne, 1969-71; v.p. internat. exploration and prodn. Shell Can., Calgary, Alta., 1972-74, Shell Oil Co., New Orleans, 1974-75; v.p. internat. exploration and prodn. Houston, 1975-78, corp. v.p. exploration, 1978-87, ret., 1987; v.p., dir., co-founder Energy Exploration Mgmt. Co., Houston, 1988-90; pres., owner Threet Energy, Inc., Houston, 1989—. Served with U.S. Army, 1953-55. Mem. Am. Assn. Petroleum Geologists, Lakeside Country Club (Houston), Rotary. Republican. Methodist.

THREET, MARTIN EDWIN, lawyer; b. El Paso, Tex., Sept. 1, 1933; s. Martin Albro and Frances Elizabeth (Mitchell) T.; m. Laura Elliott, Aug. 1, 1959; children—Martin, Melissa, Jennifer. B.A., N.Mex. Mil. Inst., 1955; LL.B., Vanderbilt U., 1959. Bar: N.Mex. 1959, U.S. Dist. Ct. N.Mex. 1959, U.S. Ct. Appeals (10th cir.) 1962. Ptnr., Threet, Ussery & Threet, Albuquerque, 1959-61; sr. ptnr. Threet, Threet & Glass, 1963, Threet, Threet, Glass & King, 1963-72, Threet, Threet, Glass, King & Maxwell, 1972-78, Threet, Threet, Glass, King & Hooe, 1978-80, Threet & King, 1980—; lectr. U. N.Mex., 1975-76. Served with AUS, 1958. Root Tilden scholar, 1956. Mem. N.Mex Trial Lawyers Assn., N.Mex. Bar Assn., Albuquerque Bar Assn., ABA, Comml. Law League Am. Democrat. Club: Newcomen Soc. Office: 6400 Uptown Blvd NE Suite 500 W Albuquerque NM 87110

THRELKELD, RICHARD DAVIS, broadcast journalist; b. Cedar Rapids, Iowa, Nov. 30, 1937; s. Robert M. and Lou Jane (Davis) T.; m. Sharon A. Adams, June 11, 1960 (div. 1983); children: Susan Anne, Julia Lynn; m. Betsy Aaron, May 15, 1983. B.A., Ripon Coll., 1959; M.S. in Journalism, Northwestern U., 1961; LHD (hon.), Ripon Coll., 1989. Editor Sta. WHAS-TV, Louisville, 1961; reporter Sta. WMT-TV, Cedar Rapids, Iowa, 1961-66; corr. CBS News, N.Y.C. and San Francisco, 1966-82; nat. corr. CBS News, 1989—; chief corr. ABC News N.Y., N.Y.C., 1982-89. Corr.: TV news documentary Defense of America, 1981 (Emmy award); TV news report Rhodesia Remembered, 1980 (Overseas Press Club award), TV news report Vietnam Remembered, 1985 (Emmy award), TV news series Status Reports, 1984 (Dupont award), TV news report Lebanon-Grenada 1983 (Overseas Press Club award). CBS News fellow, 1964. Mem. AFTRA, Radio-TV News Dirs. Assn., Sigma Delta Chi.

THRIFT, JULIANNE STILL, academic administrator; b. Barnwell, S.C.; m. Ashley Ormand Thrift; children: Lindsay, Laura. BA, U. S.C., MEd; PhD in Pub. Policy, George Washington U. Formerly asst. exec. dir. Nat. Assn. Coll. and Univ. Attys.; ombudsman U. S.C.; exec. dir. Nat. Inst. Ind. Colls. and Univs., 1982-88; exec. v.p. Nat. Assn. Ind. Colls. and Univs., Washington, 1988-91; pres. Salem Acad. and Coll., Winston-Salem, N.C., 1991—. Office: Salem Coll Office of the President Winston Salem NC 27108-0548

THRIFT, SHARRON WOODARD, secondary education program director; b. Waycross, Ga., July 18, 1962; d. Lawrence Marvin and Evon Mattie (Lee) Woodard; m. Gary Wayne Thrift, Sept. 5, 1987; children: Dustin Wayne, Zachary Lawrence. BS in Edn., U. Ga., 1983; MEd, Valdosta State Coll., 1987, EdS, 1993. Cert. bus. edn. tchr. Night sch. keyboarding instr. Waycross (Ga.)-Ware Tech., 1984-87; bus. edn. instr. Brantley County H.S., Nahunta, Ga., 1984-85, data processing coord., 1985-93, CBE coord., 1993—. Projects chairperson Blackshear (Ga.) Pilot Club, 1988-89. Mem. Nat. Bus. Edn. Assn., Ga. Bus. Edn. Assn., Profl. Assn. Ga. Educators. Republican. Baptist. Avocations: crafts, reading. Office: Brantley County HS PO Box 1239 Hwy 82 W Nahunta GA 31553

THROCKMORTON, JOAN HELEN, direct marketing consultant; b. Evanston, Ill., Apr. 11, 1931; d. Sydney L. and Anita H. (Pusheck) T.; m. Sheldon Burton Satin, June 26, 1982. B.A. with honors, Smith Coll., 1953. Mktg. exec. Lawrence Chait & Co., N.Y.C., 1965; mktg. exec. Cowles Communications, Inc., N.Y.C., 1968-69; founder, chief exec. officer Throckmorton Assocs., Inc., N.Y.C., 1970-83; pres. Joan Throckmorton, Inc., N.Y.C., 1983—; lectr. in field; instr. Direct Mktg. Assn., Sch. Continuing Edn., NYU, N.Y.C., 1985. Author: Winning Direct Response Advertising, 1986, 2d edit., 1996. Trustee Halle Ravine Com. Nature Conservancy, 1985; mem. expetition com. Outward Bound, 1980-83. Named Direct Mktg. Woman of Yr., 1986. Mem. Women's Dir. Response Group (founding mem.), Dir. Mktg. Assn. (bd. dirs. 1971-77, exec. com. 1972-77, mem. long-range planning com. 1977-78), Women's Forum, Dir. Mktg. Idea Exchange, Dir. Mktg. Creative Guild (bd. dirs. 1984-85), Jr. League Mexico City, Jr. League N.Y.C., Phi Beta Kappa. Office: Joan Throckmorton Inc PO Box 452 Pound Ridge NY 10576-0452

THRODAHL, MARK CRANDALL, medical technology company executive; b. Charleston, W.Va., Mar. 31, 1951; s. Monte Cordon and Josephine (Crandall) T.; m. Sudie Kenton, Oct. 21, 1978; children: Mary Elizabeth, Anne Katherine, Andrew Kenton. AB, Princeton U., 1973; MBA, Harvard U., Boston, 1975. Various positions Mallinckrodt, Inc., St. Louis, 1975-88; dir. corp. planning Becton Dickinson & Co., Franklin Lakes, N.J., 1988-91; pres. Nippon Becton Dickinson, Becton Dickinson & Co., Tokyo, 1991-94; sector pres. Becton Dickinson & Co., Franklin Lakes, 1994-95, sr. v.p., 1995—. Mem. Old Warson Country Club, Ivy Club. Republican. Episcopalian. Home: 38 Carteret Rd Allendale NJ 07401 Office: Becton Dickinson & Co One Becton Dr Franklin Lakes NJ 07417

THRODAHL, MONTE CORDEN, former chemical company executive; b. Mpls., Mar. 25, 1919; s. Monte Conrad and Hilda (Larson) T.; m. Josephine Crandall, Nov. 6, 1948; children: Mark Crandall, Peter Douglas. B.S., Iowa State U., 1941. With Monsanto Co., St. Louis, 1941-84; gen. mgr. internat. div. Monsanto Co., 1964-66, v.p., 1965-84, dir., 1966-84, group v.p. tech., 1974-77, sr. v.p., 1979-84; v.p., dir. Monsanto Research Corp. Fellow AIChE, AAAS, Am. Inst. Chemists; mem. NAE, Am. Chem. Soc., Comml. Devel. Assn., Soc. Chem. Industry, Old Warson Country Club, St. Louis Club, Univ. Club, Old Warson Country Club, St. Louis Club, Alpha Chi Sigma. Home: 36 Briarcliff Ladue MO 63124-1753 Office: 20 S Central Ave Saint Louis MO 63105-3317

THRONER, GUY CHARLES, JR., engineering executive, scientist, engineer, inventor, consultant; b. Mpls., Sept. 14, 1919; s. Guy Charles and Marie (Zechar) T.; m. Jean Holt, Dec. 5, 1943; children—Richard, Carol Anne, Steven. BA, Oberlin Coll., 1943; postgrad., UCLA, 1960, 61. Registered profl. engr., Calif. Br. head Naval Weapon Ctr., China Lake, Calif., 1946-53; mgr. ordnance div., mgr. weapon systems div. Aerojet Gen. Corp., Azusa, Calif., 1953-64; v.p., div. mgr. FMC Corp., San Jose, Calif., 1964-74; research dir. Vacu Blast Corp., Belmont, Calif., 1976-78; v.p., devel. mfg. Dahlman, Inc., Braham, Minn., 1978-79; mgr. ordnance systems & tech. Battelle Meml. Inst., Columbus, Ohio, 1979-85; pres. Guy C. Throner & Assocs., tech. and mgmt. cons., 1985—; dir. Omron Corp. Am., Chgo., 1976-77. Inventor, patentee indls., med. and mil. systems design. Served as officer USNR, World War II. Am. Order St. Barbara medal U.S. Army Arty, 1983, Recipient IR-100 award Indsl. Research Mag., Chgo., 1971, Congl. Commendation, 1985, also various commendations. Mem. AIAA, Am. Def. Preparedness Assn. (Bronze medal 1974, Simon award 1985), Lake Wildwood Country Club, Sigma Xi. Republican. Avocations: astronomy; photography; golf. Home and Office: 17992 Jayhawk Dr Penn Valley CA 95946-9206

THROWER, ELLEN, academic administrator. BS in Bus. Adminstn., U. N.C., Greensboro, 1975, MBA, 1978; PhD, Ga. State U., 1981; postgrad., Harvard U., 1988. Asst. prof. ins. and risk mgmt. Fla. State U., Talahassee, 1981-84; assoc. prof. ins. Drake U., Des Moines, 1984-88, dir. ins. ctr., 1985-88; pres., CEO The Coll. of Ins., N.Y.C., 1988—; prof. risk mgmt. and ins. The Coll. of Ins., 1988—; bd. dirs. Pa. Nat. Ins. Cos., United Educators, Inc., SCOR, U.S., Excel, Ltd.; mem. editl. adv. bd. Risk Mgmt. mag., 1994—; mem. adv. bd. Bermuda Found. for Ins. Studies, Internat. Ins. Found. Contbr. numerous articles to profl. jours. Bd. dirs. N.Y.C. Coun. on Econ. Edn., 1992—, Ins. Edn. Found., 1988—. Named Ins. Woman of Yr. APIW, 1993; recipient Chmn.'s award Nat. Assn. Mut. Ins. Cos., 1994. Mem. Internat. Ins. Soc., Am. Risk and Ins. Assn., Am. Mgmt. Assn., Risk and Ins. Mgmt. Soc., Soc. for Ins. Rsch., So. Risk and Ins. Assn., Western Risk and Ins. Co., Fin. Women's Assn. N.Y., Consortium. Office: The Coll of Ins 101 Murray St New York NY 10007-2165

THUERING, GEORGE LEWIS, industrial engineering educator; b. Milw., Sept. 2, 1919; s. Louis Charles and Elsie (Luetzow) T.; m. Lillian May Cline, Dec. 7, 1945 (dec.); 1 child; m. Betty L. McBride, Aug. 9, 1975. B.S., U. Wis., 1941, M.E., 1954; M.S., Pa. State U., 1949. Registered profl. engr., Pa. Mfg. engr. Lockheed Aircraft Corp., Burbank, Calif., 1941-47; supr. plant layout Lockheed Aircraft Corp., Marietta, Ga., 1951-52; mem. faculty Pa. State U., University Park, 1947—; assoc. prof. indsl. engring. Pa. State U., 1952-56, prof., 1956-82, prof. emeritus, 1982—, dir. mgmt. engring., 1961-82; cons. engring. Contbr. articles to profl. jours. Fellow Soc. Advancement Mgmt.; mem. ASME (chmn. mgmt. div. 1976-77, mem. exec. com. mgmt. div. 1973-77, chmn. papers rev. com. 1969-73, v.p. gen. engring. 1982-84), Am. Inst. Indsl. Engrs. (dir. students affairs 1972-74), Am. Soc. Engring. Edn. (chmn. indsl. engring. div. 1956-57), Sigma Xi, Tau Beta Pi, Pi Tau Sigma, Alpha Pi Mu. Home: 436 Homan Ave State College PA 16801-6336 Office: 207 Hammond Bldg University Park PA 16802-1401

THUESEN, GERALD JORGEN, industrial engineer, educator; b. Oklahoma City, July 20, 1938; s. Holger G. and Helen S. T.; m. Harriett M. Thuesen; children: Karen E., Dyan L. BS, Stanford U., 1960, MS, 1961, PhD, 1968. Engr. Pacific Telephone Co., San Francisco, 1961-62, Atlantic Richfield Co., Dallas, 1962-63; asst. prof. indsl. engring. U. Tex., Arlington, 1963, 67-68; asso. prof. indsl. and systems engring. Ga. Inst. Tech., Atlanta, 1968-76, prof., 1976—. Author: Engineering Economy, 4th edit., 1971, 5th edit., 1977, 6th edit., 1984, 7th edit., 1989, 8th edit., 1993, Economic Decision Analysis, 1974, 2d edit., 1980; assoc. editor: The Engring. Economist, 1974-80, editor, 1981-91. NASA/Am. Soc. Engring. Edn. summer faculty fellow, 1970. Fellow Inst. Indsl. Engrs. (dept. editor Trans. 1976-80, v.p. publs. 1979-80, divsn. dir. 1978-80, Wellington award 1989, Publs. award 1990), Am. Soc. Engring. Edn. (bd. dirs. 1977-79, Eugene L. Grant award 1977, 89); mem. Informs, Sigma Xi. Office: Ga Inst Tech Sch Indsl & System Engring Atlanta GA 30332

THUILLIER, RICHARD HOWARD, meteorologist; b. N.Y.C., Apr. 3, 1936; s. Howard Joseph and Louise (Schilling) T.; m. Barbara Unger (dec. 1992); children: Stephen, David, Lawrence, Daniel. BS in Physics, Fordham U., 1959; MS in Meteorology, NYU, 1963, postgrad., 1963-66. Cert. cons. meteorologist. Instr. SUNY, 1963-66; dir. of research Weather Engrs. of Panama Inc., Panama City, Rep. Panama, 1966-68; cons. Oakland, Calif., 1968—; meteorologist and chief of research and planning Bay Area Air Quality Mgmt. Dist., San Francisco, 1968-76; sr. research meteorologist SRI Internat., Menlo Park, Calif., 1976-80, Pacific Gas & Electric, San Ramon, Calif., 1980—; Note, your military record is listed in your civic section, per style. Capt. USAF, 1959-62. Mem. Am. Meteorol. Soc., (pres. Panama Canal Zone chpt. 1967-68, San Francisco Bay chpt. 1971-72, Outstanding Contributions to Advance of Applied Meteorolgy award 1993), Sigma Xi (hon.). Republican. Roman Catholic. Avocations: skiing, bowling, golf, music, art.

THULEAN, DONALD MYRON, symphony conductor; b. Wenatchee, Wash., June 24, 1929; s. Elmer Edward and Mary (Myron) T.; m. Meryl Mary Parnell, Mar. 17, 1951; children—Dorcas Marie, Mark Myron, William Norton. B.A., U. Wash., 1950, M.A. in Music, 1952; Mus.D. (hon.), Whitworth Coll., 1967. Faculty Pacific U., 1955-62; dean Pacific U. (Sch. Music), 1957-62. Assoc. conductor Portland (Ore.) Symphony, 1961-62, conductor, music dir. Spokane Symphony, 1962-84; v.p. artistic affairs, orch. svcs. Am. Symphony Orch. League, 1984—; asst. conductor Seattle Symphony, 1966-69, chorus master, Aspen Music Festival, 1957-61; artistic cons. Title III project in performing arts, Wash., 1966-68, music dir. Tamarack Music Festival, 1971. Served with AUS, 1953-55. Unitarian (trustee). Office: 1156 15th St NW Washington DC 20005-1704

THULIN, WALTER WILLIS, real estate company executive; b. Mpls., Aug. 10, 1929; s. Edwin and Henrietta Helen (Kaupp) T.; m. M. Joan Thulin, Jan. 11, 1952; children: Elizabeth, Joshua K., Edwin K., Justin F. B.Chem. Engring., U. Minn., 1952, B.B.A., 1952; M.B.A., Harvard U., 1954. V.p. internat. mktg. Internat. Flavors & Fragrances, N.Y.C., 1967-78; group v.p. Mallinckrodt, Inc., St. Louis, 1978-88; chmn. Evergreen Mgmt. Inc., Jackson, Wyo., 1989—. Home: PO Box 727 Wilson WY 83014-0727 Office: PO Box 2871 Jackson WY 83001-2871

THUMANN, ALBERT, association executive, engineer; b. Bronx, N.Y., Mar. 12, 1942; s. Albert and Ella (Josephy) T.; m. Susan Stock, Jan. 23, 1966; 1 child, Brian. BS, CUNY, 1964; MS in Elec. Engring., NYU, 1967, M.S. in Indsl. Engring, 1970. Registered profl. engr., N.Y., Ga., Ky. Project engring. mgr. Bechtel Corp., N.Y.C., Louisville, 1964-77; exec. dir., founder Assn. Energy Engrs., 1977—; Adj. prof. environmental engring. U. Louisville, 1974-75; lectr. on energy conservation. Author: Electrical Consulting-Engineering and Design, 1973, (with R.K. Miller) Secrets of Noise Control, 1976, Biorhythms and Industrial Safety, 1977, How to Patent Without a Lawyer, 1978, Electrical Design, Safety and Energy Conservation, 1978, 979, 3d edit., 1995, Energy Audit Sourcebook, 1983, Fundamentals of Energy Engineering, 1984, Introduction to Efficient Electrical Systems Design, 3d edit., 1990, (with Goldstick) Waste Heat Recovery, 1986, (with Miller) Introduction to Noise Control Engineering, 1986, Optimizing HVAC Systems, 1988, Lighting Efficiency Applications, 1988, (with James A. Bent) Project Management for Engineering and Construction, 1988, Palnt Engineers and Managers Guide to Energy Conservation, 5th edit., 1991, Handbook of Energy Engineering, 1989, 3d edit., 1994, Energy management Guide for Government Buildings, 1994, (with D. Paul Mehta) Handbook of Energy Engineering, 1995, Plant Engineers and Managers Guide to Energy Conservation, 6th edit., 1996; editor: Emerging Synthetic Fuel Industry, 1981; contbr. articles to profl. jours. Named Young Engr. of Year Ky. Soc. Profl. Engrs., 1974-75, Ky. col.; recipient Disting. Service award Assn. Energy Engrs., 1980. Mem. Nat. Soc. Profl. Engrs., Am. Soc. Assn. Execs., City Coll. Alumni Assn. Creater retng. course for unemployed aerospace engrs. Home: 931 Smoketree Dr Tucker GA 30084-1548 Office: Assn Energy Engrs 4025 Pleasantdale Rd Ste 420 Atlanta GA 30340-4260 *Where am I going and what am I doing, is a phrase which I have repeated many times. Constant appraisal of what one is doing and evaluation of this action with the goal are necessary for achieving one's objective. Salesmanship is the guiding tool which helps to obtain the objective once the course is chosen.*

THUMS, CHARLES WILLIAM, designer, consultant; b. Manitowoc, Wis., Sept. 5, 1945; s. Earl Oscar and Helen Margaret (Rusch) T. B. in Arch., Ariz. State U., 1972. Ptnr., Grafic, Tempe, Ariz., 1967-70; founder, prin. I-Squared Environ. Cons., Tempe, Ariz., 1970-78; designer and cons. design morphology, procedural programming and algorithms, 1978—. Author: (with Jonathan Craig Thums) Tempe's Grand Hotel, 1973, The Rossen House, 1975; (with Daniel Peter Aiello) Shelter and Culture, 1976; contbg. author: Tombstone Planning Guide, 5 vols., 1974. Office: PO Box 3126 Tempe AZ 85280-3126

THURBER, CLEVELAND, JR., trust banker; b. Detroit, Aug. 2, 1925; s. Cleveland and Marie Louise (Palms) T.; m. Elizabeth-Mary Hamilton, June 22, 1946; children: Cleveland III, Elizabeth King Thurber Crawford, David. Student, Purdue U.; B.A., Williams Coll., 1948. Asst. trust officer Comerica Bank-Detroit, 1958-61, trust officer, 1961-63, v.p., 1963-69, sr. v.p., 1969-81, exec. v.p., chief trust officer, 1981-89. Pres. Friends of Grosse Pointe Pub. Libr., 1971-72, Mich. Heart Assn., 1969-74; sec. United Community Svcs., 1968-70; bd. dirs. Cottage Hosp., 1970-94, United Found., 1975-89, Mich. Humane Soc., 1973-89, Elmwood Cemetery, pres., 1995; bd. dirs. Ctr. for Creative Studies, 1976-89, Wm. L. Clements Libr., Ann Arbor. With USMCR, 1943-46. Clubs: Bayview Yacht (Detroit), Yondotega (Detroit), Country (Detroit), Grosse Pointe. Home: 34 Edgemere Rd Grosse Pointe MI 48236-3709 Office: 21 Kercheval Ave Grosse Pointe MI 48236-3601

THURBER, DONALD MACDONALD DICKINSON, public relations counsel; b. Detroit, Feb. 3, 1918; s. Donald MacDonald Dickinson and Fayetta Cecelia (Crowley) T.; m. Margaret Worcester Dudley, June 6, 1964. A.B. magna cum laude, Harvard U., 1940. Pvt. tutor Detroit, 1937-39; house mgr. Cape Playhouse, Dennis, Mass., 1940; exec. sec. youth div. Democratic Nat. Com., 1940; membership sec. Harvard Club, N.Y.C., 1940; project supr. Detroit Council for Youth Service, 1941-43; rep. for Mich., Nat. Found. Infantile Paralysis, 1943-46; sec., adminstr. Wayne County (Mich.) chpt., 1946-50; exec. dir. Gov. Mich. Study Commn. on Deviated Criminal Sex Offenders, 1950-51; exec. sec. Mayor Detroit Com. Rehab. Narcotic Addicts, 1951-53; sec., asst. treas. Mich. Rotary Press, Inc., Detroit, 1953-54; pres. Mich. Rotary Press, Inc., 1954-58; exec. v.p. Pub. Relations Counselors, Inc., Detroit, 1958-61; pres. Pub. Relations Counselors, Inc., 1961—. Bd. dirs. Clan Donald Found., 1994—; mem. Mich. Crippled Children Commn., 1954-58, vice chmn., 1956-58; planning dir. Episcopal Diocese of Mich., 1958-62, mem. exec. council, 1963-66; cons. to Sec. Interior, 1962-68; mem. Nat. Park Trust Fund Bd., 1963-67; bd. regents U. Mich., 1958-63; mem. Mich. Bd. Edn., 1965-67; mem. bd. overseers com. to visit Harvard Coll., 1964-70; mem. Mich. Citizens Com. for Higher Edn. Planning, 1967-69; chmn. Wayne County Community Coll., 1968-72, trustee, 1968-74; mem. Adv. Com. on Higher Edn. Planning in Southeastern Mich., 1970-72; advisor Nat. Trust Hist. Preservation, 1972-78; bd. dirs. Nat. Park Found., 1974-80, founder and historian, 1992—; mem. adv. council to Sec. Commerce, 1976-77; former v.p. Detroit Grand Opera Assn.; mem. adv. com. Detroit Urban League; trustee Clan Donald Lands Trust, Isle of Skye, Scotland, 1979—; trustee, vice chmn. St. Gregory's Abbey Found., Three Rivers, Mich., 1984-92; trustee Mich. Hist. Ctr. Found., vice chmn., 1992—; mem. Mich. Hist. Commn., 1984-87; bd. dirs. Blue Cross-Blue Shield of Mich., 1986-92, chmn. bd., exec. com., 1988-92; Mich. exec. com. United Negro Coll. Fund; bd. dirs. Friends of U. Mich. Libr., 1988—. Mem. Detroit Symphony Orch. Hall Vol. Coun., Detroit Hist. Soc., Mich. Hist. Soc., Friends of Detroit and Grosse Pointe Pub. Librs., Mich. Natural Areas Coun., Mich. Nature Assn., Clan McDonald-U.S.A. (Gt. Lakes commr. emeritus, Mich. commr. emeritus), Ancient and Honorable Artillery Co., Soc. Colonial Wars, Soc. War of 1812, State Soc. of the Cincinnati of Pa., Mil. Order Loyal Legion U.S., Order Founders and Patriots Am., Colonial Order of Acorn, St. Nicholas Soc., Prismatic Club (Detroit), Detroit Club, Harvard Club (Ea. Mich., N.Y.C., Boston). Democrat. Episcopalian. Office: Pub Rels Counselors Inc 10 Rathbone Pl Grosse Pointe MI 48230-1914

THURBER, JOHN ALEXANDER, lawyer; b. Detroit, Nov. 9, 1939; s. John Levington and Mary Anne (D'Agostino) T.; m. Barbara Irene Brown, June 30, 1962; children: John Levington II, Sarah Jeanne. AB in History, U. Mich., 1962, JD, 1965. Bar: Ohio 1965, Mich. 1968. Assoc. Hahn, Loeser and Parks, Cleve., 1965-67, Miller, Canfield, Paddock and Stone, Birmingham, Mich., 1967-73; ptnr. Miller, Canfield, Paddock and Stone, Bloomfield Hills, Mich., 1974—. Treas. Birmingham Community House, 1971-73; pres. Birmingham Village Players, 1983-84; bd. dirs. Oakland Parks Found., Pontiac, Mich., 1984—, pres., 1989-92; mem. capital com. Lighthouse Found. Mem. Otsego Ski Club (Gaylord, Mich.). Avocations: reading, theater, walking, sports. Office: Miller Canfield Paddock & Stone 1400 N Woodward Ave Ste 100 Bloomfield Hills MI 48304-2855

THURBER, PETER PALMS, lawyer; b. Detroit, Mar. 23, 1928; s. Cleveland and Marie Louise (Palms) T.; m. Ellen Bodley Stites, Apr. 16, 1955; children—Edith Bodley, Jane Chenoweth, H. Thomas, Sarah Bartlett. B.A., Williams Coll., 1950; J.D., Harvard U., 1953. Bar: Mich., 1954. Ptnr. Miller, Canfield, Paddock and Stone, Detroit, 1953-93, of counsel, 1994—; trustee McGregor Fund, Detroit, 1979—. Bd. dirs. Detroit Symphony Orch., Inc., 1974-93; trustee Community Found. for Southeastern Mich., 1990—, Coun. Mich. Founds., 1991—. With U.S. Army, 1953-55. Fellow Am. Bar Found.; mem. ABA, Mich. Bar Assn. Roman Catholic. Club: Country of Detroit (Grosse Pointe Farms, Mich.). Avocations: reading;

traveling; athletics. Home: 28 Provencal Rd Grosse Pointe MI 48236-3038 Office: Miller Canfield Paddock & Stone 150 W Jefferson Ave Ste 2500 Detroit MI 48226-4415

THURBER, ROBERT EUGENE, physiologist, researcher; b. Bayshore, N.Y., Oct. 11, 1932; s. Hallett Elliot and Mary Jean (Winkler) T.; m. Barbara Meyer, June 24, 1953 (div. 1982); children: Robert, Joseph, Karl, Michael; m. Linda Boyd, Mar. 4, 1984; stepchildren: Janet, Barbara, Karen, Robert. BS, Holy Cross Coll., Worcester, Mass., 1954; MS, Adelphi U., 1961; PhD, U. Kans., 1964. Rsch. assoc. Brookhaven Nat. Lab., Upton, N.Y., 1956-61; rsch. asst. Iowa State U., Ames, 1961-62; asst. prof. Med. Coll. Va., Richmond, 1964-69; assoc. prof. Jefferson Med. Coll., Phila., 1969-70; prof., chmn. physiology Sch. Medicine East Carolina, Greenville, N.C., 1970-94, prof., 1994—. Contbr. articles to profl. jours. Sgt. U.S. Army, 1954-56, Korea. Predoctoral fellow USPHS, 1962, postdoctoral fellow NEH, 1977. Mem. Am. Physiol. Soc., Assn. Chairmen Depts. Physiology (councilor 1989-91), Am. Heart Assn. (pres. N.C. affiliate 1979), Greenville Country Club, River Bend Country Club. Avocations: music, sailing. Home: 108 Hyde Ct New Bern NC 28562-3724 Office: E Carolina U Sch Medicine Dept Physiology Greenville NC 27858

THURLBECK, WILLIAM MICHAEL, retired pathologist, retired medical educator; b. Johannesburg, South Africa, Sept. 7, 1929; s. William and Enid Muriel (Mears) T.; m. Elizabeth Anne Tippett, Oct. 28, 1955; children—Sarah Margaret, David William, Alison Mary. B.Sc., U. Cape Town, 1951, M.B., Ch.B., 1953. Intern Groote Schuur Hosp., Cape Town, 1955; research fellow resident in pathology Mass. Gen. Hosp. and Harvard U., 1955-61; asst. prof. to prof. pathology McGill U., 1961-73; sr. investigator Midhurst Med. Research Inst. and Royal Postgrad. Med. Sch., Eng., 1973-75; prof. pathology, head U. Man. and Health Scis. Centre, Winnipeg, 1975-80; prof. pathology U. B.C., 1981—, asso. dean research and grad. studies, 1981—, pathologist Children's Hosp., 1985—, acting head med. microbiol., 1992—; examiner in pathology Royal Coll. Physicians and Surgeons Can., 1964-70; mem. McGill Interdisciplinary Com. on Air Pollution, 1967-73; cons. Cardiovascular Research Inst., San Francisco; pulmonary diseases adv. com. Nat. Heart and Lung Inst., 1971-74; task force research planning in environ. health scis. NIH, mem. respiration and applied physiology study sect., 1981—; adv. fellow Indsl. Hygiene Found., Pitts., 1967-71, Paul Dudley White fellow in cardiology, 1960-61; Med. Research Council vis. scientist Oxford (Eng.) U., 1970-71; Schering travelling fellow Canadian Soc. Clin. Investigation, 1971. Author: Chronic Airflow Obstruction in Lung Disease, 1976, The Lung: Structure, Function and Disease, 1978; Contbr. articles to med. jours. Fellow Royal Coll. Physicians, Royal Coll. Pathologists, Am. Coll. Chest Physicians (medalist), Royal Coll. Pathology; mem. Am. Assn. Pathologists, Internat. Acad. Pathology, Path. Soc. Gt. Britain and Ireland, Canadian Soc. Clin. Investigation, Am. Thoracic Soc., Fleischner Soc. Clubs: Rondebosch Old Boys, Pluto. Home: 4094 W 37th Ave, Vancouver, BC Canada V6N 2W7

THURMAN, KAREN L., congresswoman; b. Rapid City, S.D., Jan. 12, 1951; d. Lee Searle and Donna (Altfillisch) Loveland; m. John Patrick Thurman, 1973; children: McLin Searl and Liberty Lee. BA, U. Fla., 1973. Mem. Dunnellon City Council (Fla.), 1974-82; mayor of Dunnellon, 1979-81; mem. Monroe Regional Med. Ctr. Governancy Com.; mem. Comprehensive Plan Tech. Adv. Com.; del. Fla. Dem. Conv.; Dem. Nat. Conv., 1980; mem. Regional Energy Action com.; mem. Fla. State Senate, 1982-1992; mem. 103rd-104th Congress from 5th Fla. dist., 1993—, ranking minority mem. govt. reform & oversight subcom. nat. security, internat. affairs & criminal justice, mem. com. on aging. Recipient Svc. Above Self award Dunnellon C. of C., 1980; Regional Planning Coun. Appreciation for Svc. award. Mem. Dunnellon C. of C. (dir.), Fla. Horseman's Children's Soc. (charter). Episcopalian. Office: US Ho of Reps 130 Cannon House Office Bldg Washington DC 20515-0905*

THURMAN, UMA KARUNA, actress; b. Boston, Apr. 29, 1970; d. Robert and Nena (von Schlebrugge) T.; m. Gary Oldman (div.). Appeared in films Kiss Daddy Good Night, 1987, Johnny Be Good, 1988, Dangerous Liaisons, 1988, The Adventures of Baron Munchausen, 1989, Where the Heart Is, 1990, Henry and June, 1990, Final Analysis, 1992, Jennifer Eight, 1992, Mad Dog and Glory, 1993, Even Cowgirls Get the Blues, 1993, Pulp Fiction, 1994 (Acad. award nom. Best Supporting Actress), A Month By the Lake, 1995; TV movies include Robin Hood, 1991. Office: care CAA 9830 Wilshire Blvd Beverly Hills CA 90212*

THURMAN, WILLIAM GENTRY, medical research foundation executive, pediatric hematology and oncology physician, educator; b. Jacksonville, Fla., July 1, 1928; s. Horace Edward and Theodosia (Mitchell) T.; m. Peggy Lou Brown, Aug. 11, 1949 (div. 1978); children—Andrew E., Margaret Anne, Mary Allison; m. Gabrielle Anne Martin, Jan. 22, 1980; 1 step child, Stephanie Anne. B.S., U. N.C., 1949; M.S., Tulane U. Sch. Pub. Health, 1960; M.D.C.M., McGill U., Montreal,, 1954. Prof. pediatrics Cornell U. Sch. Medicine, N.Y.C., 1962-64; prof. pediatrics U. Va., Charlottesville, 1964-73; dean sch. medicine Tulane U., New Orleans, 1973-75; provost Health Scis. Ctr. U. Oklahoma, Oklahoma City, 1975-80; pres., chief exec. officer Okla. Med. Research Found., Oklahoma City, 1979—; sr. cons. pediatrics Surgeon Gen. USAF, Washington, 1964—; mem. Diet and Nutrition Study Com., Nat. Cancer Inst., Bethesda, Md., 1969—, Profl. Edn. Com., Am. Cancer Soc., N.Y.C., 1973—. Author: (with others) Bone Tumors in Children, 1963, Pediatric Malignant Disease, 1964; contbr. articles to profl. jours. Bd. dirs. United Way, Oklahoma City, 1977—, chmn., 1994, Community Found., Oklahoma City, 1975—, ARC, Oklahoma City, 1992—; bd. dirs. C. of C., 1984—, chmn. 1995. Served with U.S. Army, 1944-46, ETO. Markle scholar, 1959-64. Fellow Am. Acad. Pediatrics (dir. 1969-72); mem. Am. Pediatric Soc., Soc. Pediatric Rsch. (councillor 1971-75), Soc. Mil. Cons., Assn. Ind. Rsch. Insts. (pres. 1985-87), Oklahoma City C. of C. (dir. 1979, chmn. 1994-95), Alpha Omega Alpha. Baptist. Club: Petroleum. Avocations: physical fitness; sailing. Home: 1213 Larchmont Ln Oklahoma City OK 73116

THURMON, THEODORE FRANCIS, medical educator; b. Baton Rouge, Oct. 20, 1937; s. Theodore Francis and Gertrude Wilhemena (Arnette) T.; m. Virginia Ruth Strange, Sept. 1, 1961 (div. Oct. 1975); children: Penelope, Suzanna; m. Susonne Annette Ursin, Aug. 8, 1981 (div. Aug. 1992); children: Sarah Eileen, Amanda Aislinn; m. Suzanne Greenwood, Sept. 2, 1992. BS, La. State U., Baton Rouge, 1960; MD, La. State U., New Orleans, 1962. Diplomate Am. Bd. Pediatrics, Am. Bd. Med. Genetics. Commd. ensign USNR, 1957; transferred to USN, 1957, advanced through grades to lt. comdr., 1967; intern naval hosp. Pensacola, Fla., 1962-63; resident in pediatrics naval hosp. Phila., 1963-65, trainee in cytogenetics St. Christopher's Hosp., 1964-65; asst. cardiology naval hosp. St. Albans, N.Y., 1965-67; resigned USN, 1968; fellow in med. genetics Johns Hopkins Hosp., Balt., 1968-69; asst. prof. La. State U. Med. Ctr., New Orleans, 1969-72, assoc. prof., 1972-78, prof., 1978-86; prof. La. State U. Med. Ctr., Shreveport, 1986—. Author: Rare Genetic Diseases, 1974, Medical Genetics Primer, 1995; contbr. articles to med. jours. Active birth defects ctr. Nat. Found./March of Dimes, New Orleans, 1969-81, La. Bd. Regents, New Orleans, 1982, La. Dept. Health, New Orleans, 1984—, La. Cancer & Lung Trust Fund, New Orleans, 1985-86. Fellow Am. Coll. Med. Genetics, Am. Acad. Pediat.; mem. AAAS, Am. Genetic Assn., Am. Soc. Human Genetics, Am. Statis. Assn., Assn. Profs. Human or Med. Genetics, La. Med. Soc., N.Y. Acad. Scis. Home: 1732 Willow Point Dr Shreveport LA 71119-4108 Office: La State U Med Sch Pediat-Genetics 1501 Kings Hwy Shreveport LA 71103-4228

THURMOND, STROM, senator; b. Edgefield, S.C., Dec. 5, 1902; s. John William and Eleanor Gertrude (Strom) T.; m. Jean Crouch, Nov. 7, 1947 (dec. Jan. 1960); m. Nancy Moore, Dec. 22, 1968; children: Nancy Moore (dec.), J. Strom, Jr., Juliana Gertrude, Paul Reynolds. B.S., Clemson Coll., 1923; 14 hon. degrees. Bar: S.C. 1930. Tchr. S.C. schs., 1923-29; city atty., county atty., supt. edn. Edgefield County, 1929-33; state senator, 1933-38, circuit judge, 1938-46, gov. of S.C., 1947-51; chmn. So. Govs. Conf., 1950; practiced in Aiken, S.C., 1951-55; U.S. senator from S.C., 1955—, pres. pro tem 104th Congress; Del. Nat. Democratic Conv., 1932, 36, 48, 52, 56, 60; chmn. S.C. dels., armed svcs. com., Judiciary Subcom. on antitrust bus. rts. and competition; mem. Dem. Nat. Com., 1948, Vets. Affairs/Sen. Rep. Policy Com.; States Rights candidate for Pres. U.S., 1948; del. Nat. Republican Conv., 1968, 72, 76. Bd. dirs. Ga.-Carolina council Boy Scouts Am. Served with AUS; attached to 82d Airborne Div. for invasion 1942-46, Europe; maj. gen. Res. Decorated Legion of Merit with oak leaf cluster, Bronze Star with V, Purple Heart, Croix de Guerre France; Cross of Order of Crown Belgium; others; recipient Congl. Medal Honor Soc. Nat. Patriots award, 1974, Presdl. Medal of Freedom, 1992. Mem. S.C. (past v.p.), ABA, Clemson Coll. Alumni Assn. (past pres.), also numerous def., vets., civic, fraternal and farm orgns. Baptist. Office: US Senate 217 Russell Senate Office Bldg Washington DC 20510*

THURSBY, JERRY GILBERT, economics educator, consultant; b. Camp Le Jeune, N.C., Aug. 6, 1947; s. Gilbert Earl and Mary Kathleen (Bailey) T.; m. Marie Sloan Currie, Mar. 11, 1972; children: James, Mary. AB, U. N.C., 1969, PhD, 1975. Asst. prof. Syracuse (N.Y.) U., 1975-78; from asst. to assoc. prof. Ohio State U., Columbus, 1978-88; prof. Purdue U., West Lafayette, Ind., 1988—. Contbr. articles to profl. jours. With U.S. Army, 1969-71. Home: 144 Creighton Rd West Lafayette IN 47906 Office: Dept Econs Kran Bldg Purdue Univ West Lafayette IN 47907

THURSTON, ALICE JANET, former college president; b. Milw., Mar. 20, 1916; d. Karl J. and Nellie Ann (Smith) Stouffer; children: Anne, Robert. B.A., Denison U., 1937; MA, Northwestern U., 1938; PhD, George Washington U., 1960. Mem. faculty dept. psychology, counselor, dean students Montgomery Coll., Takoma Park, Md., 1950-65; dir. counseling Met. Campus, Cuyahoga Community Coll., Cleve., 1965-66; dean of students Western Campus, Cuyahoga Community Coll., 1966-67; vis. lectr. U. Ill., 1968-69; dir. Inst. Research and Student Services Met. Jr. Coll. Dist., Kansas City, Mo., 1969-71; pres. Garland Jr. Coll., Boston, 1971-75, Los Angeles Valley Coll., Van Nuys, Calif., 1975-81; lectr. Pepperdine U., L.A., 1978-81, Calif. State U., Worthridge, 1984-95; mem. adv. com. grad. program student affairs Calif. State U., Northridge. Author works in field. Bd. dirs. New Dir. for Youth, Van Nuys, Calif.; mem. ministerial search com. Unitarian Ch., Studio City, Calif., 1991-92, chair caring com., 1994—. Recipient Disting. Alumnae award Denison U., 1987, Humanitarian award Juvenile Justice Connection Project, 1987. Mem. Kappa Alpha Theta, Mortar Bd. Democrat. Unitarian. Home: 13156 Crewe St North Hollywood CA 91605-4727

THURSTON, DAVID E., lawyer, general counsel; b. Hartford, Conn., Apr. 16, 1957; s. Robert Charles and Carol Jean (Demson) T.; m. Gaye Winifred Hennemuth, Oct. 3, 1987; children: Perry Bishop, Demson Collin. BA, George Washington U., 1979; JD, Cath. U., 1982. Bar: Tex. 1982, Pa. 1984; lic. real estate broker, Pa. Assoc. Johnson, Bromberg & Leeds, Dallas, 1982-84; assoc. Morgan, Lewis & Bockius, Phila., 1984-85, N.Y.C., 1985; assoc. Shea & Gould, N.Y.C., 1986-87; sr. v.p. nat. and internat. sales, gen. counsel The Binswanger Co., Phila., 1987-96; pres. Legal Realty, Inc., Wayne, Pa., 1996—. Recipient AmJur award in property Lawyers Co-op Pub. Co. Mem. ABA, Pa. Bar Assn., Tex. Bar Assn., Delaware County Bar Assn., Delaware Valley Bd. Realtors. Republican. Avocations: bicycling, swimming, golfing, computers. Office: Legal Realty Inc 125 Strafford Ave Ste 300 Wayne PA 19087

THURSTON, DONALD ALLEN, broadcasting executive; b. Gloucester, Mass., Apr. 2, 1930; s. Joseph Allen and Helen Ruth (Leach) T.; m. Oralie Alice Lane, Sept. 9, 1951; children: Corydon Leach, Carolie Lane. Grad., Mass. Radio and Telegraph, 1949; HHD (hon.), North Adams (Mass.) State Coll., 1977; LHD (hon.), Emerson Coll., 1995. Announcer, engr. Sta. WTWN, St. Johnsbury, Vt., 1949-52; v.p., gen. mgr. Sta. WIKE, Newport, Vt., 1952-60; v.p., treas., gen. mgr. Sta. WMNB, North Adams, 1960-66; pres., treas. Berkshire Broadcasting Co., Inc., North Adams, 1966—; bd. dirs. Broadcast Capital Fund, Inc., 1980-96, chmn. bd., 1981-89; dir. Berkshire Bank and Trust Co., 1967-85, Broadcast Music, Inc., N.Y.C., 1990—, chmn. bd., 1994—. Pres. No. Berkshire Indsl. Devel. Corp., 1965-67; commr. Mass. Cmty. Antenna TV Commn., 1972-74; trustee North Adams State Coll., 1991—, vice chmn. bd. trustees, 1993-96, chmn., 1996—. Recipient Laymen's award Vt. Tchrs. Assn., 1958; Laymen's award Mass. Tchrs. Assn., 1962; Abe Lincoln Merit award So. Baptist Radio and TV Commn., 1975; named Man of Yr. Vt. Assn. Broadcasters, 1978. Mem. North Adams C. of C. (Hayden award 1967, pres. 1964-67), Nat. Assn. Broadcasters (dir. 1965-69, 73-77, chmn. radio 1976-77, chmn. bd., chmn. exec. com. 1977-79, Disting. Svc. award 1980), Mass. Broadcasters Assn. (pres. 1964, Disting. Svc. award 1964, 71, 78), Taconic Golf Club (Williamston, Mass.; bd. dirs. 1975-89). Republican. Methodist. Office: 466 Curran Hwy North Adams MA 01247-3901 *My goals have been to better my community, profession and life in general because I was a positive participant, and to provide independence, a sense of responsibility and a love of humanity for my family.*

THURSTON, GEORGE BUTTE, mechanical and biomedical engineering educator; b. Austin, Tex., Oct. 8, 1924; s. Rudolph D. and Olivia Ruth (Lester) T.; m. Carol A. McWharter, Apr. 5, 1947; children—John Douglas, Mary Elizabeth. B.S., U. Tex., Austin, 1944, M.A., 1948, Ph.D., 1952. Registered profl. engr., Tex. Supr. hydroacoustics sect. Def. Research Lab., U. Tex., Austin, 1949-52; asst. prof. physics U. Wyo., Laramie, 1952-53, U. Ark., Fayetteville, 1953-54; physicist Naval Ordnance Test Sta., Inyokern, Calif., 1954-55; assoc. prof. Okla. State U., Stillwater, 1954-59; research physicist U. Mich., Ann Arbor, 1958-59; prof. Okla. State U., Ann Arbor, 1959-68; vis. scientist Centre de Recherche sur les Macromolecules, Strasbourg, France, 1963-64; prof. mech. engring. and biomed. engring. U. Tex., Austin, 1968—; vis. prof. Helmholtz Inst. fur Biomedizinische Technik, Aachen, West Germany, 1975-76; cons. for govt., industry. Contbr. articles to profl. jours. Recipient Brown U. Calculus prize, 1942; Alexander von Humboldt Found. Sr. U.S. Scientist award, 1975; NSF faculty fellow, 1963-64; numerous grants. Fellow Am. Phys. Soc., Acoustical Soc. Am.; mem. ASME, Soc. Rheology, Internat. Soc. Biorheology, Brit. Soc. Rheology, Sigma Xi, Sigma Pi Sigma. Home: 1000 Madrone Rd Austin TX 78746-4320 Office: U Tex Dept Mech Engring Austin TX 78712

THURSTON, GEORGE R., lumber company executive; b. 1942. BS, Northwestern U., 1965, MBA, 1966. With Cummins Engine Co., 1966-78; exec. v.p. fin. and treas. North Pacific Lumber Co., Portland, 1987—. Office: North Pacific Lumber Co 1505 SE Gideon St Portland OR 97202-2441*

THURSTON, MORRIS ASHCROFT, lawyer; b. Logan, Utah, May 25, 1943; s. Morris Alma and Barbara (Ashcroft) T.; m. Dawna Lyn Parrett, Sept. 10, 1966; children: Morris III, David, Ashley, Tyson. BA, Brigham Young U., 1967; JD, Harvard U., 1970. Bar: Calif. 1971, U.S. Dist. Ct. (cen. dist.) Calif. 1971, U.S. Supreme Ct. 1978. Assoc. Latham & Watkins, Los Angeles, 1970-77, ptnr., 1978—; jud. arbitrator Orange County Superior Ct., Calif., 1980—. Mem. Calif. Bar Assn., Orange County Bar Assn., Assn. Bus. Trial Lawyers. Republican. Mormon. Avocations: basketball, tennis, lit. Home: 9752 Crestview Cir Orange CA 92667-3204 Office: Latham & Watkins 650 Town Center Dr Ste 2000 Costa Mesa CA 92626-1925*

THURSTON, STEPHEN JOHN, pastor; b. Chgo., July 20, 1952; s. John Lee and Ruth (Hall) T.; m. Joyce DeVonne Hand, June 18, 1977; children: Stephen John II, Nicole D'Vaugh, Teniece Rael, Christian Avery Elijah. BA in Religion, Bishop Coll., 1975; Hon. degree, Chgo. Baptist Inst., 1986. Copastor New Covenant Missionary Bapt. Ch., Chgo., 1975-79, pastor, 1979—; corr. sec. Nat. Bapt. Conv. Am., mem. exec. com. Christian Edn. Congress; exec. v.p. Ill. Nat. Bapt. State Conv.; mem. Northwood River Dist. Bapt. Assn.; lectr. various orgns.; instr. New Covenant Bapt. Ch., Fellowship Bapt. Ch. Mng. editor The Crier (Nat. Bapt. Conv. Am. Evangelical Bd. quarterly pub.). Co-chmn. religious affairs div. Operation People United to Save Humanity (PUSH); bd. dirs. nat. alumni assn. Bishop Coll.; active NAACP; trustee, fin. chmn. Chgo. Bapt. Inst.; mem. Campus Crusade for Christ, Here's Life Black Am. Mem. Broadcast Ministers Alliance, Bapt. Ministers Conf. Chgo. (Ministerial Pioneer award). Club: Bishop Coll. (Chgo.). Office: Nat baptist Conv Am 777 S R L Thornton Fwy Ste 205 Dallas TX 75203-2900

THURSWELL, GERALD ELLIOTT, lawyer; b. Detroit, Feb. 4, 1944; s. Harry and Lilyan (Zeitlin) T.; m. Lynn Satovsky, Sept. 17, 1967 (div. Aug. 1978); children: Jennifer, Lawrence; m. Judith Linda Bendix, Sept. 2, 1978; children: Jeremy, Lindsey. LLB with distinction, Wayne State U., 1967. Bar: Mich. 1968, N.Y. 1984, D.C. 1986, Colo. 1990, Ill. 1992, U.S. Dist. Ct. (ea. dist.) Mich. 1968, U.S. Ct. Appeals (7th cir.) 1968, U.S. Supreme Ct., 1994. Student asst. to U.S. atty. Ea. Dist. Mich., Detroit, 1966; assoc. Zwerdling, Miller, Klimist & Maurer, Detroit, 1967-68; sr. ptnr. Thurswell, Chayet & Weiner, Southfield, Mich., 1968—; arbitrator Am. Arbitration Assn., Detroit, 1969—; mediator Wayne County Cir. Ct., Mich., 1983—, Oakland County Cir. Ct. Mich., 1984—, also facilitator, 1991; twp. atty. Royal Oak Twp., Mich., 1982—; lectr. Oakland County Bar Assn. People's Law Sch., 1988. Pres. Powder Horn Estates Subdiv. Assn., West Bloomfield, Mich., 1975, United Fund, West Bloomfield, 1976. Arthur F. Lederle scholar Wayne State U. Law Sch., Detroit, 1964, grad. profl. scholar Wayne State U. Law Sch., 1965, 66. Mem. Mich. Bar Assn. (investigator/arbitrator grievance bd., atty. discipline bd., chmn. hearing panel), Mich. Trial Lawyers Assn. (legis. com. on govtl. immunit, 1984), ATLA (treas. Detroit met. chpt. 1986-87, v.p. 1989-90, pres. 1991-93), Detroit Bar Assn. (lawyer referral com., panel pub. adv. com. judicial candidates), Oakland County Bar Assn. Clubs: Wabeek Country (Bloomfield Hills), Skyline (Southfield, Mich.). Home: 1781 Golf Ridge Dr S Bloomfield Hills MI 48302-1733 Office: Thurswell Chayet & Weiner 1000 Town Ctr Ste 500 Southfield MI 48075-1221

THURSZ, DANIEL, retired service organization executive, consultant; b. Casablanca, Morocco, Jan. 25, 1929; came to U.S., 1941; s. Jonathan and Franka (Gutlas) T.; m. Hadassah Neulander, Feb. 8, 1953; children—Deborah Thursz Bleiweis, David, Deena Thursz Klopman, Tamar Thursz Trulano. B.A., Queens Coll., 1949; M.S.W., Catholic U. Am., 1955, D.S.W., 1960; L.H.D. (hon.), U. Md., 1977, Balt. Hebrew U., 1990. Asso. prof. social welfare Sch. Social Service, Cath. U. Am., 1961-63; Assoc. prof. social welfare Sch. Social Work, U. Md., 1963-65; nat. asso. dir. VISTA, OEO, Washington, 1965-67; dean, prof. U. Md. Sch. Social Work and Community Planning, 1967-77; exec. v.p. B'nai B'rith Internat., Washington, 1977-87; pres., CEO, Nat. Coun. on Aging Inc., Washington, 1988-95, pres. emeritus, 1995—; Cardinal O'Boyle prof. social work Catholic U. Am.; cons. social welfare agys., mem. nat. and state commns. social welfare; internat. v.p. Internat. Fedn. Aging; bd. dirs. Sage Pubs., Beverly Hills, Calif. Author books, monographs, articles in field.; Co-editor: Meeting Human Needs, Vol. I, 1975, Vol. II, 1977, Vol. III, Reaching People, 1978, Vol. IV, Reaching the Aged, 1979. Mem. bd. visitors U. N.C., Asheville. Served with AUS, 1951-53. Alvin Johnson scholar. Mem. Acad. Certified Social Workers, Md. Welfare Conf. (pres. 1969-71), Nat. Assn. Social Workers (1st v.p. 1973-75), Conf. Jewish Communal Service (exec. com., pres. 1988-90), B'nai B'rith (hon. exec. v.p.). Jewish. Home and Office: 8605 Carlynn Dr Bethesda MD 20817-4310

THYDEN, JAMES ESKEL, diplomat, educator, UN administrator; b. L.A., Apr. 10, 1939; s. Eskel A. and Mildred Aileene (Rock) T.; m. Patricia Irene Kelsey, Dec. 15, 1959; children: Teresa Lynn, Janice Kay, James Blaine. BA in Biology, Pepperdine U., 1961; MA in Scandinavian Area Studies, U. Wash., 1992. Cert. secondary tchr., Calif., Wash. Tchr. Gompers Jr. High Sch., L.A., 1962-64; fgn. svc. officer U.S. Dept. State, Washington, 1964-90; rschr. U. Wash., Seattle, 1991-93; exec. dir. Seattle chpt. UN Assn., 1993-96; travel lectr. Cunard Lines, Royal Viking Sun, 1995. Editor govt. report, ann. human rights report, 1983-86; author, editor in-house govt. reports, documents. Dir. Office of Human Rights, 1983-86; counselor Embassy for Polit. Affairs, Am. Embassy, Oslo, Norway, 1986-90. Named Outstanding Young Man Am., 1969, Alumnus of Yr., Pepperdine U., 1984. Mem. Am. Fgn. Svc. Assn., World Affairs Coun. Seattle. Avocations: travel, reading, gardening. Home: 5631 153rd Pl SW Edmonds WA 98026-4239

THYEN, RONALD JOSEPH, furniture company executive; b. New Albany, Ind., 1937. BS, Notre Dame U., 1959. With Kimball Internat. Inc., Jasper, Ind., 1959—, exec. v.p. office furniture divsn., 1977-92; sr. exec. v.p. ops. officer, 1992—; also bd. dirs. Kimball Internat. Inc., Jasper, Ind. Home: 1407 W 31st St Jasper IN 47546-3551 Office: Kimball Internat Inc 1600 Royal St Jasper IN 47549-1001

TIAHRT, W. TODD, congressman, former state senator; b. Vermillion, S.D., June 15, 1951; s. Wilbur E. and Sara Ella Marcine (Steele) T.; m. Vicki Lyn Holland, Aug. 14, 1976; children: Jessica, John, Luke. Student, S.D. Sch. Mines & Tech., Rapid City, 1969-72; BA, Evangel Coll., 1975; MBA, S.W. Mo. State U., 1989. Property estimator Crawford & Co., Springfield, Mo., 1975-78; project engr. Zenith Electronics, Springfield, 1978-81; cost engr. Boeing, Wichita, Kans., 1981-94; proposal mgr. Boeing, Wichita, 1991-94; state senator State of Kans., Topeka, 1995—; mem. 104th Congress from 4th Kans. dist. Washington; chmn. 4th dist. Rep. party, 1990-92; exec. com. Kans. Rep. party, 1990-92, nat. security com., sci. com. Mem. Pachyderm (bd. dirs. 1991-92), Delta Sigma Phi. Republican. Home: 1329 Amity Goddard KS 67052-9999 Office: House Office Bldg 1319 Longworth Washington DC 20515-1604*

TIAN, GANG, mathematics educator. BS, Nanking U., 1982; MS, Beijing U., 1984; PhD, Harvard U., 1988. Prof. math. NYU Courant Inst. Math. and Sci., N.Y.C., 1992-95; prof. math. MIT, Cambridge, 1995—. Recipient Alan T. Waterman award NSF, 1994, Velben Geometry prize Am. Math. Soc., 1996. Office: MIT Dept Math Rm 2-172 77 Massachusetts Ave Cambridge MA 02139

TIANO, ANTHONY STEVEN, television producer, book publishing executive; b. Santa Fe, Mar. 27, 1941; s. Joseph A. and Marian (Adlesperger) T.; m. Kathleen O'Brien, Dec. 29, 1972; children: Mark A., A. Steven. BA, U. N.Mex., 1969, MA, 1971; LittD (hon.), Calif. Sch. Profl. Psychology, 1985. Dir. programming Sta. KNME-TV U. N.Mex., Albuquerque, 1968-72; sta. mgr. Sta. WHA-TV U. Wis., Madison, 1972-76; exec. dir. Sta. KETC-TV, St. Louis, 1976-78; pres., CEO KQED, Inc., San Francisco, 1978-93; chmn., CEO Santa Fe Ventures, Inc., San Francisco, 1993—. Vice-chair bd. dirs. Calif. Sch. Profl. Psychology, San Francisco, 1985-90. Mem. Nat. Assn. Pub. TV Stas. (vice chair bd. dirs. 1986). Office: Santa Fe Ventures 582 Market St Ste 1300 San Francisco CA 94104

TIBBETTS, PAMELA LEE, health facility administrator. Pres. Riverside Med. Ctr., Mpls. Office: Fairview Riverside Medical Ctr 2450 Riverside Ave Minneapolis MN 55454-1450*

TIBBITTS, THEODORE WILLIAM, horticulturist, researcher; b. La Crosse, Wis., Apr. 10, 1929; s. John Wilson and Vivian Sophia (Elver) T.; m. Allison Lou Mahan, Aug. 25, 1956 (dec. June 1975); children: Scott, Tia Anne; m. Mary Florence Olmsted, June 22, 1985. BS, U. Wis., 1950, MS, 1952, PhD, 1953. Asst prof., assoc. prof., and prof. U. Wis., Madison, 1955-96, emeritus prof., 1996—, dir. Biotron, 1987-92; sr. rsch. engr. N.Am. Aviation, L.A., 1965-66; cons. Johnson Space Ctr., Manned Spaceflight Ctr., Apollo Flights, 1969-70; vis. prof. U. Guelph, Ont., Can., 1981; mem. NASA Controlled Ecol. Life Support System Discipline Working Group, Washington, 1989—. Author: Controlled Environment Guidelines for Plant Research, 1979; co-author: Growth Chamber Manual, 1978, 1995; contbr. articles to sci. jours. Elder Covenant Presbyn. Ch., Madison, 1961-65. With U.S. Army, 1953-55. Recipient Rsch. award Dept. Sci. and Indsl. Rsch., New Zealand, 1981. Fellow Am. Soc. Hort. Sci. (assoc. editor, Marion Meadows award); mem. AAAS, Am. Inst. Biol. Sci., Internat. Hort. Soc., Potato Assn. Am., Am. Soc. Gravitational and Space Biology, Am. Soc. Plant Physiologists, Internat. Commn. of Illumination (CIE). Achievements include development of guidelines for controlled environment research, optimizing growth of potatoes for life support in space, patent for use of light-emitting diodes for irradiation of plants; establishment of causal factors for physiological disorders in vegetable species; plant experiment on Biosatellite flights 1966-67, growth chamber experiments on shuttle flight, 1992, 93, 94, 95. Office: U Wis Dept Hort Madison WI 53706

TIBBLE, DOUGLAS CLAIR, lawyer; b. Joliet, Ill., May 26, 1952. BA, DePaul U., 1974; JD, Syracuse U., 1977, MPA, 1978. Bar: Ill., U.S. Dist. Ct. (no. dist.) Ill., U.S. Ct. Appeals (7th cir.), U.S. Supreme Ct. Ptnr. Keck, Mahin & Cate, Oakbrook Terrace, Ill., 1996—. Mem. ABA, DuPage County Bar Assn., Chgo. Bar Assn. Office: Keck Mahin and Cate One MidAmerica Ctr Ste 1000 Oakbrook Terrace IL 60181

TICE, CAROL HOFF, middle school educator, consultant; b. Ashville, N.C., Oct. 6, 1931; d. Amos H. and Fern (Irvin) Hoff; m. (div.); children:

Karin E., Jonathan H. BS, Manchester Coll., North Manchester, Ind., 1954; MEd, Cornell U., 1955. Cert. tchr., Mich., N.Y., N.J. Tchr. Princeton (N.J.) Schs., 1955-60; tchr. Ann Arbor (Mich.) Schs., 1964—; dir. intergenerational programs Inst. for Study Children and Families Eastern Mich. U., Ypsilanti, 1985—; founder, pres. Lifespan Resources, Inc., Ann Arbor, 1979—; commr. U.S. Nat. Commn. Internat. Yr. of the Child, Washington, 1979-81; del. to White House Conf. on Aging, 1995. Innovator; program, Tch. Learning Intergenerational Communities, 1971; author: Guide Books and articles, Community of Caring, 1980; co-producer, Film, What We Have, 1976 (award, Milan, Italy Film Festival 1982). Trustee Blue Lake Fine Arts Camp, Twin Lake, Mich., 1975—; del. White House Conf. on Aging, 1995. Recipient Program Innovation award Mich. Dept. Edn., 1974-80, C.S. Mott Found. award, 1982, Nat. Found. Improvement in Edn. award, Washington, 1986, Disting. Alumni award Manchester Coll., 1979, A+ Break the Mold award U.S. Sec. of Edn., 1992; Ford Found. fellow, Ithaca, N.Y., 1955. Mem. AAUW (agt. 1979), Generations United (Pioneer award 1989), Optimist Club. Democrat. Presbyterian. Office: Scarlett MS 3300 Lorraine St Ann Arbor MI 48108-1970

TICE, DOUGLAS OSCAR, JR., federal judge; b. Lexington, N.C., May 2, 1933; s. Douglas Oscar Sr. and Lila Clayton (Wright) T.; m. Janet N. Capps, Feb. 28, 1959 (div. Sept. 1976); children: Douglas Oscar III, Janet E.; m. Beverley Carole Black, Aug. 8, 1982 (div. Apr. 1995). BS, U. N.C., 1955, JD, 1957. Bar: N.C. 1957, U.S. Ct. Appeals (4th cir.) 1964, Va. 1970, U.S. Dist. ct. (ea. dist.) Va. 1976, U.S. Bankruptcy Ct. (ea. dist.) Va. 1976. Exec. sec. N.C. Jud. Coun., Raleigh, 1958-59; assoc. Baucom & Adams, Raleigh, 1959-61; trial atty. Office Dist. Coun., IRS, Richmond, Va., 1961-70; corp. atty. Carlton Industries, Inc., Richmond, 1970-75; ptnr. Hubard, Tice, Marchant & Samuels, P.C., Richmond, 1975-87; judge U.S. Bankruptcy Ct., Richmond, Norfolk, Alexandria, Va., 1987—. Vice pres. Richmond Pub. Forum, 1976-80, com. chmn. Richmond Forum, Inc., 1986—; past pres. Richmond Civil War Roundtable, mem., 1965—; bd. dirs. Epilepsy Assn. Va., Inc., 1976-87. Capt. USAR, 1957-66. Mem. ABA, Va. Bar Assn., City of Richmond Bar Assn., Am. Bankruptcy Inst., Nat. Conf. Bankruptcy Judges, Old Dominion Sertoma (pres. Richmond chpt. 1967). Home: 2037 W Grace St Richmond VA 23220-2003 Office: US Bankruptcy Ct 1100 East Main St #341 Richmond VA 23219

TICE, GEORGE A(NDREW), photographer; b. Newark, Oct. 13, 1938; s. William S. and Margaret T. (Robertson) T.; m. Joanna Blaylock, 1958; m. Marie Tremmel, 1960; children: Christopher, Loretta, Lisa, Lynn, Jennifer. Instr. photography New Sch. Social Research, 1970—. One-man shows, Witkin Gallery, 1970, Met. Mus. Art, 1972, group shows include, Whitney Mus. Am. Art, 1974, Mus. Modern Art, 1979; represented in permanent collections, Mus. Modern Art, Met. Mus. Art, Art Inst. Chgo., Bibliothèque Nationale, Nihon U., Tokyo; books include Fields of Peace, 1970, Goodbye River, Goodbye, 1971, Paterson, 1972, Seacoast Maine, 1973, George A. Tice Photographs, 1953-73, 1975, Urban Landscapes, 1975, Artie Van Blarcum, 1977, Urban Romantic, 1982, Lincoln, 1984, Hometowns, 1988, Stone Walls, Grey Skies, 1991. Served with USN, 1956-59. Recipient Grand prix for best photography book of Year Arles, France, 1973; Guggenheim Found. fellow, 1973-74; Nat. Endowment for Arts fellow, 1973—; Nat. Mus. Photography and Bradford and Ilkley Community Coll. (Eng.) fellow, 1990-91. Address: 323 Gill Ln Apt 9B Iselin NJ 08830-2825

TICE, RAPHAEL DEAN, army officer; b. Topeka, Kans., Dec. 4, 1927; s. Arthur Taylor and Mamie (McDonald) T.; m. Eunice Miriam Suddarth, Dec. 23, 1946; children: Karen Ann Tice Claterbos, William Dean. B.S. in Mil. Sci., U. Md., 1963; M.S. in Bus. Adminstrn, George Washington U., 1970. Served as enlisted man U.S. Army, 1946-47; commd. 2d lt., 1947, advanced through grades to lt. gen., 1981; platoon leader and co. comdr. 1st Inf. div., W.Ger., 1949-52; co. comdr., regimental adj. 8th Inf. div., 1955-56; tng. advisor Vietnam, 1956-57; mem. staff Office of Dep. chief of Staff for Personnel, Dept. Army, 1960-63; chief personnel mgmt. div. Office of Under Sec. of Army, 1963-64; plans Officer So. Command, Panama, 1965-67; dep. brigade comdr. 3d Brigade, 4th Inf. Div., 1967; comdr. 2d Bn., 12th Inf. of 25th Inf. div., Vietnam, 1968; exec. for personnel procurement Office of Sec. Def. for Manpower and Res. Affairs, 1968-69; comdr. 1st Brigade, 1st Inf. div., 1970, chief of staff, 1971; dep. dir. mil. personnel mgmt. Dept. Army, 1972-73; comdg. gen. Berlin Brigade, 1974-76; dep. chief of staff personnel U.S. Army Europe, 1976-77; comdg. gen. 3d. Inf. div., 1977-79; dep. asst. sec. def. for mil. personnel and force mgmt. Dept. Def., 1979-85; exec. dir. Nat. Recreation and Park Assn., 1986—; spl. adviser Pres.'s Council on Phys. Fitness and Sports. Decorated Silver Star, Legion of Merit with 2 oak leaf clusters, Air medal with V and 7 oak leaf clusters, Bronze Star with V, Vietnam Cross of Gallantry with Palm, Purple Heart, Def. Disting. Service medal, Army Disting. Service medal. Mem. Assn. U.S. Army, Am. Chess Found. (hon. pres.). Home: 8655 Gateshead Rd Alexandria VA 22309-4042 Office: Nat Recreation & Park Assn 2775 S Quincy St Ste 300 Arlington VA 22206-2236

TICER, PATRICIA, state senator; m. Jack Ticer; 4 children. Grad., Sweet Briar Coll. Councilwoman City of Alexandria, Va., 1982-84, vice mayor, 1984-90, appointed mayor, 1991-92, mayor, 1992-95; state senator State of Va., 1995—, mem. agrl., conservation & natural resources com., transp. com., rehab. & social svcs. com., local govt. com., 1995—; chair COG Transp. Planning Bd., chmn. bd. dirs., 1994; mem. coordinating com. Woodrow Wilson Bridge; bd. dirs. No. Va. Transp. Commn., chmn., 1994; bd. dirs. Transp. Coordinating Coun. Founding mem. Early Childhood Devel. Commn., No. Va. Housing Coalition, Alexandria Commn. on the Arts; mem. Govs. Coun. on Child Care and Early Childhood Programs; mem. adv. coun. Alexandria Symphony Orch.; active No. Va. AIDS Mins. Mem. Nat. Assn. Regional Couns. (pres. 1994-95). Office: Rm 2007 Cith Hall 301 King St Alexandria VA 22314-3211

TICHENOR, CHARLES BECKHAM, III, federal agency computer specialist, consultant; b. Balt., Mar. 10, 1950; s. Charles Beckham II and Suzanne Nelson (Stevens) T.; m. Alison P. Walton, May 29, 1971; 1 child, Charles Beckham IV. BS in Mktg., Ohio State U., 1972; MBA, Va. Tech., 1990. Cert. function point specialist. Asst. prodn. supr. Champale Products, Norfolk, Va., 1977-80; ops. rsch. analyst IRS, Washington, 1989-93. Lt. col. USAR, ret. Mem. Mensa. Roman Catholic. Avocations: Black Belt Tae Kwon Do, amateur astronomer. Home: 6207 Cardinal Brook Ct Springfield VA 22152 Office: IRS 1111 Constitution Ave NW Washington DC 20037 also: Devel Support Ctr Inc 1625 Lindhurst Dr Ste 100 Elm Grove WI 53122

TICHENOR, DONALD KEITH, trade association administrator; b. Battle Creek, Mich., Apr. 14, 1937; s. Don Leighton and Sarah Sophia (Parry) T.; m. Dolores B.; children: Don Kenneth, Andrew Scott, Thomas Dwight. B.A., Hillsdale Coll., 1961; M.B.A., Loyola U., Chgo., 1974. Service analyst Mich. Med. Service, Detroit, 1965-66; adminstrv. asst. Port Huron (Mich.) Hosp., 1966-70; coordinator affiliated socs. Am. Hosp. Assn., Chgo., 1970-71; dir. div. membership Am. Hosp. Assn., 1971-72, dir. div. registration and membership, 1972-73, asst. dir. Bur. of Mgmt. and Planning, 1973-75, acting dir. Bur. of Mgmt. and Planning, 1975; exec. dir. Internat. Personnel Mgmt. Assn., Washington, 1975-96. Served with U.S. Army, 1958-60. Mem. Am. Soc. Assn. Execs., Greater Washington Soc. Assn. Execs.

TICHI, CECELIA, English language educator; b. Pitts., Apr. 10, 1942; d. James Francis Halbert and Mary Louise (Doherty) Tashman; m. William John Tichi, Sept. 8, 1967; children: Claire, Julia. BA, Pa. State U., 1964; MA, Johns Hopkins U., 1965; PhD, U. Calif., Davis, 1968. Asst. prof., English Boston U., 1968-75, assoc. prof., 1975-82, prof., 1982-87; prof., English Vanderbilt U., Nashville, 1987-90, William R. Kenan jr. prof., English, 1991—; cons. Nat. Ctr. Humanities, Research Triangle Park, N.C., 1992—. Author: New World New Earth, 1979, Shifting Gears, 1987, Electronic Hearth, 1991, High Lonesome, 1994; editor: The Harper American Literature, 1986. Rsch. grantee Sci. Tech. Soc., NEH, 1986, summer seminar for coll. tchrs. grantee NEH, 1996. Mem. MLA, Am. Studies Assn. (pres. 1992-93). Home: 616 Hillwood Blvd Nashville TN 37205-1314 Office: Vanderbilt U Dept English Nashville TN 37235

TIDBALL, CHARLES STANLEY, computer scientist, educator; b. Geneva, Switzerland, Apr. 15, 1928; (parents Am. citizens); s. Charles Taylor and Adele (Desmaison) T.; m. Mary Elizabeth Peters, Oct. 25, 1952. B.A., Wesleyan U., 1950; M.S. (Univ. scholar), U. Rochester, 1952; Ph.D., U. Wis., Madison, 1955; M.D. (Shattuck fellow, Van Noyes scholar), U. Chgo., 1958; LHD (hon.), Wilson Coll., 1994. Rotating intern Madison (Wis.) Gen. Hosp., 1958-59; physician I Mendota State Hosp., Madison, 1959; asst. research prof. physiology dept. George Washington U. Med. Center, Washington, 1959-63; USPHS spl. fellow George Washington U. Med. Center, 1960-61, asso. prof., acting chmn. dept., 1963-64, prof., 1964-65, chmn. dept., 1964-71, Henry D. Fry prof., 1965-84, research prof. med., 1972-80; dir. Office Computer Assisted Edn. George Washington U. Med. Ctr., 1973-75, dir. Office Computer Assisted Edn. and Svcs., 1975-78; Lucie Stern disting. vis. prof. natural scis. Mills Coll., 1980; prof. edn. George Washington U., 1982-84, dir. ednl. computing tech. program Sch. Edn., 1982-84, prof. computer medicine Med. Ctr., 1984-92, prof. emeritus computer medicine, 1992, prof. neurol. surgery, 1990-92, prof. emeritus neurol. surgery, 1992; civil surgeon Immigration and Naturalization Svc., Dept. Justice, Washington, 1986-89; disting. rsch. scholar, co-dir. Tidball Ctr. for Study Ednl. Environments Hood Coll., Frederick, Md., 1994—; trustee in residence Skidmore Coll., 1995. Author: (with others) Consolidated Index to For Thy Great Glory, 1993; editor: (with M. C. Shelesnyak) Frontiers in the Teaching of Physiology: Computer Literacy and Simulation, 1981; mem. editorial bd.: Jour. Applied Physiology, 1966-69, Jour. Computer-Based Instrn., 1974-89, Am. Jour. Physiology; assoc. editor physiology tchr. sect.; The Physiologist, 1979-85; contbr. articles to profl. jours. Trustee Cathedral Choral Soc., 1976-79, Wilson Coll., 1983-92, Everitt-Pomeroy, 1993—, Population Reference Bur., 1987-94, 96—, chmn. bd. trustees, 1992-94, sec., 1994—; lay reader St. Albans Parish, 1965-67; lay eucharistic min. Washington Nat. Cathedral, 1967-94, 94—, clergy asst., 1968—, homilist, 1977—, info. sys. specialist, 1986-93, vol. mgr. info. sys. program, 1982—; mem. commn. Episcopal Diocese Washington, 1976-78; mem. com. mgmt. YMCA Camp Letts, 1968—, chmn., 1972-75, dir., chmn. Endowment Fund, 1977—; bd. dirs. Met. YMCA, Washington, 1972-84, trustees coun., 1984-91, fin. com., 1972-93, v.p. internat. program, 1974-75, asst. treas., 1975-77, v.p., treas., 1977-79, vice chmn., 1979-80, chmn., 1980-82, pres. of found., 1991-93; bd. dirs., treas. Woodley Ensemble, 1993—; bd. dirs. Mid-Atlantic Region YMCA, 1974-83; bd. dirs., vice-chmn. Cathedral West Condo., 1983-84, chmn., 1984-87, 91-93, fin. com., 1979-94. Recipient award Washington Acad. Scis., 1967, Leader of Yr. award Met. YMCA, Washington, 1974, Red Triangle award, 1976, Service award, 1979; Dakota Indian name Am. Youth Found., 1976; Research Career Devel. award USPHS, 1961-63. Mem. Am. Physiol. Soc. (emeritus). Home: 4100 Cathedral Ave NW Washington DC 20016-3584

TIDBALL, M. ELIZABETH PETERS, physiology educator, research director; b. Anderson, Ind., Oct. 15, 1929; d. John Winton and Beatrice (Ryan) Peters; m. Charles S. Tidball, Oct. 25, 1952. BA, Mt. Holyoke Coll., 1951, LHD, 1976; MS, U. Wis., 1955, PhD, 1959; MTS summa cum laude, Wesley Theol. Sem., 1990; ScD (hon.), Wilson Coll., 1973; DSc (hon.), Trinity Coll., 1974, Cedar Crest Coll., 1977; ScD (hon.), U. of South, 1978, Goucher Coll., 1979; DSc (hon.), St. Mary-of-The-Woods Coll., 1986; LittD (hon.), Regis Coll., 1980, Coll. St. Catherine, 1980, Alverno Coll., 1989; HHD (hon.), St. Mary's Coll., 1977, Hood Coll., 1982; LLD (hon.), St. Joseph Coll., 1983; LHD (hon.), Skidmore Coll., 1984, Marymount Coll., 1985, Converse Coll., 1985, Mt. Vernon Coll., 1986. Teaching asst. physiology dept. U. Wis., 1952-55, 58-59; research asst. anatomy dept. U. Chgo., 1955-56, research asst. physiology dept., 1956-58; USPHS postdoctoral fellow NIH, Bethesda, Md., 1959-61; staff pharmacologist Hazleton Labs., Falls Church, Va., 1961; assoc. in physiology George Washington U. Med. Ctr., 1960-62; cons. Hazleton Labs., 1962; asst. research prof. dept. pharmacology George Washington U. Med. Ctr., 1962-64, assoc. research prof. dept. physiology, 1964-70, research prof., 1970-71, prof., 1971-94, prof. emeritus, 1994—; asst. dir. M of Theol. Studies program Wesley Theol Sem., 1993-94; disting. rsch. scholar Hood Coll., Frederick, Md., 1994—; co-dir. Tidball Ctr. for Study of Ednl. Environments Hood Coll., 1994—; Lucie Stern Disting. vis. prof. natural scis. Mills Coll., 1980; scholar in residence Coll. Preachers, 1984, Salem Coll., 1985, Wesley Theol. Sem., 1992; Disting. scholar in residence So. Meth. U., 1985; vis. trustee prof. Skidmore Coll., 1995; cons. FDA, 1966-67, assoc. sci. coord. sci. assocs. tng. programs, 1966-67; mem. com. on NIH tng. programs and fellowships Nat. Acad. Scis., 1972-75; faculty summer confs. Am. Youth Found., 1967-78; founder, dir. Summer Seminars for Women Am. Youth Found., 1987-95; cons. for instl. rsch. Wellesley Coll., 1974-75; exec. sec. com. on edn. and employment women in sci. and engring. Commn. on Human Resources, NRC/NAS, 1974-75, vice chmn., 1977-82; cons., staff officer NRC/Nat. Acad. Scis., 1974-75; cons. Woodrow Wilson Nat. Fellowship Found., 1975—, NSF, 1974-91; bd. mentor Assn. Governing Bds. of Univs. and Colls., 1991—, Gale Fund for the Study of Trusteeship Adv. Comm., 1992—; cons. Assn. Am. Colls. Women's Coll. Coalition Rsch. Adv. Com., 1992—; Single Gender Schooling Working Group, U.S. Dept. Edn., 1992-94; rep. to D.C. Commn. on Status of Women, 1972-75; nat. panelist Am. Coun. on Edn., 1983-90; panel mem. Congl. Office of Tech. Assessment, 1986-87; mem. fellows selection com., fellows mentor Coll. Preachers, 1992—. Columnist Trusteeship, 1993—; mem. editl. bd. Jour. Higher Edn., 1979-84, cons. editor, 1984—; mem. editl. adv. bd. Religion and Intellectual Life, 1983—; contbr. sci. articles and rsch. on edn. of women to profl. jours. Trustee Mt. Holyoke Coll., 1968-73, vice-chmn., 1972-73, trustee fellow, 1988—; trustee Hood Coll., 1972-84, 86-92, exec. com., 1974-84, 89-92; overseer Sweet Briar Coll., 1978-85; trustee Cathedral Choral Soc., 1976-90, pres. bd. trustees, 1982-84, hon. trustee, 1991—; trustee Skidmore Coll., 1988—, mem. exec. com., 1993—; mem. governing bd. Coll. of Preachers, 1979-85, chmn., 1983-85; mem. governing bd. Washington Cathedral Found., 1983-85, mem. exec com., 1983-85; bd. vis. Salem Coll., 1986-93; ctr. assoc. Nat. Resource Ctr., Girls Clubs Am., 1983—. Shattuck fellow, 1955-56; Mary E. Woolley fellow Mt. Holyoke Coll., 1958-59; USPHS postdoctoral fellow, 1959-61; recipient Alumnae Medal of Honor Mt. Holyoke Coll., 1971, Award for Valuable Contbns. Gen. Alumni Assn. George Washington U., 1982, 87, Chestnut Hill Medal for Outstanding Achievement Chestnut Hill Coll., Phila., 1987; named Outstanding Grad. The Penn Hall Sch., 1988. Mem. AAAS, Am. Physiol. Soc. (chmn. task force on women i3-80, com. on coms. 1977-80, mem. emeritus 1994—), Am. Assn. Higher Edn., Mt. Holyoke Alumnae Assn. (dir. 1966-70, 76-77), Histamine Club, Sigma Delta Epsilon, Sigma Xi. Episcopalian. Home: 4100 Cathedral Ave NW Washington DC 20016-3584

TIDMAN, DEREK ALBERT, physics researcher; b. London, Oct. 18, 1930; came to U.S., 1957; s. Albert Horace and Florence Violet (Oscar) T.; m. Pauline Harrell Tidman, Apr. 25, 1959; children: Katherine Fleming, Mark Harrell. BSc, London U., 1952; diploma, Imperial Coll. Sci. & Tech., 1956; PhD, 1956. Rsch. fellow U. Sydney, Australia, 1956-57; asst. prof. U. Chgo., Ill., 1957-60; rsch. assoc. prof. U. Md., College Park, 1961-64, rsch. prof., 1964-80; pres. GT-Devices subs. Gen. Dynamics, Alexandria, Va., 1980-94, Utron Inc., Manassas, Va., 1994—; cons. NASA Goddard Space Flight Ctr., Greenbelt, Md., 1961-69, Los Alamos Sci. Lab., 1974-78, Lawrence Livermore Lab., Calif., 1977-80. Co-author: Plasma Kinetic Theory, 1963, Shock Waves in Collisionless Plasmas, 1971; co-editor: Plasma Instabilities in Astrophysics, 1969; assoc. editor: Physics of Fluids, 1970-72, Jour. Math. Physics, 1972-74; contbr. articles to profl. jours.; patentee in field. Recipient Disting. Scientist award Md. Acad. Scis., 1965. Fellow Am. Phys. Soc.; mem. IEEE, AIAA. Office: Utron 8506 Wellington Rd Manassas VA 22110-3915

TIDWELL, GEORGE ERNEST, federal judge; b. Atlanta, Aug. 1, 1931; s. George Brown and Mary (Wooddall) T.; m. Carolyn White, July 1, 1961; children: Thomas George, Linda Carol, David Loran. LL.B., Emory U., 1954. Bar: Ga. 1954. With John J. Westmoreland Sr. and Jr., Atlanta, 1954-58, Slaton, Brookins, Robertson & Tidewell, Atlanta, 1958-66; exec. asst. atty. gen. Atlanta, 1966-68; judge Civil Ct., Fulton County, Ga., 1968-71, Superior Ct., Atlanta Jud. Circuit, 1971-79, U.S. Dist. Ct. (no. dist.) Ga., Atlanta, 1979—. Mem. ABA, State Bar Ga., Am. Judicature Soc., Atlanta Bar Assn. Office: US Dist Ct 1967 US Courthouse 75 Spring St SW Atlanta GA 30303-3309*

TIDWELL, JOSEPH PAUL, JR., technical specialist research and engineering; b. Tuscaloosa, Ala., Oct. 29, 1943; s. Joseph Paul and Jeanette (Steinwinder) T.; m. Susan Kay White, Oct. 3, 1970; children: Joseph Paul III, James Boland, Heather Loran, Shawn Damon. A.S., NYU, 1978, BS, 1984; postgrad. Murray (Ky.) State U., 1984-85; MBA Embry Riddle Aero. U., 1991. Lic. pilot rotorcraft, cert. safety mgr., safety exec. Commd. aviation ops. officer U.S. Army, 1976, advanced through grades to maj., 1985; aviation safety officer Ft. Campbell, Ky., 1982-85, Chun Chon, Korea, 1981-82; chief aviation and product safety/flight safety parts programs McDonnell Douglas Helicopter, Co., Mesa, Ariz., 1985-89, dept. mgr., supplier evaluation and requirements Quality Control div., 1989-91, sr. systems safety engr. Advanced Devel. and Tech. div., 1991-93; rsch. and engring. tech. specialist (aviation and product safety) advanced devel. and engring. divsn. McDonnell Douglas Corp., 1993—. Adj. instr. Embry Riddle Aero. Univ.; developer safety engring., safety cons., safety instr. Webelos den leader Clarksville council Cub Scouts Am., Tenn., 1983-85; asst. scout master Clarksville council Boy Scouts Am., 1983-85, scoutmaster Mesa council, 1985—. Decorated Purple Heart, Meritorious Service medal, recipient Den Leaders Tng. Key Middle Tenn. council Boy Scouts Am., 1985, Woodbadge Beads Middle Tenn. Council Boy Scouts Am., 1985. Named Scoutmaster of Yr., Mesa Dist., Theodore Roosevelt Council Boy Scouts Am., 1986, award of merit Mesa Dist. 1988.. Mem. Am. Soc. Safety Engrs. (profl.; Safety Officer of Month award 1985, chmn. awards and elections Ariz. chpt. 1985-87), Army Aviation Assn. Am. (air assault chpt. exec. treas. 1983-85, Aviation Safety Officer of Yr. award 1984), U.S. Army Warrant Officer's Assn. (Ky.-Tenn. chpt. pres. 1984-85, Disting. Service plaque 1984, Cert. of Merit for Disting. Achievement in Youth Leadership Devel. Men of Achievement, Cambridge, Eng., 1987. World Safety Orgn. (affiliate), Internat. Soc. Air Safety Investigators, S.W. Safety Congress and Exposition (bd. govs., conv. and advt. dir., vice chmn. external affairs 1985-88), Aviation Edn. Coun. of Ariz. (bd. govs.), System Safety Soc. (organizer, pres. Ariz. chpt. 1993). Republican. Roman Catholic. Lodge: WIPALA WIKI, Order of Arrow. Avocations: golfing, camping, cycling. Home: 2338 W Lindner Ave Apt 10 Mesa AZ 85202-6430 Office: McDonnell Douglas Helicopter Co 5000 E Mcdowell Rd Mesa AZ 85215-9797

TIDWELL, MOODY RUDOLPH, federal judge; b. Kansas City, Mo., Feb. 15, 1939; s. Moody R., Jr. and Dorothy T.; m. Rena Alexandra, Jan. 28, 1966; children—Gregory, Jeremy. B.A., Ohio Wesleyan U., 1961; J.D., Am. U., 1964; LL.M., George Washington U., 1972. Bar: U.S. Ct. Appeals (D.C. cir.) 1964, U.S. Dist Ct. D.C. 1965, U.S. Ct. Claims 1972, U.S. Ct. Appeals (10th cir.) 1979. Assoc. solicitor gen. law div. Dept. Interior, Washington, 1972-75, assoc. solicitor Energy and Resources div., 1975-78; assoc. solicitor Mine Health and Safety div. Dept. Labor, Washington, 1978-80; deputy solicitor, counsellor to the sec. Dept. Interior, Washington, 1981-83; judge U.S. Ct. Federal Claims, Washington, 1983—; dir., corporate sec. Keco, Inc., Cin. Pres. Pine Lake Corp., Glengary, W.Va., 1975—. Recipient Disting. Service award Sec. of Interior, 1983, Meritorious Service award Sec. of Labor, 1979. Mem. ABA, Fed. Bar Assn., D.C. Bar Assn. Office: US Ct Fed Claims 717 Madison Pl NW Washington DC 20005-1011

TIDWELL, THOMAS TINSLEY, chemistry educator; b. Atlanta, Feb. 20, 1939; s. Charles Speer and Helen (Frazier) T.; m. Sarah Huddleston, July 29, 1971. BS, Ga. Inst. Tech., 1960; AM, Harvard U., 1963, Ph.D., 1964. Research assoc. U. Calif., San Diego, 1964-65; research assoc. U. East Anglia, Norwich, Eng., 1966-67; asst. prof. U. S.C., Columbia, 1965-72; assoc. prof. U. Toronto, 1972-77, prof. chemistry, 1977—, assoc. dean, 1979-82, assoc. chair dept. chemistry, 1991-93; chair Iupac Commn. Phys. Orgn. Chem., 1994—. NATO research fellow, 1978, 83, 89; exch. scientist U.S. Acad. Sci., Bulgaria, 1982, USSR, 1989. Mem. Am. Chem. Soc., Am. Assn. Adv. Sci., Can. Soc. Chemistry. Office: U Toronto, Dept Chemistry, Toronto, ON Canada M5S 1A1

TIEBER, F. MARTIN, lawyer; b. Detroit, Mar. 26, 1950; s. Frank Martin and Sarah Jane (Lucot) T.; 1 child, Kristoffer; m. Michela Remer, Nov. 29, 1981; 1 child, Samantha. BA in English, U. Notre Dame, 1972; JD, Wayne State U., 1975. Bar: Mich. 1975, U.S. Dist. Ct. (ea. dist.) Mich. 1975, U.S. Dist. Ct. (we. dist.) Mich. 1976, U.S. Ct. Appeals (6th cir.) 1978, U.S. Supreme Ct. 1981. Rsch. asst. State Appellate Defender, Detroit, 1973-75, rsch. atty., 1975-76, staff atty., 1976-78; dir. Lansing (Mich.) office, dep. defender State Appellate Defender, 1978—; adj. prof. Thomas M. Cooley Law Sch., Lansing, 1985—. Bd. dirs. New Way In, Lansing, 1990-91, Lansing YMCA, 1993—; active Gov.'s Task Force on Prison Issues, Lansing, 1979-80, Mich. Prison Overcrowding Project, Lansing, 1981-84; commr. Mich. Justice Tng. Commn., 1995—. Mem. State Bar Mich. (coun. criminal law sect. 1986-89, chairperson defender com. 1980-82, coun. appeals practice sect. 1995—), Criminal Def. Attys. Mich. (bd. dirs. 1990—, Spl. Svc. award 1991). Avocations: guitar, cross country skiing. Office: State Appellate Defender 200 Washington Sq N 340 Business & Trade Ctr Lansing MI 48913

TIECKE, RICHARD WILLIAM, pathologist, educator, association executive; b. Muscatine, Iowa, Apr. 5, 1917; s. Harry Frederick and Nell Eola (McKibben) T. BS, U. Iowa, 1940, DDS, 1942, MS, 1947; Ph.D. pathology, U Chicago, 1949; postgrad. in pathology, U. Chgo., 1947-49. Diplomate Am. Bd. Oral Pathology (bd. dirs., past pres.). Jr. pathologist, asst. pathologist, dep. chief oral pathology div. Armed Forces Inst. Pathology, 1949-54; assoc. prof. pathology Georgetown, 1949-54; prof. pathology Northwestern U. Sch. Medicine, Chgo., 1954-85; prof. emeritus Northwestern U. Sch. Medicine, 1985—, head oral pathology, assoc. cancer coordinator, 1954-62; prof. dept. oral pathology U. Ill., 1965-80, prof. dept. oral diagnosis, 1980-84; adj. staff Northwestern Meml. Hosps., 1981-85; research fellow Hektoen Inst. Med. Research, Cook County Hosp., Chgo., 1965-80; dir. research inst. Am. Dental Assn., Chgo., 1968-71, asst. exec. dir., 1971-85; lectr. Royal Coll. Surgeons, London, 1958, Royal Coll. Surgeons, Copenhagen, Denmark, 1959, Royal Coll. Surgeons, Helsinki, Finland, 1959; cons. AMA, U.S. Naval Hosp., Great Lakes, Ill., VA Research Hosp., VA West Side Hosp., Pub. Health Hosp., Chgo., City Chgo. Bd. Health; surgeon gen. USPHS; head and neck cancer detection Nat. Center Chronic Disease Control-USPHS, Nat. Cancer Inst. NIH; cons. to surgeon gen. Army, 1969-80. Author: Physiologic Pathology of Oral Disease, 1959, Oral Pathology, 1964, Atlas on Oral Cytology, 1969, also research articles. Served from 1st lt. to col. U.S. Army and AUS, 1942-77; now col. Res. (ret.). Richard W. Tiecke Pathology Lab. named in his honor Northwestern U. Med. Ctr., 1977. Fellow Am. Acad. Oral Pathology (past pres.), Am. Coll. Dentists; mem. ADA (hon., asst. sec. coun. dental therapeutics 1962-68), Ill., Chgo. dental socs., Internat. Assn. Dental Rsch., Psi Omega, Omicron Kappa Upsilon. Home: 5 Major Aly Palm Beach FL 33480-4518

TIEDE, TOM ROBERT, journalist; b. Huron, S.D., Feb. 24, 1937; s. Leslie Albert and Rose (Allen) T.; children: Kristina Anne, Thomas Patrick. B.A. in Journalism, Wash. State U., 1959. Mem. staff Kalispell (Mont.) Daily Interlake, 1960-61, Daytona Beach (Fla.) News Jour., 1961-63; war corr. Newspaper Enterprise Assn., N.Y.C., 1964—; lectr. in field., 1965—. Author: Your Men at War, 1965, Coward, 1968, Calley: Soldier or Killer?, 1971, Welcome to Washington, Mr. Witherspoon, 1979, The Great Whale Rescue, 1986, American Tapestry: Eye Witness Accounts of the 1900's, 1988, The Man Who Discovered Pluto, 1990, Fosser, 1994. Served as lt., inf. AUS, 1960. Recipient Ernie Pyle Meml. award, 1965; Freedoms Found. award, 1966; George Washington medal, 1972. Mem. Internat. Platform Assn., Sigma Delta Chi, Lambda Chi Alpha. Roman Catholic. Clubs: Overseas Press, National Press, Nat. Headliners (award 1966 Atlantic City). Work collected by Boston U. Library. Office: NEA 1090 Vermont Ave NW Washington DC 20005-4905 Address: PO Box 1919 Mill Run Bourne Richmond Hill GA 31324

TIEDEKEN, KATHLEEN HELEN, health facilities administrator; b. Camden, N.J., Aug. 6, 1945; d. Joseph Henry and Katherine Rita (Byrne) T. RN, Our Lady of Lourdes Sch., Camden, 1966; BSN, U. Pa., 1974, MSN, 1979. RN, N.J. Staff nurse Our Lady of Lourdes Med. Ctr., Camden, 1966-68, head nurse, 1968-76, asst. dir. staffing, 1976-78; asst. dir. nursing Our Lady of Lourdes Med. Ctr., 1978-80, assoc. dir. nursing, 1980-83; assoc. exec. dir. nursing West Jersey Health System, Voorhees, N.J., 1983-87; assoc. adminstr. nursing Meml. Hosp. Burlington County, Mt. Holly, N.J., 1986-90, v.p. patient svcs., 1990-93, v.p. patient and hosp. ops., 1993-95; asst. adminstr. patient care svcs. Mediplex Rehab. Hosp., Marlton, N.J., 1995—; clin. adj., faculty nursing Widener U.; speaker in field. Contbg. author: Emotion and Reproduction, 1979, New Directions for Nursing in the '80s, 1980, Computer Applications in Nursing Education and Practice, 1992. Rsch. grantee State Dept. Health, 1990, 91; Johnson & Johnson Wharton fellow in mgmt. for nurses, 1992. Mem. ANA (cert. nursing advanced adminstrn.), Orgn. Am. Nurses Execs. (bd. dirs., chmn.

ednl. dialogue com., newsletter), N.J. State Nurses Assn. (legis. com., role of honor com. 1980-85), N.J. Bd. Nursing (ad hoc com. on unlicensed personnel role), Vol. Hosps. Am. (N.J. nursing coun.), Am. Coll. Obstetricians and Gynecologists (nurses assn.), Nat. Perinatal Assn., Sigma Theta Tau. Roman Catholic. Avocations: travel, photography, swimming, reading. Home: 1610 Beechwood Pl Clementon NJ 08021-5801 Office: Mediplex Rehab Hosp 300 Brick Rd Marlton NJ 08053

TIEDEMAN, DAVID VALENTINE, education educator; b. Americus, Ga., Aug. 12, 1919; s. Walter Dohlen and Edna M(arie) (Komfort) T.; m. Marjorie I(da) Denman, Sept. 26, 1942 (div. Jan. 2, 1973); children—David Michael, Jeffrey Denman; m. Anna Louise Miller, Jan. 6, 1973. A.B., Union Coll., Schenectady, 1941; A.M., U. Rochester, 1943; Ed.M., Harvard, 1948, Ed.D., 1949. Staff mem. NRC com. selection and tng. aircraft pilots U. Rochester, 1941-43; staff mem. test constrn. dept. Coll. Entrance Exam. Bd., 1943-44; assoc. head statistics div. Manhattan Project, 1944-46; Milton teaching fellow, instr. edn. Harvard Grad. Sch. Edn., 1946-48, Sheldon travelling fellow, 1948-49, instr. edn., 1949-51, asst. prof. edn., 1951-52, lectr. edn., 1952-55, assoc. prof., 1955-59, prof., 1959-71, assoc. dir., research assoc. Center for Research in Careers, 1963-66, also chmn. exec. com., info. system for vocat. decisions, 1966-69; prin. research scientist Palo Alto office Am. Insts. for Research, 1971-73; prof. edn. No. Ill. U., DeKalb, 1973-80; dir. ERIC Clearinghouse in Career Edn., 1973-76; coordinator Office Vocat., Tech., and Career Edn., 1978-80; prof. career and higher edn. U. So. Calif., Los Angeles, 1981-84; prof. emeritus higher and post secondary edn. U. So. Calif., 1984—; exec. dir. Nat. Inst. Advancement of Career Edn., 1981-84; pres. Internat. Coll., 1985-86; v.p. Lifecareer Found., 1985—; provost William Lyon U., 1988-91; faculty Walden U., 1992—; mem. Adv. Council on Guidance Dept. Edn. Commonwealth Mass., 1957-63; chmn. commn. on tests Coll. Entrance Exam. Bd., 1967-70; mem. advisory screening com. in edn. Council Internat. Exchange of Scholars, 1975-79, chmn., 1978-79. Co-author 5 books.; editorial assoc.: Jour. Counseling Psychology, 1957-63, Personnel and Guidance Jour., 1960-63, Character Potential: A Record of Research, 1977-82, Jour. Career Edn., 1979-85; contbr. articles to profl. jours., chpts. to books. Bd. dirs. Mass. Com. Children and Youth, 1961-63. Fellow Ctr. for Advanced Study in Behavioral Scis.; spl. fellow NIMH, 1963-64. Fellow Am. Psychol. Soc., APA (prs. divsn. counseling psychology 1965-66); mem. ACA, Nat. Career Devel. Assn. (pres. 1965-66, Eminent Career award 1979), Nat. Coun. Measurement in Edn. (pres. 1962-63), Phi Beta Kappa, Sigma Xi, Phi Delta Kappa, Phi Kappa Phi. Office: Lifecareer Ctr 1078 La Tortuga Dr Vista CA 92083-6441

TIEDEMANN, ALBERT WILLIAM, JR., chemist; b. Balt., Nov. 7, 1924; s. Albert William and Catherine (Madigan) T.; m. Mary Therese Sellmayer, Apr. 6, 1953; children: Marie Therese, Donna Elise, Albert William III, David Lawrence. BS, Loyola Coll., Balt., 1947; MS, NYU, 1949; PhD, Georgetown U., 1958. Teaching fellow N.Y. U., 1947-50; instr. chemistry Mt. St. Agnes Coll., 1950-55; chief chemist Emerson Drug div. Warner Lambert Pharm. Co., Balt., 1955-60; analytical supr. Hercules Powder Co., Allegany Ballistics Lab., Cumberland, Md., 1960-68; tech. svc. supt. Hercules Inc., Radford, Va., 1968-72; dir. Va. Div. Consol. Labs., Richmond, 1972-78; vice-chmn. Va. Toxic Substances Adv. Council, 1978-92; dep. dir. for labs. Va. Dept. Gen. Svcs., 1978-92, cons. 1992—. Mem. sci. adv. com. Longwood Coll., 1983—. Served to lt. (j.g.) USNR, 1943-46; capt. Res., 1946—. Fellow Am. Inst. Chemists; mem. Soc. Advancement Mgmt., chpt. v.p. 1983-84, chpt. pres. 1984-85), Am. Soc. Quality Control (chmn. Richmond sect. 1975-76, councilor biomed. div. 1978-80), U.S. Naval Inst., Naval Res. Assn. (dist. pres. 1954-57; nat. v.p. 1962-63, 65-69; nat. chmn. Navy Sabbath Program 1969-75; Nat. Meritorious Service award 1971, Twice a Citizen award 1978), Cen. Atlantic States Assn. Food & Drug Ofcls. (exec. bd. 1977-84, v.p. 1981-82, pres. 1982-83, CASA award 1986), Nat. Assn. Food & Drug Ofcls. (chmn. sci. and tech. com. 1981-85, sec.-treas. 1985-87), Internat. Assn. Ofcl. Analytical Chemists (editorial bd. 1986-88, bd. dirs. 1987-90), Analytical Lab. Mgrs. Assn., Royal Acad. Pharmacy (elected acad. fgn. mem. Barcelona, Spain 1989—). Home: 10511 Cherokee Rd Richmond VA 23235-1008

TIEDGE-LAFRANIER, JEANNE MARIE, editor; b. N.Y.C., July 24, 1960; d. Richard Frederick and Joan Jean (Gerardo) Tiedge; m. John Daniel Lewis Lafranier, Oct. 8, 1989; children: Katelyn Ellen, John Richard. BA, Drew U., 1982. Asst. Denise Marcil Lit. Agy., N.Y.C., 1982-84; sr. editor New Am. Libr., N.Y.C., 1984-87, Warner Books, N.Y.C., 1987-95; edito-in-chief Disticor News, Ajax, Ont., Can., 1995—. Avocation: equestrian.

TIEDJE, JAMES MICHAEL, microbiology educator, ecologist; b. Newton, Iowa, Feb. 9, 1942; married, 1965; 3 children. BS, Iowa State U., 1964; MS, Cornell U., 1966, PhD in Soil Microbiology, 1968. From asst. prof. to prof. Mich. State U., 1968-78, disting. prof., 1991—; dir. sci. and tech. ctr. microbial ecology NSF, 1988—; vis. assoc. prof. U. Ga., 1974-75; cons. NSF, 1974-77; vis. prof. U. Calif. Berkeley, 1981-82; mem. biotech. sci. adv. com. EPA, 1986-89, chair sci. adv. coun. GPA, 1988-90. Editor: Applied Microbiology, 1974—, editor-in-chief, 1980-86. Recipient Carlos J. Finley prize, UNESCO, 1993. Mem. AAAS, Am. Soc. Agronomy (Soil Sci. award 1990), Internat. Inst. Biotech., Am. Soc. Microbiology (award in applied and environ. microbiology 1992), Soil Sci. Soc. Am., Ecol. Soc. Am., Internat. Soc. Soil Sci. (chair soil biology divsn.). Achievements include research in dentrification, microbial metabolism of organic pollutants, and molecular microbiol. ecology. Office: Michigan State U Microbial Ecology Ctr 540 Plant & Soil Scis Bldg East Lansing MI 48824-1325

TIEFEL, VIRGINIA MAY, librarian; b. Detroit, May 20, 1926; d. Karl and June Garland (Young) Brenkert; m. Paul Martin Tiefel, Jan. 25, 1947; children: Paul Martin Jr., Mark Gregory. B.A. in Elem. Edn., Wayne State U., 1962; M.A. in Library Sci., U. Mich., 1968. Librarian Birmingham Schs., Mich., 1967-68; librarian S. Euclid-Lyndhurst Schs., Cleve., 1968-69; acquisitions-reference librarian Hiram Coll., Ohio, 1969-77; head undergrad. libraries Ohio State U., Columbus, 1977-84, dir. library user edn., 1978-95, faculty outreach coord., 1995—. Contbr. articles to profl. jours. Recipient Disting. Alumnus award U. Mich. Sch. Info. and Libr. Studies, 1993. Mem. ALA (v.p. Ohio sect. 1973-74, pres. 1974-75, Miriam Dudley Bibliographic Instrn. Librarian of Yr. 1986), Acad. Library Assn. Ohio (Outstanding Ohio Acad. Librarian 1984), Assn. Coll. and Research Libraries (chmn. bibliographic instrn. sect. com. on research 1983-84, chmn. com. on performance measures 1984-90). Lutheran. Home: 4956 Smoketalk Ln Westerville OH 43081-4433 Office: Ohio State U Libraries 1858 Neil Ave Columbus OH 43210-1225

TIEFEL, WILLIAM REGINALD, hotel company executive; b. Rochester, N.Y., Mar. 30, 1934; s. William Reginald and Mary Hazel (Cross) T.; m. Vada Morell, Dec. 30, 1985. Student, Williams Coll., 1952-54; B.A. with honors, Mich. State U., 1956; postgrad., Harvard Bus. Sch. Gen. mgr. Marriott Hotels, Arlington, Va., 1964-65, Saddle Brook, N.J., 1966-69, Newton, Mass., 1969-71; regional v.p. Marriott Hotels, Washington, 1971-80; corp. v.p. Marriott Corp., Washington, 1976-89; exec. v.p. Marriott Hotels and Resorts, Washington, 1980-88; pres. Marriott Hotels, Resorts and Stes., 1988—; exec. v.p., mem. exec. and growth coms. Marriott Corp., 1988—; pres. Marriott Lodging Group, 1992—. Bd. visitors Valley Forge Mil. Acad. and Jr. Coll., 1976-79, chmn., 1979, trustee, 1982-88, 89-92; chmn. Campaign for Valley Forge, 1985-88, chmn. com. on trustees, 1989-91. Mem. Am. Hotel and Motel Assn. (dir. Ednl. Inst.). Republican. Roman Catholic. Home: 2426 Wyoming Ave NW Washington DC 20008-1643 Office: Marriott Corp 1 Marriott Dr Washington DC 20058-0001

TIEGS, CHERYL, model, designer; d. Theodore and Phyllis T. Student, Calif. State U., Los Angeles. Profl. model, appearing in nat. mags., including, Time, Life, Bazaar, Sports Illustrated, Glamour; appeared weekly on ABC's Good Morning America; also appearing in TV commls., Cheryl Tiegs line of sportswear, Cheryl Tiegs nationally-distributed line of women's eyeglass frames, Cheryl Tiegs Collection of 14k Gold Jewelry, Fashion Watches, Shoes and Hosiery; author: The Way to Natural Beauty, 1980; Sports Illustrated video Aerobic Interval Training with Cheryl Tiegs. Address: care Barbara Shapiro 2 Greenwich Plz Ste 100 Greenwich CT 06830-6353

TIELKE, JAMES CLEMENS, retail and manufacturing executive; b. St. Helena, Nebr., May 15, 1931; s. Joseph Hubert and Catherine Josephine (Schmidt) T.; m. Betty Merle Adams, Apr. 18, 1953; children: P.J., Michael J., Dawn M. B.S. in Bus. Adminstrn., U. S.D., 1959, MA in Speech and Econ., 1960. Partner, Tielke Motors, Yankton, S.D., 1952-54; owner Ft. Collins Motors, Colo., 1954-56; corp. buying mgr. Montgomery Ward, Chgo., 1960-81, v.p. mdse. adminstrn., 1978-81; pres. Midwest div. Structured Approaches, Inc., 1981-82; v.p. nat. accounts Dupli-Color Products, Elk Grove Village, Ill., 1983-85; pres. Black Leaf Products Co., 1985-89; v.p. Hysan Corp., Des Plaines, Ill., 1985-89; v.p. ice melter sales Vigoro Consumer Products Corp., Kenosha, Wis., 1989—. Recipient Honors award U. S.D. Sch. Bus., 1977. Office: 4500 13th Ct Kenosha WI 53140-2790

TIEMAN, SUZANNAH BLISS, neurobiologist; b. Washington, Oct. 10, 1943; d. John Alden and Winifred Texas (Bell) Bliss; m. David George Tieman, Dec. 19, 1969. AB with honors, Cornell U., 1965; postgrad., MIT, 1965-66, Calif. Inst. Tech., 1971-72; PhD, Stanford U., 1974. Postdoctoral fellow dept. anatomy U. Calif., San Francisco, 1974-77; rsch. assoc. Neurobiology Rsch. Ctr. SUNY, Albany, 1977-90; sr. rsch. assoc., 1990—; assoc. prof. dept. biomed. scis. SUNY, Albany, 1988-95, prof., 1995—, rsch. prof. dept. biol. scis., 1990—, sr. rsch. assoc., 1990—. Contbr. articles to profl. jours., chpts. to books in field. Rsch. grantee Nat. Eye Inst., SUNY, Albany, 1979-83, NSF, SUNY, 1983-86, 88-92, 92-96; predoctoral fellow NSF, NIH, Stanford U., 1970-73, 73-74, postdoctoral fellow Nat. Eye Inst., U. Calif., San Francisco, 1974-77. Mem. AAAS, Soc. for Neurosci. (steering com. Hudson Berkshire chpt. 1980-81, pres. 1991-93), Assn. Rsch. in Vision and Ophthalmology, Am. Assn. Anatomists, Assn. Women in Sci., Fedn. Am. Socs. Exptl. Biology, Women in Neurosci., Nat. Audubon Soc., Nature Conservancy. Avocations: choral music, folk music, birding, eskimo art. Office: SUNY Neurobiology Rsch Ctr 1400 Washington Ave Albany NY 12222-0100

TIEN, CHANG-LIN, chancellor; b. Wuhan, China, July 24, 1935; came to U.S., 1956, naturalized, 1969; s. Yun Chien and Yun Di (Lee) T.; m. Di-Hwa Liu, July 25, 1959; children: Norman Chihnan, Phyllis Chihping, Christine Chihyih. BS, Nat. Taiwan U., 1955; MME, U. Louisville, 1957; MA, PhD, Princeton U., 1959; PhD (hon.), U. Louisville, 1991, U. Notre Dame, 1992, Hong Kong U. Sci. and Tech., 1993, U. Conn., 1994, U. Waterloo, Can., 1995, U. Ill., 1995. Acting asst. prof. dept. mech. engring. U. Calif., Berkeley, 1959-60, asst. prof., 1960-64, assoc. prof., 1964-68, prof., 1968-88, 90—, A. Martin Berlin prof., 1987-88, 90—, dept. chair, 1974-81, also vice chancellor for research, 1983-85; exec. vice chancellor U. Calif., Irvine, 1988-90; chancellor U. Calif., Berkeley, 1990—; chair exec. com. Internat. Ctr. for Heat and Mass Transfer, 1980-82; hon. prof., dir. Xi'an Jiatong U. Engring. Thermodynamics Rsch. Inst., 1987—; mem. adv. bd. Hong Kong U. Sci. and Tech., 1991—; chair internat. adv. panel U. Tokyo Inst. Indsl. Sci., 1995; bd. trustees Princeton (N.J.) U., 1991-95, Chiang Indsl. Charity Found., Ltd., Hong Kong, 1991—, The Asia Found., 1993—, U.S. Com. on Econ. Devel., 1994—, Carnegie Found. for Advancement of Tchg., 1994—; tech. cons. Lockheed Missiles and Space Co., GE; gov. bd. dirs. Com. of 100, 1991—; bd. dirs. Berkeley Cmty. Found., Wells Fargo Bank; active Aspen Inst. Domestic Strategy Group. Author one book; editor Internat. Commn. Heat and Mass Transfer, 1981—; editor-in-chief Exptl. Heat Transfer, 1987—; editor eleven vols.; contbr. articles to profl. jours. John Simon Guggenheim fellow, 1965, Sr. U.S. Sci. fellow Japan Soc. for Promotion of Sci., 1980; recipient Sr. U.S. Sci. award Alexander von Humboldt Found., 1979; named Most Disting. Chinese scholar, Soc. Hong Kong Scholars, 1989, Li Ka Shing Disting. Lectr., U. Hong Kong, 1994, Gordon Wu Disting. Lectr., Princeton U., 1995. Fellow AAAS (bd. dirs. 1992—), ASME (hon., chair exec. com. heat transfer divsn. 1980-81, v.p. basic engring. 1988-90, Heat Transfer Meml. award 1974, Gustus L. Larson Meml. award 1975, AIChE/ASME Max Jakob Meml. award 1981, Disting. Lectr. award 1987-89), AIAA (Thermophysics award 1977), Am. Acad. Arts and Scis. (hon.), Academia Sinica (hon., Taiwan); mem. NAE (mem. internat. affairs adv. com. 1987-90, chair mech. engring. peer com. 1989-90), Am. Soc. Engring. Edn. (mem. nat. adv. coun. 1993—), Heat Transfer Soc. Japan (hon.), Chinese Acad. Scis. (fgn. mem., Hon. Prof., Inst. Thermophysics 1981—). Office: U Calif Berkeley Chancellor's Office 200 Calif Hall 1500 Berkeley CA 94720-1500

TIEN, H. TI, biophysics and physiology educator, scientist; b. Beijing, China, Feb. 1, 1928; came to U.S., 1947; s. Fang-cheng and Wen-tsun (Chow) T.; children: Stephen, David, Adrienne, Jennifer; m. Angelica Leitmannova, 1992. B.Sc., U. Nebr., 1953; Ph.D., Temple U., 1963. Chem. engr. Allied Chem. Corp., Phila., 1953-57; med. scientist Eastern Pa. Psychiat. Inst., Phila., 1957-63; assoc. prof. Northwestern U., Boston, 1963-66; assoc. prof. Mich. State U., East Lansing, 1966-70, prof. biophysics, 1970—, chmn. dept., 1978-82; cons. Hungarian Acad. Sci., Szeged, 1975-76; rsch. prof. Acad. Sinica, Beijing, 1978; cons. prof. Sichuan U., 1984—; cons. Tianjin Econ. Tech. Devel. Area, China; external dir. Ctr. Interface Scis., Slovak Tech. U., Slovakia; cons. prof. Jilin U., Peoples Republic China; frequent lectr. many countries. Author: Bilayer Lipid Membranes, 1974; contbr. chpts. to books. Research grantee NIH, 1964—, NSF, 1978, Dept. Energy, 1980-83, U.S. Naval Rsch. Office, 1985—. Mem. AAAS, Biophys. Soc. (council 1972-75), Nat. Inst. Peer Reviewer. Research interests include membrane biophysics, bioelectrochemistry, photobiology, solar energy conversion via semiconductor septum electrochemical photovoltaic cells (SC-SEP); biomolecular electronic devices. Office: Mich State U Physiology Dept Giltner Hall East Lansing MI 48824

TIEN, PING KING, electronics engineer; b. Chekieng, China, Aug. 2, 1919; came to U.S., 1947; s. N.S. and C.S. (Yen) T.; m. Nancy N.Y. Chen, Apr. 19, 1952; children: Emily-Ju-Psia, Julia Ju-Wen. MS, Stanford U., 1948, PhD, 1951. Fellow emeritus Photonics Rsch. Lab., AT&T, Holmdel, N.J., 1990—; hon. prof. Jiao-Tong U., Shanghai, China. Editor-in-chief Internat. Jour. High Speed Electronics and Sys.; contbr. sci. and tech. articles to profl. jours. Recipient Achievement award Chinese Inst. Engrs., 1966; fellow AT&T Labs., 1983. Fellow IEEE (Morris N. Liebmann award 1979), Optical Soc. Am.; mem. Nat. Acad. Sci., Nat. Acad. Engring., Inst. Am. Physics, Acad. Sci. Republic of China, Acad. Sci. of Third World, Sigma Xi. Patentee in field. Home: 9 Carolyn Ct Holmdel NJ 07733-2070 Office: AT&T Bell Labs Holmdel NJ 07733

TIENDA, MARTA, demographer, educator; b. Tex. Ph.D. in Sociology, U. Tex., 1977. From asst. prof. to prof. rural sociology U. Wis., Madison, 1976-87; vis. prof. Stanford U., 1987; Ralph Lewis prof. sociology U. Chgo., 1987—, chmn. dept. sociology, 1994—; rsch. assoc. Population Research Ctr. Co-author: Hispanics in the U.S. Economy, 1985, Hispanic Population of the United States, 1987, Divided Opporunities, 1988; contbr. articles to profl. jours. Trustee Kaiser Family Found., Russell Sage Found., Carnegie Corp. N.Y. Guggenheim fellow. Fellow Am. Acad. Arts and Scis., Ctr. Advanced Study Behavioral Scis.; mem. Am. Sociol. Assn., Population Assn. Am., Internat. Union for the Sci. Study of Population. Office: U Chgo Dept Sociology 1126 E 59th St Chicago IL 60637-1580

TIENKEN, ARTHUR T., retired foreign service officer; b. Yonkers, N.Y., Aug. 5, 1922. B.A., Princeton U., 1947, M.A., 1949. With U.S. Fgn. Svc., 1949-87; dep. chief mission U.S. Fgn. Svc., Tunis, Tunisia, 1973-75, Addis Ababa, Ethiopia, 1975-77; Ambassador to Gabonese Republic and Democratic Republic of Sao Tome and Principe,, Libreville, Gabon, 1978-81; dir. Fgn. Svc. Assignments and Career devel. Dept. State, 1981-85, sr. insp., 1985-87, ret., 1987; diplomat-in-residence Marquette U., 1972-73. Served with U.S. Army, 1943-46.

TIERNEY, BILL, university athletic coach. Head coach Princeton Tigers, 1988—. NCAA Divsn. 1A Champions, 1992, 94; named Morris Touchstone Divsn. 1A Coach of the Yr.; elected to L.I. Lacrosse Hall of Fame, 1995. Office: Princeton U Dillon Gym Princeton NJ 08544*

TIERNEY, BRIAN PATRICK, advertising and public relations executive; b. Bryn Mawr, Pa., Feb. 21, 1957; s. James Richard and Claire Ella (Springfeld) T.; married; 2 children. BA, U. Pa., 1979; JD, Widener U., 1987. Field person Rep. Nat. Com., Washington, 1979-82, dir. incumbent programs, 1979-81, dep. dir. edn., 1981-82; polit. dir. GOPAC, Washington, 1982-83; asst. regional adminstr. U.S. SBA, Bala Cynwyd, Pa., 1983-84; pres. Tierney & Co., Phila., 1984-86; pres., chief exec. officer, Lewis, Gilman & Kynett Pub. Rels., Phila., 1986-89; pres., chief exec. officer The Tierney Group, Phila, 1989—; pres., CEO FCB/Tierney, Phila., 1994—. ann. giving chmn. Ingis House for Disabled Persons, Phila.; bd. dirs. Wilma Theater, Phila., Moore Coll. Art and Design, Phila., Sch. Bd. Archdiocese of Phila., Ave. of Arts, Inc., Phila. Police Athletic League, Phila. coun. Boy Scouts Am., fund for Phila., Phila. Festival of Arts. Mem. ABA, Pa. Bar Assn., Phila. Bar Assn., Pub. Rels. Soc. Am., St. Anthony Club, Union League. Roman Catholic. Avocation: skydiving, Bonsai gardening. Office: Foote Cone and Belding of PA Inc 200 S Broad St Fl 10 Philadelphia PA 19102-3803

TIERNEY, GORDON PAUL, real estate broker, genealogist; b. Ft. Wayne, Ind., Oct. 17, 1922; s. James Leonard and Ethele Lydia (Brown) T.; m. Carma Lillian Devine, Oct. 17, 1946; 1 child, Paul N. Student, Ind. U., 1940-41, Cath. U. Am., 1941-42; coll. tng. detachment, Clemson U., 1943. Br. mgr. Bartlett-Collins Co., Chgo., 1956-84; prin., broker Kaiser-Tierney Real Estate, Inc., Palatine, Ill., 1984-89; pres. Tierney Real Estate, Newburgh, Ind. Author: Burgess/Bryan Connection, 1978; assoc. editor Colonial Genealogist Jour., 1976-85. Served in USAC, 1943-45, China. Decorated Legion of Honor. Fellow Am. Coll. Genealogists (pres. 1977—); mem. SAR (v.p. gen. 1984-85, genealogist gen. 1981-83, Silver and Bronze medals 1978-80, Patriot medal 1976, Meritorious Svc. award 1983, Minutemen award 1984), Huguenot Soc. Ill. (state pres. 1978-80), Huguenot Soc. S.C., Nat. Huguenot Soc., Huguenot Soc. Ind. (pres. 1993-95), Nat. Geneal. Soc., Ind. Hist. Soc., Soc. Ind. Pioneers, First Families Ohio, Ohio Geneal. Soc., Va. Geneal. Soc., Md. Geneal. Soc., Augustan Soc., Gen. Soc. War 1812 (state pres. 1985), Sons and Daus. Pilgrims, Descs. Old Plymouth Colony, Mil. Order Stars and Bars, Soc. Descs. Colonial Clergy, Sons of Union Vets., Sons of Confederate Vets., Pioneer Wis. Families, Welcome Soc. Pa., Pa. Geneal. Soc., Nat. Soc. Archivists, Soc. Colonial Wars in Ill., Soc. Colonial Wars in Ind. (gov. 1992-94), Sons of Am. Colonists (nat. v.p. 1971-74), Mil. and Hospitalier Order St. Lazarus of Jerusalem, Order Descs. Ancient Planters, Hump Pilots Assn., Nat. Bd. Realtors, Ill. Bd. Realtors, Sword Bunker Hill, Tri-State Geneal. Soc., Jamestowne Soc., Baronial Order Magna Charta, Masons, Shriners, Rolling Hill Country Club. Republican. Presbyterian. Home and Office: 8766 Hanover Dr Newburgh IN 47630-9327

TIERNEY, JAMES EDWARD, attorney general; b. Bklyn., Apr. 12, 1947; s. Charles J. and Agnes V. (Quinn) T.; m. Susan Webster, Jan. 26, 1969; children: Adam, Josie, Matthew, Daniel, Kate. B.A. with highest honors, U. Maine, 1969, J.D., 1974. Bar: Maine 1974. Mem. Maine State Ho. Reps., 1972-80, majority leader, 1976-80; atty. gen. State of Maine, 1980-90; cons. state attys. gen., 1994—; bd. dirs. People for the Am. Way, Topsham, Maine, 1991-93; spl. prosecutor investigate Pa. Supreme Ct., 1992-93; mem. bd. commentators Courtroom TV Network. Wasserstein fellow Harvard Law Sch., 1992-93. Mem. Am. Judicature Soc. (bd. dirs.). Office: PO Box 417 Topsham ME 04086-0417

TIERNEY, JOHN JAMES, advertising agency executive; b. Detroit, Oct. 13, 1934; s. Edward and Rose (DeLargy) T.; m. Bernice Claire Kaminski, Nov. 12, 1978; children—Erica Lynn, John Vincent, Bradley Edward. B.A. in Bus. Adminstrn., Wayne State U., 1956, B.A. in Advt., 1956. Regional sales mgr. Rox Paint Co., Detroit, 1956-60; asst. advt. dir. Detroit Free Press, 1960-65; dir. mktg. Fretter Appliance, Livonia, Mich., 1965-70; exec. v.p. Northgate Advt., Detroit, 1970-73; 1st sr. v.p. Mars Advt., Southfield, Mich., 1973—. Sgt. U.S. Army, 1956-57. Mem. Detroit Advt. Assn., Adcraft Club of Detroit. Roman Catholic. Home: 8681 Cooley Rd Union Lake MI 48387 Office: Mars Advt Co 24209 Northwestern Hwy Southfield MI 48075-2551

TIERNEY, JOHN WILLIAM, chemical engineering educator; b. Oak Park, Ill., Dec. 29, 1923; s. John William and Agnes (Shea) T.; m. Patricia A. O'Neill, June 21, 1952; children: John, Patrick, Joseph, Paul. B.S. in Chem. Engring., Purdue U., 1947; M.S. in Chem. Engring., U. Mich., 1948; Ph.D. in Chem. Engring., Northwestern U., 1951. Sr. research engr. Pure Oil Co., Crystal Lake, Ill., 1948-53; asst. prof. Purdue U., West Lafayette, Ind., 1953-56; mgr. dept. Remington Rand Univac, St. Paul, 1956-60; assoc. prof. chem. engring. U. Pitts., 1960-62, prof., 1962—, W.K. Whiteford prof. chem. engring., 1991-94, prof. emeritus, 1995—; vis. prof. U. Técnica Federico Santa Maria, Valparaiso, Chile, 1960-62; lectr. U. Barcelona (Spain), 1968-69. Fellow AIChE (chmn. Pitts. sect. 1982, McAfee award Pitts. sect. 1995); mem. Am. Chem. Soc., Am. Soc. Engring. Edn. Home: 1330 N Sheridan Ave Pittsburgh PA 15206-1760 Office: U Pitts 1230 Benedum Hall Pittsburgh PA 15261-2212

TIERNEY, MICHAEL EDWARD, lawyer; b. N.Y., July 16, 1948; s. Michael Francis and Margret Mary (Creamer) T.; m. Alicia Mary Boldt, June 6, 1981; children: Colin, Madeleine. BA, St. Louis U., 1970, MBA, 1978, JD, 1978. Bar: Mo. Assoc., law clk. Wayne L. Millsap, P.C., St. Louis, 1977-80; staff atty. Interco. Inc., St. Louis, 1980-83; textile divsn. counsel Chromalloy Am. Corp., St. Louis, 1984-87; v.p., sec. P.N. Hirsch & Co., St. Louis, 1983-84; sr. counsel, asst. sec. Jefferson Smurfit Corp., St. Louis, 1987-92, v.p., gen. counsel, sec., 1993—. Mem. adv. bd. St. Louis Area Food Bank, 1980—. U.S. Army, Security Agy., 1970-73. Mem. Racquet Club St. Louis. Republican. Roman Catholic. Avocations: sailing, squash. Home: # 10 Twin Springs Ln Saint Louis MO 63124 Office: Jefferson Smurfit Corp 8182 Maryland Ave Saint Louis MO 63105-3786

TIERNEY, MICHAEL STEWART, newspaper editor, journalist; b. Louisville, May 20, 1952; s. James Edmund Jr. and Mary (Mullin) T.; m. Lorri Booker; children: Shannon, Meredith, Jordan. BA, U. Ky., 1973. Sports writer, asst. sports editor St. Petersburg Times, 1973-85; asst. sports editor, exec. sports editor, Olympics editor Atlanta Jour.-Constitution, 1986—, now Olympics News reporter only; mem. nat. recognized sports staffs St. Petersburg Times, Atlanta Jour.-Constitution, Assoc. Press Sports Editors. Recipient various writing awards Assoc. Press Sports Editors, Fla. Sports Writers Assn. Mem. Assoc. Press Sports Editors. Home: 457 Nelson Ferry Rd Decatur GA 30030-2323 Office: Atlanta Journal-Constitution PO Box 4689 Atlanta GA 30302-4689

TIERNEY, PATRICK JOHN, information services executive; b. Denver, Oct. 9, 1945; s. Thomas Michael and Betty Ruth (Fairall) T.; m. Lois Bruce, Jan. 1, 1980; children: Christopher, Blake. BS, U. Colo., 1967, MBA, 1970. Pres. Gould E.P.C. Div., San Diego, 1980-84, Caterpillar Capital, San Diego, 1984-85; v.p., gen. mgr. TRW Info. Svcs., Orange, Calif., 1985-91; CEO Knight-Ridder Info., Mountain View, Calif., 1991—. Mem. Info. Industry Assn. (bd. dirs. 1992—). Republican. Office: Knight-Ridder Info Inc 2440 W El Camino Real Mountain View CA 94040-1400

TIERNEY, PAUL E., JR., investment company executive; b. Feb. 18, 1943; married. Postgrad., Harvard U. With Peace Corps., Chile, 1964-66, Starwood Corp., 1969-72; v.p., gen. mgr. Continental Ill. Ltd., London, 1972-75; sr. v.p. White Weld & Co., 1975-78; mng. dir. Gollust Tierney & Oliver, Inc., 1987-90; chmn. TW Holdings, Inc., Spartanburg, S.C., 1990-92; also bd. dirs. UAL Corp., Elk Grove, Ill.; chmn. bd. Technoserve, Inc. Office: Gollust Tierney & Oliver 500 Park Ave Fl 5 New York NY 10022-1606*

TIERNEY, RAYMOND MORAN, JR., lawyer; b. Bklyn., Aug. 1, 1932; s. Raymond M. and Alice Mary (Hoag) T.; m. Kathleen Maguire, June 23, 1956; children: Kathy Snyder, Alicia Johnson, Raymond III, Michael, Christopher. BA, U. Notre Dame, 1954; LLB, Fordham U., 1961. Bar: N.J. 1962. Asst. sec. and credit loaning officer Hanover Bank, N.Y.C., 1956-61; law sec. to Hon. J.J. Francis Supreme Ct. N.J., 1961-62; assoc. Shanley & Fisher P.C., Newark, 1962-67; ptnr. Shanley & Fisher P.C., Morristown, 1967—; adj. prof. Monmouth Coll., W. Long Branch, N.J., 1985-88; master William J. Brennan Jr. Inn of Ct., 1987-92; faculty U. Va. Law Sch. Ann. Trial Inst., 1990—; speaker in field. Bd. adjustment Borough Shrewsbury, 1973-80; councilman Coun. Borough Shrewsbury, 1981-83; commr. Gateway Nat. Park Adv. Commn., 1983-86; trustee Newark Mus., 1990—, St. Peter's Coll., Jersey City, 1990—. 1st Lt. U.S. Marines, 1954-56. Recipient Trial Bar award Trial Attys. N.J., 1989, Thomas More Assn. medal Seton Hall Law Sch., 1991, William J. Brennan award U. Va. Law Trial Advocacy Inst., 1996. Fellow Am. Coll. Trial Attys., Am. Bar Found.; mem. D.C. Bar Assn., N.J. State Bar Found. (chmn. 1990-92, pres. 1992-94), N.J. State Bar Assn. (trustee 1992-94), Monmouth County Bar Assn. Office: Shanley & Fisher 131 Madison Ave Morristown NJ 07960-6086

TIERNEY, SUSAN FALLOWS, federal official; married; 2 children. BA, Scripps Coll., 1973; student, L'Institut d'Etudes Politiques, Paris; MA, Cornell U., 1976, PhD, 1980; LLD (hon.), Regis Coll. Asst. prof. U. Calif., Irvine, 1978-82; sr. economist Mass. Exec. Office Energy Resources, 1983-84; exec. dir. Mass. Energy Facilities Siting Coun., 1984-88; commr. Dept. Pub. Utilities, 1988-90, sec. environ. affairs, resources authority, 1991-93; asst. sec. energy, office of policy, planning and program evaluation Dept. Energy, Washington, 1993—; chmn. transmission task force New Eng. Gov.'s Conf. Power Planning Com.; mem. Keystone Project Electric Transmission Ind. Power Prodrs. Contbr. articles to profl. jours. Mem. New Eng. Conf. Public Utility Commrs., Nat. Assn. Regulatory Utility Commrs. (energy conservation gas com.), Electric Power Rsch. (adv. com.). Home: Dept Energy Policy 108 Hammond St Chestnut Hill MA 01267

TIERNEY, THOMAS J., business management consultant; b. San Francisco, Mar. 5, 1954; s. Ralph Thomas and Eleanor Faye (Walker) T.; m. Joy Karen McGee, Sept. 23, 1984; 1 child, Colin Mcgee. BA in Econs. with distinction, U. Calif., Davis, 1976; MBA with distinction, Harvard, 1980. Field engr. Bechtel Internat., Azrew, Algeria, 1976-78; cons. Bain & Co., San Francisco, 1980-82, mgr., 1982-83, v.p., 1983-87, exec. v.p., mng. ptnr., 1987-90, mng. dir., 1990—. Mem. campaign cabinet strategy com. United Way, San Francisco, 1987—; bd. dirs. Bay Area Coun., San Francisco, 1991—, The Nature Conservancy, San Francisco, 1991—. Recipient Winslow Meml. award U. Calif. Davis, 1976. Mem. U. Calif. Davis Alumni Assn. (dir. 1984-88), San Francisco C. of C., Harvard Bus. Sch. Alumni Assn. Roman Catholic. Avocations: biking, fishing, history. Home: 45 Old Farm Rd Wellesley MA 02181-1423

TIESZEN, RALPH LELAND, SR., internist; b. Marion, S.D., Sept. 21, 1928; s. Bernard D. and Hulda J. (Thomas) T.; m. Florence Morrill Johnson, July 25, 1952; children: Ralph Leland Jr., Stuart Carl, Stephan Lee. Student, Freeman Jr. Coll., 1946-48; BS, Wheaton Coll., 1950; postgrad., U. S.D., 1950-52; MD, Loma Linda U., 1954. Diplomate Am. Bd. Internal Medicine, Am. Bd. Geriatric Medicine. Intern L.A. County Hosp., 1954-55, resident TB and Chest, 1955-56; commd. 2d lt. med. corps. USAF, 1956, advanced through grades to maj., 1964; chief medicine hosp. USAF, Eglin AFB, 1962-64; ret. USAF, 1979; resident in internal medicine Mayo Found., Rochester, Minn., 1957-60; mem. active staff dept. internal medicine Carraway Meth. Med. Ctr., Birmingham, 1964—, dir. resident program, 1968-72, trustee, 1972-77, pres. staff, 1973-75, exec. com., fin. com., 1974-77, dir. geriatrics, 1989—; pvt. practice Norwood Clinic, Inc., Birmingham, Ala., 1964—; asst. clin. prof. medicine Med. Coll. Ala., 1965-69, asst. clin. prof. dept. endocrinology, 1969-70, clin. assoc. prof. medicine, 1970-81, clin. prof. medicine, 1981—; med. dir. Community Hosp., 1989—; mem. faculty joint commn. accreditation hosps., 1974-78; exec. com. Birmingham Regional Health Systems Agy.; investigator numerous clin. trials. Contbr. articles to profl. jours. Chmn. Birmingham String Quartet, 1970-74; v.p. ticket sales Ala. Symphony Assn., 1979, exec. com.; sec. men's com. Ala. Symphony, 1986-88, pres. 1990-91. Gen. Med. Officer USAR, 197984, comdr. U.S. Army Hosp., Birmingham, 1984-88, col., chief profl. svcs. 5th med. group, Birmingham, 1988-92, ret., 1992. Mem. ACP, AMA, Am. Thoracic Soc. (sr.), Med. Assn. State Ala., Jefferson County Med. Soc. (past bd. censors, del. to state med. assn.), Birmingham Acad. Medicine (pres. 1987-88), Birmingham Internists Soc. (pres. 1972-73). Democrat. Avocations: opera, symphony, philosophy, medical ethics, astronomy. Office: Norwood Clinic Inc PO Box 830230 1528 26th St N Birmingham AL 35234-1911

TIETJEN, JOHN HENRY, biology and oceanography educator, consultant; b. Jamaica, N.Y., June 19, 1940; s. Reinhard L. and Emma (Wilkomm) T.; m. Theresa Mary Martin, Aug., 24, 1968; children: Theresa Emma, Mary Elizabeth. BS, CCNY, 1961; PhD, U. R.I., 1966. Asst. prof. biology CCNY, N.Y.C., 1966-71, assoc. prof., 1971-75, prof., 1975—; ecol. cons. Tex. Instruments, Dallas, 1977-79, S.W. Rsch. Inst., Houston, 1978-80, Henderson and Bodwell Engrs., Bethpage, N.Y., 1982, N.E. Utilities, Hartford, Conn., 1968—, North Atlantic Energy Svc., Seabrook, N.H., 1994—. Author, co-author over 50 rsch. articles. V.p., pres. Leonia (N.J.) Bd. Edn., 1977-86. Research grantee NSF, Office Naval Research, Dept. Energy, Nat. Oceanic & Atmospheric Adminstrn. Mem. Am. Arbitration Assn., Sigma Xi. Roman Catholic. Avocations: outdoor activities, reading, travel. Office: CCNY Dept of Biology Convent Ave New York NY 10027-2604

TIETKE, WILHELM, gastroenterologist; b. Niengraben, Germany, Oct. 15, 1938; came to U.S., 1969, naturalized, 1979; s. Wilhelm and Frieda (Schmeding) T.; m. Imme Schmidt, Oct. 15, 1965; children: Cornelia, Isabel. MD, U Goettingen (West Germany), 1968. Diplomate Am. Bd. Internat. Medicine, Am. Bd. Gastroenterology. Intern Edward W. Sparrow Hosp., Lansing, Mich., 1970; resident in internal medicine Henry Ford Hosp., Detroit, 1971-73; fellow in gastroenterology, 1973-75; practice medicine specializing in gastroenterology, Huntsville, Ala., 1975—; mem. vol. faculty, cons. U. Ala., Huntsville, 1976; clin. assoc. prof. internal medicine, 1979—; v.p. Huntsville Gastroenterology Assocs., P.C., 1979—. Fellow Coll. Gastroenterology; mem. AMA, Ala. Med. Soc., Am. Coll. Physicians, Am. Soc. Gastrointestinal Endoscopy. Lutheran. Lodge: Rotary. Home: 2707 Westminister Way SE Huntsville AL 35801-2241 Office: 119 Longwood Dr Huntsville AL 35801-4205 also: PO Box 2169 Huntsville AL 35804-2169

TIETZ, DENNIS JAMES, securities executive; b. Chgo., Nov. 10, 1952; s. Carl John and Beverly Jean (Hoff) T.; m. Jennifer Yates, Sept. 17, 1980. BSBA, San Jose State U., 1975. Acct. Sutro & Co., San Francisco, 1975-76; sales rep. Bank of Am., San Francisco, 1976-77, Trans Ocean Leasing, Houston, 1977-81; pres. Cronos Capital Corp., San Francisco, 1981—; bd. dirs. C.G. Holdings, Luxembourg, 1993—. Mem. Nat. Assn. Securities Dealers (lic. securities prin.). Avocations: cross-country skiing, bicycling, reading. Office: Cronos Capital Corp 444 Market St Fl 15 San Francisco CA 94111-5325

TIETZ, NORBERT WOLFGANG, clinical chemistry educator, administrator; b. Stettin, Germany, Nov. 13, 1926; s. Joseph and Anna (Kozalla) T.; m. Gertrud Kraft, Oct. 17, 1959; children—Margaret, Kurt, Annette, Michael. Student, Tuebingen, Germany, 1945-46; D.Sc., Tech. U., Stuttgart, W.Ger., 1950. Chmn. dept. chemistry Reid Meml. Hosp., Richmond, Ind., 1956-59; prof., dir. clin. chemistry Mt. Sinai Med. Ctr. and Chgo. Med. Sch., Chgo., 1959-76, U. Ky. Med. Ctr., Lexington, 1976—; research fellow and asst. U. Munich, W.Ger., 1951-54; research fellow dept. pathology U. Chgo. and St. Luke's Hosp., Chgo., 1955-56, Rockford Meml. Hosp., Ill., 1954-55; cons. Ill. Dept. Pub. Health, 1967-76, VA Hosp., Hines, Ill., 1974-76; prof. biochemistry and pathology Rush Med. Coll., Chgo., 1975-76; vol. cons. VA Hosp., Lexington, 1976—. Editor: Fundamentals of Clinical Chemistry, 1970, 76, 87, Clinical Guide to Laboratory Tests, 1983, 90, 95, Textbook of Clinical Chemistry, 1986, A Study Guide to Clinical Chemistry, 1987, Applied Laboratory Medicine, 1992; assoc. editor: Dictionary and Encyclopedia of Laboratory Medicine and Technology, 1983; contbr. numerous articles to profl. jours. Recipient A. Dubin award Nat. Acad. Clin. Biochemistry, 1995, Disting. Internat. Svc. award Internat. Fedn. Clin. Chemistry. Fellow Acad. Clin. Lab. Physicians and Scientists, Am. Inst. Chemists; mem. Am. Assn. Clin. Chemistry (clin. chemist award 1971, award for outstanding efforts in edn. and tng. 1976, Disting. Alumnus award 1977, Steuben Bowl award 1978, Bernard F. Gerulat award N.J. chpt. 1988, award for Outstanding Contbns. to Clin. Chemistry 1989, Donald D. Van Slyke award N.Y. Met. chpt. 1989), AAAS, Am. Chem. Soc., Am. Soc. Clin. Pathologists, Man. Soc. Clin. Chemists (ann. Lectureship award 1987), Sigma Xi. Roman Catholic. Home: 2075 Bridgeport Dr Lexington KY 40502-2615 Office: U Ky Med Ctr Dept Pathology HA 645 C Lexington KY 40536

TIETZE, LUTZ FRIEDJAN, chemist, educator; b. Berlin, Mar. 14, 1942; s. Friedrich and Hete-Irene (Kruse) T.; m. Karin Krautschneider; children: Martin, Maja, Andrea, Julia. Diploma, U. Kiel, 1966, PhD, 1968; habil. for Organic Chemistry, U. Münster, 1975; DSc (hon.), U. Szeged, Hungary, 1994. Rsch. assoc. MIT, 1969-71; lectr. U. Münster, 1971-76; prof. U. Dortmund, 1977-78; full prof. and inst. dir. U. Göttingen, Göttingen, 1978—; dean and prodean U. Göttingen, 1983-87, 91-95; mem. bd. German Faculties of Chemistry. Author: Reactions and Syntheses, 1981, (translated into Japanese 1984, 2d edit., 1995, English 1989), 2d edit., 1991, Basic Course in Organic Chemistry, 1993, 2d edit., 1995; contbr. numerous articles to profl. jours.; patentee in field. Recipient Karl-Winnacker award, Hoechst AG, Germany, 1976, Lit. prize, Fonds der Chem. Industry, Germany, 1982; fellow Japan Soc. Promotion Sci. Fellow Royal Soc. Chemists; mem. Gesellschaft Deutscher Chemiker, Am. Chem. Soc., Chem. Soc. Argentina (hon.), Academia Scientiarum Göttingen. Home: Stumpfe Eiche 73, D-37077 Göttingen Germany Office: U Göttingen Inst Organic Chemistry, Tammannstrasse 2, D-37077 Göttingen Germany

TIETZE, PHYLLIS SOMERVILLE, media specialist; b. Bklyn., Aug. 5, 1941; d. Samuel Clark and Norma Helen (Vanderbeck) Somerville; m. Robert Morse Tietze, Dec. 22, 1962; children: Kevin North, Andrea Kristina. BS, U. Miami, 1962; ML, U. S.C., 1989. Rsch. asst. U. Miami Inst. Marine Sci., 1962-65; media specialist Pendleton (S.C.) High Sch., 1989—. Mem. ALA, S.C. Assn. Sch. Librs., Anderson County Libr. Assn. Presbyterian. Avocations: tennis, cross-stitch, reading mystery stories. Home: 226 Weaver Rd Pendleton SC 29670-8945 Office: Pendleton High Sch Hwy 187 Box 218 Pendleton SC 29670

TIFFANY, JOSEPH RAYMOND, II, lawyer; b. Dayton, Ohio, Feb. 5, 1949; s. Forrest Fraser and Margaret Watson (Clark) T.; m. Terri Robbins, Dec. 1, 1984. AB magna cum laude, Harvard U., 1971; MS in Internat. Relations, London Sch. Econs., 1972; JD, U. Calif., Berkeley, 1975. Bar: U.S. Dist. Ct. (no. dist.) 1975, U.S. Dist. Ct. (ea. dist.) 1977, U.S. Ct. Appeals (9th cir.) 1982. Assoc. Pillsbury, Madison & Sutro, San Francisco, 1975-82, ptnr., 1983—. Mem. ABA (antitrust, intellectual property, litigation sects.), Calif. Bar Assn., Harvard Club (bd. dirs. San Francisco chpt. 1990—). Office: Pillsbury Madison & Sutro 225 Bush St San Francisco CA 94104-4207

TIFFT, WILLIAM GRANT, astronomer; b. Derby, Conn., Apr. 5, 1932; s. William Charles and Marguerite Howe (Hubbell) T.; m. Carol Ruth Nordquist, June 1, 1957 (div. July 1964); children: Jennifer, William John; m. Janet Ann Lindner Homewood, June 2, 1965; 1 child, Amy, stepchildren: Patricia, Susan, Hollis. AB, Harvard Coll., 1954; PhD, Calif. Inst. Tech., 1958. Nat. sci. postdoctoral Australian Nat. U., Canberra, 1958-60; rsch. assoc. Vanderbilt U., Nashville, 1960-61; astronomer Lowell Obs., Flagstaff, Ariz., 1961-64; assoc. prof. U. Ariz., Tucson, 1964-73, prof., 1973—. Joint author: Revised New General Catalog, 1973; contbr. over 100 articles to profl. jours. NSF Predoctoral fellow, 1954-58, NSF Postdoctoral fellow, 1958-60; grantee NASA, NSF, ONR, Rsch. Corp. Fellow Am. Astron. Soc.; mem. Internat. Astron. Union. Achievements include discovery of redshift quantization and correlations relating to it, including variability; first to detect voids in mapping of large scale supercluster structure; investigations of three-dimensional time in cosmology and particle physics. Office: U of Arizona Dept of Astronomy Tucson AZ 85721

TIFT, MARY LOUISE, artist; b. Seattle, Jan. 2, 1913; d. John Howard and Wilhelmina (Pressler) Dreher; m. William Raymond Tift, Dec. 4, 1948. BFA cum laude, U. Wash., 1933; postgrad., Art Ctr. Coll., L.A., 1945-48, U. Calif., San Francisco, 1962-63. Art dir. Vaughn Shedd Advt., L.A., 1948; asst. prof. design Calif. Coll. Arts & Crafts, Oakland, Calif., 1949-59; coord. design dept. San Francisco Art Inst., 1959-62. Subject of cover story, Am. Artist mag., 1980, studio article, 1987; one woman shows, Gumps Gallery, San Francisco, 1977, 1986, 90, Diane Gilson Gallery, Seattle, 1978, Oreg. State U., 1981, group shows include, Brit. Biennale, Yorkshire, Eng., 1970, Grenchen Triennale, Switzerland, 1970, Polish Biennale, Crakow, 1972, Nat. Gallery, Washington, 1973, U.S.-U.K. Impressions, Eng., 1988; represented in permanent collections, Phila. Mus. Art, Bklyn. Mus., Seattle Art Mus., Library Congress, Achenbach Print Collection, San Francisco Palace Legion of Honor. Served to lt. USNR, 1943-45. Mem. Print Club Phila., World Print Council, Calif. Soc. Printmakers, Phi Beta Kappa, Lambda Rho. Christian Scientist. Studio: 275 Los Ranchitos Rd Apt 341 San Rafael CA 94903-3692

TIGAR, MICHAEL EDWARD, lawyer, educator; b. Glendale, Calif., Jan. 18, 1941; s. Charles Henry and Margaret Elizabeth (Lang) T.; m. Pamet Ayer Jones, Sept. 21, 1961 (div. Mar. 1973); children: Jon Steven, Katherine Ayer; m. Amanda G. Birrell, Feb. 16, 1980; 1 child, Elizabeth Torrey. BA in Polit. Sci., U. Calif., Berkeley, 1962, JD, 1966. Bar: D.C. 1967, U.S. Ct. Appeals (2d, 4th, 5th, 6th, 7th, 8th, 9th, 10th and D.C. cirs.), U.S. Tax Ct., U.S. Supreme Ct. 1972, N.Y. 1993. Assoc. Williams & Connolly, Washington, 1966-69; editor-in-chief Selective Svc. Law Reporter, Washington, 1967-69; acting prof. law UCLA, 1969-71; pvt. practice law Grasse, France, 1972-74; assoc. William & Connolly, Washington, 1974, ptnr., 1975-77; ptnr. Tigar & Buffone, Washington, 1977-84; prof. law U. Tex., Austin, 1984-87, Joseph D. Jamail centennial chair in law, 1987—; of counsel Haddon, Margan & Foreman, Denver, 1996—; reporter 5th Cir. Pattern Jury Instrns., Austin, 1988-90. Author: Practice Manual Selective Service Law Reporter, 1968, Law and the Rise of Capitalism, 1977, Federal Appeals: Jurisdiction and Practice, 2d edit., 1993, Examining Witnesses, 1993; contbr. articles to profl. jours. Mem. ABA (vice chair 1987-88, chair elect 1988-89, chair 1989-90 sect. litigation). Avocations: sailing, cooking. Office: PO Box 160037 Austin TX 78716-0037

TIGAY, ALAN MERRILL, editor; b. Detroit, June 23, 1947; s. Leonard and Ethel (Cooper) T.; m. Suelly Rodrigues, July 30, 1995; 1 child from previous marriage: Rafael Leonard. B.A. in Sociology, U. Mich., 1969; M.S. in Journalism, Columbia U., 1976. Feature writer United Feature Syndicate, N.Y.C., 1976-78; editor in chief Near East Report, Washington, 1978-80; exec. editor Hadassah Mag., N.Y.C., 1980—; judge Nat. Mag. Awards, 1981—, Nat. Jewish Book Awards, 1988—; adminstr. Harold U. Ribalow prize, 1983—. Editor: The Jewish Traveler, 1987, 2d edit., 1994, Myths and Facts: A Concise Record of the Arab-Israeli Conflict, 1978, 2d edit., 1980; free-lance writer various N.Y. and nat. newspapers, mags., 1972—. Pres., vol. Owners Corp., N.Y.C., 1982-86; vol. Partnership for Homeless Rodeph Sholom Winter Shelter Program, N.Y.C., 1983-85, Interfaith Hospitality Network, Montclair, N.J., 1988—. Mem. Am. Soc. Mag. Editors, Am. Jewish Press Assn. Avocation: collecting newspapers. Office: Hadassah Mag 50 W 58th St New York NY 10019-2500

TIGER, IRA PAUL, lawyer; b. Bklyn., Jan. 31, 1936; s. Sidney and Rebecca (Frankel) T.; m. Rosalind Silverman, July 4, 1957 (dec. Nov. 1972); children: Ruth, Lori; m. Ann Mae Gersh, May 5, 1974; stepchildren: Jimmie, Randy, Richard Riesenberg. B.S. in Econs., U. Pa., 1956, J.D. magna cum laude, 1959. Bar: Pa. 1960, U.S. Dist. Ct. (ea. dist.) Pa. 1960, U.S. Ct. Appeals (3d cir.) 1960, U.S. Supreme Ct. 1971. Law clk. 3d cir., 1959-60; assoc. Schnader, Harrison, Segal & Lewis, Phila., 1960-67, ptnr., 1968—, chmn. litigation dept., 1986-90, chmn. standing com. on profl. conduct, 1992—. Research editor U. Pa. Law Rev., 1958-59. Pres. Temple Sinai Synagogue, 1989-91; mem. Planning Adv. Bd. Upper Dublin Twp., 1982-87, mem. edn. adv. com., 1976-78; legal counsel Phila. Jr. C. of C., 1963-64, bd. dirs., 1962-66, sec. Jewish campus activities bd., 1971-73. Mem. ABA, Am. Judicature Soc., Inst. Jud. Adminstrn., Pa. Bar Assn., Phila. Bar Assn. (chmn. fed. cts. com. 1985), Lawyers Club Phila., Order of Coif (exec. com. Pa. chpt. 1981-83), Beta Alpha Psi, Beta Gamma Sigma. Democrat. Office: Schnader Harrison 1600 Market St Ste 3600 Philadelphia PA 19103-4252

TIGER, LIONEL, social scientist, anthropology consultant; b. Montreal, Que., Can., Feb. 5, 1937; s. Martin and Lillian (Schneider) T.; m. Virginia Conner, Aug. 19, 1964; 1 child, Sebastian Benjamin. BA, McGill U., 1957, MA, 1959; PhD, U. London, 1963. Instr. anthropology U. Ghana, Accra, 1960; asst. prof. dept. anthropology and sociology U. B.C., Vancouver, Can., 1963-68; assoc. prof. anthropology Rutgers U., New Brunswick, N.J., 1969-74, prof. anthropology, 1974—, Charles Darwin prof. anthropology, 1990—; cons., rsch. dir. Harry F. Guggenheim Found., N.Y.C., 1972-84; chmn. bd. social scientists U.S. News and World Report, 1986-88; sci. adv. bd. Am. Wine Inst., San Francisco. Author: Men in Groups, 1969, 2d. edit., 1987; (with Robin Rox) The Imperial Animal, 1971, 2d edit., 1989; (with Joseph Shepher) Women in the Kibbutz, 1975, Optimism: The Biology of Hope, 1979, 2d edit., 1994, China's Food, 1985, The Manufacture of Evil: Ethics, Evolution, and the Industrial System, 1987; editor: Female Hierarchies, 1978, (with Michael Robinson) Man and Beast Revisited, 1991, The Pursuit of Pleasure, 1992; mem. editorial bd. Social Sci. Info., Ethology and Sociobiology jour., Jour. of Social Distress and the Homeless. Bd. dirs. David R. Graham Found., Toronto, Ont., Can. Recipient W.I. Susman award for excellence in tchg., 1985, McNaughton prize for creative writing; Guggenheim fellow, 1969, rsch. fellow ASDA Found., 1985, Can. Coun., fgn. area tng. fellow Ford Found., Can. Coun.-Killam fellow for interdisciplinary rsch., Rockefeller fellow Aspen Inst., 1979, fellow H.F. Guggenheim Found, 1988-89. Fellow Royal Anthrop. Inst. (Eng.); mem. PEN (mem. exec. bd., treas. 1988-91, v.p. 1991-94), Am. Anthrop. Assn., Can. Anthrop. Assn., Can. Humanists Assn. (hon.), Soc. for Study of Evolution, Century Assn. Home: 248 W 23rd St Fl 4 New York NY 10011-2304 also: RR 2 Millbrook NY 12545-9802 Office: Rutgers U Douglas Coll New Brunswick NJ 08903-0270

TIGERMAN, STANLEY, architect, educator; b. Chgo., Sept. 20, 1930; s. Samuel Bernard and Emma Louise (Stern) T.; m. Margaret I. McCurry; children: Judson Joel, Tracy Leigh. Student, MIT, 1948-49; B.Arch., Yale U., 1960, M.Arch., 1961. Archtl. draftsman firm George Fred Keck, Chgo., 1949-50, Skidmore, Owings and Merrill, Chgo., 1957-59, Paul Rudolph, New Haven, 1959-61, Harry Weese, Chgo., 1961-62; partner firm Tigerman & Koglin, Chgo., 1962-64; prin. firm Stanley Tigerman & Assos., Chgo., 1964-82; ptnr. Tigerman Fugman McCurry, Chgo., 1982-88, Tigerman McCurry, 1988—; prof. architecture U. Ill.-Chgo., 1967-71, 80-93, dir. Sch. Architecture, 1985-93; vis. lectr. Yale U., 1974, Cornell U., Ithaca, N.Y., 1963, Cooper Union, 1970, U. Calif. at Berkeley, 1968, Cardiff (Wales) Coll., 1965, Engring. U., Bangladesh, 1967; chmn. AIA com. on design, coordinator exhbn. and book Chicago Architects, 1977; Charlotte Shepherd Davenport prof. architecture Yale U., 1979; architect-in-residence Am. Acad. in Rome, 1980; vis. prof. architecture Harvard U., 1982; William Henry Bishop Chair. prof. architecture Yale U., 1984; dir. post-professional grad. program U. Ill.-Chgo.; co-founder Archeworks, Design Lab., Chgo., 1993. Prin. works include: Fukuoka Apt. Complex, Japan, The Power House, Zion, Ill., The Preserve Clubhouse, New Buffalo, Mich., others; author: Versus, 1982, Architecture of Exile, 1988 (nominated Nat. Jewish Book awar 1989), Stanley Tigerman: Buildings and Projects, 1966-89, 1989; contbg. author: Design of the Housing Site, 1966, Chicago on Foot, 1969, Art Today, 1969, New Directions in American Architecture, 1969, Contemporary Jewelry, 1970, Urban Structures for the Future, 1972, Spaces for Living, 1973, Chicago 1930-70, 1974, Interior Spaces Designed by Architects, 1974, Housing, 1976, Chicago Architects, 1976, 100 Years of Architecture in Chicago, 1976, Architectural Graphics Primer, 1976, 86, Mies Reconsidered, 1986, Chicago Architecture 1872-1922, 1988 (designer exhbn.), others, also numerous articles in newspapers and profl. jours.; exhibited, Venice Biennale, 1976, 80; co-curator, author essay, Calif. Condition exhbn., 1982; curator, designer exhbn., author catalogue Chicago Architecture, The New Zeitgeist: In Search of Closure, 1989. Pres. Yale Arts Assn., 1969-70; mem. advisory com. Yale Archtl. Sch., 1976—; bd. dirs. Bangladesh Found. Served with USN, 1950-54. Recipient Alpha Rho Chi medal Yale, 1961, Advanced Studies in Fine Art grant Graham Fedn., 1965, Archtl. Record award, 1970, Chgo. Masonry award, 1974, Masonry gold medal, 1974, Alumni Art award Yale U., 1985, Design award for Art Inst. Chgo. Schinkel Exhbn., Am. Soc. Interior Designers, 1995. Fellow AIA (chmn. com. design 1976-77, adv. com., Disting. Svc. award Chgo. chpt. 1983, Chgo. Honor awards 1977-79, Nat. Honor award 1982, 84, 87, 91, Nat. Modern Income Housing award 1970, Nat. Homes for Better Living award 1974, 75, Ill. award 1976, Nat. award of Merit 1970, 74, 75, named to Hall of Fame 1990, Disting. Bldg. award for pvt. residence Chgo. chpt. 1991, Chgo. Interior Archtl. Award of Excellence 1981, 83, 87, 91, 92, Nat. Interior Archtl. Award of Excellence 1992-93, Chgo. Disting. Bldg. award 1971, 73, 75, 77, 79, 81, 82, 84, 85, 86, 91, 94, Italian Ceramic Tile Design award 1995, Fukuoka Urban Beautification award 1995, 6 citations of merit Chgo. chpt. 1994); mem. Phi Kappa Phi. Clubs: Arts of Chgo, Yale of N.Y.C, Century Assn. Office: Tigerman & McCurry LTD 444 N Wells St Ste 206 Chicago IL 60610-4522

TIGH, MARK STEPHEN, communications executive, engineering consultant; b. Salem, Mass., Apr. 26, 1948; s. Louis Mark II and Frances Winifred (Mitchell) T.; m. Theresa Ann Kirsher, Apr. 4, 1981; 1 child, Tanya Marcia; children: Tiffany Ann, Louis Mark III, William Sullivan. Student, Marist Coll., 1966; BS, Ga. Inst. Tech., 1966-67, 1972-76; student, West Ga. Coll., 1967, La. State U., Lafayette, 1977-78, Batelle Meml. Inst., 1981. Regional mgr. Wilson-Mankin Engrs., Atlanta, 1975-76; offshore engr. The Offshore Co., Venezuela, 1976-78; prin., CEO Mark Stephen Tigh Assocs., Atlanta, 1976-79; project engr. SP Comms., Burlingame, Calif., 1979-82; sr. engr. Aydin Systems Saudi Arabia, Riyadh, Saudi Arabia, 1982-85; v.p. Constrn. Surveillance Svcs., San Diego, 1985-87; sr. v.p. Transworld Consortium, Inc., San Francisco, 1987-92; sr. mgr. Bell South Internat., Atlanta, 1992—; cons. Royal Saudi Nat. Guard, Riyadh, 1982-86, U.S. Dept. Def., Washington, 1978—; bd. dirs. Transworld Consortium, Inc., San Francisco, Mango Internat., Inc., Sunnyvale, Calif. Author: Veet-A Nam-Ah, 1992; contbr. articles to profl. jours.; inventor of telecom equipment. Mem. San Mateo (Calif.) County Commn., 1985-92, Mott Twp. Police Res., Siskiyou County, Calif., 1982—. Sgt. USMC, 1967-72, Vietnam, maj. in Res. 1975-91. Named outstanding marine Leatherneck Mag., 1967; recipient Cross of Gallantry, 1st place design award Ga. Sheriff's Assn., 1975, 1st place cover shot Assn. Archtl. Photographers, 1981. Mem. AIA, USMC Ret. Officer's Assn., So. Bldg. Code Congress, USMC Force Recon Assn., Constrn. Specifications Inst., San Francisco C. of C., Engrs. Club. Roman Catholic. Avocations: internat. travel and photography, skiing, scuba exploration, mil. history. Home: 3855 Jettie Ct SW Lilburn GA 30247-2362 Office: Bell South Internat 1100 Peachtree St 11HO8 Atlanta GA 30309

TIGHE, JAMES C., publisher; b. Edmonton, Alta., Can., Sept. 30, 1950; s. James Donald and Ellen Grant (Drever) T.; m. Barbara C. Teske, Dec. 2, 1972; children: Teresa M., Jason M. Grad. high sch., Edmonton. Area supr. Edmonton Jour., 1969-73; circulation mgr. Thomson Newspapers, Western Can., 1973-79; dir. circulation Edmonton sun, 1979-81, gen. mgr., 1981-82; gen. mgr. UP Can., Toronto, Ont., 1982-84; pub. Calgary (Alta.) Sun, 1984-88; gen. mgr. Toronto Sun, 1988-89, pub., 1991-94, v.p. corp. planning, 1994-95; pres. Island Pub. Ltd., Can., 1995—. Office: Island Pub Ltd, 1824 Store St, Victoria, BC Canada

TIGHT, DEXTER CORWIN, lawyer; b. San Francisco, Sept. 14, 1924; s. Dexter Junkins and Marie (Corwin) T.; m. Elizabeth Callander, Apr. 20, 1951; children: Dexter C. Jr., Kathyryn Marie Loken, Steven M., David C. AB, Denison U., 1948; JD, Yale U., 1951. Bar: Calif. 1951. Assoc. Pillsbury, Madison & Sutro, San Francisco, 1953-60; gen. atty. W.P. Fuller & Co., San Francisco, 1960-61; gen. counsel Schlage Lock Co., San Francisco, 1961-77; dir. govt. affairs Crown Zellerbach Corp., San Francisco, 1977-78; sr. v.p., gen. counsel The Gap Inc., San Bruno, Calif., 1978-90, legal, internat. cons., 1990—; gen. coun. The Nature Co., 1990-96; bd. dirs. Shaw-Clayton Plastics, San Rafael, Calif., Granite Rock Co., Watsonville, Calif., Alden Lee Ins. Co. Bd. dirs., pres. San Francisco Boys' and Girls' Club; chmn. That Man May See, San Fransisco; trustee Denison U., 1978—, chmn. capital fund dr., 1988-94; trustee Calvary Presbyn. Ch., 1968, 73, elder, 1969—; elder Valley Presbyn. Ch., 1992-96. 1st lt. U.S. Army, 1943-45, 51-52. Mem. ABA, Internat. Exec. Svc. Corps., Calif. Bar Assn., San Francisco Bar Assn. (chmn. various coms.), Commonwealth Club Calif. (past bd. dirs., exec. com.), Menlo Country Club, Bohemian Club (San Francisco), Guardsman Club (1st v.p. 1961), Phi Beta Kappa. Republican. Presbyterian. Avocations: hiking, fishing, tennis, golf, photography. Home: 170 Wildwood Way Redwood City CA 94062-2352

TIGNOR, GEORGE, principal. BA in Biology, St. Mary of Plains Coll., 1969; MA in Botany, Kans. U., Lawrence, 1972; postgrad., Emporia State U., 1974-76. Sci. instr. Rosedale H.S., Kansas City, Kans., 1969-71, Washington H.S., Kansas City, 1973-74, F.L. Schlagle H.S., Kansas City, 1974-76; asst. prin., athletic dir. Wyandotte H.S., Kansas City, 1976-80; prin. Rosedale Mid. Sch., Kansas City, 1980-81, Parsons (Kans.) H.S., 1981—. Named Prin. of Yr., Nat. Assn. Secondary Sch. Prins, 1995, Kans. Prin. of Yr., Kans. Assn. Secondary Sch. Prins., 1995. Office: Parsons HS 3030 Morton Ave Parsons KS 67357-4417

TIHANY, LESLIE CHARLES, retired foreign service officer, educator; b. Hungary, Dec. 28, 1911; came to U.S., 1930; naturalized, 1940; s. Béla and Katalin (Bárody) T.; m. Elizabeth Derricott, 1936; m. 2d., Maria Dekom, 1959; children: Elizabeth, Richard, Peter. BS, Franklin and Marshall Coll., 1931; MA, Northwestern U., 1933, PhD, 1936; AM, Harvard U., 1938; PhD, U. Chgo., 1943; posdoctoral study, U. Helsinki. Rsch. fellow Am. Coun. Learned Socs., 1938-40; asst. history U. Chgo., 1941; teaching fellow Harvard U., 1942-43; prof. U. Denver, 1943; joined Fgn. Svc., Dept. State, 1943, fgn. affairs specialist, 1943-56; consul Salzburg, Austria, 1956-57,

Bombay, 1957-59; 1st sec. Am. Embassy, Beirut, 1960-61, 1st sec., chief econ. officer, 1961-65; 1st sec., chief econ. officer Am. Embassy, Saigon, Vietnam, 1965-66; pub. affairs officer Bur. Far Ea. Affairs, Dept. State, 1966; counselor of embassy, assigned Dept. State, 1966-69, internat. rels. officer Bur. European Affairs, 1966-69; Am. consul gen. Antwerp, Belgium, 1969-72; Disting. prof. humanities and social sci. No. Ky. U., 1972-76, prof. emeritus, 1976—; adj. prof. history U. Cin., 1978—; vis. prof. Ecoledes Hautes Etudes de l'Histoire et de la Philologie, Sorbonne, Paris, 1984; museological study, Paris, 1992, 93, 95. Author: History of Middle Europe, 1976, The Baranya Dispute, 1978; contbr. articles, revs. to profl. jours. Bd. dirs. Inst. Mediterranean Art and Archeology. Lt. col. USAFR, ret. Decorated comdr. Order Concordia, Rome, 1949; recipient Meritorious Honor award Dept. State, 1965; Frederick Sheldon Prize and Teaching fellow Harvard U., 1938-40. Mem. Soc. Finno-Ougrienne, Cosmos Club. Home: 218 Scenic View Dr Fort Thomas KY 41075-1245 Office: 18 E 4th St Ste 211 Cincinnati OH 45202-3706

TIJERINA, RAUL MARTIN, physics and mathematics educator; b. Brownsville, Tex., Dec. 10, 1962; s. Gregorio and Maria Olivia (Reyes) T. BS in Physics, U. North Tex., 1987; Cert. in Teaching, U. Tex., Brownsville, 1989. Cert. tchr., Tex. Math., physics tchr. U. Tex., Brownsville, 1988—; math., algebra tchr. Brownsville Ind. Sch. Dist., 1988—. Mem. Nat. Coun. Tchrs. Math., Math. Assn. Am., Am. Inst. Physics. Roman Catholic. Avocations: computers, racquetball, softball. Office: Perkins Mid Sch 4750 Austin Rd Brownsville TX 78521-5455

TILBERIS, ELIZABETH, editor-in-chief; m. Andrew Tilberis, 1971. Student, Jacob Kramer Coll. Arts, Leeds, England; BA in Eng., Leicester (Eng.) Poly. Fashion asst. British Vogue, 1970, fashion editor, 1974, exec. fashion editor, 1984, sr. fashion editor, 1986, editor-in-chief, 1987; dir. Conde Nast Pubs., 1991; editor-in-chief Harper's Bazaar, N.Y.C., 1992—. Recipient 2 Nat. Mag. awards for design, photography, 1993, Coun. Fashion Designers of Am. award, 1994. Office: Harper's Bazaar 1700 Broadway New York NY 10019-5905 also: care Susan Magrino Susan Magrino Agency 167 E 73rd St New York NY 10021-3510*

TILBURY, ROGER GRAYDON, lawyer, rancher; b. Guthrie, Okla., July 30, 1925; s. Graydon and Minnie (Lee) T.; m. Margaret Dear, June 24, 1952; 1 dau., Elizabeth Ann. B.S., U. So. Calif., 1945; J.D., U. Kans., 1949; LL.M., Columbia, 1950; postgrad., Oxford (Eng.) U., 1949. Bar: Mo. bar 1950, Oreg. bar 1953. Pvt. practice Kansas City, Mo., 1950-53, Portland, Oreg., 1953—; assoc. firm Rogers, Field, Gentry, Kansas City, Mo., 1950-53, Stern, Reiter & Day, Portland, 1953-56; ptnr. firm Roth & Tilbury, 1956-58, Tilbury & Kane, 1970-72, Haessler, Tilbury & Platten, 1978-81; pvt. practice Portland, 1981—; circuit judge pro tem., Oreg., 1972—, arbitrator and fact finder, 1973—; sec. Barrington Properties; mem. nat. panel arbitrators U.S. Mediation and Conciliation Svc.; arbitrator for N.Y. Stock Exch., Pacific Stock Exch. and Nat. Assn. Security Dealers; mediator U.S. Dist. Ct.; atty. Animal Defender League, 1969-73. Dep. election commr. Kansas City, Mo., 1952-53; bd. dirs. Multnomah Bar Found. Served to lt. (j.g.) USNR, 1943-45. Battenfeld scholar, 1943. Mem. Oreg. State Bar, Soc. Barristers, Am. Arbitration Assn., Save the Redwoods League, East African Wildlife League, Nat. Wildlife Found., Am. Trial Lawyers Assn., Delta Tau Delta, Phi Delta Phi. Home: 9310 NW Cornell Rd Portland OR 97229-6449 Office: Tilbury-Rothman Bldg 1123 SW Yamhill St Ste 101 Portland OR 97205-2106

TILEWICK, ROBERT, lawyer; b. N.Y.C., Jan. 16, 1956; s. David and Helen (Fogel) T.; m. Julia Sarah Trachtenberg, Dec. 12, 1987; children: Naomi Seana, Benjamin Solomon. BA, Columbia U., 1977; JD, Temple U., 1985. Bar: N.Y. 1986, Ct. 1993, U.S. Dist. Ct. (so. and ea. dists.) N.Y. 1988, U.S. Ct. Appeals (2d cir.) 1989, U.S. Dist. Ct. Conn. 1991. Systems analyst, cons. Personnelmetrics, Inc., N.Y.C., 1977-80, 81-82; assoc. Cravath, Swaine & Moore, N.Y.C., 1985-87, Paul, Weiss, Rifkind, Wharton & Garrison, N.Y.C., 1987-91, Wiggin & Dana, New Haven, Conn., 1991—. Co-designer race timing system for N.Y.C. Marathon, 1977-82. NIH grantee Marine Biol. Lab., Woods Hole, Mass. 1980. Mem. ABA, Am. Inns of Ct., New Haven County Bar Assn., Supreme Ct. Hist. Soc. Avocation: music. Office: Wiggin & Dana 1 Century Tower New Haven CT 06510-7013

TILGER, JUSTINE THARP, research director; b. New Point, Ind., Sept. 11, 1931; d. Joseph Riley and Marcella Lorene (King) Tharp; m. Clarence A. Tilger II, Aug. 22, 1959 (div. Nov. 1972); children: Evelyn Mary, Clarence Arthur III, Joseph Thomas. AB, U. Chgo., 1951; BA, St. Mary's Coll., Notre Dame, Ind., 1954; MA, Ind. U., 1962, PhD, 1971. Mem. Sisters of the Holy Cross, Notre Dame, 1954-58; teaching fellow Ind. U., Bloomington, 1959-61; asst. editor Ind. Mag. History, Bloomington, 1962-64; bookkeeper Touche Ross, Boston, 1974-77; mgr. account services Harvard U., Cambridge, Mass., 1977-81; dir. research and records Bentley Coll., Waltham, Mass., 1982-84; dir. support services Sta. WGBH-TV, Boston, 1985; dir. research Tufts U., Medford, Mass., 1986—; cons. Laduke Assocs., Framingham, Mass., 1972-74, New Eng. Ballet, Sudbury, Mass., 1981-82. v.p. Potter Rd. Sch. Assn., Framingham, 1968-69; chmn. vols. St. Anselm's, Sudbury, 1970-71. Mem. Coun. for Advancement and Support Edn., Assn. Records Mgmt. Adminstrs., Am. Prospect Rsch. Assn., New Eng. Devel. Rsch. Assn., Mass. Bus. and Profl. Women (sec. 1981-82), Mensa. Roman Catholic. Avocations: dramatics, travel. Home: 15 Auburn St # 6 Framingham MA 01701-4844 Office: Tufts U Dept of Research Pachard Hall Medford MA 02155

TILGHMAN, RICHARD GRANVILLE, banker; b. Norfolk, Va., Sept. 18, 1940; s. Henry Granville and Frances (Fulghum) T.; m. Alice Creech, June 28, 1969; children—Elizabeth Arrington, Caroline Harrison. B.A., U. Va., 1963. Asst. cashier United Va. Bank-Seaboard Nat., Norfolk, Va., 1968-70, asst. v.p., 1970-72; pres., chief adminstrv. officer United Va. Bank, Richmond, 1978-80; asst. v.p. United Va. Mortgage Corp., Norfolk, Va., 1972, v.p., 1972-73, pres., chief exec. officer, 1974-76; pres., chief exec. officer United Va. Leasing Corp., Richmond, Va., 1973-74; sr. v.p. bank related United Va. Bankshares, Inc., Richmond, 1976-78, exec. v.p. corp. banking, 1980-84, vice chmn., 1984-85; pres., chief exec. officer United Va. Bankshares, Inc., now Crestar Fin. Corp., Richmond, 1985—, chmn., 1986—; bd. dirs. Chesapeake Corp., Richmond, 1986—; chmn. Va. Pub. Bldg. Authority, Richmond, 1982-87; prin. Va. Bus. Coun., 1987—; mem. Fed. Adv. Coun., 1994—. Chmn. bd. dirs. Richmond Symphony, 1984-85; bd. dirs., mem. gen. adv. coun. Sheltering Arms Hosp., Richmond, 1981-89; bd. dirs. Va. Free, 1989-90, Richmond Symphony Found., 1989-91, Va. Found. Ind. Colls., 1988—, Va. Literacy Found., 1986-89; bd. govs. St. Catherine's Sch., 1989-95; bd. dirs. Va. Mus. Found., 1986-92, trustee, 1994—; trustee Randolph Macon Coll., 1985-93, Richmond Renaissance, 1986—, Colonial Williamsburg Found., 1994—; co-chmn. NCCJ. 1st lt. U.S. Army, 1963-66. Mem. Bankers Rountable (dir. 1996—), Am. Bankers Assn., Va. Bankers Assn. (bd. dirs.). Episcopalian. Clubs: Commonwealth, Country of Va. Office: Crestar Fin Corp PO Box 26665 919 E Main St Richmond VA 23219-4625

TILL, FRANKLIN L., school system administrator; b. San Diego, Jan. 20, 1947; s. Franklin L. Sr. and Luella Jane (Krough) T.; m. Barbara Jane Till, May 1, 1971; children: Marlo, Jeffrey. BA, San Diego State U., 1969, MA, 1973; EdD, U. So. Calif., 1981. Vice prin. secondary schs. San Diego United Sch. Dist., ops. mgr., prin. mid. level, dep. supt. Contbr. articles to profl. jours. Bd. dirs. YMCA, Cornerstone 2000, Weed and Seed, United Way. Recipient three PTA Hon. Svc. awards. Mem. Assn. of Calif. Sch. Adminstrs. (Disting. Leaders award), Adminstrs. Assn. Home: 5851 Torca Ct San Diego CA 92124-1020

TILL, JAMES EDGAR, scientist; b. Lloydminster, Sask., Can., Aug. 25, 1931; s. William and Gertrude Ruth (Isaac) T.; m. Marion Joyce Sinclair, June 6, 1959; children: David William, Karen Sinclair, Susan Elizabeth. BA, U. Sask., 1952, MA, 1954; PhD, Yale U., 1957. Mem. physics div. Ont. Cancer Inst., Toronto, 1957-67, div. biol. rsch., 1967-89, div. head, 1969-82, with div. epidemiology and stats., 1989—; assoc. dean U. Toronto, 1981-84, Univ. prof., 1984—. Contbr. articles on biophysics, cell biology and cancer control research to sci. jours. Recipient Gairdner Found. Internat. award, 1969, Order of Can., 1994. Fellow Royal Soc. Can.; mem. Can. Bioethics Soc. Home: 182 Briar Hill Ave, Toronto, ON Canada M4R 1H9 Office: 610 University Ave, Toronto, ON Canada M5G 2M9 *Albert Einstein said: "The most beautiful thing we can experience is the mysterious. It is the source of all true art and science." He also believed that concern for humanity must always form the chief interest of all technical endeavors—"in order that the creations of our mind shall be a blessing and not a curse to mankind." Is there a more eloquent summary of standards for the scientist than this?.*

TILLACK, THOMAS WARNER, pathologist; b. Jacksonville, Fla., Nov. 16, 1937; s. Warner S. and Charlotte G. T.; m. Lynne Anne Beam, Oct. 30, 1970; children—Jonathan Allan, Allison Anne. B.A., U. Rochester, 1959; M.D., Yale U., 1963. Diplomate: Diploma Am. Bd. Pathology. Intern Barnes Hosp., St. Louis, 1963-64; resident Barnes Hosp., 1964-66; staff asso. NIH, Bethesda, Md., 1966-69; sr. staff fellow NIH, 1969-71; asst. prof. pathology Washington U., St. Louis, 1971-73; assoc. prof. Washington U., 1973-76; Walter Reed prof., chmn. dept. pathology U. Va. Med. Center, 1976—. Served with USPHS, 1966-69. Mem. Am. Soc. Investigative Pathology, U.S. and Can. Acad. Pathology, Am. Soc. Cell Biology, Assn. Pathology Chairs, Phi Beta Kappa. Research, publs. in cell biology and pathology. Home: PO Box 376 Ivy VA 22945-0376 Office: U Va Med Ctr Dept Pathology PO Box 214 Charlottesville VA 22908-0001

TILLER, OLIVE MARIE, retired church worker; b. St. Paul, Dec. 13, 1920; d. Otto William and Myrtle Alice (Brougham) Foerster; m. Carl William Tiller, June 21, 1940; children: Robert W., Jeanne L. Peterson. BS, U. Minn., 1940. Spl. edn. tchr. Prince Georges County, Md., 1955-63; spl. asst. for profl. svcs. Kendall Demonstration Elem. Sch., Gallaudet Coll., Washington, 1971-78; spl. asst. for program Ch. Women United, N.Y.C., 1979-80; exec. asst. to gen. sec. Nat. Coun. Chs. of Christ in U.S.A., N.Y.C., 1981-87; dep. gen. sec. for coop. Christianity Am. Bapt. Chs. of U.S.A., Valley Forge, Pa., 1987-88. Author: (with Carl W. Tiller) At Calvary, 1994. Mem. Human Rels. Commn., Prince George's County, 1967-73; v.p. Am. Bapt. Chs. U.S.A., Valley Forge, 1976-77; bd. dirs. Am. Leprosy Missions, Greenville, S.C., 1981-95, Bapt. Peace Fellowship of N.Am., Memphis, 1984-95; mem. Nat. Interreligious Svc. Bd. for Conscientious Objectors, 1991—, treas., 1994—. Recipient Dahlberg Peace award Am. Bapt. Chs., 1991, Valiant Woman award Ch. Women United, 1978, Meeker award Ottawa U., 1995. Mem. Nat. Coun. Fellowship of Reconciliation. Baptist. Home: 100 Norman Dr Apt 283 Cranberry Township PA 16066-4235

TILLERY, RICHARD LEE, television executive; b. Pratt, Kans., Nov. 6, 1940; s. Donald R. and Thelma L. (Keen) T.; m. Naomi Goodman, June 7, 1967 (div. July 1984); children: Richard Craig, Mary Kathrine; m. Julia D. Rockler, June 30, 1985; 1 child, Melissa Beth. Student, Ft. Hays State U., 1958-60, 63-65. Investigative reporter, photographer, editor Sta. KZTV, Corpus Christi, Tex., 1965; asst. news dir., prodr., assignments editor, inv. reporter Sta. KIII-TV, Corpus Christi, 1970; asst. news dir., co-anchor, prodr. Sta. KRIS-TV, Corpus Christi, 1973; asst. news dir., prodr., assignment editor Sta. KETV, Omaha, 1974; news dir. Sta. KHGI-TV, Kearney, Nebr., 1976; acting news dir., exec. prodr. Sta. KWCH-TV, Wichita, Kans., 1980; exec. prodr., dir. spl. projects Sta. KENS-TV, San Antonio, 1984; freelance prodr., investigator Washington, 1986-87; coord. Newsnet satellite feed svc. CBS News, 1987-88; bur. chief The Washington Bur., Washington, 1988—; com. mem. UPI, AP, Soc. of Prof. Journalists; panelist, guest speaker in field; organizer profl. seminars in field. Bd. dirs. ARC, Campfire Girls, Boy Scouts Am., South Tex. Mental Health and Retardation. With U.S. Army, 1960-63. Recipient Pieringer award Tex. Assn. Broadcasters, Headliners award U. Tex., Gavel award Tex. Bar Assn., Sch. Bell award Tex. Classroom Tchrs. Assn., Investigative Reporting award Nat. AP, investigative reporting and regional awards from various orgns. Mem. Nebr. AP Broadcasters (past pres., regional awards), South Tex. Press Club (past v.p., regional awards), Radio and TV News Dirs. Assn. (com. mem., panelist, guest speaker). Office: The Washington Bur # 363 400 N Capitol St NW Ste 363 Washington DC 20001-1511

TILLERY-TATE, JOHNNIE LEA, mental health and geriatrics nurse; b. San Angelo, Tex., Aug. 25, 1938; d. John A. and M. Inez (Balkum) Whittenberg; m. Leon Tillery, June 1, 1957; children: Valerie Joyce, Tanya Leann; m. Don Tate, Sept. 5, 1992. Student, Angelo State U., San Angelo, 1956; diploma, San Angelo Sch. Vocat. Nursing, 1979; ASN, Eastern N.Mex. U., 1984. Cert. mental health and gerontol. nurse. Staff nurse Sterling County Hosp., 1984-87, St. Johns Hosp., 1987, Sterling County Hosp., 1989; unit supr. San Angelo State Sch. Tex. Dept. Mental Health and Mental Retardation, 1987-93; investigator, surveyor Tex. Dept. Health, 1993; nurse, surveyor, qualified mental retardation profl. Tex. Dept. Human Svcs., 1993—; nurse supr. Riverside Manor. Mem. Tex. Pub. Employees Assn., Am. Assn. Mental Retardation (nursing div.). Home: 7593 Gladiolis San Angelo TX 76901

TILLETT, SAMUEL RAYMOND, lawyer; b. Akron, Ohio, May 4, 1951. AB, Hamilton Coll., 1973; JD, Case Western Res. U., 1977. Bar: Ohio 1977, D.C. 1978, Ill. 1988. Ptnr. Mayer, Brown & Platt, Chgo.; adj. prof. law DePaul U. Coll. Law, Chgo., 1992—; trustee Village of Glencoe, Ill. Libr. Bd., 1995—. Bd. dirs. Chgo. Metro History Edn. Ctr., 1989-94. Mem. ABA, Nat. Assn. Bond Lawyers, D.C. Bar Assn., Chgo. Bar Assn. Office: Mayer Brown & Platt 190 S La Salle St Chicago IL 60603-3410

TILLEY, C. RONALD, retired gas company executive; b. Welch, W.Va., Oct. 20, 1935; s. Clarence D. and Mildred R. (Carnes) T.; m. Janice E. Tilley, Aug. 24, 1956; children: Christopher R., Cory G., Beth Ann. B.S. in Acctg., Concord Coll., 1957. Clk. rate dept. United Fuel Gas Co., Charleston, W.Va., 1957-62, rate analyst, 1962-64; engr. rate dept. Columbia Gas Service Corp., N.Y.C., 1964-71; mgr. rate dept. Columbia Gas Service Corp., Columbus, Ohio, 1971-73; dir. rate dept. Columbia Gas Service Corp., Charleston, 1973-75; v.p. corp. Columbia Gas Service Corp., Washington, 1975-80; v.p. rate Columbia Gas Service Corp., Wilmington, Del., 1980-82; sr. v.p. Columbia Gas Distbn. Cos., Columbus, 1982-85, pres., 1985-87, chmn., chief exec. officer, 1987-96; bd. dirs. BancOhio Nat. Bank. Trustee Columbus Symphony Orch., 1988—, Children's Hosp., 1989—, Columbus Mus. Art, 1990; bd. dirs. United Negro Coll. Fund, 1987—; mem., bd. dirs. Columbus Assn. Performing Acts, 1989—; chmn. Coun. on Ethics in Econs., 1992. With U.S. Army, 1958-60. Mem. Columbus Area C. of C. (bd. dirs. 1987—). Republican. Avocations: golf; reading.

TILLEY, CAROLYN BITTNER, technical information specialist; b. Washington, July 29, 1947; d. Klaud Kay and Margaret Louise (Hanson) Bittner; m. Frederick Edwin Dudley, June 18, 1985. B.S., Am. U., 1975; M.L.S., U. Md., 1976. With NIH, 1965-71; statis. research asst. Health Manpower Edn., Bethesda, Md., 1971-72; tech. info. specialist Nat. Libr. Medicine, Bethesda, Md., 1972-81, head medlars (med. lit. analysis and retrieval system) mgmt. sect., 1981—. Mem. editorial bd.: Med. Reference Services Quar. Mem. CENDI User Edn. Com., Nat. Fed. Abstracting and Info. Svc. Pub. Com. Recipient Merit award NIH, 1984, Rogers award Nat. Libr. Medicine, 1991. Mem. Med. Library Assn. Presbyterian. Avocation: horseback riding. Office: Nat Libr Medicine 8600 Rockville Pike Bethesda MD 20894-0001

TILLEY, NORWOOD CARLTON, JR., federal judge; b. Rock Hill, S.C., 1943; s. Norwood Carlton and Rebecca (Westbrook) T.; m. Greta Medlin, Sept. 25, 1970. BA, Wake Forest U., 1966, JD, 1969. Bar: N.C. 1969, U.S. Dist. Ct. (middle dist.) N.C. 1971. Law clk. to Hon. Eugene A Gordon, U.S. Dist. Judge Middle Dist. N.C., 1969-71; asst. U.S. atty. Mid. Dist. N.C., Greensboro, 1971-73, U.S. atty., 1974-77; U.S. dist. judge Mid. Dist. N.C., Durham, 1988—; ptnr. Osteen, Adams, Tilley & Walker, Greensboro, 1977-88; instr. Wake Forest U. Sch. Law, 1980. Office: US Dist Ct PO Box 3443 Greensboro NC 27402-3443*

TILLEY, RICE M(ATTHEWS), JR., lawyer; b. Ft. Worth, June 21, 1936; s. Rice Matthews Sr. and Lucille Geyer (Kelly) T.; children: Marisa Lynn, Angela Ainsworth, Lisa Scott, Rice Matthews III; m. Sandra Cooper, May 13, 1994. BA, Washington & Lee U., 1958; JD, So. Meth. U., 1961; LLM in Taxation, NYU, 1962. Bar: Tex. 1961. Mem. Law, Snakard & Gambill, Ft. Worth, 1964—. Bd. dirs. Van Cliburn Found., Ft. Worth Ballet Assn., Ft. Worth Symphony Orch. Assn.; bd. trustees Tex. Wesleyan Univ.; pres. Ft. Worth Opera Assn. Mem. State Bar Tex. (chmn. real estate, probate and trust law sect.), Ft. Worth C. of C. (chmn. bd.), Century II Club (pres.), Leadership Ft. Worth (chmn. bd. dirs.), Exch. Club of Ft. Worth (pres.). Republican. Office: Law Snakard & Gambill 500 Throckmorton St Ste 3200 Fort Worth TX 76102-3819

TILLEY, SUZANNE DENISE, education specialist; b. Corpus Christi, Tex., Sept. 14, 1963; d. Franklin Roosevelt and Sharie Jerilyn Tilley. BA in Early Childhood Edn., U. Guam, 1984; MEd, Tex. Tech. U., 1994, postgrad., 1994—. Cert. elem. tchr., Tex. Kindergarten tchr. San Angelo (Tex.) Ind. Sch. Dist., 1985-91; edn. coord. South Plains Head Start, Levelland, Tex., 1992-93; disability coord. SHAPES Head Start, Levelland, 1993-94, edn. specialist, 1994—; co-owner Opening a World of Learning for All Children, Littlefield, Tex., 1993—; presenter profl. confs., 1993-94. CPR, first aid instr. ARC, Lubbock, Tex., 1992—. Capt. USAR, 1985—. Mem. Tex. Head Start Assn., Nat. Assn. for Edn. Young Children, South Plains Assn. Edn. Young Children. Avocations: reading, creating educational activities. Home: 1031 W 7th St Littlefield TX 79339-3703 Office: SHAPES Head Start 1301 Houston St Levelland TX 79336-3313

TILLINGHAST, CHARLES CARPENTER, JR., aviation and financial consultant; b. Saxton's River, Vt., Jan. 30, 1911; s. Charles C. and Adelaide Barrows (Shaw) T.; m. Lisette Micoleau, Nov. 16, 1935; children: Charles Carpenter III, Elizabeth, Jane, Anne Shaw. Ph.B., Brown U., 1932; J.D., Columbia U., 1935; L.H.D., S.D. Sch. Mines and Tech., 1959; LL.D., Franklin Coll., 1963, U. Redlands, 1964, Brown U., 1967, Drury Coll., 1967, William Jewell Coll., 1973. Bar: N.Y. bar 1935, Mich. 1943. Assoc. Hughes, Schurman & Dwight, 1935-37; dep. asst. dist. atty. N.Y. County, 1938-40; assoc. Hughes, Richards, Hubbard & Ewing, 1940-42; ptnr. Hughes, Hubbard, Blair & Reed (and predecessor firms), N.Y.C., 1942-57; v.p., dir. The Bendix Corp., Detroit, 1957-61; pres., chief exec. officer Trans World Airlines, Inc., 1961-69, chmn. bd., chief exec. officer, 1969-76, dir., 1961-81; dir., vice chmn. bd. White Weld & Co., Inc., 1977-78; mng. dir. Merrill Lynch White Weld Capital Markets Group, 1978-82; bd. dirs. Henry Luce Found., Air Transport Assn., 1961-72, 74-75; mem. exec. com. Internat. Air Transport Assn., 1969-75. Bd. dirs. Cmty. Welfare Fund, Bronxville, 1951-53, pres., 1953; gov. Lawrence Hosp., Bronxville, 1955-59; trustee Brown U., 1954-61, 65-79, chancellor, 1968-79, fellow, 1979—; fellow Midwest Rsch. Inst., 1963-76, the Conf. Bd., 1965-76, People to People Program, 1961-70, Com. for Econ. Devel., 1967—; bd. visitors Sch. Law, Columbia U., 1962-92; bd. govs. John Carter Brown Libr., 1989-96. Mem. ABA, Assn. Bar City N.Y., Brown U. Club (N.Y.C.), Hope Club (R.I.), Sakonnet Golf Club. Home: 355 Blackstone Blvd Apt 530 Providence RI 02906-4953

TILLINGHAST, CHARLES CARPENTER, III, marketing company executive; b. N.Y.C., Nov. 16, 1936; s. Charles Carpenter, Jr. and Lisette (Micoleau) T.; m. Cynthia Branch, Sept. 28, 1974; children by previous marriage: Avery D., Charles W., David C. B.S. in Mech. Engring, Lehigh U., 1958; M.B.A., Harvard U., 1963. Asst. to dir. devel. Lehigh U., Bethlehem, Pa., 1958-61; adminstrv. asst. Boise Cascade Corp., Portland, Oreg., 1963; asst. to v.p. Boise Cascade Corp., Boise, Idaho, 1964-65; gen. mgr. office supply div. Boise Cascade Corp., 1965-67, gen. mgr. paper distbn. div., 1966, v.p. bus. products, 1967-69, sr. v.p. housing group, 1969-71, sr. v.p., 1971-73; pres. CRM div. Ziff-Davis Pub. Co., Inc., Del Mar, Calif., 1971-75; pres., treas. Value Communications, Inc., La Jolla, Calif., 1975-76; pres. Oak Tree Publs., Inc., San Diego, 1976-81; pres. Advanced Mktg. Services Inc., San Diego, 1982-94, chmn., 1994—. Served to 2d lt. AUS, 1959. Home: 1762 Nautilus St La Jolla CA 92037-6413 Office: Advanced Mktg Svcs Inc 5880 Oberlin Dr San Diego CA 92121-4735

TILLINGHAST, DAVID ROLLHAUS, lawyer; b. N.Y.C., Feb. 25, 1930; s. Charles Carpenter and Josephine Dorothy (Rollhaus) T.; m. Phyllis Van Horn, Sept. 24, 1955 (div. Jan. 1984); m. Lisa Sewell, Feb. 25, 1984; children: Gregory Barrett Sewell, Lauren Alexa. AB cum laude, Brown U., 1951; LLB cum laude, Yale U., 1954. Bar: N.Y. 1955, Oreg. 1956, U.S. Supreme Ct. 1978. Assoc. Hughes, Hubbard & Reed, N.Y.C., 1954-55, 57-61; ptnr. Hughes, Hubbard & Reed, 1961-62, 65-90; assoc. King, Miller, Anderson, Nash & Yerke, Portland, Oreg., 1955-57; spl. asst. for internat. tax affairs U.S. Dept. Treasury, Washington, 1962-65; ptnr. Chadbourne & Parke, N.Y.C., 1990—; adj. prof. Sch. Law, NYU, 1977-87; cons. UN Ctr. on Transnat. Corps., 1978-87; reporter Am. Law Inst. Project on Internat. Aspects of U.S. Income Taxation, 1982-91; cons. to reporters Am. Law Inst. Revision of Restatement of Fgn. Relations Law of U.S., 1982-83. Author: Tax Aspects of Internat. Transactions, 1978, 2d edit., 1984; contbr. articles to profl. publs. Mem. transition team Sec. of Treasury W. Michael Blumenthal, 1977. Mem. Assn. of Bar of City of N.Y. (chmn. com. on taxation 1981-83), Internat. Fiscal Assn. (v.p. U.S. br. 1983—, permanent sci. com. 1983—, vice chmn. 1993-95, chmn. 1995—), Internat. Bar Assn. (vice chmn. com. on taxation bus. law sect. 1984-86), U.S. Coun. for Internat. Bus. (com. on taxation), Tax Forum, Coun. on Fgn. Rels. Democrat. Avocations: golf; tennis. Office: Chadbourne & Parke 30 Rockefeller Plz New York NY 10112

TILLINGHAST, JOHN AVERY, utilities executive; b. N.Y.C., Apr. 30, 1927; s. Charles C. and Dorothy J. (Rollhaus) T.; m. Mabel Healy, Sept. 11, 1948; children: Katherine Brickley, Susan Trainor, Abigail Ryan. BSME, Columbia U., 1948, MS, 1949. Registered profl. engr., Ky., Ind., Mich., N.Y., Ohio, Va., W.Va., N.H. With Am. Elec. Power Service Corp., N.Y.C., 1949-79, exec. v.p. engring. and constrn., 1967-72, sr. exec. v.p., vice chmn. engring. and constrn., 1972-79; sr. v.p. tech. Wheelabrator-Frye Inc., Hampton, N.H., 1979-83, Signal Advanced Tech. Group, The Signal Cos., Hampton, N.H., 1983-85; sr. v.p. Allied-Signal Internat., Hampton, 1985-86, Sci. Applications Internat. Corp., San Diego, 1986-88; pres. TILTEC, Portsmouth, N.H, 1987-94; CEO Great Bay Power Corp., Portsmouth, 1994—. Patentee generating unit control system. Elder Reformed Ch., 1976-79. Served with USN, 1944-46. Fellow ASME; mem. IEEE, Nat. Acad. Engring.,Sigma Xi, Tau Beta Pi. Office: Great Bay Power Corp 20 Ladd St Portsmouth NH 03801-4080

TILLIS, MEL(VIN), musician, songwriter; b. Tampa, Fla., Aug. 8, 1932; m. Judy Edwards, 1979; children: Pam, Connie, Cindy, Melvin Jr., Carrie, Hannah. Student, U. Fla. Founder Sawgrass Music, Sabal Music, Tillis Tunes, Sweet Tater Tunes, Nashville. Songwriter, Cedarwood Music, Nashville, 20 years, (Named Entertainer of Year, Country Music Assn. 1976), numerous personal and TV appearances; composer over 600 songs recorded by, Webb Pierce, Ray Price, Carl Smith, Brenda Lee, Kenny Rogers, Charlie Pride, Burl Ives, George Strait, others; (with The Statesiders) 56 albums including; Mel Tillis and the Statesiders on Stage, Best of Mel Tillis, Love Revival, Welcome to Country, California Road, 1985, American Originals, 1990, Greatest Hits, 1991, Beyond the Sunset, 1993; author: Stuttering Boy, 1986. Served in USAF. Named Comedian of Yr., Country Music Assn., 1971, 73, 74, 75, 76, 77, Entertainer of Yr., 1976. Office: Mel Tillis Theater Inc PO Box 1626 2527 Hwy 248 Branson MO 65616-9999

TILLIS, PAM, country singer, songwriter; b. Plant City, Fla., 1957; d. Mel and Doris T.; divorced; 1 child, Ben; m. Bob DiPiero, Feb. 14, 1991. Student, U. Tenn. Recording artist Arista Records, 1990—. Singer, songwriter for acts including Highway 101, Gloria Gayner, Dan Seals, Chaka Kahn, Ricky Van Shelton, Suzy Bogguss, Conway Twitty; albums: Put Yourself in My Place, 1991, Homeward Looking Angel, 1992, Pam Tillis Collection, 1994, Sweethearts Dance, 1994; 1st single: Every Home Should Have One, 1981; #1 hit record Don't Tell Me What To Do, 1991. Grammy nomination, Best Country Vocal Collaboration for "Romeo" with Dolly Parton, Tanya Tucker, Billy Ray Cyrus, Kathy Mattea & Mary-Chapin Carpenter, 1994. Office: Arista Records 6 W 57th St New York NY 10019-3913

TILLMAN, ELIZABETH CARLOTTA, nurse, educator; b. Md., Aug. 31, 1929; d. Walter Monroe and Mozelle Virginia (Shugars) Brown; m. Lloyd A. Tillman, Apr. 16, 1949; children: Lloyd A. Jr., William L., Susan E. Tillman Chaires. Diploma, Md. Gen. Hosp. Sch. Nursing, 1950; student, Towson State U., U. Md., Loyola Coll., Balt., Howard C.C. RN. Psychiatric nurse Spring Grove Hosp. Ctr., Catonsville, Md., 1950; pvt. duty home health nurse Md., 1951-60; dir., tchr., nurse Doughoregan Manor Day Sch., Ellicott City, Md., 1960-80; med.-surg. nurse Woman's Hosp., Balt., 1964, Md. Gen. Hosp., Balt., 1980; nursing instr. Howard County Dept. Edn., Ellicott City, 1981-91; nursing educator Howard County Sch. Tech., 1981-91, Howard County Gen. Hosp., 1981-91; geriatric nurse Lorien Columbia (Md.) Nursing & Rehab. Ctr., 1981-91; home health nurse Md., 1992—. Mem. NEA, Md. State Tchrs. Assn., Md. Gen. Hosp. Alumni Assn., Am. Vocat. Assn.,

Health Occupations Educators, Md. Vocat. Assn., Phi Eta Sigma, Iota Lambda Sigma. Home: 10002 Reed Ln Ellicott City MD 21042-2238

TILLMAN, JOHN LEE, principal; b. Mesa, Ariz., Jan. 31, 1947; s. W.L. and Juanita (Johnson) T.; m. Judith Ann Tuxhorn, May 31, 1970; children Matthew Lee, Andrew Lee. BA, Adams State Coll., 1969, MA, 1975. Cert. tchr., Colo., Va.; cert. adminstr., Colo. Music tchr. Mountain Valley Sch., Saquache, Colo., 1969-70; dir. music Hargrave Mil. Acad., Chatham, Va., 1970-76; music tchr. Sargent Sch. Dist., Monte Vista, Colo., 1976-82; secondary prin. Sargent Sch. Dist., Monte Vista, 1982-95, dir. devel., 1995—; bd. control Colo. H.S. Activities Assn., Denver, 1990-93; alumni bd. dirs. Adams State Coll., Alamosa, Colo., 1990-93. Music dir. Calvary Bapt. Ch., Monte Vista, 1976—. Mem. Nat. Assn. Secondary Prins., Colo. Assn. Secondary Prins., Nat. Middle Assn., Colo. Assn. Sch. Execs., Colo. Music Educators Nat. Conf., Phi Delta Kappa. Baptist. Avocations: computers, music, electronics, woodworking. Office: Sargent High Sch 7090 N County Road 2 E Monte Vista CO 81144-9756

TILLMAN, JOSEPH NATHANIEL, engineering executive; b. Augusta, Ga., Aug. 1, 1926; s. Leroy and Canarie (Kelly) T.; m. Alice Lavonia Walton, Sept. 5, 1950 (dec. 1983); children: Alice Lavonia, Robert Bertram; m. Areerat Usahaviriyakit, Nov. 24, 1986. BA magna cum laude, Paine Coll., 1948; MS, Northrop U., 1975, MBA, 1976; DBA, Nova U., 1989. Dir. Rockwell Internat., Anaheim, Calif., 1958-84; pres. Tillman Enterprises, Corona, Calif., 1985—; guest lectr. UCLA, 1980-85. Contbr. articles to profl. jours. Capt. USAF, 1948-57, Korea. Recipient Presdl. Citation Nat. Assn. for Equal Opportunity in Higher Edn., 1986. Mem. Acad. Mgmt. (chmn. 1985-86), Soc. Logistics Engrs. (pres. 1985-86), Paine Coll. Alumni Assn. (v.p. 1976—), NAACP (pres. 1984-88). Avocations: duplicate bridge, travel, swimming, skiing, hiking. Office: Tillman Enterprises 1550 Rimpau Ave Trlr 45 Corona CA 91719-3206

TILLMAN, MASSIE MONROE, federal judge; b. Corpus Christi, Tex., Aug. 15, 1937; s. Clarence and Artie Lee (Stewart) T.; m. Karen Wright, July 2, 1993; children: Jeffrey Monroe, Holly. BBA, Baylor U., 1959, LLB, 1961. Bar: Tex. 1961, U.S. Dist. Ct. (no. dist.) Tex. 1961, U.S. Ct. Appeals (5th cir.) 1969, U.S. Supreme Ct. 1969; bd. cert. Personal Injury Trial Law, Tex. Ptnr. Herrick & Tillman, Ft. Worth, 1961-66; pvt. practice, Ft. Worth, 1966-70, 79-87; ptnr. Brown, Herman et al., Ft. Worth, 1970-78, Street, Swift et al., Ft. Worth, 1978-79; U.S. bankruptcy judge No. Dist. Tex., Ft. Worth Div., 1987—. Author: Tillman's Trial Guide, 1970; Comments Editor/Case Notes Editor; mem. editl. bd. Baylor Law Rev., 1960-63. Fellow Am. Bd. Trial Advocates, Tex. Bar Found.; mem. Ft. Worth/Tarrant County Bar (bd. dirs. 1969-70, v.p. 1970-71), Assn. Trial Lawyers Am., Trial Attys.'s of Am., Nat. Conf. of Bankruptcy Judges, Am. Bankruptcy Inst. Democrat. Baptist. Avocations: cutting horses, competition shotgun shooting.

TILLMAN, MURRAY HOWELL, instructional technology educator; b. Birmingham, Ala., Nov. 7, 1940; s. Gray Eddie and Ruby (Wood) T.; m. Dorris Collier Hogan, June 9, 1962; children: David Murray, Kathryn Collier. BA, Birmingham So. Coll., 1962; MS, U. Ga., 1965, PhD, 1966. Elem. sch. tchr. Muscogee County Bd. Edn., Columbus, Ga., 1961-62; rsch. assoc. R&D Ctr. U. Ga., Athens, 1966-70, asst. prof. Coll. Edn., 1970-71, assoc. prof., 1971-81, prof. instrnl. tech., 1981-93; prof. emeritus, 1993—; acting head dept. curriculum and instrn. U. Ga., Athens, 1983-84, acting head div. instrnl. support, 1983-84, head instrnl. tech., 1991-92; Co-author: Learning to Teach, 1976; author: Troubleshooting Classroom Problems, 1982; editor, author: Instructional Design, 1991. NDEA fellow, 1963-65. Mem. Am. Ednl. Rsch. Assn., Assn. Ednl. Comm. and Tech. (cert. of merit 1986), Humanities and Tech. Assn., Internat. Soc. for Performance Improvement (cert. of achievement 1989, cert. of recognition 1990). Avocations: biking, swimming, chess, music. Home: 215 Hall St Athens GA 30605-1211 Office: U Ga 607 Aderhold Hall Athens GA 30602

TILLMAN, ROLLIE, JR., university official; b. Lake Wales, Fla., Apr. 11, 1933; s. Rollie and Louise (Johnson) T.; m. Mary Windley Dunn, June 22, 1957; children—Mary Windley, Jane Guion, Rollie. BS, U. N.C., 1955; MBA, Harvard U., 1957, DBA, 1962. Rsch. asst. Harvard Bus. Sch., 1958-60; asst. prof. bus. adminstrn. U. N.C., Chapel Hill, 1960-63, assoc. prof., 1963-65, prof., 1965—, dir. MBA program, 1965-67, dir. exec. program, 1968-77, vice chancellor for univ. relations, 1978-84; trustee chmn. Kenan Inst. Pvt. Enterprise, Chapel Hill, 1985-90, chmn. bd., 1990—; dir. U. N.C. Press, Renfro Inc., Entrepreneur of Yr. Inst., Coun. Entrepreneur Devel., Good Mark Foods. Author: (with C.A. Kirkpatrick) Promotion: Persuasive Communication in Marketing, 1964, (with Luther H. Hodges, Jr.) Bank Marketing: Text and Cases, 1968. Trustee St. Mary's Coll., 1968-78; dir., pres. N.C. Mus. of Art Soc. Mem. Am. Mktg. Assn. (dir. 1967-69). Democrat. Episcopalian. Office: Kenan Inst Pvt Enterprise CB 3490 Chapel Hill NC 27599

TILLOTSON, CAROLYN, state legislator; m. John C. Tillotson. Mem. Kans. Senate, 1993—. Republican. Home: 1606 Westwood Dr Leavenworth KS 66048-6622 Office: Kans State Senate State Capitol Topeka KS 66612*

TILLSON, JOHN BRADFORD, JR., newspaper publisher; b. Paris, Tex., Dec. 21, 1944; s. John Bradford Sr. and Frances (Ragland) T.; m. Patricia Hunt, June 14, 1966 (div. June 1978); children: John, Karen; m. Cynthia Wornom, Oct. 10, 1981. BA, Denison U., Granville, Ohio, 1966. Reporter Charlotte (N.C.) News, 1969-71; reporter Dayton (Ohio) Daily News, 1971-76, city editor, 1977-80, asst. mng. editor, 1980-82, mng. editor features, 1982-84; editor Dayton Daily News and Jour. Herald, 1984-88, pub., 1988—; lectr. Am. Press Inst., Reston, Va., 1980-84. Exec. com. Vietnam Vets. Meml. Park Fund, Dayton, 1985-86; community bd. advisors Jr. League Dayton, 1986; trustee Dayton Art Inst., 1984—, Victory Theatre, 1986—; trustee Dayton Performing Arts Fund. Mem. Am. Soc. Newspaper Pub. Episcopalian. Home: 4833 Far Hills Ave Dayton OH 45429-2318 Office: Dayton Daily News 45th S Ludlow St Dayton OH 45401

TILLY, JENNIFER, actress. TV series include: Shaping Up, 1984, Bodyguard, 1990, Key West, 1993; TV movies include: Heads, 1994; films include: No Small Affair, 1984, Moving Violations, 1985, He's My Girl, 1987, Inside Out, 1987, Rented Lips, 1988, High Spirits, 1988, Johnny Be Good, 1988, Remote Control, 1988, The Fabulous Baker Boys, 1989, Let It Ride, 1989, Far From Home, 1989, Scorchers, 1991, Shadow of the Wolf, 1992, Made in America, 1993, At Home With the Webbers, 1993, Double Cross, 1994, Bullets Over Broadway, 1994 (Academy award nomination best supporting actress 1994), The Getaway, 1994. Office: SB & V 145 S Fairfax Ave Ste 310 Los Angeles CA 90036-5812*

TILLY, LOUISE AUDINO, history and sociology educator; b. Orange, N.J., Dec. 13, 1930; d. Hector and Piera (Roffino) Audino; m. Charles Tilly, Aug. 15, 1953; children: Christopher, Kathryn, Laura, Sarah. BA, Rutgers U., 1952; MA, Boston U., 1955; PhD, U. Toronto, 1974. From instr. to asst. prof. Mich. State U., East Lansing, 1972-75; from asst. prof. to prof. U. Mich., Ann Arbor, 1975-84; prof. history and sociology New Sch. for Social Rsch., N.Y.C., 1984-94, chair com. hist. studies, 1984—, Michael E. Gellert prof. history and sociology, 1994—; assoc. dir. studies Ecole des Hautes Études en Scis. Sociales, Paris, 1979, 80, 88; fellow Shelby Cullom Davis Ctr., Princeton (N.J.) U., 1978; vis. mem. Inst. for Advanced Study, Princeton, 1987-88; fellow Ctr. for Advanced Studies Behavioral Scis., 1991-92; vis. scholar Russell Sage Found., 1994-95; bd. dirs. Social Scis. Rsch. Coun., N.Y.C., 1983-86. Author: Politics and Class in Milan, 1881-1901, 1992; co-author: The Rebellious Century, 1975, Women, Work and Family, 1978, rev. edit., 1987; co-editor, co-author: Class Conflict and Collective Action, 1981, Women, Politics and Change, 1990; co-editor: The European Experience of Declining Fertility: The Quiet Revolution, 1992; also articles. Active com. on women's employment and related social issues Nat. Acad. Scis., 1981-86, chmn., co-editor report Panel on Tech. and Women's Employment, 1984-86. Grantee Rockefeller Found., 1974-76, Am. Philos. Soc., 1977-78, 85-86, Russell Sage Found., 1985-86; Guggenheim Found. fellow, 1991-92. Mem. Am. Hist. Assn. (coun. 1985-87, pres. elect. 1992, pres. 1993), Social Sci. History Assn.(pres. 1981-82), Coun. on European Studies (exec. com. 1980-83), Berkshire Conf. Women Historians. Democrat. Home: 5 E 22nd St Apt 5K New York NY 10010-5321 Office: Com on Hist Studies 80 Fifth Ave New York NY 10011-8002

TILLY, MEG, actress; b. Long Beach, Calif., Feb. 14, 1960. Actress: (films) Fame, 1980, Tex, 1982, One Dark Night, 1983, The Big Chill, 1983, Psycho II, 1983, Impulse, 1984, Agnes of God, 1985 (Academy award nomination best supporting actress 1985), Off Beat, 1986, Masquerade, 1988, The Girl in a Swing, 1988, Valmont, 1989, The Two Jakes, 1990, Leaving Normal, 1992, Body Snatchers, 1994, Sleep with Me, 1994, (TV movies) In the Best Interest of the Child, 1990, (TV series) Winnetka Road, 1993; author: Singing Songs, 1994. *

TILNEY, NICHOLAS LECHMERE, surgery educator; b. N.Y.C., Oct. 19, 1935; s. Robert Wallace and Olive van Rensallaer (Gawtry) T.; m. Henriette Beatrice London, Sept. 20, 1958 (div. 1975); children: Rebecca, Louise Moore, Victoria; m. Mary Johanna Graves, June 17, 1978. AB, Harvard U., 1958; MD, Cornell U., 1962. Surg. resident Peter Bent Brigham Hosp., Boston, 1962-71; rsch. fellow U. Oxford, Eng., 1968-69, 71-72; surg. registrar U. Glasgow, Scotland, 1972-73; asst. prof. surgery Harvard Med. Sch., Boston, 1974-76, assoc. prof. surgery, 1977-82, prof. surgery, 1983—, Francis D. Moore prof., 1992—, dir. Surg. Rsch. Lab., 1975—; dir. transplant svcs. Brigham & Womens Hosp., Boston, 1976-92, Transplant Rsch. Ctr., 1992—. Contbr. articles to profl. jours. Lt. comdr. USN, 1966-68. Fellow Royal Coll. Physicians and Surgeons (Glasgow); mem. Am. Soc. Transplant Surgeons (pres. 1995), Phi Beta Kappa. Avocation: boating. Office: Brigham and Womens Hosp 75 Francis St Boston MA 02115

TILSON, JOHN QUILLIN, lawyer; b. New Haven, Aug. 27, 1911; s. John Quillin and Marguerite (North) T.; m. Catherine E. Jackson, Sept. 14, 1934; children—John Quillin III, Thomas D., Rebecca E. Grad., Hotchkiss Sch., 1929; B.A., Yale, 1933, LL.B., 1936. Bar: Conn. bar 1936. Since practiced in New Haven; assoc. Wiggin & Dana, New Haven, 1936-48, ptnr., 1948—; lectr. hosp. law Yale Sch. Medicine, 1959—. Chmn. plan and zoning commn., Hamden, Conn., 1949-51; pres. Conn. Conf. Social Work, 1949-50; Bd. aldermen, New Haven, 1935-37; rep. Conn. Gen. Assembly, 1953; alternate Republican Nat. Conv., 1956, del., 1964; chmn. Hamden Rep. Town Com., 1964-68; Corporator Inst. Living, Hartford, 1959—; bd. dirs. New Haven Vis. Nurse Assn., New Haven United Fund; trustee Yale in China, 1936-62; bd. dirs. Yale New Haven Hosp., Yale Psychiat. Inst.; bd. dels. Am. Hosp. Assn. Served to lt. comdr. USNR, 1943-46, 51-53. Mem. ABA (del.), Conn. Bar Assn. (pres.), New Haven County Bar Assn., Quinnipiack Club, Morys Club. Home: 88 Notch Hill Rd Apt 372 North Branford CT 06471-1853 Office: Wiggin & Dana 1 Century Tower New Haven CT 06510-7013

TILSON, M(ARTIN) DAVID, surgeon, scientist; b. Texarkana, Tex., Aug. 25, 1941; s. M. David and Leta (Martin) T.; m. Joan E. Staneski, 1976; children: William Thomas, John Wainwright, Martin David III. BA, Rice U., 1963; MD, Yale U., 1967. Diplomate Am. Bd. Surgery, Nat. Bd. Med. Examiners. Surg. intern Yale U., 1967-68; resident in surgery U. New Haven, 1968-72; asst. to assoc. prof. Yale U., New Haven, 1974-83, prof., 1983-89; Alisa Mellon Bruce prof. of surgery Columbia U., N.Y.C., 1989—. Contbr. articles to profl. jours. Maj. USAF, 1972-74. Rsch. grantee NIH, 1983-94. Mem. ACS, Soc. Univ. Surgeons, Am. Surg. Assn., Soc. Vascular Surgery, Internat. Soc. Cadiovasc. Surgery, Halsted Soc. Office: St Lukes Roosevelt Hosp 1000 10th Ave New York NY 10019-1105 Home: 104 Edgemont Rd Scarsdale NY 10583

TILSON THOMAS, MICHAEL, symphony conductor; b. L.A., 1944; s. Ted and Roberta T. Studies with, Ingolf Dahl, U. So. Calif., others; student conducting, Berkshire Music Festival, Tanglewood, Mass.; student conducting (Koussevitsky prize 1968); LL.D., Hamilton Coll.; L.H.D. (hon.), D'Youville Coll., 1976. Asst. condr. Boston Symphony Orch., 1969, assoc. condr., 1970-72, prin. guest condr., 1972-74; also Berkshire Music Festival, summer 1970, 74; music dir., condr. Buffalo Philharmonic Orch., 1971-79; music dir., prin. condr. Great Woods Ctr. for Performing Arts, 1985-88; prin. condr. London Symphony Orch., 1988—; artistic dir. New World Symphony, Fla., 1988—. Condr., dir., N.Y. Philharmonic Young People's Concerts, CBS-TV, 1971-77; vis. condr. numerous orchs., U.S., Europe, Japan; chief condr. Ojai Festival, 1967, dir., 1972-77; opera debut, Cin., 1975; condr.: Am. premiere Lulu (Alban Berg), Santa Fe Opera, summer 1979; prin. guest condr., L.A. Philharm., 1981-85, Am. premiere Desert Music (Steve Reich), 1984; prin. condr. Gershwin festival London Symphony Orch., Barbcan Ctr., 1987; composer: Grace (A Song for Leonard Bernstein), 1988, Street Song (for Empire Brass Quintet), 1988, From the Diary of Anne Frank (for orchestra and narrator Audrey Hepburn and New World Symphony), 1990; commd. by UNICEF for Concerts for Life's European premiere, 1991; recording artist Sony Classical/CBS Masterworks, 1973—; co-artistic dir. Pacific Music Festival, 1990—, with Leonard Bernstein 1st ann. Pacific Music Festival, Sapporo, Japan, 1990; co-artistic dir. 2d ann. Pacific Music Festival, 1991, Salzburg Festival, 1991; conducted Mozart Requiem. Named Musician of Year, Musical Am. 1970; recipient Koussevitsky prize, 1968, Grammy award for Carmina Burana with Cleve. Orch., 1976, for Gershwin Live with Los Angeles Philharm., 1983, Grammy nomination, Best Classical Album - Debussy: Le Martyre de Saint Sebastien (with the London Symphony Orchestra), 1994. Office: 888 7th Ave Fl 37 New York NY 10106-3799 Office: San Francisco Symphony Davies Symphony Hall San Francisco CA 94102

TILTON, DAVID LLOYD, savings and loan association executive; b. Santa Barbara, Calif., Sept. 21, 1926; s. Lloyd Irving and Grace (Hart) T.; m. Mary Caroline Knudtson, June 6, 1953; children: Peter, Jennifer, Michael, Catharine. A.B., Stanford U., 1949, M.B.A., 1951. With Santa Barbara Savs. & Loan Assn., 1951-90, pres., 1965-84; now pres. Fin. Corp., Santa Barbara; trustee, chmn. Calif. Real Estate Investment Trust, 1988. Served with USNR, World War II. Mem. Calif. Savs. and Loan League (dir. 1980), Delta Chi. Home: 630 Oak Grove Dr Santa Barbara CA 93108-1402 Office: 505 Bath St Ste 102 Santa Barbara CA 93101

TILTON, GEORGE ROBERT, geochemistry educator; b. Danville, Ill., June 3, 1923; s. Edgar Josiah and Caroline Lenore (Burkmeyer) T.; m. Elizabeth Jane Foster, Feb. 7, 1948; children—Linda Ruth, Helen Elizabeth, Elaine Lee, David Foster, John Robert. Student, Blackburn Coll., 1940-42; B.S., U. Ill., 1947; Ph.D., U. Chgo., 1951; D.Sc. (hon.), Swiss Fed. Inst. Tech., Zurich, 1984. Phys. chemist Carnegie Instn., Washington, 1951-65; prof. geochemistry U. Calif.-Santa Barbara, 1965-91, emeritus, 1991—, chmn. dept. geol. scis., 1973-77; guest prof. Swiss Fed. Inst., Zurich, 1971-72; prin. investigator NSF research grant, 1965—; mem. earth scis. panel NSF, 1966-69, 82-85. Assoc. editor Jour. Geophys. Research, 1962-65, Geochimica et Cosmochimica Acta, 1973—; contbr. articles to profl. jours. Served with AUS, 1942-45. Decorated Purple Heart; recipient Sr. Scientist award Alexander von Humboldt Found., 1989. Fellow AAAS, Am. Geophys. Union, Geol. Soc. Am.; mem. Nat. Acad. Scis., Geochem. Soc. (pres. 1981), Sigma Xi. Episcopalian. Home: 3425 Madrona Dr Santa Barbara CA 93105-2652 Office: U Calif Dept Geol Scis Santa Barbara CA 93106

TILTON, GLENN F., oil company executive; b. Washington, Apr. 9, 1948. BA in Internat. Rels., U. S.C., 1970. Sales trainee U.S. mktg. ops. Texaco Inc., Washington, 1970; various assignments Texaco Inc., Washington, Pa., Conn., 1970-76; div. supr. mktg. Texaco Inc., East Brunswick, N.J., 1976-78; area mgr. resale N.Y. div. Texaco Inc., N.Y.C., 1978, asst. to gen. mgr. northeastern region, 1978-79; mktg. mgr. resale Phila. div. Texaco Inc., 1979-81; staff coord. corp. planning and econs. dept. Texaco Inc., Harrison, N.Y., 1981-83; asst. gen. mgr. sales Texaco Europe, 1983-84, gen. mgr. mktg., 1984-87; v.p. mktg. Texaco U.S.A., Houston, 1987-88; pres. Texaco Refining and Mktg. Inc., Houston, 1988-91; v.p. Texaco Inc., 1989; chmn. Texaco Ltd., 1991-92; pres. Texaco Eruope, 1992-94, Texaco USA, Houston, 1994—; sr. v.p. Texaco Inc., 1995—. Office: Texaco Inc 1111 Bagby St Houston TX 77002-2551

TILTON, JAMES FLOYD, theatrical designer, art director; b. Rochelle, Ill., July 30, 1937; s. Norval Bailey T. and Magdeline (Ripplinger) Marelli; m. Helga Strang, Dec. 26, 1962 (div. Nov. 1976). B.A., U. Iowa, 1959. Resident designer John Drew Theater, Easthampton, N.Y., 1963; prin. designer Assn. Producing Artists, N.Y.C., 1965-69, Phoenix Theatre, N.Y.C., 1970-80; freelance designer, 1963—; designer maj. indsl. shows Avon, Coca-Cola, ABC, NBC Affl., N.Y.C., 1974—; designer for TV, 1977—; designer mus. exhibits Guild Hall Mus., East Hampton, 1979—; set and lighting designer 30 Broadway shows including You Can't Take It With You,, 1965, 83, Seascape (nomination for Antoinette Perry award), 1975. Served with U.S. Army, 1960-62. Recipient Carbonelle awards, 1987, 91, 92. Mem. United Scenic Artists 829. Democrat. Roman Catholic. Office: 10 W 15th St New York NY 10011-6838

TILTON, JOHN ELVIN, mineral economics educator; b. Brownsville, Pa., Sept. 16, 1939; s. John Elvin Sr. and Margaret Julia (Renn) T.; m. Elizabeth Martha Meier, June 18, 1966; children: Margaret Ann, John Christian. AB, Princeton U., 1961; PhD in Econs., Yale U., 1965. Staff analyst Office of Sec. of Def., Washington, 1965-67; rsch. assoc. Brookings Inst., Washington, 1967-70; asst. prof. econs. U. Md., College Park, 1970-72; assoc. prof. mineral econs. Pa. State U., University Park, 1972-75, prof., 1975-85; Coulter prof. Colo. Sch. Mines, Golden, 1985-94, dir. Divsn. Econs. and Bus., 1994—; officer econ. affairs commodities divsn. UN Conf. on Trade and Devel., Geneva, 1977; leader rsch. Internat. Inst. Applied Systems Analysis, Laxenburg, Austria, 1982-84; joint dir. mineral econs. and policy Program of Resources for Future, Colo. Sch. Mines, Washington, 1982—; vice chmn. bd. mineral and energy resources NRC, Washington, 1980-83, mem. nat. materials adv. bd., 1987-89. Author: International Diffusion of Technology, 1971, The Future of Nonfuel Minerals, 1977; editor: Material Substitution, 1983, World Metal Demand, 1990, Mineral Wealth and Economic Development, 1992, View from the Helm, 1995; co-editor: Economics of Mineral Exploration, 1987, Competitiveness in Metals, 1992. Capt. U.S. Army, 1965-67. Fulbright scholar Ecole Nat. Supérieure des Mines de Paris, 1992. Mem. Am. Econ. Assn., Am. Inst. Mining Metall. and Petroleum Engrs. (Mineral Econs. award 1985), Mineral Econs. and Mgmt. Soc. (pres. 1993-94), Mining and Metall. Soc. Am. Avocations: skiing, hiking. Office: Colo Sch Mines Divsn Econs and Bus Golden CO 80401

TILTON, WEBSTER, JR., contractor; b. St. Louis, Sept. 11, 1922; s. Webster and Eleanor (Dozier) T.; student St. Marks Prep. Sch., 1936-40, Pawling Prep. Sch., 1940-42; master brewers degree, U.S. Brewers Acad., 1949; m. Grace Drew Wilson, Feb. 14, 1948 (div. Oct. 1959); 1 son, Webster III; m. 2d, Nancy McBlair Payne, Jan. 5, 1963. Asst. brewing technologist F&M Schaffer Brewing Co., Bklyn., 1948-52; factory sales rep. Cole Steel Equipment Co., N.Y.C., 1957-68; dist. sales mgr. Scantlin Electronics, Inc., Washington, 1968-70; sales rep. Comml. Washer & Dryer Sales Co., Washington, 1970-72; propr. Webster Tilton, Jr., contractor, Washington, 1972-86. Served from cadet to chief mate Mcht. Marine Res.-USNR, 1942-45. Episcopalian. Home: RD # 2 Box 634 Cooperstown NY 13326

TILY, STEPHEN BROMLEY, III, bank executive; b. Phila., July 7, 1937; s. Stephen Bromley Jr. and Edith Helen (Straub) T.; m. Janet Anita Walz, July 10, 1965; children: Deborah Powell, Stephen Bromley IV, James Charles II. BS in Econs., Washington and Jefferson Coll., 1960; postgrad., Temple U. Sch. Law, 1963. Trust officer Indsl. Valley Bank & Trust Co., Phila., 1968-71; v.p. Farmers Bank of Delaware, Wilmington, 1971-77; exec. officer G&T, Inc., Ltd., Wilmington, 1977-80; pres., COO DCG&T Co., Wilmington, 1977-91, chmn., CEO, 1991-93, chmn. emeritus, 1993—; chmn. The Declaration Group, Conshohocken, Pa., 1985—; tchr. Am. Inst. Banking, 1970-79. Capt. USAR, 1960-61. Mem. Fin. Analysts of Phila., Internat. Assn. Fin. Planning, Barnegat Light Yacht Club (commodore 1988-89, trustee 1989-92), Kimberton Fish and Game Assn., Waynesborough Country Club, Union League Club of Phila., Merion Golf Club, Ducks Unltd. Republican. Episcopalian. Office: The Declaration Group 555 North Ln Ste 6160 Conshohocken PA 19428

TIMBAN, DEMETRIO SUNGA, lawyer; b. Hamilton, Ohio, June 29, 1966; s. Demetrio R. and Teresita (Sunga) T. AB, U. Mich., 1988; JD, Boston U., 1992. Bar: Ma. 1993, N.Y. 1993. Staff atty. Bedford Stuyvesant Cmty. Legal Svcs. Corp., Bklyn., 1993—; exec. com. del. Legal Svcs. Staff Assoc. UAW, N.Y.C. Mem. N.Y. State Bar Assn. (resident landlord & tenant com.), Mass. Bar Assn., N.Y. County Lawyers Assn. Roman Catholic. Home: 2 Woodlake Ct Medford NJ 08055

TIMBERG, SIGMUND, lawyer; b. Antwerp, Belgium, Mar. 5, 1911; came to U.S., 1916, naturalized, 1921; s. Arnold and Rose (Mahler) T.; m. Eleanor Ernst, Sept. 22, 1940; children—Thomas Arnold, Bernard Mahler, Rosamund and Richard Ernst (twins). A.B., Columbia U., 1930, A.M., 1930, LL.B., 1933. Bar: N.Y. 1935, U.S. Supreme Ct. 1940, D.C. 1954. Sr. atty., solicitors' office Dept. Agr., 1933-35, chief, soil conservation sect., 1935-38; staff mem. Temporary Nat. Econ. Com., 1938-39; sr. atty. SEC, 1938-42; chief, property relations and indsl. orgn. div., reoccupation br. Bd. Econ. Warfare and Fgn. Econ. Adminstrn., 1942-44; spl. asst. to atty. gen., antitrust div. Dept. Justice, 1944-45, chief judgments and judgment enforcement sect., 1946-52; sec. UN Com. on Restrictive Bus. Practices, 1952-53; cons. UN, 1953-55, 62-64; pvt. law practice, 1954-88; prof. law Georgetown U. Law School, 1952-54; faculty Parker Sch. Comparative Law, Columbia U., 1967-80; spl. counsel Senate Mil. Affairs Subcom. on Surplus Property Legislation, 1944; mem. Mission for Econ. Affairs, Am. Embassy, London, 1945; del. Anglo-Am. Telecommunications Conf., Bermuda, 1945, Geneva Copyright Conf., 1952; cons. Senate Patents Subcom., 1961, UN Patents Study, 1962-64, OAS, 1970; mem. adv. com. on fed. policy on indsl. innovation, patent and info. policy sub com., 1978-79, adv. com. on internat. investment, tech. and devel., 1979-85. Contbr. articles on antitrust, intellectual property and internat. law to legal periodicals. Mem. ABA, D.C. Bar Assn., Internat. Bar Assn., Internat. Law Assn., Am. Soc. Internat. Law, Washington Fgn. Law Soc., Am. Law Inst., Assn. Bar City N.Y., Copyright Soc. Am., Cosmos Club (Washington), Philosophy Club (Washington). Home: 3519 Porter St NW Washington DC 20016-3177

TIMBERLAKE, CHARLES EDWARD, history educator; b. South Shore, Ky., Sept. 9, 1935; s. Howard Ellis and Mabel Viola (Collier) T.; m. Patricia Alice Perkins, Dec. 23, 1958; children: Mark Brewster, Daniel Edward, Eric Collier. BA, Berea Coll., 1957; Calif. State Teaching Credential, Claremont Grad. Sch., 1958, MA, 1962; PhD, U. Wash., 1968. Tchr. Barstow High Sch., Calif., 1959-60, Claremont City Sch., Calif., 1960-61; teaching, rsch. asst. U. Wash., Seattle, 1961-64; asst. prof. history U. Mo., Columbia, 1967-73, assoc. prof., 1973-81, prof., 1981—, asst. dir. Honors Coll., 1988-90; exch. prof. Moscow State U., 1985, U. Manchester, Eng., 1987-88; hon. prof. history Lanzhou U., People's Republic of China, 1991; edn. coord. Revalba Russian River Cruises, 1992—. Editor: Essays on Russian Liberalism, 1972, Detente: A Documentary Record, 1978, Religious and Secular Forces in Late Tsarist Russia, 1992, Profiles of Finland series, 1991-94, (microfiche) The St. Petersburg Collection of Zemstvo Publs., 1992—; contbr. chpts. to books, articles to profl. jours. Mem. Citizens Alliance for Progress, Columbia, Mo., 1969-75, pres., 1969-70; founding mem. High Edn. Rescue Operation, Mo., 1983—; mem. Columbians Against Throw-Aways, 1980-83. Fgn. Area fellow, 1965-66, Am. Coun. Learned Socs. fellow, 1978-79; NEH grantee, 1972, 79, 87. Mem. Am. Assn. Advancement Slavic Studies (bd. dirs. 1980-82, 84-86, chmn. council regional affiliates 1981-82, 85-86, chmn. permanent membership com. 1981-84), Western Slavic Conf., Am. Hist. Assn. (exec. council Conf. on Slavic and East European History 1987-89), Central Slavic Conf. (sec.-treas. 1967-68, pres. 1968-69, 76-77, 83-84, 88-89, exec. bd. 1972—, custodian archive 1972—), Mo. Conf. History (pres. 1992), State Hist. Soc. Mo., Rocky Mountain Assn. Slavic Studies. Avocations: backpacking, travel, skiing. Home: 9221 S Rte N Columbia MO 65203-9312 Office: U Mo Dept History Columbia MO 65211

TIMBERLAKE, MARSHALL, lawyer; b. Birmingham, Ala., July 25, 1939; s. Landon and Mary (Perry) T.; m. Rebecca Ann Griffin, Aug. 22, 1987; children: Sumner, Jane Ellison. BA, Washington & Lee U., 1961; JD, U. Ala., 1970. Bar: Ala. 1970, Ala. Supreme Ct. 1970, U.S. Dist. Ct. (no., so. and mid. dists.) Ala. 1970, U.S. Supreme Ct. 1976, U.S. Ct. Appeals (11th and 5th cirs.) 1981, U.S. Ct. Appeals (D.C. cir.) 1991. Assoc. Balch & Bingham Law Firm, Birmingham, 1970-76, ptnr., 1976—; pres. Legal Aid Soc., Birmingham, 1980-81; chmn. Ala. Supreme Ct. Commn. on Dispute Resolution, 1994—; trustee Ala. Dispute Resolution Found., 1995—. Pres. Ala. Drug Abuse Coun., 1994-95, dir., 1989—; v.p. Assn. Atty. Mediators, 1994—. Capt. U.S. Army, 1962-66, Vietnam. Mem. ABA, Ala. State Bar (chmn. corp. banking and bus. law sect. 1981-82, chmn. bar task force on ADR 1992-94, Spl. Merit award 1995), Birmingham Bar Assn. (chmn. ethics com. 1975-76, chmn. unauthorized practice of law com. 1976-77, chmn. spl. projects com. 1994-95), Redstone Club (bd. govs. 1977-78), Rotary (Birmingham chpt., chmn. civic club found. 1984), Beaux Arts Krewe, Mountain Brook Club. Republican. Presbyterian. Avocations: tennis, thoroughbred racing, photography. Office: Balch & Bingham 1901 6th Ave N Birmingham AL 35203-2618

TIMBERS, ROSEANN S., cultural organization administrator; b. Solomon, Alaska, June 2, 1952; d. Lloyd H. and Adrienne (Newcomb) Tarpenning; m. Bryan P. Timbers, Aug. 3, 1974; children: Gregory P., Kirsten M. AA in Acctg., Bryant & Stratton, San Jose, Calif., 1972; student, U. Alaska, 1972, 80-81. Pres. Solomon Native Corp., Nome, Alaska, 1980—, Solomon Trad. Coun., Nome, Alaska, %. Chairperson Western Alaska Coun., Nome, 1992—; treas. North Northwest Mayors Conf., Nome, 1993—; bd. dirs. Alaska Fedn. Natives, Anchorage, 1990—; v.p. Kawerak, Inc., Nome, 1986—; bd. dirs. Bering Straits Native Corp., Nome, 1986—; del. Inuit Circumpolar Conf., Anchorage, 1986—; mem. State of Alaska Gov.'s Task Force on Govt. Roles, 1990-92, Gov.'s Commn. for Adminstrn. of Justice, 1980-84. Address: PO Box 243 Nome AK 99762-0243

TIMBERS, STEPHEN BRYAN, financial services company executive; b. Madison, Wis., Aug. 8, 1944; s. James G. Timbers and Betty A. (Aalseth) Fink; m. Joan Phillips (div.); 1 child, Alexander C. A.; m. Elaine C. Mack, Nov. 17, 1990; children: Christopher B., Brendan C. AB in English Lit., Yale U., 1966; MBA, Harvard U., 1968. Portfolio strategist Mutual Life Ins. Co. of N.Y., N.Y.C., 1970-81; sr. portfolio mgr. Smith Barney, Harris Upham & Co., N.Y.C., 1981-84; chief investment officer The Portfolio Group, Inc., N.Y.C., 1984-87, Kemper Fin. Svcs., Inc., Chgo., 1987-92; pres., COO Kemper Corp., Long Grove, Ill., 1992-96; pres., CEO, CIO Zurich Kemper Investments, Inc.(acquired by Zurich Ins. Group), Chgo., 1996—; bd. dirs. Kemper Corp. and Affiliates, LTV Corp., Gillett Holdings, Inc.; trustee Kemper Mutual Funds and Seperate Accounts; mem. NYSE Panel on Market Volatility and Investor Confidence, N.Y.C., 1990. Agt. Yale Alumni Fund, Harvard Bus. Sch. Alumni Fund. With U.S. Army, 1968-70. Mem. Investment Analysts Soc. Chgo. (dir.), N.Y. Soc. Security Analysts, The Yale Club of N.Y.C., The Economic Club of Chgo. (membership com. 1990), Chgo. Club, Glen View Club, The Attic, The Racquet Club of Chgo. Office: Zurich Kemper Investments 120 S La Salle Chicago IL 60603*

TIMBERS, WILLIAM HOMER, JR., nuclear fuel company executive; b. N.Y.C., Nov. 10, 1949; s. William Homer and Charlotte McLaughlin (Tanner) T.; m. Jeannette Amalie Mattson, July 14, 1979; children: Lisa Allison, Colin Mattson, Alexander Arms. BA, Allegheny Coll., Meadville, Pa., 1972; MBA, U. Pa., 1976. Assoc. Smith Barney, Harris Upham, N.Y.C., 1976-78, 2nd v.p., 1978-80, v.p., 1980-83; mng. dir. Western region Smith Barney, Harris Upham, San Francisco, 1983-86; mng. dir. Smith Barney, Harris Upham, N.Y.C., 1986-91; pres., CEO Timbers Corp., Stamford, Conn., 1991-93; apptd. transition mgr. by U.S. Pres. William J. Clinton U.S. Enrichment Corp., Washington, 1993-94; pres., CEO U.S. Enrichment Corp., Bethesda, Md., 1994—. Mem. Nuclear Energy Inst. (mem. com. 1993—). Home: 19 Piney Glen Ct Potomac MD 20854 Office: US Enrichment Corp 6903 Rockledge Dr Bethesda MD 20817-1818

TIMINS, BONITA LEA, interior decorator; b. Scranton, Pa., Nov. 26, 1951; d. Edward Joseph and Mary Loretta (Lake) T. BS in Art Edn., Kutztown U., 1973; MA in Art Edn. magna cum laude, Marywood Coll., 1976, MA in Psychology magna cum laude, 1990; PhD in Metaphysics, Am. Internat. U., 1994. Art tchr. Scranton Sch. Dist., 1974-77; prodn. asst. Garan, Inc., N.Y.C., 1977-78, Marty Gutmacher, Inc., N.Y.C., 1979-81, R.R.J. Industries, N.Y.C., 1981-82; prodn. mgr. Double Dutch Sportswear, N.Y.C., 1982-84; MR/CLA supr. Allied Svcs., Scranton, 1984-86; home health care coord. Scranton, 1986-95; interior decorator Kurlancheek Furniture Gallery, Clarks Summit, Pa., 1995—; ind. curator, Scranton, 1992-94; chemistry tutor U. Scranton, 1994-95. Contbr. articles to profl. jours. Com. woman Dem. Party, Scranton, 1994; fundraiser Am. Cancer soc., Scranton, 1993; mem. Nat. Coun. for Geocosmic Rsch. Recipient Nightingale award Pa. Hosp. Assn., 1995, Outstanding Assoc. Mem. Cmty. Svc. award Lackawanna County Young Dems., 1996, Excellence award Sigma Theta Tau Internat. Nursing Soc., 1995. Mem. Art Student's League N.Y.C. (life), Psi Chi, Kappa Pi. Roman Catholic. Avocations: travel, costume design, oil painting. Home: 2108 Jackson St Scranton PA 18504-1610

TIMKEN, W. ROBERT, JR., manufacturing company executive; b. 1938; married. B.A., Stanford U., 1960; M.B.A., Harvard U., 1962. With Timken Co. (formerly The Timken Roller Bearing Co.), Canton, Ohio, 1962—, asst. v.p. sales, 1964-65, dir. corp. devel., 1965-68, v.p., 1968-73, vice-chmn. bd., chmn. fin. com., 1973-75, chmn. bd., chmn. fin. com., 1975—, chmn. exec. com., 1983—, also dir. Office: Timken Co 1835 Dueber Ave SW Canton OH 44706-2728*

TIMLIN, JAMES CLIFFORD, bishop; b. Scranton, Pa., Aug. 5, 1927; s. James C. and Helen E. (Norton) T. A.B., St. Mary's Sem., Balt., 1948; S.T.B., Gregorian U., Rome, Italy, 1950. Ordained priest Roman Catholic Ch., 1951; asst. pastor St. John the Evangelist Ch., Pittston, Pa., 1952-53, St. Peter's Cathedral, Scranton, Pa., 1953-66; asst. chancellor, sec. Diocese of Scranton, 1966-71, chancellor, 1971-77, aux. bishop, vicar gen., 1976-84; pastor Ch. of Nativity, Scranton, 1979-84; bishop Diocese of Scranton, 1984—. Address: 300 Wyoming Ave Scranton PA 18503-1224

TIMMER, BARBARA, lawyer; b. Holland, Mich., Dec. 13, 1946; d. John Norman and Barbara Dee (Folensbee) T. BA, Hope Coll., Holland, Mich., 1969; JD, U. Mich., 1975. Bar: Mich. 1975, U.S. Supreme Ct. Assoc. McCrosky, Libner, VanLeuven, Muskegon, Mich., 1975-78; apptd. to Mich. Women Commn. by Gov., 1976-79; staff counsel subcom. commerce, consumer & monetary affairs Ho. Govt. Ops. Com., 1979-82, 85-86; exec. v.p. NOW, 1982-84; legis. asst. to Rep. Geraldine Ferraro, 1984; atty. Office Gen. Counsel Fed. Home Loan Bank Bd., 1986-89; gen. counsel Com. on Banking, Fin. and Urban affairs U.S. Ho. of Reps., Washington, 1989-92; asst. gen. counsel, dir. govt. affairs ITT Corp., Washington, 1992-96; with Alliance Capitol, Washington, 1994—. Recipient Affordable Housing award Nat. Assn. Real Estate Brokers, 1990, Acad. of Women Achievers, YWCA, 1993. Mem. ABA (bus. law, exec. coun. adminstrv. law and regulatory practice sects.), Mich. Bar Assn., Fed. Bar Assn. (exec. coun. of banking law com.), Bar of Supreme Ct., Women in Housing and Fin. (bd. dirs. 1992-94, gen. counsel 1994—), Supreme Ct. Bar Assn., Supreme Ct. Hist. Soc. Episcopalian. Office: Alliance Capitol 1801 Irving St NW Washington DC 20010

TIMMER, MARGARET LOUISE (PEG TIMMER), educator; b. Osmond, Nebr., July 4, 1942; d. John Henry and Julia Adeline (Schilling) Borgmann; m. Charles B. Timmer, May 23, 1964 (div. June 1990); children: Jill Marie, Mark Jon. AA, N.E. Community Coll., Norfolk, Nebr., 1987; BA in Edn., K-12 art endorsement, Wayne (Nebr.) State U., 1988; MEd, Bank Street Coll./Parsons Sch. Design, N.Y.C., 1992. Cert. tchr., Nebr. Bookkeeper Goeres Electric, Osmond, 1960-61; tel. operator Northwestern Bell, Norfolk, 1961-64; with want advt. dept. Washington Post, 1964-65; saleswoman Jeannes Fashion Fabrics, Norfolk, 1970-72, Tripps, Norfolk, 1986-87; office and fin. mgr. Tim's Plumbing & Heating Inc., Norfolk, 1972-86; tchr. art Norfolk Cath. Schs., 1988—, mem. bd., 1985-88; instr. art history N.E. Community Coll., 1992—; mem. youth art bd. Norfolk Art Ctr., 1988—. One-woman show Uptown Restaurant, Norfolk, 1993, Norfolk Art Ctr., 1996; exhibited in group shows Sioux City (Iowa) Art Ctr., 1988, Columbus (Nebr.) Art Ctr., 1993. Mem. choir St. Mary's Cath. Ch., Norfolk, 1991—; mem. Norfolk Community Choir, 1991; bd. dirs. Norfolk Community Concerts Assn., 1984-87; treas. Norfolk Cath. Booster Club, 1985-86; leader 4-H, Madison County, 1973-78; judge art show Laurel (Nebr.) Women's Club, 1988. Named outstanding profl. vol. Norfolk Art Ctr., 1996. Mem. Nat. Art Edn. Assn. (presenter 1987), Nebr. Art Edn. Assn. (3d place award 1988). Avocations: watercolor and oil painting, gardening, reading, gourmet cooking, sewing. Home: Box 239 83729 Warnerville Dr Norfolk NE 68701-9758 Office: Norfolk Cath Schs 2300 Madison Ave Norfolk NE 68701-4456

TIMMER, WAYNE F., architectural firm executive. BA in Pre-Architecture with High Honors, Clemson U., 1972; MArch in Urban Design, Rice U., 1975, MArch, 1978. Registered architect, Miss.; cert. Nat. Coun. Archtl. Registration Bds. Asst. planner/programmer Caudill, Rowlett, and Scott, Architects and Engrs., Houston, 1975; sr. planner divsn. urban design Oklahoma City Dept. Planning, 1976-78; project architect Barlow and Plunkett, Architects and Engrs., Jackson, Miss., 1978-83; prin., project mgr. WFT Architects, P.A., Jackson, 1983—; adj. prof. sch. architecture Miss. State U., 1981—. Mem. adv. com. neighborhood revitalization City of Jackson, 1988, mem. history city hall com., 1990; mem. Save Hist. Burwell Ho. Com., 1990-91; mem. Jackson Hist. Preservation Commn., 1990—, chmn., 1990, 91. Rsch. fellow Rice U. Mem. AIA (miss. chpt., bd. dirs. 1992-93, sec./treas. 1994, 2d v.p. 1995, pres. elect 1996), Nat. Trust Hist. Preservation, Tau Sigma Delta, Phi Kappa Phi. Office: WFT Architects PA PO Box 12344 Jackson MS 39236-2344

TIMMERHAUS, KLAUS DIETER, chemical engineering educator; b. Mpls., Sept. 10, 1924; s. Paul P. and Elsa L. (Bever) T.; m. Jean L. Mevis, Aug. 3, 1952; 1 dau., Carol Jane. BS in Chem. Engring, U. Ill., 1948, MS, 1949, PhD, 1951. Registered profl. engr., Colo. Process design engr. Calif. Rsch. Corp., Richmond, 1952-53; extension lectr. U. Calif., Berkeley, 1952; mem. faculty U. Colo., Boulder, 1953-95, prof. chem. engring., 1961—, asso. dean engring., 1963-86, dir. engring. rsch. ctr. coll. engring., 1963-86, chmn. aerospace dept., 1979-80, chmn. chem. engring. dept., 1986-89, Patten Chair Disting. prof., 1986-89, presdl. teaching scholar, 1989—; chem. engr. cryogenics lab. Nat. Bur. Standards, Boulder, summers 1955,57,59,61; lectr. U. Calif. at L.A., 1961-62; sect. head engring. div. NSF, 1972-73; cons. in field. Bd. dirs. Colo. Engring. Expt. Sta., Inc., Engring. Measurements Co., both Boulder. Editor: Advances in Cryogenic Engineering, vols. 1-25, 1954-80; co-editor: Internat. Cryogenic Monograph Series, 1965—. Served with USNR, 1944-46. Recipient Disting. Svc. award Dept. Commerce, 1957, Samuel C. Collins award for outstanding contbns. to cryogenic tech., 1967, George Westinghouse award, 1968, Alpha Chi Sigma award for chem. engring. rsch., 1968, Meritorious Svc. award Cryogenic Engring. Conf., 1987, Disting. Pub. Svc. award NSF, 1984; named CASE Colo. Prof. of Yr., 1993. Fellow AAAS (Southwestern and Rocky Mountain divsn. Pres.' award 1989), Internat. Inst. Refrigeration (v.p. 1979-87, pres. 1987-95, U.S. nat. commn. 1983—, pres. 1983-86, W.T. Pentzer award 1989), AIChE (v.p. 1975, pres. 1976, Founders award 1978, Eminent Chem. Engr. award 1983, W.K. Lewis award 1987, F.J. Van Antwerpen award 1991, Inst. Lecture award 1995), Am. Soc. for Engring. Edn. (bd. dirs. 1986-88, 3M Chem. Engring. divsn. award 1980, Engring. Rsch. Coun. award 1990, Delos Svc. award 1991); mem. NAE, Am. Astron. Soc., Austrian Acad. Sci., Cryogenic Engring. Conf. (chmn. 1956-67, bd. dirs. 1956—), Soc. Automotive Engrs. (Ralph Teetor award 1991), Sigma Xi (v.p. 1986-87, pres. 1987-88, bd. dirs. 1981-89), Sigma Tau, Tau Beta Pi, Phi Lambda Upsilon. Home: 905 Brooklawn Dr Boulder CO 80303-2708

TIMMONS, EDWIN O'NEAL, psychologist; b. West Point, Ga., May 12, 1928; s. Robert A. and Lois O. T.; m. Mary Birmingham, June 21, 1952; children: Robert A., Laura W., Jenny O., William B. B.S., Auburn U., 1951; M.A., U. Tenn., 1956, Ph.D., 1959. Staff psychologist Tuscaloosa (Ala.) VA Hosp., 1958-59; clin. psychologist Gulfport (Miss.) VA Hosp., 1960-61; asso. prof., then Alumni prof. psychology La. State U., 1961-78, prof. bus. adminstrn. and Alumni prof. psychology, 1978-83; mem. faculty Sch. Banking of South, 1975—; prin. Timmons & Assos. (Psychol. Cons.), Baton Rouge; mem. faculty So. Meth. U. Grad. Sch. Banking, 1976-83. Author TV-based tng. series on sales, mgmt., human rels., 1979. Served with U.S. Army, 1946-48, 51-53. Mem. Am. Psychol. Assn., La. Psychol. Assn., Southeastern Psychol. Assn., AAAS, AAUP, Sigma Xi. Office: 505 L S U Ave Baton Rouge LA 70808-4643 *Assume we have a given amount of elan vital. If we overinvest it in the past, we reap guilt over what we should or shouldn't have done. If we overinvest it in the future, we gain anxiety over what may happen. How better to invest it mainly in the here-and-now, to live the most fully human life possible for each of us.*

TIMMONS, EVELYN DEERING, pharmacist; b. Durango, Colo., Sept. 29, 1926; d. Claude Elliot and Evelyn Allen (Gooch) Deering; m. Richard Palmer Timmons, Oct. 4, 1952 (div. 1968); children: Roderick Deering, Steven Palmer. BS in Chemistry and Pharmacy cum laude, U. Colo., 1948. Chief pharmacist Meml. Hosp., Phoenix, 1950-54; med. lit. rsch. librarian Hoffman-LaRoche, Inc., Nutley, N.J., 1956-57; staff pharmacist St. Joseph's Hosp., Phoenix, 1958-60; relief mgr. various ind. apothecaries, Phoenix, 1960-68; asst. then mgr. Profl. Pharmacies, Inc., Phoenix, 1968-72; mgr. then owner Mt. View Pharmacy, Phoenix and Paradise Valley, Ariz., 1972—; pres. Ariz. Apothecaries, Ltd., Phoenix, 1976—; mem. profl. adv. bd., bereavement counselor Hospice of Valley, 1983—; mem. profl. adv. bd. Upjohn Health Care and Svcs., Phoenix, 1984-86; bd. dirs. Am. Council on Pharm. Edn., Chgo., 1986-92, v.p. 1988, 89, treas., 1990-91. Author poetry; contbr. articles to profl. jours. Mem. Scottsdale (Ariz.) Fedn. Rep. Women, 1963; various other offices Rep. Fedn.; mem. platform com. State of Ariz., Nat. Rep. Conv., 1964; asst. sec. Young Rep. Nat. Fedn., 1963-65; active county and state Rep. coms.; fin. chmn. Internat. Leadership Symposium:Woman in Pharmacy, London, 1987; treas. Leadership Internat. Women Pharmacy, 1991—. Named Outstanding Young Rep. of Yr., Nat. Fedn. Young Reps., 1965, Preceptor of Yr., U. Ariz./Syntex, 1984; recipient Disting. Public Svc. award Maricopa County Med. Soc., 1962, Disting. Alumni award Wasatch Acad., 1982, Career Achievement award, 1983, Leadership and Achievement award Upjohn Labs., 1985-86, Outstanding Achievement in Profession award Merck, Sharp & Dohme, 1986, award of Merit, 1988, Disting. Coloradoan award U. Colo., 1989, Vanguard award, 1991, Pharmacist of the Yr. award Profl. Compounding Corp. of Am., 1995, 96. Fellow Am. Coll. of Apothecaries (v.p. 1982-83, pres. 1984-85; chmn. bd. dirs. 1985-86, adv. council 1986—, Chmn. of Yr. 1980-81 Victor H. Morganroth award 1985, J. Leon Lascoff award 1990); mem. Ariz. Soc. of Hosp. Pharmacists, Am. Pharm. Assn. (Daniel B. Smith award 1990, U.S. pharmacoepial conv. expert adv. com. on compounding pharms. 1992—), Ariz. Pharmacy Assn. (Svc. to Pharmacy award 1976, Pharmacist of Yr. 1981, Bowl of Hygeia 1989, 1st Innovative Pharmacy award 1994), Maricopa County Pharmacy Assn. (pres. 1977, Svc. to Pharmacy award 1977), Am. Soc. of Hosp. Pharmacists, Aux. to County Med. Soc. (pres. 1967-68), Am. Aircraft Owners and Pilots Assn., Air Safety Found., Nat. Assn. of Registered Parliamentarians, Kappa Epsilon (recipient Career Achievement award 1986, Vanguard award 1991, Unicorn award 1993). Lodge: Civinettes (pres. Scottsdale chpt. 1960-61). Avocations: flying, skiing, swimming, backpacking, hiking. Office: Mt View Pharmacy 10565 N Tatum Blvd Ste B-118 Paradise Valley AZ 85253

TIMMONS, GERALD DEAN, pediatric neurologist; b. Rensselaer, Ind., June 1, 1931; s. Homer Timmons and Tamma Mildred (Spall) Rodgers; m. Lynne Rita Matrisciano, May 29, 1982; 1 child, Deanna Lynne; children from previous marriage: Jane Christina Timmons Mitchell, Ann Elizabeth, Mary Catherine. AB, Ind. U., 1953, MD, 1956. Diplomate Am. Bd. Psychiatry and Neurology. Intern Lima (Ohio) Meml. Hosp., 1956-57; resident Ind. U. Hosp., Indpls., 1957-59, 61-62; instr. neurology dept. Ind. U., Indpls., 1962-64; practice medicine specializing in psychiatry and neurology Indpls., 1962-64; practice medicine specializing in pediatric neurology Akron, Ohio, 1964—; chief pediatric neurology Children's Hosp. Med. Ctr., Akron, 1964—; chmn. neurology subcouncil Coll. Medicine Northeastern Ohio Univs., Rootstown, 1978—; chief examiner Am. Bd. Neurology and Psychiatry. Contbr. articles to profl. and scholarly jours. Served to capt. USAF, 1959-61. Mem. Summit County Med. Soc., Ohio Med. Soc., AMA, Am. Acad. Pediatrics, Am. Acad. Neurology (practice com. 1980-86), Child Neurology Soc. (chmn. honors and awards com. 1978—), Am. Soc. Internal Medicine, Am. Electroencephalographic Soc. Republican. Methodist. Office: Akron Pediatric Neurology 300 Locust St Ste 460 Akron OH 44302-1804

TIMMONS, GLENN F., church administrator. Grn. sec. Parish Ministries Commn. of the Ch. of the Brethren. Office: Ch of the Brethren 1451 Dundee Ave Elgin IL 60120-1674

TIMMONS, STEVE (RED), volleyball player; b. Newport Beach, Calif., Nov. 29, 1958. BA in Comm., U. So. Calif., 1982. Mem. U.S.A. Nat. Olympic Volleyball Team, 1983-88, 92; founder, creator volleyball clothing Redsand, 1985—; profl. volleyball tour player U.S., Il Messaggero, Italian Profl. League, Ravenna. Recipient Gold medal Olympics, 1984, 88, Bronze medal Olympics, 1992; named Most Valuable Player U.S.A. Olympic Volleyball Team, 1984. Mem. Assn. Volleyball Profls. Career-high second at 1991 Off Shore Manhattan Beach Open, 1991; only 3-time Olympic medal winner; led U.S.A. Nat. Team to bronze medal finish Olympics, Barcelona, Spain, 1992, gold medal finishes, 1984, 88; led U.S.A. Nat. Team to first Triple Crown-1984 Olympics, 1985 World Cup, 1986 World Championships; led Il Messaggero to team title, 1991, 2d place finish, 1992; team capt. Team Cup Volleyball champions, 1992; team capt. Team Coca-Cola Superstars Competition, 1993-94. Office: c/o Assn Volleyball Profls 15260 Ventura Blvd Ste 2250 Sherman Oaks CA 91403-5352*

TIMMONS, WILLIAM EVAN, corporate executive; b. Chattanooga, Dec. 27, 1930; s. Owen Walter and Doris (Eckenrod) T.; m. Mimi Bakshian, Sept. 28, 1966; children: Karen Leigh, Kimberly Anne, William Evan. Grad., Baylor Mil. Acad., Chattanooga, 1949; B.S. in Fgn. Service, Georgetown U., 1959; postgrad., George Washington U., 1959-61. Aide to U.S. Senator Alexander Wiley, 1955-62; adminstrv. asst. to U.S. Rep. William Brock, 1963-69; dep. asst. to Pres. Richard M. Nixon, 1969-70, asst., 1970-74; asst. to Pres. Gerald R. Ford, 1974; pres. Timmons & Co. Inc., 1975-86, chmn. exec. com., 1986—; mem. Fed. Property Rev. Bd., 1972-75, Pres.'s Trade Adv. Com., 1975-80; U.S. del. to Internat. Conf. on Viet Nam, Paris, 1973. Exec. dir. Tenn. Rep. Com., 1962; mgr. Brock campaigns, 1962, 64, 66, 68; dir. congl. rels. Nixon-Agnew campaign, 1968; coord. Nixon for Pres.; Rep. Nat. Conv., Miami, Fla., 1968, 72; dir. Pres. Ford com. Rep. Nat. Conv., Kansas City, 1976; nat. conv. dir. Reagan for Pres. Com., Detroit, 1980, Dallas, 1984; mem. adv. com. Rep. Nat. Com. Conv., New Orleans, 1988, San Diego, 1996; mem. exec. com. Nat. Young Reps., 1965-67; nat. polit. dir. Reagan for Pres. Com., 1980; dep. dir. for transition Office of Pres-Elect, 1980-81; presdl. appointee U.S.-Japan Adv. Commn., 1983-85; mem. faculty Nat. Rep. campaign workshops, 1963-69; bd. dirs. Radio Free Europe/Liberty, 1975-82, Georgetown U. Ctr. Strategic and Internat. Studies, 1982-85; sr. adviser Bush for Pres. Com., New Orleans, 1988. With USAF, 1951-55. Named Outstanding Young Rep. of Year Nat. Rep. Com., 1965; recipient 1970 Ann. Achievement award Georgetown Alumni Club; citation for Disting. Service Baylor Mil. Acad. Alumni Assn., 1970. Mem. SCV, SAR, Soc. of the Cin., Soc. of Colonial Wars, Columbia Country Club, George Towne Club, F Street Club, City Club, St. Alban's Tennis Club, Masons (33d degree). Home: 4426 Garfield St NW Washington DC 20007-1142 Office: Timmons & Co 1850 K St NW Washington DC 20006-2213

TIMMONS, WILLIAM MILTON, producer, freelance writer, retired cinema arts educator, publisher, film maker; b. Houston, Apr. 21, 1933; s. Carter Charles and Gertrude Monte (Lee) T.; m. Pamela Cadorette, Dec. 24, 1975 (div. 1977). BS, U. Houston, 1958; MA, UCLA, 1961; PhD, U. So. Calif., 1975. Child actor Houston Jr. Theater, 1945-46; staff announcer Sta. KMCO, Conroe, Tex., 1951-52; prodn. asst. Sta. KUHT-TV, Houston, 1953-54, 56-57; teaching fellow UCLA, 1960-61; ops. asst. CBS-TV, Hollywood, Calif., 1961-62; prof. speech and drama Sam Houston State U., Huntsville, Tex., 1963-67; chmn. dept. cinema Los Angeles Valley Coll., Van Nuys, Calif., 1970-91, ret., 1992; prodr. Sta. KPFK, L.A., 1959-60, 83-95; pub. Acad. Assocs., L.A., 1976; proofreader, cons. Focal Press Pub. Co., N.Y.C., 1983-92. Author: Orientation to Cinema, 1986; contbr. articles to mags.; prodr., dir.: (radio programs) Campus Comments, 1963-67, numerous ednl. films, 1963—; prodr. ednl. series for cable TV, 1993—. With USNR, 1954-56. Named Hon. Tex. Ranger, State of Tex., Austin, 1946; U. Houston scholar, 1957. Mem. Mensa, U. So. Calif. Cinema-TV Alumni Assn., Red Masque Players, Secular Humanists L.A., Alpha Epsilon Rho, Delta Kappa Alpha. Democrat. Avocations: reading, writing, viewing movies.

TIMMRECK, THOMAS C., health sciences and health administration educator; b. Montpelier, Idaho, June 15, 1946; s. Archie Carl and Janone (Jensen) T.; m. Ellen Prusse, Jan. 27, 1971; children: Chad Thomas, Benjamin Brian, Julie Anne. AA, Ricks Coll., 1968; BS, Brigham Young U., 1971; MEd, Oreg. State U., 1972; MA, No. Ariz. U., 1981; PhD, U. Utah, 1976. Program dir. Cache County Aging Program, Logan, Utah, 1972-73; asst. prof. div. health edn. Tex. Tech U., Lubbock, 1976-77; asst. prof. dept. health care adminstrn. Idaho State U., Pocatello, 1977-78; program dir., asst. prof. health services program No. Ariz. U., Flagstaff, 1978-84; cons., dir. grants Beth Israel Hosp., Denver, 1985; prof. dept. health scis. and human ecology, coordinator grad. studies, coordinator health adminstrn. and planning Calif. State U., San Bernardino, 1985—; pres. Health Care Mgmt. Assocs., 1985—; presenter at nat. confs.; mem. faculty Loretto Heights Coll., Denver, Dept. Mgmt. U. Denver, Dept. Mgmt. and Health Adminstrn. U. Colo., Denver, dept. bus. adminstrn. U. Redlands (Calif.), U. So. Calif., L.A. Author: Dictionary of Health Services Management, rev. 2d edit., 1987, Health Services Cyclopedic Dictionary, 3d edit., An Introduction to Epidemiology, 1994, Handbook of Planning and Program Development for Health and Social Services, 1995; mem. editl. bd. Jour. Health Values, 1986—; contbr. numerous articles on health care adminstrn., behavioral health, gerontology and health and health edn. to profl. jours. Chmn., bd. dirs. Inland Counties Health System Agy.; mem. strategic planning com. chmn. Vis. Nurses Assn. of Inland Counties; bd. dirs. health svc. orgns. With U.S. Army, 1966-72, Vietnam. Mem. Assn. Advancement of Health Edn., Am. Acad. Mgmt., Assn. Univ. Programs in Health Care Adminstrn., Healthcare Forum. Republican. Mormon. Office: Calif State U Dept Health Scis and Human Ecology San Bernardino CA 92407

TIMMS, PETER ROWLAND, art museum administrator; b. Phila., Aug. 26, 1942; s. H. Rowland and Nancy Virginia (Shaub) T.; m. Romayne Julian Dawnay, Jan. 8, 1972; children: Matthew, Zöe, Christopher. B.A., Brown U., 1964; M.A., Harvard U., 1970, Ph.D., 1976. Instr. Internat. Coll., Beirut, Lebanon, 1967-68; dir. Fitchburg (Mass.) Art Mus., 1973—; dir. Spofford Garrison Excavations, 1978; teaching fellow Harvard U., 1969-71, MIT, 1973. Author: Flint Implements of the Old Stone Age, 1974. Mem. Fitchburg Bicentennial Com., 1974; bd. dirs. Cen. Mass. Tourist Coun., 1974-78, Fitchburg chpt. ARC, 1975-79, Spofford Garrison Excavations, 1978, 79, 80, Nashua River Watershed Assn., 1979-81, Nashua Arts and Sci. Ctr., 1983-86; trustee Applewild Sch., 1982-94, Nat. Plastics Ctr. and Mus., 1991—; pres. Fitchburg Cultural Alliance, 1979-83. Capt. USMCR, 1964-67, Vietnam. Mem. Am. Assn. Museums, Fitchburg Hist. Soc. Republican. Episcopalian. Home: 198 Lake Rd Ashburnham MA 01430-1207

TIMONEY, PETER JOSEPH, veterinarian, virologist, educator, consultant; b. Dublin, Ireland, June 5, 1941; came to U.S., 1983; s. John Francis and Evelyn Norah (Whittle) T.; m. Katherine Mary Murphy, Sept. 11, 1971; children: Peter, Caroline, Sarah, David. MVB, Nat. U., Dublin, 1964; MS, U. Ill., 1966; PhD, U. Dublin, 1974. Rsch. assoc. U. Ill., Urbana, 1964-66; rsch. officer Vet. Rsch. Lab., Abbotstown, Ireland, 1966-72; sr. rsch. officer equine diseases sect. Veterinary Rsch. Lab., Abbotstown, Ireland, 1972-79; assoc. prof. diagnostic lab., dept. microbiology Cornell U., Ithaca, N.Y., 1979-81; sci. dir. Irish Equine Ctr., Johnstown, Ireland, 1981-83; assoc. prof. virology vet. sci. dept. U. Ky., Lexington, 1983-87, prof. virology, assoc. chair for rsch., 1987-89, Frederick Van Lennep prof., 1988—, acting chair, 1989-90, chair, dir. Gluck Equine Rsch. Ctr., 1990—; cons. Daryl Labs., Inc., Santa Clara, Calif., 1981-86, Ft. Dodge (Iowa) Labs., 1986-92, 94—. Fellow Royal Coll. Vet. Surgeons, World Equine Vet. Assn. (pres. 1995—); mem. AAAS, Am. Assn. Equine Practitioners, Am. Soc. Microbiology, Am. Soc. Virology, U.S. Animal Health Assn. Avocations: reading, gardening. Office: U Ky Gluck Equine Rsch Ctr 108 Gluck Ctr Lexington KY 40506

TIMOTHY, DAVID HARRY, biology educator; b. Pitts., June 9, 1928; s. David Edgar and Harriett P. (Stein) T.; m. Marian Claire Whiteley, Sept. 5, 1953; children: Marjory J., M. Elisabeth, David W. BS, Pa. State U., 1952, MS, 1955; PhD, U. Minn., 1956. Asst. geneticist Rockefeller Found., Bogota, Colombia, 1956-58; assoc. geneticist Rockefeller Found., Bogota, 1958-61; assoc. prof. N.C. State U., Raleigh, 1961-66, prof., 1966-93, prof. emeritus, 1993—; cons. to fgn. and U.S. govts., also U.S. and internat. sci. orgns.; mem. crop adv. com. on grasses USDA, 1983-87, mem. policy adv. com., sci. and edn. grants program, 1982-84, chief scientist Sci. and Edn. Competetive Rsch. Grants Office, 1985, 86; with Nat. Plant Genetic Resources Bd., 1984-91, vice chmn., 1991; bd. dirs., treas. Genetic Resources Comms. Sys., Inc., 1985-91, pres., 1991-93; mem. bd. on agr. NAS-NRC; mem. work group on U.S. Nat. Plant Germplasm Sys., 1987-89. Co-author monographs, also author articles. With AUS, 1946-48, PTO. Grantee NSF, 1965, 78, Rockefeller Found., 1968, 69, Pioneer Hi-Bred Internat., 1982, 83. Fellow AAAS (electorate nominating com., sect. O, Agr. 1988-90), Am. Soc. Agronomy, Crop Sci. Soc. Am. (editl. bd. 1982-84, assoc. editor Crop Sci. 1982-84, Frank N. Meyer medal for plant genetic resources 1994). Home: 13 Furches St Raleigh NC 27607-7048

TIMOTHY, RAYMOND JOSEPH, television executive; b. N.Y.C., Mar. 23, 1932; s. Richard and Mary Ann (O'Connor) T.; B.A. in Polit. Sci., Queens Coll., 1954; LL.B., Bklyn. Law Sch., 1963; m. Kathleen Shanahan, May, 1964; children—Matthew, Patrick, Luke. Admitted to N.Y. bar, 1964;

various broadcasting positions, 1954-76; v.p., gen. mgr. WNBC-TV, N.Y.C., 1976-77; exec. v.p. affiliate relations NBC, N.Y.C., 1977-79, group exec. v.p., 1982-84; exec. v.p. NBC-TV Network, N.Y.C., 1979-81, pres., 1981-82; group exec. v.p. NBC Entertainment, 1984—. Active N.Y.C. affiliate Nat. Council on Alcoholism. Served with U.S. Army, 1956-58. Mem. Nat. Acad. Arts and Scis. (pres. internat. council).

TIMOTHY, ROBERT KELLER, telephone company executive; b. Gilcrest, Colo., June 27, 1918; s. Virge and Alice (Patterson) T.; m. Elaine Hurd, Oct. 23, 1941; children: Kristen, Timothy Lankester, Robert Alan. AB, U. No. Colo., 1941, LLD (hon.), 1986. High sch. sci. tchr. Ft. Lupton, Colo., 1941-42; with Mountain States Tel. & Tel. Co., 1946-83, v.p. operations, 1968-69, pres., 1970-82, chmn. bd., 1982-83, also bd. dirs.; past bd. dirs. United Bank Denver, United Banks Colo.; bd. dirs. Rocky Mountain Health Care Corp. Pres., campaign chmn. United Fund, Boise, Idaho, 1962-64; Bd. dirs. Air Force Acad. Found., Bus.-Industry Polit. Action Com., 1975-82, Luth. Med. Center, 1971-84, Nat. Safety Council, 1971-80; trustee U. Denver, 1982-89, Gates Found., 1982-89; pres. Telephone Pioneers Am., 1977-78. Served to capt., Signal Corps U.S. Army, 1943-46. Mem. Newcomen Soc. (chmn. Colo. 1980-84), Civilian/Mil. Inst. (founding bd.), Rotary, Denver Country Club, Univ. Club (Denver). Republican. Home: 2155 E Alameda Ave Denver CO 80209-2710 Office: 931 14th St Denver CO 80202-2903

TIMOUR, JOHN ARNOLD, retired librarian, medical bibliography and library science educator; b. Hartford, Conn., Jan. 20, 1926; s. John Alfred and Karin Elizabeth (Levin) T.; m. Betty Jo Lord, Mar. 23, 1952; children—Jon, David, Alan. B.A., Miami U., Oxford, Ohio, 1951; postgrad., Fla. State U., 1951-52; M.A., George Washington U., 1960; M.L.S., U. Md., 1969. Tng. and Med. Lit. Analysis and Retrieval System liaison officer Nat. Library of Medicine, Bethesda, Md., 1966-69; dir. library services Conn. Regional Med. Program-Yale U., New Haven, 1969-73; dir. Mid-Eastern Med. Library Service Coll. Physicians of Phila., 1973-75; univ. librarian Thomas Jefferson U., Phila., 1975-87; instr. U.S. Army Reserve, Hamden, Conn., 1970-73; lectr. library sci. So. Conn. State Coll., New Haven, 1970-71; adj. prof. library sci. Drexel U., Phila., 1976-78. Contbr. articles to profl. jours. Served to RM2-c USN, 1943-46, PTO; 2d lt. USAF, 1951-53, lt. col. USAR, ret. Mem. Assn. Acad. Health Sci. Libr. Dirs., Am. Med. Writers Assn. (pres. Phila. chpt. 1986-87), Med. Libr. Assn. (bd. dirs. 1978-81, Eliot prize 1974), Acad. of Health Info. Profls. (disting. mem.), Spl. Librs. Assn. (pres. Phila. chpt. 1979-80), Conn. Assn. Health Sci. Librs. (hon. life), Sigma Xi (bull. editor Jefferson chpt. 1980-86, recognition cert. 1982), Beta Phi Mu. Episcopalian. Club: Washington Yacht and Country. Avocations: golfing; sailing; chess. Home: 209 Wedgewood Dr Washington NC 27889-9688

TIMPANE, PHILIP MICHAEL, education educator, foundation official; b. Troy, N.Y., Nov. 27, 1934; s. Philip Thomas and Rita (Killeen) T.; m. Genevieve LaGrua, Nov. 30, 1957; children: Michael J., Joseph T., Paul J., David A. AB, Cath. U. Am., 1956, MA, 1964; MPA, Harvard U., 1970; LittD (hon.), Wagner Coll., 1986; LLD (hon.), Catholic U. Am., 1991. Historian Joint Chiefs of Staff Dept. Def., 1961-65; spl. asst. civil rights Office of Sec. Def., 1965-68; edn. policy planner HEW, 1968-72; sr. fellow Brookings Instn., 1972-74; dir. edn. policy ctr. Rand Corp., 1974-77; dep. dir. Nat. Inst. Edn., Washington, 1977-80; dir. Nat. Inst. Edn., 1980-81; prof. edn. Tchrs. Coll. Columbia U., N.Y.C., 1981—, dean, 1981-84, pres., 1984-94; Aspen Inst. Edn. Program, 1974-77, 87—; v.p. and sr. scholar Carnegie Found. for the Advancement of Teaching, Princeton, N.J., 1994—. Author: Corporate Interest in Public Education in the Cities, 1982; co-author: Youth Policy in Transition, 1976, Business Impact on Education and Child Development Reform, 1991; co-editor: Planned Variation in Education, 1975, Work Incentives and Income Guarantees, 1975, Ethical and Legal Issues in Social Experimentation, 1975; editor: Federal Interest in Financing Schooling, 1978. Mem. Arlington (Va.) Sch. Bd., 1972-76, chmn., 1973-74; bd. dirs. Synergos Inst., 1988—, Children's TV Workshop, 1989—, Joba for the Future, 1995—, So. Edn. Found., 1995—. Mem. Cosmos Club. Democrat. Roman Catholic. Office: Carnegie Found Advncmnt of Tchng 5 Ivy Ln Princeton NJ 08540

TIMPANO, ANNE, museum director, art historian; b. Osaka, Japan, June 17, 1950; d. A.J. and Margaret (Smith) T. BA, Coll. William and Mary, 1972; MA, George Washington U., 1983. Program mgmt. asst. Nat. Mus. Am. Art, Washington, 1977-86; dir. The Columbus (Ga.) Mus., 1986-93, DAAP Galleries, U. Cin., 1993—; grant reviewer Inst. Mus. Svcs., Washington, 1988—, Ga. Coun. for Arts, Atlanta, 1988-91. Mem. 1992 Quincentenary Commn., Columbus, 1987-92. Recipient David Lloyd Kreeger award George Washington U., 1980. Mem. Am. Assn. Mus. (surveyor mus. assessment program), Assn. of Coll. and Univ. Mus. and Galleries, Coll. Art Assn., Midwest Mus. Conf. Roman Catholic. Home: 85 Pleasant Ridge Ave Fort Mitchell KY 41017 Office: U Cin PO Box 210016 Cincinnati OH 45221-0016

TIMPERLAKE, EDWARD THOMAS, public relations executive; b. Perth Amboy, N.J., Nov. 22, 1946; s. James Elwood Timperlake Jr. and Joan Dorothy (Conkling) Maurer; m. Barbette Runckel, Aug. 10, 1969 (div. 1993; children: Tara, Kimberly. BS, U.S. Naval Acad., 1969; MBA, Cornell U., 1977. Commd. 2d lt. USMC, 1969, advanced through grades to lt. col., 1985, resigned, 1975; rsch. asst. peace studies program Cornell U., Ithaca, N.Y., 1976-77; asst. venture mgr. optical info. systems Exxon Enterprise, N.Y.C., 1977-88; sect. mgr. Analytic Svcs. Corp., Arlington, Va., 1978-81; dep. dir. Nat. Dir. Vietnam Vets. Leadership Program, The Action Agy., Washington, 1981-83; dir. mobilization plans and requirements Office of Sec. Def., Washington, 1984; campaign staff George Bush for Pres., 1988; staff asst. Dept. Navy, Washington, 1989; asst. sec. congl. and pub. affairs Dept. Vets. Affairs, Washington, 1989-91, asst. sec. pub. and intergovtl. affairs, 1991-93, appt. spl. asst. to sec. of Vets. Affairs, 1993; pres. T-9 Group, 1993—, The Battle of Normandy Found., Washington, 1994; dir. Nat. Security task force Gramm for Pres., 1995-96. Contbr. numerous articles to profl. jours. Bd. dirs. Louis Pullen Vietnam Children's Fund. Lt. col. USMCR, 1985-88, ret., 1993. Mem. Naval Acad. Alumni Assn., Army-Navy Club, U.S. Naval Sailing Squadron, N.Y. Yacht Club, Bush-Quayle Alumni Assn. Home: 317 Chesapeake Ave Annapolis MD 21403-3201 Office: Dept Vets Affairs 810 Vermont Ave NW Washington DC 20420-0001

TIMPTE, SHANNON TALBERT, public relations executive; b. Bristol, Va., Feb. 11, 1942; d. Harry Irvin and Isabella Lois (Calhoun) Talbert; m. John Chandler Hopkins, Sept. 19, 1964 (div. Dec. 1981); children: John Chandler, David Calhoun, Nancy Talbert; m. Rudolph Gerhardt Timpte, Nov. 7, 1987. BA, Fla. State U., 1963; MA in Comm. Studies, St. Mary's U., 1993. Accredited pub. rels. profl. Legal sec. Smith, Swift, Currie McGhee Hancock, Atlanta, 1964-65; mgr. proxy dept., adminstrv. asst. Courts and Co., Atlanta, 1965-68; adminstrv. asst. customer complaints Budget Rent-a-Car, San Antonio, 1968-82; sec. nuclear medicine computed tonogora div. Univ. Tex. Health Sci. Ctr., San Antonio, 1981-82; mgr. pub. rels. dept., adminstrv. asst. Barshop Enterprises, Inc., San Antonio, 1983-85; spl. asst., fundraiser legal staff State Sen. Cyndi Krier, San Antonio, 1985; with news bur., spl. programs, cmty. rels. comm./mktg., property and casualty claims comm., claims process integration comm. specialist United Svcs. Automobile Assn., San Antonio, 1985—; mem. United Svcs. Automobile Assn. Spkrs. Bur. and mentor program. Mistress of ceremonies Channel 12 TV, 1959; contbr. articles to profl. jours. Bd. dirs., newsletter editor, mem. spl. events com., image brochures and ads com., stategic plans, bench marking, comm. audits/surveys United Way, 1986-87; co-chmn. Arneson River Restoration Commn., 1985-86; bd. dirs. San Antonio Coun. on Alcoholism, 1986-87; mem. fundraising com. San Antonio Symphony; mem. illiteracy prevention com. San Antonio Target 90; active Heart of Gold Dinner Am. Heart Assn., 1994. Recipient Friend of Edn. award Northside Ind. Tchrs. Assn., 1979-80. Mem. PRSA (sec. bd. 1988-90, v.p. programs 1993, v.p. membership 1994, pres. 1995), No. San Antonio C. of C. (chmn. task force, chair bus. book libr. campaign, chair image com.), Women in Comm. (v.p. bd. 1989-90), Internat. Assn. Bus. Communicators, NAFE, Am. Mktg. Assn., Toastmasters Internat. (area gov. dist. 56 1994-95). Republican. Methodist. Avocations: tennis, genealogy, philately, Bible study. Office: USAA 9800 Fredericksburg Rd San Antonio TX 78288-0001

TINDAL, DOUGLAS, religious organization administrator. Chmn. Religious TV Assocs. Office: Religious TV Assocs, 600 Jarvis St, Toronto, ON Canada M4S 1M7

TINDALL, GEORGE BROWN, historian, educator; b. Greenville, S.C., Feb. 26, 1921; s. Goin Roscoe and Nellie Evelyn (Brown) T.; m. Carliss Blossom McGarrity, June 29, 1946; children: Bruce McGarrity, Blair Alston Mercer. AB, Furman U., 1942, LittD, 1971; MA, U. N.C., 1948, PhD, 1951. Asst. prof. history Eastern Ky. State Coll., 1950-51, U. Miss., 1951-52, Woman's Coll. of U. N.C., 1952-53, La. State U., 1953-58; assoc. prof. U. N.C., Chapel Hill, 1958-64, prof., 1964-69, Kenan prof., 1969-90, Kenan prof. emeritus, 1990—; vis. prof. Coll. of Charleston, 1951, Kyoto Am. Studies Sem., 1977; Fulbright guest prof. U. Vienna, 1967-68; mem. Inst. for Advanced Study, 1963-64; mem. Ctr. for Advanced Study in Behavioral Scies., 1979-80. Author: South Carolina Negroes, 1877-1900, 1952, The Emergence of the New South, 1913-1945, 1967 (Jules F. Landry award 1968, Mayflower Cup 1968, Lillian E. Smith award 1968, Charles S. Syndor award 1968), The Disruption of the Solid South, 1972, The Persistent Tradition in New South Politics, 1975, The Ethnic Southerners, 1976, America: A Narrative History, 1984, 4th edit., (with David Shi), 1996, Natives and Newcomers: Ethnic Southerners and Southern Ethics, 1995; editor: The Pursuit of Southern History, 1964, A Populist Reader, 1966. Guggenheim fellow, 1957-58, Social Sci. Rsch. Coun. fellow, 1959-60, Ctr. for Advanced Study in Behavioral Scis., 1979-80. Mem. Am. Hist. Assn., Hist. Soc. N.C. (pres. 1990), N.C. Lit. and Hist. Soc., Organ. Am. Historians, So. Hist. Assn. (pres. 1973). Home: 305 Burlage Cir Chapel Hill NC 27514-2703

TINDALL, GEORGE TAYLOR, neurosurgeon, educator; b. Magee, Miss., Mar. 13, 1928; s. George Earl and Lyda (Smith) T.; children: Catherine, George Taylor Jr., Suzanne, Annelle. BA, U. Miss., 1948; MD, Johns Hopkins U., 1952. Diplomate Am. Bd. Neurol. Surgery. Intern Johns Hopkins Hosp., Balt., 1952-53; resident in neurosurgery Duke U., Durham, N.C., 1955-61, asst. prof. neurosurgery, 1961-67, assoc. prof., 1967-68; chief neurosurgery Durham VA Hosp., 1961-68; prof., chief div. neurosurgery U. Tex. Med. Br., Galveston, 1968-73; prof. surgery, chief neurosurgery Emory U., Atlanta, 1973-95; pvt. practice specializing in neurosurgery Atlanta, 1973—. Capt. USAF, 1953-55. Mem. Am. Acad. Neurol. Surgery (editor Jour. 1971-74)), Am. Assn. Neurol. Surgeons (pres. 1988-89), Congress Neurol. Surgeons (pres. 1973-74), Soc. Neurol. Surgeons, Neurosurg. Soc. Am., Soc. Univ. Neurosurgeons (pres. 1966), ACS, AMA (vice chmn. coun. neurol. surgery 1972—), Ga. Med. Assn., Johns Hopkins Med. and Surg. Assn., Alpha Omega Alpha. Home: 869 Lullwater Pky NE Atlanta GA 30307-1233 Office: 1327 Clifton Rd NE Atlanta GA 30307-1013

TINDER, JOHN DANIEL, federal judge; b. Indpls., Feb. 17, 1950; s. John Glendon and Eileen M. (Foley) T.; m. Jan M. Carroll, Mar. 17, 1984. B.S., Ind. U., 1972, J.D., 1975. Bar: Ind. 19, U.S. Dist. Ct. (so. dist.) Ind. 19, U.S. Ct. Appeals (7th cir.) 19, U.S. Supreme Ct. Asst. U.S. atty. Dept. of Justice, Indpls., 1975-77; pub. defender Marion County Criminal Ct., Indpls., 1977-78; chief trial dep. Marion County Pros. Office, Indpls., 1979-82; litigation counsel Harrisone Moberly, Indpls., 1982-84; U.S. atty. U.S. Dist. Ct. (so. dist.) Ind., Indpls., 1984-87; judge U.S. Dist. Ct. (so. dist.) Ind., 1987—; adj. prof. Ind. U. Sch. of Law, Indpls., 1980—; mem. Supreme Ct. Character & Fitness Com., Ind., 1982—. Co-founder Turkey Trot Invitational Race, Indpls., 1980. Recipient Cert. of Appreciation award Bur. Alcohol, Tobacco & Firearms, Indpls., 1976; Service award Marion County Prosecutor, Indpls., 1981. Mem. ABA, Ind. State Bar Assn. (dir. criminal justice sect. 1984—), Indpls. Bar Assn., 7th Circuit Ct. Bar Assn., Fed. Bar Assn. Republican. Roman Catholic. Office: US Dist Ct 304 US Courthouse 46 E Ohio St Indianapolis IN 46204-1903*

TINDLE, JEFFREY ALAN, hospital association executive; b. Sedalia, Mo., Apr. 19, 1955; married. BS, U. Mo., 1977, M Healthcare Adminstrn., 1980. Adminstrv. resicent Audrain Med. ctr., Mexico, Mo., 1980-81; asst. adminstr. Nevada (Mo.) City Hosp., 1981-83; assoc. adminstr. Nevada City Hosp., 1983-84; exec. dir. Assn. Ind. Hosps., Kansas City, Mo., 1984-87, pres., CEO, 1987—; mem. Mark Twain Bancshares Health Bd.; bd. dirs. Cabot Westside clinic. Active various civic and cmty. orgns. Mem. Assn. Healthcare Execs., Assn. Healthcare Enterprises, Am. Coll. Healthcare Execs. (assoc.), Mo. Hosp. Assn. Office: Assn Ind Hosps 8300 Troost Ave Kansas City MO 64131

TINER, STANLEY RAY, business communications executive, former editor; b. Springhill, La., Aug. 22, 1942; s. Elmer Ray and Nannie Lea (Randolph) T.; m. Veronica Jo Thibodeaux, Dec. 31, 1966; children—Mark Gerard, Jon Stuart, Heather Nicole. B.A., La. Tech. U., 1969. City editor Texarkana Daily News, 1969-70; mng. editor Minden (La.) Press-Herald, 1970-71; chief editorial writer Shreveport (La.) Times, 1972-74; editor Shreveport Jour., 1974-88; dir. pub. affairs Arkla Inc., 1988—. Bd. dirs. Shreveport chpt. NCCJ, 1981—, Assn. of Retarded Citizens, Caddo-Bossier, La. 1974-87; chmn. Holocaust Commemoration, Shreveport, 1987; bd. dirs. La. Assn. for Blind, 1988—; chmn. La. State Exhibit Mus., 1991—. Served as sgt. USMC, 1962-66, Vietnam. Recipient Frank Allen award La.-Miss. AP, 1976; Silver Gavel award ABA, 1977; Robert F. Kennedy award, 1978; Social Justice award Social Justice Com., Shreveport, 1981; Nieman fellow Harvard U., 1985-86; Liberty Bell award Shreveport Bar Assn., 1985; award of merit AIA. Mem. Interstate Natural Gas Assn. Am. (state rels. com. 1988—), Internat. Assn. Bus. Communicators, La. Assn. Bus. and Industry (bd. dirs. 1989—), Soc. Profl. Journalists (pres. 1974, bd. dirs. 3 yrs.), La. Press Assn. (bd. dirs. 1975-77). Democrat. Baptist. Avocations: walking; photography. Office: Arkla Inc 525 Milam St Shreveport LA 71101-3539

TING, ALBERT CHIA, bioengineering researcher; b. Hong Kong, Sept. 7, 1950; came to U.S., 1957; s. William Su and Katherine Sung (Bao) T.; m. Shirley Roung Wang, July 30, 1988. BA, UCLA, 1973; MS, Calif. State U., L.A., 1975, Calif. Inst. Tech., 1977; PhD, U. Calif., San Diego, 1983. Rsch. asst. Calif. Inst. Tech., Pasadena, 1975-77, U. Calif., San Diego, 1982-83; sr. staff engr. R&D Am. Med. Optics, Irvine, Calif., 1983-86; project engr., rsch. Allergan Med. Optics, Irvine, Calif., 1987-89; sr. project engr., rsch., 1989-92, sr. project engr., engring., 1993-94; biorengr. cons. Pharmacia Iovision, Inc., Irvine, Calif., 1995—. Inventor med. and optical devices, recipient patent awards 1988, 89, 91, 92, 93; contbr. articles to sci. jours. Mem. AAAS, Biomed. Engring. Soc., Assn. for Rsch. in Vision and Ophthalmology, Biomed. Optics Soc.

TING, ROBERT YEN-YING, physicist; b. Kwei-yang, China, Mar. 8, 1942; came to U.S. 1965; s. Chi-yung and Shou-feng (Yang) T.; m. Teresa Yen-chun Ting, June 3, 1967; children: Paul H., Peggy Y. BS, Nat. Taiwan U., 1964; MS, MIT, 1967; PhD, U. Calif., San Diego, 1971. Rsch. engr. U.S. Naval Rsch. Lab., Washington, 1971-77, supervisory engr., 1977-80; supervisory physicist U.S. Naval Rsch. Lab., Orlando, Fla., 1980—; prof. George Washington U., 1972-80. Contbr. over 100 articles in rheology, polymer and acoustics to profl. jours. Fellow Acoustical Soc. Am.; mem. Am. chem. Soc., Am. Ceramics Soc., Am. Inst. Chem. Engrs. Office: US Naval Rsch Lab PO Box 568337 Orlando FL 32856-8337

TING, SAMUEL CHAO CHUNG, physicist, educator; b. Ann Arbor, Mich., Jan. 27, 1936; s. Kuan H. and Jeanne (Wong) T.; m. Susan Carol Marks, Apr. 28, 1985; children: Jeanne Min, Amy Min, Christopher M. BS in Engring., U. Mich., 1959, MS, 1960, PhD in Physics, 1962, ScD (hon.), 1978; ScD (hon.), Chinese U. Hong Kong, 1987, U. Bologna, Italy, 1988, Columbia U., 1990, U. Sci. and Tech., China, 1990, Moscow State U., 1991, U. Bucharest, Romania, 1993. Ford Found. fellow CERN (European Orgn. Nuc. Rsch.), Geneva, 1963; instr. physics Columbia U., 1964, asst. prof., 1965-67; group leader Deutsches Elektronen-Synchrotron, Hamburg, W.Ger., 1966; assoc. prof. physics MIT, Cambridge, 1967-68, prof., 1969—; Thomas Dudley Cabot Inst. prof. M.I.T., 1977—; program cons. divsn. particles and fields Am. Phys. Soc., 1970; hon. prof. Beijing Normal Coll., 1987, Jiatong U., Shanghai, 1987, U. Bologna, Italy, 1988. Assoc. editor: Nuclear Physics B, 1970; mem. editl. bd. Nuc. Instruments and Methods, Mathematical Modeling; advisor Jour. Modern Physics A; contbr. articles to profl. jours. Recipient Nobel prize in Physics, 1976, De Gasperi prize in Sci., Italian Republic, 1988, Ernest Orlando Lawrence award U.S. Govt., 1976, Eringen medal Soc. Engring. Sci., 1977, Gold medal in Sci. City of Brescia, Italy, 1988, Golden Leopard award Town of Taormina, 1988, Forum Engelberg prize, 1996; Am. Acad. Arts and Sci. fellow, 1975. Mem. NAS; mem. Pakistani Acad. Sci., Acad. Sinica, Russian Acad. Sci., Hungarian Acad. Sci., Deutsche Acad. Naturforscher Leopoldina. Office: MIT Dept Physics 51 Vassar St Cambridge MA 02139-4308

TING, SHAO KUANG, artist, educator; b. Beijing, Oct. 7, 1939; came to U.S., 1980; s. Jun Sheng and Shiang Jun (Lee) T.; m. Daxi Zhang, Oct. 8, 1968 (div. Oct. 1987); children: Angelina, Li. B degree, Ctrl. Acad. Arts & Design, Beijing, 1962. Prof. Yunnan Inst. Arts, Kunming, Peoples Republic of China, 1962-80; lectr. dept. visual arts UCLA, 1983; profl. artist Beverly Hills, Calif., 1980—; prof. Ctrl. Acad. Arts & Design, Beijing, 1992—, U. Shanghai (People's Republic of China), Sch. Fine Arts, 1992—, U. Shan Xi, Taiyuan, People's Republic of China, 1992—, Yunan Inst. Arts, 1992—. One-man shows include Ginza Art Mus., Tokyo, 1988, Studio 47 Gallery, N.Y.C., 1989, Bernheim Gallerr, Paris, 1990, Historical Mus., Beijing, 1992; exhibited in group shows at Internat. Art Expo, 1986-94, Floriade Artist, Amsterdam, The Netherlands, 1991, Exhbn. by Chinese Artists in USA, Taipei, Taiwan, 1994; prin. works include mural The Great Hall of the People, People's Republic of China, 1989-90, Mus. Shanghai, Mus. Beijing, Matsuzakaya Gallery, Nagoya, Japan. Artist World Fedn. of UN, 1993, 94, 95; artist, donator UNICEF Charity Art Bazar, Tokyo, 1990, Midwest Inundation, L.A., 1993. Recipient Best of Show award U. So. Calif., 1984; recipient Outstanding Chinese Am. Role Model award Chinese Cultural Club Orange County, 1993, Pan Pacific Performing Arts, Internat., 1993; Ting Shao Kuang Day proclaimed by Mayor of Sante Fe, 1993; recipient Golden Image award Transpacific, Face and XO mags., 1994. Mem. Chinese Artists Assn. (pres. 1992—), Pang Xunqin Art Mus. (hon. curator 1992—). Avocations: music, literature, movies. Home: 707 N Alpine Dr Beverly Hills CA 90210-3305

TINGELSTAD, JON BUNDE, physician; b. McVille, N.D., Jan. 15, 1935; s. Sophus B. and Mabelle (Bunde) T.; m. Marcia Ayers, Dec. 17, 1960; children: Paul, Catherine, David. B.A., U. N.D., 1957, B.S., 1958; M.D., Harvard U., 1960. Diplomate Am. Bd. Pediatrics. Intern Children's Hosp. Med. Ctr., Boston, 1960-61, resident, 1961-62; resident U. Colo. Med. Ctr., Denver, 1962-63; fellow in pediatric cardiology Children's Hosp., Buffalo, 1965-67; asst. prof. pediatrics Med. Coll. Va., Richmond, 1967-71, assoc. prof., 1971-76; prof., vice chmn. pediatrics East Carolina U. Sch. Medicine, Greenville, N.C., 1976-77, prof., chmn. pediatrics, 1977—. Mem. Greenville City Bd. Edn., 1978-82, chmn., 1981-82. Served to capt. USAF, 1963-65. Fellow Am. Acad. Pediatrics, Am. Coll. Cardiology; mem. AAAS, AMA, So. Soc. Pediatric Rsch., Assn. Med. Sch. Pediatric Dept. Chairmen, Am. Bd. Pediatrics (bd. dirs.), Phi Beta Kappa, Phi Eta Sigma. Home: 208 Chowan Rd Greenville NC 27858-6321 Office: E Carolina U Sch Med Dept Pediatrics Greenville NC 27858-4354

TINGLE, AUBREY JAMES, pediatric immunologist, research administrator; b. St. Paul, Alta., Can., June 28, 1943; s. Cyril Nisbet Tingle and Margaret Lucy (Fraser) Tarbuck; m. Valerie Jean Anderson, Nov. 2, 1968; children: Heather Lynn, Brian James. MD, U. Alta., Edmonton, 1967; PhD, McGill U., Montreal, Que., Can., 1974. Asst. prof. dept. pediatrics U. B.C., Vancouver, Can., 1974-79, head div. immunology dept. pediatrics, 1974-86, assoc. prof., 1979-86, prof., 1986—, prof. dept. pathology, 1986—; dir. rsch. B.C. Rsch. Inst. for Child and Family Health, Vancouver, 1992—; asst. dean rsch. Faculty of Medicine, U. B.C., Vancouver, 1992—. Fellow Royal Coll. Physicians and Surgeons Can., Soc. Pediatric Research, Am. Acad. Pediatrics; mem. Western Soc. Pediatric Research. Office: BC Childrens Hosp-Pediatrics, 4480 Oak St, Vancouver, BC Canada V6H 3V4

TINGLE, JAMES O'MALLEY, lawyer; b. N.Y.C., June 12, 1928; s. Thomas Jefferson and Mercedes (O'Malley) T. B.S., U. Mont., 1950, B.A., 1952, LL.B., 1952; LL.M., U. Mich., 1953, S.J.D., 1958. Bar: Calif. 1959, Mont. 1952, N.Y. 1961. Asst. prof. law U. Mont., Missoula, 1955-56; atty. Shell Oil Co., N.Y.C., 1957-62; assoc. Pillsbury, Madison & Sutro, San Francisco, 1962-68, ptnr., 1969—. Author: The Stockholder's Remedy of Corporate Dissolution, 1959; editor: State Antitrust Laws, 1974. Served to 1st lt. USAF, 1953-55. William W. Cook fellow U. Mich. Mem. Mont. Bar Assn., Calif. Bar Assn., ABA. Democrat. Office: Pillsbury Madison & Sutro 225 Bush St San Francisco CA 94104-4207

TINGLE, KATHY CARTWRIGHT, school administrator; b. Lexington, Ky., May 25, 1961; d. Kenneth Cartwright and Marietta (Canter) Martin; m. M. Keith Tingle, July 12, 1980; children: Marshal Keith, Alexander Kenneth. BS, Georgetown Coll., 1984, MA in Edn., 1987; Adminstrv. Endorsement, Morehead State U., 1992. Cert. instrnl supr. elem. and secondary schs. Elem. tchr. Grant County Schs., Williamstown, Ky., 1984-89; early childhood tchr. Bath County Sch., Owingsville, Ky., 1990-92, dir. spl. edn. and early childhood programs, 1992—; task force cert. of early childhood, Ky. Dept. Edn., Frankfort, 1993, assoc. Regional Svc. Ctr., 1993, early childhood cons., 1992—. Mem. Coun. for the Arts, Owingsville, 1991, Owingsville Homemakers, 1991; dir. Owingsville Community Choir, 1991—. Mem. Ky. Early Childhood Assn., So. Early Childhood Assn., ASCD, Nat. Mid. Sch. Assn., Ky. Assn. Sch. Adminstrs., Phi Delta Kappa. Democrat. Baptist. Avocations: piano, reading, theatre. Home: 181 Sherman Ct Owingsville KY 40360 Office: Bath County Bd Edn 459 W Main St Owingsville KY 40360-2018

TINGLEY, FLOYD WARREN, physician; b. Charlotte, N.C., Nov. 22, 1933; s. Floyd Warren Sr. and Janie (Suggs) T.; m. Sandra Carpenter, Aug. 20, 1955 (div. Dec. 1984); children: Sheryl Tingley Hagen, David Alan; m. Johnette Hill, Apr. 5, 1985. BA in English, Emory U., 1955, MD, 1959. Diplomate Am. Bd. Internal Medicine (bd. govs. 1986-92). Intern USAF Hosp., Lackland AFB, Tex., 1959-60; resident in internal medicine Parkland Meml. Hosp., Dallas, 1963-65, fellow in cardiology, 1965-66; pvt. practice specializing in internal medicine Arlington, Tex., 1966-88; med. dir. southwestern region Met. Life Ins. Co., Irving, Tex., 1988-90; regional practice leader William M. Mercer Inc., 1990-91; v.p., sr. med. dir. Provident Life and Accident Co., Chattanooga, 1991-92; v.p., nat. med. dir. Travelers Ins. Cos., Hartford, Conn., 1992-94; sr. v.p., chief med. officer Kemper Nat. Svcs., Plantation, Fla., 1995—; apptd. Tex. Commn. on Health Care Reimbursement Alternatives, 1987; bd. dirs. Riverside Nat. Bank, Grand Prairie, Tex. Contbr. articles to profl. jours. Pres. Arlington YMCA, 1971; chmn. budget com. Family Services, Ft. Worth, 1973; participant Health Policy Agenda for Am. People, Chgo., 1984-87; trustee Tex. Med. Liability Trust, Austin, 1987-88. Capt. USAF, 1958-63. Fellow ACP (pres. Tex. chpt. 1981); mem. AMA (chmn. sect. coun. internal medicine, 1979-88), Am. Soc. Internal Medicine (pres. 1986-87), Tex. Med. Assn. (treas. 1978-85, alt. del. to AMA 1985-91, commendation 1985), Tarrant County Med. Soc. (pres. Arlington br. 1974, del. to Tex. Med. Assn., Community Svc. award 1983). Presbyterian. Avocations: photography, sailing, gardening, computer hobbies. Home: 7588 NW 51st Pl Coral Springs FL 33067 Office: Kemper Nat Svcs Inc 1601 SW 80th Terr Plantation FL 33324-4036

TINGLEY, WALTER WATSON, computer systems manager; b. Portland, Maine, July 24, 1946; s. Edward Allen Tingley and Ruth Annie (Howard) Tuttle; m. Elizabeth A. Fletcher, May 1970 (div. 1975). BS, U. Md., 1974. Programmer analyst U.S. Ry. Assn., Washington, 1974-80, Digital Equipment Corp., Maynard, Mass., 1980-81, Interactive Mgmt. Systems, Belmont, Mass., 1981; systems designer Martin Marietta Data Systems, Greenbelt, Md., 1982-84; mgr. computer ops. Genex, Rockville, Md., 1984; system mgr. Applied Rsch. Corp., Landover, Md., 1985; programmer analyst Input/Output Computer Svcs., Washington, 1986-87, Lockheed Engring. and Scis., Las Vegas, Nev., 1987-91, Computer Profls., Inc., Los Alamos, N.Mex., 1992—. Author tech. book revs., software revs. With USAF, 1964-68. Mem. IEEE Computer Soc., Assn. Computing Machinery. Avocations: skiing, hiking, swimming. Home: PO Box 429 Los Alamos NM 87544-0429

TINKER, GRANT A., broadcasting executive; b. Stamford, Conn., Jan. 11, 1926. Student, Dartmouth Coll. With radio program dept. NBC, 1949-54; TV dept. McCann-Erickson Advt. Agy., 1954-58, Benton & Bowles Advt. Agy., 1958-61; v.p.-programs West Coast, NBC, 1961-66; v.p. in charge programming West Coast, NBC, N.Y.C., 1966-67; v.p. Universal TV, 1968-69, 20th-Fox, 1969-70; pres. Mary Tyler Moore (MTM) Enterprises, Inc., Studio City, Calif., 1970-81; chmn. bd., chief exec. officer NBC, Burbank, Calif., 1981-86; independent producer Burbank, Calif., from 1986; pres. GTG Entertainment, Culver City, Calif., from 1986. Author: (with Bud Rukeyser) Tinker in Television: From General Sarnoff to General Electric, 1994. Office: GTG Entertainment 9336 Washington Blvd Culver City CA 90232-2628

TINKER, H(AROLD) BURNHAM, chemical company executive; b. St. Louis, May 16, 1939; s. H(arold) Burnham and Emily (Barnicle) T.; m.

Barbara Ann Lydon, Feb. 20, 1965; children: Michael B., Mary K., Ann E. BS in Chemistry, St. Louis U., 1961; MS in Chemistry, U. Chgo., 1964, PhD in Chemistry, 1966. Sr. research chemist Monsanto, St. Louis, 1966-69, research specialist, 1969-73, research group leader, 1973-77, research mgr., 1977-81; tech. dir. Mooney Chems., Inc., Cleve., 1981-90, v.p. rsch. and devel., 1991-94; v.p. corp. devel., 1994—. Patentee in field; contbr. article to profl. jours. Mem. scis. adv. coun. U. Akron, 1995—. Mem. Am. Chem. Soc. (chmn. bd. St. Louis sect. 1978-79), Cleve. Assn. Rsch. Dirs. (v.p. 1989, pres. 1990, bd. dirs. 1991—). Roman Catholic. Avocation: computers. Home: 2889 Manchester Rd Cleveland OH 44122-2570 Office: OM Group Inc 3800 Terminal Tower Cleveland OH 44113-2204

TINKER, JOHN HEATH, anesthesiologist, educator; b. Cin., May 18, 1941; s. Leonard Henry and Georgia (Reeves) T.; m. Martha Iuen (div. Jan., 1989); children: Deborah H. Lynne, Karen Sue, Juliette Kay; m. Bonnie Howard, Mar. 18, 1989. BS magna cum laude, U. Cin., 1964, MS summa cum laude, 1968. Diplomate Am. Bd. Anesthesiology (sr. examiner 1976—). Surg. intern, resident Harvard Med. Sch., Peter Bent Brigham Hosp., Boston, 1969-70, resident in anesthesiology, 1970-72; cons. anesthesiology Mayo Clinic, Rochester, Minn., 1974-83, chief cardiovascular anesthesiology, 1978-83; prof. anesthesiology U. Iowa Coll. Medicine, Iowa City, 1983—, chmn. dept., 1983—; mem. pharm. scis. rev. com., NIH, Bethesda, Md., 1986—; dir. Matrix Med. Inc., Orchard Park, N.Y., 1988—; frequent guest lectr. Author: Controversies in Cardiopulmonary Bypass, 1989 (monograph award Soc. Cardiovascular Anesthsiologists); editor: Anesthesia and Analgesia, Jour. Internat. Anesthesiology Rsch. Soc., 1983—; contbr. over 185 articles to profl. jours. Maj. U.S. Army, 1972-74. NIH grantee, 1977-87. Fellow Royal Coll. Surgeons Australia; mem. Am. Soc. Anesthesiologists (active numerous coms. 1972—), Soc. Cardiovascular Anesthesiologists, Assn. Univ. Anesthetists. Avocations: fishing, golf, modeling ships and airplanes. Office: U Iowa Hosps & Clinics 450 Newton Rd Iowa City IA 52242

TINKER, MARK CHRISTIAN, producer, director; b. Stamford, Conn., Jan. 16, 1951; s. Grant Almerin Tinker and Ruth Prince Byerly Fricke; m. Kristin Harmon, Apr. 16, 1988; 1 child, James. BS, Syracuse U., 1973. Producer, dir., writer TV series: The White Shadow, 1978-81, St. Elsewhere, 1981-88 (Emmy, Peabody award, Peoples Choice award); dir. TV Movie: Babe Ruth, 1991; producer, dir. TV series: Civil Wars, 1991—. Mem. Nat. Acad. TV Arts and Scis. *

TINKER, THOMAS EATON, headmaster; b. Providence, May 24, 1941; s. George Milan and Ruth (Eaton) T.; m. Rosalyn May Silverman, Dec. 21, 1968. BA, Columbia U., 1963; MA, Brown U., 1968. English instr. Tabor Acad., Marion, Mass., 1964-66; history instr. Wheeler Sch., Providence, 1967-77; headmaster Broadmeadow Sch., Middletown, Del., 1977-82, St. Paul's Sch., Garden City, N.Y., 1982-89, The Barnard Sch., N.Y.C., 1989-93; assoc. head sch. The Day Sch., N.Y.C., 1993—; evaluator Mid. State Assn. Colls. and Schs., Phila., 1978—. Trustee Ballard Sch. Found., 1993—; bd. dirs. Univ. Club L.I., 1984-86. With USR, 1963-69. Mem. Nat. Assn. Ind. Schs., N.Y. State Assn. Ind. Schs., L.I. Episcopal Sch. Assn. (v.p./treas. 1984-89), Del. Assn. Ind. Schs. (sec. 1978-82). Episcopalian. Avocation: sailing. Home: 174 Howard Ave Rochelle Park NJ 07662-3523 Office: The Day Sch 4 E 90th St New York NY 10128

TINKHAM, MICHAEL, physicist, educator; b. Green Lake County, Wis., Feb. 23, 1928; s. Clayton Harold and LaVerna (Krause) T.; m. Mary Stephanie Merin, June 24, 1961; children: Jeffrey Michael, Christopher Gillespie. A.B., Ripon (Wis.) Coll., 1951, Sc.D. (hon.), 1976; M.S., MIT, 1951; Ph.D., 1954; M.A. (hon.), Harvard, 1966. NSF postdoctoral fellow at Clarendon Lab., Oxford (Eng.) U., 1954-55; successively research physicist, lectr., asst. prof., assoc. prof., prof. physics U. Calif. at Berkeley, 1955-66; Gordon McKay prof. applied physics Harvard U., 1966—, prof. physics, 1966-80, Rumford prof. physics, 1980—, chmn. physics dept., 1975-78; cons. to industry, 1958—; participant internat. seminars and confs.; mem. commn. on very low temperatures Internat. Union Pure and applied Physics, 1972-78; vis. Miller rsch. prof. U. Calif.-Berkeley, 1987; vis. prof. Technical Univ., Delft, The Netherlands, 1993. Author: Group Theory and Quantum Mechanics, 1964, Superconductivity, 1965, Introduction to Superconductivity, 1975, 2d edit., 1996; contbr. articles to profl. jours. Served USNR, 1945-46. Recipient award Alexander von Humboldt Found. U. Karlsruhe, W. Ger., 1978-79; NSF sr. postdoctoral fellow Cavendish lab.; vis. fellow Clare Hall Cambridge (Eng.) U., 1971-72; Guggenheim fellow, 1963-64. Fellow Am. Phys. Soc. (chmn. div. solid state physics 1966-67, Buckley prize 1974, Richtmyer lectr. 1977), AAAS; mem. Am. Acad. Arts and Scis., Nat. Acad. Scis. Home: 98 Rutledge Rd Belmont MA 02178-2633 Office: Harvard Univ Physics Dept Lyman Lab of Physics 326 Cambridge MA 02138

TINKHAM, THOMAS W., lawyer; b. Milw., June 29, 1944; s. Richard Perry and Helen (Savage) T.; m. Jackie Hauser; children: Tamara, Liza, Taylor. BS with honors, U. Wis., 1966; JD with honors, Harvard U., 1969. Ptnr. Dorsey & Whitney, Mpls., 1974—. Mem. Minn. State Bar (pres. 1991), Hennepin County Bar Assn. (pres. 1980). Office: Dorsey & Whitney 220 S 6th St Minneapolis MN 55402-4502*

TINNER, FRANZISKA PAULA, social worker, artist, designer, educator; b. Zurich, Switzerland, Sept. 18, 1944; came to U.S., 1969; d. Siegfied Albin and Gertrude Emilie (Sigg) Maier; m. Rolf Christian Tinner, Dec. 19, 1976; 1 child, Eric Francis. Student, U. Del., 1973-74, Va. Commonwealth U., 1974; BFA, U. Tenn., 1984; BA of Arts, U. Ark., Little Rock, 1991, postgrad. Lic. real estate broker. Dominican nun Ilanz, Switzerland, 1961-67; waitress London, 1967-68; governess Bryn Mawr, Pa., 1969; saleswoman, 1970-90, model, 1983; artist, designer Made For You, Kerrville, Tex. and Milw., 1984—; realtor Century 21, Milw., 1987-91; intern Birch Community Ctr., 1992-93. Designer softsculptor doll Texas Cactus Blossom, 1984. Ombudsman Action 10 Consumerline, Knoxville, Tenn., 1983-84; foster mother, Powhatan, Va., 1976-81; vol. ARC, Knoxville, 1979, Va. Home for Permanently Disabled, 1975; vol., counselor Youth For Understanding-Fgn. Exch., Powhatan, Va., 1975-77; tchr. pager/archiving host, mentor, area expert on Am. On Line; vol. Interactive Ednl. Svc. Recipient Art Display award U. Knoxville, 1983, Prof. Choice of Yr. award, 1983, Outstanding Achievemnt award TV Channel 10, Knoxville, 1984, 1st place award for paintings and crafts State Fair Va., Tenn., 1st place award Nat. Dollmakers, 1985, finalist Best of Coll. Photography, 1991, Achievement award Coll. Scholar af Am., 1991, Achievement cert. in technique of anger therapy, 1993, Achievement cert. in crisis response team tng., 1994; named One of Outstanding 1000 Women, 1995, Woman of Yr., 1995. Mem. NASW, NAFE, Milw. Bd. Realtors, Homemakers Club (pres. 1979-80), Newcomers Club, Bowlers Club (v.p.), Internat. Platform Assn. Avocations: art, cooking, teaching, writing, helping disabled and mentally ill.

TINSLEY, ADRIAN, college president; b. N.Y.C., July 6, 1937; d. Theodore A. and Mary Ethel (White) T. AB, Bryn Mawr Coll., 1958; MA, U. Wash., 1962; PhD, Cornell U., 1969. Asst. prof. English U. Md., College Park, 1968-72; dean William James Coll., Grand Valley State, Allendale, Mich., 1972-80; assoc. vice chancellor acad. affairs Minn. State U., St. Paul, 1982-85; exec. v.p., provost Glassboro (N.J.) State Coll., 1985-89; pres. Bridgewater (Mass.) State Coll., 1989—; coord. women higher edn. adminstrn. Bryn Mawr (Pa.) & Hers Summer Inst., 1977—. Editor: Women in Higher Education Administration, 1984. Office: Bridgewater State Coll Office of Pres Bridgewater MA 02325-0001

TINSLEY, BARBARA SHER, historian, educator, writer; b. Gloversville, N.Y., Apr. 29, 1938; d. Max and Ruth Ida (Shpritzer) Sher; m. William Earl Tinsley, Dec. 30, 1959; children: Claire Jennifer, Yve Hillary. BA, U. Wis., Milw., 1959; MA, U. Calif., Berkeley, 1960; PhD, Stanford U., 1983. Instr. English and French Stephens Coll., Columbia, Mo., 1963-64; instr. European history San Jose (Calif.) State U., 1969-71; prof. European history Foothill Coll., Los Altos Hills, Calif., 1974—; lectr. in English Santa Clara (Calif.) Univ., 1977-79; lectr. in western culture Stanford (Calif.) U., 1985, vis. scholar, 1989-94. Author: History and Polemics in the French Reformation: Florimond de Raemond Defender of the Church, 1992; co-author (with Lewis S. Spitz) Johann Sturm and Education, 1995; contbr. articles to profl. jours. Woodrow Wilson fellow U. Calif.-Berkeley, 1959-60; NDEA fellow Mich. State U. and Emory U., 1961, 63; Jessie Speyer fellow Stanford U., 1965-67; Fulbright fellow U. Strasbourg, 1983-84; NEH fellow Duke U., 1988, Princeton, 1995. Mem. Am. Hist. Assn., Sixteenth Century Studies Conf., YMCA. Democrat. Avocations: sewing, piano, gardening, swimming, oil painting. Home: 15550 Glen Una Dr Los Gatos CA 95030-2936

TINSLEY, JACKSON BENNETT, newspaper editor; b. Ewing, Tex., Dec. 14, 1934; s. Henry Bine and Sallie Alberta (Jackson) T.; m. Claudia Anne Miller, Oct. 3, 1965; children: Ben, Anna. B.S., Sam Houston State U., 1958. Editor Diboll News-Bull., 1953-54, Corrigan Times, 1954; reporter Lufkin News, 1952, 56; news editor Port Lavaca Wave, 1955; mem. staff Ft. Worth Star-Telegram, 1959-60, 62—, Sunday editor, 1967-71, asst. mng. editor, 1971-74, asst. to editor, 1974-75, exec. editor, 1975-82, v.p., exec. editor, 1982-86, v.p., editor, 1986-90, sr. v.p., editor, chmn., 1990—; info. asst. S.W. Bell Telephone Co., 1960-62; part time instr., editor Tex. Christian U., 1971-72. Com. chmn. United Way Tarrant County, 1970-87, gen. chmn. Tex. Gridiron Show, 1981, 93-95; bd. dirs. Safety Coun. Ft. Worth, 1975-80; pres., bd. dirs. Parenting Guidance Ctr., 1989-90. 2d lt. U.S. Army, 1959. Recipient Nat. Writing award Edn. Writers Assn., 1965, citation Tex. Conf. AAUP, 1965; named Disting. Alumnus, Sam Houston State U., 1984; named to C.E. Shuford Journalism Hall of Honor, U. North Tex., 1987. Mem. Soc. Profl. Journalists (pres. Ft. Worth chpt. 1991-92, chmn. journalism adv. com. U. North Tex. and Sam Houston State U. 1988-93), Am. Soc. Newspapers Editors, AP Mng. Editors Assn., Tex. AP Mng. Editors Assn. (pres. 1979-80), Press Club Ft. Worth (pres. 1970-71), Colonial Country Club, Ft. Worth Club, Rotary (v.p. Ft. Worth 1981, pres. 1983-84). Home: 3550 Wind River Ct Fort Worth TX 76116-9329 Office: Ft Worth Star-Telegram 400 W 7th St Fort Worth TX 76102-4701

TINSLEY, TUCK, III, book publishing executive. With Fla. School for the Deaf & Blind, St. Augustine, Fla., 1968-89; pres. American Printing House for the Blind, Louisville, 1989—. Office: Am Print House for the Blind PO Box 6085 1839 Frandfort Ave Louisville KY 40206-0085

TINSLEY, WALTON EUGENE, lawyer; b. Vanceburg, Ky., Jan. 22, 1921; s. Wilbur Walton and Sarah Edith (Frizzell) T.; m. Joy Mae Matthews, Aug. 31, 1952; children—Merry Walton Tinsley Moore, Troy Eugene, Paul Richard. E.E., U. Cin., 1943; M.S. in Aero. Engring, NYU, 1947; J.D., U. So. Calif., 1953. Bar: Calif. 1954, U.S. Supreme Ct. 1971. Practiced in Los Angeles, 1954—; mem. firm Harris, Wallen, MacDermott & Tinsley, 1958—. Author: (book) Tasmania: Stamps and Postal History, 1986. Pres. World Philatelic Exhbn., Pacific 97 Inc. Signatory Roll of Disting. Philatelists, 1983. Fellow Royal Philatelic Soc. London; mem. IEEE (assoc.), AIAA, ABA, L.A. County Bar Assn., Am. Philatelic Soc. (v.p. 1965-69, Luff award 1986), S.R., English Speaking Union (dir. L.A. br.), Mensa. Presbyterian (elder, trustee, chmn. trustees 1972). Home: 2210 Moreno Dr Los Angeles CA 90039-3044 Office: Harris Wallen MacDermott Tinsley 650 S Grand Ave Los Angeles CA 90017-3809

TINSTMAN, DALE CLINTON, food products company consultant; b. Chester, Nebr., May 19, 1919; s. Clinton Lewis and Elizabeth Golashin (Gretzinger) T.; m. Jean Sundell, Oct. 1, 1942; children: Thomas C., Nancy (Mrs. Ron Remington), Jane C. (Mrs. Stephen Kramer). BS, U. Nebr., 1941, JD, 1947. Bar: Nebr. 1947. Asst. sec., asst. mgr. investment dept. First Trust Co., Lincoln, Nebr., 1947-58; v.p., asst. treas. Securities Acceptance Corp., Omaha, financial v.p., treas. Central Nat. Ins. Group, Omaha, 1958-60; pres., treas. Tinstman & Co., Inc., Lincoln, 1960-61; exec. v.p. First Mid Am., Inc., Lincoln, 1961-68, pres., 1968-74, fin. cons., 1974—; pres., dir. Iowa Beef Processors, Inc., 1976-77, vice chmn., 1977-82, co-chmn., 1982-83, dir., cons., 1983—; chmn., dir. Eaton Tinstman Druliner, Inc., 1983—; bd. dirs. IBP, Inc.; past chmn. Nebr. Investment Council. Trustee, chmn. U. Nebr. Found.; trustee Lincoln Found., Nebr. Council Econ. Edn., Mall Corp., Smith Haye Trust. Served with USAAF, World War II, Korea; to col. Nebr. Air NG. Mem. Nebr. Bar Assn., Neb. Diplomats, Newcomen Soc. N.Am., Am. Legion, Nebr. State Chamber of Commerce, Lincoln Contry Club, Lincoln U. Club, Firethorn Country Club, Alpha Sigma Phi, Phi Delta Phi. Republican. Presbyterian (elder). Home: 40 Bishop Sq Lincoln NE 68502 Office: Ste 200 1201 O St Lincoln NE 68502

TINSTMAN, ROBERT A., construction, real estate executive. Pres. mining group Morrison Knudsen Co., Inc., Boise, Idaho, 1989-95, CEO, 1995—. Office: Morrison Knudsen Co Inc 720 Park Blvd Boise ID 83729-0001*

TINTINALLI, JUDITH ELLEN, physician; b. Detroit, 1943. MD, Wayne State U., 1969. Diplomate Am. Bd. Internal Medicine, Am. Bd. Emergency Medicine (pres. 1988-89). Intern Detroit Gen. Hosp., 1969-70, assoc. dir. emergency dept., 1974—, jr. assoc. dept. internal medicine, from 1975; resident Mich. Med. Ctr., 1971-73; instr. dept. medicine Wayne State U., 1975-76, asst. prof. emergency medicine. Mem. Am. Coll. Emergency Physicians.

TIPKA, KAREN, obstetric and women's health nurse; b. Wilmington, Del., Aug. 13, 1946; d. James Spruance and Catherine (O'Connor) T. BA in English, Immaculata Coll., Malvern, Pa., 1969; MA in Psychology, Pa. Dept. Edn., Harrisburg, 1975; postgrad., U. Del., 1995—. Tchr. English Tredyffrin/Easttown Schs., Berwyn, Pa., 1969-76; mental health asst. Psychiatric Unit, Paoli (Pa.) Meml. Hosp., 1977-78; med. asst. Internal Medicine Associates, Norristown, Pa., 1980-82; crisis counselor Chester County Crisis Intervention, Downingtown, Pa., 1979-82; staff nurse psychiatry Phila. Psychiat. Ctr., 1984; staff nurse labor/delivery Osteopathic Med. Ctr., Phila., 1985, Sacred Heart Med. Ctr., Chester, 1985-86; staff nurse high risk labor/delivery Thomas Jefferson Univ. Hosp., Phila., 1986-87; staff nurse labor/delivery Lankenau Hosp., Phila., 1987-88, Bryn Mawr (Pa.) Hosp., 1987-88; nurse clinician Caremark Women's Health, Malvern, Pa., 1992; clin. educator Holy Family Coll., Phila., 1993-94; perinatal cons., educator Toitu of Am., Wayne, Pa., 1995—; clin. adj. instr. Del. County Community Coll., Media, Pa., 1989-90; William Penn grant minority nursing tutor Gwynedd Mercy Coll., 1992; group facilitator Parkinson's Disease Support Group, Delaware County, Pa., 1989—; selected del. People to People Found. Profl. Nurse Exchange, Norway, Sweden, Czechoslovakia, 1988. Contbr. articles to profl. jours. Safety instr. Girl Scouts U.S., Chester County, 1987-88; guest speaker ethics St. Joseph's U. Grad. Sch. Health Adminstrn., Phila., 1991. U.S. Dept. Health and Human Svcs. traineeship, 1988-89; Foerderer scholar, 1983-84. Mem. ANA, NAACOG (cert.), Pa. Nurses Assn., Pa. Perinatal Soc., Phila. Perinatal Soc., ANA Coun. Maternal/Child Nurses, Am. Med. Writers Assn. Avocations: reading, sewing, gardening, cooking. Home: 119 Bishop Hollow Rd Newtown Square PA 19073-3220

TIPPEE, ROBERT THOMAS, journalist; b. St. Louis, Mar. 27, 1950; s. Howard Wayne and Mary Ellen (Thomas) T.; m. Dawn Louise Rowland, June 10, 1972; children: Elizabeth Marie, Jessica Lea. BS in Journalism, U. Tulsa, 1972. Reporter tulsa Worls, 1970-72, 76-77; sr. editor, dist. editor Oil & Gas Jour., Tulsa, 1977-90; mng. editor Oil & Gas Jour., Houston, 1990—; cons. PennWell Books, Tulsa. Author: Where's The Shortage?, 1993; co-author: The Natural Gas Industry, 2d edit., 1995; contbr. short stories to myster mags. 1st lt. USAF, 1972-76. Recipient Cert. of Merit for Editl. Writing, Am. Bus. Press, 1987, 89, Cert. of Merit for Editl./Opinion, N.Y. Bus. Press Editors, 1989. Presbyterian. Office: Oil & Gas Jour 3050 Post Oak Blvd St 200 Houston TX 77056

TIPPETT, WILLIS PAUL, JR., automotive and textile company executive, retired; b. Cin., Dec. 27, 1932; s. Willis Paul and Edna Marie (Conn) T.; m. Carlotta Prichard, Jan. 24, 1959; children: Willis Paul III, Holly. AB, Wabash Coll., 1953. Brand mgr., advt. supr. Procter & Gamble Co., Cin., 1958-64; advt. and sales promotion mgr. Ford Motor Co., Dearborn, Mich., 1964-65; gen. mktg. mgr. Ford Motor Co., 1965-69; advt. mgr. Ford Motor Co. (Ford div.), 1969-70, advt. and sales promotion mgr., 1970-72; v.p. product and mktg. Philco-Ford Corp., Phila., 1972-73; dir. sales and mktg. Ford of Europe, Inc., Brentwood, Essex, Eng., 1973-75; pres., dir. STP Corp., Ft. Lauderdale, Fla., 1975-76; exec. v.p., dir. Singer Co., N.Y.C., 1976-78; pres., chief operating officer, dir. Am. Motors Corp., Southfield, Mich., 1978-82; chmn., chief exec. officer Am. Motors Corp., Southfield, 1982-85; pres. Springs Industries, Inc., Ft. Mill, S.C., 1985-89; prin. Ann Arbor (Mich.) Ptnrs. Investment Co., 1989—; bd. dirs. Lukens, Inc., Stride Rite Corp., Just Cynthia Inc. With USN, 1953-58. Mem. Univ. Club (N.Y.).

TIPPIN, AARON, country music singer, songwriter; b. Pensacola, Fla., July 3, 1958; married; 1 child, Charla. Various positions including farm hand, welder, airplane pilot, truck driver, heavy equipment operator, factory worker; writer Acuff-Rose, 1987—; recording artist RCA, 1990—. Albums include You've Got to Stand for Something, 1991 (gold), Read Between the Lines, 1992 (platinum), Call of the Wild, 1993 (gold), Lookin' Back at Myself, 1994 (gold), Toolbox, 1995; No. 1 single There Ain't Nothing Wrong with the Radio, 1992, That's As Close As I'll Get to Lovin You; toured with Bob Hope to perform for troops during Persian Gulf War, 1991; 1st singer to perform song You've Got to Stand for Something, anthem of troops. Avocation: body-building (prize winner). Office: RCA Records Nashville 1 Music Circle Nashville TN 37203

TIPPING, WILLIAM MALCOLM, social services administrator; b. Oak Park, Ill., Mar. 31, 1931; s. William McKinley and Evelyn Amelia (Freier) T.; m. Lois A. Grife, Sept. 18, 1954 (dec. May 1986); children: William, Barbara, Robert; m. Babette J. Cumming, Oct. 10, 1987; children: Christopher Cumming, Courtney Barone. BA, Carleton Coll., Northfield, Minn., 1954. Sales rep. Gen. Mills, Inc., Mpls., 1954-56; account exec. Campbell Mithun, Inc., Mpls., 1956-63; v.p. mgmt., supr. Campbell Mithun, Inc., Mpls. and Chgo., 1965-76; account supr., v.p. Lennen & Newell, Inc., N.Y.C., 1963-65; ptnr., mgr. Heidrick & Struggles, Inc., Chgo., 1976-88; exec. v.p., chief exec. officer Am. Cancer Soc., Atlanta, 1988-91; pres. Tipping and McRae, Inc., Atlanta, 1991-93; mng. dir. Ward Howell Internat., Inc., Atlanta, 1993—. Trustee Carleton Coll., 1986-90; bd. dirs. Nat. Health Coun., N.Y.C., Ga. Conservancy, Families First; mem. fin. com. UICC, Geneva, 1990-91. Recipient Disting. Svc. award Carleton Coll., 1984. Mem. Skokie Country Club (Glencoe, Ill., pres. 1983-84), Capital City Club (Atlanta), Haig Pt. Club (Daufuskie Island, S.C.), Quechee (Vt.) Club. Republican. Episcopalian. Office: Ward Howell Internat Inc 3350 Peachtree Rd NE Ste 1600 Atlanta GA 30326-1040

TIPPINS, BEDELL A., lawyer; b. Berlin, Aug. 8, 1948. BA, Rutgers U., 1970; JD, John Marshall Law Sch., 1978. Bar: Ill. 1978. Ptnr. Keck, Mahin & Cate, Chgo. Editor-in-chief John Marshall Law Rev., 1977-78. Mem. ABA, Ill. State Bar Assn., Chgo. Bar Assn., Maritime Law Assn. U.S. Office: Keck Mahin & Cate 77 W Wacker Dr Ste 4900 Chicago IL 60601-1629

TIPPIT, JOHN HARLOW, lawyer; b. Marietta, Okla., July 22, 1916; s. Alva Ney and Edna Pearl (Harlow) T.; m. Ann Morse, Feb. 27, 1943; children—David H., Ann Maurine. B.A., U. Okla., 1940, LL.B., 1940. Bar: Okla., 1940, Colo., 1945, U.S. Supreme Ct., 1960. States atty. Love County, Okla., 1940; sole practice Denver, 1945-77, Boulder, Colo., 1978-83; ptnr. Tippit, Haskell & Welborn, Tippit & Haskell and Tippit & Whittington P.C., Boulder, 1947-48; dir. Buckingham Nat. Bank; pres., mng. ptnr. natural resources cos.; lectr. Rocky Mountain Mineral Law Found.; lectr. various legal confs. Co-author: American Law of Mining; contbr. articles to profl. jours. Vice pres. Denver council Boy Scouts Am.; pres. Red Rocks Assn.; bd. dirs., sec. Acad. Ind. Scholars. Served to lt. col. USAAF, 1940-44. Mem. ABA (chmn. sect. natural resources), Okla. Bar Assn., Colo. Bar Assn. (chmn. mineral law sect.), Denver Bar Assn. (trustee). Republican. Episcopalian. Clubs: Mile High Denver Country (Denver); Boulder Country. Home: 525 Aurora Ave Boulder CO 80302-7127 Office: 305 Park West Bldg 250 Arapahoe Ave Boulder CO 80302-5838

TIPPLES, KEITH HOWARD, research director; b. Cambridge, Eng., Feb. 4, 1936; arrived in Can., 1963; s. Arthur Lyndhurst and Violet Isobel (Brown) T.; m. Maureen Cecilia Mannall, Apr. 23, 1962; children: Neil Anthony, Megan Angela, Graham Arthur. BSc, U. Birmingham, Eng., 1959, PhD, 1962. Rsch. scientist Grain Rsch. Lab., Can. Grain Commn., Winnipeg, Man., 1964-79, dir. rsch., 1979—. Fellow Am. Assn. Cereal Chemists (bd. dirs. 1985-87, Carl Wilhelm Brabender award 1978, William F. Geddes Meml. award 1991). Avocations: choral singing, cross-country skiing, sailing, tennis, cricket. Office: Can Grain Commn Rsch Lab, 1404-303 Main St, Winnipeg, MB Canada R3C 3G8

TIPTON, CLYDE RAYMOND, JR., communications and resources development consultant; b. Cin., Nov. 13, 1921; s. Clyde Raymond and Ida Marie (Molitor) T.; m. Marian Gertrude Beushausen, Aug. 6, 1942; children: Marian Page Ashley, Robert Bruce. BS, U. Ky., 1946, MS, 1947. Research engr. Battelle Meml. Inst., Columbus, Ohio, 1947-49, sr. tech. adviser, 1951-62, coordinator corporate communications, 1969-73, v.p. communications, 1973-75, asst. to pres., 1978-79, v.p., corp. dir. communications and pub. affairs, 1979-86, ret.; staff mem. Los Alamos Sci. Lab., 1949-51; dir. research Basic, Inc., Bettsville, Ohio, 1962-64; asst. dir. Battelle Pacific N.W. Labs., Richland, Wash., 1964-69; pres., trustee Battelle Commons Co. for Community Urban Redevel., Columbus, 1975-78; cons. bus. communications and devel. Columbus, 1986—; secretariat U.S. del. 2d Internat. Conf. on Peaceful Uses Atomic Energy, Geneva, 1958; cons. U.S. AEC in Atoms for Peace Program, Tokyo, 1959, New Delhi, 1959-60, Rio de Janeiro, Brazil, 1961. Author: How to Change the World, 1982; editor: Jour. Soc. for Nondestructive Testing, 1953-57, The Reactor Handbook, Reactor Materials, vol. 3, 1955, vol. 1, 1960, Learning to Live on a Small Planet, 1974; patentee in field. Past pres. Pilot Dogs; bd. dirs., treas. Pilot Guide Dog Found. Served with U.S. Army Air Corp., 1943. U. Ky. Haggin fellow, 1947; Otterbein Coll. Sr. fellow, 1978. Mem. NSPE (past pres.), Am. Soc. Metals, Ohio Soc. Profl. Engrs. (past pres., Distin. Svc. award, Uncommon Man award, Outstanding Svc. award), Lions Club, Sigma Xi, Alpha Chi Sigma. Episcopalian. Home and Office: 6475 Strathaven Ct W Columbus OH 43085-2991

TIPTON, DANIEL L., religious organization executive. Gen. supt. Churches in Christ in Christian Union, Circleville, Ohio. Office: Chs of Christ in Christian Union Box 30 1426 Lancaster Pike Circleville OH 43113

TIPTON, E. LINWOOD, trade association executive; b. Adrian, Mo., Nov. 19, 1934; s. Harlow Acklin and Mary Catherine (Lacy) T.; m. Marjorie A. Wolford, Dec. 17, 1955 (div. June 1983); children: Kelly A., Mark A.; m. Constance E. Eaton Broadstone, Oct. 8, 1983. BS in Agriculture, U. Mo., 1955, MS in Agriculture and Econs., 1956. Economist USDA Fgn. Agy. Svc., Washington, 1956-57, Eastern Milk Prodrs., Syracuse, N.Y., 1960-62; exec. dir. Coop. Dairy Econ. Svc., Boston, 1962-65; v.p., exec. v.p., pres., chief exec. officer Internat. Dairy Foods Assn., Washington, 1965—; founder Nat. Economist Club, Washington, treas., chmn. bd., 1967-73; founder Nat. Economist Ednl. Found., Washington, treas., chmn. bd., 1969-74; chmn. bd. Petlin, Inc., Fredericksburg, Va.; expert witness congl. coms., regulatory agencies; founder Internat. Sweetener Colloquium; apptd. to Nat. Commn. Agrl. Trade and Export Policy, 1984; advisor Sec. Agriculture, U.S. Trade Rep.; co-founder, chmn. bd. restaurant/motel chain, 1967—; chmn. The Food Group, The Ice Cream and Milk Polit. Action Com., Food Processors Steering Com. on Wage and Price Stability. 1st lt. Army Fin. Corp., 1957-60. Recipient Citation of Merit U. Mo. Alumni Assn., 1988. Avocations: tennis, golf. Office: Internat Dairy Foods Assn 1250 H St NW Ste 900 Washington DC 20005-3952

TIPTON, HARRY BASIL, JR., state legislator, physician; b. Salida, Colo., Mar. 14, 1927; s. Harry Basil Sr. and Nina Belle (Hailey) T.; m. Dorothy Joan Alexander, Sept. 16, 1950; children: Leslie Louise, Harry Basil III, Robert Alexander. BA, U. Colo., 1950, MD, 1953. Diplomate Am. Bd. Family Practice. Postgrad. med. tng. Good Samaritan Hosp., Phoenix, Ariz., Maricopa County Hosp., Phoenix; prin. dir. Lander (Wyo.) Med. Clinic, 1954—; mem. Wyo. Ho. Reps., Cheyenne, 1981—, chmn. judiciary com., 1986—; cons. Indian Health Svc., Ft. Washakie, Wyo., 1968—; dir NOWCAP Family Planning, Worland, Wyo., 1975-90. Mem., pres. Fremont County Sch. Dist. # 1, Lander, 1958-78. With USMC, 1945-46, capt. USNR Med. Corps, 1950-87. Named Capt. Med. Corps. USNR, 1974. Fellow Am. Coll. Ob.-Gyn., Am. Assn. Family Practice (charter); mem. Wyo. Med. Soc. (Physician of Yr. 1989), Rotary (pres. 1960-61), Elks. Republican. Avocations: fishing, skiing, bird hunting, military history. Office: Lander Med Clin PC 745 Buena Vista Dr Lander WY 82520-3431

TIPTON, JENNIFER, lighting designer; b. Columbus, Ohio, Sept. 11, 1937; d. Samuel Ridley and Isabel (Hanson) T. B.A., Cornell U., 1958. arist in residence Nat. Theater Artist Residency Program at Wooster Group funded by the PEW Charitable Trusts, 1994; assoc. prof. lighting Yale U. Sch. of

Drama. Work includes: Paul Taylor Dance Co., Twyla Tharp and Dancers, Am. Ballet Theater, Jerome Robbins, Dana Reitz, Guthrie Theater, Hartford Stage Co., Murder Among Friends, 1975, Rex, For Colored Girls Who Consider Suicide When the Rainbow is Enuf (Drama Desk award), The Landscape of the Body, Newman Theatre, The Cherry Orchard (Drama Desk award, Tony award 1977), Agamemnon, Beaumont Theatre, Happy End, Martin Beck Theatre, Agamemnon, Delacorte Theatre, 1977, Museum, Public Theatre, Runaways, Public Theatre and Plymouth Theatre, All's Well That Ends Well, Taming of the Shrew, Delacorte Theatre, After the Season, Academy Festival Theatre, A Month in the Country, Williamstown Theatre Festival, Mikhail Baryshnikov's Don Quixote, Am. Ballet Theatre, Drinks Before Dinner, Public Theatre, The Pirates of Penzance, Public Theatre, 1978, Lunch Hour, 1980, Billy Bishop Goes to War, 1980, The Sea Gull, 1980, Sophisticated Ladies, 1981, The Wake of Jamie Foster, 1982, Uncle Vanya, 1983, Orgasmo Adulto Escapes from the Zoo, 1983, Baby with the Bathwater, 1984, Hurlyburly, 1984, Whoopie Goldberg, 1984, Endgame, 1984, Jerome Robbins' Broadway (Tony award 1989). Recipient Chgo.'s Joseph Jefferson award, 1976-77, Obie award 1979, Brandies U. Creative Arts award medal in dance, 1982, Mpls. Kudos award 1983, N.Y. Bessie award 1984, (with Dana Reitz), 1987, Guggenheim fellowship, 1986-87, Am. Theater Wing award 1989, Commonwealth award in dramatic arts, 1989, Lawrence Olivier award, 1991, Dance Magazine award, 1991, NEA Disting. Theater Artist award 1991. Home: 11 W 18th St New York NY 10011-4603

TIPTON, JOHN J., lawyer; b. Denver, Dec. 18, 1946. BS cum laude, Colo. State U., 1968; JD, U. Denver, 1974, LLM, 1978. Bar: Colo. 1975, U.S. Dist. Ct. (Colo. dist.) 1975, U.S. Ct. Appeals (10th cir.) 1975, U.S. Tax Ct. 1976, U.S. Supreme Ct. 1978. Exec. dir. Colo. Dept. Revenue, Denver, 1988-92, Colo. Dept. Adminstrn., Denver, 1990-91; cabinet officer Colo. Gov. Roy Romer, Denver, 1988-92; ptnr. Baker & Hostetler, Denver; sr. v.p., ceo, general counsel Seven Circle Resorts, Denver, CO. With USAF, 1968-72. Mem. ABA (mem. sect. econs. law practice law practice mgmt. divsn., divsn. vice chmn. 1987-89, chmn. law practice mktg. of legal svcs. group 1986-89, co-chmn. nat. mktg. conf. com. 1986-89), Colo. Bar Assn., Denver Bar Assn. (mem. sects. taxation, econs. of law practice, real property, probate and trust law), Denver Estate Planning Coun. Office: Seven Circle Resorts 1512 Larimer St Ste 300 Denver CO 80202*

TIPTON, JON PAUL, allergist; b. Lynchburg, Ohio, Nov. 8, 1934; s. Paul Alvin and Jeanette (Palmer) T.; m. Martha J. Johnson, Dec. 29, 1968; children: Nicole Ann, Paula Michelle. BS, Ohio U., 1956; MD, Ohio State U., 1960. Resident internal medicine Ohio State U. Hosps., Columbus, 1964-66; fellow in allergy and pulmonary disease Duke U. Med. Ctr., Durham, N.C., 1963-64, 66-67; pvt. practice medicine specializing in allergies Athens, Ohio, 1967-74; pvt. practice medicine specializing in allergy Marietta, Ohio, 1974—; dir. cardio respiratory therapy Marietta Meml. Hosp., 1983, med. dir. pulmonary rehab. program, chief of medicine; med. dir. Inhalation Therapy Sch. Wash. State C.C.; cons. Ohio U. Hudson Health Ctr., 1967—, Mariette Coll. Health Ctr., 1974—, United Mine Workers of Am. Funds, 1984—; med. lectr. for physicians groups; med. dir. Washington State C.C. Inhalation Therapy Sch. Vol. Marietta Rep. Hdqrs., 1978—; mem. choir St. Luke's Luth. Ch., Marietta, 1983—. Served to capt. USAF, 1961-63. Mem. Am. Acad. Allergy, Ohio State Med. Assn., Wash. County Med. Soc., Parkersburg Acad. Medicine. Republican. Methodist. Avocations: yardwork, piano, attending plays, football, children. Home: 101 Meadow Ln Marietta OH 45750-1345 Office: 100 Front St Marietta OH 45750-3142

TIPTON, KENNETH WARREN, agricultural administrator, researcher; b. Belleville, Ill., Nov. 14, 1932; s. Roscoe Roy and Martha Pearl (Davis) T.; m. Barbara Adds, Mar. 2, 1957; children: Kenneth Warren Jr., Nancy Tipton O'Neal. BS, La. State U., 1955, MS, 1959; PhD, Miss. State U., 1969. Asst. prof. Agrl. Ctr., La. State U., Baton Rouge, 1959-70, assoc. prof., 1970-75, prof., 1975—; supt. Red River Rsch. Sta., La. Agrl. Expt. Sta. Agrl. Ctr., La. State U., Bossier City, 1975-79; assoc. dir. La. Agrl. Expt. Sta. Agrl. Ctr., La. State U., Baton Rouge, 1979-89, dir. La. Agrl. Expt. Sta., vice chancellor, 1989—; mem. com. nine USDA/Coop. State Rsch. Svc., 1986-88; Expt. State Com. Orgn. Policy, 1988-91. Contbr. articles to Agronomy Jour., Jour. Econ. Entomology, Grain Sorghum Conf. Coach baseball program Am. Legion, 1969-74; scoutmaster Boy Scouts Am., Baton Rouge, 1970-75. Capt. USAF, 1955-58. Mem. Am. Soc. Agronomy, Crop Sci. Soc. Am., Coun. Agrl. Sci. Tech. Achievements include research on inheritance of fiber traits in cotton, resistance of grain sorghum hybrids to bird damage, tannin content of grain sorghum and effects of phosphorus on growth of sorghum. Home: 732 Baird Dr Baton Rouge LA 70808-5916

TIPTON, PAUL S., former college president, association executive. Joined S.J., Roman Catholic Ch., ordained priest, 1971. Pres. Spring Hill Coll., Mobile, Ala., 1972-1989, Assn. Jesuit Colls. and Univs., Washington, 1990—. Office: Assn Jesuit Colls and Univs 1 Dupont Cir NW Ste 405 Washington DC 20036-1110

TIPTON-MARTIN, TONI, newspaper editor. Food section editor, wine section editor The Cleveland Plain Dealer, Ohio. Office: Plain Dealer Pub Co 1801 Superior Ave E Cleveland OH 44114-2107

TIRANA, BARDYL RIFAT, lawyer; b. Geneva, Dec. 16, 1937; s. Rifat and Rosamond English (Walling) T.; m. Anne Prather, June 22, 1985; children by previous marriage: Kyra, Amina. A.B., Princeton U., 1959; LL.B., Columbia U., 1962. Bar: D.C. 1962, Md. 1986, N.Y. 1986. Va. 1986, Pa. 1992. Trial atty. Dept. Justice, 1962-64; assoc. Amram, Hahn & Sundlun, Washington, 1965-68; ptnr. Amram, Hahn & Sundlun, 1969-72; dir., sec. Exec. Jet Aviation, Inc., Columbus, Ohio, 1970-77, Technics, Inc., Alexandria, Va., 1971-77; ptnr. Sundlun, Tirana & Scher, Washington, 1972-77; dir. def. civil preparedness agy. Dept. Def., Washington, 1977-79, mem. armed forces policy coun., 1977-79; chmn. bd. Technics, Inc., San Jose, Calif., 1979-85; of counsel Silverstein and Mullens, Washington, 1982-84, ptnr., 1984-90; pvt. practice law Washington, 1991—. Mem.-at-large D.C. Bd. Edn., 1970-74; trustee Jimmy Carter Inaugural Trust, Washington, 1977-87; co-chmn. 1977 Presdl. Inaugural Com., 1976-77; mem. exec. adv. coun. Calif. Commn. Indsl. Innovation, 1981-82; pres. China/USA Edn. Fund, Inc., Washington, 1981—; dir. Rocky Mountain Inst., Snowmass Colo., 1982-95. Recipient medal for disting. pub. svc. Dept. Def., 1979, Fuess award Phillips Acad., 1991, Svc. Commendation award YWCA of Nat. Capital Area, 1991. Mem. N.Y.C. Racquet and Tennis Club, D.C. Met. Club. Home: 3550 Tilden St NW Washington DC 20008-3121 Office: 4401 Connecticut Ave NW Ste 606 Washington DC 20008-2322

TIRELLA, THERESA MARY, special education educator; b. Worcester, Mass., Apr. 22, 1963; d. Samuel Louis and Cecilia Barbara (Trczinski) T. BS, Northeastern U., 1986, MEd, 1989. Acting supr., childcare worker Dr. Franklin Perkins Sch., Lancaster, Mass., 1983-84; sr. recreational counselor Friendly House Inc., Worcester, 1985; adult edn. educator Action for Boston Community Devel., 1986-87; spl. edn. educator Cotting Sch., Lexington, Mass., 1987—; cons. United Cerebral Palsy, Watertown, Mass., 1993, Spl. Needs Advocacy Network Newton, Mass., 1991-93; corrd. bd. dirs. Access Now, Boston, 1991-93. Vol. mem. program planning com. Ptnrs. for Disabled Youth, Boston, 1991-94; vol. tutor Bethel Bapt. Ch., Roxbury, Mass., 1991-92, mem. youth com., 1991-92, mem. choir, 1991-92. Mem. Assn. for Suprevision and Curriculum Devel., Northeastern Univj. Women's Alumni Club, Northeastern U. Alumni Assn. Avocations: reading, graphic arts, crafts, arts, basketball. Home: 17 Seaverns Ave Jamaica Plain MA 02130-2874

TIRICO, MIKE, sportscaster; b. Whitestone, N.Y., Dec. 13, 1966; married. BA in Polit. Sci. and Broadcast Journalism, Syracuse U., 1988. Sports dir. WTVH-TV (affil. CBS), Syracuse, N.Y., 1987-91; reporter ESPN, Bristol, Conn., 1991—, host NFL Prime Monday, co-host GameDay ESPN Sports Radio, anchor SportsCenter, 1993—. Named top local sportscaster Syracuse Jour., 1989; recipient A.P. N.Y. Broadcasters award. Office: ESPN Inc Comms Dept ESPN Plz Bristol CT 06010*

TIRRELL, DAVID A., research scientist, educator; b. Jan. 10, 1953. BS in Chemistry, MIT, 1974; MS in Polymer Sci. and Engring., U. Mass., 1976, PhD in Polymer Sci. and Engring., 1978. Rsch. assoc. Kyoto U., 1978; asst. prof. chemistry Carnegie-Mellon U., 1978-82, assoc. prof. chemistry, 1982-84; assoc. prof. polymer sci. and engring. U. Mass., 1984-87, prof. polymer sci. and engring., 1987-92, Barrett prof. polymer and sci. and engring., 1992—; adj. prof. chemistry U. Mass., 1991; dir. NSF materials rsch. lab., 1991-94, dir. NSF material rsch. sci. and engring. ctr., 1994—; mem. molecular and cellular biology faculty, 1990—; vis. prog. chemistry U. Queensland, Australia, 1987, Inst. Charles Sadron, Strasbourg, 1991; mem. materials rsch. adv. com. NSF, 1988-91; chmn. com. on synthetic hierarchical structures Nat. Rsch. Coun., 1990-94, mem panel on biomolecular materials, 1991—, mem. naval rsch. lab. polymers in biosystems, Oxnard, 1994; co-chmn. grad. polymer rsch. conf. State Coll., Pa., 1994; program com. IUPAC Macromolecular Symposium, 1994; chmn. Gordon Rsch. Conf. on Chemistry of Supramolecules and Assemblies, 1995. Editor Jour. of Polymer Sci., 1988—; assoc. editor New Polymeric Materials, 1986-87; editl. bd. Indsl. and Engring. Chemistry, Product Rsch. and Devel., 1983-86, Jour. of Bioactive and Compatible Polymers, 1986—, Biomaterials, 1986—, New Polymeric Materials, 1987—, Jour. of Macromolecular Sci.-Chemistry, 1990—, Progress in Polymer Sic., 1992—, Macromolecular Reports, 1992, Materials Sci. and Engring., 1993—, Chem. and Engring. News, 1995—; contbr. articles to profl. jours. Univ. fellow, 1974-77, Alfred P. Sloan Rsch. fellow, 1982-84, Rotschild fellow Institut Curie, 1995-97; recipient Presdl. Young Investigator award, 1984-89, Fulbright Sr. scholar award, 1987. Mem. AAAS, Am. Chem. Soc., N.Y. Acad. Scis., Materials Rsch. Soc., Sigma Xi, Phi Lambda Upsilon. Office: University of Massachusetts Materials Rsch Lab Gradute Rsch Ctr Rm 701 Amherst MA 01003

TIRRELL, JOHN ALBERT, religious organization executive, consultant; b. Boston, Feb. 11, 1934; s. George Howard and Helen Sarah (Hitchings) T.; m. Helga Ruth Eisenhauer, Jan. 29, 1966; children: Steffanie Ruth, Sabina Lisette, Monica Susanne. BA in Psychology, The King's Coll., Briarcliff Manor, N.Y., 1961; MEd, U. Ariz., 1975. Various positions for several orgns., 1962-68; analyst instrnl.-ednl. systems GE, Daytona Beach, Fla., 1969-72; dir. curriculum and program devel. Brookdale C.C., Lincroft, N.J., 1972; dir. learning and faculty resources Pima C.C., Tucson, 1972-76; dir. human resources planning and devel. Miami divsn. Cyprus Copper Co., Claypool, Ariz., 1976-79; exec. dir. Calvary Missionary Fellowship, Tucson, 1983-85; interim pastor Sagauro Evang. Ch., Tucson, 1985-86; Midvale Evang. Ch. Midvale Evangelical Ch., Tucson, 1986-87; founder, pres. The Jethro Consultancy, Birmingham, Mich., 1979—; v.p. mgmt. svc. AA Gage, Ferndale, Mich., 1987-88; pastor Desert Hills Bapt. Ch., Tucson, 1993-95; mem. adv. bd. UIM Internat., Flagstaff, Ariz., 1983-92, mem. fin. com., 1983-94, sec. support svcs. field bd., 1993—, also bd. dirs.; assoc. faculty mem. Gila Pueblo Campus Ea. Ariz. Coll., Globe, 1978; adj. prof. Montclair State Coll., Upper Montclair, N.J., 1972; chmn. Mgmt. and Pers. Com. Wildwood Ranch, Inc., Howell, Mich., 1989-92; interim pres., v.p. programs, v.p. devel. Detroit Rescue Mission Ministries, 1990-92; v.p. corp. planning, tng., productivity George Instrument Co., Royal Oak. Contbr. articles to profl. jours. Mem. Ariz. Coun. for Econ. Conversion, 1992-94; mem. facilities task force Grace Evang. Free Ch., Birmingham, 1989-90, chmn. bylaws revision com., 1989-90, chmn. property devel. com., 1990-92; interim pastor Desert Hills Bapt. Ch., Tucson, 1992-93; elder 1st Evang. Free Ch., Tucson, 1979-81, 86-87, supt. Sunday sch., 1981-84, supr. adult Sunday sch., 1992-93, chmn. gen. bd., elder bd., 1979-82, short-term missions coord., missions bd., 1992-93; bd. dirs. S.W. Border dist. Evang. Free Ch. Am., 1996—, Shadow Roc Homeowners Assn., 1996—, Clearing House of Operational Resources for Christian Orgns., Royal Oak, Mich., 1991; v.p. parent-tchr. fellowship Palo Verde Christian Sch., Tucson, 1980-81. Staff sgt. USAF, 1952-56. Mem. ASTD (treas., Old Pueblo chpt. 1982, bd. dirs.-at-large 1983, Human Resources Devel. award Valley of the Sun chpt. 1977), Birmingham-Bloomfield C. of C. (mem. profl. devel. edn. com. 1987-91, mem. pub. rels. mktg. com. 1989), King's Coll. Alumni Assn. (class gov. 1988-95). Republican. Avocations: photography, Bible teaching. Home and Office: 1205 E Deer Canyon Rd Tucson AZ 85718-1069

TIRRELL, MATTHEW, chemical engineering/materials science educator; b. Phillipsburg, N.J., Sept. 5, 1950; s. Matthew Vincent Tirrell Jr. and Loraine (Wier) Gonsky; m. Pamela Lavigne, Aug. 1993. BS, Northwestern U., 1973; PhD, U. Mass., 1977. Mem. coop. edn. program Cin. Milacron Chem. Inc., 1970-72; tchg. and rsch. asst. U. Mass., Amherst, 1973-77; asst. prof. U. Minn., Mpls., 1977-81, assoc. prof., 1981-85, prof. chem. engring. and materials sci., 1985—, Shell disting. chair in chem. engring., 1986-91, acting head, 1992-93, Earl E. Bakken prof. biomed. engring., 1993—, head, 1995—; dir. Biomed. Engring. Inst., 1995—; sci. advisor BIOSYM Techs., San Diego. Author: Modeling of Polymerization Processes, 1995. John Simon Guggenheim Meml. Found. fellow, 1986. Mem. AIChE (editor jour. 1991—, Profl. Progress award 1994, Allan P. Colburn award 1985), Am. Chem. Soc., Am. Phys. Soc. (John H. Dillon medal 1987), Materials Rsch. Soc. Avocations: gourmet cooking, movies, distance running. Office: U Minn Dept Chem Engring & Mat Sci Minneapolis MN 55455

TIRRO, FRANK PASCALE, music educator, author, composer; b. Omaha, Sept. 20, 1935; s. Frank and Mary Carmela (Spensieri) T.; m. Charlene Rae Whitney, Aug. 16, 1961; children: John Andrew, Cynthia Anne. B.M.E., U. Nebr., 1960; M.M., Northwestern U., 1961; Ph.D., U. Chgo., 1974. Chmn. lab. schs. U. Chgo., 1961-70; fellow of Villa I Tatti Harvard U., Florence, Italy, 1971-72; lectr. U. Kans., Lawrence, 1972-73; asst. prof. music Duke U., 1973-74; dir. Southeastern Inst. Medieval and Renaissance Studies, Durham, N.C., 1978-80; chmn., assoc. prof. music Duke U., Durham, 1973-80; prof. Yale U., New Haven, 1980—, dean, 1980-89; reader, cons. several univ. presses; jurist Parisot Internat. Cello Competition, Sao Paolo, Brazil, 1981. Author: Jazz: A History, 1977, rev. edit., 1993, Renaissance Choirbooks in the Archive of San Petronio in Bologna, 1986, Living With Jazz, 1995, (with others) The Humanities: Cultural Roots and Continuities, 1980, 4th edit., 1992; editor: Medieval and Renaissance Studies No. 9, 1982; mem. editl. bd. Wittenberg Rev.; composer American Jazz Mass, 1960; assoc. editor Am. Nat. Biography, 1994—. Bd. dirs. New Haven Symphony, 1980-89, Neighborhood Music Sch., New Haven, 1982-89, Chamber Orch. New Eng., 1980-82, Ctr. for Black Music Rsch., 1985—. Recipient Standard Composer award Am. Soc. Composers, Authors and Pubs., 1966, Gustavus Fine Arts medal, 1988, Duke Ellington Fellow medal, 1989; travel grantee Am. Coun. Learned Socs., 1967; rsch. grantee Duke U., 1978. Mem. Am. Musicol. Soc. (council 1978-80), Coll. Music Soc. (council 1980-82, mem. exec. bd. 1984-86), Nat. Assn. Schs. of Music, Internat. Soc. Jazz Research, Renaissance Soc. Am., Mory's Club, Yale Club (N.Y.C.). Republican. Lutheran. Office: Yale U Sch Music PO Box 208246 New Haven CT 06520-8246

TIRRO, IRMA JACOBS, aerospace transportation executive; b. Miami Shores, Fla., July 3, 1935; d. Virgil Ellis and Mollie Estelle (Faircloth) Goodson; m. Jesse F. Jacobs, July, 1953 (div. 1979); 1 child, Brian Jay Jacobs; m. A.J. Tirro, Aug. 23, 1986. BA, Barry U., Miami, Fla., 1985; MA in Mgmt., Webster U., Orlando, Fla., 1994. Judicial asst. State of Fla., Titusville, Fla., 1967-81; exec. asst. to pres. Heritage Real Estate and Devel. Co., Cocoa Beach, Fla., 1981-83; various Lockheed Space Ops. Co., Titusville, Fla., 1983—; prin. Life Mgmt. Strategies, Melbourne, Fla.; human resources and orgn., tng., and devel. Recipient Manned Flight Awareness award NASA, 1991. Mem. NAFE, ASTD, Nat. Mgmt. Assn. Avocations: golfing, reading, crocheting. Home: 508 Crystal Lake Dr Melbourne FL 32940-1935

TIRYAKIAN, EDWARD ASHOD, sociology educator; b. Bronxville, N.Y., Aug. 6, 1929; s. Ashod Haroutioun and Keghinee (Agathon) T.; m. Josefina Cintron, Sept. 5, 1953; children: Edmund Carlos, Edwyn Ashod. BA summa cum laude, Princeton U., 1952; MA, Harvard U., 1954, PhD, 1956; PhD (hon.), U. Rene Descartes, Paris, 1987. Instr. Princeton U., 1956-57, asst. prof., 1957-62; lectr. Harvard U., 1962-65; assoc. prof. Duke U., Durham, N.C., 1965-67, prof., 1967—, chmn. dept. sociology and anthropology, 1969-72, dir. internat. studies, 1988-91; vis. lectr. U. Philippines, 1954-55, Bryn Mawr Coll., 1957-59; vis. scientist program Am. Sociol. Assn., 1967-70; vis. prof. Laval U., Quebec City, Que., Can., 1978, Inst. Polit. Studies, Paris, 1992; summer seminar dir. NEH, 1978, 80, 93, 89, 91, 96; lectr. Kyoto Am. Studies Summer Seminar, 1985. Author: Sociologism and Existentialism, 1962; Editor: Sociological Theory, Values and Sociocultural Change: Essays in Honor of P.A. Sorokin, 1963, The Phenomenon of Sociology, 1971, On the Margin of the Visible: Sociology, the Esoteric, and the Occult, 1974, The Global Crisis: Sociological Analyses and Responses, 1984; co-editor: Theoretical Sociology: Perspectives and Developments, 1970; New Nationalisms of the Developed West, 1985. Recipient Fulbright rsch. award, 1955; Ford faculty rsch. fellow, 1971-72. Mem. Am. Sociol. Assn., African Studies Assn., Am. Soc. for Study Religion (council 1975-78, pres. 1981-84), Assn. Internationale des Sociologues de Langue Française (v.p. 1985-88, pres. 1988-92), Soc. for Phenomenology and Existential Philosophy, Phi Beta Kappa. Clubs: Princeton, Century Assn. (N.Y.C.). Home: 16 Pascal Way Durham NC 27705-4924 *As a sociological researcher, I have sought to understand on a comparative basis the dynamics of social consciousness in the process of historical change. As a teacher, I have sought to encourage in students—undergraduates, graduates, and postgraduates— a gusto for intellectual curiosity in exploring the myriad of linkages that make up social reality, our human patrimony.*

TISCH, JAMES S., diversified holding company executive; b. Atlantic City, Jan. 2, 1953; s. Laurence A. and Wilma (Stein) T.; m. Merryl Hiat; children: Jessica, Benjamin, Samuel. BA, Cornell U., 1975; MBA, Wharton Grad. Sch., U. Pa., 1976. With Loews Corp., N.Y.C., 1977—, exec. v.p., 1987-94, pres., 1994—, also mem. mgmt. com. Pres. Fedn. Employment and Guidance Svc., N.Y.C., 1985—; trustee Dalton Sch., N.Y.C., 1985—, Mt. Sinai Med. Ctr., N.Y.C., 1988—. Office: Loews Corp 667 Madison Ave New York NY 10021-8029*

TISCH, JONATHAN MARK, hotel company executive; b. Atlantic City, Dec. 7, 1953; s. Preston Robert and Joan (Hyman) T. BA, Tufts U., 1976. Cinematographer, producer WBZ-TV, Boston, 1976-79; sales mgr. Loews Hotels, N.Y.C., 1980-81, dir. devel., 1981-82, v.p., 1982-85, exec. v.p., 1985-86, pres., 1986-89, pres., chief exec. officer, 1986—; mem. mgmt. com. Loews Corp.; bd. dirs. N.Y. Giants, 1991—. Trustee Robert Steel Found., N.Y.C., Gunnery Sch., Washington, Conn., 1983—, Tufts U., Medford, Mass., 1986—, Vice Pres.'s Residence Found., 1994; chmn. N.Y.C. host com. for Grammys, 1988, 92, 94; bd. dirs. Pediatric AIDS found.; mem. dean's adv. coun. Sch. Hotel Adminstrn., Cornell U.; chmn. Travel Bus. Roundtable; vice chair econ. devel. com. N.Y.C. Partnership, 1994—. Mem. Am. Hotel and Motel Assn. (officer 1994—), Travel Bus. Roundtable (chmn. 1995—). Clubs: Century Country (Purchase, N.Y.); Friars (N.Y.C.). Avocations: golf, tennis, skiing. Office: Loews Hotels 667 Madison Ave New York NY 10021-8029

TISCH, LAURENCE ALAN, diversified manufacturing & service executive; b. N.Y.C., Mar. 5, 1923; s. Al and Sadye (Brenner) T.; m. Wilma Stein, Oct. 31, 1948; children: Andrew, Daniel, James, Thomas. BSc cum laude, NYU, 1942; MA in Indsl. Engring, U. Pa., 1943; postgrad., Harvard Law Sch., 1946; LLD (hon.), Skidmore Coll., 1994. Pres. Tisch Hotels, Inc., N.Y.C., 1946-74; chmn. bd., co-chief exec. officer Loews Corp., N.Y.C., 1960—; pres., chief exec. officer CBS Inc., N.Y.C., 1987-1995, chmn., pres. chief exec. officer, 1990-1995, also bd. dirs., co-chmn. bd., 1994-1995; chmn. bd. dirs. CNA Fin. Corp., Chgo.; bd. dirs. Bulova Corp. subs. Loews Corp., N.Y.C., ADP Corp., Petrie Stores Corp., Federated Dept. Stores. Bd. dirs. United Jewish Appeal-Fedn.; chmn. bd. trustees NYU; trustee Met. Mus. Art, N.Y.C., N.Y. Pub. Libr. Mem. Coun. Fgn. Rels. Home: Island Dr N Manursing Island Rye NY 10580 also: Loews Corp 667 Madison Ave New York NY 10021-8029*

TISCH, PRESTON ROBERT, finance executive; b. Bklyn., Apr. 29, 1926; s. Abraham Solomon and Sayde (Brenner) T.; m. Joan Hyman, Mar. 14, 1948; children: Steven E., Laurie M., Jonathan M. Student, Bucknell U., 1943-44; B.A., U. Mich., 1948. Co-chmn., co-chief exec. officer, dir. Loews Corp., N.Y.C., 1960—; postmaster gen. U.S. Postal Svc., Washington, 1986-88; chmn., co-CEO, half owner N.Y. Football Giants, 1990—; bd. dirs. CNA Fin. Corp., Bulova Watch Co. Chmn. emeritus N.Y. Conf. and Visitors Bur., Nat. Dem. Conv., 1976, 80; trustee NYU; mem. Quadrennial Commn. on Exec., Legis. and Jud. Salaries, 1988; mem. Gov.'s Bus. Adv. Coun. for N.Y. State; pres. Citymeals on Wheels. With AUS, 1943-44. Mem. Rye Racquet Club, Century Country Club, Sigma Alpha Mu. Office: Loews Corp 667 Madison Ave New York NY 10021-8029 also: NY Giants Giants Stadium East Rutherford NJ 07073*

TISCH, RONALD IRWIN, lawyer; b. N.Y.C., Aug. 3, 1944; s. Joseph and Elsie (Rosler) T.; m. Eddi Gorewicz, July 1, 1973; children: Marissa, Courtney. BA, Bklyn. Coll., 1966; JD George Washington U., 1969; LLM, Harvard U., 1970. Bar: D.C. 1969. Appellate atty. NLRB, Washington, 1970-72; ptnr. Graham & James, Washington, 1987—. Mem. ABA, Am. Arbitration Assn., Immigration and Naturalization Lawyers Assn., Nat. Health Lawyers Assn., Order of Coif, Phi Alpha Delta. Contbr. to profl. publs. Home: 11005 Roundtable Ct Rockville MD 20852-4560 Office: Graham & James 2000 M St NW Ste 700 Washington DC 20036-3307

TISCH, STEVEN E., movie producer; b. Lakewood, N.J., Feb. 14, 1949; s. Preston Robert and Joan (Hyman) T.; m. Patricia Keast, Sept. 27, 1981 (div. July 1991); children: Hilary, William. BA, Tufts U., 1971. Pres. Tisch-Avnet Prodns., L.A., 1981-88, Steve Tisch Co., L.A., 1988—. Chmn. AIDS Project L.A., 1992-94. Office: 3815 Hughes Ave Culver City CA 90232-2715*

TISCHLER, GARY LOWELL, psychiatrist, educator; b. N.Y.C., Oct. 30, 1935; s. Louis and Dorothy (Green) T.; m. Judith Post, Aug. 18, 1957; children: Laurie Dee, Marc David, Rachel Mara. AB, Hamilton Coll., 1957; MD, U. Pa., 1961; MS, Yale U., 1975. Intern Kings County Hosp., Bklyn., 1961-62; resident in psychiatry Yale U. Sch. Medicine, New Haven, 1962-65, asst. prof., 1967-70, assoc. prof., 1970-75, prof. psychiatry, 1975-90; prof., chmn. dept. psychiatry and biobehavioral scis., dir. neuropsychiatric inst. UCLA Sch. Medicine, 1990-95; chmn. dept. psychiatry Yale U. Sch. Medicine, New Haven, 1986-87; dir. Yale Psychiatric Inst., New Haven, 1978-87; chief psychiatry Yale-New Haven Hosp., 1986-87; clin. dir. Hill-West Haven div. Conn. Mental Health Ctr., New Haven, 1968-70, dir., 1970-77; prof. psychiatry UCLA, 1990-95; prof., exec. vice chair dept. psychiatry Cornell U. Med. Coll., 1996—; dir. Westchester divsn., dir. mental health programs N.Y. Hosp., 1994—, dir. Payne Whitney Clinic, 1996—; study dir. Pres.'s Commn. on Mental Health, Washington, 1977-79; cons. Arthur D. Little Inc., Boston, 1973-75, IBM Corp., Armonk, N.Y., 1986-87; mem. profl. adv. com. Am. Med. Internat., L.A., 1984-86; mem. bd. mental health and behavioral medicine Inst. Medicine, Washington, 1986—, com. on clin. evaluation, 1990-94. Author: Quality Assurance Thru Utilization and Peer Review, 1982; editor: Patient Care Evaluation in Mental Health, 1985, Diagnosis and Classification in Psychiatry, 1987; contbr. articles to profl. jours. Mem. Gov.'s transition staff on mental health, Conn., 1975; vice chmn. Bd. Mental Health State of Conn., 1986. Served to capt. U.S. Army, 1965-67, Vietnam. Fellow Am. Psychiat. Assn., Am. Coll. Mental Health Adminstrn., Am. Assn. for Social Psychiatry, Am. Coll. Psychiatry. Home: 36 Rock Hill Rd Bedford NY 10506-1522 Office: NY Hosp-Cornell Med Ctr 21 Bloomingdale Rd White Plains NY 10605

TISCHLER, HERBERT, geologist, educator; b. Detroit, Apr. 28, 1924; s. Louis and Hermina (Leb) T.; m. Annette Zeidman, Aug. 10, 1954; children—Michael A., Robert D. B.S., Wayne U., 1950; M.A., U. Calif.-Berkeley, 1955; Ph.D., U. Mich., 1961. Instr. Wayne State U., Detroit, 1956-58; assoc. prof. No. Ill. U., DeKalb, 1958-65; prof. dept. earth scis. U. N.H., Durham, 1965—, chmn. dept., 1965-90; co-dir. No. New Eng. Jr. Sci. and Humanities Symposium, 1979—, mem. nat. adv. com., 1989-92. Trustee Mt. Washington Observatory, 1980-92. With USCG, 1943-46. Fellow Geol. Soc. Am. (sr.). Home: 36 Oyster River Rd Durham NH 03824-3029 Office: U NH Dept Earth Scis James Hall Durham NH 03824

TISDALE, DOUGLAS MICHAEL, lawyer; b. Detroit, May 3, 1949; s. Charles Walker and Violet Lucille (Battani) T.; m. Patricia Claire Brennan, Dec. 29, 1972; children: Douglas Michael, Jr., Sara Elizabeth, Margaret Patricia, Victoria Claire. BA in Psychology with honors, U. Mich., 1971, JD, 1975. Bar: Colo. 1975, U.S. Dist. Ct. Colo. 1975, U.S. Ct. Appeals (10th cir.) 1976, U.S. Supreme Ct. 1979. Law clk. to chief judge U.S. Dist. Ct. Colo., Denver, 1975-76; assoc. Brownstein Hyatt Farber & Madden, P.C. ; ptnr., dir. Brownstein Hyatt Farber & Strickland, P.C., 1976-92; shareholder Popham, Haik, Schnobrich & Kaufman, Ltd., 1992—, dir. 1995—. lectr. Law Seminars, Inc., 1984-92, Continuing Legal Edn. in Colo., Inc., 1984-93, Nat. Bus. Insts., 1985—, ABA Nat. Insts. 1988-92; Colo. Law-Related Edn. Coord., 1982-88; bd. dirs. Vail Valley Med. Ctr., 1992—. Mem. ABA (mem. litigation sect. trial evidence com. 1981—, vice chmn. real property sect. com. on enforcement of creditors rights and bankruptcy 1984-90, vice chmn.

real property sect. com. on pub. edn. concerning the lawyers role 1984-87, chmn. 1987-90, chmn. real property sect. sub-com. on foreclosures in bankruptcy 1982-90), ATLA, Colo. Bar Assn. (conv. com. 1979-88), Denver Bar Assn. (jud. adminstrn. com. 1978-89), Colo. Trial Lawyers Assn., Law Club of Denver (sec. 1984-85, v.p. 1990-91), Phi Alpha Delta, Phi Beta Kappa. Democrat. Roman Catholic. Home: 4662 S Elizabeth Ct Cherry Hills Village CO 80110-7106 Office: Popham Haik Schnobrich & Kaufman Ltd 1200 17th St Ste 2400 Denver CO 80202-5824

TISDALE, NORWOOD BOYD, lawyer; b. N.Y.C., Aug. 1, 1945; s. Wright and Mariam Norwood (Boyd) T.; m. Laurine Gardner, Aug. 5, 1972; children: Mariam Spotswood, Mary Barden, William Norwood Boyd. BA, Duke U., 1968, M Tchg., 1970, JD, 1975. Bar: N.C. 1975. Assoc. Robert E. Lock, Jacksonville, N.C., 1975-78; ptnr. Ellis, Hooper, Warlick, Waters and Morgan, Jacksonville, 1978-88; pvt. practice Jacksonville, 1988—. Pres. Greater Jacksonville-Onslow, 1985; bd. dirs. Greater Jacksonville-Onslow C. of C., Jacksonville, 1983-85; counsel Carobell Children's Home, Jacksonville, 1979—. Mem. Rotary. Avocations: soccer, golf, sailing. Office: Norwood Boyd Tisdale 400 New Bridge St Jacksonville NC 28540

TISE, LARRY EDWARD, historical organization administrator, historian; b. Winston-Salem, N.C., Dec. 6, 1942; s. Russell Edward and Lena Irene (Norman) T.; children: Larry Edward, Nicholas Allen, William Zane. A.B., Duke U., 1965, M.Div., 1968; Ph.D. (Ford Found. fellow, 1970, Research Triangle fellow, 1971), U. N.C., 1974. Part-time editor John Fries Blair, Pub., Winston-Salem, 1969-72; teaching fellow history dept. U. N.C., Chapel Hill, 1971; instr. U. N.C., 1972-73; dir. hist. publs. N.C. Bicentennial Com., 1973-74; asst. dir. N.C. Div. Archives and History, Raleigh, 1974-75; dir. N.C. Div. Archives and History, 1975-81, N.C. State Hist. Preservation officer, 1975-81; exec. dir. Pa. Hist. and Mus. Commn., 1981-87; Pa. State Hist. Preservation officer, 1981-87; dir. Am. Assn. for State and Local History, Nashville, Tenn., 1987-89; exec. dir. Benjamin Franklin Nat. Meml., Phila., 1989—; adj. prof. grad. sch. fine arts U. Pa., 1984-87; vis. prof. Vanderbilt U., 1988-89, Temple U., 1989-91; mem. Nat. Hist. Publs. and Records Commn., 1982-88; officer Preservation Action; corp. dir. Fedn. N.C. Hist. Socs., Friends of N.C. Archives, Inc., Hist. Preservation Fund of N.C., Inc., Preservation Fund of Pa., Inc., Hist. Preservation Soc. N.C., Inc., Mus. History Assocs., Inc., N.C. Inst. Applied History, Stagville Ctr. Corp., N.C., Inc. Author, co-author writings in fields of archives, hist. preservation, hist. sites and museums, history, society, religion; author: The Southern Experience in the American Revolution, 1978, The Monitor: Its Meaning and Future, 1978, Writing North Carolina History, 1979, A House Not Made with Hands, 1966, The Yadkin Melting Pot: Methodism and the Moravians in the Yadkin Valley, 1750-1850, 1968, Proslavery: The Defense of Slavery in America, 1987, A Book About Children, 1992; gen. editor: writings in fields of archives, hist. preservation, hist. sites and museums, history, society, religion including Winston-Salem in History, 13 vols, 1976; edit. bd. The Public Historian, 1980-86; editor N.C. Hist. Rev., 1974-81, Pa. Heritage, 1981-87, History News, 1987-89, Franklin Gazette, 1989—; contbr. articles to books, newsletters, publs. Recipient William R. Davie History award, 1979, Herbert L. Feis award, Am. Hist. Assn., 1989, Benjamin Franklin Nat. Meml. awards 1990; Nat. Endowment for the Humanities fellow, 1992-93. Mem. Am. Hist. Assn. (various coms.), Orgn. Am. Historians (chmn. coms.), So. Hist. Assn., Soc. Am. Archivists, Am. Assn. State and Local History (mem. council and coms.), Nat. Trust for Hist. Preservation, Nat. Assn. State Archives and Records Adminstrs. (pres. 1980-81), Nat. Conf. State Hist. Preservation Officers (bd. dirs. 1976-79, pres. 1979-81), Nat. Council on Public History (bd. dirs., exec. com. 1979-83, pres. 1983-85), N.C. Hist. Commn. (sec. 1975-81), N.C. Lit. and Hist. Assn. (sec., treas. 1977-81), Pa. Fedn. Hist. Socs. (sec. 1981-87), Internat. Cong. Disting. Awards (founder, pres. 1993—), Friends of Franklin, Inc. (exec. sec. 1989—). Methodist. Home: 705 Corinthian Ave Philadelphia PA 19130-2614

TISE, MARY SHACKELFORD, public librarian; b. Charlottesville, Va., Oct. 26, 1954; d. Alfred Colquitt and Mary Aston (Leavell) Shackelford; m. Frank Peine Tise, July 4, 1981; children: David, Gregory, Joseph. BA, U. Va., 1976; MLS, U. N.C., 1978. Libr. dir. Vaughan Meml. Libr., Galax, Va., 1978-81; reference libr. Concord Pike Libr., Wilmington, Del., 1981-83, divsn. mgr., 1989—; divsn. mgr. Claymont (Del.) Pub. Libr., 1983-89. Mem. ALA, AAUW, Del. Libr. Assn. (pres. 1989-90). Office: Concord Pike Libr 3406 Concord Pike Wilmington DE 19803-5031

TISHLER, WILLIAM HENRY, landscape architect, educator; b. Baileys Harbor, Wis., June 22, 1936; s. William John and Mary Viola (Sarter) T.; m. Betsy Lehner, Sept. 23, 1961; children—William Phillip, Robin Elizabeth. B.S. in Landscape Architecture, U. Wis., 1960; M.L.A., Harvard U., 1964. Urban planner City of Milw., 1961-62; mem. faculty dept. landscape architecture U. Wis.-Madison, 1964—; asso. Hugh A Dega & Assos. (Landscape Architects), 1964-66; prin. Land Plans Inc. (Land and Hist. Preservation Planning Cons.), Madison, 1966—; advisor emeritus Nat. Trust for Hist. Preservation; mem. Door County Land Trust, Inc., 1986-91; bd. dirs. The Hubbard Ednl. Trust. Author: American Landscape Architecture: Designers and Places, 1989; contbr. articles to profl. jours. Served with C.E., U.S. Army, 1960. Recipient Design Arts Program award NEH, 1981; Attingham (Eng.) Program fellow Soc. Archtl. Historians, 1980; Dumbarton Oaks sr. fellow, 1990. Fellow Am. Soc. Landscape Architects (Horace Cleve. Vis. Prof. U. Minn. 1993, merit award 1971, nat. honor award 1980, 89); mem. Assn. Preservation Tech., Wis. Acad. Arts, Letters and Scis., Pioneer Am. Soc., Hist. Madison (hon.), Vernacular Architecture Forum, Madison Trust for Hist. Preservation, Alliance for Hist. Landscape Preservation (founder), The Clearing Landscape Inst. (co-dir.), Phi Kappa Phi, Sigma Lambda Alpha, Sigma Nu. Lutheran. Home: 3925 Regent St Madison WI 53705-5222 Office: U Wis Dept Landscape Architecture Madison WI 53706

TISHMAN, JOHN L., realty and construction company executive; b. N.Y.C., Jan. 24, 1926; s. Louis and Rose F. (Foreman) T.; m. Suzanne Weisberg; children: Daniel R., Katherine T. Chmn., chief exec. officer. Tishman Realty & Constrn. Co., Inc., N.Y.C. Home: Mianus Riv Rd Bedford NY 10506 Office: Tishman Constrn Corp N Y 666 5th Ave New York NY 10103-0001*

TISINGER, CATHERINE ANNE, college dean; b. Winchester, Va., Apr. 6, 1936; d. Richard Martin and Irma Regina (Ohl) T. BA, Coll. Wooster, 1958; MA, U. Pa., 1962, PhD, 1970; LLD (hon.), Coll. of Elms, 1985. Provost Callison Coll., U. of Pacific, Stockton, Calif., 1971-72; v.p. Met. State U., St. Paul, 1972-75; v.p. acad. affairs S.W. State U., Marshall, Minn., 1975-76, interim pres., 1976-77; dir. Ctr. for Econ. Edn., R.I. Coll., Providence, 1979-80; v.p. acad. affairs Cen. Mo. State U., Warrensburg, Mo., 1980-84; pres. North Adams State Coll., Mass., 1984-91; dean arts and scis. Shenandoah U., Winchester, Va., 1991—; cons. North Cen. Assn. Colls. and Schs., 1980-84, New Eng. Assn. Schs. and Colls., 1978-79, 85—, Minn. Acad. Family Physicians, 1973-77; mem. adv. bd. First Agrl. Bank, North Adams, 1985-91; pres. No. Berkshire Cooperating Colls., 1986-91; v.p. Coll. Consortium for Internat. Studies, 1989-90. V.p. Med. Simulation Found., 1986-88; bd. dirs. Williamstown Concerts, 1988-91, Shawnee coun. Girl Scouts U.S., 1992-93. Mem. No. Berkshire C. of C. (bd. dirs. 1984-89, v.p. 1988-89). Avocations: fiber and textile arts, photography. Office: Shenandoah U 1460 College Dr Winchester VA 22601

TISON, JOSEPH SOUTHWOOD, food products company executive; b. Savannah, Ga., June 23, 1943; s. Henry Lawton and Edna Lucille (Williamson) T.; m. Sarah Wheeler, July 22, 1967; children: Katherine Coates, Joseph Southwood, Sarah Lawton, Robert Fletcher. BA, U. N.C., 1965; MBA, Old Dominion U., 1971; cert. exec. mgmt., Pa. State U., 1982. Mktg. assoc. Continental Can Co., N.Y.C., 1971-72; sales rep. Continental Can Co., Cin., 1972-77; dist. mgr. Continental Can Co., Atlanta, Stamford, Conn., 1977-82; nat. sales mgr. TriCoast Container Corp., Stamford, 1982-85; exec. v.p. Citrus Products Inc., N.Y.C., 1985—. Vice-chmn. Ridgefield (Conn.) Parking Authority, 1989; incorporator Ridgefield Community Ctr., 1988—. Mem. Nat. Juice Processors Assn., Internat. Apple Inst., Citrus Processors Assn. (assoc.), Dairy and Food Industries Supply Assn., Brazilian-Am. C. of C. (dir. 1987—), Citrus Assocs. N.Y. N.Y. Cotton Exchange (assoc.), Oglethorpe Club (Savannah, Ga.), Lakeside Field (South Salem, N.Y.). Republican. Episcopalian. Avocations: skiing, tennis, horticulture. Office: Citrus Products Inc 499 Park Ave New York NY 10022-1240*

TITCOMB, CALDWELL, music and theatre historian; b. Augusta, Maine, Aug. 16, 1926; s. Samuel and Lura Elizabeth (Smith) T. A.B. summa cum laude, Harvard U., 1947, M.A., 1949, Ph.D., 1952. Univ. organist Brandeis U., Waltham, Mass., 1953-70, dir. undergrad. studies music, 1956-84, curator creative arts, library, 1961-64, co-chmn. music dept., 1977-84, from instr. to prof. music, 1953-88, prof. emeritus, 1988—; drama critic Harvard Crimson, 1953-82, Bay State Banner, 1975— ; trustee Charles Playhouse, Boston, 1966-71. Editor: The Art of Fine Words, 1965, The Furies (Lucien Price), 1988; co-editor: Varieties of Black Experience at Harvard, 1986, Blacks at Harvard: A Documentary History of African-American Experience at Harvard and Radcliffe, 1993; contbr. articles to profl. jours., ency.; composer stage and film music scores. Bd. dirs. Cambridge Civic Symphony Orch., Mass., 1959-70; exec. bd. Mus. Fine Arts Friends Music, Boston, 1959-65; panelist Mass. Commn. Arts and Humanities, 1981-83; mem. selection com. Theater Hall of Fame, 1980—; juror Elliot Norton awards, 1985-94; pres. Boston Theater Awards, 1994—. With U.S. Army, 1944-46, PTO; with Mil. Intelligence Res., 1946-50. Mem. AAUP, Coll. Music Soc., Am. Theatre Critics Assn. (charter), New Eng. Theatre Conf. (adv. coun. 1961-81, coll. fellows 1981), Am. Guild Organists, Am. Musicol. Soc. (coun. 1965-67), Soc. for Ethnomusicology, Hist. Brass Soc., Signet Soc., Sonneck Soc., Phi Beta Kappa (sec. Mu chpt. Mass. 1984—). Avocations: philology; Afro-Am. history and culture. Office: Brandeis U Music Dept South St Waltham MA 02254-9110

TITE, JOHN GREGORY, secondary school educator; b. Southbridge, Mass., Sept. 20, 1941; s. Gregory Louca and Androniq (Zhidro) T. BS, U. Mass., 1963; MEd, Worcester (Mass.) State Coll., 1966; MS, Clarkson Coll. Tech., 1971. Instr. math. Grafton (Mass.) Pub. Schs., 1963-67, math. dept. chairperson, calculus instr., 1967—; adj. prof. calculus Anna Maria Coll., Paxton, Mass., 1986-88; in-svc. instr. metrics for h.s. and elem. tchrs., 1974-76; spkr. in field. Grantee NSF, 1965, 67, 75, Computer Assisted Math Project grant U. Mass., 1985-86. Mem. Assn. of Tchrs. of Math. in Mass. (pres., exhibits chmn. 1970), Nat. Coun. Supts. of Math., Nat. Coun. of Tchrs. of Math. (chmn. films and filmstrips com. 1973, chmn. sales of NCTM materials 1976), Neighborhood Assn. of Math. Dept. Heads (bd. dirs. 1976-79). Avocations: reading, traveling, walking. Home: 12 Arrowhead Ave Auburn MA 01501-2302 Office: Grafton Pub Schs 24 Providence Rd Grafton MA 01519-1178

TITILOYE, VICTORIA MOJIRAYO, pediatrics nurse; b. Okemesi Ekiti, Nigeria, Nov. 17, 1955; d. Ezekiel Ajiboye and Julianah Oyindaola (Atitebi) T. Diploma, Lagos U. Teaching Hosp., 1977; BS, SUNY, Bklyn., 1981; MA, NYU, 1983, PhD valedictory rep., 1988. Cert. occupational therapist, Nigerian nurse, RN. Asst. nursing supt. adult med. and surg. wards Wesley Guild Hosp., Unife-Complex, Ilesha, Oyo, 1977-78; sr. occupational therapist United Cerebral Palsy, Bklyn., 1982-85; occupational therapist con., Sch. for Multiply Handicapped Children, Vis. Therapist Assocs., Bklyn., 1985-89; rsch. assoc. NYU, N.Y.C., 1989-90; asst. dir. occupational therapy Cobble Hill Nursing Home, Bklyn., 1991-92; asst. prof. occupl. therapy SUNY Health Sci. Ctr., Bklyn., 1994—; dir. occupl. therapy dept. Sts. Joachim and Ann Residence, Bklyn., 1992-93; cons. drs. office occupl. therapy dept. U. Medicine and Dentistry N.J., 1993; clin. and rsch. cons. League Therapeutic Ctr., Bklyn., 1993—; rsch. cons. Kessler Inst. Rehab., East Orange, N.J., 1993—; adj. asst. prof. dept. life scis. N.Y. Inst. Tech., 1993-94; clin. and rsch. cons. League Therapeutic Ctr., Bklyn., 1993—; rep. NYU Sch. Edn., Health, Nursing and Arts Professions; reviewer articles and proposals for profl. jours. and confs. Contbr. articles to profl. jours. Food coord. Food Program for the Homeless, Sts. Ann and George, Bklyn.; reviewer conf. proposals. Recipient scholarships Nigerian govt., NYU Grad. Sch., Downstate Acad. Achievement. Mem. ANA, Am. Occupational Therapy Assn., Am. Soc. on Aging, N.Y. Acad. Scis., Nigerian Nurses Assn., MEDART Internat.

TITLE, PETER STEPHEN, lawyer; b. New Orleans, Nov. 24, 1950; s. Harold Benjamin and Beulah (Sterbcow) T.; m. Sheryl Gerber, June 14, 1981. B.A., Columbia U., 1972; J.D., Tulane U., 1975. Bar: La. 1975, U.S. Dist. Ct. (ea., we., mid. dists.) La., U.S. Ct. Appeals (5th cir.). Assoc. Sessions, Fishman, Rosenson, Boisfontaine, Nathan & Winn, New Orleans, 1975-81, ptnr., 1982—; instr. on property Tulane U., 1978; asst. examiner com. on Admissions to Bar, 1980-88, examiner, 1988—; lectr. on real estate. Author: Louisiana Real Estate Transactions, 1991. Mem. ABA, La. Bar Assn. (chmn. sect. on trust estates, probate and immovable property law 1983-84), New Orleans Bar Assn. (chmn. title examinations com., 1992-93), Rep. Am. Judicature Soc., Order of Coif, Phi Delta Phi. Jewish. Lodge: B'Nai Brith. Home: 515 Hillary St New Orleans LA 70118-3833 Office: Sessions & Fishman 201 Saint Charles Ave Fl 35 New Orleans LA 70170-1000

TITLEY, LARRY J., lawyer; b. Tecumseh, Mich., Dec. 9, 1943; s. Leroy H. and Julia B. (Ruesink) T.; m. Julia Margaret Neukom, May 23, 1970; children: Sarah Catherine, John Neukom. BA, U. Mich., 1965, JD, 1972. Bar: Va. 1973, Mich. 1973. Assoc. Hunton & Williams, Richmond, Va., 1972-73, Varnum, Riddering, Schmidt & Howlett, Grand Rapids, Mich., 1973—. Trustee Friends Pub. Mus., 1985-94; bd. dirs. Grand Rapids Pub. Mus., 1988—, pres., 1992-95; bd. dirs. Camp Optimist YMCA, 1993—, Peninsular Club, 1994—, v.p., 1996. Mem. ABA, Mich. Bar Assn., Grand Rapids Bar Assn. Home: 746 San Jose Dr SE Grand Rapids MI 49506-3418 Office: Varnum Riddering Schmidt & Howlett Bridgewater Pl PO Box 352 Grand Rapids MI 49504

TITONE, VITO JOSEPH, judge; b. Bklyn., July 5, 1929; s. Vito and Elena (Ruisi) T.; m. Margaret Anne Viola, Dec. 30, 1956; children: Stephen, Matthew, Elena Titone Hill, Elizabeth. BA, NYU, 1951; JD, St. John's U., 1956, LL.D., 1984. Bar: N.Y. 1957, U.S. Dist. Ct. (ea. and so. dists.) N.Y., 1962, U.S. Supreme Ct. 1964. Ptnr. Maltese & Titone, N.Y.C., 1957-65, Maltese, Titone & Anastasi, N.Y.C., 1965-68; assoc. counsel to pres. pro tem N.Y. State Senate, 1965; justice N.Y. State Supreme Ct, N.Y.C., 1969-75; assoc. justice appellate div. 2d dept., 1975-85; judge N.Y. State Ct. Appeals, Albany, 1985—; adj. prof. Coll. S.I., CUNY, 1969-72, St. John's U., Jamaica, N.Y., 1969-85. Contbr. articles to law jour. Bd. govs. Daytop Village Inc., N.Y.C.; bd. dirs. Boy Scouts Am. With U.S. Army, 1951-53, to col. N.Y. State Guard. Named Citizen of Yr. Daytop Village, N.Y.C., 1969, Disting. Citizen Wagner Coll., S.I., 1983, Outstanding Contbr. Camelot Substance Abuse Network, 1983; recipient citation of merit S.I. Salvation Army Adv. Bd., 1983, Rapollo award Columbian Lawyers Assn., 1983, Disting. Judiciary award Cath. Lawyers Guild Diocese of Bklyn., 1991, Disting. Svc. award N.Y. State Lawyers Assn., Justice William Brennan award N.Y. Assn. Criminal Def. Lawyers, 1993. Mem. ABA, N.Y. State Bar Assn., Richmond County Bar Assn., Supreme Ct. Justice Assn., VFW, Am. Legion (past comdr.), Charles C. Pinckney Tribute Def. Assn. of N.Y., Justinian Soc., K.C. Roman Catholic. Office: NY Ct Appeals 20 Eagle St Albany NY 12207-1004 also: 60 Bay St Fl 9 Staten Island NY 10301-2514

TITTMANN, BERNHARD RAINER, engineering science and mechanics educator; b. Moshi, Tanganjika, East Africa, Sept. 15, 1935; came to U.S., 1950, naturalized, 1956; s. Gustav and Hermine Marie (Polland) T.; m. Katharine Shower, Dec. 17, 1966; children: Christine M., Heidi E., Raymond J., Monica M., Brian P.F. BS, George Washington U., 1957; MS, UCLA, 1961, PhD, 1965. Mem. staff Hughes Aircraft Co., Culver City, Calif., 1957-65; asst. prof. UCLA, 1965-66; mem. staff Rockwell Internat., Thousand Oaks, Calif., 1966-79, dept. mgr., 1979-89; Schell prof. engring. Pa. State U., University Park, 1989—. Co-author 5 books; contbr. over 200 articles to profl. jours.; patentee in field. George Washington fellow George Washington U., 1953, Howard Hughes fellow Hughes Aircraft Co., 1957. Fellow IEEE (adminstrv. com. for ultrasonics, ferrolectrics, frequency control, nominating chmn. 1988—); mem. Acoustical Soc. Am. (tech. program mem. 1986-89), KC (4th degree), Phi Beta Kappa. Home: 2466 Sassafras Ct State College PA 16803-3366 Office: Pa State U 228C Hammond Bldg University Park PA 16802

TITUS, ALICE CESTANDINA (DINA TITUS), state legislator; b. Thomasville, Ga., May 23, 1950. AB, Coll. William and Mary, 1970; MA, U. Ga., 1973; PhD, Fla. State U., 1976. Prof. polit. sci. U. Nev., Las Vegas; mem. Nev. Senate, 1989—; alt. mem. legis. commn., 1989-91, mem., 1991-93; minority floor leader, 1993—; chmn. Nev. Humanities Com., 1984-86; mem. Eldorado Basin adv. group to Colo. River Commn.; active Gov. Commn. Bicentennial of U.S. Constn.; former mem. Gov. Commn. on Aging. Author: Bombs in the Backyard: Atomic Testing and American Politics, 1986, Battle Born: Federal-State Relations in Nevada during the 20th Century, 1989. Mem. Western Polit. Sci. Assn., Clark County Women's Dem. Club. Greek Orthodox. Home: 1637 Travois Cir Las Vegas NV 89119-6283 Office: Nev State Senate State Capitol Carson City NV 89710*

TITUS, DAVID ANSON, political science educator; b. Cleve., Dec. 2, 1934; s. Jesse Edmund and Anne (Bonnette) T.; m. Kaoru Matsumura, Sept. 3, 1960 (div. 1966); m. Rachel Thankful Roberts, Aug. 3, 1968; children: Jeffrey, Brian. B.A., Harvard U., 1956; M.A., Columbia U., 1962, Ph.D., 1970. Instr. Wesleyan U., Middletown, Conn., 1966-70, asst. prof., 1970-73, assoc. prof., 1973-79, prof. govt., 1979—, co-chmn. Coll. Social Studies, 1972-75, 81-84, 93-96, chmn. dept. govt., 1976-78, chmn. East Asian Studies Program, 1976-78, 1979-81, 1988-90; mem. staff Joint Com. Japanese Studies, N.Y.C., 1968-70; chmn. bd. dirs. Associated Kyoto Program, 1976-77, 79-82, resident dir., 1975-76, 84-85, 96-97. Author: Palace and Politics in Prewar Japan, 1974; translator: Japan's Road to the Pacific War—The Final Confrontation: Japan's Negotiations with the United States, 1941, 1994. Founder Mattabeseck Audubon Soc., Middletown, Conn., 1974. Served to lt. (j.g.) USN, 1956-58. Recipient Ansley award Columbia U. Press, 1970; vis. scholar Corpus Christi Coll., Cambridge, Eng., 1978-79, Doshisha U., Kyoto, Japan, 1987, 93. Mem. Assn. Asian Studies (council confs. 1983-86, chmn. studies program com. 1975). Home: 376 Main St Cromwell CT 06416-2305 Office: Wesleyan U Dept of Sci Ed Middletown CT 06459

TITUS, EDWARD DEPUE, psychiatrist, administrator; b. N.Y.C., May 24, 1931; s. Edward Kleinhans and Mary (Brown) Chadbourne; m. Virginia Van Den Steenhoven, Mar. 24, 1963 (div.); m. Catherine Brown, Apr. 22, 1990. BA, Occidental Coll., 1953; MS, U. Wis., 1955; MD, Stanford U., 1962; PhD, So. Calif. Psychoanalytic Inst., 1977. Mng. ptnr. Hacker Clinic Assn., Lynwood, Calif., 1968-90; chief psychiatrist parole outpatient clinic region III Calif. Dept. Corrections, L.A., 1991—; asst. clin. prof. psychiatry U. So. Calif., 1993—; chmn. dept. psychiatry St. Francis Hosp., Lynwood, 1979-80. Fellow Am. Psychiat. Assn.; mem. Calif. Med. Assn. (ho. of dels. 1981-95), So. Calif. Psychiat. Soc. (sec. 1984-85), Los Angeles County Med. Assn. (dist. pres. 1980-81, pres. sect. psychiatry 1990-92). Avocations: photography, backpacking. Office: Parole Outpatient Clinic 307 W 4th St Los Angeles CA 90013-1104

TITUS, JACK L., pathologist, educator; b. South Bend, Ind., Dec. 7, 1926; s. Loren O. and Rutha B. (Orr) T.; m. Beverly Harden, June 18, 1949; children—Jack, Elizabeth Ann Titus Engelbrecht, Michael, Matthew, Joan. B.S., Notre Dame U., 1948; M.D., Washington U., St. Louis, 1952; Ph.D., U. Minn., 1962. Practice medicine Rensselaer, Ind., 1953-57; fellow in pathology U. Minn., 1957-61; assoc. prof. pathology Mayo Grad. Sch., Rochester, Minn., 1961-72; prof. pathology Mayo Med. Sch., 1971-72, coordinator pathology tng. programs, 1964-72; W.L. Moody Jr. prof., chmn. dept. pathology Baylor Coll. Medicine, Houston, 1972-87; chief pathology service Meth. Hosp., Houston, 1972-87; pathologist-in-chief Harris County Hosp. Dist., Houston, 1972-87; chmn. dept. pathology Med. Ctr. Hosp., Conroe, Tex., 1982-87, Woodlands Community Hosp., 1984-87; dir. registry for cardiovascular diseases United Hosps., 1987-95; clin. prof. pathology U. Minn., 1987—; adj. prof. pathology Baylor Coll. Medicine, 1987—; sr. cons. in pathology U. Tex. System Cancer Ctr., Houston, 1974—. Mem. edit. bd. Circulation, 1966-72, Am. Heart Jour., 1972-77, Modern Pathology, 1987-95, Human Pathology, 1988—, Am. Jour. of Cardiovascular Pathology, 1987-94, Cardiovascular Pathology, 1991—; contbr. articles to med. jours. Served with U.S. Army, 1945-47. Recipient Billings gold medal AMA, 1968, Hoektoen gold medal, 1969, Disting. Achievement award Soc. Cardiovascular Pathology, 1993, Scholarly Achievement award Houston Soc. Clin. Pathology, 1993. Mem. Internat. Acad. Pathology, Am. Assn. Pathologists, Am. Soc. Clin. Pathologists, AAAS, AMA, Am. Heart Assn., Coll. Am. Pathologists, Minn. Med. Assn., Minn. Heart Assn., Minn. Soc. Clin. Pathologists, Ramsey County Med. Soc., Sigma Xi, Alpha Omega Alpha. Methodist. Office: 255 Smith Ave N Ste 200 Saint Paul MN 55102-2518

TITUS, ROBERT P., accounting company executive; b. 1941. Student, CUNY. CPA, N.Y. Founder Mitchell, Titus & Co., L.L.P., N.Y.C., 1973—, now vice chmn., COO, mng. ptnr. Office: Mitchell/Titus & Co 2 Park Ave New York NY 10016-5603*

TITUS, ROGER WARREN, lawyer; b. Washington, Dec. 16, 1941; s. George R. and Margaret (Merithew) T.; m. Catherine Mary Gaughen, Aug. 16, 1961; children: Paula Titus Laboy, Richard Roger, Mark William. BA, Johns Hopkins U., 1963; JD, Georgetown U., 1966. Bar: Md. 1966, D.C. 1966, U.S. Dist. Ct. Md. 1966, D.C. Dist. 1966, U.S. Ct. Appeals (4th cir.) 1966, U.S. Supreme Ct. 1970. Ptnr. Titus & Glasgow, Rockville, Md., 1966-88, Venable, Baetjer & Howard, Rockville, 1988—; asst. city atty. City of Rockville, 1966-69, city atty., 1970-82; spl. asst. Md. State Bd. of Law Examiners, 1969-72; adj. prof. law Georgetown U., Washington, 1972-78; mem. inquiry com. Atty. Grievance Commn., Annapolis, Md., 1975-80; mem. Trial Cts. Judicial Nominating Commn. Montgomery County, 1979-91; mem. standing com. on rules of practice and procedure Ct. of Appeals of Md., 1989—; mem. Appellate Jud. Nominating Commn., 1991—. Trustee Suburban Hosp., Inc., Bethesda, Md., 1986—. Fellow Am. Coll. Trial Lawyers, Am. Bar Found., Md. Bar Found. (bd. dirs. 1987—, v.p. 1990-91, pres. 1991-93); mem. ABA (del. 1987-95), Nat. Conf. Bar Pres. (mem. exec. coun. 1990-93), Md. Bar Assn. (sec. 1984-87, pres. 1988-89), Am. Judicature Soc. (bd. dirs. 1995—), Md. Mcpl. Attys. Assn. (pres. 1975), Montgomery County Bar Assn. (exec. com. 1983-84), City Tavern Club. Office: Venable Baetjer & Howard PO Box 1906 1 Church St Ste 1000 Rockville MD 20850-4158

TITUS, VICTOR ALLEN, lawyer; b. Nevada, Mo., Sept. 2, 1956; s. Charles Allen and Viola Mae (Cliffman) T.; m. Laraine Carol Cook, Oct. 13, 1974 (div. Feb. 1982); 1 child, Matthew; m. Deborah Diane Carpenter, Apr. 10, 1984; 1 child, Jacquelynn. BS, Ctrl. Mo. State U., 1978, BA, 1978; JD, U. Mo., 1981. Bar: N.Mex. 1981, U.S. Dist. Ct. N.Mex. 1981, Mo. 1982, U.S. Ct. Appeals (10th cir. 1983), U.S. Supreme Ct. 1986, Colo. 1989. Lawyer Jay L. Faurot, P.C., Farmington, N.Mex., 1981-83; ptnr. Faurot & Titus, P.C., Farmington, N.Mex., 1983-85; lawyer, sole proprietor Victor A. Titus, P.C., Farmington, N.Mex., 1985—; arbitrator in civil disputes Alternative Dispute Resolution-Arbitration; liquor lic. hearing officer City of Farmington, 1989-94. Contbr. articles to profl. jours. Adult Behind Youth, Boys & Girls Club, Farmington, 1987—; mem. hosp. adv. bd. San Juan Regional Med. Ctr., Farmington, 1988-93. Recipient San Juan County Disting. Svc. award N.Mex. Bar Assn., 1984; named one of Best Lawyers in Am., 1995-96. Mem. Assn. Trial Lawyers of Am., N.Mex. Trial Lawyers (bd. pres. 1983—, pres. 1993-94), State Bar of N.Mex. (specialization com. 1992—, legal advt. com. 1990), San Juan County Bar Assn. (pres. 1984), Natl. Assn. Criminal Def. Lawyers, Colo. Trial Lawyers. Democrat. Avocation: sports. Home: 5711 Tee Dr Farmington NM 87402-0933 Office: Victor A Titus PC 2021 E 20th St Farmington NM 87401-2516

TITZE, INGO ROLAND, physics educator; b. Hirschberg, Silesia, Germany, July 8, 1941; came to U.S. 1955; s. Kurt Herrmann and Marta Emma (Bettermann) T.; m. R. Katherine Pittard, July 19, 1969; children: Karin, Michael, Jason, Gregory. BSEE, U. Utah, 1963, MS in Elec. Engring. and Physics, 1965; Ph.D. in Physics, Brigham Young U., 1972. Rsch. engr. N. Am. Aviation, Tulsa, 1965-66, Boeing Co., Seattle, 1968-70; lectr. Calif. State Poly. U., Pomona, 1973-74; asst. prof. U. Petroleum and Minerals Dhahran, Saudi Arabia, 1974-76, Gallaudet Coll., Washington, 1976-79; disting. prof. speech sci. and voice U. Iowa, Iowa City, 1979—; cons. Bell Labs., Murray Hill, N.J., 1977-78; exec. dir. Wilbur James Gould Voice Rsch. Ctr., Denver Ctr. Performing Arts, 1983—; pres. Voice Cons. Inc., 1985—; panelist, site visitor NRC-NAS, 1984—; regular cons. divsn. rsch. grants NIH, 1986—; chmn. task force on voice Nat. Inst. Deafness and Other Comm. Disorders, 1989; adj. prof. Westminster Choir Coll., Princeton, N.J., 1989-94; dir. Nat. Ctr. for Voice and Speech, 1990—. Author: Principles of Voice Production, 1993; editor: Vocal Fold Physiology: Biomechanics, Acoustics and Phonatory Control, 1985, Vocal Fold Physiology: Frontiers in Basic Science, 1992; assoc. editor Jour. of Voice; contbr. articles to profl. jours. Adv. bd. Voice Found., N.Y.C., 1980—; young men's pres. Latter Day Saints Ch. and Boy Scouts Am., Iowa City, 1982—. Jacob Javits Neurosci. Investigator grantee NIH, 1984; recipient William and Harriot

Gould Found. award, 1983, Claude Pepper award, 1989, Quintant award Voice Found., 1990, fellow ASHA, 1992. Fellow Acoustical Soc. Am. (tech. council, awards com. 1989); mem. Am. Speech-Hearing-Lang. Assn., Nat. Assn. Tchrs. Singing (research council 1977—, editorial bd. 1986—), Internat. Assn. Research Singing (dir. publs. 1982—). Republican. Avocations: classical singing; tennis; choir directing; home building. Home: 2015 Glendale Rd Iowa City IA 52245-3217 Office: Nat Ctr for Voice & Speech Univ of Iowa 330 Wjshc Iowa City IA 52242-1012

TITZE, WOLFGANG, management consultant. Co-chmn. Gemini Cons. Inc., Morristown, N.J. Office: Gemini Cons Inc 2535 Airport Rd Morristown NJ 07960

TIZZIO, THOMAS RALPH, brokerage executive; b. Elmont, N.Y., Jan. 9, 1938; s. Anthony Thomas and Ann Marie (Pascale) T.; m. Mary Ann Gentile, Aug. 26, 1962; children: Anthony, Vincent, Thomas. BBA, Bklyn. Coll., 1962. Underwriter W.J. Roberts & Co., N.Y.C., 1957-65; sr. underwriter Atlantic Mut. Ins. Co., 1965-67; various positions AIG Am. Home Assurance Co., N.Y.C., 1967-74, sr. v.p. property underwriting, 1974-78; exec. v.p. AIG Transatlantic Reins. Co., N.Y.C., 1978-80, pres., bd. dirs., 1980-82; sr. v.p. reins. Am. Internat. Group, Inc., N.Y.C., 1982-85, pres. domestic brokerage divsn., 1985-91, pres. Brokerage divsn., 1986-91, pres., 1991—. Mem. Am. Inst. for Property and Liability Underwriters (trustee), Ins. Inst. Am. (trustee). Office: Am Internat Group Inc 70 Pine St New York NY 10270-0002

TJOFLAT, GERALD BARD, federal judge; b. Pitts., Dec. 6, 1929; s. Gerald Benjamin and Sarita (Romero-Hermoso) T.; m. Sarah Marie Pfohl, July 27, 1957; children: Gerald Bard, Marie Elizabeth Tjoflat. Student, U. Va., 1947-50, U. Cin., 1950-52; LL.B., Duke U., 1957; D.C.L. (hon.), Jacksonville U., 1978; LLD (hon.), William Mitchell Coll. Law, 1993. Bar: Fla. 1957. Individual practice law Jacksonville, Fla., 1957-68; judge 4th Jud. Cir. Ct. Fla., 1968-70, U.S. Dist. Ct. for Middle Dist. Fla., Jacksonville, 1970-75, U.S. Ct. Appeals, 5th Cir., Jacksonville, 1975-81; judge U.S. Ct. Appeals, 11th Cir., Jacksonville, 1981-89, chief judge, 1989—; mem. Adv. Corrections Coun. U.S., 1975-87, Jud. Conf. of U.S., 1989—, Fed. Jud. Ctr. Com. on Sentencing, Probation and Pretrial Svcs., 1988-90; mem. com. adminstrn. probation system Jud. Conf. of U.S., 1972-87, chmn., 1978-87; U.S. del. 6th and 7th UN Congress for Prevention of Crime and Treatment of Offenders. Hon. life mem., bd. visitors Duke U. Law Sch.; pres. North Fla. coun. Boy Scouts Am., 1976-85, chmn., 1985-90; trustee Jacksonville Marine Inst., 1976-90, Episc. H.S., Jacksonville, 1975-90; mem. vestry St. Johns Cathedral, Jacksonville, 1969-71, 73-75, 77-79, 81-83, 85-87, 93, 95-96, sr. warden, 1975, 83, 87, 91, 92. Served with AUS, 1953-55. Recipient Merit award Duke U., 1990. Mem. ABA, Fla. Bar Assn., Am. Law Inst., Am. Judicature Soc. Episcopalian. Office: US Ct Appeals PO Box 960 Jacksonville FL 32201-0960

TKACZUK, NANCY ANNE, cardiovascular services administrator; b. Cambridge, Mass., Nov. 17, 1949; d. Ralph Aubrey and Eleanor Mae (Goding) Bedley; m. John Paul Tkaczuk, Apr. 9, 1977 (div. Apr. 1983); children: Timothy Aubrey, James Paul. AS in Social Svc., Endicott Coll., 1969; ADN, Clayton Coll., 1975. Coronary care nurse New England Meml. Hosp., Wakefield, Mass., 1975; cardiac cath lab nurse Saint Josephs Hosp., Atlanta, 1976-79; dir. cardiovascular svcs. Northside Hosp., Atlanta, 1979—; founder Mitral Valve Prolapse Support, Atlanta, 1986—; BCLS instr., trainer Am. Heart Assn., 1976—, instr. ACLS, 1990—, pub. spkr., 1975—. Author: Mitral Valve Prolapse, The Heart With A Different Beat, 1986. Mem. Am. Coll. Cardiovascular Adminstrs., Atlanta Health Care Alliance. Methodist. Avocation: tennis. Home: 715 Cranberry Trail Roswell GA 30076 Office: Northside Hosp Cardiology Dept 1000 Johnson Ferry Rd NE Atlanta GA 30342

TOAL, JAMES FRANCIS, academic administrator; b. N.Y.C., June 7, 1932; s. John Joseph and Catherine (Whyte) T. MA, St. John's U., 1966; PhD, Fordham U., 1976. Cert. elem. tchr., N.Y. cert. supt., adminstrn. and supervision, English 7-12. Athletic dir., tchr. English St. Francis Prep. High Sch., N.Y.C., 1957-60; tchr. Bishop Ford High Sch., N.Y.C., 1960-66, chmn. dept. English; prin. St. Francis Central Summer High Sch., N.Y.C., 1966-73, St. Francis Prep. High Sch., N.Y.C., 1966-73; exec. v.p., assoc. prof. dept. edn. adminstrn. and supervision Grad. Sch. St. Bonaventure U., N.Y., 1976-83; pres., prof. Quincy U., Ill., 1983—; also bd. trustees; mem. Springfield Diocesan Bd. of Edn., Provincial Bd. of Edn., Franciscan Friars of Chgo. and St. Louis. Trustee Siena Coll., Loudonville, N.Y., 1977-83; bd. advisors Jamestown Community Coll., Olean, N.Y., 1979-83; bd. dirs. Am. Cancer Soc., Olean, 1981-83; mem. Mental Health Assn., 1981-83; mem. state legis. com. Commn. of Ind. Colls. and Univs., Albany. N.Y., 1980-83; mem. bd. trustees Padua Franciscan High Sch. Grantee Colgate U., 1967; grantee SUNY-Plattsburg, 1968, St. Bonaventure U., 1980. Mem. Am. Coun. on Edn., Associated Colls. of Ill., Ill. Bus. and Edn. Forum, Assn. of Governing Bds., West Ctrl. Ill. Ednl. Telecomm. Corp. (bd. dirs. exec. com., fin. com., pers. com.), Fedn. Ind. Ill. Colls. and Univs. (pub. rels. com.), Mid. States Accrediting Assn. (assoc., evaluation team for higher edn.), Nat. Assn. Secondary Sch. Prins., North Ctrl. Accrediting Assn. (evaluation team for higher edn., chair evaluation team 1986—), Soc. Coll. and U. Planning, Quincy C. of C. (transp. com. 1985-96, computer com. 1996—), Rotary, Univ. Club, KC, Phi Delta Kappa. Office: Quincy U Office of Pres 1800 College Ave Quincy IL 62301-2699

TOAL, JEAN HOEFER, lawyer, state supreme court justice; b. Columbia, S.C., Aug. 11, 1943; d. Herbert W. and Lilla (Farrell) Hoefer; m. William Thomas Toal; children: Jean Hoefer, Lilla Patrick. BA in Philosophy, Agnes Scott Coll., 1965; JD, U. S.C., 1968; LHD (hon.), Coll. Charleston, 1991; LLD (hon.), Columbia Coll., 1992. Bar: S.C. Assoc. Haynsworth, Perry, Bryant, Marion & Johnstone, 1968-70; ptnr. Belser, Baker, Barwick, Ravenel, Toal & Bender, Columbia, 1970-88; assoc. justice S.C. Supreme Ct., 1988—; mem. S.C. Human Affairs Commn., 1972-74; mem. S.C. Ho. of Reps., 1975-88, chmn. house rules com., constitutional laws subcom. house judiciary com.; mem. parish coun. and lector St. Joseph's Cath. Ch.; chair S.C. Juvenile Justice Task Force, 1992-94; chair S.C. Rhodes Scholar Selection Com., 1994. Mng. editor S.C. Law Rev., 1967-68. Bd. visitors Clemson U., 1978; trustee Columbia Mus. Art. Named Legislator of Yr. Greenville News, Woman of Yr., U. S.C.; recipient Disting. Svc. award S.C. Mcpl. Assn., Univ. Notre Dame award, 1991, Algernon Sydney Sullivan award U. S.C., 1991. Mem. John Belton O'Neill Inn of Ct., Phi Alpha Delta. Office: Supreme Ct SC PO Box 12456 Columbia SC 29211-2456

TOALE, THOMAS EDWARD, school system administrator, priest; b. Independence, Iowa, Aug. 30, 1953; s. Francis Mark and Clara R. (DePaepe) T. BS in Biology, Loras Coll., 1975, MA in Ednl. Adminstrn., 1986; MA in Theology, St. Paul Sem., 1980; PhD in Ednl. Adminstrn., U. Iowa, 1988. Ordained priest Roman Cath. Ch., 1981; cert. tchr., prin., supt., Iowa. Tchr. St. Joseph Key West, Dubuque, Iowa, 1975-77; tchr. Marquette High Sch., Bellevue, Iowa, 1981-84, prin., 1984-86; assoc. supt. Archdiocese of Dubuque, 1986-87, supt. schs., 1987—; assoc. pastor St. Joseph Ch., Bellevue, 1981-84; pastor Sts. Peter and Paul Ch., Springbrook, Iowa, 1984-86, St. Peter, Temple Hill, Cascade, Iowa, 1986—. Mem. Nat. Cath. Edn. Assn. Office: Archdiocese of Dubuque 1229 Mount Loretta Ave Dubuque IA 52003-7826

TOBACCOWALA, RISHAD, marketing professional; b. Bombay, India, 1959. BA in Maths., U. Bombay, 1979; MBA, U. Chgo., 1982. Media buyer Leo Burnett USA, Chgo., 1982-84, account supr., 1984-92, v.p., account dir. direct mkg., 1992-94, dir. interactive mktg., 1994—. Office: Leo Burnett USA 35 W Wacker Dr Chicago IL 60601*

TOBE, STEPHEN SOLOMON, zoology educator; b. Niagara-on-the-Lake, Ont., Can., Oct. 11, 1944; s. John Harold and Rose T. (Bolter) T.; m. Martha Reller. BSc, Queen's U., Kingston, Ont., 1967; MSc, York U., Toronto, Ont., 1969; PhD, McGill U., Montreal, Que., Can., 1972. Rsch. fellow U. Sussex, Eng., 1972-74; asst. prof. U. Toronto, 1974-78, assoc. prof., 1974-78, prof., 1982—, assoc. dean scis., faculty arts and sci., 1988-93, vice dean faculty arts and sci., 1995-96; vis. prof. U. Calif., Berkeley, 1981, Nat. U. Singapore, 1987, 1993-94, U. Hawaii, 1988; mem. animal biology grant selection com. Natural Scis. and Engring. Rsch. Coun. Can., 1986-89, chair, 1988-89; lectr. Internat. Congress Entomology, Vancouver, B.C., Can., 1988; cons. in hydroponics. Editor Insect Biochemistry, 1987; mem. editl. bd. Jour. Insect Physiology, 1980—, Physiol. Entomology, 1985—, Life Scis. Advances, 1987—, Gen. and Comparative Endocrinology, 1995—; contbr. chpts. to books and articles to profl. jours. Recipient Pickford medal in comparative endocrinology, 1993; E.W.R. Steacie fellow Natural Scis. and Engring. Rsch. Coun. Can., 1982-84. Fellow Royal Soc. Can., Royal Entomol. Soc.; mem. AAAS, Entomol. Soc. Can. (C. Gordon Hewitt award 1982, gold medal 1990), Entomol. Soc. Am., Soc. Exptl. Biology. Avocations: amateur radio, gardening, hydroponics. Home: 467 Soudan Ave, Toronto, ON Canada M4S 1X1 Office: U Toronto Dept Zoology, 25 Harbord St, Toronto, ON Canada M5S 1A1

TOBER, BARBARA D. (MRS. DONALD GIBBS TOBER), editor; b. Summit, N.J., Aug. 19, 1934; d. Rodney Fielding and Maude (Grebbin) Starkey; m. Donald Gibbs Tober, Apr. 5, 1973. Student, Traphagen Sch. Fashion, 1954-56, Fashion Inst. Tech., 1956-58, N.Y. Sch. Interior Design, 1964. Copy editor Vogue Pattern Book, 1958-60; beauty editor Vogue mag., 1961; dir. women's services Bartell Media Corp., 1961-66; editor-in-chief Bride's mag., N.Y.C., 1966-94; chmn. Am. Craft Mus.; pres. Acronym, Inc., N.Y.C., 1995—, The Barbara Tober Found., 1995—; dir. Gen. Brands Corp., sec.-treas.; adv. bd. Traphagen Sch.; coordinator SBA awards; Am. Craft Council Mus. Assoc., 1983—, benefit food com. chmn., 1984-87. Author: The ABC's of Beauty, 1963, China: A Cognizant Guide, 1980, The Wedding . . . The Marriage . . . And the Role of the Retailer, 1980, The Bride: A Celebration, 1984. Mem. Nat. Council on Family Relations, 1966; nat. council Lincoln Center Performing Arts, Met. Opera Guild; mem. NYU adv. bd. Women in Food Service, 1983; NYU Women's Health Symposium: Steering Com., 1983—. Recipient Alma award, 1968, Penney-Mo. award, 1972, Traphagen Alumni award, 1975, Diamond Jubilee award, 1983. Mem. Fashion Group, Nat. Home Fashions League (v.p., program chmn.), Am. Soc. Mag. Editors, Am. Soc. Interior Designers (press mem.), Intercorporate Group, Women in Communications (60 yrs. of success award N.Y. chpt. 1984), Nat. Assn. Underwater Instrs., Pan Pacific and S.E. Asia Women's Assn., Asia Soc., Japan Soc., China Inst., Internat. Side Saddle Orgn., Millbrook Hounds, Golden's Bridge Hounds, Wine and Food Soc., Chaines des Rotisseurs (chargée de press) (bd. dirs.), Dames d'Escoffier, Culinary Inst. Am. Home: 620 Park Ave New York NY 10021-6591 Office: Acronym Inc 620 Park Ave New York NY 10021-6591

TOBER, LESTER VICTOR, shoe company executive; b. St. Louis, Dec. 29, 1916; s. Abraham E.M. and Anna (Saifer) T.; m. Sylvia Isenburg, Aug. 4, 1940; children—Neil Steven, Robert Boyd, Cristie Elizabeth. B.S., U. Wis., 1935; postgrad., Washington U., 1936, U. Mo., 1936-39. Sec. Tober-Saifer Shoe Mfg. Co., St. Louis, 1955-65; v.p. Tober-Saifer Shoe Mfg. Co., 1966-68, exec. v.p., 1969-71, pres., 1974—; pres., chief exec. officer Tober Industries, Inc., 1977—. Active St. Louis Ambassadors, United Fund.; Trustee A.E. Tober Charitable Trust. Served to lt. (j.g.) USNR, 1944-46. Mem. Washington U. Eliot Soc., St. Louis Club, Mo. Athletic Club, Naples (Fla.) Pelican Bay Club, Hideaway Beach Club, Elks, Zeta Beta Tau. Republican. Jewish (pres. temple brotherhood 1957). Home: 19 Maryhill Dr Saint Louis MO 63124-1318 Office: Tober Industries Inc 1520 Washington Ave Saint Louis MO 63103-1817

TOBER, STEPHEN LLOYD, lawyer; b. Boston, May 27, 1949; s. Benjamin Arthur Tober and Lee (Hymoff) Fruman; m. Susan V. Schwartz, Dec. 22, 1973; children: Cary, Jamie. Grad., Syracuse U., 1971, JD, 1974. Bar: N.H. 1974, U.S. Dist. Ct. N.H. 1974, U.S. Supreme Ct. 1978, N.Y. 1981. Assoc. Flynn, McGuirk & Blanchard, Portsmouth, N.H., 1974-79; sole practice Portsmouth, 1979-81; ptnr. Aeschliman & Tober, Portsmouth, 1981-91; prin. Tober Law Offices, P.A., Portsmouth, 1992—; lectr. Franklin Pierce Law Ctr., Concord, N.H., 1978-80. Contbr. articles to law jours. Mem. Portsmouth Charter Commn., 1976, Portsmouth Planning Bd., 1977-81; del. N.H. Constl. Conv., Concord, 1984; city councilman, Portsmouth, 1977-81. Fellow ABA (mem. ho. dels.), Am. Bar Found., N.H. Bar Assn. (pres. 1988-89, chair com. to redraft code of profl. responsibility, Disting. Svc. award, 1986, 94); mem. ATLA (gov. 1980-86), N.H. Trial Lawyers Assn. (pres. 1977), New Eng. Bar Assn. (bd. dirs. 1988-91), Charles Doe Inns of Ct. Democrat. Jewish. Avocations: reading, tennis. Home: 55 T J Gamester Ave Portsmouth NH 03801-5871 Office: Tober Law Offices PA PO Box 1377 Portsmouth NH 03802-1377

TOBEY, ALTON STANLEY, artist; b. Middletown, Conn., Nov. 5, 1914; s. Saul Zilman and Rose (Aaronson) T.; m. Rosalyn S. Caplovitz, Sept. 24, 1950; children: David Seth, Judith Robin. BFA, Yale Sch. Fine Arts, 1937, MFA, 1946. Faculty mem. Yale Sch. of Fine Arts, New Haven, 1946-50, CCNY, N.Y.C., 1951-53; pvt. practice, 1953—; instr. Yale U. Sch. Fine Art, New Haven, City Coll., N.Y.C., 92nd St. Lexington Ave., YMHA, N.Y.C.,; now teaching privately, Larchmont, N.Y. One-man shows include Am. Ctr., Stockholm, Alliance Gallery, Copenhagen, Cape East Gallery, Provincetown, Mass., Pietrantonis Gallery, N.Y.C., Bridge Gallery, White Plains, N.Y., Burliuk Gallery, N.Y.C., Katonah (N.Y.) Gallery, Portrait Gallery, Westport, Conn., Charles Mann Gallery, N.Y.C., Casa de Aquarella, Mexico City, Alice Tully Hall, Lincoln Ctr., N.Y.C., Riverside Mus., N.Y.C., Westchester Art Soc., White Plains, N.Y., Bloomingdales, White Plains, N.Y., U. Pa., Trinity Coll., Yale Art Sch., Sarah Lawrence Coll., U. Maine; permanent collections include Met. Opera Gallery, Lincoln Ctr., N.Y., Norfolk (Va.) Mus., Mus. City of N.Y., Goshen (N.Y.) Hall of Fame, Hillandale Mus., Chadds Ford, Pa., Sea Air Space Mus., N.Y.C., Smithsonian Inst., Washington, West Point (N.Y.) Mus., MacArthur Meml., Norfolk, Va., Jewish Mus., N.Y.C., Tazewell (Va.) Mus.; limited editions include Royal Doulton Plates, London, Lucien Piccard, N.Y.C., Franklin (Pa.) Mint, Numa Ltd., Akron, Ohio; corporate collections include ABC-TV, N.Y.C., Chas. Pfizer Co., N.Y.C., Readers' Digest, Pleasantville, N.Y., Evyan Perfumes, N.Y.C., Ciba Geigy, Ardsley, N.Y., Am. Cyanamid, Bound Brook, N.J., Gen. Foods, White Plains, N.Y.; govt. and other collections include Dept. Commerce, Washington, Am. Machine & Foundry, White Plains, N.Y., Pres. Coun. on Physical Fitness & Sports, Washington, Yonkers (N.Y.) Profl. Hosp., Iona Coll., New Rochelle, N.Y., Am. Bureau of Shipping, N.Y.C., Nat. Acad., N.Y.C., St. Patrick's Cathedral, N.Y.C., St. Francis Hosp., Hartford, Conn., Elmira (N.Y.) Coll., Hofstra Coll., L.I., N.Y.; murals in public bldngs. throughout the U.S.; portraits include Albert Einstein, Pope John Paul II, Ronald Reagan, Robert Frost, Douglas MacArthur, J.F. and Robert Kennedy, Robert Merrill, E. Roland Harriman, Cardinal Cook, Golda Meir. Named Artist of the Year Westchester Council of Arts, 1987; recipient Honorary award Thornton Donovan Sch., 1989. Mem. Nat. Soc. Mural Painters (pres. emeritus 1985-89), Artists Equity N.Y. (pres. emeritus), Hudson River Contemporary Artists (pres. emeritus), Internat. Artists Assn. (v.p.), Mamaronick Artists Guild (pres. emeritus), Proto V, Abraxas, League of Present Day Artists, Fine Arts Fedn. Avocations: pre-Colombian archeology, history of art. Home and Office: 296 Murray Ave Larchmont NY 10538-1239

TOBEY, CARL WADSWORTH, retired publisher; b. Meriden, Conn., Nov. 18, 1923; s. Carl W. and Prudence (Wadsworth) T.; m. Charlotte Butterworth, Aug. 19, 1944; children: Peter Wadsworth, Carl Eric, Cheryl L. Ed., U.S. Mcht. Marine Acad. Regional sales mgr. Northeastern div. Dell Pub. Co., Inc., 1953-58; sales mgr. Dell Books, 1958-64, v.p. co., 1964-68, sr. v.p., 1968, exec. v.p., dir., 1968-76; pres. Dell Pub. Co. Inc., from 1976, chmn., 1981-83; ret., 1983; owner Greater Savannah Travel, Inc.;. With U.S. Mcht. Marine, 1943-46. Mem. Landing Club on Skidaway Island. Democrat. Congregationalist. Office: Greater Savannah Travel 12-D Bishops Ct Trustees Garden Savannah GA 31401

TOBIA, STEPHEN FRANCIS, JR., marketing professional, consultant; b. Bronx, N.Y., Jan. 14, 1955; s. Stephen Francis and Zelinda (Caruso) T.; m. Maureen Patricia Homan, Dec. 31, 1978; children: Michael, Marc. BA, U. Dayton, 1978; MA, Occidental Coll., L.A., 1980. Project mgr. L.A. C. of C., 1978-81; mgr. pub. affairs/communications Coca Cola Bottling Co., L.A., 1981-84, dir. pub. affairs, 1984; v.p. pub. affairs Beatrice Cos. Inc., L.A., 1984-86; pres. Pacific/West Communications, L.A., 1987—; mem. adv. com. Calif. Mus. Sci. & Industry, L.A., L.A. C. of C. Edn.; guest lectr. mktg. communications UCLA, 1989, 90; panelist Nat. Recycling Congress, 1990; speaker Inst. for Internat. Rsch., 1991, World Recycling Conf. and Expn., 1991. Mem. adv. com. Sch. Pub. Adminstrn., U. So. Calif., L.A., Focus on Youth; chmn. YMCA, East L.A.; bd. dirs. Big Bros. Greater L.A.; mem. Mayor Bradley's Edn. Adv. Com. Pub. Affairs fellow CORO Found., 1978-79. Mem. RecyCAL (founding chmn.), So. Calif. Business Men's Assn. (bd. dirs.), Calif./Nev. Soft Drink Assn. (bd. dirs.), Nat. Soft Drink Assn. (govt. rels. com.), L.A. Pub. Affairs Officer Assn., CORO Assn., Rotary. Office: Pacific/West Communications Group 3435 Wilshire Blvd Ste 2850 Los Angeles CA 90010-2014*

TOBIAS, ANDREW PREVIN, columnist, lecturer; b. N.Y.C., Apr. 20, 1947; s. Seth D. and Audrey J. (Landau) T. BA, Harvard U., 1968, MBA, 1972. Pres. Harvard Agys. Inc., Cambridge, Mass., 1967-68; v.p. Nat. Student Mktg. Corp., N.Y.C., 1969-70; contbg. editor N.Y. Mag., 1972-77, Esquire mag., 1977-83; columnist Playboy mag., 1982-86; contbr. Time mag., 1989—, Worth mag., 1995—. Author: The Funny Money Game, 1972, Fire and Ice, 1976, The Only Investment Guide You'll Ever Need, 1978, Getting by on $100,000 a Year and Other Sad Tales, 1980, The Invisible Bankers, 1982, Managing Your Money (software), 1984-94, Money Angles, 1984, The Only Other Investment Guide You'll Ever Need, 1987, Kids Say Don't Smoke, 1991, Auto Insurance Alert!, 1993. Recipient Gerald Loeb award, 1984, Consumer Fedn. of Am. Media Svc. award, 1993.

TOBIAS, BENJAMIN ALAN, portfolio manager, financial planner; b. Bklyn., June 4, 1951; s. Joseph M. and Alma Ruth (Schneider) T.; m. Barbara Anne Biller, July 31, 1977; children: Daniel, Rachel. BBA, CUNY, 1973. CPA, N.Y., Fla.; PFS. Sr. acct. Deloitte & Touche, N.Y.C., Miami, 1973-79; pres. Benjamin A. Tobias, P.A. d/b/a Tobias Fin. Advisors, Pembroke Pines, Fla., 1980—; adj. prof. Rollins Coll., 1996—. Author weekly newspaper column, Sun Newspapers, 1988-89. Mem. AICPAs, Fla. Inst. CPAs (com. on personal and fin. planning 1989-90, 91), Gold Coast Soc. Cert. Fin. Planners (v.p. comm. 1989-90), South Fla. Cert. Fin. Planners (pres. 1992-93, chmn. 1993-94), Inst. Cert. Fin. Planners (mem. nat. com. 1994-95), Rotary (Pembroke Pines chpt., pres. 1986-87). Office: Tobias Fin Advisors 10081 Pines Blvd Ste E-1 Pembroke Pines FL 33024-6171

TOBIAS, CHARLES HARRISON, JR., lawyer; b. Cin., Apr. 16, 1921; s. Charles Harrison and Charlotte (Westheimer) T.; m. Mary J. Kaufman, June 15, 1946; children—Jean M., Thomas Charles, Robert Charles. B.A. cum laude, Harvard U., 1943, LL.B., 1949. Bar: Ohio 1949. Assoc. firm Steer, Strauss and Adair, Cin., 1949-56; ptnr. firm Steer, Strauss, White and Tobias, Cin., 1956-90; mem. Kepley MacConnell & Eyrich, Cin., 1990-93; conf. atty. U.S. Ct. Appeals (6th crct.) Ohio, Cin., 1993—. Bd. dirs. Cin. City Charter Com., 1955-75; mem. Wyoming (Ohio) City Council, 1972-77, vice mayor, 1974-77; bd. govs., sec., past chmn. Cin. Overseers, Hebrew Union Coll.-Jewish Inst. Religion; pres. Met. Area Religious Coalition of Cin., 1977-80, Jewish Fedn. Cin., 1972-74; mem. nat. bd. govs. Am. Jewish Com., 1981-87. With USN, 1943-46. Mem. Cin. Bar Assn., Losantiville Country Club. Home: 1201 Edgecliff Pl Unit 1001 Cincinnati OH 45206 Office: US Ct Appeals Potter Stewart US Courthse 5th and Walnut St Cincinnati OH 45202

TOBIAS, JULIUS, sculptor; b. N.Y.C., Aug. 27, 1915; s. Louis and Anna (Tabachnick) T.; m. Suzanne Tobias. Student, Atelier Fernand Leger, Paris, 1949-52. Pvt. tchr., 1950-63; tchr. Morris Davidson Sch. Modern Painting, 1947-48; instr. N.Y. Inst. Tech., 1966-70; lectr. Rutgers U., Queens Coll., N.Y.C., 1966-67, Ind. U., Bloomington, 1974. One-man shows include Esther Stuttman Gallery, 1959, Bleecker Gallery, 1961, Easthampton Gallery, 1962, 10 Downtown, 1968, Max Hutchinson Gallery, 1970, 71, 72, Alessandra Gallery, 1976, 55 Mercer St. Gallery, 1976, 77, 78, 80, all N.Y.C., Zriny-Hayes Gallery, Chgo., 1979, B4A Gallery, N.Y.C., 1991, The SUNY, Stony Brook, 1992, Artemisia Gallery, Chgo., 1992, Galerie Art In, Nürnberg, Germany, 1994, 96; group shows include, Provincetown (Mass.) Art Assn., 1946, Roko Gallery, N.Y.C., 1946, Camino Gallery, N.Y.C., 1957, Polari Gallery, Woodstock, N.Y., 1957, Art USA, Coliseum, N.Y.C., 1957, Brata Gallery, N.Y.C., 1957-59, Pa. Acad. Fine Arts, 1958, Gallery Creuze, Paris, 1958, Knoedler Gallery, N.Y.C., 1959, Mus. Modern Art, traveling exhbn. in Tokyo, 1959, New Eng. Exhbn., Silvermine, Conn., 1960, De Aenlle Gallery, N.Y.C., 1961, Bleecker Gallery, N.Y.C., 1962, Staten Island Mus., N.Y.C., 1962, Allan Stone Gallery, N.Y.C., 1962, Easthampton Gallery, N.Y.C., 1962-66, Windham Coll., Putney, Vt., 1963, Rutgers U., 1966, Park Pl. Gallery, N.Y.C., 1967, Tibor Dinagy Gallery, N.Y.C., 1968, Whitney Mus. Annual, N.Y.C., 1968, Parker St. 470, Boston, 1969, Everson Mus., Syracuse, N.Y., 1972, Hunter Gallery, N.Y.C., 1981, Art Park, Lewiston, N.Y., 1981, Jan Weiss Gallery, N.Y.C., 1990, Munson-Williams-Proctor Inst., Utica, N.Y., 1995, numerous others; represented in numerous collections, Europe, N. and S.Am., also pvt. collections. Served to 1st lt. USAAF, 1942-45. Decorated D.F.C., Air medal with 3 oak leaf clusters; grantee Nat. Endowment for Arts, 1975, 81, N.Y. Coun. Found., 1971-78, Adolf and Esther Gottlieb Found., 1980, The Penny McCall Found., 1988; Guggenheim fellow, 1972-73, 78-79, N.Y. Found. for Arts fellow, 1986; recipient Oscar Williams and Gene Derwood award, 1989, award Adolph and Esther Gottlieb Found., 1991, 96, The Pollock-Krasner Found., 1991, Teh Richard A. Florsheim Art Fund. Address: 9 Great Jones St New York NY 10012-1128

TOBIAS, KAL, transportation executive; b. Bklyn., Feb. 1, 1946; m. Karen Liberty, Mar. 11, 1967; children: Kristopher, Kirk. BA, CUNY, Bklyn., 1967. Mgr. dealer devel. Volkswagon Can., Toronto, Ont., 1967-72; pres. cons. firm Toronto, Ont., Can., 1972-78; v.p. Burmah Oil Group, Toronto, Ont., Can., 1978-83; pres., C.E.O. DHL Internat. Express Ltd., Toronto, Ont., Can., 1983—, also bd. dirs., 1983—; bd. dirs DHL Customs Brokerage, Toronto, 1983—, Skyhawk Trans., Toronto, 1988—, Can. Courier Assn., pres.. 1987—, C.E.O., 1987—. Office: DHL Internat Express Ltd, 6205 Airport Rd Ste 400, Mississauga, ON Canada L4V 1E1

TOBIAS, PAUL HENRY, lawyer; b. Cin., Jan. 5, 1930; s. Charles H. and Charlotte (Westheimer) T.; 1 child, Eliza L. AB magna cum laude, Harvard U., 1951, LLB, 1958. Bar: Mass. 1958, Ohio 1962. Assoc. Stoneman & Chandler, Boston, 1958-61, Goldman & Putnick, Cin., 1962-75; ptnr. Tobias, Kraus and Torchia, Cin., 1976—; instr. U. Cin. Law Sch., 1975-77. Author: Litigating Wrongful Discharge Claims, 1987; contbr. articles to profl. jours. Mem. Cin. Bd. of Park Commrs., 1973-81, Cin. Human Rels. Commn., 1980-84, Cin. Hist. Conservation Bd., 1990-91. With U.S. Army, 1952-54. Mem. ABA, Nat. Employment Lawyers Assn. (founder), Nat. Employee Rights Inst. (chmn.), Ohio State Bar Assn., Cin. Bar Assn. (past chmn. legal aid com.), Phi Beta Kappa. Home: 15 Hill And Hollow Ln Cincinnati OH 45208-3317 Office: Tobias Kraus Torchia 911 Mercantile Libr Bldg Cincinnati OH 45202

TOBIAS, RANDALL L., pharmaceutical company executive; b. Lafayette, Ind., Mar. 20, 1942; m. Marilyn Jane Salyer, Sept. 2, 1966 (dec. May 1994); children: Paige Noelle, Todd Christopher; m. Marianne Williams, July 15, 1995; stepchildren: James Russell Ullyot, Kathryn Lee Ullyot. BS in Mktg., Ind. U., 1964; LLD (hon.), Galuedette U. Numerous positions Ind. Bell, 1964-77, Ill. Bell, 1977-81; v.p. residence mktg. sales and service AT&T, 1981-82, pres. Am. Bell Consumer Products, 1983, pres. Consumer Products, 1983-84, sr. v.p., 1984-85; chmn., CEO AT&T Comm., N.Y.C., 1985-91, AT&T Internat., Basking Ridge, N.J., 1991-93; vice chmn. bd. AT&T, N.Y.C., 1986-93; chmn., CEO Eli Lilly & Co., Indpls., 1993—; bd. dirs. Eli Lilly & Co., Kimberly-Clark, Knight-Ridder, Phillips Petroleum; active U.S.-Japan Bus. Coun., U.S.-China Bus. Coun., Indpls. Cmty. Leaders Allied for Superior Schs. Trustee Duke U.; vice chmn. Colonial Williamsburg Found.; bd. govs. Skyline Club, Indpls. Mus. Art; bd. dirs. Indpls. Symphony Orch., Ind. U. Found., Econ. Club Indpls., Indpls. Conv. and Visitors Assn.; mem. Nat. Mus. Women in Arts, Bus. Coun. Indpls. Cmty. leaders Alliance Superior Schs., U.S.-China Bus. Coun. Mem. Coun. Fgn. Rels., Indpls. Conv. and Visitors Assn. (bd. dirs.), Nat. Mus. Women in Arts, Bus. Roundtable, Meridian Hills Country Club (Indpls.), Woodstock Club, Amwell Valley Conservancy, Theta Chi. Avocations: skiing, fly fishing, shooting. Office: Eli Lilly & Co Lilly Corp Ctr Indianapolis IN 46285

TOBIAS, ROBERT MAX, labor leader, lawyer; b. Detroit, Aug. 4, 1943. BA, U. Mich., 1965, MBA, 1968; JD, George Washington U., 1969. Lawyer Nat. Treasury Employees Union, Washington, 1968-70, gen. counsel, 1970-79, exec. v.p. and gen. counsel, 1979-83, pres., 1983—; lectr. George Washington U. Law Sch., Washington, 1970-90. Contbr. articles to law revs. Sec., treas. Fed. Employee Edn. and Asst. Fund, Washington, 1986. Mem. ABA, Soc. for Labor Relations Profls. (1st Annual Union Leader award, 1987), Fed. Bar Assn., D.C. Bar Assn., Am. Arbitration Assn. (bd. dirs.).

Democrat. Episcopalian. Office: Nat Treasury Employees Union 901 E St NW Ste 600 Washington DC 20004-2037

TOBIAS, THOMAS NELSON, JR., elementary school educator; b. July 22, 1932; s. Thomas N. Sr. and Mary A. (Hanton) T.; m. Kathleen A. Black, May 28, 1964; 1 child, Amy. BA, Ea. Mich. U., 1965, MA, 1966; postgrad., Mich. State U., U. Nev. Cert. elem./secondary tchr., Mich. Tchr. Ypsilanti (Mich.) Pub. Schs., 1965—; vis. lectr. Ea. Mich. U., Ypsilanti, 1980-90; mem. edit. bd. Scholastic Pub. Co., N.Y.C. Cartoonist, Mich. Reading Jours.; author teaching materials. Vice pres. Ypsilanti Hist. Soc.; bd. dirs. Ypsilanti Heritage Found. With USAF, 1951-55. Recipient Outstanding Alumnus award Ea. Mich. U., 1985. Mem. Ypsilanti Edn. Assn. (past pres.). Office: Ypsilanti Sch Dist 1885 Packard Rd Ypsilanti MI 48197

TOBIN, BENTLEY, lawyer; b. Bklyn., N.Y., Feb. 8, 1924; s. Nathan H. and Mildred E. (Aronoff) T.; m. Nancy Gurvitz, Sept. 13, 1947; children—Patricia E., Mitchell H.; m. 2d, Beverly Ann Mucciarone, Feb. 17, 1979. B.S., CCNY, 1943; LL.B., Harvard U., 1948. Bar: N.Y. 1948, Mass. 1951, R.I. 1952. Atty. N.Y.C. Housing Authority, 1948-49; ptnr. Titiev, Greenman & Tobin, Boston, 1949-52; sr. ptnr. Tobin & Silverstein, Inc., Providence, 1952-84; ptnr. Hinckley, Allen, Tobin & Silverstein, 1984-87, Hinckley, Allen, Comen, 1987-92, Hinckley, Allen & Snyder, 1992—; chmn. bd. Landmark Health Systems, Inc. Served in USAR, 1943-46. Mem. ABA, R.I. Bar Assn., Woonsocket Bar Assn. Office: Hinckley Allen Snyder 1500 Fleet Ctr Providence RI 02903 Also: Landmark Health Systems Inc 115 Cass Ave Woonsocket RI 02895-4705

TOBIN, BRIAN, Canadian government official; b. Stephenville, Nfld., Can., Oct. 21, 1954; s. Patrick Vincent and Florence Mary (Frye) T.; m. Jodean Smith; children: Heather Elizabeth, Adam Vincent, John Joseph. Student, Meml. U. Nfld. Mem. parliament for Humber-St. Barbe-Baie Verte Ho. Commons, Can., 1980, parliamentary sec. to Min. Fisheries and Oceans, 1980-93, Min. Fisheries and Oceans, 1993-96, vice chair com. on regional devel., mem. transport, fisheries and forestry, labour, emnployment and immigration, constl. coms., spl. com. on employment opportunities for 1980s; premier Newfoundland, 1996—; past exec. asst. to Liberal leader Liberal Party Nfld. and Labrador; opposition MP; critic for forestry, employment, regional industrial expansion, privatization; critic, assoc. critic transport. Electrd chair Nat. Liberal Caucus, 1989, mem. Liberal nat. campaign, nat. platform coms. 1993. *

TOBIN, CALVIN JAY, architect; b. Boston, Feb. 15, 1927; s. David and Bertha (Tanfield) T.; m. Joan Hope Fink, July 15, 1951; children—Michael Alan, Nancy Ann. B.Arch., U. Mich., 1949. Designer, draftsman Arlen & Lowenfish (architects), N.Y.C., 1949-51; with Samuel Arlen, N.Y.C., 1951-53, Skidmore, Owings & Merrill, N.Y.C., 1953; architect Loebl, Schlossman & Bennett (architects), Chgo., 1953-57, v.p., 1953-57; v.p. Loebl, Schlossman & Hackl, 1957—; Chmn. Jewish United Fund Bldg. Trades Div., 1969; chmn. AIA and Chgo. Hosp. Council Com. of Hosp. Architecture, 1968-76. Archtl. works include Michael Reese Hosp. and Med. Ctr., 1954—, Prairie Shores Apt. Urban Redevel., 1957-62, Louis A. Weiss Meml. Hosp., Chgo., Chgo. State Hosp., Ctrl. Cmty. Hosp., Chgo., Gottlieb Meml. Hosp., Melrose Park, Ill., West Suburban Hosp., Oak Park, Ill., Thorek Hosp. and Med. Ctr., Chgo., Water Power Pl., Chgo., Christ Hosp., Oak Lawn, Greater Balt. Med. Ctr., Shriners Hosp. for Crippled Children, Chgo. Hinsdale (Ill.) Hosp., South Chgo. Cmty. Hosp., Chgo., Mt. Sinai Med. Ctr., Chgo., Alexian Bros. Med. Ctr., Elk Grove Village, Ill., Luth. Gen. Hosp., Park Ridge, Ill., Evanston (Ill.) Hosp., Resurrection Med. Ctr., Chgo., New Cook County Hosp., Chgo., also numerous apt., comml. and cmty. bldgs. Chmn. Highland Park (Ill.) Appearance Rev. Commn., 1972-73; mem. Highland Park Plan Commn., 1973-79; mem. Highland Park City Coun., 1974-89, mayor pro-tem, 1979-89; mem. Highland Park Environ. Control Commn., 1979-84, Highland Park Hist. Preservation Commn., 1982-89; bd. dirs. Highland Park Hist. Soc., Young Men's Jewish Coun., 1953-67, pres., 1967; bd. dirs. Jewish Community Ctrs. Chgo., 1973-78, bd. dirs., 1989-93; Ill. Coun. Against Handgun Violence, 1989-94; trustee Ravinia Festival Assn., 1990—. With USNR, 1945-46. Fellow AIA (2d v.p. Chgo. chpt.); mem. U. Mich. Alumni Soc. Coll. Architecture and Urban Planning (bd. govs. 1989-95), U. Mich. Alumni Assn. (bd. govs. 1990-95, v.p. 1993-95), Std. Club, Ravinia Green Country Club, Pi Lambda Phi. Jewish. Home: 814 Dean Ave Highland Park IL 60035-4749 Office: Loebl Schlossman & Hackl 130 E Randolph St Chicago IL 60601

TOBIN, CRAIG DANIEL, lawyer; b. Chgo., Aug. 17, 1954; s. Thomas Arthur and Lois (O'Connor) T. BA with honors, U. Ill., 1976; JD with high honors, Ill. Inst. Tech., 1980. Bar: Ill. 1980, U.S. Dist. Ct. (no. dist.) Ill. 1980, U.S. Dist. Ct. (no. dist.) Ind. 1986, U.S. Ct. Appeals (7th cir.) 1986, U.S. Supreme Ct. 1987. Trial atty. Cook County Pub. Defender, Chgo., 1980-82; trial atty. homicide task force Pub. Defender, Chgo., 1982-84; ptnr. Craig D. Tobin and Assocs., Chgo., 1984—; lectr. Ill. Inst. for Continuing Legal Edn., Cook County Pub. Defender, Chgo., 1983, 92, Ill. Pub. Defender Assn., 1987; instr. Nat. Inst. Trial Advocacy. Named One of Outstanding Young Men in Am., 1985. Mem. ABA, Chgo. Bar Assn., Nat. Assn. Criminal Def. Lawyers. Roman Catholic. Office: Craig D Tobin & Assocs 3 First National Plz Chicago IL 60602

TOBIN, DENNIS MICHAEL, lawyer; b. Chgo., June 3, 1948; s. Thomas Arthur and Lois (O'Connor) T.; m. Sue Wynn Henslee, June 14, 1969 (div. 1977); m. Karen Thompson, Oct. 11, 1980; children: Kyle James, Daniel Patrick. BA with honors, U. Ill., 1971; JD, Loyola U., Chgo., 1976. Bar: Ill 1976, Wis. 1989, U.S. Dist. Ct (no. dist.) Ill. 1976, U.S. Ct. Appeals (7th cir.) 1985, U.S. Supreme Ct. 1985. Trial atty. Cook County Homicide Task Force, Chgo., 1976-84; prin. Dennis M. Tobin & Assocs., Chgo., 1984—; gen. counsel Forest Health Systems and Found., Ill., Miss., Hawaii, 1986—, Manages Behavioral Care Inc., Psychiat. Ins. Co. Am. Dir. Forest Health Systems Found.; mem. Chgo. Coun. on Fgn. Rels. Mem. ABA (forum on health law), Chgo. Bar Assn. (com. on health law), Am. Soc. Law and Medicine, Ill. Assn. Criminal Def. Attys. (v.p. 1984-87), Ill. Attys. for Criminal Justice, Wis. Bar Assn., Ill. Assn. Hosp. Attys., Nat. Health Lawyers Assn., U.S. Sporting Clays Assn., Nat. Sporting Clays Assn., Gateway Gun Club. Roman Catholic. Office: Dennis M Tobin and Assocs 18-3 Dundee Rd Barrington IL 60010

TOBIN, EUGENE MARC, academic administrator; b. Newark, Mar. 23, 1947; s. Hyman and Clara (Pekersky) T.; m. Beverly Stethem Gehm, May 26, 1979; children: David Gehm, Leslie. BA in History, Rutgers U., 1968; MA in History Am. Civilization, Brandeis U., 1970, PhD in History of Am. Civilization, 1972; LLD (hon.), Hamilton Coll., 1994. Vis. instr. history Jersey City State Coll., N.J., 1972-74; vis. asst. prof. Kutztown (Pa.) State Coll., 1975-76; NEH postdoctoral fellow Vanderbilt U., Nashville, 1976-77; vis. asst. prof. Miami U., Oxford, Ohio, 1977-79, Indiana U., Bloomington, 1979-80; asst. prof. history Hamilton Coll., Clinton, N.Y., 1980-83, assoc. prof. history, 1983-88, prof. history, 1988—, dir. Am. studies program, 1983-88, chair dept. history, 1986-88, acting dean coll., 1988, dean faculty, 1989-93, pres., 1993—. Author: The Age of Urban Reform: New Perspectives on the Progressive Era, 1977, Organize or Perish: America's Independent Progressives, 1986, The National Lawyers Guild: From Roosevelt Through Reagan, 1988; contbr. articles to profl. jours: presenter numerous papers at profl. confs. With USAR, 1968-74. Recipient William Adee Whitehead award N.J. Hist. Soc., 1976; NDEA fellow, 1968-70, Rsch. grantee Am. Philos. Soc., 1978-79, 1982-83, and recipient of numerous other grants. Mem. Am. Hist. Assn., Orgn. Am. Historians. Home: 11 College Hill Rd Clinton NY 13323 Office: Hamilton Coll 198 College Hill Rd Clinton NY 13323

TOBIN, GARY A., cultural organization administrator. PhD in City and Regional Planning, U. Calif., Berkeley. Dir. Maurice and Marilyn Cohen Ctr. for Modern Jewish Studies, Waltham, Mass., Inst. Cmty. and Religion, San Francisco; rsch. on synagogue affiliation, youth programs in Jewish Cmty. Ctrs. and Jewish Family Founds. Author: Jewish Perceptions of Antisemitism, Philanthropy in the Modern Jewish Community, 1995, Church and Synagogue Affiliation. Office: Brandeis U Cohen Ctr Modern Jewish Studies Waltham MA 02254*

TOBIN, JAMES, economics educator; b. Champaign, Ill., Mar. 5, 1918; s. Louis Michael and Margaret (Edgerton) T.; m. Elizabeth Fay Ringo, Sept. 14, 1946; children: Margaret Ringo, Louis Michael, Hugh Ringo, Roger Gill. AB summa cum laude, Harvard U., 1939, MA, 1940, PhD, 1947, LLD, 1995; LLD (hon.), Syracuse U., 1967, U. Ill., 1969, Dartmouth Coll., 1970, Swarthmore Coll., 1980, New Sch. Social Research, 1982, NYU, 1982, Bates Coll., 1982, U. Hartford, 1984, Colgate U., 1984, Gustavus Adolphus Coll., 1986, Western Md. Coll., 1984, U. New Haven, 1986; Harvard U., 1995; D in Econs. (hon.), New U. Lisbon, 1980; D in Econs. (hon.), Athens U. Econ. & Bus., 1992; D in Econs. (hon.), Athens U. of Econ. and Bus., 1992; LHD (hon.), Hofstra U., 1983, Sacred Heart U., 1990; Bard Coll., 1995; D in Social Scis. honoris causa, U. Helsinki, 1986. Assoc. economist OPA, WPB, Washington, 1941-42; teaching fellow econs. Harvard U., Cambridge, Mass., 1946-47, with Soc. Fellows, 1947-50; assoc. prof. econs. Yale U., New Haven, 1950-55, prof., 1955—, Sterling prof. econs., 1957-88, prof. emeritus, 1988—; mem. Council Econ. Advisers, 1961-62, Nat. Acad. Scis. Author: National Economic Policy, 1966, Essays in Economics-Macroeconomics, vol. 1, 1972, The New Economics One Decade Older, 1974, Consumption and Econometrics, vol. 2, 1975, Asset Accumulation and Economic Activity, 1980, Theory and Policy, vol. 3, 1982, Policies for Prosperity, 1987; co-author: Two Revolutions in Economic Policy, 1987, National and International, 1996, Full Employment and Growth, 1966, Money, Credit, and Capital, 1996. Served to lt. USNR, 1942-46. Recipient Nobel prize in econs., 1981; Social Sci. Research Council faculty fellow, 1951-54; Grand cordon Order of the Sacred Treasure, Japan, 1988; Centennial medal Harvard Grad. Sch., 1989. Fellow Am. Acad. Arts and Scis., Econometric Soc. (pres. 1958), Am. Statis. Assn., Brit. Acad. (corr.); mem. Am. Philos. Soc., Am. Econ. Assn. (John Bates Clark medal 1955, v.p. 1964, pres. 1971), Acad. Scis. Portugal (fgn. assoc.), Phi Beta Kappa. Home: 117 Alden Ave New Haven CT 06515-2109 Office: Yale U Dept Econs Box 208281 New Haven CT 06520-8281

TOBIN, JAMES MICHAEL, lawyer; b. Santa Monica, Calif., Sept. 27, 1948; s. James Joseph and Glada Marie (Meisner) T.; m. Kathleen Marie Espy, Sept. 14, 1985. BA with honors, U. Calif., Riverside, 1970; JD, Georgetown U., 1974. Bar: Calif. 1974, Mich. 1987. From atty. to gen. atty. So. Pacific Co., San Francisco, 1975-82; v.p. regulatory affairs So. Pacific Communications Co., Washington, 1982-83; v.p., gen. counsel Lexitel Corp., Washington, 1983-85; v.p., gen. counsel, sec. ALC Communications Corp., Birmingham, Mich., 1985-87, sr. v.p., gen. counsel, sec., 1987-88; of counsel Morrison & Foerster, San Francisco, 1988-90, ptnr., 1990—. Mem. ABA, Calif. Bar Assn., Mich. Bar Assn., Fed. Communications Bar Assn. Republican. Unitarian. Avocations: innkeeper (DeHaven Valley Farm, Westport, Calif.), carpentry, travel. Home: 2739 Octavia St San Francisco CA 94123-4303 Office: Morrison & Foerster 345 California St San Francisco CA 94104-2635

TOBIN, JAMES ROBERT, biotechnology company executive; b. Lima, Ohio, Aug. 12, 1944; s. J. Robert and Doris L. (Hunt) T.; m. Janet Trafton, Dec. 30, 1971; children: James Robert III, Amanda Trafton. BA in Govt., Harvard U., 1966, MBA, 1968. Fin. analyst Baxter Internat., Inc., Deerfield, Ill., 1972-73, internat. contr., 1973-75; mng. dir. Japan Baxter Internat., Inc., Tokyo, 1975-77; mng. dir. Spain Baxter Internat., Inc., Valencia, 1977-80; pres. IV Sys. Divsn. Baxter Internat. Inc., Deerfield, 1981-84; group v.p. Baxter Internat., Inc., Deerfield, 1984-88, exec. v.p., 1988-92, pres., COO, 1992-94; pres., COO Biogen, 1994—; also bd. dirs.; bd. dirs. Medisense, Creative Biomolecules, Genovo. Lt. USN, 1968-72. Republican. Home: 12 Briarwood Ln Lincolnshire IL 60069-2500 Office: Biogen Inc 14 Cambridge Ctr Cambridge MA 02142-1401

TOBIN, JOAN ADELE, writer; b. N.Y.C., Nov. 24, 1930; d. William and Helen (Steinis) Butler; m. Oct. 15, 1950; children: Patricia, Michael, Eileen. Freelance editor Suffield, Conn., 1980-85; owner, pub. Paper Works, Suffield, Conn., 1984-92. Contbr. over 80 articles to Internat. Mensa Jour., OWL Nat. News, N.Y. Times, N.Y. Mensa, and others. Mem. Am. Mensa, NOW, Universalist-Unitarian Womens Fedn., Writers Group Mensa. Home: 32 Harmon Dr Suffield CT 06078-2062

TOBIN, JOHN EVERARD, retired lawyer; b. Utica, N.Y., Sept. 28, 1923; s. Michael and Julia Theresa (O'Brien) T.; m. Margaret T. Swope, June 17, 1944; children: John E. Jr., Catherine J. (dec.), Brian D., Paul C. A.B., Hamilton Coll., 1947; LL.B., Columbia U., 1950. Bar: N.Y. 1950, U.S. Supreme Ct. 1966. Practiced law N.Y.C., 1950-94; assoc. Donovan, Leisure, Newton & Irvine, 1950-59, ptnr., 1959-84; ptnr. Dorsey & Whitney, 1984-94; chief counsel subcom. administrn. internal revenue laws, ways and means com. U.S. Ho. of Reps., 1952-53; dir. Alleghany Corp. Bd. dirs. Legal Aid Soc., N.Y., 1979-85; trustee Hamilton Coll., 1974—; mem. exec. com. Lawyers Com. for Civil Rights under Law. 1st lt. USAF, 1942-46. Mem. Assn. of Bar of City of N.Y., Am. Judicature Soc., Century Assn. (N.Y.C.). Home: 100 Ackerman Ave Ho Ho Kus NJ 07423-1039

TOBIN, LOIS MOORE, home economist, educator, retired; b. Johnstown, Pa., Oct. 8, 1928; d. William B and Ida L. (Diehl) Moore; m. Warner E. Tobin, June 7, 1953 (dec.); children: Brian W., Robert E. BS, Ind. (Pa.) State Tchrs. Coll., 1951; postgrad., U. Pitts., 1952, U. Colo., 1953; MEd, Pa. State U., 1967; postgrad., Ind. U. of Pa., 1977-85. Tchr. Allegheny Valley Joint Sch. Dist., Springdale, Pa., 1951-53, Kittanning (Pa.) Sch. Dist., 1953-55, Carlisle (Pa.) Joint Sch. Dist., 1964-66, State Coll. (Pa.) Sch. Dist., 1967-73; mem. faculty Dept. Food/Nut Ind. U. of Pa., 1974, 76-77, mem. faculty Home Econs. Edn., 1979-82, coord. Single Parent-Homemaker Svc. Ctr. Vocat. Pers. Prep., 1984-91; mem. adv. com. Ind. Area Vocat.-Tech. Sch., 1981—; presenter Pa. Vocat. Edn. Conf., Seven Springs, 1985, Lancaster, 1991., treas. Pa. Home economics assn.1976-78., sec. Pa. Vac. Home Economics Edn. Assn.,1989-91. Author: (booklet) Home Economics Education Bibliography on Special Needs, 1982, Teaching Special Needs Individuals in Home Economics, 1982; contbr. articles to profl. newsletters. Sec. Ind. County Human Svcs. Coun., 1990-91; vol. Bloodmobile, 1986—; tour guide Breezedale Restoration, 1986—; pres. Calvary Ch. Women's Club, 1975-76, Ind. County Newcomer's Club, 1974, 75; elder Presbyn. Ch. Grantee Dept. Edn. Bur. of Vocat. Edn., 1980-82, 86-91, Human Svcs. Devel. Fund, 1989-91. Mem. Am. Vocat. Assn., Pa. Vocat. Assn., Nat. Trust for Hist. Preservation, Ind. County Hist. and Geneal. Soc. Avocations: swimming, travel, church choir. Home: 896 White Farm Rd Indiana PA 15701-1254

TOBIN, MICHAEL EDWARD, banker; b. Newtown Square, Pa., Jan. 17, 1926; s. Michael Joseph and Emma (Roberts) T.; m. Judith Anne Brown; children: Michael E., Allegra, Corey. B.S. in Econs, U. Pa., 1948. Cons. Philco, RCA, Ebasco Services, Inc., 1950-56; sr. cons. Arthur Young & Co., N.Y.C., 1956-59; midwest dir. cons. svcs. Arthur Young & Co., Chgo., 1959-68; pres. Midwest Stock Exch., Chgo., 1968-78; pres. Am. Nat. Bank & Trust Co., Chgo., 1978, chmn. bd., chief exec. officer, 1979-90, chmn. bd., 1990-91, ret. Served with U.S. Army, World War II, ETO.

TOBIN, PAUL EDWARD, JR., naval officer; b. Detroit, Oct. 24, 1940; s. Paul Edward and Mary Margaret (Atkinson) T.; m. Lynne Dawson Carter, June 12, 1963; children: Mary Elizabeth, Patricia Carter. BS in Naval Sci., U.S. Naval Acad., 1963; MS in Computer Sys., U.S. Naval Postgrad. Sch., 1969. Commd. ensign USN, 1963, advanced through grades to rear adm., 1988; commdg. officer USS Tattnall (DDG-19), 1979-81, USS Fox (CG-33), 1984-86; chief engr. USS Forrestal (CV-59), 1986-88; commdg. officer Surface Warfare Officers Sch., 1986-88; dir. USN Info. Sys. Mgmt., 1988-90; commdr. Western Pacific USN Info. Sys., Subic Bay, The Philippines, 1990-92; asst. chief naval pers. USN, Washington, 1992-94; vice commdr. naval edn. and tng. USN, Pensacola, Fla., 1994—. Decorated D.S.M., Legion of Merit (3). Mem. U.S. Naval Inst., Surface Navy Assn., Army Navy Country Club. Presbyterian. Avocations: classical music, running, computers, boating. Home: Quarters 4 North Ave Pensacola FL 32508 Office: CNET 250 Dallas St Pensacola FL 32508-5218*

TOBIN, ROBERT G., supermarket chain executive; b. 1938. With Stop & Shop Supermarket Co., 1960—, pres., COO, 1989-93; pres., COO Stop & Shop Cos., Braintree, Mass., 1993—, chmn., 1995—. Office: Stop & Stop Cos Inc 1385 Hancock St Quincy MA 02169

TOBIN, THOMAS F., lawyer; b. Chgo., Apr. 12, 1929. BSS, John Carroll U., 1951; JD, Loyola U., 1954. Bar: Ill. 1954. Ptnr. Connelly & Schroeder, Chgo. Office: Connelly & Schroeder 1 North Franklin Ste 1200 Chicago IL 60606

TOBIN, WILLIAM THOMAS, retail executive; b. Cleve., May 31, 1931; s. Paul William and Ellen Louise (Fenlon) T.; m. Mary Ellen Fawcett, May 22, 1976; children: William Thomas, Bradford Fenlon. B.A., Yale U., 1949-53. With M. O'Neil Co., Akron, Ohio, 1953-73; exec. v.p. M. O'Neil Co., 1973-75, pres., 1975-79; pres., chief exec. officer Kaufmann's, Pitts., 1979—. Mem. Yale Club (N.Y.C.), Portage Country Club, Rolling Rock Club, Duquesne Club, Fox Chapel Golf Club, Laurel Valley Golf Club, Pittsburgh Golf Club, Rivers Club. Office: Kaufmann's 400 5th Ave Pittsburgh PA 15219-1713

TOBIS, JEROME SANFORD, physician; b. Syracuse, N.Y., July 23, 1915; s. David George and Anna (Feinberg) T.; m. Hazel Weisbard, Sept. 18, 1938; children: David, Heather, Jonathan. B.S., CCNY, 1936; M.D., Chgo. Med. Sch., 1943. Diplomate: Am. Bd. Phys. Medicine and Rehab. Intern Knickerbocker Hosp., 1943-44; resident Bronx VA Hosp., 1946-48; med. dir. state fever therapy unit USPHS, Brookhaven, Miss., 1944-46; practice medicine N.Y.C., 1948-70; prof. dir. dept. phys. medicine and rehab. N.Y. Med. Coll., Flower and Fifth Av. Hosps., 1948-61; prof. rehab. medicine Albert Einstein Coll. of Medicine, 1963-70; chief div. rehab. medicine Montefiore Hosp., 1961-70; dir. vis. physician Met., Bird S. Coler hosps., 1952-61; prof., chmn. dept. phys. medicine and rehab. Calif. Coll. Medicine, U. Calif. at Irvine, 1970-82, prof., dir. program in geriatric medicine and gerontology, 1980-86; mem. adv. com. Acad. Geriatric Resource program, 1984-86, 95—; mem. expert med. com. Am. Rehab. Found., 1961-70; cons. Dept. Health, N.Y.C., Long Beach VA Hosp., 1970—, Fairview State Devel. Ctr., 1976—; mem. adv. coun. phys. medicine and rehab. for appeals com. Calif. Med. Assn., 1971-74, adv. com. U. Calif. Acad. Geriatric Resource Program, 1995—; NIH Internat. Fogarty fellow, hon. lectr., dept. geriatric medicine U. Birmingham, 1979-80; chair ethics com. U. Calif.-Irvine Med. Ctr., 1986—. Mem. editorial bd.: Heart and Lung, 1973-76, Geriatrics, 1975-80, Archives of Phys. Medicine and Rehab, 1958-73. Named Physician of the Year, 1957; recipient Distinguished Alumnus award Chgo. Med. Sch., 1972, Acad. award Nat. Inst. on Aging, 1981-86; named hon. faculty mem. Calif. Zeta chpt. Alpha Omega Alpha, 1981; Leavitt Meml. lectureship Baylor Coll. Medicine, 1983, Griffith Meml. lectureship Am. Geriatric Soc., 1984; Australian Coll. Rehabilitation Medicine, 1984; Jerome S. Tobis Ann. Conf. on Geriatric Medicine established in his name, U. Calif. at Irvine, 1986. Fellow ACP, Am. Coll. Cardiology; mem. AMA (mem. residency rev. com. Coun. Med. Edn. 1973), AAAS, Am. Acad. Cerebral Palsy, Am. Acad. Phys. Medicine and Rehab. (Disting. Clinician award 1993), Am. Congress Rehab. Medicine (pres. 1962), Calif. Coun. Gerontology and Geriatrics (bd. dirs. 1980-86, pres. 1985), N.Y. Acad. Medicine, N.Y. Acad. Sci., Orange County Med. Soc. Home: 1115 Goldenrod Ave Corona Del Mar CA 92625-1508 Office: U Calif Dept Phys Medicine & Rehab Irvine CA 92668

TOBISMAN, STUART PAUL, lawyer; b. Detroit, June 5, 1942; s. Nathan and Beverly (Porvin) T.; m. Karen Sue Tobisman, Aug. 8, 1965; children: Cynthia Elaine, Neal Jay. BA, UCLA, 1966; JD, U. Calif., Berkeley, 1969. Bar: Calif. 1969. Assoc. O'Melveny & Myers, L.A., 1969-77, ptnr., 1977—; dir. Burton G. Bettingen Corp. Contbr. articles to profl. jours. Trustee L.A. County Bar Assn., 1983-84. With USN, 1961-63. Fellow Am. Coll. Trust and Estate Counsel; mem. Phi Beta Kappa, Order of Coif. Office: O'Melveny & Myers 1999 Avenue Of The Stars Los Angeles CA 90067-6022

TOBITA, SHIGEO, English language educator; b. Tokyo, Dec. 22, 1927; s. Tokiwa and Tsurue (Yamada) T.; B.A., Aoyama Gakuin U., 1952; M.A., Waseda U., 1954, postgrad., 1957; m. Tomoko Mori, Sept. 30, 1957; children: Hiroko, Kyoko, Miyuki. Lectr., Aoyama Gakuin U., 1957-60, asst. prof., 1960-63; asst. prof. Otaru Coll. Commerce, 1963-69; prof. English, Chuo U., Tokyo, 1969—; rsch. scholar Carleton Coll., 1976, U. N.C., Chapel Hill, 1978-79; lectr. Keio U., 1980-92. Mem. MLA, Japan English Lit. Soc., Japan Am. Lit. Soc., Japanese Assn. Am. Studies, Japan Henry Miller Soc. (pres.). Translator: Catch-22 (Joseph Heller), 1969; Travesty (John Hawkes), 1979; Good as Gold (Joseph Heller), 1981; Neighbors (Thomas Berger), 1982, An Artist of the Floating World (Kazuo Ishiguro), 1988, Back in the World (Tobias Wolff), 1991, This Boy's Life (Tobias Wolff), 1992, The Power of Myth (Joseph Campbell), 1992; Author: An Unconventional Dictionary of English, 1994, A Guidebook of English Dictionaries, 1995; co-editor: Shogakkan-Random House English-Japanese Dictionary, 1994. Home: 6-6 Kinuta 3-chome, Setagaya-ku Tokyo 157, Japan Office: Chuo U, 742-1 Higashi-nakano Hachioji-shi, Tokyo 192-03, Japan

TOBLER, D. LEE, chemical and aerospace company executive; b. Provo, Utah, July 25, 1933; s. Donald and Louise Harriet (Shoell) T.; m. H. Darlene Thueson, Nov. 21, 1956; children—Lisa, Julianne, Curtis, Craig, Denise, Bradley. BA in Fin. and Econs., Brigham Young U., 1957; MBA in Fin., Northwestern U., 1958. Mgr. planning and econs. Exxon, N.Y.C., 1958-72; v.p., treas. Aetna Life & Casualty, Hartford, Conn., 1972-81; group v.p., chief fin. officer Zapata Corp., Houston, 1981-84; exec. v.p., chief fin. officer B.F. Goodrich Co., Akron, Ohio, 1985—; also bd. dirs. B.F. Goodrich Co., Akron. Trustee U. Akron, 1996—; exec. v.p. bd. trustees Ohio Ballet, 1995-96, trustee, 1994—, chmn. Akron Regional Devel. Bd., 1992-95, trustee, exec. com., 1990—; pres. Literacy Vols. Conn., Hartford, 1973-81; exec. bd. Sam Houston Area Boy Scouts Am., 1984. Mem. Portage Country Club (Akron). Republican. Mem. LDS Ch. Avocations: gardening; tennis; reading. Home: 16135 Warwick Rd Marshallville OH 44645 Office: BF Goodrich Co 3925 Embassy Pky Akron OH 44333-1763

TOBLER, WALDO RUDOLPH, geographer, cartographer; b. Portland, Oreg., Nov. 16, 1930; s. Verner and Hanny (Urech) T.; m. Dorothy Weix, Dec. 27, 1957 (div. 1979); children—Eric, Stephen; m. Rachel Mendenhall, Sept. 16, 1982. B.A., U. Wash., 1955, M.A., 1957, Ph.D., 1961; Dr. h.c., U. Zurich, 1988. Asst. planner Pierce County, Tacoma, 1958-59; asst. prof. to prof. U. Mich., Ann Arbor, 1961-77; prof. U. Calif., Santa Barbara, 1977-94, rsch. prof., 1994—; vis. prof. U. Minn.-Mpls., 1968, U. Zurich, Switzerland, 1973, Tech. U. Vienna, Austria, 1993; chmn. Math. Social Sci. Bd., 1974; coun. Regional Sci. Assn., 1967-69; rsch. scientist Internat. Inst. for Applied Systems Analysis, Austria, 1975. Contbr. articles on math. geography and cartography to profl. jours. Served to sgt. U.S. Army, 1948-52; ETO. Fellow Royal Geograph. Soc. (London); mem. Assn. Am. Geographers (Meritorious Svc. 1968), Assn. Computing Machinery, Am. Congress Surveying and Mapping, Nat. acad. Scis., Am. Geog. Soc. (hon., O.M. MIller Cartographic medal 1989), Nat. Ctr. for Geographic Info. and Analysis (sr. scientist NSF Ctr. 1989—), Sierra Club, Swiss (Santa Barbara pres. 1980-82, treas. 1983-85). Avocations: skiing; hiking; swimming; classical music. Office: Univ California Dept Geography Santa Barbara CA 93106

TOBUREN, LAWRENCE RICHTER, transportation company executive; b. Cleburne, Kans., July 11, 1915; s. Edward Franklin and Anna Fredericka (Richter) T.; m. Ella Joyner Brame, Dec. 16, 1942; children: Lawrence Richter Jr., William Brame, Luanne Brame, Gwendolyn Brame. Student, U. Denver, 1937-41. Dispatch clk. Continental Airlines, Denver, 1943-48; dispatcher Pacific Intermountain Express, Denver, 1948-52; dir. dispatch Pacific Intermountain Express, Oakland, Calif., 1952-57, western region ops. mgr., 1957-58; with Pilot Freight Carriers, Inc., 1958-82, exec. v.p., Winston-Salem, N.C., 1972-76, pres., 1976-81, vice chmn. bd., 1981-82, also bd. dirs., ret., 1982. Officer, pilot U.S. Army Air Corps, 1941-43. Republican. Methodist. Home: 1517 Boxthorne Ln Winston Salem NC 27106-4471

TOBY, JACKSON, sociologist, educator; b. N.Y.C., Sept. 10, 1925; s. Phineas and Anna (Weissman) T.; m. Marcia Lifshitz, Aug. 1, 1952; children: Alan Steven, Gail Afriat. B.A., Bklyn. Coll., 1946; M.A. in Econs, Harvard U., 1947, M.A. in Sociology, 1949, Ph.D. in Sociology, 1950. Research assoc. Lab. Social Relations, Harvard, 1950-51; mem. faculty Rutgers U., 1951—, prof. sociology, chmn. dept., 1961-68, dir. Inst. for Criminological Research, 1969-94; cons. Youth Devel. Program, Ford Found., 1959-63. Author: (with H.C. Bredemeier) Social Problems in America, 1960, 2d edit., 1971; contbr. numerous articles to profl. jours., pub. policy jours., N.Y. Times, Wall St. Jour., L.A. Times, Chgo. Tribune, Washington Post. Cons., Pres.'s Commn. Law Enforcement and Adminstrn. Justice, 1967. Recipient numerous research grants. Mem. Am. Sociol. Assn., Am. Soc. Criminology, Univ. Ctrs. for Rational Alternatives, Nat. Assn. Scholars. Spl. research adolescent delinquency in U.S., Sweden, Japan, other countries, on violence and dropouts in Am. public schools. Home: 17 Harrison Ave Highland Park NJ 08904-1813 Office: Rutgers U Dept Sociology Lucy Stone Hall Livingston Campus New Brunswick NJ 08903

TOCCO, JAMES, pianist; b. Detroit, Sept. 21, 1943; s. Vincenzo and Rose (Tabbita) T.; 1 child, Rhoya. Prof. music Ind. U., Bloomington, 1977-91; eminent scholar, artist-in-residence U. Cin. Coll.-Conservatory Music, 1991—; prof. Musikhochschule, Lübeck, Ger., 1990—; artistic dir. Great Lakes Chamber Music Festival, 1994—. Debut with orch., Detroit, 1956, since performed with symphony orchs. including Chgo. Symphony, Los Angeles Philharmonic, Cin. Symphony, Detroit Symphony, Nat. Symphony, Balt. Symphony, Atlanta Symphony, Denver Symphony, Montreal Symphony, London Symphony, London Philharm., Berlin Philharm., Moscow Radio-TV Orch., Amsterdam Philharmonic, Munich Philharmonic, Bavarian Radio Orch., also recitals, U.S. and abroad, and performances, CBS and NBC networks; guest performer, White House; Recs. include the complete preludes of Chopin, collected piano works of Leonard Bernstein, complete piano works of Charles Tomlinson Griffes, 4 piano sonatas of Edward MacDowell, selected piano works of Aaron Copland, complete Bach-Liszt organ transcriptions. Recipient Bronze medal Tchaikovsky Competition, Moscow 1970, Bronze medal Queen Elisabeth of Belgium Competition, Brussels 1972, 1st prize Piano Competition of Americas, Rio de Janeiro 1973, 1st prize Munich Internat. Competition 1973. Office: U Cin Coll-Conservatory Music Cincinnati OH 45221-0003

TOCCO, STEPHEN, airport administrator. Exec. dir. Boston Gen. Edward Lawrence Logan Internat. Airport. Office: Mass Port Authority 10 Park PlzAviation Dept 18th FL Boston MA 02116-3933*

TOCHIKURA, TATSUROKURO, applied microbiologist, home economics educator; b. Nagaoka, Niigata, Japan, Nov. 15, 1927; s. Tatsujiro and Fuji (Sato) T.; m. Kano Takako, Nov. 8, 1953; children: Momoyo, Tadafumi. BS in Agrl. Chemistry, Kyoto (Japan) U., 1951, PhD, 1960. Cert. indsl. microbiology and microbial biochemistry. Rsch. assoc. dept. agrl. chemistry Kyoto (Japan) U., 1956-61, assoc. prof. dept. agrl. chemistry, 1961-68, prof. dept. food sci. and tech., 1968-91, prof. emeritus, 1991; prof. home econs. Kobe (Japan) Women's U., 1991—; vis. asst. prof. Oreg. State U., 1964-65. Co-author: Microbial Production of Nucleic Acid-Related Substances, 1976, Methods in Carbohydrate Chemistry, 1980, Bioconversion of Waste Materials to Industrial Products, 1991. Mem. Am. Soc. Microbiology, Japan Bioindustry Assn., Japan Soc. for Fermentation and Bioengring., Japan Soc. for Bioscience Biotech. and Agrochemistry. Office: Kobe Womens Univ, 2-1 Aoyama Higashi-Suma, Kobe 654, Japan

TOCK, JOSEPH, lawyer; b. Cleve., Aug. 22, 1954; s. Julius Joseph and Marianna Yvonne (Carracio) T. BA, Kent State U., 1979; JD, Case Western Res. U., 1983. Bar: Ohio, 1983, U.S. Ct. Mil. Appeals, 1983, Colo. 1988. Commd. 1st lt. USAF, 1983, advanced through grades to maj., 1994; asst. staff judge advocate, chief civil law USAF, McConnell AFB, Kans., 1983-84; asst. staff judge advocate, chief civil law USAF, Yokota Air Base, Japan, 1984-85, area def. counsel 7th cir., 1985-87; dep. staff judge advocate, chief mil. justice USAF, Kelly AFB, Tex., 1987-88; dep. county atty. El Paso County, Colo., 1989-90; pvt. practice Colorado Springs, Colo., 1990-91; staff atty. Guam Legal Svcs. Corp., 1991-92; asst. atty. gen. White Collar unit Prosecution Divsn., Agana, Guam, 1992-95; 1st asst. to chief prosecutor White Collar unit Prosecution Divsn., Agana, Guam, 1994-96; asst. atty. gen. Solicitor's Divsn., Agana, Guam, 1996—; dep. staff judge advocate Peterson AFB, Colo., 1990-91, Andersen AFB, Guam, 1991—; instr. family law Pikes Peak C.C., 1990-91; lectr. Continental Security Divsn., San Antonio, 1987-88, NCO prep course, Kelly AFB, Tex., 1987-88, Profl. Mil. Edn. Ctr., Yokota Air Base, 1984-87. Mem. ABA, Internat. Legal Soc. Japan, Am. Legion, Mensa. Roman Catholic. Avocations: golf, handball, sailing, scuba. Office: Atty Gen Prosecution Divsn Jud Ctr Bldg 120 W Obrien Dr Ste 2-200E Agana GU 96910-5174

TOCKLIN, ADRIAN MARTHA, insurance company executive, lawyer; b. Coral Gables, Fla., Aug. 4, 1951; d. Kelso Hampton and Patricia Jane (Crook) Cook Atkins; m. Gary Michael Tocklin, Nov. 23, 1974. BA, George Washington U., 1972; JD, Seton Hall U., 1994. Regional claim examiner Interstate Nat. Corp., St. Petersburg, Fla., 1973-74; branch supr. Underwriter's Adjusting Co. subs. Continental Corp., Tampa, Fla., 1974-77, asst. dir. edn. tng. adminstrn., N.Y.C., 1977, asst. regional mgr. adminstrn. ops., Livingston, N.J., 1977-78, br. mgr., Paramus, N.J., 1978-80, sr. v.p. mktg., N.Y.C., Piscataway, N.J., 1980-84, regional v.p., mgr., Livingston, N.J., 1984-86, exec. v.p., 1986-88, also bd. dirs.; sr. v.p. Continental Corp., 1988-92, exec. v.p. 1992-94, pres., N.Y.C., 1994-95; pres. diversified ops. CNA Ins., Chgo., 1995—; pres. bd. dirs. U.S. Protection Indemnity Agy., Inc., N.Y.C.; bd. dirs. Underwriters Adjusting Co., Arbitration Forums, Inc., Tarrytown, N.Y., Continental Ins. Co., Sonat Corp.; v.p. Continental Risk Services, Inc., Hamilton, Bermuda, 1983-86; editor-in-chief Profl. Ins. Bulletin Update, N.Y.C., 1977-79. Mem. YWCA Acad. Women Achievers. Mem. Nat. Assn. Ins. Women (Outstanding Ins. Woman in N.Y.C.), NOW. Democrat. Lutheran. Office: CNA Ins CNA Plz Chicago IL 60685

TOD, G. ROBERT, consumer marketing executive; b. Schenectady, N.Y., July 10, 1939; s. George B. and Jane (Nicholson) T.; m. JoAnn Anderson, Oct. 24, 1964; children: G. Robert Jr., Jennifer R. BME, Rensselaer Poly. Inst., 1961; MBA, Harvard U., 1967. Group mgr. Bangor Punta Corp., Boston, 1967-69; pres., chief oper. officer and co-founder CML Group Inc., Acton, Mass., 1969—; bd. dirs. SCI Systems Inc., Huntsville, Ala., EG & G Inc., Wellesley, Mass. Co-author: (with others) Chief Executive's Handbook, 1976. Trustee Rensselaer Poly. Inst., Troy, N.Y., 1981—; bd. dirs. Emerson Hosp., Concord, Mass., 1983—; former trustee Fenn. Sch., Middlesex Sch., Concord. Capt. USAF, 1961-65. Mem. Harvard Bus. Sch. Alumni Coun. (bd. dirs. 1988-92). Home: PO Box 650 Concord MA 01742-0650 Office: CML Group Inc 524 Main St Acton MA 01720-3933

TODA, KEISHI, electronics executive; b. Tokyo, Japan, 1933. Grad., Hito Tsu Bashi U., Tokyo, 1960. Pres. Hitachi Am. LTD., Tarrytown, N.Y. Office: Hitachi America LTD 50 Prospect Ave Tarrytown NY 10591-4625*

TODARO, PATRICIA ANNE, painter, singer; b. Rockville Centre, N.Y., Feb. 24, 1933; d. Russell Norman and Grace Ruth (Eyerman) Sheidow; m. Raymond Ashman, Feb. 6, 1958 (div.); children: Robert Ashman, Richard Ashman, Kathryn Ashman. Student, Sullins Coll., 1950-51, Art Students League, 1954, Susquehanna U., 1952-54, Coll. of William and Mary, 1982-84. With programming dept. ABC, 1954-55; with travel dept. Rand, Santa Monica, Calif., 1955-56; pres. Seltzer Gallery, N.Y.C., 1986, 87. One-woman shows include Seltzer Coll., 1985-87, Seltzer Gallery, Phoenix Visual Arts Ctr., 1988, Kerr Cultural Ctr., Scottsdale, Ariz., 1989, Williamsburg Duke of Glouster Show, 1984, Albert Einstein Med. Ctr., N.Y.C., 1987, Seltzer Gallery, represented in pvt. collections Albi-France, 1986, Leo House, N.Y.C., 1986-87, Shanti-AIDS Home, Phoenix, Ariz., 1988, Unipas Gallery, N.Y.C., 1991. Recipient Silver medal Salon D'Automne, Albi, France, 1986; scholar Am. Theatre Wing, 1954-58. Mem. Am. Fedn. Musicians. Avocations: cantor and organist with church, sailing, biking.

TODD, BRUCE M., mayor. BBA in acctg., U. Tex. CPA, Tex. Former ptnr. Mueller, Todd and Co.; commr. Travis County, Tex., 1987—; mayor City of Austin, Tex., 1991—; City of Austin chair AISD/City Coun. Joint Com., Audit Com., Conv. Ctr. Com., Opportunities for Youth subcom., Joint Debt Advisory Com., Legis. Com., Judicial Com., Policy Planning and Budget Com., Downtown subcom., So. Union Gas Rate Request subcom. bd. dirs. Tex. Mcpl. League, Austin Transp. Study Com., Capital Metro Local Govt. Approval Com.; mem. Mayor's United on Safety, Crime and Law Enforcement; chairperson Balcones Canyonlands Conservation Plan; former pres. Austin-San Antonio Corridor Coun. Mem. Tex. Soc. CPAs (former mem. bd. dirs, exec. com. Austin chpt.). Address: 7629 Rockpoint Dr Austin TX 78731-1438 Office: Office of Mayor PO Box 1088 Austin TX 78767*

TODD, DAVID FENTON MICHIE, architect; b. Middletown, Ohio, Feb. 22, 1915; s. Robert Chalmers and Frances Fenton (Michie) T.; m. Suzanne Williams, Sept. 1, 1942; 1 child, Gregory F.W. A.B., Dartmouth, 1937; B.Arch., U. Mich., 1940. Draftsman J.R.F. Swanson, Birmingham, Mich., 1940-41; archtl. designer W. Ray Yount, Dayton, Ohio, 1941-42; architect Harrison, Ballard & Allen, N.Y.C., 1942-53; architect, prin. Ballard, Todd & Snibbe, N.Y.C., 1957-62, Ballard Todd Assos., 1962-66, David Todd & Assos., 1966—. Works include Manhattan Plaza, N.Y.C., Collegiate Sch, N.Y.C., Rye (N.Y.) Country Day Sch. Past chmn. bd. dirs. Leake & Watts Children's Home, N.Y.C.; chmn. N.Y.C. Landmarks Preservation Commn., 1989-90. Served to 1st lt. AUS, 1942-46. Recipient awards for tennis pavillion, Princeton U. AIA, 1962, Harry B. Rutkins Meml. award N.Y.C. AIA, 1963, Robert Treat Hotel, Newark Asn. Commerce and Industry, 1964, Manhattan Pla. Constrn. Industry Bd., 1978, Andrew Thomas Pioneer in Housing award N.Y.C. AIA, 1986, cert. of merit Mcpl. Art Soc. N.Y.C., 1991,. Fellow AIA (pres. N.Y.C. chpt. 1969-70, chmn. jury of fellows 1971, chmn. task force on housing policy 1974), Constrn. Specifications Inst. (pres. N.Y.C. chpt. 1960-61, regional dir. 1965-66). Clubs: Century Assn, Amateur Comedy. Home and Office: 134 E 95th St New York NY 10128-1705

TODD, ERICA WEYER, lawyer; b. Beacon Falls, Conn., Sept. 22, 1967; d. Richard Burton and Elizabeth Jane (Weyer) T. BA in Biology, U. Bridgeport, 1989, JD, 1992; JD, Quinnipiac Coll. Sch. Law, 1994. Bar: Conn. 1992, U.S. Dist. Ct. Conn. 1993. Assoc. Trotta, Trotta and Trotta, New Haven, 1993—; admissions counselor Quinnipiac Coll. Sch. of Law, Hamden, 1992-93. Recipient Alumni award for Svc. to Law Sch., Quinnipiac Coll. Sch. Law, 1994. Mem. ABA, Conn. Bar Assn. (exec. com. Young Lawyers divsn. 1993—), New Haven Bar Assn. (exec. com. Young Lawyers Assn. 1994—), Def. Rsch. Inst., Assn. Trial Lawyers of Am. Democrat. Roman Catholic. Avocation: golf. Home: 551 Skokorat Rd Beacon Falls CT 06403-1457 Office: Trotta Trotta & Trotta 195 Church St # 815 817 New Haven CT 06510-2009

TODD, FRANCES EILEEN, pediatrics nurse; b. Hawthorne, Calif., Aug. 20, 1950; d. James Clark and Jean Eleanor (McGinty) Nailen; m. Steven Charles Todd, Oct. 25, 1975; 1 child, Amanda Kathryn. ASN, El Camino Jr. Coll., 1974; BSN, Calif. State Coll., Long Beach, 1982, postgrad. RN, Calif.; cert. pub. health nurse, Calif.; cert. pediatric nurse practitioner; cert. pediatric advanced life support Am. Heart Assn. Nursing attendant St. Earne's Nursing Home, Inglewood, Calif., 1973; clinic nurse I Harbor-UCLA Med. Ctr., Torrance, Calif., 1974-77, evening shift relief charge nurse, clinic nurse II, 1977-85, pediatric liaison nurse, 1984-90, pediatric nurse practitioner, 1985—; steward Local Union 660, 1995—; tutor Compton (Calif.) C.C., 1988, clin. instr., 1987-88; lectr. faculty dept. pediatrics UCLA Sch. Medicine, 1980—; lectr. in field. Contbr. articles to profl. jours. Co-chair parent support group Sherrie's Schs., Lomita, Calif. Mem. Nat. Assn. Pediatric Nurse Assocs. and Practitioners, L.A. Pediatric Soc., Emergency Nurses Assn., Local 660 (shop steward), Svc. Employees Int. Union, local 660 (union steward), Peruvian Paso Horse Registry N.Am. (co-chair judge's accreditation com. 1989—, judge's Andalusian horses). Avocations: Peruvian Paso horses, orchids. Office: Harbor UCLA Med Ctr 1000 W Carson St PO Box 14-7W Torrance CA 90509

TODD, HAROLD WADE, association executive, retired air force officer; b. Chgo., Jan. 17, 1938; s. Harold Wade and Jeanne (Fayal) T.; m. Wendy Yvonne Kendrick, July 12, 1981; children by previous marriage: Hellen J. Wilson, Kenneth J., Stephen D., Joseph M., Michelle M. Adams, Mark A.; stepchildren: Jamie Y. White, James K. Mills, Timothy S. Emerson. B.S., U.S. Air Force Acad., 1959; grad., Nat. War Coll., 1975. Commd. 2d lt. U.S. Air Force, 1959, advanced through grades to maj. gen., 1982; aide to comdr. (2d Air Force (SAC)), Barksdale AFB, La., 1970-71; exec. aide to comdr.-in-chief U.S. Air Forces Europe, Germany, 1971-74; spl. asst. chief of staff USAF, 1975-76; chief Concept Devel. Div., 1976-77, chief Readiness and NATO Staff Group, Hdqrs. USAF, 1977-78; exec. asst. to chmn. Joint Chiefs Staff Washington, 1978-80; comdr. 25th region N. Am. Aerospace Def. Command McChord AFB, Wash., 1980-82; chief staff 4th Allied Tactical Air Force Heidelberg, 1982-85; commandant Air War Coll., 1985-89; vice comdr. Air U., 1985-89, ret., 1989; ind. cons. Colorado Springs, Colo., 1989-95; pres., CEO, Nat. Stroke Assn., Denver, 1995—. Founder, pres. Bossier City (La.) chpt. Nat. Assn. for Children with Learning Disabilities, 1970-71. Decorated Def. D.S.M., Air Force D.S.M. (2), Legion of Merit (2), D.F.C., Air medal (8), Air Force Commendation medal. Mem. Air Force Assn., USAF Acad. Assn. Grads., Nat. War Coll. Alumni Assn. Home: 1250 Big Valley Dr Colorado Springs CO 80919-1015

TODD, HARRY WILLIAMS, aircraft propulsion system company executive; b. Oak Park, Ill., 1922. BSME, U. So. Calif., 1947, BSIE, 1948, MBA, 1950. With Rockwell Internat., Pitts., 1947-76, former v.p. ops.; pres., chmn., chief exec. officer, bd. dirs. The L.E. Myers Co., Pitts., 1976-80; with Rohr Industries, Inc., Chula Vista, Calif., 1980-90, chief operating officer, 1980-82, pres., chief exec. officer, chmn., 1982-90, retired, 1990; mng. ptnr. Carlise Enterprises, 1990—; bd. dirs. Rohr Industries, Pacific Scientific, Helmerich & Payne, Garrett Aviation Svcs. Trustee Scripps Clinic and Rsch. Found. With U.S. Army, 1944-46. Office: Carlisle Enterprises 7777 Fay Ave La Jolla CA 92037-4327

TODD, J. C. See COOPER, JANE TODD

TODD, JAMES DALE, federal judge; b. Scotts Hill, Tenn., May 20, 1943; s. James P. and Jeanette Grace (Duck) T.; m. Jeanie M. Todd, June 26, 1965; children: James Michael, Julie Diane. BS, Lambuth Coll., 1965; M Combined Scis., U. Miss., 1968; JD, Memphis State U., 1972. Bar: Tenn. 1972, U.S. Dist. Ct. (we. dist.) Tenn. 1972, U.S. Ct. Appeals (6th cir.) 1973, U.S. Supreme Ct. 1975. Tchr. sci., chmn. sci. dept. Lyman High Sch., Longwood, Fla., 1965-68, Memphis U. Sch., 1968-72; ptnr. Waldrop, Farmer, Todd & Breen, P.A., 1972-83; cir. judge div. II 26th Jud. Dist., Jackson, Tenn., 1983-85; judge U.S. Dist. Ct. (we. dist.) Tenn., Jackson, 1985—. Named Alumnus of Yr. Lambuth Coll. Alumni Assn., 1985. Fellow Tenn. Bar Found.; mem. Fed. Judges Assn., Fed. Bar Assn., Tenn. Bar Assn., Jackson Madison County Bar Assn. (pres. 1978-79). Methodist. Office: US Dist Ct 109 S Highland Ave Jackson TN 38301-6123

TODD, JAMES HIRAM, II, management consultant; b. Oklahoma City, Nov. 2, 1942; s. Prentiss Oliver and Itillious Vener (Jackson) T.; m. Unzerlo Verginia General, June 19, 1963; 1 child, Mark A. BA, U. Okla., 1972, MA, 1986; PhD, Western Inst. Social Rsch., Berkeley, Calif., 1990. Health adminstr. Mary Mahoney Health Ctr., Spencer, Okla., 1973-76; spl. project dir. North Tulsa Ambulatory Care System, 1976-78; clin. nurse Bapt. Med. Ctr., Oklahoma City, 1979-83; pres., CEO Ednl. Resource Devel. Group, Oklahoma City, 1983-94; regional mgr. STAT Nursing Svcs., Oakland, Calif., 1986-88; rsch. prof. San Francisco State U., 1988—; adv. com. San Francisco Unified Sch. Dist., 1989-94; White House Conferee, 1975. Author: Our Home is Not the Ghetto, 1995. Fin. com. United Way, Oklahoma City, 1973-76; scout master Boy Scouts Am., Norman, Okla., 1970-72; v.p. Nat. Black Child Devel. Inst., San Francisco, 1990—; bd. dirs., congrl. cons. Nat. Assn. Cmty. Health Ctrs., Washington, 1973-78; bd. dirs. Emergency Med. Svcs. Auth., Tulsa, 1976-78. With U.S. Army, 1960. Recipient Cert. Commendation, City of Tulsa, 1978, Cert. Appreciation, U.S. Dept. Edn., 1991, proclamation award Mayor San Francisco, 1990. Mem. AAUP, Nat. Assn. Black Sch. Educators, Calif. Commonwealth, Calif. Acad. Sci., World Future Soc., Ernest W. Lyons Lodge. Democrat. Avocations: travel, reading, photograpy, bowling. Office: San Francisco State U 8 Tapia Dr San Francisco CA 94132-1717

TODD, JAMES S., surgeon, educator, medical association administrator; b. Hyannis, Mass., 1931. Intern Presbyn. Hosp., N.Y.C., 1957-58, resident in surgery, 1959-63; resident in surgery Delafield Hosp., N.Y.C., 1963; resident ob-gyn. Sloane Womens Hosp., N.Y.C., 1958-59; resident Valley Hosp., Ridgewood, N.J.; clin. asst. prof. surgery U. Medicine and Dentistry N.J., Newark; exec. v.p. AMA, 1993—; pres. AMA. Office: American Medical Assocation 515 N State St Chicago IL 60610-4320*

TODD, JAMES STILES, surgeon, professional executive association; b. Hyannis, Mass., July 9, 1931; s. Alexander Campbell and Myra Crowell (Stiles) T.; m. Marjorie Patricia Thorn, Sept. 6, 1958; children: Kendall Scott, Christopher James. AB, Harvard U., 1953, MD, 1957. Diplomate Am. Bd. Surgery. Intern Columbia-Presbyn. Med. Ctr., N.Y.C., 1957-58, resident in surgery, 1958-64; pvt. practice Ridgewood, N.J., 1964-85; asst. in surgery Columbia Coll. of Physicians & Surgeons, N.Y.C., 1964—, Columbia-Presbyn. Hosp., N.Y.C., 1964—; sr. dep. exec. v.p. AMA, Chgo., 1985—, exec. v.p., 1990—; former chmn. bd. N.J. State Med. Underwriters, Inc. Lawrenceville; cons. physician Valley Hosp., Ridgewood, 1985—. Author: (with others) DRGs for Physicians, 1983; editor: Intensive Care, 1965; contbr. articles to profl. jours. Pres. Bergen Community Blood Bank, Paramus, N.J., 1978-85; pres. bd. mgrs. County Hosp., 1978-79. Recipient Edward J. Ill Distinguished Physician award, N.J. Acad. Medicine, 1980, Disting. Svc. award N.J. Hosp. Assn., 1984. Fellow ACS; mem. Health Care Execs., Med. Soc. N.J., AMA, pres. Physician Insurers Assn. of Am., Lawrenceville, N.J., 1984-85. Republican. Avocations: clock building and repair, boating. Office: AMA 515 N State St Chicago IL 60610-4320

TODD, JAN THERESA, counselor; b. Mobile, Ala., Mar. 20, 1961; d. Joseph Thomas and Lessie Grey (Sullivan) T. BA, U. Tex., San Antonio, 1983, MA, 1992. Cert. profl. counselor; cert. provisional tchr. English tchr. Bandera (Tex.) High Sch.-Bandera (Tex.) Ind. Sch. Dist., 1987-91; counselor Yorktown (Tex.) High Sch.-Yorktown (Tex.) Ind. Sch. Dist., 1992-93, John F. Kennedy High Sch.-Edgewood Ind. Sch. Dist., San Antonio, 1993-95, Lackland Jr./Sr. H.S., Lackland Ind. Sch. Dist., San Antonio, 1995—. Mem. ACA, Tex. Counselors Assn., South Tex. Counselors Assn. Home: 9415 De Sapin San Antonio TX 78250-6308 Office: Lackland Jr/Sr HS 2460 Bong Ave Bldg 8265 San Antonio TX 78236-1244

TODD, JOHN, mathematician, educator; b. Carnacally, Ireland, May 16, 1911; came to U.S., 1947, naturalized, 1953; s. William Robert and Catherine (Stewart) T.; m. Olga Taussky, Sept. 29, 1938. B.S., Queen's U., Belfast, Ireland, 1931; research student, St. John's Coll., Cambridge (Eng.) U., 1931-33. Lectr. Queen's U., 1933-37, King's Coll., London, 1937-49; chief computation lab., then chief numerical analysis Nat. Bur. Standards, 1947-57; prof. math. Calif. Inst. Tech., 1957—; Fulbright prof. Vienna, Austria, 1965. Author, editor books on numerical analysis and tables; editor in chief: Numerische Mathematik, 1959—; assoc. editor Aequationes Mathematicae, 1967-85, 89-95, Jour. Approximation Theory, 1967-93. Mem. Am. Math. Soc., Soc. Indsl. and Applied Math., Math. Assn. Am. (gov. 1980-83). Office: Calif Inst Technology Mathematics 253 # 37 Pasadena CA 91125

TODD, JOHN DICKERSON, JR., lawyer; b. Macon, Ga., June 30, 1912; s. J.D. and Hazel (McManus) T.; m. Mellicent McWhorter, Mar. 7, 1943; children—Rosalind (Mrs. Jack Harding Tedards, Jr.), John D. Student, Va. Mil. Inst., 1930-32; LL.B., U. Ga., 1935. Bar: S.C. bar 1935. With firm Hingson & Todd, 1935-51; partner firm Leatherwood, Walker, Todd & Mann, Greenville, S.C., 1952—; now sr. partner; judge Greenville City Ct., 1939; atty. County of Greenville, 1948-56; mem. bd. bar examiners State of S.C.; chmn. S.C. Judicial Study Commn., 1995. Served to maj. AUS, 1941-45. Mem. ABA, Am. Coll. Trial Lawyers, Am. Bar Found., 4th U.S. Cir. Jud. Conf., S.C. Bar Assn. (bd. govs., pres. 1978—), Greenville Jr. C. of C. (pres.), Greenville County Bar (past pres.), Greenville Kiwanis (past pres.), Greenville Country Club (past pres.), Summit Club, Commerce Club, Phi Delta Phi, Sigma Nu. Baptist. Home: 200 Riverside Dr Greenville SC 29605-1133 Office: 100 E Coffee St Greenville SC 29601-2707

TODD, JOHN JOSEPH, lawyer; b. St. Paul, Mar. 16, 1927; s. John Alfred and Martha Agnes (Jagoe) T.; m. Dolores Jean Shanahan, Sept. 9, 1950; children: Richard M., Jane E., John P. Student, St. Thomas Coll., 1944, 46-47; B.Sci. and Law, U. Minn., 1949, LL.B., 1950. Bar: Minn. bar 1951. Practice in South St. Paul, Minn., 1951-72; partner Thuet and Todd, 1953-72; asso. justice Minn. Supreme Ct., St. Paul, 1972-85; sole practice West St. Paul, 1985-92; of counsel Brenner & Glassman Ltd., Mpls., 1992—. Served with USNR, 1945-46. Mem. Am. Bar Assn., state bar assns., Am. Legion, VFW. Home: 6689 Argenta Trl W Inver Grove MN 55077-2208 Office: Brenner & Glassman Ltd 2001 Killebrew Dr Ste 170 Minneapolis MN 55425-1884

TODD, JOHN ODELL, insurance company sales professional; b. Mpls., Nov. 12, 1902; s. Frank Chisholm and Mary Mable (Odell) T.; AB, Cornell U., 1924; CLU, Am. Coll., 1933; m. Katherine Sarah Cone, Feb. 21, 1925; children: John Odell, George Bennett. Spl. agt. Equitable Life Assurance Soc., Mpls., 1926-28; ins. broker, Mpls., 1928-31; spl. agt. Northwestern Mut. Life Ins. Co., Mpls., 1931-38, Evanston, Ill., 1938—; ptnr. H.S. Vail & Sons, Chgo., 1938-43, Vail and Todd, gen. agts. Northwestern Mut., Chgo., 1943-44; sole gen. agt., Chgo., 1944-51; pres. Todd Planning and Service Co., life ins. brokers, 1951—; founder, hon. chmn., prin. John O. Todd Orgn., Exec. Compensation Specialists and Cons., 1970-91; faculty lectr. C.L.U. Insts., U. Conn., 1952-53, U. Wis., 1955-57, U. Calif., 1956, U. Hawaii, 1966; host interviewer ednl. Films Series of the Greats, 1973-74. Pres. Evanston (Ill.) 1st. Ward Non-Partisan Civic Assn., 1956-57; trustee Evanston Hist. Soc., 1973-76; bd. dirs. First Congl Ch., Evanston, 1987-89; co-founder MDRT Charitable Found., 1959, pres., 1971, sole lifetime dir. emeritus, 1971—. Recipient Cleary award Best Gen. Agt. Devel., 1948, Golden Plate award Am. Acad. Achievement, 1969; Huebner Gold medal for contbn. to edn., 1978; named Ins. Field Man of Year, Ins. Field Pub. Co., 1965, John Newton Russell award Instn. Life Ins., 1969; Ill. Room in Hall of States dedicated to him by Am. Coll., 1981. Mem. AALU Am. Coll. John O. Nat. Assn. Life Underwriters, Assn. Advanced Life Underwriters (pres. 1963-64), Am. Coll. Life Underwriters (trustee 1957-78), Chgo. Life Underwriters Assn. (dir. 1938-41, Disting. Service award 1984), Northwestern Mut. Spl. Agts. Assn. (pres. 1955-56), Life Agy. Mgrs. Assn. (dir. 1945-48), Northwestern Mut. Assn. Agts. (pres. 1957-58, leader sr. agents 1994), Chgo. Life Trust Council, Million Dollar Round Table (pres. 1951, only 60th yr. consecutive qualifier), Top of Table (charter mem.), Psi Upsilon, Sphinx Head. Republican. Clubs: Evanston Univ.; Glen View. Author: Taxation, Inflation and Life Insurance, 1950; Ceiling Unlimited, 1965, 5th edit., 1984, Never a Dull Day, an Autobiography, 1990, A Lifetime of Opportunities, 1996; contbg. author to text Huebner Foundation, 1951, Secrets of the Master Sellers, Am. Mgmt. assn., 1987.

TODD, KATHLEEN GAIL, physician; b. Portland, Oreg., Aug. 31, 1951; d. Horace Edward and Lois Marie (Messing) T.; m. Andrew Richard Embick, March 31, 1980; children: Elizabeth Todd Embick, Margaret Todd Embick. BA, Pomona Coll., 1972; MD, Washington U., St. Louis, 1976. Diplomate Am. Bd. Family Practice. Resident U. Wash. Affiliated Hosps., Seattle, 1976-79; pvt. practice Valdez (Alaska) Med. Clinic, 1980—; chief of staff Valdez Community Hosp., 1986—. Mem. AMA, AAFP, Am. Acad. Family Practice, Alaska State Med. Assn. (counselor-at-large 1986-87). Democrat. Episcopalian. Avocations: skiing, kayaking, camping, music. Office: Valdez Med Clinic PO Box 1829 Valdez AK 99686-1829

TODD, KENNETH S., JR., parasitologist, educator; b. Three Forks, Mont., Aug. 25, 1936; s. Kenneth S. and Anna Louise (Seeman) T. BS, Mont. State U., 1962, MS, 1964; PhD, Utah State U., 1967. Asst. prof. U. Ill., Urbana, 1967-71, assoc. prof., 1971-76, prof. vet. parasitology, 1976—, chmn. div. parasitology, 1983-90, asst. head vet. pathobiology, 1984-87, prof. vet. programs in agr., 1984-94, acting head vet. pathobiology, 1987-90, head, 1990-94; prof. emeritus, 1994; affiliate scientist Ill. State Natural History Survey, 1987—; adj. prof. microbiology Mont. State U. Served with USAF, 1954-58. NSF grad. fellow, 1966-67. Mem. AVMA, Am. Assn. Vet. Parasitologists, Am. Micros. Soc., Am. Soc. Parasitologists, Am. Soc. Tropical Medicine and Hygiene, Helminthologic Soc. Washington, Midwest Conf. Parasitologists, Wildlife Disease Assn., Soc. Protozoologists. Office: Mont State U Dept Microbiology Bozeman MT 59715

TODD, MALCOLM CLIFFORD, surgeon; b. Carlyle, Ill., Apr. 10, 1913; s. Malcolm N. and Grace (Heitmeier) T.; m. Ruth Holle Schlake, June 12, 1945; 1 son, Malcolm Douglas. AB, U. Ill., 1934; MB, Northwestern U., 1934, MD, 1938; DSc (hon.), Brown U., 1975. Diplomate Am. Bd. Surgery. Intern St. Lukes Hosp., Chgo., 1937-38; resident Cook County Hosp., Chgo., 1938-41; instr. surgery Northwestern U., 1939-46; pvt. practice Long Beach, Calif., 1946-90; clin. prof. surgery U. Calif., Irvine, 1964-85, emeritus prof. surgery, 1985—; chief surgery, hon. bd. dirs. Long Beach Meml. Hosp., 1956-57, chief of staff, 1958-60; attending surgeon Long Beach VA Hosp., 1954-80, Los Angeles County Gen. Hosp., 1964-74; bd. dirs. Harbor Bank Long Beach, Spectral Diagnostics, Toronto, Ont., Can. Contbr. sci. and socio-econ. articles to med. jours. Mem. Nat. Adv. Com. on Health Manpower; U.S. del. WHO, 1970-72; dir. Calif. Health Planning Coun., 1966-74; mem. Calif. Regional Med. Programs Coun., 1968-74, Presdl. Commn. on Refugees, 1975, Long Beach Ednl. TV Bd., 1956-70; chmn.

Long Beach br. ARC, 1957-58; pres. Forward Long Beach Com., 1978—; trustee Long Beach Meml. Hosp., Sch. Medicine Morehouse U., Atlanta; chmn. Long Beach Community Svcs. Devel. Corp., 1979—; mem. health policy bd. Georgetown U.; bd. dirs. Downtown Long Beach Assocs., Medic Alert Found., Calif. Cancer Soc., Japan Am. Conf. Mayors; regent Uniformed Svcs. Health Scis. U., 1973-80; mem. Nat. Commn. Cost Health Care. Served to maj. AUS, 1942-46. Fellow ACS, Internat. Coll. Surgeons (pres. 1983-84, pres. U.S. sect. 1977), Royal Soc. Medicine, Am. Coll. Gastroenterology, Soc. Internat. Chirugie; mem. AMA (trustee 1973-76, pres. 1974-75, chmn. coun. on health manpower), Calif. Med. Assn. (pres. 1968-69), Los Angeles County Med. Soc., Long Beach Med. Soc. (pres. 1953-54), Karl A. Meyer Surg. Soc. (pres.), Long Beach C. of C. (pres. 1983), Virginia Country Club, Internat. City Club, Torch, Kiwanis, Pi Kappa Alpha (v.p. 1976). Home: 5330 E El Parque St Long Beach CA 90815-4247 Office: 2840 N Long Beach Blvd Long Beach CA 90806-1531

TODD, MARGARET LOUISE, retired secondary education educator; b. Newport News, Va., Nov. 27, 1919; d. Preson Curtis and Lydia Emos (Diggs) Watson; m. Jesse Emerson Todd, Sr., Apr. 5, 1947; children: Frances Diggs, Jesse Emerson Jr. AB, Coll. William & Mary, Williamsburg, Va., 1943; MA, Hampton U., 1978. Elem. tchr. Newport News (Va.) Sch. System, 1943-45; newspaper reporter Times-herald, 1945-46; tchr. English Goerge Wythe Jr. High, 1946-47; tchr. English Bethel High Sch., Hampton, 1970-82, ret., 1982; speaker in field and tchr. workshops. Author: (with others) Hampton From the Sea to the Stars, 1985; author: (biograph) C. Alton Lindsay: Educator and Community Leader, 1994; contbr. articles to profl. jours. Cert. lay speaker United Meth. Ch., Peninsula, 1970s-95; judge Va Forensics Debate, 1970s-82; debate coach Bethe H.S., Hampton, 1971-82. Mem. AAUW (life), Va. Ret. Tchrs. Assn. (trustee Va. conf. UM Hist. Soc.), Nat. Assn. Parliamentarians, Great Books Group, Planned Parenthood (pres. 1967-68), Hampton Hist. Found., Nat. Blackstone Coll. Alumnae Assn. (pres. 1995—). Avocations: reading, visiting historical sites, teaching, travel. Home: 909 Todds Ln Hampton VA 23666-1842

TODD, RICHARD D. R., lawyer; b. Borger, Tex., July 17, 1962; s. William H. and Linda (Brumfield) T.;m. Lisa Ann McCown, Jan. 4, 1986; 1 child, Richard Benjamin. Student, Tex. Tech. U., Lubbock, 1984; BS in Health Care Adminstrn., Wayland Bapt. U., Plainview, Tex., 1988; JD magna cum laude, Oklahoma City U., 1991. Bar: Tex. 1992, Okla. 1992, U.S. Dist. Ct. (no. dist.) Tex. 1992, U.S. Dist. Ct. (we. dist.) Okla. 1992, U.S. Ct. Appeals (5th cir.) 1993, U.S. Supreme Ct. 1995. Paramedic/ops. mgr. Amarillo (Tex.) Med. Svcs., 1982-89; legal intern Lampkin, McCaffrey & Tawwater, Oklahoma City, 1990-92; pvt. practice Borger, Tex., 1992—; barrister Am. Inn of Ct., Oklahoma City, 1990-92. Percussionist San Jacinto Orch., Amarillo, Tex. Mem. ABA, Borger Bar Assn., State Bar Tex. (pro bono coll. 1994-95), Phi Delta Phi (vice magister 1991). Baptist. Office: 605 W 3rd St Borger TX 79007-4007

TODD, ROBERT FRANKLIN, III, hematologist, educator; b. Granville, Ohio, Apr. 16, 1948; m. Susan Erhard; children: Currier Nathaniel, Andrew Joseph. AB, Duke U., 1970, PhD, 1975, MD, 1976. Diplomate Am. Bd. Internal Medicine. Intern Peter Bent Brigham Hosp., Boston, 1976-77, resident, 1977-78; fellow in oncology Sidney Farber Cancer Inst., Boston, 1978-80; clin. fellow in medicine Harvard Med. Sch., Boston, 1978-81; postdoctoral fellow divsn. tumor immunology Sidney Farber Cancer Inst., Boston, 1979-81; asst. prof. medicine Harvard Med. Sch., Boston, 1981-84; assoc. prof. internal medicine U. Mich., Ann Arbor, 1984-88, assoc. prof. cellular and molecular biology, 1985-88, assoc. dir. divsn. hematology-oncology internal medicine, 1987-91, prof. internal medicine, 1988—, assoc. chair for rsch. dept. internal medicine, 1989-91, assoc. chair dept. internal medicine, 1991-93, chief divsn. hematology-oncology dept. internal medicine, 1993—; attending physician U. Mich. Hosps., 1984—; chmn. hematology/oncology subsplty chpt. Ctrl. Soc. for Clin. Rsch., 1995—. Contbr. numerous articles to profl. jours.; patentee in field. Mem. Am. Coll. Physicians, Am. Assn. of Immunologists, Am. Assn. for Cancer Rsch., Am. Soc. of Clin. Oncology, Soc. of Leukocyte Biology (councilor 1996—), Am. Soc. of Hematology, Am. Fedn. for Clin. Rsch. (councilor midwest chpt. 1986-89), Ctrl. Soc. for Clin. Rsch. (coun. chair hematology/oncology subsplty. 1995-97), S.W. Oncology Group, Am. Soc. for Clin. Investigation, The Microcirculatory Soc., Phi Beta Kappa, Alpha Omega Alpha. Office: U of Mich Med Sch Divsn Hematology/Oncology 3119 Taubman Ctr Ann Arbor MI 48109

TODD, RONALD GARY, lawyer; b. Spokane, Wash., Dec. 12, 1946; s. Theodore H. and Dorothea I. (Swanson) T.; m. Natalie A., June 16, 1973; children: Russell E., Brian N., David E. AB, Cornell U., 1969; JD, Columbia U., 1972. Bar: N.Y. 1973, U.S. Dist. Ct. (so. and ea. dists.) N.Y. 1975, U.S. Ct. Appeals (2nd cir.) 1975, U.S. Supreme Ct. 1976, D.C. 1993. Atty. Dewey Ballantine, N.Y.C., 1973-79, Simpson Thacher & Bartlett, N.Y.C., 1980-82; atty., ptnr. Golenbock & Barell, N.Y.C., 1982-89; ptnr. Reid & Priest, N.Y.C., 1989—; instr., guest lectr. NYU Sch. Continuing Edn., 1983-90; adv. bd. Commonwealth Land Title and TransAm. Title Ins. Co., N.Y.C., 1992—. Contbr. articles to profl. jours. Pres., bd. dirs. Seven Bridges Field Club, 1982-85. Mem. ABA (real property sect. 1973—), N.Y. Bar Assn. (real property sect. 1973—), D.C. Bar Assn. (real property sect. 1992—). Avocations: instrumental music, tennis. Office: Reid & Priest 40 W 57th St New York NY 10019-4001

TODD, SHIRLEY ANN, school system administrator; b. Botetourt County, Va., May 23, 1935; d. William Leonard and Margaret Judy (Simmons) Brown; m. Thomas Byron Todd, July 7, 1962 (dec. July 1977). B.S. in Edn., Madison Coll., 1956; M.Ed., U. Va., 1971. Cert. tchr., Va. Elem. tchr. Fairfax County Sch. Bd., Fairfax, Va., 1956-66, 8th grade history tchr., 1966-71, guidance counselor James F. Cooper Mid. Sch., McLean, Va., 1971-88, dir. guidance, 1988—; chmn. mktg. Lake Anne Joint Venture, Falls Church, Va., 1979-82, mng. ptnr., 1980-82. Del. Fairfax County Republican Conv., 1985. Fellow Fairfax Edn. Assn. (mem. profl. rights and responsibilities commn. 1970-72, bd. dirs. 1968-70), Va. Edn. Assn. (mem. state com. on local assns. and urban affairs 1969-70), NEA, No. Va. Counselors Assn. (hospitality and social chmn., exec. bd. 1982-83), Va. Counselors Assn. (exec. com. 1987), Va. Sch. Counselors Assn., Am. Assn. for Counseling and Devel., Chantilly Nat. Golf and Country Club (v.p. social 1981-82, Centreville, Va.). Baptist. Avocations: golf, tennis. Home: 6543 Bay Tree Ct Falls Church VA 22041-1001 Office: James F Cooper Mid Sch 977 Balls Hill Rd Mc Lean VA 22101-2020

TODD, THOMAS ABBOTT, architect, urban designer; b. North Stonington, Conn., May 5, 1928; s. James Arnold and Isabel Nisbet (Downs) T.; m. Carol Roberts, July 7, 1956; children: Christopher, Suzannah, Cassandra. B.A., Haverford Coll., 1950; M.C.P., U. Pa., 1959, M.Arch. with honors, 1959. Designer Geddes Brecher Qualls Cunningham, Phila., 1961; chief designer Eshbach Pullinger Stevens Bruder, Phila., 1962; partner Grant & Todd, Phila., 1963, Wallace McHarg Roberts Todd, Phila., 1963-79, Wallace Roberts & Todd, Phila., 1979-91. Works include The master plan for Abuja, capitol city of, Nigeria; urban design concept, master plan and public architecture for Balt. Inner Harbor; master plan U.S. Capitol Grounds, McKeldin Sq., Balt., Norfolk waterfront design, (Va.), Atlantic City Conv. Ctr./Rail Terminal, Lower Manhattan Plan, N.Y.C., Downtown L.A. devel. Plan, plan for State facilities, Annapolis, Md., master plan Haverford Coll., 6th St Market Pl., Richmond, Va., Tredegar Galleries Valentine Mus., Richmond, Waterside Festival Market, Norfolk, Va., Liberty State Pk., Jersey City, N.J., Wiggins Waterfront State Pk., Camden, N.J., Downtown Buffalo master plan, Quadrangle Life Care Community, Haverford, Liberty Pl. master plan, Phila., long range devel. plan U. Pa., Performing Arts Ctr., Haverford Coll., Assembly Hall, Germantown Friends Sch., plan for downtown Westerly, R.I., numerous pvt. residences, landscape plans, instl. and pub. master plans; contbr. numerous articles, editorials to profl.jours. Bd. dirs. Germantown Friends Sch., Phila., 1972-74, Green St. Friends Sch., Phila., 1973-75, Phila. Maritime Mus., 1986-90, Philomel Ancient Instruments, Phila., 1986-91, Maxwell Mansion, Phila., 1983-86; v.p. Haverford Coll. Arboretum, 1983; chmn. ann. giving Haverford Coll., 1987; mem. Jamestown (R.I.) Planning Bd.; advisor Ft. Adams Found., Newport, R.I. Theophilus Parsons Chandler fellow, 1959; recipient numerous design awards. Fellow AIA; mem. Am. Inst. Cert. Planners. Republican. Quaker. Home: 118 Highland Dr Jamestown RI 02835-2900

TODD, VIRGIL HOLCOMB, clergyman, religion educator; b. Jordonia, Tenn., June 22, 1921; s. George Thurman and Nellie Mai (Dutton) T.; m. Irene Rolman, Sept. 21, 1941; 1 child, Donald Edwin. BA, Bethel Coll., 1945; BD, Cumberland Presbyn. Sem., 1947; MA, Scarritt Coll., 1948; PhD, Vanderbilt U., 1956. Ordained to ministry Presbyn. Ch., 1944. Minister Cumberland Presbyn. Chs., Tenn. and Ky., 1943-52; assoc. prof. Bethel Coll., McKenzie, Tenn., 1952-54; prof. of Old Testament Memphis Theol. Sem., 1954—; interim minister Presbyn. chs. in Tenn., Ky. and Miss., 1952—; vice-moderator Gen. Assembly Cumberland Presbyn. Ch., 1984-85, moderator, 1985-86. Author: Prophet Without Portfolio (2d Isaiah), 1972, A New Look at an Old Prophet (Ezekiel), 1977, Biblical Eschatology, 1985. Active Shelby (County) United Neighbors, Memphis, 1973-74, United Way of Greater Memphis, 1974-82. Mem. Soc. Bibl. Lit., Memphis Ministers' Assn. Democrat. Lodge: Civitan (chaplain, bd. dirs. local chpt.). Avocations: travel, golf. Office: Memphis Theol Sem 168 E Parkway S Memphis TN 38104-4340

TODD, WILLIAM BURTON, English language and literature educator; b. Chester, Pa., Apr. 11, 1919; s. William Booth and Edith Hawkins (Burton) T.; m. Ann Bowden, Nov. 23, 1969; children by previous marriage: Marilyn Chestnut Todd Guinn, Susan Linda Todd Kramer, Deborah Burton, Terence Kingsley. BA, Lehigh U., 1940, MA, 1947, LHD (hon.), 1975; PhD, U. Chgo., 1949. Prof., head dept. English, Salem (N.C.) Coll., 1949-54; asst. libr. Houghton Libr., Harvard U.; assoc. prof. English U. Tex., Austin, 1958; prof., dir. bibliog. rsch. U. Tex., 1959-82, Kerr Centennial prof. English history and culture, 1982-85, Kerr Prof. emeritus, 1985—, Ransom Ctr. scholar, 1990—; J.P.R. Lyell reader in bibliography Oxford (Eng.) U., 1969-70; Andrew D. Osbord lectr. U. Western Ont., 1978; cons. Nat. Libr. Australia, 1973; D. Nichol Smith lectr. Australian Nat. U., Canberra, 1973; Cecil Oldman Meml. lectr. Leeds (Eng.) U., 1975; mem. adv. bd. rsch. tools program NEH, 1977-78; Internat. Libr. lectr. Leipzig, Germany, 1981; Internat. Lit. lectr., Budapest, 1984; mem. nat. adv. bd. Ctr. for the Book, 1978-88. Author: New Adventures among Old Books, 1958, Prize Books: Awards Granted to Scholars, 1961, Bibliography of Edmund Burke, 1964, Directory of Printers: London 1800-1840, 1972, The White House Transcripts: An Enquiry, 1974, The Gutenberg Bible: New Evidence, 1982; editor: Goldsmith's Prospect of Society, 1954, Burke's Reflections on the Revolution in France, 1959, Thomas J. Wise Centenary Studies, 1959, (with E. Stenbock-Fermor) The Kilgour Collection of Russian Literature, 1959, Guy of Warwick, 1968, Suppressed Commentaries on the Wiseian Forgeries, 1969, Hume and the Enlightenment, 1974, (with R.H. Campbell and A.S. Skinner) Smith's Wealth of Nations, 1976, (with Paul Langford) Writings and Speeches of Burke, 1981-95, Hume's History of England, 1983-85, Papers Bibliog. Soc. Am., 1967-81, Swinburne's Character and Opinions of Dr. Johnson, 1985, (with Ann Bowden) Tauchnitz International Editions in English, 1988; contbr. articles to profl. jours. Served to maj. inf. AUS, 1941-45, ETO. Decorated Bronze Star, Purple Heart; Fulbright fellow U.K., 1952-53, Am. Coun. Learned Socs. fellow, 1961-62, Guggenheim fellow, 1965-66, vis. fellow All Souls Coll., 1970, Zachariah Poulson fellow Libr. Co. Phila., 1990, Peterson fellow Am. Antiquarian Soc., 1992; scholar-in-residence Rockefeller Conf. and Study Ctr., Villa Serbelloni, Bellagio, Italy, 1986, vis. scholar Wolfson Coll., Oxford, England, 1993; recipient Oldman Meml. award and Marc Fitch bibliography prize, 1975. Mem. MLA, Bibliog. Soc. Am. (v.p. 1981-84), Bibliog. Soc. (Eng.), Printing Hist. Soc., Johnsonians (chmn. 1985), Pvt. Librs. Assn. (Eng.) (pres. 1983-86), Assn. Internat. de Bibliophilie (France), Phi Beta Kappa. Club: Grolier. Home: 2803 Scenic Dr Austin TX 78703-1040

TODD, WILLIAM MICHAEL, lawyer; b. Cleve., Dec. 13, 1952; s. William Charles and Jennie Ann (Diana) T.; m. Sara Lynn, Jan. 4, 1986. BA, U. Notre Dame, 1973; JD, Ohio State U., 1976. Bar: Ohio 1976, U.S. Dist. Ct. (so. dist.) Ohio 1977, U.S. Supreme Ct. 1987. Assoc. Porter, Wright, Morris & Arthur, Columbus, Ohio, 1976-82, ptnr., 1983-93; ptnr. Squire, Sanders & Dempsey, Columbus, 1993—. Trustee Callvac Svcs., Columbus, 1985-91, pres. 1988. Mem. ABA (governing com. forum on health law 1988-91), Ohio Bar Assn., Columbus Bar Assn., Def. Rsch. Inst., Am. Soc. Med. Assn. Counsel, Am. Bd. Trial Advocates, Ohio Soc. Hosp. Attys., Nat. Health Lawyers Assn., Worthington Hills Country Club, Columbus Athletic Club. Roman Catholic. Avocations: music, recreational sports. Office: Squire Sanders & Dempsey 41 S High St Columbus OH 43215-6101

TODD, ZANE GREY, retired utilities executive; b. Hanson, Ky., Feb. 3, 1924; s. Marshall Elvin and Kate (McCormick) T.; m. Marysnow Stone, Feb. 8, 1950 (dec. 1983); m. Frances Z. Anderson, Jan. 6, 1984. Student, Evansville Coll., 1947-49; BS summa cum laude, Purdue U., 1951, DEng (hon.), 1979; postgrad., U. Mich., 1965; DHL, U. Indpls., 1993. Fingerprint classifier FBI, 1942-43; electric system planning engr. Indpls. Power & Light Co., 1951-56, spl. assignments supr., 1956-60, head elec. system planning, 1960-65, head substation design div., 1965-68, head distbn. engring. dept., 1968-70, asst. to v.p., 1970-72, v.p., 1972-74, exec. v.p., 1974-75, pres., 1975-81, chmn., chief exec. officer, 1976-89, dir., chmn. exec. com., 1989-94, chief exec. officer, 1981-89; chmn., pres. IPALCO Enterprises, Inc., Indpls., 1983-89, dir., chmn. exec. com., 1989-94; chmn. bd., chief exec. officer Mid-Am. Capital Resources, Inc. subs. IPALCO Enterprises, Inc., Indpls., 1984-89, also bd. dirs., 1984-94; gen. mgr. Mooresville (Ind.) Pub. Svc. Co., Inc., 1956-60; bd. dirs. Nat. City Bank Ind. (formerly Mchts. Nat. Corp.), 1975-94, Am. States Ins. Co., 1976-94; hon. dir. 500 Festival Assocs., Inc., pres. 1987. Originator probability analysis of power system reliability; contbr. articles to tech. jours. and mags. Past pres. adv. bd. St. Vincent Hosp.; bd. dirs. Commn. for Downtown, YMCA Found., Crime Stoppers Cen. Ind., Corp. Community Coun.; past chmn., bd. trustees Ind. Cen. U. (now U. Indpls.); bd. govs. Associated Colls. of Ind.; Nat. and Greater Indpls. adv. bds. Salvation Army; mem. adv. bd. Clowes Hall. Sgt. AUS, 1943-47. Recipient William Booth award Salvation Army, 1994; named Disting. Engring. Alumnus Purdue U., 1976, Outstanding Elec. Engr. Purdue U., 1992, Knight of Malta, Order of St. John of Jerusalem, 1986. Fellow IEEE (past chmn. power sys. engring. com.); mem. ASME, NSPE, Power Engring. Soc., Ind. Fiscal Policy Inst. (bd. govs.), Ind. C. of C., Indpls. C. of C., Mooresville C. of C. (past pres.), PGA Nat. Country Club, Ulen Country Club, Columbia Club, Indpls. Athletic Club (past bd. dirs.), Meridian Hills Country Club (past bd. dirs.), Skyline Club (bd. govs.), Newcomen Soc. (past chmn. Ind.), Rotary, Lions (past pres.), Eta Kappa Nu, Tau Beta Pi. Home: 7645 Randue Ct Indianapolis IN 46278-1565

TODER, ERIC JAY, economist; b. N.Y.C., Mar. 16, 1944; s. Saul and Rose (Cohen) T.; m. Susan C. Cote, Aug. 2, 1980. BS, Union Coll., 1964; MA in Econs., U. Rochester, 1967, PhD in Econs., 1971. Asst. prof. econs. Tufts U., Medford, Mass., 1968-73; sr. rsch. assoc. Charles River Assocs., Cambridge, Mass., 1973-76; fin. economist U.S. Dept. Treasury, Washington, 1976-83; dir. fin. and tax analysis U.S. Dept. Energy, Washington, 1980-81; dep. dir. Office Tax Analysis, U.S. Treasury, Washington, 1983-84; dep. asst. dir. Congl. Budget Office, Washington, 1984-88, 91-93; cons. New Zealand Treasury, Wellington, 1988-91; dep. asst. sec. tax analysis U.S. Dept. Treasury, Washington, 1993—. Author: Trade Policy and U.S. Auto Industry, 1978; contbr. to econs. publs. Mem. Am. Econ. Assn., Nat. Tax Assn., Assn. Pub. Policy Analysis and Mgmt., Washington Tax Economists Forum. Jewish. Avocations: travel, hiking, music. Office: US Dept Treasury 15th & Pennsylvania Ave NW Washington DC 20220

TODOROVIC, JOHN, chemical engineer; b. Madison, Wis., Mar. 28, 1961; s. Radmilo A. and Lillian (Djukic) T.; m. Nadja Petranin, June 29, 1991. BSChemE, Tex. A&M U., 1984; MSChemE, Rose-Hulman Inst. Tech., 1987. Process engr. GE Plastics, Pittsfield, Mass., 1989-90; sr. product devel. engr. Rexam Graphics, South Hadley, Mass., 1991—. Pres. Brazos Valley Amateur Soccer League, College Station, 1984. B. Rankovich scholarship B. Rankovich Found., 1986. Mem. AIChe (student chpt. pres. 1985), Sigma Xi, Tau Beta Pi, Alpha Chi Sigma. Serbian Orthodox. Achievements include implemented a new die coating technology that enabled a specialized product to be coated efficiently after several previous unsuccessful attempts. Office: Rexam Graphics 87 Alvord St South Hadley MA 01075

TODREAS, NEIL EMMANUEL, nuclear engineering educator; b. Peabody, Mass., Dec. 17, 1935; s. David and Anna (Gendleman) T.; m. Carol S. Schonberg, June 19, 1958; children: Timothy, Ian. B.S.M.E., Cornell U., 1958, M.S., 1958; Sc.D. in Nuclear Engring., MIT, 1966. Asst. prof. dept. nuclear engring. MIT, Cambridge, 1970-71, assoc. prof., 1971-75, prof., 1975—, Kepco prof. nuclear engring. and prof. mech. engring., 1992—, head dept. nuclear engring., 1981-89. Served to lt. (j.g.) USN, 1958-62. Named Disting. Tchr., Ruth and Joel Spira award MIT Sch. Engring., 1995; Arthur Holly Compton award Am. Nuclear Society, 1995. Fellow Am. Nuclear Soc. (Arthur Holly Compton award for outstanding educators in nuclear engring. 1995, Tech. Achievement award for outstanding contbns. to thermal hydraulics 1994), ASME; mem. Nat. Acad. Engring., Sigma Xi, Tau Beta Pi, Pi Tau Sigma. Office: MIT 77 Massachusetts Ave # 24-219 Cambridge MA 02139-4301

TODRES, ELAINE M., Canadian provincial official; married; two children. PhD in Polit. Sci., U. Pitts. Asst. dep. min. Ont. Women's Directorate Min. of Revenue, dep. min. human resources secretariat, chair civil svc. comm, dep. min. culture and comm., dep. min. culture, tourism and recreation, 1993-95, dep. solicitor gen., dep. min. correctional svcs., 1995—; spkr. in field. Editor-at-large Agy. for Instrnl. Tech.; mem. editl. bd. Can. Inst. Pub. Adminstr., 1992. Office: Ste 400 N Tower, 175 Bloor St E, Toronto, ON Canada M4W 3R8

TOEDTMAN, JAMES SMITH, newspaper editor, journalist; b. Dayton, Ohio, Dec. 1, 1941; s. James Christian and Ella Barnes (Smith) T.; m. Haydee N. Sicart, Aug. 23, 1969; children—Eric, Kristen. A.B., Coll. Wooster, 1963; postgrad., U. Queensland, Brisbane, Australia, 1964; M.Sc. in Journalism, Columbia U., 1967. Pub. dir. Coll. Wooster, Ohio, 1963, 65; reporter, city editor, Sunday news editor, Washington Bur. news editor Newsday, L.I., N.Y., 1967-79; exec. editor Boston Herald Am., 1979-82; editor Balt. News Am., 1982-86; mng. editor N.Y. Newsday, 1986—; editor N.Y. Newsday, Balt., 1986-95; Washington bur. chief N.Y. Newsday, 1995—. Recipient shared award Silurian Soc., Polk award, N.Y. Pubs. award, Pulitzer Prize, 1970, spl. citation Inter-Am. Press Assn., 1979, best editorial award Md.-Del.-D.C. Press Assn., 1984, 86; Rotary Found. fellow, 1964, Internat. fellow Columbia U., 1966-67. Mem. AP Mng. Editors, Coll. of Wooster Alumni Assn. (pres. 1980-81). Methodist. Home: 2604 Geneva Hill Ct Oakton VA 22124 Office: 1730 Pennsylvania Ave NW Washington DC 20006

TOENSING, VICTORIA, lawyer; b. Colon, Panama, Oct. 16, 1941; d. Philip William and Victoria (Brady) Long; m. Trent David Toensing, Oct. 29, 1962 (div. 1976); children: Todd Robert, Brady Cronon, Amy Victoriana; m. Joseph E. diGenova, June 27, 1981. BS in Edn., Ind. U., 1962; JD cum laude, U. Detroit, 1975. Bar: Mich. 1976, D.C. 1978. Tchr. English Milw., 1965-66; law clk. to presiding justice U.S. Ct. Appeals, Detroit, 1975-76; asst. U.S. atty. U.S. Atty.'s Office, Detroit, 1976-81; chief counsel U.S. Senate Intelligence Com., Washington, 1981-84; dep. asst. atty. gen. criminal div. Dept. Justice, Washington, 1984-88; spl. counsel Hughes Hubbard & Reed, Washington, 1988-90; ptnr. Cooter and Gell, Washington, 1990-91; ptnr., co-chmn. nat. white collar group Manatt, Phelps and Phillips, Washington, 1991-95; founding ptnr. diGenova & Toensing, Wasington, 1996—; mem. working group on corp. sanctions U.S. Sentencing Commn., 1988-89; co-chairperson Coalition for Women's Appts. Justice Judiciary Task Force, 1988-92; rep. legal expert for trial of O.J. Simpson, Am.'s Talking, legal analyst, 1995. Author: Bringing Sanity to the Insanity Defense, 1983, Mens Rea: Insanity by Another Name, 1984; contbg. author: Fighting Back: Winning The War Against Terrorism, Desk Book on White Collar Crime, 1991; contbr. articles to profl. jours. Founder, chmn. Women's Orgn. To Meet Existing Needs, Mich., 1975-79; chmn. Republican Women's Task Force, 1979-81; bd. dirs. Project on Equal Edn. Rights, Mich., 1980-81, Nat. Hist. Intelligence Mus., 1987-95, America's Talking Legal Analyst, 1995. Recipient spl. commendation Office U.S. Atty. Gen., 1980, agy. seal medallion CIA, 1986, award of achievement Alpha Chi Omega, 1992; featured on cover N.Y. Time Mag. for anti-terrorism work, April 1991. Mem. ABA (mem. standing com. on law and nat. security, mem. coun. criminal justice sect., mem. adv. com. complex crimes and litigation, vice chmn. white collar crime com., chmn. subcom. on corp. criminal liability).

TOEPFER, SUSAN JILL, editor; b. Rochester, Minn., Mar. 9, 1948; d. John Bernard and Helen Esther (Chapple) T.; m. Lorenzo Gabriel Carcaterra, May 16, 1981; children: Katherine Marie, Nicholas Gabriel. BA, Bennington Coll., 1970. Mng. editor Photoplay Mag., N.Y.C., 1971-72; freelance writer, N.Y.C., 1972-78; TV week editor N.Y. Daily News, N.Y.C., 1978-79, leisure editor, 1979-82, features editor, 1982-84, arts and entertainment editor, 1984-86, exec. mag. editor, 1986-87; sr. writer People Mag., 1987-89, sr. editor, 1989-91, asst. mng. editor, 1991-94, exec. editor, 1994—. Office: People Mag Time-Life Bldg Rockefeller Ctr New York NY 10020

TOEPKE, UTZ PETER, lawyer; b. Konigsberg, Germany, May 5, 1940; came to U.S., 1976; s. Gunter and Christel (Printz) T.; m. Beverley Beatrice Goldsworthy, Nov. 29, 1975; children: Christopher, Beatrice, Thomas. LLB, U. Hamburg, Fed. Republic Germany, 1965, Dr.jur., 1967, Assessor, 1970. Bar: Stuttgart, Fed. Republic Germany 1973, N.Y. 1978, Hamburg 1982. Assoc. Altstotter, Weisgerber, Kalb, Nuremberg, Fed. Republic Germany, 1967-70; bus. mgr. Aktiva, GmbH, Nuremberg, 1970-72; internat. counsel IBM Germany, Stuttgart, 1972-73; counsel internat. law IBM, London and Armonk, N.Y., 1973-81; ptnr. Schwartz, Klink & Schreiber, N.Y.C., 1982-86, Heimann, Hardenberg & Ptnrs., Hamburg, 1982—, Graham & James, N.Y.C., Frankfurt, Germany, 1986—; adj. prof. NYU. Contbr. articles to profl. jours. Mem. ABA (mem. antitrust internat. law sect., chmn. European law com.), Hanseatische Rechtsanwaltskammer Hamburg, Hamburgischer Anwaltsverein, Met. Club, Shore Club. Home: 919 3rd Ave # 4778 New York NY 10022 Office: Skadden Arps 919 3rd Ave New York NY 10022-3903*

TOEPLITZ, GIDEON, symphony society executive; b. Tel Aviv, Nov. 18, 1944; s. Erich and Ruth (Loeb) T.; m. Gail Ransom, Sept. 2, 1978. B.A., Hebrew U., Jerusalem, 1969; M.B.A., UCLA, 1973. Flutist, Israel Philharm. Orch., 1969-71; asst. mgr. Rochester Philharm., 1973-75; asst. mgr. Boston Symphony, 1975-79, orch. mgr., 1979-81; exec. dir. Houston Symphony Soc., 1981-87; v.p., mng. dir. Pitts. Symph. Orch., 1987—. Mem. Nat. Acad. Rec. Arts and Scis., Am. Jewish Com. (bd. dirs.). Home: 2087 Beechwood Blvd Pittsburgh PA 15217-1705

TOEVS, ALDEN LOUIS, management consultant; b. American Falls, Idaho, Jan. 25, 1949; s. Alden Louis and Wilma Christen (Coffee) T.; m. Coralie Norwood Sickels, July 20, 1974. BS, Lewis and Clark Coll., 1971; PhD, Tulane U., 1975. NSF fellow MIT Energy Lab., Boston, 1975-76; prof. econs. La. State U., Baton Rouge, 1976-77, U. Oreg., Eugene, 1978-83; dir. mortgage rsch. Morgan Stanley and Co., N.Y.C., 1983-90; mng. v.p. First Manhattan Cons. Group, N.Y.C., 1990—; vis. scholar Fed. Home Loan Bank, San Francisco, 1983, Fed. Reserve Bank, 1982; dir. capital market research U. Oreg., Eugene, 1982-83. Author: Innovations in Bond Portfolio Managements, 1983; editor, bd. dirs. Fin. Analysts Jour., 1983-95, Jour. Portfolio Mgmt., 1984-90; contbr. articles to profl. jours. Recipient Graham and Dodd scroll Fin. Analysts Fed., 1983.

TOEWS, DANIEL PETER, zoologist; b. Grande Prairie, Alta, Can., Dec. 18, 1941; married; three children. BS, U. Alta, 1963, MS, 1966; PhD in Zoology, U. B.C., 1969. Asst. prof. zoology U. Alta, 1969-71; assoc. prof. Acadia U., Wolfville, N.S., Can., 1971-80, prof. biology, 1980—. Mem. Can. Soc. Zoology, Brit. Soc. Expt. Biology. Office: Acadia University, Perry Biological Laboratories, Wolfville, NS Canada B0P 1X0 Office: Dept Biology, Acadia Univ, NS, Wolfville, Canada*

TOFEL, RICHARD JEFFREY, newspaper executive; b. N.Y.C., Feb. 17, 1957; s. Robert Leonard and Carol (Collins) T.; m. Jeanne Helen Straus, Feb. 26, 1983; children: Rachel Straus, Colin Straus. AB, Harvard U., 1979; MPP, JFK Sch. Govt., 1983; JD, Harvard U., 1983. Bar: N.Y. 1984, U.S. Dist. Ct. (so. and ea. dists.) N.Y. 1984, U.S. Ct. Appeals (2d cir.) 1987, U.S. Dist. Ct. (no. dist.) N.Y. 1988, U.S. Supreme Ct. 1990. Assoc. Patterson, Belknap, Webb & Tyler, N.Y.C., 1983-86; exec. dir. Mayor's Commn. Human Svcs. Reorganization, N.Y.C., 1984-85; assoc. Gibson, Dunn & Crutcher, N.Y.C., 1986-89; counsel Dow Jones & Co., Inc., N.Y.C., 1989-91, asst. gen. counsel, 1991-92; asst. mng. editor The Wall St. Jour., N.Y.C., 1992-95; dir. internat. devel. and adminstrn. Dow Jones & Co., Inc., N.Y.C., 1995—. Contbr. articles to profl. jours. Mem. ABA, Assn. of Bar of City of

N.Y. Democrat. Jewish. Home: 12 W 96th St # 8a-8B New York NY 10025-6509 Office: Dow Jones & Co Inc 200 Liberty St New York NY 10281-1003

TOFF, NANCY ELLEN, book editor; b. Greenburgh, N.Y., Aug. 29, 1955; d. Ira N. and Ruth (Bluthenthal) T. AB, Radcliffe Coll./Harvard U., 1976. Editor and producer Music Minus One, N.Y.C., 1973-75; researcher Time-Life Books, Alexandria, Va., 1976-80; editor & asst. producer Time-Life Music, Alexandria, Va., 1980-84; production mgr. Vanguard Recording Soc., N.Y.C., 1984-86; editor Grove's Dictionaries of Music, N.Y.C., 1984-85; v.p. & editor-in-chief Chelsea House Pubs., N.Y.C., 1986-89, v.p., dir. book devel., 1990; editorial dir. Julian Messner/Silver Burdett Press, Englewood Cliffs, N.J., 1990-91; editl. dir. children's and young adult books Oxford U. Press, N.Y.C., 1991—; editorial cons., Music Div. Lib. of Congress, 1983; hist. cons., Dept. of Musical Instruments, Met. Mus. of Art, N.Y.C., 1986. Author: The Development of the Modern Flute, 1979, The Flute Book, 1985, Georges Barrère and the Flute in America, 1994; cons. editor Flutist Quar., 1990—; contbr. articles to profl. jours.; curator Georges Barrère and the Flute in America, N.Y. Pub. Libr., 1994. Bd. dirs., Radcliffe Coll. Alumnae Assn. 1979-80. Mem. Nat. Flute Assn. (asst. sec. 1988-89, sec. 1989-90, bd. dirs. 1990-92), N.Y. Flute Club (bd. dirs. 1986—, sec. 1991-92, pres. 1992-95, 1st v.p. 1995—). Home: 309 E 87th St Apt 5H New York NY 10128-4812 Office: Oxford U Press 198 Madison Ave New York NY 10016-4314

TOFFEL, ALVIN EUGENE, corporate executive, business and governmental consultant; b. Los Angeles, July 14, 1935; s. Harry and Estelle Charlotte Toffel; m. Neile McQueen; children: Stephanie, Elizabeth, Michelle; step children: Terry, Chad. B.A., UCLA, 1957. Dir. mgmt. systems and organizational planning Rockwell Internat., 1963-69; Exec. Office for the Pres. White House, Washington, 1969-70; nat. chmn., campaign dir. McCloskey for Pres., 1971-72; polit. cons., 1971—; cons. personal bus. and govt. Norton Simon and Norton Simon, Inc., Los Angeles, 1972-80; pres. Norton Simon Found., Pasadena, Calif., 1977-80; cons. exec. asst. to pres. Twentieth Century Fox Film Corp., 1980; bd. dirs. Geometrics, Inc.; pres. So. Shellfish Inc., Atlantic Internat. Ins. Ltd., Toffel Thoroughbred Racing; lectr. mgmt. UCLA, Stanford U. Pres. Norton Simon Mus. Art, Pasadena; vice chmn. U.S. Pension Svcs., Inc. With SAC USAF, 1958-63. Recipient White House Interchange Exec. Outstanding Achievement, 1971; recipient Achievement Am. Advtg. Council, 1972. Mem. Ky. Cols., Presdl. Interchange Execs. Assn., Assn. Old Crows. Developed standard U.S. govt. program performance measurement system, aerospace engrng. techniques of program mgmt., aerospace manuals. Home and Office: 2323 Bowmont Dr Beverly Hills CA 90210-1808 *My legacy derives from my grandparents leaving the familiar to come to America. Here, anything can be accomplished if one honestly defines what he wants. It then becomes a matter of choosing among the many ways to accomplish anything. The character of the individual can be seen by the choices he makes.*

TOFIAS, ALLAN, accountant; b. Boston, Apr. 13, 1930; s. George I. and Anna (Seidel) T.; m. Arlene Shube, Aug. 30, 1981; children: Bradley Neil, Laura Jean Silver. BA, Colgate U., 1951; MBA, Harvard U., 1956. CPA, Mass. Sr. acct. Peat, Marwick, Mitchell & Co., Boston, 1956-60; mng. ptnr. Tofias, Fleishman, Shapiro & Co., P.C., Boston, 1960-96; chmn. bd., 1996—. Mem. Brookline (Mass.) Town Meeting, 1970-77, mem. fin. adv. bd., 1975-81; mem. New Eng. Bapt. Health Care Corp., 1985—; bd. dirs. West Newton YMCA, 1986-89; mem. exec. com. Boston Aid to Blind, bd. dirs., 1988—, pres., 1993-94. Lt. USNR, 1951-54. Mem. AICPA (coun. 1995—), Mass. Soc. CPA's (pres. 1995-96), Nat. CPA Group (exec. com. 1983-88, vice chmn. 1985-88), BKR Internat. (world bd. dirs. 1988—, chmn. 1994—), Wightman Tennis Club (treas. 1974-76), Newton Squash and Tennis Club (bd. dirs. 1966—), Masons. Home: 59 Monadnock Rd Wellesley MA 02181-1334 Office: Tofias Fleishman Shapiro & Co PC 205 Broadway Cambridge MA 02139-1901

TOFT, RICHARD P(AUL), title insurance executive; b. St. Louis, Sept. 20, 1936; s. Paul C. and Hazel F. T.; B.S.B.A., U. Mo., 1958; m. Marietta Von Etzdorf, Oct. 5, 1963; children—Christopher P., Douglas J. With Lincoln Nat. Life Ins. Co., 1959-73, group and pension sales mgr., 1969-73; 2d v.p. Lincoln Nat. Sales Corp., Ft. Wayne, Ind., 1973-74, v.p., 1974-80, v.p., treas., 1980-81; pres. Chgo. Title Ins. Co., 1981-82, pres., chief exec. officer Chgo. Title Ins. Co. and Chgo. Title and Trust Co., 1982—, also dir. both; dir. Lincoln Nat. Devel. Corp. Trustee, Chgo. Community Trust, 1982. Served to 2d lt. U.S. Army, 1958-59. Mem. Am. Land Title Assn. Congregationalist. Club: Union League (Chgo.). Office: Chgo Title & Trust Co 171 N Clark St Chicago IL 60601-3203

TOFT, THELMA MARILYN, secondary school educator; b. Balt., Sept. 15, 1943; d. George Edward and Thelma Iola (Smith) Trageser; m. Ronald Harry Toft, Aug. 27, 1966; 1 child, Joanna Lynn. BS in Med. Tech., Mt. St. Agnes Coll., Balt., 1965; BSE, Coll. Notre Dame, Balt., 1972; MEd, Pa. State U., 1983. Recreation dir. Villa Maria, Balt., 1961-65; blood bank supr. Wayman Park NIH, Balt., 1965-68; tchr. Sacred Heart, St. Mary's Govan's, Balt., 1968-74, Lincoln Intermediate Unit # 12, Adams County, Pa., 1979-80, York (Pa.) City Sch. Dist., 1980—; curriculum dir. M.O.E.S.T. Pa. State U., 1991-93; mem. Pa. State Consortium-Pa. Team for Improving Math. and Sci.; grant writer, speaker in field; writer sch. to work curriculum. Active Girl Scouts USA, Hanover, 1988-92, leader, 1984-87; mgmt. bd. Agrl. Indsl. Mus. Mem. ASCD, AAUW, Nat. Ptnrs. in Edn., Am. Bus. Women's Assn. (edn. com. 1992, sec. 1993, Chpt. Woman of Yr. 1994, York County Woman of Yr. 1995), Phi Delta Kappa. Democrat. Roman Catholic. Avocations: writing, marketing. Home: 30 Panther Dr Hanover PA 17331-8888

TOFTNER, RICHARD ORVILLE, engineering executive; b. Warren, Minn., Mar. 5, 1935; s. Orville Gayhart and Cora Evelyn (Anderson) T.; m. Jeanne Bredine, June 26, 1960; children: Douglas, Scott, Kristine, Kimberly, Brian. BA, U. Minn., 1966; MBA, Xavier U., 1970. Registered environ. assessor, Calif. Sr. economist Federated Dept. Stores, Inc., Cin., 1967-68; dep. dir. EPA, Washington and Cin., 1968-73; mgmt. cons. environ. affairs, products and mktg., 1973-74; prin. PEDCo Environ., Cin., 1974-80; trustee PEDCo trusts, 1974-80; pres. ROTA Mgmt., Inc., Cin., 1980-82; gen. mgr. CECOS, 1982-85, cons., 1985—; v.p. Smith, Stevens & Young, 1985-88; real estate developer, 1980—; pres., CEO Toxitrol Internat., Inc., 1988-89; dir. Environ. Svcs. Belcan Engrng. Group, Inc., Cin., 1989-92; prin. exec. cons. Resource Mgmt. Internat., Inc., 1994—; adj. prof. environ. engrng. U. Cin., 1975-86; lectr. Grad. fellowship rev. panel Office of Edn., 1978-79; advisor, cabinet-level task force Office of Gov. of P.R., 1973; pvt. investor, 1991—; bd. dirs. EnviroAudit Svcs., Inc., pres., CEO, 1992—; mem. legis. com. Ohio Chem. Coun., 1995—; subcom. Nat. Safety Coun., 1972; mem. exec. environ. briefing panels Andersen Consulting, 1991-92; nominee commr. PUCO, Ohio; chmn. Cin. City Waste Task Force, 1987-88; co-chair Hamilton County Resource Recovery Com., 1989—. Contbr. articles on mgmt. planning and environ. to periodicals, chpts. to books; inventor, developer Toxitrol Waste Minimization; inventor EnviroAudit. With AUS, 1954-57. Mem. Nat. Registry Environ. Profl. Rep., Engrng. Soc. Cin., Assn. Corp. Environ. Execs., Cin. C. of C., Global Assn. Corp. Environ. Execs. (charter), Bankers Club. Republican. Lutheran. Home: 9175 Yellowwood Dr Cincinnati OH 45251-1948 Office: 4700 Ashwood Dr Ste 100 Cincinnati OH 45241-2424

TOGAFAU, MALAETASI MAUGA, judge; b. Pago Pago, Am. Samoa, June 4, 1946; s. Sefulu Mauga Togafau and Femalua'i (Mauga) Sialo'i; m. Oreta Mapu, Dec. 10, 1977; children: Malaetasi Jr., Steve, June, Wayne, Heidi. BS, Peru Stat U., 1971; JD, Calif. Western Sch. of Law, 1974. Asst. pub. defender High Ct., Am. Samoa, 1974; legis. asst. Office of Del.-at-Large, Washington, 1975-80, U.S. Ho. of Reps., Washington, 1981-82; rep. Legislature of Am. Samoa, Am. Samoa, 1983-86; atty. Law Firm of Talalelei Tulafono, Am. Samoa, 1983-86; dist. ct. judge High Ct., Am. Samoa, 1986-93; atty. gen. Am. Samoa, 1993—. Legal counsel Dem. Party, Am. Samoa, 1985-86; chmn. budget com. Ho. of Reps., Am. Samoa, 1985-86; vice chmn., bd. dirs. Denm. Bank of Am. Samoa, 1985-86. Mem. Am. Samoa Bar Assn., Nat. Jud. Coll. Democrat. Mem. Congregation Christian Ch. Avocations: softball, long boat crew, farming. Office: Office of Atty Gen PO Box 7 Pago Pago AS 96799*

TOGASAKI, SHINOBU, computer scientist; b. San Francisco, Aug. 17, 1932; s. Kikumatsu and Sugi (Hida) T.; m. Toshiko Kawaguchi, Nov. 24, 1959; children: John Shinobu, Ann Mariko. BS in Math., Duke U., 1954; postgrad., Stanford U., 1954-56. Math. programmer IBM, 1956—; sr. programmer IBM, Palo Alto, 1970-87; mgr. applications devel. Service Bur. Corp., Palo Alto, 1961-64, sr. analyst, 1964-68; systems architect devel. lab. Service Bur. Corp., San Jose, Calif., 1968-70; chief fin. officer Robin Hood Ranch, Inc., 1976—; mgr. architecture & strategy Hewlett Packard Corp., Cupertino, Calif., 1987-89; mgr. strategic planning, 1989-93; chief architect MFA Hewlett Packard, 1993—. Mem. Am. Mgmt. Assn., AAAS, Am. Statis. Assn., Assn. Computing Machinery, Inst. Mgmt. Sci., Palo Alto C. of C., Sigma Pi Sigma. Home: 2367 Booksin Ave San Jose CA 95125-4705 Office: 19447 Pruneridge Ave Cupertino CA 95014-0609

TOGERSON, JOHN DENNIS, computer software company executive; b. Newcastle, England, July 2, 1939; arrived in Can., 1949; s. John Marius and Margaret (McLaughlin) T.; m. Donna Elizabeth Jones, Oct. 3, 1964 (div. 1972); children: Denise, Brenda, Judson; m. Patricia Willis, May 5, 1984. BME, GM Inst., Flint, Mich., 1961; MBA, York U., Toronto, Ont., 1971. Sr. prodn. engr. GM of Can., Oshawa, Ont., 1961-69; with sales, investment banking Cochran Murray, Toronto, 1969-72; pres. Unitec, Inc., Denver, 1972-79, All Seasons Properties, Denver, 1979-81, Resort Computer Corp., Denver, 1981—; mng. dir. VCC London (subs. of Resort Computer Corp.), 1992; bd. dirs. VCC London (sub. of 1st Nat. Bank U.K.), London, 1989—, mng. dir., 1992; pres., bd. dirs. Resort Mgmt. Corp., Dillon, Colo., 1980-81; presenter Assn. of Resort Developers Nat. Conv., 1993, Internat. T.S. Found. Think Tank, 1993, and others. Contbr. articles to profl. jours. Avocations: mountain biking, ice hockey. Office: Resort Computer Corp 2801 Youngfield St Ste 300 Golden CO 80401-2266

TOGNINO, JOHN NICHOLAS, financial services executive; b. N.Y.C., Sept. 20, 1938; s. Gennaro and Catherine (Barbieri) T.; m. Norma Lucille Borrelli, Nov. 7, 1959; children: Katherine Ann, John Nicholas Jr., Michael A. BA in Econs. summa cum laude, Fordham U., 1975. Instnl. sales trader A.G. Becker & Co., N.Y.C., 1970-72; trader Merill Lynch, N.Y.C., 1957-69, instnl. salesman, 1972-74, mgr. over-the-counter sales trading, 1974-83, dir. over-the-counter dept., 1983-87, dir. unlisted trading, 1987-88; mng. dir. non-dollar equities Merill Lynch, London, 1988-91; mng. dir. global equities, ret. Merill Lynch, N.Y.C., 1991-93; exec. v.p. Charles Schwab & Co., Inc., Jersey City, 1993—; bd. dirs. Nat. Assn. Security Dealers Automated Quotations Inc. Contbg. author: Market Maker Sponsorship: A Synergistic Package of Services, 1987. Pres. Ardsley (N.Y.) Rep. Club, 1967-68; mem. Ardsley Bd. Edn., 1977-84, pres. 1979; v.p. Ardsley Sch. Dist. Bd., 1978, 81; mem. exec. com. of laity Archdiocese of N.Y.C., 1988. Named Trader of Yr., Security Traders Monthly mag., 1984, Over-the-Counter Man of Yr., Equities mag., 1986. Mem. Nat. Security Traders Assn. (various offices 1981-88, chmn. fin. com. Found. 1992—), Nat. Assn. Security Dealers (bus. conduct com. 1984-86), Security Traders Assn. N.Y. (various offices 1973-83, pres. 1980-81), St. Andrews Golf Club (Hastings, N.Y.), Grey Oaks Country Club (Naples, Fla.), Alpha Sigma Lambda. Republican. Roman Catholic. Avocations: jogging, tennis, golf. Home: 114 Boulder Rdg Scarsdale NY 10583-3138 Office: Charles Schwab & Co 111 Pavonia Ave Jersey City NJ 07310-1755

TOGO, YUKIYASU, automotive executive; b. Yokohama, Kanagawa, Japan, Nov. 13, 1924; came to U.S., 1983; s. Kinji Togo and Nobuko Watanabe; m. Misako Mineta, Apr. 2, 1948; children: Yukinori, Yumi. Gen. mgr. Toyota Motor Sales, Tokyo, Japan, 1976-78, assoc. dir., 78-79, dir., 1979-80; pres. Toyota Can. Inc., Ontario, Can., 1980-82; dir. Toyota Motor Corp., Aichi, Japan, 1982, mng. dir., 1982-83; pres. Can. Auto Parts Toyota Inc., B.C., Can., 1983—; pres., chief exec. officer Toyota Motor Sales U.S.A. Inc., Torrance, Calif., 1983—; pres. Toyota Motor Credit Corp., Torrance, Calif., 1989—, Toyota Motor Ins. Svcs., Torrance, Calif., 1989—, Toyota Aviation USA Inc., Torrance, Calif., 1989—. Bd. dirs. Los Angeles World Affairs Coun., 1989. Avocations: golf, flying, skiing. Office: Toyota Motor Sales USA Inc 19001 S Western Ave Ste 2991 Torrance CA 90501-1106*

TOIBIN, COLM, journalist, writer; b. Ireland, 1955. Journalist, columnist Dublin Sunday Ind., 1985—. Author: Seeing Is Believing: Moving Statues in Ireland, 1985, (travelogue) Walking Along the Border, 1987, Homage to Barcelona, 1990, Dubliners, 1990, (novel) The South, 1990, The Trial of the Generals: Selected Journalism, 1980-90, The Heather Blazing, 1993, Soho Square 6: New Writing from Ireland, 1993; contbr. articles to profl. publs. Recipient E.M. Forster award Am. Acad. of Arts and Letters, 1995. Home: 23 Carnew St, Dublin 7, Ireland*

TOKAR, EDWARD THOMAS, manufacturing company executive; b. Passaic, N.J., June 12, 1947; s. Edward Thomas Sr. and Helen (Fabian) T.; m. Frances Deland, Sept. 30, 1972; 1 child, Adam Edward. BS with high honors, U. Md., 1969; MBA, Coll. William and Mary, 1971; postgrad., George Washington U., 1972. CPA, N.J., Md. Audit, cons. Touche Ross & Co., Washington, 1970-73; mgr. fin. div. Nat. Rural Electric Coop. Assn., Washington, 1973-77; v.p. investments Allied-Signal Inc., Morristown, N.J., 1977—; bd. dirs. Morgan Products Ltd., Noel Group Inc.; mem. bd. advisors Saugatuck Capital Co., Stamford, RFE Investment Ptnrs., Stamford, Allen Value Ptnrs.; trustee Morgan Grenfel Investment Trusts; mem. pension adv. com. N.Y. Stock Exch., N.Y.C. Trustee Newark Boys Chorus Sch., 1980-84, Coll. of William and Mary; mem. investment adv. com. Paterson Diocese Roman Cath. Ch., Clifton, N.J. Mem. AICPA, Nat. Econs. Club, Sentinel Pension Inst. (bd. advisors), Investment Tech. Symposium, Fin. Execs. Inst., CIEBA Comm. Avocations: golf, tennis. Home: 8 Sweetbriar Rd Summit NJ 07901-3256 Office: Allied-Signal Inc PO Box 1219R Morristown NJ 07962-1219

TOKER, FRANKLIN K., art history educator, archaeologist, foundation executive; b. Montreal, Apr. 29, 1944; came to U.S., 1964; naturalized, 1983; s. Maxwell Harris and Ethel (Herzberg-Serchuk) T.; m. Ellen Judith Burack, Sept. 3, 1972; children: Sarah Augusta, Maxwell, Jeffrey. BA, McGill U., Montreal, 1964; AM in Fine Arts, Oberlin Coll., 1966; PhD in Fine Arts, Harvard U., 1973. Instr. Boston Sch. Architecture, 1967; archaeol. dir. Florence (Italy) Cathedral excavations, 1969-74; A.W. Mellon vis. prof. Carnegie-Mellon U., Pitts., 1974-76, assoc. prof., 1976-80; assoc. prof. fine arts U. Pitts., 1980-87, prof., 1987—; vis. prof. U. Florence, 1988-89, U. Rome, 1991—, U. Reggio Calabria, 1996; preservation cons. The Carnegie, Pitts., 1981-83; bd. dirs. Allegheny Survey, Pitts. History and Landmarks Found., 1980-85; mem. Inst. for Advanced Study, Princeton, N.J., 1985; fellow Com. to Rescue Italian Art, Florence, 1969; fellow I Tattie-Harvard U. Ctr. for Italian Renaissance Studies, Florence, 1972. Author: Notre Dame in Montreal, 1970 (Alice Davis Hitchcock award 1971), French edit., 1981, 2d English edit., 1991, S. Reparata: l-Antica Cattedrale Fiorentina, 1974, Pittsburgh: An Urban Portrait, 1986 (Pitts. History and Landmarks Found. award 1987); contbr. articles to profl. jours. Mem. econ. devel. com. Allegheny Conf. Community Devel., Pitts., 1983-85. Kress fellow, 1965; Can. Coun. fellow, 1966; Guggenheim fellow, 1979; NEH grantee 1979, 92, NEH sr. fellow, 1985, fellow Bellagio Study and Conf. Ctr., Rockefeller Found., 1994. Mem. Coll. Art Assn. (life, Arthur Kingsley Porter prize 1980), Medieval Acad. (life), Soc. Archtl. Historians (pres., 1993-94, life mem., bd. dirs. 1985-88), Archaeol. Inst. Am., Internat. Ctr. for Medieval Art. Avocations: creative writing, photography, cycling. Home: 1521 Denniston Ave Pittsburgh PA 15217-1449 Office: U Pittsburgh Dept History Art Archi Pittsburgh PA 15260

TOKER, KAREN HARKAVY, physician; b. New Haven, Conn., Oct. 23, 1942; d. Victor M. and Nedra (Israel) Harkavy; m. Cyril Toker, Sept. 1, 1968; children: David Edward, Rachel Lee. BS in Chemistry, Coll. William and Mary, 1963; MD, Yale U., 1967. Diplomate Am. Bd. Pediatrics, 1974. Intern dept. pediatrics Bronx Mcpl. Hosp. Ctr., Albert Einstein Coll. Medicine, N.Y., 1967-68, asst. resident dept. pediatrics, 1968-69, sr. resident dept. pediatrics, 1969, 70-71, attending pediatrician, 1971-72, 73-76; pediatrician Montgomery Health Dept., Silver Springs, Md., 1976-83; pediatric cons. Head Start Program Montgomery County Pub. Schs., Rockville, Md., 1976-83; pvt. practice gen. pediatrics Rockville, 1983-89; pediatrician Nemours Children's Clinic, Jacksonville, Fla., 1991-95; med. dir. Pearl Plaza Pediatrics, Duval County Pub. Health Unit, 1995—; instr. pediatrics Albert Einstein Coll. Medicine, N.Y., 1971-74, asst. prof. pediatrics, 1974-76; clin. asst. prof. U. Fla., 1995—. Exec. bd. sec. Congregation Har Shalom, Potomac, 1989-91. Fellow Am. Acad. Pediatrics; mem. Fla. Med. Assn., Duval County Med. Soc., Ambulatory Pediatric Assn. Democrat. Jewish. Avocations: piano, opera, ballet, swimming. Home: 6030 Oakbrook Ct Ponte Vedra Beach FL 32082-2052 Office: Pearl Plaza Pediatrics 5220 N Pearl St Jacksonville FL 32208

TOKOFSKY, JERRY HERBERT, film producer; b. N.Y.C., Apr. 14, 1936; s. Julius H. and Rose (Trager) T.; m. Myrna Weinstein, Feb. 21, 1968 (div.); children: David, Peter; m. Fiammetta Bettuzzi, 1970 (div.); 1 child, Tatianna; m. Karen Oliver, Oct. 4, 1981. BS in Journalism, NYU, 1957, LLD, 1959. Talent agt. William Morris Agy., N.Y.C., 1953-59; v.p. William Morris Agy., L.A., 1959-64; exec. v.p. Columbia Pictures, L.A., 1964-69; v.p. Paramount Pictures, London, 1970; exec. v.p. MGM, London, 1971; pres. Jerry Tokofsky Prodns., L.A., 1972-82; exec. v.p. Zupnik Enterprises, L.A., 1982-92; pres. Jerry Tokofsky Entertainment, Encino, Calif., 1992—; prof. Sch. TV and Film U. So. Calif. Sch. Bus. Prodr. films: Where's Poppa, 1971, Born to Win, 1972, Dreamscape, 1985, Fear City, 1986, Wildfire, 1988, Glengarry Glen Ross, 1992, The Grass Harp, 1994, American Buffalo, 1995, Double Down, 1996, Life on Mars, 1996. With U.S. Army, 1959, res. 1959-63. Named Man of Yr. B'nai B'rith, 1981; recipient L.A. Resolution City of L.A., 1981. Mem. Variety Club Internat. Avocations: skiing, tennis, golf, chess. *Passion for family, life, work, with patience and intelligence and you have a chance to grab that winning ring.*

TOKUMARU, ROBERTA, principal. Prin. Aikahi Elem. Sch. Recipient DOE Elem. Sch. Recognition award, 1989-90. Office: Aikahi Elem Sch 281 Ilihau St Kailua HI 96734-1657

TOLAN, DAVID J., insurance corporation executive; b. Detroit, Dec. 27, 1927; s. Joseph James and Helen Barbara (Blahnik) T.; m. Roseann Biwer, Feb. 15, 1958; children: Joseph, David, Julie. AB, Haverford Coll.; JD, U. Mich.; MS, Am. Coll. Bar: Wis.; CLU. Pvt. practice atty. Milw., 1952-57; agt. Northwestern Mut. Ins. Co., Milw., 1957—; prin. Tolan, Schueller & Assoc., Ltd., Milw., 1959—; lectr. AICPAs, Am. Soc. CLUs, Wis. Bar Assn., 1975—; mem. faculty CLU Inst., 1990—. Contbr. articles to profl. jours. Pres. Young Reps. Milwaukee County, 1961; bd. dirs. United Performing Arts Fund, Milw., 1966, 91, 92, Bel Canto Chorus, Milw., 1960—; scoutmaster Boy Scouts Am., 1975-77; mem. Com. for Future of Milw., 1988. With U.S. Army, 1954-57. Recipient Disting. Svc. award Assn. Milw. Assn. Life Underwriters, 1990. Mem. Am. Soc. CLUs, Assn. Advanced Life Underwriters, Estate Counselors Forum, Mid Winter Estate Planning Coun. Republican. Roman Catholic. Club: University (Milw.). Avocations: golf, sailing, scuba, singing. Office: Tolan Schueller and Assocs 770 N Jefferson St Milwaukee WI 53202-3701

TOLAN, DAVID JOSEPH, transportation executive; b. N.Y.C., Jan. 25, 1933. BS in Marine Transp., SUNY, Bronx, 1955. Deck mcht. marine officer Alcoa Steamship Co., Bklyn., 1955-61; with Sea-Land Svc., Edison, N.J., 1961—, marine mgr. to group v.p. Ams., 1984-85; sr. v.p. labor rels. Sea-Land Corp., Edison, 1985—; bd. dirs. Shipping Industry Mut. Assurance Soc., Vt. Industry Mut. Assurance Soc., Sea-Land Svc. Inc. Trustee Christian Bros. Acad., Lyncroft, N.J., 1984-89. Recipient Good Scout award Greater N.Y. Coun., N.Y.C., 1987, Dir.'s award Fed. Mediation and Conciliation Svc., 1991, Humanitarian award Am. Cancer Soc. Schneider-Lerner Chpt., 1995; named Person of Yr. Seaman's House YMCA, 1994. Mem. Am. Maritime Assn. (pres. 1985—), Carriers Container Coun., Inc. (chmn. 1985—), Transp. Inst. (bd. dirs. 1985—), N.Y. Shipping Assn., Inc. (bd. dirs. 1978-82, 85—), Pacific Maritime Assn. (exec. com. 1979-82, 85—), Maritime Assn. of Port of N.Y./N.J. (bd. dirs. 1991-94). Office: Sea-Land Svc Inc 600 Carnegie Blvd Charlotte NC 28209

TOLAN, JAMES FRANCIS, corporate and financial communications executive, marketing consultant, financial analyst; b. Hornell, N.Y., Oct. 3, 1934; s. Edward Bartholemew and Mercedes Irene (Welden) T.; m. Dawna Marie Sheehan, Jan. 25, 1959 (dec. June 1977); children—Jeffrey, Lyn, Craig, Leslie, Lisa, Jason, Brendan, Gavin, Lauren; m. Barbara Ann Bierowski, Apr. 9, 1983; 1 child, Timothy. B.S., Canisius Coll., 1956. Stockbroker Bache & Co., Binghamton, N.Y., 1960-66; sr. analyst Value Line Investment Service, N.Y.C., 1966-68; exec. v.p. Lyle D. Gumm & Assocs., Chgo., 1968-73; nat. sales mgr. Heinold Commodities, Inc., Chgo., 1973-79; ptnr. Fin. Rels. Bd., Chgo., 1979-91; pres. Fin. Community Contact Inc, Waukegan, Ill., 1991-92; sr. v.p. O'Connor Biro & Assocs., Northbrook, Ill., 1992—; v.p. Kemper Lesnik Comm. Served to sgt. U.S. Army, 1957-58. Roman Catholic. Home: 214 Douglas Ave Waukegan IL 60085-2040 Office: Kemper Lesnik Communications 455 City Front Plz Chicago IL 60611*

TOLAND, FLORENCE WINIFRED, printing company executive, retired business educator; b. Paola, Kans., Aug. 6, 1906; d. Frederick W. and Bertha G. (Cartwright) Arzberger; BA, U. Ariz., 1935, MS in Bus. Adminstrn., 1946; m. Jess William Toland, Dec. 23, 1934 (dec. 1954); 1 child, Ronald William. Tchr. grade sch., Dos Cabezos, Willcox and Mascot, Ariz., 1925-32, jr. high and high sch., 1934-36, 38-42, amphitheater sch., Tucson; asst. prof. U. Ariz., Tucson, 1942-71, asst. prof. emeritus, 1971—; co-owner, mgr., pres. Pima Printing Co., Tucson, 1954—. Mem. Ariz. Bus. Educators Assn. (life), Nat. Bus. Educators Assn., Western Bus. Educators Assn., Pi Omega Pi, Pi Lambda Theta. Democrat. Club: Order Eastern Star. Co-author: Transcription Method Shorthand, 1946. Home: 5461 N Paseo Espejo Tucson AZ 85718-5229 Office: 110 S Park Ave Tucson AZ 85719

TOLAND, JOHN WILLARD, historian, writer; b. La Crosse, Wis., June 29, 1912; s. Ralph and Helen Chandler (Snow) T.; m. Toshiko Matsumura, Mar. 12, 1960; 1 dau., Tamiko; children by previous marriage: Diana Toland Netzer, Marcia. B.A., Williams Coll., 1936; student, Yale Drama Sch., 1936-37; L.H.D., Williams Coll., 1968, U. Alaska, 1977, Western Conn. U., 1986. Mem. adv. council Nat. Archives. Author: Ships in the Sky, 1957, Battle: The Story of the Bulge, 1959, But Not in Shame, 1961 (Best Book Fgn. Affairs award Overseas Press Club), The Dillinger Days, 1963, The Flying Tigers, 1963, The Last 100 Days, 1966 (Best Book Fgn. Affairs citation Overseas Press Club), The Battle of the Bulge, 1966, The Rising Sun, 1970 (Van Wyck Brooks award for non-fiction, Best Book Fgn. Affairs award Overseas Press Club, Pulitzer prize for non-fiction), Adolf Hitler, 1976 (Best Book Fgn. Affairs award Overseas Press Club, Gold Medal Nat. Soc. Arts and Letters), Hitler, The Pictorial Documentary of His Life, 1978, No Man's Land, 1980 (Best Book Fgn. Affairs citation Overseas Press Club), Infamy, 1982, In Mortal Combat, 1991; (novels) Gods of War, 1985, Occupation, 1987; also short stories. Served to capt. USAAF, 1942-46, 1947-49. Mem. Authors Guild, Accademia del Mediterraneo., Western Front Assn. (hon. v.p.). Home: 101 Long Ridge Rd Danbury CT 06810-8434

TOLAND, JOY E., marketing professional; b. Newark, Apr. 8, 1965; d. William D. Cartwright; m. Mark E. Toland, Sept. 10, 1988. BS, Montclair State U., 1987. Staff acct., acctg. clk., billing clk. Delta Dental Plan of N.J., Parsippany; support svc. mgr. PyMaH Corp., Flemington, N.J., 1996—; dir. mktg. Am. Multi-Svcs. Unltd., Inc., Manville, N.J. Mem. NAFE, N.J. Healthcare Cen. Svc. Assn., N.Y.C. Assn. for Cen. Svc. and Materials Mgmt. Pers., L.I. Intercounty chpt. Cen. Svc. Pers., Kiwanis (treas. Circle K 1983-84). Avocations: camping, reading.

TOLBERT, BERT MILLS, biochemist, educator; b. Twin Falls, Idaho, Jan. 15, 1921; s. Ed. and Helen (Mills) T.; m. Anne Grace Zweifler, July 20, 1959; children—Elizabeth Dawn, Margaret Anne, Caroline Joan, Sarah Helen. Student, Idaho State U., 1938-40; B.S., U. Calif. at Berkeley, 1942, Ph.D., 1945; postgrad., Fed. Inst. Tech., Zurich, Switzerland, 1952-53. Chemist Lawrence Radiation Lab., Berkeley, 1944-57; faculty U. Colo., Boulder, 1957-89, prof., 1961-89, prof. emeritus, 1989—, assoc. chmn. dept. chemistry and biochemistry, 1980-88; bd. dirs. Hauser Chem. Rsch., Boulder, 1983—; vis. prof. IAEA, Buenos Aires, Argentina, 1961-62; Biophysicist U.S. AEC, Washington, 1967-68; cons. pvt. cos, govt. agys. Author: (with others) Isotopic Carbon, 1948; contbr. (with others) articles to profl. jours. Fellow AAAS; mem. Am. Chem. Soc., Am. Soc. Biochemistry and Molecular Biology, Radiation Rsch. Soc., Soc. for Exptl. Biology and Medicine. Rsch. on organic chemistry, including use of isotopes in chemistry and biochemistry, radiation chemistry, radiation effects in protein, intermediary metabolism, metabolism of ascorbic acid, nutritional biochemistry, instrumentation in radioactivity. Home: 444 Kalmia Ave Boulder CO 80304-1732

TOLBERT, JAMES R., III, financial executive; b. Amarillo, Tex., Apr. 29, 1935; s. James R. and Mary (Noble) T.; m. Elizabeth McMahan, Dec. 26, 1956; children: James R. IV, Cannon Miles, Elizabeth Nelson, Lee Mitchener. Student, Stanford U., 1953-55; B.A., Okla. U., 1957; M.B.A., Stanford U., 1959. Vice pres. acquisitions Mid-Am. Corp., 1959-64; pres. James R. Tolbert & Assos., Inc., 1964-69; chmn. bd., treas., co-founder Holden Tolbert & Co., 1967—; sr. partner, co-founder Resource Analysis and Mgmt. Group, 1969-80; chmn., pres. First Okla. Corp., 1986—; trustee in bankruptcy Four Seasons Nursing Ctrs. of Am., Inc., 1971-72; pres., treas., chmn. bd. Anta Corp., Oklahoma City, 1972-85; bd. dirs. Bonray Drilling Corp., Sun Healthcare, Inc. Chmn. Okla. Higher Edn. Task Force, 1986, Oklahoma City Arts Coun., 1987-89; chmn. Okla. Futures Commn., 1988-90; trustee Casady Sch., 1989-94, Okla. Found. for Humanities, McGee Eye Inst.; chmn. Myriad Gardens Authority and Found. Recipient Exec. Leadership of Yr. award Oklahoma City U., 1975, 4th Ann. Dean A. McGee award, Downtown Now, 1989. Democrat. Home: 2321 Belleview Ter Oklahoma City OK 73112-7740 Office: First Okla Corp PO Box 1533 Oklahoma City OK 73101-1533

TOLBERT, NATHAN EDWARD, biochemistry educator, plant science researcher; b. Twin Falls, Idaho, May 19, 1919; s. Edward and Helen (Mills) T.; m. Evelynne Cedarlund, June 21, 1952 (dec. Nov. 1963); children—Helen, Carol, James; m. Eleanor Dalgleish, June 22, 1964. BS in Chemistry, U. Calif., Berkeley, 1941; PhD in Biochemistry, U. Wis., 1950. Prof. biochemistry Mich. State U., East Lansing, 1958-89, prof. emeritus, 1989—. Editor: Biochemistry of Plants, Vol. 1, 1980; editor 3 sci. jours.; contbr. numerous papers, revs., abstracts to profl. publs.; patentee in field. Served to capt. USAF, 1943-45, PTO. Named disting. prof. Mich. State U., 1963, Mich. Scientist of Yr., 1985; Fulbright fellow, 1969; grantee NSF, NIH. Mem. Nat. Acad. Sci., Am. Soc. Plant Physiology (pres. 1983-84, Stephen Hale award 1980), Am. Soc. Biol. Chemists, Am. Chem. Soc., Nat. Acad. Sci. Avocation: travel. Office: Mich State U Dept Biochemistry East Lansing MI 48824

TOLCHIN, JOAN GUBIN, psychiatrist, educator; b. N.Y.C., Mar. 10, 1944; d. Harold and Bella (Newman) Gubin; m. Matthew Armin Tolchin, Sept. 1, 1966; 1 child, Benjamin. AB, Vassar Coll., 1964; MD, NYU, 1972. Diplomate Am. Bd. Gen. Psychiatry, Am. Bd. Child Psychiatry. Rsch. asst. Albert Einstein Coll. Medicine, N.Y.C., 1964-68; instr. psychiatry med. coll. Cornell U., N.Y.C., 1977-78, clin. instr., 1978-86, clin. asst. prof., 1986—. Contbr. articles to profl. jours. Fellow Am. Acad. Child and Adolescent Psychiatry; mem. APA, Am. Acad. Psychoanalysis, N.Y. Coun. Child and Adolescent Psychiatry (bd. dirs. 1992-96, pres. 1994-95), Alpha Omega Alpha. Office: 35 E 84th St New York NY 10028-0871

TOLCHIN, MARTIN, newspaper reporter, author; b. N.Y.C., Sept. 20, 1928; s. Charles T. and Evelyn (Weisman) Tolchin; m. Susan Jane Goldsmith, Dec. 23, 1965; children: Charles, Karen. Student, U. Utah, 1947-49; LL.B., N.Y. Law Sch., 1951. Reporter N.Y. Times, N.Y.C., 1954-94; publisher and editor-in-chief The Hill, Washington, 1994—. Author: (with Susan Jane Tolchin) To The Victor, 1971, Clout-Woman Power and Politics, 1974, Dismantling America-The Rush to Deregulate, 1983, Buying Into America: How Foreign Money is Changing the Face of Our Nation, 1988, Selling Our Security—The Erosion of America's Assets, 1992. Served with U.S. Army, 1951-53. Recipient Schaeffer Gold Typewriter award E.M. Schaeffer Co., 1967; recipient Page One award Newspaper Guild N.Y., 1967, 69, 73, Citizens Budget Commn. award, 1967, Sigma Delta Chi award, 1973, Everett M. Dirksen award for disting. reporting of Congress, 1983. Jewish. Club: Nat. Press (Washington). Home: 5117 Wickett Ter Bethesda MD 20814-5716 Office: The Hill 733 15th St NW Washington DC 20005-2112

TOLCHIN, SUSAN JANE, public administration educator, writer; b. N.Y.C., Jan. 14, 1941; d. Jacob Nathan and Dorothy Ann (Markowitz) Goldsmith; m. Martin Tolchin, Dec. 23, 1965; children: Charles Peter, Karen Rebecca. B.A., Bryn Mawr Coll., 1961; M.A., U. Chgo., 1962; Ph.D., N.Y.U., 1968. Lectr. in polit. sci. City Coll., N.Y.C., 1963-65, Bklyn. Coll., 1965-71; adj. asst. prof. polit. sci. Seton Hall U., South Orange, N.J., 1971-73; assoc. prof. polit. sci., dir. Inst. for Women and Politics, Mt. Vernon Coll., Washington, 1975-78; prof. pub. adminstrn. George Washington U., Washington, 1978—. disting. lectr. Industrial Coll. of the Armed Forces, 1994. Author: (book) The Angry American: How Voter Rage is Changing the Nation, 1996; co-author (with Martin Tolchin): To The Victor: Political Patronage from the Clubhouse to the White House, 1971, Clout-Womanpower and Politics, 1974, Dismantling America-The Rush to Deregulate, 1983, Buying Into America-How Foreign Money Is Changing the Face of Our Nation, 1988, Selling Our Security-The Erosion of America's Assets, 1992. Bd. dirs. Cystic Fibrosis Foun., 1982—; county committeewoman Dem. Party, Montclair, N.J., 1969-73. Dilthey fellow George Washington U., 1983, Aspen Inst. fellow, 1979; named Tchr. of Yr., Mt. Vernon Coll., 1978; recipient Founder's Day award NYU, 1968. Fellow Nat. Acad. Pub. Adminstrn.; mem. Am. Polit. Sci. Assn. (pres. Women's Caucus for Polit. Sci. 1977-78), Am. Soc. Pub. Adminstrn. (chairperson sect. Natural Resources and Environ. Adminstrn. 1982-83). Democrat. Jewish. Office: George Washington U Dept Pub Adminstrn Washington DC 20052

TOLCHINSKY, PAUL DEAN, organization design psychologist; b. Cleve., Sept. 30, 1946; s. Sanford Melvin and Frances (Klein) T.; m. Laurie S. Schermer, Nov. 3, 1968 (div. Jan. 1982); m. Kathy L. Dworkin, June 19, 1988; children: Heidi E., Dana M. BA, Bowling Green State U., 1971; PhD, Purdue U., 1978. Bd. dirs. Temple Tiferth Israel, Cleve., 195. With U.S. Army, 1966-69, Vietnam. Mem. APA, Acad. Mgmt. Democrat. Jewish. Avocations: running, travel. Office: Dannemiler Tyson Assocs Box 22987 Beachwood OH 44122

TOLEDANO, RALPH DE, columnist, author, photographer; b. Internat. Zone of Tangier, Aug. 17, 1916; s. Hayim and Suzanne (Nahon) de T.; m. Nora Romaine, July 6, 1938 (div. 1964); children: James, Paul, Christopher; m. Eunice Marshall, Apr. 19, 1979. Student, Fieldston Sch., N.Y.C., 1928-34; BA, Columbia Coll., 1938; student, Cornell U., 1943. Founder, co-editor Cross-Town, 1932-33; Founder, co-editor Jazz Info., 1938-39; assoc. editor The New Leader, 1941-43; editor The Standard, 1946; mng. editor Plain Talk, 1946-47; pub. dir. Dress Joint Bd., Internat. Ladies Garment Workers Union, 1947-48; asst. editor Newsweek, 1948, nat. reports editor, 1950-60, asst. chief Washington Bur., 1956-60; syndicated columnist King Features, 1960-71, Nat. News Research Syndicate, 1971-74, Copley News Service, 1974-89, Heritage Features Syndicate, 1989-91, Creators Syndicate, 1991—; editor House Republican Leadership report Am. Mil. Strength and Strategy; chief Washington Bur., Taft Broadcasting Co., 1960-61; dir. polit. intelligence Goldwater Presdl. Campaign Com., 1963-64; contbg. editor Nat. Rev., 1960—; pres. Nat. News-Research, 1960—, Anthem Books, 1970; editor-in-chief Washington World, 1961-62; vice chmn. Am. Conserva-Union, 1965-66; mem. 20th Century Fund Task Force on Freedom Press, 1971-72. Author: Seeds of Treason, 1950, Spies, Dupes and Diplomats, 1952, Day of Reckoning, 1955, Nixon, 1956, Lament for a Generation, 1960, The Greatest Plot in History, 1963, The Winning Side, 1963, The Goldwater Story, 1964, RFK: The Man Who Would be President, 1967, America, I-Love-You, 1968, One Man Alone: Richard M. Nixon, 1969, Claude Kirk: Man and Myth, 1970, Little Cesar, 1971, J. Edgar Hoover: The Man in His Time, 1973, Hit and Run: The Ralph Nader Story, 1975, Let Our Cities Burn, 1975, Poems: You & I, 1978, Devil Take Him, 1979, The Apocrypha of Limbo (poems), 1994, Notes from the Underground: The Chambers-Toledano Letters; editor: Frontiers of Jazz, 1947; co-editor: The Conservative Papers, 1962, 64, 93; editor-in-chief: Political Success, 1968-69; mem. adv. bd.: Yale Lit. Mag, 1981-86; contbr. to nat. mags. Bd. dirs. Americans for Constitutional Action, 1966-67, Constructive Action, 1990—. With OSS, AUS, 1943-46. Recipient Freedoms Found. award, 1950, 61, 74; Americanism award VFW, 1953; Heritage Found. Disting. Journalism fellow. Mem. Internat. Mark Twain Soc. (knight), Bibl. Archeology Soc., Dutch Treat Club (N.Y.), Nat. Press Club, Naval and Mil. Club (London), Am. Philatelic Soc., NRA, Sigma Delta Chi. Office: 500 23rd St NW Washington DC 20037-2828

TOLEDO, FRANCISCO, painter, printmaker; b. Minatitlan, Oaxaca, Mex., July 17, 1940. Grad., Nat. Inst. Fine Arts, 1959. One-man shows include Martha Jackson Gallery, N.Y., 1975, Everson Mus., Syracuse, N.Y., 1980; retrospective Nat. Mus. Modern Art, Tokyo, 1974, Mus. Modern Art, Mexico City, 1976, Mus. Contemporary Art, Bogota, Colombia, 1977, Mus. Biblioteca Pape, Monslova, 1979, others. Office: c/o TwoSixtyOne Art Ste 8A 261 Broadway New York NY 10007

TOLENTINO, CASIMIRO URBANO, lawyer; b. Manila, May 18, 1949; came to U.S., 1959; s. Lucio Rubio and Florence (Jose) T.; m. Jennifer Masculino, June 5, 1982; 2 children: Casimiro Masculino, Cristina Cecelia Masculino. BA in Zoology, UCLA, 1972, JD, 1975. Bar: Calif. 1976. Gen. counsel civil rights div. HEW, Washington, 1975-76; regional atty. Agrl. Labor Relations Bd., Fresno, Calif., 1976-78; regional dir. Sacramento and San Diego, 1978-81; regional atty. Pub. Employment Relations Bd., Los Angeles, 1981; counsel, west div. Writers Guild Am., Los Angeles, 1982-84; dir. legal affairs Embassy TV, Los Angeles, 1984-86; sole practice Los Angeles, 1986-87; mediator Ctr. Dispute Resolution, Santa Monica, Calif., 1986-87; asst. chief counsel Dept. of Fair Employment and Housing, State of Calif., 1986-92, adminstrv. law judge dept. social svcs., 1992—. Editor: Letters in Exile, 1976; contbr. articles and revs. to Amerasia Jour. Chmn. adv. bd. UCLA Asian Am. Studies Ctr., 1983-90; chmn. bd. Asian Pacific Legal Ctr., L.A., 1983-93 (Decade award); pres. bd. civil svc. commrs. City of L.A., 1984-85, 90-93; bd. dirs. met. region United Way, 1987-95; bd. dirs. Rebuild L.A., 1992—; mem. Asian-Pacific Am. adv. coun. L.A. Police Commn. Mem. State Bar Calif. (exec. com. labor law sect. 1985-88), Los Angeles County Bar Assn., Minority Bar Assn. (sec. 1984-85), Philippine Lawyers of So. Calif. (pres. 1984—, Award of Merit 1982). Democrat. Roman Catholic. Avocations: history, photography, travel.

TOLER, JAMES C., electrical engineer; b. Carthage, Ark., Jan. 31, 1936. BSEE, U. Ark., 1957; MSEE, Ga. Inst. Tech., 1970. Prin. rsch. engr. Ga. Inst. Tech., Atlanta, 1966—, dir. bioengring. ctr., 1984-95, dir. ctr. rehab. tech., 1987-93, dir. biomed. interactive tech. ctr., 1995—. Fellow IEEE; mem. Bioelectromagnetics Soc. Achievements include research on interaction of electromagnetic waves with biological systems. Office: Ga Tech Inst Bioengring Office Interdisc Programs 225 North Ave NW Atlanta GA 30332-0200

TOLER, RAY EDWARD, conductor, band director; b. Detroit, Feb. 1, 1942; s. Ralph Vivian and Neva Florence (Killough) T.; m. Catherine Virginia Hoff, Aug. 15, 1964; children: Ray Edward Jr., Eric Andrew, Bryan Alan. MusB, Tex. Christian U., 1964; MA summa cum laude, Trenton State Coll., 1975; grad., Air Command and Staff Coll., Maxwell AFB, Ala., 1982, Air War Coll, Maxwell AFB, Ala., 1984. Commd. 2d lt. USAF, 1968, advanced through grades to lt. col., 1984; trombonist 539th Air Force Band USAF, Lackland AFB, Tex., 1966-68; condr., comdr. Air Force Logistics Command Band Wright-Patterson AFB, Ohio, 1968-71; condr., comdr. 13th Air Force Band of the Pacific Clark AFB, The Philippines, 1971-73, Air Force Band of the East, McGuire AFB, N.J., 1973-75; condr., comdr. Mil. Airlift Command Band Scott AFB, Ill., 1975-78; condr., comdr. Air Force Band of the West, Lackland AFB, 1978-81, Band of the Air Force Res., Robins AFB, Ga., 1982-85; chief of bands and music USAF Pentagon, Washington, 1985-88; condr. USAF Band, Washington, 1985-88; ret. USAF, 1988; dir. bands Tex. A&M U., College Station, 1988—; trombonist Ft. Worth Symphony and Opera Co., 1963-65, Stan Kenton Orch. , L.A., 1965, Dallas Symphony Orch., 1965-66; band dir. Weatherford (Tex.) High Sch., 1964-66. Condr. rec. Music of the King, 1971; condr./prodr. rec. Music of West Africa, 1977, Ready Then, Ready Now, 1982, Concert Band Classics, 1983, Recall! Step-Off on Hullabaloo, 1990, Bands of Aggieland, 1993, Texas Aggie Band Centennial, 1994, Texas A&M Univ. Symphonic Band Live At TMEA, 1995; prodr. Comin' At 'Ya, 1984; condr./composer rec. In Concert, 1985; condr. rec. The Best of the Air Force Reserve, 1988. Deacon 1st Presbyn. Ch., Fairborn, Ohio, 1970; judge Miss Am. Scholarship Pageant, 1992, 94; bd. dirs. Woodcreek Homeowners assn., College Station, 1988-91; bd. dirs. Brazor Valley Symphony Orch., College Station, 1996. Mem. Nat. Assn. Mil. Marching Bands, John Philip Sousa Found. (bd. dirs.), Coll. Band Dirs. Nat. Assn., Tex. Bandmasters Assn., Tex. Music Educators Assn., World Assn. for Symphonic Bands and Ensembles, N.Am. Band Dirs. Coordinating Coun., Internat. Mil. Music Soc., Assn. Concert Bands, USAF Ret. Band Dirs. Soc., Kappa Kappa Psi, Phi Mu Alpha Sinfonia. Republican. Methodist. Avocations: reading, crossword puzzles, fishing, computers. Office: Tex A&M U Adams Band Bldg College Station TX 77843

TOLES, EDWARD BERNARD, retired judge; b. Columbus, Ga., Sept. 17, 1909; s. Alex and Virginia Frances (Luke) T.; m. Susan Evelyn Echols, Jan. 24, 1944; 1 son, Edward Bernard. A.B., U. Ill., 1932; postgrad., Law Sch., 1932-34; J.D., Loyola U., Chgo., 1936. Bar: Ill. bar 1936. Practiced in Chgo., 1936-69; asst. atty. U.S. Housing Authority, 1939-40; asst. gen. counsel, war corr. ETO; Chgo. Defender, 1943-45; U.S. bankruptcy judge No. Dist. Ill., Chgo., 1969-87. Author: Chicago Negro Judges, 1959, Negro Federal Judges, 1960, Negro Lawyer in Crisis, 1966, Black Lawyers and Judges in the U.S, 1971, also articles.; Editor: Cook County Bar News, 1961-63; Columnist: Bench and Bar, Nat. Bar Assn. Bull, 1968-75. Recipient U.S. War Dept. award for services as war corr., 1947, Ill. Jud. Coun. award, 1988; named Sr. Counsellor, Ill. State Bar Assn., 1986,. Mem. ABA, Fed. Bar Assn., Nat. Bar Assn. (Barrister of Year award 1960, C.F. Stradford award, columnist Bench and Bar Bull., historian jud. coun. 1985—), Chgo. Bar Assn. (bd. mgrs. 1969-70), Cook County Bar Assn. (Edward H. Wright award, 1962, pres. 1960-62), 7th Circuit Bar Assn. (World Peace Through Law Bar Assn.), Am. Judicature Soc., Nat. Conf. Bankruptcy Judges, Alpha Phi Alpha, Omega Psi Phi (Ode to Excellence award 1963). Democrat. Home: 4800 S Chicago Beach Dr Chicago IL 60615-2009

TOLES, THOMAS GREGORY, editorial cartoonist; b. Buffalo, Oct. 22, 1951; s. George Edward and Rose Elizabeth (Riehle) T.; m. Gretchen Amanda Saarnijoki, May 26, 1973; children: Amanda Laurel, Seth August. B.A. in English, SUNY-Buffalo, 1973. Artist Buffalo Courier-Express, 1973-80, cartoonist, 1980-82; cartoonist Buffalo News, 1982—, UPS, 1982—, The New Republic, 1992-94, U.S. News & World Report, 1994—. Author: The Taxpayer's New Clothes, 1985, Mr. Gazoo: A Cartoon History of the Reagan Era, 1987, At Least Our Bombs Are Getting Smarter: A Cartoon Preview of the 1990's, 1991, My Elected Representatives Went to Washington, 1996; creator (comic strip) Curious Avenue, 1992. Recipient John Fischetti Editorial Cartoon award Columbia Coll., Chgo., 1984, Pulitzer Prize for editorial cartooning, 1990. Mem. Am. Assn. Editorial Cartoonists. Home: 75 Central Ave Hamburg NY 14075-6219 Office: Buffalo News 1 News Plz Buffalo NY 14203-2930

TOLIVER, LEE, mechanical engineer; b. Wildhorse, Okla., Oct. 3, 1921; s. Clinton Leslie and Mary (O'Neall) T.; m. Barbara Anne O'Reilly, Jan. 24, 1942; children: Margaret Anne, Michael Edward. BSME, U. Okla., 1942. Registered profl. engr., Ohio. Engr. Douglas Aircraft Co., Santa Monica, Calif., 1942, Oklahoma City, 1942-44; engr. Los Alamos (N.Mex.) Sci. Lab., 1946; instr. mech. engring. Ohio State U., Columbus, 1946-47; engr. Sandia Nat. Labs., Albuquerque, 1947-82; instr. computer sci. and math. U. N.Mex., Valencia County, 1982-84; number theory researcher Belen, N.Mex., 1982—. Author: (computer manuals with G. Carli, AF. Schkade) Experience with an Intelligent Remote Batch Terminal, 1972; (with C.R. Borgman, T.I. Ristine) Transmitting Data from PDP-10 to Precision Graphics, 1973, Data Transmission-PDP-10/Sykes/Precision Graphics, 1975. With Manhattan Project (Atomic Bomb) U.S. Army, 1944-46. Mem. Math. Assn. Am., Am. Math. Soc., Am. Mensa Ltd. Achievements include devel. of 44 computer programs with manuals. Home: 206 Howell St Belen NM 87002-6225

TOLK, NORMAN HENRY, physics educator; b. Idaho Falls, Idaho, Jan. 9, 1938; s. Henry and Merle (Ricks) T.; m. Marilyn Ann Neubauer, Dec. 19, 1961; children: Jeffrey S., Bentley J., David H., Rebecca E., Amy C. AB in Physics, Harvard U., 1960; PhD in Physics, Columbia U., 1966. Rsch. physicist Columbia Radiation Lab., N.Y.C., 1966, rsch. assoc., 1966-67, lectr., mem. staff, 1967-68; adj. asst. prof. Columbia U., N.Y.C., 1968-69; mem. tech. staff Bell Telephone Lab., Murray Hill, N.J., 1968-83, Bell Comms. Rsch., Murray Hill, 1984; prof. physics Vanderbilt U., Nashville, 1984—, prof. dept. radiology, 1993—; adj. prof. physics Fisk U., Nashville, 1991—; cons. Physitron, Inc., Huntsville, Ala., 1993—, Lawrence Livermore Nat. Lab., Livermore, Calif., 1995—. Editor: Inelastic Ion-Surface Collisions, 1977, Desorpion Induced by Elec. Trans., 1983, Atomic Collisions in Solids, 1986; N.Am. editor Radiation Effects and Def./Solids, 1987—; contbr. over 140 articles to profl. jours. Alexander von Humboldt sr. scientist, 1987. Fellow Am. Phys. Soc. Home: 314 Appomattox Dr Brentwood TN 37027-4955 Office: Vanderbilt U Dept Physics PO Box 1807 B Nashville TN 37202-1807

TOLL, BARBARA ELIZABETH, art gallery director; b. Phila., June 8, 1945; d. Joseph M. and Evelyn (Fogel) T. BA, Goucher Coll., 1967; MFA, Pratt Inst., 1969. Asst. dir. jr. coun. Mus. Modern Art, N.Y.C., 1969-70; dir. Hundred Acres Gallery, N.Y.C., 1971-76; curator David Rockefeller Collection, N.Y.C., 1975-81; pres., dir. Barbara Toll Fine Arts, N.Y.C., 1981-94, dir., 1994—. Bd. dirs. Parks Coun., N.Y.C., 1995—. Avocation: gardening. Office: 138 Prince St New York NY 10012

TOLL, DANIEL ROGER, corporate executive, civic leader; b. Denver, Dec. 3, 1927; s. Oliver W. and Merle D'Aubigne (Sampson) T.; m. Sue Andersen, June 15, 1963; children: Daniel Andersen, Matthew Mitchell. AB magna cum laude (Pyne prize), Princeton U., 1949; MBA with distinction, Harvard U., 1955. With Deep Rock Oil Corp., Tulsa, 1949-51, asst. mgr. product supply and distbn.; with Helmerich & Payne, Tulsa, 1955-64, roughneck, landman, exploration mgr., pipeline constrn. mgr., v.p. fin., 1961-64; with Sunray DX Oil Co., Tulsa, 1964-69, treas., v.p. corp. planning and devel.; v.p. Sun Oil Co., 1969; with Walter E. Heller Internat. Corp., Chgo., 1970-85, sr. v.p. fin., dir., 1970-80, pres., dir., 1980-85, corp. and civic dir., 1985—; bd. dirs. Brown Group, Inc., Mallinckrodt Group, Inc. (formerly IMCERA Group Inc.), Kemper Nat. Ins. Co., Lincoln Nat. Income Fund, Inc., NICOR, Inc., A.P. Green Industries Inc. Vice chmn. Tulsa Cmty. Chest, 1964-66; v.p., bd. dirs. Tulsa Opera, 1960-69; bd. dirs. Tulsa Little Theatre, 1963-69, Internat. House, Chgo., 1984-87; bd. dirs. Inroads, Inc., 1973-95, nat. vice chmn., 1982-95; bd. dirs. Area coun. Boy Scouts Am., 1976-94, pres., 1981-83; mem. Kenilworth (Ill.) Sch. Bd. Dirs. 38, 1975-81, pres., 1978-81; bd. dirs., mem. exec. com., chmn. fin. and hosp. affairs coms. Evanston (Ill.) Hosp., 1982—; bd. dirs. Chgo. Met. Planning Coun., 1989—, pres., 1991-94; bd. dirs. Northwestern Healthcare Network, Inc., 1995—; trustee Princeton U., 1990-94. Lt. (j.g.) USNR, 1951-52. Baker scholar Harvard U., 1955. Mem. Chgo. Assn. Commerce and Industry (bd. dirs. 1979-86), Chgo. Club, Comml. Club, Econ. Club, Harvard Bus. Sch. Club (past pres., bd. dirs. 1971-91), Indian Hill Club (bd. govs. 1987-90), Princeton Club (past pres., bd. dirs. 1985—), Phi Beta Kappa. Home: 1500 Sheridan Rd #10-I Wilmette IL 60091-1879 Office: 135 S La Salle St Ste 1117 Chicago IL 60603-4203

TOLL, JACK BENJAMIN, government official; b. Denver, Nov. 25, 1925; s. John B. and Vera (Calabrese) T.; m. Jean Small, Dec. 31, 1946; children: Robert John, Barbara, Susan Jean, Jack Edward, Carol. J.D., U. Denver, 1947; postgrad., Westminster Law Sch., Denver, 1950. Bar: Colo. 1950. Inland marine mgr. Gen. Adjustment Bur., Denver, 1949-53; dir. legal dept. Denver Chgo. Trucking Co., 1953-65, sec., 1965-69; dir. D.C. Internat., Inc., Denver, 1966-69; v.p. D.C. Internat., Inc., 1967-69, sec., 1965-69; gen. counsel Denver Urban Renewal Authority, 1969-71; regional counsel HUD, 1971-82; regional dir. Merit Systems Protection Bd., 1982-88; ret., 1988; judge Jefferson County, Colo., 1955-59. Republican. Home: 14020 Elderberry Rd Golden CO 80401-2014

TOLL, JOHN SAMPSON, university administrator, physics educator; b. Denver, Oct. 25, 1923; s. Oliver Wolcott and Merle d'Aubigne (Sampson) T.; m. Deborah Ann Taintor, Oct. 24, 1970; children: Dacia Merle Sampson, Caroline Taintor. BS with highest honors, Yale U., 1944; AM, Princeton U., 1948, PhD, 1952; DSc (hon.), U. Md., 1973, U. Wroclaw, Poland, 1975; LLD (hon.), Adelphi U., 1978; hon. doctorate, Fudan U., Peoples Republic China, 1987; LHD (hon.), SUNY, Stony Brook, 1990; LLD (hon.), U. Md., Eastern Shore, 1993. Mng. editor, acting chmn. Yale Sci. mag., 1943-44; with Princeton U., 1946-49, proctor fellow, 1948-49; Friends of Elementary Particle Theory Research grantee for study in France, 1950; theoretical physicist Los Alamos Sci. Lab., 1950-51; staff mem., assoc. dir. Project Matterhorn, Forrestal Rsch. Ctr., Princeton U., 1951-53; prof., chmn. physics and astronomy U. Md., 1953-65; pres., prof. physics SUNY, Stony Brook, 1965-78; pres., prof. physics U. Md., 1978-88, chancellor, 1988-89, chancellor emeritus, prof. physics, 1989—; pres. Univs. Rsch. Assn., Washington, 1989-94, Washington Coll., Chestertown, Md., 1995—; 1st dir. SUNY Chancellor's Panel on Univ. Purposes, 1970; physics cons. to editl. staff Nat. Sci. Tchrs. Assn., 1957-61; U.S. del., head sci., secretariat Internat. Conf. on High Energy Physics, 1960; mem.-at-large U.S. Nat. Com. for Internat. Union of Pure and Applied Physics, 1960-63; chmn. rsch. adv. com. on electrophysics to NASA, 1961-65; mem. gov. Md. Sci. Resources Adv. bd., 1963-65; mem., chmn. NSF adv. panel for physics, 1964-67; mem. N.Y. Gov.'s Adv. Com. Atomic Energy, 1966-70; mem. commn. plans and objectives higher edn. Am. Coun. Edn., 1966-69; mem. Hall of Records Commn., 1979-88; mem., chmn. adv. coun. Princeton Plasma Physics Lab, 1979-85; mem. Adv. Coun. of Pres.'s, Assn. of Governing Bds., 1980-88, So. Regional Edn. Bd., 1980-90; mem. exec. com. Washington/Balt. Regional Assn., 1980-89, Nat. Assn. State Univs. and Land Grant Colls., 1980-88, Ctr. for the Study of the Presidency, 1983-84; mem. univ. programs panel of energy rsch. bd. Dept. Energy, 1982-83; mem. SBHE Adv. Com., 1983-89, Md. Gov.'s Chesapeake Bay Coun., 1985; mem. resource com. State Trade Policy Coun. Gov.'s High Tech Roundtable Md. Dept. Econ. Devel., 1986-89; marine divsn. chmn. NASULGC, 1986; bd. trustees Aspen Inst. for Humanities, 1987-89; mem. Commn. on Higher Edn. Middle States Assn. Colls. and Schs., 1987; chmn. adv. panel on tech. risks and opportunities for U.S. energy supply and demand U.S. Office Tech. Assessment, 1987-91; chmn. adv. panel on internat. collaboration in def. tech., U.S. Office Tech. Assessment, 1989-91, Sea Grant Rev. Panel U.S. Dept. Commerce, 1992-96—; chair., vis. prof. Nordic Inst. Theoretical Physics, Niels Bohr Inst., Denmark, U. Lund, Sweden, 1975-76. Math. Scis. Edn. Bd., 1991-93—. Contbr. articles to sci. jours. Recipient Benjamin Barge prize in math. Yale U., 1943, George Beckwith medal for Proficiency in Astronomy, 1944, Outstanding Citizen award City of Denver, 1958, Outstanding Tchr. award U. Md. Men's League, 1965, Nat. Golden Plate award Am. Acad. Achievement, 1968, Copernicus award govt. of Poland, 1973, Stony Brook Found. award for disting. contbns. to edn., 1979, Disting. Svc. award State of Md., 1981, Silver medal Sci. U. Tokyo, 1994; named Washingtonian of Yr., 1985; John Simon Guggenheim Meml. Found. fellow Inst. Theoretical Physics U. Copenhagen, U. Lund, Sweden, 1958-59. Fellow Am. Phys. Soc., Washington Acad. Scis. (pres. 1995-96); mem. NAS, NSTA, Am. Coun. Edn. (bd. dirs. 1986-89, NAACP (life), Am. Assn. Physics Tchrs., Fedn. Am. Scientists (chmn. 1961-62), Philos. Soc. Washington, N.Y. Acad. Scis., Assn. Higher Edn., Yale U. Sci. and Engring. Assn. (award for disting. contbns. 1996), Cosmos Club, Univ. Club, Phi Beta Kappa, Sigma Xi (Sci. Achievement award 1965), Phi Kappa Phi (disting.), Omicron Delta Kappa (hon.), Sigma Pi Sigma. Achievements include research on elementary particheory; scattering. Office: U Md Dept Physics College Park MD 20742-4111 also: Washington Coll Pres's Office Chestertown MD 21620 *Throughout my life I have tried mainly to do whatever seemed most important and useful.*

TOLL, MAYNARD JOY, JR., investment banker; b. L.A., Feb. 5, 1942; s. Maynard Joy and Ethel (Coleman) T.; m. Kathryn Wiseman, Sept. 12, 1964; children: Ian Wolcott, Adam Donahue. BA, Stanford U., 1963; MA, Johns Hopkins U., 1965, PhD, 1970. Asst. prof., asst. dean faculty U. Mass., Boston, 1968-71; legis. and adminstrv. asst. Sen. Edmund Muskie, Washington, 1971-75; from asst. v.p. to mng. dir. CS First Boston, N.Y.C., 1975—. Mem. Links Club. Democrat. Episcopalian.

TOLL, PERRY MARK, lawyer; b. Kansas City, Mo., Oct. 28, 1945; s. Mark Irving and Ruth (Parker) T.; m. Mary Anne Shottenkirk, Aug. 26, 1967; children: Andrea Lynne, Hillary Anne. BS in Polit. Sci. and Econs., U. Kans., 1967, JD, 1970. Bar: Mo. 1970 1970, U.S. Dist. Ct. (we. dist.) Mo. 1970, U.S. Tax. Ct. 1979, U.S. Supreme Ct. 1979. With Shughart, Thomson & Kilroy P.C., Kansas City, 1970-94, prs., 1995—; asst. prof. deferred compensation U. Mo., Kansas City, 1979-83; bd. dirs., pres. Heart of Am. Tax Inst., Kansas City, 1975-87. Mem., chmn. Prairie Village (Kans.) Bd. Zoning Appeals, 1977-95. Mem. ABA, Mo. Bar Assn., Nat. Health Lawyers Assn., Am. Agr. Law Assn., Mo. Merchants and Mfrs. Assn., Greater Kansas City Med. Mgrs. Assn., Lawyers Assn. Kansas City, East Kans. Estate Planning Coun. (bd. dirs., pres.), Phi Kappa Tau (bd. dirs.). Office: Shughart Thomson & Kilroy 12 Wyandotte Plz 120 W 12th St Kansas City MO 64105-1902

TOLL, ROBERT IRWIN, lawyer, real estate developer; b. Elkins Park, Pa., Dec. 30, 1940; s. Albert A. and Sylvia (Steinberg) T.; m. Norma (div.); children: Laurie, Deborah; m. Jane Snyder; children: Rachel, Jacob; stepson, Joshua Goldfein. AB, Cornell U., 1963; LLB cum laude, U. Pa., 1966. Bar: Pa. 1967. Atty. Wolf, Block Schorr Solis-Cohen, Phila., 1966-67; chmn., chief exec. officer Toll Bros. Inc., Huntingdon Valley, Pa., 1967—; mem. Mayor's Coun. on Housing in Phila.; mem. bd. overseers U. Pa. Law Sch.; mem. real estate coun. Cornell U. Real Estate Coun. Bd. dirs. Pa. Campaign for Choice, Phila., Beth Sholom Synagogue, Elkins Park, Southeastern chpt. ARC; sponsor Say Yes to Edn., Phila.; mem. bd. trustees Abington Meml. Hosp. Found. Named Profl. Builder of Yr., Builder Mag., 1988. Mem. Nat. Assn. Home Builders, Philmont Country Club (Huntingdon Valley), Equity Lodge 591. Avocations: racing J/35 sailboats, tennis, skiing. Office: Toll Brothers Inc 3103 Philmont Ave Huntingdon Valley PA 19006-4225*

TOLL, SHELDON SAMUEL, lawyer; b. Phila., June 6, 1940; s. Herman and Rose (Ornstein) T.; m. Roberta Darlene Pollack, Aug. 11, 1968; children: Candice Moore, John Maitland, Kevin Scott. Bar: Pa. 1967, Mich. 1972, Ill. 1990, Tex. 1990, U.S. Dist. Ct. (ea. dist.) Pa. 1968, U.S. Ct. Appeals (3d cir.) 1970, U.S. Supreme Ct. 1971, Mich. 1972, U.S. Dist. Ct. (ea. dist.), U.S. Ct. Appeals (6th cir.) 1973, U.S. Ct. Appeals (5th cir.) 1978, U.S. Dist. Ct. (no. dist.) Calif. 1986, U.S. Ct. Appeals (9th cir.) 1987, U.S. Dist. Ct. (ea. dist.) Wis. 1989. Assoc. Montgomery, McCracken et al, Phila., 1967-72; sr. ptnr. Honigman Miller Schwartz and Cohn, Detroit, 1972—; panelist Bankruptcy Litigation Inst., N.Y.C., 1984—. Author: Pennsylvania Crime Codes, 1972, Bankruptcy Litigation Manual, 1988. Bd. dirs. Southeastern Mich. chpt. ARC, Detroit. Mem. Fed. Bar Assn. (past pres. Detroit chpt.), ABA, Pa. Bar Assn., Phila. Bar Assn., Detroit Bar Assn., Am. Bankruptcy Inst. (cert. bus. bankruptcy law specialist), Franklin (Mich.) Hills Country Club, Phi Beta Kappa. Democrat. Jewish. Office: Honigman Miller Schwartz & Cohn 2290 1st National Bldg Detroit MI 48226

TOLLE, PAT MINA, artist; b. Ann Arbor, Mich., Jan. 17, 1948; d. Charles B. Tolle and Charlene J. (Vallet) Snow; m. Dennis A. Bohn, Aug. 12, 1986; children: Koshtra B. Tolle, Kira Bohn. Student, Brooks Art Inst., Santa Barbara, Calif., 1969-72, Chouinard Art Inst., L.A., 1968. One-woman shows include Kauai (Hawaii) Regional Libr., 1978, Casa-U-Betcha, Seattle, 1991, Jackson Street Gallery, Seattle, 1992, King County Arts Commn. Gallery Program, Seattle, 1992, Julia's, Wallingford, Seattle, 1992, Cafe Forza, Seattle, 1992, Phinney Ctr. Gallery, Seattle, 1992, Gunnar Nordstrom Gallery, Kirkland, Wash., 1993—, Lynnwood Arts Coun., 1995; represented in group shows at Santa Barbara Art Mus., 1966, The Artists' Own Gallery, Santa Barbara, 1973, Hawaii Artists League, 1978, Kauai Women's Art Show, 1978, Art Kauai '79, 1979 (3 1st Pl. awards), Arts Coun. Snohomish County Gallery, Everett, Wash., 1987, Eileen Enck Gallery, Bellevue, Wash., 1987, Snohomish (Wash.) Invitational Show, 1988, Artworks Gallery, Santa Barbara, 1988, Alligator Gallery, San Francisco, 1988, A New Space Gallery, Seattle, 1988, Prima Gallery Edmonds (Wash.) Coll., 1989, Seattle Art Mus., 1989, Cheney Cowles Mus., Spokane, Wash., 1990, Pacific N.W. Arts & Crafts Fair, Bellevue, Wash., 1991, Ea. Wash. U. Gallery, Cheney, 1992, Santa Barbara Art Co., 1993, 1994 N.W. Poets and Artists Calendar Exhbn., Bainbridge Island, Wash., 1993, Arts Coun. Snohomish, Monte Cristo, Everett, Wash., 1994, Ea. Wash. U. Gallery, Cheney, 1995; represented in The Calif. Art Review, 2d edit., 1989, The Encyclopedia of Living Artists, 4th edit., 1989, Limited Ink, 1st edit., 1991.

TOLLENAERE, LAWRENCE ROBERT, retired industrial products company executive; b. Berwyn, Ill., Nov. 19, 1922; s. Cyrille and Modesta (Van Damme) T.; m. Mary Elizabeth Hansen, Aug. 14, 1948; children: Elizabeth, Homer, Stephanie, Caswell, Mary Jennifer. BS in Engring., Iowa State U., 1944, MS in Engring., 1949; MBA, U. So. Calif., 1969; LLD (hon.), Claremont Grad. Sch., 1977. Specification engr. Alumninum Co. Am., Vernon, Calif., 1946-47; asst. prof. indsl. engring. Iowa State U., Ames, 1947-50; sales rep. Am. Pipe and Constrn. Co. (name changed to AMERON 1970), South Gate, Calif., 1950-53; spl. rep. Am. Pipe and Constrn. Co. (name changed to AMERON 1970), S.Am., 1952-54; 2nd v.p., mgr. Columbian divsn. Am. Pipe and Constrn. Co. (name changed to AMERON 1970), Bogota, S.Am., 1955-57; divsn. v.p., mgr. Am. Pipe and Constrn. Co. (name changed to AMERON 1970), Calif., 1957-63; v.p. concrete pipe ops. Am. Pipe and Constrn. Co. (name changed to AMERON 1970), Monterey Park, Calif., 1963-65, pres. corp. hdqrs., 1965-67; pres., CEO Ameron Inc., Monterrey Park, Calif., 1967-89; CEO, pres. Ameron Inc., Pasadena, 1989-93, chmn. bd. dirs., 1989-94, ret., 1994; bd. dirs. Avery Dennison, Pasadena, Calif., Newhall Land and Farming Co., Valencia, Calif., The Parsons Corp., Pasadena. Trustee The Huntington Library, Art Gallery and Bot. Gardens; emeritus mem. bd. fellows Claremont U. Ctr.; bd. gov.'s Iowa State U. Found. Mem. Newcomen Soc. N.Am., Calif. C. of C. (bd. dirs. 1977-92), Jonathan Club, San Gabriel Country Club, Bohemian Club, San Francisco Club, Commanderie de Bordeaux Club, L.A. Confrerie des Chevaliers du Tastevin Club, Twilight Club, Lincoln Club, Beavers Club (past pres., hon. dir.), Valley of Montecito Club, Alpha Tau Omega. Republican. Avocations: fishing, hunting, equestrian, philately. Home: 1400 Milan Ave South Pasadena CA 91030-3930 Office: 750 E Green St Ste 301 Pasadena CA 91101

TOLLER, WILLIAM ROBERT, chemical and oil company executive; b. Ft. Smith, Ark., Aug. 10, 1930; s. Audly Sr. and Martha (Anderson) T.; m. Jo Ella Perry, June 13, 1959; children: William R. Jr., Michelle D., Gregory A. BBA, U. Ark., 1956; postgrad., Stamford U., 1971. Various positions Conoco Inc., Okla., Tex. and Colo., 1955-77; v.p. fin. and adminstrn. Continental Carbon Co., Houston, 1977-81, pres., chief exec. officer, 1981-84; v.p., gen. mgr. Concarb div. Witco Corp., Houston, 1984-86; dir., chmn. bd., chief exec. officer Witco Corp., N.Y.C., 1990—; bd. dirs. Chem. Mfrs. Assn. Mem. Rep. Nat. Com., Washington, 1988-92; bd. dirs. Internat. Ctr. for Disabled, SW Area Commerce and Industry. Mem. Am. Chem. Soc., Am. Petroleum Inst., Bus. Roundtable, U.S. C. of C. (bd. dirs.). Presbyterian. Avocations: golf, skiing. Home: 53 Ridge Brook Dr Stamford CT 06903-1234 Office: Witco 1 American Lane Greenwich CT 06831

TOLLERSON, ERNEST, newspaper editor; married; 2 children. Grad., Princeton U., Columbia U. With Wall Street Jour., N.Y.C.; gen. assignment, ct. reporter N.Y. Daily News; statehouse bur. chief Phila. Inquirer, Trenton, N.J.; with N.Y. Newsday, N.Y.C., 1986—, editl. page editor, 1990—. Recipient Silurian award, 1989. Office: NY Newsday 2 Park Ave New York NY 10016-5603

TOLLES, BRYANT FRANKLIN, JR., history and art history educator; b. Hartford, Conn., Mar. 14, 1939; s. Bryant Franklin and Grace Frances (Ludden) T.; m. Carolyn Coolidge Kimball, Sept. 15, 1962; children: Thayer Coolidge, Bryant Franklin III. BA, Yale U., 1961, MA in Teaching, 1962; PhD, Boston U., 1970. Instr. history King Sch., Stamford, Conn., 1962-63; tchr. history St. George's Sch., Newport, R.I., 1963-65; instr., asst. dean Tufts U., Medford, Mass., 1965-71; asst. dir., libr., editor publs. N.H. Hist. Soc., Concord, 1972-74; exec. dir., libr. Essex Inst., Salem, Mass., 1974-84; dir. mus. studies program, assoc. prof. history and art history U. Del., Newark, 1984—; mem. Com. for a New England Bibliography, Inc. Author: New Hampshire Architecture, 1979, Architecture in Salem, 1983, The Grand Resort Hotels of the White Mountains: A Vanishing Architectural Legacy, 1996; editor: Leadership for the Future, 1991; contr. articles to profl. jours. Trustee Mt. Washington Obs., N.H. Ford. Found. fellow Yale, 1962. Mem. Orgn. Am. Historians, Soc. Archtl. Historians, Soc. Indsl. Archaeology, Am. Assn. Mus., New Eng. Mus. Assn., Mid-Atlantic Mus. Assn., Am. Assn. for State and Local History, Wilmington Rowing Club, Appalachian Mountain Club, Univ. Barge Club (Phila.). Home: 1002 Kent Rd Wilmington DE 19807-2820 Office: U Del Mus Studies Program 301 Old Coll Newark DE 19716

TOLLETT, GLENNA BELLE, accountant, mobile home park operator; b. Graham, Ariz., Dec. 17, 1913; d. Charles Harry and Myrtle (Stapley) Spafford; m. John W. Tollett, Nov. 28, 1928; 1 child, Jackie J., 1 adopted child, Beverly Mae Malgren. Bus. cert., Lamson Coll. Office mgr, Hurley Meat Packing Co., Phoenix, 1938-42; co-owner, sec., treas. A.B.C. Enterprises, Inc., Seattle, 1942—; ptnr. Bella Investment Co., Seattle, 1962—, Four Square Investment Co., Seattle, 1969—, Warehouses Ltd., Seattle, 1970—, Tri State Partnership, Wash., Idaho, Tex., 1972—; pres. Halycon Mobile Home Park, Inc., Seattle, 1979—; co-owner, operator Martha Lake Mobile Home Park, Lynwood, Wash., 1962-73. Mem. com. Wash. Planning and Community Affairs Agy., Olympia, 1981-82, Wash. Mfg. Housing Assn. Relations Com., Olympia, 1980-84; appointed by Gov. Wash. to Mobile Home and RV Adv. Bd., 1973-79. Named to RV/Mobile Home Hall of Fame, 1980. Mem. Wash. Mobile Park Owners Assn. (legisl. chmn., lobbyist 1976-85, cons. 1984, pres. 1978-79, exec. dir. 1976-84, This is Your Life award 1979), Wash. Soc. of Assn. Execs. (Exec. Dir. Service award 1983), Mobile Home Old Timers Assn., Mobile Home Owners of Am. (sec. 1972-76, Appreciation award 1976), Nat Fire Protection Assn. (com. 1979-86), Aurora Pkwy. North C. of C.)sec. 1976-80), Fremont C. of C. Republican. Mormon. Avocations: needlework, gardening, fishing, swimming, trailering. Home: 18261 Springdale Ct NW Seattle WA 98177-3228 Office: ABC Enterprises Inc 3524 Stone Way N Seattle WA 98103-8924

TOLLETT, LELAND EDWARD, food company executive; b. Nashville, Ark., Jan. 21, 1937; s. Vergil E. and Gladys V. (Sturgis) T.; m. Betty Ruth Blew, June 2, 1961; children—Terri Lynn, Gary Dwayne. B.S.A., U. Ark., 1958, M.S.A., 1959. Dir. Research Tyson Foods, Inc., Springdale, Ark., 1959-64, gen mgr. prodn., 1965-66, v.p. prodn., 1966-80, chief operating officer, 1981-83, pres., chief operating officer, 1983-91, chief exec. officer, 1991—, vice chmn., 1993-95, chmn., 1995—, also dir.; pres., chief oper. officer Spring Valley Farms Inc., Tyson Farms Tex., Inc., Poultry Growers Inc., Lane Processing Inc., Tyson-Carolina Inc., Eagle Distbg. Inc., Lane Farms Inc., Tyson Export Sales Inc.; pres. Louis Kemp Seafood Co., Arctic Alaska Fisheries Corp., Henry House, Inc. Served with USAF, 1961-62. Mem. Nat. Broiler Council (bd. dirs. 1979—). Avocations: hunting; golfing. Home: 6 Samoset Ct Rogers AR 72758-1463 Office: Tyson Foods Inc 2210 W Oaklawn Dr Springdale AR 72762-6900*

TOLLEY, AUBREY GRANVILLE, hospital administrator; b. Lynchburg, Va., Nov. 15, 1924; married. Student, Duke U., 1942-43; M.D., U. Va., 1952. Diplomate Am. Bd. Psychiatry and Neurology. Intern St. Elizabeths Hosp., Washington, 1952-53; asst. resident psychiatry U. Va. Hosp., Charlottesville, 1953-54; resident psychiatry VA Hosp., Roanoke, Va., 1954-56; instr. U. N.C. Sch. Medicine, 1956-61, asst. prof., 1961-66, clin. asst. prof. psychiatry, 1966-72, clin. assoc. prof., 1972-76, clin. prof., 1976—; dir. psychotherapy Dorothea Dix Hosp., Raleigh, 1962-67; dir. hosp. Dorothea Dix Hosp., 1973-88; dir. resident tng. John Umstead Hosp., Butner, N.C., 1966-67; dir. profl. tng. and edn. N.C. Dept. Mental Health, Raleigh, 1967-72, asst. dir., 1972-73; Prin. investigator USPHS grant, 1957-59; cons. VA Hosp., Fayetteville, N.C., 1957-78; sr. cons., supervising faculty, community psychiatry sect. dept. psychiatry U. N.C. Sch. Medicine, 1971—; exec. sec. Multiversity Group, 1968-73. Trustee Found. Hope, Raleigh, N.C., 1984—. Served with USNR, 1943-46. Fellow Am. Psychiat. Assn. (rep. N.C. Dist. bd. 1969-82, 86—, mem. joint commn. on pub. affairs 1984-87, mem. constl. membership com. 1990—, mem. commn. on subspecialization 1990-94, Warren Williams award 1987), Am. Coll. Psychiatrists; mem. N.C., Durham-Orange County med. socs., N.C. Neuropsychiat. Assn. (pres. 1984-85), Am. Assn. Dirs. Psychiat. Residency Tng., N.C. Hosp. Assn. (life), George C. Ham Soc. (Disting. Alumni award 1992). Home and Office: 110 Laurel Hill Rd Chapel Hill NC 27514-4323

TOLLEY, EDWARD DONALD, lawyer; b. San Antonio, Jan. 31, 1950; s. Lyle Oren and Mary Theresa Tolley; m. Beth Dekle Tolley; 1 child, Edward Spencer. BBA, U. Ga., 1971, MBA, 1974, JD, 1975. Bar: Ga. 1975, U.S. Dist. Ct. (5th cir.) 1976, U.S. Supreme Ct. 1978, U.S. Ct. Appeals (11th cir.) 1981. Ptnr. Cook, Noell, Tolley and Wiggins, Athens, Ga., 1975—; lectr. various colls., univs., civic and profl. groups. Mem. Family Counseling Assn. of Athens, Inc., mem. Gov.'s Commn. on Criminal Sanctions and Correctional Facilities, 1988-90; past bd. dirs. Am. Cancer Soc.; pres. Clarke County Bd. Edn., 1992-93. Fellow Ga. Bar Found., Am. Bd. Criminal Lawyers (bd. dirs. 1987, pres.-elect 1995); mem. State Bar Ga. (chmn. law office and econ. com., bd. govs. 1985—, formal adv. opinion bd.), Ga. Trial Lawyers (v.p.), Ga. Assn. Criminal Def. Lawyers (pres. 1985, Indigent Def. award 1983, 88), Athens Bar Assn. (past pres.), Am. Judicature Soc., Fed. Bur. Assn. (treas. 1985, sec. 1983), Order of Barristers. Office: Cook Noell Tolley & Wiggins 304 E Washington St Athens GA 30601-2751

TOLLEY, JERRY RUSSELL, clinical laboratory executive; b. Goldsboro, N.C., Nov. 6, 1942; s. Elva Russell Tolley and Clara (Smith) Tolley-Bunch; m. Joan Morrison, June 8, 1965; children: Jerry R. Jr., Justin Clay. BS, East Carolina U., 1965, MEd, 1966; EdD, U. N.C., Greensboro, 1982; exec. mgmt. courses, Duke U. Tchr., coach Fayetteville (N.C.) Sr. High Sch., 1966; asst. football coach, head track and tennis coach Elon Coll., N.C., 1967-77, head football coach, 1977-81, dir. athletic sholarship fund, 1982, dir. corp. and ann. resources, 1983, coordinator Pride II Capital Campaign, 1984, assoc. dir. devel., 1985; asst. v.p. tng., nat. dir. tng. & pub. affairs Lab. Corp. of Am., Burlington, N.C., 1986—. Author: Intercollegiate History of Athletics and Elon College, 1982, American Football Coaches Guidebook to Championship Football Drills, 1985; contbg. author: 101 Winning Plays, 1977, Leadership Education: A Source Book, 1989; contbr. articles to profl. jours. Treas. Town of Elon Coll., 1984-87, mayor protem, 1988, mayor, 1990-94, 94—; convenor City County Govt. Assn., Alamance County, N.C., 1986—; mem. exec. bd. dirs. Cherokee Coun. Boy Scouts Am., 1986, Thomas E. Powell Jr. Biology Found., Alamance Found., N.C. Health & Fitness Found.; visitors Elon Coll.; mem. exec. com. Alamance County Ptnrs. in Edn. Named one of Outstanding Young Men Am., 1980, Internat. Men of Achievement, 1990, Cmty. Leaders Am., 1990, Mayors Hall of Fame, 1995; recipient Dwight D. Eisenhower award Nat. Football Hall of Fame, 1980, 81, Nat. Collegiate Football Championship award Eastman Kodak, Meritorious Svc. award Tom Sawyer-Huck Finn Tennis Classic, 1986; named Nat. Football Coach of Yr., Nat. Assn. Intercollegiate Athletics, 1980, Elon Coll. Sports Hall of Fame, East Carolina U. Athletic Hall of Fame, 1991. Mem. Am. Football Coaches Assn., Phi Delta Kappa, Sigma Delta Psi. Avocations: writing, racquet sports, jogging. Home: Box 463 1322 Westbrook Ave Elon College NC 27244 Office: Laboratory Co America 430 Spring St Burlington NC 27215-5865

TOLLEY, STEPHEN GREGORY, oceanographer; b. Huntington, W.Va., July 4, 1958; s. Gary Maurice and Wanda Gordon (Chain) T. BS, Marshall U., 1980; PhD, U. So. Fla., 1994, knight fellow, 1987-92. Rsch. asst. U. So. Fla., St. Petersburg, 1983-86; mgr., curator The Pier Aquarium, St. Petersburg, 1988-89; rsch. assoc. U. So. Fla., 1989-94, asst. prof., 1995—; cons. The Pier Aquarium, 1988, Natural History Mus., N.Y.C., 1988, Mote Marine Lab., Sarasota, Fla., 1985; treas. bd. dirs. Pier Aquarium, Inc., 1989-91. Judge Ann. State Sci. and Engring. Fair, 1990-96; sxhibit adv. St. Petersburg Hist. Mus., 1986. Mem. Am. Soc. Ichthyologists & Herpetologists, Am. Fisheries Soc., Ichthyological Soc. Japan, Oceanography Soc., Am. Inst. Fisheries Rsch. Biologists, Sigma Xi, Omicron Delta Kappa, Phi Kappa Phi. Office: U So Fla 140 7th Ave S Saint Petersburg FL 33701

TOLLIVER, DON L., dean library and media services; b. Louisville, Ill., Mar. 11, 1938; s. Edgar and Alene (Blair) T. BS in Edn., Ea. Ill. U., 1960, MS in Edn. Adminstrn., 1964; MLS, U. Ill., 1967; PhD in Adminstrn., Edn. Psychology, Purdue U., 1970. Instr. edn. media Purdue U., Lafayette, Ind., 1965-69, asst. head instrn. media research, 1969-70, head instrnl. media research, 1970-74; dean library U. Wis., Whitewater, 1974-80; asst. dir. libraries U. Mich., Ann Arbor, 1980-84; dean librs. Kent State U., Ohio, 1984—. Mem. ALA. Office: Dean Kent State U Library Kent OH 44242

TOLLIVER, URSULA DENISE, home improvement contractor, consultant; b. Balt., July 12, 1962; d. James Howard and Jennie Velma (Givan) T. BS, Morgan State U., Balt., 1984. Cert. med. lab. technician, Md. Sales assoc. AT&T IS, Balt., 1984-86; mgr. Tandy Corp., Balt., 1986-88; staff painter Community Realty Co., Beltsville, Md., 1988-90; propr. Ursa Major Enterprises, Balt., 1990—; maintenance cons. People Encouraging People, Balt., 1991—. Mem. Tau Beta Sigma. Avocation: photography.

TOLLMAN, THOMAS ANDREW, librarian; b. Omaha, Mar. 14, 1939; s. James Perry and Elizabeth (McVey) T.; m. Teresa Ramírez, Jan. 4, 1964; children: James Daniel, Lisa Maria. BA, Carleton Coll., 1960; MA, U. Chgo., 1965, U. Minn., 1974; postgrad., U. Ariz., 1977-79. Admissions counselor Carleton Coll., Northfield, Minn., 1960-62; asst. dean of coll. Carleton Coll., Northfield, 1968-73; reference libr. N.W. Mo. State U., Maryville, 1974-77; adj. instr. U. Ariz., Tucson, 1977-79; chair libr. reference dept. U. Nebr., Omaha, 1979-88, assoc. prof., reference libr., 1988—; sr. lectr. Fulbright Commn., Quito, Ecuador, 1991. Contbr. articles to profl. jours. Mem. ALA, Nebr. Libr. Assn., Spl. Librs. Assn., Assn. Coll. and Rsch. Librs., Reference and Adult Svcs. Div., Reforma, Nebr. Libr. Assn. (disting. svc. award, 1995). Mem. ALA, Nebr. Libr. Assn. (Disting. Svc. award 1995), Spl. Librs. Assn., Assn. Coll. and Rsch. Librs., Reference and Adult Svcs. Divsn., Reforma. Avocations: running, bicycling. Home: 2121 S 84th St Omaha NE 68124-2222 Office: Reference Libr U Nebr Omaha NE 68182-0237

TOLMAN, RICHARD ROBINS, zoology educator; b. Ogden, Utah, Dec. 1, 1937; s. Dale Richards and Dorothy (Robins) T.; m. Bonnie Bjornn, Aug. 18, 1964; children: David, Alicia, Brett, Matthew. BS, U. Utah, 1963, MSEd, 1964; PhD, Oreg. State U., 1969. Tchr. sci. Davis County Sch. Dist., Bountiful, Utah, 1964-66; instr. Mt. Hood C.C., Gresham, Oreg., 1968-69; staff assoc., project dir. Biol. Scis. Curriculum Study, Boulder, Colo., 1969-82; prof. zoology Brigham Young U., Provo, Utah, 1982—, chair dept. of zoology, 1994—. Contbr. articles to profl. jours. Scoutmaster Boy Scouts Am., Orem, Utah, 1992. With USAR, 1956-63. Alcuin fellow Brigham Young U., 1991. Mem. Nat. Sci. Tchrs. Assn., Utah Sci. Tchrs. Assn. (exec. sec. 1991—), Nat. Assn. for Rsch. in Sci. Teaching, Nat. Assn. of Biology Tchrs. Mem. Ch. of LDS. Avocations: whitewater rafting, hunting, fishing, hiking. Home: 174 E 1825 S Orem UT 84058-7836 Office: Brigham Young Univ Dept Zoology Provo UT 84602

TOLMIE, DONALD MCEACHERN, lawyer; b. Moline, Ill., June 21, 1928; s. Ronald Charles and Margaret Blaine (Kerr) T.; m. Joann Phillis Swanson, Aug. 15, 1953; children; David M., John K., Paul N. AB, Augustana Coll., 1950; JD, U. Ill., 1953. Bar: Ill. 1953, Va. 1968. Atty. Pa. R.R., Chgo., 1953-60; asst. gen. soliciter Pa. R.R., Phila., 1961-67; gen. atty. Norfolk & Western, Roanoke, Va., 1968; gen. soliciter Norfolk & Western, Roanoke, 1968-75, gen. counsel, 1975-82; gen. counsel Norfolk (Va.) So. Corp., 1982, v.p., gen. counsel, 1983-89. Mem. Va. Bar Assn., U.S Supreme Ct. Bar Assn., Harbor Club, Cedar Point Club. Lutheran. Home: 912 Hanover Ave Norfolk VA 23508-1227

TOLMIE, KENNETH DONALD, artist, author; b. Halifax, N.S., Can., Sept. 18, 1941; s. Archibald and Mary Evelyn (Murray) T.; m. Ruth Mackenzie, Aug. 11, 1962; children: Sarah Katherine, Jane Marianna. B.F.A., Mt. Allison U., 1962. Proprietor Tolmie Gallery, Mahone Bay, N.S., St. Albans, Vt.; Chmn. Visual Arts Ottawa, 1975-76; founding mem. Bridgetown and Area Hist. Soc., James House Mus.; bd. dirs. Art Gallery N.S. Author: (children's book) Tale of an Egg, 1974, (art book) A Rural Life: An Artist's Portrait, 1986; 3 TV documentary films produced on his work by CBC and by TV-Ont.; one-man shows include Dorothy Cameron Gallery, Toronto, 1963, Beckett Gallery, Hamilton, 1986, Kaspar Gallery, Toronto, 1988; Mt. Allison Univ. solo cross Can. touring exbn. Bridgetown Series, 1982-84; group shows include Banfer Gallery, N.Y.C., 1963, Nat. Gallery Can., Watercolors Prints and Drawing, 1964, 66, London Art Mus., Ont., 1966, Can. Soc. Graphic Art, 1973, Art Gallery N.S., 1980, 81, N.S. Art Bank, 1981; represented in permanent collections Nat. Gallery Can., Ottawa, Montreal Mus. Fine Arts, N.S. Art Bank, Art Gallery N.S., Confedn. Centre for Arts, Hirshhorn Collection, Washington, Owens Art Gallery, Mt. Allison U., Dofasco Ltd., Husky Oil Ltd., Procter & Gamble Ltd., Slater Steels Ltd., Crownx Ltd. Mem. Writer's Union Can., Writers Fedn. N.S., Visual Arts N.S. Address: PO Box 96 16 Orchard St, Mahone Bay, NS Canada B0J 2E0

TOLOR, ALEXANDER, psychologist, educator; b. Vienna, Austria, Oct. 21, 1928; s. Stanley and Josephine (Kellner) T.; m. Belle Simon, Sept. 2, 1951; children: Karen Beth, Lori Ann, Diana Susan. B.A., NYU, 1949, M.A., 1950, Ph.D., 1954. Diplomate Am. Bd. Profl. Psychologists. Grad. asst. NYU, 1950-52; intern Neurol. Inst., N.Y.C., 1952-53; clin. psychologist Neurol. Inst., 1953-55; sr. clin. psychologist Inst. of Living, Hartford, Conn., 1957-59; dir. psychol. services Fairfield Hills Hosp., Newtown, Conn., 1959-64; clinic dir. Kennedy Center, Bridgeport, Conn., 1964-65; dir. Inst. Human Devel., Fairfield U., 1965-77, assoc. prof. psychology, 1965-68, research prof. psychology, 1968-75, prof. psychology, 1975-89, dir. school psychology div., 1975-77, dir. sch. and applied psychology program, 1982-86, prof. emeritus, 1989—; practice psychology Danbury, Conn., 1960-96; clin. instr. psychology Yale U., 1963-67; cons. West Haven VA Hosp., 1962-66, Bridgeport Bd. Edn., Silver Hill Found., 1972-75, Fairfield Hills Hosp., 1973-94, Hallbrooke Hosp., 1975-92. Author: (with H.C. Schulberg) An Evaluation of the Bender-Gestalt Test, 1963, (with G.G. Brannigan) Research and Clinical Applications of the Bender-Gestalt Test, 1980, (with M. Deignan) Adjustment Problems in Children, 1984; editor: Effective Interviewing, 1985; adv. editor Jour. Cons. and Clin. Psychology; cons. editor Personality: An Internat. Jour.; contbr. articles to profl. jours. Served to 1st lt. USAF, 1955-57. Fellow Am. Psychol. Assn., Soc. Personality Assessment; mem. Conn. Psychol. Assn. (mem. council 1964, pres. 1984), Eastern Psychol. Assn., Psi Chi, Delta Phi Alpha, Beta Lambda Sigma, Phi Delta Kappa. Home: 6 Brittania Dr Danbury CT 06811-2606

TOLSON, JAY HENRY, lawyer, industrial instrument company executive; b. Phila., May 15, 1935; s. Julius Henry and Lois Carolyn Ruth (Leidich) T.; m. Elizabeth J. Fischer, Aug. 22, 1962 (dec. June 1972); children—Jon H., Carrie L., Lori D., Julie I., Karen L. B.S., Pa. State U., 1957; LL.B., Temple U., 1960, J.D., 1968. Bar: Pa. 1961. Partner Solomon, Tolson & Resnick, Phila., 1961-70; partner firm Malis, Tolson & Malis, Phila., 1970-74; chmn. exec. com. Malis, Tolson & Malis, 1972—; now chmn., CEO Fischer & Porter Co., Warminster, Pa.; pres. Fischer & Porter Co., 1974-84; dir. F&P, Australia, Belgium, Can., Eng., France, Italy, Mex., Netherlands, Spain; mem. listed co. advisory com. Am. Stock Exchange, 1979-85. Vice pres., trustee Delaware Valley Com. To Combat Huntington's Disease, pres., 1971-80; bd. dirs. Washington Sq. West Civic Assn., 1965-68; trustee Community Legal Services, Inc., Baldwin Sch., 1966-81, treas., 1978-81; trustee, mem. fin. com., chmn. audit com. Hahnemann Med. Coll. and Hosp., Phila., 1971-89; chmn. Pa. Bus. Roundtable, 1990-92, mem. policy and exec. coms.; v.p., trustee, mem. exec. com., Com. to Combat Huntington's Disease; bd. dirs., chmn. ops. com. Mfg. Svcs. Extension Ctr., 1989-93; bd. dirs. NET Ben Franklin Tech. Ctr., 1988-93; vice chmn. Bd. Mfg. Resource Ctr.; bd. dirs., chmn. labor and mgmt. coop. com. Pa. Econ. Devel. Partnership; dir. Colonial Penn Ins. With AUS, 1960-61. Mem. ABA, Pa. Bar Assn., Phila. Bar Assn. (chmn. subcom. on community legal services 1968-70, chmn. subcom. on juvenile services 1965-68), Instrument Soc. Am., Young Pres.'s Orgn., Phila. Pres.'s Orgn., World Bus. Coun., S.R. Soc. War 1812, S.A.R. Clubs: Explorers, Locust (Phila.).

TOLSON, JOHN J., editor; b. Montgomery, Ala., June 28, 1948; s. John J. and Margaret Jordan (Young) T.; m. Mary Irene Bradshaw; 1 child, Benjamin Bradshaw. AB, Princeton U., 1972; MA, Am. Univ., 1977. Instr. English and history Asheville (N.C.) Sch., 1972-74, Landon Sch., Bethesda, Md., 1974-77; free-lance writer, critic Washington, 1977-81; lit. editor The Wilson Quar., Washington, 1981-89, editor, 1989—. Author: Pilgrim in the Ruins: A Life of Walker Percy (So. Book Nonfiction award 1992-93, Hugh Holman prize for best work of criticism and scholarship 1992), 1992; contbr. essays and criticism to The New Republic, The Nation, The Scis., Washington Post, The Times Lit. Supplement, Civilization, other publs. Independent Scholars fellow NEH, Washington, 1989. Mem. Nat. Book Critics Circle. Home: 2010 N Lincoln St Arlington VA 22207-3729 Office: Wilson Quarterly 901 D St SW Washington DC 20024-2169

TOLTZIS, ROBERT JOSHUA, cardiologist; b. Phila., May 6, 1949; s. Louis and Shirley (Weiner) T.; m. Catharina Kolek, 1989; 1 child, Alexander Jonah. AB, Temple U., 1970; MD, Hahnemann U., 1974. Cert. Am. Bd. Internal Medicine, Cardiovascular Diseases. Intern, resident, fellow Peter Bent Brigham Hosp., Boston, 1974-79, Children's Hosp., Boston, 1974-79; chief of service in cardiology Nat. Heart Lung and Blood Inst., Bethesda, Md., 1980-82; assoc. prof. clin. medicine and pediatrics U. Cin., 1982—; cardiologist Christ Hosp., Cin., 1988—; fellow in medicine Harvard U., Boston, 1974-79, instr. 1979-80; dir. coronary care unit U. Hosp., Cin., 1982-88, dir. electrocardiography lab., 1988—. Fellow Am. Coll. Cardiology (coun. clin. cardiology), Am. Heart Assn., Am. Coll. Chest Physicians; mem. Am. Soc. Echocardiography, Alpha Omega Alpha. Home: 7720 Annesdale Dr Cincinnati OH 45243-4058 Office: 2123 Auburn Ave Ste 139 Cincinnati OH 45219-2966

TOMA, DONNA M., psychologist, researcher; b. Belleville, N.J., Sept. 8, 1962; d. David and Patricia (D'Amore) T. BA, U. N.C., Charlotte, 1984; MA, Seton Hall U., 1986, Yeshiva U., 1990; PhD, Yeshiva U., 1993. Cert. crisis/suicide instr.; cert. in hypnosis, psychol. testing and evaluation. Liaison, therapist Union County Psychiat. Clinic, Plainfield, N.J., 1986-88; therapist individuals, families Sch. Based Youth Svc. Program, Plainfield, 1988-90; psychologist Spofford Maximum Security Facility Juvenile Offenders, Bronx, N.Y., 1990-91, Alliance for Recovery, Belleville, 1991—, Bergen County Spl. Svcs., Ridgewood, N.J., 1991—, Contemporary Counseling Psychotherapy Inst., Teaneck, N.J., 1994—; cons. substance abuse Da-Tom Enterprises, Clark, N.J., 1986-93; cons. psychologist to TV program, 1988—; cons., expert nat. TV talk shows. Contbr. articles to profl. jours. Vol. Children's Aid Soc., N.Y.C., 1992—, Gay Men's Health Crisis, N.Y./N.J., 1993—. Mem. APA, NOW (v.p. no. N.J. chpt.), Soc. Child Devel., Menninger Found., Orthopsychiat. Soc., C. Jung Inst., Kappa Delta Pi. Avocations: triathlons, cycling, seminars.

TOMAINO, JOSEPH CARMINE, retail executive, retired postal inspector; b. Danbury, Conn., Dec. 12, 1948; s. Joseph and Lena Marie (LaCava) T.; m. Eileen Pulver (div. Nov. 1977); m. Ann C. Underriner, Sept. 20, 1986; children: Joseph Richard, Robert John. BS, Western Conn. State U., 1970; MBA, Roosevelt U., 1978, MS in Acctg., 1986. Cert. fraud examiner. Post office clk. U.S. Postal Svc., Ridgefield, Conn., 1970-71; postal inspector U.S. Postal Svc., Chgo., 1971-80, supervisory postal inspector, 1980-93; mgr. western ops. loss prevention dept. Walgreen Co., Deerfield, Ill. Mem. Am. Soc. Indsl. Security, Fed. Law Enforcement Officers Assn., Nat. Assn. Chiefs Police, Ill. Chiefs Police, Spl. Agts. Assn., Ill. Police Assn., Nat. Soc. Pub. Accts., Assn. Cert. Fraud Examiners. Office: Walgreen Co 300 Wilmot Rd Stop 3153 Deerfield IL 60015-4600

TOMAINO, MICHAEL THOMAS, lawyer; b. Utica, N.Y., Dec. 1, 1937; s. Joseph Michael and Rosemary (Fragetta) T.; m. Beverly A. Meyer, Aug. 29, 1959; children—Mark, Matthew, Andrea, Michael, Julie. B.A., Holy Cross Coll., 1959; J.D., Cornell U., 1962. Bar: N.Y. 1962, U.S. Dist. Ct. (so., ea., no. and we. dists.) N.Y., U.S. Ct. Appeals (2d., 4th and 5th cirs.), U.S. Supreme Ct. 1975. Assoc. Donovan, Leisure, Newton & Irvine, N.Y.C., 1962-64; assoc. Nixon, Hargrave, Devans & Doyle, Rochester, N.Y., 1964-70, ptnr., 1971-95; v.p., sec., gen. counsel Goulds Pumps, Inc., Fairport, N.Y., 1995—. Past pres., hon. trustee Aquinas Inst. of Rochester, 1976—. Mem. ABA, N.Y. State Bar Assn. (past chmn. com. on pub. utility law), Monroe County Bar Assn., Am. Coll. Trial Lawyers. Republican. Roman Catholic. Avocations: squash; tennis; sailing. Home: 135 Taylor Rd Honeoye Falls NY 14472-9732 Office: Goulds Pumps Inc 300 Willowbrook Office Pk Fairport NY 14450-4285

TOMAN, MARY ANN, federal official; b. Pasadena, Calif., Mar. 31, 1954; d. John James and Mary Ann Zajec T.; m. Milton Allen Miller, Sept. 10, 1988; 1 child, Mary Ann III. BA with honors, Stanford U., 1976; MBA, Harvard U., 1981. Mgmt. cons. Bain and Co., Boston, 1976-77; brand mgr. Procter & Gamble Co., Cin., 1977-79; summer assoc. E.F. Hutton, N.Y.C., 1980; head corp. planning The Burton Group, PLC, London, 1981-84; pres., founder Glendair Ltd., London, 1984-86; pres. London Cons. Group, London, Beverly Hills, Calif., 1987-88; mem. U.S. Presdl. Transition Team, Bus. and Fin., 1988-89; dep. asst. sec. commerce, automotive affairs, consumer goods U.S. Dept. Commerce, Washington, 1989-93; commr., chmn. L.A. Indsl. Devel. Authority, 1993-95; dep. treas. State of Calif., Sacramento, 1995—; bd. dirs. U.S. Coun. of Devel. Fin. Agencies, 1994—. Founder, chair Stanford U. Fundraising, London, 1983-88; chair Reps. Abroad Absentee Voter Registration, London, 1983-88; bd. dirs. Harvard Bus. Sch. Assn., London, 1984-87; vol. Bush-Quayle Campaign, 1988; trustee Bath Coll., Eng., 1988—; apptd. by Gov. Wilson to State of Calif. Econ. Devel. Adv. Coun., 1994—. Mem. Stanford Club U.K. (pres. 1983-88), Harvard Club N.Y., Harvard Club Washington. Roman Catholic. Home: 604 N Elm Dr Beverly Hills CA 90210-3421 Office: PO Box 71483 Los Angeles CA 90071

TOMAR, RUSSELL HERMAN, pathologist, educator, researcher; b. Phila., Oct. 19, 1937; s. Julius and Ethel (Weinreb) T.; m. Karen J. Kent, Aug. 29, 1965; children: Elizabeth, David. BA in Journalism, George Washington U., 1959, MD, 1963. Diplomate Am. Bd. Pathology, Am. Bd. Allergy and Immunology, Am. Bd. Immunopathology. Intern Barnes Hosp., Washington U. Sch. Medicine, 1963-64, resident in medicine, 1964-65; asst. prof. medicine SUNY, Syracuse, 1971-79, assoc. prof., 1979-88, assoc. prof. microbiology, 1980-84, prof., 1984-88, asst. prof. pathology, 1974-76, assoc. prof., 1976-83, prof., 1983-88, dir. immunopathology, 1974-88, attending physician immunodeficiency clinic, 1982-88, acting dir. microbiology, 1977-78, 82-83, interim dir. clin. pathology, 1986-87; dir. clin. labs., prof. pathology and lab. medicine U. Wis. Ctr. for Health Scis., Madison, 1988—; dir. div. lab medicine U. Wis., Madison, 1988-95, dir. immunopathology, 1995—; past mem. numerous coms. SUNY, Syracuse, U. Wis., Madison; mem. exec. com., chair and med. cons. AIDS Task Force Cen. N.Y., 1983-88. Assoc. editor Jour. Clin. Lab. Analysis; contbr. articles, rev. to profl. jours. Mem. pub. health com. Onondaga County Med. Soc., 1987-88. Lt. comdr. USPHS, 1965-67. Allergy and Immunology Div. fellow U. Pa. Fellow Coll. Am. Pathologists (diagnostics immunology rsch. com. 1993—), Am. Soc. Clin. Pathology (com. on continuing edn. immunopathology 1985-91, pathology data presentation com. 1976-79, standards com. 1995—), Am. Acad. Allergy (penicillin hypersensitivity com. 1973-77); mem. AAAS, Am. Assn. Immunologists, Am. Assn. Pathology, Acad. Clin. Lab. Physicians and Scientists (com. on rsch. 1979-81, chairperson immunology 1979), Clin. Lab. Immunology Com. (chair coun. 1991—), Clin. Immunology Soc. Office: U Wis Clinical Sci Ctr Rm B4/251 Madison WI 53792-2472

TOMAS, JEROLD F. V., business executive, management consultant; b. N.Y.C.; s. Samuel and Jean Tomas. BS, U. Bridgeport, 1968; MEd, U. Mass., 1971, D in Organizational Behavior and Mgmt., 1973. Grantee in exec. devel. Ford Found. and Carnegie Found., 1970-73; fellow Ctr. for Leadership, 1970-73; dir. edn. Young Pres.'s Orgn., Inc., N.Y.C., 1975-77; chief rsch. scientist Mgmt. Decision Lab., Grad. Sch. Bus. Administrn. NYU, 1977-78; officer, sr. cons., mgmt. and orgn. J.P. Morgan & Co., N.Y.C., 1978-80; corp. mgr. mgmt. resources planning Pfizer, Inc., N.Y.C., 1981-82; pres. TOMACO, Inc., Cons., N.Y.C., 1983—; mem. sr. faculty advanced mgmt. program Rutgers U., 1984—; sr. faculty, presenter Mgmt. Confs., U.S., Latin Am., Europe, and Asia Pacific. Contbr. articles to profl. jours. Football scholar U. Bridgeport.

TOMASH, ERWIN, retired computer equipment company executive; b. St. Paul, Nov. 17, 1921; s. Noah and Milka (Ehrlich) T.; m. Adelle Ruben, July 31, 1943; children: Judith Sarada Tomash Diffenbaugh, Barbara Ann Tomash, Bussa. B.S., U. Minn., 1943; M.S., U. Md., 1950. Instr. elec. engring. U. Minn., 1946; assoc. dir. computer devel. Univac div. Remington Rand Corp., St. Paul, 1947-51; dir. West Coast ops. Univac div. Sperry Rand Corp., L.A., 1953-55; pres. Telemeter Magnetics, Inc., L.A., 1956-60; v.p. Ampex Corp., L.A., 1961; founder, pres. Dataproducts Corp., L.A., 1962-71; chmn. bd. Dataproducts Corp., 1971-80; chmn. bd. & dir. Newport Corp., Irvine, Calif., 1982-94; chmn. exec. com. Dataproducts Corp., 1980-89; chmn. Tomash Cons., Inc., cons. to high tech. industry; chmn. bd. Tomash Pubs., pubs. computer and physics works; dir. Supershuttle Internat., Inc., L.A., Pasqua Inc., San Francisco. Founder, chmn. bd. trustees Charles Babbage Found., U. Minn.; dir. and nat. gov. Coro Found., L.A.; trustee Computer Mus., Boston; dir. L.A. Ednl. Partnership. Served to capt. Signal Corps AUS, 1943-46. Decorated Bronze Star; recipient Outstanding Grad. award U. Minn., 1983. Mem. IEEE (sr., computer entrepreneur award 1988), Assn. Computing Machinery, Am. Soc. for Technion (exec. v.p., dir.), History of Sci. Soc., Soc. for History of Tech., Assn. Internationale du Bibliophile, Grolier Club. Home: 110 S Rockingham Ave Los Angeles CA 90049-2514

TOMASI, DONALD CHARLES, architect; b. Sacramento, Calif., Oct. 24, 1956; s. Thomas M. and Anita (Migliavacca) T.; m. Loretta Elaine Goveia, Feb. 1, 1986; children: Jeffrey, Genna, Michael. AB in Architecture with honors, U. Calif., Berkeley, 1979; MArch, U. Wash., 1982. Registered architect, Calif. Project mgr. Robert Wells and Assocs., Seattle, 1982-84, Milbrandt Architects, Seattle, 1984, T.M. Tomasi Architects, Santa Rosa, Calif., 1984-86; prin. Tomasi Architects, Santa Rosa, 1986-93, Tomasi Lawry Coker De Silva Architecture, Santa Rosa, 1993—. Grad. Leadership Santa Rosa, 1992; mem. design rev. com. Sonoma County, 1988-90; chmn. Santa Rosa Design Rev. Bd., 1990—. Recipient Honor award Coalition for Adequate Sch. Housing, 1991, 93, Merit award, 1991. Mem. AIA (chpt. bd. dirs. 1990-91, Merit award 1986). Avocations: snow skiing, wine, travel.

TOMASI, THOMAS B., cell biologist, administrator; b. May 24, 1927; s. Thomas B. and Ivis (Ratazzi) T.; children: Barbara, Theodore, Anne. AB, Dartmouth Coll., Hanover, N.H., 1950; MD, U. Vt., Burlington, 1954; PhD, Rockefeller U., 1965. Intern, resident, chief resident Columbia Presbyn. Hosp., N.Y.C., 1954-58, instr. medicine, 1958-60; prof., chmn. div. exptl. medicine U. Vt., Burlington, 1960-65; prof. medicine, dir. immunology SUNY, Buffalo, 1965-73; prof., chmn. immunology dept. Mayo Med. Sch., Rochester, Minn., 1973-81; dir. Cancer Ctr., Disting. Univ. prof., chmn. dept. cell biology U. N. Mex., Albuquerque, 1981-86; pres., CEO Roswell Park Cancer Inst., Buffalo, 1986—, chmn. dept. molecular medicine. Author: The Immune System of Secretions, 1976; contbr. over 200 articles to profl. jours. Served with USN, 1945-46. Mem. Am. Soc. Cell Biology, Am. Assn. Immunologists, Am. Assn. Cancer Research, Am. Soc. Clin. Investigation, Am. Fedn. Clin. Research, Assn. Am. Physicians. Roman Catholic. Avocations: skiing, tennis, hunting, fishing, gardening. Office: Roswell Park Cancer Inst Elm And Carlton St Buffalo NY 14263-0001

TOMASKO, EDWARD A., financial planner; b. Stafford Springs, Conn., Sept. 18, 1943; s. Edward A. Sr. and Gertrude Ann (Burr) T.; m. Helen F. Flanagan, Oct. 18, 1969; children: Felicia, Joy. BA, Quinnipac Coll., 1966; MBA, Am. U., 1968. CFP. Direct mktg. & sales Iroquois Brands, Stamford, Conn., 1979-81; owner Tomasko Bus. Cons., Bethel, Conn., 1981-82; v.p. mktg. & consulting Excell Mktg., New Canaan, Conn., 1982; market mgr. Stauffer Chem., Westport, Conn., 1982-85; direct mktg. & sales Folz Vending, L.I., N.Y., 1986; registered rep. Moseley Securities, New Haven, 1987-88, Fahnestock & Co. Inc., Danbury, Conn., 1988-90; prin. Titan Value Equities, Hamden, Conn., 1990—. V.p. bd. govs. Quinnipac Coll. Mem. IAFP (pres. So. Conn. chpt. 1993—, chmn. state conf. 1992-93). Republican. Avocations: photography, choir singing. Home: 20 Spring Hill Ln Bethel CT 06801-2726 Office: Titan Value Equities 2600 Dixwell Ave Ste 1 Hamden CT 06514-1833

TOMASKY, SUSAN, federal officer; b. Morgantown, W.Va., Mar. 29, 1953; m. Ron Ungvarsky; 1 child, Victoria. BA cum laude, Univ. Ky., 1974; JD (hons.), George Washington Univ., 1979. Ptnr. Van Ness, Feldman & Curtis, Washington, 1974-76; with FERC's Office of Gen. Counsel., Washington, 1979-81; staff mem. House Com. Interstate and Fgn. Commerce, Washington, 1981-86; gen. coun. Federal Energy Regulatory Commn.,, Washington, 1993—; gen. counsel Fed. Energy Regulatory Commn., Washington, 1993—. Mem. Phi Beta Kappa. Office: Fed Energy Regulatory Commn General Counsel 888 1st St NE Rm 10A-01 Washington DC 20426*

TOMASSINI, LAWRENCE ANTHONY, accounting educator, consultant; b. San Francisco, June 12, 1945; s. Charles Pasquale and Flora Joan (Novelli) T.; m. Eve Collier, July 20, 1982; children: Nicholas Charles, Anthony Domenic, Katherine Joiner. BS, U. Santa Clara, 1967; MS, UCLA, 1969, PhD, 1974. CPA, Tex. Asst. prof. acctg. U. Tex., Austin, 1973-78, assoc. prof., 1978-83, prof., 1983-85, John Arch White prof. bus., 1985-86, Peat, Marwick, Mitchell & Co. Centennial prof. acctg., 1986-87; Arthur Young Disting. prof. acctg. U. Ill., Urbana-Champaign, 1987-90, Ernst and Young Disting. prof. acctg., 1990-93; prof., Ernst & Young scholar, chmn. dept. acct. and MIS Ohio State U., Columbus, 1993—; bd. dirs. Fermentations Inc., Austin. Contbr. articles to profl. jours. Grantee for Doctoral Dissertation AICPAs, 1971-72. Mem. AICPA, Am. Acctg. Assn. (fellowship 1971-73), Ill. Soc. CPAs, Soc. for Judgment and Decision Making (founder). Avocations: collecting fine wines, antiques, golf. Home: 2035 Tremont Rd Upper Arlngtn OH 43221-4329 Office: Ohio State U Dept Acctg & MIS 1775 S College Rd Columbus OH 43210-1309

TOMASSO, JOHN, tax specialist; b. Queens, N.Y., Apr. 28, 1955; s. Joseph A. and Angelina (Iannone) T.; m. Patrizia, Aug. 5, 1978; children: Michelle, Joseph A. BS in Acctg., Fordham U., 1977; JD, NYLS, 1980. CPA N.Y. Legal assoc. Robert Samuels, N.Y.C., 1979-80; tax assoc. Drescher Dorkin & Co., N.Y.C., 1981; tax mgr. Coopers & Lybrand, Melville, N.Y., 1981-91; dir. taxation Rexel, Inc., Coral Gables, Fla., 1991—. Office: Rexel Inc 150 Alhambra Cir Coral Gables FL 33134

TOMASSON, HELGI, dancer, choreographer, dance company executive; b. Reykjavik, Iceland, 1942; m. Marlene Rizzo, 1965; children: Kristinn, Erik. Student, Sigridur Arman, Erik Bidsted, Vera Volkova, Sch. Am. Ballet, Tivoli Pantomime Theatre, Copenhagen. With Joffrey Ballet, 1961-64; prin. dancer Harkness Ballet, 1964-70, N.Y.C. Ballet, 1970-85; artistic dir. San Francisco Ballet, 1985—, also dir. Debut with Tivoli Pantomime Theatre, 1958; created roles in A Season of Hell, 1967, Stages and Reflections, 1968, La Favorita, 1969, The Goldberg Variations, 1971, Symphony in Three Movements, 1972, Coppélia, 1974, Dybbuk Variations, 1974, Chansons Madecasses, 1975, Introduction and Allegro, 1975, Union Jack, 1976, Vienna Waltzes, 1977; choreographer Theme and Variations, Polonaise, Op. 65, 1982, Ballet d'Isoline, 1983, Menuetto (for N.Y.C. Ballet) 1984, Beads of Memory, 1985, Swan Lake, 1988, Handel-a Celebration, 1989, Sleeping Beauty, 1990, Romeo and Juliet, 1994, others. Decorated Knight Order of Falcon (Iceland), 1974, Comdr. Order of Falcon, 1990; recipient Silver medal Internat. Moscow Ballet Competition, 1969, Golden Plate award Am. Acad. Achievement, 1992, Dance Mag. award, 1992. Office: care San Francisco Ballet 455 Franklin St San Francisco CA 94102-4438

TOMASULO, VIRGINIA MERRILLS, retired lawyer; b. Belleville, Ill., Feb. 10, 1919; d. Frederick Emerson and Mary Eckert (Turner) Merrills; m. Nicholas Angelo Tomasulo, Sept. 30, 1952; m. Harrison I. Anthes, March 5, 1988. BA, Wellesley Coll., 1940; LLB (now JD), Washington U., St. Louis, 1943. Bar: Mo. 1942, U.S. Ct. Appeals (D.C. cir.) 1958, Mich. 1974, U.S. Dist. Ct. (ea. dist.) Mo. 1943, U.S. Supreme Ct. 1954, U.S. Tax Ct. 1974, U.S. Ct. Appeals (6th cir.) 1976. Atty. Dept. of Agr., St. Louis and Washington, 1943-48, Office of Solicitor, Chief Counsel's Office, IRS, Washington and Detroit, 1949-75; assoc. Baker & Hostetler, Washington, 1977-82, ptnr., 1982-89, of counsel, 1989, ret., 1989. Sec., S.W. Day Care Assn., Washington, 1971-73; mem. fin. com. Residents Assn. Village on the Green, Longwood, Fla. Mem. ABA, Mo. Bar, Fed. Bar, Village on the Green Residents Assn. (fin. com.), Wellesley Club (Ctrl. Fla.). Episcopalian. Home: 570 Village Pl Apt 300 Longwood FL 32779-6037

TOMASZ, ALEXANDER, cell biologist; b. Budapest, Hungary, Dec. 23, 1930; married; 1 child. Diploma, Pazmany Peter U., Budapest, 1953; PhD in Biochemistry, Columbia U., 1961. Rsch. assoc. cytochem. Inst. Genetics hungarian Nat. Acad., 1953-56; fellow, guest investigator in genetics Am. Cancer Soc., 1961-63; from asst. prof. to assoc. prof. genetics and biochemistry Rockefeller U., N.Y.C., 1963-77, prof. microbiology, chmn. dept., 1977—. Mem. AAAS, Am. Soc. Microbiology, Am. Soc. Cell Biology, Harvey Soc. Office: Rockefeller U Dept Biology 1230 York Ave New York NY 10021-6399*

TOMAZINIS, ANTHONY RODOFLOS, city planning educator; b. Larissa, Greece, June 24, 1929; came to U.S., 1956, naturalized, 1966; s. Rodolfos A. and Christofily (Papamargaritou) T.; m. JoAnn R. Frank, June 24, 1962; children: Christina, Marina, Alexis. BCE, Assoc. Schs. Nat. Tech. U. Greece, 1952; M of City Planning, Ga. Inst. Tech., 1959; PhD in Planning, U. Pa., 1963. Mem. faculty U. Pa., Phila., 1962—, assoc. prof. city planning, 1966-77, prof. city and regional planning and civil engring., 1977—, chmn. transp. research group, inst. environ. studies, 1969-79, dir. Transp. Studies Center, 1969-79, chmn. univ.-wide program in transp. Transp. Studies Center, 1977—, chmn. faculty senate, 1984-87; chmn. grad. liberal studies program U. Pa., 1987-92; chmn. dynamics of orgn. U. Pa., Phila., 1990—; chmn. dept. city and regional planning dept. U. Pa., 1992—; pres. A.R. Tomazinis & Assocs., Inc., 1977-90; pres. Arista Found. Inc., 1991—, chmn. dept. city and regional planning, 1993—; cons. Inst. for Internat. Edn., 1991-92; cons. transp. and urban planning; pres. ARISTA Found., 1991—; transp. planning cons. Del. Valley Regional Commn., 1965-72, Doxiadis & Assocs., Athens, Greece, 1961-64, OECD, Paris, 1970-74, Govt. Iran, 1976; mem. travel forecasting com. transp. Rsch. Bd.; Fulbright prof. city planning U. Paris, 1973-74, chmn. dept. city & regional planning, 1992—; cons. Institut de Recherche des Transports, Paris, 1973-74. Served with Greek Armed Forces, 1953-54. Decorated medal of Meritorious Acts King of Greece, 1949. Mem. Am. Inst. Cert. Planners, Inst. Transp. Engrs. (assoc. editor Jour. Advanced Transp., Transp. Planning and Tech.), Am. Hellenic League (Phila. pres. 1967-71, 81-85, dir. 1971-80), AAAS, Regional Scis. Assn., Am. Soc. Planning Ofcls., Univ. City Arts League, Fedn. Am. Hellenic Socs. of Greater Phila. (pres. 1977-79). Club: Hellenic University. Home: 379 Montgomery Ave Wynnewood PA 19096-1718 Office: U Pa Translab 3400 Walnut St Philadelphia PA 19104-3411 *What we call success in life is indeed relative to what we want in life. My deep commitment to city planning led me to seek gratification in the process of solving urban problems, planning for new cities and sections of older cities, and in educating the young and aspiring planners. Searching not for convention or compromise, the stress is on innovation and accomplishment. What others call success is for me simply a struggle to achieve the best solution possible to each given problem.*

TOMBAUGH, CLYDE WILLIAM, astronomer, educator; b. Streator, Ill., Feb. 4, 1906; s. Muron D. and Adella Pearl (Chritton) T.; m. Patricia Irene Edson, June 7, 1934; children: Annette Roberta, Alden Clyde. AB, U. Kans., 1936, MA, 1939; DSc (hon.), No. Ariz. U., 1960. Asst. Lowell Obs., Flagstaff, Ariz., 1929, asst. astronomer, 1938; instr. sci. Ariz. State Coll., Flagstaff, 1943-45; vis. asst. prof. astronomy UCLA, 1945-46; astronomer Aberdeen Ballistics Labs. Annex/White Sands Missile Range, Las Cruces, N.Mex., 1946—, chief optical measurement sect., 1948, chief research and evaluation br. planning dept. Flight Determination div., 1948-53, chief investigator search for natural satellites project, 1953-58, planetary astrophys. researcher, 1958—; research assoc. prof. astronomy N.Mex. State U., 1955-59, prof., 1965-73, prof. emeritus, 1973—, with planetary astrophysics research program, 1959—; discoverer planet Pluto, 1930, 1 globular star cluster, 1932, 5 galactic star clusters, variable stars, asteroids, clusters of galaxies; extensive search for distant planets and natural earth's satellites, studies in apparent distbn. extragalactic galaxies, geol. studies Mars' and Moon's surface features, prodn. telescope mirrors; mem. expdn. extension satellite research project, Quito, Ecuador, 1956-58; lectr. in field. Author: Out of the Darkness: the Planet Pluto, 1980; contbr. articles to profl. jours. Paul Harris fellow Rotary Internat.; Edward Emory Slosson scholar in sci. U. Kans., 1932-36; recipient Jackson-Guilt medal and gift Royal Astron. Soc. Eng., 1931, Fairbanks award Soc. Photog. Instrument Engrs., 1968, Bruce Blair award, 1965, Disting. Svc. citation U. Kans., 1966, Rittenhouse award, Phila., 1990, Golden Plate award Am. Acad. Achievement, 1991; named to White Sand Missile Range Hall of Fame, 1980, Internat. Space Hall of Fame; Clyde Tombaugh Scholars Endowment Fund established in his honor at N.Mex. State U., 1987. Fellow Soc. for Research on Meteorites, AIAA; mem. Am. Astron. Soc., Internat. Astron. Union, Astron. Soc. Pacific, Sigma Xi. Mem. Unitarian Ch. Avocations: grinding telescope mirrors, designing small telescopes. Home: PO Box 306 Mesilla Park NM 88047-0306

TOMBERLIN, WILLIAM G., principal. Prin. St. Simons (Ga.) Elem. Sch. Recipient DOE Elem. Sch. Recognition Program award, 1989-90. Office: St Simons Elem Sch 805 Ocean Blvd Saint Simons Island GA 31522

TOMBLIN, EARL RAY, state official; b. Logan County, W.Va., Mar. 15, 1952; s. Earl and Freda (Jarrell) T.; m. Joanne Jaeger, Sept. 8, 1979; 1 child, Brent Jaeger. BS, W.Va. U.; MBA, Marshall U.; postgrad., U. Charleston. Former sch. tchr., businessman; mem. W.Va. Ho. Dels., 1974-80; mem. W.Va. State Senate, 1980—, pres., 1995—; lt. gov. State of W.Va., Charleston; mem. exec. com. So. Legis. Conf. Former pres., bd. dirs. Appalachia Ednl. Lab., Inc.; mem. Logan County Devel. Authority. Mem. Kappa Alpha. Democrat. Presbyterian. Office: Capitol Bldg Rm 229M Charleston WV 25305 Address: PO Box 116 Chapmanville WV 25508*

TOMBLINSON, JAMES EDMOND, architect; b. Flint, Mich., Feb. 12, 1927; s. Carl and Edna Ethel (Spears) T.; m. Betsy Kinley, Sept. 26, 1959; children: Amy Lisa, John Timothy (dec.). B.Arch., U. Mich., 1951. Draftsman firms in Detroit, 1951-53, Flint, 1953-54, 56-57, San Francisco, 1955-56; field engr. Atlas Constructors, Morocco, 1952-53; architect Tomblinson, Harburn, & Assos., Inc. (and predecessors), Flint, 1958—; pres. Timblinson, Harburn & Assocs., Inc. (and predecessors), 1969-95, chmn. bd., 1995—; chmn. Mich. Bd. Registration Architects, 1975-77; sec. Mundy Twp. Planning Commn., 1974-85, Grand Blanc Planning Commn., City of Mich., 1985—; chmn., 1988—. Pres. Flint Beautification Commn., 1968-69; bd. dirs. Grand Blanc Beautification Commn., 1969-84; founding mem. bd. dirs. Flint YMCA, 1969-75, chmn. camp com., 1971-75; founding mem. bd. dirs. Flint Environ. Action Team, 1971-77, v.p., 1971-73; elder First Presbyn. Ch. Flint, 1983, trustee, 1986—; exec. com. Tall Pine council Boy Scouts Am., 1975—; bd. dirs. New Paths, pres., 1985-86. Served with AUS, 1945-46. Recipient various civic service awards. Fellow AIA; mem. Mich. Soc. Architects, Flint Area C. of C. Clubs: Greater Flint Jaycees (dir. 1957-63, v.p. 1963), Flint City, U. Mich. (pres. Flint chpt. 1980—). Lodge: Rotary (pres. 1984-85). Home: 686 Applegate Ln Grand Blanc MI 48439-1669 Office: THA Architects Engrs 817 E Kearsley St Flint MI 48503-1913

TOMBRELLO, THOMAS ANTHONY, JR., physics educator, consultant; b. Austin, Tex., Sept. 20, 1936; s. Thomas Anthony and Jeanette Lilian (Marcuse) T.; m. Esther Ann Hall, May 30, 1957 (div. Jan. 1976); children: Christopher Thomas, Susan Elaine, Karen Elizabeth; m. Stephanie Carhart Merton, Jan. 15, 1977; 1 stepchild, Kerstin Arusha. B.A. in Physics, Rice U., 1958, M.A., 1960, Ph.D., 1961. Research fellow in physics Calif. Inst. Tech., Pasadena, 1961-62, 64-65, asst. prof. physics, 1965-67, assoc. prof., 1967-71, prof., 1971—, tech. assessment officer, 1996—; asst. prof. Yale U., New Haven, 1963; cons. in field; disting. vis. prof. U. Calif.-Davis, 1984; v.p., dir. rsch. Schlumberger-Doll Rsch., Ridgefield, Conn., 1987-89; mem. U.S. V.P.'s Space Policy Adv. Bd., 1992; mem. scientific adv. bd. Ctr. of Nanoscale Sci. and Technology, Rice U., 1995—. Assoc. editor Nuclear Physics, 1971-91, Applications of Nuclear Physics, 1980—, Radiation Effects, 1985-88, Nuclear Instruments and Methods B, 1993—. Recipient Alexander von Humboldt award von Humboldt Stiftung, U. Frankfurt, Federal Republic of Germany, 1984-85; NSF fellow Calif. Inst. Tech. 1961-62; A.P. Sloan fellow, 1971-73. Fellow Am. Phys. Soc.; mem. AAAS, Materials Rsch. Soc., Phi Beta Kappa, Sigma Xi, Delta Phi Alpha. Avocations: reading, jogging. Democrat. Office: Calif Inst Tech Dept Physics Mail Code 91125 Pasadena CA 91125

TOMBROS, PETER GEORGE, pharmaceutical company executive; b. Oak Hill, W.Va., June 12, 1942; s. George P. and Mary Jane (Boliski) T.; m. Ann Riblett Cullen, June 12, 1965. BS, Pa. State U., 1964, MS, 1966; MBA, U. Pa., 1968. Mktg. asst. Pfizer Labs. div. Pfizer Inc., N.Y.C., 1968; asst. product mgr. Pfizer Inc., N.Y.C., 1969, product mgr., 1970-71, group product mgr., 1972-74, v.p. mktg., 1975-80; sr. v.p., gen. mgr. Roerig div. Pfizer Inc., N.Y.C., 1980-86; exec. v.p. Pfizer Pharms. div. Pfizer Inc., N.Y.C., 1986-90, v.p. corp. strategic planning, 1990-94; also corp. officer Pfizer Inc., N.Y.C.; pres., CEO Enzon, Inc., Piscataway, 1994—, also bd. dirs.; adv. panel Penn State BS/MBA, 1992—, alumni fellow Penn State, 1993; bd. dirs. Pfizer Pharm. Inc., AL Pharma Inc., Oslo, Norway. Bd. dirs. Am. Found. for Pharm. Edn., North Plainfield, N.J., 1980—, past chmn.; trustee Fisk U., Nashville, 1986—, Dominican Coll., Orangeburg, N.Y., 1987—; key campus exec. U. Pa., Phila., 1987—; trustee Bklyn. Borough Hall Restoration, 1987—; mem. corp. devel. com. Cen. Park Conservancy, N.Y.C.; bd. dirs. Vote America, 1990; bd. dirs. Cancer Care; hon. bd. mem. Reflex Sympathetic Dystrophy Assn. Am. Mem. Pharm. Mfrs. Assn. (past chmn. mktg. steering com.), Links Club, Blind Brook Club, Masons. Avocations: marathon running, golf, tennis, skiing, bridge.

TOMEH, AMIN ADNAN, geotechnical engineer, consultant; b. Damascus, Syria, Apr. 17, 1971; came to U.S., 1986; s. Adnan and Souad (Idlibi) T. BSCE, U. Pitts., 1990; MSCE, Ga. Inst. Tech., 1992. Grad. team leader researcher U. Pitts., Pitts., 1989-90; grad. rsch. asst. Ga. Inst. Tech., Atlanta, 1991-92; sr. project engr. R&D Testing & Drilling, Inc., Atlanta, 1992-94, dept. mgr. constrn. svcs., 1994-95; prin. Matrix Engring. Group, Atlanta, 1995—; civil engring. tutor U. Pitts., 1989. Mem. ASTM, Ga. Tech. Geotech. Soc. (founding, constn. com. 1991—). Achievements include replacement up to 50% of the cement used in normal weight concrete with an oil shale ash (by-product) without affecting the compressive strength; defined aggregate breaking patterns under compaction devices. Office: Matrix Engring Group Ste 525 3300 Buckeye Rd Atlanta GA 30341

TOMEI, MARISA, actress; b. Bklyn., Dec. 4, 1964. TV appearances include (series) A Different World, 1987, (films) Parker Kane, 1990; film appearances include: The Flamingo Kid, 1984, Playing for Keeps, 1986, Oscar, 1991, Zandalee, 1991, My Cousin Vinny, 1992 (Acad. award best supporting actress 1993), Chaplin, 1992, Untamed Heart, 1993, Equinox, 1993, The Paper, 1994, Only You, 1994, The Perez Family, 1994; theatre appearances include Slavs! Thinking About the Longstanding Problems of Virtue and Happiness, 1994. Office: William Morris Agy 151 S El Camino Dr Beverly Hills CA 90212-2704*

TOMEK, LAURA LINDEMANN, marketing executive; b. New Brunswick, N.J., Oct. 21, 1940; d. A. John and Jeanette (Lacey) Lindemann; m. Charles L. Tomek, Oct. 4, 1969 (div. Apr. 1990); 1 child, Gregory C. Student, U. Wis., Milw., 1958-59; BS in Mktg., U. Ariz., 1962. Market rsch. mgr. Procter & Gamble Inc., Cin., 1962-66; nat. buyer, exec. tng. mgr., market rsch. analyst Sears, Roebuck & Co., Chgo., 1966-84; hdqrs. buyer Federated Dept. Stores, Chgo., 1984-85; v.p. O'Bryan Bros., Inc., Chgo., 1985-86; cons. Mktg. Connections, Chgo., 1986-88; regional sales mgr. Fabrican, Inc., Chgo., 1988-90; counsel Crouch & Fitzgerald, Oakbrook, Ill., 1991-93; with Little Switzerland Corp., 1993-94; merchandising and mktg. cons. Mktg. Connections and Info., 1994; mktg. cons. Kraft Foods, 1994-95, Govt. of Thailand, 1995-96; mem. bd. judges Ray Coll. Design, Chgo., 1987-88, Internat. Fashion Group, 1979—. Mem. com. March of Dimes Ann. Corp. Fundraiser, Chgo., 1992. Mem. Internat. Fashion Group Assn., U. Ariz. Alumni (bd. dirs. 1990—). Avocations: skiing, sailing, boating, travel, investments. Home: 675 Lake St Oak Park IL 60301

TOMEK, WILLIAM GOODRICH, agricultural economist; b. Table Rock, Nebr., Sept. 20, 1932; s. John and Ruth Genevieve (Goodrich) T. B.S., U. Nebr., 1956, M.A., 1957; Ph.D., U. Minn., 1961. Asst. prof. Cornell U., Ithaca, N.Y., 1961-66, NSF fellow, 1965, assoc. prof. agrl. econs., 1966-70, prof., 1970—, chmn. dept. agrl. econs., 1988-93; vis. econ. USDA, 1978-79; vis. fellow Stanford U., 1968-69, U. New Eng., Australia, 1988. Author: Agricultural Product Prices, 1990; editor: Am. Jour. Agrl. Econs., 1975-77; co-editor: Chgo. Bd. Trade Rsch. Symposia, 1993—; mem. editl. bd. Jour. Futures Markets, 1992-95; contbr. articles to profl. jours. Served with U.S. Army, 1953-55. Recipient Earl Combs Jr. award Chgo. Bd. Trade Found. Mem. Am. Agrl. Econs. Assn. (pres. 1985-86), Am. Econ. Assn., Econometric Soc., Northeastern Agrl. Econs. Assn., Am. Agrl. Econs. Assn. (awards 1981, 89, fellow), Gamma Sigma Delta (rsch. award 1994). Democrat. Methodist. Office: Cornell U Warren Hall Ithaca NY 14853-7801

TOMICH, LILLIAN, lawyer; b. L.A., Mar. 28, 1935; d. Peter S. and Yovanka P. (Ivanovic) T. AA, Pasadena City Coll., 1954; BA in Polit. Sci., UCLA, 1956, cert. secondary teaching, 1957, MA, 1958; JD, U. So. Calif., 1961. Bar: Calif. Sole practice, 1961-66; house counsel Mfrs. Bank, Los Angeles, 1966; assoc. Hurley, Shaw & Tomich, San Marino, Calif., 1968-76; assoc. Driscoll & Tomich, San Marino, 1976—; dir. Continental Culture Specialists Inc., Glendale, Calif. Trustee, St. Sava Serbian Orthodox Ch., San Gabriel, Calif. Charles Fletcher Scott fellow, 1957; U. So. Calif. Law Sch. scholar, 1958. Mem. ABA, Calif. Bar Assn., Los Angeles County Bar Assn., Women Lawyers Assn., San Marino C. of C., UCLA Alumni Assn., Town Hall and World Affairs Council, Order Mast and Dagger, Iota Tau Tau, Alpha Gamma Sigma. Office: 2460 Huntington Dr San Marino CA 91108-2643

TOMIYASU, KIYO, consulting engineer; b. Las Vegas, Nev., Sept. 25, 1919; s. Yonema and Toyono (Kawamura) T.; m. Eiko Nakamizo, Aug. 31, 1947. B.S., Calif. Inst. Tech., 1940; M.S., Columbia U., 1941; M.E.S., Harvard U., 1947, Ph.D., 1948. Instr. Harvard U., 1948-49; head engring. sect. Sperry Gyroscope Co., Gt. Neck, N.Y., 1949-55; with GE, 1955-93; cons. engr. microwave techniques GE Valley Forge Space Ctr., Phila., 1969-93; with Martin Marietta Corp., Phila., 1993-95, Lockheed Martin Corp., Phila., 1995—. Author: The Laser Literature-An Annotated Guide, 1968; articles; patentee in field. Exec. bd. Friendship Hill Civic Assn., Paoli, Pa., 1972-73, pres., 1973. Recipient Steinmetz award Gen. Electric Co., 1977; Mgmt. and Data Systems fellow Martin Marietta Corp., 1993; established Tomiyasu Meml. ann. scholarship Calif. Inst. Tech., 1977. Fellow IEEE (life, hon. life mem. Microwave Theory and Techniques Soc. 1973, tech. activities bd., awards bd., publs. bd., bd. dirs. div. IV 1985-86, ednl. activities bd. 1987-88, Microwave Career award, 1981, Centennial medal 1984, Geosci. and Remote Sensing Outstanding Svc. award 1986, Microwave Disting. Svc. award 1987); mem. Am. Phys. Soc. Patents. Home: 366 Hilltop Rd Paoli PA 19301-1211 Office: Lockheed Martin Corp PO Box 8048 Philadelphia PA 19101-8048

TOMJACK, T.J., wholesale distribution executive. BBA, U. Notre Dame, 1964. With Peat Marwick Mitchell & Co., 1964-71, Potlatch Corp., 1971-85; exec. v.p. sales North Pacific Lumber Co., Portland, Oreg., 1971-85, exec. v.p., COO, 1987, pres., 1988—, chmn., CEO, 1989—. Office: North Pacific Lumber Co PO Box 3915 Portland OR 97208*

TOMJANOVICH, RUDOLPH, professional athletic coach; b. Hamtramck, Mich., Nov. 24, 1948. Scout Houston Rockets, 1981-83, asst. coach, 1983-92, head coach, 1992—. Named to Sporting News All-Am. first team, 1970; coach NBA championship team, 1994-95. Office: Houston Rockets The Summit 10 Greenway Plz Houston TX 77046-3865*

TOMKINS, ALAN, art director, production designer. Art dir.: (films) The Empire Strikes Back, 1980 (Academy award nomination best art direction 1980), The Curse of the Pink Panther, 1983, The Keep, 1983, Lassiter, 1984, Lifeforce, 1985, Haunted Honeymoon, 1986, High Spirits, 1988, A Dry White Season, 1989, (with Steve Spence) Heaven and Earth, 1991, (with Derek R. Hill) JFK, 1991, Natural Born Killers, 1994; prodn. designer: (films) National Lampoon's European Vacation, 1985, (TV movies) War and Remembrance, 1989. Office: care Art Directors Guild 11365 Ventura Blvd Ste 315 Studio City CA 91604-3148

TOMKINS, CALVIN, writer; b. Orange, N.J., Dec. 17, 1925; s. Frederick and Laura (Graves) T.; m. Grace Lloyd Fanning, Sept. 11, 1948; children: Anne Graves, Susan Temple, Spencer; m. Judy Johnston, Nov. 11, 1961 (div. Feb. 1981); m. Susan Cheever, Oct. 1, 1981; 1 child, Sarah Liley Cheever; m. Dodie Kazanjian, May 28, 1988. B.A., Princeton U., 1948. Assoc. editor Newsweek mag., N.Y.C., 1955-57, gen. editor, 1957-59; staff writer The New Yorker, N.Y.C., 1960—. Author: The Bride and The Bachelors, 1965, Merchants and Masterpieces, 1970, Living Well Is the Best Revenge, 1971, Off the Wall, 1980, Post- to Neo-, 1988. Bd. dirs. Cunningham Dance Found., N.Y.C., 1963—. Served with USN. Guggenheim fellow, 1978. Mem. Authors League Am. Inc., Pen Am. Ctr. Club: Century (N.Y.C.). Home: 145 E 74th St New York NY 10021-3225 Office: New Yorker Magazine 20 W 43rd St New York NY 10036-7400

TOMKINS, FRANK SARGENT, physicist; b. Petoskey, Mich., June 24, 1915; s. Charles Frederick and Irene Eugenie (Gouin) T.; m. Mary Ann Lynch, Jan. 6, 1964; 1 son, Frank Sargent. B.S., Kalamazoo Coll., 1937; Ph.D. (Parke-Davis fellow), Mich. State U., 1941. Physicist Buick Aviation Engine Div., Melrose Park, Ill., 1941-42; scientist Manhattan Project U. Chgo., 1943-45; sr. scientist Argonne (Ill.) Nat. Lab., 1945—, group leader, 1944—; U.S. del. 2d Internat. Conf. on Peaceful Uses Atomic Energy, 1958; cons. Bendix Corp., Cin., 1963-69; assoc. Harvard Coll. Obs., 1978—; chmn. bd. Pegasus Enterprises, Inc. Contbr. articles to sci. jours. John Simon Guggenheim fellow Laboratoire Aime-Cotton, Bellevue, France, 1960-61; Sci. Rsc. Coun. fellow Imperial Coll., London, 1975; recipient Argonne Univs. Assn. Disting. Appointment, 1975-76, Kalamazoo Coll. Disting. Achievement award, 1990. Fellow Am. Phys. Soc., Optical Soc. Am. (William F. Meggers award 1977); mem. AAAS, Societe Francaise de Physique, N.Y. Acad. Scis., Sigma Xi. Home: 11714 S 83rd Ave Palos Park IL 60464-1015 Office: 9700 Cass Ave Lemont IL 60439-4803

TOMKOVICZ, JAMES JOSEPH, law educator; b. L.A., Oct. 10, 1951; s. Anthony Edward and Vivian Marion (Coey) T.; m. Nancy Louise Abboud, June 27, 1987; children: Vivian Rose, Michelle Evelene, Henry James. BA, U. So. Calif., 1973; JD, UCLA, 1976. Bar: Calif. 1976, U.S. Dist. Ct. (so. dist.) Calif., U.S. Ct. Appeals (9th and 10th cirs.), U.S. Supreme Ct. Law clk. to Hon. Edward J. Schwartz San Diego, 1976-77; law clk. to Hon. John M. Ferren Washington, 1977-78; atty. U.S. Dept. Justice, Washington, 1979-80; assoc. prof. law U. Iowa, Iowa City, 1982-86, prof., 1986—; vis. prof. U. Iowa, Iowa City, 1981, U. Mich., Ann Arbor, 1992; adj. prof. UCLA, 1981-82. Author: (casebook) Criminal Procedure, 2d edit., 1994; contbr. articles to profl. jours. Mem. Order of Coif, Phi Beta Kappa. Democrat. Roman Catholic. Avocations: running, tennis, softball, creative writing. Office: U Iowa Coll Law Melrose & Byngton Iowa City IA 52242

TOMLIN, PATRICK LESLIE, real estate consulting executive; b. Columbia, S.C., Jan. 12, 1949; s. Donald Robert and Frances Marie (Patrick) T.; m. Deborah Lyn Lee, July 11, 1960; children: Leslie Ryann, Adam West Lee. BS in Fin., U. S.C., 1971; MPH in Biostats., U. N.C., 1975. Statistician S.C. Dept. Health, Columbia, 1970-76; sr. v.p. Columbia Mgmt. Corp., 1977-80; exec. v.p. U.S. Capitol Corp., Columbia, 1981-87; chmn. Am. Capital Holdings, Columbia, 1988-90; pres. The Paradigm Corp., Columbia, S.C., 1990—; bd. dirs. Resort Devel. Corp., Columbia. Republican. Presbyterian. Club: Capital City Club (Columbia). Avocations: fishing, basketball. Home: 121 Kenwood Ct Irmo SC 29063-9702 Office: Paradigm Corp Ste 825 1401 Main St Columbia SC 29201

TOMLINSON, ALEXANDER COOPER, investment banker, consultant; b. Haddonfield, N.J., May 13, 1922; s. Alexander Cooper and Mary Cooper (Buzby) T.; m. Elizabeth Anne brierley, Jan. 10, 1953 (div.); children: William Brierley, Deborah T. Marple, Alexander Cooper III; m. Margaret L. Dickey, Nov. 15, 1986. BS, Haverford Coll., 1943; postgrad., London Sch. Econs. and Polit. Sci., 1947-48; MBA, Harvard U., 1950; LLD (hon.), Haverford Coll., 1995. With Morgan Stanley & Co., N.Y.C., 1950-76, ptnr., 1958-76, mng. dir., 1970-76; dir., pres. Morgan Stanley Can. Ltd. div., Montreal, Que., 1972-76; chmn. exec. com. First Boston, Inc., N.Y.C., 1976-82, dir., 1976-88; pres. Nat. Planning Assn., Washington, 1982-85; exec. dir. Ctr. for Privatization, Washington, 1985-88; pres. Hungarian-Am. Enterprise Fund, Washington, 1990-93; chmn. Fund for Arts and Culture in Ctrl. and Ea. Europe, 1994—; bd. dirs. Preco Corp.; mem. U.S. adv. bd. Que. Hydro, 1984-95. Trustee Incorp. Village, Cove Neck, N.Y., 1958-72, 76-82, Cold Spring Harbor Lab., 1976-87, N.Y. Infirmary-Beekman Downtown Hosp., 1968-82, East Woods Sch., Oyster Bay, N.Y., 1962-70, Nature Conservancy, L.I., N.Y., 1970-82, Carnegie Found. for Advancement Tchg., 1984-90; bd. mgrs. Haverford Coll., 1979-92; bd. dirs. Nat. Bldg. Mus., 1987-94, Nat. Planning Assn., 1982-90, Decatur House Coun., 1990-94; chmn. Am. Friends Can., Inc., 1982-91, Harvard Bus. Sch. Fund, 1981-83. Lt. USNR, 1943-46. Mem. Coun. on Fgn. Rels., Metropolitan Club (Washington), Links (N.Y.). Home: 3314 P St NW Washington DC 20007-2701

TOMLINSON, CHARLES WESLEY, JR., advertising executive; b. West Chester, Pa., Oct. 14, 1947; s. Charles Wesley and Kathryn Elizabeth (Madeira) T.; m. Kathy Anne Petersheim, June 7, 1969 (div.); 1 child, Alan Charles (dec.); m. Carol A. Oldfield, Apr. 4, 1986; 1 stepchild, Christie. BS in Comm., Temple U., 1969. Announcer, then sales mgr., air personality sta. WCHE, West Chester, 1966-70; communications specialist West Chester Area Sch. Dist., 1970-71; freelance advt. cons., 1971-73; gen. mgr. sta. WCHE, 1973-75; gen. sales mgr. Sta. WJBR-AM/FM, Wilmington, Del., 1975-84; dir. mktg. svcs. Winner Group, Wilmington, 1984-93; dir. sales and mktg. Del. Today mag. Del. Today mag., Main Line Today mag. Suburban Mktg. Assn., Wilmington, 1994—. Past mem. exec. com. United Fund Greater West Chester. Mem. Advt. Club Phila., Chester County Chambers Commerce Assn. (1st v.p. 1981-82, pres. 1982-84), C. of C. Greater West Chester (pres. 1977). Republican. Lodges: Masons, Elks (past exalted ruler). Office: 407 Homestead Dr West Chester PA 19382-8200

TOMLINSON, GEORGE HERBERT, retired industrial company research executive; b. Fullerton, La., May 2, 1912; emigrated to Can., 1914; s. George Herbert and Irene Loretta (Nourse) T.; m. Frances Fowler, July 17, 1937; children: Peter George, David Lester, Susan Margaret Tomlinson Goff. B.A., Bishop's U., 1931; Ph.D., McGill U., 1935; D.C.L. (hon.), Bishop's U., 1986. Chief chemist Howard Smith Chem. Ltd., Cornwall, Ont., Can., 1936-39; research dir. Howard Smith Paper Mills Ltd., Cornwall, 1939-61, Domtar Ltd., Montreal, Que., 1961-70; v.p. research and environ. tech. Domtar Ltd., 1970-77, sr. sci. adv., 1977-90. Contbr. articles to profl. jours. Recipient Gov. Gen.'s Gold medal, 1931; Laureate of UN Environ. Programme Global 500, June, 1987. Fellow Royal Soc. Can., Internat. Acad. Wood Sci., Chem. Inst. Can., TAPPI (dir. 1976-79, medal 1969, hon. life mem.); mem. Am. Chem. Soc. (emeritus), Can. Pulp and Paper Assn. (hon. life mem.), Chemists Club (N.Y.). Anglican. Patentee in field. Home: 920 Perrot Blvd N, Ile Perrot, PQ Canada J7V 3K1

TOMLINSON, GUS, biology educator; b. Bon Aqua, Tenn., Apr. 30, 1933; s. Clarence Doyle and Ina Mae (Hutcheson) T.; m. Opal Aline Bowman, May 10, 1952; children—Jeffrey Lynn, Jenifer Lynne, Tracey Eileen. BS in Math, George Peabody Coll., 1958; MA in Molecular Biology, Vanderbilt U., 1961, PhD, 1962; postgrad. (Nat. Cancer Inst. fellow), Swiss Fed. Inst., Zurich, Switzerland, 1963-64. Asst. prof. biology George Peabody Coll., Nashville, 1962-63; asso. prof. biology George Peabody Coll., 1964-67, prof., 1968-80, chmn. dept. biology, 1966-80, chmn. div. natural scis., 1967-80, dir. NSF summer insts., 1966, dir. sci. leadership devel. program, 1973-74, dir. instrnl. improvement implementation program, 1974—; prof. biology Tenn. State U., Nashville, 1980—; cons. project Reach High (Tenn.) and Project MAMOS, Mo., cardiovascular edn. Bapt. Hosp., Nashville, 1971—, U.S. Corps of Engrs., 1992-93. Contbr. articles to sci. jours. Served with AUS, 1953-55. Recipient Sci. Chair award, 1978, Sci. Leadership award, 1979; Nat. Med. Scis. rsch. grantee, 1965-70, NIH, NSF rsch. grantee, 1987-91. Fellow Tenn. Acad. Sci. (exec. com. 1970—, pres. 1987, editor jour. 1970-86, Disting. Svc. award 1989); mem. Southeastern Electron Microscopic Soc., Sigma Xi. Office: Tenn State U Arts and Scis 10th And Charlotte Ave Nashville TN 37203 *I have never met anyone from whom I could not learn.*

TOMLINSON, J. RICHARD, engineering services company executive; b. Newtown, Pa., Mar. 26, 1930; s. Robert K. and Margaret (Wright) T.; m. Barbara Elizabeth Brazill, Apr. 30, 1955; children: Karin Kathleen Tomlinson Pizzitola, Kimberly Ann Tomlinson Donahue. B.A., Swarthmore Coll., 1952; postgrad., George Washington U., 1952-53, U. Mich., 1955-57, Drexel Inst. Tech., 1954-57, Am. U., 1965. Mgmt. analyst Dept. State, Washington, 1952-53; with Old Republic Life Ins. Co., Washington, 1953-54; supr. financial analysis Ford Motor Co., Detroit, 1954-61; cons. McKinsey & Co., Washington, 1961-65; v.p. finance, dir. passenger svcs. Reading Co., Phila., 1965-69; v.p. finance Rollins Internat., Inc., 1969-71; exec. v.p. Amtrak, Washington, 1972-74; ptnr. L.T. Klauder and Assocs., 1974-75, 79-83; exec. v.p. Penn Central Transp. Co., 1975-78; pres. LTK Engring. Svcs., 1984-95. Named Man of Month, Phila. C. of C., 1967. Mem. Union League, Aronomink Golf and Country Club, Phila. Aviation Country Club. Home: 451 Inveraray Rd Villanova PA 19085-1139

TOMLINSON, JAMES FRANCIS, retired news agency executive; b. Long Beach, Calif., Oct. 18, 1925; s. Lilburn Jesse and Margaret (Roemer) T.; m. Sally JoAnne Ryan, Aug. 12, 1967; children—Elizabeth Anne, Victoria Alexandra. B.A., U. Va., 1950; student, Harvard U., Grad. Sch. Arts and Scis., 1950-51; grad., Advanced Mgmt. Program, Harvard U., 1977. With A.P., 1951-92; chief bur. A.P., Newark, 1957-63; bus. news editor A.P., N.Y.C., 1963-67; dep. treas. A.P., 1967-68, treas., 1968-87, v.p., 1972-92, sec., 1978-92, asst. to pres., 1987-92. Served with AUS, 1943-46, ETO. Mem. Phi Beta Kappa, Phi Eta Sigma. Clubs: N.Y. Athletic (N.Y.C.), Harvard (N.Y.C.). Home: 222 E 71st St New York NY 10021-5134

TOMLINSON, JAMES LAWRENCE, mechanical engineer; b. Detroit, Sept. 12, 1935; s. James Emmet and Ethel Pearl (Williams) T.; m. Marilyn Joyce Peterson, Aug. 24, 1957; children: James, Mary, Robert, Susan. BSME, Mich. Tech., 1957. Registered profl. engr., Mich. Design engr. Buick Motor div. GMC, Flint, Mich., 1960-61, project engr., 1961-66, sr. project engr., 1966-71; staff analysis engr. GM Corp., Warren, Mich., 1971-82, sr. staff analysis engr., 1983-88; pres. Eastport (Mich.) Engring., Grand Blanc, Mich., 1989—. Mayor City of Grand Blanc, 1985-89, city councilman, 1969-84, police liaison/commr., 1971-82, planning adv. bd., 1978-80, planning commn., 1985-89; nat. coun. mem. Boy Scouts Am., 1979-90, 93—, regional bd. mem., 1995—, coun. commr., 1979-84, coun. v.p., 1984—, nat. camp sch. staff, 1986-88, regional camp inspector/accreditation team, 1988—; vice chmn. Genesee County Sml. Cities and Villages Assn., 1986, chmn., 1987. Capt. USAF, 1958-60. Recipient Silver Beaver Tail Pine Coun. Boy Scouts Am., 1980, Silver Antelope Ctrl. region, 1996. Mem. NSPE (treas. Flint chpt. 1968-72, Engr. of the Yr. Flint chpt. 1990), SAE (mem. com. 1992-94, 96-98), ASME (exec. bd. Saginaw Valley chpt. 1968-70), Friends of Torch Lake Twp., Inc. (pres. 1994—). United Ch. of Christ. Home: 12077 Harris Beach Rd Eastport MI 49627-0025

TOMLINSON, JOSEPH ERNEST, manufacturing company executive; b. Sycamore, Ill., Apr. 22, 1939; s. Bernie Gilbert and Elizabeth Lowe (Hoffman) T.; m. Judith Ann Worst, Sept. 20, 1969; children: Mark Joseph, Amy Ann. BS in Acctg., U. Ill., 1962. CPA. Staff acct. Price Waterhouse and Co., Chgo., 1962-65, sr. acct., 1965-69; audit mgr. Price Waterhouse and Co., Indpls., 1969-74; corp. contr. Inland Container Corp., Indpls., 1974-82, v.p., treas., contr., 1982—. Congl. chmn. Carmel Luth. Ch., Ind., 1983-86, v.p., 1988-91; mem. bd. dirs. Luth. Child and Family Svcs., Indpls., 1994—. With Ill. N.G. 1963-69. Mem. Fin. Execs. Inst. (treas. Indpls. chpt. 1986-87, sec. 1987-88, 2d v.p. 1988-89, 1st v.p. 1989-90, pres. 1990-91). Republican. Club: Crooked Stick Golf. Home: 2063 St Andrews Cir Carmel IN 46032-9547 Office: Inland Container Corp 4030 Vincennes Rd Indianapolis IN 46268-3007

TOMLINSON, KENNETH Y., periodical editor-in-chief; b. Mt. Airy, N.C., Aug. 3, 1944; s. Young and Mattie (Wingate) T.; m. Rebecca Moore, Apr. 25, 1975; children: William Moore, Lucas Young. BA in History, Randolph Macon Coll., 1966. Reporter Richmond Times Dispatch, 1965-68; corr. Reader's Digest, Pleasantville, N.Y., 1968-81, editor, 1981-82, mng. editor, 1984-85, exec. editor, 1985-90, editor-in-chief, 1990—; dir. Voice of Am., 1982-84. Co-author: History of American Prisoners of War in Vietnam, 1975. Chmn. Nat. Commn. Librs. and Info. Sci., 1986-87; active Nat. Commn. Vol. Svc., 1981-83, U.S. Bd. Internat. Broadcasting, 1987—. Episcopalian. Office: Readers Digest Road Pleasantville NY 10570-7000*

TOMLINSON, WARREN LEON, lawyer; b. Denver, Apr. 2, 1930; s. Leslie Alton and Esther (Hasler) T.; m. Lois Elaine Retallack, Aug. 8, 1953 (div. 1987); children: Stephanie Lynn Huffine, Brett Louis; m. Linda Jane Beville, May 17, 1989. BA, U. Denver, 1951; JD, NYU, 1954. Bar: Colo. 1954, U.S. Dist. Ct. Colo., U.S. Ct. Appeals (10th cir.) 1958, U.S. Supreme Ct. 1960. Assoc. Holland & Hart, Denver, 1958-63, ptnr., 1963-85, mediator, arbitrator, 1995—. Contbr. numerous articles to profl. jours. Lt. U.S. Army, 1954-58. Mem. ABA (chmn. law practice mgmt. sect. 1988-89, charter fellow Coll. of Law Practice Mgmt. 1994). Republican. Episcopalian. Avocations: skiing, white-water rafting. Home: 5017 Main Gore Dr # 4 Vail CO 81657 Office: Holland & Hart 555 17th St Ste 2900 Denver CO 80202-3929

TOMLINSON, WILLIAM HOLMES, management educator, retired army officer, b. Thornton, Ark., Apr. 12, 1922; s. Hugh Oscar and Lucy Gray (Holmes) T.; m. Dorothy Payne, June 10, 1947 (dec.); children: Jane Axtell, Lucy Gray, William Payne; m. Florence Mood Smith, May 1, 1969 (div.); m. Suzanne Scollard Gill, Mar. 16, 1977. Student, Centenary Coll., 1938-39; BS, U.S. Mil. Acad., 1943; grad. Field Arty. Sch., 1951; grad. Air Command Staff Coll., 1958; MBA, U. Ala., 1960; MS in Internat. Affairs, George Washington U., 1966; grad. U.S. Army War Coll., 1966; grad. Indsl. Coll. Armed Forces, 1968; PhD in Bus. Adminstrn., Am. U., 1974; postgrad. 56th Advanced Mgmt. Program, Harvard U., 1968, 69; BAS, U. N. Fla., 1988. Commd. 2d lt. U.S. Army, 1943, advanced through grades to col., field arty., 1966; combat svc. in Leyte and Cebu, Philippines 246 Field Arty. Bn. Americal Divsn., 1945; aide de camp, comdg. gen. 8th U.S. Army, Japan, 1945-48, ops. officer 9th Divsn. Arty., Germany, 1954-56, Office of Undersec. Army, Pentagon, Washington, 1961-64; comdr. 2d Bn., 8th Arty. and 7th Div. Arty., UN Comd. S. Korea, 1964-65; faculty Indsl. Coll. Armed Forces, Ft. McNair, Washington, 1966-72, ret., 1973; faculty U. North Fla., Jacksonville, 1972—, prof. mgmt., 1993—; vis. prof. U. Glasgow, Scotland, fall 1987; vis. lectr. Moscow Linguistics U., Plekhanov Econ. U., Ulyanovsk U., Russia, fall 1993; mem. Nat. Def. Exec. Res., Fed. Emergency Mgmt. Agy., 1976—. Co-author: International Business, Theory and Practice; contbr. articles to profl. jours. and books. Exec. bd. Jacksonville Campus Ministry, 1991—. Decorated Bronze Star, Legion of Merit, Philippine Liberation medal, Japanese Occupation; recipient Freedom Found. award, 1967-71, Sr. Profl. in Human Resources, Teaching Incentive award State Univ. Sys., 1994-95. Mem. Soc. Human Resource Mgmt., Acad. Mgmt., Indsl. Rels. Rsch. Assn., Acad. Internat. Bus., European Internat. Bus. Assn., Internat. Trade and Fin. Assn., Exec. Svc. Corps. Bd., Co. Mil. Historians., Nat. Eagle Scout Assn., Northeast Fla. Employee Svcs. Assn. (charter pres. 1987-89), West Point Soc. N. Fla. (pres. 1976-77), Mil. Order Stars and Bars (comdr. 1980-90), Army Navy Club, Fla. Yacht Club, Mason, Shriner, Rotary, Beta Gamma Sigma (pres. 1988-89), Kappa Alpha. Presbyterian (elder). Home: 1890 Shadowlawn St Jacksonville FL 32205-9430 Office: U North Fla Dept Mgmt 4567 Saint Johns Bluff Rd S Jacksonville FL 32224-2646

TOMLINSON-KEASEY, CAROL ANN, university administrator; b. Washington, Oct. 15, 1942; d. Robert Bruce and Geraldine (Howe) Tomlinson; m. Charles Blake Keasey, June 13, 1964; children: Kai Linson, Amber Lynn. BS, Pa. State U., 1964; MS, Iowa State U., 1966; PhD, U. Calif., Berkeley, 1970. Lic. psychologist, Calif. Asst. prof. psychology Trenton (N.J.) State Coll., 1969-70, Rutgers U., New Brunswick, N.J., 1970-72; prof. U. Nebr., Lincoln, 1972-77; prof. U. Calif., Riverside, 1977-92, acting dean Coll. Humanities and Social Scis., 1986-88, chmn. dept. psychology, 1989-92; vice provost for academic planning and personnel U. Calif., Davis, 1992—. Author: Child's Eye View, 1980, Child Development, 1985; also numerous chpts. to books; articles to profl. jours. Recipient Disting. Tchr. award U. Calif., 1986. Mem. APA, Soc. Rsch. in Child Devel., Riverside Aquatics Assn. (pres.). Office: Office of Provost U Calif Davis Davis CA 95616

TOMLJANOVICH, ESTHER M., judge; b. Galt, Iowa, Nov. 1, 1931; d. Chester William and Thelma L. (Brooks) Moellering; m. William S. Tomljanovich, Dec. 26, 1957; 1 child, William Brooks. AA, Itasca Jr. Coll., 1951; BSL, St. Paul Coll. Law, 1953, LLB, 1955. Bar: Minn. 1955, U.S. Dist. Ct. Minn. 1958. Asst. revisor of statutes State of Minn., St. Paul, 1957-66, revisor of statutes, 1974-77; dist. ct. judge State of Minn., Stillwater, 1977-90; assoc. justice Minn. Supreme Ct., St. Paul, 1990—. Former mem. North St. Paul Bd. Edn., Maplewood Bd. Edn., Lake Elmo Planning Commn; bd. trustees William Mitchell Coll. Law, 1995—. Mem. Minn. State Bar Assn., Bus. and Profl. Women's Assn. St. Paul (former pres.). Office: Supreme Ct MN MN Judicial Ctr Rm 423 25 Constitution Ave Saint Paul MN 55155-1500

TOMMERAASEN, MILES, college president; b. Sioux Falls, S.D., Jan. 30, 1923; m. Marilyn Fladmark, 1945; children: Marsha Tommeraasen Heimann, Mark, Miles. B.A., Morningside Coll., Sioux City, Iowa, 1943; M.B.A., Northwestern U., 1948; Ph.D., U. Nebr., Lincoln, 1964. Tchr. math. secondary sch. Canton, S.D., 1943-45; staff acct. Arthur Andersen & Co., Chgo., 1946-50; mem. faculty Morningside Coll., 1950-64, chmn. dept. econs. and bus., 1951-61, prof., 1952-64, exec. v.p., 1960-64, pres., 1978-93, pres. emeritus, 1993; prof. U. Nebr., Lincoln, 1964-78; asst. dean Coll. Bus. Adminstrn. U. Nebr., 1968-69, vice chancellor for bus. and fin., 1969-78; mem. 5 corporate bds. Bd. dirs. Siouxland Found., Sunrise Manor; mem. mayor's com. Internat. Visitors; mem. Lincoln Downtown program, United Way Bd., Symphony Bd., First Luth. Ch. Mem. Am. Acctg. Assn., Am. Inst. C.P.A.s, Iowa Soc. C.P.A.s, Nebr. Soc. C.P.A.s (dir. 1966-69), Am. Fin. Assn., Fin. Analysts Soc., Inst. Chartered Fin. Analysts, Midwest Bus. Adminstrn. Assn. (pres. 1973-74), Fin. Execs. Inst. (dir. 1975-76), Lincoln C. of C. Office: Morningside Coll 1501 Morningside Ave Sioux City IA 51106-1717

TOMMEY, CHARLES ELDON, surgeon; b. Nashville, Ark., Jan. 13, 1922; s. William Robert and America Anna (Compton) T.; m. Clara Blair Newman, Aug. 28, 1948; children: Robert, Jean, Phillip, Dale, Scott. Student, Henderson State Tchrs. Coll., 1940-42; BSM, U. Ark. Sch. Medicine, 1944, MD, 1945. Diplomate Am. Bd. Surgery. Intern City Hosp., Columbus, Ga., 1945-46; surg. resident Bapt. Hosp., Little Rock, 1948-49, VA Hosp., Cleve., 1950-54; pvt. practice surgery El Dorado, Ark., 1954—; asst. clin. instr. surgery U. Ark. Coll. Medicine. Capt. U.S. Army Med. Corps, 1943-45, 46-48. Fellow ACS. Baptist. Avocations: golf, photography. Home: 123 Glenridge Pky El Dorado AR 71730-3117 Office: Surg Clinic of S Ark 518 Thompson Ave El Dorado AR 71730-4556

TOMOVIC, MILETA MILOS, mechanical engineer; b. Belgrade, Yugoslavia, Dec. 29, 1955; came to U.s., 1979; s. Milos Nedeljko and Danica Dane (Lemaic) T.; m. Cynthia Lou Bell, Apr. 15, 1994; children: Milos, Senja. BS, U. Belgrade, 1979; MS, MIT, 1981; PhD, U. Mich., 1991. Rsch. asst. MIT, Cambridge, Mass., 1979-81, 83-85; design engr. Foundry Belgrade, 1982-83; sys. engr. Energoproject, Belgrade, 1985-86; v.p. Canyus, Inc., Que., Can., 1988—; asst. prof. Purdue U., West Lafayette, Ind., 1991—; cons. Tech. Assistance Program, 1993—. Assoc. editor Foundry, 1995, also conf. procs. in field. Grantee Purdue Rsch. Found., 1994, 95; named Key prof. Foundry Edn. Found., 1991-95. Mem. ASME (chpt. bd. dirs. 1993-95), Am. Soc. Metals (chmn. vice chair 1994-95), Am. Soc. Engring. Educators, Am. Foundrymen Soc. Christian Orthodox. Achievements include patents in areas of metalcasting refiner plates for pulp and paper industry, mill balls for cement and metal extraction industry; research on wear and impact resistant materials, new metalcasting technologies. Avocations: tennis, skiing, swimming. Home: 123 Pawnee Dr West Lafayette IN 47906 Office: Purdue U MET Dept Knoy Hall West Lafayette IN 47907

TOMPKINS, CURTIS JOHNSTON, academic administrator; b. Roanoke, Va., July 14, 1942; s. Joseph Buford and Rebecca (Johnston) T.; m. Mary Katherine Hasle, Sept. 5, 1964; children: Robert, Joseph, Rebecca. BS, Va. Poly. Inst., 1965, MS, 1967; PhD, Ga. Inst. Tech., 1971. Indsl. engr. E.I. DuPont de Nemours, Richmond, Va., 1965-67; instr. Sch. Indsl. and Systems Engring., Ga. Inst. Tech., Atlanta, 1968-71; assoc. prof. Colgate Darden Grad. Sch. Bus. Adminstrn., U. Va., Charlottesville, 1971-77; prof., chmn. dept. indsl. engring. W.Va. U., Morgantown, 1977-80, dean Coll. Engring., 1980-91; pres. Mich. Tech. U., Houghton, 1991—; mem. engring. accreditation commn. Accreditation Bd. for Engring. and Tech., 1981-86; mem. Commn. on Engring. Edn., Nat. Assn. State Univs. and Land Grant Colls., 1985-90; cons. corps., govt. agys., ednl. instns.; lectr. various univs.; mem. exec. bd. Engring. Deans Coun., 1985-89, vice chmn., 1987-89; mem. engring. adv. com., chmn. of planning com. NSF, 1988-91, chm. Mich. Univs. pres. coun., 1996—, mem. bd. dirs. Oak Ridge Associated Univs., 1996—, Pres. Coun. Assn. Governing bds. 1996—, Gov's. Workforce commn. Author: (with L.E. Grayson) Management of Public Sector and Nonprofit Organizations, 1983, (with others) Maynard's Industrial Engineering Handbook, 1992; contbr. chpt. to Ency. of Profl. Mgmt, 1978, 83. Co-chmn. W.Va. Gov.'s Coun. on Econ. Devel.; bd. dirs. Pub. Land Corp. W.Va., 1980-89; mem. faculty Nat. Acad. Voluntarism, United Way Am., 1976-91; mem. Morgantown Water Commn., 1981-87, Morgantown Utility Bd., 1987-91; mem. steering com. W.Va. Conf. on Environ., 1985-89; chmn. Monogalia County United Way, 1989-90; mem. Mich. Govs. Workforce Commn., 1996—; campaign chmn. Copper Country United Way, 1995-96; mem., bd. dirs. Oak Ridge Associated Univs., 1996—. Fellow Inst. Indsl. Engrs. (life mem., sr. v.p. publs. 1983-85, v.p. edn. and rsch. 1985-87, trustee 1983-90, pres.-elect 1987-88, pres. 1988-89), Am. Soc. Engring. Edn. (chmn. indsl. engring. div. 1981-82, v.p. pub. affairs 1985-87, bd. dirs. 1985-87, 1st v.p., exec. com., fin. com. 1986-87, pres.-elect 1989-90, pres. 1990-91); mem. Am. Assn. Engring. Soc. (bd. govs. 1987-90, exec. com. 1987-90, sec.-treas. 1989-90), Jr. Engring. Tech. Soc. (bd. dirs. 1988-91), Nat. Soc. for Sci., Tech. and Society (bd. dirs. 1991—), Internat. Hall of Fame of Sci. and Engring. (hon. trustee), Sigma Xi, Phi Kappa Phi, Tau Beta Pi, Alpha Pi Mu. Methodist. Home: 2 Woodland Rd Houghton MI 49931-9746 Office: Mich Tech U 1400 Townsend Dr Houghton MI 49931-1200

TOMPKINS, JAMES ARTHUR, consulting firm executive, industrial engineer; b. Chgo., Dec. 8, 1946; s. Carroll Arthur and Evelyn Angela (Smith) T.; m. Sharon Marie Steffens, Aug. 17, 1968; children: Tiffany, Jamie, Jimmy. BS in Indsl. Engring., Purdue U., 1969, MS in Indsl. Engring., 1970, PhD, 1972. Sr. scientist Rsch. Triangle Inst., Raleigh, N.C., 1975-77; prof. N.C. State U., Raleigh, 1975-78; pres. Tompkins Assocs. Inc., Raleigh, 1978—; dir. Material Handling Edn. Found., 1990. Author: Facilities Planning, 1984 (best book 1984), Winning Manufacturing, 1989, others; editor: Warehouse Handbook, 1988; contbr. numerous articles to profl. jours. Recipient Reed Apple award Material Handling Inst., 1985, numerous others. Mem. Inst. Indsl. Engrs. (pres. 1990), Internat. Materials Mgmt. Soc. (pres. 1986), Coll. Industry Coun. on Material Handling Edn. (pres. 1984). Republican. Office: Tompkins Assocs Inc 2809 E Millbrook Rd Ste 200 Raleigh NC 27604-2849

TOMPKINS, JAMES RICHARD, special education educator; b. Camden, N.J., Jan. 17, 1935; s. Leo Joseph and Cecelia Nichols; children: Tim, Mark. BA cum laude, Mt. St. Mary's Coll., 1959; postgrad., U. Mich., 1960; MA, Niagara U., 1961; PhD, Cath. U., 1971. Coord. unit on edn. of emotionally disturbed Bur. Edn. Handicapped-USOE, Washington, 1966-71; asst. prof. U. N.C., Chapel Hill, 1971-72; exec. dir. N.C. Govs. Advocacy Commn., Raleigh, 1972-74; prof. spl. edn. Appalachian State U., Boone, N.C., 1974—; cons. edn. of disturbed children N.C. Dept. Human Resources. Contbr. articles to profl. jours. Mem. Coun. Exceptional Children, Coun. Children with Behavior Disorders, Coun. Career Devel., Give Youth a Chance Inc., Arts and Humanities for the Handicapped, N.C. Tchr. Preparation Programs for Emotionally Disturbed Children. Home: 117 Meadowbrook Ln Deep Gap NC 28618-9713

TOMPKINS, JOHN ANDREW, school system administrator. Supt. Salina (Kans.) Unified Sch. Dist. 305. State finalist Supt. of Yr. award, 1992. Office: Salina Unified Sch Dist 305 PO Box 797 Salina KS 67402-0797

TOMPKINS, JOSEPH BUFORD, JR., lawyer; b. Roanoke, Va., Apr. 4, 1950; s. Joseph Buford and Rebecca Louise (Johnston) T.; m. Nancy Powell Wilson, Feb. 6, 1993; children: Edward Graves, Claiborne Forbes; 1 stepchild, Clayton Tate Wilson. BA in Politics summa cum laude, Washington and Lee U., 1971; M.P.P. in Pub. Policy, Harvard U., 1975, JD, 1975. Bar: Va. 1975, U.S. Dist. Ct. D.C. 1982, U.S. Ct. Appeals (D.C. cir.) 1976, U.S. Ct. Appeals (5th cir.) 1977, U.S. Ct. Appeals (11th cir.) 1982, U.S. Ct. Appeals (3d cir.) 1983, U.S. Ct. Appeals (6th cir.) 1985, U.S. Ct. Appeals (7th cir.) 1991, U.S. Ct. Appeals (4th cir.) 1993, U.S. Supreme Ct. 1977. Assoc. Sidley & Austin, Washington, 1975-79, ptnr., 1982—; assoc. dir. Office of Policy and Mgmt. Analysis, criminal div. U.S. Dept Justice, Washington, 1979-81, dep. chief fraud sect. criminal div., 1981-82. Contbr. articles to legal publs. Mem. Va. Bd. of Health Professions, Richmond, Va., 1984-92, vice chmn., 1984-86, chmn., 1986-88, 90-91. Recipient Spl. Commendation, U.S. Dept. Justice, 1981. Mem. ABA (criminal justice sect., mem. white collar crime com., 1980—, chmn. task force on computer crime 1982-92), Va. Bar Assn., D.C. Bar Assn., Fed. Bar Assn., Phi Beta Kappa. Democrat. Methodist. Home: 8146 Wellington Rd Alexandria VA 22308-1214 Office: Sidley & Austin 1722 I St NW Washington DC 20006-3705

TOMPKINS, ROBERT GEORGE, physician; b. Portland, Oreg., May 29, 1923; s. George Henry and Minnie (Davies) T.; m. Rosemarie Nowicki, June 6, 1948 (dec. 1960); children: Timothy Michael, Mary Eileen, George Henry, Robert George. B.S., U. Wash., 1943; M.B., Northwestern U., 1947; M.D., 1949; M.S., U. Minn., 1954. Diplomate Am. Bd. Internal Medicine. Intern King County Hosp., Seattle, 1948-49; resident King County Hosp., 1949-50; fellow, 1st asst. Mayo Found., Rochester, Minn., 1950-54; practice medicine specializing in cardiology and internal medicine Tulsa, 1954—; mem. staff St. Francis Hosp., chief staff, 1964, med. dir., 1968-86; clin. prof. medicine Tulsa Med. Coll. and U. Okla. Med. Coll.; v.p., med. dir. Wiliam K. Warren Med. Rsch. Inst., med. chmn. Guatemala Mission Hosp., Diocese Oklahoma City and Tulsa; coord. planning program Okla. Regional Med. Program; mem. Tulsa Health and Hosp. Planning Coun.; bd. dirs. Okla. Ctr. Molecular Medicine; med. dir. Laureate Hosp. Rsch. Inst.; pres. Tulsa Med. Edn. Found., 1980-82; bd. dirs. Laureate Psychiatric Clinic and Hosp.; founding mem. bd. dirs. Am. Bank and Trust, Tulsa. Contbr. articles to profl. jours; editor: Jour. Okla. State Med. Assn, 1974-86. Pres. Oklahoma Cath. Health Conf., 1981-82; bd. dirs. St. Francis Hosp., Tulsa. Decorated Knight of the Grand Cross (Equestrian Order Holy Sepulchre of Jerusalem, Knight (Sovereign Mil. Order of Malta); recipient Dean's award U. Okla., 1991, diploma of Merit and Honor, Municipality of Santiago, Atitlau, Guatemala. Fellow ACP, Royal Coll. Medicine, Am. Coll. Cardiology; mem. AAAS, AMA, Am. Diabetic Assn., Am. Acad. Med. Dirs. (bd. dirs.), Am. Heart Assn., Tulsa County Heart Assn. (pres. 1959), Am. Rheumatism Assn., Mayo Alumni Assn., KC, Alpha Kappa Kappa. Home: 6551 S Darlington Ave Tulsa OK 74136-2002 Office: 6465 S Yale Ave Tulsa OK 74136-7822

TOMPKINS, RONALD K., surgeon; b. Malta, Ohio, Oct. 14, 1934; s. Kenneth Steidley and Mildred Lillian (Loomis) T.; m. Suzanne Colbert, June 9, 1956; children—Gregory Alan, Teresa Susan, Geoffrey Stuart. B.A., Ohio U., 1956; M.D., Johns Hopkins U., 1960; M.S., Ohio State U., 1968; DSc (hon.), U. Bordeaux, 1995. Diplomate: Am. Bd. Surgery. Intern in surgery Ohio State U., 1960-61, resident in surgery, 1964-68, adminstrv. chief resident in surgery, 1968-69, NIH trainee in acad. surgery, instr. physiol. chemistry, 1966-69; asst. prof. surgery UCLA, 1969-73, asso. prof., 1973-79, prof., 1979—, chmn. basic surg. tng. program, 1970-79, asst. dean student affairs, 1979-82, chief div. gen. surgery, 1982-88, chief gastrointestinal surgery, 1986—, assoc. dean, 1988-91; cons. VA Hosps. Editor-in-chief World Jour. Surgery, 1993—. Served with M.C. USAF, 1961-64. NIH grantee, 1968-70; John A. Hartford Found. grantee, 1970-79; Royal Soc. Medicine Eng. travelling fellow, 1976-77. Fellow ACS; mem. Am. Surg. Assn., Am. Gastroenterol. Assn., Am. Fedn. Clin. Rsch. Am. Inst. Nutrition, AMA, Assn. Acad. Surgery, Pacific Coast Surg. Assn. (recorder 1986-91, pres. 1995), Soc. Clin. Surgery, Soc. Surgery Alimentary Tract (sec. 1982-85, pres.-elect 1985, pres. 1986, chmn. bd. trustees 1987), Soc. Univ. Surgeons, Societe Internationale de Chirurgie (U.S. chpt. sec. 1990-94, pres. 1996—), Internat. Biliary Assn. (pres. 1979-81), Bay Surg. Soc., L.A. Surg. Soc. (pres. 1981), ACS (So. Calif. chpt. pres. 1987), Robert M. Zollinger/Ohio State U. Surg. Soc. (pres. 1988-90), Phi Beta Kappa, Sigma Xi, Alpha Omega Alpha, Delta Tau Delta. Republican. Research, numerous publs. in gastrointestinal surgery and gastrointestinal metabolism and biochemistry. Office: Dept of Surgery University of California Los Angeles CA 90024

TOMPKINS, TAIN PENDLETON, foreign service official; b. Phila., Apr. 2, 1943; s. Pendleton Souther and Louise Agnes (Mertz) T.; m. Grace Muller, Feb. 26, 1981; children: Ann Louise, Heather Ashley Muller. BA in English, Washington & Lee U., 1964; MA in Internat. Rels., Johns Hopkins U., 1968, MA in English, 1970. Commd. Fgn. Svc., 1969; 3d sec. Am. Consulate, Can Tho, South Vietnam, 1970-71, Am. Embassy, Lisbon, Portugal, 1972-74; ceasefire observer Am. Consulate, Can Tho, South Vietnam, 1974; staff asst. U.S. Dept. State, Washington, 1974-75; fellow Inst. Politics Harvard U., Cambridge, Mass., 1976; 2d sec. Am. Embassy, Beirut, Lebanon, 1977-80; staff asst. Office of Les Aspin, Washington, 1980-81; dep. dir. staff secretariat U.S. Dept. State, 1981-83; 2d sec. Am. Embassy, Harare, Zimbabwe, 1983-85; 1st sec. Am. Embassy, Canberra, Australia, 1987-91; dep. chief of mission Am. Embassy, Bridgetown, Barbados, 1992-95; coun. Econ. Affairs Am. Embassy, Tel Aviv, Israel, 1995—; diplomat in residence U. Tex., Austin, 1991-92. Co-editor: The Challenge of NAFTA, 1992. Mem. Army and Navy Club, Phi Beta Kappa Assoc. Episcopalian. Avocations: tennis, reading. Office: Am Embassy PSC 98 Box 100 APO AE 09830

TOMPSETT, WILLIAM C., lawyer; b. N.Y.C., Dec. 22, 1948. BA, Haverford Coll., 1970; JD, Cornell U., 1974. Bar: Pa. 1974, Ill. 1978. Ptnr. Mayor, Brown & Platt, Chgo. Mem. ABA, Chgo. Bar Assn. Office: Mayer Brown & Platt 190 S La Salle St Chicago IL 60603-3410*

TOMPSON, MARIAN LEONARD, professional society administrator; b. Chgo., Dec. 5, 1929; d. Charles Clark and Marie Christine (Bernardini) Leonard; m. Clement R. Tompson, May 7, 1949 (dec. 1981); children: Melanie Tompson Kandler, Deborah Tompson Mikolajczak, Allison Tompson Fagerholm, Laurel Tompson Davies, Sheila Tompson Dorsey, Brian, Philip. Student public and parochial schs., Chgo. and Franklin Park, Ill. Co-founder La Leche League (Internat.), Franklin Park, 1956; pres. La Leche League (Internat.), 1956-80, dir., 1956—, pres. emeritus, 1990—; exec. dir. Alternative Birth Crisis Coalition, 1981-85; cons. WHO; bd. dirs. North Am. Soc. Psychosomatic Ob-Gyn, Natural Birth and Natural Parenting, 1981-83; mem. adv. bd. Nat. Assn. Parents and Profls. for Safe Alternatives in Childbirth, Am. Acad. Husband-Coached Childbirth; mem. adv. bd. Fellowship of Christian Midwives; mem. profl. adv. bd. Home Oriented Maternity Experience; guest lectr. Harvard U. Med. Sch., UCLA Sch. Public Health, U. Antioquia Med. Sch., Medellin, Columbia, U. Ill. Sch. Medicine, Chgo., U. W.I., Jamaica, U. N.C., Nat. Coll. of Chiropractic, Am. Coll. Nurse Midwives, U. Parma, Italy, Inst. Psychology, Rome, Rockford (Ill.) Sch. Medicine, Northwestern U. Sch. Medicine; mem. family com. Ill. Commn. on Status of Women, 1976-85; mem. perinatal adv. com. Ill. Dept. Pub. Health, 1980-83; mem. adv. bd. Internat. Nutrition Communication Service, 1980—; bd. cons. We Can, 1984—; exec. adv. bd. United Resources for Family Health and Support, 1985-86. Author: (with others) Safe Alternatives in Childbirth, 1976, 21st Century Obstetrics Now!, 1977, The Womanly Art of Breastfeeding, 3d edit., 1981, Five Standards for Safe Childbearing, 1981, But Doctor, About That Shot..., 1988, Breast Feeding, 5th edit., 1991; author prefaces and forwards in 10 books; columnist La Leche League News, 1958-80; columnist People's Doctor Newsletter, 1977-88, mem. adv. bd., cons., 1988-92; assoc. editor Child and Family Quar., 1967—; mem. med. adv. bd. East West Jour., 1980—; also articles. Recipient Gold medal of honor Centro de Rehabilitacao Nossa Senhora da Gloria, 1975, Night of 100 Stars III Achiever award Actors Fund Am., 1990. Mem. Nat. Assn. Postpartum Care Svcs. (adv. bd.), Chgo. Cmty. Midwives (adv. bd.). Office: 1400 N Meacham Rd Schaumburg IL 60173-4808

TOMS, MICHAEL ANTHONY, broadcast journalist; b. Washington, June 7, 1940; s. Austin Herman Toms and Margaret Dorothy (Pitcher) Slavinsky; m. Justine Willis, Dec. 16, 1972; children: Michael Anthony, Robert Welch. Student, U. Miami, 1959-60, U. Va., 1961-63; postgrad., Calif. Inst. Integral Studies, San Francisco, 1973-75; DrTheology, Sem. St. Basil the Great, Sydney, Australia, 1981; DHL (hon.), U. Humanistic Studies, San Diego, 1983. Field govt. rep. VariTyper Corp., Washington, 1960-64; sales mgr. VariTyper Corp., San Francisco, 1964-67; regional sales mgr. VariTyper Corp., San Bernardino, 1967-68; pres. Creative Mktg. Assocs., San Francisco, 1968-73; chmn. bd. The Response Mktg. Group, San Francisco, 1971-73; CEO Michael A. Toms & Assocs., San Francisco, 1973-76; pres. New Dimensions Found., San Francisco, 1973—; sr. acquisitions editor Harper Collins, San Francisco, 1989-95; exec. prodr., host nat. pub. radio interview series New Dimensions, 1980—; chmn. bd. emeritus Calif. Inst. Integral Studies, San Francisco, 1979-83; exec. dir. Audio Inds., Inc., San Francisco, 1981-83; adj. prof. Marylhurst Coll. Grad. Sch. of Bus., 1993—, Union Grad. Sch., 1994—; founder, CEO New Dimensions Broadcasting Network, 1994—; exec. editor New Dimensions Book Series, 1993—; mem. bd. dirs. KQED, Inc., San Francisco, 1980-83, Green Earth Found., 1989—, KZYX-FM, Mendocino County, Calif., 1989-91; mem. bd. adv. The Great Round, 1989—. Author: Worlds Beyond, 1978, The New Healers, 1980, An Open Life, 1988, At The Leading Edge, 1991. Mem. Task Force to Promote Self Esteem and Personal and Social Responsibility, Mendocino County, Calif., 1988-89; mem. internat. adv. bd. Radio for Peace Internat. Mem. Internat. Assn. for Socially Responsible Radio (founding dir. 1991—). Avocations: travel, writing, reading. Home: PO Box 1029 Ukiah CA 95482-1029 Office: New Dimensions Found PO Box 569 Ukiah CA 95482

TOMSETH, VICTOR L., ambassador; b. Eugene, Oreg., Apr. 14, 1941; s. Hersey F. and Lyla I. (Currant) T.; m. Wallapa Charoenrath, Sept. 1, 1968; 2 children. BA in History, U. Oreg., 1963; student in Thai lang., Fgn. Svc. Inst., 1966-67; MA in History, U. Mich., 1966; student, Cornell U., 1972-73; student in Persian lang., Fgn. Svc. Inst., 1975-76, student exec. seminar in nat. and internat. affairs, 1981. Vol. Peace Corps, Nepal, 1964-65; joined Fgn. Svc., 1966; polit.-mil. officer Am. Embassy, Bangkok, 1967-68, staff asst. to amb., 1969-70, polit. officer, 1970-71, dep. chief of mission, 1989-92; vice consul U.S. Consulate Gen., Chiang Mai, Thailand, 1967, Udorn, Thailand, 1968-69; prin. officer U.S. Consulate Gen., Shiraz, Iran, 1976-79; mem. bd. examiners Dept. State, Washington, 1971-72, country officer for Thailand, 1973-75; dir. India, Nepal and Sri Lanka affairs Dept. State, 1982-84, dir. Thailand and Burma affairs, Bur. East Asian and Pacific affairs, 1986-89; polit. counselor Am. Embassy, Tehran, Iran, 1979-81; dep. chief of mission Am. Embassy, Colombo, Sri Lanka, 1984-86; U.S. amb. to Laos Am. Embassy, Vientiane, 1993—; diplomat-in-residence N.C. Consortium for Internat./Intercultural Edn., 1992-93. Active Am. Mus. Natural History. Mem. Asia Soc., Oreg. Winegrowers Assn., Sr. Seminar Alumni Assn., Westwood Country Club (Vienna, Va.). Office: AMEMB Vientiane Box V APO AP 96546

TOMSICH, ROBERT J., heavy machinery manufacturing executive. Chmn. Blaw Knox Corp., Pitts. *

TOMSOVIC, EDWARD JOSEPH, college dean; b. San Francisco, 1922. MD, U. Calif., 1946. Intern Franklin Hosp., San Francisco, 1946-47, asst. resident internal medicine, 1948; pediatric intern Bellevue Hosp., N.Y.C., 1948-49, asst. resident in pediatrics, 1949-50; chief med. service 109th Field Hosp., Salzburg, Austria, 1950-52, chief pediatrician, 1954; chief pediatrician Madigan Army Hosp., Tacoma, Wash., 1954-59, Walter Reed Army Inst. Rsch., Washington, 1959-60; staff Walter Reed Gen. Hosp., Washington, 1960-61, chief pediatrician, 1961-62; chief pediatrician USA Tripler Gen. Hosp., Honolulu, 1963-66, Letterman Gen. Hosp., San Francisco, 1966-69; dir. div. pediatrics Orange (Calif.) County Med. Ctr., 1969-72, med. dir., 1972-76; med. dir. U. Calif.-Irvine Med. Ctr., 1976-79; dean Coll. Medicine, U. Okla., Tulsa, 1979-91, prof. pediatrics, 1979-93, prof. emeritus, 1993—, med. dir. devel. support program, 1991-93; assoc. clin. prof. pediatrics Georgetown U., Washington, 1961-62; clin. prof. U. Calif., Irvine, 1969-77, adj. prof., 1977-79, asst. dean for hosp. profl. affairs, 1972-79. Served to col., M.C., U.S. Army, 1950-69. Fellow Am. Acad. Pediatrics, ACP; mem. AMA, Assn. Mil. Surgeons of U.S., So. Med. Assn., Okla. State Med. Assn.

TON, L. EUGENE, church official. Exec. min. Ind. Bapt. Conv., Indpls. Office: American Baptist Churches 1350 N Delaware St Indianapolis IN 46202-2415

TONDEL, LAWRENCE CHAPMAN, lawyer; b. N.Y.C., Apr. 9, 1946; s. Lyman Mark and Jean (Basch) T.; m. Sharyn A. Smith, Aug. 3, 1974; children: Michael Lawrence, Kathryn Chapman. Student, The Lawrenceville Sch., 1964; AB, Wesleyan U., 1968; JD, U. Mich., 1971. N.Y. 1972. Assoc. Brown & Wood, N.Y.C., 1971-79, ptnr., 1980—; chmn. Internat. Bus. Comm. Ann. Internat. Forum on Offshore Funds, 1993-96. Trustee Elisabeth Morrow Sch., Englewood, N.J., 1988-93. Mem. ABA, Am. Law Inst., Am. Bar Found., Assn. Bar City N.Y. Republican. Episcopalian. Office: Brown & Wood 1 World Trade Ctr New York NY 10048-0202

TONDEUR, PHILIPPE MAURICE, mathematician, educator; b. Zurich, Switzerland, Dec. 7, 1932; came to U.S., 1964, naturalized, 1974; s. Jean and Simone (Lapaire) T.; m. Claire-Lise Ballansat, Dec. 20, 1965. Ph.D., U. Zurich, 1961. Rsch. fellow U. Paris, 1961-63; lectr. math. U. Zurich, 1963-64, U. Buenos Aires, 1964, Harvard U., Cambridge, Mass., 1964-65, U. Calif., Berkeley, 1965-66; asso. prof. Wesleyan U., Middletown, Conn., 1966-68, U. Ill., Urbana, 1968-70; prof. U. Ill., 1970—; vis. prof. Auckland U., 1968, Eidg. Techn. Hochschule U. Heidelberg, 1973, U. Zurich, 1982, U. Rome, 1984, Ecole Polytechnique, Paris, 1987, U. Santiago de Compostela, 1987, Max Planck Inst., 1987, U. Leuven, Belgium, 1990, Keio U., Yokohama, Japan, 1993; assoc. mem. Ctr. Advanced Study U. Ill., 1977-78, 91-92. Contbr. articles to profl. jours. Recipient fellowships Swiss Nat. Sci. Found., fellowships Harvard U., fellowships U. Ill. Mem. Am. Math. Soc., Schweiz Math. Gesellschaft, Société Math. de France. Office: Math Dept U Ill Urbana IL 61801

TONE, JEFFREY R., lawyer; b. Oak Park, Ill., Mar. 27, 1953. AB cum laude, Princeton U., 1975; JD summa cum laude, U. Ill., 1978. Bar: Ill. 1978. Law clk. to Hon. Prentice H. Marshall U.S. Dist. Ct. (no. dist.), Ill., 1978-80; law clk. to Hon. John Paul Stevens U.S. Supreme Ct., 1980-81; ptnr. Sidley & Austin, Chgo. Office: Sidley & Austin 1 First Nat Plz Chicago IL 60603*

TONE, KENNETH EDWARD, lawyer; b. Tiffin, Ohio, July 15, 1930; s. Harry Frederick and Lucille (Wahl) T.; m. Mary Zeitzheim, July 19, 1954; children: Mary Robin Buechlein, Tygh Mathew. B.S., Miami U., Oxford, Ohio, 1950; LL.B., J.D., Ohio No. U., 1953. Bar: Ohio 1953, Fed. Ct. 1955, U.S. Supreme Ct. 1962. Practice in Sandusky, Ohio, 1953—; ptnr. firm Tone, Maddrell, Eastman, Grubbe, McGory & Vermeeren, 1960—; solicitor Village of Bay View, Ohio, also Village of Milan, Ohio, 1955-60; spl. legal counsel to atty. gen. Ohio, 1971-84; acting judge Sandusky Mcpl. Ct. Author: Sandusky Civil Service Rules, 1955-56, Your Budget and You, 1966, History of Tone Family, 1409-1978, 1978. Sec. Sandusky Planning and Zoning Commn., 1956-65, Sandusky Zoning Code Bd. Appeals, 1956-65, Sandusky Bldg. Code Bd. Appeals, 1956-65, Sandusky Civil Service Commn., 1953-72; mem. Sandusky City Charter Revision Com., 1954-55, 64; chmn. Erie County Bd. Visitors to Public Instns., 1976-82; mem. Erie County Democratic Exec. Com. and Central Com., 1962-70; bd. dirs. Goodwill Industries, 1969-79; bd. dirs. Vols. of Am., 1955-63, v.p., 1959-60, pres., 1960-62; bd. dirs., drive chmn., legal counsel Erie County chpt. Am. Heart Assn., 1956-58; chmn. Heart Ball, 1969; bd. dirs., v.p. Sandusky Area council Girl Scouts U.S.A., 1956-59; trustee Sandusky chpt. Am. Cancer Soc., 1958-60, pres., 1960; exec. bd. Firelands Area council Boy Scouts Am., 1985-92. Served with USNR, 1950-52. Mem. ABA, Ohio Bar Assn. (probate and trust com. 1964-74), Erie County Bar Assn. (pres. 1978), Fed. Bar Assn., Am. Judicature Soc., Sandusky Area C. of C. (steering, legis. coms.), Sandusky Jaycees (past treas., v.p., dir., parliamentarian), N. Central Ohio Arts Council, Internat. Platform Assn., AMVETS (life), Ohio Fire Chiefs Assn. (hon.), Ohio Protective Assn. (hon.), Nat. Eagle Scout Assn., Sandusky Power Squadron (comdr. 1981), Ohio Geneal. Soc., Phi Kappa Tau, Delta Theta Phi. Mem. United Ch. Christ (past mem. consistory). Clubs: Ski (founder), Torch (founder), Sandusky Yacht (commodore 1973), Interlake Yachting Assn. Lodges: Grotto, Elks, Masons, Shriners, Internat. Order Blue Gavel (chpt. pres. 1981, dist. 9 pres. 1984, internat. northeastern v.p. 1984-86). Home: 587 Bimini Dr Sandusky OH 44870-3942 Office: 1401 Cleveland Rd Sandusky OH 44870-4216

TONE, MICHAEL P., lawyer; b. Washington, Aug. 31, 1949. BA, Denison U., 1971; JD, U. S.C., 1974. Bar: Ill. 1974; U.S. Ct. Appeals; U.S. Dist. Ct. Atty. Peterson & Ross, Chgo.; now ptnr. Wilson, Elser, Oskowitz, Edelman & Dieker. Mem. ABA, Ill. State Bar Assn. Office: Wilson, Elser, Moskowitz, Edelman, Dieker 120 North LaSalle Sel2600 Chicago IL 60602*

TONE, PHILIP WILLIS, lawyer, former federal judge; b. Chgo., Apr. 9, 1923; s. Elmer James and Frances (Willis) T.; m. Gretchen Altfillisch, Mar. 10, 1945; children: Michael P., Jeffrey R., Susan A. B.A., U. Iowa, 1943, J.D., 1948; grad. fellow, Yale Law Sch., 1948. Bar: Iowa 1948, Ill. 1950, D.C. 1950. Law clk. Justice Wiley B. Rutledge, Supreme Ct. U.S., Washington, 1948-49; assoc. firm Covington & Burling, Washington, 1949-50; assoc., ptnr. firm Jenner & Block, Chgo., 1950-72, 80—; judge U.S. Dist. Ct., Chgo., 1972-74, U.S. Ct. Appeals (7th cir.), Chgo., 1974-80; spl. counsel Nat. Commn. on Causes and Prevention of Violence, 1968-69, U.S. Senate sub-com. to investigate individuals representing interests of fgn. govts., 1980; Chmn. Ill. Supreme Ct. Rules Com., 1968-71, sec., 1963-68; mem. Com. on Jud. Br. of Jud. Conf. of U.S., 1987-91; gen. counsel U.S. Golf Assn., 1988-92; mem. Fed. Jud. Fellows Commn., 1986-92; chmn. Fed. Jud. Ctr. Found. Contbr. articles to legal periodicals. Served with AUS, 1943-46. Fellow Am. Coll. Trial Lawyers (regent 1984-87, pres. 1988-89); mem. ABA, Am. Bar Found., Am. Law Inst., Ill. Bar Assn. (bd. govs. 1960-64), Chgo. Bar Assn. (bd. mgrs. 1966-69), Am. Judicature Soc., Law Club Chgo. (pres. 1979-80), Legal Club Chgo. Office: Jenner & Block 1 E IBM Plz Chicago IL 60611

TONEGAWA, SUSUMU, biology educator; b. Nagoya, Japan, Sept. 5, 1939; came to U.S., 1963; s. Tsutomu and Miyoko (Masuko) T.; m. Mayumi Yoshinari, Sept. 28, 1985; children: Hidde, Hanna, Satto. BS, Kyoto U., Japan, 1963; PhD, U. Calif., San Diego, 1968. Rsch. asst. U. Calif., San Diego, 1963-64, teaching asst., 1964-68; mem. Basel (Switzerland) Inst. Immunology, 1971-81; prof. biology MIT, Cambridge, 1981—; investigator Howard Hughes Med. Inst., 1988—; dir. MIT Ctr. for Memory and Learning, 1994; professorship Amgen, Inc., 1994. Editorial bd. Jour. Molecular and Cellular Immunology. Decorated Order of Culture, Emperor of Japan; recipient Cloetta prize, 1978, Avery Landsteiner prize Gesselschaft für Immunologie, 1981, Louisa Gross Horwitz prize Columbia U., 1982, award Gardiner Found. Internat., Toronto, Ont., Can., 1983, Robert Koch Found. prize, Bonn., Fed. Republic Germany, 1986, co-recipient Albert Lasker Med. Rsch. award, 1987, Nobel prize in Physiology or Medicine, 1987; named Person with Cultural Merit Japanese Govt., 1983. Mem. NAS (fgn. assoc.), Am. Assn. Immunologists (hon.), Scandinavian Soc. Immunology (hon.). Office: MIT 77 Massachusetts Ave Cambridge MA 02139-4301

TONELLO-STUART, ENRICA MARIA, political economist; b. Monza, Italy; d. Alessandro P. and Maddalena M. (Marangoni) Tonello; m. Albert

E. Smith; m. Charles L. Stuart. BA in Internat. Affairs, Econs., U. Colo., 1961; MA, Claremont Grad. Sch., 1966, PhD, 1971. Sales mgr. Met. Life Ins. Co., 1974-79; pres., CEO, ETS R&D, Inc., Palos Verdes Peninsula, Calif., 1977—; dean internat. studies program Union U., L.A. and Tokyo; lectr. internat. affairs and mktg. UCLA Ext., Union U. Pub., editor Tomorrow Outline Jour., 1963—, The Monitor, 1988; pub. World Regionalism-An Ecological Analysis, 1971, A Proposal for the Reorganization of the United Nations, 1966, The Persuasion Technocracy, Its Forms, Techniques and Potentials, 1966, The Role of the Multinationals in the Emerging Globalism, 1978; developed the theory of social ecology and econsociometry. Organizer 1st family assistance program Langley FB Tractical Air Command, 1956-58. Recipient vol. svc. award VA, 1956-58, ARC svc. award, 1950-58. Mem. Corp. Planners Assn. (treas. 1974-79), Investigative Reporters and Editors, World Future Soc. (pres. 1974-75), Asian Bus. League, Chinese Am. Assn. (life), Japan Am. Assn., L.A. World Trade Ctr., Palos Verdes C. of C. (legis. com.), L.A. Press Club (bd. dirs.), Zonta (chmn. internat. com. South Bay), Pi Sigma Alpha. Avocations: writing, collecting old books and maps, community service, travel.

TONER, MICHAEL F., journalist; b. LeMars, Iowa, Mar. 17, 1944; s. Francis F. and Mary Ann (Delaney) T.; m. Patricia L. Asleson, Aug. 28, 1966; children: Susan Michelle, Sharon Lynn. BA cum laude, U. Iowa, 1966; postgrad., U. Okla., Peru; MS cum laude, Northwestern U., 1967. Reporter UPI, Chgo., 1966-67; bur. chief Miami Herald, Key West, Fla., 1967-68, reporter, 1968-69, asst. city editor, 1970-72; sci./environ. writer Miami (Fla) Herald, 1973-84; sci. editor Atlanta Journal and Constitution, 1984-91, sci. writer, 1991—. Co-author: Florida by Paddle and Pack, 1979; contbr. articles to mags. Recipient Pulitzer Prize for explanatory journalism, 1993; Stanford U. profl. journalism fellow, 1973. Avocations: hiking, swimming, photography, stamp collecting, cooking. Office: Atlanta Journal and Constn 72 Marietta St NW Atlanta GA 30303-2804

TONER, WALTER JOSEPH, JR., transportation engineer, financial consultant; b. Rutherford, N.J., July 22, 1921; s. Walter Joseph Toner and Rhea Virginia Carell; m. Barbara Jean Francis, Sept. 11, 1943; children: Sherry Francis, Walter J. III. Student, Wesleyan U., 1938-39; BS in Engring., U.S. Naval Acad., 1942. Profl. engr. Engring. mgr. Bethlehem Steel Corp., Boston, 1946-75; nuclear cons. Stone & Webster, Boston, 1975-77; v.p. project devel. & mgmt. Sverdrup Corp., Boston, 1977-86; cons., v.p., T.Y. Lin Internat., Boston, 1986—; v.p. Performance Index, Inc., 1991—. Lt. USN, 1942-46. Fellow Soc. Am. Mil. Engrs. (nat. trustee, v.p. 1978-85, life); mem. ASCE (life), DAV, Am. Consulting Engrs. Coun., Am. Railway Engrs. Assn., Boston Soc. Civil Engrs., Transp. Rsch. Bd., U.S. Naval Acad. Alumni Assn. (life, nat. trustee), U.S. Naval Inst. (life), Wardroom Club, Bass River Yacht Club (chair race com.), Wrinkle Point Beach Assn., Masons. Episcopalian. Office: Box 617 37 Garfield Ln West Dennis MA 02670-0617

TONEY, ANTHONY, artist; b. Gloversville, N.Y., June 28, 1913; s. Michael and Susan (Betor) T.; m. Edna Amadon Greenfield, apr. 8, 1947 (dec. Apr. 1993); children: Anita, Karen, Adele Susan. B.F.A., Syracuse U., 1934; M.A., Columbia Tchrs. Coll., 1952, Ed.D., 1955. Instr. art Stevenson Sch., N.Y.C., 1948-52, Hofstra Coll., Hempstead, N.Y., 1953-55, New Sch. Social Research, 1953-96, No. Westchester Ctr. for Arts, Mt. Kisco, N.Y., 1980—; vis. artist Brandeis U., spring 1973, 74. Executed mural Gloversville (N.Y.) High Schs., 1937, Bowne Hall, 1967, Brockway Cafeteria Syracuse U, 1971; one-man shows Wakefield Gallery, 1941, Santa Barbara Mus., 1942, Artists Gallery, 1948, A.C.A. Gallery, 1949, 51, 54, 55, 57, 59, 62, 64, 68, 70, 72, 75, 77, 79, 81, 83, 87, Syracuse Mus., Roswell Mus., Kansas City Art Inst., U. N.Mex., 1956, Berkshire Mus., 1957, 60, S.I. Mus., Rochester Inst. Tech., 1958, U. So. Ill., Tyringham (Mass.) Gallery, 1960, 61, 66, Katonah Gallery, 1982-83, Albany Inst. History and Art, Lenox (Mass.) Art Gallery, Cayuga Mus., Auburn, N.Y., 1959, Harbor Gallery, L.I., N.Y., 1965, Dutchess C.C., Fordham Coll., 1967, Pace Coll., 1968, New Sch. for Social Rsch., 1970, 77, 83, St. Mary's Coll. Md., 1974, Bridge Gallery, White Plains, N.Y., 1975, Virginia Barrett Gallery, 1978, 80, 86, Amphora, La Jolla, Calif., 1979, Nardin Gallery, Crossriver, N.Y., 1986, Retrospective ACA Gallery, 1987, Rutgers U., 1987, Rose Mus., Brandeis U., 1987, No. Westchester Ctr. for the Arts, 1988, Juniper Gallery, Napa (Calif.) Art Ctr., 1991, Rasmussen Art Gallery, Angwin, Calif., 1991, Herbert Johnson, Cornell Mus., 1991, Notre Dame U., 1991, Tchrs. Coll.-Columbia U., N.Y.C., 1994 (Audubon Artists Annual prize 1994), others; exhibited many group shows including Syracuse Mus., Whitney Mus., U. Ill., U. Nebr., Carnegie Biennial, Pa. Acad., Nat. Acad., Walker Art Center, Nat. Inst. Arts and Letters, Am. Acad. Arts and Letters, Katonah Gallery, St. Lawrence U., Purchase Coll., Brandeis U., Westminster Coll., Rutgers U., Corcoran Biennial, Butler Inst. Am. Art, Youngstown, Ohio, 1979-80, Staatliche Galerie, Moritazburg Halle, Fed. Republic, Germany, 1990, Im Gemeente, J.K. Vanreekum-Museum Apeldoorn, Niederlande, 1991, Autier Gallery, Piermont, N.Y., 1992, Peel Gallery, Danbi, Vt., 1993, Nardin Galleries, Somers, N.Y., 1993-94, Triton Mus. Art, Santa Clara, Calif., 1994; works in permanent collections, U. Ill., Ind. Fine Arts Ctr., Ohio Wesleyan U., Wichita State U. Mus., U. Wyo. Mus. Art, Norton Gallery (Fla.), New Britain (Conn.) Mus., Whitney Mus., Tchrs. Coll. Columbia U., Nat. Acad., Chrysler Mus. at, Norfolk, Montgomery Community Coll., S.I. Mus., Berkshire Mus., Butler Inst. Am. Art, Hofstra Coll., No. Westchester Hosp. Ctr., Lenin Mus., USSR, Anti-War Show, Berlin, New Soc. Fine Arts, No. Westchester Ctr. for the Arts, Bklyn. Mus., Herbert Johnson, Notre Dame, Cornell U., Fordham U., Skidmore Coll., Bennington Coll., SUNY, Fleming Hall Mus. U. Vt., City Hall, Gloversville, N.Y., Katonah (N.Y.) Libr., New Eng. Ctr. Contemporary Art, Putnam Art Coun., The State Mus. N.J., Bklyn. Mus., also pvt. collections; freelance comml. artist, 1945-50; author: Creative Painting and Drawing, 1968, Painting and Drawing, 1978, Leonardo; also articles.; editor: 150 Masterpieces of Drawing, 1963; contbr. to The Tune of the Calliope, 1958, Family Creative Workshop, 1975, The Palette and the Flame, 1979, Funk and Wagnalls Ency., 1980, Political Affairs, 1985. Served as sgt. AUS, 1942-45. Served in Abraham Lincoln Brigade, Spain, 1938-39. Decorated D.F.C. with clusters, Air medal with clusters; recipient purchase prize U. Ill., 1950, 1st prize Artists Equity Assn., 1952, Emily Lowe award, 1955, Mickewiecz Art Competition 1st prize, 1956, Purchase prize S.I. Mus., 1957, Ranger purchase Nat. Acad., 1966, 76, Childe Hassam purchase prize Nat. Inst. Arts and Letters, 1967, 76, Mintz Meml. award, 1974, Benjamin Altman Figure prize Nat. Acad., 1975, 80, Eggers Sr. Alumni awardSyracuse U., 1989, Disting. Alumnus award Tchrs. Coll., Columbia U., 1991, 3 1st prizes Putnam Arts Coun., 1994. Mem. NEA, Nat. Soc. Mural Painters (treas. 1973-74), Artists Equity Assn. (nat. dir. 1952-56, 71-72, sec. nat. bd. 1956-57, exec. bd. N.Y. chpt. 1960-62, 71-72), Audubon Artists (mem. bd. 1959, 75-78, Grumbacher award 1954, medal of honor Nat. Show 1967, 75, 87, Judy Brenne Meml. award 1981, Ann. Emily Lowe award 1983, Ralph Fabri award 1984, Ann. Robert Phillips Meml. award 1988, Len G. Everett Meml. award 1989, 91, Silver medal 1993, Stephen Hirsch Meml. award 1995), Nat. Acad. (mem. coun., asst. corr. sec. 1978—, membership com. 1988—), Coll. Art Assn., Kappa Delta Pi. Home: 16 Hampton Pl Katonah NY 10536-1402 *I consider persistent struggle in the context of as much awareness of all possible factors of key importance. It is necessary to be as whole as possible in one's understanding of self, life, society and one's individual endeavor. One's goal must be the survival of life, the earth and solar system that makes it possible, and the solution of the problems that threaten human survival and perhaps all existence as we know it.*

TONG, ALEX WAIMING, immunologist; b. Hong Kong, Apr. 8, 1952; came to U.S., 1970; s. Robert S. and Agnes M. (Cheng) T.; m. Susan J. Radtke, May 23, 1980 (div. Mar. 1988); 1 child, Nicole L.; m. S. Quay Mercer, May 13, 1995. BA in Biology, U. Oreg., 1973; PhD in Microbiology and Immunology, Oreg. Health Scis. U., 1980. Undergrad. teaching asst. biology dept. U. Oreg., Eugene, 1972-73; rsch. asst. dept. microbiology and immunology Oreg. Health Scis. U., Portland, 1975-80, teaching asst. Sch. Medicine, 1977-78, rsch. assoc. dept. micrology and immunology, 1981-82; postdoctoral fellow Surg. Rsch. Lab. Portland VA Med. Ctr., 1980-82; rsch. assoc. in immunology Charles A. Sammons Cancer Ctr., Baylor U. Med. Ctr., Dallas, 1982-86; assoc. dir. immunology lab. Baylor U. Med. Ctr., Dallas, Tex., 1986—; asst. prof. Inst. Biomed. Studies, Baylor U., Waco, 1988—; prin. investigator Nat. Cancer Inst., Bethesda, Md., 1994—; adj. faculty immunology grad. studies program U. Tex. Southwestern Med. Ctr., Dallas, 1982—. Contbr. articles to profl. jours. Tatar rsch. fellow Med. Rsch. Found. Oreg., Portland, 1981-83. Mem. Am. Assn. Immunologists, Am. Assn. Cancer Rsch., Am. Soc. Hematology, Clin. Immunology Soc., Japan Karate Assn. Dallas (dir.), Internat. Traditional Karate Fedn. (cert. coach 1990—, cert. referee 1988—), Am. Amateur Karate Fedn. (dir. S.W. region). Democrat. Avocations: traditional karate, alpine skiing, scuba diving. Office: Baylor U Med Ctr Cancer Immunology Rsch Lab 3500 Gaston Ave Dallas TX 75246-2045

TONG, HING, mathematician, educator; b. Canton, China, Feb. 16, 1922; s. Shen-Beu and Fung-Kam (Cheng) T.; m. Mary Josephine Powderly, Aug. 19, 1956; children—Christopher Hing, Mary Elizabeth, William Joseph, Jane Frances, James John. A.B., U. Pa., 1943; Ph.D., Columbia, 1947; M.A. (hon.), Wesleyan U., Middletown, Conn., 1961. NRC postdoctoral fellow Inst. Advanced Study, Princeton, 1947-48; lectr. Canton (China) U., 1949; Cutting travelling fellow Inst. Henri Poincare, Paris, France, 1950-51; asst. prof. Reed Coll., 1952-53; vis. asst. prof. Barnard Coll., 1953-54; mem. faculty Wesleyan U., 1954-67, prof. math., 1960-67, chmn. dept., 1962-64; prof. math. Fordham U., Bronx, N.Y., 1966—; chmn. dept. Fordham U., 1967-74; mem. U.S. subcom. World Orgn. Gen. Systems and Cybernetics. Contbr. profl. jours. Mem. Phi Beta Kappa, Sigma Xi. Home: 725 Cooper Ave Oradell NJ 07649-2334 Office: Math Dept Fordham U Bronx NY 10458

TONGES, MARY CRABTREE, nurse executive; b. Dixon, Ill.; d. John Charles and Marion Rita (Shields) Crabtree; m. James Alan Tonges, may 21, 1983; children: Christina Mary, James John. BSN, U. Iowa, 1973; MSN, U. Ill., Chgo., 1977; MBA, Baruch Coll., 1994. Cert. in nursing adminstrn. Asst. dir. med.-surg. nursing St. Joseph Hosp., Chgo., 1977-78; dir. specialty nursing Northwestern Meml. Hosp., Chgo., 1979-82; v.p. nursing Clara Maass Med. Ctr., Belleville, N.J., 1983-86, Robert Wood Johnson U. Hosp., New Brunswick, N.J., 1987-91; cons. Ctr. for Case Mgmt., Inc., South Natick, Mass., 1991—. Contbr. articles to profl. jours. Commonwealth Fund nurse exec. fellow, 1991. Mem. Am. Orgn. Nurse Execs., Orgn.Nursing Execs. N.J., Nat. Forum Women Health Care Leaders, Sigma Theta Tau. Home: 8 Fairfield St Montclair NJ 07042-4114

TONGUE, PAUL GRAHAM, financial executive; b. Phila., Dec. 30, 1932; s. George Paul and Florence Amelia (Kogel) T.; m. Marjorie Joan Meyers, May 26, 1954; children: Suzanne Marjorie, Douglas Paul. BS in Commerce, Drexel U., 1957; MBA, NYU, 1965. With Chase Manhattan Bank, N.Y.C., 1957-87; chmn. Plus Systems Inc., Denver, 1985; pres. Eppley-Tongue Assocs., Inc., Towson, Md., 1988—; exec. v.p. Veritas Venture Inc., Scotch Plains, N.J., 1990-91; cons. Prime Care Sys., Inc., Newport News, Va., 1995—; chmn. Plus Systems Inc., Denver, 1984-85; bd. dirs. PrimeCare Systems, Inc., Newport News, Va. Pres. Our Saviour Luth. Ch., Manhasset, N.Y., 1984; bd. dirs. Nassau Symphony Orch. With U.S. Army, 1954-55. Mem. Ford's Colony Country Club. Avocations: golf, classical music.

TONGUE, WILLIAM WALTER, economics and business consultant, educator emeritus; b. Worcester, Mass., May 24, 1915; s. Walter Ernest and Lena (Brown) T.; m. Beverly Harriet Cohan, Dec. 26, 1936; children—Barbara Tongue Duggan, Kathleen Tongue Alligood. A.B., Dartmouth, 1937, M.C.S., 1938; Ph.D., U. Chgo., 1947. Jr. acct. Price, Waterhouse & Co. (C.P.A.'s), N.Y.C., 1938; instr. Coe Coll., Cedar Rapids, Iowa, 1941-42; spl. cons. OSS, 1942; financial economist Fed. Res. Bank Chgo., 1942-44; economist Jewel Companies, Inc., Chgo., 1944-64; prof. econs. and finance U. Ill. Chgo. Circle, 1965-80; prof. emeritus, 1980—; econ. cons. LaSalle Nat. Bank, Chgo., 1968-91; mem. com. CNA Fin. Separate Fund B.; dir. St. Joseph Light & Power Co., Mo., 1965-86; trustee Signode Employees' Savings and Profit Sharing Trust Fund, 1980-89. Author articles; contbr.: to books including How We Can Halt Inflation and Still Keep Our Jobs, 1974. Bd. dirs., v.p. research and statistics Chgo. Assn. Commerce and Industry, 1968-69. Mem. Nat. Assn. Bus. Economists (pres. 1962-63), Conf. Bus. Economists, Am. Statis. Assn. (pres. Chgo. chpt. 1951-52), Econ. Club Chgo., Investment Analysts Assn. Chgo., Inst. Chartered Fin. Analysts (chartered fin. analyst 1963), Midwest Fin. Assn. (pres. 1972-73). Home and Office: 212 Shoreline Dr Park Ridge IL 60068-2934

TONJES, MARIAN JEANNETTE BENTON, education educator; b. Rockville Center, N.Y., Feb. 16, 1929; d. Millard Warren and Felicia E. (Tyler) Benton; m. Charles F. Tonjes (div. 1965); children: Jeffrey Charles, Kenneth Warren. BA, U. N.Mex., 1951, cert., 1966, MA, 1969; EdD, U. Miami, 1975. Dir. recreation Stuyvesant Town Housing Project, N.Y.C., 1951-53; tchr. music., phys. edn. Sunset Mesa Day Sch., Albuquerque, 1953-54; tchr. remedial reading Zia Elem. Sch., Albuquerque, 1965-67; tchr. secondary devel. reading Rio Grande High Sch., Albuquerque, 1967-69; rsch. asst. reading Southwestern Coop. Ednl. Lab., Albuquerque, 1969-71; assoc. dir., vis. instr. Fla. Ctr. Tchr. Tng. Materials U. Miami, 1971-72; asst. prof. U.S. Internat. U., San Diego, 1972-75; prof. edn. Western Wash. U., Bellingham, 1975-94, dir. summer study, 1979-94, prof. emerita, 1994—; dir. summer study at Oriel Coll. Oxford (Eng.) U., Bellingham, 1975-94; reading supr. Manzanita Ctr. U. N.Mex., Albuquerque, 1968; vis. prof. adult edn. Palomar (Calif.) Jr. Coll., 1974; vis. prof. U. Guam, Mangilao, 1989-90; speaker, cons. in field; invited guest Russian Reading Assn., Moscow, 1992; part-time prof. U. N.Mex., Albuquerque, 1995—. Author: (with Miles V. Zintz) Teaching Reading/Thinking Study Skills in Content Classrooms, 3d edit., 1992, Secondary Reading, Writing and Learning, 1991; contbr. articles to profl. jours. Tng. Tchr. Trainers grantee, 1975; NDEA fellow Okla. State U., 1969. Mem. Am. Reading Forum (chmn. bd. dirs. 1983-85), Adult and Adolescent Literacy Confs. (spkr. 1991-94), Internat. Reading Assn. (mem. travel, interchange and study tours com. 1984-86, mem. non-print media nd reading com. 1980-83, workshop dir. S.W. regional confs. 1982, mem. com. internat. devel. N.Am. 1991-96, Outstanding Tchrs. Educator 1988-90), U.K. Reading Assn. (spkr. 1977-93), European Conf. in Reading (spkr. Berlin 1989, Edinburgh 1991, Malmo 1993, Budapest 1995), European Coun. Internat. Schs. (The Hague, spkr. 1993), World Congress in Reading Buenos Aires (spkr. 1994), PEO (past chpt. pres.), Phi Delta Kappa, Delta Delta Delta. Avocations: miniatures, tennis, bridge, art, travel.

TONKENS, REBECCA A., maternal women's health nurse; b. Searcy, Ark., Dec. 17, 1943; d. William T. and Velda M. (Goodloe) McAfee; m. Richard E. Morris, June 24, 1960 (div. Nov. 1980); children: Terri L. Morris Bomar, Toni L. Morris Carroll; m. Solvin W. Tonkens, Dec. 22, 1986. LPN, Area Vocat. Tech. Sch., Kansas City, Kans., 1973; ADN, Kansas City C.C., 1980; BSN, Webster U., 1992. RN, Kans., Mo. Area Vocat. Tech. Sch.; Staff nurse Providence-St. Margaret Hosp., Kansas City, 1973-80; indsl. nurse, office mgr. Kansas City Indsl. Clinic, 1980-81; staff nurse Bethany Med. Ctr., Kansas City, 1981—; active community rels. diabetes unit Bethany Med. Ctr., 1983-86. Officer, v.p., bd. dirs. Cambridge Townhouse Assn., Leawood, Kans., 1989-92; chaperone Rose Bud (Ark.) Band at Presdl. Inauguration, Washington, 1992; mem. adv. bd. Kansas City Kans. C.C. Day Care Ctr.; vol. Habitat for Humanity, Salvation Army, others. Recipient Cert. of Appreciation, Salvation Army, 1994. Mem. ANA, Am. Coll. Occupational and Environ. Medicine (aux.). Episcopalian. Home and Office: 12861 Cambridge Ter Leawood KS 66209-1634

TONKIN, HUMPHREY RICHARD, academic administrator; b. Truro, Cornwall, Eng., Dec. 2, 1939; came to U.S., 1962; s. George Leslie and Lorna Winifred (Sandry) T.; m. Sandra Julie Winberg, Mar. 9, 1968 (div. 1981); m. Jane Spencer Edwards, Oct. 1, 1983; 1 child, Sebastian George. BA, St. John's Coll., Cambridge, Eng., 1962, MA, 1966; AM, Harvard U., 1966, PhD, 1966. Asst. prof. English U. Pa., Phila., 1966-71, assoc. prof., 1971-80, prof., 1980-83, vice-provost undergrad. studies, 1971-75, coord. internat. programs, 1977-83, master Stouffer Coll. House, 1980-83; pres. State Univ. Coll., Potsdam, N.Y., 1983-88, U. Hartford, Conn., 1989—; vis. prof. English Columbia U., N.Y.C., 1980-81; exec. dir. Ctr. Rsch. and Documentation on World Lang. Problems, Rotterdam and Hartford, 1974—. N.Am. editor: Lang. Problems and Lang. Planning; author: (bibliography) Sir Walter Raleigh, 1971, Esperanto and International Language Problems, 4th edit., 1977, Spenser's Courteous Pastoral, 1972, (with Jane Edwards) The World in the Curriculum, 1981, The Faerie Queene, 1989, (with Allison Keef) Language in Religion, 1989, Esperanto: Language, Literature and Community, 1993; contbr. articles, studies, revs. to profl. jours. Pres. Pa. Coun. Internat. Edn., 1980-81; bd. dirs. World Affairs Coun. Phila., 1979-83, Am. Forum, 1985—, Zamenhof Found., 1987-94, Hartford Symphony Orch., 1989—, World Affairs Coun. Conn., 1989—, Greater Hartford Arts Coun., 1989—; chmn. Coun. Internat. Exch. Scholars, 1991-95, Esperantic Studies Found., 1991—, Partnership for Svc.-Learning, 1991-96. Recipient Lindback award for disting. teaching, 1970; Frank Knox fellow Harvard U., 1962-66; Guggenheim fellow, 1974. Fellow Acad. Esperanto; mem. Universal Esperanto Assn. (pres. 1974-80, 86-89, rep. to UN 1974-83, hon. com. 1995—), Spenser Soc. (pres. 1983-84, former dir.), Internat. Acad. Scis. San Marino, Conn. Acad. Arts and Scis., Greater Hartford C. of C., Cosmos Club, Hartford Golf Club, Hartford Club. Home: 85 Bloomfield Ave Hartford CT 06105-1007 Office: U Hartford Office of Pres 200 Bloomfield Ave Hartford CT 06117

TONKIN, LEO SAMPSON, educational foundation administrator; b. Suffern, N.Y., Apr. 2, 1937; s. Leo S. and Ann (Petrone) T. A.B., Johns Hopkins, 1959; postgrad., Sch. Advanced Internat. Studies, 1962-63; J.D., Harvard, 1962; Dr. Pedagogy, St. Thomas Aquinas Coll., 1973. Legis. asst. to U.S. Congressman; then Sen. Charles McC. Mathias, Jr., of Md., 1962-63; asso. counsel U.S. Ho. of Reps. Select Com. on Govt. Research, 1964; spl. cons. Ho. Spl. Subcom. on Edn., 1965-66; exec. dir. D.C. Commrs. Council on Higher Edn., 1965-66; pres. Leo S. Tonkin Assos., Inc., 1966—; founder, dir., chmn. bd. Washington Workshops Found., 1967—; Mem. White House Conf. on Edn., 1965, White House Conf. on Youth, 1971; spl. asst. to chmn. U.S. Ho. of Reps. Select Com. on Crime, 1972; mem. bd. plebe sponsors U.S. Naval Acad., 1977—; v.p. London Fedn. Boys' Clubs, 1980—; mem. adv. panel Nat. Commn. for Protection of Human Subjects of Biomed. and Behavioral Research, HEW, 1976-77. Contbr. articles to mags. Bd. dirs. Washington Choral Arts Soc., 1971-73, Nat. Coordinating Council on Drug Edn., 1973, Nat. Student Ednl. Fund, 1974—; chmn. Wall Street Seminar Found., 1978—; chmn. bd. trustees St. Thomas Aquinas Coll., 1966-73, continuing trustee, 1973-78, trustee, chmn. emeritus, 1978—; chmn. bd. trustees City of Phila. Govt. Honors Program; trustee Southeastern U., 1966-73; asso. bd. trustees Immaculata Coll., 1966-73; mem. advisory bd. Pub. Affairs and Govt. Degree Program, Mt. Vernon Coll., 1971-74; bd. dirs. YMCA, Washington, 1969-71. Recipient Americanism award, Valley Forge Freedoms Found, 1973. Mem. Johns Hopkins Alumni Assn. of Washington (pres. 1969-72). Clubs: Georgetown (Washington), City Tavern (Washington), Nat. Press (Washington), Capitol Hill (Washington), Capitol Yacht (Washington); Harvard (N.Y.C.). Home: 4368 Sunset Ct Warrenton VA 20187 Office: 3222 N St NW Washington DC 20007-2849

TONKONOGY, JOSEPH MOSES, physician, neuropsychiatrist, researcher; b. Belaya Tserkov, Kiev, Ukraine, Oct. 22, 1925; cmae to U.S., 1979, naturalized, 1985; s. Moysey Iosifovich and Beyla (Gdalievna (Schvachkina) T.; married; children: Vitaly, Milla, Bella. MD, Military Med. Acad., Leningrad, USSR, 1947; PhD, All Union Acad. Med. Sci., Moscow, 1956; DSc, 1st Med. Inst., Leningrad, 1966. From asst. to assoc. prof. The Bechterev Inst., Leningrad, 1956-66, prof., chmn., 1966-78; assoc. Boston U. Sch. Medicine, 1980-81; physician VA Med. Ctr., Northampton, Mass., 1981-87; assoc. prof. U. Mass. Med. Ctr., Worcester, 1987-95, prof., 1995—; dir. neuropsychiatry svc. Worcester State Hosp., Mass., 1989—. Author: Introduction to Clinical Neuropsychology, 1973, Vascular Aphasia, 1986; editor: Problems of Contemporary Psychoneurology, 1966, Psychological Experiment in Psychiatry and Neurology, 1969, Mathematical Methods in Psychiatry and Neurology, 1971, Current Problems of Clinical Psychology, 1975; cons.: (book) Soviet Military Psychiatry, 1986; contbr. numerous articles to profl. jours. Capt. Med. Corps, Germany, 1947-48. Recipient The Bechterev Prize, All Union Acad. Med. Scis., Moscow, 1974. Fellow The Royal Soc. Medicine (U.K.); mem. Am. Neuropsychiat. Assn., Am. Acad. Neurology, Internat. Neuropsychol. Soc., Soc. Neurosci., Internat. Psychogeriatric Soc. Jewish. Office: U Mass Med Ctr Dept of Psychiatry 55 Lake Ave N Worcester MA 01655-0002

TONKS, ROBERT STANLEY, pharmacology and therapeutics educator, former university dean; b. Aberystwyth, Wales; emigrated to Can., 1973; s. Robert Patrick Dennis and Prudence Violet (Williams) T.; m. Diana Mary Cownie; children: Pamela Mary, Julia Rosalind, Robert Michael, Sara Katharine. Student, U. Coll. of South Wales, Welsh Coll. Pharmacy; B.Pharm., Welsh Nat. Sch. Medicine, Cardiff, Ph.D. Organon postdoctoral fellow Med. Sch., Cardiff, Nat. Health Service postdoctoral fellow; Nat. Health Service sr. fellow Cardiff and Nevill Hall Hosp., Abergavenny; lectr. pharmacology U. Wales, Cardiff, 1958-72; vis. fellow Claude Bernard Research Assn., Faculté de Medicine, Paris, 1959; sr. lectr. pharmacology and therapeutics Med. Sch. and U. Wales Hosp., Cardiff, 1972-73; dir., prof. Coll. Pharmacy, Dalhousie U., Halifax, N.S., Can., 1973-77, dean Faculty of Health Professions, 1977-88, prof. geriatric pharmaco-therapeutics, 1988—, acting head divsn. geriatric medicine, 1991-94; cons. pharm. industry in U.K., Govt. of N.B., Can., Health and Welfare Dept. Can.; advisor health manpower Govt. of N.S.; coordinator N.E. Can./Am. Health Coun. co-chmn., 1974-91; mem. Health and Welfare Personnel Career Rev. Com.; pharm. scis. grants com. Med. Rsch. Council Can., chmn.; mem. rev. com. health protection br. fed. govt. div. pharm. chemistry, Can.; chmn. advisory com. N.B. Minister of Health; mem. joint com. on devel. rsch. in nursing Med. Rsch. Coun.-Nat. Health Rsch. Devel. Program; mem. nat. adv. panel on risk/benefit mgmt. of drugs. Contbr. articles on pharmacology and pathology to profl. jours. Fellow Pharm. Soc. Gt. Britain, Inst. Biology; mem. Brit. Pharmacol. Soc., Internat. Soc. Thrombosis and Haemostasis, Canadian Soc. Clin. Investigation, Soc. Pharm. Medicine, Can. Assn. on Gerontology, Gerontol. Soc. Am., Am. Soc. Clin. Pharm. and Therapeutics, Can. Soc. Hosp. Pharmacy (hon.), N.B. Pharm. Soc. (hon.), N.S. Pharm. Soc. (cert. of merit, coord. drug and med. supplies Ethiopia airlift), Med. Soc. N.S. (task force on pharmacare), Welsh Cultural Soc. (past pres.). Anglican. Mailing Address: 62 Kingsway Dr, Stillwater Lake, NS Canada B3Z 1G3 Office: Dalhousie U, Coburg Rd, Halifax, NS Canada

TONKYN, RICHARD GEORGE, retired oil and gas company executive, researcher, consultant; b. Portland, Oreg., Mar. 26, 1927; s. William James and Gladys (Campbell) T.; m. Carol Joan Sloan, May 29, 1948 (div. 1976); children: Michael Stephen, Paula Ruth, David William, John Campbell, James Lewis, Russell George; m. Barbara Ann Friedman, May 27, 1982. BA, Reed Coll., 1948; MA, U. Oreg., 1951; PhD, U. Wash., 1960. Registered patent agt., U.S. Patent and Trademark Office. Chemist Titanium Metals Corp., Henderson, Nev., 1952-54, Allegheny Ludlum Steel, Brackenridge, Pa., 1954-55; rsch. engr. Boeing Airplane Co., Seattle, 1955-59; chemist, project scientist Union Carbide Corp., Bound Brook, N.J., 1961-69; mgr. rsch., group leader Betz Labs., Inc., Trevose, Pa., 1969-76; v.p. rsch. and devel. Mogul div. The Dexter Corp., Chagrin Falls, Ohio, 1976-85, Petrolite Corp., St. Louis, 1985-92. Patentee in field. NSF fellow, 1959, 60-61. Mem. Am. Chem. Soc., Indsl. Rsch. Inst., Cooling Tower Inst. (bd. dirs. 1982-85, pres. 1985), Physical and Chem. Soc., Sigma Xi, Phi Lambda Upsilon. Avocations: tennis, golf.

TONN, ELVERNE MERYL, pediatric dentist, dental benefits consultant; b. Stockton, Calif., Dec. 10, 1929; s. Emanuel M. and Lorna Darlene (Bryant) T.; m. Ann G. Richardson, Oct. 28, 1951; children: James Edward, Susan Elaine Tonn Yee. AA, La Sierra U., Riverside, Calif., 1949; DDS, U. So. Calif., 1955; BS, Regents Coll., U. State N.Y., 1984. Lic. dentist; cert. tchr., Calif., dental ins. cons. Pediatric dentist, assoc. Walker Dental Group, Long Beach, Calif., 1957-59, Children's Dental Clinic, Sunnyvale, Calif., 1959-61; pediatric dentist in pvt. practice Mountain View, Calif., 1961-72; from clin. instr. to assoc. prof. U. Pacific, San Francisco, 1964-84; pediatric dentist, ptnr. Pediatric Dentistry Assocs., Los Altos, Calif., 1972-83; assoc. prof. U. Calif., San Francisco, 1984-86; pediatric dentist, ptnr. Valley Oak Dental Group, Manteca, Calif., 1987—; ; pediatric dental cons. Delta Dental Plan, San Francisco, 1985—; chief dental staff El Camino Hosp., Mountain View, 1964-65, 84-85; lectr. in field. Weekly columnist Manteca Bull., 1987-92; producer 2 teaching videos, 1986; contbr. articles to profl. jours. Lectr. to elem. students on dental health Manteca Unified Sch. Dist., 1982-92; dental health screener Elem. Schs., San Joaquin County Pub. Health, 1989-92; dental cons. Interplast program Stanford U. Sch. Medicine. Capt. U.S. Army, 1955-57. Fellow Internat. Coll. Dentists, Internat. Assn. Pediatric Dentistry, Internat. Assn. Dental Rsch., Fedn. Dentaire Internationale, Am. Acad. Pediatric Dentistry, Am. Coll. Dentists, Royal Soc. Health (Eng.), Acad. of Dentistry for Handicapped, Pierre Fauchard Acad., Acad. Dental Materials; mem. ADA, Am. Assn. Dentists Children, Am. Assn. Dental Cons., Calif. Dental Assn., Calif. Soc. Dentistry for Children (pres. 1968), Calif. Soc. Pediatric Dentists, N.Y. Acad. Scis., Calif. Acad. Sci., Rotary Internat., Am. Bd. Quality Assurance and Utilization Rev. Physicians, Nat. Assn. for Healthcare Quality. Republican. Avocations: photography, travel, history. Home: 374 Laurelwood Cir Manteca CA 95336-7122 Office: Valley Oak Dental Group Inc 1507 W Yosemite Ave Manteca CA 95337

TONN, ROBERT JAMES, entomologist; b. Watertown, Wis., June 23, 1927; s. Harry James and Elise (Foogman) T.; m. Noemi C. Tonn; children: Sigrid M., Monica E. BS, Colo. State U., 1949, MS, 1950; MPH, Okla. Med. Sch., 1963; PhD, Okla. State U., 1959. Rsch. assoc La. State U., Costa Rica/New Orleans, 1961-63; dir. Taunton Field Sta., Taunton, Mass., 1963-65; chief PMO unit WHO, various locations, 1965-87; adj. prof. of parasitology U. Tex.-El Paso, 1988—; cons. USAID/VBC, 1987—. Contbr. numerous articles to profl. jours. Mem. Am. Soc. Tropical Medicine, Soc. Vector Ecology (pres. 1984), Am. Mosquito Control Assn., U.S./ Mex. Border Health Assn., Royal Soc. Tropical Medicine and Hygiene, Masons. Congregationalist. Home: RR 3 Box 505 Park Rapids MN 56470-9363

TONN, SHERI JEANNE, chemistry educator, dean; b. Dallas, May 13, 1949; d. Harvey C. Bartel and Jeanne Marie (Siddall) Shelton; m. Jeffrey F. Tonn, Aug. 22, 1971. BS in Chemistry, Oreg. State U., 1971; PhD in Chemistry, Northwestern U., 1976; postgrad., U. Minn., 1976-79. Asst. prof. chemistry Pacific Luth. U., Tacoma, 1979-84, assoc. prof. chemistry, 1984-93, prof. chemistry, 1993—, dean natural sci., 1993—; mem. adv. com. Simpson Tacoma Kraft, 1993—. Co-founder, bd. dirs. Citizens for a Healthy Bay, 1991—, past pres.; bd. dirs. People for Puget Sound, Seattle, 1992—; mem. Puget Sound Water Quality Authority, Olympia, Wash., 1985-96; mem. adv. com. State of Wash. Environment 2010, Olympia, 1990-92; bd. trustees Associated Western Univs., Salt Lake City, 1995—, chair elect, 1996; faculty sponsor and state bd. MESA, Wash., 1993—. Eisenhower grantee, 1994, 95, NSF grantee, 1981, 90, 95, Murdock Charitable Trust grantee, 1995—. Mem. Am. Chem. Soc. (various local sect. offices 1971—), N.Y. Acad. Scis., Sigma Xi, Iota Sigma Pi. Avocations: canoeing, scuba diving, sailing. Home: 1201 Garfield St S Tacoma WA 98444 Office: Pacific Luth U Dept Chemistry Tacoma WA 98447

TONNOS, ANTHONY, bishop; b. Port Colborne, Ont., Can., Aug. 1, 1935. Ordained priest Roman Cath. Ch., 1961. Bishop Archdiocese of Hamilton, Ont., Can., 1984—. Office: Roman Catholic Church-Canada, 700 King St W, Hamilton, ON Canada L8P 1C7

TONRY, RICHARD ALVIN, lawyer, pecan farmer; b. New Orleans, June 25, 1935; s. Richard Gordon and Dolores Theresa (Kroger) T.; m. Joy Ann Willmouth, Feb. 3, 1950; children: Richard A., Tara Ann, Cullen Adair. BA magna cum laude, Spring Hill Coll., Mobile, Ala., 1961, M Philosophy summa cum laude, 1962; JD, Loyola U. of South, New Orleans, 1967. Bar: La. 1967, U.S. Dist. Ct. (ea. dist.) La. 1967, U.S. Ct. Appeals (5th cir.) 1972, U.S. Supreme Ct. 1972. Ptnr. McBride & Tonry, Arabi, La., 1967-73, Tonry & Mumphrey, Chalmette, La., 1973-90; mem. La. Ho. of Reps., 1976, U.S. Ho. Reps., Washington, 1977; ptnr. Tonry & Ginart, Chalmette, 1990—; pecan farmer, Lumberton, Miss., 1991—. Chmn. Heart Fund of St. Bernard, Chalmettee, 1971-73. Named Outstanding Young Man of St. Bernard, St. Bernard Jaycees, 1973. Mem. ABA, ATLA, La. Bar Assn. (ho. of dels. 1973-74), La. Trial Lawyers Assn. (bd. dirs. 1972-75). Democrat. Roman Catholic. Avocations: hunting, gardening. Home: 1177 W Main Ave Lumberton MS 39455-8335

TONSETH, RALPH G., airport executive. Dir. aviation San Jose (Calif.) Airport. Office: San Jose Airport 1661 Airport Rd Ste C-205 San Jose CA 95110-1285*

TONTZ, ROBERT L., government official; b. Guthrie, Okla., May 18, 1917; s. John and Mabel (Johnson) T.; m. Hazel D. Crothers, June 10, 1944; children: John W., Brenda Kay. BS, Okla. State U., 1940, PhD, 1952; MS, Iowa State U., 1941. Asst. agrl. economist U. Tenn., 1942; assoc. agrl. economist U.S. Dept. Agr., Washington, 1942-45, agrl. economist, 1956-68, supervisory agrl. economist, 1971-80; agrl. statistician U.S. Dept. Commerce, Washington, 1946; asst. prof. Okla. State U., 1947-55; internat. economist Dept. State, Paris, 1968-71; econ. cons. Nat. Assn. Fed. and State Employees, 1980—. Editor: Foreign Agricultural Trade: Selected Readings, 1966; contbr. numerous econ. studies to profl. jours.; sr. joint author: Memberships of General Farmers' Organizations, United States, 1965-89, 1991, U.S. Agricultural Organizations The Voices of Organized Agriculture, 1991, Historical Statistics of Memberships of General Farmers' Organizations United States, 1874-1991, 1992, Organized Agriculture in the United States, 1992. Elder, chmn. bd. dirs. Christian Ch., Falls Church, Va. Recipient Superior Svc. award U.S. Dept. Agr., 1965, 75, Blue Ribbon award, 1972. Mem. Nat. Orgn. Fed.-State Employees (pres. 1988-92), Sigma Xi, Phi Kappa Phi, Alpha Phi Sigma, Alpha Zeta, Phi Eta Sigma. Home: 8712 Braeburn Dr Annandale VA 22003-3970

TOOHEY, BRIAN FREDERICK, lawyer; b. Niagara Falls, N.Y., Dec. 14, 1944; s. Matthew Frederick and Marilyn Gertrude (Hoag) T.; m. Mary Elizabeth Monihan; children: Maureen Elizabeth, Matthew Sheridan, Margaret Monihan, Mary Catherine. BS, Niagara U., 1966; JD, Cornell U., 1969. Bar: N.Y. 1969, N.Mex. 1978, Ohio 1980. Ptnr. Cohen, Swados, Wright, Hanifin & Bradford, Buffalo, 1973-77; pvt. practice, Santa Fe, 1977-79; of counsel Jones, Day, Reavis & Pogue, Cleve., 1979-80, ptnr., 1981—. Mem. Citizens League Greater Cleve., 1982—. Lt. JAG Corps, USNR, 1970-73. Mem. ABA, N.Y. State Bar Assn., State Bar N.Mex., Ohio State Bar Assn., Greater Cleve. Bar Assn. Roman Catholic. Home: 25 Pepper Creek Dr Cleveland OH 44124-5279 Office: Jones Day Reavis & Pogue N Point 901 Lakeside Ave Cleveland OH 44114-1190

TOOHEY, DANIEL WEAVER, lawyer; b. St. Louis, Feb. 5, 1940; s. Jerome Vincent and Marion (Weaver) T.; m. Anne Iva Latta, Aug. 14, 1966; children: Bridget Toohey Keefe, Sean Kirkpatrick. AB, St. Louis U., 1961, JD, 1964. Prodr., dir. Sta. KETC-TV, St. Louis, 1961-64; gen. atty. FCC, Washington, 1964-65; assoc. lawyer Welch & Morgan, Washington, 1965-66; assoc. lawyer Dow, Lohnes & Albertson, Washington, 1966-71, ptnr., 1971—; mng. ptnr. Dow Lohnes & Albertson, Washington, 1985-91; Henry Marsh prof. U. Mich., Ann Arbor, 1984, vis. prof., 1985-86; dir. Bur. Nat. Affairs, Inc., Washington. Author: Legal Problems in Broadcasting, 1974; contbr. articles to profl. jours.; mem. editorial adv. bd. Pub. Telecom. Rev., 1973-81. Mem. adv. com. Ohio State Awards, 1984-94; trustee Legal Aid Soc. D.C., 1984—, pres., 1991-93; trustee Washington Opera, 1986-90; bd. dirs., corp. sec. Volunteer: Nat. Ctr., 1986-92; trustee Shakespeare Theatre Washington, 1987—, vice chmn., gen. counsel, 1991—; Washington trustee Fed. City Coun., 1987—, mem. exec. com., 1991—; mem. crime task force Greater Washington Bd. Trade, 1989-90, mem. regional affairs com., 1990—, gen. counsel, 1993-96. Mem. Nat. Assn. Coll. and Univ. Attys., D.C. Bar Assn. (bd. dirs. 1976-77), Econ. Club Washington, Met. Club Washington, Columbia Country Club. Roman Catholic. Avocations: reading, writing, golf, hunting. Office: Dow Lohnes & Albertson 1255 23rd St NW Ste 500 Washington DC 20037-1125

TOOHEY, JAMES KEVIN, lawyer; b. Evanston, Ill., July 16, 1944; s. John Joseph and Ruth Regina (Cassidy) T.; m. Julie Marie Crane, Nov. 1, 1969 (div. Aug. 1977); children: Julie Colleen, Jeanne Christine; m. Anne Margaret Boettigheimer, May 28, 1983; children: James Robert, Kevin John, Casey Anne. BBA, U. Notre Dame, 1966; JD, Northwestern U., 1969. Bar: Ill. 1969, U.S. Dist. Ct. (no. dist.) Ill. 1971, U.S. Dist. Ct. (ctrl. dist.) Ill. 1991, U.S. Ct. Appeals (7th cir.) 1972, U.S. Ct. Appeals (8th cir.) 1975, U.S. Supreme Ct. 1988. Assoc. Taylor, Miller, Magner, Sprowl & Hutchings, Chgo., 1970-71, Ross, Hardies, O'Keefe, Babcock & Parsons, Chgo., 1974-77; asst. U.S. atty. Office U.S. Atty., Chgo., 1971-74; ptnr. Ross & Hardies, Chgo., 1978—. Bd. dirs., commr. Edgebrook Sauganash Athletic Assn., 1993—. Mem. Ill. Bar Assn., Soc. Trial Lawyers, Assn. Advancement of Automotive Medicine, Ill. Assn. Defense Attys., Trial Lawyers Club Chgo. Office: Ross & Hardies 150 N Michigan Ave Ste 2500 Chicago IL 60601-7525

TOOHEY, MARGARET LOUISE, journal editor, researcher; b. Torrington, Conn., Mar. 18, 1925; d. Erwin Byron and Lucy Lucille (Duigou) Gabarée; m. John Michael Toohey, Nov. 25, 1950 (div. Jan. 1972); children: John Michael Jr., Michele Louise Toohey Parsons. BS, U. Rochester, 1974, MA in English, 1978, PhD in English, 1987. Rsch. asst. Sch. Medicine Psychiatry Dept. Yale U., New Haven, 1950-57; rsch. asst., adminstr. adult psychiatry NIMH, Bethesda, Md., 1957-71; data analyst coord. Psychiatry Dept., U. Rochester, 1973-74, rsch. assoc., 1977—; tech. editor Family Process, Vernon, N.J., 1986—, Family Systems Medicine, N.Y.C., 1990-95, Families, Sys. & Health, Vernon, 1996—, Family Systems & Health, Vernon, N.J., 1996—. Contbr. articles to profl. jours., books. Mem. MLA. Democrat. Office: U Rochester Dept Psychiatry Rm 1-9011 300 Crittenden Blvd Rochester NY 14642-8409

TOOHIG, TIMOTHY E., physicist; b. Lawrence, Mass., Feb. 17, 1928; s. Timothy Michael and Catherine Marie (Walsh) T. BS in Physics, Boston Coll., 1947; MS in Optics, U. Rochester, 1953; PhD in Physics, Johns Hopkins U., 1962; Licentiate in Philosophy, Weston Coll., 1957. Ordained priest Soc. Jesus, 1965. Rsch. asst. Johns Hopkins U., 1957-62, rsch. assoc., 1962-63; physicist 200 Be V project Lawrence Berkeley Lab., 1964-66; physicist Brookhaven Nat. Lab., 1967-70; physicist, various positions Fermi Nat. Accelerator Lab., 1970-89; physicist superconducting supercollider Ctrl. Design Group, 1984-89, dep. head conventional systems divsn.; physicist SSC Lab., 1989-94, dep. head conventional construction divsn.; chaplain Seton Hall High Sch., Patchogue, N.Y., 1967-70, St. Joseph High Sch., Westchester, Ill., 1971-89. Sgt. U.S. Army, 1946-47. Fellow Jesuit Inst. Boston Coll., 1994. Mem. Am. Phys. Soc. Roman Catholic. Achievements include discovery of eta meson. Measurement of pi meson and k meson form factors. Demonstration of charged particle steering by crystals. Demonstration of the existence of channeling radiation from crystals. Home: Jesuit Cmty Boston Coll Chestnut Hill MA 02167-3802 Office: 102 College Rd Chestnut Hill MA 02167-3847

TOOKER, CARL E., department store executive; b. Allegan, Mich., 1947. Grad., Ferris State Coll., 1970. Chmn. Filene's subs. May Dept. Stores, Boston; pres., CEO Stage Stores Inc., Houston. Office: Specialty Retailers Inc 10201 Main St Houston TX 77025-5229*

TOOKER, GARY LAMARR, electronics company executive; b. Shelby, Ohio, May 25, 1939; s. William Henry and Frances Ione (Melick) T.; m. Diane Rae Kreider, Aug. 4, 1962; children: Lisa, Michael. B.S.E.E., Ariz. State U., 1962. With Motorola Inc., Phoenix, 1962—, v.p., gen. mgr. internat. semicondr. div., 1980-81, v.p., gen. mgr. semicondr. products sector, 1981-82, sr. v.p., gen. mgr. semicondr. products sector, 1982-83; exec. v.p., gen. mgr. semicondr. products sector Motorola Inc., 1983-86; sr. exec. v.p., chief corp. staff officer Motorola Inc., Schaumburg, Ill., 1986-88, sr. exec. v.p., chief operating officer, 1988-90, pres., chief oper. officer, 1990-93, chief exec. officer, 1993—, also bd. of dirs., now vice chmn., chief exec. officer; mem. engring. adv. council Ariz. State U., Tempe, 1982-86. Bd. dirs. Scottsdale (Ariz.) Boys Club, 1980-86, Jr. Achievement Chgo., 1988—; chief crusader, major. corp. group United Way, Chgo., 1988—; mem. alumni bd., mem. Found. bd. Ariz. State U., 1991—. Named Outstanding Alumni of Yr., Ariz. State U., 1983. Mem. IEEE, Am. Mgmt. Assn., Semicondr. Industry Assn. (bd. dirs. 1981-86, chmn. bd. 1982-86), Ariz. Assn. Industries (bd. dirs. 1981-86), Am. Electronics Assn. (bd. dirs. 1988—, chmn. bd. 1991), Econ. Club of Chgo., Elec. Mfrs. Club. Republican. Office: Motorola Inc 1303 E Algonquin Rd Schaumburg IL 60196-4041*

TOOKER, GEORGE, artist; b. Bklyn., Aug. 5, 1920; s. George Clair and Angela Montejo (Roura) T. BA, Harvard U., 1942; student, Art Students League, N.Y.C., 1943-44. Instr. Art Students League, N.Y., 1965-68. One man shows include Edwin Hewitt Gallery, 1951, 55, Robert Isaacson Gallery, 1960, 62, Durlacher Bros., 1964, 67, Hopkins Center at Dartmouth Coll., 1967, Fine Arts Mus., San Francisco, 1974, Mus. Contemporary Art, Chgo., 1974, Whitney Mus., N.Y.C., 1975, Indpls. Mus. Art, 1975; exhibited in group shows at Whitney Mus., 1947-50, 53, 55-58, 61, 64, 65, 67, 75, Venice Biennale, 1956, Art Inst. Chgo., 1951, 52, 54, 59, Inst. Contemporary Arts, London, 1950, Va. Mus., 1954, 62, Pa. Acad., 1966, Marisa Del Re Gallery, 1985, 88, 92, Spoleto Festival, Gibbes Mus. Art, Charleston, S.C., 1987, Robert Hall Fleming Mus. U. Vt., 1987, Marsh Gallery, U. Richmond, Va., 1989, Addison Gallery of Am. Art, 1994; represented permanent collections at Smithsonian Nat. Mus. of Am. Art, Smithsonian Hirshhorn Mus., Whitney Mus., Dartmouth Coll., Met. Mus., Walker Art Center, Mus. Modern Art, S.C. Johnson & Sons, Inc., Art, U.S.A., Sara Roby Fund Collection Am. Art, Addison Gallery, Ariz. State Univ. Gallery, Bklyn. Mus. Columbus (Ohio) Mus. Recipient Vt. gov.'s award for excellence in arts, 1983; Grantee Nat. Inst. Arts and Letters, 1960. Mem. NAD., Acad. Arts and Letters. Address: PO Box 385 Hartland VT 05048-0385 Office: care Marisa del Re Gallery 41 East 57th St New York NY 10022

TOOKEY, ROBERT CLARENCE, consulting actuary; b. Santa Monica, Calif., Mar. 21, 1925; s. Clarence Hall and Minerva Maconachie (Anderson) T.; BS, Calif. Inst. Tech., 1945; MS, U. Mich., 1947; m. Marcia Louise Hickman, Sept. 15, 1956; children: John Hall, Jennifer Louise, Thomas Anderson. With Prudential Ins. Co. Am., Newark, 1947-49; assoc. actuary in group Pacific Mut. Life Ins. Co., Los Angeles, 1949-55; asst. v.p. in charge reins. sales and service for 17 western states Lincoln Nat. Life Ins. Co., Ft. Wayne, Ind., 1955-61; dir. actuarial services Peat, Marwick, Mitchell & Co., Chgo., 1961-63; mng. partner So. Calif. office Milliman & Robertson, cons. actuaries, Pasadena, 1963-76; pres. Robert Tookey Assos., Inc., 1977—. Committeeman troop 501 Boy Scouts Am., 1969-72. Served to lt. (j.g.) USNR, 1943-45, 51-52. Fellow Soc. Actuaries, Conf. Consulting Actuaries; mem. Am. Acad. Actuaries, Pacific States Actuarial Club, Pacific Ins. Conf., Rotary Club (Pasadena), Union League Club (Chgo.). Home and Office: 3950 San Augustine Dr Glendale CA 91206-1232 also: PO Box 646 La Canada Flintridge CA 91012-0646

TOOLAN, BRIAN PAUL, newspaper editor; b. Carbondale, Pa., June 29, 1950; s. Walter William and Elizabeth (Cleary) T.; m. Maureen Ellen Connolly, Sept. 7, 1974; children: Brendan, Seamus, Bridget, Colin, Molly. BA in English, St. Bonaventure U., Olean, N.Y., 1972. Reporter Scranton (Pa.) Tribune, 1972-79; copy editor Dayton (Ohio) Jour. Herald, 1979-81; layout editor Balt. News Am., 1981; copy editor Phila. Daily News, 1982-84, sports editor, 1984-89, asst. mng. editor, 1989-91, mng. editor, 1991—. Mem. AP Mng. Editors, Am. Soc. Newspaper Editors, Pa. Soc. Newspaper Editors (dir. 1989-92). Roman Catholic. Office: Phila Daily News 400 N Broad St Philadelphia PA 19130-4015

TOOLE, DAVID GEORGE, pulp and paper products executive; b. Winnipeg, Man., Can., Apr. 22, 1942; s. George Toole; m. Bette Lynn Smith, Aug. 28, 1965; children: Jennifer, Simon. BSME, U. Man., 1964; MS in Adminstrv. Scis., The City U., London, 1968. Mem. corp. devel. Can. Pacific Ltd., Montreal, 1975-79, dir. fin. analysis, 1983-89, v.p. fin. analysis and planning, 1989-90; gen. mgr. Can. Pacific Ltd., Bermuda, 1979-83; sr. v.p., chief fin. officer Can. Pacific Forest Products Ltd., Montreal, 1990-94; pres. White Paper Group. Avenor Inc., Montreal, 1994—. Mem. Alpine Club Can. (sec.), Viking Ski Club (past pres.). Home: 18 Plumstead Ct, Etobicoke, ON Canada M9A 1V5 Office: 2 Kenview Blvd, Brampton, ON Canada L6T 5EH

TOOLE, JAMES FRANCIS, medical educator; b. Atlanta, Mar. 22, 1925; s. Walter O'Brien and Helen (Whitehurst) T.; m. Patricia Anne Wooldridge, Oct. 25, 1952; children: William, Anne, James, Douglas Sean. BA, Princeton U., 1947; MD, Cornell U., 1949; LLB, LaSalle Extension U., 1962. Intern, then resident internal medicine and neurology U. Pa. Hosp., Nat. Hosp., London, Eng., 1953-58; mem. faculty U. Pa. Sch. Medicine, 1958-62; prof. neurology, chmn. dept. Bowman Gray Sch. Medicine Wake Forest U., 1962-83; vis. prof. neuroscis. U. Calif. at San Diego, 1969-70; vis. scholar Oxford U., 1989; mem. Nat. Bd. Med. Examiners, 1970-76; mem. task force arteriosclerosis Nat. Heart Lung & Blood Inst., 1970-81; chmn. 6th and 7th Princeton confs. cerebrovascular diseases; cons. epidemiology WHO, Japan, 1971, 73, 93, USSR, 1968, Ivory Coast, 1977, Japan, 1993; mem. Lasker Awards com., 1976-77; chmn. neuropharmacologic drugs com. FDA, 1979; co-chair Commn. on Presdl. Disability, 1994—; cons. NASA, 1966. Author: Cerebrovascular Diseases, 4th edit., 1990; editor: Current Concepts in Cerebrovascular Disease, 1969-73, Jour. Neurol. Sci., 1990—; mem. editorial bd. Annals Internal Medicine, 1968-75, Stroke, 1972-91, Jour. AMA, 1975-77, Ann. Neurology, 1980-86, Jour. Neurol. Soc., 1990; mem. editorial bd. Jour. of Neurology, 1985-89. Pres. N.C. Heart Assn., 1976-77. Served with AUS, 1950-51; flight surgeon USNR, 1951-53. Decorated Bronze Star with V, Combat Med. badge. Fellow ACP (life), AAAS (life); mem. AMA, Am. Clin. and Climatol Assn. (life), Am. Heart Assn. (chmn. com. ethics 1970-75), Am. Physiol. Soc., Am. Neurol. Assn. (sec.-treas. 1978-82, pres. 1984-85, archivist, historian 1988—), World Fedn. Neurology (sec.-treas. 1982-89, mgmt. com. 1990—), Am. Acad. Neurology, Am. Soc. Neuroimaging (pres. 1992-94), Internat. Stroke Soc. (exec. com. 1989—, program chmn. 1992), Nat. Stroke Assn. (bd. dirs. 1993—, exec. com. 1994—, co-chmn. Commn. on U.S. Presdl. Disability 1994—); hon. mem. Assn. Brit. Neurologists, German Neurol. Soc., Austrian Soc. Neurology, Irish Neurol. Assn. Home: 1836 Virginia Rd Winston Salem NC 27104-2316

TOOLE, WILLIAM BELL, III, college dean, writer; b. Augusta, Ga., Sept. 23, 1930; s. William Bell Jr. and Mary Anita (Haverstick) T.; m. Katie Ruth Durham, June 7, 1954; children: Laurel Anita Toole Smith, William Durham. BA, Presbyn. Coll., Clinton, S.C., 1954; MA, Vanderbilt U., 1955, PhD in English, 1963. From instr. to asst. prof. English Presbyn. Coll., 1955-58; instr. English Vanderbilt U., Nashville, 1960-63; asst. prof. English N.C. State U., Raleigh, 1963-66, assoc. prof., 1966-71, prof., 1971—, asst. dean Sch. Humanities and Social Scis., 1971-72, assoc. dean, 1972-84, dean, 1984—; mem. nat. bd. cons. NEH, 1979—. Author: Shakespeare's Problem Plays: Studies in Form and Meaning, 1966; contbr. short stories to Wis. Rev., Pembroke Mag., So. Humanities Rev., Crucible, St. Andrews Rev., New Laurel Rev., others; contbr. articles to profl. jours. Bd. dirs. Friends of the Libr., Friends of the Gallery; trustee Triangle Univs. Ctr. for Advanced Studies. Served with U.S. Army, 1948-49. Named to Acad. of Outstanding Tchrs., 1967; Carnegie Found. scholar, 1954-55; So. fellow, 1959-60. Mem. Phi Beta Kappa, Alpha Kappa Psi, Phi Kappa Phi. Avocation: tennis. Home: 2515 Kenmore Dr Raleigh NC 27608 Office: NC State U Box 8101 Raleigh NC 27605

TOOMAJIAN, WILLIAM MARTIN, lawyer; b. Troy, N.Y., Sept. 26, 1943; s. Leo R. and Elizabeth (Gundrum) T.; children: Andrew, Philip. AB, Hamilton Coll., 1965; JD, U. Mich., 1968; LLM, N.Y.U., 1975. Bar: N.Y. 1968, Ohio 1978. Mem. firm Cadwalader, Wickersham & Taft, N.Y.C., 1971-77, Baker & Hostetler, Cleve., 1977—. Served to lt. USCG, 1968-71. Mem. ABA, Ohio Bar Assn., Cleve. Bar Assn., Cleve. Tax Club. Home: 3582 Lytle Rd Cleveland OH 44122-4908 Office: Baker & Hostetler 3200 National City Ctr 1900 E 9th St Cleveland OH 44114-3401

TOOMBS, CATHY WEST, assistant principal; b. Lafayette, Tenn., Dec. 9, 1954; d. Frank and Eudrice Estelle (Russell) West; m. Paul E. Toombs, Jr., June 18, 1977. BS, Mid. Tenn. State U., 1975, MEd, 1986, EdS, 1991; postgrad., Tenn. State U. Cert. tchr. English, speech, adminstrn., supervision, Tenn. Tchr. spl. edn. Eastside Elem. Sch., McMinnville, Tenn., 1975-76; tchr. English, speech, drama Mt. Juliet (Tenn.) H.S., 1976-90; dir. continuing studies Mid. Tenn. State U., Murfreesboro, 1990-94; asst. prin. Lebanon (Tenn.) H.S., 1994—. Mem. ASCD, Tenn. Assn. Supervision and Curriculum Devel., Alpha Delta Kappa, Phi Kappa Phi. Home: PO Box 595 Mount Juliet TN 37122-0595 Office: Lebanon HS 415 Harding Dr Lebanon TN 37087-3925

TOOMBS, KENNETH ELDRIDGE, librarian; b. Colonial Heights, Va., Aug. 25, 1928; s. Garnett Eldridge and Susie W. (Bryant) T.; m. Ada Teresa Hornsby, Aug. 29, 1949; children—Susan Elizabeth Shealy, Cheri Lynn Morris, Teresa Ann Heilman. A.A., Tenn. Wesleyan Coll., 1950; B.S., Tenn. Poly. Inst., 1951; M.A., U. Va., 1955; M.L.S., Rutgers U., 1956; student, La. State U., 1961-63. Reference asst. Alderman Library, U. Va., 1954-55; research asst. Grad. Sch . Library Sci., Rutgers U., 1955-56; mem. staff and faculty La. State U., 1956-63, asst. dir. charge pub. services, 1962-63; dir. libraries, prof. library sci. U. Southwestern La., 1963-67; dir. libraries U. S.C., Columbia, 1967—; bd. dirs. Southeastern Library Network, 1967-88; disting. dir. of librs. emeritus U. S.C., Columbia, 1988—; vice chmn. Southeastern Library Network, 1973-74, 83-84, chmn., 1974-75, treas., 1984-85; libr. cons. for bldgs. and adminstrn. for 60 colls. and univs. in past 30 yrs.; chmn. librarians sect. La. Coll. Conf., 1965-67; mem. Bd. La. Libr. Examiners, 1966-67; participant Libr. Mgmt. Inst., U. Wash., Seattle, 1969, Libr. Bldg. Problems Inst., UCLA, 1970. Contbr. articles to profl. jours.; editor: Bull. La. Library Assn, 1959-62; mng. editor: SW La. Jour, 1963-67; adv. bd.: Linguistic Atlas Am. Treas. Wesley Found.; v.p. Am. Field Services Internat. Scholarships; bd. dirs. U. S.C. Ednl. Found., 1975-82; Danforth assoc., 1967—; AIA/ALA Bldg. Awards Jury, 1987. Served to 1st lt. AUS, 1946-47, 51-53. Mem. ALA (life), La. Library Assn. (parliamentarian 1962-63, 66-67), Southeastern Library Assn. (Life mem., exec. bd. 1981-85, Rothrock award 1978), Southwestern Library Assn., S.C. Library Assn. (Life mem., pres. 1976, exec. bd. 1981-85), Assn. Southeastern Research Libraries (chmn. 1973-75, adv. com. to OCLC 1979-84), AAUP (sec.), La. Hist. Assn., La. Tchrs. Assn., Soc. Tympanuchus Cupido Pinnatus, South Caroliniana Soc., Nat. Library Bldg. Consultants List (chmn. 1981-84), Tenn. Squire. Methodist. Clubs: Mason (Shriner), Kiwanis. Home: 16 Garden Springs Rd Columbia SC 29209-1716

TOOMEY, JEANNE ELIZABETH, animal activist; b. N.Y.C., Aug. 22, 1921; d. Edward Aloysius and Anna Margaret (O'Grady) Toomey; m. Peter Terranova, Sept. 28, 1951 (dec. 1968); children: Peter Terranova, Sheila Terranova Beasley. Student, Hofstra U., 1938-40; student law sch., Fordham U., 1940-41; BA, Southampton Coll., 1976; postgrad., Monmouth Coll., 1978-79. Reporter, columnist Bklyn. Daily Eagle, 1943-52; with The Fitzgeralds, NBC Radio, N.Y.C., 1952-53; reporter, writer King Features Syndicate, N.Y.C., 1953-55; reporter, columnist N.Y. Jour.-Am., N.Y.C., 1955-61; newsman AP, N.Y.C., 1963-64; stringer; columnist News Tribune, Woodbridge, N.J., 1976-86; editor Calexico (Calif.) Chronicle, 1987-88; editor community sect. Asbury Park (N.J.) Press, 1988; pres., dir. Last Post Animal Sanctuary, Falls Village, Conn., 1991—. Author: Murder in the Hamptons, 1994. Named Woman of the Yr. N.Y. Women's Press Club, 1960. Mem. Newswomen's Club of N.Y., Overseas Press Club, N.Y. Press Club, Silurians. Roman Catholic. Home and Office: 95 Belden St Falls Village CT 06031-1113

TOOMEY, SHEILA CRAWFORD, education educator, consultant; b. Beckley, W.Va., Mar. 1, 1943; d. Roger and Ruth (Ashworth) Crawford; m. Lloyd E. Johnston, June 4, 1966 (dec. Dec. 1988); 1 child, Jacqueline De Vries; m. James E. Toomey, Feb. 10, 1989. BA, Tenn. Tech. U., 1963; MA in Christian Edn., Seabury Western Theol. Sem., 1965; MS in Curriculum and Instrn., U. Tenn., Martin, 1989; EdD in Instrn. and Curriculum Leadership, U. Memphis, 1994; postgrad., San Jose State U., U. Calif., Berkeley, U. Utah, Tex. Woman's U. Cert. tchr., Tenn. Dir. Christian edn. St. Luke's Episcopal Ch., Rochester, Minn., 1965-66; elem. tchr. Santa Catalina Sch. Girls, 1967-69, Rowland-Hall St. Mark's Sch., Salt Lake City, 1968-69, Union City (Tenn.) Christian Sch., 1984-87; libr. Dept. Edn. U. Tenn. at Martin, 1987-89; rsch. asst. U. Memphis, 1989-92, adj. prof., 1996; prof., edn. dept. chair Lane Coll., Jackson, Tenn., 1992-94; reading tchr., drama club sponsor Ashland (Miss.) Mid. Sch., 1994-95; workshop presenter Jackson, Tenn., 1989—; ednl. cons. Masco, Jackson, 1995—; adj. prof. Shelby State C.C., 1995; tng. devel. coord. Delta Faucet Tenn., 1995—; homebound tchr. Jackson-Madison County Schs., 1996—; adj. prof. Shelby State C.C., 1995, U. Memphis, 1996; mem. campus All Stars, Honda, Jackson, 1992-93. Contbr. articles to profl. jours. Mem. Am. Counseling Assn., Tenn. ASCD, Assn. for Case Method Rsch., DAR, Nat. Libr. Assn., Ch. and Synagogue Libr. Assn., AAUW, Order Eastern Star (worthy matron 1980-89), Sigma Tau Delta, Kappa Delta Pi. Anglican. Home: 137-2 Birchwood Ln Jackson TN 38305-2508

TOOMEY, THOMAS MURRAY, lawyer; b. Washington, Dec. 9, 1923; s. Vincent L. and Catherine V. (McCann) T.; m. Grace Donohoe, June 22, 1948; children: Isabelle Marie Toomey Hessick, Helen Marie, Mary Louise, Thomas Murray. Student, Duke U., 1943-44, Catholic U. Am., 1942-43, 47-49; J.D., Catholic U. Am., 1949. Bar: D.C. 1949, Md. 1952. Sole practice Washington and Md., 1949—; bd. dirs. Allied Capital Corp. and subs., Washington and Vero Beach, Fla., Fed. Ctr. Plz. Corp., Donohoe Cos., Inc., Washington, Nat. Capital Bank, Washington. Chmn. aviation and transp. coms. Met. Washington Bd. Trade, 1954-76, bd. dirs., 1962-77; chmn. dedication Dulles Internat. Airport, 1962; trustee Cath. U. Am., 1981—; founding trustee Heights Sch. Served to 1st lt. USMC, 1942-46, 50-52. Recipient Ann. Alumni Achievement award Cath. U., 1977, Most Disting. Alumnus award St. John's Coll. High Sch. D.C., 1994. Mem. ABA, D.C. Bar Assn., Md. Bar Assn., Bar Assn. D.C., Am. Judicature Soc., Comml. Law League Am., Friendly Sons St. Patrick (pre. 1983), Sovereign Mil. Order of Malta (Fed. Assn. U.S.A.), Congl. Golf and Country Club, Kenwood Golf and Country Club, Univ. Club, Army and Navy Club, Tower Club, Lago Mar Beach Club. Home: 6204 Garnett Dr Bethesda MD 20815-6618 also: 2000 S Ocean Dr Apt 1410 Fort Lauderdale FL 33316-3813 Office: 4701 Sangamore Rd Bethesda MD 20816-2508

TOOMRE, ALAR, applied mathematician, theoretical astronomer; b. Rakvere, Estonia, Feb. 5, 1937; came to U.S., 1949, naturalized, 1955; s. Elmar and Linda (Aghen) T.; m. Joyce Stetson, June 15, 1958; children—Lars, Erik, Anya. B.S. in Aero. Engring., B.S. in Physics, MIT, 1957; Ph.D. in Fluid Mechanics, U. Manchester, Eng., 1960. C.L.E. Moore instr. math. dept. MIT, Cambridge, 1960-62; asst. prof. applied math. MIT, 1963-65, assoc. prof., 1965-70, prof., 1970—; fellow Inst. for Advanced Study, Princeton, N.J., 1962-63. Contbr. articles to profl. jours. Guggenheim fellow, 1969-70, MacArthur fellow, 1984-89; Fairchild scholar, 1975, Marshall scholar, 1957-60. Fellow AAAS; mem. Am. Astron. Soc. (Dirk Brouwer award 1993), Internat. Astron. Union, Am. Acad. Arts and Scis., Nat. Acad. Scis. Office: MIT 77 Massachusetts Ave Rm 2-371 Cambridge MA 02139-4301

TOON, MALCOLM, former ambassador; b. Troy, N.Y., July 4, 1916; s. George and Margaret Harcomb (Broadfoot) T.; m. Elizabeth Jane Taylor, Aug. 28, 1943; children: Barbara, Alan, Nancy. A.B., Tufts U., 1937, LL.D. (hon.), 1977; M.A., Fletcher Sch. Law and Diplomacy, 1939; student, Middlebury Coll., 1950, Harvard U., 1950-51; LL.D. (hon.), Middlebury Coll., 1978, Drexel U., 1980, Am. Coll. Switzerland, 1985, Grove City Coll., 1990. Fgn. service officer, 1946-79; assigned successively Warsaw, Budapest, Moscow, Rome, Berlin, Washington, 1946-60; assigned Am. embassy, London, 1960-63; counselor political affairs Am. embassy, Moscow, 1963-67; with Dept. of State, Washington, 1967-69; ambassador to Czechoslovakia, 1969-71, to Yugoslavia, 1971-75, to Israel, 1975-76, to USSR, 1976-79; mem. U.S. del. Nuclear Test Conf., Geneva, 1958-59, Four Power Working Group, Washington, London, Paris, 1959, Fgn. Ministers Conf., Geneva, 1969, Ten Nation Disarmament Com., Geneva, 1960; mem. SALT II del., 1977-79, U.S.-Soviet Summit Conf., Vienna, 1979; Brennen prof. U. N.C., Asheville, 1981; Finch prof. Miami U., Oxford, Ohio, 1982; Allis-Chalmers chair Marquette U., Milw., 1982. Trustee emeritus Tufts U.; bd. visitors Fletcher Sch. Law and Diplomacy, 1992; chmn. U.S. Delegation to Joint U.S. Russian Commn. on POW's, MIA's. Served from ensign to lt. comdr. USNR, 1942-46. Recipient Freedom Leadership award Hillsdale Coll., 1980, Valley Forge Freedom award, 1981, Disting. Honor award Dept. State, 1980, Wallace award, 1984, Gold medal Nat. Inst. of Social Scis., 1987, Degree of Prof., Acad. Natural Scis. of the Russian Fedn., 1996. Home: 375 Pee Dee Rd Southern Pines NC 28387-2118

TOOR, HERBERT LAWRENCE, chemical engineering educator, researcher; b. Pitts., June 22, 1927; s. Matthew G. and Jean (Mogul) T.; m. Elizabeth Margaret Weir, Dec. 1950; children: Helen Mary, John Weir, William Ramsay. BS, Drexel U., 1948; MS, Northwestern U., 1950, PhD, 1952. Rsch. chemist Monsanto Chems., Ltd., 1952-53; asst. prof. Carnegie Mellon U., Pitts., 1953-57, assoc. prof., 1957-61, prof., 1961—, head chem. engring dept., 1967-70, dean Carnegie Inst. Tech., 1970-79, Mobay prof. chem. engring., 1980-92, Mobay prof. chem. engring. emeritus, 1992—; vis. UNESCO prof. U. Madras, India, 1962-63. Contbr. numerous articles to tech. jours. With USNR, 1944-45. Recipient merit award Northwestern U. Alumni, 1973. Fellow AAAS, Am. Inst. Chem. Engrs. (Colburn award 1964); mem. NAE.

TOOT, JOSEPH F., JR., bearing manufacturing company executive; b. 1935; married. AB, Princeton U., 1957; postgrad., Harvard U. Grad. Sch. Bus. Adminstrn., 1961. With Timken Co., Canton, Ohio, 1962—; dep. mgr. Timken (France) Co., 1965-67; v.p. internat. div. Timken Co., Canton, 1967-68, corp. v.p., then exec. v.p., 1968-79, pres., 1979—, also bd. dirs.; bd. dirs. Rockwell Internat. Mem. Am. Iron and Steel Inst. Office: Timken Co 1835 Dueber Ave SW Canton OH 44706-2728

TOOTE, GLORIA E. A., developer, lawyer, columnist; b. N.Y.C.; d. Frederick A. and Lillie M. (Tooks) Toote. Student, Howard U., 1949-51; J.D., NYU, 1954; LL.M., Columbia U., 1956. Bar: N.Y. 1955, U.S. Dist. Ct. (so. and ea. dists.) N.Y. 1956, U.S. Supreme Ct. 1956. With firm Greenbaum, Wolff & Ernst, 1957; mem. editorial staff Time mag., 1957-58; asst. gen. counsel N.Y. State Workmen's Compensation Bd., 1958-64; pres. Toote Town Pub. Co. and Town Sound Studios, Inc., 1966-70; asst. dir. Action Agy., 1971-73; asst. sec. Dept. HUD, 1973-75; vice chmn. Pres.'s Adv. Council on Pvt. Sector Initiatives, 1983-85; housing developer, 1976—; pres. Trea Estates and Enterprises, Inc.; newspaper columnist; chairperson The Policy Coun. Former bd. dirs. Citizens for the Republic, Nat. Black United Fund, Exec. Women in Govt., Am. Arbitration Assn., Consumer Alert; bd. overseers Hoover Inst., 1985-95; vice chair Nat. Polit. Congress of Black Women, 1984-92; former mem. Coun. Econ. Affairs, Rep. Nat. Com.; pres. N.Y.C. Black Rep. Coun.; exec. trustee Polit. Action Com. for Equality; mem. NYNEX Consumer Adv. Coun., 1995—. Recipient citations Nat. Bus. League, Alpha Kappa Alpha, U.S. C. of C., Nat. Assn. Black Women Attys. Mem. N.Y. Fedn. Civil Svc. Orgns., Nat. Assn. Real Estate Brokers, Nat. Fed. Mortgage Assn. (bd. dirs. 1992), Nat. Citizens Participation Coun., Nat. Bar Assn.,Delta Sigma Theta. Address: 282 W 137th St New York NY 10030-2439

TOPAZ, MURIEL, dance educator; b. Phila., May 7, 1932; d. Joseph Topaz and Rhea Rebecca Rosenbloom; m. Jacob Druckman, June 5, 1954; children: Karen Druckman Jeanneret, Daniel Druckman. Student, NYU, 1950-51; studies with Martha Graham, Antony Tudor, The Juilliard Sch., 1951-54; student, Dance Notation Bur., N.Y.C., 1954-56. Mem. faculty The Juilliard Sch., N.Y.C., 1959-70, dir. dance div., 1985-92; exec. dir. Dance Notation Bur., 1978-85; co-chmn. First Internat. Congress on Movement Notation Bur., Israel, 1984, 2d Internat. Congress, Hong Kong, 1990; chmn. artistic com. Dance Notation Bur.; adjudicator Reginal Dance/Am., Mid-States 1980, Pacific 1981, N.E. 1996. Author: Changes and New Developments in Labanotation, 1966, Intermediate Reading Studies, 1972, Choreography and Dance: The Notation Issue, 1988, Alvin Ailey, An American Visionary, 1995, Elementary Labanotation, A Study Guide, 1996; co-author: (with Hackney & Manno) Elementary Study Guide, 1970, Elementary Reading Studies, 1970, (with Edelson) Readings in Modern Dance, 1972; author, editor Young Dancer sect. Dance Mag.; editl. cons. Choreography and Dance, Dance Studies; reconstructor: Lilac Garden (Milw. Ballet), Continuo (Paris Conservatory, N.C. Sch. Arts), Notator Moor's Pavane. Mem. May O'Donnell Hon. Com., 1979; chmn. dance panel N.Y. State Coun. on Arts, 1982-83; assessor Can. Coun., 1987; auditor NEA, 1989—; chmn. Internat. Coun. Kinetography Laban; panel chair Am. Dancing, Kennedy Ctr. Recipient fgn. travel grant Inst. Internat. Edn., 1967.

TOPAZIO, LAWRENCE PETER, special education educator; b. Waterbury, Conn., Apr. 6, 1948; s. Nicholas Angelo and Stella Veronica (Lagownik) T.; m. Maureen Ellen Hanlon; children: Nicholas, Michael. BS in Elem. Edn., So. Conn. State U., New Haven, 1971; MS in Spl. Edn., So. Conn. State U., 1978. Cert. tchr. learning disabilities K-12. Tchr., spl. edn. tchr. Stadley Roush Sch., Danbury, Conn., 1972-83; tchr. resource rm. Danbury H.S., 1983—. Pres. Wolcott (Conn.) Spl. Edn. PTA, 1993—. Mem. NEA, Coun. Exceptional Children, Conn. Assn. Children with Learning Disabilities, Conn. State PTA, Conn. Parent Advocacy Ctr. Home: 62 Woodward Dr Wolcott CT 06716-2823

TOPAZIO, VIRGIL WILLIAM, university official; b. Middletown, Conn., Mar. 27, 1915; s. Concetto and Corradina (Rizzo) T.; m. Juwil E. Child, July 28, 1941; 1 dau., Jula Diane. B.A., Wesleyan U., Middletown; M.A., Columbia U., 1947, Ph.D., 1951. Lectr. Columbia U., 1947-48; from instr. to prof. French lit. U. Rochester, 1948-65; prof. French, chmn. dept. Rice U., 1965-67, dean humanities and social scis., 1967—, also acad. v.p.; Favrot chair in French lit., 1973; Fulbright vis. lectr. U. Rennes, France, 1964-65. Author: D'Holbach's Moral Philosophy, 1956, Voltaire: A Critical Study of His Major Works, 1967. Served with AUS, 1945-46. Decorated Palmes Academiques France, 1966, 76. Mem. Alliance Francaise (pres. 1963-65), Modern Lang. Assn. (pres. 18th century sect. 1965), Council Fgn. Langs. (v.p. 1967-68). Home: 3 Knoll Pines Ct The Woodlands TX 77381-2690

TOPE, DWIGHT HAROLD, retired management consultant; b. Grand Junction, Colo., Aug. 29, 1918; s. Richard E. and Elizabeth (Jones) T.; m. Carolyn Stagg, Apr. 29, 1949; children: Stephen R., Chris L. AS, Mesa Coll., 1940; student, George Washington U. With Fgn. Funds Control, a Div. of U.S. Treasury Dept.; staff adjuster Fire Cos. Adjustment Bur., Denver, Albuquerque, 1946-48; br. mgr. Gen. Adjustment Bur., Deming, N.Mex., 1948-50; spl. agt. Cliff Kealey State Agy., Albuquerque, 1950-56; pres. Dwight Tope State Agy., Inc., Albuquerque, 1956-84; with Fgn. Funds Control divsn. U.S. Dept. Treasury, Albuquerque; sr. cons. Dwight Tope State Agy., Inc., Albuquerque, 1985-87. Mem. adv. bd. Salvation Army, Albuquerque, 1974—, Meals on Wheels, 1987—; past chmn. bd., pres. Presbyn. Heart Inst., Albuquerque, 1977—. Maj. Coast Arty. Anti-Aircraft, 1941-45. Mem. N.Mex. Ins. Assn. (past chmn.), Ins. Info. Inst. (past chmn.), N.Mex. Surplus Lines Assn. (past pres.), Air Force Assn., Assn. of U.S. Army, Am. Legion, Albuquerque C. of C. (mil. rels. com.), Rotary, Masons, Shriners, Albuquerque Country Club, Petroleum Club. Republican. Avocations: boating, fishing, hunting. Home: 1812 Stanford Dr NE Albuquerque NM 87106-2538 Office: 8100 Mountain Rd NE Ste 204E Albuquerque NM 87110-7833

TOPEL, DAVID G., agricultural studies educator; b. Lake Mills, Wis., Oct. 24, 1937; m. Jackie Topel. BS, U. Wis., 1960; MS, Kans. State U., 1962; PhD, Mich. State U., 1965. Assoc. prof. animal sci. and food tech. Iowa State U., Ames, 1967-73, prof. animal sci. and food tech., 1973-79, dean Coll. Agr., 1988—, dir. agr. and home econs. experiment sta., 1988—; prof., head dept. Auburn U., Ames, 1979-88; cons., presenter, lectr. in field; mem. Gov. of Iowa's Sci. Adv. Coun., 1990—, Gov. of Iowa's Livestock Revitalization Task Force, 1993—; chair Gov.'s Environ. Agr. Com., 1994; mem. Iowa Corn Promotion Bd.; mem. faculty Royal Vet. and Agrl. U., Denmark, 1971-72, 90; vis. prof. Nat. Taiwan U., 1972. Author: The Pork Industry - Problems and Progress, 1968. Secretariat World Food Prize, Iowa State U., Ames, 1991—. Fulbright-Hays scholar Royal Vet. and Agrl. U., 1971-72; recipient award of merit Knights of Ak-Sar-Ben, 1973, Commr.'s award Agrl. Commr. Republic of China, 1977, disting. Achievement award Block and Bridle Club, 1979, Ala. Cattlemen's Assn.,1 984, Hon. State Farmer Degree, Ala., 1986, Harry L. Rudnick Educator's award Nat. Assn. Meat Purveyors, 1989; named hon. prof. Ukrainian State Agrl. U., 1993. Mem. AAAS, Am. Meat Sci. Assn., Am. Soc. Animal Sci. (Disting. Rsch. award in meat sci. 1979), Inst. Food Tech., Iowa Crop Improvement Assn., Iowa State Dairy Assn., Iowa Farm Bur. Fedn. (ex-officio), Iowa Pork Prodrs. Assn. (ex-officio), Iowa Beef Industry Coun., Nat. Coun. for Agrl. Rsch., Mid-Am. Internat. Agrl. Consortium (pres. 1991-92), Extension and Tchg. (pres. North Ctrl. Region 1992), Nat. Assn. State Univs. and Land-Grant Colls. (chair bd. agr. 1993, mem. commn. on food, environ. and renewable resources 1992—), Ukrainian Acad. Agrl. Scis., Sigma Xi (Outstanding Achievement award Iowa chpt. 1993), Alpha Zeta, Gamma Sigma Delta. Presbyterian. Avocations: fishing, golf. Home: 2630 Meadow Glen Rd Ames IA 50014 Office: Iowa State U 122 Curtiss Hall Ames IA 50011

TOPEL, DAVID LOUIS, lawyer; b. Wilmington, Del., June 16, 1953; s. Henry and Phyllis Lee (Parkes) T. BA, U. Del., 1975; JD, Widener U., 1978. Bar: Pa. 1979, U.S. Dist. Ct. (ea. dist.) Pa. 1980, U.S. Ct. Appeals (3d cir.) 1980. Trial atty. major trials divsn. City Solicitor's Office of Phila., 1979-82; assoc. Obermayer Rebmann Maxwell & Hippel, Phila., 1982-84; ptnr. Sprecher Felix Visco Hutchison & Young, Phila., 1984-89; sole practice Phila., 1989—; guest lectr. Thomas Jefferson Univ. Hosp., Phila., 1983-87. Editor, pub. (mag.) Progress Notes, 1983-89. Recipient Outstanding Alumnus award Widener U. Sch. Law, 1984; nationally ranked swimmer U.S. Masters Swimming Assn. Mem. Pa. Bar Assn., Am. Soc. Law & Medicine, Pi Sigma Alpha. Avocations: screenwriting. Office: 212 Monroe St Philadelphia PA 19147-9999

TOPELIUS, KATHLEEN E., lawyer; b. July 15, 1948. BA, U. Conn., 1970; JD, Cath. U. Am., 1978. Bar: D.C. 1978, U.S. Supreme Ct. 1988. Atty. office of gen. counsel Fed. Home Loan Bank Bd., 1978-80; ptnr. Morgan, Lewis & Bockius, Washington, 1985-93, Bryan Cave, Washington, 1993—. Office: Bryan Cave 700 13th St NW Washington DC 20005-3960

TOPERZER, THOMAS RAYMOND, art museum director; b. Pitts., Aug. 12, 1939; s. Raymond Otto and Blodwyn (Roberts) T.; m. Carol Jane Reece, June 2, 1961; children: Scott Thomas, Max Otto. Student, West Liberty (W.Va.) State Coll., 1959, Sterling (Kans.) Coll., 1959-61; AB, Southwestern Coll., 1963; MFA, U. Nebr., 1970. Dir. Blanden Meml. Art Mus., Fort Dodge, Iowa, 1970-71, Rochester (Minn.) Art Ctr., 1971-72; curator univ. art gallery Ill. State U., Normal, 1972-73, asst. dir. univ. mus., 1972-73, dir. univ. art mus. and CVA art galleries, 1973-82; coordinator div. fine arts Bethel Coll., St. Paul, 1982-84; dir. Fred Jones Jr. Mus. Art, U. Okla., Norman, 1984—; arts cons. to various corps., Minn., Ill. and Okla., 1972—. Nelle Cochran Woods fellow U. Nebr., 1969-70. Mem. Assn. Coll. and U. Mus. and Galleries (mem. exec. com. 1986—), Am. Assn. Mus., Coll. Art Assn. Office: Fred Jones Jr Mus Art U Okla 410 W Boyd St Norman OK 73069-4851

TOPEY, ISHMAEL ALOYSIUS, urban planner; b. Port Henderson, St. Catherine, Jamaica, Nov. 10, 1926; s. Ferdinand Aloysius and Amy (Brown) T.; m. Dulcie Rose Clarke, Feb. 24, 1960; children: Patrick F., Robert I., Amy L., George A. AA in Bus. Adminstrn., Wayne County C.C., 1983; BBA, U. Detroit, 1985; MA in Labor Rels., Wayne State U., Detroit, 1987. Cert. profl. cons./advisor; cert. adminstrv. mgr. Mgr. Sea Food Club, Jamaica, West Indies, 1960-75; tchr. Detroit Pub. Schs., 1986-87; urban renewal asst. City of Detroit, 1987—; founder Inter-Galactic Enterprises, Inc., Detroit, 1990—; creator of human math.; econ. devel. specialist; cons. in field. Creator Topeyology Sys. of Speedy Learning, 1987; author: Letter to Stephen Hawking, Debunking the Bell Curve, History of Intelligence. Co-recipient Papal Citation for Social Work, 1985; Jesuit Founders scholar U. Detroit, 1984. Mem. Am. Planning Assn., Buckminster Fuller Inst., World Future Soc. Home: 15700 Mapleridge St Detroit MI 48205-3031 Office: City of Detroit City County Bldg Ste 150 Detroit MI 48226

TOPIK, STEVEN CURTIS, history educator; b. Montebello, Calif., Aug. 6, 1949; s. Kurt and Gertrude Irene (Kriszanich) T.; m. Martha Jane Marcy, Feb. 3, 1979; children: Julia, Natalia. BA, U. Calif., San Diego, 1971; MA, U. Tex., 1973, PhD, 1978. Asst. prof. Universidade Fed. Fluminense, Rio de Janeiro, 1978-81, vis. prof., 1984; asst. prof. Colgate U., Hamilton, N.Y., 1981-84; vis. prof. Univ. Ibero Americana, Mexico City, 1982; prof. U. Calif., Irvine, 1984—; vis. prof. Ecols des Hautes Etudes en Sci. Social, Paris, 1990; cons. in field; mem. editorial com. U. Calif. Press, Berkeley, 1987-89. Author: The Political Economy of the Brazilian State, 1987, Trade and Gunboats, The United States and Brazil in the Age of Empire, 1996; contbr. articles, revs. to profl. publs. Mem. Mayor's Adv. Bd. on Sister Cities, Irvine, 1989-90; mem. adv. bd. Orange County (Calif.) Com. on Latin Am., 1989-90. Fellow NEH, 1987, 89-90, Rockefeller Found., 1977, Social Sci. Rsch. Coun. Mexico City, 1982-83, Fulbright-Hayes Found., 1978-79, 84, U. Calif., 1988-89. Mem. Latin Am. Studies Assn., Am. Hist. Assn., Conf. Latin Am. History (com. on hist. statistics, com. on projects and publs., chair Brazilian studies com. 1988-90), Pacific Coast Coun. on Latin Am. Studies (bd. govs. 1987-90).

TOPILOW, CARL S., symphony conductor; b. Jersey City, N.J., Mar. 14, 1947; s. Jacob Topilow and Pearl (Roth) Topilow Josephs; m. Shirley; 1 child, Jenny Michelle. B.Mus., Manhattan Sch. of Music, 1968, M.Mus., 1969. Exxon/Arts Endowment Condr. Denver Symphony Orch., 1976-79, asst. condr., 1979-80; mus. dir. Denver Chamber Orch., 1976-81, Denver Youth Orch., 1977-80, Grand Junction Symphony, Colo., 1977-80, Nat. Repertory Orch., Breckenridge, Colo., 1978—; dir. orchs. Cleve. Inst. Mus., 1981—, condr. Summit Brass 1986—, Cleve. Pops Orch., 1995—. Recipient Conducting fellowship Nat. Orch. Assn., N.Y.C., 1972-75, Aspen Mus. Festival, Colo., 1976; winner 1st place Balt. Symphony Conducting Competition, Md., 1976.

TOPINKA, JUDY BAAR, state official; b. Riverside, Ill., Jan. 16, 1944; d. William Daniel and Lillian Mary (Shuss) Baar; 1 child, Joseph Baar. BS, Northwestern U., 1966. Features editor, reporter, columnist Life Newspapers, Berwyn and LaGrange, Ill., 1966-77; with Forest Park (Ill.) Rev. and Westchester News, 1976-77; coord. spl. events dept. fedn. comm., AMA, 1978-80; rsch. analyst Senator Leonard Becker, 1978-79; mem. Ill. Ho. of Reps., 1981-84; mem. Ill. Senate, 1985-94; treas. State of Ill., Springfield, 1995—; former mem. judiciary com., former chmn. senate health and welfare com.; former mem. fin. instn. com.; former co-chmn. Citizens Coun. on Econ. Devel.; former co-chmn. U.S. Commn. for Preservation of Am.'s Heritage Abroad, serves on legis. ref. bur.; former mem. minority bus. resource ctr. adv. com. U.S. Dept. Transp.; former mem. adv. bd. Nat. Inst. Justice. Founder, pres., bd. dirs. West Suburban Exec. Breakfast Club, from 1976; chmn. Ill. Ethnics for Reagan-Bush, 1984, Bush-Quayle 1988; spokesman Nat. Coun. State Legislatures Health Com.; former mem nat. adv. coun. health professions edn. HHS; mem., GOP chairwoman Legis. Audit Commn. of Cook County; chmn. Riverside Twp. Regular Republican Orgn., 1994—. Recipient Outstanding Civilian Svc. medal, Molly Pitcher award, Abraham Lincoln award, Silver Eagle award U.S. Army and N.G. Office: JR Thompson Ctr 100 W Randolph St Ste 15-600 Chicago IL 60601-3220

TOPOL, CLIVE M., lawyer; b. Chgo., Feb. 16, 1949. BS, U. Ill., 1971, JD, 1975. Bar: Ill. 1975. Ptnr. Winston & Strawn, Chgo. Mem. Ill. State Bar Assn., Chgo. Bar Assn. Office: Winston & Strawn 35 W Wacker Dr Chicago IL 60601-1614*

TOPOL, ROBERT MARTIN, retired financial services executive; b. N.Y.C., Mar. 9, 1925; s. Morris and Pearl Topol; m. D'Vera Greene, Oct. 10, 1948; children—Clifford M., Gail S., Martha E. B.A., NYU, 1948. Ptnr. Greene & Co., N.Y.C., 1948-71; dir. Harris Upham & Co, N.Y.C., 1971-76; exec. v.p., dir. Shearson Lehman Bros., N.Y.C., 1976-94; ret., 1995. Served with USMC, 1943-46. Mem. Security Traders N.Y., Nat. Security Traders Assn., N.Y. Security Dealers Assn. (gov. 1961-77), Securities Industry Assn. (v.p. 1981-94), Investment Co. Inst., Chevalier Chaine de Rotisseurs, Hampshire Country Club. Republican. Jewish. Home: 825 Orienta Ave Mamaroneck NY 10543-4314 Office: Smith Barney & Co Inc White Plains NY 10604

TOPP, GEORGE CLARKE, soil physicist; b. Canfield, Ont., Can., Nov. 12, 1937; s. G. Ernest and Rhea L. (Mehlenbacher) T.; m. Eleanor Bruce, Dec. 29, 1962; children: Karen, Bruce, Brenda. BS in Agr., U. Toronto, Ont., 1959; MSc, U. Wis., 1962, PhD, 1964. Rsch. asst. U. Wis., Madison, 1959-64; rsch. assoc. U. Ill., Urbana, 1964-65; rsch. scientist Land Resource Rsch. Ctr., Ottawa, Ont., 1965-87, rsch. mgr., 1987-91; rsch. scientist land resource div. Agr. Can., Ottawa, 1991—; sessional lectr. Carleton U., Ottawa, 1975-78; vis. assoc. prof. U. Sask., Saskatoon, Can., 1980; vis. scientist Divsns. Environment, Mechanics and Soils Commonwealth Sci. and Indsl. Rsch. Orgn., Canberra, Australia, 1992-93; cons. Can. Internat. Devel. Agy., Islamabad, Pakistan, 1985, Hyderabad, India, 1986, Campinas, Sao Paulo, Brazil, 1988. Editor: Soil Physical Measurements, 1992. Chmn. Ottawa West End Community Chaplaincy, 1984-87, bd. dirs., 1991-92; chmn. Bells Corners United Ch., Nepean, Ont., 1987-89. Fellow Can. Soc. Soil Sci. (sec. 1969-72, pres. 1978), Soil Sci. Soc. Am. (bd. dirs. 1990-91); mem. Am. Geophys. Union. Mem. United Ch. of Canada. Avocations: cross-country skiing, canoeing, sailing. Home: 45 Foothills Dr, Nepean, ON Canada K2H 6K6 Office: Agriculture Canada, 960 Carling Ave, Ottawa, ON Canada K1A 0C6

TOPP, SUSAN HLYWA, lawyer; b. Detroit, Oct. 9, 1956; d. Michael Leo and Lucy Stella (Rusak) Hlywa; m. Robert Elwin Topp, July 25, 1985; children: Matthew, Sarah, Michael and Jamie (triplets). BS in Edn. cum laude, Ctrl. Mich. U., 1978; JD cum laude, Wayne State U., Detroit, 1991. Bar: Mich. 1992, U.S. Dist. Ct. (ea. dist.) Mich. 1992. Conservation officer Mich. Dept. Natural Resources, Pontiac, 1980-88; environ. conservation officer Mich. Dept. Natural Resources, Livonia, 1988-93; pvt. practice law Gaylord, Mich., 1993; ptnr. Rolinski & Topp, PLC, Gaylord, 1993-95; assoc. Plunkett & Cooney, P.C., Gaylord, 1995—; ct. apptd. to represent abused children Probate Ct., Gaylord, 1993—. Recipient Am. Jurisprudence award Wayne State U., 1987, Trial Advocacy award, 1988. Mem. ABA (nat. resources and environ. law com.), Mich. State Bar Assn. (environ. law sect.), AAUW, Mich. C. of C. Roman Catholic. Avocations: backpacking, skiing, scuba diving, back-country camping, canoeing. Office: Plunkett & Cooney PC Hidden Valley Exec Ctr PO Box 280 Gaylord MI 49735

TOPPING, DONALD M., English language professional, educaor; b. 1929. BA, U. Ky., 1954, MA, 1956; PhD, Mich. State U., 1963. Asst. prof. English Territorial Coll. Guam, 1956-58, asst. prof. and chmn. English dept., 1960-62; instr. English Mich. State U., East Lansing, 1959-60; instr. English Lang. Inst. U. Hawaii, Honolulu, 1962-64, TESL coord. Peace Corps Tng. Ctr., 1962-63, lang. coord., 1963-66, asst. prof. linguistics, 1964-69, assoc. prof. linguistics, dir. Pacific/Asian Linguistic Inst, 1969-74, prof. linguistics, dir. Social Sci. Rsch. Inst., 1974—, dir. PEACESAT Project, 1981—; mem. NDEA Inst. on TESL, Coll. of Guam, summer 1965; linguistics cons. Officer of Internat. Programs, U. Hawaii, 1966-68, project coord. Micronesian Lang. Materials Project, 1967; prin. investigator Chamorro Dictionary Project, NSF, 1968; specialist in linguistics SEAMEO Regional English Lang. Ctr., Singapore, 1968-69; prin. investigator Micronesian Linguistics Rsch. Project, 1970-74; linguistics cons. Chamorro Bilingual Edn. Project on Guam and Rota, Mariana Islands, 1971-74; prin. investigator Palauan-English Dictionary Project, 1973-74, Bilingual Edn. Project for Micronesia, 1974-77, Access to Govt. Through Neighborhood Bds., HEW, 1977-79, Pacific Area Lang. Materials Devel. Ctr., 1977-83, Carolinian-English Dictionary Project, Trust Territory Govt., 1981-83, Salish Lexicography Project, NEH, 1985-92, Integrated Approach to Hawaii's Drug Policy Issues, Robert Wood Johnson Found., 1994—. Editl. bd. Oceanic Linguistics: Spl. Publs., 1969—, Pacific Islands Monograph Series, 1981—, ISLA: A Jour. of Micronesian Studies, 1992—; editor SSRI Monograph Series, 1974—, PALI Lang. Series: Micronesia, 1974—; co-author: (with D. Crowley) Lessons in Indonesian, 1964; author: Spoken Chamorro, 1969, Chamorro Reference Grammar, 1973, A Chamorro Dictionary, 1975, Spoken Chamorro, rev. edit., 1980; contbr. articles to profl. jours. Office: U Hawaii at Manoa Social Science Rsch Inst Porteus Hall 2424 Maile Way Honolulu HI 96822

TOPPING, JOHN CARRUTHERS, JR., environmental organization administrator, lawyer; b. Wilkinsburg, Pa., Apr. 18, 1943; s. John Carruthers and Barbara Anne (Murray) T.; m. Linda Marie Thompson, Dec. 1, 1974; children: John Carruthers III, Elizabeth Barrett, Alexandra LaMotte. AB, Dartmouth Coll., 1964; JD, Yale U., 1967. Bar: Mass. 1967, D.C. 1968. Counsel Adv. Coun. for Minority Enterprise, Washington, 1970-73, staff dir., 1972-73; chief counsel office minority bus. enterprise U.S. Dept. Commerce, Washington, 1973-76; ptnr. Topping and Sherer, Washington, 1977-82; cons. U.S. EPA, Washington, 1982-83, staff dir. office air and radiation, 1983-86; ptnr. Topping & Swillinger, Washington, 1986-87; pres. Climate Inst., Washington, 1986—. Co-author: Southern Republicanism and the New South, 1966, Clean Air Handbook, 1987; editor: Preparing for Climate Change, 1988, Coping with Climate Change, 1989. Mem. D.C. adv. com. to U.S. Commn. on Civil Rights, 1974—; pres. Ripon Soc. Washington, 1978-80. Capt. USAF, 1968-70. Recipient Pres.'s award Nat. Bar Assn., 1976. Republican. Presbyterian. Home: 220 Maryland Ave NE Washington DC 20002-5704 Office: Climate Inst 324 4th St NE Washington DC 20002-5821 *The challenge of democracy is to represent the interests of generations yet to be born. The world in which they will live depends on decisions we make today.*

TOPPING, NORMAN HAWKINS, former university chancellor; b. Flat River, Mo., Jan. 12, 1908; s. Moses H. and Charlotte Amanda (Blue) T.; m. Helen Rummens, Sept. 2, 1930 (dec. Aug. 1989); children—Brian, Linda. A.B., U. So. Calif., 1933, M.D., 1936. Diplomate: Am. Bd. Preventive Medicine and Pub. Health. Intern USPHS marine hosps., San Francisco, Seattle; mem. staff NIH, Bethesda, Md., 1937-52; asst. chief div. infectious diseases NIH, 1946-48; asst. surgeon gen. USPHS; asso. dir. NIH, 1948-52; v.p. for med. affairs U. Pa., 1952-58; pres. U. So. Calif., 1958-70, chancellor, 1970-80, chancellor emeritus, 1980—; engaged in med. research, viral and rickettsial diseases, 1937-48; mem. com. on virus research and epidemiology Nat. Found. Infantile Paralysis, 1950-56, chmn., 1956-58; mem. research com. Nat. Found., chmn., 1958-77; pres. Am. Soc. Tropical Medicine, 1949. Author articles on typhus, Rocky Mountain spotted fever, Q fever, pub. health. Pres. So. Calif. Rapid Transit Dist., 1971-73. Recipient Bailey K. Ashford award, 1943; Wash. Acad. Sci. award, 1944; U.S.A. Typhus Commn. medal, 1945. Mem. A.A.A.S., Assn. Am. Physicians, Am. Epidemiological Soc., Soc. Exptl. Biology and Medicine. Home and Office: 100 S Plymouth Blvd Los Angeles CA 90004-3836

TOPPING, PETER, historian, educator; b. Milw., May 13, 1916; s. William P. and Anastasia (Makri) Topitzes; m. Eva V. Catafygiotu, June 20, 1951; 1 son, John Themis. B.A., U. Wis., 1937, M.A., 1938; postgrad., U. Cin., 1939-40; Ph.D., U. Pa., 1942. Instr. history U. Wis., 1943-44, Northwestern U., 1944-45; asst. prof. history U. Calif.-Santa Barbara, 1948-53; librarian Gennadeion Am. Sch. Classical Studies, Athens, Greece, 1953-60, mem.

mng. com., 1961—; vis. assoc. prof. history, library cons. U. Pa., 1960-61; assoc. prof. history, later Greek studies U. Cin., 1961-64, prof., 1964-67, Charles Phelps Taft prof., 1967-78; fellow Grad. Sch., 1972—; sr. research assoc. Dumbarton Oaks Rsch. Libr. and Collection, Washington, 1978-84; mem. bd. scholars Dumbarton Oaks Center for Byzantine Studies, 1972-74, mem. sr. fellows, 1979-86, hon. sr. research assoc., 1984—; interpreting officer U.S. staff Allied Mission to Observe Greek Elections, 1946; mem. exec. com. Frank L. Weil Inst. in Religion and Humanities, 1964-78. Author: Feudal Institutions as Revealed in the Assizes of Romania, 1949, (with Jean Longnon) Documents sur le régime des terres dans la principauté de Moreé au XIVme siècle, 1969, Studies on Latin Greece A.D. 1205-1715, 1977; contbr. articles, revs. to hist. jours. Advanced fellow Belgian Am. Edn. Found., 1947-48; Fulbright sr. research awardee Greece, 1950-51; sr. fellow NEH, 1974-75. Mem. Am. Hist. Assn., Mediaeval Acad. Am., Soc. Byzantine Studies (Athens, Greece) (hon.), Modern Greek Studies Assn., Phi Beta Kappa. Democrat. Mem. Greek Orthodox Ch. Home: 1823 Rupert St Mc Lean VA 22101-5434

TOPPING, SEYMOUR, publishing executive, educator; b. N.Y.C., Dec. 11, 1921; s. Joseph and Anna (Seidman) Topolsky; m. Audrey Elaine Ronning, Nov. 10, 1949; children: Susan, Karen, Lesley, Rebecca, Joanna. B.J., U. Mo., 1943; Litt.D. (hon.), Rider Coll., 1983. With I.N.S. (China civil war), 1946-47; with AP, 1948-59; corr. AP, Berlin, 1957-59; mem. staff N.Y. Times, 1959-93; chief corr. N.Y. Times, Moscow, 1960-63, Southeast Asia, 1963-66; fgn. editor N.Y. Times, 1966-69, asst. mng. editor, 1969-76, dep. mng. editor, 1976-77, mng. editor, 1977-86; dir. editorial devel. N.Y. Times Regional Newspapers, 1987-93; pres. Am. Soc. Newspaper Editors, 1992-93; prof. Grad. Sch. Journalism Columbia U., N.Y.C., 1993—; Sanpaolo prof. internat. journalism, 1994—; adminstr. Pulitzer Prizes Columbia U., N.Y.C., 1993—; adviser Ctr. Fgn. Journalists, Found. Am. Comm.; juror Pulitzer Prize com.; lectr. in field. Author: Journey Between Two Chinas, 1972. Spl. advisor to Sec.-Gen. UN to Earth Summit, Rio de Janeiro, 1992; mem. Nat. Com. U.S.-China Rels.; bd. dirs. Lamont-Doherty Earth Obs. Served with inf. AUS, 1943-46, PTO. Mem. Coun. Fgn. Rels., Asia Soc., Am. Soc. Newspaper Editors, Internat. Press Inst. (Am. com., bd. dirs.), Century Assn. Home: 5 Heathcote Rd Scarsdale NY 10583-4413

TORAN, KAY DEAN, social services director; b. Birmingham, Ala., Nov. 21, 1942; d. Benjamin and Mary Rose Dean; children: Traci Rossi, John D. Toran. BA, U. Portland, 1964; MSW, Portland State U., 1970. Asst. prof. social work Portland (Oreg.) State U., 1971-76; mgr. Adult and Family Svcs., Salem, Oreg., 1976-79; asst. gov. Office of Gov., Salem, 1979-87; adminstr. purchasing divsn. Dept. Gen. Svcs., Salem, 1987-90; regional adminstr. Children's Svcs. Divsn., Portland, 1991-94, adminstr., 1994—; pres. Walker Inst., Portland, 1990-94, Portland chapter Links, Inc., 1990-92. Bd. trustees Catlin Gabel Sch., Portland, 1980-84, Portland State U. Found., 1980-87; bd. dirs. Oreg. Law Found., 1990-93. Office: Svcs to Childen & Families 500 Summer St NE Salem OR 97310-0101

TORBERT, CLEMENT CLAY, JR., state supreme court justice; b. Opelika, Ala., Aug. 31, 1929; s. Clement Clay Sr. and Lynda (Meadows) T.; m. Gene Hurt, May 2, 1952; children: Mary Dixon, Gene Shealy, Clement Clay III. Student, U.S. Naval Acad., 1948-49; B.S., Auburn U., 1951; postgrad., U. Md., 1952; LL.B., U. Ala., 1954. Bar: Ala. 1954. Practiced in Opelika, 1954-77, city judge, 1954-58; partner firm Samford, Torbert, Denson & Horsley, 1959-74; chief justice Ala. Supreme Ct., 1977-89; ptnr. firm Maynard, Cooper & Gale, 1990—; past chmn. Ala. Jud. Study Commn., Jud. Coordination Com.; past pres. Conf. Chief Justices; supervisory bd. Ala. Law Enforcement Planning Agy., 1977-83; bd. dirs. Ala. Criminal Justice Info. Systems, Nat. Inst. for Dispute Resolution, First Nat. Bank Opelika, State Justice Inst., 1986-92; mem. panel of arbitrators Am. Arbitration Assn.; panelist-at-large Ctr. for Pub. Resources; held Leslie S. Wright Chair of Law, Cumberland Sch. Law, 1989, John Sparkman Chair, U. Ala. Sch. Law. Mem. Ala. Ho. of Reps., 1958-62, Ala. Senate, 1966-70, 74-77. Served to capt. USAF, 1952-53. Elected to Ala. Acad. of Honor, 1979; recipient Disting. Svc. award Nat. Ctr. for State Cts., 1989, 1989 award, Am. Judges Assn. Mem. Am. Judicature Soc., Farrah Law Soc., Phi Delta Phi, Phi Kappa Phi, Alpha Tau Omega. Methodist. Lodge: Kiwanis. Home: 611 Terracewood Dr Opelika AL 36801-3850 Office: One Commerce St Ste 302 Montgomery AL 36104

TORBERT, PRESTON M., lawyer; b. Greenwich, Conn., Aug. 9, 1943. AB magna cum laude, Princeton U., 1966; MA, U. Chgo., 1970, PhD, 1973; JD, Harvard U., 1974. Bar: Ill. 1974. Ptnr. Baker & McKenzie, Chgo. Office: Baker & McKenzie 1 Prudential Plz 130 E Randolph St Chicago IL 60601*

TORCIVIA, BENEDICT J., SR., construction company executive; b. Passaic, N.J., Sept. 8, 1929; s. Joseph and Felicia (Latteri) T.; m. Elvira Venneri, June 20, 1953; children—Benedict J., Joseph A. B.S. in Archtl. Engring., Catholic U. Am., 1951. Registered profl. engr., N.H. Estimator, project mgr. Arthur Venneri Co., Westfield, N.J., 1951-60, v.p., asst. to pres., 1960-63, pres., 1963-65; pres., treas. Torcon, Inc., Westfield, 1965-84, pres., treas., chief exec. officer, 1984-89, chmn. bd., chief exec. officer, 1990—. Trustee bd. overseers N.J. Inst. Tech., Newark, 1980—; trustee Found. U. Medicine and Dentistry N.J., Newark, 1985-88; regent St. Peter's Coll., Jersey City, 1972-80; No. N.J. Area chmn. U.S. Olympic Com., 1984—; exec. com. March of Dimes, Monmouth County, N.J., 1985, N.J. unit NCCJ, 1985; trustee Kidney Fund of N.J., Union County, 1980-85, The Pingry Sch., 1987—. Recipient Ann. Alumni Achievement in Engring. award Cath. U. Am., Washington, 1978, Humanitarian and Brotherhood award N.J. chpt. Nat. Conf. Christians and Jews, 1990; named Constrn. Man of Yr., N.J. Ready Mixed Concrete Assn., 1981, Gen. Contractor of Yr. N.J. chpt. Am. Subcontractors Assn., 1974, 82, Constrn. Mgr. of Yr., 1989. Mem. Constrn. Congress (pres. 1983-85), Union County Bldg. Contractors Assn. (pres. 1975-83), Am. Concrete Inst., Bldg. Contractors Assn. N.J. (pres. 1981-82), N.J. Alliance for Action (trustee 1980—), Navesink Country Club, Jupiter Hills Club, MetedeconK Country Club. Roman Catholic. Avocations: golf; reading. Office: Torcon Inc PO Box 609 214 E Grove St Westfield NJ 07090-1657*

TORCIVIA, BENEDICT JOSEPH, JR., construction company executive; b. Buffalo, July 5, 1957; s. Benedict Joseph and Elvira (Venneri) T.; m. Judith Anne Hlavenka, May 2, 1981; children: Benedict III, Brian, Christopher, Leigh Ann. BS in Bus., Lehigh U., 1979; lic. in real estate, Union Coll., 1980. Lic. in real estate. Exec. v.p., chief oper. officer Torcon, Inc., Westfield, N.J., 1979—, exec. v.p., 1979—. Bd. dirs. N.J. Alliance for Action. Mem. Bldg. Contrs. Assn. N.J. (trustee), Constrn. Mgmt. Com., Assoc. Gen. Contrs. Am. (com. mem.), Waterfront Invest (bd. advisors), Navesink Country Club (Middletown, N.J.), Atlantic City Country Club. Roman Catholic. Office: Torcon Inc 214 E Grove St Westfield NJ 07091*

TORDOFF, HARRISON BRUCE, retired zoologist, educator; b. Mechanicville, N.Y., Feb. 8, 1923; s. Harry F. and Ethel M. (Dormandy) T.; m. Jean Van Nostrand, July 3, 1946; children: Jeffrey, James. B.S., Cornell U., 1946; M.A., U. Mich., 1949, Ph.D., 1952. Curator Inst. of Jamaica, Kingston, 1946-47; instr. U. Kans., 1950-52, asst. prof., 1952-57, assoc. prof., 1957; asst. prof. U. Mich., 1957-59, assoc. prof., 1959-62, prof., 1962-70; former dir. Bell Mus. Natural History; prof. ecology U. Minn., Mpls., 1970-91, dean coll. biol. scis., 1986-87. Contbr. articles in ornithology to profl. jours. Served with USAF, 1942-45. Decorated D.F.C., 17 Air medals. Fellow Am. Ornithologists Union (pres. 1978-80); mem. Nature Conservancy (chmn. bd. Minn. chpt. 1975-77), Wilson Ornithol. Soc. (editor 1952-54), Cooper Ornithol. Soc. Home: 6 Chickadee Ln North Oaks Saint Paul MN 55127 Office: 100 Ecology 1987 Upper Buford Cir Saint Paul MN 55108-6097

TOREN, ROBERT, photojournalist; b. Grand Rapids, Mich., Oct. 9, 1915; s. Clarence J. and Helen (Holcomb) T.; student Winona Sch. Profl. Photography, 1957, West Coast Sch. Photography, 1959-62; m. Miriam Jeanette Smith, July 17, 1940. Photographer, Harris and Ewing, Washington, 1938-39, Versluis Studios, Grand Rapids, Mich., 1939-43, prodn. mgr., 1940-43; owner, photographer Toren Galleries, San Francisco, 1946-70; photographer Combat Tribes of World, Rich Lee Orgn., 1978-84, Darien jungle expdn. Am. Motors, 1979; feature writer Auburn (Calif.) Jour., El Dorado Gazette, 1983-87, Georgetown Gazette, 1983-96. One man shows various univs.; prints in permanent collections: Photog. Hall of Fame, Coyote Point Mus., San Mateo County Hist. Mus.; photog. column San Mateo Times, Georgetown Gazette; lectr. Am. Pres. Lines, Coll. San Mateo, Peninsula Art Assn., Mendicino Art Ctr. Historian City of Foster City; vice chmn. Art Commn. Foster City. Trustee, West Coast Sch.; bd. dirs. Foster City Art League, Hillbarn Theatre, San Mateo County Arts Council; mem. art com. San Mateo County Fair, 1979-87; coord., dir. Georgetown (Calif.) Mountain Mus., 1982-88; founding pres. Music on The Divide, 1989; founder Georgetown CA. Ragtime Concerts, 1996; pres. El Dorado County Arts Coun. Served from pvt. to staff sgt. AUS, 1943-46. Mem. Calif. Writers (br. pres.), Profl. Photographers Am. Presbyn. Author: Peninsula Wilderness. Illustrator: The Tainted Tree, 1963. Editor: The Evolution of Portraiture, 1965; The Western Way of Portraiture, 1965, Conquest of the Darien, 1984, Two Cities, 1996. Home: 3140 Cascade Trl Cool CA 95614-2615

TORESCO, DONALD, automotive executive; b. 1936. With Dom's Auto Sales, Inc., Plainfield, N.J., 1958-91; CEO Toresco Enterprises, Springfield, N.J., 1984—. Office: 170 Rte 22 E Springfield NJ 07081

TORFFIELD, MARVIN, artist; b. Bklyn., July 25, 1943; s. Barnett Philip and Rina (Shapiro) T. B.F.A., Pratt Inst., 1965; M.F.A., Yale U., 1970. Vis. fellow Advanced Ctr. Visual Studies, MIT, 1970; rsch. fellow Harvard U., 1972. One man shows include Jewish Mus. N.Y., 1969, The Seagram Pla., N.Y.C., 1973, Whitney Mus. Am. Art., 1973-74, Paula Cooper Gallery, 1977, Central Park, 1980, Leo Castelli Gallery, 1983, 35th IDCA, 1985, Sert Gallery, Harvard U., 1986; represented in group shows. Mem. Rolling Stones Steel Wheels Tour, N.Am., Japan, Europe, 1989-90. Patentee in field. Fellow Nat. Endowment for Arts, 1970, Guggenheim Found., 1975; Pollock-Krasner Found. grantee, 1986-87; MacDowell Colony residency, Peterborough, N.H., 1988—. Office: PO Box 292 Canal Sta New York NY 10013

TORGERSEN, PAUL ERNEST, academic administrator, educator; b. N.Y.C., Oct. 13, 1931; s. Elnar and Frances (Hansen) T.; m. Dorothea Hildegarde Zuschlag, Sept. 11, 1954; children: Karen Elizabeth, Janis Elaine, James Einar. BS, Lehigh U., 1953, DEng, 1994; MS, Ohio State U., 1956, PhD, 1959. Grad. tchg. asst. Ohio State U., Columbus, 1957, instr., 1957-59; asst. to assoc. prof. Okla. State U., Stillwater, 1959-66; prof., dept. head, dean Coll. Engring. Va. Tech, Blacksburg, 1967-93, pres., 1993—; dir. Roanoke (Va.) Electric Steel, 1986—, Pressure Sys., Hampton, Va., 1988—, Fistr Union Va., Roanoke, 1994—. Author 5 books. Mem. Gov. Charles Robb's Policy Adv. Com. on High Tech., Richmond, Va., 1984-85; rep. So. State Energy Bd., Richmond, 1986-90. 1st lt. USAF, 1953-55. Fellow Am. Soc. Engring. Edn. (Lamme medal 1994), Inst. Indsl. Engring; mem. Nat. Acad. Engring. Avocation: tennis. Office: Va Tech 210 Burruss Hall Blacksburg VA 24061

TORGERSEN, TORWALD HAROLD, architect, designer; b. Chgo., Sept. 2, 1929; s. Peder and Hansine Malene (Hansen) T.; m. Dorothy Darlene Peterson, June 22, 1963. B.S. in Archtl. Engring. with honors, U. Ill., 1951. Lic. architect Ill., D.C., real estate broker, Ill., interior designer, Ill.; retistered architect Nat. Coun. Archtl. Registration Bds. Ptnr. Coyle & Torgersen (Architects-Engrs.), Washington, Chgo. and Joliet, Ill., 1955-56; project coord. Skidmore, Owings & Merrill, Chgo., 1956-60; corp. architect, dir. architecture, constrn. and interiors Container Corp. Am., Chgo., 1960-86; prin. in charge of orgn. and adminstrn. Jack Train Assocs. Inc., Chgo., 1987-88; cons. Torwald H. Torgersen, AIA, FASID, Chgo., 1988—; guest lectr. U. Wis. Capt. USNR, 1951-82. Recipient Top Ten Design award Factory mag., 1964. Fellow Am. Soc. Interior Designers; mem. AIA, Naval Res. Assn., Ill. Naval Militia, Am. Arbitration Assn., Am. Soc. Mil. Engrs., Paper Industry Mgmt. Assn. (hon.), Sports Car Club Am., Nat. Eagle Scout Assn. Club: 20 Fathoms. Home and Office: 3750 N Lake Shore Dr Chicago IL 60613-4238

TORGERSON, DAVID FRANKLYN, chemist, research facility administrator; b. Winnipeg, Man., July 11, 1942; m. Dale Rae Evans, May 28, 1966; children: Kristen, Dara, Shauna. BSc with honors, U. Man., 1965, MSc, 1966; PhD, McMaster U., 1969; postgrad., Nat. Def. Coll., Kingston, Ont., 1987-88. Rsch. scientist cyclotron inst. Tex. A&M Univ., College Station, 1969-76; rsch. scientist cyclotron inst. Atomic Energy Can. Ltd. Rsch., Pinawa, Man., 1976-78, head containment analysis sect., 1978-79, head br. rsch. chemistry, 1979-84, dir. reactor safety rsch., 1984-89, v.p. environ. sci. and waste mgmt., 1989-91; v.p. reactor devel. Atomic Energy Can. Ltd. Rsch., Chalk River, Ont., 1991-95; acting pres. Atomic Energy Can. Ltd. Rsch., Ottawa, Ont., 1994; v.p. rsch., product devel. Atomic Energy Can. Ltd., 1995—; chmn. prin. working group Orgn. Econ. Cooperation and Devel./Com. Safety Nuclear Installation, Paris, 1985-87, chmn. task force on source terms, 1986-87. Contbr. articles to profl. jours. Scholar Dow Chem. Can., 1966, Nat. Rsch. Coun. Can., 1967-69. Fellow Chem. Inst. Can. (chmn. Man. sect. 1982, regional councillor 1983), Can. Nuclear Soc. Office: Atomic Energy Can Ltd, Chalk River Labs, Chalk River, ON Canada K0J 1J0

TORGET, ARNE O., electrical engineer; b. Cathlamet, Wash., Oct. 10, 1916; s. John B. and Anna J. (Olson) T.; m. Dorothy M. Lackie, Aug. 30, 1941; children: Kathleen, James, Thomas. BSEE, U. Wash., 1940. Registered profl. elec. engr., Calif. Design engr. Boeing, Seattle, 1940-41, asst. group engr., 1941-46; design specialist N.Am. Aviation, L.A., 1946-50, 60-64, elec. supr., 1950-55; design specialist Rocketdyne N.Am. Aviation, Canoga Park, Calif., 1955-60; design specialist Space Div. Rockwell Internat., Downey, Calif., 1964-79; commr. Wahkiakum Count Pub. Utility, Cathlamet, 1985—; Bd. dirs. Wash. Pub. Utility Dist. Utility Systems, Seattle, 1985—, Wash. Pub. Power Supply System, Richland, 1987—, Wash. Pub. Utility Dist. Assn., Seattle, 1985—. Mem. AAAS, IEEE, Elks. Republican. Roman Catholic. Home: 166 E Sunny Sands Rd Cathlamet WA 98612-9708 Office: Wahkiakum County Pub Utilities Dist 45 Riv St Cathlamet WA 98612

TORGOW, EUGENE N., electrical engineer; b. Bronx, N.Y., Nov. 26, 1925; s. Frank and Blanche Anita (Revzin) T.; m. Cynthia Silver, Mar. 19, 1950; children: Joan, Martha, Ellen. BSEE, Cooper Union, 1946; MSEE, Poly. Inst. Bklyn., 1949; Engr. in E.E., Poly. Inst. N.Y., 1980; postgrad. UCLA, 1983. Rsch. assoc., sect. leader Microwave Research Inst., Poly. Inst. Bklyn., 1947-51, 53-60, instr., 1954-59; mgr. microwave lab. A.B. Dumont Labs, East Patterson, N.J., 1951-53; chief engr., mgr. microwave products Dorne & Margolin, Inc., Westbury, L.I., N.Y., 1960-64; chief engr., dir. research, dir. mktg. Rantec div. Emerson Electric, Calabasas, Calif., 1964-68; with Missile Systems Group, Hughes Aircraft Co., Canoga Park, Calif., 1968-85. assoc. labs. mgr., 1981-85; cons. various electronics firms, N.Y.C., 1956-59; cons., 1986—; lectr. Calif. State U., Northridge, 1986-91. Contbr. articles to profl. jours.; patentee in field. Mem. Fair Housing Coun., San Fernando Valley, L.A., 1967—; mem. L.A. County Mus. Assn., 1976—. Served with USAAF, 1946-47. Recipient Engr. '85 Merit award San Fernando Valley Engrs. Coun., 1985. Fellow Inst. for Advancement Engring., IEEE (life); mem. WINCON (bd. dirs. 1984-89, chmn. bd. dirs. 1988-89), Microwave Theory and Techniques Soc. of IEEE (pres. 1966, mem. adminstrn. com. 1962-72, Svc. award 1978), Accreditation Bd. Engring. and Tech. (mem. engring. accreditation com. 1994—), Hughes Mgmt. Club (edn. chmn. 1979-80), Sigma Xi. Democrat. Office: 9531 Donna Ave Northridge CA 91324-1816

TORIAN, HENRY, automotive executive. CEO Tasha. Office: 43285 Auto Mall Circle Fremont CA 94538

TORIBARA, TAFT YUTAKA, radiation biologist, biophysicist, chemist, toxicologist; b. Seattle, Apr. 10, 1917; s. Minekichi and Hisano (Miyata) T.; m. Masako Ono., Aug. 28, 1948; children—Lynne Suzanne, Neil Willard. BS in Chem. Engring. summa cum laude, U. Wash., 1938, M.S. in Chem. Engring, 1939; Ph.D., U. Mich., 1942. Rsch. chemist dept. engring. rsch. U. Mich., 1942-48; from asst. prof. to prof. radiation biology and biophysics Sch. Medicine and Dentistry, U. Rochester, N.Y., 1948-89, prof. emeritus toxicology in biophysics, 1989-93; prof. emeritus dept. environ. medicine, 1993—; cons. in field. Editor: Modern Techniques for the Detection and Measurement of Environmental Pollutants, 1978, Polluted Rain, 1980; contbr. articles to profl. jours. Chmn. advancement com. Boy Scouts Am., 1964-67; pres. Jr. High Family Faculty Forum, 1964-66; mem. Gates Library Bd., 1965-75, pres., 1972-74. NIH Spl. Rsch. fellow, 1960-61. Mem. Am. Chem. Soc., AAAS. Inventor ultrafiltration apparatus, 1953. Home: 54 Timpat Dr Rochester NY 14624-2928 Office: EHSC U Rochester Med Ctr Rochester NY 14642 *My life might be summarized by the statement, "Adversity is not always bad".*

TORII, SHUKO, psychology educator; b. Toyohashi, Aichi-ken, Japan, Apr. 5, 1930; m. Toshiko Mochizuki, June 19, 1975. BA, U. Tokyo, 1954, MA, 1956, PhD, 1964. Rsch. asst. Tokyo Inst. Tech., 1959-61, U. Tokyo, 1961-65; assoc. prof. Tokyo U. Agr. Tech., 1965-70; rsch. assoc. U. Mich., Ann Arbor, 1966-68; rsch. assoc. Inst. Molecular Biophysics Fla. State U., 1968-69; from assoc. prof. to prof. psychology U. Tokyo, 1970-91; prof. U. Sacred Heart, Tokyo, 1991—. Author: The World of Vision, 1979, Psychology of Vision, 1982, Visual Perception in the Congenitally or Early Blinded after Surgery, 1992; author, editor: Perception, 1983, Visually Handicapped and Technology of Sensory Substitution, 1984, The Visually Handicapped and Their Cognitive Activity, 1993. Mem. Japanese Psychonomic Soc. (assoc. editor 1981-88, editor 1988-96, pres. 1996—), Japanese Psychol. Assn. (mem. editorial com. 1987-89, editor 1989-92), Optical Soc. Am., Assn. Rsch. in Vision and Ophthalmology. Home: 2-17-26-204 Takada, Toshima, Tokyo 171, Japan Office: U Sacred Heart, 4-3-1 Hiroo, Shibuya Tokyo 150, Japan

TORKELSON, JODIE RAE, executive branch staff member; b. Cudahy, Wis., May 13, 1958; d. Wallace Keith and Delores Helen (Hagen) T. BA in Polit. Sci., Moorhead State U., 1980. Staff asst. Congressman Richard Nolan, Washington, 1980-81; office mgr. Congressman Leon E. Panetta, Washington, 1981-86, adminstrv. asst., 1988-89; acting exec. dir. Life Underwriters for Lutheran Charities, Mpls., 1986-88; dir. adminstrn. com. on budget U.S. Ho. of Reps., Washington, 1989-93, assoc. dir. for adminstrn. Office of Mgmt. and Budget, 1993-94; asst. to pres. for mgmt. and adminstrn. The White House, Washington, 1994—. Lutheran. Office: The White House Office Mgmt & Adminstrn Old Executive Office Bldg Washington DC 20503

TORKILDSEN, PETER G., congressman; b. Milw., Jan. 28, 1958; s. Robert Allan and Mary Ellen (Hill) T.; m. Gail Bloomgarden, Jan. 1996. BA, U. Mass., 1980; MPA, Harvard U., 1990. Mem. Mass. House of reps., from 1985, 103rd Congress from 6th Mass. dist., 1993—. Chmn. Danvers (Mass.) Rep. Town Com., 1983-88; mem. Danvers Town Meeting, 1983-85, Mass. Rep. State Com., Boston, 1984-93. Mem. Am. Legis. Exchange Council, Mass. Legislator's Assn., Nat. Rep. Legislator Assn. Roman Catholic. Lodge: Sons of Norway. Home: 12 Spruce St Danvers MA 01923-2613 Office: US House of Reps 120 Cannon Bldg Washington DC 20515-0003

TORKPO, BETTYE JEWELL, kindergarten educator; b. Dumas, Ark.; d. Etherine (Jackson) James; m. George K. Torkpo, Apr. 19, 1977. Cert. group tchr., Essex County Coll., Newark, N.J., 1985, AA, 1993; diploma, Phillips Bus. Sch., East Orange, N.J., 1990. Student tchr. Mattie Jackson D.C. presch., Okla. City, 1976; housekeeper Holiday Inn, Livingston, N.J., 1977-78; subst. tchr. State of N.J. C.D.C., East Orange, 1978; tchr.'s aide Orange (N.J.) Daycare, 1978-79; housekeeper Rsorts Hotel-Casino, Atlantic City, N.J., 1979-82; tchr. Mustard Seed C.C., Newark, 1986-89; tchr. The Urban League of Essex County, Newark, 1989-90, kindergarten tchr., 1992; tchr.'s asst. Newark Pre-Sch. Coun., 1991-92. Head usher, pres. fellowship com. Imani Bapt. Ch. of Christ Inc. Democrat. Baptist. Avocations: reading, teaching, writing, poetry, church, security investigation. Home: 410 Prospect St East Orange NJ 07017-3311

TORLEY, JOHN FREDERIC, iron and steel company executive; b. Pitts., June 5, 1911; s. Walter Anderson and Emma Katherine (Hacker) T.; m. Leona Helen Depp, Oct. 5, 1940; children: Lois Leona, Jane Mildred. BS in Mech. Engring., Carnegie-Mellon U., 1940; Indsl. Engr., Youngstown U., 1948. Registered profl. engr., Pa. V.p. Midland Ross Co., Sharon, Pa., Phoenix and Chgo., 1946-61; chmn. Amcast Corp., Ohio, 1961-80, also bd. dirs.; chmn. bd. Morris Bean & Co., Yellow Springs, Ohio, 1992—; bd. dirs. Monarch Machine Tool Co., Ponderosa Systems Inc., Van Dyne Crotty Corp. Chmn. Air Force Mus. Found. Served with USNR, World War II; comdr. Res. Mem. ASME. Office: 1515 Kettering Towers Dayton OH 45423

TORME, MEL(VIN) (HOWARD TORME), musician, jazz vocalist; b. Chgo., Sept. 13, 1925; m. Janette Scott (div.); 2 children. Studied drums at age seven. Acted in radio soap operas; sang with Buddy Rogers, other name bands during early years; toured with Chico Marx band, 1942-43; motion picture debut in Higher and Higher, 1943; other motion picture appearances include Pardon My Rhythm, 1944, Words and Music, 1948, Walk Like a Dragon, 1960, A Man Called Adam, 1966, The Land of No Return; leader vocal group, Mel-Tones, Calif.; solo singer, 1947—, co-founder Producers Group Ltd., 1982; numerous compositions including County Fair; solo singer Vaudeville Tour, Eng., 1956, 57; recs. include Live at the Maisonette, Mel Torme and Friends, Recorded at Marty, Back in Town, Songs of New York, Swings Shubert Alley, That's All, Easy to Remember, Velvet Fog, Songs About Love, Round Midnight, Together Again, The London Sessions, 1992, Mel Torme in Hollywood, 1992, Nothing Without You, 1993, Christmas Songs, 1993, Sixteen Most Requested Songs, 1993, Sing, Sing, Sing: Live at the Fujitsu-Concord Jazz Festival, 1993, Jazz 'Round Midnight, 1994, A Tribute to Bing Crosby, 1994; author: The Other Side of the Rainbow, 1970, autobiography It Wasn't All Velvet, 1988. Recipient Grammy award Best Male Jazz Vocal Performance, 1983, 84. Address: care Prappas Co 9201 Wilshire Blvd Ste 204 Beverly Hills CA 90210-5513

TORN, RIP (ELMORE RUAL TORN, JR.), actor, director; b. Temple, Tex., Feb. 6, 1931; s. Elmore and Thelma (Spacek) T.; m. Ann Wedgeworth, Jan. 15, 1955 (div.); 1 dau., Danae; m. Geraldine Page; children: Angelica, Anthony, Jonathan. Student, Tex. A & M Coll., 1948-50; B.S.F.A., U. Tex. Performances include: (stage) Cat on a Hot Tin Roof, 1955, Orpheus Descending, 1958, Chaparral, 1958 (Theatre World award 1959), Sweet Bird of Youth, 1959, on tour, 1960, Daughter of Silence, 1961, Macbeth, 1962, Desire Under the Elms, 1963, Strange Interlude, 1963, Blues for Mr. Charlie, 1964, The Kitchen, 1966, The Country Girl, 1966, The Deer Park, 1967 (Obie award), The Cuban Thing, 1968, The Honest-to-God Schnozzola, 1969, Dream of a Blacklisted Actor, 1969, The Dance of Death, 1970-71, The Marriage Proposal, 1971, Marriage and Money, 1971, Barbary Shore, The Little Foxes, 1974, The Father, 1975, The Glass Menagerie, 1975, Fever for Life, 1975, Creditors, 1977, Night Shift, 1977, Seduced, 1979, Anna Christie, 1992; (motion pictures) Baby Doll, 1956, A Face in the Crowd, 1957, Time Limit, 1957, Pork Chop Hill, 1959, King of Kings, 1961, Hero's Island, 1962, Sweet Bird of Youth, 1962, Critic's Choice, 1963, The Cincinnati Kid, 1965, One Spy Too Many, 1966, Beach Red, 1967, You're a Big Boy Now, 1967, Beyond the Law, 1968, Sol Madrid, 1968, Coming Apart, 1969, Tropic of Cancer, 1970, Slaughter, 1972, Payday, 1973, Crazy Joe, 1974, Birch Interval, 1976, Maidstone, The Man Who Fell to Earth, 1976, Nasty Habits, 1977, Coma, 1978, The Seduction of Joe Tynan, 1979, First Family, 1980, Heartland, 1980, One Trick Pony, 1980; Jinxed, 1982, Airplane II: The Sequel, 1982, The Beastmaster, 1982, A Stranger is Watching, 1982, Cross Creek, 1983, City Heat, 1984, Misunderstood, 1984, Night Shadows, 1984, Song Writer, 1984, Flashpoint, 1984, Summer Rental, 1985, Beer, 1985, Extreme Prejudice, 1987, Defending Your Life, 1991, Beautiful Dreamers, 1992, Hard Promises, 1992, Robocop 3, 1993, Where the Rivers Flow North, 1994, How to Make an American Quilt, 1995; (TV films and miniseries) Two Plays, 1971, The President's Plane Is Missing, 1973, The FBI Versus the Ku Klux Klan, 1975, Song of Myself, 1976, Betrayal, 1976, The Gift of Love, 1978, Blind Ambition, 1979, A Shining Season, 1979, Sophia Loren: Her Own Story, 1980, Rape and Marriage: The Rideout Case, 1980, The Blue and the Gray, 1982, When She Says No, 1984, Dream West, 1986, April Morning, 1988, Sweet Bird of Youth, 1989, By Dawn's Early Light, 1990, Another Pair of Aces: Three of a Kind, 1991, My Son Johnny, 1991, Death Hits the Jackpot, 1991, T-Bone and Weasel, 1992, A Mother's Right: The Elizabeth Morgan Story, 1993, Dead Ahead: The Exxon Valdez Disaster, 1992; (TV series) The Larry Sanders Show, HBO, 1992— (Emmy nominee for best supporting actor 1993, 94, Cable Ace award for best supporting actor 1994); dir. plays: The Beard, 1968 (Obie award), Look Away, 1973. Mem. AFTRA, SAG, Actors Equity Assn., Actors' Studio (bd. dirs., prodn. bd., 1st chmn. founding com.), Dirs. Guild Am. *

TORNABENE, RUSSELL C., communications executive; b. Gary, Ind., Sept. 18, 1923; s. Samuel Tornabene and Marion (LaVorci) Roush; m. Audrey F. Shankey, June 21, 1952; children—Joseph, Leigh, David, Lynn. A.A., Gary Jr. Coll., 1941, 46-47; B.A., Ind. U., 1949, M.A., 1950. Radio, TV newswriter WRC-AM-TV, Washington, 1951-55; network supr. NBC Network News, Washington, 1955-61; network gen. mgr. NBC Network News, NYC, 1961-75; v.p. NBC News, NYC, 1975-81; exec. officer Soc. Profl. Journalists, Chgo., 1981-87; Midwest dir. Exec. TV Workshop, Chgo., 1987-96; pres. Russell Communications Cons., 1996—. Contbr. articles on news to mags. and newspapers. Mem. N.Y. Catholic Archdiocese Sch. Bd., N.Y.C., 1972. Recipient Disting. Service award, Sigma Delta Chi, 1949; Ernie Pyle scholar, 1949. Mem. Acad. TV Arts and Scis., Radio TV News Dirs. Assn. Club: Overseas Press (former v.p.). Avocation: photography. Office: 626 Sheridan Sq # 2 Evanston IL 60202-3156

TORNABENE, THOMAS GUY, microbiologist, researcher, administrator; b. Cecil, Pa., May 6, 1937; s. Guy Thomas and Helen (Skarupa) T.; m. Maria D. Butos, June 10, 1962 (div. May 1974); children; Elene D., Demi E., Joanna M.; m. Kristi S. Broadwater, Nov. 5, 1977; children: Kari J., Miki A., Talia C. BS in Biology, St. Edwards U., 1959; MS in Immunology, U. Houston, 1962, PhD in Biol. Chemistry, 1967. Postdoctoral fellow NRC, Ottawa, Ont., Can., 1967-68; asst. prof. Colo. State U., Ft. Collins, 1968-73, assoc. prof., 1973-78, prof., 1978-81; dir., prof. Ga. Inst. Tech., Atlanta, 1981-90, assoc. dean, 1990-95, prof., 1981—. Contbr. articles to profl. jours., chpts. to books in field. Mem. Am. Soc. Microbiology. Office: Ga Inst Tech Sch Applied Biology Atlanta GA 30332-0230

TORNATORE-MORSE, KATHLEEN MARY, pharmacy educator; b. Oneida, N.Y., Feb. 25, 1955; d. James Joseph and Concetta Barbara (Crimi) T.; m. Gene Morse; two children. BS in Pharmacy cum laude, Union U., 1978; PharmD, SUNY, Buffalo, 1981. Registered pharmacist, N.Y. Hosp. pharmacy residency U. Nebr. Med. Ctr., Omaha, 1978-79; pharmacist Health Care Plan, West Seneca, N.Y., 1979-80; lab. instr. Profl. Practice Lab. Sch. of Pharmacy SUNY, Buffalo, 1979-80, instr. in pharmacology nurse practitioner program, 1982-85, 87-91, clin. pharmacokinetics fellow, 1983-85, clin. instr. Sch. of Pharmacy, 1981-83, rsch. asst. prof. pharmacy Sch. of Pharmacy, 1985-87, asst. prof. pharmacy, 1987-90, clin. asst. prof. pharmacy, 1990-91, asst. prof. pharmacy, 1991-95; assoc. prof. pharmacy, 1995—; lectr. and presenter in field; pharmacokinetics cons. VA Med. Ctr., Buffalo, 1986-91; curriculum com. mem. Sch. of Pharmacy, SUNY, Buffalo, 1990-91, mem. Ctr. for Clin. Pharmacy Rsch., 1989—, mem. substance abuse com., 1990—, mem. Doctor of Pharmacy Student Rsch. com., 1987—, mem. curriculum com. Doctor of Pharmacy program, 1984-86, mem. policy and implementation com., 1984-86; quality assurance com. Buffalo Gen. Hosp. Corp., 1981-82, investigational rev. bd., 1982-83; mem. med. adv. com. West N.Y. Kidney Found., 1994—. Contbr. chpts. to Textbook of Pharmacology, 1991; contbr. numerous articles to profl. jours. including Transplantation, Clin. Pharmacology and Therapeutics, Clin. Nephrology, Clin. Transplantation, others. Recipient Outstanding Young Women of Am. award, 1984, Achievement award Albany Coll. Pharmacy, 1984; grantee Upjohn, 1984-86, 88, 90-91, 93, 95. Mem. AAAS, AAUW, Internat. Soc. Immunopharmacology, Am. Coll. Clin. Pharmacy, (mem. devel. and steering com. N.Y. state chpt. 1990-91, other coms. 1991-93), Am. Soc. Hosp. Pharmacists, Am. Assn. Colls. Pharmacy, Am. Fedn. Aging Rsch., Rho Chi. Office: SUNY Sch of Pharmacy Dept Pharmacy Practice 313 Cooke Hall Buffalo NY 14260-1200

TORNEK, TERRY E., real estate executive; b. Bklyn., Nov. 23, 1945; s. Allen Vernon and Gertrude (Slotkin) T.; m. Maria Elizabeth Mascoli, June 25, 1967; children: Joshua, Jessica, Rachel. BA, Princeton U., 1967; MS in Urban Planning, Columbia U., 1971. Urban renewal rep. U.S. Dept. HUD, N.Y.C., 1968-69; prin. planner, dir. Planning Dept., Springfield, Mass., 1971-75; dir. Planning Dept., Pasadena, Calif., 1982-84; adminstr. Pioneer Valley Transit Authority, Springfield, 1975-79; v.p., gen. mgr. Cannon Planning & Devel., Springfield, 1979-82; dir. devel. BWC Devel., L.A., 1984-87; exec. v.p. Haseko (Calif.) Inc., L.A., 1987—. City councillor Springfield (Mass.) City Coun., 1976-77; bd. dirs. Springfield (Mass.) Action Commn., 1975-80; bd. dirs., v.p. Pasadena (Calif.) Neighborhood Housing Svcs., 1982-88. Home: 4910 Burgoyne Ln La Canada CA 91011-3717 Office: Haseko (Calif) Inc 350 S Figueroa St Ste 601 Los Angeles CA 90071-1102

TORNQVIST, ERIK GUSTAV MARKUS, chemical engineer, research scientist; b. Lund, Sweden, Jan. 13, 1924; came to U.S., 1951; s. Gustav Ivar and Anne Marie (Lassen) T.; m. Linnéa Dagmar Lindborg, June 28, 1969; children: Gunvor, Karin, Carl-Erik. MSChemE, Royal Inst. Tech., Stockholm, 1948; MS in Biochemistry, U. Wis., 1953, PhD in Biochemistry/Organic Chemistry, 1955. Registered engr., Sweden. 1st rsch. asst. div. food chemistry Royal Inst. Tech., 1949-51; rsch. asst. dept. biochemistry U. Wis., Madison, 1951-55; rsch. chemist chem. divsn. Esso Rsch. and Engring. Co., Linden, N.J., 1955-58, rsch. assoc., 1958-66, sr. rsch. assoc., 1966-72; sr. rsch. assoc. Exxon Chem. Co., Tech., Linden, 1972-86; internat. cons. Watchung, N.J., 1986-90; pres. PolymErik, Inc., Watchung, 1990—; vis prof. Royal Inst. Tech., 1987; invited prin. speaker Scandinavian Day, Chautauqua (N.Y.) Instn., 1983, 87; invited speaker, chmn. numerous nat. and internat. meetings. Co-editor: Polymer Chemistry of Synthetic Elastomers, 2 vols., 1968, 69; patentee in field; contbr. articles to profl. jours., chpts. to books. Treas. United Swedish Socs., N.Y.C., 1972-86, Swedish Sch. Assn. N.J., 1988-91; bd. govs. Am. Swedish Hist. Mus., Phila., 1974-89; trustee New Sweden Co., Bridgeton, N.J., 1986-89, Kalmar Nyckel Found., Wilmington, Del., 1987—; bd. dirs. Watchung Hills Soccer Assn., Watchung/Warren, N.J., 1989—. Recipient award 1st Nat. Inventors Day, 1973, gold Bicentennial medal King of Sweden, 1980, John Hanson award for excellence in pub. svc. Am.-Swedish Cultural Found., Mpls., 1981, citation Swedish Coun. of Am., 1983, cert. of appreciation Swedish New Sweden '88 Com., 1989; grad. fellow Roos' Found., Stockholm, 1949, 51, Govt. of Sweden, 1948, State Coun. for Technol. Rsch., Stockholm, 1949, Adelsköld fellow Royal Acad. Sci., 1951, 53, Univ. fellow Sweden-Am. Found., Stockholm, 1951. Mem. N.Y. Acad. Scis., Am. Chem. Soc., Swedish Soc. Chem. Engrs., Swedish Assn. Grad. Engrs., Internat. Union Pure and Applied Chemistry (affiliate), Am. Soc. Swedish Engrs. (life, sec. 1965-68, pres. 1968-72, John Ericsson Gold medal 1984), John Ericsson Soc., Wis. Alumni Assn. (life), KTH Alumni, Swedish-Am. C.of C., Swedish Colonial Soc. (hon. gov. Ad Vitam 1982, gov. 1977-82, 86-89), Am. Scandinavian Soc., Vasa Order Am., Svensk I Världen (life), Schlaraffia, Swedish Ski Club (pres. 1972-74), Phi Lambda Upsilon, Sigma Xi. Lutheran. Avocations: skiing, music, photography, historical research and writing. Home and Office: 38 Mareu Dr Watchung NJ 07060-5025

TOROK, MARGARET LOUISE, insurance company executive; b. Detroit, June 22, 1922; d. Perl Edward Ensor and Mary (Seggie) Armstrong; m. Leslie A. Torok, Aug. 14, 1952; 1 child, Margaret Mary Ryan. Lic. Ins. Agy. Ins. agy. Grendel-Wittbold Ins., Southgate, Mich., 1961-68, corp. officer, 1968-72; pres. of corp. Grendel-Wittbold Ins., Southgate, 1972—; bd. dirs. Ind. Ins. Agts. of Mich., Lansing, 1984-92, Ind. Ins. Agts. of Wayne County, Dearborn, 1979—, pres. 1978. Bd. dirs. So. Wayne County C. of C., Taylor, 1975, 1st vice chair, 1995; bd. dirs. City of Southgate Tax Increment Finance Authority Dist. and Econ. Devel. Commn.; leadership chmn. YMCA, Wyandotte, 1980—, Downriver Cmty. Alliance; lay chmn. Cath. Svc. Appeal for Archdiocese of Detroit, 1989; co-chair fundraiser Sacred Heart Ch.; mem. bd. MESC Employers Com., 1991—; mem. com., bd. New Workforce Devel. Com. (gov. appt., charter mem.). Recipient Capital award Ind. Ins. Agents of Mich., 1988, Amb. award, 1994, Woman of Yr. AAUW, 1994, Salute to Excellence award Downriver Coun. of Arts, 1993-94, Chmn. of Yr. award MESC Job Svc. Employers Com., 1991, Robert Stewart award Wyandotte Svc. Club Coun., 1994. Mem. Wyandotte Yacht Club, Soroptimist Club of Wyandotte Southgate Taylor (pres. 1984-86, Advancing Status Women award 1988, Soroptimist of Yr. award 1993-94). Roman Catholic. Office: Grendel Wittbold Agy Inc 12850 Eureka Rd Southgate MI 48195-1344

TORQUATO, SALVATORE, civil engineering educator; b. Falerna, Calabria, Italy, Feb. 10, 1954; came to U.S., 1955; s. Vincent and Palma (Vaccaro) T.; m. Kim Tracey Hoberock, Nov. 8, 1975; 1 child, Michelle. BSME, Syracuse U., 1975; MSME, SUNY, Stony Brook, 1977, PhD in Mech. Engring., 1980. Rsch. engr. Grumman Aerospace Corp., Bethpage, N.Y., 1975-78; rsch. asst. dept. mech. engring. SUNY, Stony Brook, 1978-80; asst. prof. dept. mech. engring. GM Inst., Flint, Mich., 1981-82; from asst. to assoc. prof. depts. mech., aerospace & chem. engring. N.C. State U., Raleigh, 1982-90, prof. depts. mech., aerospace & chem. engring., 1991-92; prof. Civil Engring. Princeton (N.J.) U., 1992—; vis. prof. Courant Inst. Math. Scis., N.Y.C., 1990-91; cons. Eastman Kodak, Rochester, N.Y., 1989—. Contbr. articles to profl. jours. Grumman Masters fellow, 1975-77; grantee NSF, 1982—, U.S. Dept. Energy, 1986—; recipient Engring. Rsch. Achievement award Alcoa Co., 1987, Disting. Engring. Rsch. award, 1989, Gustus L. Larson Meml. award, 1994. Fellow ASME; mem. Am. Inst. Chem. Engrs., Am. Phys. Soc., Soc. Engring. Sci., Soc. for Indsl. and Applied Math. Avocations: racquetball, reading. Office: Princeton U Princeton Materials Inst Depts Civ Eng & Oper Rsch Princeton NJ 08544

TORRANCE, ELLIS PAUL, psychologist, educator; b. Milledgeville, Ga., Oct. 8, 1915; s. Ellis Watson and Jimmie Pearl (Ennis) T.; m. Jessie Pansy Nigh, Nov. 25, 1959 (dec. Nov. 1988). B.A., Mercer U., 1940; M.A., U. Minn., 1944; Ph.D., U. Mich., 1951. Tchr. Midway Vocational High Sch., Milledgeville, 1936-37; tchr., counselor Ga. Mil. Coll., 1937-40, prin., 1941-44; counselor student counseling bur. U. Minn., 1945; counselor counseling bur. Kans. State Coll., 1946-48, dir., 1949-51; dir. survival research field unit Stead AFB, Nev., 1951-57; dir. Bur. Ednl. Research, 1958-64; prof. ednl. psychology U. Minn., 1958-66; chmn., prof. dept. ednl. psychology U. Ga., 1966-78, Alumni Found. disting. prof., 1974-85; Alumni Found. disting. prof. emeritus, 1985—; advisor Torrance Ctr. for Creative Studies, U. Ga. Author: Torrance Tests of Creative Thinking, Thinking Creatively in Action and Movement, Style of Learning and Thinking, and Sounds and Images; contbr. articles to jours., mags., books. Trustee Creative Edn. Found.; founder Nat. Future Problem Solving Problem and Bowl, Nat. Scenario Writing Contest. Fellow Am. Psychol. Assn.; mem. Am. Ednl. Rsch. Assn., Am Soc. Group Psychotherapy and Psychodrama, Creative Edn. Leadership Coun., Nat. Assn. Gifted Children, Am. Creativity Assn., Phi Delta Kappa. Baptist. Home: 183 Cherokee Ave Athens GA 30606-4305

TORRAS, JOSEPH HILL, pulp and paper company executive; b. Americus, Ga., Nov. 14, 1924; s. Fernando Joseph and Nell Wilson (Hill) T.; m. Mary Ravenel Robertson, Sept. 20, 1952; children: Mary Martin, Fernanda Maria, Joseph Hill. S.B., Yale U., 1948; M.B.A., Harvard U., 1950. Asst. to fin. v.p. Seatrian Lines, Inc., 1950-51; with St. Regis Paper Co., 1951-60, sales mgr. printing papers div., 1956-60; exec. v.p. Brown Co., Boston, 1960-64; pres., chmn. bd. Premoid Corp., West Springfield, Mass., 1964-87; pres. Precon, Inc., Ludlow, 1967-87, Lincoln Pulp & Paper Co., Lincoln, Maine, 1968—, Astro Tissue Co., Battleboro, Vt., 1968-72; chmn. bd. Whitman Products, Ltd., West Warwick, R.I., 1976-89; pres., chief exec. officer Preco Corp., Amherst, Mass., 1976—; chmn. Lincoln (Maine) Pulp and Paper Co., 1989—; bd. dirs. Bay Banks, Inc., Boston; chmn. Ea. Fine Paper Inc., Brewer, Maine; adv. dir. Liberty Mut. Ins. Mem. Mass. Gov.'s Bus. Adv. Coun., 1985-88, devel. bd. Yale U., 1989—; bd. govs. Mass. Gen. Hosp.; bd. dirs. Mass. Taxpayers Assn., 1976-86, U. Maine Pulp and Paper Found., 1981—; trustee Hist. Deerfield, 1990—, Piedmont Coll., Ga., 1991—. Lt. (j.g.), aviator USNR, 1943-46. Mem. Tissue Paper Mfrs. Assn. (dir. 1963-64), Am. Pulp and Paper Mill Supts. Assn., Salesman's Assn. Paper Industry, NAM (dir. 1981-85), Colony Club. Independent. Office: Preco Corp 100 University Dr Amherst MA 01002-2232

TORRE, CAROLYN TALLEY, pediatric nurse practitioner; b. Spokane, Wash., Mar. 31, 1946; d. James P. and Jean H. (Talley) Green; m. Louis P. Torre, Aug. 29, 1970; children: Erin, Colin. BSN summa cum laude, U. Wash., 1969; MA, NYU, 1975; PNP cert., Rutgers Coll. Nursing, 1975. Cert. pediatric nurse practitioner. Lectr. in phys. assessment Rutgers Coll. Nursing, Newark, asst. prof., 1975-78, 80-85; PNP Rutgers Student Health Svcs., New Brunswick, N.J., 1977-88, Rsch. Found. for Mental Hygiene, N.Y.C.; PNP, project dir. child health and progress study U. Pa., Phila., 1988-95; PNP Princeton Child Health Conf., 1992—; with Princeton U. Student Health Svcs., 1996—. Contbr. articles to profl. jours. Recipient Adminstrv. award Rutgers Student Health Svcs., 1986; grantee Rutgers Student Health Svcs., 1985, NAACOG/AWHONN, 1992. Mem. AWHONN, ANA, N.J. State Nurses Assn. (Appreciation award for svc. 1992), Nat. Assn. Pediat. Nurse Assocs. and Practitioners, Am. Coll. Nurse Practitioners, Phi Beta Kappa.

TORRE, DOUGLAS PAUL, dermatologist; b. New Orleans, Feb. 6, 1919; s. Peter and Jeanne Renee (Mottram) T.; m. Sylvia Elizabeth Stenmark, Apr. 22, 1954 (div. May 1977); children—Eric, Jeanne; m. Catherine Babcock, May 28, 1977. BS, Tulane U., 1940, MD, 1943; postgrad., Cornell U., 1946-50. Intern Phila. Gen. Hosp., 1943-44; fellow Cornell U. Med. Coll.-N.Y. Hosp., 1946-50; practice medicine, specializing in dermatology N.Y.C., 1946—; instr. Cornell U. Med. Coll., N.Y.C., 1950-55; from asst. to assoc. prof. Cornell U. Med. Coll., 1956-65, clin. prof. dermatology, 1966-95, clin. prof. emeritus dermatology, 1995—; attending physician N.Y. Hosp.; cons. Meml. Hosp. Contbr. articles to profl. jours. and chpts. to textbooks. Served to lt., M.C. USNR, 1944-46, PTO. Mem. AMA, Am. Acad. Dermatology, Soc. Investigative Dermatology, Atlantic Dermatology Assn (pres. 1969), N.Y. Dermatology Assn. (pres. 1969, 79), Am. Soc. Dermatol. Surgery (v.p. 1979, pres. 1980-81), Am. Coll. Cryosurgery (pres. 1982-83), N.Y. Acad. Medicine, Phi Beta Kappa, Delta Tau Delta. Club: University (N.Y.C.). Home: 122 Rowayton Ave Norwalk CT 06853-1409 Office: 320 E 65th St New York NY 10021-6743

TORREANO, JOHN FRANCIS, painter, sculptor; b. Flint, Mich., Aug. 17, 1941. BFA, Cranbrook Acad. Art, 1963; MFA, Ohio State U., 1967. Prin. works exhibited in numerous one-man shows including Scott Hanson Gallery, N.Y.C., 1989, Shea & Beker Gallery, N.Y.C., 1989, 90, Susanne Hilberry Gallery, Birmingham, Mich., 1990, Shea & Beker Gallery, 1990, Dart Gallerym Chgo., 1990, Hypo Bank, N.Y., 1992, Post Minimalism 1979-1990 An Extended Harvest Genouese Gallery, Boston, 1990, Painting Between the Paradigms Part IV: A Category of Objects as Yet Unnamed, Penine Hart Gallery, N.Y., With the Grain: Contemporary Panel Painting, Whitney Mus. Am. Art, Stamford, Conn., 1990; exhibited in group shows including Margo Leavin Gallery, L.A., 1990, Laforet Mus., Havajuku, Japan, Pleasure, Hallwalls, Buffalo, N.Y., 1991, many others. Grantee Nat. Endowment for Arts, 1978-79, fellow, 1982-83, 89-90, John Simon Guggenheim Meml. Found., 1991, N.Y. Found. Arts, 1991. Office: 103 Franklin St New York NY 10013-2911

TORREGROSSA, JOSEPH ANTHONY, lawyer; b. Bklyn., Sept. 23, 1944; s. Joseph and Marie (Faraone) T.; m. Ann S. Gormally, July 11, 1970; children—Brennan, Maresa. A.B., Villanova U., 1966, J.D., 1969. Bar: N.Y. 1970, Pa. 1971, U.S. Dist. Ct. (ea. dist.) Pa. 1971, U.S. Ct. Appeals (3d cir.) 1973, U.S. Supreme Ct. 1975. Law Clk. to judge U.S. Dist. Ct. (ea. dist.) Pa., 1969-71; assoc. Morgan, Lewis & Bockius, Phila., 1971-77; ptnr. Morgan, Lewis & Bockius, Phila., 1977—; lectr. in field. Mem. Phila. Bar Assn., Pa. Bar Assn., ABA. Office: Morgan Lewis & Bockius 2000 One Logan Sq Philadelphia PA 19103

TORRENCE, GWEN, Olympic athlete. 2d place NCAA 100, 1985; 7th place USA/Mobil 100, 1985; 5th place USA/Mobil 200, 1985; champion NCAA 100, 1987, NCAA 200, 1987; 5th place U.S. World Championships 200; winner of sprints World Univ. Games; winner Pan Am. Games 200, 1987; 3rd place in both 100 and 200 Olympic Trials, 1988; 2d place USA/Mobil 100, 1991; winner USA/Mobil 200, 1991; gold medalist 200 Meter, Barcelona, Spain, 1992; winner Mobil Grand Prix 100 meters, 1993. Achievements include 5th place world ranking at 200 meters Track & Field News, 1987, ranked number 3 sprinter in the world, 1991, ranked 3rd place in world in the 100, 1993, ranked 2d place in world in the 200, 1993, ranked 4th place in world in the 400, 1993. *

TORRENCE, ROSETTA LENA, educational consultant; b. New Rochelle, N.Y., Nov. 3, 1948; d. Stanley Livinston and Evelyn Ann Phillips; m. John Wesley Torrence, Sept. 14, 1981. BA in Edn. cum laude, Bklyn. Coll., 1974. Instr. Dept. Def.-Kadena Air Base, Okinawa, Japan, 1984-86, Halifax C.C., Weldon, N.C., 1986-88; dir. The Ednl. Workshop, Richmond, Va., 1989—; ednl. cons. Philip Morris, USA (EDTC), Richmond, 1989—, Juvenile and Domestic Rels. Dist. Ct., Richmond, 1993—, Jack & Jill, Inc., Richmond, 1994—; dir. Sound-It-Out The Easy Way, Inc., 1995—. Author: (booklet, cassette) Sound-It-Out The Easy Way Phonics Program, 1989, (workbook, cassette) Sound-It-Out The Easy Way Pre-Phonics Workbook, 1993, Sound-It-Out The Easy Way: The Syllables Workbook, 1993, Sound-It-Out The Easy Way Phonics Readers, 1993. Spokesperson Concerned Business & Residents of South Side Community Group, Richmond, 1993. Baptist. Avocations: reading, writing, teaching, swimming, yoga. Home and Office: The Ednl Workshop 1818 Stockton St Richmond VA 23224-3762

TORRENZANO, RICHARD, public affairs executive. BS, N.Y. Inst. Tech., 1972, LittD (hon.), 1990; postgrad., Standford U. With N.Y. Stock Exch., N.Y.C., 1981-91, sr. v.p. and chief spokesman, mem. mgmt. com., 1991-93; sr. v.p. and dir. corp. affairs SmithKline Beecham, London; CEO, The Torrenzano Group Ltd., N.Y.C., 1994—; coord. Pres. Reagan's Bd. Advisors on Pvt. Sector Initiatives, Washington, 1986-89; mem. pvt. sector adv. com. USIA, Washington, 1983-92; coord. program USSR-N.Y. Stock Exch., Moscow, 1990; lectr. in field. Contbr. articles to profl. jours. Trustee N.Y. Inst. Tech., 1985—. Recipient Silver Anvil award Pub. Rels. Soc. Am. Mem. Royal Soc. Medicine (London), Internat. Pub. Rels. Assn., Nat. Press Club (Washington), N.Y. Press Club, Knights of Malta. Office: The Torrenzano Group Ltd Ste 1400 551 Fifth Ave New York NY 10176

TORRES, CYNTHIA ANN, banker; b. Glendale, Calif., Sept. 24, 1958; d. Adolph and Ruth Ann (Smith) T.; m. Michael Victor Gisser, Mar. 11, 1989; children: Spencer Williams Gisser, David Westfall Torres Gisser. AB, Harvard U., 1980, MBA, 1984. Research assoc. Bain & Co., Boston, 1980-82; assoc. Goldman, Sachs & Co., N.Y.C., 1984-88, v.p., 1988; v.p. First Interstate Bancorp, L.A., 1989-92; dir. Fidelity Investments Mgmt. (H.K.) Ltd., Hong Kong, 1993—. Mem. judiciary rev. bd. Bus. Sch. Harvard U., Boston, 1983-84. Rockefeller Found. scholar, 1976; Harvard U. Ctr. for Internat. Affairs fellow, 1979-80; recipient Leadership award Johnson and Johnson, 1980; by Council for Opportunity in Grad. Mgmt. Edn. fellow, 1982-84. Mem. Acad. Polit. Sci., Asia Soc., Fin. Women's Assn. Hong Kong (bd. dirs.), Harvard Club of Hong Kong. Avocation: sportswriting. Office: Fidelity Investments Mgmt, 16/F Citibank Tower 3 Garden Rd, Hong Kong Hong Kong

TORRES, EDWIN, state judge, writer; b. N.Y., 1931; s. Edelmiro and Ramona T.; m. Vickie; 4 children. Degree, City Coll., N.Y., Bklyn. Law Sch. Asst. dist. atty. complaints bur., then homicide bur. Manhattan Dist. Atty's. Office, 1958-61; appt. judge Criminal Ct. Bench, N.Y. State Supreme Ct., 1980—. Author: Carlito's Way, 1975, After Hours, 1979, Q & A, 1977. Office: NY Supreme Ct 12th Judicial Dist 100 Centre St New York NY 10013-4308

TORRES, ERNEST C., federal judge; b. 1941. AB, Dartmouth Coll., 1963; JD, Duke U., 1968. Assoc. Hinckley, Allen, Salisbury & Parsons, 1968-74; ptnr. Saunders & Torres, 1974-80; assoc. justice R.I. Superior Ct., 1980-85; asst. v.p. Aetna Life and Casualty, 1985-86; ptnr. Tillinghast, Collins & Graham, 1986-87; judge U.S. Dist. Ct. R.I., Providence, 1988—; pres. East Greenwich (R.I.) Town Coun., 1972-74; state rep. R.I. Ho. of Reps., 1975-80, dep. minority leader, 1977-80. Recipient Disting. Svc. award Jaycees, 1974; named Man of Yr., Prince Henry Soc. R.I., 1988, Prince Henry Soc. Mass., 1995; Alfred P. Sloan scholar Dartmouth Coll. Mem. ABA, ATLA, R.I. Bar Assn., Jaycees (Dist. Svc. award 1974), Prince Henry Soc. of R.I., Prince Henry Soc. of Mass. Office: US Dist Ct 1 Exch Ter 216 Federal St Providence RI 02903

TORRES, ESTEBAN EDWARD, congressman, business executive; b. Miami, Ariz., Jan. 27, 1930; s. Esteban Torres and Rena Baron (Gomez) T.; m. Arcy Sanchez, Jan. 22, 1955; children: Carmen D'Arcy, Rena Denise, Camille Bianca, Selina Andre, Esteban Adrian. Student, East Los Angeles Coll., 1960, Calif. State U., Los Angeles, 1963, U. Md., 1965, Am. U., 1966; PhD (hon.), Nat. U., 1987. Chief steward United Auto Workers, local 230, 1954-63, dir. polit. com., 1963; organizer, internat. rep. United Auto Workers (local 230), Washington, 1964; asst. dir. Internat. Affairs Dept., 1975-77; dir. Inter-Am. Bureau for Latin Am., Caribbean, 1965-67; exec. dir. E. Los Angeles Community Union (TELACU), 1967-74; U.S. ambassador to UNESCO, Paris, 1977-79; chmn. Geneva Grp., 1977-78; chmn. U.S. del. Gen. Conf., 1978; spl. asst. to pres. U.S., dir. White House Office Hispanic Affairs, 1979-81; mem. 98th-103rd Congresses from 34th Dist. Calif., 1983—, mem. appropriations com., subcom. fgn. ops., subcom. military constrn.; campaign coordinator Jerry Brown for Gov., 1974; Hispanic coordinator Los Angeles County campaign Jimmy Carter for Pres., 1976; mem. Sec. of State Adv. Group, 1979-81; v.p. Nat. Congress Community Econ. Devel., 1973-74; pres. Congress Mex.-Am. Unity, 1970-71, Los Angeles Plaza de la Raza Cultural Center, 1974; dir. Nat. Com. on Citizens Broadcasting, 1977; cons. U.S. Congress office of tech. assessment, 1976-77; del to U.S. Congress European Parliament meetings, 1984—; ofcl. congl. observer Geneva Arms Control Talks; chmn. Congl. Hispanic Caucus, 1987; speaker Wrights Del. to USSR, 1987; Dem. dep. Whip, 1990. Contbr. numerous articles to profl. jours. Co-chmn. Nat. Hispanic Dems., 1988—; chmn. Japan-Hispanic Inst. Inc.; bd. visitors Sch. Architecture U. Calif. at Los Angeles, 1971-73; bd. dirs. Los Angeles County Econ. Devel. Com., 1972-75, Internat. Devel. Conf., 1976-78. Served in AUS, 1949-53, ETO. Recipient various awards for public service. Mem. Americans for Dem. Action (exec. bd. 1975-77), VFW Post 6315, Pico Rivera, Calif., Am. Legion Post 0272, Montebello, Calif. Office: House of Representatives Rayburn Bldg Rm 2368 Washington DC 20515-0005*

TORRES, RALPH CHON, minister; b. San José, Calif., Oct. 18, 1948; s. Chon Poncé and Dora (Grijalva) T.; m. Pamela Ellen Hansen, Mar. 6, 1971; children: Chon, Brita, Samuel, Sarah. BTh, L.I.F.E. Bible Coll., L.A., 1970. Ordained to ministry Internat. Ch. of the Foursquare Gospel, 1981. Missionary asst. Internat. Ch. of Foursquare Gospel, Mexicali, Mex., 1970; youth pastor Internat. Ch. of Foursquare Gospel, Redondo Beach, Calif., 1971-72, Pueblo, Colo., 1972-74; sr. pastor Internat. Ch. of Foursquare Gospel, Pasadena, Calif., 1984—; youth pastor Ch. on the Way, Van Nuys, Calif., 1975-84; asst., dir. children's camps, Jr. and Sr. High camps for So. Calif. Dist. Foursquare Chs., 1978—; tchr. L.I.F.E. Bible Coll., L.A., 1979-86; bd. dirs. Holy Ghost Repair Svc., Hollywood, Calif., Centrum of Hollywood, Christians in Govt., L.A., Camp Cedar Crest, Running Springs, Calif.; bd. dirs., speaker Mainstream Inc., Tacoma, 1978-83. Composer: Kids of the Kingdom, 1976. Mem. Prop. 98 Sch. Report Card Com., Pasadena, 1989-90; adv. com. Marshall Fundamental Sch., Pasadena, 1989-90, Pasadena Unified Sch. Dist., 1990—. Recipient commendation for svc. Mayor of Pasadena, 1990. Office: Pasadena Foursquare Ch 174 Harkness Ave Pasadena CA 91106-2007

TORRES-AYBAR, FRANCISCO GUALBERTO, medical educator; b. San Juan, P.R., July 12, 1934; s. Francisco and Maria (Aybar) Torres; m. Elga Arroyo; children: Elga, JoAnn Marie. BS, U. P.R., 1956; MD, U. Barcelona, Spain, 1963. Diplomate Am. Bd. Pediatrics. Chief pediatric cardiology Ponce (P.R.) Dist. Hosp., 1970-91, chmn. dept. pediatrics, 1971-91, med. dir., 1980, prog. dir. pediatric tng. prog., 1970-91; prof., chmn. dept. pediatrics Cath. Univ. Sch. of Medicine, Ponce, 1978-80; chmn., dept. pediatrics Damas Hosp., Ponce, 1985—; prof., chmn. dept. pediatrics Ponce Sch. of Medicine, 1980—. Mem. editl. bd. Sci.-Ciencia jour., ponce, 1975-95; contbr. articles to profl. jours. Fellow Am. Acad. Pediatrics, Am. Coll. Physicians, Am. Coll. Cardiology, Am. Coll. Internat. Physicians, British Royal Soc. Health, InterAm. Coll. Physicians and Surgeons; mem. AAUP, Phi Delta Kappa. Republican. Roman Catholic. Home: A26 Jacaranda Ponce PR 00731 Office: 13 Calle Mayor Ponce PR 00731-5025

TORRES-GIL, FERNANDO M., federal official; b. Salinas, Calif., June 24, 1948. BA in Polit. Sci., San Jose State U., 1970; MSW, Brandeis U., 1972, PhD, 1976. Spl. asst. to sec. Dept. Health, Edn. and Welfare, Washington, 1978-79; spl. asst. to sec. Dept. Health and Human Svcs., Washington, 1979-80, asst. sec. for aging, 1993—; prof. gerontology and pub. adminstrn. U. So. Calif., 1981-91, assoc. dir. Nat. Resource Ctr. on Minority Aging Populations, 1988-92, prof. social welfare, 1991-93; staff dir. Select Com. on Aging, U.S. Ho. of Reps., Washington, 1985-87. Contbr. articles to profl. jours. White House fellow, 1978-79. Mem. Am. Soc. Aging (pres. 1989-92). Office: Dept Health and Human Svcs 200 Independence Ave SW Washington DC 20201-0001

TORRES-LABAWLD, JOSE DIMAS, institutional research director, service company executive, educator; b. Luquillo, P.R., Mar. 25, 1932; s. Antonio Torres Herrera and Maria S. (Labawld) Torres; m. Patricia Ann

Zaccaria, Apr. 18, 1959; children: Peter, Michelle, Mary E., Patrick, David, Gwendolyn, Christopher. BA cum laude, Inter-Am. U., San German, P.R., 1957; MPA, Syracuse U., 1959; postgrad., U. Notre Dame, 1961-62; PhD, Ohio State U., 1973; postgrad., Dartmouth Coll., 1995. Mgmt. ofcl., adminstr. U.S. state dept. Point IV program Office of Pers., Office of Gov., San Juan, P.R., 1959-61; lectr. Ind. U., South Bend, 1963-64; lectr. NDEA Knox Coll., Galesburg, Ill., 1965; instr. Ohio U., Athens, 1965-69; rsch. assoc. Mershon Ctr. Ohio State U., Columbus, 1970-71; dir. dept. gen. studies Hocking Coll., Nelsonville, Ohio, 1973-75, dir. instl. rsch., 1975—; pres. IMSA, Inc., Athens, 1981—; bus. cons. IMSA, Inc., 1981—. Coord. youth for understanding internat. exchg. program U.S. State Dept., 1966-70; cand. Athens County Cen. Com. Dem., 1974; chmn. fin. com. Ohio U. Christ the King Parish, 1992-96; dir. Transnational Bus. Program, U.S., Mexico, Can., 1995—. Cpl. U.S. Army, Korea, 1951-53. Commonwealth of P.R. fellow Syracuse U., 1959; Hocking Coll. scholar, 1990. Mem. Am. Arbitration Assn., Assn. for Instnl. Rsch., U.S. Hispanic C. of C., World Trade Club, Columbus Area C. of C., VFW, Lions (pres. Athens chpt. 1984), Am. Legion, Phi Alpha Theta. Roman Catholic. Avocations: tennis, golf, piano, painting, chess. Home: 15 Grand Park Blvd Athens OH 45701-1438

TORRES MEDINA, EMILIO, oncologist, consultant; b. Mexico, Aug. 8, 1934; s. Manuel Torres and Juana Medina; m. Luisa Torres Dec. 6, 1966; children: Patricia, Ana Luisa, Veronica, Jesus Manuel. MD, U. Mex., 1958-64. Cert. Consejo Mexicano de Radioterapia and Consejo Mexicano de Oncologia. Internist Hosp. of Nutrition, Mex., 1965-67; oncologist Hosp. of Oncology, Mex., 1967-70; chief dept. radiation Clin. of Parque, Chih, Mexico, 1970-80, chief of med. edn., 1974-78; chief dept. radiation Centro Oncologico del Norte, Juarez, Mexico, 1981-95; chief. of med. edn. I.S.S.S.T.E., Juarez, Mexico, 1984-85; oncologist I.S.S.S.T.E., Juarez, 1981-85; oncology prof. Uach Y Uacj, Juarez, Mexico, 1981-92; mem. med. coun. Pensiones Civiles del Edo., Juarez, Chih., 1985-90; med. dir. Pensionesl Civiles del Edo., Juarez, Chih., 1982-88, Electronic Diagnosis of Juarez, 1981-92; oncologist cons. Gen. Hosp. of Juarez City, 1988-95. Author: Policitemia on Rats by Hemolizates, 1965, Alkil beta-d Glicosias on Human Lymphs, 1970. Advisor Juarez Cancer Soc., 1986-95. Mem. ASTRO, ASCO, Soc. Mex. Est. Oncol. Capitulo Chihuahua (pres. 1990-92), Soc. Medicina Interna Cd. Juarez (pres. 1992). Office: Centro Oncologico del Norte, Plutarco Elias Calles 1235, 32350 Juarez Mexico

TORRES OLIVER, JUAN FREMIOT, bishop; b. San German, P.R., Oct. 28, 1925; s. Luis N. and Amalia (Oliver) Torres. B.A., St. John's Seminary, 1944-50; M.A. Musicology, Catholic U., 1952; LL.B., U. of P.R., 1959; LL.M., St. John's U., 1964, LL.D., 1995. Ordained priest Roman Cath. Ch., 1950. Instr. Catholic U., Ponce, P.R., 1952-56; vice-chancellor Diocesan Curia, 1961-64; prof., assoc. dean Catholic U. Sch. of Law, Ponce, P.R., 1961-64; bishop of Ponce P.R., 1964—; grand chancellor Pontifical Cath. U. P.R., Ponce, 1964—; pres. P.R. Episcopal Conf. 1982-94; Grand Prior, P.R. lieutenancy of Equestrian Order of the Holy Sepulchre of Jerusalem, 1984—. Decorated Cross of Order Juan Pablo Duarte, Dominican Republic. mem. Academia de Artes y Ciencias; Phi Alpha Delta. Office: Obispado de Ponce Apartado 205 Sta 6 Ponce PR 00732*

TORREY, BARBARA BOYLE, research council administrator; b. Pensacola, Fla., Nov. 27, 1941; d. Peter F. and Elsie (Hansen) Boyle; m. E. Fuller Torrey, Mar. 23, 1968; children: Michael, Martha. BA, Stanford U., 1963, MS, 1970. Vol. Peace Corps, Tanzania, 1963-65; fiscal economist Office Mgmt. and Budget, Washington, 1970-80; dept. asst. sec. HHS, Washington, 1980-81; dir. Ctr. for Internat. Rsch., Census Bur., Washington, 1984-92; pres. Population Reference Bur., Washington, 1992-93; exec. dir. Commn. on Behavioral and Social Scis. and Edn., NRC, NAS, Washington, 1993—; bd. dirs. Luxembourg Income Study, 1984—. Co-editor: The Vulnerable, 1987, Population and Land Use, 1992; contbr. articles to profl. jours. Mem. Population Assn. Am. (bd. dirs. 1993—). Office: NRC 2101 Constitution Ave NW Washington DC 20418-0007

TORREY, CLAUDIA OLIVIA, lawyer; b. Nashville, June 10, 1958; d. Claude Adolphus and Rubye Mayette (Prigmore) T. BA in Econ., Syracuse U., 1980; JD, N.Y. Law Sch., 1985. Bar: N.Y. State 1988. Legal intern Costello, Cooney & Fearon, Syracuse, N.Y., 1979; legal clk. First Am. Corp., Nashville, 1981; legal asst. James I. Meyerson, N.Y.C., 1982-85; jud. law clk. N.Y. State Supreme Ct., N.Y.C., 1985; interim project supr., legal asst. CUNY Ctrl. Office, 1985-86; legal analyst Rosenman & Colin Law Firm, N.Y.C., 1986-87; asst. counsel N.Y. State Legis., Albany, 1988-90; atty., cons. pvt. practice, Nashville, Cookeville, Tenn., 1991—; bd. mem. Children's Corner Day Care Ctr., Albany, N.Y., 1989-90. Ch. rep. FOCUS exec. coun. Westminster Presbyn. Ch., Albany, 1990; v.p. dormitory coun., flr. rep. Syracuse U., 1977-79. Mem. ABA (young lawyers divsn. liaison to ABA forum on health law 1994-96), N.Y. State Bar Assn., Alpha Kappa Alpha (Syracuse U. chpt. treas. 1977-78, pres. 1979). Avocations: singing, piano, harp, tennis, art. Home and Office: PO Box 150234 Nashville TN 37215-0234

TORREY, DAVID LEONARD, investment banker; b. Ottawa, Ont., Can., Oct. 6, 1931; s. Arthur Starratt and Josephine Edith (Leonard) T.; divorced; children: Heather Torrey Murphy, John Winthrop, Diana Bruce, Arthur Bruce, David Molson. BA in Econs., St. Lawrence U., 1953; diploma, Grad. Sch. Bus., U. Western Ont., 1954. With Pitfield Mackay Ross Ltd., Toronto, Ont., Can., 1954-84; v.p. Pitfield Mackay Ross Ltd., 1963-73, sr. v.p., 1973-80, vice chmn., 1980-82, pres., 1982-84, also bd. dirs.; vice chmn. Dominion Securities, Inc., 1984-88, RBC Dominion Securities, Inc., 1988-91; chmn. Montreal Stock Exch., 1971-73, Phillips Cables Ltd., 1991-96; bd. dirs. Total Petroleum N.Am. Ltd., Wajax Ltd., Can. Stubbins Engring. and Mfg. Co. Ltd., Provigo Inc., Cuddy Internat., Inc.; mem. adv. bd. I.C.I. Can., Inc.; mem. coun. Montreal Bd. Trade, 1971-72. Chmn. Montreal Downtown YMCA, 1972-74; trustee St. Lawrence U.; bd. dirs. Montreal Gen. Hosp. Found. Mem. Investment Bankers Assn. (gov. 1971-72), Securities Industries Assn. (bd. govs. 1972-73), Multiple Sclerosis Can. (past pres., bd. dirs.), Beta Theta Pi. Clubs: Montreal Badminton and Squash, Royal Montreal Golf, Mt. Royal (Montreal); Toronto. Home: 389 Carlyle Ave, Montreal, PQ Canada H3R 1T3 Office: PO Box 6001, 1 Pl Ville Marie Ste 7S, Montreal, PQ Canada H3C 3A9

TORREY, RICHARD FRANK, utility executive; b. Saratoga Springs, N.Y., Dec. 31, 1926; s. Reginald Frank and Marian (Currey) T.; m. Betty Louise Stetson, July 2, 1949; children: Patricia Ann Torrey Simpkins, Carol Louise Torrey Kress, Barbara Jean Torrey Friedman. BA cum laude, Syracuse U., 1951. News reporter Syracuse (N.Y.) Post Standard, 1947-51; pub. rels. account exec. Syracuse, 1951-53; home sec. 35th Congl. Dist., Syracuse, 1952-53; exec. sec. to mayor Syracuse, 1954-58; dir. area devel. Niagara Mohawk Power Corp., Syracuse, 1958-66; comml. v.p. Niagara Mohawk Power Corp., Buffalo, 1966-68; adminstrv. v.p. Niagara Mohawk Power Corp., 1968-72, v.p., gen. mgr., 1972-76; sr. v.p. Niagara Mohawk Power Corp., Syracuse, 1976-88, ret., 1988; pres. Can. Niagara Power Co. Ltd., Niagara Falls, Ont., Can., 1968-88, dir., 1968-89; pres., dir. Caragh Investments Ltd., 1981-85; pres. Opinac Investments Ltd., Toronto, 1982-88, bd. dirs., 1982-89; pres. Opinac Energy Ltd., Calgary, Alta., 1983-88, bd. dirs., 1983-89. Pres. Syracuse USO, 1959-61, mem. nat. coun., 1959-62, 68-74; co-chmn. Ctrl. N.Y. Interim Coun. Regional Planning, 1965-66; gen. chmn. Dunbar-Huntington Bldg. Fund, Syracuse, 1963; state campaign chmn. N.Y. Job Devel. Authority, 1961; gen. chmn. United Way of Buffalo and Erie County, 1971; mem. Syracuse U. Corp. Adv. Coun., 1972-76; turstee Elmcrest Children's Ctr., 1962-63, Camp Good Will, Syracuse, 1964-66, Syracuse Area Coun. Chs., 1959-64; bd. dirs. United Way Buffalo and Erie County, 1967-76, Greater Buffalo Devel. Found., Kenmore Mercy Hosp., 1970-76, Crouse Irving Meml. Hosp. Found., 1978-87, Nat. Kidney Found., 1987-89, Venice (Fla.) Hosp. Found., 1992—, vice chmn. 1995—; bd. dirs. Plantation Cmty. Found., Venice, 1989, pres., 1990-93, pres. emeritus, 1993—; mem. bd. adv. Sisters of St. Joseph, 1967-76; elder Trinity Presbyn. Ch., Venice, 1992-94; assoc. mem. Dewitt Cmty. Ch. Served with Air Corps U.S. Army, 1944-47. Recipient Syracuse Young Man of Yr. award, 1962; Outstanding Citizen award Buffalo Evening News, 1973. Mem. Empire State (v.p., bd. dirs. 1963-80), Buffalo Area (v.p. 1968-72, bd. dirs. 1968-76, pres. 1972-73, chmn. bd. 1973-74, Man of Yr. 1974) C. of C., Associated Industries of N.Y. (bd. dirs. 1978-80), Bus. Coun. N.Y. (bd. dirs. 1980-82), Mfrs. Assn. Cen. N.Y. (bd. dirs. 1977-88), Augusta Villa Assn. (bd. dirs. 1989-92), Buffalo Club (past 2d v.p., dir.), Syracuse Century Club (gov. 1980-83), Onondaga Golf Club, Plantation Golf and Country Club, Automobile Club Western N.Y.(bd. dirs. 1971-73, pres. 1973), N.Y.S. Automobile Assn. (dir. 1975-76). Home and Office: 705 Carnoustie Ter Venice FL 34293-4349

TORREZ, NAOMI ELIZABETH, copyright review editor, librarian; b. Scranton, Pa., July 3, 1939; d. Sterling E. and Naomi (Reynolds) Hess; m. Lupe F. Torrez, Dec. 23, 1961; children: Sterling Edward, Stanley Marshall. BA, U. Ariz., 1961; MA, U. Calif., Berkeley, 1964, MLS, 1970; DRE, Golden State Sch. Theology, Oakland, Calif., 1988; cert. in travel industry, Vista C.C., 1993. Libr. asst. Oakland Pub. Libr., 1966-67, U. Calif. Libr., Berkeley, 1967-70; tutor-couns. Sonoma State Hosp., Eldridge, Calif., 1973-77, libr. tech. asst., 1977-79; health scis. libr. Kaiser Hosp., Vallejo, Calif., 1979-87; copyright rev. editor Kaiser Dept. Med. Editing, Oakland, 1987—; former instr. Bay Cities Bible Inst., Oakland, Golden State Sch. Theology, Oakland; instr. Calif. Theol. Inst., 1996—; participant Statewide Latino Congress, 1994. Author: Not in My Pew, 1990, GSST Research Manual, 1990; contbr. to Co-op Low Cost Cookbook, 1965. Active Albany 75th Anniversary Com., 1983, Women's Health Initiative, 1995—; officer Ariz. Fedn. of the Blind, Calif. Coun. of the Blind, 1959-66. Woodrow Wilson fellow, 1961; winner Nat. Spelling Bee, 1953; Nat. Merit scholar, 1957-61. Mem. Kaiser Permanente Latino Assn., Kaiser Affirmative Action Com., Kaiser Health Edn. Com., K.P. Regional Librs. Group (chair 1988), Phi Beta Kappa, Phi Kappa Phi. Baptist. Office: Kaiser Dept Med Editing 1800 Harrison St Fl 16 Oakland CA 94612-3429

TORRIANI-GORINI, ANNAMARIA, microbiologist; b. Milan, Italy, Dec. 19, 1918; came to U.S., 1955, naturalized, 1962; d. Carlo and Ada (Forti) Torriani; m. Luigi Gorini (dec. Aug. 1976); 1 child, Daniel. PhD, U. Milan, Italy, 1942. Research assoc. Istituto Ronzoni Chimica-Biochimica, Milan, 1942-48; charge de recherche Institut Pasteur, Paris, 1948-56; research assoc. NYU, 1956-58, Harvard U., Cambridge, Mass., 1958-60; research assoc. MIT, Cambridge, 1960-71, assoc. prof. microbiology, 1971-76, prof., 1976—; prof. emerita, 1989. Recipient NIH Career award, 1962-72; Fulbright fellow, 1956-58. Mem. Am. Soc. Microbiology, Am. Soc. Genetics, Am. Soc. Biochemistry, Soc. Française de Microbiologie (hon.). Home: 115 Longwood Ave Brookline MA 02146-6625 Office: MIT Dept of Biology 68-371 Cambridge MA 02139

TORRICELLI, ROBERT G., congressman; b. Paterson, N.J., Aug. 26, 1951. BA, Rutgers U., 1974, JD, 1977; MPA, Harvard U., 1980. Bar: N.J. 1978. Dep. legis. counsel Office Gov. N.J., 1975-77; counsel to Vice Pres. Mondale, Washington, 1978-81; pvt. practice Washington, 1981-82; mem. 98th-104th Congresses from 9th Dist. N.J., Washington, 1983—; ranking minority mem. internat. rels. subcom. on the western hemisphere, mem. select com. intelligence. Mem. bd. govs. Rutgers U., 1977-83. Mem. ABA, N.J. Bar Assn. Democrat. Office: US Ho of Reps 1026 Longworth Washington DC 20515-3009

TORRUELLA, JUAN R., federal judge; b. 1933. BS in Bus. and Fin., U. Pa., 1954; LLB, Boston U., 1957; LLM, U. Va., 1984; MPA, U. P.R., 1984; LLD, St. John's U., 1995. Judge U.S. Dist. Ct. P.R., San Juan, 1974-82, chief judge, 1982-84; judge U.S. Ct. Appeals (1st cir.), San Juan, 1984-94, chief judge, 1994—; former mem. jud. conf. com. on the Adminstrn. of the Fed. Magistrate Sys; mem. jud. conf. com. on Internat. Jud. Reform. Mem. ABA, Fed. Bar Assn., Assn. Labor Rels. Practitioners P.R. and V.I., D.C. Bar Assn., P.R. Bar Assn. Office: US Ct Appeals PO Box 3671 San Juan PR 00904 also: US Ct Appeals (1st cir) Boston MA 02109*

TORSHEN, JEROME HAROLD, lawyer; b. Chgo., Nov. 27, 1929; s. Jack and Lillian (Futterman) T.; m. Kay Pomerance, June 19, 1966; children: Jonathan, Jacqueline. BS, Northwestern U., 1951; JD, Harvard U., 1955. Bar: Ill. 1955, U.S. Dist. Ct. (no. dist.) Ill. 1955, U.S. Ct. Appeals (7th cir.) 1958, (8th cir.) 1961, (9th and D.C. cirs.) 1972, U.S. Supreme Ct. 1972. Assoc. Clausen, Hirsh & Miller, Chgo., 1955-62; pres. Jerome H. Torshen, Ltd., Chgo., 1963-87, Torshen, Schoenfield & Spreyer Ltd., Chgo., 1987-93, Torshen, Spreyer & Garmisa, Ltd., Chgo., 1994—; spl. asst. atty. gen. Ill., 1965-70; assoc. counsel Spl. Commn. Ill. Supreme Ct., 1969; counsel Ill. Legis. Redistricting Commn., 1971-72; spl. state's atty. Cook County, Ill., 1979-81, 83-86; spl. counsel Met. San. Dist. Greater Chgo., 1977-81, 84-88. Contbr. articles to profl. jours. Counsel Cook County Dem. Cen. Com., Chgo., 1982-87; bd. dirs. Jewish Family and Community Svc., Parents' Coun. Washington U., St. Louis, 1988-92; mem. collectors' group Mus. Contemporary Art; sustaining fellow Art Int. Chgo. Served with U.S. Army, 1951-52. Recipient Torch of Learning award Am. Friends of Hebrew U., 1985, Outstanding Civic Duty award, Union League Club of Chgo., 1967. Fellow Am. Coll. Trial Lawyers; mem. ABA, Chgo. Bar Assn. (commn. on jud. evaluation 1986-90), Bar Assn. 7th Cir. Appellate Lawyers Assn. (founder, pres. 1976-77), Decalogue Soc., Standard Club, Sixty Club of Chgo. Office: 105 W Adams St Ste 3200 Chicago IL 60603-6201

TORTO, RAYMOND GERALD, economist; b. Lynn, Mass., Dec. 16, 1941; s. Edward Dante and Lucy (Petrucci) T.; m. Linn Torto; children: Stephanie, Pamela, Nathaniel. AB, Boston Coll., 1963, MA, 1967, PhD, 1969. Prof. econs. U. Mass., Boston, 1970-96; spl. asst. to mayor for tax policy City of Boston, 1976-80, commr. assessing, 1980-82; pres. Torto Wheaton and Assocs., Boston, 1982-86; prin. CB Comml./Torto Wheaton Rsch., Boston, 1987—; sr. fellow., dir. McCormack Inst. U. Mass., Boston, 1984-95; bd. dirs. Boston Mcpl. Rsch. Bur., Assoc. Ind. of Mass. Author: The Rich Get Richer and the Rest Pay Taxes, 1974, Money and Financial Institutions, 1981, Property Tax Reevaluation, 1983. Chmn. fiscal issues study group Commonwealth of Mass., 1988-90. Mem. Am. Soc. Real Estate Councilors, Am. Real Estate Soc., Lambda Alpha Soc., Corinthian Yacht Club. Avocations: sailing, squash, gardening. Home: 38 Foster St Marblehead MA 01945-3645 Office: CB Comml/Torto Wheaton Rsch 200 High St Boston MA 02110-3036

TORTORICI, PETER FRANK, television executive; b. N.Y.C., June 19, 1949; s. Tony F. and May (Augello); m. Susan Kay Dupar, June 21, 1986; children: Caitlin, Dayna, Thomas. BA, Ohio State U., 1971; JD, St. John's U., 1974. Sr. counsel grievance com. 2nd & 11th Jud. Dists., Bklyn., 1974-80; prodn. asst. ABC Sports, N.Y.C., 1980; dir. program acquisitions CBS Sports, N.Y.C., 1981-83, v.p. program planning and devel., 1983-86, v.p. programming, 1986-87; sr. v.p. program planning CBS Entertainment, L.A., 1987-91; exec. v.p. CBS Entertainment, 1991-94, pres., 1994-95; exec. producer, sr. exec. The Carsey-Werner Co., 1996—. Writer (TV show) Tour de France, 1987 (Emmy nomination). Mem. Hollywood Radio TV Soc. (bd. dirs. 1990-92, pres. 1994). Avocations: golf, skiing, music, N.Y. sports teams. Home: 1148 Napoli Dr Pacific Palisades CA 90272-3112 Office: Carsey-Werner Co Bldg 3 4024 Radford Ave Studio City CA 91604

TORY, JOHN A., newspaper publishing executive. Dep. chmn. The Thomson Co., Toronto, Ont., Can. Office: Thomson Newspaper Inc 3150 Des Plaines Ave Des Plaines IL 60018-4205 also: The Thomson Corporation, Toronto Dominion Ctr Box 24, Toronto, ON Canada M5K 1A1

TOSCANO, JAMES VINCENT, medical institute administration; b. Passaic, N.J., Aug. 8, 1937; s. William V. and Mary A. (DeNigris) T.; m. Sharon Lee Bowers; children: Shawn, Lauren, David Brendan, Dania. A.B. summa cum laude, Rutgers U., 1959; M.A., Yale U., 1960. Lectr. Wharton Sch., U. Pa., 1961-64; chief opinion analyst Pa. Opinion Poll, 1962-64; mng. dir. World Press Inst., St. Paul, 1964-68; exec. dir. World Press Inst., 1968-72; dir. devel. Macalester Coll., St. Paul, 1972-74; v.p. resource devel. and public affairs Mpls. Soc. Fine Arts, 1974-79; pres. Minn. Mus. Art, 1979-81; exec. v.p. Park Nicollet Med. Found., 1981-95; corp. sec. Park Nicollet Med. Ctr., 1983-86; sr. v.p. Am. Med. Ctrs., Inc., 1985-87; exec. v.p. Inst. for Rsch. and Edn. Health Sys. Minn., Mpls., 1996—; also bd. dirs. Inst. for Rsch. and Edn., Health Sys. Minn.; adj. prof. sch. of mgmt. U. St. Thomas, 1989—. Author: The Chief Elected Official in the Penjerdel Region, 1964; co-author, co-editor: The Integration of Political Communities, 1964. Bd. dirs., faculty mem. World Press Ins., 1972—; bd. dirs., chmn. Southside Newspaper Mpls., 1975-79; chmn. com. to improve student behavior St. Paul Pub. Schs., 1977-79; bd. dirs. Planned Parenthood St. Paul, 1965-72; emeritus dir. Help Enable Alcoholics Receive Treatment; mem. St. Paul Heritage Preservation Commn., 1979-82, vice chmn., 1981; mem. Citizens Adv. Com. on Cable Comm.; bd. dirs. Citizens League, 1980, Park Nicollet Med. Found., 1981-95, African-Am. Culture Ctr., 1979-82, Minn. Composers Forum, 1981-85, St. Paul Chamber Orch., 1976-80, 83-89, United Theol. Sem., 1985-88; bd. dirs. affiliates, mem. exec. com. Med. Alley Assn., 1986—; mem. task force on tech. assessment Med. Alley, 1992-93; mem. health affairs adv. com. Acad. Health Ctr. U. Minn., 1988-95; bd. dirs. Mother Cabrini House, 1985-92, Minn. Civil Justice Coalition, 1987-91, also chmn.; chmn. Gov.'s Task Force on Health Care Promotion, 1985-86, mem. Gov.'s Com. Promotion Health Care Resources, 1986-87; chmn. bd. Minn. Fin. Counseling Svcs., Inc., 1990-93; mem. task force cost effectiveness Med. Alley, 1994-95. Mem. Minn. Newspaper Found. (bd. dirs. 1987-92), Minn. Coun. Nonprofits (bd. dirs. 1989-95, bd. mem. Plymouth Music series 1993-96, alt. Minn. Healthcare Commn., 1993-95, mem. Minn. Healthcare Commn., 1995—, chair task force on med. edn. and rsch. costs 1994-96; chair com. on med. rsch. and edn. costs, 1996—, liaison health tech. adv. com. 1993), Skylight Club, Informal Club. Address: 1982 Summit Ave Saint Paul MN 55105-1460 Office: Inst for Rsch and Edn Health Sys Minn 3800 Park Nicollet Blvd Minneapolis MN 55416

TOSCANO, PETER RALPH, economics educator; b. N.Y.C., Mar. 20, 1920; s. Luigi and Maria (Cosentino) T.; m. Margo Frances Ledee, Aug. 5, 1950; children: Louis, Ellyn. MA, U. Chgo., 1950, PhD, 1954. Instr. U. Conn., Storrs, 1951-52, Lehigh U., Bethlehem, Pa., 1953-55; asst. prof. Rockford (Ill.) Coll., 1955-57, U. Wash., Seattle, 1957-58, Rensselaer Poly. Inst., Troy, N.Y., 1958-60, Lake Forest (Ill.) Coll., 1960-62, U. Wis., Milw., 1962-65; assoc. prof. So. Ill. U., Macomb, 1965-68; prof. econs. Loyola U., Chgo., 1968-84, prof. emeritus, 1984—. Translator On Money (Della Moneta), 1977. Sgt. U.S. Army, 1942-46, PTO. Mem. Am. Econ. Assn., Econ. History Assn., History of Econs. Soc. Democrat. Roman Catholic. Avocations: U.S. foreign policy, foreign affairs. Home: 600 N Mcclurg Ct Apt 1911 A Chicago IL 60611-3025

TOSCANO, SAMUEL, JR., wholesale distribution executive; b. 1948. With Manhattan Drug Co. and Hillside (N.J.) Drug Co., 1967-72; with Neuman Distributors, Inc., Ridgefield, N.J., 1972—, mgr. sales, dir. sales, v.p. sales, CEO, 1979—. Office: 175 Railroad Ave Ridgefield NJ 07657

TOSKES, PHILLIP PAUL, physician, educator, clinical researcher; b. Balt., Md., Jan. 4, 1940; s. John F. and Mary R. (Vonelli) T.; m. Patricia A. Sponsel, June 3, 1961; children: Tammy Lynn Price, Tracey Lynn, Steven D. BA, Johns Hopkins U., 1961; MD, U. Md., 1965. Diplomate Am. Bd. Internal Medicine (bd. dirs.), Am. Bd. Gastroenterology. Intern, resident U. Md. Hosp., Balt., 1965-68; fellow in gastroenterology Hosp. U. Pa., Phila., 1968-70; asst. prof. medicine U. Fla., Gainesville, 1973-75, assoc. prof. medicine, 1975-78, prof. medicine, 1978—, dir. divsn. gastro, hepatology, 1978—; chief gastro sect. Gainesville VA Med. Ctr., 1973-92; mem. adv. bd. Lederle Labs, Pearl River, N.Y., 1986—, Solvay Labs, Marietta, Ga., 1990—, Martek Inc., Columbia, Md., 1991—; chmn. Nat. Digestive Disease Adv. Bd., Washington, 1992-94. Author chpts. to books. Maj. U.S. Army, 1970-73. Recipient Disting. Achievement award Can. Gastroenterol. Assn., 1982. Fellow ACP (Meade Johnson scholar 1966-68); mem. Am. Soc. Clin. Investigation, Am. Fedn. Clin. Rsch., Am. Gastroenterol. Assn. Avocations: travel, swimming, boating. Home: 202 NW 114th Way Gainesville FL 32607-1122 Office: U Fla Box 100214 1600 SW Archer Rd Gainesville FL 32610

TOSTESON, DANIEL CHARLES, physiologist, medical school dean; b. Milw., Feb. 5, 1925; s. Alexis H. and Dilys (Bodycombe) T.; m. Penelope Kinsley, Dec. 17, 1949 (div. 1969); children: Carrie Marias, Heather Tosteson, Tor, Zoe Losada; m. Magdalena Tieffenberg, July 8, 1969; children: Joshua, Ingrid. Student, Harvard U., 1942-44, MD, 1949; DSc (hon.), U. Copenhagen, 1979; Dr. hon. causa, U. Liege, 1983; DSc (hon.), Med. Coll. Wis., 1984, NYU, 1992; DHL (hon.), Johns Hopkins U., 1993; Dr. honoris causa, Cath. U. Louvain, 1996, Duke U., 1996, Emory U., 1996. Fellow physiology Harvard Med. Sch., 1947-48; intern, then asst. resident medicine Presbyn. Hosp., N.Y.C., 1949-51; research fellow medicine Brookhaven Nat. Lab., 1951-53; lab. kidney and electrolyte metabolism Nat. Heart Inst., 1953-55, 57; research fellow biol. isotope research lab. Nat. Heart Inst., Copenhagen, 1955-56; research fellow Physiol. Lab., Cambridge, Eng., 1956-57; assoc. prof. physiology Washington U. Sch. Medicine, St. Louis, 1958-61; prof., chmn. dept. physiology and pharmacology Duke U. Sch. Medicine, 1961-75, James B. Duke Distinguished prof., 1971-75; dean div. biol. scis., dean Pritzker Sch. Medicine U. Chgo., Lowell T. Coggleshall prof. med. scis., v.p. for Med. Center, 1975-77; dean and Caroline Shields Walker prof. physiology Harvard Med. Sch., Boston, 1977—; pres. Med. Center Harvard Med. Sch., 1977; mem. molecular biology panel NSF, 1959-62; cons. sci. rev. com. NIH, 1964-67, nat. adv. gen. med. scis. coun., 1982-86; mem. U.S. Office Tech. Assessment, 1976; ethics adv. bd. HEW, 1977-80; nat. adv. gen. med. scis. coun. NIH, 1982—; mem. governing bd. NRC, 1977; mem. sci. com. Found. pour l'Etude du Systeme Nerveux Central et Peripherique, 1982—; nat. adv. com. biomed. scis. PEW Scholars Program, 1984-87. Mem. Inst. Medicine NAS (coun. 1975-78, adv. bd. PEW scholars program 1984-85), AAAS, Am. Physiol. Soc. (council 1967-75, pres. 1973-74), Soc. Gen. Physiologists (pres. 1968-69), Biophys. Soc. (council 1970-73), Assn. Am. Med. Colls. (chmn. coun. acad. socs. 1969-70, chmn. assembly 1973-74, chmn. physician supply task force 1988—, Abraham Flexner award 1991), Assn. Am. Physicians, Red Cell Club, Soc. Health and Human Values, Danish Royal Soc. (fellow), Alpha Omega Alpha. Spl. research cellular transport processes, red cell membranes. Office: Harvard Med Sch 25 Shattuck St Boston MA 02115-6027

TOTA, FRANK PETER, educational administrator; b. Hoboken, N.J., Dec. 28, 1938; s. Frank and Jeanette (Grimaldi) T.; m. Eileen Virginia Dolan, Aug. 3, 1968; children: Frank, Christopher. BA, N.J. State Coll., 1960; MA, Columbia U., 1962; EdD, Columbia U., 1986. Tchr., coordinator pub. schs., Englewood, N.J., 1960-65; head lang. arts dept. pub. schs., Bedford, N.Y., 1965-70; dir. secondary and elem. edn. pub. schs., New Rochelle, N.Y., 1970-73; supt. for instrn., pub. schs., Rochester, N.Y., 1973-81; supt. schs., Roanoke, Va., 1981—; adj. prof. VPI, SU, guest lectr. Cambridge U. (Eng.), 1983. Bd. dirs. Roanoke Symphony Orch., United Way Roanoke Valley, Arts Council Roanoke Valley. Recipient Nat. Conf. Christians and Jews award, 1985, Leadership for Learning awd., Am. Assn. of School Administrators, 1993. Mem. Am. Assn. Sch. Adminstrs., Nat. Sch. Bds. Assn., Va. Urban Schs. Assn. (pres. 1991, exec. bd. mid-urban supts. northeast and mid-Atlantic region), Assn. for Supervision and Curriculum Devel., Nat. Forensic League, Roanoke C. of C., Phi Delta Kappa, Kappa Delta Pi, Delta Upsilon. Roman Catholic. Lodge: Rotary (chmn. youth com. Roanoke 1983-84). Home: 14 Crosshill Rd Hartsdale NY 10530-3014 Office: Roanoke City Pub Schs PO Box 13145 40 Douglas Ave NW Roanoke VA 24012-4699 also: Roanoke CSD PO Box 13145 Roanoke VA 24031-3145

TOTENBERG, NINA, journalist; b. N.Y.C., Jan. 14, 1944; d. Roman and Melanie (Shroder) T.; m. Floyd Haskell, Feb. 3, 1979. Student, Boston U.; LLD (hon.), Haverford Coll., Chatham Coll., Gonzaga U., Northeastern U., St. Mary's, SUNY; LHD, Lebanon Valley Coll., Westfield State Coll. Reporter Boston Record Am., 1965, Peabody Times, 1967, Nat. Observer, 1968-71, Newtimes, 1973, Nat. Pub. Radio, Washington, 1974—, Inside Washington, 1992—; reporter Nightline ABC, 1993—. contbr. articles to N.Y. Times Mag., Harvard Law Rev., Christian Sci. Monitor, N.Y. Mag., Parade. Recipient Alfred I. Dupont award Columbia U., 1988, George Foster Peabook award, 1991, George Polk award, 1991, Joan Barne award, 1991, Silver Gavel award ABA, 1991, Woman of Courage award Women in Film, 1991, Athena award, 1994. Mem. Sigma Delta Chi. Office: Nightline 1717 Desales St NW Washington DC 20036-4401

TOTENBERG, ROMAN, violinist, music educator; b. Lodz, Poland, Jan. 1, 1911; came to U.S., 1935; s. Adam and Stanislava (Vinaver) T.; m. Melanie Shroder, July 30, 1941; children: Nina, Jill, Amy. Grad., Chopin Sch. Music, Warsaw, Poland, 1928, Hochschule für Music, Berlin, 1931, Paris Inst. Instrumental Music, 1933. Head violin dept. Peabody Conservatory, Balt., 1943-44, Mannes Coll. Music, N.Y.C., 1951-57; chmn. string dept. Boston U., 1962-78, prof., 1978—, co-chmn. string dept.; Prin. soloist, dir. chamber music Interstate Broadcasting Co., N.Y.C., 1937-42; prin. soloist, head string dept. Music Acad. West, Santa Barbara, Calif., summers 1948-51; with Music Assocs., Aspen, Colo., summers 1951-62; dir. Totenberg Instrumental Ensemble, 1953-60; George Miller vis. prof. U. Ill., 1960-61; head string dept. Boston U. Tanglewood Inst., summers 1966-74; performer, tchr. Kneisel Hall Festival, Blue Hill, Maine, 1975—, acting dir., 1984-87; dir. Longy Sch. Music, Cambridge, Mass., 1978-85; judge Paganini, Wieniawski, Carnegie Hall competitions, Kreisler and Japan Internat. Competition. Performer worldwide concerts and tours; rec. artist with Vanguard, DGG, Mus. Heritage Soc. records, Titanic compact disk, Omega Records, VGR Records. Chmn. Music Project, Newton Tricentenary, 1988. Recipient Mendelssohn prize, 1932, Wieniawski Soc. medal, 1970, Eugene Ysaye Soc. medal, 1975, Polish Nat. medal of Cultural Achievement, 1988. Mem. Am. String Tchrs. Assn. (named Artist-Tchr. of yr. 1983), AAUP, Music Tchrs. Nat. Assn., Phi Kappa Lambda. Avocations: photography, tennis. Office: Boston U 855 Commonwealth Ave Boston MA 02215-1303 *Devotion to human values expressed through music as well as through daily activities in public life.*

TOTH, JAMES JOSEPH, power systems engineer; b. Perth Amboy, N.J.; s. James J. and Lucille J. Toth; m. Cynthia L. Camfield; children: Jennifer, James. BE with honor, Stevens Inst. Tech., Hoboken, N.J., 1976; ME, Rensselaer Poly. Inst., Troy, N.Y., 1977; student, Ga. Inst. Tech., 1977-82. Registered profl. engr., Ga., N.C., S.C., Va. Project engr. Westinghouse Elec. Corp., Pitts., 1982-84; power sys. engr. Westinghouse Elec. Corp., Atlanta, 1984-86; powersys. engr. GE Co., Charlotte, N.C., 1986-95; sr. power sys. engr. ABB Svc., Inc., Charlotte, 1995—. Contbr. articles to jour. IEEE. Sec. Newell Sch. Adv. Team, Charlotte, 1994; corr. sec. Reid Park PTA, Charlotte, 1994-95, pres., 1995-96. Faculty fellow Rensselaer Poly. Inst., 1976-77. Mem. IEEE, NSPE, GE Elfun Soc. Achievements include research in harmonic analysis program, optimal var compensation allocation program. Home: 7026 Leaves Ln Charlotte NC 28213-5746 Office: ABB Svc Inc 10820 H Independence Pt Pky Matthews NC 28105

TOTH, ROBERT CHARLES, polling consultant, journalist; b. Blakely, Pa., Dec. 24, 1928; s. John and Tillie (Szuch) T.; m. Paula Goldberg, Apr. 12, 1954; children: Jessica, Jennifer, John. B.S. in Chem. Engring., Washington U., St. Louis, 1952; M.S. in Journalism, Columbia U., 1955; postgrad., Harvard U., 1960-61. Started as engr. in Army Ordnance Dept., 1952-54; reporter Providence Jour., 1955-57; sci. reporter N.Y. Herald Tribune, 1957-62, N.Y. Times, 1962-63; mem. staff Los Angeles Times, 1963-93; bur. chief Los Angeles Times, London, 1965-70; diplomatic corr. Los Angeles Times, 1970-71, White House corr., 1972-74; bur. chief Los Angeles Times, Moscow, 1974-77; nat. security corr. Washington bur. Los Angeles Times, 1977-93; cons. opinion poll in U.S. and abroad by Times Mirror Ctr. (now Pew Rsch. Ctr.) for People and Press, 1990, sr. assoc., 1993—. Served with USMC, 1946-48. Recipient Overseas Press Club award, 1977, Sigma Delta Chi award, 1977, George Polk award in Journalism for fgn. reporting L.I. U., 1978, Columbia U. Alumni award, 1978, Wienthal award Fgn. Service Inst., Georgetown U., 1986, Edwin N. Hood award Nat. Press Club, 1986; Pulitzer Travelling scholar, 1955; Nieman fellow Harvard U., 1960-61. Mem. Coun. on Fgn. Rels. Home: 21 Primrose St Chevy Chase MD 20815-4228 Office: Pew Rsch Ctr 1875 I St NW Washington DC 20006-5409

TOTLIS, GUST JOHN, title insurance company executive; b. Highwood, Ill., May 15, 1939; s. John Chris and Agape (Galelis) T.; m. Joyce Elaine Edholm, June 5, 1960; children: Kenneth Chris, Charles Gust. BA, Lake Forest Coll., 1962; MBA, U. Chgo., 1964. Fin. planning mgr. Gen. Foods Corp., Battle Creek, Mich., 1964-68; fin. analyst Irving Trust Co., N.Y.C., 1968-69, asst. sec., 1969-71, asst. v.p., 1971-72, v.p., 1972-75; corp. contr. Irving Bank Corp., N.Y.C., 1975-82; exec. v.p., CFO Fidelity Union Bancorp, Newark, 1982-85, Star Banc Corp (formerly First Nat. Cin. Corp.), Cin., 1985-93; sr. v.p., CFO Chgo. Title and Trust Co., 1993—; bd. dirs. Ticor Title Ins. Co., Security Union Title Ins. Co. Adv. bd. dirs., treas. Salvation Army, Cin., 1987-93; bd. dirs., pres. Cin. Chamber Orch., 1988-93; pres. May Festival Assn., 1988-93; v.p. Spl. Olympics, 1990-93; vice chmn. United Way, 1991-94; bd. trustees Cin. Inst. Fine Arts, 1991-93. Mem. Fin. Execs. Inst., Univ. club, Kenwood Country Club, Univ. Club Chgo. Presbyterian. Home: 111 E Bellevue Pl Chicago IL 60611-1115

TOTMAN, CONRAD DAVIS, history educator; b. Conway, Mass., Jan. 5, 1934; s. Raymond Smith and Mildred Edna (Kingsbury) T.; m. Michiko Ikegami, Jan. 21, 1958; children: Kathleen Junko, Christopher Ken. B.A., U. Mass., 1958; M.A., Harvard U., 1960, Ph.D., 1964. Asst. prof. U. Calif., Santa Barbara, 1964-66; asst. prof. Northwestern U., Evanston, Ill., 1966-68; assoc. prof. Northwestern U., 1968-72, prof. Japanese history, 1972-84, chmn. dept. history, 1977-80; prof. Japanese history Yale U., New Haven, 1984—; chmn. Council on East Asian Studies, Yale U., 1985-88, acting chmn. Dept. History, 1989-90; prof. Kyoto Ctr. for Japanese Studies, 1992-93. Author: Politics in the Tokugawa Bakufu 1600-1843, 1967, paperback edit., 1988, The Collapse of the Tokugawa Bakufu 1862-1868, 1979 (John K. Fairbank prize Am. Hist. Assn. 1981), Japan Before Perry: A Short History, 1981, Tokugawa Ieyasu: Shogun, 1983, The Origins of Japan's Modern Forests, 1985, The Green Archipelago: Forestry in Preindustrial Japan, 1989, Early Modern Japan, 1993, paperback edit., 1995, The Lumber Industry in Early Modern Japan, 1995. Served with U.S. Army, 1953-56. Recipient Carstensen prize for essay Agrl. History Soc., 1982; Woodrow Wilson nat. fellow, 1958-59; Social Sci. Research Council-Am. Council Learned Socs. fellow, 1968-69; NEH sr. fellow, 1972-73; Fulbright-Hays research grantee, 1968-69; Japan Found. grantee, 1981-82. Mem. Assn. Asian Studies (N.E. Asia coun. 1977-80, chmn. 1978-80, exec. com. 1978-80, pres. New Eng. Conf. 1985-86, coun. of confs. 1992-95), Forest History Soc. Office: Yale U Dept History New Haven CT 06520

TOTO, MARY, elementary and secondary education educator; b. Phila., Mar. 12, 1922; d. John and Piacentina (Rossi) T. BS in Edn., Temple U., 1943; MS in Edn., U. Pa., 1951; MS in Libr. Sci., Villanova U., 1963. Cert. elem. and secondary tchr., Pa. Tchr. Phila. Sch. Dist., 1943-81; MS in LS. Mem. Dem. Nat. Com., 1995, 96. Mem. NEA, AAUW, LWV, Phila. Fedn. Tchrs., Columbus Forum Lodge, Nationalities Svc. Ctr. of Phila., Italian Folk Art Fedn. of Am., Nat. Assn. Retired Tchrs., Pa. Assn. Sch. Retirees, Pa. Edn. Assn., Womens Internat. League Peace and Freedom, United We Stand Am. Roman Catholic. Avocations: needlework, interior decorating, folk dancing, travel. Home: 1210 W Ritner St Philadelphia PA 19148-3524

TOTTEN, GEORGE OAKLEY, III, political science educator; b. Washington, July 21, 1922; s. George Oakley Totten Jr. and Vicken (von Post) Totten Barrois; m. Astrid Maria Anderson, June, 1948 (dec. Apr. 26, 1975); children: Vicken Yuriko, Linnea Catherine; m. Lilia Huiying Li, July 1, 1976; 1 child, Blanche Maluk Lemes. Cert., U. Mich., 1943; AB, Columbia U., 1946, AM, 1949; MA, Yale U., 1950, PhD, 1954; docentur i japanologi, U. Stockholm, 1977. Lectr. Columbia U., N.Y.C., 1954-55; asst. prof. MIT, Cambridge, 1958-59, Boston U., 1959-61; assoc. prof. U. R.I., Kingston, 1961-64; assoc. prof. polit. sci. U. So. Calif., L.A., 1965-68, prof., 1968-92, chmn. dept., 1980-86, prof. emeritus, 1992—; dir., founder Calif. Pvt. Univs. and Colls. Yr.-in-Japan program Weseda U., 1967-73; dir. East Asian Studies Ctr., 1974-77; 1st dir. USC-UCLA Joint East Asian Studies Ctr., 1976-77; sr. affiliated scholar Ctr. for Multiethnic and Transnat. Studies, 1993—; vis. prof. U. Stockholm, 1977-79, 1st dir. Ctr. Pacific Asia Studies, 1985-89, sr. counselor bd. dirs., 1989—. Author: Social Democratic Movement in Prewar Japan, 1966, chinese edit., 1987; co-author: Socialist Parties in Postwar Japan, 1966, Japan and the New Ocean Regime, 1984; author, editor: Helen Snow's Song of Ariran, 1973, Korean edit., 1991, Chinese edit., 1993; author, co-editor: Developing Nations: quest for a Model, 1970, Japanese edit., 1975, china's Economic Reform: Administering the Introduction of the Market Mechanism, 1992, Community in Crisis: Korean American. . ., 1994; co-translator: Chien Mu's Traditional Government in Imperial China, 1982; contbr. The Politics of Divided Nations, 1991, Chinese edit., 1995. Mem. U.S.-China People's Friendship Assn., Washington, 1974—; mem. Com. on U.S.-China Relations, N.Y.C., 1975—; chmn. L.A.-Pusan Sister City Assn., L.A., 1976-77; bd. dirs. L.A.-Guangzhou Sister City Assn., 1982—, Japan-Am. Soc. L.A., 1981—; mem. nat. adv. com. Japan Am. Student Conf., 1984—, Assn. of Korean Pol. Studies in N.Am., 1992—; coun. mem. China Soc. for People's Friendship Studies, Beijing, 1991—. 1st lt. AUS, 1942-46, PTO. Recipient Plaque for program on Korean studies Consulate Gen. of Republic of Korea, 1975, Disting. Emeritus award U. So. Calif., 1996; Social Sci. Rsch. Coun. fellow, 1952-53; Ford Found. grantee, 1955-58, NSF grantee, 1979-81, Korea Found. grantee, 1993, Rebuild L.A. grantee, 1993, Philippine Liberation medal, 1994. Mem. Assn. Asian Studies, Am. Polit. Sci. Assn., Asia Soc., Internat. Polit. Sci. Assn., Internat. Studies Assn., Japanese Polit. Sci. Assn., European Assn. Japanese Studies, U. So. Calif. Faculty Ctr., Phi Beta Delta (founding mem. Beta Kappa chpt. 1993—). Episcopalian. Home: 5129 Village Grn Los Angeles CA 90016-5205 Office: U So Calif Ctr Multiethic & Transnat Studies GFS 344 Los Angeles CA 90089-1694 *The two main driving forces in my life have been a desire for world peace and a fascination with Asia. I try to work for the reduction and eventual abolition of armaments and a world-wide decision making process. Within countries, especially my own, I try to promote democracy. I think it can be promoted in both capitalist and socialist nations, and can be compatible with modified communist ideology but not with fascism. Since childhood I have tried to work for friendship with Asian nations, especially China, Japan and Korea. My research has been on better understanding their politics, history and culture.*

TOTTEN, GLORIA JEAN (DOLLY TOTTEN), real estate executive, financial consultant; b. Port Huron, Mich., Sept. 23, 1943; d. Lewis Elmer and Inez Eugenia (Houston) King; m. Donald Ray Totten, Feb. 5, 1961 (div. Apr. 1981); children: D. Erik, Angela J. Totten Sales, Kymberly D. Totten DiVita. Student, Patricia Stevens Sch., Detroit, 1976-79, Gold Coast Sch., West Palm Beach, Fla., 1988; degree in mktg., St. Clair County Coll., Port Huron, Mich., 1979. Lic. real estate saleswoman, Fla., Mich. Demonstrator, saleswoman Hoover Co., 1969-75; instr., promoter Port Huron Sch. Bus., 1973-75; real estate borker Select Realty, Port Huron, 1979-81, Earn Keim Realty, Port Huron, 1981-83, Schweitzer's Better Homes and Gardens, Marysville, Mich., 1983-86, Coldwell Banker Property Concepts Corp., North Palm Beach, Fla., 1986-94; pres., broker, owner Dolly Totten Real Estate Inc., West Palm Beach, Fla., 1994—; model, instr. Patricia Stevens Modeling Sch., Troy, Mich., 1972-75; beauty cons. Mary Ky Cosmetics, 1982—. Grantee Mich. State U., 1972. Mem. Nat. Assn. Realtors, North Palm Beach Rd. Realtors, Million Dollar Club (Port Huron chpt.), Women's Coun. Realtors (co-founder Port Huron chpt.). Avocations: singing, acting, dancing, horticulture, crafts. Home and Office: 515 Evergreen Dr West Palm Beach FL 33403

TOTTEN, RANDOLPH FOWLER, lawyer; b. Washington, June 20, 1943; s. Arthur Irving and Margaret Holland (Ross) T.; m. Virginia Hunton, July 31, 1965; children—Louise, Fitz, Caroline. B.A., Yale U., 1965; LL.B., U. Va., 1968. Bar: Va. 1968. Law clk. to Justice Gordon, Va. Supreme Ct. Appeals, Richmond, 1968-69; from assoc. to mem. Hunton & Williams, Richmond., 1969—; dir. Mid-Atlantic Holdings, Inc. Chmn., Richmond Community High Sch., 1979-81; mem. exec. com. Christchurch Sch., 1982—; trustee Church Schs. Episcopal Diocese Va., 1974—, mem. standing com., 1984—. Mem. ABA, Va. Bar Assn. Clubs: Country of Va., Commonwealth. Bd. editors Va. Law Rev. Office: Hunton & Williams Riverfront Plz 951 E Byrd St Richmond VA 23219-4040*

TOTTER, JOHN RANDOLPH, biochemist; b. Saragossa, Tex., Jan. 7, 1914; s. Mathias and Agnes (Smith) T.; m. Elizabeth Margaret Van Sant, Aug. 6, 1938; children—Lorena E. Totter Barfuss, Anita Ruth, John Alan. B.A., U. Wyo., 1934, M.A., 1935; Ph.D., State U. Iowa, 1938. Instr. biochemistry U. W.Va., 1938-39; instr. biochemistry Ark. Sch. Medicine, 1939-42, asst. prof., 1942-45, asso. prof., 1945-52; chemist Oak Ridge Nat. Lab., 1952-56; biochemist AEC, Washington, 1956-58; vis. staff mem. U. of Republic, Montevideo, Uruguay, 1958-60; prof. biochemistry, chmn. div. biol. scis. U. Ga., 1960-62; asst. dir. for biol. scis. div. biology and medicine U.S. AEC, 1962-67, dir., 1967-72, asso. dir. for research, 1963-67; asso. dir. biomed. and environ. scis. Oak Ridge Nat. Lab., 1972-74; vis. staff mem. Inst. for Energy Analysis, Oak Ridge Asso. Univs., 1976-79, staff mem., 1979-87, ret., 1987; Participant nutritional survey, Alaska, 1947. Mem. Am. Chem Soc., Am. Soc. Biol. Chemists, Soc. for Exptl. Biology and Medicine (chmn. S.W. sect. 1950), Sigma Xi. Home: 360 Laboratory Rd Apt 517 Oak Ridge TN 37830-6851 Office: Med Scis Div Oak Ridge Assoc Univs Oak Ridge TN 37830

TOUBORG, MARGARET EARLEY BOWERS, non-profit executive; b. Rome, N.Y., Aug. 12, 1941; d. George Thomas and Margaret Earley (Brown) Bowers; m. Jens Touborg, Sept. 9, 1961 (div. 1985); children: Margaret Earley, Anne Touborg Zimmer, Sarah Touborg Moyers, Peter Nicolai. AB magna cum laude, Radcliffe Coll., 1965; MEd, Harvard U., 1984. Asst. to pres. Radcliffe Coll., Cambridge, Mass., 1984-86, exec. asst. to pres., 1986-87, dir. corp. and found. relations, 1988-89; pres. U. Cape Town Fund, Inc., N.Y.C., 1989—; sr. project dir. Open Soc. Scholars Fund, N.Y.C., 1989—; bd. dirs. Technoserve, Inc. Trustee The Trinity Sch., N.Y.C., 1994—, Bemis Lectr. Series, Lincoln, Mass., 1982-85; nat. cons. Schlesinger Libr. on History of Women in Am., 1995—; assoc. chmn. edn. div. United Way Mass., 1986; mem. South African adv. com. New Eng. Bd. Higher Edn., 1987—. Mem. Harvard Club N.Y.C., Phi Beta Kappa (chmn. com. hon. membership 1976-94). Episcopalian. Office: 441 Lexington Ave New York NY 10017-3910

TOUBY, RICHARD, lawyer; b. Sioux City, Iowa, Nov. 17, 1924; s. Louis and Rebecca (Keck) T.; m. Marion Lascher, Aug. 6, 1949; children: Jill Diane, Kim Paula. LLB, U. Miami, 1948; LLM, Duke U., 1950. Bar: Fla. 1948. Faculty U. Miami, Coral Gables, Fla., 1948-63; mem. 8th Air Force Meml. Assn., 1948—. 1st Lt. USAF, 1943-45. Office: 19 W Flagler St Ste 907 Miami FL 33130

TOUHILL, BLANCHE MARIE, university chancellor, history-education educator; b. St. Louis, Mo., July 1, 1931; d. Robert and Margaret (Walsh) Van Dillen; m. Joseph M. Touhill, Aug. 29, 1959. BA in History, St. Louis U., 1953, MA in Geography, 1954, PhD in History, 1962. Prof. history and edn. U. Mo., St. Louis, 1965-73, assoc. dean faculties, 1974-76, assoc. vice chancellor for acad. affairs, 1976-87, vice chancellor, 1987-90, chancellor, 1991—; bd. dirs. Boatmen's Nat. Bank of St. Louis, Barnes-Jewish Christian Health Hosps. Conglomerate. Author: William Smith O'Brien and His Irish Revolutionary Companions in Penal Exile, 1981, The Emerging University UM-St. Louis, 1963-83, 1985; editor: Readings in American History, 1970, Varieties of Ireland, 1976; adv. editor Victorian Periodicals Rev. Bd. dirs. Sister City Internat., Am. Coun. Fgn. Rels., St. Louis Forum, Network Bd., Mo. State Hist. Soc., 1989—, Mo. Bot. Garden, 1980, St. Louis Symphony Soc., 1993—. Named Outstanding Educator St. Louis chpt. Urban League, 1976; recipient Leadership award St. Louis YWCA, 1986. Mem. Nat. Assn. State Univs. and Land Grant Colls. (exec. com. 1988—), Am. Com. on Irish Studies (pres. 1991—), Phi Kappa Phi, Alpha Sigma Lambda. Office: U Missouri- St Louis Office of the Chancellor 8001 Natural Bridge Rd Saint Louis MO 63121-4499

TOULMIN, PRIESTLEY, geologist; b. Birmingham, Ala., June 5, 1930; s. Priestley and Catharine Augusta (Carey) T.; m. Martha Jane Slason, Aug. 30, 1952; children: Catharine Bosier (Mrs. Robert G. Gibson), Priestley Chewning. A.B., Harvard U., 1951, Ph.D., 1959; M.S., U. Colo., 1953. With U.S. Geol. Survey, Washington, 1953-56, 57-89; staff geologist for exptl. geology U.S. Geol. Survey, 1966, chief br. exptl. geochemistry, 1966-71, geologist geologic div., 1971-89; geologist geologic div. U.S. Geol. Survey, Reston, Va., 1974-89, ret., 1989; also leader inorganic chemistry team NASA (Viking Project); adj. prof. Columbia U., 1966; research asso. in geochemistry Calif. Inst. Tech., 1976-77; vis. lectr. Am. Geol. Inst.; dir. petrogenesis and mineral resources program NSF, 1985; bd. dirs., treas. 28th Internat. Geol. Congress, 1985-86;. Mng. sci. editor Geochemistry Internat., 1965-68; assoc. editor Am. Mineralogist, 1974-76; contbr. articles to profl. jours. Mem. advisory com. spl. edn., Alexandria, Va., 1977-80. Recipient Exceptional Service medal NASA, 1977; Meritorious Service award U.S. Dept. Interior, 1978. Fellow Geol. Soc. Am., Mineral Soc. Am. (bd. assoc. editors 1974-76), Soc. Econ. Geologists; mem. AAAS, Geol. Soc. Washington (2d v.p. 1977, councillor 1973-74, 90-91, 1st v.p. 1981, pres. 1982), Am. Geophys. Union, Soc. Mayflower Descs., S.R., SAR, Soc. Colonial Wars (D.C.), Aztec Club of 1847, Cosmos Club (pres. 1993-94), Sigma Xi, Sigma Gamma Epsilon. Home: 418 Summers Dr Alexandria VA 22301-2449 Office: PO Box 183 Alexandria VA 22313-0183

TOULMIN, STEPHEN EDELSTON, humanities educator; b. London, Mar. 25, 1922. BA in Math. and Physics, King's Coll., Cambridge, Eng., 1942; PhD, King's Coll., 1948; D Tech. (hon.), Royal Inst. Tech., Stockholm, 1991. Lectr. in philosophy of sci. Oxford U., Eng., 1949-55; prof., chmn. dept. of philosophy U. Leeds, Yorkshire, Eng., 1955-59; dir. unit for history of ideas Nuffield Found., London, 1960-65; prof. history of ideas and philosophy Brandeis U., Waltham, Mass., 1965-69; prof. philosophy Mich. State U., East Lansing, 1969-72; prof. humanities U. Calif., Santa Cruz, 1972-73; prof. com. social thought U. Chgo., 1973-86; Avalon prof. humanities Northwestern U., Evanston, Ill., 1986-92, Avalon prof. emeritus, 1992—; Henry R. Luce prof.Ctr. Multiethnic and Transnational Studies U. So. Calif., L.A., 1993—; vis. prof. U. Melbourne, Australia, 1954-55, Stanford U., 1959, Columbia U., N.Y.C., 1960, Hebrew U., Jerusalem, 1964, U. South Fla., 1972, Dartmouth Coll., 1979, SUNY, Plattsburgh, 1980, Colo. Coll., 1980, 82, MacMaster U., 1983, Harvard Project Physics Grad. Sch. Edn., Harvard U., 1965; counselor Smithsonian Inst., Washington, 1967-77; cons., staff mem. Nat. Commn. Protection Human Subjects Biomed. Behavioral Rsch., 1975-78; sr. vis. scholar, fellow Inst. Soc. Ethics and Life Scis., Hastings-on-Hudson, N.Y., 1981—; regent's lectr. U. Calif. Med. Sch., Davis, 1985; Mary Flexner lectr. Bryn Mawr Coll., 1977; Reyerson lectr. U. Chgo., 1979, John Nuveen lectr., 1980; Tate-Wilson lectr. So. Meth. U., 1980; Or Emet lectr. Osgoode Hall Law Sch., 1981; McDermott lectr. U. Dallas, 1985; lectr. Sigma Xi, 1965-66, Phi Beta Kappa, 1978-79, Phi Beta Kappa-AAAS, 1984; guest prof. social and human scis. Wolfgang Goethe Universitat, Frankfurt, Germany, 1987; vis. fellow Internationales Forschungszentrum Kulturwissenschaften (IFK), Vienna, Austria, 1995—. Author: The Place of Reason in Ethics, 1949, The Philosophy of Science: an Introduction, 1953, The Uses of Argument, 1958, Foresight and Understanding, 1961, Human Understanding, vol. 1, 1972, Knowing and Acting, 1976, The Return to Cosmology, 1982, Cosmopolis, 1989; (with J. Goodfield) The Fabric of the Heavens, 1961, The Architecture of Matter, 1963, The Discovery of Time, 1965; (with A. Janik) Wittgenstein's Vienna, 1973; (with R. Rieke and A. Janik) An Introduction to Reasoning, 1978; (with A. Jonsen) The Abuse of Casuistry, 1987; contbr. numerous sci. articles to profl. jours. Recipient Honor Cross 1st class (Austria), 1991; Getty Ctr. for History of Art and Humanities scholar, 1985-86, First Book of the Year prize Am. Soc. Social Philosophy, 1992; Ctr. for Psychosocial Studies fellow, 1974-76. Fellow Am. Acad. Arts and Scis. Office: U So Calif CMTS GFS 344 Los Angeles CA 90089-1694

TOULOUSE, ROBERT BARTELL, retired college administrator; b. Wellsville, Mo., May 8, 1918; s. Walter Eaton and Emma (Schmidt) T.; m. Virginia Lee Danford, Aug. 7, 1948; children—Samuel Phillip, Robert Bartell. Student, Central Coll., 1935-37; B.S., U. Mo., 1939, M.Ed., 1947, Ed.D., 1948. Tchr. sci. and social studies, high sch. Mountain View, Mo., 1939-41; asst. prof. to prof. U. North Tex., 1949-54, dean Grad. Sch., 1954-82, v.p., from 1982; now ret. Contbr. articles profl. jours. State sponsor Future Tchrs. Am. Served from pvt. to lt. col. AUS, World War II. Mem. Assn. Tex. Grad. Schs. (pres.), Assn. Coll. Tchr. Edn. (v.p.), Tex. Assn. Audio-Visual Edn. Dirs. (v.p.), AAUP, NEA, Phi Delta Kappa. Democrat. Methodist. Club: Kiwanis (pres.). Home: 1218 Emerson Ln Denton TX 76201-1104

TOUMEY, HUBERT JOHN (HUGH TOUMEY), textile company executive; b. N.Y.C.; s. William Joseph and Mary Veronica (Drury) T.; m. Dorothy A. Henry, Oct. 16, 1954; children: Donald Joseph, Kenneth Drury. A.B., Fordham U., 1936; M.B.A., Harvard, 1938. With Cannon Mills, Inc., 1938-81, v.p., mgr. towel sales, 1959-60, v.p., gen. sales mgr., 1960-62, exec. v.p., 1962-67, pres., chief adminstrv. and mktg. officer, 1967-81, chmn., chief exec. officer, 1978-81, also dir.; dir. Cannon Mills Co.; Mem. mktg. com. Am. Textile Mfrs. Inst., 1967-81, chmn., 1977-78. Trustee Coll. Mt. St. Vincent, Riverdale, N.Y., 1977-89, chmn., 1979-88. Mem. Assn. Knights of Malta. Home: 29 Bank St Leefair E New Canaan CT 06840

TOUPIN, HAROLD OVID, chemical company executive; b. Hibbing, Minn., Jan. 21, 1927; s. Ovid Pascal and Ellen (Holt) T.; m. Edna F. Sallila, Feb. 8, 1948 (div. Feb. 1973); m. Colleen Beverly Lange, Apr. 18, 1981; children: James, Ronald. BS, U. Minn., 1954, MA, 1955, postgrad, 1968; PhD (hon.), Internat. Acad. Color, Las Vegas, Nev., 1982, U. Mont., 1990. Mgr. Firestone Tire Co., East Los Angeles, Calif., 1948-51; dir. vocat. edn. Hopkins (Minn.) Pub. Schs., 1955-75; with research and devel. Power-o-Peat Co., Gilbert, Minn., 1966-67; chief exec. officer, cons. Color Specialties Inc., Mpls., 1976—; pres., founder travel, meeting planners svc. co., 1990; bd. dirs. Vu-tek Inc., St. Paul, Airport Auto Sales, St. Paul, Color Specialties of Nev., Las Vegas, Instant Air Inc., Mpls., Freedom Fin.; cons. Runs Hot Cons. Service, 1966-75. Contbr. articles to profl. jours. Bd. dirs. Hopkins Jaycees, 1958-60. Served with USAAF, 1944-47. Mem. Am. Assn. Mfrs., Internat. Assn. Color, Nat. Ret. Tchrs. Assn., Am. Assn. Self Employeed, Met. Area Dist. Edn. Instrs. Assn. (pres.), Mpls. C. of C. (Super Bowl com. 1992), Am. Legion, VFW. Democrat. Roman Catholic. Lodge: Lions (sec. Hopkins club 1956-76). Avocations: traveling, golfing, writing. Office: Color Specialities Inc 6405 Cedar Ave S Minneapolis MN 55423-1836

TOUR, ROBERT LOUIS, ophthalmologist; b. Sheffield, Ala., Dec. 30, 1918; s. R.S. and Marguerite (Meyer) T.; m. Mona Marie Elien, Oct. 3, 1992. Chem.E., U. Cin., 1942, M.D., 1950. Intern, U. Chgo. Clinics, 1950-51; resident U. Calif. Med. Center-San Francisco, 1951-54; practice medicine, specializing in ophthalmology, occupational medicine and plasmapheresis, San Francisco, 1954-76, Fairbanks, Alaska, 1976-79, Phoenix, 1979—; clin. prof. ophthalmology U. Calif.-San Francisco, 1974-76. Maj. AUS, 1942-45. Diplomate Am. Bd. Ophthalmology. Fellow ACS, Am. Acad. Ophthalmology; mem. AMA, MENSA, Ariz. Ophthal. Soc., Phoenix Ophthal. Soc., Calif. Assn. Ophthalmology, Contact Lens Assn. Ophthalmologists, Pacific Coast Oto-Ophthal. Soc., Ariz. Med. Assn., Maricopa County Med. Soc. , F.C. Cordes Eye Soc., Masons, K.T., Lions, Shriners, Sigma Xi, Nu Sigma Nu, Alpha Tau Omega, Tau Beta Pi, Alpha Omega Alpha, Phi Lambda Upsilon, Omicron Delta Kappa, Kappa Kappa Psi. Home: 2201 E Palmaire Ave Phoenix AZ 85020-5633

TOURLENTES, THOMAS THEODORE, psychiatrist; b. Chgo., Dec. 7, 1922; s. Theodore A. and Mary (Xenostathy) T.; m. Mona Belle Land, Sept. 9, 1956; children: Theodore W., Stephen C., Elizabeth A. BS, U. Chgo., 1945, MD, 1947. Diplomate Am. Bd. Psychiatry and Neurology (sr. examiner 1964-88, 90). Intern Cook County Hosp., Chgo., 1947-48; resident psychiatry Downey (Ill.) VA Hosp., 1948-51; practice medicine specializing in psychiatry Chgo., 1952, Camp Atterbury, Ind., 1953, Ft. Carson, Colo., 1954, Galesburg, Ill., 1955-71; staff psychiatrist Chgo. VA Clinic, 1952; clin. instr. psychiatry Med. Sch., Northwestern U., 1952; dir. mental hygiene consultation service Camp Atterbury, 1953-54, Ft. Carson, 1953-54; asst. supt. Galesburg State Research Hosp., 1954-58, supt., 1958-71; dir. Comprehensive Community Mental Health Ctr. Rock Island and Mercer Counties; dir. psychiat. services Franciscan Hosp., 1971-85; chief mental health services VA Outpatient Clinic, Peoria, Ill., 1985-88; clin. prof. psychiatry U. Ill., Chgo. and Peoria, 1955—; preceptor in hosp. adminstrn. State U. Iowa, Iowa City, 1958-64; councilor, del. Ill. Psychiat. Soc.; chmn. liaison com. Am. Hosp. and Psychiat. Assns., 1978-79, chmn. Quality Care Bd., Ill. Dept. Mental Health, 1995—. Contbr. articles profl. jours. Mem. Gov. Ill. Com. Employment Handicapped, 1962-64; zone dir. Ill. Dept. Mental Health, Peoria, 1964-71; mem. Spl. Survey Joint Commn. Accreditation Hosps.; chmn. Commn. Cert. Psychiat. Adminstrs., 1979-81; pres. Knox-Galesburg Symphony Soc., 1966-68; bd. dirs. Galesburg Civic Music Assn., pres., 1968-70; chair Knox county United Way Campaign, 1989; pres. Civic Art Ctr., 1990-92. Capt. M.C. AUS, 1952-54. Fellow AAAS, AMA, Am. Psychiat. Assn. (chair hosp. and cmty. psychiatry award bd. 1989-90), Am. Coll. Psychiatrists, Am. Coll. Mental Health Adminstrs.; mem. Ill. Med. Soc. (chmn. aging com. 1968-71, coun. on mental health and addictions 1987-89), chair mental health substance abuse com. 1987-89), Ill. Psychiat. Soc. (pres. 1969-70), Am. Pub. Health Assn., Soc. Biol. Psychiatry, Ill. Hosp. Assn. (trustee 1968-70), Am. Coll. Hosp. Adminstrs., Assn. for Rsch. Nervous and Mental, Am. Assn. Psychiat. Adminstrs. (pres. 1980). Home and Office: 138 Valley View Rd Galesburg IL 61401-8524 *Feeling useful and needed is the greatest recognition and reward.*

TOURNAS, METHODIOS (METHODIOS OF BOSTON), bishop, academic administrator; b. N.Y.C., Nov. 19, 1946; s. Vasilios and Stavroula (Stavropoulos) T. B.A., Hellenic Coll., Brookline, Mass., 1968; M.Div., Coll. of Holy Cross, 1971; S.T.M., Boston U., 1972, D.D. (hon.), 1985. Ordained priest Greek Orthodox Ch., 1979. Archdeacon Greek Orthodox Archdiocese, N.Y.C., 1973-79, aux. bishop, 1982-84; priest St. Spyridon Ch., N.Y.C., 1980-82; bishop Greek Orthodox Diocese of Boston, 1984—; pres. Hellenic Coll., Holy Cross Greek Orthodox Sch. Theology, Brookline, Mass., 1989—. Trustee Hellenic Coll. Inc. Mem. Nat. Coun. Chs. Office: Greek Orthodox Diocese Boston 162 Goddard Ave Brookline MA 02146-7414 also: Hellenic Coll 50 Goddard Ave Brookline MA 02146-7415

TOURNILLON, NICHOLAS BRADY, trade finance, international investments company executive; b. New Orleans, Sept. 1, 1933; s. Samuel C. and Anna Mae (Brady) T.; m. Audrey Nicosia, Dec. 15, 1956; children: Brady, Linda, Tracy, Jeffrey, Gregory, Lori. B.A., Southeastern La. U., 1958; M.B.A., La. State U., 1960. Loan officer Export Import Bank U.S., Washington, 1960-66; adminstrv. asst. to exec. officers Atlantic Gulf & Pacific Co. of Manila, 1966-68; asst. treas. GTE Internat., Stamford, Conn., 1968-76, treas., 1976-86, v.p., 1978-86; pres. GTE Fin. Corp., 1984-86; asst. treas. GTE Corp., 1985-86; chmn., chief exec. officer Am. and Internat. Investment Corp., 1986—; mgr. Dir. Trade and Investment Advisors Ltd., Hungary, 1992—; bd. dirs. Global Access Corp.; mem. internat. adv. bd. Union Trust Co.; advisor on export fin. to Office of Pres. (U.S. Trade Rep.). Past chmn. Conn. Dist. Export Council of US Dept. Commerce; mem. monetary com. U.S. Council Internat. Bus.; bd. dirs. Nat. Fgn. Trade Council. Served with USNR, 1953-54, Korea. Named Outstanding Alumnus of Yr., Southeastern La. U., 1976. Mem. Soc. Internat. Treasurers, Acad. Internat. Bus., Phi Kappa Phi. Home: Midwood Dr Greenwich CT 06831-4400 Office: Am and Internat Investment Corp 25 Midwood Dr Greenwich CT 06831-4412 *Perseverance is an often mentioned but never overrated quality—the quality that prevents the substitution of expediency for excellence. Throughout life, persevering effort has been responsible for converting ideas and talents into results and recognition.*

TOURTELLOTTE, CHARLES DEE, physician, educator; b. Kalamazoo, Aug. 28, 1931; s. Dee and Helen May (Lotz) T.; m. Barbara Richwine, June 25, 1955; children: Daniel DeWitt, Elizabeth Anne, William Charles, Scott David. AB, Johns Hopkins U., 1953; MS in Biochemistry, MD, Temple U., 1957. Diplomate Am. Bd. Internal Medicine. Intern, resident in medicine U. Mich. Hosp., Ann Arbor, 1957-60; fellow in rheumatology Temple U. Hosp., Phila., 1960-61; fellow in biochemistry Rockefeller U., N.Y.C., 1961-63; faculty Sch. Medicine, Temple U., 1963—, prof. medicine, 1972—; chief rheumatology Temple U. Hosp., 1966—, pres. med. staff, bd. govs., 1984-86; dir. Greater Delaware Valley Arthritis Control Program, 1974-77; pres. Eastern Pa. chpt. Arthritis Found., 1972-74; mem. active/cons. staff 10 area and regional hosps. Contbr. chpts. to textbooks, articles to profl. jours.; Editorial Bd.: Arthritis and Rheumatism, 1969-77, 19th-24th Rheumatism Revs, 1969-81. Mem. Haddonfield (N.J.) Bd. Edn., 1968-74, pres., 1974; mem. Borough of Haddonfield Environ. Comm., 1975-87, chmn., 1977-85; mem. Haddonfield Civic Assn., 1963—; South N.J. chmn. Johns Hopkins U. Alumni Schs. Com., 1975-90; trustee Bobby Fulton Meml. Fund, 1979—. Served with AUS, 1953-61. Helen Hay Whitney Found. fellow, 1962-63; Arthritis Found. fellow, 1963-66. Fellow ACP, Phila. Coll. Physicians, Am. Coll. Rheumatology (founding fellow); mem. AMA, Am. Fedn. for Clin. Rsch., Am. Soc. Internal Medicine, Pa. Soc. Internal Medicine, Pa. Med. Soc., Phila. County Med. Soc., Babcock Surg. Soc., Phila. Rheumatism Soc. (pres. 1968-69), Pa. Rheumatology Soc. (founding pres. 1985-86), N.J. Soc. of Pa., Huguenot Soc. Pa., Tavistock County Club (N.J.), Little Egg Harbor Yacht Club, Med. Club of Phila. (bd. dirs. 1991—), Diamond Club (Yale U.), Sigma Xi, Alpha Omega Alpha, Delta Upsilon, Phi Chi. Republican. Presbyterian. Clubs: Tavistock Country (N.J.); Little Egg Harbor Yacht, Med. of Phila. (bd. dirs. 1991—); Johns Hopkins; Diamond (Temple U.). Home: 6 Lane of Acres Haddonfield NJ 08033-3505 Office: Temple Univ Hosp Philadelphia PA 19140-5192

TOURTELLOTTE, WALLACE WILLIAM, neurologist; b. Great Falls, Mont., Sept. 13, 1924; s. Nathaniel Mills and Frances Victoria (Charlton) T.; m. Jean Esther Toncray, Feb. 14, 1953; children: Wallace William, George Mills, James Millard, Warren Gerard. PhB, BS, U. Chgo., 1945, PhD, 1948, MD, 1951. Intern Strong Meml. Hosp. U. Rochester (N.Y.) Sch. Medicine and Dentistry, 1951-54; resident in neurology U. Mich. Med. Ctr., Ann Arbor, 1954-57, asst. prof. neurology, 1957-59, assoc. prof., 1959-66, prof., 1966-71; prof., vice chmn. dept. neurology UCLA, 1971—; chief neurology service West Los Angeles VA Med. Ctr., 1971—; vis. assoc. prof. Washington U., St. Louis, 1963-64; mem. med. adv. bd. Nat. Multiple Sclerosis Soc., 1968—, So. Calif. Multiple Sclerosis Socs., 1972—; dir. Multiple Sclerosis Rsch. and Treatment Ctr., Nat. Neurol. Rsch. Specimen Bank, 1971—. Author: Multiple Sclerosis, Clinical and Pathogenetic Basis, 1997; mem. editorial bd. Jour. Neurol. Sci., Revue Neurologica, Italian Jour. Neurol. Sci., Multiple Sclerosis Jour. Lt. (j.g.) M.C., USN, 1952-54. Recipient Disting. Alumni Service award U. Chgo., 1982. Fellow Am. Acad. Neurology (S. Weir Mitchell Neurology Reseach award 1959); mem. AAUP, Am. Neurol. Assn. (counselor 1982—, v.p. 1992), World Fedn. Neurology (founding mem.), Am. Assn. Neuropathologists, Internat. Soc. Neurochemsitry (founding mem.), Am. Soc. Pharmacology and Exptl. Therapeutics, Am. Soc. Neurochemistry (founding mem.), Soc. Neurosci., Conferie de la Chaine des Rotisseur (chevalier Los Angeles chpt.), Argentier du Baillage de Los Angeles, Ordre Mondial des Gourmets Degustateurs Etats-Unis, Pasadena Wine and Food Soc., Physician Wine & Food Soc., Soc. Med. Friends of Wine, Sigma Xi. Republican. Presbyterian. Home: 1140 Tellem Dr Pacific Palisades CA 90272-2244 Office: West Los Angeles VA Med Ctr 11301 Wilshire Blvd Los Angeles CA 90073

TOURTILLOTT, ELEANOR ALICE, nurse, educational consultant; b. North Hampton, N.H., Mar. 28, 1909; d. Herbert Shaw and Sarah (Fife) T. Diploma Melrose Hosp. Sch. Nursing, Melrose, Mass., 1930; BS, Columbia U., 1948, MA, 1949; edn. specialist Wayne State U., 1962. RN. Gen. pvt. duty nurse, Melrose, Mass., 1930-35; obstet. supr. Samaritan Hosp., Troy, N.Y., 1935-36, Meml. Hosp., Niagara Falls, N.Y., 1937-38, Lawrence Meml. Hosp., New London, Conn., 1939-42, New Eng. Hosp. for Women and Children, Boston, 1942-43; dir. H. W. Smith Sch. Practical Nursing, Syracuse, N.Y., 1949-53; founder, dir. assoc. degree nursing program Henry Ford Community Coll., Dearborn, Mich., 1953-74; dir. pioneering use of learning techs. via mixed media USPHS, 1966-71; prin. cons., initial coord. Wayne State U. Coll. Nursing, Detroit, 1975-78; cons. curriculum design, modular devel., instructional media Tourtillott Cons., Inc., Dearborn, Mich., 1974—; condr. numerous workshops on curriculum design, instructional media at various colls., 1966—; mem. Mich. Bd. Nursing, 1966-73, chmn., 1970-72, mem. rev. com. for constrn. nurse tng. facilities, div. nursing USPHS, 1967-70, mem. nat. adv. coun. on nurse tng., Dept. Health Edn. and Welfare, 1972-76. Author: Commitment-A Lost Characteristic, 1982; contbg. co-author: Patient Assessment-History and Physical Examination, 1975-78; contbr. chpts., articles, speeches to profl. publs. Served to capt. Nurse Corps, U.S. Army, 1943-47; ETO. Recipient Disting. Alumnae award Tchrs. Coll. Columbia U., 1974, Spl. tribute 77th Legislature Mich., 1974, Disting. Alumnae award Wayne State U., 1975, Disting. Service award Henry Ford Community Coll., 1982; established and endowed Eleanor Tourtillott Outstanding Student Nurse of Yr. award at Henry Ford C.C., 1993. Mem. DAR, ANA, Nat. League Nursing (chmn. steering com. dept. assoc. degree programs 1965-67, bd. dirs. 1965-67, 71-73, mem. assembly constituent leagues 1971-73, council assoc. degree programs citation 1974, Mildred Montag Excellence in Leadership award coun. assoc. degree programs 1994), Mich. League for Nursing (pres. 1969-71), Mich. Acad. Sci., Arts and Letters, Am. Legion, Tchrs. Coll. Alumnae Assn., Wayne State U. Alumnae Assn., Phi Lambda Theta, Kappa Delta Pi.

TOUSEY, RICHARD, physicist; b. Somerville, Mass., May 18, 1908; s. Coleman and Adella Richards (Hill) T.; m. Ruth Lowe, June 29, 1932; 1 dau., Joanna. A.B., Tufts U., 1928, Sc.D. (hon.), 1961; A.M., Harvard, 1929; Ph.D., 1933. Instr. physics Harvard, 1933-36, tutor div. phys. scis., 1934-36; research instr. Tufts U., 1936-41; physicist U.S. Naval Research Lab. optics div., 1941-58, head instrument sect., 1942-45, head micron waves br., 1945-58, head rocket spectroscopy br., atmosphere and astrophysics div., 1958-67, space sci. div., 1967-78, cons., 1978—; Mem. com. vision Armed Forces-NRC, 1944—; line spectra of elements com. NRC, 1960-72; mem. Rocket and Satellite Research Panel, 1958—; mem. astronomy subcom. space sci. steering com. NASA, 1960-62, mem. solar physics subcom., 1969-71; prin. investigator expts. including Skylab; mem. com. aeronomy Internat. Union Geodesy and Geophysics, 1958—; U.S. nat. com. Internat. Comm. Optics, 1960-66; mem. sci. steering com. Project Vanguard, 1956-58; mem. adv. com. to office sci. personnel Nat. Acad. Scis.-NRC, 1969-72. Contbr. articles to sci. jours. and books. Bayard Cutting fellow Harvard, 1931-33, 35-36; recipient Meritorious Civilian Service award U.S. Navy, 1945; E.O. Hulburt award Naval Research Labs., 1958; Progress medal photog. Soc. Am., 1959; Prix Ancel Soc. Francaise de Photographie, 1962; Henry Draper medal Nat. Acad. Scis., 1963; Navy award for distinguished achievement in sci, 1963; Eddington medal, 1964; NASA medal for exceptional sci. achievement, 1974; George Darwin lectr. Royal Astron. Soc., 1963. Fellow Am. Acad. Arts and Scis., Am. Phys. Soc., Optical Soc. Am. (dir. 1953-57, Frederic Ives medal 1960), Am. Geophys. Union; mem. Internat. Acad. Astronautics, Nat. Acad. Scis., Am. Astron. Soc. (v.p. 1964-66, Henry Norris Russell lectr. 1966, George Ellery Hale award 1992), Soc. Applied Spectroscopy, AAAS, Am. Geophys. Union, Philos. Soc. Washington, Internat. Astron. Union, Nuttall Ornithol. Club, Audubon Naturalists Soc., Phi Beta Kappa, Sigma Xi, Theta Delta Chi. Home: 10450 Lottsford Rd Apt 231 Bowie MD 20721-2742 Office: US Naval Research Lab Washington DC 20375

TOUSIGNANT, GUY, international organization commander. Comdr. UN Assistance Mission to Rwanda, Kigali. Office: Dept Peace-keeping Ops Rm S-3727-B United Nations New York NY 10017

TOUSIGNANT, JACQUES, human resources executive, lawyer; b. Montreal, Que., Can., Sept. 20, 1948. JD, Sherbrooke U., Que., 1975. Assoc. law firm Pouliot Mercure & Assocs., Montreal, Que., 1975-85; dir. assoc. law firm Montreal Trans. Soc., Montreal, Que., 1985-87; v.p. La Presse Ltee, Montreal, Que., 1987—. Mem. Can. Bar Assn., Que. Bar Assn. Office: La Presse, 7 Rue St Jacques, Montreal, PQ Canada H2Y 1K9

TOUSSAINT, ALLEN RICHARD, recording studio executive, composer, pianist; b. New Orleans, Jan. 14, 1938; s. Clarence Matthew and Naomi (Neville) T.; children: Naomi, Clarence, Alison. Student pub. and pvt. schs., New Orleans. Pres. Sea-Saint Recording Studios, Inc., New Orleans; lectr. in field. Pianist for, Shirley & Lee, 1957, U.S. Army Soldiers Choir, 1963-65; recorded albums Tousan-Wild Sounds of New Orleans, 1958, Life, Love & Faith, 1972, Southern Nights, 1975, Motion, 1978, Connected, 1996; founder, v.p. recorded albums, Sansu Enterprises, Inc., from 1965, pres., Sea-Saint Rec. Studio, Inc., New Orleans, Marsaint Music, Inc., NYNO Music, Inc.; composer: songs Southern Nights (Country Music Assn. Song of Yr., Broadcast Music, Inc., citation of achievement), The Greatest Love, The Optimism Blues, Viva La Money, Whipped Cream, With You In Mind, Working In A Coal Mine, Yes We Can, Can, All These Things, (Broadcast Music, Inc. citation of achievement); stage (Broadway) performer, dir., choreographer, The High Rollers Social and Pleasure Club, 1992; performer, New Orleans Jazz Festival, annually. Served with U.S. Army, 1963-65. Mem. Broadcast Music, Inc., Am. Fedn. Musicians, Contemporary Arts Ctr. Office: Sea-Saint Rec Studio Inc 3809 Clematis St New Orleans LA 70122-4801

TOUSTER, SAUL, law educator; b. Bklyn., Oct. 12, 1925; s. Ben and Bertha (Landau) T.; m. Helen Davidson, Nov. 23, 1954 (div. 1967); children: Natasha Ann, Jonathan Bach; m. Irene Tayler, Jan. 14, 1978. A.B. magna cum laude, Harvard U., 1944, J.D., 1948. Bar: N.Y. 1949. Practiced in N.Y.C., 1949-55; prof. law SUNY-Buffalo, 1955-69, asst. to pres., 1966-68, mem. adj. faculty in medicine, edn., psychology, 1964-69; prof. law and social scis. State Coll. at Old Westbury, 1969-71; prof., provost, acad. v.p. CCNY, 1971-73; acting pres. Richmond Coll. City U. N.Y., 1973-74; prof. law CUNY Grad. Sch. also John Jay Coll. of Criminal Justice, 1974-80; prof., dir. legal studies, humanities, professions programs Brandeis U., Waltham, Mass., 1980-93, prof. emeritus, 1993; legis. cons. N.Y. State Law Rev. Commn., 1956-61; vis. prof. U. Brussels, summer, 1968, Boston Coll. Law Sch., 1994. Author: Still Lives and Other Lives, 1966 (Devins Meml. prize 1966); Contbr. articles to legal periodicals. Served to lt. (j.g.) USNR, 1944-46. NEH fellow, 1978; Am. Bar Found. Legal History fellow, 1977-78. Mem. Internat. Inst. Boston (bd. dirs.), Phi Beta Kappa. Home: 180 Beacon St Boston MA 02116-1401 Office: Legal Studies Program Brandeis U Waltham MA 02254

TOVAR, CAROLE L., real estate management administrator; b. Toppenish, Wash., May 19, 1940; d. Harold Max and Gertrude Louisa (Spicer) Smith; m. Duane E. Clark, Aug. 1959 (div. 1963); 1 child, David Allen; m. Vance William Gribble, May 19, 1966 (div. 1989), m. Conrad T. Tovar, June 25, 1992. Student, Seattle Pacific Coll. Cert. profl. exec.; cert. profl. of occupancy. With B.F. Shearer, Seattle, 1959-60, Standard Oil, Seattle, 1960-62, Seattle Platen Co., 1962-70; ptnr. West Coast Platen, Los Angeles, 1970-87, Waldorf Towers Apts., Seattle, 1970—, Cascade Golf Course, North Bend, Wash., 1970-88; co-owner Pacific Wholesale Office Equipment, Seattle and L.A., 1972-87; owner Pacific Wholesale Office Equip., Seattle, L.A. and San Pablo, Calif., 1988-92, Pac Electronic Service Ctr., Commerce and San Pablo, Calif., 1988-90, Waldorf Mgmt. Co. dba Tovar Mgmt. Co., 1988—; Tovar Properties, 1993—. Mem. Nat. Ctr. Housing Mgmt. (cert. occupancy specialist), Assisted Housing Mgmt. Assn. (nat. cert., Wash. bd. dirs., pres. 1996—). Methodist. Avocations: genealogy, music, low income housing for seniors. Office: 706 Pike St Seattle WA 98101-2301

TOVISH, HAROLD, sculptor; b. N.Y.C., July 31, 1921; s. Louis Goodman and Anna (Treffman) T.; m. Marianna Pineda Packard, Jan. 14, 1946; children: Margo, Aaron, Nina. Student, WPA Art Project, 1938-40, Columbia U., 1940-43, Ossip Zadkine Sch. Drawing and Sculpture, Paris, France, 1949-50, Acad. De La Grande Chaumiere, Paris, 1950-51. Tchr. sculpture N.Y. State Coll. Ceramics, 1947-49, U. Minn., 1951-54, Sch. of Boston Mus., 1957-66; sculptor in residence Am. Acad. in, Rome, 1966; prof. art Boston U., 1971-85, prof. emeritus, 1986—; vos. prof. U. Hawaii, 1969-70. Group exhbns. include Met. Mus. of Art, 1943, Toledo Mus. Art, 1948, Galerie 8, 1949, Walker Art Center, 1951, Mpls. Inst. Art, 1953, San Francisco Art Assn., 1953, Whitney Mus. Am. Art, 1954, 58, 60, 64, 80, 28th Venice Biennial, 1956, Mus. Modern Art, 1960, Chgo. Art Inst., 1960, Carnegie Internat, 1960, Am. Fedn. Art, 1964, Decordova Mus., 1964, Internat. Exhbn. of Contemporary Medal, Paris, 1967, Boston Visual Artists Union Gallery, 1975, Boston U., 1975, 78, Colby Coll., 1975, Inst. Contemporary Art, Boston, 1975, 76, Skowhegan Sch., 1975, NYU, 1976, Boston Mus. Fine Arts, 1977, Nat. Mus. Am. Art, 1987, Nat. Acad. Design, 1987, DeCordova Mus., 1987, Howard Yezersky Gallery, 1988; one-man shows include, Walker Art Center, 1953, Swetzoff Gallery, Boston, 1957, 60, 65, Dintenfass Gallery, N.Y.C., 1965, 72, Addison Gallery Am. Art, Andover, Mass., 1965, Alpha Gallery, Boston, 1968, 73, 86, Terry Dintenfass, Inc., N.Y.C., 1980, 85, Boston U., 1980, retrospective exhibit, Wheaton Coll., 1967, Howard Yezerski Gallery, Boston, 1993, 95; survey exhibit, Solomon Guggenheim Meml. Mus., 1968, Fed. Res. Bank, Boston, 1991; retrospective exhbn. Addison Gallery Am. Art, 1988; survey exhibit Muscarelle Mus., Williamsburg, Va., 1990; represented in permanent collections Phila. Mus. Art, Whitney Mus. Am. Art, Walker Art Center, Mpls. Inst. Art, Addison Gallery Am. Art, Chgo. Art Inst., Mus. Modern Art, Boston Mus. Fine Art, Guggenheim Mus., Worcester Mus. Art, Hirshhorn Collection, Sara Roby Found., Colby Coll., Muscarelle Mus. William & Mary Coll., Williamsburg, Va., Nat. Gallery Am. Art, Minn. Gallery Art, Nat. Mus. Am. Art, Boston Pub. Library; (Recipient 1st prize sculpture Boston Arts Festival 1957, 1st prize drawing 1958, award Am. Inst. Arts and Letters 1971, sculpture grantee Am. Inst. Arts and Letters 1960). Guggenheim fellow, 1967; research fellow Center for Advanced Visual Studies, MIT, 1967-68. Assoc. mem. NAD.

TOWBIN, A(BRAHAM) ROBERT, investment banker; b. N.Y.C., May 26, 1935; s. Harold Clay and Minna (Berlin) T.; m. Jacqueline de Chollet; children: Minna Joyce Pinger, Abraham Robert Jr., Zachary Harold. B.A., Dartmouth Coll., 1957. With Asiel & Co., N.Y.C., 1958-59; with L.F. Rothschild, Unterberg, Towbin Holdings, Inc. (merged with C.E. Unterberg, Towbin Co. 1977), N.Y.C., 1959-86, vice chmn., 1961-86; mng. dir. Lehman Bros. (formerly Shearson Lehman Bros., Inc.), N.Y., 1987-94; pres. Russian Am. Enterprise Fund., N.Y.C., 1994-95; vice chmn. U.S. Russian Investment Fund, N.Y.C., 1995; mng. dir. Unterberg Harris, N.Y.C., 1995—; bd. dirs. Bradley Real Estate, Inc., Gerber Sci. Inc., Globalstar Telecom. Ltd., K&F Industries, Very Spl. Arts, Columbus New Millenium Fund, 1994. Hon. mem. N.Y. State Coun. Arts.; bd. dirs. St. David's Sch., Marymount Sch. Mem. Securities Industry Assn., Bond Club N.Y., Stock Exch. Luncheon Club, Harmonie Club (N.Y.C.), Nat. Golf Links Am., N.Y. Yacht, Antigua Yacht Club, Chelsea Art Club (London), Century Assn. Home: 1010 5th Ave New York NY 10028-0130 Office: Unterberg Harris 10 E 50th St New York NY 10022

TOWE, THOMAS EDWARD, lawyer; b. Cherokee, Iowa, June 25, 1937; s. Edward and Florence (Tow) T.; m. Ruth James, Aug. 21, 1960; children: James Thomas, Kristofer Edward. Student, U. Paris, 1956, BA, Earlham Coll., 1959; LLB, U. Mont., 1962; LLM, Georgetown U., 1965. Ptnr. Towe, Ball, Enright, Mackey & Sommerfeld, Billings, Mont., 1967—; legislator Mont. House of Rep., Billings, 1971-75, Mont. State Senate, Billings, 1975-87, 91-94; served on various coms. Mont. Senate, 1975-87, 91-94. Contbr. articles to law revs. Mem. Alternatives, Inc., Halfway House, Billing, 1977—, pres., 1985-86; mem. adv. com. Mont. Crime Control Bd., 1973-78, Youth Justice Coun., 1981-83; mem. State Dem. Exec. Com., 1969-73; candidate for Congress, 1976; bd. dirs. Mont. Consumer Affairs Coun., Regl. Cmty. Svcs. for the Devel. Disabled, 1975-77, Rimrock Guidance Found., 1975-80, Vols. of Am., Billings, 1984-89, Youth Dynamics Inc., 1989—, Zoo Mont., 1985—, Inst. for Peace Studies, 1993—, Mont. State Parks Assn., 1993—. Capt. U.S. Army, 1962-65. Mem. Mont. Bar Assn., Yellowstone County Bar Assn., Am. Hereford Assn., Billings C. of C. Mem. Soc. of Friends. Avocation: outdoor recreation. Home: 2739 Gregory Dr S Billings MT 59102-0509 Office: 2525 6th Ave N Billings MT 59101-1338

TOWELL, WILLIAM EARNEST, forester, former association executive; b. St. James, Mo., June 11, 1916; s. Esco Joel and Margaret (Pinto) T.; m. Virginia Ruth Dotter, Aug. 31, 1940; children: Jane Towell Darrough, Linda Towell Pinney. B.S. in Forestry, U. Mich., 1938, M.S. in Silviculture, 1938; D.Sc. (hon.), U. Mo., 1981. With Mo. Dept. Conservation, 1938-67, dir., 1957-67; exec. v.p. Am. Forestry Assn., Washington, 1967-78; adj. prof. forestry N.C. State U., 1979—. Mem. Pres.'s Water Pollution Control Adv. Bd., 1963-66, Sec. Agr. Wildlife Adv.Bd., 1965-69, Lewis and Clark Trail Commn., 1965-67; mem. conservation com. Boy Scouts Am., 1968-78, nat. chmn., 1975-78; nat. chmn. project SOAR, 1970-74; adv. mem. com. interrelations wildlife and agr. NAS, 1965-70, mem. adv. team to Indonesia, 1972; mem. Cradle of Forestry Advisory Commn., Dept. Agr., 1971-76; conservation cons. Walt Disney Prodns., 1969-78; chmn. exec. com. Internat. Assn. Fish and Wildlife Agys., 1964-65, pres., 1965-66; mem. exec. com. Fontana Conservation Roundup, 1969-80; mem. exec. com. Nat. Resources Coun. Am., 1968-78, chmn., 1975-77; bd. dirs. Nat. Wildlife Fedn., 1979-87; Forest History Soc., 1978-88;; mem. study panel Fishery Mgmt. Nat. Marine Fisheries Svc. NOAA, U.S. Dept. Commerce, 1986; mem. adv. bd. Wild Horse and Burro dept. U.S. Dept. of Interior, 1986-87; mem. diocesan coun., past sr. warden Episcopal Ch., pres. The Village Chapel, Pinehurst, N.C., 1988, 91. Lt. USNR, 1943-46. Recipient Merit de Agrico medal France, 1970; Conservationist of Year award Nat. Wildlife Fedn., 1976; Disting. Service award U. Mich. Sch. Natural Resources Alumni Soc., 1978; Lifetime Achievement award Nat. Assn. State Foresters, 1978; John Aston Warder Medal Am. Forestry Assn., 1982; J. Sterling Morton award Nat. Arbor Day Found., 1984. Fellow Soc. Am. Foresters (chmn. Ozark sect. 1950, v.p. 1982-83, pres. 1984, Sir William Schlich Meml. medal 1978); mem. Kiwanis. Democrat. Home: 4 Village Green Cir Southern Pines NC 28387-3209

TOWER, HORACE LINWOOD, III, consumer products company executive; b. New Haven, July 16, 1932; s. Horace Linwood, Jr. and Madeline Elizabeth (Davin) T.; m. Elizabeth Wright, Dec. 29, 1956; children: Cynthia, William, John. BA, Cornell U., 1955, MBA, 1960; DHL (hon.), Westfield (Mass.) State Coll., 1984. With Procter & Gamble Corp., Cin., 1960-62; mgmt. cons. Booz, Allen & Hamilton, N.Y.C., 1962-63; with Gen. Foods Corp., White Plains, N.Y., 1963-67, pres. Maxwell home divsn., 1963-78, pres., CEO, 1978-90; pres., CEO, Stanhome Inc., Westfield, Mass., 1978-90, chmn., 1982—; bd. dirs. Stanhome Inc., Tambrands, Inc., Stanley Park; formerly bd. dirs. Forman Cos. Capt. USAF, 1956-59. Mem. Air Force Assn., Sabre Pilots Assn., Thimble Island Sailing and Lit. Soc., Stony Creek Boating Club, Pi Kappa Phi, Sigma Gamma Epsilon. Office: Stanhome Inc 333 Western Ave Westfield MA 01085-1629

TOWERS, BERNARD LEONARD, medical educator; b. Preston, Eng., Aug. 20, 1922; s. Thomas Francis and Isabella Ellen (Dobson) T.; m. Carole Ilene Lieberman (div. 1992); 1 child, Tiffany Sabrina; children from previous marriage: Helena Marianne, Celia Marguerite, Julie Carole. M.B., Ch.B., U. Liverpool, 1947; M.A., U. Cambridge, 1954. House surgeon Royal Infirmary, Liverpool, 1947; lectr. U. Bristol, 1949-50, U. Wales, 1950-54, Cambridge U., 1954-70; fellow Jesus Coll., 1957-70, steward, 1961-64, tutor, 1964-69; dir. med. studies, 1964-70; prof. pediatrics UCLA, 1971-84, prof. anatomy, 1971-91, prof. psychiatry, 1983-91, prof. emeritus anatomy and psychiatry, 1991—, convenor, moderator medicine and soc. forum, 1974-89; pvt. practice integrative medicine, 1991—; co-dir. Program in Medicine, Law and Human Values, 1977-84; cons. Inst. Human Values in Medicine, 1971-84; adv. bd. Am. Teilhard Assn. for Future of Man, 1971—; v.p. Teilhard Centre for Future Man, London, 1974—. Author: Teilhard de Chardin, 1966, Naked Ape or Homo Sapiens?, 1969, Concerning Teilhard, 1969; also articles, chpts. on sci. and philosophy.; Editor anat. sect.: Brit. Abstracts Med. Scis, 1954-56, Teilhard Study Library, 1966-70; adv. bd.: Jour. Medicine and Philosophy, 1974-84. Served to capt. RAMC, 1947-49. NIH grantee, 1974-78; NEH grantee, 1977-83. Fellow Cambridge Philos. Soc., Royal Soc. Medicine; mem. Brit. Soc. History of Medicine, Soc. Health and Human Values (pres. 1977-78), Anat. Soc. G.B., Worshipful Soc. Apothecaries London, Am. Assn. for Study Mental Imagery, Western Assn. Physicians, Societe Europeene de Culture Venise. Office: 436 N Bedford Dr Ste 302 Beverly Hills CA 90210-4320

TOWERY, CURTIS KENT, lawyer; b. Hugoton, Kans., Jan. 29, 1954; s. Clyde D. and Jo June (Curtis) T. BA, Trinity U., 1976; JD, U. Okla., 1979; LLM in Taxation, Boston U., 1989. Mem. Curtis & Blanton, Pauls Valley, Okla., 1980-81; lawyer land and legal dept. Trigg Drilling Co., Oklahoma City, 1981-82; adminstrv. law judge Okla. Corp. Commn., Oklahoma City, 1982-85; counsel Curtis & Blanton, Pauls Valley, Okla., 1985-88; adminstrv. law judge Okla. Dept. Mines, Oklahoma City, 1985-88, assoc. gen. counsel, 1989-92; contracts and purchasing adminstr., atty. Okla. Turnpike Authority, Oklahoma City, 1992-93; asst. gen. counsel Okla. Corp. Commn., 1993—; bd. dirs. First Nat. Bank Pauls Valley, 1983-88. Assoc. bd. Okla. Mus. Art, 1985-88, Okla. Symphony Orch., 1987-92; assoc. bd. Ballet Okla., 1987-92, sec., 1990-91, v.p., 1988-89. Mem. ABA, Okla. Bar Assn., Am. Assn. Petroleum Landmen, Internat. Assn. Energy Economist, Phi Alpha Delta, Sigma Nu. Democrat. Presbyterian. Clubs: Young Men's Dinner Club (Oklahoma City), Faculty House. Lodges: Rotary, Elks. Avocations: flying, golf, traveling, investment analysis. Home: PO Box 14891 Oklahoma City OK 73113-0891 Office: Jim Thorpe Bldg 2101 N Lincoln Blvd Oklahoma City OK 73105-4904

TOWERY, MATTHEW ALLEN, SR., lawyer; b. Atlanta, Dec. 6, 1959; s. Maurice Jean and Joan (Gilleland) T.; m. Marilea Jean Taglia; children: Matthew Allen Jr., Katherine Alexandra. M of Philosophy, Cambridge (Eng.) U., 1984; JD cum laude, Stetson U., 1987. Bar: Ga. Speechwriter, spl. asst. to Mack F. Mattingly U.S. Senate, Washington, 1981-82; ptnr. Towery, Thompson, Gulliver, and Bunch, Atlanta, 1987-92; mem. Ga. Ho. Reps., 1993—; of counsel Long Aldridge and norman, Atlanta, 1995—; trustee Southeastern Legal Found., Atlanta, Pace Acad.; overseer coll. law Stetson U. Author: Power in the South, 1984. Rep. nominee for lt. gov. State of Ga., 1990. Recipient Nat. Bicentenniel Debate Champion award Nat. Bicentennial Commn., 1976-77; named Nat. Freshman Legis. of Yr., Nat. Rep. Party, 1993. Mem. Ga. Bar Assn., Atlanta Bar Assn., Oxford-Cambridge Club, Cherokee Town and Country Club, Nat. Color Graphics, Inc. (chmn. 1993—), Friends of Newt Gingrich (chmn. campaign com. 1992—).

TOWEY, RICHARD EDWARD, economics educator; b. Mount Kisco, N.Y., Sept. 22, 1928; s. William Joseph and Anna Margaret (Rumse) T.; m. Mary Ann Franusich, June 12, 1954 (dec. Mar. 1988); 1 child, John Patrick; m. Lorraine T. Miller, July 21, 1990. BS, U. San Francisco, 1954; MA, U. Calif., Berkeley, 1957, PhD, 1967. Economist Fed. Res. Bank of San Francisco, 1957-60; prof. econs. Oreg. State U., Corvallis, 1962-93, emeritus prof., 1993—; economist Fed. Deposit Ins. Corp., Washington, 1968-70. Cpl. U.S. Army, 1948-49, 1950-51. Earhart fellow U. Calif., Berkeley, 1961-62. Mem. Am. Econ. Assn., Am. Fin. Assn., Western Econ. Assn. Roman Catholic. Office: Oreg State Univ Dept. Econ Corvallis OR 97331

TOWLE, LAIRD CHARLES, book publisher; b. Exeter, N.H., Sept. 13, 1933; s. Gerald Charles and Wilma Lois (Buzzell) T.; m. Marlene Ann Towne, Apr. 14, 1956; children: Karen Lee, Joel Andrew, Glenn Corbett, Leslie Kim. BS in Physics, U. N.H., 1955, MS in Physics, 1958; PhD, U. Va., 1962. Rsch. physicist AVCO Corp., Wilmington, Mass., 1962-63, Allis Chalmers Corp., West Allis, Wis., 1963-67; section head Naval Rsch. Lab., Washington, 1967-77, project mgr., 1977-81; chief exec. officer Heritage Books, Inc., Bowie, Md., 1981—. Author: N.H. Genealogical Research

Guide, 1973, The Descendants of William Brown and Isabella Kennedy, 1992; editor: Genealogical Periodical Annual Index, 1974—; contbr. articles to profl. jours. Pres. NRL Fed. Credit Union, Washington, 1970-71, treas., 1972-84; pres. Prince George's County General Soc., Bowie, 1970-71; mem. Bowie Adv. Planning Bd., 1987-91. Mem. Nat. Geneal. Soc., N.E. Historic Geneal. Soc., Prince George's County General Soc., Sigma Xi. Avocations: genealogical research, sailing, gardening. Home: 3602 Maureen Ln Bowie MD 20715-2936 Office: Heritage Books Inc 1540 Pointer Ridge Pl Bowie MD 20716-1859

TOWLE, LELAND HILL, government official; b. Boston, Mar. 29, 1931; s. Leland and Bertha Mary (Hill) T.; m. Carol Peterson, June 5, 1953; children—Peter Kimball, Gretchen Towle Maynard, Michele. B.S., U. N.H., 1952; M.S., M.I.T., 1953; Cert. in Bus. and Mgmt, U. Calif., Berkeley, 1962. Nuclear chemist Stanford Research Inst., Menlo Park, Calif., 1956-59; community systems economist, economist, nuclear economist Stanford Research Inst., 1959-68, mgr. health scis. research, 1968-74; asst. dir. Nat. Center for Alcohol Edn., Arlington, Va., 1974-75; cons. Medicine in the Pub. Interest, Washington, 1975, Internat. Ctr. for Alcohol Policies, 1995—; vis. scientist Nat. Inst. on Alcohol Abuse and Alcoholism, Rockville, Md., 1975-76, dep. dir. office of program devel. and analysis, 1976-77, assoc. dir. office of program devel. and analysis, 1977-81, dir. internat. and intergovtl. affairs, 1981-95; cons. regional and med. programs. Contbr. articles to profl. jours. Bd. dirs. Med. Resources Found., Palo Alto, Calif., 1972-73. Served with USAF, 1952-56. Mem. Am. Pub. Health Assn., Sci. Research Soc. Am., Am. Nuclear Soc., Am. Chem. Soc., Sigma Xi, Phi Kappa Phi. Home: Rt 663 Burgess VA 22432

TOWLES, DONALD BLACKBURN, retired newspaper publishing executive; b. Lawrenceburg, Ky., Sept. 10, 1927; s. Joseph Sterling and Marjorie (Blackburn) T.; m. Geraldine Gooch, Dec. 20, 1947 (dec. Nov. 1980); children: Sally Blackburn Towles Clark, Rebecca Neale Towles Brown; m. Julia Mason, Dec. 3, 1981. A.B. in Journalism, U. Ky., 1948. Asst. dir. publicity, editor In Ky. Mag. Commonwealth of Ky., Frankfort, 1948-55; pub. service mgr. Courier-Jour. and Louisville Times Co., Louisville, 1956-66, dir. pub. service and promotion, 1966-71, v.p., 1974-92, v.p., dir. circulation, 1971-76, v.p., dir. pub. affairs, 1976-92. Author: The Press of Kentucky 1787-1994; editor: Newspaper Promotion Handbook, 1983. Pres. Heritage Corp. of Louisville, 1982-85; chmn. Louisville area chpt. ARC, 1987-89; chmn. program adv. com. Louisville Devel. Program, 1971-80; mem. adv. bd. Salvation Army; bd. dirs. Louisville Med. Ctr., Thos. D. Clark Found., Christian Church Homes of Ky., Sr. Citizens East. With U.S. Army, 1952-54, Korea. Recipient Comty. Svc. award Louisville Devel. Com., 1980; named Outstanding Chpt. Vol. Louisville area chpt. ARC, 1993, Outstanding State Vol., 1994; inducted into Ky. Journalism Hall of Fame, 1992. Mem. Internat. Newspaper Promotion Assn. (pres. 1980-82, Silver Shovel 1983), Ky. Press Assn. (pres. 1982, Pres.'s Cup Leadership 1982, Disting. Comty. Svc. award 1987), Journalism Alumni Assn. U. Ky. (pres. 1979-94, Outstanding Alumnus award 1976, All-Am. Alumni award 1994), Soc. Profl. Journalists (pres. Louisville chpt. 1991-92). Democrat. Disciple of Christ. Home: 3536 Norbourne Blvd Louisville KY 40207-3753

TOWNE, L. STANTON, lawyer; b. Chgo., July 16, 1952. BS, Columbia U., JD, 1976. Bar: N.Y. 1977, Ill. 1991. Ptnr. McDermott, Will & Emery, Chgo. Mem. ABA, Assn. Bar City N.Y., N.Y. State Bar Assn. Office: McDermott Will & Emery 227 W Monroe St Chicago IL 60606-5016*

TOWNE, ROBERT, screenwriter; b. 1936; m. Luisa Towne; 2 children. Student, Pomona State Coll. Screenplays include The Last Woman on Earth, 1960, The Tomb of Ligeia, 1965, Villa Rides, 1968, The Last Detail, 1973, Chinatown, 1974 (Acad. award best original screenplay), (with Warren Beatty) Shampoo, 1974 (Acad. award best original screenplay), (with Paul Schrader) The Yazuka, 1975, (also prodr., dir.) Personal Best, 1981, 1981, (with Michael Austin) Greystoke, 1984, (also dir.) Tequila Sunrise, 1988, The Two Jakes, 1990, Days of Thunder, 1990, The Firm, 1992. Office: Creative Artists Agy 9830 Wilshire Blvd Beverly Hills CA 90212-1804

TOWNES, BOBBY JOE, travel agency executive; b. Pickens, S.C., Aug. 29, 1932; s. James Harold and Coda Lenora (Nations) T.; m. Addie Elise Ray, May 2, 1956; children: John William, Robert Scott. Assoc. BA, Mars Hill (N.C.) Jr. Coll., 1952; BA, Furman U., Greenville, S.C., 1955; diploma, Grad. Sch. Banking, Rutgers U., 1969. V.p. Peoples Nat. Bank, Greenville, 1954-73; exec. v.p. Community Bank, Greenville, 1973-76; pres. Piedmont Travel, Inc., Greenville, 1976-93, chmn., 1993—; mng. ptnr. Long Beach Properties, 1992—; chmn. Greenville World of Travel, 1976-80; pres. Piedco Assocs., Greenville, 1973—; mng. ptnr. Cutter Joint Ventures, Hilton Head, S.C., 1972—; pres. Piedco II, 1992—; chmn. Boutique Ltd., 1971-75; instr. Am. Inst. Banking, 1964-70, Charter Life Underwriters, Greenville, 1968; mem. adv. com. KLM Dutch Airlines, Atlanta, 1982, System One Automation, Miami, Fla., 1980, Eastern Airlines, Miami, 1983-87; mem. adv. bd. Mars Plus Data Systems, Miami, 1976-79. Author: Independent Bank Survival, 1968, Townes and Allied Families, 1995. Chmn. United Way, Greenville, 1973; v.p. ARC, Greenville, 1970, Cancer Soc., Greenville, 1966; v.p. Furman U. Alumni Bd., Greenville, 1968-70, Furman U. Paladin Bd., Greenville, 1972-74; mem. Furman U. Com. for Self Study, Greenville, 1976; com. Gov.'s Econ. Coun., Columbia, S.C., 1972; v.p., mem. founders com. Cmty. Concerts, Greenville, 1976; pres. YMCA Youth Guides, Greenville, 1970; v.p., organizer Centurian Club, 1978. Recipient Sertuma Internat. Disting. Club Pres. award, 1967, Outstanding Young Mem. of Am. award, 1968. Mem. Am. Inst. Banking (pres. 1964, bd. dirs. 1966), Young Bankers S.C. (bd. dirs. 1965), S.C. Bankers Assn. (bd. dirs. 1969), Greenville Wine Soc. (pres., organzer 1968, 72), S.C. Hist. Soc., Greenville County Hist. Soc., Poinsett Club, Commerce Club, Colonial Club (v.p. 1989, pres. 1991), Sertoma (v.p. 1982, Gold Honor club 1967). Republican. Episcopalian. Avocation: genealogy. Home: 14 Selwyn Dr Greenville SC 29615-1727

TOWNES, CHARLES HARD, physics educator; b. Greenville, S.C., July 28, 1915; s. Henry Keith and Ellen Sumter (Hard) T.; m. Frances H. Brown, May 4, 1941; children: Linda Lewis, Ellen Screven, Carla Keith, Holly Robinson. B.A., B.S., Furman U., 1935; M.A., Duke U., 1937; Ph.D., Calif. Inst. Tech., 1939. Mem. tech. staff Bell Telephone Lab., 1939-47; assoc. prof. physics Columbia U., 1948-50, prof. physics, 1950-61; exec. dir. Columbia Radiation Lab., 1950-52, chmn. physics dept., 1952-55; provost and prof. physics MIT, 1961-66, Inst. prof., 1966-67; v.p., dir. research Inst. Def. Analyses, Washington, 1959-61; prof. physics U. Calif., Berkeley, 1967-86, 94, prof. physics emeritus, 1986-94, prof. grad. sch., 1994—; Guggenheim fellow, 1955-56; Fulbright lectr. U. Paris, 1955-56, U. Tokyo, 1956; lectr., 1955, 60; dir. Enrico Fermi Internat. Sch. Physics, 1963; Richtmeyer lectr. Am. Phys. Soc., 1959; Scott lectr. U. Cambridge, 1963; Centennial lectr. U. Toronto, 1967; Lincoln lectr., 1972-73, Halley lectr., 1976, Krishman lectr., 1992, Nishina lectr., 1992; dir. Gen. Motors Corp., 1973-86; mem. Pres.'s Sci. Adv. Com., 1966-69, vice chmn., 1967-69; chmn. sci. and tech. adv. com. for manned space flight NASA, 1964-69; mem. Pres.'s Com. on Sci. and Tech., 1976; researcher on nuclear and molecular structure, quantum electronics, interstellar molecules, radio and infrared astrophysics. Author: (with A.L. Schawlow) Microwave Spectroscopy, 1955; author, co-editor: Quantum Electronics, 1960, Quantum Electronics and Coherent Light, 1964; editorial bd.; Rev. Sci. Instruments, 1950-52, Phys. Rev., 1951-53, Jour. Molecular Spectroscopy, 1957-60, Procs. Nat. Acad. Scis., 1978-84; contbr. articles to sci. publs.; patentee masers and lasers. Trustee Calif. Inst. Tech., Carnegie Instn. of Washington, Grad. Theol. Union, Calif. Acad. Scis.; mem. corp. Woods Hole Oceanographic Instn. Decorated officier Légion d'Honneur (France); recipient numerous hon. degrees and awards including Nobel prize for physics, 1964; Stuart Ballantine medal Franklin Inst., 1959, 62; Thomas Young medal and prize Inst. Physics and Phys. Soc., Eng., 1963; Disting. Public Service medal NASA, 1969; Wilhelm Exner award Austria, 1970; Niels Bohr Internat. Gold medal, 1979; Nat. Sci. medal, 1983, Berkeley citation U. Calif., 1986; named to Nat. Inventors Hall of Fame, 1976, Engring. and Sci. Hall of Fame, 1983; recipient Common Wealth award, 1993, ADION medal Observatory Nice, 1995. Fellow IEEE (life, Medal of Honor 1967), Am. Phys. Soc. (pres. 1967, Plyler prize 1977), Optical Soc. Am. (hon., Mees medal 1968, Frederic Ives medal 1996), Indian Nat. Sci. Acad., Calif. Acad. Scis.; mem. NAS (coun. 1968-72, 78-81, chmn. space sci. bd. 1970-73, Comstock award 1959), Am. Philos. Soc., Am. Astron. Soc., Am. Acad. Arts and Scis., Royal Soc. (fgn. mem.), Russian Acad. Scis. (fgn. mem.), Pontifical Acad. Scis., Max-Planck Inst. for Physics and Astrophysics (fgn. mem.). Office: U Calif Dept Physics Berkeley CA 94720

TOWNES, PHILIP LEONARD, pediatrician, educator; b. Salem, Mass., Feb. 18, 1927; s. Saul and Lillian (Kravetsky) T.; m. Marjorie Joan Greenstone, Aug. 27, 1956; children: Elizabeth Ann, Susan Jane, David Andrew. A.B., Harvard, 1948; Ph.D., U. Rochester, 1952, M.D., 1959. Diplomate: Am. Bd. Pediatrics, Am. Bd. Med. Genetics. Intern Strong Meml. Hosp., Rochester, 1959-60; asst. resident Strong Meml. Hosp., 1963, chief resident pediatrics, 1965; mem. faculty U. Rochester Sch. Medicine, 1952-79, prof. pediatrics, 1969-79; prof. anatomy (genetics), chmn. div. genetics, dir. Genetic Clinic, 1966-79; prof. pediatrics U. Mass. Sch. Medicine, 1979—, dir. Genetic Clinic, 1979—, dir. Cytogenetics Lab., 1981—; pediatrician Strong Meml. Hosp.; cons. attending Newark State Hosp., Genesee Hosp.; hon. research asst. Univ. Coll., London, Eng., 1965-66; mem. adv. com. for genetics services Mass. Dept. Pub. Health, 1979—, chmn. com., 1982—; mem. steering com. New Eng. Regional Genetics Group, 1981—. Contbr. articles to med. jours. Mem. com. qualifications cytogenetics N.Y. State Dept. Health, 1968-74; bd. dirs. Monroe County chpt. Nat. Found., 1965-79, chmn. med. adv. com., 1967-79, hon. bd. dirs., 1979—, also cons.; trustee Seven Hills Found., 1996—. USPHS predoctoral fellow, 1951-52; sr. research fellow, 1960-61; research career devel. award, 1961-66. Mem. Am. Acad. Pediatrics, Am. Assn. Anatomists, Soc. Pediatric Research, Am. Soc. Human Genetics, Am. Pediatric Soc., Teratology Soc., Sigma Xi, Alpha Omega Alpha. Home: 14 Spring Valley Rd Worcester MA 01609-1151

TOWNLEY, JON, production company creative director. BFA, Ohio State U., 1976. Formerly dir. design Cranston/Csuri Prodns.; creative dir. MetroLight Studios, L.A., 1987—; designer, dir. numerous TV and film projects; designer animation storyboards HBO, ESPN, NBC Sports, Nat. TV comml., and feature film effects. Recipient various awards Broadcast Designers Assn., Broadcast Promotion and Mktg. Execs., Internat. Film & TV Festival of N.Y., Nicograph, Emmy Acad. of TV Arts and Scis. Office: Metrolight Studios 5724 W 3rd St Ste 400 Los Angeles CA 90036-3078

TOWNLEY, ROBERT GORDON, medical educator; b. Omaha, Nebr., July 27, 1928. MD, Creighton U., 1955. Pvt. practice in internal medicine and allerty Physicians Clinic, Omaha, 1960-62; attending staff mem. Douglas County Hosp., Omaha, 1960-62; instr. dept. medicine and allergy Creighton U., Omaha, 1960-62; asst. prof. medicine Creighton U., 1966-69, assoc. prof. medicine and microbiology, 1969-74, chief allergy sect., 1969—, prof. medicine, prof. microbiology, 1974—; instr. dept. medicine and allergy U. Colo. Med. Sch., 1962-66; asst. chief dept. asthma-allergy Nat. Jewish Hosp., Denver, 1962-66; mem. presdl. task NHLI, 1973-74. Editor three books on allergic diseases; contbr. numerous articles to profl. publs. Lederle fellow, 1954. Fellow Am. Acad. Asthma, Allergy and Immunology; mem. Am. Thoracic Soc., Nebr. Thoracic Soc. (pres. 1970). Office: Creighton U Allergic Disease Ctr Dept Medicine Omaha NE 68178

TOWNS, EDOLPHUS, congressman; b. Chadbourn, N.C., July 21, 1934; m. Gwendolyn Forbes, 1960; children: Darryl, Deidra. B.S., N.C. A & T State U., Greensboro, 1956; M.S.W., Adelphi U., Garden City, N.Y., 1973; PhD (hon.), N.C. A&T, Shaw U. Tchr. Medgar Evers Coll., Bklyn., N.Y.C. Pub. Schs.; dep. hosp. adminstr., 1965-71; dep. pres. Borough of Bklyn., 1976-82; mem. 98th-104th Congresses from 11th (now 10th) N.Y. dist., Washington, D.C., 1982—; ranking minority mem. subcom. Human Resources and Intergovt. Affairs; mem. Commerce com. Mem. adv. council Boy Scouts Am.; active Salvation Army. Served with U.S. Army, 1956-58. Named to Acad. of Distinction Adelphi U. Mem. Kiwanis, Phi Beta Sigma. Democrat. Office: US Ho of Reps 2232 Rayburn Ho Office Bldg Washington DC 20515*

TOWNSEND, ANN VAN DEVANTER, foundation administrator, art historian; b. Washington, June 20, 1936; d. John Ward and Ellen Keys (Ramsey) Cutler; m. Willis Van Devanter, Dec. 27, 1958 (div. May 1974); 1 child, Susan Earling Van Devanter (Mrs. John Philip Newell); m. Lewis Raynham Townsend, Dec. 10, 1983. BA, Brown U., 1958; MA, George Washington U., 1975. Grantsmanship ctr. cert. Guest curator Balt. Mus. Art, 1971-77; dir. cultural affairs Chevy Chase (Md.) Savs. & Loan, Inc., 1978-81; dir. spl. partnership projects NEA, Washington, 1982-83; founding pres. The Trust for Mus. Exhbns., Washington, 1984—; organizer over 60 nat. and internat. mus. exhbns. for more than 200 mus. Co-author: Self-Portraits of American Artists, 1670-1973, 1974; author: Anywhere So Long As There Be Freedom, 1975, Two Hundred Years of American Painting, 1976; contbr. articles to mags. U.S. commr. Cagnes-Sur-Mer Internat. Afts Festival, France, 1977, 78; mem. women's com. Washington Opera, 1993—; bd. dirs. Friends of Corcoran Gallery of Art, Washington, 1975-76, Strathmore Hall Arts Ctr., Rockville, Md., 1978-80, Am. Swedish Hist. Mus., Phila., 1987-89, U.S. Com. World Fedn. Friends of Mus., 1995—. Acad. grad. fellow Johns Hopkins Sch. Advanced Internat. Studies, 1958. Mem. Nat. Soc. Arts & Letters, Am. News Women's Club, Soc. Women Goegraphers, Sulgrave Club. Episcopalian. Avocations: backgammon, gourmet cooking, ballroom dancing. Office: The Trust for Mus Exhbns 1424 16th St Ste 502 Washington DC 20036-2211

TOWNSEND, CHARLES EDWARD, Slavic languages educator; b. New Rochelle, N.Y., Sept. 29, 1932; s. Charles Edward and Lois (Fukushima) T.; m. Janet Linner, Sept. 18, 1957; children: Erica, Sylvia, Louise. B.A., Yale U., 1954; M.A., Harvard U., 1960, Ph.D., 1962. Instr., then asst. prof. Harvard U., 1962-66; mem. faculty Princeton U., 1966—, dir. Critical Langs. Program, 1968-70, prof. Slavic langs., 1971—, chmn. dept., 1970—. Author: Russian Word Formation, 1968, Continuing With Russian, 1970, Memoirs of Princess Natalja Borisovna Dolgorukaja, 1977, Czech Through Russian, 1981, A Description of Spoken Prague Czech, 1990, Russian Readings for Close Analysis, 1993, Common and Comparative Slavic, 1956. Served with U.S. Army, 1955-58. IREX grantee, 1968, 89; Fulbright grantee, 1954-55, 71, 83, 88; Ford Found. fellow, 1958-60; NDEA fellow, 1960-62. Mem. Am. Coun. Tchrs. Russian, Am. Assn. Tchrs. Slavic and East European Langs. (Disting. Contbn. to Profession award), N.Am. Assn. Tchrs. Czech (pres. 1992-94), Am. Assn. Advancement Slavic Studies, Linguistic Soc. Czech Republic (hon.), Czechoslovak Soc. Arts. and Scis., Phi Beta Kappa. Home: 145 Hickory Ct Princeton NJ 08540-3434 Office: Princeton U Dept Slavic Langs 028 E Pyne Princeton NJ 08544-3810

TOWNSEND, CHARLES H., publishing executive. Pub. Glamour, Conde Nast Pub. Inc., N.Y.C.; exec. v.p. Conde Nast Pub. Inc., N.Y.C. Office: Conde Nast Publication Inc. 350 Madison Ave New York NY 10017-3704*

TOWNSEND, EARL CUNNINGHAM, JR., lawyer, writer; b. Indpls., Nov. 9, 1914; s. Earl Cunningham and Besse (Kuhn) T.; m. Emily Macnab, Apr. 3, 1947 (dec. Mar. 1988); children: Starr, Vicki M. (Mrs. Christopher Katterjohn), Julia E. (Mrs. Edward Goodrich Dunn Jr.), Earl Cunningham III, Clyde G. Student, De Pauw U., 1932-34; AB, U. Mich., 1936, JD, 1939. Bar: Ind. 1939, Mich. 1973, U.S. Supreme Ct. 1973, U.S. Ct. Appeals (4th, 5th, 6th, 7th cirs.), U.S. Dist. Ct. (no. and so. dists.) Ind., U.S. Dist. Ct. (ea. dist.) Va., U.S. Dist. Ct. (ea. dist.) Mich. Sr. ptnr. Townsend & Townsend, Indpls., 1941-64, Townsend, Hovde & Townsend, Indpls., 1964-84, Townsend & Townsend, Indpls., 1984—; dep. prosecutor, Marion County, Ind., 1942-44; radio-TV announcer WIRE, WFBM, WFBM-TV, Indpls., 1940-53, 1st TV announcer Indpls. 500 mile race, 1949, 50; Big Ten basketball referee, 1940-47; lectr. trial tactics U. Notre Dame, Ind. U., U. Mich., 1968-79; chmn. faculty seminar on personal injury trials Ind. U. Sch. Law, U. Notre Dame Sch. Law, Valparaiso Sch. Law, 1981; mem. Com. to Revise Ind. Supreme Ct. Pattern Jury Instrns., 1975-83; lectr. Trial Lawyers 30 Yrs. Inst., 1986; counsel atty gen., 1988-92. Author: Birdstones of the North American Indian, 1959; editor: Am. Assn. Trial Lawyers Am. Jour., 1964-88; contbr. articles to legal and archeol. jours.; composer (waltz) Moon of Halloween. Trustee Cathedral High Sch., Indpls., Eiteljorg Mus. Am. Indian and Western Art, Cale J. Holder Scholarship Found. Ind. U. Law Sch.; life trustee, bd. dirs., mem. fin. and bldg. coms. Indpls. Mus. Art; life trustee Ind. State Mus.; founder, dir. Meridian St. Found.; mem. dean's coun. Ind. U.; founder, life fellow Roscoe Pound/Am. Trial Lawyers Found., Harvard U.; fellow Meth. Hosp. Found. Recipient Ind. Univ. Writers Conf. award, 1960, Hanson H. Anderson medal of honor Arsenal Tech. Schs., Indpls., 1971; named to Coun. Sagamores of Wabash, 1969; Rector scholar, 1934, Ind. Basketball Hall of Fame; hon. chief Black River-Swan Creek Saginaw-Chippewa Indian tribe. Fellow Internat. Acad. Trial Lawyers, Internat. Soc. Barristers, Ind. Bar Found. (life trustee, disting. fellow award); mem. ASCAP, ABA (com. on trial techniques 1964-76, aviation and space 1977—), Assn. Trial Lawyers Am. (v.p.), Ind. State Bar Assn. (Golden Career award 1989), Indpls. Bar Found. (disting. charter 1986), Ind. Trial Lawyers Assn. (pres. 1965, pres. Coll. Fellows 1984-90, Lifetime Achievement award 1992), Am. Bd. Trial Advs. (diplomate, pres. Ind. chpt. 1980-86), Am. Arbitration Assn. (nat. arbitrators panel), Am. Judicature Soc., State Bar of Mich. (Champion of Justice award 1989), Roscommon County Bar Assn., 34th Jud. Cir. Bar Assn., Bar Assn. 7th Fed. Cir. (bd. govs. 1966-68), Mich. Trial Lawyers Assn., Soc. Mayflower Descendants (gov. 1947-49), Ind. Hist. Soc., Marion County/Indpls. Hist. Soc. (bd. dirs.), Key Biscayne C. of C., U. Mich. Pres. Club, U. Mich. Victors Club (founder, charter mem.), Trowel and Brush Soc. (hon.), Genuine Indian Relic Soc. (founder, pres., chmn. frauds com.), The Players Club, Key Biscayne Yacht Club, Columbia Club, Indpls. Athletic Club, Masons (33 degree), Shriners, Delta Kappa Epsilon, Phi Kappa Phi. Republican. Methodist. Avocations: art, Indian relics. Home: 5008 N Meridian St Indianapolis IN 46208-2624

TOWNSEND, FRANK MARION, pathology educator; b. Stamford, Tex., Oct. 29, 1914; s. Frank M. and Beatrice (House) T.; m. Gerda Eberlein, 1940 (dec. div. 1944); 1 son, Frank M.; m. Ann Graf, Aug. 25, 1951; 1 son, Robert N. Student, San Antonio Coll., 1931-32, U. Tex., 1932-34; MD, Tulane U., 1938. Diplomate: Am. Bd. Pathology. Intern Polyclinic Hosp., N.Y.C., 1939-40; commd. 1st lt. M.C., U.S. Army, 1940, advanced through grades to lt. col., 1946; resident instr. pathology Washington U., 1945-47; trans. to USAF, 1949, advanced through grades to col., 1956; instr. pathology Coll. Medicine, U. Nebr., 1947-48; asso. pathologist Scott and White Clinic, Temple, Tex., 1948-49; asso. prof. pathology Med. Br. U. Tex., Galveston, 1949-59; flight surgeon USAF, 1950-65; dir. labs. USAF Hosp. (now Wilford Hall USAF Hosp.), Lackland AFB, Tex., 1950-54; cons. pathology Office of Surgeon Gen. Hdqrs. USAF, Washington, 1954-63, chief cons. group Office of Surgeon Gen. Hdqrs., 1954-55; dep. dir. Armed Forces Inst. Pathology, Washington, 1955-59; dir. Armed Forces Inst. Pathology, 1959-63; vice comdr. aerospace med. divsn. Air Force Systems Command, 1963-65; ret., 1965; practice medicine specializing in pathology San Antonio, 1965—; dir. labs. San Antonio State Chest Hosp.; consulting pathologist Tex. Dept. Health hosps., 1965-72; clin. prof. pathology U. Tex. Med. Sch., San Antonio, 1969-72; prof., chmn. dept. pathology Health Sci. Ctr. U. Tex. Med. Sch., 1972-86, emeritus chmn., prof., 1986—; cons. U. Tex. Cancer Ctr.-M.D. Anderson Hosp., 1966-80, NASA, 1967-75; mem. adv. bd. cancer WHO, 1958-75; mem. Armed Forces Epidemiology Bd., 1983-91; bd. govs. Armed Forces Inst. Pathology, 1984-95. Mem. editorial bd. Tex. Med. Jour., 1978-86; contbr. articles to med. jours. Mem. adv. coun. Civil War Centennial Commn., 1960-65; bd. dirs. Alamo Area Sci. Fair, 1967-73. Decorated D.S.M., Legion of Merit; recipient Founders medal Assn. Mil. Surgeons, 1961. Recipient Comdr.'s award Armed Forces Epidemiol. Bd., 1990; F.M. Townsend Chair of Pathology endowed in his honor by faculty of Dept. Pathology, U. Tex. Health Sci. Ctr., 1987. Fellow ACP, Coll. Am. Pathologists (edn. advisor on accreditation, commr. lab. accreditation South Ctrl. States region 1971-84), Am. Soc. Clin. Pathologists (Ward Burdick award 1983), Aerospace Med. Assn. (H.G. Mosely award 1962); mem. AMA, AAAS, Tex. Med. Assn., Internat. Acad. Aviation and Space Medicine, Tex. Soc. Pathologists (Caldwell award 1971), Am. Assn. Pathologists, Internat. Acad. Pathology, Acad. Clin. Lab. Physicians and Scientists, Soc. Med. Cons. to Armed Forces, Torch Club. Home: PO Box 77 Harwood TX 78632-0077 Office: U Tex Health Sci Ctr Dept Pathology 7703 Floyd Curl Dr San Antonio TX 78284-7750

TOWNSEND, GREG, professional football player; b. Los Angeles, Calif., Nov. 3, 1961. Student, Long Beach City Coll., Tex. Christian U. Defensive end L.A. Raiders, 1983—. Named defensive end The Sporting News NFL All-Pro team, 1990. Played in Pro Bowl, 1990, 91, in Super Bowl XVIII, 1983. Office: L A Raiders 332 Center St El Segundo CA 90245-4047

TOWNSEND, HAROLD GUYON, JR., publishing company executive; b. Chgo., Apr. 11, 1924; s. Harold Guyon and Anne Louise (Robb) T.; AB, Cornell U., 1948; m. Margaret Jeanne Keller, July 28, 1951; children: Jessica, Julie, Harold Guyon III. Advt. salesman Chgo. Tribune, 1948-51; gen. mgr. Keller-Heartt Co., Clarendon Hills, Ill., 1951-62; pub. Santa Clara (Calif.) Jour., 1962-64; chmn. bd. dirs., pub. Dispatch-Tribune newspaper Townsend Communications, Inc., Kansas City, Mo., 1964—. Chmn., Suburban Newspaper Research Commn., 1974—; dir. Certified Audit Bur. of Circulation, 1968-72. del. Rep. Nat. Conv., 1960; chmn. Mission Hills Rep. Com., 1966-77; bd. dirs. Kansas City Jr. Achievement, 1966-68, Kansas City council Girl Scouts U.S.A., 1969-71, Kansas City council Boy Scouts Am., 1974, Kansas City chpt. ARC, 1973-79, Kansas City Starlight Theater, Clay County (Mo.) Indsl. Commn.; treas., trustee Park Coll., Parkville, Mo., 1970-78. Mem. adv. com. North Kansas City Hosp.; bd. dirs. Taxpayers Research of Mo., 1978—, Nelson Gallery Friends of Art, 1980-85. Served with inf. AUS, World War II. Mem. Kansas City Advt. and Sales Club, Kansas City Press Club, Suburban Press Found. (pres. 1969-71), Suburban Newspapers Am. (pres. 1976-77), Kansas City Printing Industries Assn. (pres., dir.), Printing Industries of Am. (pres. non-heatset web sect. 1980-82), North Kansas City C. of C. (dir., pres. 1964-70), Univ. Assocs. (treas. 1977-80), Sigma Delta Chi, Pi Delta Epsilon, Phi Kappa Psi. Clubs: University (treas. 1977); Indian Hills Country; Hinsdale (Ill.) Golf; Field (Sarasota, Fla.). Home: 23 Compton Ct Prairie Village KS 66208 Office: 7007 NE Parvin Rd Kansas City MO 64117-1532

TOWNSEND, JAMES WILLIS, computer scientist; b. Evansville, Ind., Sept. 9, 1936; s. James Franklin and Elma Elizabeth (Galloway) T.; m. Leona Jean York, Apr. 20, 1958; 1 child, Eric Wayne. BS in Arts and Scis., Ball State U., 1962; PhD, Iowa State U., 1970. Rsch. technologist Neuromuscular div. Mead Johnson, Evansville, 1957-60; chief instr. Zoology dept. Iowa State U., Ames, 1965-67; asst. prof. Ind. State U., Evansville, 1967-72; cons. electron microscopy Mead Johnson Rsch. Ctr., Evansville, 1971-73; mgr. neurosci. Neurosci. Lab., Kans. State U., Manhattan, 1974-76; head electron microscopy Nat. Ctr. for Toxicology Rsch., Jefferson, Ark., 1976-82; dir. electron microscopy U. Ark. Med. Sci., Little Rock, 1982-87; dir. computer ops. pathology dept. Univ. Hosp., Little Rock, 1987—; workshop presenter Am. Soc. Clin. Pathology, 1980-81, Nat. Soc. Histotechnologists, 1984-88. With USAF, 1957. Contbr. articles to profl. jours.; reviewer Scanning Electron Microscopy, 1977-78. Nat. Def. fellowship NDEA, Iowa State U., 1962-65; recipient Chgo. Tribune award Chicago Tribune, 1955. Mem. Sigma Xi, Sigma Zeta. Baptist. Avocations: genealogy, American Civil War. Home: 4 Breeds Hill Ct Little Rock AR 72211-2514 Office: Univ Ark for Med Sci Dept Pathology Slot 517 4301 W Markham St Little Rock AR 72205-7101

TOWNSEND, JANE KALTENBACH, zoologist, educator; b. Chgo., Dec. 21, 1922; B.S., Beloit Coll., 1944; M.A., U. Wis., 1946; Ph.D., U. Iowa, 1950; m. 1966. Asst. in zoology U. Wis., 1944-47; asst., instr. U. Iowa, 1948-50; asst., project assoc. in pathology U. Wis., 1950-53; Am. Cancer Soc. research fellow Wenner-Grens Inst., Stockholm, 1953-56; asst. prof. zoology Northwestern U., 1956-58; asst. prof. to assoc. prof. zoology Mt. Holyoke Coll., South Hadley, Mass., 1958-70, prof., 1970-93, chmn. biol. scis., 1980-86, prof. emeritus, 1993—. Fellow AAAS (sec. sect. biol. sci. 1974-78); mem. Am. Assn. Anatomists, Am. Inst. Biol. Scis., Am. Soc. Zoologists, Soc. Experimental Biology and Medicine, Soc. Devel. Biology, Corp. of Marine Biol. Lab., Sigma Xi, Phi Beta Kappa. Office: Mount Holyoke Coll Dept Biology South Hadley MA 01075

TOWNSEND, JEFFREY, production designer. Prodn. designer: (films) Baby, It's You, 1983, Old Enough, 1984, Reckless, 1984, After Hours, 1985, Maid to Order, 1987, The Fabulous Baker Boys, 1989, Straight Talk, 1993, Sleepless in Seattle, 1993. Office: care Lawrence Mirisch The Mirisch Agency 10100 Santa Monica Blvd Ste 700 Los Angeles CA 90067-4011

TOWNSEND, JOHN MICHAEL, lawyer; b. West Point, N.Y., Mar. 21, 1947; s. John D. and Vera (Nachman) T.; m. Frances M. Fragos, Oct. 8, 1994; 1 child, James E. BA, Yale U., 1968, JD, 1971. Bar: N.Y. 1972, U.S. Dist. Ct. (so. and ea. dists.) N.Y. 1975, U.S. Ct. Appeals (2nd cir.) 1975, U.S. Supreme Ct. 1975, U.S. Ct. Appeals (8th cir.) 1982, U.S. Ct. Appeals (7th and 10th cirs.) 1986, D.C. 1990, U.S. Dist. Ct. D.C. 1990, U.S. Ct.

Appeals (D.C. cir.) 1990, U.S. Ct. Appeals (4th cir.) 1991. Assoc. Hughes Hubbard & Reed, N.Y.C., 1971-73, 1975-80, ptnr., 1980; assoc. Hughes Hubbard & Reed, Paris, 1973-74; arbitrator U.S. Dist. Ct. (ea. dist.) N.Y., Am. Arbitration Assn., bd. dirs.; trustee U.S. Coun. Internat. Bus. 1st lt. USAR, 1971-75. Mem. ABA, Internat. Bar Assn., Assn. of Bar of City of N.Y., N.Y. Lawyers for Pub. Interest, D.C. Bar Assn., Union Internat. des Advs., Univ. Club (Washington), Yale Club (N.Y.C.). Democrat. Episcopalian. Office: Hughes Hubbard & Reed 1300 I St NW Washington DC 20005-3306

TOWNSEND, JOHN WILLIAM, JR., physicist, retired federal aerospace agency executive; b. Washington, Mar. 19, 1924; s. John William and Elenore (Eby) T.; m. Mary Irene Lewis, Feb. 7, 1948; children: Bruce Alan, Nancy Dewitt, John William III, Megan Lewis. BA, Williams Coll., 1947, MA, 1949, ScD, 1961. With Naval Research Lab., 1949-55, br. head, 1955-58; with NASA, 1958-68, dep. dir. Goddard Space Flight Ctr., 1965-68; dep. adminstrn. Environmental Scis. Services Adminstrn., 1968-70; asso. adminstr. Nat. Oceanic and Atmospheric Adminstrn., 1970-77; pres. Fairchild Space and Electronics Co., 1977-82; v.p. Fairchild Industries, 1979-85; pres. Fairchild Space Co., 1983-85; sr. v.p. Fairchild Industries, 1985-87; chmn. bd. Am. Satellite Co., 1985, sr. v.p., exec. aerospace group, 1987, exec. v.p., 1987; dir. NASA Goddard Space Flight Ctr., 1987-90; ret., 1990; mem. U.S. Rocket, Satellite Rsch. Panel, 1950-60; chmn. space applications bd. NRC, 1985-87; bd. dirs., trustee Telos Corp., 1990-92; mem. adv. bd. Loral Corp., 1990-92; mem. coms. NRC, 1990—; bd. dirs CTA, Inc. Author numerous papers, reports in field. Pres. town council, Forest Heights, Md., 1951-55. Served with USAAF, 1943-46. Recipient Profl. Achievement award Engrs. and Architects Day, 1957; Meritorious Civilian Service award Navy Dept., 1957; Outstanding Leadership medal NASA, 1962; Distinguished Service medal, 1971, 90; recipient Arthur S. Fleming award Fed. Govt., 1963. Fellow AIAA, AAAS, Am. Meteorol. Soc.; mem. NAE (com. 1990—), Am. Phys. Soc., Am. Geophys. Union. (fin. com. 1991—), Internat. Astronautical Fedn. (mem., trustee internat., acad. astronautics), Sigma Xi. Home: 15810 Comus Rd Clarksburg MD 20871-9169

TOWNSEND, KATHLEEN KENNEDY, state official; m. David Townsend; children: Meaghan, Maeve, Kate, Kerry. BA cum laude, Harvard U.; JD, U. N.Mex. Former dep. asst. atty. gen. U.S. Dept. Justice, Washington; lt. gov. State of Md., 1994—; tchr. U. Md., Balt. County, Essex. C.C., Dundalk C.C., U. Pa.; past exec. dir. Md. Student Svcs. Alliance; chair so. region Nat. Conf. Lt. Govs., oversight com. Peobody Inst.; expert adv. bd. Export-Import Bank U.S. Editor U. N.Mex. Law Rev. Founder Robert F. Kennedy Human Rights award. Recipient 4 hon. degrees. Office: Lt Gov State House 100 State Cir Annapolis MD 21401-1925*

TOWNSEND, KENNETH ROSS, priest; b. Holly Grove, Ala., Oct. 31, 1927; s. James Ernest and Mary H. (Jordan) T.; m. Irene Fogleman, Mar. 18, 1951; children; Marietta, Martha, Kenneth Ross, Elizabeth. AB, Birmingham South Coll., 1956; postgrad., Union Theol. Sem., 1960-63; MDiv, Va. Theol. Sem., 1964. Ordained priest Episcopal Ch., 1965. Pastor meth. chs. N.C. and Va. Confs., 1954-63; priest Bath Priest Parish, Dinwiddie, Va., 1964-69, St. Paul's Ch., Vanceboro, N.C., 1969-89; supply priest Olivet Ch., Franconia, Va., 1989—; lectr. philosophy Richard Bland Coll. of Coll. William and Mary, Williamsburg, Va., 1966-68; del. to synod Province IV, 1973; mem. liturgical com. Episcopal Diocese of East Carolina, Wilmington, N.C., 1971-82, mem. prison commn., 1984. Writer, painter. Supply priest Sacramental Min. to Deaf Congregation, Olivet Episcopal Ch., Franconia, Va. With USN, 1945-46. Mem. Delta Sigma Phi. Address: 2521 Paxton St Lake Ridge Woodbridge VA 22192 ***Yearning for self fulfillment in a better world is the 'mother of the will' to be and to accomplish. By this will we define ourselves. This will identifies our goals in work and relationships. Such a self concept informs our minds as to what is right and correct. The yearning, the will, the goals and accomplishment are thinkable and obtainable. The world awaits our resolve.***

TOWNSEND, LEROY B., chemistry educator, university administrator, researcher; b. Lubbock, Tex., Dec. 20, 1933; s. L.B. and Ocie Mae (McBride) T.; m. Sammy Beames, Sept. 15, 1953; children: Lisa Loree, LeRoy Byron. BA in Chemistry and Math., N.Mex. Highlands U.-Las Vegas, 1955, MS, 1957; PhD, Ariz. State U.-Tempe, 1965. Assoc. prof. medicinal chemistry U. Utah, Salt Lake City, 1971-75, prof., 1975-78, adj. prof. chemistry, 1975-78; prof. medicinal chemistry U. Mich., Ann Arbor, 1979—, Albert B. Prescott prof. medicinal chemistry, 1985—, prof. chemistry, 1979—, chmn., 1979—, dir. interdept. grad. program in medicinal chemistry, 1979—; chmn. drug discovery and devel. program Comprehensive Cancer Ctr.; mem. cancer rsch. com. Nat. Cancer Inst., 1979—, com. on devel. treatments for rare genetic disease dept. human genetics; mem. nat. adv. com. on AIDS to NIAID; mem. steering com. on chemotherapy of malaria WHO; mem. study sect. on chemotherapy of cancer Nat. Am. Cancer Soc.; mem. Am. Cancer Soc. study sect. drug devel.. hematology and pathology; various ad hoc site visit teams Nat. Cancer Inst.; chmn. purines and pyrimidines Gordon Rsch. Conf.; chmn. Nat. Medicinal Chemistry Symposium; pres. Internat. Congress Heterocyclic Chemistry; participant symposia in field; lectr. various nat. and internat. sci. congresses. Contbr. articles to profl. jours.; assoc. editor Internat. Jour. Heterocyclic Chemistry; mem. editorial bd. Jour. Carbohydrates, Nucleosides, Nucleotides, Jour. Nucleosides and Nucleotides, Jour. Chinese Pharm. Soc., Jour. Medicinal Chemistry. Recipient Smissman-Bristol Myers-Squibb award in medicinal chemistry; various grants; named Disting. prof. MAGB. Fellow AAAS; mem. Am. Chem. Soc. (chmn., counsilor medicinal chemistry div.), Internat. Soc. Heterocyclic Chemistry (treas., pres. 1973-79), Nat. Am. Chem. Soc. (chmn. divsn. of medicinal chemistry), Sigma Xi, Phi Kappa Phi. Home: 3317 E Dobson Pl Ann Arbor MI 48105-2583 Office: U Mich Coll Pharmacy Coll Pharmacy 4563 Pharmacy CC Little Bldg Ann Arbor MI 48109

TOWNSEND, LINDA LADD, mental health nurse; b. Louisville, Apr. 26, 1948; d. Samuel Clyde and Mary Elizabeth (Denton) Ladd; m. Stanley Allen Oliver, June 7, 1970 (div. 1978); 1 child, Aaron; m. Warren Terry Townsend Jr., Jan. 1, 1979; children: Mark, Amy, Sarah. Student, Catherine Spalding Coll., 1966-67; BSN, Murray State U., 1970; MS in Psychiat./Mental Health Nursing, Tex. Woman's U., 1976. RN, Tex., Ky.; lic. advanced nurse practitioner, profl. counselor, marriage and family therapist, Tex.; cert. group psychotherapist. Charge nurse med. and pediatric units Murray (Ky.)-Calloway County Hosp., 1970-71; team leader surg./renal transplant unit VA Hosp., Nashville, 1971-73; team leader, charge nurse gen. med.-surg. unit Providence Hosp., Waco, Tex., 1973-74; outpatient therapist Mental Hygiene Clinic, Ft. Hood, Tex., 1975-76; outpatient nurse therapist Ctrl. Counties Ctr. for Mental Health/Mental Retardation, Copperas Cove & Lampasas, Tex., 1977-80; psychiat. nurse clin. specialist, marriage/family therapist Profl. Counseling Svc., Copperas Cove, 1979—; cons. Metroplex Hosp. and Pavilion, Killeen, Tex., 1980—, Woods Psychiat. Inst., Killeen, 1987—. Founding mem. Family Outreach of Coryell County, Copperas Cove, 1986—, also past pres. and past sec.; founding mem. Partnership for a Drug and Violence-Free Copperas Cove, vol. music therapist at local nursing home. Recipient Mary M. Roberts Writing award Am. Jour. of Nursing, 1970; named Mem. of Yr.-Vol., Family Outreach of Coryell County. Mem. ANA (cert. clin. specialist in adult psychiat. and mental health nursing, cert. clin. specialist in child and adolescent psychiat./mental health nursing), AAUW (v.p. membership, past bd. dirs., sec.-treas.), Tex. Nurses Assn., Tex. Peer Assistance Program for Nurses (advocate), Am. Group Psychotherapy Assn. (cert.), Learning Disabilities Assn., Inst. for Humanities at Salado, Sigma Theta Tau. Democrat. Methodist. Avocations: genealogy, camping, nature activities, music, sports. Home: RR 1 Box 253-E Kempner TX 76539-9502 Office: Profl Counseling Svc 806 E Avenue D Ste F Copperas Cove TX 76522-2231

TOWNSEND, MARJORIE RHODES, aerospace engineer, business executive; b. Washington, Mar. 12, 1930; d. Lewis Boling and Marjorie Olive (Trees) Rhodes; m. Charles Eby Townsend, June 7, 1948; children: Charles Eby Jr., Lewis Rhodes, John Cunningham, Richard Leo. BEE, George Washington U., 1951. Electronic scientist Naval Rsch. Lab., Washington, 1951-59; rsch. engr. to sect. head Goddard Space Flight Ctr.-NASA, Greenbelt, Md., 1959-65, tech. asst. to chief systems divsn., 1965-66, project mgr. small astronomy satellites, 1966-75, project mgr. applications explorer missions, 1975-76, mgr. preliminary systems design group, 1976-80; aerospace and electronics cons. Washington, 1980-83; v.p. systems devel. Space Am., 1983-84; aerospace cons. Washington, 1984-90; dir. space systems engring. BDM Internat., Inc., Washington, 1990-91; dir. space applications BDM ESC, Washington, 1991-92; sr. prin. staff mem. BDM Fed., Inc., Washington, 1992-93; areospace cons., Washington, 1993—. Patentee digital telemetry system. Decorated Knight Italian Republic Order, 1972; recipient Fed. Women's award, 1973, EUR award for Culture, 1974, Engr. Alumni Achievement award George Washington U., 1975, Gen. Alumni Achievement award George Washington U., 1976, Exceptional Svc. medal NASA, 1971, Outstanding Leadership medal NASA, 1980, Eye-of-the-Needle award NASA, 1991. Fellow IEEE (chmn. Washington sect. 1974-75), AIAA (chmn. nat. capitol sect. 1985), AAAS (coun. del. 1985-88), Washington Acad. Sci. (pres. 1980-81); mem. Internat. Acad. Astronautics, Am. Geophys. Union, Soc. Women Engrs., Wing of Aerospace Med. Assn., Inc. (hon.), DAR, Daus. Colonial Wars, Mensa, Sigma Kappa, Sigma Delta Epsilon. Republican. Episcopalian. Home and Office: 3529 Tilden St NW Washington DC 20008-3194

TOWNSEND, MILES AVERILL, aerospace and mechanical engineering educator; b. Buffalo, N.Y., Apr. 16, 1935; s. Francis Devere and Sylvia (Wolpa) T.; children: Kathleen Townsend Hastings, Melissa, Stephen, Joel, Philip. BA, Stanford U., 1955; BS MechE, U. Mich., 1958; advanced cert., U. Ill., 1963, MS in Theoretical and Applied Mechanics, 1967; PhD, U. Wis., 1971. Registered profl. engr., Ill., Wis., Tenn., Ont. Project engr. Sundstrand, Rockford, Ill., 1959-63, Twin Disc Inc., Rockford, 1963-65, 67-68; sr. engr. Westinghouse Electric Corp., Sunnyvale, Calif., 1965-67; instr., fellow U. Wis., Madison, 1968-71; assoc. prof. U. Toronto, Ont., Can., 1971-74; prof. mech. engring. Vanderbilt U., Nashville, 1974-81; Wilson prof. mech. and aerospace engring. U. Va., Charlottesville, 1982—, chmn. dept., 1982-91; ptnr., v.p. Endev Ltd., Can. and U.S., 1972—; cons. in field. Contbr. numerous articles to profl. jours.; 7 patents in field. Recipient numerous research grants and contracts. Fellow ASME (mem. coun. on engring., productivity com., tech. editor Jour. Mech. Design); mem. AAAS, N.Y. Acad. Scis., Sigma Xi, Phi Kappa Phi, Pi Tau Sigma. Avocations: running, reading, music. Home: 221 Harvest Dr Charlottesville VA 22903-4850 Office: U Va Dept Mech and Aerospace Engring Thornton Hall Charlottesville VA 22903-2442

TOWNSEND, PALMER WILSON, chemical engineer, consultant; b. Bronx, N.Y., Aug. 1, 1926; s. Atwood Halsey and Mildred Brower (Wilson) T.; m. Helen Anne Lydecker, Feb. 6, 1949; children: Janet M., Martha L., Andrew W., Amy E., Rebecca L. AB in Chemistry, Dartmouth Coll., 1947; BSChemE, Columbia U., 1947, MSChemE, 1948, PhDChemE, 1956. Instr. chem. engring. Columbia U., N.Y.C., 1948-53; sr. engr. pilot plant divsn. Air Reduction Co., Inc., Murray Hill, N.J. and N.Y.C., 1953-56, sect. head chem. engring. divsn., 1957-61, asst. dir., 1961-1964, mgr. exptl. engring., cen. engring. dept., 1964-66, asst. to group v.p., 1966-67, dir. comml. devel. Chem. and Plastics divsn., 1967-70; dir. comml. devel. Plastics divsn. Allied Chem. Corp., 1970-72; cons. Berkeley Heights, N.J., 1972—. Editor phys. sci. sect. Good Reading, 1956, 60, 64; contbr. articles to profl. jours. With USNR, 1944-46. DuPont fellow, 1951. Mem. Am. Inst. Chem. Engrs., Am. Chem. Soc., Soc. Plastic Engrs., Soc. Plastics Industries, Assn. Cons. Chemists and Chem. Engrs. (pres. 1991-92), Sigma Xi, Phi Lambda Upsilon, Theta Tau. Congregationalist. Achievements include patents for processes for trifluorethyl vinyl ether, trifluoro ethanol, cryogenic composition of matter, carbon dioxide snow; development of molding approach for the plastic spacers used in superconducting magnets for ISAbelle and the Superconducting Super Collider; establishment of rigid PVC molding materials in the Bell Telephone System; invention of improved processes for production of fluorochemical intermediates to anesthetic agents; research on plastics development and processes, chemicals and monomers, energy development, polyvinyl chloride resin production and market applications. Home and Office: 93 Continental Road Morris Plains NJ 07950

TOWNSEND, PAUL BRORSTROM, editor; b. Port Washington, N.Y., Feb. 22, 1919; s. Richard Edwin and Alice (Brorstrom) T.; BA, Hobart Coll., 1940; JD, Columbia U., 1943; LHD, Hofstra U., 1971; LLD, Dowling Coll., 1984; m. Terry De Marco, Dec. 8, 1961; children: Wendy, Tobin, Kim. Bar: N.Y. 1946. Sales mgr. Creative Mailing Svc., 1946-47; sales and advt. dir. Corydon M. Johnson Co., 1947-50; pres. Townsend & Willis, pub. rels. counsel, 1951-54; ptnr. Tex McCrary Inc., 1955-57; devel. cons. North Shore Hosp., 1949-66; exec. dir. L.I. Fund, 1951-59; editor L.I. Bus. News, 1957—; ptnr. L.I. Communicating Svcs., 1959—; pres. L.I. Stage, 1984-86; comm. counsel L.I. Midsuffolk Bus. Action, 1968—. Trustee North Shore Univ. Hosp. With CIC, U.S. Army, 1943-45. Fellow Poly. Inst. N.Y., 1980. Mem. Deepdale Club. Office: 2150 Smithtown Ave Ronkonkoma NY 11779-7348

TOWNSEND, PHILIP W., JR., library director; b. Phila., Aug. 14, 1949; s. Philip Walsh and Eleanor (Clay) T.; m. Mary Rasmussen, Aug., 1973; children: Grace, Philip, Erica. BA, U. Utah, 1973; MSLS, Villanova U., 1988. Libr. dir. Valley Forge Mil. Coll., Wayne, Pa., 1985—. Capt. U.S. Army Res., 1973-83. Avocations: pipe major Washington Meml. Pipe Band. Office: Valley Forge Mil Coll Office of Libr 1001 Eagle Rd Wayne PA 19087-3694

TOWNSEND, P(RESTON) COLEMAN, agricultural business executive; b. Salisbury, Md., Dec. 27, 1945; s. Preston Coleman and Rachel (Morris) T.; m. Susan Marshall, Dec. 8, 1981. B.S., U. Del., 1969. Chmn., CEO Townsends, Inc., Millsboro, Del., 1969—. Bd. visitors Del. State U. Mem. Nat. Broiler Council (bd. dirs.). Republican. Office: Townsends Inc Route 24 PO Box 468 Millsboro DE 19966

TOWNSEND, ROBERT, film director; b. Chgo., Feb. 6, 1957; s. Robert and Shirley (Jenkins) T. Actor: (stage) Take It From the Top, 1979, Bones, 1980, (films) Cooley High, 1974, Willie and Phil, 1980, Streets of Fire, 1983, A Soldier's Story, 1983, American Flyers, 1984, Odd Jobs, 1984, Ratboy, 1985, The Mighty Quinn, 1989, That's Adequate, 1990, (t.v. movies) Women At West Point, 1979, Senior Trip!, 1981, In Love With an Older Woman, 1982; actor, prod., dir., co-writer: (films) Hollywood Shuffle, 1987, The Five Heartbeats, 1990, The Meteor Man, 1993; dir.: (films) Eddie Murphy Raw, 1987; stand-up comedian: (t.v. spls.) Robert Townsend and His Partners in Crime, Take No Prisoners, Robert Townsend and His Partners in Crime II.TV series: Townsend Television, 1992, The Parent 'Hood, 1995. Office: Tinsel Townsend 8033 W Sunset Blvd Ste 890 Los Angeles CA 90046-2427 also: CAA 9830 Wilshire Blvd Beverly Hills CA 90212-1804

TOWNSEND, ROBERT J., lawyer; b. Charlotte, Mich., Nov. 11, 1938; s. Robert Wright and Rhea Lucille (Jennings) T.; m. Thea E. Kolb, Aug. 1, 1964; children: Melissa, Bradley. BA, Mich. State U., 1960; LLD, Harvard U., 1963. Bar: Ohio 1964, U.S. Dist. Ct. (so. dist.) Ohio 1964, U.S. Ct. Appeals (6th cir.) 1971, U.S. Supreme Ct. 1992. Assoc. Taft, Shettinus & Hollister, Cin., 1963-72, ptnr., 1972—; dir. Employers Resource Assn., Cin., 1989—. Dir. Jobs for Cin. Grads., 1990—. With U.S. Army, 1963-64, 68-69. Office: 1800 Star Bank Ctr 425 Walnut St Cincinnati OH 45202-3904

TOWNSEND, SUSAN ELAINE, social service institute administrator, hostage survival consultant; b. Phila., Sept. 5, 1946; d. William Harrison and Eleanor Irene (Fox) Rogers; m. John Holt Townsend, May 1, 1976. BS in Secondary Edn., West Chester State U., 1968; MBA, Nat. U., 1978; PhD in Human Behavior, La Jolla U., 1984. Biology tchr. Methacton Sch. Dist., Fairview Village, Pa., 1968-70; bus. mgr., analyst prof. La Jolla Research Corp., San Diego, 1977-79; pastoral asst. Christ Ctr. Bible Therapy, San Diego, 1980-82, also bd. dirs.; v.p., pub. relations World Outreach Ctr. of Faith, San Diego, 1981-82, also bd. dirs.; owner, pres., cons. Townsend Research Inst., San Diego, 1983-89; teaching assoc. La Jolla U. Continuing Edn., 1985-86, adminstr., assoc. registrar, adj. faculty, 1990. Author: Hostage Survival-Resisting the Dynamics of Captivity, 1983; contbr. articles to profl. jours. Instr. USN Advanced Survival Evasion Resistance Escape Sch., 1986-89; security officer Shield Security, San Diego, 1991-92; bd. dirs. Christ Fellowship Ch. of San Diego, 1987-96, music dir., 1992—; religious vol. Met. Correctional Ctr., San Diego, 1983-89, San Diego County Jail Ministries, 1978—, scheduling coord., 1993—. Comdr. USN, 1970-76, USNR, 1976-93. Mem. Naval Res. Assn. (life), Res. Officers Assn. (outstanding Jr. Officer of Yr. Calif. chpt. 1982), Navy League U.S. (life), West Chester U. ALumni Assn., Nat. U. Alumni Assn. (life), La Jolla U. Alumni Assn., Gen. Fedn. Women;s Clubs (pres. Peninsula Woman's Club 1983-85, pres. Peninsula Woman's Club 1994-96, pres. Parliamentary Law Club 1984-86, 96—, res. sec. Past Pres.' Assn. 1994-96), Calif. Fedn. Women's Clubs (v.p.-at-large San Diego dist. 25 1982-84, rec. sec. 1994-96, 1st v.p./dean of chmn. 1996—).

TOWNSEND, TERRY, publishing executive; b. Camden, N.J., Dec. 14, 1920; d. Anthony and Rose DeMarco; BA, Duke U., 1942; LHD (hon.) Dowling Coll., 1991; m. Paul Brorstrom Townsend, Dec. 8, 1961; 1 son, Kim. Pub. rels. dir. North Shore Univ. Hosp., Manhasset, N.Y., 1955-68; pres. Theatre Soc. L.I., 1968-70; pres. Townsend Comm. Bur., Ronkonkoma, N.Y., 1970—, L.I. Communicating Service, Ronkonkoma, 1977—; columnist, writer L.I./Bus., Ronkonkoma, 1970-75; pub. L.I. Bus. News, 1978—; v.p. Parr Meadows Racetrack, Yaphank, N.Y., 1977. Assoc. trustee North Shore U. Hosp., 1968—; bd. govs. Adelphi U. Friends Fin. Edn., 1978-85; chmn. ann. archtl. awards competition N.Y. Inst. Tech., 1970-83; trustee Dowling Coll., 1994—, L.I. Fine Arts Mus., 1984-85; pub. broadcasting Sta. WLIW TV, Garden City, L.I., N.Y., 1990-93; bd. dirs. Family Svc. Assn. Nassau County, 1982-92; dinner chmn. L.I. 400 Ball, 1987; bd. trustees Dowling Coll., 1994—; trustee Mus. at Stony Brook, 1994—. Recipient Media award 110 Center Bus. and Profl. Women, 1977, Enterprise award Friends of Fin. Edn., 1981, L.I. Loves Bus. Showcase Salute, 1982, Community Svc. award N.Y. Diabetes Assn., 1983, Disting. Long Islander in Communications award L.I. United Epilepsy Assn., 1984, Spl. award Dowling Coll. Spring Tribute, 1989, Disting. Svc. award Episcopal Health Svcs., 1989, Disting. Citizen award Dowling Coll., 1991, Gilbert Tilles award Nat. Assn. Fundraising Execs., 1994; named First Lady of L.I., L.I. Public Relations Assn., 1973, L.I. Woman of Yr. L.I. Assn. Action Com., 1989. Office: LI Bus News 2150 Smithtown Ave Ronkonkoma NY 11779-7348

TOWNSEND, THOMAS PERKINS, former mining company executive; b. Bryn Mawr, Pa., Mar. 28, 1917; s. John and Mildred (Perkins) T.; m. Laura M. Trench, Sept. 14, 1940; children: Joanne Townsend Taber, Hunter, Elizabeth Townsend Ballinger. B.S. in Econs., U. Pa., 1939; postgrad., Harvard U., 1944. C.P.A., Pa. Sr. acct. Price Waterhouse & Co., 1945-48; treas., dir. Fox Products Co., 1948-53, Wilcolator Co., 1953-55; staff acct. Tex. Gulf Sulphur Co., N.Y.C., 1955-57; asst. treas. Tex. Gulf Sulphur Co., 1958-61, v.p., controller, 1961-62, v.p., treas., 1962-64, v.p. internat. ops., 1964-68; exec. v.p. Bosco Middle East Oil Corp., Greenwich, Conn., 1968-69; pres. Conn. Real Estate Corp., Greenwich, 1969-70, also bd. dirs., 1969—; v.p. finance Rosaria Resources Corp., N.Y.C., 1970-81; treas. Unidyne Corp., 1984-85; cons. AMAX, Inc., 1981-85; bd. dirs. Thermal Exploration Corp., Carlin Gold Co. Chmn. nat. com. for employment youth Nat. Child Labor Com., 1968-70; trustee, pres. South Kent Sch.; trustee Soc. to Advance Retarded, Norwalk, Conn.; bd. dirs. United Way of Tri-State, Denison Pequotsegos Nature Ctr.; mem. New Canaan Bd. Fin., Conn., 1985-89 . Served to lt. (s.g.) Supply Corps, USNR, World War II. Mem. Am. Inst. Accts., N.Y. State Soc. CPAs, Fin. Execs. Inst., Mason's Island Yacht Club, Off Soundings Club. Episcopalian (treas., vestryman 1960-72, 87-95). Home: 9 Kensington Ct Mystic CT 06355-3116 *The principal goal in my life has been to be a straight dealer, to be honest in thought, word and deed. It has paid off for me. Crooked dealing may make more money, but it does not lead to a happier life. One must live by his God.*

TOWNSEND, WARDELL C., JR., federal agency administrator; b. Balt., Oct. 16, 1952; s. Wardell Clinton Sr. and Toyoko Yonamine; m. Diane Martin, 1979; 4 children. BS in Psychology and Social Welfare, Western Carolina U., 1975; MSW with distinction, W.Va. U., 1977. Project dir. Congressman Jamie Clarke, Washington, 1983-85, Congressman Doug Applegate, Washington, 1985-87; from legis. dir. to adminstrv. asst./chief of staff Congressman Mike Espy, Washington, 1987-93; sr. adv. Presdl. Transition Team, Washington, 1992-93; asst. sec. adminstrn. USDA, Washington, 1993—. Former group counselor Boys Club, Asheville, N.C.; former health educator, outreach coord. Assn. Sickle Cell Disease, Charlotte, N.C.; former planning and devel. mgr. Human Resource Devel. Found., Morgantown, W.Va.; former dir. Community Devel. Dept., Henderson County, N.C.; former bus. mgr. Cherokee Minority Bus. Devel. Ctr., Asheville, N.C.; bd. dirs. Shepherd's Table, Inc., 1985-88, chmn. pub. rels. com., 1986-87; sr. warden ministry Ascension Episc. Ch., Silver Spring, Md., 1986-90, vestry mem., treas., chmn. fin. com., chmn. rector search com.; mem. diocesan investment com. Episc. Diocese Washington, 1991—; active YMCA, Silver Spring, 1988—. Mem. NASW, Adminstrv. Assts. Assn. (bd. dirs. 1991, 92, v.p. 1992), Coun. African-Am. Adminstrv. Assts., Acad. Cert. Social Workers, Global Leders for the Soutn, House Adminstrv. Assts. Alumni Assn. (bd. dirs. 1994). Office: Dept Agriculture Office Asst Sec Administrn 14th & Independence Ave SW Washington DC 20250-0002*

TOWNSEND-BUTTERWORTH, DIANA BARNARD, educational consultant, author; b. Albany, N.Y., Dec. 12; d. Barnard and Marjorie (Bradley) Townsend; m. J. Warner Butterworth, Jan. 23, 1969; children: James, Diana. AB, Harvard-Radcliffe Coll., 1960; MA, Tchrs. Coll., Columbia U., 1971. Tchr. St. Bernard's Sch., N.Y.C., 1963-78, head of lower sch. English, 1965-71, head of jr. sch., 1971-78; assoc. dir. Early Care Ctr., N.Y.C., 1984-87; acad. advisor Columbia Coll., N.Y.C., 1987-88; ednl. cons., lectr. N.Y.C., 1988—; dir. parent involvement initiative Dept. Continuing Profl. Edn., Tchrs. Coll., Columbia U., 1996, chmn. devel. com. alumni coun. Tchrs. Coll., 1994—; chmn. sub-com. Harvard schs. com. Harvard Coll., Cambridge, Mass., 1975—. Author: Preschool and Your Child: What You Should Know, 1995, Your Child's First School, 1992 (Parent's Choice award 1992), (book chpt.) Handbook of Clinical Assessment of Children and Adolescents; contbr. articles to ednl. publs. and jours. Mem. women's health symposium steering com. N.Y. Hosp., N.Y.C., 1988—. Mem. Assn. Lower Sch. Heads (co-founder 1975), Alumni Coun. Tchrs. Coll. (com. chair 1993-95), Harvard Faculty Club. Avocations: skiing, hiking, swimming, theatre, reading. Home: 1170 5th Ave New York NY 10029-6527

TOWNSHEND, PETER, musician, composer, singer; b. London, England, May 19, 1945. Co-founder (with Keith Moon, Roger Daltry, John Entwhistle), guitarist, composer music and lyrics for musical group, The Who (originally called The High Numbers, The Detours), 1964-82; composer: (rock operas) Tommy, 1969 (Tony Award, Best Score - Broadway prodn., 1993), Quadrophenia, 1973, (other albums) The Who Sings My Generation, 1965, Happy Jack, 1966, The Who Sell Out, 1967, Magic Bus: The Who on Tour (U.S. only), Live At Leeds, 1970, Who's Next, 1971, The Who By Numbers, 1975, Who Are You, 1978, Face Dances, 1981, It's Hard, 1982, Join Together, 1990; compositions including Behind Blue Eyes, I'm Free, Who Are You, My Generation, The Kids Are Alright, Bargain, Pure and Easy, Won't Get Fooled Again, Pinball Wizard, We're Not Gonna Take It, Dreaming From the Waist, Emminence Front, Nothing Is Everything (Let's See Action), Slit Skirts, Give Blood, Let My Love Open the Door, Cats in the Cupboard, English Boy; producer: films The Kids Are Alright, 1979, Quadrophenia, 1979, (with The Who) Meaty, Beaty, Big and Bouncy, 1971, Odds and Sods, 1974, The Kids Are Alright, 1979, Hooligans, 1981, Who's Missing, 1986, Two's Missing, 1987, Who's Better Who's Best, 1989, Who's Missing. 1986; solo albums include Who Came First, 1972, (with Ronnie Lane) Rough Mix, 1977, Secret Policeman's Ball, 1980, Empty Glass, 1980, All the Best Cowboys Have Chinese Eyes, 1982, Scoop, 1983, White City, 1985, Another Scoop, 1986, Deep End Live, 1987, The Iron Man, 1989, Psychoderelect, 1993, Psychoderelict, 1993; rec. 13 albums with The Who; author (short stories) Horse's Neck, 1985; musical dir. (film and soundtrack) Tommy, 1975 (Oscar award nomination 1975); Broadway musical The Who's Tommy (Tony awd., best original score), 1993. Office: care Entertainment Corp Am 99 Park 16th Ave New York NY 10016

TOY, ARTHUR DOCK FON, chemist; b. Canton, China, Sept. 13, 1915; came to U.S., 1927, naturalized, 1952; s. Yam Hong and Suei Hao (Loui) T.; m. Hui-I Liang, Sept. 5, 1942; children: Larry, Alan, Howard. Student, Joliet Jr. Coll., 1935-37; B.S., U. Ill., 1939, M.S., 1940, Ph.D. (Sigma Xi fellow, U. Ill. fellow), 1942. Research chemist Victor Chem. Works, Chicago Heights, Ill., 1942-52; dir. organic research Victor Chem. Works, 1952-59, asso. dir. research, 1959-63, dir. research, 1963-65; vis. scientist Cambridge U., Eng., 1965-66; sr. scientist Stauffer Chem. Co., Westport, Conn., 1965-68; mgr. splty. dept. Stauffer Chem. Co., 1968-72, chief scientist, 1972-74; dir. Eastern Research Ctr., 1975-78, dir. research, 1979-80; cons. Stamford, Conn., 1980—; cons. dept. chemistry Manhattan Coll., 1982-85; internat. sci. bd. Internat. Conf. Phosphorus Chemistry, 1974-80. Author: Phosphorus

Chemistry in Everyday Living, 1976, 2d edit. (with Edward N. Walsh), 1987, The Chemistry of Phosphorus, 1975; contbr. articles to sci. jours.; holder 83 patents in field; researcher on organic phosphorus compounds for plastic applications, on allyl aryl-phosphonate flame resistant plastics, on economic processes for synthesis of organic phosphorus intermediates, on phosphorus insecticides, on aquo ammono phosphoric acids, on organic reaction mechanisms, and on new reactions leading to the formation of carbon to phosphorus bonds. Recipient Disting. Alumnus award Joliet Jr. Coll., 1985, Eli Whitney award Conn. Patent Law Assn., 1988; honoree of Symposium Phosphorus Chemistry in Am., 1991, at 202d Am. Chem. Soc. nat. meeting. Fellow AAAS; mem. Am. Chem. Soc. (chmn. N.Y. chpt. 1974-76, councilor 1973-87, Outstanding Svc. award 1978), Royal Soc. Chemistry (London), Westchester Chem. Soc. (chmn. 1970-71), Conn. Acad. Sci. and Engring., Chinese-Am. Chem. Soc., Phi Beta Kappa, Sigma Xi. Home: 14 Katydid Ln Stamford CT 06903-4813 *In the area of human interaction, I find that clear communication is of utmost importance in that we are not what we think we are but what others perceive us tobe.*

TOY, CHARLES DAVID, lawyer; b. N.Y.C., June 29, 1955; s. Frank H.F. and Louise S.K. (Louie) T.; m. Sandra Lynn Youla, Mar. 10, 1984. BA cum laude, Harvard U., 1977, JD, 1980. Bar: N.Y. 1981. Assoc. Milbank, Tweed, Hadley & McCloy, N.Y.C., 1980-84; assoc. Kaye, Scholer, Fierman, Hays & Handler, Hong Kong, 1984-88, ptnr., 1989-91; ptnr. Kaye, Scholer, Fierman, Hays & Handler, N.Y.C., 1991-93; v.p., gen. counsel Overseas Pvt. Investment Corp., Washington, 1993—, v.p., fin., 1995-96; spkr. seminars Bus. Internat., 1985, 96, Asia Conf., 1988, Korea Fgn. Trade Assn., 1989, 90, World Trade Inst., 1992, U. Pa., 1993, 94, 95, Washington Internat. Trade Assn., 1993, Am. Conf. Inst., 1994, 95, Am. Soc. Internat. Law, 1994, Small Bus. Exporters Assn., 1994, Inst. for Infrastructure Fin., 1995, Assn. Bar City of N.Y., 1995, Infocast, 1995, Calif. Coun. Internat. Trade, 1995, World Econ. Devel. Congress, 1995, Baker & McKenzie Ann. Mtg. Client Conf., 1995, Corp. Legal Times Roundtable, 1995, Ctr. for Bus. Intelligence, 1995. Contbg. editor Taxes and Investment in Asia and the Pacific, 1985, Tax News Svc., 1986—, Bull. for Internat. Fiscal Documentation, 1986—; bd. editors Strategic Alliance Alert, 1994—. Mem. ABA (spkr. seminar 1994, 95), Am. Arbitration Assn., N.Y. State Bar Assn., Assn. Bar City of N.Y., Nat. Asian Pacific Am. Bar Assn., Asian Am. Bar Assn. N.Y., Asia Soc., Hong Kong Assn. N.Y., Harvard Law Sch. Assn., Harvard Club (N.Y.C. and Washington), Am. Club (Hong Kong), Ladies Recreation Club (Hong Kong), Phi Beta Kappa. Democrat. Roman Catholic. Office: Overseas Pvt Investment Corp 1100 New York Ave NW Washington DC 20527-0001

TOY, PEARL TAK-CHU YAU, transfusion medicine physician; b. Hong Kong, July 31, 1947; came to U.S., 1965; d. Tse-Wah Yau and Grace Liang; m. Larry Toy, Dec. 12, 1970; 1 child, Jennifer. BA, Smith Coll., 1969; MD, Stanford U., 1973. From asst. prof. to assoc. prof. dept. lab. medicine U. Calif. Sch. Medicine, San Francisco, 1980-91, prof. dept. lab. medicine, 1991—; chief blood bank and donor ctr. Moffitt-Long Hosp., U. Calif., San Francisco, 1991—; chair expert panel on autologous transfusion NIH, Bethesda, Md., 1988-94, chair rsch. tng. rev. com., 1992. Contbr. articles to profl. jours., chpts. to books. Recipient numerous grants NIH, 1983—. Mem. Phi Beta Kappa, Sigma Xi, Alpha Omega Alpha. Achievements include research in autologous blood transfusion; blood transfusions.

TOYER, RICHARD HENRY, accountant; b. Snohomish, Wash., Aug. 6, 1944; s. Henry James Toyer and Bertha Maud (Darrow) Gilmore; m. Jean Ann Moore, July 1, 1966; 1 child, David K. BS in Acctg., Cen. Wash. U., 1973. CPA. Staff acct. Moss, Adams and Co., Everett, Wash., 1973-74, sr. staff acct., 1975-77; prin. Toyer and Assocs., CPAs Inc., PS, Everett, Wash., 1977—. Mayor City of Lake Stevens, Wash., 1983-91, city councilman, 1977-83; state treas. Wash. Jaycees, 1975-76; mem. Snohomish County Estate Planning Coun.; chmn. Snohomish County Subregional Coun., 1981-82; exec. bd. Puget Sound Regional Coun.,1 981-83; chmn. City of Everett Navy Rev. Task Force, 1987-88, Shonomish County HUD policy adv. bd., 1982-91; chmn. Snohomish County Cities and Towns, 1983-84, Snohomish County Transp. Authority, 1987-89, Snohomish County Dept. Emergency Mgmt., 1981-91, Snohomish County Tomorrow Steering Com., 1989-91; treas. Lake Stevens Aquafest, 1983-84; sponsor Miss Lake Stevens Pageant, 1983-84; bd. dirs., treas. Josephine Sunset Home, 1993-94; bd. dirs. Vols. of Am., 1995—. Sgt. U.S. Army, 1965-67, Vietnam. Mem. AICPA, Wash. Soc. CPAs, Everett C. of C. (treas. 1990-94), Marysville C. of C., Lake Stevens C. of C. (charter), Rotary (charter). Lutheran. Home: 15128 76th St SE Snohomish WA 98290-6150 Office: 3705 Colby Ave Everett WA 98201

TOYOMURA, DENNIS TAKESHI, architect; b. Honolulu, July 6, 1926; s. Sansuke Fujimoto and Take T.; m. Akiko Charlotte Nakamura, May 27, 1949; children—Wayne J., Gerald F., Amy J., Lyle D. BS in Archtl. Engring., Chgo. Tech. Coll., 1949; cert., U. Ill., Chgo., 1950, 53, 54; student, Ill. Inst. Tech., Chgo., 1953-54; cert., U. Hawaii-Dept. Def., Honolulu, 1966-67, 73. Lic. architect, Ill. 1954, Hawaii 1963, real estate broker Ill., 1957; cert. fallout shelter analyst Dept. Def., cert. analyst multi-disaster design Dept. Def., cert. value engr. NavFacEngCom, Gen. Svc. Adminstrn., EPA, Fed. Housing Agy., U.S. Corps. of Engrs., cert. arbitrator Hawaii. Designer, draftsman James M. Turner, Hammond, Ind., 1950-51, Wimberly and Cook, Honolulu, 1952, Gregg, Briggs & Foley, Chgo., 1952-54; architect Holabird, Root & Burgee, Chgo., 1954-55, Loebl, Schlossman & Bennett, Chgo., 1955-62; prin. Honolulu, 1963—; juror Walt Disney Imagi-Nations, U. Hawaii's Imagineering Design Competition, Manoa, 1993, Engring. Excellence awards Cons. Engring. Coun., Hawaii, 1987; cons. Aloha Tower Devel. Corp., State of Hawaii Project Devel. Evaluation Team, 1989, archl. cons. 1991—; mem. Provost Selection Interview Com., Leeward C.C., U. Hawaii, 1987; design profl. conciliation panelist Dept. of Commerce and Consumer Affairs, State of Hawaii, 1983, 84; archtl. design examiner Nat. Coun. of Archtl. Registration Bd., State of Hawaii, 1974-78; cons. Honolulu Redevel. Agy., City and County of Honolulu, 1967-71; sec., dir. Maiko of Hawaii, Honolulu, 1972-74, Pacific Canal of Hawaii, 1972; mem. steering com. IX world conf. World Futures Studies Fedn., U. Hawaii, 1986; conf. organizer pub. forum 10th Hawaii Conf. in High Energy Physics, U. Hawaii, 1985, 60th Ann. Nat. Coun. of Archtl. Registration Bd. Conv., Maui, Hawaii, 1981, Hawaii State Bd. Conv. steering com.; del. Nat. Credential Com., NCARB, 1981, 125th Nat. AIA Com., Honolulu, 1982, HS/AIA Conv. Com., steering com., budget and fin. chmn., treas., 1981-82; apptd. Arbitration Panel State of Hawaii Lemon Law, 1995; commr. Hawaii Housing Authority, 1994—; mem. Nat. Assn. Housing and Redevel. Ofcls., 1994—; mem. legis. adv. com. Hawaii State Legis., 1990-93; vice chmn. Rsch. Corp. U. Hawaii, 1991-94, bd. dirs. 1986—; commr. Hawaii State Found. on Culture and the Arts, 1982-86, Gov.'s Com. on Hawaii Econ. Future, 1984; archtl. mem. Bd. Registration for Profl. Engrs., Architects, Land Surveyors and Landscape Architects, State of Hawaii, 1974-82, sec. 1980, vice chmn. 1981, chmn., 1982; mem. Nat. Coun. Engring. Examiners, 1974-82; mem. Nat. Coun. Archtl. Registration Bds., Western region del. 1974-82, nat. del. 1974-82. Editor, pub.: (directory) Japanese Companies Registered to do Business in Hawaii, 1991. Del. commr. state assembly Synod of Ill., United Presbyn. Ch. U.S.A., 1958, alt. del. commr. nat. gen. assembly, 1958, del. commr. L.A. Presbytery, 1965; mem. bd. session 2d Presbyn. Ch., Chgo., 1956-62, trustee, 1958-62; trustee lst Presbyn. Ch., Honolulu, 1964-66, 69-72, sec., 1965, bd. sessions, 1964-72, 74-79; founding assoc. Hawaii Loa Coll., Kaneohe, 1964; mem. adv. commn. drafting tech. Leeward Community Coll., U. Hawaii, 1965—; bd. dirs. Lyon Arboretum Assn., U. Hawaii, 1976-77, treas.,1976. With AUS, 1945-46. Recipient Human Resources of U.S.A. award Am. Bicentennial Rsch. Inst., 1973, Outstanding Citizen Recognition award Cons. Engrs. Coun. Hawaii, 1975, cert. appreciation Gov. Hawaii, 1982, 86, 89, commendation Hawaii Ho. of Reps. and Senate, 1983, 90, 91, cert. appreciation Leeward C.C., U. Hawaii Adv. Com., 1971-86, 87—, medal for peace Albert Einstein Internat. Acad. Found., 1990, commendation resolution Honolulu Japanese C. of C., 1991, Recognition award Consulting Engrs. Coun., 1995. Fellow AIA (Coll. Fellows 1983, bd. dirs. Hawaii Soc. 1973-74, treas. 1975, pres. Hawaii Coun. 1990, Pres.'s Mahalo award 1981, Fellows medal 1983, govt. affairs award 1996); mem. AAAS (life), ASTM, Am. Arbitration Assn. (mem. paf arbitrators, 1983—), Nat. Assn. Housing & Redevelopment Ofcls., Acad. Polit. Sci. (life), Am. Acad. Polit. and Social Scis., N.Y. Acad. Scis. (life), Chgo. Art Inst., Chgo. Natural History Mus., Honolulu Acad. Arts (life), Nat. Geog. Soc. (life), Coun. Ednl. Facility Planners Internat. (bd. govs. N.W. region 1980-86, 89—), Bldg. Rsch. Inst. (adv. bd. of Nat. Acad. Sci.), Ill. Assn. Professions, Constrn. Specifications Inst. (charter mem. Hawaii), Constrn. Industry Legis. Orgn. (bd. dirs. 1973-81, 83—, treas. 1976-77, v.p. 1990-91, pres. 1991-93), Japan-Am. Soc., Hawaii State C. of C. (bd. dirs. 1984-87), U. Hawaii Kokua O'Hui, O'Nahe Popo (bd. dirs. 1984-88), Hawaii-Pacific Rim Soc. (bd. trustees 1988—, sec. 1991—), Malolo Mariners Club (purser 1964, skipper 1965, Hawaii), Alpha Lambda Rho, Kappa Sigma Kappa. Home: 2602 Manoa Rd Honolulu HI 96822-1703 Office: 1370 Kapiolani Blvd Honolulu HI 96814-3604

TOZER, W. JAMES, JR., investment company executive; b. Salt Lake City, Feb. 9, 1941; s. W. James and Virginia (Somerville) T.; m. Elizabeth Farran, July 30, 1965; children: Farran Virginia, Katharine Coppins. B.A. cum laude, Trinity Coll., 1963; M.B.A., Harvard U., 1965. Investment officer First Nat. City Overseas Investment Corp., N.Y.C., 1965-70; v.p. corp. devel. Citicorp, N.Y.C., 1970-71; sr. v.p. and head Citicorp Subs. Group, 1971-74; sr. v.p., gen. mgr., head Merchant Banking Group, 1974-75, sr. v.p., gen. mgr. N.Y. banking div., 1975-77; sr. exec. v.p., dir. and head investment banking div. Shearson Hayden Stone, Inc., N.Y.C., 1978-79; exec. v.p. Marine Midland Bank and Marine Midland Banks, Inc., 1979-80, sr. exec. v.p. ops., fin. and strategic staff units, 1980-85, mem. office of chmn., sector exec. corp., instl. and internat. banking, 1985-87; chmn. Mountain West Banking Corp., Denver, 1988-89; pres., chief operating officer Prudential-Bache Securities, Inc., N.Y.C., 1989-90; mng. dir. Vectra Mgmt. Group, 1990-93; pres., CEO Lincolnshire Mgmt., Inc., N.Y.C., 1993-94; mng. dir. Vectra Mgmt. Group, 1995—; trustee Mktg. Sci. Inst., 1975-78; bd. dirs. Vectra Banking Corp., Trans-Wasatch Co., Credentials Svcs. Internat. Chmn. bd. Fellows Trinity Coll., 1972-78; trustee, treas. Community Service Soc., 1976-87; mem. Securities Industry Assn., 1977-78; mem. Citizens Budget Commn., 1986—; adv. council Atlanta U. Sch. Bus. Adminstrn., 1985-89. Mem. N.Y. State Bankers Assn. (legis. policy com. 1981-87), Assn. Res. City Bankers (govt. rels. com. 1984-87), Am. Bankers Assn. (govt. rels. coun. 1985-87), Economic Club, University Club, Bond of N.Y. Club, Millbrook Club, Mashomack Club, River Club (N.Y.C.). Home: 1112 Park Ave New York NY 10128-1235 Office: 65 E 55th St New York NY 10022-3219

TOZER, WILLIAM EVANS, entomologist, educator; b. Binghamton, N.Y., July 7, 1947; s. William Evans and Gertrude Genevieve (Lewis) T. BS in Natural Sci., Niagara U., 1969; MS in Biology, Ball State U., 1979; PhD in Entomology, U. Calif., Berkeley, 1986. Cert. C.C. biology and zoology tchr. Calif. Jr. H.S. sci. and English tchr. St. Patricks Sch., Corning, N.Y., 1969-71; tchg. asst. biology Ball State U., Muncie, Ind., 1974-76; pvt. practice biol. eviron. cons. Berkeley, Calif., 1976-79, 86-88; rsch. asst. U. Calf., Berkeley, 1979-86; dept. head edn. and tng. U.S. Navy Disease Vector Ecology and Control Ctr., Poulsbo, Wash., 1988—; mem., acting chmn. San Francisco Bay Area Mosquito Control Coun., Alameda, 1988-96; com. mem. Armed Forces Pest Mgmt. Bd., Washington, 1994—. Editor (field handbook) Navy Environmental Health Center, 1994; contbr. articles to profl. jours. With U.S. Army, 1971-73. Mem. Am. Entomol. Soc., Sigma Xi. Achievements include first to publish evidence for underwater behavioral thermoregulation in adult insects. Avocations: photography, tennis, hiking, bicycling, softball. Home: 1407 NW Santa Fe Lane # 304 Silverdale WA 98383 Office: USN Disease Vector Ecol Control Ctr 19950 Seventh Ave NE # 201 Poulsbo WA 98370

TRABITZ, EUGENE LEONARD, aerospace company executive; b. Cleve., Aug. 13, 1937; s. Emanuel and Anna (Berman) T.; m. Caryl Lee Rine, Dec. 22, 1963 (div. Aug. 1981); children: Claire Marie, Honey Caryl; m. Kathryn Lynn Bates, Sept. 24, 1983; 1 stepchild, Paul Francis Rager. BA, Ohio State U., 1965. Enlisted USAF, 1954, advanced through grades to maj.; served as crew commdr. 91st Stragetic Missile Div., Minot, S.D., 1968-70; intelligence officer Fgn. Tech. Div., Dayton, Ohio, 1970-73; dir. external affairs Aero Systems Div., Dayton, 1973-75; program mgr. Air Force Armament Div., Valparaiso, Fla., 1975-80; dir. ship ops. Air Force Ea. Test Range, Satellite Beach, Fla., 1980-83; dep. program mgr. Air Force Satellite Text Ctr., Sunnyvale, Calif., 1983-84; ret., 1984; sr. staff engr. Ultrasystems Inc., 1984-86; pres. TAWD Systems Inc., Palo Alto, Calif., 1986-92, Am. Telenetics Co., San Mateo, Calif., 1992—; cons. Space Applications Corp., Sunnyvale, 1986-87, Litton Computer Svcs., Mountain View, Calif., 1987-91, Battelle Meml. Inst. Columbus, 1993—. V.p. Bd. County Mental Health Clinic, Ft. Walton Beach, Fla., 1973-75. Decorated Bronze Star. Mem. DAV (life), World Affairs Coun., U.S. Space Found. (charter), Air Force Assn. (life), Assn. Old Crows, Nat. Sojourners, Commonwealth Club Calif., Masons (32 degree). Avocations: golf, tennis, racketball, sailing, bridge. Home: 425 Anchor Rd Apt 317 San Mateo CA 94404-1058

TRACANNA, KIM, elementary and secondary physical education educator; b. Washington, Pa., Nov. 3, 1960; d. Frank and Mary Lou (Nardi) T. BSEd in Health and PE, Slippery Rock U., 1982; MS, U. N.C., 1985. Cert. health and physical edn. tchr. K-12, Fla., CPR, Advanced First Aid, ARC. Instr. PE Young World, Inc., Greensboro, N.C.; instr. PE and Health Beth-Ctr. Elem. Sch., Fredericktown, Pa.; rsch. asst. Physical Edn. Dept. U. N.C., Greensboro; instr. phys. edn., health coord. Lakeside Elem. Sch., Orange Park, Fla., 1986—; mem. exec. bd. dirs. Fla. Striders CORE Team Curriculum Coun. Active in civic orgns., bd. dirs. Clay County Tchrs. Acad. Excellence, 1994—. Recipient World Fellowship award for Outstanding Young Scholar, 1987, cert. of Outstanding Achievment in Elem. PE, 1987, Supt.'s Cert. of Achievement Clay County Sch. Bd., 1987, Gov.'s Leadership award, 1988, Unsung Hero of Yr. award, Jacksonville Track Club, 1989; named to Young Profl. Hall of Fame, 1987. Mem. AAHPERD, Fla. Alliance for Health, Phys. Edn., Recreation and Dance (Profl. Recognition award 1995), Am. Running and Fitness Assn., Clay County Reading Coun., Clay County Edn. Assn., Nat. Assn. for Edn. of Young Children, Nat. Assn. for Sports and Phys. Edn., Nat. Assn. for Girls and Women in Sports, Phi Epsilon Kappa (Outstanding PE Major award 1982), Sigma Sigma Kappa.

TRACEY, EDWARD JOHN, physician, surgeon; b. Norwalk, Conn., July 26, 1931; s. Edward John and Clara (Hammond) T.; m. Ann Marie Schenk, Sept. 7, 1957; children: Sharon, Scott. BA, Yale U., 1954; MD, N.Y. Med. Coll., N.Y.C., 1958. Diplomate Am. Bd. Surgery. Intern Bellevue Hosp., N.Y.C., 1958-59; resident in surgery NYU-Bellevue Med. Ctr., N.Y.C., 1958-63; attending surgeon Norwalk (Conn.) Hosp., 1965—, asst. dir. dept. surgery, 1975-82, chief of staff, 1982-85, chief sect. gen. surgery, 1989-95, trustee, 1972, 82-85, 92—; dir., physician support svcs., 1995—. Lt. comdr. USNR, 1963-65. Mem. ACS, AMA, Conn. Med. Soc., Fairfield County Med. Soc., Norwalk Med. Soc. (pres. 1976-77). Clubs: Cath. (Norwalk, Conn., pres. 1974-75), Shore and country (Norwalk, Conn.). Home: 124 East Ave Norwalk CT 06851-5713

TRACEY, JAY WALTER, JR., retired lawyer; b. Rocky Ford, Colo., June 13, 1925; s. Jay Walter and Margaret Louise (Bish) T.; m. Elizabeth Longfellow Henry, Nov. 1, 1952 (div. July 1988); children: Jay Walter III, William H., Anne E., John B.; m. Elizabeth Folk Flinn, Apr. 22, 1989. BS, Yale U., 1949; LLB, Harvard U., 1952. Bar: Colo. 1952, U.S. Dist. Ct. Colo. 1952, U.S. Ct. Appeals (10th cir.) 1958. Assoc. Holland & Hart, Denver, 1952-57, ptnr., 1957-71, 72-89; pres. Von Frellick Assocs., Inc., Denver, 1971-72; dir. Ctr. for Dispute Resolution, Denver, 1984-88. Councilman, City of Cherry Hills Village (Colo.), 1965-70, mayor pro tem, 1966-70, mem. Home Rule Charter Conv., 1966; trustee Denver Country Day Sch., 1967-70. With U.S. Army, 1943-46. Decorated Purple Heart. Mem. ABA, Colo. Bar Assn., Denver Bar Assn., Colo. Yale Assn. (pres. 1971-72), Assn. Yale Alumni (del. 1975-78), Harvard Law Sch. Assn. Colo. (pres. 1962-63), Harvard Law Sch. Assn. (v.p. 1963-64), Univ. Club (pres. 1967-69) Denver Country Club, Mile High Club, Round Hill Club (Greenwich, Conn.), Denver Rotary (sec. 1979-80, bd. dirs. 1980-82, 1st v.p. 1981-82). Republican. Episcopalian. Office: 555 17th St Ste 3200 Denver CO 80202-3929

TRACEY, MARGARET, dancer; b. Pueblo, Colo.. Student, Sch. Am. Ballet, 1982. With corps de ballet N.Y.C. Ballet, 1986-88, soloist, 1989-91, prin., 1991. Featured in ballets (Balanchine) Ivesiana, Tarantella, The Nutcracker, Symphony in C, Jewels, Square Dance, Tschaikovsky Pas de Deux, Tschaikovsky Suite No. 3, Vienna Waltzes, Apollo, Ballo Della Regina, Divertimento No. 15, Donizetti Variations, Harlequinade, A Midsummer Night's Dream, Sonatine, La Source, Stars and Stripes, Symphony in Three Movements, Valse Fantaisie, Western Symphony, Who Cares?, (Robbins) Afternoon of a Faun, The Four Seasons, The Goldberg Variations, (Martins) Les Petits Riens, Mozart Serenade, Fearful Symmetries, Zakouski, Sleeping Beauty, (Anderson) Baroque Variations; also appeared in N.Y.C. Ballet's Blanchine Celebration, 1993; toured in Europe, Asia. Recipient U.S.A. award Princess Grace Found., 1985-86; scholar Atlantic Richfield Found., 1982-85. Office: NYC Ballet NY State Theater Lincoln Ctr Plaza New York NY 10023

TRACEY, VALERIE LEWIS, special education educator; b. N.Y.C., Dec. 20, 1953; d. Alvin Walter and Vida Arlene (Davies) Lewis; m. Steven William Tracey, Aug. 15, 1981; children: Sean Michael, Heather Brianna. BS, So. Conn. State U., 1975, MS, 1981. Cert. tchr. spl. edn., phys. edn. Tchr. phys. edn. Danbury (Conn.) Pub. Schs., 1975-79, tchr. spl. edn., 1980—. Recipient Recognition award Coun. Exceptional Children, 1991. Mem. ASCD, Phi Delta Kappa. Home: 13 Hawthorne Hill Rd Newtown CT 06470-1404 Office: Rogers Park Mid Sch 21 Memorial Dr Danbury CT 06810

TRACHSEL, WILLIAM HENRY, corporate lawyer; b. El Paso, Tex., Apr. 20, 1943. BS in Aerospace Engring., U. Fla., 1965; JD, U. Conn., 1971. Bar: Conn. 1971. With United Tech. Corp., Hartford, Conn., 1965-86, v.p., sec. and dep. gen. counsel, 1993—. Mem. ABA, Am. Corp. Counsel Assn. Office: United Tech Corp United Tech Bldg Hartford CT 06101

TRACHT, DAVID ADAMS, petroleum products consultant; b. Ft. Worth, Oct. 2, 1916; s. Glenwood Alonzo and Virginia Bell (Evans) T.; m. Thedz Evelyn Johnson, July 25, 1941 (div. Oct. 1973); m. Margie Virginia Estonson, June 29, 1979; 1 child, Delene Spencer. BA, U. Redlands, 1939; postgrad. in chem. engring., U. Houston, Baytown, 1962. Inspector ship tanks Esso Std. Oil Co., Baytown, Tex., 1942-61; marine chemist Homble co., Baytown, 1942-61; sr. staff coord. Exxon, Benicia, Calif., 1969-78; v.p. Urich Oil Co., Whittier, Calif., 1977-85; cons. gasoline blending, aviation gas, jet fuel Sevedz Oil Co., 1985-94; adv. bd. Conte Costa County Jr. Coll., Martinez, Calif., 1974-78; cons. pet products blending, 1984-89. Vice pres. Boy Scouts Am.; lt. gov. Kiwanis, pres., 1974. Fellow Inst. for Advancement of Engring.; mem. ASTM (D2 com.), So. Calif. Soc. of Engrs., Soc. of Automotive Engrs. (chmn. So. Calif.), Nat. Pet Refining Assn., Internat. Std. Orgn. Republican. Methodist. Avocations: football, basketball officiating. Home: 4692 Barcelona Way Oceanside CA 92056-5106

TRACHTENBERG, MATTHEW J., bank holding company executive; b. N.Y.C., June 20, 1953; s. Mark Trachtenberg and Joanne Horne. BA magna cum laude, NYU, 1974; JD, Bklyn. Law Sch., 1977; MBA in Fin., Fordham U., 1982. Bar: N.Y. 1979. Mgmt. trainee Mfrs. Hanover Trust Co., N.Y.C., 1977-78, credit analyst, 1978-79, corp. banking rep., 1979-80, asst. sec., 1980-82, asst. v.p., 1982, v.p., 1982-86, v.p., corp. sec., 1987-92; v.p., corp. sec. Mfrs. Hanover Corp., N.Y.C., 1987-92; dir. Mfrs. Hanover Found., 1987-92; v.p., sec. regional bd. Chem. Bank, N.Y.C., 1992-96; v.p., dep. corp. sec. Chem. Banking Corp., N.Y.C., 1992-96, Chem. Bank, 1992-96; sec. Chem. Bank Regional Bd., 1992-96; v.p. Chem. Bank, 1992-96, Chem. Banking Corp., 1992-96; v.p. asst. corp. sec. Chase Manhattan Corp., N.Y.C., 1996—, Chase Manhattan Bank, N.Y.C., 1996—. Bd. dirs., treas. Nat. Orch. Assn.; bd. dirs. Joffrey Ballet, N.Y. Eye and Ear Infirmary; pres. U.S.O. of Met. N.Y.; chmn. Manhattan direct svcs. com. Lighthouse for the Blind. N.Y. State Regents scholar. Mem. N.Y. State Bar Assn., Am. Soc. Corp. Secs., Phi Beta Kappa, Pi Sigma Alpha. Avocations: music, fishing, painting, writing. Office: Chase Manhattan Corp 270 Park Ave New York NY 10017-2014

TRACHTENBERG, STEPHEN JOEL, university president; b. Bklyn., Dec. 14, 1937; s. Oscar M. and Shoshana G. (Weinstock) T.; m. Francine Zorn, June 24, 1971; children: Adam Maccabee, Ben-Lev. BA, Columbia U., 1959; JD, Yale U., 1962; M in Pub. Adminstrn., Harvard U., 1966; LHD (hon.), Trinity Coll., 1986; HHD (hon.), U. Hartford, 1989; LLD (hon.), Hanyang U., Seoul, 1990, Richmond Coll., London, 1995; DPA (hon.), Kyonggi U., Seoul, 1994. Bar: N.Y. 1964, U.S. Supreme Ct. 1967. Atty. AEC, 1962-65; legis. asst. to Congressman John Brademas of Ind., Washington, 1965; tutor law Harvard Coll., also; teaching fellow edn. and pub. policy J.F. Kennedy Grad. Sch. Govt., Harvard U., 1965-66; spl. asst. to U.S. edn. commr. Office of Edn., HEW, Washington, 1966-68; asso. prof. polit. sci. Boston U., 1969-77, asso. dean, 1969-70, dean, 1970-74, assoc. v.p., co-counsel, 1974-76, v.p. acad. services, 1976-77; pres., prof. pub. adminstrn. U. Hartford, Conn., 1977-88, George Washington U., Washington, 1988—; mem. adv. bd. Ednl. Record; bd. dirs. Consortium of Univs. Washington Met. Area; mem. coun. on competitiveness, mem. Fed. City Coun.; peer reviewer NCAA Com. on Athletics Cert.; bd. dirs. Loctite Corp., NationsBank, NationsBank Trust Co., Greater Washington Bd. Trade, Nat. Edn. Telecom. Orgn., Washington Rsch. Libr. Consortium. Mem. editl. bd. Jour. Higher Edn. Mgmt.; consulting editor Jour. Edn.; contbr. articles to profl. jours. Bd. dirs. Urban League, Washington; mem. D.C. Mayor's Bus. Adv. Coun., Jewish Hist. Soc. Am., Jewish Pub. Soc. Am.; mem. exec. panel Chief Naval Ops.; bd. overseers List Coll. Jewish Theol. Sem. Am. Winston Churchill fellow Eng., 1969; named Outstanding Young Person, Boston Jr. C. of C., 1970, One of 100 Young Leaders, Acad. Am. Council Learning, 1978, Alumnus of Yr. James Madison High Sch., Bklyn., 1982, one of Fifty Outstanding Alumni Problem Solvers Harvard's John F. Kennedy Sch. Government, 1987; recipient Myrtle Wreath award Hadassah, 1982, Scopus award Am. Friends of Hebrew U., 1986, assoc. fellow Morse Coll. Yale U., 1980, Human Rels. award NCCJ, 1987, award NAACP, 1988, citation Conn. Bar Assn., 1988, Univ. medal of highest honor Kyung Hee U., Seoul, Korea, 1990, Martin Luther King, Jr. Internat. Salute award, 1992, Hannah G. Solomon award Nat. Coun. Jewish Women, 1992, Father of Yr. award Washington Urban League, 1993, Univ. Pres. medal Kyonggi U., Seoul, 1993, Am. Czech and Slovak Assn. Merit award, 1993, John Jay award Columbia U., 1995, Spirit of Democracy award Am. Jewish Congress, 1995, Newcomen Soc. award, 1995, Disting. Achievement medal Greenberg Ctr. for Judaic Studies U. Hartford, 1995. Mem. Am. Assn. Univ. Adminstrs., N.Y. Acad. Scis., Internat. Assn. Univ. Pres. (N.Am. coun., v.p., Mount Vernon Adv. Coun. for 1999), Coun. Fgn. Rels., Sr. Soc. Sachems, Retail Cattleman's Assn. (adv. coun.), Masons, Scottish Rite Freemasonry (33d degree), Harvard Club (N.Y.C.), Tumblebrook Country Club (Bloomfield, Conn.), Cosmos Club (Washington), Univ. Club (Washington), 1925 F St. Club (Washington), Phi Beta Kappa, Pi Alpha Alpha. Office: George Washington U Office of President Washington DC 20052

TRACHTMAN, JERRY H., lawyer; b. Phila., Aug. 10, 1945. BSEE, Pa. State U., 1967; JD, U. Fla., 1976. Bar: Fla. 1976, U.S. Dist. Ct. (mid. dist.) Fla. 1978, U.S. Supreme Ct. 1980, U.S. Ct. Appeals (11th cir.) 1989; cert. aviation law. Elec. engr. N.Am. Aviation, Columbus, Ohio, 1967-68; Apollo spacecraft systems engr. N.Am. Aviation, Kennedy Space Ctr., Fla., 1968-71; Skylab project engr. Martin Marietta, Kennedy Space Ctr., 1971-74; pvt. practice Satellite Beach, Fla., 1976-80; atty., mng. ptnr. Trachtman and Henderson, P.A., Melbourne, Fla., 1980—; adj. prof. aviation law Fla. Inst. Tech., Melbourne, 1983-90; mem. adv. bd. Kaiser Coll., Melbourne, 1994—. Recipient Apollo achievement award NASA. Mem. ATLA, Fla. Bar Assn. (chmn. aviation law com. 1995, vice chmn. 1993-95), Lawyer-Pilots Bar Assn., NTSB Bar Assn. (founder 1984—), Acad. Fla. Trial Lawyers. Office: Ste 201 1990 W New Haven Ave Melbourne FL 32904

TRACI, DONALD PHILIP, retired lawyer; b. Cleve., Mar. 13, 1927; m. Lillian Traci Calafiore; 11 children. BS cum laude, Coll. of the Holy Cross, Worcester, Mass., 1950; JD magna cum laude, Clevé. State U., 1955; LLD (hon.), U. Urbino, Italy, 1989. Bar: Ohio 1955, U.S. Dist. Ct. (no. and so. dists.) Ohio 1955, U.S. Ct. Appeals (3d, 6th and 7th cirs.), U.S. Dist. Ct. (we. and ea. dists.) Pa., U.S. Supreme Ct. 1965. Ptnr. Spangenberg, Shibley, Traci, Lancione & Liber, Cleve., 1955-95; lectr. York U., Toronto, Ont., Can., Case Western Res. U., Cleve. Marshall Law Sch., U. Mich., Akron U., U. Cin., Ohio No. U., Harvard U. Trustee Cath. Charities Diocese of Cleve., past pres. Bd. Cath. Edn.; former chmn. bd. regents St. Ignatius H.S., Cleve.; mem. pres.'s coun. Coll. of Holy Cross; Eucharist min. St. Rose of Lima Ch. With USN, 1945-46. Fellow Am. Coll. Trial Lawyers, Internat. Acad. Trial Lawyers (past pres.), Am. Bd. Trial Advocacy; mem. ABA, ATLA (trustee Lambert Chair Found., lectr. trial practice), Ohio State Bar Assn. (lectr. trial practice), Ohio Acad. Trial Lawyers (past chmn. rules seminar, lectr. trial practice), Cuyahoga County Bar Assn. (lectr. trial practice), Cleve. Acad. Trial Lawyers (lectr. trial practice), Trial Lawyers for Pub. Justice (sustaining founder), Cleve. Bar Assn. (chmn. Advocacy Inst., trustee, CLE com., jud. selection com., spl. justice ctr. com., fed. ct., common pleas ct. and ct.

appeals com., pres. 1986), Jud. Conf. U.S. 6th Cir. Ct. (life), Jud. Conf. 8th Jud. Dist. Ohio life), Knights of Malta, Delta Theta Phi. Home: 10416 Lake Ave Cleveland OH 44102-1206 Office: 2400 National City Ctr Cleveland OH 44114

TRACT, MARC MITCHELL, lawyer; b. N.Y.C., Sept. 20, 1959; s. Harold Michael and Natalie Ann (Meyerowitz) T.; m. Sharon Beth Widrow; children: Melissa Hope, Harrison Michael. BA in Biology, Ithaca Coll., 1981; JD, Pepperdine U., 1984. Bar: N.Y. 1985, N.J. 1985, D.C. 1986. Assoc. Kroll & Tract, N.Y.C., 1985-90, ptnr., 1990-94; ptnr. Rosenman & Colin LLP, N.Y.C., 1994—; bd. dirs. Sorema N.Am. Reinsurance Co., N.Y.C., Colonia Ins. Co., N.Y.C., Folksamerica Reinsurance Co., N.Y.C., Navigators Group Inc., N.Y.C., Fortress Ins. Co. Am., N.Y.C., N.Y. Surety Co., Great Neck, N.Y., Chatham Reinsurance Corp., San Francisco, Nordstern Ins. Co. Am., N.Y.C., Colonia Underwriters Ins. Co., Ft. Smith, Ark., Alliance Ins. Co. Am., N.Y.C., London Assurance Am. Inc., N.Y.C., The Marine Indemnity Ins. Co. Am., N.Y.C., Sea Ins. Co. Am., N.Y.C., Sun Ins. Office Am., N.Y.C., The Mercantile & Gen. Reinsurance Co. Am., N.Y.C., 400 East 85th St. Realty Corp., N.Y.C. Mem. ABA, Assn. of Bar of City of N.Y. (com. on ins.), N.Y. State Bar Assn., N.J. State Bar Assn., N.Y. County Lawyers Assn., Am. Coun. Germany, Old Westbury Golf and Country Club, Met. Club, Econ. Club N.Y. Office: Rosenman & Colin LLP 575 Madison Ave New York NY 10022-2511

TRACY, ALLEN WAYNE, manufacturing company executive; b. Windsor, Vt., July 25, 1943; s. J. Wayne and Helen (Bernard) T.; m. Karla Noelte, Dec. 14, 1968; children: Tania, Tara. BA, U. Vt., 1965; MBA cum laude, Boston U., 1974. Retail salesman Exxon Corp., Boston, 1965-72; mfg. mgr. Leonard Silver Mfg. Co., Inc., Boston, 1974-78, v.p. ops., 1979-81; pres. OESM Corp., N.Y.C., 1978-81; pres. Gold Lance Inc., Houston, 1981-91, also bd. dirs.; v.p. ops. Town & Country Corp., 1989-92; sr. v.p. L.G. Balfour Co., 1990-92; asst. to pres. Syratech Corp., Boston, 1993; dir. ops. Goldman-Kolber Co., Inc., Norwood, Mass., 1994; exec. v.p., COO George H. Fuller & Son Co., Inc., Pawtucket, R.I., 1994—; bd. dirs. Verilyte Gold, Inc., L.G. Balfour Co., Inc. Mem. Bd. Selectmen, Town of Ashland, 1977-78; chmn. Ashland Study Town Govt. Com., 1976-77; vice chmn. ch. council Federated Ch. of Ashland, 1979-80, chmn., 1981; bd. dirs. Nottingham Forest Civic Assn., 1986. Served with U.S. Army, 1965-68. Mem. Nottingham Forest Club (Houston, bd. dirs. 1986), Beta Gamma Sigma. Home: 455 Prospect St Seekonk MA 02771-1503 Office: George H. Fuller & Son Co Inc 151 Exchange St Pawtucket RI 02860-2210 *The key to economic and social mobility is education. Education, however must be coupled with perseverance, diligence, hard work and a genuine appreciation of the efforts of all the people that one interacts with.*

TRACY, BARBARA MARIE, lawyer; b. Mpls., Oct. 13, 1945; d. Thomas A. and Ruth C. (Roby) T. BA, U. Minn., 1971; JD, U. Okla., 1980. Bar: Okla. 1980, U.S. Dist. Ct. (we. dist.) Okla. 1980, U.S. Dist. Ct. (no. dist.) Tex. 1991, U.S. Supreme Ct. 1988, U.S. Dist. Ct. (ea. dist.) Tex. 1995. Assoc. Pierce, Couch, Hendrickson, Johnston & Baysinger, Oklahoma City, 1980-82; ptnr. Rizley & Tracy, Sayre, Okla., 1982-84; pvt. practice Oklahoma City, 1984-90; gen. atty. U.S. Army Corps Engrs., Ft. Worth, 1991—. Mem. citizens adv. bd. O'Donoghue Rehab. Inst., Oklahoma City. Mem. ABA, Okla. Bar Assn., Fed. Bar Assn., Internat. Tng. in Commn. (pres. Ace Club chpt.). Democrat. Roman Catholic. Avocations: photography, flying, water sports. Office: 819 Taylor St Fort Worth TX 76102-6114

TRACY, CAROL COUSINS, foundation executive, former educator; b. N.Y.C., Jan. 31, 1943; d. James Franklin and Ruth (Hubbard) Cousins; m. William Ferber Tracy, Feb. 14, 1963; children: Lisa, Scott, Jennifer. BA, Duke U., 1965. Cert. educator, math. Tchr. Thrasher Sch., Signal Mountain, Tenn., 1967-69; tchr., math. Girls Prep. Sch., Chattanooga, 1980-91; exec. dir. Psi Beta, Chattanooga, 1981—; fin. officer Psi Chi, 1991—. Vol., bd. dirs. Jr. League, Chattanooga, 1973-83; tutor Inner City, Chattanooga, 1974-75, 88-90; sec., vol. Allied Arts, Chattanooga; publicity LWV; v.p., pres. Chattanooga Ballet Bd., 1991—; sec., bd. dirs. Signal Mountain Libr. Avocations: skiing, reading, roller blading. Home: 1500 Lyndhurst Dr Chattanooga TN 37405-3121 Office: Psi Beta Psi Chi Ste B 407 E 5th St Chattanooga TN 37403

TRACY, DAVID, theology educator; b. Yonkers, N.Y., Jan. 6, 1939. Licentiate in Theology, Gregorian U., Rome, 1964, Doctorate in Theology, 1969; hon. doctorate, U. of the South, 1982, Cath. Theol. Union, 1990; LHD (hon.), Rosary Coll., 1992, Fairfield U., 1993, Williams Coll., 1994, Fontbonne Coll., 1995, St. Xavier U., 1996. Instr. theology Cath. U. Am., Washington, 1967-69; prof. theology Divinity Sch., U. Chgo., 1969—, prof. com. analysis of ideas and methods, 1981—, Disting. Svc. prof., 1985, Andrew Thomas Greeley and Grace McNichols Greeley Disting. Svc. prof. Cath. studies, 1987, prof. com. social thought, 1990—; lectr. Beijing Inst. Sci. Study of Religion, Trinity Coll., Dublin, Gregorian U., Rome, World Coun. Chs., Geneva, Cath. U., Leuven, Belgium, Union Theol. Sem., Princeton Theol. Sem., numerous U.S. univs. including Harvard, Yale, Fordham, Notre Dame, Vanderbilt, So. Meth., Xavier, Marquette. Author: The Achievement of Bernard Lonergan, 1970, Blessed Rage for Order: The New Pluralism in Theology, 1975, The Analogical Imagination: Christian Theology and the Context of Pluralism, 1981, Plurality and Ambiguity: Hermeneutics, Religion and Hope, 1987, Religion and the Public Realm, 1987; co-author: (with John Cobb) Talking About God, 1983, (with Stephen Happel) The Catholic Vision, 1983, (with Robert M. Grant) A Short History of the Interpretation of the Bible, 1984; co-editor: (with Hans Küng and Johann Baptist Metz) Towards Vatican III: The Work That Needs to be Done, (with H. Küng) Theologie-Wohin?. German edit., 1983, English edit., 1985, (with Hans Küng) Paradigm Change in Theology, 1989; editor or co-editor various spl. vols. for Jour. Religion, Concilium jour.; co-editor Jour. Religious Studies Rev., Commonweal; past mem. editorial bd. Jour. Am. Acad. Religion, Theol. Studies jour.; current editorial bd. Theology Today, Jour. Pastoral Psychology; contbr. articles to scholarly and popular jours. including Jour. Religion, Theology Today, Critical Inquiry, Daedalus, Jour. Am. Acad. Religion, New Republic, N.Y. Times Book Rev., Christian Century. Mem. Am. Acad. Arts and Scis., Am. Acad. Religion, Am. Theol. Soc., Cath. Theol. Soc. Am. (pres. 1977-78). Office: U Chgo The Divinity Sch 1025 E 58th St Chicago IL 60637-1509

TRACY, JAMES DONALD, historian; b. St. Louis, Feb. 14, 1938; s. Leo W. and Marguerite M. (Meehan) T.; m. Nancy Ann McBride, Sept. 6, 1968 (div. 1993); children: Patrick, Samuel, Mary Ann. BA, St. Louis U., 1959; MAS, Johns Hopkins U., 1960; MA, Notre Dame U., 1961; PhD, Princeton U., 1967. Instr. U. Mich., 1964-66; instr. to prof. history U. Minn., Mpls., 1966—, dept. chmn., 1988-91; vis. prof. U. Leiden, Netherlands, spring 1987. Author: Erasmus: The Growth of a Mind, 1972, The Politics of Erasmus: A Pacifist Intellectual and His Political Milieu, 1979, True Ocean Found; Paludanus' Letters on Dutch Voyages to the Kara Sea, 1980, A Financial Revolution in the Habsburg Netherlands: Renten and Renteniers in the County of Holland, 1515-1565, 1985, Holland under Habsburg Rule: The Formation of a Body Politic, 1506-1566, 1990, Erasmus of the Low Countries, 1996; editor: Luther and the Modern State in Germany, 1986, The Rise of Merchant Empires: Long Distance Trade in the Early Modern Era, 1350-1750, 1990, The Political Economy of Merchant Empires: Long Distance Trade and State Power in the Early Modern World, 1991, (with T.A. Brady and H.O. Oberman) Handbook of European History in the Late Middle Ages, Renaissance and Reformation, Vol. 1, 1994, Vol. 2, 1995; mem. editl. bd. Sixteenth Century Jour., 1979—. Guggenheim fellow, 1972-73; NEH summer grantee, 1977, 85; Fulbright rsch. grantee, Belgium, 1979, Netherlands, 1980; resident fellow Netherlands Inst. for Advanced Studies, 1993-94. Fellow Netherlands Inst. for Advanced Studies; mem. Am. Cath. Hist. Soc., Soc. Reformation Rsch., 16th Century Studies Conf. (pres. 1995-96). Republican. Roman Catholic. Home: 63 Avon St S Apt 33 Saint Paul MN 55105-3336 Office: U Minn 614 Social Sci Bldg Minneapolis MN 55455

TRACY, JAMES JARED, JR., accountant, law firm administrator; b. Cleve., Jan. 17, 1929; s. James Jared and Florence (Comey) T.; m. Elizabeth Jane Bourne, June 30, 1953 (div. 1988); children: Jane Mackintosh, Elizabeth Boyd, James Jared IV, Margaret Gardiner; m. Judith Anne Cooper, Feb. 18, 1989. AB, Harvard U., 1950, MBA, 1953. CPA, Ohio. Acct., mgr. Price Waterhouse & Co., Cleve., 1953-65; treas., CFO Clevite Corp., Cleve., 1965-69; asst. treas. Republic Steel Corp., Cleve., 1969-70, treas., 1970-75; v.p., treas. Johns-Manville Corp., Denver, 1976-81; v.p., treas., CFO I. T. Corp., L.A., 1981-82; exec. dir. Hufstedler, Miller, Carlson & Beardsley, L.A., 1983-84, Shank, Irwin & Conant, Dallas, 1984-85, Pachter, Gold & Schaffer, L.A., 1985-86; v.p., sr. cons. Right Assocs., L.A., 1987-91; dir. adminstrn. Larson & Burnham, Oakland, Calif., 1991-95; retired Larson & Burnham, 1995; adminstrv. dir. Law Offices of Thomas E. Miller, Newport Beach, Calif., 1996—; trustee and v.p. Miss Hall's Sch., Pittsfield, Mass., 1970-78; dir. Union Commerce Bank, Cleve., 1971-76; adv. bd. mem. Arkwright-Boston Ins. Co., Boston, 1976-81. Trustee and v.p. Cleve. Soc. for Blind, 1965-76; trustee Western Res. Hist. Soc., Cleve., 1972-76; treas. St. Peters by the Sea Presbyn. Ch., Palos Verdes, Calif., 1981-91. Recipient Alumni award Harvard U., Denver, 1981. Mem. AICPA, Ohio Soc. CPAs, Assn. Legal Adminstrs., Nat. Assn. Realtors, Piedmont Montclair Rotary Club (pres. 1995-96), Harvard Club San Francisco, Harvard Bus. Sch. Club No. Calif. Avocations: sailing, golf, gardening, railroad layouts. Home: 180 Lombardy Ln Orinda CA 94563-1126

TRACY, JANET RUTH, legal educator, librarian; b. Denison, Iowa, July 16, 1941; d. L. M. and Grace (Harvey) T.; m. Rodd Mc Cormick Reynolds, Feb. 15, 1975 (dec. June 1993); children: Alexander, Lee. BA, U. Oreg., 1963; ML, U. Wash., 1964; JD, Harvard U., 1969. Bar: N.Y. 1970. Reference libr. Harvard Coll. Librs., Cambridge, Mass., 1964-66; assoc. Kelley Drye & Warren, N.Y.C., 1969-71; dir. data base design Mead Data Ctrl., Inc., N.Y.C., 1971-75; dir. rsch. Mvpl. Employees Legal Svc. Fund, N.Y.C., 1975-76; from asst. to assoc. prof. N.Y. Law Sch., N.Y.C., 1976-82; asst. libr. dir. Law Libr. Columbia U., N.Y.C., 1982-86; prof., law libr. dir. Fordham U., N.Y.C., 1986—; chmn. Conf. Law Librs. Jesuit Univs., 1988-89. Co-author: Professional Staffing and Job Security in Academic Law Libraries, 1989. Recipient Catalog Automation award Winston Found., 1990, 91, 92. Home: 285 Riverside Dr New York NY 10025-5276 Office: Fordham U Sch of Law 140 W 62nd St New York NY 10023-7407

TRACY, MARY E., principal. Prin. Holy Names Acad. Recipient Blue Ribbon Sch. award, 1990-91. Office: Holy Names Acad 728 21st Ave E Seattle WA 98112-4022

TRACY, MICHAEL CAMERON, choreographer, performer; b. Florence, Italy, Feb. 1, 1952; s. Stanley B. and Elizabeth Lee (McIntosh) T. B.A. Magna cum laude, Dartmouth Coll., 1973. Instr. Yale U., New Haven, Conn., 1992—. Artistic dir. Pilobolus Dance Theatre, Washington, Conn., 1974—; choreographer Die Zauberflöte, European prodn. with John Eliot Gardiner's Monteverdi Choir and Orch., 1995; co-choreographer: Ciona, 1974, Monkshood's Farewell, 1975, Untitled, 1976, Day Two, 1980, Pyramid of the Moon, 1994, The Doubling Cube, 1995. Recipient Berlin Critics award, 1975, New Eng. Theatre Conf. prize, 1977, Brandeis award, 1978, Excellence in Arts award Conn. Commn. on the Arts, 1981; sr. fellow Dartmouth Coll., 1973. Office: PO Box 388 Washington Depot CT 06794-0388

TRACY, ROBERT (EDWARD), English language educator, poetry translator; b. Woburn, Mass., Nov. 23, 1928; s. Hubert William and Vera Mary (Hurley) T.; m. Rebecca Garrison, Aug. 26, 1956; children: Jessica Janes, Hugh Garrison, Dominick O'Donovan. AB in Greek with honors, Boston Coll., 1950; MA, Harvard U., 1954, PhD, 1960. Teaching fellow Harvard U., Cambridge, Mass., 1954-58; instr. Carleton Coll., Northfield, Minn., 1958-60; from asst. prof. English, to assoc. prof., then prof. U. Calif., Berkeley, 1960-89, prof. English and Celtic Studies, 1989—, assoc. dir. Dickens Project, 1994-95; vis. prof., Bruern fellow in Am. studies U. Leeds, Eng., 1965-66; vis. prof., Leverhulme fellow Trinity Coll., Dublin, 1971-72; vis. Kathryn W. Davis prof. slavic studies Wellesley (Mass.) Coll., 1979; Charles Mills Gayley lectr. U. Calif., Berkeley, 1989-90; vis. prof. Anglo-Irish lit. Trinity Coll., 1995-96. Author: Trollope's Later Novels, 1978; translator (poems by Osip Mandelstam): Stone, 1981, 2d edit., 1991; editor J.M Synge's The Aran Islands, 1962, The Way We Live Now (Anthony Trollope), 1974, The Macdermots of Ballycloran (Anthony Trollope), 1989, Nina Balatka and Linda Tressel (Anthony Trollope), 1991, In A Glass Darkly (Sheridan Le Fanu) 1993, Rhapsody in Stephen's Green (Flann O'Brien), 1994; adv. editor The Recorder, 1985—, LIT (Lit., Interpretation, Theory), 1989—; contbr. articles and revs. to numerous jours. including Shakespeare Quarterly, So. Rev., Nineteenth-Century Fiction, Eire-Ireland, Irish Literary Supplement, others; poetry translations in New Orleans Rev., Poetry, N.Y. Rev. of Books, others. Appointed mem. cultural panel San Francisco-Cork Sister City Com. Fulbright travel grantee, 1965-66; recipient humanities research fellowships U. Calif., Berkeley, 1962, 69, 78, 81, 86, 92; Guggenheim fellow, 1981-82. Mem. MLA, Philol. Assn. Pacific Coast, Am. Conf. for Irish Studies, Internat. Assn. for Study of Anglo-Irish Lit. Avocation: exploring western Ireland and no. Calif. Office: U Calif Dept English Berkeley CA 94720

TRACY, THOMAS MILES, international health organization official; b. Great Barrington, Mass., July 8, 1936; s. Thomas Paul and Marion (Miles) T.; m. June Betts, June 17, 1967; children: Miles Christopher, Keir Thomas John. B.A., Colgate U., 1958; M.A., Stanford U., 1959; M.B.A., Columbia U., 1973. Fgn. service officer Dept. State, Washington, 1960-84; counselor Am. Embassy, Moscow, 1975-78, Bonn, Germany, 1978-79; asst. sec. Dept. State, Washington, 1979-83; chief adminstrn. Pan Am./WHO, Washington, 1983—; v.p. Pan-Am. Health and Edn. Found. Trustee, treas. Chelsea Sch.; treas. Pam Am. Health and Edn. Found. With U.S. Army, 1959-60. Recipient Superior Honor award Dept. State, 1978. Mem. Am. Fgn. Svc. Assn. (dir. 1970-72), Am. Fgn. Svc. Protective Assn. (dir. 1988—), Am. Fgn. Svc. Protective Found. (sec., treas.). Home: 5902 Devonshire Dr Bethesda MD 20816-3416 Office: Pan Am WHO 525 23rd St NW Washington DC 20037-2847

TRACY, TRACY FAIRCLOTH, special education educator; b. Washington, Aug. 22, 1961; d. James Claybert and Esther (Harrell) Faircloth; m. Charles Randall Tracy, Aug. 16, 1986; children: James Wren, Corissa Estelle. BS in Spl. Edn.-Mental Retardation, Old Dominion U., 1983. Tchr. Newport News (Va.) Pub. Schs., 1983—, community-based instruction specialist, 1992—. Leader Camp Fire, Inc., Newport News, 1983-92; vol. Newport News Spl. Olympics, 1984—, treas., 1987—; mem. Warwick PTA, Va. PTA, Nat. PTA. Recipient Award for Outstanding Svc. Newport News Spl. Olympics, 1986, 88, 90, Citizenship award Denbigh Kiwanis, 1988, Appreciation award Hampton-Newport News Cmty. Svcs. Bd. Mem. Assn. for Retarded Citizens, Coun. for Exceptional Children, Student Coun. for Exceptional Children (pres. 1982-83), Va. Reading Coun., Newport News Reading Coun., Internat. Reading Assn., Kappa Delta Pi (Nu Eta chpt.), Alpha Chi. Democrat. Methodist. Avocations: arts and crafts, swimming, walking. Home: 4708 Harlequin Way Chesapeake VA 23321-1247 Office: Warwick High Sch 51 Copeland Ln Newport News VA 23601-2309

TRADER, JOSEPH EDGAR, orthopedic surgeon; b. Milw., Nov. 2, 1946; s. Edgar Joseph and Dorothy Elizabeth (Senzig) T.; m. Janet Louise Burzycki, Sept. 23, 1972 (div. Nov. 1987); children: James, Jonathan, Ann Elizabeth; m. Rhonda Sue Schultz, May 26, 1990. Student, Marquette U., 1964-67; MD, Med. Coll. Wis., 1971. Diplomate Am. Bd. Orthopaedic Surgery. Emergency rm. physician columbia, St. Joseph's Hosps., Milw., 1972-76; orthopaedic surgeon Orthopaedic Assn., Manitowoc, Wis., 1978—; exec. com. Holy Family Meml. Med. Ctr., Manitowoc, 1985—, chief-of-staff, 1994—, ethics com., 1995, bd. dirs. Mem., former pres., bd. dirs. Holy Innocents Men's Choir; county del. State Med. Soc. Charitable Sci. and Edn. Found.; mem. adv. bd. Manitowoc Area Cath. Schs. Endowment Fund. Fellow Am. Acad. Orthopaedic Surgeons (orthopaedic rsch. and edn. found. state com.), ACS; mem. AMA, Wis. State Med. Soc. (del. gov. affairs com.), Wis. Orthopaedic Soc., Midwest Orthopaedic Soc., Milw. Orthopaedic Soc., Phi Delta Epsilon, Psi Chi, Crown & Anchor. Roman Catholic. Club: Manitowoc Yacht. Avocations: singing, piano, scuba diving, tennis, skiing, sailing. Home: 1021 Memorial Dr Manitowoc WI 54220-2242 Office: Orthopaedic Assocs 501 N 10th St Manitowoc WI 54220-4039

TRAEGER, CHARLES HENRY, III, lawyer; b. Bethlehem, Pa., Sept. 30, 1942; s. Charles Henry Jr. and Dorothy Shelly (Weinberger) T.; m. Carole Lynn DeGraff, Feb. 20, 1972; children: Chad, Erin, Seth, Anna, Claire, Benjamin. AB, Coll. William and Mary, 1964; JD, Stanford U., 1967. Bar: Calif. 1967, N.Y. 1972, Mass. 1976, Ariz. 1980. Assoc. Milbank, Tweed, Hadley & McCloy, N.Y.C., 1967, 71-76; v.p., gen. counsel Shawmut Corp., Boston, 1976-80, Shawmut Bank of Boston, N.A., 1976-80; assoc. Snell & Wilmer, Phoenix, 1980-83, ptnr., 1983-91; v.p., asst. gen. counsel Bank One Ariz. N.A., Phoenix, 1991-95. Contbr. Stanford Law Rev. Lt. comdr. USNR, 1968-71. Phi Beta Kappa. Republican. Mem. LDS Ch.

TRAFFORD, ABIGAIL, editor, writer, columnist; b. N.Y.C., July 14, 1940; d. William Bradford and Abigail (Sard) T.; children from previous marriage: Abigail, Victoria, Brett; m. Donald Lloyd Neff, Nov. 25, 1989. BA cum laude, Bryn Mawr Coll., 1962. Researcher Nat. Geog. Soc., Washington, 1964-67; tchr. Hermansberg Mission, Northern Ter., Australia, 1967-68; spl. corr. Time mag., The Washington Post, Houston, 1969-74; writer, asst. mng. editor U.S. News & World Report, Washington, 1975-86; health editor The Washington Post, 1986—; syndicated columnist Universal Press Syndicate. Author: Crazy Time: Surviving Divorce and Building a New Life, 1982, revised edit., 1992. Journalism fellow Harvard Sch. Pub. Health, 1980. Mem. Nat. Press Club, Washington Press Club Found. (bd. mem. 1989—, pres. 1993-95). Home: 2600 Upton St NW Washington DC 20008-3826 Office: The Washington Post 1150 15th St NW Washington DC 20071-0001

TRAFICANT, JAMES A., JR., congressman; b. Youngstown, Ohio, May 8, 1941; s. James A. and Agnes T. Traficant; m. Patricia Coppa; children: Robin, Elizabeth. B.S., U. Pitts., 1963, M.S., 1973; M.S., Youngstown State U., 1976. Exec. dir. Mahoning County Drug Program, Ohio, 1971-81; sheriff Mahoning County, Ohio, 1981-85; mem. 99th-104th Congresses from 17th Ohio dist., Washington, D.C., 1985—; ranking minority mem. transp. and infrastructure subcom. on Coast Guard and maritime transp., mem. sci. com. Office: US House of Reps Office of House Members 2446 Rayburn Bldg Ofc Washington DC 20515-0005

TRAFTON, STEPHEN J., banking executive; b. Mt. Vernon, Wash., Sept. 17, 1946; m. Diane Trafton; children: John, Roland. BS in Zoology, Wash. State U., 1968. V.p., mgr. dept. money market Seattle-First Nat. Bank, 1968-79; v.p., mgr. bank consulting group Donaldson Lufkin Jennrette, N.Y.C., 1980; exec. v.p., treas. Gibraltar Savings Bank, L.A., 1980-84; banking cons., 1984-86; v.p., treas. Hibernia Bank, San Francisco, 1986-88; sr. v.p., treas. Goldome Bank, Buffalo, N.Y., 1988-90; sr. exec. v.p., CFO Glenfed Inc., 1990-91, vice chmn., CFO, 1991—, pres., 1992—; sr. exec. v.p., CFO Glendale Fed. Bank, 1990-91, vice chmn., CFO, 1991, pres., COO, 1991-92, chmn. bd., pres., CEO, 1992—, also bd. dirs. Mem. Phi Eta Sigma. Office: Glendale Fed Bank 414 Central Ave Glendale CA 91203*

TRAGER, ALAN MARTIN, financial services company executive; b. N.Y.C., Apr. 21, 1947; s. Sidney C. and Alice N. T.; m. Katherine Jones, Sept. 15, 1974; children: Carolyn, David. AB in Liberal Arts, Syracuse U., 1970; MPA, Harvard U., 1972. Sr. project mgr. Bur. of Budget City of N.Y., 1972-74; mgr. planning Pfizer Pharms., N.Y.C., 1974-78; mng. dir. Morgan Stanley, N.Y.C., 1978-91; pres. AMT Capital Advisers, Inc., N.Y.C., 1991—; speaker numerous industry confs. Contbr. articles to profl. jours. Mem. Harvard Club N.Y. Home: 175 Riverside Dr New York NY 10024-1616 Office: AMT Capital Advisers Inc 600 Fifth Ave Fl 26 New York NY 10020

TRAGER, DAVID G., federal judge; b. Mt. Vernon, N.Y., Dec. 23, 1937; s. Sol and Clara (Friedman) T.; m. Roberta E. Weisbrod, May 2, 1972; children: Mara Emet, Josiah Samuel, Naomi Gabrielle. B.A., Columbia Coll., 1959; LL.B., Harvard U., 1962. Bar: N.Y. Assoc. Berman & Frost, 1963-65, Butler, Jablow & Geller, 1965-67; asst. corp. counsel Appeals Div. City of N.Y., 1967; law clk. Judge Kenneth B. Keating, N.Y. State Ct. Appeals, 1968-69; asst. U.S. atty. chief, appeals div., 1970-72; U.S. atty. Ea. Dist. N.Y., Bklyn., 1974-78; prof. Bklyn. Law Sch., 1972-94, dean, 1983-94; judge U.S. Dist. Ct. (ea. dist.) N.Y., Bklyn., 1994—; chmn. Mayor's Com. on Judiciary, 1982-89, N.Y. State Temp. Commn. on Investigation, 1983-90. Mem. N.Y.C. Charter Rev. Commn., 1986-89. With U.S. Army, 1962. Mem. ABA, N.Y. State Bar Assn., Assn. Bar City N.Y., Fed. Bar Council (pres. 1986-88), Am. Law Inst., Am. Judicature Soc. Office: US Courthouse 225 Cadman Plz E Brooklyn NY 11201-1818

TRAGER, MICHAEL DAVID, lawyer; b. N.Y.C., Feb. 15, 1959; s. Philip and Ina (Shulkin) T.; m. Mariella Gonzalez, Sept. 12, 1987; children: Nicholas, Alexander. BA, Wesleyan U., Middletown, Conn., 1981; JD, Boston U., 1985. Bar: Mass. 1985, Conn. 1986, Fla. 1988, D.C. 1989. Staff atty. enforcement divsn. Securities & Exchange Com., Washington, 1985-87; assoc. Morgan, Lewis & Bockius, Miami, Fla., 1987-88; participating assoc. Fulbright & Jaworski, Washington, 1989-92; ptnr. Trager & Trager, Washington, 1992-93; of counsel Fulbright & Jaworski, Washington, 1993-94, ptnr., 1995—. Bd. dirs. Jewish Nat. Fund-Mid-Atlantic Region, 1993—. Mem. ABA (bus. law sect. fed. regulation securities com. and civil litigation and SEC enforcement matters subcom., litigation sect. securities litigation com. and SEC enforcement subcom., class action and derivative litigation com. and securities litigation subcom.), D.C. Bar Assn. (corp., fin. and securities law sect. corp. counsel and planning group for broker-dealer programs 1992-94, broker-dealer regulation com.), Conn. Bar Assn. (corp. counsel, corps. and other bus. orgns. sects.), Fla. Bar Assn., Mass. Bar Assn. Office: Fulbright & Jaworski 801 Pennsylvania Ave NW Washington DC 20004-2615

TRAGER, PHILIP, photographer, lawyer; b. Bridgeport, Conn., Feb. 27, 1935; s. Bernard Harold and Mina (Rubenstein) T.; m. Ina Louise Shulkin, Sept. 2, 1957; children: Michael, Julie. B.A., Wesleyan U., Middletown, Conn., 1956; J.D., Columbia U., 1960. Bar: Conn. 1960, N.Y. 1981, U.S. Supreme Ct. 1963. With Trager & Trager, P.C., Fairfield, Conn., 1960—. One-man shows Wesleyan U. Davison Art Ctr., 1970, 74, 81, 87, 92, Balt. Mus. Art, 1977, Mus. City of N.Y., 1980, Witkin Gallery, 1973, 80, 86, Jacobs Pillow, 1992, 93, Drew U., 1993, Recontres Internationales de Photographie, Arles, France, 1994, Mus. Photog. Arts, 1994, Photog. Resource Ctr., Boston, 1995; exhibited in group shows, including Yale U. Art Gallery, 1979, Santa Barbara (Calif.) Mus. Art, 1979, Internat. Ctr. Photography, 1987, N.Y. State Mus., Albany, 1982, Bklyn. Mus., 1989, Bibliothèque Nationale, Paris, 1982, NYU, 1985; represented in permanent collections Balt. Mus. Art, Corcoran Gallery Art, Met. Mus. Art, Mus. Modern Art, New Orleans Mus. Art, Yale U. Gallery Art; author: Echoes of Silence, 1972, Photographs of Architecture, 1980 (Book of Yr., Am. Inst. Graphic Arts), Wesleyan Photographs, 9182, The Villas Palladio, 1986, Dancers, 1992. Bd. dirs. Bridgeport Hosp., 1985-95, Bridgeport Hosp. Found., 1993-95, New Eng. Found. for Arts, 1988-95. Recipient Lay Person award Conn. Soc. Architects, 1980; recipient Disting. Alumnus award Wesleyan U., 1981. Mem. ABA, Conn. Bar Assn. Home: 20 Rolling Ridge Rd Fairfield CT 06430-2254 Office: Trager and Trager PC 1305 Post Rd Fairfield CT 06430-6016

TRAGER, WILLIAM, biology educator; b. Newark, Mar. 20, 1910; s. Leon and Anna (Emilfork) T.; m. Ida Sosnow, June 16, 1935; children—Leslie, Carolyn, Lillian. B.S., Rutgers U., 1930, Sc.D. (hon.), 1965; M.A., Harvard U., 1931, Ph.D., 1933; Sc.D. (hon.), Rockefeller U., 1987. Fellow Rockefeller U., N.Y.C., 1934-35, mem. faculty, 1935—, assoc. prof., 1950-64, prof. biology, 1964-81, prof. emeritus, 1981—; guest investigator West African Inst. Trypanosomiasis Research, 1958-59, Nigerian Inst. Trypanosomiasis Research, 1973-74; vis. prof. Fla. State U., 1962, U. P.R. Med. Sch., 1963, U. Mex. Med. Sch., 1965; mem. study sect. parasitology and tropical medicine Nat. Inst. Allergy and Infectious Diseases, 1954-58, 67-70, mem. tng. grant com., 1961-64, mem. microbiology and infectious diseases adv. com., 1978-79; mem. malaria commn. Armed Forces Epidemiol. Bd., 1965-73; mem. study group parasitic diseases Walter Reed Army Inst. Research, 1977-79; chmn. sci. adv. council Liberian Inst. Tropical Medicine, 1965-66; rapporteur 6th, 7th Congresses Tropical Medicine; pres. Am. Found. for Tropical Medicine, 1966-69; mem. steering com. Malaria Immunology Group, WHO, 1977-80; cons. WHO, Bangkok, 1978, Panama, 1979, Shanghai, 1979; hon. pres. Asia and Pacific Conf. on Malaria, 1985. Author: Symbiosis, 1970, Living Together: The Biology of Animal Parasitism, 1986; editor Jour. Protozoology, 1954-65; contbr. articles on insect physiology and exptl. parasitology to profl. jours. Served to capt. AUS, 1943-45. Recipient Leuckart medal Deutsche Gesellschaft fur Parasitologie, 1982, First Rameshwardas Birla Internat. award in Medicine, 1982, Darling medal WHO, Manson medal Royal Soc. Tropical Medicine and Hygiene, 1986, Prince Mahidol award in Med. Sci., 1994; fellow NRC, 1933-34, Guggenheim Found., 1973-74, Avivah Zuckerman fellow Kuvin Ctr. Infections and Tropical Diseases, Hebrew U., 1982. Fellow AAAS, N.Y. Acad. Scis.; mem. Nat. Acad. Sci., Am. Soc. Parasitologist (council 1956-57, v.p. 1973, pres. 1974), Soc. Protozoologists (pres. 1960-61), Am. Soc. Tropical Medicine and Hygiene (pres. 1978-79, Le Prince medal 1991). Office: Rockefeller U York Ave At 66th St New York NY 10021

TRAGOS, GEORGE EURIPEDES, lawyer; b. Chgo., July 15, 1949; s. Euripedes G. and Eugene G. (Gatziolis) T.; m. Donna Marie Thalassites, Nov. 18, 1978; children: Louise, Gina, Peter. BA, Fla. State U., 1971, JD, 1974; Bar: Fla., U.S. Dist. Ct. (mid., so. dists.) Fla., U.S. Dist. Ct. (we. dist.) Tenn., U.S. Ct. Appeals (5th, 11th cirs.). Legis. aide Fla. Ho. of Reps., 1972-73, tax analyst tax and fin. com., 1973-74; chief, felony asst. states atty. State of Fla., Clearwater, 1974-78; partner firm Case, Kimpton, Tragos & Burke, P.A., Clearwater Beach, 1978-83; chief criminal div. U.S. Atty.'s Office for Middle Dist. Fla., Tampa, 1983-85; lead trial asst. Pres. Organized Criminal Task Force, Tampa, 1985; sole practice, Clearwater, 1985—. Contbr. articles to profl. jours. and frequent lectr. Mem. Clearwater Bar (pres. 1994, chmn. criminal procedure com. 1979—), Fla. Bar Assn. (chmn. fed. practice com. 1986, treas. exec. coun. criminal law sect., chmn. bar evidence com. 1990), Fla. Assn. Criminal Def. Lawyers (pres. 1991), Fla. Acad. Trial Lawyers, Am. Trail Lawyers Assn., Fla. State U. Alumni Assn. Law Sch., (bd. dirs.), Tampa Bay Fed. Bar Assn. (v.p. 1989), Clearwater Beach Jaycees (pres. 1979), Fla. U. Gold Key Club (pres. 1972), Ahepa. Democrat. Mem. Greek Orthodox Ch. Avocations: boating, tennis. Office: 600 Cleveland St Ste 700 Clearwater FL 34615-4158

TRAHANT, MARK NEIL, newspaper editor; b. Pocatello, Idaho, Aug. 13, 1957; s. Neil Walter Trahant and Sharon Dianne (Murray) Empey; m. Lenora Ann Begay, Nov. 2, 1991; children: Marvin Sam, Elias Begay. Student, Idaho State U., 1975. Editor Sho-Ban News, Ft. Hall, Ind., 1977-79; pub. info. officer U.S. Bur. Indian Affairs, Washington, 1979-80; freelance writer Washington, 1980-83; pub. Navajo Times Today, Widow Rock, Ariz., 1983-87; reporter Ariz. Republic, Phoenix, 1989-91; pres., pub. Navajo Nation Today, Window Rock, 1991-92; exec. news editor Salt Lake Tribune, Salt Lake City, 1992—; bd. dirs. Robert C. Maynard Inst. for Journalism Edn.; mem. nat. adv. bd. Poynter Inst. for Media Studies; vis. scholar Freedom Forum's First Amendment Ctr., Vanderbilt U. Author: Pictures of Our Nobler Selves: A History of Native American Journalism, 1995; contbg. author: A Circle of Nations. Founding bd. dirs. UNITY '94. Mem. Native Am. Journalists Assn. (past pres.), Am. Soc. Newspaper Editors. Office: Salt Lake Tribune 143 S Main St Salt Lake City UT 84111-1917

TRAHERN, JOSEPH BAXTER, JR., humanities educator; b. Clarksville, Tenn., Feb. 20, 1937; s. Joseph Baxter and Margaret Dancey (Fort) T.; m. Marjorie Elizabeth Hawkins, Aug. 29, 1958; children: Sarah Margaret, Joseph Baxter III. BA, Vanderbilt U., 1958, MA, 1959; MA, Princeton U., 1962, PhD, 1963. Asst. prof. English U. Ill., Urbana, 1963-71, assoc. prof., 1971-78, acting head dept., 1976-77; prof. English U. Tenn., Knoxville, 1978—, head dept. English, 1978-88, exec. asst. to chancellor, 1989-90, acting vice chancellor for acad. affairs, 1990-92; mem. adv. coun. dept. English Princeton U., 1982—, chair, 1984-92. Editor: (annotated bibliography) Year's Work in Old English Studies, 1986—; Standardizing English: Essays in the History of Language Change, 1989; assoc. editor Old English Newsletter, 1986—; contbr. articles on Old English language and lit. to profl. jours. Trustee Webb Sch. Knoxville, 1981-87. Served to 2d lt. U.S. Army, 1958-59. Fulbright fellow Worcester Coll., Oxford, Eng., 1962-63. Mem. MLA (exec. com. Old English divsn. 1982-86), South Atlantic MLA (exec. com. 1993-95), Medieval Acad. Am. (Haskins medal com. 1987-90), New Chaucer Soc., South Atlantic Assn. Depts. English (exec. com. 1986-88), Internat. Soc. Anglo-Saxonists (adv. bd. 1988-91), Phi Beta Kappa (chpt. pres. 1985-86). Democrat. Methodist. Home: 3920 Topside Rd Knoxville TN 37920-6043 Office: U Tenn Dept English Knoxville TN 37996-0430

TRAICOFF, GEORGE, college president; b. Elyria, Ohio, May 16, 1932; s. George and Lena (Szaroff) T.; m. Diane C. Schneider, Dec. 28, 1965; children: George Scott, Paula Jane, Amy Jo. BS, Miami U., Oxford, Ohio, 1954; MEd, Kent State U., 1959; EdD, Ind. U., 1967. Tchr. bus. LaGrange (Ohio) High Sch., 1956-57, Elyria High Sch., 1956-57; instr., coord. Ind. U., 1959-60, Ohio State U., 1960-63; prof., head dept. No. Mich. U., Marquette, 1963-66, dir. program gen. studies, 1966-67; dean community svcs. Cuyahoga Community Coll., Cleve., 1967-73; pres. North Shore Community Coll., Danvers, Mass., 1973—; pres. New Eng. Jr. Community and Tech. Coll. Coun.; vice chmn. regional employment bd. Pvt. Industry Coun.; bd. dirs. Century Bank and Trust Co. With U.S. Army, 1954-56. Mem. Am. Assn. Community and Jr. Colls., Nat. Coun. Community Svcs. (past pres.), Mass. Adminstrs. Community Colls., Mass. Community Coll. Assn. (treas.). Episcopalian. Office: North Shore Community Coll 1 Ferncroft Rd Danvers MA 01923-4017

TRAIN, HARRY DEPUE, II, retired naval officer; b. Washington, Nov. 5, 1927; s. Harold Cecil and May (Philipps) T.; m. Catharine Peck Kinnear, July 8, 1950; children: Louise Lucas, Catharine Philipps, Elizabeth Langdon, Cecilia Spencer. B.S., U.S. Naval Acad., 1949. Commd. ensign U.S. Navy, 1949, advanced through grades to adm., 1978; comdr. Cruiser-Destroyer Flotilla 8, 1971-72; dir. internat. security affairs East Asia and Pacific Region Office Asst. Sec. Def., 1972-73; dir. Systems Analysis Div., Office Chief Naval Ops., 1973-74; dir. joint staff Orgn. Joint Chiefs of Staff, 1974-76; comdr. U.S. 6th Fleet, 1976-78; comdr.-in-chief U.S. Atlantic Fleet and supreme allied comdr. Atlantic, 1978-82, ret., 1982; mgr. Hampton Rds. Ops., Sci. Applications Internat. Corp.; bd. dirs. Aydin Corp.; bd. trustees Inst. for Def. Analyses. Bd. dirs. Am. Cancer Soc., Inc. Decorated D.S.M. with 3 gold stars, Def. Disting. Svc. medal, Legion of Merit with 3 gold stars, Meritorious Svc. medal, Joint Svcs. Commendation medal, Navy Commendation medal; comdr. Order Republic of Tunisia; Order Naval Merit Brazil; Pedro Campbell medal Uruguay; Order of Pres. of Republic Chile; decorated Portuguese Mil. Order Christ; Netherlands Order Orange-Nassau; German Order Merit; French Legion of Honor; Colombian Naval Order Admiral Padilla; Mex. Order Spl. Merit; sr. fellow Flag and Gen. Officers Course, Nat. Def. U. Mem. U.S. Naval Inst., Coun. on Fgn. Rels., Def. Sci. Study Group (sr. mentor). Clubs: Columbia Country (Chevy Chase, Md.), Town Point (chmn. bd. govs.). Home: # 10 401 College Pl Norfolk VA 23510

TRAIN, JOHN, investment counselor, writer, government official; b. N.Y.C., May 25, 1928; s. Arthur Cheney and Helen (Coster) T.; m. Maria Teresa Cini di Pianzano, 1961 (div. 1976); children: Helen, Nina, Lisa; m. Frances Cheston, July 23, 1977. BA magna cum laude, Harvard U., 1950, MA, 1951. Founder, mng. editor Paris Rev., 1952-54; staff Asst. Sec. Army, Washington, 1954-56; assoc. de Vegh & Co., 1956-58; chmn. Train, Smith Counsel (and predecessor firms), N.Y.C., 1958-94, chmn. emeritus, 1995—; co-chmn., then dir. ICAP, S.A., Athens, 1964—; pres. Chateau Malescasse, Lamarque-Margaux, Bordeaux, France, 1970-81; columnist Forbes mag., 1977-83, Harvard mag., 1983-95, Wall St. Jour., 1984—, Worth Mag., Boston, 1991-93, Town and Country mag., 1994-95, Fin. Times, London, 1994—; bd. dirs. African Devel. Found., Washington, 1988-94; bd. dirs. Bulgarian-Am. Enterprise Fund, Washington, Genesis Funds, London, Internat. Rescue Com., N.Y.C.; bd. govs. East-West Ctr., Hawaii, 1993—; chmn. Montrose Advisors, N.Y.C., 1992—; overseer Nat. Endowment for Democracy Internat. Forum for Democratic Studies, 1995—. Author: Dance of the Money Bees, 1973, Remarkable Names, 1977, Even More Remarkable Names, 1979, Remarkable Occurrences, 1978, Remarkable Words, 1980, The Money Masters, 1980, Remarkable Relatives, 1971, Preserving Capital, 1983, Famous Financial Fiascos, 1984, John Train's Most Remarkable Names, 1985, The Midas Touch, 1987, The New Money Masters, 1989, Valsalva's Maneuver, 1989, John Train's Most Remarkable Occurences, 1990, Wit, 1991, Love, 1993, The Craft of Investing, 1994; various articles. Chmn. Italian Emergency Relief Com., 1976-77; pres. Afghanistan Relief Com., 1986-95; trustee Harvard Lampoon, Cambridge, Mass., 1974-90, World Monuments Fund, 1988-92; chmn. Free Elections Project, 1990, Brit. Mus. Nat. Hist. Internat. Trust, 1990—; trustee Am. U. Bulgaria, 1996—. With U.S. Army, 1954-56. Decorated commendatore Ordine del Merito della Repubblica, commendatore Ordine Della Solidarieta (Italy). Mem. Order Colonial Lords of Manors, The Pilgrims, Century Club, Racquet and Tennis Club, Met. Club (Washington), Brooks's Club (London), Beefsteak Club (London), Travellers Club (Paris). Office: 667 Madison Ave New York NY 10021-8029

TRAIN, RUSSELL ERROL, environmentalist; b. Jamestown, R.I., June 4, 1920; s. Charles R. and Errol C. (Brown) T.; m. Aileen Bowdoin, May 27, 1954; children—Nancy, Emily, Bowdoin, Errol. A.B., Princeton U., 1941, LL.D. (hon.), 1970; JD, Columbia U., 1948, LL.D. (hon.), 1970; LL.D. (hon.), Bates Coll., 1970, Drexel U., 1970; D.E. (hon.), Worcester Poly. Inst., 1970, U. Md., 1975; Sc.D. (hon.), St. Mary's Coll., 1970, Clarkson Coll. Tech., 1973, Salem Coll., 1975, Southwestern U., 1976, Mich. State U., 1976; D.C.L. (hon.), U. of South, 1973. Bar: D.C. bar 1949. Atty. staff joint com. on internal revenue taxation U.S. Congress, 1949-53; chief counsel Ways and Means Com., U.S. Ho. of Reps., 1953-54, minority adviser, 1955-56; asst. to sec., head legal adv. staff Treasury Dept., 1956-57; judge U.S. Tax Ct., 1957-65; pres. Conservation Found., 1965-69; also trustee; undersec. Dept. Interior, 1969-70; chmn. Council on Environ. Quality, 1970-73; adminstr. EPA, Washington, 1973-77; sr. assoc. Conservation Found., 1977; pres., chief exec. officer World Wildlife Fund, Washington, 1978-85, chmn. bd., 1985-94; chmn. bd. Conservation Found., 1985-90, Nat. Commn. on the Environment, 1991-93; chmn. Nat. Coun. World Wildlife Found., Washington; chief exec. Washington Nat. Monument Assn.; mem. Nat. Water Commn., 1968; head U.S. del. UN Conf. Human Environment, 1972; rep. Internat. Whaling Commn., 1972, other internat. confs.; dir. Applied Energy Services Inc.; mem. Pres.'s adv. com. on trade and trade negotiations, 1991-93. Trustee emeritus African Wildlife Found.; bd. dirs. Am. Conservation Assn., Found. Philippine Environ., King Mahendra Trust for Nature Conservation in Nepal; bd. dirs. Served to maj., F.A. AUS, 1941-46. Decorated Order of Golden Ark (The Netherlands); recipient Albert Schweitzer medal Animal Welfare Inst., 1972; Aldo Leopold medal Wildlife Soc., 1975; Conservationist of Yr. award Nat. Wildlife Fedn., 1974; John and Alice Tyler Ecology award, 1978; Freese award ASCE, 1978; Public Welfare award Nat. Acad. Scis., 1981; Elizabeth Haub prize in internat. environ. law, 1981, Lindbergh award, 1985, Environ. Law Inst. award, 1986; conservationist of yr. award Nat. Wildlife Fedn., 1986; Presidential Medal of Freedom, 1991. Mem. Council Fgn. Relations, Washington Inst. Fgn. Affairs, Atlantic Coun. Office: World Wildlife Fund 1250 24th St NW Washington DC 20037-1124

TRAINA, ALBERT SALVATORE, publishing executive; b. Bklyn., Apr. 30, 1927; s. Salvatore and Guilia (LeBarbara) T.; m. Vail Devereux, June 27, 1957; children—Caroline Vail, Robert Brooks. B.S. (N.Y. State War Service scholar), Seton Hall U., 1950; postgrad., Columbia U., 1950-51; M.B.A., NYU, 1954. Circulation promotion advt. space salesman Fairchild Publs., N.Y.C., 1951-53; Eastern advt. mgr. Modern Bride mag. Ziff-Davis, N.Y.C., 1953-58; advt. mgr. Bride and Home mag. Hearst Mags., N.Y.C., 1958-60; pub. Bride and Home mag. Hearst Mags., 1960-64; pub. Sports Afield mag., 1964-65, Town and Country mag., 1965-67, Harpers Bazaar mag., 1967-70; pres., chief exec. officer Bartell Media Corp., 1970-74; pres. Ziff-Davis Mag. Network, 1974-76, group v.p., 1976-78; sr. v.p. Ziff-Davis Pub. Co., 1978-81; pres. Ziff-Davis Consumer Mag., 1981-85; exec. v.p. mags. CBS, N.Y.C., 1985; pres. Traina Assocs., N.Y.C., 1985—. Mem. Scarsdale Bi-Partisan Com., 1975-78; bd. dirs. Crane Berkeley Assn., 1978-88, pres., 1983-84; mem. nat. bd. dirs., chmn. comms. com., treas. Goodwill Industries of Am., 1979—, chmn. bd., 1988-92; bd. dirs. Goodwill Industries of N.Y., 1983—. With USNR, 1945-46. Mem. NYU Grad. Sch. Bus. Adminstrn. Alumni Assn., NYU Alumni Fedn. (comms. com. 1970-73), Fox Meadow Tennis Club (Scarsdale), Union League Club (N.Y.C.). Home: RR 1 Box 201 Chebeague Island ME 04017

TRAINA, JEFFREY FRANCIS, orthopedic surgeon; b. Nagoya, Japan, Apr. 17, 1956; s. Vincent L. and Carol A. (Anselmo) T.; m. Kathy Traina, Oct. 7, 1981; children: Kristin, Kourtney. B in Gen. Studies, U. Mich., 1975; MD, So. Ill. U., 1978. Intern Emory U./Grady Meml. Hosp., Atlanta, 1978-79; resident Wake Forest U./N.C. Bapt. Hosp., Winston-Salem, N.C., 1979-83; orthopedic instr. Bowman-Gray Med. Sch., Salem, N.C., 1979-83; rsch. fellow Med. Sch. Harvard U., Boston, 1983-84; asst. prof. U. Tex. Med. Sch., Houston, 1984-86; clin. asst. prof. Coll. Medicine U. Ill., Peoria, 1987—; orthopedic surgeon U. Tex. Med. Sch., Houston, 1984-86, Orthopaedic Assocs., Peoria, 1986-89, Heartland Orthopedic Inst., Peoria, 1989-91, Assoc. Orthopaedic Surgeons, Ltd., Peoria, 1992—. Contbr. articles to profl. jours. Recipient Nat. Rsch. Svc. award, 1983; biomed. rsch. support grantee U. Tex., 1985. Mem. AMA, AAAS, N.Y. Acad. Scis., Orthopaedic Rsch. Soc., Peoria Med. Soc., Ill. State Med. Soc., Am. Acad. Orthopaedic Surgeons, Ill. Orthopaedic Soc., Assn. for Arthritic Hip and Knee Surgery, Bowman-Gray Orthopaedic Alumni Assn. Home: 5618 N Prospect Rd Peoria IL 61614-4324 Office: Assoc Orthopaedic Surgeons 2805 N Knoxville Ave Peoria IL 61604-2869

TRAINA, RICHARD PAUL, academic administrator; b. San Francisco, June 3, 1937; s. Frank Ignatius and Isabelle (Thomas) T.; m. Margaret Bradley Warner, June 6, 1959; children: Cristina Traina Hutchison, Michelle Traina Riecke, Matthew Warner, Michael Derek. B.A., U. Santa Clara, 1958; M.A., U. Calif.-Berkeley, 1960, Ph.D., 1964. Instr. history Wabash Coll., Crawfordsville, Ind., 1963-64, asst. prof., 1964-68, assoc. prof., 1968-74, dean, 1969-74; dean, prof. Franklin & Marshall Coll., Lancaster, Pa., 1974-81, acad. v.p., dean, 1981-84; pres. Clark U., Worcester, Mass., 1984—. Author: American Diplomacy and the Spanish Civil War, 1968; co-editor: (with A. Rappaport) Present in the Past, 1972. Mem. Orgns. of Am. Historians, Soc. for Values in Higher Edn. Democrat. Roman Catholic. Home: 80 William St Worcester MA 01609-2138 Office: Clark U 950 Main St Worcester MA 01610-1400

TRAINOR, BERNARD EDMUND, educator, journalist, retired military officer; b. N.Y.C., Sept. 2, 1928; s. Joseph Patrick and Ann Veronica (Whelan) T.; m. Margaret Ann Hamilton, June 13, 1959; children: Kathleen Marie, Theresa Ann, Eileen Cecile, Claire Hamilton. BS, Coll. of Holy Cross, 1951; MA, U. Colo., 1963, postgrad., 1970—; ed., Air War Coll., Montgomery, Ala., 1969-70. Commd. 2nd lt. USMC, 1951, advanced through grades to lt. gen., 1983; inf. comdr. USMC, Korea, 1952; assigned to USS Columbus USMC, 1953-55, mem. staff Marine Corps Hdqrs., 1955-58, with exch. office Royal Marine Commandos, 1958-59, inf. comdr. 1st Marine divsn., 1959-61; asst. prof. naval sci. U. Colo., Boulder, 1961-64; assigned to Marine Corps Command and Staff Coll., 1964-65; adv. Republic of Vietnam, 1965-66; instr. Marine Corps Command and Staff Coll., 1966-69; bn. comdr. Vietnam, 1970-71; staff officer Hdqrs. Marine Corps, Washington, 1970-71; dir. First Marine Corps Dist., N.Y.C., 1974-76; asst. depot comdr. Marine Corps Recruit Depot, Parris Island, S.C., 1976-78; dir. Edn. Ctr., Quantico, Va., 1978-81; dep. chief of staff for plans, policies and ops. Hdqrs. Marine Corps, 1981-85; cons., 1985—; mil. corr. N.Y. Times, 1986-90; dir. nat. security program Kennedy Sch. Govt. Harvard U., Cambridge, Mass., 1990—. Author: History of the U.S. Marine Corps, 1968, The Generals' War, 1995; contbg. author: American Defense Annual, 1990, Defense Beat, 1991, After the Storm, 1992, The Almanac of Seapower, 1993, Newsmen and National Defense, 1991, Perspectives on Warfighting, 1992; mem. editl. adv. bd. Naval War Coll. Rev., Harvard Jour. Internat. Affairs; mem. editl. bd. Amphibious Warfare Rev.; contbr. articles to profl. jours. Mem. adv. bd. to pres. of Naval War Coll.; mil. analyst NBC News; rsch. bd. dirs. Inst. for Fgn. Policy Analysis. Decorated D.S.M., Legion of Merit with two oak leaf cluster, Bronze Star, Navy Commendation medal with two gold stars, others; recipient Anderson Meml. award Air War Coll., 1970. Mem. Naval Inst., Internat. Inst. Strategic Studies, Marine Corps Assn., Coun. Fgn. Rels., World Affairs Coun., Army-Navy Club. Roman Catholic. Home: 80 Potter Pond Lexington MA 02173-8250 Office: Harvard U Kennedy Sch Govt 79 JFK St Cambridge MA 02138-5801

TRAINOR, HOWARD ALLEN, newspaper editor; b. Moncton, New Brunswick, Canada, Apr. 13, 1943; s. Francis Adrian and Mary Agnes (Rae) T.; m. Patricia Louise O'Brien, Nov. 16, 1962 (div. 1979); children: Alayna, Angela, Leslee, Darlene; m. Carol Joan LeBlanc, Nov. 10, 1983; 1 child, Adam James Nelson. Sports writer Moncton (N.B.) Times, Canada, 1961-65, news editor, 1966-74; editor, translator Jour. l'Avenir, Sept-Isles, Que, Canada, 1965; gen. mgr. Brunswick Downs Rack Track, Moncton, N.B., Canada, 1974-76; sports news dir. Stas. CKCW and CFQM-Radio, Moncton, N.B., Canada, 1974-79; sports editor Telegraph Jour., Saint Johns, N.B., Canada, 1979-80, news editor, 1980-87; mgn. editor Evening Times-Globe, Saint Johns, N.B., Canada, 1987-93, dir. comm., 1993—; chmn. Atlantic Region News Study Com., 1966-74. Bd. dirs. East End Boys Club, Moncton, 1966-68; active Coun. Maritime Premiers Task Force on Harness Racing, 1992—; chmn. Harness Task Force on Casinos, 1990—. Mem. Can. Mgn. Editors Assn. (bd. dirs.), The Can. Press (bd. dirs.), U.S. Trotting Assn. (bd. dirs. 1986-90, 93-95). Roman Catholic. Home: 47 Jennings Dr, Fredericton, NB Canada E3B 4Y9 Office: Comm New Brunswick, PO Box 6000, Fredericton, NB Canada E3B 5H1

TRAINOR, JOHN FELIX, retired economics educator; b. Mpls., Dec. 1, 1921; s. James Patrick and Myra Catherine (Pauly) T.; m. Margaret Dolores Pudenz, July 3, 1965 (dec. 1977); children: John Anthony, Patrick James. BA cum laude, Coll. St. Thomas, 1943; MA, U. Minn., 1950; PhD, Wash. State U., 1970. Instr. high sch. Mpls., 1946-47; instr. Coll. St. Thomas, 1949-50; v.p. Trainor Candy Co., Mpls., 1949-56; instr., asst. prof. econs. Rockhurst Coll., Kansas City, Mo., 1956-62; instr. Wash. State U., Pullman, 1966-67; asst. prof. Moorhead (Minn.) State U., 1967-70, assoc. prof. econs., 1971-87, prof. econ., 1988-89, chmn. dept. econs., 1981-89; prof. emeritus, 1989—. Author: (with Frank J. Kottke) The Nursing Home Industry in the State of Washington, 1968. Ensign to Lt. (j.g.) USNR, 1943-46, ETO. Mem. Minn. Econs. Assn. (pres. 1976-77), Assn. Social Econs., Omicron Delta Epsilon. Roman Catholic. Home: 1333 4th Ave S Moorhead MN 56560-2971

TRAINOR, LILLIAN (MIDGE TRAINOR), elections official, campaign consultant; b. Norma, N.J., Oct. 30, 1936; d. Loenell Lesley and Lillie Ara (Kenyon) Barber; m. Arthur James Trainor, Mar. 9, 1959; children: Michael, Arthur, Lynn Marie. Student pub. schs., Pleasantville, N.J. Chair Burlington County Bd. Elections, Mount Holly, N.J., 1978-81, commr. of registration, 1981-83, chair, 1983-90; dir. N.J. Div. Elections, 1990-94. Vice chair, mem. exec. bd. Burlington County Dem. Com., 1977-90, 94—; chair Southampton Twp. Dem. County Com., 1976-79, 94—, Bd. County Convassers, Burlington County, 1978-90; v.p. Southeastern Dem. Coalition, 1977-87; mgr. Florio for Gov. Campaign, N.J., 1981, Carter for Pres. Campaign, Burlington County area, 1980; del. Dem. Nat. Conv., 1984, 88; coord. Women for Florio Gubanatorial campaign, 1989. Served with WAC, 1955-57. Mem. Nat. Assn. State Election Dirs., N.J. State Assn. Election Ofcls., VFW Aux. Club: Big Six (pres. 1973-79). Avocations: accordian, piano, birdwatching, reading. Home: PO Box 2266 Vincentown NJ 08088-2266

TRAISMAN, HOWARD SEVIN, pediatrician; b. Chgo., Mar. 18, 1923; s. Alfred Stanley and Sara (Sevin) T.; m. Regina Gallagher, Feb. 29, 1956; children—Barry D. Lifschultz, Edward S., Kenneth N. B.S. in Chemistry, Northwestern U., 1943, M.B., 1946, M.D., 1947. Intern Cook County Hosp., Chgo., 1946-47; resident in pediatrics Children's Meml. Hosp., Chgo., 1949-51; attending physician div. endocrinology Children's Meml. Hosp., 1951—; mem. faculty Northwestern U. Med. Sch., 1951—, prof. pediatrics, 1973—. Author articles in field, chpts. in books. Served to capt. M.C. AUS, 1943-46, 47-49. Mem. Am. Diabetes Assn. (Disting. Service award 1976), Am. Pediatric Soc., Am. Acad. Pediatrics, Endocrine Soc., Lawson Wilkins Pediatric Endocrine Soc., AMA, Midwest Soc. Pediatric Research, Ill. Med. Soc., Chgo. Pediatric Soc., Chgo. Med. Soc., Inst. Medicine Chgo. Democrat. Jewish. Office: 1325 Howard St Evanston IL 60202-3766

TRAISTER, ROBERT EDWIN, naval officer, engineer; b. Haverhill, Mass., Sept. 15, 1937; s. Frank and Anne (Schlafman) T.; m. Janet Weinberger; children: James, Jeffrey. Student, Bowdoin Coll., 1955-56; BS, U.S. Naval Acad., Annapolis, Md., 1960; MSME, U.S. Naval Postgrad. Sch., Monterey, Calif., 1967. Commd. ensign USN, 1960, advanced through grades to rear adm., 1988; surface warfare officer, chief engr. USS William R. Rush, 1962-64; ship supt. Puget Sound Naval Shipyard, Bremerton, Wash., 1969-72, shipbuilding/repair/prodns. officer, 1982-86; chief engr. USS Springfield, USS Little Rock, 1972-75; trials officer Office Comdr. Naval Sea Systems, DD963 PRGM, Washington, 1975-78; comdg. officer Pearl Harbor (Hawaii) Naval Shipyard, 1986-88; maintenance officer Office Comdr. in Chief Pacific Fleet, Pearl Harbor, 1988-90; dep. comdr. surface ships Naval Sea Systems Command, Washington, 1990-94; dir. projects and site svcs. Westinghouse Hanford Corp., Richland, Wash., 1994—. Decorated Legion of Merit. Mem. Am. Soc. Naval Engrs. Assn., Am. Def. Preparedness Assn. (bd. dirs. 1990-92), U.S. Naval Acad. Alumni Assn. (pres. 1989-90), Bowdoin Coll. Alumni Assn., Army/Navy Country Club, Meadows Spring Country Club. Avocations: photography, sports. Office: Westinghouse Hanford Co Richland WA 99352

TRAMMELL, ELGIN MALLETTE, lawyer; b. Mobile, Ala., July 19, 1952; s. Robert William and Odessa (Ellis) T.; m. Deborah Carr; children: Elgin Mallette Jr., Patsy Chiffa, Charles Gulley. AA, L.A. Community Coll. Atty. ABA, 1992-94, Damu's Legal Svcs., L.A., 1994—. Organizer gang peace treaty L.A. Bloods/Crips, 1992; candidate L.A. City Coun. 12th Dist. Democrat. Muslim. Avocations: fishing, hunting, horseback riding, oration, civic volunteer duty. Office: Damu's Legal Svcs Lake View Terrace CA 91342

TRAMMELL, GEORGE THOMAS, physics educator; b. Marshall, Tex., Feb. 5, 1923; s. George Thomas and Cordelia (Whitsitt) T.; children: Peter, David, Susan, Jonathon. BA, Rice Inst., 1944; PhD, Cornell U., 1950. Physicist Oak Ridge Nat. Lab., 1950-61; prof. physics Rice U., Houston, 1961—; vis. prof. Tech. U., Munich, Fed. Republic Germany, 1967-68; vis. scientist Internat. Laue-Langevin Inst., Grenoble, France, 1975-76. Contbr. articles to profl. jours. Lt. (j.g.) USNR, 1944-46. Fellow Am. Phys. Soc. Office: Rice U Dept Physics PO Box 1892 Houston TX 77251-1892

TRAMMELL, HERBERT EUGENE, physicist, laboratory executive; b. Laurel, Miss., Apr. 19, 1927; s. Homer Lee and Evie Louisa (Breazeale) T.; m. Jane Walker, Dec. 28, 1948; children—Carmen, Bert, Lisa, Brian. B.A. in Physics, U. Miss., 1947, M.A., 1948. With Nuclear div. Union Carbide, Oak Ridge, 1949-89, mgr. barrier devel. programs, 1967-69, dir. gaseous diffusion devel. div., 1969-77; dir. engring. tech. div. Oak Ridge Nat. Lab., 1977-89, ret., 1989; with Martin Marietta Energy Systems, 1983-89. Bd. dirs. Emory Valley Sch. for Retarded Children, 1962-68, v.p., 1966-68; mem. Tenn. Med. Malpractice Rev. Bd., 1974-80; active PTA. Served with U.S. Navy, 1944-45. Methodist. Club: Rotary (pres. 1980-81). Home: 901 Johnson St Key West FL 33040-4745

TRAMONTINE, JOHN O., lawyer; b. Iron Mountain, Mich., Sept. 21, 1932; s. Orlando F. and Susan M. (Hollar) T.; m. Nancy A. McCabe, July 14, 1956; 1 child, Margaret A. BSChemE, U. Notre Dame, 1955; postgrad., Georgetown U., 1956-58; LLB, NYU, 1960. Bar: N.Y. 1960, U.S. Dist. Ct. (no. dist.) Ill. 1963, U.S. Dist. Ct. (so. and ea. dists.) N.Y. 1965, U.S. Ct. Appeals (2d and 5th cirs.) 1967, U.S. Supreme Ct. 1970, U.S. Ct. Appeals (8th cir.) 1970, (3d cir.) 1973, (7th cir.) 1976, (fed. cir.) 1979, U.S. Dist. Ct. (we. dist.) N.Y. 1981. Examiner U.S. Patent Office, 1956-58; patent agt. Arthur, Dry & Dole, N.Y.C., 1958-60; assoc. Arthur, Dry, Kalish, Taylor & Wood, N.Y.C., 1960-62, Wolfe, Hubbard, Voit & Osann, Chgo., 1962-63; assoc. Fish & Neave, N.Y.C., 1963-70, ptnr., 1970—. 2nd lt. USMCR, 1955. Fellow Am. Coll. Trial Lawyers, Am. Bar Found.; mem. ABA, Assn. of Bar of City of N.Y. (chmn. patent com. 1974-77), Fed. Cir. Bar Assn., N.Y. Intellectual Property Law Assn. (pres. 1985-86), St. Andrews Golf Club (sec. 1981-83). Office: Fish & Neave 1251 Avenue Of The Americas New York NY 10020-1104

TRAN, JACK NHUAN NGOC, gas and oil reservoir engineer; b. Quang Binh, Vietnam, Sept. 21, 1933; came to U.S., 1975; s. Dieu Ngoc and Ly Thi (Nguyen) T.; m. Tamie Nguyen, July 25, 1990; children: Andy Nguyen, Quoc Dung, Anh Nga Huyen, Ephram Anh Dung, John Hung Dung. BS, U. San Francisco, 1977, MBA, 1978. With Republic of Vietnam Mil., 1952-67; cadet Rep. Vietnam Mil. Acad., Dalat, 1952-53; 1st lt., co. comdr. 1st Republic of Vietnam Bn., South Vietnam, 1953-54; editor-in-chief Republic of Vietnam Revs., Saigon, 1955-57; commandant Republic of Vietnam Aerial Photo Ctr., Saigon, 1958-61, Republic of Vietnam Mil. Intelligence Sch., Caymai and Saigon, 1962-67; mem. Republic of Vietnam Senate, 1967-73; v.p. The Meteco Corp., Saigon, Vietnam, 1971-72; pres., chmn. bd. Meteco-Vinageco Co., Saigon, 1972-75; air photo analyst Std. Oil Co., San Francisco, 1975-79; gas and oil engr. Chevron Oil Co., San Francisco, 1980—; col. U.S. Intelligence, Calif., 1980-90. Author: Flower in the Battle Field, 1956, Geological Survey of the Kndu, CA, 1982, Beluga River Oil Development, 1984, The Military Life, 1992; editor-in-chief Chien-Si Quoc-Gia Mag. Recipient Hon. Key of the City, City of Omaha, Nebr., 1989, Hon. Citizen City of Fayetteville, N.C., 1969; Resolution of Recognition, Senate of State of Hawaii, 1969, Senate of State of Tex., 1969. Mem. The U. of San Francisco Alumni Assn., Rotary Internat. Roman Catholic. Avocations:

swimming, music, reading, traveling. Home: 1418 Lundy Ave San Jose CA 95131-3310

TRAN, LONG TRIEU, industrial engineer; b. Saigon, Vietnam, Oct. 10, 1956; came to U.S., 1973; s. Nguyen Dinh and Thiet Thi (Nguyen) T.; m. Khanh Thi-Hong Phan, Aug. 3, 1988. BS in Mech. Engring. with honors, U. Kans., 1976; MS in Mech. Engring., MIT, 1980; MBA in Bus. Adminstrn. with honors, U. Louisville, 1993. Cert. quality engr.; cert. mfg. engr.; cert. project mgmt. profl. Tchg. asst. U. Kans., 1975-76, U. Calif., Berkeley, 1977; rsch. asst. Lawrence Berkeley Labs., 1977, MIT, 1977-80; libr. staff Harvard U. Med. Sch. Libr., 1977-78; mem. staff New England Deaconess Hosp., Boston, 1978-80; prodn. programming engr. GE, Cleve., 1980-81; advanced mfg. engr. GE, Louisville, 1981-82, quality sys. engr., 1982-84, quality control engr., 1984-86, sr. quality info. equipment engr., 1986-89, sr. quality indsl. engr., 1990-94, sr. supplier tech. assistance engr., 1995—; exec. advisor Jr. Achievement Inc., Louisville, 1983-84; monitor/reader Rec. for the Blind, 1994—; fundraiser The Dream Factory Inc., 1994—. Vol. NCCJ, 1994—, Clothe-A-Child, 1993—, Dare-To-Care, 1994—, Ronald McDonald House, 1994—. Mem. AAAS, ASME, Am. Soc. Quality Control, Computer and Automated Sys. Assn. (charter), Robot Inst. Am., Robotics Internat. (charter), Soc. Mfg. Engrs. (sr.), Instrument Soc. Am. (sr.), Am. Mgmt. Assn., N.Y. Acad. Scis., Internat. Platform Assn., Indsl. Computing Soc. (founding), Project Mgmt. Inst., Nat. Pks. Conservation Assn., U.S. Libr. Congress Assocs. (founding), Sigma Xi, Pi Tau Sigma, Tau Beta Pi, Phi Kappa Phi, Beta Gamma Sigma. Republican. Achievements include research on grinding processes and material surface analysis, also manufacturing project management. Home: 3423 Brookhollow Dr Louisville KY 40220-5009 Office: GE GE AP2-117 Louisville KY 40225

TRANCHINA, FRANK PETER, JR., lawyer; b. New Orleans, July 18, 1953; s. Frank P. and Effie (Volpe) T.; m. Susan Kendrick, Sept. 28, 1995. BA, Loyola U., New Orleans, 1976, JD, 1979. Bar: La. 1979, U.S. Ct. Appeals (5th cir.) 1981, Calif. 1994. Assoc. Law Offices Guy W. Olano, Jr., Kenner, La., 1979-86, Satterlee, Mestayer & Freeman, New Orleans, 1986-88; ptnr. Tranchina & Martinez, A.P.L.C., New Orleans, 1988—; lectr. in field, 1989—; asst. grader for civil code I, La. Bar Exam., 1989—. Contbr. articles to legal jours. Fellow Am. Acad. Matrimonial Lawyers (bd. cert. family law specialist La.); mem. ABA (trial techniques com. family law sect., law practice mgmt. com.), La. State Bar (chmn. CLE family law sect. 1989-90, treas. 1990, vice chmn. 1991-92, chmn. 1992-94), New Orleans Bar Assn., Toastmasters (pres. Metairie, La. 1981-84), Jefferson Parish Bar Assn. (chmn. CLE 1989-90, 91-92 domistic rels. sect.). Home: 3120 48th St Metairie LA 70001 Office: 601 Poydras St Ste 2025 New Orleans LA 70130

TRANI, EUGENE PAUL, academic administrator, educator; b. Bklyn., Nov. 2, 1939; s. Frank Joseph and Rose Gertrude (Kelly) T.; m. Lois Elizabeth Quigley, June 2, 1962; children: Anne Chapman, Frank. BA in History with honors, U. Notre Dame, 1961; MA, Ind. U., 1963, PhD, 1966. Instr. history Ohio State U., Columbus, 1965-67; asst. prof. So. Ill. U., Carbondale, 1967-71, assoc. prof., 1971-75, prof., 1975-76; asst. v.p. acad. affairs, prof. U. Nebr., 1976-80; prof., vice chancellor acad. affairs U. Mo. Kansas City, 1980-86; prof., v.p. acad. affairs U. Wis. System, 1986-90; pres. Va. Commonwealth U., 1990—; pres., bd. dirs. Va. Biotechnology Rsch. Park, 1992—; vis. asst. prof. U. Wis. Milw., 1969; bd. dirs. Crestar Bank Richmond Met. Bd., Crestar Fin. Corp., Lawyers Title Corp., Innovative Tech. Authority; cons. various univ. presses, jours., govtl. agys.; advisor gov. La., Okla. State Regents Higher Edn.; mem. commn. Internat. Edn. Am. Coun. Higher Ed., 1991—; bd. gov. Ctr. Russian Am. Bus., Washington, 1993—; bd. advisors Inst. for U.S. Studies, I. London, 1993—; adv. coun. mem. Coun. on Grad. Studies and Rsch., U. Notre Dame, 1994—. Author, editor: Concerns of a Conservative Democrat, 1968, The Treaty of Portsmouth: An Adventure in American Diplomacy, 1969, The Secretaries of the Department of the Interior, 1849-69, 1975, (with David Wilson) The Presidency of Warren G. Harding, 3d edit., 1989; contbr. articles to profl. jours., newspapers; book reviewer. Permanent mem. Coun. Fgn. Rels., N.Y.C., 1979—; bd. dirs. Richmond Ballet, 1991—, NCCJ, Richmond, 1991—, Va. Spl. Olympics, 1991—, YMCA of Greater Richmond, 19926, Richmond Renaissance, 1992—, Met. Found., 1992-95; mem. U.S. Savs. Bond Vol. Com., chmn. higher edn. area, 1992, 93; adv. bd. Greater Richmond chpt. ARC, 1992—. Fellow Russian and East European Inst., 1964-65, Nat. Hist. Publs. Commn., 1969-70, Woodrow Wilson Internat. Ctr. Scholars, 1972-73, So. Ill. U. Sabbatical Leave, 1975-76, Coun. Internat. Exchange Scholars, 1981, U. Mo. Faculty, 1981; grantee U.S. Dept. Interior Rsch., 1965, 66, So. Ill. U. Office Rsch. and Projects, 1967-74, Am. Philos. Soc., 1968, 72, So. Ill U. Summer Rsch. 1970, 72, 75, Lilly Endowment, 1975-76, Sloan Commn. Govt. and Higher Edn., 1978, U.S. Info. Agy. Am. Participants Program, 1984, 85, 86, 88, 90; recipient Younger Humanist award NEH, 1972-73, Leadership and Achievement award Ctrl. Richmond Assn., 1992. Mem. Internat. Inst. Strategic Studies, Am. Assn. Advancement Slavic Studies, Orgn. Am. Historians, Soc. Historians Am. Fgn. Rels., Met. Richmond C. of C. (bd. dirs. 1991—), Va. Ctr. for Innovative Tech., Ctrl. Richmond Assn. (leadership award, 1992), Phi Kappa Phi. Roman Catholic. Avocations: reading, travel, basketball, golf. Office: Va Commonwealth U Box 842512 910 W Franklin St Richmond VA 23284-2512

TRANK, DOUGLAS MONTY, rhetoric and speech communications educator; b. Lincoln, Nebr., Sept. 8, 1944; s. Walter John and Hazel Elaine (Stegeman) T.; children: Heather Nicole, Jessica Celeste; m. Christine Marie Quinn, 1992. BA in English, U. Nebr., Kearney, 1967, MS in Comm., 1970; PhD in Comm., U. Utah, 1973. Tchr. Ogallala (Nebr.) High Sch., 1967-70; teaching fellow in communications U. Utah, Salt Lake City, 1970-72; prof. communications Old Dominion U., Norfolk, Va., 1972-74; prof. rhetoric and edn. U. Iowa, Iowa City, 1974—, chmn. rhetoric dept., 1984-89; chmn. bd. control athletics, faculty senate, mem. ednl. policy com., faculty adv. com., faculty assembly, exec. com. U. Iowa. Author book, chpts. books, monographs; editor Communication Edn., 1993-96; assoc. editor Communication Studies; contbr. articles to profl. jours. Recipient Admiral award Ace Adventures, Inc., Iowa, 1987, Hemingway prize, 1992. Mem. Speech Communication Assn., Iowa Communication Assn. (pres. 1980-82, editor 1977-81, mem. jour. editorial bd.), Cen. States Communication Assn. (pres. 1990-91), Fedn. Iowa Speech Orgns. (pres. 1977-79), Iowa City Optimist Club (dir. 1982-89, pres. 1987-88). Democrat. Avocations: ice sailing, hunting, fishing, canoeing. Office: U Iowa Dept Rhetoric Iowa City IA 52242

TRANQUADA, ROBERT ERNEST, medical educator, physician; b. Los Angeles, Aug. 27, 1930; s. Ernest Alvro and Katharine (Jacobus) T.; m. Janet Martin, Aug. 31, 1951; children: John Martin, James Robert, Katherine Anne. B.A., Pomona Coll., 1951; M.D., Stanford U., 1955; D.Sc. (hon.), Worcester Poly. Inst., 1985. Diplomate Am. Bd. Internal Medicine. Intern in medicine UCLA Med. Center, 1955-56, resident in medicine, 1956-57; resident Los Angeles VA Hosp., 1957-58; fellow in diabetes and metabolic diseases UCLA, 1958-59; fellow in diabetes U. So. Calif., 1959-60, asst. prof. medicine, 1960-63, assoc. prof., 1964-68, chmn. dept. community medicine, 1967-70; med. dir. Los Angeles County/U. So. Calif. Med. Center, 1969-74; regional dir. Central Region, Los Angeles County Dept. Health Services, 1974-76; assoc. dean UCLA Sch. Medicine, 1976-79; chancellor and dean U. Mass. Med. Sch., 1979-86; dean U. So. Calif. Sch. Medicine, 1986-91; prof. medicine U. So. Calif., L.A., 1986-92, Norman Topping/Nat. Med. Enterprises prof. medicine and pub. policy, 1992—. mem., chair L.A. County Task Force on Health Care Access, 1992-94. Trustee Pomona Coll., 1969—, vice chmn., 1987-91, chmn. 1991—; mem. bd. fellows Claremont U. Ct., 1971-79, 91—; corporator Worcester Art Mus., 1980-86; bd. dirs. Nat. Med. Fellowships, Inc., 1973—, chmn. 1980-85; trustee Charles Drew U. Med. and Sci., 1968-79, 86-95, Orthopaedic Hosp., 1986-91, Barlow Hosp., 1987-89; bd. dirs. Worcester Acad., 1984-86, Worcester County Inst. for Savs., 1982-86, U. So. Calif. Univ. Hosp., 1988-91, Alliance for Childrens Rights, 1991-95; bd. dirs. Good Hope Med. Found., 1994—; mem. Ind. Commn. on L.A. Police Dept., 1991-92; mem. governing bd. L.A. County Local Initiative Health Authority, 1994—. Milbank faculty fellow, 1967-72. Fellow AAAS, Am. Antiquarian Soc.; mem. AMA, Am. Diabetes Assn., Western Soc. Clin. Investigation, Los Angeles County Med. Assn., Los Angeles Acad. Medicine, Calif. Med. Assn., Inst. Medicine of Nat. Acad. Scis., Phi Beta Kappa, Sigma Xi, Alpha Omega Alpha. Office: U So Calif VKC # 368A Los Angeles CA 90089-0041

TRAN-SON-TAY, ROGER, mechanical engineer educator; b. Saigon, Vietnam, Jan. 1, 1955; came to U.S., 1979; s. Dominique and Pauline (Tran-Thi-Tri) Tran-Son-Tay; m. Doan Bui, Nov. 17, 1984; children: Heather, Anthony. BSME, Ecole Superieure des, Transports et Propulsion, Orleans, France, 1978; MS in Biomed. Engring., U. Tech. de Compiegne, 1979; DSc in Mech. Engring., Washington U., St. Louis, 1983. Rsch. assoc. Dept. Biophysics U. So. Calif., L.A., 1983-84; sr. rsch. assoc. Chem. Engring. Rice U., Houston, 1984-86; asst. prof., assoc. prof., adj. assoc. prof. Mech. Engring. Duke U., Durham, N.C., 1986—; assoc. prof. Aerospace Engring., Mechanics and Engring. Sci. U. Fla., Gainesville, 1993—. Co-editor: Cell Mechanics and Cellular Engineering, 1994; reviewer NIH, Bethesda, 1993; co-inventor Magneto-Acoustic Ball Microrheometer; contbr. chpts. in books. Mem. ASME, Soc. Rheology, Biophys. Soc., Biomed. Engr. Soc. Achievements include building a modified cone/plate viscometer in order to study cell damage and lysis. Office: U Fla Dept Aerospace Engr 231 Aerospace Bldg Gainesville FL 32611

TRANSOU, LYNDA LEW, advertising art administrator; b. Atlanta, Dec. 11, 1949; d. Lewis Cole Transou and Ann Lynette (Taylor) Putnam; m. Lue Gregg Loso, Oct. 25, 1991. B.F.A. cum laude, U. Tex.-Austin, 1971. Art dir., The Pitluk Group, San Antonio, 1971, Campbell, McQuien & Lawson, Dallas, 1973-74, Bozell & Jacobs, Dallas, 1974-75; art dir., ptnr. The Assocs., Dallas, 1975-77; art dir. Belo Broadcasting, Dallas, 1977-80; creative dir., v.p. Allday & Assocs., Dallas, 1980-85; owner Lynda Transou Advt. & Design, 1986—. Recipient Merit award N.Y. Art Dirs. Show, 1980; Gold award Dallas Ad League, 1980, Silver award, 1980, Bronze award, 1981, 82, 2 Merit awards Houston Art Dirs. Club, 1978-86; Merit award Broadcast Designers Assn., 1980, 82; Merit awards Dallas Ad League, 1978, 87; Silver award Houston Art Dirs. Show; Gold award Tex. Pub. Relations Assn., 1982, 85; Gold award N.Y. One Show, 1982, Creativity award Art Direction mag., 1986, Print award Regional Design Annual, 1988, Telly Finalist, 1987. Mem. Am. Inst. Graphic Arts, Dallas Soc. Visual Communications (Bronze award 1980, Merit awards, 1978-86), Delta Gamma (historian 1969-70).

TRAPASSO, JOSEPH ANGELO, secondary school educator, coach; b. Albany, N.Y., July 17, 1951; s. Joseph Angelo and Patricia Mary (Vennard) T.; m. Darcie Jo Turner, Apr. 16, 1993; 1 child, Stephanie Anne. BA in Bus. Econs., LeMoyne Coll., 1973; postgrad., U. Albany, 1974-75, St. Rose Coll., 1975-76. Phys. edn. tchr. Cathedral Acad., Albany, N.Y., 1974-75; bus. tchr., jr. varsity basketball coach Cardinal McCloskey H.S., Albany, N.Y., 1975-76; bus. tchr., dept. chmn. Cath. Ctrl. H.S., Troy, N.Y., 1976—, varsity tennis coach, 1977-79, head and asst. basketball coach, 1978, 80, 82, bus. dept. chairperson, 1984—, N.Y. State mock trial tchr., coach, 1985—, acad. sports advisor, 1990-91, 92, faculty senate pres., 1994—; asst. tennis coach U. Albany, 1994—. Basketball coach Cathedral Acad., Albany, 1974-75; head tennis coach Siena Coll., Loudonville, N.Y., 1979-94; trustee Guilderland (N.Y.) Town Libr., 1987-88; tennis dir. Guilderland Parks and Recreation, summers 1980, 81, 82; tournament dir. women's tennis N.Y. State Divsn. III Athletic Assn., 1984, 85, 86. Named Mock Trial County Champion, Rensalaer N.Y. Bar Assn., 1980s, 90s. Mem. NCAA, Nat. Bus. Educator Assn. Am., Bus. and Mktg. Educators Assn. Capital Dist., Intercollegiate Tennis Assn., U.S. Tennis Assn. Avocations: tennis, jogging, writing poetry, listening to music, reading short stories. Home and Office: 25 Parkwood St Albany NY 12203-3625

TRAPOLIN, FRANK WINTER, retired insurance executive; b. New Orleans, Jan. 29, 1913; s. John Baptiste and Florence Bertha (Winter) T.; BS in Econs., Loyola U. of South, New Orleans, 1935; cert. official U.S.A. Track & Field. m. Thelma Mae Mouledoux, Oct. 27, 1937; children: Timothy, Patricia Couret, Jane Oaksmith, Anne Britt. Agt., Godchaux & Mayer, New Orleans, 1935-42, 46-51; pres. Trapolin-Couret Ins. Agy., Inc., New Orleans, 1953-92, 92-93; v.p. Gillis, Ellis & Baker, Inc., New Orleans, 1993-94, ret., 1994; mem. faculty Loyola U.; TV lectr., seamanship instr. Coast Guard Aux., New Orleans Former pres. Cath. Human Rels. Commn. Greater New Orleans, Associated Cath. Charities New Orleans, Maryland Dr. Homeowners Assn., Loyola U. Alumni Assn.; former chmn. adv. bd. Ursuline Nuns New Orleans, New Orleans Juvenile Cts.; former scoutmaster Boy Scouts Am., former chmn. Boy Scout troop com.; former v.p. Cmty. Rels. Coun. Greater New Orleans, New Orleans Jr. C.of C., La. Interch. Conf.; former trustee United Fund Greater New Orleans Area; treas. emeritus La. Interchurch Conference, dir. emeritus Catholic Book Store Found., tng. officer 8th Coast Guard Dist. Aux.; former mem. adv. bd. Coll. Bus. Adminstrn., Loyola U., Mother-house of Sisters of Holy Family, Immaculate Conception Cath. Ch.; group captain Manresa Retreats, 1947—; former bd. dirs. St. John Berchman Orphanage, New Orleans Interfaith Conf., St. Elizabeth's Home for Girls, Cath. Book Store Found., Manresa Retreat House; adv. bd. New Orleans Track Club; founder, Serra Run for Vocations; bd. dirs. Audubon Blvd. Assn. Served with USN, 1942-46, 51-53, capt. Res. ret. Recipient Merit cert. City of New Orleans, 1972; Order of St. Louis, 1976; lector Catholic Ch., 1964-87; eucharistic min., 1986—. Mem. La. Assn. Ins. Agts., Nat. Assn. Ins. Agts., New Orleans Ins. Exch., Navy League, Mil. Order World Wars, Greater New Orleans Exec. Assn. (pres. 1985, named Exec. of the Year 1985, lifetime hon. mem.), New Orleans Photog. Soc., Sierra Club, Blue Key. Democrat. Roman Catholic. Clubs: Sertoma (pres. New Orleans 1955-56), Serra (pres. New Orleans 1973-74), Internat. House, New Orleans Track, Greater New Orleans Runners Assn., New Orleans Yacht, Pass Christian Yacht. Lodge: KC (4 deg.). Patentee gunnery, tng. and machinery devices for USN. Home: 119 Audubon Blvd New Orleans LA 70118-5538

TRAPP, FRANK ANDERSON, art educator; b. Pitts., June 13, 1922; s. Frank Louis and Mary (Anderson) T. BA, Carnegie Inst. Tech., 1943; AM, Harvard, 1947, Ph.D., 1952; AM (hon.), Amherst U., 1963. Teaching fellow Harvard (also resident tutor Adams House), 1948-51; mem. faculty Williams Coll., 1951-56; mem. faculty Amherst (Mass.) Coll., 1956-92, prof. art, 1963-92, William R. Mead prof., 1976-89, Arms prof., 1989-92, dir. Mead Art Mus., 1969-89; rsch. assoc. fine arts U. Pitts., 1994—; vis. Mellon prof. dept. fine arts U. Pitts., 1979-80. Author: The Attainment of Delacroix, 1970, Peter Blume, 1987, The Grand Tradition: British Art in the Amherst College Collection, 1988 (with others) Clarence Holbrook Carter, 1989; contbg. author and editor Mead Mus. Publs.; contbr. articles to profl. jours. Served with AUS, 1943-46, PTO. Fulbright grantee, 1949-50; Belgian-Am. Ednl. Found. fellow, 1954; Nat. Endowment for the Humanities sr. fellow, 1971-72. Home: 4609 Bayard St Apt 51 Pittsburgh PA 15213-2735

TRAPP, JAMES MCCREERY, lawyer; b. Macomb, Ill., Aug. 11, 1934. BA, Knox Coll., 1956; JD, U. Mich., 1961. Bar: Ill. 1961. Ptnr. McDermott, Will & Emery, Chgo. Chmn. Ill. Inst. Continuing Legal Edn., 1978-79, bd. dirs., 1980-86, pres., 1984-85. Fellow Am. Coll. Trust and Estate Coun. (Ill. chmn. 1980-83, nat. regent 1983—, treas. 1989-90, sec. 1990-91, v.p. 1991-92, pres.-elect 1992-93, pres. 1993-94, exec. com. 1986-94), Am. Bar Found., Ill. Bar Found.; mem. ABA, Ill. State Bar Assn., Chgo. Bar Assn. (chair trust law com. 1972-73, com. on coms. 1972-74), Internat. Acad. Estate and Trust Law, Am. Law Inst. (pres.), Chgo. Estate Planning Coun. Office: McDermott Will & Emery 227 W Monroe St Chicago IL 60606-5096

TRAPPE, JAMES MARTIN, mycologist; b. Spokane, Wash., Aug. 16, 1931; s. Martin Carl and Esther Louise (Koss) T.; m. Beverly Joan Reller, Dec. 27, 1963; children: Matthew, Erica, John, Angela. B.S., U. Wash., 1953, Ph.D., 1962; M.F., SUNY, Syracuse, 1955. With U.S. Forest Service, 1954-85; prin. mycologist, project leader Pacific N.W. Forest and Range Experiment Sta., Corvallis, Oreg., 1965-85; mem. faculty Oreg. State U., Corvallis, 1965—; prof. botany-plant pathology and forest sci. Oreg. State U., 1977—; co-chmn. Corvallis FISH, 1971-73. Editor Convictions mag.; contbr. articles to profl. jours. Recipient Civil Rights Accomplishment award U.S. Forest Svc., 1979, Civil Liberties award ACLU, 1990, Barrington Moore Meml. award Soc. Am. Foresters, 1995; grantee NSF, 1971—, Am. Philos. Soc., 1968-72, Sigma Xi, 1968-72, U.S. Spain Joint Com. Sci. and Tech. Cooperation, 1985-87, Indo-Am. Sci. and Tech. Initiative, 1984-91. Fellow AAAS; mem. Mycological Soc. Am. (council 1976-77, program chmn. 1976-77, v.p. 1984-85, pres. 1986-87), N.W. Sci. Assn. (past pres., Outstanding Scientist award 1991), Oreg. Acad. Sci., Oreg. Mycological Soc. (hon. life), Soc. Mex. de Micologia, Japanese Mycological Soc., Brit. Mycological Soc., N.Am. Truffling Soc. (hon. life). Home: 2165 NW Maser Pl Corvallis OR 97330 Office: Oreg State U Dept Forest Sci Corvallis OR 97331-7501

TRASK, THOMAS EDWARD, religious organization administrator; b. Brainard, Minn., Mar. 23, 1936; m. Shirley Burkhart; children: Kimberly, Bradley, Todd, Tom. BA, North Ctrl. Bible Coll., 1956, DDiv (hon.), 1994. Ordained min. Assemblies of God, 1958. Pastor First Assembly of God, Hibbing, Minn., 1956-60; pastor First Assembly of God, Vicksburg, Mich., 1960-64; Mich. dist. A/G youth leader First Assembly of God, 1964-68; sr. pastor Saginaw (Mich.) First Assembly of God, 1968-73, Brightmoor Tabernacle, Southfield, Mich., 1976-88; supt. Mich. Dist. Coun., Dearborn, 1973-76; gen. treas. The Gen. Coun. Assemblies of God, Springfield, Mo., 1988-93; gen. supt. The Gen. Coun. Assemblies of God, Springfield, Mich., 1993—. Co-author: Back to the Altar: A Call to Spiritual Awakening, 1994, Back to the Word, A Call to Biblical Authority, 1996. Office: Assemblies of God 1445 N Boonville Ave Springfield MO 65802-1894

TRAUB, J(OSEPH) F(REDERICK), computer scientist, educator; b. June 24, 1932; m. Pamela Ann McCorduck, Dec. 6, 1969; children: Claudia Renee, Hillary Anne. B.S., CCNY, 1954; Ph.D., Columbia U., 1959. Mem. tech. staff Bell Labs., Murray Hill, N.J., 1959-70; prof. computer sci. and math., head dept. computer sci. Carnegie-Mellon U., Pitts., 1971-79; Edwin Howard Armstrong prof. computer sci., chmn. dept., prof. math. Columbia U., 1979-86; prof. computer sci. Princeton (N.J.) U., 1986-87; pres. John Von Neumann Nat. Supercomputer Ctr., Consortium for Sci. Computing, Princeton, 1986-87; Edwin Howard Armstrong prof., chmn. dept. computer sci., prof. math. Columbia U., N.Y.C., 1987-89, Edwin Howard Armstrong prof. computer sci., math., 1989—; dir. N.Y. State Ctr. Computers and Info. Systems, 1982-88; disting. lectr. MIT, 1977; vis. Mackay prof. U. Calif., Berkeley, 1978-79; cons. Hewlett-Packard, 1982, IBM, 1984, Schlumberger, 1986; mem. pres.'s adv. com. computer sci. Stanford U., 1972-75, chmn., 1975-76; mem. adv. com. Fed. Jud. Center; mem. sci. council I.R.I.A., Paris, 1976-80; mem. central steering com., computing sci. and engring. research study NSF, also liaison to panel on theoretical computer sci. and panel on numerical comp., 1974-80; mem. adv. com. Carnegie-Mellon Inst. Research, 1978-79; mem. applied math. div. rev. com. Argonne Nat. Lab., 1973-75; mem. adv. com. math. and computer sci. NSF, 1978-80; chmn. computer sci. and tech. bd. NRC, 1986-90; chmn. computer sci. and telecommunications bd. NRC, 1990-92; trustee Columbia U. Press, 1983-85; founding chair Spl. Interest Group on Numerical Math., 1965-71. Author: Iterative Methods for the Solution of Equations, 1964, Russian edit., 1985; (with H. Wozniakowski) A General Theory of Optimal Algorithms, 1980, Russian edit., 1983; (with G. Wasilkowski and H. Wozniakowski) Information, Uncertainty, Complexity, 1983, Information-Based Complexity, 1988; editor: Complexity of Sequential and Parallel Numerical Algorithms, 1973, Analytical Computational Complexity, 1976, Algorithms and Complexity: New Directions and Recent Results, 1976, Jour. Assn. Computing Machinery, 1970-76, Transactions on Math. Software, 1974-76, Jour. Computer and Sys. Scis., 1973-86, Internat. Jour. on Computers and Math. with Applications, 1974—, Cohabiting With Computers, 1985; founding editor Jour. Complexity, 1985—, Ann. Rev. Computer Sci., 1986-92; assoc. editor Complexity, 1995—. Sherman Fairchild Disting. scholar Calif. Inst. Tech., 1991, 92; recipient Award for Disting. Svc. to Computing Rsch. Computer Rsch. Assn., 1992, Lezione Lincee Acad. Nazionale dei Lincei, 1993, Sr. Scientist award Alexander Von Humboldt Found., 1992—. Fellow AAAS (coun. 1971-74), ACM (chmn. award com. 1974-76); mem. IEEE (Emanuel R. Piore Gold medal 1991), NAE (membership com. for computer sci., elec. engring. and control 1986-87, membership com. for computer sci. and engring. 1987-91, presdl. search com. 1993-94), Conf. Bd. Math. Scis. (coun. 1971-74), Soc. Indsl. and Applied Math., Am. Math. Soc., N.Y. Acad. Sci. (exec. com., bd. govs. 1987-89), Nat. Acad. Sci. (mem. study on high performance computing and comm. 1994-95). Office: Columbia University Dept Computer Sci New York NY 10027

TRAUB, RICHARD KENNETH, lawyer; b. Lakewood, N.J., Aug. 4, 1950; s. Harold W. and Muriel N. (Zurlin) T.; m. Barbara Lynn Wright, July 9, 1972; children: Russell S., Melissa L. BBA, U. Miami, Coral Gables, Fla., 1972, JD cum laude, 1975. Bar: Fla. 1975, N.Y. 1976, N.J. 1976, U.S. Dist. Ct. N.J. 1976, U.S. Supreme Ct. 1979, U.S. Dist. Ct. (ea. & so. dists.) N.Y. 1981. Ptnr. Wilson, Elser, Moskowitz, Edelman & Dicker, N.Y.C., 1975-95, Traub Eglin Lieberman Straus, Hawthorne, N.Y., 1996—; ptnr. Time for Patty Stables, N.J., 1992—; officer, dir. X-Ray Duplications, Inc., N.J.; ptnr., founder Fractured Greetings, N.J., 1993—, mem., lectr. Fedn. Ins. and Corp. Counsel, 1993—, mem. admissions com., industry cooperation ins. coverage and ADR coms.; lectr. Inst. for Internat. Rsch., Washington, 1988, Engring. News Record Constrn. Claims Conf., 1991. Author: Legal and Professional Aspects of Construction Management, 1990; contbr. articles to profl. jours. Bd. dirs. Pop Warner Football Assn., Holmdel, N.J., 1989—. Mem. ABA (forum com. on constrn. industry 1989, tort and ins. practice sect. 1985—, computer litigation sect.), N.Y. State Bar Assn., N.J. Bar Assn., Fla. Bar Assn., Fedn. Ins. and Corp. Counsel (spkr. ins. coverage sect., mem. ins. coverage and industry coop. sects., mem. admissions com.). Office: Traub Eglin Lieberman et al Mid-Westchester Exec Park Three Skyline Dr Hawthorne NY 10532

TRAUGER, DONALD BYRON, nuclear engineering laboratory administrator; b. Exeter, Nebr., June 29, 1920; s. Charles C. and Ethel L. (Downey) T.; m. Elaine Causey, Sept. 2, 1945; children: Byron Roscoe, Thomas Charles. A.B., Nebr. Wesleyan U., 1942, D.Sc. (hon.), 1974; postgrad., Columbia U., 1942-46, U. Tenn., 1946-49; D.Sc. (hon.), Tenn. Wesleyan Coll., 1977. Supr. test equipment devel. Manhattan Dist. Project, 1942-46; supr. Devel. Lab., Oak Ridge Gaseous Diffusion Plant, 1946-54; with Oak Ridge Nat. Lab., 1954-93, assoc. dir. nuclear and engring. technologies, 1970-84, sr. staff asst. to dir., 1984-93; cons. in energy tech., 1993—. Editorial advisor Anns. Nuclear Engring, 1973—; design features editor sect. IV Nuclear Safety Jour., 1989—. Mem. Oak Ridge Bd. Edn., 1961-67; pres. Oak Ridge PTA Coun., 1969-70, Oak Ridge Parents Adv. Coun., 1958-59; chmn. exec. com., trustee Tenn. Wesleyan Coll., 1976-81, chmn. bd. govs., 1986-90, chmn. bd. trustees, 1990-93. Recipient Alumni Achievement award Nebr. Wesleyan U., 1962. Fellow Am. Nuclear Soc. (chmn. planning com. 1981-83); mem. AAAS, Am. Phys. Soc., Sigma Xi (pres. Oak Ridge chpt. 1987-88), Sigma Pi Sigma. Methodist. Club: Rotary. Office: PO Box 2008 Oak Ridge TN 37831-6254

TRAUGH, DONALD GEORGE, III, secondary education educator; b. Tucson, Aug. 5, 1950; s. Donald G. Jr. and Leatrice (Rhodes) Traugh-Long; m. Brenda Kay Kreischer, June 14, 1975; children: Jonathan P., Brandon M. AB in Edn., Fairmont (W.Va.) State U., 1974; MEd in Social Studies, Bloomsburg (Pa.) State U., 1980. Cert. tchr., Pa. Tchr. social studies Bloomsburg Area Sch. Dist., 1974—, chmn. dept. social studies, 1978—; co-chair social studies curriculum staff Bloomsburg Area Sch. Dist., 1984—. Vol. firefighter Catawissa (Pa.) Hose Co. 1, 1969—, chief dept., 1987—; mem. Catawissa Borough Coun., 1977-89, v.p., 1987-89. Mem. NEA, Pa. Edn. Assn., Bloomsburg Area Edn. Assn., Nat. Coun. Social Studies, Mid. States Assn. Social Studies, Pa. Coun. Social Studies, Nat. Fire Protection Assn., Keystone State Fire Chiefs Assn., Pi Gamma Mu, Delta Sigma Phi. Democrat. Lutheran. Avocations: coaching football, hunting, fishing, scouting, gardening. Home: 503 E Main St Catawissa PA 17820-1030 Office: Bloomsburg HS 1200 Railroad St Bloomsburg PA 17815-3613

TRAUGOTT, ELIZABETH CLOSS, linguistics educator and researcher; b. Bristol, Eng., Apr. 9, 1939; d. August and Hannah M.M. (Priebsch) Closs; m. John L. Traugott, Sept. 26, 1967; 1 dau., Isabel. BA in English, Oxford U., Eng., 1960; PhD in English lang., U. Calif., Berkeley, 1964. Asst. prof. English U. Calif., Berkeley, 1964-70; lectr. U. East Africa, Tanzania, 1965-66, U. York, Eng., 1966-67; lectr., then assoc. prof. linguistics and English Stanford U., Calif., 1970-77, prof., 1977—, chmn. linguistics dept., 1980-85; vice provost, dean grad. studies Stanford U., 1985-91, mem. grad. record examinations bd., 1989-93, mem. test of English as a fgn. lang. bd., 1989-91, chmn. test of English as a fgn. lang. bd., 1991-92; mem. higher edn. funding coun. Eng. Assessment Panel, 1996. Author: A History of English Syntax, 1972, (with Mary Pratt) Linguistics for Students of Literature, 1980, (with Paul Hopper) Grammaticalization, 1993; editor: (with ter Meulen, Reilly, Ferguson) On Conditionals, 1986, (with Heine) Approaches to Grammaticalization, 2 vols., 1991; contbr. numerous articles to profl. jours. Am. Coun. Learned Socs. fellow, 1975-76, Guggenheim fellow, 1983-84, Ctr. Advanced Study of Behavioral Scis. fellow, 1983-84. Mem. MLA, AAUP, AAUW, Linguistics Soc. Am. (pres. 1987, sec.-treas. 1994—), Internat. Soc. Hist. Linguistic (pres. 1979-81). Office: Stanford Univ Dept Linguistics Bldg 460 Stanford CA 94305-2150

TRAUM, JEROME S., lawyer; b. Newark, Sept. 26, 1935; s. Max and Evelyn (Fein) T.; m. Lynda Sturner, Apr. 16, 1972; children: David, Norman, Daniel, Edward. A.B., U. Mich., 1956, J.D. with distinction, 1959. Bar: N.Y. 1960, U.S. Supreme Ct. 1976. Assoc. Chadbourne, Parke, Whiteside & Wolff, N.Y.C., 1959-62; assoc. to ptnr. Spear and Hill, N.Y.C., 1962-67; ptnr. Janklow and Traum, N.Y.C., 1967-89; v.p., then pres. Morton L. Janklow Assocs., Inc., lit. agy., 1977-89; gen. ptnr. investment bankers The Blackstone Group, N.Y.C., 1989-91; of counsel Proskauer, Rose, Goetz & Mendelsohn, N.Y.C., 1991-95; ptnr. Moses & Singer, N.Y.C., 1995—; adj. prof. fed. securities regulation Syracuse U. Coll. Law, 1975; bd. dirs. Interep Nat. Radio Sales, Inc. Bd. dirs. McCaffery & McCall, Inc., 1987-90, Open Channel, 1971-77, Call for Action, 1978-83, Playwright's Forum, Inc., 1981—, Penny McCall Found., Inc., 1987—; trustee Jose Limon Dance Found., 1968. Mem. Assn. of Bar of City of N.Y., ABA (com. fed. regulation securities), Order of Coif. Home: 111 W 67th St Apt 30C New York NY 10023 Office: Moses & Singer 1301 Ave of Americas New York NY 10019-6076

TRAUSCHT, DONALD C., security services executive; b. 1933. BA, St. Mary's Coll., 1955; MBA, U. Chgo., 1959. With Langevin Co., 1959-67; with Borg Warner Corp., 1967—, v.p. bus. devel. and acquisitions, 1978-82, v.p. corp. planning, 1982-87, v.p. finance and strategy, 1987, COO, pres., CEO, COO, 1992-93; chair, CEO Borg-Warner Security Corp., Chgo., 1993—; bd. dirs. Thiokol Corp., Bluebird Corp., Borg-Warner Automotive, Inc, IMO Industries, Inc., Esco Electronics Corp., Borg-Warner Security Corp. Office: Borg-Warner Security Corp 200 S Michigan Ave Chicago IL 60604-2402

TRAUTMAN, DONALD W., bishop; b. Buffalo, June 24, 1936. Ed., Our Lady of Angels Sem., Niagara Falls, N.Y., Theology Faculty, Innsbruck, Austria, Pontifical Biblical Inst., Rome, Cath. U., St. Thomas Aquinas U., Rome. Ordained priest Roman Cath. Ch., 1962, consecrated bishop, 1985. Titular bishop of Sassura and aux. bishop Diocese of Buffalo, 1985; bishop Erie, Pa., 1990—; Episc. moderator Diocesan Fiscal Mgmt. Conf.; mem. com. on doctrine and migration Nat. Conf. Cath. Bishops; chmn. Bishops' Liturgy Com. Home: 205 W 9th St Erie PA 16501-1304 Address: St Mark's Ctr PO Box 10397 Erie PA 16514-0397

TRAUTMAN, HERMAN LOUIS, lawyer, educator; b. Columbus, Ind., Sept. 26, 1911; s. Theodore H. and Emma (Guckenberger) T.; m. Marian Lucille Green, Sept. 1, 1940; children: Stephen M., Pamela C.; LLB with distinction Ind. U., 1937, BA, 1946, JD with distinction, 1946; postgrad., NYU, 1953, Ford Found. faculty fellow, Harvard U., 1954-55. Bar: Ind. 1937, U.S. Tax Ct., U.S. Ct. Appeals (6th cir.) Tenn. Sole practice, Evansville, Ind., 1937-43; pres. Crescent Coal Co., Evansville, 1941-43; prof. law U. Ala. Tuscaloosa, 1946-49; prof. law Vanderbilt U., 1949—, prof. law emeritus, 1977; NYU vis. prof., 1955, U. Mich., Ann Arbor, 1963-64; ptnr. Trautman & Trautman, Nashville, 1976-85; sole practice, Nashville, 1986—. Served to lt. comdr. USN, 1943-46. Mem. ABA, Am. Law Inst., Tenn. Bar Assn., Nashville Bar Assn., Nat. Conf. Jud. Adminstrs., Estate Planning Coun., Order of Coif, Phi Gamma Delta, Belle Meade Club, Univ. Club, Kiwanis. Methodist. Address: 5100 Stanford Dr Nashville TN 37215-4230

TRAUTMAN, WILLIAM ELLSWORTH, lawyer; b. San Francisco, Nov. 27, 1940; s. Gerald H. and Doris Joy (Tucker) T.; m. Dorothy Williamson, June 17, 1962; children: Darcey, Torey. AB, U. Calif., Berkeley, 1962, LLB, 1965. Bar: Calif. U.S. Supreme Ct., Calif. Dist. Ct., U.S. Ct. Appeals (9th and fed. cirs.). Assoc. Chickering & Gregory, San Francisco, 1965-71, ptnr., 1972-81; ptnr. Brobeck, Phleger & Harrison, San Francisco, 1981—, mng. ptnr., 1992-96, litigation dept. chair, 1984-91. Pres. Oakland (Calif.) Mus. Assn., 1981-83; mem. profl. ethics com. State Bar Calif., 1974-77. Fellow Am. Coll. Trial Lawyers; mem. Legal Aid Soc. (bd. dirs. 1982-93, pres. 1985-88), Bar Assn. San Francisco (bd. dirs. 1972-73), Calif. Barristers (bd. dirs., v.p.), Barrister's Club of San Francisco (v.p. 1973). Office: Brobeck Phleger & Harrison 1 Market San Francisco CA 94105

TRAUTMANN, CHARLES HOME, museum director, civil engineer; b. Pawtucket, R.I., Jan. 6, 1952; s. Homer Frank and Gail (Greenhalgh) T.; m. Nancy Lawson Morton, May 7, 1977; children: Nina Morton, Eric Morton. BA cum laude, Amherst Coll., 1974; MSCE, MS in Geology, Stanford U., 1976; PhD in Civil Engring., Cornell U., 1983. Registered profl. engr.; cert. profl. geologist. Geologist Geotech. Engrs., Inc., Winchester, Mass., 1976-79; grad. rsch. asst. Cornell U., Ithaca, N.Y., 1979-83; rsch. assoc. Cornell U., Ithaca, 1983-88, sr. rsch. assoc., 1988-94; adj. assoc. prof. civil and environ. engring., 1994—; exec. dir. Sciencenter, Ithaca, 1990—; cons. engr., geologist, pvt. practice, Ithaca, 1983—. Contbr. over 60 articles to profl. jours. Bd. dirs. Ithaca Montessori Sch., 1984-91, pres., 1984-86, trustee, 1995—; pres. Forest Home Assn., Ithaca, 1989-90; pres., bd. trustees 1st Meth. Ch., Ithaca, 1984-87; mem. adv. bd. Paleontol. Rsch. Inst., 1993—, Cayuga Nature Ctr., 1993—; bd. dirs. Tompkins County Area Devel., 1995—. Rsch. fellow Alexander von Humboldt Found., 1987-88; named Engr. of Yr., N.Y. State Soc. Profl. Engrs. So. Tier Sect., 1996. Mem. ASCE (pres. Ithaca sect. 1993-94, Engr. of Yr. award Ithaca sect. 1995), AAAS, Assn. Engring. Geologists, Am. Inst. Profl. Geologists, Nat. Assn. Sci. Tchrs., Assn. Sci.-Tech. Ctrs., Sci. Tchrs. Assn. N.Y. State (exec. com. 1994-95), Am. Assn. Mus., N.Y. State Sci. and Tech. Mus. Consortium (v.p. 1993-95, pres. 1995—), Nat. Eagle Scout Assn., Sigma Xi, Chi Epsilon. Office: Sciencenter 601 1st St Ithaca NY 14850-3507

TRAUTMANN, THOMAS ROGER, history and anthropology educator; b. Madison, Wis., May 27, 1940; s. Milton and Esther Florence (Trachte) T.; m. Marcella Hauolilani Choy, Sept. 25, 1962; children: Theodore William, Robert Arthur. BA, Beloit Coll., 1962; PhD, U. London, 1968. Lectr. in history Sch. Oriental and African Studies, U. London, 1965-68; asst. prof. history U. Mich., Ann Arbor, 1968-71, assoc. prof., 1971-77, prof., 1977—, Richard Hudson rsch. prof., 1979, prof. history and anthropology, 1984—, chmn. dept. history, 1987-90, Steelcase rsch. prof., 1993-94. Author: Kautilya and the Arthasastra, 1971, Dravidian Kinship, 1981, Lewis Henry Morgan and the Invention of Kinship, 1987, (with K.S. Kabelac) The Library of Lewis Henry Morgan, 1994 (with Diane Owen Hughes) Time: Histories and Ethnologies, 1995; mem. editl. bd. Comparative Studies in Soc. and History; contbr. various articles on India, kinship and history of anthropology. Sr. Humanist fellow NEH, 1984. Fellow Royal Asiatic Soc.; mem. Am. Anthrop. Assn., Assn. Asian Studies, Am. Oriental Soc., Am. Inst. Indian Studies (trustee, sr. rsch. fellow in India 1985), Phi Beta Kappa. Office: U Mich Dept History Ann Arbor MI 48109-1045

TRAUTWEIN, GEORGE WILLIAM, conductor; b. Chgo., Aug. 5, 1927; s. William Jacob and Hilda (Martin) T.; m. Barbara Wilson, Jan. 20, 1955; children: Paul Martin, Matthew Richard. MusB, Oberlin Conservatory, Ohio, 1951; MusM, Cleve. Inst. Music, 1955; MusD, Ind. U., 1961. mem. faculty U. Minn., U. Tex., Austin, Armstrong (Ga.) State Coll.; arts cons. Nat. Endowment Arts. Violinist Indpls. Symphony Orch., 1947-48, Balt. Symphony Orch., 1951-52, Nat. Symphony Orch., Washington, 1952-53, Cleve. Orch., 1953-57, Chautauqua Symphony Orch., N.Y., 1953-59, Camerata Acad., Salzburg, 1957-58, Mozarteum Orch., Salzburg, 1958 (Fulbright grantee 1958), assoc. condr. Dallas Symphony Orch., 1962-66, Mpls. Symphony, 1966-73; music dir. S.D. Symphony, 1971-75, Internat. Congress Strings, Ohio, 1973-75; music dir., condr. Savannah (Ga.) Symphony Orch., 1974-77; music adv., prin. guest condr. Evansville (Ind.) Philharm., 1979-80; music dir., condr. RIAS Edn. Network, Berlin, 1979, Tucson Symphony Orch., 1977-81; artistic dir., condr. Piedmont Chamber Orch.; prin. condr. Internat. Music program; dir. orchestral programs, N.C. Sch. of Arts, 1981-83; dir. instrumental ensembles, Wake Forest U., 1983—, dir. Artists series, 1985—; guest appearances with orchs., U.S., Germany, Sweden, France, Rumania, Jugoslavia, Portugal, Hong Kong, India, P.R., Mex. Adv. bd. Avery Fisher Found., N.Y.C. Served with USN, 1948-49. Recipient Orpheus award Phi Mu Alpha, 1971, ASCAP award, 1979, 82, World Peace award Ministry of World Harmony, 1983; Fulbright grantee Mozarteum, Salzburg, 1958; Sr. Fulbright lectr., India, 1989-90. Mem. Am. Fedn. Musicians, Chamber Music Soc. Am., Sir Thomas Beecham Soc., Erich Wolfgang Korngold Soc., Wilhelm Furtwaengler Soc., Literacy Initiative Assn., Am. String Tchrs. Assn. Avocations: chamber music, art reproduction, Indian ragas, Scandinavian cuisine. Office: Wake Forest U PO Box 7411 Winston Salem NC 27109-7411

TRAVAGLINI, RAYMOND DOMINIC, corporate executive; b. Greenville, Pa., May 3, 1928; s. Perugino and Mary Ann (DiFalco) T.; children: Alan, Lynne, Debbie, Kimberly, Kristine. LHD (hon.), Youngstown State U., 1993. Mgr. Kroger Co., Meadville, Pa., 1949-62; owner Suburban Water Conditioning, Warren, Ohio, 1962-65; ptnr. Sanray Corp., Meadville, 1965—; bd. dirs. Bank One, Youngstown, Ohio. Bd. dirs. Butler Inst. Am. Art, Youngstown, Mahoning Valley Econ. Devel. Corp.; mem. Base Comty. Coun. Dept. Air Force. Named Man of Yr. Boys' Towns of Italy, 1979, Italian Scholarship League, 1984, Mahoning Valley County Econ. Devel. Corp., 1985, Nat. Italian-Am. Sports Hall of Fame, 1992; recipient Disting. Citizen award Youngstown State U. Alumni Assn., 1993. Office: Sanray Corp 1323 Youngstown Warren Rd Niles OH 44446-4616

TRAVANTI, DANIEL JOHN, actor; b. Kenosha, Wis., Mar. 7, 1940; s. John and Elvira (DeAngelis) T. BA, U. Wis.; MA, Loyola Marymount, L.A. Performances include: (TV movies) The Love War, 1970, Adam, 1983, Aurora, 1984, Murrow, 1986, Adam: His Song Continues, 1986, I Never Sang for My Father, 1988, A Case of Libel, Howard Beach: Making the Case for Murder, 1989, Fellow Traveler, 1990, Tagget, 1991, Eyes of a Witness, 1991; (TV series) appeared as Capt. Frank Furillo in Hill Street Blues, 1981-87, Missing Persons, 1993-94; (films) St Ives, 1976, Midnight Crossing, 1988, Millenium, 1989, Megaville, 1991, Weep No More My Lady, 1993, Siao Yu, 1994, Who Killed Teddy Bear, 1994, Just Cause, 1995; (stage) Othello, Who's Afraid of Virginia Woolf?, The Taming of the Shrew, I Never Sang for My Father, Only Kidding, Les Liaisons Dangereuses, A Touch of the Poet. Gen. Motors fellow U. Wis., 1958-61; Woodrow Wilson fellow, 1961; Yale U. Sch. Drama, 1961-62; recipient Emmy award for role as Capt. Frank Furillo in Hill Street Blues, 1981, 82; Golden Globe award, 1981.

TRAVELSTEAD, CHESTER COLEMAN, former educational administrator; b. Franklin, Ky., Sept. 25, 1911; s. Conley and Nelle (Gooch) T.; m. Marita Hawley, Aug. 1, 1936; children—Coleman, Jimmie. A.B., Western Ky. State Coll., Bowling Green, 1933; M.Music, Northwestern U., 1947; Ph.D., U. Ky., 1950; D.Hum., Morehead (Ky.) State U., 1975; Ph.D., John F. Kennedy U., Buenos Aires, 1975; LHD, U. N.Mex., 1980. Tchr., prin. rural and consol. schs. Mecklenberg County, Va., 1931-32, 33-35; tchr. gen. sci., math., music Picadome High Sch., Lexington, Ky., 1935-37; dir. music Henry Clay High Sch., Lexington, 1937-42; personnel supr. Lexington Signal Dept., Dept. War, 1942-43; supr. music Lexington pub. schs., 1945-47; rep. Investors Diversified Services, Inc., 1947-48; coordinator in-service tchr. edn. Ky. Dept. Edn., 1950-51; asst. prof. edn., asst. dean Coll. Edn., U. Ga., Athens, 1951-53; dean Sch. Edn., U. S.C., Columbia, 1953-56; dean Coll. Edn. U. N.Mex., Albuquerque, 1956-68; v.p. acad. affairs U. N.Mex., 1968-76, provost, 1976-77; Mem. Nat. Council Accreditation Tchr. Edn., 1960-66, chmn., 1963-65. Author books; contbr. articles in field to profl. jours. Pres. bd. dirs. N.Mex. Symphony Orch., 1977-78, 84-85; treas. U.S. Senator Jeff Bingaman's re-election campaign, 1988-93. With USNR, 1943-45; PTO. Mem. NEA, Nat. Soc. Study Edn., Soc. Advancement Edn., AAUP, Phi Kappa Phi, Phi Delta Kappa., Kappa Delta Pi. Home: 320 Fontana Pl NE Albuquerque NM 87108-1167

TRAVER, COURTLAND LEE, lawyer; b. New Haven, Sept. 20, 1935; s. Courtland L. Sr. and Bertha (Wilmot) T.; (div.); children: Lee, Kim, Amy. BA, U. Conn., 1957; LLB, Georgetown U., 1966. Bar: D.C. 1966, Va. 1967. Law clk. to presiding justice Ct. of Gen. Sessions, Washington, Va., 1965-66; clk. U.S. Ct. Appeals (D.C. cir.), Washington, 1966-67; ptnr. McGuire, Woods, Battle & Boothe, McLean, 1967—. Contbr. articles on real estate law to jours. Lt., pilot USN, 1957-63. Mem. ABA (various coms.), Va. State Bar Assn. (chmn. real estate com.), D.C. Bar Assn., Va. Bar Assn. (chmn. real estate sect.). Home: 4755 40th St N Arlington VA 22207 Office: McGuire Woods Battle & Boothe 8280 Greensboro Dr Ste 900 Mc Lean VA 22102-3892

TRAVER, ROBERT WILLIAM, SR., management consultant, author, lecturer, engineer; b. Waterbury, Conn., Oct. 13, 1930; s. Alfred Matthew Sr. and Dorothy Viola (Thomson) T.; m. Eleanor Jean Finnemore (div. Feb. 1963); children: Robert William Jr., Jeffrey Matthew, Elizabeth; m. Valarie Jane Mason. B in Mech. Engring., Clarkson U., 1955; MBA, U. Mass., 1963. Registered profl. engr., N.Y. Quality control engr. Gen. Electric Co., Pittsfield, Mass., 1955-62; mgr. reliability and quality assurance Tansitor Electronics, Inc., Bennington, Vt., 1962-65; sr. cons. Rath & Strong, Inc., Lexington, Mass., 1965-70; regional mgr. TAC, Inc., Albany, N.Y., 1970-72; dist. mgr. IDS, Inc., Albany, 1972-81; v.p. Reddy, Traver & Woods, Inc., Lexington, 1981-96; owner Traver Assocs., Averill Pk., N.Y., 1996—; participant in ednl. exch. with Peoples Republic of China, 1985, Australia and New Zealand, 1986. Author: Manufacturing Solutions for Consistent Quality and Reliability; contbr. articles to profl. jours. Chmn. lake com. Crooked Lake Improvement Assn., Averill Park, N.Y., 1973-74; v.p. Sand Lake (N.Y.) Businessmen's Assn., 1974-76. With U.S. Army, 1950. Fellow Am. Soc. for Quality Control; mem. Inst. Mgmt. Cons., Trout Unltd. Republican. Congregationalist. Avocations: fishing, gardening, hockey. Home and Office: Twin Lions On Crooked Lk Averill Park NY 12018

TRAVERS, CAROL, mathematics educator; b. Oil City, Pa., July 10, 1941; d. Philip Patrick and Frances Mary (McNamara) Healy; divorced; children: William. Joseph, Bruce, Rose. BS in Elem. Edn., State U. Pa., 1962; MS in Elem. Edn., SUNY, Brockport, 1977. Tchr. elem. sch. Lincoln-Garfield Sch., New Castle, Pa., 1962-64; tchr. Mohawk Area Schs., Mt. Jackson, Pa., 1964-65; tchr. nursery sch. Learn 'N' Play Sch., Middleport, N.Y., 1970-77; tchr. remedial reading Royalton-Hartland, Middleport, N.Y., 1977-80; tchr. remedial reading, remedial math Middleport Elem. Sch., 1980—; co-chair bldg. team Sch. Bldg. Team, Middleport, 1989-91, 94-95; mem. computer coun. Roy-Hart Dist., Middleport, 1981—, chmn. prof. coun.; rep. Math. Standards Support Group, Lockport, N.Y., 1990—. Co-author/editor:)booklet) Child Study Team, 1989. Mem. Nat. Coun. Math. Tchrs., N.Y. State Maths. Tchrs., Assn. Compensatory Educators, PTA. Democrat. Roman Catholic. Avocations: model railroading, travel, sewing, home remodeling. Office: Middleport Elem Sch State St Middleport NY 14105

TRAVERSE, ALFRED, palynology educator, clergyman; b. Port Hill, P.E.I., Can., Sept. 7, 1925; s. Alfred Freeman and Pearle (Akerley) T.; m. Elizabeth Jane Insley, June 30, 1951; children: Paul, Martha, John, Celia. S.B., Harvard U., 1946, A.M., 1948, Ph.D., 1951; cert. in Botany, Kings Coll., Cambridge, Eng., 1947; M.Div., Episcopal Theol. Sem. S.W., 1965. Teaching fellow Harvard U., 1947-51; coal technologist U.S. Bur. Mines, Grand Forks, N.D., 1951-55; head Fuels Microscopy Lab., Denver, 1955; palynologist Shell Devel. Co., Houston, 1955-62; cons. palynologist Austin, Tex., 1962-65; asst. prof. geology U. Tex., Austin, 1965-66; assoc. prof. geology and biology Pa. State U., University Park, 1966-70; prof. palynology Pa. State U., 1970—; ordained to ministry Episcopal Ch., 1965; asst. priest St. Matthew's Ch., Austin, 1965-66, St. Paul's Ch., Philipsburg, Pa., 1966-75, Christuskirche (Old Cath.), Zurich, Switzerland, 1980-81; vicar St. John's Ch., Huntingdon, Pa., 1975-80; adj. prof. geobiology Juniata Coll., 1977-82; guest prof. Geol. Inst., Swiss Fed. Tech. Inst., Zurich, 1980-81; councillor Internat. Commn. Palynology, 1973-77, 80—, pres., 1977-80, archivist, historian, 1986—; on-bd. scientist Glomar Challenger, 1975; Fulbright prof. Senckenberg Rsch. Inst., Frankfurt, 1992. Author: Paleopalynology, 1988, Sedimentation of Organic Particles, 1994; mem. editl. bd. Catalog Fossil Spores and Pollen, 1957-66, editor-in-chief, 1966-76; palynological editor: Palaeontographica, 1989-95. Recipient Best Paper award Am. Assn. Stratigraphic Palynologists, 1973, Internat. prize Palaeobot. Soc. India, 1990-91, Korrespondierendes Mitglied, Senckenbergische Naturforschende Gesellschaft, 1992—; NSF rsch. grantee, 1966-87. Fellow AAAS, Geol. Soc. Am.; mem. Bot. Soc. Am. (sec.-treas. paleobot. sect. 1957-60, chmn. sect. 1960-61), Internat. Assn. Plant Taxonomists (sec. com. fossil plants 1969-93), Am. Assn. Stratigraphic Palynologists (sec.-treas. 1967-70, pres. 1970-71, chmn. type collections com. 1989-91), Internat. Fedn. Palynol. Soc. (pres. 1976-80, archivist 1980—). Home: RR 2 Box 390 Huntingdon PA 16652-9209 Office: 435 Deike Bldg University Park PA 16802

TRAVIS, ANDREW DAVID, lawyer; b. Washington, Mar. 23, 1944; s. Don Carlos Jr. and Nevenna (Tsanoff) T. BA, Rice U., 1966; JD, U. Tex., 1969. Bar: Tex. 1969. Sole practice Houston, 1971-75; atty. Allright Corp. (formerly Allright Auto Parks Inc.), Houston, 1975-82, v.p., legal counsel, 1982—. Mem. ABA, Tex. Bar Assn., Houston Bar Assn. Home: 307 Timber Terrace Rd Houston TX 77024-5602 Office: Allright Corp 1111 Fannin St Ste 1300 Houston TX 77002-6923

TRAVIS, DEMPSEY JEROME, real estate executive, mortgage banker; b. Chgo., Feb. 25, 1920; s. Louis and Mittie (Strickland) T.; m. Moselynne Hardwick, Sept. 17, 1949. B.A., Roosevelt U., 1949; grad., Sch. Mortgage Banking, Northwestern U., 1969; D.Econs., Olive Harvey Coll., 1974; D.B.A. (hon.), Daniel Hale Williams U., Chgo., 1976; PhD (hon.), Kennedy-King Coll., 1982. Cert. property mgr.; cert. real estate counselor. Pres. Travis Realty Co., Chgo., 1949—, Urban Rsch. Press, 1969—. Author: Don't Stop Me Now, 1970, An Autobiography of Black Chicago, 1981, An Autobiography of Black Jazz, 1983, An Autobiography of Black Politics, 1987, Real Estate is the Gold in Your Future, 1988, Harold: The People's Mayor, 1989, Racism: American Style a Corporate Gift, 1990, I Refuse to Learn to Fail, 1992, Views From the Back of the Bus During World War II and Beyond, 1995, The Duke Ellington Primer, 1996. Trustee Northwestern Meml. Hosp., Chgo., Chgo. Hist. Soc., Auditorium Theater, Chgo., Roosevelt U. With AUS, 1942-46. Recipient award Soc. Midland Authors, 1982, Chgo. Art Deco Soc., 1985. Mem. United Mortgage Bankers Assn. Am. (pres. 1961-74), Dearborn Real Estate Bd. (pres. 1957-59, 70-71), Nat. Assn. Real Estate Brokers (1st v.p. 1959-60), Inst. Real Estate Mgmt., Soc. Profl. Journalists, Soc. Midland Authors (pres. 1988-90), NAACP (pres. Chgo. 1959-60), Beta Gamma Sigma, Lambda Alpha. Clubs: Economics, Forty of Chgo., Assembly (Chgo.). Office: Travis Realty Co 840 E 87th St Chicago IL 60619-6242 *I refuse to learn to fail.*

TRAVIS, J. FRANK, manufacturing company executive; b. Atlanta, Mar. 12, 1936; s. L. Earl and Willene E. (Brisendine) T.; m. Eleanor Jackson, Aug. 26, 1961; children: T. Eric, J. Gregory. BSME, Auburn U., 1959; postgrad., So. Tex. Coll. Law, 1964-66. Various engring. and managerial positions Ingersoll-Rand Co., Woodcliff Lake, N.J., 1959-89; corp. v.p. Ingersoll-Rand Co., Woodcliff Lake, 1990-94, exec. v.p., 1994—; pres. Ingersoll Air Co. Group, 1989-90, Ingersoll-Torrington Group, 1990-94; bd. dirs. Nat. Assn. Mfrs., Washington, N.Am. Com., Washington. Home: 21 Breezy Knoll Avon CT 06001 Office: Ingersoll-Rand Co 200 Chestnut Ridge Rd Woodcliff Lake NJ 07675

TRAVIS, JEREMY, federal official, think tank executive. BA in Am. Studies cum laude, Yale Coll.; MPA, NYU, JD cum laude. Spl. counsel to first dep. mayor and asst. dir. law svcs. City of N.Y., spl. advisor to mayor; chief counsel to subcom on criminal justice U.S. Ho. of Reps., Washington; dep. commr. for legal matters N.Y.C. Police Dept.; dir. Nat. Inst. Justice, Washington, 1994—; exec. dir. N.Y.C. Criminal Justice Agy., Victim/Witness Assistance Project Vera Inst. Justice; lectr. N.Y. Law Sch., NYU, Yale Coll. Marden and Marshall fellow in criminal law NYU Sch. Law, Arthur Garfield Hays fellow in Civil Liberties. Contbr. articles to law rev. and profl. jours. Office: Nat Inst Justice 633 Indiana Ave NW Washington DC 20531

TRAVIS, LAWRENCE ALLAN, accountant; b. Bloomington, Ill., Sept. 17, 1942; s. Willard Burns and Florence May (Harvey) T.; m. Katy Quinones, Apr. 16, 1965 (div. Feb. 1978); children: Lawrence Allan Jr., Matthew B.; m. Kathleen Lucas, May 20, 1995. BS in Bus. Edn., Ill. State U., 1968; MA in Pub. Adminstrn., Sangamon State U., Springfield, Ill., 1976. CPA, Ill. Staff acct. Alexander Grant & Co., Chgo., 1969; internal auditor State Farm Ins., Bloomington, 1969-73; dep. dir. Ill. Dept. Ins., Springfield, 1973-74; audit mgr. Ill. Auditor Gen., Springfield, 1974-81; pres. Lawrence Travis & Co., P.C., CPAs, Virden, Normal, Springfield, Ill., 1979—; also bd. dirs. Lawrence Travis & Co., P.C., CPAs, Virden, Normal, Springfield; v.p., bd. dirs. Virden Broadcasting Corp., 1986-95; pres., bd. dirs. Travco, Inc., Virden, Ka-Lar Enterprises, Inc., Springfield; v.p., bd. dirs. Carlinville Broadcasting Corp., Miller Comm., Inc.; registered rep. Terra Securities Corp. Mem. Ill. Common Cause, Springfield. Mem. AICPA, Assn. Govt. Accts., Ill. CPA Soc., Internat. Platform Assn., Nat. Space Soc., Smithsonian Assocs., World Future Soc., Internat. Traders. Democrat. Roman Catholic. Avocation: sports. Home: 2409 Idlewild Dr Springfield IL 62704-5403 Office: 1700 S 1st St Springfield IL 62704

TRAVIS, LUCINDA LOUISE, product designer, writer, editor; b. Holdrege, Nebr., June 28, 1948; d. Dale Edward Travis and Betty Louise (Watts) Travis McCreadie. Cultural diploma, U. Stranieri di Perugia, Italy, 1969, ITESM, Monterey, Mex., 1969, U. Granada, Spain, 1971; BA in Italian, UCLA, 1970; cultural diploma, U. Salamanca, Spain, 1971; BA in Spanish with high honors, Calif. State Coll., San Bernardino, 1972; MEd., U. Hawaii, 1975. Cert. secondary tchr., Calif. Producer, dir. promotions, programming Hawaii Pub. TV KHET, Honolulu, 1972-78; producer, writer Direcion Gen. Radio, TV y Cinemagrafia del Gobierno de Mex., Mexico City, 1978-80; dir. World's Children's Art Exhbn., L.A., 1983-89; coord. grant applications ind. filmmaker program Am. Film Inst., L.A., 1982-87; creative/pub. rels. specialist Ohio Art, Bryan, 1987-90; product designer Hama, Inc., Nokøbing Mors, Denmark, 1991—; editor Wee Deliver newsletter for Office of Literacy U.S. Postal Svc., Washington, 1991-93; instr. Payap Coll., Chiang Mai, Thailand, 1983, 84; designer, curator traveling mus. exhibit Gumby Exhibit, 1991-92; programming cons. Internat. Mass-Comm. Svc., Kvinesdal, Norway, 1984. Author: (poetry) Aire y Alma, 1971, Animation: A Resource Book, 1986; co-editor: Film/Television: Grants, Scholarships and Special Programs, 1985; patentee beading system for craft market. Speaker for various svc. and ednl. orgns.; Bible study tchr. Presbyn. and Bapt. Chs., Ontario, Calif., Bryan, Ohio, 1982-91; vol. missionary refugee work Am. Bapt. Chs., Thailand. Calif. Arts Coun. grantee, 1985. Mem. Alpha Gamma Delta. Avocations: skiing, ice skating, tennis, topiary, foreign languages.

TRAVIS, MARTIN BICE, political scientist, educator; b. Iron Mountain, Mich., Sept. 22, 1917; s. Martin Bice and Helen (Carrett) T.; m. Olivia Brewster Taylor, Nov. 29, 1942; children: Elizabeth Nichols (Mrs. Usama Mugharbil), Helen Willard. A.B., Amherst Coll., 1939; student, Heidelberg (Germany) U., 1937; M.A., Fletcher Sch. Law and Diplomacy, 1940; Ph.D., U. Chgo., 1948. Asst. prof. internat. relations Syracuse U., 1948-49; asst. prof. polit. sci. Duke U., 1949-52; asst. prof., then asso. prof. polit. sci. Stanford U., 1953-61; prof. polit. sci. SUNY-Stony Brook, 1961-92; coordinator SUNY Program Am. U., Beirut, Lebanon, 1972-73; chmn. dept., 1961-68; dir. Inst. Am. Studies SUNY-Stony Brook, 1965-93; vis. prof. Sch. Internat. Affairs, Columbia, 1956-57; vis. summer prof. U. Guadalajara, Mex., 1959, 62, U. Wash., 1961; Bd. dirs. State U N.Y. Inst. Am. Studies in France, 1966-77; cons. to industry. Author: (with E.E. Robinson) Powers of the President in Foreign Affairs, 1966; Co-editor, contbr.: (with Philip W. Buck) Control of Foreign Relations in Modern Nations, 1957; bd. editors: Western Polit. Quar, 1956-58; adv. bd.: Almanac of Current World Leaders, 1957—; editorial critic for book pubs. Mem. sch. bd., Cold Spring Harbor, N.Y., 1965-71, v.p. 1967-68, pres. 1968-69; trustee Village of Laurel Hollow, 1983—, police com., 1983-85, mayor, 1985-95; established Martin B. Travis Scholarship fund for pre-law majors at SUNY, Stonybrook, 1995. Grantee Ford Found. 1960-61. Mem. Coun. Fgn. Rels., Phi Delta Theta, Phi Delta Kappa. Home: 533 Cold Spring Rd Syosset NY 11791-1206 Office: Dept Polit Science Suny Stony Brook NY 11794

TRAVIS, NANCY, actress; b. New York, NY, Sept. 21, 1961. BA, NYU. stage appearances include: Brighton Beach Memoirs (touring prodn.), It's Hard to Be a Jew, 1984, I'm Not Rappaport, 1986, The Signal Season of Dummy Hoy, 1987-88; television appearances include: High School Narc, 1985, Malice in Wonderland, 1985, Harem, 1986, I'll Be Home for Christmas, 1988, Almost Perfect, 1995—; films include: Three Men and a Baby, 1987, Eight Men Out, 1988, Married to the Mob, 1988, Air America, 1990, Internal Affairs, 1990, Loose Cannons, 1990, Three Men and a Little Lady, 1990, Passed Away, 1992, Chaplin, 1992, The Vanishing, 1993, So I Married an Ax Murderer, 1993, Greedy, 1994, Fluke, 1995, Destiny Turns On the Radio, 1995.

TRAVIS, NEIL, film editor. Editor: (TV movies) Roots, 1977 (Emmy award outstanding film editing of drama series for Part 1 1977), The Atlanta

Child Murders, 1985, Shannon's Deal, 1989, (films) Jaws II, 1978, The Idolmaker, 1980, Second Thoughts, 1983, The Philadelphia Experiment, 1984, Cujo, 1984, Marie, 1985, No Way Out, 1987, Cocktail, 1988, Dances with Wolves, 1990 (Academy award best film editing 1990), Patriot Games, 1992, Bopha!, 1993, Clear and Present Danger, 1994, Outbreak, 1995, Moll Flanders, 1996. Address: 19426 Hatteras St Tarzana CA 91356

TRAVIS, RANDY BRUCE, musician; b. Monroe, N.C., 1959; married. Musician Country City U.S.A., 1977-82, Nashville Palace, 1982-85. Rec. artist Warner Bros. Records, 1985—; albums include debut Storms of Life, 1986 (Album of Yr., Acad. Country Music 1987, Album of Yr., Music City News 1987), Always & Forever, 1987 (Album of Yr., Country Music Assn. 1987), Old 8x10, 1988, No Holdin' Back, 1989, An Old Time Christmas, 1989, Heroes and Friends, 1990, High Lonesome, 1991, Greatest Hits, 1992, Wind in the Wire, 1993, This is Me, 1994; songs include On the Other Hand (Best Song, Acad. Country Music 1987, Best Single, Acad. Country Music 1987, Single of Yr., Music City News 1987), Diggin' Up Bones, No Place Like Home, Forever and Ever, Amen (Single of Yr., Song of Yr.,Country Music Assn. 1987, Best Country Record, AMOA Jukebox 1987), I Won't Need You Anymore, No Holding Back, 1989; film appearances include: Frank and Jesse, 1994. Named Top Male Vocalist, Acad. Country Music, 1987, Male Vocalist of Yr., Music City News, 1987, Star of Tomorrow, Music City News, 1987, Male Vocalist of Yr., Country Music Assn., 1987, Entertainer of Yr. Music City News, 1988, Male Artist of Yr., 1988, Favorite Entertainer, Favorite Entertainer, Nashville Network Viewers Choice Awards, 1988; recipient Horizon award Country Music Assn., 1986, Grammy award, 1987, Am. Music award, best country album, 1988, Am. Music award, best country single, 1988, Country Music Assn. best male vocalist, 1988. Mem. Grand Ole Opry.

TRAVIS, SHIRLEY LOUISE, nursing administrator; b. Falls City, Nebr., July 16, 1950; d. Vernon J. and Gladys E. (Veach) Gerweck; children: Stacy, Kimberly. Diploma, Clarkson Coll. Nursing, Omaha, 1971; BS, Coll. St. Francis, Joliet, Ill., 1982; MSA, Ctrl. Mich. U., 1992. RN. Staff nurse Lincoln (Nebr.) Gen. Hosp., 1971-73, head nurse, 1973-74, staff asst., 1974-76, dir. nursing, 1976-87, v.p., 1987—; chair ADN, LPN S.E. Cmty. Coll. Bd., Lincoln, 1976—. Alumni Leadership Lincoln, 1992—. Mem. ANA (cert. nurse adminstr. 1985, 90), Am. Orgn. Nurse Execs., Nebr. Nurses Assn. (conv. del. 1992—), Nebr. Orgn. Nurse Execs. (pres., Nurse Exec. Leadership award 1994). Avocations: reading, walking, swimming. Home: 6900 Pike Pl Lincoln NE 68516-1571

TRAVIS, VANCE KENNETH, petroleum business executive; b. Coriander, Sask., Can., Jan. 30, 1926; s. Roy Hazen and Etta Orilla (Anderson) T.; m. Louise Mary, Nov. 30, 1948 (div. 1979); children: Stuart, Shirley, Gordon, Donald, Marian; m. Mildred Elaine, June 29, 1979; stepchildren: Susan, Nancy, Gordon, Sandra, Karen. Chmn. bd. Turbo Resources Ltd., 1970-83, Challenger Internat., 1977-83, Bankeno Mines Ltd., 1977-83, Queenston Gold Mines Ltd., Toronto, Ont., Can., 1977-84, Health Risk Mgmt. Inc., Mpls., 1984-86, Triad Internat. Inc., 1985—; dir. Health Resource Mgmt. Ltd., Edmonton, 1990—; bd. dirs. Vencap Equities Alta. Ltd., Edmonton, 1981-86, L.K. Resources Ltd., Calgary, 1973-84. Mem. Young. Pres.'s Orgn., Calgary, 1964-76, World Pres. Orgn. Recipient Presdl. pin Jr. Achievement, 1963, Best Pitcher award Petroleum Fastball League, 1955. Clubs: Calgary Petroleum, Ranchmen's. Office: Triad Internat Inc, 4600 5th St NE # 200, Calgary, AB Canada T2E 7C3 also: Health Resource Mgmt Ltd, 10104-103rd Ave Ste 800, Edmonton, AB Canada T5J 4R5 also: Med Tech Computer Systems, 3015 5th Ave NE Ste 150, Calgary Can T2A6T8

TRAVISANO, FRANK PETER, professional management consultant, business broker; b. Newark, Feb. 5, 1921; s. Peter Fountain and Carmela Elizabeth (Tellone) T.; m. Nancy Jean Drees; children: Peter, Thomas, James, Theresa, Patricia. BS in Bus., Rutgers U., 1943, postgrad. in mktg., 1945, postgrad. in real estate, 1946; Cert. Computers, morris C.C., Morris County, Randolph, 1985. Cert. profl. mgmt. cons. Various to pres. Rochester Lubricator Co., Newark, 1943-71, Franklin Hosp. Equipment Co., Newark, 1955-71, Acme Plating Works, Newark, 1961-72, Micro Machine Co., Union, N.J., 1962-72, Darwin Phoenix Co., Cranbury, N.J., 1972—, Darwin Safety Packaging Co., Cranbury, 1986—; exec. v.p. Logos Group, Chester, N.J., 1987—; mktg. mgr. Artisan Controls Corp., Parsippany, N.J., 1991—; mktg. cons. First Occupational Ctr. of N.J.; cons. dir. TPI Inc., Lodi, N.J., 1991—; sr. cons. Solutions Group, Madison, N.J., 1991—; cons. OM Internat., 1982—, Man-Roland PPI, 1985—, Superior MPM Plastics, 1990—; mktg. cons. First Occupl. Ctr. N.J., 1996—. Inventor in field of hosp. products and saftety packaging materials. Co-founder Essexfields Youthful Offenders Program, pres. 1965. Recipient various svc. awards Rutgers U. Mem. Inst. Chem. Physics (chmn. bd. dirs. 1993—), Rutgers U. Alumni Assn. (bd. dirs., pres. 1966-67), Kiwanis (bd. dirs.), Newark Execs. Assn. (pres. 1960). Avocations: inventions in field.

TRAVIS-JASPERING, MARGARET ROSE, artist, educator; b. St. Louis, Dec. 1, 1950; d. George Thomas and Margaret Lina (Black) Travis; 1 child from previous marriage, Jo Anne Urian; m. Richard W. Jaspering, Jan. 31, 1989; children: Wendy E., Mandy E., Sarah M., Chloe K. BFA, Lindenwood Coll., 1980, postgrad., 1981; postgrad., U. Mo., St. Louis, 1980, U. Mo., Columbia, 1981. Cert. art edn. tchr. K-12. Tchr. Troy and Winfield (Mo.) Schs., 1979-80, Silex (Mo.) Schs., 1980-81, Wentzville (Mo.) Schs., 1981-86, Wright City (Mo.) Schs., 1984-90; artist, tchr., owner Jasmar Studios and Gallery, Foristell, Mo., 1987—; instr. adult painting workshops, 1985—. Exhibited in group shows at Harry Henderson Gallery, Lindenwood Colls., 1976-80, Grand Gallery South, Belleville Ceramic Show, 1987 (Best of Show, 4 1st pl. awards), Internat. Ceramic Conv. and Show, 1988 (Best of Show, Best of Category, 5 1st pl. awards), Greater St. Louis Ceramic Assn. Show, 1988 (Best of Show, 1st pl. award), 76th Ann. Sculpture and Fine Crafts, 1989, Black and White Show, 1989, U. Mo., Chancellor's Residence, 1988-90, St. Charles Artists Guild, 1989 (Best of Show), Nat. Invitational of Am. Contemporary Art, 1993; contbr. catalog, mags. Organizer Art for Animals fundraiser Animal Welfare Assn., Warren City, Mo., 1993; active St. Charles Artists Guild, 1987-89. Dept. scholar in art Lindenwood Colls., 1976-80, art scholar Dept. Exhbn., 1965-67-69. Mem. St. Louis Artists Coalition (3d divsn.), Art St. Louis. Roman Catholic. Avocations: gardening, swimming, breeding Yorkshire terriers and Pekingnese. Office: Jasmar Studios and Gallery PO Box 147 Archer Rd Foristell MO 63348-0147

TRAVOLTA, JOHN, actor; b. Englewood, N.J., Feb. 18, 1954; s. Salvatore and Helen (Burke) T.; m. Kelly Preston; one child, Jett. Appeared in TV series Welcome Back Kotter, 1975-77; TV movies: The Boy in the Plastic Bubble, 1976; films: Carrie, 1976, Saturday Night Fever, 1977 (Best Actor award Nat. Bd. Rev., 1977, Best Actor Acad. award nominee 1977, Best Actor 1st runner up Nat. Soc. Film Critics 1977, Best Actor 2nd runner up N.Y. Film Critics Circle 1977), Grease, 1978 (Golden Globe World Film Favorite 1978), Moment-By-Moment, 1979, Urban Cowboy, 1980, Blow Out, 1981, Staying Alive, 1983 (Male/Box Office Star of Yr., Nat. Assn. Theatre Owners ShowEast 1983), Two of a Kind, 1983, Perfect, 1985, The Dumb Waiter, 1987, The Experts, 1989, Chains of Gold, 1980, Look Who's Talking, 1989 (Male/Box Office Star of Yr., Nat. Assn. Theatre Owners ShowEast 1989), Look Who's Talking Too, 1990, The Tender, 1991, Shout, 1991, Look Who's Talking Now, 1993, Pulp Fiction, 1994 (Best Actor Acad. award nominee 1994, Best Actor award nominee Brit. Acad. Film and TV Arts 1994, Golden Globe Best Actor award nominee 1994, Best Actor award nominee SAG 1994, Best Actor award nominee Chgo. Film Critics 1994, Best Actor award nominee Comedy awards 1994, Best Actor award L.A. Film Critics 1994, Best Actor award Stockholm Film Festival 1993, Best Actor award London Film Critics Cir. 1994), Get Shorty, 1995, White Man's Burden, 1995, Broken Arrow, 1995; author: Staying Fit, 1984; rec. artist album, 1976, 77. Recipient Best Male Vocalist Billboard award, 1976, Best Male Vocalist award Record World and Music Retail mag., 1976, Best Actor Golden Apple award Cue mag., Juno award Can. Acad. Rec. Arts and Scis., 1978; nominated Best New Male Star Women's Press Club, 1976; named Man of Yr., Hasty Pudding Club, Harvard U., 1981.

TRAWICK, LEONARD MOSES, English educator; b. Decatur, Ala., July 4, 1933; s. Leonard M. and Frances (Earle) T.; m. Kerstin Ekfelt, July 16, 1960; children: Eleanor, Matthew. BA, U. of South, 1955; MA in English, U. Chgo., 1956; PhD in English, Harvard U., 1961. Asst. prof. Columbia U., N.Y.C., 1961-69; from assoc. prof. to prof. English Cleve. State U., 1969—; editor Poetry Ctr., Cleve. State U., 1971—, dir., 1990-92. Editor: Backgrounds of Romanticism, 1968, World, Self, Poem, 1990, (poems) Beastmorfs, 1994; editor, prin. translator: German Literature of the Romantic Era and Age of Goethe, 1993; author (opera libretto) Mary Stuart: A Queen Betrayed, 1991; founding editor mag. The Gamut, 1980-92 (Ohioana award for Editl. Excellence 1991). Recipient Individual Artist award Ohio Arts Coun., 1980; Ohioana Poetry award, 1994. Office: Cleve State U Dept English Cleveland OH 44115

TRAXLER, WILLIAM BYRD, retired lawyer; b. Greenville, S.C., July 10, 1912; s. David Byrd and Mary Willey (Gatling) T. Student The Citadel, 1929-30, U. Tex., 1930-32; JD, George Washington U., 1940. Bar: D.C. 1940, S.C. 1940, U.S. Ct. Appeals (4th cir.) 1960. Ptnr. Hinson, Traxler and Hamer, Greenville, 1950-58, Rainey, Fant, Traxler and Horton, 1958-60; sole practice, Greenville, 1960-94; ret., 1994. Bd. dirs. Phyllis Wheatly Assn., 1954, Vis. Nurse Assn., Greenville, 1957-59, United Way, Greenville, 1976; vice-chmn. bd. health City of Greenville, 1960-68; life mem. The Citadel Endowment Fund; prosecutor So. Bavaria Mil. Govt., asst. in reopening German civil cts. Capt. U.S. Army, 1942-46. Recipient Alumni Achievement award George Washington U., 1946. Fellow S.C. Bar Found.; mem. S.C. State Bar Assn., Greenville County Bar Assn. (pres. 1976), Greenville C. of C. (Chmn. of Yr. 1967, chmn. taxation com.), Law Sci. Acad., George Washington U. Law Assn. (life), Phi Alpha Delta (justice 1939), Beta Theta Pi, Torch Club (pres. 1956), Greenville Country Club (bd. govs. 1982-85). Author: Military Government in Germany, 1960, Political Third Parties, 1968, History of the Fourteenth Amendment, 1974, The Jury Numbers Game, 1976, Medieval Harmony, 1982, Presumptions of Life and Death, 1989. Home: 100 Trails End Greenville SC 29607-1741

TRAXLER, WILLIAM BYRD, JR., federal judge; b. Greenville, S.C., May 1, 1948; s. William Byrd and Bettie (Wooten) T.; m. Patricia Alford, Aug. 21, 1971; children: William Byrd III, James McCall. BA, Davidson Coll., 1970; JD, U. S.C., 1973. Assoc. William Byrd Traxler, Greenville, 1973-75; asst. solicitor 13th Jud. Ct., Greenville, 1975-78, dep. solicitor, 1978-81, solicitor, 1981-85, resident crct. judge, 1985-92; U.S. Dist. judge Dist. of S.C., Greenville, 1992—. Recipient Outstanding Svc. award Solicitors Assn., S.C., 1987, Leadership award Probation, Parole & Pardon Svcs., S.C., 1990. Office: US Dist Ct 300 E Washington St Greenville SC 29601-2800

TRAYLOR, ANGELIKA, stained glass artist; b. Munich, Bavaria, Germany, Aug. 24, 1942; came to U.S., 1959; d. Walther Artur Ferdinand and Berta Kreszentia (Boeck) Klau; m. Lindsay Montgomery Donaldson, June 10, 1959 (div. 1970); 1 child, Cameron Maria Greta; m. Samuel William Traylor III, June 12, 1970. Student, Pvt. Handelsschule Morawetz Jr. Coll., Munich, 1958. came to U.S., 1959;. Freelance artist, 1980—; Works featured in profl. jours. including the Daylily Jour., 1987, Design Jour., South Korea, 1989, The Traveler's Guide to American Crafts, 1990, Florida Mag., 1991, Florida TODAY, 1993, Melbourne Times, 1994, The Orbiter, 1996. Works featured in profl. jours. including the Daylily Jour., 1987, Design Jour., South Korea, 1989, The Traveler's Guide to American Crafts, 1990, Florida Mag., 1991, Florida TODAY, 1993, Melbourne Times, 1994, The Orbiter, 1996. Recipient Fragile Art award Glass Art mag., 1982, 1st Yr. Exhibitor award Stained Glass Assn. Am., 1984, 2d pl. Non-figurative Composition award Vitraux des USA, 1985, Best of Show Stained Glass Assn. Am., 1989, 3d pl., 1989, Merit award George Plimpton All-Star Space Coast Art Open, 1994; named Hist. Woman of Brevard Brevard Cultural Alliance, 1991, one of 200 Best Am. Craftsmen Early Am. Life mag., 1994, 95. Home and Office: 100 Poinciana Dr Melbourne FL 32937

TRAYLOR, JOAN SADLER, interior design educator; b. Pique, Ohio; d. Carl E. and Mary E. (Bond) Sadler; children: Douglas Traylor, Michelle Traylor. BS in Interior Design and Art, Western Ky. U., 1981, MS in Interior Design, 1984. Interior designer Interiors By Biggers, Glasgow, Ky., 1981-83; teaching fellow Western Ky. U., Bowling Green, 1983-84, instr. interior design, 1985; asst. prof. interior design U. So. Miss., Hattiesburg, 1985-91, assoc. prof. interior design, 1991—, interior design program coord., 1990—; prof. Brit. studies abroad program, 1989—; presenter profl. assn. meetings. Contbr. articles and abstracts to profl. publs. Mem., officer Warren County Arts Alliance, Bowling Green, 1977-85; mem. Jr. Woman's Club, Bowling Green, 1970-76. Mem. Interior Design Educators Coun., Am. Soc. Interior Design Educators Coun., Am. Soc. Interior Designers (La. chpt. presdl. citation 1991), Inst. Bus. Designers (officer Delta chpt. 1992-94), Nat. Trust for Hist. Preservation, New Orleans Preservation Resource Ctr., Hattiesburg Hist. Soc., Designed Comm. Assn., Internat. Interior Design Assn. (Miss. dir. 1994—), Phi Upsilon Omicron, Phi Delta Kappa, Delta Kappa Gamma. Avocations: travel, drawing and painting, textile design. Home: 315 Woodshire Dr Hattiesburg MS 39402 Office: U So Miss SS Box 5035 Hattiesburg MS 39406-5035

TRAYLOR, ORBA FOREST, economist, lawyer, educator; b. Providence, Ky., June 16, 1910; s. Eddie Ewing and Dillie (Stuart) T.; m. Josephine Zananiri, Nov. 17, 1945; children—Joseph Marion, Robert Forest, John Christopher. B.A., Western Ky. U., 1930; M.A., U. Ky., 1932, Ph.D., 1948; J.D., Northwestern U., 1936. Bar: Ky. 1941. Head dept. econs. Ashland Coll., 1935-36; legal asst. trust dept. 1st Nat. Bank, Chgo., 1936-37; assoc. prof. econs., sociology Western Ky. U., 1938-40; research asst. Bur. Bus. Research, U. Ky., 1939; research dir. Ky. Legislative Council, 1939-41; dir. research and statistics Ky. Dept. Welfare, 1941; assoc. econ. analyst div. tax research U.S. Treasury Dept., 1942; acting chief acctg. UNRRA, Balkan Mission, 1944-45; asst. prof. econs. and bus. U. Denver, 1946-47, U. Mo., 1947-50; tax specialist, asst. econ. commr. ECA, Greece, 1950-53; coordinator exec. devel. programs Ordnance Corps, Dept. Army, 1954; pub. fin. expert UN; lectr. fin. adminstrn. Inst. Pub. Adminstrn., Egypt, 1954-56; exec. asst. to lt. gov. Ky. Legislative Research Commn., Frankfort, 1956-58; commr. fin. State of Ky., Frankfort, 1958-59; dir. finance Office High Commr., Ryukyu Islands, 1960-64; dir. econ. affairs Office High Commr., 1964-65; prof. econs. and pub. adminstrn. U. Ala., Huntsville, 1965-75; chmn. dept. bus. and pub. adminstrn. U. Ala., 1966-68, chmn. econs., 1968-70; vis. prof. pub. adminstrn. San Diego State U., 1975-76, Western Ky. U., 1976-77; fin. economist AID, U.S. State Dept., 1977-78; adj. prof. Ala. A&M U., 1978-81, N.Y. U. and Rider Coll., 1981-82, Columbia Coll., 1982—; cons. economist Am. Tech. Services, Inc., 1982-91; cons. ops. research Johns Hopkins U., 1957-61; fiscal cons. various orgns.; vis. lectr. econs. various univs. and colls.; lectr. U. Md. Far East Div., 1960-65, Ala. A&M U., 1976-77, Fla. Inst. Tech., 1977; sr. adv. Bank of Ryukyus, 1960-65, Joint Fgn. Investment Bd., 1964-65; chmn. bd. Ryukyuan Devel. Loan Corp., 1960-65, Joint Petroleum Bd., 1960-65; counsellor Oak Ridge Asso. Univs., 1966-67. Mem. editorial bd.: Public Adminstrn. Rev, 1973-79; contbr. articles to profl. publs. Mem. Ala. Edn. Study Commn. Fin. Task Force, 1968-69; chmn. fin. com. Top of Ala. Health Planning Agy., 1974-75; mem. adv. com. Ala. Legislature, 1981-94. With AUS, 1942-46; lt. col. Res. (ret.). Mem. Am. So. econs. assns., Am. Soc. for Pub. Adminstrn. (council 1973-75), Am., Ky. bar assns., Nat. Tax Assn. (dir. 1971-74), local C. of C., Res. Officers Assn., Mil. Order World Wars, Beta Gamma Sigma, Delta Sigma Pi. Democrat. Baptist. Club: Rotary. Address: 216 Westmoreland Ave SE Huntsville AL 35801-2726

TRAYLOR, ROBERT ARTHUR, lawyer; b. Syracuse, N.Y., Jan. 15, 1949; s. Robert Arthur and Julie Elizabeth (McNulty) T.; m. Bonita Lynn Schmidt, Nov. 26, 1977. BS, LeMoyne Coll., 1970; JD cum laude, Syracuse U., 1975. Bar: N.Y., U.S. Dist. Ct. (no. dist.) N.Y., U.S. Tax Ct. Atty. Love, Balducci & Scaccia, Syracuse, N.Y., 1976-77; estate tax atty. IRS, Syracuse, 1977-81; atty. Scaccia Law Firm, Syracuse, 1981—. Contbr. articles to profl. jours. Of counsel The Saint Ann Sch., Syracuse, 1981—, mem. coordinating com. Vision 2000 1994—). With U.S. Army, 1970-72. Recipient Outstanding Acctg. award Fin. Execs. Inst.-Syracuse Chpt., 1972, Cert. Achievement, Commanding Gen.-VII Corps., U.S. Army, 1972, Am. Jurisprudence award Adminstrv. Law, 1975. Mem. ABA, Onondaga County Bar Assn. (vol. lawyer program 1993—, Vol. Lawyer of Month 1994), World Wildlife Fedn. Republican. Roman Catholic. Avocations: motorsports, military history, Catholic education. Home: 112 Knowland Dr Liverpool NY 13090-3130 Office: Scaccia Law Firm Ste 402 State Tower Bldg Syracuse NY 13202

TRAYNHAM, JAMES GIBSON, chemist, educator; b. Broxton, Ga., Aug. 5, 1925; s. James G. and Eddie Louise (Greer) T.; m. Margaret A. Egert, 1948; children: David F., Peter C.; m. Gresdna A. Doty, 1980. Student, South Ga. Coll., 1942-43; B.S., U. N.C., 1946; Ph.D., Northwestern U., 1950. Instr. Northwestern U., 1949-50; asst. prof. Denison U., 1950-53; mem. faculty La. State U., Baton Rouge, 1953—; prof. chemistry La. State U., 1963-88, prof. emeritus, 1988—, chmn. dept. chemistry, 1968-73, vice chancellor for advanced studies and rsch., dean Grad. Sch., 1973-81; postdoctoral research fellow Ohio State U., 1951-53. Author: Organic Nomenclature: A Programmed Introduction, 1966, 4th edit., 1991; editor: Essays on the History of Organic Chemistry, 1987; contbr. articles to profl. jours. Bd. dirs. Council Grad. Schs. in U.S., 1981. Recipient Petroleum Research Fund-Am. Chem. Soc. Type D award Eidg. Technische Hochschule, Zurich, Switzerland, 1959-60; Charles E. Coates award Baton Rouge sects. Am. Chem. Soc. and Am. Inst. Chem. Engrs., 1965; NATO sr. fellow in sci. Universität des Saarlandes, Saarbrücken, Fed. Republic Germany, 1972. Mem. Am. Chem. Soc. (councilor, past chmn. Baton Rouge sect., chmn. divsn. history of chemistry 1988), La. Acad. Sci., Internat. Union Pure and Applied Chemistry (titular mem. commn. on nomenclature of organic chemistry, sec. 1994—), Phi Beta Kappa, Sigma Xi, Phi Lambda Upsilon, Phi Kappa Phi (past pres. La. State U. chpt.). Home: 628 Polytech Dr Baton Rouge LA 70808-4755

TRAYNOR, HARRY SHEEHY, engineering consultant; b. Lexington, Ky., Sept. 4, 1911; s. John Hanrahan and Augusta (Sheehy) T.; m. Helen Mae Ingalls, June 28, 1941; children: Martha Ingalls (Mrs. Paul J. Sweeney), Harry Sheehy. B.S. in Mech. Engring., U. Ky., 1935. Test engr. Aerofin Corp., Newark, 1935; air conditioning, refrigeration engr. Carrier Corp., Syracuse, N.Y., 1935-42; pres., gen mgr. Regent Knitting Co., Inc., Syracuse, N.Y., 1946-50; contract sales mgr. Remington Corp., Auburn, N.Y., 1950-54; spl. asst. to gen. mgr., asst. gen. mgr. adminstrn. AEC, 1954-64, asst. to gen. mgr., 1964-71; asst. to dean Grad. Sch. U. Ky., Lexington, 1972-73; cons. Inst. Mining and Minerals Research, 1974-79, Ky. Center for Energy Research, 1976-78; ret., 1971; mem. U.S. Intelligence Bd., 1954-64; exec. officer U.S. del. Internat. Conf. on Peaceful Uses of Atomic Energy, Geneva, 1955. Chmn. Met. Environ. Improvement Commn., Lexington, 1975; mem. U. Ky. Rsch. Found., SCORE, 1987-89. Col., C.E. AUS, 1952. Decorated Legion of Merit; recipient Disting. Alumni award U. Ky., 1965. Mem. ASHRAE (asso.), AAAS, Ky. Hist. Soc., Pi Kappa Alpha, Pi Tau Sigma. Roman Catholic. Clubs: Lafayette (Lexington), Kiwanis (Lexington), Spindletop (Lexington). Home: 1336 Prather Rd Lexington KY 40502-2421

TRAYNOR, J. MICHAEL, lawyer; b. Oakland, Calif., Oct. 25, 1934; s. Roger J. and Madeleine (Lackmann) T.; m. Shirley Williams, Feb. 11, 1956; children: Kathleen Traynor Millard, Elizabeth Traynor Fowler, Thomas. B.A., U. Calif., Berkeley, 1955; J.D., Harvard U., 1960. Bar: Calif. 1961, U.S. Supreme Ct. 1966. Dep. atty. gen. State of Calif., San Francisco, 1961-63; spl. counsel Calif. Senate Com. on Local Govt., Sacramento, 1963; assoc. firm Cooley Godward Castro Huddleson & Tatum, San Francisco, 1963-69, ptnr., 1969—; adviser 3d Restatement of Unfair Competition, 3d Restatement of Torts; Product D Liability, 1992—, Apportionment, 1994—, 1988 Revs. 2d Restatement of Conflict of Laws, 2d Restatement of Restitution, 1981-85; lectr. U. Calif. Boalt Hall Sch. Law, Berkeley, 1982-89, 1996—; chmn. Sierra Club Legal Defense Fund, 1989-91, pres. 1991-92, trustee. Mem. bd. overseers Inst. for Civil Justice The RAND Corp., 1991—; bd. dirs. Environ. Law Inst., 1992—. Served to 1st lt. USMC, 1955-57. Fellow AAAS, Am. Bar Found. (life); mem. Am. Law Inst. (coun. 1985—, 2d v.p. 1993—), Bar Assn. San Francisco (pres. 1973). Home: 3131 Eton Ave Berkeley CA 94705-2713 Office: Cooley Godward Castro Huddleson & Tatum 1 Maritime Plz Ste 2000 San Francisco CA 94111-3510

TRAYNOR, SEAN GABRIAL, manufacturing executive; b. Waterford, Ireland, Jan. 6, 1950; came to U.S., 1974; s. Sean Gerard and Norah Mary (Gower) T.; m. Geraldine Margaret Turner, Aug. 21, 1974; children: Kevin, Patrick, Tara. BA in Chemistry magna cum laude, Trinity Coll., 1971, PhD in Chemistry, 1974. Rsch. chemist SCM Glidco Organics, 1975, mgr. devel., 1980, dir. devel. and engring., 1984, dir. mktg., 1986, v.p. sales and mktg., 1986-93; chmn., CEO Garden State Tanning Inc., King of Prussia, Pa., 1993—; bd. dirs. Leather Industries Am. Co-author: (chpt.) Chemistry of Turpentine, 1989; contbr. over 30 articles to profl. jours. Pres. Irish Cultural Assn., Jacksonville, Fla., 1980. Recipient Exec. Achievement award Hanson Industries, 1990. Fellow Am. Inst. Chemists, Am. Chem. Soc.; mem. Anethole Task Force (co-chmn. 1989-92), Rotary (bd. dirs. Jacksonville chpt. 1991-92). Achievements include 12 patents in field organic chemistry. Office: Garden State Tanning Inc 630 Freedom Bus Ctr King Of Prussia PA 19406

TRCZINSKI, ROBERT A., public relations executive. Ptnr., treas. Fin. Rels. Bd., Chgo. Office: Fin Rels Bd John Hancock Ctr 875 N Michigan Ave Chicago IL 60611-1779*

TREACY, GERALD BERNARD, lawyer; b. Newark, July 29, 1951; s. Gerald B. Sr. and Mabel L. (Nesbitt) T.; m. Joyce M. Biazzo, Apr. 6, 1974. BA summa cum laude, Rider Coll., 1973; JD, UCLA, 1981. Bar: Calif. 1981, Wash. 1982, D.C. 1995. Tchr. English Arthur L. Johnson Regional High Sch., Clark, N.J., 1973-77; assoc. Gibson, Dunn & Crutcher, L.A., 1981-82; ptnr. Perkins Coie, Bellevue, Wash., 1982-94, McGuire Woods Battle & Boothe, McLean, Va., 1994-96; McGuire Woods Battle & Boothe, Bellevue, Wash.; ptnr. Egger, Betts, Sherwood, Austin & Treacy, Bellevue, Wash., 1996—; chmn. bd. dirs. estate planning adv. bd. U. Wash., Seattle, 1990-92; presenter TV Seminar, Where There's a Will, PBS affiliate. Author: Washington Guardianship Law, Administration and Litigation, 1988, supplemented, 1991, 2d edit., 1992, supplemented, 1993, 96. Mem. endowment fund com. United Way, Seattle, 1987-89, exec. com. Washington Planned Giving Coun., 1993—; bd. dirs., mem. adv. bd. ARC, Seattle, 1985-89, Arthritis Gift, 1987-89, Seattle Symphony, 1992—. Mem. Eastside King County Estate Planning Coun., Order of Coif. Avocations: photography, hiking, ethnic and classical music, poetry, host/writer Gilbert & Sullivan radio show. Office: Egger Betts Sherwood Austin & Treacy 500 108th Ave NE Ste 2300 Bellevue WA 98004

TREADWAY, DOUGLAS MORSE, academic administrator; b. San Diego, Apr. 23, 1942; s. Thelma Lillian (Lindsay) T.; m. Carole Rae Culp, June 5, 1964; children: Christine, Paul. BA, Calif. Western U., 1964; MT, Claremont Grad. Sch., 1967; PhD, Northwestern U., 1971. Asst. dean students Northwestern U., Evanston, Ill., 1969-71; asst. prof. psychology U.S. Internat. Univ., Maui, Hawaii, 1971-73; dir. coop. edn. Maui Community Coll., 1973-74; dean of students Ea. Oreg. State Coll., La Grande, 1974-79, dean continuing edn., 1979-85; pres. Western Mont. Coll., Dillon, 1985-87, S.W. State U., Marshall, Minn., 1987-91; chancellor N.D. U. System, 1991-94; supt., pres. Shasta Coll., Redding, Calif., 1994—; chmn. Nat. Conf. Rural Edn., Washington, 1987; mem. rsch. coun. USDA. Author: Higher Education in Rural America, 1985; contbr. numerous articles on higher edn. and rural programs to profl. jours. Mem. Big Bros., Maui, 1971-74. Mem. Am. Assn. Higher Edn., Am. Assn. State Colls. and Univs., Nat. Univ. Continuing Edn. Assn. Republican. Methodist. Lodge: Rotary. Avocations: swimming, fishing, hunting. Home: 13310 Pala Mesa Circle Redding CA 96003

TREADWAY, JAMES CURRAN, investment company executive, lawyer, former government official; b. Anderson, S.C., May 21, 1943; s. James C. and Maxine (Hall) T.; m. Susan Pepper Davis, Sept. 6, 1969; children: Elizabeth Pepper Hall, Caroline Worrell Harper. A.B., U. Ga., 1964; JD summa cum laude, Washington and Lee U., 1967. Bar: Ga. 1967, Mass. 1968, D.C. 1970. Assoc. Candler, Cox, McClain & Andrews, Atlanta, 1967-68, Gadsby & Hannah, Boston and Washington, 1968-72; ptnr. Dickstein, Shapiro & Morin, Washington, 1972-82; commr. SEC, Washington, 1982-85; ptnr. Baker & Botts, Washington, 1985-87; exec. v.p. PaineWebber Group Inc., N.Y.C., 1987—; chmn. Nat. Commn. on Fraudulent Fin. Reporting, 1985-87. Mem. Mass. Bar Assn., Ga. Bar Assn., D.C. Bar Assn., Chevy Chase (Md.) Club, Bedford (N.Y.) Golf and Tennis Club, City Tavern Club, Met. Club, Univ. Club (Washignton), Verbank Hunting and Fishing Club (Uniondale N.Y.; dir. 1995—), Order of Coif, Phi Beta Kapap, Omicron Delta Kappa. Republican. Roman Catholic. Home: Laurel Ledge RD 4

Croton Lake Rd Bedford Corners NY 10549 Office: PaineWebber Group Inc 1285 Ave Of The Americas New York NY 10019-6028

TREADWAY, JOHN DAVID, history educator; b. San Bernardino, Calif., June 30, 1950; s. Emery Russell and Mabel A. (Batchelor) T.; m. Sandra Gioia, Sept. 4, 1976; 1 child, Robyn. BA summa cum laude, Fla. State U., 1972; PhD, U. Va., 1980. Prof. History U. Richmond, Va., 1980—; vis. prof. U. Belgrade, 1990. Author: The Falcon and the Eagle, 1983; co-editor: The Soviet Union under Gorbachev, 1987; editor Ind. Slavic Studies/ Balkanistica, 1991-92; book reviewer Am. Hist. Rev., Historian, Choice, Slavic Rev., Serbian Studies, et al.; contbr. articles to profl. jours. Recipient Disting. Educator award U. Richmond, 1985, 88, 91, 95, Outstanding faculty award Va., 1993; fellow ITT Internat., 1975-76, Fulbright, 1985, 90, Woodrow Wilson Ctr., 1989; grantee NDFL, 1976-77, ACLS, 1981, Internat. Rsch. and Exch. Bd., 1981. Mem. Am. Hist. Assn., Southern Hist. Assn. (Snell prize 1985-87), Va. Hist. Soc., Am. Assn. for Advancement Slavic Studies, Am. Assn. Southeast European Studies (pres. 1987-89), North Am. Soc. Serbian Studies (exec. com. 1985-88), Library Svc. and Construction Act Adv. Coun., Va. Social Sci. Assn. (exec. bd. 1987-89), Am. Com. to Promote Studies of History of Habsburg Monarchy. Lutheran. Home: 8201 Gaylord Rd Richmond VA 23229-4121 Office: U Richmond Dept History Richmond VA 23173

TREADWAY-DILLMON, LINDA LEE, athletic trainer, actress; b. Woodbury, N.J., June 4, 1950; d. Leo Elmer and Ona Lee (Wyckoff) Treadway; m. Randall Kenneth Dillmon, June 19, 1982. BS in Health, Phys. Edn. & Recreation, West Chester State Coll., 1972, MS in Health and Phys. Edn., 1975; postgrad., Ctrl. Mich. U., 1978; Police Officer Stds. Tng. cert. complaint dispatcher, Goldenwest Coll., 1982. Cert. in safety edn. West Chester State Coll.; cert. EMT, Am. Acad. Orthopaedic Surgeons. Grad. asst., instr., asst. athletic trainer West Chester (Pa.) State Coll., 1972-76; asst. prof., program dir., asst. athletic trainer Ctrl. Mich. U., Mt. Pleasant, 1976-80; police dispatcher City of Westminster, Calif., 1980-89; oncology unit sec. Children's Hosp. Orange County, Orange, Calif., 1989—. Stuntwoman, actress United Stunt Artists, SAG, L.A., 1982—; dancer Disneyland, Anaheim, Calif., 1988—; contbr. articles to profl. jours. Athletic trainer U.S. Olympic Women's Track and Field Trials, Frederick, Md., 1972, AAU Jr. World Wrestling Championships, Mt. Pleasant, Mich., 1977, Mich. Spl. Olympics, Mt. Pleasant, 1977, 78, 79. Named Outstanding Phys. Educator, Delta Psi Kappa, Ctrl. Mich. U., 1980, Outstanding Young Woman of Am., 1984; named to Disneyland Entertainment Hall of Fame, 1995. Mem. SAG, Nat. Athletic Trainers Assn. (cert., women and athletic tng. ad hoc com. 1974-75, placement com. 1974-79, program dirs. coun. 1976-80, ethics com. 1977-80, visitation team 1978-80), U.S. Field Hockey Assn. (player), Pacific S.W. Field Hockey Assn. (player, Nat. Champion 1980, 81, 82), L.A. Field Hockey Assn. (player), Swing Shift Dance Team (dancer). Presbyterian. Avocations: flying, piano, athletics, stitchery, travel. Home: 15400 Belgrade St Apt 152 Westminster CA 92683-6962 Office: Childrens Hosp Orange County 455 S Main St Orange CA 92668-3835

TREADWELL, ALEXANDER F., state official; b. London, Mar. 25, 1946; m. Libby, 1970; children: Carrie, Zach. BA, U. N.C. Sec. of state State of N.Y. Office: 162 Washington Ave Albany NY 12231-0001

TREADWELL, HUGH WILSON, publishing executive; b. Waurika, Okla., Nov. 21, 1921; s. Hugh and Jessie Ellen (Cogdell) T.; m. Edith Albena Doolittle, June 20, 1959; children—Pamela, Hugh, Cynthia. B.A., U. Okla., 1949, M.A., 1952; diploma in French Studies (Rotary Found. fellow), Institut de Touraine, U. Poitiers, France, 1950. Asst. editor internat. lit. quar. Books Abroad, U. Okla., 1952-53; field rep. coll. dept. The Macmillan Co., 1953-60, Holt, Rinehart & Winston, Inc., Okla. and Tex., 1960-62; mgr. coll. programs in fgn. lang. dept. Holt, Rinehart & Winston, Inc., N.Y.C., 1962-67; sr. editor coll. dept. Random House-Knopf, N.Y.C., 1967-72; dir. U. N.Mex. Press, Albuquerque, 1973-80, Tex. Western Press, U. Tex., El Paso, 1981-85; pvt. practice cons., 1985—; field rep. coll. dept. W. W. Norton & Co., Tex., N.Mex., Okla., 1988-93; instr. ESL El Paso C.C., 1994—; instr. French U. Okla., 1952-53; Industry rep. Nat. Com. Support of Fgn. Langs., 1971. Pres. El Paso Council for Internat. Visitors, 1987-88. Served with USAAF, 1943-46. Decorated Air medal. Mem. Phi Beta Kappa. Democrat. Club: Alliance Francaise (El Paso). Home: 6832 La Cadena Dr El Paso TX 79912-2810 *In my mind, the pursuit of happiness has always been bound up with the pursuit of knowledge—knowledge not in a purely abstract sense, but purposeful knowledge humanely applied. The professions of teaching and publishing, if practiced in the light of the highest ethical standards associated with each, make this pursuit possible and offer the greatest satisfaction to those who view life as I do. I consider myself fortunate to have served in both of these professions.*

TREANOR, CHARLES EDWARD, scientist; b. Buffalo, Oct. 22, 1924; s. William Michael and Margaret Mary (Powers) T.; m. Ruth Ziegelmaier, Jan. 28, 1950; children: Timothy, John, Peter, Michael, Melissa. B.A., U. Minn., 1947; Ph.D., U. Buffalo, 1956. Instr. physics U. Buffalo, 1952-53; physicist Cornell Aero. Lab., Buffalo, 1954-68, head aerodynamic research dept., 1968-78; v.p. phys. sci. group Calspan Corp., Buffalo, 1978-83, v.p., chief scientist, 1983-90; pres. CTSA, Inc., 1990—. Contbr. articles to profl. jours. Patentee in field. Served to lt. U.S. Army, 1943-46. Recipient C.C. Furnas award SUNY, Buffalo, 1989. Fellow Am. Phys. Soc. (div. chmn. 1977), AIAA (com. chmn. 1975-76, 87-89, Fluid and Plasma Dynamics award 1978); mem. NAE. Home: 140 Segsbury Rd Buffalo NY 14221-3425 Office: Calspan UB Rsch Ctr 4455 Genesee St PO Box 400 Buffalo NY 14225

TREANOR, HELEN JUNE, nursing administrator, geriatrics professional; b. Battle Creek, Mich., Dec. 22, 1931; d. Antoine Joseph and Helen June (Jevnem) Hudon; m. Richard Clifford Treanor, Aug. 8, 1953; children: Kathleen, Theresa, Peggy, Michael, John, Sharon, Thomas. Diploma, U. Ill./Cook Co. Sch. Nursing, 1953; BS, Barat Coll., 1986; MBA, Lake Forest Grad. Sch., 1990. RN, CNA, Ill.; cert. nursing home adminstr., Ill., 1992. Staff nurse McNeal Meml. Hosp., Berwyn, Ill., 1953-55, Lake Forest (Ill.) Hosp., 1977-79; staff nurse, head nurse Good Shepherd Hosp., Barrington, Ill., 1979-87; pres., CEO N.W. Suburban Microfilm, Inc., Arlington Heights, Ill., 1987-91; dir. nursing and aux. svcs. Libertyville (Ill.) Manor Rehab. and Healthcare Ctr., 1991—; adv. bd. Lake County Vocat. Sch., Grayslake, Ill., 1992—. Pres. Friends of the Ela Area Libr., Lake Zurich, 1976-77, St. Frances de Sales Women's Orgn., Lake Zurich, Ill., 1970's. Mem. Nat. Assn. Dirs. Nursing Adminstrn. Avocations: aerobics, walking, gardening, reading, writing. Home: 21539 W Boschome Dr Kildeer IL 60047 Office: Libertyville Manor Rehab and Healthcare Ctr 610 Peterson Rd Libertyville IL 60048

TREAS, JUDITH KAY, sociology educator; b. Phoenix, Jan. 2, 1947; d. John Joseph and Hope Catherine (Thomas) Jennings; m. Benjamin C. Treas II, May 14, 1969; children: Stella, Evan. BA, Pitzer Coll., Claremont, Calif., 1969; MA, UCLA, 1972, PhD, 1976. Instr. U. So. Calif., L.A., 1974-75, asst. prof., 1975-81, assoc. prof., 1981-87, dept. chair, 1984-89, prof., 1987-89; prof. U. Calif., Irvine, 1989, dept. chair, 1989-94; bd. overseers Gen. Social Survey, 1986-88; cons. social sci. and population study sect. NIH, 1989-92. Contbr. articles to profl. jours. Trustee Pitzer Coll., 1977-79. Recipient Rsch. award NSF, 1978-81, 84-91, NIH, 1979-81; Univ. scholar U. So. Calif., 1982-83. Fellow Gerontological Assn. Am.; mem. Golden Key (hon.), Am. Sociol. Assn., Population Assn. Am., Internat. Union for Sci. Study Population. Office: U Calif-Irvine Dept Sociology Irvine CA 92717

TREASTER, JOSEPH B. (BLAND), journalist; b. Mt. Union, Pa., May 19, 1941; s. Ellsworth F. and Anna Katherine (Chalupka) T.; m. Barbara A. Gluck, June 6, 1970 (div. Aug. 1976); m. .Barbara J. Dill, Feb. 24, 1990; 1 child, Chloe Qiao Xing. BA, U. Miami, 1965; student, Sorbonne, Paris, 1971, San Francisco de Marroquin, Guatemala, 1988. Reporter Miami (Fla.) Herald, 1963; staff asst. Saigon bur. N.Y. Times, 1965-67, Vietnam corr., 1968-69, 72-74; reporter N.Y. Times, N.Y.C., 1969-70; chief Conn. bur. N.Y. Times, 1970-72, investigative reporter N.J. bur., 1974-75, crime/youth violence writer, 1975-76, rewrite desk and spl. assignments to Washington, L.Am. and Mid. East, 1976-84, chief Caribbean bur., 1984-90, drug policy corr., 1990—; freelance corr. Atlantic Monthly, Rolling Stone, The Nation, others; fellow Poynter Inst., St. Petersburg, Fla., 1993, U. Nev. Bus. Journalism, 1995; Knight-Bagehot fellow in econs. and bus. Columbia U., 1995-96. Co-author: No Hiding Place: Inside Report on the Hostage Crisis (in Iran), 1981; contbg. author: Encyclopedia Britannica, Insight Guide to Caribbean, Youth Violence, 1992. Served with U.S. Army, 1963-65, Vietnam. Recipient Page One award N.Y. Newspaper Guild, 1977, 79; Tom Wallace award Inter-Am. Press Assn., 1980, citation and awards Overseas Press Club Am., 1977, 80, 85, News Analysis award Soc. of Silurians, 1993, Casey medal for meritorious journalism U. Md., 1995, others; Poynter fellow Yale U., 1975. Mem. Mystery Writers Am. Avocations: skiing, sport fishing, running, bicycling. Office: NY Times 229 W 43rd St New York NY 10036-3913

TREASURE, JOHN ALBERT PENBERTHY, advertising executive; b. Usk, Monmouthshire, Eng., June 20, 1924; s. Harold Paul and Constance (Shapl) T.; m. Valerie Bell, Apr. 1954; children—Jonathan, Julian, Simon. Ph.D., Cambridge U., 1956. Research officer Brit. Market Research Bur., Ltd., London, 1952-56; mng. dir. Brit. Market Research Bur., Ltd., 1957-60; dir. research and mktg. J. Walter Thompson Co., Ltd., London, 1960-66; chmn. J. Walter Thompson Co., Ltd., 1967-77, John Treasure and Partners, London, 1981-83; dean City U. Bus. Sch., London, 1978-81; vice chmn. Saatchi & Saatchi Advt. Ltd., 1983-89; chmn. Taylor Nelson AGB plc, 1992—. Contbr. articles to profl. jours. Friend Royal Coll. Physicians; trustee Found. for Bus. Responsibilities. Fellow Inst. Practitioners in Advt. (past pres.); mem. Market Research Soc. (past pres.). Home: 20 Queensberry House, Friars Ln, Richmond, Surrey TW9 1NT, England Office: Taylor Nelson AGB, AGB House, West Gate, Hanger Ln, London W5 1UA, England

TREAT, JAMES J., accountant, business executive; b. Pittsfield, Mass., May 8, 1942; s. Orion F. and Gladdis A. (Whittsley) T.; m. Marcelle Joanne Felker, Sept. 8, 1967; children: James Matthew, Jessica Ann. BS, Butler U., 1965; student, U. New Haven, 1969-79, MIT, 1976. Cost acctg. mgr. Sperry Products, Inc., Danbury, Conn., 1969-70; chief acct. Automation Industries, Inc., Danbury, 1970-73, asst. controller, 1974-75, group controller, 1976-80; controller Nuclear Energy Services Inc., Danbury, 1975-76; gen. mgr. Conam Inspection, Midland, Tex., 1980-81; v.p. Conam Inspection, Longview, Tex., 1981-84; co-owner, v.p. Longview Inspection, Inc., 1984-90; pres., 1990-95; v.p. ops. Longview Holdings, Inc., 1995—; treas. Automation Fedn. Credit Union, Danbury, 1973-75, v.p., 1975-80. Inventor (with others) ultrasonic testing device, 1986. Fund raiser YMCA, Danbury, 1978, dir. regional YMCA, Danbury, 1978-79; fin. chmn. United Meth. Ch., Hallsville, Tex., 1984-85. Served with USN, 1965-69. Mem. Am. Welding Soc., Nat. Assn. Accts., Am. Soc. Nondestructive Testing, Nondestructive Mgmt. Assn. Avocations: sports, collectibles. *

TREAT, JOHN ELTING, management consultant; b. Evanston, Ill., June 20, 1946; s. Carlin Alexander and Marjorie Ann (Mayland) T.; adopted s. Howard Elting Jr.; m. Barbara Laflin, May 27, 1984; children: Charles, Luli, Tyler. BA, Princeton U., 1967; MA, Johns Hopkins U., 1969. Legis. asst. U.S. Senate, 1966; assoc. ops. officer Office of Sec., U.S. Dept. State, 1971-73; research coordinator Presdl.-Congressional Commn. on Orgn. of Govt. for Conduct of Fgn. Policy, Washington, 1973-74; dir. research trade U.S. Fed. Energy Adminstrn., Washington, 1974-78; dep. asst. sec. U.S. Dept. Energy, Washington, 1979-80; staff mem. Nat. Security Council, 1980-81; sr. v.p. N.Y. Merc. Exchange, N.Y.C., 1981-82, pres., 1982-84; ptnr. Bear Stearns & Co., Los Angeles, 1984-85; exec. pub. Petroleum Intelligence Weekly, N.Y.C., 1985-87; pres. Regent Internat., Washington and The Hague, 1987-89; v.p., ptnr. Booz, Allen & Hamilton, Inc., San Francisco, 1989—. Chmn. spl. gifts Am. Cancer Soc., 1983; chmn. bd. dirs. Mirror Repertory Co., 1987—; trustee, mem. exec. com., chmn. corp. rels. com. No. Calif. World Affairs Coun.; mem. San Francisco Fgn. Rels. com.; bd. trustees Am. U. of Cairo. With USNR, 1969-71. Decorated AF Commendation medal; Ford Found. European Area Travel grantee, 1972; Woodrow Wilson fellow, 1967; McConnell fellow, 1966. Mem. Coun. Fgn. Rels., Internat. Assn. for Energy Econs. Democrat. Unitarian. Clubs: Colonial (Princeton, N.J.), St. Francis Yacht Club, Bankers (San Francisco). Home: 42 San Carlos Ave Sausalito CA 94965-2048

TREAT, LAWRENCE, author; b. N.Y.C., Dec. 21, 1903; s. Henry and Daisy (Stein) Goldstone; m. Rose Ehrenfreund, 1943. B.A., Dartmouth Coll., 1924; LL.B., Columbia U., 1927. Author: fiction Run Far, Run Fast, 1937, B as in Banshee, 1940, D as in Dead, 1941, H as in Hangman, 1942, O as in Omen, 1943, The Leatherman, 1944, V as in Victim, 1945, H as in Hunted, 1946, Q as in Quicksand, 1947, Over the Edge, 1948, F as in Flight, 1948, Trial and Terror, 1949, Big Shot, 1951, Weep for a Wanton, 1956, Lady, Drop Dead, 1960, Venus Unarmed, 1961, P as in Police, 1970, True Crime With Judge Norbert Ehrenfreund: You're the Jury, 1992; originator of police procedurals and pictorial mysteries, Bringing Sherlock Home, 1931, Crime and Puzzlement, 1981, Crime and Puzzlement 2, 1982, You're the Detective, 1983, The Clue Armchair Detective, 1983, Crime and Puzzlement 3, 1988, Cherchez le Coupable, 1 and 2, 1989, Crime and Puzzlement, My Cousin Phoebe, 1991, Crime and Puzzlement on Martha's Vineyard, 1993; editor: Murder in Mind, 1967; The Mystery Writer's Handbook, 1976, A Special Kind of Crime, 1982; contbr. numerous short stories to mags. including Alfred Hitchcock's Mystery Mag., Ellery Queen's Mystery Mag., Red Book, others, also numerous anthologies. Recipient Ceremonial sword Mystery Writers Japan, 1961, Edgar Allan Poe award Mystery Writers of Am., 1965, 78, Spl. Edgar Allan Poe award for story in Alfred Hitchcock TV Hour, 1986; prize Internat. Crime Writer's Conv., Stockholm, 1981. Mem. Mystery Writers Am. (founder, past pres.), Boston Author's Club, Crime Writers' Assn., Phi Beta Kappa. Office: RFD Box 475A Edgartown MA 02539 also: care Vicky Bijur 333 W End Ave New York NY 10023-8128

TREBEK, ALEX, television game show host; b. Sudbury, Ont., Can., July 22, 1940; came to U.S., 1973; s. George Edward and Lucille (Lagace) T.; m. Elaine Callei (div. 1981); m. Jean Currivan, Apr. 30, 1990; 2 children. BA and PhB, U. Ottawa, Ont., 1961. Staff announcer CBC, Toronto, Ont., 1961-73; game show host Wizard of Odds for NBC, Calif., 1973-74, High Rollers for NBC, Calif., 1974-79, Stars on Ice for Can. TV, 1974-77, $128, 000 Question for Global TV, Can., 1976-77, Double Dare for CBS, Calif., 1977-78, Battle Stars for NBC, Calif., 1981-82; game show host, producer Jeopardy!, Calif., 1984-87, game show host 1987—; game show host Classic Concentration, Calif., 1987-90, To Tell the Truth, 1991. film appearances include: Short Cuts, 1993. Mem. Screen Actors Guild, AFTRA, Assn. Can. TV and Radio Artists. Roman Catholic. Avocations: golf, hockey, tennis, water skiing. Office: Jeopardy! 1020 W Washington Blvd Culver City CA 90232

TREBILCOTT, JAMES JOSEPH, former utility executive; b. Kansas City, Mo., June 20, 1917; s. William Henry and Catherine (Curran) T.; m. Maureen E. Ball, Dec. 16, 1944; children: Katherine, Michael, Ronald. B.S., U. Mo., 1938; postgrad., Harvard U., 1942, Mass. Inst. Tech., 1942, U. Mich., 1952. With Pub. Service Co., Okla., 1946-48, Mich. Wis. Pipe Line Co., Detroit, 1948-80; v.p., chief ops. officer, dir. Mich. Wis. Pipe Line Co., 1960-72, exec. v.p., dir., 1973-80; exec. v.p. Am. Nat. Resources Co., 1980-82; pres., dir. Am. Nat. Service Co., 1980-82, Worldwide Profl. Mgmt., 1982—; chmn. Thermo Electric Co., 1982-87; v.p., chief ops. officer, dir. Am. La. Pipe Line Co., Detroit, 1960-66; v.p., dir. Am. Natural Gas Prodn. Co., 1962-80; exec. v.p., dir. Am. Nat. Alaskan Co., 1979-80, pres., dir., 1981-82; chmn. Oumic Thermo-Electric Co.; pres., dir. Am. Nat. LNG Corp., ANR LaSalle LNG Transmission Corp., ANR Elba LNG Transmission Corp., all 1979-82, Mich. Med. Properties, 1985—; exec. v.p., dir. Energy Conversion Devices Inc., 1983-87; dir. Gt. Lakes Gas Transmission Co., St. Clair Group Money Market Funds. Served to capt. USAAF, 1942-46. Mem. Engring. Soc. Detroit, Greater Detroit Bd. Commerce, Detroit Econ. Club, Newcomen Soc., Am. Gas Assn., Midwest Gas Assn. (chmn.), So. Gas Assn., Ind. Natural Gas Assn., Internat. Gas. Union (com. mem.). Clubs: Detroit Athletic, Detroit, Detroit Golf, Circumnavigators (pres., dir.) (Detroit). Lodges: K.C., Rotary (Detroit). Home: 3 Alger Pl Grosse Pointe MI 48230-1908

TREBLE, GERRY, religious organization leader. BA, U. W.O., 1974, MEd, 1980. Tchr. Muron Heights Pub. Sch., 1966-68; tchr., adminstr. Leo LaCroix, Ont., Can., 1968-69; tchr. Riverview Pub. Sch., 1970-72, libr., 1972-73; guidance counselor Pearson Sr. Pub. Sch., 1973-78; resource counsellor Chippewa Pub. Sch., 1979-80; tchr. area learning resource Pearson Sr. Pub. Sch., 1980-81, vice prin., 1984-85; prin. Mcdonald.Townahand Pub. Schs., 1989, Knollwood Park Pub. Sch., 1995—. Office: 60 Logan Ave, London Ont, Canada NS4 2P8

TRECKELO, RICHARD M., lawyer; b. Elkhart, Ind., Oct. 22, 1926; s. Frank J. and Mary (Ferro) T.; m. Anne Kosick, June 25, 1955; children: Marla Treckelo Buck, Mary Treckelo Lucchesi. AB, U. Mich., 1951, JD, 1953. Bar: Ind. 1953, U.S. Dist. Ct. (no. and so. dists.) Ind. Pvt. practice, Elkhart, 1953-70; ptnr. Elkhart, South Bend, Indpls., Ft. Wayne, Washington, Elkhart, South Bend, Indpls., Ft. Wayne, 1971-91; of counsel Elkhart, South Bend, Indpls., Ft. Wayne, Chgo., Washington, Elkhart, South Bend, Indpls., Ft. Wayne, Chgo., 1992—; sec. Skyline Corp., Elkhart, 1959-94, bd. dirs., 1961-91. Bd. dirs. Elkhart Gen. Hosp. Found., Elkhart Park Found.; co-chmn. Elkhart Constl. Bicentennial Commn. Served with USAF, 1945-46. Mem. ABA, Elkhart City Bar Assn. (pres. 1975), Ind. Bar Assn., Elkhart County Bar Assn., Pres.'s Club (U. Mich.), Christiana Country Club, Rotary. Republican. Office: Barnes & Thornburg 301 S Main St Ste 305 Elkhart IN 46516-3119

TREDENNICK, STEVEN BURROUGHS, lawyer; b. Newport News, Va., June 26, 1943; s. John C. and Jacqueline (Burroughs) T.; m. D. Diane French, June 11, 1966; children: Steven Randolph, Christopher Scott. BA, U. Tex., El Paso, 1965; JD, U. Va., 1968; cert., Coll. for Fin. Planning, 1984. Bar: Tex. 1970, N.Mex. 1984. Assoc. Goodman, Hallmark & Akard, El Paso, Tex., 1972-74; pvt. practice Steven Tredennick, P.C., El Paso, 1974-79; sr. shareholder Mayfield and Perrenot, P.C., El Paso, 1979—; mem. U.S.-Mex. task force Atlantic coun. of U.S., Washington, 1985. Editor newsletter Franchising in the Americas. Chmn. Sun Bowl luncheon Rotary Club of El Paso, 1993-94; chmn. Tex. Lyceum Assn., 1989; chmn. various coms. U. Tex., El Paso, 1980—; sponsor, spkr., writer The Franchise Ctr., 1993-95. Capt. U.S. Army, 1968-72. Recipient Rising Star of Tex. award Tex. Bus. Mag., 1983; named to Best Lawyers in Am., Woodward/White, Inc., 1995—. Fellow Tex. Bar Found. (life); mem. ABA, El Paso Bar Assn. (past program chair 1972—), State Bar of Va. (assoc.). Episcopalian. Avocations: physical fitness, reading, volunteer work. Home: 6221 Bandolero Dr El Paso TX 79912-1922 Office: Mayfield and Perrenot PC 300 E Main Dr Fl 5 El Paso TX 79901-1372

TREDWAY, THOMAS, college president; b. North Tonawanda, N.Y., Sept. 4, 1935; s. Harold and Melanya (Scorby) T.; m. Catherine Craft, Jan. 12, 1991; children: Daniel John, Rebecca Elizabeth. BA, Augustana Coll., 1957; MA, U. Ill., 1958; BD, Garrett Theol. Sem., 1961; PhD, Northwestern U., 1964. Instr. history Augustana Coll., Rock Island, Ill., 1964-65, asst. prof., 1965-69, assoc. prof., 1969-71, prof., 1971—, v.p. acad affairs, 1970-75, pres., 1975—; vis. prof. ch. history Waterloo Lutheran Sem., 1967-68. Mem. Am. Hist. Assn., Am. Soc. Ch. History, Phi Beta Kappa, Omicron Delta Kappa. Lutheran. Office: Augustana Coll Office of President 639 38th St Rock Island IL 61201-2210

TREE, DAVID L., advertising agency executive. Formerly sr. v.p., creative dir. D'Arcy Masius Benton & Bowles, Inc., N.Y.C.; chmn., corp. chief creative officer Campbell Mithun Esty, 1989—. Office: Campbell Mithun Esty 222 S 9th St Minneapolis MN 55402-3389*

TREE, MICHAEL, violinist, violist, educator; b. Newark, Feb. 19, 1934; s. Samuel and Sada (Rothman) Applebaum; m. Johanna Kreck, Sept. 8, 1966; children: Konrad Efrem, Anna Louise. Diploma, Curtis Inst. Music, Phila., 1955; DFA (hon.), U. South Fla., 1975, SUNY, Binghamton, 1985. Faculty Harpur Coll., Binghamton, 1965-70, Curtis Inst. Music, 1970—, U. Md., College Park, 1981—, St. Louis Conservatory Music, 1982-88, Rutgers U., 1988—, Manhattan Sch. Music, 1993—; co-artistic dir. Phila. Chamber Orch., 1985-88; Misha Elman chair Manhattan Sch. Music, 1991. Violin recital debut at Carnegie Hall, 1954; soloist with major orchs. and at maj. internat. festivals, 1958—; founding mem. Guarneri String Quartet, 1964—, rec. artist for Philips, RCA, Columbia, Nonesuch, Vanguard, Sony Classics records. Recipient Seal of Recognition City of N.Y., 1982. Avocations: hiking, tennis. Home: 45 E 89th St New York NY 10128-1251 Office: care Herbert Barrett Mgmt Inc 1776 Broadway New York NY 10019-2002

TREECE, JOHN W., lawyer; b. Madison, Wis., Oct. 2, 1952. BA magna cum laude, Harvard U., 1975; JD, Columbia U., 1978. Bar: Ill. 1978. Ptnr. Sidley & Austin, Chgo. With Army NG, 1972-78. Harlan Fiske Stone scholar. Office: Sidley & Austin 1 First Nat Plz Chicago IL 60603*

TREFFERT, DAROLD ALLEN, psychiatrist, author, hospital director; b. Fond du Lac, Wis., Mar. 12, 1933; s. Walter O. and Emma (Leu) T.; m. Dorothy Marie Sorgatz, June 11, 1955; children: Jon, Joni, Jill, Jay. B.S., U. Wis., 1955, M.D., 1958. Diplomate: Am. Bd. Psychiatry and Neurology. Resident in psychiatry U. Wis. Med. Sch., 1959-62, assoc. clin. prof. psychiatry, 1965—; chief children's unit Winnebago (Wis.) Mental Health Inst., 1962-64, supt., 1964-79; supt. Central State Hosp., Waupun, Wis., 1977-78; dir. Dodge County Mental Health Center, Juneau, Wis., 1964-74; mem. staff St. Agnes Hosp., Fond du Lac, 1963—; exec. dir. Fond du Lac County Mental Health Center, 1979-92; chmn. Controlled Substances Bd. Wis.; mem. critical health problems com. Wis. Dept. Pub. Instrn., med. examining bd. State of Wis. Author: Extraordinary People: Understanding Savant Syndrome, 1989, edits. in U.S., U.K., Italy, Japan, The Netherlands, Sweden; autism cons. (movie) Rainman, 1988. Fellow Am. Coll. Psychiatrists; mem. AMA, Wis. Med. Soc. (pres. 1979-80), Wis. Psychiat. Assn. (pres.), Am. Assn. Psychiat. Adminstrs. (pres.), Alpha Omega Alpha. Home: W 4065 Maplewood Ln Fond Du Lac WI 54935-9562 Office: 481 E Division St Fond Du Lac WI 54935-3775 *People often spend too much time regretting what they are not and far too little time savoring that which they are.*

TREFFINGER, KARL EDWARD, architectural firm executive; b. Columbus, Ohio, Oct. 21, 1927; s. Raymond Hartman and Eldred (Ruffner) T.; m. Beverly Jean Beck, Mar. 21, 1957 (dec. 1994); children: Kathy Anne, Julia Frances Wirth, Karl Raymond, Frederick Charles. BA, Yale U., 1948, MArch, 1952. Registered arch. Calif., Oreg. Wash., Nev., Ohio, Ill., Fla., Okla.; cert. Nat. Coun. Archtl. Registration Bds. Draftsman Stanley Morse, Denver, 1955-56; pvt. practice Columbus, Ohio, 1956-57; apprentice Edward Durrell Stone, Palo Alto, Calif., 1957-58; designer Wurster, Bernardi and Emmons, San Francisco, 1959-60; arch. Karl Treffinger & Assoc., San Francisco, 1960-78; prin. Treffinger, Walz and MacLeod, San Francisco and San Rafael, Calif., 1978-92. Prin. works include Harbor Point Beach Club, Strawberry Peninsula, Calif., Telegraph Hill Apts., San Francisco, Peninsula Squash Club, San Mateo, Calif., Sheraton Inn-Walden, Schaumburg, Ill., Court of Flags Complex, Orlando, Fla., Growers Sq., Walnut Creek, Calif. Walden Office Sq., Schaumburg, Wescot Internat., San Rafael, Treffinger, Walz & MacLeod Offices, San Rafael, Remillard Brick Yard, Larkspur, Calif., Walden Market Sq. Project, Schaumburg, Walden, Schaumburg, Walden Lakes, Bensenville, Ill., Smith Ranch Master Plan, San Rafael, Bon Air Project, Greenbrae, Calif., Ridgeland Devel. Project, Marin City, Calif., condominiums, townhouses, apts.; contbr. articles to profl. jours. Lt. USN, 1952-55, Korea. Recipient civic awards for design excellence. Fellow AIA (corp., pres. No. Calif. chpt. 1974, sec. Calif. coun., awards design excellence). Home: 700 SW Schaeffer Rd West Linn OR 97068-9644

TREFIL, JAMES S., physicist, educator; b. Chgo., Sept. 10, 1938; s. Stanley James and Sylvia (Mestek) T.; m. Elinor Pletka; children: James Karel, STefan; m. Jeanne L. Waples, Oct. 17, 1972; children: Dominique, Flora, Tomas. BS, U. Ill., 1960; BA, MA, Oxford (Eng.) U., 1962; MS, Stanford U., 1964, PhD, 1966. Rsch. assoc. Stanford (Calif.) Linear Accelerator Ctr., 1966; Air Force Office Sci. Rsch. postdoctoral fellow CERN, Geneva, 1966-67; asst. prof. physics U. Ill., Urbana, 1968-70; assoc. prof. physics U. Va., Charlottesville, 1970-75, prof. physics, 1975-87, Univ. prof. physics, 1987; C.J. Robinson prof. physics George Mason U., Fairfax, Va., 1987—; sci. adv. bd. Nat. Pub. Radio; sci. cons. Smithsonian Mag.; tech. cons. Am. Heritage Dictionary. Author: Dictionary of Cultural Literacy, 1988, 2d edit., 1993, Reading the Mind of God, 1989, Science Matters, 1991, Facts of Life: Science and the Abortion Controversy, 1992, A Scientist in the City, 1994, The Sciences: An Integrated Approach, 1995. NSF fellow Stanford U., 1966; recipient Sci. Journalism award AAAS-Westinghouse, 1983; John Simon Guggenheim fellow, 1987-88; Marshall scholar Oxford U., 1962. Fellow Am. Phys. Soc., World Econ. Forum. Office: George Mason U 207 E Bldg Fairfax VA 22030

TREFRY, ROBERT J., healthcare administrator; b. Springfield, Vt., Mar. 29, 1947; married. Bachelors' degree, Ga. Inst. Tech., 1970; Masters' degree, George Washington U., 1974. With Greater Southeast Community Hosp., Washington, 1973, adminstrv. asst., 1973-74, asst. adminstr., 1974-79; sr. v.p. North Kansas City (Mo.) Community Hosp., 1979-83; exec. v.p., chief exec. officer St. Agnes Hosp., White Plains, N.Y., 1983-88; exec. v.p., chief operating officer Carle Found. Hosp., Urbana, Ill., 1988-91; exec. v.p., chief oper. officer Bridgeport (Conn.) Hosp., 1991-94, pres., CEO, 1994—. With U.S. mil. 1970-71. Office: Bridgeport Hosp 267 Grant St Bridgeport CT 06610-2870

TREGOE, BENJAMIN BAINBRIDGE, management consultant, researcher; b. San Francisco, Dec. 23, 1927; s. Benjamin Bainbridge and Marianne (West) T.; m. Jeannette Sylvia Gill, Aug. 4, 1956; children: Cynthia West, Elizabeth Gill, Benjamin Bainbridge III. BA, Whittier Coll., 1951, HHD (hon.), 1990; PhD, Harvard U., 1957. Rsch. assoc. Rand Corp., Santa Monica, Calif., 1955-58; co-founder Kepner-Tregoe, Inc., Princeton, N.J., 1958—, also chmn. bd. dirs.; lectr. UCLA, Westwood, 1956-57, UCLA, 1955-58; bd. dirs. J.M. Smucker Co., Orrville, Ohio, World Affairs Coun. of Phila., 1992—; mem. exec. com., bd. dirs. Nat. Alliance Bus., Washington; pres., founder Bainbridge Ednl. Found., 1993. Author: The Rational Manager, 1965, The New Rational Manager, 1980, Top Management Strategy, 1980, Vision in Action, 1989. Trustee Whittier Coll., 1980—, St. Simon's-by-the-Sea, Mantoloking, N.J., 1988—, Princeton Day Sch., 1976-85; chmn. adv. com. grad. sch. arts and scis. Harvard U., Cambridge, Mass., 1994—; bd. dirs. Princeton U. Libr., 1986-89, YWCA Exec. Assn., Princeton, 1975-86; elder Nassau Presbyn. Ch., Princeton, 1990—. With USMC, 1946-47. Mem. Chief Execs. Orgn., World Affairs Coun. (bd. dirs. Phila.), ASTD (dir. 1975-79), Harvard Club N.Y.C., Harvard Club Princeton (dir. 1987-89), Nassau Club, BayHead Yacht Club, Mantoloking Yacht Club. Republican. Avocations: skiing, swimming, reading, fly fishing. Office: Kepner-Tregoe Inc 17 Research Rd PO Box 704 Princeton NJ 08542-0704

TREGURTHA, PAUL RICHARD, marine transportation and construction materials company executive; b. Orange, N.J., 1935; married. BSME, Cornell U., 1958; MBA, Harvard U., 1963. V.p., controller Brown & Sharpe Mfg. Co., 1969-71; v.p. fin. Moore McCormack Resources, Inc., Stamford, Conn., 1971-73, exec. v.p. fin., 1973-78, pres., chief operating officer, from 1978, pres., chief exec. officer, chmn., 1987-88; chmn., co-owner Mormac Marine Group, Inc., Stamford, 1988—; vice chmn., co-owner The Interlake Steamship Co., 1988—; chmn. Meridian Aggregates Acquisitions, Inc., Moran Transp. Co., 1994—; bd. dirs. Fleet Financial Group, Brown and Sharpe Mfg., FPL Group, Inc. Trustee Cornell U., Ithaca, N.Y.; trustee Tchrs. Ins. and Annuity Assn. Served to 1st lt. USAF, 1958-61. Named Baker Scholar, Harvard U., 1963. Office: Mormac Marine Group Inc Three Landmark Sq Stamford CT 06901

TREIBL, HANS GEORGE, industrial chemist; b. Vienna, Austria, Aug. 7, 1914; came to U.S., 1950; s. Robert and Ida (Salzer) T.; m. Gertrude Schacherl, Nov. 22, 1951. PhD in Engring., States Rsch. Inst. Organic Ind, Vienna, 1935; Culturate Doctorate in Chemistry (hon.), World U., 1984. Analytical chemist United Labs. of Austrian Health Dept., Vienna, 1937-38; petrochemist Cathay Oil Co., Shanghai, 1939-49; assayer, supr. Luscar (Alta., Can.) Oil Co., 1949-50; chief chemist Hydrocarbon Chems., Newark, 1951-57; rsch. chemist Diamond Alkali, Newark, 1957-58; dir. rsch., chief chemist Std. Chlorine Chem. Co., Inc., Kearney, N.J., 1958-83, rsch. dir., 1979—; mem. product rsch. panel Chem. Engring. Mag., 1970-71. Contbr. articles to Encyclopedia of Industrial Chemical Analysis, 1972. Recipient Cert. of Merit Dictionary of Internat. Biography, 1979. Fellow AIChE (emeritus), Am. Chem. Soc. Achievements include research on chlorination of aromatic hydrocarbons and naphthalene, kinetics of catalysts in halogenations of aromatic hydrocarbons. Home: Century Village 1002 Newport G Deerfield Beach FL 33442

TREIGER, IRWIN LOUIS, lawyer; b. Seattle, Sept. 10, 1934; s. Sam S. and Rose (Steinberg) T.; m. Betty Lou Friedlander, Aug. 18, 1957; children: Louis H., Karen I., Kenneth B. BA, U. Wash., 1955, JD, 1957; LLM in Taxation, NYU, 1958. Bar: Wash. 1958, D.C. 1982, U.S. Dist. Ct. (we. dist.) Wash., U.S. Ct. Appeals (9th cir.), U.S. Supreme Ct. Assoc. Bogle & Gates, Seattle, 1958-63, ptnr., 1964—; chmn., 1986-94. Pres. Jewish Fedn. Greater Seattle, 1993-95; chmn. Mayor's Symphony Panel, 1986, Corp. Coun. for the Arts, 1987-88; pres. Seattle Symphony Found., 1986—; trustee, co-chmn. Cornish Coll. of the Arts, 1990—; trustee The Seattle Found., 1992—, Samis Found., 1989—; chmn. King County Baseball Pk. Commn., 1995. Fellow Am. Coll. Tax Counsel; mem. ABA (chmn. taxation sect. 1988-89, sect. del. 1990—), Wash. State Bar Assn. (chmn. taxation sect. 1975), Greater Seattle C. of C. (chmn. 1993-94), Seattle Rotary Svc. Found. (v.p. 1995—). Jewish. Office: Bogle & Gates 601 Union St Seattle WA 98101-2327

TREIMAN, SAM BARD, physics educator; b. Chgo., May 27, 1925; s. Abraham and Sarah (Bard) T.; m. Joan Little, Dec. 27, 1952; children—Rebecca, Katherine, Thomas. Student, Northwestern U., 1942-44; S.B., U. Chgo., 1948, S.M., 1949, Ph.D., 1952. Mem. faculty Princeton U., 1952—, instr., 1952-54, asst. prof., 1954-58, assoc. prof., 1958-63, prof. physics, 1963—, Eugene Higgins prof., 1976—, chmn. dept., 1981-87, chmn. univ. rsch. bd., 1988—. Author: (with M. Grossjean) Formal Scattering Theory, 1960, (with R. Jackiw and D.J. Gross) Current Algebra and Its Applications, 1972; Contbr. articles to profl. jours. Served with USNR, 1944-46. Recipient Oersted medal Am. Assn. Physics Tchrs. Mem. NAS, Am. Phys. Soc., Am. Acad. Arts and Scis. Home: 60 Mccosh Cir Princeton NJ 08540-5627

TREISTER, GEORGE MARVIN, lawyer; b. Oxnard, Calif., Sept. 5, 1923; s. Isadore Harry and Augusta Lee (Bloom) T.; m. Jane Goldberg, Jan. 24, 1946; children: Laura, Neil, Adam, Dana. B.S., UCLA, 1943; LL.B., Yale U., 1949. Bar: Calif. 1950. Law clk. to chief justice Calif. Supreme Ct., 1949-50; law clk. to Assoc. Justice Hugo L. Black U. S. Supreme Ct., 1950-51; asst. U.S. atty. So. Dist. Calif., 1951-53; dep. atty. gen. Calif., 1953; practiced in Los Angeles, 1953—; mem. Stutman, Treister and Glatt, 1953—; instr. U. So. Calif. Law Sch., 1954—, Stanford U. Law Sch., 1977-81; mem., former vice chmn. Nat. Bankruptcy Conf.; former mem. adv. com. on bankruptcy rules Jud. Conf. U.S. Contbr. articles to profl. jours. Served with USNR, 1943-46. Mem. Am. Law Inst., Am. Judicature Soc. Home: 1201 Neil Creek Rd Ashland OR 97520-9778 Office: 3699 Wilshire Blvd Los Angeles CA 90010-2719

TREITEL, DAVID HENRY, financial consultant; b. Lynn, Mass., Apr. 22, 1954; s. Henry David and Lotte (Elkeses) T.; m. Madelynn Drimmer, Sept. 1982 (div. Oct. 1988); m. Amy Gail Granowitz, Apr. 18, 1990. BA in Econs. with honors, Middlebury Coll., 1976; MBA, Columbia U., 1978. Sr. assoc. Simat Helliesen & Eichner, Inc., N.Y.C., 1980-84, 1980-84, v.p., 1984-88, sr. v.p., 1988-90, exec. v.p., 1990-95; pres. Simat Helliesen & Eichner, Inc., N.Y.C., 1995—; bd. dirs. Midwest Express Airlines, Milw. Contbr. articles to profl. jours. Mem. The Wings Club. Republican. Avocations: golf, tournament bridge, travel. Home: 190 E Seventy Second St New York NY 10021 Office: Simat Helliesen & Eichner 90 Park Ave New York NY 10016*

TRELEASE, ALLEN WILLIAM, historian, educator; b. Boulder, Colo., Jan. 31, 1928; s. William, Jr. and Helen (Waldo) T.; children—William C. (dec. 1990), Mary E., John A. A.B., U. Ill., 1950, M.A., 1951; Ph.D., Harvard U., 1955. Mem. faculty Wells Coll., Aurora, N.Y., 1955-67; prof. history Wells Coll., 1965-67, chmn. dept. history and govt., 1963-67; prof. history U. N.C., Greensboro, 1967-94, head dept., 1984-92, prof. emeritus, 1994—. Author: Indian Affairs in Colonial New York: The Seventeenth Century, 1960, White Terror: The Ku Klux Klan Conspiracy and Southern Reconstruction, 1971, Reconstruction: The Great Experiment, 1971, The North Carolina Railroad, 1849-1871, and the Modernization of North Carolina, 1991, Changing Assignments: A Pictorial History of the U. of N.C. at Greensboro, 1991. Mem. Am., So. Hist. assns., Orgn. Am. Historians, Hist. Soc. N.C. (pres. 1986-87), AAUP, Phi Beta Kappa, Phi Kappa Phi, Phi Eta Sigma, Phi Kappa Psi.

TRELEAVEN, PHILLIPS ALBERT, retired publishing company executive; b. Oak Park, Ill., July 20, 1928; s. Harry William and Mary Elizabeth (Gregory) T. BA, Duke U., 1950; AM, Boston U., 1959; DBA (hon.), Unity Coll., 1988; graduate gemologist, Gemological Inst. Am., 1994. With G. K. Hall & Co., Boston, 1956-60, 61-67, 69-79; pres. G. K. Hall & Co., 1969-78, chmn. bd., 1970-78; underwriter mcpl. bonds Scharff & Jones, New Orleans, 1959-61; instr. in polit. economy Boston U., 1967-69; vis. lectr. econs. Unity Coll., 1979-90; owner Odyssey Hill Farms, Thorndike, Maine, 1971-75; pres., pub. Thorndike Press, 1977-87, chmn. bd. dirs., 1988-89; pres. pubs./info. group Sr. Svc. Corp., 1987-89; bd. dirs. Marco Polo Pasta House, Inc., 1989-92, pres., 1991-92. Selectman, Thorndike, 1979-81; trustee Unity Coll., 1985-90, 92—, chmn., 1988-90. Served with AUS, 1950-53. Mem. Phi Beta Kappa. Home: PO Box 40 Thorndike ME 04986-0040 *The biggest blunders I have made in my life have usually resulted from taking myself or my circumstances too seriously.*

TRELFA, RICHARD THOMAS, paper company executive; b. Alpena, Mich., July 5, 1918; s. Fred R. and Mable (Hagen) T.; m. Heidi Brigitte Ruckstuhl, Dec. 3, 1965; children: Thomas W., Barbara E., Jeffrey C., Michael F. B.S., U. Mich., 1940. With Hercules Powder Co., 1941-52, Watervliet Paper Co., Mich., 1952-58; exec. v.p., treas., dir. Perkins-Goodwin Co., Inc., N.Y.C., 1958-70; v.p., treas., chief fin. officer Perkins-Goodwin Co., Inc., 1970, sr. v.p., 1974—82; chmn. bd. Elcon, Inc., Houston, 1983-91, also bd. dirs., 1983-93; vice chmn. bd. B.S. & W Whiteley Ltd., Eng., 1983-88; bd. dirs. B.S. & W Whiteley Ltd.; treas., dir. Kennebec River Pulp & Paper Co., Madison, Maine, 1967-69, chmn. bd., treas., 1969-72, chmn. bd., mem. exec. com., 1972-73, dir., mem. exec. com., 1973-75; pres. Castle & Overton (Can.) Ltd., 1971-82; chmn. bd. EHV Weidmann Industries, Inc., St. Johnsbury, Vt., 1974-84, Franconia Paper Co. Inc., Lincoln, N.H., 1978-80; bd. dirs. Elcon Mgmt. Svcs. Co., chmn. bd. 1984-91, Old Forge Pulp and Paper Co., chmn. bd. 1985-91; N.H. State rpe. to Gen. Ctr., 1990—; water commr. Lisbon, N.H., 1990—, selectman, Lisbon, 1995—. Fellow Am. Soc. Quality Control, TAPPI (former div. chmn., dir.); mem. Paper Industry Mgmt. Assn. (former div. chmn.), Am. Inst. Chem. Engrs., Am. Chem. Soc., Soc. Rheology. Republican. Club: U. Mich. Lodge: Masons. Home: Northey Rd PO Box 245 Lisbon NH 03585-0245 Office: 46 Main St Saint Johnsbury VT 05819-0403

TREMAIN, ALAN, hotel executive; b. Kent, England, Aug. 18, 1935; came to U.S., 1966; s. Archibalt and Elizabeth (Morris) T.; divorced; 1 child, Warren. Grad., Westminster Hotel Sch., 1952, Canterbury Sch. Econs., 1962; LL.B., La Salle Sch., Chgo., 1971. Chef de Pertie Grosvenor House, London, 1954-55; food and beverage mgr. Peninsula, Hong Kong, 1956-57; gen. mgr. Warners Hotel, also The Russley, Christchurch, New Zealand, 1958-64, Menzies, Sydney, Australia, 1964-65, Empress Hotel, Vancouver, B.C., Can., 1966-69; pres. Planned Food Facilities (Internat.) Ltd., Toronto, 1970-72; resident mgr. Sheraton Boston, 1972; mng. dir. Copley Plaza Hotel, Boston, 1972—; chmn. Hotels of Distinction, Inc., Boston. Author: A Guide to the Fine Art of Living, 1963, A Meal for To-Night, 1965. Decorated officer Order Brit. Empire (U.K.); recipient Culinary Merit award from Cercle Epicurien Mondel, Paris, 1956. Fellow Hotel and Catering Inst. (U.K.); founding mem. Internat. Soc. Chefs de Cuisine (chmn. 1954). Clubs: Mason, Montreal Badminton and Squash, The Beach Club, Palm Beach, Les Ambs., London, Rolls Royce Owners. Address: Hotels of Distinction Inc 380 S County Rd 200 Palm Beach FL 33480

TREMAIN, RICHARD DEAN, vocational educator; b. Pittsburg, Kans., Sept. 18, 1954; s. Gerald Dean and Shirley Nell (Dye) T.; m. Judy Elaine Weathers, Dec. 23, 1972; children: Curtis Shane, Kimberly Jane. BS, Pittsburg State U., 1987, MS, 1992. Cert. tchr. secondary, post-secondary welding; cert. welding inspector, cert. bldg. adminstrn. Welder Poli-Tron, Inc., Pittsburg, 1972-73, Atlas Steel, Oswego, Kans., 1973-74, Sauder Tank & Tower, Emporia, Kans., 1974-75, Pittsburg Steel, 1975-77; instr. Kans. State Sch. for Deaf, Olathe, 1977-87, Johnson County Area Vocat. Sch., Olathe, 1987—. Mem. Kans. N.G., 1972-94; mem. adv. com. Johnson County C.C., Overland Park, Kans., 1993—. Recipient Erickson Trophy, N.G. Bur., 1984, Disting. Grad. award N.G. Assn. Kans., 1984; decorated Army Commendation medal (2). Mem. NEA, Kans. Edn. Assn., Nat. Vocat. Assn., Kans. Vocat. Assn. (dist. v.p. 1990-91), Am. Welding Soc. (scholarship com. 1993—), Kans. Sch. for Deaf Edn. Assn. (pres. 1984-85), Masons (3d degree), Kappa Delta Pi. Republican. Avocations: hunting, fishing, water skiing, snow skiing, softball. Home: 2325 W Post Oak Rd Olathe KS 66061-5064 Office: Johnson County Tech Edn Ctr 311 E Park St Olathe KS 66061-5407

TREMAINE, SCOTT DUNCAN, astrophysicist; b. Toronto, Ont., Can., May 25, 1950; s. Vincent Joseph and Beatrice Delphine (Sharp) T. BSc, McMaster U., Hamilton, Ont., 1971; PhD, Princeton U., 1975. Postdoctoral fellow Calif. Inst. Tech., Pasadena, 1975-77; rsch. assoc. Inst. Astronomy, Cambridge, Eng., 1977-78; long-term mem. Inst. for Advanced Study, Princeton, N.J., 1978-81; assoc. prof. MIT, Cambridge, 1981-85; prof., dir. Canadian Inst. for Theoretical Astrophysics U. Toronto, 1985—. Author: Galactic Dynamics, 1987; contbr. articles to profl. jours. E.W.R. Steacie fellow Natural Scis. and Engring. Rsch. Coun., 1988; recipient H.B. Warner prize Am. Astron. Soc., 1983, Steacie prize, 1989, C.S. Beals award Canadian Astron. Soc., 1990, Rutherford medal Royal Soc. Can., 1990. Fellow Royal Soc. London, Royal Soc. Can.; mem. Am. Acad. Arts and Scis. (fgn. hon.). Office: U Toronto-CITA McLennan Lab, 60 St George St, Toronto, ON Canada M5S 3H8

TREMBLAY, ANDRE GABRIEL, lawyer, educator; b. Jonquiere, Que., Can., Nov. 10, 1937; s. Jean-Charles T. and Julienne (Tremblay) Laberge; children: Jean-Francois, Frederic, Alexandre Reynold. B.A., U. Laval-Que. Can., 1959, LL.L., 1962; D.E.S. in Law, U. Ottawa-Ont. Can., 1964, LL.D., 1966. Bar: Que. 1963. Asst., law U. Ottawa, 1966-70; assoc. U. Montreal, Que., 1970-75, prof., 1972—, pres. Gen. Assn. Profs.; dir. Pub. Law Ctr., Que., 1972-76, vice dean Sch. Law, 1982-86; dir. grad. studies U. Ottawa, 1968-70; pres. Com. on Human Rights, Montreal, 1981—; legal adv. to bar, govts., law firms, cos. Can., 1972—; sr. Constl. adviser to Que. Govt., 1986-92; pres. Prof.'s Union, U. Montreal, 1995. Author: Les competences legislatives, 1967 (1st prize Govt. of Que. 1968), Precis de droit municipal, 1973, Precis de droit constitutionnel, 1982, Droitconstitutionnel-Principles, 1993, La Revision Constitution Nelle, 1995; contbr. articles, chpts. to legal publs. Sec. Polit. Chmn., Que. Liberal Party, Montreal, 1977-81; mem. observer's mission, Internat. Commn. Jurists, Geneva, 1981—, mem. coun. Can. sect., Ottawa, 1981—; v.p. Can. Human Rights Found., Montreal, 1982—. Mem. Assn. Can. Law Tchrs. (pres. Ottawa Chpt. 1974-75). Christian Scientist. Office: Faculty Law U Montreal, CP 6201 succ A, Montreal, PQ Canada H3C 3T1

TREMBLAY, ANDRÉ-MARIE, physicist; b. Montreal, Que., Can., Jan. 2, 1953; m. Marié à Guylaine Séguin; children: Noémie, Rachel. BSc, U. Montreal, 1974; PhD, MIT, 1978. With Energie Atomique du Can. Limitée, 1973-74, MIT, Boston, 1974-75, Inst. de Recherche de l'Hydro-Que., 1976, Cornell U., Ithaca, N.Y., 1978-80; prof. physics U. Sherbrooke, Que., 1980—, dir. Rsch. Ctr. Physics of Solids, 1991—; cons. Cornell U., 1981, Ohio State U., 1982, IBM, 1984; vis. scientist Cornell U., 1986-87; vis. rsch. physicist Inst. for Theoretical Physics, Santa Barbara, Calif., 1989, 96; vis. scientist Brookhaven (N.Y.) Nat. Lab, 1984; assoc. prof. U. Provence, France, 1982, 83. Contbr. articles to profl. pubs. Recipient Herzberg medal Can. Assn. Physics, Steacie prize Natural Scis. and Engring. Rsch. Coun., 1987; Killam fellow, 1992-94. Mem. Can. Inst. Advanced Rsch. Office: Sherbrooke U, Dept Physics, Sherbrooke, PQ Canada J1K 2R1

TREMBLAY, MARC ADÉLARD, anthropologist, educator; b. Les Eboulements, Que., Can., Apr. 24, 1922; s. Willie and Laurette (Tremblay) T.; m. Jacqueline Cyr, Dec. 27, 1949; children: Geneviève, Lorraine, Marc, Colette, Dominique, Suzanne. A.B., U. Montreal, 1944, L.S.A., 1948; M.A., Laval U., 1950; Ph.D., Cornell U., 1954; PhD (hon.), Ottawa U., 1982, Guelph U., 1983, U. N. B.C., 1994, Carleton U., 1995. Research asso. Cornell U., 1953-56; mem. faculty Laval U., 1956-93, prof. anthropology, 1963-68, 81-93, prof. emeritus, 1994, vice dean social scis., 1968-71, dean Grad. Sch., 1971-79, also mem. univ. council.; pres. Quebec Coun. Social Rsch., 1987-91; dir. Inuit and Circupolar Study Group, Laval U., 1991-93. Author 25 books and monographs in social scis., about 200 articles. Recipient Que. Lit. prize, 1965, Innis-Gerin prize Royal Soc. Can., 1979, Molson prize Can. Coun., 1987, Prix Marcel Vincent ACFAS, 1988, Contbn. exceptionnelle Societé de sociologie et d'anthropolotie, 1990, Esdras Minville award Soc. St.-Jean Baptiste, 1991; named Officer of Order of Can., 1980, Gt. Officer of Order of Que., 1995; named to Internat. Order of Merit, Internat. Biog. Inst., Cambridge, Eng., 1990. Mem. Royal Soc. Can. (pres. 1981-84), Acad. des Scis. Morales et Politiques (sec.), Rsch. Inst. Pub. Policy, Am. Anthrop. Assn. (past fellow), Can. Soc. Applied Anthropology, Can. Sociology and Anthropology Assn. (founding pres.), Can. Ethnology Soc. (past pres.), Assn. Can. Univs. for Northern Studies (past pres.), Assn. Internat. Sociology, Societe des savants et sci. Can. (v.p.). Home: 835 N Orléans St, Sainte Foy, PQ Canada G1X 3J4 Office: Laval Univ, Dept Anthropology, Quebec, PQ Canada G1K 7P4

TREMBLAY, MARY DENISE, administrator, educator; b. Lowell, Mass., Aug. 29, 1951; d. Romeo D. and Marion A. (Metivier) Martel; m. Richard J. Tremblay; children: Richard Jr., Christopher, Miriam. BA in Edn., U. Mass., 1973; MEd, Rivier Coll., 1990. Instr. U. Mass., Lowell; instr. Spl. Needs Program, Lowell, asst. dir., dir.; tchr. St. Joseph's Sch., Lowell; dir. PMA Devel. Ctr., Hudson, N.H., Chapel Sch., Nashua, N.H.; mem. adv. bd. Chapel Sch., N.H. Tech. Inst., Nashua, Child Care Network, Nashua. Mem. Nat. Assn. Edn. Young Children, N.H. Assn. Edn. Young Children (bd. sec. 1994-95, mem. adv. bd.), Assn. Childhood Edn. Internat. Avocations: painting, crafts, archery, antiques, music. Office: Chapel Sch 3 Lutheran Dr Nashua NH 03063-2909

TREMBLAY, RICHARD E., psychology educator; b. Nov. 23, 1944. BA, U. Ottawa, Can., 1966; MPsed, U. Montreal, 1970; PhD, U. London, 1976. Asst. prof. U. Montreal, 1976-81, assoc. prof., 1981-86, prof., 1986—; psychologist St. Charles Psychiat. Hosp., Joliette, Can., 1966-69, Boscoville, Montreal, Can., 1967-70, Phillippe Pinel Psychiat. Inst., Montreal, 1970-73; chmn. Sch. of Psycho-Edn., Faculty of Arts and Scis., U. Montreal, 1986-90; invited prof. ethology lab. U. Rennes I, 1993-94, dept. psychology U. Jyväskylä, Finland, 1991; invited scientist psychophysiology lab. U. Franche-Com., 1982-83; presenter in field. Author: (with others) Preventing Antisocial Behavior from Birth to Adolescence, 1992, Les enfants agressifs: Perspective Development Interculturelle, 1992, Famille, Inadaption et Intervention, 1991, Human Development and Criminal Behavior: New Ways of Advancing Knowledge, 1992, Les Relations Entre Enfants, 1988, Le Traitement des Adolescents Deltingquants, 1985, Ethologie de Development de l'enfant, 1985, Face to Face with Giftedness, 1983; contbr. chpts. to books and numerous articles to profl. jours. Recipient Beccaria award Quebec Soc. of Criminology, 1988; recipient numerous grants. Mem. AAAS, Internat. Soc. for the Study of Behavioral Devel. (exec. com. 1994—), Internat. Soc. for Rsch. on Agression (coun. mem. 1992-96), Am. Soc. of Criminology, Assn. Canadienne-Française pour l'Avancement des Scis., Can. Psychol. Assn., European Assn. for Psychology and Law, Internat. soc. for Human Theology, N.Y. Acad. Scis., soc. for Rsch. in Child Devel. Office: Rsch Unit on Children's Psych, 750 Gouin E / CP6128 A, Montreal, PQ Canada H2C 1A6

TREMBLAY, RODRIGUE, economics educator; b. Matane, Que., Can., Oct. 13, 1939; s. George and Germaine (St. Louis) T.; m. Carol Howard, Sept. 5, 1964; children: Jean-Paul, Alain, Joanne. BA, Laval U., Quebec City, 1961; BS in Econs., U. de Montreal (Que.), 1963; MA in Econs., Stanford U., 1965, PhD in Econs., 1968. Prof. Univ. de Montreal, 1967—; mem. nat. assembly Parliament of Que., 1976-81; min. industry and commerce Govt. of Que., 1976-79; mem. arbitrage panel Can.-U.S. Free Trade Agreement Ottawa (Can.) and Washington, 1989—. Woodrow Wilson Found. fellow, 1964-65. Mem. N.Am. Econs. and Fin. Assn. (pres. 1986-87). Office: U Montreal, Dept of Economics, Montreal, PQ Canada H3C 3J7

TREMBLY, CRISTY, television executive; b. Oakland, Md., July 11, 1958; d. Charles Dee and Mary Louise (Cassidy) T. BA in Russian, German and Linguistics cum laude, W.Va. U., 1978, BS in Journalism, 1978, MS in Broadcast Journalism, 1979; advanced cert. travel, West L.A. Coll., 1982; advanced cert. recording engring., Soundmaster Schs., North Hollywood, Calif., 1985. Videotape engr. Sta. WWVU-TV, Morgantown, W.Va., 1976-80; announcer, engr. Sta. WVVW Radio, Grafton, W.Va., 1979; tech. dir., videotape supr. Sta. KMEX-TV, L.A., 1980-85; broadcast supr. Sta. KADY-TV, Oxnard, Calif., 1988-89; news tech. dir. Sta. KVEA-TV, Glendale, Calif., 1985-89; asst. editor, videotape technician CBS TV Network, Hollywood, Calif., 1989-90; videotape supr. Sta. KCBS-TV, Hollywood, 1990-91, mgr. electronic news gathering ops., 1991-92; studio mgr., engr.-in-charge CBS TV Network, Hollywood, 1992—; radio operator KJ6BX Malibu Disaster Comm., 1987—. Producer (TV show) The Mountain Scene, 1976-78. Sr. orgn. pres. Children of the Am. Revolution, Malibu, Calif., 1992—; chmn. adminstrv. coun. Malibu United Meth. Ch., 1994-96; sec., mem. adv. com. Tamassee (S.C.) Sch., 1992—; vol. Ch. Coun., L.A. Riot Rebldg., Homeless shelter work, VA Hosps., Mus. docent; sponsor 3 overseas foster children. Recipient Outstanding Young Woman of Am., 1988, Asst. editor Emmy award Young and the Restless, 1989-90, Golden Mike award Radio/TV News assn., 1991, 92. Mem. DAR (state chmn. jr. membership 1987-88, state chmn. scholarships 1992-94, state chmn. jr. contest 1994-96, others, Malibu chpt. regent 1991, state chmn. motion pictures radio and TV Calif. 1988-90, Mex. 1990—, Nat. Outstanding Jr. 1993, nat. vice chmn. broadcast media 1995—), Am. Women in Radio and TV (so. Calif. bd. 1984-85, 93-95, pres.-elect 1995-96), Soc. Profl. Journalists, Women in Comms., Travelers Century Club (program chair 1987—), Acad. TV Arts and Scis. (pres. 1996-97, exec. com. electronic prodn. 1992—), Mensa (life), Beta Sigma Phi. Democrat. Methodist. Avocations: singing, cooking, travel, genealogy, languages. Home: 2901 Searidge St Malibu CA 90265-2969 Office: CBS TV City 7800 Beverly Blvd Los Angeles CA 90036-2165

TREMBLY, DENNIS MICHAEL, musician; b. Long Beach, Calif., Apr. 16, 1947; s. Fred Lel and Jewel Fern (Bouldin) T. Student, Juilliard Sch. Music, 1965-68. Asst. adj. prof. U. So. Calif., 1981—. Bass player, 1959—, with Los Angeles Philharmonic Orch., 1970-73, co-prin. bass, 1973—. Recipient 2d pl. Internat. Solo Bass competition, Isle of Man, 1978. Mem. Internat. Soc. Bassists. Office: L A Philharm Orch 135 N Grand Ave Los Angeles CA 90012-3013

TREML, VLADIMIR GUY, economist, educator; b. Kharkov, USSR, Mar. 27, 1929; came to U.S., 1950, naturalized, 1953; s. Guy Alexey and Lydia Vladimir (Timofeev) T.; m. Emma Miro, July 12, 1952; children—Irene Treml Cagney, Tatiana, Alexey. B.A. in Econs, Bklyn. Coll., 1955; M.A. in Econs, Columbia U., 1956; Ph.D. in Econs, U. N.C., 1963. Dept. supr. Bache & Co., N.Y.C., 1953-58; research asso. Inst. for Social Scis., U. N.C., Chapel Hill, 1958-61; asso. prof. econs. Franklin and Marshall Coll., 1961-66; research asso. Inst. Study USSR, Munich, Germany, 1966-67; prof. econs. Duke U., 1967—; dir. Ctr. for Slavic Studies U.S. Dept. Edn. of Duke U., 1991—; cons. in field; expert Dept. Commerce, other fed. agys., 1971—; vis. Ford research prof. U. Calif., Berkeley, 1984-85; vis. research prof. U. Hokkaido, Sapporo, Japan, 1985. Author: (with others) Structure of the Soviet Economy, 1972, Input-Output Analysis and the Soviet Economy, 1975; contbr. reports to pubs. of Joint Econ. Com., U.S. Congress; contbr. articles to profl. publs.; editor: Soviet Economic Statistics, 1972; editor, contbg. author: Studies in Soviet Input-Output Analysis, 1977, Alcohol in the USSR, 1982; contbg. editor: Soviet Economy Jour. Trustee Nat. Council for Soviet and East European Research, Inc., Washington, 1978-84. Served with USMC, 1951-53. Ford Found. grantee, 1972-81, Dept. Def.-Advanced Rsch. Project Agy. grantee, 1975-76, Dept. State grantee, 1976-77, Dept. Def. grantee, 1985-90, Georgetown U. grantee, 1984-86, Olin Found. grantee, 1989; Fulbright fellow Moscow U., 1992. Mem. So. Econ. Assn., Am. Econ. Assn., Assn. Comparative Econ. Studies (exec. com. 1972-74), Am. Assn. Advancement Slavic Studies, So. Conf. on Slavic Studies (pres. 1977-78), Phi Beta Kappa. Democrat. Eastern Orthodox. Home: 603 Longleaf Dr Chapel Hill NC 27514-3039

TREMPER, KEVIN KEEFE, anesthesiologist, educator; b. Phila., Jan. 5, 1948; s. Henry Stever and Sheila Tremper; m. Amy Louise Opheim, Dec. 19, 1987; children: Theodore Tyler, Connor Keefe. BSChemE, U. Denver, 1971; MS in Chem. Engring., U. Calif., Berkeley, 1973, PhD in Chem. Engring., 1975; MD, U. Calif., Irvine, 1978. Diplomate Am. Bd. Anesthesiologists; lic. physician, Mich., Calif. Intern/surg. resident Harbor/UCLA Med. Ctr., 1978-79, surg. ICU rsch. fellow, 1979-81; resident in anesthesiology UCLA

Sch. Medicine, 1981-83; asst. prof. anesthesiology U. Calif., Irvine, 1983-84, assoc. prof., chmn. dept. anesthesiology, 1984-90; prof., chmn. dept. anesthesiology U. Mich., Ann Arbor, 1991—; extensive lectr. in field. Editl. bd. Anesthesiology News, Critical Care Medicine, Jour. Clin. Monitoring, Jour. Clin. Anesthesia, Seminars in Anesthesia, Jour. Intensive Care Monitoring, 1986-88; reviewer for AIChE Jour., Anesthesiology, Anesthesia and Analgesia, Chest, Critical Care Medicine, IEEE Transactions, Jour. Applied Psychology, Jour. Clin. Engring., Jour. Clin. Anesthesia, Pediatrics, Pediatric Rsch., Obstetrics and Gynecology, Med. Instrumentation, Sugery; contbr. 89 articles and 500 abstracts to profl. jours., 33 chpts. to books; author: Perfluorochem. Oxygen Transport, 1985, Advances in Oxygen Monitoring, 1987. With USAR, 1971-77. Fellow Am. Coll. Chest Physicians, Am. Coll. Anesthesiologists; mem. AMA, Am. Soc. Anesthesiologists (chmn. subcom. on equip., monitoring and engring. tech. 1992—, adj. mem. com. on sci. papers 1992—), Internat. Anesthesia Rsch. Soc., Mich. Soc. Anesthesiologists, Internat. Soc. of Oxygen Transport to Tissue, Am. Soc. Critical Care Anesthesiologists, Calif. Med. Assn. (sci. adv. panel 1984-90), Orange County Anesthesia Soc. (treas. 1985-86, pres. 1986-87), Alpha Omega Alpha. Republican. Home: 7227 Pleasant Lake Rd Ann Arbor MI 48103 Office: U of Mich Med Sch 1301 Catherine St Ann Arbor MI 48109-0600

TRENBERTH, KEVIN EDWARD, atmospheric scientist; b. Christchurch, New Zealand, Nov. 8, 1944; came to U.S., 1977; s. Edward Maurice and Ngaira Ivy (Eyre) T.; m. Gail Neville Thompson, Mar. 21, 1970; children: Annika Gail, Angela Dawn. BSc with honors, U. Canterbury, Christchurch, 1966; ScD, MIT, 1972. Meteorologist New Zealand Meteorol. Service, Wellington, 1966-76, supt. dynamic meteorology, 1976-77; assoc. prof. meteorology U. Ill., Urbana, 1977-82, prof., 1982-84; scientist Nat. Ctr. Atmospheric Research, Boulder, Colo., 1984-86, sr. scientist, 1986—, leader empirical studies group, 1987, head sect. climate analysis, 1987—; dep. dir. climate and global dynamics divsn. Nat. Ctr. Atmospheric Rsch., Boulder, Colo., 1991-95; mem. joint sci. com. for world climate programme, com. climate changes and the ocean Tropical Oceans Global Atmosphere Program Sci. Steering Group, 1990-94; mem. Climate Variability and Predictability Sci. Steering Group, 1995—, co-chair, 1996—. Editor: Climate System Modeling, 1992, Earth Interactions, 1996—; contbr. articles to profl. jours. Grantee NSF, NOAA, NASA. Fellow Am. Meteorol. Soc. (editor sci. jour. 1981-86, com. chmn. 1985-87, Editor's award 1989), AAAS (coun. del. sect. atmosphere and hydrosphere sci. 1993—), Royal Soc. New Zealand (hon.); mem. NAS (earth scis. com. 1982-85, tropical oceans global atmosphere adv. panel 1984-87, polar rsch. bd. 1986-90, climate rsch. com. 1987-90, global oceans atmosphere land sys. panel 1994—), Atmosphere Obs. Panel of Globe Climate Observing Sys., Meterol. Soc. New Zealand. Home: 1445 Landis Ct Boulder CO 80303-1122 Office: Nat Ctr Atmospheric Research PO Box 3000 Boulder CO 80307-3000

TRENCH, WILLIAM FREDERICK, mathematics educator; b. Trenton, N.J., July 31, 1931; s. George Daniel and Anna Elizabeth (Taylor) T.; m. Lucille Ann Marasco, Dec. 26, 1954 (div. Dec. 1978); children: Joseph William, Randolph Clifford, John Frederick, Gina Margaret; m. Beverly Joan Busenshut, Nov. 22, 1980. B.A. in Math., Lehigh U., 1953; A.M., U. Pa., 1955, Ph.D., 1958. Applied mathematician Moore Sch. Elec. Engring., U. Pa., 1953-56; with Gen. Electric Corp., Phila., 1956-57, Philco Corp., Phila., 1957-59, RCA, Moorestown, N.J., 1959-64; assoc. prof. math. Drexel U., Phila., 1964-67; prof. Drexel U., 1967-86; Andrew G. Cowles disting. prof. math. Trinity U., San Antonio, 1986—. Author: Advanced Calculus, 1971, (with Bernard Kolman) Elementary Multivariable Calculus, 1971, Multivariable Calculus with Linear Algebra and Series, 1972; contbr. rsch. articles in numerical analysis, ordinary differential equations, smoothing, prediction and spl. functions to profl. jours. Mem. Math. Assn. Am., Am. Math. Soc., Soc. Indsl. and Applied Math., Phi Beta Kappa, Eta Kappa Nu, Pi Mu Epsilon. Achievements include development of Trench's Algorithm for inversion of finite Toeplitz matrices, of fast algorithms for computing eigenvalues of structured matrices, of asymptotic theory of solutions of nonlinear functional differential equations under mild integral smallness conditions. Home: 211 W Rosewood Ave San Antonio TX 78212-2332 also: 413 Lake Dr Divide CO 80814-9612 Office: Dept Math Trinity U 215 Stadium Dr San Antonio TX 78212

TRENNEPOHL, GARY LEE, finance educator, consultant; b. Detroit, Dec. 6, 1946; s. Leo Donald and Wilma Mae (Tiensvold) T.; m. Sandra K. Yeager, June 9, 1968; children: Paige E., Adrienne A. BS, U. Tulsa, 1968; MBA, Utah State U., 1971; PhD, Tex. Tech U., 1976. Asst. prof. aero. studies Tex. Tech U., Lubbock, 1972-74; asst. prof. fin. Ariz. State U., Tempe, 1977-80, assoc. prof., 1980-82; prof. U. Mo., Columbia, 1982-86, dir. Sch. Bus., 1984-86; prof. fin., dept. head Tex. A&M U., College Station, 1986-91, assoc. dean Coll. Bus., 1991-93, Peters prof. fin., 1992—, exec. assoc. dean, 1994-95; dean Coll. Bus. Okla. State U., Stillwater, 1995—; mem. faculty Options Inst., Chgo. Bd. Options Exchange, 1987—. Author: An Introduction to Financial Management, 1984, Investment Management, 1993; assoc. editor Jour. Fin. Research, 1983—, Rev. Bus. Studies, 1992—; contbr. chpts. Encyclopedia of Investments; contbr. articles to profl. jours. Capt. USAF, 1968-72. Decorated Commendation medal with oak leaf cluster, Vietnam Svc. medal. Mem. Fin. Mgmt. Assn. (v.p. program 1993, pres. 1993-94), So. Fin. Assn., Southwestern Fin. Assn. (bd. dirs. 1983-84, pres. 1986), Midwest Fin. Assn. (bd. dirs. 1985-89). Republican. Lutheran. Office: Okla State U 201 Business Bldg Stillwater OK 74078

TRENT, CLYDE NATHANIEL, legal assistant; b. Pitts., Nov. 25, 1945; s. Isaiah and Grace Sarah (Massie) T.; m. Mary Julia Kelly, Nov. 22, 1974; children: Robert, Nathaniel. BA, U. Pitts., 1979; paralegal cert., Pa. State U., 1984; AS, C.C. Allegheny, Monroeville, Pa., 1986; paralegal cert., U. Pitts., 1987. Letter carrier U.S. Postal Svc., Pitts., 1968-80; legal asst. Strassburger & McKenna, Pitts., 1980-85, Feldstein Law Office, Pitts., 1985-90, Elderly Citizens Ctr., Mt. Lebanon, Pa., 1990-91; claims examiner Office Econ. Security, Pitts., 1991—; adv. bd. mem. Legal Intellect, Inc., Monroeville, 1988—. Mem. Western Pa. Hist. Soc., Pitts., 1993—. With U.S. Army, 1965-67. Mem. Am. Criminal Justice, Pitts. Paralegal Assn. (com. 1990), Pa. State Alumni (vol. 1986-94), Lambda Alpha Epsilon (pres. 1979-80), Phi Theta Kappa. Avocations: horseback riding, student pilot, cooking, historical research.

TRENT, DARRELL M., academic and corporate executive; b. Neosho, Mo., Aug. 2, 1938; s. Clarence Melvin and Edna Ruth T.; m. Judith Mercy Turner; children: Darrell Michael, Derek Montgomery, Mercy Ruth. A.B., Stanford U., 1961; postgrad., Internat. Law Sch., The Hague, Netherlands, summer 1961, Wharton Grad. Sch. Bus., U. Pa., summer 1962; M.B.A., Columbia U., 1964. Owner, mgr. Trent Enterprises, Kans. and Mo., 1963-66; pres., chief exec. officer N.Am. Carmen, Ltd., Del., 1965-68, Assoc. Stores, Inc., Okla., 1967-69, Plaza Supermarkets, Inc., Kans., 1966-69, Food Service, Inc., Kans., 1966-69, Supermarkets, Inc., Kans., 1966-69, Acton Devel. Co., Inc., Kans., 1966-81; research/writer Nixon for Pres., 1968; staff dir. for personnel Presdl. Transition, 1968-69; commr. Property Mgmt. and Disposal Service, GSA, 1969; dep. asst. to Pres. U.S., 1969-70; exec. dir. Property Rev. Bd., Exec. Office of Pres., 1969-73; dep. dir. Office Emergency Preparedness, 1970-72, acting dir., 1973; mem. Cost of Living Council, 1973, Oil Policy Com., 1973; chmn. Joint Bd. Fuel Supply and Fuel Transp., 1973; mem. NSC, 1973; chmn. Pres.'s Adv. Council CD, 1973; U.S. mem. NATO Sr. Civil Emergency Planning Com., 1973; sr. research fellow Hoover Inst., Stanford U., 1974-81, 89—, assoc. dir., 1974-81, bd. overseers, 1985-89; dep. campaign mgr. Citizens for Reagan, 1976; dep. campaign mgr., cons. Reagan for Pres. Com., 1979-80, sr. policy advisor, 1980; dir. Office Policy Coordination, Presdl. Transition, 1980-81; U.S. alt. rep. Nato Com. Challenges of Modern Soc., 1982-83; dep. sec. U.S. Dept. Transp., 1981-82, acting sec., 1982-83; chmn. U.S. del. European Civil Aviation Com. with rank ambassador, 1983-88; chmn. Action Devel. Corp., Inc., 1988—; chmn., chief exec. officer Rollins Environ. Svcs., Inc., 1983-88, TEC Systems, Inc., 1990-91, Clean Earth Techs., Inc., 1992—; chmn. Fed. Home Loan Bank Pitts., 1983-91; cons. ACDA, 1974-81, HUD, 1974, Dept. Commerce, 1974-76; bd. advisors Chronicle Info. Svcs., Inc., 1984-87. Author: The U.S. and Transnational Terrorism, 1980, Transportation: Policy, Goals, Accomplishments, 1984; co-author: Terrorism: Threat, Reality, Response, 1979; contbr. articles to profl. pubis. Bd. regents Pepperdine U., 1985—; bd. dirs. Found. Teach Econs., 1988-90; dep. chmn. Ronald Reagan Presdl. Found., 1985-88. Mem. Mt. Pelerin Soc. Republican. Methodist. Club: Bohemian. Office: 1325 N Pegram St Alexandria VA 22305

TRENT, DONALD STEPHEN, thermo fluids engineer; b. Cloverdale, Oreg., Mar. 29, 1935; s. James Charles and Emma (Bauer) T.; (div. Jan., 1986); children: Steve, Lynn Trent Woolridge, Greg; m. Alta Mae Brown, Aug. 20, 1994. BSAE, Oregon State U., 1962, MSME, 1964, PhD in Mech. Engring., 1972. Chief scientist Battelle Meml. Inst., Richland, Wash., 1965-96; retired, 1996; courtesy prof. Oreg. State U., Corvallis, 1987—; rsch. affiliate MIT, Cambridge, Mass., 1990—; mem. tchg. staff Wash. State U., Richland, 1991—; vis. U. Md., College Park, 1995—. Sgt. U.S. Army, 1958-61. Recipient Fed. Lab. Consortium award, 1992. Mem. ASME, Phi Kappa Phi, Sigma Xi. Achievements include patent on a heat pipe; 2 copyrights on computational fluid dynamics software. Home: 721 Lynnwood Loop Richland WA 99352

TRENT, LUTHER E., airport executive, state agency executive. Dir. airports Okalhoma City Dept. Airports. Office: Will Rogers World Airport 7100 Terminal Dr Box 937 Oklahoma City OK 73159*

TRENT, ROBERT HAROLD, business educator; b. Norfolk, Va., Aug. 3, 1933; s. Floyd Murton and Myrtle Eugenia (White) T.; m. Joanne Bell, Aug. 17, 1951; 1 child, John Thomas. B.S., U. Richmond, 1963; Ph.D., U. N.C., 1968. Asst. prof. U. N.C., Chapel Hill, 1968-69; assoc. prof. commerce McIntire Sch. Commerce U. Va., Charlottesville, 1970-74, prof. commerce, 1975-84, Ralph A. Beeton prof. free enterprise, 1985-91; C. & P. Telephone Co. prof. commerce U. Va., Charlottesville, 1991—. Co-author: Marketing Decision Making, 1976, 4th edit., 1988; editor: Developments in Management Information Systems, 1974. Mem. Inst. Mgmt. Scis., Soc. Info. Mgmt., Assn. Comp. Machinery, Decision Scis. Inst., Beta Gamma Sigma, Omicron Delta Kappa. Office: U Va Monroe Hall Charlottesville VA 22903

TRENT, WARREN C., mechanical engineer; b. Boswell, Okla., Feb. 22, 1921; s. Clem and Fannie Edora (Greer) T.; m. Ruth Magdalene Potts, Apr. 2, 1948; 1 child, Paul Dudley. BSME, Okla. State U., 1943; MSME, Purdue U., 1948. Engr. Boeing Airplane Co., Seattle, 1943-45; instr. Okla. State U., Stillwater, 1946-47; rsch. engr. Kans. State U., Manhattan, 1948-51; mgr. sect. LTV Aerospace, Dallas, 1951-65; dir. engring. tech. McDonnell Douglas, St. Louis, 1965-77; owner Trent Assocs., Tyler, Tex., 1977-93; CEO Trent Techs., Inc., Tyler, 1993—; cons. Rockwell Internat., El Segundo, Calif., 1982-87; lectr. Navy Aviation Exec. Inst., Washington, 1973-76. Patentee in field. Arbitrator Better Bus. Bur., Tyler, 1985—. With USN, 1945-46. Fellow AIAA (assoc.); mem. ASHRAE, Tex. Profl. Engrs., Mo. Profl. Engrs. Republican. Baptist. Avocations: bridge, golf. Home: 1410 Woodlands Dr Tyler TX 75703-5718 Office: Trent Techs Inc 535 WSW Loop 323 Ste 301 Tyler TX 75701

TRENT, WENDELL CAMPBELL, business owner; b. Sneedville, Tenn., Nov. 1, 1940; s. William Campbell and Inez Hall (Daugherty) T.; m. Donna Lee Posey, May 31, 1964. BA, Berea Coll, 1963; MPH, UCLA, 1971; D in Pub. Adminstrn., Nova U., 1980. Asst. USPHS, UCLA, 1969; pres. Lockwood MacDonald Hosp., Petoskey, Mich., 1971-75, Allegan Gen. Hosp., Mich., 1975-79, Bethany Meth. Hosp., Chgo. 1979-84, St. Ansgar Hosp., Moorhead, Minn., 1984-85; pres. Meml. Hosp., Lawrenceville, Ill., 1985-89; midwest devel. dir. Brim Healthcare, 1989-90; prin. Larson & Trent Assocs., Sumner, Ill., 1990—; mem. Gov.'s Health Care Task Force; mem. Govs. Com. on Healthcare. Contbr. articles to profl. jours. Maj. USAF, 1963-69. Decorated Bronze Star. Fellow Am. Coll. Hosp. Adminstrs. (article of year com.); mem. Rotary, Kiwanis. Republican. Presbyterian. Avocations: photography, amateur radio. Home: RR 1 Box 120 Sumner IL 62466-9704

TREPPLER, IRENE ESTHER, state senator; b. St. Louis County, Mo., Oct. 13, 1926; d. Martin H. and Julia C. (Bender) Hagemann; student Meramec Community Coll., 1972; m. Walter J. Treppler, Aug. 18, 1950; children: John M., Steven A., Diane V. Anderson, Walter W. Payroll chief USAF Aero. Chart Plant, 1943-51; enumerator U.S. Census Bur., St. Louis, 1960, crew leader, 1970; mem. Mo. Ho. of Reps., Jefferson City, 1972-84; mem. Mo. Senate, Jefferson City, 1985—; chmn. Minority Caucus, 1991-92. ActiveGravois Twp. Rep. Club, Concord Twp. Rep. Club; alt. del. Rep. Nat. Conv., 1976, 84. Recipient Spirit Enterprise award Mo. C. of C., 1992, Appreciation award Mo. State Med. Assn., Nat. Otto Nuttli Earthquake Hazard Mitigation award, 1993, Disting. Legislator award Cmty. Colls. Mo., 1995; named Concord Twp. Rep. of Yr., 1992. Mem. Nat. Order Women Legislators (rec. sec. 1981-82, pres. 1985), Nat. Fedn. Rep. Women. Mem. Evangelical Ch. Office: Mo State Senate Rm 433 Jefferson City MO 65101

TRESCOTT, SARA LOU, water resources engineer; b. Frederick, Md., Nov. 17, 1954; d. Norton James and Mabel Elizabeth (Hall) T.; m. R. Jeffrey Franklin, Oct. 8, 1983. AA, Catonsville C.C., Balt., 1974; BA in Biol. Sci., U. Md., Balt., 1980. Sanitarian Md. Dept. Health & Mental Hygiene, Greenbelt, 1982; indsl. hygienist Md. Dept. Licensing & Regualtion, Balt., 1982-85; from water resources engr. to chief dredging div. Md. Dept. Natural Resources, Annapolis, 1985-92; chief navigation div. Md. Dept. Natural Resources, Stevensville, 1992-96, chief ops. & maintenance, 1996—; chair adv. bd. EEO, Annapolis, 1990-92; tech. com. Nat. Mgmt. Info. Systems, Balt., 1983. Contbr. articles to profl. jours. Mem. ASCE, County Engrs. Assn. Md. Democrat. Achievements include research in beneficial uses of dredged material; development of technology for hydrographic surveying, providing Md. with an improved waterway transportation network. Home: PO Box 22 Woodbine MD 21797-0022 Office: DNR Navigation div 305 Marine Academy Dr Stevensville MD 21666-2859

TRESELER, KATHLEEN MORRISON, retired nursing educator; b. Tacoma, Wash., Apr. 28, 1925; d. Charles T. and Elizabeth M. (McDermott) Morrison; m. Donald K. Treseler, July, 1949; children: Michael S., C. Maureen, Patrick A. BS, Seattle Coll., 1946; MSN, U. Wash., 1966. Prof. Seattle U. Sch. Nursing, 1968-91, prof. emeritus, 1991—. Author: Clinical Laboratory and Diagnostic Tests, 1982, 3d edit., 1995. Home: 17401 17th Pl NE Shoreline WA 98155-5201

TRESMONTAN-STITT, OLYMPIA DAVIS, clinical counselor, psychotherapy educator, consultant; b. Boston, Nov. 27, 1925; d. Peter Konstantin and Mary (Hazimanolis) Davis; B.S., Simmons Coll., 1946; M.A., Wayne State U., 1960; Ph.D. (Schaefer Found. grantee), U. Calif., Berkeley, 1971; m. Dion Marc Tresmontan, Sept. 15, 1957 (dec. Mar. 1961); m. 2d, Robert Baker Stitt, Mar. 21, 1974. Lic. clin. counselor. Child welfare worker San Francisco Dept. Social Service, 1964-66; sensitivity tng. NSF Sci. Curriculum Improvement Study, U. Calif., Berkeley, 1967-68; individual practice psychol. counseling, San Francisco, 1971-92, individual practice clin. counselor, Morrill, Maine, 1995—; dir. Studio Ten Services, San Francisco, Promise for Children, San Francisco, 1981-88; tchr. U. Calif. extension at San Francisco, 1971-72, Chapman Coll. Grad. Program in Counseling, Travis AFB, 1971-74; clin. cons. Childworth Learning Ctr., San Francisco, 1976-80; cons. project rape response Queen's Bench Found., San Francisco, 1977; adjunct instr. Unity Coll., Maine, 1992; adv. bd. Childrens' Multicultural Mus., San Francisco, 1988-92. Active Women's Heritage Mus., Palo Alto, Calif., 1991-92, Friends of Belfast (Maine) Free Libr., 1993—, Friends of the San Francisco Pub. Libr., 1971-92, 95—; bd. dirs. Childworth Learning Center, 1976-80. Mem. Am. Psychol. Assn., Am. Orthopsychiat. Assn., Calif. Assn. Marriage, Family and Child Therapists. Author: (with J. Morris) The Evaluation of A Compensatory Education Program, 1967; (Karplus edit.) What is Curriculum Evaluation, Six Answers, 1968. Home: RR 1 Box 632 Morrill ME 04952-9709

TRESNOWSKI, BERNARD RICHARD, retired health insurance company executive; b. Chgo., Oct. 14, 1932; s. Al and Luella (Stewart) T.; m. Beverly Ann Gesmond, Nov. 26, 1955; children: Linda, Judy, Mark, Tom, MaryBeth, David; m. Leanne Patricia Irish, Aug. 1985; 1 child, Megan. B.S., U. Mich., 1955; M.P.H. in Hosp. Adminstrn, U. Pitts., 1958; postgrad., U. Chgo. Second asst. adminstr., then asst. adminstr. Albert Einstein Med. Center, Phila., 1958-61; research asso. U. Mich., 1961-62; assoc. adminstr. St. Joseph Mercy Hosp., Pontiac, Mich., 1963-67; sr. v.p. Blue Cross Assn., Chgo., 1967-78; exec. v.p. Blue Cross Assn., 1977-78; exec. v.p. Blue Cross and Blue Shield Assn., Chgo., 1978-81, pres., 1981-94; ret. Blue Cross and Blue Shield Assn., 1994; mem. Health Adminstrs. Study Soc. Author articles in field. Mem. Am. Hosp. Assn., Am. Coll. Health Care Execs., Am. Pub. Welfare Assn., Health Mgmt. Edn. Assn., Soc. Health Svc. Adminstrs., Internat. Found. Employee Benefit Plans, Internat. Fedn. Vol. Health Svc. Funds. (pres.), Am. Health Planning Assn., The Conf. Bd.

TRESTMAN, FRANK D., distribution company executive; b. Mpls., Sept. 3, 1934; s. Saul and Rose (Hyster) T.; m. Carol Lynn Wasserman, Apr. 3, 1960; children—Lisa Ellen, Jill Susan. B.B.A. with high distinction, U. Minn., 1955. Exec. v.p., treas. Napco Industries, Inc., Mpls., 1965-74, pres., dir., 1974-84; chmn, CEO Mass Merchandisers, Inc., Hopkins, Minn., 1984-86; pres. Trestman Enterprises, Golden Valley, Minn., 1987—; bd. dirs. Best Buy Co., Mpls., Western Container Corp., Mpls., Insignia Systems, Inc., T.C.F. Industries. Mem. bd. govs. Mt. Sinai Hosp., Mpls., 1978-91, Abbott Northwestern Hosp., 1993—; chmn. bd. trustees Mpls. Fedn. Endowment Fund. With USN, 1957-58. Jewish. Clubs: Oak Ridge Country (Hopkins); Presidents Country (West Palm Beach, Fla.). Home: 4544 Woodridge Rd Minnetonka MN 55345-3936 Office: Trestman Enterprises 5500 Wayzata Blvd Ste 1045 Minneapolis MN 55416-1241

TREU, JESSE ISAIAH, venture capitalist; b. N.Y.C., Apr. 10, 1947. BS, Rensselaer Poly. Inst., 1968; MS, Princeton U., 1971, PhD, 1973. Physicist, liaison sci. components, materials group Gen. Electric Co., Schenectady, N.Y., 1973-77; tech. dir. Technicon Corp., Tarrytown, N.Y., 1977-82; v.p. Channing Weinberg-CW Ventures, N.Y.C., 1982-85; gen. ptnr. Domain Assocs., Princeton, N.J., 1986—. Office: Domain Assocs 1 Palmer Sq Princeton NJ 08542-3718

TREUHOLD, CHARLES RICHARD, retired investment banker; b. Bklyn., May 24, 1930; s. Eugene and Selma (Straus) T.; m. Kerstin Margareta Nevrell, July 28, 1956; 1 child, Robert Charles. BA, Yale U., 1952; postgrad., U. Paris, 1955-56. Syndicate assoc. Lehman Bros., N.Y.C., 1956-61; syndicate mgr. Paribas Corp., N.Y.C., 1961-66; sr. v.p., syndicate mgr. Arnhold & S. Bleichroeder, Inc., N.Y.C., 1966-95. Editor: Bawl St. Jour., 1977, 88. Lt. (j.g.) USN, 1952-55). Mem. Assn. Internat. Bond Dealers (bd. dirs. 1979-86), Bond Club N.Y. (gov. 1988-95), Union Club. Home: 200 E 66th St New York NY 10021-6728

TREUMANN, WILLIAM BORGEN, university dean; b. Grafton, N.D., Feb. 26, 1916; s. William King and Dagny Helen (Borgen) T.; m. Mildred Elizabeth Jenkins, Aug. 14, 1948; children—Richard Roy, Robert Evan, Beverly Kay. B.S., U. N.D., 1942; M.A., U. Ill., 1944, Ph.D., 1947. Teaching asst. chemistry U. Ill., 1942-45, teaching asst. math., 1945-46, vis. prof., summers 1948-50; from asst. prof. to prof. chemistry N.D. State U., 1946-55; mem. faculty Moorhead (Minn.) State U., 1960—, prof. chemistry, 1962—, asso. dean acad. affairs, 1968-70, dean faculty math. and sci., 1970—. Contbr. to profl. jours. Research Corp. Am. grantee, 1954; Minn. U. Bd. grantee, 1967. Fellow Am. Inst. Chemists; mem. Am. Chem. Soc., Am. Assn. U. Profs., Minn. Acad. Sci., Fedn. Am. Scientists, Phi Beta Kappa, Sigma Xi. Home: One 2nd St S Apt 5-204 Fargo ND 58103-1921 Office: Math Dept Moorhead State U Moorhead MN 56560

TREUTING, EDNA GANNON, retired nursing administrator; b. New Orleans, Dec. 16, 1925; d. Alphonse Joseph and Clara Josephine (David) Gannon; m. August Raymond Treuting, Sept. 4, 1948 (dec.); children: Keith, Karen Treuting Stein, Madeline Treuting LeBlanc, Jaime Treuting Gonzales, Jay (dec.). Diploma, Charity Hosp. Sch. Nursing, New Orleans, 1946; BS in Nursing Edn., La. State U., 1953; MPH, Tulane U., 1972, DPH, 1978. RN, La.; cert. family nurse practitioner Tulane U. Head nurse premature nursery Charity Hosp., New Orleans, 1946-47, head nurse pediatrics, 1947-49; instr. pediatrics Charity Hosp. Sch. Nursing, New Orleans, 1949-52, 54, instr., LPN, 1953; pvt. duty Touro, Hotel Dieu, New Orleans, 1957-59; instr. maternal and child health La. State U. Sch. Nursing, New Orleans, 1960, 65, 69-71; from instr. to prof., sect. head Tulane Sch. Pub. Health and Tropical Medicine, New Orleans, 1972-83; dean, prof. Our Lady Holy Cross Coll. Nursing Div., New Orleans, 1983-84; chief nurse Dept. Health and Hosp., New Orleans, 1987-94; region IV nurse practitioner Baylor U., Health Edn. and Welfare, 1974-76; citizen amb. to South Am. People to People, 1979; presentor U. Hawaii Pub. Health and Nursing, 1977; planner, advisor, reviewer continuing edn. U. Tenn., Memphis, 1990-95. Author, editor: Occupation Health Nursing, 1979; sect. head, prin. investigator Practitioner Programs Family and Pediatric, 1973-83; item writer Nurse Practitioners, Community Health and Occupational Nursing, 1974-80; mem. editl. bd. to sci. jours. and Nurse Practitioner Jour. Pres. Oti-Mrs. Internat., New Orleans, 1955-68; sponsor bd. dirs. Holy Cross H.S. Treuting Scholarship, New Orleans, 1966—; hurricane and disaster nurse ARC, New Orleans, 1966-77; v.p. Pandora Carnival Club, New Orleans, 1968-78; alternate state health dept. Commn. Nursing Supply and Demand by Legislation, 1991-94; planner, presentor La. State Rsch. Day, 1990-92. Named outstanding woman in the mainstream world's fair women of achievement, 1984. Mem. New Orleans Dist. Nurses Assn. (First J.B. Hickey Meml. Community award 1985, Great 100 Nurse-First Yr. 1987), La. Pub. Health Assn. (Dr. C.B. White Merritorious Diligent Svc. 1990), La. Nurse Practitioners Assn.(Edna Treuting scholarship named in her honor), Tulane U. Alumni Assn. (past pres.), Tulane Med. Alumni Assn. (past pres.), Delta Omega (past pres. nat.,Eta chpts.), Sigma Theta Tau (Epsilon Nu chpt.). Republican. Roman Catholic. Avocations: traveling, dancing, swimming, photography, reading. Home: 1914 Marlin Dr Mandeville LA 70448-1069

TREVES, SAMUEL BLAIN, geologist, educator, administrator; b. Detroit, Sept. 11, 1925; s. Samuel and Stella (Stork) T.; m. Jane Patricia Mitoray, Nov. 24, 1960; children: John Samuel, David Samuel. BS, Mich. Tech. U., 1951; postgrad., U. Otago, New Zealand, 1953-54; MS, U. Idaho, 1953; PhD, Ohio State U., 1959. Geologist Ford Motor Co., 1951, Idaho Bur. Mines and Geology, 1952, Otago Catchment Bd., 1953-54; mem. faculty U. Nebr., Lincoln, 1958—, prof. geology, 1966, chmn. dept., 1964-70, 74-89, assoc. dean Coll. Arts and Scis., 1989—; curator geology Nebr. State Mus., 1964—; participant expdns. to Antarctica and Greenland, 1960-61,63, 65, 70, annually 72-76. Rsch. and pubis. on geology of igneous and metamorphic rocks of Idaho, New Zealand, Mich., Antarctica, Nebr., Can., Greenland with emphasis on origin of Precambrian granite complexes and basaltic volcanic rocks. Fulbright scholar U. Otago, New Zealand, 1953-54. Fellow Geol. Soc. Am., AAAS, Explorers Club; mem. Am. Mineral Soc., Sigma Xi, Tau Beta Pi, Sigma Gamma Epsilon. Home: 1710 B St Lincoln NE 68502-1524

TREVETT, KENNETH PARKHURST, lawyer; b. Boston, Sept. 22, 1947; s. Laurence Davies and Naomi (Smith) T.; m. Barbara Kent, June 10, 1978; stepchildren: Kimberly, Dennison, Tanya. BA in English (hon.), Colgate U., 1969; JD cum laude, Suffolk U., 1979. Bar: Mass. 1980, U.S. Dist. Ct. Mass. 1980, Maine 1983. With office of pub. affairs Sec. of State, Commonwealth of Mass., Boston, 1978; asst. dean for adminstrn. Tufts U. Sch. Vet. Medicine, Boston, 1979-82; asst. to dir., house counsel The Jackson Lab., Bar Harbor, Maine, 1982-89; gen. counsel Dana-Farber Cancer Inst., Boston, 1989-96; pvt. practice, 1996—. Co-author: An Evaluation of the De-institutionalization of the Massachusetts Department of Youth Services, 1972; co-developer: (ednl. CD-ROM on licensing) Technology Transfer Series; contbr. several invited papers on legal and ethical aspects of biotech. and medicine. Mem. Gov.'s Tech. Strategy Task Force, Augusta, Maine, 1983-84, Maine Sci. and Tech. Commn., 1988-89; trustee 2d v.p., Mt. Desert Island Hosp., 1984-89; 1st v.p. Assn. Ind. Rsch. Insts., 1990-92, pres., 1993-95. Named one of Outstanding Young Men of Am., 1981. Democrat. Unitarian. Avocations: golf, writing. Home and Office: 390 Commonwealth Ave # 711 Boston MA 02215-2826

TREVILLIAN, WALLACE DABNEY, economics educator, retired dean; b. Charlottesville, Va., May 1, 1918; s. Robert Carr and Mary Anna (Perry) T.; m. Mary Lou McEachern Moody, Nov. 28, 1963; children: Malcolm McEachern, Edward Dabney. BS, U. Va., 1940, MA, 1947, PhD, 1954; postgrad., U. Calif., 1950-51. Mem. faculty Clemson (S.C.) U., 1947—, successively instr. econs., asst. prof., assoc. prof., 1947-55, prof. econs., head dept. indsl. mgmt., 1955-63, founding dean Coll. Commerce and Industry, 1963-80, prof., dean emeritus, 1983—; vis. scholar U. Sussex, Eng., 1980—; mem. Regional Export Expansion Council, 1965-77; sec. commn. on edn. for bus. professions Nat. Assn. State Univs. and Land-Grant Colls., 1975-77; pres. Nat. Council for Textile Edn., 1978-80. Master sgt. AUS, 1941-45. Mem. St. Andrews Soc. Upper S.C., Newcomen Soc., Thomas Jefferson Soc. of Alumni U. Va. Mem. Cradle Episcopalian Ch. Home: PO Box 1258 Clemson SC 29633-1258

TREVIÑO, FERNANDO MANUEL, professional society administrator; b. Brownsville, Tex., Aug. 20, 1949; s. Manuel Emilio and Consuelo Ivern

(Galindo) T.; m. Dorothy Dell Bullock, Mar. 1, 1980 (div. Mar.1990); m. Lorene Samora Treviño, Feb. 14, 1992; 1 child, Gabriela Alejandra. BS, U. Houston, 1971; MPH, U. Tex., Houston, 1975; PhD, U. Tex., Galveston, 1979. Sr. scientist AMA, Chgo., 1986-88; assoc. prof. U. Tex. Med. Br., Galveston, 1988-94, dir. Ctr. for Cross-Cultural Rsch., 1989-94; prof. and dean S.W. Tex. State U., San Marcos, 1991-93; exec. dir. APHA, Washington, 1993—; pres. World Fedn. Pub. Health Assns., Geneva, Switzerland, 1995—. Exec. editor Am. Jour. Pub. Health, 1993—. Mem.Interncultural Cancer Coun., 1995—. Capt. U.S. Army, 1971-79. Recipient Disting. Author award Jour. Allied Health, 1995. Fellow Royal Soc. Health (hon.); mem. Nat. Medicine/Pub. Health Initiative (co-chair 1994—). Avocations: photography, motorcycles, camping. Home: 5308 Wilson Ln Bethesda MD 20814 Office: American Public Health Assn 1015 15th St NW Washington DC 20005

TREVINO, JERRY ROSALEZ, secondary school principal; b. Mathis, Tex., July 9, 1943; s. Geronimo R. and Hilaria (Rosalez) T.; m. Juanita Escalante, Jan. 1, 1985; 1 child, John-Michael. BA, U. Houston, 1967, MEd, 1974; PhD, Kennedy-Western U., 1988; postgrad., U. Tex., Odessa, 1988-92. Cert. tchr., adminstr., supt., Tex. Tchr. N.E. Houston Sch. Dist., 1966-70, pub. rels. officer, 1970-72, asst. prin., 1972-76; tchr. Harris County Dept. Edn., Houston, 1968-72, Austin (Tex.) Ind. Sch. Dist., 1977-87; asst. prin. Tex. Youth Commn., Pyote, 1987-91, prin., 1991—; Title VII project dir. U.S. Dept. Edn., Pyote, 1988-96; instr. Austin C.C., 1980-84, chair, Prin. Coun. for Edn. of Lang. Minority Students, S.W. Ednl. Devel. Lab., Austin. Editor newsletter The Flyer, 1970-72; contbr. articles to profl. publs. Mem. Community Adv. Coun., Pyote, 1987—; mem. Tex. Children's Mental Health Plan, Monahans, Tex., 1991—; mem. planning com. Permian Basin Quality Work Force, Midland, Tex., 1992—; mem. Supt.'s Coun., Pyote, 1987—. Named Outstanding Adminstr. of Permian Basin (Golden Apple award) Permian Basin Private Industry Coun., 1994. Mem. ASCD, Nat. Assn. for Bilingual Edn., Am. Biog. Inst. (rsch. bd. advisors 1992—, Recognition plaque 1992, diploma of honor 1992, Commemorative Medal of Honor). Presbyterian. Avocations: flying, travel, reading, landscaping. Home: 12009 Rotherham Dr Austin TX 78753 Office: Tex Youth Commn PO Box 415 Pyote TX 79777-0415

TREVINO, LEE BUCK, professional golfer; b. Dallas, Dec. 1, 1939; s. Joe and Juanita (Barrett) T.; m. Claudia Bove; children: Richard Lee, Lesley Ann, Tony Lee, Troy Liana, Olivia Leigh, Daniel Lee. Ed. pub. schs. Head profl. Hardy's Driving Range, Dallas, 1961-65; asst. profl. Horizon Hills Country Club, El Paso, Tex., 1966-67; chmn. bd. Lee Trevino Enterprises, Inc., 1967—. Hon. chmn. Christmas Seal campaign, 1969-72, sports ambassador, 1971; mem. Pres.'s Conf. on Phys. Fitness and Sports; grand marshal Sun Carnival Parade, 1969-70, 71-72; mem. sports com. Nat. Multiple Sclerosis Soc. Served with USMCR, 1956-60. Recipient Hickok Belt award, 1971; named Golf Rookie of Yr., 1967, PGA Player of Yr., 1971, Tex. Pro Athlete of Yr., 1970, Gold Tee award, 1971, AP Pro Athlete of Yr., 1971, Player of Yr. Golf Mag., 1971, Sportsman of Yr. Sports Illustrated, 1971, PGA Sr. Tour Players of Yr., 1990, 92, 94, Internat. Sports Personality of Yr. Brit. Broadcasting Assn., 1971, Rookie and Player of Yr., Sr. PGA Tour, 1990; mem. Tex. Hall of Fame, Am. Golf Hall of Fame, World Golf Hall of Fame. Tournament winner Tex. Open, 1965, 66, N.Mex. Open, 1966, U.S. Open, 1968, 71, Amana Open, 1968, 69, Hawaiian Open, 1968, Tucson Open, 1969, 70, World Cup, 1969, 71, Nat. Airlines Open, 1970, Brit. Open, 1971, 72, Canadian Open 1971, 77, 79, Can. PGA, 1979, Danny Thomas-Memphis Classic, 1971, 72, 80, Tallahassee Open, 1971, Sahara Invitational, 1971, St. Louis Classic, 1972, Hartford Open, 1972, Jackie Gleason Classic, 1973, Doral-Eastern Open, 1973, Mexican Open, 1973, 75, Chrysler Classic, Australia, 1973, PGA Championship, 1974, 84, World Series Golf, 1974, Greater New Orleans Open, 1974, Fla. Citrus Open, 1975, Colonial Nat. Invitational, 1976, 78, Colgate Mixed Team Matches, 1979, Brit. Masters, 1985, U.S. Sr. Open, 1990; King Hassan Moroccan trophy II, 1977; Lancome trophy Benson & Hedges, 1978, 80; 1st golfer to have scored four sub-par rounds in U.S. Open Competition, 1968; leading Money winner, 1970, 2d pl. money winner 1971, 1972; Vardon trophy winner, 1970 1972, 74, 80; Can. PGA, 1983; PGA Seniors Championship, 1994; capt. Ryder Cup Matches, 1985; first golfer to have scored 4 sub-par rounds in PGA competition. Office: 5757 Alpha Rd Ste 620 Dallas TX 75240-4668

TREVISAN, MAURIZIO, epidemiologist, researcher; b. Naples, Italy, Jan. 31, 1952; came to U.S., 1979; s. Ilario and Bianca (Bruni) T.; m. Lisa Monagle, Dec. 22, 1983; children: Simona, Alessia, Stefan. MD magna cum laude, U. Naples, Italy, 1977; MS, SUNY, Buffalo, 1989. Cert. in medicine and surgery, Italy, 1977, diabetes and metabolic disease, Italy, 1980. Resident dept. internal medicine Med. Sch. U. Naples, 1977-79; rsch. fellow dept. community health and preventive medicine Med. Sch. Northwestern U., 1979-82; co-prin. investigator, dir. Cellular Ion Transport Lab Project Gubbio, U. Naples, 1983-85; asst. prof. dept. social and preventive medicine SUNY, Buffalo, 1985-88, clinical asst. prof. dept. family medicine, 1988-89, assoc. prof. dept. social and preventive medicine, 1988-92, clinical assoc. prof. nutrition program, 1989-94, assoc. prof. dept. family medicine, 1989-94, interim chair dept social and preventive medicine, 1991-92, prof. and chmn. dept. social and preventive medicine, 1993—, prof. dept. family medicine, 1994—; prin. investigator Women's Health Initiative WNY Vanguard Clin. Ctr., 1993—; vis. physician dept. physiology Harvard Med. Sch., 1982; cons. inst. internal medicine and metabolic disease rsch. U. Naples, 1982-85; adj. asst. prof. dept. cmty. health and preventive medicine Northwestern U. Med. Sch., 1987—; adj. prof. nutrition program SUNY, Buffalo, 1994—. Fellow Am. Heart Assn. Coun. on Epidemiology. Recipient Rsch. Career Devel. award NIH, 1989-94. Mem. Epidemiol. Soc. Achievements include population-based epidemiological investigation of ion transport abnormalities as risk factors for essential hypertension. Office: SUNY Buffalo Dept Social & Preventive Medicine 270 Farber Hall Buffalo NY 14214

TREVOR, ALEXANDER BRUEN, computer company executive; b. N.Y.C., Apr. 12, 1945; s. John B. Jr. and Evelyn (Bruen) T.; m. Ellen Ruth Armstrong, Sept. 21, 1974; children: Anne Wood, Alexander Jay Bruen. BS, Yale U., 1967; MS, U. Ariz., 1971. Rsch. asst. U. Ariz., Tucson, 1971; systems analyst CompuServe Inc., Columbus, Ohio, 1971-73, dir. systems, 1973-74, v.p., 1974-81, exec. v.p., chief tech. officer, 1981-96, also bd. dirs., 1985-96. Author (software program) CB Simulator, 1980. Trustee Trudeau Inst., Saranac Lake, N.Y., Aviation Safety Inst., Worthington, Ohio. 1st lt. Signal Corps, U.S. Army, 1968-70, Vietnam. Decorated Bronze Star. Mem. IEEE, Assn. for Computing Machinery, SAR (N.Y.), Union Club (N.Y.), Scioto Country Club. Republican. Episcopalian. Office: 910 Clayton Dr Worthington OH 43085

TREVOR, BRONSON, economist; b. N.Y.C., Nov. 12, 1910; s. John Bond and Caroline Murray (Wilmerding) T.; A.B., Columbia Coll., 1931; m. Eleanor Darlington Fisher, Nov. 8, 1946; children—Eleanor, Bronson, Caroline. Own bus., 1931—; dir., asst. sec. Northwestern Terminal R.R., 1952-58; chmn. bd. Texinia Corp., 1959-92. Former dir. chmn. fin. com. Gen. Hosp. of Saranac Lake mem. Council for Agrl. and Chemurgic Research, Am. Forestry Assn. Mem. Republican County Com. of N.Y. County, 1937-39; leader in primary election campaigns N.Y. County, 1937, 38, 39 to free local Rep. party orgn. from leftwing affiliations. Served with U.S. Army, 1942, World War II. Mem. S.A.R., Soc. Colonial Wars. Clubs: Union, Knickerbocker, Racquet and Tennis, Piping Rock, Bath and Tennis. Author: (pamphlet) The United States Gold Purchase Program, 1941; also numerous articles on econ. subjects. Home: Heron Ln Paul Smiths NY 12970 Office: PO Box 182 Oyster Bay NY 11771-0182

TREVOR, KIRK DAVID NIELL, orchestra conductor, cellist; b. London, Feb. 8, 1952. Student, Dartington Coll., 1968-69; grad. with distinction, Guildhall Sch. Music and Drama, 1974; student, N.C. Sch. Arts, 1975-77. Asst. condr. Guildhall Opera Sch., 1973-74; music dir. Youth Symphony of Carolinas, 1978-82; music dir., condr. Knoxville (Tenn.) Symphony Orch., 1984—; chief condr. Martinu Philharmonic Czech Rep., 1995—; assoc. condr. Charlotte (N.C.) Symphony Orch., 1978-82, Exxon Art Endowment and Dallas Symphony, 1982-85; former resident condr. Dallas Symphony; dir. music Indpls. Chamber Orch., 1988—; instr. U. Tenn., 1985—; guest condr. U.S., S.Am., USSR, Czech Republic, Poland, Romania, Switzerland; tchr. Condrs. Symphonic Workshop in Zlin, Czech Republic, 1991—, Artistic Dir. Recipient Libottom Meml. prize, 1972, Kappilis Condr. prize, 1974, Toussant prize, 1974; winner Am. Condrs. Program, 1990; Fulbright Exchange grantee U.K. and U.S. Dept. State, 1975, Am. Condrs. Program grantee, 1990. Mem. Condrs. Guild, Am. Symphony Orch. League. Office: Knoxville Symphony Orch 623 Market St Ste 600 Knoxville TN 37902-2204

TREVOR, LEIGH BARRY, lawyer; b. Galesburg, Ill., Aug. 29, 1934; s. Dean Spaulding and Jean Elizabeth (Barry) T.; m. Mary Witherell, Aug. 8, 1978; children: John W. Hoffman, Ann Kete, Stephen S., Julia B. Kramer, Elizabeth P. Grad., Phillips Acad., 1952; AB magna cum laude, Harvard U., 1956, LLB, 1962. Bar: Ohio 1963, U.S. Dist. Ct. D.C. 1970. Assoc. Jones, Day, Reavis & Pogue, Cleve., 1962-68, ptnr., 1969—, ptnr.-in-charge, 1990-93; dir., sec. Dix & Eaton, Inc., Cleve.; lectr. on hostile corp. takeovers, other corp. law topics. Contbr. articles to profl. jours. Trustee, sec. State Troopers of Ohio, 1985—; pres. Stakeholders in Am., Mpls., 1987-88; trustee Cleveland State U. Found., 1990-94, Gt. Lakes Theater Festival, 1991-94. Lt. (j.g.) USN, 1956-59. Fellow Ohio State Bar Found.; mem. Ohio State Bar Assn. (mem. tender offer subcom. 1982—, corp. governance subcom. 1986—, chmn. corp. law com. 1989-91, coun. of dels. 1991—), Cleve. Bar Assn., D.C. Bar Assn., Nat. Investor Rels. Inst. (bd. dirs. local chpt. 1985-92, pres. Cleve.-Akron chpt. 1990-91), Phi Beta Kappa. Republican. Episcopalian. Home: 3 Hidden Vly Rocky River OH 44116-1143 Office: Jones Day Reavis & Pogue 901 Lakeside Ave E Cleveland OH 44114-1116

TREXLER, EDGAR RAY, minister, editor; b. Salisbury, N.C., Sept. 17, 1937; s. Edgar Ray and Eula Belle (Farmer) T.; m. Emily Louise Kees, Aug. 21, 1960; children—David Ray, Mark Raymond, Karen Emily. AB, Lenoir-Rhyne Coll., 1959, LittD, 1978; MDiv, Luth. Theol. So. Sem., 1962; MA, Syracuse U., 1964; postgrad., Boston U., 1960, Luth. World Fedn. Study Project, Geneva, 1977, 81; LittD (hon.), Midland Coll., 1990; DD, Wittenberg U., 1994. Ordained to ministry United Luth. Ch. Am., 1962; pastor St. John's Luth. Ch., Lyons, N.Y., 1962-65; features editor Luth. Mag., Phila., 1965-72, assoc. editor, 1972-78, editor, 1978-87; editor Luth. Mag., Chgo., 1988—; sec. Commn. Ch. Papers, Luth. Ch. Am., 1971-72, mem. staff team communications, 1972-78; chmn. Interch. Features, 1971-76; chmn. postal affairs com. Assoc. Ch. Press, 1983-90, Work Group on New Ch. Periodical, 1985-86; Evangelical Luth. Ch. Am. Cabinet of Execs., 1988—. Author: Ways to Wake Up Your Church, 1969, Creative Congregations, 1972, The New Face of Missions, 1973, Mission in a New World, 1977, LWF/6, 1978, Anatomy of a Merger, 1991; mem. editorial adv. bd. The New World, Roman Cath. Archdiocese of Chgo., 1994—. Pres. Lyons Council Chs., 1964; trustee Lenoir Rhyne Coll., 1975-84. Recipient Disting. Alumnus award Lenoir-Rhyne Coll., 1991, Disting. Svc. award Newberry Coll., 1992, Bachman award for disting. leadership Luth. Theol. So. Sem., 1993, award of merit for editorials Assoc. Ch. Press, 1991, award of merit for articles in mission mags. Assoc. Ch. Press, 1974. Mem. Nat. Luth. Editors Assn. (pres. 1975-77). Home: 1401 Sequoia Rd Naperville IL 60540-6391 Office: Luth Mag 8765 W Higgins Rd Chicago IL 60631-4101

TREXLER, SUZANNE FRANCES, geriatrics nurse; b. Harrisburg, Pa., Feb. 8, 1963; d. Walter Richard and Catherine Frances (Mourawski) Markham; m. Barry Kenneth Trexler, Nov. 9, 1991; children: William Chester, Brittany Nancy, Katye Iona. LPN, Harrisburg Stelton Highs, Sch. Practical Nursing, 1984; ADN, Harrisburg (Pa.) Area C.C., 1984; BA in Long Term Care Adminstrn., St. Joseph Coll., 1994, postgrad., 1994—; BSN, York (Pa.) Coll., 1996. Nurse ICU and critical care unit Meml. Hosp., York, Pa., 1987-88; staff nurse emergency dept. Polyclinic Med. Ctr., Harrisburg, 1988-91; assoc. prof. Nat. Edn. Ctr.-Jr. Coll., Harrisburg, 1991; dir. nursing Camp Hill (Pa.) Care Ctr., 1991-92; resident assessment supr. Susquehanna Ctr., Harrisburg, 1992-94; dir. nursing Susquehanna Luth. Village, Millersburg, Pa., 1994-95; asst. adminstr. Dauphin Manor, Harrisburg, 1995—; ACLS, CPR instr. Am. Heart Assn., Harrisburg, 1989—; BCLS, CPR instr. ARC, Harrisburg, 1992—; RN, paramedic Lebanon (Pa.) County First Aide and Safety Patrol, 1992—. Sec. Little People PTA, Harrisburg, 1991-92; pres. Student Human Resource Mgmt. Club, York (Pa.) Coll., 1992—. Recipient Nurse of Hope award Am. Cancer Soc., Dauphin County, Harrisburg, 1983-84. Mem. AACN, Pa. Nurses Assn., Pa. Dir. Nursing Assn. for Long Term Care, PANPHA (advocate). Roman Catholic. Avocations: ceramics, ballet, flute. Office: Dauphen Manor Paxton St Harrisburg PA 17111

TREYBIG, JAMES G., computer company executive; b. Clarendon, TX, 1940. BS, Rice U., 1963; MBA, Stanford, 1968. Mkgt. mgr. Hewlett-Packard Co., 1968-72; with Kleiner and Perkins, 1972-74; with Tandem Computer Inc., Cupertino, Calif., 1974—, now pres., chief exec. officer, dir. Office: Tandem Computers Inc 19333 Vallco Pky Cupertino CA 95014-2506*

TREYNOR, JACK LAWRENCE, financial advisor, educator; b. Council Bluffs, Iowa, Feb. 21, 1930; s. Jack Vernon and Alice (Cavin) T.; m. Elizabeth Glassmeyer, Aug. 29, 1968; children: Elizabeth Childs, Wendy F.C., Thomas Pirrie. BA, Haverford Coll., 1951; MBA with distinction, Harvard U., 1955; postgrad., MIT, 1962-63. Jr. faculty Harvard U. Sch. Bus., Cambridge, Mass., 1955-56; ops. research staff Arthur D. Little, Cambridge, 1956-66; mgr. computer applications Merrill Lynch, N.Y.C., 1966-69; editor Fin. Analysts Jour., N.Y.C., 1969-81; chief investment officer Treynor-Arbit Assocs., Chgo., 1981-85; assoc. vis. prof. dept. of fin. and bus. econs. U. So. Calif., Los Angeles, 1985-88; pres. Treynor Capital Mgmt., Palos Verdes Estates, Calif.; gen. ptnr., trustee, dir. certain mutual funds Eaton Vance, 1970—. Author: (with Patrick Regan and William Priest) The Financial Reality of Pension Funding Under ERISA, 1976; mem. editl. bd. Fin. Analysts Jour., 1969—; co-author and contbr. numerous articles in fin. jours. (Graham and Dodd Scroll award 1968, 82, twice in 1987, Graham and Dodd Plaque for best paper in Fin. Analysts Jour. 1981). Trustee Fin. Analysts Research Found., 1970-85; mem. vis. com. Grad. Sch. Bus. Adminstrn. U. Chgo., 1984-89. Served with U.S. Army, 1951-53. Fellow Inst. for Quantitative Rsch. in Fin. (disting., bd. dirs. 1970—); mem. Fin. Analysts Fedn. (Nicholas Molodovsky award 1985), Am. Fin. Assn. (bd. dirs. 1979-81), Haverford Varsity Club, Longwood Cricket Club (Chestnut Hill, Mass.), N.Y. Athletic Club, Manursing Island Club (Rye, N.Y.), Winter Club (Lake Forest, Ill.),), Palos Verdes Tennis Club, Palos Verdes Beach and Athletic Club. Episcopalian. Avocations: jazz piano, sports cars, antique trains.

TREYZ, JOSEPH HENRY, librarian; b. Binghamton, N.Y., Nov. 23, 1926; s. Joseph Henry and Edna Belle (Leonard) T. B.A., Oberlin Coll., 1950; postgrad., Harvard U., 1951; M.L.S., Columbia U., 1952. Circulation asst. N.Y. Acad. Medicine Library, 1950-51; cataloger Columbia Libraries, N.Y.C., 1951-53, Stevens Inst. Tech., Hoboken, N.J., 1953-54; adminstrv. asst. Yale Library, 1955, asst. head catalogue dept., 1955-61; head new campuses program U. Calif., La Jolla, 1961-65; asst. dir. U. Mich. Library, Ann Arbor, 1965-71; dir. libraries U. Wis., Madison, 1971-83, asst. to chancellor, 1983-85; sec.-treas. L.D. Repos, Inc., 1985-87, pres., 1987—; univ. rep. Consumer Reaction Project for Catalog Card Reprodn. Study, 1961; condr. survey tech. services Fordham U. Libraries, 1967-69, Brandeis U. Libraries, 1970-71; mem. Wis. Gov.'s Com. on Library Devel., 1973-81, Wis. com. Library Services and Constrn. Act, 1979-81; del. U.S. Mission to China on Libraries, 1979. Author: Books for College Libraries, 1967, also articles. Bd. dirs. Wis. Center for Theatre Research. Served with AUS, 1945-46. Mem. Universal Serials and Book Exchange (v.p. 1976, pres., chmn. bd. dirs. 1977), ALA (councilor 1970-74, 77-81, chmn. various coms. 1967-69, recipient Melvil Dewey medal 1970), Assn. Research Libraries (commn. orgn. materials, dir. 1975-78), Midlnet (v.p. 1978-79, pres. 1979-80), Assn. Coll. and Research Libraries (chmn. editorial bd. Choice 1968-70), Wis. Library Consortium (pres. 1975-76), Wis. Assn. Acad. Libraries (chmn. 1973-74), Council U. Wis. Librarians (chmn. 1975-76, 79-80, 81-83), Wis. Library Assn. (bd. dirs. 1973-74, mem. White House Conf. com. 1977-78), Madison Area Library Council (v.p. 1973-74), Mich. Library Assn. (chmn. tech. services sect. 1968-69), N.Y. Tech. Services Librarians (pres. 1959-60). Methodist. Home: 801 N Venetian Dr Miami FL 33139-1007

TREZEK, GEORGE JAMES, mechanical engineer; b. Chgo., July 10, 1937; s. George A. T.; m. Joan A. Arcieri, Aug. 18, 1962; children: Wendy Marie, Keith R., Cynthia Ann. B.M.E., Gen. Motors Inst., 1960; M.S., U. Ill., 1962, Ph.D., 1965. Asst. prof. mech. engring. Northwestern U., 1965; asst. prof. U. Calif., Berkeley, 1966-70, assoc. prof., 1970-74, prof., 1974-90, prof. emeritus, 1990—; v.p. R&D Greenfield Environ.; dir. recycling ops. BKK Corp., 1990-96; pres. Trezek Group, Inc., 1996—; cons. to industry, state and fed. govtl. agys. Contbr. numerous articles on heat transfer, bio-engring. and environ. engring., solid waste mgmt. and hazardous waste mgmt., heavy metals treatment tech., marine sediments remediation, plastics recycling tech. to profl. jours. Mem. ASME, ASTM. Roman Catholic. Home: 2210 Canyon Oak Ln Danville CA 94506-2014

TREZISE, PHILIP HAROLD, government official; b. Calumet, Mich., May 27, 1912; s. Norman and Emma (Anderson) T.; m. Ruth Elenor Dorsey, Nov. 26, 1938; children: John Dorsey, David Philip. A.B., U. Mich., 1936, M.A., 1939; student, Nat. War Coll., 1949-50. Research asso. U. Mich., 1940-41; fellow Social Sci. Research Council, 1941-42; ofcl. Office Def. Transportation, 1942-43; with Dept. State, 1946-71; advisor U.S. delegation to U.N. Commn. on Indonesian question, 1948, cons. report to Pres. on fgn. econ. policy, 1950; dep. dir. Office Intelligence Research, intelligence activities, 1952-55, mem. policy planning staff, 1956-57; minister econ. affairs Am. embassy, Tokyo, 1957-61; dep. asst. sec. for econ. affairs Dept. State, 1961-65; U.S. ambassador to OECD, Paris, France, 1966-69; asst. sec. state econ. affairs, 1969-71; mem. Washington Policy Council Internat. Mgmt. and Devel. Inst., Trilateral Commn., 1976-83; sr. fellow Brookings Instn., 1971—; Adj. prof. dept. polit. sci. Columbia U., 1978; Dir. Bank of Tokyo Trust Co., 1976, Atlantic Council; mem. Nat. Commn. Supplies and Shortages, 1975-76. Contbg. editor: Yomiuri Shimbun, 1979-86. Pres. Japan-Am. Soc., 1973-76. Served as lt. OSS USNR, 1943-46. Decorated Order of Rising Sun (Japan); recipient Pres.'s award for disting. fed. civilian svc., 1965, Disting. Honor award Dept. State, 1971, Disting. Alumnus award U. Mich., 1980. Mem. Council Fgn. Relations, Phi Beta Kappa. Episcopalian. Club: Internat. Nat. Economists (Washington). Home: 6900 Broxburn Dr Bethesda MD 20817-4716 Office: 1775 Massachusetts Ave NW Washington DC 20036-2188

TREZZA, ALPHONSE FIORE, librarian, educator; b. Phila., Dec. 27, 1920; s. Vincent and Amalia (Ferrara) T.; m. Mildred Di Pietro, May 19, 1945; children: Carol Ann Trezza Johnston, Alphonse Fiore. B.S., U. Pa., 1948, M.S., 1950, postgrad.; librarian cert., Drexel Inst., 1949. Page Free Library, Phila., 1940-41, 45-48; library asst. Free Library, 1948-49; cataloger, asst. reference librarian Villanova U., 1949-50, instr., 1956-60; head circulation dept. U. Pa. Library, 1950-56; lectr. Drexel Inst. Sch. Library Sci., 1951-60; editor Cath. Library world, 1956-60; exec. sec. Cath. Library Assn., 1956-60; assoc. exec. dir. ALA, exec. sec. library adminstrn. div., 1960-67, assoc. dir. adminstrv. services, 1967-69; dir. Ill. State Library, Springfield, 1969-74; lectr. Grad. Sch. Library and Info. Sci., Cath. U., 1975-82; exec. dir. Nat. Commn. on Libraries and Info. Scis., Washington, 1974-80; dir. intergovt. library Cooperation Project Fed. Library Com./Library of Congress, Washington, 1980-82; assoc. prof. Sch. Library and Info. Studies Fla. State U., Tallahassee, 1982-87, prof., 1987-93, emeritus prof., 1993—; mem. Ill. Library LSCA TITLE I-II Adv. Commn., 1963-69; mem. network devel. com. Library of Congress, 1977-82; bd. visitors Sch. Library and Info. Sci., U. Pitts., 1977-80; cons. Becker & Hayes, Inc., 1980-84, King Research, Inc., 1981-82; mem. planning com and steering com. Fla. Gov.'s Conf. on Library and Info. Svcs., 1988-91. Nat. chmn. Cath. Book Week, 1954-56; pres. Joliet Diocesan Bd. Edn., 1966-68; Democratic committeeman, Lombard, Ill., 1961-69; auditor Borough of Norwood (Pa.), 1958-60. Served to 1st lt. USAAF, 1942-45. Decorated Air medal; recipient Ofcl. commendation White House Conf. on Libr. and Info. Svc., 1979. Mem. ALA (coun. 1973-82, 88-92, mem. exec. bd. 1974-79, chmn. stats. coordinating com. 1970-74, mem. pub. com. 1975-78, 81-83, 87-89, chmn. adv. com. interface, 1979-83, chmn. membership com. 1983-84, chmn. nominating com. 1988-89, mem. legis. com. 1989-91, adv. bd. ALA Yearbook 1976-91, Assn. Specialized and Coop. Library Agys. legis. com., 1987-89, ad hoc com. White House Conf. on Libr. and Info. Svcs. 1989-91, chmn. awards com. 1990-92, Exceptional Achievement award 1981, J.B. Lippincott award 1989), Cath. Library Assn. (life, adv. coun. 1960—), Ill. Library Assn. (chmn. legis.-library devel. com. 1964-69, mem. exec. bd., libr's. citation 1974), Fla. Library Assn. (bd. dirs. 1987-93, pres. 1991-92, intellectual freedom com., chmn. com. on Fla. Librs. publ., editor, publ. com., planning com., 1991, site com.), Continuing Libr. Edn. Network and Exchange (pres. 1982-83), Internat. Fedn. Library Assns. and Institutions (statistics standing com. 1976-85, planning com.), Coun. Nat. Library Assns. (chmn. 1959-61), Assn. Coll. and Research Librarians (pres. Phila. chpt. 1953-55), Drexel Inst. Library Sch. Alumni Assn. (pres. 1955-56, exec. bd. 1956-60, chmn. chief officers State Library Agys. 1973-74), Chgo. Library Club (pres. 1969), Assn. Library and Info. Sci. Edn. (govt. relation com. 1985-87), Drexel U. Alumni Assn. (Outstanding Alumnus award 1963), Kappa Phi Kappa (chpt. pres. 1948), Beta Phi Mu (hon.). Lodge: K.C. Office: Fla State U Sch Libr and Info Studies Tallahassee FL 32306 *You can't do anything alone. You need support and you need opposition. Opposition provides you with challenge. Challenge brings out the best in you.*

TRIANTAFYLLOU, MICHAEL STEFANOS, ocean engineering educator; b. Athens, Greece, Oct. 27, 1951; came to U.S., 1974; s. Stefanos M. and Penelopi I. (Koutras) T.; m. Joan L. Kimball, Sept. 22, 1985; children: Stefanos R., Kimon K. MS in Ocean Engring., MIT, 1977, MSME, 1977, ScD, 1979. Rsch. assoc. MIT, Cambridge, Mass., 1978-79, asst. prof., 1979-83, assoc. prof., 1983-86, tenured assoc. prof., 1986-90, prof., dir. ocean engring. testing tank, 1990—; vis. scientist Woods Hole (Mass.) Oceanographic Inst., 1990—. Featured cover Scientific American; contbr. articles to profl. jours. Rsch. grantee OFfice NAval Rsch., Office Naval Tech., NSF, Doherty Found. Dept. Commerce, 1979—. Mem. Internat. Soc. Offshore and Polar Engrs. (founding mem.), Soc. Naval Architects and Marine Engrs. (papers com., vice chmn. OC-2 com.), Am. Phys. Soc. Office: MIT 77 Massachusetts Ave Rm 5-323 Cambridge MA 02139-4301

TRIANTAPHYLLOU, HEDWIG HIRSCHMANN, plant pathologist; b. Fuerth, Bavaria, Germany, Jan. 16, 1927; came to U.S., 1954; d. Friedrich and Ferdinandine (Schonleben) Hirschmann; m. Anastasios Christos Triantaphyllou, July 9, 1960; 1 child, Christos F. PhD, U. Erlangen, Erlangen, Germany, 1951. From tech. asst. to prof. N.C. State Univ., Raleigh, N.C., 1954-92, ret. Contbr. articles to profl. jours., chpts. to books in field. Recipient rsch. award Soc. Sigma Xi, 1962, Ruth Allen award Am. Phytopathol. Soc., 1993, Soc. Nematologists fellowship, 1981. Mem. Helminthological Soc. Wash., Soc. European Nematologists, Soc. of Nematologists, Soc. Sigma Xi. Avocations: sailing, music, piano. Office: N C State U Dept Plant Pathology Box 7616 Raleigh NC 27695-7616

TRIARHOU, LAZAROS CONSTANTINOS, neurobiologist, educator; b. Thessaloniki, Greece, June 23, 1957; s. Constantinos and Penelope (Georgiades) Triarhou. MD, Aristotelian U., Thessaloniki, 1981; MSc in Neurosci., U. Rochester, 1984; PhD in Neurobiology, Ind.-Purdue U., 1987. Rsch. asst. in neurosci. Ctr. for Brain Rsch., U. Rochester, N.Y., 1981-84; postdoctoral fellow in neuropathology and neurobiology Ind. U. Med. Ctr., Indpls., 1984-88, asst. prof. neuropathology and med. neurobiology, 1988-94; assoc. prof., 1994—; Mem. Internat. Parliament for Safety and Peace (dep. 1991—). Referee Brain Rsch., Exptl. Neurology, Cell Transplantation; contbr. numerous sci. reports to profl. jours. including Arch. Neurology, Experientia, Proc. Nat. Acad. Sci. USA, Jour. Comparative Neurology, Anatomy and Embryology, Nature Med., others. Recipient Honourable Weil award Am. Assn. Neuropathologists, 1987, First award U.S. Dept. of HHS, 1990, Scientific award in medicine Bodossaki Found., 1995. Fellow Am. Soc. Neural Transplantation; mem. Brit. Brain Rsch. Orgn., Soc. for Neurosci. (mem. exec. com. Indpls. chpt. 1986-88), European Brain and Behaviour Soc., European Neurosci. Assn., Internat. Brain Rsch. Orgn., Hellenic Soc. for Neurosci., Med. Assn. Thessaloniki, N.Y. Acad. Scis., World Fedn. Neuroscientists, John Shaw Billings History of Medicine Soc., Internat. Union Psychol. Sci. Achievements include research in structural and ontogenetic neuroscience, central nervous system regeneration and neurobiology of intracerebral transplantation. Office: Ind U Sch Medicine Med. Sci Bldg A-128 Indianapolis IN 46202

TRÍAS-MONGE, JOSE, lawyer, former territory supreme court chief justice; b. San Juan, P.R., May 5, 1920; s. José and Belén Monge; m. Jane G. Trías, June 3, 1943; children: Jose Enrique, Peter James, Arturo Trías. B.A., U. P.R., 1940; M.A., Harvard U., 1943, LL.B., 1944; J.S.D., Yale U., 1947. Bar: P.R. 1945, U.S. Supreme Ct 1949. Teaching fellow Harvard U., 1943-44; practiced law San Juan, 1950-52, 57-74; atty. gen. P.R., 1953-57; chief justice Supreme Ct. P.R., San Juan, 1974-85; of counsel Trías, Acevedo & Otero, San Juan, 1989—; mem. P.R. Constl. Conv., 1951-52, Inter-Am.

Juridical Commn., OAS, 1966-67; pres. P.R. Acad. Legislation and Jurisprudence, 1985—; lectr. U. P.R., 1947-49. Author: El Sistema Judicial de Puerto Rico, 1978, La Crisis del Derecho en Puerto Rico, 1979, Historia Constitucional de Puerto Rico, Vol. I, 1980, Vol. II, 1981, Vol. III, 1982, Vol. IV, 1983, Vol. V, 1994; Sociedad, Derecho y Justicia, 1985, El Choque de Dos Culturas Juridicas en Puerto Rico, 1991. Mem. nat. com. ACLU, 1958-74; v.p. Festival Casals, Inc., 1957-69, 73-74; trustee U. P.R., 1962-72. Mem. Bar Assn. P.R., ABA, Soc. de Legislation Comparée, French Acad. Comparative Law, Royal Acad. Spanish Lang. (life). Roman Catholic. Office: PO Box 366283 San Juan PR 00936-6283

TRIBBLE, RICHARD WALTER, brokerage executive; b. San Diego, Oct. 19, 1948; s. Walter Perrin and Catherine Janet (Miller) T.; m. Joan Catherine Sliter, June 26, 1980. BS, U. Ala., Tuscaloosa, 1968; student, Gulf Coast Sch. Drilling Practices, U. Southwestern La., 1977. Stockbroker Shearson, Am. Express, Washington, 1971-76; ind. oil and gas investment sales, Falls Church, Va., 1976-77; pres. Monroe & Keusink, Inc., Falls Church and Columbus, Ohio, 1977-87; instnl. investment officer FCA Asset Mgmt., 1983-85; fin. cons. Merrill Lynch Pierce, Fenner & Smith, Inc., Phoenix, 1987—, cert. fin. mgr., 1989—, sr. fin. cons., 1992—, asst. v.p., 1993—. Served with USMC, 1969-70. Republican. Methodist. Office: 2525 E Camelback Rd Phoenix AZ 85016-4219

TRIBETT, BRENDA DIANE BELL, religious organization administrator; b. Richmond, Va., Oct. 3, 1947; d. Ervin George Jr. and Claudia (Miller) Bell; m. Louis Tribett Jr., Sept. 2, 1967 (div. 1973); 1 child, Diondrea Nichelle. BS in Juvenile Justice, Va. Commonwealth U., 1978; MA in Legal Studies, Antioch Sch. Law, 1981; MA in Christian Edn., Presbyn. Sch. Christian Edn., 1991, EdS in Christian Edn., 1992. Ch. sec., youth coord. Mt. Olive Bapt. Ch., Richmond, 1973-89; acad. skills coord. Va. Union U., Richmond, 1987-89; ESL/adult basic edn. tchr. Richmond Pub. Schs., 1982-92; dir. Joseph Nash Multicultural Ctr., Richmond, 1990-92; exec. dir. Christian edn. Prog. Nat. Bapt. Conv., Washington, 1992—; workshop facilitator Bapt. Gen. Conv., Richmond, 1974-92, mem. leadership team, 1980-92; cons. Commonwealth Girl Scouts, Richmond, 1988; tchr. Adult Basic Edn., 1991-92. Named one of 100 Most Influential Black Women, Koinonia Ind. Meth. Ch., 1993; Educator's fellow Ecumenical Resource Ctr. Mem. Nat. Coun. Chs., Religious Edn. Assn. Democrat. Avocations: jogging, reading, cooking, skating. Office: Prog Nat Bapt Conv Inc Dept of Christian Edn 601 50th St NE Washington DC 20019-5499

TRIBLE, PAUL SEWARD, JR., former United States senator; b. Balt., Dec. 29, 1946; s. Paul Seward and Katherine (Schilpp) T.; m. Rosemary Dunaway; children: Mary Katherine, Paul Seward III. B.A., Hampden-Sydney Coll., 1968; J.D., Washington and Lee U., Lexington, Va., 1971. Bar: Va. 1971. Law clk. to U.S. dist. judge Albert V. Bryan, Jr., 1971-72; asst. U.S. atty. Office U.S. Atty. Eastern Dist. Va., 1972-74; commonwealth's atty. Essex County, Va., 1974-76; U.S. Congressman 1st Va. Dist., Washington, 1976-82; U.S. Senator from Va., 1982-89; of counsel Shuttleworth, Ruloff & Giordano, 1989-95; pres. Jefferson Group, Washington, 1991-95, Christopher Newport U., Newport News, Va., 1996—. Mem.: Washington and Lee Law Rev. Republican. Episcopalian. Office: Christopher Newport Univ Office of President 50 Shoe Lane Newport News VA 23606

TRIBUS, MYRON, quality counselor, engineer, educator; b. San Francisco, Oct. 30, 1921; s. Edward and Marie D. (Kramer) T.; m. Sue Davis, Aug. 30, 1945; children—Louanne, Kamala. B.S. in Chemistry, U. Calif. at Berkeley, 1942; Ph.D. in Engring, U. Calif. at Los Angeles, 1949; D.Sc. (hon.), Rockford (Ill.) Coll., 1965, Oakland (Mich.) U., 1971. Registered profl. engr., Mass. Instr. to prof. engring. U. Calif. at Los Angeles, 1946-61; dir. aircraft icing research U. Mich., 1951-54; dean engring. Thayer Sch. Engring., Dartmouth Coll., 1961-69; asst. sec. sci. and tech. Dept. Commerce, Washington, 1969-70; sr. v.p. tech. and engring. info. tech. group Xerox Corp., Rochester, N.Y., 1970-74; dir. Center for Advanced Engring. Study, Mass. Inst. Tech., Cambridge, 1974-86; cons. in quality mgmt., 1986—; dir. rsch., co-founder Exergy, Inc., Hayward, Calif., 1987—; cons. heat transfer Gen. Electric Co., 1950; cons. Fed. Office Saline Water; tech. adv. bd. Dept. Commerce; adviser to NATO, 1953; mem. Nat. Adv. Com. Oceans and Atmosphere, 1971-72; bd. dirs. Exergy, Inc., Hayward, Calif. Author: Thermostatics and Thermodynamics, 1961, Rational Descriptions, Decisions and Designs, 1969; Contbr. articles to profl. jours. Bd. govs. Technion, Haifa, Israel, 1973-84. Served to capt. USAAF, 1942-46. Recipient Thurman H. Bane award Inst. Aero. Scis., 1945, Wright Bros. medal Soc. Automotive Engrs., 1945; Alfred Noble prize Engring. Socs., 1952, Robert Fletcher awrd Thayer Sch. Engring., Dartmouth Coll., 1994; named UCLA Alumnus of Yr., 1972. Mem. ASME, IEEE, NSPE, Am. Soc. Engring. Edn. Home: 350 Britto Ter Fremont CA 94539-3824 Office: Exergy Inc 22320 Foothill Blvd Hayward CA 94541-2700

TRICARICO, JOSEPH ARCHANGELO, lawyer; b. N.Y.C., May 6, 1940; s. Nicholas and Frances Tricarico; m. Mildred Grandi, Feb. 12, 1972; 1 child, Nicholas. BS, St. Johns U., 1963, JD, 1967. V.p. trust counsel U.S. Trust Co. N.Y., N.Y.C., 1973—. Author: Generation-Skipping Transfers: A Primer, 1984. Pro bono arbitrator small claims ct. Civil Ct. of City of N.Y., S.I., 1981—; trustee Eger Health Care Ctr., S.I., 1990—. Mem. ABA (com. bus. law 1990—, vice chair com. generation-skipping transfers 1993—, com. taxation 1984—), Am. Corp. Counsel Assn. (com. securities litigation 1991—, com. environ. law 1992—), N.Y. Bankers Assn. (spl. counsel trust legis. and regulatory com. 1991—), N.Y. Bar Assn., N.Y. County Lawyers Assn. (com. legislation 1989—). Office: US Trust Co NY 114 W 47th St New York NY 10036-1510

TRICE, WILLIAM HENRY, paper company executive; b. Geneva, N.Y., Apr. 4, 1933; s. Clyde H. T.; m. Sandra Clayton, July 16, 1955; children—Russell, Amy. B.S. in Forestry, State U. N.Y., 1955; M.S., Inst. Paper Chemistry, Appleton, Wis., 1960, Ph.D., 1963. With Union Camp Corp., 1963—, tech. dir. bleached div., 1972-74; v.p., corp. tech. dir. research and devel. Union Camp Corp., Wayne, N.J., 1974-79; sr. v.p. tech. Union Camp Corp., 1979-85, exec. v.p., 1985—; chmn. bd. dirs. Bush Boake Allen, Inc. Trustee, pres. Western Mich. U.-Paper Tech. Found., Syracuse Pulp and Paper Found. With USAF, 1955-57. Fellow TAAPI (bd. dirs. 1978-81), Indsl. Rsch. Inst. (alt. rep.), Inst. Paper Sci. and Tech. (trustee, exec. commn. alumni assn.). Home: 6 Hanover Rd Mountain Lakes NJ 07046-1004 Office: Union Camp Corp 1600 Valley Rd Wayne NJ 07470-2043

TRICHEL, MARY LYDIA, middle school educator; b. Rosenberg, Tex., Feb. 2, 1957; d. Henry John and Henrietta (Jurek) Pavlicek; m. Keith Trichel, Aug. 8, 1981; children: Daniel, Nicholas. BS cum laude, Tex. A & M U., 1980. Cert. tchr., Tex. Social studies tchr. grades 6, 7 and 8 St. Francis de Sales, Houston, 1980-81; English tchr. grades 7 and 8 Dean Morgan Jr. High, Casper, Wyo., 1983-86; English and journalism tchr. grades 9 and 11 Tecumseh (Okla.) High Sch., 1987; English tchr. grade 6 Christa McAuliffe Middle Sch., Houston, 1988-92; tchr. Tex. history grade 7, journalism grade 8 Lake Olympia Middle Sch., Missouri City, Tex., 1991-92; tchr. social studies 6th grade Lake Olympia Mid. Sch. Ft. Bend Ind. Sch. Dist., 1993—. Recipient teaching awards. Mem. Nat. Coun. Tchrs. English, Nat. Coun. Tchrs. Social Studies, Am. Fedn. Tchrs. Avocations: desktop publishing, scuba diving, traveling. Home: 3707 Pin Oak Ct Missouri City TX 77459-7018

TRICK, ANN LOUISE, accountant; b. Jefferson Parish, La.; d. Claybourne and Avis Margaret (Middleton) Waldrop; m. Joseph Michael Trick, Dec. 28, 1982 (div.); children: Philip Michael, Justin Anthony, Kristen Alicia. BA, Tex. Tech. U., 1979; M of Profl. Acctg., U. Tex., Arlington, 1992. CPA. Acct. exec., office mgr. DBG & H, Dallas, 1979-80; bus. mgr. Creative Microsystems, Inc., Dayton, Ohio, 1980-81; office mgr. Sinclair & Rush, Inc., Arlington, 1981-83, Norand Corp., Arlington, 1983-84; acct. Price Waterhouse, Ft. Worth, 1992—. SERVA vol. Arlington Ind. Sch. Dist., 1990-91; den leader Cub Scout Pack 389, Arlington, 1992-93; mem. bd. fin. All Saints Luth. Ch. Recipient Scholarship Cert. of Merit, Inst. Cert. Mgmt. Accts., 1991; scholar Am. Women's Soc. CPAs, 1991, Mid Cities Assn. CPAs, 1991. Mem. Am. Soc. Women Accts., Tex. Soc. CPAs, Inst. Mgmt. Accts. (assoc. dir. acad. rels. 1991-92, dir. acad. rels. 1992-93), Beta Alpha Psi, Beta Gamma Sigma. Office: Price Waterhouse 1700 City Ctr Tower III 301 Commerce St Fort Worth TX 76102-4140

TRICK, TIMOTHY NOEL, electrical and computer engineering educator, researcher; b. Dayton, Ohio, July 14, 1939; s. Edmund Louis and Roberta Elizabeth (Heckel) T.; m. Dorothe Lee Jacobs, Feb. 18, 1958; children: Patricia, Michael, Thomas, William, Gregory, Andrew. BSEE, U. Dayton, 1961; MSEE, Purdue U., 1962, PhD, 1966. Instr. Purdue U., West Lafayette, Ind., 1963-65; asst. prof. elec. and computer engring. U. Ill., Urbana, 1965-70, assoc. prof., 1970-75, prof., 1975—, dir. Coordinated Sci. Lab., 1984-86, head dept. elec. and computer engring., 1985-95. Author: Introduction to Circuit Analysis, 1978. Fellow IEEE (bd. dirs. 1986-89, v.p. publs. 1988-89, Guillemin-Cauer award 1976, Centennial medal 1984, Meritorious Svc. award 1987); mem. NSPE, Circuits and Sys. Soc. of IEEE (pres. 1979, Van Valkenburg award 1994), Am. Soc. Engring. Educators. Roman Catholic. Avocations: hiking, camping. Office: U Ill Dept Elec & Computer Engring 1406 W Green St Urbana IL 61801-2918

TRICOLES, GUS PETER, electromagnetics engineer, physicist, consultant; b. San Francisco, Oct. 18, 1931; s. Constantine Peter and Eugenia (Elias) T.; m. Beverly Mildred Ralsky, Dec. 20, 1953 (dec. Dec. 1974); children: Rosanne, Robin; m. Aileen Irma Aronson, Apr. 1, 1980 (div. June 1980). BA in Physics, UCLA, 1955; MS in Applied Math., San Diego State U., 1958; MS in Applied Physics, U. Calif., San Diego, 1962, PhD in Applied Physics, 1971. Engr. Convair div. Gen. Dynamics, San Diego, 1955-59, engr. Electronics div., 1962-75, engring. mgr. Electronics div., 1975-89, sr. engring. staff specialist, 1989-92; engr. Smyth Rsch. Assn., San Diego, 1959-61; rsch. asst. Scripps Instn. Oceanography, La Jolla, Calif., 1961-62; sr. engring. staff specialist G.D.E. Systems, Inc., San Diego, 1992—; cons. Ga. Inst. Tech., Atlanta, 1972, 79-80, Transco Industries, L.A., 1973, Aero Geo Industries, San Antonio, 1980-82, Vantage Assocs., San Diego, 1988; rsch. reviewer NRC, NAS, Boulder, Colo., 1986-88. Author: (with others) Radome Engineering Handbook, 1970, Antenna Handbook, 1988; contbr. articles to profl. jours.; holder 18 patents. With USN, 1952-53. Fellow IEEE (antenna standards com. 1980—, advancement com. 1988), Optical Soc. Am. (local sect. v.p. 1966); mem. N.Y. Acad. Scis., Am. Geophys. Union. Avocations: woodworking, photography. Home: 4633 Euclid Ave San Diego CA 92115-3226 Office: GDE Sys Inc PO Box 92150 San Diego CA 92150-9009

TRIECE, ANNE GALLAGHER, magazine publisher; b. Bklyn., July 1, 1955; d. Anthony J. and Mary Ann (Clines) Gallagher; m. David Mark Triece, Nov. 3, 1990. BBA cum laude, CUNY, 1978. Media planner Isidore Lefkowitz Elgort, N.Y.C., 1978-80; sr. media supr. Ted Bates Advt., N.Y.C., 1980-83; account mgr. Prevention mag., N.Y.C., 1983-85; N.Y. mgr. Home mag., N.Y.C., 1985-92; assoc. pub. Met. Home mag., N.Y.C., 1992—. Coord. Arts Program for Homeless, N.Y.C., 1994. Recipient advt. excellence award Knapp Comm., 1985. Mem. Advt. Women N.Y. (commendation 1985). Roman Catholic. Avocations: scuba diving, tennis, skiing.

TRIENENS, HOWARD JOSEPH, lawyer; b. Chgo., Sept. 13, 1923; s. Joseph Herman and Myrtle (Wilsberg) T.; m. Paula Miller, Aug. 27, 1946; children: John, Thomas, Nancy. BS, Northwestern U., 1945; JD, 1949. Bar: Ill. 1949, N.Y. 1980, U.S. Dist. Ct. (no. dist.) Ill. 1949, U.S. Dist. Ct. (so. and ea. dists.) N.Y. 1980, U.S. Ct. Appeals (2d, 3d, 7th, 9th, 10th, 11th and D.C. cirs.), U.S. Surpeme Ct. 1954. Assoc. firm Sidley, Austin, Burgess & Harper, Chgo., 1949-50; law clk. to Chief Justice Vinson, 1950-52; assoc. Sidley, Austin, Burgess & Smith, Chgo., 1952-56; ptnr. Sidley & Austin, Chgo., 1956—; v.p., gen. counsel AT&T, 1980-86. Trustee Northwestern U., 1967—. With USAAF, 1943-46. Mem. ABA, Ill. Bar Assn., Chgo. Bar Assn., N.Y. State Bar Assn., Am. Coll. Trial Lawyers, Legal Club (Chgo.), Law Club (Chgo.), Chgo. Club, Casino Club (Chgo.), Mid-Day Club, Skokie Country Club, Shoreacres Club, Glen View Club (Golf, Ill.), Met. Club (Washington), Old Elm Country Club, Sigma Chi. Democrat. Home: 690 Longwood Ave Glencoe IL 60022-1761 Office: Sidley & Austin 1 First National Plz Chicago IL 60603

TRIER, JERRY STEVEN, gastroenterologist, educator; b. Frankfurt, Germany, Apr. 12, 1933; came to U.S., 1938, naturalized, 1943; s. Kurt J. and Alice L. (Cahn) T.; m. Laurel M. Bryan, June 8, 1957; children: Stanley, Jeryl, Stephen. M.D., U. Wash., 1957; M.A. (hon.), Harvard U., 1973. Diplomate: Am. Bd. Internal Medicine. Intern U. Rochester, N.Y., 1957-58; resident in medicine U. Rochester, 1958-59; clin. asso. Nat. Cancer Inst., Bethesda, Md., 1959-61; trainee in gastroenterology U. Wash., Seattle, 1961-63; asst. prof. medicine U. Wis., Madison, 1963-67; asso. prof. U. N.Mex., Albuquerque, 1967-69, Boston U., 1969-73, Harvard U. Med. Sch., Cambridge, Mass., 1973-76; prof. Harvard U. Med. Sch., 1976—; sr. physician Brigham and Women's Hosp.; cons. Sidney Farber Cancer Ctr., Boston VA Hosp., W. Roxbury VA Hosp. Nat. Inst. Diabetes and Digestive and Kidney Disease; adv. coun. NIH, 1986-90. Editor: Internal Medicine; mem. editorial bd.; Anatomical Record, 1969—, Gastroenterology, assoc. editor, 1971-77, mem. editorial bd., 1967-71, 78-83, 93—, chmn., 1988-93, Am. Jour. Medicine, 1978-87, Current Opinion in Gastroenterology, 1990—; contbr. articles to chpts. on gastrointestinal histology, pathology, devel. and disease to med. jours. and books. Served as surgeon USPHS, 1959-61. USPHS/NIH grantee, 1963-94. Mem. Am. Soc. Clin. Investigation, Assn. Am. Physicians, Am. Gastroent. Assn. (pres. 1985-86), Am. Soc. Cell Biology, Am. Fedn. Clin. Research. Home: 119 Pine St Weston MA 02193-1178 Office: Brigham and Women's Hosp 75 Francis St Boston MA 02115-6110

TRIEWEILER, TERRY NICHOLAS, justice; b. Dubuque, Iowa, Mar. 21, 1948; s. George Nicholas and Anne Marie (Oastern) T.; m. Carol M. Jacobson, Aug. 11, 1972; children: Kathryn Anne, Christina Marie, Anna Theresa. BA, Drake U., 1970, JD, 1972. Bar: Iowa 1973, Wash. 1973, U.S. Dist. Ct. (so. dist.) Iowa 1973, U.S. Dist. Ct. (we. dist.) Wash. 1973, Mont. 1975, U.S. Dist. Ct. Mont. 1977. Staff atty. Polk County Legal Services, Des Moines, 1973; assoc. Hullin, Roberts, Mines, Fite & Riveland, Seattle, 1973-75, Morrison & Hedman, Whitefish, Mont., 1975-77; sole practice, Whitefish; justice Mont. Supreme Ct., Helena, 1991—; lectr. U. Mont. Law Sch., 1981—; mem. com. to amend civil proc. rules Mont. Supreme Ct., Helena, 1984, commn. to draft pattern jury instrns., 1985; mem. Gov.'s Adv. Com. on Amendment to Work Compensation Act, adv. com. Mont. Work Compensation Ct. Mem. ABA, Mont. Bar Assn. (pres. 1986-87), Wash. Bar Assn., Iowa Bar Assn., Assn. Trial Lawyers Am., Mont. Trial Lawyers Assn. (dir., pres.). Democrat. Roman Catholic. Home: 1615 Virginia Dale St Helena MT 59601-5823 Office: Mont Supreme Ct 414 Justice Bldg 215 N Sanders St Rm 323 Helena MT 59620 also: 215 N Sanders St Helena MT 59620*

TRIFFIN, NICHOLAS, law librarian, law educator; b. Boston, May 30, 1942; s. Robert and Lois (Brandt) T.; m. Mary M. Bertolet, June 1, 1965 (div. June 1975); children: Amyk (dec.), A. Robert; m. Madeleine J. Wilken, May 30, 1981. BA cum laude, Yale U., 1965, JD, 1968; MLS, Rutgers U., 1978. Bar: N.Y. 1969, Conn. 1973, U.S. Dist. Ct. Conn. 1973, U.S. Ct. Appeals (2nd cir.) 1973, U.S. Tax Ct. 1974. Assoc. Willkie Farr & Gallagher, N.Y.C., 1968-70; dean students Johnson (Vt.) State Coll., 1970-72; assoc. Di Sesa & Evans, New Haven, 1972-76; head pub. services, instr. law U. Conn., W. Hartford, 1977-81; law library dir., assoc. prof. Hamline U., St. Paul, 1982-84; dir. law library, prof. Pace U., White Plains, N.Y., 1984—; bd. dirs. Hale Found.; bd. advisors Oceana Pub., Inc., 1987-95; chief info. svcs. Inst. Internat. Comml. Law, 1993-94, dir., 1994—; adj. prof. Hartford Coll., 1978-80. Author: Law Books Published, 1984-95, Law Books in Print, 5th edit., 1987, 6th edit., 1991, 7th edit., 1995, Law Books in Review, 1984-92, Drafting History of the Federal Rules of Criminal Procedure, 1991; columnist Law Libr. Jour., 1983-84. Justice of the Peace, Conn., 1976-78. Mem. Am. Assn. Law Librs. (chmn. reader svcs. spl. interest sect. 1982-83, chmn. legal history and rare books spl. interest sect. 1991-92, chmn. constn. and bylaws com. 1994-95), Westchester Acad. Libr. Dirs. Orgn., Inc. (v.p. 1990-91, pres. 1991-92, exec. bd. dirs. 1992-94), Law Libr. New Eng. (pres. 1981-82), Minn. Assn. Law Librs. (v.p. 1983-84), Westchester Libr. Assn. (exec. bd. 1990-91), Inclusion Body Myositis Assn., Mory's Club, Beta Phi Mu. Mem. Soc. of Friends. Avocations: kayaking, rare books, opera. Office: Pace U Law Sch 78 N Broadway White Plains NY 10603-3710 *Society delights in putting barriers between people. Our greatest task is to remove these barriers - to use every encounter with others as an opportunity to empathise and to expand the horizons of our understanding - and to see that fundamentally we are all one.*

TRIGERE, PAULINE, fashion designer; b. Paris, Nov. 4, 1912; came to U.S., 1937, naturalized, 1942; d. Alexandre and Cecile (Coriene) Trigere; children: Jean-Pierre, Philippe Radley. Student, Victor Hugo Coll., Paris. Began career at Martial et Armand, Paris, 1937; became asst. designer at Hattie Carnegie, N.Y.C.; started House of Trigere, N.Y.C., 1942. Recipient Coty Am. Fashion Critics award, 1994, Return award, 1951, Neiman-Marcus award, 1950, Cotton award Nat. Cotton Coun., 1959, award Filene's, 1959, Coty Hall of Fame award, 1959, Silver medal City of Paris, 1972, medal of Vermeil City of Paris, 1982, Lifetime Achievement award, 1992, Nat. Arts Club award, 1993, Coun. of Fashion Designers Lifetime Achievement award Lincoln Ctr., 1994; celebrated 50 yrs. in the bus. at Fashion Inst. Tech., 1992. Office: Trigere Inc 498 7th Ave New York NY 10018-6701

TRIGG, GLYN RAY, guidance counelor, educational administrator; b. Canton, Miss., Apr. 21, 1964; s. Bruce L. and Eunice W. (Davis) T. BS in Social and Rehabilitative Svcs., U. So. Miss., 1991. Cert. phys. edn. tchr., guidance counselor, Miss. Alcohol-drug counselor, intervention-prevention counselor S.W. Miss. Mental Health, McComb, 1992-93; guidance counselor, tchr. phys. edn., coach Porter's Chapel Acad., Vicksburg, Miss., 1993—, interim hedmaster, 1994—. Bell ringer Salvation Army, Vicksburg, 1993; organizer, activities chmn. Eagle Fest, Porter's Chapel Patron's Club, 1994. Named Jaycee of Month, Hattiesburg Jaycees, 1991, recipient cert. of merit, Jacke Eckerd svc. award. Mem. Jackson Jaycees (2d dir. 1990-92, Jaycee of Month 1992), Kiwanis (faculty advisor Key Club 1993-94). Baptist. Home: 5402 66th St Apt 1024 Lubbock TX 79424

TRIGG, PAUL REGINALD, JR., lawyer; b. Lewistown, Mont., Mar. 25, 1913; s. Paul Reginald and Opal Stella (Fay) T.; m. Helen Ruth Leake, Dec. 25, 1938; children: Paul Reginald III, Mary Adra. BA, Grinnell Coll., 1935; JD, U. Mich., 1938. Bar: Mich. 1938. Practiced law in Detroit; ptnr. Dykema, Gossett (and predecessor), 1938—. Mem. ABA, Mich. Bar Assn., Detroit Bar Assn., Detroit Country Club, Yondotega Club. Clubs: Detroit, Detroit Country, Yondotega.

TRIGG, ROGER HUGH, philosophy educator; b. Pontypridd, Wales, Aug. 14, 1941; s. Ivor and Muriel Grace (Collins) T.; m. Julia Gibbs, July 12, 1972; children: Nicholas (dec.), Alison. MA, Oxford U., Eng., 1967, DPhil, 1968. From lectr. to sr. lectr. then reader U. Warwick, Coventry, Eng., 1966-87, prof. philosophy, 1987—, chmn. dept. philosophy, 1984-91, 94-95; dir. Ctr. for Rsch. in Philosophy and Lit., Coventry, 1985-91; vis. fellow St. Cross Coll., Oxford U., 1986-87, 91-92; vis. fellow Harris Manchester Coll., Oxford U., 1996; Stanton lectr. in Philosophy of Religion U. Cambridge, 1996-97. Author: Pain and Emotion, 1970, Reason and Commitment, 1973, Reality At Risk, 1980, The Shaping of Man, 1982, Understanding Social Science, 1985, Ideas of Human Nature, 1988, Rationality and Science, 1993. Justice of the Peace, Warwickshire, Eng., 1981-91. Mem. Brit. Soc. for Philosophy of Religion (pres. 1993-96), Royal Inst. Philosophy (of coun.), Mind Assn. (pres. 1997-98). Office: U Warwick, Dept Philosophy, Coventry West Midlands CV4 7AL, England

TRIGGER, BRUCE GRAHAM, anthropology educator; b. Cambridge (formerly Preston), Ont., Can., June 18, 1937; s. John Wesley and Gertrude Elizabeth (Graham) T.; m. Barbara Marian Welch, Dec. 7, 1968; children: Isabel Marian, Rosalyn Theodora. BA, U. Toronto, 1959; PhD, Yale U., 1964; DSc (hon.), U. N.B., 1987; LittD (hon.), U. Waterloo, 1990; LLD (hon.), U. Western Ont., 1995. Asst. prof. Northwestern U., 1963-64; asst. prof. McGill U., 1964-67, assoc. prof., 1967-69, prof. anthropology, 1969—, chmn. dept., 1970-75; bd. govs., 1996—; V.G. Childe Meml. lectr. U. London, 1982; Harry Hawthorn Disting. lectr., 1988; Disting. lectr. in archaeology Am. Anthrop. Assn., 1990; Disting. vis. prof. Am. U. in Cairo, 1992, Newman lectr., 1995. Author: History and Settlement in Lower Nubia, 1965, Beyond History, 1968, The Huron: Farmers of the North, 1969, 2d edit., 1990, Cartier's Hochelaga, 1972, Nubia Under the Pharaohs, 1976, The Children of Aataentsic, 1976, Time and Traditions, 1978, Gordon Childe: Revolutions in Archaeology, 1980, Natives and Newcomers, 1985, A History of Archaeological Thought, 1989, Early Civilizations, 1993; vol. editor: Handbook of North American Indians, Vol. 15, 1978; editor Native and Northern Series. Recipient Can. Silver Jubilee medal, 1977, Cornplanter medal, 1979, John Porter prize, 1987, Prix Victor-Barbeau Acad. Canadienne-française, 1991, Prix Leon-Gérin (Prix du Québec), 1991, James R. Wiseman Book award Archaeol. Inst. Am., 1991; Woodrow Wilson fellow, 1959-60, Woodrow Wilson dissertation fellow, 1962-63, Can. Coun. Leave fellow, 1968-69, 76-77, Killam rsch. fellow Can. Coun., 1970-71, 90, 91, leave fellow Social Scis. and Humanities Rsch. Coun. of Can., 1983. Fellow Royal Soc. Can. (Innis-Gerin medal 1985), Soc. Antiquaries of Scotland (hon.); mem. Prehistoric Soc. U.K. (hon.), Huron Great Turtle Clan (adopted), Sigma Xi. Home: Apt 603, 3495 Mountain St, Montreal, PQ Canada H3G 2A5 Office: McGill U Dept Anthropology, 855 Sherbrooke St W, Montreal, PQ Canada H3A 2T7

TRIGGER, KENNETH JAMES, manufacturing engineering educator; b. Carsonville, Mich., Sept. 6, 1910; married, 1939; 3 children. BS, Mich. State U., 1933, MS, 1935, ME, 1943. Asst. Mich. State Coll., 1933-34, instr. mech. engring., 1935-36; instr. mech. engring. Swarthmore (Pa.) Coll., 1937-38, Lehigh (Pa.) U., 1938-39; assoc. U. Ill., Urbana, 1939-45, from asst. prof. to prof., 1945-70, prof. mech. and indsl. engring.; cons. nuclear divsn. Union Carbide Corp., Continental Can Co., Aeroprojects Inc., Atlantic Richfield Co., numerous others. Fellow Soc. Mfg. Engrs. (medal 1959), Am. Soc. Mech. Engrs. (life), (Blackall award 1957, William T. Ennor Mfg. Tech. award 1992), Am. Soc. Metals (life); mem. Am. Soc. Engring. Edn. Achievements include research in metal cutting and machinability, physical metallurgy, cutting termperatures and temperature distribution in cutting of metals and mechanism of tool wear. Office: U Illinois Dept Mech Engr Indust Engr 140 1206 W Green St Urbana IL 61801-2906

TRIGGLE, DAVID JOHN, university dean, consultant; b. U.K., Apr. 5, 1935; came to U.S., 1962; s. William John and Maud F. (Henderson) T.; m. Ann. M. Jones, Sept. 22, 1959; children: Andrew B., Jocelyn A. BSc in Chemistry, U. Southampton, United Kingdom, 1956; PhD, U. Hull, United Kingdom, 1959. Research fellow U. Ottawa, Ont., Can., 1959-61, U. London, 1961-62; asst. prof. SUNY Sch. of Pharmacy, Buffalo, 1962-65, assoc. prof., 1965-69, prof., 1985-95, chmn. dept., 1971-85, dean, 1985-95, Disting. prof., vice-provost for grad. edn., 1990—. Author: Chemical Aspects of Autonomic Nervous System, 1965, Neurotransmitter-Receptor Interactions, 1971, Chemical Pharmacology of the Synapse, 1976. Recipient Volwiler Rsch. Achievement award Am. Assn. Colls. Pharmacy, 1988, 89, George Koepf award Biomed. Rsch. Med. Found. Buffalo, 1994. Fellow AAAS; mem. Am. Chem. Soc., Am. Soc. Pharmacology and Therapeutics (Otto Krayer award), Soc. Neurosci., Brit. Pharmacology Soc. Office: SUNY Grad Sch 410 Capen Buffalo NY 14260

TRIGIANO, LUCIEN LEWIS, physician; b. Easton, Pa., Feb. 9, 1926; s. Nicholas and Angeline (Lewis) T.; children: Lynn Anita, Glenn Larry, Robert Nicholas. Student Tex. Christian U., 1944-45, Ohio U., 1943-44, 46-47, Milligan Coll., 1944, Northwestern U., 1945, Temple U., 1948-52. Intern, Meml. Hosp., Johnstown, Pa., 1952-53; resident Lee Hosp., Johnstown, 1953-54; gen. practice, Johnstown, 1953-59; med. dir. Pa. Rehab. Center, Johnstown, 1959-62, chief phys. medicine and rehab., 1964-70; fellow phys. medicine and rehab. N.Y. Inst. Phys. Medicine and Rehab., 1962-64; dir. rehab. medicine Lee Hosp., 1964-71, Ralph K. Davies Med. Center, San Francisco, 1973-75, St. Joseph's Hosp., San Francisco, 1975-78, St. Francis Meml. Hosp., San Francisco, 1978-83; asst. prof. phys. medicine and rehab. Temple U. Sch. Medicine; founder Disability Alert. Served with USNR, 1944-46. Diplomate Am. Bd. Phys. Medicine and Rehab. Mem. AMA, A.C.P., Pa., San Francisco County Med. socs., Am. Acad. Phys. Medicine and Rehab., Am. Congress Phys. Medicine, Calif. Acad. Phys. Medicine, Nat. Rehab. Assn., Babcock Surg. Soc. Author various med. articles. Home: 1050 North Point St San Francisco CA 94109-8302 Office: 1150 Bush St Ste 4B San Francisco CA 94109-5920

TRILLIN, CALVIN MARSHALL, writer, columnist; b. Kansas City, Mo., Dec. 5, 1935; s. Abe and Edyth T.; m. Alice Stewart, Aug. 13, 1965; children: Abigail, Sarah Stewart. BA, Yale U., 1957; DLitt (hon.), Beloit Coll., 1987; LHD (hon.), Albertus Magnus Coll., 1990. Reporter, writer Time mag., 1960-63; staff writer New Yorker mag., 1963—; columnist Nation mag., 1978-85; syndicated columnist, 1986—; trustee N.Y. Pub. Libr. Author: An Education in Georgia, 1964, Barnett Frummer is an Unbloomed Flower, 1969, U.S. Journal, 1971, American Fried, 1974, Runestruck, 1977, Alice, Let's Eat, 1978, Floater, 1980, Uncivil Liberties, 1982, Third Helpings, 1983, Killings, 1984, With All Disrespect, 1985, If You Can't Say Something Nice, 1987, Travels With Alice, 1989, Enough's Enough, 1990, American Stories, 1991, Remembering Denny, 1993, Deadline Poet, 1994, Too Soon to Tell, 1995; author, performer one-man show Calvin Trillin's Uncle Sam, Am. Place Theatre, N.Y.C., 1988, Calvin Trillin's Words, No Music, Am. Place Theatre, 1990. Office: care New Yorker 20 W 43rd St New York NY 10036-7400

TRILLING, DIANA, writer; b. N.Y.C., July 21, 1905; d. Joseph and Sadie Helene (Forbert) Rubin; m. Lionel Trilling, June 12, 1929; 1 son, James Lionel. A.B., Radcliffe Coll., 1925. Fiction critic: The Nation, 1941-49; free-lance writer on lit., social and polit. subjects, 1949—; author: Claremont Essays, 1964, We Must March My Darlings, 1977, Reviewing The Forties, 1978, Mrs. Harris: The Death of the Scarsdale Diet Doctor, 1981, The Beginning of the Journey: The Marriage of Diana and Lionel Trilling, 1993; contbr. numerous articles to mags.; Editor: Viking Portable D. H. Lawrence, 1947, Selected Letters of D. H. Lawrence, 1958, Uniform Edition of the Works of Lionel Trilling, 1978-80. Guggenheim fellow, 1950-51, 91-92; Rockefeller-NEH grantee, 1977-79. Fellow Am. Acad. Arts and Scis.; mem. Phi Beta Kappa (hon.).

TRILLING, DONALD R., federal agency administrator; b. Phila., Jan. 23, 1928; s. David Morris and Shirley (Siskin) T.; m. Jane Hunter, June 6, 1954 (div.); m. Shirley Morlan, Aug. 8, 1975; children: Jeffrey, James, Terry, Greg, Randy. BA in Economics, U. Pa., 1956, MA in Economics, 1959, PhD in Bus. Applied Economics, 1969. Mgr. mgmt. scis. Westinghouse Electric Corp., Pitts., 1967-69; dir. Washington ops. Westinghouse Pub. Mgmt. Svc., 1969-73; dir. policy rev., office sec. U.S. Dept. Transp., Washington, 1973-81; acting dep. asst. sec. policy office OST, Washington, 1978-79; exec. asst. to dep. sec. U.S. Dept. Transp., Washington, 1981-83; dir. environ. and safety policy office OST, Washington, 1986-92; mgr. industry policy Commercial Space Trans., Washington, 1983-86; acting dir. Comml. Space Transp., Washington, 1992-93; dir., environ. and safety office OST, 1994—. Co-author: (handbook) New Horizons for Air Traveler, 1991. 1st lt. US Army, 1950-53, Korea. Decorated Bronze Star, 1953. Mem. AIAA, Nat. Economists Club. Republican. Home: 5903 Mount Eagle Dr Apt 1418 Alexandria VA 22303-2532 Office: Dept of Transp Environ Energy and Safety 400 7th St SW Washington DC 20590-0001

TRILLING, GEORGE HENRY, physicist, educator; b. Bialystok, Poland, Sept. 18, 1930; came to U.S., 1941; s. Max and Eugenie (Walfisz) T.; m. Madeleine Alice Monic, June 26, 1955; children: Stephen, Yvonne, David. BS, Calif. Inst. Tech., Pasadena, 1951, PhD, 1955. Research fellow Calif. Inst. Tech., Pasadena, 1955-56; Fulbright post-doctoral fellow Ecole Polytechnique, Paris, 1956-57; asst. to assoc. prof. U. Mich., Ann Arbor, 1957-60; assoc. to prof. dept. physics U. Calif., Berkeley, 1960—. Fellow Am. Phys. Soc., Am. Acad. Arts and Scis.; mem. NAS. Research in high energy physics. Office: Lawrence Berkeley Lab Berkeley CA 94720

TRILLING, HELEN REGINA, lawyer; b. Boston, May 13, 1950; d. Charles Alexander and A. Lillian Trilling. AB magna cum laude, Radcliffe Coll., 1973; JD, Harvard U., 1976. Bar: Mass. 1977, U.S. Dist. Ct. Mass. 1978, U.S. Supreme Ct. 1980, D.C. 1984, U.S. Ct. Appeals (10th cir.) 1984. Asst. gen. counsel Blue Cross/Blue Shield, Boston, 1976-79; sp. asst. to gen. counsel HHS, Washington, 1979-83; assoc. Hogan & Hartson, Washington, 1983-86, ptnr., 1987—. Mem. ABA (health law forum com.), Nat. Health Lawyers Assn., Women and Health Roundtable, Women's Legal Def. Fund, Wash. Council Lawyers.

TRILLING, LEON, aeronautical engineering educator; b. Bialystok, Poland, July 15, 1924; came to U.S., 1940, naturalized, 1946; s. Oswald and Regina (Zakhejm) T.; m. Edna Yuval, Feb. 17, 1946; children: Alex R., Roger S. B.S., Calif. Inst. Tech., 1944, M.S., 1946, Ph.D., 1948. Research fellow Calif. Inst. Tech., 1948- 50; Fulbright scholar U. Paris, 1950-51, vis. prof., 1963-64; mem. faculty MIT, Cambridge, 1951—, prof. aeros. and astronautics, 1962-94, prof. emeritus, 1994—, mem. coun. on primary and secondary edn., 1992—; mem. Program in Sci. Tech. and Society, Engring. Edn. Mission to Soviet Union, 1958; vis. prof. Delft Tech. U., 1974-75; vis. prof. engring. Carleton Coll., 1987;. Pres. Met. Com. Ednl. Opportunity, 1967-70, Council for Understanding of Tech. in Human Affairs, 1984—. Guggenheim fellow, 1963-64. Fellow AAAS. Home: 180 Beacon St Boston MA 02116-1401 Office: MIT 77 Massachusetts Ave Cambridge MA 02139-4301

TRIM, DONALD ROY, consulting engineer; b. Saginaw, Mich., June 23, 1937; s. Roy E. and Agnes (Kontranowski) T.; m. Dorothy Mae Franek, Aug. 11, 1962; children—Jeffrey D., Gregory S., Christopher M. B.S. in Civil Engring., U. Mich., 1959. Registered profl. engr., Mich., Ohio, Fla.; registered land surveyor, Mich. Engr., Francis Engring., Saginaw, 1959-64, Edwin M. Orr, Inc., Dearborn, Mich., 1964-66; pres. Wade-Trim Group, Plymouth, Mich., 1966—; pres. Wade-Trim Inc., Tampa, Fla., 1984—. Vice pres. Plymouth Canton Basketball Assn., 1980-84; bd. govs. Greater Mich. Found., Lansing, 1983-85. Mem. Nat. Soc. Profl. Engrs., Cons. Engrs. Council Mich. (dir. 1972-73, pres. 1983-84), Am. Cons. Engrs. Council (v.p. 1986-88), Am. Waterworks Assn. Roman Catholic. Office: Wade-Trim Group PO Box 701428 Plymouth MI 48170-0964

TRIMBLE, CHARLES R., electronics executive; b. 1941. BS in Engring., Calif. Inst. Tech., 1963, MS in Elec. Engring., 1964. Mgr. integrated circuit rsch. and devel. Hewlett-Packard Co., Santa Clara, Calif., 1964-78; pres., CEO Trimble Navigation Ltd., Sunnyvale, Calif., 1978—; now chmn. Trimble Navigation Ltd., Sunnyvale, CA. Recipient Piper Gen. Aviation award Am. Inst. Aeronautics and Astronautics, 1994. Office: Trimble Navigation Limited 585 N Mary Ave Sunnyvale CA 94086-2905*

TRIMBLE, GEORGE SIMPSON, industrial executive; b. Phila., Oct. 12, 1915; s. George Simpson and Edna Mae (Mytinger) T.; m. Janet Anna Bogue, Apr. 15, 1939; children: Robert Bogue, Frank George. S.B., Mass. Inst. Tech., 1936. With The Martin Co., Balt., 1937-67; successively draftsman, design engr., chief fluid dynamics, mgr. aerodynamics, mgr. advanced design, v.p. advanced design The Martin Co., 1937-55, v.p. engring., 1955-60, v.p. advanced programs, 1960-67; dir. Advanced Manned Missions Program, NASA, Washington, 1967; dep. dir. Johnson Spacecraft Center, Houston, 1967-69; pres., dir. Bunker Ramo Corp., Oak Brook, Ill., 1970-80; dir. Richardson Co., Des Plaines, Ill., 1978-82, Martin Marietta Corp., 1970-78; owner, pres. Carefree Engine Co. (Ariz.), 1981—; cons. Sci. Adv. Bd. Aero Vehicle Panel, 1959-61, Office Dir. Def., Research and Engring. Trustee Devereux Found., 1968—, chmn. bd. trustees, 1976-79. Fellow AIAA; mem. Tau Beta Pi. Home: PO Box 1355 Carefree AZ 85377-1355 Office: Carefree Engine Co Carefree AZ 83577

TRIMBLE, JAMES T., JR., federal judge; b. Bunkie, La., Sept. 13, 1932; s. James T. Sr. and Mabel (McNabb) T.; m. Murel Elise Biles, Aug. 18, 1956; children: Lise Ann Reed, Mary Olive Beacham, Martha McNabb Elliott, Sarah Palmer Trimble. Attended, U. Southwestern La. (formerly Southwestern La. Inst.), 1950-52; BA in Law, La. State U., 1955, JD, 1956. Bar: La. 1956. With Gist, Murchison & Gist (now Gist, Methvin, Hughes & Munsterman), 1959-78, Trimble, Percy, Smith, Wilson, Foote, Walker & Honeycutt, 1979-86; U.S. magistrate U.S. Dist. Ct. (we. dist.) La., 1986-91, judge, 1991—. Lt. USAF, 1956-59. Mem. Fed. Judges Assn., Southwest La. Bar Assn., La. Bar Assn., La. Bar Found. Avocations: jogging, gardening, tennis. Office: 611 Broad St Ste 237 Lake Charles LA 70601-4380

TRIMBLE, KATHLEEN LOUISE, library director; b. Reading, Pa., Oct. 10, 1949; d. Melvin Blackburn and Ruth Louise (Kreitz) T.; m. Richard Harvey Greenberg, May 20, 1984; children: Max, Jacob. BA, U. Toledo, 1972, MLS, 1979. Librarian II Toledo Blade, 1971-75, librarian I, 1975-78, asst. head librarian, 1976-78, head librarian, 1978-82; mgr. library info. U.S. News and World Report, Washington, 1982-83, library dir., 1983—. Recipient Henebry award News Divsn., 1993. Mem. Spl. Libraries Assn. (dir. newspaper div. 1978-80, sec.-treas. 1979-81). Jewish. Office: US News & World Report 2400 N St NW Washington DC 20037-1153

TRIMBLE, PAUL JOSEPH, retired lawyer; b. Springfield, Mass., Oct. 9, 1930; s. Peter Paul and Bernnese (Myrick) T.; m. Suzanne Hrudka; children: Troy, Derrick, Andrew. B.A., Am. Internat. U., Springfield, Mass., 1952; LL.B., U. Tex., Austin, 1955. Bar: Calif., Tex., Ill., Alaska. Counsel Mobil Oil Corp., Joliet, Ill., 1964-72; assoc. counsel Fluor Corp., Irvine, Calif., 1972-73, corp. counsel, 1973-74, sr. corp. counsel, 1974, asst. gen. counsel, 1974-80, gen. counsel, 1980-82, sr. v.p., gen. counsel, 1982-96, sr. v.p. law, gen. counsel, 1984-96, corp. sec., 1992-96. Mem. ABA, Calif. Bar Assn., Tex. Bar Assn., Ill. Bar Assn., Alaska Bar Assn. Republican.

TRIMBLE, PHILLIP RICHARD, law educator; b. Springfield, Ohio, Nov. 12, 1937; s. Melvin R. and Dorothy (Lang) T.; m. Stephanie Gardner, July 20, 1963 (div. 1977); children: John, William. BA, Ohio U., 1958; MA, Tufts U., 1959; JD, Harvard U., 1963. Bar: NY 1964. Legal writing instr. U. Calif., Berkeley, 1963-64; assoc. Cravath, Swaine & Moore, N.Y.C., 1964-70; staff mem. senate fgn. rels. com. Dept. State, Washington, 1971-72, asst. legal adviser, 1973-78; counsel to the mayor N.Y.C., 1978; dep. mayor N.Y.C., 1979; U.S. ambassador Nepal, 1980-81; prof. law UCLA, 1981—; mem. exec. com. Asia Soc. So. Calif. Ctr., L.A., 1981-94; vis. prof. law Stanford U., 1988-89, U. Mich., 1995-96; U.S. panelist under U.S.-Can. Free Trade Agreement; cons. ACDA, 1989-92. Mem. bd. editors Am. Jour. Internat. Law. Fellow Explorers Club; mem. Am. Soc. Internat. Law, Am. Alpine Club (bd. dirs. 1978-87). Democrat. Avocation: mountaineering. Office: UCLA Law Sch 405 Hilgard Ave Los Angeles CA 90095-1301

TRIMBLE, PRESTON ALBERT, retired judge; b. Salina, Okla., Aug. 27, 1930; s. James Albert and Winnie Louella (Walker) T.; m. Patricia Ann Beadle; children: Todd, Beth, Amy. B.A., U. Okla., 1956, LL.B., 1960. Bar: Okla. 1960. Practice law, 1960; asst. county atty. Cleveland County, Okla., 1960-62; county atty., 1962-67, dist. atty., 1967-79, dist. judge, 1979-91; spl. instr. S.W. Center Law Enforcement Edn.; cons. prosecution mgmt. Mem. Jud. Council Okla.; chmn. Okla. Corrections Workshop; mem. planning com. Nat. Inst. Crime and Delinquency; mem. com. on multi-agy. problems in criminal justice Appellate Judges Conf. Bd. dirs. Okla. U. Crisis Ctr., 1970—, ARC, Lake Murray Conservation Assn.; trustee Nat. Assn. Pretrial Svc. Agys. Resource Ctr., Sarkeys Found., 1994—. With USNR, 1948-52; col. USAFR. Mem. Okla., Cleveland County bar assns., Nat. Dist. Attys. Assn. (past pres.), Okla. Dist. Attys. Assn. (past pres.), Nat. Coll. Dist. Attys. (bd. regents), Am. Legion. Democrat. Methodist. Club: Lion. Home: 1886 Trailview Dr Norman OK 73072-6655 Office: 231 S Peters Ave Norman OK 73069-6035 *An elected public official must remember that the people own his position and he only holds it in trust for them.*

TRIMBLE, STANLEY WAYNE, hydrology and geography educator; b. Columbia, Tenn., Dec. 8, 1940; s. Stanley Drake and Clara Faye (Smith) T.; m. Alice Erle Gunn, Aug. 16, 1964; children: Alicia Anne, Jennifer Lusanne. BS, U. North Ala., 1964; MA, U. Ga., 1970, PhD, 1973. Asst. prof. hydrology and geography U. Wis., Milw., 1972-75; from assoc. prof. to prof. UCLA, 1975—; vis. asst. prof. U. Chgo., 1978, vis. assoc. prof., 1981, vis. prof. environ. geography, 1990—; vis. lectr. U. London, 1985; hydrologist U.S. Geol. Survey, 1974-84; vis. prof. U. Vienna, 1994; Frost lectr. Brit. Geomorphological Rsch. Group, Durham, Eng., 1994; vis. rsch. lectr. Oxford U., 1995; Fulbright scholar in U.K., 1995; vis. fellow Keble Coll., Oxford U., 1995 member, committee on watershed mang. National Academy of Sciences, 1996—. Author: Culturally Accelerated Sedimentation on the Middle Georgia Piedmont, 1971, Man-Induced Erosion on the Southern Piedmont, 1700-1970, 1974, Soil Conservation and the Reduction, 1982, Sediment Characteristics of Tennessee Streams, 1984; joint editor: Catena, 1995—; contbr. articles to profl. jours. Served to 1st lt. U.S. Army, 1963-65. Grantee U.S. Geol. Survey, Washington, 1974-79, Wis. Dept. Natural Resources, Madison, 1978, 82, 93, 94, 95, NSF, Washington, 1976, Agrl. Rsch. Svc. of USDA, Washington, 1972, Nat. Geographic Soc., 1993. Mem. NAS (com. on watershed mgmt.), Assn. Am. Geographers, Am. Geophys. Union, Soil Conservation Soc. Am., Brit. Geomorphol. Rsch. Group, Sigma Xi. Republican. Avocations: historic houses, documentation and restoration. Office: UCLA Dept Geography 405 Hilgard Ave Los Angeles CA 90024-1301

TRIMBLE, THOMAS JAMES, utility company executive, lawyer; b. Carters Creek, Tenn., Sept. 3, 1931; s. John Elijah and Mittie (Rountree) T.; m. Glenna Kay Jones, Sept. 3, 1957; children: James Jefferson, Julie Kay. BA, David Lipscomb U., 1953; JD, Vanderbilt U., 1956; LLM, NYU, 1959. Bar: Tenn. 1956, Ariz. 1961, U.S. Dist. Ct. Ariz. 1961, U.S. Dist. Ct. D.C. 1963, U.S. Ct. Appeals (10th cir.) 1971, U.S. Supreme Ct. 1972, U.S. Ct. Appeals (9th cir.) 1975. From assoc. to ptnr. Jennings, Strouss & Salmon, Phoenix, 1960-85, mng. ptnr., 1985-87; sr. v.p., gen. counsel, corp. sec. S.W. Gas Corp., Las Vegas, Nev., 1987—, gen. counsel, 1987-92; corp. sec. Primerit Bank, 1990-92, pres., 1994-96; exec. v.p. Energy Ins. (Bermuda) Ltd., 1992-94, bd. dirs., 1992—; bd. dirs. Energy Ins. Mut. Ltd., vice chmn., 1992-94, chmn., 1994-96. Mem. editorial bd. Vanderbilt U. Law Rev., 1954-56. Mem. Pepperdine U. Bd. Regents, Malibu, Calif., 1981—, sec., 1982—, mem. exec. com., 1982-89; bd. visitors Pepperdine Sch. Law, Malibu; pres. Big Sisters Ariz., Phoenix, 1975, bd. dirs., 1970-76; chmn. Sunnydale Children's Home, Phoenix, 1966-69, bd. dirs., 1965-75; pres. Clearwater Hills Improvement Assn., Phoenix, 1977-79, bd. dirs., 1975-80; trustee Nev. Sch. of Arts, 1988-92, chmn., 1989-90. 1st lt. JAGC, USAF, 1957-60. Fellow Ariz. Bar Assn. (editorial bd. Jour. 1975-80), Am. Gas Assn. (legal sect. mng. com. 1987—), Order of Coif, Spanish Trail Country Club (Las Vegas), Southshore Golf Club (Las Vegas), Kiwanis (pres. Phoenix 1972-73), Phi Delta Phi. Republican. Mem. Ch. Christ. Home: 5104 Turnberry Ln Las Vegas NV 89113-1394 Office: SW Gas Corp PO Box 98510 5241 Spring Mountain Rd Las Vegas NV 89150-8510

TRIMBLE, VANCE HENRY, retired newspaper editor; b. Harrison, Ark., July 6, 1913; s. Guy L. and Josephine (Crump) T.; m. Elzene Miller, Jan. 9, 1932; 1 dau., Carol Ann. Student pub. schs., Wewoka, Okla. Cub reporter Okemah (Okla.) Daily Leader, 1928; worked various newspapers in Okmulgee, Muskogee, Tulsa and, Okla.; successively reporter, rewrite man, city editor Houston Press, 1939-50, mng. editor, 1950-55; news editor Scripps-Howard Newspaper Alliance, Washington, 1955-63; editor Ky. Post and Times-Star, Covington, 1963-79. Author: The Uncertain Miracle, 1974, Sam M. Walton, 1990, (biography) E.W. Scripps, 1992, Frederick Smith of Federal Express, 1993, An Empire Undone: Rise and Fall of Chris Whittle, 1995; co-author: Happy Chandler Autobiography, 1989; editor: Scripps-Howard Handbook, 1981. Trustee Scripps-Howard Found., 1974-79. Recipient Pulitzer prize for nat. reporting, 1960, Raymond Clapper award, 1960, Sigma Delta Chi award for disting. Washington correspondence, 1960, Frank Luther Mott award for journalism book rsch. U. Mo., 1993; named to Okla. Journalism Hall of Fame, 1974. Mem. Am. Soc. Newspaper Editors. Baptist. Clubs: Nat. Press (Washington); Press (Houston); Cincinnati, Ft. Mitchell Country. Home: 1013 Sunset Rd Covington KY 41011-1168

TRIMBLE, WILLIAM CATTELL, JR., lawyer; b. Buenos Aires, Argentina, Feb. 7, 1935; s. William Cattell and Nancy Gordon (Carroll) T.; m. Barbara Janney, June 19, 1960; children: William C., Margery M. Kennelly. A.B., Princeton U., 1958; LL.B., U. Md., 1964. Bar: Md. 1965. With firm Ober, Grimes & Shriver, Balt., 1965-87, ptnr., 1970-87, mng. ptnr., 1973-77; counsel Semmes, Bowen & Semmes, Balt., 1987—; mem. Gov.'s Commn. to Revise Annotated Code of Md., 1975-83. Pres. bd. trustees Valley Sch., 1968-73; trustee Garrison Forest Sch., 1975-95, Gilman Sch. 1980-84; hon. consul of The Netherlands, 1986—. Lt. USNR, 1958-61. Mem. Am., Md., Balt. bar assns. Episcopalian. Clubs: Colonial (Princeton); Md, Greenspring Valley Hunt, Soc. of Cin. Home: 409 Chattolanee Hill Rd Owings Mills MD 21117-4318 Office: 16th Fl 250 W Pratt St Baltimore MD 21201

TRIMMER, HAROLD SHARP, JR., lawyer, international telecommunications consultant; b. Somerville, N.J., July 27, 1938; s. Harold Sharp and Mary Elizabeth (Knox) T. B.A., Wesleyan U., 1960; J.D., Harvard U., 1963. Instr. law UCLA, 1963-64; Congl. fellow Am. Polit. Sci. Assn., Washington, 1964-65; assoc. Royall, Koegel & Rogers, Washington and N.Y.C., 1965-66, McCutchen, Doyle, Brown & Enersen, San Francisco, 1966-69; with GSA, Washington, 1969-75; exec. asst. to adminstr. GSA, 1969-70, asst. adminstr., 1970-72, commr. automated data and telecommunications, 1972-73, assoc. adminstr. fed. mgmt. policy, 1973, gen. counsel, 1974-75; sec., gen. counsel Garfinckel, Brooks Bros., Miller & Rhoads, Inc., Washington, 1976-82, v.p., 1979-82; v.p. internat. MCI Communications Corp., Washington, 1982-83, v.p. regulatory policy, 1983-84, v.p. fin. and adminstrn. M.A. div., 1984-86, v.p. govt. systems, 1986-87; pres. Pacific div. MCI Communications Corp., San Francisco, 1987-89, sr. v.p. internat. devel., 1990-91; cons. internat. telecom., 1991—. Trustee World Affairs Council No. Calif., 1969-70, Wesleyan U., 1971-74. George F. Baker scholar. Mem. State Bar Calif., Phi Beta Kappa. Home: 169 Filbert Ave Sausalito CA 94965-1846

TRIMMIER, ROSCOE, JR., lawyer; b. Charlotte, N.C., July 22, 1944; s. Roscoe and Susie Elizabeth (Stitt) T.; divorced; 1 child, Leigh Snowden. AB, Harvard U., 1971, JD, 1974. Bar: Mass. 1974, U.S. Dist. Ct. Mass. 1975, U.S. Ct. Appeals (1st cir.) 1975, U.S. Supreme Ct. 1979, U.S. Claims Ct. 1983. Assoc. Ropes & Gray, Boston, 1974-83, ptnr., 1983—; mem. hearing com. Bd. Bar Overseers, 1983-89; bd. dirs., v.p. Family Counseling & Guidance Ctr., Inc., Boston, 1980-93; overseer Mus. of Sci., 1981-93; mem. exec. com. Jud. Nominating Commn., 1991—; corp. mem. Mass. Gen. Hosp., 1992—; overseer N.E Med. Ctr. Hosps., 1992—. Served to 1st lt. U.S. Army, 1965-68. Fellow Am. Bar Found. (life), Mass. Bar Found. (life), Am. Coll. Trial Lawyers; mem. ABA, Mass. Bar Assn., Boston Bar Assn., Mass. Soc. for Prevention of Cruelty to Children, Mass. Black Lawyers Assn. (life). Home: 1265 Beacon St Brookline MA 02146-5243 Office: Ropes & Gray 1 International Pl Boston MA 02110-2600

TRINH, VICTOR, small business owner; b. Vientiane, Laos, Apr. 7, 1941; came to U.S., 1975; naturalized, 1981; s. Thu and Mao (Nguyen) T.; m. Tuyet Mai Nguyen, Jan. 19, 1972; children: Nancy H., Wiliam Q. Grad. high sch., Vientiane. Electronic assembler Anilam Electronics, Miami, Fla., 1978-80; owner Kim-Do Food, Pitts., 1981-85, Jensen Food Mart, Houston, 1986—; pub. Vic Pub., Houston, 1993—. Author: Student Assignments Notebook, 1993. Avocations: biking, swimming. Office: 7202 Jensen Dr Houston TX 77093-8705

TRINKAUS, JOHN PHILIP, cell and developmental biologist; b. Rockville Centre, N.Y., May 23, 1918; s. Charles Edward and Fransiska Magdalena (Krueger) T.; m. Madeleine Francine Marguerite Bazin, Oct. 6, 1963; children: Gregor, Tanya, Erik. B.A. with honors and high distinction in Biology, Wesleyan U., Middletown, Conn., 1940; M.A. (Cramer fellow in genetics), Columbia U., 1941; Ph.D., Johns Hopkins U., 1948. Mem. faculty Yale U., New Haven, 1948—; prof. cell. and devel. biology Yale U., 1964—, dir. grad. studies in biology, 1965, master of Branford Coll., 1966-73, also dir. undergrad. studies in biology, prof. emeritus biology, 1988—, sr. rsch. scientist, 1988—; chmn. Gordon Rsch. Conf. on Cell Contact and Movement, 1979; mem. staff embryology course Woods Hole (Mass.) Marine Biol. Lab., 1953-57, 78, trustee, 1991—; mem. space biology adv. panel NASA, 1976-79; lectr. internat. symposia, including Internat. Inst. Embryology, Moscow, 1969, Ciba, London, 1972, Devl. Biol Fishes, Tampa, 1979, 500th anniversary U. Uppsala, Sweden, 1977, Conf. on Malignancy, Keystone, Colo., 1979, Conf. on Cell Behaviour, London, 1982 and Oxford, 1987, Gastrulation, Louisville, 1982, Biol. Fundulus, Phila., 1983, Conf. Cell Traffic, Zurich, 1984, Cellular Basis of Morphogenesis, Woods Hole, 1988, Experimental Embryology of Aquatic Plants and Animals, Banyuls-sur-Mer, 1989, Gastrulation: Movements, Patterns and Molecules, Bodega Bay, 1990, Cytoskeleton. in Devel. Biology, Kingston, Ont., 1991, Gastrulation, Brighton, U.K., 1992, Devl. and Genetics of Zebrafish, Cold Spring Harbor, 1994, Soc. Devel. Biology, La Jolla, 1995. Author: Cells into Organs-The Forces that Shape the Embryo, 1969, 2d rev. edit., 1984, On the Mechanism of Metazoan Cell Movements, 1976; also articles on cell motility, invasiveness, morphogenesis, gastrulation and differentiation; assoc. editor: Jour. Exptl. Zoology, 1964-68. Served to capt. USAAF, 1942-46. Recipient citation for distinction in scholarship and teaching Wesleyan U., 1960; John Simon Guggenheim fellow Coll. de France, 1959-60; NSF grantee, 1952-76; NIH grantee, 1974—; Merit award NIH, 1987-96. Mem. Am. Soc. Zoologists, Am. Soc. Cell Biology, Am. Soc. Developmental Biology (Edwin Grant Conklin medal 1995), Internat. Inst. Embryology, ACLU, Phi Beta Kappa, Sigma Xi. Clubs: Yale (N.Y.C.); Mory's. Home: Moose Hill Rd Guilford CT 06437-2356 Office: Osborn Meml Lab Yale Univ Dept Biology New Haven CT 06520

TRINKUS, LAIMA MARY, special education educator; b. Chgo., Mar. 6, 1950; d. Steven and Antonia (Ambrasas) Trinkus. BS in Sociology, Daemen Coll., Buffalo, 1974; MS in Behavioral Sci. Spl. Edn., SUNY, Buffalo, 1987. Cert. spl. edn. tchr., N.Y. Tchr. aide Cantalician Ctr. for Learning, Buffalo, 1975-78, tchr. spl. edn., 1978-85; tchr. spl. edn. Erie I Bd. Coop. Edn. Svcs., Lancaster, N.Y., 1985—. Vol. Spl. Olympics, Buffalo, 1976—. Home: 9821 Greiner Rd Clarence NY 14031

TRIO, EDWARD ALAN, lawyer, accountant; b. Newark, N.J., Dec. 29, 1952; s. Edward B. and Dorothy J. (Salvia) T.; m. Patricia Ann Sherwood, June 19, 1982; children: Edward Joseph, Michael John. B.B.A., U. Notre Dame, 1974; J.D., Hamline U., St. Paul, 1977; LL.M. in Taxation with honors, Chgo.-Kent Coll. Law, 1984. Bar: Ill. 1977, U.S. Dist. Ct. (no. dist.) Ill. 1977, U.S. Tax Ct. 1979, U.S. Supreme Ct. 1984. C.P.A. Staff auditor Donald E. Bark, C.P.A., Arlington Heights, Ill., 1972-77; assoc. Graf & Gulbrandsen, Morton Grove, Ill., 1977-80; ptnr. Schneider, Graf & Trio, Morton Grove, 1980-82; tax specialist Deloitte Haskins & Sells, Chgo., 1982-85; assoc. Gould & Ratner, Chgo., 1985-90, ptnr., 1991—. Mem. ABA, AICPA, Ill. State Bar Assn., Chgo. Bar Assn., KC. Roman Catholic. Home: 909 N Derbyshire Ave Arlington Heights IL 60004-5776 Office: Gould & Ratner 222 N La Salle St Chicago IL 60601-1086

TRIOLO, PETER, advertising agency executive, marketing educator, consultant; b. N.Y.C., Feb. 20, 1927; s. Antonino and Cira T.; m. Audrey Sullivan, Aug. 7, 1954; children—Stuart, Bruce, Ellen, Leslie. A.B., Adelphi U., Garden City, N.Y., 1952; exec. program, Columbia U. Grad. Sch. Bus., 1966. Vice pres. Ogilvy & Mather, Inc., N.Y.C., 1958-64; sr. v.p. Ketchum, MacLeod & Grove Inc., Pitts. and N.Y.C., 1964-68; founder, exec. v.p. Marketronics Inc., N.Y.C., 1968-72; chief adminstrv. officer Rosenfeld, Sirowitz & Lawson Inc., N.Y.C., 1972-76; sr. v.p., media dir. William Esty Co., Inc., N.Y.C., 1976-87; cons. Internat. Exec. Svc. Corps, Stamford, Conn., 1987—; adj. prof. mktg. Baruch Coll., City U. N.Y., 1980-86, Fordham U., N.Y.C., 1987—. Guest editor: Mktg. and Media Decisions, 1967. Served with USAAF, 1945-47. Mem. Assn. Nat. Advertisers (TV workshops), Advt. Age Media Workshops Faculty, Mktg. and Media Decisions Faculty.

TRIPATHY, SUKANT KISHORE, chemistry educator; b. Chakradharpur, Bihar, India, Aug. 4, 1952; came to U.S., 1976; s. Jyotish C. and Usha (Pani) T.; m. Susan Thomson, Sept. 5, 1981; children: Sheila, Aneil. MS, I.I.T. Kharagpur, 1974; PhD, Case Western Res. U., 1981. Tech. staff mem. GTE Labs., Waltham, Mass., 1981-83; rsch. mgr. GTE Labs., Waltham, 1983-86; assoc. prof. chemistry U. Lowell, Mass., 1986-87; prof. chemistry U. Lowell, 1987—; dir. ctr. advanced materials U. Mass., Lowell, 1992-94, vice chancellor for acad. affairs, 1994—; dir. Molecular Technologies, Inc., Lowell, 1987—. Contbr. over 200 articles to profl. jours. Mem. AAAS, Am. Chem. Soc. (Carl S. Marvel Creative Polymer Chemistry award 1993), Am. Phys. Soc., Sigma Xi, MRS, SPE. Achievements include 20 patents. Home: 8 Northbriar Rd Acton MA 01720-5826 Office: U Mass Ctr for Advanced Materials 1 University Ave Lowell MA 01854-2881

TRIPLEHORN, CHARLES A., entomology educator, insects curator; b. Bluffton, Ohio, Oct. 27, 1927; s. Murray E. and Alice Irene (Lora) T.; m. Wanda Elaine Neiswander, June 12, 1949 (dec. Nov. 1985); children: Bradley Alyn, Bruce Wayne; m. Linda Sue Parsons, July 11, 1987. B.Sc., Ohio State U., 1949, M.S., 1952; Ph.D., Cornell U., 1957. Asst. prof. entomology U. Del., Newark, 1952-54; teaching asst. entomology Cornell U., Ithaca, N.Y., 1954-57; asst. prof. entomology Ohio Agrl. Research and Devel. Ctr., Wooster, Ohio, 1957-61; asst. prof. entomology Ohio State U., Columbus, 1961-62, assoc. prof. entomology, 1962-66, prof. entomology, 1966-92, prof. emeritus, 1992—; econ. entomologist U.S. AID/Brazil, Piracicaba, Sao Paulo, 1964-66; vis. curator Can. Nat. Collection, Ottawa, Ont., 1977. Co-author: Introduction to the Study of Insects, 6th edit., 1989. Cubmaster Boy Scouts Am., Wooster, Ohio, 1959-60, scoutmaster, Columbus, 1971-72;

football coach Upper Arlington Football Assn., Ohio, 1968-71. Grantee Am. Philos. Soc., 1963, NSF, 1979, 85. Mem. Entomol. Soc. Am. (pres. 1985), Coleopterists Soc. (pres. 1976), Royal Entomol. Soc. London, Entomol. Soc. Washington, Sigma Xi, Gamma Sigma Delta. Republican. Methodist. Club: Wheaton (pres.). Avocations: sports; music; reading; writing. Home: 3943 Medford Sq Hilliard OH 43026-2219 Office: Mus Biol Diversity Div Insects The Ohio State University 1315 Kinnear Rd Columbus OH 43212-1157

TRIPLETT, ARLENE ANN, travel company executive; b. Portland, Oreg., Jan. 21, 1942; d. Vincent Michael and Lorraine Catherine (Starr) Jakovich; m. William Karrol Triplett, Jan. 27, 1962; children: Stephen Michael, Patricia Ann. B.A. in Bus. Adminstrn., U. Calif., Berkeley, 1963. Budgets and reports analyst Cutter Labs., Berkeley, 1963-66; controller Citizens for Reagan, 1975-76; dir. adminstrn. Republican. Nat. Com., 1977-80; asst. sec. Dept. Commerce, Washington, 1981-83; assoc. dir. mgmt. Office Mgmt. and Budget, Exec. Office of Pres., Washington, 1983-85; prin. assoc. McManis Assocs., Inc., 1985-87, v.p., 1987-89, sr. v.p., 1989-93; v.p. Am. Tours Internat., Inc., L.A., 1993—, exec. v.p., 1994—. Roman Catholic. Office: Am Tours Internat Inc 6053 W Century Blvd Los Angeles CA 90045-5323

TRIPLETT, E. EUGENE, editor; b. LaJolla, Calif., Mar. 12, 1949; s. Erbin Eugene Triplett and Marjorie Ann (Aldrich) Heath; m. Vannie Carol Crow, July 19, 1968; 1 child, Aaron Eugene. BA in Journalism, Ctrl. State U., 1975. Reporter, columnist The Okla. Jour., Oklahoma City, 1976-80; entertainment editor The Daily Oklahoman, Oklahoma City, 1981-85, asst. city editor, 1985-89, city editor, 1989—. Comm. com. Okla. Heart Assn., 1989-92. With U.S. Army, 1969-71, Vietnam. Recipient 1st. Place Feature Writing award Soc. Profl. Journalist, 1987, 2nd. Place Feature Writing award AP/One, 1988. Mem. AP/Okla. News Exec. (pres.-elect 1994-95, pres. 1995-96). Democrat. Avocations: collecting recorded music, feature films, vintage TV shows. Home: 2821 Tealwood Dr Oklahoma City OK 73120-1777 Office: The Daily Oklahoman 9000 Broadway Ext Oklahoma City OK 73114-3708

TRIPLETT, KELLY B., chemist; b. Cin.. BA, Northwestern U., 1968; PhD in Chemistry, U. Mich., 1974. Rsch. assoc. Mich. State U., 1974-76; rsch. chemist Stauffer Chem. Co., Dobbs Ferry, N.Y., 1976-78, supr., 1978-82, tech. mgr., 1982-84, bus. mgr., 1984-87; program mgr., bus. mgr. Akzo Chem. Inc., Dobbs Ferry, N.Y., 1987-90, mgr. rsch. ctr., 1990—, dir. rsch., 1992—; v.p. Akzo Nobel Ctrl. Rsch., 1994. Mem. Am. Chem. Soc., Indsl. Rsch. Inst. Achievements include development of new research and development methodologies; research in new polymerization products and process, organometallics and transition metal chemistries; investigation of chemical routes to advanced ceramics. Office: Akzo Nobel Chems Inc 1 Livingstone Ave Dobbs Ferry NY 10522-3401

TRIPLETT, LOREN O., religious organization administrator; b. San Jose, Calif., July 5, 1926; m. Mildred Triplett; children: Donald, Debora, Marcus, Timothy. Grad., Bethany Bible Coll., 1946; student, Ctrl. Bible Coll., Evangel Coll., Dade Jr. Coll. Ordained min. Assemblies of God, 1950.. Pastor various orgns., Oreg. and Nebr., 1947-54; missionary Life Pubs., Nicaragua, 1954-73; field dir. Divsn. Fgn. Missions, Springfield, Mo., 1973-89; exec. dir. Divsn. Fgn. Ministries, Springfield, Mo., 1990—. Contbr. articles to profl. jours. Office: Assemblies of God 1445 N Boonville Ave Springfield MO 65802-1894

TRIPODI, LOUIS ANTHONY, advertising agency executive; b. N.Y.C., July 7, 1931; m. Mary Gail Ennis; children: Pascal, William, Louis, James, Stephen, Michela, Gian, Christian, Blanid, Theresa, Michael. B.A., Bklyn. Coll., 1952. Dir. corp. pub. relations Kenyon & Eckhardt, N.Y.C., 1965-68; sr. v.p., corp. dir. pub. relations Needham Harper Worldwide, N.Y.C., 1968-87; exec. v.p., corp. dir. pub. affairs DDB Needham Worldwide, N.Y.C., 1987—. Mem. ASCAP, Am. Assn. Advt. Agys. (chmn. pub. relations com. 1982-83), Am. Advt. Fedn. (chmn. pub. relations com.). Home: 565 Kiowa Dr Franklin Lakes NJ 07417-1208 Office: DDB Needham Worldwide Inc 437 Madison Ave New York NY 10022-7001

TRIPOLE, MARTIN R., religion educator, priest; b. Penn Yan, N.Y., June 14, 1935; s. James and Mary T. BA, Fordham U., 1957, MPhil, 1963; postgrad., Syracuse U., 1957-58; ThM, Woodstock Coll., 1968; STD, Inst. Catholique de Paris, 1972. Joined S.J., Roman Cath. Ch., 1958, ordained priest, 1967. Instr. Bellarmine Coll., Plattsburg, N.Y., 1957-58, Le Moyne Coll., Syracuse, N.Y., 1962-64; asst. prof. Marquette U., Milw., 1974-75; assoc. prof. St. Joseph's U., Phila., 1972—; instr. St. Agnes Coll., Balt., 1967. Author: Jesus Event and Our Response, 1980, Faith Beyond Justice: Widening the Perspective, 1994; contbr. articles to profl. jours. Mem. Am. Acad. Religion, Cath. Theol. Soc. Am., Coll. Theol. Soc. Roman Catholic. Home: 5600 City Ave Philadelphia PA 19131-1308 Office: St Josephs Univ 5600 City Line Ave Philadelphia PA 19131-1308

TRIPP, FREDERICK GERALD, investment advisor; b. Chgo., Oct. 1, 1936; s. Gerald F. and Kathryn Ann (Siebold) T.; m. Terry Anne Shull, Aug. 26, 1967; children: Mark A., Karin M., Tracy L. Clark, Tricia L., Patrick G. BS in Econs., Purdue U., 1958; MBA, Lehigh U., 1964; PhD, The Am. U., 1972. Sr. v.p. CRI, Inc., Rockville, Md., 1979-82, Security Pacific, Inc., Seattle, 1982-83; pres. Frederick G. Tripp & Assocs., Inc., Rockville, 1983—; instr. Troy State U., 1965-67, Am. U., 1975-77, Indsl. Coll. Armed Forces, 1975-80; mem. pres.'s coun. Investment Mgmt. and Rsch., Inc., 1985—. Pres. Doctoral Assn., The Am. U., 1973. Maj. U.S. Army, 1958-67, Vietnam. Mem. Internat. Assn. Fin. Planning, Investment Mgmt. Cons. Assn., Sigma Pi. Methodist. Avocations: skiing, boating, racquetball. Office: Frederick G Tripp & Assocs 3200 Tower Oaks Blvd # 300 Rockville MD 20852-4216

TRIPP, KAREN BRYANT, lawyer; b. Rocky Mount, N.C., Sept. 2, 1955; d. Bryant and Katherine Rebecca (Watkins) Tripp; m. Robert Mark Burleson, June 25, 1977 (div. 1996). BA, U. N.C., 1976; JD, U. Ala., 1981. Bar: Tex. 1981, U.S. Dist. Ct. (so. dist.) Tex. 1982, U.S. Dist. Ct. (ea. dist.) Tex. 1991, U.S. Ct. Appeals (fed. cir.) 1983, U.S. Supreme Ct. 1994. Law clk. Tucker, Gray & Espy, Tuscaloosa, Ala., 1978-81, to presiding justice Ala. Supreme Ct., Montgomery, summer 1980; atty. Exxon Prodn. Rsch. Co., Houston, 1981-86, coord. tech. transfer, 1986-87; assoc. Arnold, White and Durkee, Attys. at Law, Houston, 1988-93, shareholder, 1994—. Editor: Intellectual Property Law Review, 1996; contbr. articles to profl. jours.; editor Intellectual Property Law Rev., 1995. Recipient Am. Jurisprudence award U. Ala., 1980, Dean's award, 1981. Mem. ABA (intellectual property law section, ethics com. 1992-95), Houston Bar Assn. (interprofl. rels. com. 1988-90), Houston Intellectual Property Lawyers Assn. (mem. outstanding inventor com. 1982-84, chmn. 1994-95, chmn. student edn. com. 1986, sec. 1987-88, chmn. awards com. 1988-89, chmn. program com. 1988-91, 95-96, treas. 1991-92, bd. dirs. 1992-94, nominations com. 1993, 96), Tex. Bar Assn. (antitrust law com. 1984-85, chmn. Internat. Law com. of Intellectual Property Law Sect. 1987-88, internat. transfer tech. com. 1983-84), Am. Intellectual Property Lawyers Assn. (mem. patent law com. 1995), Women in Tech. (founder), Phi Alpha Delta (clk. 1980). Democrat. Episcopalian. Office: Arnold White & Durkee PO Box 4433 Houston TX 77210-4433

TRIPP, LUKE SAMUEL, educator; b. Atoka, Tenn., Feb. 6, 1941; s. Luke Samuel and Dorothy Mae (Watson) T.; m. Hedwidge Mary Bruyns, Aug. 21, 1989; children: Ruth, Azania, Comrade. BS, Wayne State U., 1966; MA, U. Mich., 1974, PhD, 1980. Computer programmer No. Elec. Co., Montreal, Que., Can., 1966-68; tchr. elem. sch. math. Santa Maria Edn. Ctr., Detroit, 1969-70; instr. black studies Wayne County C.C., Detroit, 1971-72; tchr. secondary sch. sci. Cmty. Skills Ctr., Ann Arbor, Mich., 1971-73; dir. grad. rsch. U. Mich., Ann Arbor, 1977-80; asst. prof. U. Ill., Champaign, 1981-82, So. Ill. U., Carbondale, 1982-89; from asst. prof. to prof. social sci. St. Cloud (Minn.) State U., 1989-95, prof., 1995—; co-founder, coord. Faculty/Staff Color Caucus, St. Cloud, 1989—; founder, dir. Human Rights Coputhon, St. Cloud, 1989-91, So. Ill. Anti-Aparthied Coalition, Carbondale, 1984-87. Dir. polit. edn. Nat. Black Ind. Polit. Party, Ann Arbor, 1980-81; co-founder, mem. exec. bd. Labor Defense League, Detroit, 1970-71, League Revolutionary Black Workers, Detroit, 1968-70; coord. Nat. Black Econ. Devel. Conf., Detroit, 1969-70; student activist SNCC, Detroit, 1960-65. Mem. Nat. Coun. Black Studies, Assn. Study Afro-Am. Life and History. Office: St Cloud State U 720 4th Ave S Saint Cloud MN 56301-4442

TRIPP, SUSAN GERWE, museum director; b. Balt., Dec. 28, 1945; d. Earl Joseph and Maria Elizabeth (Wise) Gerwe; m. David Enders Tripp, June 9, 1977. BS, U. Md., 1967. Home econs. tchr. Balt. County Pub. Sch. Sys., 1967-74; curator of art Johns Hopkins U., Balt., 1974-76; curator of art, archivist Johns Hopkins U., 1976-78, instr. evening coll., 1978-84, dir. univ. collections, 1979-91; supr., instr. art history Goucher Coll., Notre Dame U., Balt., 1977-86; dir. docent tng. Homewood Mus., Balt., 1987-89; exec. dir. Old Westbury (N.Y.) Gardens, 1992-96; writer Stuyvesant, N.Y., 1996—; dir. Homewood Restoration Adv. Com., 1983-92, Evergreen Restoration Adv. Com., 1988-92; lectr. in field. Co-author: The Garrett Collection of Japanese Art, 1993 (NEA Grant 1980), Contbr. articles to profl. jours. Trustee Columbia County Hist. Soc., 1996—. Recipient Hist. Preservation award Balt. Heritage, Inc., 1988, 91, Rsch. award Am. Soc. Interior Designers, 1991. Mem. Am. Assn. Bot. Gardens and Arboreta, Netsuke Kenkyokai Japanese Cir. of Art, Oreintal Ceramic Soc., Balt. Mus. Art, Oreintal Ceramic Soc. Hong Kong, Assn. of Frick Art Ref. Libr. So. Garden Hist. Soc., Furniture History Soc., N.Y. Zool. Soc., Am. Assn. Mus. John Hopkins U. Falcuty Club., Omicron Nu. Avocations: architecture, archaeology, Chinese ceramics, historical restoration. Office: PO Box G Stuyvesant NY 12173

TRIPP, SUSAN LYNN, small business owner; b. Long Beach, Calif., May 1, 1953; d. Fred Robert and Marion Mary (Swales) Mulker; m. Gary Elliot Wolf, July 3, 1977 (div. Aug. 1986); 1 child, Daniel Gary; m. Robert Rolan Tripp, Mar.22, 1987. BA in Liberal Arts, San Jose State U., 1976. Cert. tchr., Calif. Dir.. San Jose (Calif.) State Housing, 1975-77; dir. Wonderland Presch., San Jose, 1978; tchr. Hillbrook Sch., Los Gatos, Calif., 1979-87; owner, mgr. TeleVet, San Jose, 1987-90; mgr. La Mirada Animal Hosp., Santa Fe Springs, Calif., 1989-90, owner, mgr., 1990—; spkr. Vet. Mgmt. Co., Ft. Collins, Colo., 1992, Ebell Club, La Mirada, 1993; cons., 1993; TV appearances include La Mirada Cable, 1993. Author: Sex is Good, Abuse is Wrong, 1986-93. Pub. safety commr. La Mirada, Calif., 1993—; campaign chair Sch. Bd. candidate, 1993; coord. Neighborhood Watch Program, La Mirada, 1993; chair Com. to Elect Pat Ruiz, La Mirada, 1993; mem. La Mirada Gang Task Force, 1993-94, La Mirada Disaster Steering Com., 1993-94; elder Cmty. Presbyn. Ch., La Mirada, 1994. Mem. La Mirada C. of C. Avocation: pets, hiking, travel, computer, advertising. Office: La Mirada Animal Hosp 13914 Rosecrans Ave Santa Fe Springs CA 90670-5210

TRIPP, THOMAS NEAL, lawyer, political consultant; b. Evanston, Ill., June 19, 1942; s. Gerald Frederick and Kathryn Ann (Siebold) T.; m. Ellen Marie Larrimer, Apr. 16, 1966; children: David Larrimer, Bradford Douglas, Corinne Catherine. BA cum laude, Mich. State U., 1964; JD, George Washington U., 1967. Bar: Ohio 1967, U.S. Ct. Mil. Appeals 1968, U.S. Supreme Ct. 1968, Wyo. 1991. Pvt. practice law, Columbus, Ohio, 1969—, Wilson, Wyo., 1991—; real estate developer, Columbus, 1969—; chmn. bd. Black Sheep Enterprises, Columbus, 1969—; polit. cons. David A. Keene & Assocs., Washington, 1986—; vice chmn. bd. Sun Valley-Elkhorn Assn., Idaho, 1983-85, chmn. 1986-91; vice chmn. Sawtooth Sports, Ketchum, Idaho, 1983-85; legal counsel Wallace F. Ackley Co., Columbus, 1973—; bd. dirs. KWRP Broadcasting Corp., 1986-91; presiding judge Ohio Mock Trial Competition, 1986-94; bd. dirs. U.S. Master's Swimming, Ohio, 1988-91, 94—; bd. dirs. U.S. Prison Industries (apptd. former pres. Bush 1992), Zero Population Growth, 1993; mem. small bus. adv. coun. FCC (apptd. former pres. Bush 1992); dep. spl. adv. to the pres. North Am. Free Trade Agreement (apptd. Pres. Clinton 1993). Trustee Americans for Responsible Govt., Washington, GOPAC; mem. Peace Corps Adv. Council, 1981-85; mem. U.S. Commn. on Trade Policy and Negotiations, 1985-88; campaign mgr., fin. chmn. Charles Rockwell Saxbe, Ohio Ho. of Reps., 1974, 76, 78, 80; campaign mgr. George Bush for Pres., 1980, nat. dep. field dir., 1980; mem. alumni admissions council Mich. State U., 1984—, George Washington U., 1988—; regional co-chmn. Reagan-Bush, 1984, mem. nat. fin. com., 1984; mem. Victory '84 fin. com.; mem. Victory '88 fin. com. Bush-Quayle; co-chmn. Ohio Lawyers for Bush/Quayle, 1988; Rep. candidate 2d U.S. Congl. Dist., Idaho, 1988; transition dir. Ohio Sec. of State, 1990-91; mem., bd. trustees Columbus Acad. Pvt. Co-ed Secondary Sch., 1991-94; chair bd. dirs. T.R.E.E. Coalition, 1991—. Served to 1st lt. U.S. Army, 1967-69. Fellow Pi Sigma Alpha; Vietnam Vet. Am., Phi Delta Phi. Republican. Avocations: athletics, writing, political essays. Home: 5420 Clark State Rd Columbus OH 43230-1956

TRIPPE, KENNETH ALVIN BATTERSHILL, shipping industry executive; b. Kansas City, Mo., Jan. 3, 1933; s. Alvin C. and Blanche (Battershill) T.; m. Jane Muir Mitchell, June 11, 1955 (dec. Jan. 1988); children: Kenneth, Tracy, Robert; m. Josphine M. Kling, May, 12, 1990. B.S. in Bus. Adminstrn, Kans. U., 1955; LL.B., U. Mo., 1958; postdoctoral mgmt. program, MIT, 1972. Bar: Mo. 1958. With Miss. River Corp., St. Louis, 1958-68, asst. sec., 1958-64, sec., 1964-65, asst. to pres., 1965-68; asst. treas. Internat. Utilities Corp. (name IU Internat. Corp. 1973), Phila., 1968-69; asst. treas. corporate and internat. fin. Internat. Utilities Corp. (name IU Internat. Corp. 1973), 1970-72, v.p., treas., 1972-75; exec. v.p., dir. subs. Gotaas-Larsen Shipping Corp., 1975-77, pres., chief exec. officer, dir., 1977-82; founder, chmn. Cruiseship Info. Systems Inc., Coral Gables, Fla., 1982-91, Cruise Brokers Inc., 1990—, Trippe & Co., 1990—; dir. The Herzfeld Caribbean Basin Fund; v.p. fin. Kans. Gas & Electric Co., Wichita, 1969-70. Patentee cruise info. and booking data processing system. Mem. Mo. Bar Assn., Fisher Island Club, Union League N.Y.C., Phi Delta Phi, Sigma Chi. Republican. Episcopalian. Home and Office: 2134 Fisher Island Dr Fisher Island FL 33109

TRIPPET, SUSAN ELAINE, nursing educator; b. Princeton, Ind., Nov. 3, 1946; d. Charles Kightly and Isabel (Key) T. AA, Ind. U., Indpls., 1971, MS in Nursing, 1983; DS in Nursing, U. Ala., Birmingham, 1988. Lectr. Ind. U., Indpls., 1976-83, asst. prof., 1983-84; CNS perinatal div. U. Hosps., Birmingham, 1984-85; assoc. prof. U. So. Miss., Hattiesurg, 1988-94; pres. D.J.S. Resources P.A., 1995—; pres. D.J.S. Resources P.A.; various presentations on older women, relationship issues, mothers & daughters, and therapeutic use of music. Mem. Am. Nursing Assn., So. Nursing Rsch. Soc., Internat. Coun. Women's Health Issues, Sigma Theta Tau, Sigma Tau Delta.

TRIPPLEHORN, JEANNE, actress; b. Tulsa, Okla., 1963; d. Tommy and Suzanne (Ferguson) T. Student, Juilliard Sch. Appeared in (theatre off-Broadway) The Big Funk, 1990, 'Tis Pity She's A Whore, 1992; (film) Basic Instinct, 1991, The Firm, 1993, The Night We Never Met, 1993, Reality Bites, 1994, Waterworld, 1995. *

TRISKA, JAN FRANCIS, retired political science educator; b. Prague, Czechoslovakia, Jan. 26, 1922; came to U.S., 1948, naturalized, 1955; s. Jan and Bozena (Kubiznak) T.; m. Carmel Lena Burastero, Aug. 26, 1951; children: Mark Lawrence, John William. J.U.D., Charles U., Prague, 1948; LL.M., Yale U., 1950, J.S.D., 1952; Ph.D., Harvard U., 1957. Co-dir. Soviet treaties Hoover Instn., Stanford, Calif., 1956-58; lectr. dept. polit. sci. U. Calif.-Berkeley, 1957-58; asst. prof. Cornell U., Ithaca, N.Y., 1958-60; assoc. prof. Stanford U., Calif., 1960-65, prof. polit. sci., 1965-89, assoc. chmn. dept., 1965-66, 68-69, 71-72, 74-75, emeritus prof. polit. sci., 1990—. Co-author: (with Slusser) The Theory, Law and Policy of Soviet Treaties, 1962, (with Finley) Soviet Foreign Policy, 1968, (with Cocks) Political Development and Political Change in Eastern Europe, 1977, (with Ike, North) The World of Superpowers, 1981, (with Gati) Blue Collar Workers in Eastern Europe, 1981, Dominant Powers and Subordinate States, 1986; bd. editors: East European Quar. Comparative Politics, Internat. Jour. Sociology, Jour. Comparative Politics, Studies in Comparative Communism, Soviet Statutes and Decisions, Documents in Communist Affairs. Recipient Rsch. award Ford Found., 1963-68, Josef Hlavka Commemorative medal Czechoslovak Acad. Scis., 1992, M.A. Comenius 1592-1992 Meml. medal Czechoslovak Pedagogical Mus., Prague, 1991; fellow NSF, 1971-72, Sen. Fulbright fellow, 1973-74, Woodrow Wilson fellow Internat. Ctr. for Scholars, 1980-81. Mem. Am. Polit. Sci. Assn. (sec. pres. conf. on communist studies 1970-76), Assn. Advancement Slavic Studies (bd. dirs. 1975-83), Am. Soc. Internat. Law (exec. coun. 1964-67), Czechoslovak Soc. Arts and Scis. (pres. 1978-80, 90-92), Inst. for Human Scis. Vienna (acting for Commn. European Communities, Brussels, com. experts on transformation of nat. higher edn. and rsch. system in Ctrl. Europe, Brussels 1991—). Democrat. Club: Fly Fishers (Palo Alto, Calif.). Home: 720 Vine St Menlo Park CA 94025-6154 Office: Stanford U Dept Polit Sci Stanford CA 94305

TRITES, DONALD GEORGE, human service consultant; b. Boston, Sept. 26, 1941; s. George Herman and Ada Christena (Patten) T.; m. Ruth Ann Lewis, June 15, 1963 (div. 1987); children: Sarah Jeanne, Amy Bray; m. Beverly Jean Baker, Apr. 8, 1989; children: Erica Christena, Philip Jameson Granville. AB, Colgate U., 1963; EdM, Tufts U., 1964; PhD, Syracuse U., 1976. Thcr., then chair history dept. Hamilton (Mass.)-Wenham Regionial High Sch., 1964-70; instr. div. ednl. studies Emory U., Atlanta, 1973-76; asst. prof. ednl. studies Emory U., 1976-81, vis. faculty, 1981-86; exec. dir. Ga. Advocacy Office, Inc., Atlanta, 1981-86, Devel. Svcs. Strafford County, Inc., Dover, N.H., 1986-95; founder, pres. Jebdas Consulting, Eliot, Maine, 1995—; program mgr. Mental Retardation and Substance Abuse Svcs. State of Maine, 1996—; cons. in human svc. mgmt. and evaluation, U.S. and Europe, 1978—. Editor, author: The College and A Human Future, 1986; contbr. articles to profl.publs. Deacon, First Bapt. Ch., Melrose, Mass., 1968-69, Syracuse, N.Y., 1972-73; deacon, Cen. Congl. Ch., Atlanta, 1984-86. Mem. Assn. for Persons with Severe Handicaps, Delta Upsilon. Democrat. Mem. United Ch. of Christ. Avocations: reading, gardening. Home: 42 Rollingwood Rd Eliot ME 03903-1508 Office: Dept Mental Health & Mental Retardation 40 State House Sta Augusta ME 04333-0040

TRITT, TRAVIS, country music singer, songwriter; b. Marietta, Ga., 1963. Recording artist Warner Bros., 1990—. Albums include Country Club, 1990 (platinum), It's All About to Change, 1991 (platinum), T-R-O-U-B-L-E, 1992 (platinum), A Travis Tritt Christmas: Loving Time of the Year, 1992 (with Marty Stuart, Hank Williams Jr., Waylon Jennings) Ten Feet Tall and Bulletproof, 1994; #1 singles The Whiskey Ain't Workin' (Grammy award with Marty Stuart 1993), Here's a Quarter (Call Someone Who Cares), Anymore, Can I Trust You with my Heart; author: (with Michael Bane) 10 Foot Tall and Bullet Proof, 1994. Named Billboard's Top New Male Country Artist, 1990; recipient Horizon award Country Music Assn., 1991, (with Marty Stuart) Vocal Event of Yr. award Country Music Assn., 1992; inductee Grand Ole Opry, 1992. Office: Warner Bros Records 3300 Warner Blvd Burbank CA 91505-4632

TRITTEN, JAMES JOHN, national security educator; b. Yonkers, N.Y., Oct. 3, 1945; s. James Hanley and Jennie (Szucs) T.; m. Kathleen Tritten, (div. 1983); children: Kimberly, James John Jr.; m. Jasmine Clark, Dec. 29, 1990. BA in Internat. Studies, Am. U., 1971; MA in Internat. Affairs, Fla. State U., 1978; AM in Internat. Rels., U. So. Calif., L.A., 1982, PhD in Internat. Rels., 1984. Commd. officer USN, 1967, advanced through grades to commdr., 1981; joint strategic plans officer Office of the Chief of Naval Ops., Washington, 1984-85; asst. dir. net assessment Office of the Sec. of Def., Washington, 1985-86; chmn. dept. nat. security affairs Naval Postgrad. Sch., Monterey, Calif., 1986-89; ret. USN, 1989; assoc. prof. nat. security affairs Naval Postgrad. Sch., Monterey, 1989-93; spl. asst. to comdr. Naval Doctrine Command, Norfolk, Va., 1993-96; dir. exercise and tng. U.S. Atlantic Command, Suffolk, VA, 1996—; cons. Rand Corp., Santa Monica, Calif., 1982-84; with Nat. Security Rsch., Fairfax, Va., 1992, AmerInd, Alexandria, Va., 1996—. Author: Soviet Naval Forces and Nuclear Warfare, 1986, Our New National Security Strategy, 1992 (George Washington honor medal 1991); co-author: Doctrine Reader, 1996; co-editor: Reconstituting National Defense, 1992; contbr. chpts. to books, articles to profl. jours. Mem. Adv. Bd. on Alcohol Related Problems, Monterey County, Calif., 1987-90; bd., officer Leadership Monterey (Calif.) Peninsula, 1989-92, Carmel Valley (Calif.) Property Owners Assn., 1989-91; commr. Airport Land Use Commn., Monterey County, 1990-93, mem. Nat Eagle Scout Assn. Decorated Def. Superior Svc. medal Sec. Def., Washington, 1986, Meritorious Svc. medal Sec. Navy, Monterey, 1989, Navy Civilian Supr. Svc. medal, 1996; recipient Alfred Thayer Mahan award for literary achievement Navy League of U.S., Arlington, Va., 1986. Mem. Mil. Ops. Rsch. Soc. (v.p. 1990-91), U.S. Naval Inst. (Silver and Bronze medals), Pi Sigma Alpha, Pi Gamma Mu. Republican. Presbyterian. Avocations: hiking, camping. Office: USACOM Analysis and Simulation Ctr Ste 2170 116 Lakeview Pkwy Suffolk VA 23435-2697

TRITTER, RICHARD PAUL, strategic consulting executive; b. Boston, Sept. 30, 1945; s. Herman Louis and Rose (Greenblatt) T.; 1 child, Melissa Rosanne; m. Marcy Lynn Kroll, June 17, 1984; children: Matthew Alexander, Rachel Danielle, Adam Levi. AB, Columbia Coll., N.Y.C., 1967; JD, Northeastern U., 1976. Bar: Mass. 1977, U.S. Supreme Ct. 1980. Mktg. mgr./cons. Digital Equipment Corp., Merrimack, N.H., 1979-81, 83-86; nat. dir. high-tech. industry program Coopers & Lybrand, Boston, 1981-83; pres. Video/Demo Ctrs., Inc., Burlington, Mass., 1986-88; v.p. bus. devel. Info. Resources, Inc., Boston, 1988-91; dir. facilitation consulting methodologies Arthur Andersen, Boston, 1991-93; dir. self-assessment practices Arthur Andersen, Chgo., 1993—; panelist MIT Enterprise Forum, Cambridge, 1983-89; pres. Somali Lobster Exports Co., 1995. Creator software application Compliance Testing and Verification, 1981. UN rep. Jubaland Relief and Rehab. Soc., Somalia; dir. Save Somalia Livestock Campaign, 1993. Recipient Better Govt. award Pioineer Inst. for Pub. Policy Rsch., Boston. Facilitated meetings between opposing clans in the Juba region of southern Somali; initiated lobster export project with cooperation of Gen. Omar Jess, Col. Ahmed Hashi and other Somali leaders. Home: 2000 Arrow Ln Deerfield IL 60015 Office: Arthur Andersen LLP 33 W Monroe St Chicago IL 60603-5302

TRIVEDI, SUDHIR K., computer science educator, researcher; b. Agra, India, Dec. 5, 1959; came to U.S., 1987; s. Sewa Ram and Sarala Dewi (Misra) T. MS in Math., Agra U., India, 1981, MPhil in Math., 1982, PhD in Math., 1985; PhD in Computer Sci., La. State U., 1993. Rsch. fellow Coun. Scientific and Indsl. Rsch., India, 1982-87; teaching asst. in computer sci. dept. La. State U., 1988-93; asst. prof. in computer sci. Southern U., Baton Rouge, 1993—; teaching asst. in math. Agra U., India, 1984-85, 85-86; rsch. asst. Robotics Rsch. Lab., La. State U., 1993. Mem. IEEE, IEEE Computer Soc., Assn. Computing Machinery (reviewer 32d and 33d S.E. Conf.), Soc. Indsl. and Applied Math. (session chmn. 7th conf. on discrete math.), Indian Math. Soc., N.Y. Acad. Scis., Upsilon Pi Epsilon. Home: 3000 July St Apt 140 Baton Rouge LA 70808-2045 Office: Southern U. PO Box 9221 Baton Rouge LA 70813

TRIVELPIECE, ALVIN WILLIAM, physicist, corporate executive; b. Stockton, Calif., Mar. 15, 1931; s. Alvin Stevens and Mae (Hughes) T.; m. Shirley Ann Ross, Mar. 23, 1953; children: Craig Evan, Steve Edward, Keith Eric. B.S., Calif. Poly. Coll., San Luis Obispo, 1953; M.S., Calif. Inst. Tech., 1955, Ph.D., 1958. Fulbright scholar Delft (Netherlands) U., 1958-59; asst. prof., then assoc. prof. U. Calif. at Berkeley, 1959-66; prof. physics U. Md., 1966-76; on leave as asst. dir. for research div. controlled thermonuclear research AEC, Washington, 1973-75; v.p. Maxwell Labs. Inc., San Diego, 1976-78; corp. v.p. Sci. Applications, Inc., La Jolla, Calif., 1978-81; dir. Office of Energy Research, U.S. Dept. Energy, Washington, 1981-87; exec. officer AAAS, Washington, 1987-88; pres., dir. Oak Ridge (Tenn.) Nat. Lab., 1988—; v.p. Martin Marietta Energy Systems, 1988-95, Lockheed Martin Energy Systems, 1996—; pres. Lockheed Martin Energy Rsch. Corp., 1996—; head del. joint NAS and Soviet Acad. Scis. mtg. and conf. on energy and global ecol. problems, USSR, 1989; chmn. math. scis. ednl. bd. NAS, 1990-93, chmn. coordinating coun. for edn., 1990-93; chmn. coordinating coun. for edn. NRC, 1991-93, mem. Commn. on Phys. Scis., Math. and Applications, 1993—; bd. dirs. Bausch & Lomb, Inc., Rochester, N.Y.; mem. Tenn. Sci. and Tech. Adv. Commn., 1993-96, chmn., 1996—; adv. com. Federal Networking Coun., 1992-96. Author: Slow Wave Propagation in Plasma Wave Guides, 1966, Principles of Plasma Physics, 1973; also articles. Named Disting. Alumnus, Calif. Inst. Tech., Pasadena, Calif., 1987; recipient U.S. Sec. of Energy's Gold medal for Disting. Svc., 1986, Outstanding Engr. award IEEE Region 3, 1995; Guggenheim fellow, 1966. Fellow AAAS, IEEE (Outstanding Engr. award region 3 1995), Am. Phys. Soc.; mem. AAUP, NAE, Am. Nuclear Soc., Am. Assn. Physics Tchrs., Capital Hill Club, Nat. Press Club, Sigma Xi. Achievements include patents in field. Home: 8 Rivers Run Way Oak Ridge TN 37830-9004 Office: Oak Ridge Nat Lab Office of Dir PO Box 2008 Oak Ridge TN 37831-6255

TRODDEN, STEPHEN ANTHONY, federal agency administrator; b. Washington, D.C., Dec. 13, 1939; s. Stephen Albertson and Margaret Mary (Myers) T.; m. Regina Lee Miller, Dec. 26, 1962; children: Mark Andrew, Sharon Ruth. BS in Engring., U. Mich., 1962; JD, Georgetown U., 1965. Bar: Va. 1965. Indsl. engr. U.S. Army Materiel Command, 1962-66; staff officer missile systems U.S. Army Missile Command, 1966-69; tech. advisor, budget analyst Directorate for Procurement, Office of Sec. Def., 1969-73; dep. dir. R & D Office Asst. Sec. Defense, 1973-75, dep. dir., 1975-81, dir. procurement, 1981-83; dir. major acquisition programs Dept. Defense, 1983-86; asst. insp. gen. auditing Office of Insp. Gen., 1986-90; insp. gen. Dept. Vets. Affairs, 1990—; chmn. inspection com. Pres. Coun. Integrity and Efficiency, Washington, 1990-94. Lay dir. No. Va. Cursillo Movement, 1988-91. Recipient Meritorious Civilian Svc. award Sec. Defense, Washington, 1983, Disting. Civilian Svc. award, 1990, Meritorious Exec. Pres. rank award U.S. Govt., 1990. Mem. Va. State Bar. Avocations: basketball, jogging, beach, reading, bicycling. Office: IG Dept Vets Affairs 810 Vermont Ave NW Washington DC 20420-0001*

TROELSTRA, ARNE, physics educator; b. Zelhem, The Netherlands, Mar. 30, 1935; came to U.S., 1965; m. Louise M. Van de Meent; 1 child, Catherine. BS in Physics and Math., Utrecht U., The Netherlands, 1955, MS in Physics, 1958, PhD in Physics, 1964. Rsch. scientist Applied Physics Rsch. TNO, Soesterberg, The Netherlands, 1959-65; assoc. prof. U. Ill., Chgo., 1965-69; assoc. prof. Rice U., Houston, 1969-76, prof., 1976-80; instr. physics Okla. Sch. Sci. and Math., Oklahoma City, 1989—. Postdoctoral fellow NATO, MIT, 1962-63. Home: 501 NE 15th St Oklahoma City OK 73104-1221 Office: Okla Sch Sci and Math 1141 N Lincoln Blvd Oklahoma City OK 73104-2847

TROEN, PHILIP, physician, educator; b. Portland, Maine, Nov. 24, 1925; s. Ben and Gertrude (Cope) T.; m. Betty Ann Zelig, Mar. 22, 1953 (dec.); children: Mark Lawrence, Bruce Robert, Gail Sheri. A.B., Harvard U., 1944, M.D., 1948. Diplomate: Nat. Bd. Med. Examiners, Am. Bd. Internal Medicine. Intern Boston City Hosp., 1948-49, asst. resident in medicine, 1949-50; resident in medicine Beth Israel Hosp., Boston, 1950, 52-53; chief resident Beth Israel Hosp., 1953-54, asst. in medicine, 1955-56, USPHS research fellow, 1955-56, assoc. in med. research, 1956-64, assoc. in medicine, 1956-58, asst. vis. physician, 1959-64; teaching fellow Harvard Med. Sch., 1952-53, asst. in medicine, 1953-54, research fellow, 1955-56, instr. medicine, 1956-59, asso. in medicine, 1959-60, asst. prof., 1960-64; prof. medicine U. Pitts. Sch. Medicine, 1964—, assoc. chmn. dept. medicine, 1969-79, vice chmn. dept. medicine, 1979-90, interim chief divsn. of endocrinology and metabolism, 1995—, physician in chief Montefiore Univ. Hosp., 1964-90, physician in chief emeritus, 1990—; sci. counselor NIH, key cons. contraceptive devel. br., 1980; sci. counselor rev. Intramural Reproductive Biology Program, Nat. Inst. Child Health and Human Devel., 1977; cons. male fertility and infertility Nat. Inst. Occupational Safety and Health, 1977; mem. med. res. service merit rev. bd. in endocrinology VA, 1979-82; mem. contract rev. com. Nat. Inst. Child Health and Human Devel., 1975-84, chmn., 1976-89, reviewer intramural site visit devel. endocrinology br., 1983, 87; mem. endocrinologic and metabolic drugs adv. com. FDA, 1984-88, chmn. 1987-88; mem. expert advisor panel on occupational health, WHO, 1987—. Mem. editorial bd. Jour. Andrology, Jour. Clin. Endocrinology and Metabolism, Internat. Jour. Andrology, Andrologia; contbr. articles to profl. jours. Served to capt. M.C., AUS, 1950-52. Fellow in endocrinology and metabolism Mayo Clinic, Rochester, Minn., 1954-55; Kendall-Hench research fellow, 1955; Ziskind teaching fellow, 1956-59; Med. Found. Greater Boston research fellow, 1959-63; Guggenheim fellow Stockholm, 1960-61. Mem. AAAS, Assn. Am. Physicians, Am. Soc. Clin. Investigation, Am. Soc. for Biochemistry and Molecular Biology, Am. Fedn. Clin. Rsch., Am. Soc. Andrology (program and publs. com., exec. coun., 1977-79, v.p. 1979-80, pres. 1980-81, chmn. publ. com. 1990-93, Disting. Andrologist award 1991, Disting. Svc. award 1996), Internat. Soc. Andrology (sec. 1981-89, pres. 1989-93), Endocrine Soc. (publ. com. 1984-90, chmn. 1987-90), N.Y. Acad. Scis., Ctrl. Soc. Clin. Rsch., Soc. Study of Reproduction. Office: Montefiore U Hosp U Pitts Med Ctr 200 Lothrop St Pittsburgh PA 15213-2546

TROGANI, MONICA, ballet mistress; b. Newark, Sept. 2, 1963; m. Jay Brooker, July 3, 1993. Grad. high sch., 1980. Ballet dancer N.J. Ballet, West Orange, 1980-83; field asst., coder Reichman Rsch., Inc., N.Y.C., 1984-86; ballet mistress, prin. dancer Dance Theatre of L.I., Port Washington, N.Y., 1984-88; exec. sec. programming dept. The First N.Y. Internat. Festival of the Arts, N.Y.C., 1987-89; guest regisseur Alta. Ballet, Edmonton, Can., 1988-89, ballet mistress, asst. to artistic dir., 1989-93; guest regisseur Ballet du Nord, Roubaix, France, 1991, Dance Theatre of Harlem, N.Y.C., 1993-94; ballet mistress Les Grands Ballets Canadiens, Montreal, 1994—. Avocation: singing. Office: Les Grands Ballets Canadien, 4816 Rue Rivard, Montreal, PQ Canada H2J 2N6

TROGDON, DEWEY LEONARD, JR., textile executive; b. Summerfield, N.C., Feb. 17, 1932; s. Dewey Leonard and Ethel (Miller) T.; m. Barbara Jean Ayers, Sept. 10, 1955; children: Mark, Leonard. AB in Econs., Guilford Coll., 1958; postgrad., U. N.C., 1967-68, U. Va., 1970, Advanced Mgmt. Program, Harvard U., 1978. With Cone Mills Corp., Greensboro, 1958—, staff asst. to chief exec. officer, 1970-74, exec. v.p., 1978, pres., 1979—, chief exec. officer, 1980-90, chmn., 1981—; pres. subs. co. Otto B. May, 1974-78; v.p. Cone Mills Mktg. Co., 1977-78; dir. First Union Corp. With USNR, 1949-53. Mem. Am. Textile Mfrs. Inst. (pres. 1986-87), N.C. Textile Mfrs. Assn. (past pres., dir.). Methodist. Office: Cone Mills Corp 3101 N Elm St PO Box 26540 Greensboro NC 27415-6540*

TROIDL, RICHARD JOHN, banker; b. Buffalo, July 2, 1944; s. Henry Albert and Lola Julian (Davern) T.; m. Diane Budney, Nov. 20, 1982; children: Nicholas, Holly. AAS, SUNY, Buffalo, 1973. Sr. v.p. Empire Am. Fed. Savs. Bank, Buffalo, 1969-93; pres. Express Svcs. of Am., Inc., Las Vegas, Nev., 1993—. With U.S. Army, 1965-71. Home: 6120 W Tropicana #A16 Las Vegas NV 89103-4694 Office: Express Svcs Am Inc 6120 W Tropicana Ave Ste A-16 Las Vegas NV 89103-4694

TROLANDER, HARDY WILCOX, engineering executive, consultant; b. Chgo., June 2, 1921; s. Elmer Wilcox and Freda Marie (Zobel) T.; m. Imogen Davenport, July 3, 1946; children: Megan, Patricia. BS in Engring., Antioch Coll., 1947. Instr. Antioch Coll., Yellow Springs, Ohio, 1947-48; co-founder, CEO Yellow Springs Instrument Co., Inc., 1948-86; dir., co-founder Cook Design Ctr., Dartmouth Coll., Hanover, N.H., 1975-88; bd. dirs. Deban Inc., Yellow Springs. Contbr. articles to profl. jours.; patentee in field. Co-founder, trustee Yellow Springs Community Found., 1974-83; trustee Autioch Coll., 1968-74, chmn. bd., 1972-74; trustee Engring. and Sci. Found., Dayton, 1982—, Engring. and Sci. Hall of Fame, 1994—; bd. dirs. united Way Greater Dayton Area, 1984-92. 1st lt. U.S. Army Air Corps., 1943-46. Named Outstanding Engr., Dayton Affiliate Socs., 1967, 89. Fellow Dayton Engrs. Club; mem. ACLU, Nat. Acad. Engring., Amnesty Internat. Democrat. Avocations: restoring antique radios and automobiles. Home and Office: 1475 President St Yellow Springs OH 45387-1326

TROLINGER, JAMES DAVIS, laser scientist; b. Shelbyville, Tenn., Mar. 2, 1940; s. Winston Perry and Euna Mae (Davis) T.; children: James D. Jr., Kristina Lin, Jonathan P. BS, U. Tenn., 1963; MS, La. State U., 1964; PhD, U. Tenn., 1967. Scientist Sverdrup Tech., Tullahoma, Tenn., 1967-73, Sci. Applications, Tullahoma, 1973-75; chief scientist, founder Spectron, Costa Mesa, Calif., 1975-88; gen. ptnr., founder MetroLaser, Irvine, Calif., 1988—; cons. Adv. Group for Aerospace R & D, NATO, Chatillon, France, 1985-88. Recipient George W. Goddard award Internat. Soc. Optical Engring., 1992. Home: 3417 Wimbledon Way Costa Mesa CA 92626-1645 Office: MetroLaser 18006 Sky Park Cir Irvine CA 92714-6429

TROLLER, FRED, graphic designer, painter, visual consultant, educator; b. Zurich, Switzerland, Dec. 12, 1930; came to U.S., 1961; s. Albert and Katherina (Iseli) T.; m. Beatrice Stocklin, Nov. 22, 1952; children—Simon, Meret. B.A. in Graphic Design, Kunstgewerbeschule, Zurich, 1950. Art dir. Geigy Corp., Ardsley, N.Y., 1961-66; pres. Fred Troller Assocs., Visual Communications Cons., Rye, N.Y., 1966—; chmn., prof. design div. design Sch. Art and Design N.Y. State Coll. Ceramics at Alfred U., 1991—. Author and illustrator articles. Served to pvt. 1st class Inf. Swiss Army, 1949-60. Mem. Am. Inst. Graphic Arts, Alliance Graphique Internationale. Home & Office: Fred Troller Assocs 12 Harbor Ln Rye NY 10580-2213

TROMBINO, ROGER A., investment banker; b. Kenosha, Wis., Sept. 23, 1939; s. Paul and Lena T.; m. Joann M. Buchholtz, 1961; children: Tracey, Suzanne, Steven. B.S., U. Wis., 1962. CPA. Audit mgr. Ernst & Young, Chgo., 1962-73; sr. v.p., exec. officer Norin Corp./Norris Cos., Miami, Fla., 1973-85; executor, trustee Norris Group, Miami, 1986-92; mng. dir. AIBC Investment Bank, Miami, 1993-95; exec. v.p., COO West Indies Sugar Corp., 1996—. Chmn. bd. Bon Secours Hosp., Miami, 1979-94. Mem. AICPA. Club: Riviera Country.

TRONFELD, JAY, lawyer; b. Phila.; s. Sidney I. and Cecilia (Zalkin) T.; m. Caren Herzberg, Aug. 30, 1970; children: Andrew Clinton, Caye Margaret. BA, U. Richmond, 1966; JD, U. Tenn., 1971. Bar: Va. Law clk. Doumar, Pincus, Knight & Harlan, Norfolk, Va., 1971; lawyer Donmar, Pinens, Knight & Harlan, Norfolk, Va., 1971-72; pres. Jay Tronfeld & Assoc., Richmond, Va., 1972—; pres. Richmond Trial Lawyers Assn., 1991-92; lectr. in field. Served with USAF Res., 1967. Mem. ABA, Am. Trial Lawyers Assn., Va. Trial Lawyers Assn., Richmond Bar Assn. Avocations: fishing, gardening, traveling. Office: Jay Tronfeld and Assoc 4020 W Broad St Richmond VA 23230-3916

TRONVOLD, LINDA JEAN, occupational therapist; b. Yankton, S.D., Dec. 8, 1950; m. Marvis D. Tronvold, July 7, 1976; children: Marcie, Tami, Kristi, Bradley, Cindy. Student, Mt. Marty Coll., 1989; AS, Kirkwood Community Coll., Cedar Rapids, Iowa, 1989; BS, Creighton U., 1991. Registered occupl. therapist, S.D., Neb., Iowa. Psychiatric aide S.D. Human Svcs. Ctr., Yankton, 1969-74, mental health technician, 1974-85, occupl. therapist asst., 1985-89, occupl. therapist, 1991-92; mem. edn. svc. unit Human Svcs. Ctr., Yankton, 1991-93; asst. program dir. occupl. therapy Western Iowa Tech. C.C., Dakota Dunes, S.D., 1993—; dir. occupl. therapy Nova Care, Inc., 1993—; guest speaker Creighton U., Omaha, U. S.D., Vermillion; mem. student staff Upward Bound, Omaha, 1989-91,. Scout leader Boy Scouts Am., Hartington, Nebr., 1977-80, Girl Scouts USA, Yankton, 1986-89; Sunday sch. tchr. United Ch. of Christ, Yankton, 1984-88; mem. spl. populations staff YWCA, Cedar Rapids, Iowa, 1987-88. Mem. Am. Occupl. Therapy Assn., S.D. Occupl. Therapy Assn., Nebr. Occupl. Therapy Assn., Iowa Occupl. Therapy Assn., Creighton U. Student Occupl. Therapy Assn., VFW Aux., Sq. Dance Club (pres. 1979-81), Alpha Tri Ota Club. Avocations: camping, cake decorating, swimming, dancing, sewing. Home: 705 Broadway St Yankton SD 57078-3923 Office: 350 W Anchor Dr Ste 500 Dakota Dunes SD 57049-5153

TROOBOFF, PETER DENNIS, lawyer; b. Balt., June 22, 1942; s. Benjamin M. and Rebecca C. (Cohen) T.; m. Rhoda Morss, Aug. 10, 1969; children: Hannah, Abigail. BA cum laude, Columbia U., 1964; LLB cum laude, Harvard U., 1967; LLM, London Sch. Econs., 1968; diploma cum laude, Hague (Netherlands) Acad. Internat. Law, 1968. Bar: N.Y. 1968, D.C. 1970. Rsch. assoc., Harvard U. Law Sch., 1968-69; asst. to exec. editor for The Advocates, Sta. WGBH-TV, Boston, 1969; assoc. Covington & Burling, Washington, 1969-75, ptnr., 1975—; lectr., dir. seminars The Hague Acad. Internat. Law, 1972, 82, lectr., 1986, mem. curatorium, 1991—; lectr. The Hague Acad. External Programn Beijing, 1987, Harare, 1993, internat. orgns. U. Va. Sch. Law, 1973; head U.S. del. 3d Inter-Am. Specialized Conf. Pvt. Internat. Law, La Paz, Bolivia, 1984; mem. U.S. del. Hague Conf. private internat. law, 1993; mem. sec. of state adv. com. private internat. law, 1990—. Frank Knox Meml. fellow. Mem. Coun. Fgn. Rels., Am. Soc. Internat. Law (pres. 1990-92, bd. editors Am. Jour. of Internat. Law 1980-92, 94—, hon. v.p. 1992—), Internat. Law Assn., Washington Inst. Fgn. Affairs. Club: Cosmos, City (Washington). Contbr. chpts., articles to profl. publs.; editor: Law and Responsibility in Warfare-The Vietnam Experience, 1975. Office: Covington & Burling PO Box 7566 1201 Pennsylvania Ave NW Washington DC 20044

TROOST, BRADLEY TODD, neurologist, educator; b. Mankato, Minn., July 5, 1937; s. Henry Bradley and Elizabeth (Todd) T.; m. Elizabeth Gail Godet, Apr. 17, 1976; children: Elizabeth Claire, Laurie Anne. BS with honors in Biophysics, Yale U., 1959; MD, Harvard U., 1963. Diplomate Am. Bd. Psychiatry and Neurology. Intern, Colo. Gen. Hosp., Denver, 1963-64; resident in neurology U. Colo., Denver, 1966-69; NIH fellow in neuro-ophthalmology U. Calif.-San Francisco, 1969-70; asst. prof. U. Miami (Fla.), 1970-76; assoc. prof. U. Pitts., 1976-80; prof. Case Western Res. U., Cleve., 1980-83; prof., chmn. dept. neurology Bowman Gray Sch. Medicine, Winston-Salem, N.C., 1983—; chief dept. neurology VA med. ctrs., Pitts., Cleve. Bd. dirs. Greater Miami Epilepsy Found., 1973-76. Served to capt. U.S. Army, 1964-66. Fellow Am. Acad. Neurology; mem. Am. Neurol. Assn., Am. Assn. Univ. Profs. Neurology (pres.-elect), Barany Soc. Republican. Episcopalian. Contbr. numerous articles to profl. publs.

TROSINO, VINCENT JOSEPH, insurance company executive; b. Upland, Pa., Nov. 19, 1940; s. Sylvester N. and Stella Trosino; m. Patricia Ann Gibney, June 18, 1960; children: Laura, Valerie, Vincent Jr. BS in Psychology, Villanova U., 1962; MS in Psychology, Ill. State U., 1973. Ops. supr. State Farm Mut. Auto Ins. Co., Springfield, Pa., 1962-67; personnel mgr. State Farm Mut. Auto Ins. Co., Bloomington, Ill., 1970-72, dir. personnel, 1972-74, corp. v.p., 1986-87, exec. v.p., 1987—, COO, 1990—; also bd. dirs.; vice-chmn. bd. dirs. State Farm Mut. Auto Ins. Co., Costa Mesa, Calif., 1995, dep. regional v.p., 1976-80; regional v.p. State Farm Mut. Auto Ins. Co., Wayne, N.J., 1981-85; bd. dirs. State Farm Fire & Casualty Co., State Farm Life Ins. Co., State Farm Internat. Services, State Farm Investment Mgmt. Corp., all Bloomington. Bd. dirs. Chilton Hosp., Pompton Lakes, N.J., 1982-85, Jr. Achievement, McLean County, Ill., 1971, McLean County Law and Justice Com., 1970, McLean County Alcohol and Drug Assistance Corp., 1970-74, The Brookings Inst., Washington, 1996. Mem. N.J. Ins. News Svc. (pres. 1984-85, bd. dirs.), N.J. Joint Underwriting Assn. (bd. dirs. 1982-85), Jud. Inquiry Bd. State of Ill. (apptd. by Gov. Edgar, 1992—). Avocations: trout fishing, tennis, golf. Office: State Farm Ins Cos 1 State Farm Plz Bloomington IL 61710-0001

TROST, BARRY MARTIN, chemist, educator; b. Phila., June 13, 1941; s. Joseph and Esther T.; m. Susan Paula Shapiro, Nov. 25, 1967; children: Aaron David, Carey Daniel. B.A. cum laude, U. Pa., 1962; Ph.D., MIT, 1965; D (hon.), U. Claude Bernard, Lyons, France, 1994. Mem. faculty U. Wis., Madison, 1965—, prof. chemistry, 1969—, Evan P. and Marion Helfaer prof. chemistry, from 1976; Vilas rsch. prof. chemistry U. Wis.; prof. chemistry Stanford U., 1987—, Tamaki prof. humanities and scis., 1990; cons. Merck, Sharp & Dohme, E.I. duPont de Nemours.; Chem. Soc. centenary lectr., 1982. Author: Problems in Spectroscopy, 1967, Sulfur Ylides, 1975; editor-in-chief Comprehensive Organic Synthesis, 1991—, Chem-Tracts/Organic Chemistry, 1993—; editor: Structure and Reactivity Concepts in Organic Chemistry series, 1972—; assoc. editor Jour. Am. Chem. Soc., 1974-80; mem. editl. bd. Organic Reactions Series, 1971—, Chemistry A European Jour., 1995—, Sci. of Synthesis, Houben-Weyl Methods of Molecular Transformations, 1995—; contbr. numerous articles to profl. jours. Recipient Dreyfus Found. Tech.-Scholar award, 1970, 77, Creative Work in Synthetic Organic Chemistry award, 1981, Baekland medal, 1981, Alexander von Humboldt award, 1984, Guenther award, 1990, Janssen prize, 1990, Roger Adams award Am. Chem. Soc. 1995; named Chem. Pioneer, Am. Inst. Chemists, 1983; NSF fellow, 1963-65, Sloan Found. fellow, 1967-69, Am. Swiss Found. fellow, 1975—; Cope scholar, 1989. Mem. AAAS, Am. Chem. Soc. (award in pure chemistry 1977, Roger Adams award 1995), Nat. Acad. Scis., Am. Acad. Arts and Scis., Chem. Soc. London. Office: Stanford U Dept Chemistry Stanford CA 94305

TROST, CARLISLE ALBERT HERMAN, retired naval officer; b. Valmeyer, Ill., Apr. 24, 1930; s. Elmer Herman and Luella Caroline (Hoffman) T.; m. Pauline Louise Haley, May 1, 1954; children—Carl, Laura Lee, Steven, Kathleen. Student, Washington U., St. Louis, 1948-49; B.S., U.S. Naval Acad., 1953; Olmsted scholar, U. Freiburg, W. Ger., 1960-62. Commd. ensign U.S. Navy, 1953, advanced through grades to adm., 1985; exec. officer U.S.S. Scorpion, 1962-63, U.S.S. Von Steuben, 1963-65; mil. asst. to Dep. Sec. Def., 1965-68; comdg. officer U.S.S. Sam Rayburn, 1968-69; staff Comdr. Sub Force Atlantic, 1969-70; exec. asst. to Sec. Navy, 1970-73; comdr. Submarine Group Five, 1973-74; asst. chief Bur. Naval Personnel, 1974-76; dir. systems analysis div. Office Chief Naval Ops., Washington, 1976-78; dep. comdr.-in-chief U.S. Pacific Fleet, 1978-80; comdr. U.S. Seventh Fleet, 1980-81; dir. Navy program planning Office Chief Naval Ops., 1981-85; comdr.-in-chief U.S. Atlantic Fleet, 1985-86, chief naval ops., 1986-90; bd. dirs. Lockheed Martin Corp., La. Land and Exploration, Gen. Pub. Utility Corp., GPU Nuclear Corp., Bird-Johnson Co., Gen. Dynamics Corp., Precision Components Corp. Trustee U.S. Naval Acad. Found. Decorated Def. D.S.M. with cluster, Navy D.S.M. with 2 clusters, Army D.S.M., Air Force D.S.M., Legion of Merit with 2 oak leaf clusters, Navy Achievement medal, Def. Disting. Svc. medal; named Outstanding Young Man of Am. Nat. Jr. C. of C., 1964. Mem. U.S. Naval Inst., U.S. Naval Alumni Assn. (trustee). Episcopalian. Home: 10405 Windsor View Dr Rockville MD 20854-4025

TROST, J. RONALD, lawyer; b. Fresno, Calif., Nov. 27, 1932; s. David Trost and Betty (Shapiro) Buno; m. Florence Stern; children: Gregory, Larry, Leslie, Jacqueline. BA, Rice U., 1954; JD, U. Tex., 1957. Bar: Tex. 1957, D.C. 1960, Calif. 1963, N.Y. 1994. With U.S. Dept. Justice, Washington, 1957-59; pvt. practice law Washington, 1959-62; pvt. practice L.A., 1963—; ptnr. Sidley & Austin, L.A., 1980—; adj. prof. law UCLA; instr. law U. So. Calif., Los Angeles. Contbr. articles to law revs. and jours.; contbg. editor Collier on Bankruptcy. Served with U.S. Army, 1957-63. Mem. ABA, Am. Law Inst., Nat. Bankruptcy Conf. Office: Sidley & Austin 875 3rd Ave New York NY 10022-6225

TROSTEL, MICHAEL FREDERICK, architect; b. Balt., May 19, 1931; s. Louis Jacob and Katharine (Fisher) T. BArch, U. Pa., 1954, MArch, 1957; diploma, Ecole des Beaux Arts, Fontainebleau, France, 1957. Registered architect, Md., D.C., Va. Draftsman Taylor & Fisher, Balt., 1958-59, Fisher, Nes, Campbell & Ptnrs., Balt., 1959-60; assoc. James R. Edmunds, Jr., Balt., 1960-73; v.p. Edmunds & Hyde, Balt., 1973-81; prin. Michael F. Trostel, FAIA, Balt., 1981-94, Trostel & Pearre, 1995—; mem. adv. bd. Md. House and Garden Pilgrimage, 1982—; archtl. advisor Hammond-Harwood House Assn., 1988-94. Author: Mount Clare, 1981, Domestic Maryland Architecture, 1984, Wines and Other Potables in Maryland, 1987, Mondawmin: Baltimore's Last Country Estate, 1991; editor Architect's Report mag., 1963-65. Bd. dirs. Balt. Heritage, Inc., 1970-73, Am. Wing Balt. Mus. Art, 1994—; mem. art commn. City of Balt., 1972-80, chmn., 1978-80; mem. gov.'s com. for Nat. Register Hist. Places, State of Md., 1984—, vice-chmn., 1987-92, chmn., 1993, 95. Recipient Award of Excellence, Balt. Bldg. Congress, 1980, 83, 87, Honor award Balt. Heritage, 1986, 90, Commendation award Preservation Md., 1986, 90, Preservation award Md. Hist. Trust, 1991, 92. Fellow AIA (mem. com. on hist. preservation); mem. Soc. for Preservation of Md. Antiques (bd. dirs. 1965-68, 81-84, sec. 1968-79), Nat. Trust for Hist. Preservation (mem. bd. advisors 1990—, Honor award 1992), Assn. for Preservation of Tech., Soc. Archtl. Historians, Vernacular Architecture Form, Soc. Colonial Wars, Md. Club. Home and Office: 1307 Bolton St Baltimore MD 21217-4102

TROSTEN, LEONARD MORSE, lawyer; b. Bklyn., Jan. 25, 1932; s. David and Anne Bertha (Belkin) T.; m. Arthea Howell Dickson, Aug. 21, 1954 (dec. Jan. 1978); children: Amanda Trosten-Bloom, Jessica Trosten Forrest; m. Addie Jane Tyner Harris, Jan. 12, 1979; children: Hope Harris Pampillonia, Arthur F.M. Harris. A.B., Columbia U., 1953, LL.B., 1955. Bar: N.Y. 1955, D.C. 1965. Assoc. Dwight, Royall, Harris, Koegel & Caskey, N.Y.C., 1955-58; with Office of Gen. Counsel AEC, Washington, 1958-64; staff counsel Joint Congrl. Com. on Atomic Energy, Washington, 1964-67; ptnr. LeBoeuf, Lamb, Leiby & MacRae, Washington, 1968-90, of counsel, 1991—. Contbr. articles to profl. jours.; editor Columbia Law Rev., 1953-55. Mem. University Club (Washington), Columbia Country Club (Chevy Chase, Md.), First City Club (Savannah, Ga.), The Landings Club (Savannah, Ga.), Rotary, Phi Beta Kappa. Republican. Episcopalian. Avocations: bridge, walking, bowling. Home: 3 Mainsail Crossing Savannah GA 31411-2723 Office: LeBoeuf Lamb Greene MacRae 1875 Connecticut Ave NW Washington DC 20009-5728

TROSTORFF, ALEXANDER PETER, lawyer; b. Queens, N.Y., Apr. 6, 1951; s. Peter W. and Cecilia (Rott) T.; m. Danielle Lombardo, June 30, 1984. BA, Davidson Coll., 1973; JD, Washington U., 1976; LLM in Taxation, Georgetown U., 1981. Bar: N.Y. 1978, La. 1981. Tax law specialist IRS, Washington, 1978-80; assoc. Jones, Walker, Waechter, Poitevant, Carrere & Denegre, New Orleans, 1980-84, ptnr., 1984—. Lutheran. Avocations: tennis, basketball, golf. Home: 1414 Eleonore St New Orleans LA 70115-4318 Office: Jones Walker Waechter Poitevant Carrere & Denegre 201 Saint Charles Ave New Orleans LA 70170-1000

TROTMAN, ALEXANDER J., automobile manufacturing company executive; b. 1933; married. MBA, Mich. State U., 1972. Various positions Ford Motor Co., Europe, 1955-69, Dearborn, Mich., 1969-71, dir. sales and mktg. planning, 1971-72, exec. dir. product planning and research, 1972-75, chief car planning mgr. Car Product Devel. Group, 1975-77, exec. dir. ops. planning, 1977-78, asst. gen. mgr. truck and recreational products ops., 1978-79, corp. v.p., from 1979, mgr. truck ops. Ford of Europe, Inc., then pres. Ford Asia-Pacific Inc., 1983-84, pres., chmn. Ford of Europe, Inc., from 1984, then exec. v.p. No. Am. auto ops., now chmn. bd., pres., CEO, dir. Ford Motor Co., 1993—; bd. dirs. IBM Corp., Armonk, N.Y. Served with RAF, 1951-55. Office: Ford Motor Co The American Rd Dearborn MI 48121*

TROTT, SABERT SCOTT, II, marketing professional; b. Concord, N.C., Nov. 21, 1941; s. Sabert Scott and Mary Welker (Crooks) T.; m. Brenda Lee Bost, Nov. 27, 1964; children—Sabert Scott III, David Lee. B.S. in Textile Tech., N.C. State U., 1964; M.B.A., U. N.C., 1969. Mgr. trainee Cannon Mills Co., Kannapolis, N.C., 1969-70, mktg. mgr., 1970-75, v.p. mktg., 1975-82, sr. v.p. mktg., 1982-86, dir. telemktg. and premium sales, 1987-89; mgr. spl. markets, mktg. & sales Fieldcrest Cannon Inc., mktg. mgr., telemarketing sales mgr., 1989-92; v.p. mktg. and sales Spencer's Inc., Mt. Airy, N.C., 1992-93; v.p. mktg. Carpenter Co., Richmond, Va., 1994—. Chmn. Cabarrus-Rowan Parks and Recreation Commn., N.C., 1982-86; mem. Cabarrus County Parks and Recreation Commn., N.C., 1980-88; Rep. candidate County Commr., Cabarrus County, 1990; bd. dirs. Cabarrus Meml. Hosp., 1992, N.C. Ctr. for Applied Textile Tech.; vestryman local Episcopal ch., 1988-93. Capt. U.S. Army, 1965-70. Decorated Commendation medal (2). Republican. Lodge: Rotary. Avocations: canoeing; rafting; golf; basketball; racquetball. Home: 2607 Helmsley Ct Midlothian VA 23113 Office: Carpenter Co 5016 Monument Ave Richmond VA 23230

TROTT, STEPHEN SPANGLER, federal judge, musician; b. Glen Ridge, N.J., Dec. 12, 1939; s. David Herman and Virginia (Spangler) T.; divorced; children: Christina, Shelley. B.A., Wesleyan U., 1962; LL.B., Harvard U., 1965; LLD (hon.), Santa Clara U., 1992. Bar: Calif. 1966, U.S. Dist. Ct. (cen. dist.) Calif. 1966, U.S. Ct. Appeals (9th cir.) 1983, U.S. Supreme Ct. 1984. Guitarist, mem. The Highwaymen, 1958—; dep. dist. atty. Los Angeles County Dist. Atty.'s Office, Los Angeles, 1966-75; chief dep. dist. atty. Los Angeles County Dist. Atty.'s Office, 1975-79; U.S. dist. atty. Central Dist. Calif., Los Angeles, 1981-83; asst. atty. gen. criminal div. Dept. Justice, Washington, 1983-86; mem. faculty Nat. Coll. Dist. Attys., Houston, 1973—; chmn. central dist. Calif. Law Enforcement Coordinating Com., Houston, 1981-83; coordinator Los Angeles-Nev. Drug Enforcement Task Force, 1982-83; assoc. atty. gen. Justice Dept., Washington, 1986-88; chmn. U.S. Interpol, 1986-88; judge U.S. Ct. of Appeals 9th Cir., Boise, Idaho, 1988—; chmn. U.S. Interpol. Trustee Wesleyan U., 1984-87; bd. dirs. Children's Home Soc., Idaho, 1990—, Boise Philharm. Assn., 1995—. Recipient Gold record as singer-guitarist for Michael Row the Boat Ashore, 1961, Disting. Faculty award Nat. Coll. Dist. Attys., 1977. Mem. Am. Coll. Trial Lawyers, Wilderness Fly Fishers Club (pres. 1975-77), Brentwood Racing Pigeon Club (pres. 1977-82), Magic Castle, Internat. Brotherhood Magicians, Idaho Classic Guitar Soc. (founder, pres. 1989—). Republican. Office: US Ct Appeals 9th Cir 666 US Courthouse 550 W Fort St Boise ID 83724-0101

TROTTA, FRANK PAUL, JR., lawyer; b. New Rochelle, N.Y., Jan. 19, 1955; s. Frank Anthony Trotta and Lorraine Burigo. BA, SUNY, Albany, 1975; JD, Union U., Albany, 1978; LLM, NYU, 1986; MBA, Columbia U., 1992. Bar: N.Y., D.C. 1985, Conn. 1988, Pa. 1991, U.S. Dist. Ct. (no. and we. dists.) N.Y. 1979, U.S. Ct. Mil. Appeals 1979, U.S. Dist. Ct. (so. and ea. dists.) N.Y. 1980, U.S. Ct. Internat. Trade 1980, U.S. Tax Ct. 1982, U.S. Supreme Ct. 1982, U.S. Ct. Appeals (D.C. cir.) 1983, U.S. Ct. Customs and Patent Appeals 1984. Assoc. Weil, Gotshal & Manges, N.Y.C., 1978-81; gen. counsel Lehrman for Gov., N.Y.C., 1981-82; pvt. practice Washington, N.Y.C., 1981-86, New Rochelle, 1981-92, Greenwich, Conn., 1986—; bd. dirs. Numbercrunchers Inc., Sound Investments, Clinton, Conn., Lehrman, Bell Mueller Cannon Inc., Arlington, Va.; mng. dir. N.Y. Consultancy, New Rochelle, 1981—; gen. counsel L.E. Lehrman Corp., Washington, 1982—, sec., treas., 1983—, COO, 1986—; gen. counsel Citizens for Am., Washington, 1983-87, sec., treas., 1985-87; sec., v.p., treas. Monroe Corp., Harrisburg, Pa., 1985-86, pres., 1986-90; bd. govs. Fund for Justice and Edn.,

1987-90, ABA, 1987-90; bd. advs. U.S. Fed. Small Bus., Schenectady, N.Y., 1985-95; mem. faculty Practicing Law Inst., 1979; governing mem. Nat. Jud. Coll., 1987-90, Am. Bar Endowment, 1987-90, ABRA Pension Fund, 1987-90; chmn. bd. adv. Inst. for Non-for-Profit Mgmt., Columbia U. Grad. Sch. Bus., 1992-95; devel. com. Greenwich Cath. Sch., 1994-96; chair fin. com. St. Mary's Parish, Greenwich, 1994—. Author: Lois Lane's On Hold: What a Lawyer Should Do if a Reporter Calls, 1987; (with others) Federal Regulation of Consumer Credit, 1979; co-editor: Finishing First: A Campaign Manual, 1983, Starting and Organizing a Business-A Legal & Tax Guide for Small Business; legal corr. The Westchester Eagle. Mem. nat. com. Cath. Campaign Am.; chmn. New Rochelle Rep. Party, 1982-85. Named one of Outstanding Young Men Am., 1976. Fellow Am. Bar Found. (life); mem. N.Y. State Bar Assn. (assn. pub. rels. com., banking law com. bus. law sect., election law com., task force on solo and small practices), Am. Arbitration Assn., Guild of Cath. Lawyers (ethics com.), Mensa Internat., Pro-Life Athletes (dinner com.), Columbian Lawyers Westchester (bd. dirs.), Knights of Malta. Avocations: computers, politics, magic. Address: 53 Bote Rd Greenwich CT 06830-4828

TROTTER, F(REDERICK) THOMAS, retired academic administrator; b. L.A., Apr. 17, 1926; s. Fred B. and Hazel (Thomas) T.; m. Gania Demaree, June 27, 1953; children—Ruth Elizabeth, Paula Anne (dec.), Tania, Mary. AB, Occidental Coll., 1950, DD, 1968; STB, Boston U., 1953, PhD, 1958; LHD, Ill. Wesleyan U., 1974, Cornell Coll., 1985, Westmar Coll., 1987; LLD, U. Pacific, 1978, Wesleyan Coll., 1981; EdD, Columbia Coll., 1984; LittD, Alaska Pacific U., 1987. Exec. sec. Boston U. Student Christian Assn., 1951-54; ordained elder Calif.-Pacific, Methodist Ch., 1953; pastor Montclair (Calif.) Meth. Ch., 1956-59; lectr. So. Calif. Sch. Theology at Claremont, 1957-59, instr., 1959-60, asst. prof., 1960-63, assoc. prof., 1963-66, prof., 1966, dean, 1961; prof. religion and arts, dean Sch. Theology Claremont, 1961-73; mem. Bd. Higher Edn. and Ministry, United Meth. Ch., 1972-73, gen. sec., 1973-87; pres. Alaska Pacific U., Anchorage, 1988-95; ret., 1995; dir. Inst. for Antiquity and Christianity at Claremont. Author: Jesus and the Historian, 1968, Loving God with One's Mind, 1987, weekly column local newspapers; editor-at-large: Christian Century, 1969-84. Trustee Dillard U. Served with USAAF, 1944-46. Kent fellow Soc. for Values in Higher Edn., 1954; Dempster fellow Meth. Ch., 1954. Mem. Rotary Internat. (Anchorage Downtown), Commonwealth North. Home: 75-136 Kiowa Dr Indian Wells CA 92210

TROTTER, HAYNIE SEAY, lawyer; b. Clarksville, Va., Feb. 24, 1931; s. William Augustus and Frances (Seay) T.; m. Marguerite Stapleford, Feb. 6, 1958; (dec. Feb. 1981); children: Richard Haynie, Frances Patricia; m. Katrin Gunnarsdottir, May 31, 1986. AB, Coll. of William & Mary, 1952; LLB, U. Va., 1957. Bar: Va. 1957, U.S. Dist. Ct. (ea. dist.) Va. 1957, U.S. Ct. Appeals (4th cir.) 1963, U.S. Supreme Ct. 1963. Sole practice Vienna, Va., 1957-58; assoc. William C. Bauknight, Fairfax, Va., 1958-59; ptnr. Bauknight, Williams, Swann & Trotter, Fairfax, 1959-61, Bauknight, Prichard, McCandlish & Williams, Fairfax, 1961-71, Boothe, Prichard & Dudley, McLean, Va., 1971-87, McGuire, Woods, Battle & Boothe, 1987—; bd. trustees Nat. Hosp. Orthopaedics and rehab., Alexandria, Va., 1981-93; bd. dirs. Network Health Plan, Alexandria. Mem. ABA, Va. Bar Assn., Fairfax Bar Assn., Assn. Trial Lawyers Am. Republican. Episcopalian. Avocations: tennis, fishing. Home: 9185 Old Dominion Dr Mc Lean VA 22102-1018 Office: McGuire Woods Battle & Boothe 8280 Greensboro Dr Ste 900 Mc Lean VA 22102-3807

TROTTER, HERMAN EAGER, JR. (HERMAN TROTTER), music critic; b. Providence, Sept. 25, 1925; s. Herman Eager, Sr. and Shelley Fern (Jones) T.; m. Johanne Marguerite Haberstro, Sept. 22, 1956; children: Kim Avery. Holly Anne. Joy Caroline. BA, Yale U., 1946. Pub. utility sec. analyst Mass. Mut. Life Ins. Co., Springfield, 1947-51; sales engr. B-I-F Industries, Providence, 1951-56; asst. sec. Buffalo Batt and Felt Co, Depew, N.Y., 1956-68; account exec. Harold Warner Advt., Buffalo, N.Y., 1968-77; freelance music critic Buffalo News, 1968-77, staff music critic, 1977—. Contbr. articles to profl. and popular jours. Program annotator Buffalo Philharm., 1964-70. Lt. (j.g.) USN, 1943-46, PTO. Mem. Music Critics Assn. (v.p. 1988-93). Avocations: skiing, record collecting. Home: 125 Edward St No 1 J Buffalo NY 14201 Office: The Buffalo News PO Box 100 Buffalo NY 14240-0100

TROTTER, LESLIE EARL, operations research educator, consultant; b. Muskogee, Okla., Nov. 17, 1943; s. Leslie Earl and Sylvia Helene (Freeze) T.; m. Jomi Tuggle, July 19, 1968; children: Colleen Nicole, Eamonn Scott. AB in Math., Princeton U., 1965; MS in Indsl. and Systems Engring., Ga. Inst. Tech., 1971; PhD in Ops. Rsch., Cornell U., 1973. Sci. computer programmer Lockheed-Ga. Co., Marietta, 1965-68; computer applications analyst Control Data Corp., Atlanta, 1968-70; postdoctoral rsch. assoc. Math. Rsch. Ctr., U. Wis., Madison, 1973; asst. prof. Yale U. Sch. Orgn. and Mgmt., New Haven, 1974-75; assoc. prof. ops. rsch. Cornell U. Sch. Ops. Rsch. and Indsl. Engring., Ithaca, N.Y., 1975-84, dir. of Sch., 1983-87, prof., 1984—; dir. Advanced Computational Optimization Lab. Cornell Theory Ctr., 1995—; vis. prof. Bonn (Germany) U., 1977-79, math. dept. E.P.F.L., Lausanne, Switzerland, 1984-85, 91-92, Math. Inst., Augsburg (Germany) U., 1987-88; vis. cons. Bell Labs., Holmdel, N.J., 1981. Editor optimization area Jour. Ops. Rsch., 1982-87; contbr. numerous articles to profl. jours. Recipient tchg. excellence awards Cornell U., 1977, 81, 93, 94, sr. U.S. scientist award Alexander von Humboldt Found., Germany, 1988; numerous rsch. grants NSF, 1974—. Mem. Ops. Rsch. Soc. Am., Math. Programming Soc. (treas. 1988-94), Soc. for Indsl. and Applied Math. Avocations: running, skiing, music. Home: 161 Highgate Rd Ithaca NY 14850-1469 Office: Cornell U Sch Ops Rsch Engring Rhodes Hall Ithaca NY 14853

TROTTER, THOMAS ROBERT, lawyer; b. Akron, Ohio, Apr. 11, 1949; s. Fred and Josephine (Daley) T. BA, Ohio U., 1971; JD, Tulane U., 1975. Bar: Ohio 1975, U.S. Dist. Ct. (no. dist.) Ohio 1975. Assoc. Squire, Sanders & Dempsey, Cleve., 1975-80; mem. Buckingham, Doolittle & Burroughs, Akron, 1980—; chair taxation and legis. com. Akron Regional Devel. Bd., 1988-95. Trustee Akron Symphony Orch., 1984-93, Cascade CDC, Inc., Akron, 1983—, Akron/Summit Solid Waste Mgmt. Authority, 1994—, Weathervane Cmty. Playhouse, 1996—. Mem. ABA, Ohio Bar Assn. (chair local govt. law com.), Akron Bar Assn., Cleve. Bar Assn., Nat. Assn. Bond Lawyers, Sigma Alpha Epsilon. Democrat. Home: 589 Avalon Akron OH 44320-2048 Office: Buckingham Doolittle & Burroughs PO Box 1500 50 S Main St Akron OH 44308-1828

TROTTI, JOHN BOONE, librarian, educator; b. Asheville, N.C., Dec. 11, 1935; s. Clarence Trotti and Janice Trotti Lyon; m. Joan Thompson, June 12, 1957; children: Elizabeth, Margaret, Michael. BA, Davidson Coll., 1957; BD cum laude, Union Theol. Sem. Va., 1960; MA, Yale U., 1961, PhD, 1964; MLS, U. N.C., 1964. Ordained to ministry Presbyn. Ch. in the U.S., 1964; instr. O.T. Yale Div. Sch., 1961-62; minister ch. Altavista, Va., 1964-68; asst. prof. religion Randolph Macon Woman's Coll., Lynchburg, Va., 1965-68; asst. librarian, asst. prof. Union Theol. Sem. Va., 1968-70, librarian, 1970—, assoc. prof. bibliography, 1972-80, prof. bibliography, 1980—; mem. library adv. com., Va.; mem. Va. State Networking Users Adv. Council, 1983-88; pres. Altavista Area Ministerial Assn., 1967. Author: Lesser Festivals 2, 1980; editor: Aids to a Theological Library, 1977; editor: Scholar's Choice, Building a Pastor's Library, 1991; contbr. articles to religious and profl. jours., ch. sch. curriculum. Trustee Stillman Coll., 1969-78, Richmond Baptist Theological Seminary, 1989—; bd. dirs. Hist. Found. Presbyn. and Ref. Chs., 1979-86. Mem. Am. Theol. Library Assn. (exec. com. 1971-74, 78-79, pres. 1977-78), Va. Library Assn., Presbyterian Library Assn. (pres. 1973), Soc. Bibl. Lit., Beta Phi Mu. Home: 1222 Rennie Ave Richmond VA 23227-4723 Office: 3401 Brook Rd Richmond VA 23227-4514 *Life is a gift from God to be expended with zest, joy, and a concern for others. In our free society achieving an education appropriate for one's vocation involves seizing opportunities when they come and much hard work. An effective education puts one more, not less, in touch with our common humanity.*

TROTTIER, BRYAN JOHN, professional sports team coach, former professional hockey player; b. Val Marie, Sask., Can., July 17, 1956; s. Eldon J. and Mary (Gardner) T.; m. Laura Lynn Theis, July 14, 1976; children-:Bryan John, Lindsay Ann. Student public schs., Val Marie; student, Swift Current Comprehensive High Sch. Mem. N.Y. Islanders Hockey Club, Farmingdale, 1975-90; owner, operator Bryan Trottier Skating Acad., Port Washington, N.Y.; player Pitts. Penguins, 1990-93; asst. coach Pittsburgh Penguins, 1993—; hockey cons. Right Guard Corp., Phila; spokesman 1980 Winter Olympics, Lake Placid, N.Y.; pres. NHL Player's Assn. Recipient Calder Meml. trophy as Rookie of Yr. Nat. Hockey League, 1976; Hart Meml. trophy as Most Valuable Player, 1979; Art Ross trophy as Leading Scorer; Conn Smythe trophy as Most Valuable Player in Nat. Hockey League Playoffs, 1979-80. Office: Pitts Penguins Civic Arena Gate 9 Pittsburgh PA 15219*

TROUBETZKOY, ALEXIS SERGE, foundation administrator, educator; b. Paris, Mar. 6, 1934; came to U.S., 1936; s. Serge G. and Luba A. (Obolensky) T.; m. Helene de Klebnikoff, July 8, 1967; children: Anne, Andrew. BA, Sir George William U., 1958; grad. diploma in Edn., Bishop's U., 1960. Tchr. Stanstead Coll., 1959-60, Bishop's Coll. Sch., Lennoxville, Que., Can., 1960-66; registrar St. Stephen's Sch., Rome, 1966-68; asst. headmaster Appleby Coll., Oakville, Ont., Can., 1968-71, headmaster, 1981-87; headmaster Selwyn House Sch., Montreal, Que., 1971-81, Toronto (Ont.) French Sch., 1987-92; exec. dir. Tolstoy Found., N.Y.C., 1992-95; county rep. I.O.C.C., Moscow, 1995—. Author: The Road to Balaklava, 1986. Regent Cathedral St. John the Divine, N.Y.C.; bd. overseers CARE, N.Y.C.; mem. lt.-gov.'s conservation award selection com., Ont.; active Sir Edmund Hillary Found. Mem. Can. Assn. Internat. Affairs (pres. Sherbrooke br. 1964-66), Assn. Russian-Am. Scholars, Can. Assn. Ind. Schs. (pres. 1980-81), European Coun. Internat. Schs., Quebec Assn. Ind. Schs. (pres. 1979-81), Amities Internat. Napoleoniennes. Mem. Orthodox Ch. in Am. Avocations: hist. reading and writing, music. Home: 50 Rosehill Ave #1611, Toronto, ON Canada M4T 1G6

TROUNSTINE, PHILIP J., editor, journalist; b. Cin., July 30, 1949; s. Henry P. and Amy May (Joseph) Trounstine; children: Jessica, David; m. Deborah Williams, May 1, 1993; children: Amy, Ryan, Patrick Wilkes. Student, U. Vt., 1967-68, Stanford U., 1968-70; BA in Journalism, San Jose State U., 1975. Graphic artist Eric Printing, San Jose, Calif., 1972-75; reporter Indpls. Star, Ind., 1975-78; reporter San Jose Mercury News, Calif., 1978-83, editoral writer, 1983-86, political editor, 1986—. Co-author: Movers & Shakers: The Study of Community Power, 1981. Creator, writer SPJ Gridiron Show, San Jose, 1981-91. Pulliam fellow, 1975, Duke U., 1991, J.S. Knight Stanford U., 1993-94. Mem. Soc. Profl. Journalist (mem. nat. ethics com. 1993—). Jewish. Avocations: golf, fishing. Home: 960 Asbury St San Jose CA 95126-1805 Office: San Jose Mercury News 750 Ridder Park Dr San Jose CA 95131-2432

TROUP, THOMAS JAMES, electronics company executive; b. Council Bluffs, Iowa, Sept. 4, 1923; s. Ralph Leslie and Ruth (Beaumont) T.; m. Marjory Alice Suelflow, Feb. 2, 1946; children: Robert, Patricia Alice, James Thomas. B.Sc. in Chem. Engring, U. Wis., 1945; M.B.A. with high distinction, Harvard U., 1952. With Internat. Minerals & Chem. Corp., 1945-53; asst. to gen. mgr. Internat. Minerals & Chem. Corp., Chgo., 1950-53; sales rep. Foxboro Co., Los Angeles, 1949-50; with W.R. Grace Co., 1954-68; v.p. chem. group W.R. Grace Co., N.Y.C., 1965-68; treas. Burr-Brown Corp., Tucson, 1968-71; dir. Burr-Brown Research Co., 1967—, vice-chmn., 1981—; v.p., treas. Akzona, Inc., Asheville, N.C., 1971-82; bd. dirs. Dynamics Research Corp., Wilmington, Mass. Mem. Biltmore Forest Country Club (Asheville), Red Fox Country Club (Tryon, N.C.), Farmers Club (London), Ventana Golf and Racquet Club (Tucson, Tucson Country Club. Home & Office: 7278 E Camino Valle Verde Tucson AZ 85715-3408

TROUPE, TERRY LEE, contracting & distribution holding company executive; b. Ephrata, Pa., Apr. 17, 1947; s. Jacob I. and Mary J. (Shober) T.; m. Judy A. Hagy, May 28, 1966; children—Todd L., Brenda R. B.S., Pa. State U. CPA, Conn. Auditor Arthur Andersen & Co., Hartford, Conn., 1969-73; exec. v.p., chief fin. officer Am. Bank and Trust Co. Pa., Reading, 1973-85; vice chmn. Meridian Bancorp, Inc., Reading, 1985-92; v.p., CFO Irex Corp., Lancaster, Pa., 1993—. Mem. adv. bd. Pa. State U., Berks Campus. Mem. AICPA, Fin. Execs. Inst., Construction Financial Mgmt. Assoc. (bd. dirs. Ctrl. Pa. chpt.). Republican. Mem. United Ch. of Christ. Avocations: sailing, skiing, tennis, golf. Office: Irex Corp PO Box 1268 120 N Lime St Lancaster PA 17608

TROUSDALE, STEPHEN RICHARD, newspaper editor; b. L.A., May 29, 1963; s. Richard Gardner Trousdale and Geraldine Barbara Wisdom. AB, Stanford U., 1985. News editor L.A. Daily Commerce, 1986-87; edit. page editor L.A. Daily Jour., 1987-89, mng. editor, 1989—. Mem. Soc. Profl. Journalists (pres. L.A. chpt.), AP Mng. Editors, Calif. Soc. Newspaper Editors, Soc. Newspaper Design, Toastmasters Internat. Avocation: skiing, karate. Home: 10933 Huston St Apt 203 North Hollywood CA 91601-5135 Office: LA Daily Jour 915 E 1st St Los Angeles CA 90012-4050

TROUT, CHARLES HATHAWAY, historian, educator; b. Seattle, Nov. 3, 1935; s. Charles Whyron and Elizabeth (Hathaway) T.; m. Margot Stevens, Dec. 30, 1961 (div. 1983); children: Nicholas H., Benjamin C.; m. Katherine Taylor Griffiths, Oct. 6, 1984. B.A., Amherst Coll., 1957; M.A., Columbia U., 1961, Ph.D., 1972. History instr. Hill Sch., Pottstown, Pa., 1958-59, Philips Exeter Acad., (N.H.), 1960-69; prof. history Mt. Holyoke Coll., South Hadley, Mass., 1969-80; provost, dean faculty Colgate U., Hamilton, N.Y., 1980-90; pres. Washington Coll., Chestertown, Md., 1990-95; prof. history U. Nairobi, 1996—; vis. prof. U. Mass. Labor Rels. and Rsch. Ctr., 1974-80. Author: Boston, The Great Depression, and the New Deal. Trustee Md. Citizens for the Arts, Chesapeake Bay Maritime Mus., Pickering Creek Environ. Ctr. Columbia U. Pres.'s scholar, 1959-60; NEH rsch. fellow, 1975-76; Charles Warren fellow Harvard U., 1978-79. Democrat. Episcopalian. Home: 109 S Mill St Chestertown MD 21620 Office: Washington Coll Office of President Chestertown MD 21620-1197

TROUT, MAURICE ELMORE, foreign service officer; b. Clifton Hill, Mo., Sept. 17, 1917; s. David McCamel and Charlotte Temple (Woods) T.; m. Margie Marie Mueller, Aug. 24, 1943; children—Richard Willis, Babette Yvonne. B.A., Hillsdale Coll., 1939; M.A. in Pub. Adminstrn, St. Louis U., 1948, Ph.D. in Polit. Sci, 1950. Joined U.S. Fgn. Service, 1950; assigned Paris, France, 1950-52, Vienna, Austria, 1952-55, London, Eng., 1955-59, Vientiane, Laos, 1959-61; with Office Exec. Dir. Bur. Far Eastern Affairs, Dept. State, Washington, 1961-65; Am. consulate gen. Munich, Germany, 1965-69; 1st sec., consul Am. embassy, Bangkok, Thailand, 1969-72; dep. office dir. Bur. Politico-Mil. Affairs, Dept. State, Washington, 1972-75; Dept. State advisor Armed Forces Staff Coll., Norfolk, Va., 1975-77. Bd. dirs. Internat. Sch., Bangkok, 1970-72. Served with USCG, 1939-45; capt. USAFR, 1951-55. Recipient Achievement award diplomacy and internat. affairs Hillsdale Coll., 1962. Mem. Am. Fgn. Service Assn., Diplomatic and Consular Officer, Delta Tau Delta, Delta Theta Phi, Pi Gamma Mu. Home: 6203 Hardy Dr Mc Lean VA 22101-3114

TROUT, MONROE EUGENE, hospital systems executive; b. Harrisburg, Pa., Apr. 5, 1931; s. David Michael and Florence Margaret (Kashner) T.; m. Sandra Louise Lemke, June 11, 1960; children: Monroe Eugene, Timothy William. AB, U. Pa., 1953, MD, 1957; LLB, Dickinson Sch. of Law, 1964, JD, 1969; LLD (hon.), Dickinson Sch. Law, 1996, Bloomfield Coll., 1994. Intern Great Lakes (Ill.) Naval Hosp., 1957-58; resident in internal medicine Portsmouth (Va.) Naval Hosp., 1959-61; chief med. dept. Harrisburg State Hosp., 1961-64; dir. drug regulatory affairs Pfizer, Inc., N.Y.C., 1964-68; v.p., med. dir. Winthrop Labs., N.Y.C., 1968-70; med. dir. Sterling Drug, Inc., N.Y.C., 1970-74, v.p., dir. med. affairs, 1974-78, sr. v.p., dir. med. affairs, bd. dirs., mem. exec. com., 1978-86; pres., CEO Am. Healthcare Sys., Inc., 1986-95, chmn., 1987-95; also bd. dirs. Am. Healthcare Systems, Inc.; chmn. emeritus Am. Healthcare Sys., Inc., 1995—; interim CEO Cytran Inc., 1996—; bd. dirs. Baxter Internat., SAIC, Gensia, Inc., West Co., Inc., Cytyc, Inc.; chmn. bd. dirs. Am. Excess Ins. ltd., 1990-95; adj. assoc. prof. Bklyn. Coll. Pharmacy; spl. lectr. legal medicine, trustee Dickinson Sch. Law, 1970-93; trustee Ariz. State U. Sch. Health Adminstrn., 1988-91; mem. Sterling Winthrop Rsch. Bd., 1977-86, Joint Commn. Prescription Drug Use, 1976-80; sec. Commn. on Med. Malpractice, HEW, 1971-73, cons., 1974; co-chmn. San Diego County Health Commn., 1992-94; dir. Biotransplantation, Inc., 1994-95. Mem. editl. bd. Hosp. Formulary Mgmt., 1969-79, Forensic Sci., 1971—, Jour. Legal Medicine, 1973-79, Reg. Tox. and Pharmac, 1981-87, Med. Malpractice Prevention, 1985—; editl. reviewer Annals of Internal Medicine; contbr. articles to profl. jours. Exec. com. White House Mini Conf. on Aging, 1980; Rep. dist. leader, New Canaan, Conn., 1966-68; active Nat. Health Adv. Bd. AAA, N.Y. State Commn. Substance Abuse, 1978-80, Town Coun., New Canaan, 1978-86, vice chmn., 1985-86; bd. dirs. New Canaan Interchurch Svc. Com., 1965-69, Athletes Kidney Found., Circle in Sq. Theatre Inc., 1984-86; trustee U. Calif.-San Diego Thornton Hosp. and Med. Ctr., Albany Med. Coll., 1977-86, St. Vincent DePaul Ctr. for the Homeless, 1987-90, Cleve. Clinic, 1971-87; trustee, vice chmn. Morehouse Med. Sch., 1980-89; assoc. trustee U. Pa.; bd. visitors U. Pa. Sch. Nursing, 1988-92; pres. U. Calif.-San Diego Edn. Bd. Trustees, 1994—; vice chmn. Med. Commn. for Food and Shelter, Inc.; chmn. bd. Am. Coll. Legal Medicine Found., 1983-87; chmn. Internat. B'nai B'rith Dinner, 1989, 94. Recipient Alumni award of merit U. Pa., 1953, Disting. Alumni award Dickinson Sch. Law, 1989, Nat. Healthcare award Internat. B'nai B'rith, 1991, Entrepreneur of Yr. award San Diego, 1994, Horatio Alger award 1995, Salvation Army Tradition of Caring award 1996; named to Hon. Order Ky. Cols., Tenn. Cols. Fellow Am. Coll. Legal Medicine (v.p., pres., bd. govs.); mem. AMA (Physician's Recognition awards 1969, 72, 76, 82, 85, 88, 92), Med. Execs. (pres. 1975-76), Delta Tau Delta (Alumni Achievement award 1996). Lutheran. Office: Box 8052 Rancho Santa Fe CA 92067

TROUTMAN, E. MAC, federal judge; b. Greenwood Township, Pa., Jan. 7, 1915; s. Emmett Theodore and Kathryn (Holman) T.; m. Margaret Petrick, Nov. 23, 1944; children—Jane A., Jean K. A.B., Dickinson Coll., 1934, LL.B., 1936. Bar: Pa. 1937. With Phila. and Reading Coal and Iron Co., 1937-58, gen. counsel, 1954-58; gen. atty. Phila. and Reading Corp., 1958-67; gen. counsel Reading Anthracite Co., 1958-61, Reserve Carbon Corp., 1961-66, So. Carbon Corp., 1966-67; solicitor Blue Mountain Sch. Dist., 1963-67, Blue Mountain Area Sch. Authority, 1963-67, Orwigsburg Municipal Authority, 1966-67, Am. Bank and Trust Co., Reading and Pottsville, Pa., 1957-67; exec. sec., gen. counsel Pa. Self-Insurers Assn., 1962-67; U.S. judge Eastern Dist. Pa., from 1967, now sr. judge. Bd. dirs. Greater Pottsville Indsl. Devel. Corp., 1963-67, Pa. C. of C., 1955-65, Greater Pottsville Area C. of C., 1961-64, Orwigsburg Community Meml. Assn., 1950-66, Schuylkill County Soc. Crippled Children, 1945-67; v.p., dir. Pottsville Hosp. and Warne Clinic, 1960-67. Served with AUS, World War II. Mem. ABA, Pa. Bar Assn., Schuylkill County Bar Assn. (vice chancellor 1955-57, chmn. jud. vacancies and unauthorized practice coms. 1960, chmn. medico-legal com. 1963-65). Lutheran (pres. coun. 1961—). Club: Lion (bd. dirs. Orwigsburg 1964). Home: Kimmel's Rd Orwigsburg PA 17961 Office: US District Ct The Madison Bldg 400 Washington St Rm 400 Reading PA 19601-3908

TROUTMAN, GEORGE WILLIAM, consulting firm executive, geological consultant; b. Brandenburg, Ky., Aug. 8, 1949; s. George I. and Ellen G. (Parker) T.; m. Marcia Lyn Roseman, Aug. 14, 1971; children—Nancy, Anthony, Janet, David, Barbara, Jonathan. Student Murray State U., 1967-68; B.S. in Geology, Western Ky. U., 1974. Geophys. engr. Birdwell div. Seismograph Service Corp., Ohio, Pa., W.Va., 1974-77; geologist Consolidated Natural Gas, Clarksburg, W.Va., 1977-79; exploration geologist Mountain Fuel Supply Corp., Denver, 1979-80; regional exploration geologist Al-Aquitaine Exploration, Ltd., Denver, 1980-81; sr. staff geologist Resources Investment Corp., Denver, 1981-82; geol. mgr. Petro-Lewis Corp., MCR, Oklahoma City, 1982-84; pres., geologist Troutman Geol. & Assocs., Edmond, Okla., 1984—.Served with USN, 1968-70. Mem. Am. Assn. Petroleum Geologists (cert.), Soc. Profl. Well Log Analysts, Oklahoma City Geol. Soc. (exec. com. 1985-86, editor Shale Shaker Digest XI 1982-85, treas. 1987-88, v.p. 1988-89), Kans. Geol. Soc., Rocky Mountain Assn. Geologists, Ardmore Geol. Soc., New Orleans Geol. Soc., Computer Oriented Geol. SOc., Geophysical Soc. of Oklahoma City. Republican. Mem. Ch. of Jesus Christ of Latter-day Saints. Office: Troutman Geological & Assocs 4406 Karen Dr Edmond OK 73013-8124

TROUTMAN, RONALD R., electrical engineer; b. Lewisburg, Pa., Oct. 4, 1940; m. Roy Marlin and Dorothy Irene (Savidge) T.; m. Gail McCarthy Owen, July 30, 1966; children: Kelby Scott, Ramsay Owen. BS, MIT, 1962; PhD, NYU, 1966. Staff engr. gen. tech. div. IBM, Essex Junction, Vt., 1969-73, adv. engr., 1973-81, sr. engr., 1981-87; sr. engr. IBM T.J. Watson Rsch. Ctr., Yorktown Heights, N.Y., 1987-91, engring. staff mem., 1991—; Fellow MIT Ctr. for Advanced Engring. Studies, Cambridge, 1983-84. Author: Latchup in CMOS Technology: The Problem and Its Cure, 1966; contbr. over 60 articles to profl. jours. Lt. USN, 1966-68. Fellow IEEE; mem. IBM Acad. of Tech. Achievements include patents on random access memory design, semiconductor technology development, others; analysis and characterization of short channel effects, subthreshold behavior and hot electron phenomena in field-effect transistors, modeling and control of latchup in CMOS technology, management of TFT/LCD materials and devices research and of TFT/LCD array tester development. Home: 38 Deer Hill Dr Ridgefield CT 06877-5308 Office: IBM TJ Watson Rsch Ctr PO Box 218 Yorktown Heights NY 10598-0218

TROUTWINE-BRAUN, CHARLOTTE TEMPERLEY, psychologist, educator, writer; b. Newton, Mass., Nov. 27, 1906; d. Joseph and Libbie (Kempton) Temperley; m. Arklay S. Richards, Nov. 28, 1928 (div. 1942); children: Whitman Albin, Lincoln Kempton, Sylvia Caroline; m. Harry Troutwine, May 3, 1945 (div. 1954); m. Charles E. McCrum, 1961 (div. 1965); m. Lester Lewis Walsh, Feb. 16, 1968 (div. Feb. 1972); m. George Braun, Feb. 6, 1975 (dec. Oct. 1975). BS, Simmons Coll., 1927; postgrad. Boston U., 1947-49; MA, Northeastern U., 1966; BES, Internat. Ch. Ageless Wisdom, 1981. Pvt. sec. pres. Hygrade Sylvania Electric Corp. Salem, Mass., 1927-28; pvt. and dept. exec. sec. Dr. Stanley Cobb, Bullard prof. neuropathology Harvard U. Med. Sch., 1928-31; part-time caseworker Friends of Framingham Reformatory, 1928-31, others, 1931-51; organizer, exec. dir. Postgrad. Med. Inst. under Mass. Med. Soc., Boston, 1951-57; mgr. Postgrad. Information Services, Lederle Labs. div. Am. Cyanamid Co., Pearl River, N.Y., 1957-61; exec. dir. postgrad. med. edn., Hahnemann Med. Coll. and Hosp. also exec. dir. Mary Bailey Inst. Cardiovascular Research, 1961; counselor, tchr. psychology Holliston High Sch., 1965-66. Counselor Falmouth (Mass.) High Sch., 1966-74; psychotherapist Hallgarth Clinic, 1974-75. Speaker for Am. Epilepsy League. Mem. Mass. Tchrs. Assn. (life), Spiritual Frontiers Assn. (life), N.E.A. (life), Nat. Ret. Tchrs. Assn. (life), Nat. Assn. Sch. Counselors (charter, life), Assn. Research Enlightenment, Soc. Mayflower Descs. (life), Simmons Coll. Alumnae Assn., AAUW, Med. Soc. Execs. Assn. (emeritus), Am. Soc. Psychical Research, States Med. Postgrad. Assn. (past sec.), Mass. Psychol. Assn. (life), Spiritual Frontiers Fellowship (life), World Fedn. Healers (healer mem.), Mass. Healers Assn. Author: Practicing the Silence, 1978, 5th edit., 1992, Open Windows, 1994; contbr. numerous articles in med., spiritual and psychol. fields. Mem. Soc. of Friends. Home: 83 Falmouth Ct Bedford MA 01730-2912

TROWBRIDGE, ALEXANDER BUEL, JR., corporate director, consultant; b. Englewood, N.J., Dec. 12, 1929; s. Alexander Buel and Julie (Chamberlain) T.; m. Eleanor Hutzler, Apr. 18, 1981; children by previous marriage: Stephen C., Corrin S., Kimberly. Grad., Phillips Acad., Andover, Mass., 1947; AB cum laude, Princeton U., 1951; LLD (hon.), D'Youville Coll., 1967, Hofstra U., 1968, Hobart Coll., William Smith Coll., 1975. With Calif. Tex. Oil Co., 1954-59; ops. mgr. Esso Standard Oil S.A. Ltd., Panama C.Z., 1959-61; div. mgr. Esso Standard Oil S.A. Ltd., El Salvador, 1961-63; pres. Esso Standard Oil Co., P.R., 1963-65; asst. sec. commerce for domestic and internat. bus. U.S., 1965-67; sec. of commerce, 1967-68; pres. Am. Mgmt. Assn., N.Y.C., 1968-70, The Conf. Bd., Inc., N.Y.C., 1970-76; vice chmn. bd. Allied Chem. Corp., 1976-80; bd. dirs. NAM, Washington, 1978—, pres., 1980-90; bd. dirs. New Eng. Mut. Life Ins. Co., PHH Corp., WMX Technologies, Inc., Rouse Co., Harris Corp., Gillette Co., Sun Resorts Internat. Ltd., Warburg Pincus Funds, Sun Co. Inc., ICOS Corp. Trustee Phillips Acad., Andover, Mass.; mem. Pres.'s Task Force on Pvt. Sector Initiatives, Nat. Commn. on Social Security Reform, 1982; mem. Nat. Commn. on Exec., Legis. and Jud. Salaries, 1985, Nat. Commn. on Pub. Svcs.; mem. Competitiveness Policy Coun., 1991. With USMCR, 1951-53, maj. Res. Decorated Bronze Star with combat V; recipient Arthur Flemming award, 1966, Pres.'s E cert. for export service, 1968, Bryce Harlow award for Bus.-Govt. Rels., 1988. Mem. Coun. Fgn. Rels., Met. Club, Georgetown Club, Univ. Club. Home: 1823 23rd St NW Washington DC 20008-4030 Office: 1317 F St NW Ste 500 Washington DC 20004

TROWBRIDGE, DALE BRIAN, educator; b. Glendale, Calif., May 17, 1940; s. Dale Beverly and Alison Amelia (Goldsborough) T.; m. Helen Elaine Turner, July 2, 1966; children: Katelin Elizabeth, David Brian. BA, Whittier Coll., 1961; MS, U. Calif., Berkeley, 1964, PhD, 1970. Chemist

Aerojet Gen., Azusa, Calif., 1961-62; chemistry tchr. Berkeley (Calif.) High Sch., 1964-66; prof., chemistry dept. chmn. Sonoma State U., Rohnert Park, Calif., 1969—; vis. prof. chemistry U. Calif., Berkeley, 1970-74, 88; rsch. assoc. Cambridge U., 1978. Contbr. articles to profl. jours. Mem. Am. Chem. Soc., AAAS, Internat. Platform Assn., Sigma Xi. Home: 6039 Elsa Ave Rohnert Park CA 94928-2246 Office: Sonoma State U 1801 E Cotati Ave Rohnert Park CA 94928-3613

TROWBRIDGE, JOHN PARKS, physician, joint treatment, chelation therapy; b. Dinuba, Calif., Mar. 24, 1947; s. John Parks Sr. and Claire Dovie (Noroian) T.; m. Evelyn Anne Parker, Apr. 20, 1996; children: Sharla Tyann, Lyndi Kendyll. AB in Biol. Scis., Stanford U., 1970; MD, Case Western Res. U., 1976; postgrad., Fla. Inst. Tech., 1983-85. Diplomate in Preventive Medicine, Am. Bd. Chelation Therapy (examiner for bd. 1987—), Am. Bd. Biologic Reconstructive Therapy (examiner for bd. 1994—), Nat. Bd. Med. Examiners. Intern in gen. surgery Mt. Zion Hosp. & Med. Ctr., San Francisco, 1976-77; resident in urol. surgery U. Tex. Health Sci. Ctr., Houston, 1977-78; pvt. med. practice Pain Relief Ctr. for Arthritis and Sports Injuries, Health Recovery Ctr. (formerly Ctr. for Health Enhancement), Humble, Tex., 1978—; chief corp. med. cons. Tex. Internat. Airlines, Houston, 1981-83; indsl. med. cons. to several heavy and light mfg. and svc. cos., Houston, 1979-84; immunology research asst. Stanford U. Med. Ctr., Stanford, Calif., 1967-70; night lab. supr. Kaiser Found. Hosp., Redwood City, Calif., 1971-72; advisor to bd. dirs. Am. Inst. Med. Preventics, Laguna Hills, Calif., 1988-90; featured lectr. profl. and civic orgns., U.S., 1983—; sr. aviation med. examiner FAA, 1983-96, rep. to Chelation Protocol Coun., 1996—. Co-author: The Yeast Syndrome, 1986, Chelation Therapy, 1985, 2d edit., 1990, Yeast Related Illnesses, 1987, Do What You Want to Do, 1996; contbr. Challenging Orthodoxy: America's Top Medical Preventives Speak Out, 1991; edit. adv. bd. mem. nat. health and wellness newsletters, and jours., 1990—; contbr. articles to profl. jours. Adv. bd. mem. Tex. Chamber Orchestra, Houston, 1979-80; med. dir. Humble unit Am. Cancer Soc., 1980-81; med. cons. personal fitness program Lake Houston YMCA, 1981-83. Nat. Merit scholar, 1965-69, Calif. State scholar, 1967-69; recipient Resolution of Commendation house of dels., 1974 Am. Podiatry Assn., Spl. Profl. Svc. Citation bd. trustees, 1976, Am. Podiatry Students Assn. Fellow Am. Acad. Neurol. and Orthopaedic Surgery, Am. Soc. for Laser Medicine and Surgery, Am. Coll. Advancement in Medicine (v.p. 1987-89, pres.-elect 1989-91); mem. AMA, Am. Coll. Preventive Medicine, Am. Preventive Med. Assn. (charter, bd. dirs.), Am. Acad. Environ. Medicine, Am. Soc. Gen. Laser Surgery, Nat. Health Fedn. (chmn. bd. govs. 1989), Am. Acad. Thermology, Am. Assn. Nutritional Cons., Am. Soc. Life Extension Physicians (founding), Am. Assn. Physicians and Surgeons, Tex. Med. Assn., Harris County Med. Soc., Houston Acad. Medicine, Aerospace Med. Assn., N.Y. Acad. Scis., Internat. Acad. Bariatric Medicine, Med. Acad. Rheumatoid Disease, Huxley Inst. for Biosocial Rsch., Great Lakes Assn. Clin. Medicine (med. rsch. instnl. rev. bd., v.p. 1993-94, pres. 1994-95), Soc. for Orthomolecular Medicine, Delta Chi. Avocations: private piloting, computer applications, personal watercraft. Office: Pain Relief Ctr Arthritis and Sports Injuries 9816 Memorial Blvd Ste 205 Humble TX 77338-4206

TROWBRIDGE, PHILLIP EDMUND, surgeon, educator; b. Hartford, Conn., Oct. 17, 1930; s. John Henry and Isabelle Story (Warner) T.; m. Fay Elaine Russell, June 23, 1956; children: Kimberly, Heather, Allison, John, David. BA, Trinity Coll., 1952; postgrad., Harvard U., 1955; MD, Tufts Med. Sch., 1959. Diplomate Am. Bd. Surgery. Intern Hartford Hosp., 1959-60, resident in gen. surgery, 1960-65, from mem. surg. staff to sr. surgeon, 1965—; clin. asst. prof. Surgery U. Conn. Med. Sch., Farmington, 1986—; adj. asst. prof. Surgery Dartmouth Med. Sch., Hanover, N.H., 1986—. Contbr. 17 articles to profl. jours. Corporator Hartford Sem., Hartford, 1975-77, 86—, trustee, 1977-86; dir. West Hartford Street Ministry, 1974-79. With USAF, 1952-54. Mem. ACS, Hartford Med. Soc. (pres. 1988, trustee 1989-93, Loving Cup award 1994), Am. Soc. Gen. Surgeons (chmn. Conn. chpt. 1993—), New Eng. Surg. Soc., New Eng. Cancer Soc., Internat. Surg. Soc., Soc. for Surgery Alimentary Tract. Republican. American Baptist. Avocations: golf, tennis, skiing, photography, painting. Home: 11 Lucy Way Simsbury CT 06070-2534 Office: 85 Seymour St Hartford CT 06106-5501

TROWBRIDGE, RONALD LEE, college admininstrator; b. Ft. Wayne, Ind., Dec. 4, 1937; s. Perry and Arola May (Erb) T.; m. Pamela Gay Chapman, Aug. 11, 1962; children: Andrew Lee, Stephen Scott, Elizabeth Chapman. BA, U. Mich., 1960, MA, 1962, PhD in English Lang. and Lit., 1967. Prof. English Ea. Mich. U., Ypsilanti, 1965-78; v.p. Hillsdale (Mich.) Coll., 1978-81, 90—; assoc. dir. U.S. Info. Agy., Washington, 1981-86; dir. fed. and internat. programs Commn. on Bicentennial of U.S. Constitution, Washington, 1986-88, staff dir., 1988-90. Contbr. articles to profl. jours. Mem. Ann Arbor (Mich.) City Coun., 1975-79. Recipient George Washington Honor medal Freedoms Found. Valley Forge, 1979. Mem. Mont Pelerin Soc., Phila. Soc. Republican. Presbyterian. Avocations: politics, writing, speaking. Home: 1500 Lake Pleasant Rd S Osseo MI 49266-9636 Office: Hillsdale Coll Office of the Vice Pres Hillsdale MI 49242

TROWBRIDGE, THOMAS, JR., mortgage banking company executive; b. Troy, N.Y., June 28, 1938; s. of Thomas and Elberta (Wood) T.; m. Delinda Bryan, July 3, 1965; children: Elisabeth Tacy, Wendy Bryan. BA, Yale U., 1960; MBA, Harvard U., 1965. V.p. James W. Rouse & Co., Balt., 1965-66, Washington, 1966-68, San Francisco, 1968-73, 76-78; pres. Rouse Investing Co., Columbia, Md., 1973-76, Trowbridge, Kieselhorst & Co., San Francisco, 1978—. Bd. dirs. Columbia Assn., 1975-76; trustee, treas. The Head-Royce Sch., Oakland, Calif., 1980-84; trustee, pres. Gen. Alumni Assn. Phillips Exeter Acad., 1984-90. Lt. USNR, 1960-63. Mem. Urban Land Inst., Calif. Mortgage Bankers Assn. (bd. dirs. 1991—, pres. 1996—), Mortgage Bankers Assn. Am. (bd. govs. 1993—), Olympic Club, Pacific Union Club, Lambda Alpha Internat. Republican. Presbyterian. Avocations: running, golf. Home: 4 Ridge Ln Orinda CA 94563-1318 Office: Trowbridge Kieselhorst & Co 555 California St Ste 2850 San Francisco CA 94104-1604

TROXEL, DONALD EUGENE, electrical engineering educator; b. Trenton, N.J., Mar. 11, 1934; s. Shirley Monroe and Emma Ruth (Marvel) T.; m. Eileen Millicent Cronk, Aug. 23, 1963; children: Gregory, Jocelyn, Andrea. BS, Rutgers U., 1956; SM, MIT, 1960, PhD, 1962. Ford Found. postdoctoral fellow, asst. prof. MIT, Cambridge, Mass., 1962-64, asst. prof. dept. elec. engring., 1964-67, assoc. prof., 1967-85, prof. elec. engring., 1985—; asst. prof. Tufts U., Medford, Mass., 1963; bd. dirs. ECRM, Inc., Tewksbury, Mass. 1st lt. U.S. Army, 1956-58. Mem. IEEE (sr. mem., Leonard G. Abraham Prize Paper award 1971), Assn. for Computing Machinery, Sigma Xi, Tau Beta Pi, Eta Kappa Nu, Pi Mu Epsilon. Home: 4 Madison St Belmont MA 02178-3536 Office: MIT 77 Massachusetts Ave # 36-287 Cambridge MA 02139-4301

TROXELL, RAYMOND ROBERT, JR., college administrator; b. Easton, Pa., July 11, 1932; s. Raymond Robert and Mary Jane (Cooney) T.; m. Barbara Lou Foulk, Aug. 11, 1955; children: Gayle L., Pamella A., Lynn R. BA in Polit. Sci., Lafayette Coll., 1956; MA in Internat. Rel., Lehigh U., 1960, MS in Adminstrn., 1964; PhD in Adminstrn., Southwestern U., 1974. Tchr./prin., curriculum coord. Easton (Pa.) Area High Sch., 1956-66; asst. supt. West York Area, York, Pa., 1966-67; supt. West York Area, 1967-79, Windber (Pa.) Schs., 1979-82; gen. edn. coord., life experience coord., dean grad. sch., mgmt. coord., prof. Tampa (Fla.) Coll., 1982—; vis. prof. Western Md. Coll., Westminster, 1967-82; model schs. dir. Pa. Consortium, 1975-82; cons. in field; evaluator U.S. Office Edn., Washington, 1973—; lectr. in field; conductor workshops/seminars in field; participant edn. seminar in eastern Europe, Siberia, USSR. Author: Administrative Accountability, 1977, Successful Negotiations, 1979, New Trends in Supervision, 1981, Performance Based Curriculum, 1982, Institutional Effectiveness; contbr. articles to profl. jours. Active various charitable orgns. Mott Found. grantee, Ford Found. grantee; recipient Valley Forge Freedoms Found. award, Am. Educators medal, Outstanding Tchrs. award. Mem. Am. Assn. Sch. Adminstrs., Assn. for Supervision and Curriculum Devel., Coun. on Basic Edn., Am. Acad. Polit. and Social Sci., Ctr. for Study of the Presidency, Nat. Assn. Secondary Sch. Prins., Nat. Sch. Bds. Assn., Am. Judicature Soc., Am. Mgmt. Assn., Coun. for Adult Experiential Learning, U.S. Office of Edn. Fund for the Improvement of Postsecondary Edn., Lehigh Valley Grad. Sch. Edn. Alumni coun., Soc. Ednl. Adminstrs. of Lehigh U., Kappa Phi Kappa, Phi Delta Kappa. Lutheran. Avocations: golf, swimming, writing, hiking, travel. Home: 4664 56th Ave N Saint Petersburg FL 33714-1625 Office: Tampa College 3319 W Hillsborough Ave Tampa FL 33614-5801

TROY, ANTHONY FRANCIS, lawyer; b. Hartford, Conn., Apr. 16, 1941; children: Anthony John, Francis Gerard II. BA in Govt., St. Michael's Coll., Vt., 1963; LLB, T.C. Williams, U. Richmond, Richmond, Va., 1966. Bar: Va. 1966, D.C. 1972, U.S. Dist. Ct. (ea. dist.) Va. 1966, U.S. Dist. Ct. (we. dist.) Va. 1967, U.S. Ct. Appeals (4th cir.) 1967, U.S. Supreme Ct. 1969. Asst. atty. gen. Commonwealth of Va., Richmond, 1966-72, dep. atty. gen., 1974-75, chief dep. atty. gen., 1975-76, atty. gen., 1977-78; assoc. Colson & Shapiro, Washington, 1972-74; ptnr. Mays & Valentine, Richmond, 1978—. Contbr. articles to profl. jours. Trustee Sci. Mus. Va. Home: 1814 Park Ave Richmond VA 23220-2832 Office: Mays & Valentine 1111 East Main St PO Box 1122 Richmond VA 23218-1122

TROY, FREDERIC ARTHUR, II, medical biochemistry educator; b. Evanston, Ill., Feb. 16, 1937; s. Charles McGregor and Virginia Lane (Minto) T.; m. Linda Ann Price, Mar. 23, 1959; children: Karen M., Janet R. BS, Washington U., St. Louis, 1961; PhD, Purdue U., 1966; postdoctoral, Johns Hopkins U., 1968. Asst. prof. U. Calif. Sch. Medicine, Davis, 1968-74, assoc. prof., 1974-80, prof., 1980—, chmn., 1991-94; vis. prof. Karolinska Inst. Med. Sch., Stockholm, 1976-77; cons. NIH, Bethesda, Md., 1974—, NSF, Washington, 1975—, Damon Runyon Cancer Found., N.Y.C., 1980-81, VA, Washington, 1984-88. Mem. editl. bd. Jour. Biol. Chem., 1988—, Glycobiol., 1990—; contbr. articles to profl. jours. Recipient Research Cancer Devel. award Nat. Cancer Inst., 1975-80; Eleanor Roosevelt Internat. Cancer fellow Am. Cancer Soc., 1976-77. Mem. AAAS, Am. Soc. Biol. Chemistry and Molecular Biology, Am. Assn. Cancer Rsch., Am. Chem. Soc., Am. Soc. Enologists, Biochemistry Soc., Biophysics Soc., Am. Fedn. for Clin. Rsch., N.Y. Acad. Scis., Soc. for Glycobiol. (pres. 1991-92), Am. Med. and Grad. Sch. Dept. Biochem. (pres.-elect 1995—), Sigma Xi. Office: U Calif Sch Medicine Davis CA 95616

TROY, J. EDWARD, bishop; b. Chatham, N.B., Can., Sept. 2, 1931; s. J. Thomas and Lilian Mary (Barry) T. BA, St. Francis Xavier U., Antigonish, N.S., 1951; lic. philosophy, Louvain (Belgium) U., 1953, PhD, 1962; BD, Holy Heart Sem., Halifax, N.S., 1959; LLD (hons), St. Thomas U., Fredericton, N.B., 1985. Ordained priest Roman Cath. Ch., 1959. Prof. philosophy St. Thomas U., Chatham, N.B., 1959-63; commd. Canadian Armed Forces, 1963, advanced through grades to col., 1979, ret., 1984, chaplain, 1963-84; dir. personnel adminstrn. Can. Forces Chaplaincy, Ottowa, Ont., 1981-84; bishop Roman Cath. Ch., St. John, N.B., 1984—; episcopal promoter Apostleship of the Sea, Can., 1985—. Columnist New Freeman newpaper, 1984—. Chancellor St. Thomas U., 1986—. Mem. Canadian Conf. Cath. Bishops, Anglican/Roman Cath. Dialogue. Avocations: reading, bird watching. Office: Diocese St John, 1 Bayard Dr, Saint John's, NF Canada E2L 3L5

TROY, JOSEPH FREED, lawyer; b. Wilkes-Barre, Pa., Aug. 16, 1938; s. Sergei and Shirley Jean T.; m. Brigitta Ann Balos, June 9, 1962; children: Darcy Kendall, Austin Remy. BA, Yale U., 1960; LLB, Harvard U., 1963. Bar: Calif. 1964, D.C. 1979. Assoc. Hindin, McKittrick & Marsh, Beverly Hills, Calif., 1964-68, ptnr., 1968-70; pres. Troy & Gould, Los Angeles, 1970—; lectr. Calif. Continuing Edn. of Bar, 1972-80, 94; dir. Amerigon Inc., 1993—, Movie Gallery, Inc., 1994-96, Digital Video Systems, Inc., 1996—. Author: Let's Go: A Student Guide to Europe, 1962, Accountability of Corporate Management; co-author: Protecting Corporate Officers and Directors from Liability, 1994. Pres. L.A. Chamber Orch. Soc., 1968-75, chmn. bd. dirs., 1975-78, vice chmn. bd. dirs., 1978-81; bd. dirs. Music Ctr. Opera Assn., 1972—, v.p., mem. exec. com., 1987—; hon. consul of Tunisia, L.A., 1984-88; pres. Internat. Festival Soc.; bd. dirs. Brentwood Pk. Property Owners Assn., 1988-93. Reid Hall fellow U. Paris, 1958. Mem. ABA, Calif. State Bar Assn. (chmn. bus. ct. com.), D.C. Bar Assn., L.A. County Bar Assn. (chmn. bus. and corp. law sect. 1977-78), French Am. C. of C. U.S. (exec. v.p. 1983-85), French Am. C. of C. L.A. (pres. 1982-84), Wine and Food Soc. So. Calif. Inc. (sec., bd. dirs.), Beach Club, Calif. Club. Office: 1801 Century Park E Ste 1600 Los Angeles CA 90067-2318

TROYER, ALVAH FORREST, seed corn company executive, plant breeder; b. LaFontaine, Ind., May 30, 1929; s. Alvah Forrest and Lottie (Waggoner) T.; m. Joyce Ann Wigner, Sept. 22, 1950; children: Anne, Barbara, Catherine, Daniel. B.S., Purdue U., 1954; M.S., U. Ill., 1956; Ph.D., U. Minn., 1964. Research assoc. U. Ill., Urbana, 1955-56; research fellow U. Minn., St. Paul, 1956-58; research sta. mgr. Pioneer Hi-Bred Internat., Inc., Mankato, Minn., 1958-65, research coordinator, 1965-77; dir. research and devel. Pfizer Genetics, St. Louis, 1977-81, v.p. and dir. research and devel., 1981-82; v.p. research and devel. DEKALB Plant Genetics, Ill., 1982-93; cons.Hybrid Seed Divsn. Cargill, Mpls., 1993—; researcher corn breeding, econ. botany, crop physiology, increasing genetic diversity, recent corn evolution. Contbr. articles to numerous publs.; developer of popular corn inbred lines and hybrids. Master sgt. U.S. Army, 1951-53, Korea. Recipient Nat. Coun. Comml. Plant Breeders Genetics and Plant Breeding award, 1992. Fellow AAAS, Am. Soc. Agronomy, Crop Sci. Soc. Am.; mem. Am. Genetic Assn., Genetic Soc. Am., N.Y. Acad. Sci., CAST, Sigma Xi, Gamma Sigma Delta, Alpha Zeta, Lambda Chi Alpha, Gamma Alpha, VFW. Methodist. Lodge: Masons. Home: 611 Joanne Ln De Kalb IL 60115-1862

TROYER, LEROY SETH, architect; b. Middlebury, Ind., Nov. 23, 1937; s. Seth and Nancy (Miller) T.; m. Phyllis Eigsti, May 24, 1958; children: Terry, Ronald, Donald. BArch, U. Notre Dame, 1971. Prin. LeRoy Troyer and Assocs., South Bend, 1971; sr. ptnr. LeRoy Troyer and Assocs., Mishawaka, Ind., 1977; pres. Southfield, Inc., 1988, The Troyer Group, Inc., Mishawaka, 1988—; bd. dirs. Lead Devel., Inc. Recipient numerous local, state and nat. awards and honors. Past pres. Environic Found. Internat., Inc.; bd. dirs. Habitat for Humanity Internat. Americus, 1987-91, Coalition for Christian Colls. and Univs., 1991-96, Habitat for Humanity St. Joseph County, Ind., 1992—; mem. adv. bd. Archtl. Sch., Andrews U., Berrien Springs, Mich., 1986—; bd. dirs. Bethel Coll., Mishawaka, Housing Devel. Corp., South Bend, CONNECT, South Bend. Fellow AIA (practice mgmt. com., chmn. 1983-84), Ind. Soc. Architects, Mennonite Econ. Devel. Assn. Internat. (chmn. bd. 1987-91). Avocations: photography, travel, reading, art, woodworking. Home: 1442 Deerfield Ct South Bend IN 46614-6429 Office: The Troyer Group Inc 415 Lincoln Way E Mishawaka IN 46544-2213

TROYER, LISA LYNN, marketing and activities director; b. Washington, Mar. 26, 1964; d. Jarnot DeVere and Virginia Mae (Holmes) T. AA in Mktg. Mgmt., Prince George's Community Coll, 1985; B in Gen. Studies, U. Md., 1987; postgrad., Abilene Christian U., 1993—. Staff asst. U.S. House Reps., Washington, 1987-88; adminstrv. coord. Nuclear Info. & Resource Svc., Washington, 1988-89; residential child devel. specialist Country Acres, Gilsum, N.H., 1989-90; program asst. NSF, Washington, 1990-92; mktg. and activities dir. Springvale Ter., Silver Spring, Md., 1992-93; grad. asst. Tex. Del. of the White House Conf. on Aging, 1994—; mission team mem. S.E. Asia Global Campaign Project, summer 1994; bd. dirs. Employees Assn.; prin. rep. EEO Coun., Washington, 1991; sch. outreach vol. NSF Rep., Washington, 1991. Assoc. editor: Children of the American Revolution National Magazine, 1981-82, nat. pubs. chmn., 1982-83. bd. dirs. Prince George's County Chpt. ARC, Hyattsville, 1981-82; polit. intern Gary Hart's Pres. Campaign, 1983-84; del. Md. Young Democrats, Largo, 1984-85; pres. student program bd. Prince George's Community Coll., Largo, 1984-85, bd. trustees mem., 1985-86; active City's Human Resource League Com., Bowie, Md., 1987-89; coord. Laotian refugee camp rescue mission Ch. of Christ, Silver Spring, Md., 1989, youth coord.; vol. Silver Spring Soup Kitchen. Mem. NAFE, U. Md. Alumni Assn., Prince George's Community Coll. Alumni Assn. (v.p., 1985-86, bd. dirs., 1985-91), Alpha Delta Pi Alumni Assn. Democrat. Avocations: writing romance novels, politics, working with abused/neglected teens, music, doll collecting. Office: Abilene Christian U Abilene TX 79699

TROYER, THOMAS ALFRED, lawyer; b. Omaha, Aug. 15, 1933; s. Robert Raymond and Dorothy (Darlow) T.; m. Sally Jean Brown, June 28, 1958; children: Kenneth D., Robert C., Virginia D., Thomas C. BA, Harvard U., 1955; JD, U. Mich., 1958. Bar: Colo. 1958, U.S. Ct. Appeals (D.C. cir.) 1967. Assoc. Holme, Roberts, More & Owen, Denver, 1958-61; USAF, Denver, 1961-62; trial atty. U.S. Dept. Justice, Washington, 1962-64; mem. legal staff Asst. Sec. Treasury for Tax Policy, Washington, 1964-66; assoc. tax legis. counsel U.S. Dept. Treasury, Washington, 1966-67; mem. Caplin & Drysdale, Washington, 1967—; pres. Stern Fund, N.Y.C., 1985-86; bd. dirs., Children's Def. Fund, Washington, Mineral Policy Ctr., Washington, Am. Tax Policy Inst., Washington; mem. bd. trustees Natural Resources Def. Coun., N.Y.C., 1977—, Carnegie Corp., N.Y.C., 1983-91, Found. Nat. Capital Region, 1992—. Contbr. numerous articles to profl. jours. Bd. dirs. Common Cause, Washington, 1980-83; mem. Treasury Adv. Commn. on Pvt. Philanthropy and Pub. Needs, Washington, 1976-77; mem. adv. group to Commr. Internal Rev., Washington, 1978-80; mem. com. of visitors U. Mich. Law Sch., Ann Arbor, 1982—; mem. IRS Commr.'s Exempt Orgn. Adv. Group, Washington, 1987-90. Fellow Am. Bar Found., Am. Coll. Tax Counsel; mem. ABA (vice chmn. govt. rels. tax sect. 1989-91, commn. on homelessness and poverty 1992-94), Coun. for Excellence in Govt., Am. Law Inst. Democrat. Home: 16 Primrose St Chevy Chase MD 20815-4229 Office: Caplin & Drysdale Chartered 1 Thomas Cir NW Washington DC 20005-5802

TROZZOLO, ANTHONY MARION, chemistry educator; b. Chgo., Jan. 11, 1930; s. Pasquale and Francesca (Vercillo) T.; m. Doris C. Stoffregen, Oct. 8, 1955; children: Thomas, Susan, Patricia, Michael, Lisa, Laura. BS, Ill. Inst. Tech., 1950; MS, U. Chgo., 1957, PhD, 1960. Asst. chemist Chgo. Midway Labs., 1952-53; assoc. chemist Armour Rsch. Found., Chgo., 1953-56; mem. tech. staff Bell Labs., Murray Hill, N.J., 1959-75; Charles L. Huisking prof. chemistry U. Notre Dame, 1975-92, Charles L. Huisking prof. emeritus, 1992—, asst. dean Coll. Sci., 1993—, P.C. Reilly lectr., 1972, Hesburgh Alumni lectr., 1986, Disting. lectr. sci., 1986; vis. prof. Columbia U., N.Y.C., 1971, U. Colo., 1981, Katholieke U. Leuven, Belgium, 1983, Max Planck Inst. für Strahlenchemie, Mülheim/Ruhr, Fed. Republic Germany, 1990; vis. lectr. Academia Sinica, 1984, 85; Phillips lectr. U. Okla., 1971; C.L. Brown lectr. Rutgers U., 1975; Sigma Xi lectr. Bowling Green U., 1976, Abbott Labs., 1978; M. Faraday lectr. No. Ill. U., 1976; F.O. Butler lectr. S.D. State U., 1978; Chevron lectr. U. Nev., Reno, 1983; plenary lectr. various internat. confs.; founder, chmn. Gordon Conf. on Organic Photochemistry, 1964; trustee Gordon Rsch. Confs., 1988-92; cons. various chem. cos. Assoc. editor Jour. Am. Chem. Soc., 1975-76; editor Chem. Revs., 1977-84; editorial adv. bd. Accounts of Chem. Rsch., 1977-85; cons. editor Encyclopedia of Science and Technology, 1982-92; contbr. articles to profl. jours.; patentee in field. Fellow AEC, 1951, NSF, 1957-59. Fellow N.Y. Acad. Scis. (chmn. chem. scis. sect. 1969-70, Halpern award in photochemistry 1980), AAAS, Am. Inst. Chemists (Student award 1950); mem. AAUP, Am. Chem. Soc. (Disting. Svc. award St. Joseph Valley sect. 1979, Coronado lectr. 1980, 93, N.Y. state lectr. 1993, Hoosier lectr. 1995, Ozark lectr. 1995), Sigma Xi. Roman Catholic. Home: 1329 E Washington St South Bend IN 46617-3340 Office: U Notre Dame Sch Medicine Notre Dame IN 46556

TRPIS, MILAN, vector biologist, scientist, educator; b. Mojsova Lucka, Slovakia, Dec. 20, 1930; came to U.S., 1971, naturalized, 1977; s. Gaspar and Anna (Sevcikova) T.; m. Ludmila Tonkovic, Dec. 15, 1956; children: Martin, Peter, Katarina. M.S., Comenius U., Bratislava, 1956; Ph.D., Charles U., Prague, 1960. Research asst. Slovak Acad. Sci., Bratislava, 1953-56; sci. asst. Slovak Acad. Sci., 1956-60, scientist, 1960-62, ind. scientist, 1962-69; ecologist-entomologist East Africa-Aedes Rsch. Unit West Africa-Aedes Rsch. Unit, WHO, Dar es Salaam, Tanzania, 1969-71; asst. faculty fellow dept. biology U. Notre Dame, 1971-73, assoc. faculty fellow, 1973-74; assoc. prof. med. entomology Johns Hopkins U. Sch. Hygiene and Pub. Health, 1974-78, prof., 1978—, dir. labs. med. entomology; med. entomology; rsch. assoc. U. Ill., Urbana, 1966-67, Can. Dept. Agr., Lethbridge, Alta., 1967-68; dir. Biol. Rsch. Inst. Am., 1971-79; external dir. rsch. Liberian Inst. Biomed. Rsch., 1981—; dir. AID project on transmission of river blindness in areas of Liberia and Sierra Leone; dir. WHO rsch. grant; tech. adv. com. AID Vector Biology and Control Project, 1986-91; dir. Johns Hopkins U./Fed. U. Tech. Akure Onchocerciasis Project in Nigeria, 1991-94, Johns Hopkins U./Organisation de Coordination et de Cooperation pour la Lutte les Grandes Endemies-Pierre Richet Inst. Onchocerciasis Project, Bouakè, Ivory Coast, 1993-96; dir. Johns Hopkins U./Pierre Richet Inst./ ORSTOM onchocerciasis project in Ivory Coast, 1993-96; trainer doctoral students, Africa, Asia, Cen. Am., 1979—. Editor: Jour. Biologia, 1956-71, Jour. Entomol. Problems, 1960-72; zool. sect.: Jour. Biol. Works, 1960-71; Contbr. articles to profl. jours. Dir. WHO project on prophylactic drugs for river blindness, Liberia, 1985-87. Recipient Slovak Acad. Sci., 1st prize for research project. Mem. AAUP, AAAS, Am. Inst. Biol. Soci., Am. Mosquito Control Assn., Am. Soc. Parasitologists, Helminthol. Soc. Washington, Am. Soc. Tropical Medicine and Hygiene, Entomol. Soc. Am., Am. Genetic Assn., Soc. of Vector Ecology, N.Y. Acad. Scis., Johns Hopkins U. Tropical Medicine Club, Smithsonian Assocs., Royal Soc. Tropical Medicine and Hygiene, Royal Entomol. Soc. of London, Sigma Xi, Delta Omega (Alpha chpt.). Home: 1504 Ivy Hill Rd Cockeysville MD 21030-1418 Office: Johns Hopkins U 615 N Wolfe St Baltimore MD 21205-2103

TRSTENSKY, SISTER JOMARY, hospital administrator; b. Springfield, Ill., June 12, 1938. BA, Marillac Coll., 1970; MA, Catholic U. of Am., 1972, Ohio State U., 1984. Nursing coord. St. John's Hosp., Springfield, Ill., 1962-65; head nurse St. Mary's Hosp., Streator, Ill., 1965-68; clin. specialist St. John's Hosp., Springfield, Ill., 1972-76; mgr. human resources Sisters Health System, Springfield, Ill., 1976-82; resident Mercy Health Ctr., Dubuque, Iowa, 1983; asst. adminstr. St. Vincent Hosp., Green Bay, Wis., 1984-88; exec. v.p. Hosp. Sisters Health System, Springfield, Ill., 1988-89, pres., CEO, 1989—. Home: 2101 Shabbona Dr Springfield IL 62702-1338 Office: Hosp Sisters Health System PO Box 19431 Springfield IL 62794-9431*

TRUBIN, JOHN, lawyer; b. East Orange, N.J., Aug. 1, 1917; s. Albert J. and Fanny (Babetch) T.; m. Edna Glassman, June 24, 1945; children—Priscilla Jo, Andrew James. Student, Johns Hopkins U., 1935-36, Coll. City N.Y., 1936-39; J.D., N.Y.U., 1943. Bar: N.Y. 1943. Asso. firm Strauss, Reich & Boyer, N.Y.C., 1943-46; pvt. practice N.Y.C., 1946-48; asst. atty. gen. N.Y. State, 1948-50; law sec. to Surrogate George Frankenthaler, 1950-53; chief counsel to Moreland Act Commn. on Workmen's Compensation, N.Y.C., 1953-54; first asst. atty. gen. N.Y. State, 1955-57; partner firm Trubin Sillcocks Edelman and Knapp, N.Y.C., 1958-84; counsel firm Parker Chapin Flattau & Klimpl., 1984-86; pvt. practice N.Y.C., 1986-90; mem. chief investigative counsel N.Y. State Senate Com. on Investigation, 1986-90; mem. N.Y.C. Housing Authority, 1990-94; commr. N.Y.C. Tax Appeals Tribunal, 1994—; mem. com. on character and fitness First Jud. Dept., 1976—. Trustee-at-large Fedn. Jewish Philanthropies; trustee N.Y.C. Police Found., Inc.; bd. dirs. Citizen's Com. for N.Y.C., Inc.; bd. overseers Center for N.Y.C. Affairs, New Sch. for Social Research; bd. dirs. United Jewish Appeal Greater N.Y. Mem. N.Y. County Lawyers Assn. (dir. 1967-73), Assn. Bar City N.Y., N.Y. State, Am. bar assns., Am. Judicature Soc. Home: 26 E 10th St New York NY 10003-5945 Office: 1 Centre St #2400 New York NY 10007-2516

TRUBY, JOHN LOUIS, computer, management and trucking consultant; b. New Kensington, Pa., Nov. 28, 1933; s. George N. Sr. and Bertha (Deyber) T.; m. Mary Ann Holmes, Dec. 10, 1952 (dec.); children: Leslie Ann, Jacque Lee, Barbara Holmes. BBA cum laude, U. Pitts., 1959. Fin. analyst Union R.R., East Pittsburgh, Pa., 1959-64; adminstrn. mgr. Westvaco, Luke, Md., 1964-70; controller Lehigh Portland Cement Co., Allentown, Pa., 1970-72; v.p. finance Lehigh Portland Cement Co., 1972-74; pres. J. Truby Co., Zanesville, Ohio, 1974—, Truby Enterprises, Inc., Zanesville, 1981—, TruCom Inc., 1989—. Past pres. Keyser Jaycees, Mineral County Sch. Bd. Levy; class of 1959 agt. U. Pitts.; v.p., treas. Zanesville Habitat for Humanity; elder Cen. Presbyn. Ch. 1st lt. AUS, 1953-56. Named Outstanding Personality of the South, 1967. Mem. Am. Inst. Individual Investors, Fin. Execs. Inst., Zanesville Country Club. Home: 225 W Willow Dr Zanesville OH 43701-1252 Office: PO Box 2519 Zanesville OH 43702-2519

TRUCANO, MICHAEL, lawyer; b. Washington, May 28, 1945; s. Peter Joseph and Fern Margaret (Bauer) T.; m. Doreen E. Struck, 1969; children: Michael, David. BA, Carleton Coll., 1967; JD, NYU, 1970. Assoc. Dorsey & Whitney, Mpls., 1970-75, ptnr., 1976—. Office: Dorsey & Whitney 220 S 6th St Minneapolis MN 55402-4502

TRUCE, WILLIAM EVERETT, chemist, educator; b. Chgo., Sept. 30, 1917; s. Stanley C. and Frances (Novak) T.; m. Eloise Joyce McBroom, June 16, 1940; children—Nancy Jane, Roger William. B.S., U. Ill., 1939; Ph.D., Northwestern U., 1943. Mem. faculty Purdue U., 1946-88, prof. chemistry, 1956-88, prof. chemistry emeritus, 1988—, asst. dean Grad. Sch., 1963-66; Mem. numerous univ. dept. and profl. coms.; chmn. various profl. meetings. Co-author book; contbr. articles to profl. jours., chpts. to books. Guggenheim fellow Oxford U., 1957. Mem. Am. Chem. Soc., Phi Beta Kappa. Research in new methods of synthesis, devel. new kinds of compounds and reactions. Home: 156 Creighton Rd West Lafayette IN 47906-2102 Office: Purdue U Dept Chemistry Lafayette IN 47907

TRUCKSIS, THERESA A., library director; b. Hubbard, Ohio, Sept. 1, 1924; d. Peter and Carmella (DiSilverio) Pagliasotti; m. Robert C. Trucksis, May 29, 1948 (dec. May 1980); children: M. Laura, Anne, Michele, Patricia, David, Robert, Claire, Peter; m. Philip P. Hickey, Oct. 19, 1985 (dec. May 1993). BS in Edn., Youngstown Coll., 1945; postgrad., Youngstown State U., 1968-71; MLS, Kent State U., 1972. Psychometrist Youngstown (Ohio) Coll., 1946-49; instr. ltd. svc. Youngstown State U., 1968-71; libr. Pub. Libr. Youngstown & Mahoning County, Youngstown, 1972-73, asst. dept. head, 1973-74, asst. dir., 1985-89, dir., 1989—; dir. NOLA Regional Libr. System, Youngstown, 1974-85. Contbr. articles to profl. jours. Mem. bd. Hubbard Sch. Dist., 1980-85. Mem. ALA, Ohio Libr. Assn. (bd. dirs. 1979-81), Pub. Libr. Assn. Office: Pub Libr Youngstown & Mahoning County 305 Wick Ave Youngstown OH 44503-1003

TRUDEAU, GARRETSON BEEKMAN (GARRY TRUDEAU), cartoonist; b. N.Y.C., 1948; m. Jane Pauley, June 14, 1980; children: 1 son, Ross, 1 dau., Rachel (twins). M.F.A., Yale U., 1970, D.H.L., 1976. Artist graphics studio, New Haven, CT; syndicated cartoonist, writer. Creator: comic strip Doonesbury; syndicated nationwide comic strip; author: Still a Few Bugs in the System, 1972, The President is a Lot Smarter Than You Think, 1973, But This War Had Such Promise, 1973, Call Me When You Find America, 1973, Guilty, Guilty, Guilty, 1974, Joanie, 1974, The Doonesbury Chronicles, 1975, What Do We Have for the Witnesses, Johnnie?, 1975, Dare to Be Great, Ms. Caucus, 1975, Wouldn't A Gremlin Have Been More Sensible?, 1975, We'll Take it From Here, Sarge, 1975, Speaking of Inalienable Rights, Amy..., 1976, You're Never Too Old for Nuts and Berries, 1976, An Especially Tricky People, 1977, As the Kid Goes For Broke, 1977, Stalking the Perfect Tan, 1978, Any Grooming Hints for Your Fans, Rollie?, 1978, Doonesbury's Greatest Hits, 1978, But The Pension Fund was Just Sitting There, 1979, We're Not Out of the Woods Yet, 1979, A Tad Overweight, but Violet Eyes to Die For, 1980, And That's My Final Offer!, 1980, The People's Doonesbury, 1981, He's Never Heard of You, Either, 1981, In Search of Reagan's Brain, 1981, Ask for May, Settle for June, 1982, Unfortunately, She Was Also Wired for Sound, 1982, Adjectives Will Cost You Extra, 1982, Gotta Run, My Government is Collapsing, 1982, The Wreck of the Rusty Nail, 1983, You Give Great Meeting, Sid, 1983, Guess Who Fish Face, 1983, It's Supposed to be Yellow Pinhead: Selected Cartoons From Ask For May, Settle For June, Vol. I, 1983, Do All Birders Have Bedrooms, 1983, Farewell to Alms, 1984, Doonesbury Dossier: The Reagan Years, 1984, Doonesbury: A Musical Comedy, 1984, Check Your Egos at the Door, 1985, That's Doctor Sinatra, You Little Bimbo, 1986, Death of a Party Animal, 1986, Doonesbury Deluxe: Selected Glances Askance, 1987, Downtown Doonesbury, 1987, Calling Dr. Whoopee, 1987, The Doonesbury Desk Diary 1988, 1987, Talking Bout My G-G-Generation, 1988, We're Eating More Beets, 1988, Read My Lips, Make My Day, Eat Quiche & Die! A Doonesbury Collection, 1989, Small Collection, 1989, The Doonesbury Stamp Album, 1990, 1990, Recycled Doonesbury: Second Thoughts on a Gilded Age, 1990, You're Smokin' Now, Mr. Butts! A Doonesbury Book, 1990, Welcome to Club Scud: A Doonesbury Book, 1991, The Portable Doonesbury, 1993, In Search of Cigarette Holder Man: A Doonesbury Book, 1994, Doonesbury Nation, 1995; co-author: Talks From the Margaret Mead Taproom, 1979; contbr.: (with Nicholas von Hoffman) publs. including The People's Doonesbury; many others (recipient Pulitzer prize 1975); plays include: Doonesbury, 1983, Rapmaster Ronnie, A Partisan Review (with Elizabeth Swados), 1984. Pulitzer Prize for Editorial Cartooning, 1975.

TRUDEAU, GARRY See TRUDEAU, GARRETSON BEEKMAN

TRUDEAU, PIERRE ELLIOTT, lawyer, former Canadian prime minister; b. Montreal, Que., Can., Oct. 18, 1919; s. Charles-Emile and Grace (Elliott) T.; m. Margaret Sinclair, Mar. 4, 1971 (div.); children: Justin Pierre, Alexandre Emmanuel, Michel Charles-Emile. B.A., Jean de Brebeuf Coll., Montreal, 1940; LL.L., U. Montreal, 1943; M.A., Harvard U., 1946; student, Ecole des Sciences Politiques, Paris, London Sch. Econs.; LLD (hon.), U. Alta., 1968, Queen's U., Kingston, 1968, U. Ottawa, 1974, Duke U., 1974, U. Keio, Japan, 1976, St. Xavier U., N.S., 1982, Notre Dame U., 1982, Dalhousie U., 1983, McGill U., 1985, U. B.C., 1986, U. Montreal, 1987, U. East Asia, Macau, 1987, Mt. Allison U., 1989, U. Toronto, 1991; LittD (hon.), U. Moncton, 1969. Bar: Que. 1944, Ont. 1967; created Queen's counsel 1969. Practiced law in Montreal, 1952—; jr. economist staff Privy Coun., Ottawa, Ont., Can., 1949; assoc. prof. law, mem. Inst. Pub. Law U. Montreal, 1961-65; former mem. Ho. of Commons, from 1965; parliamentary sec. to prime minister, 1966-67; minister justice, atty. gen. Can., 1967-68; leader Liberal party, from 1968; prime minister Can., 1968-79, 80-84; leader of opposition in parliament, 1979-80, mem. Privy Council., from 1979; mem. Heenan Blaikie and predecessor firms, 1984—; co-founder Cité Libre (monthly rev.); del. France-Can. Interparliamentary Assn., 1966, UN, 1966. Author: Towards a Just Society: The Trudeau Years, 1990, Memoirs, 1993, The Canadian Way: Shaping Canada's Foreign Policy, 1968-84, Ivan Head and Pierre Trudeau, 1995. Decorated Order of Companions of Honor (Gt. Britain). Recipient Order of Merit U. Montreal, 1975, Berkeley citation U. Calif., 1977, Family of Man award N.Y.C. Council Chs., 1981, Ralston prize Faculty of Law Stanford U., Calif., 1990; Albert Einstein Internat. Peace prize, 1984; named Freeman of City of London, 1975, Companion of Honour, 1984, Companion of the Order of Can., 1985, hon. dean Faculty of Law U. Poitiers, France, 1975; hon. fellow London Sch. Econs., 1968. Mem. Canadian Bar Assn., Montreal Civil Liberties Union, Royal Soc. Can. Liberal. Roman Catholic. Office: Heenan Blaikie y Assocs Bur 2500, 1250 boul René-Lévesque Ouest, Montreal, PQ Canada H3B 4Y1

TRUDEL, MARC J., botanist. PhD, Cornell U. Prof. plant physiology and horticulture Laval U., former dean sch. agrl. and food scis., dir. gen. continuing edn. Office: Universite Laval, Ctr Continuing Edn, Quebec, PQ Canada G1K 7P4

TRUDNAK, STEPHEN JOSEPH, landscape architect; b. Nanticoke, Pa., Feb. 25, 1947; s. Stephen Adam and Marcella (Levulis) T.; m. Arden Batchelder Weill, Sept. 6, 1980. BS in Landscape Architecture, Pa. State U., 1970. Jr. landscape architect Kling Partnership, Phila., 1970-72; landscape architect firm Keith French Assocs., Washington, 1972-73; head dept. landscape architecture Linganore Center Design, Frederick, Md., 1973-74; head dept. landscape architecture Toups and Loiederman, Rockville, Md., 1974-76; project landscape architect Dade County Transit Improvement Program, Kaiser Transit Group, So. Calif. Rapid Transit Dist., Metro Rail Transit Cons.; v.p. Harry Weese & Assocs., Ltd., Miami, Fla., 1976-84; v.p. landscape architecture Canin Assocs., Orlando, Fla., 1984-87; dir. planning and design Bonita Bay Properties Inc., Bonita Springs, Fla., 1987-91; prin. Stephen J. Trudnak, P.A., Landscape Architecture and Land Planning, 1991—. V.p. bd. dirs. Koreshan State Hist. Site, 1989-94; mem. 'not for profit' com. Bonita Springs Cmty. Redevel. Agy., 1994—. Fellow Am. Soc. Landscape Architects (pres. Fla. chpt. 1983, chpt. adv. bd. 1984-85, elections task force 1986, publs. task force 1987, trustee 1987-89, membership task force, chmn. 1989-90, nat. v.p. chpt. and mem. svcs. 1992-94, non-dues revenue task force 1994-95), Nat. Xeriscape Coun. (Fla. steering com.), Nat. Speleol. Soc. SCARAB; mem. Bonita Springs C. of C. (chair beautification com. 1991-92, 1994-95, bd. dirs. 1995—). Home: 554 104th Ave N Naples FL 33963-3225 Office: 3461 Bonita Bay Blvd Bonita Springs FL 33923-4384

TRUE, EDWARD KEENE, architectural engineer; b. Boston, July 12, 1915; s. Edward Payson and Laura Keene (Darling) T.; m. Mildred Louise Richenburg, Aug. 31, 1940; children: Edward Bartlett, Robert Payson, Peter Keene, James Duncan. B.S., MIT, 1939. Engr. Concrete Steel Co., Boston, 1939-40; instr. architecture U. Oreg., 1940-42; sr. engr. Raytheon Mfg. Co., Waltham, Mass., 1943-45; mem. faculty Grad. Sch. Design, Harvard U., 1945-76, prof. architecture, 1958-76; trustee, mem. bd. investment Middlesex Savs. Banks, Natick, Mass., 1954-88; cons. engr. and architect, 1947-59; ptnr. Souza and True, engrs., Cambridge, 1959—; engr. Souza and True Inc., 1970, pres., 1970-86; chmn. bd. Souza, True and Ptnrs. Inc., 1986—. Mem. Concord Planning Bd., 1948-58, chmn., 1954-58; mem. Concord Bd. Appeals, 1959-668, chmn., 1959-61; mem. Concord Bd. Selectmen, 1970-766, chmn., 1972-73; mem. exec. com. Mass. League of Cities and Towns, 1974-76, Searsport Yacht Club; pres. Hist. Soc./Hope, Maine, 1994-95. Home: PO Box 483 Searsport ME 04974-0483 Office: 653 Mount Auburn St Watertown MA 02172-2017

TRUE, JEAN DURLAND, entrepreneur, oil company executive; b. Olney, Ill., Nov. 27, 1915; d. Clyde Earl and Harriet Louise (Brayton) Durland; m. Henry Alfonso True, Jr., Mar. 20, 1938; children: Tamma Jean (Mrs. Donald G. Hatten), Henry Alfonso III, Diemer Durland, David Lanmon. Student, Mont. State U., 1935-36. Ptnr. True Drilling Co., Casper, Wyo., 1951—, True Oil Co., Casper, 1951-94, Eighty-Eight Oil Co., 1955-94, True Geothermal Energy Co., 1980—, True Ranches, 1981-94; officer, dir. White Stallion Ranch, Inc., Tucson, Smokey Oil Co., Casper. Mem. steering com. YMCA, Casper, 1954-55, bd. dirs., 1956-58; mem. bd. dirs. Gottsche Rehab. Ctr., Thermopolis, Wyo., 1966-93, mem. exec. bd. 1966-93, v.p., 1973-90; mem. adv. bd. for adult edn. U. Wyo., 1966-68; mem. Ft. Casper Commn., Casper, 1973-79; bd. dirs. Mus. of Rockies, Bozeman, Mont., 1983-87, bd. dirs. Nicolaysen Art Mus., 1988-93; mem. Nat. Fedn. Rep. Women's Clubs; del. Rep. nat. conv., 1972; trustee Trooper Found., 1995—. Mem. Rocky Mountain Oil and Gas Assn., Casper Area C. of C., Alpha Gamma Delta, Casper Country Club, Petroleum Club (Casper). Episcopalian. Office: Rivercross Rd PO Box 2360 Casper WY 82602-2360

TRUE, RICHARD BROWNELL, scientist; b. Framingham, Mass., Apr. 4, 1943; s. Charles Richard and Marjorie Brownell (Clapp) T.; m. Sarah Jellison, Feb. 5, 1966; children: Christopher Edmund, Jonathan Richard. BSEE, Brown U., 1966; MS in Microwave Engring., U. Conn., 1968, PhD in Electrophysics, 1972. Elec. engr. Raytheon Co., Inc., Portsmouth, R.I., 1966; lectr., rschr. U. Conn., Storrs, 1966-72; tech. cons., elec. engr. Microwave Assocs., Inc., Burlington, Mass., 1972-73; sr. engr., dept. analyst Litton Systems, Inc., San Carlos, Calif., 1973-78, sr. scientist, 1978-90, chief scientist, 1990—; cons. True Sci., Sunnyvale, 1985—; bd. dirs. AFTER Program U. Utah, 1980-85, chmn. recruiting brochure, 1981, organizer spl. topics course, 1982, 83, lectr. spl. topics course, 1982-86, indsl. thesis advisor, 1982-87; bd. dirs. AFTER Program Stanford U., 1979-81, organizer spl. topics course, 1980, 81, lectr. spl. topics course, 1978-81, indsl. thesis advisor, 1978-81. Patentee in field; contbr. articles to profl. jours. and papers to meetings. Recipient Paul Rappaport award for best paper of yr. in IEEE Electron Devices Soc. publ., 1987, Litton Industries Corp. Advanced Tech. award for electron beam dynamics software, 1992; NDEA fellow, 1967-70, NSF fellow, 1970-71. Fellow IEEE (mem. advminstrv. com. electron devices soc. 1988-94, assoc. editor IEEE Transactions on Electron Devices 1986-90, Paul Rappaport award electron devices soc. 1987); mem. Sigma Xi. Home: 1760 Karameos Dr Sunnyvale CA 94087-5226 Office: Litton Systems Inc 960 Industrial Rd San Carlos CA 94070-4116 *Focus is everything.*

TRUE, ROY JOE, lawyer; b. Shreveport, La., Feb. 20, 1938; s. Collins B. and Lula Mae (Cady) T.; m. Patsy Jean Hudsmith, Aug. 29, 1959; children: Andrea Alane, Alyssa Anne, Ashley Alisbeth. Student, Centenary Coll., 1957; BS, Tex. Christian U., 1961; LLB, So. Meth. U., 1963, postgrad., 1968-69. Bar: Tex. 1963. Pvt. practice Dallas, 1963—; pres. Invesco Internat. Corp., 1969-70, True & Sewell and predecessor firms, 1975—; bus. adviser, counselor Mickey Mantle, 1969-95; dir. The Mickey Mantle Found. Editorial bd.: Southwestern Law Jour, 1962-63. Served with AUS, 1956. Mem. Am., Dallas bar assns., Tex. Assn. Bank Counsel, Phi Alpha Delta. Home: 5601 Ursula Ln Dallas TX 75229-6429 Office: 8080 N Central Expy Fl 9 Dallas TX 75206-1806

TRUEBA, FERNANDO, film director and producer, screenwriter; b. Madrid, Jan. 18, 1955; s. Maximo Rodriguez and Palmira Trueba; m. Cristina Huete, Oct. 8, 1982; 1 child, Jonas-Groucho. Film critic El Pais, newspaper, Madrid, 1976-79; editor, dir. Casablanca, film mag., Madrid, 1981-83. Dir., screenwriter Opera Prima, 1980 (Silver Hugo award Chgo. Film Festival 1980), Mientras el Cuerpo Aguante, 1982, Sal Gorda, 1983, Se Infiel y No Mires con Quien, 1985, El Año de Las Luces, 1986 (Silver Bear award Berlin Film Festival 1987), The Mad Monkey, 1989, Belle époque, 1992 (Academy Award, Best Foreign Language Film, 1993); producer, screenwriter A Contratiempo, 1981, De Tripas Corazon, 1984, La Mujer de tu Vida, 1988-89; producer Lulu de Noche, 1985, El Juego Mas Divertido, 1987, Earth Magicians, 1989—, Amo tu cama rica, 1991, Alas de mariposa, 1991 (Concha of Gold award San Sebastian Film Festival 1991), Sublet, 1992; also dir. short films. Mem. Acad. Motion Pictures Spain (pres. 1988). Home: Bueso Pineda 29, 28043 Madrid Spain Office: Antonio Cavero 37, 28043 Madrid Spain

TRUEBLOOD, ALAN STUBBS, former modern language educator; b. Haverford, Pa., May 3, 1917; s. Howard M. and Louise (Nyitray) T. B.A., Harvard U., 1938, M.A., 1941, Ph.D., 1951; M.A. (hon.), Brown U., 1957. Ednl. dir. Chile-U.S. Cultural Inst., Santiago, 1942-43; mem. faculty Brown U., 1947—, prof. Spanish, 1963-82, prof. comparative lit., 1972-82, adj. prof., 1982-87, prof. emeritus, 1987—, chmn. dept. Hispanic and Italian studies, 1967-72, chmn. dept. comparative lit., 1973-77; Fulbright lectr. Am. studies, Colombia, 1972; Sr. Resident scholar Merton Coll., Oxford (Eng.) U., 1973. Author: Experience and Artistic Expression in Lope de Vega, 1974, Antonio Machado, Selected Poems, 1982, (with E. Honig) Lope de Vega, La Dorotea, 1985, Letter and Spirit in Hispanic Writers: Selected Essays, 1986, A Sor Juana Anthology, 1988; transl. Gongora (Picasso), 1985, Garcia Lorca, Complete Poems, 1991, Selected Poems, 1995, Songs, Lament for Ignacio Sanchez Mejias, Villegas, Colombia from the Air, 1993, Villegas, The Route of Humboldt: Colombia and Venezuela, 2 vols., 1994. Served to lt. USNR, 1943-46. Fulbright research scholar Chile, 1958; Guggenheim fellow, 1965-66; Nat. Endowment for Humanities grantee, 1977-81; recipient Spanish Govt. award Order of Isabel la Catolica, 1990. Home: 54 Willow Ave Little Compton RI 02837-1532 Office: Brown U PO Box 1961 Providence RI 02912-1961

TRUEBLOOD, HARRY ALBERT, JR., oil company executive; b. Wichita Falls, Tex., Aug. 28, 1925; s. Harry A. and Marguerite (Barnhart) T.; m. Lucile Bernard, Jan. 22, 1953; children: Katherine T. Astin, John B. Student, Tex. A&M Coll., 1942-43; BS in Petroleum Engring., U. Tex., 1948. Petroleum engr. Cal. Co., 1948-51; chief engr. McDermott & Barnhart Co., Colo., Tex., 1951-52; cons. petroleum and geol. engr. Denver, 1952-55; pres. Colo. Western Exploration Inc., Denver, 1955-58; pres. Consol. Oil and Gas., Inc., 1958-88, chmn. bd., chief exec. officer, 1969-88; chmn. bd., chief exec. officer Princeville Devel. Corp., 1979-87, pres., 1984-86; chmn. bd., chief exec. officer Columbus Energy Corp., 1983—; chmn. bd., CEO, Princeville Airways, Inc., 1979-87; pres. CEC Resources, Ltd., 1984—. With USNR, 1944-46, ensign, 1949-52. Mem. Soc. Petroleum Engrs., Am. Petroleum Inst., World Bus. Council and Chief Execs. Orgn. (bd. dirs.), Ind. Petroleum Assn. Am. (exec. com.), Natural Gas Supply Assn. (exec. com.), Denver Petroleum Club, Cherry Hills Country Club, Univ. Club, One Hundred Club. Roman Catholic. Home: 2800 S University Blvd Apt 82 Denver CO 80210-6056 Office: Columbus Energy Corp 1660 Lincoln St Ste 2400 Denver CO 80264-2401

TRUEBLOOD, PAUL GRAHAM, retired English educator, author, editor; b. Macksburg, Iowa, Oct. 21, 1905; s. Charles E. and Adele (Graham) T.; m. Helen Churchill, Aug. 19, 1931; children—Anne Williams, Susan Stuart. BA, Willamette U., 1928; MA, Duke U., 1930, Ph.D., 1935; Litt.D. (hon.), Willamette U., 1984. Instr. Friends U., 1931-34; English master Mohonk Sch. Boys, Lake Mohonk, N.Y., 1935-37; instr. U. Idaho, 1937-40; asso. prof. Stockton Coll., 1940-46; asst. prof. U. Wash., 1947-52; vis. prof. U. Oreg., 1954-55; prof. English, head dept. Willamette U., 1955-70, prof. emeritus, 1971—; vis. lectr. U. B.C., summer 1963. Author: The Flowering of Byron's Genius, 2d edit. 1962, Lord Byron, 2d edit, 1977; Editor: Byron's Political and Cultural Influence in Nineteeth-Century Europe: A Symposium, 1981; Contbr. to charter issues Keats-Shelley Jour, 1952, Byron Jour, 1973. Pendle Hill fellow, 1934-35; fellow Am. Council Learned Socs., 1952-53; recipient Disting. Alumni citation Willamette U., 1975. Mem. MLA, Keats-Shelley Assn. Am., Philol. Assn. Pacific Coast (exec. com. 1964-65), Byron Soc. (founding mem. Am. com. 1973, bd. dirs. 1975, delivered lecture to Byron Soc. in Ho. of Lords 1975). Home: Capitol Manor 1955 Dallas Hwy NW Apt 903 Salem OR 97304-4496

TRUEHEART, HARRY PARKER, III, lawyer; b. Rochester, N.Y., Mar. 27, 1944; s. Harry Parker and Bertha (Hendryx) T.; m. Karen Ellingson, June 26, 1965; children: Eric Parker, Kathryn Marie. BA, Harvard U., also JD. Bar: N.Y. 1970, Fla. 1975. Assoc. Nixon, Hargrave, Devans & Doyle, Rochester, 1969-77, ptnr., 1977—; spkr. fed. ct. practice, 1979-83; mng. ptnr., 1995—; arbitrator, mediator Ctr. Pub. Resources, Inst. Dispute Resolution, Am. Arbitration Assn. Trustee Sta WXXI Broadcasting, The Greater Rochester Metro C. of C.; bd. dirs. Rochester Downtown Devel. Corp., High Tech. of Rochester, Inc., Park Ridge Found. Mem. ABA, N.Y. State Bar Assn. (chair comml. and fed. litigation sect. 1992-93, house of del.), Monroe County Bar Assn., Fed. Bar Coun (v.p.), Am. Arbitration Assn. Co-author: Federal Civil Practice; contbr. articles on fed. ct. litigation, microfilm records, profl. liability in connection with use of computers to profl. jours. Office: Nixon Hargrave Devans & Doyle Clinton Sq Rochester NY 14604 also: Nixon Hargrave Devans & Doyle 437 Madison Ave New York NY 10022

TRUEHEART, WILLIAM E., academic administrator; b. Stamford, Conn., July 10, 1942. BA in Polit. Sci., U. Conn., 1966; MPA, Harvard U., 1973, EdD in Edn. and Social Policy, 1979. Asst. dir. admissions U. Conn., Storrs, 1966-68, Am. Coun. on Edn. fellow, 1968-69, asst. to pres., 1969-70, dean undergrad. acad. affairs Liberal Arts and Scis., 1970-72; asst. dean, dir. MPA program John F. Kennedy Sch. Govt. Harvard U., Cambridge, Mass., 1979-83; assoc. sec. to univ. Office Governing Bds. Harvard U., Cambridge, 1983-86; exec. v.p. Bryant Coll., Smithfield, R.I., 1986-89, pres., 1989—; cons. Arthur D. Little, Inc., 1974-75, Lincoln U., Pa., 1977, Mary Reynolds Babcock Found., 1979-80, Ford Found., 1979-80, 82, Lilly Endowment, 1982, Nat. Pk. Svc., 1983; bd. dirs. Fleet Nat. Bank, New Eng. Edn. Loan Mktg. Corp., Nellie Mae, Inc., Lifespan, Narragansett Electric; expert witness U.S. vs. Ala. ct. case, HEW vs. N.C. adminstrv. hearing; mem. adv. bd. Dorcas Place, Assn. Governing Bds; with Roxbury Comprehensive Cmty. Health Ctr., Boston, 1984-87, Blackstone Valley Devel. Found., 1990-93, Woodshole Oceanog. Instn., 1991-94. Author: (with George Weathersby) Production Function Analysis in Higher Education: General Methodology and Applications to Four Year Black Colleges, 1977; contbr. articles to profl. jours. Trustee Pub. Edn. Fund, 1987-93, Bryant Coll., 1981-86, Pomfret (Conn.) Sch., 1972-76; rep. Consortium on Fin. Higher Edn., 1983-86; bd. visitors, vice chmn. Fed. Emergency Mgmt. Inst., 1986-88; chmn. exec. bd., prin. architect Conn. Talent Assistance Coop., 1967-68. Littauer, Travelli fellow John F. Kennedy Sch. Govt. Harvard U., Ford Found. fellow Harvard U. Mem. R.I. Commodores (bd. dirs. 1991), R.I. Ind. Higher Edn. Assn. (chmn. 1995—). Office: Bryant Coll Office of Pres Smithfield RI 02917-1284

TRUEHILL, MARSHALL, JR., minister; b. New Orleans, Sept. 5, 1948; s. Marshall Truehill and Inez Gray Williams; adopted s. Elizabeth (May) T.; m. Mary Ola Williams, Dec. 20, 1969 (div. 1972); m. Valli Maria Dobard, July 22, 1972; children: Briana Traci, Marshall III, Jessica, Quentin. B in Music Edn., Xavier U., 1973; BTh, Christian Bible Coll., 1979; MDiv, Orleans Bapt. Theol. Sem., 1986; D Ministry, New Orleans Bapt. Theol. Seminary, 1990; postgrad., U. New Orleans. Ordained to ministry Bapt. Ch., 1980; cert. tchr., La. Tchr. Orleans Parish Sch. Bd., New Orleans, 1973-78, Delgado Community Coll., New Orleans, 1975-78; pastor Faith in Action Bapt. Ch., New Orleans, 1982—; founder, dir. Faith in Action Evangel. Team, New Orleans, 1977—; lectr. Nat. Bapt. Conv. on Congl. Evangelism, New Orleans, 1977-79; cons. So. Bapt. Conv. Home Mission Bd., La., 1986—. Bd. dirs. Project New Orleans, 1983—. Democrat. Avocations: computers, aquariums, interior decorating, aerobics. Office: Faith in Action Evang Team 2544 Onzaga St New Orleans LA 70119-2344 *The greatest investment one can make in this life is an investment in the life of another person. That is the only investment with eternal value.*

TRUEMAN, WALTER, retired advertising agency executive; b. N.Y.C., Oct. 20, 1928; s. David Frank and Bertha H. T.; m. Enid Prussman, Nov. 7, 1953; children—Beth, Deborah, Glenn, Richard. B.A., N.Y. U., 1951. Advt. services dir. Pepsi-Cola Co., Purchase, N.Y., 1966-74; advt. dir. Royal Crown Cola Co., Columbus, GA., 1974-76; sr. v.p., creative mgr. SSC&B, Inc., N.Y.C., 1976-81; sr. v.p., dir. creative ops. McCann-Erickson, N.Y.C., 1981-87; seminar leader, guest speaker in field. Exec. v.p. H.S. Richards Boys Club, Yonkers, N.Y., 1972-74. Served with AUS, 1946-48. Jewish. Home: 11 Balint Dr Yonkers NY 10710-3942 Office: 485 Lexington Ave New York NY 10017-2630

TRUEMAN, WILLIAM PETER MAIN, broadcaster, newspaper columnist; b. Sackville, N.B., Can., Dec. 25, 1934; s. Albert William and Jean Alberta (Miller) T.; m. Eleanor Joy Wark, Dec. 22, 1956; children: Anne, Mark, Victoria. Student, U. N.B., 1951-54. UN corr. Montreal Star, 1957-62, Washington corr., 1962-65; Parliamentary corr. Toronto Star, Ottawa, Ont., 1965-67; nat. dir. UN Assn. in Can., 1967-68; nat. news writer CBC, Toronto, 1968-69; exec. producer news, head network news CBC, 1969-72; freelance reporter, 1972-73; anchorman Global TV News, Don Mills, Ont., 1974-88; free lance broadcaster, 1988—; media critic Toronto Star's Starweek mag., 1988—; Kingston Whig-Standard, 1989—. Host, writer Canadian Discovery Channel TV series Great Canadian Parks, 1995—. Recipient Bowater award for journalism, 1962, Sam Ross award, 1983.

TRUEMPER, JOHN JAMES, JR., retired architect; b. Helena, Ark., June 18, 1924; s. John James and Mary Ann (Jacob) T.; m. Julia Clare Wood, Nov. 21, 1956; children: Zachary Wood, John James III, Ann Rutland Penick. BS in Arch., U. Ill., 1950; DHL (hon.), Lyon Coll., 1995. With archtl. firm Cromwell, Truemper, Levy, Thompson, Woodsmall Inc. (and predecessors), Little Rock, 1950-94; v.p. Cromwell, Truemper, Levy, Thompson, Woodsmall Inc. (and predecessors), 1972-74, pres., 1974-81, chmn. bd., 1980-89; ret., 1994; mem. Ark. Bd. Architects, 1974-82. Prin. works include Ark. system for edn. and tng. mentally retarded, 1956-78, Winrock Farm, Morrilton, Ark., 1953-58, Ark. State Parks, 1955-75, Ark. Power & Light Co., 1961-89, Lyon Coll., Batesville, 1983-94; author: A Century of Service, 1885-1985, 1985. Pres. Ark. Arts Ctr., 1979, chmn. bd., 1980; mem. Little Rock Bldg. Code Bd. Appeals, 1961-86, chmn., 1971-86; mem. Ark. Hist. Preservtion Rev. Bd.; bd. dirs. Little Rock Met. YMCA, 1975-84; mem. Friends of Libr. Bd., U. Ark., Little Rock, 1989, pres. 1995. With USAAF, 1943-46. Recipient Winthrop Rockefeller Meml. award Ark. Arts Center, 1980. Fellow AIA, Greater Little Rock C. of C. (dir. 1979-88). Roman Catholic. Home: 5216 Crestwood Dr Little Rock AR 72207-5404

TRUESDALE, GERALD LYNN, plastic and reconstructive surgeon; b. High Point, N.C., Aug. 3, 1949; s. Gonzales and Emma Dorothy (Allen) T.; m. Althea Ellen Sample, May 27, 1978; children: Gerard Lynn, Jessica Lynne. BS, Morehouse coll., 1971; MD, U. Chgo., 1975; LLD (hon.), A&T State U., 1995. Intern gen. surgery Emory U., 1975-78; resident gen. and plastic surgery Tulane Med. Ctr., 1978-82; pres. Greensboro (N.C.) Plastic Surg. Assocs. P.A., 1982—; bd. dirs. Greensboro Nat. Bank, 1989-92. Bd. dirs. N.C. A&T U. Found., Greensboro, 1988—, Natural Sci. Ctr., Greensboro, 1980—, N.C. A&T State Found., Greensboro Day Sch., Ctr. for Creative Leadership, Nat. Bank Greensboro; program chmn. Greensboro Men's Club, 1990; pres. Ea. Music Festival, 1992. Recipient Disting. Svc. award Morehouse Med. Sch., 1989, Bennett Coll., 1990, A&T State U., 1992; named Physician of Yr., Greensboro Med. Soc., 1992. Mem. AMA, NAACP (life, Greensboro chpt.), Greater Greensboro Med. Soc. (past pres.), Med. Splty. Jour. Club Greensboro, Beta Pi Phi, Sigma Pi Phi. Home: 502 Staunton Dr Greensboro NC 27410-6071 Office: Greensboro Plastic Surg Assocs PA 901 N Elm St Greensboro NC 27401-1512

TRUESDALE, JOHN CUSHMAN, government executive; b. Grand Rapids, Mich., July 17, 1921; s. John Cushman and Hazel (Christianson) T.; m. Karin A. Nelson, Feb. 10, 1957; children—John Cushman, Charles N., Margaret E., Andrew C. A.B., Grinnell Coll., 1942; M.S., Cornell U., 1948; J.D., Georgetown U., 1972. Bar: Md. bar 1972, D.C. bar 1973. Field examiner NLRB, Buffalo and New Orleans, 1948-52; adminstrv. analyst NLRB, Washington, 1952-57, assoc. exec. sec., 1963-68; dep. exec. sec.

NLRB, 1968-72, exec. sec., 1972-77, 81-94, mem., 1977-81, 94, 95; dir. info., dir. World Data Center/Rockets and Satellites, IGY, Nat. Acad. Scis., Washington, 1957-63. Served with USCG, 1942-46. Recipient Presdl. award Pres. of U.S., 1988. Mem. ABA, D.C. Bar Assn., Assn. Labor Rels. Agys. (pres. 1992-93). Democrat. Congregationalist. Office: Nat Labor Rels Bd 1099 14th St NW Washington DC 20570-0001

TRUESDELL, CLIFFORD AMBROSE, III, author, editor; b. Los Angeles, Feb. 18, 1919; s. Clifford Ambrose and Yetta Helen (Walker) T.; m. Beverly Poland, Nov. 18, 1939 (dec.); 1 child, Clifford Ambrose IV; m. Charlotte Janice Brudno, Sept. 16, 1951. B.S. in Math, Calif. Inst. Tech., 1941, B.S. in Physics, 1941, M.S., 1942; cert. in mechanics, Brown U., 1942; Ph.D. in Math, Princeton U., 1943; Dott. ing. h.c., Politecnico di Milano, 1965; D.Sc., Tulane U., 1976; Fil.D. (hon.), Uppsala U., 1979; Dr.Phil. (hon.), Basel U., 1979; Dottore di Matematica (hon.), U. Ferrara, 1992. Asst. in history, debating and math. Calif. Inst. Tech., Pasadena, 1940-42; asst. in mechanics Brown U., Providence, 1942; instr. math. Princeton U., 1942-43, U. Mich., Ann Arbor, 1943-44; mem. staff radiation lab. MIT, Cambridge, 1944-46; chief theoretical mechanics subdiv. U.S. Naval Ordnance Lab., White Oak, Md., 1946-48; head theoretical mechanics sect. U.S. Naval Rsch. Lab., Washington, 1948-51; prof. math. Ind. U., Bloomington, 1950-61; prof. rational mechanics Johns Hopkins U., Balt., 1961-89, prof. emeritus, 1989—; hon. prof. applied math. and mechanics Shanghai Inst., 1985. Author or co-author 25 books including Mechanical Foundations, 1952, Kinematics of Vorticity, 1954, Classical Field Theories, 1960, Rational Mechanics of Flexible or Elastic Bodies 1638-1788, 1960, Nonlinear Field Theories of Mechanics, 1965, 2d edit., 1992, Essays in the History of Mechanics, 1968, Rational Thermodynamics, 1969, 2d edit., 1984, Introduction to Rational Elasticity, 1973, Rational Continuum Mechanics, 1977, 2d edit., 1991, Concepts and Logic of Classical Thermodynamics, 1977, Maxwell's Kinetic Theory, 1980, Tragicomical History of Thermodynamics, 1980; An Idiot's Fugitive Essays on Science, 1984, Great Scientists of Old as Heretics in "The Scientific Method", 1987; co-founder, co-editor: Jour. Rational Mechanics and Analysis, 1952-56; editor or co-editor: Leonhardi Euleri Opera Omnia Series II, vols. 11-13, 18, 19, 1952-71; co-editor: Handbuch der Physik, vols. 6a, 8-9, 1956-74; founder, editor: Archive for Rational Mechanics and Analysis, 1957-67; co-editor, 1967-85, editor, 1985-89; founder, editor Archive for History of Exact Sciences, 1960—, Springer Tracts in Natural Philosophy, 1962-66; co-editor, 1967-78, editor, 1979—; editorial bd.: Rendiconti del Circolo Matematico di Palermo, 1971—; Annali della Scuola Normale Superiore, Pisa, 1974—, Meccanica, 1974—, Bollettino di Storia delle Scienze Matematiche, 1979—, Speculations in Science and Technology, 1980-87. Recipient Euler medal USSR Acad. Sci, 1958, 83, Bingham medal Soc. of Rheology, 1963, gold medal and internat. prize Modesto Panetti, Accademia di Scienze di Torino, 1967; Birkhoff prize Am. Math. Soc., 1978; Ordine del Cherubino U. Pisa, Italy, 1978; Guggenheim fellow, 1957; NSF Sr. Postdoctoral fellow, 1960-61; Japan Soc. Sci. fellow, 1981, U.S. Sr. Scientist award Alexander von Humboldt Stiftung, Fed. Republic of Germany, 1986. Fellow Am. Acad. Arts and Scis.; mem. Soc. for Natural Philosophy (founding mem., dir. 1963-85), Socio Onorario dell'Accademia Nazionale di Scienze, Lettere ed Arti (Modena, Italy), Académie Internationale d'Histoire des Sciences (Paris, France), Istituto Lombardo Accademia di Scienze e Lettere (Milano, Italy), Istituto Veneto di Scienze, Lettere ed Arti (Venice, Italy), Accademia delle Scienze dell'Istituto di Bologna (Italy), Accademia Nazionale dei Lincei (Rome, Italy), Académia Brasileira de Ciencias, Académie Internationale de Philosophie des Sciences (Bruxelles, Belgium), Accademia delle Scienze di Torino (Italy), Polish Soc. Theoretical and Applied Mechanics (hon. fgn. mem.), Regia Societas Scientiarum Upsaliensis (Sweden). Home: 4007 Greenway Baltimore MD 21218-1153 Office: Johns Hopkins Univ Computer Sci Rm 222 New Engring Bldg Baltimore MD 21218

TRUESDELL, WESLEY EDWIN, public relations and investor relations consultant; b. Bklyn., Dec. 16, 1927; s. Wesley Edwin and Anna Josephine (Gippert) R.; m. Mabel Johnsen, Oct. 4, 1957. BBA, St. John's U., Jamaica, N.Y., 1956. With Doremus & Co. (advt. and pub. rels.), N.Y.C., 1953-88; v.p. Doremus & Co., 1969-74; dir. Doremus & Co. (advt. and pub. rels.), 1970-88, sr. v.p., mgr. public relations dept., 1974-81, exec. v.p., 1981-88, mem. exec. com., 1978-88, chmn. profit sharing com., 1975-81; dir. Creamer, Dickson, Basford (subs. EuroRSCG, Paris), N.Y.C., 1988-91, exec. v.p., gen. mgr., 1988-89, dep. chmn., 1989-91, also bd. dirs.; pres. The W.E. Truesdell Co., 1991—. Contbg. author: Dealing With The Business and Financial Media, 1989, Dartnell's Public Relations Handbook, 1996; contbr. articles profl. jours. V.p. S.I. Citizens Planning Com., 1965-72; trustee S.I. Inst. Arts and Scis., 1970-88; chmn. High Rock Park Conservation Ctr., 1970-75. Master sgt. USAR, 1950-52, Korea. Mem. Pub. Rels. Soc. Am. (editor newsletter Fin. Communications Report 1990—), Nat. Investor Rels. Inst. (pres. N.Y.C. chpt. 1979-80), Women Execs. in Pub. Rels. (bd. dirs. 1993—), Downtown-Lower Manhattan Assn. (dir. 1975-88), Profl. Communicators N.Y., Bklyn. Tech. Rsch. Found. Inc. (bd. dirs. 1988—). Republican. Home: Silver Ct Staten Island NY 10301-3420 Office: The W E Truesdell Co 200 Park Ave Fl 26 New York NY 10166

TRUETT, HAROLD JOSEPH, III (TIM TRUETT), lawyer; b. Alameda, Calif., Feb. 13, 1946; s. Harold Joseph and Lois Lucille (Mellin) T.; 1 child, Harold Joseph IV; m. Anna V. Billante, Oct. 1, 1983; 1 child, James S. Carstensen. BA, U. San Francisco, 1968, JD, 1975. Bar: Calif. 1975, Hawaii 1987, U.S. Dist. Ct. (ea., so., no., and cen. dists.) Calif. 1976, Hawaii 1987, U.S. Ct. Appeals (9th cir.) 1980, U.S. Supreme Ct. 1988, U.S. Ct. Fed. Claims, 1995. Assoc. Hoberg, Finger et al, San Francisco, 1975-78, Bledsoe, Smith et al, San Francisco, 1979-80, Abramson & Bianco, San Francisco, 1980-83; mem. Ingram & Truett, San Rafael, 1983-90; prin. Law Office of H.J. Tim Truett, San Francisco, 1991-93, Winchell & Truett, San Francisco, 1994—; lectr. trial practice Am. Coll. Legal Medicine, 1989, 90, Calif. Continuing Edn. of the Bar. Bd. dirs. Shining Star Found. 1991—, Marin County, Calif.; mem. Marin Dem. Coun., San Rafael, 1983-90. Lt., aviator USN, 1967-74. Mem. ABA, Hawaii Bar Assn., Assn. Trial Lawyers Am., Calif. Bar Assn. (com. for adminstrn. of justice, conf. of dels.), San Francisco Bar Assn., Calif. Trial Lawyers Assn., Lawyers Pilots Assn. Roman Catholic. Home: 2622 Leavenworth St San Francisco CA 94133-1614

TRUEX, DOROTHY ADINE, retired university administrator; b. Sedalia, Mo., Oct. 6, 1915; d. Chester Morrison and Madge (Nicholson) T. AB, William Jewell Coll., 1936; MA, U. Mo., 1937; EdD, Columbia U., 1956. Asst. dean women N.W. Mo. State U., Maryville, 1939-43; dean women N.W. Mo. State U., 1943-45, Mercer U., Macon, Ga., 1945-47, U. Okla., Norman, 1947-69; assoc. prof. U. Okla., 1969-72, dir. rsch. and program devel., 1969-74, prof. edn., 1972-74, dir. grad. program in student pers. svcs., 1969-74; vice chancellor for student affairs U. Ark., Little Rock, 1974-83; alumni specialist U. Ark., 1983-84, acad. adviser, 1984-87; exec. bd. N. Cen. Assn. Schs. and Colls., 1977-83. Mem. Nat. Assn. Women Deans, Adminstrs. and Counselors (pres. 1973-74), So. Coll. Pers. Assn. (pres. 1970), Okla. Coll. Pers. Assn. (pres. 1972-73), William Jewell Coll. Alumni Assn. (pres. 1970-73), Pi Beta Phi, Alpha Lambda Delta, Mortar Bd., Sigma Tau Delta, Cardinal Key, Gamma Alpha Chi, Kappa Delta Pi, Pi Lambda Theta, Alpha Psi Omega, Pi Gamma Mu, Delta Kappa Gamma, Phi Delta Kappa, Phi Kappa Phi. (nat. v.p. 1986-89). Avocation: novelist. Home: 14300 Chenal Pky Apt 7422 Little Rock AR 72211-5819

TRUEX, DUANE PHILLIP, III, museum executive; b. Syracuse, N.Y., Aug. 30, 1947; s. Duane Phillip and Dorothy Jean (Ricketts) T.; m. Brenda Truex; children: Duane Phillip IV, Adriane Michelle, Sarah Jeanne. BFA in Music, Ithaca Coll., 1969; postgrad. in bus. adminstrn. Okla. State U., 1969-72; MBA, SUNY-Binghamton, 1984, now PhD candidate in computer sci. and info. systems. Dir. allied arts programs Okla. State U., 1969-72; dir. public relations Kansas City (Mo.) Philharm., 1972-73; exec. dir. Baton Rouge Symphony, 1973-76; exec. dir. Arts and Humanities Council Greater Baton Rouge, 1973-78; exec. dir. Roberson Ctr. Arts and Scis., Binghamton, N.Y., 1978-83; dir. M.B.A./arts adminstr. program SUNY-Binghamton, 1984-85, lectr. mgmt. info. systems, 1985—; cons. in field. Contbr. articles to profl. publs. Bd. dirs. Alliance La. Arts and Artists, 1977-78, Binghamton Gen. Hosp. Found., 1980. Mem. Am. Assn. Mus., N.Y. State Assn. Mus. (sec. bd. dirs.), Nat. Assn. Community Arts Agys., Am. Council on Arts, N.Y. State Assembly Community Arts Agys. (studio sch. and art gallery 1985—), Phi Mu Alpha, Beta Gamma Sigma. Republican. Home: 5 1/2 Hayden St Binghamton NY 13905-3508 Office: 30 Front St Binghamton NY 13905-4704

TRUHLAR, DONALD GENE, chemist, educator; b. Chgo., Feb. 27, 1944; s. John Joseph and Lucille Marie (Vancura) T.; m. Jane Teresa Gust, Aug. 28, 1965; children: Sara Elizabeth, Stephanie Marie. BA in Chemistry summa cum laude, St. Mary's Coll., Winona, Minn., 1965; PhD in Chemistry, Calif. Inst. Tech., 1970. Asst. prof. chemistry and chem. physics U. Minn., Mpls, 1969-72; assoc. prof. U. Minn., Mpls., 1972-76, prof., 1976-93, Inst. of Tech. prof., 1993—; cons. Los Alamos Sci. Lab.; vis. fellow Joint Inst. for Lab. Astrophysics, 1975-76; sci. dir. Minn. Supercomputer Inst., 1987-88, dir., 1988—. Editor Theoretica Chimica Acta, 1985—, Computer Physics Comms., 1986—, Topics Phys. Chemistry, 1992—, Understanding Chem. Reactivity, 1990-92, Internat. Jour. Modern Physics C, 1994—; mem. editorial bd. Jour. Chem. Physics, 1978-80, Chem. Physics Letters, 1982—, Jour. Phys. Chemistry, 1985-87, Advances in Chem. Physics, 1993—, IEEE Computational Sci. and Engring., 1994—, Internat. Jour. Quantum Chemistry, 1996—. Ruhland Walzer Meml. scholar, 1961-62; John Stauffer fellow, 1965-66, NDEA fellow, 1966-68, Alfred P. Sloan Found. fellow, 1973-77; grantee NSF, 1971—, NASA, 1987-95, U.S. Dept. Energy, 1979—, NIST, 1995—. Fellow AAAS, Am. Phys. Soc.; mem. Am. Chem. Soc. (sec.-treas. theoretical chemistry subdivsn. 1980-89, councilor 1985-87, editor jour. 1984—). Achievements include research, numerous publications in field. Home: 5033 Thomas Ave S Minneapolis MN 55410-2240 Office: U Minn Minn Supercomputer Inst 1200 Washington Ave S Minneapolis MN 55415-1227

TRUHLSEN, STANLEY MARSHALL, physician, educator; b. Herman, Nebr., Nov. 13, 1920; s. Henry and Lola Mollie (Marshall) T.; m. Ruth Haney, June 2, 1943 (dec. Dec. 1976); children: William, Nancy, Stanley M., Barbara; m. Dorothy D. Johnson, Jan 10, 1981. AB, U. Nebr., 1941, MD, 1944. Diplomate Am. Bd. Ophthalmology. Intern Albany (N.Y.) Hosp., 1944-45; resident Barnes Hosp., St. Louis, 1948-51; practice medicine specializing in ophthalmology Omaha, 1951—; mem. staff U. Nebr., Clarkson, Immanuel; pres. med. staff Immanuel Hosp., 1961, Clarkson Hosp., 1972-73; prof. ophthalmology U. Nebr. Coll. Medicine, 1974-81, clin. prof., 1981-93, interim chmn. dept. ophthalmology, 1989-90; dir. Nebr. Blue Cross and Blue Shield, 1971-95, vice chmn. bd., 1986-96; dir. Health Planning Council Midlands, 1972-75, Clarkson Hosp., 1974-76, Nebr. Soc. Prevention Blindness., Lions Eye Bank of Nebr., 1983-91. Trustee Omaha Home of Boys, 1966—, Brownell Talbot Sch., 1966-69, Omaha Citizens Assbmely, 1972—, U. Nebr. Found., 1985—, Action Internat., Inc., 1994-96. With AUS, 1946-48. Recipient Alumni Achievement award U. Nebr., 1986, Disting. Alumnus Achievement award U. Nebr. Med. Ctr., 1989, Ann. Hon. awards for civic and community contbns.; named Omaha Health Citizen of Yr., 1989; named King Aksarben XCI for outstanding contbns. to Nebr. community, 1985. Fellow ACS (bd. govs. 1985-91); mem. Am. Ophthal. Soc. (asst. editor transactions 1973-79, editor 1979-84, coun. 1987-92, v.p. 1994, pres. 1995), Am. Acad. Ophthalmology and Otolaryngology (assoc. editor transactions 1968-75, editor 1975-80), Am. Acad. Ophthamology (1st v.p. 1981, pres. 1983, vice chmn. AAO Found. 1992—), Nebr. Acad. Ophthalmology (pres. 1975), Am. Eye Study Club (pres. 1962), Omaha Med. Soc. (pres. 1973), Omaha Country Club (pres. 1977-78), U. Nebr. Med. Ctr. Alumni Assn. (pres. 1958), Masons, Rotary (pres. local club 1981-82), Sigma Xi, Alpha Omega Alpha, Sigma Nu, Phi Rho Sigma. Republican. Home: 10086 Fieldcrest Dr Omaha NE 68114-4939

TRUINI PALOMBA, MARIA GIUSEPPINA, supreme court lawyer, judge; b. Borbona, Ri-Latium, Italy, Aug. 25, 1935; d. Costanzo and Ezia (Giorgi) Truini; m. Emilio Palomba, Jan. 11, 1964; children: Francesco Maria, Giovanna Palomba. Degree in Law, State U. Rome, 1960. Tchr. State High Sch., Rieti, Italy, 1955-84; local magistrate Rieti, Italy, 1974-86; judge Fiscal Commn., Rieti, Italy, 1974—. Author: La Cucina Sabina, 1991; contbr. articles to profl. jours. Mem. drug Prevention Assn., L'Aquila, 1979—; hon. guard Nat. Inst. Royal Tombs of Pantheon, Rome, 1980—. Decorated Cavalier of the Merit of the Italian Rep., 1984, Lady of the Order of Chivalry of the Holy Sepulchre of Jerusalem, Grand Master Cardinal, 1990; mem. Italian Red cross, 1986—, patroness, 1978; vol. UNICEF. Mem. Nat. Civil Lawyers Union (dist. pres. Rieti, nat. councillor 1990—), Italian Women Jurists Assn. (dist. pres Rieti and nat. councillor 1990—), Internat. Assn. of Lawyers, Eurojuris Internat. Geie, Italian Acad. Cooking (nat. cons. 1974, dist. del.), Italian Women's Mgmt. Assn., Italian Women's Nat. Coun., Amnesty Internat. Lawyers, Aeroclub (pres. 1992-93), Rotary (councillor 1994-95). Avocations: travel, cinema, theatre, cooking, volleyball. Home and Office: A Gherardi 70, 02100 Rieti Italy

TRUITT, ANNE DEAN, artist; b. Balt., Mar. 16, 1921; d. Duncan Witt and Louisa Folsom (Williams) Dean; m. James McConnell Truitt, Sept. 19, 1947 (div.); children—Alexandra, Mary McConnell, Samuel Rogers. B.A., Bryn Mawr Coll., 1943; postgrad., Inst. Contemporary Art, Washington, 1948-50. Exhibited in one woman shows at Andre Emmerich Gallery, N.Y.C., 1963, 65, 69, 75, 80, 86, 91, Minami Gallery, Tokyo, 1964, 67, Balt. Mus. Art, 1969, 75, 92, Pyramid Galleries, Washington, 1971, 73, 75, 77, Whitney Mus. Am. Art, N.Y.C., 1973-74, Corcoran Gallery, Washington, 1974, Osuna Gallery, Washington, 1979, 81, 86, 89, 91-92, Neuberger Mus., Purchase N.Y., 1986; exhibited in group shows at Balt. Mus. Art, 1970, 72-73, 82, Whitney Mus. Am. Art, 1970-71, 72, 77, Phillips Collection, Washington, 1971-72, Pyramid Galleries, 1972, 73, Mus. Contemporary Art, Chgo., 1974, 77, Indpls. Mus. Art, 1974, Nat. Gallery Art, Washington, 1974, Corcoran Gallery Art, Washington, 1975, numerous others; translator: (with C.J. Hill) Marcel Proust and Deliverance from Time (Bermaine Brée), 1955; author: Daybook: The Journal of an Artist, 1982, Turn: The Journal of an Artist, 1986, Prospect: The Journal of an Artist, 1996. Guggenheim fellow, 1970; Nat. Endowment for Arts fellow, 1971, 77; Australia Council for Arts fellow, 1981. Home: 3506 35th St NW Washington DC 20016-3114

TRUITT, RICHARD HUNT, public relations agency executive; b. Chgo., June 12, 1932; s. Richard Braeme and Cleon (Johnson) T.; m. Ruth Young, Oct. 4, 1958 (div. June 1983); children: Susan, Thomas, Stephen. B.S. in Polit. Sci., Northwestern U., 1953, M.S. in Journalism, 1957. Reporter, editor Chgo. Tribune, 1957-59; account exec. Carl Byoir & Assocs., Inc., N.Y.C., 1959-67, v.p., 1967-75, sr. v.p., 1975-76, group v.p., 1976-78, exec. v.p., 1978-85; pres. Doremus Pub. Relations, N.Y.C., 1985-91, Arnold & Truitt, N.Y.C., 1992—; adj. assoc. prof. Mgmt. Inst., NYU, k1992—. Author: Strategic Public Relations Counseling, 1987, (with others) History of U.S. Marine Corps Reserve, 1965; chmn. editl. bd.: The Strategist, 1995—; contbg. editor Pub. Relations Quar.; contbr. articles on pub. rels. counseling to profl. jours. Pres. Winnebago Day Sch., Menasha, Wis., 1969; mem. bd. edn., Neenah, Wis., 1970-71; v.p. Ind. Soc., Chgo., 1976—. Served to maj. USMC, 1953-55, Korea, Japan. Recipient CeeBee award Carl Byoir & Assocs., 1974. Fellow PRSA; mem. Pub. Relations Soc. Am. (sec.-treas. Counselors Acad. 1982, chmn. 1983, chmn. ann. conf. 1985, Silver Anvil award 1973, 74, Thoth award Washington chpt. 1973, elected fellow 1991). Republican. Clubs: Norwalk Yacht (Conn.); N.Y. Yacht; Internat. (Washington). Avocations: sculpting; sailboat racing. Home: 27 Craw Ave Rowayton CT 06853-1608 Office: Arnold & Truitt 530 Fifth Ave New York NY 10036

TRUITT, SHIRLEY ANN BOWDLE, middle school educator; b. Cambridge, Md., July 14, 1933; d. Thomas Woodrow and Sarah Virginia (Corkran) Bowdle; m. Herman James Truitt, June 19, 1955; children: Jennie Ann Knapp, Thomas Lee, Sarah Jane. BS, Salisbury (Md.) State Coll., 1955, MEd, 1977. Cert. reading specialist, elem. tchr., Md., Del. Tchr. North Salisbury Elem. Sch., Salisbury, 1955-57, Selbyville (Del.) Elem. Sch., 1963-64, Whaleyville (Md.) Elem. Sch., 1965-67, Phillip C. Showell Sch., Selbyville, 1970-73; reading specialist Selbyville Mid. Sch., 1974-91; lang. arts and math. tchr. Sussex Ctrl. Mid. Sch., Millsboro, Del., 1991—; cooperating tchr. Wilmington Coll., 1996, adv. bd., 1995—. Sec. Worcester County Recreation and Parks Commn., 1972-84; pres. United Meth. Ch., Whaleyville; troop leader Girl Scouts U.S., Berlin, Md., 1968-73; mem. adv. com. Wilmington Coll. Named Tchr. of Yr., Indian River Sch. Dist., 1973, 94, recipient Supts. award, 1993. Mem. AAUW (pres. Salisbury 1988—), Nat. Assn. Secondary Sch. Prins., Del. State Reading Assn. (pres. 1980-81), Sussex County Orgn. Reading (pres. 1977, 86), Alpha Delta Kappa (pres. 1986), Phi Delta Kappa (charter mem. eastern shore chpt.). Avocations: collecting clocks, growing orchids. Home: 11517 Dale Rd Whaleyville MD 21872-2026

TRUITT, WILLIAM HARVEY, private school educator; b. Alton, Ill., May 27, 1935; s. Howard Earl and Mary Margaret (Haper) T.; m. Janetha Mitchell, Aug. 5, 1961; children: Joy Elizabeth, Janita Ann. BA, Principia Coll., 1957; MA, So. Ill. U., 1964. Headmaster Forman Schs., Litchfield, Conn.; prin. upper and lower sch. The Principia, St. Louis, headmaster. Mem. NASSP, Mo. Assn. Secondary Prins., St. Louis Ind. Sch. Heads, Mo. Ind. Schs. (pres. 1983-84), Am. Coun. for Am. Pvt. Edn. (v.p. 1983-84), North Cen. Accrediting Assn. (exec. bd. dirs. 1988-91). Home: 13201 Clayton Rd Saint Louis MO 63131-1002

TRUJILLO, ANGELINA, endocrinologist; b. Long Beach, Calif.. BA in Psychology, Chapman Coll., 1974; postgrad., U. Colo., 1974-75, MD, 1979. Resident in internal medicine Kern Med. Ctr., Bakersfield, Calif., 1979-82; fellow in endocrinology UCLA, Sepulveda, Calif., 1982-84, chief resident dept. internal medicine, 1985-86; chief diabetes clinic Sepulveda (Calif.) VA Med. Ctr., 1986-89; physician specialist Olive View Med. Ctr., Sylmar, Calif., 1989; chief divsn. endocrinology U. S.D. Sch. Medicine, Sioux Falls, 1990—; coord. R&D Royal C. Johnson VA Med. Ctr., Sioux Falls, 1993—; adj. instr. UCLA, 1982-84, adj. asst. prof. medicine, 1985-89, clin. asst. prof. family medicine, 1994—; asst. prof. U. S.D. Sch. Medicine, 1990-94, assoc. prof., 1994—, assoc. dir. internal medicine residency program, 1992-95; spkr. in field. Mental health vol. Counselor/Lompoc Mental Health, Washington, 1971; bd. dirs. Lompoc (Calif.) Assn. Retarded Citizens, 1973-74, Santa Barbara Health Planning Com., Lompoc, 1974; vol. counselor Pike's Peak Mental Health Assn., 1974-75; hot line counselor Terros, Colorado Springs, Colo., 1974-75; 5th grade catechist tchr. Our Lady of Perpetual Help, Valencia, Calif., 1984-89; pub. spkr. in diabetes, women and heart disease. Grantee NIH, 1986-89, 91-92, Am. Diabetes Assn., 1985-87, Pfizer, Inc., 1990-91, Nat. Heart, Lung, and Blood Inst., 1994—, Bristol-Myers Squibb, 1994. Mem. ACP, Am. Fedn. Clin. Rsch. (med. sch. rep., endo/metabolism subspecialty coun.), Am. Soc. Hypertension, Am. Diabetes Assn., Assn. Program Dirs. in Internal Medicine, Assn. Clerkship Dirs. in Internal Medicine, S.D. State Med. Assn., Seventh Dist. Med. Soc., Wilderness Med. Soc. (mem. environ. coun.). Office: U SD Sioux Falls Med Rsch Ctr 2501 W 22nd St Sioux Falls SD 57105*

TRUJILLO, LORENZO A., lawyer; b. Denver, Aug. 10, 1951; s. Filbert G. and Marie O. (Duran) T.; children: Javier Antonio, Lorenzo Feliciano. BA, U. Colo., 1972, MA, 1974, postgrad.; EdD, U. San Francisco, 1979; JD, U. Colo., 1993. Bar: Colo. 1994, U.S. Dist. Ct. Colo. 1994, U.S. Ct. Appeals (10th cir.) 1994; cert. edn. tchr., prin., supt., Colo., Calif. Exec. assoc. Inter-Am. Rsch. Assocs., Rosslyn, Va., 1980-82; exec. dir. humanities Jefferson County Pub. Schs., Golden, Colo., 1982—; pvt. practice edn. cons. Lakewood, Colo., 1992-93; gen. corp. counsel Am. Achievement Schs., Inc., Lakewood, Colo., 1994—; atty. Frie, Arndt & Trujillo Law Firm, Arvada, Colo., 1994-95, ptnr., 1995—; co-chair Mellon fellowships The Coll. Bd., N.Y.C., 1987-93; cons. U.S.I.A. Fulbright Tchr. Exch. Program, Washington, 1987-93; editorial advisor Harcourt, Brace, Jovanovich Pub., Orlando, Fla., 1988-93. Contbr. numerous articles to profl. jours. Mem. panel of arbitrators Am. Arbitration Assn., 1994. Recipient Legal Aid Clinic Acad. award Colo. Bar Assn., 1993, Pro Bono award, 1993, Loyola U. Acad. award, 1993, Gov.'s award for excellence in the arts State of Colo., 1996. Mem. Colo. chpt. Am. Assn. Tchrs. of Spanish and Portuguese (pres. 1985-88), Am. Immigration Lawyers Assn., Nat. Sch. Bds. Coun. Sch. Attys., Nat. Assn. Judiciary Interpreters and Translators, Colo. Bar Assn. (family law sect., probate and trust sect.), Colo. Lawyers Com. on Sch. Discipline, Interdisciplinary Com. on Child Custody, Soc. Security Benefits Panel, U. San Francisco Alumni Assn. (founder, pres. 1987-90), Phi Delta Kappa (chair internat. edn. com. 1988-89), Phi Alpha Delta. Avocation: violinist. Home: 1556 S Van Dyke Way Lakewood CO 80228-3917 Office: Frie Arndt & Trujillo 7400 Wadsworth Blvd Ste 201 Arvada CO 80003

TRUJILLO, MICHAEL JOSEPH, elementary school principal; b. L.A., May 14, 1939; s. Damacio and Helen (Rubalcava) T.; m. Yolanda Flores, June 23, 1973; children: Roberto Miguel, Antonio Miguel. BA in Spanish, Iona Coll., 1961; MA in Counseling Psychology, Santa Clara U., 1973. Cert. tchr., adminstr., supr., pupil pers., Calif. Tchr. St. Laurence H.S., Chgo., 1961-62, Christian Bros. H.S., Butte, Mont., 1962-64, Damien Meml. H.S., Honolulu, 1964-68, St. Patrick's H.S., Vallejo, Calif., 1968-71; jr. H.S. tchr., elem. sch. counselor, vice prin. jr. H.S. Pajaro Valley Unified Sch. Dist., Watsonville, Calif., 1971-77; elem. sch. prin. Natividad Sch. Salinas (Calif.) City Sch. Dist., 1977—; cons., presenter in planning for year round edn. Bd. dirs. North Monterey Unified Sch. Dist., Moss Landing, Calif., 1983-91. Recipient Cert. of Recognition, Calif. Senator Henry Mello, 1992. Mem. ASCD, Calif. Assn. Yr. Round Edn. (pres. 1994-95), Nat. Assn. Yr. Round Edn., Assn. Calif. Sch. Adminstrs., Nat. Assn. Elem. Sch. Prins. Democrat. Roman Catholic. Home: 14597 Charter Oak Blvd Salinas CA 93907-1015 Office: Natividad Sch 1465 Modoc Ave Salinas CA 93906-3003

TRUJILLO, SANDRA SUE, nurse; b. Circle, Mont., July 5, 1945; d. Theodore Ward and Ethel Marie (Wilhelm) Keeland; m. Michael Savoie, June 1966 (div. Jan. 1980); children: Nichola, Helena, Jodi, Kevin; m. George N. Trujillo, Mar. 1984 (dec. May 1994). ADN, Mont. State U., 1966; BSN, U. N.Mex., 1991; MSN, Tex. A&M U., 1996—. Staff psychiat. nurse Mont. State Hosp., Warm Springs, 1966-81; critical care staff nurse Betsy Johnson Hosp., Dunn, N.C., 1981-82, Calais (Maine) Regional Hosp., 1982-83, Rumford (Maine) Cmty. Hosp., 1983-84, Albemarle Hosp., Elizabeth City, N.C., 1984-86; charge nurse, nurse mgr. St. Vincent Hosp., Sante Fe, 1986-91; nurse mgr. McAllen (Tex.) Med. Ctr., 1991-93; head nurse Scott & White Hosp., Temple, Tex., 1993—. Mem. Oncology Nurse Soc., Sigma Theta Tau. Home: PO Box 5255 Temple TX 76505-5255 Office: Scott & White Meml Hosp 2401 S 31st Temple TX 76505

TRUKENBROD, WILLIAM SELLERY, banker; b. Orange, N.J., June 19, 1939. B.B.A., U. Wis., 1961; M.B.A., U. Chgo., 1969. Account officer No. Trust Co., Chgo., 1962-71, v.p., 1972-81, sr. v.p., 1981-94, exec. v.p., 1994—. Chmn. Bannockburn (Ill.) Plan Commn., 1979-89, trustee, 1989-91, pres. bd. trustees, 1991—; bd. dirs. Bank Rsch. Ctr., 1988—, Chgo. Crime Commn., 1994—, Pilsen Devel. Corp., 1993—. Mem. Am. Inst. Banking, Alumni Bd. U. Wis. Bus. Sch. (emeritus), Tennaqua Club (Deerfield, Ill.), Univ. Club (bd. dirs. 1985-88), Econ. Club (Chgo.). Republican. Episcopalian. Avocations: tennis; skiing. Office: No Trust Co 50 S La Salle St Chicago IL 60603-1003

TRULL, FRANCINE SUE, research foundation administrator, lobbyist; b. Lawrence, Mass., Sept. 14, 1950; d. Irving M. and Shirley Ann (Barenboim) Leoff; m. David J. Trull, Oct. 22, 1978 (div. 1985). BA cum laude, Boston U., 1972; MA, Tufts U., 1980. Dir. extramural programs Tufts Dental Sch., Boston, 1972-76; asst. dir. office health planning Tufts U., Boston, 1976-80; assoc. dir. Nat. Health Professions Placement Network, Boston, 1978-80; pres. Nat. Assn. Biomed. Research, Washington, 1980—, Found. for Biomed. Research, Washington, 1981—; v.p. govt. affairs Capitol Assocs., Inc., Washington, 1987-94; pres. Policy Directions, Inc., 1995—; chair, bd. dirs. Biomed. Resources Found., Inc., 1995—. Sponsor UNICEF, Washington, 1985-86. Jewish. Avocations: horseback riding, racquetball. Office: Nat Assn Biomedical Rsch 818 Connecticut Ave NW Ste 303 Washington DC 20006-2702

TRULUCK, JAMES PAUL, JR., dentist, vintner; b. Florence, S.C., Feb. 6, 1933; s. James Paul and Catherine Lydia (Nesmith) TruL.; m. Kay Bowen (dec. Oct. 1981); children: James Paul III, David Bowen, Catherine Ann; m. Amelia Nickels Calhoun, Apr. 26, 1983; 1 child, George Calhoun. BS, Clemson (S.C.) U., 1954; DMD, U. Louisville, 1958. Pvt. practice Lake City, S.C., 1960—; founder, pres. TruLuck Vineyards & Winery, Lake City, 1976, Chateau TruLuck Natural Water Co., Lake City, 1990. Member bd. advisors Clemson U., 1978-84; mem. bd. visitors Coker Coll., Hartsville, S.C., 1978-84; pres., bd. dirs. Lions, Lake City, 1960-73; chmn. Greater Lake City Lake Commn., 1967-84. Capt. USAF, 1958-67. Recipient S.C. Bus. and Arts Partnership award S.C. State Arts Commn., 1988. Mem. ADA, Am. Assn. Vinters (bd. dirs. 1982-86), Am. Wine Soc. (nat. judge 1982-88), Am. Soc. Clin. Hypnosis (emeritus), Internat. Acad. Laser Dentistry (chartered), S.C. Dental Assn., Florence County Dental Assn., Soc. First Families of S.C. (exec. sec. 1991—), Descs. Colonial Govs. of Am., Descs. Magna Carta Barons Runnymede, Soc. Gem Cutters Am. Episcopalian. Avocations: genealogy, gemealogy, tennis, sailing, writing. Home: 1036

Mccutcheon Rd Lake City SC 29560-5616 Office: 125 Epp St Lake City SC 29560-2449

TRULY, RICHARD H., academic administrator, former federal agency administrator; b. Fayette, Miss., Nov. 12, 1937; s. James B. Truly; m. Colleen Hanner; children: Richard, Michael, Daniel, Bennett, Lee Margaret. B.Aero. Engring., Ga. Inst. Tech., 1959. Commd. ensign U.S. Navy, 1959; advanced through grades to rear adm., assigned Fighter Squadron 33, served in U.S.S. Intrepid, served in U.S.S. Enterprise; astronaut Manned Orbiting Lab. Program USAF, 1965-69; astronaut NASA, from 1969, comdr. Columbia Flight 2, 1981; comdr. Columbia Flight 2 Challenger Flight 3, 1983; dir. Space Shuttle program, 1986-89; adminstr. NASA, 1989-92; now v.p., dir. Georgia Tech Rsch. Inst., Atlanta, Ga. Recipient Robert H. Goddard Astronautics award AIAA, 1990. Office: Georgia Inst Tech Georgia Tech Rsch Inst 400 Tenth St Atlanta GA 30332

TRUMAN, EDWARD CRANE, real estate manager, consultant, composer; b. Des Moines, Dec. 28, 1915; s. Wright Edward and Annie Louise (Cate) T.; m. Maxine LeVon Hemping, June 28, 1947 (dec. Apr. 1983); 1 child, Robert E.C. Student, UCLA, 1966, 72; BA in English, Immaculate Heart Coll., 1978; MA in Psychology, U. Redlands, 1980. Asst. program dir. Cowles Broadcasting, Des Moines, 1938-44; pub. rels. writer Armed Forces Radio Svcs., Hollywood, Calif., 1944-46; staff musician Don Lee Mut. Radio, Hollywood, Calif., 1946-48, ABC-TV, Hollywood, Calif., 1948-53; music dir., composer TV series NBC-TV, Burbank, Calif., 1955-60; freelance organist, composer Hollywood, 1960—; real estate property mgr., owner, 1974—; bd. dirs. Gen. Affiliates U. Calif. Santa Barbara, chair scholarship com., 1988—; founder Artasia Seminars, L.A., 1972-75. Composer: Matinee, 1956, Broadcast Mood Music, Bowie Knife, 1958, Songs for Builders, 1960. Endowment grantor in religious studies U. Calif., Santa Barbara, 1984—, mem. president's cir., 1993—; endowment grantor in religious studies Drake U., Des Moines, 1994, mem. president's cir., 1995—; mem. judging panels acad. advancement program UCLA, 1994—. Recipient citation Dept. Edn., 1976, commendation City Atty. Office, L.A., 1993. Mem. Nat. Acad. TV Arts and Scis. (Emmy panels, music br.), Pacific Pioneer Broadcasters (bd. dirs. 1988-91, Golden Circle award 1991), Musician's Union (asst. to pres. Local 47 1969-77). Democrat. Episcopalian. Avocations: stamp and coin collecting, biking. Home: 1826 Jewett Dr Los Angeles CA 90046-7702 Office: Compass-Am Group 1826 Jewett Dr Los Angeles CA 90046

TRUMAN, MARGARET, author; b. Independence, Mo., Feb. 17, 1924; d. Harry S. (32nd Pres. U.S.) and Bess (Wallace) T.; m. E. Clifton Daniel Jr., Apr. 21, 1956; children: Clifton T., William, Harrison, Thomas. LHD, Wake Forest U., 1972; HHD, Rockhurst Coll., 1976. Concert singer, 1947-54, actess, broadcaster, author, 1954—; author: Souvenir, 1956, White House Pets, 1969, Harry S. Truman, 1973, Women of Courage, 1976, Murder in the White House, 1980, Murder on Capitol Hill, 1981, Letters from Father, 1981, Murder in the Supreme Ct., 1982, Murder in the Smithsonian, 1983, Murder on Embassy Row, 1985, Murder at the FBI, 1985, Muder in Georgetown, 1986, Bess W. Truman, 1986, Murder in the CIA, 1987, Muder at the Kennedy Center, 1989, Murder in the National Cathedral, 1990, Murder at the Pentagon, 1992, Murder on the Potomac, 1994, First Ladies, 1995; editor: Where the Buck Stops: The Personal and Private Writings of Harry S. Truman, 1989. Trustee and v.p. Harry S. Truman Inst.; sec. bd. trustees Harry S. Truman Found.

TRUMBLE, ROBERT ROY, business educator; b. Wabeno, Wis., Mar. 21, 1940; s. Clarence Lincoln and Celia (Ward) T.; children: Eric, Monica. BA, Hamline U., 1962; MA, U. Minn., 1963, PhD, 1971. Vol. Peace Corps., Lima, Peru, 1963-65; mgr. Latin Am. programs U. Minn., Mpls., 1965-67; asst. dir. internat. programs Cooperative League USA, Washington, 1967-69; program dir. Ops. Research Inc., Washington, 1969-71; chief party Ohio State U., Caracas, Venezuela, 1971-72; div. dir. NIH, Bethesda, Md., 1972-76; sect. head NSF, Washington, 1976-84; dean grad. sch. mgmt. Kent (Ohio) State U., 1984-88; dean sch. bus. Va. Commonwealth U., Richmond, 1988-93; dir. Va. Labor Studies Ctr., 1993—; adj. faculty George Washington U., Washington, 1976-84; pres. Ctr. for Applied Studies, Kent, 1971—; CEO Trumble Investments, St. Croix, V.I., 1987—; bd. dirs. Cen. Allied Ent., Willmar, Minn. Contbr. articles to profl. jours. U.S. State Dept. grantee, 1971-72, State of Ohio grantee, 1986-87. Mem. Am. Assembly Collegiate Schs. Bus., Indsl. Relations Research Assn., Ohio Bus. Deans, Fgn. Policy Assn. (Outstanding Young Person 1968), Mensa, LWV (fin. com. 1987), Delta Sigma Pi, Beta Gamma Sigma, Phi Gamma Mu, Tau Kappa Epsilon (trustee 1960—). Presbyterian. Avocations: Spanish lang., sports, music, painting. Home: 8101 Spencely Pl Richmond VA 23229-8426 Office: VCU Sch of Bus 1015 Floyd Ave Richmond VA 23284-4000

TRUMBULL, DOUGLAS, film director, writer, creator special effects; b. Apr. 8, 1942. Created spl. effects for films including: 2001: A Space Odyssey, 1968, Silent Running, 1971 (also dir.), Close Encounters of the Third Kind, 1977, Star Trek, 1979, Blade Runner, 1982, Brainstorm, 1983 (also prodr., dir.), Spaced Invaders, 1990; inventor Showscan process. Address: c/o Larry Goldberg Goldberg, Nagler & Schnieder 9460 Wilshire Blvd Beverly Hills CA 90212

TRUMBULL, RICHARD, psychologist; b. Johnstown, N.Y., Apr. 6, 1916; s. Milton Elmer and Hazel (Busse) T.; m. Alice Esther McDaniel, June 17, 1939; children—Judith Trumbull Townsend, Joanne Trumbull Titus, Janice Trumbull Smith, Joyce Ellen Trumbull Setzer. A.B., Union Coll., 1937; M.S., Union U., 1939; Ph.D., Syracuse U., 1951. Asst. prof. psychology Green Mountain Jr. Coll., Poultney, Vt., 1939-41; chmn. dept. psychology, 46-49; lectr. Syracuse U., 1941-43; chmn. undergrad. program psychology, 49-51; mem. research staff Sch. Aviation Medicine, U.S. Navy, 1951-53, asst. head physiol. psychology br., Office of Naval Research, 1953-54, head, 1954-61, dir. psychol. scis., 1961-67; dir. research Office Naval Research, Washington, 1967-70; dep. exec. officer AAAS, 1970-74; exec. dir. Am. Inst. Biol. Scis., Arlington, Va., 1974-79, Renewable Natural Resources Found., Bethesda, Md., 1979-80; chmn. adv. group on human factors NATO; research advisory com. NASA; surgeon gen. advisory com. FAA. Author: Research and Its Management, 1984; joint editor: Sensory Deprivation, 1961, Psychological Stress: Issues in Research, 1966, The Dynamics of Stress, 1986, Scientific Freedom and Responsibility in Psychology, Science and Human Affairs, 1994; contbr. articles to profl. jours. Trustee Green Mountain Jr. Coll., Biol. Scis. Info. Service. Served with USNR, 1943-46, 51-53. Recipient Navy Distinguished Civilian Service award, 1961, Longacre award in aerospace medicine, 1966; Sustained Super Accomplishment award, 1966. Mem. AAAS, Aerospace Med. Assn., Natural Resources Council Am. (sec. 1977), Sigma Xi. Home: 4708 N Chelsea Ln Bethesda MD 20814-3714

TRUMKA, RICHARD LOUIS, labor leader, lawyer; b. Waynesburg, Pa., July 24, 1949; s. Frank Richard and Eola Elizabeth (Bertugli) T.; m. Barbara Vidovich, Nov. 27, 1982; 1 child, Richard L. BS, Pa. State U., 1971; JD, Villanova U., 1974. Bar: U.S. Dist. Ct. (D.C.) 1974, U.S. Ct. Appeals (3d, 4th and D.C. cirs.) 1975, U.S. Supreme Ct. 1979. Atty. United Mine Workers Am., Washington, 1974-77, 78-79, internat. pres., 1982-95; miner, operator Jones & Laughlin Steel, Nemacolin, Pa., 1977-78, 79-81; internat. exec. bd. Dist. 4 United Mine Workers Am., Masontown, Pa., 1981-82; sec. treas. AFL-CIO, Washington, 1995—; bd. dirs. Am. Coal Found.; mem. Nat. Coal Council, 1985. Trustee Pa. State U. Recipient Labor Responsibility Award, Martin Luther King Ctr. for Nonviolent Social Change, 1990. Democrat. Roman Catholic. Office: AFL-CIO 815 16th St NW Washington DC 20006*

TRUMP, DONALD JOHN, real estate developer; b. N.Y.C., 1946; s. Fred C. and Mary Trump; m. Ivana Zelnicek, 1977 (div. 1991); children: Donald Jr., Ivanka, Eric; m. Marla Maples, Dec. 20, 1993; one child, Tiffany. Student, Fordham U.; BA, U. Pa., 1968. Pres. Trump Orgn., N.Y.C.; owner Trump Enterprises Inc., N.Y.C., The Trump Corp., N.Y.C., Trump Devel. Co., N.Y.C., Wembly Realty Inc., Park South Co., Land Corp. of Calif., Plaza Hotel, Trump Tower, Trump Parc, Trump Palace, all N.Y.C., Trump Pla., Trump Castle, Trump Taj Mahal, casinos, hotels, Atlantic City, West Side Rail Yards to be devel. as Riverside South, N.Y.C. Author: The Art of the Deal, 1987, Surviving at the Top, 1990. Co-chmn. N.Y. Vietnam Vets. Meml. Fund; founding mem. constrn. com. Cathedral of St. John the Divine; mem. N.Y. Citizens Tax Coun., Fifth Ave Assn., Realty Found. of N.Y., Met. Mus. of Art's Real Estate Coun.; bd. dirs. Police Athletic League; mem. adv. bd. Lenox Hill Hosp., United Cerebral Palsy; spl. advisor to Pres.'s Coun. on Phys. Fitness and Sports; mem. N.Y. Sportsplex Commn.; bd. of overseers Wharton Sch.; mem. adv. bd. Wharton Real Estate Ctr.; bd. dirs. Fred C. Trump Found.; chmn. N.Y. citizens com. 78th Ann. NAACP Conv., 1987. Recipient Entrepreneur of Yr. award Wharton Entrepreneurial Club, 1984, Ellis Island Medal of Honor, 1986; inducted Wharton Hall of Fame.

TRUNDLE, W(INFIELD) SCOTT, publishing executive newspaper; b. Maryville, Tenn., Mar. 24, 1939; s. Winfield Scott and Alice (Smith) T.; m. Elizabeth Latshaw, Oct. 14, 1989; children: Stephen, Allison. B.A., Vanderbilt U., 1961, J.D., 1967. Bar: Tenn. 1967. Spl. agt. U.S. Secret Service, 1963-66; asso. to partner firm Hunter, Smith, Davis & Norris, Kingsport, Tenn., 1967-72; pub. Kingsport (Tenn.) Times-News, 1972-78; pres. Greensboro (N.C.) Daily News, 1978-80; exec. v.p. Jefferson Pilot Publs., Inc., Greensboro and Clearwater, Fla., 1980-82; v.p., bus. mgr. Tampa Tribune (Fla.), 1982-91; sr. v.p. Hillsborough Community Coll., 1991-93; publisher Ogden (Utah) Standard Examiner, 1993—; assoc. prof. E. Tenn. State U., 1973-77. Bd. dirs. Downtown Ogden, Inc.; trustee Utah Opera. Mem. Tenn. Bar Assn., Utah Press Assn. (v.p., bd. dirs.), Weber Ogden C. of C. (bd. dirs.). Methodist. Home: 1580 Maule Dr Ogden UT 84403-0413 Office: Ogden Publ Corp 455 23d St PO Box 951 Ogden UT 84402

TRUOG, DEAN-DANIEL WESLEY, philosophy educator, consultant; b. Denver, Apr. 1, 1938; s. George Calvin and Zelma Elizabeth (Bennett) T.; m. Dorothy Anne Harding, May 31, 1961; children: David Robert, Denise Dawne. Student, Bethel Coll., 1960-61, L'Abri Fellowship Found., Switzerland, 1967-68; diploma in Bible and Leadership Devel., The Navigators Internat. Tng. Inst., 1968; BA in European History, U. Colo., 1971; Diploma in Gen. Univ. Studies in French Civilization, U. Strasbourg, France, 1977; MA in Liberal Edn., St. John's Coll., 1986; M of Liberal Arts in History of Sci., Harvard U., 1987; postgrad., Boston U., 1987-93. Sr. resident adv. U. Colo., Boulder, 1964-65; rep., tutor, lectr. biblical studies and practical christianity The Navigators, 1965-93; rep. for greater Washington area, 1965-67; training asst. The Navigators, Colorado Springs, Colo., 1968; rep. at U. Colo. The Navigators, Boulder, 1968-70, No. Colo. dir., 1970-71; spl. adv. The Navigators, Birmingham, Eng., 1971-72; rep. at large The Navigators, Boulder, Colo., 1979-80; founding dir., pres. Les Navigateurs, France, 1972-84; v.p. Les Navigateurs, France, 1984-85, rep. to U. Strasbourg, 1973-79, rep. to U. Grenoble, 1980-85; sr. teaching fellow in non-deptmental studies Harvard U., Cambridge, Mass., 1987-90; founding pres., life mgmt. cons./counselor Cornerstone Inst. for Values and Relationships, 1990—; v.p. U.S.-Bulgaria Inst., Cambridge, 1991—; spl. cons. to mems. U.S. Congress, 1993—; tutor North House, Harvard U., 1987-91; founding chmn. Harvard Christian Assocs., 1987-92; spkr., tchr. profl. confs.; designer, dir. leadership devel. programs, Boston, Washington, Colo., Austria, France, Switzerland. With USN, 1958-59. Mem. AAAS, History of Sci. Soc., Am. Sci. Affiliation, Soc. Christian Philosophers, Assn. for Religion and Intellectual Llife, Inst. on Religion in Age of Sci., Ctr. for Theology and Natural Scis., Nat. Assn. Scholars, Rotary. Presbyterian. Avocations: cycling, gardening, skiing, tennis, reading. Home and Office: 15 Sheridan Rd Swampscott MA 01907-2046

TRURAN, JAMES WELLINGTON, JR., astrophysicist; b. Brewster, N.Y., July 12, 1940; s. James Wellington and Suzanne (Foglesong) T.; m. Carol Kay Dell'Acy, June 26, 1965; children—Elaina Michelle, Diana Lee, Anastasia Elizabeth. B.A. in Physics, Cornell U., 1961; M.S. in Physics, Yale U., 1963, Ph.D. in Physics, 1966. Postdoctoral rsch. assoc. NAS-NRC Goddard Inst. Space Studies, NASA, N.Y.C., 1965-67; asst. prof. physics Belfer Grad. Sch. Sci., Yeshiva U., 1967-70; rsch. fellow in physics Calif. Inst. Tech., 1968-69; assoc. prof. Belfer Grad. Sch. Sci., Yeshiva U., 1970-72, prof., 1972-73; prof. astronomy U. Ill., Urbana, 1973-91; sr. vis. fellow, Guggenheim Meml. Found. fellow Inst. Astronomy, U. Cambridge, Eng., 1979-80; trustee Aspen Ctr. Physics, 1979-85, 91-93, v.p., 1985-88; assoc. U. Ill. Center for Advanced Study, 1979-80, 86-87; prof. astronomy astrophysics U. Chgo., 1991—; Alexander von Humboldt-Stiftung sr. scientist Max-Plank Inst., Munich, Germany, 1986-87, 94. Contbr. articles to profl. jours.; co-editor: Nucleosynthesis, 1968, Nucleosynthesis— Challenges and New Developments, 1985, Nuclear Astrophysics, 1987; editor: Physics Letters B, 1974-80. Co-recipient Yale Sci. and Engring. Assn. annual award for advancement basic or applied sci., 1980. Fellow AAAS, Am. Phys. Soc.; mem. Am. Astron. Soc., Am. Phys. Soc., Internat. Astron. Union. Home: 210 Wysteria Dr Olympia Fields IL 60461-1202 Office: U Chgo Dept Astronomy Astrophysics 5640 S Ellis Ave Chicago IL 60637-1433

TRUS, BENES LOUIS, structural chemist; b. Tyler, Tex., May 9, 1946; s. Joseph N. and Ruthie (Mosier) T.; m. Susan Gale Evans, Apr. 23, 1972; children—Aaron Baram, Anthony Phillip. B.S. cum laude with honors, Tulane U., 1968; Ph.D., Calif. Inst. Tech., 1972. Jane Coffin Childs postdoctoral fellow Calif. Inst. Tech., Pasadena, 1972-75; research fellow NIH, Bethesda, Md., 1975-77, sr. research fellow, 1977-80, research chemist, 1980-93; chief image processing rsch. sect., computational biosci. and engring. lab., computer rsch. and tech. divsn. NIH, 1993—; mem. steering com. NIH wide image processing group, Bethesda, 1984— (NIH Dirs. award, 1987, 94). Contbr. articles to profl. jours., chpt. to book. Tulane U. scholar and fellow 1965-68. Mem. Am. Crystallographic Assn., Chesapeake Soc. for Microscopy, Microscope Soc. Am., N.Y. Acad. Scis., Phi Beta Kappa, Sigma Xi. Mem. NIH 1986-88 Marathon Team (1st Place Marine Corps Marathon, Govt. Team Competition 1986, 3d place 1987, 88, 2d place Masters Team, 1993). Clubs: Montgomery County Road Runners, NIH Health's Angels Running. Avocations: music, running, carpentry. Office: NIH Rm 2033 Bethesda MD 20892

TRUSHEIM, H. EDWIN, insurance executive; b. Chgo., May 3, 1927; s. H. Edwin and Lucy (Genslein) T.; m. Ruth M. Campbell; children—John E., Mark R. BS in Edn., Concordia Tchrs. Coll., Chgo., 1948; MA in Polit. Sci., Northwestern U., 1955; postgrad. in polit. sci. and econs., Washington U., St. Louis, 1951-54. With Gen. Am. Life Ins. Co., St. Louis, v.p., 1966-67, sr. v.p., 1974, exec. v.p., 1974-79, pres., 1979—, also chief exec. officer, 1981—, chmn., 1986—; chmn. bd. Fed. Res. Bank of St. Louis; bd. dirs. Am. Coun. Life Ins., Washington. Bd. dirs. Angelica Corp., St. Louis, Civic Progress, St. Louis, United Way Greater St. Louis. Office: Gen Am Life Ins Co 700 Market St Saint Louis MO 63101-1829*

TRUSKOSKI, ELAINE BARBARA, executive secretary; b. Torrington, Conn., July 19, 1947; d. Edward John and Wanda Mary (Tokarz) Drenzyk; m. Mark Lucian Truskoski, June 6, 1970; children: Ryan Thomas, Jason Todd. Student, Cambridge Sch. Bus./Broadcast, Boston. Prodn. asst. ESPN, Bristol, Conn., 1981, exec. sec., 1982-87, 1993—. Active Coalition to Stop Gun Violence, Washington, 1992. Named to 20 Great Am. Women, McCall's Mag., 1993. Mem. Conn. NOW (Alice-Paul award 1992), Nat. NOW. Roman Catholic. Avocations: tennis, reading. Home: 205 Wildcat Hill Rd Harwinton CT 06791-2509 Office: ESPN 935 Middle St Bristol CT 06010-1000

TRUSKOWSKI, JOHN BUDD, lawyer; b. Chgo., Dec. 3, 1945; s. Casimer T. and Jewell S. (Kirk) T.; m. Karen Lee Sloss, Mar. 21, 1970; children: Philip K., Jennifer B. BS, U. Ill., 1967; JD, U. Chgo., 1970. Bar: Ill. 1970, U.S. Dist. Ct. (no. dist.) Ill. 1970, U.S. Tax Ct. 1977. Assoc. Keck, Mahin & Cate, Chgo., 1970-71, 74-78, ptnr., 1978—. Author, editor Callaghan's Federal Tax Guide, 1987. Served to lt, USNR, 1971-74. Mem. ABA, Ill. State Bar Assn., Chgo. Bar Assn. Republican. Presbyterian. Avocations: model railroading, stamp collecting. Home: 251 Kimberly Ln Lake Forest IL 60045-3862 Office: Keck Mahin & Cate 77 W Wacker Dr 49th Fl Chicago IL 60601

TRUSSELL, CHARLES TAIT, columnist; b. Balt., May 9, 1925; s. Charles Prescott and Beatrice (Tait) T.; m. Woodley Grizzard, Dec. 27, 1953 (div. 1990); children: Galen Tait, Thomas Marshall; m. Nancy Rathbun Billington, Dec. 19, 1990. B.A. in Journalism, Washington and Lee U., 1949. Reporter St. Petersburg (Fla.) Times, also; writer Congl. Quar. News Features, 1951-54; reporter Wall St. Jour., 1954-56, Washington Evening Star, 1956; asso. editor Nation's Business mag., 1956-64, mng. editor, 1964-69; sr. editor Congressional Quar., Inc., 1969-70; dir. pub. relations and advt. Investment Co. Inst., Washington, 1970-72; free-lance writer, real estate investor, 1972-74; v.p. Am. Forest Inst., Washington, 1974-79, sr. v.p., 1980-81; v.p. Am. Enterprise Inst., 1981-86; dir. communications Constitution Bicentennial Commn., 1986-88; freelance writer, columnist, 1988—. Producer: documentary record album The Best of Washington Humor, 1963; author: Beating the Competition, 1992; editor: (with others) Successful Management, 1964, (with Paul Hencke) Dear NASA Please Send Me a Rocket, 1964. Served with USNR, 1944-46. Recipient Loeb Spl. Achievement award for mags. U. Conn., 1961, Benjamin Fine Journalism award, 1992. Mem. Washington Assembly (exec. com. 1961-65, chmn. 1965), Country Club of Mt. Dora, Beta Theta Pi. Home: 6014 Spring Creek Ct Mount Dora FL 32757-6952

TRUSSELL, R(OBERT) RHODES, environmental engineer; b. National City, Calif; s. Robert L. and Margaret (Kessing) T.; m. Elizabeth Shane, Nov. 26, 1969; children: Robert Shane, Charles Bryan. BSCE, U. Calif.-Berkeley, 1966, MS, 1967, PhD, 1972. With Montgomery Watson, Inc. (formerly J.M. Montgomery Cons. Engrs.), Pasadena, Calif., 1972—, v.p., 1977, sr. v.p., 1986, dir. applied tech., 1988-92, sr. v.p., dir. of corp. devel., 1992— Mem. com. on water treatment chems. Nat. Acad. Sci., 1980-82, mem. com. 3d part cert., 1982-83, com. on irrigation-induced water quality problems, 1985-88, Am. Water Work Commn. on mixing of water treatment chems., 1988-90; mem. U.S./German rsch. com. on corrosion of water systems, 1984-85; mem. U.S./Dutch rsch. com. on organics in water, 1982-83; mem. U.S./USSR rsch. com. on water treatment, 1985-88, U.S./E.C. Com. Corrosion in Water, 1992-94. Mem. joint editl. bd. Standards Methods for Examination of Water and Wastewater, 1980-89; mem. editl. adv. bd. Environ. and Sci. and Tech., 1977-83; contbr. articles to profl. publs. Mem. AIChE, NAE, Nat. Acad. Engrs., Water Works Assn. (mem. editl. adv. bd. jour. 1987-94, EPA sci. adv. bd. com. on drinking water 1988-91, 94—, cons. radon disinfectant by products 1993, cons. on disinfection and disinfection byproducts 1994), Internat. Water Supply Assn. (U.S. rep. to standing com. on water quality and treatment 1990-94, chmn. com. on disinfection and mem. sci. and tech. coun. 1994—), Water Pollution Control Fedn., Internat. Water Pollution Rsch. Assn., Am. Chem. Soc., Nat. Assn. Corrosion Engrs., Sigma Xi. Office: Montgomery Watson 300 N Lake Ave Ste 1200 Pasadena CA 91101-4106

TRUST, TREVOR JOHN, microbiology educator and researcher; b. Melbourne, Australia, June 24, 1942. BSc, U. Melbourne, Australia, 1964; MSc, U. Melbourne, 1966, PhD in Microbiology, 1969. Lectr. microbiology Royal Melbourne Inst. Tech., Australia, 1969; from asst. prof. to assoc. prof., 1969-80; prof. microbiology U. Victoria, B.C., Can., 1981-95; v.p. Astra Rsch. Ctr. Boston, Inc., Cambridge, Mass., 1995—; vis. rsch. fellow Southampton Fac. Med., 1977-78. Mem. Can. Soc. Microbiology, Am. Soc. Microbiology, Brit. Soc. Gen. Microbiology. Achievements include research in fish diseases, in gastrointestinal diseases; molecular basis for bacterial virulence and immunogenicity; campylobacter, helicobacter, aeromonas; development of therapeutic agents for heliocobacter pylori. Office: Astra Rsch Ctr Boston Inc 128 Sidney St Cambridge MA 02139

TRUSTMAN, BENJAMIN ARTHUR, lawyer; b. June 14, 1902; s. Israel and Pessie (Rubin) T.; m. Julia Bertha Myerson, July 31, 1927; children: Alan Robert, Phyllis Anne (Mrs. Robert W. Gelfman). A.B. summa cum laude, Harvard U., 1922, J.D., 1925; Sc.D. (hon.), Lowell Coll., 1964; fellow, Brandeis U. Bar: Mass. 1925, Fla. 1953. Asso. Nutter, McClennen & Fish (and predecessor), Boston, 1925-34; mem. firm Nutter, McClennen & Fish (and predecessor), 1934-77; past dir. Wm. Filene's Sons Co., Shawmut Corp., Shawmut Bank of Boston N.A. Co-author: Town Meeting Time, 1962, 2d edit., 1964. Former hon. life dir. Lincoln and Therese Filene Found.; former mem. corp. Eye Research Inst. of Retina Found.; former trustee Met. Mus., Coral Gables, Fla.; former dir. John F. Kennedy Ctr. Performing Arts, Washington; hon. life mem., patron bd. visitors dept. prints and drawings, life overseer, donor Prints and Drawings Gallery, Boston Mus. Fine Arts; donor Daumier Print Dept. Brandeis U.; former elective town moderator, Brookline, Mass.; donor Trustman Art Gallery and Trustman travelling fellowships, Simmons Coll., Boston; past chmn. Brookline Housing Authority; past mem. nat. adv. council Am. Assn. Jewish Edn.; past mem. adv. council Lincoln Filene Ctr. Law in Social Studies Project, Tufts U.; former dir. United Community Services Met. Boston; founder Trustman Travelling Fellowships Harvard U., donor Trustman Scholarship Fund, Harvard Law Sch.; life trustee, past pres. Hebrew Coll., Boston; donor Trustman Lecture Hall, John F. Kennedy Sch. Govt., Harvard U.; life trustee, past chmn. bd. mgrs., past pres. Combined Jewish Philanthropies Greater Boston; life trustee, past chmn. bd. mgrs., former v.p., donor, bd. dirs. meeting rm. Beth Israel Hosp. Assn., Boston; founding mem. Mass. Council Arts and Humanities; past mem. bd. visitors Lowell Coll. Recipient Nat. Brotherhood award NCCJ, 1964; Benjamin A. Trustman Apts. dedicated by Brookline Housing Authority, 1975. Mem. Harvard U. Law Sch. Assn. (life), Am., Mass., Fla. Boston bar assns., Am. Law Inst. (life), Am. Jewish Hist. Soc. (patron, life), Nat. Phi Beta Kappa Assos. (life), Phi Beta Kappa (Harvard Alpha chpt.). Jewish (trustee temple). Clubs: Miami Shores Country; Harvard (Miami) (dir.). Leading collector works of Honoré Daumier. Home: 1700 NE 105th St Apt 119 Miami FL 33138

TRUSTY, ROY LEE, former oil company executive; b. Paris, Ark., Nov. 27, 1924; s. Bennie Otis and Katy Jane (Williamson) T.; m. Caroline Sue Thibaut, Nov. 23, 1950; children: Rebecca Sue, Sara Elizabeth, Jane Ellen, Roy Lee. B.S. in Chem. Engring, La. State U., 1949. Engr. Esso Standard Oil Co., Baton Rouge, 1949-61; mgr. Humble Oil and Refining Co., Houston, 1961-64, Standard Oil of N.J., N.Y.C., 1964-68; pres. Lago Oil and Transp. Co. Ltd., Aruba, Netherlands Antilles, 1970-73; various exec. positions Exxon Co. U.S.A., Houston, 1973-76, sec., 1976-83; trustee, exec. dir. Exec. Service Corps, Houston, 1983-92. Served with U.S. Army, 1943-46, ETO. Republican. Methodist. Home: PO Box 103 Round Top TX 78954-0103

TRUTA, MARIANNE PATRICIA, oral and maxillofacial surgeon, educator, author; b. N.Y.C., Apr. 28, 1951; d. John J. and Helen Patricia (Donnelly) T.; m. William Christopher Donlon, May 28, 1983; 1 child Sean Liam Riobard Donlon. BS, St. John's U., 1974; DMD, SUNY, Stonybrook, 1977. Intern The Mt. Sinai Med. Ctr., N.Y.C., 1977-78, resident, 1978-80, chief resident, 1980-81; asst. prof. U. of the Pacific, San Francisco, 1983-85, clin. asst. prof., 1985-94; asst. dir. Facial Pain Rsch. Ctr., San Francisco, 1986-92; pvt. practice oral and maxillofacial surgery Peninsula Maxillofacial Surgery, South San Francisco, Calif., 1985—, Burlingame, Calif., 1988—, Redwood City, Calif., 1990-95, San Carlos, Calif., 1995—. Contbr. articles to profl. jours., chpts. to textbooks. Mem. Am. Assn. Oral Maxillofacial Surgeons, Am. Dental Soc. Anesthesiology, Am. Soc. Cosmetic Surgery, Am. Assn. Women Dentists, Western Soc. Oral Maxillofacial Surgeons, No. Calif. Soc. Oral Maxillofacial Surgeons, San Mateo County Dental Soc. (bd. dirs. 1995). Office: Peninsula Maxillofacial Surgery 1860 El Camino Real Ste 300 Burlingame CA 94010-3114

TRUTTER, JOHN THOMAS, consulting company executive; b. Springfield, Ill., Apr. 18, 1920; s. Frank Louis and Frances (Mischler) T.; m. Edith English Woods II, June 17, 1950; children: Edith English II, Jonathan Woods. BA, U. Ill., 1942; postgrad., Northwestern U., 1947-50, U. Chgo., 1947-50; LHD (hon.), Lincoln Coll., 1986. Various positions Ill. Bell, Chgo., 1946-58, gen. traffic mgr., from asst. v.p. pub. rels. to gen. mgr., 1958-69, v.p. pub. rels., 1969-71, v.p. operator svcs., 1971-80, v.p. community affairs, 1980-85; mem. hdqs. staff AT&T, N.Y.C., 1955-57; pres. John T. Trutter Co., Inc., Chgo., 1985—; pres., CEO Chgo. Conv. and Visitors Bur., 1985-88; pres. Chgo. Tourism Coun., 1988-90; mem. adv. bd. The Alford Group, Chgo., 1984—, Bozell-Worldwide, Chgo., 1994-96; chancellor Lincoln Acad. of Ill., 1985—. Co-author: Handling Barriers in Communication, 1957, The Governor Takes a Bride, 1977. Past chmn., life trustee Jane Addams Hull House Assn.; hon. chmn. United Cerebral Palsy Assn. Greater Chgo., chmn. Canal Corridor Assn., 1991—; bd. dirs. Chgo. Crime Commn., Abraham Lincoln Assn., Lyric Opera Chgo.; v.p. English Speaking Union, 1989-91, bd. govs., 1980—; chmn. bd. City Colls. Chgo. Found., 1987-91; past chmn. Children's Home and Aid Soc. Ill.; v.p. City Club Chgo.; treas. Chgo. United, 1970-85; mem. Ill. Econ. Devel. Commn., 1985; past presiding co-chmn. NCCJ; v.p., bd. dirs. Ill. Humane Soc. Found.; numerous others; bd. govs. Northwestern U. Libr. Coun., 1984—; trustee Lincoln (Ill.) Coll., 1987-90, Mundelein Coll., 1988-91; mem. sch. problems coun. State Ill. Assembly, 1985-91, spl. commn. on adminstrn. of justice in Cook County,

1986-92. Lt. col. U.S. Army. Decorated Legion of Merit; recipient Laureate award State of Ill., 1980, Outstanding Exec. Leader award Am. Soc. Fundraisers, Humanitarian of Yr. award, New Directions award SSMD, 1987, Jane Addams award The Hull House Assn., 1991. Mem. Pub. Rels. Soc. Am., Sangamon County Hist. Soc. (founder, past pres.), Ill. State Hist. Soc. (pres. 1985-87), Coun. on Ill. History (chmn. 1991—), U. Ill. Alumni Assn. (bd. dirs. 1990-94), Tavern Club, Econ. Club, Mid-Am. Club, Alpha Sigma Phi (Nat. Merit Achievement award 1994), Phi Delta Phi, founding chm. Evanston Historical Soc. advisory council 1995—.

TRYBUL, THEODORE N., education educator; b. Chgo., Apr. 12, 1935; s. Theodore and Sophie T.; m. (dec.); children: Adreienne, Barbie, Cathy, Diane, Elizabeth, Teddy. BS, U. Ill., 1957; MS, U. N.Mex., 1963; DSc, George Washington U., 1976. Registered profl. engr., D.C. Dir. SES, ES-IV Fed. Govt., Washington, 1966-83; prof. George Washington U., Washington, 1983-94, Tex. Grad. Sch., Corpus Christi, Tex., 1994—; adv. bd. NSF, Nat. Acad. Engring., NIH, Surgeon Gens. Office. Contbr. articles to profl. jours. Officer Corpus Christi C. of C., Neuces Club, Millionaires Club, CC Town Club. Col. U.S. Army, 1957. Fellow ASME, Soc. for Computer Simulation, Health Care Execs., Sir Isaac Walton, Audubonn Soc., Sierra Club; mem. Pi Tau Sigma, Phi Betta Kappa, Kappa Mu Epsilon, Sigma Xi. Avocations: golf, tennis, fishing, mountain climbing. Office: Tex Grad Sch 14514 Cabana E Corpus Christi TX 78418

TRYBUS, RAYMOND J., higher education executive, psychologist; b. Chgo., Jan. 9, 1944; s. Fred and Cecilia (Liszka) T.; m. Sandra A. Noone, Aug. 19, 1967; children: David, Nicole. BS, St. Louis U., 1965, MS, 1970, PhD, 1971. Lic. psychologist, Md., D.C., Calif. Clin. psychologist Jewish Vocat. Svc., St. Louis, 1968-71; clin. psychologist Gallaudet U., Washington, 1971-72, rsch. psychologist, 1972-74, dir. demographic studies, 1974-78, dean grad. studies and rsch., 1978-88; provost, prof. psychology Calif. Sch. of Profl. Psychology, 1988—, chancellor, 1992—; dir. Rehab. Rsch. and Tng. Ctr., 1994—; mem. Sci. Rev. Bd. Dept. Vets. Affairs Rehab. Rsch. and Devel. Program, 1991—; cons. Mental Health Ctr. for Deaf, Lanham, Md., 1982-88, Congl. Rsch. Svc., 1982-84, McGill U. Nat. Study Hearing Impairment in Can., 1984-88. Contbg. author: The Future of Mental Health Services for the Deaf, 1978, Hearing-impaired Children and Youth with Devel. Disabilities, 1985; editor Jour. Am. Deafness and Rehab. Assn., 1988-91. Grantee NIMH, Nat. Inst. Disability and Rehab. Rsch., Spencer Found., Tex. Edn. Agy., W.K. Kellogg Found. Mem. APA, Am. Assn. Univ. Adminstrs., Calif. Psychol. Assn. (pres. div. edn. and tng. 1990-92), San Diego Psychol. Assn., Am. Coun. Edn., Am. Deafness and Rehab. Assn., Am. Assn. Higher Edn., Am. Psychol. Soc. Roman Catholic. Home: 6342 Cibola Rd San Diego CA 92120-2124 Office: 6160 Cornerstone Ct E San Diego CA 92121-3725

TRYGG, STEVE LENNART, advertising executive; b. Ludvika, Sweden, Sept. 19, 1947; came to U.S., 1982; s. Lennart Tore Roland and Ingrid Linnea (Widěn) T.; m. Karin Margareta Hammarstrand, May 31, 1969; children: Tobias, Jenny, Carl. övningselev, Sch. Visual Arts, Stockholm, 1967; cert. interpretation, Tolkskolan (Swedish Army Lang. Sch.), Uppsala, Sweden, 1968; Kandidat in Philosophy, Stockholm U., 1970. Copywriter Anderson & Lembke, Stockholm, 1970-72, pres., creative dir., 1977-82; pres., creative dir. Anderson & Lembke, Stamford, 1985—; creative dir. Lenskog & Co., Stockholm, 1972-77; v.p., creative dir. Anderson Lembke Welinder, Stamford, Conn., 1982-85; mem. specialist adv. bd. ADS mag. Recipient over 60 internat. and nat. advt. awards including The One Show, Clio, Andy, Guldägg. Lutheran. Avocations: boating, carpentry. Home: 74 Gardiner St Darien CT 06820-5114 Office: Anderson & Lembke Inc 79 Fifth Ave # 17 New York NY 10003-3034*

TRYGSTAD, LAWRENCE BENSON, lawyer; b. Holton, Mich., Mar. 22, 1937. BA, U. Mich., 1959; JD, U. So. Calif., 1967. Bar: Calif. 1968, U.S. Supreme Ct. 1974. Legal counsel Calif. Tchrs. Assn., United Tchrs. L.A., L.A., 1968-71; ptnr. Trygstad & Odell, L.A., 1971-80; pres. Trygstad Law Corp., L.A., 1980—; instr., tchr. negotiation U. Calif.-Northridge; panelist TV shows Law and the Teacher. Bd. dirs. George Washington Carver Found., L.A. Mem. ABA, Calif. Bar Assn., L.A. County Bar Assn., Calif. Trial Lawyers Assn., L.A. Trial Lawyers Assn., Nat. Orgn. Lawyers for Edn. Assns., Am. Trial Lawyers Assn., Phi Alpha Delta. Home: 4209 Aleman Dr Tarzana CA 91356-5405 Office: 1880 Century Park E Bldg 404 Los Angeles CA 90067-1604

TRYHANE, GERALD, newspaper publishing executive. V.p. finance New York Newsday, N.Y.C. Office: New York Newsday 2 Park Ave New York NY 10016-5603

TRYTEK, DAVID DOUGLAS, insurance company executive; b. Cleve., Jan. 18, 1955; s. Edmund Trytek and Mary Elaine Salzwedel Blech; m. Lorie Ann Stone, Apr. 10, 1982; children: Dane, Douglas. BS in BA, Bowling Green (Ohio) State U., 1977. Claims adjuster Liberty Mus. Ins. Co., Toledo, 1977-80; claims supr. Liberty Mus. Ins. Co., Milw., 1980-85; spl. claims examiner Liberty Mus. Ins. Co., Boston, 1986-89; claims mgr. Liberty Mus. Ins. Co., Green Bay, Wis., 1989-93; tech. svcs. mgr. Liberty Mut. Ins. Co., Milw., 1993-95; regional field investigations supr. Liberty Mutual Ins. Co., Milw., 1996—; arbitrator Inter-Co. Arbitration Com., Milw., 1984-85. Coach Toledo Optimists Youth Hockey Assn., 1979-80, Wauwatosa (Wis.) Recreation Dept., 1980-85, YMCA Youth Baseball, 1994; alt. Worker's Compensation divsn. Ins. Adv. Com., Madison, Wis., 1994l youth baseball and football coach, Sussex, Wis., 1995. Mem. Exptl. Aircraft Assn., Air Force Assn., Warbirds of Am., USA Hockey Inc. Avocations: camping, ice hockey, golf, military aircraft. Office: Liberty Mutual Ins PO Box 0915 15700 W Bluemound Rd Brookfield WI 53008

TRYTHALL, HARRY GILBERT, music educator, composer; b. Knoxville, Tenn., Oct. 28, 1930; s. Harry Gilbert and Clara Hannah (Akre) T.; m. Jean Marie Slater, Dec. 28, 1951 (div. 1976); children: Linda Marie, Karen Elizabeth; m. Carol King, Sept. 19, 1985. BA, U. Tenn., 1951; MusM, Northwestern U., 1952; DMA, Cornell U., 1960. Asst. prof. music Knox Coll., Galesburg, Ill., 1960-64; prof. music theory and composition George Peabody Coll. Tchrs., Nashville, 1964-75; dean Creative Arts Ctr., 1975-81; prof. music W.Va. U., Morgantown, 1975—; pres. Luxikon Music, Pandora-Synthe Records, Westover, W.Va., 1983—. Author: Principles and Practice of Electronic Music, 1974, Eighteenth Century Counterpoint, 1993, Sixteenth Century Counterpoint, 1994; past mem. editorial bd. Music Educators Jour.; composer orchestral music, chamber and electronic music. With USAF, 1953-57. Home: 41 W Main St Morgantown WV 26505-4561 Office: Pandora-Synthe Records PO Box 2281 Westover WV 26502-2281

TRZEBIATOWSKI, GREGORY L., education educator; b. Buena Vista, Wis., May 19, 1937; s. Bert Bernard and Amelia O. (Brychell) T.; m. Maxine Eder, June 18, 1960 (dec. Sept. 1991); children: Peggy, Heidi, Molly; m. Ana Virginia Mangili Godoy, June 5, 1992; children: Gregory L., Jr., Thomas John. BS, U. Wis., Stout, 1959; PhD, Mich. State U., 1967. Tchr. Madison (Wis.) Pub. Schs., 1959-62; asst. prof. U. So. Calif., Los Angeles, 1965-67; from asst. to assoc. prof. Coll. Edn. Ohio State U., Columbus, 1967-74, prof. edn. Coll. Edn., 1974-92, asst. dean, 1970-77, assoc. dean med. and grad. edn., Coll. Medicine, 1978-87, prof. emeritus, 1992; rector, pres., chief exec. officer The Thomas Jefferson Sch., Concepción, Chile; dir. Office Geriatrics and Gerontology, 1985-92, Alzheimer's Disease Rsch. Ctr., 1987-92, Ohio State U.; cons. U. Concepcion, Chile, 1979—, Meml. Hosp. Union County, Marysville, Ohio, 1978-87; mem. peer rev. com. Nat. Cancer Inst., Bethesda, Md., 1979-84; cons., sci. rev. com. Pan Am. Health Orgn., Rio de Janeiro, 1978-82; pres., CEO Inmobiliaria Monticello S.A., Talcahauno, Chile. Author: Medical Education for the 21st Century, 1985; contbr. articles to profl. jours. V.p. Friends of Upper Arlington (Ohio) Library, 1987, pres. 1988-91; bd. dirs. Ohio State U. Friends of Library, 1987-92. Recipient Stout Medallion, U. Wis., 1959, Outstanding Alumni award Mich State U., 1979, Disting. Alumni award U. Wis. Stout, 1980; named hon. prof. U. Concepcion, Chile, 1981. Mem. Am. Assn. Sch. Adminstrs., Alzheimer's Assn. (trustee Columbus chpt. 1988-92), Am. Fedn. Aging Research (bd. dirs. Ohio affiliate 1988-92), Phi Beta Delta (pres. Hon. Soc. for Internat. Scholars Ohio State U. 1989-90, nat. pres. 1990-91). Roman Catholic. Avocations: bicycling, jogging, woodworking, collecting books. Home: Casilla #2532, Concepcion Chile Office: Thomas Jefferson Sch, Avenida Jorge Alessandri #26, Casilla 2532 Concepcion Chile

TRZETRZELEWSKA, BASIA See BASIA

TSAI, STEPHEN WEI-TUN, aeronautical educator; b. Beijing, China, July 6, 1929; U.S. citizen; married; two children. BE, Yale U., 1952, D in Mech. Engring., 1961. Project engr. Foster Wheeler Corp., 1952-58; dept. mgr. material rsch. aeronutronic divsn. Philco Corp., 1961-66; prof. engring. Wash. U., 1966-68; chief scientist Air Force Material Lab., Wright-Patterson AFB, 1968-76, scientist, 1976—; lectr. U. Calif., L.A., 1965-66; affiliate prof. Washington U., 1968—; Battelle vis. prof. Ohio State U., 1969. Edito-in-chief Jour. Composite Materials, 1966; editor Internat. Jour. Fibre Sci. and Tech., 1968—. Mem. AIAA, ASm. Phys. Soc., Soc. Rheol., Nat. Acad. Engring., Sigma Xi. Office: Stanford University Dept Aeronautics & Astronautics Stanford CA 94305*

TSAI, WEN-YING, sculptor, painter, engineer; b. Xiamen, Fujian, China, Oct. 13, 1928; came to U.S., 1950, naturalized, 1962; s. Chen-Dak and Ching-Miau (Chen) T.; m. Pei-De Chang, Aug. 7, 1968; children: Lun-Yi and Ming Yi (twins). Student, Ta Tung U., 1947-49; BSME, U. Mich., 1953; postgrad., Art Students League N.Y., 1953-57, Faculty Polit. and Social Sci., New Sch., 1956-58. cons. engr., 1953-63; project mgr. Cosentini Assocs., 1962-63; project engr. Guy B. Panero, Engrs., 1956-60. Creator cybernetic sculpture based on prin. harmonic motion, stroboscopic effects; one-man shows include, Ruth Sherman Gallery, N.Y.C., 1961, Amel Gallery, N.Y.C., 1964, 65, Howard Wise Gallery, N.Y.C., 1968, Kaiser Wilhelm Mus. Haus Lange, Krefeld, Germany, 1970, Hayden Gallery of MIT, Cambridge, Ont. Sci. Centre, Toronto, Can., 1971, Corcoran Gallery Art, 1972, Denise René Gallery, 1972, 73, Musée d'Art Contemporain, Montreal, 1973, Museo de Arte Contemporáneo, Caracas, 1975, Wildenstein Art Center, Houston, 1978, Museo de Bellas Artes, Caracas, 1978, Hong Kong Mus. Art, 1979, Isetan Mus. Art, Tokyo, 1980, Galerie Denise René, Paris, 1983, Nat. Mus. History, Taipei, Taiwan, 1989, Taiwan Mus. of Art, Taichung, 1990; represented maj. internat. exhbns., also numerous group exhbns., in permanent collections, Centre Georges Pompidou, Paris; Tate Gallery, London, Albright-Knox Gallery, Buffalo Mus., Addison Gallery Am. Art, Andover, Mass., Museo de Arte Contemporáneo, Caracas, Museo de Bellas Artes, Caracas, Whitney Mus., Chrysler Art Mus., Orlando Sci. Ctr., MIT, Hayden Gallery, Kaiser Wilhelm Mus., Mus. Modern Art, Israel Mus., Jerusalem, Artware, Kunst und Elektronik, Honnover-Messe, Great Exploration-The Hands on Mus., Taiwan Mus. Art, Saibu Gas Mus., Nagoya City Mus., Mus. fü Holographie, Kanagawa Sci. Pk., Hong Kong Sci. Mus., others; commd. works include: fountain at Land Mark, Hong Kong, 1980, , water sculpture at Shell Tower, Singapore, 1982, cybernetic upward falling fountains (2), Paris; creator spatial dynamic hydro-cybernetic systems for 42d Internat. Exhbn. Art-La Biennale di Venezia, 1986, Digital Visions-Computers and Art, Everson Mus. of Art, 1987, Contemporary Arts Ctr. Cin., 1987, IBM Gallery of Sci. and Art, N.Y.C., 1988, Phenomena Art Expo, Fukuoka, Japan, 1989, Artec '91, Wonderland of Sci.-Art Kanagawa Internat. Art Sci. Exhbn., Kawasaki, Japan, 1989, Vienna Messe-Wiener Festwochen, 1989, Kanagawa Internat. Art & Sci. Exhbn., Kawasaki, Japan, 1989, Artec 91, Internat. Biennale in Nagoya, Japan, 1991 (Artec Grand Prix winner); creator first CD-ROM version of cybernetic sculpture, 1995, Info-Art Kwang Ju Internat. Biennale Korea, Osaka Triennale, 1995—, Internet Graphics Gallery, 1995; featured: Art for Tomorrow-The 21st Century, CBS-TV, 1969, Video Variation, WGBH-TV, 1971, Science and Art, Japan TV Man Union, 1982, Art and Sci.-Innovation, Sta. WNET-TV, 1988, The World of Wen-Ying Tsai, Taiwan Pub. TV, 1991. John Hay Whitney fellow, 1963; MacDowell fellow, 1965; fellow Center Advanced Visual Studies, MIT, 1969, 70. Inventor upward falling fountain, computer mural, multiple light computer array, utilizing environ. feedback control system.

TSALIKIAN, EVA, physician; b. Piraeus, Greece, June 22, 1949; came to U.S., 1974; d. Vartan and Arousiak (Kasparian) T. M.D., U. Athens, 1973. Research fellow U. Calif.-San Francisco, 1974-76; resident pediatrics Children's Hosp., Pitts., 1976-78, fellow endocrinology, 1978-80; research fellow Mayo Clinic, Rochester, Minn., 1980-83; asst. prof. dept. pediatrics U. Iowa, Iowa City, 1983—. Fellow Juvenile Diabetes Found., 1978-80, Heinz Nutrition Found., 1980-81; recipient Young Physician award AMA, 1977. Mem. Am. Diabetes Assn. Home: 1217 Dolen Pl Iowa City IA 52246-4524 Office: U Iowa Dept Pediatrics Iowa City IA 52242

TSAO, GEORGE T., chemical engineer, educator; b. Nanking, China, Dec. 4, 1931; married; 3 children. BSc, Nat. Taiwan U., 1953; MSc, U. Fla., 1956; PhD in Chem. Engring., U. Mich., 1960. Asst. prof. physics Olivet Coll., 1959-60; chem. engr. Merck & Co., Inc., 1960-61; rsch. chemist TVA, 1961-62; sect. leader hydrolisys and fermentation, rsch. dept. Union Starch & Refining Co. divsn. Miles Labs., Inc., 1962-65, asst. rsch. dir., 1965-66; from assoc. prof. to prof. chem. engring. Iowa State U., 1966-77; prof. chem. engring. Purdue U., West Lafayette, Ind., 1977—, dir. Lab. Renewable Resources Engring. Recipient John Ericsson award Dept. Energy, 1989. Mem. AIChE, Am. Chem. Soc., Am. Soc. Engring. Edn. Office: Purdue U Lab Renewable Resources Engring 1295 Potter Bldg West Lafayette IN 47907*

TSAPOGAS, MAKIS J., surgeon; b. Athens, Greece, May 7, 1926; m. Lily Philossopoulou. M.D., U. Athens, 1954; MChir magna cum laude, U. London, 1960, DSc, 1967, PhD (hon.), 1991; DM (hon.), U. France, 1993. Intern Ryhope Gen. Hosp., Durham, Eng., 1954-55; resident in surgery Meml. Hosp., London, 1955-56, London Jewish Hosp., 1956, Blackburn Royal Infirmary, 1957-58; resident in surgery Aberdeen Royal Infirmary Med. Sch., Scotland, 1958-59, sr. resident in surgery, 1959-60; research fellow King's Coll. Hosp. Med. Sch., U. London, 1960-61, lectr. in surgery, 1961-63, chief resident in vascular and gen. surgery, 1961-63, sr. lectr. in surgery, 1963-67, attending surgeon, 1963-67; attending surgeon Albany Med. Center, N.Y., 1967-75; assoc. prof. surgery Albany Med. Coll., 1967-70, prof. surgery, 1970-75; chief surg. dept. VA Hosp., Albany, 1967-73; adj. prof. biomed. scis. Rensselaer Poly. Inst., 1970-80; chmn. dept. surgery Ellis Hosp., Schenectady, 1973-75; cons. surgeon St. Clare's Sunnyview, Glenridge and VA hosps., 1973-75, UN, 1993—; prof. surgery, chief vascular surgery Rutgers Med. Sch., 1976; prof. surgery Sch. Medicine, SUNY-Stony Brook, 1977—; also attending surgeon Univ. Hosp.; founding dir. NE Regional Med. Edn. Ctr., Northport, N.Y., 1976—; Hunterian prof. Royal Coll. Surgeons Eng., 1964—; academician (c.m.) Acad. Athens, 1984—; advisor WHO, 1987—, Inst. Internat. Edn., 1993—; vis. prof. Univs. London, Athens, Salonica, Patras, Ioannina, Alexandroupolis, Crete, Nice, Alexandria, 1980—; cons. devel. program UN, 1993—. Contbr. chpts. to books, articles to med. jours. Fellow ACS; mem. Internat. Soc. Surgery, Central Surg. Assn., Soc. Vascular Surgery, Internat. Cardiovascular Soc., Vascular Surg. Soc. Gt. Britain and Ireland (founding mem.), Surg. Research Soc. Gt. Britain and Ireland, Nat. Assn. VA Chiefs of Staff, Assn. VA Surgeons, Brit. Med. Assn., Hellenic Surg. Soc., Hellenic Med. Assn., Pan Am. Med. Assn., Assn. Am. Med. Colls., N.Y. Regional Vascular Soc. (founding mem., councillor), Ea. Vascular Soc. Home and Office: PO Box 457 Northport NY 11768-0457

TSCHANTZ, BRUCE ALLEN, civil engineer, educator; b. Akron, Ohio, Sept. 15, 1938; s. Miles Emerson and Gladys Marcella (Krichbaum) T.; m. Penelope Ann Ford, Dec. 20, 1962; children: Peter Allen, Michael Ford. BS, Ohio No. U., 1960; MS, N.Mex. State U., 1962, ScD, 1965. Registered profl. engr., Ohio, Tenn., Va. San. engr. Bur. Indian Affairs, Albuquerque, 1962-63; civil engr. White Sands (N.Mex.) Missile Range, 1965; asst. prof. civil engring. U. Tenn., Knoxville, 1965-69; asso. prof. U. Tenn., 1969-74, prof., 1974—, M. E. Brooks Disting. prof., 1978, R.N. Condra Disting. prof.; acting dir. Tenn. Water Resources Rsch. Ctr., 1991-94; cons. hydrologist U.S. Geol. Survey, Noxville, 1973-76; cons. Exec. Office of Pres., Office Sci. Tech. POlicy, Washington, 1977-80, Tenn. Dept. Transp., 1976—, Tenn. Dept. Conservation, 1978; chief fed. dam safety FEd. Emergency Mgmt. Agy., Washington, 1979-80; mem. Tenn. Gov.'s Adv. Com. on Dams, 1972; adviser, cons. Coun. of State Govts., Lexington, Ky.; mem. U.S. Com. on Large Dams; mem. bd. on radioactive waste mgmt. NAS/NRC; mem. Ward Valley, Calif. Commn. on Low Level Radioactive Waste. Contbr. articles on dam safety, flood control, hydrologic impacts of strip mining to profl. jours., chpts. to books. Recipient Robert Fulton Engring. Prof. award, 1980, Outstanding Tchr. award, 1985, 89, 91, 92, 93, 94, President's award Assn. State Dam Safety Ofcls., 1986, Centennial Outstanding Alumnis award N.Mex. State U., 1988, Engring. Coll. Leon and Nancy Cole Outstanding Tchg. award, 1995, Quality Tchg. award, 1995, 96, Outstanding Svc. Award, 1996. Mem. ASCE (Faculty of Year award Student chpt. 1968), Am. Soc. Engring. Edn. (civil engr. chmn. S.E. sect. 1972, Dow Chem. award 1969, Western Electric award 1980), Nat. Soc. Profl. Engrs., Tenn. Soc. Profl. Engrs. (v.p., pres. Knoxville br. 1973-75), U.S. Com. on Large Dams, Knoxville Tech. Soc. (Knoxville Young Engr. award 1970), N.Mex. Acad. Civil Engring., Sigma Xi, Tau Beta Pi, Chi Epsilon. Home: 1508 Meeting House Rd Knoxville TN 37931-4427 Office: U Tenn 63 Perkins Hall Knoxville TN 37996

TSCHERNY, GEORGE, graphic designer; b. Budapest, Hungary, July 12, 1924; s. Mendel and Bella (Heimann) T.; m. Sonia Katz, July 7, 1950; children—Nadia, Carla. Student, Pratt Inst., Bklyn., 1947-50. Staff designer Donald Deskey & Assocs., N.Y.C., 1950-53; designer, assoc. George Nelson & Assocs., N.Y.C., 1953-55; pres. George Tscherny, Inc., N.Y.C., 1955—; instr. Pratt Inst., Bklyn., 1956, bd. advisors, 1979; instr. Sch. Visual Arts, N.Y.C., 1955-64; curriculum cons. Phila. Coll. Art, 1967; Mellon vis. prof. Cooper Union, N.Y., 1978. Retrospective exhbn. Visual Art Mus., N.Y.C., 1992; exhibited in group shows, Germany, 1962-67, Italy, 1974, U.S., 1975; represented in permanent collections Mus. Modern Art, N.Y.C., Cooper Hewitt Mus., N.Y.C., Libr. of Congress, Washington, Kunstgewerbeschule der Stadt Zurich. Contbr. design svcs. to UN Assn., Sta. WNET Pub. TV, Am. Lung Assn., Peace Corps, Cystic Fibrosis Found., L.I. State Park Commn. With U.S. Army, 1943-46, ETO. Recipient numerous awards, Am. Inst. Graphic Arts medal, 1988, Art Dirs. Club N.Y., N.Y. Type Dirs. Club; Silver medal Warsaw Biennale, 1976. Mem. Am. Inst. Graphic Arts (pres. 1966-68), Alliance Graphique Internationale. Office: 238 E 72nd St New York NY 10021-4571

TSCHETTER, PATRICIA LINN BARRETT, investor, oil producer; b. Denver, May 9, 1960; d. Arthur Eames Wright Barrett and Patricia Ruth Pickens; m. Robert Alan Tschetter, Jan. 9, 1988. BBA, BA, So. Meth. U., 1982; MBA, U. Dallas, 1984; MS, Tex. Woman's U., 1993. Investor, ind. oil prodr. Houston and Dallas, 1981—; interpreter Automatic Radius Mgmt., Dallas, 1984; exec. asst. Pickens Energy Corp., Dallas, 1984-87; artist, designer Moroch & Assocs., Dallas, 1988; staff therapist Galaxy Ctr., Garland, Tex., 1991-93; pres. Krazy Karrot, Inc., Dallas, 1993—, Tschetter Properties, Ltd., 1993—; student therapist Marriage and Family Clinic, Tex. Woman's U., Denton, 1990; student intern Galaxy Ctr., Garland, 1990-91. Author: Comparative Analysis of Marital Satisfaction Between Alcoholic and Nonalcoholic Couples, 1993, (design) Theta Kat, 1982. Ct. advocate The Family Place, Dallas, 1988-91. Mem. Nat. Soc. Magna Charta Dames, Nat. Soc. Daughters of the Am. Revolution, 1993—, Soc. of Colonial Dames of XVII Century, Metroplex Early Birds, Classic Thunderbird Club Internat., Sigma Iota Epsilon, Sigma Delta Pi (v.p. 1980), Delta Sigma Pi.

TSCHINKEL, ANDREW JOSEPH, JR., law librarian; b. Catskill, N.Y., Aug. 8, 1952; s. Andrew Joseph and Marie Frances (O'Connor) T.; m. Frances K. Quigley, Nov. 4, 1989. BA summa cum laude, St. John's Coll., Jamaica, N.Y., 1975, MLS, 1977; MBA, Fordham U., 1983. Grad. asst. div. libr. sci. St. John's Coll., Jamaica, 1975-77, asst. law libr., 1977-79, adj. law librarian, 1983-87; head librarian Christ the King High Sch., Middle Village, N.Y., 1979-80; sr. law librarian Bklyn. Supreme Ct., 1980-81; prin. law librarian N.Y. Supreme Ct., Jamaica, 1981—. Recipient Pub. Svc. award Queens Borough Pres. and N.Y. Tel. Co., 1986; named Alumnus of Yr. Grad. Sch. Arts & Scis. Divsn. Libr. & Info. Sci. St. John's U., 1993. Mem. Am. Assn. Law Librs., Law Libr. Assn. Greater N.Y., Elks, Beta Phi Mu. Republican. Office: NY Supreme Ct Libr 88-11 Sutphin Blvd Jamaica NY 11435-3716

TSCHIRHART, PAUL M., corporate lawyer. BS, UNotre Dame, 1963; JD, Wayne State U., 1968. Bar: Mich. 1968, D.C. 1971, Ill. 1978. Hearing counsel Fed. Maritime Commn., 1968-69; assoc. Coles and Goertner, Washington, 1969-71, Bebchick Sher & Kushnick, Washington, 1971-73; asst. U.S. Atty. Office of the U.S. Atty., Washington, 1973-76; sr. trial atty.civil divsn. U.S. Dept. Justice, 1976-77; sr. counsel United Airlines, Park Ridge, N.J., 1982-86; sr. v.p., gen. counsel The Hertz Corp., Park Ridge, 1986—. Office: Hertz Corp 225 Brae Blvd Park Ridge NJ 07656-1870

TSCHOEPE, THOMAS, bishop; b. Pilot Point, Tex., Dec. 17, 1915; s. Louis and Catherine (Sloan) T. Student, St. Thomas Sch. Pilot Point, 1930, Pontifical Coll. Josephinum, Worthington, Ohio, 1943. Ordained priest Roman Cath. Ch., 1943; asst. pastor in Ft. Worth, 1943-46, Sherman, Tex., 1946-48, Dallas, 1948-53; adminstr. St. Patrick Ch., Dallas, 1953-56; pastor St. Augustine Ch., Dallas, 1956-62, Sacred Heart Cathedral, Dallas, 1962-65; bishop San Angelo, Tex., 1966-69; bishop Dallas, 1969-90, ret. bishop, 1990; asst. pastor St. Joseph Parish, Waxahachie, Tex., 1990—. Home and Office: St Joseph Ch PO Box 190 504 E Marvin St Waxahachie TX 75165-3406

TSCHUMI, BERNARD, dean; b. Lausanne, Switzerland, Jan. 25, 1944. BArch, Fed. Inst. Tech., Zurich, Switzerland, 1969. Tchr. Archtl. Assn., London, 1970-80, Inst. Architecture and Urban Studies, N.Y.C., 1976, Princeton U. Sch. Architecture, 1980-81, Cooper Union, 1980-83; dean Columbia U. Grad. Sch. Architecture, Planning & Preservation, N.Y.C.; head firm Bernard Tschumi Architects, N.Y.C. and Paris; Davenport vis. prof. architecture. Contbr.: The Manhattan Transcripts, 1981, Architecture and Disjunction, 1994, Event Cities, 1994, Bernard Tschumi: Architecture and Event, 1994. Recipient 1st prize for design of new Sch. of Architecture, Paris, 1994. Office: Grad Sch Architecture Planning & Preservation 116 St & Broadway New York NY 10027*

TSE, EDMUND SZE-WING, insurance company executive; b. Hong Kong, Jan. 2, 1938; s. Kai-Sum and Chao-Sui (Chui) T.; m. Peggy Pik-Kin Wai, Dec. 18, 1965; children: Ada Koon-Hang, Elaine Koon-Ming. BA, U. Hong Kong, 1960; diploma, Life Ins. Agy. Mgmt. Assn., 1972, Stanford U., 1980. Mng. supr. Nan Shan Life Ins. Co., Ltd., Taipei, Taiwan, 1970-74, pres., mng. dir., 1975-83; chmn. Nan Shan Life Ins. Co., Ltd., 1990; various positions Am. Internat. Assurance Co., Ltd., Hong Kong, 1961-70, pres., CEO, 1983—, also bd. dirs.; pres., dir. Am. Internat. Assurance Co. (Bermuda), Ltd.; exec. v.p. life ins. Am. Internat. Group Inc., N.Y., 1991—, bd. dirs., 1996—; bd. dirs. Australian Am. Assurance Co. Ltd., dep. chmn., 1987—; bd. dirs., dep. chmn. Australian Am. Superannuation Co., Ltd.; chmn. Nan Shan Life Ins. Co., Ltd., 1990—; vice-chmn. Philippine Am. Life Ins. Co.; pres., chmn. bd. dirs. Green Heights Inc., Panama; dir. Met. Land Co., Ltd., Hong Kong; mem. ins. adv. com. Govt. of Hong Kong, 1988; bd. dirs. Am. Internat. Data Ctr. Ltd., USI Far East Corp., Life Ins. Mktg. & Rsch. Assn., Inc.; chmn. Universal Fin. Co., others. Active Project Hope, AIA Found.; trustee The Harvard Club of Hong Kong. Mem. Gen. Ins. Coun. Hong Kong (chmn. 1989-90, chmn. legis. subcom. 1988-89), Hong Kong Fedn. Inst. (dep. chmn. 1991-92, chmn. 1992-93), Chief Execs. Orgn. (U.S.), Pacific Ins. Conf. (nat. area chmn. 1985—), Bus. and Profls. Fedn. Hong Kong (mem. exec. com., fin. specialist group 1993—), Pres. Orgn. (U.S.). Home: 10C Headland Rd, Repulse Bay Hong Kong Office: Am Internat Assurance Co Lt, No 1 Stubbs Rd, Hong Kong Hong Kong

TSE, HARLEY Y., immunologist, educator; b. China, July 17, 1947; s. Toncheuk and Hou-Ying (Choy) T.; m. Kwai-Fong Chui, Jan. 13, 1979; children—Kevin Y., Alan C., Leslie W. B.S. with honors, Calif. Inst. Tech., 1972; Ph.D., U. Calif.-San Diego, 1977; M.B.A., Rutgers U., 1986. Fellow Arthritis Found., NIH, Bethesda, Md., 1977-80; sr. research immunologist Merck Sharp & Dohme Research Lab., Rahway, N.J., 1980-83, research fellow, 1983-86; adj. asst. prof. Columbia U., 1981-84 ; assoc. prof. Wayne State U. Sch. Medicine, 1986—. Contbr. articles to profl. jours. Bd. dirs. Chinese Social Service Center, San Diego, 1975. Recipient NIH Rsch. Career Devel. award, 1992—; Calif. Biochem. Research fellow, 1975, Arthritis Found. fellow, 1977-80; NIH grantee, Nat. Multiple Sclerosis Soc. grantee, 1988—. Mem. Am. Assn. Immunologists,, NIH Immunological Sci. Study Sec., 1995—, Chinese Student Assn. (pres. 1974-76)., Soc. Chinese Bioscientist in Am., Detroit Immunological Soc. (pres. 1989-91). Roman Catholic. Home: 5393 Tequesta Dr West Bloomfield MI 48323-2351 Office: Wayne State U Sch Medicine 540 E Canfield St Detroit MI 48201-1928

TSE, STEPHEN YUNG NIEN, insurance executive; b. Shanghai, China, Feb. 14, 1931; came to U.S., 1949; s. Koong Kai and Teh-Ying Koo T.; m. Margaret Miray Lock, Sept. 7, 1957; children: Chida, Chiming, Chiyung, Chikai. Student Ripon Coll., 1951-52; BBA, U. Wis., 1955. V.p. investments Am. Internat. Assurance Co., Hong Kong, 1962-64, fin. v.p., 1964-70;

v.p. fgn. investments Am. Internat. Group, Inc., N.Y.C., 1971-82, sr. v.p., 1982—; pres., CEO AIG Assocs., 1986—; bd. dirs. Am. Internat. Assurance Co., Tai Ping Carpets Internat. Ltd., Worldwide Looms, Ltd., AIG Realty Inc., C.V. Starr & Co., Inc. Mem. Sky Club, India House Club, Hong Kong Country Club, Am. Club of Hong Kong, Royal Hong Kong Golf Club, Beta Theta Pi. Office: Am Internat Group Inc 70 Pine St New York NY 10270-0002

TSENG, TSUNG-CHE, plant pathologist, educator; b. Tianan Hsein, Republic of China, Jan. 2, 1937; s. Wen-Kue and Ching-Hong (Chang) T.; m. Tsu-Huey Yang, Oct. 5, 1963. BS, Nat. Taiwan U., Taipei, Republic of China, 1961; MS, Cornell U., 1968; PhD, U. Mass., 1973. Rsch. technician U.S. Naval Med. Rsch. Unit, Taipei, 1962-63; rsch. asst. Inst. of Botany, Academia Sinica, Taipei, 1963-69, asst. rsch. fellow, 1969-73; grad. asst. dept. plant pathology U. Mass., 1971-73; assoc. rsch. fellow Inst. of Botany, Academia Sinica, Taipei, 1973-77, rsch. fellow, 1977—; assoc. prof. Nat. Taiwan U., Taipei, 1973-77, prof., 1977—; advisor Indsl. Rsch. Lab., Hsinchu, Republic of China, 1981-82, Nat. Bur. Stds., Ministry of Econ. Assn., Taipei, 1991—, Nat. Labs. of Foods and Drugs, Dept. Health, Execuitide Yuan, Taipei, 1986-88. Editor-in-chief Plant Protection Bull., 1976-78; editor Botanical Bull., Acad. Sinica, 1978—; patentee monoclonal antibody, 1991. Res. officer Taiwan Army, 1961-62. Fellow Nat. Sci. Coun., 1970-72, French Govt., 1981-82; recipient Disting. Rsch. award Nat. Sci. Coun., 1988, 90, 91. Mem. AAAS, Internat. Union Biological Scis., Internat. Union Toxicology, N.Y. Acad. Scis., Mycol. Soc. Republic of China (editor 1985—). Avocations: reading, writing, music, sports. Home: 2F 9, Alley 8, Ln 158, Pa-Teh Rd Sec 3, Taipei Taiwan Office: Academia Sinica, Inst of Botany, Taipei Taiwan

TSIAPERA, MARIA, linguistics educator; b. Cyprus, July 26, 1935; naturalized, 1964; d. Anastasis and Aphrodite T.; m. Jeff Beaubier, May 1, 1969; 1 dau., Nike Tsiapera. B.A., U. Tex., Austin, 1957, M.A., 1959, Ph.D., 1963. Asst. prof. linguistics Fresno (Calif.) State U., 1964-66; asst. prof. U. N.C., Chapel Hill, 1966-67, assoc. prof., chmn. dept., 1967-72, prof., chmn., 1972-73, prof., 1973—. Author: Maronite Cypriot Arabic, 1969, Generative Studies in Historical Linguistics, 1971; The Port-Royal Grammar: Sources and Influences, 1993; contbr. articles to profl. jours. NSF travel grantee, 1977; U. N.C. research grantee, 1967, 69, 72, 74, 77. Mem. Linguistic Soc. Am. (exec. com.), Southeastern Conf. Linguistics (founder, pres.), Am. Oriental Soc., Modern Greek Studies Assn., Am. Assn. Tchrs. Arabic, N.Am. Assn. for History of Lang. Scis. (v.p., pres.-elect 1992). Democrat. Greek Orthodox. Research on history and philosophy of linguistics and human scis. since 1660. Home: 1051 Burning Tree Dr Chapel Hill NC 27514-5657 Office: U NC Dept Linguistics Chapel Hill NC 27514

TSIEN, RICHARD WINYU, biology educator; b. Tating, Kweichow, People's Republic China, Mar. 3, 1945; s. Hsue-Chu and Yi-Ying (Li) T.; m. Julia Shiang; children: Sara Shiang-Ming, Gregory Shiang-An, Alexa Tsien-Shiang. BS, MIT, 1965, MS, 1966; DPhil, Oxford U., Eng., 1970. Rsch. student Eaton Peabody Lab. Auditory, Physiology, Mass. Eye and Ear Infirmary, 1966; asst. prof. dept. physiology, Yale U. Sch. Medicine, New Haven, 1970-74, assoc. prof., 1974-79, prof., 1979-88; George D. Smith prof. molecular and cellular physiology Stanford (Calif.) U., 1988—, chmn. dept., 1988—; established investigator Am. Heart Assn., 1974-79. Author: Electric Current Flow in Excitable Cells, 1975. Recipient Otsuka award Internat. Soc. Heart Rsch., 1985; Rhodes Scholar, 1966; Weir Rsch. fellow, 1966-70 Univ. Coll., Oxford, 1966-70, lecturing fellow Balliol Coll., Oxford, 1969-70. Mem. Soc. Gen. Physiologists (pres. 1988), Biophys. Soc. (Kenneth S. Cole award 1985), Soc. for Neurosci. Democrat. Home: 866 Tolman Dr Palo Alto CA 94305-1026 Office: Stanford U Dept Molecular and Cellular Physiology 300 Pasteur Dr Stanford CA 94305*

TSINA, RICHARD VASIL, chemistry educator; b. Boston, Aug. 13, 1941; s. Vasil Anastas and Theodora (Kasuli) T.; m. Irene Wang, Nov. 28, 1970; children: Lesley, Katherine. BA, Boston U., 1963; MA, Duke U., 1965; PhD, Tufts U., 1968. Asst. prof. chemistry Rutgers U., New Brunswick, N.J., 1970-73; v.p. Sultra Corp., N.Y.C., 1973-76; dean continuing edn. Cogswell Coll., San Francisco, 1976-79; asst. dean U. Calif., Berkeley, 1990-95, vice chmn. engring. ext., 1982-85, chmn., 1995—, dir. tech. programs, 1995—. Contbr. articles to profl. jours. Mem. IEEE (chmn. San Francisco sect. 1984-85, chmn. fin. coun. 1985-86, meritorious achievement award in continuing edn. 1995), Am. Chem. Soc. (chair continuing edn. adv. com. 1995—), Sigma Xi, Tau Beta Pi (eminent engr. com.). Home: 1424 Dana Ave Palo Alto CA 94301-3149 Office: U Calif Continuing Edn Engring 1995 University Ave #7010 Berkeley CA 94704-1450

TSIRPANLIS, CONSTANTINE N., theology, philosophy, classic and history educator; b. Kos, Greece, Mar. 18, 1935; came to U.S., 1957; m. Sophia Pappas, July 12, 1975; children: Kalliope-Chrysoula, Nike. BA, STM, lic. in theology magna cum laude, Halke Theol. Sem., Istanbul, Turkey, 1957; ThM, Harvard U., 1962; ThD, Union Theol. Sem., 1963; MA, Columbia U., 1966, PhD, 1970; PhD, Fordham U., 1973. Instr., organizer Greek-Am. communities, 1958-63; founder, chmn., prof. modern Greek studies NYU, 1963-70; prof. world history N.Y. Inst. Tech. N.Y.C. and Delaware County Coll., Media, Pa., 1967-75; disting. prof. theology, history, ecumenism, Greek studies Union Theol. Sem., Barrytown, N.Y., 1976—; chmn., prof. classics Collegiate Sch., N.Y.C., 1967-69; prof. modern Greek lang. and lit. New Sch. for Social Rsch., N.Y.C., 1968-70; prof. classical mythology Hunter Coll. CUNY, 1968-70. Author numerous books including A Short History of the Greek Language, 1966, rev. edit., 1970, A Modern Greek Reader for Americans, 1967, rev. edit., 1968, A Modern Greek Idiom and Phrase Book, 1978, Mark Eugenicus, 1979, N. Cabasilas, 1979, Greek Patristic Theology, 9 vols.; editor The Patristic and Byzantine Rev., 1981—; contbr. articles to profl. jours. Decorated Medal of Nat. Rebirth 1821 (Greece), medals of Byzentine nobility, including count, baron, G. chevalier, Gt. Prior of N.Am., medal of Accademia Ferdinandea, medals of DEEL. Mem. Am. Soc. Neohellenic Studies (founder, v.p.), Pan Dodecanisian Fedn. U.S., Am. Hist. Assn., Am. Philog. Assn., Am. Acad. Medieval Studies, Internat. Assn. Byzantine Studies, Am. Philos. Assn., N.Am. Patristic Soc., Hellenic Philog. Assn., Am. Soc. Papyrologists, Am. Inst. Patristic-Byzantine Studies (pres., founder), Justinianum Oikoumenikon R.C. (pres., founder). Home: 12 Minuet Ln Kingston NY 12401-9801 Office: Union Theol Sem 10 Dock Rd Barrytown NY 12507

TSIVIDIS, YANNIS P., electrical engineering educator; b. Piraeus, Greece, Dec. 22, 1946; came to U.S., 1970; s. Pelopidas I. and Maria (Filippa) T. BS, U. Minn., 1972; MS, U. Calif., Berkeley, 1973, PhD, 1976. Asst. prof. elec. engring. Columbia U., N.Y.C., 1976-81, assoc. prof., 1981-84, prof., 1984—; prof. Nat. Tech. U., Athens, Greece, 1992-95; cons. AT&T Bell Labs., Murray Hill, N.J., 1977-88. Author: Operation and Modeling of the Mos Transistor, 1987, Mixed Analog-Digital VLSI Devices and Technology, 1996; co-editor: Design of Mos VLSI Circuits for Telecommunications, 1985, Integrated Continuous-Time Filters, 1993, Design of Analog-Digital VLSI Circuits for Telecommunications and Signal Processing, 1994; contbr. over 100 articles to profl. jours.; patentee in field. Recipient best paper award European Solid State Cirs. Conf., 1986, Great Tchr. award Columbia U., 1991. Fellow IEEE (Baker best paper award 1984, Darlington award 1987). Office: Columbia Univ Dept Elec Engring New York NY 10027

TSO, TIEN CHIOH, federal agency official, plant physiologist; b. Hupeh, China, July 25, 1917; came to U.S., 1947, naturalized, 1961; s. Ya Fu and Suhwa (Wang) T.; m. Margaret Lu, Aug. 28, 1949; children: Elizabeth, Paul. B.S., Nanking U., China, 1941, M.S., 1944; Ph.D., Pa. State U., 1950; postgrad., Oak Ridge Inst. Nuclear Studies. Supt. exptl. farm Ministry Social Affairs, China, 1944-46; exec. sec. Tobacco Improvement Bur., 1946-47; research chemist Gen. Cigar Research Lab., 1950-51; with U.S. Dept. Agr., 1952—; prin. plant physiologist crop research div. Agrl. Research Service, Beltsville, Md., 1964-66; leader tobacco quality investigations, tobacco and sugar crops research br. Agrl. Research Service, 1966-71, chief tobacco lab., 1972-83, sr. exec. service, 1974-83, collaborator, 1984—; exec. dir. Internat. Devel. and Edn. in Agr. and Life Scis., 1984—; cons. Nat. Cancer Inst., Ky. Tobacco Health Rsch. Inst., China Nat. Tobacco Corp., Philippine Tobacco Rsch. Ctr., Philip Morris Tobacco Corp. Author: Physiology and Biochemistry of Tobacco Plants, 1972, Production, Physiology and Biochemistry of Tobacco Plants, 1991; contbg. author: Ann. Rev. Plant Physiology, Vol. 9, 1958, The Chemistry of Tobacco and Tobacco Smoke, 1972, Toward Less Harmful Cigarettes, 1968, 71, 75, 80; editor: Structural and Functional Aspects of Phytochemistry, 1972, Recent Advances in Tobacco Science, vol. 1, 1975. Fellow AAAS, Am. Soc. Agronomy (chmn. colloquium on agr. and life scis. in China 1983, 84, 85, 86, 87, 88-89), Am. Inst. Chemists; mem. Am. Chem. Soc., Am. Soc. Plant Physiologists, Phytochem. Soc. N.Am. (pres. 1971, life mem.), Tobacco Chemists Rsch. Conf. (symposium chmn. 1965, 79, chmn. 1975, 83), World Conf. Smoking and Health (sect. chmn. 1967, 71, 75), Tobacco Workers Conf., N.Y. Acad. Scis., Interagy. Smoking and Health Forum (chmn. 1979-83), Nat. Coordinating Com. on Tobacco-Related Rsch., Sigma Xi, Gamma Sigma Delta. Research publs. on establishment of loci of alkaloid formation, biosynthetic pathway, interconversion and fate of alkaloids in tobacco plants, chem. composition as affected by macro and micro elements, homogenized leaf curing, health-related factors including mycotoxins and phenolics. Home: 4306 Yates Rd Beltsville MD 20705-2758 Office: Beltsville Agr Rsch Ctr Bldg 005 Beltsville MD 20705 also: Ideals Inc 5010 Sunnyside Ave Beltsville MD 20705-2320 *We are thankful to those fools. They are the only ones who dare to dream of something new and seemingly impossible.*

TSOI, EDWARD TZE MING, architect, interior designer, urban planner; b. New Orleans, Aug. 7, 1943; s. Edward Mong Yok and Ruby Liu Wei (Hsia) T.; m. Louise Smoyer, June 15, 1968; children: Laura Li Ling, Alison Li Mei. BArch, MIT, 1966; MArch, U. Pa., 1968, M in City Planning, 1968, cert. in urban design, 1969. Registered architect, Mass., La. Assoc. Sert/Jackson & Assocs., Cambridge, Mass., 1969-76; assoc. prin. Skidmore Owings & Merrill, Boston, 1976-83; prin. Tsoi/Kobus & Assocs., Inc., Cambridge, 1983—, pres., 1985-89, 93—; instr. Sch. Design, Harvard U., Cambridge, 1980-84. Designer Marine Resource Ctr., 1994. Chmn. Arlington (Mass.) Redevel. Bd., 1972—; chmn. 1st parish Unitarian Universalist Ch., Arlington, 1990; pres. bd. dirs. Cambridge Salvation Army, 1990-94; mem. Boston Civic Design Commn., 1993—. Recipient Best New Med. Facility award Symposium on Healthcare, 1993, Grand Honor award Assn. Gen. Contractors, 1993, award Lotus Devel. Corp. landscape award Urban Design, 1991, nat. award for renovation Ford Model T plant ULI. Fellow AIA; mem. Boston Soc. Architects (pres. 1993-94). Democrat. Avocations: windsurfing, boating, woodworking, carpentry. Home: 16 Devereaux St Arlington MA 02174-8114 Office: Tsoi/Kobus & Assocs Inc PO Box 9114 Cambridge MA 02238-9114

TSONGAS, PAUL EFTHEMIOS, lawyer, former senator; b. Lowell, Mass., Feb. 14, 1941; s. Efthemios and Katina Tsongas; m. Nicola Sauvage, Dec. 21, 1969; children: Ashley, Katina, Molly. BA, Dartmouth Coll., 1962; LLB, Yale U., 1967. Bar: Mass. Tng. coord. Peace Corps, W.I., 1967-68; mem. Gov.'s Com. on Law Enforcement, 1968-69; dep. asst. atty. gen. Mass., 1969-71; pvt. practice, 1971-74; mem. 94th-95th Congresses from 5th Mass. dist., 1975-79; U.S. senator from Mass., 1979-85; ptnr. Foley, Hoag & Eliot, Boston, 1985—; Dem. candidate for U.S. pres., 1992; mem. energy and natural resources com., mem. com. on small bus., mem. fgn. rels. com., co-chmn. ad-hoc Congl. monitoring group on So. Africa. Author: The Road From Here, 1981, Heading Home, 1984, A Call to Economic Arms, 1992, Journey of Purpose, 1996. Vol. Peace Corps, Ethiopia, 1962-64; city councillor City of Lowell, 1969-72; county commr. Middlesex County, 1973-74; chmn. Mass. Bd. Regents of Higher Edn., 1989-91; bd. govs. Am. Stock Exch. Democrat. Greek Orthodox. Office: Foley Hoag & Eliot 1 Post Office Sq Boston MA 02109-2103

TSORIS, STEPHEN A., lawyer; b. Milw., July 26, 1957; s. Athan John Tsoris and Lillian Marian (Ribish) Groothousen; m. Elizabeth Mintor Lennihan, June 25, 1983. BA, Marquette U., 1979; JD, Cornell U., 1982. Bar: Ill. 1982, U.S. Dist. Ct. (no. dist.) Ill. 1982. Assoc. Jenner & Block, Chgo., 1982-84; assoc. McDermott, Will & emery, Chgo., 1984-87, ptnr., 1988—. Author (note) Great Britain's Protection of Trading Interests, 1982, Act: The Claw and the Lever, 1982; editor-in-chief Cornell Internat. Law Jour., Ithaca, N.Y., 1981-82. Mem. ABA, Chgo. Bar Assn. (chmn. corp. law com. 1992-93). Office: McDermott Will & Emery 227 W Monroe St Chicago IL 60606-5016

TSOU, TANG, political science educator, researcher; b. Canton, Guangdong, China, Dec. 10, 1918; came to U.S., 1941; s. Lu and Chien-yun (Hsu) T.; m. Yi-chuang Lu. BA, Nat. Southwest Associated U., Kunming, Yunnan, China, 1940; PhD, U. Chgo., 1951. Rsch. assoc. Ctr. for Study Am. Fgn. Policy, U. Chgo., 1955-62, asst. prof. dept. polit. sci., 1959-62, assoc. prof., 1962-66, prof., 1966-84, Homer J. Livingston prof., 1984-88, Homer J. Livingston prof. emeritus, 1989—; bd. dirs. Nat. Com. on U.S.-China Rels., N.Y.C., 1971-87, emeritus, 1987—; mem. Joint Com. on Contemporary China, Social Sci. Rsch. Coun. and Am. Coun. Learned Socs., 1972-74. Author: America's Failure in China, 1963 (Gordon J. Laing prize 1965), The Cultural Revolution and Post-Mao Reforms, 1986, Chinese Politics in the Twentieth-Century: Macrohistory and Micro-mechanisms, 1994; co-editor, co-author: China in Crisis, 1968; mem. editorial bd. World Politics, China Quarterly, Asian Survey, Modern China; contbr. articles to profl. jours. Named Hon. Prof. Peking U., Beijing, 1986; rsch. grantee Joint Com. on Contemporary China, Social Sci. Rsch. Coun. and Am. Coun. Learned Socs., 1962-63, 68-69, 75-76; fellow Rockefeller Found., 1966-67, Luce Found., 1982-83. Mem. Am. Polit. Sci. Assn. Office: U Chgo Dept Polit Sci 5828 S University Ave Chicago IL 60637-1515

TSOUCALAS, NICHOLAS, federal judge; b. N.Y.C., Aug. 24, 1926; s. George Michael and Maria (Monogenis) T.; m. Catherine Aravantinos, Nov. 21, 1954; children: Stephenie, Georgia. BSBA, Kent State U., 1949; LLB, N.Y. Law Sch., 1951. Bar: N.Y. 1953. Sole practice, N.Y.C., 1953-55, 59-68; asst. U.S. atty. So. Dist. N.Y., 1955-59; judge Criminal Ct., City of N.Y., 1968-86; acting supreme ct. judge State of N.Y., N.Y.C., 1975-82; judge U.S. Ct. Internat. Trade, N.Y.C., 1986—. Dist. leader Republican Party N.Y. County, N.Y.C., 1961-68; mem. Rep. Exec. Com., N.Y.C., 1961-68. Served with USN, 1944-46, 51-52. Recipient Proficiency in Constl. Law award N.Y. Law Sch., N.Y.C., 1951, Man of Yr. award St. Paul Soc., N.Y.C., 1971. Mem. ABA, N.Y. County Lawyers Assn., Queens County Bar Assn., Fed. Bar Assn., Greek Am. Lawyers Assn., Am. Hellenic Ednl. Prog. Assn. Republican. Greek Orthodox. Lodges: Parthenon, Masons. Avocations: basketball, racquetball, stamp collecting, walking, dancing. Office: US Ct Internat Trade 1 Federal Plz New York NY 10278-0001*

TSOULFANIDIS, NICHOLAS, nuclear engineering educator; b. Ioannina, Greece, May 6, 1938; came to U.S., 1963; s. Stephen and Aristea (Ganiou) T.; m. Zizeta Koutsombidou, June 21, 1964; children: Stephen, Lena. BS in Physics, U. Athens, Greece, 1960; MS in Nuclear Engring., U. Ill., 1965, PhD in Nuclear Engring., 1968. Registered profl. engr., Mo. Prof. nuclear engring. U. Mo., Rolla, 1968—, vice chancellor acad. affairs, 1985-86, asst. dean School of Mines and Metallurgy, 1989—; sr. engr. Gen. Atomic Co., San Diego, 1974-75; engr. Ark. Power and Light Co., 1976-80; researcher Cadarache France, 1986-87. Author: Measurement and Detection of Radiation, 1984, 2d edit. 1995; co-author: Nuclear Fuel Analysis and Management, 1990. Electric Power Research Inst. grantee, 1980-84. Mem. Am. Nuclear Soc. (chmn. radiation protection shielding div. 1987-88), Health Physics Soc., Nat. Soc. Profl. Engring., Rotary. Office: U of Mo Rolla Dept Nuc Engring 1870 Miner Cir Engring Rolla MO 65409-0170

TSUBAKI, ANDREW TAKAHISA, theater director, educator; b. Chiyoda-ku, Tokyo, Japan, Nov. 29, 1931; s. Ken and Yasu (Oyama) T.; m. Lilly Yuri, Aug. 3, 1963; children: Arthur Yuichi, Philip Takeshi. BA in English, Tokyo Gakugei U., Tokyo, Japan, 1954; postgrad. in Drama, U. Saskatchewan, Saskatoon, Canada, 1958-59; MFA in Theatre Arts, Tex. Christian U., 1961; PhD in Speech & Drama, U. Ill., 1967. Tchr. Bunkyo-ku 4th Jr. High Sch., Tokyo, Japan, 1954-58; instr., scene designer Bowling Green (Ohio) State U., 1964-68; asst. prof. speech & drama U. Kans., Lawrence, 1968-73, assoc. prof., 1973-79; visiting assoc. prof. Carleton Coll., Northfield, Minn., 1974; lectr. Tsuda U., Tokyo, Japan, 1975; visiting assoc. prof. theatre Tel-Aviv (Israel) U., 1975-76; visiting prof. theatre Mo. Repertory Theatre, Kansas City, Mo., 1976, Nat. Sch. Drama, New Delhi, India, 1983; prof. theatre, film, east Asian Languages and Cultures U. Kans., Lawrence, 1979—; dir. Internat. Theatre Studies Ctr., U. Kans., Lawrence, 1971—, Operation Internat. Classical Theatre, 1988—; Benedict disting. vis. prof. Asian studies Carleton Coll., 1993; area editor Asian Theatre Jour., U. Hawaii, Honolulu, 1982-94; chmn. East Asian Langs. and Cultures, U. Kans., Lawrence, 1983-90; mem. editl. bd. Studies in Am. Drama, Oxford, Miss., 1985—. Dir. plays Kanjincho, 1973, Rashomon, 1976, 96, King Lear, 1985, Fujito and Shimizu, 1985, Hippolytus, 1990, Busu and the Missing Lamb (Japan) 1992, Suehirogari and Sumidagawa, 1992, 93, Tea, 1995; choreographed Antigone (Greece), 1987, Hamlet (Germany), 1989, The Resistible Rise of Auturo Ui, 1991, Man and the Masses (Germany), 1993, The Children of Fate (Hungary), 1994, The Great Theatre of the World (Germany); editor Theatre Companies of the World, 1986; contbg. author to Indian Theatre: Traditions of Performance, 1990; contbr. 7 entries in Japanese Traditional plays to the Internat. Dictionary of Theatre, vol. 1, 1992, vol. 2, 1994. Recipient World Univ. Svc. Scholarship U. Saskatchewan, 1958-59, University fellow U. Ill., 1961-62, Rsch. fellow The Japan Found., 1974-75, 90, Rsch. Fulbright grantee, 1983. Mem. Am. Theatre Assn., Asian Theatre Program (chair 1976-79), Assn. for Asian Studies, Assn. Kans. Theatres., Assn. Kans. Theatres U/C Div. (chmn. 1980-82), Assn. for Theatre in Higher Edn., Assn. for Asian Performance. Democrat. Buddhist. Avocations: Ki-Aikido (3d Dan), photography, travel. Home: 924 Holiday Dr Lawrence KS 66049-3005 Office: U Kans Theatre And Film Lawrence KS 66045

TSUBOUCHI, DAVID H., Canadian provincial official. BA in English, York U.; LLB, Osgoode Hall Law Sch. Ward 5 councillor Town of Markham, 1988-94; sr. ptnr. Tsubouchi & Nichols & Assocs., 1994-95; apptd. Min. of Cmty. and Social Svcs. Ont. Progressive Conservative Govt., 1995—; chmn. planning and devel. com., econ. alliance com., indsl. and corp. devel. com. Markham Hist. Mus. Named Optimist of Yr., 1985-86; recipient Air Can. Heart of Gold award, 1988; granted Coat of Arms, Gov. Gen.'s Office, 1993. Office: Hepburn Block, Queens Park, Toronto, ON Canada M7A 1E9

TSUCHIYA, KEN, computer engineer; b. Iiyama, Japan, Dec. 30, 1947; came to U.S., 1967; s. Junzo and Fumi (Shiozaki) T.; m. Viviane M. Clausset, Oct. 6, 1973; 1 child, Aimee. BSEE, U. Minn., 1972. Registered profl. engr., Minn. Design, develop engr. Avionics Honeywell Co., Mpls., 1973-80; sys. design engr. Gen. Mills Co., Mpls., 1980; sr. design engr. Def. Honeywell Co., Mpls., 1980-83; prin. engr., cons. Unisys Co., St. Paul, 1983—. Patentee in field. Mem. IEEE, Minn. Profl. Engring. Soc. Avocations: travel, skiing, fishing, bicycling. Home: 1425 N Innsbuck Dr Fridley MN 55432

TSUEI, CHANG CHYI, physicist; b. Wi-hai-wi, Shantong, China, July 16, 1937; came to U.S., 1962; s. Yu Zuen and Ai-nan (Chiang) T.; m. Holly Yung Chen; children: Albert, Angela, Nancy. BSME, Nat. Taiwan U., Taipei, 1960; MS in Materials Sci., Calif. Inst. Tech., 1963, PhD in Materials Sci., 1966. Rsch. fellow in materials sci. Calif. Inst. Tech., Pasadena, 1966-69, sr. rsch. fellow, 1969-72, sr. rsch. assoc. in applied physics, 1972-73; mem. rsch. staff Thomas J. Watson Rsch. Ctr. IBM, Yorktown Heights, N.Y., 1973-79, acting mgr. superconductivity, 1974-75, mgr. physics of amorphous materials, 1979-83, mgr. physics of structured materials, 1983-93, project leader physics of superconductivity, 1993—; vis. scholar in applied physics Harvard U., Cambridge, Mass., summer 1980, Stanford (Calif.) U., 1982-83. Contbr. chpts. to: Amorphous Magnetism, 1973, Rapidly Quenched Metals, 1976, Amorphous Magnetism II, 1977, Thin Film Phenomena—Interfaces and Interaction, 1978, Superconductor Materials Science: Metallurgy, Fabrication and Applications, 1981, Magnetic Monopoles, 1983, 3 chpts. with others; contbr. entry on amorphous superconductors to Ency. Materials Sci. and Engring., 1986; contbr. numerous articles to sci. jours. Recipient Max Planck Rsch. prize Max Planck Soc., Alexander von Humboldt Found. Germany award for achievement, 1992. Fellow Am. Phys. Soc.; mem. Chinese Phys. Soc. (life), Chinese Soc. Materials Sci. (life). Achievements include pioneering work ferromagnetism in amorphous metals, discovery of collective flux pinning in superconductors; of effect of thermodynamic fluctuations on electrical conductivity above Tc; of a quadratic temperature dependence of in-plane normal state resistivity in electron-doped Cu oxides; first direct observation of the half-integer flux quantum effect providing strong evidence for d-wave pairing symmetry in high-temperature superconductors; rsch. in fundamental study of electrical and magnetic properties of solids. Office: IBM Thmas J Watson Rsch Ctr PO Box 218 Yorktown Heights NY 10598

TSUI, LAP-CHEE, molecular genetics educator; b. Shanghai, Dec. 21, 1950; arrived in Can., 1981; s. Jing Lue Hsue and Hui Ching Wang; m. Ellen Lan Fong, Feb. 11, 1977; children: Eugene, Felix. BS, Chinese U. Hong Kong, 1972, MPhil, 1974, DSc (hon.), 1991; PhD, U. Pitts., 1979; DCL (hon.), U. King's Coll., Halifax, N.S., Can., 1991; DSc (hon.), U. N.B., Can., 1991; DLL (hon.), U. St. Francis Xavier, Antigonish, N.S., Can., 1994. Postdoctoral investigator Oak Ridge (Tenn.) Nat. Lab., 1979-80; postdoctoral fellow Hosp. for Sick Children, Toronto, Ont., Can., 1981-83; asst. prof. depts. genetics and med. genetics Hosp. for Sick Children and U. Toronto, 1983-88, assoc. prof., 1988-90; prof., Sellers chair cystic fibrosis rsch., 1990—, univ. prof., 1994—; chmn. chromosome 7 subcom. Human Gene Mapping Workshop, 1986—; mem. mammalian genetics study sect. NIH, Bethesda, Md., 1988-93; dir. Cystic Fibrosis Rsch. Ctr., Hosp. for Sick Children Spl. Rsch. Ctr., 1994—; scientist Med. Rsch. Coun. Can., 1989—; advisor European Jour. Human Genetics, 1992—, Molecular Medicine Today, 1995—. Editor Cytogenetics and Cell Genetics, 1988-92, Internat. Jour. Genome Rsch., 1990—; assoc. editor Am. Jour. Human Genetics, 1990-93, Genomics, 1994—; mem. editl. bd. Mammalian Genome, 1990, Clin. Genetics, 1991—, Human Molecular Genetics, 1991—; communicating editor Human Mutation, 1995—, Molec. Medicine Today; contbr. over 200 articles to sci. jours.; co-discoverer cystic firbrosis gene, 1989. Trustee Edn. Found., Fedn. Chinese Canadian Profls., Toronto, 1987—. Recipient Paul di Sant Agnese Disting. Achievement award Cystic Fibrosis Found., 1989, Gold medal of honor Pharm. Mfrs. Assn. Can., 1989, award of excellence Genetics Soc. Can., 1990, Gairdner Internat. award 1990, Cresson medal Franklin Inst., 1992, E. Mead Johnson award, 1992, Disting. Scientist award The Canadian Soc. Clin. Investigators, 1992, Canadian Conf. medal 1992, Sarstedt Rsch. prize, 1993, Sanremo Internat. award for Genetic Rsch., 1993, J.P. Lecocq prize Inst. de France, 1994, Henry Frieson award The Canadian Soc. for Clin. Investigation and the Royal Coll. of Physicians and Surgeons of Can.; named scholar Can. Cystic Fibrosis Found., 1984-86. Fellow Royal Soc. Can., Royal Soc. London, Academia Sinica; mem. Human Genome Orgn., Am. Soc. Human Genetics. Office: Hosp for Sick Children, 555 University Ave, Toronto, ON Canada M5G 1XG

TSUI, SOO HING, research consultant; b. Hong Kong, Aug. 2, 1959; came to U.S., 1985; d. Sik Tin and Yuk Kam (Cheung) T. BSW cum laude, Nat. Taiwan U., 1983; MSW cum laude, Columbia U., 1987, postgrad., 1992—. Cert. social worker, N.Y. Dir. cmty. handicapped ctr. Taipei, Taiwan, 1983-85; dir. youth recreational program N.Y., 1986; social work dept. supr. St. Margaret's House, N.Y.C., 1987-89; chief bilingual sch. social work N.Y.C. Bd. Edn., 1990-93, rsch. cons., 1993—; chief rsch. cons. N.Y.C. Dept. Transp., 1993—. Union social work regional rep. N.Y.C. Bd. Edn., 1990-93, citywide bilingual social work rep., 1991-93, citywide social work budget allocation comms. rep., 1992-93; mem. planning com. social work bd. Asian Am. Comms., N.Y.C., 1991-95; mem. conf. planning com. bd. Amb. For Christ, Boston, 1991-93; coord. doctoral colloquial com. bd. Scholarship Coun. Social Work Edn., Columbia U., N.Y.C., 1992-94. Nat. Acad. scholar, 1987-88; recipient Nat. Acad. award, 1979-83; Nat. Rsch. fellow Sch. Coun. on Social Work Edn., 1992-94. Mem. Nat. Assn. Asian/Am. Edn. (bilingual social worker). Home: 507 W 113th St Apt 22 New York NY 10025-8070

TSUKIJI, RICHARD ISAO, international marketing and financial services consultant; b. Salt Lake City, Jan. 31, 1946; s. Isamu and Mitsuie (Hayashi) T.; children: Angela Jo, Richard Michael. Grad. Sacramento City Coll., 1966; AA, U. Pacific, McGeorge Sch. Law, 1970-72. Grocery mgr. Food Mart, Inc., Sacramento, 1963-65; agy. supr. Takehara Ins. Agy., Sacramento, 1965-68; sales rep. Kraft Foods Co., Sacramento, 1969-71; sales mgr. Olivetti Corp., Sacramento, 1972-73; co-founder Mktg. Devel. and Mgmt. Coll., Sacramento, 1973, pres., 1973-74; pres. Richard Tsukiji Corp., Sacramento, 1974-77; CEO, chmn. bd. Assocs. Investment Group, Sacramento, 1978-82 ; chmn. bd. RichColor Corp. Sacramento, 1978-83, E.J. Sub Factories, Inc., Elk Grove, Calif., 1978-81; gen. agt. Comml. Bankers Life Ins. Co., 1974-82; chmn. bd. Phoenix Industries, Inc., Carson City, Nev., 1981-84, Databank, Inc., Roseburg, Oreg., 1982-83; pres. Computers, Etc. Corp., Carson City,

1982-84; regional v.p. U.S. BankCard Group, Salem, Oreg., 1993-95; pres. Richard Tsukiji Comm., Inc., Sacramento, 1993—; CEO RTC Wireless,Inc., 1994—, Bonaventure Group, Inc., Wilmington, Del., 1995—; bd. dirs. Michton, Inc., Pontiac, Mich., Hunt & Johnson, Inc., Phoenix Group, Melbourne, A.N.D. Corp., New Orleans, ET World Travel, Salt Lake City, Utah, Bonaventure Group, Inc., Wilmington, Del., Royal Am. Bank, Cayman Islands; exec. v.p. Edco Corp., Glide, Oreg., 1982-94; chmn. bd. Computer Edn. Resource Ctr., 1983-90, Bonaventure, Inc., Roseburg, 1984-91, RTC Wireless Group, Inc., Oakland, Calif., 1995—; editor ST World, Melrose, Oreg., 1985-88, publisher, 1988-91; editor ST World Reseller, 1988-91. Mem. Yolo County Oral Rev. Bd., 1975-76; bd. dirs. Valley Area Constrn. Opportunity Program, 1972-76, chmn., 1976-77; bd. dirs. Douglas County Citizens Community Involvement, 1980-82; bd. dirs. Computer Edn. Found., Sacramento, 1983-93, Access Sacramento Cable Television, 1993, Heart to Heart Found., 1993; chmn. pub. rels. Sacramento Asian Pacific C. of C., 1993—; bd. dirs. Chinese Am. Coun. Sacramento, 1994—; mem. Asian Cmty. Ctr., 1994—, Sacramento Chinese Cmty. Svc. Ctr., 1994—; bd. dirs. ARC Sacramento-Sierra chpt., 1995—, No. Calif. Asian Peace Officers Assn., 1995—, Sacramento Chinese Cmty. Svc. Ctr., 1995—, Japanese Am. Citizens League, 1995—; democratic precinct committeeman, Melrose, Oreg., 1982-86; appt. mem. adv. coun. Sacramento City Minority/Women Bus. Enterprise, 1995; bd. dirs., v.p. Orgn. Chinese Ams., Inc., 1996. Served with U.S. Army, 1962-63. Recipient Commendation, Calif. Senate, 1978. Mem. Internat. Assn. Fin. Planners, Associated Gen. Contractors, VIC-20 Users Group (pres. Roseburg 1983-84), Atari Computer Enthusiasts (pres. Sacramento 1983-85), U.S. Commodore Council (pres. Natl. 1984-85), Sacramento Jaycees (dir. 1977-78), Orgn. Chinese Ams. (v.p. Sacramento chpt. 1995—), Asian Alliance, Japanese Am. Citizens League, Sacramento Urban League. Democrat. Roman Catholic. Office: 9 Heathfield Rd Unit #1, Coolum Beach 4573, Queensland Australia also: 1530-16th St Sacramento CA 95814

TSUMURA, YUMIKO, Japanese language and culture educator, consultant; b. Gobo City, Wakayama, Japan, Mar. 8, 1939; came to the U.S., 1972; s. Yoshio and Masako (Moriguchi) T.; m. Motoi Umano, Apr. 13, 1961 (dec. Apr. 1962); 1 child, Junko; m. Samuel B. Grolmes, Mar. 2, 1969. BA, Kwansei Gakuin U., Nishinomiya, Japan, 1961, MA, 1965, postgrad., 1965-66; MFA, U. Iowa, 1968. Lectr. Baika Women's Coll., Osaka, Japan, 1970-72, Calif. State U., San Jose, 1973-74, U. Santa Clara, Calif., 1975-77, West Valley Coll., Saratoga, Calif., 1974-79; assoc. prof. Foothill Coll., Los Altos Hills, Calif., 1974—; asst. prof. Coll. San Mateo, Calif., 1975—; asst. prof. Japanese lang. and culture, shodo Cañada Coll., Redwood City, Calif., 1974—; U.S.-Japan intercultural cons. Apple Computer, Inc., Cupertino, Calif., 1984—, NASA Ames Rsch. Ctr., Mountain View, Calif., 1987-93, Hewlett Packard Co., Santa Clara, 1992—, Kobe Steel U.S.A., Inc., San Jose, 1992—. Co-translator: (with Sam Grolmes) (Japanese poetry and fiction) New Directions Annual, 1970-74; contbr. poetry to lit. jours., 1967—. Artist rep. Junko Tsumura, Igor Scedrov piano cello duo Cultural Comm. and Cons., Palo Alto, 1988—; lectr. and demonstrator on Shodo Galerija Foruma Mladih, Varazdin, Croatia, 1993; bd. dirs. Japanese Cultural Ctr., Foothill Coll., 1994. Honor scholar Kwansei Gakuin U., Nishinomiya, 1958-59; Travel grantee Fulbright-Hayes Commn., Tokyo, 1966, Internat. Peace Scholarship grantee P.E.O. Internat. Peace Fund, Des Moines, 1967-68. Mem. No. Calif. Tchrs. Assn. Avocations: poetry, Shodo ink brush art, classical music, dance, cooking. Home: 723 Torreya Ct Palo Alto CA 94303-4160 Office: Foothill Coll 4000 Middlefield Rd Palo Alto CA 94303-4739

TSUNEJI, NAGAI, pharmaceutics educator; b. Shikishima, Gumma, Japan, June 10, 1933; s. Ushinosuke and Take (Kogure) N.; m. Kiyoko Usui, May 5, 1964. BS, U. of Tokyo, 1956, MS, 1958, PhD, 1961. Lic. pharmacist. Rsch. and teaching assoc. U. of Tokyo, 1961-71; postdoct. fellow Columbia U., N.Y.C., 1965-66, U. Mich., Ann Arbor, 1966-67; prof. pharmaceutics Hoshi U., Tokyo, 1971—; Chmn. bd. trustees The Nagai Found., Tokyo, 1986—; dir. FIP Found. for Edn. and Rsch., The Hague, The Netherlands, 1983—, Iwaki Found., Tokyo, 1985—. Author numerous books, papers and articles in field; inventor 55 patents. Trustee Hoshi U., Tokyo, 1979-91; mem. adv. com. Ministry of Health and Welfare, Tokyo, 1967-83, Ministry of Fgn. Affairs, Tokyo, 1981-87, Ministry of Edn. Culture and Sci., Tokyo, 1981-83; spl. mem. Japan Accredidation Assn., Tokyo, 1981—. Recipient Japan Invention prize Japan Invention Assn., Tokyo, 1984, Most Prestigious Rsch. prize Pharm. Soc. Japan, Tokyo, 1987; William Evans fellow U. Otago, Duneden, New Zealand, 1993. Mem. Acad. Pharm. Sci. and Tech. (founding pres. 1985-87), Internat. Pharm. Fedn. (v.p. 1986-94, Host-Madsen medal 1986), Controlled Release Soc. (del., pres. 1996—), Japan Soc. Drug Delivery (pres., chmn. bd. dirs. 1994—), Soc. of Cyclodextrins Japan (founding pres.), Internat. House of Japan. Avocations: kabuki, music, antiques. Home: 1-23-10-103 Hon-Komagome, Bunkyo-ku, Tokyo 113, Japan Office: Hoshi U Dept Pharmaceutics, 2-4-41 Ebara, Shinagawa-ku, Tokyo 142, Japan

TSUNG, CHRISTINE CHAI-YI, financial executive, treasuruer; b. Nanking, China, Mar. 23, 1948; came to U.S., 1970; d. Chi-Huang Tsung and Siao-Tuan Huang; m. Icheng Wu, Aug. 14, 1971 (div. Dec. 1989); m. Jerome Chen, Aug. 10, 1990; children: Jonathan, Julia. BBA, Nat. Taiwan U., Taipei, 1970; postgrad., Washington U., St. Louis, 1970-71; MBA, U. Mo., 1973. Acct. Capital Land Co., St. Louis, 1972-74; chief acct. Servis Equipment Co., Inc., Dallas, 1974-75; acctg. supr. Calif. Microwave, Sunnyale, 1975-76; budget and sales mgr. Columbia Pictures TV Internat., Burbank, Calif., 1976-77; acctg. mgr. Husquarna, San Diego, 1977-82; sr. acct. City of Poway, Calif., 1982-88, fin. mgr., 1988-95; pres., treas. Jade Poly Investment, San Diego, 1989—; cons. assoc. Metro Properties, San Diego, 1989—. Tchr. San Diego North County Chinese Sch., 1985-86; v.p. San Diego Chinese Culture Assn., 1982-86, bd. dirs., 1988-90, 93-94. Mem. Govt. Fin. Officers Assn. (Cert. of Achievement 1988-94), Calif. Soc. Mcpl. Fin. Officers (standing com. membership devel., Cert. of Award 1988-94), Mcpl. Treas. Assn. U.S. and Can., Taiwanese C. of C. of N.Am. (bd. dirs. 1994-95). Avocations: traveling, swimming, tennis, golf, reading. Home: 18766 Aceituno St San Diego CA 92128-1564 Office: Jade Poly Investments PO Box 302 Poway CA 92064-0302

TSUNG-DAO LEE, physicist, educator; b. Shanghai, China, Nov. 25, 1926; s. Tsing-Kong L. and Ming-Chang (Chang); m. Jeannette Chin, June 3, 1950; children: James, Stephen. Student, Nat. Chekiang U., Kweichow, China, 1943-44, Nat. S.W. Assoc. U., Kunming, China, 1945-46; PhD, U. Chgo., 1950; DSc (hon.), Princeton U., 1958; LLD (hon.), Chinese U., Hong Kong, 1969; DSc (hon.), CCNY, 1978. Research assoc. in astronomy U. Chgo., 1950; research assoc., lectr. physics U. Calif., Berkeley, 1950-51; mem. Inst. for Advanced Study, Princeton (N.J.) U., 1951-53, prof. physics, 1960-63; asst. prof. Columbia U., N.Y.C., 1953-55, assoc. prof., 1955-56, prof., 1956-60, 63—, adj. prof., 1960-62, Enrico Fermi prof. physics, 1963—, Univ. prof., 1984—; Loeb lectr. Harvard U., Cambridge, Mass., 1957, 64. Editor: Weak Interactions and High Energy Nutrino Physics, 1966, Particle Physics and Introduction to Field Theory, 1981. Decorated grande ufficiale Order of Merit (Italy); recipient Albert Einstein Sci. award Yeshiva U., 1957, (with Chen Ning Yang) Nobel prize in physics, 1957, Ettore Majorana-Erice-Sci. for Peace prize, 1990. Mem. NAS, Acad. Sinica, Am. Acad. Arts and Scis., Am. Philos. Soc., Acad. Nazionale dei Lincei, Acad. Sci. China. Office: Columbia U Dept Physics Morningside Heights New York NY 10027*

TU, JOHN, engineering executive; b. 1941. With Motorola Co., Wiesbaden, Germany, 1966-74; pres. Tu Devel., L.A., 1975-82, Camintonn Corp., Santa Ana, Calif., 1982-85; v.p., gen. mgr. AST Rsch., Irvine, Calif., 1985-87; pres. Newgen Systems Corp., Fountain Valley, Calif., 1987—; CEO Kingston Tech., Fountain Valley, 1988—. Office: 17600 Newhope St Fountain Valley CA 92708

TU, WEI-MING, historian, philosopher, writer; b. Kunming, Yunnan, China, Feb. 26, 1940; came to U.S., 1962, naturalized, 1976; s. Shou-tsin (Wellington) and Shu-li (Sonia Ou-yang) T.; m. Helen I-yu Hsiao, Aug. 24, 1963 (div.); 1 son, Eugene L.; m. Rosanne V. Hall, Mar. 17, 1982; children: A. Yalun, Mariana Mei-ling B., Rosa Wen-yun. B.A., Tunghai U., 1961; M.A., Harvard U., 1963; Ph.D., 1968. Vis lectr. humanities Tunghai (Taiwan) U., 1966-67; vis. lectr. East Asian studies Princeton U., 1967-68, asst. prof., 1968-71; asst. prof. history U. Calif., Berkeley, 1971-73, assoc. prof., 1973-77, prof., from 1977; vis. prof. Chinese history and philosophy Harvard U., 1981-82, prof. Chinese history and philosophy, 1982—, chmn. com. on study of religion, 1984-87, chmn. dept. East Asian langs. and civilizations, 1991-92, coord. Dialogue of Civilizations, 1990-93; dir. Inst. Culture and Communication, East-West Ctr., Honolulu, 1990-91; vis. prof. dept. philosophy Peking U., 1985; disting. vis. prof. depts. philosophy and history Taiwan U., 1988; 10th Ch'ien Mu lectr. New Asia Coll., The Chinese U. of Hong Kong, 1989; 1st Henry Chai lectr. Hong Kong U., 1989; vis. prof. Ecole Pratique des Hautes Etudes, U. Paris, 1991; bd. dirs. Inst. Advanced Rsch. in Asian Sci. and Medicine, 1993—; trustee Adironack Work-Study Project, Inc., 1990—; chmn. adv. bd. Inst. Literature and Philosophy, Academia Sinica, 1993—; gov. Inst. East Asian Political Economy, Singapore, 1983-93; pres. Contemporary Mag., Taiwan, 1986—; acad. adviser Chinese Culture Acad., Beijing; vice-chmn. Internat. Confician Assn., Beijing, 1994, Annual Freeman Lectr. Wesleyan U., 1982; assembly speaker Grinnell Coll., 1983; commencement speaker Grad. Theol. Union at Berkeley, 1990; keynote speaker alumni conf. East-West Ctr., Bangkok, 1990; GET lectr. Bal State U., 1991; panelist 1st World Chinese Enterprises Conv., Singapore, 1991; Paul Desjardins Meml. lectr. Haverford Coll., 1992; baccalaureate speaker Swarthmore Coll., 1993; co-moderator seminar, the Chineses in the Global Community, Aspen Inst., 1994; guest prof. Wuhan U.; dir. Harvard Yenchnig Inst., 1996—. Author: Neo-Confucian Thought in Action—Wang Yang-ming's Youth, 1976, Centrality and Commonality—An Essay on Chung-Yung, 1976, Humanity and Self-Cultivation—Essays in Confucian Thought, 1980, Confucian Ethics Today: The Singapore Challenge, 1984, Confucian Thought: Selfhood as Creative Transformation, 1985, The Way, Learning, and Politics: Perspective on the Confucian Intellectual, 1988, Toward the "Third Epoch" of Confucian Humanism: Problems and Prospects (in Chinese), 1989, A Reflection on Confucian Self-Consciousness (in Chinese), 1990, The Modern Spirit and the Confucian Tradition (in Chinese), 1993; editor: The Triadic Tension: Confucian Ethics, Max Weber and Industrial East Asia, 1991, The Confucian World Observed, 1992, The Living Tree: Changing Meaning of Being Chinese, 1993, China in Transformation, 1994, Confucian Traditions in East Asian Modernity, 1996; mem. editorial bd. Asian Thought and Soc., 1976—, Harvard Jour. Asiatic Studies, 1983, Philosophy East and West, 1984—, The Twenty-First Century (Chinese), Contemporary (Chinese); columnist Commonwealth (Chinese); contbr. articles Philosophy East and West, Jour. Asian Studies, Daedalus, The Monist, Chinese lang. jours. and newspapers. Am. Council Learned Socs. fellow, 1968-69; research grantee Center East Asian Studies, Harvard U., 1968-69; research grantee Humanities Council Princeton U., 1970-71; research grantee U. Calif., 1973-74; sr. scholar Com. on Scholarly Communication with People's Republic of China Nat. Acad. Scis., 1980-81; Fulbright-Hays research scholar Peking U., 1985; interviewed by Bill Moyer in World of Ideas, 1991. Fellow Am. Acad. Arts and Scis. (exec com. fundamentalism project 1988—), Soc. for Study of Value in Higher Edn.; mem. Am. Soc. for the Study Religion, Assn. Asian Studies (dir. 1971-75), Am. Hist. Assn., Soc. Asian and Comparatie Philosophy, Am. Acad. Religion, Conf. Study of Polit. Thought, AAAS, Asia Soc. N.Y. (assoc. China Council). Office: Harvard U Dept East Asian Langs and Civilizations Cambridge MA 02138 *As an all-embracing humanist tradition, Confucianism seeks to find integrated and holistic solutions to socio-political problems. One of its core ideas is self-cultivation, signifying that the way to universal peace takes personal knowledge as the point of departure. Learning to be human, in the Confucian perspective, entails an unceasing spiritual transformation. This quest for self-realization involves an ever-expanding circle of human-relatedness. It is not simply a search for one's own inner spirituality but a concern for the establishment of a fiduciary community for humankind as a whole.*

TUAN, CHRISTOPHER YOUNG-BEE, structural engineer, researcher; b. Taipei, Taiwan, Republic of China, Apr. 15, 1954; came to U.S., 1977; s. Chang-Yi and Hsiao-I (Chang) T.; m. Deborah Lynn Tollander, Nov. 25, 1989; children: Christopher Brandon, Sean Robert, Benjamin Alexander. BS, Nat. Taiwan U., Taipei City, 1977; MS, U. Wis., 1979, PhD, 1983. Registered profl. engr., Nebr., Tex. Assoc. prof. U. Nebr., Lincoln, 1983-89; sr. engr. Wilfred Baker Engring., Inc., San Antonio, 1989-91, Applied Rsch. Assocs., Inc., Panama City, Fla., 1991—; mem. solar dish rev. panel Sandia Nat. Lab., Albuquerque, 1987; cons. TELTECH, Inc., Mpls., 1990—. Contbr. articles to profl. jours. Mem. ASCE (mem. loading guide group 1985-88), Soc. Am. Mil. Engrs., Prestressed Concrete Inst. (seismic com. 1988), Sigma Xi, Chi Epsilon, Phi Kappa Phi. Achievements include designing of a passive airblast attenuator under sponsorship of U.S. Army Corps of Engineers. Avocations: basketball, volleyball, table tennis, camping. Home: 7709 Betty Louise Dr Panama City FL 32404

TUAN, SAN FU, theoretical physics, political science educator; b. Tientsin, China, May 14, 1932; came to U.S., 1954; naturalized, 1967; s. Mao Lan and Lu Kung (Tao) T.; m. Loretta Kan, Dec. 15, 1963; children: Katherine Tsung Yen, Melinda Tsung Tao, Priscilla Tsung Pei, David Tsung Lien. BA, U. Oxford, Eng., 1954, MA, 1958; PhD, U. Calif. at Berkeley, 1958. Rsch. assoc. U. Chgo., 1958-60; asst. prof. Brown U., R.I., 1960-62; assoc. prof. Purdue U., 1962-65; prof. physics U. Hawaii, Honolulu, 1966—; vis. prof. physics U. Hawaii, 1965-66, Purdue U., 1973, Beijing U. and Inst. Theoretical Physics, 1979-80, U. Wis.-Madison, spring 1982; vis. scientist Inst. Theoretical Physics Acad. Sinica, 1987, Inst. Physics Academia Sinica, Taipei, City Poly., Hong Kong, Inst. High Energy Physics Acad. Sinica, Beijing, fall 1993, Weizmann Inst., Rehovot, spring 1994; mem. Inst. Advanced Study, Princeton, 1966, 72; prin. investigator Theoretical High Energy Program AEC, 1967-80; cons. Argonne Nat. Lab., 1963-70; dir. Hawaii Topical Conf. in Particle Physics, 1967, 69, 73, 75, 77; vis. lectr. Bariloche Summer Sch., Argentina, 1969-70, U.S.-China Sci. Coop. Program NSF, 1970-71; participant exploratory mission to China U. Hawaii-China Sci. Coop., 1973. Editor: Modern Quantum Mechanics, 1985, rev. edit., 1994; co-editor Procs. of Hawaii Topical Confs. in Particle Physics, 1967, 69, 73, 75, 77, Procs. of 10th Hawaii Conf. in High Energy Physics, 1985; reviewer Math. Rev., 1962-70, Phys. Rev., 1963—); contbr. articles to profl. jours. Coord. State Hawaii on initial planning for projected Internat. Sci. Found., 1970; mem. Hawaii Gov.'s Alt. Energy Sources Com., 1974. John S. Guggenheim fellow, 1965-66; Mackinnon scholar Magdalen Coll., Oxford, 1951-54. Fellow Am. Phys. Soc.; mem. Phi Beta Kappa. Home: 3634 Woodlawn Terrace Pl Honolulu HI 96822-1475 Office: U Hawaii Dept Physics 2505 Correa Rd Honolulu HI 96822-2219

TUAZON, JESUS OCAMPO, electrical engineer, educator, consultant; b. Manila, Jan. 2, 1940; came to U.S., 1963; s. Filomeno and Patrocino (Ocampo) T.; m. Norma Mamangun, Oct. 12, 1963; children: Maria, Noel, Norman, Mary, Michelle. BSEE, Mapua Inst., Manila, 1962; MSEE, Iowa State U., 1965, PhD, 1969. Elec. prof. Calif. State U., Fullerton, Calif., 1969—; scientist Jet Propulsion Lab., Pasadena, Calif., 1984—; computer cons. Hughes Aircraft, Fullerton, 1977, Gen. Dynamic, Pomona, Calif., 1983, U.S. Naval Weapon Sta., Seal Beach, Calif., 1978-83. Author of papers for profl. confs. Mem. IEEE, Am. Assn. Engring Educators. Democrat. Roman Catholic. Avocations: jogging, swimming, chess. Home: 816 S Verona St Anaheim CA 92804-4035 Office: Calif State Univ 800 N State College Blvd Fullerton CA 92631-3547 also: Jet Propulsion Lab 4800 Oak Grove Dr Pasadena CA 91109-8001

TUBB, JAMES CLARENCE, lawyer; b. Corsicana, Tex.; s. Cullen Louis and Sarah Elmore (Chapman) T.; m. Suzanne Alice Smith, Nov. 22, 1954; children: James Richard, Sara Elizabeth, Daniel Chapman. BA, So. Meth. U., 1951, JD, 1954. Bar: Tex. 1954, U.S. Dist. Ct. (no. dist.) Tex. 1955, U.S. Ct. Appeals (5th cir.) 1959, U.S. Supreme Ct. 1978; cert. comml. real estate specialist; lic. Tex. real estate broker; cert. mediator Dallas Bar Assn., 1989. With legal dept. Schlumberger Well Surveying Corp., Houston, 1954-55; claims atty. Franklin Am. Ins. Co., Dallas, 1957-58; ptnr. Vial, Hamilton, Koch, Tubb & Knox and predecessor firm Akin, Vial, Hamilton, Koch & Tubb, Dallas, 1958-84; dir., ptnr. Winstead, McGuire, Sechrest & Minick, Dallas, 1984-90; pvt. practice Dallas, 1990—; guest lectr. on real estate broker liability Real Estate Ctr., Tex. A&M U., 1987. Bd. dirs. Christian Concern Found., 1965-71, bd. deacons, 1972-78; ruling elder Highland Park Presbyn. Ch., Dallas, 1978-84, 88-91; mem. permanent jud. commn. Grace Presbytery, 1984-90; bd. dirs. Am. Diabetes Assn. Dallas County affiliate, 1991-95. 1st lt. JAGC, SAC, USAF, 1955-57, 1st lt. USAFR, ret. Recipient Outstanding Student award Student Bar Assn., 1954. Fellow Tex. Bar Found.; mem. ABA (chmn. comml. law com. gen. practice sect. 1982-84, real estate probate and trust law sect.), Tex. Bus. Law Found., Tex. Bar Assn., Am. Arbitration Assn., Soc. Profls. in Dispute Resolution, Dallas Country Club, Dallas County Rep. Men's Club (sec. 1978-79). Home: 3407 Haynie Ave Dallas TX 75205-1842 Office: 5956 Sherry Ln Ste 1000 Dallas TX 75225-8021

TUBBS, MICKI MARIE, nursing administrator; b. Lorain, Ohio, June 29, 1956; d. Albert James and Katherine (Zahratka) McDermott; m. Terry P. Tubbs, Aug. 6, 1977; children: Anthony, Alison, Adam. Diploma nursing, Providence Hosp. Sch. Nursing, 1977; BSN, Ursuline Coll., 1983; MBA, Baldwin Wallace Coll., 1991. Cert. RN hospice. Charge nurse surg. St. Joseph Hosp. and Health Ctr., Lorain, Ohio, 1977-81, staff nurse ICU, 1981-86, home care case mgr., 1986-88, dir. of hospice, 1988-93; pres., CEO New Life Hospice, Elyria, Ohio, 1993—. Mem. Leadership Lorain County, 1994—. Named Woman of Achievement YWCA, 1989. Mem. Hospice Nurses Assn. (pres. nat. office 1993—, v.p. 1991-93), Ohio Hospice Orgn. (v.p. state office 1994—, bd. dirs. 1992—), Hospice Nurses Assn. (pres., bd. dirs.), Nat. Bd. for Certification of Hospice Nurses, Ohio Hospice Orgn. (bd. dirs., v.p. 1992—), Am. Cancer Soc. (com. mem. 1988—). Avocations: tennis, basketball, coaching, reading. Office: New Life Inc 5255 N Abbe Rd Elyria OH 44035

TUBESING, RICHARD LEE, library director; b. Kansas City, Mo., Nov. 25, 1937; s. Clarence and Letha (Thacker) T. BA, Yale U., 1959; MA, U. Chgo., 1969; MSL, Western Mich. U., 1972. Asst. to dir. U. Louisville, 1972-73; reference libr. Ga. Tech. Libr., Atlanta, 1973-76; head bus. and sci. Atlanta Pub. Libr., 1976-79; libr. dir. Lewis U., Romeoville, Ill., 1979-81; collection devel. coord. U. Toledo Libr., 1981-86; libr. dir. Coll. of the Southwest, Hobbs, N.Mex., 1986-89; libr. dir., dir. libr. sci. program Glenville (W.Va.) State Coll., 1989—. Author: Architectural Preservation, 1978, Architectural Preservation and Urban Renovation, 1982. Program coord. Lea County Archaeol. Soc., Hobbs, 1987-89. Lt. j.g. USNR, 1960-63. Mem. W.Va. Libr. Assn., Lea County Libr. Assn. (v.p. 1987-88, pres. 1988-89). Avocation: collecting primitive and peasant art. Home: Rte 76 Box 17 Glenville WV 26351 Office: Glenville State Coll Robert F Kidd Libr Glenville WV 26351

TUBMAN, WILLIAM CHARLES, lawyer; b. N.Y.C., Mar. 16, 1932; s. William Thomas and Ellen Veronica (Griffin) T.; m. Dorothy Rita Krug, Aug. 15, 1964; children: William Charles Jr., Thomas Davison, Matthew Griffin. BS, Fordham U., 1953, JD, 1960; postdoctoral, NYU Sch. Law, 1960-61. Bar: N.Y. 1960, U.S. Ct. Appeals (2d cir.) 1966, U.S. Supreme Ct. 1967, U.S. Ct. Customs and Patent Appeals 1971. Auditor Peat, Marwick Mitchell & Co., N.Y.C., 1956-60; sr. counsel Kennecott Corp., N.Y.C., 1960-82; sr. counsel Phelps Dodge Corp., N.Y.C., 1982-85, sec., 1985-95, v.p., 1987-95; pres. Phelps Dodge Found., Phoenix, 1988-95. Author: Legal Status of Minerals Beyond the Continental Shelf, 1966. Mem. scholarship adv. coun. U. Ariz., 1990-92; active Big Bros., Inc., N.Y.C., 1963-73; trustee Phoenix Art Mus., 1989-94; bd. dirs. St. Joseph Hosp. Found., 1994—, chmn., 1994-95; bd. dirs. The Phoenix Symphony, 1994-95. Recipient Cert. Disting. Service, Big Brothers Inc., 1968. Mem. ABA, N.Y. State Bar Assn., Maricopa County Bar Assn. Democrat. Roman Catholic.

TUCCI, JOSEPH M., computer software and services executive; b. 1947. BA, Manhattan Coll.; MBA, Columbia U. With Sperry Corp., 1970-86; pres. U.S. ops. Unisys Corp., 1986-90; exec. v.p. ops. Wang Labs., Inc., 1990-93; chmn. bd., CEO Wang Labs., Inc., Lowell, Mass., 1993—. Office: Wang Labs Inc 600 Technology Park Dr Billerica MA 01821

TUCCI, MARK A., state agency administrator; b. Trenton, N.J., Dec. 14, 1950; s. William F. and Theresa M. (Miccio) T.; m. Carolyn J. Bilecki, July 10, 1971; children: Nicholas A., Anthony M., Vincent J. BS, Trenton State Coll., 1972, MEd, 1978; cert. pub. mgr., Rutgers U. Cert. N.J. chief sch. adminstr., prin., supr., tchr. of deaf, tchr. of handicapped, N.J. Tchr. of deaf Katzenbach Sch. for the Deaf, West Trenton, N.J., 1972-82; spl. asst. to supt. Katzenbach Sch. for the Deaf, West Trenton, 1982-85; exec. asst. to asst. commr. edn. N.J. Dept. Edn., Trenton, 1985-87; chief of enterprise license bur. N.J. Casino Control Commn., Atlantic City, 1987-91, dir. organizational devel., 1991—, dir. adminstrn., 1992-93; examiner N.J. Quality Achievement Award Program, 1993, sr. examiner, 1994; judge N.J. Exemplary State and Local Awards Program, 1994—; chmn. N.J. Quality Achievement Award Focus Group, 1994-96. Mem. editorial bd. periodical for Trenton chpt. Phi Delta Kappa, 1986-88; columnist Total Quality Management, 1994; contbr. articles to profl. pubs. Chmn. bd. trustees AIDS Support Found., Inc., 1995; cub scout leader Trenton chpt. Boy Scouts Am., 1981-84, mem. dist. com. Jersey Shore Coun., 1995-96; pres. Katzenbach (N.J.) chpt. N.J. State Enployees' Assn., 1979; co-chair adv. coun. Mercer County Spl. Edn. Assn., 1984; mem. bus. adv. coun. Atlantic Cmty. Coll., 1990—; chmn. bd. trustees AIDS Support Found., Inc., 1994—. Mem. Cert. Pub. Mgrs. Soc. N.J. (fellow trustee), Phi Delta Kappa, Kappa Delta Pi. Roman Catholic. Avocations: reading, journalism, martial arts, photography, songwriting. Home: 273 Neptune Dr Manahawkin NJ 08050-5026 Office: NJ Casino Control Commn Tennessee Ave Atlantic City NJ 08401-4602

TUCHMAN, AVRAHAM, physicist, researcher; b. N.Y.C., July 1, 1935; s. Max and Rebecca (Brick) T.; m. Sylvia Crystal, Dec. 26, 1957; children: Davida, Ari, Sima, Pnina. BA, Yeshiva U., 1956; PhD, MIT, 1963. Scientist, group leader to sect. chief Avco Rsch. and Advanced Devel., Wilmington, Mass., 1963; prin. scientist, staff scientist to prin. staff scientist Avco Systems Div., Wilmington; chief scientist Textron Def. Systems, Wilmington, 1988-93; owner, sr. cons. physicist Added Value Innovations (AVI), Brookline, Mass., 1994—; vis. prof. Weizmann Inst. Sci., Rehovot, Israel, 1974, 78, 82. Contbr. numerous articles to profl. jours. Founder, pres. Kehilla Day Camp of Jewish Community Ctrs., Westwood, Mass., 1975-86; chmn. Brookline (Mass.) Traffic Commn., 1975-81; pres. Mikvah Rescue Svc., Brighton, Mass., 1969-77; pres. Temple Beth Avraham, Brookline, 1969—. Recpient award for outstanding cantorial artistry Am. Soc. Forktwangers, Detroit, 1970. Fellow AIAA (sr.). Avocations: computers, gardening, softball, homecraft. Office: AVI 138 Tappan St Brookline MA 02146-5818

TUCHMAN, MAURICE SIMON, library director; b. Bklyn., Sept. 14, 1936; s. William and Rose (Luria) T.; m. Helene Lillian Bodner, Aug. 30, 1959; children: Joel Aron, Miriam Auri. BA, CUNY, 1958; MLS, Columbia U., 1959; B Hebrew Lit., Jewish Theol. Sem., N.Y.C., 1964; D of Arts in LS, Simmons Coll., 1979. Cataloger. svcs. Buffalo and Erie County, 1959-60; asst. libr. N.Y. State Maritime Coll., Ft. Schuyler, 1962-64; libr. cons. Mid-Hudson Librs., Poughkeepsie, N.Y., 1964-66; libr. dir. Hebrew Coll., Brookline, Mass., 1966—; book appraiser, Auburndale, Mass., 1980—; book reviewer Libr. Jour., 1970—. With U.S. Army, 1960-62. N.Y. Regents scholar, 1959. Mem. ALA, Assn. Jewish Librs., Coun. Archives and Rsch. Librs. Jewish Studies, Ch. and Synagogue Libr. Assn. (pres. 1974-75), Fenway Libr. Consortium (coord. 1980-82, treas. 1990—). Home: 16 Duffield Rd Newton MA 02166-1004 Office: Hebrew Coll 43 Hawes St Brookline MA 02146-5412 *It is our most difficult task and our greatest accomplishment to reach our potential as a thinking and ethical human being.*

TUCHMAN, PHYLLIS, critic; b. Passaic, N.J., Jan. 4, 1947; d. Jack and Evelyn (Sugarman) T. BA, Boston U., 1968; MA, NYU, 1973. Independent critic N.Y.C., 1968—; adj. lectr. Hunter Coll., CUNY, N.Y.C., 1976-79; vis. prof. Williams Coll., Williamstown, Mass., 1981-83; v.p. Art Table, N.Y.C., 1984-87; curator Six in Bronze Williams Coll. Mus. Art & Tour, 1985, Big Litte Sculpture, 1988, Drawing Redux San Jose Mus. Art & Tour, 1992. Author: George Segal, 1983; contbr. articles to profl. jours. Art Critics grantee NEA, 1978-79; vis. fellow Princeton U., NEH, 1980. Mem. Internat. Assn. Art Critics (Am. sect. pres. 1986-89). Home: 340 E 80th St New York NY 10021

TUCHMANN, ROBERT, lawyer; b. N.Y.C., July 7, 1946; s. Frederick C. and Hildegard (Jung) T.; m. Naomi R. Walfish, June 1, 1969; children; David, Paul. AB, Oberlin Coll., 1967; JD, Harvard U., 1971. Bar: Mass. 1971, U.S. Dist. Ct. Mass. 1971. Assoc. Hale and Dorr, Boston, 1971-76, jr. ptnr., 1976-80, sr. ptnr., 1980—; lectr. Mass. Continuing Legal Edn., 1976—. Pres. Project Bread-The Walk for Hunger, Boston, 1990—; mem. com. Oberlin Coll., 1990; chair Ctrl. Artery Environ. Oversight Com., 1992—; mem. New Fed. Courthouse Task Force, 1993—. Mem. Boston Bar Assn. (com. chairperson 1977-81), Mass. Conveyancers Assn. (com. chairperson 1984-89), Abstract Club. Office: Hale and Dorr 60 State St Boston MA 02109-1803

TUCK, EDWARD HALLAM, lawyer; b. Brussels, June 27, 1927; s. William Hallam and Hilda (Bunge) T.; m. Liliane Solmsen, June 8, 1978; children by previous marriage—Edward, Jessica, Matthew. B.A., Princeton U., 1950; LL.B., Harvard Law Sch., 1953. Bar: N.Y. Assoc. Shearman & Sterling, N.Y.C., 1953-62, ptnr., 1962-86, of counsel, 1986—; bd. dirs. The French-Am. Found.; bd. dirs. Lafarge Corp., Comml. Bank. Bd. dirs. Belgian Am. Ednl. Found., Fgn. Policy Discussion Group, Am. Assn. for Internat. Commn. of Jurists; trustee French Inst. Alliance Francaise; chmn. bd. North Country Sch., Inc., 1974-78, The Drawing Ctr., Gateway Citizens Com., 1972-74; pres. The Parks Council, 1970-74; chmn. N.Y. State Parks and Recreation Commn., City of N.Y., 1971-76. Served with USN, 1945-46. Mem. Assn. Bar City N.Y., Coun. on Fgn. Rels., Racquet and Tennis Club, The Brook Club, The Ivy Club, Pilgrims, Soc. of the Cin. Episcopalian. Office: Shearman & Sterling 599 Lexington Ave New York NY 10022-6030

TUCK, GRAYSON EDWIN, real estate agent, former natural gas transmission executive; b. Richmond, Va., May 11, 1927; s. Bernard Okly and Erma (Wiltshire) T.; m. Rosalie Scroggs, June 6, 1947; children—Janice Lorrain, Kenneth Edwin, Carol Lynn. B.S., U. Richmond, 1950. Payroll clk., cost clk. Gen. Baking Co., Richmond, 1948-51; jr. accountant Commonwealth Natural Gas Corp., Richmond, 1951-55; sr. accountant Commonwealth Natural Gas Corp., 1956-57, accounting supr., 1957-58, asst. treas., 1959-62, asst. sec., asst. treas., 1963-64, treas., asst. sec., 1965-77; treas. Commonwealth Natural Resources, Inc., 1977-81, CNG Transmission Co. subs., 1977-79; sec.-treas. Air Pollution Control Products, Inc., Richmond, 1970-73; asst. treas., asst. sec. Commonwealth Gas Distbn. Corp., Richmond, 1969-79; mgr. taxes and cash mgmt. Commonwealth Gas Pipeline Corp., subs. Columbia Gas System Inc., 1981-86; investor, realtor Bill Eudailey & Co., 1986—. Active Boy Scouts Am., 1965-69; bd. dirs. Henrico Area Mental Health Retardation Services, 1983-85. Served with USNR, 1945-46. Mem. Nat. Assn. Accts. (assoc. dir. 1963-64). Presbyn. (deacon 1958-86, elder 1986—, treas. 1968-70). Home: 2923 Oakland Ave Richmond VA 23228-5827 Office: 6401 Mallory Dr Richmond VA 23226-2911

TUCK, JOHN CHATFIELD, former federal agency administrator, public policy advisor; b. Dayton, Ohio, May 28, 1945; m. Jane McDonough; 3 children. BS, Georgetown U., 1967. Various positions as asst. to Rep. leaders Ho. of Reps., Washington, 1974-77, chief Rep. floor ops., 1977-81; asst. sec. to majority U.S. Senate, 1981-86, spl. asst. then dep. asst. to pres. for legis. affairs, 1986-87; dep. asst. to Pres. of U.S. and exec. asst. to chief of staff Office Chief of Staff, The White Ho., 1987-88; asst. to Pres. and dir. Office Chief of Staff, 1988-89; under sec. Dept. Energy, Washington, 1989-92; sr. pub. policy advisor Baker, Donelson, Bearman & Caldwell, Washington, 1992—. With USN, 1968-73, ret. capt. USNR, 1973-94. Office: Baker Donelson Bearman & Caldwell 801 Pennsylvania Ave NW Washington DC 20004-2615

TUCK, RUSSELL R., JR., past college president; b. June 9, 1934; m. Marjorie Gay Tuck; children: Russell R. III, Catherine Elizabeth. BS in Chemistry, Union U., 1956; MS in Biology, Vanderbilt U., 1957, PhD in Curriculum and Instrn., 1971; study, Wash. U., 1960-61. Instr. biology, asst. coordinator Korean Tchr. Edn. Program George Peabody Coll. Vanderbilt U., Nashville, 1957-59; tchr. biology, chmn. sci. dept. University City (Mo.) Sr. High Sch., 1960-63, from asst. prin. to prin., 1963-70; prin. Parkway North Sr. High Sch., St. Louis County, Mo., 1971-78; asst. supt. Parkway Sch. Dist., St. Louis County, 1979-81, assoc. supt., 1981-84; pres. Calif. Bapt. Coll., Riverside, 1984-95, pres. emeritus, 1995—. Contbr. articles to profl. jours. Bd. dirs. Opera Assn.; pres. Riverside County chpt. ARC, 1989-90; active Bapt. Ch., local hosp. assn. bd., local edn. com.; World Affairs Coun. Mem. Calif. Bapt. Hist. Soc. (bd. dirs.), Calif. Bapt. Devel. Found. (bd. dirs.), Am. Assn. Sch. Adminstrs., Inland Empire Higher Edn. Coun. (pres. 1987-88), Kappa Delta Pi, Phi Delta Kappa. Lodge: Rotary.

TUCKER, ALAN CURTISS, mathematics educator; b. Princeton, N.J., July 6, 1943; s. Albert William and Alice Judson (Curtiss) W.; m. Amanda Almira Zeisler, Aug. 31, 1968; children: Lisa, Kathryn. BA, Harvard U., 1965; MS, Stanford U., 1967, PhD, 1969. Asst. prof. applied math. SUNY, Stony Brook, 1970-73, assoc. prof. applied math., 1973-78, prof. applied math., chmn., 1978-89, SUNY Disting. Teaching prof., 1989—; vis. asst. prof. math. U. Wis., Madison, 1969-70; vis. assoc. prof. computer sci. U. Calif., San Diego, 1976-77; vis. prof. ops. research Stanford U., 1983-84; cons. Sloan Found., 1981-85; acad. cons. 40 colls. and univs. Author: Applied Combinatorics, 1980, Unified Introduction to Linear Algebra, 1987, Linear Algebra, 1993; assoc. editor Math. Monthly, 1977-81, Applied Maths. Letters, 1986—; contbr. 45 rsch. articles to profl. jours. Ga. U. Consortium Disting. Visitor, 1982; NSF grantee, 1972-86. Mem. Math. Assn. Am. (chmn. publs. 1982-86, editor Studies in Math. series 1979-86, v.p. 1988-90, chmn. ednl. coun. 1990—, Disting. Tchr. award 1994), U.S. Commn. Math. Instrn., Am. Math. Soc., Ops. Rsch. Soc. Am., Soc. Indsl. Applied Maths., Sigma Xi (chpt. pres. 1987—). Home: 36 Woodfield Rd Stony Brook NY 11790-1112 Office: SUNY At Stony Brook Dept Of Math Stats Stony Brook NY 11794

TUCKER, ALAN DAVID, publisher; b. Erie, Pa., Mar. 9, 1936; s. Meredith LaDue and Monica (Klocko) T.; m. Kiyoko Iizuka, Feb. 8, 1963; 1 child, Kumi Tucker. A.B., Princeton U., 1957. Assoc. editor Hawthorn Books, N.Y.C., 1964-66; editor John Day Co., Inc., N.Y.C., 1966-72; mng. editor David McKay Co., Inc., N.Y.C., 1972-75, v.p., 1975-78, exec. v.p., editorial dir., 1978-84; editorial dir. Fodor's Travel Guides, Inc., N.Y.C., 1978-84; producer, Penguin Travel Guides and other publs. N.Y.C., 1984-91; gen. editor Berlitz Travellers Guides, N.Y.C., 1991-95; sr. analyst Genesis Group Assocs., Montclair, N.J., 1995—. Served to USNR, 1957-60. Mem. Soc. Am. Travel Writers, N.Y. Travel Writers Assn. Office: 186 Riverside Dr New York NY 10024-1007

TUCKER, ALLEN BROWN, JR., computer science educator; b. Worcester, Mass., Feb. 19, 1942; s. Allen Brown and Louise (Woodberry) T.; m. Maida Somerville, Dec. 18, 1965; children: Jennifer, Brian. BA, Wesleyan U., Middletown, Conn., 1963; MS, Northwestern U., 1969, PhD, 1970. Asst. prof. computer sci. U. Mo., Rolla, 1970-71; asst. prof. computer sci. Georgetown U., Washington, 1971-76, assoc. prof., chmn., 1976-83; MacArthur prof., chmn. Colgate U., Hamilton, N.Y., 1983-88, assoc. dean faculty, 1986-88; prof. Bowdoin Coll., Brunswick, Maine, 1988—; dir. acad. computing Georgetown U., 1976-83; cons. in field, 1976—. Author: Programming Languages, 1977, 2d rev. edit., 1986, Text Processing, 1979, Computer Science: A Second Course, 1988, Fundamentals of Computing I, 1992, 2d edit., 1995, Fundamentals of Computing II, 1993, 2d edit., 1995; assoc. editor Jour. of Computer Langs., 1979—, Jour. of Machine Translation, 1986—; contbr. articles to profl. jours. NSF fellow, 1984-86, ACM fellow, 1994—, Fulbright lectureship, 1986, 92. Fellow Assn. for Computing Machinery (Outstanding Contbn. award 1991); mem. Computer Soc. of IEEE, N.Y. Acad. Scis., Sigma Xi. Democrat. Episcopalian. Avocations: squash, golf, jogging, music, travel. Home: 1 Boody St Brunswick ME 04011-3005 Office: Bowdoin Coll Dept of Computer Sci Brunswick ME 04011

TUCKER, ALVIN LEROY, government official; b. Bklyn., Sept. 7, 1938; s. Alvin Leroy and Alveria (Klune) T.; m. Jacqueline Twiggs, Aug. 27, 1966; children: Hazel, Pluma, Jacqueline, Alvin. BS, U. Md., 1965. CPA, Md.; cert. internal auditor, govt. fin. mgr. Auditor Dept. Army, Washington, 1965-67; dep. insp. gen. HUD, Washington, 1986-89; auditor Dept. Def., Washington, 1967-72, budget analyst, 1972-79, dir. tng. and edn., 1979-83, dep. asst. insp. gen., 1983-86, dep. comptr., 1989-94, dep. CFO, 1991—, chmn. concessions com., 1989—; mem. steering com. Joint Fin. Mgmt. Improvement Program, 1990-93; mem. CFO's Coun., 1989—, chmn. fin. sys. com., 1989—; mem. Fed. Acctg. Stds. Adv. Bd., 1991—. With U.S. Army, 1958-61. Mem. AICPA, Am. Soc. Mil. Comptrs., Assn. Govt. Accts. (nat. exec. com. 1993-94), Kiwanis (club pres. 1981-82, 86-87). Avocation: genealogy. Office: Undersec of Def (Comptr) Pentagon Rm 3E831 Washington DC 20301

TUCKER, ANNETTE BAUER, paleontologist; b. Phila., Aug. 29, 1942; d. Edward Ewing and Margaret (McConnell) Bauer; m. John Michael Tucker, Apr. 24, 1965; children: John Michael Jr., Jennifer Michelle, Jannette Mari. BS in Geology, Kent State U., 1985, MS in Geology, 1988, PhD in Geology, 1995. Rsch. asst. Kent (Ohio) State U., 1986-87, teaching fellow, 1988-92, temporary asst. prof., 1994—; summer intern Amoco Oil Co., Houston, 1988. Contbr. articles to profl. jours. Sec. Oaks of Aurora (Ohio) Assn., 1994-95. Amoco Found. Masters fellow Kent State U., 1987-88, Univ. fellow Kent State U., 1992, William B. Smith fellow Kent State U., 1994. Mem. Biol. Soc. Wash., Paleontol. Soc., Crustacean Soc., Sigma Xi (assoc.), Sigma Gamma Epsilon (pres. 1985-86). Avocations: golf, tennis, scuba, hiking, birdwatching, travel, piano. Home: 143 Royal Oak Dr Aurora OH 44202-8225 Office: Kent State U Dept Geology Kent OH 44242

TUCKER, ARLIE G., manufacturing executive; b. 1939. Pres. Haulpak Division, Peoria, Ill., 1964-90; with Komatsu Dresser Co., Lincolnshire, Ill., 1990-91, chmn., CEO, 1991—. Office: Komatsu Dresser Co 200 Tri State Intl Lincolnshire IL 60069-4407*

TUCKER, BOBBY GLENN, minister; b. Grand Saline, Tex., Sept. 11, 1954; s. Glen Burton and Edna LaFaye (Phillips) T. BS, Tex. A&M U., 1979; student, Southwestern Bapt. Theol., Seminary, Ft. Worth, 1980-83. Minister of music and youth First Missionary Bapt. Ch., Terrell, Tex., 1980; minister of youth Farley St. Bapt. Ch., Waxahachie, Tex., 1980-83; assoc. pastor First Bapt. Ch., Magnolia, Ark., 1983-86; youth ministry cons. Dept. Ch. Ministries Bapt. Missionary Assn. of Am., Waxahachie, 1986-87; exec. dir. Nat. Youth Dept. Bapt. Missionary Assn. of Am., Texarkana, Tex., 1987—; dir. Nat. Christian Youth Leadership Conf., Washington, 1984-87; trustee Found. for Christian Youth Leadership, 1983—; cons. to denominational curriculum com., 1987—. Named Outstanding Young Religious Leader, Jaycees, Magnolia, 1986, Outstanding Young Man of Am., 1976. Republican. Home: PO Box 871 College Station TX 77841-0871 Office: National Youth Dept PO Box 3376 Texarkana TX 75504-3376

TUCKER, BOWEN HAYWARD, lawyer; b. Providence, Apr. 13, 1938; s. Stuart Hayward and Ardelle Chase (Drabble) T.; m. Jan Louise Brown, Aug. 26, 1961; children: Stefan Kendric Slade, Catherine Kendra Gordon. AB in Math., Brown U., 1959; JD, U. Mich., 1962. Bar: R.I. 1963, Ill. 1967, U.S. Supreme Ct. 1970. Assoc. Hinckley & Allen, Providence, 1962-66; sr. atty. Caterpillar, Inc., Peoria, Ill., 1966-72; counsel FMC Corp., Chgo., 1972-82, sr. litigation counsel, 1982—. Chmn. legal process task force Chgo. Residential Sch. Study Com., 1973-74, mem. Commn. on Children, 1983-85, Ill. Com. on Rights of Minors, 1974-77, Com. on Youth and the Law, 1977-79; mem. White House Conf. on Children, ednl. svcs. subcom., 1979-80; chairperson Youth Employment Task Force, 1982-83; mem. citizens com. on Juvenile Ct. (Cook County), 1978-94, chmn. detention subcom., 1982-94; mem. econ. effects adv. com. Rand Inst. Civil Justice, 1990-92. 1st lt. U.S. Army, 1962-69. Mem. ABA, Am. Law Inst., Ill. State Bar Assn., R.I. Bar Assn., Chgo. (chmn. com. on juvenile law, 1976-77), Engine Mfrs. Assn. (chmn. legal com. 1972), Constrn. Industry Mfrs. Assn. (exec. com. of Lawyers' Coun. 1972, 1975-79, vice chmn. 1977, chmn. 1978-79), Mfrs. Alliance (products liability coun. 1974-95, vice chmn. 1981-83, chmn. 1983-85), Product Liability Adv. Coun. (bd. dirs. 1986—, exec. com. 1990—, vice chmn. 1991-93, chmn. 1993-95), ACLU (bd. dirs. Ill. div. 1970-79, exec. com. 1973-79, sec. 1975-77), Am. Arbitration Assn. (mem panel of arbitrators 1985—), Phi Alph Delta. Club: Brown Univ. of Chgo. (nat. alumni schs. program 1973-85, v.p. 1980-81, pres. 1981-86). Home: 107 W Noyes St Arlington Heights IL 60005-3747 Office: 200 E Randolph St Ste 6700 Chicago IL 60601-6436

TUCKER, CYNTHIA ANNE, journalist; b. Monroeville, Ala., Mar. 13, 1955; m. Michael Pierce, Dec. 26, 1987 (div. 1989). BA, Auburn U., 1976. Reporter The Atlanta Jour., 1976-80, editorial writer, columnist, 1983-86; reporter The Phila. Inquirer, 1980-82; assoc. editorial page editor The Atlanta Constitution, 1986-91, editorial page editor, 1992—. Bd. dirs. ARC, 1989-93, Families First, 1988—, Internat. Women's Media Found., 1994—. Nieman fellow Harvard U., 1988-89. Mem. Am. Soc. Newspaper Editors. Mem. United Ch. Christ. Office: Atlanta Jounal Constitution 72 Marietta St NW Atlanta GA 30303

TUCKER, CYNTHIA DELORES NOTTAGE (MRS. WILLIAM M. TUCKER), political party official, former state official; b. Phila., Oct. 4, 1927; d. Whitfield and Captilda (Gardiner) Nottage; m. William M. Tucker, July 21, 1951. Student, Temple U., Pa. State U., U. Pa.; student hon. degrees, Villa Maria Coll., Erie, Pa., 1972, Morris Coll., Sumter, S.C., 1976. Sec. of state Commonwealth of Pa., Harrisburg, 1971-77; nat. pres. Fedn. Democratic Women, 1979-81; v.p. Pa. chpt. NAACP, nat. v.p. bd. trustees; mem. nat. adv. bd. Nat. Women's Polit. Caucus; now chair Black Caucus Nat. Dem. Com.; mem., vice chair Pa. Black Dem. Com., 1966—; chair Women for Dem. Action, 1967—; founding vice chair Nat. Polit. Congress of Black Women, Inc., 1984-92, nat. chair, 1992—; sec., mem. Phila. Zoning Bd. Adjustment, 1968-70; vice chair Pa. Dem. State Com., 1970-76; mem. exec. com. Dem. Nat. Com., 1972-76; Dem. candidate lt. gov., Pa., 1978; v.p. Phila. Tribune Newspaper. Del. to White Ho. Conf. on Civil Rights; bd. dirs. Phila. YWCA, New Sch. Music, Martin Luther King Ctr. for Social Change; pres., founder Phila. Martin Luther King Assn.; mem. Commonwealth bd. Med. Coll. Pa.; bd. assocs. Messiah Coll.; founder, pres. Bethune-DuBois Fund. Recipient Svc. and Achievement award NAACP, 1964, Phila. Tribune Charities Ann. award, Cmty. Svc. award Opportunities Industrialization Ctr., Emma V. Kelley Achievement award Nat. Elks, 1971, Lincoln U. Nat. Leadership award, 1993, Cmty. Svc. award Quaker City chpt. B'nai B'rith; named Best Dressed Woman of Yr., Ebony mag., One of 100 Most Influential Black Ams., 1973-77; included in 1996 People mag.'s list of Twenty-Five Most Intriguing People. Mem. Nat. Assn. Secs. State (v.p.), Bus. and Profl. Women's Club, Links (dir.), Alpha Kappa Alpha (hon.). Home: 6700 Lincoln Dr Philadelphia PA 19119-3155

TUCKER, DAVID, newspaper editor. Sports editor Phila. Inquirer, now city editor. Office: Phila Inquirer 400 N Broad St Philadelphia PA 19130-4015

TUCKER, DON EUGENE, retired lawyer; b. Rockbridge, Ohio, Feb. 3, 1928; s. Beryl Hollis and Ruth (Primmer) T.; m. Elizabeth Jane Parke, Aug. 2, 1950; children: Janet Elizabeth, Kerry Jane, Richard Parke. B.A., Aurora Coll., 1951; LL.B., Yale, 1956. Bar: Ohio 1956. Since practiced in Youngstown, Ohio; assoc. Manchester, Bennett, Powers & Ullman, 1956-62, ptnr., 1962-73, of counsel, 1973-87; gen. counsel Comml. Intertech Corp., Youngstown, 1973-75, v.p., gen. counsel, 1975-83, also dir., sr. v.p., gen. counsel, 1983-87, sr. v.p., 1987-93; ret., 1993; bd. dirs. Bank One of Youngstown Ohio. Solicitor Village of Poland, Ohio, 1961-63; former chmn. bd., pres., trustee United Cerebral Palsy Assn., Youngstown and Mahoning County; trustee Mahoning County Tb and Health Assn.; former trustee, pres. Indsl. Info. Inst.; former pres., trustee Ea. Ohio Lung Assn.; trustee, former chmn. Cmty. Corp.; trustee, former pres. Butler Inst. Am. Art. With USMCR, 1946-48, 51-53. Mem. Ohio Bar Assn., Mahoning County Bar Assn. (pres. 1972, trustee 1970-73), Youngstown Area C. of C. (chmn. bd. dirs. 1979). Methodist. Home: 7850 W Garfield Rd Salem OH 44460-9274 Office: Comml Intertech Corp PO Box 239 Youngstown OH 44501-0239

TUCKER, EDWIN WALLACE, law educator; b. N.Y.C., Feb. 25, 1927; s. Benjamin and May Tucker; m. Gladys Lipschutz, Sept. 14, 1952; children: Sherwin M., Pamela A. BA, NYU, 1948; LLB, Harvard U., 1951; LLM, N.Y. Law Sch., 1963, JSD, 1964; MA, Trinity Coll., Hartford, Conn., 1967. Bar: N.Y. 1955, U.S. Dist. Ct. (ea. and so. dists.) N.Y. 1958, U.S. Ct. Appeals (2d cir.) 1958, U.S. Supreme Ct. 1960. Pvt. practice, N.Y.C., 1955-63; Disting. Alumni prof. and prof. bus. law U. Conn., Storrs, 1963—, mem. bd. editors occasional paper and monograph series, 1966-70. Author: Adjudication of Social Issues, 1971, 2d edit., 1977, Legal Regulation of the Environment, 1972, Administrative Agencies, Regulation of Enterprise, and Individual Liberties, 1975, CPA Law Review, 1985; co-author: The Legal and Ethical Environment of Business, 1992; book rev. editor Am. Bus. Law Jour., 1964-65, adv. editor, 1974—; co-editor Am. Bus. Jour., 1965-73; mem. editl. bd. Am. Jour. Small Bus., 1979-86; editor Jour. Legal Studies Edn., 1983-85, editor-in-chief, 1985-87, adv. editor, 1987—; mem. bd. editors North Atlantic Regional Bus. Law Rev., 1984—. With USAF, 1951-55. Recipient medal of excellence Am. Bus. Law Assn., 1979. Mem. Acad. Legal Studies in Bus., North Atlantic Regional Bus. Law Assn. Home: 11 Eastwood Rd Storrs Mansfield CT 06268-2401

TUCKER, FRANCES LAUGHRIDGE, civic worker; b. Anderson, S.C., Dec. 4, 1916; d. John Franklin and Sallie V. (Cowart) Laughridge; m. Russell Hatch Tucker, Aug. 30, 1946 (dec. Aug. 1977); children—Russell Hatch, Pamela Tucker (dec.). Student U. Conn., 1970, Sacred Heart U., Fairfield, Conn., 1977, 79, Fairfield U., 1978, U. S.C., 1984. Sec. to atty., Asheville, N.C., 1935-37; sec. to gen. mgr. Ga. Talc Mining & Mfg., Asheville, 1937-42; sec. engrng. dept. E.I. duPont de Nemours, Wilmington, Del., 1942-46. Chmn. radio com. D.C. chpt. ARC, 1947-48, bd. dirs., chmn. pub. rels. Westport-Weston Ct. chpt., 1968-73, mem. adv. coun. ARC Ct. Divsn., 1973-80, chmn. pub. rels., Hilton Head Island, S.C., 1981-84, 89-92, chmn. pub. rels. bloodmobile, Hilton Head Island, 1984-89; bd. dirs., mem. pub. relations com. United Fund, Westport-Weston, Conn., 1968-69, bd. dirs. Beaufort County chpt. ARC, 1982-87, 89-92; mem. media communications St. Luke's Episcopal Ch., Hilton Head Island, 1980-94, office vol., 1995—; with Hilton Head Hosp. Aux., 1984-89. Mem. Sea Pines Country Club. Home: 13 Willow Oak Rd Hilton Head Island SC 29928-5926

TUCKER, FREDERICK THOMAS, electronics company executive; b. Herkimer, N.Y., May 27, 1940; s. Edmond and Martha R. (Rich) T.; m. Mary McDonald; children: Michael, Lisa. BSEE, Rochester Inst. Tech., 1963. Coop. student designer Delco Products div. Gen. Motors, Rochester, N.Y., 1960-65; salesman Motorola, N.Y., N.J., Conn., 1965-70; prodn. engr. Motorola, Phoenix, 1970-73, prodn. mgr., 1973-78, from ops. mgr. to v.p., div. ops., 1978-79, v.p., gen. mgr. power products div., 1981-84; v.p., gen. mgr. bipolar i.c. div. Motorola, 1984-87; corp. v.p., asst. gen. mgr. automotive and indsl. electronics group Motorola, Schaumburg, Ill., 1987-88; sr. v.p., gen. mgr. Motorola, Northbrook, Ill., 1988-92, exec. v.p., gen. mgr. automotive and inds. electronics group, 1992-93; exec. v.p., gen. mgr. automotive, energy and controls group, 1993—. Patentee in field. Bd. dirs. Jr. Achievement Chgo.; trustee Rochester Inst. Tech., 1986. Named Disting. Alumnus Coll. Engring., Rochester Inst. Tech., 1983; Alumni Honor Roll of Excellence, Rochester Inst. Tech., 1986. Mem. ITS Am. (chmn. bd. 1993). Republican. Lutheran. Office: Motorola Inc 4000 Commercial Ave Northbrook IL 60062-1829

TUCKER, GARDINER LUTTRELL, physicist, former paper company executive; b. N.Y.C., June 9, 1925; s. Ernest Eckford and Katherine May (Luttrell) T.; m. Helen Caldwell Harwell, July 24, 1954; children: Patricia Leigh Tucker Stroh, Gardiner Luttrell, James Busbee. A.B. with honors and spl. distinction in Math. and Physics, Columbia U., 1947, PhD in Physics, 1953. Dir. research IBM, Yorktown Heights, N.Y., 1963-67; dep. dir. research and engrng. U.S. Dept. Def., Washington, 1967-69, prin. dept. dir. research and engrng., 1969-70, asst. sec. def. systems analysis, 1970-73; asst. sec. gen. def. support NATO, Brussels, 1973-76; v.p. sci. and tech. Internat. Paper Co., N.Y.C., 1976-85. Contbr. articles to profl. jours.; patentee in field. Bd. dirs. Schola Cantorum of N.Y., 1985-91. Recipient Disting. Civilian Service award Dept. Def., 1972. Mem. Phi Beta Kappa, Sigma Xi. Democrat. Episcopalian. Home: 13 Quarter Mile Rd Westport CT 06880-1422

TUCKER, GARLAND SCOTT, III, investment banker; b. Raleigh, N.C., June 17, 1947; s. Garland Scott Jr. and Jean Smith (Barnes) T.; m. Greyson Conrad Shuff, Jan. 15, 1972; children—Greyson Carrington, Elizabeth Bradford. B.S. magna cum laude, Washington and Lee U., 1969; M.B.A., Harvard U., 1972. V.p. Tucker Furniture Co., Wilson, N.C., 1972-76; corp. fin. assoc. Investment Corp. of Va., Norfolk, 1976-78; v.p., to pres., chief exec. officer Carolina Securities Corp., Raleigh, N.C., 1978-88; v.p. corp. banking and fin. Chem. Bank, N.Y.C., 1988-90; pres. First Travelcorp., Inc., Raleigh, 1990—; Mem. N.Y. Stock Exchange, 1983-88; mem. regional firms adv. com. N.Y. Stock Exchange, 1984-87. Dir. Raleigh Rescue Mission, 1980-83; vestry Christ Episcopal Ch., Raleigh, 1981-84; bd. advisors NCO Investors, N.Y.C, 1991—; trustee N.C. Mus. Art Found., 1990—, Chatham Hall Sch., Penick Episcopal Home for Aging, 1992—, Trinity Episc. Sem., Pitts., FOCUS, N.Y.C. Mem. Carolina Securities Corp. (bd. dirs. 1979-88), Securities Industry Assn. (bd. dirs. Mid-Atlantic region 1981-82, 84-88, regional firms com. 1983-86), Raleigh C. of C. (bd. dirs. 1984-86), Phi Beta Kappa. Republican. Clubs: Capital City, Carolina Country (Raleigh); Harvard of N.Y.C., Roaring Gap Club. Home: 2327 Lake Dr Raleigh NC 27609-7667 Office: First Travelcorp Inc 4513 Creedmoor Rd Raleigh NC 27612-3815

TUCKER, GARY JAY, physician, educator; b. Cleve., Mar. 6, 1934; s. Isadore Martin and Blanche Hanna (Luftig) T.; m. Sharon Ruth Pobby, June 10, 1956; children: Adam, Clare. AB, Oberlin Coll., 1956; MD, Case Western Res. U., 1960; postdoctoral fellow, Yale U., 1961-64; MA (hon.), Dartmouth Coll., 1977. Diplomate Am. Bd. Psychiatry and Neurology. Asst. prof. psychiatry Sch. Medicine Yale U., New Haven, 1967-70, assoc. prof. psychiatry, 1970-71; with Dartmouth Med. Sch., Hanover, N.H., 1971-85, prof. psychiatry, 1974-85, chmn. dept., 1978-85; prof., chmn. psychiatry and behavioral scis. Sch. Med. U. Wash., Seattle, 1985—; bd. dirs. Am. Bd. Psychiatry and Neurology. Co-author: Rational Hospital Psychiatry, 1974, Behavioral Neurology, 1985; contbr. articles to profl. jours. Lt. Commdr. USN, 1964-67. Fellow Am. Psychiat. Assn.; mem. W. Coast Coll. Biol. Psychiatry, Sigma Xi, Alpha Omega Alpha. Democrat. Jewish. Avocations: photography, motorcycles. Office: Univ of Washington Dept of Psychiatry RP-10 Seattle WA 98195

TUCKER, H. RICHARD, oil company executive; b. Streator, Ill., Oct. 2, 1936; s. H.L. and Dorothy A. (Miller) T.; children by previous marriage: Randall R., Brian A.; m. Cheryl L. Kirk, Jan. 14, 1984. BS in Chem. Engring., Purdue U., 1958; MBA, Northwestern U., 1962. Project engr. crude oil supply Amoco Corp., Chgo., 1958-64, specialist product supply, 1965-66, coord. fgn. crude oil supply, 1967-68; coord. orgn. planning Amoco Internat. Corp., Chgo., 1969-70; coord. orgn. planning Amoco Corp., Chgo., 1970-72, mgr. adminstrv. svcs., 1972-84, mgr. real estate svcs., 1984-86, coord. spl. studies, 1986-89, dir. quality mgmt., 1989-92; mgr. cost mgmt., 1992-94; v.p. Amoco Realty Co., 1984-91, Amoco Devel. Co., 1984-91. Mem. adv. com. Sch. Bd. Wheaton, Ill., 1966; mem. Citizen's Nominating Com., Wheaton, 1972; leader Boy Scouts Am., Wheaton, 1979-82; dir. Oak Brook Colony Condominium Assn., 1992-94. Mem. Westhaven Home Owners Assn. (pres. 1965-67), Phi Eta Sigma, Omega Chi Epsilon, Beta Gamma Sigma, Tau Beta Pi. Avocations: tennis, bridge, hiking.

TUCKER, HOWARD MCKELDIN, investment banker, consultant; b. Washington, Apr. 1, 1930; s. Howard Newell and Bessie Draper (McKeldin) T.; m. Julia Spencer Merrell, Feb. 1, 1952; children: Deborah, Mark, Alexander, H. David; m. Megan Evans, Aug. 17, 1979. BA, U. Va., 1954; MBA, NYU, 1956. CFA. Pension investment dept. J.P. Morgan & Co., N.Y.C., 1954-61; registered rep.-analyst Mackall & Coe, Washington, 1962-69; dir. internat. dept., analyst Legg Mason Wood Walker & Co., Washington, 1969-79; with Govt. Rsch. Corp./Nat. Jour., 1979-82, Potomac Asset Mgmt., 1982-91; ptnr., mng. dir. Capital Insights Group, Washington, 1992—; cons. County Natwest (Washington Analysis Corp.), 1985-90; bd. dirs. Monarch Enterprises, Inc., Uniflight, Inc., Sci. Mgmt. Assocs., Inc., Jeffrey Bigelow Assocs.; mem. task force on balance-of-payments U.S. Dept. Treasury, 1967—; co-organizer U.S.-Ger. Parliamentary Exchange, 1980-82; observer OECD, 1980-82; spl. overseas visitor Australian Govt., 1982. Author: Literature in Medicine; writer London Investment Jour.; contbr. articles to fin. jours. Trustee Nat. Cathedral Sch. for Girls, 1972-78; chmn. Missionary Devel. Fund Episcopal Diocese of D.C., 1974; vestryman Christ Episcopal Ch., Georgetown, 1962-65; mem. chpt. Washington Nat. Cathedral, 1966-72; del. Va. Republican Conv., 1968; dir. Washington Area Con. Chs., 1962-65; co-dir. Andover-Exeter Washington Intern Program, 1976-86; patron West Europe program Woodrow Wilson Ctr., 1985-86. Served with USNR, 1950-56. Mem. Washington Soc. Investment Analysts, Nat. Economists Club, Cogswell Soc. Clubs: Naval and Mil. (London), Nat. Press, Georgetown Visitation Tennis, Saints and Sinners, Dumplings Yacht Club, Beta Theta Pi. Home: 4 Potomac Ct Alexandria VA 22314-3821 Office: Capital Insights Group 1700 K St NW Ste 1200 Washington DC 20006-3817

TUCKER, JACK RANDOLPH, JR., architectural firm executive; b. Little Rock, Feb. 6, 1939. BArch, BA, U. Ark., 1963. Registered arch., Ark., Tenn.; cert. Nat. Coun. Archtl. Registration Bds. Designer, draftsman, field inspector U. Ark., 1962-64, 66-68; arch., planner Peace Corps, Tunisia, 1964-66; designer, project mgr. Roy P. Harrover and Assocs. Archs., Memphis, 1968-79; prin. Jack. R. Tucker, Jr., Arch., Memphis, 1979-82; prin., owner Jack R. Tucker Jr. and Assocs., Memphis, 1982—. Mem. Shelby County mayor's task force The Econs. of Amenity, 1983; pres. Downtown

Neighborhood Assn., 1984, also mem. exec. bd.; mem. exec. bd. Memphis Heritage; mem. selection com., mem. pub. works com. Center City Commn. Policy Com. Downtown Devel. Plan; chmn. Memphis Landmarks Commn.; bd. dirs. Greater Memphis State; mem. profl. adv. bd. U. Ark. Sch. Architecture; active Brooks Meml. Art Gallery, Downtown Transit Task Force, Union Ave. Task Force, Mud Island Found. Support Group. Recipient 30 awards for design. Fellow AIA (past pres. Memphis chpt., Francis Gassner award Memphis chpt. 1994). Office: 81 S Front St Memphis TN 38103-2905

TUCKER, JACK WILLIAM ANDREW, writer, film editor; b. Portland, Oreg., May 1, 1944; s. Admyrl Foster and Aileen Eloise (McDaniels) T. BA in English, Portland State U., 1964. Film editor MGM TV, Culver City, Calif., 1984-86, Cannon Film Group, Beverly Hills, Calif., 1988, Columbia TV, Burbank, Calif., 1988, Paramount Pictures, Hollywood, Calif., 1990—. Editor: (TV) Winds of War, 1982 (Emmy award nominee 1983), The Fifth Missile, 1986, 240-Robert, 1979, Flatbed Annie and Sweetpie, 1979, (films) Shogun, 1980, Salsa, 1988, They're Playing with Fire, 1983, Viper, 1988, Nightmare on Elm Street IV, 1988, Distortions, 1987, Diplomatic Immunity, 1991, Illusions, 1992, Double-O-Kid, 1993, A Million to Juan, 1994, Cinemeditor mag. Sgt. USAF, 1964-68, Vietnam. Mem. NATAS, Am. Cinema Editors (former bd. dirs., treas. 1993—).

TUCKER, JAMES RAYMOND, elementary education educator; b. Pueblo, Colo., Apr. 18, 1944; s. James George and Pauline F. (Sena) T.; m. Kathie Owens; 1 child, Brittany. BA, U. So. Colo., 1966; MA, U. No. Colo., 1990, postgrad., 1991. Tchr. Sinclair Mid. Sch., Englewood, Colo., 1971-93, Denver Pub. Schs., 1993—; co-dir. Nick Bolleteri Tennis Acad., Boulder, Colo., 1986; head tennis coach Englewood High Sch., 1971—. Sgt. U.S. Army, 1967-70. Mem. NEA, U.S. Profl. Tennis Assn., U.S. Profl. Tennis Registry, Internat. Platform Assn., Colo. Edn. Assn., Meadow Creek Tennis and Fitness, Colo. H.S. Coaches Assn. (Achievement award 1989, 92, Tchr. of Yr. 1973, 78, 86, Coach of Yr. 1986, 87, 90, 93, Franklin award 1988, 89). Home: 2316 S Harlan Ct Denver CO 80227-3962

TUCKER, JANET PIKE, employment agency owner; b. Mercedes, Tex., Aug. 21, 1944; d. Herbert McDowell and Marjorie Evelyn (Hale) Pike; m. Edwin Hal Tucker, Sept. 28, 1966; children: Stephanie Anne, Gregory McDowell. BA, Trinity U., San Antonio, 1966. Cert. tchr., Tex., N.Mex. Tchr. San Antonio Ind. Sch. Dist., 1966, Weslaco (Tex.) Ind. Sch. Dist., 1968-69, Farmington (N.Mex.) Ind. Sch. Dist., 1978-82; exec. dir. San Juan United Way, Farmington, 1982-83; co-owner Horizons Travel, Farmington, 1983-84; owner, pres. Temporarily Yours, Inc., Farmington, 1984—. Bd. dirs., v.p. Four Corners Opera Assn., Farmington, 1978-82; bd. dirs., div. head San Juan United Way, Farmington, 1984-85; bd. dirs. San Juan Coll. Found., Farmington, 1985—; pres. Anasazi Pageant Found., Farmington, 1988—; bd. dirs. FIDS/San Juan Econ. Devel. Svcs., 1986—; mem. N.Mex. Pvt. Industry Coun., 1987-92; bd. dirs. Assn. of Commerce and Industry. Named Citizen of Yr. C. of C., 1990. Mem. N.Mex. Assn. Pers. Cons., Nat. Assn. Pers. Cons., Nat. Assn. Temp. Svcs., Assn. Commerce and Industry, Nat. Fedn. Ind. Bus., Rotary (bd. dirs. Farmington chpt. 1989—). Republican. Methodist. Avocations: golf, skiing, reading, volunteer work. Office: Temporarily Yours Inc 111 N Behrend Ave Farmington NM 87401-8413

TUCKER, JOHN MARK, librarian, educator; b. Natchez, Miss., Oct. 25, 1945; s. Paul Marlin and Edith (Upton) T.; m. Barbara Ann Wilson, Mar. 22, 1968. BA, David Lipscomb Coll., 1967; MLS, George Peabody Coll. Tchrs., 1968, specialist in edn., 1972; PhD, U. Ill., 1983. Head libr. Freed-Hardeman Coll., Henderson, Tenn., 1968-71; reference libr. Wabash Coll., Crawfordsville, Ind., 1973-79; reference libr. Purdue U., West Lafayette, Ind., 1979-82, asst. prof. libr. sci., 1979-85, assoc. prof. libr. sci., 1985-89, sr. reference libr. Humanities, Social Sci. and Edn. Libr., 1982-90, prof. libr. sci., 1989—, libr. Humanities, Social Sci. and Edn. Libr., 1990—; grantee com. on instnl. coop. NEH, 1991-94. Co-editor: Reference Services and Library Education, 1983, User Instruction in Academic Libraries, 1986, American Library History, 1989; contbr. articles to profl. publs. Thomas S. Wilmeth grantee for innovative excellence, 1988, Frederick B. Artz rsch. grantee Oberlin Coll. Archives, 1991; Coun. on Libr. Resources rsch. fellow, 1990. Mem. ALA (chair Libr. History Round Table 1993-94), Assn. for Bibliography of History, Assn. Coll. and Rsch. Librs., Disciples of Christ Hist. Soc., Soc. for Historians of the Gilded Age and Prog. Era, So. Hist. Assn., Friends of Univ. Ill. Libr., Phi Kappa Phi, Beta Phi Mu. Democrat. Mem. Chs. of Christ. Home: 1055 Southernview Dr S Lafayette IN 47905-3797 Office: Purdue U Humanities Social Sci & Edn Libr 1530 Stewart Center West Lafayette IN 47907-1530

TUCKER, L. DAN, lawyer; b. El Dorado, Ark., Oct. 23, 1936; s. Floyd A. and Harriet Kathleen (Graves) T.; m. Katherine Washburn, June 21, 1958; children: Laurie Tucker Diaz, Dana Tucker Kleine. BS in Chem. Engring., U. Okla., 1959, LLB, 1962. Bar: Okla. 1962, Tex. 1972. Patent atty. Phillps Petroleum Co., Bartlesville, Okla., 1964-67, Monsanto Co., St. Louis, 1967-70; patent mgr. Monsanto Co., Texas City, Tex., 1970-74; ptnr. Hubbard, Tucker & Harris, Dallas, 1974-94, Harris, Tucker & Hardin, Dallas, 1994—. 1st lt. U.S. Army, 1962-64. Republican. Episcopalian. Avocations: fishing, hunting, traveling. Office: Harris Tucker & Hardin PC 2100 Galleria Tower I Dallas TX 75240

TUCKER, LOUIS LEONARD, historical society administrator; b. Rockville, Conn., Dec. 6, 1927; s. Joseph and Dora (Conn) T.; m. Beverley Jones, Mar. 27, 1953; children—Mark T., Lance K. B.A., U. Wash., 1952, M.A., 1954, Ph.D., 1957. Instr. history U. Calif., Davis, 1958; fellow Inst. Early Am. History and Culture, Williamsburg, Va., 1958-60; instr. history Coll. William and Mary, 1958-60; dir. Cin. Hist. Soc., 1960-66; asst. commr., state historian of N.Y., N.Y State Edn. Dept., 1966-76; also dir. N.Y. State Bicentennial Commn., 1969-76; dir. Mass. Hist. Soc., Boston, 1977—. Author: Puritan Protagonist, 1962, Cincinnati During Civil War, 1962, Cincinnati's Citizen Crusaders, 1967, Our Travels, 1968, Cincinnati: Students Guide to Local History, 1969, James Allen, Jr.: From Elkins to Washington, 1969, Connecticut's Seminary of Sedition, Yale College, 1974, Clio's Consort: Jeremy Belknap and the Founding of the Massachusetts Historical Society, 1990. Dir. Shaker Mus., 1967-74; dir. Am. Heritage Co., 1973-75. Served with AUS, 1946-47. Winston Churchill fellow, 1969. Mem. Am. Assn. State and Local History (pres. 1972-74). Home: 11 Colburn Rd Wellesley MA 02181-3019 Office: Massachusetts Historical Society 1154 Boylston St Boston MA 02215-3695

TUCKER, MARCUS OTHELLO, judge; b. Santa Monica, Calif., Nov. 12, 1934; s. Marcus Othello Sr. and Essie Louvonia (McLendon) T.; m. Indira Hale, May 29, 1965; 1 child, Angelique. BA, U. So. Calif., 1956; JD, Howard U., 1960. Bar: Calif. 1962, U.S. Dist. Ct. (cen. dist.) Calif. 1962, U.S. Ct. Appeals (9th cir.) 1965, U.S. Ct. Internat. Trade 1970, U.S. Supreme Ct. 1971. Pvt. practice, Santa Monica, 1962-63, 67-74; dep. atty. City of Santa Monica, 1963-65; asst. atty. U.S. Dist. Ct. (Cen. Dist.) Calif., 1965-67; commr. L.A. Superior Ct., 1974-76; judge mcpl. ct. Long Beach (Calif.) Jud. Dist., 1976-85; judge superior ct. L.A. Jud. Dist., 1985—; supervising judge L.A. County Dependency Ct. L.A. Superior Ct., 1991-92, presiding judge Juvenile divsn., 1993-94; asst. prof. law Pacific U., Long Beach, 1984, 86; justice pro tem U.S. Ct. Appeals (2d cir.), 1981; exec. com. Superior Ct. of L.A. County, 1995—. Mem. editorial staff Howard U. Law Sch. Jour., 1959-60. Pres. Community Rehab. Industries Found., Long Beach, 1983-86, Legal Aid Found., L.A., 1976-77; bd. dirs. Long Beach coun. Boy Scouts Am., 1978-92. With U.S. Army, 1960-66. Named Judge of Yr. Juvenile Cts. Bar Assn., 1986, Disting. Jurist Long Beach Trial Trauma Coun., 1987, Honoree in Law Handy Community Ctr., L.A., 1987, Bernard S. Jefferson Jurist of Yr. John M. Langston Bar Assn. Black Lawyers, 1990, Judge of Yr. Long Beach Bar Assn., 1993; recipient award for Law-Related Edn. Constl. Rights Found./L.A. County Bar Assn., 1992. Mem. ABA, Calif. Judges Assn. (chmn. juvenile law com. 1986-87), Langston Bar Assn. (pres. bd. dirs. 1972, 73), Calif. Assn. Black Lawyers, Santa Monica Bay Dist. Bar Assn. (treas. 1969-71), Am. Inns of Ct., Selden Soc. Avocations: comparative law, traveling. Office: 201 Centre Plaza Dr Ste 3 Monterey Park CA 91754-2142

TUCKER, MICHAEL, actor; b. Balt., Feb. 6, 1944; m. Jill Eikenberry, 1973. Grad., Carnegie-Mellon Univ., 1966. Theatre appearances include Long Wharf Theatre, Milw. Repertory Theatre, 1960's, Arena Stage, Washington, 1970, N.Y. Shakespeare Fest. prodn. of A Comedy of Errors, 1976; Broadway appearances include Trelawney of the Wells, Moonchildren, The Goodbye People; feature films include Purple Rose of Cairo, Diner, An Unmarried Woman, The Eyes of Laura Mars, Radio Days, Tin Men, Checking Out, For Love or Money, D2: The Mighty Ducks; TV work includes regular role on series L.A. Law, NBC; also TV movies Assault and Matrimony, Day One, Spy, Too Young to Die?, Casey's Gift: For Love of a Child, The Secret Life of Archie's Wife, In the Nick of Time, A Town Torn Apart. Office: Artist Group 10100 Santa Monica Blvd Ste 2490 Los Angeles CA 90067*

TUCKER, MICHAEL, elementary school principal. Prin. Grace Abbott Elem. Sch., Omaha. Recipient Elem. Sch. Recognition award U.S. Dept. Edn., 1989-90. Office: Grace Abbott Elem Sch 1313 N 156th St Omaha NE 68118-2371

TUCKER, MICHAEL LANE, lawyer; b. Feb. 13, 1955; s. Robert Lane and Bonnie Jean (Childers) T.; m. Paula Jane Arrowood, Nov. 22, 1975; children: Melissa, Amy, Laura. BA in Polit. Sci., Wright State U., 1977; JD, U. Dayton, 1980. Bar: Ohio 1980, U.S. Dist. Ct. (so. dist.) 1980, U.S. Ct. Appeals (6th cir.) 1988. Assoc. Brannon & Cox Law Offices, Dayton, Ohio, 1980-84, Brannon & Hall Law Offices, Dayton, 1984-87; ptnr. Brannon, Hall & Tucker, Dayton, 1987-90, Hall, Tucker & Fullenkamp, Dayton, 1990-93, Hall, Tucker, Fullenkamp & Singer, Dayton, 1993—. Office: Hall Tucker Fullenkamp & Singer 131 N Ludlow St Ste 1000 Dayton OH 45402-1104

TUCKER, PAUL WILLIAM, retired petroleum company executive; b. Liberty, Mo., Dec. 21, 1921; s. Nova William and Georgia May (Cuthbertson) T.; m. Beverly Caryl Livingston, June 2, 1943; children: Ann Caryl Tucker Worland, Linda Tucker Smith. B.S., William Jewell Coll., 1942, LL.D., 1968, DSc, 1992; M.S. in Chemistry, La. State U., 1944; Ph.D. in Chemistry, (George Breon fellow), U. Mo., 1948; postgrad., U. Ill., 1946. Registered profl engr., Okla. Chemist, spectroscopist Tenn. Eastman Corp., Oak Ridge, 1944-46; chemist Phillips Petroleum Co., Bartlesville, Okla., 1948-49; tech. rep. Phillips Petroleum Co., 1949-60, asst. dir. public affairs, 1960-62; mng. dir. U.K. Ltd., London, 1962-68; v.p. gas and gas liquids U.K. Ltd., Europe-Africa, London, 1969-73; v.p. gas and gas liquids public affairs and govt. relations Europe-Africa, London, 1973-74; mgr. internat. gas and gas liquids Bartlesville, 1974-78; v.p. gas and gas liquids div., natural resources group, 1978-80, v.p. gas and gas liquids group, 1980-85. Contbr. articles to profl. jours. Recipient Disting. Services award N.Mex. Petroleum Industries Com., 1956, Citation of Achievement William Jewell Coll., 1979. Fellow Inst. Petroleum (U.K.), Instn. Gas Engrs. (U.K.); mem. NSPE (life), Am. Chem. Soc. (emeritus), Okla. Soc. Profl. Engrs., Hillcrest Country Club, Sigma Xi, Alpha Chi Sigma, Phi Lambda Upsilon. Republican. Baptist.

TUCKER, RANDOLPH WADSWORTH, engineering executive; b. Highland Pk., Ill., Dec. 3, 1949; s. Thomas Keith and Nancy Ellen (Jung) T.; m. Jean Marjorie Zenk, June 30, 1973 (div. 1991); 1 child, Nicholas Randolph; m. Lori Kaye Hicks, June 21, 1991. BS in Fire Protection Engring., Ill. Inst. Tech., 1972; M in Mgmt., Northwestern U., 1979. Registered profl. engr., Ill., Tex., Fla., La., Ga. With Ins. Svcs. Office of Ill., Chgo., 1972-74, bldg. insp., fire protection cons., 1972-74; with Rolf Jensen & Assocs., Inc., Deerfield, Ill., 1974—, cons. engr., 1974-77, mktg. mgr., 1977-81, mgr. Houston office, 1981-83, v.p. engring. mgr. Houston, 1983-89, v.p., tech. officer for Atlanta, Houston, N.Y.C., and Washington offices, 1989-90, sr. v.p., 1990-94, sr. v.p. internat. devel., 1994—; mem. adv. coun. Tex. State Fire Marshal, Austin, 1983-91; Dept. of Justice/Nat. Inst. Corrections cons. to Tex. Commn. on Jail Stds., 1993—. Editorial advisor Rusting Publs., N.Y.C., 1981—, Cahners Pub., 1993—; author articles in field. V.p. Juvenile Fire Setters Program, Houston, 1982-84; assoc. mem. Internat. Devel. Rsch. Coun., Urban Land Inst. Named one of Outstanding Young Men Am., U.S. Jaycees, 1981. Mem. AIA (profl. affiliate), Soc. Fire Protection Engrs. (chmn. nat. qualifications bd. 1985, pres. Houston chpt. 1983-84), Soc. Mktg. Profl. Svcs. (pres. Houston chpt. 1985, nat. pres. 1989-90), Nat. Fire Protection Assn., Internat. Conf. Bldg. Ofcls., Soc. Bldg. Code Cong. Internat., Inc., Bldg. Ofcls. Assn. Tex., Tex. Soc. Architects (profl. affiliate), Internat. Devel. Rsch. Coun., Houston C. of C. (vice chmn. fire protection com. 1983, govt. rels. com. 1984—), Aircraft Owners and Pilots Assn., Waller Country Club. Republican. Episcopalian. Avocations: flying, golf. Office: Rolf Jensen & Assoc Inc 13831 Northwest Fwy Ste 330 Houston TX 77040-5215

TUCKER, RICHARD BLACKBURN, III, lawyer; b. Pitts., Oct. 28, 1943; s. Richard B. Jr. and Alice (Reed) T.; m. Dorothy Dohoney, Aug. 24, 1974; 1 child, R. Wade. BA, U. Va., 1965; JD, Columbia U., 1968. Bar: Pa. 1970, R.I. 1971, U.S. Supreme Ct. 1984. Vista vol. Greater Kansas City (Mo.) Legal Aid & Defender Soc., 1968-69; atty. R.I. Legal Svcs., Providence, 1970-76, Tucker Arensberg, P.C., Pitts., 1976—. Active western Pa. chpt. Nat. Hemophilia Found., Pitts., 1976-82. Mem. Pa. Bar Assn., Allegheny County Bar Assn. (vice-chmn. appellate practice com. 1994-95, chmn., 1996—). Democrat. Episcopalian. Avocations: tennis, skiing. Home: 217 Edgeworth Ln Sewickley PA 15143 Office: Tucker Arensberg PC 1500 One PPG Pl Pittsburgh PA 15222

TUCKER, RICHARD LEE, civil engineer, educator; b. Wichita Falls, Tex., July 19, 1935; s. Floyd Alfred and Zula Florence (Morris) T.; m. Shirley Sue Tucker, Sept. 1, 1956; children: Brian Alfred, Karen Leigh. BCE, U. Tex., 1958, MCE, 1960, PhD in Civil Engring., 1963. Registered profl. engr., Tex. Instr. civil engring. U. Tex., 1960-62; from asst. prof. to prof. U. Tex., Arlington, 1962-74, assoc. dean engring., 1963-74; v.p Luther Hill & Assoc., Inc., Dallas, 1974-76; C.T. Wells prof. project mgmt. U. Tex., Austin, from 1976, dir. Constrn. Industry Inst., from 1983, dir. Constrn. Engring. and Project Mgmt. Program, 1976—; pres. Tucker and Tucker Cons., Inc., Austin, 1976—. Contbr. numerous articles and papers to profl. jours. Recipient Erwin C. Perry award, Coll. Engring., U. Tex., 1978, Faculty Excellence award, 1986, Joe J. King Profl. Engring. Achievement award, 1990, Disting. Engring. Grad., 1994; Ronald Reagan award for Individual Initiative, Constrn. Industry Inst., 1991; named Outstanding Young Engr., Tex. Soc. Profl. Engrs., 1965, Outstanding Young Man, City of Arlington, 1967; Michael Scott Endowed Rsch. fellow Inst. for Constructive Capitalism, 1990-91. Fellow ASCE (R.L. Peurifoy award 1986, Thomas Fitch Rowland prize 1987, Tex. sect. award of honor 1990); mem. NSPE (Constrn. Engring. Educator award of the Profl. Engrs. in Constrn. 1993), Nat. Acad. Engring., NRC, Soc. Am. Mil. Engrs., The Moles (hon.). Baptist. Office: Univ Tex Coll Engring Constrn Industry Inst 3208 Red River St Ste 300 Austin TX 78705-2650

TUCKER, RICHARD LEE, financial executive; b. Boston, Jan. 16, 1940; s. Frank Lee and Dorothy (Mansell) T.; m. Melinda Nichols, 1970 (div. 1987); children: Anne P., John M.; m. Elizabeth M. Lyne, 1988; children: Christopher B., William M. AB, Harvard U., 1962. CFA. Portfolio mgr. Scudder Stevens & Clark, Boston, 1963-72, v.p. investments, 1972-80; sr. v.p., mgr. trust div. The Boston Co., 1980-86; supervising portfolio mgr., v.p. Trinity Investment Mgmt. Corp., Boston, 1986—, mng. dir., 1992—; dir. Data Gen. Corp., 1994—. Trustee Phillips Exeter (N.H.) Acad., 1975-86. Served with U.S. Army, 1962-63. Mem. Inst. Chartered Fin. Analysts, Somerset Club (pres.), The Country Club (Brookline). Home: 23 Woodman Rd Chestnut Hill MA 02167-1221 Office: Trinity Investment Mgmt 75 Park Plz Boston MA 02116-3934

TUCKER, ROBERT DENNARD, health care products executive; b. Tifton, Ga., July 18, 1933; s. Robert Buck and Ethel Margaret (Dennard) T.; m. Peggy Angelyn Smith, June 23, 1957; children: Robert Barron, Jennifer Lee. BBA, Ga. State U., 1958. With sales and sales mgmt. Johnson & Johnson Inc., New Brunswick, N.J., 1958-68; v.p., gen. mgr. ASR Med. Industries, N.Y.C., 1968-72, Howmedica Suture div. Pfizer Inc., N.Y.C., 1972-75; exec. v.p., chief operating officer R. P. Scherer Corp., Detroit, 1976-79; pres., chief operating officer Scherer Sci. Inc., Atlanta, 1980-95, also bd. dirs.; chmn., chief exec. officer Scherer Health Care Inc., Atlanta, 1980-95, also bd. dirs.; bd. dirs. Nat. Travel Mgmt., Atlanta Biofor Inc., Waverly, Pa., Clean Air Corp. Am., Atlanta, U.S. Environ. Compliance Corp., Atlanta, Body Care Inc., Atlanta; chmn., CEO Throwleigh Techs., LLC, 1995—. Pub: Tuckers of Devon, 1983; author, pub.: Descendants of William Tucker of Throwleigh, Devon. Chmn. bd. Health Industries Mfrs. Assn. polit. action com., Washington, 1983-85; trustee, past pres. Ga. Horse Found., Atlanta; trustee Brenau Coll., Gainesville, Ga., 1985—. Served with USN, 1951-54, Korea. Decorated Knight of Malta, Imperial Russian Order of St. John; recipient Disting. Service award Brenau Coll., 1987. Mem. Nat. Assn. Mfrs., Health Industries Mfrs. Assn. (bd. dirs. 1979-86, disting. service recognition 1981, 86), Pharm. Mfrs. Assn., Thoroughbred Owners and Breeders Assn. Ky. and Ga. (Man of Yr. 1984). Republican. Methodist. Clubs: Cherokee (Atlanta); Big Canoe (Ga.). Avocations: scuba diving, tennis, genealogical research. Home: 405 Townsend Pl NW Atlanta GA 30327-3037 Office: Scherer Healthcare Inc 2859 Paces Ferry Rd NW Ste 300 Atlanta GA 30339-5701

TUCKER, SHIRLEY LOIS COTTER, botany educator, researcher; b. St. Paul, Apr. 4, 1927; d. Ralph U. and Myra C. (Knutson) Cotter; m. Kenneth W. Tucker, Aug. 22, 1953. BA, U. Minn., 1949, MS, 1951; PhD, U. Calif., Davis, 1956. Asst. prof. botany La. State U., Baton Rouge, 1967-71, assoc. prof., 1971-76, prof., 1976-82, Boyd prof., 1982-95, prof. emerita, 1995—; adj. prof. dept. biology U. Calif., Santa Barbara, 1995—. Co-editor: Aspects of Floral Development, 1988, Advances in Legume Systematics, Vol. 6, 1994; Contbr. more than 90 articles on plant devel. to profl. jours. Fellow Linnean Soc., London, 1975—; Fulbright fellow Eng., 1952-53. Mem. Bot. Soc. Am. (v.p. 1979, program chmn. 1975-78, pres.-elect 1986-87, pres. 1987-88, Merit award 1989), Am. Bryological and Lichenological Soc., Brit. Lichenological Soc., Am. Inst. Biol. Scis., Am. Soc. Plant Taxonomists (pres.-elect 1994-95, pres. 1995-96), Phi Beta Kappa, Sigma Xi. Home: 3987 Primavera Rd Santa Barbara CA 93110 Office: Dept Biology (EEMB) U Calif Santa Barbara CA 93106

TUCKER, STANLEY R., headmaster. Headmaster Girls Prep. Sch., Chattanooga. Office: Girls Prep Sch 200 Barton Ave PO Box 4736 Chattanooga TN 37405

TUCKER, STEFAN FRANKLIN, lawyer; b. Detroit, Dec. 31, 1938. Assoc. in Bus., Flint Jr. Community Coll., 1958; BBA, U. Mich., 1960, JD, 1963. Bar: U.S. Dist. Ct. D.C. 1964, U.S. Ct. Appeals (D.C. cir.) 1964, U.S. Ct. Claims 1964, U.S. Tax Ct. 1964. Clk. to judge U.S. Tax Ct., Washington, 1963-64; assoc. Arent, Fox, Kintner, Plotkin & Kahn, Washington, 1964-69, ptnr., 1970-74; ptnr. Tucker, Flyer & Lewis, Washington, 1975—; profl. lectr. law George Washington U. Nat. Law Ctr., 1970—; adj. prof. law Georgetown U. Law Ctr., 1990—; adj. profl. lectr. law U. Miami Law Ctr., 1975-78; mem. adv. com. Ann. Inst. Estate Planning, U. Miami, 1978-91; trustee Mass. Sch. Law, Andover, 1989—, chmn. bd. trustees, 1989-95; mem. visitors com. U. Mich. Law Sch., 1989—. Author: Tax Planning for Real Estate Transactions, 1989; mem. editorial bd. Taxation for Lawyers, 1972—; mem. adv. bd. Bur. Nat. Affairs Housing and Devel. Reporter, 1973-76, Mertens on Federal Income Taxation, 1985—, The Tax Times, 1986-87; mem. editorial adv. bd. Jour. Real Estate Taxation, 1975—, Practical Real Estate Lawyer, 1984—. Mem. nat. com. U. Mich. Law Sch. Fund, 1972-78. Mem. ABA (tax sect., chmn. real estate tax problems com. 1977-79, chmn. continuing legal edn. com. 1984-86, coun. mem. 1987-91, vice chmn. com. ops. 1991-93), Fed. Bar Assn., D.C. Bar Assn. (taxation div., steering com. 1980-82), Nat. Trust Hist. Preservation (com. legal svcs. 1978-85). Office: 1615 L St NW Ste 400 Washington DC 20036-5610 *I believe that each person has an obligation to share with others, whether through teaching, lecturing or writing, the knowledge and experience gained through his life's work. Such sharing provides a greater reward than monetary gain can ever provide.*

TUCKER, STEPHEN LAWRENCE, health administration educator, consultant; b. Cin., Oct. 18, 1940; s. Lawrence Henry and Blanche Virginia (Greenwood) T.; m. Lucille Frances Dinda, June 15, 1968; children: Gregory Lawrence, David John. BA, Dartmouth Coll., 1962; MBA, Xavier U., Cin., 1966; D Bus. Adminstrn., George Washington U., 1970. Adminstrv. asst. Presbyn.-U. Pa. Med. Ctr., Phila., 1966-67; assoc. adminstr. Harrisburg (Pa.) Hosp., 1970-73; assoc. prof. Xavier U., 1973-76; dept. chmn. Trinity U., San Antonio, 1976-81, prof. healthcare adminstrn., 1981-87, 94—, dean, 1987-94; cons. on healthcare adminstrn., San Antonio, 1976—. Co-author: Analysis Manual for Hospital Information Systems, 1980; contbr. articles to profl. jours., chpts. to books. Bd. dirs. Bexar County Mental Health and Mental Retardation Ctr., San Antonio, 1979-85; bd. dirs., chmn. S.W. Neuropsychiat. Inst., San Antonio, 1986-92. 1st lt. U.S. Army, 1962-64. Recipient Disting. Alumni Svc. award Xavier U., 1984; fellow Accrediting Commn. Grad. Edn. in Hosp. Adminstrn., 1974, WHO, Eng., 1975. Fellow Am. Coll. Healthcare Execs. (various coms. 1966—); mem. Soc. for Healthcare Planning and Mktg. (bd. dirs. 1983-86). Home: 347 Tophill Rd San Antonio OH 78209 Office: Trinity U Dept of Hlth Adm 715 Stadium Dr San Antonio TX 78212-3104

TUCKER, TANYA DENISE, singer; b. Seminole, Tex., Oct. 10, 1958; d. Beau and Juanita Tucker; children: Presley, Beau Grayson. Regular on Lew King Show; rec. artist formerly with Columbia Records, MCA Records, Capital Records; albums include Tear Me Apart, Chagnes, Delta Dawn, Dreamlovers, Here's Some Love, TNT, Girls Like Me, Greatest Hits, 1989, Greatest Hits (1972-75), Greatest Hits Encore, 1990, Greatest Country Hits, 1991, Greatest Hits 1990-92, 1993, Love Me Like You Use To, 1987, Strong Enough to Bend, 1988, Tanya Tucker Live, Tennessee Woman, 1990, What Do I Do With Me, 1991, (with Delbert McClinton) Can't Run From Youself, 1992, Soon, 1993, Fire to Fire, 1994, TV appearances include A Country Christmas, 1979, The Georgia Peaches, 1980; actress: (mini-series) The Rebels, 1979, (film) Jeremiah Johnson, 1968. Recipient: Country Music Assn. award, 1991, female vocalist of the year; 2 Grammy nominations, 1994. Office: Tanya Tucker Inc 5200 Maryland Way Ste 202 Brentwood TN 37027

TUCKER, THOMAS JAMES, investment manager; b. Atlanta, Sept. 5, 1929; s. Thomas Tudor and Carol (Govan) T.; m. Margaret Guerard. B.A., U. of the South, 1952. With CIT Corp, N.Y.C., 1957-72; pres., chief exec. officer AmSouth Fin. Corp., Birmingham, Ala., 1972-82; chmn. bd. AmSouth Fin. Corp., 1982, also dir., 1972-93; exec. v.p. AmSouth Bank N.A., Birmingham, 1982-93, chief credit officer, 1992; ret. Tucker Investments, Birmingham, 1993, prin., 1994—; exec. v.p. AmSouth Bankcorp, Birmingham, 1982-93; bd. dirs. Alabanc Properties Corp., Birmingham, chmn., 1991-93; bd. dirs. Birmingham Broadway Series Inc. Contbr. articles on credit and leasing to trade jours.; photographer gen. interest mags., 1970—. Bd. dirs. Birmingham Community Devel. Corp.; chmn. bd., 1990-93. 1st lt. USAF, 1952-56. Mem. Vulcan Trail Assn., Birmingham Art Mus. Assn., Birmingham Canoe Club (bd. dirs. 1990—), Photography Guild, Shades Valley Camera Club, Cahaba River Soc. (adv. bd. 1991-92, bd. dirs. 1993), Ala. Growth Strategies Task Force, Regional Open Space and Trails Alliance, The Club, Jefferson Club, Summit Club. Episcopalian. Avocations: photography, high altitude hiking, white water canoeing. Home and Office: Tucker Investments 4132 Old Leeds Rd Birmingham AL 35213-3210

TUCKER, THOMAS RANDALL, public relations executive; b. Indpls., Aug. 6, 1931; s. Ovie Allen and Oris Aleen (Robertson) T.; A.B., Franklin Coll., 1953; m. Evelyn Marie Armuth, Aug. 9, 1953; children—Grant, Roger, Richard. Grad. asst. U. Minn., 1953-54; dir. admissions, registrar Franklin Coll., 1954-57; with Cummins Engine Co., Inc., Columbus, Ind., 1957; dir. pub. relations, 1968-88; pub. rels. cons. Mem. Bd. Sch. Trustees Bartholomew County, Ind., 1966-72, pres., 1968-69; mem. Ind. State Bd. Edn., 1977-89; treas. Bartholomew County Rep. Cen. Com., 1960-80; mem. Columbus Area Visitor Info. and Promotion Commn.; chmn. Columbus 2000; trustee, chmn. ednl. policy com. of bd. trustees Franklin Coll.; bd. dirs. The Hoosier Salon. Mem. Pub. Relations Soc. Am., Columbus (Ind.) C. of C. (Community Service award 1986), Kappa Tau Alpha, Phi Delta Theta, Sigma Delta Chi. Lutheran. Lodge: Rotary. Home: 4380 N Riverside Dr Columbus IN 47203-1123 Office: Box 3005 Columbus IN 47202

TUCKER, WATSON BILLOPP, lawyer; b. Dobbs Ferry, N.Y., Nov. 16, 1940; s. Watson Billopp and Mary (Prema) T.; m. Ann Bryant Cramer, June 19, 1981; children: Robin, Craig, Christopher, Alexander, John. BS, Northwestern U., Evanston, Ill., 1962; JD, Northwestern U., 1965. Bar: Ill. 1965, U.S. Dist. Ct. (no. dist.) Ill. 1966, U.S. Supreme Ct. 1971, U.S. Dist. Ct. (no. dist.) N.Y. 1976, U.S. Ct. Appeals (7th cir.) 1970, U.S. Ct. Appeals (2d cir.) 1976, U.S. Ct. Appeals (3d cir.) 1981. Ptnr. Mayer, Brown & Platt, Chgo., 1965—. Fellow Am. Coll. Trial Lawyers. Office: Mayer Brown & Platt 190 S La Salle St Chicago IL 60603-3410

TUCKER, WILLIAM EDWARD, academic administrator, minister; b. Charlotte, N.C., June 22, 1932; s. Cecil Edward and Ethel Elizabeth (Godley) T.; m. Ruby Jean Jones, Apr. 8, 1955; children: Janet Sue, William Edward, Gordon Vance. BA, Barton Coll., Wilson, N.C., 1953, LLD (hon.), 1978; BD, Tex. Christian U., 1956; MA, Yale U., 1958, PhD, 1960; LHD (hon.), Chapman Coll., 1981; DH (hon.), Bethany Coll., 1982; DD (hon.), Austin Coll., 1985; LHD (hon.), Kentucky Wesleyan Coll., 1989. Ordained to ministry Disciples of Christ Ch., 1956; prof. Barton Coll., 1959-66, chmn. dept. religion and philosophy, 1961-66; mem. faculty Brite Div. Sch., Tex. Christian U., 1966-76, prof. ch. history, 1969-76, dean, 1971-76, chancellor, 1979—; pres. Bethany (W.Va.) Coll., 1976-79; dir. Justin Industries, Inc., Tandy Corp., Brown and Lupton Found.; mem. gen. bd. Christian Ch. (Disciples of Christ), 1971-74, 75-87, adminstrv. com., 1975-81, chmn. theol. edn. commn., 1972-73, mem. exec. com., chmn. bd. higher edn., 1975-77; dir. Christian Ch. Found., 1980-83; moderator Christian Ch. (Disciples of Christ), 1983-85. Author: J.H. Garrison and Disciples of Christ, 1964, (with others) Journey in Faith: A History of the Christian Church (Disciples of Christ), 1975; also articles. Bd. dirs. Ft. Worth Symphony Orch. Assn., 1980—, Van Cliburn Internat. Piano Competition, 1981—. Mem. Newcomen Soc. N.Am. Coll. Football Assn. (chmn. bd. 1993-96), Exch. Club, Phi Beta Kappa. Home: 2900 Simondale Dr Fort Worth TX 76109-1250 Office: Tex Christian U Office of Chancellor Fort Worth TX 76129

TUCKER, WILLIAM P., lawyer, writer; b. Kingston, N.Y., Jan. 26, 1932; s. Philip and Mary (McGowan) T.; m. Dolores F. Beaudoin, June 10, 1961; children: Andrew M., Thomas B., Mary A. BA with honors, Hunter Coll., 1958; JD with honors, St. John's U., 1962. Bar: N.Y. 1962, U.S. Dist. Ct. (ea. dist.) N.Y. 1962, Fla. 1980. Assoc. Mendes & Mount, N.Y.C., 1962-63; ptnr. Cullen and Dykman, Bklyn. and Garden City, N.Y., 1963—; gen. counsel Broadway Nat. Bank, Roosevelt Savs. Bank, Olympian Bank, GreenPoint Bank, Ridgewood Savs. Bank, Atlantic Liberty Savs., F.A., Bethpage Fed. Credit Union, Episcopal Health Svcs., Inc., St. John's Episocpal Hosp., Smithtown, St. John's Home for the Aged and Blind, St. John's Episcopal Nursing Home, Wartburg Luth. Svcs., Luth. Ctr. for the Aging, Martin Luther Apartments, Inc., Interfaith Med. Ctr.; spl. counsel OCI Mortgage Corp., FBG Mortgage Svcs., Bklyn. C. of C., Downtown Bklyn. Bus. Assoc., Marine Midland Bank, N.A., Bank of N.Y., Chem. Bank, Nat. Westminster Bank, Travelers Mortgage Svcs., Cititrust, North Fork Bank, Am. Express Credit Union, Mcpl. Credit Union. Mem. Selective Svc. Bd.; past pres. St. Vincent Ferrer Home Sch. Assn.; del. Diocesan Union Holy Name Socs.; mem. coun. St. Johns's U.; mem. coun. of regents St. Francis Coll., Bklyn.; bd. dirs. Faith Home Found. Mem. N.Y. State Bar Assn. (real estate exec. com.), Fla. Bar Assn., Savs. Banks Lawyers Assn. of Bklyn., N.Y. Land Title Assn., Suffolk County Bar Assn., Savs. Bank Assn. N.Y. State (law com.), Bklyn. Mpcl. Club, Knight of Malta. Avocations: co-owner Bellingham Giants baseball team. Home: 23 Bunker Hill Dr Huntington NY 11743-5705 Office: Cullen and Dykman 100 Quentin Roosevelt Blvd Garden City NY 11530-4843 Office: One Gateway Ctr Newark NJ 07102 also: 177 Montague St Brooklyn NY 11201-3633

TUCKER, WILLIAM VINCENT, vocational evaluator, former college president; b. Beatrice, Nebr., May 23, 1934; s. Casimir Augustine and Mary Margaret (Carmichael) T.; m. Marian Elizabeth Cooper, Aug. 9, 1958; children: Catherine, Jean, Rose Marie, Alan. B.A., Benedictine Coll., 1955; M.S., Emporia State U., 1963; Ed.D., U. S.D., 1968. Tchr. Kelly (Kans.) High Sch., 1958-61; grad. asst. Emporia State U., 1960-61, instr., 1961-63; instr. Briar Cliff Coll., 1963-65, asst. prof. ednl. psychology, assoc. prof., 1968-70, prof., 1970-71, acad. v.p., 1967-71; pres., prof. St. Mary of the Plains Coll., 1971-75; pres. Mt. Marty Coll., 1975-83; sr. devel. rep. State of S.D., 1983-84; pres. Greater Huron Devel. Corp., 1984-87; owner Career Devel., Inc., 1987—; cons. Social Security Adminstrn., 1962—; vocat. evaluator Goodwill Rehab., 1992—. Contbr. articles on ednl. rehab., placement of physically handicapped to profl. jours. Trustee Dodge City Area Hosp. Assn., Kans.; chmn. bd. Colls. of Mid Am.; pres. S.D. Found. Private Colls. Served with U.S. Army, 1955-57. Mem. Am. Econ. Devel. Council, Yankton C. of C. (dir.), Phi Delta Kappa. Roman Catholic. Clubs: Elks, Rotary. Home: 2605 W 37th St Sioux Falls SD 57105-5201

TUCKER-KETO, CLAUDIA A., academic administrator; b. Phila., Jan. 24, 1948; d. Arthur and Erma (Miller) Tucker; m. Clement T. Keto (div. 1993); children: Victor Lefa, James Lefanyana (twins). BA, Temple U., 1982. With adminstrv. office Pa. Supreme Ct., Phila.; coll. adminstr., family resource specialist Camden County Coll., Blackwood, N.J.; coord. women's programs Camden County Dept. Health and Human Svcs., Camden, N.J. mem. ethics com. Dist. IV Supreme Ct., 1993-95. Legis. chairwoman N.J. Fed. Dem. Women, Trenton, N.J.; mem. planning com. U.S. Dept. Labor Women's Bur. Region II, N.Y.; commr. N.J. Martin Luther King Jr. Organization, Trenton; bd. dir. N.J. Women's Summit, Sicklerville, N.J.; chairwomen Camden County Commn. on Women, N.J. Recipient Women in Bus. award Nat. Hookup of Black Women, 1992, Outstanding Svc. to Women award African Am. Women's Network, 1994. Mem. AAUW. Baptist. Home: 133-4 Kirkbride Rd Voorhees NJ 08043 also: Commn on Women Court House/ Adminstrv Bldg 5th and Market Sts Camden NJ 08104-1935

TUCKMAN, BRUCE WAYNE, educational psychologist, educator, researcher; b. N.Y.C., Nov. 24, 1938; s. Jack Stanley and Sophie Sylvia (Goldberg) T.; children: Blair Z., Bret A. BS, Rensselaer Poly. Inst., 1960; MA, Princeton U., 1962, PhD, 1963. Rsch. assoc. Princeton (N.J.) U., 1963; rsch. psychologist Naval Med. Rsch. Inst., Bethesda, Md., 1963-65; assoc. prof. edn. Rutgers U., New Brunswick, N.J., 1965-78; dir. Bur. Research and Devel.-Rutgers U., New Brunswick, 1975-78; dean Coll. Edn. Baruch Coll., CUNY, 1978-82; sr. rsch. fellow CUNY, 1982-83; dean Coll. Edn. Fla. State U., Tallahassee, 1983-85, prof., 1985—. Author: Preparing to Teach the Disadvantaged, 1969 (N.J. Assn. Tchrs. of English Author's award 1969), Conducting Educational Research, 1972, 4th rev. edit., 1994 (Phi Delta Kappa Rsch. award 1973), Evaluating Instructional Programs, 1979, 2d rev. edit., 1985, Analyzing and Designing Educational Research, 1979, Effective College Management, 1987, Testing for Teachers, 1988; (novel) Long Road to Boston, 1988, Educational Psychology: From Theory to Application, 1992. Rsch. dir. Task Force on Competency Standards, Trenton, N.J., 1976. N.Y. State Regents scholar, 1956; Kappa Nu grad. scholar, 1960; NIMH predoctoral fellow, 1961, 62; Rutgers U. faculty study fellow, 1974-75;. Fellow APA, Am. Psychol. Soc.; mem. am. Ednl. Rsch. Assn., Phi Delta Kappa.

TUCKSON, REED V., university president. Pres. Charles R. Drew U., L.A. Office: Charles R Drew U Office of President 1621 E 120th St Los Angeles CA 90059-3025

TUCKWELL, BARRY EMMANUEL, musician, music educator; b. Melbourne, Australia, Mar. 5, 1931; s. Charles Robert and Elizabeth (Hill) T.; children: David Michael, Jane Madeleine, Thomas James; m. Susan Levitan, June 21, 1992. Grad., Sydney (Australia) State Conservatorium; DMus (hon.), Sydney U., Australia, 1994. Prof. French horn Royal Acad. Music, 1962-74; mem. mgmt. com. London Symphony Orch. Trust, 1963-68; mem. faculty congregation arts Dartmouth Coll., 1968-69; guest prof. Harvard U., Yale U., others. With Melbourne, Sydney, Halle, Scottish Nat. and Bournemouth symphony orchs., 1947-55; solo French horn, London Symphony Orch., 1955-68; tchr., soloist and chamber music player, 1968—, mem. Chamber Music Soc. of Lincoln Ctr., N.Y.C., 1974-81, dir. London Symphony Orch. Ltd., 1957-68, chmn., 1961-68, mem. Tuckwell Wind Ensemble, Tuckwell Wind Quintet, Tuckwell Horn Quartet, chief condr. Tasmanian Symphony Orch., 1980, condr., music dir. Md. Symphony Orch., 1982—, res. artist for RCA, CRI, Angel, London, Argo.; author: Playing the Horn, 1978, The Horn, 1983; editor: Horn Lit. for G. Schirmer, Inc; leader ann. French horn workshop, Fla. State U., Claremont Music Festival, 1970-71. Decorated Order Brit. Empire; companion Order of Australia; recipient Harriet Cohen Meml. medal for soloists, 1968. Fellow Royal Coll. Music, Royal Soc. arts; mem. Internat. Horn Soc. (hon., pres. 1969-77, 92-94), Royal Acad. Music (hon.), Guildhall Sch. Music (hon.). Address: 13140 Fountain Head Rd Hagerstown MD 21742-2839

TUDOR, DONALD NORRIS, state government administrator; b. Raleigh, N.C., Mar. 15, 1947; s. Owen Shell and Rubelle Catherine (Norris) T.; m. Melba Elaine Buckner Spencer, Aug. 15, 1970 (div. Apr. 1988); children: James Dwight, Lauren Burdette, William Brandon Norris; m. Leah Annette McNeely, Apr. 2, 1994. BS, East Carolina U., 1969; MPA, Golden Gate U., 1976. Urban planner Gov.'s Office, Columbia, S.C., 1969-71; dir. planning orgn. Santee-Wateree Regional Planning Coun., Sumter, S.C., 1971-78; exec. asst. Inter-Agy. Coun. on Pub. Transp., Columbia, 1978-79; dir. transp. policy Gov.'s Office, Columbia, 1979-86; dir. trans. cons. Carter Goble Assocs., Columbia, 1986-90; pub. transit cons. Donald Tudor Assocs., Columbia, 1990-91; sr. exec. asst. for support svcs. S.C. Dept. Edn., Columbia, 1991—; charter chmn. Nat. Transp. Acctg. Consortium, Lansing, Mich., 1980-86; mem. bd. dirs. Southeastern Pupil Transp. Conf. Mem. adminstrv. bd. Shandon United Meth. Ch., Columbia, 1988-91, 93—; bd. dirs. Internat. Trade Conf., Charleston, S.C., 1982-92, Inter-Modal Transp. Program, Coll. of Charleston, 1982-92. Decorated Order of the Palmetto, Gov. of S.C., 1986; recipient ann. award Transp. Assn. S.C., 1986. Mem. AICP, S.C. Assn. Pupil Transp. (pres. 1995—), Nat. Assn. State Dirs. Pupil Transp. Svcs. Avocations: home repair, reading, travel. Home: 833 Adger Rd Columbia SC 29205 Office: SC Dept Edn 1429 Senate St Columbia SC 29201-3730

TUDOS, RUTH LILLIAN, retired nurse; b. Bridgeton, N.J., Sept. 19, 1922; d. Redmon Faucett and Helen (Wells) T. RN, Lincoln Sch. for Nurses, Bronx, N.Y., 1947; BA in Sociology, Marymount Coll., 1977. Head nurse Lincoln Hosp. and Mental Health Ctr., Bronx, 1947-94; retired, 1995. Vol. Ex Drug Addicts, N.Y.C., 1973-77, Ex Prisoners, N.Y.C., 1977-79. Recipient plaques Ednl., 1992, Lincoln Black History Com., 1994. Mem. N.Y. State Nurses Assn., Lincoln Sch. for Nursing Alumni, Marymount Coll. Alumni Assn., Alpha Kappa Alpha (philacter 1991-95). Avocation: collecting antiques. Home: 596 Edgecombe Ave New York NY 10032-4333

TUDRYN, JOYCE MARIE, professional society administrator; b. Holyoke, Mass., July 27, 1959; d. Edward William and Frances Katherine (Bajor) T.; m. William Wallace Friberger III, Sept. 18, 1982; 1 child, Kristen. BS in Comm., Syracuse U., 1981. Asst. editor Nat. Assn. Broadcasters, Washington, 1981-83; dir. programs Internat. Radio and TV Soc. Found., N.Y.C., 1983-87; assoc. exec. dir. Internat. Radio and TV Soc., N.Y.C., 1988-94, exec. dir., 1994—; spkr. in field; nat. adv. bd. Alpha Epsilon Rho Broadcasting Soc., 1988-91, 93-94, hon. trustee, 1994—; v.p. Corp. for Ednl. Radio and TV, 1988-94. Editor-in-chief IRTS News, 1983—; columnist TV Facts, Figures and Film mag., 1983-88. Recipient Mass. Kodak Photography award, 1977; S.I. Newhouse scholar Syracuse U., 1980-81. Mem. N.Y. Media Roundtable, Gamma Phi Beta. Avocations: photography. Home: 602 Bennington Dr Union NJ 07083-9104 Office: Internat Radio and TV Soc Found Ste 1714 420 Lexington Ave New York NY 10170-1799

TUELL, JACK MARVIN, retired bishop; b. Tacoma, Nov. 14, 1923; s. Frank Harry and Anne Helen (Bertelson) T.; m. Marjorie Ida Beadles, June 17, 1946; children—Jacqueline, Cynthia, James. B.S., U. Wash., 1947, LL.B., 1948; S.T.B., Boston U., 1955; M.A., U. Puget Sound, 1961, DHS, 1990; D.D., Pacific Sch. Religion, 1966; LLD, Alaska Pacific U., 1980. Bar: Wash. 1948; ordained to ministry Meth. Ch., 1955. Practice law with firm Holte & Tuell, Edmonds, Wash., 1948-50; pastor Grace Meth. Ch., Everett, Wash., 1950-52, South Tewksbury Meth. Ch., Tewksbury, Mass., 1952-55, Lakewood Meth. Ch., Tacoma, 1955-61; dist. supt. Puget Sound dist. Meth. Ch., Everett, 1961-67; pastor 1st United Meth. Ch., Vancouver, Wash., 1967-72; bishop United Meth. Ch., Portland, Oreg., 1972-80, Calif.-Pacific Conf., United Meth. Ch., L.A., 1980-92; interim sr. pastor First United Meth. Ch., Boise, Idaho, 1995; Mem. gen. conf. United Meth. Ch., 1964, 66, 68, 70, 72; pres. coun. of Bishops United Meth. Ch., 1989-90. Author: The Organization of the United Methodist Church, 1970, 7th edit. 1993. Pres. Tacoma U.S.O., 1959-61, Vancouver YMCA, 1968; v.p. Ft. Vancouver Seamens Cnt., 1969-72; vice chmn. Vancouver Human Rels. Commn., 1970-72; pres. Oreg. Coun. Alcohol Problems, 1972-76; trustee U. Puget Sound, 1961-73, Vancouver Meml. Hosp., 1967-72, Alaska Meth. U., Anchorage, 1972-80, Willamette U., Salem, Oreg., 1972-80, Willamette View Manor, Portland, 1972-80, Rogue Valley Manor, Medford, Oreg., 1972-76, Sch. Theology at Claremont, Calif., 1980-92, Methodist Hosp., Arcadia, Calif., 1983-92; pres. nat. div. bd. global ministries United Meth. Ch., 1972-76, pres. ecumenical and interreligious concerns div., 1976-80, Commn. on Christian Unity and interreligious concerns, 1980-84, Gen. Bd. of Pensions,1984-92, Calif. Coun. Alcohol Problems, 1985-88. Jacob Sleeper fellow, 1955. Mem. Lions. Home and Office: 2697 S North Bluff Rd Greenbank WA 98253-9713

TUERFF, JAMES RODRICK, insurance company executive; b. Gary, Ind., Jan. 17, 1941; m. Julie K. Luttinen; children: Brian J., Kevin A., Jeffrey J., Gregory S. BA in Econs., St. Joseph's Coll., 1963. CLU. Asst. v.p. Life and Casualty Ins. Co., Nashville, 1967-75; v.p. Commonwealth Life Ins. Co., Louisville, 1975-77; v.p. Am. Gen. Life Ins. Co., Houston, 1977-78, sr. v.p., exec. v.p., 1979-83; v.p. Am. Gen. Corp., Houston, 1978-79, exec. v.p., 1983-88, pres., chief exec. officer Gulf Life Ins. Co., 1988-90; pres., chief exec. officer Am. Gen. Life and Accident Ins. Co., Nashville, 1990-93, also bd. dirs.; pres. Am. Gen. Corp., Houston, 1993—; mem. adv. com. to bd. trustees, St. Joseph's Coll.; bd. dir. YMCA Greater Houston, Sam Huston Coun. Boy Scouts Am., St. Joseph Hosp. Found., Am. Coun. Life Ins. Fellow Life Mgmt. Inst. Soc. Houston (life). Republican. Roman Catholic. Office: Am Gen Corp 2929 Allen Pky Houston TX 77019-2197*

TUFARO, RICHARD CHASE, lawyer; b. N.Y.C., July 9, 1944; s. Frank P. and Stephania A. (Maida) T.; m. Helen M. Tufaro, June 25, 1977; children: Mary C., Edward F., Paul R., Cynthia M. AB magna cum laude, Dartmouth Coll., 1965; LLB cum laude, Harvard U., 1968. Bar: N.Y. 1969, D.C. 1992, Md. 1994; U.S. Dist. Ct. (so. dist.) N.Y. 1973, U.S. Dist. Ct. (ea. dist.) N.Y. 1978, U.S. Dist Ct. (D.C. dist.), 1994; U.S. Ct. Apls. (2d cir.) 1973, (5th cir.) 1976, (9th cir.) 1979, (6th cir.) 1980, (4th cir.), 1995; U.S. Ct. Claims, 1985, U.S. Ct. Appeals (3d cir.) 1990, U.S. Ct. Appeals (D.C. cir.) 1992; U.S. Sup. Ct., 1975. Law clk. Appellate-Div. N.Y. State, N.Y.C., 1970-71, assoc. Milbank, Tweed, Hadley & McCloy, N.Y.C., 1971-72, adminstrv. asst. White House Domestic Coun., Washington, 1972-73, assoc. Milbank, Tweed, Hadley & McCloy, N.Y.C., 1973-77, ptnr. 1978—. Served to capt. U.S. Army, 1968-70. Decorated Bronze Star with oak leaf cluster. Mem. ABA, Am. Mgmt. Assn., Phi Beta Kappa. Home: 7109 Heathwood Ct Bethesda MD 20817-2915 Office: 1825 I St NW Ste 1100 Washington DC 20006-5403

TUFT, MARY ANN, executive search firm executive; b. Easton, Pa., Oct. 11, 1934; d. Ben and Elizabeth (Reibman) T. BS, West Chester (Pa.) State Coll., 1956; MA, Lehigh U., 1960. Cert. assn. exec. Nat. trainer Girl Scouts U.S.A., N.Y.C., 1965-68; cons. Nat. League for Nursing, N.Y.C., 1968-69; exec. dir. Nat. Student Nurses Assn., N.Y.C., 1970-85; mem. Commn. on Dietetic Registration, Am. Dietetic Assn., 1981-85; pres. Specialized Cons. Ltd., 1983-85; exec. dir. Radiol. Soc. N.Am., Oak Brook, Ill., 1985-88; pres. Tuft & Assocs., Inc., 1989—. Bd. dirs. Nurses House, Inc., 1981-85; bd. dirs. Chgo. Sinai Cong., 1987-91, v.p., 1988. Mary Ann Tuft Scholarship Fund named in her honor Found. Nat. Student Nurses Assn.; Kepner-Tregoe scholar, 1966. Mem. ALA (pub. mem. com. on accreditation 1993-95), Am. Soc. AAssn. Execs. (bd. dirs. 1980-83, trustee for cert. 1980-83, vice chmn. 1983-84), N.Y. Soc. Assn. Execs. (pres. 1978-79, bd. dirs. 1975-78, 1st Outstanding Exec. award 1982), Continuing Care Accreditation Assn. (bd. dirs. 1983-85), Specialized Cons. in Nursing (faculty).

TUFTE, EDWARD ROLF, statistics educator, publisher; b. Kansas City, Mo., Mar. 14, 1942; s. Edward E. and Virginia (James) T.; m. Inge Druckrey. BS, Stanford U., 1963, MS, 1964; PhD, Yale U., 1968; HHD (hon.), Cooper Union, 1992, Conn. Coll., 1995. Asst. prof. pub. policy Princeton U., 1967-71, assoc. prof., 1971-74, prof., 1974-77; prof. polit. sci., stats., computer sci. and graphic design Yale U., New Haven, 1977—; pres. Graphics Press, Cheshire, 1983—; cons. in field; mem. com. on nat. stats. NRC, 1979-84. Author: Quantitative Analysis of Social Problems, 1970, Size and Democracy, 1973, Data Analysis, 1974, Political Control of the Economy, 1978 (Kammerer award 1979, Citation Classic 1989), The Visual Display of Quantitative Information, 1983 (Citation Classic 1992), Envisioning Information, 1990. Pres. Cheshire Neighborhood Assn., 1984-87. Recipient Best Graphic Design award Internat. Design, 1990, Wittenborn award, 1991, Best Book Design award Assn. Ind. Publs., Computer Press Assn. award, 1991, Sci. award Phi Beta Kappa, 1991; Ctr. for Advanced Study in Behavioral Scis. fellow, 1973-74; Guggenheim fellow, 1977. Fellow Am. Acad. Arts and Scis., Am. Statis. Assn. Office: Yale U PO Box 208301 New Haven CT 06520-8301

TUFTE, OBERT NORMAN, retired research executive; b. Northfield, Minn., May 30, 1932; s. Ole Nels and Stella Josephine (Lundene) T.; m. Doris Helen Wisbroecker, Dec. 29, 1956; children: Keith, Brian, Stephen, Jon. BA in Physics, St. Olaf Coll., 1954; PhD in Physics, Northwestern U., 1960. Rsch. scientist Honeywell Inc., Hopkins, Minn., 1960-69; rsch. mgr. Honeywell Inc., Bloomington, Minn., 1969-84; rsch. fellow Honeywell Inc., Bloomington, 1984-87, chief scientist, 1987-93; ret., 1994. Contbr. articles to profl. jours., 1960-88; inventor 7 U.S. patents, 1962-89. Mem. IEEE (sr.), Am. Phys. Soc., Sigma Xi. Home: 14937 Manitou Rd NE Prior Lake MN 55372-1114

TUFTS, DONALD WINSTON, electrical engineering educator; b. Yonkers, N.Y., Mar. 5, 1933; s. Fletcher Gorham Tufts and Myrtle (Ayers) Gordon; m. Barbara Michelsen, Mar. 24, 1956; children: Cynthia Tufts Anderson, David Jost, John Lawrence. MS; Diploma, The Hotchkiss Sch., Lakeville, Conn., 1951; BA, Williams Coll., 1955; BS, MS, MIT, 1957, DSc, 1960. Engr. Sanders Assocs., Nashua, N.H., summer 1960; cons. Sanders Assocs., Nashua, 1960—; asst. prof. applied math. Harvard U., Cambridge, Mass., 1960-67; prof. elec. engring. and computer sci. U. R.I., 1967—; cons. NASA, AT&T, others, 1966-75. Contbg. author books, papers in field. Chmn. East Greenwich (R.I.) Sch. Commn., 1976, 77; bd. dirs. East Greenwich Acad. Found., 1989-91. Recipient Bell Fellowship AT&T, 1957-60, Rsch. award URI, 1987, 90. Fellow IEEE (chmn. providence sect. 1985-87, 93—, CNEC div. 1990-91); mem. Assn. Computer Mach., Tau Beta Pi, Sigma Si, Eta Kappa Nu. Democrat. Unitarian. Achievements include four patents and one patents pending. Home: 490 Carrs Pond Rd East Greenwich RI 02818-1007 Office: Univ RI 199 Kelly Hall Kingston RI 02881

TUFTY, HAROLD GUILFORD, editor, publisher; b. Chgo., Sept. 1, 1922; s. Harold and Esther (Van Wagoner) T.; m. Barbara Jean Taeusch, Dec. 29, 1948; children: Christopher, Karen, Steven. BME, U. Va., 1949; postgrad., Sorbonne/Alliance Franciase, 1949-50. Corr. Tufty News Svc., Washington, 1946—; reporter Denver Post, 1949-51; European corr. Denver Post, Paris, 1951-52; pub. rels. Grant Advt., N.Y.C., 1953-55; info. officer U.S. Info. Agy., Madras, India, 1955-58, Bombay, India, 1958-59; pub. affairs officer, press attache U.S. Info. Agy., Conakry, Guinea, 1960, Abidjan, Ivory Coast, 1961-62; dir. French speaking African programs Peace Corps, Washington, 1963-64; pres. Tufty & Assoc., Washington, 1964—; bureau chief Tufty News Svc., Washington, 1984—; comml. pilot, single engine, land and sea, 1947—; mem. media staff conf. on civil rights White House, Washington, 1964; cons. U.S. Senate Com. Pub. Works, Washington, 1966-80; dir. The Ad Agy., Inc., Washington, 1970-78; pres. The Value Found., Washington, 1979—; congl. value engring. witness, testimony rschr., 1967—; presenter value engring. workshops in Bombay, Madras, Delhi, Hyderabad, Bangalore, and Calcutta; mem. U.S. Senate Press Gallery, 1980—, White House Corrs. Ann's, 1980—. Author: Compendium on Value Engineering, 1983, rev. 2d edit., 1989; editor, pub. Value Engring. and Mgmt. Digest, 1972—; columnist Interactions, 1988—. Nat. v.p. Soc. Am. Value Engrs., Washington, 1970-72; bd. dirs. SAVE Nat. Capital, Washington, 1964—, chmn., 1973—, congl. receptions; founding dir., asst. sec. Lower Cacapon River Com., 1995. Lt. USN, 1944-46. Recipient Capital Honor award SAVE, 1971, Disting. Svc. award SAVE, 1977-78, Fallon Value-In-Life award SAVE, 1994. Fellow Soc. Am. Value Engrs. (nat. pres. 1990-92); mem. Nat. Dem. Club. Avocations: reading, understanding my computer, haiku, chess, instructing sailing using aerodynamic principles. Home: 3812 Livingston St NW Washington DC 20015-2803 Office: Tufty Comm Co 2107 National Press Bldg Washington DC 20045

TUGGLE, FRANCIS DOUGLAS, management educator; b. Portsmouth, Va., Jan. 19, 1943; s. Francis Joyner and Florence Eleanor (Dahlgren) T.; m. Mary Ann Tredway, June 3, 1967; children: Wendy Elizabeth, Laura Michelle. SB, MIT, 1964; MS, Carnegie-Mellon U., 1967, PhD, 1971. Prof. bus. adminstrn. and computer sci. U. Kans., Lawrence, 1968-78; Jesse H. Jones prof. mgmt. Rice U., Houston, 1978-90; dean Kogod Coll. Bus. Adminstrn., Am. U., Washington, 1990—; bd. dirs. Equus II, Inc., Houston, Internat. Expert Sys. Inc., Houston; mem. coun. acad. advisors Bryce Harlow Found., 1994—; dir.-at-large Inst. for Ops. Rsch. and Mgmt. Scis., 1995. Author: How to Program a Computer, 1975, Organizational Processes, 1978. Com. chmn. United Way Tex. Gulf Coast, Houston, 1985-88. Ford Found. fellowship, 1966. Mem. AAAS, Inst. for Ops. Rsch. and Mgmt. Scis. (bd. dirs. 1995, v.p. 1992-94), Am. Assn. Artificial Intelligence, Assn. for Computing Machinery, Acad. of Mgmt., Sigma Xi, Beta Gamma Sigma, Alpha Kappa Psi. Episcopalian. Avocations: golf, bicycling, jogging. Home: 4709 Ft Sumner Dr Bethesda MD 20816-2466 Office: Am U Kogod Coll Bus Adminstrn 4400 Massachusetts Ave NW Washington DC 20016-8044

TUGGLE, JESSIE LLOYD, professional football player; b. Spalding County, Ga., Feb. 14, 1965. Student, Valdosta State Coll. Linebacker Atlanta Falcons, 1987—. Selected to Pro Bowl, 1992, 94. Office: Atlanta Falcons 2745 Burnette Rd Suwanee GA 30174

TUINEI, MARK PULEMAU, professional football player; b. Nanakuli, Hawaii, Mar. 31, 1960. Student, Univ. Calif., Univ. Hawaii. Offensive tackle Dalls Cowboys, 1983—. Selected to Pro Bowl, 1994; Dalls Cowboys Super Bowl Champions, 1992, 93. Office: One Cowboys Pkwy Irving TX 75063

TUKE, ROBERT DUDLEY, lawyer, educator; b. Rochester, N.Y., Dec. 5, 1947; s. Theodore Robert and Doris Jean (Smith) T.; m. Susan Devereux Cummins, June 21, 1969; children: Andrew, Sarah. BA with distinction, U. Va., 1969; JD, Vanderbilt U., 1976. Bar: Tenn. 1976, U.S. Dist. Ct. (mid. dist.) Tenn. 1976, U.S. Ct. Appeals (6th cir.) 1976, U.S. Ct. Appeals (4th cir.) 1978, U.S. Ct. Appeals (fed. cir.) 1993, U.S. Supreme Ct. 1986, U.S. Ct. Internat. Trade 1993. Assoc. Farris, Warfield & Kanaday, Nashville, 1976-79, ptnr., 1980-94; ptnr. Tuke Yopp & Sweeney, Nashville, 1994—; lectr. laaw Vanderbilt U. Law Sch., Nashville; mem. AMA Drs.' Adv. Network. Author: (with others) Tennessee Practice, 1992; contbr. articles to profl. jours. Mem. Tenn. Adoption Law Study Commn., Metro CATV Com.; chmn. Hist. Nashville, Inc., 1982; bd. dirs. March of Dimes, Nashville, 1983. Capt. USMC, 1969-73. Decorated Cross of Gallantry; Patrick Wilson Merit scholar. Mem. ABA, Nat. Health Law Assn., Nat. Assn. Bond Lawyers, Am. Acad. Adoption Attys., Tenn. Bar Assn., Nashville Bar Assn., Nashville C. of C. (chmn. govt. coun.), Order of Coif. Democrat. Episcopalian. Avocations: rowing, running, cycling, hiking, travel. Office: NationsBank Plz 414 Union St Ste 1100 Nashville TN 37219

TUKEY, HAROLD BRADFORD, JR., horticulture educator; b. Geneva, N.Y., May 29, 1934; s. Harold Bradford and Ruth (Schweigert) T.; m. Helen Dunbar Parker, June 25, 1955; children: Ruth Thurbon, Carol Tukey Schwartz, Harold Bradford. B.S., Mich. State U., 1955, M.S., 1956, Ph.D., 1958. Research asst. South Haven Expt. Sta., Mich., 1955; AEC grad. research asst. Mich. State U., 1955-58; NSF fellow Calif. Inst. Tech, 1958-59; asst. prof. dept. floriculture and ornamental horticulture Cornell U., Ithaca, N.Y., 1959-64, assoc. prof., 1964-70, prof., 1970-80; prof. urban horticulture U. Wash., Seattle, 1980—, dir. Arboreta, 1980-92, dir. Ctr. Urban Horticulture, 1980-92; cons. Internat. Bonsai mag., Electric Power Rsch. Inst., P.R. Nuclear Ctr., 1965-66; mem. adv. com. Seattle-U. Wash. Arboretum and Bot. Garden, 1980-92, vice chmn., 1982, chmn., 1986-87; vis. scholar U. Nebr., 1982; vis. prof. U. Calif., Davis, 1973; lectr. U. Western Sydney-Hawkesburg U. Melbourne, Victoria Coll. Agrl. and Horticulture, 1995; Hill prof. U. Minn., 1996; mem. various coms. Nat. Acad. Scis.-NRC; bd. dirs. Arbor Fund Bloedel Res., 1980-92, pres., 1983-84. Mem. editorial bd. Jour. Environ. Horticulture, Arboretum Bull. Mem. nat. adv. com. USDA, 1990—; pres. Ithaca PTA; troop advisor Boy Scouts Am., Ithaca. Lt. U.S. Army, 1958. Recipient B.Y. Morrison award USDA, 1987; NSF fellow, 1958-59; named to Lansing (Mich.) Sports Hall of Fame, 1987; grantee NSF, 1962, 75, Bot. Soc. Am., 1964; hon. dr. Portuguese Soc. Hort., 1985. Fellow Am. Soc. Hort. Sci. (dir. 1970-71); mem. Internat. Soc. Hort. Sci. (U.S. del. to coun. 1971-90, chmn. commn. for amateur horticulture 1974-83, exec. com. 1974-90, v.p. 1978-82, pres. 1982-86, past pres. 1986-90, chmn. comm. Urban Horticulture 1990—, hon. mem. 1994), Wash. State Nursery and Landscape Assn. (hon. mem. 1995), Internat. Plant Propagators Soc. (hon., ea. region dir. 1969-71, v.p. 1972, pres. 1973, internat. pres. 1976), Am. Hort. Soc. (dir. 1972-81, exec. com. 1974-81, v.p. 1978-80, citation of merit 1981), Royal Hort. Soc. (London) (v.p. hon. 1993—), Bot. Soc. Am., N.W.

Horticulture Soc. (dir. 1980-92), Arboretum Found. (dir. 1980-92), Rotary, Sigma Xi, Alpha Zeta, Phi Kappa Phi, Pi Alpha Xi, Xi Sigma Pi. Presbyterian. Home: 3300 E St Andrews Way Seattle WA 98112-3750 Office: U Wash Ctr Urban Horticulture Box 354115 Seattle WA 98195

TUKEY, LOREN DAVENPORT, pomology educator, researcher; b. Geneva, N.Y., Dec. 4, 1921; s. Harold Bradford and Margaret (Davenport) T.; m. Louise Arleyne Young, Feb. 2, 1952; children: David Davenport, Barbara Ann Tukey Shea. B.S., Mich. State U., 1943, M.S., 1947; Ph.D., Ohio State U., 1952. Asst. prof. pomology Pa. State U., University Park, 1950-57, assoc. prof., 1957-66, prof., 1966-91, prof. emeritus pomology, 1991—; fruit rsch. cons. Nat. Inst. Agrl. Tech., Argentina, 1965-70; rsch. cons. Instituto Interamericano Cooperacion Agricultura, Argentina, 1988; rsch. cons. cocoa Malaysian Agr. Rsch. and Devel. Inst., Malaysia, 1993. Editor: Pa. State Hort. Revs., 1962-91; assoc. editor: Jour. Hort. Sci. (Eng.), 1978-92; researcher numerous publs. in field. Bd. dirs. State College chpt. ARC, 1963-82; mem. Borough of State College Traffic Commn., 1976-80. Served to capt. Q.M.C., U.S. Army, 1943-46, ETO. Named Outstanding Horticulturist State Hort. Assn. Pa., 1986; recipient Milo Gibson award N.Am. Fruit Explorers, 1989. Fellow Am. Soc. Hort. Sci., AAAS; mem. Internat. Soc. Hort. Sci., Am. Soc. Plant Physiologists, Plant Growth Regulator Soc. Am., Am. Pomological Soc. (sec. 1968-74, Paul Howe Shepard award 1964, treas. and bus. mgr. 1968-89), Internat. Dwarf Fruit Tree Assn. (Svc. and Leadership award 1988), Academie d'Agriculture de France (corr.), Brit. Soc. for Plant Growth Regulation, Sigma Xi, Gamma Sigma Delta (pres. chpt. 1967-68), Phi Epsilon Phi, Theta Chi, Rotary (pres. State Coll. 1971-72, Paul Harris fellow). Republican. Presbyterian. Growth and development of tree fruits: growth regulating chemicals, environ. factors in fruit sizing, orchard productivity, intensive orchard systems and rootstocks. Developer of Penn State low-trellis hedgerow system for apple culture. Home: 549 Glenn Rd State College PA 16803-3473 Office: 103 Tyson Bldg University Park PA 16802-4200

TULAFONO, TOGIOLA T.A., senator; b. Aunu'u Island, American Samoa, Feb. 28, 1947; s. Aitu and Silika (Vaatu'itu'i) T.; m. Maryann Taufaasau Mauga, Sept. 17, 1984; children: Puataunofo, Olita, Cherianne, Emema, Timoteo, Rosie. Grad., Honolulu Police Acad., 1967; BA, Chadron State Coll., 1970; JD, Washburn U., 1975. Bar: Kans., Am. Samoa. Police instr. Am. Samoa Police Dept., Pago Pago, 1967; adminstrv. asst. Sec. of Samoan Affairs, Pago Pago, 1970-71; legal asst. Atty. Gen., Pago Pago, 1971-72; assoc. Law Offices of George A. Wray, Pago Pago, 1975-77; v.p. South Pacific Island Airways, Pago Pago, 1977-79; judge Dist. Ct. of Am. Samoa, Pago Pago, 1979-80; chmn. bd. dirs. Am. Samoa Power Authority, Pago Pago, 1978-80; mem. Am. Samoa Senate, Pago Pago, 1981-85, 89—; pres. Nayram Samoa, Ltd., Pago Pago, 1985-88; chmn. Senate Investigation Com., 1993—. Chmn. Bd. Higher Edn., Am. Samoa, 1993—; bd. dirs. Am. Samoa Jr. Golfers' Assn.; deacon Sailele Congrl. Ch. Mem. ATLA, Am. Samoa Bar Assn., Kans. Bar Assn., Samoa Profl. Golfer's Assn. (pres. 1985-87), Am. Samoa Golf Assn. (pres.). Democrat. Congregationalist. Home: PO Box Ppe Pago Pago AS 96799-9733

TULCHIN, DAVID BRUCE, lawyer; b. N.Y.C., Dec. 2, 1947; s. Philip Tulchin and Mary (Weiner) Black; m. Nora Barrett, Aug. 20, 1972; children: Rachel, Daniel, Laura. BA, U. Rochester, 1970; JD, Harvard U., 1973. Bar: N.Y. 1974, U.S. Dist. Ct. (so. & ea. dists.) N.Y. 1975, U.S. Ct. Appeals (2d cir.) 1975, U.S. Supreme Ct. 1977, U.S. Ct. Appeals (5th cir.) 1978, U.S. Ct. Appeals (1st & 6th cirs.) 1984, U.S. Dist. Ct. (no. dist.) Ohio 1984, U.S. Ct. Appeals (3d, 4th & Fed. cirs.) 1988, U.S. Ct. Appeals (7th cir.) 1991. Law clk. to Judge Frederick V.P. Bryan U.S. Dist. Ct. So. Dist. N.Y., N.Y.C., 1973-75; assoc. Sullivan & Cromwell, N.Y.C., 1975-82, ptnr., 1982—. Mem. ABA, Assn. Bar of City of N.Y., Fed. Bar Coun., N.Y. State Bar Assn., Fed. Cir. Bar Assn. Office: Sullivan & Cromwell 125 Broad St New York NY 10004-2400

TULCHIN, STANLEY, banker, lecturer, author, business reorganization consultant. Founder, chmn. bd. Stanley Tulchin Assocs., Westbury, N.Y., 1955-95; bd. dirs. N.Y. Inst. Credit, Topps Corp., PCA Internat.; founder, chmn. Reprise Capital Corp. Recipient Leadership in Credit Edn. award N.Y. Inst. Credit, 1990. Mem. Comml. Law League Am. (Pres.' Cup award 1975, past bd. govs., vice-chmn. bd. editors Comml. Law Jour., bd. dirs. Fund for Pub. Edn.), Nat. Assn. Credit Mgmt. Office: Stanley Tulchin Assocs 400 Post Ave PO Box 185 Westbury NY 11590

TULEY, RICHARD W., manufacturing executive. CEO Motor Wheel Corp., Okemos, Mich. Office: Motor Wheel Corp 2501 Woodlake Cir Okemos MI 48864

TULL, DONALD STANLEY, marketing educator; b. Mo., Oct. 28, 1924; s. Raymond Edgar and Ethel (Stanley) T.; m. Marjorie Ann Dobbie, May 15, 1948; children: Susan Margaret, David Dobbie, Brooks William. S.B., U. Chgo., 1948, M.B.A., 1949, Ph.D., 1956. Analyst U.S. Steel Corp., 1949-50; instr. U. Wash., 1950-52; mgr. adminstrn. N.Am. Aviation, 1954-61; prof. mktg. Calif. State U., Fullerton, 1961-67; dean Sch. Bus. Adminstrn. and Econs., 1966-67; prof. mktg. Coll. Mgmt. and Bus. U. Oreg., 1967-90, chmn. dept. mktg., transp. and bus. environment, 1967-69, 73-81. Author: (with P.E. Green and G.S. Albaum) Research for Marketing Decisions, 1987, (with G.S. Albaum) Survey Research, 1973, (with L.R. Kahle) Marketing Management, 1989, (with D.I. Hawkins) Marketing Research: Measurement and Method, 1993, Essentials of Marketing Research, 1994. Served to lt. (j.g.) USNR, 1943-46. Mem. AAUP (pres. 1978-79), Beta Gamma Sigma. Home: 2310 Trillium St Eugene OR 97405-1343

TULL, JOHN E., JR., federal agency administrator; b. Lonoke, Ark., Mar. 15, 1925; s. John E. and Nettie (Frohlich) T.; m. Mary Ybarrondo, Sept. 7, 1952; children: John E. Tull, III, Elizabeth Tull Landers, Mary Tull Eldridge. BS in Commerce, U. N.C. Apptd. commr. by presdl. nom. Commodity Futures Trading Commn., 1993—; mem., chmn. Ark. State Planning Bd.; pres. Ark. Rice Coun., Nat. Rice Coun.; chmn. bd. dirs. European subcom. Nat. Rice Coun.; chmn. Govs. Rail Safety Com.; mem. adv. bd. agr. Cattleman's Found.; mem. bd. dirs. Bayou Metro Irrigation Dist., U.S. Rice Found.; mem. adv. bd. First Comml. Bank Cabot, Ark. Lt. U.S. Navy. Mem. Ark. Seed Growers Assn. (pres.), Ark. Cattlemen's Assn. (pres.), Ark. Soybean Assn. (pres.), Trade's Rice Working Group (mem. chgo. bd.), Gamma Sigma Delta (hon.). Presbyterian. Office: Commodity Futures Trading Commn 2033 K St NW Rm 801 Washington DC 20581

TULL, THERESA ANNE, ambassador; b. Runnemede, N.J., Oct. 2, 1936; d. John James and Anna Cecelia (Paull) T. B.A., U. Md., 1972; M.A., U. Mich., 1973; postgrad., Nat. War Coll., Washington, 1980. Fgn. svc. officer Dept. State, Washington, 1963, Brussels, 1965-67, Saigon, 1968-70; dep. prin. officer Am. Consulate General, Danang, Vietnam, 1973-75; prin. officer Cebu, Philippines, 1977-79; dir. office human rights, 1980-83; charge d'affaires Am. Embassy, Vientiane, Laos, 1983-86; Dept. State Senior Seminar, 1986-87; ambassador to Guyana, 1987-90; diplomat-in-residence Lincoln U., Pa., 1990-91; dir. office regional affairs, bur. East Asian & Pacific affairs Dept. State, Washington, 1991-93; amb. to Brunei Bandar Seri Begawan, 1993—. Recipient Civilian Service award Dept. of State, 1970, Superior Honor award, 1977. Mem. Am. Fgn. Svc. Assn. Home: care Waldis 416 N Washington Ave Moorestown NJ 08057-2411 Office: Am Embassy Box B APO AP 96440 also: Am Embassy, Bandar Seri Begawan, Brunei Darussalam

TULL, WILLIS CLAYTON, JR., librarian; b. Crisfield, Md., Feb. 22, 1931; s. Willis Clayton and Agnes Virginia (Milbourne) T.; m. Taeko Itoi, Dec. 18, 1952. Student, U. Balt., 1948, Johns Hopkins U., 1956; BS, Towson (Md.) State Coll., 1957; MLS, Rutgers U., 1962; postgrad., Miami U., Oxford, Ohio, 1979. Editorial clk. 500th Mil. Intelligence Svc. Group, Tokyo, 1952-53; tchr. Hereford Jr.-Sr. High Sch., Parkton, Md., 1957-59; aide Enoch Pratt Free Libr., Balt., 1959-61, profl. asst., 1962-64; coord. adult svcs. Washington County Free Libr., Hagerstown, Md., 1964-67; asst. area libr. Eastern Shore Area Libr., Salisbury, Md., 1967; br. libr. Balt. County Pub. Libr., Pikesville, Md., 1968-71; asst. area br. libr. Balt. County Pub. Libr., Essex, Md., 1971-72; sr. info. specialist Balt. County Pub. Libr., Catonsville, Md., 1972-87; on-line supr. Balt. County Pub. Libr., Towson, Md., 1988-89; sr. info. specialist Balt. County Pub. Libr., Reisterstown, Md., 1989-90; exec. dir. Milbourne and Tull Rsch. Ctr., 1991—. Contbr. to profl. and geneal. jours. Mem. Rep. Cen. Com. Balt. County, 1971-72. With U.S. Army, 1949-52. Mem. Nat. Congress Patriotic Orgns. (founding fellow), Habitat for Humanity Internat., Internat. Rescue Com., Heritage Found., Inst. Religion and Democracy, Freedom to Read Foun., Freedom House, Nat. Assn. Scholars, Assn. of Lit. Scholars and Critics, Nat. Ctr. for Neighborhood Enterprise, Md. Libr. Assn. (chmn. intellectual freedom com. 1969-70), Johns Hopkins Assocs., Md. Assn. Adult Edn. (coord. Western Md. region 1965-67), Unitarian and Universalist Geneal. Soc. (founder, bd. dirs. 1971-87), Md. Geneal. Soc., Sons and Daus. of the Pilgrims, Descendants of Early Quakers, Soc. War of 1812, SAR, St. George's Soc. Balt., Ea. Shore Soc. Balt. City, Balt. Coun. Fgn. Affairs, Star Spangled Banner Flag House Assn., Md. Coalition Against Crime, Empower Am., Woodrow Wilson Internat. Ctr. Scholars, Ancient and Hon. Mech. Co. Balt., Nature Conservancy, Ctr. Study Popular Culture, Media Rsch. Ctr., World Future Soc., U.S. Holocaust Meml. Mus., Kappa Delta Pi. Home and Office: 10605 Lakespring Way Cockeysville Hunt Valley MD 21030-2818

TULLER, HARRY LOUIS, materials science and engineering educator. BS, Columbia U., 1966, MS, 1967, DSc in Engring., 1973. Rsch. assoc. physics Technion, Haifa, Israel, 1974-75; from asst. to assoc. prof. materials sci. and engring. MIT, Cambridge, 1975-81, prof. materials sci. and engring., 1981—; dir. Crystal Physics and Electroceramics Lab., Cambridge, 1985—; vis. prof. U. Pierre et Marie Curie, Paris, 1990; faculty chair Sumitomo Electric Industries, 1992. Co-editor: High Temperature Superconductors, 1988, Electroceramics and Solid State Ionics, 1988, Science and Technology of Fast Ion Conductors, 1989, Sold State Ionics, 1992; series editor: Electronic Materials: Science and Technology. Fulbright travel grantee, 1990. Fellow Am. Ceramic Soc. (N.E. chair 1983); mem. IEEE, Electrochem. Soc. (co-organizer 1st and 2d internat. symposium ionic and mixed conducting ceramics 1991, 94), Materials Rsch. Soc., Am. Phys. Soc. Jewish. Avocations: photography, gardening. Office: MIT 77 Massachusetts Ave Rm 13-3126 Cambridge MA 02139-4301

TULLIS, EDWARD LEWIS, retired bishop; b. Cin., Mar. 9, 1917; s. Ashar Spence and Priscilla (Daugherty) T.; m. Mary Jane Talley, Sept. 25, 1937; children: Frank Loyd, Jane Allen (Mrs. William Nelson Offutt IV). AB, Ky. Wesleyan Coll., 1939, LHD, 1975; BD, Louisville Presbyn. Theol. Sem., 1947; DD, Union Coll., Barbourville, Ky., 1954, Wofford Coll., 1976; LHD, Claflin Coll., 1976, Lambuth Coll., 1984. Ordained to ministry Methodist Ch., 1941; service in chs. Frenchburg, Ky., 1937-39, Lawrenceburg, Ky., 1939-44; asso. pastor 4th Ave. Meth. Ch., Louisville, 1944-47, Irvine, Ky., 1947-49; asso. sec. ch. extension sect. Bd. Missions, Meth. Ch., Louisville, 1949-52; pastor First Meth. Ch., Frankfort, Ky., 1952-61, Ashland, Ky., 1961-72; resident bishop United Meth. Ch., Columbia, S.C., 1972-80, Nashville area, 1980-84; ret. United Meth. Ch., 1984; instr. Bible Ky. Wesleyan Coll., 1947-48; instr. Louisville Presbyn. Theol. Sem., 1949-52; mem. Meth. Gen. Conf., 1956, 60, 64, 66, 68, 70, 72, Southeastern Jurisdictional Conf., 1952, 56, 60, 64, 68, 72, bd. mgrs. Bd. Missions, 1962-72, mem. bd. discipleship, 1972-80, v.p. Gen. Council on Fin. and Adminstrn., 1980-84; Chaplain Ky. Gen. Assembly, 1952-61; chmn. Frankfort Com. Human Rights, 1956-61, Mayor's Advisory Com. Human Relations, Ashland, 1968-72. Author: Shaping the Church from the Mind of Christ, 1984. Contbr. articles to religious jours. Sec., bd. dirs. Magee Christian Edn. Found.; trustee Emory U., 1973-80, Alaska Meth. U., 1965-70, Ky. Wesleyan Coll., Martin Coll., Lambuth Coll., McKendree Manor, Meth. Hosps., Memphis, Lake Junaluska Assembly, 1966-88; chair adv. bd. Found. for Evangelism, United Meth. Ch., 1991—. Recipient Outstanding Citizen award Frankfort VFW, 1961, Mayor's award for outstanding service. Ashland, 1971. Club: Kiwanis. Home: PO Box 754 Lake Junaluska NC 28745-0754

TULLIS, JOHN LEDBETTER, retired wholesale distributing company executive; b. Quanah, Tex., May 9, 1911; s. John Ledbetter and Coral (Horton) T.; m. Bettye Bishop Winston, Mar. 22, 1980; children—Tom, Jeff, Alan Winston. B.S. in Elec. Engring. U. Tex., Austin, 1933. With AMF, Inc. and predecessors, 1947-74, pres., chief oper. officer, 1967-74; gen. mgr. Interstate Electric Co., Inc., Shreveport, La., 1974-83, ret., 1983; cons. in field. Chmn. devel. council Schumpert Med. Center, Shreveport, 1974-82; mem. chancellor's council U. Tex., Austin, 1974—. Recipient Disting. Engring. Grad. award U. Tex., Austin, 1963. Mem. Tex. Hist. Assn. Methodist. Clubs: Shreveport Country, Shreveport. Home: 1806 Hunter Cir Shreveport LA 71119-4104

TULLOCH, GEORGE SHERLOCK, JR., electrical equipment distribution company executive, lawyer; b. Bklyn., Aug. 18, 1932; s. George Sherlock and Dorothy (Gooch) T.; m. Edyth Benson Woodroofe, June 16, 1956; children: Michael, Daniel, Lindsay. BA in History, Amherst Coll., 1954; LLB, U. Mich., 1959. Bar: N.Y. 1960, Mo. 1983. Assoc. Breed, Abbott & Morgan, N.Y.C., 1959-66; sec., asst. gen. counsel Westvaco Corp., N.Y.C., 1966-78; v.p., sec., gen. counsel, dir. Graybar Electric Co., N.Y.C., 1978—. Dir. World Affairs Coun., St. Louis. 1st lt. USMCR, 1954-56. Mem. ABA, Assn. Bar City N.Y., Met. St. Louis Bar Assn., Am. Soc. Corp. Secs. Home: 4954 Lindell Blvd Saint Louis MO 63108-1500 Office: Graybar Electric Co Inc 34 N Meramec Ave PO Box 7231 Saint Louis MO 63177

TULLOS, HUGH SIMPSON, orthopedic surgeon, educator; b. Waco, Tex., Aug. 7, 1935; s. Hugh Simpson and Roberta (Thomas) T.; m. Marcelle Gaye Unger; children: Paul R., Hugh S. III. Student, Vanderbilt U., 1952-55; MD, MS in Cancer Biology, Baylor U., 1960. Diplomate Am. Bd. Orthopaedic Surgeons (examiner 1974—). Intern Jefferson Davis Hosp., Houston, 1960-61; gen. surgery resident Baylor Coll. Medicine, Houston, 1961-62, orthopedic surgery resident, 1964-67; successively asst. instr., instr., asst. prof. to assoc. prof. Div. Orthopedic Surgery, Baylor Coll. Medicine, 1967-75; pvt. practice Fonden Orthopedic Group, Houston, 1967-88; head div. orthopedic surgery Tex. Med. Ctr., Houston, 1989—, Wilhemina Barnhart chmn., prof. dept. orthopedic surgery, 1991—; chief orthopedic svc. Meth. Hosp., Houston, 1974, Ben Taub Gen. Hosp., Houston, 1974; clin. assoc. prof. dept. surgery U. Tex. Med. Sch. Health Sci. Ctr., Houston, 1975; vis. lectr. sports medicine symposium Hosp. for Joint Diseases, N.Y.C., 1982; vis. prof. Peruvian Orthopaedic Soc., 1978, U. Miami Sch. Medicine, 1979, Health Sci. Ctr., Tex. Tech U., 1983, Rex Dively Lecturship, Kansas City, Mo., 1985; presenter numerous instructional courses, profl. symposia, meetings; Murray S. Danforth surgeon-in-chief pro tempore Brown U., R.I. Hosp., Providence, Nov., 1988. Author: (with others) Principles of Sport Medicine, 1984, The Elbow, 1985, Injuries to the Throwing Arm, 1985, Art of Total Hip Arthoplasty, 1987, other books, also Instructional Course Lectures Am. Acad. Orthopaedic Surgeons, vols. 25, 33, 1984, 86; editorial bd. Jour. of Arthroplasty, 1988; bd. assoc. editors Clin. Orthopaedics and Related Rsch., 1986—; cons. to editor Tex. Medicine; contbr. numerous articles, abstracts to profl. jours.; presenter exhibits, films med. meetings. Patentee orthopedic devices. Capt. U.S. Army, 1961-63. Fellow Am. Acad. Orthopaedic Surgeons (bd. dirs. 1976, sec. com. sports medicinew 1974-81, com. instructional courses 1987—, chmn. 1988; mem. AMA, Am. Orthopaedic Assn., Am. Orthopaedic Soc. Sports Medicine (founding, chmn. nominating com. 1980, chmn. ann. meeteing 1982), Assn. Bone and Joint Surgeons, Assn. Orthopaedic Chmn., Clin. Orthopaedic Soc., Harris County Med. Soc., Houston Orthopaedic Assn., Houston Surg. Soc., Internat. Congress Knee Surgeons, Internat. Soc. of the Knee (founding, bd. dirs. 1983-88, sec.-treas. 1989), Mid-Am. Orthopaedic Assn., Orthopaedic Rsch. Soc., Pan Am. Med. Assn., Soc. Am. Shoulder and Elbow Surgeons, 20th Century Orthopaedic Soc. (chmn. ann. meeting 1987), Tex. Soc. Athletic Team Physicians (pres. 1978), Tex. Med. Assn., Tex. Orthopaedic Assn., Tex. Rheumatism Soc., The Knee Soc., Baylor Orthopaedic Alumni Assn. (pres. 1970—). Office: Tex Med Ctr Div Orthopedic Surgery 6565 Fannin St Ste 2525 Houston TX 77030-2704

TULLOS, JOHN BAXTER, banker; b. Morton, Miss., Dec. 3, 1915; s. William Baxter and Mell (Roberts) T.; m. Maxine Stone, Sept. 20, 1941. Student, Miss. Coll., 1934, Am. Inst. Bank, Jackson, Miss., 1936-40, Sch. Banking South, La. State U., 1955-57. With Trustmark Nat. Bank, Jackson, 1935-88; exec. agt. Trustmark Corp. (formerly 1st Capital Corp.); faculty Sch. Banking South La. State U.; 1st pres. Miss. Young Bankers Assn.; mem. Miss. Valley World Trade Council, 1965—; mem. La.-Miss. Regional Export Expansion Council div. U.S. Dept. Commerce, 1967-74; vice-chmn. Ala.-Miss. Dist. Export Council, 1975-80; chmn. Miss. Dist. Export Council, 1980-85. Former chmn. budget com. United Givers Fund. Served with AUS, World War II. Mem. Miss. Bankers Assn. (past chmn. operations/automation com.). Methodist. Clubs: Lion, Capitol City Petroleum. Home: 8 Eastbrooke St Jackson MS 39216-4714 Office: PO Box 2343 Jackson MS 39225-2343

TULLY, DANIEL PATRICK, financial services executive; b. 1932; married. BBA, St. Johns U., 1953. With Merrill Lynch, Pierce, Fenner & Smith, N.Y.C., 1955—, mem. acctg. dept., 1955-59, acct. exec. trainee, 1959-63, asst. to mgr. Stamford, Conn. office, 1963-70, mgr., 1970-71, v.p., 1971-79, dir. individual sales, 1976-79, exec. v.p., 1979-82, pres. individual services group, 1982-84, pres. consumer mktg., from 1984; pres., COO Merrill Lynch & Co., Inc., N.Y.C., 1985; former exec. v.p. Merrill Lynch & Co. (parent), N.Y.C., 1979, CEO, chmn. bd., 1992—, chmn., CEO, pres., 1993—. Served U.S. Army, 1953-55. Office: Merrill Lynch & Co Inc World Fin Ctr No Tower 250 Vesey St New York NY 10281-1332

TULLY, DARROW, newspaper publisher; b. Charleston, W.Va., Feb. 27, 1932; s. William Albert and Dora (McCann) T.; m. Victoria Lynn Werner; children: Bonnie Tully Paul, Michael Andrew. Student, Purdue U., 1951; BA in Journalism, St. Joseph's Coll., 1972; PhD in Journalism (hon.), Calumet (Ind.) Coll., 1975. V.p., gen. mgr. Stas. WDSM-AM-FM and WDSM-TV, Duluth, Minn., 1956-59; bus. mgr. Duluth Herald & News Tribune, 1960-62; gen. mgr. St. Paul Dispatch & Pioneer Press, 1962-66; pub. Gary (Ind.) Post-Tribune, 1966-73; v.p., pub. Wichita (Kans.) Eagle & Beacon, 1973-75; pres. San Francisco Newspaper Agy., 1975-78; exec. v.p., pub. Ariz. Republic & Phoenix Gazette, 1978-85; editor., pub., chief exec. officer Ojai (Calif.) Valley News, 1987-90; pres., pub., CEO Beacon Comms., Acton, Mass., 1990-92; asst. to pres. newspaper divsn. Chronicle Pub. Co., 1992-94. Author: Minority Representation in the Media, 1968. Trustee Calumet Coll. Recipient Disting. Achievement award Ariz. State U., 1982, Disting. Journalist award No. Ariz. U./AP, 1983, 1st Pl. Editorial Writing award Ariz. Planned Parenthood, 1983. Mem. Am. Soc. Newspaper Editors, Soc. Profl. Journalists. Office: 3001 Barret Ave Plant City FL 33567-7278

TULLY, JOHN CHARLES, research chemical physicist; b. N.Y.C., May 17, 1942; s. Harry V. and Pauline (Fischer) T.; m. Mary Ellen Thomsen, Jan. 23, 1971; children: John Thomsen, Elizabeth Anne, Stephen Thomsen. BS, Yale U., 1964; PhD, U. Chgo., 1968. NSF postdoctoral fellow U. Colo. and Yale U., 1968-70; mem. tech. staff AT&T Bell Labs., Murray Hill, N.J., 1970-82, disting. mem. tech. staff, 1982-85, head phys. chemistry rsch. dept., 1985-90, head materials chem. rsch. dept., 1990—; vis. prof. Princeton (N.J.) U., 1981-82, Harvard U., Cambridge, Mass., 1991. Contbr. articles to sci. jours.; author, prodr. movie Dynamics of Gas-Surfact Interactions, 1979. NSF predoctoral fellow, 1965-68. Fellow AAAS, Am. Phys. Soc. (chem. physics exec. com. 1983-86); mem. Am. Chem. Soc., chmn. theoretical chemistry subdiv. 1991-92, phys. chemistry div. 1993-94, (Peter Debye award 1995) Sigma Xi. Achievements include patent on Method and Apparatus for Surface Characterization Utilizing Radiation from Desorbed Particles; fundamental theoretical contributions towards atomic leval understanding of chemical reaction dynamics. Office: AT&T Bell Labs 1D346 600 Mountain Ave New Providence NJ 07974

TULLY, MICHAEL J., JR., state senator; b. N.Y.C., June 23, 1933; s. Michael and Elizabeth (Carpenter) T.; children: Michael, Christpher, Maura, Brian. JD, St. John's U.; DHL (hon.) N.Y. Inst. Tech., 1994. Asst. dist. atty. Nassau County; town councilman Town of North Hempstead, Manhasset, N.Y., 1967-71, town supr., 1971-82; senator State of N.Y., Roslyn, 1982—; chmn. senate water resources com.; mem. coun. healthcare fin.; mem. health com. Nat. Conf. State Legislators; mem. coun. state govts.' Health Policy Task Force. Bd. dirs. NCCJ, Am. Com. on Italian Migration, Manhasset-Great Neck Econ. Opportunity Commn.; adv. bd. Assn. for Help of Retarded Children; mem. Am. Legis. Exchange Coun. Served with U.S. Army, USAR. Recipient Hon. Law Enforcement Man of Year award, Nassau County Police Dept. Detectives Assn., 1984, Outstanding Cmty. Svc. award, United Jewish Y's L.I., Frank A. Gulotta Criminal Justice award, Former Asst. Dist. Atty.'s Assn., 1980 award, 1976, 1975, medal for assistance Displaced Homemakers, 1988, Pres.' medal N.Y. Inst. Tech., 1988, Leadership award N/S Health Systems Agy., 1988, Health Care Leader Yr. award N.C. Helath Facilities Assn., 1992, plaque Am. Acad. Pediatrics, Med. Soc. N.Y. State, Am. Coll. Obstetrics and Gynecologists, 1992, Legislator of Yr. award, Legislative Leadership award Am. Coll. Emergency Physicians, 1994. Lodge: K.C., Ancient Order of Hibernians, Order Sons of Italy, Elks (New Hyde Park past exalted ruler). Republican. Roman Catholic. Avocations: golf; reading. Office: NY State Senate 201 Expressway Plz 1 Roslyn Heights NY 11577

TULLY, SUSAN BALSLEY, pediatrician, educator; b. San Francisco, July 12, 1941; d. Gerard E. Balsley Sr. and Norma Lilla (Hand) Carey; m. William P. Tully, June 19, 1965; children: Michael William, Stephen Gerard. BA in Premed. Studies, UCLA, 1963, MD, 1966. Diplomate Am. Bd. Pediatrics, Am. Bd. Pediatric Emergency Medicine. Intern L.A. County-U. So. Calif. Med. Ctr., 1966-67, jr. resident pediatrics, 1967-68; staff pediatrician, part-time Permanente Med. Group, Oakland, Calif., 1968; sr. resident pediatrics Kaiser Found. Hosp., Oakland, 1968-69; sr. resident pediatrics Bernalillo County Med. Ctr., Albuquerque, 1969-70, chief resident pediatric outpatient dept., 1970; instr. pediatrics, asst. dir. outpatient dept. U. N.Mex. Sch. Medicine, 1971-72; asst. prof. pediatrics, dir. (ambulatory pediatrics) U. Calif., Irvine, 1972-76, asst. prof. clin. pediatrics, vice chair med. edn., 1977-79; staff pediatrician Ross-Loos Med. Group, Buena Park, Calif., 1976-77; assoc. prof. clin. pediatrics and emergency medicine U. So. Calif. Sch. Medicine, 1979-86; dir. pediatric emergency dept. L.A. County/U. So. Calif. Med. Ctr., 1979-87; prof. clin. pediatrics and emergency medicine U. So. Calif. Sch. Medicine, 1986-89; dir. ambulatory pediatrics L.A. County/U. So. Calif. Med. Ctr., 1987-89, L.A. County-Olive View/UCLA Med. Ctr., 1989—; clin. prof. pediatrics U. Calif., L.A., 1989-93, prof. clin. pediatrics, 1993—; pediatric toxicology cons. L.A. County Regional Poison Control Ctr. Med. Adv. Bd., 1981—; faculty exec. com., clin. faculty rep. UCLA Sch. Medicine, 1992-93, strategic planning action com. subcom. on ednl. structure, 1992-93, dept. pediatrics alliance-wide rev. and appraisal com., 1992-93, steering com., 1993—; pediatric liaison dept. emergency medicine Olive View/UCLA Med. Ctr., 1989—, dir. lead poisoning clinic, 1993—, L.A. County Dept. Health Svcs., 1990—; mem. quality assurance com. L.A. County Community Health Plan, 1986-89; mem. survey team pediatric emergency svcs. L.A. Pediatric Soc., 1984-86; mem. adv. bd. preventive health project U. Affiliated Program Children's Hosp. L.A., 1981-83; active numerous coms. Author: (with K.E. Zenk) Pediatric Nurse Practitioner Formulary, 1979; (with W.A. Wingert) Pediatric Emergency Medicine: Concepts and Clinical Practice, 1992; (with others) Educational Guidelines for Ambulatory/General Pediatrics Fellowship Training, 1992, Physician's Resource Guide for Water Safety Education, 1994; reviewer Pediatrics, 1985-89; editorial cons. Advanced Pediatric Life Support Course and Manual, 1988-89; dept. editor Pediatric Pearls Jour. Am. Acad. Physician Assts., 1989-94; tech. cons., reviewer Healthlink TV Am. Acad. Pediatrics, 1991; reviewer Pediatric Emergency Care, 1992—; question writer sub-bd. pediatric emergency medicine Am. Bd. Pediatrics, 1993—; cons. to lay media NBC Nightly News, Woman's Day, Sesame Street Parents, Parenting, Los Angeles Times; author numerous abstracts; contbr. articles to profl. jours. cons. spl. edn. programs Orange County Bd. Edn., 1972-79; mem. Orange County Health Planning Coun., 1973-79; co-chairperson Orange County Child Health and Disability Prevention Program Bd., 1975-76; mem. Orange County Child Abuse Consultation Team, 1977-79; mem. project adv. bd. Family Focussed "Buckle Up" Project, Safety Belt Safe, U.S.A., 1989—; Fellow Am. Acad. Pediatrics (life, active numerous sects. and coms., active Calif. chpt.); mem. APHA, Ambulatory Pediatric Assn., L.A. Pediatric Soc. (life), L.A. Area Child Passenger Safety Assn. Democrat. Avocations: art needlework, reading. Office: Olive View UCLA Med Ctr Pediatrics 3A108 14445 Olive View Dr Sylmar CA 91342-1495

TULLY, THOMAS ALOIS, building materials executive, consultant, educator; b. Dubuque, Iowa, Nov. 11, 1940; s. Thomas Aloysius and Marjorie Mae (Fosselman) T.; m. Joan Vonnetta Dubay, Nov. 30, 1963; children: Thomas Paul, Maureen Elizabeth. BA, Loras Coll., 1962; postgrad., Georgetown U., 1963-66; MPA, Harvard U., 1968. Mgmt. trainee Office of Sec. Def., Washington, 1962-63, fgn. affairs officer, 1963-70; v.p. Dubuque Lumber Co., 1970-84, pres., 1984-91; pres. Tully's, 1991-92, LBM Mktg. Assocs., Inc., 1992—; adj. instr. Divine Word Coll., 1971, Loras Coll., 1972; adj. instr. Clarke Coll., 1987-89, instr., 1989-91, asst. prof., 1992—, chmn.

dept. acctg. and bus., 1993—, dir. small bus. inst., 1994—; pres. Hills and Dales Child Devel. Ctr., Inc., 1992—; mem. bd. trustees Alverno Apts., 1995—. Mem. Dubuque Human Rights Commn., 1974-75, chmn., 1975, Iowa State Com. for Employer Support of Guard and Res. Forces, 1988—; city councilman, Dubuque, 1975-79; bd. dirs. League Iowa Municipalites, 1977-79; mayor City of Dubuque, 1978; vice chmn. Iowa Temporary State Land Pres. Policy Com., 1978-79; pres. N.E. Iowa Regional Coordinating Council, 1985-93, East Cen. Intergovtl. Assn. Bus. Growth, Inc., 1987—, chmn., 1993—; bd. dirs. Pvt. Industry Council of Dubuque and Delaware Counties, Inc., 1983-86; trustee Divine Word Coll., 1986—; pres. Barn Community Theatre, 1988-89; chmn. bd. trustees United Way Svcs. of Dubuque, 1990, campaign chmn., 1991, bd. mem., 1980-94. Recipient Meritorious Civilian Svc. award Sec. of Def., 1970, Gov.'s Vol. award, 1989. Mem. Nat. Lumber and Bldg. Material Dealers Assn. (exec. com. 1988-90), Iowa Lumbermen's Assn. (pres. 1984, chmn. legis. com. 1985-90), Northwestern Lumbermen Assn. (bd. dirs. 1984-87, 2d v.p. 1988, 1st v.p. 1989-90, pres. 1990-91). Democrat. Roman Catholic. Home: 838 Stone Ridge Pl Dubuque IA 52001-1362 Office: LBM Mktg Assocs PO Box 771 Dubuque IA 52004-0771

TULSKY, ALEX SOL, physician; b. Chgo., Aug. 10, 1911; s. Solomon and Clara (Tarnipolsky) T.; m. Klara Glottmann, July 20, 1948; children—Shayne Lee, Steven Henry, Asher Arthur, James Aaron. B.S., U. Ill., 1932, M.D., 1934. Intern Michael Reese Hosp., Chgo., 1934-36; attending obstetrician and gynecologist Michael Reese Hosp., 1938—, pres. med. staff, 1962-64; house officer Bklyn. Jewish Hosp., 1937-38; pvt. practice Chgo., 1938—; clin. prof. obstetrics and gynecology Abraham Lincoln Sch. Medicine, U. Ill., 1980—. Served to lt. col. M.C. AUS, 1941-45. Decorated Bronze Star. Mem. A.M.A., Chgo., Ill. med. socs., Chgo. Gynecol. Soc., Chgo. Inst. Medicine, Chgo. Oriental Inst., Pan Am. Med. Assn., Chgo. Soc. History Medicine. Home: 442 W Wellington Ave Chicago IL 60657-5804 Office: 111 N Wabash Ave Chicago IL 60602

TULSKY, FREDRIC NEAL, journalist; b. Chgo., Sept. 30, 1950; s. George and Helen (Mailick) T.; m. Kim Rennard, June 20, 1971; children: Eric George, Elizabeth Rose. B.J., U. Mo., 1972; J.D. cum laude, Temple U., Phila., 1984. Bar: Pa. 1984. Reporter Saginaw News, Mich., 1973-74, Port Huron Times Herald, Mich., 1974-75, Jackson Clarion-Ledger, Miss., 1975-78, Los Angeles Herald Examiner, 1978-79, Phila. Inquirer, 1979-93; mng. editor Ctr. for Investigative Reporting, San Francisco, 1993-94, exec. dir., 1994; reporter L.A. Times, 1995—; adj. prof. urban studies U. Pa., 1990-93. Recipient nat. awards including Robert F. Kennedy Found. award, 1979, Heywood Broun award Newspaper Guild, 1978, Disting. Svc. medal Sigma Delta Chi, 1978, Pub. Svc. award AP Mng. Editors, 1978, Silver Gavel award ABA, 1979, 87, Pulitzer prize for investigative reporting, 1987, Pub. Svc. award Nat. Headliners Club, 1987; Nieman fellow Harvard U., 1989. Mem. Investigative Reporters and Editors (pres. 1988-91, chair 1991-93), Reporters Com. for Freedom of Press, Kappa Tau Alpha. Office: LA Times 388 Market St Fl 12 San Francisco CA 94111-5311

TULVING, ENDEL, psychologist, educator; b. Estonia, May 26, 1927; s. Johannes and Linda T.; m. Ruth Mikkelsaar, June 24, 1950; children: Elo Ann, Linda. BA, U. Toronto, Ont., Can., 1953, MA, 1954; PhD, Harvard U., 1957; MA (hon.), Yale U., 1969; FD (hon.), U. Umea (Sweden), 1982; DLitt (hon.), U. Waterloo, 1987, Laurentian U., 1988; D Psychology (hon.), U. Tartu, Estonia, 1991. Lectr. U. Toronto, 1956-59, asst. prof., 1959-62, asso. prof., 1962-65; prof., 1965-70; prof. psychology Yale U., New Haven, 1970-75; prof. psychology U. Toronto, 1972-85, chmn. dept., 1974-80, univ. prof., 1985-92, Univ. prof. emeritus psychology, 1992—; vis. scholar U. Calif., Berkeley, 1964-65; fellow Ctr. Advanced Study in Behavioral Scis., Stanford, Calif., 1972-73; Commonwealth vis. prof. Oxford (Eng.) U., 1977-78; Tanenbaum chair in cognitive neurosci. Rotman Rsch. Inst. of Baycrest Ctr., Can., 1992—; disting. prof. neurosci., disting. prof. psychology U. Calif., Davis, 1993—. Author: Elements of Episodic Memory, 1983; editor Jour. Verbal Leaning and Verbal Behavior, 1969-72, Psychol. Rsch., 1976-88; co-editor: Organization of Memory, 1972, Memory Systems 1994, 1994; mem. editl. bd. Oxford Psychology Series, 1979-95; contbr. numerous articles on memory to sci. jours. Recipient Izaak Walton Killam Meml. prize Can. Coun., 1994, Meml. scholar, 1976-77, Gold medal award for life achievemnt in psychol. sci. Am. Psychol. Found., 1994; Guggenheim fellow, 1987-88. Fellow Can. Psychol. Assn. (disting. sci. contbn. award 1983), APA (disting. sci. contbn. award 1983, William James fellow), Royal Soc. Can., AAAS (fgn. hon.), Soc. Exptl. Psychologists (Warren medal 1982), Royal Soc. London; mem. NAS (fgn. assoc.), Soc. for Neuroscis., Psychonomic Soc. (governing bd. 1974-80), Royal Swedish Acad. Scis. (fgn.), Cognitive Neurosci. Soc. Home: 45 Baby Point Crescent, Toronto, ON Canada M6S 2B7 Office: Rotman Rsch Inst of Baycrest Ctr, Bathurst St, North York, ON Canada M6A 2E1

TUMAN, WALTER VLADIMIR, Russian language educator, researcher; b. Heidelberg, Germany, Jan. 21, 1946; came to U.S., 1949; s. Val Alexander Tuman and Valida (Zedins) Grasis; m. Helena Eugenia Makarowsky, June 6, 1970; children: Gregory Vladimir, Larissa Alexandra. BA, Fordham U., 1967; MS in Russian, Linguistics, Georgetown U., 1970, PhD in Russian, 1975. Supr. Russian dept. Def. Lang. Inst., Washington, 1972-75; developer course-curriculum Def. Lang. Inst., Monterey, Calif., 1975-78; asst. prof. Russian Hollins (Va.) Coll., 1978-84; dir. fgn. lang. lab. La. State U., Baton Rouge, 1984-90; assoc. prof., coord. Russian program Thunderbird Campus Am. Grad. Sch. Internat. Mgmt., Glendale, Ariz., 1990-95, prof., 1995—; cons. various univs.; grant participant, cons. US AID Consortia Am. Buss., NIS, 1993—, U.S. Commerce Dept., Nizhny Novgorod, Volgograd, Am. Bus. Ctrs., 1994—. Author: Think Russian: Level I, 1993; editor: A Bibliography of Computer-Aided Language Learning, 1986; contbg. editor Jour. Ednl. Techniques and Techs., 1987—; mem. editl. bd.: Jour. Lang. in Internat. Bus.; author book revs., computer programs, conf. presentations; contbr. articles to profl. jours. Georgetown U. fellow, 1969; recipient Prof.'s Exch. award Internat. Rsch. and Exchs. Bd. (USSR), 1979; Mednick Meml. Fund grantee Va. Found. for Ind. Colls. (Australia), 1983, Apple Computer grantee, 1989, U.S. Dept. Edn. grantee Ctr. Internat. Bus. Edn. and Rsch., 1993—. Mem. Am. Assn. Tchrs. Slavic and East European Langs. (v.p. 1981-84, founder Monterey, Calif. chpt.), Am. Coun. on the Teaching Fgn. Langs., Am. Coun. Tchrs. (bd. dirs. 1992—), Internat. Assn. Learning Lab. Dirs., Assn. Internat. Linguistique Appliquée. Russian Orthodox. Office: Am Grad Sch Internat Mgmt 59th and Greenway Glendale AZ 85306

TUMAY, MEHMET TANER, geotechnical consultant, educator, research director; b. Ankara, Turkey, Feb. 2, 1937; came to U.S., 1959; s. Bedrettin and Muhterem (Uybadin) T.; m. Karen Nuttycombe, June 15, 1962; children: Peri, Suna. BS in Civil Engring., Robert Coll. Sch. Engring. (Turkey), 1959; MCE, U. Va., 1961; postgrad. UCLA, 1963-64; PhD, Tech. U. Istanbul (Turkey), 1971; Fugro-Cesco postdoctoral research fellow U. Fla., Gainesville, 1975-76. Instr. civil engring. U. Va., Charlottesville, 1961-62; asst. prof. civil engring. U. Louisville, 1962-63; teaching fellow UCLA, 1963-64; asst. prof. civil engring. Robert Coll. Sch. Engring., Istanbul, 1966-71; assoc. prof. dept. civil engring. Bogazici U., Istanbul, 1971-75; assoc. prof. then prof. civil engring., coord. geotech. engring. La. State U., Baton Rouge, 1976—; adv. prof. U. Vicosa, Minas Gerais, Brazil, 1991—, Tongji U., Shanghai, China, 1991—; dir. Geomechanics Program NSF, Washington, 1990-94; dir. rsch. Louisiana Transp. Rsch. Ctr., Baton Rouge, 1994—; maitre de conferences Ecole Nationale des Ponts et Chaussees, Paris, 1980—; geotech. cons. Sauti, Spa, Cons. Engrs., Italy, 1969-72, SOFRETU-RATP, Paris, 1972-73, D.E.A., Cons. Engrs., Istanbul, 1974-75, BOTEK, Ltd., Istanbul, 1975—, Senler-Campbell Assos., Louisville, 1979—, Fugro Gulf-Geogulf, Houston, 1980—; cons. UN Devel. Program, 1982-84, 87; cons. in field. Contbr. articles to profl. jours. AID scholar, 1975-76; lic. civil engr., La., Ga., S.C., Turkish Chamber of Civil Engring; French Ministry External Relations scholar, 1982. Fellow ASCE; mem. Am. Soc. Engring. Edn., ASTM, La. Engring. Soc., Turkish Soil Mechanics Group (charter), Turkish Chamber Civil Engrs., Internat. Soc. Soil Mechanics and Found. Engring., Sigma Xi, Chi Epsilon, Tau Beta Pi. Home: 1915 W Magna Carta Pl Baton Rouge LA 70815-5521 Office: La State U La Transp Rsch Ctr Dept Civil Engring Baton Rouge LA 70808

TUMMALA, RAO RAMAMOHANA, engineering educator; b. Nandamuru, India, Feb. 15, 1942; came to U.S., 1966; s. Venkateswara Rao and Subbamma (Paladugu) T.; m. Anne Mitran, Dec. 30, 1966; children: Dinesh, Vijay, Suneel. BSc, Loyola Coll., Vijayawada, India, 1961; BE, Indian Inst. of Sci., 1963; MS, Queen's U., Kingston, Can., 1964; PhD, U. Ill., 1968. IBM fellow, 1984-93; process engr. Norton Co., Niagara Falls, Can., 1965-66; rsch. asst. U. Ill., Urbana, 1966-68; staff engr. IBM Corp., East Fishkill, N.Y., 1968-70, adv. engr., 1970-76, sr. engr., 1976-84, fellow, 1984—, dir., 1987-89; Pettit chair prof. Ga. Inst. Tech., Atlanta, 1993—; mem. selection com. Inventors Hall of Fame, Washington, 1984—. Contbr. articles to profl. jours.; patentee in field. Mem. adv. bd. U. Ill., Urbana, 1980-83; chmn. adv. bd. U. Calif., Berkeley, 1987-89, MIT, Cambridge, 1990-93. Recipient Disting. Alumni award U. Ill., 1991, David Sarnoff award IEEE, John Wagnon award; named one of 50 in U.S. in indsl. policy Industry Week. Fellow IEEE, Am. Ceramic Soc.; mem. NAE. Avocations: tennis, golf, skiing, international travel. Home: 1748 Tilling Way Stone Mountain GA 30087-2329 Office: Ga Inst Tech MARC Ctr Atlanta GA 30332-0560

TUMMINELLO, STEPHEN CHARLES, consumer electronics manufacturing executive; b. Paterson, N.J., Nov. 7, 1936. Grad., Fairleigh Dickinson U., 1958. Former pres. N.Am. Philips Lighting Corp.; exec. v.p., former v.p., group exec. Philips Electronics N.Am. Corp. (formerly N.Am. Philips Corp.), 1984-90; pres., chief exec. officer Philips Electronics N.Am. Corp. (formerly N.Am. Philips Corp.), N.Y.C., 1990—. Office: Philips Electronics N Am Corp 100 E 42nd St New York NY 10017-5613

TUMPOWSKY, IRA BRUCE, advertising agency executive; b. N.Y.C., Sept. 24, 1938; s. Mortimer Herbert and Pearl (Weissberger) T.; m. Audrey Francine Klieger, Jan. 13, 1963; children: Jeffrey Lon, Andrew Keith, Brian Peter. BS in Mktg., NYU, 1961. Media buyer Lennen & Newell, N.Y.C., 1962-65; media supr. Young & Rubicam, N.Y.C., 1965-71; v.p., media dir. Young & Rubicam, Houston, 1971-79, sr. v.p., group supr., 1980-88; sr. v.p., group media dir. Young & Rubicam, N.Y.C., 1988—; sr. v.p., media dir. Wunderman, Ricotta & Kline, N.Y.C., 1979-80. Writer, speaker: (cable TV conv.) The Love Triangle, 1982-88, pres. 1988-88). V.p. bd. trustees Temple Israel, Westport, Conn., 1982-88. With U.S. Army, 1961-67. Named to NYU Student Hall of Fame, 1961. Mem. Bus. Publs. Audit (Edward Bill award 1980), Alpha Delta Sigma. Democrat. Jewish. Avocations: tennis, gardening. Home: 25 Colony Rd Westport CT 06880-3703 Office: Young & Rubicam 285 Madison Ave New York NY 10017-6401

TUNE, TOMMY (THOMAS JAMES TUNE), musical theater director, dancer, choreographer, actor; b. Wichita Falls, Tex., Feb. 28, 1939; s. Jim P. and Eva Mae (Clark) T. Student, Lon Morris Jr. Coll., 1958-59; BFA, U. Tex., 1962; postgrad., U. Houston, 1962-63. Dancer, choreographer, dir. various prodns., N.Y.C., 1963—. Dancer (Broadway prodns.): Baker Street, 1965, A Joyful Noise, 1966, How Now Dow Jones, 1967, Seesaw, 1973 (Tony award Best Featured Actor musical 1974), (films): Hello Dolly, 1968, The Boyfriend, 1971; dir., choreographer Broadway prodns.: The Best Little Whorehouse in Texas, 1978 (Tony award nominations Best Dir. musical 1979, Best Choreography 1979, Drama Desk award Best Dir. musical 1979), A Day in Hollywood/A Night in the Ukraine, 1980 (Tony award Best Choreography 1980, Tony award nomination Best Dir. musical 1980, Drama Desk awards Best Musical Staging, 1980, Best Choreography 1980), Nine, 1982 (Drama Desk award Best Dir. musical 1982, Tony award Best Dir. musical 1982, Tony award nomination Best Choreography 1982), Grand Hotel, 1989 (Tony awards Best Choreography 1990, Best Dir. 1990, Drama Desk awards Best Choreography 1990, Best Dir. musical 1990); dir., actor, choreographer My One and Only, 1983 (Tony awards Best Actor musical 1983, Best Choreography 1983, Tony award nomination Best Dir. musical 1983, Drama Desk award Outstanding Choreography 1983), The Will Rogers Follies, 1990 (Tony awards Best Choreography 1991, Best Dir. 1991, Drama Desk award Best Choreography 1991); tour Bye, Bye Birdie, 1991-92; dir. Broadway prodn.: Stepping Out, 1987; dir. Off-Broadway prodns.: The Club, 1976 (Obie award 1977), Sunset, 1977, Cloud 9, 1981 (Drama Desk award Best Dir. 1982, Obie award Disting. Direction 1982); performed in the USSR, 1988. Recipient Drama League Musical Achievement award, 1990. Mem. Dirs. Guild Am., Stage Soc. Dirs. and Choreographers, Actors Equity Assn. Office: care Internat Creative Mgmt 40 W 57th St New York NY 10019-4001

TUNG, FRANK YAO-TSUNG, microbiologist educator; b. Tainan, Taiwan, Republic of China, Feb. 6, 1958; came to U.S., 1984; m. Man-Hwa Do, July 10, 1982; children: Kuang-Tsung, Jack. BS, Tunghai U., Taichung, Taiwan, Republic of China, 1980; MS, Nat. Yangming U., Taipei, Taiwan, 1984; PhD, U. Tenn., 1987. Postdoctoral fellow Harvard U., Boston, 1988-90; asst. prof. U. Fla., Gainesville, 1990-94, U. Pitts., 1994—. Contbr. articles to profl. jours. Recipient Rsch. awards NIH, 1991-96, Am. Cancer Soc., 1994-95. Mem. Am. Soc. Microbiology. Office: U Pittsburgh Rm 439 130 Desoto St Pittsburgh PA 15261

TUNG, KO-YUNG, lawyer; b. Peking, Peoples Republic China, Feb. 20, 1947; came to U.S., 1964; s. Tien-chung and Hung-Fang (Wong) T.; m. Alison Heydt, Feb. 2, 1975; children: Vanessa, Adrian, Cameron, Gregory. BA, Harvard U., 1969; JD, U. Tokyo, 1971. Bar: N.Y., 1973. Assoc. Debevoise & Plimpton, N.Y.C., 1973-76; ptnr. Tung, Drabkin & Boynton, N.Y.C., 1976-84, O'Melveny & Myers, N.Y.C., 1985—; adj. assoc. prof. sch. law NYU, 1974-88. mem. Coun. on Fgn. Rels., N.Y.C., 1986—, The Brookings Inst., 1990, Overseas Devel. Coun., Washington, 1990—, The Japan Soc., 1990, Asia Soc., 1994—; N.Am. mem. Trilateral Commn., N.Y.C., 1990—; chmn., bd. govs. East West Ctr., Honolulu, 1990—; U.S. Nat. Commn. for Pacific Econ. Cooperation, 1991—; bd. dirs. Asian Am. Legal Def. and Edn. Fund, 1990. Law Faculty fellow Harvard U., 1993. Mem. Phi Beta Kappa. Office: O'Melveny & Myers Citicorp Ctr 153 E 53rd St New York NY 10022-4602

TUNG, PHOEBUS CHE-SE, biomedical educator; b. Nanking, China, Nov. 19, 1948; s. Cheng and Nai-Tsai (Ku) T.; m. Chang-Chu Fu, Aug. 3, 1975; children: Chen-Wen, Chen-Li. MD, Nat. Def. Med. Ctr., Taipei, Taiwan, 1975; PhD in Pharmacology, Vanderbilt U., 1983. Diplomate in medicine. Tchg. asst. Dept. Physiol. and Biophysics, Taipei, 1975-78; tchg. asst. dept. pharmacology Nat. Def. Med. Ctr., Taipei, 1978-79, assoc. prof. dept. pharmacology, 1984-88, prof. dept. pharmacology, 1988-89, prof. dept. physiology and biophysics, 1989-91, prof., chmn. dept. physiology and biophysics, 1991—; rsch. assoc. Dept. Medicine and Pharmacology, Nashville, 1983-84; vis. scientist dept. pharmacology Karolinska Inst., Sweden, 1988-89; jointed prof. dept. biomed. engring Chung-Yuan Christian U., Taipei, 1990-92; trustee Chinese Soc. Pharmacology, Taiwan, 1984—, Chinese Soc. Neurosci., Taiwan, 1991—; cons. Bur. of Drug, Dept. Agr., Taiwan, 1986—. Col. Chinese Army, 1969—. Hrafn Sveinbjarnarson Postdoctoral fellow, Nashville, 1983-84; Rsch. grantee Nat. Sci. Coun., Taiwan, 1984—; Karolinska Inst. fellow, Sweden, 1988-89. Mem. Am. Autonomic Soc., Am. Soc. for Pharmacology and Exptl. Therapeutics, Chinese Physiol. Soc., The Planetary Soc. Avocations: traveling, reading, mountain hiking, watching movies. Office: Nat Def Med Ctr Physiology, PO Box 90048-503, Taipei Taiwan

TUNG, ROSALIE LAM, business educator, consultant; b. Shanghai, China, Dec. 2, 1948; came to U.S., 1975; d. Andrew Yan-Fu and Pauline Wai-Kam (Cheung) Lam. BA (Univ. scholar), York U., 1972; MBA, U. B.C., 1974, PhD in Bus. Adminstrn. (Univ. fellow, Seagram Bus. fellow, H.R. MacMillan Family fellow), 1977; m. Byron Poon-Yan Tung, June 17, 1972; 1 child, Michele Christine. Lectr. diploma div. U. B.C., 1975, lectr. exec. devel. program, 1975; asst. prof. mgmt. grad. sch. mgmt. U. Oreg., Eugene, 1977-80; assoc. prof. U. Pa. , Phila. 1981-86; prof., dir. internat. bus. ctr. U. Wis., Milw., 1986-90; endowed chaired prof. Simon Fraser U., 1991—; vis. scholar U. Manchester (Eng.) Inst. Sci. and Tech., 1980; vis. prof. UCLA, 1981, Harvard U., 1988, Copenhagen Bus. Sch., 1995, Chinese U. Hong Kong, 1996; Wis. disting. prof. U. Wis. System, 1988-90, Ming and Stella Wong chair in internat. bus., 1991—. Mem. Acad. Internat. Bus. (mem. exec. bd., treas. 1985-86), Acad. Mgmt. (bd. govs. 1987-89), Internat. Assn. Applied Psychology, Am. Arbitration Assn. (comml. panel arbitrators). Author: Management Practices in China, 1980, U.S.-China Trade Negotiations, 1982, Chinese Industrial Society After Mao, 1982, Business Negotiations with the Japanese, 1984, Key to Japan's Economic Strength: Human Power, 1984, The New Expatriates: Managing Human Resources Abroad, 1988; editor: Strategic Management in the U.S. and Japan, 1987, International Management in International Library of Business and Management Series, 1994, Internat. Encyclopedia Bus. & Mgmt., 1996. Oppehheimer Bros. Found. fellow, 1973-74, U. B.C. fellow, 1974-75, H.R. MacMillan Found. fellow, 1975-77; named Wis. Disting. Prof., 1988, Ming and Stella Wong Prof., 1991. Roman Catholic; recipient Leonore Rowe Williams award U. Pa., 1990, U. B.C. Alumni 75th Anniversary award, 1990. Avocation: creative writing. Office: Simon Fraser U, Faculty Bus Adminstrn, Burnaby, BC Canada V5A 1S6

TUNG, SHIH-MING SAMUEL, medical physicist; b. Taipei, Aug. 18, 1954; came to U.S., 1983; s. Yao-Ching and Chen-Ping (Yen) T.; m. Hilda Tung, Oct. 16, 1983; children: Margaret, David. BS in Nuclear Engring., Nat. Tsing Hua U., Hsinchu, Taiwan, 1976, MS in Nuclear Engring., 1980; MS in Radiol. Sci., U. Colo. Health Sci. Ctr., Denver, 1985. Cert. Am. Bd. Radiology, Taiwan Nat. Bd. Health Physics; lic. med. physicist, Tex. Med. physicist Chung Gung Meml. Hosp., Taipei, 1980-81; health physicist Atomic Energy Coun., Taipei, 1981-83; physicist, radiation safety officer Bishop Clarkson Meml. Hosp., Omaha, 1986-89; med. physicist U. Tes. MD Anderson Cancer Ctr., Houston, 1989—. Contbr. articles to profl. jours. Mem. Am. Assn. Physicists in Medicine, Health Physics Soc. Baptist. Achievements include patent for Tungsten shields for electron beam treatment; avocations: church choir, reading. Home: 12710 Water Oak Dr Missouri City TX 77489-3902 Office: U Tex MD Anderson Cancer Ctr 1515 Holcombe Blvd # 94 Houston TX 77030-4009

TUNG, THEODORE HSCHUM, banker, economist; b. Beijing, Aug. 28, 1934; came to U.S., 1959; s. R. T. and C. (Lin) Dong; m. Patricia C. Hsu, Dec. 24, 1966; children: Candice H., Roderick. BA, Nat. Taiwan U., Taipei, 1956; MBA, U. Okla., 1962; PhD, U. Pa., 1965. Asst. prof. econs. Colo. State U., Ft. Collins, 1964-66, U. Pa., Phila., 1966-68; economist Bank of N.Y., N.Y.C., 1968-70; v.p., economist Continental Bank, Chgo., 1971-80; v.p., chief economist Cen. Nat. Bank, Cleve., 1980-83; sr. v.p., chief economist Nat. City Corp., Cleve., 1983—; cons. economist Richard Howes & Assocs., Washington, 1966-68. Co-author: General Theory: Economic, Social, Political and Regional, 1966; author Nat. City Corp.'s fin. letter, 1983—. Bd. dirs. Family Health Assn., Cleve., 1987-89. Grantee USDA, 1964-66. Mem. Nat. Assn. Bus. Economists, Am. Econs. Assn. Home: 3735 Middle Post Ln Cleveland OH 44116-3935 Office: Nat City Corp 1900 E 9th St Cleveland OH 44114-3401

TUNGATE, DAVID E., lawyer, educator; b. Columbus, Ohio, Apr. 22, 1945; s. Ernest O. and Diantha (Woltz) T.; m. Mary Ann V. Montaleone, Jan. 27, 1968; children: David, Melissa. BA, U. Ill., Champaign, 1967, JD, 1970. Bar: U.S. Dist. Ct. (we. dist.) Pa. 1970, Superior Ct. Pa., 1971, Supreme Ct. Pa., 1971, U.S. Ct. Appeals (3d cir.) 1973, U.S. Ct. Claims 1987, U.S. Dist. Ct (ea. dist.) Wis. 1989, U.S. Ct. Appeals (fed. cir.) 1990. Assoc. Eckert, Seamans, Cherin & Mellott, Pitts., 1976-75, ptnr., 1976—; bd. dirs. Rokop Corp., Pitts.; adj. prof. Carnegie Mellon U., Pitts., 1991—. Contbr. articles to profl. jours.; author bus. book revs. Pitts. Post-Gazette, 1986—. Chmn. Zoning Hearing Bd. Upper St. Clair, 1991—. Mem. ABA, Penn. Bar Assn., Allegheny County Bar Assn. Office: Eckert Seamans Cherin & Mellott 42d Fl USX Tower 600 Grant St Pittsburgh PA 15219-2702

TUNHEIM, JERALD ARDEN, academic administrator, physics educator; b. Claremont, S.D., Sept. 3, 1940; s. Johannes and Annie (Ness) T.; m. Patricia Ann Witham, June 7, 1963; children: Jon, Angie, Alec. BS in Engring. Physics, S.D. State U., 1962, MS in Physics, 1964; PhD in Physics, Okla. State U., 1968. Vis. scientist Sandia Corp., Albuquerque, 1970-71, Ames (Iowa) AEC Labs., 1972; asst. prof. S.D. State U., Brookings, 1968-73, assoc. prof., 1973-78, prof., 1978-80, prof., head physics dept., 1980-85; dean Ea. Wash. U., Cheney, 1985-87; pres. Dakota State U., Madison, S.D., 1987—; bd. dirs. NSF Systemic Initiative. Co-author: Elementary Particles and Unitary Symmetry, 1966, Quantum Field Theory, 1966; contbr. articles to profl.jours. Bd. dirs. Madison Devel. Corp., 1988—. Grantee USDA, 1987-88, S.D. Govt. Office Edn. Devel., 1988-89, U.S. Dept. Edn., Eisenhower Program, 1985-86, 87-90, 92-93, 95-96, U.S. Dept. Edn. Math. and Sci. Program, 1989-92; named Tchr. of Yr. S.D. State U., 1972. Mem. NSPE, Am. Phys. Soc., Am. Assn. Physics Tchrs., Madison C. of C. (bd. dirs. 1990—), Rotary. Republican. Lutheran. Office: Dakota State U Office of President 820 N Washington Ave Madison SD 57042-1799

TUNLEY, NAOMI LOUISE, retired nurse administrator; b. Henryretta, Okla., Jan. 10, 1936; d. Alexander and Ludia Bell (Franklin) T. BSN, Dillard U., 1958; MA, U. Mo., Kansas City, 1974. RN, Okla. Staff nurse, assoc. chief nursing svc. Oklahoma City VA Med. Ctr., 1958-65; instr. Iowa Luth. Hosp. Sch. Nursing, Des Moines, 1965-66; charge nurse emergency rm. Mercy Hosp., Iowa City, Iowa, 1966-67; charge nurse, assoc. chief nursing svc. Kansas City (Mo.) VA Med. Ctr., 1967-76, charge nurse neurol. unit, 1976-79, nurse mgr. orthopedic unit, 1979-80, nurse mgr. substance abuse unit, 1980-94; ret., 1994; equal employment opportunity counselor Kansas City (Mo.) VA Med. Ctr., 1976-86; trustee Nat. Coun. Alcohol and Other Drugs, Kansas City, 1986-90. Vol. Am. Cancer Soc., Kansas City, 1971-79, March of Dimes, Kansas City, 1971-79; big sister Big Bros.-Sisters Am., Kansas City, 1974-84. Mem. ARC, Sigma Theta Tau. Avocations: fishing, golf, tennis. Home: 3120 Poplar Ave Kansas City MO 64128-1803

TUNLEY, ROUL, author; b. Chgo., May 12, 1912; s. Joseph Hartley and Lillian (Boyd) T. BA, Yale, 1934. Reporter N.Y. Herald Tribune, 1934-37; asst. circulation mgr. Look mag., 1937-39; syndicated columnist, 1939-41; mem. English faculty Yale, 1946-47; fellow Jonathan Edwards Coll., 1946—; dir. editorial promotion Look mag., 1948-50; staff writer, assoc. editor Am. mag., 1951-56; asst. mng. editor Woman's Home Companion, 1956; assoc. editor Sat. Eve. Post, 1961-63. Author: Kids, Crime and Chaos, 1962, The American Health Scandal, 1966, (with Anne Wahle) Ordeal by Fire, 1966; frequent contbr. to nat. mags. including Reader's Digest, 1951—. Lt. comdr. USNR, 1942-45. Mem. Authors Guild (coun.), Elizabethan Club (adjoining chmn.). Address: PO Box T Stockton NJ 08559-0993

TUNNER, WILLIAM SAMS, urological surgeon; b. San Antonio, Nov. 14, 1933; s. William Henry and Sarah Margaret (Sams) T.; m. Sallie Berry Woodul, Dec. 4, 1965; children: William Woodul, Jonathan Sams. Student Washington and Lee U., 1952-55; MD, U. Va., 1960. Diplomate Am. Bd. Urology. Intern in surgery, then asst. surg. resident Duke Hosp., 1960-62; fellow cancer surgery Cancer Inst. NIH, Bethesda, Md., 1962-64; resident in urol. surgery Cornell-N.Y. Hosp., 1964-68, fellow transplantation, dialysis and biochemistry, instr. surgery, 1968-70; asst. prof. urol. surgery U. Tex. Med. Sch., San Antonio, 1970-72; pvt. practice medicine specializing in pediatric and adult urology, Richmond, Va., 1972—; mem. staff Henrico County St. Marys Hosp., Chippenham, Johnston-Willis hosps.; asst. clin. prof. urology Med. Coll. Va., 1972—. Valentine research fellow, 1970-72; grantee Hearst Research Found., 1970-72. Fellow ACS, (past pres. Va. chpt., gov.-at-large), Am. Acad. Pediatrics (affiliate); mem. AMA, SocietéInternationalde Urologié, Transplantation Soc., Soc. Pediatric Urology, Am. Urol. Assn., Am. Nephrology Assn., SR, Country Club of Va., Deep Runt Hunt Club, Alpha Epsilon Delta, Beta Theta Pi. Episcopalian. Contbr. articles to med. jours., films. Home: Braedon Farm 1240 Shallow Well Rd Manakin Sabot VA 23103-2300 Office: St Mary's Hosp Profl Bldg 5855 Bremo Rd Richmond VA 23226-1926

TUNNESSEN, WALTER WILLIAM, JR., pediatrician; b. Hazleton, Pa., July 25, 1939; s. Walter William and Grace Louise (Schaller) T.; m. Nancy Louise Layton, Aug. 24, 1963; children: Walter William III, Anne L. BA, Lafayette Coll., Easton, Pa., 1961; MD, U. Pa., 1965. Diplomate Am. Bd. Pediatrics (bd. dirs. 1986—). Resident Children's Hosp. of Phila., 1965-67; chief resident in pediatrics Hosp. U. Pa., Phila., 1967-68; isntr., dir. newborn nurseries Hosp. U. Pa./U. Pa. Sch. Medicine, Phila., 1970-72; from asst. prof. to assoc. prof. pediatrics SUNY Health Sci. Ctr., Syracuse, 1972-81, prof. pediat., 1981, acting chair dept., 1985-86; assoc. prof. pediatrics and dermatology Johns Hopkins U. Sch. Medicine, Balt., 1986-90, dir. pediatric dermatology, dir. pediatric diagnostic clinic, 1986-90; assoc. chmn. for med. edn. Children's Hosp. of Phila., 1990-95; prof. pediatrics U. Pa. Sch. Medicine, Phila., 1990-95; sr. v.p. Am. Bd. Pediatrics, Chapel Hill, N.C., 1995—; Robert Wood Johnson clin. Scholar Yale U. Sch. Medicine, New Haven, 1978-79; mem. Nat. Bd. Med. Examiners, 1989-91; mem. sci. bd. Nat. Found. for Ectodermal Dysplasia, 1989-93. Author: Signs and Symptons in Pediatrics, 1983, 2d edit., 1988; editor monthly jour. sects.

Capt. USAF, 1968-70. Mem. Am. Acad. Pediats. (sect. on dermatology exec. com. 1993-95), Soc. for Peidat. Dermatology (pres. 1988-89, bd. dirs.), Am. Pediat. Soc. Avocation: furniture refinishing. Office: Am Bd Pediatrics 111 Silver Cedar Ct Chapel Hill NC 27514-1651

TUNNEY, JOHN VARICK, lawyer, former senator; b. N.Y.C., June 26, 1934; s. Gene and Mary (Lauder) T.; m. Kathinka Osborne, April 1977; children: Edward Eugene, Mark Andrew, Arianne Sprengers, Tara Theodora. B.A. in Anthropology, Yale, 1956; J.D., U. Va., 1959; student, Acad. Internat. Law, The Hague, Netherlands, 1957. Bar: N.Y. 1959, Calif. 1963, Va. 1963. With firm Cahill, Gordon, Reindel & Ohl, N.Y.C., 1959-60; tchr. bus. law U. Calif., Riverside, 1961-62; practice law Riverside, 1963—; mem. 89th-91st Congresses from Calif. 38th Dist., U.S. Senate from Calif., 1971-77; mem. firm Manatt, Phelps, Rothenberg & Tunney, Los Angeles, 1977-86; chmn. bd. Cloverleaf Group, Inc., Los Angeles, 1986—; gen. ptnr. Sun Valley Ventures, 1994—; chmn. bd. Enterprise Plan, Inc., chmn. bd. Trusted Brands Inc.; bd. dirs. Prospect Group Inc., Garnet Resources Corp., Ill. Central Railroad, The Forschner Group, Inc., Foamax Internat. Trustee Westminster Sch., St. Matthews Sch.; bd. visitors Loyola Law Sch.; vice chmn. Limited Incomes Housing Corp.; mem. Lawyers Adv. Council. Constl. Rights Found., Citizens Rsch. Found., Commn. on Soviet Jewry. Served to capt. USAF, 1960-63. Chubb fellow Yale U., 1967. Mem. Am. Bar Assn. Democrat. Episcopalian. Office: 1819 Ocean Ave Santa Monica CA 90401-3223

TUNNICLIFF, DAVID GEORGE, civil engineer; b. Ord, Nebr., Sept. 18, 1931; s. George Thomas and Ada Ellen (Ward) T.; m. Elaine Jean Interrante, Oct. 17, 1959 (div.); children: Martha Allison Tunnicliff Loeb, Vivian Jean Tunnicliff Perez; m. Joan Elizabeth Duchesneau, Oct. 25, 1975. BS, U. Nebr., 1954; MS, Cornell U., 1958; PhD, U. Mich., 1972. Registered profl. engr., Nebr., Mass. Engr. Nebr. Dept. Rds., Lincoln, 1954-60; asst. prof., then assoc. prof. Wayne State U., Detroit, 1960-67; chief tech. svcs. Warren Bros. Co., Cambridge, Mass., 1967-79; prin., cons. engr. D.G. Tunnicliff, Cons. Engr., Omaha, 1979—. Contbr. to profl. publs. Rep. precinct del., Detroit, 1965-66. With U.S. Army, 1955-56. Mem. ASTM (chair subcom. 1973-94), ASCE, Assn. Asphalt Paving Tech. (bd. dirs. 1976-78), Transp. Rsch. Bd. (com. chair 1983-89). Mem. Evangel. Covenant Ch. Home & Office: DG Tunnicliff Cons Engr 9624 Larimore Ave Omaha NE 68134-3038

TUNNICLIFFE, WILLIAM WARREN, graphics company executive; b. Washington, Apr. 22, 1922; s. Homer Warren and Christine (Hobbs) T.; m. Ruth Loretto Loftus, June 23, 1951; children: Peter Warren, Virginia Warren, Elizabeth Loftus, William Loftus. BEE, Worcester Poly., 1943; MA in Engring. Scis. and Applied Physics, Harvard U., 1951. Staff mem. MIT Radiation Lab., 1943-44; head electronics sect. Boston U. Optical Research Lab., 1946-51; electronics engr. Barkley & Dexter Labs. Inc., Fitchburg, Mass., 1953-55; mgr. Eastern engring. office Offner Electronics Inc., Somerville, Mass., 1955-56; systems engr., project mgr., program mgr. Raytheon Co., Wayland, Mass., 1956-63; v.p. Info. Dynamics Corp., Reading, Mass., 1963-65; program mgr. Courier Citizen Co., Lowell, Mass., 1965-68, v.p., 1969-72; nat. sales mgr. Graphic Services, an Am. Standard Co., Warren, Mich., 1972, pres., 1973-74; gen. mgr. Woodland Communications Co. subs. W.E. Andrews Co., Bedford, Mass., 1975; program dir. prepress systems Graphic Communications Computer Assn., Arlington, Va., 1976-77; v.p. Walter T. Armstrong, Phila., 1977-78; program mgr. Bobst Graphic Inc. (subs. Bobst SA, Lausanne, Switzerland), Bohemia, N.Y., 1979, dir. market research, 1979-80, dir. market mgmt. and research, 1980, mktg. mgr., 1980-81; mktg. mgr. Graphics Arts div. Imlac Corp. subs. Hazeltine, Needham, Mass., 1981; account exec. Altertext Inc., Boston, 1982-83; v.p. info. techs. Graphic Communications Assn., Arlington, 1983-85; pres. Tunnicliffe Assocs. Inc., Winchester, Mass., 1974—; cons. Raytheon Co., 1964-66, Courier-Citizen Co., 1972, Chrysler Corp., 1974, Bobst Graphic Inc., 1981, Printing Industries of Am. Inc., 1985-86, Aspen Systems Corp., 1986-87, Oak Ridge Nat. Lab., 1986-87, Xyvision Inc., 1987, Interleaf Inc., 1987-88, Sci. Typographers, Inc., 1990—; printing industry rep. concerning the Standard Generalized Markup Lang. (SGML) to Joint Industry-Dept. Def. Task Force on Computer-Aided Acquisitions & Logistic Support, 1983-85, the Internat. Orgn. for Standardization and corr. coms. of Am. Nat. Standards Inst./Computer & Bus. Equipment Mfrs. Assn., 1983-85 and The Assn. Am. Pubs., 1983-85. Bd. dirs. Horace L. and Florence E. Mayer Found., Inc., Balt.; organizing chmn. bd. dirs. Printing Rsch. Inst. for New Tech., Inc., Washington, 1968-69, chmn. bd., pres., 1970-74. Lt. (j.g.) USNR, 1944-46, lt., 1951-53, capt., 1953-82. Recipient Walter Sherman Gifford Jr. Trophy; also numerous industry awards related to SGML, including recognition award Printing Inds. of Am., Inc., 1983, Gutenberg award Printing Inds. of Am., Inc., 1984, Tekkie award Graphic Communications Assn., 1986, 25th Anniversary-recognition award Can. Govt. Printing Office, 1967. Mem. Am. Soc. Info. Scis., Armed Forces Communications and Electronics Assn., Assn. Computing Machinery, IEEE, Internat. Word Processing Assn., Nat. Micrographics Assn., Nat. Soc. Profl. Engrs., Soc. Info. Display, Soc. Motion Picture and TV Engrs., Soc. Scholarly Pub., Inst. Printing (London), Printing Industries Am., Graphic Communications Computer Assn. (chmn. character generation com. 1967-74, dir. 1970-74, v.p. 1973-74), Printing Industries New Eng. (co-chmn. computer conf. 1967), Nat. Composition Assn., Research and Engring. Council of Graphic Arts Industry, Am. Def. Preparedness Assn., Naval Res. Assn., Res. Officers Assn., Retired Officers Assn., Standard Generalized Markup Lang. Users' Group (hon. mem.), U.S. Naval Inst., Sci. Research Soc. Am., Sigma Xi. Club: Harvard (Boston). Home and Office: 39 Central St Winchester MA 01890-2629 also: 759 E Washington Rd Hillsboro NH 03244-4007

TUOHEY, MARK HENRY, III, lawyer; b. Rochester, N.Y., Sept. 27, 1946; s. Mark Henry T.; m. Martha; children—Brendan, Sean, Devin. B.A. in History, St. Bonaventure U., 1968; J.D., Fordham U., 1973. Bar: D.C. 1973, U.S. Supreme Ct. 1980, U.S. Ct. Appeals (D.C. cir.) 1974, U.S. Dist. Ct. D.C. 1974, N.Y. 1984. Asst. U.S. atty. U.S. Atty.'s Office, Washington, 1973-77; spl. trial counsel U.S. Dept. Justice, Washington, 1977-79; spl. counsel to U.S. Atty. Gen., Washington, 1979; ptnr. Vinson & Elkins, Washington; dep. ind. counsel Whitewater Investigation, 1993-94. Served to 1st lt. U.S. Army, 1970-71. Fellow Am. Law Inst., Am. Bar Found. (bd. dirs. 1980-85), Am. Coll. Trial Lawyers; mem. ABA (litigation sect. coun. 1980-90, chair standing com. on continuing edn. of bar, chair 1980-85, Am. Law Inst./ABA com. on continuing profl. edn. 1983—), D.C. Bar (pres. 1993—, bd. govs. 1988—), Jud. Conf. U.S. Ct. Appeals (D.C. cir.), Wm. Bryant Inn of Ct. (master). Home: 1655 Kalmia Rd NW Washington DC 20012-1125 Office: Vinson & Elkins The Willard Office Bldg 1455 Pennsylvania Ave NW Washington DC 20004

TUOHY, WILLIAM, correspondent; b. Chgo., Oct. 1, 1926; s. John Marshall and Lolita (Klaus) T.; m. Mary Ellyn Dufek, 1955 (div.); m. Johanna Iselin 1964 (div.); 1 child, Cyril Iselin. BS, Northwestern U., 1951. Reporter, night city editor San Francisco Chronicle, 1952-59; assoc. editor, nat. polit. corr., fgn. corr. Newsweek mag., 1959-66; Vietnam corr. L.A. Times, 1966-68; Middle East corr. L.A. Times, Beirut, 1969-71; bur. chief L.A. Times, Rome, 1971-77, London, 1977-85, Bonn, Fed. Republic Germany, 1985-90; European security corr. L.A. Times, London, 1990—. Author: Dangerous Company, 1987. Served with USNR, 1944-46. Recipient Nat. Headliner award for Vietnam bur. coverage, 1965, Pulitzer prize internat. reporting (Vietnam), 1969, Overseas Press Club award for best internat. reporting (Middle East), 1970, various others.

TUPPER, CHARLES JOHN, physician, educator; b. Miami, Ariz., Mar. 7, 1920; s. Charles Ralph and Grace (Alexander) T.; m. Mary Hewes, Aug. 4, 1942; children: Mary Elizabeth, Charles John. B.A. in Zoology, San Diego State Coll., 1943; M.D., U. Nebr., 1948. Diplomate: Am. Bd. Internal Medicine. Intern U. Mich. Hosp., Ann Arbor, 1948-49; asst. resident U. Mich. Hosp., 1949-50, resident, 1950-51, jr. clin. instr., 1951-52; pvt. practice specializing in internal medicine Ann Arbor, 1954-66; practice medicine specializing internal medicine Davis, Calif., 1966—; rsch. asst. Inst. Indsl. Health, U. Mich., 1951-52, rsch. assoc., 1954-56, instr. internal medicine, 1954-56, asst. prof., 1956-59, assoc. prof., 1959-66, sec. Med. Sch., 1957-59, asst. dean, 1959-61, assoc. dean, 1961-66, dir. periodic health appraisal program univ. faculty, 1956-66; prof. internal medicine Sch. Medicine U. Calif., Davis, 1966-90, prof. emeritus cmty. health & family medicine, 1990—, dean, 1966-80, prof. cmty. health, 1980-90, prof. family practice, 1981-90, acting chair cmty. health, 1989-91, 94-95; mem. adv. bd. Golden State Svcs. Dir. consultation services U. Mich. Health Service, 1956-66, 73-76; pres. Calif. Med. Assn., 1979-80; vice chmn. U. Calif. Davis Found., 1993—, Sacramento Regional Found., 1993. Served from 1st lt. to capt. USAF, 1952-54. Fellow ACP; mem. AMA (trustee 1985-89, pres. elect 1989-90, pres. 1990-91, immediate past pres. 1991-92, chmn. coun. sci. affairs 1977-79, coun. sect. med. schs. 1977-78), Internat., Am., Calif. socs. internal medicine, Am. Coll. Health Assn., Assn. Am. Med. Colls., Am. Assn. Automotive Medicine, Yolo County Med. soc., Calif. Med. Assn. (pres. 1979-80, chmn. sci. bd. 1970-78, chmn. liaison to state bar com., chmn. com. on state legislation 1975-85, del. to AMA 1975-85), Sci. Rsch. Club. Club: El Macero Country (dir.). Home: PO Box 2007 El Macero CA 95618-0007 Office: U Calif Med Sch Dept Cmty Health Davis CA 95616

TURAJ, FRANK, university dean, literature and film educator; b. Derby, Conn., May 31, 1934; children: Kristyn, Julie. B.A., U. Conn., 1959, M.A., 1960; Ph.D., Brown U., 1968. Instr. George Washington U., 1962-65; asst. prof. lit. Am. U., Washington, 1965-68, assoc. prof., 1969-74, prof., 1975—, chmn. dept. lit., 1974-76, acting dean Coll. Arts and Scis., 1976-77, dean, 1977-85, founder Am. studies program, 1970, cinema studies program, 1975; Polish exchange and Italian study program Am. U. Author: H.L. Mencken and American Literature, 1968, The Modern Cinema of Poland, 1988; (with others) Post New Wave Cinema in the Soviet Union and Eastern Europe, 1988; co-writer and co-producer: USIA documentary The Impact of Film, 1973. Served with USAF, 1951-55. Recipient Disting. Teaching award Am. U., 1968, Media Achievement award Perspectives mag., Washington, 1980, medal for svc. to Polish culture Govt. of Poland, 1981, Spl. award Polish Filmmakers Assn., 1983, Presdl. citation Am. U., 1985; Disting. Svc. medal Adam Mickiewicz U., Poznan, Poland, 1986, Spl. 70th Ann. of Univ. award, 1989. Mem. Am. Assn. Higher Edn., Am. Assn. Slavic Studies, Assn. Am. Colls., Polish Inst. Arts and Scis. (bd. dirs.). Office: Am Univ Dept of Literature 4400 Massachusetts Ave NW Washington DC 20016-8001

TURANO, DAVID A., lawyer; b. Ashtabula, Ohio, Sept. 9, 1946; s. Egidio A. and Mary Agnes (Bartko) T.; m. Karen J. Emmel, Aug. 29, 1970; children: Aaron, Thad, Bethen, Kyle. BS, Kent State U., 1968; JD, Ohio State U., 1971. Bar: Ohio 1971. Staff atty. The Pub. Utilities Commn. Ohio, Columbus, 1971-72; assoc., then ptnr. George, Greek, King, McMahon and Mcconnaughey, Columbus, 1972-79; ptnr. Baker & Hostetler, Columbus, 1979—. Mem. ABA, Ohio State Bar Assn., Columbus Bar Assn., Transp. Lawyers Assn. Roman Catholic. Office: Baker & Hostetler 65 E State St Columbus OH 43215-4213

TURANO, EMANUEL NICOLAS, architect; b. Bklyn., Mar. 1, 1917; s. Dominick and Ann (Girordi) T.; m. Sybyl Rosmarin, July 1, 1951; children: Lisa, Laurie, Leslie. Cert. in architecture, Cooper Union, 1941, Profl. Achievement citation (hon. Ph.D.), 1964; BArch, Harvard, 1947, MArch, 1963. Designer Skidmore, Owings & Merrill, 1947-50; chief design Kelly & Gruzen, N.Y.C., 1950-52; prin. E.N. Turano (architects and planners), N.Y.C., 1952—; dir. T-4 Studios, N.Y.C., 1965; tchr. 3d, 4th, 5th and master studios Pratt Inst., Bklyn., 1959-62; archtl. instr. 4th yr. studio Columbia, N.Y.C., 1959-60; Cons. HUD, 1963-67, Sussex Woodlands, Inc., N.J., 1963-66. Mem. Boca Raton (Fla.) Bd. Adjustments and Appeals, 1979—; chmn. Boca Raton Code Enforcement Bd. Served with USAAF, 1941-45, PTO. Decorated D.F.C., Air medal. Recipient several awards including Pub. Housing Authority awards, Archtl. award excellence for Pan Am. Passenger Terminal Bldg., Archtl. award excellence for Am. Inst. Steel Constrn., 1961; Fulbright fellow, 1950. Fellow AIA (exec. com. N.Y.C. 1962-66); mem. N.Y. State Assn. Architects, Nat. Inst. Archtl. Edn. (past sec. treas.), N.Y. Soc. Architects, Municipal Art Soc., Cooper Union Alumni Assn. (gov. 1964-67), Cooper Union Adv. Council (chmn. edn. com. 1957-59). Home and Office: 1900 Isabel Rd Este Boca Raton FL 33486-6734

TURBEVILLE, GUS, emeritus college president; b. Turbeville, S.C., Jan. 20, 1923; s. William Jasper and Ila Lucile (Morris) T.; m. Joanne Beverly Johnson, June 7, 1950; children—David Baxter, William Jackson, Sara Ellen. B.A., Vanderbilt U., 1944; M.A., La. State U., 1946; Ph.D., Mich. State U., 1948; LL.D., Columbia Coll., 1982. Head sociology dept. U. Minn., Duluth, 1948-53; pres. Northland Coll., Ashland, Wis., 1953-61; chmn. sociology dept. U. Wis., Superior, 1962-69; pres. Coker Coll., Hartsville, S.C., 1969-74, Emerson Coll., Boston, 1975-78, William Penn Coll., Oskaloosa, Iowa, 1979-84; pres. emeritus William Penn Coll., Oskaloosa, Iowa, 1984—. Co-author: Social problems, 1955; If You Smoke, What Have You?, 1970; The Best of Pogo, 1982; contbr. articles to profl. jours. Bd. dirs. St. Joseph's Hosp., Superior, Wis., 1960-69, Intercomputer Communications Corp., Phoenix, 1970-79. Fellow Am. Sociol. Assn. Quaker. Lodge: Rotary (Ashland, Wis. and Hartsville, S.C.). Avocations: hiking; swimming; reading; writing; philately. Home: 1350 SW 13th Dr Boca Raton FL 33486-5367

TURBEVILLE, ROBERT MORRIS, engineering executive; b. Cleve., May 2, 1951; s. Wilfred and Patricia Alice (Lamb) T.; m. Lisa Edelman, Apr. 2, 1977; children: Adam, Dennis, Diana. Student, Drew U., London, 1971-72; BA in History, W. Va. Wesleyan, 1973. Mgmt. trainee U.S. Steel, Pitts., 1973-74, foreman, 1975-79; mgr. standard products Heyl & Patterson, Inc., Pitts., 1979-83, sales mgr. to gen. mgr., 1983-88, v.p., 1988-91, pres., CEO, 1991—; dir. Heyl & Patterson, Inc., Pitts., 1988—; chmn. Bridge & Crane Inspection, Inc., Pitts., 1990—. Asst. leader Cub Scouts Am., Pitts., 1991—; coach Mt. Lebanon Soccer Assn., Pitts., 1990—. Mem. AIME, Coal Prep. Adv. Bd. (co-chmn. 1985-89), Process Equipment Mfrs. Assn., Young Pres. Orgn. Republican. Methodist. Avocations: car restoration, travel, music. Office: Heyl & Patterson Inc PO Box 36 Pittsburgh PA 15230-0036

TURBIDY, JOHN BERRY, investor, management consultant; b. Rome, Ga., Oct. 18, 1928; s. Joseph Leo and Louyse (Berry) T.; m. Joan Marsales, Dec. 19, 1958; children: John Berry, Trevor Martin. Grad., Darlington Sch., 1945; B.A., Duke U., 1950; postgrad., NYU, 1952, Emory U., 1954-56. Pers. positions Lockheed Aircraft, Marietta, Ga., 1951-56; gen. mgmt. cons. McKinsey & Co., N.Y.C. and London, 1956-63; v.p. adminstrn. ITT Europe, Inc., Brussels, 1963, v.p., group exec. European consumer products, 1964-65, v.p., group exec. for No. Europe, 1965-67; corp. v.p. adminstrn. Celanese Corp., N.Y.C., 1967-68; pres., mng. dir. SIACE, SP.A. subs., Milan, Italy, 1968-69; chmn. bd., pres. Vecta Group, Kalamazoo, Mich., 1970-74; v.p. corp. devel. IU Internat. Corp., Phila., 1974-76, sr. v.p., 1976-77, exec. v.p., 1978-83; exec. v.p. Pitcairn Inc., Jenkintown, Pa., 1984-85; pres., chief exec. officer Pitcairn Fin. Mgmt. Group, 1986-89; chmn. Office John Turbidy, 1990—. Bd. dirs. Statute of Liberty Ellis Island Found. Served with USNR, 1952. Club: Merion Cricket. Address: 7 Hillside Pl Fair Haven NJ 07704

TURBIN, RICHARD, lawyer; b. N.Y.C., Dec. 25, 1944; s. William and Ruth (Fiedler) T.; m. Rai Saint Chu-Turbin, June 12, 1976; children—Laurel Mei, Derek Andrew. B.A. magna cum laude, Cornell U., 1966; J.D., Harvard U., 1969. Bar: Hawaii 1971, U.S. Dist. Ct. Hawaii 1971. Asst. atty. gen. Western Samoa, Apia, 1969-70; dep. pub. defender Pub. Defender's Office, Honolulu, 1970-74; dir. Legal Aid Soc. Hawaii, Kaneohe, 1974-75; sr. atty., pres. Law Offices Richard Turbin, Honolulu, 1975—; legal counsel Hawaii Crime Commn., 1980-81. Co-author: Pacific; author: Medical Malpractice, Handling Emergency Medical Cases, 1991; editor Harvard Civil Rights-Civil Liberties Law Rev., 1969. Legal counsel Democratic Party, Honolulu County, 1981-82; elected Neighborhood Bd., 1985, elected chair, 1990-93; bd. dirs. Hawaii chpt. ACLU, 1974-78. East-West Ctr. grantee, 1971, 72. Mem. Hawaii Bar Assn., ABA (chair internat. torts and ins. law and practice com., mem. governing coun.), Am. Trial Lawyers Assn., Hawaii Trial Lawyers Assn. (bd. govs.), Hawaii Jaycees (legal counsel 1981-82), Chinese Jaycees Honolulu (legal counsel 1980-81), Honolulu Tennis League (undefeated player 1983). Jewish. Club: Hawaii Harlequin Rugby (sec., legal counsel 1978-82). Lodge: Elks. Home: 4557 Kolohala St Honolulu HI 96816-4953 Office: 737 Bishop St Ste 1850 Honolulu HI 96813-3209

TURCO, LEWIS PUTNAM, English educator; b. Buffalo, N.Y., May 2, 1934; s. Luigi and May Laura (Putnam) T.; m. Jean Cate Houdlette, May 29, 1934; children: Melora Ann, Christopher Cameron. BA, U. Conn., 1959; MA, U. Iowa, 1962. Instr. Cleve. State U., 1960-64; asst. prof. Hillsdale (Mich.) Coll., 1964-65; asst. prof. to full prof. SUNY, Oswego, 1965—, poet-in-residence, 1995; grad. asst. English, U. Conn., 1959; editorial asst. Writer's Workshop, U. Iowa, 1959-60; vis. prof. SUNY, Potsdam, 1968-69; Bingham Poet in Residence, U. Louisville, 1982; Writer in Residence, Ashland U., 1991; founding dir. Cleve. State U. Poetry Ctr., 1962, program in writing arts, SUNY Oswego, 1968. Author: First Poems, 1960, Awaken, Bells Falling: Poems 1959-67, 1968, The Inhabitant, 1970, Pocoangelini: A Fantography and Other Poems, 1971, American Still Lifes, 1981, numerous other poetry books including The Shifting Web: New and Selected Poems, 1989; author numerous non-fiction books including The Book of Forms: A Handbook of Poetics, 1968, The New Book of Forms, 1986, Visions and Revisions of American Poetry, 1986, Dialogue, 1989, Emily Dickinson, Woman of Letters, 1993, others; articles. Sec. City of Oswego Charter Revision Commn., 1990-91; active Oswego Opera Theater Chorus, Oswego Festival Chorus, 1986—. With USN, 1952-56. Recipient scholarship Meriden Record-Jour. Pub. Co., U. Conn., 1957-58, 58-59, Disting. Alumnus award, 1992, Melville Cane award Poetry Soc. Am., 1986, others; resident fellowships Yaddo Found., 1959, 77, Faculty fellowships Rsch. Found. of SUNY, 1966-67, 69, 71, 73, 78; grant-in-aid, 1969; inducted into Meridan Hall of Fame, 1983. Home: PO Box 362 Oswego NY 13126-0362 Office: SUNY College 39A Swetman Hall Oswego NY 13126

TURCO, RICHARD PETER, atmospheric scientist; b. N.Y.C., Mar. 9, 1943; s. Salvatore Joseph and Mary Louise (Cuocolo) T.; m. Barbara Marie Bren, July 1, 1967 (div. Sept. 1990); 1 child, Richard Cameron; m. Linda Stevenson Newman, July 27, 1991. BSEE, Rutgers U., 1965; PhDEE and Physics, U. Ill., 1971. Research fellow Ames Research Ctr., NASA, Moffett Field, Calif., 1971; research scientist R&D Assocs., Los Angeles, 1971-88; prof. UCLA, 1988—, Disting. Faculty Rsch. lectr., 1992—, dept. chair, 1993—; founding dir. Inst. of the Environment, 1995—. Author: Environmental Consequences of Nuclear War, 1986, (with Carl Sagan) A Path Where No Man Thought: Nuclear Winter and the End of the Arms Race, 1990, Earth Under Seige: From Air Pollution to Global Change, 1995; proposed nuclear winter theory, 1983. Recipient H. Julian Allen award NASA, 1983, 88, Peace Garden award U. N.D., 1984, Leo Szilard award Am. Phys. Soc., 1985; MacArthur Found. fellow, 1986. Mem. Am. Geophys. Union (pres. atmospheric scis. sect. 1992-94, assoc. editor Jour. Geophys. Rsch. 1982-91, fellow 1993), Sigma Xi. Avocations: hiking, handball.

TURCOTTE, DONALD LAWSON, geophysical sciences educator; b. Bellingham, Wash., Apr. 22, 1932; s. Lawson Phillip and Eva (Pearson) T.; m. Joan Meredith Luecke, May 17, 1957; children: Phillip Lawson, Stephen Bradford. BS, Calif. Inst. Tech., 1954, PhD, 1958; M in Aero. Engring., Cornell U., 1955. Asst. prof. aero. engring. U.S. Naval Postgrad. Sch., Monterey, Calif., 1958-59; asst. prof. aero. engring. Cornell U., Ithaca, N.Y., 1959-63; assoc. prof. Cornell U., 1963-67, prof., 1967-73, prof. geol. scis., 1973-85, Maxwell Upson prof., 1985—, chmn., 1981-90. Author: (with others) Statistical Thermodynamics, 1963, Space Propulsion, 1965, Geodynamics, 1982, Fractals and Chaos in Geology and Geophysics, 1992. Trustee U. Space Research Assn., 1975-79. NSF sr. postdoctoral research fellow, 1965-66; Guggenheim fellow, 1972-73; Recipient Charles A. Whitten award Am. Geophysical Union, 1995. Mem. Am. Geophys. Union (Charles A. Whitten Medal, 1995), Geol. Soc. Am. (Day medal 1982), Seismol. Soc. Am., Nat. Acad. Scis., Am. Acad. Arts and Scis. Club: Ithaca Country. Home: 703 Cayuga Heights Rd Ithaca NY 14850-1463 Office: Cornell U Snee Hall Ithaca NY 14853

TURCOTTE, JEAN-CLAUDE CARDINAL, archbishop; b. Montreal, Que., Can., June 26, 1936; s. Paul-Émile and Rita (Gravel) T. Attended, U. Catholique de Lille, France; DD (hon.), McGill U. Grand Seminaire of Montreal Lic. Theology, ordained priest Roman Catholic Ch., consecrated bishop. Aux. bishop Diocese of Montreal, Que., Can., 1982-90, archbishop, 1990—; cardinal Diocese of Montreal, Que., Can., 1994. Home: 1071 de la Cathedrale St, Montreal QC Canada H3B 2V4 Office: Diocese de Montreal, 2000 rue Sherbrooke ouest, Montreal, PQ Canada H3H 1G4

TURCOTTE, JEREMIAH GEORGE, physician, surgery educator; b. Detroit, Jan. 20, 1933; s. Vincent Joseph and Margaret Campau (Meldrum) T.; m. Claire Mary Lenz, July 5, 1958; children: Elizabeth Margaret, Sarah Lenz, John Jeremiah, Claire Meldrum. BS with high distinction, U. Mich., 1955, MD cum laude, 1957. Diplomate Am. Bd. Surgery (dir. 1982-88); added qualification in surg. critical care, 1986. Intern U. Mich. Med. Ctr., 1957-58, resident in surgery, 1958-60, 61-63; research asst. USPHS grant U. Mich. surgery dept., 1960-61; mem. faculty U. Mich. Med. Sch., 1963—, prof. surgery, 1971—, chmn. dept., 1974-87, head sect. gen. surgery, 1974-81; mem. residency rev. com. for surgery Am. Coun. for Grad. Med. Edn., 1980-86; dir. Transplant and Health Policy Ctr., U. Mich., 1985-95, dir. Organ Transplant Ctr. and Liver Transplant Program, 1984—; chmn. ethics com. United Network for Organ Sharing, 1987-91. Author 8 books, 51 book chpts. contbr. some 185 articles to profl. jours. Recipient Henry Russell award U. Mich., 1970, Mich. State Med. Soc. award, 1991. Fellow ACS (gov. 1982-92, pres. Mich. chpt. 1979-80); mem. Transplantation Soc. Mich. (pres. 1973-75), Assn. Acad. Surgeons, Am. Surg. Assn., Soc. Univ. Surgeons, Internat. Transplantation Soc., Ctrl. Surg. Assn. (pres. 1990-91), Midwest Surg. Assn., Am. Gastroenterol. Assn., Western Surg. Assn., Soc. Surgery Alimentary Tract, Am. Soc. Transplant Surgeons (pres. 1979-80, chmn. ethics com. 1991-94), Frederick A. Coller Soc. (pres. 1982-83), Am. Trauma Soc. (founder), Halsted Soc., Mich. State Med. Soc. (Pres.'s award 1991), Am. Liver Found., Am. Coun. on Transplantation (bd. dirs. 1987-90), Ctrl. Surg. Assn. Found. (executor and sec. 1992—). Roman Catholic. Home: One Regent Dr Ann Arbor MI 48104-1738

TURCZYN-TOLES, DOREEN MARIE, pharmaceutical consultant; b. Chelsea, Mass., Aug. 5, 1958; d. Francis Henry and Rosalie (Lomba) Turczyn; m. Ronald Eugene Toles, Oct. 19, 1986. BA cum laude, Boston U., 1981; MA, U. Chgo., 1984. Programming subcontr. Abbott Labs., Abbott Park, Ill., 1983-84; programmer, analyst Nat. Opinion Research Ctr., Chgo., 1984-88; statis. computing analyst G.D. Searle & Co., Skokie, Ill., 1988-90; supr. Parke-Davis Pharms., Ann Arbor, Mich., 1990-92; mgr. applications programming Univax Biologics, Inc., Rockville, Md., 1993-95; asst. project dir. Apache Med. Sys., Inc., McLean, Va., 1995—. Mem. Nat. Assn. Female Execs., NOW. Democrat. Roman Catholic.

TURE, NORMAN BERNARD, public policy research organization executive; b. Cleve., Sept. 8, 1923; s. Albert Abel and Anne T.; m. Donna Jeanne Cramer, Oct. 23, 1979; children: Martha Elizabeth, Peter Douglas, Heather, Julianne, Keli, Anne Claire. Student, Ohio State U., 1941-43; M.A., U. Chgo., 1947, Ph.D. in Econs., 1968. Mem. staff Treasury Dept., 1951-55, Joint Econ. Com., 1955-61, Nat. Bur. Econ. Research, 1961-68, Planning Research Corp., 1968-71; pres. Norman B. Ture, Inc., Washington, 1971-80, Inst. Research Econs. Taxation, Washington, 1977-80; undersec. tax and econ. affairs Treasury Dept., 1981-82; pres. Inst. Research on Econs. of Taxation, 1983—. Author: Accelerated Depreciation in the United States 1954-60, 1967, Tax Policy, Capital Formation, and Productivity, 1973, The Future of Private Pension Plans, 1976, The Effects of Tax Policy on Capital Formation, 1977, Wealth Redistribution and the Income Tax, 1978, The Value Added Tax: Facts and Fancies, 1979, Measuring the Benefits and Costs of Section 936. Served with AUS, 1943-44. Republican. Roman Catholic. Club: Capitol Hill. Office: 1300 19th St NW Ste 240 Washington DC 20036-1609

TURECK, ROSALYN, concert performer, author, editor, educator; b. Chgo., Dec. 14, 1914; d. Samuel and Mary (Lipson) T.; (w. 1964). Piano studies with Sophia Brilliant-Liven, Chgo., 1925-29; with Jan Chiapusso, 1929-31; harpsichord studies with Gavin Williamson, Chgo., 1931-32; piano studies with Olga Samaroff, N.Y.C., 1931-35; BA cum laude, The Juilliard Sch. Music, 1935; MusD (hon.), Colby Coll., 1964, Roosevelt U., 1968, Wilson Coll., 1968, Oxford U., Eng., 1977, Music and Arts Inst., San Francisco, 1987. Mem. faculty Phila. Conservatory Music, 1935-42, Mannes Sch., N.Y.C., 1940-44, Juilliard Sch. Music, N.Y.C., 1943-55, Columbia U., N.Y.C., 1953-55; prof. music, lectr.; regents prof. U. Calif., San Diego, 1966, prof. music, 1966-74; vis. prof. Washington U., St. Louis, 1963-64, U. Md., 1981-85, Yale U., 1991-93; vis. fellow St. Hilda's Coll., Oxford (Eng.) U., 1974, hon. life fellow, 1974—; vis. fellow Wolfson Coll., Oxford, 1975—; lectr. numerous ednl. instns., U.S., Eng., Spain, Denmark, Holland, Can., Israel, Brazil, Argentina, Chile; lectr. Royal Inst. Great Britain, 1993, Boston U., 1993, 94, Smithsonian Instn., 1994, Rockefeller U., 1994, U. Calif., Santa Barbara, 1995, Hebrew U., Israel, Royal Inst. Gt. Britain, London, U. Southampton, Oxford U., 1993; 10th Internat. Congress Logic, Methodology and Philosophy Sci., 1995; founder Composers of Today, 1949-53; soc. for performance internat. contemporary music, founder, dir. Tureck

Bach Players, London, 1957, N.Y.C., 1981; founder, dir. Internat. Bach Soc., Inst. for Bach Studies, 1968 ; founder, dir. Tureck Bach Inst., Inc., 1981, Symposia 1968-86, Tureck Bach Rsch. Found., Oxford, U.K., 1994; First Ann. Symposium, Structure: Principles and Applications in the Sciences and Music, 1995. Debut solo recital, Chgo., 1924; soloist Ravinia Park, Chgo., 1926, 2 all-Bachrecitals, Chgo., 1930; N.Y.C. debut Carnegie Hall with Phila. Orch., 1936; series 6 all-Bach recitals, Town Hall, N.Y.C., 1937, ann. series 3 all-Bach recitals, N.Y.C., 1944-54, 59—, ann. U.S.-Can. tours, 1937—; European debut Copenhagen, 1947; extensive ann. European tours; continuing ann. concert tours, recitals, master classes in Spain, Italy, Russia, Eng., Germany, U.S., 1995; world tours in Far East, India, Australia, Europe, 1971, S.Am., 1986, 87, 88, 89, 91, 92, Europe, Israel, Turkey, Spain, 1986-90, Argentina, Chile, 1989, 90, 91, 92, Casals Festival, 1991; N.Y.C. series Met. Mus. Art and Carnegie Hall, 1969—; numerous solo recitals including N.Y.C., 1992, Mostly Mozart Festival, Lincoln Ctr., N.Y.C. , 1994; appeared with leading orchs. U.S., Can., Europe, South Africa, S.Am., Israeli; condr., soloist Collegium Musicum, Copenhagen, 1957, London Philharm. Orch., 1959—, N.Y. Philharm., 1960, Tureck Bach Players, London, 1960-72, San Antonio Symphony, Okla. Symphony, 1962, Scottish Nat. Symphony, Edinburg, Glasgow, 1963, Israel Philharm., Tel Aviv, Haifa and Kol Israel orchs., 1963, Glyndebourne Internat. Bach Soc. Orch., N.Y.C., 1967—, Kans. City Philharm., 1968, Washington Nat. Symphony, 1970, Madrid Chamber Orch., 1970, Israel Festival, Internat. Bach Soc. Orchs., 1967, 69, 70, Carnegie Hall, N.Y., 1975-86, St. Louis Symphony Orch., 1981; Bach festivals cities, Eng., Ireland, Spain, 1959—, Carnegie Hall Ann. Series, N.Y.C., 1975—; TV series Well-Tempered Clavier, Book I, Granada TV, Eng., 1961; BBC series Well-Tempered Clavier, Books 1 and 2, 1976; numerous TV appearances, U.S., 1961—, including Wm. F. Buckley's Firing Line, 1970, 85, 87, 89, Today Show, Camera Three, Bach recitals on piano, harpsichord, clavichord, antique and electronic instruments, 1963—; video concert Teatro Colon, Buenos Aires, 1992; recs. for HMV, Odeon, Decca, Columbia Masterworks., Everest, Allegro, Sony, Video Artists Internat., 1993—, R. Tureck Plays Bach, Goldberg Variations, Great Solo Works Vol. 1 and 2, Live at the Teatro Colon, The R. Tureck Collection, vol. 1 The Young Firebrand, vol. 2 The Young Visionary, Tribute to a Key ; author: Introduction to the Performance of Bach, 3 vols., 1960, Authenticity, 1994, J.S. Bach and Number, Symmetries and Other Relationships, Music and Mathematics, 1995; contbr. articles to various mags.; editor Bach-Sarabande, C minor, 1960, Tureck Bach Urtext Series: Italian Concerto, 1983, 2d edit., 1991, Lute Suite, E minor, 1984, C minor, 1985, Schirmer Music, Inc., Carl Fischer Paginini-Tureck: Moto Perpetuo, A. Scarlatti: Air and Gavotte; films: Fantasy and Fugue: Rosalyn Tureck Plays Bach, 1972, Rosalyn Tureck plays on Harpsichord and Organ, 1977, Joy of Bach, 1978, Camera 3: Bach on the Frontier of the Future, CBS film, Ephesus, Turkey, 1985. Decorated Officers Cross of the Order of Merit, Fed. Republic Germany, 1979; recipient 1st prize Greater Chgo. Piano Playing Tournament, 1928, 1st Town Hall Endowment award, 1937, Phi Beta award, 1946; named Schubert Meml. Contest winner, 1935, Nat. Fedn. Music Clubs Competition winner, 1935, Musician of Yr., Music Tchrs. Nat. Assn., 1987; NEH grantee. Fellow Guildhall Sch. Music and Drama (hon.); mem. Royal Mus. Assn. London, Am. Musicological Soc., Inc. Soc. Musicians (London), Royal Philharmonic Soc. London, Sebastian Bach de Belgique (hon.), Am. Bach Soc., Oxford Soc. Clubs: Century (N.Y.C., Oxford and Cambridge, London), Bohemians (N.Y.C.) (hon.). Office: care Christa Phelps, Lies Askonas Ltd 6 Henrietta St, London WC2 EALA, England also: Tureck Bach Rsch Found, Windrush House Davenant Rd, Oxford OX2 8BX, England *My work in Bach is not a specialization, although concentration on a single composer may seemingly give that impression. It spreads to performance on antique instruments, harpsichord, clavichord, fortepiano, to the contemporary piano and electronic Moog, to the organ, to conducting. My work embraces scholarly research in original sources of manuscript notetexts, period treatises, studies in concepts of form and structure ranging from the far east to medieval, renaissance and baroque culture as well as those concepts which emerge from the 19th and 20th centuries. The years of concertizing in compositions of all periods—pre-Bach, romantic, contemporary, and electronic music and scholarly studies in these fields—have all brought a rich tapestry of understanding to the magisterial requirements for interpreting music of a past era authentically and significantly as a contemporary artist.*

TUREK, SONIA FAY, journalist; b. N.Y.C., Aug. 2, 1949; d. Louis and Julia (Liebson) T.; m. Gilbert Curtis, June 18, 1995. BA in English, CCNY, 1970; MSLS, Drexel U., 1972; MS in Journalism, Boston U., 1979. Children's libr. Wissahickon Valley Pub. Libr., Ambler, Pa., 1973; supr. children's svcs. Somerville Pub. Libr., 1973-78; stringer The Watertown (Mass.) Sun, 1979, The Bedford (Mass.) Minuteman, 1979; reporter The Middlesex News, Framingham, Mass., 1979-82, county bur. chief, 1982-83; reporter The Boston Herald, 1983, asst. city editor, city editor, 1985-86, asst. mng. editor features, 1986-89, asst. mng. editor Sunday, 1989-93, dep. mng. editor, arts and features, 1993—; tchr. Cambridge (Mass.) Ctr. for Adult Edn., 1982, 83; adj. prof. Boston U., 1986; travel writer The Boston Herald, 1984-88, wine columnist, 1984—. Avocations: wine and food, travel, sailing. Office: The Boston Herald One Herald Sq Boston MA 02106

TUREKIAN, KARL KAREKIN, geochemistry educator; b. N.Y.C., Oct. 25, 1927; s. Vaughan Thomas and Victoria (Guleserian) T.; m. Arax Roxanne Hagopian, Apr. 22, 1962; children: Karla Ann, Vaughan Charles. A.B., Wheaton (Ill.) Coll., 1949; M.A., Columbia U., 1951, Ph.D., 1955; DSc (hon.), SUNY, Stony Brook, 1989. Lectr. geology Columbia U., 1953-54, rsch. assoc. Lamont-Doherty Earth Obs., 1954-56; faculty, asst. prof. Yale U., 1956-61, assoc. prof., 1961-65, prof. geology and geophysics, 1965-72, Henry Barnard Davis prof. geology and geophysics, 1972-85, Benjamin Silliman prof., 1985—, chmn. dept., 1982-88, curator meteorites, archaeology coun., dir. Ctr. for the Study of Global Change; chmn. studies in the environment, 1992-93; cons. Pres.'s Commn. Marine Sci. Engring. and Resources, 1967-68; oceanography panel NSF, 1968-70; NASA exobiology panel Am. Inst. Biol. Scientists, 1966-69; mem. NAS-NRC climate rsch. bd., 1977-80, ocean sci. bd., 1979-82, ocean studies bd., 1989-92, bd. on global change, 1992-95, Com. Phys. Scis., Math. Resources, 1986-90, Com. Geoscis., Environment, Resources, 1990-92; mem. group experts sci. aspects Marine Pollution UN, 1971-73. Author: Oceans, 1968, 2d edit., 1976, Chemistry of the Earth, 1972, (with B.J. Skinner) Man and the Ocean, 1973, (with C.K. Drake, J. Imbrie and J.A. Knauss) Oceanography, 1978, Global Environmental Change, 1996. Served with USNR, 1945-46. Guggenheim fellow Cambridge U., 1962-63; Fairchild Disting. scholar Calif. Inst. Tech., 1988. Fellow AAAS, Geol. Soc. Am., Meteoritical Soc., Am. Geophys. Union, Am. Acad. Arts and Scis.; mem. NAS, Am. Chem. Soc., Geochem. Soc. (pres. 1975-76, V.M. Goldschmidt medal 1989), Sigma Xi (pres. Yale chpt. 1961-62). Home: 555 Skiff St North Haven CT 06473-3013 Office: Yale U Dept Geology and Geophysics PO Box 208109 New Haven CT 06520-8109

TURGEON, EDGAR LYNN, economics educator; b. Mitchell, S.D., Aug. 26, 1920; s. Edgar Franklin and Margie (Fellows) T.; m. Livia Racko, Oct. 13, 1950 (div. 1988); 1 child, Danielle Kim. AB, U. Calif., Berkeley, 1942, MA, 1948; PhD, Columbia U., 1959. With Rand Corp., Santa Monica, Calif., 1950-57; prof. econs. Hofstra U., Hempstead, N.Y., 1957-90, prof. emeritus, 1991—; Fulbright lectr. Moscow State U., 1978, Acad. for Fgn. Trade, Moscow, 1991. Author: The Contrasting Economies, 1963, The Advanced Capitalist System, 1980, State and Discrimination, 1989, Bastard Keynesianism, 1996. Lt. USN, 1942-46, PTO. Home: 30 Duncan Rd Hempstead NY 11550-4616 Office: Hofstra U Dept Econs Hempstead NY 11550

TURILLO, MICHAEL JOSEPH, JR., management consultant; b. Hartford, Conn., Aug. 22, 1947; s. Michael Joseph and Alice (Vargas) T.; m. Deborah Sherburne; children: Stephanie, Christopher. BS, Providence Coll., 1969; MBA, Syracuse U., 1972; MS, U. Mass., 1973. Cons. Peat, Marwick, Mitchell & Co. (name changed to KPMG Peat Marwick), Boston, 1974-77, mgr., 1977-82, ptnr., 1982—, nat. cons. practice dir. for fin. svc. cos., 1985-91; chmn. Internat. Mgmt. Cons. Practice Com. on Banking and Fin., 1986—; nat. ptnr.-in-charge Fin. Svcs.-Specialized Cons., 1990-93, Capital Strategies, 1995—, nat. lead ptnr. in charge Global Capital Group, 1993-94. Com. mem. United Way, Boston, 1981-83; trustee Elliot Montessori, South Natick, Mass., 1984-85; dir. Greater Boston coun. Boy Scouts Am., 1988—. Capt. U.S. Army, 1969-71, Vietnam. Decorated Bronze Star. Mem. Bank Mktg. Assn., Assn. Planning Execs., Assn. Corp. Planners, Beta Gamma Sigma. Roman Catholic. Avocations: tennis, photography, travel, golf. Home: 47 South St Natick MA 01760-5526 Office: KPMG Peat Marwick 99 High St Boston MA 02110 also: 345 Park Ave New York NY 10154-0004

TURINO, GERARD MICHAEL, physician, medical scientist, educator; b. N.Y.C., May 16, 1924; s. Michael and Lucy (Arciero) T.; m. Dorothy Estes, Aug. 25, 1951; children: Peter, Phillip, James. A.B., Princeton U., 1945; M.D., Columbia U., 1948. Diplomate: Am. Bd. Internal Medicine. Intern Columbia U., Bellevue Hosp., 1948-49, asst. resident in medicine, 1949-50; resident in medicine New Haven Hosp., 1950-51; chief resident in medicine Columbia U. div. Bellevue Hosp., 1953-54; sr. fellow N.Y. Heart Assn., 1956-60; career investigator Health Research Council City of N.Y., 1961-71; asst. prof. medicine Columbia U., 1960-67, assoc. prof., 1967-72, prof. medicine, 1973-83, John H. Keating prof. medicine, 1983—; mem. staff Presbyn. Hosp., N.Y.C., 1960—; attending physician Presbyn. Hosp., 1983—; dir. med. svcs. St. Lukes-Roosevelt Hosp., N.Y.C., 1983-92; cons. on sci. affairs Am. Thoracic Soc., 1992—; mem. sci. adv. com. Nat. Heart, Lung, and Blood Inst., Am. Lung Assn., Am. Heart Assn., N.Y. Lung Assn., N.Y. Heart Assn.; mem. staff divsn. med. sci. Nat. Rsch. Coun., Washington; cons. VA Hosp., East Orange, N.J., 1962-67; cons. in medicine Englewood (N.J.) Hosp., Hackensack (N.J.) Hosp., pres.-elect Am. Bur. Med. Advancement in China, 1994, pres., 1994—. Contbr. articles to med. jours. Mem. Bd. Edn., Alpine, N.J., 1960-67. Served to capt. USAF, 1951-53. Recipient Joseph Mather Smith prize Columbia U., 1965, Alumni medal, 1983; Silver medal Alumni Assn. Coll. Physicians and Surgeons Columbia U., 1979, gold medal, 1986. Fellow AAAS; mem. Assn. Am. Physicians, Am. Soc. Clin. Investigation, Harvey Soc., Am. Thoracic Soc. (pres. 1987-88), Am. Fedn. Clin. Rsch., Am. Physiol. Soc. (chmn. steering com. respiration sect.), Am. Heart Assn. (award of merit 1980, Disting. Achievement award 1989, bd. dirs.), N.Y. Heart Assn. (pres. 1981-83, dir.), N.Y. Lung Assn. (dir.), N.Y. Med.-Surg. Soc. (pres. 1995), N.Y. Clin. Soc., Princeton Club (N.Y.C.), Maidstone Club, Devon Yacht Club, Century Assn. Club. Home: 66 E 79th St New York NY 10021-0217 Office: St Lukes-Roosevelt Hosp W 114th St and Amsterdam Ave New York NY 10025

TURINSKY, PAUL JOSEF, nuclear engineer, educator; b. Hoboken, N.J., Oct. 20, 1944; s. Paul J. and Wilma A. (Budig) T.; m. Karen Ann DeLuca, Aug. 29, 1966; children: Grant Dean, Beth Noelle. BS, U. R.I., 1966; MSE, U. Mich., 1967, PhD, 1970; MBA, U. Pitts., 1979. Asst. prof. Rensselaer Poly. Inst., Troy, N.Y., 1971-73; engr., mgr. nuclear design Westinghouse Elec. Corp., Pitts., 1973-78, mgr. core devel., 1978-80; head dept. nuclear engring. N.C. State U., Raleigh, 1980-88, prof., 1980—, dir. Electric Power Rsch. Ctr., 1989—; pres. Nuclear Fuel Mgmt. Assocs., 1994—; bd. dirs. Quantum Rsch. Svcs.; cons. Electric Power Rsch. Inst., Palo Alto, Calif., 1980—, Sci. Applications Internat. Corp., 1990-92, U.S. Dept. of Energy, 1993; tech. specialist Internat. Atomic Energy Agy., Vienna, Austria, 1982—; mem. nuclear safety rev. bd. Duke Power Co., Charlotte, N.C., 1986—. Author: (with others) CRC Handbook of Nuclear Reactor Calculations, 1986; contbr. more than 90 articles to tech. jours. Recipient Oustanding Tchr. award N.C. State U., 1985, Alcoa Disting. Rschr. award, 1993, Supercomputer award IBM, 1991. Fellow Am. Nuc. Soc. (chmn. reactor physics divsn. 1987-88, chmn. math. and computer divsn. 1995-96, Mark Mills award 1971, bd. dirs. 1990-93); mem. AAAS (mem. math. com.), IEEE Computer Soc., Am. Soc. Engring. Educators (chmn. nuc. engring. divsn. 1984-85, Glenn Murphy award 1990), Edison Electric Inst. (Power Engring. Educator award 1992), Soc. Indsl. and Applied Math. Office: NC State U Dept Nuclear Engring PO Box 7909 Raleigh NC 27695-7909

TURK, AUSTIN THEODORE, sociology educator; b. Gainesville, Ga., May 28, 1934; s. Hollis Theodore and Ruth (Vandiver) T.; m. Janet Stuart Irving, Oct. 4, 1957 (div. 1977); children: Catherine, Jennifer; m. Ruth-Ellen Marie Grimes, July 27, 1985. BA cum laude, U. Ga., 1956; MA, U. Ky., 1959; PhD, U. Wis., 1962. Acting instr. sociology U. Wis., Madison, 1961-62; from instr. to prof. sociology Ind. U., Bloomington, 1962-74; prof. U. Toronto, Can., 1974-88; prof. U. Calif., Riverside, 1988—, chmn. dept. sociology, 1989-94; interim dir. Robert B. Presley Ctr. for Crime and Justice Studies, 1994-95. Author: Criminality and Legal Order, 1969, Political Criminality, 1982; gen. editor crime and justice series SUNY Press, Albany, 1990—; contbr. articles to jours. in field. Mem. Calif. Mus. Photography, 1988—, Citizens Univ. Com., 1990—. Recipient Paul Tappan award Western Soc. Criminology, 1989. Fellow Am. Soc. Criminology (pres. 1984-85); mem. Am. Sociol. Assn. (chair criminology sect. 1975-76), Law and Soc. Assn. (trustee 1982-85), Acad. Criminal Justice Scis. Democrat. Avocations: gardening, reading, swimming, tennis. Office: Dept Sociology U Calif Riverside Riverside CA 92521

TURK, JAMES CLINTON, federal judge; b. Roanoke, Va., May 3, 1923; s. James Alexander and Geneva (Richardson) T.; m. Barbara Duncan, Aug. 21, 1954; children—Ramona Leah, James Clinton, Robert Malcolm Duncan, Mary Elizabeth, David Michael. A.B., Roanoke Coll., 1949; L.L.B., Washington and Lee U., 1952. Bar: Va. bar 1952. Assoc. Dalton & Poff, Radford, Va., 1952-53; ptnr. Dalton, Poff & Turk, Radford, 1953-72; U.S. senator from Va., 1959-72; judge U.S. Dist. Ct. (we. dist.) Va., Roanoke, 1972-73, chief judge, 1973—; dir. 1st & Mchts. Nat. Bank of Radford. Mem. Va. Senate, from 1959, minority leader.; Trustee Radford Community Hosp., 1959—. Served with AUS, 1943-46. Mem. Order of Coif, Phi Beta Kappa, Omicron Delta Kappa. Baptist (deacon). Home: 1002 Walker Dr Radford VA 24141-3018 Office: US Dist Ct 246 Franklin Rd SW # 220 Roanoke VA 24011-2204

TURK, PATRICIA AVEDON, dance company executive. Gen. mgr. N.Y.C. Ballet. Office: NYC Ballet New York State Theatre 20 Lincoln Center Plz New York NY 10023-6913

TURK, RICHARD ERRINGTON, retired psychiatrist; b. Staten Island, N.Y., Oct. 6, 1925; s. Richard Jason and Marian (Errington) T.; m. Dec. 30, 1948 (widowed Dec. 23, 1978); children: Stephanie, Jeffrey, Alan. BS, Dartmouth Coll., 1945; MD, Johns Hopkins Med. Sch., 1948. Diplomate Am. Bd. Psychiatry. Intern Highland-Alameda County Hosp., Oakland, Calif., 1948-49; resident Herrick Meml. Hosp., Berkeley, Calif., 1949-50; fellow psychiatry Harvard Med. Sch., Boston, 1950-51, 53-54; clin. instr. UCLA Med. Sch., 1954-70; pvt. practice psychiatry Berkeley, 1954-85; pvt. practice, Walnut Creek, Calif., 1972-88; staff Herrick Meml. Hosp., 1954-85, Walnut Creek Hosp., 1972-88, John Muir Meml. Hosp., Walnut Creek, 1980-88. Capt. USAF, 1951-53, Korea. Mem. AMA, Am. Psychiat. Assn., No. Calif. Psychiat. Assn., Calif. Med. Assn., Alameda-Contra Costa County Med. Assn. Avocations: travel, bicycling, boating, car camping.

TURK, RUDY HENRY, artist, retired museum director; b. Sheboygan, Wis., June 24, 1927; s. Rudolph Anton and Mary Gertrude (Stanisha) T.; m. Wanda Lee Borders, Aug. 4, 1956; children: Tracy Lynn, Maria Teresa, Andrew Borders, Jennifer Wells. BS in Edn., U. Wis., 1949; MA in History, U. Tenn., 1951; postgrad., Ind. U., 1952-56. Instr. art history, gallery dir. U. Mont., Missoula, 1957-60; dir. Richmond (Calif.) Art Ctr., 1960-65; asst. dir. San Diego Mus. Art, 1965-67; dir. Ariz. State U. Art Mus., 1967-92; from assoc. prof. to prof. art Ariz. State U., 1967-77; art cons. Yares Gallery, Scottsdale, Ariz., 1993—. Painer, paintings exhibited in solo and group exhbns. including Stable of Udinotti Gallery, Scottsdale, 1970—; mus. cons., juror, art cons., art lectr.; author: (with Cross and Lamm) The Search for Personal Freedom, 2 vols., 1972, 76, 80, 85, Merrill Mahaffey: Monumental Landscapes, 1979, (with others) Scholder, 1983, also commentaries and critiques. Bd. dirs. Chandler Arts Com., 1987-89, Friends of Mex. Art, Ariz., 1986-96, pres. 1988-90; mem. Tempe Arts Com., 1987-89, Ariz. Living Treasures Com., 1988-93; bd. dirs. Ariz. Mus. for Youth, 1993—; mem. adv. bd. Tempe Hist. Mus., 1995—. Recipient merit award Calif. Coll. Arts and Crafts, 1965, Senator's Cultural award State of Ariz., 1987, Golden Crate award Western Assn. Art Mus., 1974, Ariz. Gov.'s Art award, 1992; named Hon. Ariz. Designer Craftsman, 1975; named dir. emeritus Ariz. State U. Art Mus., 1992, Rudy Turk Gallery at Ariz. State U. Art Mus. named in his honor, 1992; Fulbright scholar U. Paris, 1956-57; hon. fellow Am. Craft Coun., 1988. Mem. Nat. Coun. Edn. Ceramic Arts (hon. mem. coun. 1991), Phi Alpha Theta, Phi Kappa Phi. Democrat. Home: 760 E Courtney Ln Tempe AZ 85284-4003 Office: Ariz State U Art Museum Tempe AZ 85287-2911

TURK, S. MAYNARD, lawyer; b. Roanoke County, Va., Oct. 14, 1925; s. James Alexander and Geneva (Richardson) T.; m. Patricia A. Tucker, June 1, 1957; children—Heather F., William A., Thomas M.T. B.A. in Econs., Roanoke Coll., 1949; LL.B., Washington and Lee U., 1952. Bar: Va. 1951, Del. 1961, U.S. Patent and Trademark Office 1975. With Hercules Inc., 1954-90; sr. counsel Hercules Inc., Wilmington, Del., 1966-70, sr. patent counsel, 1972, dir. patent dept., 1972-76, gen. counsel, 1976-90, sec., 1980-82, v.p., 1982—, also bd. dirs.; of counsel Morris, Nichols, Arsht & Tunnel, Wilmington, 1990—; bar examiner State of Del. Bd. Examiners, 1987-91. Mem. Assn. Gen. Counsel, ABA, Phila. Patent Law Assn., Mfg. Chemists Assn. (legal adv. com.), Atlantic Legal Found. (bd. dirs.), Southwestern Legal Found. (adv. bd.), Licensing Execs. Soc., N.A.M., Assn. Corp. Patent Counsel (emeritus), Nat. Security Indsl. Assn. Home: PO Box 3958 Wilmington DE 19807-0958 Office: Morris Nichols Arsht & Tunnell 1201 N Market St Wilmington DE 19801-1147

TURK, STANLEY MARTIN, advertising agency executive; b. Newark, N.J., June 4, 1934; s. Jack and Sylvia (Rachmiel) T.; m. Helga Louise Haberle, Dec. 1, 1962; children: Russell, Laura. BS, Purdue U., 1956; MBS, UCLA, 1989. Sr. account exec. Cunningham & Walsh Advt. Agy., N.Y.C., 1964-68; mgr., v.p. Meltzer Aaron & Lemon, N.Y.C. and San Francisco, 1968-70; pres. Promotion Devel. Specialists, N.Y.C., 1970-75; sr. v.p., ptnr. Chalek & Dreyer, N.Y.C., 1975-80; exec. v.p. Korhausen & Calene, N.Y.C., 1980-88; pres. The Turk Group, N.Y.C., 1991—; tchr. N.Y. Inst. Advt., N.Y.C., 1968-75. Capt. U.S. Army, 1958-60. Recipient Jesse Neal award Am. Bus. Publs. Assn., 1963. Mem. Nat. Assn. Chain Drug Stores, Am. Mktg. Assn. (Effie award 1982). Office: The Turk Group 200 Clearbrook Rd Elmsford NY 10523

TURKEL, STANLEY, hotel consultant, management executive; b. N.Y.C., Sept. 2, 1925; s. Nathan and Mollie (Kurtzman) Turkeltaub; m. Barbara Bell, June 12, 1955 (div. Apr. 1971); children: Marc Alexander, Allison Lee; m. Rima Sokoloff, Apr. 26, 1971; stepchildren: Joshua Bernard Forrest, Benay Debra Forrest. BS, NYU, 1947; MBA, St. Johns U., Jamaica, N.Y., 1980. Laundry cons. Victor Kramer Co. Inc., N.Y.C., 1952-59; v.p., space planner Michael Saphier Assocs., N.Y.C., 1959-62; with spl. hotel svcs. Loews Hotel Corp., N.Y.C., 1962-63; res. mgr. Americana Hotel, N.Y.C., 1963-64; gen. mgr. Drake Hotel, N.Y.C., 1964-66; mng. dir. Summit Hotel, N.Y.C., 1966-67; product line mgr. hotels ITT, N.Y.C., 1968-73; pres. Stanley Turkel Co., Hotel Cons., N.Y.C., 1973—; mem. faculty NYU Ctr. Hospitality, Tourism and Travel Adminstrn. Contbr. articles to N.Y. Times, Wall St. Jour., N.Y. NEwsday, Washington Post, Crain's N.Y. Bus., N.Y. Observer, Smithsonian Mag., N.Y. Mag., N.Y. Post, N.Y. Daily News, Hotel and Motel Mgmt., World's-Eye View, Cornell Quar., Lodging Hospitality, Lodging Mag., Hotel & Resort Industry, The Bottomline, Ariz. Hospitality Trends, FIU Hospitality Rev. Mem. free speech assn. com. ACLU. With USAAF, 1943-45. Mem. Am. Hotel and Motel Assn. (MHS cert.), Internat. Soc. Hospitality Cons. (ISHC cert.), Civic Affairs Forum (chmn. 1987-93), City Club N.Y. (trustee 1964—, pres. 1966-68, chmn. 1977-88, chmn. exec. com. 1988-91). Avocations: Reconstruction period of Am. history, civic affairs, autograph collecting, tennis. Office: 10 Rockefeller Plz Ste 1250 New York NY 10020-1903 *As a lifelong civil libertarian, I have learned to cherish the first amendment which provides protection for unpopular speech. We should not carve out exceptions to the first amendment because we are disgusted by vile language or racist epithets.*

TURKELSON, JULIE ANN, gerontological nurse; b. Cin., Apr. 25, 1961; d. Norman Billy and Shirley Bell (Dixon) T. Diploma, Bethesda Hosp. Sch. Nursing, Cin., 1983; BSN summa cum laude, U. Cin., 1991, MSN, 1994. RN, Ohio; cert. gerontol. clin. nurse specialist. Charge nurse Drake Hosp., Cin., 1983-88; charge nurse ICU Mercy Hosp., Cin., 1988-91; rsch. asst. U. Cin., 1990-92; asst. dir. of nursing Mercy St. Theresa Ctr., 1991-93, dir. of nursing, 1993—; developer dementia unit, asst. in devel. of continuum of care for retired citizens Mercy St. Theresa Ctr., quality assurance coord., 1990-94. Avocations: crafts, outdoor activities, sports. Home: 4373 Mckeever Pike Williamsburg OH 45176-9702 Office: Mercy St Theresa Ctr 7010 Rowan Hill Dr Cincinnati OH 45227-3313

TURKEVICH, ANTHONY LEONID, chemist, educator; b. N.Y.C., July 23, 1916; s. Leonid Jerome and Anna (Chervinsky) T.; m. Ireene Podlesak, Sept. 20, 1948; children: Leonid, Darya. B.A., Dartmouth Coll., 1937, D.Sc., 1971; Ph.D., Princeton U., 1940. Research assoc. spectroscopy physics dept. U. Chgo., 1940-41; asst. prof., research on nuclear transformations Enrico Fermi Inst. and chemistry dept., 1946-48, assoc. prof., 1948-53, prof., 1953-86, James Franck prof. chemistry, 1965-70, Distinguished Ser. prof., 1970-86, prof. emeritus, 1986; war research Manhattan Project, Columbia U., 1942-43, U. Chgo., 1943-45, Los Alamos Sci. Lab., 1945-46; Participant test first nuclear bomb, Alamagordo, N.Mex., 1945, in theoretical work on and test of thermonuclear reactions, 1945—, chem. analysis of moon, 1967—; cons. to AEC Labs.; fellow Los Alamos Sci. Lab., 1972—. Del. Geneva Conf. on Nuclear Test Suspension, 1958, 59. Recipient E.O. Lawrence Meml. award AEC, 1962; Atoms for Peace award, 1969. Fellow Am. Phys. Soc.; mem. N.Y. Acad. Sci. (Pregel award 1988), AAAS, Am. Chem. Soc. (nuclear applications award 1972), Am. Acad. Arts and Scis. Mem. Russian Orthodox Greek Cath. Ch. Clubs: Quadrangle, Cosmos. Home: 175 Briarwood Loop Oak Brook IL 60521-8713 Office: U Chicago Dept Chemistry 5640 S Ellis Ave Chicago IL 60637-1433

TURKIN, MARSHALL WILLIAM, symphony orchestra, festival and opera administrator, arranger, composer; b. Chgo., Apr. 1, 1926; 4 children. Student, U. Kans., 1946-48; Mus. B. in Music Composition, Northwestern U., 1950, Mus. M., 1951; postgrad., Juilliard Sch. Music, Columbia U., U. Ind. Record rev. columnist, classical music commentator, gen. mgr., Honolulu Symphony and Opera Co., 1959-66; orch. festival mgr., Ravinia Festival for Chgo. Symphony, 1966-68; founding mgr.; Blossom Festival for Cleve. Orch., 1968-70; gen. mgr. Detroit Symphony, 1970-73, exec. dir., 1973-79, mng. dir., Pitts. Symphony Orch., 1979-88; gen. dir. Hawaii Opera Theatre, Honolulu, 1988-91. Served with USN, World War II. Avocations: jazz musician, newspaper music critic.

TURLEY, CLARENCE M., JR., finance company executive; b. 1928. Grad., Washington U., St. Louis. With Turley Corp., St. Louis, 1950-72; vice chmn. bd. dirs. Turley-Martin Co., Inc., St. Louis, 1972—; chmn. Roosevelt Fin. Group, Chesterfield, Mo., 1991—; v. chmn. Colliers, Turley, Martin, St. Louis. Office: Colliers Turley Martin 700 Corp Park Dr Saint Louis MO 63105*

TURLEY, LINDA, lawyer; b. Altus, Okla., July 16, 1958; d. Windle and Shirley (Lacey) Turley; m. Thomas J. Stutz, Mar. 30, 1985; 1 child, Lacey. BS, Georgetown U., 1980; JD with honors, U. Tex., 1983. Bar: Tex. 1983; bd. cert. in personal injury trial law. Atty., head product liability dept. Law Offices of Windle Turley, P.C., Dallas, 1986-95; sole practitioner Dallas, 1995—; mem. task force on Tex. rules of civil procedure Tex. Supreme Ct., 1992-93. Mem. ATLA (bd. govs. 1993—, chair women trial lawyers' caucus 1989-90, chmn.-elect product liability sect. 1995-96), Tex. Trial Lawyers Assn. (bd. dirs. 1989—). Office: 6440 N Central Expy Ste 610 Dallas TX 75206

TURLEY, MICHAEL ROY, lawyer; b. St. Louis, Mar. 7, 1945; s. W. Richard and Mary Jeanne (Ogle) T.; m. Patricia Ederle, Aug. 21, 1968; children: James, Alisyn. AB, Princeton U., 1967; JD, Mo. U., 1970. Bar: Mo. 1970, U.S. Dist. Ct. (ea. dist.) Mo. 1975. Assoc. Lewis, Rice & Fingersh (formerly Lewis & Rice), St. Louis, 1970-71, 74-80, ptnr., 1980—; bd. dirs. Mo. Innovation Ctr.-St. Louis, St. Louis Mfg. Resource Ctr. Mem. Planning and Zoning Commn., Jefferson County, 1987—. Mem. ABA, Mo. Bar Assn., St. Louis Met. Bar Assn., Princeton Club. Episcopalian. Office: Lewis Rice & Fingersh 500 N Broadway Ste 2000 Saint Louis MO 63102-2130

TURLEY, STEWART, retail company executive; b. Mt. Sterling, Ky., July 20, 1934; s. R. Joe and Mavis S. Turley; m. Linda A. Mulholland; children from previous marriage: Carol, Karen. Student, Rollins Coll., 1952-53, U. Ky., 1953-55. Plant mgr. Crown Cork & Seal Co., Orlando (Fla.), Phila., 1955-66; mgr. non-drug ops., dir. corporate employee rels. and spl. svcs. Eckerd Corp. (formerly Jack Eckerd Corp.), Clearwater, Fla., 1966-68; v.p. Eckerd Corp., Clearwater, Fla., 1968-71, sr. v.p., 1971-74; dir. Jack Eckerd Corp., Clearwater, Fla., 1971—, pres., chief exec. officer, 1974-96, chmn. bd., 1975—; bd. dirs. Sprint Corp., Barnett Banks, Inc., Springs Industries, Inc.

Trustee Eckerd Coll., St. Petersburg, US Ski Team. Mem. Fla. Coun. Econ. Ed. (bd. dirs.), Nat. Assn. Chain Drug Stores (bd. dirs., chmn. bd. 1978-79, 88-89), Fla. Coun. 100 (vice chmn.), World Pres.'s Orgn., Chief Execs. Orgn., Carlouel Yacht Club, Belleair Country Club, Bayou Club, Eagle Springs Golf Club, Kappa Alpha. Office: Eckerd Corp PO Box 4689 Clearwater FL 34618-4689

TURLINGTON, CHRISTY, model; b. Walnut Creek, Calif., Jan. 2, 1969; d. Dwain and Elizabeth T. With Ford Models, Inc., 1985; model Calvin Klein, 1986; face of Calvin Klein's Eternity Fragrance, 1988—; with Maybelline Cosmetics, 1992; rep. (abroad) Ford Models, Paris; beauty spread with Vogue, 1987; has worked with Herb Ritts, Patrick Demarchelier, Steven Meisel; has worked for Anne Klein, Michael Kors, Chanel, Perry Ellis; appeared in George Michael's "Freedom" video. Office: Ford Models Inc 344 E 59th St New York NY 10022-1570

TURMAN, GEORGE, former lieutenant governor; b. Missoula, Mont., June 25, 1928; s. George Fugett and Corinne (McDonald) T.; m. Kathleen Hager, Mar. 1951; children: Marcia, Linda, George Douglas, John, Laura. BA, U. Mont., 1951. Various positions Fed. Res. Bank of San Francisco, 1954-64; mayor City of Missoula, 1970-72; mem. Mont. Ho. of Reps. from (Dist. 18), 1973-74; Mont. Pub. Service commr. (Dist. 5), 1975-80; lt. gov. State of Mont., 1981-88, resigned; apptd. Pacific N.W. Electric Power Planning and Conservation Coun., 1988; pres. Nat. Ctr. for Appropriate Tech., Butte, Mont., 1989—; sr. advisor, adj. staff mem., dir. New Horizon Techs., Inc., 1995. With U.S. Army, 1951-58. Decorated Combat Inf. badge. Home: 1525 Gerald Ave Missoula MT 59801-4227

TURMEL, JEAN BERNARD, banker; b. Lac Etchemin, Que., Can., Dec. 17, 1944; s. Joseph N. and Rose Marie (Chabot) T.; m. Lorraine Louise Langevin, June 4, 1966; children—Andree, Elaine, Johanne. B.Commerce, Laval U., Quebec, Can., 1966, M.C.S., 1967. Salesman Macmillan Bloedel, Montreal and Vancouver, Can., 1967-68; money market trader Dominion Securities, Montreal, Que., 1968-78, Merrill Lynch Can., Montreal and Toronto, Can., 1978-81; v.p. treasury Nat. Bank Can., Montreal, 1981-83, sr. v.p. treasury and exchange, 1983-86; exec. v.p. treasury, 1986-89, sr. exec. v.p., 1989—; chmn. bd. Trust Gen. du Can., 1993—, Nat. Bank Securitiesm, Inc., Levesque Beaubien & Co.; bd. dirs. Levesque Beaubien, Natcan Investment Mgmt., Inc., Cartons St.-Laurent; outside adviser investment com.: Assn. Bienfaisance et Retraite de communauté urbaine de Montreal; City of Montreal Pension Plan. Liberal. Roman Catholic. Avocations: music, golf, fishing, stamp collecting. Office: Nat Bank Can, 600 ouest de la Gauchetière, Montreal, PQ Canada H3B 4L2

TURNAGE, FRED DOUGLAS, lawyer; b. Ayden, N.C., Sept. 24, 1920; s. Fred C. and Lou (Johnson) T.; m. Margaret Futrell, Aug. 21, 1943 (div. Nov. 1980); children: Betty Lou Griffith, Douglas C.; m. Elizabeth Louisa Turnage, Jan. 23, 1981. Grad. Naval Sch. on Far Eastern Civil Affairs, Princeton U., 1945; LLB, Wake Forest U., 1948, LLD, 1970. Bar: N.C. 1948, U.S. Supreme Ct. 1953, U.S. Dist. Ct. D.C. 1965, U.S. Ct. Appeals (D.C. cir.) 1967, U.S. Ct. Appeals (4th and 7th cirs.) 1979. Trial atty. antitrust div. U.S. Dept. Justice, Kansas City, Mo., 1948-51; sr. trial atty. antitrust div. U.S. Dept. Justice, Washington, 1951-65, spl. asst. to atty. gen., 1965; sr. ptnr. Cleary, Gottlieb, Steen & Hamilton, Washington, 1968—; lectr. continuing legal edn. courses, 1973-77. Contbr. articles to profl. jours. Bd. Visitors Wake Forest U. Sch. Law, Winston-Salem, N.C., 1980—. Served to 1st lt. AUS, 1942-46. Recipient Disting. Service in Law citation Wake Forest U., 1979. Mem. ABA (antitrust and litigation sects.), Fed. Bar Assn., Adv. Bd. Antitrust Bulletin, Wake Forest U. Alumni Assn. (pres. 1977), Nat. Lawyers Clubs. Methodist. Avocations: fishing, golf, writing. Home: 209 N Liberty St Arlington VA 22203-1050 Office: 1752 N St NW Washington DC 20036-2806

TURNAGE, JEAN A., state supreme court chief justice; b. St. Ignatius, Mont., Mar. 10, 1926. JD, Mont. State U., 1951; D Laws and Letters (non.), U. Mont., 1995. Bar: Mont. 1951, U.S. Supreme Ct. 1963. Formerly ptnr. Turnage, McNeil & Mercer, Polson, Mont.; formerly Mont. State senator from 13th Dist.; pres. Mont. State Senate, 1981-83; chief justice Supreme Ct. Mont., 1985—. Mem. Mont. State Bar Assn., Nat. Conf. Chief Justices (past pres.), Nat. Ctr. State Courts (past chair). Office: Mont Supreme Ct 215 N Sanders St Helena MT 59601-4522

TURNBAUGH, ROY CARROLL, archivist; b. Peoria, Ill., Oct. 16, 1945; s. Roy Carroll and Zora (Alexander) T.; m. Donna Marie Chase, Mar. 28, 1970; children: Andrew, Peter. BA, Aurora Coll., 1969; AM, U. Ill., 1973, PhD, 1977. Asst. prof. U. Ill., Urbana, 1977-78; archivist Ill. State Archives, Springfield, 1978-85; dir. Oreg. State Archives, Salem, 1985—. Office: Oreg State Archives 800 Summer St NE Salem OR 97310-1347

TURNBULL, ADAM MICHAEL GORDON, financial executive, accountant; b. Dumfries, Scotland, Dec. 29, 1935; emigrated to Canada, 1977; s. Robert Wilson and Catherine Russell (Strang) T.; m. Karen Margaret Walker, June 12, 1965; children: Candida Louise, Andrew Robert. M.A., Edinburgh U., 1956, LL.B., 1958. Chartered acct., Scotland, 1960. With Price Waterhouse, Paris, 1960-62, U.S. Time Corp., France and U.S., 1962-64; group chief acct. Formica Internat. Ltd., London, 1965-70; group fin. dir. Donald Macpherson Group Ltd., London, 1970-77; controller, asst. treas. Indal Ltd., Weston, Ont., Can., 1978-81; controller Indal Inc., Weston, 1978-81; v.p., treas. Indal Ltd., Weston, Ont., Can., 1981-90; v.p. fin., CFO, Hawker Siddeley Can. Inc., Mississauga, Ont., Can., 1990-94, sr. v.p. fin., CFO, 1994—. Mem. Inst. Chartered Accts. Scotland. Home: 2610 Hammond Rd, Mississauga, ON Canada L5K 2M3 Office: Hawker Siddeley Can Inc, 3 Robert Speck Pkwy, Mississauga, ON Canada L4Z 2G5

TURNBULL, ANN PATTERSON, special education educator, consultant; b. Tuscaloosa, Ala., Oct. 19, 1947; d. H. F. and Mary (Boone) Patterson; m. H. Rutherford Turnbull III, Mar. 23, 1974; children: Jay, Amy, Kate. BS in Edn., U. Ga., 1968; MEd, Auburn U., 1971; EdD, U. Ala., 1972. Asst. prof. U. N.C., Chapel Hill, 1972-80; prof., co-dir. Beach Ctr. U. Kans., Lawrence, 1980—; cons. Dept. Edn., Washington, 1987—, Australian Soc. for Study of Intellectual Disability, Adelaide and Washington, 1990. Author: Disability and the Family, 1989, Exceptional Lives: Special Education in Today's Schools, 1995, Families, Professionals and Exceptionality, 1996. Recipient Rose Kennedy Internat. Leadership award, Kennedy Found., 1990; Joseph P. Kennedy Jr. Found. fellow, 1987-88. Mem. Am. Assn. on Mental Retardation (bd. dirs. 1986-88), Assn. for Retarded Citizens (named Educator of Yr. 1982), Zero to Three: Nat. Ctr. for Infants and Toddlers (bd. dirs. 1993-96), Internat. League Socs. for Persons with Mental Handicap (com. chair 1986-90). Democrat. Avocations: travel, exercise. Home: 1636 Alvamar Dr Lawrence KS 66047-1714 Office: Univ Kans Beach Ctr 3111 Haworth Hall Lawrence KS 66044-7516

TURNBULL, DAVID JOHN (CHIEF PIERCING EYES-PENN), cultural association executive; b. Hornell, N.Y., May 18, 1930; s. Gerald and Dorothy Esther (Badgley) T.; m. Martha Lillian Crouse, Aug. 12, 1949 (div. 1960); children: Garry David, Mary Jane Stuhr, Dorothy Grace Houde; m. Frances Early Spring Vickery, May 4, 1985. Degree in ministry, Elim Bible Coll., 1964. Dir. pub. rels. Elim Bible Inst., Lima, N.Y., 1960-61; pastor Eagle Harbor (N.Y.) Ch., 1962-65, South Lima (N.Y.) Gospel Ch., 1962-66; ind. ins. agent, 1965-82; chief, counselor, performer weddings and funerals Pan-Am. Indian Assn., Nocatee, Fla., 1980—, pub. Pan.-Am. Indian Assn. News, 1984—; pastor Cherokee Bapt. Ch., Arcadia, Fla., 1994. Mem. Ministerial Assn. Libertarian. Mem. LDS Ch. Avocation: experimental gardening. Home and Office: 2596 SE Durrance St Arcadia FL 33821*

TURNBULL, FRED GERDES, electronics engineer; b. Oakland, Calif., Apr. 12, 1931; s. Fred and Gertrude Turnbull; m. Nancy Greene, Aug. 22, 1959; children: Fred, David. BSEE, U. Calif., Berkeley, 1953, MSEE, 1959. Electronics engr. corp. rsch. devel. ctr. GE, Schenectady, N.Y., 1959-93; cons. Scotia, N.Y., 1993—. Co-author: Power Electronic Control Of AC Motors, 1988. Lt. (j.g.) USN, 1954-57. Fellow IEEE; assoc. mem. Sigma Xi.

TURNBULL, GORDON KEITH, metal company executive, metallurgical engineer; b. Cleve., Nov. 10, 1935; s. Gordon Gideon and Florence May (Felton) T.; m. Sally Ann Ewing, June 15, 1957; children: Kenneth Scott, Stephen James, Lynne Ann, June Patricia, James Robert. BS in Metall. Engring., Case Western Res. U., 1957, MS in Metall. Engring., 1959, PhD in Phys. Metallurgy, 1962. Engr. then sr. engr. casting and forgings div., Cleve. Research ALCOA, 1962-67, sr. metallurgist quality assurance, Cleve. Forge Plant, 1967-68; group leader fabricating metallurgy div. ALCOA Tech. Ctr., Pitts., 1968-71, sect. head, mgr. ingot casting div., 1971-78, mgr. fabricating metallurgy div., 1978-79, asst. dir. finishes engring. properties and design, 1979-80; mgr. bus. planning services, corp. planning dept. ALCOA, Pitts., 1980-82, dir. tech. planning, 1982-86, v.p. tech. planning, 1986-91, exec. v.p. strategic analysis/planning and info., 1991—. Patentee method of not compacting titanium powder. Governing bd. Allegheny Ctr. Christian & Missionary Alliance Ch., Pitts. Mem. AIME, ASM, Nat. Acad. Engring., Am. Foundrymen's Soc., Rsch. Bd., Sigma Xi. Avocation: hockey. Home: 550 Fairview Rd Pittsburgh PA 15238-1745 Office: Aluminum Co Am 1501 Alcoa Bldg 31st Fl Pittsburgh PA 15219-1819

TURNBULL, H. RUTHERFORD, III, law educator, lawyer; b. N.Y.C., Sept. 22, 1937; s. Henry R. and Ruth (White) T.; m. Mary M. Slingluff, Apr. 4, 1964 (div. 1972); m. Ann Patterson, Mar. 23, 1974; children: Jay, Amy, Katherine. BA, Johns Hopkins U., 1959; LLB with hon., U. Md., 1964; LLM, Harvard U., 1969. Bar: Md., N.C. Law clerk to Hon. Emory H. Niles Supreme Bench Balt. City, 1959-60; law clerk to Hon. Roszel C. Thomsen U.S. Dist. Ct. Md., 1962-63; assoc. Piper & Marbury, Balt., 1964-67; prof. Inst. Govt. U. N.C., Chapel Hill, 1969-80, U. Kans., Lawrence, 1980—. Editor-in-chief Md. Law Review. Cons., author, lectr., co-dir. Beach Ctr. on Families and Disability, U. Kans.; pres. Full Citizenship Inc., Lawrence, 1987-93; spl. staff-fellow U.S. Senate subcom. on disability policy, Washington, 1987-88; bd. dirs. Camphill Assn. N.Am., Inc., 1985-87; trustee Judge David L. Bazelon Ctr. Mental Health Law, 1993-96. With U.S. Army, 1960-65. Recipient Nat. Leadership award Nat. Assn. Pvt. Residential Resources, 1988, Nat. Leadership award Internat. Coun. for Exceptional Children, 1996; Public Policy fellow Joseph P. Kennedy, Jr. Found., 1987-88. Fellow Am. Assn. on Mental Retardation (pres. 1985-86); mem. ABA (chmn. disability law commn. 1991-95), U.S.A. Assn. for Retarded Citizens (sec. 1981-83), Assn. for Persons with Severe Handicaps (treas. 1988), Nat. Assn. Rehab. Rsch. and Tng. Ctrs. (chair govt. affairs com. 1990-93), Internat. Assn. Scientific Study of Mental Deficiency, Internat. League of Assns. for Persons with Mental Handicaps, Johns Hopkins U. Alumni Assn. Democrat. Episcopalian. Home: 1636 Alvamar Dr Lawrence KS 66047-1714 Office: U Kans 3111 Haworth Hall Lawrence KS 66045

TURNBULL, JOHN CAMERON, pharmacist, consultant; b. Regina, Sask., Can., Sept. 5, 1923; s. Cameron Joseph and Lillian Irene (Pentz) T.; m. Hazel Evelyn Rockwell, July 31, 1948; children—Lillian Elizabeth, John Rockwell, Jocelyn Hazel. B.S. in Pharmacy, U. Sask., 1949. Pharmacist with village and city pharmacies, 1945-50; supr. pharm. services Dept. Pub. Health, Province of Sask., Regina, 1950-52; ops. mgr. Nat. Drugs, Ltd., Winnipeg, and Saskatoon, 1953; exec. dir. Can. Pharm. Assn., Toronto, Ont., 1953-78; sec.-treas., mng. dir. Canadian Pharm. Realty Co. Ltd.; mem. provisional bd. Pharmacare Ltd.; registrar-treas. Pharmacy Examining Bd. of Can., 1963-68, mem. bd., 1963-78; pharmacy cons., dir. drug service Ministry of Health, Barbados, 1979-84; staff assoc. Mgmt. Scis. for Health, Boston, 1984-85; cons. logistics and pharms. USAID, East Caribbean, PanAm. Health Orgn./WHO (Belize, Cen. Am.), 1985—. Chmn. Govt.'s Spl. Com. on Acetylsalicylic Poisonings, 1967; mem. Emergency Health Services Advisory Com. Served to squadron leader RCAF, 1941-45. Decorated D.F.C., Order of Can.; recipient Can. Centennial medal, 1967, Queen's Jubilee medal, 1977, Can. 125th Anniversary medal, 1992, John C. Turnbull rsch. ann. award in socio-econs. pharmacy established in his honor Can. Pharm. Assn., 1990. Mem. Fedn. Internationale Pharmaceutique (v.p.), Inst. of Assn. Execs. (hon. life), Conf. on Pharmacy Registrars of Can. (sec.), Commonwealth Pharm. Assn. (coun. 1969-78); hon. mem. Am., Canadian, Saskatchewan, B.C., Alta., Ont., Man., N.S. Pharm. Assns., Sask. Pharm. Assn., Ont. Pharmacists Assn., Canadian Soc. Hosp. Pharmacists, Rho Pi Phi. Mem. United Ch. of Canada. Club: Bayview Country (past dir.). Home: 40 Banstock Dr, North York, ON Canada M2K 2H6

TURNBULL, JOHN NEIL, retired chemical company executive; b. South Shields, U.K., Feb. 13, 1940; s. John Smith and Kathleen Bernadette (Higgins) T.; m. Aloysia Lindemann, Feb. 9, 1966; children: John Michael, David Stephen. BSChemE with honors, Kings Coll./Univ. Durham, Eng., 1961. Chartered engr., U.K. Process engr. Brit. Petroleum PLC, Sunbury, Eng., 1961-64; engr. Deutsche B.P., Dinslaken, Fed. Republic Germany, 1964-66; rsch. project mgr. Brit. Petroleum PLC, Sunbury, 1967-70; prodn. mgr. BP Chems., Port Talbot, Eng., 1975-80; pres. BP Chems. Suisse, Geneva, 1982-84; dir. BP Chems., London, 1984-89, dep. chief exec. officer, 1991-93; pres. BP Chems., Cleve., 1989-91; cons. in field. Patentee in field; contbr. articles to profl. jours. Bd. dirs. Playhouse Square Found., Cleve., 1990, The Internat. Forum, Phila., 1995—. Fellow Instn. Chem. Engrs., Royal Acad. Engring. Avocations: skiing, theatre, reading, walking, music.

TURNBULL, RENALDO, professional football player; b. St. Thomas, V.I., Jan. 5, 1966. Degree in Comm., W.Va. U. Linebacker New Orleans Saints, 1990—. Named to Pro Bowl Team, 1993. Office: New Orleans Saints 6928 Saints Dr Metairie LA 70003-5151

TURNBULL, ROBERT SCOTT, manufacturing company executive; b. North Dumfries, Ont., Can., Dec. 19, 1929; s. Leslie William and Marjorie Clara (Scott) T.; m. Dawna Rose Sinclair, Feb. 17, 1956. Sr. Matriculation, Galt U., Ont., 1950; M.T.C., U. Western Ont., 1975. Credit mgr Can. Gen. Tower, Cambridge, Ont., 1951-53, gen. acct., 1953-62, comptroller, 1962-68, v.p. mktg., 1968-78, v.p., gen. mgr., 1978-80, pres., 1980—, also bd. dirs. Mem. Chem. Fabrics and Films Assn. (bd. dirs.), Soc. Plastics Industry (bd. dirs.), Japan Soc. (bd. dirs.). Home: 26 Lansdowne Rd S, Cambridge, ON Canada N1S 2T3 Office: Can Gen Tower, 52 Middleton St, Cambridge, ON Canada N1R 5T6

TURNBULL, WILLIAM, JR., architect; b. N.Y.C., Apr. 1, 1935; s. William and Elizabeth (Howe) T. A.B., Princeton U., 1956, M.F.A. in Architecture, 1959; student, Ecole des Beaux Arts Fontainebleau, 1956. With Skidmore, Owings & Merrill, San Francisco, 1960-63; founding ptnr. Moore, Lyndon, Turnbull, Whitaker, 1962; partner-in-charge Moore, Turnbull (San Francisco office), 1965-69; mem. design group Pres.'s Adv. Coun. Pennsylvania Ave., 1963; lectr. U. Calif.-Berkeley, 1965-69; vis. prof. U. Oreg., 1966-68; dir. MLTW/Turnbull Assocs., 1970-83; dir. William Turnbull Assocs., 1983—; lectr. Stanford U., 1974-77, vis. design critic MIT, 1975, U. Calif., Berkeley, 1977-81, 95; Mobil vis. design critic Yale U., 1982, Bishop vis. prof. archtl. design, 1986; Hyde prof. excellence U. Nebr., 1994; design cons. Formica Corp., 1977-84, World Savs. and Loan, 1976-95; mem. design rev. bd. U. Calif., San Diego, 1988-93, City of Sausalito, Calif., 1976-77. Author: Global Architecture Series: Moore, Lyndon, Turnbull & Whitaker: The Sea Ranch, The Sea Ranch Details, The Poetics of Gardens, 1988; illustrator: The Place of Houses; prin. works include Sea Ranch Condominium I, 1965, Sea Ranch Swim Tennis Club, 1966, Lovejoy Fountain Plaza, Portland (assoc. architect), Faculty Club at U. Calif.-Santa Barbara, Kresge Coll. at U. Calif.-Santa Cruz, Biloxi (Miss.) Library, Am. Club, Hong Kong, Ariz. State U. Sonora Ctr., Tempe, Foothill Student Housing, U. Calif., Berkeley, Mountain View City Hall and Community Theater, Calif.; mem. editorial adv. bd. Architecture California, 1986-92. Mem. tech. adv. com. Calif. Legislature Joint Com. Open Space Lands, 1968-71; mem. regional honor awards (90) jury AIA, 1968—, nat. honor awards jury, 1969, chmn. jury, 1977, 1988; chmn. jury C.E. honor award, 1973, 79; mem. Progressive Architecture Honor Awards Jury, 1975, Pres.'s Jury for Nat. Design Excellence, 1984; bd. dirs. Pub. Sculpture Pub. Places, 1981-85. Served with AUS, 1959-60. Recipient Calif. Gov. award Planned Communities, 1966, citation Progressive Architecture Design awards, 1962-66, 68-70, 81, 1st honor award, 1971, 74, 1st honor award Homes for Better Living, 1963, Merit award, 1966; Honor award Western Home awards, 1961-62, 63, 66-67, 88, 89, 93, 95; Merit award, 1966-67; House of Yr. award Archtl. Record, 1961, 67, 69, 70, 72, 83; award of Honor San Francisco Art Commn., 1982; Am. Wood Coun. Design award, 1984, Honor award, 1985, 89, 92, 93, 94; Firm of Yr. award Calif. Coun. AIA, 1986, Maybeck award, 1993, cited for continuous distinctive practice of architecture in Calif. by an individual; Am. Wood Coun. Merit award, 1991; Honor award San Francisco AIA, 1988, 91, 93. Fellow AIA (dir. chpt. 1981, Nat. Honor award 1967, 68, 73, 79, 90, 91, 95, award of merit Bay Region honor awards 1963, 67, 7, 78, 82, Nat. 25 Yr. Honor award 1991), Am. Acad. in Rome. Office: William Turnbull Assocs Pier 1 1/2 The Embarcadero San Francisco CA 94111

TURNDORF, HERMAN, anesthesiologist, educator; b. Paterson, N.J., Dec. 22, 1930; s. Charles R. and Ruth (Blumberg) T.; m. Sietske Huisman, Nov. 24, 1957; children: David, Michael Pieter. A.B., Oberlin Coll., 1952; M.D., U. Pa., 1956. Diplomate: Am. Bd. Anesthesiology. Instr. anesthesiology U. Pa. Hosp., 1957-59; asst. anesthetist med. sch. Harvard U., Mass. Gen. Hosp., Boston, 1961-63; assoc. attending anesthesiologist, asst. dir. dept. anesthesiology Mt. Sinai Hosp., N.Y.C., 1963-70; clin. prof. anesthesiology Mt. Sinai Hosp., 1966-70; prof., chmn. dept. anesthesiology W.Va. U. Sch. Medicine and Med. Center, Morgantown, 1970-74, NYU Sch. Medicine, 1974—; dir. anesthesiology NYU Hosp., 1974—; pres. med. bd., med. dir. Bellevue Hosp. Med. Center, 1990—; cons. in anesthesiology Manhattan VA Hosp., Armed Forces Sch. Medicine, 1974-77. Co-author: Anesthesia and Neurosurgery, 2d edit., 1986, Trauma, Anesthesia and Intensive Care, 1990; contbr. articles to profl. jours. Served to lt. M.C. USNR, 1959-61. Fellow Am. Coll. Chest Physicians, Am. Coll. Anesthesiologists (bd. govs. 1977-85, chmn. bd. govs. 1984), N.Y. Acad. Medicine; mem. AMA, Am. Soc. Anesthesiologists, Assn. Univ. Anesthetists, Internat. Soc. Study of Pain, Soc. Acad. Anesthesia Chairmen, Soc. Critical Care Medicine, Soc. Neurosutgical Anesthesia and Neurologic Supportive Care, N.Y. Acad. Scis., N.Y. State Soc. Anesthesiologists. Home: 105 Harbor Dr Unit 118 Stamford CT 06902-7456 Office: NY Univ Dept Anesthesiology 550 1st Ave New York NY 10016-6481

TURNDORF, JAMIE, clinical psychologist; b. Boston, July 12, 1958; d. Gary Owen and Sharon (Sandow) T.; m. Emile Jean Pin, Jan. 2, 1988. AB in Am. Culture, Vassar Coll., 1980; MSW, Adelphi U., 1983; PhD, Calif. Coast U., 1994. Lic. social worker, N.Y. Pvt. practice psychology N.Y.C. and Millbrook, N.Y., 1981—; lead creative movement and psychodrama program Lincoln Farms Work Camp, Roscoe, N.Y., 1976; with Astor Child Guidance Clinic, Poughkeepsie, N.Y., 1982-83; leader various pgroups Braig House Hosp., Beacon, N.Y., 1982-87, developer, dir.eating disorders program, 1984-86; founder, dir. INC.TIMACY, 1990—, J.T. Developers, Inc., Poughkeepsie, 1983-91; dir. Hudson Valley br. Ctr. for Advancement Group Studies, Ctr. for Emotional Comm., Millbrook, 1990—. Author: (with Emile Jean Pin) The Pleasure of Your Company: A Socio-Psychological Analysis of Modern Sociability, 1985; columnist Dr. Love various newspapers; host Ask Dr. Love, Sta. WEVD, N.Y.C., 1992; creator, inventor LoveQuest: The Game of Finding Mr. Right, 1990 (one of best new games award Fun and Games mag. 1991). Mem. NASW, N.Y. State Soc. Clin. Social Work Psychotherapists. Avocations: house restoration, opera singing, antiques. Home and Office: PO Box 475 Millbrook NY 12545-0475

TURNER, ALMON RICHARD, art historian, educator; b. New Bedford, Mass., July 28, 1932; s. Louis Alexander and Margaret (Mather) T.; m. Jane Beebe; children: Louis Hamilton, David Alexander. AB, Princeton U., 1955, MFA, 1958, PhD, 1959. Instr. in fine arts U. Mich., Ann Arbor, 1959-60; from instr. to prof. art and archaeology Princeton (N.J.) U., 1960-68; prof. fine arts Middlebury (Vt.) Coll., 1968-74, dean faculty, 1970-74; prof. fine arts, pres. Grinnell (Iowa) Coll., 1975-79; prof., dir. Inst. Fine Arts NYU, N.Y.C., 1979-82, dean faculty arts and scis., 1982-85, prof. dept. fine arts, 1985—, dir. N.Y. Inst. Humanities, 1986-93, Paulette Goddard prof. in arts and humanities, 1994—. Author: Vision of Landscape in Renaissance Italy, 1966, 73, (With G. Andres and J. Hunisak) Art of Florence (L'Art de Florence), 1988 (prix 1989), Inventing Leonardo, 1993. Mem. Coll. Art Assn., Century Assn., N.J. Aubudon Soc. (1st v.p. 1990-93, pres. 1993—), Phi Beta Kappa. Democrat. Unitarian Universalist. Avocations: birding, photography. Home: PO Box 2322 Cape May NJ 08204-7322 Office: NYU Dept Of Fine Arts New York NY 10003

TURNER, ARTHUR CAMPBELL, political science educator, author; b. Glasgow, Scotland, May 19, 1918; naturalized, 1958; s. Malcolm and Robina Arthur (Miller) T.; m. Anne Gordzialkowska, Jan. 21, 1950; 1 child, Nadine (Mrs. M.J. O'Sullivan). M.A. with 1st class honors, U. Glasgow, 1941; B.A. with 1st class honors in Modern History, Queen's Coll., Oxford U., 1943, M.A., 1947, B.Litt., 1948, M.Litt., 1979; Ph.D., U. Calif., Berkeley, 1951. Lectr. history U. Glasgow, 1945-51; asst. prof. history U. Toronto, 1951-53; Commonwealth Fund fellow U. Calif., Berkeley, 1948-50, vis. prof., summers 1950, 66, 71, 78; assoc. prof. polit. sci. U. Calif., Riverside, 1953-58, prof., 1958—, chmn. div. social scis., 1953-61, dean grad. div., 1960-61, chmn. dept. polit. sci., 1961-66; prof. internat. relations, govt. Claremont Grad. Sch., part-time 1962-72; vis. prof. UCLA, 1967, Pomona Coll., 1977; Exec. com. Inst. World Affairs, 1960—, dir., 1965. Author: The Post-War House of Commons, 1942, Free Speech and Broadcasting, 1944, Mr. Buchan, Writer: A Life of the First Lord Tweedsmuir, 1949, Scottish Home Rule, 1952, Bulwark of the West: Implications and Problems of NATO, 1953, Towards European Integration, 1953, Pakistan: The Impossible Made Real, 1957, The Unique Partnership: Britain and the United States, 1971; co-author: Control of Foreign Relations, 1957, (with L. Freedman) Tension Areas in World Affairs, 1964, The Regionalization of Warfare, 1985, Power and Ideology in the Middle East, 1988, Fights of Fancy: Armed Conflict in Science Fiction, 1993; contbr.: Ency. Americana Annual, 1957—; mem. editorial com. U. Calif. Press, 1959-65, 80-83, 90, chmn., U. Calif. Press, 1962-65. Recipient Cecil prize, 1939, Blackwell prize U. Aberdeen, 1943, 51; Wilton Park fellow, 1966, 76, Santa Barbara Seminar on Arms Control fellow, 1983; Rockefeller rsch. grantee Cambridge, Eng., 1959-60, NSF travel grantee Geneva, Switzerland, 1964. Mem. Am. Soc. Internat. Law, Am., Canadian hist. assns., Am. Polit. Sci. Assn., Hist. Assn. (Eng.)., Phi Beta Kappa. Republican. Home: 1992 Rincon Ave Riverside CA 92506-1628 Office: U Calif Dept Polit Sci Riverside CA 92521 *It is now popular to say that we are nothing but the playthings of large, impersonal forces. Actually people, and peoples, bring most of their troubles on themselves. Our success and happiness are, to a large extent, in our own hands.*

TURNER, ARTHUR EDWARD, college administrator; b. Hemlock, Mich., Jan. 31, 1931; s. Alvin S. and Grace E. (Champlain) T.; m. Johann M. Jordan, May 10, 1953; children: Steven Arthur, Michael Scott, Kathryn Jo. BS, Alma (Mich.) Coll., 1952; MEd, Wayne State U., 1954; postgrad., Cen. Mich. U., U. Mich.; LLD, Ashland Coll., 1968; HUD, Colegio Americano de Quito, Ecuador, 1968; LLD, Northwood U., Cedar Hill, Tex., 1984. Admissions counselor Alma Coll., 1952-53, dir. admissions, alumni relations, 1953-59; co-founder Northwood U., Midland, Mich., 1959, 1st pres., 1959-74, chmn. bd., chief exec. officer, trustee, 1974-78, chmn. bd. trustees, 1978-82. Founder, lay minister Presbyn. Ch., Alma, 1956-59; trustee Epilepsy Found., Palm Beach, Fla., 1982; bd. dirs. Margaret Chase Smith Libr., Skowhegan, Maine, 1978, Salvation Army, 1989. Recipient People of Peru award, 1966, Horatio Alger award Horatio Alger Assn., 1981, Great Ams. award Internat. City of Care Fund, 1989, Internat. Freedom of Mobility award Nat. Automobile Dealers Assn., 1986; named one of Outstanding Young Americans, U.S. Jaycees, 1965. Mem. Palm Beach Round Table (chmn. bd.), Midland Country Club, Beach Club, Gov.'s Club (Palm Beach, Fla.), Masons (33 deg.), Shriners, Rotary, Alpha Psi Omega, Phi Phi Alpha. Home: 340 S Ocean Blvd Palm Beach FL 33480 Office: Northwood U Office of Trustees West Palm Beach FL 33409

TURNER, BERT S., construction executive; b. 1921. Grad., La. State U., 1943, Harvard U., 1949. With Esso Standard Oil Co., 1946-57, Nichols Constrn. Inc., Baton Rouge, 1957-61, Nichols Constrn. Corp., Baton Rouge, 1961—; chief exec. officer Turner Industries Ltd., Baton Rouge. Office: Turner Inds Ltd PO Box 2750 Baton Rouge LA 70821*

TURNER, BILLIE B., chemical company executive; b. Whitesboro, TX, 1930. BS, Tex. A&M U., 1952. V.p. Internat. Minerals & Chem. Corp., Northbrook, Ill., 1954-87; chmn., pres., ceo IMC Fertilizer Inc Group, Northbrook, Ill., 1987-93; chmn. IMC Global Inc. (formerly IMC Fertilizer Inc. Group), 1993—. Served with U.S. Army, 1952-54. Office: IMC Global Inc 2100 Sanders Rd Northbrook IL 60062-6139

TURNER, BILLIE LEE, botanist, educator; b. Yoakum, Tex., Feb. 22, 1925; s. James Madison and Julia Irene (Harper) T.; m. Virginia Ruth Mathis, Sept. 27, 1944 (div. Feb. 1968); children: Billie Lee, Matt Warnock; m. Pauline Henderson, Oct. 22, 1969 (div. Jan. 1975); m. Gayle Langford,

Apr. 18, 1980; children (adopted)—Roy P., Robert L. B.S., Sul Ross State Coll., 1949; M.S., So. Meth. U., 1950; Ph.D., Wash. State U., 1953. Teaching asst. botany dept. Wash. State U., 1951-53; instr. botany dept. U. Tex., Austin, 1953; asst. prof. U. Tex., 1954-58, asso. prof., 1958-61, prof., 1961—, now S.F. Blake prof. botany, chmn., 1967-75, dir. Plant Resources Ctr., 1957—; Asso. investigator ecol. study vegetation of, Africa, U. Ariz., Office Naval Research, 1956-57; vis. prof. U. Mont., summers 1971, 73, U. Mass., 1974. Author: Vegetational Changes in Africa Over a Third of a Century, 1959, Leguminosae of Texas, 1960, Biochemical Systematics, 1963, Chemotaxonomy of Leguminosae, 1972, Biology and Chemistry of Compositae, 1977, Plant Chemosystematics, 1984; Asso. editor: Southwestern Naturalist, 1959—. Served to 1st lt. USAAF, 1943-47. NSF postdoctoral fellow U. Liverpool, 1965-66. Mem. Bot. Soc. Am. (sec. 1958-59, 60-64, v.p. 1969), Tex. Acad. Sci., Southwestern Assn. Naturalists (pres. 1967, gov.), Am. Soc. Plant Taxonomists (Asa Gray award 1991), Internat. Assn. Plant Taxonomists, Soc. Study Evolution, Phi Beta Kappa, Sigma Xi. Office: U Tex Plant Resources Ctr Main Bldg 228 Austin TX 78712

TURNER, CAL, SR. (H. CALISTER TURNER), discount stores executive; widowed. With Neely Harwell Co., 1931-36; operated Retail Goods Store, 1936-39; with Dollar Gen. Corp., Scottsville, Ky., from 1939, chmn. emeritus, bd. dirs. Office: Dollar Gen Corp 427 Beech St Scottsville KY 42164-1670*

TURNER, CATHY, Olympic athlete; b. Apr. 10, 1962. BS in Computer Sys., No. Mich. U., 1991. Gold medal 500 meter short-track speedskating Albertville Olympic Games, 1992, also silver medal 3000 meters relay, 1992; Star made in Am. tour Ice Capades, 1992-93; Gold medalist 500 meter speedskating Winter Olympics, Lillehammer, Norway, 1994, Bronze medalist 3000 meter relay, 1994; owner, pres. Cathy Turner's Empire Fitness; motivational spkr. Profl. singer, songwriter, actress. Olympic recordholder 500 meter speedskate: 45.98. Address: US Olympic Committee 1750 E Boulder St Colorado Springs CO 80909-5724

TURNER, CHRISTOPHER, medical educator. BS in Psychology, U. Wis., 1973; MS in Audiology, U. Minn., 1979, PhD of Hearing Sci., 1982. Rsch. assoc. U. Minn., Mpls., 1972-82; asst. prof. U. Alta., Can., 1982-83; asst. prof. Syracuse (N.Y.) U., 1983-87, assoc. prof., 1987—. Contbr. articles to profl. jours. Grantee Sigma Xi, 1984, Deafness Rsch. Found., 1985-87, 88-89, NIH, 1986—, Air Force Office Sci. Rsch., 1989. Mem. Acoustical Soc. Am., Assn. Rsch. in Otolaryngology, Am. Speech, Lang. and Hearing Assn. Office: Univ Iowa Wendell Johnson Speech & Hearing Ctr Iowa City IA 52242

TURNER, CRAIG, journalist; b. Pasadena, Calif., May 24, 1949; s. Donald Leslie and Dorothy A. (Kupseck) T.; m. Ellen Bevier, Oct. 10, 1973 (div. Dec. 1983); m. Joyce Huyett, Sept. 10, 1988. BS in Journalism, San Jose State U., 1971. Reporter L.A. Times, Orange County, Calif., 1971-79; asst. city editor L.A. Times, San Diego, 1979-83; asst. met. editor L.A. Times, L.A., 1983-89, met. editor, 1989-93; fgn. corr. L.A. Times, Toronto, Ont., 1994—. Co-recipient Pulitzer Prize for journalism, 1993, George Polk award Long Island U., 1993. Mem. Soc. Profl. Journalists. Episcopalian. Avocations: outdoor activities, travel, theatre. Office: Los Angeles Times, 890 Yonge St St 400, Toronto, ON Canada M4W 3P4

TURNER, DAVID REUBEN, publisher, author; b. N.Y.C., Dec. 9, 1915; s. Charles and Eva (Turner) Moskowitz; m. Ann Louise Perkins, Apr. 29, 1946 (div. 1976); children—Eve (Mrs. William Watters), Ruth. B.S., Coll. City N.Y., 1936, M.S. in Edn, 1937. Co-founder Arco Pub. Co., N.Y.C., 1937; pub., dir. Arco Pub. Co., 1937-78; v.p. parent co. Prentice-Hall, Inc., 1979-80; pres. Turner Pub., 1980-92; pub. cons. under Ford Found. contract Burma Translation Soc., Rangoon, 1959-60. Author: more than 300 books on tests and testing, including High School Equivalency Diploma Tests, 1951, 75, How to Win a Scholarship, 1955, Scoring High On College Entrance Tests, 1969, 71, Food Service Supervisor, 1968, Bank Examiner, 1968, Accountant-Auditor, 1960, 77, Officer Candidate Tests, 1978, Professional-Administrative Career Exams, 1979, English Grammar and Usage for Test-Takers, 1976, College Level Examination Program, 1979. Adviser bd. publs. Union Am. Hebrew Congregations. Home and Office: 13 Glengary Rd Croton On Hudson NY 10520-2139

TURNER, DOUGLAS LAIRD, writer, editor, columnist; b. Buffalo, N.Y., Jan. 5, 1932; s. Henry Albert and Effie Donna (McIndoo) T.; m. Mary Joan Hassett, July 17, 1962; children: Christopher Henry, Mary Julia, Albert William. BA, Brown U., 1954; postgrad., Stanford U., 1968. Reporter Buffalo (N.Y.) Courier-Express, 1957-60, state capital corr., 1960-64, fin. editor, 1964, city editor, 1964-70, exec. editor, 1971-80, Washington bur. chief, 1981-82; Washington corr. Buffalo (N.Y.) Evening News, 1982, Washington columnist, 1983, Washington bur. chief, 1989—; publs. com. Canisius Coll., Buffalo, 1975-80; founders' com. Niagara Frontier Chpt. Profl. Journalism Soc., N.Y. State Commn. on Pub. Access to Records, 1976-81; mem. cmty. adv. coun. State U. Buffalo, N.Y., 1976-79. Mem. U.S. Olympic Rowing Team, 1956; founder Erie County Forensic Psychiatry Svc., Buffalo, 1975, Area Leadership Group, Buffalo, 1977-79. Spl. agt. U.S. Army Counter Intelligence Corps, 1956-57. Nation champion four-oared shell with cox, 1956; winner Hanlan Trophy, Royal Can. Henley Regatta, 1956; recipient numerous awards Am. Newspaper Guild, N.Y. State Associated Press Assn., personal citations Erie County Legislature, N.Y. State Assembly, Buffalo Common Coun. Mem. Nat. Press Club (former gov. 1988), Potomac Boat Club, Occoquan Boat Club. Roman Catholic. Avocations: classical guitar, piano, voice, rowing, sailing. Home: 7923 Saint George Ct Springfield VA 22153-2741 Office: Buffalo News Washington Bur 1141 National Press Building Washington DC 20045-2101

TURNER, E. DEANE, lawyer; b. Auburn, N.Y., Aug. 4, 1928; s. Alfred Edward and Bertha (Deane) T.; A.B. summa cum laude, Princeton U., 1950; LL.B. cum laude, Harvard U., 1953. Bar: N.Y. 1953. Assoc., Dewey Ballantine and predecessor firms, N.Y.C., 1953-63, ptnr., 1963—, of counsel, 1991-93; treas. Harvard Law Sch. Assn. N.Y.C., 1964-83. Elder, trustee Brick Presbyn. Ch., N.Y.C., 1976—, pres. bd. trustees, 1988-90; mem. com. to adminstr. James N. Jarvie Endowment, 1993—. Fellow Am. Coll. Investment Counsel; mem. ABA, N.Y. Bar Assn., Union Club, John's Island Club, Phi Beta Kappa. Republican. Home: 1120 5th Ave New York NY 10128-0144 also: 381 Lloyds Ln Johns Island Vero Beach FL 32963 Office: Dewey Ballantine 1301 Avenue Of The Americas New York NY 10019-6092

TURNER, ED SIMS, broadcast executive, writer; b. Bartlesville, Okla., Sept. 25, 1935; s. Ed and Dee (Sims) T.; m. Beth Coburn, June 25, 1964; 1 child, Christopher. BA in Journalism, U. Okla., 1957. Producer, dir. documentary films Okla U., Norman, 1957-59; reporter Sta. KWTV, Oklahoma City, 1959-64; v.p. news Sta. WTTG, Washington, 1966-68; v.p. news and pub. affairs Metromedia, N.Y.C., 1968-74; v.p. news United Press Internat. TV News, N.Y.C., 1975; news producer CBS, N.Y.C., 1975-78; news dir. Sta. KWTV, Oklahoma City, 1978-79; managing editor Cable News Network, Atlanta, 1979-81, exec. producer, 1982, chief Wash. bur., 1983, exec. v.p., 1984—; spl. instr. Okla. U., 1968, Mary Mount Coll., N.Y.C., 1978. Dir. ednl. documentary (Best Documentary award Cannes Film Festival 1958); creative producer (TV spl.) Crossfire; creator, engr. (TV spl.) Novak Reports. Press sec. Bud Wilkinson for U.S. Senate campaign, 1964-65. Recipient Best Reporting award UPI, 1959-64, 8 Emmys, 1966-72, Channels mag. Award of Excellence, 1987, Peabody awards, 1983, 87, 89, 91, 6 Ace awards for cable excellence; named Producer of Yr. Millmeter mag., 1984, Outstanding Alumni, Okla. U. Sch. Journalism, 1985, One of 25 Who Count in TV/Motion Picture Industry, View mag., 1986. Mem. Radio TV News Dirs. Assn., Sigma Delta Chi (nat. reporting awards 1963), Phi Gamma Delta. Republican. Office: CNN One CNN Ctr PO Box 105366 Atlanta GA 30348

TURNER, EDWIN LEWIS, astronomy educator, researcher; b. Knoxville, Tenn., May 3, 1949; s. George Lewis and Gladys Love (Gregory) T.; m. Joyce Beldon, Aug. 15, 1971; children: Alexander, Daniel. SB in Physics, MIT, 1971; PhD in Astronomy, Calif. Inst. Tech., 1975. Fellow Inst. for Advance Study, Princeton, N.J., 1975-76; asst. prof. dept. astronomy Harvard U., Cambridge, Mass., 1977-78; asst. prof. dept. astrophysics Princeton U., 1978-81, Alfred P. Sloan Found. Rsch. fellow, 1980-84, assoc. prof., 1981-86, prof., 1986—, assoc. chmn., 1988-95; acting chmn. dept. astronomy Harvard U., Cambridge, 1995—; counselor Space Telescope Inst. Counsel, Balt., 1989—; vis. prof. Nat. Astron. Obs., Japan, Tokyo, 1990; dir. Apache Point Obs. 3.5 meter Telescope, 1995—. Contbr. over 100 articles to astron. publs. Bd. dirs. Assn. Univs. for Rsch. in Astronomy, Inc., Tucson, 1980-89. Mem. Internat. Astron. Union, Am. Astron. Assn. Achievements include research in galaxy masses, cosmic structure formation, quasars, gravitational lenses, and cosmology. Office: Princeton U Obs Ivy Ln Princeton NJ 08544-0001

TURNER, ELIZABETH ADAMS NOBLE (BETTY TURNER), healthcare executive, former mayor; b. Yonkers, N.Y., May 18, 1931; d. James Kendrick and Orrel (Baldwin) Noble; m. Jack Rice Turner, July 11, 1953; children: Jay Kendrick, Randall Ray. BA, Vassar Coll., 1953; MA, Tex. A&I U., 1964. Ednl. cons. Noble & Noble Pub. Co., N.Y.C., 1956-67; psychometrist Corpus Christi Guidance Ctr., 1967-70; psychologist Corpus Christi State Sch., 1970-72, dir. programs, asst. supt., 1972, dir. devel. and vol. svc., 1972-76, dir. rsch. and tng., 1977-79, psychologist Tex. Mental Health and Mental Retardation, 1970-79; pres. Turner Co., 1979—; program cons. Tex. Dept. Mental Health and Mental Retardation, 1979-85; mayor pro tem. Corpus Christi, 1981-85, mayor, 1987-91; CEO, pres. Corpus Christi C. of C., 1991-94; v.p. bus. and govt. rels. ctrl. and south Tex. divsns. Columbia Healthcare Corp., 1994—. Dir. alumni Corpus Christi State U., 1976-77; coord. vols. Summer Head Start Program, Corpus Christi, 1967; chmn. spl. gifts coml United Way, Corpus Christi, 1970; mem. Corpus Christi City Coun., 1979-91; family founded Barnes and Noble, N.Y.C.; with Leadership Corpus Christi II; founder Com. of 100 and Goals for Corpus Christi; pres. USO; bd. dirs. Coastal Bends Coun. Govts., Corpus Christi Mus., Harbor Playhouse, Communities in Schs., Del Mar Coll. Found., Pres.' Coun., Food Bank, Salvation Army, Jr. League; bd. govs. Southside Community Hosp., 1987-93, Gulfway Nat. Bank, 1985-92, Bayview Hosp., 1992—, strategic planning com. Meml. Hosp., 1992, Tex. Capital Network Bd., 1992—, Humana Hosp., Rehab. Hosp. South Tex., Admiral Tex. Navy; apptd. Gov.'s Commn. for Women, 1984-85, Leadership Tex. Class I; founder Goals for Corpus Christi, Bay Area Sports Assn., Assn. Coastal Bend Mayor's Alliance; founder Mayor's Commn. on the Disabled, Mayor's Task Force on the Homeless; active Port Aransas Cmty. Ch. Recipient Love award YWCA, 1970, Y's Women and Men in Careers award, 1988, Commander's Award for Pub. Svc. U.S. Army, Scroll of Honor award Navy League, award Tex. Hwy. Dept., Road Hand award Tex. Hwy. Commn., 1989; named Corpus Christi Newsmaker of Yr., 1987. Mem. Tex. Psychol. Assn. (pres., mem. exec. bd.), Psychol. Assn. (pres., founder), Tex. Mcpl. League (bd. dir.), Corpus Christi C. of C. (pres., CEO), Jr. League Corpus Christi, Tex. Bookman's Assn., Tex. Assn. Realtors, Kappa Kappa Gamma, Corpus Christi Town Club, Corpus Christi Yacht Club, Jr. Cotillion Club. Home: 4600 Ocean Dr Apt 801 Corpus Christi TX 78412-2543

TURNER, ELVIN L., retired educational administrator; b. Springfield, Ohio, Jan. 9, 1938; s. Willie and Jinada (Lawson) T.; m. Betty Jo Breckinridge, June 11, 1966 (div. Jan. 1972); 1 child, Anthony; m. Carrie Johnson, Aug. 3, 1972; 1 child, Brenetta Bell. BS in Biology and Chemistry, Knoxville (Tenn.) Coll., 1962; MEd, U. Cin., 1968; postgrad., Nova U., Ft. Lauderdale, Fla., 1973, Kensington U., Glendale, Calif., 1993—. Cert. secondary prin., tchr., Ohio. Spl. edn. tchr. Cin. Pub. Schs., 1965-69, coord. spl. edn., 1969-72, asst. prin., 1972-78, prin., 1978-90, asst. prin., 1990-93; part-time adj. prof. Mt. St. Joseph (Ohio) Coll., 1987-88; mem. adv. com. Millcreek Psychiat. Ctr. for Children, Cin., 1988-89. Bd. dirs. Big Bros./Big Sisters, Cin., 1973; mem. bd. deacons New Hope Bapt. Ch., Hamilton, Ohio, 1993; Sunday sch. tchr. Bethel AME Ch., Lebanon, Ohio, 1996. Recipient plaques and grants. Mem. Nat. Assn. for Secondary Sch. Prins., Ohio Assn. for Secondary Sch. Prins., Knoxville Coll. Alumni Assn., Phi Delta Kappa, Alpha Phi Alpha. Avocations: bowling, golf, reading, travel. Home: 7886 Bobolink Dr Cincinnati OH 45224-1104

TURNER, ERIC RAY, professional football player. Safety Cleveland Browns, 1991—. Selected to Pro Bowl, 1994; tied for lead in interceptions (9), 1994. Office: c/o Cleveland Browns 80 First Ave Berea OH 44017-1269*

TURNER, EUGENE ANDREW, manufacturing executive; b. Bridgeton, N.J., Aug. 7, 1928; s. Benjamin Homer and Pearl Irene (Wolbert) T.; m. Paula Ann Webb, 1987; children: Mary Ann, John-Reed. BA, Rutgers U., 1966; student, Columbia U., 1980. With Owens Ill., 1950-73, regional mgr. West Coast, 1970-73; v.p. adminstrn. Midland Glass Co., Cliffwood, N.J., 1973-76, pres., chief operating officer, 1981-82, also bd. dirs.; v.p., gen. mgr. Anchor Hocking Corp., Lancaster, Ohio, 1976-81; dir. ops. Theo Chem. Labs., Tampa, Fla., 1988-90, Profit Counselors Inc, Sarasota, Fla., 1990-94; pres. Profit Sys. Inc., Oklahoma City, 1994—; mng. cons. 1987-88. Mem. Harbor Island Club, Seaview Country Club, Navesink Country Club. Home: 1103 Tedford Way Oklahoma City OK 73116-6006 *Take time to learn the chosen business then develop credibility by doing what you say you will do.*

TURNER, EVAN HOPKINS, retired art museum director; b. Orono, Maine, Nov. 8, 1927; s. Albert Morton and Percie Trowbridge (Hopkins) T.; m. Brenda Winthrop Bowman, May 12, 1956; children: John, Jennifer. A.B. cum laude, Harvard U., 1949, M.A., 1950, Ph.D., 1954. Head docent svc. Fogg Mus., Cambridge, Mass., 1950-51; curator Robbins Art Collection of Prints, Arlington, Mass., 1951; teaching fellow fine arts Harvard U., 1951-52; lectr., research asst. Frick Collection, N.Y.C., 1953-56; gen. curator, asst. dir. Wadsworth Atheneum, Hartford, Conn., 1956-59; dir. Montreal Mus. Fine Arts, Que., Can., 1959-64, Phila. Mus. Art, 1964-77, Ackland Art Mus., 1978-83, Cleve. Mus. Art, 1983-93; adj. prof. art history U. Pa., U. N.C., Chapel Hill, 1978-83; disting. vis. prof. Oberlin Coll., 1993—. Mem. Assn. Art Mus. Dirs., Coll. Art Assn. Am., Am. Mus. Assn., Century Assn. Club. Home: 3071 N Park Blvd Cleveland OH 44118-4114

TURNER, FLORENCE FRANCES, ceramist; b. Detroit, Mar. 9, 1926; d. Paul Pokrywka and Catherine Gagal; m. Dwight Robert Turner, Oct. 23, 1948; children: Thomas Michael, Nancy Louise, Richard Scott, Garry Robert. Student, Oakland C.C., Royal Oak, Mich., 1975-85, U. Ariz., Yuma, 1985, U. Las Vegas, 1989—. Pres., founder Nev. Clay Guild, Henderson, 1990-94, mem. adv. bd., 1994—; workshop leader Greenfield Village, Dearborn, Mich., 1977-78, Plymouth (Mich.) Hist. Soc., 1979, Las Vegas Sch. System, 1989-90, Detroit Met. area, 1977-85. Bd. dirs. Las Vegas Art Mus., 1987-91; corr. sec. So. Nev. Creative Art Ctr., Las Vegas, 1990-94. Mem. Las Vegas Gem Club, Nev. Camera Club, Golden Key, Phi Kappa Phi. Avocations: photography, collecting gems, travel. Office: Nev Clay Guild PO Box 50004 Henderson NV 89016-0004

TURNER, FRANK MILLER, historian, educator; b. Springfield, Ohio, Oct. 31, 1944; s. Ronald O. and Mary Elizabeth (Miller) T.; m. Margaret Good, Aug. 26, 1967 (div. 1981); m. Nancy Rash, July 29, 1984 (dec. Mar. 1995). BA, Coll. of William and Mary, 1966; MPhil, Yale U., 1970, PhD, 1971; LHD (hon.), Coll. William and Mary, 1991. Asst. prof. Yale U., New Haven, Conn., 1972-77, assoc. prof., 1977-82, prof., 1982—, provost, 1988-92. Author: Between Science and Religion, 1974, The Greek Heritage in Victorian Britain, 1981, Contesting Cultural Authority: Essays in Victorial Intellectual Life, 1993; co-author: The Western Heritage, 1979, 83, 87, 91, 94, Heritage of World Civilizations, 1985, 90, 93. Guggenheim fellowship, 1983; recipient Brit. Coun. prize Conf. on Brit. Studies, 1982, Yale Press Gov.'s award, 1983. Office: Yale U History Dept PO Box 1504a West Haven CT 06520-3554

TURNER, FRANKLIN DELTON, bishop; b. Norwood, N.C., July 19, 1933; s. James T. and Dora (Streeter) T.; m. Barbara Dickerson, July 6, 1963; children: Jennifer, Kimberly, Franklin. AB, Livingstone Coll., 1956, DD (hon.), 1993; MDiv, Yale U., 1965; DD (hon.), Berkeley Div. Sch., Yale U., 1977. Ordained deacon and priest Episcopal Ch., 1965, consecrated bishop, 1988. Vicar Epighany Ch., Diocese of Dallas, 1965-66; rector St. George's Ch., Diocese of Washington, 1966-72; officer nat. staff Episcopal Ch. Ctr., N.Y.C., 1972-83; mem. bishop's staff for congl. devel. Episcopal Diocese of Pa., Phila., 1983-86, suffragan bishop, 1988—. Author: Black Leaders in the Episcopal Church, 1975. 1st lt. U.S. Army, 1966-72. Office: Diocese of Pa 240 S 4th St Philadelphia PA 19106-3722

TURNER, GENE, religious organization administrator. Dir. Dept. of Governing Body Ecumenical and Agy. Relationship of the Presbyn. Ch., USA, Louisville. Office: Presbyterian Church 100 Witherspoon St Louisville KY 40202-1396

TURNER, GEORGE PEARCE, consulting company executive; b. Dallas, Aug. 22, 1915; s. Fred Horatio and Florence (Phillips) T.; m. June Lori Haney, Feb. 4, 1943 (div. 1976); children: Bruce Haney, Brian Phillips, Mark Richardson; m. Kathryn Blank Hauf, June 1976. Student, U. Tex., 1932-33, 35-36, 40-41, So. Methodist U., 1934; BA in Internat. Rels. cum laude, U. So. Calif., 1962, MS in Internat. Pub. Adminstrn. summa cum laude, 1966; PhD in Econs. and Internat. Rels., Columbia Pacific U., 1982, PhD in Pub. Adminstrn. and Internat. Rels., 1985. Archtl. designer L.A., 1946-48; prin. Lieburg & Turner (cons. engrs.), Pasadena, Calif., 1947-48; pres. Radiant Heat Engring., Inc., Pasadena, 1948-53; exec. asst. to dir. fgn. subsidiaries S.Am. Fluor Corp. Ltd., L.A., 1953-54; mem. exec. staff Coast Fed. Savs. & Loan Assn., 1954-55; exec. staff Holmes & Narver, Inc., L.A., 1955-61; mgr. project devel. S.Am. ops. Southwestern Engring. Co., L.A., 1962; pres. Haney Devel. Corp., 1964-90, Fomento e Inversiones Quisqueyanos C. por A., Santo Domingo de Guzman, Dominican Republic, 1967—; gen. mgr. for Venezuelan ops. Hale Internat. Inc., Caracas, 1970-71; dir., mgr. Consortium Lomas de La Lagunita, Caracas, 1970, Consortium Desarrollos Urbanos, Valencia, Venezuela, 1970; pres. Haney Investment Corp. (HANCO), 1974-90, Casa FOMIQ, 1978—, Caribbean Vagabond Ltd., Grand Cayman Island, B.W.I., 1981-90, Kay Pearce & Turner, Ltd., Newtown Square, Pa., 1981—; sec. Integrated Industries of Atlantic County, N.J.; gen. ptnr. N.Y. Ave. Parking Assocs., Atlantic City, 1980-91; adviser, provisional pres., Dominican Republic, 1965-66, constl. pres. of republic, 1966-68; projects programmer Nat. Planning Inst. Peru Tri-Partite Mission, 1962-65; ofcl. OAS adviser Nat. Office Tourism Dominican Republic, 1966-67, Nat. Office Cultural Patrimony, Liga Mcpl. Dominicana, 1967-68; cons., dir. projects, programming, tech. matters Mission Recovery and Rehab., Dominican Republic, 1965-67; dep. dir. Tech. Assistance Mission Dominican Republic, 1967-68; cons. assignments for program assistance Inter-Am. Tng. Ctr., Fed. U. Ceara, Brazil; OAS adviser on tech. assistance to Chile, Argentina, Uruguay, Peru, Brazil, 1962-68; cons. Wildwood Ocean Towers, N.J., 1969-70, Capital Investment Devel. Corp., Downing Ctr., Downingtown, Pa., 1971-77; dir. for Project Monitor and owners agt., hosp. tower Hahnemann Med. U. and Hosp., Phila., 1975-78; pres. Urban Planning and Devel. Corp., Exton, Pa., 1978-79; cons., corp. sec., v.p. Constrn. Devel. and Properties Mgmt. Group, Integrated Industries Inc., Exton, 1978-80; ltd. ptnr. Marsh Creek Assocs. Two, 1985—; apptd. to faculty Columbia Pacific U., 1987; cons. internat. consortium for multi-billion dollar econ. devel. program with projects in countries of Pacific Rim and Ea. Europe, 1993-95; established Casa FOMIQ awards program, 1995. Author: An Analysis of the Economy of El Salvador, 1961, The Alliance for Progress: Concept Versus Structure, 1966, Some Observations on the Decade of the 1960s - U.S. vis-a-vis Latin America, 1982, Latin American Odyssey, 1985, Third Generation, 1990, Growing Up Male in America: With the Prince Charming Mystique, 1993; pub., editor Fountain of Age, The Jour. of Casa FOMIQ, 1995; contbr. articles to profl. publs. With USAF, 1941-45. Decorated OAS Medal of Honor; recipient Citation for Valiant Svc. in Dominican Republic, 1965-66, Ofcl. OAS Commendation for Program Contbns., Peru, Dominican Republic, Brazil, Venezuela, 1969. Mem. Delta Phi Epsilon, Alpha Sigma Lambda. Home: 8 Fox Run Ln Newtown Square PA 19073-1004 Office: Kay Pearce & Turner Ltd PO Box 419 Newtown Square PA 19073-0419

TURNER, GERALD PHILLIP, hospital administrator; b. Winnipeg, Man., Can., May 13, 1930; s. Lorry and Shirley (Litman) Turbovsky; m. Clare Henteleff, June 12, 1955 (dec.); children: Robin Joy, Neil Lindsay, Daryl Lyon; m. Donna Ireland, May 22, 1994. B.Sc. in Pharmacy, U. Man., Winnipeg, 1953; Diploma in Hosp. Adminstrn., U. Toronto, Ont., Can., 1955. Asst. adminstr. Mt. Sinai Hosp., Toronto, 1955-62; assoc. adminstr. Mt. Sinai Hosp., 1962-66, adminstr., 1966-74, exec. dir., 1974-84, pres., chief exec. officer, 1984-93, pres. emeritus, 1993—; exec. v.p. Mt. Sinai Inst., Toronto, 1976-86; pres. Mt. Sinai Hosp. Found. (formerly Inst.), Toronto, 1987-88, vice chmn., 1988—; assoc. prof. health adminstrn. U. Toronto, 1971-90, prof., 1990—; chmn. rsch. bd. Samuel Lunenfeld Rsch. Inst. Author: (with Joseph Mapa) The Choice is Yours: Making Canada's Medical System Work for You, 1981; co-editor: (with Joseph Mapa) Humanizing Hospital Care, 1979; Humanistic Health Care: Issues for Caregivers, 1988. Recipient Queen's Silver Jubilee medal, Pres.'s Achievement award, Extendicare award, Toronto Chpt. award for Disting. Svcs., Can. Coll. Health Svc. Execs., 1993. Fellow Am. Coll. Healthcare Execs., Can. Coll. Health Service Execs. (founder mem., cert. mem.), Ont. Hosp. Assn. (chmn. elect 1986-87, chmn. 1987-88). Office: Mt Sinai Hospital, 600 University Ave, Toronto, ON Canada M5G 1X5

TURNER, GLORIA TOWNSEND BURKE, social services association executive; b. Lumberton, N.C., Nov. 16, 1938; d. John B. and Alice (Haite) Townsend; m. James Rae Burke, June 3, 1957 (dec. 1974); children: William H., Sonya Kyle; m. Robert R. Turner,June 23, 1977. Student, U. S.C., 1974; degree in nursing, York Tech. Coll./U. S.C., 1976. RN, S.C. Staff nurse, head nurse York Gen. Hosp., Rock Hill, S.C., 1976-78; head med. dept., indsl. nursing J.P. Stevens Plant, Rock Hill, 1976-78; hsop., nursing home auditor S.C. Med. Found., Columbia, 1978-79; exec. dir. Kershaw County Coun. on Aging, Camden, S.C., 1979-93; mgr. med. floor Conway (S.C.) Hosp., 1993—; bd. dirs. S.C. Fedn. Older Ams., 1988-95; mem. state adv. com. on Alzheimers, Columbia, 1984—; trustee Kershaw County Meml. Hosp., Camden, 1989-93. Mem. Camden C. of C., Rotary. Methodist. Avocations: reading, watching football and basketball, travel. Home: 147 Dusty Trail Ln Surfside Beach SC 29575

TURNER, HAL WESLEY, state agency administrator; b. Winchester, Mass., Nov. 18, 1932; s. Wesley Francis and Anna Louise (Hodgkins) T.; m. Jean Marie Turner; children: Julie, Karen. BA, U. Sioux Falls, S.D., 1955. Cert. Govtl. Fin. Mgr. Mem. tech. and mgmt. staff Boeing Computer Svcs., Seattle, 1958-69; mgr. prodn. systems Kennecott Copper Corp., Salt Lake City, 1970-71; dir. MIS State of Idaho, Boise, 1971-74, adminstr. of budget, 1974-77; sales assoc. White Riedel Realtors, Boise, 1978-81; chief dep. Idaho State Controller's Office, Boise, 1981—; pres., Student Loan Fund Idaho, Inc., Fruitland, 1978—. Mem. Boise Samaritan Village Health Facility Adv. Bd.; region 4 chmn. Idaho Com. for Employer Support of Guard and Res. With U.S. Army, 1955-57. Mem. Nat. Assn. State Auditor's Comptr. and Treas., Nat. Assn. Govtl. Accts., Elks, Broadmore Country Club. Democrat. Methodist. Avocations: golf, racquetball. Home: 3512 S Brookshore Pl Boise ID 83706-5582 Office: State Contrs Office PO Box 83720 Boise ID 83720-0002

TURNER, HAROLD EDWARD, education educator; b. Hamilton, Ill., Nov. 22, 1921; s. Edward Jesse and Beulah May (White) T.; m. Catherine Skeeters, Apr. 5, 1946; children: Michele Turner Nimerick, Thomas, Barbara Turner McMahon, Krista Turner Landgraf. A.B., Carthage Coll., 1950; M.S., U. Ill. - Urbana, 1951, Ed.D. (George Peabody fellow), 1956. Tchr., Taylorville Jr. High Sch., Ill., 1951-52, Moline Jr. High Sch., Ill., 1952-54; dir. elem. edn. Jefferson County, Colo., 1955-57; prin. Jefferson County High Sch., 1957-60; asst. prof. edn. N. Tex. State U., Denton, 1960-63; asst. supt. curriculum Sacramento City Schs., 1963-66; asso. prof., chmn. dept. curriculum and instrn. U. Mo. - St. Louis, 1966-69, prof., 1971-85, prof. emeritus, 1985—, chmn. dept. adminstrn., founds., secondary edn., 1977-78, dept. chmn., 1983-85; vis. prof. Adams State Coll., Alamosa, Colo., 1959, U. Ga., Athens, 1981-82; adj. prof. NYU, 1965, U. Ill., 1980; cons. various sch. dists., Tex., Mo.; spl. cons. Mo. State Dept. Edn., 1973. Author: (with Adolph Unruh) Supervision for Change and Innovation, 1970; contbr. articles to profl. jours. Served with USNR, 1942-46. Mem. Profs. Supervision. Presbyterian (elder). Home: 3155 S Calle Pueblo Green Valley AZ 85614-1058 Office: U Mo St Louis Sch Edn 8001 Natural Bridge Rd Saint Louis MO 63121-4401

TURNER, HARRY EDWARD, lawyer; b. Mt. Vernon, Ohio, Dec. 25, 1927; s. Paul Hamilton and Harriett (Krafft) T.; m. Shirley Marilyn Eggert, July 8, 1950; children: Harry Edward, Thomas Frederick. B.A., Baldwin Wallace Coll., 1951; J.D., Ohio No. U., 1954. Bar: Ohio 1954, U.S. Supreme Ct. 1966. Practice in Mt. Vernon, 1954—; state rep. Ohio Gen. Assembly, 1973-85; solicitor Mt. Vernon, 1958-62; Prosecutor Mt. Vernon Municipal Ct., 1955-58. Mem. Mt. Vernon City Sch. Bd., 1964-70, pres., 1965-70;

trustee Ohio Sch. Bd. Assn., 1968-70, Hannah Browning Home, 1987—, Sta. Break/Commn. on Planning Svcs., 1989-95; mem. Knox County Pub. Defender Commn., 1987-91. With USN, 1946-47. Mem. Ohio State Bar Assn., Knox County Bar Assn. (pres. 1970), Alpha Sigma Phi, Sigma Delta Kappa. Republican. Lutheran. Home: 400 E Vine St Mount Vernon OH 43050-3442 Office: 118 E High St Mount Vernon OH 43050-3402

TURNER, HARRY WOODRUFF, lawyer; b. Blairsville, Pa., May 2, 1939; s. James McKinnie and Dorothy Elizabeth (Tittle) T.; m. Mary Elizabeth Phelan, Dec. 30, 1972; children: James William, David Woodruff. AB, U. Pitts., 1961; JD, Harvard U., 1964. Bar: Pa., 1965, U.S. Supreme Ct., 1979. Assoc. Kirkpatrick & Lockhart, Pitts., 1964-71, ptnr., 1971—; bd. dirs., sec. Imperial Harbor Corp., 1968—, IH Utility Co., 1975—, IH Properties Co., 1980-87; mem. Fed. Jud. Selection Commn. Pa., 1995—. Trustee U. Pitts., 1995—, Wilson Coll., Chambersburg, Pa., 1978-89, Aspinwall Baseball Assn., 1985—; trustee, sec. Adoptive Rights Coun.; pres. U. Pitts. Nat. Alumni Assn., 1990-91; alt. del. Rep. Nat. Conv., Miami, 1968, Houston, 1992; trustee, v.p. Torrance (Pa.) State Hosp., 1969-73; trustee ann. giving fund Pitts. 1982-95; chair distbn. com. William L. Benz Found., 1985—; bd. dirs. Pitts. divsn. Am. Heart Assn., 1993—. Mem. ABA, Pa. Bar Assn., Am. Law Inst., Internat. Acad. Trial Lawyers, Allegheny County Bar Assn., Allegheny County Acad. Trial Lawyers, SAR (v.p. 1994), Fox Chapel Golf Club, Duquesne Club, Harvard-Yale-Princeton Club, Univ. Club, Allegheny Club. Presbyterian. Office: Kirkpatrick & Lockhart 1500 Oliver Bldg Pittsburgh PA 15222-2404

TURNER, HENRY A., political science educator, author; b. King City, Mo., Jan. 2, 1919; s. Henry A. and Bessie Marie (Claxton) T.; m. Mary Margaret Tilton, May 23, 1943; children—John Andrew, Nancy Ellen, Stephen Heald. B.S., N.W. Mo. State U., 1939; M.A., Mo. U., 1941; Ph.D., U. Chgo., 1950. Jr. coll. instr., 1940-42; instr. Iowa State U., 1945-46; from instr. to assoc. prof. U. Calif.-Santa Barbara, 1948-62, prof., 1962—, chmn. dept. polit. sci., 1960-65, acad. vice chancellor, 1971-73; mem. summer faculty U. Mo., 1951, U. Nebr, 1956, U. Calif.-Berkeley, 1958; vis. prof. polit. sci. U. Khartoum, Sudan, 1962-63; Fulbright lectr. U. Witwatersrand, Republic South Africa, 1968, U. Teheran, Iran, 1974; cons. Bur. Budget, 1953; mem. staff White House, 1953. Author: (with J.A. Vieg) The Government and Politics of California, 4th edit., 1971, American Democracy: State and Local Government, 1968, 2d edit., 1970; co-author: American Democracy in World Perspective, 1967, 5th edit., 1980, The Wilson Influence on Public Administration, 1990; editor: Politics in the United States, 1955; contbr. articles to profl. jours. Staff mem. Democratic Nat. Com., 1952. Served from ensign to lt. USNR, 1942-45. Mem. Am. Polit. Sci. Assn., Western Polit. Sci. Assn. Home: 703 Foxen Dr Santa Barbara CA 93105-2516

TURNER, HENRY BROWN, finance executive; b. N.Y.C., Sept. 3, 1936; s. Henry Brown III and Gertrude (Adams) T.; m. Sarah Jean Thomas, June 7, 1958 (div.); children: Laura Eleanor, Steven Bristow, Nancy Carolyn. A.B., Duke U., 1958; M.B.A., Harvard U., 1962. Controller Fin. Corp. of Ariz., Phoenix, 1962-64; treas., dir. corporate planning Star-Kist Foods, Terminal Island, Calif., 1964-67; dir., 1st v.p. Mitchum, Jones & Templeton, Los Angeles, 1967-73; asst. sec. Dept. Commerce, Washington, 1973-74; v.p. fin. N-Ren Corp., Cin., 1975-76; v.p. Oppenheimer & Co., N.Y.C., 1976-78; exec. v.p., mng. dir. corporate fin. Shearson Hayden Stone Inc., N.Y.C., 1978-79; sr. mng. dir. Ardshiel Inc., 1980-81, pres., 1981-93, chmn. emeritus, 1994—; vis. lectr. U. Va. Sch. of Bus.; bd. dirs. MacDonald & Co., Pembrook Mgmt., Inc., Golden State Vitners, Inc., Cellu-Tissue Corp., Wrangler Ft. McDowell Adventures McDowell Indian Reservation, Phoenix. Sponsor Jr. Achievement, 1964-67. Served to lt. USNR, 1958-60. Coll. Men's Club scholar Westfield, N.J., 1954-55. Mem. Fed. Govt. Accountants Assn. (hon.), Duke Washington Club, Omicron Delta Kappa.

TURNER, HESTER HILL, management consultant; b. San Antonio, Jan. 31, 1917; d. Orvin A. and Edna Lee (Guerguin) Hill; m. William Hoag Turner, Mar. 7, 1939 (div. Aug. 1957); children: William Hoag, John Daniel, Mary Lee, Jane Livingston (Mrs. S. Thomas Toleno). B.S., Our Lady of Lake U., 1938; M.A., S.W. Tex. State Coll., 1940; J.D., U. Ariz., 1945; Ed.D., Oreg. State U., 1956; L.H.D. (hon.), Drury Coll., Our Lady of the Lake, Salem Coll. Faculty Lewis and Clark Coll., Portland, 1947-66, dean students, 1961-66; nat. exec. dir. Camp Fire Girls, Inc., Kansas City, Mo., 1966-79; vis. instr. Oreg. State U., Western Wash. Coll., Portland State Coll.; dir. profl. services Oreg. Edn. Assn., Portland, 1959-61. Contbr. articles and chpts. to profl. publs. Mem. Oreg. Commn. on Status of Women, 1964-66; del. White House Conf. on Status of Women, 1965; mem. Portland met. steering com. OEO, 1965-66, Nat. Citizens Adv. Com. Vocat. Rehab., 1966-68; mem. Def. Adv. Com. Women in Services, 1966-69, chmn., 1968-69; mem. N.Y. State Vocat. Rehab. Planning Council, 1967-68; trustee Council for Advancement and Support of Edn.; chmn. Accreditation Commn., Nat. Home Study Council, 1983-89; mem. Army Adv. Council on ROTC Affairs, 1974-75; bd. dirs. Nat. Wildlife Fedn., 1982-88, Yosemite Inst., 1983-90; bd. dirs. Lincoln Found. and Lincoln Inst. Land Planning, 1983-89, New Century Conservation Trust, Inc., 1992—. Recipient Dept. Def. medal for disting. pub. service, 1970; named Disting. Citizen U. Ariz. Mem. NEA, Oreg. Assn. Health and Phys. Edn. (pres. 1959-60), Oreg. Bar Assn., Ariz. Bar Assn., Am. Forestry Assn. (v.p. 1977-79, pres. 1980-82), Forest History Soc. (pres. 1991-93), Gemological Inst. Am. (bd. dirs. 1989-92), Phi Kappa Phi, Delta Kappa Gamma. Home and Office: 601 E 20th St New York NY 10010-7622 *One learns to make decisions only by making them. All adults who care about young people are presented with a special challenge: If we want to help them become responsible adults, we must have both the courage to stand for our own beliefs, and the faith to allow them to discover their own.*

TURNER, HUGH JOSEPH, JR., lawyer; b. Paterson, N.J., Oct. 5, 1945; s. Hugh Joseph and Louise (Sullivan) T.; m. Charlene Chiappetta, Feb. 11, 1983. BS, Boston U., 1967; JD, U. Miami, Coral Gables, Fla., 1975. Bar: Fla. 1975, U.S. Dist. Ct. (so. & mid. dists.) Fla. 1975, U.S. Ct. Appeals (11th cir.) 1981, U.S. Supreme Ct. 1984. Tchr. Browne & Nichols, Cambridge, Mass., 1968-72; ptnr. Smathers & Thompson, Miami, Fla., 1981-87, Kelley Drye & Warren, Miami, 1987-93, English, McCaughan & O'Bryan, Ft. Lauderdale, 1993—; chmn. Fla. Bar internat. law sect., 1988-89. Contbg. author book on internat. dispute resolution Fla. Bar, 1989; contbr. articles to profl. jours. Bd. dirs. Japan Soc. South Fla., Miami, 1989—. Mem. ABA, Def. Rsch. Inst., Internat. Bar Assn. Avocation: running. Office: English McCaughan O'Bryan 100 NE 3rd Ave Fort Lauderdale FL 33301-1176

TURNER, JAMES THOMAS, judge; b. Clifton Forge, Va., Mar. 12, 1938; s. James Thomas and Ruth (Greene) T.; m. Patricia Sue Renfrow, July 8, 1962; 1 child, James Thomas. BA, Wake Forest Coll., 1960; JD, U. Va., 1965. Bars: Va. 1965, U.S. Ct. Appeals (4th and fed. cirs.), U.S. Supreme Ct. Assoc. firm Williams, Worrell, Kelly & Greer, Norfolk, Va., 1965, ptnr., 1971-79; U.S. magistrate U.S. Dist. Ct., Eastern Dist. Va., Norfolk, 1979-87; judge, U.S. Ct. Fed. Claims, 1987—. Mem. ABA, FBA, Va. Bar Assn., Norfolk and Portsmouth Bar Assn. (sec. 1975-79). Office: US Ct Fed Claims 717 Madison Pl NW Washington DC 20005-1011

TURNER, JAMES WESLEY, minister, former church administrator; b. Hampton, Va., May 30, 1914; s. James Hugh Turner and Lizzie Emma Moger; m. Ruth Clark Brown, Sept. 28, 1940; children: James Wedford, Susan Clark. BA, Randolph-Macon Coll., 1937, DD, 1961; MDiv, Emory U., 1940. Ordained to ministry Meth. Ch., 1940. Pastor Meth. Ch., Richmond, Va., 1940-82; dir. program coun. United Meth. Ch., Richmond, 1976-82; dist. supt. United Meth. Ch., Arlington, Va., 1971-76; chmn. fin. Va. Conf. Credit Union, Inc., 1954—; pres. Chaplain Svc. Va., Richmond; mem. bd. ordained ministry, Richmond, 1989—. Vice pres. Robert E. Lee coun. Boy Scouts Am., 1978—; mem. allocation panel United Way Greater Richmond, 1987-95. Recipient Gold medal Freedom Found., 1967, Silver Beaver award Boy Scouts Am., 1980. Mem. Masons. Avocations: photography, golf, travel. Home and Office: 10201 Glendye Rd Richmond VA 23235-2122

TURNER, JANE ANN, federal agent; b. Rapid City, S.D., Aug. 26, 1951; d. John Owen and Wilma Veona (Thompson) T.; 1 child, Victoria Thompson. BA, Carroll Coll., 1973; student forensic psychology, John Jay Sch. Criminal Justice, N.Y.C., 1985-87. Spl. agt. FBI, Seattle and N.Y.C., 1978-87; sr. resident spl. agt. FBI, Minot, N.D., 1987—; spkr., instr. FBI, Seattle, N.Y.C. and Minot, 1978—, Psychol. Profiler, 1983—. Mem. Minot Commn. on the Status of Women, 1991-93. Mem. Gen. Fedn. Women's Clubs (v.p. 1992-93), Women in Law Enforcement, N.D. Peace Officer Assn., Optimist Club. Office: FBI PO Box 968 Fed Bldg Minot ND 58701

TURNER, JANET SULLIVAN, painter; b. Gardiner, Maine, Nov. 15, 1935; d. Clayton Jefferson and Frances (Leighton) Sullivan; m. Terry Turner, Oct. 6, 1956; children: Lisa Turner Reid, Michael Ross, Jonathan Brett. BA cum laude, Mich. State U., 1956; student, Haystack Mountain Sch. rep. Am. Women in Art, UN World Conf. on Women, Nairobi, Kenya, 1995. One-artist shows include San Diego Art Inst., 1971, Villanova (Pa.) U. Gallery, 1982, Pa. State U. Gallery, Middletown, 1985, Temple U. Gallery, 1986, Widener U. Art Mus., Chester, Pa., 1987, 94, Rosemont Coll., Pa., 1995; group shows include Del. Art Mus., Wilmington, 1978, Woodmere Art Mus., Phila., 1980, Port of History Mus., Phila., 1984, Allentown Art Mus., 1984, Trenton (N.J.) City Mus. Ellarslie Open VIII, 1989, Ammo Gallery, Bklyn., 1989, Pa. State Mus., Harrisburg, 1990-94, Galeria Mesa, Ariz., 1991, Del. Ctr. for Contemporary Arts, Wilmington, 1992, Holter Mus., Helena, Mont., 1992, S.w. Tex. State U., San Marcos, 1993, Fla. State U. Mus., Tallahassee, 1993, Newark Mus., 1993, U. Del., 1994, 1st St. Gallery, N.Y.C., 1994, Noyes Mus., N.J., 1995, Sande Webster Gallery, Phila. 1995, 96; represented in permanent collections Nat. Mus. Women in Arts, Washington, Mich. State U., East Lansing, ARA Svcs. Inc., Phila., Blue Cross/Blue Shield, Phila., am. Nat. Bank and Trust co., Rockford, Ill., Burroughs Corp., Lisle, Ill., State Mus. Pa., Harrisburg, Bryn Mawr (Pa.) Coll., Rosemont Coll., Villanova (Pa.) Coll.; contbg. writer and art critic Art Matters, Phila., 1987. Bd. dirs. Rittenhouse Sq. Fine Arts Ann., Phila., 1984-86. Recipient 2d pl. award San Diego Art Inst. 19th Ann. Exhbn., 1971, award of merit Pavilion Gallery, Mt. Holly, N.J., 1991, 3d pl. Katonah Mus. of Art, N.Y., 1992, purchase award State Mus. of Pa., Harrisburg, 1992. Mem. Artists Equity (bd. dirs. 1985-86, 1st v.p. Phila. 1986-87, newsletter editor 1985-86, pres. 1987-88), Phila. Watercolor Club, Delta Phi Delta. Republican. Roman Catholic. Home and Studio: 88 Cambridge Dr Glen Mills PA 19342-1545

TURNER, JANINE, actress; b. Lincoln, Nebr., Dec. 6, 1963; d. Janice Gaunt. Appearences include (TV) Behind the Screen, 1981-82, General Hospital, 1982-83, Northern Exposure, 1990-95 (Hollywood Fgn. Press Assn. award 1992, Emmy award nominee 1993), (films) Young Doctors in Love, 1982, Knights of the City, 1985, Tai-Pan, 1986, Monkey Shines: An Experiment in Fear, 1988, Steel Magnolias, 1988, The Ambulance, 1990, Cliffhanger, 1993. Office: CAA 9830 Wilshire Blvd Beverly Hills CA 90212-1804*

TURNER, JEAN-LOUISE, public relations executive; b. Washington, Sept. 29, 1942; d. Fletcher Wood and Mary Louise (Gant) T.; student Howard U., 1959-62; B.A., Fed. City Coll., 1970; M.A., 1972; children—Nathaniel Anthony Landry, Mark Andrew Landry. Coordinator public relations Sta. WRC-TV, Washington, 1969; adminstr. prodn., 1970-72; mgmt. trainee NBC, Washington, 1972; producer spls. Sta. WRC-TV, 1972-76, asso. producer documentaries, 1972-76; mgr. community affairs and public affairs, host Sta. WRC/WKYS, Washington, 1976-78, producer WRC 1978-79; media rep. PEPCO, Washington, 1979-81; press aide D.C. City Council, 1981-82; dir. pub. relations LaMancha, Inc., 1983-84; v.p. Talisman Assocs., 1984—. cons. Jafra Skin Care, 1994; Judge Gabriel awards; mem. media panel D.C. Arts and Humanities Commn.; bd. dirs. Epilepsy Found. Am.; pres. parish coun. St. Francis de Sales Roman Cath. Ch., 1993, 94—; career role model St. Anthony's High Sch. Recipient Hallmark award Jr. Achievement, 1976, Public Service award Washington Area Council Alcoholism and Drug Abuse, 1977; Public Interest award Council Better Bus. Burs. Inc., 1977. Mem. Capital Press Club, Washington Assn. Black Journalists, Nat. Acad. TV Arts and Scis., Nat. Assn. Public Continuing Adult Edn., Anchor Mental Health Assn. (bd. dirs., chmn. 1992-94, Award of Appreciation 1994), Washington Women's Forum (charter), Alpha Kappa Alpha. Roman Catholic. Editorial bd. NAPCAE Exchange, 1979-81. Home: 2715 31st Pl NE Washington DC 20018-1601 Office: 4005 20th St NE Washington DC 20018

TURNER, JEROME, federal judge; b. Memphis, Feb. 18, 1942; s. Cooper and Eugenia (Morrison) T.; m. Shirley Broadhead, Oct. 18, 1969 (div. July 1986); children: Alexandra Cox, Christian Annette; m. Kay Farese, Aug. 22, 1987. BA, Washington and Lee U., 1964, LLB cum laude, 1966. Bar: Tenn. 1966. Law clk. to judge U.S. Dist. Ct., Memphis, 1966-67; assoc. Canada, Russell & Turner, Memphis, 1967-73, ptnr., 1974-78; ptnr. Wildman, Harrold, Allen, Dixon & McDonnell, Memphis, 1978-87; judge U.S. Dist. Ct. (we. Dist.) Tenn., Memphis, 1988—. Author: Law Rev. Comment, Washington and Lee Law Rev., 1964, 65; editor: Law Rev., 1966. Treas. Elect Don Sundquist to Congress Com., 1981-82, Reelect Don Sundquist to Congress Com., 1983-86. Fellow Tenn. Bar Found.; mem. ABA, Memphis and Shelby County Bar Found. (bd. dirs. 1982-83, 87), Memphis and Shelby County Bar Assn. (pres. 1988, treas. 1984, bd. dirs. 1978-79), Fed. Bar Assn., Tenn. Bar Assn., Leo Bearman Sr. Am. Inn of Ct. (pres. 1995-96), Order of Coif, Omicron Delta Kappa. Roman Catholic. Avocations: hunting, tennis, reading, gardening. Office: Clifford Davis Fed Bldg Ste 1111 167 N Main St Memphis TN 38103-1830

TURNER, JOHN GOSNEY, insurance company executive; b. Springfield, Mass., Oct. 3, 1939; s. John William and Clarence Oma (Gosney) T.; m. Leslie Corrigan, June 23, 1962; children: John Fredric, Mary Leslie, James Gosney, Andrew William. B.A., Amherst Coll., 1961; student, Advanced Mgmt. Program, Harvard U., 1980. Assoc. actuary Monarch Life Ins. Co., Springfield, Mass., 1961-67; group actuary Northwestern Nat. Life Ins. Co., Mpls., 1967-75, sr. v.p. group, 1975-79, sr. v.p., chief actuary, 1979-81, exec. v.p., chief actuary, 1981-83, pres., chief operating officer, 1983—, chmn., CEO; dir. NWNL Reins. Co., NWNL Gen. No. Life, North Atlantic Life Ins. Co. N.Y. Trustee Abbott-Northwestern Hosps., Evans Sch. Found.; chmn. Minn. Trustees of the Evans Scholars Found. Fellow Soc. Actuaries; mem. Am. Acad. Actuaries, Western Golf Assn. (dir.), Minn. Golf Assn. Club: Minikahda (Mpls.). Office: Northwestern Nat Life Ins Co PO Box 20 20 Washington Ave S Minneapolis MN 55401*

TURNER, JOHN NAPIER, former prime minister of Canada, legislator; b. Richmond, Eng., June 7, 1929; s. Leonard and Phyllis (Gregory) T.; m. Geills McCrae Kilgour, May 11, 1963; children: Elizabeth, Michael, David, Andrew. BA with honors in Polit. Sci., U. B.C., Can., 1949; BA, Oxford U., Eng., 1951, BCL, 1952; MA, Oxford U., 1957; postgrad., U. Paris, 1952-53; LLD (hon.), U. New Brunswick, 1968, York U., Toronto, 1969, U. B.C., 1994; D. of Civil Law (hon.), Mt. Allison U., N.B., 1980. Bar: Eng. 1953, Que. 1954, Ont. 1968, B.C. 1969, Y.T. 1969, N.W.T. 1969, Barbados 1969, Trinidad 1969. With Stikeman, Elliot, Tamaki, Mercier and Turner, Montreal, Que., 1953-65, McMillan Binch, Toronto, 1976-84; M.P. for St. Lawrence-St. George Montreal, 1962-68, Ottawa-Carleton, 1968-75; parliamentary sec. to Minister of Northern Affairs and Nat. Resources, 1963-65; minister without portfolio, 1965-67; registrar-gen. Govt. of Can., 1967-68, minister of consumer and corp. affairs, 1968, solicitor-gen., 1968, minister of justice and atty.-gen. of Can., 1968-72, minister of fin., 1972-75, prime minister of Can., 1984; leader Liberal Party Can., 1984-90; mem. parliament Vancouver Quadra, 1984-93; Miller Thomson Toronto; created Queen's Counsel, Ontario and Quebec, 1968; former positions include minister without portfolio, registrar gen., minister consumer and corp. affairs, solicitor gen., minister justice and atty. gen., minister fin. Author: Senate of Canada, 1961, Politics of Purpose, 1968. Can. Track Field Champion, 1948; mem. English Track and Field Team, 1950-51. Appointed Companion of Order of Can., 1995. Mem. Eng. Bar Assn., Grey's Inn London, Bar. Assns. of Ont., Que., B.C., Barbados, Trinidad, Mt. Royal Club, Montreal Racquet Club, Cercle Universitaire d'Ottawa Club, Aylmer (Que.) Country Club, Queen's Club, Badminton and Racquet Club, York Club, The Vancouver Club. Liberal. Roman Catholic. Avocations: tennis, canoeing, skiing. Home: 27 Dunloe Rd, Toronto, ON Canada M4V 2W4 Office: Miller Thomson, 20 Queen St W Box 27 Ste 2700, Toronto, ON Canada M5H 3S1

TURNER, JOHN SIDNEY, JR., otolaryngologist, educator; b. Bainbridgw, Ga., July 25, 1930; s. John Sidney and Rose Lee (Rogers) T.; m. Betty Jane Tigner, June 5, 1955; children: Elizabeth, Rebecca, Jan Marie. BS, Emory U., 1952, MD, 1955. Diplomate Am. Bd. Otolaryngology. Intern U. Va. Hosp., 1955-56; resident in otolaryngology Duke U. Med. Ctr., 1958-61; prof. otolaryngology Emory U., Atlanta, 1961-95, chmn. dept., 1961-95; cons. Healthcare Partnership Cons., Atlanta, 1995—; ear specialist, chief otolaryngology Emory Clinic, 1961-95; area cons. in field U.S. 3d Army, 1962-69; assoc. dir. heart disease control program Fla. Bd. Health, 1956-58; Ga. state chmn. Deafness Rsch. Found., 1968—; v.p. Clifton Casualty Ins. Co., Atlanta, 1975-95. Mem. internat. editl. bd. Drugs Jour., 1982—, Ethicals in Med. Progress, 1982—, Dialogue Jour., 1988-95; mem. editl. bd. Otolaryngolog—Head and Neck Surgery, 1991; contbr. chpts. to books, articles to profl. jours. With USPHS, 1956-58. Recipient Appreciation award Children of Fulton County and Fulton County Health Dept., 1975, Citation for Disting. Svc., Fla. divsn. Am. Cancer Soc., 1957, Lester A. Brown award Ga. Soc. Otolaryngology—Head and Neck Surgery, 1995. Mem. AMA, So. Med. Assn. (chmn. otolaryngology sect. 1974, cert. of appreciation 1974), Am. Acad. Otolaryngology--Head and Neck Surgery (Honor award 1994), Triological Soc. (v.p., chmn. so. sect. 1991—), Am. Acad. Otolaryngic Allergy, Ga. Soc. Otolaryngology (pres. 1973), Med. Assn. Ga., Med. Assn. Atlanta, Assn. Acad. Depts. Otolaryngology, Optimists (pres. Atlanta 1975), Alpha Omega Alpha. Democrat. Methodist. Home: 1388 Council Bluff Dr NE Atlanta GA 30345-4132

TURNER, KAREN ELAINE, pastor; b. Chgo., Jan. 29, 1953; d. Washington Sylvester and Geraldine (Price) T. BA, Ill. Wesleyan U., 1974. Ordained to Ch. of God ministry; cert. tchr., Ill. Ins. agt. Washington Nat., Evanston, Ill., 1977-79; group ins. exec. sales Bankers Life, Des Moines, 1979-81; tchr. St. James Acad., Chgo., 1984, Chgo. Bd. Edn., 1989-91; tchr., office adminstr. Ahead Christian Ctr., Chgo., 1989—; pastor Ch. of God Ch., Chgo., 1990—. Coord. Ahead Adult Literacy Program, Chgo., 1991—. Mem. NAFE, internat. Platform Assn. Avocations: reading, sewing. Office: Ch of God 1459 E 69th St Chicago IL 60637-4863

TURNER, KATHLEEN, actress; b. Springfield, Mo., June 19, 1954; m. Jay Weiss, 1984; 1 child, Rachel Ann. Student, Cen. Sch. of Speech and Drama, London, Southwest Mo. State U.; BFA, U. Md. various theater roles, Broadway debut: Gemini, 1978, Cat on a Hot Tin Roof, 1990, Indiscretions, 1995; appeared in TV series The Doctors, 1977; films include Body Heat, 1981, A Breed Apart, 1982, The Man With Two Brains, 1983, Crimes of Passion, 1984, Romancing the Stone, 1984, Prizzi's Honor (Golden Globe award for best actress), 1985, The Jewel of the Nile, 1985, Peggy Sue Got Married, (D.W. Griffith award for best actress, Oscar nomination for best actress) 1986, Julia and Julia, 1988, Switching Channels, 1988, Who Framed Roger Rabbit, 1988, Accidental Tourist, 1988, The War of the Roses, 1989. V.I. Warshawski, 1991, Undercover Blues, 1993, House of Cards, 1993, Serial Mom, 1994, Naked in New York, 1994; dir. (Showtime Cable movie) Leslie's Folly, 1994; also performed in radio shows with the BBC, 1992, 93. Office: ICM 8942 Wilshire Blvd Beverly Hills CA 90211*

TURNER, KATHLEEN J., communication educator, consultant; b. Canton, Ohio, Jan. 8, 1952; d. Josiah Shelden Turner and Anne Alexander; m. Raymond Sprague, May 30, 1981. BA in Speech Comm., English summa cum laude, U. Kans., 1974; MA in Comm., Purdue U., 1976, PhD in Comm., 1978. Teaching asst. Purdue U., Lafayette, Ind., 1976-78; asst. prof. Denison U., Granville, Ohio, 1978-79, U. Notre Dame, South Bend, Ind., 1979-85; vis. assoc. prof. U. Tulsa, 1985-86; assoc. prof. Tulane U., New Orleans, La., 1986—; also chair dept. comm., 1992—; mem. comm. course and curriculum com. U. Tulsa, 1985-86; mem. com. comm. program curriculum U. Notre Dame, 1979-80, com. for redesigned comm. curriculum, 1983-84; mem. jr. yr. abroad com. Tulane U., 1987-88, Am. studies com., 1987-88, Univ. Coll. com. on bus. studies, 1988-91, univ. senate, 1989-91, search com. for v.p. devel., 1989, juror 5th yr. architecture student thesis reviews, 1987, 88, 89, 90, chair univ. senate com. on devel., 1991-94, women's studies com., 1986-91, com. Newcomb Ctr. for Rsch. on Women, 1988-90; lectr. numerous seminars; presenter numerous workshops. Author: Lyndon Johnson's Dual War: Vietnam and the Press, 1985, paperback, 1986; contbr. chpts. and articles numerous books; book and jour. reviewer; contbr. articles to profl. jours. Invited to 16th Air Force Acad. Assembly, 1974; recipient Paul B. Lawson award U. Kans., 1973, Allen Crafton scholarship U. Kans., 1972-73, 73-74, fellowship Purdue U., 1974-75, 75-76; Residential fellow Tulane U., 1992—, Newcomb fellow Tulane U., 1989—. Mem. Speech Comm. Assn. (life, rsch. bd. 1990-93, short course selection com. 1992-93), Ctrl. States Comm. Assn. (life, chair fin. com. 1984-85), So. States Comm. Assn. (chair rhetoric and pub. address div. 1992-93, editor So. Speech Comm. Jour. 1988-89), Ctr. for Study of Presidency. Home: 2412 Jay St New Orleans LA 70122-4310 Office: Tulane Univ Dept Comm New Orleans LA 70118

TURNER, LARRY WILLIAM, agricultural engineer, educator; b. Cin., Dec. 18, 1954; s. Roy Obertate and Martha Lucille (McNeely) T.; m. Lois V. Lynch, Oct. 23, 1976; children: Molly Elizabeth, Amy Rebekah, Clay Matthew. BS, Purdue U., 1976, MS in Agrl. Engring., 1978; PhD, U. Ky., 1984. Lic. profl. engr., 1980. Grad. instr. Purdue U., West Lafayette, Ind., 1976-78; cons. engr. Turner Engring., Rising Sun, Ind., 1980-81; extension agrl. engr. U. Ky., Lexington, 1978-80, rsch. specialist, 1981-84, asst. extension prof., 1984-89, assoc. extension prof., 1989-94, extension prof., 1994—; vis. scientist Silsoe Rsch. Inst., England, 1992-93; cons. Smith Constrn., State of Ky. Contbr. articles to profl. jours. Chmn. bd. Christ United Meth. Ch., Lexington, 1980, lay leader, 1983; evangelism chmn. St. Andrew's United Meth. Ch., 1989-90, chmn. bd., 1990-91. Mem. Am. Soc. of Agrl. Engrs., Am. Soc. of Heating, Refrigerating and Air Conditioning Engrs., Tau Beta Pi, Alpha Epsilon, Phi Kappa Phi, Gamma Sigma Delta. Republican. Methodist. Avocations: painting, drawing, fishing, basketball. Office: U Ky Agrl Engring Dept Lexington KY 40546-0276

TURNER, LEE, travel company executive; b. 1952. BS, Worcester Polytechnic Inst., 1974; MBA, Dartmouth, 1976. With Baxter Healthcare, Deerfield, Ill., 1976-79, 82-87, Southeastern Pub. Svc. Co., Miami Beach, Fla., 1979-82; exec. v.p., CFO BTI Ams., Inc., Northbrook, Ill., 1987—. Office: BTI Ams Inc 400 Skokie Blvd Fl 8 Northbrook IL 60062-2887

TURNER, LEE S., JR., civil engineer, consultant, former utilities executive; b. Dallas, Nov. 5, 1926; s. James A. and Fay Sims; m. Donetta Mae Johnson, Jan. 17, 1947. BCE, Tex. A&M U., 1948; JD, So. Meth. U., 1957. Engr. Dallas Power & Light Co., 1948, various exec. positions, pres., chief exec., 1967-76; dir. Tex. Utilities Co., 1967-82; exec. v.p. Tex. Utilities Co., Dallas, 1976-84; cons., 1989—. Trustee Com. for Econ. Devel., Southwestern Med. Found.; past pres., bd. dirs. Dallas Citizens Coun.; bd. dirs. So. Meth. U. Found. for Sci. and Engring.; past chmn. Children's Med. Ctr.; past chmn. United Way, YMCA, Community Coun. of Greater Dallas; past pres. Greater Dallas Ahead, Inc., Dallas Assembly. With U.S. Army, 1945-46. Mem. ABA, Am. Arbitration Assn. Presbyterian.

TURNER, LISA PHILLIPS, human resources executive; b. Waltham, Mass., Apr. 10, 1951; d. James Sinclair and Virginia (Heathcote) T. BA in Edn. and Philosophy magna cum laude, Washington Coll., Chestertown, Md., 1974; AS in Electronics Tech., AA in Engring., Palm Beach Jr. Coll., 1982; MBA, Nova U., 1986, DSc, 1989; PhD, Kennedy Western U., 1990. Cert. pers. adminstr., quality engr., human resource profl.; lic. USCG capt.; lic. pvt. pilot FAA. Founder, pres. Turner's Bicycle Svc., Inc., Delray Beach, Fla., 1975-80; electronics engr., quality engr. Audio Engring. and Video Arts, Boca Raton, 1980-81; tech. writing instr. Palm Beach Jr. Coll., Lake Worth, Fla., 1981-82; adminstr. tng. and devel. Mitel Inc., Boca Raton, 1982-88; mgr. communications and employee rels. Modular Computer Systems, Inc., Ft. Lauderdale, Fla., 1988-89; U.S. mktg. project mgr. Mitel, Inc., Boca Raton, Fla., 1990-91; v.p. human resources Connectronics, Inc., Ft. Lauderdale, Fla., 1991-93; mgr. human resources Sensormatic Electronics Corp., Boca Raton, Fla., 1993—. With USCG Aux. Mem. ASTD, Am. Soc. for Pers. Adminstrn., Internat. Assn. Quality Cirs., Am. Soc. Quality Control, Fla. Employment Mgmt. Assn., Am. Acad. Mgmt., Employment Assn. Fla., Am. Capts. Assn., Citizens Police Acad., Aircraft Owners and Pilot's Assn., Exptl. Aircraft Assn., Fla. Aero. Club. Home: 1358 Farifax Cir E Lantana FL 33462-7412 Office: Sensormatic Electronics Corp 6600 Congress Ave Boca Raton FL 33487-1213

TURNER, LOYD LEONARD, advertising executive, public relations executive; b. Claude, Tex., Nov. 5, 1917; s. James R. and Maude (Brown) T.; m. Lee Madeleine Barr, Apr. 13, 1944; children: Terry Lee, Loyd

Lee. Student, Tex. Tech. U., 1935-36, Okla. Bapt. U., 1936-37; BA, Baylor U., 1939, MA, 1940; postgrad., U. Pa., 1940-42. Instr. dept. English U. Pa., Phila., 1940-42; pub. relations coordinator Consol. Vultee Aircraft Corp., San Diego, 1946-48; dir. pub. relations Consol. Vultee Aircraft Corp., Fort Worth, 1948-53; asst. to pres. Fort Worth div. Gen. Dynamics Corp., 1953-72; exec. asst. to pres. and chmn. bd. Tandy Corp., Fort Worth, 1972-76; v.p. Tandy Corp., 1976-85; sr. v.p. Witherspoon and Assocs., Inc., Fort Worth, 1986—, also bd. dirs.; mem. Gov.'s Com. on Public Sch. Edn., Tex., 1966-69; pres. Tex. Council Major Sch. Dists., 1968-69. Author: The ABC of Clear Writing, 1954. Bd. dirs. Tarrant County chpt. ARC, 1956-59; bd. dirs. Pub. Communication Found. for North Tex., 1970-76, Tex. Com. Pub. Edn., 1961-69; bd. dirs. Ft. Worth Child Study Ctr., 1974-81, 85-88, v.p., 1986-88; bd. dirs. Parenting Guidance Ctr., 1976-78, Longhorn coun. Boy Scouts Am., 1976-91, One Broadway Plaza, 1978-88; planning and research coun. United Way, Tarrant County, 1976-80; bd. dirs. Casa Manana Musicals, 1978—, pres., 1978-80; bd. dirs. Fort Worth Citizens Organized Against Crime, 1976-90, vice chmn., 1978-89; bd. dirs. Jr. Achievement Tarrant County, 1982-87, North Central chpt. March of Dimes, 1983-84; mem. Christian edn. coordinating bd. Bapt. Gen. Conv., Tex., 1976-80; trustee Ft. Worth Pub. Libr. Bd., 1953-63, pres., 1958-63; trustee Ft. Worth Bd. Edn., 1959-71, pres., 1965-71; trustee Baylor U., Waco, Tex., 1980-89. Served with USAAF, 1942-46. Named Library Trustee of Yr. Tex. Library Assn., 1961; Paul Harris fellow Rotary Internat., 1983; recipient Silver Beaver award Boy Scouts Am., 1986. Mem. Pub. Relations Soc. Am. (pres. N.Tex. chpt. 1977), Pub. Rel. Soc. Am. (Paul M. Lund Pub. Service award 1980), Nat. Mgmt. Assn., Tex. Congress of Parents and Tchrs. (hon. life mem.), West Tex. C. of C. (bd. dirs. 1982-87, v.p. 1985-87, Leadership award 1966, 69), NEA (pres. Best Bd. of Large Sch. Systems in U.S. 1968), Tex. Assn. of Sch. Bds. (bd. dirs. 1966-71, Outstanding Service award 1971), Advt. Club of Fort Worth (pres. 1977-78), Air Force Assn. (Spl. citation 1962), Assn. for Higher Edn. of N. Tex. (vice chmn. 1979-82), Fort Worth C. of C. (bd. dirs. 1974-76, 78-81, 83-87, vice chmn. 1985-87), Arts Council of Fort Worth (dir. 1973-75, 80-89), Tex. Assn. Bus. (bd. dirs. 1977-82, 83-86), Tex. Research League (bd. dirs. 1979-87), Baylor U. Devel. Council (pres. 1975-77), Baylor U. Alumni Assn. (bd. dirs. 1958-61), Fort Worth Safety Council (bd. dirs. 1980-83), Am. Advt. Fedn. (Silver Medal award 1981), Soc. Profl. Journalists (pres. Fort Worth chpt. 1961-62). Baptist. Clubs: Admirals, Bear, Frog. Lodge: Rotary (pres. 1974-75; William B. Todd Service Above Self award 1987). Home: 3717 Echo Trl Fort Worth TX 76109-3432 Office: Witherspoon and Assocs Inc 1000 W Weatherford St Fort Worth TX 76102-1842

TURNER, LYNNE ALISON (MRS. PAUL H. SINGER), harpist; b. St. Louis, July 31, 1941; d. Sol and Evelyn (Klein) T.; m. Paul H. Singer, June 2, 1963; children: Bennett Lloyd, Rachel E. Singer Sullivan. Degree with high honors, Paris Conservatory Music (Premier Prix Hors Concours-Harp), 1959-60; studied with Pierre Jamet. lectr. in field. Harpist Chgo. Symphony Orch., 1962—, acting prin. harpist, 1994—; soloist Chgo. Symphony Orch., Israel Philharm. Orch., other maj. orchs. in U.S. and Europe, also chamber groups; founding mem. L'Ensemble Recamier, The Chgo. Duo (harp and violin); instr. harp Sch. Music, DePaul U., Chgo., 1976-86; instr. harp Lake Forest Coll., 1988-90; instr. pvt. students. Recipient 1st prize 2d Internat. Harp Competition, Israel, 1962. Mem. Am. Harp Soc., Chgo. Hist. Soc. (costume com.), Women's Assn. Chgo. Symphony Orch., Antiquarian Soc. Art Inst. Chgo., Internat. Visitors Ctr. Chgo., Chgo. Arts Club, The Casino Club. Avocations: gardening, decorating, collecting antiques. Office: Orch Hall 220 S Michigan Ave Chicago IL 60604-2508

TURNER, MALCOLM ELIJAH, biomathematician, educator; b. Atlanta, May 27, 1929; s. Malcolm Elijah and Margaret (Parker) T.; m. Ann Clay Bowers, Sept. 16, 1948; children: Malcolm Elijah IV, Allison Ann, Clay Shumate, Margaret Jean; m. Rachel Patricia Farmer, Feb. 1, 1968; children: Aleta van Riper, Leila Samantha, Alexis St. John, Walter McCamy. Student, Emory U., 1947-48; B.A., Duke U., 1952; M.Exptl. Stats., N.C. State U., 1955, Ph.D., 1959. Analytical statistician Communicable Disease Center, USPHS, Atlanta, 1953; rsch. assoc. U. Cin., 1955, asst. prof., 1955-58; asst. statistician N.C. State U., Raleigh, 1957-58; assoc. prof. Med. Coll. Va., Richmond, 1958-63, chmn. div. biometry, 1959-63; prof., chmn. dept. statistics and biometry Emory U., Atlanta, 1963-69; chmn. dept. biomath., prof. biostats. and biomath. U. Ala., Birmingham, 1970-82, prof. biostats. and biomath., 1982—; instr. summers Yale U., 1966, U. Calif. at Berkeley, 1971, Vanderbilt U., 1975; prof. U. Kans., 1968-69; vis. prof. Atlanta U., 1969; cons. to industry. Mem. editorial bd. So. Med. Jour., 1990—; contbr. articles to profl. jours. Fellow Ala. Acad. Sci., Am. Statis. Assn. (hon.), AAAS (hon.); mem. AAUP, AMA (affiliate), Biometrics Soc. (mng. editor Biometrics 1962-69), Soc. for Indsl. and Applied Math., Mensa, Sigma Xi, Phi Kappa Phi, Phi Delta Theta, Phi Sigma. Home: 1734 Tecumseh Trl Pelham AL 35124-1012 *The logic of induction is the quest.*

TURNER, MARGERY AUSTIN, government agency administrator; b. Ithaca, N.Y., July 10, 1955; d. William Weaver and Elizabeth Jane (Hallstrum) Austin; m. James Charles Turner, Aug. 26, 1979; children: James Austin, Benjamin Phillip. BA, Cornell U., 1977; M Urban Planning, George Washington U., 1984. Rschr. Urban Inst., Washington, 1977-88, dir. housing rsch., 1988-93; dep. asst. sec. for rsch. U.S. Dept. HUD, Washington, 1993—. Author: Housing Market Impacts of Rent Control, 1990; co-author: Urban Housing in the 1980's, 1985, Future U.S. Housing Policy, 1987, Opportunities Denied, Opportunities Diminished, 1991, Housing Markets and Residential Mobility, 1993. Mem., coach Boys and Girls Club, Camp Springs, Md., 1990—. Mem. Lambda Alpha.

TURNER, MARSHALL CHITTENDEN, JR., venture capitalist; b. Santa Monica, Calif., 1941; s. Marshall C. and Winifred K. Turner; m. Ann Curran, 1965; children: Erin, Benjamin, Brian. BSME, Stanford U., 1964, MS in Product Design, 1965; MBA with distinction, Harvard U., 1970. Indsl. designer Mattel Toy Co., Hawthorne, Calif., 1965; rsch. engr. GM Def. Rsch. Lab., Santa Barbara, Calif., 1965-66; med. engr. NIH, Bethesda, Md., 1966-68; White House fellow Washington, 1970-71; asst. to dep. adminstr. EPA, Washington, 1971-73; assoc. Crocker Assocs., L.P., San Francisco, 1973-75; v.p. fin., COO Sierra R.R., 1973-75; pres., chmn. bd. dirs. Liquid Crystal Tech., Inc., San Leandro, Calif., 1975-80; gen. ptnr. Taylor & Turner Assocs., Ltd., San Francisco, 1981—; bd. dirs. DuPont Photomasks, Inc., Alliance Tech. Fund, N.Y., Remanco Internat., Inc., Wilmington, Mass.; bd. dirs., past chmn. bd. dirs. Corp. Pub. Broadcasting, Washington. Contbr. articles to profl. jours. Bd. dirs. Sta. KQED, Inc., San Francisco, 1977-87, chmn., 1985-87, acting CEO, 1993; trustee Reed Union Sch. dist., Tiburon, Calif., 1977-81, chmn., 1979-81; bd. dirs. George Lucas Ednl. Found., San Rafael, Calif., 1992—, PBS, Alexandria, Va., 1993—, PBS Enterprises, Inc., 1992—; trustee Mus. TV and Radio, N.Y.C., 1991-92. Lt. USPHS, 1966-68. Recipient Creative design award Machinery Inst., 1965. Avocations: fly fishing, theatrical set design. Office: Penthouse 10 220 Montgomery St San Francisco CA 94104-3402

TURNER, MARTA DAWN, youth program specialist; b. Morgantown, W.V., Oct. 7, 1954; d. Trubie Lemard and Dorothy Genevieve (Helmick) T.; m. David Michael Dunning, Mar. 1, 1980. Student, Royal Acad. Dramatic Art, London, 1975; BA with honors, Chatham Coll., 1976; grad. cert. in arts adminstrn., Adelphi U., 1982; MA Devel. Drama, Hunter Coll., 1988. Cert. video prodn. specialist. Asst. dir. Riverside Communications, N.Y.C., 1985-88; dir. drama, video youth environ. group Water Proof, Cornell Coop. Extension, 1989-91; playwright, dir. Awareness Players, The Disabled Theatre of Maine, 1993-95. Exec. prodr. video projects including Hispanic City Sounds, Time for Peace, Home, Home in Inwood, 1985—; asst. dir., dir. video series Riverside at Worship, 1985-88. Bd. dirs. Trinity Presbyn. Ch., N.Y.C., 1980-90, Am. Diabetes Assn., 1986-87. Avocations: swimming, Scrabble, karate, Marilyn Monroe fan/memoribilia collection. Home and Office: 818 Ohio St Apt 90 Bangor ME 04401-3100

TURNER, MARY ALICE, elementary school educator; b. Birmingham, Ala., Aug. 8, 1946; d. Henry and Elzona (Griffin) Johnson; m. Raymond Carver Turner, July 6, 1968; 1 child, Taunya Nicole. BS in Edn., Ala. A&M U., 1968, MEd, 1992. Cert. tchr. home econs. edn., elem. edn., early childhood edn. Elem. tchr. Huntsville (Ala.) City Schs., 1969—. Mem. Parent/Sch./Tchr. adv. bd. Ridgecrest Elem. Sch., Huntsville, 1978; tchr. rep. PTA, Rolling Hills Elem. Sch., Huntsville, 1988-93. Recipient Award for Dedicated Svc. Rolling Hills PTA, 1988. Mem. ASCD, NEA, Ala. Edn. Assn., Huntsville Edn. Assn. (sch. rep. 1969-96, mem. budget com., rule and regulations com. review), Ala. Reading Assn., Alpha Kappa Alpha. Democrat. Baptist. Avocations: needlepoint, sewing, reading, public speaking. Home: 6508 Mercator Dr NW Huntsville AL 35810-1361 Office: Rolling Hills Elem Sch 2901 Hilltop Ter NW Huntsville AL 35810-1862

TURNER, MARY JANE, educational administrator; b. Colorado Springs, Colo., June 1, 1923; d. David Edward and Ina Mabel (Campbell) Nickelson; m. Harold Adair Turner, Feb. 15, 1945 (dec.); children: Mary Ann, Harold Adair III. BA in Polit. Sci., U. Colo., 1947, MPA in Pub. Adminstrn., 1968, PhD in Polit. Sci., 1978. Secondary tchr. Canon City (Colo.) Sch. Dist., 1950-53; tchr. assoc. in polit. sci. U. Colo., Denver, 1968-70, Boulder, 1970-71; rsch. asst. Social Sci. Edn. Consortium, Boulder, 1971, staff assoc., 1972-77; dir. Colo. Legal Edn. Program, Boulder, 1977-84; assoc. dir. Ctr. for Civic Edn., Calabasas, Calif., 1984-88; dir. Close Up Found., Alexandria, Va., 1988-92; sr. edn. advisor Close Up Found., Arlington, Va., 1992—. Author: Political Science in the New Social Studies, 1972; co-author: American Government: Principles and Practices, 1983, 4th edit., 1996; Civics: Citizens in Action, 1986, 2d edit., 1990, U.S. Government Resource Book, 1989. Mem. Nat. Coun. for Social Studies (chair nominations 1983-84, chair bicentennial com. 1986), Social Sci. Edn. Consortium (pres. 1986-87, bd. dirs. 1984-87), Pi Lambda Theta, Pi Sigma Alpha. Democrat. Presbyterian. Office: Close Up Found 44 Canal Center Plz Alexandria VA 22314-1592

TURNER, MICHAEL GRISWOLD, advertising executive, writer; b. Pitts., Mar. 2, 1925; s. James Jewett and Madelaine Eunice (Griswold) T.; m. Elizabeth Anne Tufel, Sept. 8, 1951; children: Jason A., Michael G., Nanci S. Turner Steveson, James A., Craig C., Ashley S. BA cum laude, Princeton U., 1949. Rsch. asst. to mgmt. supr. Benton & Bowles, N.Y.C., 1950-60; dir. Benton & Bowles, London, 1960-63; mgmt. supr. Benton & Bowles, N.Y.C., 1963-66; exec. v.p., dir. Ogilvy & Mather, N.Y.C., 1966-70, Houston, 1970-85, Washington, 1985-86; vice chmn. Earle Palmer Brown, Bethesda, Md., 1986-91, Atlanta, 1986-91; chmn. Turner & Turner Comm., Inc., Atlanta, 1992—; cons. and lectr. in field. Contbr. articles to trade jours. With USNR, 1943-46, PTO. Mem. Gipsy Trail Club (vice commodore 1968-70), Bay Head Yacht Club (N.J.). Home: 750 Olde Clubs Dr Alpharetta GA 30202-6890 Office: Turner & Turner Comm Inc 906 East Ave Mantoloking NJ 08738

TURNER, MICHAEL STANLEY, physics educator; b. L.A., July 29, 1949; s. Paul Joseph and Janet Mary (Lindholm) T.; m. Terri Lee Shields, Aug. 1978 (div. Sept. 1980); m. Barbara Lynn Ahlberg, Sept. 10, 1988; children: Rachel Mary, Joseph Lucien. BS in Physics, Calif. Inst. Tech., 1971; MS in Physics, Stanford U., 1973, PhD in Physics, 1978. Enrico Fermi fellow U. Chgo., 1978-80, from asst. to assoc. prof., 1980-85, prof., 1985—; scientist Fermi Nat. Accelerator Lab, Batavia, Ill., 1983—; trustee Aspen (Colo.) Ctr. Physics, 1984—, pres., 1989-93; Halley lectr. Oxford U., 1994. Author: (with E.W. Kolb) The Early Universe, 1990; contbr. over 150 articles to profl. jours. Sloan fellow A.P. Sloan Found., 1983-88. Fellow Am. Acad. Arts and Scis., Am. Phys. Soc. (mem. exec. bd. 1992-94, chmn. publ. oversight com. 1993-94); mem. Am. Astron. Soc. (Helen B. Warner prize 1984), Internat. Astron. Union, Sigma Xi. Office: U Chgo Enrico Fermi Inst 5640 S Ellis Ave Chicago IL 60637-1433

TURNER, MILDRED EDITH, day care owner; b. Winnebago, Wis., Jan. 11, 1926; d. Jewett Candfield and Angeline Mary (Long) T. BS, State Tchrs. Coll., 1949; MS of Edn., U. Wis., Milw., 1962; postgrad., U. Wis., Oshkosh, 1965-70. Cert. tchr., Wis. Tchr. Winnebago County, Omro, Wis., 1945-47, Plymouth (Wis.) Pub. Schs., 1949-51, Ripon (Wis.) Pub. Schs., 1951-53, Omro Pub. Schs., 1953-88; instr. U. Wis., Oshkosh, 1971, supervising tchr. of student tchrs., 1970-91; owner, operator Wee Care Children's Ctr., Omro, 1974—. Contbr. articles to newspapers, profl. publs., children's books. Acolyte coord. Algoma Blvd. United Meth. Ch.; supt. Sunday sch., pianist, choir dir., ch. music dir. Eureka/Waukau United Meth. Ch.; sub-dist. children's dir. Watertown sub-dist. United Meth. Ch. Mem. Ret. Tchrs. Assn. Winnebago County, Ret. Tchrs. Assn. Omro, Fox Valley Assn. for Edn. of Young Children, Word and Pen Christian Writers (sec.-treas.), Alumni Assn. U. Wis. Oshkosh), Alumni Assn. Omro (treas.), Odd Fellows (past noble grand Rebekah lodge), Omro Study Club (past pres.). Avocation: collecting nativity sets. Home and Office: Wee Care Childrens Ctr 305 E Scott St Omro WI 54963-1707

TURNER, NORV, professional football coach. Head coach Washington Redskins, 1994—. Office: Washington Redskins PO Box 17247 Washington DC 20041-0247

TURNER, PETER MERRICK, retired manufacturing company executive; b. Toronto, Ont., Can., July 4, 1931; s. William Ian MacKenzie and Marjorie (Merrick) T.; m. Beverley Brophey, Sept. 13, 1958 (dec.); children: Peter Merrick, Christopher Harold, David MacKenzie; m. Alix Johanna Houston, Aug. 17, 1991. BASc, U. Toronto, 1954; MBA, Harvard U., 1956. Staff asst. controllers dept. Bridgeport Brass Co., Conn., 1956-57; sec. treas. Perkins Paper Products Co., Montreal, Que., Can., 1957-58; with Texaco Can. Ltd., Montreal, 1958-68, treas., 1966-68; dir. budgeting and planning, corp. devel. Molson Breweries Can. Ltd., Montreal, 1968—; v.p. planning Molson Breweries Can. Ltd., 1968-70; v.p. corp. devel. Molson Industries Ltd., Toronto, 1970-72; exec. v.p. Bennett Pump Inc., Muskegon, Mich., 1972-73, pres., chief exec. officer, 1973-78; v.p. corp. planning and devel. Sealed Power Corp., Muskegon, 1978-83, group v.p. internat., 1981-83, group v.p. Gen. Products Group, 1984-89; v.p. bus. devel. SPX Corp., Muskegon, 1989-91, v.p. ops., 1991-92, v.p. corp. planning and devel., 1992-94; ret., 1994; bd. dirs. Grand Trunk Corp., Grand Trunk Western Ry., Domestic Four Leasing Corp.; lectr. extension dept. McGill U., 1960-67, Grand Valley State Coll., 1979. Gen. chmn. red shield appeal Montreal Salvation Army, 1969-70; chmn. McGill Assocs., Montreal, 1969-70; bd. dirs. Hackley Hosp., 1975-94, West Shore Symphony Orch., 1976-94; bd. dirs. Muskegon C.C. Found., 1976-94. Mem. Mount Royal Club, Granite Club, Lake O'Hara Trail Club, Zeta Psi. Episcopalian. Home: 45 Heath St W, Toronto, ON Canada M4V 2M6

TURNER, PHILIP MICHAEL, university official and dean, author; b. West Acton, Mass., Nov. 26, 1948; s. William Albert and Evelyn Olena (Peterson) T.; m. Lis Jane VanderBeke, Aug. 16, 1969; children: Gabrielle, Adrienne. BS in Edn., Boston State Coll., 1970; MS, U. Wis. at La Crosse, 1972; MSLS, East Tex. State U., 1977, EdD, 1977. Tchr. math. Edgewood Jr. High Sch., Merritt Island, Fla., 1969-71; ptnr. Video Guide Prodn. Co., Denver, 1973; libr. media specialist Edison Jr. High Sch., Green Bay, Wis., 1973-76; prof. libr. sci. U. Ala., Tuscaloosa, 1977-88; dean Grad. Sch. Libr. and Info. Studies, asst. vice chancellor for acad. affairs U. Ala. System, Tuscaloosa, 1988—. Author: Handbook for In-School Media Personnel, 1980, Helping Teachers Teach, 1985, 2d edit., 1993, Casebook for Helping Teachers Teach, 1988. Vol. Meals on Wheels, Tuscaloosa, 1987—. Recipient Outstanding Commitment To Teaching award U. Ala. Alumni Assn., 1979, Outstanding Svc. award Ala. Libr. and Media Prodrs., 1987, publ. award Div. Sch. Libr. Media Specialist, 1987, award for mng. info. tech., 1994, Ala. Libr. Assn. Disting. Svc. award, 1996; named Libr. of Yr., Beta Phi Mu, 1991. Mem. ALA, Assn. Sch. Librs. (chair rsch. com. 1987-90, bd. dirs. 1990-94), Assn. for Ednl. Comm. and Tech. (chair evaluation com. 1979). Unitarian. Office: Univ Ala Sch Libr and Info Studies PO Box 870252 Tuscaloosa AL 35487-0252

TURNER, RALPH HERBERT, sociologist, educator; b. Effingham, Ill., Dec. 15, 1919; s. Herbert Turner and Hilda Pearl (Bohn) T.; m. Christine Elizabeth Hanks, Nov. 2, 1943; children: Lowell Ralph, Cheryl Christine. B.A., U So. Calif., 1941, M.A., 1942; postgrad., U. Wis., 1942-43; Ph.D., U. Chgo., 1948. Rsch. assoc. Am. Coun. Race Relations, 1947-48; faculty UCLA, 1948—, prof. sociology and anthropology, 1959-90, prof. emeritus, 1990—, chmn. dept. sociology, 1963-68; chmn. Acad. Senate U. Calif. System, 1983-84; bd. dirs. Founds. Fund for Rsch. in Psychiatry; vis. summer prof. U. Wash., 1960, U. Hawaii, 1962; vis. scholar Australian Nat. U., 1972; vis. prof. U. Ga., 1975, Ben Gurion U., Israel, 1983; vis. fellow Nuffield Coll. Oxford U., 1980; disting. vis. prof. Am. U., Cairo, Egypt, 1983; adj. prof. China Acad. Social Scis., Beijing, People's Republic China, 1986; faculty rsch. lectr. UCLA, 1986-87. Author: (with L. Killian) Collective Behavior, 1957, 2d edit., 1972, 3d edit., 1987, The Social Context of Ambition, 1964, Robert Park on Social Control and Collective Behavior, 1967, Family Interaction, 1970, Earthquake Prediction and Public Policy, 1975, (with J. Nigg, D. Paz, B. Young) Community Response to Earthquake Threat in So. Calif., 1980, (with J. Nigg and D. Paz) Waiting for Disaster, 1986; editl. cons., 1959-62; editor: Sociometry, 1962-64; acting editor: Ann. Rev. of Sociology, 1977-78; assoc. editor, 1978-79, editor, 1980-86; adv. editor: Am. Jour. Sociology, 1954-56, Sociology and Social Rsch., 1961-74; editl. staff: Am. Sociol. Rev., 1955-56; assoc. editor: Social Problems, 1959-62, 67-69; cons. editor: Sociol. Inquiry, 1968-73, Western Sociol. Rev., 1975-79; mem. editl. bd. Mass Emergencies, 1975-79, Internat. Jour. Crit. Sociology, 1974-76, Symbolic Interaction, 1977-90, 95—. Mem. behavioral scis. study sect. NIH, 1961-66, chmn., 1963-64; dir.-at-large Social Sci. Rsch. Coun., 1965-66; chmn. panel on pub. policy implications of earthquake predictions Nat. Acad. Scis., 1974-75, also mem. earthquake study del. to Peoples Republic of China, 1976; mem. policy adv. bd. So. Calif. Earthquake Preparedness program, 1987-92, mem. com. social edn. and action L.A. Presbytery, 1954-56. Served to lt. (j.g.) USNR, 1943-46. Recipient Faculty prize Coll. Letters and Scis. UCLA, 1985; Faculty Rsch. fellow Social Sci. Rsch. Coun., 1953-56; Sr. Fulbright scholar U.K., 1956-57; Guggenheim fellow, U.K., 1964-65. Mem. AAAS (exch. del. to China 1988), AAUP, Am. Sociol. Assn. (coun. 1959-64, chmn. social psychology sect. 1960-61, pres. 1968-69, chmn. sect. theoretical sociology 1973-74, chmn. collective behavior and social movements sect. 1983-84, Cooley-Mead award 1987), Pacific Sociol. Assn. (pres. 1957), Internat. Sociol. Assn. (coun. 1974-82, v.p. 1978-82), Soc. Study Social Problems (exec. com. 1962-63), Soc. for Study Symbolic Interaction (pres. 1982-83, Charles Horton Cooley award 1978, George Herbert Mead award 1990), Sociol. Rsch. Assn. (pres. 1989-90), Am. Coun. of Learned Soc. (exec. com. of coun. 1990-93), UCLA Emeriti Assn. (pres. 1992-93). Home: 1126 Chautauqua Blvd Pacific Palisades CA 90272-3808 Office: UCLA 405 Hilgard Ave Los Angeles CA 90024-1301

TURNER, ROBERT COMRIE, composer; b. Montreal, Que., Can., June 6, 1920; s. William Thomson and Myrtle Wellsteed (Snowdon) T.; m. Sara Nan Scott, June 30, 1949; children: Alden, Martin, Carolyn. BM, McGill U., 1943, MusD, 1953; student, Royal Coll. Music, 1947-48; MusM, George Peabody Coll. Tchrs., 1950. Sr. music producer Canadian Broadcasting Corp., Vancouver, B.C., 1952-68; lectr. in music U. B.C., Vancouver, 1955-57; asst. prof. music Acadia U., Wolfville, N.S., Can., 1968-69; prof. composition U. Manitoba, Winnipeg, 1969-85; prof. emeritus U. Manitoba, 1985—. Over 70 compositions including Opening Night: A Theatre Overture, 1955, The Third Day (Easter Cantata), 1962, Symphony for Strings, 1960, Capriccio Concertante, 1975, Third String Quartet, 1975, opera The Brideship, 1967, Trio Transition for Violin Cello and Piano, 1969, The Phoenix and the Turtle, 1964, Concerto for Two Pianos and Orchestra, 1971, Johann's Gift to Christmas, 1972, Eidolons, 1972, Variations on the Prairie Settler's Song, 1974, From a Different Country, 1976, Lament for Linos, 1978, Amoroso Canto, 1978, Shadow Pieces I (after Joseph Cornell), 1981, opera Vile Shadows, 1983, Symphony in One Movement, 1983, Encounters I-IX, 1984, Time for Three, 1985, Playhouse Music, 1986, Concerto for Viola and Orchestra, 1987, Shades of Autumn, 1987, Manitoba Memoir, 1989, Third Symphony, 1990, a Group of Seven, 1991, The River of Time, 1994, House of Shadows, 1994, Four "Last Songs", 1995; All-Turner concert, 1989, Canada House, London; com. mem. Vancouver Internat. Festival; adjudicator Met. and San Francisco Opera auditions; MacDowell Colony resident, 1987. Served with Royal Can. Air Force, 1943-45. Recipient Commemorative medal for 125th Anniversary of Confedn. of Can., 1993; overseas scholar Royal Coll. Music, 1947-48; fellow Can. Coun., 1966-67; grantee Man. Arts Coun., 1982-83, 85, Can. Coun. Artists, 1990-92. Mem. Soc. Composers, Authors and Music Pubrs. of Can., Can. League Composers, Can. Music Ctr., MacDowell Colony.

TURNER, ROBERT EDWARD, psychiatrist, educator; b. Hamilton, Ont., Can., June 8, 1926; s. Robert William and Alice May (Johnson) T.; m. Gene Anne Stewart, Sept. 27, 1952; children: Margaret, John, Robert, Richard. B.A. with honors in Zoology and Chemistry, McMaster U., 1948; M.D., U. Toronto, 1952. Intern Hamilton Gen. Hosp., 1952-53; resident Bristol (Eng.) Mental Hosps. Group, 1953-55; practice medicine specializing in psychiatry Toronto, Ont.; dir. Forensic Clinic Toronto Psychiat. Hosp., 1958-66; sr. psychiatrist forensic service Clarke Inst. Psychiatry, Toronto, 1966; chief forensic service Clarke Inst. Psychiatry, 1967-69, med. dir., 1969-76; asst. prof. dept. psychiatry U. Toronto, 1964-68, prof., 1973-77, prof. forensic psychiatry, 1977-91, prof. emeritus, 1991—; cons. in psychiatry Law Reform Commn. Can., 1972-85; staff psychiatrist, 1987—; dir. Met. Toronto Forensic Service, 1977-87; hon. cons. Clarke Inst. Psychiatry, 1991—. Author: Pedophilia and Exhibitionism, 1964; contbr. articles on psychiatry and law to profl. jours. Pres. Kenneth G. Gray Found., 1971—; mem. legal task force Com. on Mental Health Svcs. for Ont., Ont. Coun. Health, 1978-79; dep. warden Cathedral Ch. of St. James, Toronto, 1978-79, 92-94, rector's warden, 1994-96; bd. dirs. Clin. Inst. Addiction Rsch. foun. Ont., 1973-86, chmn., 1985-86; bd. dirs. Addiction Rsch. Found., 1982-86. Fellow Royal Coll. Physicians and Surgeons Can., Am. Psychiat. Assn. (life), Can. Psychiat. Assn. (life, bd. dirs. 1974-77), Ont. Psychiat. Assn. (life, pres. 1975-76), Can. Med. Assn., Ont. Med. Assn., Med.-Legal Soc. Toronto (coun. 1979-82), Royal Coll. Psychiatrists. Home: 18 Rolph Rd, Toronto, ON Canada M4G 3M6 Office: U Toronto Dept Psychiatry, 250 College St, Toronto, ON Canada M5T 1R8

TURNER, ROBERT FOSTER, lawyer, educator, former government official, writer; b. Atlanta, Feb. 14, 1944; s. Edwin Witcher and Martha Frances (Williams) T. AB, Ind. U., Bloomington, 1968; postgrad., Stanford U., 1972-73; JD, U. Va., 1981. Bar: Va. 1982, U.S. Supreme Ct. 1986. Rsch. assoc., pub. affairs fellow Hoover Instn. on War, Revolution and Peace, Stanford U., 1971-74; spl. asst., legis. asst. U.S. Sen. Robert P. Griffin, 1974-79; assoc. dir. Ctr. for Nat. Security Law U. Va., Charlottesville, 1981, 87—; sr. fellow, 1985-86; spl. asst. undersec. for policy Dept. Def., 1981-82; counsel Pres.'s Intelligence Oversight Bd., White House, 1982-84; prin. dep. asst. sec. for legis. and intergovtl. affairs Dept. State, 1984-85; pres. U.S. Inst. Peace, Washington, 1986-87; lectr. in law and in govt. and fgn. affairs U. Va., Charlottesville, 1988-93, assoc. prof., 1993—; Charles H. Stockton prof. internat. law Naval War Coll., 1994-95. Author: Myths of the Vietnam War: The Pentagon Papers Reconsidered, 1972, Vietnamese Communism: Its Origins and Development, 1975, The War Powers Resolution: Its Implementation in Theory and Practice, 1983, Nicaragua v. United States: A Look at the Facts, 1987, Repealing the War Powers Resolution: Restoring the Rule of Law in U.S. Foreign Policy, 1991, (with John Norton Moore) The Legal Structure of Defense Organization, 1986, International Law and the Brezhnev Doctrine, 1987, Readings on International Law, 1995, (with John Norton Moore and Frederick Tipson) National Security Law, 1990, (with John Norton Moore and Guy B. Roberts) National Security Law Documents, 1995; contbr. articles to profl. jours. and newspapers. Pres. Endowment of U.S. Inst. Peace, 1986-87; trustee Intercollegiate Studies Inst., 1986-92. Capt. U.S. Army, 1968-71, Vietnam. Grantee Hoover Press, 1972, Earhart Found., 1980, 1989-90, Inst. Edtl. Affairs, 1980, Carthage Found., 1980. Mem. ABA (chmn. com. on exec.-congl. rels., sec. internat. law and practice 1983-86, adv. com. on law and nat. security 1984-86, standing com. on law and nat. security 1986-92, chmn. 1989-92, editor ABA Nat. Security Law Report 1992—), Bd. Rsch. Cons., Inst. Fgn. Policy Analysis, Mensa, Am. Soc. Internat. Law, Nat. Eagle Scout Assn., Coun. on Fgn. Rels. Home: RR 18 Box 59 Charlottesville VA 22911-9819 Office: Univ Va Sch of Law Ctr for Nat Security Law Charlottesville VA 22903-1789

TURNER, ROBERT GERALD, academic administrator; b. Atlanta, Tex., Nov. 25, 1945; s. Robert B. and Oreta Lois (Porter) T.; m. Gail Oliver, Dec. 21, 1968; children: Angela Jan, Jessica Diane. AA, Lubbock Christian Coll., 1966, LLD (hon.), 1985; LLD (hon.), Pepperdine U., 1989; BS, Abilene Christian U., 1968; MA, U. Tex., 1970, PhD, 1975. Tchr. Weatherford High Sch., Tex., 1968-69; tchr. Lanier High Sch., Austin, Tex., 1969-70; instr. psychology San Antonio Coll., 1970-72; instr. Prairie View A & M U., Tex., 1973-75; asst. prof. psychology Pepperdine U., Malibu, Calif., 1975-78, assoc. prof. psychology, 1978-79, dir. testing, 1975-76, chmn. social sci. div., 1976-78, assoc. v.p. univ. affairs, 1979; assoc. prof. psychology U. Okla., Norman, 1979-84, exec. asst. to pres., 1979-81, acting provost, 1982, v.p. exec. affairs, 1981-84; chancellor U. Miss., University, 1984-95; pres. So. Meth. U., Dallas, 1995—; Pres. Southeastern Conf., 1985-87; rsch. asst. Tex. Adoption Study, 1973-75; mem. Pepperdine U., 1994-95; mem. Commn. on Telecomm., Nat. Assn. State Univs. and Land-Grant Colls., 1985-86, chmn. Commn. on Edn. for Tchg. Profession, 1990-91; mem. Pres.'s Commn., NCAA, 1989-92, chmn., 1991-92; mem. Knight Commn. on Intercollegiate Athletics, 1991-95; chmn. pres. coun. Miss. Assn. Colls., 1985-86; mem. def. adv. com. Svc.

Acad. Athletic Programs, 1992—. Author: (with L. Willerman) Readings About Individual and Group Differences, 1979. Contbr. articles to profl. jours. Dir. area 2, Miss. Econ. Coun.; bd. dirs. First Miss. Corp., 1987; mem. Yocona Area coun. Boy Scouts Am. NIMH grantee, 1972; recipient Outstanding Alumni award Abilene Christian U., 1989, Communicator of Yr. award Toastmasters Club, 1987; named Miss. Amb., 1986; inducted New Boston High Sch. Athletic Hall of Fame, 1993. Mem. Young Pres. Orgn., Coun. on Competitiveness, Am. Inst. Pub. Svc. (bd. nominators 1989), Sigma Xi, Beta Alpha Psi, Phi Theta Kappa, Alpha Chi, Phi Kappa Phi. Mem. Ch. of Christ. Avocations: tennis; golf; reading; traveling. Office: So Meth Univ Office of the Pres Dallas TX 75275

TURNER, ROBERT HAL, telecommunications and computer executive; b. Kingsport, Tenn., July 12, 1948; s. Robert Harold Sr. and Mattie Louise (Gambrell) T.; m. Bonnie Carolotte Cromer, June 22, 1969; children: Robert H. III, Christopher Albert. BS in Mktg., U. S.C., 1972, MBA, 1973. Founder Bojangles Restaurants, Columbia, S.C., 1973-77; account exec. So. Bell Tel., Columbia, 1977-80, industry mgr., 1980-81; tng. mgr. AT&T, Denver, 1981-82; area sales support mgr. AT&T, N.Y.C., 1983-85; region mgr. South Cen. Bell Advanced Sys., New Orleans, 1985-87; v.p. Bell South Comm. Holdings, Inc., Atlanta, 1987; exec. v.p. Norlite Computer Sys., Kanata, Ont., Can., 1988; pres. Insightguide, N.Y.C., 1989-90; pres., CEO PTT Telecom Netherlands U.S., Inc., N.Y.C., 1991-93; CEO Telezone Corp., Toronto, Ont., Can., 1994—. Lutheran. Avocations: running, Alpine skiing, reading.

TURNER, ROBERT J. (JIM TURNER), lawyer; b. Oklahoma City, Apr. 9, 1934; s. Bob and Frances L. (Wasson) T.; m. Mary A. Sochor, July 5, 1958; children: Lisa A., Mark A. B.A., Okla. U., 1956, LL.B., 1960. Bar: Okla. 1960; U.S. Dist. Ct. (we. dist.) Okla., U.S. Ct. Appeals (10th cir.), U.S. Supreme Ct. Asst. mcpl. counselor City of Oklahoma City, 1961-62; asst. county atty. Oklahoma County, 1963-64; ptnr. Turner, Turner, Green & Braun, 1969—. Served to capt. U.S. Army, 1957. Mem. Okla. State Bar Assn. (pres. 1984, gov. 1980-82), Coll. Am. Trial Lawyers, Oklahoma County Bar (pres. 1978-79), Okla. Trial Lawyers, Assn. Trial Lawyers Am., Nat. Assn. Criminal Def. Lawyers. Democrat. Address: 4920 NW 36th St Oklahoma City OK 73122-2326

TURNER, ROBERT J., surgeon; b. Granada, Miss., Nov. 1, 1929; s. Robert Joseph and Edith Irene (Pearson) T.; m. Ellise Brown Weldon, Aug. 8, 1953; children: Ruth Stinsen, Laura Brown, Weldon, Stephanie, Jennifer, Kenneth. BS, La. State U., Baton Rouge, 1950; MD, La. State U., New Orleans, 1954. Diplomate Am. Bd. Surgery. Pvt. practice surgery Ft. Worth, Tex., 1964—; chief of surgery John Peter Smith Hosp., Ft. Worth, 1974-79; chief of staff St. Joseph Hosp., Ft. Worth, 1987-88; pres. R.J. White Lecture Found., Ft. Worth. Contbr. articles to profl. jours. Pres. Am. Cancer Soc., Ft. Worth, 1975; bd. dirs. Streams & Valleys, Ft. Worth, Ft. Worth Theater, 1989—. Maj. USAF, 1959-64. Decorated Air Force Commendation medal. Fellow ACS (pres. 1988-89); mem. Tex. Surg. Soc., Tex. Med. Assn., Ft. Worth Surg. Soc. (pres. 1979-80), Western Surg. Assn., River Crest Country Club, Ft. Worth Club. Episcopalian. Avocations: golf, travel, racquetball, art, writing, medical history. Home: 1905 Highland Park Cir Fort Worth TX 76107-3653 Office: 1350 S Main St Fort Worth TX 76104-7611

TURNER, ROBERT LLOYD, state legislator; b. Columbus, Miss., Sept. 14, 1947; s. Roosevelt and Beatrice (Hargrove) T.; m. Gloria Harrell; children: Roosevelt, Robert, Ryan. BS, U. Wis., Racine, 1976. Mgr. French Quarter Restaurant, Racine, 1989; legislator Wis. State Assembly, Madison, 1990—, chmn. transp. com. bldg. commn., mem. ways and means com., hwy. com., elections, correction & constitution com., excise fees and license com.; br. sales mgr. ETG Temporaries, Inc., Racine, 1989—; pub. Communicator News, Racine, 1989—; v.p. Racine Raider Football Team. State chmn. Dem. Black Polit. Caucus, Madison; pres. Bd. Health, Racine; chmn. Wis. State Elections Bd., Madison, 1990; alderman Racine City Coun., 1976—; chair Econ. Devel. Com., Racine; regional dir. Badger State Games, Racine; active Pvt. Industry Coun. Southeastern Wis., 1988-89, bd. dirs. Racine County Youth Sports Assn.; active Racine Juneteenth Day Com., bd. advisors Big Bros./Big Sisters. Sgt. USAF, 1967-71, Vietnam. Decorated Commendation medal; named Man of Yr. 2d Missionary Bapt. Ch., 1983. Mem. Urban League (pres. bd. dirs.), NAACP (2d v.p.), VFW, Am. Legion, Masons, Shriners. Home: 36 McKinley Ave Racine WI 53404-3414 Office: Wis Assembly PO Box 8953 Madison WI 53708-8953

TURNER, ROSS JAMES, investment corporation executive; b. Winnipeg, Man., Can., May 1, 1930; permanent U.S. resident, 1980; s. James Valentine and Gretta H. (Ross) T.; children: Ralph, Rick, Tracy. U. Man. Extension, 1951, Banff Sch. Advanced Mgmt., 1956. Various sr. operating and mgmt. positions Genstar Corp., San Francisco, 1961-76, chmn./pres., CEO, 1976-86, also bd. dirs.; chmn. Genstar Investment Corp., San Francisco, 1987—; bd. dirs. Rio Algom Ltd., Great-West Life & Annuity Ins. Co., Blue Shield of Calif., Guy F. Atkinson Co. of Calif. Fellow Soc. Mgmt. Accts. Can.; mem. Toronto Club, Pacific Union Club, Rancho Santa Fe Golf Club, Peninsula Golf and Country Club. Office: Genstar Investment Corp Metro Tower Ste 1170 950 Tower Ln Foster City CA 94404-2121

TURNER, SCOTT MACNEELY, lawyer; b. Clinton, N.Y., Nov. 8, 1948; s. Frederick George and Ruth Alys (Thomas) T.; m. Susan Lynn Funkhouser, June 20, 1970; children: Katherine, Benjamin, Robert. AB with honors, Colgate Univ., N.Y., 1970; JD magna cum laude, Washington & Lee, Va., 1973. Bar: N.Y. 1974, U.S. Dist. Ct. (we. dist.) N.Y. 1974, U.S. Ct. Appeals (2d cir.) N.Y. 1987, (3d cir.) N.Y. 1988. Assoc. Nixon Hargrave Devans & Doyle, Rochester, N.Y., 1973-80, ptnr., 1981—; chmn. environ. practice group Nixon Hargrove Devans & Doyle, 1984—; chmn. legis. regulatory affairs com. Internat. Gas Turbine Inst. Atlanta, 1993-95. Editor: (Book) N.Y. Environmental Law Handbook, 1993. Bd. dirs. Park Ridge Hosp., Rochester, N.Y., 1992—, Park Ridge Found., Rochester, 1987-92, Monroe County Cmty. Svcs. Bd., Rochester, 1992-95; town leader Ogden Rep. Party, Spencerport, N.Y., 1981-86. Capt. USAR, 1972-73. Mem. Air & Waste Mgmt. Assn. (chmn. legal com. 1984-88), N.Y. State Bar Assn. (environ. sect., co-chmn. solid and hazardous waste com. 1982-94). Republican. Congregationalist. Home: 408 Dewey St Churchville NY 14428-9103 Office: Nixon Hargrave Devans & Doyle Clinton Sq PO Box 1051 Rochester NY 14603-1051

TURNER, STANSFIELD, former government official, lecturer, writer, teacher; b. Chgo., Dec. 1, 1923; s. Oliver Stansfield and Wilhelmina Josephine (Wagner) T.; m. Eli Karin Gilbert, Mar. 16. 1985. Student, Amherst Coll., 1941-43, DCL, 1975; BS, U.S. Naval Acad., 1946; MA (Rhodes scholar), Oxford U., 1950; LHD, Sierra Nev. Coll., 1984; HumD, Roger Williams Coll., 1975; DSc in Edn, Bryant Coll., 1977; LLD, Salve Regina Coll., 1977, The Citadel, 1980, Pace U., 1980. Ensign USN, 1946, advanced through grades to adm., 1975, ret., 1979; served primarily in destroyers; comdr. U.S.S. Horne, guided missile cruiser, 1967-68; aide to Sec. Navy; comdr. carrier task group 6th Fleet, 1970-71; dir. systems analysis div. Office Chief Naval Ops., Navy Dept., Washington, 1971-72; pres. Naval War Coll., Newport, R.I., 1972-74; comdr. U.S. Second Fleet, 1974-75; comdr.-in-chief Allied Forces So. Europe, NATO, 1975-77; dir. CIA, Washington, 1977-81; John M. Olin Disting. prof. nat. security U.S. Mil. Acad., West Point, 1989-90; prof. U. Md. Grad. Sch. Pub. Affairs, 1991—; sr. rsch. fellow Norwegian Nobel Inst., Oslo, Norway, 1995-96. Author: Secrecy and Democracy, 1985, Terrorism and Democracy, 1991. Decorated Nat. Security medal, Legion of Merit, Bronze Star. Home and Office: 1320 Skipwith Rd Mc Lean VA 22101-1834

TURNER, SYLVESTER, state legislator, lawyer; b. Houston, Sept. 27, 1954; 1 child, Ashley Paige. BA in Polit. Sci., U. Houston; JD, Harvard U. Assoc. Fulbright & Jaworski, Houston, 1980-83; owner firm Barnes & Turner, Houston, 1983—; mem. Tex. Ho. of Reps., Austin, 1988—; mem. appropriations and calendars coms.; vice-chair state affairs. Candidate for mayor City of Houston, 1991; active Negro Coll. Fund, Houston Met. Ministries, Houston-Galveston Area Food Bank, Acres Homes War on Drugs Com., Brookhollow Bapt. Ch.. Named Rookie of Yr., Tex. Monthly, Legislator of Yr. and One of the Ten Best Legislators, Houston Police Patrolman's Union, Rising Star, Harris County Dems., Outstanding Houstonian, Houston Jaycees, 1990. Office: Texas House Reps PO Box 2910 Austin TX 78768-2910 also: PO Box 2910 Austin TX 78768-2910

TURNER, TED (ROBERT EDWARD TURNER), television executive; b. Cin., Nov. 19, 1938; s. Robert Edward and Florence (Rooney) T.; m. Judy Nye (div.), m. Jane Shirley Smith, June 1965 (div. 1988); children: Beau, Rhett, Jennie; children by previous marriage: Laura Lee, Robert Edward IV; m. Jane Fonda, Dec. 21, 1991. Grad. in classics, Brown U.; DSc in Commerce (hon.), Drexel U., 1982; LLD (hon.), Samford U., 1982, Atlanta U., 1984; D Entrepreneurial Sci. (hon.), Cen. New Eng. Coll. Tech., 1983; D in Pub. Adminstrn. (hon.), Mass. Maritime Acad., 1984; D in Bus. Adminstrn. (hon.), U. Charleston, 1985. Account exec. Turner Advt. Co., Atlanta, 1961-63, pres., chief oper. officer, 1963-70; pres., chmn. bd. Turner Broadcasting System, Inc., Atlanta, 1970—; bd. of dirs. Atlanta Hawks, Atlanta; owner Atlanta Braves, Atlanta. Chmn. bd. Better World Soc., Washington, 1985-90; bd. dirs. Martin Luther King Ctr., Atlanta. Won America's Cup in his yacht Courageous, 1977; named Yachtsman of Yr. 4 times.Recipient Outstanding Entrepreneur of Yr. award Sales Mktg. and Mgmt. Mag., 1979, Salesman of Yr. award Sales and Mktg. Execs., 1980, Pvt. Enterprise Exemplar medal, Freedoms Found. at Valley Forge, 1980, Communicator of Yr. award Pub. Rels. Soc. Am., 1981, Communicator of Yr. award N.Y. Broadcasters, 1981, Internat. Communicator of Yr. award Sales and Mktg. Execs., 1981, Nat. News Media award VFW, 1981, Disting. Svc. in Telecommunications award Ohio U. Coll. Communication, 1982, Carr Van Anda award Ohio U. Sch. Journalism, 1982, Spl. award Edinburgh Internat. TV Festival, Scotland, 1982, Media Awareness award United Vietnam Vets. Orgn., 1983, Bd. Govs. award Atlanta chpt. NATAS, 1982, Spl. Olympics award Spl. Olympics Com., 1983, Dinner of Champions award Ga. chpt., Multiple Sclerosis Soc., 1983, Praca Spl. Merit award N.Y. Puerto Rican Assn. for Community Affairs, 1983, World Telecommunications Pioneer award, N.Y. State Broadcasters Assn., 1984, Golden Plate award Am. Acad. Achievement, 1984, Outstanding Supporter Boy Scouting award Nat. Boy Scout Coun., 1984, Silver Satellite award Am. Women in Radio and TV, Lifetime Achievement award N.Y. Internat. Film and TV Festival, 1984, Corp. Star of Yr. award Nat. Leukemia Soc., 1985, Disting. Achievement award U. Georgia, 1985, Tree of Life award Jewish Nat. Fund, 1985, Bus. Exec. of Yr. award Ga. Security Dealers Assn., 1985, Life Achievement award Popular Culture Assn., 1986, George Washingtonn Disting. Patriot award S.R., 1986, Mo. Honor medal Sch. Journalism, U. Mo., 1987, Golden Ace award Nat. Cable TV Acad., 1987 Sol Taishoff award Nat. Press Found., 1988, Citizen Diplomat award Ctr. for Soviet-Am. Dialogue, 1988, Chmn.'s award Cable Advt. Bur., 1988, Directorate award NATAS, 1989, Paul White award Radio and TV News Dirs. Assn., 1989 Bus. Marketer of Yr. Am. Mktg. Assn., 1989, Disting. Svc. award Simon Wiesenthal Ctr., 1990, Glasnost award Vols. Am. and Soviet Life mag., 1990, numerous others; inducted into Hall of Fame, Promotion and Mktg. Assn., 1980, Dubuque (Iowa) Bus. Hall of Fame, 1983, Nat. Assn. for Sport and Phys. Edn. Hall of Fame, 1986. Mem. Nat. Cable TV Assn. (Pres.'s award 1979, 89, Ace Spl. Recognition award 1980), NAACP (life, bd. dirs. Atlanta chpt., Regional Employer of Yr. award 1976), Nat. Audubon Soc., Cousteau Soc., Bay Area Cable Club (hon.). Avocations: sailing, fishing. Office: Turner Broadcasting 1 CNN Ctr PO Box 105366 Atlanta GA 30348-5366

TURNER, TERRY MADISON, architect; b. Bastrop, La., Apr. 5, 1938; s. Eugene Campbell and Anna Pauline (Terry) T.; m. Mary Alice Fischer, June 20, 1964; children: Mat Madison, Paul Alison, William Terry. BBA, Memphis State U., 1958; BS in Archtl. Scis., Washington U., St. Louis, 1961, BArch, 1963. Registered architect, Mo., N.C.A.R.B. Asst. prof. Sch. Architecture Auburn (Ala.) U., 1965-66, U. Va., Charlottesville, 1966-69; chief architect HUD-FHA, St. Louis, 1969-79; prin. Terry M. Turner, Architect, Clayton, Mo., 1979—; CEO Westminster Apts., Inc., St. Louis, 1993—. Regent Harris-Stowe State Coll., St. Louis, 1992—. 1st lt. USAR, 1963-70. Republican. Episcopalian. Avocation: reading. Home and Office: 50 Hillvale Dr Clayton MO 63105

TURNER, THOMAS MARSHALL, telecommunications executive, consultant; b. Cumberland, Md., Aug. 17, 1951; s. James Richard and Laura Roselie (Durst) T. BS in Indsl. Tech. and Mgmt., U. Md., 1973, MA in Indsl. Tech. and Mgmt., 1980. Grad. asst U. Md., College Park, 1975-76; sales assoc., gen. mgr. Equity Trades Reality, Riverdale, Md., 1976-83; account exec. RCA Corp., Greenbelt, Md., 1983; sr. telecommunications cons. CMC, Inc., Washington, 1984-86, ORS Assoc., McLean, Va., 1986-87; owner, pres. T-1 Communications, Boca Raton, Fla., 1987—; cons. Marriott Corp., Bethesda, Md., 1990—, Group Health, Inc., N.Y.C., 1991-92, Colgate-Palmolive Co., 1993-94, State of Md., 1993, Trump Corp., 1993, Martin-Marietta, 1994, Matsushita, 1994, Montgomery Wards, 1994, Nabisco Foods, 1994, Harris Corp., 1995, Urban League, 1995, EDS, 1995—, Chem. Bank, 1996—; grad. asst. instr. Dale Carnegie Inst., 1992. Contbr. articles to profl. jours. Vol. ARC, Riverdale, Md., 1977-80; instr. Jr. Achievement Bus. Co-op, Rockville, Md., 1979-82. Recipient Highest Achievment award Dale Carnegie Inst., 1989. Mem. Am. Soc. Tng. and Devel., Telecommunications Mgrs. Assn. of Capital Area, Toastmasters, Sigma Alpha Epsilon Alumni Assn.

TURNER, THOMAS PATRICK, architect; b. Gaffney, S.C., May 13, 1926; s. Thomas Patrick and Lily Mae (Clarke) T.; m. Lola Ann Love, Aug. 17, 1950; children: Sheryl A., Thomas P. III, A. Bryan. BS in Archtl. Engring., Clemson U., 1951, postgrad., 1952. Registered architect; lic. real estate broker; lic. contractor. Draftsman John H. Truluck, Walterboro, S.C., 1951-52, M.R. Marsh, Charlotte, N.C., 1953-55; architect in tng. Holroyd, Folk and Gray, Charlotte, 1955-57; architect A.G. Odell & Assocs., Charlotte, 1957-77; pres., owner ADEP Architects, Charlotte, 1977—. Precinct chmn. Dem. Party, 1993-94; elder Myers Park Presbyn. Ch. With U.S. Navy, 1943-45. Fellow AIA (nat. bd. dirs. 1987—, v.p. 1990, pres. Charlotte sect. 1966), N.C. Inst. Architects (bd. dirs. 1970, 71, 76, 77, v.p. 1972-73, pres. 1985), Rotary. Office: ADEP Architects 401 S Independence Blvd Ste 72 Charlotte NC 28204-2623

TURNER, THOMAS WILLIAM, lawyer; b. Indpls., Nov. 17, 1946; s. Tal Andy and Mary Etta (Eddleman) T.; m. Judith Ann Stewart, Mar. 14, 1970; children: Laura Marie, Brian Christopher. AB, Ball State U., 1969; JD cum laude, Wayne State U., 1974. Bar: Mich. 1974, Ind. 1975, Fla. 1985. Trial atty. criminal div. fraud sect. U.S. Dept. Justice, Washington, 1974-78; 1st asst. atty. U.S. Dept. Justice, Springfield, 1978-81; asst. atty. U.S. Dept. Justice, Indpls., 1981-83; managing asst. atty. U.S. Dept. Justice, Orlando, Fla., 1983-86; sole practice Orlando, 1986-91, pvt. practice, 1991—; asst. U.S. atty. U. S. Dept. Justice, Orlando. Mem. Orange County bar Assn., Am. Inns of Ct., Delta Theta Phi. Republican. Methodist. Home: 4800 S Saint Brides Cir Orlando FL 32812-5980 Office: 201 Federal Bldg 80 N Hughey Ave Orlando FL 32801-2231

TURNER, TINA (ANNA MAE BULLOCK), singer; b. Brownsville, Tenn., Nov. 26, 1939; m. Ike Turner, 1956 (div. 1978); children: Craig, Ike Jr., Michael, Ronald. Singer with Ike Turner Kings of Rhythm, and Ike and Tina Turner Revue; appeared in films: Gimme Shelter, 1970, Soul to Soul, 1971, Tommy, 1975, Mad Max Beyond Thunderdome, 1985, Break Every Rule, 1986; concert tours of Europe, 1966, Japan and Africa, 1971; albums with Ike Turner include Hunter, 1970, Ike and Tina Show II, Ike and Tina Show, 1966, Ike and Tina Turner, Bad Dreams, 1973, Ike and Tina Turner Greatest Hits, vol. 1,2 and 3, 1989, Greatest Hits, 1990, Proud Mary, 1991, The Ike and Tina Turner Collection, 1993; solo albums include Let Me Touch Your Mind, 1972, Tina Turns the Country On, 1974, Acid Queen, 1975, Love Explosion, 1977, Rough, 1978, Airwaves, 1979, Private Dancer, 1984, Break Every Rule, 1986, Tina Live In Europe, 1988, Foreign Affair, 1989, Simply the Best, 1991, What's Love Got to Do With It? (soundtrack), 1993, The Collected Recordings: Sixties to Nine Ties, with others, 1994; performed with USA for Africa on song We are The World, 1985; author (autobiography) I, Tina, 1985 (filmed as What's Love Got To Do With It?, 1993). Recipient Grammy award, 1972, 85 (three), 86, Grammy nomination (Best Pop Female Vocal) for "I Don't Wanna Fight", 1994; inducted into Rock and Roll Hall of Fame, 1991. Address: care CAA 9830 Wilshire Blvd Beverly Hills CA 90212-1804

TURNER, WADE SLOVER, biochemist, pilot; b. Terre Haute, Ind., Dec. 21, 1965; s. Howard Royce and Euleta (Slover) T. BS, Ind. State U., 1987, MS, 1990. Registered environ. profl., Ind.; cert. PADI advanced and night scuba diver. Lab. mgr., biochemist Foxfire Environ., Inc., Jasonville, Ind., 1990-92; gen. mgr. Turner Farms, Inc., Shelburn, Ind., 1992-94; biochemist, flight instr. NASA-Marshall & U.S. Space Ctrs., Huntsville, Ala., 1993-95; pilot Am. Trans Air, Inc., Terre Haute, 1992-94; spl. ops. analyst, USNR, Wright Patterson AFB, 1995—; instr. NRA, Shelburn, 1994—; chemistry instr. Ind. State U., 1989, 90; physics instr. Indiana State U., 1995—. Contbr. articles to profl. publs. including Protein Kinase C Signal Transduction in Microgravity. Lt. (j.g.) USNR. Collegiate scholar Ind. State U., 1985, 86, 92, 93, Nat. Deans List scholar, 1984-88. Fellow Phi Kappa Phi; mem. Am. Assn. Airport Execs., Am. Legion, Ruritan Club, Sigma Xi, Alpha Eta Rho. Achievements include Protein Kinase C research in Nb2 lymphocytes; presentations to EPA on multi-million dollar environmental projects; laboratory work for Space Station Freedom project at NASA, special operations in USNR. Avocations: shooting, flying, jogging, golf, tennis. Home: 1502 E Mill St Shelburn IN 47879 Office: Office of Naval Intelligence Area A Bldg 856 Wright Patterson AFB OH 45433-5619

TURNER, WALLACE L., reporter; b. Titusville, Fla., Mar. 15, 1921; s. Clyde H. and Ina B. (Wallace) T.; m. Pearl Burk, June 12, 1943; children: Kathleen Turner, Elizabeth Turner Everett. B.J., U. Mo., 1943; postgrad. (Nieman fellow), Harvard U., 1958-59. Reporter Springfield (Mo.) Daily News, 1943, Portland Oregonian, 1943-59; news dir. Sta. KPTV, Portland, 1959-61; asst. sec. HEW, Washington, 1961-62; reporter N.Y. Times, San Francisco, 1962—; bur. chief N.Y. Times, 1970-85, Seattle bur. chief, 1985-88. Author: Gamblers Money, 1965, The Morman Establishment, 1967. Recipient Heywood Broun award for reporting, 1952, 56; Pulitzer Prize for reporting, 1957. Office: Box 99269 Magnolia Sta Seattle WA 98199-4260

TURNER, WARREN AUSTIN, state legislator; b. Berkeley, Calif., Dec. 21, 1926; s. Warren Mortimer and Rebecca Oline (Noer) T.; m. Beverly Daune Mackay, Mar. 29, 1952; children: Daune Scott, Warren Adair, Alan Corey. BA, U. Calif., Berkeley, 1950, BS, 1952, MPH, 1958. Pub. acct. Price Waterhouse, San Francisco, 1951-52, AW Blackman, Las Vegas, Nev., 1952-56; asst. adminstr. Marin Gen. Hosp., San Rafael, Calif., 1958-60; assoc. dir. UCLA Hosp., 1960-68; founding adminstr. Walter O. Boswell Meml. Hosp., Sun City, Ariz., 1968-81; pres. Sun Health Corp., 1981-89; mem. Ariz. Senate, Phoenix, 1993—, chmn. rules com., vice chair health com., mem. appropriations, family svcs. and transp. com., 1995—; chmn. appropriation subcom. K-12, C.C.'s and natural resources. With USN, 1944-46. Mem Ariz. Acad., Rotary Internat. Republican. Avocations: breeding and showing Siamese cats, fishing, mining. Home: 18432 W Glendale Ave Waddell AZ 85355-9737 Office: Ariz State Senate Capital Complex Phoenix AZ 85007

TURNER, WILLIAM BENJAMIN, electrical engineer; b. Bklyn., Sept. 23, 1929; s. Jacob Joshua and Mollie (Klein) T. BEE, CCNY, 1955; MBA, NYU, 1964; DD (hon.), UCLA, 1978. Cert. tchr., N.Y. Chief engr. Esan Electronic Labs., Fla. and N.Y., 1969—; cons. in field, 1965—. Author: Theology-The Quintessence of Science, 1981, Nothing and Non-Existence, 1986, Hyper Light Speed Technology, 1992, Outer Space Communications, 1994, Eulogy for Our Dying World, 1994, Advanced Concepts and Limitations in Science, 1994. Sgt. U.S. Army, 1951-53, Korea. Decorated Bronze Star. Mem. Mensa, Boynton Beach C. of C. Achievements include invention of the world's fastest computers, advanced concepts in time theory, development of multi-dimensional geometry theory of the universe, development new physics method that exceeds speed of light, research into hyper light speed communications equipment to probe far off regions of outer space, research into the physics of the human thinking process. Home and Office: 429 Seaview Ave Palm Beach FL 33480-4109

TURNER, WILLIAM COCHRANE, international management consultant; b. Red Oak, Iowa, May 27, 1929; s. James Lyman and Josephine (Cochrane) T.; m. Cynthia Dunbar, July 16, 1955; children: Scott Christopher, Craig Dunbar, Douglas Gordon. BS, Northwestern U., 1952, LLD (hon.), Am. Grad. Sch. Internat. Mgmt., 1993. Pres., chmn. bd. dirs. Western Mgmt. Cons., Inc., Phoenix, 1955-74, Western Mgmt. Cons. Europe, S.A., Brussels, 1968-74; U.S. amb., permanent rep. OECD, Paris, 1974-77, vice chmn. exec. com., 1976-77, U.S. rep. Energy Policy Com., 1976-77, mem. U.S. dels. internat. meetings, 1974-77; mem. western internat. trade group U.S. Dept. Commerce, 1972-74; chmn., CEO Argyle Atlantic Corp., Phoenix, 1977—; chmn. European adv. coun., 1981-88, Asia Pacific adv. coun. AT&T Internat., 1981-88; founding mem. Pacific Coun. Internat. Policy, L.A., 1995—; mem. U.S.-Japan Bus. Coun., Washington, 1987-93, European adv. coun. IBM World Trade Europe/Mid. East/Africa Corp., 1977-80; mem. Asia Pacific adv. coun. Am. Can Co., Greenwich, Conn., 1981-85, GE of Brazil adv. coun. GE Co., Coral Gables, Fla., 1979-81, Caterpillar of Brazil adv. coun. Caterpillar Tractor Co., Peoria, Ill., 1979-84, Caterpillar Asia Pacific Adv. Coun., 1984-90, U.S. adv. com. Trade Negotiations, 1982-84; bd. dirs. Goodyear Tire & Rubber Co., Akron, Ohio, Rural/Metro Corp., Microtest, Inc., Phoenix; chmn. bd. dirs. GO Wireless Internat. Ltd., Melbourne, Fla., 1995—; chmn. internat. adv. coun. Avon Products, Inc., N.Y.C., 1985—; mem. Spencer Stuart adv. coun. Spencer Stuart and Assocs., N.Y.C., 1984-90; chmn., mem. internat. adv. coun. Advanced Semiconductor Materials Internat. NV., Bilthoven, The Netherlands, 1985-88; bd. dirs. The Atlantic Coun. of U.S., Washington, 1977-92; co-chmn. internat. adv. bd. Univ. of Nations, Kona, Hawaii, 1985—; bd. dirs. World Wildlife Fund/U.S., 1983-85, World Wildlife Fund/The Conservation Found., 1985-89, Nat. Coun., 1989-95; bd. govs. Joseph H. Lauder Inst. Mgmt. and Internat. Studies, U. Pa., 1983—; trustee Heard Mus., Phoenix, 1983-86, mem. nat. adv. bd., 1986-93; trustee Am. Grad. Sch. Internat. Mgmt., 1972—, chmn. bd. trustees, 1987-89; bd. govs. Atlantic Inst. Internat. Affairs, Paris, 1977-88; adv. bd. Ctr. Strategic and Internat. Studies, Georgetown U., 1977-81; dir. Atlantic Inst. Found., Inc., N.Y.C., 1984-90; mem. European Cmty.-U.S. Businessmen's Coun., 1978-79; bd. govs. Am. Hosp. of Paris, 1974-77; trustee Nat. Symphony Orch. Assn., Washington, 1973-83, Am. Sch., Paris, 1976-77, Orme Sch., Mayer, Ariz., 1970-74, Phoenix Country Day Sch., 1971-74; mem. nat. coun. Salk Inst., 1978-82; mem. U.S. Adv. Com. Internat. Edn. and Cultural Affairs, 1969-74; nat. rev. bd. Ctr. Cultural and Tech. Interchange between East and West, 1970-74; mem. vestry Am. Cathedral, Paris, 1976-77; pres., bd. dirs. Phoenix Symphony Assn., 1969-70; chmn. Ariz. Joint Econ. Devel. Com., 1967-68; exec. com., bd. dirs. Ariz. Dept. Econ. Planning and Devel., 1968-70; chmn. bd. Ariz. Crippled Children's Services, 1964-65; treas. Ariz. Rep. Com., 1956-57; chmn. Ariz. Young Rep. League, 1955-56; chmn. bd. Mercy Ships Internat., Inc., A Ministry of Youth With A Mission, Lindale, Tex., 1985—; mem. trade and environment com. Nat. Adv. Coun. for Environ. Policy and Tech.-U.S. EPA, Washington, 1991-95; dir. exec. com., chmn. internat. com. Ariz. Econ. Coun., Phoenix, 1989-93; dir. exec. com. Orgn. for Free Trade and Devel., Phoenix, 1991-93; chmn. Internat. Adv. Coun. Plasma Tech., Inc., Sante Fe, 1992—. Recipient East-West Ctr. Disting. Svc. award, 1977. Mem. U.S. Coun. Internat. Bus. (trustee, exec. com.), Coun. Fgn. Rels., Coun. of Am. Ambs. (vice chmn. bd.), Nat. Adv. Coun. on Bus. Edn., Coun. Internat. Edn. Exchange, Greater Phoenix Leadership, Govs. Strategic Partnership Econ. Devel., Phoenix, 1992-95, Met. Club, Links Club (N.Y.C.), Plaza Club (Phoenix), Paradise Valley (Ariz.) Country Club. Episcopalian. Office: 4350 E Camelback Rd Ste 240B Phoenix AZ 85018-2722

TURNER, WILLIAM WEYAND, author; b. Buffalo, N.Y., Apr. 14, 1927; s. William Peter and Magdalen (Weyand) T.; m. Margaret Peiffer, Sept. 12, 1964; children: Mark Peter, Lori Ann. BS, Canisius Coll., 1949. Spl. agt. in various field offices FBI, 1951-61; free-lance writer Calif., 1963—; sr. editor Ramparts Mag., San Francisco, 1967—; investigator and cons. Nat. Wiretap Commn., 1975; U.S. del. J.F.K. Internat. Seminar, Rio de Janeiro, 1995. Author: The Police Establishment, 1968, Invisible Witness: The Use and Abuse of the New Technology of Crime Investigation, 1968, Hoover's F.B.I.: The Men and the Myth, 1970, Power on the Right, 1971, (with Warren Hinckle and Eliot Asinof) The Ten Second Jailbreak, 1973, (with John Christian) The Assassination of Robert F. Kennedy, 1978, (with Warren Hinckle) The Fish is Red: The Story of the Secret War Against Castro, 1981, updated, expanded, retitled as Deadly Secrets: The CIA-Mafia War Against Castro and the Assassination of JFK, 1992; contbg. author: Investigating the FBI, 1973; contbr. articles to popular mags. Dem. candidate for U.S. Congress, 1968. Served with USN, 1945-46. Mem. Authors Guild, Internat. Platform Assn., Press Club of San Francisco. Roman Catholic. Avocation: tennis. Home and Office: 163 Mark Twain Ave San Rafael CA 94903-2820

TURNER, WILLIAM WILSON, hospital administrator; b. Valley Mills, Tex., Apr. 21, 1916; s. Will S. and Nettie A. (Vickrey) T.; m. Wilma David, Feb. 22, 1945; 1 child, Elizabeth Ann. B.B.A., Baylor U., 1938; postgrad., Grad. Sch. Bus., Northwestern U., 1939. Bus. mgr. Hillcrest Meml. Hosp., Waco, Tex., 1941-47; asst. adminstr. Meml. Bapt. Hosp. (name changed to Meml. Hosp. System), Houston, 1947-50; adminstr. Meml. Bapt. Hosp. (name changed to Meml. Hosp. System), 1955-63, exec. dir. hosp. system, 1963-71, pres. system, 1971-81, pres. emeritus, cons., 1981—; adminstr. Bapt. Hosp., Alexandria, La., 1950-54, Miss. Bapt. Hosp., Jackson, 1954-55; hon. life dir. Blue Cross-Blue Shield Tex., Group Life and Health Ins. Co.; mem. Council on Manpower and Edn., 1974-77. Served to lt. USNR, 1942-45, PTO, ATO. Recipient Collier award for distinguished hosp. adminstrn., 1974, Tex. Assn. Hosp. Governing Bds. Founders award, 1980, Meml. Stewardship award, 1992. Fellow Am. Coll. Hosp. Adminstrs.; mem. Am. Prostestant Hosp. Assn. (del. 1970—, council ch.-hosp. relations 1962-66, council on edn. 1972-75, Hosp. Adminstrn. award 1979), Am. Hosp. Assn. (del. 1969-75), Tex. Hosp. Assn. (trustee 1961-68, treas. 1969, pres. 1971-72), Bapt. Hosp. Assn. (past pres., trustee), Houston Area Hosp. Assn. (past pres.), Mental Health Assn. Houston (profl. adv. com.), Tex. Assn. Hosp. Accountants (past pres., disting. life mem.), Houston Area Hosp. Council (past pres.), Houston C. of C., Tex. League Nursing (dir. 1961-63), Delta Sigma Pi. Baptist (deacon). Lodge: Masons. Developer satellite hosp. concept. Home: 7480 Beechnut St Apt 303 Houston TX 77074-4507 Office: 7737 Southwest Fwy Ste 595 Houston TX 77074-1800

TURNHEIM, PALMER, banker; b. S.I., N.Y., June 30, 1921; s. Gustav and Helga (Hansen) T.; m. Gloria Freer, June 1948 (dec.); 1 child, Joy Karen. BS magna cum laude, NYU, 1960; Am. Inst. Banking, 1947; grad., Stonier Grad. Sch. Banking, Rutgers U., 1958, Advanced Mgmt. Program, Harvard, 1962. Asst. mgr. credit dept. Chase Nat. Bank, 1951-55, asst. treas., 1955; asst. v.p. Chase Manhattan Bank, N.Y.C., 1956-61; v.p. Chase Manhattan Bank, 1961-71, sr. v.p., 1971-86; sr. v.p. Chase Manhattan Capital Markets Corp.; exec. v.p. 1st Fidelity Bank, Newark, 1990-95, First Union Bank, Newark, 1996—; instr. mgmt. decision lab. Stern Grad. Sch. Bus. NYU, 1986—; pres. Chasex Asso cs., Inc. Author: International Finance Corporation, 1958. Nat. pres. United Cerebral Palsy Assns., Inc., 1967-70; dir. United Cerebral Palsy Research and Ednl. Found.; Mem. U.S. govt. com. on cash mgmt. Gen. Services Adminstrn., Washington, Am. Bankers Assn. task force advising Dept. Energy on gasoline rationing, 1979-81; Bd. dirs. Fund for Theol. Edn., 1957-84, N.Y. Inst. Credit, 1971-84. Served with USAAF, 1942-46. Mem. N.Y. State Bankers Assn. (dir. 1972-75), N.Y.U. Stern Sch. Bus. Alumni Assn. (pres. 1982-83), N.Y.U. Alumni Fedn. (v.p., dir., mem. alumni coun.), Am. Legion, Beta Gamma Sigma, Phi Alpha Kappa. Lutheran. Clubs: Harvard Bus. Sch., Union League, NYU Fin. (pres., dir. 1982-83). Home: 23 Oak Ln Mountain Lakes NJ 07046-1311

TURNLEY, DAVID CARL, photojournalist; b. Fort Wayne, Ind., June 22, 1955; s. William Loyd and Elizabeth Ann (Protsman) T.; m. Karin Nicolette, Apr. 15, 1989. BA in French, U. Mich., 1977; student, Sorbonne, Paris, 1975; DMus (hon.), Keele (Eng.) U., 1991. Staff photogapher Sliger Home Newspapers, Northville, Mich., 1978-80, Detroit Free Press, 1980—; European based photographic corr. Detroit Free Press/Black Star Paris, 1988—. Author: Why Are They Weeping? South Africans under Aparthied, 1988, Beijing Spring, 1989, Moments of Revolution: Eastern Europe, 1990; artist London Decca Records. Recipient Canon essay award for S. African coverage, 1985, World Press Picture of Yr. award for Earthquake in Armenia, 1988, Robert Capa Gold medal for China, Romania coverage, 1990, Pulitzer prize for China, E. Europe coverage, 1990. Office: Detroit Free Press 321 W Lafayette Blvd Detroit MI 48226-2705*

TURNLUND, JUDITH RAE, nutrition scientist; b. St. Paul, Sept. 28, 1936; d. Victor Emanuel and Vida Mae (Priddy) Hanson; m. Richard Wayne Turnlund, Nov. 9, 1957; children: Michael Wayne, Mark Richard, Todd Hanson. BS in Chemistry and Psychology, Gustavus Adolphus Coll., 1958; PhD in Nutrition, U. Calif., Berkeley, 1978. Registered dietitian. Postdoctoral fellow U. Calif., Berkeley, 1978-80, lectr., 1984-92, adj. assoc. prof., 1989—; rsch. nutrition scientist Western Regional Rsch. Ctr./Western Human Nutrition Ctr., USDA, San Francisco and Albany, Calif., 1980—, rsch. leader, 1993—; vis. asst. prof. Am. U. Beirut, Lebanon, 1979, 80. Editor: Stable Isotopes in Nutrition, 1984; contbr. articles to profl. jours. Recipient Cert. of Merit, USDA/ARS, 1984, 1993, Disting. Alumni citation Gustavus Adolphus Coll., 1988, Am. Inst. Nutrition's Lederle award in Human Nutrition, 1996; USDA grantee, 1982-90, Nat. Dairy Coun. grantee, 1986. Mem. Am. Inst. Nutrition (Lederle award in human nutrition 1996), Am. Soc. Clin. Nutrition, Am. Dietetic Assn. Home: 2276 Great Hwy San Francisco CA 94116-1555 Office: USDA/ARS PO Box 29997 San Francisco CA 94129-0997

TURNOFF, WILLIAM CHARLES, judge; b. Phila., Nov. 19, 1948; s. David and Frieda (Kleiman) T.; m. Joy Rahinsky, Aug., 1971; children: Wendy, Dana. A.B. cum laude, Franklin and Marshall Coll., 1970; J.D., Cornell U., 1973. Bar: Pa. 1973, Fla. 1977, U.S. Dist. Ct. (ea. dist.) Pa. 1973, U.S. Dist. Ct. (so. dist.) Fla. 1980; U.S. Ct. Appeals (5th cir.) 1980, U.S. Ct. Appeals (11th cir.) 1981. Asst. dist. atty., Phila., 1973-80; asst. U.S. atty. office of U.S. Atty., Miami, Fla., 1980-86, chief maj. crimes sect., 1982-86; apptd. magistrate judge U.S. Dist. Ct. (so. dist.) Fla., 1986—, chief magistrate judge, 1994—. Chmn. Fla. Bar Grievance Com., 1985-86. Recipient Judicial Distinction award Miami chpt. Fla. Assn. Criminal Defense Lawyers, 1992. Mem. B'nai B'rith (pres. bench-bar unit 1991-92), Phi Beta Kappa.

TURNOVSKY, STEPHEN JOHN, economics educator; b. Wellington, New Zealand, Apr. 5, 1941; came to U.S., 1981; s. Frederick and Liselotte Felicitas (Wodak) T.; m. Michelle Henriette Louise Roos, Jan. 21, 1967; children: Geoffrey George, Jacqueline Liselotte. BA, Victoria U., Wellington, 1962, MA with honors, 1963; PhD, Harvard U., 1968. Asst. prof. econs. U. Pa., Phila., 1968-71; assoc. prof. U. Toronto, Ont., Can., 1971-72; prof. Australian Nat. U., Canberra, 1972-82; IBE disting. prof. econs. U. Ill., Champaign, 1982-87; prof. econs. U. Wash., Seattle, 1987—, chmn. dept., 1990-95; Castor prof., 1993—; rsch. assoc. Nat. Bur. Econ. Rsch., Cambridge, Mass., 1983-93. Author: Macroeconomic Analysis and Statistical Policy, 1977, International Macroeconomic Stabilization Policy, 1990, Methods of Macroeconomic Dynamics, 1995; mem. editl. bd. several jours.; contbr. numerous articles to profl. jours. Fellow Econometric Soc., Acad. Social Scis. in Australia; mem. Soc. Econ. Dynamics and Control (pres. 1982-84, editor Jour. Econ. Dynamics and Control 1981-87, 95—). Avocations: skiing, hiking, music. Home: 6053 NE Kelden Pl Seattle WA 98105-2045 Office: U Wash Coll Arts and Scis Dept Econs 301 Savery Hall Seattle WA 98195

TURNQUIST, PAUL KENNETH, agricultural engineer, educator; b. Lindsborg, Kans., Jan. 3, 1935; s. Leonard Otto and Myrtle Edith (Ryding) T.; m. Peggy Ann James, Dec. 22, 1962; children: Todd, Scott, Greg. BS Agrl. Engring., Kans. State U., 1957; MS in agrl. engring., Okla. State U., 1961, PhD agrl. engring., 1965. Registered profl. engr., Okla. Rsch. engr. Caterpillar Tractor Co., Peoria, Ill., 1957; instr., asst. prof. Okla. State U., Stillwater, 1958-62; assoc. prof., prof. S.D. State U., Brookings, 1964-76; prof., dept. head Auburn (Ala.) U., 1977—; mem. ABET Engring. Accreditation Commn., 1992—. Co-author: Tractors & Their Power Units, 1989; contbr. articles to profl. jours. Fellow Am. Soc. Agrl. Engrs. (life, trustee found. 1990-93, bd. dirs. edn. com. 1992-94); mem. NSPE, Am. Soc. for Engring. Edn., Coun. Forest Engrs., Sigma Xi. Methodist. Home: 1216 Nixon Dr Auburn AL 36830-6302

TURO, JOANN K., psychoanalyst, psychotherapist, consultant; b. Westerly, R.I., Feb. 13, 1938; d. Angelo and Anna Josephine (Drew) T. BS in Biology and Chemistry, U. R.I., 1959; MA in Human Rels. and Psychology, Ohio U., 1964; postgrad., NYU, 1966-71, N.Y. Freudian Inst., N.Y.C., 1977-85, Mental Health Inst., N.Y.C., 1977-80. Rsch. asst. biochemistry studies on schizophrenia Harvard U. Med. Sch., Boston, 1959-60; indsl. psychology asst. studies on managerial success N.Y. Telephone Co., N.Y.C., 1964-66; staff psychologist Testing and Advisement Ctr. NYU, 1966-70; psychology intern Kings County Hosp., Bklyn., 1970-71; staff psychologist M.D.C. Psychol. Svcs., N.Y.C., 1971-72; clin. dir. Greenwich House Substance Abuse Clinic, N.Y.C., 1973-76; cons. psychotherapist Mental Health Consultation Ctr., N.Y.C., 1977-82; pvt. practice psychoanlysis and psychotherapy N.Y.C., 1981—; mental health cons. Bklyn. Ctr. for Psychotherapy, 1976-78; with Psychoanaltyic Consultation Svcs., 1994—; presenter in field. Mem. Itnernat. Psychoanalytic Assn. (cert., presenter fall meeting 1995), Soc. for Personality Assessment (cert.), N.Y. Freudian Soc. (cert., co-chmn. grad. com. 1985-86, mem. continuing edn. com. 1986—, pub. rels. com. 1992-93, psychoanalytic consult svc. 1994—, tng. and supr. psychoanalyst 1995), N.Y. Coun. Psychoanalytic Psychotherapists (cert.), Met. Assn. for Coll. Mental Health Practitoners (cert.). Office: 175 W 12th St Apt 9H New York NY 10011-8221

TURO, RON, lawyer; b. Fort Wayne, Ind., Apr. 2, 1955; s. John B. and Joan L. (Gluntz) T.; m. Claire Teresa Fetterman T., May 24, 1980; children: Andrew Jacob, Patricia Erin. BA in History with honors, Pa. State U., 1978; JD, Dickinson Sch. Law, 1981. Bar: Pa. 1981, U.S. Dist. (mid. dist.) Pa. 1982, U.S. Supreme Ct. 1987, U.S. Ct. Appeals (3d cir.) 1989. Ast. pub. defender Cumberland County, Carlisle, Pa., 1981-84; ptnr. Griffie & Turo, Carlisle, 1984-89; pvt. practice Carlisle, 1989—. Founder West Shore Police Recognition Dinner, Camp Hill, Pa., 1985—; bd. dirs. Carlisle Econ. Devel. Com., Carlisle, 1988-91; parliamentarian Cumberland County Rep. Party, Carlisle, 1988-89; mem. Nat. Cath. Com. on Scouting, 1988-92; chmn. Region III, Pa., N.J., 1993-95, parliamentarian and legal coun., 1991—; mem. Big Bros./Big Sisters Carlisle select com., 1993—; bd. dirs. AHEDD, Inc., 1993-94, vice chmn. 1994-95, chmn., 1995—. Recipient St. George Emblem Boy Scouts Am., Harrisburg, Pa., 1983, Golden AAD Emblem, 1989. Mem. Nat. Assn. Criminal Def. Lawyers, Pa. Bar Assn., Pa. Assn. Criminal Def. Lawyers, Cumberland County Bar Assn. (social chmn. 1985—), Dickinson Sch. Law Alumni Orgn. (bd. dirs. 1987—), Trinity H.S. Alumni Orgn. (pres. 1988-90), Mensa (local sec. 1990-92, editor 1992-95), KC (pres. Capital area chpt. 1989, Knight of Yr. 1981, Grand Knight 1985-87, 93-95). Republican. Roman Catholic. Avocations: politics, scouting, scuba diving, travel. Home: 539 Baltimore Pike Mount Holly Springs PA 17065 Office: 32 S Bedford St Carlisle PA 17013-3302

TUROCK, BETTY JANE, library and information science educator, educational association administrator; b. Scranton, Pa., June 12; d. David and Ruth Carolyn (Sweetser) Argust; BA magna cum laude (Charles Weston scholar), Syracuse U., 1955; postgrad. (scholar) U. Pa., 1956; MLS, Rutgers U., 1970, PhD, 1981; m. Frank M. Turock, June 16, 1956; children: David L., B. Drew. Library and materials coordinator Holmdel (N.J.) Public Schs., 1963-65; story-teller Wheaton (Ill.) Public Library, 1965-67; ednl. media specialist Alhambra Public Sch., Phoenix, 1967-70; br. librarian, area librarian, head extension service Forsyth County Public Library System, Winston-Salem, N.C., 1970-73; asst. dir. Montclair (N.J.) Public Library, 1973-75, dir., 1975-77; asst. dir. Monroe County Library System, Rochester, N.Y., 1978-81; asst. prof. Rutgers U. Grad. Sch. Communications, Info. and Library Studies, 1981-87, assoc. prof. 1987-93, prof. 1994—, dept. chair, 1989-95, dir. MLS program, 1990-95; vis. prof. Rutgers U. Grad. Sch. Library and Info. Studies, 1980-81; adviser U.S. Dept. Edn. Office of Libr. Programs, 1988-89. Trustee, Raritan Twp. (N.J.) Public Library, 1961-62, Keystone Coll., 1991—, Freedom to Read Found., 1994—, Libs. for the Future, 1994—, Fund for Am.'s Libs., 1995; mem. Bd. Edn. Raritan Twp., 1962-66; mem. Title VII Adv. Bd., Montclair Public Schs., 1975-77; ALA coord. Task Force on Women, 1978-80, mem. action coun.; treas. Social Responsibilities Round Table, 1978-82. Recipient N.J. Libr. Leadership award, 1994; named Woman of Yr., Raritan-Holmdel Woman's Club, 1975. Mem. AAUP, Am. Soc. Info. Sci., Assn. Libr. and Info. Sci. Edn., Am. Libr. Assn. (pres. 1995—, pres.-elect 1994-95, exec. bd. 1991—, coun. 1988—), Rutgers U. Grad. Sch. Library and Info. Studies Alumni Assn. (pres. 1977-78, Disting. Alumni award 1994), Phi Theta Kappa, Psi Chi, Beta Phi Mu, Pi Beta Phi. Unitarian. Author: Serving Older Adults, 1983, Creating a Financial Plan, 1992; editor: The Bottom Line, 1984—; contbr. articles to profl. jours. Home: 39 Highwood Rd Somerset NJ 08873-1834 Office: Rutgers U 4 Huntington St New Brunswick NJ 08901-1071

TUROK, PAUL HARRIS, composer, music reviewer; b. N.Y.C., Dec. 3, 1929; s. Joseph and Esther (Pashman) T.; m. Susan Kay Frucht, Mar. 24, 1967. BA, Queens Coll., N.Y.C., 1950; MA, U. Calif., Berkeley, 1951; MS, Baruch Coll., 1986. Music dir. Sta. KPFA, Berkeley, 1955-56; lectr. CCNY, 1959-63; vis. prof. Williams Coll., Williamstown, Mass., 1963-64; music critic New York Herald-Tribune, 1964-65; critic, columnist Music Jour., New York, 1964-79, Ovation mag., New York, 1980—; critic, contbr. New York Times, 1984—, Sta. WQXR, First Hearing, New York, 1985—; pub. Turok's Choice, 1990—. Composer musical compositions, premiered Indpls. Symphony, 1971, Louisville Orch., 1973, Cleve. Orch., 1973, Phila Orch., 1976; opera Richard III, 1975, Sousa Overture, 1976, Lanier Songs, 1978, English Horn Quintet, 1982, Cello Sonata, 1984, Organ Toccata, 1984, Tourist Music, 1985, String Quartet No. 4, 1986, Rhapsody for Band, 1987, Piano Dance, 1988, Violin Sonata, 1989, From Sholem Aleichem, 1990, Abac for trumpet and organ, 1990, Partita for three winds, 1991, Concerto for two violins and orchestra, 1991, Piano Trio, 1992, C.C. 6 for bassoon and orchestra, 1992, Fantasy for 4 flutes and piano, 4 hands, 1994, Clap, Cluck, Count: Three Interactive Proverbs for Chidren and Orchestra, 1995. Served with U.S. Army, 1953-55. Hertz travelling scholar, U. Calif., 1956-58; Grammy nominee 1992, 93. Jewish. Avocations: world travel, computing.

TUROV, DANIEL, financial writer, investment executive; b. Bklyn., Jan. 15, 1947; s. Bernard and Mildred (Stevelman) T.; B.A. in Econs., CCNY, 1969; m. Rosalyn B. Kalishock, Aug. 25, 1968 (dec.); children: Joshua Nathaniel, Steven Russell. Registered investment advisor. Account exec. Walston & Co., 1969-72, Thomson McKinnon Securities, 1972-75; sr. v.p. Faulkner Dawkins & Sullivan, 1975-77, Cowen & Co., N.Y.C., 1977-80; dir. Turov Investment Group div. Moore & Schley, Cameron & Co., N.Y.C., 1980-82; v.p. Dean Witter Reynolds, Inc., 1982-83, sr. v.p., 1983-84; pres. Just Right Comm., 1992—; chmn. Philtrum Advt. Corp., 1982-84. Author: (monthly) Turov on INvestments and Hedging, 1972-80, monthly; investment column Best Buys Mag., 1982-83; editor New Innovations Pub. Corp., 1979-86, Turov on Timing, 1993—; contbr. articles to profl. jours. and newspapers. Mem. faculty N.Y. Inst. Fin., New Sch. Social Research; mem. panel The Wall St. Transcript's Option Roundtable; speaker in field. Office: Just Right Comm 154 Whippoorwill Ln Oak Ridge TN 37830-8645

TUROW, JOSEPH GREGORY, communication educator; b. Bklyn., Apr. 5, 1950; s. Abraham and Danuta (Chaikin) T.; m. Judith Anne Forrest, June 17, 1979; children: Jonathan, Marissa, Rebecca. BA, U. Pa., 1971, MA, 1973, PhD, 1976. Asst. prof. Purdue U., West Lafayette, Ind., 1976-86; from assoc. prof. to prof. comms. U. Pa., 1986—. Author: Getting Books to Children, 1979, Entertainment, Education and the Hard Sell, 1981, Media Industries, 1984, Playing Doctor, 1989, Media Systems in Society, 1992. Recipient Russell Nye award Popular Culture Assn., 1982; NEH grantee, 1986, 94; FCC grantee, 1978. Mem. Speech Comm. Assn. (divsn. head 1987), Internat. Comm. Assn. (divsn. chair 1995—), Phi Beta Kappa. Avocation: viewing residential architecture. Office: U Pa Annenberg Sch Philadelphia PA 19104

TUROW, SCOTT F., lawyer, author; b. Chgo., Apr. 12, 1949; s. David D. and Rita (Pastron) T.; m. Annette Weisberg, Apr. 4, 1971; 3 children. BA magna cum laude, Amherst Coll., 1970; MA, Stanford U., 1974; JD cum laude, Harvard U., 1978. Bar: Ill. 1978, U.S. Dist. Ct. (no. dist.) Ill. 1978, U.S. Ct. Appeals (7th cir.) 1979. Asst. U.S. atty. U.S. Ct. Appeals (7th dist.), Chgo., 1978-86; ptnr. Sonnenschein Nath & Rosenthal, Chgo., 1986—; E. H. Jones lectr. Stanford U., 1972-75. Author: One L.: An Inside Account of Life in the First Year at Harvard Law School, 1977, Presumed Innocent, 1987 (Silver Dagger award Crime Writers Assn. 1988), The Burden of Proof, 1990, Pleading Guilty, 1993; contbr. articles to profl. jours. Edith Mirrielees fellow, 1972. Mem. Chgo. Bar Assn., Fed. Bar Assn., Chgo. Coun. of Lawyers. Office: Sonnenschein Nath Rosenthal Ste 8000 Sears Tower 233 S Wacker Dr Chicago IL 60606*

TURPEN, LOUIS A., airport terminal executive. Pres., CEO Lester B. Pearson Internat. Airport, Toronto, Ont., Can.; dir., San Francisco Airports Commn.

TURPEN, MICHAEL CRAIG, lawyer; b. Tulsa, Nov. 10, 1949; s. Wallace Kendall and Marjorie Allyce (Kinkaid) T.; m. Susan Lynn Haugor; children: Sean Michael, Patrick Michael, Sarah Allyce. BS in History Edn., U. Tulsa, 1972, JD, 1974. Bar: Okla. 1975. Legal advisor Muskogee Police Dept., Okla., 1975-76; asst. dist. atty. City of Muskogee, 1976, dist. atty., 1977-82; atty. gen. State of Okla., 1983-87; ptnr. Riggs, Abney, Neal & Turpen, Oklahoma City, 1987—; conf. speaker; mem. Okla. Spl. Legis. Com. on Criminal Justice System, 1978-79; adj. prof. bus. law N.E. Okla. State U.-Tahlequah, 1977; adj. prof. criminal law Connors State Coll., 1977-79. Author: Police-Prosecutor Training Manual, 1975; contbr. articles to profl. jours. Mem. Gov.'s Alts. to Incarceration Com., 1980-81; bd. dirs. Call Rape, Inc., Okla. Acad. State Goods; apptd. by Pres. Clinton JFK Performing Arts Ctr. Adv. Bd.; vice chmn. Okla. Crime Commn., 1980-81; commr. Okla. State Bur. Investigation, 1978-79; bd. dirs., coach Muskogee Green Country Girls Softball Assn.; mem. Muskogee H.S. Booster Club; mem., coach Muskogee Knothole League Boys Baseball Assn.; mem. Muskogee County Human Soc., Muskogee County Women's Dem. Club; hon. mem. Okla. Hwy. Patrol, 1980; co-chmn. Clinton/Gore Okla., 1992, Al Gore for Pres., 1988; chmn. State Dem. Party Okla. Recipient Maurice Merrill Golden Quill award Okla. Bar Jour., 1981, Donald Santarelli award Nat. Orgn. Victim Assistance, Toronto, 1981, Mayor's commendation City of Muskogee, 1976, Mayor's commendation City of Owasso, 1975, $10,000 Cash award Found. for Improvement Justice, Inc., Achievement award Found. for Improvement Justice, Inc., 1986; named Outstanding Young Oklahoman, Okla. Jayeees, 1979, Outstanding Young Lawyer, Okla. Bar Assn., 1975, Outstanding Young Man, Muskogee Jaycees, 1979, One of Ten Outstanding Nat. Leaders in field of victim rights, Nat. Orgn. for Victim Assistance, 1986, One of Men and Women Under 40 Who are Changing Nation, Esquire Mag., 1985. Mem. ABA, Okla. Bar Assn., Muskogee County Bar Assn. (past sec.), Okla. Dist. Attys. Assn. (pres. 1980-81, bd. dirs.), Tulsa U. Alumni Assn., Rotary, Tulsa U. Hurricane Club, Fraternal Order of Police. Presbyterian. Office: Riggs Abney Neal & Turpen Ste 101 5801 Broadway Ext Oklahoma City OK 73118-7489 also: 502 W 6th St Tulsa OK 74119-1016

TURPIN, CHERYL NIDO, retail executive; b. Port Huron, Mich., Sept. 13, 1947; d. James N. and Lillian Mary (Forbes) N.; m. James M. Turpin, Apr. 26, 1980; children: Nicholas Nido, Jessica Rose. BA in English and Philosophy, U. Mich., 1969. Buyer, div. mdse. mgr. Rike's, Dayton, Ohio, 1969-74; div. mdse. mgr. Gimbels, Phila., 1974-75; v.p., gen. mdse. mgr. Weinstock's, Sacramento, 1975-78, chmn., chief exec. officer, 1982—; exec. v.p. Broadway Dept. Stores, Los Angeles, 1978-82. Mem. adv. bd. Sacramento Area Spl. Olympics, 1982—; bd. dirs. Sacramento Area United Way, 1985—, mem. Com. of 200, Sacramento YWCA, 1985-87, Pvt. Industry Coun. Sacramento, 1984-85. Recipient YWCA Outstanding Woman award, Sacramento, 1985, Disting. Bus. Woman's award, Sacramento C. of C., 1984-85. Mem. Fashion Group, Calif. C. of C. (bd. dirs.), The Trusteeship. Avocation: skiing. Office: Ltd Lndn-Pris NY Inc PO Box 16528 Columbus OH 43216-6528*

TURPIN, DAVID HOWARD, biologist, educator; b. Duncan, B.C., Can., July 14, 1956; s. George Howard and Marilyn Elizabeth (Jones) T.; m. S. Laurene Clark, Oct. 4, 1985; children: Chantal, Joshua. BSc in Biology, U. B.C., 1977, PhD in Botany, Oceanography, 1980. Post-doctoral rsch. fellow Natural Sci. & Engring. Coun., 1980-81; rsch. assoc. Simon Fraser U., 1980; v.p. Sigma Resource Cons., Vancouver, B.C., 1980-81; from asst. prof. to assoc. prof. Queen's U., Kingston, Ont., Can., 1981-90; prof. biology Queen's U., Kingston, Ont., 1990-91, dean arts & sci., 1993-95, vice prin. acad., 1993—; prof., head botany U. B.C., 1991-93; invited speaker profl. meetings, univs. worldwide. Co-editor: Plant Physiology, Biochemistry and Molecular Biology, 1990, 2nd edit., 1996; mem. editl. bd. Jour. Physiology, 1992-96, Plant Physiology, 1988-92, Plant Cell and Environment, 1994—, Jour., Exptl. Botany, 1995—; contbr. chpts. to books; author numerous articles, conf. procs. V.p. Great Lakes Tomorrow, 1986-90; mem. program com. Great Lakes Course-Ont. Sci. Ctr., 1988; Kingston City rep. Cataraqui Regional Conservation Authority, 1984-86. Recipient Excellence in Teaching Alumni award Queen's U., 1989, Outstanding Alumni award U. B.C., 1990, Darbaker prize in phycology Am. Bot. Assn., 1991; Natural Sci. and Engring. Rsch. Can. E.W.R. Stacie Meml. fellow, 1989-90; Capt. T.S. Byrne Meml. scholar U. B.C., 1980; postgrad. scholar Natural Scis. and Engring. Rsch. Coun., 1979-81, Edith Ashton Meml. scholar U. B.C., 1979, Nat. Rsch. Coun. scholar, 1978-79; Natural Scis. and Engring. Rsch. Coun. grantee, 1982—. Mem. Phycological Soc. Am., Am. Soc. Limnology & Oceanography, Can. Soc. Plant Physiologists (C.D. Nelson award 1989), Am. Soc. Plant Physiologists (cert. recognition 1992). Office: Queen's Univ, Office of Vice Prin (Acad), 239 Richardson Hall, Kingston, ON Canada K7L 3N6

TURPIN, JOSEPH OVILA, counselor, educator; b. Rockford, Ill., July 11, 1943; s. D. John and Mona Belle (Albright) T.; m. Hester R. Thompson, June 26, 1969; children: Matthew, Michael. AB in Sociology, Ind. U., 1965, MS in Mental Retardation, 1966, postgrad., 1966-67; PhD in Rehab. Psychology, U. Wis., 1986. Rsch. assoc. Ind. U., Bloomington, 1966-67; instr. U. Wis. Parkside Extension, Kenosha, 1967-71; tchr. Kenosha Unified Sch. Dist., 1967-71; coord. Racine area Gov.'s Com. on Spl. Learning State of Wis. Dept. Adminstrn., 1971-73; dir. Racine County Comprehensive Mental Health, Mental Retardation, Alcohol and Other Drug Abuse Svcs. Bd, 1973-78; vocat. cons., counselor supr. Industrial Injury Clinic, Neenah, Wis., 1978-83; owner, vocat. expert Vocat. Counseling Svc., Inc., Madison, Wis., 1983-88; teaching intern, counseling supr., student tchr. supr. U. Wis., Madison, 1983-86; asst. prof. rehab. counselor edn. Ohio U., Athens, 1986-89; assoc. prof. rehab. counseling program Calif. State U., San Bernardino, 1989-94, prof. rehab. counseling program, 1994—, coord. rehab. counseling program, 1990-94; mem. sch. psychologist exam. com. Dept. Edn. State of Ohio, 1989; rschr., presenter, cons. in field. Contbr. articles to profl. pubs. Bd. dirs. United Cerebral Palsy of Racine County, 1969-73, Children's House, Inc., Racine, 1971-73, Ctrl. Ohio Regional Coun. on Alcoholism, 1987-89, Inland Caregivers Resource Ctr., 1993—, Health and Hosp. Planning Com. of Racine County, 1976; treas. Cub Scout Pack # 68, Boy Scouts Am., Neenah, 1981-83, Whitcomb Village Assn., Inc., 1984; bd. dirs. Aquinas H.S., 1992-94, pres. 1994; H.S. liaison West Point Parents Club of Inland Empire, 1992-94; budget rev. com. United Fund Racine County, 1975. Grantee Rehab. Svcs. Adminstrn., 1985-88, Ohio U., 1987-88, Ohio U. Coll. Osteo. Medicine and Coll. Edn., 1989, Office Spl. Edn. and Rehab., 1989-92. Mem. ACA (pub. policy and legis. com. 1992-94, various subcoms.), APA, San Bernardino Area Mental Health Assn. (bd. dirs.), Am. Rehab. Counseling Assn. (exec. coun. 1992—, ethics com. 1990-91, chair coun. on profl. preparation and stds. 1992—), Nat. Rehab. Counseling Assn. (bd. dirs. 1993-94, chmn. grievance com., pres.-elect 1996). Office: Calif State U 5500 University Pky San Bernardino CA 92407-2318

TURRELL, EUGENE SNOW, retired psychiatrist; b. Hyattsville, Md., Feb. 27, 1919; m. Denise Deuprey, Dec. 26, 1942 (div. Jan. 1976); children: David Hillyer, Gregory Sherman (dec.); m. Zenobia A. Hopper, Apr. 16, 1988; stepchildren: Elizabeth Ann Crofoot, Mary Jane Cooper. BS, Ind. U., 1939, MD, 1947. Diplomate Am. Bd. Psychiatry and Neurology. Intern Peter Bent Brigham Hosp., Boston, 1947-48; resident physician Kandakee (Ill.) State Hosp., 1948-49; clin. asst. psychiatry U. Calif., San Francisco, 1949-51; asst. prof. Ind. U. Sch. Medicine, 1952-53, assoc. prof., 1953-58; prof., chmn. dept. psychiatry Marquette U. Sch. Medicine, 1958-63, clin. prof. psychiatry, 1963-69; lectr. U. Calif., San Francisco, 1969-75; assoc. prof. Ind. U., 1975-80, prof., 1980-89, prof. emeritus, 1989—; dean emeritus San Diego County Psychiat. Hosp., 1995—, 1995—; assoc. clin. prof. U. Calif., San Diego, 1991-95; ret., 1995; mem., bd. dirs. Community Addictions Svcs. Agy, Indpls., 1975-79, pres. bd., 1976-77. Contr. articles to profl. jours. Lt. USNR, 1950-52. Recipient Certs. of Appreciation Office Sci. Rsch. and Devel., 1945, VA, 1964, Ind. U. Found., 1966. Fellow Am. Psychiat. Assn. (life); mem. AMA (Physician's Recognition award 1978-96), AAAS, Calif. State Med. Assn., Calif. State Psychiat. Assn., San Diego County Med. Soc., San Diego County Soc. Psychiat. Physicians, Sigma Xi, Alpha Omega Alpha. Democrat. Episcopalian. Avocations: tennis, motorcycling, bridge, literature, arts.

TURRELL, RICHARD HORTON, SR., retired banker; b. Kingston, Pa., Apr. 9, 1925; s. George Henry and Margaret (Clark) T.; m. Sally Wolfe, May 28, 1955; children: Richard H. Jr., David C., Douglas W. (dec.). Student, Cornell U., 1943; BS in Commerce, Washington and Lee U., 1949. Rep. sales Del. Lackawanna and Western Coal Co., Phila., 1949-51; asst. to pres. N.Y.C., 1951-58; broker Auchincloss Parker & Redpath, N.Y.C., 1958-61; mgr. investments Fiduciary Trust Co. Internat., N.Y.C., 1961-94, v.p., 1968-94, sr. v.p., 1968-94, sec., 1971-84; asst. sec. Blue Coal Corp., N.Y.C., 1953-

58; v.p., bd. dirs. Pine Raleigh (N.C.) Corp., 1966-93. Trustee, overseer Simon's Rock of Bard Coll., Gt. Barrington, Mass., 1968-93; trustee Monmouth Coll., West Long Branch, N.J., 1980—, chmn. bd. trustees, 1989-92; chmn. Millburn-Short Hills (N.J.) Rep. Com., 1973-78; trustee Children's Specialized Hosp. Found., Mountainside, N.J., 1989-95. With Signal Corps, U.S. Army, 1943-46, PTO. Named Disting. Alumnus, Washington and Lee U., 1986. Mem. Baltusrol Golf Club (Springfield, N.J., gov. 1977), Capitol Hill Club (Washington), Turtle Creek Club (Tequesta, Fla.), Masons, Irem Temple Aaonms, Phi Beta Kappa, Phi Eta Sigma, Alpha Kappa Psi, Omicron Delta Kappa (hon.), Beta Gamma Sigma, Phi Delta Theta. Presbyterian. Avocations: golf, history, education. Home: 114 Turtle Creek Dr Tequesta FL 33469-1547

TURRENTINE, HOWARD BOYD, federal judge; b. Escondido, Calif., Jan. 22, 1914; s. Howard and Veda Lillian (Maxfield) T.; m. Virginia Jacobsen, May 13, 1965 (dec.); children: Howard Robert, Terry Beverly; m. Marlene Lipsey, Nov. 1, 1992. AB, San Diego State Coll., 1936; LLB, U. So. Calif., 1939. Bar: Calif. 1939. Practiced in San Diego, 1939-68; judge Superior Ct. County of San Diego, 1968-70, U.S. Dist. Ct. (so. dist.) Calif., Calif.; sr. judge U.S. Dist. Ct. (so. dist.) Calif., San Diego, 1970—. Served with USNR, 1941-45. Mem. ABA, Fed. Bar Assn., Am. Judicature Soc. Office: US Dist Ct 940 Front St San Diego CA 92101-8909

TURRENTINE, STANLEY WILLIAM, musician; b. Pitts., Apr. 5, 1934; m. Shirley Scott. Plays tenor saxophone; played with, Ray Charles, 1952, Earl Bostic, 1953, Max Roach, 1959-60; led group with wife, organist Shirley Scott, 1960-71; solo artist thereafter; rec. numerous albums including: Straight Ahead, 1985, Turrentine Again, Tender Togetherness!, Betcha Use the Stairs, What About You?, West Side Highway, Night Wings, The Man with the Sad Face, Everybody Come on Out, Have You Ever Seen the Rain?, In the Pocket, Pieces of Dreams, Salt Song, Cherry, Don't Mess with Mr. T., The Sugar Man, Sugar, Another Story, Common Touch, Always Something There, Easy Walker, The Spoiler, Rough'n Tumble, Joyride, Hustlin', A Chip Off the Old Block, Never Let Me Go, Jubelee Shouts, That's Where It's At, Dearly Beloved, Up at Minton's, Blue Hour, Ain't No Way, Mr. Natural, In Memory Of, New Time Shuffle, Straight Ahead, Wonderland, The Best of Stanley Turrentine, 1989, More Than A Mood, 1993. Office: care Associated Booking Corp 1955 Broadway New York NY 10023-6504

TURRI, JOSEPH A., lawyer; b. Seneca Falls, N.Y., July 24, 1943; s. Louis Arthur and Assunta (Faiola) T.; m. Susan Ruth Testa, Dec. 29, 1975; 1 child, Michael James. BA, SUNY, Buffalo, 1965; JD, Cornell U., 1970. Bar: N.Y. 1971, U.S. Dist Ct. (we. dist.) N.Y. 1971, U.S. Supreme Ct. 1974. Ptnr. Harris, Beach & Wilcox, Rochester, N.Y., 1970—; mgmt. ptnrs. com. Harris, Beach & Wilcox, Rochester, 1991—, chmn. constrn. law dept., 1992—, chmn. litigation dept., 1994-96; bd. dirs. Thousand Island Park Corp., N.Y., Castle Bay Ltd., Rochester, N.Y.; arbitrator Am. Arbitration Assn., Syracuse, 1985—. Bd. dirs. Rochester Downtown Devel. Corp., 1992—. Mem. N.Y. Bar Assn., Monroe County Bar Assn., Assn. Gen. Contractors, Met. Forum (trustee). Avocations: horseback riding, antique wooden boats. Home: 110 Merriman St Rochester NY 14607-1506 Office: Harris Beach & Wilcox 130 Main St E Rochester NY 14604-1620

TURRO, NICHOLAS JOHN, chemistry educator; b. Middletown, Conn., May 18, 1938; s. Nicholas John and Philomena (Russo) T.; m. Sandra Jean Misenti, Aug. 6, 1960; children: Cynthia Suzanne, Claire Melinda. BA, Wesleyan U., 1960, DSc (hon.), 1984; PhD, Calif. Inst. Tech., 1963. Instr. chemistry Columbia U., N.Y.C., 1964-65, asst. prof., 1965-67, assoc. prof., 1967-69, prof. chemistry, 1969—, William P. Schweitzer prof. chemistry, 1982—, chmn. chemistry dept., 1981-84; Cons. E.I. duPont de Nemours and Co., Inc. Author: Molecular Photochemistry, 1965, Vol. 2, 1970, Vol. 3, 1971, (with A.A. Lamola) Energy Transfer and Organic Photochemistry, 1971, Modern Molecular Photochemistry, 1978; mem. editl. bd. Langmuir Ency. Phys. Sci. and Tech., Jour. Reactive Intermediates. Fellow NSF, Alfred P. Sloan Found., Guggenheim fellow, Oxford U., 1985; recipient Eastman Kodak award for excellence in grad. rsch. pure chemistry, 1973, E.O. Lawrence U.S. Dept. Energy, 1983, Porter medal European Photochem. Soc., Inter-Am. Photochem Soc., 1994, Havinga medal Leiden, The Netherlands, 1994, Disting. Alumni award Calif. Inst. Tech., 1996. Mem. NAS, Am. Chem. Soc. (mem. editl. bd. jour. 1984—, Harrison Howe award Rochester, N.Y. sect. 1986, Arthur C. Cope award 1986, Fresenius award 1973, award for pure chemistry 1974, James Flack Norris award 1987), Am. Acad. Arts and Scis., Chem. Soc. (London), N.Y. Acad. Scis. (Freda and Gregory Halpern award in photochemistry 1977), Inter-Am. Photochemistry Soc. (award 1991, 94), European Photo-Chem. Assn. (Porter medal), Phi Beta Kappa, Sigma Xi. Office: Columbia U 3030 Broadway New York NY 10027

TURSI, CARL THOMAS, lawyer; b. Mt. Vernon, N.Y., July 28, 1941; s. Frank Carl and Rose Lucy (Viggiano) T. AB, Colgate U., 1963; LLB, Harvard U., 1966. Bar: N.Y. 1967. Atty. Cahill Gordon, N.Y.C., 1967-71, Donovan Leisure, N.Y.C., 1971-76; v.p., sec. Amerada Hess Corp., N.Y.C., 1976—. Mem. N.Y. State Bar Assn. Home: 20 Beekman Pl New York NY 10022-8032 Office: Amerada Hess Corp 1185 Ave Of The Americas New York NY 10036-2601

TURSI, FRANK VINCENT, journalist; b. Bklyn., Apr. 30, 1951; s. Dominick and Grace (Berardi) T.; m. Doris Ann Foster, Nov. 12, 1973; 1 child, Diana. BA in English, East Carolina U., 1973. Reporter Clemmons (N.C.) Courier, 1973-74, Key Biscayne (Fla.) Island News, 1974-75; news editor Coral Gables (Fla.) Times-Guide, 1975-77; sports writer, copy editor Miami (Fla.) Herald, 1977-79; sports writer, copy editor Winston-Salem (N.C.) Jour., 1979-81, copy editor, layout editor, 1981-85, med./sci. reporter, 1985-88, spl. projects reporter, 1988—. Author: Where the Land Meets the Sea, 1990, Winston-Salem: A History, 1994, Magnolia Trees and Pulitzer Prizes: A History of the Winston-Salem Journal, 1996. Pres. Old Meadowbrook Homeowners Assn., 1991-92; mem. Winston-Salem Mayor's Com. for Handicapped, 1989-90; vol. camp counselor Muscular Dystrophy Assn. Recipient Media award N.C. chpt. Am. Planning Assn., 1987, Environ. Media award for Excellence N.C. Sierra Club, 1987, Conservation Communicator award N.C. Wildlife Fedn., 1988. Roman Catholic. Home: 3851 Willowood Dr Clemmons NC 27012 Office: Winston Salem Journal 418 N Marshall St Winston Salem NC 27102

TURTELL, NEAL TIMOTHY, librarian; b. N.Y.C., Nov. 1, 1949; s. Richard Roland and Ann Grace (Glover) T. AB, Fordham U., 1971; MLS, Pratt Inst., 1975. Cataloger-libr. Ford Found., N.Y.C., 1972-75, U.S. Dept. Transp., Washington, 1975-77; spl. projects libr. Smithsonian Instn., Washington, 1977-81, chief catalogue records, 1981-82; asst. dir. tech. svcs. U. Wis., Oshkosh, 1982-83, asst. prof. libr. sci., 1982-83; asst. chief libr. Nat. Gallery of Art, Washington, 1983-87, exec. libr., 1987—. Contbr. to book revs. Libr. Jour., 1972-75, exhbn. catalogue. Bd. trustees Pyramid Atlantic Ctr. for Printmaking and the Art of the Book, Riverdale, Md., 1988—, v.p. bd. trustees, 1991—. Mem. Art Librs. Soc. N.Am., Rsch. Librs. Group (steering com. for art and architecture 1988-89), Grolier Club. Home: 1631-B S Hayes Arlington VA 22202 Office: Nat Gallery of Art 4th & Constitution Ave NW Washington DC 20565-0001

TURTURRO, JOHN, actor; b. Brooklyn, Feb. 28, 1957; s. Nicholas and Katherine Turturro; m. Katherine Borowitz; 1 child, Amadeo. Grad., SUNY (New Paltz), 1978; student, Yale Drama Sch. Worked in regional theater and off-Broadway in Danny and the Deep Blue Sea (Obie award 1985), Men Without Dates, Tooth of the Crime, La Puta Vida, Chaos and Hard Times, The Bald Soprano, Of Mice and Men, The Resistable Rise of Arturo Ui, 1991; appeared in Broadway prodn. Death of a Salesman, 1984; appeared in films Raging Bull, 1980, The Flamingo Kid, 1984, To Live and Die in L.A., 1985, Desperately Seeking Susan, 1985, Hannah and Her Sisters, 1986, Gung Ho, 1986, Offbeat, 1986, The Color of Money, 1986, The Sicilian, 1987, Five Corners, 1988, Do the Right Thing, 1989, Miller's Crossing, 1990, Men of Respect, Mo Better Blues, 1990, Jungle Fever, 1991, Barton Fink, 1991 (winner best actor award, Cannes Film Festival, 1991, David Donatello award Montreal Film Festival-Best Actor), Backtrack, 1991, Brain Donors, 1992, Fearless, 1993, Being Human, 1994, Quiz Show, 1994, Search and Destroy, 1995, Unstrung Heroes, 1995; film dir. (debut) Mac (Camera d'Or award Cannes Film Festival, 1992), Sugartime, Grace of My Heart, Box of Moonlight, The Truce. Office: care ICM 8942 Wilshire Blvd Beverly Hills CA 90211

TUSCHMAN, JAMES MARSHALL, lawyer; b. Toledo, Nov. 28, 1941; s. Chester and Harriet (Harris) T.; m. Ina S. Cheloff, Sept. 2, 1967; children: Chad Michael, Jon Stephen, Sari Anne. BS in Bus., Miami U., Oxford, Ohio, 1963; JD, Ohio State U., 1966. Bar: Ohio 1966, U.S. Ct. Appeals (6th and 7th cirs.), U.S. Supreme Ct. Assoc. Shumaker, Loop & Kendrick, Toledo, 1966-84, ptnr. 1970-84; co-founder, chmn. ops. com. Jacobson Maynard Tuschman & Kalur, Toledo, Cleve., Cin., Columbus, Youngstown and Dayton, Ohio, Morgantown, W.Va. and Louisville, Kansas City, Mo., Columbia, Md., St. Louis, Phila., 1984—; chmn. bd., sec. Tuschman Steel Co., Toledo, 1969-76; vice chmn. bd. Kripke Tuschman Industries, Inc., 1977-85, dir. 1977-86; chmn. bd., sec. Toledo Steel Supply Co., 1969-86; ptnr. Starr Ave. Co., Toledo, 1969-86; bd. dirs. Capital Holdings Inc., Toledo, Capital Bank, Toledo, Fetal Devel. Eval., Ltd., Toledo. Mem. bd. trustees U. Toledo; past trustee, chmn. fin. com., former treas. Maumee Valley Country Day Sch.; past trustee, v.p., treas. Temple B'nai Israel, 1984-88. Fellow Internat. Soc. Barristers; mem. ABA, Am. Bd. Trial Advocates, Ohio Bar Assn., Toledo Bar Assn., Def. Rsch. and Trial Lawyers Assn., Ohio Civil Trial Lawyers Assn., Toledo Club, Inverness Country Club, Zeta Beta Tau, Phi Delta Phi. Home: 2579 Olde Brookside Rd Toledo OH 43615-2233 Office: 333 N Summit St Toledo OH 43604-2617

TUSHER, THOMAS WILLIAM, apparel company executive; b. Oakland, Calif., Apr. 5, 1941; s. William C. and Betty J. (Brown) T.; m. Pauline B. Kensett, Jan. 1, 1967; children: Gregory Malcolm, Michael Scott. B.A., U. Calif., Berkeley, 1963; M.B.A., Stanford U., 1965. Asst. to v.p. internat. Colgate Palmolive Co., N.Y.C., 1965-67; product mgr. Colgate-Palmolive P.R., 1967-68; supt. corp. planning Levi Strauss & Co., San Francisco, 1969; pres. Levi Strauss Internat., 1977-84; sr. v.p. Levi Straus & Co., before 1984, exec. v.p., chief operating officer, dir., from 1984, now pres., chief oper. officer; regional gen. mgr., Australia/N.Z., Levi Strauss Australia, 1970-74; area gen. mgr. Levi Strauss No. Europe, London, 1974-75; pres. European div. Levi Strauss Internat., San Francisco, 1976; dir. various subs's. Levi Strauss Internat.; dir. Gt. Western Garment Co., Can. Bd. dirs. Calif. Council Internat. Trade, 1977—, U. Calif. Grad. Bus. Sch. Served with Intelligence Corps. USAR, 1966-67. Mem. San Francisco C. of C. (dir.). Republican. Presbyterian. Clubs: World Trade, Bay. Office: Levi Strauss & Co 1155 Battery St San Francisco CA 94111-1230*

TUSHINGHAM, (ARLOTTE) DOUGLAS, museum administrator; b. Toronto, Ont., Can., Jan. 19, 1914; s. Arthur Douglas and Lottie Elizabeth (Betts) T.; m. Margaret McAndrew Thomson, Apr. 9, 1948; children: Margaret Elizabeth, Ian Douglas. B.A., U. Toronto, 1936; B.D., U. Chgo., 1941, Ph.D., 1948, LL.D., 1982. Instr. U. Chgo., 1948-51; ann. prof. Am. Sch. Oriental Research, Jerusalem, 1951-52; dir. Am. Sch. Oriental Research, 1952-53; assoc. prof. Queen's U., 1953-55; head art and archaeology div. Royal Ont. Mus., Toronto, 1955-64; chief archaeologist Royal Ont. Mus., 1964-79, head Jerusalem project, 1979—, trustee, 1984-90; prof. emeritus dept. Nr. Eastern studies U. Toronto, Ont., 1955-79; Asst. dir. Jericho Excavations, 1952, 53, 56; dir. Dhiban Excavations, 1952-53; assoc. dir. Jerusalem Excavations, 1962-67; mem. Toronto Hist. Bd., 1960—, chmn., 1967-73. Author: (with V.B. Meen) Crown Jewels of Iran, 1968, (with Denis Baly) Atlas of the Biblical World, 1971, The Excavations at Dibon (Dhībân) in Moab, 1952-53, 1972, Gold for the Gods, 1976, Ancient Peruvian Metalworking, 1979, Excavations in Jerusalem, I, 1985. Served as lt. Royal Canadian Navy, 1942-45. Fellow Soc. Antiquaries of London, Royal Soc. Can., Canadian Museums Assn. (pres. 1964, 65), Archaeol. Inst. Am. Home: Apt 501, 20 Baif Blvd, Richmond Hill, ON Canada L4C 8T1

TUSHMAN, J. LAWRENCE, wholesale distribution executive. CEO Sherwood Food Distbrs., Detroit. Office: Sherwood Food Distributors 18615 Sherwood Ave Detroit MI 48234

TUSHNET, MARK VICTOR, law educator, associate dean; b. Newark, N.J., Nov. 18, 1945; s. Leonard and Fannie (Brandchaft) T.; m. Elizabeth Alexander, Aug. 23, 1969; children: Rebecca, Laura. BA magna cum laude, Harvard U., 1967; JD, MA in History, Yale U., 1971. Law clk. for Judge George Edwards, Detroit, 1971-72; law clerk for Justice Thurgood Marshall $D, Washington, 1972-73; prof. U. Wis. Law Sch., 1973-81; prof. Georgetown U. Law Ctr., Washington, 1981—, assoc. dean rsch. and scholarship; vis. prof. U. Tex., 1977-78, U. So. Calif., 1989, U. Chgo., 1994. Author: (with Stone, Seidman and Sunstein) Constitutional Law, 1986, 2nd ed., 1991, (with Fink) Federal Jurisdiction: Policy and Practice, 1984, 2nd ed., 1987, The American Law of Slavery, 1981, The NAACP's Legal Strategy Against Segregated Education 1925-1950, 1987 (Littleton-Griswold prize Am. Hist. Assn.), Red, White, and Blue: A Critical Analysis of Constitutional Law, 1988; editor: Comparative Constitutional Federalism: Europe and America, 1990, Making Civil Rights Law: Thurgood Marshall and the Supreme Ct., 1936-61, 1994; contbr. articles to profl. jours. Jewish. Office: Georgetown U Law Ctr 600 New Jersey Ave NW Washington DC 20001-2075

TUSIANI, JOSEPH, foreign language educator, author; b. Foggia, Italy, Jan. 14, 1924; came to U.S., 1947, naturalized, 1956; s. Michael and Maria (Pisone) T. Dottore in Lettere summa cum laude, U. Naples, 1947, Litt.D., 1971. Lectr. in Italian lit. Hunter Coll., 1950-62; chmn. Italian dept. Coll. Mt. St. Vincent, 1948-71; vis. assoc. prof. NYU, 1956-64, CUNY, 1971-83; prof. Herbert H. Lehman Coll., 1971-83; NDEA vis. prof. Italian Conn. State Coll., 1962. Author: Dante in Licenza, 1952, Two Critical Essays on Emily Dickinson, 1952, Poesia Missionaria in Inghilterra Ed America, 1953, Sonettisti Americani, 1954, Melos Cordis; poems in Latin, 1955, Lo Speco Celeste, 1956, Odi Sacre; poems, 1958, The Complete Poems of Michelangelo, 1960, Rind and All, 1962, Lust and Liberty (The Poems of Machiavelli), 1963, The Fifth Season, 1963, Dante's Inferno (Introducted to Young People), 1964, Envoy from Heaven, 1965, Dante's Purgatorio (Indroduced to Young People), 1969, Dante's Paradise (Introduced to Young People), 1970, Tasso's Jerusalem Delivered; verse transl., 1970, Boccaccio's Nymphs of Fiesole, 1971, Italian Poets of the Renaissance, 1971, From Marino to Marinetti, 1973, The Age of Dante, 1973, America the Free, 1976, Tireca Tàreca, 1978, Tasso's Creation of the World, 1982, Rosa Rosarum, poems in Latin, 1984, In Exilio Rerum, poems in Latin, 1985; poems, 1978, Gente Mia and Other Poems, 1978; (au obiography) La Parola Difficile, vol. I, 1988, (poems in Latin) Confinia Lucis et Umbrae; La Parola Nuova, vol. II, 1991, La parola antica, vol. III, 1992, (poems in Italian) Il Ritorno, 1992, Bronx America, 1992, Annemale Parlante, 1994, Carmina Latina, 1994, Le Poesie Inglesi di G.A. Borgese, 1995. Recipient Greenwood prize for poetry in England, 1956, outstanding tchr. award, 1969, cavaliere ufficiale Italian Republic, 1973, Leonardo Covello's educator award, 1980, Leone di San Marco award, 1982, Avis award, 1983, Joseph Tusiani scholarship fund established in his honor at Lehman Coll., 1983, Congl. medal merit, 1984, Progresso medal liberty, 1986, gold plaque City Hall San Marco, 1986, outstanding tchr. award Am. Assn. Tchrs. Italian, 1986, Renoir literary award, 1988; Joseph Tusiani, Poet, Translator, Humanist (An Internat. Homage), 1995, Enrico Fermi award, 1995; Melvin Jones fellow, 1995. Mem. Poetry Soc. Am. (v.p.), Cath. Poetry Soc. Am. (dir. 1958, Spirit gold medal 1968). Home: 2140 Tomlinson Ave Bronx NY 10461-1202 *Strange how this continually re-edited Who's Who forces one to work and achieve.*

TUTEN, RICHARD LAMAR, professional football player; b. Perry, Fla., Jan. 5, 1965. BS in Econs., Fla. State U., 1986. Mem. Phila. Eagles, 1989, Buffalo Bills, 1990; punter Seattle Seahawks, 1991—. Named to NFL Pro Bowl, 1994. Office: Seattle Seahawks 11220 NE 53d St Kirkland WA 98033

TUTHILL, JOHN WILLS, former diplomat, educator; b. Montclair, N.J., Nov. 10, 1910; s. Oliver Bailey and Louise Jerolomen (Wills) T.; m. Erna Lueders, July 3, 1937; children: Carol Anne (dec.), David. S.B., Coll. William and Mary, 1932, LL.D., 1978; M.B.A., N.Y. U., 1936; A.M., Harvard U., 1943; LL.D., MacMurray Coll., 1967. Teller First Nat. Bank, Paterson, N.J., 1932-34; corporate trust adminstr. Bankers Trust Co. N.Y., 1934-36; investment counsel Fiduciary Counsel, N.Y.C., 1936-37; instr. Northeastern U., 1937-39, asst. prof. banking and finance, 1939-40; apptd. fgn. service officer Dept. State, 1940; served as vice counsul Windsor, Ont., Can., 1940-41, Mazatlan, Mexico, 1942; 3d sec. embassy Ottawa, Ont., 1942-44; sec. mission Office U.S. Polit. Adviser SHAEF, 1944-45; sec. mission and Am. Mil. Govt. for Germany, 1945-47, Am. consul, 1947; asst. chief shipping div. Dept. State, 1948, adviser, 1949; counselor of embassy Stockholm, 1949-51; spl. asst. ambassador London, 1952; dep. dir. Office Econ. Affairs, Bonn, W. Ger., 1952-54, USOM, Bonn, 1954; dir. USOM, 1954-56, counselor of embassy for econ. affairs, 1955-56; counselor embassy for econ. affairs with personal rank of minister Paris, 1956-59; dir. Office European Regional Affairs, Dept. State, 1959; minister-counselor econ. affairs U.S. Mission to NATO, European Regional Orgns., U.S.; rep. prep. com. for OECD; also dep. U.S. rep. OEEC, 1960; U.S. rep. OECD with personal rank of ambassador, 1960-62; U.S. ambassador to European Communities, 1962-66, Brazil, 1966-69; prof. internat. politics Johns Hopkins U., Bologna Center, Italy, 1969; pres. Salzburg Seminar in Am. Studies, Cambridge, Mass., 1977-85; vis. fellow Woodrow Wilson Nat. Fellowship Found., Princeton, 1978-80; exec. dir., trustee The Am.-Austrian Found., 1985-88. Author: Some Things to Some Men: Serving in the Foreign Service, 1995. Gov. Atlantic Inst. for Internat. Affairs, Paris, 1969-86, dir. gen. 1969-76. Recipient All Am. Silver Anniversary award Sports Illustrated, 1956; named to Athletic Hall of Fame Coll. William and Mary, 1979; Dir. Gen.'s Cup Dept. State, 1983. Mem. N.Y. Coun. Fgn. Rels., Washington Inst. Fgn. Policy, Am. Acad. Diplomacy (bd. dirs.), Jean Monnet Coun. (bd. dirs. 1985-95), Harvard Club (N.Y.C.), Cosmos Club (Washington), Flat Hat of William and Mary, Omicron Delta Kappa, Theta Delta Chi. Home: 2801 New Mexico Ave NW Washington DC 20007-3921

TUTHILL, WALTER WARREN, retail executive; b. Madison, N.J., Nov. 28, 1941; s. Walter Warren and Elizabeth Emma (Kniskern) T.; m. Barbara Ann Stephens, Apr. 22, 1967. BSBA, U. N.C., 1964. CPA, N.Y., N.J., N.C.; cert. info systems auditor, cert. internal auditor. Sr. mgr. Price Waterhouse, N.Y.C., 1964-77; dir. internal audit Carter Hawley Hale Stores Inc., L.A., 1977-82, gen. auditor, 1982-85, v.p., 1985-94; v.p. retail control Broadway Stores, Inc., L.A., 1994—; lectr. in field. Contbr. articles to profl. jours. Pres. Twin W Rescue Squad, Princeton Junction, N.J., 1976-77. Mem. AICPA, N.Y. Soc. CPA's, Am. Statis. Assn., Am. Acctg. Assn., Inst. Internal Auditors, Nat. Retail Mchts. Assn. (chmn. bd. internal audit group 1982-84, bd. dirs.), EDP Auditors Assn. Avocations: travel, computers, classical music. Office: Broadway Stores Inc 3880 N Mission Rd Los Angeles CA 90031-3179 *Life is what happens when we're planning something else.*

TUTTLE, CLIFFORD HORACE, JR., electronics manufacturing company executive; b. Teaneck, N.J., Aug. 3, 1930; s. Clifford Horace Sr. and Mary (Rodman) T.; m. Martha M. Greene, Apr. 23, 1952; children: Deborah Tuttle Fox, Michael R., Sandra, Mary Tuttle Faucher. BA in Psychology, Amherst, 1952. V.p. mktg. Vitramon, Inc., Monroe, Conn., 1957-63; pres. Mktg. Assistance, Inc., Weston, Mass., 1963-70; v.p. mktg. AVX Corp., New Bedford, Mass., 1970-72; pres., chmn. Aerovox, Inc., New Bedford, 1973—; chmn. Electronic Industries Assn., Washington, 1994-95; bd. dirs. NBB Bank; mem. exec. com. New Bedford Inst. for Savs. Trustee St. Luke's Hosp., New Bedford, 1984—. Served to lt. USCG, 1953-55. Mem. IEEE, C. of C. (v.p. New Bedford chpt. 1982-89). Republican. Avocation: boating. Office: Aerovox Inc 370 Faunce Corner Rd North Dartmouth MA 02747-1257

TUTTLE, DAVID BAUMAN, data processing executive; b. N.Y.C., Oct. 25, 1948; s. John Bauman and Charlotte (Root) T.; m. Mildred Suzanne Lamb, May 5, 1973 (div. May 1978); m. Nancy Viola Caraber, Mar. 14, 1981; children: Jason David, John Paul. Student, MIT, 1966-69. Assoc., sr. assoc. programer IBM Cambridge (Mass.) Sci. Ctr., 1968-71; staff programmer IBM VM/370 Devel., Burlington, Mass., 1971-76; sr. prin. S/W engr. Digital Equipment Corp., Maynard, Mass., 1976-78; mgr. Cambridge Telecom/GTE Telenet, Burlington, 1978-81; sr. scientist GTE Telenet, Burlington, 1981-84, chief scientist, 1984-85; sr. tech. cons. Prime Computer, Inc., Framingham, Mass., 1985-86; prin. tech. cons. Prime Computer, Inc., Framingham, 1986-89; sr. rsch. engr. Ungermann-Bass Inc., Andover, Mass., 1990-91; chief engr. Ungermann-Bass, Inc., Andover, Mass., 1991-93; cons. engr. Augment Sys., Inc., Bedford, Mass., 1993-95; chief tech. officer Augment Systems Inc., Westford, Mass., 1995—; strategy forum del. Corp. for Open Systems, McLean, Va., 1986-89, architecture com. mem., 1989, strategy forum nominating com., 1986-87; patent rev. com. Prime Computer, Inc., 1985-89. Co-author and editor: 3270 Display System Protocol, 1981, 83, Hotline BSC Access Method, 1970. Donor mem. Smithsonian Inst., Washington, 1980—. Mem. IEEE, IEEE Computer Soc., Nat. Space Soc. (life mem.), The Cousteau Soc., USS Constitution Mus. Assn., Black and Blues of Killington (treas. 1986-89), Mandala Folk Dance Ensemble (dancer 1970-73). Republican. Presbyterian. Avocations: Duplicate Bridge (life master, Am. Contract Bridge League, 1983), alpine skiing. Home: 27 Heather Dr Reading MA 01867-3961 Office: Augment Sys Inc 2 Robbins Rd Westford MA 01886-4113

TUTTLE, FRANK JAMES, bank executive; b. N.Y.C., Apr. 17, 1941; s. Franklin B. and Esther (Leeming) T.; m. Nora Veress, June 27, 1964; children: Franklin, Thomas, Christopher. BA, Denison U., 1963; MBA, Suny, Albany, 1970. Various positions Key Bank N.A., Albany, 1970—, sr. adminstrv. v.p., 1980-89; sr. v.p. KeyCorp, Cleve., 1989—. Served to capt. USAF, 1963-68. Clubs: Old Chatham Hunt (N.Y.) (pres. 1982-85). Office: Key Corp 127 Public Sq Cleveland OH 44114-1216

TUTTLE, JON F., lawyer; b. Cin., 1940. BSEE, Ohio U., 1964; JD, U. Pitts., 1969. Bar: Minn. 1969, U.S. Dist. Ct. (Minn. dist.) 1970, U.S. Ct. Appeals (7th and 8th cirs.) 1970, U.S. Supreme Ct. 1970, U.S. Ct. Appeals (5th and fed. cirs.) 1973, D.C. 1985. Mng. ptnr. Dorsey & Whitney, Washington; instr. legal writing U. Minn., 1970-73; adj. prof. law William Mitchell Coll., 1974-80. Mng. editor, mem. editorial bd. U. Pitts. Law Rev., 1968-69. Mem. ABA (mem. intellectual property law sect.), Minn. State Bar Assn. (mem. sect. coun., computer law sect. 1983-88), ITC Trial Bar Assn. Office: Dorsey & Whitney 1330 Connecticut Ave NW Ste 20 Washington DC 20036-1704*

TUTTLE, MARTHA BENEDICT, artist; b. Cin., Feb. 4, 1916; d. Harris Miller and Florence Stevens (McCrea) Benedict; m. Richard Salway Tuttle, June 3, 1939; children: Richard, Jr., McCrea Benedict (dec.), Martha (dec.), Elisabeth Hall. Grad. high sch., Cin.; student, Art Acad. Cin. V.p. Barg Bottling Co., Inc., Cin., 1948-80. One-woman shows include KKAE Gallery, 1963, Univ. Club, 1967, Miller Gallery, 1971, St. Clements, N.Y., 1973, Livingston Lodge, 1974, Holly Hill Antiques, 1979, Peterson Gallery, 1983, Art Acad. Cin., 1984, Closson Gallery, 1986, Camargo Gallery, 1992; represented in permanent collection Cin. Art Mus. Tchr. Sunday sch. Grace Episcopal Ch. and Indian Hill Ch., Cin., 1953-75; shareholder Cin. Art Mus.; founder partnership to save the William and Phebe Betts House; donor with partnership to The Nat. Soc. Colonial Dames of Am. the William and Phebe Betts House for establishing a Rsch. Ctr. Mem. Soc. Colonial Dames Am. (bd. dirs. 1976-89), Camargo Club, Univ. Club. Republican. Home: 5825 Drewry Farm Ln Cincinnati OH 45243-3441

TUTTLE, VIOLET MYREL, elementary school educator; b. Grassy Meadows, W.Va., Aug. 28, 1938; d. Alva Huston and Ila Myrel (Bowles) Fitzwater; m. Donald Silas Tuttle, Sept. 16, 1956; children: Donna Hope McCase, Donald Marion. AS, W.Va. State Coll., 1973, BS, 1975; postgrad., W.Va. U., 1985-92, MEd, 1983. Cert. elem. and secondary sch. tchr., W.Va. Tchr. aide Mary Ingles Sch. Kanawha County Schs., Tad, W.Va., 1969-75; tchr. Chelyan (W.Va.) Sch. Kanawha County Schs., 1975-86, tchr. Belle (W.Va.) Sch., 1986-94, v.p. PTA, 1991-92, computer specialist, 1987-93; tchr. evaluation com. Elk Elem. Ctr., Charleston, 1994—; tchr. evaluation com. Elk Elem. ctr., Charleston, 1994—, faculty senate treas., 1995—. Mem. Christian edn. bd. dirs. Judson Bapt. Ch., 1986-87, vacation Bible sch. dir., 1986-88; mem. Kanawha County Rep. exec. bd., 1995—; treas. Faculty Senate. Mem. Belle Women's Club (historian 1994—), Alpha Delta Kappa (v.p. Theta chpt. 1990-91, pres. 1992-94, corr. sec. 1994-96, Kanawha dist. coun. v.p. 1994—), Kanawha Coun. Tchrs. Math. Avocations: reading, travel, crafts, walking. Home: 786 Campbells Creek Dr Charleston WV 25306-6735 Office: Elk Elem Ctr 3320 Pennsylvania Ave Charleston WV 25302-4632

TUTTLE, WILLIAM G(ILBERT) T(OWNSEND), JR., research executive; b. Portsmouth, Va., Nov. 26, 1935; s. William Gilbert and Edith Inez (Ritter) T.; m. Helen Lynn Warren, Dec. 27, 1959; children: Lynn, Robert,

Jonathan. B.S., U.S. Mil. Acad., 1958; M.B.A., Harvard U., 1963. Commd. 2d lt. U.S. Army, 1958, advanced through grades to gen., 1989; dir. combat service support (Office Combat Devels., Hdqrs. Tng. and Doctrine Command), Ft. Monroe, Va., 1976-77; comdr. 3d Armored Div. Support Command Frankfurt, W. Ger., 1977-79; comdr. Mil. Traffic Mgmt. Command Eastern Area Bayonne, N.J., 1979-81; dir. force mgmt. Hdqrs. Dept. Army, Washington, 1981-82; chief policy and programs br. Supreme Hdqrs. Allied Powers Europe, 1982-84; comdr. U.S. Army Operational Test and Evaluation Agy., 1984-86; dep. comdg. gen. Logistics, Tng. and Doctrine Command and comdg. gen. U.S. Army Logistics Ctr., Ft. Lee, Va., 1986-89; comdg. gen. U.S. Army Materiel Command, Alexandria, Va., 1989-92; ret., 1992; pres., CEO, bd. trustees Logistics Mgmt. Inst., McLean, Va., 1993—; U.S. Army Kermit Roosevelt lectr., 1991; bd. dirs. Procurement Round Table; mem. bd. advisors Nat. Contract Mgmt. Assn.; cons. to Def. Sci. Bd. Prin., Coun. on Excellence in Govt.; nat. councillor Atlantic Coun. Decorated Def., USAF, USN, USA, D.S.M. (3), Bronze Star (3), Legion of Merit, Def. Superior Service medal. Mem. Nat. Def. Transp. Assn., Assn. U.S. Army (Pres.'s award 1992). Lutheran. Office: Logistics Mgmt Inst 2000 Corporate Rdg Mc Lean VA 22102-7805

TUTTLE, WILLIAM MCCULLOUGH, JR., history educator; b. Detroit, Oct. 7, 1937; s. William McCullough and Geneva (Duvall) T.; m. Linda Lee Stumpp, Dec. 12, 1959 (div.); children: William McCullough III, Catharine D., Andrew S.; m. Kathryn Nemeth, May 6, 1995. BA, Denison U., 1959; MA, U. Wis., 1964, PhD, 1967. Faculty mem. U. Kans., Lawrence, 1967—, prof. history, 1975—, intra-univ. prof., 1982-83; sr. fellow in So. and Negro history Johns Hopkins U., 1969-70; Charles Warren fellow Harvard U., Cambridge, Mass., 1972-73; vis. prof. U. Sc., Columbia, 1980; assoc. fellow Stanford Humanities Ctr., 1983-84; research assoc. U. Calif., Berkeley, 1986-88; vis. scholar Radcliffe Coll., 1993-94. Author: Race Riot: Chicago in the Red Summer of 1919, 1970, W.E.B. Du Bois, 1973, (with David M. Katzman) Plain Folk, 1982, (with others) A People and A Nation, 1982, 4th edit., 1994, "Daddy's Gone to War": The Second World War in the Lives of America's Children, 1993; contbr. chpts. to books, numerous articles to profl. jours. Dem. precinct committeeman, Lawrence, 1980-90. Lt. USAF, 1959-62. Recipient Merit award Am. Assn. for State and Local History, 1972; Younger Humanist fellow NEH, 1972-73, Guggenheim fellow, 1975-76, NEH fellow, 1983-84, rsch. fellow Hall Ctr., 1990; grantee Evans, 1975-76, Beveridge, 1982, NEH, 1986-89. Mem. Soc. Am. Historians (elected), Am. Hist. Assn., Orgn. Am. Historians, Am. Studies Assn., So. Hist. Assn., Lawrence Trout Club, Golden Key (hon.), Omicron Delta Kappa, Phi Beta Delta, Phi Gamma Delta. Home: 713 Louisiana St Lawrence KS 66044-2339 Office: U Kans Dept History Lawrence KS 66045

TUTTLETON, JAMES WESLEY, English educator; b. St. Louis, Aug. 19, 1934; s. Clarence M. and Nora Belle (Sutt) T. B.A., Harding U., Searcy, Ark., 1955; M.A., U. N.C., 1957, Ph.D., 1963. Instr. Clemson U., S.C., 1956-59, U. N.C., Chapel Hill, 1962-63; asst. prof. U. Wis., Madison, 1963-68; assoc. prof. English NYU, N.Y.C., 1968-74, prof., 1974—, chmn. dept., 1974-83; assoc. dean Grad Sch. Arts & Scis. NYU, 1988-89. Author: The Novel of Manners in America, 1972, Thomas Wentworth Higginson, 1978; editor: The American (Henry James), 1978, Washington Irving: History, Tales and Sketches, 1983, Voyages and Discoveries of the Companions of Columbus (Washington Irving), 1986, The Sweetest Impression of Life: The James Family and Italy, 1990, Edith Wharton: The Contemporary Reviews, 1992, Washington Irving: The Critical Reaction, 1993, Vital Signs: Essays on American Literature and Criticism, 1996. Served with USAFR, 1956-63. Mem. Century Assn. Home: 37 Washington Square W 11-D New York NY 10011 Office: NYU Dept English New York NY 10003

TUTUN, EDWARD H., retired retail executive; b. Boston, Jan. 26, 1924; s. J.J. and Esther L. T.; m. Joan M. Bocoffer, Oct. 23, 1953. B.S. in chem. Engring., Northeastern U., 1947. V.p. W.R. Grace & Co., N.Y.C., 1978-82, sr. v.p., 1982-83, exec. v.p., 1983-87, ret., 1987; vice chmn. Herman's Sporting Goods, Inc., Cartaret, N.J., 1983. Served with USAAF, 1942-45, ETO. Mem. Nat. Retail Mchts. Assn. (dir. 1983), DIY Inst. (dir. 1983). Club: N.Y. Yacht (N.Y.C.). Home: 544 Pinellas Bayway S Tierra Verde FL 33715-1966 also: 237 Guinea Rd Stamford CT 06903-3722 Office: WR Grace & Co 1114 Avenue Of The Americas New York NY 10036-7703

TUTWILER, CHARLES RICHARD (DICK TUTWILER), insurance company executive; b. Charleston, W.Va., Dec. 26, 1946; s. Jacob Oliver and Mary Helen (Nesbet) T.; m. Linda Ann Julia, Oct. 6, 1979; 1 child, Richard Patrick. BBA, Marshall U., 1973. Various positions Travelers Ins. Co., Tampa, Fla., 1973-83; property ops. pres. Charles R. Tutwiler & Assocs., Inc., Tampa, 1983—. Editor/pub. (newsletter) Jour. for Ins. Loss Adjusting, 1989, Quar. Update F.A.P.I.A., 1993. Mem. Clara Barton Soc. Red Cross, Tampa, 1993. With USAF, 1965-69. Mem. Am. Arbitration Assn., Soc. of Claim Law Assn., Nat. and State Assn. of Pub. Ins. Adjustors, Tampa Bay Exec. Assn. (bd. dirs. 1990—), Fla. Assn. of Pub. Ins. Adjustors (com. chmn. 1993), Community Assn. Inst., The John Marshall Soc. (Marshall U.). Avocations: boating, jogging, scuba diving, family. Office: Ste 720 2203 N Lois Ave Tampa FL 33607 Home: 17517 Mallard Ct Lutz FL 33549-5559

TUYAKBAEV, ZHARMAKHAN AITBAJEVICH, prosecutor; b. Kazgurt District, South Kazakhstan Region, Kazakhstan, Nov. 22, 1947; s. Aitbaj and Tynyn (Kenshymbaeva) T.; m. Bagila Nagometovna Aptaeva, May 19, 1972; children: Aziza, Tchingiz, Adilzhan. Degree, Kazakh State U., Almaty, Kazakhstan, 1971. Cert. lawyer. Asst. chief inquiry dept. Office of the Prosecutor, South Kazakhstan Region, Tchimkent, Kazakhstan, 1971-78; with South Kazakhstan Region Office, Tchimkent, Kazakhstan, 1978-81; dep. to gen. prosecutor Office of the Prosecutor, Republic of Kazakhstan, Almaty, Kazakhstan, 1981-87; prosecutor of Atyrau Office of the Prosecutor, Atyrau Region, Atyrau, Kazakhstan, 1987-90; gen. prosecutor Office of the Prosecutor, Republic of Kazakhstan, Atyrau, Kazakhstan, 1990—; dep. of Oblast Soviet Atyrau Region, Atyrau, 1989-91; dep. Parlament of Kazakhstan Supreme Coun. of Kazakhstan, Almaty, 1990-93. Recipient Devoted Work medal USSR, 1982, Honorary Worker badge USSR, 1984; named State Counsellor of Justice Republic of Kazakhstan, 1982. Avocation: tennis. Home: Internationalnaya Street 120-16, Almaty Kazakhstan Office: Embassy of Kazakhstan 3421 Massachusetts Ave NW Washington DC 20007-1446

TUZLA, KEMAL, mechanical engineer, scientist; b. Adapazari, Sakarya, Turkey, Feb. 23, 1943; came to U.S., 1974; s. Hayrettin and Muberra (Horozlu) T.; m. Asuman Fatma Cokmez. MME, Istanbul (Turkey) Tech. U., 1966, PhD in Mech. Engring., 1972. Instr. Istanbul Tech. U., 1966-72, asst. prof., 1974, assoc. prof., 1978-81; instr. Air Force Coll., Istanbul, 1973-74; rsch. asst. prof. U. Wash., Seattle, 1974-78; sr. rsch. scientist Lehigh U., Bethlehem, Pa., 1981—; mem. organizing com. 2d Thermal Sci. Conf., Istanbul; 1979, 3d Conf., Trabzon, Turkey, 1981; cons. Goodyear Tire & Rubber Co., Akron, Ohio, 1984-86, Exxon Nuclear, Richland, Wash., 1985-88. Editor Proc. 2d Thermal Sci. Conf., 1979; contbr. articles in area of thermal scis. to profl. jours. Co-founder Turkish Am. Cultural Assn., Seattle, 1977. Rsch. grantee Goodyear Tire & Rubber Co., 1985-86, Los Alamos (N.Mex.) Nat. Lab., 1989-91, Ben Franklin Tech. Ctr., Bethlehem, 1989-96, Gas Rsch. Inst., 1987-91, Elec. Power Rsch. Inst., 1991-94. Mem. ASHRAE, AIChE. Achievements include research in heat transfer in two-phase flows, boiling, fluidized beds, electronic components and nuclear safety. Avocations: skiing, tennis, chess, bridge. Home: 96 Valley Park S Bethlehem PA 18018-1360 Office: Lehigh U Chem Engring Iacocca Hall 111 Research Dr Bethlehem PA 18015-4732

TWA, CRAIGHTON OLIVER, utility company executive; b. Drumheller, Alta., Can., Oct. 15, 1937; s. Joe Philander and Freda Alice (Fowler) T.; m. Irene Adam, May 7, 1960; children: Tracy, Robert, Carey. BSEE, U. Alta., Edmonton, 1959. Registered profl. engr., Alta. Engr. Can. Utilities Ltd., Edmonton, 1959-80; v.p. customer svcs. Alta Power Ltd., Edmonton, 1980-85, sr. v.p., gen. mgr., 1985-86, pres., 1986-93; pres. CU Power div. Can. Utilities Ltd., Edmonton, 1988-93; exec. v.p. Can. Utilities Ltd., Edmonton, 1994—, Can. Utilities Ltd. and ATCO Ltd. Office of the Chmn., 1995—; bd. dirs. Alta. Power ltd., CU Power Internat. Ltd., Northland Utilitiess Enterprises Ltd., The Yukon Elec. Co. Ltd., Thames Power Ltd., Frontec Logistics Corp., Can. Western Natural Gas Co. Ltd., Northwestern Utilities Ltd. Mem. Assn. Profl. Engrs., Geologists and Geophysicists Alta. Office: ATCO Ltd, 1600 909-11th Ave SW, Calgary, AB Canada T2R 1N6

TWADDLE, ANDREW CHRISTIAN, sociology educator; b. Hartford, Conn., Apr. 21, 1938; s. Paul Holmes and Ruth Bridenbaugh (Christian) T.; m. Sarah A. Wolcott, June 15, 1963; children: Lisa, Kristin. AB, Bucknell U., 1961; MA, U. Conn., 1963; PhD, Brown U., 1968. Instr. sociology Coll. of Holy Cross, Worcester, Mass., 1966-67; instr. preventive medicine Harvard U. Med. Sch., Boston, 1967-69; asst. prof. sociology and community medicine U. Pa., Phila., 1969-71; assoc. prof. sociology and family and community medicine U. Mo., Columbia, 1971-74, prof. sociology, 1974—, chmn. dept., 1988-93; guest prof. U. Göteborg, Sweden, 1978-79; Fulbright rsch. fellow Linköping U., Sweden, 1993; guest rschr. Uppsala U., Sweden, 1993. Author: Sickness Behavior and the Sick Role, 1979; co-author: A Sociology of Health, 1987, Disease, Illness and Sickness, 1994, Salvaging Medical Care, 1994. Chair Columbia Bd. Health, 1980-83. Recipient John Kosa Meml. prize Pergamon Press, Eng., 1974. Mem. Internat. Sociol. Assn., Am. Sociol. Assn., Midwest Sociol. Soc., Muleskinners Club (v.p. 1985-87, 94—). Democrat. Unitarian-Universalist. Avocations: genealogy, sailing. Home: 919 Edgewood Ave Columbia MO 65203-2823 Office: U Mo Dept Sociology 109 Sociology Columbia MO 65211

TWAIN, SHANIA, country musician; b. Windsor, Can.. Recs. include Shania Twain, The Woman in Me (Album of Yr. Canadian Country Music Awards, 1995, Female Video Artist of Yr. ABC Radio Networks Country Music Awards, 1995, Album of Yr. Acad. Country Music Awards, 1996, Grammy award for Best Country Album 1996). Recipient Rising Star award Country Music TV/Europe, 1993, Favorite New Country Artist Am. Music Awards, 1995, Female Vocalist award Canadian Country Music Awards, 1995, Outstanding New Artist award RPM's Big Country Awards, 1995, Top New Female Vocalist award Acad. of Country Music Awards, 1996, Favorite New Country Artist award Blockbuster Entertainment Awards, 1996, Female Artist of Yr. Country Music TV/Europe, 1996, Internat. Rising Star award Gt. British Country Music Awards, 1996, Country Female Vocalist award Juno, 1996, Entertainer of Yr. award Juno, 1996, others. Office: Mercury Nashville 66 Music Sq W Nashville TN 37203

TWARDOWICZ, STANLEY JAN, artist, photographer; b. Detroit, July 8, 1917; s. Joseph and Anna Ligenski; m. Lillian Dodson, Mar. 15, 1971. Student, Meinzinger Art Sch., Detroit, 1940-44, Skowhegan (Maine) Sch. Painting and Sculpture, summer 1946. Instr. Ohio State U., 1946-51; prof. Hofstra U., 1965-87. Exhibited paintings Mus. Modern Art, Guggenheim Mus., Whitney Mus., Art Inst. Chgo., Carnegie Internat., Pa. Acad. Fine Arts, Am. Acad. Arts and Letters, Houston Mus., Milw. Art Ctr., Peridot Gallery, N.Y.C., others; retrospective exhbns. Hecksher Mus., Huntington, N.Y., 1974, Emily Lowe Gallery, Hempstead, N.Y., 1979, 40 Yr. Retrospective of Paintings Firehouse Gallery, Garden City, N.Y.; exhibited photographs Images Gallery, N.Y.C., one man show: Odeon Gallery, Sag Harbor, N.Y., 1993, Ursala Lanning Gallery, Columbus, Ohio, 1995; represented in permanent collections Mus. Modern Art, L.A. County Mus., Newark Mus., Milw. Art Ctr., Ball State Tchrs. Coll., Harvard U., Vassar Coll., Hirshhorn Mus. and Sculpture Garden, others. Guggenheim fellow, 1956. Home: 133 Crooked Hill Rd Huntington NY 11743-3811

TWARDY, STANLEY ALBERT, JR., lawyer; b. Trenton, N.J., Sept. 13, 1951; s. Stanley Albert Twardy and Dorothy M. Stonaker. BS with honors, Trinity Coll., 1973; JD, U. Va., 1976; LLM, Georgetown U., 1980. Bar: Conn. 1976, D.C. 1978, U.S. Supreme Ct. 1979, U.S. Ct. Appeals (2d cir.) 1984. Assoc. Whitman & Ransom, Greenwich, Conn., 1976-77; counsel com. on small bus. U.S. Senate, 1977-79, counsel to Senator Lowell Weicker Jr., 1979-80; ptnr. Silver, Golub & Sandak, Stamford, Conn., 1980-85; U.S. atty. Dist. of Conn., New Haven, 1985-91; chief of staff Office of Gov. Lowell Weicker, Conn., 1991-93; ptnr. Day, Berry & Howard, Stamford, Conn., 1993—. Mem. vestry St. John's Episcopal Ch., Stamford, 1983-86; bd. dirs. Drugs Don't Work!, 1989-93, 94—, chmn. program com., 1989-91; mem. nat. alumni exec. com. Trinity Coll., 1985-90, mem. athletic adv. com., 1992—; bd. dirs. Spl. Olympics World Summer Games Organizing Com., Inc., 1993-95, Easter Seals Rehab. Ctr. S.W. Conn., Inc., 1993—; chmn. City of Stamford Police Chief Selection Panel, 1993-94; mem. area adv. com. U. Conn. at Stamford, 1993—; mem. strategic planning mgmt. com. U. Conn., 1993-95; bd. dirs. Stamford Hosp. Health Found.; trustee Trinity Coll. Mem. ABA, Conn. Bar Assn., Assn. Trial Lawyers Am., Conn. Trial Lawyers Assn., Phi Beta Kappa. Office: One Canterbury Green Stamford CT 06901

TWARDZIK, DAVE, professional basketball team executive; b. Middletown, Pa.; m. Kathe Twardzik; children: Monika, Matthew. Student, Old Dominion U. Profl. basketball player Virginia Squires, 1972-76; profl. basketball player Portland (Oreg.) Trail Blazers, 1976-81, dir. cmty. rels., radio analyst, account exec., 1981-86; asst. basketball coach Indiana Pacers, Indpls., 1986-89, L.A. Clippers, 1989-90; scouting dir., dir. player pers. Charlotte (N.C.) Hornets, 1990-95; gen. mgr. Golden State Warriors, Oakland, Calif., 1995—. Avocations: fishing, hunting. Office: Oakland Coliseum Arena 700 Coliseum Way Oakland CA 94621-1918

TWAROG, SOPHIA NORA, economist; b. Columbus, Ohio, Nov. 29, 1964; d. Leon I. and Katherine (Foster) T.; m. Alberto Klaas, July 2, 1993; 1 child, Kevin Leon Twarog Klaas. BA in Econs. magna cum laude, U. Notre Dame, Ind., 1987; MA in Economics, Ohio State U., 1989, PhD in Economics, 1993. Intern Ctr. of Concern, Washington; vol. in Ctr. America Sisters of the Assumption, Phila., 1987-88; vol. in India Christian Found. for Children & Aging, Kansas City, Mo., 1988; rsch. cons. Nat. Bur. Econ. Rsch., Cambridge, Mass., 1990; grad. teaching assoc. Ohio State U., Columbus, 1989-91; econ. affairs officer UN Conf. on Trade and Devel., Geneva, 1993—; contbd. to preparation of UN Internat. Symposium on Trade Efficiency, Columbus, 1994. Contbr. articles to books. Founder, pres. Overseas Devel. Network-U. Notre Dame, 1986-87; chmn. First Ann. Great Hunger Clean-up, South Bend, Ind., 1987; chmn., co-chmn. Third World Awareness Week, U. Notre Dame, 1986, 87. Recipient Glenna R. Joyce scholar Joyce Found., 1983-87, John W. Gardner Leadership award U. Notre Dame, 1987; U. Multi-Yr. fellow Ohio State U., 1988, 92, rsch. fellow Rheinische Friedrich-Wilhelms U., Bonn, 1990-91, Dice fellow Ohio State U., 1993. Mem. Am. Econ. Assn., Phi Beta Kappa, Phi Kappa Phi. Avocations: traveling, hiking, stained glass artwork, silk painting, salsa dancing, reading. Home: 182 Oakland Park Ave Columbus OH 43214-4122 Office: UN Conf on Trade & Devel, Palais Des Nations, Ch 1211 Geneva 10, Switzerland

TWAY, STEPHEN EDWARD, marketing communications executive, consultant; b. Chillicothe, Ohio, May 13, 1943; s. Rollin E. and Marjorie E. (Householder) T.; children: John Rollin, Matthew James. BS in Bus., Miami U., Oxford, Ohio, 1965. With Marine Midland Grace Trust, 1965-66, Huntington Nat. Bank, 1968-74; ptnr. Tway Lumber Co., 1974-84; owner Indsl. Grade Photography, Columbus, Ohio, 1986—; v.p., creative dir. Veda Gilp Assocs., Columbus, 1984—. Contbr. over 200 articles to profl. jours.; numerous pub. photos. With U.S. Army, 1966-68. Mem. Profl. Photographers Am., Columbus Computer Soc., Sanyo Users of Cen. Ohio. Avocation: gourmet cooking, oenology, collecting antiques. Office: Veda Gilp Assocs 937 S 3rd St Columbus OH 43206-2542

TWEEDIE, RICHARD LEWIS, statistics educator, consultant; b. Leeton, NSW, Australia, Aug. 22, 1947; came to U.S., 1991; s. Lewis Chabaud and Nel (Dahlenburg) T.; m. Catherine Robertson, Sept. 13, 1971; 1 child, Marianne Louise Robertson. BA, Australian Nat. U., Canberra, 1968, MA, 1969, DSc, 1986; PhD, Cambridge (Eng.) U., 1972. Sr. rsch. scientist Commonwealth Sci. and Indsl. Rsch. Orgn., Canberra, 1974-77; prin. rsch. scientist Commonwealth Sci. and Indsl. Rsch. Orgn., Melbourne, Australia, 1979-81; assoc. prof. U. Western Australia, Perth, 1978; gen. mgr. Siromath Pty. Ltd., Sydney, Australia, 1981-83, mng. dir., 1983-87; prof., dean Bond U., Gold Coast, Australia, 1987-91; prof. stats. Colo. State U., Ft. Collins, 1991—, chair dept. stats., 1992—. Author: Markov Chains and Stochastic Stability, 1993; also over 90 articles. Fellow Inst. Math. Stats., Internat. Statis. Inst.; mem. Statis. Soc. Australia (pres. 1984-85). Avocations: squash, science fiction. Office: Colo State U Dept Stats Fort Collins CO 80523-1877

TWEEDY, ROBERT HUGH, equipment company executive; b. Mt. Pleasant, Iowa, Mar. 24, 1928; s. Robert and Olatha (Miller) T.; B.S. in Agrl. Engring., Iowa State U., 1952; m. Genevieve Strauss, Aug. 15, 1969; children—Bruce, Mark; 1 stepdau., Mary Ellen Francis. Sr. engr. John Deere Waterloo Tractor Works, Waterloo, Iowa, 1953-64; mktg. rep. U.S. Steel Corp., Pitts., 1964-68; mgr. product planning agrl. equipment div. Allis-Chalmers Corp., Milw., 1969-76, mgr. strategic bus. planning Agrl. Equipment Co., 1976-85; mgr. strategic bus. planning Deutz-Allis Corp., 1985-89; project mgr. AGCO Corp., Batavia, Ill., 1989-94; retired, 1994; chmn. agrl. research com. Farm and Indsl. Equipment Inst., Chgo., 1974-76, mem. safety policy adv. com., 1972-89; mem. farm conf. Nat. Safety Council, Chgo., 1973-89; mem. industry sector adv. com. No. 16, U.S. Dept. Commerce, 1982-85; bd. dirs. C.V. Riley Meml. Found. Recipient citation in engring. Iowa State U., 1983. Fellow Am. Soc. Agrl. Engrs. (v.p. 1974-78, pres. 1981-82, gen. chmn. hdqrs. bldg. project 1968-70; chmn. Found. Trustees 1983-88, Wis. Engr. of Year award 1980, McCormick-Case Gold medal 1989); mem. Soc. Automotive Engrs., Masons. Patentee in field. Home: 1340 Bonnie Ln Brookfield WI 53045-5423

TWENTYMAN, LEE, foreign service officer, economist; b. Cortland, N.Y., June 12, 1947; s. Gerald L. and Esther (Forbes) T. BS, Cornell U., 1969; MS, U. Md., 1973. Mktg. specialist Export Mktg. Svc., USDA, Washington, 1973; internat. devel. intern U.S. AID, Asuncion, Paraguay, 1973-75; capital projects officer U.S. AID, Santiago, Chile, 1975-76; dir. devel. resources U.S. AID, Lima, Peru, 1976-81; dir. Food for Peace U.S. AID, Washington, 1981-83; dir. for Lebanon U.S. AID, Beirut, 1983-84; dep. dir. for Thailand U.S. AID, Bangkok, 1984-88; dep. dir. for Indonesia U.S. AID, Jakarta, 1988-91; AID dir. to Cambodia U.S. AID, Phnom Penh, 1991—. Mem. Royal Bangkok Sports Club. Address: PO Box 1418 Sarasota FL 34230

TWERSKY, VICTOR, mathematical physicist, educator; b. Lublin, Poland, Aug. 10, 1923; came to U.S., 1928, naturalized, 1940; s. Israel and Gertrude (Levinson) T.; m. Shirley Fine, Feb. 26, 1950; children: Lori, Mark, Nina. B.S., CCNY, 1947; A.M., Columbia U., 1948; Ph.D., N.Y. U., 1950. Assoc. guidance project, biology dept. CCNY, 1946-49; teaching asst. physics N.Y. U., 1949; research assoc. electromagnetic theory Courant Inst. Math. Scis., 1950-53; assoc. Nuclear Devel. Assos., 1951-53; with Sylvania Electric-Gen. Telephone Electronics, 1953-66; head research Electronic Def. Labs., 1958-66, Electronics Systems-West, 1964-66; prof. math. U. Ill. at Chgo., 1966-90, prof. emeritus, 1991; lectr. Stanford U., 1956-58; vis. prof. Technion-Israel Inst. Tech., Haifa, 1962-63, Hebrew U., Jerusalem, summer 1972, Tel Aviv U., summer 1972, Weizmann Inst. Sci., Rehovoth, 1979, Ben-Gurion U., Beersheva, 1979, Stanford U., 1972, 73, 79-80, summers 1967-89, vis. scholar, 1991-96, others; summer mem. Courant Inst. Math. Scis., 1963; assoc. Ctr. for Advanced Study, U. Ill., 1969-70; cons. in field. Editor jours. in field.; contbr. articles to profl. jours. Mem. tech. research com. Am. Found. for Blind, 1947-49; mem. Sch. Math. Study Group, 1964-66, U.S. com. B, Internat. Sci. Radio Union; mem.-at-large Conf. Bd. Math. Scis., 1975-77. Served with AUS, 1943-46. Guggenheim fellow, 1972-73, 79-80. Fellow AAAS, Am. Phys. Soc., Acoustical Soc. Am., Optical Soc. Am. (dir.-at-large 1961), IEEE; mem. Am. Math Soc., Soc. Indsl. and Applied Math., Sci. Research So. Am. (pres. Sequoia br. 1958). Address: 14848 Manuella Rd Los Altos CA 94022-2026

TWICHELL, CHASE, poet; b. New Haven, Conn., Aug. 20, 1950; d. Charles P. and Ann (Chase) T. BA, Trinity Coll., Hartford, 1973; MFA, U. Iowa, 1976. Editor Pennyroyal Pr., W. Hatfield, Mass., 1976-84; assoc. prof. English U. Ala., 1984-88; asst. prof. Hampshire Coll., 1983-84; co-editor Alabama Poetry Series, 1984-88; lectr. Princeton U., 1990—. Author: (poetry) Northern Spy, 1981, The Odds, 1986, Perdido, 1991, The Ghost of Eden, 1995; editor: The Practice of Poetry, 1992, Borderlands, 1993. Recipient Acad. award in lit. Am. Acad. Arts and Letters, 1994; Nat. Endowment for Arts fellow, 1987, 93, Guggenheim fellow, 1990. Office: Princeton U Creative Writing Program 185 Nassau St Princeton NJ 08540

TWIFORD, TRAVIS W., school system administrator. Supt. Elizabeth City-Pasquotank Schs., Elizabeth City, N.C. Recipient Nat. Superintendent of the Yr. awd., North Carolina, Am. Assn. of School Administrators, 1992. Office: Elizabeth City Pasquotank Schs PO Box 2247 1200 Halstead Blvd Elizabeth City NC 27909

TWIGG-SMITH, THURSTON, newspaper publisher; b. Honolulu, Aug. 17, 1921; s. William and Margaret Carter (Thurston) Twigg-S.; m. Bessie Bell, June 9, 1942 (div. Feb. 1983); children: Elizabeth, Thurston, William, Margaret, Evelyn; m. Laila Roster, Feb. 22, 1983 (div. Dec. 1994); m. Sharon Smith, Feb. 28, 1996. B.Engring., Yale U., 1942. With Honolulu Advertiser, 1946—, mng. editor, 1954-60, asst. bus. mgr., 1960-61, pub., 1961-86; pres., dir., chief exec. officer Honolulu Advertiser, Inc., 1962-93, chmn., 1993—; chmn., dir., CEO Persis Corp.; bd. dirs. Atalanta/Sosnoff Capital Corp., N.Y. Trustee Punahou Sch., Old Sturbridge Inc., Honolulu Acad. Arts, The Contemporary Mus., Hawaii, Mus. Contemporary Art, L.A., The Skowhegan Sch., Maine, Yale Art Gallery, New Haven, Philatelic Found., N.Y., Whitney Mus. Am. Art, N.Y. Maj. AUS, 1942-46. Mem. Honolulu C. of C., Waialae Country Club, Pacific Club, Oaho Country Club, Outrigger Canoe Club. Office: Persis Corp PO Box 3110 96802 605 Kapiolani Blvd Honolulu HI 96813

TWINAME, B. GAYLE, nursing educator, mental health nurse; b. White Plains, N.Y.; d. James Dean and Beatrice DeNike (Hunter) T. BSN, U. North Fla., 1978; MSN, Med. Coll. Ga., 1979; MEd, Lamar U., 1985; PhD, Tex. Woman's U., 1992. Cert. CGP Registry of Group Psychotherapists. Assoc. prof. Lamar U., Beaumont, Tex., 1979—; adv. bd. Rape & Suicide Crisis, Beaumont, 1984-92; cons. Bapt. Hosp. Southeast Tex., Beaumont, 1990-93; bd. dirs. Triangle AIDS Network. Author: (with others) Statistical Analysis, 1994; contbr. articles to profl. jours. Mem. ANA (cert. CS), Am. Psychiat. Nurses Assn., Tex. Nurses Assn. (rec. sec. 1988-90), Tex. AIDS Network, Assn. of Nurses in AIDS Care, Mensa, Kappa Kappa, Sigma Theta Tau (counselor 1990-94). Avocations: computers, creative writing, farming, reading, exercise. Office: Lamar U P O Box 22122 Beaumont TX 77720-2122

TWINAME, JOHN DEAN, minister, health care executive; b. Mt. Kisco, N.Y., Dec. 27, 1931; s. C.G. and Constance Jean (Ulmer) T.; m. Carolyn Anderson, Aug. 6, 1955; children: Karen, Jeanne, Julia. A.B., Cornell U., 1953; M.B.A., Harvard U., 1957; M.Div., Union Theol. Sem., 1983. Ordained to ministry Presbyn. Ch. 1983. Sales rep. Am. Hosp. Supply Corp., Evanston, Ill., 1957-60; dir. product research Am. Hosp. Supply Corp., 1961, sales mgr., 1962, asst. to div. pres., 1963, product mgr., 1964, mktg. mgr., 1965-67, mktg. v.p., 1968-69; dep. adminstr. Social and Rehab. Service, HEW, Washington, 1969-70; adminstr. Social and Rehab. Service, HEW, 1970-73; adminstr. Office Health Office Health, Cost of Living Coun., 1973-74; pvt. cons. Mott-McDonald Assocs., Inc., Washington, 1974-76, pres., 1976-78; exec. v.p. Am. Health Found., N.Y.C., 1978-81; co-pres. HealthCare Chaplaincy, Inc., N.Y.C., 1983-93, co-chair exec. com., 1993-94, life trustee, 1995—; voting mem. Empire Blue Cross/Blue Shield, 1994. Chmn. bd. Chgo. Bus.-Indsl. Project, 1967-68, People to People Com. for Handicapped, 1976-78, Bauman Bible Telecasts, Inc., 1976-80; treas. U.S. com. Internat. Council Social Welfare, 1977-80; sec. bd. dirs. U.S. Council Internat. Year of Disabled Persons, 1979-81; founding bd. mem. Am. Paralysis Assn. (formerly Paralysis Cure Research), 1976-83; bd. dirs. Epilepsy Found. Am., 1978-85, N.Y. Regional Transplant Program, 1988-92; mem. pres. coun. United Hosp. Fund, 1991—. 1st lt. AUS, 1953-55. Recipient Disting. Svc. award Coll. Chaplains, 1992, Baker scholar, Harvard U. Home: 163 Harbor Rd Southport CT 06490-1320 Office: HealthCare Chaplaincy Inc 307 E 60th St New York NY 10022

TWINING, BEVERLY A., critical care nurse; b. Glen Cove, N.Y., May 10, 1944; d. Harold C. and Lois (Linton) T. RN, Meth. Hosp. of Bklyn., 1965; student in nursing, SUNY, Stony Brook, 1993. Charge nurse Winthrop Hosp., Mineola, N.Y., Cen. Gen. Hosp., Plainview, N.Y., Mather Meml. Hosp., Port Jefferson, N.Y., Sunrest Nursing Home, Port Jefferson; pvt. duty nurse CNR Agy., L.I. Mem. ACCN, N.Y. State Nurses Assn. Address: PO Box 571 Mount Sinai NY 11766-0571

TWINING, CHARLES HAILE, ambassador; b. Balt., Nov. 1, 1940; s. Charles Haile and Martha R. (Caples) T.; m. Irene Verann Metz, May 30, 1995; children: Daniel, Steven. BA, U. Va., 1962; MA, Johns Hopkins U., 1964; postgrad., Cornell U., 1977-78. Joined Fgn. Svc., Dept. State, Washington, 1964; former dep. chief of mission Am. Embassy, Cotonou; former prin. officer Am. Embassy, Douala; former dep. chief of mission Am. Embassy, Ouagadougou, Burkina Faso; former dir. Office of Vietnam, Laos and Cambodia Dept. State, Washington; amb. to Cambodia Phnom Penh, 1993—; Contbr.: Cambodia: 1975-78, 1990. Office: Dept State Washington DC 20520

TWINING, LYNNE DIANNE, psychotherapist, researcher, writer; b. Midland, Mich., Aug. 14, 1951; d. James and Dorothy Twining; m. Alan Howard Mass. BA in Psychology, Oakland U., 1974; MSW, Wayne State U., 1977; MA in Psychology, Yeshiva U., 1993. Diplomate Am. Bd. Clin. Social Work; cert. Bklyn. Inst. Psychotherapy and Psychoanalysis. Social work supr. non-profit orgn., Detroit, 1977-83; co-founder, co-dir. Women Psychotherapists Bklyn., 1986—; pvt. practice Bklyn. and N.Y.C., 1987—; psychotherapy rschr. Beth Israel Med. Ctr., N.Y.C., 1992—. Author: (with other) Metro Detroit Guide, 1975; contbg. editor: Detroit Guide, 1983; asst. prodr. docudrama Home; columnist Bklyn. Woman; contbr. articles to profl. jours., papers to profl. confs. Bd. dirs. Progressive Artists and Educators Coalition, Detroit, 1977-79. Fellow Am. Orthopsychiat. Assn.; mem. NASW (diplomate), ACLU (sec. exec. bd. Mich. chpt. 1982-83), Internat. Fedn. Psychoanalytical Edn., N.Y. Acad. Scis., Soc. for Psychotherapy Rsch., Nat. Trust for Hist. Preservation, Tng. Inst. Mental Health Practitioners, Nat. Assn. Advancement Psychoanalysis (affiliate), Women Psychotherapists Bklyn. (founding mem.), Amnesty Internat. (freedom writer), Acad. Cert. Social Workers, Bklyn. Inst. Psychotherapy and Psychoanalysis Grad. Assn (mem. steering com.). Avocations: comparative literature, contemporary dance, jazz. Office: 55 Eastern Pky Apt 3A Brooklyn NY 11238-5913

TWISDALE, HAROLD WINFRED, dentist; b. Roanoke Rapids, N.C., Apr. 28, 1933; s. James Robert and Elma (Smith) T.; m. Barbara Ann Edmonds, Aug. 2, 1958 (div. Apr. 1974); children: Harold Winfred, Leigh Ann.; m. Frances Jean Winstead, July 1983. B.S. in Dentistry, U. N.C., 1955, D.D.S., 1958. Individual practice dentistry Charlotte, N.C., 1961—; head, dept. dental prosthetics Meml. Hosp., 1964-66; lectr. dental subjects.; pres., gen. mgr. WCTU-TV, Charlotte Telecasters, Inc., 1967-69, WATU-TV, Augusta, Ga., Augusta Telecasters, Inc., 1968-69, Television Presentations, Inc., Charlotte, 1967-69; partner Twisdale and Steel Assos., Charlotte, 1965-70; propr. Twisdale Enterprises, Charlotte, 1965-70; Pres. Memphis Telecasters, Inc., 1966-76, Va. Telecasters, Inc., Richmond, 1966—, Durham-Raleigh Telecasters, Inc., Durham, N.C., 1966-70, Gentil Elite, Inc., 1979—. Transp. chmn. Miss N.C. Pageant, 1965; v.p. N.C. Jaycees, 1963-64; Trustee Boys Home, Lake Waccomaw, N.C., 1966-67. Served to capt. USAF, 1958-60. Recipient various awards Charlotte Jaycees, 1962-66. Mem. ADA, N.C. Dental Found., N.C. Dental Soc., Charlotte Dental Soc. (chmn. various coms. 1961—), Am. Analgesia Soc., Internat. Analgesic Soc. (dir. 1980-85), N.C. Dental Soc. Anesthesiology (v.p. 1983-84), Charlotte Analgesia Study Club (co-founder 1970), N.C. 2d Dist. Dental Soc., Metrolina Dental Soc. (founder 1994, pres. 1994-95), U. N.C. Dental Alumni Assn., Southeastern Analgesia Soc. (founder 1972, pres. 1972-74), Lambda Chi Alpha, Delta Sigma Delta. Republican. Methodist. Home: 4212 Burning Tree Dr 2221 Streatley Ln Matthews NC 28105-6648 Office: 6623 Executive Circle #110 PO Box 25528 Charlotte NC 28212 *I must give the full credit for any achievement I might have accomplished in life to my mother and father. They not only provided me the means and direction one needs to make even the slightest accomplishment in our mortal life, but most of all, they gave me love, understanding, and a sense of values. These values have never deserted me, nor have they been compromised, even in the darkest hours of depression or during the brightest times of accomplishment. They have been my steady companions.*

TWISS, JOHN R., JR., federal government agency executive; b. N.Y.C., Sept. 16, 1938; s. John R. and Edith Jordan (Liddell) T.; m. Mary Hawthorne Sheldon, Jan. 20, 1973; children: John Stewart, Alison McIntosh, Emily Ellsworth. BA, Yale U., 1961. Polar rschr. U.S. Govt., 1961-63; NSF rep. in charge U.S. Sci. Programs in Antarctica, 1964-65; mem. staff internat. divsn. Smith Kline & French Labs., 1966-67; v.p. EPC Labs., 1967-68; sci. leader So. Ocean expdn. NSF, 1968-69, spl. asst. to head Internat. Decade Ocean Exploration, 1970-74; exec. dir. Marine Mammal Commn., Washington, 1974—; mem. strategic adv. coun. Sch. Forestry and Environ. Studies Yale U., New Haven, 1990—, assoc. fellow Branford Coll., 1990—; mem. adminstrv. bd. Michael C. Rockefeller Meml. fellowship Harvard U., 1991—; chmn. bd. dirs. Kokrobitey Sch., Ghana, 1992—; bd. overseers Leadership Decisions Inst., 1992—; lectr., cons. in field; mem. numerous adv. coms. and U.S. dels. V.p. Turkey Run Citizens Assn., 1989-92, pres., 1994—. Mem. ASPA, Met. Club, Army and Navy Club, Squadron A Club, Ends of the Earth Club. Office: Marine Mammal Commn Rm 512 1825 Connecticut Ave NW Ste 512 Washington DC 20009-5708

TWISS, PAGE CHARLES, geology educator; b. Columbus, Ohio, Jan. 2, 1929; s. George Ransom and Blanche (Olin) T.; m. Nancy Homer Hubbard, Aug. 29, 1954; children—Stephen Ransom, Catherine Grace, Thomas Stuart. B.S. in Geology, Kans. State U., 1950, M.S., 1955; Ph.D., U. Tex. at Austin, 1959. Mem. faculty dept. geology Kans. State U., Manhattan, 1959-95, prof. emeritus, 1995—; assoc. prof. Kans. State U., 1964-69, prof., 1969-95; prof. emeritus Kans. State U., Manhattan, 1995—; also head dept. Kans. State U., 1968-77; geologist agrl. research service U.S. Dept. Agr., 1966-68; research scientist U. Tex., Austin, 1966-67. Contbr. articles to profl. jours. Chmn. Manhattan Council Human Relations, 1960-61; vice pres. Riley County Democratic Club, 1970-71; mem. Dem. Precinct Com., Manhattan, 1970-72, 74-80. Served with USAAF, 1951-53. Fellow Pan Am. Petroleum Found., 1957-58; Shell Found. fellow, 1958-59. Fellow Geol. Soc. Am. (chmn. south cen. sect. 1972-73, 95, sec.-treas. 1980-89, vice-chmn. 1994-95, chmn. 1995-96); mem. Am. Assn. Petroleum Geologists (geologic maps com. 1968-70), Soc. Econ. Paleontologists and Minerologists, Kans. Acad. Sci. (mem. rsch. awards com. 1966-70, assoc. editor 1977-92), AAAS, Am. Soc. Archaeology, Clay Minerals Soc., Kans. Geol. Soc., W. Tex. Geol. Soc., Am. Soc. Agronomy, Soil Sci. Soc. Am., Internat. Soc. Soil Sci., Internat. Assn. Sedimentologists, Assn. Internationale pour l'Etude des Argiles, Am. Quaternary Assn., AAUP (chpt. v.p. 1971-72, chpt. pres. 1972-73), Nat. Assn. Geology Tchrs., Mineral. Soc. Am., Soc. Phytolith Rsch. (organizing com. 1990-92, mem.-at-large, exec. com. 1992-93, pres.-elect 1993-94, pres. 1994-95, past pres. 1995-96), Sigma Xi, Sigma Gamma Epsilon, Gamma Sigma Delta. Home: 2327 Bailey Dr Manhattan KS 66502-2733

TWITCHELL, E. EUGENE, lawyer; b. Salt Lake City, Mar. 4, 1932; s. Irvin A. and E. Alberta (Davis) T.; m. Joyce A. Newey, Aug. 9, 1957 (div. May 1989); children: Robert R., Lauren E., David J., Michael S.; m. Linda Sue Wilson, 1991; children: Bonnie Wilson, Jimmy Wilson, Benjamin Wilson, Stefanie Wilson. Student, Brigham Young U., 1954-55; BA, Calif. State U., Long Beach, 1959; JD, UCLA, 1966. Bar: Mich. 1977, U.S. Dist. Ct. (ea. dist.) Mich., U.S. Supreme Ct. 1987. Contract adminstr. Rockwell No. Am. Aviation, Seal Beach, Calif., 1966-68; sr. contracts adminstr. McDonnell Douglas Corp., Long Beach, Calif., 1968-73; in-house counsel Albert C. Martin & Assocs., L.A., 1973-77; instr. bus. law Golden West Coll., Huntington Beach, 1973-74; corp. counsel, corp. sec. Barton Malow Co., Southfield, Mich., 1977—; mem. Detroit EEO Forum, 1983-87. Pres. Corona (Calif.) Musical Theater, 1975-76; dist. chmn. Boy Scouts of Am.-North Trails, Oakland County, Mich., 1978-80; treas. Barton Malow PAC, Southfield, 1983—. Sgt. USAF, 1950-52. Mem. ABA, Mich. Bar Assn., Am. Arbitration Assn. (arbitrator Detroit area 1985—), Am. Corp. Counsel Assn. (v.p., dir. 1983—). Republican. LDS. Avocations: cartooning, painting, karate, music, theatre, writing. Office: Barton Malow Co 27777 Franklin Rd #800 Southfield MI 48034

TWITCHELL, THEODORE GRANT, music educator and composer; b. Melrose, Kans., Jan. 26, 1928; s. Curtis and Sarah Frances (Lane) T.; m. Rebecca Janis Goldsmith, Nov. 18, 1989; stepchildren: Ralph Norman, Russell Norman, Dawn Jiricek. AA in Music, L.A. City Coll., 1949; BA in Social Studies, Calif. State U., L.A., 1951, MA in Secondary Edn., 1955; EdD in Secondary and Higher Edn., U. So. Calif., L.A., 1964. Tchr. Barstow (Calif.) Union High Sch., 1952, Burbank (Calif.) Unified Sch. Dist., 1954-66; dean instrn., dir. evening divsn., dir. summer sessions, 1966-69; pres. Palo Verde Coll., Blythe, Calif., 1969-70; adult tchr. L.A. Unified Sch. Dist., 1977-78; faculty Columbia West U., L.A., 1993—; pvt. English tutor, 1979—. Composer: The Gettysburg Address, Tidewater, The Pride of Monticello, Labor Day March, Valley Forge, Normandy Prayer, Christmas in L.A., L.A., Overture to Tidewater, The Joy of Snow, Walt Whitman and Friends, over 90 others; contbr. articles to profl. jours.; author: Dear Mr. President, 1982, Courage, Conflict and Love, 1988, The Magnificent Odyssey of Michael Young, 1992. With U.S. Army, 1952-53. Recipient Coll. Faculty Senate Award for Achievements for the coll., Palo Verde Coll., Student Body award. Mem. Cmty. Coll. Pres.'s Assn., Am. Assn. Composers, Authors and Pubs., Calif. PTA (hon. life mem.), Rho Delta Chi. Republican. Methodist. Avocations: music, writing, travel, hiking, photography. Home: 2737 Montrose Ave Apt 10 Montrose CA 91020-1318

TWOMEY, ELIZABETH M., education commissioner; b. Lynn, Mass.; d. Hugh E. and Theresa A. (Callahan) Molloy; children: Ann, Paula, Charles. AB, Emmanuel Coll., 1959; MEd, Mass. State Coll., 1964; EdD, Boston Coll., 1982; LLB (hon.), Notre Dame, Manchester, N.H., 1984. Elem. sch. tchr. Lynn (Mass.) Pub. Schs., 1959-63; English tchr. Reading (Mass.) Pub. Schs., 1973-75, prin., 1975-81, vice prin., 1981-82; supt. Lincoln (Mass.) Pub. Schs., 1982-88; assoc. commr. Dept. Edn., Quincy, Mass., 1988-92; dep. commr. Dept. Edn., Concord, N.H., 1992-94, commr., 1994—. Trustee Emmanuel Coll., Boston, 1975-85, U. N.H., Durham, 1994—. Recipient Disting. Alumni award Emmanuel Coll. Avocations: walking, reading, gardening. Office: Dept Edn 101 Pleasant St Concord NH 03301-3852

TWOMLEY, BRUCE CLARKE, commissioner, lawyer; b. Selma, Ala., Jan. 23, 1945; s. Robert Clarke and Eleanor Jane (Wood) Anderson T.; m. Sara Jane Minton, June 13, 1979; children: Christopher Mario, Jonathan Marion. BA in Philosophy, Northwestern U., 1967; LLM, U. Calif., San Francisco, 1970; postgrad. Nat. Jud. Coll., Reno, Nev., 1983, 88. Bar: Calif. 1972, Alaska 1973, U.S. Dist. Ct. Alaska, 1973, U.S. Ct. Appeals (9th cir.) 1982. VISTA vol., Anchorage, 1972-73; lawyer Alaska Legal Services Corp., Anchorage, 1973-82; commr. Alaska Comml. Fisheries Entry Commn., Juneau, 1982-83, chmn., 1983—; mem. Gov.'s Fisheries Cabinet, 1983—, Child Support Enforcement Divsn. Rural Task Force, 1985—, Alaska Fedn. of Natives Task Force on IRS and Alaska Native Fishermen, 1994; cons. IRS, Sta. WNED-TV, Buffalo, 1988; presenter in field. Contbr.: Limited Access Management: A Guidebook to Conservation, 1993. Recipient Alaska Legal Services Disting. Service award, 1983, 92. Mem. Bristol Bay Native Assn. (blue ribbon commn. on ltd. entry 1994—), Juneau Racquet Club (adv. bd. 1989—), Kappa Sigma (pres. interfraternity council 1966-67). Home: PO Box 20972 Juneau AK 99802-0972 Office: Alaska Comml Fisheries Entry Commn 8800 Glacier Hwy Ste 109 Juneau AK 99801-8079

TWORECKE, FRANK, retail company executive; b. Munich, Nov. 2, 1946; came to U.S., 1948; s. Leo and Rose (Lewis) T.; children: Adrian, Jacob, Matthew. BS, Cornell U., 1968; MBA, Syracuse U., 1972. Buyer Abraham & Straus, N.Y.C., 1972-77; v.p. Lord & Taylor, N.Y.C., 1977-80; exec. v.p. John Wannamaker, Phila., 1980-87; pres., CEO, Oxford Sweater Co., Stratford, Pa., 1987-90; sr. v.p. Federated Dept. Stores, Cin., 1990-94; pres. MGRE Enterprises Inc., Joppa, Md., 1994—. Bd. dirs. Maccabiah Games, Phila., 1980-88; bd. dirs., mem. U.S. com. Sports for Israel, Phila., 1980-90. Mem. Cornell U. Alumni Assn., Caves Valley Golf Club. Avocations: tennis, golf, running, travel. Office: MGRE Enterprises Inc 3300 Joppa Way Joppa MD 21085-3205

TWYMAN, JACK, wholesale grocery company executive, management services company executive; b. May 11, 1934; married. Ed., U. Cin. Basketball player Cin. Royals, 1955-67; announcer ABC, 1967-72; vice-chmn. Super Food Services, Inc., Dayton, Ohio, from 1972, formerly pres., chief operating officer, now chmn., chief exec. officer. Office: Super Food Svcs Inc 3233 Newmark Dr Miamisburg OH 45342*

TYABJI, HATIM AHMEDI, computer systems company executive; b. Bombay, Mar. 12, 1945; came to U.S., 1967, naturalized, 1976.; came to U.S., 1967, naturalized;. BSEE, Coll. Engring., Poona, India, 1967; MSEE, SUNY, Buffalo, 1969; MBA in Internat. Fin., Syracuse U., 1975; grad. exec. program, Stanford U., 1981. Program mgr. Mohawk Data Scis. Corp., Herkimer, N.Y., 1969-73; pres. Info. Systems Products and Techs. Group, Sperry Corp. (now Unisys Corp.), Roseville, Minn., 1973-86; chmn., pres., CEO VeriFone, Inc., Redwood City, Calif., 1986—. Contbr. articles to profl. publs. Islam. Avocations: skiing, tennis. Office: VeriFone Inc 3 Lagoon Dr Redwood City CA 94065-1565*

TYDINGS, JOSEPH DAVIES, lawyer, former senator; b. Asheville, N.C., May 4, 1928; s. Millard E. and Eleanor (Davies) T.; children: Mary Tydings Smith, Millard E. II, Emlen, Eleanor Davies, Alexandra. Grad., McDonogh (Md.) Sch., 1946; B.A., U. Md., 1951, LL.B., 1953. Bar: Md. bar 1952. Assoc. firm Tydings, Sauerwein, Benson & Boyd, Balt., 1952-57; ptnr. Tydings & Rosenberg, Balt., 1958-61; U.S. atty. Dist. Md., 1961-64; U.S. senator from Md., 1965-71; ptnr. Danzansky, Dickey, Tydings, Quint & Gordon, Washington, 1971-81, Anderson, Kill, Olick and Oshinsky, Washington, 1988—; spl. sr. cons. UN Fund for Population Activities, 1971-91; Del., Internat. Penal Conf., Bellagio, Italy, 1963, Interpol Conf., Helsinki, 1963, Mexican-U.S. Interparliamentary Conf., Mexico City, 1965, Council Intergovtl. Com. for European Migration, Geneva, 1966, NATO Assembly, Brussels, 1968, Atlantic Conf., P.R., 1970; bd. regents U. Md., 1974-83, vice chmn. 1978-81, chmn. 1981-83, co-chmn. population crisis com. 1971—. Mem. Md. Ho. of Dels. from Hartford Country, 1955-61; campaign mgr. for John F. Kennedy in Md. Primary, 1960. Served with AUS, 1946-48, ETO. Cited as outstanding legislator Md. Press Corr., 1961; named One of 10 Outstanding Young Men Balt. Jr. Assn. Commerce, 1962; recipient August Volmer award Am. Soc. Criminology, 1969; Nat. Brotherhood citation Washington chpt. NCCJ, 1970; Margaret Sanger award for distinguished pub. service Planned Parenthood-World Population. Mem. ABA, D.C. Bar Assn., Md. Bar Assn., Center Club, Univ. Club, Elkridge-Hartford Hunt Club, Met. Club, Chevy Chase Club, Md. Club, Lotos Club. Democrat. Episcopalian. Office: Anderson Kill Olick & Oshinsky 2000 Pennsylvania Ave NW Suite 7500 Washington DC 20006

TYER, TRAVIS EARL, librarian; b. Lorenzo, Tex., Oct. 23, 1930; s. Charlie Earl and Juanita (Travis) T.; m. Alma Lois Davis, Nov. 6, 1951; children: Alan Ross, Juanita Linn. BS, Abilene Christian U., 1952; BLS, U. North Tex., 1959; AdM in LS, Fla. State U., 1969, postgrad., 1969-71. Librarian, tchr. pub. schs. Gail, Lubbock, and Seminole, Tex., 1952-61; with Dallas Pub. Library, 1961-66, coordinator young adult services, 1962-66; library dir. Lubbock Pub. Library, 1966, Lubbock City-County Libraries, 1967-68; grad. library sch. faculty-state personnel coordinator Emporia (Kans.) State U., 1971-72; sr. cons. profl. devel. Ill. State Library, Springfield, 1972-80; exec. dir. Great River Libr. Sys., Quincy, Ill., 1980-94; cons. pub. rels. and comm. Alliance Libr. Sys., Quincy, 1994—; lectr. summer workshops Tex. Woman's U., U. Okla., U. Utah, Fla. State U., U. North Tex.; adj. faculty U. Mo., 1986-89; cons. in field; mem. adv. com. Ill. State Libr., 1984-87, 93—; pres. Resource Sharing Alliance West Ctrl. Ill., Inc., 1981-94, sec., 1994—; pres. Ill. Libr. System Dirs. Orgn., 1992-94. Contbr. articles to library jours. Inductee U. North Tex. Libr. and Info. Sci. Hall of Fame, 1990. Mem. ALA, Ill. Libr. Assn., Med. Libr. Assn., Ill. Ctr. for the Book, Friends of Librs. U.S.A., U. North Tex. Sch. Libr. and Info. Sci. (life), Friends Lubbock City-County Librs. (life), Assn. Ednl. Comm. and Tech., Ill. Assn. for Ednl. Comm. and Tech., Ill. Sch. Libr. MEdia Assn. Democrat. Mem. Ch. of Christ. Home: 2008 Arrowood Ct Quincy IL 62301-8961 Office: 515 York St Quincy IL 62301-3997

TYERS, GEDDES FRANK OWEN, surgeon; b. Giroux, Man., Can., Nov. 6, 1935; s. William Frederick and Catherine Marguerite (Stoddart) T.; m. Phyllis Amelia Randall, May 14, 1960; children: Randall Geddes, Owen Frank. M.D., U. B.C., 1962. Research and teaching fellow pharmacology U. B.C. Faculty Medicine, 1959-60; intern Vancouver Gen. Hosp., Vancouver, B.C., 1962-63; from asst. instr. to instr. surgery U. Pa. Med. Sch., 1963-68; asst. prof., then assoc. prof. surgery Pa. State U. Coll. Medicine, Hershey, 1970-77; prof., chief div. cardiovascular and thoracic surgery U. Tex. Med. Br., Galveston, 1977-79; prof., head div. cardiovascular and thoracic surgery U. B.C. Faculty Medicine, 1979—; cons. pacemaker power sources, telemetry monitoring cardiac pacemakers, med. device reliability; dir. tng. program cardiovasc. and thoracic surgery, chmn. residency tng. com.; mem. adv. com. on med. devices Health and Welfare Can., 1993-94. Mem. editorial bd. Jour. Investigative Surgery, 1995—, assoc. editor, 1996—. Recipient 1st prize essay contest Phila. Acad. Surgery, 1966, 1st prize essay contest Pa. Assn. Thoracic Surgery, 1977; Hamish Haney MacIntosh Meml. prize Dr. W.A. Whitelaw scholarship, 1962. Fellow ACS, Royal Coll. Surgeons Can. (nucleus com. cardiovascular surgery), Am. Heart Assn. (coun. cardiovascular surgery), Am. Coll. Cardiology; mem. Am. Surg. Assn., N.Am. Soc. Pacing and Electrophysiology (founder), Am. Assn. Thoracic Surgery (reviewer JTCS), Can. Cardiovascular Soc. (med. devices com.), Soc. Univ Surgeons, Can Med. Assn., Soc. Vascular Surgery, Assn. Acad. Surgery, Western Thoracic Surg. Soc., Internat. Cardiac Pacing and Electrophysiology Soc. (bd. dirs.). Patentee in field. Office: Vancouver Hosp, 700 W 10th Ave Fl C-314, Vancouver, BC Canada V5Z 4E5

TYGIEL, MARTI (MARTHA TYGIEL), instrumental music educator; b. Bklyn., June 28, 1940; d. Gustave and Rose (Gross) T. MusB, Manhattan Sch. Music, 1960, MusM, 1961. Lic. music tchr., N.Y.; lic. tchr. orchestral music, N.Y.C. Tchr. orchestral music N.Y.C. Bd. Edn., 1961-66; dir. promotion Carl Fischer, Inc., N.Y.C., 1966-67, dir. edn., 1979-81; ind. tchr. violin N.Y.C., 1961—; dir. instrumental music, orch., condr., band condr. Horace Mann Sch., Riverdale, N.Y., 1986—. Mem. Music Educators Nat. Conf., Am. String Tchrs. Assn., N.Y. State Sch. Music Assn., Chamber Music Assocs. Home: 600 W 246th St Apt 1102 Bronx NY 10471-3624 Office: Horace Mann Sch 4440 Tibbett Ave Bronx NY 10471-3416

TYGRETT, HOWARD VOLNEY, JR., lawyer; b. Lake Charles, La., Jan. 12, 1940; s. Howard Volney and Hazel (Wheeler) T.; m. Linda Lee; children: Carroll Diane, Howard V. III. BA, Williams Coll., 1961; LLB, So. Methodist U., 1964. Bar: Tex. 1964. Gen. atty. SEC, 1964-65; law clk. to chief judge U.S. Dist. Ct. No. Dist. Tex., 1965-67; partner Tygrett & Walker (and predecessors), Dallas, 1968—. Bd. dirs. Routh St. Center, 1976-83, Theatre Three, 1974-75, Shakespeare Festival, 1978-81, Suicide and Crisis Ctr., 1983-86. Mem. ABA, Tex. Bar Assn., Dallas Bar Assn., Civitan (lt. gov. Tex. dist. 1976-77, gov. 1979-90), Delta Phi, Delta Theta Phi. Episcopalian. Home: 8530 Jourdan Way Dallas TX 75225-3214 Office: Tygrett & Walker 8111 Preston Rd Ste 600 Dallas TX 75225-6315

TYKESON, DONALD ERWIN, broadcasting executive; b. Portland, Oreg., Apr. 11, 1927; s. O. Ansel and Hillie Martha (Haveman) T.; m. Rilda Margaret Steigleder, July 1, 1950; children: Ellen, Amy, Eric. BS, U. Oreg., 1951. V.p., dir. Liberty Communications, Inc., Eugene, Oreg., 1963-67, pres., chief exec. officer, dir., 1967-83; pres. Bend Cable Communications, Inc., 1983—; chmn. bd. Telecomm Systems, Inc., 1983—, Telecomm Svcs. Inc., 1988—; Ctrl. Oreg. Cable Advt., Inc., 1992—; pres. Northwest TV Inc., 1985—. Bd. dirs. Nat. Coalition Rsch. in Neurol. and Communicative Disorders, 1984-89, Sacred Heart Med. Ctr. Found., 1995—; chmn. Nat. Coalition in Rsch. pub. and govt. info. com., 1986-89, C-SPAN, 1980-89; mem. bus. adv. coun. U. Oreg. Coll. Bus. Adminstrn., 1973—; vice-chmn. we. area Nat. Multiple Sclerosis Soc., 1983—, dir., mem. rsch. and med. programs com., 1986—; trustee Eugene Art Found., 1980-85, Oreg. Health Scis. U. Found., 1988-91, mem. investment com., 1992—; mem. Oreg. Investment Coun. State of Oreg., vice chmn., 1988-92. Mem. Nat. Assn. Broadcasters, Nat. Cable TV Assn. (dir. 1976-83), Chief Execs. Orgn., Vintage Club (pres. Custom Lot Assn. 1992—), Country Club Eugene (dir. 1975-77, sec. 1976—, v.p. 1977), Multnomah Athletic Club, Arlington Club, Rotary, Elks. Home: 447 Spyglass Dr Eugene OR 97401-2091 Office: PO Box 70006 Eugene OR 97401-0101

TYL, NOEL JAN, baritone, astrologer; b. West Chester, Pa., Dec. 31, 1936. BA, Harvard U., 1958. Bus. mgr. Houston Grand Opera Assn., 1958-60; account exec. Ruder and Finn Pub. Rels., N.Y.C., 1960-62; profl. astrologer, 1970—; editor Astrology Now mag., 1974-79; pres. Tyl Assocs., Inc. pub. rels. and advt., 1980-89; media spokesman; internat. lectr., locations including U.S., Moscow, London, Oslo, Copenhagen, Berlin, Amsterdam, The Netherlands, Toronto, Ont., Tel Aviv, Bologna. Winner Am. Opera Auditions, 1964; opera singer U.S. and Europe, 1964-80; Wagner specialist; appearances include Vienna State Opera, Düsseldorf, Rome, Milan, Barcelona, N.Y.C. Opera, also throughout U.S.; author: Principles and Practice of Astrology, 12 vols., 1973-75, Teaching and Study Guide, 1976, The Horoscope as Identity, 1974, Holistic Astrology, 1980, Prediction in Astrology, 1991, Synthesis and Counseling in Astrology, 1994. Home: 17005 E Player Ct Fountain Hills AZ 85268

TYLER, ANNE (MRS. TAGHI M. MODARRESSI), author; b. Mpls., Oct. 25, 1941; d. Lloyd Parry and Phyllis (Mahon) T.; m. Taghi M. Modarressi, May 3, 1963; children: Tezh, Mitra. B.A., Duke U., 1961; postgrad., Columbia U., 1962. Author: If Morning Ever Comes, 1964, The Tin Can Tree, 1965, A Slipping-Down Life, 1970, The Clock Winder, 1972, Celestial Navigation, 1974, Searching for Caleb, 1976, Earthly Possessions, 1977, Morgan's Passing, 1980, Dinner at the Homesick Restaurant, 1982, The Accidental Tourist, 1985, Breathing Lessons, 1988 (Pulitzer Prize for fiction 1989), Saint Maybe, 1991, (juvenile) Tumble Tower, 1993, Ladder of Years, 1995; contbr. short stories to nat. mags. Home: 222 Tunbridge Rd Baltimore MD 21212-3422

TYLER, BARBARA A., museum director. Exec. dir., CEO McMichael Can. Art Collection, Kleinburg, Ont. Office: McMichael Can Art Collect, Islington Ave, Kleinburg, ON Canada L0J 1C0*

TYLER, CARL WALTER, JR., physician, health research administrator; b. Washington, Aug. 22, 1933; s. Carl Walter and Elva Louise (Harlan) T.; m. Elma Hermione Matthias, June 23, 1956 (dec. Dec. 1991); children: Virginia Louise, Laureen, Jeffrey Alan, Cynthia T. Crenshaw. A.B., Oberlin Coll., 1955; M.D., Case-Western Res. U., 1959. Diplomate Am. Bd. Ob-Gyn. Rotating intern Univ. Hosps. of Cleve., 1959-60, resident in ob-gyn, 1960-64; med. officer USPHS, 1964; obstetrician-gynecologist USPHS Indian Health Service, Tahlequah, Okla., 1964-66; epidemic intelligence service officer Bur. Epidemiology, Ctrs. for Disease Control, Atlanta, 1966-67; dir. family planning evaluation div. Bur. Epidemiology, Ctrs. for Disease Control, 1967-80, asst. dir. for sci., 1980-82, acting dir. Ctr. for Health Promotion and Edn., 1982, dir. epidemiology program office, 1982-88, med. epidemiologist Office of Dir., 1988-90, asst. dir. for acad. programs, pub. health practice program office, 1990—; clin. assoc. prof. ob.-gyn. Emory U. Sch. Medicine, Atlanta; clin. asst. prof. ob-gyn Emory U. Sch. Medicine, Atlanta, 1966-80, clin. assoc. prof., 1980—, also clin. assoc. prof. preventive medicine and community health, adj. assoc. prof. sociology Coll. Arts and Scis., 1977-90; adj. assoc. prof. pub. health Sch. Pub. Health, 1990—; clin. prof. pub. health and community medicine Morehouse Sch. Medicine, Atlanta, 1990—; mem. Nat. Sleep Disorders Rsch. Commn., 1990—; mem. adv. com. on oral contraception WHO, Geneva, 1974-77, mem. adv. com. maternal and child health, 1982-88; lectr. in field. Editor: (monograph) Venereal Infections; assoc. editor: Maxcy-Rosenau Textbook of Public Health and Preventive Medicine, 13th edit., 1992; contbr. articles to profl. jours. Chmn. Dekalb County Schs. com. on instruction programs, subcom. on health, phys. edn. and safety, (Ga.), 1967-68; active Ga. State Soccer Coaches Assn., Atlanta, 1973-79, DeKalb County YMCA. Josiah Macy Found. fellow, 1956-58; NIH grantee, 1961-64; recipient Superior Service award, 1974, Meritorious Service medal USPHS, 1984, Disting. Service medal, 1988; Carl S. Shultz Population award APHA, 1976, medal of Excellence Ctrs. for Disease Control, 1984. Fellow Am. Coll. Ob-Gyn (chmn. community health com. 1974-77), Am. Coll. Preventive Medicine, Am. Coll. Epidemiol.; mem. Am. Epidemiologic Soc., Internat. Epidemiologic Assn., Assn. Tchrs. Preventive Medicine (bd. dirs. 1988-89), Am. Pub. Health Assn. (governing council 1976-78), Assn. Planned Parenthood Profls., Population Assn. Am., Sierra Club. Avocations: photography; camping. Office: HHS Ctrs for Disease Control Mailstop E-42 1600 E Clifton Rd NE Atlanta GA 30333

TYLER, DAVID EARL, veterinary medical educator; b. Carlisle, Iowa, July 12, 1928; s. Guy Earl and Beatrice Virginia (Slack) T.; m. Alice LaVon Smith, Sept. 6, 1952; children: John William, Anne Elizabeth. B.S., Iowa State U., 1953, D.V.M., 1957, Ph.D., 1963; M.S., Purdue U., 1960. Instr. dept. vet. sci. Purdue U., 1957-60; asst. prof. dept. pathology Coll. Vet. Medicine, Iowa State U., 1960-63, assoc. prof., 1963-66; prof., head dept. pathology and parasitology Coll. Vet. Medicine, U. Ga., 1966-71, head dept. pathology, 1971-79, prof., 1971-91, prof. emeritus, 1991—, ret., 1991; co-founder internat. vet. pathology slide bank, 1984, co-dir., 1984—; apptd. discussant Charles L. Davis Found. for Advancement Vet. Pathology, 1977-91. Cub Scout master, 1967-69, scout com. chmn., 1970-72; elder Disciples of Christ Ch., 1968—, chmn. ch. bd., 1973-74, 92-94; mem. citizens com. to County Bd. Edn., 1968-70; bd. dirs. Christian Coll., Ga., 1974-77. With

AUS, 1946-48. Recipient Borden award Gail Borden Co., 1956, Norden Disting. Teaching award Norden Labs., 1964, 69, 81, 85, 91, Prof. of Yr. award Coll. Vet. Medicine, Iowa State U., 1965, Outstanding Prof. award Coll. Vet. Medicine, U. Ga., 1970, 76, 80-81, 83, 86, 87-88, 90, Joshia Meigs Teaching award, 1985, Stange award Coll. Vet. Med., Iowa State U., 1987, Phi Zeta Teaching award, 1985, N.Am. Outstanding Tchr. award, 1991, Omicron Delta Kappa Outstanding Prof. award U. Ga., 1981, Harold W. Casey award C.L. Davis Found., 1995. Mem. AVMA, Farm House, Am. Coll. Vet. Pathologists (mem. council 1975-77, exam. com. 1982-85), Am. Assn. Vet. Med. Colls. (chmn. com. teaching-learning materials 1975-77), Nat. Program for Instructional Devel. in Vet. Pathology (adv. com. 1976-77), Aghon, Sigma Xi, Phi Eta Sigma, Alpha Zeta, Gamma Sigma Delta, Phi Kappa Phi, Phi Zeta (chpt. sec.-treas. 1982-84), Omega Tau Sigma. Home: 160 Sunny Brook Dr Athens GA 30605-3348

TYLER, GAIL MADELEINE, nurse; b. Dhahran, Saudi Arabia, Nov. 21, 1953 (parents Am. citizens); d. Louis Rogers and Nona Jean (Henderson) Tyler; m. Alan J. Moore, Sept. 29, 1990; 1 child, Sean James. AS, Front Range C.C., Westminster, Colo., 1979; BS in Nursing, U. Wyo., 1989. RN. Ward sec. Valley View Hosp., Thornton, Colo., 1975-79; nurse Scott and White Hosp., Temple, Tex., 1979-83, Meml. Hosp. Laramie County, Cheyenne, Wyo., 1983-89; dir. DePaul Home Health, 1989-91; field staff nurse Poudre Valley Hosp. Home Care, 1991—. Avocations: collecting internat. dolls, sewing, reading, travel.

TYLER, GEORGE LEONARD, electrical engineering educator; b. Bartow, Fla., Oct. 18, 1940; s. George Leonard and Mable Leona (Bethea) T.; m. Joanne Lynne Phelps, Nov. 17, 1977; children: Virginia L., Matthew L. BEE, Ga. Inst. Tech., 1963; MS, Stanford U., 1964, PhD in Elec. Engring., 1967. Engr. Lockheed Aircraft Corp., Marietta, Ga., 1963; rsch. assoc. Ctr. for Radar Astronomy, Stanford (Calif.) U., 1967-69, rsch. engr., 1969-72, sr. rsch. assoc., 1972-74, rsch. prof. elec. engring., 1974-90, prof., 1990—, dir. Space, Telecom. and Radiosci. Lab., 1993—; cons. SRI-Internat., NASA, Jet Propulsion Lab., also other orgns., 1972—; mem. com. on planetary exploration of space sci. bd. NAS, 1983-87, mem. naval studies bd. panel on advanced radar tech., 1990-91. Contbr. over 150 articles to sci. jours., chpts. to books. Recipient Medal for Exceptional Sci. Achievement, NASA, 1977, 81, 86, Pub. Svc. medal, 1992; fellow NSF, 1964-66. Fellow IEEE; mem. Am. Geophys. Union, Am. Astron. Soc., Internat. Astron. Union, Internat. Radio Sci. Union, Electromagnetics Acad., Phi Kappa Phi, Tau Beta Pi. Achievements include co-discovery of Crab Nebula pulsar, first high-resolution measurement of the directional spectrum of the sea, development and application of occultation technique for outer planets, measurement of Titan's atmosphere. Office: Stanford U Ctr for Radar Astronomy Dept Elec Engring Stanford CA 94305-9515

TYLER, H. RICHARD, physician; b. Bklyn., Oct. 16, 1927; s. Max M. and Beatrice F. T.; m. Joyce Colby, June 17, 1951; children—Kenneth, Karen, Douglas, Lori. AB, Syracuse U., 1947; BS in Medicine, Washington U., 1951, MD, 1951; MA (hon.), Harvard U., 1989. Diplomate Am. Bd. Neurology and Psychiatry. Intern Peter Bent Brigham Hosp., Boston, 1951-52; resident in neurology Boston City Hosp., 1952-54; public health fellow Neurol. Inst., Queen's Sq., London, Salpêtrière, Paris, 1954-55; asst. in pediatrics and neurology Johns Hopkins Hosp., Balt., 1955-56; neurologist Peter Bent Brigham Hosp., Boston, 1956-74; asst. in neurology Harvard Med. Sch., Boston, 1956-59; assoc. in neurology Harvard Med. Sch., 1959-61, instr., 1961-64, asst. prof., 1964-68, assoc. prof., 1968-73, prof., 1974—; sr. physician Brigham and Women's Hosp., Boston, 1974—, dir. neurol. svc., 1979-88. Co-editor: Current Neurology I and II, 1979, 80; mem. editorial bd.: Jour. Neurology, 1979-84, Classics on Neurology and Neurosurgery Libr., 1983—; contbr. articles in field to profl. jours. Trustee Brookline Pub. Library, 1970—, chmn. bd. trustees, 1985-86, 90-91. Served with U.S. Army, 1946-47. Mem. Am. Neurol. Assn., Am. Acad. Neurology, Mass. Med. Soc. Office: 1 Brookline Pl Brookline MA 02146-7224

TYLER, HAROLD RUSSELL, JR., lawyer, former government official; b. Utica, N.Y., May 14, 1922; s. Harold Russell and Elizabeth (Glenn) T.; m. Barbara L. Eaton, Sept. 10, 1949; children: Bradley E., John R., Sheila B. Grad., Philips Exeter Acad., 1939; AB, Princeton U., 1943; LLB, Columbia U., 1949. Bar: N.Y. 1950. Pvt. practice N.Y.C., 1950-53, 55-60; mem. firm Gilbert & Segall, 1957-60, 61-62; asst. U.S. atty., 1953-55, asst. atty. gen. U.S. charge civil rights div., 1960-61; commr. N.Y.-N.J. Waterfront Comm., 1961-62; U.S. dist. judge So. Dist., N.Y., 1962-75; dep. atty. gen. U.S., 1975-77; mem. firm Patterson, Belknap, Webb & Tyler, N.Y.C., 1977—; adj. prof. NYU Law Sch., 1966-75, Albany (N.Y.) Law Sch., 1991—; vis. lectr. Inst. Criminology, Cambridge, 1968; vice chmn. Adminstrv. Conf. USA, 1975-77. Bd. dirs. Fed. Jud. Center, Washington, 1968-72; trustee Practising Law Inst., N.Y.C.; chmn. William Nelson Cromwell Found., Law Center Found. Home: 2 Beekman Pl New York NY 10022-8058 Office: Patterson Belknap Webb & Tyler 1133 Avenue Of The Americas New York NY 10036-6710

TYLER, JOHN RANDOLPH, lawyer; b. Canandaigua, N.Y., Aug. 3, 1934; s. John Randolph and Helen McGregor (Tewinkle) T.; m. Carroll Smith, Apr. 1, 1962 (div. Sept. 28, 1981); children: John R. III, Carroll Barrett; m. Janet MacAdam, June 5, 1982. BA cum laude, Amherst Coll., 1956; JD, Harvard U., 1963. Bar: N.Y. 1983. Assoc. Nixon, Hargrave, Devans & Doyle, Rochester, N.Y., 1963-70, ptnr., 1971—. Contbr. articles to profl. jours. Bd. dirs. Geva Theater, 1990—, treas., 1993-96, Flower City Habitat, 1992—. Lt. USNR, 1956-59. Mem. ABA, N.Y. State Bar Assn. (chmn. exec. com. bus. corp. banking sect. 1981-82, ho. of dels. 1984-87, 95-97, opinion com. 1986—), Chi Psi. Republican. Episcopalian. Clubs: Genesee Valley (Rochester); Ski Valley (Naples, N.Y.) (bd. dirs. 1980-83). Avocations: sailing, skiing, environ. matters. Home: 25 Oak Ln Rochester NY 14610-3133 Office: Nixon Hargrave Devans & Doyle PO Box 1951 PO Box 1951 Clinton Sq Rochester NY 14604-1729

TYLER, LLOYD JOHN, lawyer; b. Aurora, Ill., May 28, 1924; s. Lloyd J. and Dorothy M. (Curtis) T.; m. Inez Chappell Busener, Feb. 25, 1970; children by previous marriage: Barbara Tyler Miller, John R., Benjamin C., Robert B., Amy C. B.A., Beloit Coll., 1948; J.D., U. Mich., 1951. Bar: Ill., Mich. bars 1951. Mem. firm Sears, Streit, Tyler and Dreyer and (predecessors), Aurora, Ill., 1951-62, Tyler and Hughes (P.A.), Aurora, 1962—; lectr., speaker on profl. subjects, 1964—. Contbr. chpts. to profl. books, articles to profl. jours. Democratic precinct committeeman, 1954-59; mem. Batavia (Ill.) Sch. Bd., 1959-62. Served with USAAF, 1943-46. Fellow Am. Bar Found.; mem. Am. Bar Assn. (Ho. of Dels. 1975-79), Ill. Bar Assn. (gov. 1970-78, pres. 1978-79, chmn. legislative com. 1980, task force on alternative forms of legal service 1981-82, long range planning com. 1982-88, fed. judiciary appointment com. 1984-90, spl. com. on merit selection 1987—), Ill. Bar Found. (pres. 1972-75), Ill. Inst. Continuing Legal Edn. (dir. 1971-75, 77-79), Ill. Lawyers Polit. Action Com. (trustee 1982—, chmn. 1987-88), Soc. Trial Lawyers Ill., Appellate Lawyers Assn., Phi Beta Kappa, Omicron Delta Kappa. Presbyterian. Home: 701 Fargo Blvd Geneva IL 60134-3227 Office: Tyler and Hughes PO Box 4425 Aurora IL 60507-4425

TYLER, NOEL, geological researcher and educator; b. Johannesburg, South Africa, Dec. 6, 1950; came to U.S., 1978; s. Paul and Lorna (Timms) T.; m. Erica E. Forster, Jan. 27, 1976; children: Kristin, Caroline. BSc, U. Witwatersrand, South Africa, 1975, BSc with honours, 1976, MSc in Geology cum laude, 1978; PhD, Colo. State U., 1981. Rsch. officer Econ. Geology rsch. unit U. Witwatersrand, 1976-78; rsch. assoc. Bur. Econ. Geology, U. Tex., Austin, 1981-85, rsch. scientist, 1985-91, lectr. dept. geol. scis., 1988—, assoc. dir. oil resources, 1991-94, dir., Tex. state geologist, 1994—; cons. BP, Mobil, Texaco, Chevron, Dept. Energy, Petrobras, So. Oil Exploration Corp., others, 1986—; adj. prof. Curtin U. Tech., Perth, Australia, 1995—. Author reports, monographs, brochures, pamphlets and bulls.; contbr. chpts. to books, articles to profl. jours. Colo. Fellowship Fund fellow, 1980, Jim and Gladys Taylor Edn. Trust scholar, 1978-80; grantee Coun. for Sci. and Indsl. Rsch. Bursary, 1975, Johannesburg Consol. Investment Corp., 1976-77; named Disting. Alumnus for 1994 Coll. of Forestry and Natural Resources, Colo. State U. Fellow Geol. Soc. Am.; mem. Am. Assn. Petroleum Geologists, Soc. Petroleum Engrs., Soc. Econ. Paleontologists and Mineralogists. Avocations: boating, hiking, squash, tennis. Office: Bur Econ Geology University Sta Box X Austin TX 78713

TYLER, PRISCILLA, retired English language and education educator; b. Cleve., Oct. 23, 1908; d. Ralph Sargent and Alice Lorraine (Campbell) T. BA in Latin and Greek, Radcliffe Coll., 1932; MA in Edn., Case Western Res. U., 1934, PhD in English, 1953; LLD (hon.), Carleton U., Ottawa, Ont., Can., 1993. Parole officer, case worker Cleve. Sch. for Girls, 1934-35; tchr. English, Latin and French Cleveland Heights (Ohio) Pub. Schs., 1935-45; instr. to asst. prof. English Flora Stone Mather Coll., Cleve., 1945-59, asst. dean, 1957-59; asst. prof. edn., head dept. English Sch. of Edn. Harvard U., Cambridge, Mass., 1959-63; assoc. prof. English, U. Ill., Champaign-Urbana, 1963-67, dir. freshman rhetoric, 1966-67; prof. edn. and English U. Mo., Kansas City, 1967-78, prof. emeritus, 1978—; instr. N.S. (Can.) Dept. Edn., Halifax, summers 1972-73; condr. numerous seminars; former lectr. U. Calif., Berkeley, U. Chgo., Purdue U., U. Mo., Columbia, U. Nebr., Emory U., Fresno State U., Calif. State U., Hayward, San Jose State Coll., Mills Coll., Ala., Tift Coll., Ga., Va. Poly. Inst. and Midwestern U., Tex. Editor: Harpers Modern Classics, 19 vols., 1963, Writers the Other Side of the Horizon, 1964, (with Maree Brooks) Inupiat Paitot, 1974; co-author introduction and co-editor: (with Maree Brooks) Sevukakmet, Ways of Life on St. Lawrence Island (Helen Slwooko Carius), 1979, The Epic of Qayaq, 1995 (Lela Kiana); interviewed authors, Jan Carew, Guyana, George Lamming, Barbados, Christopher Okigbo, Nigeria; also articles. Mem. Ohio Gov.'s Com. on Employment of Physically Handicapped, 1957; mem. Friends of Art of Carleton U., Nelson Atkins Mus. Art, Kansas City, Ottawa (Kans.) Art Gallery, Friends of Libr., Ottawa. Recipient Outstanding Achievement and Contbns. in Field of Edn. award Western Res. U., 1962, Disting. Alumna award Laurel Sch., Cleve., 1994; Priscilla Tyler Endowment Fund named in her honor Case Western Res. U., 1980. Mem. MLA, NEA, Archaeol. Inst. Am., Nat. Coun. Tchrs. English (v.p. 1963, mem. com. on history of the profession 1965-68, Commn. on Composition 1968-71, trustee Rsch. Found. 1970-78, Disting. Svc. award 1978), Conf. on Coll. Composition and Comm. (pres. 1963), Arctic Inst. N.Am., Inuit Art Found., Franklin County Hist. Assn., Calif. Assn. Tchrs. English (hon.. Curriculum Commn. Ctrl. Calif.), Delta Kappa Gamma (pres. Upsilon chpt. 1950-52). Democrat. Presbyterian. Avocations: collecting rare books of American and English grammar, Inuit art, and books pertaining to Inuit art, history and culture, travel. Home: 4213 Kentucky Ter Ottawa KS 66067-8715

TYLER, RICHARD, fashion designer; b. Sunshine, Australia, Sept. 22, 1950; m. Doris Taylor (div.); 1 child, Sheridan; m. Lisa Trafficante, 1989; 1 child, Edward Charles. Prin. Zippity-doo-dah, Melbourne, Australia, 1968-80, Tyler-Trafficante, L.A., 1988—; design dir. Anne Klein Collection, N.Y.C., 1993-94; designer Richard Tyler Collections for Men & Women. Recipient New Fashion Talent Perry Ellis award Coun. Fashion Designers Am., 1993, Womenswear Designer of Yr. award, 1994, Perry Ellis award for new fashion talent in menswear, 1995. Office: 1617 E 7th St Los Angeles CA 90021

TYLER, RONNIE CURTIS, historian; b. Temple, Tex., Dec. 29, 1941; s. Jasper J. and Melba Curtis (James) T.; m. Paula Eyrich, Aug. 24, 1974. BSE, Abilene (Tex.) Christian Coll., 1964; MA, Tex. Christian U., 1966, PhD (Univ. fellow), 1968; DHL, Austin Coll., 1986. Instr. history Austin Coll., Sherman, Tex., 1967-68; asst. prof. Austin Coll., 1968-69; asst. dir. collections and programs Amon Carter Mus., Ft. Worth, 1969-86; dir. Tex. State Hist. Assn., 1986—; prof. history U. Tex., Austin, 1986—; adj. prof. history Tex. Christian U., 1971-72; cons. visual materials Western. Am. art. Author: Santiago Vidaurri and the Confederacy, 1973, The Big Bend: The Last Texas Frontier, 1975, The Image of America in Caricature and Cartoon, 1975, The Cowboy, 1975, The Mexican War: A Lithographic Record, 1974, The Rodeo Photographs of John Addison Stryker, 1978, Visions of America: Pioneer Artists in a New Land, 1983, Views of Texas: The Watercolors of Sarah Ann Hardinge, 1852-56, 1988, Nature's Classics: John James Audubon's Birds and Animals, 1992, Audubon's Great National Work: The Royal Octave Edition of the Birds of America, 1993, Prints of the West, 1994; (with Paula Eyrich Tyler) Texas Museums: A Guidebook, 1983; editor: (with Lawrence R. Murphy) The Slave Narratives of Texas, 1974, Posada's Mexico, 1979, Alfred Jacob Miller: Artist on the Oregon, 1982, Wanderings in the Southwest in 1855 (J.D.B. Stillman), 1990. Pres. Tarrant County (Tex.) Hist. Soc., 1975-77. Good Neighbor Commn. scholar Instituto Tecnologico Monterrey, Mex., 1967; Am. Philos. Soc. grantee, 1970-71; recipient H. Bailey Carroll award, 1974; Coral H. Tullis award, 1976. Mem. Am. Antiquarian Soc., Tex. Inst. Letters (Friends of Dallas Pub. Libr. award), Philos. Soc. Tex. (sec. 1990—), Phi Beta Kappa. Home: 4400 Balcones Dr Austin TX 78731-5710 Office: Ctr Studies Tex Hist 2/306 Richardson Hall University Station Austin TX 78712

TYLER, STEVEN, singer; b. Yonkers, N.Y., Mar. 26, 1948; children: Liv, Mia. Lead singer Aerosmith, 1970—. Albums include Aerosmith, 1973, Get Your Wings, 1974, Toys in the Attic, 1975, Rocks, 1976, Pure Gold, 1976, Draw the Line, 1977, Live Bootleg, 1978, A Night in the Ruts, 1979, Greatest Hits, 1980, Rock in a Hard Place, 1982, Done with Mirrors, 1986, Classics Live, 1986, Permanent Vacation, 1987, Gems, 1989, Pump, 1989, Pandora's Box, 1991, Get a Grip, 1993, Big Ones, 1994, Box of Fire, 1994. recipient w/Aerosmith: MTV Video of the Year for "Cryin'", 1994, Grammy award Best Rock Group. Office: c/o Aerosmith Geffen/GDC Records 9130 W Sunset Blvd Los Angeles CA 90069-3110*

TYLER, W(ILLIAM) ED, printing company executive; b. Cleve., Nov. 3, 1952; s. Ralph Tyler and Edith (Green) Kauer; m. Vickie Sue Boggs, Feb. 7, 1976; children: Stacia Leigh, Adam William. BS in Elec. Engring., Ind. Inst. Tech., 1974; MBA, Ind. U., 1977; postgrad., Harvard U., 1981; postgrad. in bus., Baruch U., 1988. Electronic engr. to various mgmt. positions R.R. Donnelley & Sons Co., Warsaw, Ind., 1974-89; group pres. R.R. Donnelley & Sons Co., N.Y.C., 1989—, sector pres., 1993—. Office: R R Donnelley & Sons Co 77 W Wacker Dr Chicago IL 60601-1629

TYLER, WILLIAM HOWARD, JR., advertising executive, educator; b. Elizabethtown, Tenn., May 21, 1932; s. William Howard and Ethel Margaret (Schueler) T.; m. Margery Moss, Aug. 31, 1957; children: William James, Daniel Moss. Student, Iowa State U., 1950-52, U. Iowa, 1952; AB in Lit., BJ in Advt., U. Mo., 1958, MA in Journalism, 1966. Advt. mgr. Rolla (Mo.) Daily News, 1958-59; instr. sch. journalism U. Mo., Columbia, 1959-61; copy writer, then v.p. copy dir. D'Arcy Advt. Agy., St. Louis, 1961-67; writer, producer, creative supr. Gardner Advt. Co., St. Louis, 1967-69; sr. v.p., creative dir. D'Arcy, McManus, Masius, St. Louis, 1969-77; exec. v.p., creative dir. Larson Bateman Advt. Agy., Santa Barbara, Calif., 1977-80; v.p. advt. Pizza Hut, Inc., Wichita, Kans., 1980-82; v.p., creative dir. Frye-Sills/Y&R, Denver, 1980; exec. v.p., creative dir. Gardner Advt. Co., St. Louis, 1982-88; exec. v.p., ptnr., creative dir. Parker Group, St. Louis, 1988-91; pres. TYLERtoo Advt./Communications, St. Louis, 1991—; assoc. prof. St. Louis U., 1993—. Mng. editor St. Louis Advt. Mag., 1992-95. Trustee Blackburn Coll., Carlinville, Ill., 1983-84; bd. advisors U. Mo. Journalism Sch., 1986-91. 1st lt. USMC, 1952-55, Korea. Mem. St. Louis Advt. and Mktg. Assn. (bd. dirs. 1987-90), U. Mo. Alumni Assn. (bd. dirs. 1969-70, publs. com. 1990-93), St. Louis Ind. Prodn. Profls., St. Louis Radio Profls. Episcopalian. Office: Tylertoo Advt/Communications 13705 Corrington Ct Chesterfield MO 63017

TYLEY, KRISTI SUZANN, elementary school educator; b. Garden Grove, Calif., Mar. 19, 1970; d. Stephen James and Jeanne Frances (Prelesnik) T. BA in Liberal Studies, San Francisco State U., 1992, credentials in multiple subject edn., 1993. Cert. elem. tchr., Calif., crosscultural lang. acquisition devel. Tchg. asst. San Francisco State U., 1988-92; substitute tchr. Newark (Calif.) Unified Sch. Dist., 1992-93, New Haven Unified Sch. Dist., Union City, Calif., 1992-93; tchr. after-sch. program Milpitas (Calif.) Unified Sch. Dist., 1993, substitute tchr., tchr. 2nd grade, 1994, tchr. 4th and 5th grades, 1994-95; tchr. 1st grade Newark (Calif.) Unified Sch. Dist., 1995—; after-sch. tutor Chpt. 1 program Milpitas Unified Sch. Dist., 1994-95. Mem. Calif. Tchrs. Assn., San Mateo County Math and Sci. Coun. Democrat. Avocations: exercise, weight training, bicycling, reading, theatre. Home: 3750 Tamayo St #130 Fremont CA 94536

TYMM, WILLIAM E., lawyer; b. Chgo., Jan. 17, 1945. BS, DePaul U., 1967, JD, 1970. Bar: Ill. 1970. Ptnr. Kirkland & Ellis, Chgo. *

TYMON, LEO F., JR., banker; b. Jersey City, June 2, 1942; s. Leo F. and Mary E. (Sutton) T.; m. Marie-France Leveque, June 18, 1966; 3 children. AB, St. Peter's Coll., Jersey City, 1963; postgrad., Pace U. Trainee to group sr. v.p. First Jersey Nat. Bank (name changed to Nat. Westminster Bank N.J. 1988), Jersey City, 1967—. Served to 1st lt. U.S. Army, 1964-66. Mem. Robert Morris Assocs. Roman Catholic. Office: Natwest Bancorp 10 Exchange Pl Jersey City NJ 07302-3905

TYNCH, DAVID RAY, lawyer; b. Portsmouth, Va., June 8, 1947; s. John and Inez (Conner) T.; m. April Diane Smith, May 15, 1971; children: Ashley Dawn, Alisa Christine, David Arthur. BS, Old Dominion U., 1971; JD, St. Mary's U., San Antonio, 1981; LLM, So. Meth. U., 1983. Bar: Tex. 1982, Va. 1983. Tchr. City of Portsmouth, 1971-72; salesman/mktg. Smithfield (Va.) Foods, 1972-73; assoc. Leighton & Hood, San Antonio, 1980-82, Hofheimer, Nusbaum, McPhaul & Brenner, Norfolk, Va., 1983-86; mng. ptnr., lawyer Cooper, Spong & Davis, P.C., Portsmouth, 1986—; dir. Nat. 1099, Virginia Beach, Va., 1989—, Nat. Lawyers Locate Svc., Virginia Beach, 1995, Cenit Bank FSB, Norfolk, 1994—, Homestead Savs. Bank, Portsmouth, 1985-94. Dir. Ports Events, Inc., Portsmouth, 1990—, Maryview Found., Portsmouth, 1991—, Portsmouth Schs. Found., 1991—, Urban Partnership State of Va., 1994; dir., sec. Portsmouth Partnership, 1990—; commr. City of Portsmouth Mcpl. Fin. Commn., 1986-95; commr., chmn. City of Portsmouth Parking Authority, 1989-95. Maj. USAF, 1973-79. Mem. ABA, Va. State Bar Assn., Norfolk-Portsmouth Bar Assn., Portsmouth C. of C. (dir., chmn. 1993), Portsmouth Sports Club (dir., pres. 1991). Methodist. Avocations: golf, boating. Home: 3502 Cardinal Ln Portsmouth VA 23703 Office: Cooper Spong & Davis PC 500 Ctrl Fidelity Bank Bldg PO Box 1475 Portsmouth VA 23705

TYNDALL, DAVID GORDON, business educator; b. Bangalore, India, Nov. 19, 1919; s. Joseph and Gladys E. (Pickering) T.; m. Margaret Patricia Davies, Apr. 4, 1942; children: Caroline Lee, David Gordon, Benjamin. B.Comm., U. Toronto, 1940, M.A., 1941; Ph.D., U. Calif., 1948. Asst. prof. bus. adminstrn. Cornell U., Ithaca, N.Y., 1947-49; assoc. prof. Carnegie-Mellon U., Pitts., 1949-53; assoc. prof., dir. analytical studies U. Calif., Berkeley, 1955-67; lectr. U. Calif., 1979-82; v.p. fin. and adminstrn., investment officer U. Alta., Edmonton, 1967-74; prof. fin., 1974-79; investment adv. Berkeley, 1979—. Served with Royal Can. Air Force, 1942-45. Fulbright fellow, 1952. Unitarian-Buddhist. Home: 88 Clarewood Ln Oakland CA 94618-2243 Office: 2718 Telegraph Ave Ste 102 Berkeley CA 94705-1142

TYNDALL, RICHARD LAWRENCE, microbiologist, researcher; b. Mt. Joy, Pa., Mar. 29, 1933; s. William Leroy and Reba May (Ream) T.; m. Thelma Mae Sherk, June 19, 1955; children: Sharon Tyndall Headley, Michael L., Sandra Tyndall Holland. BS in Microbiology, Pa. State U., 1955, MS in Microbiology, 1959, PhD in Microbiology, 1961. Rsch. staff biology div. Oak Ridge (Tenn.) Nat. Lab., 1961-73; rsch. staff med. div. Oak Ridge Assoc. Univs., 1973-76; assoc. prof. rsch. zoology dept. U. Tenn., Knoxville, 1976-87; adj. rsch. assoc. Biology and Environ. Scis. div. Oak Ridge Nat. Lab., 1976-87; rsch. staff mem. Health and Safety Rsch. div. Oak Ridge Nat. Lab., 1988—; founder, CEO Microbial Monitoring, Clinton, Tenn., 1985—; co-founder Reprotech Inc., Knoxville, 1981; cons. in field. Contbr. numerous articles to profl. jours.; patentee in field. Mem. com. for control of Legionella, State of Wis. With U.S. Army, 1955-57. AEC postdoctoral fellow. Fellow Am. Acad. Microbiology; mem. AAAS, ASHRAE (subcom. on Legionella), Am. Soc. Microbiology, Phi Sigma, Gamma Sigma Delta (awards). Methodist. Avocations: travel, humor, jazz, the Arts. Home: 209 Woodland View Rd Clinton TN 37716

TYNER, BESSIE HUBBARD, mechanical engineer, mathematician; b. Fayetteville, N.C., Sept. 23, 1961; d. Kenneth Brigman and Ellen Merle H.; m. Kenneth Blake Tyner. BSME, N.C. State U., 1983, MME, 1985, BS in Applied Math., 1989, M in Pub. Admin., 1993. Registered profl. engr., N.C. Mech. engr. N.C. State Univ., Raleigh, 1985-94, asst. phys. plant dir. for design svcs., 1994-95; supr. capital improvement svcs. N.C. State U., Raleigh, 1995—; spl. engr. cons. United Daughters of Confederacy, Raleigh, 1989—; mem. faculty Indsl. Ventilation Conf., N.C. State U. Author: Marriage and Death Notices, 1991, (with others) NCSU Guidelines for Construction, 1988, 91. Editor Cumberland County Geneal. Soc., Fayetteville, 1991-93. Recipient Disting. Svc. award N.C. State U., 1994. Mem. DAR (sec. 1991—), ASHRAE, NSPE, ASME (chpt. historian 1987-88), N.C. Soc. Engrs. (Order of Engr. 1987), Order of Crown of Charlemagne, Jamestowne Soc., Nat. Soc. Daus. Colonial Wars, Nat. Soc. Daus. Founders and Patriots Am., Nat. Soc. Descs. Colonial Clerty, N.C. State U. Pipes and Drums, Tau Beta Pi, Pi Alpha Alpha. Republican. Avocations: hist. rsch., genealogy, calligraphy, electronics, marquetry. Home: 116 E Ransom St Fuquay Varina NC 27526-2426 Office: NC State U Phys Plant Campus Box 7219 Raleigh NC 27695

TYNER, HOWARD A., newspaper editor, journalist; b. Milw., May 30, 1943; s. Howard Arthur and Katharine Elizabeth Tyner; m. Elizabeth Jane Adams, May 3, 1969; children: Sophie Elizabeth, Ian Adams. BA, Carleton Coll., 1965; MSJ, Northwestern U., 1967. Sports editor Chippewa Herald-Telegram, Chippewa Falls, Wis., 1965-66; fgn. corr. UPI, Europe, 1967-77; with Chgo. Tribune, 1977—; fgn. corr. Chgo. Tribune, Moscow, 1982-85; fgn. editor Chgo. Tribune, Chgo., 1985-88, asst. mng. editor, 1988-90, dep. mng. editor, 1990-92, assoc. editor, 1992-93, editor, 1993—; mem. adv. bd. Alfred Friendly Press Fellowships, Washington, 1988—; mem. exec. bd. World Press Inst., 1994—. Home: 2700 Park Pl Evanston IL 60201-1337 Office: Chgo Tribune Co 435 N Michigan Ave Chicago IL 60611-4001*

TYNER, LEE REICHELDERFER, lawyer; b. Annapolis, Md., Mar. 12, 1946; d. Thomas Elmer and Eleanor Frances (Leland) Reichelderfer; m. Carl Frederick Tyner, Aug. 31, 1968; children: Michael Frederick, Rachel Christine, Elizabeth Frances. BA, St. John's Coll., 1968; MS, U. Wash., 1970; JD, George Washington U., 1975. Bar: Wash., D.C., U.S. Dist. Ct. (D.C.), U.S. Ct. Appeals (4th cir., 1st cir., 9th cir., D.C. cir., 5th cir., 8th cir., 11th cir., 10th cir.), U.S. Ct. Claims, U.S. Supreme Ct. Profl. staff U.S. Senate Commerce Com., Washington, 1970-72; trial atty. Land and Natural Resources div. U.S. Dept. Justice, Washington, 1975-85; atty. Office of Gen. Counsel U.S. EPA, Washington, 1985—. Bd. dirs. Grace Episcopal Day Sch., Silver Spring, Md., 1987-89; den leader, cubmaster Boy Scouts Am., Silver Spring, 1987-91. Recipient Bronze medals, U.S. EPA, 1988, 92. Mem. Order of the Coif. Episcopalian. Home: 1416 Geranium St NW Washington DC 20012-1518 Office: US EPA 401 M St SW Washington DC 20460-0001

TYNER, MCCOY, jazz pianist, composer; b. Phila., 1938. Mem. Art Farmer and Benny Golson's Jazztet, 1959, John Coltrane Quartet, 1960-65; ind. pianist, 1965—. Rec. artist: (with John Coltrane) A Love Supreme, Live at the Village Vanguard, Coltrane, Meditations, (solo albums) Reaching Fourth, The Real McCoy, Time for Tyner, Extensions, Asante, Tender Moments, (with Jackie McLean) It's About Time, Echoes of a Friend, Enlightenment, Atlantis, Passion Dance, Together, 4 x 4, 13th House, Dimensions. Recipient Best Jazz Instrumental Performance, Individual or Group Grammy award, 1996. Office: care Abby Hoffer Enterprises 233 1/2 E 48th St New York NY 10017-1538*

TYNER, NEAL EDWARD, retired insurance company executive; b. Grand Island, Nebr., Jan. 30, 1930; s. Edward Raymond and Lydia Dorothea (Kruse) T.; children: Karen Tyner Redrow, Morgan. BBA, U. Nebr., 1956. Jr. analyst Bankers Life Nebr., Lincoln, 1956-62, asst. v.p. securities, 1962-67, v.p. securities, treas., 1967-69, fin. v.p., treas., 1970-72, sr. v.p. fin., treas., 1972-83, pres., chief exec. officer, 1983-87, chmn., pres., chief exec. officer, 1987-88, chmn., CEO, 1988-95; bd. dirs. Union Bank & Trust Co., Austins Steaks & Saloon; chmn. emeritus Ameritas Life Ins. Corp. Trustee U. Nebr. Found., Lincoln Found., Investment Banking Inst., NYU; bd. govs. Nebr. Wesleyan U. Capt. USMC, 1950-54, Korea. Fellow CFAs; mem. Omaha/Lincoln Soc. Fin. Analysts, Paradise Valley Country Club. Lutheran. Avocations: tennis, computers. Office: Ameritas Life Ins Corp Ste 324 6940 O St Lincoln NE 68510

TYNER, WALLACE EDWARD, economics educator; b. Orange, Tex., Mar. 21, 1945; s. Richard D. and Jeanne (Gullahorn) T.; m. Jean M. Young, May 2, 1970; children: Davis, Jeffrey. BS in Chemistry, Tex. Christian U., 1966; MA in Econs., U. Md., 1972, PhD in Econs., 1977. Vol. Peace Corps., India, 1966-68; math, sci., ednl. skill desk chief Peace Corps., Washington,

1968-70; grad. teacher asst. U. Md., Balt., 1971-73; assoc. scientist Earth Satellite Corp., Washington, 1973-74; rsch. assoc. Cornell U., Ithaca, N.Y., 1974-77; asst. prof., assoc. prof. natural resource econs. and policy Purdue U., West Lafayette, Ind., 1977-84, prof., asst. dept. head, 1983-88, dept. head, 1989—; cons. UN Food and Agrl. Orgn., Rome, Office Tech. Assessment, Washington, U.S. Dept. Interior, Washington, OECD, Paris, World Bank, Washington, USDA, Washington. Author: Energy Resources and Economic Development in India, 1978, A Perspective on U.S. Farm Problems and Agricultural Policy, 1987. Mem. Am. Assn. Agrl. Economists, Am. Econs. Assn., Internat. Assn. Energy Economists, Assn. Environmental and Resource Economists, Sigma Xi, Gamma Sigma Delta. Home: 116 Arrowhead Dr West Lafayette IN 47906-2105 Office: Purdue U Krannert Bldg West Lafayette IN 47907-1145

TYNES, THEODORE ARCHIBALD, educational administrator; b. Portsmouth, Va., Sept. 24, 1932; s. Theodore Archibald and Mildred Antonette (Lee) T.; m. Bettye Clayton, June, 1955 (div. June 1970); children: Karen A. Culbert, David Lee, Tammy Alecia Simpers; m. Cassandra Washington, Nov. 17, 1989; 1 child, Jordan Alexandria. BS in Edn., W.Va. State Coll., 1954; postgrad., Calif. State U., L.A., 1959, Mt. San Antonio Coll, 1962, Chaffey Coll., 1962, Azusa Pacific Coll., 1967; MA in Ednl. Adminstrn., U. Calif., Berkeley, 1969; PhD in Adminstrn. and Mgmt., Columbia Pacific U., 1989. Tchr., athletic dir., coach Walker Grant High Sch., Fredericksburg, Va., 1958-59; dir. programs and aquatics L.A. Times Boys Club, L.A., 1959-62; tchr., dir. recreation, acting edn. supr. youth tng. sch. Calif. Youth Authority, Chino, 1962-68; tchr., dir. drug abuse program Benjamin Franklin Jr. High Sch., San Francisco, 1968-70; asst. prin. Pomona (Calif.) High Sch., 1970-72; prin. Garey High Sch., Pomona, 1972-75; adminstrv. asst. to supt. Bd. Edn., East Orange, N.J.; asst. to commr. U.S. Dept. Edn., Washington; Rockefeller fellow, supt. adminstrv. intern Rockefeller Found., N.Y.C., 1975-76; supervising state coord. sch. programs Office Essex County Supt. N.J. State Dept. Edn., East Orange, 1976-77; rsch. asst., dir. tech. assistance career info. system U. Oreg., Eugene, 1977-79; dir. ednl. placement U. Calif., Irvine, 1979; prin. edn. svcs. Woodrow Wilson Rehab. Ctr., Fisherville, Va., 1980-87; med. courier Urology Inc., Richmond, Va., 1988-90; vice prin. Ithaca (N.Y.) High Sch., 1991—; cons. Fielder and Assocs., Berkeley, 1969-80, Jefferson High Sch., Portland, Oreg., 1970, U. Calif., Berkeley, 1972, U. Calif., Riverside, 1972, Calif. Luth. Coll., 1972, Compton Unified Sch. Dist., 1973, Goleta Unified Schs., 1973, Rialto Sch. Dist., 1973, Grant Union Sch. Dist., Sacramento, Calif., 1973-75, San Mateo Sch. Dist., Tri Dist. Drug Abuse project, 1973, North Ward Cultural Ctr., Newark, N.J., 1976, Nat. Career Conf., Denver, 1978, Opportunities Indulstrialization Ctrs. Am., Phila., Bklyn., Detroit, Poughkeepsie, N.Y., 1980, Tynes & Assocs., 1988; lectr. seminar San Francisco City Coll., 1968-69. Author various curricula, monitoring procedures, grants. 1965—. City commr. Human Rels., Pomona, Calif., 1972-74; pres. San Antonio League, Calif., 1972-75. With USAF, 1954-57. Named Coach of Yr. L.A. Times Boys Club, 1959; fellow Rockefeller Found., 1975; recipient Administrv. award for Excellence Woodrow Wilson Rehab., 1987. Mem. NAACP, Am. Assn. Sch. Adminstrs., Nat. Assn. Secondary Sch. Prins., Nat Alliance Black Sch. Adminstrs., Assn. Supervision and Career Devel., Assn. Ednl. Data Systems., Assn. Calif. Sch. Adminstrs., Va. Govtl. Employees Assn., Va. Rehab. Assn., South Bay Pers. Guidance Assn., Pomona Adminstrs. Assn., Ithaca Prins. Assn., Fisherville Ruritan, Phi Delta Kappa, Omega Psi Phi (Basilius Pi Rho chpt. 1965). Democrat. Episcopalian. Avocations: video and still photogrpahy, music, art, sports. Home: 102 Sherwood Dr Waynesboro VA 22980-9286

TYNG, ANNE GRISWOLD, architect; b. Kuling, Kiangsi, China, July 14, 1920; d. Walworth and Ethel Atkinson (Arens) T. (parents Am. citizens); 1 child, Alexandra Stevens. AB, Radcliffe Coll., 1942; M of Architecture, Harvard U., 1944; PhD, U. Pa., 1975. Assoc. Stonorov & Kahn, Architects, 1945-47; assoc. Louis I. Kahn Architect, 1947-73; pvt. practice architecture Phila., 1973—; adj. assoc. prof. architecture U. Pa. Grad. Sch. Fine Arts, 1968—; assoc. cons. architect Phila. Planning Commn. and Phila. Redevel. Plan, 1954; vis. disting. prof. Pratt Inst., 1979-81, vis. critic architecture, 1969; vis. critic architecture Rensselaer Poly. Inst., 1969, 78, Carnegie Mellon U., 1970, Drexel U., 1972-73, Cooper Union, 1974-75, U. Tex., Austin, 1976; lectr. Archtl. Assn., London, Xian U., China, Bath U., Eng., Mexico City, Hong Kong U., 1989, Baltic Summer Sch., Architecture and Planning, Tallinn, Estonia, Parnu, Estonia, 1993; panel spkr. Nat. Conv. Am. Inst. Architects, N.Y.C., 1988, also numerous univs., throughout U.S. and Can.; asst. leader People to People Archtl. del. to China, 1983; vis. artist Am. Acad., Rome, 1995. Subject of films Anne G. Tyng at Parsons Sch. of Design, 1972, Anne G. Tyng at U. of Minn., 1974, Connecting, 1976, Forming the Future, 1977; work included in Smithsonian Travelling Exhbn., 1979-81, 82, Louis I. Kahn: In the Realm of Architecture, 1990-94; contbr. articles to profl. publs.; prin. works include Walworth Tyng Farmhouse (Hon. mention award Phila. chpt. AIA 1953); builder (with G. Yanchenko) Probability Pyramid. Fellow Graham Found. for Advanced Study in Fine Arts, 1965, 79-81. Fellow AIA (Brunner grantee N.Y. chpt. 1964, 83, dir., mem. exec. bd. dirs. Phila. chpt. 1976-78, John Harbeson Disting. Svc. award Phila. chpt. 1991); mem. Nat. Acad. Design (nat. academician), C.G. Jung Ctr. Phila. (planning com. 1979—), Form Forum (co-founder, planning com. 1978—). Democrat. Episcopalian. Home: 2511 Waverly St Philadelphia PA 19146-1049 Office: Univ Pa Dept Architecture Grad Sch Fine Arts Philadelphia PA 19107

TYRE, NORMAN RONALD, lawyer; b. Boston, Aug. 28, 1910; s. Samuel and Fannie (Spector) T.; m. Margery Cayton, Mar. 10, 1935; children: Joy Tyre Coburn, Patricia Ann Tyre Tanenbaum. BA with gt. distinction, Stanford, 1930; LLB, Harvard U., 1933. Bar: Calif. 1933. Practiced in L.A., 1933—; mem. Gang, Tyre, Ramer & Brown, Inc. and predecessor firm Gang, Tyre & Brown, 1941—; v.p., dir. Motion Picture and TV Tax Inst. Named Beverly Hills Bar Assn. Entertainment Law Sect. Lawyer of Yr., 1990. Mem. Hillcrest Country Club. Home: 801 N Linden Dr Beverly Hills CA 90210-3007 Office: Gang Tyre Ramer & Brown Inc 132 S Rodeo Dr Beverly Hills CA 90212

TYREE, ALAN DEAN, clergyman; b. Kansas City, Mo., Dec. 14, 1929; s. Clarence Tillman and Avis Ora (Gross) T.; m. Gladys Louise Omohundro, Nov. 23, 1951; children: Lawrence Wayne, Jonathan Tama, Sharon Avis. B.A., U. Iowa, 1950; postgrad., U. Mo.-Columbia, 1956-58, U. Mo.-Kansas City, 1961-62. Ordained min. Reorganized Ch. of Jesus Christ of Latter Day Saints, 1947; appointee min. Lawrence, Kans., 1950-52; mission adminstr. (Mission Sanito), French Polynesia, 1953-64; regional adminstr. Denver, 1964-66; mem. Council Twelve Apostles, Independence, Mo., 1966-82; sec. Council Twelve Apostles, 1980-82, mem. First Presidency, 1982-92; ret. First Presidency, 1992; mem. Joint Coun. and Bd. Appropriations, 1966-92; originator music appreciation broadcasts Radio Tahiti, 1962-64, Mission Sanito Radio Ministry, 1960-64; instr. Music/Arts Inst., 1992—, Met. C.C.'s, 1994—. Editor: Cantiques des Saints French-Tahitian hymnal, 1965, Exploring the Faith: A Study of Basic Christian Beliefs, 1987; mem. editing com.: Hymns of the Saints, 1981; author: The Gospel Graced by a People: A Biography of Persons in Tahiti, 1993, Evan Fry: Proclaimer of Good News, 1995, Priesthood: For Other's Sake, 1996. Bd. dirs. Outreach Internat. Found., 1979-82, mem. corp. body, 1982-92; mem. corp. body Independence Regional Health Ctr., 1982-92, v.p., 1983-92, bd. dirs., 1984-93; mem. bd. publs. Herald House, 1984-92; mem. corp. body restoration Trail Found., 1982-92; chmn. Temple Art Com., 1988-94; bd. dirs. Independence Symphony Orch., 1992-96, pres., 1995-96; mem. human rels. commn. city of Independence, 1995—. Recipient Elbert A. Smith Meml. award for publ. articles, 1968, 72. Mem. Phi Beta Kappa, Phi Eta Sigma. Home and Office: 3408 S Trail Ridge Dr Independence MO 64055-1984

TYREE, LEWIS, JR., retired compressed gas company executive, inventor, technical consultant; b. Lexington, Va., July 25, 1922; s. Lewis Sr. and Winifred (West) T.; m. Dorothy A. Hinchcliff, Aug. 21, 1948; children: Elizabeth Hinchcliff, Lewis III, Dorothy Scott. Student, Washington & Lee U., 1939-40; BS, MIT, 1947. Cryogenic engr. Joy Mfg. Co., Michigan City, Ind., 1947-49; v.p. Hinchcliff Motor Service, Chgo., 1949-53; cons. engr. Cryogenic Products, Chgo., 1953-76, Liquid Carbonic Corp., Chgo., 1960-76; exec. v.p. Liquid Carbonic Industries, Chgo., 1976-87; bd. dirs. Liquid Carbonic Industries, Chgo., Worldwide Cryogenics (MVE), New Prague, Minn. Patentee in cryogenics. Served to 1st lt. U.S. Army, 1943-46, PTO. Mem. Soc. Cin., ASME, Am. Soc. Heating, Refrigeration, and Air Conditioning Engring., Hinsdale Golf Club, Lexington Golf and Country Club. Republican. Episcopalian. Home: Mulberry Hill Liberty Hall Rd Lexington VA 24450-1703

TYRELL, LORNE S., dean. Dean U. Alberta. Office: U Alberta, Faculty Medicine, 2J2 Ma Kenzie Health Sci, Edmonton, Canada T6G 2R7

TYRER, JOHN LLOYD, retired headmaster; b. Brockton, Mass., Jan. 16, 1928; s. Lloyd Perkins and Dorothy (Nicholson) T.; m. Jeanne Irene Dunning, June 7, 1952; children: Alison Jane, John Lloyd, David Dunning, Jill Anne. A.B., Bowdoin Coll., 1949; M.A., Middlebury (Vt.) Coll., 1959. Tchr. Wilbraham (Mass.) Acad., 1949-53; tchr., adminstr. Hill Sch., Pottstown, Pa., 1953-64; headmaster Asheville (N.C.) Sch., 1964-92; headmaster emeritus, 1994—; cons. Ind. Ednl. Svcs., 1994—; mem. adv. bd. Warren Wilson Coll., 1972-87. Bd. dirs. Asheville Cmty. Concert Assn., 1970-93, chmn., 1988-90; bd. dirs. Asheville Country Day Sch., 1965-68, A Better Chance, 1988-92, St. Genevieve/Gibbons Hall Sch., 1970-77, Webb Sch., Tenn., 1986-89, Ind. Ednl. Svcs., 1970-75, Coun. Religion in Ind. Schs., 1969-78, ASSIST, 1991—, chmn., 1996—; bd. dirs. Myers Cmty. Concert Assn., 1993—, Lit. Vols. of Am., Lee County, Fla., 1995—. With U.S. Army, 1946-47. Mem. Nat. Assn. Ind. Schs. (bd. dirs., chmn. com. on boarding schs., chmn. membership com.), So. Assn. Ind. Schs. (pres., bd. dirs.), Mid.-South Assn. Ind. Schs. (bd. dirs.), N.C. Assn. Ind. Schs. (pres., bd. dirs.), Headmasters Assn., So. Headmasters Assn., English-Speaking Union (bd. dirs., pres. Asheville br., chmn. secondary sch. exchange com.), Theta Delta Chi. Episcopalian. Home: 1353 Kingswood Ct Fort Myers FL 33919-1927

TYROLER, HERMAN ALFRED, epidemiologist. Grad., NYU Sch. medicine. Lic. to practice, N.C. Prof., now alumni disting. prof. dept. epidemiology U. N.C. Mem. Inst. of Medicine, Nat. Acad. Scis. Office: U NC Dept Epidemiology Chapel Hill NC 27514

TYRRELL, GERALD GETTYS, banker; b. Canton, China, Dec. 27, 1938; came to U.S., 1940.; s. Gerald Fraser and Virginia Lee (Gettys) T.; m. Jane Haldeman, June 1961 (div. Aug. 1975); children: Gerald F., Jane N., Robert M.; m. Elizabeth Ann Drautman, Mar. 31, 1978. BA, Yale U., 1960; MA, Rutgers U., 1971. Cert. real estate financier. With 1st Nat. Bank of Louisville, 1961-89, sr. v.p., 1975-81, exec. v.p., 1981-89; pres., chmn. Churchill Mortgage Corp., 1975-77; chief fin. cons. City of Louisville Office of Downtown Devel., 1989—. Author: A Positive Approach to Financing Black Business, 1972. Trustee, treas. Patton Mus., Ft. Knox, Ky., 1970; treas. Soc. Colonial Wars in Commonwealth of Ky., 1970; mem. exec. bd. Boy Scouts Am., 1983; bd. dirs. The Louisville Orch., 1984. Served to capt. U.S. Army, 1960-68. Recipient Disting. Service Ribbon Ky. Nat. Guard, 1966. Mem. Robert Morris Assocs., Nat. Soc. Real Estate Fin. (bd. govs). Democrat. Clubs: Louisville Country, Pendennis. Avocations: fine wines, tennis. Office: City of Louisville Office Downtown Devel 600 W Main St Ste 300 Louisville KY 40202

TYRRELL, ROBERT EMMETT, JR., editor-in-chief, writer; b. Chgo., Dec. 14, 1943; s. R. Emmett and Patricia (Rogers) T.; m. Judy Mathews Tyrrell, Feb. 12, 1972 (div. Dec. 1989); children: Patrick, Kathryn, Anne. BA, Ind. U., 1965, MA, 1967. Editor-in-chief The Am. Spectator, Arlington, Va., 1967—; pres. Am. Spectator Ednl. Found., Arlington, Va., 1967—. Editor: Network News Treatment of the 1972 Democratic Presidential Candidates, 1972, The Future That Doesn't Work, 1977, Orthodoxy, 1987; author: Public Nuisances, 1979, The Liberal Crack-Up, 1984, The Conservative Crack-Up, 1992, Boy Clinton: The Biography, 1996; writer nationally syndicated polit. column. Recipient Am. Eagle award Invest in Am. Coun., 1977; named Greatest Pub. Svc. Performed by an American 35 Years or Under award Am. Inst. for Pub. Svc., 1977, Ten Most Outstanding Young Men in Am., Jaycees, 1978. Roman Catholic. Avocations: handball, fishing, listening to classical music, reading. Office: The American Spectator 2020 14th St N Ste 750 Arlington VA 22201-2515

TYSON, CICELY, actress; b. N.Y.C., Dec. 19, 1933; d. William and Theodosia Tyson; m. Miles Davis, 1981 (div.). Student, N.Y. U., Actors Studio; hon. doctorates, Atlanta U., Loyola U., Lincoln U. Former sec., model; cofounder Dance Theatre of Harlem; bd. dirs. Urban Gateways. Stage appearances include: The Blacks, 1961-63, off-Broadway, Moon on a Rainbow Shawl, 1962-63, Tiger, Tiger, Burning Bright, Broadway; films include: Twelve Angry Men, 1957, Odds Against Tomorrow, 1959, The Last Angry Man, 1959, A Man Called Adam, 1966, The Comedians, 1967, The Heart is a Lonely Hunter, 1968, Sounder, 1972 (Best Actress, Atlanta Film Festival, Nat. Soc. Film Critics, Acad. award nominee, Best Actress, Emmy award, Best Actress in a spl., 1973), The Blue Bird, 1976, The River Niger, 1976, A Hero Ain't Nothin' but a Sandwich, 1978, The Concorde-Airport 79, 1979, Bustin' Loose, 1981, Fried Green Tomatoes, 1991, Jefferson in Paris, 1995; TV appearances include: (series) East Side, West Side, 1963, Sweet Justice, 1994-95; (films) Marriage: Year One, 1971, The Autobiography of Miss Jane Pittman, 1974, Just an Old Sweet Song, 1976, Wilma, 1977, Roots, 1977, A Woman Called Moses, 1978, King, 1978, The Marva Collins Story, 1981, Benny's Place, 1982, Playing With Fire, 1985, Samaritan: The Mitch Snyder Story, 1986, Acceptable Risks, 1986, Intimate Encounters, 1986, The Women of Brewster Place, 1989, Heat Wave, 1990, Winner Takes All, 1990, The Kid Who Loved Christmas, 1990, When No One Would Listen, 1992, Duplicates, 1993, House of Secrets, 1993, Oldest Living Confederate Widow Tells All, 1994 (Emmy Awd., Best Supporting Actress - Miniseries); other appearances include: Wednesday Night Out, 1972, Marlo Thomas and Friends in Free to Be...You and Me, 1974, CBS: On the Air, 1978, Liberty Weekend, 1986, The Blessings of Liberty, 1987, Without Borders, 1989, Visions of Freedom: A Time Television Special, 1990, Clippers, 1991, A Century of Women, 1994. Trustee Human Family Inst.; trustee Am. Film Inst. Recipient Vernon Price award, 1962; also awards NAACP Nat. Council Negro Women; Capitol Press award. Address: care CAA 9830 Wilshire Blvd Beverly Hills CA 90212-1804*

TYSON, DONALD JOHN, food company executive; b. Olathe, Kans., Apr. 21, 1930; s. John W. and Mildred (Ernst) T.; m. Twilla Jean Womochil, Aug. 24, 1952; children: John H., Cheryl J., Carla A. Student, U. Ark. Plant mgr. Tyson Foods, Inc., Springdale, Ark., 1951-55, pres., 1955-67, chmn., chief exec. officer, 1967-95, sr. chmn., 1995—; chief exec. officer Eagle Distbg. Inc., Tyson Export Sales Inc., Poultry Growers Inc., Tyson Carolina Inc., Spring Valley Farms Inc., Lane Processing Inc., Lane Farms Inc. Lodge: Elks. Home: 2210 W Oaklawn Dr Springdale AR 72762-6900 Office: Tyson Foods Inc PO Box 2020 Springdale AR 72765-2020*

TYSON, GAIL L., health federation administrator; b. Havre de Grace, Md., Dec. 28, 1954; d. William Alva Way and Virginia Lorena Tyson; m. Joseph Matthew Pease, May 17, 1986; 1 child, Loren Juliette Tyson Pease. BA, Dickinson Coll., 1976. Dir. edn. Harrisburg (Pa.) Area Rape Crisis Ctr., 1976-77; community response specialist CONTACT Harrisburg, 1978-81, asst. dir., 1981-85; pub. info. coord. Dauphin County Human Svcs., Harrisburg, 1985-87; unit exec. dir. Am. Cancer Soc., Harrisburg, 1988-92; exec. dir. Nat. Voluntary Health Agys. Pa. Com., Harrisburg, 1992—; v.p. Human Svcs. Program, 1987. Mem. adv. com. Harrisburg Area C.C., 1985-87; mem. adv. bd. Ret. Sr. Vol. Program, Harrisburg, 1986-88, sec., 1987; lifetime mem. Girl Scouts U.S., bd. dirs. Hemlock coun., 1977-91, v.p., 1982-88, pres., 1988-91, chmn. diversity task force, 1992. Recipient Thanks badge Hemlock coun. Girl Scouts U.S., 1991. Mem. Wheel and Chain Hon. Soc. Methodist. Office: Nat Voluntary Health Agy Pa Ste 2-C 4775 Linglestown Rd Harrisburg PA 17112

TYSON, H. MICHAEL, retired bank executive; b. Houston, Aug. 16, 1938; s. Howard Ellis and Myrle (Daunoy) T.; m. Judith O. Gilbert, June 24, 1960; children: H. Michael II, Michelle Lee. B.B.A. cum laude, U. Tex., 1962; postgrad., Stonier Grad Sch. Banking, Rutgers U., 1974. Personnel mgr. Foods div. Anderson Clayton Co., Dallas, 1962-70; exec. v.p. adminstrn. Tex. Commerce Bancshares, Houston, 1970-79; v.p. fin. and adminstrn., chief fin. officer, dir. Houston Chronicle Pub. Co., 1979-87; vice chmn., dir. Tex. Commerce Bank-Houston; exec. v.p., exec. trust officer Tex. Commerce Bancshares, 1987-95; dir. Paranet Inc., Assoc. Bldg. Svcs. Bd. dirs. Harris County Heritage Soc., Houston Symphony, Tax Rsch. Assn., Sam Houston coun. Boy Scouts Am., Houston Festival Found., Lighthouse for the Blind, Goodwill Industries; trustee Gulf Coast United Way, McCullough Found.; chmn. The Houston Parks Bd. Served with USMCR, 1961-67. Mem. Houston C. of C. (com. chmn.), Pers. Round Table, Am. Newspaper Pub. Assn., Houston Indsl. Rels. Group, Fin. Execs. Inst. (bd. dirs.), Internat. Newspaper Fin. Execs., Houston Club (dir., pres.), River Oaks Country Club (dir.), Inns of Ct. Methodist.

TYSON, HARRY JAMES, investment banker; b. Bklyn., Aug. 17, 1945; s. George William and Eileen Regina (Dunphy) T.; m. Sarah Lorretta Halloran, Mar. 9, 1969; children: Kelly J., Stacey L., Harry D. BS in Math., St. Francis Coll., Brooklyn Heights, N.Y., 1968. Analyst Smith Barney, Harris Upham & Co., N.Y.C., 1968, 2d v.p., 1974-76, v.p., 1976-78, 1st v.p., 1978-83, sr. v.p., 1983-90, mem. bd. dirs., 1987-90, exec. v.p., 1990-92; mng. dir. Dillon Read & Co. Inc., N.Y.C., 1992—, also bd. dirs., 1992—. Author: Harah's Universal Bond Basis Converter, 1970. Mem. Assn. for Help Retarded Children, Nassau, N.Y., 1987—, N.Y. Zool. Soc., 1978—, St. Christopher Ottille Guardian Club, Nassau, 1987—. Trans. named Deal of the Yr., Inst. Investor, 1984, 85. Mem. Govt. Fin. Officers Assn., P.R. C. of C. (bd. dirs. 1990-92), N.Y. Athletic Club, North Hempstead Country Club. Republican. Roman Catholic. Avocations: skiing, tennis, golf. Office: Dillon Read & Co Inc 535 Madison Ave New York NY 10022-4212

TYSON, HELEN FLYNN, civic leader; b. Wilmington, N.C.; d. Walter Thomas and Fannie Elizabeth (Smith) Flynn; Student Guilford Coll., Am. U., Washington; m. James Franklin Tyson, Dec. 25, 1940 (dec.). U.S. Civil Svc. auditor, Disbursing Office, AUS, Ft. Bragg, N.C., 1935-46, chief clerical asst. Disbursing Office, Pope AFB, N.C., 1946-49, asst. budget and acctg. officer, 1949-55, supervisory budget officer hdqrs. Mil. Transport Command, USAF, 1955-57, budget analyst Hdqrs. USAF, Washington, 1957-74, ret. Active Arlington Com. 100, Ft. Belvoir, Salvation Army Women's Aux., Inter-Svc. Club Coun. of Arlington. Recipient awards U.S. Treasury, 1945, 46, U.S. State Dept., 1970, Good Neighbor award Ft. Belvoir Civilian-Mil. Adv. Coun., 1978; awards U.S. First Army, 1973, ARC, 1977; named Arlington Woman of Yr., 1975; recipient Cert. of Recognition, 1981, Vol. Activists award Greater Washington Met. Area, 1981. Mem. NAFE, Nat. Fedn. Bus. and Profl. Women's Clubs, Am. Assn. Ret. Fed. Employees (hon.), Am. Soc. Mil. Comptrs. (hon., Outstanding Mem. award Washington chpt. 1988), Am. Inst. Parliamentarians, Guilford Coll. Alumni Assn., N.C. Soc. Washington, Altrusa Internat. Home: 4900 N Old Dominion Dr Arlington VA 22207-2834

TYSON, KENNETH ROBERT THOMAS, surgeon, educator; b. Houston, July 30, 1936; s. Howard Ellis and Myrle Henrietta (Daunoy) T.; m. Sue Ann Delahoussaye, Nov. 20, 1971; children: Deborah, Kenneth, Michael, Jill. B.A., U. Tex., 1956; M.D., U. Tex. Med. Br., 1960. Diplomate: Am. Bd. Surgery, Am. Bd. Thoracic Surgery. Intern Ind. U. Med. Ctr., Indpls., 1960-61; resident in gen. and thoracic surgery Ind. U. Med. Center, 1961-66; resident in pediatric surgery Children's Hosp. Med. Center, Boston, 1966-67; chief pediatric gen., thoracic surgery U. Tex. Med. Br., Galveston, 1967-80; asst. prof. surgery U. Tex. Med. Br., 1967-71, asso. prof., 1971-75, prof., 1975-80; surgeon-in-chief Child Health Center, 1974-80; clin. prof. surgery U. Calif., Davis, 1980-91, U. Tex. Med. Br., Galveston, 1991—. Contbr. articles to profl. jours. Fellow A.C.S., Am. Acad. Pediatrics, Am. Coll. Cardiology; mem. Am. Assn. Thoracic Surgery, Soc. Surgery Alimentary Tract, So. Thoracic Surg. Assn., Am. Pediatric Surg. Assn., Soc. Univ. Surgeons, So. Surg. Assn., Pacific Coast Surg. Assn., Sigma Xi, Alpha Omega Alpha, Delta Kappa Epsilon, Alpha Kappa Kappa. Episcopalian. Home: 7126 Las Ventanas Dr Austin TX 78731-1814 Office: U Tex Med Br Dept Pediatric Surgery Galveston TX 77550

TYSON, KIRK W. M., business consultant; b. Jackson, Mich., July 2, 1952; s. George Carlton and Wilma Marion (Barnes) T.; m. Janice Lynn Lorimer, Aug. 25, 1979 (div. Dec. 1984); m. Kathryn Margit Kennell, June 24, 1986; 1 child, Robert. BBA, Western Mich. U., 1974; MBA, DePaul U., Chgo., 1982. CPA, Ill.; cert. mgmt. cons., 1985. Bus. cons. Arthur Andersen & Co., Chgo., 1974-84; v.p. cons. First Chgo. Corp., 1984; chmn. Kirk Tyson Internat., Lisle, Ill., 1984—. Author: Business Intelligence: Putting It All Together, 1986, Competitor Intelligence: Manual and Guide, 1990, Competition in the 21st Century, 1996. Pres., Chgo. Jr. Assn. Commerce and Industry Found., 1977-79; active Easter Seals Soc., 1977, Am. Blind Skiing Found., 1977-78, Jr. Achievement, 1976-77, United Way Met. Chgo., 1979-80, Urban Gateways, 1975; Rep. Precinct Committeeman Downers Grove township, precinct 114, 1985-88; treas. St. Charles H.S. Football Booster Club, 1994-95. Fellow Soc. Competitive Intelligence Profls.; mem. Am. Inst. CPAs, Ill. Soc. CPAs, The Strategic Leadership Forum, Assn. Global Strategic Info., Inst. Mgmt. Cons., Am. Mktg. Assn., Assn. for Corp. Growth, Global Bus. Devel. Alliance, Alpha Kappa Psi (Disting. Alumni Svc. award 1982). Office: Kirk Tyson International Ltd 4343 Commerce Ct Ste 615 Lisle IL 60532-3619

TYSON, LAURA D'ANDREA, economist, government adviser, educator; b. Bayonne, N.J., June 28, 1947; m. Erik Tarloff; 1 child, Elliot. BA, Smith Coll., 1969; Ph.D., Mass. Inst. Tech., 1974. Prof. econ. and bus. adm. U. Calif., Berkeley, 1978—; chmn. Pres.'s Coun. Econ. Advisors, Washington, 1993-95; nat. econ. advisor to Pres. U.S. Nat. Econ. Coun., Washington, 1995—; dir. Inst. of Internat. Studies and Research, Univ. of Calif., Berkeley Roundtable on the Internat. Economics, Univ. of Calif.; visiting scholar Inst. for Internat. Economics; Subcom. on a global Economic Strategy for the U.S.. Editor: (with John Zysman) American Industry in International Competition, 1983, (with Ellen Comisso) Power, Purpose and Collective Choice: Economic Strategy in Socialist States, 1986, (with William Dickens and John Zysman) The Dynamics of Trade, 1988, (with Chalmers Johnson and John Zysman) Politics and Productivity: The Real Story of How Japan Works, 1989, Who's Bashing Whom? Trade Conflict in High Technology Industries, 1992. Office: Nat Econ Coun 2d Fl West Wing The White House Washington DC 20500

TYSON, LUCILLE A., administrator. AS, Middlesex County Coll.; BA, Wheaton Coll.; MSW, Rutgers U. Cert. gerontol. nurse. Dir. N.J. Parkinson Info. & Referral Ctr. Robert Wood Johnson U. Hosp., New Brunswick, N.J.; human svcs. planner Middlesex County Dept. Human Svcs., New Brunswick; dir., right to know regulations Roosevelt Hosp., Edison, N.J.; dir., quality assurance Cen. N.J. Jewish Home for Aged, Somerset, N.J. Mem. Piscataway (N.J.) Twp. Coun., 1990—; mem. rev./appeals com. Middlesex County Dept. Human Svcs., 1992—; bd. dirs. Metlar Ho. Found.; mcpl. dir. Piscataway Rep. Orgn., 1995—; county committeewoman Middlesex County Rep. Orgn., 1995—. Mem. ANA, NASW, N.J. Nurses Assn., Assn. Quality Assurance Profls. N.J., Geriatric Inst. N.J.

TYSON, MIKE G., professional boxer; b. N.Y.C., June 30, 1966; s. John Kilpatrick and Lorna Tyson; m. Robin Givens, Feb. 7, 1988 (div. Feb. 1989);. Defeated Trevor Berbick to win World Boxing Coun. Heavyweight Title, Nov. 1986, defeated James Smith to win World Boxing Assn. Heavyweight Title, 1987, defeated Tony Tucker to win Internat. Boxing Fedn. Heavyweight Title, Aug. 1987, defeated Michael Spinks to win Internat. Boxing Fedn. Heavyweight Title, June 1988, undisputed heavyweight champion 1988-90 (defeated by James "Buster" Douglas), defeated Frank Bruno to win WBC Heavyweight Title, 1996; commentator for Showtime. Hon. sports chmn. Cystic Fibrosis Assn. N.Y., 1987—, Young Adult Inst., N.Y.C., 1987—. Youngest heavyweight champion in history. Office: Don King Prodns 871 W Oakland Park Blvd Fort Lauderdale FL 33311*

TYSON-AUTRY, CARRIE EULA, legislative consultant, researcher, small business owner; b. Fayetteville, N.C., July 13, 1943; d. Henry McMillan II and Adeline Amelia (Williams) Tyson. BA in Social Studies and Lang. Edn., U. N.C., 1974, MA in Adminstrn., 1992; postgrad., U. Sterling, Scotland, 1978, Coll. Charleston, 1986-87; postgrad., doctoral candidate, Fayetteville State U., 1995—. Cert. tchr., N.C., S.C. Legislative aide, cons. N.C. Gen. Assembley, Raleigh, 1957-86; tchr. various states, 1963-88; rschr. U. N.C., Chapel Hill, 1991—; columnist Orkney, Scotland, 1992—; instr. Pope Air Force Base (CIC), Pope AFB (CTC), 1995—; mem. N.C. joint legis. com. edn., 1976-80; mem. N.C. gov. adv. com. exceptional children, 1977-78; gov. state coord. task force on reading, 1977; U.S. del. to world congr. edn., Scotland, 1978; mem. gov. conf. rural edn., Hilton Head, S.C., 1987. Author: Marlboro County Handbook, 1982-86; developer various curricula, 1977-88. Mem. adminstrv. campaign staff numerous nat. and state candidates; active St. John's Episc. Ch. With U.S. Army, 1973-77. Grantee

GED, 1974-75. Mem. ASCD, Am. Heritage Assn., Scotland's Land Trust Soc., Scottish-Am. Geneol. Soc., Nat. Trust Hist. Preservation, Smithsonian Soc., Mus. Cape Fear (docent), Mensa, Phi Delta Kappa. Republican. Avocations: furniture restoration, reading. Home: Grays Creek RR7 Box 284 Fayetteville NC 28306-9535

TYTELL, JOHN, humanities educator, writer; b. Antwerp, Belgium, May 17, 1939; came to U.S., 1941; s. Charles and Lena (Gano) T.; m. Mellon Gregori, May 28, 1967. BA, CCNY, 1961; MA, NYU, 1963, PhD, 1968. Grad. reader NYU, 1963-67; lectr. Queens Coll., N.Y.C., 1963-68, assoc. prof., 1968-73, 1973-76, prof. English, 1977—; exec. editor Am. Book Rev., 1979—; vis. prof. Rutgers U., 1980, U. Paris, 1983; cons. Nat. Humanities Faculty, Ga., 1978—. Author: The American Experience, 1970, Naked Angels, 1976, Ezra Pound: The Solitary Volcano, 1987, Passionate Lives, 1991, The Living Theatre: Art, Exile and Outrage, 1995; contbr. articles to mags. including Am. Scholar, Partisan Rev., Vanity Fair, Fame. NEH fellow, 1974. Home: 69 Perry St New York NY 10014-3297 Office: Queens College Flushing NY 11367

TYTLER, LINDA JEAN, communications and public affairs executive; b. Rochester, N.Y., Aug. 31, 1947; d. Frederick Easton and Marian Elizabeth (Allen) T.; m. George Stephen Dragnich, May 2, 1970 (div. July 1976); m. James Douglas Fisher, Oct. 7, 1994. AS, So. Sem., Buena Vista, Va., 1967; student U. Va., 1973; student in pub. adminstrn. U. N. Mex., 1981-82. Spl. asst. to Congressman John Buchanan, Washington, 1971-75; legis. analyst U.S. Senator Robert Griffin, Washington, 1975-77; ops. supr. Pres. Ford Com., Washington, 1976; office mgr. U.S. Senator Pete Domenici Re-election, Albuquerque, 1977; pub. info. officer S.W. Community Health Service, Albuquerque, 1978-83; cons. pub. relations and mktg., Albuquerque, 1983-84; account exec. Rick Johnson & Co., Inc., Albuquerque, 1983-84; dir. mktg. and communications St. Joseph Healthcare Corp., 1984-88; mktg. and bus. devel. cons., 1987-90; mgr. communications and pub. affairs Def. Avionics Systems div., Honeywell Inc., 1990—; sgt. N.Mex. Mounted Patrol, 1993—; mem. N.Mex. Ho. of Reps., Santa Fe, 1983-95, ret. 1995, vice chmn. appropriations and fin. com., 1985-86, interim com. on children and youth, 1985-86, mem. consumer and pub. affairs com., transp. com., 1992-95; chmn. Rep. Caucus, 1985-88; chmn. legis. campaign com. Rep. Com.; del. to Republic of China, Am. Council of Young Polit. Leaders, 1988. Bd. dirs. N. Mex. chpt. ARC, Albuquerque, 1984. Recipient award N.Mex. Advt. Fedn., Albuquerque, 1981, 82, 85, 86, 87. Mem. Am. Soc. Hosp. Pub. Rels. (cert.), Nat. Advt. Fedn., Soc. Hosp. Planning and Mktg., Am. Mktg. Assn., N.Mex. Assn. Commerce and Industry (bd. dirs.), Republican. Baptist.

TYUNAITIS, PATRICIA ANN, elementary school educator; b. Kenosha, Wis., Feb. 15, 1942; d. John Anton and Antoinette (Tunkieicz) T. BS, Alverno U., 1966; MAT, Webster U., 1982; postgrad., Walden U., 1994—. Cert. elem., secondary tchr., Wis. Tchr. St. John the Bapt. Sch., Johnsburg, Wis., 1964-67, St. Matthew's Sch., Campbellsport, Wis., 1967-68, St. Monica's Sch., Whitefish Bay, Wis., 1968-71; math. tchr. New Holstein (Wis.) Elem. Sch., 1971—, mem. sch. restructuring com., 1994; adj. prof. Silver Lake Coll., Manitowoc, Wic., 1993—, Marian Coll., Fond du Lac, Wis., 1993—. Mem. performance assessment tng. team Dept. Pub. Instrn., Madison, Wis., 1992—. Recipient Herb Kohl award for excellence in teaching State of Wis., 1991. Mem. ASCD, Nat. Coun. Tchrs. Math., Math. Assn. Am., Nat. Assn. Tchrs. Am., New Holstein Edn. Assn., Wis. Math. Coun., Optimist Club (coord. local forensic contest 1991—, sch. coach Odyssey of the Mind 1986—, sch. coord. Odyssey of the Mind 1992, regional dir. Stevens Point chpt. 1992—). Home: N 10335 Hwy 151 Malone WI 53049 Office: New Holstein Elem Sch 2226 Park Ave New Holstein WI 53061-1008

TZAGOURNIS, MANUEL, physician, educator, university administrator; b. Youngstown, Ohio; came to Oct. 20, 1934,; s. Adam and Argiro T.; m. Madeline Jean Kalos, Aug. 30, 1958; children: Adam, Alice, Ellen, Jack George. B.S., Ohio State U., 1956, M.D., 1960, M.S., 1967. Intern Phila. Gen. Hosp., 1960-61; resident Ohio State U., Columbus, 1961-63, chief med. resident, 1966-67, instr., 1967-68, asst. prof., 1968-70, assoc. prof., 1970-74, prof., 1974—, asst. dean Sch. Medicine, 1973-75, assoc. dean, med. dirs. hosps., 1975-80, v.p. health scis., dean of medicine, 1981-95; gen. practice medicine Columbus, 1967—; mem. staff Ohio State U. Hosps./James Cancer Hosp. & Rsch. Ctr.; mem. Coalition for Cost Effective Health Services Edn. and Research Group State of Ohio, 1983. Contbg. author: textbook Endocrinology, 1974, Clinical Diabetes: Modern Management, 1980; co-author: Diabetes Mellitus, 1983, 88. Citation Ohio State Senate Resolution No. 984, 1989. Capt. U.S. Army, 1962-64. Recipient Homeric Order of Ahepa Cleve. chpt., 1976, Phys. of Yr. award Hellenic Med. Soc. N.Y., 1989; citations Ohio State Senate and Ho. of Reps., 1975, 83. Mem. AMA (med. edn. coun. 1993—), Am. Red Cross (vice chair ctrl. Ohio 1996—), Franklin County Acad. Medicine, Assn. Am. Med. Colls., Assn. of Acad. Health Ctrs., Deans' Council. Mem. Greek Orthodox Ch. Home: 4335 Sawmill Rd Columbus OH 43220-2243 Office: Ohio State U Coll Medicine 200 Meiling Hall 370 W 9th Ave Columbus OH 43210-1238

TZALLAS, NIOVE, painter; b. Jannina, Greece, Jan. 26, 1938; d. George and Kaliroi (Papastergiou) Georgopoulos; m. Neocosmos Tzallas, Aug. 21, 1959. Student, Athens Sch. Beaux Arts, 1955-58, Atelier Andre Lhote, France, 1958-59, Cen. Sch. Arts and Crafts, Eng., 1959-61. One-woman shows at Paris, 1962, Rome, 1963, Gallery Royal Soc. Painters, London, 1964, Gallery du Damier, Paris, 1968, Gallery U. Paris, 1969, 72, Mus. de Havre, France, 1971, Galerie Vallombreuse, Biarritz, France, 1974, Gallery Mouffe, Paris, 1975, Gallery Bernheim-Jeune, Paris, 1982, BH Corner Gallery, London, 1985, 86, Everarts Galerie, Paris, 1988, 90, 93, Montserrat Gallery, N.Y., 1994, Galerie Art Present, Paris, 1996; exhibited in floating exhbns. aboard S.S. Pegassos, S.S. Semiramis, 1966, S.S. Olympia, 1967; exhibited in group shows at Salon des Independents, Grand Palais des Champs Elysees, 1973-95, Grand Prix Internat. de la Baie des Anges, Nice, France, Galerie Riviera, Nice, 1974, Galerie Blaise St. Maurice, Paris, 1974-77, Galerie l'Arthotèque, Monte Carlo, 1975, Salon Populiste, Paris, 1975, Maison de la Culture à Ville-neuve-la Garenne, 1976-77,, Ctr. Cultural de Mussidan, Dordogne, France, 1977, The Breakers Gallery, Palm Beach, Fla., 1976-78, Ctr. European Delobbe à Olloy Sur Viroin, Belgium, 1978, Galerie la Roue, Paris, 1978-79, Salon de l'Art Libre, Paris, 1978-79, Festival d'Art Graphique d'Osaka, Japan, 1983-84, Metropolis Galerie Internat. D'Art, Geneva, 1984, Mus. Luxembourg, Paris, L'Union des Femmes Peintres et Sculpteurs, 1981, 82, Galerie Hautefeuille, Paris, 1988-9, Galerie, Quincampoix, Paris, 1989, Espace Delpha, Paris, 1989, Espace Laser, Paris, 1989, Galerie Jules Salles, Nimes, France, 1993, Salon de Academie Culturelle Internationale des Artistes de France de la ville de Gimont, 1993. Home: 15 Ekalis St, 145 61 Kifissia, Attica Greece Studio: 13 Pericleous Stavrou str, 115 24 Athens Greece

TZIMAS, NICHOLAS ACHILLES, orthopedic surgeon, educator; b. Greece, Apr. 18, 1928; came to U.S., 1955, naturalized, 1960; s. Archilles Nicholas and Evanthia B. (Exarchou) T.; m. Helen J. Papastylopoulos, Apr. 22, 1958; children: Yvonne, Christina. M.D., U. Athens, Greece, 1952. Intern St. Mary's Hosp., Hoboken, N.J., 1955-56; resident in gen. surgery Misericordia Hosp., N.Y.C.; resident in orthopedic surgery Bellevue Hosp., N.Y.C., 1957-60; instr. orthopedic surgery N.Y. U. Sch. Medicine, 1961-63, asst. clin. prof., 1963-65, asso. clin. prof., 1965-71; clin. prof., 1971—; mem. staff Univ. and Bellevue Hosps.; chief children's orthopedics, 1966—; orthopedic cons. Inst. Rehab. Medicine, N.Y. U., 1966—, St. Agnes Hosp., White Plains, N.Y., 1972—; advisory com. Bur. Handicapped Children, N.Y.C., 1975—; spl. invitations for teaching, Osaka, Japan, 1970, Jerusalem, 1974, São Paolo, Brazil, 1976, Taranto, Italy, 1977, Bari, Italy, 1978, Barquisimeto, Venezuela, 1979, Bogotá, Colombia, 1983, Buenos Aires, Argentina, 1983. Author articles on spina bifida child mgmt. Served with M.C. Greek Army, 1952-55. Named ofcl. Knight of Italian Republic, 1979. Fellow Am., Internat. colls. surgeons; mem. N.Y. Acad. Medicine, N.Y. State, N.Y. County med. socs., Am. Acad. Orthopedic Surgeons, Am. Congress Rehab. Medicine, Am. Acad. Cerebral Palsy. Mem. Greek Orthodox Ch., Archon of the Ecumenical Patriarchate of Constantinople. Home: 33 Edgewood St Tenafly NJ 07670-2909 Office: 530 1st Ave New York NY 10016-6402

TZIMOPOULOS, NICHOLAS D., science and mathematics education specialist; b. Eptachorion, Greece, Feb. 19, 1941; came to U.S., 1956; s. Demetrius and Soultana (Davos) T. BA in Chemistry and Math., U. N.H., 1965; MS in Analytical Chemistry, Boston Coll., 1967, PhD in Phys. Chemistry, 1971. Dir. research So. N.H. Services, Manchester, 1978-80; prof. phys. chemistry U. Northern Fla., Jacksonville, 1981-82; chmn. math and sci. The Bartram Sch., Jacksonville, Fla., 1980-83; prof. chemistry Valencia Community Coll., Orlando, Fla., 1983-84; dir. sci. edn. Schs. of the Tarrytowns, North Tarrytown, N.Y., 1984-91; dir. sci., math. and tech. Lexington (Mass.) Pub. Schs., 1989—. Author: Modified Null-Point Potentiometry, 1967, Irreversible Processes, 1971, mathematics-Science Curricula, 1982, Modern Chemistry, 1990, 93, Life, Earth, Physical Sciences, 1987, 90, General Sciences Books 1 and 2, 1987, 90, The Next Generation: Teachers Resources Curriculum Guide, 1993, The Stuff of Dreams: Teachers Resource Curriculum Guide, 1993. N.H. rep. N.E. Metric Action Council, 1978-80; Tufts U. del. New Eng. Energy Congress, 1978; liaison Kiwanis Regional Sci. and Engring. Fair, Jacksonville, 1983; founder N.H. Legis. Acad. Sci. and Tech., Concord, 1980. Recipient Outstanding commendations in sci. achievement Internat. Sci. and Engring. Fair, 1986, CMA Catalyst award, 1987, N.Y. State Presdl. award for excellence in sci. and math., 1989. Fellow Sigma Xi; mem. AAAS, ASCD, Am. Chem. Soc. (Fla. congl. del. 1984, treas. Fla. sect. 1983, 84, chmn. Jacksonville sect. 1982-83, dir. Westchester County, N.Y. sub-sect. 1986—, high sch. exams. com. 1982-86, Outstanding Chemistry Tchr. Fla. 1982, S.E. U.S. 1983, Nichols award 1986), N.Y. Acad. Sci., Fla. Acad. Sci., Nat. Sci. Tchrs. Assn., Greek Orthodox Youth Assn. (pres. Manchester, N.H. 1963-65). Democrat. Avocations: photography, classical music, guitar, travel, soccer.

UBELL, DONALD PAUL, lawyer; b. Rome, N.Y., Dec. 16, 1945; s. Carl C. and Mary (De Cristo) U.; m. Nancy Sting, Aug. 23, 1969; children: Brian Donald, Matthew Lee, Karen Elizabeth. AB, U. N.C., 1967; JD, U. Mich., 1969. Bar: Mich. 1970, Ga. 1984, N.C. 1993. Rsch. atty. Mich. Ct. Appeals, 1969-71, asst. clk., 1971-73; dir. Pros. Attys. Appellate Svc., Lansing, Mich., 1973-74; commr. Mich. Supreme Ct., Lansing, 1974-83; ptnr. Kutak Rock, Atlanta, 1983-93, Parker, Poe, Adams & Bernstein L.L.P., Charlotte, N.C., 1993—; adj. prof. law Thomas M. Cooley Law Sch., 1972-79; jud. fellow U.S. Supreme Ct., 1979-80. Contbr. articles to profl. jours. Mem. ABA (coun. young lawyers div. 1976-78, coun. legal edn. and admissions to bar sect. 1977-78, consortium profl. competence 1983-84, bd. dirs. gen. practice sect. 1986-87, budget officer 1986-89, standing com. on continuing edn. of bar 1991-94), Mich. Bar Assn. (rep. assembly 1972-76, 78-79, bd. commrs. 1978-79, chmn. young lawyers sect. 1978-79), Ga. Bar Assn., N.C. Bar Assn., Phi Beta Kappa, Phi Eta Sigma. Office: Parker Poe Adams & Bernstein LLP 2500 Charlotte Pl Charlotte NC 28244

UBELL, EARL, magazine health editor; b. Bklyn., June 21, 1926; s. Charles and Hilda (Kramer) U.; m. Shirley Leitman, Feb. 12, 1949; children—Lori Ellen, Michael Charles. B.S., CCNY, 1948. With N.Y. Herald Tribune, 1943-66, successively messenger, asst. sec. to mng. editor, reporter, 1943-53, sci. editor, 1953-66, syndicated columnist, 1956-66; sci. commentator MBS, 1958-59; spl. sci. editor WNEW, N.Y., 1962; health and sci. editor WCBS-TV, N.Y.C., 1966-72, 78-95; health editor PARADE mag., 1983—. Dir. TV news NBC News, N.Y.C., 1972-76; producer spl. broadcasts TV news, 1976-78; producer documentaries Medicine in America, 1977, Escape from Madness, 1977; author: The World of Push and Pull, 1964, The World of The Living, 1965, The World of Candle and Color, 1969, How to Save Your Life, 1972, (with Carol C. Flax) Mother/Father/You, 1980. Pres. Council Advancement Sci. Writing, Inc., 1960-66, bd. dirs., 1960—; chmn. Center Modern Dance Edn., Inc., 1962-82; pres. North Jersey Cultural Council, 1966-72; bd. dirs. Dance Notation Bur., 1968—, chmn. bd., 1975-94; bd. dirs. Sex Info. and Edn. Council U.S., 1967-69, YMHA, Bergen County, 1968-73, Nat. Center Health Edn., 1977. Served as aviation radioman USNR, 1944-46. Recipient Mental Health Bell award N.Y. State Soc. Mental Health, 1957, Albert Lasker med. journalism award, 1958, Nat. Assn. Mental Health award for radio program, 1962, Sci. Writers award Am. Psychol. Found., 1965, Westinghouse award AAAS, 1960, Empire State award, 1963, TV Reporting award N.Y. Assoc. Press, 1969, 71, N.Y. Emmy award, 1971, Samuelson award N.Y. League for Hard of Hearing, Legal-Med. award Milton Helpern Library of Legal Medicine, Spl. Achievement award Deadline Club, 1982, Disting. Contbn. award, 1983, Nat. Media award Am. Diabetes Assn., 1985, N.Y. State Mental Health Council award, 1987, Ann. Svc. award Dance Notation Bur., 1990. Mem. Nat. Assn. Sci. Writers (pres. 1960-61), Nuclear Energy Writers Assn. (pres. 1965-66), Phi Beta Kappa (pres. Gamma chpt. 1976-77). *I learn something new, in depth, every 5 years—x-ray crystallography, French, statistics, polling, stock market—I am refreshed.*

UBELL, ROBERT NEIL, editor, publisher, consultant, literary agent; b. Bklyn., Sept. 14, 1938; s. Charles and Hilda (Kramer) U.; m. Rosalyn Deutsche, Sept. 24, 1976; children: Jennifer, Elizabeth. B.A., Bklyn. Coll., 1961; student, Acad. Fine Arts, Rome, Italy, 1959-60, City U. N.Y., 1961-62, Pratt Graphic Arts Workshop, N.Y.C., 1972-73. Asso. editor Nuclear Industry, Atomic Industrial Forum, 1962-64; editor Plenum Pub. Corp., N.Y.C., 1965-68; sr. editor Plenum Pub. Corp., 1968-70, v.p., editor in chief, 1970-76; editor The Sciences, N.Y. Acad. Scis., N.Y.C., 1976-79; Am. pub. Nature, N.Y.C., 1979-83; founding pub. Bio/Tech., 1983; pres. Robert Ubell Assocs., N.Y.C., 1983—, BioMedNet, Inc., 1996—. Author: (with Marvin Leiner) Children are the Revolution, 1974, Negotiating Networked Licensing Agreements (with Mark Tesoriero), 1995; editor Nature Directory of Biologicals, 1981, Physics Today Buyer's Guide, 1984-89; exec. editor: Linguistics: The Cambridge Survey, 1987-88, Pre-Med Handbook, 1986, International Encyclopedia of the Social Sciences, Vol. 19, 1991, Encyclopedia of Astronomy and Astrophysics, 1991, Triumph of Discovery, 1995, Encyclopedia of Climate and Weather, 1996; cons. editor ISI Press, 1985-87, Am. Inst. of Physics Book Program, 1986—; Am. Chem. Soc. Book Program, 1989; cons. pub. Computers in Physics, 1987-91; series editor Masters of Modern Physics, 1991—, Creators of Modern Chemistry, 1994-95, Sci. Am. Focus, 1995-96; contbr. articles to profl. jours. Mem. AAAS, N.Y. Acad. Scis., Nat. Assn. Sci. Writers, Soc. Scholarly Pubs. Office: Robert Ubell Assocs Inc 111 8th Ave New York NY 10011-5201

UBERALL, HERBERT MICHAEL STEFAN, physicist, educator; b. Neunkirchen, Austria, Oct. 14, 1931; came to U.S., 1953, naturalized, 1963; s. Michael and Stefanie (Hacker) U.; m. Reyna Tosta, 1981; children by previous marriage: Bernadette Chauvallon, Bertrand. Ph.D., U. Vienna, Austria, 1953, Cornell U., 1956; PhD (honoris causa), U. Le Havre, France, 1987. Staff mem. Signal Corps. Labs., Ft. Monmouth, N.J., 1953-54; research asst. Cornell U., 1954-56; research fellow Nuclear Physics Research Lab., U. Liverpool, Eng., 1956-57; Ford Found. fellow CERN, Geneva, Switzerland, 1957-58; research physicist Carnegie Inst. Tech., Pitts., 1958-60; asst. prof. U. Mich., Ann Arbor, 1960-64; assoc. prof. Cath. U. Am., Washington, 1964-65, prof. physics, 1965-84, prof. emeritus, 1984—; vis. prof. U. Paris VII Jussieu, 1984-85, U. Le Havre, 1990, 92, 94, U. Bordeaux, 1993, 95, U. Aix-Marseille II and Lab. Mech. Acoustics, 1995; cons. Naval Rsch. Lab., Washington, 1966—. Author: Electron Scattering from Complex Nuclei, 1971; co-author: Giant Resonance Phenomena, 1980, Nuclear Pion Photoproduction, 1991; editor: Acoustic Resonance Scattering, 1992; co-editor: Long Distance Neutrino Detection, 1979, Classical and Quantum Dynamics, 1991, Coherent Radiation Sources, 1985, Coherent Radiation Processes in Strong Fields, 1991, Radar Target Imaging, 1994; contbr. 300 articles to profl. jours. Recipient Achievement award Washington Acad. Scis., 1984. Fellow IEEE, Am. Phys. Soc., Acoustical Soc. Am., Washington Acad. Scis.; mem. AAUP, Am. Acad. Mech., Electromagnetics Acad., Internat. Union Radio Sci. Home: 5101 River Rd Apt 1417 Bethesda MD 20816-1571 Office: Catholic U Dept Physics Washington DC 20064

UBEROI, MAHINDER SINGH, aerospace engineering educator; b. Delhi, India, Mar. 13, 1924; came to U.S., 1945, naturalized, 1960; s. Kirpal Singh and Sulaksha (Kosher) U. B.S., Punjab U., Lahore, India, 1944; M.S., Calif. Inst. Tech., 1946; D.Eng., Johns Hopkins U., 1952. Registered profl. engr. Mem. faculty U. Mich., Ann Arbor, 1953-63, prof. aeros., 1959-63, vis. prof., 1963-64; prof. aerospace engring. U. Colo., Boulder, 1963—, chmn. dept. aerospace engring., 1963-75; fellow F. Joint Inst. for Lab. Astrophysics, Boulder, 1963-74; hon. research fellow Harvard U., 1975-76; invited prof. U. Que., Can., 1972-74. Author numerous rsch. publs. on dynamics of ionized and neutral gases and liquids with and without chem. reactions, gravity and electromagnetic fields; editor Cosmic Gas Dynamics, 1974. Council mem. Ednl. TV Channel 6, Inc., Denver, 1963-66. Guggenheim fellow Royal Inst. Tech., Stockholm, Sweden, 1958; exchange scientist U.S. Nat. Acad. Scis.; exchange scientist Soviet Acad. Scis., 1966. Mem. Am. Phys. Soc., Tau Beta Pi. Home: 819 6th St Boulder CO 80302-7418

UBINGER, JOHN W., JR., lawyer; b. Pitts., Jan. 31, 1949. BBA, Ohio U., 1970; JD, U. Notre Dame, 1973. Bar: Pa. 1973. Ptnr. Jones, Day, Reavis & Pogue, Pitts.; instr. environ. dispute resolution Duquesne U. Sec. Pa. Environ. Coun., chmn. task force on reuse of indsl. sites, 1994-95; bd. dirs., treas. Allegheny Land Trust; adv. com. Allegheny County Dept. Air Pollution Control, Allegheny County Contaminated Sites Redevel. Study, 1994-95. Mem. ABA (natural resources, energy and environ. law sect.) Pa. Bar Assn. (chmn. environ., mineral and natural resources law sect. 1990-91), Allegheny County Bar Assn. (chmn. environ. law sect. 1991), Air and Waste Mgmt. Assn. (chmn. We. Pa. Sect. 1989-90), Environ. Law Inst. (assoc.). Office: Jones Day Reavis & Pogue 1 Mellon Bank Ct 500 Grant St Pittsburgh PA 15219-2502

UBOSI, ANGIE NONYGLUM, nutrition center executive, consultant; b. Enugu, Nigeria, Aug. 12, 1952; came to U.S., 1978, naturalized, 1978; d. Thomas and Nwaobonne (Ukagi) U.; m. Williams Clearame, Nov. 8, 1984. BS, U. Ark., 1982; BA in Bus., McNeese State U., 1983; postgrad., Donsbech U., 1984—. Registered nutrition cons. Officer, Dept. Customs, Nigeria, 1973-78; mgr. Nutrition, Little Rock, 1978-82; pres. Angie Internat. Nutrition Ctr., Inc., Lake Charles, La., 1982-86, Nutritional Motivation, Lake Charles, 1983—. Author poetry. Pres. Lake Charles chpt. Am. Cancer Soc., 1982—; vol. Edn. Therapy Ctr., Lake Charles, 1986. Mem. NAFE (network dir. 1983-85), Am. Nutritional Med. Assn., Internat. Trade Orgn., Nat. Health Assn. (pres. Lake Charles chpt. 1983—). Address: 1421 Ruth Pl Decatur GA 30035-1130

UBUKA, TOSHIHIKO, biochemistry educator; b. Kagaminocho, Okayama, Japan, Jan. 31, 1934; s. Yoshio and Shigeko (Hashimoto) U.; m. Satoko Iwamiya, Oct. 18, 1960; children: Takayoshi, Hiromi, Atsue. MD, Okayama U., 1959, PhD, 1964. With Okayama U., 1964-73, asst. prof., 1973-80, assoc. prof. Med. Sch., 1980-81, prof. Med. Sch., 1981—; rsch. assoc. Med. Coll. Cornell U., N.Y.C., 1968-71. Co-author: Methods in Enzymology, vol. 143, 1987; editor Acta Med Okayama, 1980—, Physiol Chem Phys and Med NMR, 1982—, Amino Acids, 1991—; chief editor Acta Med Okayama, 1987-90. Fellow Japanese Biochem. Soc., Japanese Soc. Nutrition and Food Sci.; mem. AAAS, N.Y. Acad. Scis., Internat. Soc. Amino Acid Rsch., Soc. Study Inborn Errors Metabolism, The Protein Soc. Achievements include research in sulfur biochemistry, sulfur nutrition, cysteine metabolism in mammals, protein modification with mixed disulfides, inborn errors of cysteine metabolism. Home: 527-1 Nishikarakawa, Okayama 701-12, Japan Office: Okayama U Med Sch Dept Biochemistry, 2-5-1 Shikatacho, Okayama 700, Japan

UCCELLO, VINCENZA AGATHA, artist, director, educator emerita; b. Hartford, Conn., May 11, 1921; d. Salvatore and Josephine (Bordonaro) U. B.S., St. Joseph Coll., West Hartford, Conn., 1956; M.A. in Liberal Studies, Wesleyan U., 1961; M.F.A., Villa Schifanoia, Florence, Italy, 1963. Tchr. art Glastonbury High Sch., Conn., 1957-61, East Hartford Pub. Schs., Conn., 1963-64; prof. fine arts St. Joseph Coll., 1964—, chmn. dept. fine arts, 1967-85, acting curator, dir. coll. art collections, 1978—. One-woman shows Villa Schifanoia, Florence, 1963, St. Joseph Coll., 1965, 81, Pump House Gallery, Hartford, Conn., 1986; group shows Am. Painters in Paris Exhbn., Nat. Print and Drawing Exhbn., Ohio U., Athens, Ball State U., Muncie, Ind., Austin Art Ctr., Trinity Coll., Hartford, Munson Gallery, New Haven; represented in permanent collections St. Joseph Coll., N.Y. Pub. Libr., Ctr. for Book Arts, Conn. Nat. Bank, Hartford; pvt. collections. Recipient Harper Meml. award in painting, 1969; fellow Venice Artists Workshop, 1965; Yale U. fellow Andrew U. Mellon Found., 1980; second prize Atria Gallery Blues Show, Disting. Alumnae award St. Joseph Coll. Mem. Coll. Art Assn. Am. Conn. Women Artists (pres. 1974-76), Canton Artists Guild, Am. Assn. Mus. Home: 51 Hilltop Dr West Hartford CT 06107-1434

UCHIDA, IRENE AYAKO, cytogenetics educator, researcher; b. Vancouver, B.C., Can., Apr. 8, 1917; d. Sentaro and Shizuko (Takano) U. BA, U. Toronto, Ont., Can., 1946, PhD, 1951. Rsch. assoc. Hosp. Sick Children, Toronto, 1951-59; dir. med. genetics Children's Hosp., Winnipeg, Man., Can., 1960-69; asst. prof. U. Man., 1963-67, assoc. prof., 1967-69; dir. cytogenetics lab. McMaster U. Med. Ctr., Hamilton, Ont., 1969-91; prof. pediatrics, pathology McMaster U., 1969-85, prof. emeritus, 1985—; dir. cytogenetics Oshawa (Ont.) Gen. Hosp., 1991-95; mem. sci. adv. com. Inst. for Basic Research, Staten Island, N.Y., 1984—; vis. scientist Med. Research Council Can., U. London and Harwell Radiobiol. Research Unit, 1969; vis. prof. Med. Research Council Can., U. Western Ont., 1973. Author medcom slide tape series, 1987; contbr. articles to profl. jours. and chpts. to books. Mem. Sci. Council Can., Ottawa, 1970-73; mem. adv. com. Ont. Ministry Health, Toronto, 1979-85. Decorated officer Order of Can.; recipient Woman of Yr. award Women's Advt. Sales Club, 1963, Woman of Century award Nat. Coun. Jewish Women, 1967, achievement award Altrusa Club, 1969; Ramsay Wright scholar, 1947; fellow Rockefeller Found., 1959; grantee Nat. Found. March of Dimes, 1962-69, 71-77, NIH, 1962-69, 89-91, Nat. Heart, Lung and Blood Inst., 1977-79. Fellow Can. Coll. Med. Geneticists (emeritus 1992, Founder's award 1995), Am. Coll. Med. Genetics (emeritus 1993); mem. Am. Soc. Human Genetics (pres. 1968), Peruvian Soc. Med. Genetics (hon.). Office: McMaster U, 1200 Main St W, Hamilton, ON Canada L8N 3Z5

UCHITELLE, LOUIS, journalist; b. N.Y.C., Mar. 21, 1932; s. Abraham and Alice Lee (Cronbach) U.; m. Joan Eva Shapiro, Oct. 7, 1966; children: Isabel Anne, Jennifer Emily. B.A., U. Mich., 1954. Reporter Mt. Vernon (N.Y.) Daily Argus, 1955-57; with AP, 1957-80; fgn. corr. and bur. chief AP, San Juan, P.R., 1964-67, Buenos Aires, 1967-73; supervising editor AP Newsfeatures, N.Y.C., 1974-76; bus. news editor AP, 1977-80; asst. bus. and fin. editor N.Y. Times, 1980-87, econ. writer, 1987—; instr. journalism Sch. Gen. Studies, Columbia U., 1976-89. Home: 11 Ridgecrest W Scarsdale NY 10583-2046 Office: NY Times 229 W 43rd St New York NY 10036-3913

UCHRIN, CHRISTOPHER GEORGE, environmental scientist; b. South Amboy, N.J., Oct. 27, 1950; s. George Christopher and Annette Rose Marie (Skokan) U. B in Civil Engring., Manhattan Coll., 1972, M. in Environ. Engring., 1974; PhD in Environ. Engring., U. Mich., 1980. Registered profl. engring. N.Y. Environ. engr. U.S. EPA, N.Y.C., 1972-77; Rackham fellow U. Mich., Ann Arbor, Mich., 1977-78, rsch. asst., 1978-80; asst. prof. Rutgers U., New Brunswick, N.J., 1980-86, assoc. prof., 1986-90, prof. environ. sci., 1990—; chair dept. environ. sci. Rutgers U., New Brunswick, 1991-94, dir. grad. program in environ. sci., 1986-91; co-dir. Joint PhD Program in Exposure Assessment, Rutgers U. & UMDNJ/Robert Wood Johnson Med. Sch., 1991—. Mem. ASCE, Am. Chem. Soc., Water Environment Fedn., Am. Soc. for Materials, Soc. Environ. Toxicology and Chemistry, N.J. Acad. Sci. (pres. 1991-92), Sigma Xi. Office: Rutgers U Dept Environ Sci PO Box 231 New Brunswick NJ 08903

UCKO, DAVID ALAN, museum director; b. N.Y.C., July 9, 1948; s. Lawrence L. and Helen H. U.; m. Barbara Alice Clark, Aug. 13, 1977; 1 child, Aaron. BA, Columbia Coll., N.Y.C., 1969; PhD, MIT, 1972. Asst. prof. chemistry Hostos Community Coll., CUNY, Bronx, 1972-76; asst. prof. chemistry Antioch Coll., Yellow Springs, Ohio, 1976-79, assoc. prof. chemistry, 1979; rsch. coord. Mus. Sci. and Industry, Chgo., 1979-80, dir. sci., 1981-87, v.p., 1986-87; dep. dir. Calif. Mus. Sci. and Industry, L.A., 1987-90; pres. Kansas City (Mo.) Mus., 1990—; rsch. assoc. chemistry dept. Columbia U., 1973-76; rsch. assoc., assoc. prof. dept. edn. U. Chgo., 1982-87; adj. staff scientist C.F. Kettering Rsch. Lab., Yellow Springs, 1977-79. Author: (book) Basics for Chemistry, 1982, Living Chemistry, 2d edit., 1986; contbr. articles to profl. jours.; host, producer (radio program) Science Alive!, 1983-87; developer numerous mus. exhibits. V.p., bd. dirs. Heritage League Greater Kansas City, 1991-92; mem. Mid-Am. Regional coun., Regional Amenities Task Force, Kansas City, 1990—, Nat. Mus. Svc. Bd., 1996; bd. dirs. Cultural Alliance Greater Kansas City, Mus. Without Walls. Woodrow Wilson fellow, 1969, NIH postdoctoral fellow, 1972; grantee NSF, NEH, U.S. Dept. Edn., Ill. Humanities Coun., 1976-88; recipient Up and Comers award Jr. Achievement of Mid.-Am., 1992. Fellow AAAS (at-large sect. Y 1987-93); mem. Assn. Sci. Tech. Ctrs. (publs. com. 1984-94, chmn. 1988-94, ethics com. 1994-95, legis. com. chmn. 1996—), Greater Kansas City C. of C. (edn. com. 1993—), Alpha Sigma Nu (hon.). Home: 1007 W

66th St Kansas City MO 64113-1815 Office: Kansas City Mus 3218 Gladstone Blvd Kansas City MO 64123-1111

UCLES, MAUREEN ELLEN, bilingual educator; b. Portsmouth, Ohio, Dec. 7, 1966; d. Harold Edwin and Betty Rosemary (Scherer) Stamper; m. Jose Armando Ucles, May 17, 1993. BS in Elem. Edn., Franciscan U., Steubenville, Ohio, 1989; bilingual endorsement, U. Tex., El Paso, 1993. Cert. bilingual, ESL 1-12 elem, 6-12 history secondary tchr. Jr. high volleyball and basketball coach Aquinas Elem. Sch., Steubenville, 1987-90; tchr. 8th grade Holy Rosary Elem. Sch., Steubenville, 1990; tchr. 5th, 6th, 7th and 8th grade St. Agnes Elem. Sch., Mingo Junction, Ohio, 1990; varsity volleyball coach Notre Dame H.S., Portsmouth, Ohio, 1990; day camp dir. Portsmouth YMCA, 1990; vol., tchr.-trainer U.S. Peace Corps, Honduras, Ctrl. Am., 1990-92; tchr. 1st grade New Orleans Pub. Sch., 1992-93; tchr. 3rd grade bilingual Ysleta Ind. Sch. Dist., El Paso, 1993—. Peace Corps fellow U. Tex., El Paso, 1993-94. Mem. Assn. Tex. Profl. Educators. Roman Catholic. Avocations: poetry, dancing, travel, sports, music. Home: 1750 N Lee Trevino Dr El Paso TX 79936-4524 Office: Dolphin Ter Elem Sch 9790 Pickerel Dr El Paso TX 79924-5613

UDALL, CALVIN HUNT, lawyer; b. St. Johns, Ariz., Oct. 23, 1923; s. Grover C. and Dora (Sherwood) U.; m. Doris Fuss, Dec. 11, 1943; children: Fredric, Margaret Udall Moses, Julie (Mrs. Blair M. Nash), Lucinda (Mrs. Douglas Johnson), Tina Udall Rodriguez. LL.B., U. Ariz., 1948. Bar: Ariz. 1948. Ptnr. Fennemore Craig, 1953—; Ariz. spl. counsel Arizona v. California, 1954-62; mem. Coun. on Legal Edn. Opportunity, 1983-93. Mem. cast Phoenix Mus. Theatre, 1959-65. Fellow Am. Bar Found. (bd. dirs. 1986-89, fellows chmn. 1988-89), Ariz. Bar Found. (Disting. Svc. award 1993), Am. Coll. Trial Lawyers; mem. ABA (ho. dels. 1962-92, bd. govs. 1981-84, exec. com. 1983-84, chmn. task force on minorities 1984-86), Maricopa County Bar Assn. (pres. 1957, Disting. Pub. Svc. award 1986), State Bar Ariz. (bd. govs. 1960-65), Ariz. Law Coll. Assn. (founding bd. dirs. 1967-80, pres. 1978-79, U. Ariz. Disting. Citizen award 1984, bd. visitors 1991—). Office: Fennemore Craig One Renaissance Sq 2 N Central Ave Ste 2200 Phoenix AZ 85004-4406

UDALL, THOMAS, state attorney general; b. Tucson, May 18, 1948; s. Stewart and Lee Udall; m. Jill Z. Cooper; 1 child, Amanda Cooper. BA, Prescott Coll., 1970; LLB, Cambridge U., Eng., 1975; JD, U. N.Mex., 1977. Law clk. to Hon. Oliver Seth U.S. Ct. Appeals (10th cir.), Santa Fe, 1977-78; asst. U.S. atty. U.S. Atty.'s Office, 1978-81; pvt. practice Santa Fe, 1981-83; chief counsel N.Mex. Health & Environ. Dept., 1983-84; ptnr. Miller, Stratvert, Togerson & Schlenker, P.A., Albuquerque, 1985-90; atty. gen. State of N.Mex., 1990—. Dem. candidate U.S. Ho. Reps., 1988; past pres. Rio Chama Preservation Trust; mem. N.Mex. Environ. Improvement Bd., 1986-87; bd. dirs. La Compania de Teatro de Albuquerque, Santa Fe Chamber Music Festival, Law Fund. Mem. Kiwanis. Office: Atty Gen Office PO Box 1508 Galisteo St Santa Fe NM 87504-1508

UDASHEN, ROBERT N., lawyer; b. Amarillo, Tex., June 10, 1953; s. Leo Joe and Esther K. (Klugsberg) U.; m. Dale Lynn Sandgarten, Aug. 15, 1976. BA with high honors, U. Tex., 1974, JD, 1977. Bar: Tex. 1977, U.S. Ct. Appeals (5th cir.) 1978, U.S. Dist. Ct. (no. and so. dists.) Tex. 1978, U.S. Ct. Appeals (11th cir.) 1981, U.S. Supreme Ct. 1981, U.S. Dist. Ct. (ea. dist.) Tex. 1989, U.S. Dist. Ct. (we. dist.) Tex. 1991. Staff atty. Staff Counsel for Inmates, Huntsville, Tex., 1977-79; assoc., ptnr. Crowder, Mattox & Udashen, Dallas, 1979-85; ptnr. Udashen & Goldstucker, Dallas, 1985-87; pvt. practice, 1987-94; ptnr. Milner, Lobel, Goranson, Sorrels, Udashen & Wells, Dallas, 1995—; bd. dirs. Open, Inc., Dallas. Contbr. articles to profl. publs. Adv. bd. Coalition for Safer Dallas, 1994. Mem. State Bar Tex. (penal code com. 1992-93), Nat. Assn. Criminal Def. Lawyers, Tex. Criminal Def. Lawyers Assn., Dallas Criminal Def. Lawyers Assn. Office: Milner Lobel Goranson Sorrels Udashen & Wells 2515 Mckinney Ave # 21 Dallas TX 75201-1978

UDELL, JON R., editor, author; b. Phila., Dec. 3, 1956; s. Eugene and Anita (Magistro) U.; m. Luann Maria Huber, June 26, 1982; children: Robin, Douglas. BA in English, U. Mich., 1979; MA in Writing, Johns Hopkins U., 1985. Software engr. Lotus Devel. Corp., Cambridge, Mass., 1987-88; exec. editor for new media BYTE mag., Peterborough, N.H., 1988—. Developer web site The BYTE Site, 1995-96; columnist The BYTE Network Project, 1995-96. Office: BYTE 1 Phoenix Mill Ln Peterborough NH 03458

UDELL, RICHARD, lawyer; b. Bklyn., Dec. 27, 1932; s. Alvin and Gertrude (Langsam) U.; BA, Reed Coll., 1955; LLB, U. Pa., 1958; m. Marguerite Hartshorne, July 3, 1955; children: Benjamin Alan, Edward H. Bar: N.Y. 1958, Fla. 1984. Pvt. practice, N.Y.C., 1959-65; counsel RCA Records, N.Y.C., 1965-69; assoc. firm Machat & Kronfeld, N.Y.C., 1969-71; counsel Famous Music Corp., N.Y.C., 1971-72, Random House, Inc. subs. RCA, N.Y.C., 1972-75; gen. counsel Simon & Schuster, Inc., subs. Gulf & Western Industries, Inc., N.Y.C., 1975-77; adminstrv. v.p., chief counsel Harcourt Brace Jovanovich, Inc., N.Y.C., 1977-92; v.p. gen. coun. McGraw Hill Sch. Pub. Co., 1992—. Mem. Bar Assn. City N.Y., Orange County Bar Assn., Fla. Bar Assn. Jewish. Office: McGraw-Hill Sch Pub Co 1221 Avenue Of The Americas New York NY 10020-1001

UDENFRIEND, SIDNEY, biochemist; b. N.Y.C., Apr. 5, 1918; s. Max and Esther (Tabak) U.; m. Shirley Frances Reidel, June 20, 1943; children: Aliza, Elliot. B.S., Coll. City N.Y., 1939; M.S., N.Y. U., 1942, Ph.D., 1948; D.Sc. honoris causa, N.Y. Med. Coll., 1974, Coll. Medicine and Dentistry of N.J., 1979, Mt. Sinai Sch. Medicine, City U. N.Y., 1981. Lab. asst. N.Y.C. Dept. Health, 1940-42; jr. chemist NYU Rsch. Svc., 1942-43, asst. chemist, 1943-44, research chemist, 1944-46; research asst. Med. Sch., 1946-47, instr., 1947-48; instr. Washington U. Med. Sch., 1948-50; biochemist Nat. Heart Inst., Bethesda, Md., 1950-53; head sect. cellular pharmacology lab. chem. pharmacology Nat. Heart Inst., 1953-56, chief lab. clin. biochemistry, 1956-68; dir. Roche Inst. Molecular Biology, N.J., 1968-83, head lab. molecular neurobiology, 1983—; professorial lectr. George Washington U., 1962-69; adj. prof. human genetics and devel. dept. Columbia U., 1969—; adj. prof. dept. biochemistry City U. N.Y., 1968—; dept. pharmacology Emory U., 1976-78; adj. prof. biochemistry Cornell U. Med. Sch., 1982—; mem. sci. adv. bd. Scripps Clinic and Research Found., 1974-78; mem. adv. com. to dir. NIH, 1976-78; mem. Sci. Adv. Com. for Cystic Fibrosis; mem. adv. council of sci. and engring. City U. N.Y., 1980—; mem. sci. adv. com. Mass. Gen. Hosp., 1980-84. Trustee Wistar Inst., 1968-71; mem. adv. bd. Weizmann Inst. Sci., 1978-79, bd. govs., 1979—. Recipient Cert. of Merit for studies on malignant carcinoid A.M.A., 1956, Arthur S. Flemming award, 1958; City of Hope research award, 1975; NIH fellow St. Mary's Hosp. Med. Sch., London, Eng., 1957; Harvey lectr., 1964; recipient Superior Service award Dept. HEW, 1965, Distinguished Service award, 1966; Gairdner Found. award, 1967; Heinrich Waelsch lectr. in neurosci., 1978; recipient Townsend Harris medal CCNY Alumni Assn., 1979; Rudolph Virchow gold medal, 1979; Chauncey Leake lectr. U. Calif., 1980. Fellow N.Y. Acad. Scis. (trustee 1978—); mem. NAS, AAAS, Am. Soc. Biol. Chemists, Am. Soc. Pharmacology and Exptl. Therapeutics (sec.), Soc. Exptl. Biology and Medicine, Am. Assn. Clin. Chemists (Van Slyke award 1967, Ames award 1969), Am. Chem. Soc. (Hillebrand award 1962, Torald Sollmann award 1975), Am. Acad. Arts and Scis., Japanese Pharmacol. Soc. (hon.), Japanese Biochem. Soc. (hon.), Czechoslovak Pharmacology Soc. (hon.), Congress Internat. Neuropsychopharmacologists (hon.), Instituto de Investigaciones Citológicas (corr.) (Spain), Phi Beta Kappa, Sigma Xi. Office: Roche Inst Nutley NJ 07110

UDEVITZ, NORMAN, publishing executive; b. Cheyenne, Wyo., Jan. 22, 1929; s. Jay and Edith (Stienberg) U.; m. Marsha Rae Dinner, Dec. 17, 1960; children: Jane, Kathryn, Andrew. Student, U. Colo., 1946-49. With Cheyenne Newspapers Inc. Cheyenne, 1949-54; editor-pub. Wyo. Buffalo, Cheyenne, 1954-63; account supr. Tilds & Cantz Advt. Agy., L.A., 1963-66; exec. v.p. Fitzgerald, Maahs & Miller, L.A., 1966-71; staff writer The Denver Post, 1971-88; dir. pubs. Am. Water Works Assn., Denver, 1988—. Sgt. USNG, 1950-53. Named Colo.'s Outstanding Journalist, U. Colo., 1977; recipient Pulitzer Prize Gold medal Columbia U., 1986. Mem. Investigative Reporters and Editors Inc., (bd. dirs. 1978-80, 81-83), The Newspaper Guild (McWilliams award 1976, 77). Jewish. Home: 4677 E Euclid Ave Littleton CO 80121-3224 Office: Am Water Works Assn 6666 W Quincy Ave Denver CO 80235-3011

UDICK, ROBERT ALAN, political science and media educator; b. Bellvue, Nebr., Nov. 27, 1957; s. Earl Walter Udick and Rosemarie (Hicks) Richards. BA in History, La. State U., 1980, MA in Polit. Sci., 1983; PhD in Social Scis., Syracuse U., 1994. Rsch. asst. Inst. Govt. Rsch. La. State U., Baton Rouge, 1981-83; Blueprint editor and labor studies coord. Inst. Human Rels. Loyola U., New Orleans, 1983-87; rsch. asst., program coord. Ctr. for Study of Citizenship Syracuse (N.Y.) U., 1987-89, rsch. assoc. social sci. program Maxwell Sch. Citizenship, 1988-91; univ. senator, univ. senate hon. degrees com. Syracuse (N.Y.) U., N.Y., 1992-93; univ. senate affirmative action grievance handling com. Syracuse (N.Y.) U., 1992-93, grad. study ad hoc parking and transit com., 1992-93, grad. student rep. to bd. trustees, 1991-92; vis. prof. polit. sci. Colgate U., Hamilton, N.Y., 1994, La. State U., 1994—; presented papers at Assn. for Edn. in Journalism and Mass. Comm., Ga. State U., Atlanta, 1993, Nat. Social Sci. Assn., Memphis, 1991, Orlando, Fla., 1992, New Orleans, 1994, N.Y. State Polit. Sci. Assn., Buffalo, 1992. Founding editor The Pulse, 1989-91, Maxwell Progress, 1989-91; contbr. articles to profl. jours. Bd. dirs. New Orleans Progressive Alliance, 1985-87. Mem. Assn. for Edn. in Journalism and Mass Comm., Nat. Social Sci. Assn., Educators for Social Responsibity (nat. bd. dirs. 1987-89).

UDLER, RUBIN JAKOVLEVITCH, linguist; b. Braila, Muntenia, Romania, Sept. 27, 1925; came to U.S., 1992; s. Jakov Aronovitch and Dina Vladimirovna (Gleizer) U.; m. Malka Il'initchna Alexenberg, July 8, 1956; children: Arthur, Angela. B Philol. Sci., U. Chernovtsy, Ukrainian S.S.R., 1951; M Philol. Sci., USSR Acad. Scis., Moscow, 1961; D Philol. Sci., USSR Acad. Scis., Leningrad, 1974. Dep. chmn. fgn. langs. dept. Chernovtsy State Pedagogical Inst., 1951-56; jr. sci. researcher dialectology sect. Moldavian br. USSR Acad. Scis., Kishinev, Moldavian S.S.R., 1956-61; chief dialectology and exptl. phonetics sect. Moldavian Acad. Scis., Kishinev, Moldavian S.S.R., 1961-80, chief dialectology and history of lang. sect., 1980-86, chief dialectology and linguistic geography dept., 1986-92, dep. of academician-sec. of social studies dept., 1989-92; ctr. assoc. U. Ctr. for Internat. Studies U. Pitts., 1994—; translator Soviet Bucovina newspaper, Chernovtsy, 1951-52; mem. editl. bd. Moldavian Lang. and Lit., 1961-91, Jour. of Linguistics and Study of Lit., 1991-92; sr. sci. rschr. All-Union Cert. Com., Moscow, 1963. Author: Moldavian Dialects of the Chernovtsy Area Consonantism, 1964, Dialectological Division of the Moldavian Language, Parts 1 and 2, 1976; co-author: The Moldavian Linguistic Atlas, 4 parts, 1968-73, Dialectological Dictionary, 5 vols., 1985-86, Dialectological Texts, 6 parts, 1969-87, The Historical Grammar of the Moldavian Language, 1964, Notes on Modern Moldavian Literary Language, 1967, Moldavian Dialectology, 1976, The Carpathian Dialectological Atlas, 5 vols., 1987-93; author more than 230 pub. works; mng. editor, co-editor approximately 60 monographs, dictionaries, atlases, collection of dialectological texts, collection of articles, theses, brochures with total volume of more than 1235 editl. sheets. Corr. mem. Moldavian Acad. Scis. Presidium of Moldavian Acad. Scis.; mem. MLA, Am. Soc. Romanian Studies. Jewish. Avocations: collecting old books, coins, travel. Home: 1535 Shady Ave Pittsburgh PA 15217-1455 Office: Univ Ctr Internat Studies U Pitts 41 G40 Forbes Quadrangle Pittsburgh PA 15260

UDRY, J. RICHARD, sociology educator; b. Covington, Ky., Oct. 12, 1928. BS in Sociology, Northwestern U., 1950; MA in Social Sci., Long Beach State Coll., 1956; PhD in Sociology, U. So. Calif., 1960. Instr. Chaffey Coll., 1960-62; asst. prof. Calif. State Poly. Coll., 1962-65; assoc. prof. maternal and child health and sociology U. N.C., Chapel Hill, 1965-69, prof., 1969—, dir. demographic rsch. unit Carolina Population Ctr., 1973-77, dir. Carolina Popluation Ctr., 1977-92, Kenan prof., 1992—. Author: The Social Context of Marriage, 1966, 3rd edit., 1974, The Media and Family Planning, 1974; editor: (with Earl Huyck) The Demographic Evaluation of Domestic Family Planning Programs, 1975; contbr. over 120 articles and reports ot profl. publs. Mem. AAAS, APHA, Am. Sociol. Assn., Population Assn. Am., Nat. Coun. on Family Rels., Sociol. Rsch. Assn. Office: U NC Carolina Population Ctr Univ Sq CB 8120 Chapel Hill NC 27516-3997

UDVARHELYI, GEORGE BELA, neurosurgery educator emeritus, cultural affairs administrator; b. Budapest, Hungary, May 14, 1920; came to U.S., 1955; s. Bela and Margaret (Bakacs) U.; m. Elspeth Mary Campbell, July 24, 1956; children: Ian Steven, Susan Margaret, Jane Elizabeth. BS, St. Stephen Coll., 1938; MD, U. Budapest, 1944, U. Buenos Aires, 1952; D honoris causa, Semmelweis Med. Sch., Budapest, 1988. Diplomate Am. Bd. Neurol. Surgery. Intern resident in surgery Red Cross Hosp./11th Mil. Hosp., Budapest, 1942-44; asst. resident Neurol. Univ. Clinic, Budapest, 1944-46; postdoctoral fellow U. Vienna, Austria, 1946-47; fgn. asst. Psychiat. Clinic, U. Berne, Switzerland, 1947-48; asst. resident in neurosurgery Hosp. Espanol, Cordoba, Argentina, 1948-50; resident neurosurgeon Inst. Neurosurgery, U. Buenos Aires, 1950-53; asst. Neurolsurgical Clinic, U. Cologne, Fed. Republic Germany, 1953-54; registrar Royal Infirmary, Edinburgh, Scotland, 1954-55; from fellow to full prof. Johns Hopkins U., Balt., 1955-84, prof. emeritus, dir. cultural affairs, 1984—, assoc. prof. radiology, 1963-84, Phi Beta Kappa lectr., 1980; neurosurg. cons. Social Security Adminstrn., Balt., 1962-89, Disability Determination Svc., Balt., 1991—; vis. prof., guest lectr. U. Va., Charlottesville, 1977, Children's Hosp. Ea. Ont., Ottawa, Can., 1977, U. Salzburg, Austria, 1981, U. Vienna, Austria, 1983, Mayo Clinic, Rochester, Minn., 1983, U. Cape Town, Republic of South Africa, 1984, U. Porto, Portugal, 1985; vis. prof. Temple U., Phila., 1979, U. Vt., Burlington, 1980, Aukland (New Zealand) Gen. Hosp., 1989, George Washington U., 1991, U. Mainz, Fed. Republic Germany, 1991, numerous others; lectr. in field. Contbr. numerous articles to profl. jours., book chpts. Mem. program com. Balt. Symphony Orch., 1972-80, edn. com. Walters Art Gallery, Balt., 1985-88. Recipient Lincoln award Am. Hungarian Found., 1980; Humanities grantee NEH, 1984-91. Fellow ACS; mem. AAUP, Am. Assn. Neurol. Surgeons (life, Humanitarian award 1991), Congress Neurol. Surgeons (sr.), Am. Assn. Neuropathologists, Pan-Am. Med. Assn., Soc. Brit. Neurol. Surgeons (corr.), Pavlovian Soc. N.Am., German Neurol. Soc. (corr.), Internat. Soc. Pediatric Neurosurgery (founding), Hungarian Neurosurg. Soc. (corr.), Argentine Acad. Sci. (corr.), Am. Soc. for Laser Medicine and Surgery (charter), Johns Hopkins Med. Assn., Johns Hopkins Faculty Club, 14 West Hamilton Club (chair steering com. 1977-83), Cosmos Club (chair program subcom. 1991—), Landsdowne Club (London), Alpha Omega Alpha. Roman Catholic. Avocations: music, literature, travel, chess. Home and Office: 111 Hamlet Hill Rd # 1414 Baltimore MD 21210-9999

UECKER, BOB, actor, radio announcer, former baseball player, TV personality; b. Milw., Jan. 26, 1935; m. Judy Uecker. Major league baseball player Milw. Braves, Nat. League, 1962, 63; major league baseball player St. Louis Cardinals, 1964, 65, Phila. Phillies, 1966-67, Atlanta Braves, 1967; radio-TV announcer Milw. Brewers, 1971—; commentator ABC Monday Night Baseball, 1976-82. Co-star TV series Mr. Belvedere, ABC-TV, 1985—; guest TV appearances include: Late Night with David Letterman, The Tonight Show, Midnight Special; also numerous commls.; author: Catcher in the Wry, 1985; films include: Major League, 1989, Major League 2, 1994. Office: Metropolitan Talent Agency 4526 Wilshire Blvd Los Angeles CA 90010*

UEHLEIN, E(DWARD) CARL, JR., lawyer; b. Boston, May 7, 1941; s. Edward Carl and Elizabeth (Thatcher) U.; m. Judith Taylor, June 16, 1962; children: Christine, Sara. Student, Bowdoin Coll., Brunswick, Maine, 1958-59; BA, Swarthmore Coll., 1962; LLB, Boston Coll., 1965. Bar: Mass. 1965, D.C. 1968. Atty. Nat. Labor Relations Bd., Atlanta, 1965-68; assoc. Morgan, Lewis & Bockius, Washington, 1968-71; exec. asst. to sec. U.S. Dept. Labor, Washington, 1971-73; ptnr. Morgan Lewis & Bockius, Washington, 1973—; sec.-treas. Carlou Corp., Wilmington, Del., 1969-71. Fellow Ford Found., 1961. Mem. ABA, FBA, D.C. Bar Assn., Belle Haven Country Club, Ballybunion Golf Club, Royal Dornoch Golf Club. Republican. Avocations: travel, golf, reading. Office: Morgan Lewis & Bockius 1800 M St NW Washington DC 20036-5802

UEHLING, BARBARA STANER, educational administrator; b. Wichita, Kans., June 12, 1932; d. Roy W. and Mary Elizabeth (Hilt) Staner; children: Jeffrey Steven, David Edward. B.A., U. Wichita, 1954; M.A., Northwestern U., 1956, Ph.D., 1958; hon. degree, Drury Coll., 1978; LLD (hon.), Ohio State U., 1980. Mem. psychology faculty Oglethorpe U., Atlanta, 1959-64, Emory U., Atlanta, 1966-69; adj. prof. U. R.I., Kingston, 1970-72; dean Roger Williams Coll., Bristol, R.I., 1972-74; dean arts scis. Ill. State U., Normal, 1974-76; provost U. Okla., Norman, 1976-78; chancellor U. Mo.-Columbia, 1978-86, U. Calif., Santa Barbara, 1987-94; sr. vis. fellow Am. Council Edn., 1987; exec. dir. bus./higher edn. forum, 1994-95; mem. Pacific Rim Pub. U. Pres. Conf., 1990-92; exec. dir. Bus. and Higher Edn. Forum, Washington, 1995—; cons. North Ctr. Accreditation Assn., 1974-86; mem. nat. educator adv. com. to Compt. Gen. of U.S., 1978-79; mem. Commn. on Mil.-Higher Edn. Rels., 1978-79, Am.Coun. on Edn., bd. dirs. 1979-83, treas., 1982-83, mem. Bus.-Higher Edn. Forum, 1980-94, exec. com. 1991-94; Commn. on Internat. Edn., 1992-94, vice chair 1993; bd. dirs. Coun. of Postsecondary Edn., 1986-87, 90-93, Meredith Corp., 1980—; mem. Transatlantic Dialogue, PEW Found., 1991-93. Author: Women in Academe: Steps to Greater Equality, 1979; editorial bd. Jour. Higher Edn. Mgmt., 1986—; contbr. articles to profl. jours. Bd. dirs., chmn. Nat. Ctr. Higher Edn. Mgmt. Sys., 1977-80; trustee Carnegie Found. for Advancement of Teaching, 1980-86, Santa Barbara Med. Found. Clinic, 1989-94; bd. dirs. Resources for the Futrue, 1985-94; mem. select com. on athletics NCAA, 1983-84, also mem. presdl. commn.; mem. Nat. Coun. on Edn. Rsch., 1980-82. Social Sci. Research Council fellow, 1954-55; NSF fellow, 1956-57; NIMH postdoctoral research fellow, 1964-67; named one of 100 Young Leaders of Acad. Change Mag. and ACE, 1978; recipient Alumni Achievement award Wichita State U., 1978, Alumnae award Northwestern U., 1985, Excellence in Edn. award Pi Lambda Theta, 1989. Mem. Am. Assn. Higher Edn. (bd. dirs. 1974-77, pres. 1977-78), Western Coll. Assn. (pres.-elect 1988-89,k pres. 1990-92), Golden Key, Sigma Xi. Office: Bus-Higher Edn Forum One Dupont Cir Ste 250 Washington DC 20036

UEHLINGER, JOHN CLARK, marketing executive; b. Annapolis, Md., June 28, 1929; s. Archibald Emil and Maran Hazel (Clark) U.; m. Patsy Ann Stewart, Jan. 24, 1959 (dec. Jan. 9, 1991); children: James Williamson, Jennifer Ann, David Douglas, Sarah Elizabeth, Susannah Rachel; m. Gloria Kent Haggard, Sept. 19, 1992. BA, George Washington U., Washington, 1951; MS in Mgmt., USN Postgrad. Sch., Monterey, Calif., 1966; postgrad., Naval War Coll., Newport, R.I., 1970-71, George Washington U., Washington, 1972-73. Cert. pers. subspecialist, USN. Commd. ensign USN, 1951, advanced through grades to comdr., 1973; comdg. officer USS Moctobi, 1960-62, USS Alfred A. Cunningham, 1969-70; adminstrv. officer Leonard Wood Meml., Washington, 1973-77; asst. exec. dir. Am. Congress on Surveying and Mapping, Falls Church, Va., 1977-81, exec. dir., treas., 1981-86; mktg. dir. Systems, Analyses, Instrumentation and Devel., Inc., Falls Church, 1986—. Mem. Alexandria Rep. City Com., 1978-84. Recipient Sec. of Navy Commendation medal, 1969. Mem. Delta Tau Delta.

UELAND, SIGURD, JR., lawyer; b. Mpls., June 1, 1937; s. Sigurd and Harriet (Scofield) U.; m. Harriet Moulton, Dec. 27, 1963; children: Scott, Leif, Tora, Sigurd III. B.A., Yale U., 1959; LL.B., U. Minn., 1962. Bar: Minn. 1963. Asso. firm Neville, Johnson & Thompson, Mpls., 1963-67; corp. atty. Whirlpool Corp., Benton Harbor, Mich., 1968-69, Honeywell Inc., Mpls., 1969—; sec. Honeywell Inc., 1977—, asst. gen. counsel, 1980—, v.p., 1983—. Mem. ABA, Am. Soc. Corp. Secs. (chmn. 1996-97), Minn. Bar Assn., Hennepin County Bar Assn. Congregationalist. Home: 8206 Norman Creek Trl Bloomington MN 55437-3814 Office: Honeywell Plz Minneapolis MN 55408

UELSMANN, JERRY NORMAN, photographer; b. Detroit, June 11, 1934; s. Norman Charles and Florence Gertrude (Crossman) U. B.F.A., Rochester (N.Y.) Inst. Tech., 1957; M.S., Ind. U., 1958, M.F.A., 1960. Mem. faculty U. Fla., Gainesville, 1960—; grad. research prof. photography U. Fla., 1974—; William A. Reedy meml. lectr. Rochester Inst. Tech., 1988; mem. Kodak Ednl. Adv. Coun., 1987-90. One-man exhbns. include, Mus. Modern Art, N.Y.C., 1967, Art Inst. Chgo., 1972, Phila. Mus. Art, 1970, San Francisco Mus. Modern Art, 1977, The Crown Gallery, Houston, 1978, Worchester (Mass.) Art Mus., 1978, Nova Gallery, Vancouver, B.C., Can., 1979, Photographers Gallery, South Yarra, Australia, 1979, Columbia Coll., Chgo., 1980, Impressions Gallery of Photography, London, 1980, Atlanta Gallery of Photography, 1980, Deja Vue Gallery, Toronto, Ont., Can., Stephen White Gallery, Los Angeles, 1980, Baker Art Gallery, Kansas City, Mo., 1981, JEB Gallery, Inc., Providence, 1981, Eclipse Gallery, Boulder, Colo., 1982, Keystone Gallery, Santa Barbara, Calif., 1982, Images Gallery, Cin., 1982, Virginia Miller Galleries, Coral Gables, Fla., 1983, Weston Gallery, Carmel, Calif., 1983, G.H. Dalsheimer Gallery, Balt., 1983, Silver Images Gallery, Seattle, 1984, Cultural Ctr. of U.S.A., Istanbul, Turkey, 1984, Susan Spiritus Gallery, Newport Beach, Calif., 1984, 87, Daytona Beach (Fla.) Community Coll., 1985, Scheinbaum & Russek Gallery, Santa Fe, 1985, Boston Athenaeum, 1985, U. Fla., Gainesville, 1986, Mus. Fine Arts, St. Petersburg, 1986, Wesleyan U., Middleton, Conn., 1986, Gallery for Fine Photography, New Orleans, 1986, Gail Severn Gallery, Ketchum, Idaho, 1987, Photo Forum Gallery, Pitts., 1987, Carl Solway Gallery, Cin., 1987, Cheekwood Fine Arts Ctr., Nashville, 1988, 89, 90, Galerie Zur Stockeregg, Zurich, 1988, A Gallery for Fine Photography, New Orleans, 1989, Jacques Baruch Gallery, Ltd., Chgo., 1989, Dayton Art Inst., 1990, Kennesaw State Coll., Marietta, Ga., 1990, Spectrum Gallery, Rochester, N.Y., 1990, Fay Gold Gallery, Atlanta, 1991, Orange County Ctr. Contemporary Art, Santa Ana, Calif., 1991, Witkin Gallery, N.Y.C., 1991, Fla. Sch. of Arts, Palatka, 1992, Joslyn Art Mus., Omaha, 1992, Gallery at City Hall, Orlando, Fla., 1992, Ctr. Photographic Art, Carmel, Calif., 1992, Morgan Gallery, Kans. City, Mo., 1993, Photo Gallery Internat., Tokyo, 1993, Robert Klein Gallery, Boston, 1993, others; retrospective Harn Mus. Art U. Fla., 1994; rep. permanent collections, Mus. Modern Art, Nat. Gallery Can., Victoria and Albert Mus., London, Fogg Mus. at Harvard U., Mus. Fine Arts, Boston., George Eastman House, Rochester, N.Y., Art Inst. Chgo., Phila. Mus. Art, Mpls. Art Inst., San Francisco Mus. Modern Art, Ctr. for Creative Photography, Tucson, Moderna Museet, Stockholm, Royal Photog. Soc., London, Bibliotheque Nat., Paris, Musee Reattu, Arles, France, Nat. Gallery Australia, Melbourne, Nihon U., Tokyo, Art Mus., Ind. U., Bloomington, Princeton (N.J.) U. Art Mus., Nat. Mus. Am. Art, Washington, Chgo. Ctr. for Contemporary Photography, Chgo., Nat. Mus. Modern Art, Kyoto, Japan, Seattle Art Mus., Gallery of Modern Art of Nat. Galleries Scotland, Polaroid Collection, Cambridge, Mass., St. Petersburg (Fla.) Mus. Art, Tampa (Fla.) Mus. Art, Tokyo Met. Mus. Photography, Danforth Mus. Art, Framingham, Mass., Met. Mus. Art N.Y. (poster made of one photograph 1988); subject of monograph: Jerry N. Uelsmann, 1970, Jerry N. Uelsmann: Silver Meditations, 1975, Jerry N. Uelsmann Twenty-five Years: A Retrospective, 1982, Uelsmann/Yosemite, 1996; author: Process and Perception, 1985, Photo-Synthesis, 1992. Recipient Photographer award for Outstanding Achievement Photographic Soc. Japan, 1992, First Place Photographic Book of Yr. award Maine Photographic Workshops, Rockport, 1992; NEA photographer's fellow, 1972, U. Fla. grantee, 1971, Guggenheim fellow, 1967; inducted into the Fla. Artists Hall of Fame, 1994. Fellow Royal Photog. Soc. Gt. Britain; mem. Soc. Photog. Edn. (a founder, bd. dirs.), Friends of Photography, Internat. Mus. Photography at George Eastman House. Home: 5701 SW 17th Dr Gainesville FL 32608-5365 Office: Art Dept Univ Fla Gainesville FL 32611

UENO, EDWARD ISAO, environmental science educator; b. Numazu-shi, Japan, Nov. 28, 1938; s. Hirokichi and Sei (Sajiki) Saito; m. Taeko Ueno, Apr. 8, 1970; children: Mikako, Masanobu. BSc, Tokai U., 1961; MSc, Meiji U., 1963, PhD, 1966. Ednl. official Ministry of Edn., Tokyo, 1966—; vis. prof. Tech. U., Braunschweig, Germany, 1975-78, Tex. Tech. U., Lubbock, 1980; res. R&D group of intense neutron source U. Tokyo, 1980-89, rep. of fusion sci. group, 1989—; vis. prof. FM Tokyo Broadcasting Sta., 1981; adviser policy planning com. Japanese Govt., 1994, Hitoyoshi City, 1994. Author: Energy and Resources, 1992, 93, Waste and Resource, 1994, 95, Ekoshisutemu Noho no Kiseki (The Miracle based on Agricultural Method of Microbiological Ecosystems), 1995; contbr. numerous articles to profl. jours. Dozenten fellow Alexander von Humboldt Found., 1975; spl. rsch. grant Ministry of Edn., 1980, grants-in-aid for scientific rsch., 1981. Mem. AAAS, Inst. for Ecosystem Agr. (chief sec. 1992—), Soc. for the Study to Design Water (dir. 1993—), Soc. of Waste and Resource Rsch. (mgr. 1994—), The Inst. for Eco and Economy System (pres. 1995—), Club of Fusion Sci. (chief dir. 1983—), Vereinigung der Humboldtlaner in Japan. Avocations: go, karate, traveling, reading, writing. Office: The Club of Fusion Sci, 3-1-17-903 Sendagi, Bunkyo 113, Japan

UENO, HIROSHI, biochemist; b. Sakai, Osaka, Japan, Dec. 9, 1950; s. Haruko (Hachihama) U.; m. Yumiko Matsuzaki, Feb. 11, 1978; 1 child, Leo Dale. BE, Kyoto U., 1974; MA, Brandeis U., 1976; PhD in Biochemistry, Iowa State U., 1982. Rsch. assoc. Rockefeller U., N.Y.C., 1982-83, Rockefeller Found. fellow, 1984-85, asst. prof. biochemistry, 1986—; assoc. prof. dept. agrl. chemistry Kyoto (Japan) U., 1993—; summer investigator Woods Hole Marine Biology Lab., 1984—; vis. scientist Population Coun., 1984—; mem. ad hoc com. Nat. Heart, Lung and Blood Inst., NIH, Bethesda, Md., 1987—; mem. organizing com. 8th Internat. Congress on Vitamin B6 and Carbonyl Catalysis, Osaka, 1990; vis. prof. Kumamoto U., Japan, 1990. Recipient Molly Berns Meml. Investigator, Am. Heart Assn., 1989—. Mem. Am. Soc. Biochemistry and Molecular Biology, Am. Chem. Soc., Harvey Soc., N.Y. Acad. Scis. Research in chemistry of Gossypol, transaminases, hemoglobins. Office: Kyoto U Faculty Agr, Dept Agrl Chemistry, Sakyo 606-01, Japan

UENO, TOMIKO F., forestry company executive; b. Mie, Japan, May 26, 1930; d. Fusataro and Masuye (Higashi) U.; m. Kohei Ueno, Nov. 20, 1953; children: Fusako, Takuro, Toyotsugu. AB, Tokyo Kaseigakuin U., 1952. Pres., chief exec. officer Ueno Corp., Tokyo, 1975—; bd. dirs. Ueno Ringyo Ltd., Tokyo. Mem. Forestland Owners Assn. Japan. Avocations: travel, cooking. Office: Ueno Ringyo Ltd, 5-17 Fuyuki, Koto-ku, Tokyo 135, Japan

UFFELMAN, MALCOLM RUCJ, electronics company executive, electrical engineer; b. Clarksville, Tenn., Oct. 22, 1935; s. Malcolm C. and Margaret Lillian (Davidson) U.; m. Sarah White Barksdale, June 11, 1957; children: Malcolm Rucj Jr., Katharina White, Davidson Barksdale, Jefferson Churchill. BS, Vanderbilt U., 1957; MS, George Washington U., 1963. Engr. Melpar, Inc., Falls Church, Va., 1957-60; v.p. Scope, Inc., Reston, Va., 1960-73; sr. cons. MRI, Inc., McLean, Va., 1973-78; v.p. Racal Communications Inc., Rockville, Md., 1978-80; sr. cons. MRJ, Inc., Fairfax, Va., 1980-82; v.p., gen. mgr., Ctr. Advanced Planning and Analysis E-Systems Inc., Fairfax, 1982-96; v.p. Constellation Comm., Inc., Fairfax, 1996—; pvt. practice patent agt., Vienna, Va., 1975—. Contbr. numerous articles to profl. jours.; holder 7 patents in field. Scoutmaster Troop 183 Boy Scouts Am., Oakton, Va., 1973-79. Capt. USAR, 1957-69. Fellow IEEE, AIAA (assoc.); mem. N.Y. Acad. Scis., Assn. Old Crows, Navy League, Cosmos Club (Washington). Republican. Episcopalian. Avocations: tennis, sailing, fishing, reading, travel. Office: Constellation Comm 10530 Rosehaven St Fairfax VA 22030-2840

UFFORD, CHARLES WILBUR, JR., lawyer; b. Princeton, N.J., July 8, 1931; m. Isabel Letitia Wheeler, May 20, 1961; children: Eleanor Morris Ufford Léger, Catherine Latourette Ufford-Chase, Alison Wistar Ufford Salem. BA cum laude (Francis H. Burr scholar), Harvard U., 1953, LLB, 1959; postgrad. (Lionel de Jersey Harvard studentship), Cambridge U., Eng., 1953-54. Bar: N.Y. 1961, U.S. Tax Ct. 1963. Assoc. Riggs, Ferris & Geer, N.Y.C., 1959-61; assoc. Jackson, Nash, Brophy, Barringer & Brooks, 1961-69, ptnr., 1969-78; ptnr. Skadden, Arps, Slate, Meagher & Flom, N.Y.C., 1978-92, of counsel, 1993—. Contbr. articles to legal jours. Trustee Nat. Squash Racquets Ednl. Found., N.Y.C., 1972-81; mem. Princeton monthly meeting Soc. of Friends, clk., 1986-88. Nat. Intercollegiate Squash Racquets champion, 1952-53; mem. NCAA All-Am. Soccer 1st team, 1952. Fellow Am. Coll. Trust and Estate Counsel (transfer tax study com. 1990-93); mem. ABA, N.Y. Bar Assn. (chmn. trusts and estates law sect. 1984), Assn. Bar City N.Y., N.Y. State Office of Ct. Adminstrn. (Surrogates Ct. Adv. Com., 1994—), Internat. Acad. Trusts and Estates Law, U.S. Squash Racquets Assn. (hon. life; trustee endowment fund 1984-96), Internat. Lawn Tennis club U.S.A. (dir. 1982—). Home: 150 Mercer St Princeton NJ 08540-6827 Office: Skadden Arps Slate Meagher & Flom 919 3rd Ave New York NY 10022 *Integrity, perseverance, compassion and humor are all very well--but the key is to be blessed by a Divine Improvidence.*

UFIMTSEV, PYOTR YAKOVLEVICH, physicist, electrical engineer, educator; b. Ust'-Charyshskaya Pristan', Altai Region, Russia, July 8, 1931; s. Yakov Fedorovich and Vasilisa Vasil'evna (Toropchina) U.; m. Tatiana Vladimirovna Sinelschikova; children: Ivan, Vladimir. Grad., Odessa State U., USSR, 1954; PhD, Cen. Rsch. Inst. of Radio Industry, Moscow, 1959; DSc, St. Petersburg State U., Russia, 1970. Engr., sr. engr., sr. scientist Cen. Rsch. Inst. of Radio Industry, Moscow, 1954-73; sr. scientist Inst. Radio Engring. & Electronics Acad. Scis., Moscow, 1973-90; vis. prof., adj. prof. UCLA, 1990—; mem. Sci. Bd. of Radio Waves, Acad. Scis., Moscow, 1960-90. Author: Method of Edge Waves in the Physical Theory of Diffraction, 1962; contbr. articles to profl. jours. Recipient USSR State Prize, Moscow, 1990, Leroy Randle Grumman medal for outstanding sci. achievement, N.Y.C., 1991. Mem. AIAA, IEEE, Electromagnetics Acad. (U.S.), A.S. Popov Sci. Tech. Soc. Radio Engring., Electronics & Telecommunication (Russia). Achievements include origination of the Physical Theory of Diffraction, used for design of American stealth aircrafts and ships; for radar-cross-section calculation, and antenna design. Office: UCLA Dept Elec Engring 405 Hilgard Ave Los Angeles CA 90095-1594

UGHETTA, WILLIAM CASPER, lawyer, manufacturing company executive; b. N.Y.C., Feb. 8, 1933; s. Casper and Frieda (Bohland) U.; m. Mary L. Lusk, Aug. 10, 1957; children: William C., Robert L., Edward F., Mark R. A.B., Princeton U, 1954; LL.B, Harvard U., 1959. Bar: N.Y. 1959. Assoc. Shearman & Sterling, N.Y.C., 1959-67; asst. sec. Corning Glass Works, N.Y., 1968-70, sec., counsel, 1971-72, v.p., gen. counsel, 1972-82, sr. v.p., gen. counsel, 1983—; bd. dirs. Corning Internat. Corp., Siecor Corp., Corning Europe Inc., Corning France, Chemung Canal Trust Co. Bd. dirs. Steuben Area coun. Boy Scouts Am.; officer Corning Mus. Glass, Corning Glass Works Found.; trustee Corning Community Coll. Served to lt. (j.g.) U.S. Navy, 1954-56. Mem. Assn. Bar. City N.Y., ABA, N.Y. State Bar Assn., Am. Corp. Counsel Assn. (trustee 1982-85). Clubs: Princeton (N.Y.C.), Univ. (N.Y.C.); Corning Country. Home: 13 North Rd Corning NY 14830-3235 Office: Corning Inc 1 Riverfront Plz Corning NY 14831-0001

UHDE, GEORGE IRVIN, physician; b. Richmond, Ind., Mar. 20, 1912; s. Walter Richard and Anna Margaret (Hoopes) U.; m. Maurine Elizabeth Whitley, July 27, 1935; children—Saundra Uhde Seelig, Thomas Whitley, Michael, Janice. M.D., Duke U., 1936. Diplomate: Am. Bd. Otolaryngology. Intern Reading (Pa.) Hosp., 1936-37, resident in medicine, 1937-38; resident in otolaryngology Balt. Eye, Ear, Nose and Throat Hosp., 1938-40, U. Oreg. Med. Sch., Portland, 1945-47; practice medicine specializing in otolaryngology Louisville, 1948—; asst. prof. otolaryngology U. Louisville Med. Sch., 1945-62, prof. surgery (otolaryngology), head dept., 1963-92, prof. emeritus, 1992—, dir. otolaryngology services, 1963—; mem. staffs Meth., Norton's-Children's, Jewish, St. Joseph's, St. Anthony's, St. Mary and Elizabeth's hosps.; cons. Ky. Surg. Tb Hosp., Hazlewood, VA Hosp., Louisville, U. Louisville Speech and Hearing Center. Author 4 books.; Contbr. articles to profl. jours. Bd. dirs. Easter Seal Speech and Hearing Ctr. Lt. col. M.C. U.S. Army, 1940-45, ETO, Gen. Isenhower staff, 1943-45. Recipient Disting. Service award U. Louisville, 1972. Fellow A.C.S., Am. Acad. Ophthalmology and Otolaryngology, So. Med. Soc.; mem. N.Y. Acad. Scis., Am. Coll. Allergists, Am. Acad. Facial Plastic and Reconstructive Surgery, AAAS, Assn. U. Otolaryngologists, AAUP, Assn. Mil. Surgeons U.S., Am. Laryngol., Rhinol. and Otol. Soc., Am. Audiology Soc., Soc. Clin. Ecology, Am. Soc. Otolaryngology Allergy, Centurian Otol. Research Soc. (Ky. rep.), Am. Council Otolaryngology (Ky. rep. 1968—), Hoopes Quaker Found., SAR (life), Gen. Soc. Colonial Wars (hereditary mem.), Alpha Kappa Kappa. Democrat. Methodist. Clubs: Filson, Big Spring Country, Jefferson. Home: 708 Circle Hill Rd Louisville KY 40207-3627 Office: Med Towers Louisville KY 40202

UHER, RICHARD A., physicist, educator; b. McKeesport, Pa., June 8, 1939; s. John Richard and Josephine Constance (Stewart) U.; m. Janice Joy Smith, June 17, 1961; children: Christopher Richard, Keith David, Michaeleen Marie. BS in Physics, Carnegie Mellon U., 1961, MS in Physics, 1963, PhD, 1966. Project mgr. Westinghouse Electric Corp., Pitts., 1968-75; dep. dir. Transp. Rsch. Inst. Carnegie Mellon U., Pitts., 1975-78, dir. Rail Systems Ctr., 1978—, dir. High Speed Grand Transp. Ctr., 1988—. Contbr. numerous articles, reports to profl. jours. Mem. ASME, ASCE, Am. Inst. Physics, Assn. R.R. Engrs., Inst. Electrical & Electronic Engrs. (chmn. land transp. com. 1979-80). Avocations: walking, cycling, genealogy. Office: Carnegie Mellon U Rail Sys Ctr PO Box 2950 700 Technology Dr Pittsburgh PA 15230-2950

UHLENBECK, KAREN KESKULLA, mathematician, educator; b. Cleve., Aug. 24, 1942; d. Arnold Edward and Carolyn Elizabeth (Windeler) Keskulla; m. Olke Cornelis, June 12, 1965 (div.). BS in Math., U. Mich., 1964; PhD in Math., Brandeis U., 1968. Instr. math. MIT, Cambridge, 1968-69; lectr. U. Calif., Berkeley, 1969-71; asst. prof., then assoc. prof. U. Ill., Urbana, 1971-76; assoc. prof., then prof. U. Ill., Chgo., 1977-83; prof. U. Chgo., 1983-88; Sid W. Richardson Found. Regents' Chair in Math. U. Tex., 1988—; spkr. plenary address Internat. Conress Maths., 1990; mem. com. women on sci. and engring. NRC, 1992-94; mem. steering com., dir. mentoring program for women Inst. for Advanced Study/Park City Math. Inst. Author: Instantons and Four Manifolds, 1984. Contbr. articles to profl. jours. Recipient Commonwealth award for Sci. and Invention, PNC Bank, 1995; NSF grad. fellow, 1964-68, Sloan Found. fellow, 1974-76, MacArthur Found. fellow, 1983-88. Mem. AAAS, NAS, Alumni Assn. U. Mich. (Alumnae of Yr. 1984), Am. Math. Soc., Assn. Women in Math., Phi Beta Kappa. Avocations: gardening, canoeing, hiking. Office: U Tex Dept Math Austin TX 78712

UHLENHUTH, EBERHARD HENRY, psychiatrist, educator; b. Balt., Sept. 15, 1927; s. Eduard Carl Adolph and Elisabeth (Baier) U.; m. Helen Virginia Lyman, June 20, 1952; children: Kim Lyman, Karen Jane, Eric Rolf. BS in Chemistry, Yale U., 1947; MD, Johns Hopkins U., 1951. Intern Harborview Hosp., Seattle, 1951-52; resident in psychiatry Johns Hopkins Hosp., Balt., 1952-56; asst. psychiatrist in charge outpatient dept. Johns Hopkins Hosp., 1956-61, psychiatrist in charge, 1961-62; chief adult psychiatry clinic U. Chgo. Hosps. Clinics, 1968-76; instr. psychiatry Johns Hopkins U., 1956-59, asst. prof., 1959-67, assoc. prof., 1967-68; assoc. prof. U. Chgo., 1968-73, prof., 1973-85, acting chmn., 1983-85; prof. psychiatry U. N.Mex., Albuquerque, 1985—, vice chmn. for edn., 1991-94; cons. in field; mem. clin. psychopharmacology rsch. rev. com. NIMH, 1968-72, treatment devel. and assessment rev. com., 1987; mem. psychopharmacology adv. com. FDA, 1974-78; mem. adv. group to Treatment of Depression Collaborative Rsch. Program, NIMH, 1978-92; study rev. com. Xanax Discontinuation Program, The UpJohn Co., 1988-92, Nat. Adv. Coun. on Drug Abuse, NIDA, 1989-92, Coop. Studies Evaluation Com., VA, 1989-92. Mem. editl. bd. Jour. Affective Disorders, 1978—, Psychiatry Rsch., 1979—, Behavioral Medicine, 1982—, Neuropsychopharmacology, 1992-94, Exptl. and Clin. Psychopharmacology, 1992—, Anxiety, 1993—; contbr. articles to profl. jours. Recipient Research Career Devel. award USPHS, 1962-68, Research Scientist award, 1976-81. Fellow Am. Coll. Neuropsychopharmacology (pres. 1986), Am. Psychiat. Assn., Am. Psychopath. Assn.; mem. Balt.-Washington Soc. for Psychoanalysis, Collegium Internat. Neuro-Psychopharmacologicum, Psychiat. Rsch. Soc. Office: U NMex Dept Psychiatry 2400 Tucker NE Albuquerque NM 87131

UHLER, WALTER CHARLES, government official, writer, reviewer; b. Lebanon, Pa., Feb. 23, 1948; s. Victor Cornelius and Barbara Jean (Malin) U.; m. Judy Ann Sherk, Aug. 7, 1967 (div. 1984); children: Terry Allen, Matthew David. Life partner: Carol A. DePrisco. BA in Polit. Sci. cum laude, Pa. State U., 1973, BA in Russian cum laude, 1973, cert. Russian area, 1973, MPA, 1992. Tchg. asst. Pa. State U., University Park, 1975-76; procurement agt. Naval Aviation Supply Office, Phila., 1976-80; contracts adminstr. GSA, Phila., 1980-81; contracting officer Def. Logistics Agy., Phila., 1981-86, corp. contracting officer, 1986-94; chief fin. svcs., 1993—; regional cons. Def. Logistics Agy., L.A., 1985-86; nat. cons. Def. Logistics Agy., Cameron Station, Va., 1989-90; participant Air Force Intelligence Conf. on Soviet Affairs, Arlington, Va., 1988; spkr. on contracts DOD Conf., Cleve., 1988, on restructuring costs, Memphis, 1994; chmn. Ann. Nat. Conf. Contracting Officers and Auditors, 1987-93; mem. Citizen Amb. Archivists' Del. to Russia and Poland, 1995. Contbr. articles to profl. jours. Baseball coach Valley Athletic Assn., Bensalem, Pa., 1979-88, basketball coach, 1980-85, coord., 1981; tutor Ctr. for Literacy, Phila., 1991-93, Project GIVE, Phila., 1995—. With U.S. Army, 1966-71. Recipient Comdrs. Excellence award Defense Contract Mgmt. Area Ops., 1993. Mem. Am. Assn. for Advancement Slavic Studies, Am. Def. Preparedness Assn., Acad. Polit. Sci., Phila. Writers Orgn., Am. Acad. of Polit. and Social Scis., Friends of the Free Libr. of Phila. Democrat. Avocations: history, literature, Pa. State U. football. Office: DCNC Phila DCMDE-GDTC PO Box 7699 Philadelphia PA 19101-7699

UHLIR, ARTHUR, JR., electrical engineer, university administrator; b. Chgo., Feb. 2, 1926; s. Arthur and Helene (Houghteling) U.; m. Ingeborg Williams, July 24, 1954; children—Steven, Donald, David. B.S., Ill. Inst. Tech., 1945, M.S. in Chem. Engring, 1948; S.M. in Physics, U. Chgo., 1950, Ph.D. in Physics, 1952. Process analyst Douglas Aircraft, Chgo., 1945; asst. engr. Armour Research Found., Chgo., 1945-48; mem. tech. staff Bell Telephone Labs., Murray Hill, N.J., 1951-58; dir. semi- condr. research and devel., mgr. semicondr. div., group v.p. engring. Microwave Assos., Inc., Burlington, Mass., 1958-69; dir. research Computer Metrics, Rochelle Park, N.J., 1969-73; prof. elec. engring. Tufts U., Medford, Mass., 1970-94; chmn. dept. elec. engring. Tufts U., 1970-75, dean of engring., 1973-80. AEC fellow, 1949-51. Fellow IEEE, AAAS; mem. Am. Phys. Soc., Sigma Xi. Home: 45 Kendal Common Rd Weston MA 02193-2159 Office: Elec Engring Dept Tufts Univ Medford MA 02155

UHLMANN, FREDERICK GODFREY, commodity and securities broker; b. Chgo., Dec. 31, 1929; s. Richard F. and Rosamond G. (Goldman) U.; m. Virginia Lee Strauss, July 24, 1951; children: Richard, Thomas, Virginia, Karen, Elizabeth. B.A., Washington and Lee U., 1951. Ptnr. Uhlmann Grain Co., Chgo., 1951-61; v.p. Uhlmann & Co., Inc., Chgo., 1961-65; sr. v.p. H. Hentz & Co., Chgo., 1965-73, Drexel Burnham Lambert Inc., Chgo., 1973-84; exec. v.p., dir. bus. futures Dean Witter Reynolds Inc., Chgo., 1984-85; sr. v.p., mgr. commodity dept. Bear, Stearns & Co., Inc., Chgo., 1985-88; exec. v.p. Rodman & Renshaw, Inc., 1988-95; sr. v.p. LIT-Divsn. of First Options Inc., Chgo., 1995—; chmn. Chgo Bd. Trade, 1973-74. Trustee Highland Park Hosp., Ill.; bd. dirs. Dist. 113 H.S. Found., 1990—. Mem. Nat. Futures Assn. (dir. 1981—), Futures Industry Assn. (bd. dirs., chmn. 1975-76). Clubs: Lake Shore Country (Glencoe, Ill.) (dir.); Standard (Chgo.). Home: 783 Whitehaven Ln Highland Park IL 60035-3656

UHRICH, RICHARD BECKLEY, hospital executive, physician; b. Pitts., June 11, 1932; s. Leroy Earl and Mabel Hoffer (Beckley) U.; m. Susan Kay Manning, May 25, 1985; children by previous marriage—Mark, Karen, Kimberly. BS, Allegheny Coll., 1954; MD, U. Pa., 1958; MPH, U. Calif.-Berkeley, 1966. Diplomate: Am. Bd. Preventive Medicine. Intern Lancaster Gen. Hosp., (Pa.), 1958-59; commd. asst. surg. USPHS, 1959, advanced through grades to med. dir., 1967; resident U. Calif., 1965-66; various adminstrv. positions regional and service unit levels Indian Health Services, until 1971; dir. div. programs ops. Indian Health Service, Health Services Adminstrn. USPHS, Washington, 1971-73; assoc. dir. div. profl. resources Office Internat. Health, Office Asst. Sec. for Health, HEW, Washington, 1973-74; assoc. dir. for program devel. and coordination Office Internat. Health, 1974-78; dir. Phoenix Indian Med. Ctr. and Phoenix Services Unit, 1978-81, ret., 1982; sr. adminstr. Good Samaritan Med Ctr., Phoenix, 1981-82, chief exec. officer, 1982-89; v.p. for managed care programs Samaritan Health Svcs., Phoenix, 1989-90; cons. health care systems Phoenix, 1990-93; dir. S.E. Asia, internat. dir. Med. Ambs. Internat., Modesto, Calif., 1993-95, ret., 1995; mem. Phoenix Regional Hosp. Coun., 1981-88, pres., 1982-83; bd. dirs. Med. Ctr. Redevel. Corp., Phoenix; v.p. Samaritan Redevel. Corp., 1983-88. Bd. dirs. Phoenix Symphony Orch., 1984-89, Ariz. Sr. Olympics Bd., 1985-89. Recipient Meritorious Service medal USPHS, 1973; recipient citation USPHS, 1973, Commd. Officers award, 1981. Mem. Ariz. Hosp. Assn. (bd. dirs. 1980-86, chmn. council on planning 1980-81, council on human resources 1982-83, council on patient care 1983-84, fin. com. 1984-86), Am. Coll. Health Care Adminstrs., Am. Pub. Health Assn., Christian Med. Soc.

UHRIG, ROBERT EUGENE, nuclear engineer, educator; b. Raymond, Ill., Aug. 6, 1928; s. John Matthew and Anna LaDonna (Fireman) U.; m. Paula Margaret Schnepf, Nov. 27, 1954; children: Robert John, Joseph Charles, Mary Catherine, Charles William, Jean Marie, Thomas Paul, Frederick James. B.S. with honors, U. Ill., 1948; M.S. Iowa State U, 1950, Ph.D., 1954; grad. Advanced Mgmt. Program, Harvard U., 1976. Registered profl. engr., Iowa, Fla. Instr. engring. mechanics Iowa State U., 1948-51; assoc. engr., research asst. Inst. Atomic Research (at univ.), 1951-54, assoc. prof. engring. mechanics and nuclear engring., also group leader, 1956-60; prof. nuclear engring., chmn. dept. U. Fla., Gainesville, 1960-68; on leave U. Fla., 1967-68, dean Coll. Engring., 1968-73; dean emeritus, 1989—; dep. asst. dir. research Dept. Def., Washington, 1967-68; dir. nuclear affairs Fla. Power & Light Co., Miami, 1973-74; v.p. for nuclear affairs Fla. Power & Light Co., 1974-75, v.p. nuclear and gen. engring., 1976-78, v.p. advanced systems and tech., 1978-86; disting. prof. engring. U. Tenn., Knoxville, 1986—; disting. scientist Oak Ridge Nat. Lab., 1986—; Rep. Dept. Def. to com. on acad. sci. and engring. Fed. Council Sci. and Tech., 1967; chmn. engring. adv. com. NSF, 1972-73; bd. dirs. Engring. Council Profl. Devel., 1968-72; mem. commn. edn. for engring. profession Nat. Assn. State Univs. and Land Grant Colls., 1969-72. Author: Random Noise Techniques in Nuclear Reactor Systems, 1970, trans. into Russian, 1974; co-author: (with Lefteri H. Tsoukalas) Fuzzy and Neural Approaches in Engineering, 1996. Served to 1st lt. USAF; instr. engring. mechanics U.S. Mil. Acad. 1954-56. Recipient Sec. of Def. Civilian Service award, 1968, Outstanding Alumni award U. Ill. Coll. Engring., 1970, Alumni Profl. Achievement award Iowa State U., 1972, President's medallion U. Fla., 1973; Disting. Achievement citation Iowa State U. Alumni Assn., 1980, Glenn Murphy awd., Am. Soc. for Engineering Education, 1992. Fellow ASME (life, Richards Meml. award 1969), AAAS, Am. Nuclear Soc. (chmn. edn. com. 1962-64, chmn. tech. group for edn. 1964-66, dir. 1965-68, exec. com. bd. 1966-68); mem. Am. Soc. Engring. Edn. (pres. S.E. sect. 1972-73, chmn. nuclear engring. divsn. 1966-67, 88-89, rsch. award S.E. sect. 1962, Glenn Murphy award as Outstanding Educator 1992), John Henry Newman Honor Soc., Sigma Xi, Tau Beta Pi, Phi Mu Epsilon, Pi Tau Sigma, Phi Kappa Phi. Home: 113 Connors Dr Oak Ridge TN 37830-7662 Office: U Tenn Pasqua Nuclear Engring Bldg Knoxville TN 37996-2300

UHRY, ALFRED FOX, playwright; b. Atlanta, Dec. 3, 1936; s. Ralph Kahn and Alene (Fox) U.; m. Joanna Kellogg; children: Emily Uhry Rhea, Elizabeth Uhry MacCurrach, Katharine, Nell. BA, Brown U., 1958. worked with composer Frank Loesser, 1960-63; instr. Eng., drama Calhoun High Sch., 1963-80; instr. lyric writing NYU, 1985-88. Author: (play) Driving Miss Daisy, 1987 (Drama Desk award nomination for best play 1987, Pulitzer Prize for drama 1988, L.A. Drama Critics Circle award for best play 1989); (musicals) Chapeau, 1977, (adapter) Little Johnny Jones, 1982, (adapter) Follow Thru, 1984; (lyrics) Here's Where I Belong, 1968, Swing, 1980; (lyrics, libretto) The Robber Bridegroom, 1978 (Drama Desk award nomination for best play 1975, Tony award nomination for best book of a musical 1976), America's Sweetheart, 1985; (screenplays) Mystic Pizza, 1988, Driving Miss Daisy, 1989 (Academy award for best adapted screenplay 1989, WGA award 1989), Rich in Love, 1993. Mem. Dramatists Guild (coun. 1989—, Elizabeth Martow prize 1987). Office: care Flora Roberts 157 W 57th St Ph A New York NY 10019-2210

UICKER, JAMES LEO, mechanical engineer; b. Detroit, Feb. 5, 1943; s. John Joseph and Elizabeth Josephine (Flint) U.; divorced; children: James, John, Mary, William, Martha, Margaret; m. Suzanne Rock, Oct. 13, 1995. BSME, U. Detroit, 1966; MS in Mech. Engring., Pa. State U., 1971. Registered profl. engr., Mich. Grad. asst. Pa. State U., Univ. Pk., 1969-71; fuel engr. to combustion engr. Nat. Steel Great Lakes Div., Ecorse, Mich., 1971-79; sr. engr. rotating equipment Detroit Edison, 1979—. Treas. Birmingham (Mich.) PTO, 1985, Boy Scouts Am., Southfield, Mich., 1986; pres. Block Club, Southfield, 1989; v.p. Parent Group, Bloomfield Hills, 1989. 1st lt. U.S. Army, 1967-69 Vietnam. Mem. ASME, NSPE, Engring. Soc. Detroit, Vibration Inst. Republican. Roman Catholic. Avocations: camping, photography, wood working, fishing. Home: 1485 Mack Rd Leonard MI 48367 Office: Detroit Edison 200 Second Ave 547 GO Detroit MI 48226 Office: Detroit Edison 2000 Second Ave 547 GO Detroit MI 48226

UICKER, JOSEPH BERNARD, engineering company executive; b. State College, Pa., Mar. 29, 1940; s. John Joseph and Elizabeth Josephine (Flint) U.; m. Mary Catherine Howze, June 5, 1965 (div. Oct. 1971); children: Patricia, Suzanne; m. Janet Ann Ballman, Sept. 22, 1973. B.S.M.E., U. Detroit, 1963, M.S., 1965. Registered profl. engr., Mich. Engr., Smith Hinchman & Grylls, Detroit, 1964-72, chief mech. engr. health facilities, 1972-73, asst. dir. health facilities, 1973-75, v.p., dir. mech. engring., 1975-82, v.p., dir. profl. staff, 1983—, also dir.; dir. Smith Group, Detroit, 1984—. Served to capt. U.S. Army, 1966-67. Mem. Nat. Soc. Profl. Engrs., ASME, ASHRAE, Soc. Am. Mil. Engrs. Clubs: Engring. Soc., Athletic (Detroit). Avocations: golf; photography; gardening. Home: 15250 Knolson St Livonia MI 48154-4736 Office: Smith Group Inc 150 W Jefferson Ave Detroit MI 48226-4415

UITTI, KARL DAVID, language educator; b. Calumet, Mich., Dec. 10, 1933; s. Karl Abram and Joy (Weidelman) U.; m. Maria Esther Clark, Feb. 15, 1953 (div. Feb. 1973); children: Maria Elisabeth, Karl Gerard (dec.); m. Michelle Alice Freeman, Mar. 13, 1974; children: David Charles, Jacob Christian. AB, U. Calif., Berkeley, 1952; AM, U. Calif., Berkley, 1952, PhD, 1959; postgrad., Nancy and Bordeaux U., 1952-54. Instr. Princeton U., 1959-61, asst. prof., 1961-65, class of 1936 preceptor, 1963-66, assoc. prof., 1965-68, prof., 1968—, John N. Woodhull prof. modern langs., 1978—, chmn. dept. Romance langs., 1972-78; vis. prof. Universidad de P.R., U. Pa., Queens Coll., U. Iowa, U. Wash., Rutgers U., UCLA, Johns Hopkins U., École Normale Superieure de Saint-Cloud, de Sévres, Paris, U. Warwick, England; corr. Romance Philology, 1970-85; NEH dir. summer seminars for coll. tchrs., 1983, 87, 94, cons., 1976-78, bd. dirs.; bd. dirs. Alumni Coll. Princeton U., Paris, Fontevraud, France. Author: The Concept of Self in the Symoblist Novel, 1961, La Passion Littéraire de Remy de Gourmont, 1962, Linguistics and Literary Theory, 1969, Story, Myth and Celebration in Old French Narrative Poetry (1050-1200), 1973, (with A. Foulet) Chrétien de Troyes, Le Chevalier de la Charrette, 1989, Letteratura europea: dalle origini a Dante, 1993, Chrétien de Troyes, Le Chevalier au Lion, 1994, Chrétien de Troyes Revisited, 1995; contbr. numerous articles and revs. to scholarly jours.; editor: Edward C. Armstrong Monographs on Medieval Literature; mem. edit. bd. Romance Philology, French Forum; mem. adv. coun. Dictionary of the Middle Ages. Chmn. bd. elders Luth. Ch. of Messiah, Princeton, N.J., 1978-81. With AUS, 1954-56. Decorated officier des Palmes Académiques, France; Guggenheim fellow, 1964-65, sr. fellow Nat. Endowment for Humanities, 1974-75, vis. fellow All Souls Coll., Oxford (Eng.) U., 1975. Mem. MLA, Linguistic Soc. Am., Medieval Acad. Am. Société de linguistique romane, Phi Beta Kappa. Club: Codrington (Oxford, Eng.). Home: 50 Grover Ave Princeton NJ 08540-3654 Office: Dept Romance Langs and Lits Princeton U 309 E Pyne Princeton NJ 08544-5264

UKROP, JAMES E., retail executive; b. 1937. Pres., CEO Ukrop's Super Markets Inc., 1958—. Office: Udrop's Super Markets Inc 600 Southlake Blvd Richmond VA 23236-3922 Office: 600 Southlake Blvd Richmond VA 23236*

UKROPINA, JAMES R., lawyer; b. Fresno, Calif., Sept. 10, 1937; s. Robert J. and Persida (Angelich) U.; m. Priscilla Lois Brandenburg, June 16, 1962. A.B., Stanford U., 1959, M.B.A., 1961; LL.B., U. So. Calif., 1965. Bar: Calif. 1966, D.C. 1980. Assoc. firm O'Melveny & Myers, Los Angeles, 1965-72, ptnr., 1972-80, 92—; exec. v.p., gen. counsel Santa Fe Internat. Corp., Alhambra, Calif., 1980-84, dir., 1981-86; exec. v.p., gen. counsel Pacific Enterprises, Los Angeles, 1984-86, pres. and dir., 1986-89, chmn. bd. and chief exec. officer, 1989-91; bd. dirs. Lockheed Martin Corp., Pacific Mut. Life Ins. Co., Calif. Club. Editor in chief So. Calif. Law Rev, 1964-65. Trustee Stanford U. Mem. ABA, Calif. Bar Assn., Los Angeles County Bar Assn., Annandale Golf Club, Calif. Club, Beta Theta Pi. Office: O'Melveny & Myers 400 S Hope St Los Angeles CA 90071-2801

ULABY, FAWWAZ TAYSSIR, electrical engineering and computer science educator, research center administrator; b. Damascus, Syria, Feb. 4, 1943; came to U.S. 1964; s. Tayssir Kamel and Makram (Ard) U.; m. Mary Ann Hammond, Aug. 28, 1968; children: Neda, Aziza, Laith. BS in Physics, Am. U. Beirut, 1964; MSEE, U. Tex., 1966, PhDEE, 1968. Asst. prof. elec. and computer engring. U. Kans., Lawrence, 1968-71, assoc. prof., 1971-76, prof., 1976-84; prof. elec. engring. and computer sci. U. Mich., Ann Arbor, 1984—, dir. NASA Ctr. for Space Terahertz Tech., 1988—, Williams Disting. prof., 1993—. Author: Microwave Remote Sensing, Vol. 1, 1981, Vol. 2, 1982, Vol. 3, 1986, Radar Polarimetry, 1990. Recipient Kuwait prize in applied scis. Govt. of Kuwait, 1987, NASA Group Achievement award, 1990. Fellow IEEE (gen. chmn. internat. symposium 1981, Disting. Achievement award 1983, Centennial medal 1984); mem. IEEE Geosci. and Remote Sensing Soc. (exec. editor jour., pres. 1979-81), Internat. Union Radio Sci., Nat. Acad. Engring. Avocations: flying kites, racketball. Office: U Mich 3228 EECS 1301 Beal Ave Ann Arbor MI 48109-2122

ULAM, ADAM B., history and political science educator; b. Lwow, Poland, Apr. 8, 1922; came to U.S., 1939, naturalized, 1949; s. Jozef and Anna (Auerbach) U.; children—Alexander Stanislaw, Joseph Howard. A.B., Brown U., 1943, LL.D.(hon.), 1983; Ph.D., Harvard U., 1947. Mem. Harvard U., Cambridge, Mass., 1947—; prof. govt. Harvard U., 1959-92, Gurney prof. history and polit. sci., 1979-92, prof. emeritus, 1992—, rsch. assoc. Russian Rsch. Ctr., 1948—, ctr. dir., 1973-76, 80-92, mem. exec. com. Russian research ctr., 1968—. Author numerous books including: The Bolsheviks and Lenin, 1965, Stalin, 1972, 2nd edit., 1987, Expansion and Coexistence, 1973, The Unfinished Revolution, rev. edit., 1979, The Kirov Affair, 1988, Dangerous Relations: The Soviet Union in World Politics, 1970-1982, 1983, The Communists: The Story of Power and Lost Illusions, 1948-91, 1992. Guggenheim fellow, 1956, 69, Rockefeller fellow, 1957, 60. Mem. Am. Acad. Arts and Scis., Am. Philos. Soc. Clubs: The Signet, Harvard U. Eliot House (assoc.) (Cambridge). Avocation: tennis. Office: Harvard U Russian Rsch Ctr 1727 Cambridge St Cambridge MA 02138-3016

ULANOFF, STANLEY M., communications executive; b. Bklyn., May 30, 1922; s. Samuel H. and Minnie (Druss) U.; m. Bernice Mayer, June 15, 1947; children: Roger, Amy Ulanoff Christie, Lisa M. Ulanoff Peddie, Dory Ulanoff Kennedy. BA in Journalism, U. Iowa, 1943; MBA in Mktg., Hofstra U., 1955; PhD in Comm., NYU, 1968. Asst. to pres. SUNY, Stony Brook, 1962-64; prof. mktg., head advt., sales promotion & pub. rels. divsn. Baruch Coll. (CUNY), N.Y., 1964-86; pres. Viewmark Prodns. Inc. d.b.a. Advisions, 1986—; cons. U.S. Dept. Def., Grosset & Dunlap pubs., Siebel/Mohr, U.S. Postal Svc.; cons, asst. to pres. Compton Advt.; arbitrator N.Y. Stock Exch., Nat. Assn. Securities Dealers. Author or editor 28 books including Handbook of Sales and Promotion, also mags., newspaper articles, rsch. papers; prodr. over 50 video documentaries. 2nd lt. U.S. Army, 1945; Brig. gen. USAR, 1942-84. Decorated Chevalier dans l'Ordre des Palmes Academique, Republic of France, Legion of Merit, Meritorious Svc. medal, Army Commendation medal, Army Achievement medal, Silver Conspicuous Svc. Cross, State of N.Y.; named VIP (Very Important Prof.) Splty. Adv. Assn. Internat. (2); Am. Advt. Assn. fellow, Eastman-Kodak fellow in film prodn.; Lewis Kleid Direct Mail Advt. scholar. Mem. Mil. Intelligence Res. Soc. (pres.), Res. Officers Assn. (pres.). Office: 17 The Serpentine Roslyn NY 11576-1736

ULANOV, BARRY, author, educator; b. N.Y.C., Apr. 10, 1918; s. Nathan A. and Jeanette (Askwith) U.; m. Joan Bel Geddes, Dec. 16, 1939; children—Anne, Nicholas, Katherine; m. Ann Belford, Aug. 21, 1968; 1 son, Alexander. A.B., Columbia U., 1939, Ph.D., 1955; Litt.D., Villanova U., 1965. Editor Swing mag., 1939-41, Listen mag., 1940-42, Metronome mag., 1943-55, Metronome Yearbook, 1950-55; columnist Down Beat mag., 1955-58; instr. English Princeton U., 1950-51; instr. English Barnard Coll., 1951-56, asst. prof., 1956-59, assoc. prof., 1959-66, McIntosh prof., 1986-88, prof., 1966-88, McIntosh prof. emeritus, 1988—, chmn. English dept., 1967-71, 79-82, chmn. program in the arts, 1975-79, 82-88; adj. prof. religion Columbia U., 1966; assoc. editor The Bridge Yearbook of Inst. Judaeo-Christian studies, 1955-68; lectr. in psychiatry and religion Union Theol. Sem., 1992—. Author: The Recorded Music of W.A. Mozart, 1942, Duke Ellington, 1946, The Incredible Crosby, 1948, A History of Jazz in America, 1952, A Handbook of Jazz, 1957, Sources and Resources, 1960, Death: A Book of Preparation and Consolation, 1959, Makers of the Modern Theater, 1961, The Way of St. Alphonsus Liguori, 1961, Seeds of Hope in the Modern World, 1962, (with Robert C. Roby) Introduction to the Drama, 1962, Contemporary Catholic Thought, 1963, The Two Worlds of American Art, 1965, The Making of a Modern Saint, 1966, (with James B. Hall) Modern Culture and the Arts, 1967, 72, Where Swing Came From, 1970, Swing Lives!, 1972, (with Ann Ulanov) Religion and the Unconscious, 1975, (with Ann Ulanov) Primary Speech: A Psychology of Prayer, 1982, (with Ann Ulanov) Cinderella and Her Sisters: The Envied and the Envying, 1983, The Prayers of St. Augustine, 1984; (with Ann Ulanov) The Witch and The Clown: Two Archetypes of Human Sexuality, 1986, Essay in Men and Women: Sexual Ethics in Turbulent Times, 1989, (with Ann Ulanov) The Healing Imagination, 1991, Jung and the Outside World, 1992, (with Ann Ulanov) Transforming Sexuality: The Archetypal World of Anima and Animus, 1994; co-translator: (with Joan Ulanov) The Last Essays of George Bernanos, 1955, (with Frank Tauritz) Joy Out of Sorrow, (by Mere Marie des Douleurs), 1958; co-editor Jour. Religion and Health, 1994—. Bd. dirs. Gandy Brody Sch., 1980—, C.G. Jung Found., 1992-94. Guggenheim fellow, 1962-63. Mem. Conf. Anglican Theologians, St. Thomas More Soc. (pres. 1955-56, 64-65), Cath. Renascence Soc. (pres. 1960-66), Conf. on Humanities (sec. 1957-58, chmn. 1958-59), Medieval Acad., Renaissance Soc., PEN, The Keys (vice chmn. 1959).

ULBRECHT, JAROMIR JOSEF, chemical engineer; b. Ostrava, Czechoslovakia, Dec. 16, 1928; s. Josef and Leopolda U.; m. Vera Krafneter, July 10, 1952; children: Jan Stanislav, Magdalena Vera. Ing., Czech Inst. Tech., Prague, 1952, Ph.D., 1958. Dept. head Research div. synthetic rubber co. Zlin, Czechoslovakia, 1958-63; head lab. engring. rheology Czechoslovak Acad. Scis., Prague, 1963-68; prof. chem. engring. U. Salford, Eng., 1968-78; prof., chmn. dept. chem. engring. SUNY, Buffalo, 1978-83; chief div. chem. process metrology Nat. Bur. Standards, Washington, 1984-88; dep. dir. office tech. evaluation and assessment Nat. Inst. Standards and Tech. (formerly Nat. Bur. Standards), Washington, 1989-90, dir. tech. programs, tech. svcs., 1991-94; pres. OFI Tech Svcs., Rockville, Md., 1994—. Author: Non-Newtonian Liquids, 1967, Mixing of Liquids by Mechanical Agitation, 1985, Process Sensing and Diagnostics, 1989, Competitiveness of the U.S. Chemical Industry in International Markets, 1990; editor: Chemical Engineering Communications, 1976-86; contbr. numerous articles to profl. jours. Recipient Outstanding Scholarship award Czech Acad. Scis., 1965, 67; Alexander von Humboldt fellow, 1967. Fellow Am. Inst. Chem. Engrs.; mem. Soc. Rheology, Am. Chem. Soc., Czech Acad. Engring. (hon. fgn.), Sigma Xi. Office: OFI Tech Svcs Inc 2407 McCormick Rd Rockville MD 20850

ULBRICHT, ROBERT E., lawyer, savings and loan executive; b. Chgo., Dec. 1, 1930; s. Emil Albert and Vivian June (Knight) U.; m. Betty Anne Charleson, June 20, 1953; 1 dau., Christine Anne. A.B., U. Ill., 1952, M.A., 1953; J.D., U. Chgo., 1958. Bar: Ill. 1958, U.S. Dist. Ct. (no. dist.) Ill. 1959. Research atty. Am. Bar Found., Chgo., 1957-59; asst. trust counsel Continental Ill. Nat. Bank & Trust Co., Chgo., 1959-60; assoc. law firm Cummings and Wyman, Chgo., 1960-68; gen. counsel, sec., sr. v.p. Bell Fed. Savs. & Loan Assn., Chgo., 1968—; gen. counsel, sec. sr. v.p., Bell Bancorp., Inc., Chgo., 1991—. instr. Aurora Coll., Coll. DuPage. Mem. nominating com. Dist. 41 Sch. Bd., 1970-71, vice chmn., 1971; chmn. dist. area fund raising Glen Ellyn council Girl Scouts Am., 1970. Bd. dirs. Glen Ellyn (Ill.) Pub. Library, 1979-85, pres., 1983-84. Served with AUS, 1953-55. Mem. Chgo. Bar Assn., Ill. Bar Assn., ABA. Clubs: Glen Oak Country, Glen Ellyn Tennis. Bd. editors Chgo. Bar Record, 1970-73; contbr. articles to legal jours. Office: Bell Bancorp Inc 79 W Monroe St Chicago IL 60603-4901

ULCHAKER, STANLEY LOUIS, public relations consultant; b. Cleve., July 6, 1938; s. Stanley and Anna (Zaletal) U.; m. Margaret Eleanor, Aug. 5, 1961; children: Margaret Mary, James C. B in Social Sci., John Carroll U., 1960. Reporter, clk. Cleve. Plain Dealer, 1957-61; reporter Fairchild Publs., Cleve., 1961-62; account exec. Edward Howard & Co., Cleve., 1962-69, v.p., 1969-72, sr. v.p., 1972-77, exec. v.p., 1977-86, pres., chief exec. officer, 1987-89, chmn., chief exec. officer, 1989—. Mem. Pub. Relations Soc. Am. (pres. Greater Cleve. chpt. 1993). Office: Edward Howard & Co 1 Erieview Plz Fl 7 Cleveland OH 44114-1715*

ULENE, ARTHUR LAWRENCE, physician, journalist; b. Montreal, Que., Can., July 13, 1936; s. John and Fay (Steinman) U.; m. Priscilla Jacobson, Dec. 18, 1960; children: Douglas, Valerie, Steven. BA, UCLA, 1957, MD, 1962; DSc (hon.), Georgetown U., 1987. Diplomate Am. Bd. Ob-Gyn. Intern in internal medicine UCLA Hosp., 1962-63, resident in ob./gyn., 1963-67; asst. prof. ob-gyn Sch. Medicine U. So. Calif., L.A., 1970-85, assoc. clin. prof. Sch. of Medicine, 1985-90, clin. prof., 1990—; commendator med. Today show Sta. NBC-TV, 1978-91; commentator Home Show Sta. ABC-TV, 1991—; chmn. Feeling Fine programs, L.A., 1984—; health commentator Sta. KABC, L.A., 1980—, Sta. WLS, Chgo., 1985—. Author: Feeling Fine, 1977, Bring Out the Best in Your Body, 1987, Count Out Cholesterol, 1988, Count Out Cholesterol Cookbook, 1989; author 17 health audiotapes, 1987-90; writer TV syndicated reports. Chmn., trustee Norris Cancer Hosp. and Rsch. Inst. U. So. Calif., 1989—. Maj. US Army, 1967-70. Fellow Am. Coll. Obstetricians and Gynecologists. Avocations: sailing, skiing.

ULERICH, WILLIAM KEENER, publishing company executive; b. Latrobe, Pa., Apr. 18, 1910; s. William Wesley and Anna (Keener) U.; m. Edith O. Orton, May 26, 1934 (div. 1950); 1 dau., Constance K.; m. Althea M. Jones, Aug. 23, 1950. A.B., Pa. State U., 1931; LL.D., Dickinson Sch. Law, 1977. Editor Daily Times, State College, Pa., 1931-45; assoc. prof. journalism Pa. State U., 1934-45; pub. Clearfield (Pa.) Daily Progress, 1946; chmn. bd. dirs., chief exec. officer Prog. Pub. Co., Inc., Clearfield, Pa.; dir. emeritus County Nat. Bank, Clearfield. Bd. dirs., past pres. Clearfield Meml. Hosp.; trustee Pa. State U., 1952-57, 64-85, v.p. bd. trustees, 1973-76, pres. bd. trustees, 1976-79, pres. emeritus, 1985. Served with AUS, World War II. Mem. Pa. Newspaper Pubs. Assn. (pres. 1952). Methodist. Home: 724 S 2nd St Clearfield PA 16830-1904 Office: 206 E Locust St Clearfield PA 16830-2423

ULETT, GEORGE ANDREW, psychiatrist; b. Needham, Mass., Jan. 10, 1918; s. George Andrew and Mabel Elizabeth (Caswell) U.; m. Pearl Carolyn Lawrence; children: Richard Carlton, Judith Anne, Carol Lynn. BA in Psychology, Stanford U., 1940; MS in Anatomy, U. Oreg., 1943, PhD in Anatomy, 1944, MD, 1944. Diplomate Am. Bd. Psychiatry and Neurology. Asst. psychiatrist Barnes Hosp., St. Louis, 1950-64; med. dir. Malcolm Bliss Hosp., St. Louis, 1951-61; dir. Mo. Div. Mental Health, Jefferson City, Mo., 1962-72; prof., chair Mo. Inst. Psychiatry, St. Louis, 1964-73; dir. psychiatry Deaconess Hosp., St. Louis, 1973-94; interim dir. Mo. Inst. of Mental Health, St. Louis, 1990-91; assoc. dir. for policy and ethics Mo. Inst. of Mental Health, 1991-94; clin. prof. dept. family and cmty. medicine St. Louis U. Sch. Medicine, 1995—; mem. adv. coun. Mental Health Assn. St. Louis, 1965-66, 69-70, mem. profl. adv. com., 1965; chair health and hosp. com. Health & Welfare Coun. St. Louis, 1960; mem. alcohol rev. com., psychopharmacology study sect., alcoholism study sect., 1993, grants rev. com. for alternative medicine NIMH, Rockville, Md.; prof. psychiatry Washington U. Sch. Medicine, St. Louis, 1956-61; clin. prof. cmty. and family medicine St. Louis U. Sch. Medicine, 1981-89, U. Mo. Sch. Medicine, 1990—. Author eight books; contbr. over 200 articles to profl. jours. Capt. U.S. Air Force, 1946-47. Recipient Ann. award Mo. Assn. for Mental Health, 1966, Recognition award, 1970, AMA Honorable Mention award Foster Com. Exhibit, 1974, Pax Mundi Fellowship award for profl. excellence, 1989; named hon. mem. Turkish Coll. Neuropharmacology, 1969. Fellow Am. Psychiat. Assn.; mem. Am. Soc. Acupuncture (past pres.), Am. Soc. of Med. Psychiatry (past pres.), Mo. Acad. Psychiatry (past pres.). Office: Mo Inst Mental Health 5247 Fyler Ave Saint Louis MO 63139-1300

ULEVICH, NEAL HIRSH, photojournalist; b. Milw., June 18, 1946; s. Ben and Lea Jean (Klitsner) U.; m. Maureen Ann Vaughan, Sept. 25, 1974; children: Jacob Vaughan, Sarah Beatrice. B.A. in Journalism, U. Wis., 1968. Reporter A.P., 1968-69, photographer, photo editor, 1971-78, Asia photo editor, 1978-83; freelance writer, Vietnam, Hong Kong, 1969-71; fellow in journalism U. Wis.-Madison, 1971-72. Recipient Pulitzer prize for news photography, 1977. Jewish. Home: 2841 Perry St Denver CO 80212-1442

ULLBERG, KENT JEAN, sculptor; b. Gothenburg, Sweden, July 15, 1945; came to U.S., 1974; s. Jean Wilgot and Kerstin Aina (Axelson) U.; m. Veerle Rufina Vermeir, May 5, 1978; children: Robert, Gerald. Diploma in sculpture, Swedish State Sch. Art, 1966. Cert. conservator German Assn. Museology. Curator Nat. Mus. and Art Gallery, Botswana, Africa, 1971-74; curator III Mus. Natural History, Denver, 1974-75. Sculptor: monument Lincoln Ctr. Eagle, Dallas, 1981, Wind in the Sails, Corpus Christi, Tex., 1983, Genesee Eagle, Mumford, N.Y., 1984, Deinonychus Dinosaurs, Phila., 1987, Whooping Cranes Fountain, Washington, 1989, Broward Conv. Ctr., Fountain, Ft. Lauderdale, Fla., Rudor Monument bronze, Stockholm, 1991, Monumental Triptych Art Mus. South Tex., 1993, Bird Mountain Telecom. Hdqs., Stockholm, 1994, Christ Monument, Corpus Christi, 1995. Recipient Gold medal Tex. Rangers Hall of Fame, 1980; named Master Wildlife Artist, 1987. Fellow Nat. Sculpture Soc. (Percival Dietsch award 1979, gold medal 1983, Hering award 1993), NAD (academician 1990, Barnett prize 1975, Speyer prize 1995), Nat. Acad. Western Art (gold medal 1981, 82, 88, 90), Am. Soc. Marine Artists; mem. Soc. Animal Artists (medal of merit 1979, 80, 82, 87), Allied Artists of Am. (N.Y. Silver medal 1989), Soc. for Wildlife Art of the Nations. Home: 14337 Aquarius St Corpus Christi TX 78418-6003

ULLERY, PATRICIA ANNE, marketing professional; b. Casper, Wyo., July 13, 1949; d. Warren James and Nella Marie (Hammack) U.; m. Royce Edward Gilpatric, Apr. 1, 1968 (div. 1992); children: Royce Edward Gilpatric II, Eric Wynn Gilpatric. AA, Oakland C.C., Auburn Hills, Mich., 1978; student, Oakland U., 1979; BS in Internat. Bus. and Econs., Regis U., 1992; postgrad., U. Colo., 1994—. Divsn. editor Richardson Vick, Inc., Phila., 1979-81; dir. mktg. Rocky Mountain region Flack & Kurtz, Denver, 1982-86; dir. mktg. western region M.A. Mortenson Co., Denver, 1986-88; dir. mktg. Associated Gen. Contractors Colo., Denver, 1990-91; mgr. comml. devel. Cybercon Corp., Denver, 1992—; mem. real estate coun. U. Colo.; bd. dirs. Lower Downtown Dist., Inc., mktg. com., 1993-94. Mem. steering com. Great City Symposium '84, Urban Design Forum, Met. Denver's Great Neighborhoods, 1985, Parks and Pub. Spaces, 1986, bd. dirs. 1986-89; chair New Denver Airport design conf., 1987; mem. mktg. and mgmt. com. lower downtown task force Downtown Plan, 1986; mem. comprehensive plan land use/urban design task force City of Denver, 1987-88; bd. dirs. Community Housing Svcs., 1994; mem. Downtown Denver, Inc., 1982—. Recipient Outstanding Bus. Comm. Merit award Internat. Assn. Bus. Communicators, 1982, Fifty for Colo. award Colo. Assn. for Commerce and Industry, 1988, Ace Constrn. Excellence award Associated Gen. Contractors Colo., 1988, 91, Bus. in Arts award COlo. Bus. Com. for Arts, 1991. Mem. Soc. for Mktg. Profl. Svcs. (publicity chair Colo. chpt. 1984, v.p. 1985, pres. 1986, chair editorial com. Marketer, 1986-87, nat. bd. dirs. 1987-90, Leonardo award 1986), Ctrl. City Opera House Assn. (bd. dirs., pres. OperaPros 1993-94). Republican. Methodist. Avocations: skiing, golf, hiking, gardening, piano/. Home: 7880 W Woodard Dr Denver CO 80227-2438 Office: Cybercon Corp 1050 17th St Ste 1800 Denver CO 80265-1801

ULLIAN, JOSEPH SILBERT, philosophy educator; b. Ann Arbor, Mich., Nov. 9, 1930; s. Hyman Benjamin and Frieda G. (Silbert) U. AB, Harvard U., 1952, AM, 1953, PhD, 1957. Instr. philosophy Stanford U., Calif., 1957-58; asst. prof. philosophy Johns Hopkins U., Balt., 1958-60; vis. asst. prof. philosophy U. Pa., Phila., 1959-60, rsch. assoc. in linguistics, 1961-62; vis. asst. prof. philosophy U. Chgo., 1962-63; asst. prof. U. Calif., Santa Barbara, 1964-66; assoc. prof. Washington U., St. Louis, 1965-70, prof., 1970—; lectr. U. Calif., Berkeley, 1961; cons. Rsch. Directorate System Devel. Corp., Santa Monica, Calif., 1962-70. Co-author: The Web of Belief, 1970, 2d edit., 1978; contbr. articles to profl. jours. Mem. Am. Philos. Assn., Assn. for Symbolic Logic (exec. com. 1974-77), Am. Soc. for Aesthetics, Phi Beta Kappa. Democrat. Avocations: sports, theatre, music. Home: 984 Tornoe Rd Santa Barbara CA 93105-2229 Office: Washington U Dept Philosophy 1 Brookings Dr Saint Louis MO 63130-4899

ULLMAN, EDWIN FISHER, research chemist; b. Chgo., July 19, 1930; s. Harold P. and Jane F. Ullman; m. Elizabeth J. Finlay, June 26, 1954; children—Becky L., Linda J. BA, Reed Coll., 1952; MA, Harvard U., 1954, PhD, 1956. Research chemist Lederle Labs., Am. Cyanamid, Pearl River, N.Y., 1955-60; group leader central research div. Am. Cyanamid, Stamford, Conn., 1960-66; sci. dir. Synvar Research Inst., Palo Alto, Calif., 1966-70; v.p., dir. research Syva Co., Palo Alto, 1970-95; v.p., dir. rsch. Behring Diagnostics Inc., San Jose, Calif., 1995—; mem. sci. adv. bd. EnSys Inc., Research Triangle Park, N.C., 1992—; mem. adv. bd. San Francisco State U. Coll. of Sci. and Engring., 1994-96. Edit. bd.: Jour. Organic Chemistry, 1969-74, Jour. Immunoassay, 1979—, Jour. Clin. Lab., Analysis, 1986-87; contbr. articles to sci. jours. Patentee in field. NSF predoctoral fellow, 1952-53; U.S. Rubber Co. fellow, 1954-55. Recipient Clin. Ligand Assay Soc. Mallinckrodt award, 1981, Can. Soc. Clin. Chemists Health Group award, 1982, Inventor of Yr. award Peninsula Patent Law Assn., 1987. Fellow AAAS; mem. Am. Chem. Soc., Am. Assn. Clin. Chemists (Van Slyke award N.Y. sect. 1984, No. Calif. sect. award 1991), Am. Soc. Biol. Chemists, Clin. Ligand Assay Soc., Phi Beta Kappa. Office: Behring Diagnostics Inc PO Box 49013 San Jose CA 95161-9013

ULLMAN, JEFFREY DAVID, computer science educator; b. N.Y.C., Nov. 22, 1942; s. Seymour and Nedra L. (Hart) U.; m. Holly E., Nov. 19, 1967; children: Peter, Scott, Jonathan. B.S., Columbia U., 1963; Ph.D., Princeton U., 1966; Ph.D. hon., U. Brussels, 1975, U. Paris-Dauphine, 1992. Mem. tech. staff Bell Labs., Murray Hill, N.J., 1966-69; cons. Bell Labs., 1969-89; prof. elec. engring., computer sci. Princeton U., 1969-79; prof. computer sci. Stanford (Calif.) U., 1979—, chmn. dep., 1990-94, Stanford W. Ascherman prof. computer sci., 1994—; cons. Bell Labs., 1969-79; mem. computer sci. adv. panel NSF, 1974-77, mem. info., robotics and intelligent sys. adv. panel, 1986-88; mem. exam. com. for computer sci. grad. record exam. Ednl. Testing Svc., 1978-86; cons. editor Computer Sci. Press, 1982-95; chmn. doctoral rating com. for computer sci. N.Y. State Regents, 1989-93. Author: Principles of Database and Knowledge-Base Systems, 1988, 89, (2 vols.), (with A.V. Aho and J.E. Hopcroft) Data Structures and Algorithms, 1983, (with J.E. Hopcroft) Introduction to Automata Theory, Languages and Computation, 1979, (with A.V. Aho, R. Sethi) Compilers: Principles, Techniques and Tools, 1986, (with A.V. Aho) Foundations of Computer Science, 1992, Elements of ML Programming, 1994. Guggenheim fellow, 1989. Fellow Assn. Computing Machinery (coun. 1978-80); mem. NAE, Spl. Interest Group on Automata and Computability Theory (sec.-treas. 1973-77), Spl. Interest Group on Mgmt. Data (vice chn. 1983-95), Computing Rsch. Assn. (bd. dirs. 1994—). Home: 1023 Cathcart Way Palo Alto CA 94305-1048 Office: Stanford U 332 Margaret Jacks Hall Stanford CA 94305

ULLMAN, LEO SOLOMON, lawyer; b. Amsterdam, The Netherlands, July 14, 1939; s. Frank Leo and Emily (Konyn) U.; m. Katharine Laura Marbut, Aug. 27, 1960; children: Laura, Susan, Valerie, Frank. AB, Harvard U., 1961, JD, Columbia U. Sch. of Law, 1964, MBA, Columbia U. Grad. Sch. Bus., 1964. Bar: N.Y. 1966, U.S. Ct. Claims 1966, U.S. Tax Ct. 1969, U.S. Customs Ct. 1970. Assoc. Sullivan & Cromwell, N.Y.C., 1965-68; pres. and mem. Ullman, Miller & Wrubel and predecessors, N.Y.C., 1970-81; mem. Reid & Priest, 1984-91, of counsel, 1991-92; of counsel Schnader, Harrison, Segal & Lewis, N.Y.C., 1993—; adj. prof. internat. bus. NYU, 1972-77; lectr., panelist profl. organs. programs; chmn. Amvest Properties, Inc., SKR Mgmt., Inc., Brentway Mgmt., Inc. Mem. Port Washington (N.Y.) Bd. Edn., 1970-73, pres. 1972-73; dir. Found. for Jewish Hist. Mus. in Amsterdam, Inc.; chmn. bd. dirs. Anne Frank Ctr., U.S.A. Served with USMCR, 1959-65. Co-recipient Community Service Award, Port Washington, 1981; Harlan Fiske Stone scholar, Columbia Law Sch., 1963. Mem. ABA (tax sect. com. U.S. taxation of fgn. persons), N.Y. State Bar Assn. (tax sect. com. internat. trade and investment). Clubs: Harvard, Netherlands. Editor: European Taxation, Internat. Bur. Fiscal Documentation, Amsterdam, 1964-65; founding editor: Taxation of Private Investment Income in Europe; co-author Investeringen in Onroerend Goed in de Verenigde Staten, 1982; contbr. articles to profl. publs. Home: Seacoast Ln Sands Point NY 11050-1230 Office: Schnader Harrison Segal & Lewis 330 Madison Ave New York NY 10017-5001

ULLMAN, LOUIS JAY, financial executive; b. N.Y.C., Sept. 3, 1931; s. Abraham and Clara (Matava) U.; m. Doris Betty Weiner, Sept. 26, 1954; children: Barbara, Alan, Howard. BBA, U. Cin., 1954. CPA, Ohio. Auditor Alexander Grant & Co., Cin., 1957-60; pres. Internat. TV, Cin., 1960-62; mgmt. cons. Alexander Grant & Co., Cin., 1962-63; dir., sr. v.p. fin. Frisch's Restaurants, Inc., Cin., 1963—. former Chmn. bd. trustees Better Bus. Bur., Cin.; pres. United Jewish Cemeteries; former pres. Isaac M. Wise Temple. Mem. AICPA (mem. task force on start-up costs), Ohio Soc. CPAs. Jewish. Office: Frischs Restaurants Inc 2800 Gilbert Ave Cincinnati OH 45206-1206

ULLMAN, MYRON EDWARD, III, retail executive; b. Youngstown, Ohio, Nov. 26, 1946; s. Myron Edward Jr. and June (Cunningham) U.; m. Cathy Emmons, June 20, 1969; children: Myron Cayce, Denver Tryan, Peter Brynt, Benjamin Kyrk, Kathryn Kwynn. BS in Indsl. Mgmt., U. Cin., 1969; postgrad. Inst. Ednl. Mgmt., Harvard U., 1977. Internat. account mgr. IBM Corp., Cin., 1969-76; v.p. bus. affairs U. Cin., 1976-81; White House fellow The White House, Washington, 1981-82; exec. v.p. Sanger Harris div. Federated Stores, Dallas, 1982-86; mgr. dir., chief oper. officer Wharf Holdings Ltd., Hong Kong, 1986-88; chmn., CEO, dir. R.H. Macy & Co. Inc., N.Y.C., 1986-95; dir. Federated Dept. Stores, Inc.; chmn., CEO, dir. DFS Group Ltd., San Francisco, 1995—; mng. dir. Lane Crawford Ltd., Hong Kong, 1986-88; bd. advisors Gt. Traditions Corp., Cin.; dep. chmn. Omni Hotels, Hampton, N.H., 1988; vice chmn. bd. dirs. Mercy Ships Internat. Internat. v.p. U. Cin. Alumni Assn., 1980—; bd. dirs. Nat. Multiple Sclerosis Soc., N.Y.C.; bd. dirs. Brunswick Sch., Greenwich, Conn., U. Cin. Found., Lincoln Ctr. Devel. Mem. White House Fellow Alumni Assn., Econ. Club N.Y.C. (bd. dirs., exec. com. 1993—), Nat. Retail Fedn. (vice chmn., bd. dirs., exec. com. 1993—), Delta Tau Delta (treas. 1967-68). Republican. Office: DFS Group Ltd 655 Montgomery St San Francisco CA 94111-2635

ULLMAN, RICHARD HENRY, political science educator; b. Balt., Dec. 12, 1933; s. Jerome E. and Frances (Oppenheimer) U.; m. Margaret Yoma Crosfield, July 4, 1959 (div.); children: Claire Frances, Jennifer Margaret; m. Susan Sorrell, May 6, 1977 (div.); m. Gail Marie Morgan, Dec. 24, 1983. A.B., Harvard U., 1955; B. Phil., Oxford (Eng.) U., 1957, D.Phil., 1960. Rsch. fellow European history and politics St. Antony's Coll., Oxford U., 1958-59; instr. govt. Harvard U., 1960-63, asst. prof., 1963-65; assoc. prof. politics and internat. affairs Princeton (N.J.) U., 1965-69, prof., 1969-77, 79—, David K.E. Bruce prof. internat. affairs, 1988—; George Eastman vis. prof. Oxford U., 1991-92; mem. policy planning staff Office Asst. Sec. Def., 1967-68; mem. staff Nat. Security Coun., Exec. Office Pres., 1967; dir. studies Coun. Fgn. Rels., 1973-76, dir. 1980's project, 1974-77. Author: Intervention and the War, 1961, Britain and the Russian Civil War, November 1918-January 1920, 1968, The Anglo-Soviet Accord, 1972, vols. I, II and III Anglo-Soviet Relations, 1917-21, Securing Europe, 1991; editor: Fgn. Policy Jour., 1978-80, Western Europe and the Crisis in U.S.-Soviet Relations, 1987, (with others) Theory and Policy in International Relations, 1972; mem. editorial bd. N.Y. Times, 1977-78; contbr. articles to profl. jours. Chmn. bd. trustees World Peace Found., Boston, 1980-84, 95—. Rhodes scholar, 1955-58; recipient George Louis Beer prize Am. Hist. Assn., 1969. Fellow Am. Acad. Arts and Scis.; mem. Coun. Fgn. Rels., Internat. Inst. Strategic Studies. Home: 12 Maple St Princeton NJ 08542-3852 Office: Ctr Internat Studies Bendheim Hall Princeton Univ Princeton NJ 08544-1022

ULLMAN, TRACEY, actress, singer; b. Slough, Eng., Dec. 30, 1959; m. Allan McKeown, 1984; children: Mabel Ellen, John Albert Victor. Student, Itaia Conti Stage Sch., London. Appeared in plays Gigi, Elvis, Grease, The Rocky Horror Show, Four in a Million, 1981 (London Theatre Critics award), The Taming of the Shrew, 1990, The Big Love, (one-woman stage show) 1991; films include The Young Visitors, 1984, Give My Regards to Broad Street, 1984, Plenty, 1985, Jumpin' Jack Flash, 1986, I Love You To Death, 1990, Household Saints, 1993, I'll Do Anything, 1994, Bullets over Broadway, 1994, Ready to Wear (Prêt-à-Porter), 1994; Brit. TV shows include Three of a Kind, A Kick Up the Eighties, Girls on Top; actress TV series: The Tracey Ullman Show, from 1987-90 (Emmy award Best Performance, Outstanding Writing, 1990, Golden Globe award Best Actress, 1987); album You Broke My Heart in Seventeen Places (Gold album). Recipient Brit. Acad. award, 1983, Am. Comedy award, 1988, 90, 91, Emmy award for Best Performance in a Variety/Music Series for "Tracey Ullman Takes on New York", 1994. Office: Creative Artists Agy Inc 9830 Wilshire Blvd Beverly Hills CA 90212-1804*

ULLMANN, LIV, actress; b. Tokyo, Japan, Dec. 16, 1938; d. Viggo and Janna (Lund) U.; m. Hans Stang, 1960 (div. 1965); 1 dau., Linn, by Ingmar Bergman; m. Donald Saunders, Sept. 7, 1985. Student pub. sch.; studies with dramatic coach, London, Eng.; 8 hon. doctoral degrees in arts and humanities. Starred in Diary of Anne Frank, repertory troup, Stavanger, Norway; became established actress of classic stage and film roles in Norway; appeared as Ingmar Bergman's leading lady in film Persona, 1966;

many other films directed by Bergman; also films in U.S., Can., Mex., France, Italy, Germany, S.Am., Switzerland, England; starred as Nora in A Doll's House in N.Y. Shakespeare Festival prodn. Vivian Beaumont Theater, Lincoln Ctr., N.Y.C.; appeared on Broadway in Anna Christie, 1977, I Remember Mama, 1979, Ghosts, other stage appearances include Old Times, West End, London, 1985-86, Mother Courage, Nat. Theatre, Oslo, Norway; dir. Sofie, 1992; author: Changing, 1977, translated into over 20 langs (Book-of-Month Club), Choices, 1984, translated into over 20 langs. Ofcl. goodwill ambassador UNICEF, 1980—. Decorated officier of Arts and Letters, France, The Order of St. Olaf, King of Norway; recipient Dag Hammarskjold Hon. medal; named best actress by either N.Y. Film Critics or Nat. Soc. Film Critics U.S. for 6 yrs. in a row.

ULLMARK, HANS, advertising agency executive; b. Stockholm, Sept. 2, 1946; came to U.S., 1984; s. Gustaf and Britten (Jansson) U.; m. Marie-Louise, July 2, 1977; children: Louise, Christian. M in Psychology, Stockholm U., 1971. Tchr. Bus. Sch. Stockholm, 1971-73; media planner Anderson & Lembke Group, Stockholm, 1973-74, media dir., 1974-75, account supr., 1975-76, v.p. account services, 1976-79; pres. Ehrenstrahle/BBDO, Stockholm, 1979-84; v.p. account services Anderson & Lembke, Inc., Stamford, Conn., 1984-88, pres., 1988—. Author, editor: Direct Marketing Handbook, 1979. Mem. Swedish Direct Mktg. Assn. (bd. dirs. 1977-82). Avocations: tennis, skiing, reading, sailing. Office: Anderson & Lembke Inc 135 Main St 21st Fl San Francisco CA 94105*

ULLOA, JUSTO CELSO, Spanish educator; b. Havana, Cuba, Oct. 20, 1942; came to U.S., 1960; s. Derby Celso Ulloa and Margo (Hernandez) Usame; m. Leonor Rosario Alvarez, July 17, 1971; children: Sandra Leonor, Justin Alfonso. BS, Fla. State U., 1966; MA, U. Ga., 1969; PhD, U. Ky., 1973. With Va. Poly. Inst. and State U., Blacksburg, 1972-74, asst. prof., 1974-79, prof., 1987—; vis. prof. U. Ky., Lexington, Spring 1989. Author: Graded Spanish Reader, 1981, 2d edit., 1987, Lezama Lima y sus Lectores: guia y compendio bibliografico, 1987; assoc. editor, book rev. editor Critica Hispanica, 1979—; editor-in-chief Cuban Literary Studies, 1990. Recipient Acad. Teaching Excellence, Va. Tech., 1992, Alumni Teaching award, 1992. Mem. South Atlantic MLA, Mountain Interstate Fgn. Lang. Conf. (v.p. 1975-76, 82-83, pres. 1976-77, 83-84, 92-93), Order of the Discoverers, Phi Kappa Phi, Sigma Delta Pi (state dir. 1976-86, v.p. 1986-90). Office: Va Poly Inst and State U Dept Fgn Lang Lit Blacksburg VA 24061-0225

ULLRICH, JOHN FREDERICK, diversified manufacturing company executive; b. Kalamazoo, Aug. 27, 1940; s. Frederick John and Opal Louise (Confer) U.; m. Susan K. Brundage, July 16, 1962; children: Frederick, Kathryn, Amy. BS in Engring. Physics, U. Mich. 1962, MS in Nuclear Engring., 1963, PhD in Nuc. Engring., 1967. Mgr. ignition systems dept. Ford Motor Co., Dearborn, Mich., 1975-76, mgr. vehicle evaluation, 1976-77, exec. engr. elec. and electronics div., 1977-79; v.p. sci. and tech. Internat. Harvester Co., Hinsdale, Ill., 1979-81, v.p. components engring. and devel., 1981-82, v.p. quality and reliability, 1982-83, v.p. mfg. engine and foundry div., 1983-86; v.p. strategic mgmt. Ex-Cell-o Corp., Troy, Mich., 1986, group v.p. Textron, Inc., Providence, R.I., 1987, v.p. ethics and environ. affairs, 1987-88; v.p. tech. and support svcs. Masco Corp., Taylor, Mich., 1988—. Mem. Mich. Rep. State Ctrl. Com., 1971-75; chmn. Reps. of Dearborn, 1972-74; alt. del. Rep. Nat. Conv., 1972; mem. bd. regents Ea. Mich. U., 1974-79, trustee Ea. Mich. U. Found., 1990—; mem. nat. adv. bd. Coll. Engring., U. Mich., corp. rels. and nat. campaign coms. U. Mich., 1981—, alumni mem. Coll. Engring. planning com., 1993-94, mem. bd. govs., 1995—; divsn. chmn. Chgo. United Way, 1983, Detroit United Way, 1986; mem. guarantor's com. Goodman Theatre, Chgo., 1980-83; mem. editorial adv. bd. Mfg. Engring. Mag., 1983-90; mem. nat. adv. bd. Nat. Kidney Found., 1989-95; mem. corp. devel. com. Univ. Mus. Soc., Univ. Mich. Mus. Art, Rackham Grad. Sch., 1990—; pres. Ann Arbor Art Assn., 1993-95, bd. dirs. 1993—; bd. dirs. Ind. Tech. Inst., 1993—, Ann Arbor Hands on Mus., 1994—, Mich. Artrain, 1995—, ERim, 1995—. Named Outstanding Alumnus, 1984, Alumni Soc. award, 1992; recipient Cmty. Svc. award Ford Motor Co., 1969, 73. Mem. Soc. Automotive Engrs., Soc. Mfg. Engrs., Engring. Soc. Detroit (chmn. membership com. 1989-90, Cmty. Svc. award 1991, bd. dirs. 1992—, treas. 1994-95, gen. chair IPC 1995, v.p. 1995—), Barton Hills Country Club, Hinsdale Golf Club, L'Arbre Croche Club, Sigma Xi, Tau Beta Pi, Kappa Kappa Psi. Republican. Presbyterian. Office: Masco Corp 21001 Van Born Rd Taylor MI 48180-1340

ULLRICH, LINDA J., medical technologist; b. Rockford, Ill., May 10, 1944; d. Glenn H. and R. Catherine (Mathews) Person; m. John R. Brody, June 11, 1966 (div. July 1978); children: Kevin R. Brody, Keith A. Brody; m. Sterling O. Ullrich Sr., Mar. 10, 1979; stepchildren: Sterling O. Jr., Eugene, Lee Anna, Michelle. BA, Thiel Coll., 1966; MPA, Kent State U., 1993, postgrad., 1996—. Cert. med. tech., specialist in hematology. Staff med. tech. Sharon (Pa.) Gen. Hosp., 1966-76; supervisor hematology, coagulation, urinalysis sects. Sharon Regional Health Sys. (formerly Sharon Gen. Hosp.), 1976-96, lab. mgr., 1996—; edn. coord. Beaver County C.C., Pa., 1976-80; tech. supr. lab. Cancer Care Ctr., Hermitage, Pa., 1993—; adj. prof. Thiel Coll., Greenville, Pa., 1994-95; com. mem. Sharon Regional Health Sys., 1990—. Merit badge counselor, com. mem. Troop 67 Boy Scouts Am., Newton Falls, Ohio, 1982-95. Lutheran. Avocations: bicycling, hiking, knitting, reading. Home: 1577 Wilson Ave Newton Falls OH 44444 Office: Sharon Regional Health Sys 740 E State St Sharon PA 16146

ULLRICH, ROBERT ALBERT, business management educator; b. Port Jefferson, N.Y., Mar. 25, 1939; s. Albert Herman and Marie Kathryn (Miller) U.; divorced; children: Karl Albert, Eleanor Marie. BS, U.S. Mcht. Marine Acad., 1960; MBA, Tulane U., 1964; D in Bus. Adminstrn., Washington U., 1968. Marine engr. Lykes Bros. Steamship Co., New Orleans, 1960-62; trainee IBM Corp., New Orleans, 1964-65; sr. rsch. officer London Sch. Econs., 1968-69; prof. Vanderbilt U., Nashville, 1969-88; dean Clark U., Worcester, Mass., 1988—. Author: Motivation Methods, 1981, Robotics Primer, 1983; co-author: Organization Theory and Design, 1980; editor: The American Work Force, 1984. Lt. j.g. USNR, 1960-66. Mem. Beta Gamma Sigma. Office: Grad School Management Clark University 950 Main St Worcester MA 01610-1400

ULLRICH, ROXIE ANN, special education educator; b. Ft. Dodge, Iowa, Nov. 10, 1951; d. Rocco William and Mary Veronica (Casady) Jackowell; m. Thomas Earl Ullrich, Aug. 10, 1974; children: Holly Ann, Anthony Joseph. BA, Creighton U., 1973; MA in Teaching, Morningside Coll., 1991. Cert. tchr., Iowa. Tchr. Corpus Christi Sch., Ft. Dodge, Iowa, 1973-74, Westwood Community Schs., Sloan, Iowa, 1974-80, Sioux City Community Schs., 1987—. Cert. judge Iowa High Sch. Speech Assn., Des Moines, 1975—. Mem. Am. Paint Horse Assn., Am. Quarter Horse Assn., Sioux City Hist. Assn., M.I. Hummel Club, Phi Delta Kappa. Avocations: doll collector, plate collector, horse-back riding. Home: 819 Brown St Sloan IA 51055

ULMAN, LOUIS JAY, lawyer; b. Balt., Mar. 24, 1946; s. Erwin Ira And Rose (Clayman) U.; m. Diana Lynn Milford, Aug. 17, 1969; children: Kenneth, Douglas. BA, Dickinson Coll., 1967; JD, Am. U., 1970. Bar: Md. 1970. Assoc. Ulman & Cohan, Balt., 1970-75; ptnr. Ulman & Ulman, Balt., 1975-80, Weinberg & Green, Columbia, Md., 1980-92; prin. Hodes, Ulman, Pessin & Katz, Columbia, 1992—; adj. prof. law Washington Coll. of Law, Am. U. Pres. Santa Claus Anonymous, Balt., 1975; mem. Howard County Bd. Social Svc., Ellicott City, Md., 1990. Mem. Md. State Bar Assn. (com. on rels. with fin. profls. 1985-92), Howard County Bar Assn., Internat. Assn. for Fin. Planning. Democrat. Jewish. Office: 10500 Little Patuxent Pky Columbia MD 21044-3542

ULMER, ALFRED CONRAD, investment banker; b. Jacksonville, Fla., Aug. 26, 1916; s. Alfred C. and Ruth Clementine (Porter) U.; m. Doris Lee Bridges, June 20, 1942 (div.); children: Alfred Conrad III, James G. (dec.), Marguerite, Nicholas Courtland; m. Roberta Riva Schreiber, Mar. 22, 1983 (div.). Grad., Hill School, 1935; A.B., Princeton U., 1939. Reporter Jacksonville (Fla.) Jour., 1935-37; pub. rels. staff Benton & Bowles (advt. agy.), 1939-41; attaché Am. Embassy, Vienna, 1945-47, Madrid, 1948-50; 1st sec. embassy, spl. asst. to amb. Am. Embassy, Athens, Greece, 1953-55; cons. Far Eastern Affairs, Dept. State, 1955-58; 1st. sec. embassy, spl. asst. to amb. Paris, France, 1958-62; dir. Niarchos (London) Ltd., 1962-68; gen. ptnr. Devon Securities, 1969-72; mng. dir. Jesup and Lamont Internat. Ltd., London, 1972-75; with Lombard, Odier et Cie, Geneva, 1975-82; pres. Lombard Odier (Bermuda) Ltd., 1975-93. Lt. comdr. USNR, 1941-45. Decorated Bronze Star; comdr. Order of Phoenix, Greece. Mem. Boodle's Club (London), Knickerbocker Club (N.Y.C.). Presbyterian. Home: 5420 Connecticut Ave NW Washington DC 20015-2813

ULMER, FRANCES ANN, state official; b. Madison, Wis., Feb. 1, 1947; m. Bill Council; children: Amy, Louis. BA in Econs. and Polit. Sci., U. Wis.; JD with honors, Wis. Sch. Law. Polit. advisor Gov. Jay Hammond, Alaska, 1973-83; former mayor City of Juneau, Alaska; mem. 4 terms, minority leader Alaska Ho. Reps.; lt. gov. State of Alaska, 1995—. Home: 1700 Angus Way Juneau AK 99801-1411 Office: State Capitol PO Box 110015 Juneau AK 99811

ULMER, MELVILLE JACK, economist, educator; b. N.Y.C., May 17, 1911; s. Saul and Lillian (Ulmer) U.; m. Naomi Zinken, June 1, 1937; children: Melville Paul, Stephanie Marie. BS, NYU, 1937, MA, 1938; Ph.D., Columbia, 1948. Writer N.Y. Am., 1930-37; chief, price research sect. Bur. Labor Statistics, 1940-45; sr. economist Smaller War Plants Corp., 1945; chief financial analysis sect. Dept. Commerce, 1946-48; editor Survey of Current Bus., 1948-50; asso. prof. econs. Am. U., 1950-52, prof., 1952-61, chmn. dept., 1953-61; prof. econs. U. Md., 1961-86, emeritus prof., 1986—; vis. prof. econs. Netherlands Sch. Econ., Rotterdam, 1958-59, 65-66; research asso. Nat. Bur. Econ. Research, 1950-60; cons. OAS, 1954, Dept. Commerce, 1955, Gen. Services Adminstrn., 1957, Dept. State, 1962, Bur. Budget, 1967-69. Author: numerous books including The Economic Theory of Cost of Living Index Numbers, 1949, Trends and Cycles in Capital Formation by U.S. Railroads, 1870-1950, 1954, Economics: Theory and Practice, 2d edit., 1965, Capital in Transportation, Communications and Pub. Utilities, 1960, The Welfare State: U.S.A. 1969, The Theory and Measurement of International Price Competitiveness, 1969; co-author: (with John M. Blair) Wartime Prices, 1944, (with C. Wright Mills) Small Business and Civic Welfare, 1946; contbg. editor: The New Republic, 1970-80; contbr. articles in Am. Econ. Rev., Jour. Am. Statis. Assn., Commentary, Atlantic Monthly, Challenge, Am. Spectator, Pub. Interest, Jour. of Econ. Issues, also others. Recipient Sr. Fulbright award, 1958, 65, Medal of Honor Free U. of Brussels, 1986; Merrill Found. fellow, 1957; Wilton Park fellow Gt. Britain, 1966; Peoples Coll. fellow Denmark, 1966; Nuffield fellow Can., 1971; Nat. Endowment for Humanities sr. fellow, 1973; NSF grantee, 1973; State Dept. econ. specialist grantee, 1977, 78. Fellow AAAS; mem. Am. Econ. Assn., Am. Statis. Assn., Econometric Soc., Assn. Evolutionary Econs. (exec. bd.), Atlantic Econ. Soc. (disting assoc.), Artus Soc., Pi Gamma Mu. Club: Cosmos (Washington). Home: 10401 River Rd Potomac MD 20854-4912 Office: U Md Dept Econs College Park MD 20742 *Failure must be taken as an instructive experience that aids in exposing the pitfalls to achievement.*

ULMER, MELVILLE PAUL, physics and astronomy educator; b. Washington, Mar. 12, 1943; s. Melville Jack and Naomi Louise (Zinkin) U.; m. Patricia Elifson, Dec. 28, 1968; children: Andrew Todd, Jeremy John, Rachel Ann. BA, Johns Hopkins U., 1965; PhD, U. Wis., 1970. Asst. research U. Calif., San Diego, 1970-74; astrophysicist Harvard Smithsonian Ctr. for Astrophysics, Cambridge, Mass., 1974-76; asst. prof. Dept. Physics and Astoronomy, Northwestern U., Evanston, Ill., 1976-82, assoc. prof., 1982-87, dir. astrophysics program, 1982—, prof., 1987—; dir. Lindheimer and Dearborn Obs. Northwestern U., 1982—; co-investigator on Gamma Ray Ob. experiment and Orbiting Solar Ob. 7. Contbr. articles to profl. jours. Fellow Am. Phys. Soc.; mem. Am. Astron. Soc., Soc. Photo-optical Instrumentation Engrs., Internat. Astron. Union. Home: 2021 Noyes St Evanston IL 60201-2556 Office: Northwestern U Dearborn Obs 2145 Sheridan Rd Evanston IL 60208-0834

ULMER, SHIRLEY SIDNEY, political science educator, researcher, consultant; b. North, S.C., Apr. 15, 1923; s. Shirley S. and Anna R. (Reed) U.; m. Margaret Anel Lipscomb, Mar. 18, 1946; children: Margaret, William, Susan, John, Mary. BA cum laude, Furman U., 1952, LLD (hon.), 1981; MA, Duke U., 1954, PhD, 1956. Rockefeller fellow Duke U., 1952-53, instr. polit. sci., 1954-55, Ottis Greene fellow, 1955-56; instr. U. Houston, summer 1956; mem. faculty Mich. State U., 1956-63, asst. prof., 1956-59, assoc. prof. polit. sci., 1960-63, chmn. dept., 1961-62; prof. polit. sci., chmn. dept. U. Ky., Lexington, 1963-69, Disting. prof. arts and scis., 1975-76, Alumni prof., 1978-88, alumni prof. emeritus, 1988—; mem. polit. sci. panel NSF, 1968-70; chmn. bd. overseers NSF Supreme Ct. data base project, 1984-87; vis. prof. SUNY, Buffalo, summer 1969, U. Wis.-Milw., summer, 1974, Ariz. State U., 1980; lectr. in field. Author: Military Justice and the Right to Counsel, 1971, Courts as Small and Not so Small Groups, 1971, Supreme Court Policy Making and Constitutional Law, 1986; editor: Introductory Readings in Political Behavior, 1961, Political Decision Making, 1969, Courts, Law and Judicial Processes, 1981; Contbr. articles to profl. jours. Served with USAAF, 1942-45, PTO. Decorated Air medal with 4 oak leaf clusters, Phila. Liberation medal; recipient Sang award for outstanding contbns. to grad. edn., 1973-74, Outstanding Polit. Sci. Tchr. award Pi Sigma Alpha, 1983, 87; Social Sci. Rsch. Coun. fellow, summers 1958, 67; NSF grantee, 1969-71, 78-82, 87-90. Mem. Am. Polit. Sci. Assn. (editorial assoc. rev. 1963-67), So. Polit. Sci. Assn. (exec. council 1965-68, v.p. 1966-67, pres. 1971-72), editorial bd. jour. (1965-72), Midwest Polit. Sci. Assn. (editorial bd. jour. 1963-64, 84-85), Ky. Polit. Sci. Assn. (v.p. 1966-67), Inter-Univ. Consortium Polit. Research (exec. council 1966-67, council chmn. 1967-68), Omicron Delta Kappa, Phi Beta Kappa. Home: 1701 Williamsburg Rd Lexington KY 40504-2013

ULMER, WALTER FRANCIS, JR., consultant, former army officer; b. Bangor, Maine, Apr. 2, 1929; married; 3 children. BS in Engring., U.S. Mil. Acad., 1952; M of Regional Planning, Pa. State U., 1973. Commd. 2d lt. U.S. Army, 1952, advanced through grades to lt. gen., 1982; dep. comdr. U.S. Army Armor Ctr., Ft. Knox, Ky., 1974-75; commandant-of cadets U.S. Mil. Acad., West Point, N.Y., 1975-77; dir. human resources devel. U.S. Army, Washington, 1978-79; comdr. 3d Armored Div., Frankfurt, Germany, 1979-82; comdg. gen. III Corps and Ft. Hood, Tex., 1982-85, ret., 1985; pres., CEO Ctr. for Creative Leadership, Greensboro, N.C., 1985-94; ind. cons., 1995—; lectr. in field. Contbr. articles to profl. jours. Home: 250 Riverbay Dr Moneta VA 24121-3138

ULRICH, GLADYS MARJORIE, printing company executive; b. Chgo., Dec. 18, 1932; d. Harry Pikal and Rose Barbara (Vojta) Albert; m. William John Ulrich, Dec. 4, 1954; children: Valerie Lynn, Mark Robert, Laura Ann. Student, Gregg Coll., 1950-52. Owner, CEO Insty-Prints, Arlington Heights, Ill., 1978—; pres., owner Insty-Prints, Elk Grove Village, Ill., 1986—; mem. pres. coun. Insty-Prints, Mpls., 1987-90, nat. adv. governing com., 1987—. Organizer blood drive ARC/Cancer Soc., Elk Grove Village, 1970. Mem. Women's Resource Assn. (pres. 1988-89), Bus. & Profl. Women Assn. Republican. Avocation: travel. Office: Insty-Prints 2355 E Oakton St Arlington Heights IL 60005-4817

ULRICH, LARS, drummer. Drummer Metallica, 1981—. Albums include Kill 'em All, 1983, Ride the Lightning, 1984, Master of Puppets, 1986, ...And Justice for All, 1988, Metallica, 1991, Live Sh*t: Binge and Purge, 1993, Garage Days Re-visited. Recipient Grammy award, 1990, 91. Office: c/o Metallica Elektra Records 75 Rockefeller Plz New York NY 10019-6908

ULRICH, LAUREL THATCHER, historian, educator; b. Sugar City, Idaho, July 11, 1938; d. John Kenneth and Alice (Siddoway) Thatcher; m. Gael Dennis Ulrich, Sept. 22, 1958; children: Karl, Melinda, Nathan, Thatcher, Amy. BA in English, U. Utah, 1960; MA in English, Simmons Coll., 1971; PhD in History, U. N.H., 1980. Asst. prof. humanities U. N.H., Durham, 1980-84, asst. prof. history, 1985-88, assoc. prof. history, 1988-91, prof. history, 1991-95; prof. history and women's studies Harvard U., Cambridge, Mass., 1995—; audiocourse cons. Annenberg Found.; cons., participating humanist numerous exhibits, pub. programs, other projects; project humanist Warner (N.H.) Women's Oral History Project; bd. editors William & Mary Quar., 1989-91, Winterthur Portfolio, 1991—. Author: Good Wives: Image and Reality in the Lives of Women in Northern New England, 1650-1750, 1982, A Midwife's Tale: The Life of Martha Ballard Based on Her Diary, 1785-1812, 1990 (Pulitzer Prize for history 1991); contbr. articles, abstracts, essays and revs. to profl. publs. Coun. mem. Inst. Early Am. History and Culture, 1989-91; trustee Strawberry Banke Mus., 1987-93. John Simon Guggenheim fellow, 1991-92, NEH fellow, 1982, 84-85; women's studies rsch. grantee Woodrow Wilson Fellowship Found., 1979; co-recipient Best Book award Berkshire Conf. Women's Historians, 1990; recipient Best Book award Soc. for History of Early Republic, 1990, John S. Dunning prize and Joan Kelly Meml. prize Am. Hist. Assn., 1990, Bancroft Prize for Am. History, 1991. Mem. Orgn. Am. Historians (nominating com. 1992—, ABC-Clio award com. 1989), Am. Hist. Assn. (rsch. coun. 1993-96). Office: Harvard U Dept History Robinson Hall Cambridge MA 02138

ULRICH, MAX MARSH, executive search consultant; b. Kokomo, Ind., Mar. 21, 1925; s. Max Dan and Esther Stone (Marsh) U.; m. Mary Ellen Fisher, Sept. 12, 1950; children—Max Dwight, Jeanne Nanette; m. Geraldine A. Kidd, Jan. 25, 1973; 1 child, Amanda Marsh. B.S., U.S. Mil. Acad., 1946; M.S. in Civil Engring, Mass. Inst. Tech., 1951. Comd. 2d lt. C.E. U.S. Army, 1946, advanced through grades to capt., 1950; resigned, 1954; asst. to mng. dir. Edison Electric Inst., 1954-58; with Consol. Edison Co., N.Y.C., 1958-71; asst. v.p. Consol. Edison Co., 1962-63, v.p. charge advt. and pub. relations, 1963-67, v.p. customer service, 1968-69, v.p. Bklyn. div., 1969-71; prin., dir. Ward Howell Internat. Inc., N.Y.C., 1971-74; pres., chief exec. officer Ward Howell Internat. Inc., 1974-84, chmn., chief exec. officer, 1984-88; pres. Ward Howell Internat. Group, Inc., 1988-92, cons., 1992—. Mem. Sigma Xi. Home: 2 Kingswood Dr Orangeburg NY 10962-1806 Office: Ward Howell Internat Inc 99 Park Ave New York NY 10016

ULRICH, PAUL GRAHAM, lawyer, author, publisher, editor; b. Spokane, Wash., Nov. 29, 1938; s. Donald Gunn and Kathryn (Vandercook) U.; m. Kathleen Nelson Smith, July 30, 1982; children—Kathleen Elizabeth, Marilee Rae, Michael Graham. BA with high honors, U. Mont., 1961; JD, Stanford U., 1964. Bar: Calif. 1965, Ariz. 1966, U.S. Supreme Ct. 1969, U.S. Ct. Appeals (9th cir.) 1965, U.S. Ct. Appeals (5th cir.) 1981. Law clk. judge U.S. Ct. Appeals, 9th Circuit, San Francisco, 1964-65; assoc. firm Lewis and Roca, Phoenix, 1965-70; ptnr. Lewis and Roca, 1970-85; pres. Paul G. Ulrich P.C., Phoenix, 1985-92, Ulrich, Thompson & Kessler, P.C., 1992-94, Ulrich & Kessler, P.C., Phoenix, 1994-95, Ulrich, Kessler & Anger, P.C., Phoenix, 1995—; owner Pathway Enterprises, 1985-91; judge pro tem Divsn. 1, Ariz. Ct. Appeals, Phoenix, 1986; instr. Thunderbird Grad. Sch. Internat. Mgmt., 1968-69, Ariz. State U. Coll. Law, 1970-73, 78, Scottsdale C.C., 1975-77, also continuing legal edn. seminars. Author and pub.: Applying Management and Motivation Concepts to Law Offices, 1985; editor, contbr.: Arizona Appellate Handbook, 1978—, Working With Legal Assistants, 1980, 81, Future Directions for Law Office Management, 1982, People in the Law Office, 1985-86; co-author, pub.: Arizona Healthcare Professional Liability Handbook, 1992, supplement, 1994, Arizona Healthcare Professional Liability Defense Manual, 1995, Arizona Healthcare Professional Liability Updated Newsletter, 1992—; co-author: Federal Appellate Practice Guide: Ninth Circuit, 1994, supplement, 1996; contbg. editor Law Office Econs. and Mgmt., 1984—, Life, Law and the Pursuit of Balance, 1996. Mem. Ariz. Supreme Ct. Task Force on Ct. Orgn. and Adminstrn., 1988-89; mem. com. on appellate cts. Ariz. Supreme Ct., 1990-91; bd. visitors Stanford U. Law Sch., 1974-77; adv. com. legal assisting program Phoenix Coll., 1985-95. With U.S. Army, 1956. Recipient continuing legal edn. award State Bar Ariz., 1978, 86, 90, Harrison Tweed spl. merit award Am. Law Inst./ABA, 1987. Fellow Ariz. Bar Found. (founding 1985—); mem. ABA (chmn. selection and utilization of staff pers. com., econs. of law sect. 1979-81, mem. standing com. legal assts. 1982-86, co-chmn. joint project on appellate handbooks 1983-85, co-chmn. fed. appellate handbook project 1985-88, chmn. com. on liaison with non-lawyers orgns. Econs. of Law Practice sect. 1985-86), Am. Acad. Appellate Lawyers, Am. Law Inst., Am. Judicature Soc. (Spl. Merit citation 1987), Ariz. Bar Assn. (chmn. econs. of law practice com. 1980-81, co-chmn. lower ct. improvement com. 1982-85, co-chmn. Ariz. appellate handbook project 1976—), Coll. Law Practice Mgmt., Maricopa County Bar Assn. (bd. dirs. 1994-96), Calif. Bar Assn., Phi Kappa Phi, Phi Alpha Delta, Sigma Phi Epsilon. Democrat. Home: 6536 N 10th Pl Phoenix AZ 85014 Office: 3030 N Central Ave Ste 1000 Phoenix AZ 85012-2717

ULRICH, PETER HENRY, banker; b. Munich, Germany, Nov. 24, 1922; s. Hans George and Hella (Muschweck) U.; m. Carol A. Peek, Oct. 21, 1944; children: Carol Jean (Mrs. D. Scott Hewes), Patricia Diane (Mrs. Damon Eberhart), Peter James. Student, Northwestern U., 1941-42, U. Iowa, 1943, Sch. Mortgage Banking, 1954-56. Lic. real estate broker, cert. mortgage banker; cert. rev. appraiser; cert. mortgage underwriter. Escrow officer Security Title Ins. Co., Riverside, Calif., 1946-53; asst. cashier Citizens Nat. Trust & Savs., Riverside, 1953-57; v.p. Security First Nat. Bank, Riverside, 1957-63; sr. v.p. Bank of Calif. (N.A.), Los Angeles, 1963-72; pres. Ban Cal Mortgage Co., 1972-74, Ban Cal Tri-State Mortgage Co., 1974-75; cons., 1975-76; pres., dir. Beneficial Standard Mortgage Co., 1976-88; real estate cons., 1988—; instr. real estate and bus. San Bernardino Valley Coll., Riverside City Coll., Pasadena City Coll. Pres. Residential Rsch. Com. So. Calif., 1965, Riverside Opera Assn., 1956-59, Riverside Symphony Soc., 1959-61; trustee Idyllwild Arts Found., 1957—, pres., 1970-73, sec., 1986-87; mem. adv. bd. Salvation Army, 1959—, vice chmn., 1971-74, chmn., 1975; chmn. Harbor Light Com., 1965-68; convocator Calif. Luth. U., 1976-80, 81-83, regent, 1981-90; bd. dirs. Guild Opera Co., 1983—, v.p., 1991—; bd. dirs. Lark Ellen Lions Charities, 1976—, prse., 1987-90, 94—; treas. Opera Buffs, 1983—; mem. Arcadia Beautiful Commn., 1989-95, vice chair, 1991-92, chmn., 1992-93; trustee Calif. Luth. Edn. Found., 1989—; bd. dirs. Arcadia Tournament Roses Assn., 1994—, Arcadia Heart Assn., 1995—, vice chair, 1996; mem. Arcadia City Coun., 1995—. Served with AUS, 1943-46. Recipient Resolution of Commendation Riverside City Council, 1963; Resolution of Appreciation Los Angeles City Council, 1968, 1973. Mem. Nat. Mortgage Bankers Assn. (chmn. Life Ins. Co. com. 1986-87), Calif. Mortgage Bankers Assn. (sec. 1965, dir. 1972-75), So. Calif. Mortgage Bankers Assn. (dir. 1975, 80-81, v.p. 1982, pres. 1983), Indland Empire Mortgage Bankers Assn. (pres. 1962, hon. dir.), Assn. Real Estate Execs. (sec. 1967-71, pres. 1974-75, v.p. 1995—). Lutheran. Home: 447 Fairview Ave Unit 2 Arcadia CA 91007-6877 Office: 201 S Lake Ave Ste 409 Pasadena CA 91101-3016 *Being of foreign birth, I particularly appreciate and cherish the American way of life. I am grateful for the opportunities which it has afforded me. I also feel strongly that we who have had the benefit of these opportunities owe something in return to our communities and to our country. I have tried to the best of my abilities to conduct myself and my business affairs in an honorable and forthright manner, thus helping to preserve what I feel is still the best life style in the world.*

ULRICH, RICHARD WILLIAM, finance executive; b. Toledo, Oct. 30, 1950; s. Richard William Josef and Vera (Bender) U.; m. Pamela Ann Momenee, Apr. 19, 1974; 1 child, Nathanial Richard James. BBA, U. Toledo, 1973; postgrad., Stanford U., 1987. CPA, Ill. Sr. acct. Assocs. Mgmt. Co., South Bend, Ind., 1973-76; acquisition analyst Assocs. Fin. Svcs., South Bend, 1975-76; sr. v.p., contr. Assocs. Comml. Corp., Chgo., 1976-87; sr. v.p. corp. fin. Assocs. Corp. N.Am., Dallas, 1987—. Mem. AICPA, Ill. CPA Soc.

ULRICH, ROBERT GARDNER, retail food chain executive, lawyer; b. Evanston, Ill., May 6, 1935; s. Charles Clemens and Nell Clare (Stanley) U.; m. Diane Mary Granzin, June 6, 1964; children—Robert Jeffrey, Laura Elizabeth, Meredith Christine. LL.B. (Law Rev. key), Marquette U., Milw., 1960. Bar: Wis. 1960, Ill. 1960, N.Y. 1981. Law clk. to fed. dist. judge Milw., 1961-62; atty. S.C. Johnson & Son, Inc., Racine, Wis., 1962-65, Motorola, Inc., Franklin Park, Ill., 1965-68; atty., then asst. gen. counsel Jewel Cos., Inc., Melrose Park, Ill., 1968-75; v.p., gen. counsel Gt. Atlantic & Pacific Tea Co., Inc., Montvale, N.J., 1975—; sr. v.p., gen. counsel Gt. Atlantic & Pacific Tea Co., Inc., 1981—. Mem. Am. Bar Assn., N.Y. State Bar Assn. Home: 500 Weymouth Dr Wyckoff NJ 07481-1217 Office: Gt Atlantic & Pacific Tea Co Box 418 2 Paragon Dr Montvale NJ 07645-1718

ULRICH, ROBERT GENE, judge; b. St. Louis, Nov. 23, 1941; s. Henry George Ulrich and Wanda Ruth (Engram) Webb; m. JoAnn Demark, July 3, 1965; children—Jill Elizabeth, Jane Ashley. B.A., William Jewell Coll., 1963; J.D., U. Mo.-Kansas City, 1969; LLM, U. Mo., 1972. Bar: Mo. 1969. Assoc. Von Erdmannsdorff, Voigts & Kuhlman, North Kansas City, Mo., 1969-72; pvt. practice Raytown, Mo., 1972; asst. U.S. atty. Dept. Justice, Kansas City and Springfield, Mo., 1973-76, 78-81; ptnr. Pine & Ulrich, Warrensburg, Mo., 1976-77; litigation atty. Shifran, Treiman, et al., Clayton, Mo., 1977-78; U.S. atty. We. Dist. Mo., Kansas City, 1981-89; judge Mo. Ct.

Appeals (we. dist.), Kansas City, 1989—; mem. U.S. Atty. Gen.'s Econ. Crime Council, 1983-89 , Atty. Gen.'s Adv. Com. of U.S. Attys., chmn. 1986-89, adv. com. U.S. Ct. Appeals (8th cir.), 1983-86. Appointed mem. steering com. Protect our Children Campaign, Gov. of Mo., chmn. legis. subcom., 1985; mem. resource bd., personnel mgmt. bd. Dept. Justice, 1985-89; trustee Liberty Meml. Assn., 1989—; vice chmn. Orgn. Crime Drug Enforcement Task Force Nat. Program, Dept. Justice, 1987-89. Col. USMC, 1963-66. Mem. Am. Judicature Soc., Inst. Jud. Adminstrn., Mo. Bar Assn., Kansas City Met. Bar Assn., Marine Corps Res. Officers' Assn. (exec. councillor 1986-87), U. Mo.-Kansas City Law Sch. Alumni Assn. (v.p. 1994-95, pres. 1995—). Office: Missouri Ct Appeals 1300 Oak St Kansas City MO 64106-2904

ULRICH, ROBERT J., retail discount chain stores executive; b. 1944. Grad., U. Minn., 1967, Stanford U., 1978. Chmn., chief exec. officer, dir. Dayton Hudson Corp.; with Dayton Hudson Corp., Mpls., 1967—, exec. v.p. dept. stores divsn., 1981-84, pres. dept. stores divsn., 1984-87, chmn., CEO Target stores divsn., 1987-93, dir., 1993—, chmn, CEO, 1994—. Office: Dayton Hudson Corp 777 Nicollet Mall Minneapolis MN 55402*

ULRICH, RUSSELL DEAN, osteopathic physician; b. LaPorte, Ind., Apr. 15, 1947; s. Russell Denzel and Betty Faye (Higgins) U.; m. Evelyn Kay Gove, July 14, 1967; children—Tonya Kay, Nolan Dean, Bryce Alan. B.A. in Religion, Wesleyan Holiness Coll., Phoenix, 1970; B.A. in Psychology, U. Ariz., 1974; D.O., Coll. Osteo. Medicine and Surgery, Des Moines, 1978. Tchr., Montezuma Schs., Cottonwood, Ariz., 1970-72; intern William Beaumont Army Med. Ctr., 1978-79; gen. practice medicine Piedmont Med. Clinic, Ala., 1982-85, Piedmont Family Practice Ctr., 1985—; asst. chief of staff Piedmont Hosp., 1983-84, chief of staff, 1984-92. Med. adviser Piedmont Rescue Squad, 1982—; mem. Calhoun County Disaster Preparedness Com., Anniston, Ala., 1984—; bd. dirs. Hobe Sound Bible Coll., Dayspring Ministries. Served to capt. U.S. Army, 1978-82. Mem. AMA (Physician's Recognition award 1982, 85, 89, 92, 95), Am. Osteo. Assn., Ala. Osteopathic Med. Assn. (sec.- treas. 1988—). Republican. Methodist. Home: 932 Maple Ln Jacksonville AL 36265-9804 Office: Piedmont Family Practice Ctr PO Box 450 800 W Memorial Dr Piedmont AL 36272-1930

ULRICH, THEODORE ALBERT, lawyer; b. Spokane, Wash., Jan. 1, 1943; s. Herbert Roy and Martha (Hoffman) Ulrich; m. Nancy Allison, May 30, 1966; children: Donald Wayne, Frederick Albert. BS cum laude, U.S. Mcht. Marine Acad., 1965; JD cum laude, Fordham U., 1970; LLM, NYU, 1974. Bar: N.Y. 1971, U.S. Ct. Appeals (2nd cir.) 1971, U.S. Supreme Ct. 1974, U.S. Ct. Claims 1977, U.S. Customs Ct. 1978, U.S. Ct. Internat. Trade 1981, U.S. Ct. Appeals (5th cir.) 1988, U.S. Ct. Appeals (D.C. cir.) 1992, Colo. 1993, U.S. Ct. Appeals (10 cir.) 1994. Mng. clk. U.S. Dept. Justice, N.Y.C., 1968-69, law clk. to federal dist. judge, 1969-70; assoc. Cadwalader, Wickersham & Taft, N.Y.C., 1970-80, ptnr., 1980-94; ptnr. Popham, Haik, Schnobrich & Kaufman, Ltd., Denver, 1994-96. Author, editor Fordham Law Rev., 1969. Leader Boy Scouts Am., Nassau County, N.Y., 1984-94, Denver, 1994—. Lt. comdr. USCGR, 1965-86. Mem. ABA, Colo. Bar, Denver Bar, Maritime Law Assn., Am. Soc. Internat. Law, Soc. Naval Architects and Marine Engrs., U.S. Naval Inst., Am. Arbitration Assn.

ULRICH, WERNER, patent lawyer; b. Munich, Germany, Mar. 12, 1931; came to U.S., 1940, naturalized, 1945; s. Karl Justus and Grete (Rosenthal) U.; m. Ursula Wolff, June 28, 1959; children—Greta, Kenneth. B.S., Columbia U., 1952, M.S. (NSF fellow 1952-53), 1953, Dr.Engring. Sci., 1957; M.B.A., U. Chgo., 1975; J.D., Loyola U., Chgo, 1985. Bar: Ill., 1985. With AT&T Bell Labs, Naperville, Ill., 1953-95; head electronics switching dept. AT&T Bell Labs., Naperville, Ill., 1964-68; dir. Advanced Switching Tech., Naperville, 1968-77, head maintenance architecture dept., 1977-81; sr. atty. Intellectual Property Law Orgn., Naperville, 1981-95; vis. lectr. U. Calif., Berkeley, 1966-67. Inventor of over 20 telecommunications inventions; patentee electronic switching systems. Fellow IEEE; mem. ABA, Ill. State Bar Assn., Am. Intellectual Property Law Assn., Tau Beta Pi, Beta Gamma Sigma. Office: 434 Maple St Glen Ellyn IL 60137-3826

ULRICH, WERNER RICHARD, union education administrator; b. N.Y.C., Sept. 26, 1941; s. Werner and Erna (Schreiner) U.; m. Marie Sciacca, July 18, 1965; children: Kenneth, Clifford, Richard. AAS, Voorhees Tech. Inst., 1969; BA, SUNY, Old Westbury, 1985; MS, N.Y. Inst. Tech., 1990. Mechanic "A" Con Edison of N.Y., N.Y.C., 1963-68; apprentice steamfitter Steamfitters', Local Union # 638, Long Island City, N.Y., 1968-73, journeyman steamfitter, 1973-85; dir. edn. Steamfitters' Edn. Fund, N.Y.C., 1985—. Blood dr. coord. Steamfitters', Local Union # 638, Long Island City, 1987—; usher, capt. Holy Name of Mary Roman Cath. Ch., 1984—; mem. steering coun. L.I. Women's Coun., 1992—; skilled worker emeritus N.Y. State Tng. Partnership Coun., 1993—; mem. S.I. Job Svc. Employer Com., 1993—. With U.S. Army, 1959-62. Recipient John J. Theobald award N.Y. Inst. Tech., 1989, Commr.'s award N.Y. State Dept. Labor, 1991, L.I. Women's award L.I. Women's Coun., 1991, N.Y. State Gov.'s cert. of Appreciation, 1994. Mem. ASME, Nat. Fire Protection Assn., U.S. Apprenticeship Assn., Am. Legion, KC. Avocations: horticulture. Office: 48-03 32nd Pl Long Island City NY 11101-2517

ULSHEN, MARTIN HOWARD, pediatric gastroenterologist, researcher; b. N.Y.C., Mar. 5, 1944; s. Lawrence F. and Dorothy C. Ulshen; divorced; children: Sarah Powell, Daniel; m. Sue Ellen McRae, Dec. 17, 1988. BA, U. Rochester, 1965, MD, 1969. Diplomate Am. Bd. Pediat., sub-bd. gastroenterology. Intern U. N.C., 1969-70; resident U. Colo., 1972-74, fellow in pediat. gastroenterology, 1974-75; fellow in pediat. gastroenterology Childrens Hosp., Boston, 1975-77; prof. U. N.C., Chapel Hill, 1977—. Assoc. editor Jour. Pediat.; med. editor Pediat. Gastroenterology, Am. Bd. Pediat.; contbr. articles to profl. jours. With USPHS, 1970-72. Office: U NC Dept Pediatrics CB # 7220 Chapel Hill NC 27599-7220

ULTAN, LLOYD, historian; b. Bronx, N.Y., Feb. 16, 1938; s. Louis and Sophie U. BA cum laude, Hunter Coll., 1959; MA, Columbia U., 1960. Assoc. Edward Williams Coll. Fairleigh Dickinson U., Hackensack, N.J., 1964-74; asst. prof. history Edward Williams Coll. Fairleigh Dickinson U., Hackensack, 1974-75, assoc. prof. Edward Williams Coll., 1975-83, prof. Edward Williams Coll., 1983—; cons. in field. Editor Bronx County Hist. Soc. Pres., 1981—; author: The Beautiful Bronx, 1920-50, 1979, Legacy of the Revolution: The Valentine-Varian House, 1983, The Bronx in the Innocent Years, 1890-1925, 1985, The Presidents of the United States, 1989, The Bronx in the Frontier Era: From the Beginning to 1696, 1993, The Bronx: It Was Only Yesterday, 1935-65, 1993; contbr. Ency. N.Y. City, 1995, Roots of the Republic, Vol. VI, 1996. Gen. sec. Bronx Civic League, 1964-67; v.p. bd. trustees Bronx County Hist. Soc., 1965-67, 77-84, curator, 1968-71, pres., 1971-76, historian, 1986—; founding mem., bd. dir. Bronx Coun. on Arts, 1968-71; chmn. Bronx County Bicentennial Commn., 1973-76, Bronx Borough Pres.'s Bicentennial Adv. Com., 1974-76; vice chmn. Commn. Celebrating 350 Yr. of the Bronx, 1989; program guidelines com. N.Y.C. Dept. Cultural Affairs, 1976-77; bd. dirs. Nat. Shrine Bill of Rights, Mt. Vernon, N.Y., 1983—; mem. N.Y.C. Com. on Cultural Concerns, 1982-88; bd. sponsors Historic Preservation com. St. Ann's Ch. Morrisania, 1987—; bd. dirs. 91 Van Cortlandt Owners Corp., 1986—. Recipient Fairleigh Dickinson U. 15-Yr. award, 1979, 20-Yr. award, 1984, 25-Yr. award, 1989, 30-Yr. award, 1994, Outstanding Tchr. of Yr. award, 1994; named to Hunter Coll. Alumni Hall of Fame, 1974; N.Y. State Regents Coll. Teaching fellow, 1959. Mem. AAUP (v.p. Teaneck chpt. 1992-93, sec. coun. of FDU chpts. 1992-93), Am. Hist. Assn., N.Y. Hist. Soc., Phi Alpha Theta, Alpha Chi Alpha, Sigma Lambda. Home and Office: 91 Van Cortlandt Ave W Bronx NY 10463-2712 *Transmitting the heritage of the past to the youth and to the mature adult, either through the spoken or written word, not only ensures that the civilization we inherited will be passed on, it will also warn people about earlier mistakes that should now be shunned and will, hopefully, inspire them to add their own positive contribution. I believe I am continuing to perform this service.*

ULTMANN, JOHN ERNEST, physician, educator; b. Vienna, Austria, Jan. 6, 1925; came to U.S., 1938, naturalized, 1943; s. Oskar and Hedwig (Schechter) U.; m. Ruth E. Layton, May 25, 1952; children: Monica, Michelle, Barry. Student, Bklyn. Coll., 1946, Oberlin Coll., 1946-48; M.D., Columbia U., 1952; Dr honoris causa, Heidelberg U., Fed. Republic Germany, 1986, Vienna U., Austria, 1991. Diplomate Nat. Bd. Med. Examiners, Am. Bd. Internal Medicine. Intern N.Y. Hosp.-Cornell Med. Center, N.Y.C., 1952-53; resident N.Y. Hosp., 1953-55; Am. Cancer Soc. fellow in hematology Columbia, 1955-56; practice medicine specializing in internal medicine N.Y.C., 1956-68, Chgo., 1968—; mem. staff Francis Delafield Hosp., 1955-68, Presbyn. Hosp., 1956-68, Bellevue Hosp., 1961-68; career scientist Health Research Council City N.Y., 1959-68; cons. Harlem Hosp., N.Y.C., 1966-68; dir. clin. oncology Franklin McLean Meml. Research Inst., 1968-91; prof. medicine Sch. Medicine U. Chgo., 1970—, dir. Cancer Rsch. Ctr., 1973-91, assoc. dir., 1991-94, dir. emeritus, 1994—, dean for rsch. and devel., 1978-88; hon. prof. Cancer Inst. Chinese Acad. Med. Scis., People's Republic of China, 1988; chmn. bd. sci. counselors div. cancer treatment Nat. Cancer Inst., 1976-80, mem. bd. sci. counselors div. cancer prevention and control, 1985-88; mem. adv. bd. Cancer Control to Gov. of Ill., 1976-93, chmn., 1985-93. Asso. editor: Cancer Research, 1974-78; editorial bd.: Annals Internal Medicine, 1974-81, Blood, 1975-77; cons. editor: Am. Jour. Medicine, 1975—; Contbr. articles to profl. jours. Bd. dirs. Assn. Am. Cancer Insts., 1974-75, pres.-elect, 1983-84, pres., 1984-85, chmn. bd., 1985-86; bd. dirs. at-large Ill. div. Am. Cancer Soc., 1976-79; trustee Ill. Cancer Coun., 1976-93; chmn. Nat. Coalition for Cancer Rsch., 1985-90. With AUS, 1943-46. Fellow A.C.P., Inst. Medicine Chgo.; mem. Am. Fedn. Clin. Investigation, Soc. Study Blood, Am. Assn. Cancer Rsch., Am. Socs. Hematology, AAUP, AAAS, Harvey Soc., Am. Soc. Clin. Oncology (dir. 1978-83, pres.-elect 1980-81, pres. 1981-82, past pres. 1982-83), Chgo. Soc. Internal Medicine, Central Soc. Clin. Rsch., Sociedad Chilena de Cancerologia, Sociedad Chilena de Hematologia, Phi Beta Kappa, Alpha Omega Alpha. Home: 5632 S Harper Ave Chicago IL 60637-1872 Office: U Chgo Cancer Rsch Ctr 5841 S Maryland Ave Chicago IL 60637-1463

UMAN, MARTIN ALLAN, electrical engineering educator, researcher, consultant; b. Tampa, Fla., July 3, 1936; s. Morrice S. and Edith G. (Brown) U.; m. Dorit Brigitta Kalbas, Mar. 6, 1962; children: Jon, Mara, Derek. BS in Engring., Princeton U., 1957, MA, 1959, PhD, 1961. Assoc. prof. elec. engring. U. Ariz., Tucson, 1961-65; fellow physicist Westinghouse Rsch. Labs., Pitts., 1965-71; prof. dept. elec. and computer engring. U. Fla., Gainesville, 1971-91, prof., chmn. dept., 1991—; pres. Lightning Location & Protection, Inc., Tucson, 1975-83; mem. Internat. Commn. on Atmospheric Electricity, 1975-92; cons. Boeing Aircraft, Patrick AFB, Mobil Oil Corp., McDonnell Douglas, United Techs., IBM, Flamex Corp., NOAA, NASA, No. Telecom Can., Tampa Cable TV, Bonneville Power Adminstrn., Martin Marietta, Sandia Nat. Labs., Walt Disney World, SRI, other cos. Author: Introduction to Plasma Physics, 1964, Lightning, 1969, rev. edit., 1984, Understanding Lightning, 1971, All About Lightning, 1986, The Lightning Discharge, 1987; also over 130 articles; assoc. editor Jour. Geophys. Rsch., 1980-83; patentee in field. Mem. senate U. Fla., 1988-90, 93—, bd. dirs. div. sponsored rsch., 1989-91. Recipient Outstanding Svc. award Coll. Engring. U. Fla., 1975, Disting. Faculty award Blue Key, 1979-80, Outstanding Tchr. award, 1985-86, Faculty Advisor award, 1986, 88, Tchr.-Scholar of Yr. award, 1988-89; editor's citation Jour. Geophys. Rsch., 1989, Outstanding Fla. Scientist award Fla. Acad. Scis., 1991, Group Achievement award for Galileo Probe Spacecraft NASA, 1992; rsch. grantee various orgns. Fellow IEEE (com. mem. working group on lightning performance distbn. ins. 1979—, working group on estimating performance transmission ins. 1985—, Heinrich Hertz medal 1996), Am. Geophys. Union, Am. Meteorol. Soc.

UMANS, ALVIN ROBERT, manufacturing company executive; b. N.Y.C., Mar. 11, 1927; s. Louis and Ethel (Banner) U.; m. Nancy Jo Zadek, June 28, 1953 (div.); children: Kathi Lee Umans Lind, Craig Joseph; m. Madeleine Sayer, Sept. 21, 1985; 1 child, Valentine Brett. Student, U. Rochester, 1945. Sales mgr. Textile Mills Co., Chgo., 1954-56; regional sales mgr. Reflector Hardware Corp., Melrose Park, Ill., 1956-58; nat. sales mgr. Reflector Hardware Corp., 1959-62, v.p., 1962-65, pres., treas., dir., 1965-92; pres., CEO RHC/Spacemaster Corp., 1992—; chmn. bd. dirs., Garcy Corp., Ala.; v.p., bd. dirs. Goer Mfg. Co., Inc., Charleston, S.C.; chmn. Discovery Plastics, Oreg.; pres., treas., dir. Spacemaster Corp., Del.; chmn. Morgan Marshall Industries, Inc., Ill., Capitol Hardware, Inc., Ill.; dir., v.p. Spartan Showcase Inc., Mo.; dir. Adams Comm., Chgo.; bd. dirs. Monroe Comm., Chgo. Trustee Mt. Sinai Hosp. Med. Ctr., Chgo., chmn. bd., 1987-89; trustee Schwab Rehab. Hosp., Chgo., chmn. bd., 1987-89; dir., chmn. Sinai Health Sys., Chgo., 1995—; mem. Cook County Bur. Adv. Com., 1994—; bd. dirs. Milton & Rose Zadek Fund, 1965-78; governing bd. mem. Cinema/Chgo., 1988-89. Served with AUS, 1945-46. Mem. Nat. Assn. Store Fixture Mfrs. (dir. 1969-70), Chgo. Pres.'s Orgn. Club: Standard (Chgo.). Home: 132 E Delaware Pl Chicago IL 60611 Office: RHC/Spacemaster Corp 1400 N 25th Ave Melrose Park IL 60160-3001

UMBDENSTOCK, JUDY JEAN, physical education educator, real estate agent, farmer, entrepreneur; b. Aurora, Ill., Feb. 12, 1952; d. Alfred Aloyuisious and Mary Emma (Orha) U. AA, Elgin (Ill.) Community Coll., 1972, AS, 1973; BA, Aurora U., 1977; grad., Robert Allens Wealth Tng. 2000, 1991; grad. real estate course, Profl. Edn. Inst., 1991. Cert. phys. edn. tchr., secondary edn. tchr.; lic. real estate salesperson, Ill. Tchr. phys. edn., varsity head coach volleyball and track St. Laurence Sch., Elgin, 1970-75; asst. coach varsity basketball East Aurora High Sch., 1976-77; jr. varsity coach softball St. Charles (Ill.) High Sch., 1978-79, phys. edn. tchr., 1978-79; head coach volleyball/basketball, tchr. algebra and geometry Canton Jr. H.S., Streamwood, Ill., 1979-82; varsity coach volleyball and softball Elgin High Sch., 1982-85, phys. edn. tchr., 1982-86, jr. varsity basketball coach, 1983-84; tchr. elem. phys. edn. Sch. Dist. U-46 Heritage Elem. Sch., Streamwood, 1986—, Parkwood Elem. Sch., Hanover Park, Ill., 1986—; substitute tchr. Elgin, St. Charles and Burlington (Ill.) H.S., 1977-78; Ill. H.S. rated sports referee Elgin and St. Charles Area H.S., 1970-85; cons. Draft and Carriage Horse Assn., Kane County, 1981—; owner Umbdenstock Country Feed & Seed Store, Elgin, 1988-94; owner/ptnr. Jud Enterprises, 1992—; real estate agent Century 21 New Heritage Inc., 1994—. Leader, youth counselor 4-H (farming and animal husbandry), Northern Ill. area, 1970—; campaign supporter state and local Reps. for re-election, Kane county, 1974-86. Served with U.S. Army, 1976-77, with USNR, 1981-87. Scholar Elgin Panhellenic Soc., 1972. Mem. NEA, NAFE, Ill. Edn. Assn., Nat. Farmers Orgn. (pub. relations 1967-80), Airplane Owners and Pilots Assn., Am. Assn. Health, Phys. Edn. and Recreation, Elgin Tchrs. Assn., South Elgin Bus. Assn., Elgin Assn. Realtors, Nat. Wildlife Assn., Nat. Audubon Soc., Disabled Am. Vet. Comdr. Club, People for the Ethnic Treatment Animals, Ill. Coaches Orgn., Am. Draft Horse Assn., Kane County Tchrs. Credit Union, Kane County Farm Bureau. Clubs: Barrington (Ill.) Carriage, 99's Women's Pilot Assn. Home: 8n129 Umbdenstock Rd Elgin IL 60123-8828 Office: Sch Dist U-46 E Chicago St Elgin IL 60120-5522 also: Century 21 New Heritage Inc 41 N McLean Blvd Elgin IL 60123

UMBREIT, WAYNE WILLIAM, bacteriologist, educator; b. Markesan, Wis., May 1, 1913; s. William Traugott and Augusta (Abendroth) U.; m. Doris McQuade, July 31, 1937; children: Dorayne Loreda, Jay Nicholas, Thomas Hayden. B.A., U. Wis., 1934, M.S., 1936, Ph.D., 1939. Instr. soil microbiology Rutgers U., 1937-38; faculty U. Wis., Madison, 1938-44; asst. prof. bacteriology and chemistry U. Wis., 1941-44; faculty Cornell U., 1944-47, prof. bacteriology, 1946-47; head dept. enzyme chemistry Merck Inst., Rahway, N.J., 1947-58; asso. dir., 1958; chmn. dept. bacteriology Rutgers U., New Brunswick, N.J., 1958-75; prof. microbiology, dir. grad. programs Rutgers U., 1969-83, prof. emeritus microbiology, 1983—; dir. labs. So. Br. Watershed Assn., 1983-89. Author: (with Burris, Stauffer) Manometric Techniques, 1945, 5th edit., 1972, (with Oginsky) An Introduction to Bacterial Physiology, 1954, Metabolic Maps, 1960, Modern Microbiology, 1962, Essentials of Bacterial Physiology, 1976; Editor: Advances in Applied Microbiology, vols. 1-10, 1959-68; Contbr. articles to profl. jours. Recipient Biochem. Congress Symposium medal Paris, France, 1952. Fellow Am. Acad. Microbiology, N.Y. Acad. Sci., A.A.A.S.; mem. Am. Soc. for Microbiology (Eli Lilly award in bacteriology 1947, Carski Found. award for distinguished teaching 1968), Soc. Biol. Chemists, Am. Chem. Soc., Theobald Smith Soc. (Waksman award in microbiology 1957, past pres.), AAUP, Sigma Xi. Home: 826 Covered Bridge Rd Holland PA 18966

UMEBAYASHI, CLYDE S., lawyer; b. Honolulu, Sept. 2, 1947; s. Robert S. and Dorothy C. Umebayashi; m. Cheryl J. Much, June 27, 1975. BBA in Travel Industry Mgmt., U. Hawaii, 1969, JD, 1980. Spl. dept. atty. gen. Labor and Indsl. Rels. Appeals Bd., Honolulu, 1980-81; atty., dir., shareholder Kessner Duca Umebayashi Bain & Matsunaga, Honolulu, 1981—; commr. Hawaii Criminal Justice Commn. Bd. dirs. Wesley Found., Honolulu, 1993—. Mem. Hawaii State Bar Assn. Office: Kessner Duca Umebayashi 220 S King St Fl 19 Honolulu HI 96813-4526

UMFLEET, LLOYD TRUMAN, electrical engineering technology educator; b. Grangeville, Idaho, June 2, 1944; s. Lloyd Truman Sr. and Bessie Viola (MacKay) U.; m. Ruth Ann Strickland, Oct. 26, 1968. BSEE, U. Mo., 1966; MSIM, Poly. Inst. Bklyn., 1971; M in Engring., U. Colo., 1988. Registered profl. engr., Tex. Asst. engr. Union Electric, St. Louis, 1966; elec. engr. Power Authority State of N.Y., N.Y.C., 1967-68, Consol. Edison, N.Y.C., 1968-71; ind. engring. cons. Toledo, 1971-76; chief elec. engr. Goldston Engring., Inc., Corpus Christi, Tex., 1976-80; mgr. elec. engring. Berry Engring., Inc., Corpus Christi, 1980-84; instr. elec. tech. Bee County Coll., Beeville, Tex., 1984-86; asst. prof. Del Mar Coll., Corpus Christi, 1988—; cons. engring. Ctrl. Power and Light, Corpus Christi, 1991, 92, INDTECH, Inc., Corpus Christi, 1994, 95. Mem. IEEE (sr.), Am. Soc. Engring. Edn., Instrument Soc. Am., Rockport Sailing Club (commodore 1982). Achievements include development of universal power circle for educational purposes. Office: Del Mar Coll 101 Baldwin Corpus Christi TX 78404

UMMER, JAMES WALTER, lawyer; b. Pitts., July 16, 1945; s. Walter B. and Rose P. (Gerhardt) U.; m. Janet Sue Young, Dec. 21, 1968; children: James Bradley, Benjamin F. BA, Thiel Coll., 1967; JD, Duke U., 1972. Bar: Pa. 1972. Trust officer Pitts. Nat. Bank, 1972-75; tax atty., shareholder Buchanan Ingersoll P.C., Pitts., 1975-92; prin. Hirtle, Callaghan & Co., Pitts., 1992-93; with Babst, Calland, Clements and Zomnir, Pitts., 1993—; mng. dir. Morgan Franklin & Co., Pitts., Golf Course Cons., Orlando, Fla. Trustee Thiel Coll., Greenville, Pa., 1984—, The Rehab. Inst. Pitts., 1984—, Snee-Reinhardt Charitable Found., Pitts., 1987—. Fellow Am. Coll. Probate Counsel; mem. Estate Planning Coun. Western Pa. (pres. 1986-87), Tax Club (Pitts.), Duquesne Club, Rolling Rock Club, Oakmont Country Club. Republican. Presbyterian. Home: 200 Woodland Farms Rd Pittsburgh PA 15238-2024 Office: Babst, Calland, Clements & Zomnir 2 Gateway Ctr Fl 8 Pittsburgh PA 15222-1402

UMMINGER, BRUCE LYNN, government official, scientist, educator; b. Dayton, Ohio, Apr. 10, 1941; s. Frederick William and Elnora Mae (Waltemathe) U.; m. Judith Lackey Bryant, Dec. 17, 1966; children: Alison Grace, April Lynn. BS magna cum laude with honors in biology, Yale U., 1963, MS, 1966, MPhil, 1968, PhD, 1969; postgrad., U. Calif., Berkeley, 1963-64; cert. univ. adminstrv./mgmt. tng. program, U. Cin., 1975; cert., Fed. Exec. Inst., 1984. Asst. prof. dept. biol. scis. U. Cin., 1969-73, assoc. prof. dept. biol. scis., 1973-75, acting head dept. biol. scis., 1973-75, prof. dept. biol. scis., 1975-81, dir. grad. affairs, 1978-79; program dir. regulatory biology program NSF, Washington, 1979-84, dept. dir. cellular biosci. divsn., 1984-89, mem. sr. exec. svc., 1984—, acting divsn. dir., 1985-87, 88-89, divsn. dir. cellular biosci. divsn., 1989-91, divsn. dir. integrative biology and neurosci. divsn., 1991—; sr. advisor on health policy Office of Internat. Health Policy Dept. State, Washington, 1988; sr. advisor on biodiversity Smithsonian Instn., 1993-94; exec. sec. Nat. Sci. Bd. Com. on Ctrs. and Individual Investigator Awards, 1986-88; mem. NSF rev. panel Exptl. Program to Stimulate Competitive Rsch., 1989, Rsch. Improvement in Minority Instns., 1986, 87, U.S.-India Coop. Rsch. Program, 1981-82, U.S.-India Exchange of Scholars Program, 1979-81; vice chmn. biotech. rsch. subcom. Fed. Coord. Coun. on Sci. Engring. and Tech., Office Sci. and Tech. Policy, 1991-94; exec. sec. subcom. biodiversity and ecosystem dynamics, com. on environment and natural resources Nat. Sci. and Tech. Coun., 1994; mem. group nat. experts on safety in biotech., OECD, 1988-89; mem. sr. exec. panel Exec. Potential Program, Office Pers. Mgmt., 1988-89; mem. space shuttle proposal rev. panel in life scis. NASA, 1978, rsch. assocs. in space biology award com., 1985-91, chmn. cell and devel. biology discipline working group, space biology program, 1990-91, chmn. gravitational biology panel, NASA Specialized Ctrs. Rsch. and Tng., 1990, chmn. NASA specialized ctrs. rsch. and tng. peer rev. panel, 1995, mem. exec. steering com. in life scis., 1991; mem. gravitational biology facility sci. working group, 1992-95, mem. space sta. biol. rsch. project sci. working group, 1995-96; mem. NASA neurolab. steering com., 1993; mem. panel study biol. diversity, Bd. Sci. and Tech. Internat. Devel. NRC, 1989; exec. sec. adv. planning bd. Nat. Biodiversity Info. Ctr., Smithsonian Instn., 1993-94; mem. adv. screening com. in life scis. Coun. for Internat. Exchange of Scholars, 1978-81; liaison rep. nat. heart, lung and blood adv. coun. NIH, 1979-87, nat. adv. child health. Author book chpts. and contbr. articles to profl. jours.; assoc. editor Jour. Exptl. Zoology, 1977-79; editorial adv. bd. Gen. and Comparative Endocrinology, 1982. Mem. world mission com. Ch. of the Redeemer, New Haven, 1967-68; Sunday Sch. steering com. Calvary Episcopal Ch., Cin., 1972-73; sr. acolyte, 1972-77, adult edn. com., 1975-76; deacon Faith Presbyn. Ch., Springfield, Va., 1996—; adv. com. mem. Wakefield H.S., 1991-92, PTA exec. bd., 1991-93; sci. adv. com. Arlington Pub. Schs., 1987-92, adv. coun. on instrn., 1991-92; adv. bd. mem. Campbell Comml. Coll., Cin., 1977-79. Recipient George Rieveschl, Jr. Rsch. award U. Cin., 1973, Outstanding Performance award and Sustained Superior Performance NSF, 1981, spl. achievement award 1985, Sr. Exec. Svc. Performance award 1986, 87, 90, 91, Presdl. Rank Meritorious Exec. award 1992; U. Cin. Grad. Sch. fellow 1977—, NSF fellow 1964; rsch. grantee NSF 1971-79. Fellow AAAS (coun. 1980-83, 89-90, mem. program com. for 1989 ann. meeting 1988, chairperson-elect sect. G-Biol. Scis. 1987-88, chairperson 1988-89, ret. 1989-90), N.Y. Acad. Scis.; mem. Am. Soc. Zoologists (sec., mem. exec. com. 1979-81, chmn. nominating com. 1981, sec. divsn. of comparative physiology and biochemistry 1976-77, chmn. Congl. Sci. Fellow Program com. 1986-89, mem. 1991-93), Am. Physiol. Soc. (pro adv. com. 1978-81, program exec. com., 1983-86, mem. steering com., comparative pysiology sect. 1978-81, sec. Am. Physiol. Soc.-Am. Soc. Zoologists Task Force on Comparative Physiology 1977-78), Am. Inst. Biol. Scis. (chmn. selection com. congl. fellow liaisons com. 1991), Am. Soc. for Gravitational and Space Biology, Sr. Execs. Assn., Assn. of Yale Alumni (del. 1990-93), Mory's Assn., Yale Club (Washington), Masons (32 degree), K.T. Shriners, Sigma Xi (Disting. Rsch. award U. Cin. chpt. 1973, pres. U. Cin. chpt. 1977-79), Mensa. Achievements include development of science policy in biodiversity, space biology, integrative biology, neuroscience, and biotechnology; research in low temperature biology, in comparative physiology, endocrinology and biochemistry of fish, and in visual orientation of crustacea. Home: 4087B S Four Mile Run Dr Arlington VA 22204-5604 Office: NSF Divsn Integrative Biology and Neuroscience 4201 Wilson Blvd Arlington VA 22230-0001

UNAKAR, NALIN JAYANTILAL, biological sciences educator; b. Karachi, Sindh, Pakistan, Mar. 26, 1935; came to U.S., 1961; s. Jayantilal Virshankar and Malati Jaswantrai (Buch) U.; m. Nita Shantilal Mankad; children: Rita, Rupa. BS, Gujerat U., Bhavnagar, India, 1955; MSc, Bombay U., 1961; PhD, Brown U., 1965. Research asst. Indian Cancer Research Ctr., Bombay, 1955-61; USPHS trainee in biology Brown U., Providence, 1961-65; research assoc. in pathology U. Toronto, Ont., Can., 1965-66; asst. prof. biology Oakland U., Rochester, Mich., 1966-69, assoc. prof., 1969-74, prof., chmn. biology dept., 1974-87; prof., 1974—; adj. prof. biomed. scis. Oakland U., Rochester, Mich., 1984—; mem. coop. cataract research group Nat. Eye Inst., Bethesda, Md., 1977—; mem. visual scis. study sect. NIH, Bethesda, 1982-86, mem. cataract panel, 1980—. Mem. vis. bd. Lehigh U., Bethlehem, Pa., 1986-89. Grantee Nat. Cancer Inst., NIH, 1967-70, Nat. Eye Inst., NIH, 1976—. Mem. AAAS, Am. Soc. Cell Biology, Assn. Rsch. in Vision and Ophthalmology, Sigma Xi. Home: 2822 Rhineberry Rd Rochester Hls MI 48309-1912 Office: Oakland U Dept Of Biol Scis Rochester MI 48309

UNANUE, EMIL RAPHAEL, immunopathologist; b. Havana, Cuba, Sept. 13, 1934; married, 1965; 3 children. B.Sc., Inst. Secondary Edn., 1952; M.D., U. Havana Sch. Medicine, Cuba, 1960; M.A., Harvard U., 1974. Assoc. exptl. pathology Scripps Clin. and Research Found., 1960-70; intern in pathology Presbyn. Univ. Hosp., Pitts., 1961-62; research fellow in exptl. pathology Scripps Clin. and Research Found., 1962-65; research fellow immunology Nat. Inst. Med. Research, London, 1966-68; from asst. prof. to assoc. prof. pathology Harvard U. Med. Sch., Boston, 1971-74, prof., 1974-77, Mallinckrodt prof. immunopathology, 1977—; prof., chmn. dept. pathology Washington U. Sch. Medicine, St. Louis, 1988—. Recipient T. Duckett Jones award, Helen Hay Whitney Found., 1968, Park-Davis award, Am. Soc. Exptl. Pathology, 1973, Albert Lasker Award for Basic Med. Rsch., 1995. Office: Washington U Sch Medicine Dept of Pathology PO Box 8188 Saint Louis MO 63156-8188

UNANUE, JOSEPH, food products executive. Chmn., CEO Goya Foods, Secaucus, NJ. Office: Goya Foods Inc 100 Seaview Dr Secaucus NJ 07094-1800*

UNDE, MADHAVJI (MARK) ANANT, welding specialist engineering executive; b. Pune, India, June 28, 1934; came to U.S., 1974; s. Anant Narasinh Unde and Laxmibai A. U.; m. Dhanawanti B. Joshi, June 11, 1982 (div. Oct. 1983); 1 child, Abhijeet. M.I.E., Instn. Engrs., Calcutta, India, 1973; M.I.Prod.E., Instn. Prodn. Engrs., London, 1972; MS in Welding, Ohio State U., 1978. Chartered engr. Divsn. welding engr. Fruehauf Corp.; tool engr. Danly Machine/Ingersoll Milling Machines, Inc.; mechanical engr. Sacramento Army Depot; pres. Calif. Consulting Engrs., Sacramento. Inventor In Process Stress Relief, Equivalent Heat Sink Process for welding; patents in mechanisms, welding, casting and non-destructive testing. Recipient Presdl. award Advanced Rsch. Project Agy., 1994. Office: Calif Consulting Engrs 1980 Watt Ave Sacramento CA 95825

UNDERBERG, ALAN JACK, lawyer; b. Rochester, N.Y., Oct. 12, 1929; s. Henry and Anne (Landau) U.; m. Joyce Wisbaum, Oct. 19, 1952; children: Mark A., Amy Allen, Lisa Hamburg, Kathryn Zimmerman. BS, Cornell U., 1951; JD, Harvard U., 1956. Bar: N.Y. 1956, U.S. Dist. Ct. (we. dist.) N.Y. 1957, U.S. Supreme Ct. 1961. Ptnr. Underberg & Kessler, Rochester, 1963—; cons. to Commn. on Govt. Procurement, Washington,. 1970-71. Commr., co-founder Monroe County Human Rels. Commn., Rochester, 1961-64; trustee The Harley Sch., Rochester, 1972-75; mem. bd. mgrs. Meml. Art Gallery, Rochester, 1978—, pres. 1990-92; mem. N.Y. State Bd. Equalization and Assessment, Albany, 1976-84; mem. Nat. Pk Sys. Adv. Bd., Dept. Interior, 1981-85, chmn. 1983-84; bd. govs. the Genesee Hosp., Rochester, 1984—, chmn. 1987-89; chmn. The Genesee Hosp. Health Sys., Inc., 1989-94; vice chmn. Greater Rochester Health Sys., Inc., 1994-96, chmn. 1996—; bd. dirs. Managerial Econs. Rsch. Ctr., William E. Simon Grad. Sch. Bus. Adminstrn.; bd. trustees U. Rochester, 1986, mem. exec. com. 1988—; chmn. U. Rochester Assocs., 1976-77; bd. dirs. YMCA Greater Rochester, 1980-86, mem. exec. com. 1982-86. 1st lt. USAF, 1951-53. Mem. ABA, Monroe County Bar Assn. (bd. dirs. Found. 1985-88), N.Y. Bar Assn. (lectr. continuing legal edn. program 1962-69, com. corp. law, banking, corp. and bus. law sect. 1963—), Genesee Valley Club (pres. 1985-87), Country Club Rochester, Cornell Club N.Y.C., Harvard Club N.Y.C. Avocations: golf, tennis, skiing. Office: Underberg & Kessler 1800 Chase Sq Rochester NY 14604-1910

UNDERBERG, MARK ALAN, lawyer; b. Niagara Falls, N.Y., July 9, 1955; s. Alan Jack and Joyce Love (Wisbaum) U.; m. Diane Englander, Mar. 22, 1986; children: Andrew Englander, James Englander. BA, Cornell U., 1977, JD, 1981. Bar: N.Y. 1981. Law clk. to chief judge U.S. Ct. Appeals (3d cir.), Wilmington, Del., 1981-82; assoc. Debevoise & Plimpton, N.Y.C., 1982-87; mng. dir., dep. gen. counsel Henley Group, Inc., N.Y.C., 1987-90, mng. dir., gen. counsel, 1990-92; v.p., gen. counsel Abex Inc., Hampton, N.H., 1992-95; v.p., gen. counsel Fisher Sci. Internat. Inc., Hampton, N.H., 1991—. Editor-in-chief Cornell Law Rev., 1980-81. Mem. ABA, Assn. of Bar of City of N.Y., Genesee Valley Club, University Club. Office: Fisher Scientific Internat 375 Park Ave Ste 2001 New York NY 10152

UNDERCOFLER, J(ONAS) CLAYTON, lawyer; b. Phila., June 11, 1940; s. Jonas Clayton and Margaret (Huff) U.; m. Lesley Mowlds, Aug. 28, 1965; children: James C., Randall T. BS, Drexel U., 1962; JD, Villanova U., 1966. Bar: Pa. 1967. Law clk. Judge Thomas J. Clary, Phila., 1966-67; assoc. Clark, Ladner, Fortenbaugh & Young, Phila., 1967-69; asst. U.S. atty. U.S. Atty.'s Office, Phila., 1969-76, U.S. atty., 1976; vis. assoc. prof. Villanova (Pa.) U., 1976-77; mem. Undercofler & Hannum, West Chester, Pa., 1977, Dilworth, Paxon, Kalish & Kauffman, Phila., 1977-86, Saul, Ewing, Remick & Saul, Phila., 1986—; mem. Civil Justice Reform Act Adv. Group, Phila., 1991—. Chmn. Southeastern Pa. Transp. Authority, 1988-93; chmn. Citizens Crime Commn., Delaware Valley, 1992; bd. dirs. Greater Phila. First, 1995—. Named Citizen of the Yr. Delaware Valley March of Dimes, 1991. Fellow Am. Coll. Trial Lawyers; mem. ABA, Fed. Bar Assn. (Outstanding Younger Fed. Lawyer 1973), Phila. Bar Assn., Pa. Bar Assn., nat. Assn. of Former U.S. Attys., Greater Phila. C. of C. Office: Saul Ewing Remick & Saul 3800 Centre Square W Philadelphia PA 19102

UNDERDOWN, DAVID EDWARD, historian, educator; b. Wells, Eng., Aug. 19, 1925; s. John Percival and Ethel Mary (Gell) U. B.A., U. Oxford, 1950, M.A., 1951; M.A., Yale U., 1952; B.Litt., U. Oxford, 1953; D.Litt. hon., U. of South, 1981. Asst. prof. U. of South, Sewanee, Tenn., 1953-58, assoc. prof., 1958-62; then assoc. prof. U. Va., Charlottesville, 1962-68; prof. Brown U., Providence, 1968-85, Munro-Goodwin Wilkinson prof., 1978-85; vis. prof. Yale U., New Haven, 1979; prof. Yale U., 1986-94, George Burton Adams prof., 1994—; dir. Yale Ctr. Parliamentary History; vis. Mellon prof. Inst. for Advanced Study, 1988-89; vis. fellow All Souls Coll., Oxford, 1992; Ford's lectr. Oxford U., 1992. Author: Royalist Conspiracy in England, 1960, Pride's Purge, 1971, Somerset in the Civil War and Interregnum, 1973, Revel, Riot and Rebellion, 1985, Fire from Heaven, 1992. Guggenheim fellow, 1964-65, 91-92, fellow Am. Coun. Learned Socs., 1973-74, NEH fellow, 1980-81. Fellow Royal Hist. Soc., Brit. Acad. (corrs.); mem. Am. Hist. Assn., Conf. Brit. Studies. Office: Yale U Dept History New Haven CT 06520

UNDERHILL, ANNE BARBARA, astrophysicist; b. Vancouver, B.C., Can., June 12, 1920; d. Frederic Clare and Irene Anna (Creery) U. BA, U. B.C., 1942, MA, 1944, DSc (hon.), 1992; PhD, U. Chgo., 1948; DSc (hon.), York U., Toronto, Ont., 1969. Sci. officer Dominion Astrophys. Obs., Victoria, B.C., 1949-62; prof. astrophysics U. Utrecht, The Netherlands, 1962-70; lab chief Goddard Space Flight Ctr./NASA, Greenbelt, Md., 1970-77, sr. scientist, 1978-85; hon. prof. U. B.C., Vancouver, 1985—. Author: The Early-type Stars, 1966; author/editor: B Stars with and without Emission Lines, 1982, O, Of and Wolf-Rayet Stars, 1988; contbr. articles to profl. jours. Fellow NRC, 1948, Can. Fedn. Univ. Women, 1944, 47. Fellow Royal Soc. Can., Royal Astron. Soc.; mem. Internat. Astron. Union (pres. commn. #36 1963-66), Am. Astron. Soc., Can. Astron. Soc. Anglican. Avocation: church choir singing. Office: U BC, Dept Geophysics & Astronomy, Vancouver, BC Canada V6T 1Z4

UNDERHILL, JACOB BERRY, III, retired insurance company executive; b. N.Y.C., Oct. 25, 1926; s. Jacob Berry, Jr. and Dorothy Louise (Quinn) U.; m. Cynthia Jane Lovejoy, Sept. 9, 1950 (div. Sept. 1962); children: David Lovejoy, Kate Howell Underhill Kerwin, Benedict Quinn; m. Lois Beachy, Nov. 2, 1963 (div. July 1987); m. Betsy F. Ashton, Oct. 17, 1987. Grad., Phillips Exeter Acad., 1944; A.B., Princeton U., 1950. Editor Courier & Freeman, Potsdam, N.Y., 1950-53; reporter Democrat & Chronicle, Rochester, N.Y., 1953-56; chief editorial writer St. Petersburg (Fla.) Times, 1956-59; asso. editor McGraw Hill Publ. Co., N.Y.C., 1959-61, Newsweek, N.Y.C., 1961-63; asst. press sec. to Gov. N.Y., 1963-67; dep. supt., 1st dep. supt. State N.Y. Ins. Dept., 1967-72; v.p., sr. v.p., exec. v.p., dir., vice chmn. bd., pres. N.Y. Life Ins. Co., N.Y.C., 1972-86. Chmn. bd. dirs. Manhattan Eye, Ear and Throat Hosp.; trustee emeritus Nat. Trust for Hist. Preservation. With USNR, 1944-46. Mem. Players Club, Links Club, Piping Rock Club (Locust Valley, N.Y.). Home: 410 E 57th St New York NY 10022-3059

UNDERHILL, LINN B., photographer; b. Aug. 8, 1936; d. O. Dwight and Carol Francis (Shuey) Baldwin; m. William Webb Underhill, June 20, 1956 (div. Aug. 1979); children: Sarah Underhill-Hval, Joseph Underhill-Cady, Katherine; m. Catherine Ann Carter, Aug. 17, 1991. MFA in Photographic Studies, SUNY, Buffalo, 1982; student, U. Calif. Berkeley, 1953-56, San Francisco Art Inst, 1956-57, U. Rochester, N.Y., 1977; BFA in Photography, Alfred (N.Y.) U., 1978. Self-employed portrait and wedding photographer, 1970-74; instr. Alfred U., 1972-74; intern Internat. Mus. Photography, George Eastman House, 1977; coord. Copy Ctr. Visual Studies Workshop, 1979-81, coord. Summer Inst., 1981, conservation technician Rsch. Ctr. Print Collection, 1981-82, coord. Rsch. Ctr., 1982-84, instr. photo-print processes, visual books and bookbinding, 1980-81; assoc. faculty, tutor Empire State Coll., Rochester, 1982; faculty N.Y. State Summer Sch. Arts, Sch. Film/Media, 1983; asst. prof. dept. visual arts Mason Gross Sch. of Arts, Rutgers U., New Brunswick, N.Y., 1988-89; instr. photography divsn. internat. programs abroad Syracuse U., Florence, Italy, 1990; asst. prof. dept. art media studies Coll. Visual and Performing Arts, Syracuse U., 1992—; artist-in residence Light Work, Syracuse, N.Y., 1983; lectr. Phila. Coll. Art, 1983; panelist N.Y. Found. Arts, Artists' Fellowship Program, 1985; symposium panelist Williams Coll., Williamstown, Mass., 1986, Hunter Coll., N.Y., 1986; guest lectr. women's studies program SUNY Binghamton, 1986; panelist visual artists' fellowship program, photography panel Nat. Endowment for Arts, 1988; vis. artist, lectr. Calif. Inst. Arts, Valencia, Calif., 1988; lectr. C.E.P.A. Gallery, Buffalo, 1989, N.Y. Summer Sch. for Arts, Buffalo, 1990, Cazenovia (N.Y.) Coll., 1990; vis. artist, lectr. U. Ill., Urbana-Champaign, 1990, Md. Inst. Coll. Art, Balt., 1991, R.I. Sch. Design, Providence, 1991, Hartwick Coll., Oneonta, N.Y., 1993; panelist Syracuse (N.Y.) U., 1991; lectr. U. Arts, Phila., 1992; juror 7th Nat. Photography Competition, N.Mex. Photographer, 1993; lectr. Gallery of Sch. of Photographic Arts and Scis., Rochester Inst. Tech., 1994, Boliou Art Ctr., Carleton Coll., Northfield, Minn., 1994; spkr., panelist Binghamton (N.Y.) U., 1995; adj. faculty fine arts dept. Coll. Graphic Arts and Photography, Rochester Inst. Tech., 1981-82, Tompkins Cortland Cmty. Coll., Dryden, N.Y., 1985-87, dept. art and art history and women's studies program SUNY, Binghamton 1985-88, cinema and photography dept. Sch. Comm. Ithaca (N.Y.) Coll., 1985-88; vis. lectr. Cornell U., 1987; vis. asst. prof. dept. art and art history Colgate U., Hamilton, N.Y., 1994. One-woman shows include Light Work, Syracuse, 1984, C.E.P.A. Gallery, Buffalo, 1989, Mednick Gallery, U. of Arts, Phila., 1992, Work Space Gallery, U. Colo., Boulder, 1993, SPAS Gallery, Rochester Inst. Tech., 1993, Boliou Art Ctr., Carleton Coll., Northfield, 1994; exhibited in group shows at Pratt Manhattan Ctr., N.Y.C., 1980, Pyramid Gallery, Rochester, 1980, 84, Spaces Gallery, Cleve., 1980, Sch. of Art Inst., Chgo., 1981, Wright State U., Dayton, Ohio, 1982, Chatauqua (N.Y.) Art Assn. Galleries, 1982, Montgomery Gallery, Pomona Coll., Claremont, Calif., 1983, San Francisco Camerawork, 1984, Coop. Gallery, Wakefield, R.I., 1984, Chapman Art Gallery, Cazenovia (N.Y.) Coll., 1984, Everson Mus. Art, Syracuse, 1985, Handwerker Gallery, Ithaca Coll., 1985, 86, Mpls. Coll. Art and Design, 1986, L.A. Mcpl. Art Gallery, 1987, U. Wis., Milw. Art Mus. Fine Arts Galleries and Conf. Ctr. of Golda Meir Libr., 1987, Village Gate Art Ctr., Rochester, 1987, Robert Menschel Photography Gallery, Syracuse, 1987, N.Y. State Mus., Albany, Burchfield Art Ctr., Buffalo, Nat. Mus. Women in Arts, Washington, Coll. Art Gallery, Coll. New Paltz, N.Y., 1989-90, Andrea Ruggieri Gallery, Washington, 1990, Joe and Emily Lowe Art Gallery, Syracuse U., 1990, Artists' Space, N.Y.C., 1991, Fine Arts Gallery, Ind. U., Bloomington, 1991, Toroto PhotographersWorkshop, 1992, 494 Gallery, N.Y.C., 1992, Barrett House Galleries, Poughkeepsie, N.Y., 1993, Visual Studies Workshop Galleries, Rochester, 1994, Ohio U., Athens, 1995; curator various exhbns.; condr. various workshops. Grantee NYSCA and Visual Studies Workshop, 1982, Colgate U. Rsch. Coun., 1993; recipient Visual Artist's fellowship Nat. Endowment for Arts, 1984, 90, Photographer's fellowship N.Y. Found. for Arts, 1989. Avocation: gardening. Office: Colgate U Dept Art and Art History 13 Oak Dr Hamilton NY 13346

UNDERHILL, ROBERT ALAN, consumer products company executive; b. Columbus, Ohio, June 9, 1944; s. Robert Alan and Grace Ruth (Smith) U.; m. Lynn Louise Stentz, Oct. 18, 1963; children: Robert Alan III, Richard Louis. Student, Case Western Res. U., 1962-64, Ohio State U., 1965. With tech. svc. dept. Gen. Tire & Rubber Co., Akron, Ohio, 1966-69; quality control engr. Edmont-Wilson Co., Canton, Ohio, 1969-70; mgr. quality assurance Pharmaseal Labs., Massillon, Ohio, 1970-72; mgr. R&D Internat. Playtex Corp., Paramus, N.J., 1972-78; mgr. R&D Kimberly-Clark Corp., Neenah, Wis., 1978-80, dir. R&D, 1980-83, v.p. R&D, 1983-93, sr. v.p. R&D, sr. tech. officer, 1994—; trustee United Health Group, 1994—, mem. exec. com., 1996—, treas., 1996—, chmn. compensation com., 1994—; trustee Novus Health Group, 1993-94; bd. dirs. Appleton (Wis.) Med. Ctr., 1993—. Patentee (U.S. and fgn.) med. device. Mem. exec. bd. Bay Lakes Coun. Boy Scouts Am., 1988-92; bd. dirs. Outagamie County (Wis.) chpt. ARC, 1993—, chmn. nominations com., 1993—, mem. exec. com., 1994—, sec., 1994—; bd. dirs. Cmty. Blood Ctr., Appleton, Wis., 1996—. Mem. Riverview Country Club, Pi Delta Epsilon. Republican. Avocations: stock market investment analysis, travel. Home: 1225 W Cedar St Appleton WI 54914-5567 Office: Kimberly-Clark Corp 2100 Winchester Rd Neenah WI 54956-9317 also: 1400 Holcomb Bridge Rd Roswell GA 30076-2190

UNDERWEISER, IRWIN PHILIP, mining company executive, lawyer; b. N.Y.C., Jan. 3, 1929; s. Harry and Edith (Gladstein) U.; m. Beatrice J. Kortchmar, Aug. 17, 1959; children: Rosanne, Marian, Jeffrey. B.A., CCNY, 1950; LL.D., Fordham U., 1954; LL.M., NYU, 1961. Bar: N.Y. 1954. With firm Scribner & Miller, N.Y.C., 1951-54, 56-62; partner firm Feuerstein & Underweiser, 1962-73, Underweiser & Fuchs, 1973-77, Underweiser & Underweiser, 1977—; v.p., sec. Sunshine Mining Co., Kellogg, Idaho, 1965-70, chmn. bd., 1970-78, pres., 1971-74, 77, v.p., 1977-83; vice chmn., dir. Underwriters Bank and Trust Co., N.Y.C., 1969-73; dir. Anchor Post Products, Inc. Bd. dirs. Silver Inst. Inc.; gen. counsel, mem. bus. council Friends City Center Music and Drama, N.Y.C., 1966-67; pres. W. Quaker Ridge Assn., 1969-70; treas. Scarsdale Neighborhood Assn. Presidents, 1970-71. Served with AUS, 1954-56. Mem. Am., N.Y. State bar assns., Bar Assn. City N.Y., Phi Beta Kappa, Phi Alpha Theta. Home: 7 Rural Dr Scarsdale NY 10583-7701 Office: 405 Park Ave New York NY 10022-4405

UNDERWOOD, BERNARD EDWARD, religious organization administrator; b. Bluefield, W.Va., Oct. 26, 1925; s. W. B. and Annie Theresa (Bain) U.; m. Esther Parramore, Dec. 22, 1947; children: Paul, Karen, Pam. BA, Emmanuel Coll., Franklin Springs, Ga., 1947; MA, Marshall U., 1954. Lic. to ministry Pentecostal Holiness Ch., 1942; ordained, 1944. Mem. Pentecostal Holiness Youth Soc. bd. Va. conf. Pentecostal Holiness Ch., Kingsport, Tenn., 1946-53; Christian edn. dir. Pentecostal Holiness Ch., Va. Conf., 1951-60, asst. supt., 1958-64; supt. Va. conf. Pentecostal Holiness Ch., Roanoke, 1964-69, 74-78; exec. dir. world missions Pentecostal Holiness Ch., Oklahoma City, 1969-73, 77-89, vice chmn., 1981-89, gen. supt., 1989—. Author: Gifts of the Spirit, 1967, Spiritual Gifts: Ministries and Manifestations, 1984, 16 New Testament Principles for World Evangelization, 1988; contbr. numerous articles to profl. jours. Phi Alpha Theta scholar, 1954. Mem. Nat. Assn. Evangelicals (mem. exec. com. 1989—), Pentecostal Fellowship N.Am. (pres. 1991—), Pentecostal Renewal Svcs. (chmn. 1987—), Evang. Fgn. Missions Assn. (bd. adminstrn. 1981—). Republican. Avocation: reading. Office: Pentecostal Holiness Ch PO Box 12609 Oklahoma City OK 73157-2609

UNDERWOOD, CECIL H., company executive, past governor of West Virginia; b. Josephs Mills, W.Va., Nov. 5, 1922; s. Silas and Della (Forrester) U.; m. Hovah Hall, July 25, 1948; children: Cecilia A., Craig Hall, Sharon. AB, Salem (W.Va.) Coll., 1943; AM, W.Va. U., 1952; AM research fellow, Amelia Earhart Found., Ann Arbor, Mich., 1954-56; LLD, Marietta (Ohio) Coll., 1957, Bethany (W.Va.) Coll., 1957, W.Va. U., 1957, W.Va. Inst. Tech., 1957, W.Va. State Coll., 1961, Concord Coll., 1960; D of Humanics, Salem Coll., 1957; Dr. Pub. Adminstrn., W.Va. Wesleyan Coll., 1958; LHD (hon.), Shepherd Coll., 1964; LittD, Western New Eng. Coll., 1969. Tchr. high sch., 1943-46; mem. staff Marietta Coll., 1946-50; v.p. Salem Coll., 1950-56; gov. State of W.Va., 1957-61; v.p. Island Creek Coal Co., 1961-64; dir. civic affairs Monsanto Co., 1965-67, v.p., 1967; pres. Cecil H. Underwood Assocs., 1965-80, Franswood Corp., 1968-75, Bethany (W.Va.) Coll., 1972-75, Princess Coals, Inc., Huntington, 1978-81, Morgantown (W.Va.) Indsl. Park, Inc., 1983—, Software Valley, 1989-92, Mon View Heights of W.Va., 1993—; field underwriter N.Y. Life Ins. Co., 1976-78;, 1994; chmn. bd. Princess Coals, Inc., Huntington, 1981-83; sec. bd. dirs. Huntington Fed. Savs. and Loan Assn.; bd. dirs. Huntington Found. Mem. W.Va. Ho. Dels., 1944-56, minority floor leader, 1949, 51, 53, 55; Mem. exec. com. Gov.'s Conf., 1959; chmn. So. Regional Edn. Bd., 1959-60; Pres. Young Republican League of W.Va., 1946-50; parliamentarian Young Rep. Nat. Conv., Boston, 1951; del.-at-large Rep. Nat. Conv., 1960, 64, 72, 76, 80, 84, 88, temporary chmn., 1960; Chmn. bd. dirs. W.Va. Found. Ind. Colls., Appalachian Regional Hosps.; chmn. bd. dirs. W.Va. div. Am. Cancer Soc., nat. bd. dirs., chmn. nat. crusade com., 1976-77, chmn. com. on legacies and planned giving, 1979; chmn. bd. dirs. Salem Coll., 1978-89, Salem Teikyo U., 1989—; bd. dirs. Higher Edn. Loan Program of W.Va., 1980-94; chair W.Va. Coun. on Vocat. Edn., 1982—; chair W.Va. State Coll. System, 1991; regional vice chmn. Boy Scouts Am., 1961-67. With U.S. Army Enlisted Res. Corps, 1942-43. Mem. Nat. Assn. State Coun. Vocat. Edn. (pres. 1994—), Masons, Shriners, Elks, Rotary, Sigma Phi Epsilon, Pi Kappa Delta. Methodist. Home: 609 13th Ave Huntington WV 25701-3227 Office: PO Box 2685 Huntington WV 25726-2685

UNDERWOOD, GERALD TIMOTHY, business consultant; b. Nogales, Ariz., June 15, 1928; s. Timothy Irve and Ellen Christine (Rentzmann) U.; m. Marie Lois Steadman, Aug. 7, 1949; children: Lynn Gaye Underwood Gordon, Keri Ann Underwood Horrell. B. Engring., U. So. Calif., L.A., 1951. Mgr. factory sys. Deere & Co., Dubuque, Iowa, 1966-70, mgr. product engring. svcs., 1970-75; mgr. mgmt. devel. Deere & Co., Moline, Ill., 1975-77; factory mgr. Deere & Co., Monterrey, Mex., 1977-79; mgr. corp. engring. stds. Deere & Co., Moline, 1979-81, dir. engring. resource planning, 1981-84; dep. dir. internat. trade SBA, 1983; dir. metric program, dir. internat. programs E.A. divsn., U.S. Dept. Commerce, Washington, 1984-91; pres. INTRX Assocs., Trophy Club, Tex., 1991—; mgr. PC coord. Deere & Co. Europe, Mannheim, Germany, 1960-65, sys. analyst, Moline, 1958-60; sys. mgr./PC mgr. Beckman Instruments, Fullerton, Calif., 1954-58, Statham Labs., Santa Monica, Calif., 1951-54. Contbr. articles to profl. jours. Pres. Dubuque Cmty. Sch. Bd., 1974-75; steering com. YMCA of Washington, 1987; scout leader Boy Scouts Am., Fullerton, 1955. Recipient Bronze Medal award U.S. Dept. Commerce, Washington, 1989. Mem. ASTM, Soc. Automotive Engrs., Am. Soc. Agrl. Engrs., Am. Nat. Metric Coun. (pres. 1991-93, Presdl. award 1991), Am. Legion. Republican. Achievements include patent on hydraulic fitting protective device (closure). Avocations: hiking, investing, computer work, golf, fluent Spanish and German.

UNDERWOOD, JANE HAINLINE HAMMONS, anthropologist, educator; b. Ft. Bliss, Tex., Oct. 30, 1931; d. Frank and Lydia (Williams) Hammons; m. Van K. Hainline, Oct. 20, 1947 (div. 1966); children: Michael K., Susan J.; m. John W. Underwood, July 4, 1968; 1 dau., Anne K. A.A., Imperial Valley Coll., 1957; B.A., U. Calif., Riverside, 1960; M.A., UCLA, 1962, Ph.D., 1964. Asst. prof. U. Calif., Riverside, 1963-68; research anthropology Yap Islands, 1964, 65-66; prof. anthropology U. Ariz., Tucson, 1968—; assoc. dean Grad. Coll. U. Ariz., 1979-80, asst. provost for grad. studies, 1980-82, acting dir. Sch. Health Related Professions, 1980-82, asst. v.p. research, assoc. dean Grad. Coll., 1982-87; assoc. Micronesian Area Research Ctr., 1987—. Contbr. articles to profl. jours. Woodrow Wilson fellow, 1960-61; UCR Jr. Faculty fellow, 1968. Fellow AAAS; mem. Am. Asns. Phys. Anthropologists (v.p. 1980-82), Assn. Study Human Biology, Pacific Sci. Assn. (life), Assn. for Study Social Biology (bd. dirs. 1996—), Sigma Xi (pres. U. Ariz. chpt. 1991-92). Home: 2228 E 4th St Tucson AZ 85719-5118 Office: Dept Anthropology U Ariz Tucson AZ 85721

UNDERWOOD, JOANNA DEHAVEN, environmental research and education organizations president; b. N.Y.C., May 25, 1940; d. Louis Ivan and Helen (Guiterman) U.; m. Saul Lambert, July 31, 1982; stepchildren: Jonathan Whitty, Katherine Aviva. BA, Bryn Mawr Coll., 1962; Diplome d'etudes de Civilisation francaise with honors, Sorbonne U., Paris, 1965. Audio-visual dir. Planned Parenthood World Population, N.Y.C., 1968-70; co-dir. Council on Econ. Priorities, N.Y.C., 1970-73; founder, pres. INFORM, Inc., N.Y.C., 1973—; bd. dirs. N.Y. State Energy R&D Authority, Albany, Hampshire Rsch. Inst., Clean Sites, Rocky Mtn. Inst., Keystone Ctr.; mem. Dow Environ. Adv. Coun., 1992-96; awards com. Pres.'s Coun. on Environ. Quality, 1991; mem. eco-efficiency task force Pres.'s Coun. on Sustainable Devel., 1995. Author (with others) Voices from the Environmental Movement: Perspectives for a New Era, 1991; co-author: Paper Profits, 1971; editor: The Price of Power, 1972; contbr. articles to profl. jours. Circle of dirs. Planned Parenthood of N.Y.C. Recipient U.S. EPA Environ. Achievement award, 1987, 92. Home: 138 E 13th St New York NY 10003-5306 Office: Inform Inc 120 Wall St Fl 16 New York NY 10005-3904

UNDERWOOD, MARTHA JANE MENKE, artist, educator; b. Quincy, Ill., Nov. 28, 1934; d. Francis Norman Menke and Ruth Rosemary (Wells) Zoller; divorced; children: Leslie, Stephen. BA, Scripps Coll., 1956; MFA, Otis Art Inst., 1958. Cert. adult edn. and post secondary tchr. Designer staineglass windows Wallis-Wiley Studio, Pasadena, Calif., 1959-60; mural asst., designer Millard Sheets Murals, Inc., Claremont, Calif., 1960-68; art instr. adult edn. Monrovia, Pomona and Claremont Sch. Dists., Calif., 1967-69; prof. art Chaffey C.C., Alta Loma, Calif., 1970—; free lance illustrator Claremont, 1975—, watercolorist, 1970—; lectr. and demonstrator in field. Contbr. photographs to: How to Create Your Own Designs, 1968, Weaving Without Loom, 1969; illustrator: Opening a Can of Words, 1994, coloring books about baseball team mascots, 1995, 96; contbr. illustrations to Wayfarers Jour. Active Citizens for Saving Bonelli Park, San Dimas, Calif., 1991; co-chmn. Recording for the Blind annual fundraiser, Upland, Calif., 1995, 96. Recipient Strathmore award, 1985, Grumbacher award, 1990, 92, 95; Faculty Initiated Projects Program grantee, 1991-92. Mem. Associated Artists, Riverside Art Alliance, Soc. Children's Book Writers and Illustrators. Avocations: travel, bicycle touring, languages, history. Office: Chaffey Coll 5885 Haven Ave Alta Loma CA 91737-3002

UNDERWOOD, PAUL BENJAMIN, obstetrician, educator; b. Greer, S.C., Aug. 8, 1934; s. Paul Benjamin and Gladys (Guest) U.; m. Peggy Joyce Outen, July 7, 1957; children: Paul Benjamin III, Mary Barton. MD, Med. U. S.C., 1959. Diplomate Am. Bd. Ob-Gyn, Am. Bd. Gynecol. Oncology. Intern Med. U. S.C., Charleston, 1959-60, resident, 1960-64; fellow M.D. Anderson Hosp. and Tumor Inst., Houston, 1966-67; asst. prof. U. S.C., 1967-70, assoc. prof., 1970-74, prof., 1974-79; chmn. dept. ob-gyn U. Va. Sch. Medicine, Charlottesville, 1979—. Contbr. numerous articles to med. jours. With USN, 1964-66. Recipient Alumni of Yr. award Med. U. S.C., 1989. Mem. Am. Coll. Ob-Gyn., Soc. Gynecol. Oncologists (coun. 1972-75, v.p. 1977-78, pres. 1983), Am. Assn. Ob-Gyn. (sec. 1992-95), Felix Rutledge Soc. (pres. 1977), Am. Gynecol. Club (pres. 1996), So. Med. Soc., Charlottesville Med. Soc., S.C. Ob-Gyn. Soc., Thegos Soc., Alpha Omega Alpha. Office: U Va School Medicine Med Ctr PO Box 387 Charlottesville VA 22908

UNDERWOOD, RICHARD ALLAN, English language educator; b. Plymouth, Mich., Mar. 28, 1933; s. Harold Raymond and Yvonne Clara (Foster) U.; m. Sandra Jane Hayes, Nov. 17, 1962; 1 child, Eric Michael. BA, U. Mich., 1955, MA, 1967, PhD, 1970. Asst. prof. Clemson (S.C.) U., 1970-77, assoc. prof., 1977-84, prof. English, 1984—. Author: A Little Bit of Love, 1963, Shakespeare's "The Phoenix and Turtle": A Survey of Scholarship, 1974, Shakespeare on Love: The Poems and the Plays, 1985, The Two Noble Kinsmen and Its Beginnings, 1993; translator: En Smula Karlek, 1969, 81; editor: Phoenix with a Bayonet: A Journalist's Interim Report on the Greek Revolution (by Bayard Stockton), 1971. 1st lt. U.S. Army, 1955-57. Fellow Bread Loaf Writers Conf., 1963; vis. scholar Rackham Sch. Grad. Studies, U. Mich., 1983-85, 90-91, 91-92, 92-93, 93-94. Avocation: piano music. Home: 106 Blue Ridge Dr Clemson SC 29631-1713 Office: Clemson U 809 Strode Clemson SC 29631-1436

UNDERWOOD, ROBERT ANACLETUS, congressional delegate, university official; b. Tamuning, Guam, July 13, 1948; m. Lorraine Aguilar; 5 children. BA with honors in History, Calif. State U., 1969, MA in History, 1971; cert. edn. adminstrn., U. Guam, 1976; DEd, U. So. Calif., 1987. Loader, sorter United Parcel Svc., L.A., 1966-72; tchr. George Washington High Sch., 1972-74, asst. prin. for bus. and student pers., 1974-76; asst. and acting prin. Inarajan Jr. High Sch., 1976; instr., dir. bilingual bicultural tng. program U. Guam, 1976-81, asst. prof., 1981-83, dir. bilingual edn. assistance for Micronesia project, 1983-88, dean Coll. Edn., 1988-90, acad. v.p., 1990—; del. 104th Congress from Guam, 1993—; part-time curriculum writer Guam Bilingual Edn. Project, 1973-76; chair Chamorro Lang. Commn., 1979-90. Named citizen of yr. Nat. Assn. Bus. Execs., 1996.55adr. Roman Catholic. Office: US Ho Reps 424 Cannon Ho Office Bldg Washington DC 20515-5301

UNDERWOOD, ROBERT LEIGH, venture capitalist; b. Paducah, Ky., Dec. 31, 1944; s. Robert Humphreys and Nancy Wells (Jessup) U.; BS with gt. distinction (Alcoa scholar), Stanford U., 1965, MS (NASA fellow), 1966, PhD (NSF fellow), 1968; MBA, Santa Clara U., 1970; m. Susan Lynn Doscher, May 22, 1976; children: Elizabeth Leigh, Dana Whitney, George Gregory. Rsch. scientist, project leader Lockheed Missiles & Space Co., Sunnyvale, Calif., 1967-71; spl. asst. for engring. scis. Office Sec., Dept. Transp., Washington, 1971-73; sr. mgmt. assoc. Office Mgmt. and Budget, Exec. Office Pres., 1973; with TRW Inc., L.A., 1973-79, dir. retail nat.

accounts, 1977-78, dir. product planning and devel., 1978-79; pres., CEO OMEX, Santa Clara, Calif., 1980-82; v.p. Heizer Corp., Chgo., 1979-85; v.p. No. Trust Co., pres. No. Capital Corp., Chgo., 1985-86; mng. ptnr. ISSS Ventures, 1986-88; exec. v.p. N.Am. Bus. Devel. Co., Chgo., 1988—; dir. various pvt. and pub. portfolio cos., MECC 1991-96; mem. adv. com. indsl. innovation NSF; mem. sch. bd. Avoca Dist. 37, 1990—; mem. adv. bd. Leavey Sch. Bus. & Adminstrn. Santa Clara U., 1995—. Mem. IEEE, Sigma Xi, Phi Beta Kappa, Tau Beta Pi, Beta Gamma Sigma. Elder, Presbyterian Ch., 1978-79. Clubs: Union League Chgo., Chgo. Club; Manasquan River Yacht (Brielle, N.J.); Indian Hill (Winnetka, Ill.). Contbr. articles to profl. jours. Home: 59 Woodley Rd Winnetka IL 60093-3748 Office: 135 S La Salle St Chicago IL 60603-4105

UNDERWOOD, SANDRA JANE, planning and management director; b. Highland Park, Mich., Dec. 14, 1941; d. Donald Earl and Delores Irene (Campbell) Hayes; m. Richard Allan Underwood, Nov. 17, 1962; 1 child, Eric Michael. BA in Polit. Sci. and Pub. Adminstrn., Stephens Coll. Data mgr., rsch. analyst, div. bus. and fin. Clemson (S.C.) U., 1977-81, higher edn. project adminstr., planning/budgets, 1981-84, planning and rsch. coord., planning/budgets, 1984-86, dir. mgmt. svcs., 1986-88, asst. to v.p. bus. and fin., 1988-90, dir. univ. planning, 1989-90, dir. strategic planning and quality mgmt., 1990—; cons. colls. and univs. S.C. and Calif., 1989—. Author: Economic Development in S.C.--The Research University Link, 1987; co-editor: Alternatives for Growth, 1978. W.K. Kellogg Found. co-grantee, 1994. Mem. Am. Mgmt. Assn., World Future Soc., Assn. Women Profls., Soc. Coll. and Univ. Planning, Clemson Lions (bd. dirs. 1991-92). Avocations: poetry, philosophy, chaos theory. Home: 111 Lakeview Cir Clemson SC 29631-1713 Office: Clemson U 201 Brackett Hall Clemson SC 29634-5160

UNDERWOOD, STEVEN CLARK, publishing executive; b. Arlington Heights, Ill., Dec. 1, 1960; s. Donald William and Mary Frances (Clark) U. BBA, U. Tex., 1982, MBA, 1987; JD, So. Meth. U., 1985. Bar: Tex. 1985. Sr. fin. analyst CBS, Inc., N.Y.C., 1987-89; assoc. bus. mgr. Supplementary Edn. Group Simon & Schuster, Englewood Cliffs, N.J., 1989-90; bus. mgr. Fearon/Janus/Quercus divsn. Simon & Schuster, Belmont, Calif., 1990-92, pres. Fearon/Janus/Quercus divsn., 1992-93; pres. Globe Fearon divsn. Simon & Schuster, Upper Saddle River, N.J., 1993-96; dir. of bus. devel. Secondary Edn. Group, Simon and Schuster, Upper Saddle River, N.J., 1996—. Mem. ABA, Am. Mgmt. Assn. (pres.'s assn.), Assn. Am. Pubs., Nat. Eagle Scout Assn., Coll. Bus. Adminstrn. Found., Tex. Bar Assn., Tex. Alumni Assn., U. Tex. Century Club, Alpha Phi Omega, Beta Gamma Sigma, Phi Kappa Phi, Phi Eta Sigma, Golden Key. Republican. Methodist. Avocations: sailing, scuba diving, camping, rafting. Home: 123 Magnolia Rd Ramsey NJ 07446-1145

UNDERWOOD, VERNON O., JR., grocery stores executive; b. 1940. With Youngs Market Co., L.A., pres., from 1976, chmn. bd., 1989—, also chief exec. officer. Office: Young's Market Co 2164 N Batavia St Orange CA 92665*

UNDLIN, CHARLES THOMAS, banker; b. Madison, Minn., Mar. 4, 1928; s. Jennings C. and Alice M. (Berg) U.; m. Lois M. Anderson, June 23, 1953; children: Sarah, Mary Lee, Margaret, Thomas. BA, St. Olaf Coll., 1950. Asst. cashier Northwestern State Bank, Osseo, Minn., 1950-55, N.W. Bancorp., Mpls., 1955-57, Security Bank & Trust Co., Owatonna, Minn., 1957-59, Norwest Bank Black Hills, Rapid City, S.D., 1959-67; pres. and chief exec. officer Norwest Bank S.D., Rapid City, 1967-84, vice-chmn., 1984-85; pres. Norwest Bank Nebr., Omaha, 1985-88, also bd. dirs.; vice-chmn. Rushmore State Bank, Rapid City, 1988—; bd. dirs. Black Hills Corp., Homestake Mining Co. Past bd. dirs. Children's Hosp., Omaha, 1986. Sgt. U.S. Army, 1951-52. Mem. S.D. Bankers Assn. (past pres.), Arrowhead Country Club. Republican. Lutheran. Avocations: golf, skiing, fishing. Office: Rushmore State Bank PO Box 2290 Rapid City SD 57709-2290

UNGACTA, MALISSA SUMAGAYSAY, software engineer; b. Agana, Guam, July 3, 1967; d. Renerio Ong and Irene Acfalle (Salas) S. BS in Info. Sci., U. Hawaii, 1989; MS in Info. Tech. Mgmt., Johns Hopkins U., 1992. Cert. power builder developer assoc. Programmer, analyst Facilities Mgmt. Office, Honolulu, 1987-89, Data House Inc., Honolulu, 1989-90, ANSTEC Inc., Fairfax, Md., 1990-93; software specialist, project leader HJ Ford Assocs. Inc., Crystal City, Va., 1993-94; software cons. McDonnell Douglas Tech. Svcs., 1994—. Mem. NAFE. Avocations: tennis, running, computers. Home: PO Box 1546 Agana GU 96910-1546 Office: McDonnell Douglas 1807 Park 270 Ste 500 Saint Louis MO 63146-4021 also: 4554 Laclede Ave Apt 107 Saint Louis MO 63108-2145

UNGAR, ERIC EDWARD, mechanical engineer; b. Vienna, Austria, Nov. 12, 1926; came to U.S. 1939; s. Irwin Isidor and Sabina (Schlesinger) U.; m. Goldie Edna Becker, July 1, 1951; children: Judith Fishman, Susan Green, Ellen Borgenicht, Sharon Ungar Lane. BSME, Washington U., St. Louis, 1951; MS, U. N.Mex., 1954; Eng.Sc.D., NYU, 1957. Aero-ordnance engr. Sandia Corp., Albuquerque, 1951-53; research scientist/asst. prof. NYU, 1953-58; chief cons. engr. Bolt Beranek & Newman, Inc., Cambridge, Mass., 1958—; chief engrng. scientist Acentech Inc., Cambridge, part-time 1993—. Co-author: Structure-Borne Sound, 1973, 2nd edit. 1988; contbr. articles to profl. jours., chpts. to books. 1st lt. U.S. Army, 1945-48; ETO. Recipient Per Bruel Gold Medal for Noise Control and Acoustics, Am. Soc. of Mechanicl Engineers, 1994. Fellow ASME (life; chmn. design engrng. divsn. 1978-80, Centennial medallion 1981, Per Bruel Gold medal for noise control and acoustics 1994), AIAA (assoc.), Acoustical Soc. Am. (pres. 1991-92, Trent-Crede Silver medal 1983); mem. Inst. for Noise Control and Engrng. (bd. cert., pres. 1985). Home: 15 Considine Rd Newton MA 02159-3603 Office: BBN Systems & Tech 10 Moulton St Cambridge MA 02138-1119

UNGAR, IRWIN ALLAN, botany educator; b. N.Y.C., Jan. 21, 1934; s. Isador and Gertrude (Fageles) U.; m. Ana Celia Del Cid, Aug. 10, 1959; children: Steven, Sandra, Sharon. BS, CCNY, 1955; MA, U. Kans., Lawrence, 1957, PhD, 1961. Instr., U. R.I., Kingston, 1961-62; asst. prof. Quincy Coll., Ill., 1962-66; asst. prof. Ohio U., Athens, 1966-69, assoc. prof., 1969-74, prof. botany, 1974—, chmn. dept., 1984-89—, dir. Dysart Woods Lab., 1985—, dir. Environ. Studies Program, 1991-95; vis. prof. dept. plant scis. and vis. fellow Wolfson Coll., Oxford U., Eng., 1990-91; panelist Nat. Sea Grant Program, 1984; grant proposal reviewer NSF, 1980-95; manuscript reviewer Am. Jour. Botany, 1972-96, Bot. Gazette, 1976-96; contbr. articles to profl. jours. NSF grantee, 1974-76, 76-78, 80-83, 94-95, rsch. grantee Petroleum Environ. Rsch. Forum, 1992-96. Fellow Ohio Acad. Sci.; mem. AAAS, Am. Inst. Biol. Scis., Bot. Soc. Am., Ecol. Soc. Am., Sigma Xi. Home: 44 Walker St Athens OH 45701-2252 Office: Ohio Univ Dept Of Botany Athens OH 45701

UNGAR, MANYA SHAYON, volunteer, education consultant; b. N.Y.C., May 30, 1928; d. Samuel and Ethel M. (Liese) Shayon; m. Harry Fireman Ungar, June 25, 1950; children: Paul Benedict, Michael Shayon. BA, Mills Coll., 1950. Actress TV and radio NBC, CBS, N.Y.C., 1950-58; founder chpt. AFS, Scotch Plains-Fanwood, N.J., 1958-60; vol. project dir. Boy Scouts Am., Plainfield, N.J., 1958-61; founder, co-dir. Summer Theater Workshop, Scotch Plains, 1967-78; legis. v.p. N.J. State PTA, 1977-79, pres., 1979-81; legis. v.p. Nat. PTA, Chgo., 1981-85, 1st v.p., 1985-87, pres., 1987-89; Mem. arts edn. adv. panel Nat. Endowment Arts, Washington, 1988-91, panel Nat. Inst. Work and Learning, 1988-91; adv. coun. Nat. Panel Drug Free Schs., Washington, 1989-91, edn. adv. bd. NBC, 1988-92, PBS, 1988-91, Scholastic, Inc., 1990-94; bd. dirs. Math. Sci. Edn. Bd., 1988-92. Trustee N.J. Children's Specialized Hosp., 1990—, N.J. Pub. Edn. Inst., 1987—; mem. adv. coun. Natural Resources Def. Coun., Mothers and Others, 1990—; mem. geography assessment adv. coun. Nat. Assessment Edn. Progress, 1991-92, mem. nat. oversite commn. on geog. stds., 1992-94; mem. N.J. Basic Skills Coun., 1990-94; chmn. N.J. Math. Coalition, 1994—; mem. accreditation com. APA, 1992—; mem. tchr. programs adv. panel Ednl. Testing Svc., 1990-94; mem. external rev. com. Ctr. Disease Control Preventing Risk Behaviors in Adolescents, 1993; voters svc. dir. N.J. LWV, 1995—; bd. dirs. Washington Rock Girl Scout Coun., 1995—. Manya Shayon Ungar Scholarship and Auditorium named in her honor, 1989; named Outstanding Citizen N.J. Jaycees, 1979, Scotch Plains Twp., 1989, 92, State of N.J., 1987, Bd. of Freeholders, 1987; named life mem. nat. PTA, 45 state PTAs. Mem. LWV (chmn. voters svc. Westfield area 1991-95). Avocations: piano, acting, singing, recording talking books. Home: 10 Brandywine Ct Scotch Plains NJ 07076-2550

UNGAR, ROSELVA MAY, primary and elementary educator; b. Detroit, Oct. 31, 1926; d. John and Elva (Mutchler) Rushton; m. Kenneth Sawyer Goodman, Dec. 26, 1946 (div. 1950); m. Fred Ungar, June 22, 1952 (div. 1977); children: Daniel Brian, Carol Leslie, Lisa Maya. Student, U. Mich., 1946-48, UCLA, UCLA; postgrad., Pacific Oaks Coll. Recreation dir. Detroit City Parks and Recreation, L.A. Bd. Edn., 1946-50; tchr. L.A. Unified Sch. Dist., 1950-51, 84—, mentor tchr. elem. edn., 1988-94; tchr. head start Found. Early Childhood Edn., L.A., 1965-73; staff organizer Early Childhood Fedn. Local 1475 AFT, L.A., 1973-79; staff rep. Calif. Fedn. Tchrs., L.A., 1979-83. contbr. articles to profl. jours. Com. mem. Gov's Adv. Com. Child Care, L.A., 1980-93; mem. Nat. Parks and Conservation Assn., Washington, 1988—, Sierra Club, 1985—; vol. So. Calif. Libr. Social Studies, L.A., 1989—; charter mem. Mus. Am. Indian Smithsonian Inst., 1994—; Nat. Ctr. Early Childhood Workforce Children's Def. Fund, Southwest Mus., Ctr. Sci in Pub. Interest, Internat. League for Peace and Freedom, ACLU, So. Poverty Law Ctr., Meiklejohn Civil Liberties Inst. Mem. Calif. Assn. Bilingual Edn., So. Calif. Assn. Edn. Young Children, Early Childhood Fedn. (pres. emeritus 1979—), United Tchrs. L.A. (chpt. chair 1984—, east area dir. and UTLA bd. dirs. 1996—), Coalition Labor Union Women (bd. mem. 1980-86). Avocations: guitar, folk songs, hiking. Home: 3131 Hamilton Way Los Angeles CA 90026-2107 Office: Glen Alta Sch LA Unified Sch Dist 3410 Sierra St Los Angeles CA 90031

UNGARO, EMANUEL MATTEOTTI, fashion designer; b. Aix-en-Provence, France, Feb. 13, 1933; s. Cosimo and Concetta (Casalino) U.; m. Laura; 1 dau. Student, Lycée, Aix-en-Provence, 1943-50. Worked with father as tailor Aix-en-Provence, 1951-54; then for Camps Paris, 1955-57; with Cristobal Balenciaga, Paris, 1957-64, dir. Balenciaga br., Madrid, 1958-60; worked for André Courrèges, Paris, 1964; ind. couturier, Paris, 1965. Designer of both couture and ready-to-wear men's and women's fashions; also fragrance designer since 1977. Office: 2 Ave Montaigne, F 75008 Paris France also: 650 5th Ave Fl 20 New York NY 10019-6108

UNGARO, JOSEPH MICHAEL, newspaper publishing executive, consultant; b. Providence, Nov. 4, 1930; s. Rocco and Lucy (Mott) U.; m. Evelyn Short, Apr. 15, 1961; children: Elizabeth Anne, Joseph Michael, Ellen Lucia. B.A., Providence Coll., 1952; M.S. in Journalism, Columbia, 1953. With Providence Jour.-Bull., 1951-73, mng. editor Evening Bull., 1967-72; mng. editor Eve. Bull., also dir. planning and devel. Providence Jour. and Bull., 1972-73; mng. editor Westchester-Rockland Newspapers, White Plains, N.Y., 1974-75, v.p., exec. editor, 1975-84, pres., gen. mgr., 1984-86, pres., publisher, 1986-90; pres., chief exec. officer Detroit Newspaper Agy., 1990-91; cons., 1991—. Mem. Am. Newspaper Pubs. Assn. (past chmn. research inst., conv. program com.), Am. Soc. Newspaper Editors, AP Mng. Editors Assn. (past pres.). Home: 379 Pond Shore Dr Charlestown RI 02813-2031

UNGARO, SUSAN KELLIHER, magazine editor. Editor-in-chief Family Circle mag., N.Y.C. Office: Family Circle 110 5th Ave New York NY 10011-5601*

UNGARO-BENAGES, URSULA MANCUSI, federal judge; b. Miami Beach, Fla., Jan. 29, 1951; d. Ludivico Mancusi-Ungaro and Ursula Berliner; m. Michael A. Benages, Mar., 1988. Student, Smith Coll., 1968-70; BA in English Lit., U. Miami, 1973; JD, U. Fla., 1975. Bar: Fla. 1975. Assoc. Frates, Floyd, Pearson et al, Miami, 1976-78, Blackwell, Walker, Gray et al, Miami, 1978-80, Finley, Kumble, Heine et al, Miami, 1980-85, Sparber, Shevin, Shapo et al, Miami, 1985-87; cir. judge State of Fla., Miami, 1987-92; U.S. dist. judge Miami, 1992—; mem. Fla. Supreme Ct. Race & Ethnic & Racial Bias Study Commn., Fla., 1989-92, St. Thomas U. Inns of Ct., Miami, 1991-92. Bd. dirs. United Family & Children's Svcs., Miami, 1981-82; mem. City of Miami Task Force, 1991-92. Mem. ABA, Fed. Judges Assn., Fla. Assn. Women Lawyers, Dade County Bar Assn., Eugene Spellman Inns of Ct. U. Miami. Office: US Dist Ct 300 NE 1st Ave Ste 243 Miami FL 33132-2135

UNGER, BARBARA, poet, educator; b. N.Y.C., Oct. 2, 1932; d. David and Florence (Schuchalter) Frankel; m. Bernard Unger, 1954 (div. 1976); m. Theodore Sakano, 1987. B.A., CCNY, 1955, M.A., 1957; advanced cert. NYU, 1970; children: Deborah, Suzanne. Grad. asst. Yeshiva U., 1962-63; edn. editor County Citizen, Rockland County, N.Y., 1960-63; tchr. English, N.Y.C. Pub. Schs., 1955-58, Nyack (N.Y.) High Sch., 1963-67; guidance counselor Ardsley (N.Y.) High Sch., 1967-69; prof. English, Rockland Community Coll., Suffern, N.Y., 1969—; poetry fellow Squaw Valley Community of Writers, 1980; writer-in-residence Rockland Ctr. for Arts, 1986. Author: (poetry) Basement, 1975, Learning to Fox Trot, 1989, The Man Who Burned Money, 1980, Inside the Wind, 1986, Blue Depression Glass in Troika One, 1991; (fiction) Dying for Uncle Ray, 1990; contbr. poetry to over 50 lit. mags., including: Kans. Quar., Carolina Quar., Beloit Poetry Jour., Minn. Rev., Poet and Critic, The Nation, Poetry Now, Invisible City, Thirteenth Moon, So. Poetry Rev., Mass. Rev., Nebr. Rev., Wis. Rev., So. Humanities Rev., Denver Quarterly, Mississippi Valley REv., The G.W. Rev. Wordsmith; contbr. to Anthology Mag. Verse, Yearbook Am. Poetry, 1984, 89; contbr. poetry (anthologies) Two Worlds Walking, Life on the Line, Looking for Home, 80 on the Eighties, Disenchantments, Women and Work, If I Had a Hammer, Sexual Harassment: Women Speak Out; contbr. fiction to True to Life Adventure Stories, Midstream, Esprit, Beloit Fiction Jour., Am. Fiction '89 and numerous others; poetry reading in colls. and libraries throught N.Y. and elsewhere; critical reviewer Contact II. Ragdale Found. fellow, 1985, 86, 89, SUNY Creative Writing fellow, 1981-82, Edna St. Vincent Millay Colony fellow, 1984, Djerassi Found. fellow, 1991, Hambidge Ctr. for Creative Arts and Scis. fellow, 1988; NEH grantee, 1975. Recipient Goodman Poetry award, 1989, Anna Davidson Rosenberg award Judah Magnes Mus., 1989, Roberts Writing award, 1990, New Letters Literary awards, 1990; finalist Am. Fiction Competition, 1989, W.Va. Writing Competition, 1982, John Williams Narrative Poetry Competition, 1992; honorable mention Chester Jones Nat. Poetry Contest. Mem. Poets and Writers, Poetry Soc. Am., Writers' Community. Office: Rockland Community Coll 145 College Rd Suffern NY 10901-3611

UNGER, GERE NATHAN, physician, lawyer; b. Monticello, N.Y., May 15, 1949; s. Jessie Aaron and Shirley (Rosenstein) U.; m. Alicen J. McGowan, July 21, 1990; children: Elijah, Breena, Ari, Sasha, Arlen. JD, Bernadean U., 1979; MD, Inst. Polytecnico, Mexico City, 1986; D Phys. Medicine, Met. U., Mexico City, 1987; postgrad., Boston U., 1993, Harvard Law Sch., 1994-95. Dipomate Am. Bd. Forensic Examiners, Am. Bd. Med. Legal Analysis in Medicine and Surgery, Am. Bd. Forensic Medicine. Med. dir. Vietnam Vets. Post-Traumatic Stress Disorder Program, 1988-90; emergency rm. physician, cons. in medicaid fraud Bronx (N.Y.)-Lebanon Hosp., 1990—; clin. legal medicine Paladin Profl. Group, P.A., Palm Beach, Fla., 1992—; mediator, arbitrator, negotiator World Intellectual Property Orgn., 1994; mem. peer rev. com. Nat. Inst. on Disability and Rehab. Rsch., Office Spl. Edn., U.S. Dept. Edn., 1993; mem. clin. ethics com. Inst. Medecine Legale et de Medecine Sociale, Strasbourg, France, 1994; mem. surg. critical care com. Am. Soc. Critical Care Medicine, 1992; N.Y. state capt. Am. Trial Lawyers Exch., 1992. Editl. rev. bd. Am. Bd. Forensic Examiners, 1993, Jour. Neurol. and Orthopaedic Medicine and Surgery, 1993. Commandant Broward County Marine Corps League, 1995—. With USMC, 1968-72. Fellow Internat. Coll. Surgeons (mem. ethics com. 1994, mem. emergency response program Ea. region 1994), Am. Acad. Neurol. and Orthopaedic Surgeons, Am. Coll. Legal Medicine; mem. ABA, ATLA, FBA (mem. health com., rep. ABA 1994, chmn. med. malpractice/tort com. and FBA liaison to AMA), Nat. Coll. Advocacy, Internat. Bar Assn., Am. Coll. Physician Execs. (chair forum on law and med. mgmt. 1995), Kennedy Inst. Ethics, Nat. Health Lawyers Assn. Avocations: flying, boating. Office: Ste 9 235 S County Rd Palm Beach FL 33480

UNGER, IRWIN, historian, educator; b. Bklyn., May 2, 1927; s. Elias C. and Mary (Roth) U.; m. Bernate Myra Spaet, Feb. 1956 (div.); children—Brooke David, Miles Jeremy, Paul Joshua; m. Debi Irene Weisstein, May 11, 1970; stepchildren—Anthony Allen, Elizabeth Sarah. B.Social Scis., City Coll. N.Y., 1948; M.A., Columbia, 1949, Ph.D., 1958; student, U. Wash., 1949-51. Instr. Columbia, 1956-58; vis. lectr. U. P.R., 1958-59; asst. prof. Long Beach (Calif.) State Coll., 1959-62; assoc. prof. U. Calif., Davis, 1962-66; prof. history NYU, NYC, 1966—. Author: The Greenback Era: A Social and Political History of American Finance: 1865-1879, 1964, The Movement: A History of the American New Left, 1974, (with Debi Unger) The Vulnerable Years: The United States, 1896-1917, Turning Point: 1968, 1988, The Best of Intentions: The Rise and Fall of the Great Society Programs, 1996. Served with AUS, 1952-54. Recipient Pulitzer prize for history, 1965; Guggenheim fellow, 1972-73, Rockefeller humanities fellow, 1980-81, Harry Frank Guggenheim fellow, 1987-88. Home: 473 W End Ave New York NY 10024-4934

UNGER, PAUL WALTER, soil scientist; b. Winchester, Tex., Sept. 10, 1931; s. Edwin Herman and Elsie Anna (Schmidt) U.; m. Barbara Charlene Dutton, Sept. 13, 1960; children: Gary Robert, Paula Dianne. BS, Tex. A&M U., 1961; MS, Colo. State U., 1963, PhD, 1966. Soil scientist USDA Agrl. Rsch. Svc., Bushland, Tex., 1965-81, soil scientist/rsch. leader, 1981-87, supervisory soil scientist/rsch. leader, 1987-93, soil scientist, 1993—; cons. Food and Agrl. Orgn. UN, Rome, 1986. Author or co-author bulls. and articles; co-editor conf. proc.; editor book. With U.S. Army, 1952-55. Recipient Disting. Svc. award Great Plains Agrl. Coun., 1984; named Scientist of Yr., USDA-Agrl. Rsch. Svc., So. Plains Area, 1987. Fellow Am. Soc. Agronomy (selection com. 1988-89), Soil Sci. Soc. Am. (assoc. editor 1977-82, divsn. chmn. 1986, mem. selection com. 1994-95, Applied Rsch. award 1991), Soil and Water Conservation Soc. (various local and state offices, photography awards 1990-92); mem. Internat. Soil Tillage Rsch. Orgn., Internat. Soil Sci. Soc., World Assn. Soil and Water Conservation, Coun. Agrl. Sci. and Tech. Lutheran. Avocations: photography, gardening, woodworking. Office: USDA Agrl Rsch Svc PO Box 10 Bushland TX 79012-0010

UNGER, PETER KENNETH, philosophy educator; b. N.Y.C., Apr. 25, 1942; s. Sidney and Naomi (Fein) U.; m. Susan Gill, June 2, 1977; 1 child, Andrew. BA, Swarthmore Coll., 1962; DPhil, Oxford U., Eng., 1966. Instr. U. Wis., Madison, 1965-66, asst. prof., 1966-70, assoc. prof., 1970-72; assoc. prof. NYU, N.Y.C., 1972-75, prof., 1975—. Author: Ignorance, 1975, Philosophical Relativity, 1984, Identity, Consciousness and Value, 1990, Living High and Letting Die, 1996; contbr. articles to profl. jours. Guggenheim fellow, 1974, NEH fellow, 1993. Mem. Am. Philos. Assn., Oxfam Am. (mem. N.Y. com.). Democrat. Home: 100 Bleecker St New York NY 10012-2202 Office: Dept Philosophy NYU 503 Main Bldg Washington Sq New York NY 10003

UNGER, PETER VAN BUREN, lawyer; b. Cin., Nov. 15, 1957; s. Sherman Edward and Polly Van Buren (Taylor) U.; m. Laura Meth Simone, June 29, 1991. BA in History, Polit. Sci., Miami U., Oxford, Ohio, 1980; JD, U. Cin., 1983; LLM in Securities, Georgetown U., 1987. Bar: Ohio 1984, D.C. 1985, U.S. Supreme Ct. 1991. Law clk. chief judge U.S. Dist. Ct. (so. dist.) Fla., Ft. Lauderdale, 1983-85; trail atty. enforcement div. SEC, N.Y.C., 1986-88; assoc. Fulbright & Jaworski, Washington, 1988-89, participating assoc., 1990-94, ptnr., 1995—. Mem. ABA (bus. law sect., com. fed. regulation of securities, sub-com. on civil litigation and SEC enforcement matters 1989—, litigation sect. com. on securities litigation sub-com. on SEC enforcement practice 1990—). Home: 3308 N St NW Washington DC 20007-2807 Office: Fulbright & Jaworski 801 Pennsylvania Ave NW Washington DC 20004-2615

UNGER, RICHARD WATSON, history educator; b. Huntington, W.Va., Dec. 23, 1942; s. Abraham I. and Marion Patterson (Simons) U.; m. Katharine Lawrence, June 4, 1966; 1 child, Emily Patterson. BA, Haverford Coll., Pa., 1963; AM, U. Chgo., 1965; MA, Yale U., 1967, MPhil, 1969, Ph.D., 1971. Prof. dept. history U. B.C., Vancouver, Can., 1969—. Author: Dutch Shipbuilding Before 1800, 1978; The Ship in the Medieval Economy, 600-1600, 1980; The Art of Medieval Technology: The Image of Noah the Shipbuilder, 1991; editor: Cogs, Caravels and Galleons, 1994; co-editor: Nautical Archaeology: Progress and Public Responsibility, 1984; co-editor Studies in Medieval and Renaissance History, 1978-95; contbr. articles to profl. jours. Trustee Vancouver Maritime Mus., 1979-83. Mem. Medieval Assn. Pacific (pres. 1994-96), Econ. History Soc., Soc. Nautical Rsch. Office: U BC, Dept of History, Vancouver, BC Canada V6T 1Z1

UNGER, ROBERTA MARIE, special education educator; b. Oakland, Calif., Apr. 22, 1944; d. Lowber and Roberta June (Hedrick) Randolph; m. William Mitchell Unger, Jr., June 29, 1970; 1 child by previous marriage, Diana Marie Holt; 1 child, William Mitchell III. BA in Edn., San Francisco State U., 1965; postgrad., Utah State U., 1967, Frostburg (Md.) State U., 1973, 84; MA in Ednl. Adminstrn., W.Va. U., 1984. Cert. tchr., Calif., Utah, Md., W.Va.; cert. elem. tchr., supervising tchr. assoc., English tchr., gifted edn., learning disabilities behavior disorders, pre-sch. tchr., mentally impaired, W.Va.. Tchr. 2nd grade North Park Elem. Sch., Box Elder County, Utah, 1965-67; tchr. spl. edn. emotionally disturbed grades 5-8 Centre St. Sch., Allegany County, Md., 1967-68; tchr. 3rd grade Dennett Rd. Elem. Sch., Garrett County, Md., 1968-69; tchr. 2d & 3rd grades Grantsville Elem. Sch., Garrett County, Md., 1969-70; tchr. 1-6 grades spl. and regular edn. Short Gap Elem. Sch., Mineral County, W.Va., 1970-77; supervising tchr. W.Va. U., Morgantown, 1973-76; tchr. summer satellite program gifted edn. Frostburg State U., 1985; tchr. spl. edn. Frankfort H.S., Ridgeley, W.Va., 1977—, collaborative and consulting spl. edn. tchr., 1983—; collaborative and cons. spl. edn. tchr., 1983—; mem. gifted edn. del. to USSR, Siberia, Hungary, 1991, China, 1991; tech. chmn. Frankfort H.S. Former vol. San Francisco Hosp.; past usher Oakland Civic Light Opera Assn.; mem. Cmty. Concert Assn., Allied Arts Coun., St. Thomas Woman's Study Group, No. Maidu Tribe Calif. Native Ams., Frostburg Cmty. Orch., Md., 1968; dir. youth program 7-12th grades Emmanuel Episc. Ch., Cumberland, Md., Sunday sch. tchr.; coach Oddyssey of the Mind, 1987—; club sponsor Ski Club, AFS, Classic Club. Grantee W.Va. Dept. Edn., 1986, 87, 89-91. Mem. NEA, W.Va. Edn. Assn., Mineral County Edn. Assn. (past bldg. rep., past dept. chair, spl. edn., past county chair mentally impaired, past chair county secondary integrative colaboration com., chmn. County integrative collaboration consultation spl. edn. svc. grades 6-12), Nat. Coun. for Exceptional Children (nat. conv. presenter 1989, 92, 93, 95), W.Va. State Coun. for Exceptional Children (Mem. of Yr. award 1991, yr. award 1991, conf. presenter 1984—, sec. 1990-93, v.p. 1993, pres.-elect 1994, pres. 1995-96, newsletter editor 1995—, pres. divsn. mental retardation 1994-95, pres. chair state conv., 1993—, coun. exceptional children MRDD membership com. 1995—, coun. exceptional children DLD multicultural com. 1995—, W.Va. subdivsn. mental retardation devel. disabilties organizing chair 1992-93), Coun. for Exceptional Children (v.p. W.Va. divsn. learning disabilties 1988, membership chmn. 1988-89, pres. 1990, newsletter editor divsn. learning disabilities 1991—, sec. Coun. Exceptional Children Am. Indian caucus 1989—, del. nat. conv. 1990—), Am. Indian Soc. Washington, Allegany County Hist. Soc., Mineral County Hist. Soc., Maidu Mooretown Rancheria. Episcopalian. Avocations: playing piano and cello, skiing, painting, sewing, collecting operating farmette antiques. Office: Frankfort High Sch RR 3 Box 169 Ridgeley WV 26753-9510

UNGER, RONALD LAWRENCE, lawyer; b. Flushing, N.Y., June 8, 1930; s. Joseph and Rose (Weinstein) U.; m. Benita Kronish, July 11, 1954; children: Paul S., Thomas A. A.B., Bucknell U., 1951; LL.B., Harvard U., 1954. Office: Kaye Scholer Fierman Hays & Handler 425 Park Ave New York NY 10022-3598 Address: 605 Park Ave Apt 16C New York NY 10021-7018

UNGER, SONJA FRANZ, package company executive, travel consultant, ceramist; b. Zagreb, Croatia, former Yugoslavia, Oct. 28, 1921; came to U.S., 1947; d. Karl Dragutin and Elisabeth (Bihler) Franz; m. Paul A. Unger, Jan. 2, 1947; children: Alan, Gerald, Tamara. BS in Engring., U. Zagreb, 1944, MS in Architecture, 1945. City planner Ministry of Constrn., Zagreb, 1945-47; architect John Graham, Washington, 1947-53; corp. sec., designer The Unger Co., Cleve., 1953-94; travel cons. Kollander World Travel, Cleve., 1985—; vis. com. mem. Case Western Res. U., Cleve. Mem. citizens adv. com. Juvenile Ct. Cuyahoga County, Ohio; asst. sec. Glenville Neighborhood Ctr., Cleve.; vice chmn., sec. Cuyahoga County Dem. Exec. Com., Cleve.; ward leader Shaker Heights Dem. Party, 1958-78; forelady Grand Jury Cuyahoga County; v.p. Nationalities Svcs. Ctr., Cleve.; mem. Cercle Cult. Francaises. Recipient Golden Door award Nationalities Svcs. Ctr., 1975,

Community Svc. award Cuyahoga County Commrs., 1975; Sonja F. Unger Day proclaimed by Mayor of Cleve., 1975. Mme. Il Cenacolo Italiano (pres.), Croatian Found. of Am. (v.p.), Am. Croating Acad. Club (v.p.), Print Club of Cleve., Cleve. Skating Club, Cleve. Playhouse Club, City Club of Cleve., Cleve. Blue Book.

UNGER, STEPHEN HERBERT, electrical engineer, computer scientist; b. N.Y.C., July 7, 1931; s. Julius I. and Rebecca (Cooper) U.; m. Marion Ruth Baker, Apr. 8, 1960 (div. July 1978); children—Donald N., Debra Susan; m. Shirley Aronson, July 5, 1986. B.E.E., Poly. Inst. Bklyn., 1952; S.M., MIT, 1953, Sc.D., 1957. Research asst. MIT Rsch. Lab. of Electronics, 1954-57; mem. tech. staff Bell Telephone Labs., Whippany, N.J., 1957-61; assoc. prof. elec. engring. and computer sci. Columbia U., 1961-68, prof., 1968—, prof. computer sci., 1980—; vis. prof. U. Calif.-Berkeley, 1967; vis. prof. computer sci. Danish Tech. U., Lyngby, 1974-75; sr. research assoc. Center for Policy Research, N.Y.C., 1970-74; cons. in field. Author: Asynchronous Sequential Switching Circuits, 1969, Controlling Technology: Ethics and the Responsible Engineer, 1982, rev. 1994, The Essence of Logic Circuits, 1989; rschr., contbr. numerous articles on computer sci. Bd. dirs. Morris County Urban League, N.J., 1959-60. Guggenheim fellow,1967, IEEE fellow, 1975, AAAS fellow, 1989; NSF grantee, 1966-70, 71-74, 79-81. Mem. IEEE (chmn. Com. on Social Implications Tech. working group on ethics and employment practices 1971-78, chmn. 1979-80, U.S. Activities Bd. ethics com. 1987-92, bd. dirs. 1995-96, ethics com. 1995—, editl. bd. Spectrum 1995—, Centennial medal 1984, Disting. Contbns. Engring. Professionalism award 1987), AAAS (mem. com. on sci. freedom and responsibility 1981-84), IEEE Soc. on Social Implications Tech. (adminstrv. com. 1983-91, 93-96, pres. 1985-86), AAUP, Assn. Computing Machinery, Sigma Xi, Eta Kappa Nu, Tau Beta Pi. Patentee parallel data processing apparatus. Home: 135 Van Houten Flds West Nyack NY 10994-2525 Office: Columbia U Dept Computer Sci New York NY 10027 *Unless, in doubtful situations, we act as though good may triumph, it surely won't.*

UNGERS, OSWALD M., architect, educator; b. Kaisersesch, Germany, July 12, 1926; came to U.S., 1969; s. Anton and Maria (Michels) U.; m. Liselotte Gabler, July 4, 1956; children: Simon, Sibylle, Sophia. Diploma Tng., Tech. U., Karlsruhe, Germany, 1950. Archtl. practice Cologne, Germany, 1950-62, Berlin, 1962-69, Itahaca, N.Y., 1969—; prof. architecture Tech. U. Berlin, 1963-73, dean faculty architecture, 1965-67; prof. architecture emeritus Cornell U., Ithaca, 1968—; chmn. dept. Cornell U., 1968-74; vis. prof. Harvard U., 1972, 77, UCLA, 1973; prof. emeritus Kunstakademie Dusseldorf, 1986-90; organizer 1st and 2d Berlin Summer Acads. for Architecture. Author: (with wife) Megastructure in Habitation; also numerous articles on architecture to internat. mags., numerous chpts. in books; subject of O.M. Ungers 1951-94, Bauten und Projekte; exhibited in biennale, Venice, Italy, 1976, also Berlin, London, N.Y.C.; prin. works include Mus. Architecture, Frankfurt, high rise bldg. and gallery, Frankfurt, Alfred-Wegener-Institut für Polarforschung, Bremerhaven, Badische Landesbibliôthek, Karlsruhe, Supreme Ct., Karlsruhe, family court Berlin-Kreuzberg, art mus. Hamburg, Bayerische Hypotheken-und Wechselbank Düsseldorf, thermae mus. Trier, German Embassy Residential Washington, Friedrichstadt-Passagen Berlin, new fair building, Berlin. Recipient prizes in several urban design competitions, BDA Prize, GroBer, 1987, Prix Rhénan d'Architecture, 1989. Mem. AIA, Acad. di San Luca (Rome), BDA Berlin (hon.), Moscow Br. Internat. Acad. Architecture. Research on cast optimisation in large-scale housing, urban pattern devel. in N.Y. State, subsystems of cities. Designer large-scale pub. housing projects in Germany. Office: 60 Belvederestrasse, 50933 Cologne Germany also: Marienstrasse 10, 10117 Berlin Germany also: 17 Jay St New York NY 10013-2818

UNIS, RICHARD L., state supreme court justice; b. Portland, Oreg., June 11, 1928. Grad., U. Va., U. Oreg. Bar: Oreg. 1954, U.S. Dist. Ct. Oreg. 1957, U.S. Ct. Appeals (9th cir.) 1960, U.S. Supreme Ct. 1965. Judge Portland Mcpl. Ct., 1968-71; judge Multnomah County Dist. Ct., 1972-76, presiding judge, 1972-74; former judge Oreg. Cir. Ct. 4th Judicial Dist., 1977; former sr. dep. city atty. City of Portland; adj. prof. of local govt. law and evidence Lewis & Clark Coll. Northwestern Sch. Law, 1969-76, 77—; faculty mem. The Nat. Judicial Coll., 1971—; former faculty mem. Am. Acad. Judicial Edn. Author: Procedure and Instructions in Traffic Court Cases, 1970, 101 Questions and Answers on Preliminary Hearings, 1974. Bd. dirs. Oreg. Free from Drug Abuse; mem. Oreg. Adv. Com. on Evidence Law Revision, chmn. subcom., 1974-79. Maj. USAFR, JAGC, ret. Recipient Meritorius Svc.award U. Oregon sch. Law, 1988; named Legal Citizen of Yr. Oreg. Law Related Edn., 1987; inducted into The Nat. Judicial Coll. Hall of Honor, 1988. Mem. Am. Judicature Soc. (bd. dirs. 1975), Am. Judges Assn., Multnomah Bar Found., Oregon Judicial Conf. (chmn. Oreg. Judicial Coll. 1973-80, legis. com. 1976—, exec. com. of judicial edn. com., judicial conduct com.), N.Am. Judges Assn. (tenure, selection and compensation judges com.), Dist. Ct. Judges of Oreg. (v.p., chmn. edn. com.), Nat. Conf. Spl. Ct. Judges (exec. com.), Oreg. State Bar (judicial adminstrn. com., sec. local govt. com., com. on continuing certification, uniform jury instrn. com., exec. com. criminal law sect., trial practice sect. standards and certification com., past chmn., among others), Oreg. Trial Lawyers Assn. (named Judge of Yr. 1984). Office: Oreg Supreme Ct Supreme Ct Bldg Salem OR 97310

UNKLESBAY, ATHEL GLYDE, geologist, educator; b. Byesville, Ohio, Feb. 11, 1914; s. Howard Ray and Madaline (Archer) U.; m. Wanda Eileen Strauch, Sept. 14, 1940 (dec. 1971); children: Kenneth, Marjorie, Carolyn, Allen; m. Mary Wheeler Myhre, June 8, 1973 (dec. 1980). A.B., Marietta Coll., 1938, D.Sc. (hon.), 1977; M.A., State U. Iowa, 1940, Ph.D., 1942. Geologist U.S. Geol. Survey, 1942-45, Iowa Geol. Survey, 1945-46; asst. prof. Colgate, 1946-47; mem. faculty U. Mo., Columbia, 1947—; prof. geology U. Mo., 1954—, chmn. dept., 1959-67, v.p. adminstrn., 1967-79; exec. dir. Am. Geol. Inst., 1979-85; cons. in field. Author: Geology of Boone County, 1952, Common Fossils of Missouri, 1955, Pennsylvanian Cephalopods of Oklahoma, 1962, Missouri Geology, 1992; also articles. Mem. Columbia Bd. Edn., 1954-70, Columbia Parks and Recreation Commn., 1954-57. Wilton Park fellow, 1968, 72, 76. Mem. Am. Assn. Petroleum Geologists, Paleontol. Soc. Am., Geol. Soc. Am., Nat. Assn. Geology Tchrs., Kiwanis. Methodist. Home: 37 Broadway Village Dr Apt G Columbia MO 65201-8662

UNPINGCO, JOHN WALTER SABLAN, federal judge; b. 1950. BA, St. Louis U., 1972; MBA, JD, NYU, 1976; LLM, Georgetown U., 1983. Bar: Guam 1977, D.C. 1983, Calif. 1992. Atty. Ferenz, Bramhall, Williams & Gruskin, Guam, 1976-77; atty. Office Staff Judge Advocate USAF, 1977-85, 85-87; counsel Office U.S. Naval Air Warfare Ctr., China Lake, Calif., 1987-92; fed. judge U.S. Dist. Ct. (Guam dist.), 1992—; part-time instr. U. Md. Far East divsn., Yokota Air Base, Tokyo, 1983-87, European divsn., RAF Mildenhall, Suffolk, U.K., 1979-82. Mem. ABA, State Bar Calif., Guam Bar Assn., Internat. Legal Soc. Japan, D.C. Bar Assn., NWC Community Fed. Credit Union (bd. dirs. 1991-92). Office: Pacific News Bldg 238 Archbishop FC Flores St 6th Fl Agana GU 96910

UNRUH, JAMES ARLEN, business machines company executive; b. Goodrich, N.D., Mar. 22, 1941; m. Candice Leigh Voight, Apr. 28, 1984. BSBA, Jamestown Coll., 1963; MBA, U. Denver, 1964. Dir. corp. planning and analysis Fairchild Camera & Instrument, Calif., 1974-76, v.p. treasury and corp. devel., 1976-79, v.p. fin., 1979-80; v.p. fin. Memorex Corp., Santa Clara, Calif., 1980-82; v.p. fin. Burroughs Corp. (now known as Unisys Corp.), Detroit, 1982-84, sr. v.p. fin., 1984-86, exec. v.p. fin., 1986, exec. v.p., 1986-89, pres., chief oper. officer, 1989-90, pres., chief exec. officer, 1990-91, chmn. bd. dirs., chief exec. officer, 1991—; mem. exec. com. Computer Systems Policy Project; mem. Pres.'s Nat. Telecomms. Security Adv. Com. Vice chmn. Greater Phila. First Corp.; bd. trustees Jamestown Coll., N.C.; chmn. Franklin Inst.; bd. overseers Wharton Sch. Bus., U. Pa. Mem. Greater Phila. C. of C. (exec. com.). Office: Unisys Corp Township Line & Union Mtg Blue Bell PA 19422

UNRUH, LEON DALE, newspaper editor; b. Larned, Kans., Dec. 26, 1956; s. Elgie Larey Unruh and Anita Faye Byers; m. Margaret E. Jones, Apr. 30, 1988; 1 child, Samuel A. BS in Journalism, U. Kans., 1979. Copy editor Austin (Tex.) Am.-Statesman, 1979-83; copy desk chief Wichita (Kans.) Eagle-Beacon, 1983-86; asst. news editor Dallas Morning News, 1986-90; travel editor Anchorage Daily News, 1990—; co-owner Birchbark Press, 1995—; freelance coll. textbook editor Harcourt Brace & Co., The Dryden Press, 1989—. Vol. Dallas Soc. Visually Impaired Children, 1986-90; active Alaska Photographic Ctr. Mem. Soc. Newspaper Design (Excellence award 1992, 94). Office: Anchorage Daily News 1001 Northway Dr Anchorage AK 99508-2030

UNRUH, WILLIAM G., physics educator, researcher; b. Winnipeg, Man., Can., Aug. 28, 1945; m. Patricia Truman, Apr. 19, 1974; 1 child, Daniel B. B.Sc. (hon.), U. Man., Winnipeg, 1967; M.A., Princeton U., 1969, Ph.D., 1971. Postdoctoral fellow NRC Can., London, Eng., 1971-72; Miller fellow U. Calif., Berkeley, 1973-74; asst. prof. McMaster U., Hamilton, Ont., Can., 1974-76; asst. prof. to prof. physics U. B.C., Vancouver, Can., 1976—; rsch. fellow Can. Inst. Advanced Rsch., Toronto, Ont., 1986—, dir. Cosmology Program, 1986—. Contbr. tech. papers to profl. publs. Rutherford Meml. fellow Royal Soc. Can., 1971; Alfred P. Sloan rsch. fellow U. B.C., 1978-80; Steacie fellow Nat. Sci. and Eng. Rsch. Coun., 1984-86; Japan Soc. Promotion Sci. sr. fellow Japan, 1986; recipient Rutherford medal Royal Soc. Can., 19982, Hertzberg medal Can. Assn. Physicists, 1983, Steacie medal, 1984, Medal of Achievement, 1995; recipient Gold medal B.C. Sci. Coun., 1991, Killam prize in Nat. Sci., 1996; Rutherford lectr. Royal Soc. Can. to Royal Soc. London, 1985. Fellow Royal Soc. Can.; mem. Canadian Assn. Physicists (Medal of Achievement, 1995). Office: Univ BC Dept Physics, 6224 Agricultural Rd, Vancouver, BC Canada V60 2A6

UNSELD, WESTLEY SISSEL, professional sports team executive, former professional basketball coach, former professional basketball player; b. Louisville, Mar. 14, 1946; m. Connie Martin; children: Kimberly, Westley. Student, U. Louisville, 1964-68. Basketball player Balt. Bullets (name changed to Washington Bullets), 1968-81; v.p. Washington Bullets, 1981-94, head coach, 1988-94, exec. v.p., 1994—. Office: Washington Bullets USAir Arena Landover MD 20785*

UNSELL, LLOYD NEAL, energy organization executive, former journalist; b. Henryetta, Okla., May 12, 1922; s. John William and Rhoda Elizabeth (Martinez) U.; m. Nettie Marie Rogers, Sept. 24, 1944 (dec.); children: Lloyd Neal, Jonna Kay Unsell Wilhelm, James Allan (dec.). Student, U. Ill., Kalamazoo Coll., 1942-43. Mem. editorial staff Tulsa Daily World, 1947-48; successively staff writer, dir. communications, v.p. pub. affairs, exec. v.p., pres. and chief exec. officer Ind. Petroleum Assn. Am., Washington, 1948-87; chmn. selection com. for Milburn Petty award Am. Petroleum Inst.-Assn. Petroleum Writers, 1972-86. Author reports and articles in field. Co-chmn. corp. adv. com. Vietnam Vets. Meml., 1981-82. Served with U.S. Army, 1942-46, ETO, PTO. Recipient Spl. award as outstanding petroleum industry communicator Assn. Petroleum Writers, 1960, Russell B. Brown Meml. award, 1981, Robert J. Enright award Am. Petroleum Inst./Assn. Petroleum Writers, 1986, Disting. Service award Nat. Energy Resources Orgn., 1987; named Hon. Chief Roughneck U.S. petroleum industry, 1986. Mem. Nat. Press Club, Rocky Mountain Oil and Gas Assn. (hon. life), The Jefferson Energy Found. (co-founder 1987). Republican. Baptist. Club: Washington Golf and Country. Home: Point Breeze Rd Coltons Point MD 20626 Office: 1101 16th St NW 5th Fl Washington DC 20036

UNSER, AL, professional auto racer; b. Albuquerque, May 29, 1939; s. Jerry H. and Mary C. (Craven) U.; m. Wanda Jesperson, Apr. 22, 1958 (div.); children: Mary Linda, Debra Ann, Alfred; m. Karen Barnes, Nov. 22, 1977 (div.). Auto racer U.S. Auto Club, Speedway, Ind., 1964-94. Placed 3d in nat. standings, 1968, 2d in 1969, 77, 78, 1st in 1970, 4th in 1976; winner Indpls. 500, 1970, 71, 78, 87, Pocono 500, 1976, 78, Ont. 500, 1977, 78; placed 3d in U.S. Auto Club Sports Car Club Am. Formula 5000, 1975, 2d place, 1976; Internat. Race of Champions champion, 1978; 2d pl. Indpls. Motor Speedway, 1983; CART/PPG Indy Car champion, 1983, 85. Home: 7625 Central Ave NW Albuquerque NM 87121-2115*

UNSER, ALFRED, JR., professional race car driver; b. Apr. 19, 1962; s. Al Sr. U.; m. Shelley Unser; children: Al, Cody, Shannon. Runner-up Indpls. 500, 1989. Winner Indianpolis 500 1992, 94, Indy Car Champion 1990, 94; 1981 SCCA Super Vee Champion, 1986 24 Hours of Daytona winner and IROC champion, 1987 24 Hours of Daytona winner, 1988 IROC champion, 1990 Driver of Yr.; named ABC's Wide World of Sports, 1994 Athlete of Yr.; recipient ESPN's ESPY award for Auto Racing Performer of the Yr., 1994; winner 8 out of 16 Indy car races, 1994, 31 car career victories and 7 career poles. Office: c/o US Auto Club 4910 W 16th St Speedway IN 46224-5703

UNSER, BOBBY (ROBERT WILLIAM UNSER), professional auto racer, television commentator; b. Albuquerque, Feb. 20, 1934; s. Jerry and Mary (Craven) U.; m. Barbara Schumacher, 1953 (div. 1966); m. Norma Davis, 1967 (div. 1970); m. Marsha Sale, Oct. 20, 1976; children: Bobby Jr., Cyndi, Robby, Jeri. Former modified stock car race driver; now driver profl. racing cars; commentator ABC, 1987—; cons. Expert Accident Reconstructionist, U.S., 1985—. Co-author: The Unbelievable Unsers, 1970, The Bobby Unser Story, 1978, Unser: An American Family Portrait, 1988. Served with USAF, 1953-56. Recipient 1st pl. Indy 500 award U.S. Auto Club, 1968, 75, 81, 1st pl. Calif. 500 award U.S. Auto Club, 1974, 76, 79, 80, 1st pl. Pocono 500 award Championship Auto Racing Teams, Pa., 1980; named U.S. Auto Club Nat. Driving Champion, 1969, 75, Martini and Rossi Driver of Yr., 1974. Avocations: snowmobiling, motorbiking. Home and Office: 656 N Macdonald St Mesa AZ 85201-5020*

UNSWORTH, RICHARD PRESTON, minister, school administrator; b. Vineland, N.J., Feb. 7, 1927; s. Joseph Lewis and Laura (MacMillan) U.; m. Joy Merritt, Aug. 20, 1949; children: Sarah, John, Mary, Lucy. BA, Princeton U., 1948; BD, Yale U., 1954; ThM, Harvard U., 1963; STD, Dickinson Coll., 1971; LHD, Washington and Jefferson Coll., 1971; LLD, Smith Coll., 1992. Ordained to ministry Presbyn. Ch., 1953. Tchr. Bible and English Mt. Hermon Sch., 1948-50; asst. chaplain Yale U., New Haven, Conn., 1950-54; chaplain, assoc. prof. Smith Coll., Northampton, Mass., 1954-64, chaplain, prof. religion, 1967-80; dean William Jewett Tucker Found. and prof. religion Dartmouth (N.H.) Coll., 1963-67; headmaster Northfield (Mass.) Mt. Hermon Sch., 1980-88, pres., 1989-91, headmaster emeritus, 1991—; headmaster Berkshire Sch., Sheffield, Mass., 1991-96; interim dean of the chapel Smith Coll., 1996—; pres. Critical Langs. and Area Studies Consortium, 1987—; bd. dirs. Bank of New Eng.-West, 1984-90; cons. Ednl. Assocs., Inc., 1967-69, U.S. Office Edn., 1969-77. Author: Sexuality and the Human Community, 1970, Dignity and Exploitation: Christian Reflections on Images of Sex in the 1970s, 1974, A Century of Religion at Smith College, 1975, (with Arnold Kenseth) Prayers for Worship Leaders, 1978; contbg. author; Sex Edn. and the Schs., 1967. Leader Operation Crossroads Africa unit, Nigeria, 1961, mem. adv. bd., 1961-66; mem. adminstrv. com. Student Christian Movement New Eng., 1964; mem. Mass. unit So. Christian Leadership conf., 1968; trustee Conf. on Religion in Ind. Schs., 1961-63; pres. Am. Friends of Coll. Cevenol, France, 1957-63, 90-94, Am. rep., 1958-82; trustee Mt. Holyoke Coll., 1982-89, chair, 1984-89, chmn. emeritus, 1989—, Am. Sch. Tangier, Morocco, 1982-87, Eaglebrook Sch., 1992—, Mus. Sci., Boston, 1993-95; bd. dirs. Family Planning Coun. Western Mass., 1972-81; bd. dirs. Ind. Schs. Assn. Mass., 1992-96. Mem. AAUP, Nat. Assn. Coll. and Univ. Chaplains, Am. Acad. Religion, Assn. Ind. Schs. New Eng. (pres. 1993—), Headmasters Assn. Home: PO Box 514 Northampton MA 01061 Office: Chapel Smith Coll Northampton MA 01063

UNTENER, KENNETH E., bishop; b. Detroit, Aug. 3, 1937. Ed., Sacred Heart Sem., Detroit, St. John's Provincial Sem., Plymouth, Mich., Gregorian U., Rome. Ordained priest Roman Cath. Ch., 1963, ordained bishop, 1980. Bishop Diocese of Saginaw, Mich., 1980—. Office: Chancery Office 5800 Weiss St Saginaw MI 48603-2762*

UNTERBERGER, BETTY MILLER, history educator, writer; b. Glasgow, Scotland, Dec. 27, 1923; d. Joseph C. and Leah Miller; m. Robert Ruppe, July 29, 1944; children: Glen, Gail, Gregg. B.A., Syracuse U., N.Y., 1943; M.A., Harvard U., 1946; Ph.D., Duke U., 1950. Asst. prof. E. Carolina U., Greenville, 1948-50; assoc. prof., dir. liberal arts ctr. Whittier Coll., Calif., 1954-61; assoc. prof. Calif. State U.-Fullerton, 1961-65, prof., chmn. grad. studies, 1965-68; prof. Tex. A&M U., College Station, 1968—; vis. prof. U. Hawaii, Honolulu, summer 1967, Peking U., Beijing, 1988; vis. disting. prof. U. Calif., Irvine, 1987—, Patricia and Bookman Peters prof. history, 1991—; vis. prof. Charles U., Prague, Czechoslovakia, summer 1992; mem. adv. com. fgn. rels. U.S. Dept. State, 1977-81, chair, 1981; mem. hist. adv. com. U.S. Dept. Army, 1980-82, USN, 1991—; mem. Nat. Hist. Publs. and Records Commn., 1980-84. Author: America's Siberian Expedition 1918-1920: A Study of National Policy, 1956, 69 (Pacific Coast award Am. Hist. Assn. 1956); editor: American Intervention in the Russian Civil War, 1969, Intervention Against Communism: Did the U.S. Try to Overthrow the Soviet Government, 1918-20, 1986, The United States, Revolutionary Russia and the Rise of Czechoslovakia, 1989; contbr.: Woodrow Wilson and Revolutionary World, 1982; editorial adv. bd.: The Papers of Woodrow Wilson, Princeton U., 1982-92; bd. editors: Diplomatic History, 1981-84, Red River Valley Hist. Rev., 1975-84. Trustee Am. Inst. Pakistan Studies, Villanova U., Pa., 1981—, sec., 1989-92; mem. League of Women Voters. Woodrow Wilson Found. fellow, 1979; recipient Disting. Univ. Tchr. award State of Calif. Legislature, 1966. Mem. LWV, NOW, AAUW, Am. Hist. Assn. (chair 1982-83, nominating com. 1980-83), Orgn. Am. Historians (govt. relations com.), Soc. Historians of Am. Fgn. Relations (exec. council 1978-81, 86-89, govt. relations com. 1982-84, v.p. 1985, pres. 1986, co-winner Myrna F. Bernath prize 1991), Am. Soc. for Advancement Slavic Studies, Coordinating Com. on Women in Hist. Profession, Rocky Mountain Assn. Slavic Studies (program chair 1973, v.p. 1973-74), So. Hist. Assn., Asian Studies Assn., Assn. Third World Studies, Czechoslovak Soc. Arts and Scis., Czechoslovak History Conf., Women's Fgn. Policy Coun., Beyond War, Peace History Soc., Sierra Club, Phi Beta Kappa, Phi Beta Delta. Office: Tex A&M U College Station TX 77843

UNTERMAN, THOMAS E., lawyer; b. Newport, R.I., Oct. 23, 1944; s. Martin D. and Ruth (Marcus) U.; m. Janet M. Mead, Sept. 27, 1980; children: Rebecca, Amy. AB, Princeton U., 1966; JD, U. Chgo., 1969. Bar: Calif. 1970. Assoc. Orrick, Herrington & Sutcliffe, San Francisco, 1969-75, ptnr., 1975-86; ptnr. Morrison & Foerster, San Francisco, 1986-92; sr. v.p., gen. counsel The Times Mirror Co., L.A., 1992-95; sr. v.p., CFO The Times Mirror Co., L.a., 1995—. Democrat. Jewish. Office: The Times Mirror Co Times Mirror Sq Los Angeles CA 90053

UNTHANK, G. WIX, federal judge; b. Tway, Ky., June 14, 1923; s. Green Ward and Estell (Howard) U.; m. Marilyn Elizabeth Ward, Feb. 28, 1953. J.D., U. Miami, Fla., 1950. Bar: Ky. 1950. Judge Harlan County, 1950-57; asst. U.S. atty., Lexington, Ky., 1966-69; commonwealth atty. Harlan, 1970-80; judge U.S. Dist. Ct. (ea. dist.) Ky., Pikeville, 1980-88; sr. judge U.S. Dist. Ct. (ea. dist.) Ky., London, 1988—. Served with AUS, 1940-45, ETO. Decorated Purple Heart, Bronze Star, Combat Inf. badge. Mem. ABA, Am. Judicature Soc., Ky. Bar Assn., Fla. Bar Assn. Democrat. Presbyterian. Office: Sr Judge's Chambers PO Box 5112 London KY 40745-5112

UNTHANK, TESSA See **NELSON-HUMPHRIES, TESSA**

UOTILA, URHO ANTTI KALEVI, geodesist, educator; b. Pöytyä, Finland, Feb. 22, 1923; came to U.S., 1951, naturalized, 1957; s. Antti Samuli and Vera Justina (Kyto) U.; m. Helena Vanhakartano, Aug. 6, 1949; children: Heidi, Kirsi, Elizabeth, Julie, Trina, Caroline. B.S., Finland's Inst. Tech., 1946, M.S., 1949; Ph.D., Ohio State U., 1959. Surveyor, geodesist Finnish Govt., 1944-46, 46-51; geodesist Swedish Govt., 1946; research asst. Ohio State U., 1952-53, research assoc., 1953-58, research supr., 1959-88, lectr. in geodesy, 1955-57, asst. prof., 1959-62, assoc. prof., 1962-65, chmn. dept. geodetic sci., 1964-84, prof., 1965-89, chmn., prof. emeritus, 1989—; mem. Solar Eclipse Expdn. to Greenland, 1954; Mem. adv. panel on geodesy U.S. Coast and Geodetic Survey, Nat. Acad. Sci., 1964-66; mem. geodesy and cartography working group, space sci. steering com. NASA, 1965-67, mem. geodesy/cartography working group, summer conf. lunar exploration and sci., 1965, mem. geodesy and cartography adv. subcom., 1967-72; mem. ad hoc com. on N.Am. datum div. earth scis. Nat. Acad. Scis.-N.A.E., 1968-70; bd. dirs. Internat. Gravity Bur., France, 1975-83; mem. com. on geodesy Nat. Acad. Scis., 1975-78. Mem. editorial adv. com.: Advances in Geophysics, 1968-77; Contbr. articles to profl. jours., encys. Served with Finnish Army, 1942-44. Recipient Kaarina and W.A. Heiskanen award, 1962, Apollo Achievement award NASA, 1969, Disting. Svc. award Surveyor's Inst. Sri Lanka, Earle J. Fennell award Am. Congress on Surveying and Mapping, 1989. Fellow Am. Geophys. Union (v.p. geodesy sect. 1964-68, pres. 1968-70), Am. Congress Surveying and Mapping (nat. dir. 1970-73, 2d v.p. 1977-78, pres.-elect 1978-79, pres. 1979-80), Internat. Assn. Geodesy (pres. spl. study group 5.30 1967-71, pres. sect. V 1971-75, exec. com. 1971-79); mem. Am. Assn. Geodetic Surveying (pres. 1984-86), Am. Soc. Photogrammetry, Can. Inst. Surveying, Univs. Space Research Assn. (trustee 1973-75), Finnish Nat. Acad. Scis. (fgn.), Profl. Land Surveyors Ohio (hon.), Ala. Soc. Profl. Land Surveyors (hon.), Tenn. Assn. Profl. Surveyors (hon.). Research in geometric geodesy, phys. geodesy and statis. analysis of data. Home: 4329 Shelbourne Ln Columbus OH 43220-4243 Office: Ohio State U Dept Geodetic Science and Surveying 1958 Neil Ave Columbus OH 43210-1247

UPADHYAY, YOGENDRA NATH, physician, educator; b. Gorakhpur, India, Dec. 21, 1938; came to U.S., 1963; s. Murlidhar and Vansraji (Pande) U.; m. Cecile R. Yonish; children: Asha, Sameer, Sanjay. MB, BS, All India Inst. Med. Scis., New Delhi, 1962. Diplomate Am. Bd. Psychiatry and Neurology, Am. Bd. Pediatrics. Instr. in pediatrics Johns Hopkins U. Sch. Medicine, Balt., 1969-71; fellow in child psychiatry Johns Hopkins Hosp./Johns Hopkins U., Balt., 1971-72; resident, then sr. resident in psychiatry Albert Einstein Coll. Medicine/Bronx Mcpl. Hosp. Ctr., 1972-74, fellow in child psychiatry, 1974-75; chief, partial hosp. program for children, dept. psychiatry Brookdale Hosp., Bklyn., 1976-77; med. dir. West Nassau Mental Health Ctr., Franklin Sq., N.Y., 1977-80; asst. prof. clin. psychiatry SUNY, Stony Brook, 1978-92; dir. child and adolescent psychiatry Nassau County Med. Ctr., East Meadow, N.Y., 1980-92; sr. psychiatrist South Oaks Hosp., Amityville, N.Y., 1992—, pres. med. staff, 1995—, pres. medical staff, 1995—. Fellow Am. Psychiat. Assn. 9cons. task force treatments psychiat. disorders 1989—), Am. Acad. Child and Adolescent Psychiatry, Allmsonians of Am. (founding pres. 1982-86). Office: 400 Sunrise Hwy Amityville NY 11701-2508

UPATNIEKS, JURIS, optical engineer, researcher, educator; b. Riga, Latvia, May 7, 1936; came to U.S., 1951; s. Karlis and Eleonora (Jegers) U.; m. Ilze Induss, July 13, 1968; children: Ivars, Ansis. BSEE, U. Akron, Ohio, 1960; MSEE, U. Mich., 1965. Rsch. asst., then rsch. assoc. Willow Run Labs. U. Mich., Ann Arbor, 1960-69; rsch. engr. Inst. Sci. and Tech., U. Mich., Ann Arbor, 1969-72, Environ. Rsch. Inst. Mich., Ann Arbor, 1973-93; sr. engr. Applied Optics, Ann Arbor, 1993—; lectr. elec. engring. dept. U. Mich., 1971-73, adj. assoc. prof. elec. engring. and computer sci. dept., 1974—. Contbr. articles to profl. jours.; patentee in field. 2d lt. U.S. Army, 1961-62. Recipient Holley medal ASME, 1976, Inventor of Yr. award Assn. for Advancement Invention and Innovation, 1976. Fellow Optical Soc. Am. (R.W. Wood prize 1975), Soc. Photographic Instrumentation Engrs. (Robert Gordon award 1965), Am. Latvian Assn., Acad. Soc. Austrums, Latvian Acad. Sci. (elected 1991). Avocations: camping, gardening, hiking. Office: Applied Optics 2662 Valley Dr Ann Arbor MI 48103-2748

UPBIN, HAL JAY, consumer products executive; b. Bronx, N.Y., Jan. 15, 1939; s. David and Evelyn (Sloan) U.; m. Shari Kiesler, May 29, 1960; children: Edward, Elyse, Danielle. BBA, Pace Coll., 1961. CPA, N.Y. Tax sr. Peat, Marwick, Mitchell & Co., N.Y.C., 1961-65; tax mgr. Price Waterhouse & Co., N.Y.C., 1965-71; dir. taxes Wheelabrator-Frye Inc., N.Y.C., 1971-72, treas., 1972-74; pres. Wheelabrator Fin. Corp., N.Y.C., 1974-75; v.p., chief fin. officer Chase Manhattan Mortgage and Realty Trust (became Triton Group Ltd. 1980), N.Y.C., 1975-76, pres., 1976-78, pres., chmn., 1978-83, also dir.; chmn., pres., dir. Isomedics, 1983-85; chmn., pres. Fifth Ave. Cards, Inc., Fifth Retail Corp., Ashby's Stores, Ashby's Outlet Stores, 1984-88; bd. dirs. Stacy Industries, 1984-88; vice chmn. Am. Recreation Products, St. Louis, 1985-88, vice chmn., pres., 1988—, chmn., 1992—; v.p. corp. devel., chmn. acquistion com. Kellwood Co., Chesterfield, Mo., 1990—, exec. v.p. corp. devel., chmn. acquistion com., 1992—, pres., COO, 1994—; pres., COO, dir. Kellwood Co., Chesterfield, 1995—. Alumni advisor to bd. trustees Pace U.; past pres. Jewish Temple. Mem. AICPA, N.Y. State Soc. CPA's, Franklin Jaycees (v.p.). Home: 625 S Skinker Blvd Saint Louis MO 63105 Office: Kellwood Co PO Box 14374 Saint Louis MO 63178

UPBIN, SHARI, theatrical producer, director, agent, educator; b. N.Y.C.; children: Edward, Elyse, Danielle. Master tap instr. Talent mgr. Goldstar Talent Mgmt., Inc., N.Y.C., 1989-91; guest tchr. Total Theatre Lab., N.Y.C.; faculty Nat. Shakespeare Conservatory, N.Y. Asst. dir. 1st Black-Hispanic Shakespeare prodn. Julius Ceasar, Coriolanus at Pub. Theatre, N.Y., 1979; dir., choreographer Matter of Opinion, Players Theatre, N.Y., 1980, Side by Side, Sondheim Forum Theatre, N.J., 1981 (Nominated Best Dir. of Season N.J. Theatre Critics); producer, dir. Vincent, The Passions of Van Gogh, N.Y., 1981; producer Bojangles, The Life of Bill Robinson, Broadway, 1984, Captain America, nat. Am. tour, Virtual Theatre, 1996; dir. Fiddler on the Roof, Cabaret, Life with Father, Roar of the Grease Paint, regional theatre, 1979-82; co-producer One Mo' Time, Village Gate, N.Y., nat. and internat. tour.; producer/dir. off-Broadway musical Flypaper, 1991-92, Women on Their Own, Things My Mother Never Told Me, Theatre East, N.Y. Founded Queens Playhouse, N.Y., Children's Theatre, Flushing, N.Y.; mem. Willy Mays' Found. Drug Abused Children. Recipient Jaycees Service award Jr. Miss Pageants Franklin Twp., N.J., 1976. Mem. League Profl. Theatre Women (pres.), Soc. Stage Dirs. and Choreographers, Actors Equity Assn., Villagers Barn Theatre (1st woman pres.), N.Y. Womens Agenda (bd. dirs.). Address: The Bristol 300 E 56th St New York NY 10022

UPCHURCH, PAUL, principal. Prin. Centerfield Elem. Sch., Crestwood, Ky. Recipient DOW Elem. Sch. Recognition award, 1989-90. Office: Centerfield Elem Sch 4512 S Highway 393 Crestwood KY 40014-9288

UPDEGRAFF SPLETH, ANN L., church executive, pastor; b. Newark, Ohio, Sept. 15, 1949; d. John C. and Lela V. (Mervine) Updegraff; m. Randall Alan Spleth; children: Andrew Alan, Claire Campbell. BA, Transylvania Coll., 1971; MDiv, Vanderbilt U., 1974; DMin, Claremont Sch. Theology, 1985. Ordained min. Christian Ch. (Disciples of Christ), 1973. Assoc. min. First Christian Ch., New Castle, Ind., 1974-75, Sacramento, 1975-78; sr. assoc. regional min. Pacific S.W. region Christian Ch., L.A., 1978-85; exec. v.p. Divsn. Homeland Ministries, Indpls., 1985-89, pres., 1990—. Author: Youth Ministry Manual, 1980; co-author: Congregation: Sign of Hope, 1989, Worship and Spiritual Life, 1992; editor Vanguard, 1990—; contbr. articles to profl. jours. Founding mem. Profl. Women's Forum, L.A., 1978-85. Mem. Ind. Soc. of Washington. Democrat. Home: 8961 Sawmill Ct Indianapolis IN 46236-9171 Office: United Christian Missionary Society 130 E Washington St Indianapolis IN 46204-3615

UPDEGRAFT, KENNETH E., JR., lawyer; b. Ft. Meade, Md., Sept. 30, 1946. BSBA, Am. U., 1967; MS, U. Pa., 1968; LLB, U. Va., 1971. Bar: Ohio 1971; CPA, Va. Ptnr. Jones, Day, Reavis & Pogue, Cleve. Fellow Am. Coll. Tax Counsel; mem. ABA (chmn. natural resources com. 1987-89). Office: Jones Day Reavis & Pogue North Point 901 Lakeside Ave E Cleveland OH 44114-1116*

UPDIKE, HELEN HILL, economist, investment manager, financial planner; b. N.Y.C., Mar. 27, 1941; d. Benjamin Harvey and Helen (Gray) Hill; m. Charles Bruce Updike, Sept. 7, 1963 (div. 1989); children: Edith Hill, Nancy Lamar. B.A., Hood Coll., 1962; Ph.D., SUNY, Stony Brook, 1978; postgrad., Harvard U., 1986. Asst. prof. Suffolk U., Boston, 1965-67; lectr. SUNY-Stony Brook, 1969-75, vis. asst. prof., 1977-78; asst. prof. U. Mass., Boston, 1975-77; asst. prof. Hofstra U., Hempstead, N.Y., 1978-85, assoc. prof., 1985-90, chmn. dept. econs. and geography, 1981-84; assoc. dean Hofstra Coll. Hofstra U., 1984-87; pres. Interfid Capital Corp., 1987—; dir. McCrory Corp., 1987—; cons. on econ. policy, 1973—. Author: The National Banks and American Economic Development, 1870-1900, 1985. Trustee, v.p. L.I. Forum for Tech., 1979-85; trustee Madeira Sch., Greenway, Va., 1984-88, N.Y. Outward Bound, 1988—; mem. nat. adv. bd. Outward Bound USA, 1984-92. Mem. AAAS, Cosmopolitan Club, Cold Spring Harbor Beach Club. Office: Interfid Capital Corp 27th Fl 150 E 58th St Fl 27 New York NY 10155-0001

UPDIKE, JOHN HOYER, writer; b. Shillington, Pa., Mar. 18, 1932; s. Wesley R. and Linda G. (Hoyer) U.; m. Mary E. Pennington, June 26, 1953 (div. 1976); children: Elizabeth, David, Michael, Miranda; m. Martha Bernhard, Sept. 30, 1977. AB, Harvard U., 1954; student, Ruskin Sch. Drawing and Fine Art, 1954-55. With New Yorker mag., N.Y.C., 1955-57. Author: (fiction) The Poorhouse Fair, 1959 (Richard and Hinda Rosenthal Found. award Am. Acad. and Nat. Inst. Arts and Letters 1960), The Same Door, 1959, Rabbit, Run, 1960, Pigeon Feathers, 1962, The Centaur, 1963 (Nat. Book award 1963, Prix Medicis Etranger 1966), Olinger Stories, 1964, Of the Farm, 1965, The Music School, 1966, Couples, 1968, Bech: A Book, 1970, Rabbit Redux, 1971, Museums and Women, 1972, Warm Wine, 1973, A Month of Sundays, 1975, Marry Me, 1976, Couples, 1976, The Coup, 1978, From the Journal of a Leper, 1978, Problems, 1979, Too Far to Go: The Maples Stories, 1979 (Am. Book award nomination 1980), Three Illuminations in the Life of an American Author, 1979, Your Lover Just Called: Stories of Joan and Richard Maple, 1980, The Chaste Planet, 1980, Rabbit Is Rich, 1981 (Pulitzer prize for fiction 1982, Nat. Book Critics Circle award 1982, Am. Book award 1982), Invasion of the Book Envelopes, 1981, Bech Is Back, 1982, The Beloved, 1982, The Witches of Eastwick, 1984, Confessions of a Wild Bore, 1984, Roger's Version, 1986 (Nat. Book Critics Circle award nomination 1986), Trust Me, 1987, More Stately Mansions, 1987, S., 1988, Rabbit at Rest, 1990 (Pulitzer prize for fiction 1991, Nat. Book Critics Circle award 1991), Memories of the Ford Administration, 1992, Brazil, 1994, The Afterlife, 1994, In the Beauty of the Lilies, 1996, (poetry) The Carpentered Hen and Other Tame Creatures, 1958, Telephone Poles, 1963, A Child's Calendar, 1965, The Angels, 1968, Bath after Sailing, 1968, Midpoint, 1969, Seventy Poems, 1972, Six Poems, 1973, Tossing and Turning, 1977, Sixteen Sonnets, 1979, Five Poems, 1980, Spring Trio, 1982, Jester's Dozen, 1984, Facing Nature, 1985, Collected Poems 1953-1993, 1993, A Helpful Alphabet of Friendly Objects, 1995, (play) Buchanan Dying, 1974, (non-fiction) Assorted Prose, 1965, On Meeting Authors, 1968, Three Texts from Early Ipswich, 1968, A Good Place, 1973, Picked-Up Pieces, 1975, Hub Fans Bid Kid Adieu, 1977, Talk from the Fifties, 1979, Ego and Art in Walt Whitman, 1980, Hawthorne's Creed, 1981, Hugging the Shore, 1983 (Nat. Book Critics Circle award 1984), Emersonianism, 1984, Just Looking, 1989, Self-Consciousness, 1989, Odd Jobs, 1991; adapter: (librettos) The Magic Flute, 1962, The Ring, 1964, (plays) Bottom's Dream, 1969; author words and music: (with Gunther Schuller) The Fisherman and His Wife, 1970; editor: Pens and Needles, 1970, (with S. Ravenel) The Best American Short Stories 1984, 1984. Recipient O. Henry First Short Story award, 1966, 91, MacDowell medal for literature, 1981, Medal of Honor for literature Nat. Arts Club, 1984, PEN/Malamud Meml. prize PEN/Faulker award Found., 1988, Nat. Medal of Arts, 1989; Guggenheim fellow, 1959. Mem. AAAL, Am. Acad. Arts. and Scis. Democrat. Episcopalian.

UPGREN, ARTHUR REINHOLD, JR., astronomer, educator, outdoor lighting consultant; b. Mpls., Feb. 21, 1933; s. Arthur Reinhold and Marion (Andrews) U.; m. Joan Koswoski, Jan. 7, 1967; 1 child, Amy Joan. BA, U. Minn., 1955; MS, U. Mich., 1958; PhD, Case Western Res. U., 1961. Research assoc. Swarthmore Coll., Pa., 1961-63; astronomer U.S. Naval Obs., Washington, 1963-66; asst. prof. Wesleyan U., Middletown, Conn., 1966-73, assoc. prof., 1973-81, dir. Van Vleck Obs., 1973-93, John Monroe Van Vleck prof., 1981—, chmn. dept. astronomy, 1968-86, 90-93; v.p. Fund Astrophys. Research, N.Y.C., 1973—, chmn. grants com., 1985—; vis. lectr. U. Md., 1964-66, George Washington U., 1965-66, Thames Sci. Ctr., New London, Conn., 1990, 92; vis. prof. Yale U., 1979-80, 95—; adj. prof. U. Fla., 1984—; outdoor lighting cons. Wesleyan U., 1991—, Vt. State Agy. Natural Resources, 1993-94; reviewer books in astronomy, meteorology, classical music and urban demographics. Editor: The Nearby Stars and the Stellar Luminosity Function, 1983, Mapping the Sky-Past Heritage and Future Directions, 1988, Star Catalogues: A Centennial Tribute to A.N. Vyssotsky, 1989, Fundamentals of Astronomy, 1990, Precision Photometry: Astrophysics of the Galaxy, 1991, Objective Prism and Other Surveys, 1991, Databases for Galactic Structure, 1993, Hot Stars in the Halo, 1994, New Developments in Array Technology and Applications, 1995. Conn. state chair New Eng. Light Pollution Adv. Group, 1994—. Grantee NSF, 1967—. Fellow Royal Astron. Soc.; mem. Internat. Astron. Union (commn. v.p. 1982-85, pres. commn. 24 1985-88), Am. Astron. Soc. (Harlow Shapley lectr. 1977—, vice-chmn. dynamical astronomy div. 1988-89, chmn. 1989-90), Astron. Soc. Pacific, Illumniating Engring. Soc. N.Am., Internat. Dark Sky Assn., Sigma Xi. Office: Van Vleck Obs Wesleyan U Middletown CT 06459-0123

UPHOFF, JAMES KENT, education educator; b. Hebron, Nebr., Sept. 1, 1937; s. Ernest John and Alice Marie (Dutcher) U.; m. Harriet Lucille Martin, Aug. 6, 1962; 1 child, Nicholas James. BA, Hastings Coll., 1959; MEd, U. Nebr., 1962, EdD, 1967. Tchr., Walnut Jr. High Sch., Grand Island, Nebr., 1959-65, dept. chmn., 1962-65; instr. dept. edn. U. Nebr., Lincoln, 1965-66; curriculum intern Bellevue (Nebr.) Pub. Schs., 1966-67; asst. prof. edn. Wright State U., Dayton, Ohio, 1967-70, assoc. prof., 1970-75, prof. edn., 1975—, co-dir. pub. edn. religion studies ctr., 1972-75, dean br. campuses, 1974-79, dir. lab. experiences, 1982-91, chmn. dept. tchr. edn., 1994—, dir. coll. student svcs., 1994—, dir. profl. field experiences, 1995—; vis. prof. U. Dayton, 1968-69. Author: (with others) Summer Children: Ready or Not For School, 4th edit., 1986; School Readiness and Transition Programs: Real Facts from Real Schools, 1990, 2nd edit., 1995; editor: Dialogues on Develop. Curriculum K and I, 1987, Changing to a Developmentally Appropriate Curriculum-Successfully: 4 Case Studies, 1989; weekly columnist Oakwood Register newspaper, monthly columnist Dayton Parent newspaper. Recipient Disting. Rsch. award Coll. Edn. and Human Svcs. Wright State U., 1988, 91, Deans' award, 1991; Phi Delta Kappa scholar, 1969; Malone fellow in Arab Islamic studies, 1989. Bd. dirs. pub. edn. fund Dayton Found., 1985—; mem. Luth. Ch. coun., 1987-90, chair 1988-90; mem. Oakwood City Schs. Bd. Edn., 1989—, v.p., 1994-95, pres., 1996—. Mem. Am. Ednl. Rsch. Assn., Nat. Coun. Tchrs. English, Western Ohio Edn. Assn. (pres. 1974-75, exec. com. 1979-85), Assn. Supervision and Curriculum Devel. (dir. 1974-79, editor early childhood network 1989—, editor pub. edn. and religion network 1992—), Assn. Tchr. Educators, Assn. Childhood Edn. Internat., Ohio Assn. Supervision and Curriculum Devel. (v.p. 1972-73), Nat. Coun. Social Studies, Ohio Coun. Social Studies, Am. Edn. Rsch. Assn., Ohio Sch. Bds. Assn. (chair rules com. 1993-94, mem. policy and legislation com. 1994—, Achievement award 1995, bd. trustees 1996—), Nat. Assn. Edn. Young Children, Dayton Area Coun. Social Studies (pres. (1970-71, 85-87), Ohio Assn. Edn. Young Children (com. chair 1992-95), Dayton Assn. for Young Children (exec. bd. 1988-94), LWV Greater Dayton (edn. dir. 1981-85), Ohio Council Chs. (edn. com. 1973-75), Optimists Club (pres. 1983-85, sec./treas. 1988—), Golden Key (chpt. advisor 1991—), Phi Delta Kappa (chpt. pres. 1983-84, chpt. advisor 1988-94), Kappa Delta Pi. Republican. Home: 150 Spirea Dr Dayton OH 45419-3409 Office: Wright State U 322 Millett Edn Dayton OH 45435

UPLEDGER, JOHN EDWIN, osteopath, physician; b. Detroit, Feb. 10, 1932; s. Edwin Chauncey and Eleanor Bernice (Cave) U.; m. divorced; children from previous marriage: Leslie, John, Mark, Michael; m. Dianne Lucille Dennison, Nov. 23, 1970 (div. 1994). BA, Wayne State U, 1953; DO, Kirkville Coll. Osteo. Surgery; DSc, Medicine Alternativa, Sri Lanka, 1987. Pvt. practice Clearwater, Fla., 1964-75; prof. biomechs. Mich. State U., East Lansing, 1975-82; med.dir., clin. researcher Unity Ctr. for Health, Edn. and Rsch., West Palm Beach, Fla., 1982-85; clin.dir. Upledger Inst., Upledger Found., Palm Beach Gardens, Fla., 1985—; mem. adv. coun. NIH Office of Alt. Medicine, 1993-95. Author: Craniosacral Therapy, Vol. I-II, 1982, 85, Somato Emotional Release and Beyond, 1990, A Brain is Born, 1995; contbr. articles to profl. jours. Bd. dirs. Cleatwater/St. Petersburg Free Clinics, Fla., 1968-75. Fellow Am. Acad. Osteopathy; mem. Soc. Osteopathes (acad. fellow 1978). Achievements include craniosacral therapy; somato emotional release; therapist-patient electrocircuitry; neurocircuitry redevel. Office: Upledger Inst 11211 Prosperity Farms Rd West Palm Beach FL 33410-3446

UPPMAN, THEODOR, concert and opera singer, voice educator; b. San Jose, Calif., Jan. 12, 1920; s. John August and Hulda Maria (Thörnström) U.; m. Jean Seward, Jan. 31, 1943; children: Margot, Michael. Student, Coll. of Pacific, 1938-39, Curtis Inst. Music, 1939-41, Stanford U., 1941-42, U. So. Calif., 1948-50. mem. profl. com. regional auditions Met. Opera; voice faculty Mannes Coll. Music, 1977—, Manhattan Sch. Music, 1988—; tchr. master classes Britten-Pears Sch. Advanced Mus. Studies, 1985—, Glimmerglass Opera, Cooperstown, N.Y., 1990, 93, Opera Theatre of St. Louis, 1993, Steans Inst. at Ravinia Festival, 1995; dir. vocal dept. Music Acad. of the West, Santa Barbara, Calif., 1988. Profl. debut as baritone, No. Calif. Symphony, 1941, appeared with, San Francisco Symphony, 1947; performed in: Pelleas et Melisande, City Ctr. Opera Co., N.Y., 1948; debut, San Francisco Opera Co., 1948, N.Y. recital, Times Hall, 1950; appeared: title role Billy Budd opera premiere, Royal Opera House, London, Eng., 1951, Theatre des Champs Elysees, Paris, France, 1952; performed in: Billy Budd, NBC-TV Opera Theatre, 1952, Pelleas et Melisande, Met. Opera Co., 1953-62, Magic Flute, 1956-77, La Perichole, 1956-71, Don Giovanni, 1957-73, Madam Butterfly, 1961-78, Cosi fan Tutte, 1962-71, L'Italiana in Algeri, 1973-75; world premieres of Floyd's The Passion of Jonathan Wade, N.Y.C. Opera, 1962, Villa Lobos' Yerma, Santa Fe Opera, 1971, Pasatieri's Black Widow, Seattle Opera, 1972, Barab's Philip Marshall, Chautauqua, 1974; Aix en Provence Festival, summer 1964, Aldeburgh Festival, summer 1975, Chgo. Lyric Opera debut, 1964, War Requiem by Britten, Dallas, Cleve., Cin. orchs., 1965, Damnation of Faust, N.Y. Philharmonic, 1966; Am. premiere: Billy Budd, Chgo. Lyric Opera, 1970, Death in Venice (Britten), Geneva Opera, 1983; World premiere: A Quiet Place (Bernstein), Houston Opera, 1983, A Quiet Place, LaScala, 1984, A Quiet Place, Vienna Staatsoper, 1986; recordings include world premiere broadcast Billy Budd, 1951; concert opera symphony appearances throughout, U.S., also radio, TV. Hon. dir. Britten-Pears Sch. for Advanced Mus. Studies, 1987—. With U.S. Army, 1943-46, World War II. Recipient 1st prize Atwater Kent Found. Auditions, Gainsborough Found. award, 1947. Address: 201 W 86th St New York NY 10024-3328

UPPOOR, RAJENDRA, pharmaceutical scientist, educator, researcher; b. Ripponpete, Karnataka, India, Feb. 11, 1960; came to U.S., 1989; s. Vittal Kamath and Suvarna Vittal U.; m. VenKata Ramana K. Sista, Oct. 31, 1995. B in Pharmacy, Govt. Coll. of Pharmacy, Bangalore, India, 1981, M in Pharmacy, 1984; diploma in pharmaceutical tech., State U. Ghent, Belgium, 1986; PhD, Med. U. of S.C., Charleston, 1995. Registered pharmacist Karnataka State Pharmacy Coun., India. Prodn. mgr. Gururaj Micropulverizers, Bangalore, India, 1979-85; student trainee Burroughs Wellcome (India), Bombay, 1981; trainee supr. Eskaylab India, Bangalore, 1982; asst. prof. St. John's Pharmacy Coll., Bangalore, 1984-85; mktg. officer Associated Capsules, Bombay, 1985-87; devel. officer Sci. Tech. Ctr., Bombay, 1986-87; pharmacist Ministry of Health, Riyadh, Saudi Arabia, 1987-88; rsch. asst. Med. U. of S.C., Charleston, 1989-94; cons. Ohmeda PPD, Inc., Murray Hill, N.J., 1994; sr. scientist Ohmeda PPD, Inc., Murray Hill, 1994—. Pres. Internat. Student Orgn. Med. Univ. S.C., Charleston, 1991-92; gen. sec. Pharm. Soc. The Gov. Coll. of Pharmacy, Bangalore, India. 1983-84; student rep. in Indian schs. and colls., 1966-84. Grantee Univ. Frants Commn. scholarship Govt. of India, 1982-84; Recipient Nat. Merit scholarship Govt. of India, 1975-81, Internat. fellowship WHO, Geneva, State U. Ghent, Belgium, 1986; Ohmeda Pres'. award, 1995. Mem. Am. Assn. Pharm. Scientists, Vivekananda Kendra Yoga Therapy and Rsch. Ctr.(instr. 1981-82, life mem.), National Cadet Corps (Naval Wing), India, 1972-77; Sigma Xi, Rho Chi. Achievements include concentric coating technique/application for sustained release of drugs; application of glucose oxidase-catalase as an antioxidant system in pharmaceutical solutions; formulation, product development, scale-up and manufacturing of lipid emulsions for intravenous use, freeze drying of pharmaceuticals. Avocations: philately, travel, religions, history, photography. Home: 76 Southgate Rd Apt 1A Murray Hill NJ 07974 Office: Ohmeda PPD Inc 100 Mountain Ave New Providence NJ 07974

UPRIGHT, DIANE WARNER, art dealer; b. Cleve.; d. Rodney Upright and Shirley (Warner) Lavine. Student, Wellesley Coll., 1965-67; BA, U. Pitts., 1969; MA, U. Mich., 1973, PhD, 1976. Asst. prof. U. Va., Charlottesville, 1976-78; assoc. prof. Harvard U., Cambridge, Mass., 1978-83; sr. curator Ft. Worth Art Mus., 1984-86; dir. Jan Krugier Gallery, N.Y.C., 1986-90; sr. v.p., head contemporary art dept. Christie's, N.Y.C., 1990-95; pres. Diane Upright Fine Arts, N.Y.C., 1995—; trustee Aldrich Mus. Contemporary Art, Ridgefield, Conn. Author: Morris Louis: The Complete Paintings, 1979, Ellsworth Kelly: Works on Paper, 1987, various exhbn. catalogues; contbr. articles to art jours. Mem. Art Table, Inc. Office: Diane Upright Fine Arts 20 East 68th St New York NY 10021

UPSHAW, DAWN, soprano; b. Nashville, Tenn., July 17, 1960. BA, Ill. Wesleyan Univ., 1982; MA, Manhattan Sch. Music, 1984; studied with Jan DeGaetani at Aspen, Colo., Music Sch. Recitalist, opera singer; sang in 1983 premiere performance, Sancta Susanna (Hindemith); with Met. Opera, 1985—; other appearances include Salzburg Festival, 1987, Aix-en-Provence, 1988-89; recordings include Ariadne auf. Naxos, Mass in G (Schubert), Knoxville Summer of 1915, The Girl With Orange Lips (songs for solo voice and chamber ensemble). Winner Young Concert Artist auditions; co-winner, Naumburg Competition, N.Y.C., 1985. Office: CAMI ARBIB Div 165 W 57th St New York NY 10019-2201 also: Electra Nonesuch c/o Electra Entertainment WEA 111 N Hollywood Way Burbank CA 91505

UPSHAW, GENE, sports association executive; b. Robstown, Tex., Aug. 15, 1945; s. Eugene and Cora (Riley) U.; 1 son, Eugene; m. Teresa Buich, 1986; 1 son, Justin. B.S., Tex. A&I U., 1968; postgrad., Calif. State U., 1969, Golden Gate U., 1980. Player Los Angeles (formerly Oakland) Raiders, 1967-82; player rep.-alt. NFL Players Assn., Oakland, Calif., 1970-76, mem. exec. com., 1976—, exec. dir., 1980—; ptnr. Gene Upshaw & Assocs., Mgmt. Cons. Firm, Oakland, 1970-78. Mem. Calif. Gov.'s Council Wellness and Phys. Fitness; mem. Calif. Bd. Govs. for Community Colls.; former planning commr. Alameda County, Calif., coordinator voter registration and fund raising. Served with U.S. Army, 1967-73. Named Offensive Lineman of Yr., Am. Football Conf., 1973, 74, 77; named Lineman of Yr., NFL, 1977, Pro Bowl selection 6 times, All Pro selection Sporting News, 1967-77, All Pro selection UPI, 1967-77, All Pro selection AP, 1967-77, All Pro selection TV Guide, 1967-77, All Pro selection Profl. Football Writers, 1967-77; mem. NFL Championship Team, 1976, 1980; recipient Byron (Whizzer) White Humanitarian award NFL Players Assn., 1980, A. Philip Randolph A. Philip Randolph Inst., 1982. Mem. Alpha Phi Alpha. Democrat. Baptist. Office: Fedn Professional Athletes 2021 L St NW Fl 6 Washington DC 20036-4909

UPSHAW, HARRY STEPHAN, psychology educator; b. Birmingham, Ala., July 10, 1926; s. N.H. and Florence (Arnold) U.; m. Paula Binyon, June 18, 1950; children: Alan Binyon, Phyllis, David Arnold, Stephan Lipner. Student, U. Ala., 1946-47; A.B., U. Chgo., 1949; M.A., Northwestern U., 1951; Ph.D., U. N.C., 1956. Asst prof. psychology U. Ala., 1954-57; spl. instr. psychology Simmons Coll., Boston, 1957-58; research asso. Ednl. Research Corp., Cambridge, Mass., 1957-58; asst. prof., then assoc. prof. pub. health U. N.C., 1958-61, lectr., assoc. prof. psychology, 1958-64, rsch. prof. psychology, 1991—; assoc. prof. Bryn Mawr (Pa.) Coll., 1964-65; assoc. prof., then prof. emeritus psychology U. Ill., Chgo., 1965-91, prof. emeritus, 1991—, dept. head, 1968-72; assoc. dir. Office of Social Sci. Rsch., 1981-87; guest prof. U. Mannheim, Germany, 1975, Fulbright scholar Technische Universitaet Berlin, 1978-79; vis. scholar Inst. for Rsch. in Social Sci., U. N.C., 1991-92. Editorial cons., Jour. Exptl. Social Psychology, Research in Personality, Jour. Applied Social Psychology, Jour. Personality Social Psychology; Contbr. articles to profl. jours. Served with AUS, 1944-46. Fellow Am. Psychol. Assn., Soc. Exptl. Social Psychol. Home: 209 Kirkwood Dr Chapel Hill NC 27514-5136

UPSHAW, LISA GAYE, business computer systems analyst; b. Alamogordo, N.Mex., June 27, 1959; d. James Leroy Upshaw and Margaret (Shackelford) Carrell; m. Michael J. Zamora, Nov. 3, 1976 (div. July 1983); 1 child, Jeremy Brandon; m. Eddie Gonzalez, Mar. 19, 1984 (div. 1989). BS in Bus. Computer Systems, U. N.Mex., 1983. Govt. and large account system analyst Office Systems, Alburquerque, 1982-84; sr. system analyst, nat. accounts mgr. Bell Atlantic/CompuShop, Houston, 1984-89; nat. account mgr. CompuCom Systems, Inc., Houston, 1988—, mem. president's coun., 1988-89; br. mgr. CompuCom Systems, Inc., Atlanta, 1990-93, nat. sales mgt., 1993—; cons. Bell Atlantic President's Club, Dallas, 1986-87, 88, Bell Atlantic Leaders Club, 1986-89. Chmn. publicity Ronald McDonald House, Alburquerque, 1982, chairwoman spl. events, 1983; chairwoman Rep. Vol. Community, Houston, 1986; sponsor Houston Ballet, Theatre of Arts, Fundraising Heart Assn. Mem. NAFE (network dir. 1987-88), Assn. Info. System Profls., Houston Area League Personal Computer Specialists, NOW, VFW, CompuCom Leaders Club. Avocations: tennis, golf, traveling, ballet. Home: 3551 Robinson Rd Marietta GA 30068-2445

UPSON, DONALD V., financial executive; b. Hutchinson, Kans., Feb. 8, 1934; s. William Ernest and Luella Beatrice (Hutchison) U.; m. Janis Carol Anderson, Sept. 16, 1956; children: Mark Steven, Brent William. B.S., Kans. State U., 1956. C.P.A. With Peat, Marwick, Mitchell & Co., 1956, 60-81, ptnr., 1974-81; exec. v.p., dir. internal audit Del E. Webb Corp., Phoenix, 1981-85; mgr. info. systems Tiernay Turbines Inc., Phoenix, 1986; chief fin. officer Schomac Corp., Tucson, 1986-88; adminstr. U. Ariz., Tucson, 1988-90; pres., chief exec. officer Ariz. Commerce Bank, Tucson, 1990-91; chief fin. officer O'Connor, Cavanagh, Anderson, Westover, Killingsworth & Beshears, P.A., Phoenix, 1991-94; fin. cons., 1995—. Pres. Community Orgn. for Drug Abuse, Alcohol and Mental Health Services, Inc., 1977-78; bd. dis. Phoenix council Boy Scouts Am., elder Presbyterian Ch. Served to lt. USAF, 1956-59. Mem. Am. Inst. C.P.A.s, Ariz. Soc. C.P.A.s, Beta Theta Pi (pres. 1955-56). Republican. Home and Office: 407 W Stacey Ln Tempe AZ 85284-3956

UPSON, STUART BARNARD, advertising agency executive; b. Cin., Apr. 14, 1925; s. Mark and Alice (Barnard) U.; m. Barbara Jussen, Nov. 2, 1946; children: Marguerite Nichols, Anne Marcus, Stuart Barnard. BS, Yale U., 1945. With Dancer, Fitzgerald, Sample, Inc., N.Y.C., 1946—, sr. v.p., 1963-66, exec. v.p., 1966-67, pres., 1967-74, chmn., 1974-86; chmn. DFS-Dorland, N.Y.C., 1986-87, Saatchi & Saatchi Advt. Inc., N.Y.C., 1987—; bd. dirs. Manhattan Life Ins. Co. Bd. dirs. Fresh Air Fund, N.Y., Advt. Coun. With USNR, 1943-46. Mem. St. Elmo Soc. Clubs: Wee Burn Country (Darien); Sky (N.Y.C.); Blind Brook, Pine Valley Golf. Home: 16 Wrenfield Ln Darien CT 06820-2201 Office: Saatchi & Saatchi Advt Inc 375 Hudson St New York NY 10014-3658

UPSON, THOMAS FISHER, state legislator, lawyer; b. Waterbury, Conn., Sept. 30, 1941; s. J. Warren and Grace (Fisher) U.; m. Barbara Secor (div. Jan. 1979); children: Secor, Chauncey Julius. BA in History, Washington and Jefferson Coll., 1963; LLB, U. Conn., 1968. Bar: Conn., 1969, U.S. Dist. Ct. (2d dist.), 1969. Lawyer Upson & Secor, Waterbury, 1969-70, 74-76; lawyer, spl. asst. U.S. Dept. Commerce, Washington, 1970-72; lawyer, spl. asst. to adminstr. GSA, Washington, 1973-74; dir. admissions St. Margaret's McTernan Sch., Waterbury, 1977-78; with div. spl. revenue State of Conn., Hartford, 1978-82; assoc. Moynahan & Ruskin, Waterbury, 1979-8l; pvt. practice Upson & Daly, Waterbury, 1981—; mem. Conn. Senate, Hartford, 1985—, dep. majority leader, chmn. jud. com., 1995—. Moderator 1st Congl. Ch., Waterbury, 1986-91; bd. dirs. Easter Seals-United Way, Waterbury, 1984-88; mem. Conn. Rep. Ctrl. com., 1983-91; dir. Mattatuck Mus., 1993—. Mem. ABA, Conn. Bar Assn., Waterbury Bar Assn., SAR, Soc. Colonial Wars, Phi Gamma Delta. Republican. Congregationalist. Lodge: Kiwanis (former pres., lt. gov. SW New Eng. dist.), Elks. Avocations; hiking, music, history. Home: 10-1 827 Oronoke Rd Waterbury CT 06708-3940 Office: Conn Senate Capitol Bldg Hartford CT 06106 also: 52 Holmes Ave Waterbury CT 06710-2412

UPTON, ARTHUR CANFIELD, experimental pathologist, educator; b. Ann Arbor, Mich., Feb. 27, 1923; s. Herbert Hawkes and Ellen (Canfield) U.; m. Elizabeth Bache Perry, Mar. 1, 1946; children: Rebecca A., Melissa P., Bradley C. Grad., Phillips Acad., Andover, Mass., 1941; BA, U. Mich., 1944, MD, 1946. Intern Univ. Hosp., Ann Arbor, 1947; resident Univ. Hosp., 1948-49; instr. pathology U. Mich. Med. Sch., 1950-51; pathologist Oak Ridge (Tenn.) Nat. Lab., 1951-54, chief pathology-physiology sect., 1954-69; prof. pathology SUNY Med. Sch. at Stony Brook, 1969-77, chmn. dept. pathology, 1969-70, dean Sch. Basic Health Scis., 1970-75; dir. Nat. Cancer Inst., Bethesda, Md., 1977-79; prof., chmn. dept. environ. medicine NYU Med. Sch., N.Y.C., 1980-92, prof. emeritus, 1993—; clin. prof. radiology U. N.Mex. Sch. Medicine, 1993—; clin. prof. environ. and cmty. medicine U. Medicine and Dentistry N.J.-Robert Wood Johnson Med. Sch., 1995—; attending pathologist Brookhaven Nat. Lab., 1969-77; dir. Inst. Environ. Medicine, Med. Sch., NYU, 1980-91; mem. various coms. nat. and internat. orgns.; lectr. in field. Assoc. editor: Cancer Research; mem. editorial bd.: Internat. Union Against Cancer. Served with AUS, 1943-46. Recipient Ernest Orlando Lawrence award for atomic field, 1965, Comfort-Crookshank award for cancer rsch. Inst. Med., NAS, 1979, Claude M. Fuess award 1980, Sarah L. Poilley award for pub. health, 1983, CHUMS Physician of Yr. award 1985, Basic Cell Rsch. in Cytology Lectureship award 1985, Fred W. Stewart award, 1986, Ramazzini award, 1986, Lovelace Med. Found. award, 1993; Sigma Xi nat. lectr., 1989-91. Fellow Soc. Risk Analysis, N.Y. Acad. Sci.; mem. Am. Assn. Pathologists and Bacteriologists, Internat. Acad. Pathology, Inst. Medicine NAS, Radiation Rsch. Soc. (councilor 1963-64, pres. 1965-66), Internat. Assn. Radiation Rsch. (pres.

1983-87), Am. Assn. Cancer Rsch. (pres. 1963-64), Am. Soc. Exptl. Pathology (pres. 1967-68), AAAS, Gerontol. Soc., Sci. Rsch. Soc. Am., Soc. Exptl. Biology and Medicine, Peruvian Oncology Soc. (hon.), Japan Cancer Assn. (hon.), N.Y. State Health Rsch. Coun. (chmn. 1982-90), Internat. Assn. Radiation Rsch. (pres. 1983-87), Assn. Univ. Environ. Health Sci. Ctrs. (pres. 1982-90), Ramazzini Inst. (pres. 1992—), Phi Beta Kappa, Phi Gamma Delta, Alpha Omega Alpha, Nu Sigma Nu, Sigma Xi. Achievements include research on pathology of radiation injury and endocrine glands, on cancer, on carcinogenesis, on experimental leukemia, on aging. Home: Apt 12B 401 E 86th St New York NY 10028 Office: 681 Freylinghuysen Rd Piscataway NJ 08855-1179

UPTON, ARTHUR EDWARD, lawyer; b. N.Y.C., Aug. 30, 1934; s. Arthur Joseph and Helene Clara (Heblich) U.; m. Patricia Ann Fleming, Aug. 17, 1957; children: Kevin, Brian, Kerry, Maureen. BS in Acctg., Fordham U., 1956; JD, St. John's U., N.Y.C., 1965. Bar: N.Y. 1967, U.S. Dist. Ct. (ea. and so. dist.) 1967, U.S. Tax Ct. 1967. Pvt. practice Syosset, N.Y., 1974-82, 87-91; ptnr. Golden, Upton & Wexler, Lynbrook, N.Y., 1982-87; sr. ptnr. Upton, Cohen & Slamowitz, Syosset, 1991—. Bd. dirs. St. Mary's Children and Family Ctr., Syosset, 1993—; bd. overseers Lynn U., Boca Raton, Fla., 1994—. Mem. ABA, N.Y. State Bar Assn., Nassau County Bar Assn., K.C. (past grand knight). Republican. Roman Catholic. Avocations: theatre, reading, travel, sports. Home: 4 Hunt Dr Jericho NY 11753-1142 Office: Upton Cohen Slamowitz 485 Underhill Blvd Syosset NY 11791-3434

UPTON, FREDERICK STEPHEN, congressman; b. St. Joseph, Mich., Apr. 23, 1953; s. Stephen E. and Elizabeth Brooks (Vial) U.; m. Amey Richmond Rulon-Miller, Nov. 5, 1983; 2 children. BA in Journalism, U. Mich., 1975. Staff asst. to Congressman David A. Stockman, Washington, 1976-81; legis. asst. Office Mgmt. and Budget, Washington, 1981-83, dep. dir. legis. affairs, 1983-84, dir. legis. affairs, 1984-85; mem. 100th-104th Congresses from 4th (now 6th) Mich. dist., Washington, 1986—; mem. commerce com. Field mgr. Stockman for Congress, St. Joseph, 1975; campaign mgr. Globensky for Congress, St. Joseph, 1981. Republican. Office: US House of Reps 2333 Rayburn Bldg Washington DC 20515*

UPTON, HOWARD B., JR., management writer, lawyer; b. Tahlequah, Okla., May 17, 1922; s. Howard B. and Marjorie (Ross) U.; m. Jean Devereaux, June 14, 1945; children—Pamela, Barbara, Martha, Brian. BA, U. Okla., 1943, LLB, 1948. Cert. assn. exec. Dir. indsl. relations Western Petroleum Refiners Assn., Tulsa, 1948-51; exec. v.p. Petroleum Equipment Inst., Tulsa, 1951-87; dir. Telex Corp., Tulsa, 1972-88; mgmt. columnist Inflight Mag. of Southwest Airlines, 1988-93; lectr. dept. engring. profl. devel. U. Wis., 1988—, U. Alaska, Fairbanks, 1991—. Frequent contbr. to Wall St. Jour. Dir. Tulsa Zoo Friends, Inc., 1993—. Mem. Am. Soc. Assn. Execs. (bd. dirs. 1964-68, Gold Circle award 1977, 82), Okla. Bar Assn., Mens Forum of Tulsa. Republican. Home: 5133 E 25th Ct Tulsa OK 74114-3749 Office: Upton Comm PO Box 4634 Tulsa OK 74159-0634

UPTON, KATHRYN ANN, emergency trauma nurse; b. Ft. Smith, Ark., Dec. 13, 1955; d. William A. and Kathryn (Derrickson) U. BSN, U. Tex., Arlington, 1986. Cert. CEN, ACLS, BLS, PALS, trauma nurse core certification. Commd. ensign USN, 1987-89, advanced through grades to lt., 1989-90; staff nurse med.-surg. USN San Diego Balboa, 1987-88, relief charge/staff emergency rm., 1988-90; staff nurse neonatal ICU USN Bethesda (Md.) Nat. Naval Med. Ctr., 1990-91; staff nurse burn ICU/emergency rm. USNS Comfort-Persian Gulf, 1990-91; asst. charge nurse USN Nat. Naval Med. Ctr., Bethesda, 1991-92; ret. USN, Ft. Lauderdale, Fla., 1992; trauma nurse Broward Gen. Trauma Ctr., Ft. Lauderdale, Fla., 1992-94; nurse mgr. ambulatory care Miami Vets. Adminstn. Hosp., Miami, 1994—. Decorated Meritorious Unit Commendation, Navy Commendation medal, Nat. Def. medal, SW Asia medal, Kuwait Liberation medal, Sea Svc. medal, Combat Action ribbon, Battle "E" ribbon. Avocations: teaching adults reading, swimming, interior design.

UPTON, LORRAINE FRANCES, elementary education educator; b. Balt., Dec. 26, 1947; d. Meyer and Adeline (Kanstor) Cohen; m. Michael K. Upton, Sept. 25, 1970; 1 child, Matthew Colin. BS, Boston U., 1969; MEd, Temple U., 1974. Cert. elem. tchr., reading specialist, Pa. VISTA employee Brighton, Mass., 1968; tchr. Boston Pub. Sch. Dist., 1969-70, tchr. 3d grade, 1971-94; tchr. 4th grade Neshaminy Sch. Dist., Langhorne, Pa., 1995—; instr. The Learning Mag., The Reading Teaching. Contbr. articles to profl. jours. Active social outreach programs; minority inspector during polit. elections, Yardley, Pa.; instr. Learning Mag., The Reading Tchr. Recipient Gift of Time tribute Am. Family Inst. Pa., 1992; Harold C. Case scholar Boston U., 1969. Mem. Internat. Reading Assn., Internat. Platform Assn. Home: 5 Beechwood Ln Yardley PA 19067 Office: Samuel Everett Elem Sch Forsythia Dr Levittown PA 19056

UPTON, RICHARD THOMAS, artist; b. Hartford, Conn., May 26, 1931; s. Ray Granville and Helen Marie (Colla) U.; 1 son, Richard Thomas, II. BFA, U. Conn., 1960; MFA, Ind. U., 1963. Artist-in-residence Artists for the Environ., Del. Water Gap, 1972, UGA Program Abroad, Corona, Italy, 1982-85. Exhbns. include E'stampe Contemporaine, Galerie Mansart, Bibliot Nat., France, 1969, 74, L'estampe aujourd'hui, 1973-78, Sala Internat., Palacio de Bellas Artes, Mexico City, 1969, Sept. Graveures un Sculpteur de Medailles, Mus. Deonon, Chalon-Sur Saone, France, 1973, Brit. Internat. Print Biennale, U.S. sect. touring Eng., 1973, Del. Water Gap, Corcoran Gallery Art, Washington, 1975, Everson Mus. Art, Syracuse, N.Y., 1975, Nat. Collection Prints and Poetry, Library of Congress, 1976-77, U. Ga., Palazzo Vignoti, Cortona, Italy, retrospective prints from, Atelier 17, Paris, 1977, Okla. Art Center, Oklahoma City, 1977, Tweed Mus. Art, Duluth, Minn., 1977, Weatherspoon Art Gallery, Greensboro, N.C., 1977, Chiesadi San Stae, Venice, Italy, 1989, Grey Gallery, N.Y.C., 1990, Everson Mus. of Art, Krannert Mus. Art, 1990—, Paysage Demoralise: Landscape at the End of the Century, Grey Art Gallery and Study Ctr., N.Y.C., 1990, Tuscany Rediscovered: Richard Upton at Cortona, Everson Mus. Art, Syracuse, 1991, Richard Upton: Italian Landscapes, Krannert Art Mus., Champaign, Ill., 1992, The Italian Landscapes: Richard Upton at Cortona, Mus. Am. Art, New Britain, Conn., 1992, Richard Upton: Ten Years of Italian Landscapes, James Michener Art Mus., Pa., 1994, Phila. Art Alliance, 1994, Condeso/Lawler Gallery, N.Y.C., 1995; represented in permanent collections Nat. Mus. of Am. Art at Smithsonian Instn., Mus. Modern Art, N.Y.C., Victoria and Albert Mus., London, Bibliot Nat., Paris, Montreal Mus. Fine Arts; commns. include Eros Thanatos Suite (German poem and woodcuts), Interlaken Corp., Providence, 1967, Salamovka Poster, Okla. Art Ctr., 1974, (with poems by Stanley Kunitz) River Road Suite, 1976; suite of drawing Robert Lowell at 66, 1977; suite of drawings Salmagundi mag. for humanities; The Anxious Landscape, paintings, drawings Bellarmine Coll., Louisville, 1989. With USNR, 1950-54. Recipient designer award Interlaken Corp., 1967; subject of monograph Richard Upton and the Rhetoric of Landscape, Paul Hayes Tucker, U. Mass., U. Wash. Press; fellow Fulbright Found., 1964, Ballinglen Arts Found., Ireland, 1994; grantee Nat. Endowment for Arts Artists for Environ., 1972, Richard Florsheim Fund, 1992; elected to Nat. Acad. of Design, 1995. Home: 113 Regent St Saratoga Springs NY 12866-4323 Office: Skidmore Coll Art Dept Saratoga Springs NY 12866

URAKAMI, AKIO, manufacturing company executive; b. Tokyo, Apr. 17, 1942; came to U.S., 1991; s. Yutaka and Tomiko (Nagai) U.; m. Keiko Tanaka, Feb. 7, 1971; children: Yuji, Masako, Kota. BS, Tokyo Inst. Tech., 1965; MS, Northwestern U., 1967, PhD, 1970. Rsch. engr. Ryobi Ltd., Hiroshima, Japan, 1970-72, corp. planning mgr., 1972-76, v.p. internat., 1976-84, exec. v.p., 1984-91; chmn., pres. Ryobi N.Am., Inc., Easley, S.C., 1991—; mem. pres.'s adv. coun. Clemson (S.C.) u., 1992—. Trustee The Urakami Found., Hiroshima, 1978—; bd. dirs. Japan Am. Assn. of We. S.C., Greenville, 1992—. Mem. Keizai Doyu Kai. Office: Ryobi NAm Inc PO Box 1947 101 Grace Dr Easley SC 29641-1947

URAL, OKTAY, civil engineering educator. BA in Math., Trinity U., 1956; BS in Civil Engring., Tex. A&M U.; MSCE, U. Tenn., 1959; PhD in Civil Engring., N.C. State U., 1964; BSCE, 1958. Asst. prof. U. Mo., Rolla, 1967-69, assoc. prof., 1969-73, prof., 1973, founding dir. Inst. for Interdisciplinary Housing Studies; prof. Fla. Internat. U., Miami, 1973—, founding dir. constrn. div. Coll. Engring. and Applied Scis., dir. Inst. Housing and Bldg.; lectr. various univs.; chmn., dir., 30 nat. and internat. confs.; bd. dirs. Internat. Found. Earth Constrn., Internat. Coun. Bldg. Rsch. Studies and Documentation, Rotterdam, The Netherlands, 1978-80; mem. sci. adv. panel UN Disaster Relief Orgn.; pres. Turkish Housing Authorit, advisor to prime min. Turkish Republic, 1990-92. Author: Matrix Operations and Use of Computers in Structural Engineering, 1971, Finite Element Method: Basic Concepts and Applications, 1973, A Systematic Approach to Basic Utilities in Developing Countries, 1974, Construction of Lower-Cost Housing, 1980; editor-in-chief Internat. Jour. Housing Sci. and Its Applications, 1977—; editor 22 vols. of sci. congress procs.; contbr. articles to profl. jours. Grantee HUD, Washington, Com. on Banking and Currency, U.S. Ho. of Reps., NSF, Fla. Power and Light Co., Fla. Internat. U. Found., Inc., Dept. Edn., State Fla.; recipient Medail de Vermeil for Experts, Govt. France. Fellow ASCE (chmn. structures com. on electronic computation edn. com., urban planning and devel. div. housing com., control group, Harland Bartholomew award); mem. Internat. Assn. Housing Sci. (pres.), Am. Soc. Engring. Edn. (internat. com.), Sigma Xi, Tau Beta Pi, Phi Kappa Phi, Chi Epsilon. Home: 3608 Anderson Rd Coral Gables FL 33134-7053 Office: Fla Internat U Internat Inst Housing & Bldg Civil Engring Dept Miami FL 33199

URAM, GERALD ROBERT, lawyer; b. Newark, July 11, 1941; s. Arthur George and Mildred (Stein) U.; m. Melissa Gordon, May 27, 1995; children: Michael, Alison, Carolyn Gordon Lewis. BA, Dartmouth Coll., 1963; LLB, Yale U., 1967. Bar: N.Y. 1967. Assoc. Paul, Weiss, Rifkind, Wharton & Garrison, N.Y.C., 1967-74; v.p., corp. counsel Prudential Bldg. Maintenance Corp., N.Y.C., 1974; ptnr. Davis & Gilbert, N.Y.C., 1974—; lectr. N.Y. Law Sch. Bd. dirs. St. Francis Friends of Poor, Inc. Mem. ABA, N.Y. State Bar Assn., Assn. Bar City of N.Y. Contbr. to profl. publs. Office: 1740 Broadway Fl 3 New York NY 10019-4315

URATO, BARBRA CASALE, entrepreneur; b. Newark, Oct. 10, 1941; d. Dominick Anthony and Concetta (Castrichini) Casale; m. John Joseph Urato, June 20, 1965; children: Concetta U. Graves, Gina E., Joseph D. Student, Seton Hall U., 1961-63. File clk. Martin Gelber Esquire, Newark, 1956-58; policy typist Aetna Casualty Ins., Newark, 1959-61; sec. to dean Seton Hall U., South Orange, N.J., 1961-63; paralegal sec. Judge Robert A. McKinley, Newark, 1963-65, Joseph Garrubbo, Esquire, Newark, 1965-66; office mgr. Valiant I.M.C., Hackensack, N.J., 1971-73; asst. pers. mgr. Degussa Inc., Teterboro, N.J., 1975-78; night mgr. The Ferryboat Restaurant, River Edge, N.J., 1976-78; mgr. Fratello's and Ventilini's, Hilton Head, S.C., 1978-80; day mgr. Ramada Inn Restaurant, Paramus, N.J., 1980-81; mgr. Gottlieb's Bakery, Hilton Head, 1982-83; asst. mgr. closing dept. Hilton Head Mortgage Co., 1983-84; owner, mgr. All Cleaning Svc., Hilton Head, 1984—; owner Hilton Head Investigations, 1990-93, Hilton Head Island, 1990-92; owner Aaction Investigators, 1992-94. Mem. NAFE, Profl. Women of Hilton Head, Assn. for Rsch. and Enlightenment, Rosicrucian Order. Roman Catholic. Avocations: metaphysics, music, gardening, dancing. Office: PO Box 4953 Hilton Head Island SC 29938

URBACH, FREDERICK, physician, educator; b. Vienna, Austria, Sept. 6, 1922; s. Erich and Josepha (Kronstein) U.; m. Nancy Ann Phillips, Dec. 20, 1952; children: Erich J., Gregory M., Andrew D. AB cum laude, U. Pa., 1943; MD, Jefferson Med. Coll., 1946; MD (hon.), U. Göttingen, Fed. Republic Germany, 1987. Diplomate: Am. Bd. Dermatology. Intern Jefferson Hosp., 1946-47; fellow in dermatology U. Pa. Hosp., 1949-52; fellow pediatric dermatology Children's Hosp., Phila., 1950-52; asst. vis. physician Phila. Gen. Hosp., Skin and Cancer Hosp., U. Pa. Hosp., 1952-54; assoc. chief cancer research (dermatology) Roswell Park Meml. Inst., Buffalo, 1954-55, chief cancer research (dermatology), 1955-58; asst. med. dir. Skin and Cancer Hosp. Phila., 1958-67, med. dir., 1967-88; research prof. physiology U. Buffalo Grad. Sch., 1955-58; assoc. prof. dermatology Temple U. Sch. Medicine, 1958-60, prof. research dermatology, 1960-67, chmn. dept. dermatology, 1967-88; dir. Ctr. for Photobiology, 1977-89, prof. dermatology emeritus, 1989—; dep. dir. Health Rsch. Inc., Buffalo, 1954-58; mem. U.S. nat. com. photo-biology Nat. Acad. Sci., 1973-80. Author: The Biology of Cutaneous Cancer, 1963, The Biologic Effects of Ultraviolet Radiation, 1969, (with Parrish, Anderson and Pitts) UVA, 1978; (with Gange) Biologic Effects of UVA Radiation, 1985, Responses to UVA Radiation, 1992; contbr. articles to profl. jours. Served with AUS, 1943-46; with USAAF, 1947-49. Recipient Ritter Meml. medal German Dermatology Soc., 1980. Fellow AAAS, N.Y. Acad. Sci.; mem. AMA, ACP, FACP, Am. Soc. Photobiology (councilor 1973-76, pres. 1977), Am. Assn. Cancer Rsch. Soc. Exptl. Biology and Medicine, Internat. Soc. Tropical Dermatology, Internat. Assn. Photobiology (v.p. 1976-79, pres. 1980-84, Finsen medal 1992); hon. mem. Danish Soc. Dermatology, Swedish Soc. Dermatology (Hellerstoöm medal 1977), Polish Soc. Dermatology, Austrian Soc. Dermatology, German Soc. Dermatology, Philippine Soc. Dermatology. Research epidemiology of cancer, photobiology, phototherapy. Home: 438 Clairemont Rd Villanova PA 19085-1706 Office: Temple Med Practices 220 Commerce Dr Fort Washington PA 19034-2404

URBAN, CARLYLE WOODROW, retired lawyer; b. Beverly, Kans., Dec. 14, 1914; s. Joseph William and Anna Bell (Murphy) U.; m. Lois Ball, June 10, 1946 (dec. Mar. 1987); children: Elizabeth Anne Urban Alexander, Michael Joseph; m. Zara Walker, Feb. 11, 1989. Student, Kans. Wesleyan U., 1931-33; LL.B., U. Tex., Austin, 1941. Bar: Tex. 1941. Practiced in Austin, 1941-42, Houston, 1944-86; assoc. firm Powell, Wirtz, Rauhut & Gideon, Austin, 1941-42; partner firms Elledge, Urban & Bruce, Houston, 1944-62, Urban & Coolidge, Houston, 1963-85. Scoutmaster Sam Houston Area council Boy Scouts Am., 1959-61; Precinct committeeman Harris County (Tex.) Democratic Exec. Com., 1957-63. Served with USAAF, 1942-44. Mem. Order of Coif, Delta Theta Phi. Methodist (trustee, chmn. bd. trustees dist. conf.). Lodge: Lion. Home: 1610 Stonegate Dr Cleburne TX 76031-4554 *Have we done our children any favor by making life easier for them than for us as parents? I think not. I fear we have done our children a disservice by depriving them of the "right to struggle". We have created an environment of leniency. Being required to suffer the consequences of failure has gone out of fashion. Even our courts have pursued a policy of leniency. If our system is to be preserved, I sincerely believe that greater respect must be given to personal self-discipline, pride in personal achievement and excellence of performance.*

URBAN, CATHLEEN ANDREA, graphic designer, software developer; b. Elizabeth, N.J., June 7, 1947; d. Emil Martin and Susan (Rahoche) Cupec; m. Walter Robert Urban, Nov. 5, 1966; children: Karen Louise, Kimberly Ann. Student, Rutgers U., 1965-66, 91-93; AS in Computer Info. Systems, Raritan Valley Community Coll., North Branch, N.J., 1990, AAS in Computer Programming, 1990. Office mgr. K-Mart Corp., Somerville, N.J., 1987-90; software developer Bell Communications Rsch., Piscataway, N.J., 1990-93, sys. tech. support cons., 1993-94; software developer Bell Comm. Rsch., Piscataway, 1994-96, software quality assurance tester, 1996—; graphic designer, owner CathiCards, Inc., Neshanic Station, N.J., 1995—. Leader Somerset County 4-H Program, Bridgewater, 1978-87. Mem. NAFE, AAUW, Nat. Space Soc., Internat. Platform Assn., Internat. Guild Candle Artisans, Golden Key Honor Soc., Phi Theta Kappa. Roman Catholic. Avocations: science fiction, reading, showing Siberian Huskies, candle making. Home: 570 Amwell Rd Neshanic Station NJ 08853-3404 Office: Bell Comm Rsch 444 Hoes Ln Piscataway NJ 08854-4104

URBAN, FRANK HENRY, retired dermatologist, state legislator; b. St. Louis, May 24, 1930; s. Frank and Helen Gertrude (Zingsheim) U.; m. Lois Elaine Thurwachter, June 18, 1954 (dec. 1991); children: James, Barbara, Michael, Mark, David, Bruce, John; m. Kathryn Calvert Bloomberg, Nov. 28, 1992. BS in Med. Sci., U. Wis., 1951, MD, 1954; MS, U. Minn., 1960. Diplomate Am. Bd. Dermatology. Intern Beaumont Army Hosp., El Paso, 1954-55; resident Mayo Clinic, Rochester, Minn., 1957-60; pvt. practice dermatology Wauwatosa, Wis., 1960-93; asst. clin. prof. Med. Coll. Wis., Wauwatosa, 1964—; mem. Wis. State Assembly, Madison, 1989—. Trustee Village Bd. of Elm Grove, Wis., 1985-87, pres., 1987-89; bd. dirs. ARC of Greater Milw.; pres. Friends U. Wis.-Milw. Sch. Edn., 1995—, bd. dirs.; hon. mem. Potawatomi coun. Boy Scouts Am., pres., 1974-76. Recipient Silver Beaver award East Cen. Region Boy Scouts Am., 1972, Silver Antelope award, 1979, Civic Leadership award State Med. Soc. Wis., 1990, Disting. Svc. award U. Wis. Med. Sch. Alumni Assn., 1991. Fellow Am. Acad. Dermatology; mem. Wis. Dermatol. Soc. (pres. 1969-70), Wis. State Med. Soc. (dir. 1987-92, 93—), Milw. County Med. Soc. (caucus chmn. 1987-92, pres.-elect 1992-93, pres. 1993-94), Brookfield C. of C. (Outstanding Mem. award 1992). Republican. Roman Catholic. Avocations: walking, photography, toy trains, music. Office: State Capitol PO Box 8953 Madison WI 53708-8953

URBAN, GILBERT WILLIAM, banker; b. Silver Lake, Minn., Oct. 20, 1928; s. William and Alice (Polak) U.; m. Elvera Mattson, Feb. 23, 1954; children: Lisa Alice Marie, Leann Kay. BBA, U. Minn., 1949. Sr. acct. Price Waterhouse and Co., Chgo., 1949-50; chief acct. Calif. Bank, L.A., 1950-51; asst. contr. 1st Nat. Bank, Mpls., 1951-63, contr., 1963-69; v.p., cashier La. Nat. Bank, Baton Rouge, 1969-73, v.p. assets and liabilities, 1973-86; sr. v.p. fin. policy Premier Bancorp Inc., Baton Rouge, 1986—; instr. evening sch. U. Minn., 1956-69, La. State U., 1970—, So. U., Baton Rouge, 1989—; instr. Nat. Assn. Bank Auditors and Contrs. Sch., U. Wis., 1960-63, sect. leader, 1963-69; chmn. dept. controllership Bank Adminstrn. Inst., 1970—; course coord. Banking Sch. of South, 1970, 79—. Mem. Beta Alpha Psi, Alpha Kappa Psi. Lutheran. Office: Premier Bank PO Box 1511 Baton Rouge LA 70821-1511

URBAN, GLEN L., management educator; b. Wausau, Wis., Apr. 15, 1940. BSME, U. Wis., 1963, MBA, 1964; PhD, Northwestern U., 1966. Asst. prof. MIT, Cambridge, Mass., 1966-70, assoc. prof., 1970-77, prof. mktg. and mgmt. sci., 1977—, Dai-Ichi Kangyo Bank prof. mgmt., 1987-93, dep. dean Sloan Sch. Mgmt., 1987-91, co-dir. Internat. Ctr. for Rsch. on Mgmt. of Tech., 1992-93, dean Sloan Sch. Mgmt., 1993—; co-founder Mgmt. Decision Systems, Inc., 1970, Mgmt. Sci. for Health, Inc., 1972, Mktg. Tech. Interface, Inc., 1991. Author: (with D.B. Montgomery) Management Science in Marketing, 1969, (with J.R. Hauser and N. Dholakia) Essentials of New Product Development, 1987, (with Steven H. Star) Advanced Marketing Stragety: Phenomena, Analysis and Decisions, 1991, Design and Marketing of New Products, 2d edit., 1993; mem. editl. bd. Mktg. Sci.; reviewer for Mgmt. Sci. (Best Paper award 1986), Jour. Mktg. Rsch. (O'Dell award 1983, 88), Ops. Rsch.; contbr. over 30 articles to profl. jours. Mem. Inst. Mgmt. Sci., Ops. Rsch. Soc. Am., Am. Mktg. Assn. (Converse award for Lifetime Achievements in Mktg. 1996). Office: MIT Sloan Sch Mgmt 50 Memorial Dr # E52 473 Cambridge MA 02142-1347

URBAN, HENRY ZELLER, newspaperman; b. Buffalo, July 11, 1920; s. George Pennock and Florence Lenhard (Zeller) U.; m. Ruth deMoss Wickwire, Apr. 28, 1948; children: Ruth Robinson Urban Smith, Florence de Moss Urban Hunn, Henry Zeller, Ward Wickwire. Grad., Hotchkiss Sch., 1939; B.S., Yale U., 1943. Treas. George Urban Milling Co., 1946-53; with Buffalo Eve. News, 1953—, asst. bus. mgr., 1957-62, bus. mgr., 1962-71, treas., dir., 1971-74, pres., pub., 1974-83; dir. G. F. Zellers Sons, Inc., 1948-53. Bd. dirs. Travelers Aid Soc., 1953-59, Buffalo Fine Arts Acad., 1960-63, 73-76, 82-85, 86-89, YMCA, 1955-68; trustee Elmwood-Franklin Sch., 1967-70; trustee Canisius Coll., 1977-83, bd. regents, 1972-78; adv. bd. Medaille Coll., 1968-83; chmn. parents council Hamilton Coll., 1977. Served to lt. USNR, 1942-46. Mem. Buffalo C. of C., N.Y. State Pubs. Assn. (dir. 1970-73, 76-79). Clubs: Mid-day (Buffalo), Tennis and Squash (Buffalo), Buffalo (Buffalo), Buffalo Country (Buffalo), Saturn (Buffalo), Pack (Buffalo); Sankaty Head (Nantucket); Nantucket Yacht. Home: 57 Tudor Pl Buffalo NY 14222-1615 Office: 1 News Plz Buffalo NY 14203-2930

URBAN, JAMES ARTHUR, lawyer; b. West Palm Beach, Fla., Feb. 18, 1927; s. Arthur Joseph and Elsie Elizabeth (Wespeaker) U.; m. Alice Burmah Steed, June 21, 1952; children: James Arthur, Katherine Elizabeth. A.B., Duke U., 1950; J.D. with high honors, U. Fla., 1953. Bar: Fla. 1953. Of counsel Carlton, Fields, Ward, Emmanuel, Smith, & Cutler (P.A.), Orlando, Fla.; dir. Fla. Legal Services, Inc., 1975-76. Bd. visitors Coll. Law Fla. State U., Tallahassee, 1973-79, mem. council advisers, 1975-79; mem. pres.'s council U. Fla., Gainesville, 1976-77; charter mem. Indsl. Devel. Commn. Mid-Fla., 1977—. Served with U.S. Army, 1945-47. Recipient Outstanding Alumnus award U. Fla. Law Rev. Alumni Assn., 1975. Fellow Am. Coll. Trust and Estate Counsel, Am. Coll. Real Estate Lawyers, Am. Bar Found.; mem. ABA (Ho. of Dels. 1976-80), Am. Law Inst., Fla. Bar Assn. (bd. dirs. 1975-84, pres. 1977-79), Nat. Conf. Bar Founds. (bd. dirs. 1979-90), Orlando C. of C. (bd. dirs. 1971-73), Phi Kappa Phi, Theta Chi. Episcopalian. Clubs: Rotary (Orlando), Citrus (Orlando), Univ., Country (Orlando). Home: 1614 Pepperidge Dr Orlando FL 32806-1524 Office: Carlton Fields Ward Emmanuel Smith & Cutler PA PO Box 1171 Orlando FL 32802-1171 also: 1601 CNA Tower Orlando FL 32801

URBAN, JOHN S., engineering company executive; b. Newark, July 1, 1933; s. John Urban and Julia (Ostenski) Cahoon; m. Janet Ann Scott, June 23, 1956; children: Debra Sue Urban Doolittle, John Stanley, Gregg Scott, Jeffrey Scott. BS in Civil Engring., N.J. Inst. Tech., 1956. Registered profl. engr., N.Y., N.J., Mass., Pa., Del., Ga. Jr. engr. Edwards & Kelcey, 1956-59, engr., 1959-61, sr. engr., 1961-65, prin. engr., 1965-69, with, 1969-71, asst. v.p., 1971-74, v.p., 1974-84, sr. v.p., 1984-88, exec. v.p., 1988-90, pres., CEO, 1990-94, chmn., 1994—. Mem. bd. overseers N.J. Inst. Tech. With Army, 1957. Fellow ASCE (mem. hwy. divsn. rsch. com., Robert Ridgeway award), Am. Consulting Engrs. Coun.; mem. Am. Rd. & Transp. Builders Assn. (planning and design divsn. dir.), Soc. Am. Mil. Engrs., N.Y. Assn. Consulting Engrs. (mem. transp. com.), N.J. Soc. Profl. Engrs., N.J. Alliance Action (bd. dirs.), N.J. C. of C. (mem. transp. com.), Consulting Engrs. Coun. N.J. (past pres.), Regional Plan Assn. (mem. N.J. com.), Internat. Bridge, Tunnel and Turnpike Assn. (mem. engring. design com.), Scotch Ball Assn., Basking Ridge Golf Club (pres.), Highlander Club (N.J. Inst. Tech., chmn.). Avocations: gardening, photography, golfing. Office: Edwards and Kelcey Inc Box 1936 299 Madison Ave Morristown NJ 07962

URBAN, JOSEPH JAROSLAV, engineer, consultant; b. Chocen, Czechoslovakia, Mar. 11, 1922; came to U.S., 1955; s. Josef and Ludmila (Moravcova) U.; children: Hedvika Urban Heinicke, Richard Bruce. Diploma in engring., U. Prague, Czechoslovakia, 1948; postgrad., U. Toronto, 1952-55. Registered profl. engr., Can. Mgr. Urban Mfg., Chocen, 1942-48; prof. Masaryk U., Nuernberg, Fed. Republic Gemany, 1951; designer C.A. Meadows Cons. Engrs., Toronto, 1952-55, Rondo Devel. Corp., Stamford, Conn., 1955-58; designer, chief engr., v.p. Huck Co. Inc. Engrs., Montvale, N.J., 1958-72, also bd. dirs.; pvt. practice cons. engr. Pleasantville, N.Y., 1972—; exec. cons. Crown Cork and Seal Co. Inc., Phila., 1972—. Designer various types of machines for U.S. govt. and U.S. industries-printing presses, book binding and can mfg. equipment; patentee in field. Recipient World War II decoration Field Marshall Alexander, 1945. Mem. Czechoslovakian Acad. Art and Sci., Moose, KC. Roman Catholic. Avocations: protection of wildlife, naturalist, painting, classical music, fine art collector.

URBAN, PATRICIA A., former elementary school educator; b. Chgo., Oct. 15, 1932; d. Clifford and Caroline (Viegi) Brocken; m. Francis C. Urban, Oct. 20, 1956; children: Jim, David, Anthony, Mary Joan, Barbara, Margaret, Judy, Sharon, Jennifer. BA, Rosary Coll., River Forest, Ill., 1954; MS in Edn., Chgo. State U., 1979; MEd, Loyola U., Chgo., 1986. Cert. tchr., reading tchr., Ill. Tchr. St. Joseph Ch. Sch., Summit, Ill., 1954-56; profl. reading tutor Loyola U., 1987-90; tchr. social studies and reading Dist. 104 Schs., Summit, 1974-94; ret., 1994. Named. Dist. 104 Tchr. of Yr., 1987. Mem. ASCD, Internat. Reading Assn., Am. Fedn. Tchrs., West Suburban Tchrs. Union, Alpha Upsilon Alpha. Home: 1019 Walter St Lemont IL 60439-3290

URBAN, RICHARD, newspaper editor. Metro editor Cleveland Plain Dealer. Office: Cleveland Plain Dealer 1801 Superior Ave E Cleveland OH 44114-2107

URBAN, STANLEY T., hospital administrator; b. Buffalo, Jan. 29, 1945; married. BA, Boston Coll., 1966; MBA, Xavier U., 1969. Adminstrv. resident Colo. Gen. Hosp., Denver, 1968-69; adminstr. Colo. Psychiatric Hosp., Denver, 1969-72; asst. dir. Colo. Gen. Hosp., Denver, 1972-73, assoc. dir., 1973-76; adminstr. Oreg. Health Scis. U. Hosp., Portland, Oreg., 1976-80; dep. adminstr. St. Vincent Hosp. and Med. Ctr., Portland, Oreg., 1980-85; sr. v.p. Franciscan Health System, Aston, Pa., 1985-90, exec. v.p., 1990-92; pres., CEO Sisters of Charity Health Care Systems, Houston, 1992—. Bd. dirs. Carondelet Health Sys.; chair bd. dirs. Meml./Sisters of Charity Heal h Network. Mem. Am. Coll. Healthcare Execs., Am. Hosp. Assn., Tex. Hosp. Assn., Catholic Health Assn. Home: 161 Grogans Point Rd The

Woodlands TX 77380-4605 Office: Sisters Charity Incarnate World Health Care System 2600 North Loop W Houston TX 77092-8916

URBAN, THOMAS NELSON, agricultural products company executive; b. 1934; married. MBA, Harvard U., 1960. Began at Pioneer Hi-Bred Internat., Inc., Des Moines, 1960, now chmn., pres., also bd. dirs.; mayor Des Moines, 1968-71. Office: Pioneer Hi-Bred Internat Inc 700 Capitol Sq Des Moines IA 50309-2331*

URBANETTI, JOHN SUTHERLAND, internist, consultant; b. Mineola, N.Y., Aug. 14, 1943; s. Anthony Joseph and Mildred S. U.; m. Linda J. Sample, July 16, 1978; children: Andrew, Alexis. AB, Johns Hopkins U., 1964, MD, 1967. Diplomate Am. Bd. Internal Medicine and Pulmonary Diseases. Internal medicine intern Johns Hopkins Hosp., Balt., 1967-68, internal medicine resident, 1968-69; fellow in pulmonary cardiology McGill U., Montreal, Can., 1971-74; asst. prof. medicine and dir. pulmonary lab. Tufts New Eng. Med. Ctr. Hosp., Boston, 1974-80; asst. prof. clin. medicine and pulmonary diseases Yale U., New Haven, Conn., 1980—; cons. toxic inhalation US Surgeon Gen., U.S. Army, USN, USAF, 1974—. Author: (books) Carbon Monoxide Poisoning, 1980, Pulmonary Management of Surgical Patients, 1982, Battlefield Chemical Inhalation, 1988; contbr. articles to profl. jours. Capt. USAF, 1969-71. Recipient Commdr's award for pub. svc. U.S. Army, 1990. Fellow Royal Coll. Physicians and Surgeons (Can.), Am. Coll. Physicians, Am. Coll. Chest Physicians; mem. Am. Thoracic Soc., Aerospace Medicine Soc. Avocation: swimming. Office: Southeastern Pulmonary Assocs 155 Montauk Ave New London CT 06320-4842

URBANIAK, JAMES RANDOLPH, orthopedic surgeon; b. Fairmont, W.Va., May 15, 1936; s. Cecil and Patricia (Morgan) U.; m. Martha Helen Shawger, Dec. 20, 1970; children: Julie Kathleen, Michael James. BS, U. Ky., 1958; MD, Duke U., 1962. Diplomate Am. Bd. Orthop. Surgery, Am. Bd. Hand Surgery. Intern Duke U., Durham, N.C., 1962-63; resident in orthopaedic surgery Duke U. Hosps., Durham, N.C., 1965-69; asst. prof. Div. Orthopaedic Surgery, Duke U., Durham, 1969-73, assoc. prof., 1973-77, prof., 1977—, chief, 1985—; chief orthopaedics VA Med. Ctr., Durham, 1969-76; dir. replantation team, orthopaedic research Duke U. Med. Ctr. Editor: Microsurgery, 1987; co-editor: AAOS Symposium Microsurgery, 1979; contbr. over 110 articles to profl. jours. and 30 chpts. to books. Served to lt. comdr. USN, 1963-65. Camp Orthopaedic Travel fellow, 1968, Am. Orthopaedic Assn. Travel fellow; named N.C. Physician of Yr., 1985; recipient Disting. Alumni award U. Ky., 1985. Mem. Am. Soc. Reconstructive Microsurgery (founder, pres. 1985), Am. Soc. for Surgery of Hand (sec. 1985—), Am. Bd. Orthopaedic Surgery (bd. dirs. 1985, pres.-elect. 1988—), Joint Com. of Surgery of Hand (chmn. exam. com. 1986), Am. Orthopaedic Assn., Am. Acad. Orthopaedic Surgeons, Eastern Orthopaedic Assn. (pres. 1981), Phi Beta Kappa, Alpha Omega Alpha. Avocations: golf, skiing, sports. Home: 2600 Vintage Hill Ct Durham NC 27712-9492 Office: Duke U Med Ctr Box 2912 Durham NC 27710*

URBANIK, THOMAS, II, research civil engineer; b. Oceanside, N.Y., Feb. 15, 1946; s. John George and Helen Rita (Waterhouse) U.; m. Cynthia Ellen Myers, Feb. 23, 1948; children: Michael T., Steven J. BS, N.Y. State Coll. Forestry, 1968; BSCE, Syracuse U., 1969; MSCE, Purdue U., 1971; PhD, Tex. A&M U., 1982. Registered profl. engr., Mich., Tex. Traffic engr. City of Ann Arbor (Mich.), 1971-76; rsch. engr. Tex. A&M U., College Station, 1977—; cons. Battelle Pacific N.W. Labs., Richland, Wash., 1987—, Fed. Hwy. Adminstrn., Washington; mem. steering com. on advanced traffic mgmt. sys. Intelligent Transp. Soc. Am. Mem. ASCE, Inst. Transp. Engrs., Transp. Rsch. Bd. (assoc.). Republican. Lutheran. Office: Tex A&M U Tex Transp Inst College Station TX 77843

URBANOWSKI, FRANK, publishing company executive; b. Balt., Mar. 5, 1936; s. Frank and Tofilla (Jakubik) U.; m. Julia Blocksman; children: Alexandra, Tasha. B.S. in Ceramic Engring., Va. Poly. Inst.; postgrad., Columbia U. Rep. Ronald Press, 1960-61; editor coll. dept. Macmillan Co., 1961-66; editorial dir. Glencoe Press, 1966-68, v.p., 1968-72, pub., 1972-73; dir. market planning Ednl. Testing Service, 1973-75; dir. Mass. Inst. Tech. Press, Cambridge, 1975—; chmn. exec. council Profl. Scholarly Publs. div., 1979-81; bd. dirs. Cambridge Insight Meditation Ctr., 1985—. Mem. Am. Assn. Pubs. (dir. 1979-81), Assn. Am. Univ. Press (dir. 1979-81, pres. 1990-91), Cambridge Boat Club. Home: 129 Franklin St Cambridge MA 02139 also: Mountain Rd Cornwall VT 05753 Office: MIT Press 55 Hayward St Cambridge MA 02142-1315

URBIK, JEROME ANTHONY, financial consultant; b. Chgo., Oct. 30, 1929; s. Anthony Frank and Sophie Elizabeth (Stripeikis) U.; m. Barbara Jean Chamernik, Sept. 1956; children: Laura M. Kern, Michael A., Anthony J., Mary L. King, John T., Maria M. BA in Philosophy, St. Mary's Coll., Techny, Ill., 1953; CLU degree, Am. Coll., 1970, ChFC degree, 1979. CLU, Chartered Fin. Cons. Field underwriter MONY Fin. Svcs., Chgo., 1955-59; merchandising specialist Mut. of N.Y., N.Y.C., 1959; pvt. practice brokerage cons. Northfield, Ill., 1960-64; CEO Hinsdale (Ill.) Assocs. Fin. Svcs. Corp., 1964—; v.p. Interstate Coll. Personology, San Diego, 1982-87; pres. Gen. Agts. Mgrs. Conf., 1967-68. Mem. publ. com. Crisis mag., Washington, 1989—; contbr. articles on industry to profl. jours.; mem. editl. bd. Leaders mag., 1981-90. Mem. adv. coun. Congressman Henry Hyde, Nat. Rep. Com., Washington; mem. Small Bus. Devel. Ctr. exec. bd. advisors Lewis U., Lockport, Ill., 1987-90; exec. coord. Legatus (Cath. CEO) Bd. dirs. United Rep. Fund, 1987-92; bd. advisors Am. Life League, Washington; bd. dirs. Nat. Coalition Reps. for Life. Named Small Bus. Acct. of Yr. for State of Ill. SBA, 1987. Mem. Am. Soc. CLUs, Am. Life League (bd. advisers), Chgo. Orchestral Assn., Chgo. Lyric Opera. Roman Catholic. Avocations: reading, writing, power boating, classical music. Home: 474 South St Elmhurst IL 60126-4120 Office: Hinsdale Assoc Fin Svc Corp 15 Spinning Wheel Dr # 414 Hinsdale IL 60521-3541

URBINA, MANUEL, II, legal research historian, history educator; b. Rodriguez, Nuevo Leon, Mex., Sept. 23, 1939; came to U.S., 1947; s. Manuel and Irene (Salce) de Urbina. BA, Howard Payne Coll., 1962; postgrad., Nat. Autonoma U. Mex., Mexico City, 1963-64; MA, U. Tex., 1967, PhD, 1976; postgrad., Cambridge (Eng.) U., 1982; JD, U. Houston, 1983. Prof. Latin Am. history Coll. of the Mainland, Texas City, Tex., 1967—; founder, curator Urbina Mus. History of Mex., Houston, 1990—; chmn., legal counsel Urbina Found., Houston, 1985—; chmn., CEO Urbina Pub. Co. Inc., Houston and Mexico City, 1985—. Editor, interviewer history videos, oral history interviews with participants in the Mexican Revolution. Founder Cinco de Mayo Assn., Galveston County, Tex., 1976; founder, faculty sponsor Mex. Am. Student Assn., Coll. of Mainlan, 1974—. Named Hispanic of Yr. Galveston County League of United Latin Am. Citizens, 1982; NEH grantee, 1971-72; U.S. Dept. State scholar diplomat, 1979. Mem. League of United Latin Am. Citizens, Tex. State Hist. Assn., Howard Payne U. Alumni Assn., U. Houston Law Alumni Assn., Interam. C. of C. Democrat. Baptist. Avocations: reading, research, travel, trumpet playing, volunteer work. Home: 889 Old Genoa Red Bluff Rd Houston TX 77034-4010 Office: Museo Urbina de Historia de Mexico 889 Old Genoa Red Bluff Rd Houston TX 77034-4010

URBOM, WARREN KEITH, federal judge; b. Atlanta, Nebr., Dec. 17, 1925; s. Clarence Andrew and Anna Myrl (Irelan) U.; m. Joyce Marie Crawford, Aug. 19, 1951; children: Kim Marie, Randall Crawford, Allison Lee, Joy Renee. AB with highest distinction, Nebr. Wesleyan U., 1950, LLD (hon.), 1984; JD with distinction, U. Mich., 1953. Bar: Nebr. 1953. Mem. firm Baylor, Evnen, Baylor, Urbom, & Curtiss, Lincoln, Nebr., 1953-70; judge U.S. Dist. Ct. Nebr., 1970—; chief judge U.S. Dist. Ct. Dist. Nebr., 1972-86, sr. judge, 1991—; mem. com. on practice and procedure Nebr. Supreme Ct., 1965-95; mem. subcom. on fed. jurisdiction Jud. Conf. U.S., 1975-83; adj. instr. trial advocacy U. Nebr. Coll. Law, 1979-90; bd. dirs. Fed. Jud. Ctr., 1982-86; chmn. com. on orientation newly apptd. dist. judges Fed. Jud. Ctr., 1986-89; mem. 8th Cir. Com. on Model Criminal and Civil Jury Instrns., 1983—; mem. adv. com. on alternative sentences U.S. Sentencing Com., 1989-91. Contbr. articles to profl. jours. Trustee St. Paul Sch. Theology, Kansas City, Mo., 1986-89; active United Methodist Ch. (bd. mgrs., bd. global ministries 1972-76, gen. com. on status and role of women, 1988—, gen. conf. 1972, 76, 80, 88, 92, 96); pres. Lincoln YMCA, 1965-67; bd. govs. Nebr. Wesleyan U., chmn. 1975-80. With AUS, 1944-46. Recipient Medal of Honor, Nebr. Wesleyan U. Alumni Assn., 1983. Fellow Am. Coll. Trial Lawyers; mem. ABA, Nebr. Bar Assn. (ho. of dels. 1966-70, Outstanding Legal Educator award 1990), Lincoln Bar Assn. (Liberty Bell award 1993, pres. 1968-69), Kiwanis (Disting. Svc. award 1993), Masons (33 deg.), Am. Inns of Ct. (Lewis F. Powell Jr. award for Professionalism and Ethics 1995). Methodist. Home: 4421 Ridgeview Dr Lincoln NE 68516-1516 Office: US Dist Ct 586 Fed Bldg 100 Centennial Mall N Lincoln NE 68508-3804

URCIUOLI, J. ARTHUR, investment executive; b. Syracuse, N.Y., Nov. 13, 1937; s. Joseph R. and Nicoletta Anne (Phillips) U.; m. Margaret Jane Forelli, Aug. 13, 1966; children: Karen Sloan, Christian J.A. B.S., St. Lawrence U., 1959; J.D., Georgetown U., 1966; grad. Advanced Mgmt. Program, Harvard Bus. Sch., 1982. Bar: N.Y. 1966. Atty. Brown, Wood, Fuller, Caldwell & Ivey, N.Y.C., 1966-69; internat. investment banker, dir. internat. fin. Merrill Lynch, N.Y.C., Paris, 1970-78; pres. Merrill Lynch Internat., 1978-82; chmn. Merrill Lynch Internat. Bank, London; dir. banking div. Merrill Lynch Capital Markets, 1980-84; dir. Merrill Lynch Bus. Fin. Services, Merrill Lynch Co., 1984-93; dir. mktg. group Merrill Lynch Pvt. Client, 1993—. Contbr. articles to profl. jours. Trustee St. Lawrence U., 1976-89, Bruce Mus., Greenwich, Conn., 1990-94; bd. dirs. United Way, Greenwich, 1978-81. Capt. USMC, 1959-63. Mem. Securities Assn. (chmn. sales and mktg. com. 1987-89), River Club (N.Y.C.), N.Y. Yacht Club, Riverside (Conn.) Yacht Club, Rocky Point Club (Old Greenwich, Conn.). Republican. Congregationalist. Clubs: River (N.Y.C.); N.Y. Yacht, Riverside (Conn.) Yacht; Rocky Point (Old Greenwich, Conn.). Office: Merrill Lynch 800 Scudders Mill Rd Plainsboro NJ 08536-1606

URDANG, ALEXANDRA, book publishing executive; b. N.Y.C., June 29, 1956; d. Laurence Urdang and Irena (Ehrlich) Urdang de Tour. BA in English Lit., U. Conn., 1977. Customer svc. and fulfillment mgr. Universe Books, N.Y.C., 1978-79, sales mgr., assoc. mktg. mgr., 1980-82; asst. v.p., dir. spl. sales Macmillan Pub. Co., N.Y.C., 1982-88; v.p. new markets Warner Books, Inc., N.Y.C., 1988—. Avocations: architecture, art, antiques. Office: Warner Books Inc Time and Life Bldg 1271 Avenue Of The Americas New York NY 10020

URDANG, LAURENCE, lexicographer, publisher; b. N.Y.C., Mar. 21, 1927; s. Harry Rudman and Annabel (Schafran) U.; m. Irena B. Ehrlich vel Sluszny, May 23, 1952 (div.); children: Nicole Severyn, Alexandra Stefanie. B.S., Columbia U., 1954, postgrad., 1954-58. Lectr. gen. linguistics NYU, 1956-61; assoc. editor dictionary dept. Funk & Wagnalls, Inc., N.Y.C., 1957; reference editor Random House, Inc., N.Y.C., 1957-61, dir. reference dept., 1962-69; pres. Laurence Urdang, Inc., Old Lyme, Conn. and Aylesbury, Eng., 1969—; chmn. bd. Laurence Urdang Assocs., Ltd., Aylesbury, 1969-78; editor Verbatim, Old Lyme and Aylesbury, 1974—. Compiler, editor, author numerous books; mng. editor: Random House Unabridged Dictionary, 1966; editor in chief: Random House College Dictionary, 1968, Random House Dictionary of Synonyms and Antonyms, 1960, N.Y. Times Everyday Reader's Dictionary of Misunderstood, Misused, Mispronounced Words, 1972, 2d edit., 1985, Editor, Verbatim, The Language Quar., 1974, Dictionary of Advertising Terms, 1977, Official Associated Press Almanac, 1976, Hammond Almanac, 1977, Picturesque Expressions, 1980, 2d edit., 1985, Illustrated Children's Dictionary, 1979, Basic Dictionary of Synonyms and Antonyms, 1979, 2d edit., 1986, The Synonym Finder, 1979, Collins English Dictionary, 1979, Verbatim: Vols. I, II, 1978, Vols. III, IV, V, VI and Index, 1981, -Ologies & -Isms, 1978, 81, 86, Twentieth Century American Nicknames, 1979, A Treasury of Biblical Quotations, 1980, The Timetables of American History, 1981, Mosby's Medical and Nursing Dictionary, 1983, Allusions, 1982, 86, Modifiers, 1982, Suffixes, 1982, Prefixes, 1984, Holidays and Anniversaries, 1985, Slogans, 1985, Mottoes, 1986, Numerical Allusions, 1986, Names and Nicknames of Places and Things, 1987, Loanwords Dictionary, 1987, The Whole Ball of Wax, 1988, The Dictionary of Confusable Words, 1988, A Fine Kettle of Fish, 1990, The Oxford Thesaurus, 1992, The Oxford Desk Dictionary, 1995, The Oxford Desk Thesaurus, 1995, Warner Dictionary, 1996, Warner Thesaurus, 1996. Served with USNR, 1944-45. Mem. Linguistic Soc. Am., Am. Name Soc., Am. Dialect Soc., Brit. Name Soc., Assn. Computational Linguistics, Dictionary Soc. N.Am., Soc. Indexers, Euralex. Clubs: Athenaeum, Naval (London); Century Assn.

URENECK, LOUIS ADAM, newspaper editor, newspaper executive; b. New Brunswick, N.J., Dec. 28, 1950; s. Eugene and Helen (Kallas) U.; m. Patricia Yeager, Nov. 1974; children: Elizabeth, Adam. BA, U. N.H., 1972. Reporter Providence Jour.-Bull., 1972-73; reporter Press Herald and Maine Sunday Telegram, Portland, 1974-75, copy editor, 1975-76, asst. city editor, 1976-82, mng. editor, 1982-87, asst. exec. editor, 1987-89, exec. editor, 1989-93; editor, v.p. Press Hearld and Maine Sunday Telegram, Portland, 1993—; tchr. U. So. Maine, Portland, summers 1993, 94, 95; editor-in-residence Nieman Found., Harvard U., 1994-95. Contbr. articles to profl. jours. Mem. alumni publs. com. U. N.H., Durham, 1991-96; founding mem. Maine Quality Ctr., Skowhegan, 1992. Mem. Am. Soc. Newspaper Editors (chmn. new media com. 1995-96), New Eng. Newspaper Assn. (chmn. editl. com. 1992—), New Eng. AP News Execs. Assn. (pres. 1985). Episcopalian. Avocations: outdoors activities. Home: 88 Lodman St Portland ME 04103 Office: The Portland Newspapers 390 Congress St Portland ME 04101

URENOVITCH, JOSEPH VICTOR, chemical company executive; b. Freeland, Pa., Nov. 21, 1937; s. Joseph Charles and Victoria (Zike) U.; m. MaryJane Walsh, Sept. 5, 1959; children: Sharon, Lori, Joseph, Michael. BA in Chemistry, U. Pa., 1959, PhD, 1963. Postdoctoral resident U. Wis., Madison, 1964; rsch. scientist Olin Mathieson Chem. Corp., New Haven, 1964-65; sect. mgr. Air Products and Chems., Trexlertown, Pa., 1965-70, gen. mgr. splty. chems., 1970-80; v.p. R & D Atlas Powder Co., Tamaqua, Pa., 1980-91; v.p. U.P.R.&T ICI Explosives, Mcmasterville, Can., 1991—. Mem. Am. Chem. Soc., Soc. Explosives Engrs. Republican. Roman Catholic. Office: Tamaqua Tech Ctr PO Box 577 Tamaqua PA 18252-0577

URESTI, RONDA VEVERKA, elementary bilingual education educator; b. Newton, Iowa, May 23, 1963; d. Terry Joe and Carol Jean VeVerka; m. Eulalio Uresti, Dec. 18, 1993. BA in Elem. Edn., Ctrl. U., 1994. Instr. mentally challenged adults Progress Ind., Newton, 1989-94; bilingual tchr. San Carlos Elem., Edinburg, Tex., 1994—; mem. adv. bd. J & E Opporation, Edcouch, Tex., 1989-94; 1st grade curriculum writer, Edinburg Sch. Dist., 1995, 96, mem. assessment adv. com., 1996, mem. tech. com., 1996. Grantee Jasper Charter Am. Bus. Women's Assn., Newton, 1992, 93. Mem. Ind. Order of Odd Fellows Rebekah Lodge (sec. 1992—). Mem. Church of Christ. Avocations: quarter horses, hunting, fishing. Home: PO Box 1454 Edcouch TX 78538-1454

URHAUSEN, JAMES NICHOLAS, real estate developer, construction executive; b. Berwyn, Ill., Oct. 6, 1943; s. Jack Nicholas and Florence Frances (Stalzer) U.; m. Philomena Anne Malizia, July 16, 1966 (div. 1980); children: Kristen Anne, James Nicholas III; m. Anne Siegert, July 22, 1983; children: Bradley James, Samantha Elise. BA, St. Procopius Coll., Lisle, Ill., 1965. High sch. tchr. Nazareth Acad., LaGrange Park, Ill., 1965-66; asst. village mgr. Village of Hinsdale, Ill., 1966-69; village mgr. Village of Oak Brook, Ill., 1969-73; v.p., sec.-treas. Collins Devel. Corp., St. Charles, Ill., 1973-80; exec. v.p. Westway Constrn. Corp., St. Charles, Ill., 1980-84, pres., chief exec. officer, 1984—; guest lectr. No. Ill. U., Dekalb, 1976—; expert witness Ill. Dept. of Transp., Chgo., 1976—; dir. Harris Bank/St. Charles, Ill., 1992—. Chmn. Hotel Baker Bd. Gov.'s St. Charles, 1982-84, Bd. of Fire and Police Commmrs., St. Charles, 1986—; mem. 708 Comty. Mental Health Bd., St. Charles, 1986—, Kane County Selective Svc. Sys. Bd., St. Charles, 1981—, Kane County Solid Waste Adv. Com., Geneva, 1990—, Metra Citizen's Adv. Bd., 1993—; bd. dirs. Neighborhood Improvement Assn., St. Charles Twp., 1992—, pres., 1996—; bd. dirs. Delnor Comty. Hosp. Found., 1993—, Glenwood Sch. for Boys, 1996—. Mem. Home Bldrs. Assn. Greater Chgo. (dir. 1989—), Nat. Assn. Home Bldrs., No. Ill. Home Bldrs. Assn., Fox Valley Polit. Action Group, St. Charles C. of C. (amb. 1988, Community Devel. award 1989, Charlemagne award 1993). Republican. Roman Catholic. Avocations: golf, rail photography, power boating, model trains. Home: 3103 Greenwood Ln Saint Charles IL 60175-5627 Office: Westway Constrn Corp 440 S 3d St Saint Charles IL 60174-5535

URI, GEORGE WOLFSOHN, accountant; b. San Francisco, Dec. 8, 1920; s. George Washington and Ruby Uri; m. Pamela O'Keefe, May 15, 1961. AB, Stanford U., 1941, IA, 1943, MBA, 1946; postgrad., U. Leeds, Eng., 1945. CPA, Calif.; Chartered Fin. Planner; ChFC; Accredited Estate Planner. Mem. acctg., econs. and stats. depts. Shell Oil Co., Inc., San Francisco, 1946-48; ptnr. Irelan, Uri, Mayer & Sheppie, San Francisco; pres. F. Uri & Co., Inc.; instr. acctg. and econs. Golden Gate Univ., 1949-50. Contbr. articles to profl. jours. Chmn. San Rafael Redevel. Adv. Com., 1977-78, mem., 1978-91, mem. emeritus, 1991— ; bd. dirs. San Francisco Planning and Urban Renewal Assn., 1958-60. Served with AUS, 1942-46, to col. Res. (ret.). Recipient Key Man award San Francisco Jr. C. of C.; Meritorious Service medal Sec. of Army, 1978. Mem. AICPA (hon.), Inst. Mgmt. Scis. (treas. No. Calif. chpt. 1961-62), Calif. Soc. CPAs (hon.; sec.-treas. San Francisco chpt. 1956-57, dir. 1961-63, state dir. 1964-66, mem. Forbes medal com. 1968-69, chmn. 1969-71), Am. Econs. Assn., Inst. Mgmt. Accts., San Francisco Estate Planning Coun. (dir. 1965-68, Am. Soc. Mil. Comptrollers, Execs. Assn. San Francisco (pres. 1965-66), Inst. Cert. Mgmt. Accts. (cert. mgmt. acctg., Disting. Performance cert. 1978), Inst. Cert. Fin. Planners, Am. Soc. CLUs and ChFC, World Trade Club (San Francisco), Commonwealth Club (quar. chmn. 1971), Stanford (San Francisco; dir. 1990—), Army and Navy (Washignton). Home: 11 McNear Dr San Rafael CA 94901-1545 Office: 160 Pine St Ste 710 San Francisco CA 94111-5530

URICH, ROBERT, actor; b. Toronto, Ohio, Dec. 19, 1947; m. Heather Menzies; 2 children. B.A. in Radio and TV Communications, Fla. State U.; M.A. in Communications Mgmt., Mich. State U., 1971. Formerly sales account sta. exec. WGN, Chgo. 1st stage appearance in Lovers and Other Strangers, Pheasant Run Playhouse, other appearances at Ivanhoe Theatre, Chgo., Arlington Park (Ill.) Theatre, Burt Reynolds Theatre, Jupiter, Fla., 1983; TV appearances in series Bob and Carol and Ted and Alice, 1973, S.W.A.T, 1975-76, Tabitha, 1977-78, Soap, 1977-78; star of TV series Vega$, 1978-81, Gavilan, 1982, Spenser for Hire, 1985-88, American Dreamer, 1990, It Had to be You, 1993; other TV appearances include Fighting Back, 1980, miniseries Princess Daisy, 1983, Amerika, 1987; TV movies include Bunco, 1977, Leave Yesterday Behind, 1978, Vega$, 1978, When She Was Bad, 1979, Killing at Hell's Gate, 1981, Take Your Best Shot, 1982, Invitation to Hell, 1984, April Morning, 1988, She Knows Too Much, 1989, Murder by Night, 1989, Night Walk, 1989, Blind Faith, 1990, A Quiet Little Neighborhood, A Perfect Little Murder, 1990, Stranger At My Door, 1991, ...And Then She Was Gone, 1991, Survive the Savage Sea, 1992, Blind Man's Bluff, 1992, Double Edge, 1992, Revolver, 1992, Deadly Relations, 1993, Spenser: Ceremony, 1993; motion pictures include Magnum Force, 1973, Endangered Species, 1981, Ice Pirates, 1983, Turk 182!, 1985. Mem. Bd. Regents Cath. U. Recipient Best Actor nomination Golden Globe awards, 1980-81; People's Choice awards, 1980; named Best Actor, Bravo awards, Germany, 1980. Office: care ICM 8942 Wilshire Blvd Beverly Hills CA 90211*

URIE, JOHN JAMES, lawyer, retired Canadian federal judge; b. Guelph, Ont., Can., Jan. 2, 1920; s. G. Norman and Jane A. U.; m. Dorothy Elizabeth James.; children: David, Janet, Alison. B.Commerce, Queen's U.; LL.B., Osgoode Hall Law Sch. Bar: Ont. 1948. Ptnr. firm Burke-Robertson, Urie, Weller & Chadwick, Ottawa, Ont., 1948-73; judge Fed. Ct. Can., Ottawa, 1973-90; counsel Scott and Aylen, Ottawa, 1991—; gen. counsel to Joint Com. of Senate and House of Commons on Consumer Credit; chmn. planning com. First Nat. Conf. on Law, Ottawa, 1972; judge Ct. Martial Appeal Ct., 1973-90. Past pres. County of Carleton Law Assn.; past v.p. Children's Aid Soc.; past pres. Eastern Profl. Hockey League. Served with Cameron Highlanders of Ottawa Can. Army, 1942-45. Mem. Royal Can. Mil. Inst., Phi Delta Phi. Mem. United Ch. of Canada. Clubs: Cameron Highlanders of Ottawa Assoc. (Ottawa), Ottawa Hunt and Golf (Ottawa), Rideau (Ottawa). Office: Scott and Aylen, 60 Queen St, Ottawa, ON Canada K1P 5Y7

URIOSTE, FRANK J., film editor. Cert. Am. Cinema Editors. Films include Whatever Happened to Aunt Alice, The Grissom Gang, Boys in Company C, Fast Break, Loving Couples, Jazz Singer, The Entity, Trenchcoat, Amityville 3-D, Conan II, The Destroyer, Red Sonja, The Hitcher, Robocop (Acad. award nomination), Total Recall, Basic Instinct, Cliffhanger, (co-editor) Midway, Hoosiers, Die Hard (Acad. award nomination). Office: care Lawrence Mirisch The Mirisch Agency 10100 Santa Monica Blvd Ste 700 Los Angeles CA 90067-4011 also: 1610 Highland Ave Glendale CA 91202-1260

URIS, LEON MARCUS, author; b. Balt., Aug. 3, 1924; s. Wolf William and Anna (Blumberg) U.; m. Betty Katherine Beck, Jan. 5, 1945 (div. 1968); children: Karen Lynn, Mark Jay, Michael Cady; m. Margery Edwards, 1968 (dec. 1969); m. Jill Peabody, Feb. 15, 1970; 1 child, Rachael Jackson. Ed., Balt. City Coll.; hon. doctorate, U. Colo., 1976, Santa Clara U., 1977, Wittenberg U., 1980, Lincoln Coll., 1985. Author: Battle Cry, 1953, The Angry Hills, 1955, Exodus, 1957, Exodus Revisited,1959, Mila 18, 1960 (Calif. Literature Silver Medal award 1962), Armageddon, 1964 (Calif. Literature Gold Medal award 1965), Topaz, 1967, The Third Temple, 1967, QB VII, 1970, Ireland: A Terrible Beauty, 1975, Trinity, 1976, (with Jill Uris) Jerusalem, Song of Songs, 1981, The Haj, 1984, Mitla Pass, 1988, Redemption, 1995; screenwriter: (films) Battle Cry, 1954, Gunfight at the O.K. Corral, 1957; adaptor: (musical play) Ari, 1971. Served with USMCR, 1942-46. Recipient Daroff Meml. award, 1959, John F. Kennedy medal Irish/Am. Soc. of N.Y., 1977, Eire Soc. of Boston Gold medal, 1978, Jobotinsky medal State of Israel, 1980, Scopus award Hebrew U. of Jerusalem, 1981; Nat. Inst. Arts and Letters grantee, 1959; Hall fellow (with Jill Uris) Concord Academy, 1980.

URKOWITZ, MICHAEL, banker; b. Bronx, N.Y., June 18, 1943; s. David and Esther (Levy) U.; m. Eleanor Naomi Dreazen, July 2, 1966; children—Brian, Denise. B.Engring., CCNY, 1965, M.M.E., 1967. Project engr. Lunar Module program Grumman Corp., Bethpage, N.Y., 1964-72; asst. to dep. commr. for housing code compliance, project mgr. City of N.Y., 1972-74; 2d v.p. Chase Manhattan Bank, N.Y.C., 1974-77, v.p. group exec. ops. dept., money transfer group, 1977-80, sr. v.p., 1980—, group exec. internat. bank services, 1981-82, product and prodn. risk mgmt. exec., 1982-85, exec. v.p., corp. ops. and systems exec., 1985-87; sector exec. Chase InfoServ Internat., N.Y.C., 1987-95; exec. consumer products integration and technology Retail Banking Tech., N.Y.C., 1995—; bd. mem. Depository Trust Co., N.Y.C., 1992-95; bd. dirs. CEDEL, Luxembourg, 1992—; lectr. CCNY, 1967-68. Contbg. author: Thermal Control and Radiation, 1972. Mem. adv. bd. N.Y.C. chpt. Salvation Army, 1989—. Mem. Tau Beta Pi, Pi Tau Sigma. Office: Chase Manhattan Corp 1 Chase Manhattan Plz Fl 17 New York NY 10081-1000 *Working against my own standards as opposed to the standards set by others, provides the greater challenge but yields greater satisfaction.*

URMER, DIANE HEDDA, management firm executive, financial officer; b. Bklyn., Dec. 15, 1934; d. Leo and Helen Sarah (Perlman) Leverant; m. Albert Heinz Urmer, Sept. 2, 1952; children: Michelle, Cynthia, Carl. Student U. Tex., 1951-52, Washington U., St. Louis, 1962-63; BA in Psychology, Calif. State U.-Northridge, 1969. Asst. auditor Tex. State Bank, Austin, 1952-55; v.p., contr. Enki Corp., Sepulveda, Calif., 1966-70, also dir., 1987—; v.p., fin. Cambia Way Hosp., Walnut Creek, Calif., 1973-78; v.p., contr. Enki Health & Rsch. Sys., Inc., Reseda, Calif., 1978—, also dir. Contbr. articles to profl. jours. Pres. Northridge PTA, 1971; chmn. Northridge Citizens Adv. Council, 1972-73. Mem. Women in Mgmt. Club: Tex. Execs. Avocations: bowling, sailing, handcrafts, golf. Office: Enki Health and Rsch Systems Inc 21601 Devonshire St Chatsworth CA 91311-2946

URMY, NORMAN B., hospital administrator; b. Ft. Smith, Ark., June 26, 1944; married. BA, Williams Coll., 1966; MA, U. Chgo., 1969. Various positions Mass. Gen. Hosp., Boston, 1966-67; adminstrv. resident NYU Med. Ctr., 1968, adminstrv. asst., 1969-70, asst. adminstr., 1970-76, assoc. adminstr., 1976-79, adminstr., v.p. ops., 1979-82; exec. dir. Vanderbilt Univ. Hosp. & Clinic, Nashville, 1985—. Mem. ACHE. Office: Vanderbilt U Hosp & Clinic 1161 21st Ave S Nashville TN 37203*

UROFSKY, MELVIN IRVING, historian, educator; b. N.Y.C., Feb. 7, 1939; s. Philip and Sylvia (Passow) U.; m. Susan Linda Miller, Aug. 27, 1961; children: Philip Eric, Robert Ian. AB, Columbia U., 1961, MA, 1962,

PhD, 1968; JD, U. Va., 1983. Instr. history Ohio State U., 1964-67; asst. prof. history and edn., then asst. dean SUNY, Albany, 1967-74; prof. history Va. Commonwealth U., Richmond, 1974—; Harrison vis. prof. Coll. William and Mary, 1990-91; adj. prof. law U. Richmond, 1989—. Author: Big Steel and Wilson Adminstration, 1969, Why Teachers Strike, 1970, A Mindo of One Piece, 1971, American Zionizm from Herzl to The Holocaust, 1976, We Are One!, 1978, Louis D. Brandeis and the Progressive Tradition, 1980, A Voice that Spoke for Justice: The Life and Times of Stephen S. Wise, 1981, The Supreme Court, the Bill of Rights and the Law, 1986, A March of Liberty, 1987, The Douglas Letters, 1987; A Continuity of Change, 1990, A Conflict of Rights, 1991, Felix Frankfurter, 1991, Letting Go, 1993, The Court in Transition, 1996; co-editor: Brandeis Letters, 5 vols., 1971-78, Half Brother, Half Son, 1991. Chmn. exec. com. Zionist Academic Council, 1976-79; mem. nat. bd. Am. Zionist Fedn., 1976-79; co-chmn. Am. Zionist Ideological Commn., 1976-78; nat. bd. Assn. Reform Zionists Am., 1978-84. Mershon Found. fellow, 1965, sr. rsch. fellow NEH, 1976-77; recipient Kaplun award Jewish Book Coun., 1976; grantee NEH, Am. Coun. Learned Socs.; NEH scholar-in-residence, 1994-95, univ. award for excellence, 1995. Mem. Am. Jewish Hist. Soc. (chmn. acad. coun. 1979-83), Am. Legal History Soc. (bd. dirs., exec. com. 1991—), Orgn. Am. Historians, Va. Hist. Soc. (trustee 1992—). Office: Va Commonwealth U Dept History Richmond VA 23284-2001

UROWSKY, RICHARD J., lawyer; b. N.Y.C., June 28, 1946; s. Jacob and Anne (Granick) U. BA, Yale U., 1967, JD, 1972; BPhil, Oxford U., Eng., 1970. Bar: N.Y. 1973, U.S. Dist. Ct. (so. dist.) N.Y. 1973, U.S. Ct. Appeals (2d cir.) 1973, U.S. Supreme Ct. 1977. Law clk. to Justice Reed U.S. Supreme Ct., Washington, 1972-73; assoc. Sullivan & Cromwell, N.Y.C., 1973-80, ptnr., 1980—. Mem. ABA, Assn. of the Bar of the City of N.Y., Fed. Bar Coun., N.Y. County Lawyers Assn., Yale Club. Office: Sullivan & Cromwell 125 Broad St New York NY 10004-2400

URQUHART, GLEN TAYLOR, investment and development executive; b. Pitts., Nov. 10, 1948; s. George Taylor and Bernice (Wasserman) U.; m. Angela Margaret Boleyn, Dec. 3, 1977; children—Robert Andrew, Caroline. B.S., U. Va., 1971. Fin. mgr. Victor Wilburn & Assocs., Washington, 1972-74; v.p. Chantilly Devel. Corp., Va., 1976-79; pres. Urquhart & Co., Inc., Washington, 1979—; chmn. Nat. Capital Planning Commn., Washington, 1983—; dir. Pennsylvania Ave. Devel. Corp., Washington, 1983—; mem. Council Govts., Washington, 1983—; trustee Fed. City Council, Washington, 1983—. Mem. Com. for Dulles, Dulles Internat. Airport, Washington, 1983—; active, founding mem. Ctr. Internat. Security Studies, Washington, 1984—, World Strategy Network, Washington, 1984—; mem. U.S. Global Strategy Coun., Washington, 1984—; bd. dirs. Am. Def. Found., Washington, 1984—; mem. bd. endowment Comty. Leadership, 1989—. Republican. Avocation: flying. Office: Urquhart & Co 7601 Lewinsville Rd Mc Lean VA 22102

URQUHART, JOHN, medical researcher, educator; b. Pitts., Apr. 24, 1934; s. John and Wilma Nelda (Martin) U.; m. Joan Cooley, Dec. 28, 1957; children: Elizabeth Urquhart Vdovjak, John Christopher (dec. 1965), Robert Malcolm, Thomas Jubal. BA with honors, Rice U., 1955; MD with honors, Harvard U., 1959. Lic. physician, Calif. Walter B. Cannon fellow in physiology Harvard Med. Sch., Boston, 1956, Josiah Macy, Jr. fellow, 1956-58, 59-61; intern in surgery Mass. Gen. Hosp., Boston, 1959-60, asst. resident, 1960-61; investigator Nat. Heart Inst., NIH, Bethesda, Md., 1961-63; asst. prof. physiology U. Pitts. Sch. Medicine, 1963-66, assoc. prof., 1966-68, prof., 1968-70; prof. biomed. engring. U. So. Calif., L.A., 1970-71; prin. scientist ALZA Corp., Palo Alto, Calif., 1970-86, dir. biol. scis., 1971-74, pres. research div., 1974-78, dir., 1976-78, chief scientist, 1978-82, sr. v.p., 1978-85; co-founder APREX Corp., Fremont, Calif., pres., 1986-88, dir. 1986-95, chmn., 1988-91, chief scientist, 1988-95; vis. prof. pharmacology U. Limburg Sch. Medicine, Maastricht, The Netherlands, 1984-85, vis. prof. pharmaco-epidemiology, 1986-91; prof. pharmaco-epidemiology, 1992—; adj. prof. pharm. scis. U. Calif.-San Francisco, 1984—; mem. dir.'s adv. com. NIH, 1986-88; Boerhaave lectr. U. Leiden, The Netherlands, 1991, 94, 95. Co-author: Risk Watch, 1984; contbr. numerous articles to sci. jours.; patentee therapeutic systems for controlled drug delivery and regimen compliance monitoring (43). Trustee GMI Engring. and Mgmt. Inst., Flint, Mich., 1983—. Served with USPHS, 1961-63. NIH grantee, 1963-70; Bowditch lectr. Am. Physiol. Soc., 1969. Mem. Biomed. Engring. Soc. (pres. 1976), Boyleston Med. Soc., Internat. Soc. Pharmaco-epidemiology, Am. Soc. Clinical Pharmacology and Therapeutics, Soc. for Clinical Trials, Endocrine Soc., Saturday Morning club Palo Alto., Am. Physiol. Soc., Soc. Risk Analysis. Home and Office: 975 Hamilton Ave Palo Alto CA 94301-2213

URQUHART, JOHN ALEXANDER, management consultant; b. Savannah, Ga., Aug. 26, 1928; s. George Walter and Helen Catherine (Ruwe) U.; m. Mary Anne Harvey, Apr. 23, 1954; children: Jane Harvey Urquhart Lowe, John Alexander. B.S. in Ind. Engring., Va. Poly. Inst. and State U., 1948. Registered profl. engr., Mass. With GE, 1949-90, sr. v.p. Indsl. & Power Systems, exec. v.p. Power Systems Sector, exec. v.p. Internat. Sector; vice chmn. Enron Corp., 1991—; bd. dirs. Aquarion Co., Enron Corp., Hubbell, Inc., TECO Energy Inc., The Weir Group, PLC. Mem. Brit.-N.Am. com. Fgn. Policy Assn.; trustee Am. U. of Cairo, ASME Found., Inc. 1st lt. C.E., U.S. Army, 1952-54. Mem. ASME, Country Club of Fairfield, Black Rock Yacht Club (Bridgeport, Conn.), Peguot Yacht Club (Southport, Conn.), Philanthropic Lodge (Marblehead, Mass.). Office: 111 Beach Rd Fairfield CT 06430-6668

URQUHART, SALLY ANN, environmental scientist, chemist; b. Omaha, June 8, 1946; d. Howard E. and Mary Josephine (Johnson) Lee; m. Henry O. Urquhart, July 31, 1968; children: Mary L. Urquhart Kelly, Andrew L. BS in Chemistry, U. Tex., Arlington, 1968; MS in Environ. Scis., U. Tex., Dallas, 1986. Registered environ. mgr.; lic. asbestos mgmt. planner, Tex.; Asbestos Hazard Emergency Response Act accredited inspector, mgmt. planner, project designer. Rsch. asst. U. Tex. Dallas, Richardson, 1980-82; high sch. sci. tchr. Allen (Tex.) Ind. Sch. Dist., 1983-87; hazardous materials specialist Dallas Area Rapid Transit, 1987-90, environ. compliance officer, 1990-94, environmental compliance coordination officer, 1994-95; pres. Comprehensive Environ. Svcs. Inc., Dallas, 1995—. Pres. Beacon Sunday Sch. Spring Valley United Meth. Ch., Dallas, 1987, adminstrv. bd. dirs., 1989, com. status and role of women, 1992. Scholar Richardson (Tex.) Br. AAUW, 1980. Mem. Am. Inst. Chemists, Am. Chem. Soc., Am. Soc. Safety Engrs., Am. Indsl. Hygiene Assn., Am. Conf. Govtl. Indsl. Hygienists (assoc.), Nat. Registry Environ. Profls., Soc. Tex. Environ. Profls. (sec./treas. Dallas chpt. 1994, v.p. Dallas chpt. 1996), U. Tex.-Dallas Alumnae Assn. (com. 1992-94). Avocations: jewelry design, counted cross stitching. Home: 310 Sallie Cir Richardson TX 75081-4229 Office: Comprehensive Environ Scvs Inc PO Box 1206 Dallas TX 75221-1206

URQUHART, TONY, artist, educator; b. Niagara Falls, Ont., Can., Apr. 9, 1934; s. Archer Marsh and Maryon Louise (Morse) U.; m. Madeline Mary Jennings, July 1958 (div. 1976); children: Allyson, Robin, Marsh, Aidan; m. Mary Jane Carter Keele, May 1976; 1 dau., Emily. B.F.A., U. Buffalo, 1958. Artist-in-residence U. Western Ont., London, 1960-63, 64-65, asst. prof. fine arts, 1967-70, assoc. prof., 1970-72; prof. fine art U. Waterloo, Ont., 1972—, chmn. dept., 1977-79, 82-85, 94-96; lectr. McMaster U., Hamilton, Ont., 1966-67. One-man shows Winnipeg Art Gallery, 1959, Walker Art Gallery, Mpls., 1960, Richard Demarco Gallery, Edinburgh, Scotland, 1975, group shows, Pitts. Biennial, 1958, Guggenheim Internat., N.Y.C., 1958, Art of the Ams. and Spain, Madrid, Barcelona, Rome, Paris, 1964, Nat. Gallery Can., Toronto, 1972, Mus. Modern Art, Paris, 1976; represented permanent collections, Nat. Gallery Can., Art Gallery, Ont., Fed. Art Bank of Ottawa, Montreal Mus., Vancouver Art Gallery, Mus. Modern Art, Victoria and Albert Mus., London, Museo Civico, Lugano, Switzerland; chmn., Jack Chambers Meml. Found., 1978-85; resident artist, Kitchener-Waterloo Art Gallery, Kitchener, Ont., 1981-83; illustrator: The Broken Ark: A Book of Beasts, 1969, I Am Walking in the Garden of His Imaginary Palace by Jane Urquhart, 1982, False Shuffles by Jane Urquhart, 1982, (50 drawings) Cells of Ourselves (text G.M. Dault), 1989, Memories of a Governor General's Daughter, 1990, Warbrain: poems by Stuart MacKinnon, 1994. Recipient Edits, I Arts Coun., Ont., 1974, Kilchener Waterloo Visual Arts award, 1994; winner Nat. Outdoor Sculpture Competition MacDonald Stewart Art Ctr., 1987; appointed mem. Order of Can., 1995; grantee Can. Coun. award, 1963, 79, travel trantee, 1967, 69, 70, 74, 75, 76, 88, 91, project cost grantee, 1981, 82, short-term grantee, 1991, All Can. Coun. Mem. Can. Artists Representation (founding, sec. 1968-71). Office: Dept Fine Arts U Waterloo, Waterloo, ON Canada N2L 3G1

URRY, DAN WESLEY, research biophysicist, educator, science facility administrator; b. Salt Lake City, Sept. 14, 1935; m. Janet Mills, July 1957 (div. Oct. 1970); children: Weston, Douglas (dec.), David; m. Kathleen Lake, June 8, 1974; 1 child, Kelley Danielle. BA, U. Utah, 1960, PhD in Phys. Chemistry, 1964. Postdoctoral fellow U. Utah, 1964, Harvard U., Cambridge, Mass., 1964-65; vis. investigator Chem. Biodynamics Lab. U. Calif.-Berkeley, 1965-66; prof. lectr. dept. biochemistry U. Chgo., 1967-70; prof. biochemistry U. Ala., Birmingham, 1970—, dir. molecular biophysics div., Lab. Molecular Biology, 1970-72, dir. lab., 1972—; vis. prof. U. Padua, Italy, 1977, U. Palermo, Italy, 1988; chmn. Bioelastics Inc.; gen. ptnr. Bioelastics Rsch. Ltd., 1989—; disting. faculty lectr. U. Ala., Birmingham, 1987. Contbr. numerous articles to sci. publs. Recipient Alexander von Humboldt Found. preis, 1979-80, Wright A. Gardner award Ala. Acad. of Sci., 1991; named 1988 Scientist of the Yr., R&D mag.; one of 1000 Most cited scientists all disciplines worldwide, 1981; one of 10 most cited within discipline of biophysics, 1982. Fellow Am. Inst. Med. and Biol. Engring.; mem. AAAS, Am. Soc. Biol. Chemistry, Am. Chem. Soc., Biophys. Soc. Home: 2423 Vestavia Dr Birmingham AL 35216-1333 Office: U Ala at Birmingham 1670 University Blvd # 300 Birmingham AL 35233-1709

URRY, GRANT WAYNE, chemistry educator; b. Salt Lake City, Mar. 12, 1926; s. Herbert William and Emma (Swanner) U.; m. Lillian Alibertini, Sept. 4, 1946; children—Lisa, Claudia, Serena, Anthony. S.B., U. Chgo., 1947, Ph.D., 1953. Research asst., then research assoc. U. Chgo., 1949-53, research assoc., asst. prof., 1954-55; asst. prof. Washington U., St. Louis, 1955-58; assoc. prof. Purdue U., Lafayette, Ind., 1958-64, prof., 1964-68; prof. chemistry Tufts U., Medford, Mass., 1968-92, Robinson prof. chemistry, 1970-92, chmn. dept., 1968-73, Robinson prof. emeritus chemistry, 1992—. Alfred P. Sloan fellow, 1956-58. Fellow N.Y. Acad. Scis., Am. Inst. Chemists, AAAS; mem. Am. Chem. Soc., Am. Soc. Sci. Glassblowers, Fedn. Am. Scientists, Sigma Xi, Phi Lambda Upsilon. Office: Tufts U Dept Chemistry Medford MA 02155

URSACHE, VICTORIN (HIS EMINENCE THE MOST REVEREND ARCHBISHOP VICTORIN), archbishop; b. Manastioara-Siret, Dist. of Suceava, Romania, 1912. Grad., State Lyceum of Siret; L.Th., U. Cernauti, Romania; postgrad., Bibl. Inst. Jerusalem. Ordained deacon Romanian Orthodox Ch., 1937, ordained priest, 1937. Consecrated bishop Romanian Orthodox Ch., 1966, elevated to archbishop, 1973; prof. religion Orthodox Lyceum of the Romanian Orthodox Metropolis of Cernautsi, 1936-37; prof. theology Seminary of Neamtzu Monastery, 1937-46, asst. dir. sem., 1937-40, dir. sem., superior of monastery, 1940-44; rep. Romanian Orthodox Ch. at Holy Places in, Jerusalem, 1946-56; bishop Romanian Orthodox Missionary Episcopate in Am., 1966-73; archbishop Romanian Orthodox Archdiocese in Am., 1973—; Mem. Holy Synod, Romanian Orthodox Ch. of Romania; bd. dirs. U.S. Conf., World Council Chs.; mem. central com.; mem. Standing Conf. Canonical Orthodox Bishops in, Ams. Editor: Locurile Sfinte. Address: Romanian Orthodox Ch in Am 19959 Riopelle St Detroit MI 48203-1249

URSHAN, NATHANIEL ANDREW, minister, church administrator; b. St. Paul, Aug. 29, 1920; s. Andrew David and Mildred (Hammergren) U.; m. Jean Louise Habig, Oct. 1, 1941; children: Sharon, Annette, Nathaniel, Andrew. Student, Columbia U., 1936-39; DTh (hon.), Gateway Coll. Evangelism, 1976. Ordained to ministry United Pentecostal Ch. Internat. Evangelist, 1941-44; assoc. pastor Royal Oak, Mich., 1944-46, N.Y.C., 1947-48, Indpls., 1948-49; pastor Calvary Tabernacle, Indpls., 1949-78; presbyter Ind. Dist. United Pentecostal Chs., 1950-77; asst. gen. supt. United Pentecostal Ch. Internat., 1971-77; gen. supt. United Pentecostal Ch. Internat., Hazelwood, Mo., 1977—; host radio show Harvestime, 1961-78, 81—; chaplain Ind. Ho. of Reps., 1972. Author: Consider Him, 1962, These Men Are Not Drunk, 1964, Book of Sermons of the Baptism of the Holy Spirit, 1968, Major Bible Prophecy, 1971. Mem. internat. com. YMCA, 1958-79, bd. dirs. Indpls. chpt. 1961-79, world service chmn. Region L., 1969-71; chmn. Heart Fund Campaign, 1968-69; mem. screening com. Marion County Reps., Ind., 1973-74; chmn. Ministerial Com. of Richard Lugar for May of Indpls., 1968, William Hudnut for Mayor, 1975; bd. dirs. Little Red Door, Cancer Soc. Indpls., 1974-77. Recipient gold and brass medallion Heart Fund., Indpls., 1968-69; Nathaniel A. Urshan Day named in his honor, Nov. 3, 1979, Mayor Hudnut, Indpls. Mem. Indpls. Ministerial Assn. Office: United Pentecostal Ch Internat 8855 Dunn Rd Hazelwood MO 63042-2212

URSTADT, CHARLES, real estate executive; b. N.Y.C., Oct. 27, 1928; s. Charles G. and Claire C. (Jordan) U.; m. Elinor McClure Funk, Mar. 23, 1957; children: Charles Deane, Catherine Urstadt Biddle. BA, Dartmouth Coll., 1949, MBA, 1951; LLB, Cornell U., 1953; LLD honors. Pace U., 1990. Bar: N.Y. Assoc., Nevius Brett & Kellogg, N.Y.C., 1953-58; asst. sec. Webb & Knapp, Inc., N.Y.C., 1958-63; v.p., sec., counsel Alcoa Residences, Inc., N.Y.C., 1963-67; commr. N.Y. State Div. Housing and Community Renewal, N.Y.C., 1967-73 ; chmn., Battery Park City Authority, N.Y.C. 1968-78; chmn. bd., pres., dir. Urstadt Property Co. Inc. (formerly Pearce, Urstadt, Mayer & Greer, Inc.), N.Y.C., 1979—; trustee HRE Properties (formerly Hubbard Real Estate Investments), N.Y.C., 1975—, chmn., 1986—, pres., chief exec. officer, 1989—; trustee Tchrs. Ins. and Annuity Corp., 1985—; N.Y. Trustee, Pace U., 1973—; mem. fin. com. N.Y. Rep. State Com., 1981—, del. Rep. Nat. Conv., 1988; mem. Gov.'s Task Force on N.Y. Housing, 1988-90; bd. dirs. N.Y.C. Partnership, Inc., 1984-93, chmn. Realty Found. of N.Y., 1989-95; chmn. N.Y. State Statue of Liberty Celebration Found., 1983-84, N.Y. State Housing Fin. Agy., 1969, Tri-State Regional Planning Commn., 1969-70; mem. Pres.'s Commn. on Housing, 1981-82, others. Lt. USNR, 1954-56. Recipient Man of Yr. award Realty Found. N.Y., 1979. Exec. v.p. Assoc. Builders and Owners Greater N.Y., dir. 1979—. Mem. Nat. Soc. Real Estate Fin. Mem. Reformed Church. Clubs: Links, Union League (N.Y.C.); Siwanoy Country (Bronxville); Bohemian (San Francisco). Office: HRE Properties 321 Railroad Ave Greenwich CT 06830

URSU, JOHN JOSEPH, lawyer; b. 1939. BA, U. Mich., 1962, JD, 1965. Bar: Mich. 1966, Ky. 1970, Minn. 1972. Trial atty. FTC, 1965-67; staff mem. Pres.'s Commn. on Civil Disorders, 1967; advisor to commr. FTC, 1968-69; legal counsel GE, 1969-72; divsn. atty. 3M, 1972-74, sr. atty., 1974-76, assoc. counsel, 1976-81, asst. gen. counsel, 1981-86, assoc. gen. counsel, 1986-90, dep. gen. counsel, 1990-92, gen. counsel, 1992-93; v.p. legal affairs & gen. counsel 3M, St. Paul, 1993—; adj. faculty William Mitchell Coll. Law, 1978-82. Office: 3M Exec Offices 3M Ctr 200-14W-07 Saint Paul MN 55144-1000

USCHEEK, DAVID PETROVICH, chemist; b. University Heights, Ohio, July 9, 1937; s. Peter Ivanovich and Marie (Ocasek) U. BS, Case Western Res. U., 1959. Chemist The Glidden Co., Cleve., 1963-67, Mobil Chem. Co., Cleve., 1967-71, Limbacher Coatings, Cleve., 1971-72, Continental Products, Euclid, Ohio, 1972-80, Body Bros. Paint Corp., Bedford, Ohio, 1980-83, Harrison Paint Corp., Canton, Ohio, 1983-88, Akron (Ohio) Paint and Varnish, 1988-95; with Ritrama Duramark, 1995—; cons. The Analyst, Chardon, Ohio, 1991—. Mem. Am. Chem. Soc., Internat. Union of Pure and Applied Chemists, N.Y. Acad. Scis. Achievements include rsch. on EPA compliant waterborne and high solids coatings with abnormally low volatile organic compound content, high performance corrosion inhibitive water-based primers and topcoats for industrial applications. Home: 8602 Auburn Rd Chardon OH 44024-8711 Office: Ritrama Duramark 341 Eddy Rd Cleveland OH 44108

USDIN, BARBARA TOMMIE, information system designer; b. Phila., May 16, 1954; d. Earl and Vera (Rudin) U. BA, Coe Coll., 1976; M of Info. Sci., Drexel U., 1978. Lexicographer Aspen Systems, Rockville, Md., 1978-82, info. systems designer, 1982-90; cons. ATLIS Cons. Group, Rockville, Md., 1990-94, v.p., 1994—. Office: ATLIS Consulting Group Inc 6011 Executive Blvd Rockville MD 20852-3804

USDIN, GENE LEONARD, physician, psychiatrist; b. N.Y.C., Jan. 31, 1922; s. I. L. and Eva (Miller) U.; m. Cecile Weil, Nov. 8, 1947; children: Cecile Catherine Burka, Linda Ann, Steven William, Thomas Michael. Student, U. N.C., 1939-40, U. Fla., 1940-41; B.S., Tulane U., 1943; M.D., 1946. Diplomate: Am. Bd. Psychiatry and Neurology (asst. examiner, 1956—), Am. Bd. Legal Medicine. Intern Touro Infirmary, New Orleans, 1946-47; resident psychiatry Cin. Gen. Hosp., 1949-51; fellow psychiatry Tulane Sch. Medicine, 1951-52; pvt. practice psychiatry New Orleans, 1952-86; asst. prof. clin. psychiatry Tulane U., 1959-62, assoc. clin. prof., 1962-67; assoc. clin. prof. La. State U., 1967-71, clin. prof., 1971—; sr. psychiatrist Ochsner Clinic, 1986—; prof. Notre Dame Sem., 1969-75; chief div. neurology and psychiatry Touro Infirmary, New Orleans, 1962-66; dir. psychiat. services Touro Infirmary, 1966-71; McLaughlin-Gallie vis. prof. Royal Coll. Physicians and Surgeons of Can., 1983; Robert O. Jones lectr. Atlantic Maritime Provinces Psychiat. Assn. (Can.), 1976; sr. psychiatrist DePaul and Charity Hosps.; sr. psychiat. cons. Oshsner Med. Found., New Orleans, 1980-85, Timberlawn Psychiat. Hosp., Dallas, 1979-93; chmn. psychiat. cons. com. Am. Bar Found., 1970-73; mem. nat. psychiatric adv. bd. Achievement and Guidance Ctrs. Am., Inc., 1991-92. Editor in chief Psychiatry Digest, 1964-71, 75-79, Psychiatry Digest (Europe), 1981-92, ACP-Psychiatric Update, 1980-94, co-editor, 1994-95, editor 1995—; editor Medilex Digest of Psychiatry, 1980—; mem. editorial bd. Academic Psychiatry, 1989-92, Mental Hygiene, 1969-76, Clin. Medicine, 1965-71, 75-88, Med. Digest, 1965-71, Jour. Hosp. and Community Psychiatry, 1975, chmn., 1980-81, Jour. Psychiat. Edn., 1975-89, Am. Jour. Family Therapy, 1978—, Am. Jour. Social Psychiatry, 1981-87, Swiss Med. Digest, Psychiatry, 1981—, Extracta Medica Practica Psychiatrie, 1981—, Behavioral Scis. and the Law, 1982-92, Dynamic Psychotherapy, 1982-90, Psychiat. Medicine, 1982-88, Advances in Therapy, 1983—, Clin. Psychiatry News, 1983-92, Contemporary Psychiatry, 1984-93, Health Disease, 1986—, The Psychiat. Times, 1985—, Clinical Advances in the Treatment of Psychiatric Disorders, 1987—, Jour. Ottawa Med. Sch, 1976-90, Psychiatry Bookshelf, 1976-78, Women's Psychiat. Health, 1992—; mem. internat. adv. bd. Jour. Psicopatologia, Madrid, 1989-94; editor: Psychoneurosis and Schizophrenia, 1966, Practical Lectures in Psychiatry for the Medical Practitioner, 1966, Adolescence: Care and Counseling, 1967, Perspectives on Violence, 1972, (with Peter A. Martin and A.W. Swipe) A Physician in the General Practice of Psychiatry, 1970, The Psychiatric Forum, 1973, Sleep Research and Clinical Practice, 1973, Psychiatry: Education and Image, 1973, Overview of the Psychotherapies, 1975, Schizophrenia: Biological and Psychological Perspective, 1976, Depression: Clinical, Biological and Psychological Perspectives, 1977, Psychiatric Medicine, 1977, (with Charles K. Hofling) Aging: The Process and the People, 1978, (with Jerry M. Lewis, II) Psychiatry in General Medical Practice, 1979, (with David R. Hawkins) The Office Guide to Sleep Disorders, 1980, (with Jerry M. Lewis) Treatment Planning in Psychiatry, 1982; Contbr. articles to profl. jours. Bd. trustees United Fund Greater New Orleans, 1966-70. Served to lt. (j.g.) USNR, 1947-49. Recipient Physician of Yr. award Orleans Parish Med. Soc., 1984, Outstanding Alumni Lectr. award Tulane U. Sch. Medicine, 1986, Seymour Pollack Disting. Svc. award Am. Acad. Psychiatry and the Law, 1988, Outstanding Contbrn. to Social Psychiatry award Am. Assn. for Social Psychiatry, 1993; named Psychiatrist of Yr., La. Psychiat. Med. Assn., 1994. Fellow Am. Psychiat. Assn. (chmn. com. on psychiatry and law 1964-68, mem. com. on ethics 1970-74, com. on membership 1970-74, com. on evaluation svcs. bd. 1974-77, com. on pub. affairs 1976-78, chmn. ad hoc com. on election procedures, 1980-81, trustee at large81, coun. on internat. affairs 1986-91, sec. gen. Interamerican Coun. of Psychiatric Orgns. 1990—, recipient 3d ann. Certificate of Recognition for Excellence in Med. Student Edn. 1993, Warren Williams award, 1995), So. Psychiat. Assn. (bd. regents 1969-72, chmn. 1971-72, pres. 1973-74), La. Psychiat. Assn. (past pres.), Am. Coll. Psychiatrists (bd. regents 1967-70, pres. 1978-79, E.B. Bowis award for Outstanding Contbns. 1973, Disting. Service award for Oustanding Contbns. in Am. Psychiatry 1980), Acad. Psychosomatic Medicine (mem. exec. council 1974-76), New Orleans Soc. Psychiatry and Neurology (past pres.), Group Advancement Psychiatry (bd. dirs. 1970-77, treas. 1973-77), Am. Assn. Social Psychiatry (pres. 1986-88), World Assn. for Social Psychiatry (exec. coun. 1988-90); mem. La. Med. Soc. (chmn. com. on mental health 1966-70), Orleans Parish Med. Soc., Nat. Assn. Mental Health (mem. profl. advisory counc. 1968-75), Inst. of Mental Hygiene (pres. 1978-79). Home: 3 Newcomb Blvd New Orleans LA 70118-5527 Office: Dept Psychiatry Ochsner Clinic 1514 Jefferson Hwy New Orleans LA 70121-2429

USEEM, JOHN HEARLD, sociologist, anthropologist; b. Buffalo, N.Y., Oct. 15, 1910; s. Abram and Sema (Ross) Usem; m. Ruth Marie Hill, June 6, 1940; children: Michael, Howard, Bert. B.A., UCLA, 1934; student, Harvard U., 1934-36; Ph.D., U. Wis., 1939. Prof. U. S.D., 1939-42; vis. lectr. Barnard Coll., Columbia U., 1946; assoc. prof. U. Wis., 1946-49; prof. sociology and anthropology Mich. State U., 1949-81, prof. emeritus, 1981—, head dept., 1958-65; lectr., cons. Fgn. Svc. Inst., U.S. Dept. State, 1950—; cons. Nat. Inst. Growth and Devel.; mem. adv. com. Edward W. Hazen Found., Social Sci. Rsch. Coun., NIMH, Conf. Bd. Assoc. Rsch. Coun.; sr. fellow East-West Ctr., 1972, mem. internat. adv. panel, 1978-79; rsch. on transnat. roles of higher educated in periods of internat. conflict and change. Author: The Western-Educated Man in India, 1955; contbg. author: Human Problems in Technological Change, 1952, Cultural Patterns and Technical Change, 1953, Reconstituting the Human Community, 1972, Bonds Without Bondage, 1979, study Abroad: The Experiences of American Undergraduates in Western Europe and in the United States, 1990; contbr. articles to profl. jours. Bd. govs. Arctic Inst. Served as lt. USNR, World War II; mil. gov. in South Pacific. Recipient Mich. State U. Disting. Faculty award, 1962, Disting. Scholar award in internat., cultural and sci. affairs Internat. Soc. Ednl., Cultural and Sci. Interchange, 1979, Disting. Profl. Service award North Central Sociol. Assn., 1982, Research in Internat. Ednl. Exchange, Council on Internat. Ednl. Exchange, 1986. Mem. Am. Sociol. Assn., Am. Anthrop. Assn., North Central Sociol. Assn. (pres. 1971), Soc. Applied Anthropology, Sociol. Research Assn., Soc. Study Social Problems (chmn. internat. div., Lee Founders' award for disting. career 1987), Central States Anthrop. Soc., Phi Beta Kappa, Phi Kappa Phi, Alpha Kappa Delta, Pi Gamma Mu, Pi Sigma Alpha. Home: 227 Chesterfield Pky East Lansing MI 48823-4110

USEEM, RUTH HILL, sociology educator; b. Hamilton, Ohio, May 31, 1915; d. William E. and Anna E. (Starlin) Hill; m. John Hearld Useem, June 6, 1940; children: Michael, Howard Sheldon, Bert. B.A., Miami U., Oxford, Ohio, 1936; Ph.D., U. Wis., 1947. Asst. prof. Queens Coll., N.Y.C., 1942-43, 1944-45; research cons. Mich. State U., East Lansing, 1951-52; instr. Mich. State U., 1952-58, asst. prof., 1958-60, asso. prof., 1960-70, prof. sociology and edn., 1970-85; Sr. fellow East-West Center, 1970. Author: (with J. Useem) The Western-Educated Man in India, 1955, (with F. Kempf) Psychology: Dynamics of Behavior in Nursing; contbr. articles to profl. jours. Disting. scholar Internat. Soc. Ednl., Cultural and Sci. Interchanges, 1979; recipient Excellence award Mich. State U. Faculty Women's Assn., 1979, award for Research in Internat. Ednl. Exchange, Council Internat. Ednl. Exchange, 1986; Edward W. Hazen Found. grantee India, 1952-53, 58; Edward W. Hazen Found. grantee Philippines, 1968-75; recipient Lee Founders' award for disting. career Soc. for Study of Social Problems, 1987, Pioneering Rsch. on Third Culture Kids award Global Nomads Internat., 1988. Mem. Am. Sociol. Assn. (council 1973-75, com. on cons. 1975-76, com. world sociology 1975-77, com. nominations 1979-81, liaison AAAS com. 1986-87), North Cen. Sociol. Assn. (council 1976-77, v.p./program chmn. 1977-78, pres. 1979-80, Disting. Profl. Service award 1984), Sociologists for Women in Soc., Soc. Internat. Edn., Tng. and Research (council 1978-81), Internat. Soc. Ednl., Cultural and Sci. Interchanges, Sociol. Research Assn., Mortar Bd.; fellow Am. Anthrop. Assn. Home: 227 Chesterfield Pky East Lansing MI 48823-4110

USELMANN, CATHERINE ROSE (KIT USELMANN), small business owner, network marketer, behavioral researcher; b. Madison, Wis., Sept. 17, 1960; d. Richard Lewis and Evelyn Mae (Parr) U. AA, Madison Area Tech. Coll., 1982; BA in Sociology, U. Wis., 1984, MA in Rsch. and Analysis, 1985; DD (hon.), Charter Ecumenical Ministries Internat., 1994. Pub. utility rate analyst Pub. Svc. Commn. Wis., Madison, 1986-89; rsch. mgr. Wis. Lottery, Madison, 1989-90; energy cons. HBRS, Inc., Madison, 1990-91; sr. cons., project mgr. XENERGY, Inc., Burlington, Mass., 1991-93; pres. CRU Prodns., Madison, 1993—; exec. Nutrition For Life Internat., Houston, 1995—, Trudeau Mktg. Group, Chgo., 1995—; team coord. I-Team, Cyberspace, 1996—; Leaders Club, Columbus, Ohio, 1995—; speaker Nat. Assn. Regulatory Utility Commrs., 1987-89; contbg. mem., speaker Assn. for Demand-Side Mgmt. Profls., 1991-93. Univ. rep. operating com. Mall/Concourse, Madison, 1982-84; lobbyist Inst. for Rsch. Poverty, Madison, 1984;

activist, mem. People for Ethical Treatment Animals, Washington, 1989—. Mem. Fin. Independence Assn., U. Wis. Alumni Assn., Badger Quarter Horse Assn. (life). Lakota. Avocations: gourmet cooking, stamp and coin collecting, theater. Home and Office: 3753 Robin Hood Way Madison WI 53704-6243

USELTON, JAMES CLAYTON, engineering executive; b. Tullahoma, Tenn., Oct. 2, 1939; s. Hubert and Edna Mae (Fagg) U.; m. Janice Marie Widner, Oct. 30, 1959; children: Debra Leigh, Clayton Seth, Arnold Jay. BS, U. Tenn., 1962; MS, U. Tenn. Space Inst., Tullahoma, 1966, postgrad., 1966-70. Registered profl. engr. Tenn., Mo., Fla., Mich., Tex., Mass., Ohio. Project engr. Sverdrup Tech., Inc., Tullahoma, 1962-70, lead engr., 1971-74, asst. br. mgr., 1974-77, br. mgr., 1978-79, dir., 1979-81, v.p., 1981-85, sr. v.p., 1985-86, exec. v.p., 1986-88; exec. v.p., dir. Sverdrup Corp., Maryland Heights, Mo., 1989-95, pres., 1996—; pres., CEO Sverdrup Investments, Inc., Maryland Heights, Mo., 1992—; chmn. Sverdrup Tech., Inc., Tullahoma, Tenn., 1993—; bd. dirs. Trans Fin. Bank, Tullahoma. Contbr. articles to profl. jours. Fellow AIAA (assoc.); mem. Nat. Mgmt. Assn. Methodist. Avocations: golf, skiing. Home: 16333 Wilson Farm Dr Chesterfield MO 63005-4542 Office: Sverdrup Corp 13723 Riverport Dr Maryland Heights MO 63043

USHER, ELIZABETH REUTER (MRS. WILLIAM A. SCAR), retired librarian; b. Seward, Nebr.; d. Paul and Elizabeth (Meyer) Reuter; m. Harry Thomas Usher, Feb. 25, 1950; m. William Arthur Scar, Mar. 28, 1992. Diploma, Concordia Tchrs. Coll., Seward, Litt.D. (hon.), 1981; B.S. in Edn., U. Nebr., 1942; B.S. in library Sci., U. Ill., 1944. Tchr. Zion Luth. Sch., Platte Center, Nebr. and; St. Paul's Luth. Sch., Paterson, N.J.; library asst. charge res. book reading room U. Nebr., 1942-43; asst. circulation librarian Mich. State U., 1944-45; librarian Cranbrook Acad. Art, Bloomfield Hills, Mich., 1945-48; catalog and reference librarian Met. Mus. Art, N.Y.C., 1948-53; head cataloger and reference librarian Met. Mus. Art, 1953-54, asst. librarian, 1954-61, chief of art reference library, 1961-68, chief librarian, Thomas J. Watson Library, 1968-80, chief librarian emeritus, 1980—, acting librarian, 1954-57. Contbr. articles to profl. periodicals, library publs. Trustee N.Y. Met. Reference and Research Library Agy., 1968-80, sec. to bd., 1971-77, v.p., 1977-80; 1st v.p. Heritage Village Library, 1982-88, 91-92, pres., 1988-91, 95—. Mem. Spl. Libraries Assn. (pres. 1967-68, dir. 1960-63, 66-69, Hall of Fame 1980—), Coll. Art Assn. (chmn. libraries session 1972-73), N.Y. Library Club, Archons of Colophon (convener 1980-82), Heritage Village Rep. Club (pres. 1992-95), Philanthropic Ednl. Orgn. (v.p. chpt. Q 1994—). Lutheran. Home: 711B Heritage Vlg Southbury CT 06488-1606

USHER, SIR LEONARD GRAY, retired news association executive; b. Paeroa, New Zealand, May 29, 1907; s. Robert and Mary Elizabeth (Johnston) U.; m. Mary Gertrude Lockie, Nov. 30, 1940 (div. 1962); children: Lala Athene Frazer, Miles Gray; m. Jane Hammond Derne, July 11, 1962 (dec. 1984). Tchrs. certificate, Auckland Tng. Coll., 1926-27; B.A., Auckland U., 1934. Headmaster schs. Fiji, 1930-43; pub. relations officer Govt. of Fiji, 1943-56; exec. dir. Fiji Times & Herald, Suva, 1956-73; dir. Fiji Times & Herald, 1973-77; editor Fiji Times, 1958-73; organizing dir. Pacific Islands News Assn., 1974-85, councillor, life mem., 1985—; chmn. bd. Fiji Devel. Bank, 1978-82, Suva Stock Exch., 1979-92, Island Lottlers Ltd., Fiji, 1980-86; dep. chmn. Nat. Bank Fiji, 1974-82; bd. dirs. Connoisseur Products (Pacific) Ltd., Bus. Mgmt. Group Ltd., Mt. Pleasant Ltd. Mem. Fiji Broadcasting Commn., 1954-56, Fiji Visitors Bur., 1953-56; pres. Fiji Bd. Fire Commrs., 1967-70, 75-76; councillor Suva, 1962-71, 75-77, mayor, 1967-70, 75-76; mem. council U. South Pacific, 1975-78; trustee Fiji Crippled Children Soc., 1965—, pres., 1971-74; sec. Fiji Press Council, 1986-94; chmn. Fiji Coll. Honour, 1995—. Served with inf. Fiji Army, 1942-45. Decorated comdr. and knight comdr. Order Brit. Empire. Mem. Commonwealth Trust (sec. Fiji), Fiji Arts Club (pres.), Royal Suva Yacht Club, 1961. Methodist. Clubs: Masons (master Fiji 1949-50, 74-75), United Grand Lodge Eng. (past grand, dir. ceremonies 1991), Defence (life mem., trustee), Fiji Arts (pres., life mem., trustee), United (life mem., trustee) (Suva), Royal Automobile (Sydney). Home: GPO Box 13250, Suva Fiji Office: 24 Des Voeux Rd, GPO Box 13250, Suva Fiji *I would like to be worthy of C.E. Montague's tribute to three friends: "They were not ruled by fear or desire, and you could believe what they said".*

USHER, PHYLLIS LAND, state official; b. Winona, Miss., Aug. 29, 1944; d. Sandy Kenneth and Ruth (Cottingham) L.; m. William A. Usher (dec. Dec. 1993). B.S., U. So. Miss., Hattiesburg, 1967; M.S. (Title II-B fellow 1968-69), U. Tenn., Knoxville, 1969; postgrad. Purdue U., Ind. U., Utah State U. Librarian, Natchez (Miss.)-Adams County schs., 1967-68; materials specialist Fulton County Bd. Edn., Atlanta, 1969-71; cons. div. instructional media Ind. Dept. Public Instrn., Indpls., 1971-74, dir. div., 1974-82, dir. fed. resources and sch. improvement, 1982-85; acting assoc. supt. Ind. Dept. Edn., 1985; sr. officer Ctr. for Sch. Improvement, Ind. Dept. Edn., 1985—; pres. bd. dirs. INCOLSA, mcpl. corp., 1980-82; pres., owner Usher Funeral Home, Inc.; mem. task force sch. Libraries Nat. Commn. Libraries and Info. Sci.; dir., pres. NURC; cons. in field. Mem. Gov. Inst. Conf. Children and Youth Task Force. Recipient citation Internat. Reading Assn., 1975. Mem. ALA, Nat. Assn. State Ednl. Media Profls., West Deanery Bd. Edn., Indpls. Archdioces, Delta Kappa Gamma. Adv. bd. Booklist. Office: Room 229 State House Indianapolis IN 46204

USHER, THOMAS JAMES, steel executive, energy executive; b. Reading, Pa., Sept. 11, 1942; s. Paul T. and Mary (Leonard) U.; m. Sandra L. Mort, Aug. 14, 1965; children—Leanne, Jimmy, Lauren. B.S. in Indsl. Engring., U. Pitts., 1964, M.S. in Ops. and Research, 1965, Ph.D. in Systems Engring., 1971. Indsl. engr. U. S. Steel Corp., Pitts., 1966-76, asst. gen. supt., 1975-78; asst. div. supt. U. S. Steel Corp., Gary, Ind., 1978-81; asst. to pres., mng. dir. facility planning and engring. U. S. Steel Corp., Pitts., 1982-83, v.p. engring., 1982-83, pres., 1991; pres. U.S. Steel Mining Co., Inc., Pitts., 1983-84, v.p. engring. steel, 1984—, sr. v.p. steel ops., 1984—, exec. v.p. heavy products steel divsn., 1986-89, pres. steel divsn., 1990; pres., COO USX Corp., Pitts., 1994—, chmn., CEO, 1995—. Mem. Leadership Pitts., 1984; trustee Multiple Sclerosis, Pitts., 1985; chmn. Allegheny Trails council Boy Scouts Am., Pitts., 1985, United Way, Pitts., 1985; chmn. U.S.-Korea Bus. Coun., 1993—, U.S.-Japan Bus. Coun.; trustee U. Pitts., 1994—; The Bus. Roundtable Nat. Flag Found., 1995. Mem. Am. Iron and Steel Engrs. (bd. dirs. 1984-85), Am. Iron and Steel Inst., Dinamo/Ovia (bd. dirs. 1985). Clubs: Rolling Rock, Duquesne, Laurel Valley, Double Eagle, Oakmont. Avocations: golf; tennis; racquetball; scuba diving; swimming. Home: 840 12th St Oakmont PA 15139-1151 Office: USX Corp Room 6170 600 Grant St Pittsburgh PA 15219-4776

USHIJIMA, JOHN TAKEJI, state senator, lawyer; b. Hilo, Hawaii, Mar. 13, 1924; s. Buhachi and Sano (Nitahara) U.; m. Margaret Kunishige, June 6, 1954. B.A., Grinnell Coll., 1950; J.D., George Washington U., 1952. Bar: Hawaii, 1953. Ptnr. Pence & Ushijima, Hilo, 1953-61, Ushijima & Nakamoto, Hilo, 1961-69; mem. Hawaii Senate, 1959—, pres. pro tem, 1974—; bd. dirs. Cyanotech Corp., Woodinville, Wash. Bd. dirs. Waiakea Settlement YMCA. With AUS, 1943-46, ETO. Mem. Am. Bar Assn., Phi Delta Phi. Democrat. Home: 114 Melani St Hilo HI 96720-2766 Office: 192 Kapiolani St Hilo HI 96720-2687

USSERY, LUANNE, communications consultant; b. Kershaw, S.C., Feb. 20, 1938; d. Ralph Thurston and Mary Elizabeth (Haile) U. B.A., Winthrop Coll., 1959. Assoc. editor Kershaw News-Era, 1959-61; advt. saleswoman Nonpareil newspaper, Coun. Bluffs, Iowa, 1961-67; mag. editor Mutual of Omaha-United of Omaha Ins. Co., 1968-78, asst. v.p., 1978-82, 2d v.p., 1982-87. Editor: The Presbyterian, Presbytery of Missouri River Valley, Omaha, 1984-88, Presbyterian Times, Providence Presbytery, Rock Hill, S.C., 1990-93, co-editor 1993—; weekly columnist Kershaw News Era, 1988-92. Elder, clk. of session First Presbyn. Ch. U.S.A., Coun. Bluffs, 1974-88, Beaver Creek Presbyn. Ch., Kershaw, 1990-92; chair communications com. Presbytery of Missouri River Valley, 1985-87, moderator, 1988; trustee Christian Home Assn./Children's Sq. U.S.A., Coun. Bluffs, 1985-88, Internat. Assn. Bus. Communicators (pres. Omaha chpt. 1972, Communicator of Yr. award Omaha chpt. 1973).

USTINOV, SIR PETER ALEXANDER, actor, director, writer; b. London, Apr. 16, 1921; s. Iona and Nadia (Benois) U.; m. Isolda Denham, 1940 (div.); 1 child, Tamara; m. Suzanne Cloutier, Feb. 15, 1954 (div. 1971); children: Pavla, Igor, Andrea; m. Hélène du Lau d'Allemans, 1972. Student, Westminster Sch., London, Mr. Gibbs Prep. Sch., London, London Theatre Sch.; D.Mus. (hon.), Cleve. Inst. Music, 1967; LL.D. (hon.), U. Dundee, 1969, LaSalle Coll. of Phila., 1971, U. Ottawa, 1991; Litt.D. (hon.), U. Lancaster, 1972; Doctorate (hon.), U. Toronto, 1984, 95; LHD (hon.), Georgetown U., 1988; Doctorate (hon.), Free U. Brussels, 1995. Stage appearances include The Wood Demon, 1938, The Bishop of Limpopoland, 1939, Madame Liselotte Beethoven-Fink, 1939, White Cargo, Rookery Nook, Laburnum Grove, Pygmalion, 1939, First Night, 1940, Swinging the Gate, 1940, Fishing For Shadows, 1940, Hermione Gingold Revue, 1940, Diversion No. 1 Revue, 1940, Squaring the Circle, 1941, Crime and Punishment, 1946, Frenzy, 1948, Love in Albania, 1949, The Love of Four Colonels, 1951-52 (N.Y. Critics award, Donaldson award), Romanoff and Juliet, 1956 (Evening Standard drama award), Photo Finish, 1962, 63, The Unknown Soldier and His Wife, 1968, 73, Who's Who in Hell, 1974, King Lear, 1979, 80, Beethoven's Tenth, 1983, 83-84, 87-88; currently appearing worldwide in An Evening with Peter Ustinov; film appearances include One of Our Aircraft Is Missing, 1941, The Way Ahead, 1944, Private Angelo, 1949, Odette, 1950, Quo Vadis (Acad. award nomination for Best Supporting Actor), 1950, Hotel Sahara, 1952, Beau Brummel, 1953-54, The Egyptian, 1954, We're No Angels, 1955, Lola Montez, 1955, The Spies, 1955, An Angel Flew Over Brooklyn, 1955, I Girovaghi, 1955, The Sundowners, 1960, Spartacus, 1960-61 (Acad. award for Best Supporting Actor), Romanoff and Juliet, 1961, Billy Budd, 1962, Topkapi, 1963, John Goldfarb, Please Come Home!, 1964, Blackbeard's Ghost, 1967, The Comedians, 1967, Hot Millions, 1968, Viva Max, 1969, Hammersmith Is Out, 1971, Big Truck and Poor Clare, 1971, One of Our Dinosaurs Is Missing, 1974, Logan's Run, 1975, Treasure of Matecumba, 1975, The Last Remake of Beau Geste, 1976, Purple Taxi, 1977, Death on the Nile, 1977, The Thief of Baghdad, 1978, Ashanti, 1979, Charlie Chan and the Curse of the Dragon Queen, 1980, Evil Under the Sun, 1981, Memed, My Hawk, 1982, Appointment With Death, 1988, The French Revolution, 1989, Lorenzo's Oil, 1992, The Phoenix and The Magic Carpet, 1993; dir.: (plays) Squaring the Circle, 1941, Love in Albania, 1949, No Sign of the Dove, 1952, A Fiddle at the Wedding, 1952, Romanoff and Juliet, 1956, Photo Finish, 1962, 64, Half Way Up the Tree, 1967, The Unknown Soldier and His Wife, 1968, 73, (operas) L'Heure Espagnole (Ravel), Covent Garden, 1962, Gianni Schicchi (Puccini), Covent Garden, 1962, Erwartung (Schoenberg), Covent Garden, 1962, The Magic Flute (Mozart), Hamburg Opera, 1968; dir., scenery and costume designer: Don Giovanni (Mozart), Edinburgh Festival, 1973; dir., producer, set and costume designer: Don Quichotte (Massenet), Paris Opera, 1973; dir., producer: The Brigands (Offenbach), The German Opera, Berlin, 1978; dir., writer libretto: The Marriage (Moussorgsky), Piccola Scala, 1981; dir.: Mavra and The Flood (Stravinsky), Piccola Scala, 1982, Katja Kabanowa (Janacek), Hamburg Opera, 1985, The Marriage of Figaro, Mozarteum and the Hamburg Opera, 1987, Jolanthe (Tchaikovsky) and Francesca da Rimini (Rachmaninoff), Dresden Opera, 1993; appeared on radio, London (BBC), Germany, Belgium, Rome, Paris, N.Y.C., Hollywood; TV appearances include In All Directions (host, producer, co-star), BBC, History of Europe, BBC, Einstein's Universe, PBS and BBC, 1979, Barefoot in Athens (Emmy award), Storm in Summer (Emmy award), The American Revolution, CBS (George Peabody award), Omnibus (Emmy award), The Well Tempered Bach (Emmy award nomination), PBS, 1984, 13 at Dinner, CBS, 1985, Deadman's Folly, CBS, 1985, Peter Ustinov's Russia, 1985, Appointment with Death, 1987, Around the World in Eighty Days, NBC, 1988-89, Secret Identity of Jack the Ripper, 1989-90, Monet: Legacy of Light, 1990, Ustinov Aboard the Orient Express, 1991-92, Ustinov Meets Pavarotti, 1993, Inside the Vatican, 1994, The Old Curiosity Shop, 1995, Haydn Gala, 1995, documentaries on Thailand and Hong Kong, 1995, an Evening with Sir Peter Ustinov, 1995, Russia Now, 1995, Paths of the Gods, 1996, occasional political commentaries, BBC; recordings include Mock Mozart, The Grand Prix of Gibraltar, Peter and the Wolf (directed by Herbert Von Karajan), Nutcracker Suite, The Soldier's Tale (Stravinsky) (with Jean Cocteau), Hary Janos (Kodaly), London Symphony Orch., The Little Prince (St. Exupéry), (narration) Grandpa, Babar and Father Christmas, The Old Man of Lochnagar, Grandpa, Peter Ustinov Reads the Orchestra; author: (plays) Fishing for Shadows, 1940, House of Regrets, 1942, Blow Your Own Trumpet, 1943, Beyond, 1943, The Banbury Nose, 1944, The Tragedy of Good Intentions, 1945, The Indifferent Shepherd, 1948, Frenzy, 1948, The Man in the Raincoat, 1949, The Moment of Truth, 1951, The Love of Four Colonels, 1951, High Balcony, 1952, No Sign of the Dove, 1953, Romanoff and Juliet, 1956, The Empty Chair, 1956, Paris Not So Gay, 1958, Photo Finish, 1962, The Life in My Hands, 1964, The Unknown Soldier and His Wife, 1967, Halfway Up the Tree, 1967, Who's Who in Hell, 1974, Overheard, 1981, Beethoven's Tenth, 1983, 87-88, others, (films) The Way Ahead (with Eric Ambler), 1942-43, School for Secrets, 1946, Vice Versa, 1947, Private Angelo, 1949, Romanoff and Juliet, 1961, Billy Budd (with DeWitt Bodeen), 1962-63, The Lady L (with Ira Wallach), 1964, Hot Millions (with Ira Wallach), 1968, Memed, My Hawk, 1982, (cartoon) We Were Only Human, 1960, (short stories) Add a Dash of Pity, 1960, Frontiers of the Sea, 1966, (novels) The Loser, 1961, Krumnagel, 1971, The Disinformer, 1989, The Old Man and Mr. Smith, 1991, (autobiography) Dear Me, 1977, My Russia, 1983, Ustinov in Russia, 1987, Ustinov at Large, 1991, Still at Large, 1993, Quotable Ustinov, 1995. Chancellor U. Durham, 1992; pres. World Federalist Movement, 1992. With Brit. Army, 1942-46. Decorated Comdr. Order of Brit. Empire, 1975, Commandeur des Arts et Lettres, 1985, Knight of the Realm, 1990; recipient Disting. Svc. award UNICEF, 1978, Prix de la Butte, 1978, Best Actor award Variety Club Gt. Britain, 1979, medal of Honor Charles U. (Prague), 1991, Britannia award, 1992, Critic's Circle award, 1993, German Cultural award, 1994, German Bambi, 1994, Internat. Child Survival award, 1995, Rudolph Valentino award, 1995, Norman Cousins Global Governance award, 1995; named rector U. Dundee, 1971-73; elected to Acad. Fine Arts Paris, 1988. Address: 17 Onslow Sq, London SW7 3NJ, England

UTELL, MARK J., medical educator; b. N.Y.C., July 25, 1946; m. Lois Brooks; 1 child, Michael Jon. BA cum laude, Dartmouth Coll., 1968; MD, Tufts U., 1972. Diplomate Am. Bd. Internal Medicine. Intern St. Elizabeth's Hosp., Boston, 1972-73, resident in internal medicine, 1973-75; from instr. to prof. sch. medicine U. Rochester, N.Y., 1975-92; prof. sch. medicine U. Rochester, 1992—; dir. respiratory and med. ICUs Strong Meml. Hosp., Rochester, 1977-89, mem. intensive care com., 1977-87; co-dir. pulmonary and CCU sch. medicine U. Rochester, 1984-91, occupl. medicine program, 1988—, assoc. chmn. clin. affairs dept. environ. medicine, 1992—, dir. occupl. and environ. medicine divsn., 1992—; cons. VA, 1977—, EPA, 1980, 84, 94—, mem. sci. adv. bd., 1987, chmn. clean air sci. adv. com., 1988, 89, chmn. search com., 1989, mem. rev. panel, 1989; reviewer site visit com. NIH, 1982, outside reviewer respiratory and applied physiology sect., 1982, ad hoc reviewer, 1983; mem. spl. study sect. Nat. Inst. Environ. Health Scis., 1984, reviewer, 1986, 89, 90, 91, mem. task force, 1991, mem. external adv. com., 1994; mem. health rsch. com. Health Effects Inst., 1985-94; mem. N.Y. State Commr.'s Panel on Tuberculosis, Syracuse, 1988; mem. commn. life scis. NRC, NAS, 1989; mem. panel airborne particulate matter in spacecraft NASA, 1987, mem. environ. health scis. working group, 1993—. Co-author: Inhalation Toxicology of Air Pollution: Clinical Research Considerations, 1985, Susceptibility to Inhaled Pollutants, 1989; co-editor: Advances in Controlled Clinical Inhalation Studies, 1993; mem. editl. bd. Jour. Aerosol Medicine, Inhalation Technology; guest reviewer various jours.; contbr. over 100 articles to profl. jours. Bd. dirs. Am. Lung Assn. N.Y. State, 1986-88. Grantee NASA, Nat. Inst. Environ. Health Scis., Nat. Heart Lung and Blood Inst., Elec. Power Rsch. Inst., Ctr. Indoor Air Rsch., Dow Corning Corp., Allied Signal, Inc. Fellow AAAS, ACP, Am. Coll. Chest Physicians (mem. steering com. sect. environ. occupl. health 1983-87, assessment asthma in workplace com. 1994); mem. Am. Physiol. Soc., Am. Thoracic Soc. (chmn. scientific assembly on environ. and occupl. health 1987, mem. planning com., 1992-94, respiratory protective guidelines com., 1993—, other coms.), Am. Coll. Occupl. Environ. Medicine, Ea. Sect. Am. Thoracic Soc., N.Y. Trudeau Soc. (pres. 1986). Home: 16 Framingham Ln Pittsford NY 14534 Office: Dept Medicine Pulmonary CCU Box 692 U Rochester Sch Medicine Rochester NY 14642-8692*

UTHMAN, BASIM MOHAMMAD, neurologist, epileptologist, consultant; b. Tripoli, Lebanon, Sept. 25, 1958; came to the U.S., 1984; s. Mohammad Assa'ad and Mariam Mohammad (Moukalled) U. BSc, Am. U. Beirut, 1978, MD, 1984. Diplomate Am. Bd. Psychiatry and Neurology, Am. Bd. Clin. Neurophysiology. Intern Am. Univ. Beirut Med Ctr., Lebanon, 1983-84; resident in neurologyDept. Neurology U. Cin., 1984-87, preceptor, 1987-88, clin. fellow in neurophysiology, epilepsy, 1987-88; clin. rsch. fellow in epilepsy, neurophysiology and neuropharmacology U. Fla., Gainesville, 1988-90, clin. instr., 1990-91; vis. assoc. prof. dept. neurology U. Fla., 1991-92; asst. prof. dept. neurology, brain inst. U. Fla., Gainesville, 1992-96, assoc. prof. dept. neurology, brain inst., 1996—; staff neurologist VA Med. Ctr., Gainesville, 1990—, asst. chief neurology svc., dir. status epilepticus team, 1990-95, contracting officers tech. rep., 1990-92, acting chief neurology svc., 1993, dir. clin. neurophysiology lab. EEG/EP, 1991—; chmn. Adminstrv. Bd. Investigation VA Med. Ctr., Gainesville, 1993; attending epideptologist Shands Hosp., 1993—; permanent mem. U. Fla. Instnl. Rev. Bd. Health Sci. Ctr., 1994—. Ad hoc referee U.S. Pharmacopeial Conv., 1988-89, Drug Evaluations, 1990, Epilepsia, 1990—, Jour. Neuroimaging, 1990—, Drugs, 1993—; contbr. articles to profl. jours., chpts. to books. Active emergency blood donation campaign, Beirut, 1982-83, worker war disaster plan, 1982-83; vol. Lebanese Red Cross, Beirut, 1982-83; organizer children's med. ednl. presentations, 1984; profl. adv. bd. Epilspsy Found. Fla., 1992-93, chmn., 1993—. A.S. Khalidi scholar Am. U. Beirut, 1978, Azeez B. Ajloini scholar, 1979, Tamari-Saab scholar, 1979, Dr. Haddad, 1980; fellow Bowman Gray Med. Sch., Winston-Salem, N.C., 1987; grantee Epilepsy Rsch. Found. Fla., 1988-90, Cyberonics, 1989—, Coop. Studies Program Coordinating Ctr., 1990—, VA Affairs Med. Ctr. Allotment, 1991-92, Abbott Labs., 1991—, U. Fla., 1991-92, Ceiba-Geigy, 1991-94, U. Fla. Brain Inst., 1992, Parke-Davis 1993—. Mem. AMA, Am. Acad. Neurology, Am. Epilepsy Soc., Am. Sleep Disorders Assn., Am. Electroencephalographic Soc., Am. Soc. Neurophysiological Monitoring, Am. Coll. Internat. Physicians, Nat. Stroke Assn., So. Clin. Neurol. Soc., So. Electroencephalographic Soc., Fla. Med. Assn., Alachua County Med. Soc., Nat. and Internat. Spkrs. Bur. (Parke-Davis, Marion Merryl Dow, Burroughs Wellcome, Abbott Labs., Ciba-Geigy, Cyberonics 1993—). Moslem. Avocations: tennis, cooking, traveling, jogging, music. Office: VA Med Ctr-Neurology Svc 127 1601 SW Archer Rd Gainesville FL 32608-1135

UTHOFF, DETLEF, ophthalmologist; b. Mülheim an der Ruhr, Germany, May 7, 1942; m. Anke Uthoff; children: Phillip, Nicolas, Daniel, Moritz, Antonia. Grad. with recognition, U. Kiel, Germany, 1971. Med. asst. univ. clinic, surg. clin., pediatric clinic, univ. gynecol. clinic, ear-nose-and-throat clinic U. Kiel, 1967-69; med. asst. St. Elisabeth Clinic, Kiel, 1967-69; med. asst. Rsch. Inst. Borstel, 1967-69, sci. asst., 1969-71; locum med. leader gen. sect. Dist.-Clinic Heide, 1971-72; pvt. practice, 1972; med. asst. clinic ophthalmology U. Kiel, 1975-79; sr. cons. eye sect. Flechsig Kiel Clinic, 1980-85; med. dir. Eye Hosp. Kiel-Bellevue, 1985—; rschr. micro-surgery and plastic surgery fields of ophthalmology Manhatten Eye Hosp., N.Y.C., 1979-80, Pollack Eye Hosp., Gainsville, 1979-80, Iliff Eye Hosp., Balt., 1979-80; chmn. bd. Inst. for Systemrsch. Health World Healthiness Orgn., 1985-86; habilitation, prof. U. Tel-Aviv. Contbr. numerous articles to profl. jours. German Rsch. Cmty. scholar U. Kiel, 1972-75. Fellow Internat. Eye Found. Am.; mem. AAAS, Am. Intraocular Implant Soc., Am. Soc. Cataract and Refractive Surgery, German Ophthalmology Soc., Profl. Orgn. Ophthalmologists in Germany, German Soc. Plastic and Recovering Surgery, German Soc. for Intraocularlens Implantation, Geman Soc. for Socialpädiatry, N.Y. Acad. Scis., European Refractice Surgery Soc., Internat. Soc. Ocular Surgeons, Soc. for Immunology (sci. advisor), Retinologic Soc., Julius Hirschberg Soc., Soc. Francaise d'Ophtalmologie, Inst. for Health Investigation (chmn. bd.), Internat. Assn. of Ocular Surgeons. Office: Augenklinik Kiel-Bellevue, Lindenallee 21, 24105 Kiel Germany

UTIGER, ROBERT DAVID, medical editor; b. Bridgeport, Conn., July 14, 1931; s. David Alfred and Aldine (Frey) U.; m. Sally Baldwin, Nov. 27, 1953; children: Jane, David, Nancy. A.B., Williams Coll., 1953; M.D., Washington U., 1957. Intern, resident in medicine Barnes Hosp., St. Louis, 1957-61; investigator Nat. Cancer Inst., Bethesda, Md., 1961-63; asst. prof. medicine Washington U. Sch. Medicine, 1963-69; assoc. prof. U. Pa. Sch. Medicine, Phila., 1969-73; prof. U. Pa. Sch. Medicine, 1973-79; prof. medicine U. N.C. Sch. Medicine, Chapel Hill, 1979-89; clin. prof. medicine Harvard Med. Sch., Boston, 1989—; dep. editor New Eng. Jour. Medicine, Boston, 1989—. Editor-in-chief: Jour. Clin. Endocrinology and Metabolism, 1983-89. Mem. Am. Soc. Clin. Investigation, Assn. Am. Physicians, Nat. Bd. Med. Examiners, Endocrine Soc., Phi Beta Kappa, Alpha Omega Alpha. Office: New Eng Jour Medicine 10 Shattuck St Boston MA 02115-6011

UTKU, SENOL, civil engineer, computer science educator; b. Suruc, Turkey, Nov. 23, 1931; s. Sukru and Sukufe (Gumus) U.; m. Bisulay Bereket, May 9, 1964; children: Ayda, Sinan. Dipl. Ing., Istanbul Tech. U., 1954; M.S., MIT, 1959, Sc.D., 1960. Civil engr., Istanbul, Turkey. Research engr. IBM, 1959-60; asst. prof. structural engring MIT, 1960-62; assoc. prof. Middle East Tech U., Ankara, Turkey, 1962-63; exec. dir. Computation Ctr., Istanbul Tech. U., 1963-65; mem. tech. staff Jet Propulsion Lab., Pasadena, Calif., 1965-70; assoc. prof. civil engring Duke U., Durham, N.C., 1970-72, prof., 1972-79, prof. civil engring., prof. computer sci., 1979—, dir. undergrad. studies, 1980-87, dir. grad. studies, 1987-89. Author: Linear Analysis of Discrete Structures, 1991, Theory of Adaptive Structures (Static Part), 1995; co-author: Dynamics of Offshore Structures, 1984, Finite Element Handbook, 1987, Elementary Structural Analysis, 4th edit., 1991, Parallel Processing in Computational Mechanics, 1993, Intelligent Structural Systems, 1992; contbr. articles to profl. jours. Fulbright scholar, 1957; recipient Pres.'s fund Calif. Inst. Tech., 1981, award NASA, 1969, 71, 77, 84, 86, 87, Internat. Joint Rsch. award NSF, 1991-92. Fellow ASCE; mem. Acad. Mechanics, Fulbright Assn., Am. Soc. for Engring. Edn., Sigma Xi, Chi Epsilon. Home: 1843 Woodburn Rd Durham NC 27705-5754 Office: Duke U 134 Hudson Hall Durham NC 27708

UTLAUT, WILLIAM FREDERICK, electrical engineer; b. Sterling, Colo., July 26, 1922; s. Frederick Ernst and Francis Ruth Hanna U.; m. Jeanne Elizabeth Pomeroy, Aug. 4, 1946; children—Mark William, Niles Frederick, Paige Elizabeth. Utlaut Moore. B.S.E.E., U. Colo., 1944, M.S.E.E., 1950, Ph.D. in Elec. Engring, 1966; diploma, Naval Radar Sch., 1945. Engr. Gen. Electric Co., Schenectady, 1946-48, Nat. Bur. Standards, Boulder, Colo., 1952-53; instr. U. Colo., 1948-52, 53-54; dir. Inst. for Telecommunications Scis., U.S. Dept. Commerce, Boulder, 1954—; assoc. adminstr. Nat. Telecom and Info. Adminstrn., Boulder, 1980—; chmn. U.S. study group 1, Internat. Radio Consultative Com., 1975—, mem. U.S. nat. com., 1970-81; mem. electromagnetic wave propagation panel, adv. group aerospace research and devel. NATO, 1978-81, adv. com. Nat. Research Council, 1986—; chmn. ANSI-ECSA tech. com. on Integrated Services Digital Network, 1984—, U.S. nat. com. Internat. Consultative Com. on Telegraph and Telephone Joint Working Party, 1986—. Guest co-editor spl. joint issue: IEEE Trans. on Spectrum Mgmt, 1981, IEEE Trans. on Communications, 1975; guest editor spl. issue: Radio Sci, 1974; contbr. numerous articles to profl. jours. Bd. dirs. YMCA, 1955—; mem. bd. mgmt. 1st Congl. Ch., 1960-66, 78—; mem. engring. devel. council U. Colo., 1969-81. Served in USN, 1943-46. Recipient Gold medal U.S. Dept. Commerce, 1971, 95, Disting. Engring. Alumnus award U. Colo., 1973. Fellow IEEE (Harry Dimond Meml. award leadership radio sci. and engring. 1989, Presdl. Rank award 1990, 96, policy bd. Comm. Soc.), Internat. Sci. Radio Union, Am. Nat. Stds. Inst., Exch. Carriers Stds. Assn. Office: Inst for Telecom Scis US Dept Commerce 325 Broadway St Boulder CO 80303-3328

UTLEY, F. KNOWLTON, library director, educator; b. Northampton, Mass., May 4, 1935; s. Frederick K. and Florence E. (Moore) U.; m. Faith E. Green, July 2, 1960; children: Richard F., Stephen R., David E. BS, Castleton State Coll., 1960; MA, U. Conn., 1967; EdD, Boston U., 1979; MLS, U. Ala., 1983. Tchr. indsl. arts Montpelier (Vt.) High Sch., 1960-61, Southwick (Mass.) High Sch., 1961-63; tchr., drafting instr. Putnam (Conn.) High Sch., 1963-68; media specialist Cen. Conn. State U., New Britain, 1968-69, dir. media svcs., 1969-72; doctoral teaching fellow Boston U., 1972-73; dir. libr., media svcs. Manchester (Mass.) Pub. Schs., 1973-79; assoc. prof. libr. scis. U. Maine, Farmington, 1979-80; dir. grad. program libr. media Livingston (Ala.) U., 1980-83; dir. libr. media svcs. Am. Internat. Coll., Springfield, Mass., 1983—; pres. C/W Mars-Ctrl. and Western Mass. Auto. Res., 1987-88; chmn. bd. dirs. Cooperating Librs. of Great Springfield, 1988-89; chmn. bd. dirs. Western Mass. Media Coun., 1991-93. Mem. ALA, Assn./Edn. Comm. and Tech. New Eng. Edn. Media Assn., New Eng. Libr. Assn., Mass. Sch. Libr. Media Assn., Mass. Libr. Assn., Phi Delta Kappa. Home: 11 Canal Dr Belchertown MA 01007-9224 Office: Am Internat Coll 1000 State St Springfield MA 01109-3151

UTLEY, JOHN EDDY, automotive supplies executive; b. Evanston, Ill., Feb. 20, 1941; s. John Eddy and Grace Millicent (Turnock) U.; m. Frances Elizabeth von Maur, Aug. 17, 1963; children: John Eddy III, Josephine Laurel Shaya, Robin Frances. BS in Indsl. Engring., U. Mich., 1964; MBA, Wayne State U., 1972. Sales engr. The Timken Co., Canton, Ohio, 1964-73, dist. mgr., 1973-78, asst. gen. mgr., 1978-82; v.p. sales and mktg. Kelsey-Hayes Co., Romulus, Mich., 1982-84, pres. auto group, 1984-88, pres., chief operating officer, 1988-89, vice chmn., 1989-92; chmn., CEO, 1992-94; chmn. Hayes Wheels Internat., 1993—; sr. v.p. Varity Corp.; pres. Automotive Original Equipment Mgrs. Assn., Detroit, 1987; bd. dirs. Walbro Corp. Mem. Soc. Automotive Engrs. (nat. chmn. passenger car meeting 1984), Bloomfield Hills Country Club. Republican. Methodist. Avocations: golf, tennis, boating. Office: Kelsey-Hayes Co 11878 Hubbard St Livonia MI 48150-1733*

UTROSKA, WILLIAM ROBERT, veterinarian; b. Greenwood, Miss., Oct. 21, 1946; s. Robert Julius and Ruth (McNeal) U.; m. Dian Anderson, Aug. 3, 1968; 1 child, Amy Elizabeth. BS, Miss. State U., 1968; DVM, Auburn U., 1971. Diplomate Am. Bd. Vet. Practitioners. Staff veterinarian Animal Hosp.-Brooks Rd., Memphis, 1971-73, Whitehaven Animal Hosp., Memphis, 1973-75; owner, operator Stateline Animal Clin., Southaven, Miss., 1975—; cons. VIP Products/Pet Chems., Memphis, 1984. Contbr. articles to profl. jours. Alderman City of Southaven, 1989—, mem. planning commn., 1980-89. Mem. Exchange Club (pres. 1978). Republican. Methodist. Avocations: flight instructor, golf. Home: 577 Litchfield Pl Southaven MS 38671-5926 Office: Stateline Animal Clin 100 Guthrie Dr Southaven MS 38671-5828

UTT, GLENN S., JR., motel investments and biotech industry company executive; b. Neodesha, Kans., Aug. 7, 1926; s. Glenn S. and Reba Pauline (White) U.; m. Mary Lou Ford, Aug. 8, 1948; 1 child, Jan A. B.S.E.E., BSBA, Kans. State U., 1949; M.B.A., Harvard U., 1951. Salesman Drexel Furniture Co., N.C., 1951-55; v.p. Booz Allen & Hamilton, Chgo. and Zurich, Switzerland, 1955-62; exec. v.p. Abbott Labs., North Chicago, Ill., 1962-83, also dir., ret., 1983; chmn. bd. Glendon Enterprises, Iron Mountain, Mich., Janmar Enterprises, Minocqua, Wis., Marjan Inc., Houghton, Mich., U.P. Hotel Group Inc., Houghton; bd. dirs. Sugen, Inc., Redwood City, Calif. Co-author: Lalique Perfume Bottles, 1990. Alderman City of Lake Forest, Ill., 1972-76, chmn. recreational bd., 1975-78; mem. exec. com. Lake County Republican Fedn., Waukegan, Ill., 1974-83. With USN, 1944-46. Mem. Beta Theta Pi. Avocations: antiques; objects of art. Home: PO Box 292 Palm Desert CA 92261-0292 Office: Janmar Enterprises PO Box 575 Minocqua WI 54548-0575

UTTAL, WILLIAM R(EICHENSTEIN), psychology and engineering educator, research scientist; b. Mineola, N.Y., Mar. 24, 1931; s. Joseph and Claire (Reichenstein) U.; m. Michiye Nishimura, Dec. 20, 1954; children: Taneil, Lynet, Lisa. Student, Miami U. Oxford, Ohio, 1947-48; B.S. in Physics, U. Cin., 1951; Ph.D. in Exptl. Psychology and Biophysics, Ohio State U., 1957. Staff Psychologist, mgr. behavioral sci. group IBM Research Center, Yorktown Heights, N.Y., 1957-63; assoc. prof. U. Mich., Ann Arbor, 1963-68, prof. psychology, 1968-86, research scientist, 1963-86, prof. emeritus, 1986—; grad. affiliate faculty dept. psychology U. Hawaii, 1986—; research scientist Naval Ocean Systems Ctr.-Hawaii Lab., Kailua, 1985-88; prof., chmn. dept. psychology Ariz. State U., Tempe, 1988-92, prof. dept. indsl. and mgmt. systems engring., 1992—, affiliated prof., Dept. of Computer Sci. and Engring., 1993—; vis. prof. Kyoto (Japan) Prefectural Med. U., 1965-66, Sensory Sci. Lab., U. Hawaii, 1968, 73, U. Western Australia, 1970-71, U. Hawaii, 1978-79, 80-81, U. Auckland, 1996; pres. Nat. Conf. on On-Line Uses Computers in Psychology, 1974. Author: Real Time Computers: Techniques and Applications in the Psychological Sciences, 1968, Generative Computer Assisted Instruction in Analytic Geometry, 1972, The Psychobiology of Sensory Coding, 1973, Cellular Neurophysiology and Integration: An Interpretive Introductin, 1975, An Autocorrelation Theory of Visual Form Detection, 1975, The Psychobiology of Mind, 1978, A Taxonomy of Visual Processes, 1981, Visual Form Detection in Three Dimensional Space, 1983, Principles of Psychobiology, 1983, The Detection of Nonplanar Surfaces in Visual Space, 1985, The Perception of Dotted Forms, 1987, On Seeing Forms, 1988, The Swimmer: A Computational Model of a Perceptual Motor System, 1992; also numerous articles; editor: Readings in Sensory Coding, 1972; assoc. editor Behavioral Research Method and Instrn., 1968-90, Computing: Archives for Electronic Computing, 1963-75, Jour. Exptl. Psychology: Perception and Performance, 1974-79; cons. editor Jour. Exptl. Psychology: Applied, 1994—. Served to 2d lt. USAF, 1951-53. USPHS spl. postdoctoral fellow, 1965-66; NIMH research scientist award, 1971-76. Fellow AAAS, Am. Psychol. Soc. (charter), Soc. Exptl. Psychologists (chmn. 1994-95); mem. Psychonomics Soc. Patentee in field. Office: Ariz State U Dept Indsl and Mgmt Systems Engring Tempe AZ 85287-1104

UTTER, ROBERT FRENCH, retired state supreme court justice; b. Seattle, June 19, 1930; s. John and Besse (French) U.; m. Elizabeth J. Stevenson, Dec. 28, 1953; children: Kimberly, Kirk, John. BS, U. Wash., 1952; LLB, 1954. Bar: Wash. 1954. Pros. atty. King County, Wash., 1955-57; individual practice law Seattle, 1957-59; ct. commr. King County Superior Ct., 1959-64, judge, 1964-69; judge Wash. State Ct. Appeals, 1969-71; judge Wash. State Supreme Ct., 1971-95, chief justice, 1979-81; ret., 1995; lectr. in field, leader comparative law tour People's Republic of China, 1986, 87, 88, 91, USSR, 1989; adj. prof. constl. law U. Puget Sound, 1987, 88, 89, 90, 91, 92, 93, 94; cons. CEELI, 1991, 93—, USIA, 1992; visitor to Kazakhstand and Kyrgystan Judiciary, 1993, 94, 95; lectr. to Albanian Judiciary, 1994, 95. Editor books on real property and appellate practice. Pres., founder Big Brother Assn., Seattle, 1955-67; pres., founder Job Therapy Inc., 1963-71; mem. exec. com. Conf. of Chief Justices, 1979-80, 81-86; pres. Thurston County Big Bros./Big Sisters, 1984; lectr. Soviet Acad. Moscow, 1991; USIA visitor to comment on jud. system, Latvia, 1992, Kazakstan, 1993-94,. Named Alumnus of Yr., Linfield Coll., 1973, Disting. Jud. Scholar, U. Ind., 1987, Judge of Yr., Wash. State Trial Lawyers, 1989, Outstanding Judge, Wash. State Bar Assn., 1990, Outstanding Judge, Seattle-King County Bar Assn., 1992, Conder-Faulkner lectr. U. Wash. Sch. Law, 1995, Disting. Alumnus Sch. Law U. Wash., 1995. Mem. ABA (commentator on proposed constns. of Albania, Bulgaria, Romania, Russia, Lithuania, Azerbaijan, Uzbekistan, Byelarus, Kazakhstan & Ukraine), Am. Judicature Soc. (Herbert Harley award 1983, sec. 1987—, chmn. bd. dirs., mem. exec. com.), Order of Coif. Baptist.

UVEGES, GEORGE, company executive; b. Cleve., Jan. 2, 1948; s. George and Irene (Merker) U.; m. Reneé Butler, July 30, 1971; children: Tom, Paul. BBA, Cleve. State U., 1970; MBA, Baldwin-Wallace U., 1978. CPA, Ohio. Sr. audit mgr. Ernst & Whinney, Cleve., 1971-85; treas., corp. controller Invacare Corp., Elyria, Ohio, 1985-91; CFO, v.p. adminstrn. GI Plastek, Elyria, 1991—. With U.S. Army, 1970-71. Mem. AICPA, Ohio Soc. CPAs, Fin. Execs. Inst., Cleve. State U. Alumni Assn. (pres. 1984-85). Republican. Roman Catholic. Office: GI Plastek Olive & Taylors Sts Elyria OH 44035

UVENA, FRANK JOHN, retired printing company executive, lawyer; b. Ernest, Pa., Feb. 2, 1934. AB, Ohio U., Athens, 1959; LLB, Ohio State U., Columbus, 1963. Bar: Ill. 1963. Assoc. firm McDermott, Will & Emery, Chgo., 1963-68; atty. R.R. Donnelley & Sons, Chgo., 1968-75, v.p., gen. counsel, 1975-84, sr. v.p. law and corp. staffs, 1984-95. Bd. dirs. Infant Welfare League Chgo., 1995, Am. Liver Soc., Chgo., 1996. With AUS, 1954-56. Mem. AMA, Ill. Bar Assn., Chgo. Bar Assn., Union League Club.

UWAKAH, ONYEBUCHI TIMOTHY, export company executive; b. Akoli-Imenyi, Abia, Nigeria, Aug. 25, 1942; came to U.S., 1981; s. Timothy Ikeocha and Rebecca Nwayinnaya (Ejimele) U.; m. ugonma Onyebuchi Nwankwo, Aug. 31, 1986; children: Obinna, Uzoma, Ikenna. BA, Golden Gate U., 1983, MPA, 1984, PhD, 1991. Officer Dept. of Agr., Owerri, Nigeria, 1977-81; asst. to pres. N.W. Equity Corp., San Francisco, 1985-87; pres. Manuman, Ltd., San Francisco, 1990—; examiner State Employment Devel. Dept., Oakland, Calif., 1993—. Vol. ops. analyst City of Oakland, 1991-92; mem. Mayor Jordan's Transit Team, San Francisco, 1991, San Francisco State U. Ctr. Profl. Devel., 1992—; bd. dirs. Loren Miller Homes, Inc., San Francisco, 1992—. Capt. Biafra Army, 1968-70. Mem. Am. Soc. Pub. Adminstrn., Agrl. Soc. Nigeria, Golden Gate U. Justice Club (sec. 1982-83). Methodist. Avocations: tennis, reading, guest speaking, gardening, community activities. Home: 954 Buchanan St San Francisco CA 94102-4117

UYEDA, SEIYA, geophysics educator; b. Tokyo, Nov. 28, 1929; s. Seiichi and Hatsuo (Okino) U.; m. Mutsuko Kosaka, July 6, 1952; children: Taro, Makiko, Naoko. BS, U. Tokyo, 1952, DSc, 1958; DSc (hon.), U. Athens, Greece, 1996. Rsch. assoc. Earthquake Rsch. Inst. U. Tokyo, 1957-64, assoc. prof. Geophys. Inst., 1964-69, prof. Earthquake Rsch. Inst., 1969-90; prof. dept. marine sci. and tech. Tokai U., Shimizu, Japan, 1990-94, dir. earthquake prediction rsch. ctr., 1995—; prof. Tex. A&M U, College Station, 1990-95, disting. lectr. Geodynamics Rsch. Inst., 1996—. Author: Debate About the Earth, 1966, Island Arcs, 1973, The New View of the Earth, 1978. Recipient Tanakadte prize Soc. Terrestial Magnetism and Electricity, 1955, Acad. prize, Japan Acad., 1987, G.P. Woollard award Geol. Soc. Am., 1989, Matsumae Prize for Academic Accomplishment, Tokai Univ., 1992. Fellow AAAS (hon.), Nat. Acad. Sci. (fgn. assoc., A Agassiz medal 1972), Russian Acad. Scis. (fgn.), Geol. Soc. London (hon.), European Union Geoscis. (hon.), Am. Geophys. Union (Walter Bucher medal 1991); mem. Am. Acad. Arts and Scis. (fgn.), Soc. Geology France (assoc.). Home: 2-39-6 Daizawa, Setagaya-ku, Tokyo 155, Japan Office: Tokai U, 3-20-1, Orido, Shimizu 424, Japan also: Tex A&M U Geodynamics Rsch Inst College Station TX 77843

UYEHARA, CATHERINE FAY TAKAKO (YAMAUCHI), physiologist, educator, pharmacologist; b. Honolulu, Dec. 20, 1959; d. Thomas Takashi and Eiko (Haraguchi) Uyehara; m. Alan Hisao Yamauchi, Feb. 17, 1990. BS, Yale U., 1981; PhD in Physiology, U. Hawaii, Honolulu, 1987. Postdoctoral fellow SmithKline Beecham Pharms., King of Prussia, Pa., 1987-89; asst. prof. in pediatrics U. Hawaii John Burns Sch. Medicine, Honolulu, 1991—; rsch. pharmacologist Kapiolani Med. Ctr. for Women and Children, Honolulu, 1990—; statis. cons. dept. clin. investigation Tripler Army Med. Ctr., Honolulu, 1984-87, 89—, chief rsch. pharmacology sect., 1991—, dir. coop. rsch. and devel. projects, 1995—; asst. prof. pharmacology U. Hawaii John A. Burns Sch. Medicine, 1993—; grad. faculty Interdisciplinary Biomed. Sci. program, 1995—. Contbr. articles to profl. jours. Mem. Am. Fedn. Clin. Rsch., Am. Physiol. Soc., Soc. Uniformed Endocrinologists, Endocrine Soc., We. Soc. Pediatric Rsch., N.Y. Acad. Scis. Democrat. Mem. Christian Ch. Avocations: swimming, diving, crafts, horticulture, music. Office: Tripler Army Med Ctr Dept Clin Investigation MCHK-CI 1 Jarrett White Rd Bldg 40 Rm 131 Honolulu HI 96859-5000

UYEHARA, OTTO ARTHUR, mechanical engineering educator emeritus, consultant; b. Hanford, Calif., Sept. 9, 1916; s. Rikichi and Umi (Nakayama) U.; m. Chisako Suda, Aug. 12, 1945; children: Otto Kenneth, Susan Joy Uyehara Schultheiss, Emi Ryu Uyehara-Stewart. BS, U. Wis., 1942, MS, 1943, PhD, 1946. Postdoctoral fellow U. Wis., Madison, 1945-46, rsch. assoc., 1946-47, asst. prof., then assoc. prof., 1949-57, prof., 1957-82, prof. emeritus, 1982—; pvt. practice cons. Anaheim, Calif., 1985—; mem. sci. adv. com. Eclin Corp., Branford, Conn., 1980—. Recipient Sci. Achievement award Japan Soc. Automotive Engrs, Internal Combustion Engine award ASME, 1994. FEllow Soc. Automotive Engrs.; mem. ASME (internal combustion divsn., Internal Combustion award 1994), Japan Soc. Mech. Engrs. (hon.). Home: 544 S Bond St Anaheim CA 92805-4823

UYETANI, TATSUYA AKI, electronics company executive; b. Tokyo, Apr. 12, 1940; s. Toyoma and Mieko Uyetani; m. Harue Uyetani, Apr. 6, 1968; children: Keiichiro, Masashi. BS, Keio U., Tokyo, 1963. Registered engr., Japan. Systems engr. Toshiba Corp., Tokyo, 1963-75, engring. mgr., 1975-83; head Software Tech. Ctr., Fuji Xerox, Tokyo, 1984-89, head sys. bus., 1989-92, with corp. tech. dept., 1992-94; chmn., CEO FX Palo Alto (Lab.) Inc., 1995—. Author: Introduction to Process Computer Control, 1972; editor: Local Area Network, 1985. Recipient 25th Ohm tech. prize Ohm, Tokyo, 1977. Mem. IEEE, ACM, Assn. Computing Machinery, Commonwealth Club. Avocations: golf, swimming, stamp collecting. Office: FX Palo Alto Lab Inc 3400 Hillview Ave PAHV-403 Palo Alto CA 94304

UYGUR, MUSTAFA ETI, materials and mechanical engineering educator; b. Kayseri, Turkey, Jan. 22, 1941; s. Ali and Mumine (Oktay) U.; m. Selime Kobakci, Dec. 16, 1971; children: Ayse, Esra, Zeynep, Ali. BSME, Mid. East Tech. U., Ankara, Turkey, 1963, MSc in Mech. Engring., 1964; MSc in Engring., Purdue U., 1967; PhD in Materials Sci. & Engring., Mid. East Tech. U., Ankara, Turkey, 1971. Rsch. assoc. Am. Oil Co. Rsch. Labs., Whiting, Ind., 1967; instr. Mid. East Tech. U., Ankara, Turkey, 1967-71, asst. prof., 1971-77, assoc. prof., 1977-84; prof. Gazi U., Ankara, Turkey, 1984-90; prof. mech. engring. dept. King Saud U., Riyadh, Saudi Arabia, 1990—; asst. chmn. materials sci. and engring. dept. Mid. East Tech. U., Ankara, 1977-80; dep. dean faculty tech. edn. Gazi U., Ankara, 1984-86, mem. coll. coun., grad. coll. coun., univ. senate, 1984-90; tech. & sci. advisor to dep. Min. of Nat. Def., Def. Industries Devel. Adminstrn., Ankara, 1987-90. Author: Dynamic NDT of Materials, 1976, 83, Glossary of Powder Metallurgy Terms, 1982, X-Ray Crystallography, 1983; editor-in-chief: Science-Research-Technology Five-Year Main Plan, 1988; contbr. 60 papers to profl. jours. and conf. procs.; supr. for devel. of many ednl. computer programs. Mem. specialization com. on nonferrous materials State Planning Orgn., Ankara, 1982, chmn. specialization com. on transfer of high tech. and employment, 1987-88, mem. specialization on sci. rsch., tech., 1987-88, chmn. edit. com. on sci., rsch., tech., 1988. Lt. (engr.) Turkish Army Tech. Svc.-Weapons Dept., 1973-74. Scholar Turkish Iron-Steel Works, 1963-64; rsch. grantee Turkish Sci. Rsch. Coun., 1971-73. Mem. Internat. Plansee Soc. Powder Metallurgy, Internat. Soc. Crystallographers, Am. Powder Metallurgy Inst. Internat., Am. Soc. for Metals Internat., Am. Soc. for Metals Internat.-Metall. Soc. Avocations: reading in all areas, listening to music, computers and programming, swimming, bowling. Office: King Saud U Coll Engring-Mech Engring Dept, PO Box 800, 11421 Riyadh Saudi Arabia

UYTENGSU, WILFRED, food products executive. CEO GF Industries. Office: Sunshine Biscuits Inc 100 Woodbridge Center Dr Woodbridge NJ 07095-1125 also: GF Industries Inc 930 98th Ave Oakland CA 94603*

UYTERHOEVEN, HUGO EMIL ROBERT, business educator and consultant; b. Eindhoven, The Netherlands, Aug. 6, 1931; came to U.S., 1955, naturalized, 1967; s. Willem and An (Von der Nahmer) U.; children: Monique, An, Sonia, Laura. D Iur, U. Zurich, 1955; D in law, U. Ghent, 1955; MBA, Harvard U., 1957, DBA, 1963. Mem. faculty Grad. Sch. Bus. Adminstrn. Harvard U., 1960—, Timken prof. bus. adminstrn. Grad. Sch. Bus. Adminstrn., 1974—, sr. assoc. dean Grad. Sch. Bus. Adminstrn., 1980-89; bd. dirs. Brown, Boveri & Co. Ltd., The Stanley Works, Harcourt Gen., Inc., Ciga-Geigy, AG, Bombardier, Inc., Ecolab, Inc.; mem. internat. adv. coun. Degussa Corp. Author: (with others) Strategy and Organization: Text and Cases in General Management, 1973, 2d edit., 1977, Business Policy, 8th edit., 1995. Mem. Planning Bd. Weston (Mass.), 1969-72, Conservation Commn., 1972-76; pres. Weston Forest and Trail Assn., 1970-77; trustee Concord Acad., 1982-88. Belgian-Am. Ednl. Found. fellow, 1955-57. Office: Harvard U Sch Bus Boston MA 02163

UZAN, BERNARD FRANCK, general and artistic director; b. Tunis, Tunisia, Dec. 5, 1944; arrived in Can., 1988; s. Henri and Elise Gabrielle (Pansieri) U.; m. Diana Soviero, Nov. 9, 1984. PhD, Paris U., 1968. Gen. & artistic dir. Théâtre français d'Amérique, Boston, 1973-83, Tulsa Opera, 1987-88, L'Opéra de Montreal, Que., Can., 1988—; adminstr., exec. dir. Alliance français de Boston, 1974-83; stage dir.: U.S.: Detroit, Dallas, Phila., L.A.; Can.: Montreal, Toronto, Vancouver; Europe: Monte-Carlo, Zurich, Palermo, Turin. Office: L'Opéra de Montréal, 260 de Maisonneuve W, Montreal, PQ Canada H2X 1Y9

UZMAN, BETTY GEREN, pathologist, retired educator; b. Fort Smith, Ark., Nov. 17, 1922; d. Benton Asbury and Myra Estelle (Petty) Geren; m. L. Lahut Uzman, Dec. 17, 1955 (dec.); 1 dau., Betty Tuba. Student, Fort Smith Jr. Coll., 1939-40; B.S., U. Ark., 1942; M.D., Washington U., 1945; postgrad., M.I.T., 1948-50; M.A. (hon.), Harvard U., 1967. Intern Childrens Hosp., Boston, 1945-46; resident in pathology Barnes Hosp., St. Louis, 1946-48; Am. Cancer Soc. research fellow MIT, Cambridge, Mass., 1948-50; chief biol. ultrastructure and exptl. pathology Children's Cancer Research Found., Boston, 1950-71; instr. Harvard Med. Sch., Boston, 1949-53, assoc., 1953-56, research assoc., 1956-67, assoc. prof., 1967-71, prof., 1971-72; head research dept. Sparks Regional Med. Center, Fort Smith, 1972-74; prof. pathology La. State U., Shreveport, 1974-77, U. Tenn., Memphis, 1978-89; assoc. chief staff rsch. VA, Shreveport, 1974-77; staff pathologist VA, Memphis, 1978-89, chief lab. svc., 1986-87; chief field ops., spl. asst. to dir. VA Central Office, Washington, 1978-79, dir. med. rsch. svcs., 1979-80; chmn. pathology A Study sect. NIH, 1973-76; cons. to sci. dir. Children's Cancer Rsch. Found., Boston, 1971-73; mem. adv. com. on prevention, diagnosis and treatment Am. Cancer Soc., 1970-73, 77-80; mem. adv. bd. Office Regeneration Rsch., VA, 1985-89; disting. vis. investigator Inst. Venezolano Investigation Cientificas, Caracas, 1972-74. Decorated Order of Andres Bello 1st class Venezuela; recipient Weinstein award United Cerebral Palsy, 1964; Am. Cancer Soc. research fellow, 1948-50. Mem. AAAS, Am. Soc. Cell Biology, Soc. Devel. Biology, Am. Acad. Neurology (assoc.), Am. Soc. Neurochemistry, Microscopy Soc. Am. (Diatome poster award 1985), Internat. Acad. Pathology, Am. Assn. Neuropathology (assoc.), Soc. Neurosci., Am. Assn. Cancer Rsch. Home and Office: Geren Farm 16048 E State Highway 197 Scranton AR 72863-9271

UZSOY, PATRICIA J., nursing educator and administrator; b. Corning, Ark.; m. Namik K. Diploma, Mo. Bapt. Hosp. Sch. Nursing, St. Louis, 1960; BSN, Washington U., St. Louis, 1962; MEd, Lynchburg Coll., 1977, EdS, 1981; MS in Nursing, U. Va., 1987. RN, Va. Dir. sch. nursing Lynchburg (Va.) Gen. Hosp., dir. Mem. ANA, NLN, Va. Nurses Assn. (Nurse of Yr. dist. III 1987).

UZZELL-BAGGETT, KARON LYNETTE, air force officer; b. Goldsboro, N.C., Apr. 28, 1964; d. Jesse Lee and Ernestine Smith (Merriweathers) Uzzell; m. Ronald Walter Baggett, July 26, 1990; stepchildren: Christina, Brian, Adam. BS, U. N.C., 1986; postgrad., U. Md., 1993-96. Commd. 2d lt. USAF, 1986, advanced through grades to capt., 1990; exec. officer 6ACCS USAF, Langley AFB, Va., 1986-88; ops. tng. officer 7393MUNSS USAF, Murted AFD, Turkey, 1988-89; command and control officer 52FW USAF, Spangdahlem AB, Germany, 1989-92; SENEX mission dir. 89AW USAF, Andrews AFB, Md., 1992-95, deputy chief classified control Office Sec. Def., 1995—. Emergency med. technician Orange County Rescue Squad, Hillsborough, N.C., 1985-86; treas. Melwood PTA, Upper Marlboro, Md., 1994—; meml. vol. Women in Mil. Svc., Washington, 1993—; entitlements vol. Whitman Walker Clinic, Washington, 1993—. Mem. Women in Mil. Svc. for Am., Southern Poverty Law Ctr. Democrat. Baptist. Avocations: running, weightlifting, sewing, cross stitching, gardening. Home: 10704 Tyrone Dr Upper Marlboro MD 20772-4631

VAADIA, BOAZ, sculptor; b. Petah-Tiqva, Israel, Nov. 13, 1951; s. Nissim and Rivka Vaadia; m. Kim Turner, Sept. 10, 1989; children: Rebecca Danielle, Sara Madeline. Student, Avni Inst. Fine Art, Tel Aviv, 1971. vis. artist Appalachian State U., Boone, N.C., 1982; resident Internat. Tel-Hai '80 Internat. Meeting, Israel, 1980. One-person shows include O.K. Harris Works of Art, N.Y.C., 1986, 88, 89, 94, Helander Gallery, Palm Beach, Fla., 1988, Jewish Mus., N.Y.C., 1988-89, Hokin Kaufman Gallery, Chgo., 1989, 90, Fay Gold Gallery, 1993, Allene Lapides Gallery, Santa Fe, 1995, Jaffe Baker Gallery, Fla., 1996, others; exhibited group shows at Helander Gallery, 1989-90, Utsukushi-ga-hara Open Air Mus., Japan, 1994, First Lady's Sculpture Garden, White House, 1995, more. Grantee NEA, 1988, Ariana Found. for Arts, 1986, Artists Space, 1983, Am.-Israel Cultural Found., 1975-76, Am. the Beautiful Fund, Palisades Interstate Park, 1977; Beeckman scholar, 1976-77. Home: 475 Broadway # 7flr New York NY 10013-5905 Studio: 104 Berry St Brooklyn NY 11211-2806

VACANO, JOST, cinematographer. Cinematographer: (films) Soldier of Orange, 1977, Spetters, 1980, Das Boot, 1981, The Neverending Story, 1984, 52 Pick-up, 1986, Robocop, 1987, Rocket Gibraltar, 1988, Total Recall, 1990, Untamed Heart, 1993. Office: care Spyros Skouras Sanford Skouras Gross & Assocs 1015 Gayley Ave Fl 3 Los Angeles CA 90024-3424

VACCA, JOHN JOSEPH, JR., television executive; b. Chgo., Apr. 7, 1922; s. John Joseph and Caroline (Bain) V.; m. Alice Isabel Ure, May 2, 1944; children: John Joseph, Dawn Susan, Kim Frances. Student, Northwestern U., 1940-42, Internat. Corr. Schs., 1950-54, Harvard U., 1966. Editor, Midwest Times, Chgo., 1940-41; with prodn. dept. NBC Radio, 1946-47; news dir. sta. KECK, Odessa, Tex., 1947-49; chief announcer sta. KECK, 1948-49; program mgr. KOSA-Radio, Odessa, 1949-55; sta. mgr. KOSA-TV, 1955-61, gen. mgr., 1962-72; v.p., dir. Trigg Vaughn Stas., Inc., Odessa, 1962-67; sec. Odessa Broadcasting Co., 1950-72; asst. sec. Doubleday Broadcasting Co., 1967-77, v.p., 1967-75, sr. v.p., 1975-77; gen. mgr. KDTV, Dallas, 1972-73; TV cons. Dallas, 1978—; v.p., dir., gen. mgr. Heart O'Texas Broadcasting, Waco, Tex., 1978-83; v.p. Dunn Prodns., Inc., Dallas, 1984-88, pres., 1989-92; ind. TV producer Dallas, 1992—. Author: Seven Keys to Success, 1981. Bd. dirs. Odessa Community Chest, 1964-72, Better Bus. Bur., 1956-72; campaign maj. ARC, 1951-72; publicity adviser Ector County chpt. Nat. Found. for Infantile Paralysis, 1949-72; campaign coordinator Civic Music Assn., 1950-72; sponsor, adviser Permian Playhouse, 1959-72, v.p., bd. dirs., 1971-72, City councilman, Odessa, 1962-64; Bd. dirs. Am. Cancer Soc. Served with USAAF, 1942-46. Recipient Zeus award Epsilon Sigma Alpha, 1971. Mem. Nat., Tex. assns. broadcasters, Tex. AP Broadcasters Assn., Advt. Club Odessa (pres. 1960-61, dir. 1960-63), C. of C. (publicity adviser 1950-72), Holy Name Soc. Roman Catholic. Club: K.C. (sec. Odessa 1950-51). Home and Office: 646 Harvest Hill St Lewisville TX 75067-3588 *A philosophy of service, personal and through broadcasting, coupled with a sincere approach to excellent Human Relations have formed the keystone of my career. Consistent honesty and a constant effort to give and produce much more than required have always been guiding principles. My goals have been set with flexible policies to implement them, ever mindful that 'change' is an integral part of life and progress.*

VACCARO, LOUIS CHARLES, college president; b. L. A., July 25, 1930; s. Louis Charles and Louise (Vinciguerra) V.; m. Jean Hudak, Jan. 29, 1955 (div. Aug. 1983); children: Mary Lou, Theresa, Victoria, Frances, Michelle, Justin; m. Linda Lasher, July, 1987. A.B., U. So. Calif., 1957, M.Ed., 1961; M.A., Calif. State U.-Northridge, 1960; Ph.D., Mich. State U., 1963; Litt.D. (hon.), St. Martin's Coll., Olympia, Wash., 1969; L.H.D. (hon.), Vt. Coll. of Norwich U., Montpelier, 1978; LLD (hon.), Coll. of St. Rose, Albany, N.Y., 1996. Asst. to v.p. acad. affairs Marquette U., Milw., 1963-67; v.p. acad. affairs U. Portland, Oreg., 1967-70; pres. Marycrest Coll., Davenport, Iowa, 1970-72, Colby-Sawyer Coll., New London, N.H., 1972-77, Siena Heights Coll., Adrian, Mich., 1977-83, Coll. of St. Rose, 1983—; bd. dirs. Inst. Internat. Edn., N.Y.C., Key Bank Trust Corp., Albany. Author: Notes from a College President, 1976, Planning in Small Colleges, 1979, In Search of Wisdom, 1994; editor: Student Freedom in American Higher Education, 1969, Reshaping American Higher Education, 1969. Bd. dirs. Albany Strategic Planning, 1983—, Albany Symphony Orch., 1984—; mem. Tricentennial Commn. City of Albany, 1986—; chmn. Bicentennial Commn. U.S. Constn. City of Albany, 1987. Served with USAF, 1951-52. W. K. Kellogg Found. fellow Mich. State U., East Lansing, 1961-63; Exxon Found. grantee, 1975. Mem. Nat. Cath. Edn. Assn. (exec. com., chair bd. dirs.), Hudson-Mohawk Consortium Colls., Ft. Orange Club, Univ. Club. Roman Catholic. Avocations: reading; walking; Italian cooking; travel; racquet sports. Home: 90 S Manning Blvd Albany NY 12203-1733 Office: Coll St Rose 432 Western Ave Albany NY 12203-1419

VACCARO, RALPH FRANCIS, marine biologist; b. West Somerville, Mass., Apr. 30, 1919; s. Angelo Ralph and Adelaide (Alberlini) V.; m. Martha Ann Walsh, Apr. 19, 1955; children: Christopher Ralph, Adelaide Marie, John Michael, Mark Joseph, Thomas James (dec.), Peter Anthony. B.S., Tufts U., 1941; M.P.H., MIT, 1943. Sanitary engring. aide Commonwealth of Mass., Boston, 1946-47; pub. health bacteriologist Assn. Am. Railroads, Balt., 1947-48; sr. rsch. scientist Woods Hole Oceanographic Inst. (Mass.), 1948-86, chmn. dept. biol., 1984-85; cons. environ. quality; assoc. math.-sci. staff Falmouth (Mass.) High Sch., 1989—. Patentee in field. Served with USPHS, 1956—; served with U.S. Army, 1943-46. Mem. Am. Soc. Limnology and Oceanography, AAAS. Republican. Roman Catholic. Home: PO Box 245 West Falmouth MA 02574-0245

VACCO, DENNIS C., state attorney general; b. Buffalo, Aug. 16, 1952; s. Carmen A. and Mildred V.; m. Adrianne Venczel (div.). BA, Colgate U., 1974; JD, SUNY, Buffalo, 1978. Bar: N.Y. 1978, Fed. Ct. 1978, 82. Asst. dist. atty. Office of Erie County Dist. Atty., Buffalo, 1978-82, chief G.J.

bureau, 1982-88; U.S. Atty. We. Dist. N.Y. Buffalo, 1988—; now Atty. Gen. State of New York, Albany; chmn. Atty. Gen.'s Environ. Subcom., Atty. Gen.'s Subcom. on Organized Crime and Violent Crime; mem. Nat. Environ. Enforcement Coun. Co-chair Erie County Community Commn. on Alcohol and Substance Abuse; bd. dirs. United Way of Erie County. Recipient Environ. Enforcement Leadership award Atty. Gen. Dept. of Justice, Washington, 1991. Mem. N.Y. State Bar Assn., Erie County Bar Assn., Nat. Dist. Attys. Assn., N.Y. State Dist. Attys. Assn., NCCJ, Hamburg Devel. Corp., 100 Club of Buffalo, U. Buuffalo Law Alumni Assn. (bd. dirs.). Republican. Roman Catholic. Avocations: travel, sports. Office: Off of Atty Gen State Capitol Rm 220 Albany NY 12224*

VACHHER, PREHLAD SINGH, psychiatrist; b. Rawalpindi, Punjab, Pakistan, Nov. 30, 1933; came to U.S., 1960; s. Thakar Singh and Harbans Kaur (Ghai) V.; m. Margaret Mary Begley, Oct. 9, 1963; children: Paul, Sheila, Mary Ann, Eileen, Mark. Grad., Khalsa Coll., India, 1950; MD, Panjab U., Amritsar, India, 1956. Diplomate Am. Bd. Psychiatry. Staff N.J. State Hosp., Trenton, 1965-66, Wayne County Gen. Hosp., Eloise, Mich., 1966-68; pvt. practice Livonia, Mich., 1966-75, Woodstock, Va., 1991—; pres. Vachher Psychiat. Ctr., P.C., Livonia, 1975-91; dir. community psychiatry Northville (Mich.) State Hosp., 1968-71; cons. staff Kingswood Hosp., Ferndale, Mich., 1967-72, Annapolis Hosp., Wayne, 1967-88, St. Joseph Mercy Hosp., Ann Arbor, 1970-89; westland staff Margaret Montgomery Hosp., 1988-91; bd. dirs. Oakland Rental Housing Assn., 1990-91; med. dir. mental health unit Shenandoan County Meml. Hosp., Woodstock, Va., 1991-94. Mem. Am. Psychiat. Assn., Va. Psychiat. Soc., Sikh Physicians in Mich. (bd. dirs. 1987), Canton C. of C. (pres. 1975), Sikh Bus. Profl. Coun. (pres. 1988—), Rotary (Canton and Plymouth, Mich., Woodstock), Prince William County C. of C. Office: 14573 Potomac Mills Rd Woodbridge VA 22192

VACHON, LOUIS, psychiatrist, educator; b. Montreal, June 15, 1932; m. Monique Blain, June 25, 1960; children: Philip, Dominique. BA, U. Montreal, 1952, MD, 1958. Diplomate Am. Bd. Psychiatry and Neurology. Intern Hotel Dieu de Montreal, Que., 1957-58, resident in psychiatry, 1958-61; intern Hotel Dieu de Montreal, 1957-58; psychiat. resident Instiut Albert Prevost, Montreal, 1958-61; sr. physician Medfield (Mass.) State Hosp., 1961-62; rsch. assoc., then instr. Boston U. Med. Sch., 1962-68, asst. prof., then assoc. prof., 1968-87, interim chmn. div. psychiatry, 1985-87, prof., chmn. div. psychiatry, 1987—; dir. psychiatry outpatient svc. Univ. Hosp., Boston, 1978-85, interim psychiatrist-in-chief, 1985-87, psychiatrist-in-chief, vis. physician in psychiatry, 1987—. Contbg. author: Comprehensive Textbook of Psychiatry, 1989. Fellow Am. Psychiat. Assn.; mem. Boston Psychoanalytic Soc. Inst. (faculty 1983—, pres.-elect 1990), Am. Psychoanalytic Assn., Internat. Psychoanalytic Assn., Mass. Psychiat. Soc. (sec. 1990—), Am. Psychosomatic Soc., Mass. Med. Soc., Boston. Office: Boston U Sch Medicine 720 Harrison Ave Rm 914 Boston MA 02118-2334

VACHON, LOUIS-ALBERT CARDINAL, archbishop; b. St. Frederic, Que., Can., Feb. 4, 1912; s. Napoleon and Alexandrine (Gilbert) V. D.Ph., Laval U., 1947, hon. degree, 1982; D.Th., St. Thomas Aquinas U., Rome, 1949; hon. degrees, U. Montreal, McGill and Victoria, 1964, Guelph U., 1966, Moncton U., 1967, Bishop's, Queen's and Strasbourg U., 1968, U. Notre Dame, 1971, Carleton U., 1972, Laval U., 1982. Superior Grand Seminaire Québec, 1955-59; superior gen. Le Séminaire de Qué., 1960-77; prof. philosophy Laval U., 1941-47, prof. theology, 1949-55, vice-rector, 1959-60, rector, 1960-72; protonotary apostolic, 1963-77, aux. bishop of Que., 1977-81, archbishop of Que. and primate of Can., 1981-90, apptd. Cardinal with title St. Paul of the Cross, 1985; Past pres. Corp. Laval U. Med. Centre; mem. Sacred Congregation for Clergy, Vatican, 1986—; adminstrv. bd. Nat. Order of Qué., 1985—, Can. Conf. Cath. Bishops, 1981—. Author: Espérance et Présomption, 1958, Verité et Liberte, 1962, Unité de l'universite, 1962, Apostolat de l'universitaire catholique, 1963, Memorial, 1963, Communauté universitaire, 1963, Progres de l'universite et consentement populaire, 1964, Responsabilite collective des universitaires, 1964, Les humanites aujourd'hui, 1966, Excellence et loyauté des universitaires, 1969, Pastoral Letters, 1981—. Hon. pres. La Société des etudes grecques et latines du Québec; assoc. mem. bd. Quebec Symphony Orch.; bd. govs. Laval U. Found. Decorated officier de l'Ordre de la Fidelité française, companion Order of Can., du Conseil de langue française, Ordre nat. du Qué., officier de la Légion d'honneur, France. Fellow Royal Soc. Can.; mem. Canadian Assn. French Lang. Educators (pres. 1970-72), Assn. Univs. and Colls. Can. (pres. 1965-66), Conf. Rectors and Prins. Que. Univs. (pres. 1965-68), Internat. Assn. Univs. (dep. mem. adminstrv. bd. 1965-70), Assn. des universites partiellement ou entierement de langue française (adminstrv. bd. 1961-69), Internat. Fedn. Cath. Univs. (adminstrv. bd. 1963-70), Ordre des francophones d'Amérique. *

VACHON, MARILYN ANN, retired insurance company executive; b. Fort Wayne, Ind., Dec. 12, 1924; d. Robert J. and Maude (Shaffer) V. Asst. treas Lincoln Nat. Life Ins. Co., Fort Wayne, Ind., 1961-87, asst. v.p., 1973-87; sec. Lincoln Nat. Life Ins. Co., Fort Wayne, 1980-87; asst. sec. Lincoln Nat. Corp., Fort Wayne, 1977-80, asst. treas., 1977-87, sec., 1980-87. Home: 1825 Cortland Ave Fort Wayne IN 46808-2446

VACHON, ROGATIEN ROSAIRE (ROGIE VACHON), professional hockey team executive; b. Palmarolle, Que., Can., Sept. 8, 1945; m. Nicole Vachon; children: Nicholas, Jade, Mary Joy. Goaltender Montreal (Que.) Canadiens, NHL, 1966-72, Los Angeles Kings, NHL, 1972-78, Detroit Red Wings, NHL, 1978-80, Boston Bruins, 1980-82; asst. coach Los Angeles Kings, 1982-84, gen. mgr., 1984—, alt. gov., now asst. to chmn. Co-recipient Vezina Trophy, 1968. Office: care Los Angeles Kings PO Box 17013 3900 W Manchester Blvd Inglewood CA 90305*

VACHON, SERGE JEAN, bank executive; b. Montreal, Que., Can., May 15, 1939; s. Adrien Joseph and Helene Marie (Contre) V. M.Econ. Sci., U. Montreal, 1963; diploma, Inst. IMF, Washington, 1966. Asst. prof. U. Montreal, Que., Can., 1962-63; adviser to gov. Bank of Can., Ottawa, Ont., 1980—, officer, 1981-83; chmn. Can. Payments Assn., Ottawa, Ont., 1981—. Recipient 1st prize Best Thesis in Econs. and Fin. Montreal Stock Exchange, 1963; recipient medal Lt. Gov. Que., 1963; Can. Council fellow, 1964. Mem. Societe Canadienne de Science Economique (dir. 1975-77). Roman Catholic. Club: Cercle Universitaire (Ottawa, Ont., Can.).

VACIK, JAMES PAUL, university administrator; b. North Judson, Ind., Nov. 30, 1931; s. George J. and Elsie E. (Paulsen) V.; m. Dorothy M. Nobles, Dec. 27, 1967; children: Deborah, Pamella, James, Stephen, Joshua, Jonathan. BS in Pharmacy, Purdue U., 1955, MS in Medicinal Chemistry, 1957, PhD in Bionucleonics, 1959. Cert. hazard control mgr.; registered biosafety profl., registered pharmacist, Ind., N.D., Ala. Asst. prof. bionucleonics dept. Purdue U., Lafayette, Ind., 1959-60; assoc. prof., dept. chmn. pharm. chemistry & bionucleonics N.D. State U., Fargo, 1960-63; prof., dept. chmn. pharm. chemistry & bionucleonics N.D. State U., 1963-76; assoc. prof. pharmacology Univ. S. Ala., Mobile, 1976-82; adj. prof., dir. environ. safety Univ. S. Ala., 1982—; Pub. Health Svc. grant dir. N.D. State U., Fargo, 1963-71; VA Hosp. cons. VA Hosp. System, Washington, 1966; vis. prof. Nat. Reactor Testing Sta., Idaho Falls, Idaho, 1968; pvt. cons. to various indsl. firms, 1970—. Contbr. articles to profl. Mem., first dir. "Showboat on the Red," Jaycees, Fargo, 1965. With U.S. Army, 1949-52, ETO. Named Outstanding Educator Am., Fuller & Dees, Washington, 1975. Mem. Am. Chem. Soc., Am. Pharm. Assn., Health Physics Soc. (chmn. com.), Am. Biol. Safety Assn. (bd. dirs. 1985-87), Health Physics Soc. (pres., treas., bd. dirs. Ala chpt. 1977—, pres., bd. dirs. N. Ctrl. chpt. 1969—), Masons. Baptist. Avocations: camping, fishing, woodworking. Home: 1220 Vendome Dr W Mobile AL 36609-3326 Office: U South Ala CC CB 307 University Blvd N Mobile AL 36688-3053

VACKETTA, CARL LEE, lawyer; b. Danville, Ill., Aug. 3, 1941; s. Peter G. and Julia M. (Columbus) V. BS, U. Ill., 1963, JD, 1965. Bar: Ill. 1965, D.C. 1968, U.S. Dist. Ct. D.C. 1968, U.S. Ct. Fed. Claims 1968, U.S. Supreme Ct. 1970. Tax lawyer GM, Detroit, 1965-66; ptnr. Sellers, Conner & Cuneo, Washington, 1968-74, Pettit & Martin, Washington, 1974-95, Piper & Marbury, Washington, 1995—; adj. prof. law Georgetown U., 1971—. Capt. U.S. Army, 1966-68. Fellow ABA (sec. pub. contract law sect. 1978-79, coun. 1979-82, contract law sect. 1993), Nat. Contract Mgmt. Assn.; mem. Fed. Bar Assn., D.C. Bar Assn., Nat. Assn. Purchasing Mgrs. Roman Catholic. Club: University (Washington). Co-author: Government Contract Default Termination, 1991, 93, 95; co-editor Extraordinary Contractual Relief Reporter, 1974—. Office: Piper & Marbury 7th Fl 1200 19th St NW Washington DC 20036-2430 also: Piper & Marbury 11th Fl 36 S Charles St Baltimore MD 21201

VADEN, FRANK SAMUEL, III, lawyer, engineer; b. San Antonio, Nov. 13, 1934; s. Frank Samuel Jr. and Helen Alyne (Roberts) V.; m. Caroline Chittenden Gerdes, Feb. 20, 1960; children; Christina Louise (Mrs. Eugene Linton), Olivia Anne (Mrs. Warren Augenstein), Cecilia Claire (Mrs. Scott Johnson). BSEE and BS in Indsl. Engring., Tex. A&M U., 1957; JD, So. Meth. U., 1963. Bar: Tex. 1963, U.S. Dist. Ct. (we. and so. dists.) Tex. 1963, U.S. Ct. Appeals (5th, 9th, 11th and Fed. cirs.) 1963, U.S. Supreme Ct. 1986; registered U.S. Patent and Trademark Office 1964. Assoc. Arnold & Roylance, Houston, 1963-66; ptnr. Arnold, White & Durkee, Houston, 1966-73, mng. ptnr., 1973-78; prin. Frank S. Vaden III, P.C., Houston, 1978-80; sr. ptnr. Vaden, Eickenroht & Thompson, L.L.P., Houston, 1980—; bd. dirs. Phoenix Annydrous, Inc., Houston; lectr. in field. Author: Invention Protection for Practicing Engineers, 1971; contbr. numerous articles to profl. jours. Capt. S.C., U.S. Army, 1957-67. Fellow Tex. Bar Found. (sustaining), Houston Bar Found. (sustaining); mem. ABA (mem. standing com. on spceelization), Tex. Bar Assn. (chair intellectual property law sec. 1984-85), Houston Bar Assn., Am. Intellectual Property Law Assn., Houston Intellectual Property Law Assn. (pres. 1985-86), U.S. Trademark Assn., Licensing Exec. Soc. (chmn. Houston chpt. 1987-88). Republican. Episcopalian. Office: Vaden Eickenroht & Thompson 1 Riverway Ste 1100 Houston TX 77056-1903

VADNAIS, ALFRED WILLIAM, lawyer; b. Pawtucket, R.I., Nov. 25, 1935; s. Edmund L. and Hilda W. (Winn) V.; m. Joan Bernice Markowski, Feb. 1, 1959; children—Alison J., Arlene J., Elisabeth Ann. B.A., Hofstra U., 1958; LL.B., Syracuse U., 1961. Bar: R.I. 1961, Tenn. 1972, U.S. Ct. Appeals (6th cir.) 1973, U.S. Ct. Appeals (4th cir.) 1978, U.S. Ct. Appeals (2d cir.) 1980, U.S. Supreme Ct. 1980, Pa. 1981, U.S. Dist. Ct. (we. dist.) Pa. 1982, U.S. Ct. Appeals (3d cir.) 1984. Labor atty., chief counsel Westinghouse Electric Co., Pitts., 1965-72; ptnr. Humphreys, Hutcheson & Moseley, Chattanooga, Tenn., 1972-81; ptnr. Eckert, Seamans, Cherin & Mellott, Pitts., 1981-93, chmn. labor-employment dept. Served to 1st lt. U.S. Army, 1961-63. Mem. ABA, Tenn. Bar Assn., Pa. Bar Assn., Allegheny County Bar Assn., Pitts. C. of C. Republican. Roman Catholic. Clubs: Pitts. Field, Pittsburgh. Office: Long Cove Club 30 Long Brow Rd Hilton Head Island SC 29928-3312

VADUS, GLORIA A., document examiner; b. Forrestville, Pa.. Diploma, Cole Sch. Graphology, Calif., 1978; BA in Psychology Counseling, Columbia Pacific U., 1981, MA in Psychology, 1982; diploma handwriting expert, Edith Eisenberg, Bethesda, Md., 1991. Cert. Am. Acad. Graphology, Washington, 1978, tchr. Coun. Graphological Socs., 1980; ct. qualified document examiner; registered graphologist; cert. behavioral profiling and cert. questioned documents, diplomate Am. Bd. Forensic Examiners, 1993, 94. Pres., owner Graphinc, Inc., 1976—; accredited instr. graphology Montgomery County Schs., Md., 1978; instr. Psychogram Centre, 1978-85; testifier superior and probate cts. Author numerous studies, papers, and environ. articles in field. Chmn. Letter of Hope for POW's; vol. Montgomery County, 1987-88. Recipient Gold Nib Analyst of Yr. award, 1982, Dancing Fan award Marine Tech. Soc., Japan, 1991, Spl. award U.S./Japan Marine Facilities Panel, 1978-94, Valuable Contbn. Japanese Panel UJNR/MFP, 1994; named Woman of Yr. ABI, 1990, 93-96, IBC, 1992-93, 95-96. Fellow Am. Bd. Forensic Examiners (Outstanding Contrbn. cert.); mem. Am. Handwriting Analysis Found. (cert., pres. 1982-84, chmn. rsch. com., adv. bd. 1981-86, chmn. nominations com. 1985-86, officiator 1986, mem. policy planning and ethics com. 1986-91, ethics chmn. 1989-91, chmn., past pres. adv. bd. 1989-91), Nat. Forensic Ctr., Nat. Assn. Document Examiners (ethics hearing bd. 1986, chmn. nominations com. 1987-88, elections chmn. 1988, parliamentarian 1988-92), Internat. Platform Assn., Soc. Francaise de Graphologie, Nat. Writers Club, Meninnger Found., Soroptimist Interant. (v.p., nom. pres.), Nat. Capital Jaguars Club Am. (judge 1976-86), Henry Hicks Garden Club (v.p., judge, chmn. flower shows), Sierra Club. Home: 8500 Timber Hill Ln Potomac MD 20854-4237

VADZEMNIEKS, MICHAEL LESTER, plastics company executive; b. Buffalo, Oct. 31, 1955; s. Olgerts and Linda Lou (Evans) V. Assoc. Archtl. Tech., Williamsport (Pa.) Cmty. Coll., 1975. Plant mgr. Engineered Plastics, Inc., Lake City, Pa., 1977-83; prodn. supr. Hoover Universal, Erie, Pa., 1983-84; engring. mgr. OEM/Erie, Inc., 1984-88; plant mgr. PHB-Molding Divsn., Fairview, Pa., 1988-93; gen. mgr. Springfield Plastics, Inc., East Springfield, Pa., 1993—. Founding trustee Old Lake Rd. Summer, East Springfield, Pa., 1986; pres., trustee City Trust, 1987-89; dir. Lake Erie Cmty. Fed. Credit Union (pres. 1989-95); organist, pianist Federated Ch., 1988-95. Mem. Northwestern Sportsmen's Club (treas. 1990-95). Republican. Avocations: music performance-piano, downhill skiing, gourmet cooking, carpentry, gardening. Home: 13478 Old Lake Rd East Springfield PA 16411 Office: Springfield Plastics Inc 3247 Rt 215 East Springfield PA 16411

VAETH, AGATHA MIN-CHUN FANG, quality assurance nurse, wellness consultant, home health nurse; b. Beijing, Feb. 19, 1935; d. Yung-Cheng and Wen-Pu (Cheng) Fang; m. Randy H. Vaeth, July 20, 1971; children: David Sun, Elizabeth Cheng, Philip Cheng. Diploma, Mary View Hosp. Sch. Nursing, Portsmouth, Va., 1959; student, Okla. State U., 1969-73; BS, St. Joseph's Coll., North Windham, Maine, 1986, postgrad., 1989—; postgrad., La. State U., 1986. Staff nurse, charge nurse Stillwater (Okla.) Mcpl. Hosp.; clin. nurse USIHH Hosp., Pawnee, Okla.; clin. nurse, relief supr. Gillis W. Long Hansen's Disease Ctr., Carville, La., supervisory clin. nurse; wellness cons. Translator video cassettes on Hansens Disease; illustrator herpetology lab manuel; art exhbns. at Barton Rouge Art & Artist Guild, 1976-77. Recipient Outstanding Performance award GWLHD, PHS, DHHS, 1991, 1993, High Quality Performance award, 1978, Dedicated Svc. to Clin. Br. award, 1981, Outstanding Nurses award Baton Rouge Dist. Nurses' Assn., 1994. Fellow Internat. Biog. Assn. (life); mem. ANA, AAUW, La. Nurses Assn., Baton Rouge Nurses Assn., Am. Coll. Health Execs. Avocations: ballroom dancing, swimming, travel, painting, writing. Home: 1274 Marilyn Dr Baton Rouge LA 70815-4928

VAETH, NANCY ANN, sales executive; b. Mineola, N.Y., Oct. 21, 1954; d. Jerome Marcus and Mary Teresa (MacStoker) V. B.A., Syracuse U., 1976. Advt. salesperson Sta. WEZG/WSOQ, Syracuse, N.Y., 1976-78, KMJQ, Houston, 1978-80; advt. salesperson Sta. WPLX/KLIF, Dallas, 1980-81, nat. sales mgr., 1981-82, gen. sales mgr., 1982—. Republican. Roman Catholic. Office: Sta KRBE-AM 9801 Westheimer Rd Ste 700 Houston TX 77042-3955*

VAGELOS, PINDAROS ROY, pharmaceutical company executive; b. Westfield, N.J., Oct. 8, 1929; s. Roy John and Marianthi (Lambrinides) V.; m. Diana Touliatos, July 10, 1955; children: Randall, Cynthia, Andrew, Ellen. AB, U. Pa., 1950; MD, Columbia U., 1954; DSc (hon.), Washington U., 1980, Brown U., 1982, U. Medicine and Dentistry of N.J., 1984, NYU, 1989, Columbia U., 1990; LLD (hon.), Princeton U., 1990; LHD (hon.), Rutgers U., 1991; DSc (hon.), N.J. Inst. Tech., 1992, SUNY, 1994. Intern medicine Mass. Gen. Hosp., 1954-55, asst. resident medicine, 1955-56; surgeon Lab. Cellular Physiology, NIH, 1956-59; surgeon Lab. Biochemistry, 1959-64, head sect. comparative biochemistry, 1964-66; prof. biochemistry, chmn. dept. biol. chemistry Washington U. Sch. Medicine, St. Louis, 1966-75; dir. div. biology and biomed. scis. Washington U. Sch. Medicine, 1973-75; sr. v.p. research Merck, Sharp & Dohme Research Labs., Rahway, N.J., 1975-76, pres., 1976-84; corp. sr. v.p. Merck & Co., Inc., Rahway, N.J., 1982-84, exec. v.p., 1984-85, CEO, 1985-86, chmn., CEO, 1986-94, also bd. dirs.; chmn. Regeneron Pharms., Inc., Tarrytown, N.Y., 1995—; mem. Inst. Medicine, NAS, 1974—; chmn. sci. adv. bd. Ctr. for Advanced Biotech. and Medicine, 1985-94; bd. dirs. Estee Lauder, Prudential Ins. Co., PepsiCo, Inc., McDonnell Douglas Corp. Trustee U. Pa., 1988—, chmn. bd., 1994—; trustee Rockefeller U., 1976-94, Danforth Found., 1978—; mem. President's Commn. on Environ. Quality, 1991-93, Adv. Com. Trade Policy and Negotiations, 1992-94, Bus. Coun., 1987—; bd. mng. dirs. Met. Opera Assn., Inc., 1989-95; bd. dirs. N.J. Performing Arts Ctr., 1989—, co-chmn , 1992. Recipient award for chemistry in svc. to soc., NAS, 1995, Pupin medal, 1995. Mem. Am. Chem. Soc. (Enzyme Chemistry award 1967), Am. Soc. Biol. Chemists, Nat. Acad. Scis., Am. Acad. Arts and Scis., Am. Philosophical Soc., Bus. Roundtable (policy com. 1987-94). Avocations: jogging, tennis, sculling. Discoverer of acyl-carrier protein. Home: 82 Mosle Rd Far Hills NJ 07931-2228 Office: Regeneron Pharms Inc 777 Old Saw Mill River Rd Tarrytown NY 10591-6700

VAGET, HANS RUDOLF, language professional, educator; b. Marienbad, Czekoslovakia, Feb. 2, 1938; came to U.S., 1964; s. Hans Ernst and Berta (Isop) V.; m. Ann Leone; children: Melanie Claudine, Erec Alexander. MA, U. Tübingen, Fed. Republic Germany, 1964; PhD, Columbia U., 1969. Instr. Columbia U., N.Y.C., 1964-67; from instr. to prof. Smith Coll., Northampton, Mass., 1967—; vis. prof. U. Calif., Irvine, 1979, Columbia U., 1985, Princeton U., 1986-87, Yale U., 1991, U. Hamburg, 1992. Author: Dilettantismus bei Goethe, 1971, Goethe. Der Mann von 60 Jahren, 1982, Thomas-Mann Kommentar, 1984; author, editor: Briefwechsel T. Mann-Agnes Meyer, 1992; contbr. articles to profl. and ednl. publs. Recipient Thomas Mann-Medaille, 1994; grantee NEH, 1985, Am. Coun. Learned Socs., 1986. Mem. MLA, Assn. Tchrs. of German, Deutsche Schillergesellschaft, Thomas-Mann-Gesellschaft, Goethe Soc. N.Am. (co-founder), Wagner Soc., Am. Musicol. Soc. Office: Smith Coll Dept German Northampton MA 01063-0001

VAGLIANO, ALEXANDER MARINO, banker; b. Paris, France, Mar. 15, 1927; came to U.S., 1940, naturalized, 1945; s. Andre M. and Barbara (Allen) V.; children: Barbara A., Andre M., Justin C. Grad., St. Paul's Sch., Concord, N.H., 1944; B.A., Harvard, 1949, LL.B. cum laude, 1952. Bar: N.Y. bar 1952. Asso. firm White & Case, N.Y.C., 1952-58; asst. treas. J.P. Morgan & Co., Inc., N.Y.C., 1959; v.p. Morgan Guaranty Trust Co., N.Y.C., 1959-62, 65-66; sr. v.p. Morgan Guaranty Trust Co., 1968-76, exec. v.p., 1976-81; chief exec. officer Banca Vonwiller, Milan, Italy, 1967-68; chmn. Morgan Guaranty Internat. Finance Corp., 1976-81, J.P. Morgan Overseas Capital Corp., 1976-81; ptnr. Price Waterhouse and Ptnrs., 1983-85; chmn. Sunset Ridge Farm, Inc., 1983—, Michelin Fin. Corp., Greenville, S.C., 1985—; chmn. bd. advisors Equity Linked Investors, N.Y.C., 1985—; pres. The N.Y. Farmers, 1992-94; bd. dirs. Optimum Resource, S.C., Holographics, Inc., N.Y., Ea. States Exposition; dir. office of capital devel. and fin. Near East and South Asia, AID, 1963-65; adviser Yale Econ. Growth Ctr., 1973—, NYU Inst. French Studies, 1979—; trustee Coun. for Excellence in Govt., 1990—. Pres. Parks Council N.Y.C., 1971-73; bd. dirs. French Am. Found. , N.Y.C., 1986—; gov. The Atlantic Inst. Internt. Affairs, 1986-90. Served with AUS, 1945-47. Mem. Council Fgn. Relations. Clubs: Brook (N.Y.C.); Travellers (Paris). Home and Office: Sunset Ridge Farm Inc Norfolk CT 06058

VAGTS, DETLEV FREDERICK, lawyer, educator; b. Washington, Feb. 13, 1929; s. Alfred and Miriam (Beard) V.; m. Dorothy Larkin, Dec. 11, 1954; children: Karen, Lydia. Grad., Taft Sch., 1945; AB, Harvard U., 1948, LLB, 1951. Bar: Mass. 1961. Assoc. Cahill, Gordon, Reindel & Ohl, N.Y.C., 1951-53, 56-59; asst. prof. law Harvard Law Sch., 1959-62, prof., 1962—, Eli Goldston prof., 1981-84, Bemis prof., 1984—; counselor internat. law Dept. State, 1976-77. Author: (with others) Transnational Legal Problems, 1968, 4th edit., 1994, Basic Corporation Law, 1973, 3d edit., 1989; editor: (with others) Secured Transactions Under the Uniform Commercial Code, 1963-64; assoc. reporter: (with others) Restatement of Foreign Relations Law; book rev. editor Am. Jour. Internat. Law, 1986-93, co-editor-in-chief, 1993—. 1st lt. USAF, 1953-56. Recipient Max Planck Rsch. award, 1991. Mem. ABA, Am. Soc. Internat. Law, Coun. Fgn. Rels., Phi Beta Kappa. Home: 29 Follen St Cambridge MA 02138-3502 Office: Sch Law Harvard U Cambridge MA 02138

VAGUE, JEAN MARIE, physician; b. Draguignan, France, Nov. 25, 1911; s. Victor Francois and Marie (Voiron) V.; m. Denise Marie Jouve, Sept. 3, 1936; children: Philippe, Thierry, Irene (Mrs. Claude Juhan), Maurice. Baccalaureat, Cath. Coll., Aix en Provence, France, 1928; MD, Marseilles (France) U., 1935. Intern, Hotel Dieu Conception, Marseilles, 1930, resident, 1932-39; practice medicine specializing in endocrinology, Marseilles, 1943—; assoc. prof. Marseilles U., 1946-57, prof., clinic endocrinology, 1957—. Dir. Ctr. Alimentary Hygiene and Prophylaxis Nutrition Diseases Nat. Rys. Mediterranean region, 1958—; expert chronic degenerative diseases (diabetes) WHO, 1962—. Served to lt. French Army, 1939-40. Decorated Cross Legion Honor, Acad. Palms, knight pub. health, knight mil. merit, War Cross. Mem. Endocrine Soc. U.S., Am. Diabetes Assn., Royal Soc. Medicine (London), European Assn. for Study Diabetes, Spanish, Italian, French (past pres.) socs. endocrinology, French Acad. Medicine, Spanish Acad. Medicine, Italian Acad. Medicine, Belgian Acad. Medicine, French Lang. Diabetes Assn. (past pres.). Author: Human Sexual Differentiation, 1953, Notions of Endocrinology, 1965, Obesities, 1991, Dawn on Iaboc's Ford, History of Man, History of Men, 1993, others. Achievements include first identification of the metabolic and vascular complications of android obesity and their mechanism; research in demonstration of diabetogenic and atherogenic power of obesity with topographic distbn. fat in upper and deep part of body, evolution of android diabetogenic obesity from 1st stage of efficacious hyperinsulinism to less efficacious hyperinsulinism and hypoinsulinism-neurogerminal degeneration, degenerative lesions of germinal epithelium and nervous system. Home: 6 Prado Parc, 411 Ave du Prado, 13008 Marseille France Office: Hopital U Timone Clin Endocrinologique, Blvd Jean-Moulin, 13385 Marseille France

VAHAVIOLOS, SOTIRIOS JOHN, electrical engineer, scientist, corporate executive; b. Mistra, Greece, Apr. 16, 1946; s. John Apostolos and Athanasia (Pavlakos) V.; m. Aspasia Felice Nessas, June 1, 1969; children: Athanasia, Athena, Kristy. BSEE, Fairleigh Dickinson U., 1970; MSEE, Columbia U., 1972, M in Philosophy, 1975, PhDEE, 1976. Mem. tech. staff Bell Telephone Labs., Princeton, N.J., 1970-75, supr., 1975-76, dept. head, 1976-78; founder, pres., CEO Phys. Acoustics Corp., Princeton, 1978—, MISTRAS Holdings Corp., Princeton, 1984—; adviser Greece Ministry Def., Athens, 1986-88; bd. dirs. Orthosonics, Inc., N.Y.C.; chmn. policy com. Internat. Com. of Nondestructive Testing. Contbr. more than 100 papers to profl. publs. 13 U.S. patents, 7 fgn. patentsin field. Bd. dirs. Holy Cross Greek Orthodox Sch. Theology, Boston, 1989—; pres. bd of trustees St. George Greek Orthodox Cmty., Trenton, N.J.; adv. bd. Trenton State Coll., N.J., 1983—; chmn. Princeton sect. United Fund, 1976-78. Recipient Spartan Merit award Spartan World Soc., 1987, Entrepreneur of Yr. award Arthur Young/Inc. Mag., N.J., 1989. Fellow IEEE (Centennial medal award 1984, Dr. Ing Eugene Mittlemen Achievement award 1993), Am. Soc. Nondestructive Testing (bus. and fin. com. 1984-87, 88—, bd. dirs. 1985, sec. 1989, treas. 1990, v.p. 1991, pres. 1992, chmn. bd. 1993, chmn. internat. com. nondestructive testing 1994—, chmn. internat. com. on nondestructive testing, editor handbook on Acoustic Emission 1988), Acoustic Emission Working Group; mem. ASTM, IEEE Indsl. Electronics Soc. (sr. mem. adminstrv. com. 1988, founder, v.p. conf. 1974-78, 2d prize Student Paper Contest 1970, Outstanding Young Engr. award 1984, editor Trans. on Indsl. Electronics 1976-82), N.Y. Acad. Scis. Independent. Greek Orthodox. Avocations: bird hunting, soccer, technical writing, gardening. Home: 7 Ridgeview Rd Princeton NJ 08540-7601 Office: Phys Acoustics Corp PO Box 3135 Princeton NJ 08543-3135

VAI, STEVE, guitarist; b. Carle Place, NY, June 6, 1960; married; 1 child. Student, Berklee Coll. of Music. Transcriber & stunt guitarist for Frank Zappa, 1979-83; guitarist Alcatrazz, 1984, David Lee Roth, 1986-89, Whitesnake, 1990; solo artist, 1991—. albums include Flex-able, 1984, Passion & Warfare, 1990, Sex & Religion, 1994; (with Frank Zappa) Tinsel Town Rebellion, 1980, You Are What You Is, 1981, The Man From Utopia, 1982, Ship Arriving Too Late to Save a Drowning Witch, 1983, Them or Us, 1984; (with Alcatrazz) Disturbing the Peace, 1984; (with David Lee Roth) Eat 'Em and Smile, 1986, Skyscraper, 1988; (with Whitesnake) Slip of the Tongue, 1990, (with Frank Zappa) Shut Up N' Play Yer Guitar, 1986, (with Shanker) The Epidemics; film appearances include: Crossroads, 1986. Recipient Rock Instrumental Grammy Award for "Sofa" from Zappa's Universe, 1993. Office: c/o Relativity Records 18707 Henderson Ave Hollis NY 11423-3133

VAIA, CHERYL LYNN, consultant; b. Newark, Ohio, Sept. 13, 1955; d. James Lee V. and Barbara N. (Barber) Canter; m. Herbert S. Bresler, Aug. 1, 1982; children: Reuben, Marika. BA, Capital U., 1977; MS, Wright State

U., 1980. Economist Dept. Energy, Columbus, Ohio, 1979-80; econ. analyst Energy & Environ. Analysis, Arlington, Va., 1980-83; analyst, sys. analyst, mgr., dir., v.p. Orkand Corp., Silver Spring, Md., 1983-93; dir. fed. sys. KCM Cons., Inc., Greenbelt, Md., 1993-94; ind. cons., 1994—; instr. Capital U., Columbus, 1980. Pres. Crofton (Md.) Meadows Home Owners Assn., 1984-85, sec., 1983. Mem. APHA, Am. Statis. Assn., Am. Mgmt. Contractors Assn., Women in Technology. Democrat. Jewish. Avocations: gardening, hiking. Home and Office: 2610 E Broad St Bexley OH 43209-1862

VAIL, IRIS JENNINGS, civic worker; b. N.Y.C., July 2, 1928; d. Lawrence K. and Beatrice (Black) Jennings; grad. Miss Porters Sch., Farmington, Conn.; m. Thomas V.H. Vail, Sept. 15, 1951; children: Siri J., Thomas V.H. Jr., Lawrence J.W. Exec. com. Garden Club Cleve., 1962-93; mem. women's coun. Western Res. Hist. Soc., 1960—, Cleve. Mus. Art, 1953—; chmn. Childrens Garden Fair, 1966-75, Public Square Dinner, 1975; bd. dirs. Garden Center Greater Cleve., 1963-77; trustee Cleve. Zool. Soc., 1971—; mem. Ohio Arts Coun., 1974-76, pub. sq. com. Greater Cleve. Growth Assn., 1976-93, pub. sq. preservation and maintenance com. Cleve. Found., 1989-93, chmn. pub. sq. planting com., 1993. Recipient Amy Angell Collier Montague medal Garden Club Am., 1976, Ohio Gov.'s award, 1977. Chagrin Valley Hunt Club, Cypress Point Club, Kirtland Country Club, Colony Club, Women's City of Cleve. Club (Margaret A. Ireland award). Home: 14950 County Line Rd Chagrin Falls OH 44022

VAIL, MICHAEL EDWARD, viticulturist, agronomist; b. Beech Grove, Ind., June 28, 1963; s. Charles and Kitty Belle (Soukup) V. BS, Purdue U., 1986; MS, U. Calif., Davis, 1990. Cert. profl. agronomist Am. Registry of Cert. Profls. in Agronomy Crops and Soils. Soils technician Purdue U., West Lafayette, Ind., 1981-83; botany technician Purdue U., West Lafayette, 1983, rsch. assoc., 1983-86, tchg. asst., 1986; rsch. asst. U. Calif., Davis, 1986-89; viticulture prodn. specialist Crop Care Assocs., Inc., St. Helena, Calif., 1989-92; viticulturist Vino Farms Inc., Healdsburg, Calif., 1992—; herbicide rsch. intern Monsanto Ag Products Co., St. Louis, summer 1985; rsch. intern PPG Industries, Inc., Indpls., summer 1986; invited spkr. U. Calif., Davis, 1989, cooperator, 1991-95; radiation safety officer Vino Farms, Inc., Lodi, Calif., 1992-95; mem. rsch. com. Lodi-Woodbridge Wine Grape Commn. Contbr. articles to profl. jours. Mem. Am. Phytopathol. Soc., Am. Soc. Agronomy, Am. Soc. for Enology and Viticulture (pesticide subcom. 1992-95), Sonoma County Vineyard Tech. Group, Lodi-Woodbridge Winegrape Commn. (rsch. com.), Sigma Xi, Alpha Zeta. Achievements include developed a new technique to quantify grape cluster tightness. Avocations: winemaking, international travel, gardening. Home: 9417 Lazy Creek Dr Windsor CA 95492 Office: Vino Farms Inc 10651 Eastside Rd Healdsburg CA 95448

VAIL, VAN HORN, German language educator; b. Buffalo, Dec. 23, 1934; s. Curtis Churchill and Faith Newbrook (Ely) V.; m. Michele Juliette Edelstein, May 5, 1969; 1 son, Mark Curtis. B.A., U. Wash., 1956; M.A., Princeton U., 1961, Ph.D., 1964. Instr. Princeton U., 1962-65, asst. prof., 1965-66; asst. prof. German Middlebury (Vt.) Coll., 1966-69, assoc. prof., 1969-75, prof., 1975—; chmn. dept. Middlebury Coll., Vt., 1970-73, 87-88; dir. studies Middlebury Sch. in Germany Middlebury Coll., 1967-68, 70-71, 74-75, 85-86, 88-89, 92-93, 95-96; mem. nat. screening com. Fulbright Scholarships, 1979-81. Author: German in Review, 1967, 2d edit., 1986, Der Weg zum Lesen, 1967, 2d edit., 1974, 3d edit., 1986, Modern German, 1971, 2d edit., 1978, 3d edit., 1992, Tonio Kröger als Weg zur Literatur, 1974, Workbook for Modern German, 1992. Served to 1st lt. M.I., U.S. Army, 1956-58. Fulbright scholar U. Heidelberg, 1958-59. Mem. MLA. Home: Cider Mill Rd Middlebury VT 05753 Office: Middlebury Coll Middlebury VT 05753

VAIL, WILLIAM LLOYD, minister, marriage and family therapist; b. Sheldon, Iowa, May 7, 1946; s. Arthur Gordon and Ivadell (Carry) V.; m. Melvina Janette Wood, Dec. 22, 1967; 1 child, Noah William. BS, Pacific Christian Coll., 1968, M in Psychology, 1993; M in History, Calif. Grad. Sch. Theology, 1971, PhD, 1972. Ordained minister, 1968; registered MFCC, 1993—. Youth min. Rexland Christian Ch., Bakersfield, Calif., 1966-67; assoc. min. First Christian Ch., Tujunga, Calif., 1967-73; pastor First Christian Ch., Los Gatos, Calif., 1973-85, Anaheim, Calif., 1985-86, Palmdale, Calif., 1987—; instr. San Jose (Calif.) Bible Coll., 1982-84, IberoAm. Inst., Maipu, Chile, 1995; psychotherapist Advanced Counseling, Lancaster, Calif., 1992—. Author: Contact Bible Study, 1978, Mission II, 1995, The Master's Plan, 1995. Mem. Palmdale Sunrise Rotary Club (past pres. 1989—). Home: 40544 Via Verdad Palmdale CA 93551 Office: First Christian Ch 38678 15th St E Palmdale CA 93550

VAILLANCOURT, DONALD CHARLES, corporate communications executive; b. Newark, Dec. 30, 1943; s. Vincent J. and Margaret Kathleen (Pasch) V.; A.A., Thomas Edison Coll., 1975, B.A., 1976; M.A., William Paterson Coll. of N.J., 1982; J.D., Pace Sch. Law, 1985; m. Dianne Daugherty, Oct. 2, 1987. Bar: N.J. 1985, U.S. Dist. Ct. N.J., 1985, Ala. 1986, U.S. Supreme Ct., 1990. Reporter, Newark Star Ledger, 1962-64; night editor UPI, Newark, 1964-65; reporter, editor Newark News, 1965-71; asst. dir. pub. rels. Grand Union Co., Wayne, N.J., 1971-75, dir. pub. rels., 1975-76, dir. corp. communications and consumer affairs, 1976-80, v.p. corp. communications and consumer affairs, 1980-85, corp. v.p., officer corp. communications and consumer affairs, 1985—. Former chmn. family council Essex County Geriatrics Center. Recipient Honor award Food Edn., Cornell U., 1975. Mem. Food Mktg. Inst. (govt. rels. com.), N.Y. State Food Mchts. Assn. (chmn. bd. dirs., govt. rels. com.), N.J. Food Council (former chmn.), N.J. C. of C. (pub. rels. com.). Episcopalian. Home: 180 Camelot Gate Bears Nest Village Park Ridge NJ 07656-2609 Office: 201 Willowbrook Blvd Wayne NJ 07470-7025

VAILLANCOURT, JEAN-GUY, sociology educator; b. Chelmsford, Ont., Can., May 24, 1937; s. Royal A. and Marie (Lavallée) V.; m. Pauline Hansen, June 6, 1966 (div. 1983); 1 child, Véronique. BA magna cum laude, Laurentian U., Sudbury, Ont., 1957; licenciate in philosophy, Faculté des Jésuites, Montreal, Que., Can., 1961; licentiate in sociology, Gregorian U., Rome, 1964; PhD in Sociology, U. Calif., Berkeley, 1975. Lectr. St. Boniface (Man.) Coll., Can., 1964-65; asst. prof. U. de Montréal, Que., Can., 1969-76, assoc. prof., 1976-83, prof. sociology, 1983—, chmn. dept., 1984-87; mem. consultative com. Can. ambassador for disarmament, Ottawa, Ont., 1984-91, consultative com. on environ. Hydro-Que., 1984-90. Author: Papal Power, 1980, Essais d'écosociologie, 1982; co-editor: Le processus èlectoral au Québec, 1976, Roots of Peace, 1986, Environment et dèvelopement Problemes Socio-Politiques, 1991, Getio de l'environment, èthique et sociètè, 1992, Instituer le dèvelopement durable, 1994, Aspects sociaux des precipitations acides au Quebec, 1994, La recherche sociale en environment Nouveaux paradigmes, 1996; editor-in-chief Sociologie et Sociètès, 1978-87. Mem. coun. City of Dunham, Que., 1976-80; bd. dirs. Oxfam-Que., 1976-79, Can. Inst. Internat. Peace and Security, Ottawa, Ont., 1986-89, European Univ. Ctr. for Peace Studies, Burg Schlaining, Burgenland, Austria, 1989-93, Club 2/3, 1995—. Grantee Counseil de Recherche en science sociale du Quebec, 1982, FCAR, 1989—, Social Sci. Rsch. Coun., 1983-86, 90-96, Can. Inst. Internat. Peace and Security, 1985, 91; fellow Can. Coun., 1965-68. Mem. Internat. Sociol. Assn., Assn. Can. des sociologues et anthropologues de langue francaise, Sci. for Peace, Pugwash, Group 78. Roman Catholic. Avocations: tree farming, travelling. Home: 953 Cherrier # 2, Montréal, PQ Canada H2L 1J2 Office: U Montreal, Dept Sociology, Montreal, PQ Canada H3C 3J7

VAILLANT, GEORGE EMAN, psychiatrist; b. N.Y.C., June 16, 1934; s. George Clapp and Mary Suzannah (Beck) V.; m. Leigh McCullough, Dec. 4, 1993; children: George Emery, John Holden, Henry Greenough, Anne Liberty, Caroline Joanna. A.B., Harvard U., 1955, M.D., 1959; postgrad., Boston Psychoanalytic Inst., 1967-76. Resident in psychiatry Mass. Mental Health Center, Boston, 1960-63; from asst. prof. to asso. prof. psychiatry Tufts U. Sch. Medicine, 1966-71; asso. prof. psychiatry Harvard Med. Sch., 1971-77, prof., 1977-82, 93—; dir. tng. Cambridge (Mass.) Hosp., 1976-81, Mass. Mental Health Center, Boston, 1981-83; prof. Dartmouth Sch. Medicine, 1983-92; dir. study of adult devel. Harvard U. Health Services, 1972—. Author: Adaptation to Life, 1977, Natural History of Alcoholism, 1983, Wisdom of the Ego, 1993; contbr. articles to profl. jours. Served with USPHS, 1963-65. Fellow Center for Advanced Study in Behavioral Scis., 1978-79. Fellow Am. Psychiat. Assn.; mem. Boston Psychoanalytic Soc. Episcopalian. Home: 943 High St Dedham MA 02026-4220 Office: Brigham Women's Hosp 75 Francis St Boston MA 02115-6110

VAINSTEIN, ROSE, librarian, educator; b. Edmonton, Alta., Can., Jan. 7, 1920; d. Rabbi Nathan and Jane (Simenstein) V. A.B., Miami U., Oxford, Ohio, 1941; B.L.S., Western Res. U., 1942; M.S., U. Ill., 1952. Jr. librarian Cuyahoga County Library, Cleve., 1942-43; young people's librarian Bklyn. Public Library, 1943-44; br. librarian Contra Costa County Library, Martinez, Calif., 1948-51; library cons. Calif. State Library, Sacramento, 1953-55; head extension dept. Gary (Ind.) Public and Lake County Library, 1955-57; public library specialist U.S. Office Edn., Washington, 1957-61; asso. prof. Sch. Librarianship, U. B.C., Vancouver, 1961-64; dir. Bloomfield Twp. Pub. Library, Bloomfield Hills, Mich., 1964-68; prof. library sci. U. Mich., Ann Arbor, 1968-82, Margaret Mann prof. emeritus, 1982—; dir. Middle Mgmt. Inst. for Pub. Librs., 1969, 1st Margaret Mann Disting. prof. libr. sci., 1974—; libr. U.S. Armed Forces U.S., Hawaii, Japan, 1944-48; dir. B.C. (Can.) Pub. Librs. Rsch. Study, 1963-64; mem. steering com. Kendal Corp. Strategic Planning and Orgnl. Devel. Project Phase II, 1993. Contbr. articles to profl. jours. Mem. Jewish Community Coun. of Washtenaw County, Mich., 1981-84; bd. dirs. Jewish Community Ctr., 1986-89; mem. geriatric svcs. steering com. U. Mich. Med. Ctr., 1988-89. Fulbright Research scholar Eng., 1952-53; Council on Library Resources fellow, 1974-75; scholar-in-residence Sch. Librarianship, U. B.C., 1981. Mem. ALA (chmn. public libr. stds. com. 1969-73, chmn. public libr. activities com. 1974-76, mem. coun. 1975-79, mem. coun. budget assembly 1977-79, chmn. nominating com. 1976-77), Mich., Canadian library assns., U. Mich. Women's Rsch. Club (treas. 1971-72, chmn. loan fund com. 1976-79, Spl. 75th Anniversary award 1978), LWV, Hadassah (life, co-chmn. study group Ann Arbor chpt. 1982-83), Crossland Residents Assn. (bd. dirs. 1992-94, chair genealogy study group 1990-95, forum com. 1990-93, treas. 1992-93, long range planning group 1993-94, pres. 1995-96), Phi Beta Kappa (Alumnus mem. Iota of Ohio chpt. 1976), Beta Phi Mu (dir. 1974-77). Home: Apt 179 Crosslands Kennett Square PA 19348-2019

VAIRA, PETER FRANCIS, lawyer; b. McKeesport, Pa., Mar. 5, 1937; s. Peter Francis and Mary Louise (Bedogne) V.; m. Mary Hohler, 1981. B.A., Duquesne U., 1959, J.D., 1962. Bar: Pa. 1963, D.C. 1968, Ill. 1984, U.S. Ct. Appeals (D.C. cir.) 1964, Ill. Supreme Ct. Ill. 1984, U.S. Dist. Ct. (no. dist.) Ill., U.S. Dist. Ct. (ea. dist.) Pa. Atty. Chgo. Strike Force, Justice Dept., 1968-72; atty. in charge Phila. Strike Force, 1972-73, Chgo. Strike Force on Organized Crime, 1973-78; U.S. atty. Phila., 1978-83; ptnr. firm Lord Bissel & Brook, Chgo., 1983-86; ptnr. Fox, Rothschild, O'Brien & Frankel, Phila., 1986-90, Buchanan Ingersoll, Phila., 1990-92, Vaira & Assocs., Phila., 1992-93, Vaira, Backstrom & Riley, Phila., 1993—; exec. dir. Pres.'s Commn. on Organized Crime, 1983; ind. hearing officer Laborers Internat. Union N.Am., 1995—. Author: Corporate Responses to Grant Jury Investigation, 1984, Pennsylvania Federal Practice Rules, 1996; contbr. articles to profl. jours. Mem. Mayor's Search Com. for Police Commr., Phila., 1992. Served with USNR, 1963-68. Recipient Spl. Commendation award Justice Dept., 1976. Fellow Am. Coll. Trial Lawyers (chmn. criminal procedure com.); mem. ABA (mem. criminal justice coun. 1986), Am. Law Inst., Union League, Phila. Country Club. Office: Vaira Backstrom & Riley 1600 Market St Ste 2650 Philadelphia PA 19103-7240

VAIRO, ROBERT JOHN, insurance company executive; b. Bklyn., Sept. 27, 1930; s. John and Antonietta (DeRose) V.; m. Carol P. Andross, Apr. 8, 1951 (div. Feb. 1979); children: Robert J., Gregory J.; m. Inge R. Buhlbecker, Feb. 20, 1979. Student, Coll. Ins., N.Y.C., 1953-62; Exec. Program in Bus. Adminstrn., Columbia U., 1973. CPCU. Under asst. mgr. Atlantic Cos., N.Y.C., 1952-62; underwriter mgr., v.p. Fireman's Fund Ins. Co., N.Y.C., 1962-75; v.p., sr. v.p. underwriting C & F Ins. Cos., Morristown, N.J., 1975-79; exec. v.p., pres. U.S. Ins. Group, Morristown, N.J., 1979-82; chmn., chief exec. officer C & F Underwriters Group and The North River Ins. Co., Morristown, N.J., 1982-86; pres., chief oper. officer Crum and Forster, Inc., Morristown, 1987-88, pres., chief exec. officer, 1988-90, chmn., pres., chief exec. officer, 1990-92, also bd. dirs.; chmn. Ins. Services Office, N.Y.C., 1983, Am. Ins. Assn., Washington, 1990. Pres. Lincoln Park City Council, N.J., 1971-76. Served with USMC, 1951-53. Mem. Soc. CPCUs, Am. Inst. for Chartered Property Casualty Underwriters (dir., chmn. 1991-92), Desert Highlands Golf Club. Roman Catholic. Home: Apt 451 10040 E Happy Valley Rd Scottsdale AZ 85255-2388

VAISHNAVI, VIJAY KUMAR, computer science educator, researcher; b. Srinagar, Kashmir, India, Mar. 25, 1948; came to U.S., 1980; s. Nand Lal and Prabhawati (Hakhu) V.; m. Kirti Ganju, July 17, 1972; children: Sandeep, Neil. BEE, Regional Engring. Coll., Srinagar, 1969; MEE, Indian Inst. Tech., India, 1972, PhD, 1976. Asst. prof. IIT Kanpur, 1973-77; postdoctoral fellow McMaster U., Hamilton, Ont., Can., 1977-79; vis. asst. prof. Concordia U., Montreal, 1979-80; asst. prof. Ohio U., Athens, 1980-81; assoc. prof. Ga. State U., Atlanta, 1981-87, prof., 1987—; vis. scientist U. Dortmund, Fed. Republic Germany, 1980; cons. AT&T, others, 1990—; rsch. dir. COMSOFT, 1990—. Contbr. articles to profl. jours. Recipient rsch. grants; collegiate faculty recognition, Coll. of Bus. Adminstrn., Ga. State U., Atlanta, 1989, 93. Mem. Assn. for Computing Machinery, Computer Soc. of IEEE (software engring. tech. com.), IEEE (sr.). Avocations: reading, gardening, table-tennis. Office: Ga State U Computer Info Systems Dept PO Box 4015 Atlanta GA 30302-4015

VAITKEVICIUS, VAINUTIS KAZYS, foundation administrator, medical educator; b. Kaunas, Lithuanie, Jan. 12, 1927; came to U.S., 1951; s. Henrikas and Camille Vaitkevicius; m. Ingeborg Jausen; children: Eva, Henri, Peter, Camille, Walter, Martin. Diploma, Lithuanian Coll., Eichstett, Germany, 1946; MD, J.W. Goethe U., Frankfurt, Germany, 1951. Diplomate Am. Bd. Internal Medicine, Am. Bd. Med. Oncology. Intern Grace Hosp., Detroit, 1951-52, resident, 1955-56; resident Detroit Receiving Hosp., 1956-58; fellow in cancer rsch. Detroit Inst. Cancer Rsch., 1958-59; from asst. to assoc. prof. medicine sch. medicine Wayne State U., Detroit, 1962-72, prof., 1972—, dir. divsn. conjoint svcs. and curricula oncology, 1966-72, chmn. dept. oncology, 1972-82, chmn. dept. internal medicine, 1982-89; clin. dir. Detroit Inst. Cancer Rsch., 1962-66; acting chief medicine Detroit Gen. Hosp., 1970-71; chief divsn. medicine Grace Hosp., 1973-76; chief oncology Harper-Grace Hosps., Detroit, 1977-82, chief medicine, 1982-89; assoc. dir. clin. activities Comprehensive Cancer Ctr. Met. Detroit, 1978-82; physician-in-chief Detroit Med. Ctr., 1982-89; pres. Mich. Cancer Found., Detroit, 1991-95; pres. emeritus, bd. dirs. B.A. Karmanos Cancer Ctr., 1995—; mem. com. human and animal experimentation Wayne State U., 1968-73, chmn., 1971-73, mem. presdl. selection adv. com., 1981, mem. univ. coun., 1981-83, mem. budget com. of univ. coun., 1981-83, mem. presdl. com. cancer programs, 1981—; mem. Nat. Colorectal Cancer Adv. Com., 1971-73, Com. Evaluate Cancer Curricula Am. Med. Schs., 1971-79; mem. exec. com. S.W. Cancer Chemotherapy Study Group, 1972-73; mem. evaluation adv. coun. Southeastern Regional Cancer Programs, 1972-74; chmn. gastrointestinal com. S.W. Oncology Group, 1974-79; mem. exec. bd. Wayne State U./U. Mich. Inst. Gerontology, 1975-86; mem. oper. com. Comprehensive Cancer Ctr. Met. Detroit, 1978—; mem. commd. jury Saint-Vincent Internat. Prize Med. Scis., Rome, 1979, 83; chmn. coun. dept. chairmen sch. medicine Wayne State U., 1979-81, mem. dean's coun. grad. med. edn. program, 1983-89, mem. dean's rev. com., 1986, mem. pharmacy and medicine task force, 1986, chmn. radiation oncology search com., 1987; mem. med. staff fin. and budget com. Harper-Grace Hosps., 1983-84, mem. gerontology svcs. planning com., 1984-87, chmn. NMR adv. com., 1984—; mem. transplantation com. Detroit Med. Ctr., 1985-86, mem. med. bd., 1985-89, chmn. task force cancer programs, 1987; presenter in field. Contbr. chpts. to books and articles to profl. jours.; mem. adv. bd. Cancer Treatment Reports, 1980-82. Mem. exec. com. bd. trustees Mich. Cancer Found., 1975-85; mem. blood svc. ops. com. ARC Southeastern Mich., 1981-84; bd. dirs. Wayne County unit Am. Cancer Soc., 1976-79; trustee Hospice Southeastern Mich., 1991—; mem. Nat. Cancer Adv. Bd., 1994—. Capt. U.S. Army, 1953-55. Recipient Life award Am. Cancer Soc. Met. Detroit, 1981, Mercy Medallion, 1983, Tree-of-Life award Nat. Jewish Fedn., 1987, Michiganian-of-Yr. award The Detroit News, 1987, Hospice Humanitarian award, 1989; inductee Internat. Heritage Hall of Fame, Inst. Met. Detroit, 1989; honored by Am. Cancer Soc., 1989, Weizmann Inst. Sci., 1992. Mem. AAAS, ACP, Am. Assn. Cancer Rsch., Am. Fedn. Clin. Rsch., Am. Soc. Hematology, Am. Soc. Clin. Oncology (mem. program com. 1981), Am. Assn. Cancer Edn. (mem. exec. coun. 1971—, pres. 1976-77), Mich. State Med. Soc. (mem. cancer com. 1965-73, Flag award 1992), N.Y. Acad. Scis., Mich. Soc. Internal Medicine, Wayne County Med. Soc. (mem. del. body 1981-87, mem. task force referral edn. 1986, mem. physician tech. svcs. 1986—), Detroit Physiol. Soc., Detroit Acad. Medicine, Ctrl. Soc. Clin. Rsch., James Ewing Soc., Aesculapian Soc. (hon.), Alpha Omega Alpha, Phi Lambda Kappa (hon.). Office: Harper Hosp 3990 John R Detroit MI 48201

VAITUKAITIS, JUDITH LOUISE, medical research administrator; b. Hartford, Conn., Aug. 29, 1940; d. Albert George and Julia Joan (Vaznikaitis) V. BS, Tufts U., 1962; MD, Boston U., 1966. Investigator, med. officer reproductive rsch. Nat. Inst. Child Health and Human Devel., NIH, Bethesda, Md., 1971-74; assoc. dir. clin. rsch. Nat. Ctr. Rsch. Resources NIH, Bethesda, Md., 1986-91, dir. gen. clin. rsch. ctr., 1986-91, dep. dir. extramural rsch., 1991; acting dir. Nat. Ctr. Rsch. Resources NIH, Bethesda, 1991-92, dir., 1993—; from assoc. prof. to prof. medicine Sch. Medicine Boston U., 1974-86, assoc. prof. physiology, 1975-80, assoc. prof. ob-gyn., 1977-80, program. dir. gen. clin. rsch. ctr., 1977-86, prof. physiology, 1980-86; head sect. endocrinology and metabolism Boston City Hosp., 1974-86. Mem. editorial bd. Jour. Clin. Endocrin. and Metabolism, 1973-80, Proc. Soc. Exptl. Biol. and Medicine, 1978-87, Endocrine Rsch., 1984-88. Author: Clinical Reproductive Neuroendocrinology, 1982; contbr. articles to profl. jours. Recipient Disting. Alumna award Sch. Medicine, Boston U., 1983, Mallincrodt award for Inv. Rsch. Clin. Radiossay Soc., 1980. Mem. Am. Fedn. Clin. Rsch., Endocrine Soc., Am. Soc. Clin. Rsch., Soc. Exptl. Biology and Medicine, Assn. Am. Physicians. Office: Nat Ctr Rsch Resources NIH Bldg 12A Rm 4007 12 South Dr MSC 5662 Bethesda MD 20892-5662

VAJK, HUGO, manufacturing executive; b. Ljubljana, Slovenia, Mar. 26, 1928; emigrated to Can., 1947, naturalized, 1953; s. Hugo and Magda (Slatnar) V.; m. Barbara Lois Hallin, June 13, 1953; children: Tanja Astrid, Hugo Anthony, Madeleine Louise, Anita Marie, Nicolette Cecile, Moira Suzanne. Student, Institut Polytechnique, Grenoble, France, 1947; B.Eng. with honors, McGill U., Montreal, 1951; M.S., Carnegie Mellon U., Pitts., 1953. Product mgr. Joy Mfg. Co., Buffalo, 1957-59; dir. gen. Joy Mfg. Co., Paris, 1960-63; with Massey-Ferguson Ltd., 1964-78; pres. Moteurs Perkins S.A., Paris, 1964-65, Massey-Ferguson Ltd., Paris, 1966-69; v.p. logistics parent co. Massey-Ferguson Ltd., Toronto, 1970-72, exec. v.p., 1973-78; dir. GEC Inc., subs. Gen. Electric Co., Eng., 1979; chmn. English Electric Corp., Elmsford, N.Y., 1979; with Garret Corp. div. Signal Cos., 1980-84; v.p. Garrett Automotive Products; pres. Garrett Automotive Group, Allied-Signal, Inc., 1985-87; chmn. Inovatek Advisors, Inc., Tarpon Springs, Fla., 1988—; pres. ATM Communications Internat., Inc., Wilmington, Del., 1991—. Mem. ASME, Soc. Automotive Engrs., Assn. Profl. Engrs. Ont., Inst. Mgmt. Sci., Inst. Dirs., Inst. Mgmt. Cons., Nat. Assn. Corp. Dirs., Univ. Club (Toronto), Royal Can. Yacht Club (Toronto), Union Interaliée (Paris), Yacht Club de France (Paris), Royal Thames Yacht Club (London). Office: Inovatek Advisors Inc Ste 200 6 905 Martin Luther King Jr Tarpon Springs FL 34689-4827

VAJTAY, STEPHEN MICHAEL, JR., lawyer; b. New Brunswick, N.J., Mar. 18, 1958; s. Stephen Michael and Veronica Gizella (Fehèr) V.; m. Gabriella Katherine Soltèsz, Aug. 5, 1989; children: Stephen, Andrew, Gregory. BA, Rutgers U., 1980; JD, Georgetown U., 1983; LLM, NYU, 1989. Bar: N.J. 1984, U.S. Tax Ct. 1985. Assoc. McCarter and English, Newark, N.J., 1983-91, ptnr., 1991—; chmn. bd. trustees Hungarian Scout Assn. in Exteris, Garfield, N.J., 1985—; trustee Partnership for a Drug-Free N.J., Inc., Montclair, 1993—; adj. prof. law Seton Hall U. Sch. Law, Newark, 1995—; speaker at lectrs. and seminars, 1992, 93. Contbr. articles to profl. jours. Mem. Bd. of Adjustment, New Brunswick, N.J., 1993—. Mem. ABA, N.J. Bar Assn., Tax sect. N.J. Bar Assn., Essex County Bar Assn., Phi Beta Kappa. Roman Catholic. Office: McCarter and English Four Gateway Ctr 100 Mulberry St Newark NJ 07102

VAKERICS, THOMAS VINCENT, lawyer; b. Lorain, Ohio, Mar. 26, 1944; s. Paul Peter and Margaret Theresa (Dobos) V.; m. Kathryn Ida Rogers, Aug. 7,1965; children: Meredith Vakerics Ehler, Mitchell Thomas. BA, Bowling Green State U., 1965; JD with honors, George Washington U., 1968. Bar: U.S. Dist. Ct. D.C. 1968, U.S. Ct. Appeals (D.C. cir.) 1969, U.S. Supreme Ct. 1974, U.S. Ct. Internat. Trade 1982, U.S. Ct. Appeals (Fed. cir.) 1982. Antitrust trial atty. FTC, Washington, 1969-73; assoc. Gore, Cladouhos & Brashares, Washington, 1973-75; ptnr. O'Connor & Hannan, Washington, 1975-84, Bayh, Tabbert & Capehart, Washington, 1984-86, Morgan, Lewis & Bockius, Washington, 1986-88, Winthrop, Stimson, Putnam & Roberts, Washington, 1988-94, Perkins Coie, 1994—; vis. prof. Nihon U., Tokyo, 1981-88. Author: Antitrust Basics, 1985, Antidumping, Countervailing Duty and Other Trade Actions, 1987; contbr. articles to profl. jours. Mem. ABA (vice chmn. internat. antitrust law com. sect. internat. law and practice 1992-95), Internat. Bar Assn., D.C. Bar Assn., Solar Energy Rsch. Inst. (editl. adv. bd. Solar Energy Law Reporter 1979-82), Order of Coif, Phi Delta Phi, Pi Sigma Alpha, Phi Alpha Delta, Sigma Chi. Democrat. Roman Catholic. Home: 12820 Tewksbury Dr Herndon VA 22071-2427 Office: Perkins Coie 607 14th St NW # 800 Washington DC 20005

VAKY, VIRON PETER, diplomacy educator, former foreign service officer; b. Tex., Sept. 13, 1925; m. Luann Colburn. BS, Georgetown U., 1947; MA, U. Chgo., 1948. Vocat. appraiser VA, Washington, 1948-49; joined Fgn. Svc. Dept. of State, Washington, 1949; consular officer Guayaquil, Ecuador, 1949-51; econ. officer Buenos Aires, 1951-54; internat. rels. officer Washington, 1955-57, info. specialist, 1958-59; polit.officer Bogota, Colombia, 1959-61; detailed to Nat. War Coll., 1963-64; counsellor-dep. chief mission Guatemala, 1964-67; mem. Policy Planning Coun. Dept. of State, 1967-68; dep. asst. sec. Bur. Inter-Am. Affairs, 1968-69, acting asst. sec., 1969; detailed to NSC, 1969-70; diplomat-in-residence Georgetown U., Washington, 1970-71; ambassador to San Jose, Costa Rica, 1972-74, Bogota, Colombia, 1974-76, Caracas, Venezuela, 1976-78; asst. sec. Inter-Am. Affairs Washington, 1978-89; sr. assoc. Carnegie Endowment for Internat. Peace, Washington, 1985-92; asst. dean, rsch. prof. diplomacy Sch. Fgn. Svc., Georgetown U., Washington, 1980-84, adj. prof. diplomacy, 1985-95; sr. fellow Inter-Am. Dialogue, Washington, 1994—. With U.S. Army, 1944-46.

VALADE, ALAN MICHAEL, lawyer; b. Berwyn, Ill., Jan. 26, 1952; s. Merle F. and Vera M. (Gildersleave) V.; m. June 17, 1978. BA, U. Mich., 1974; JD, Wayne State U., 1977; LLM in Taxation, NYU, 1978. Bar: Mich. 1978, Fla. 1987. Assoc. Kemp, Klein, Endelman & Beer, Birmingham, Mich., 1978-79; shareholder Valade, MacKinnon & Higgins, P.C., Detroit, 1979-84, Schwendener & Valade, P.C., Mason, Mich., 1985-91; ptnr. Honigman Miller Schwartz and Cohn, Lansing, Mich., 1991—. Co-author: The Michigan Single Business Tax, 1991; contbr. articles to profl. jours. Mem. ABA, State Bar Mich. (chmn. state and local tax com. 1991, tax. coun. 1989-92), State Bar Fla., Oak Pointe Country Club. Avocations: reading, traveling, running, skiing. Office: Honigman Miller Schwartz & Cohn 222 Washington Sq N Ste 400 Lansing MI 48933-1800

VALADE, ROBERT CHARLES, apparel company executive; b. Detroit, Apr. 19, 1926; s. Cyril K. and Marion I. (Anderson) V.; m. Gretchen Carhartt, Sept. 18, 1948; children: Gretchen Garth, Mark R. Degree in bus. adminstrn., Mich. State U., 1947. Salesman Royal Typewriter, Detroit, 1947-50; v.p. Carhartt Inc., Detroit, 1950-59; pres., CEO Carhartt Inc., Dearborn, Mich., 1959—; bd. dirs. Rep. Bank S.E., Grosse Pointe, Mich. with USN, 1944-46, PTO. Mem. World Pres.'s Orgn. (bd. dirs. 1980-82), Detroit Racquet Club (pres. 1950-54), Country Club Detroit, Fiddle Sticks Country Club (Ft. Myers, Fla.). Republican. Roman Catholic. Avocations: golf, hunting, fishing.

VALBERG, LESLIE STEPHEN, medical educator, physician, researcher; b. Churchbridge, Sask., Can., June 3, 1930; s. John Stephen and Rose (Vikfusson) V.; m. Barbara Tolhurst, Sept. 14, 1954; children: John, Stephanie, Bill. M.D., C.M., Queens U., 1954, M.S.C., 1958. Cert. internal medicine specialist Royal Coll. Physicians and Surgeons of Can. Asst. prof. Queens U. Kingston, Ont., Can., from 1960—, prof., until 1975; prof. medicine U. Western Ont., London, 1975-95, chmn. dept., 1975-85; dean faculty of medicine U. Western Ont., 1985-92; prof. emeritus, 1995—; cons. Univ. Hosp., 1975-95; prof. emeritus U. We. Ont., London, Can., 1995—. Rsch. Assoc. Med. Council of Can., 1960-65. Fellow Royal Coll. Physicians and Surgeons; mem. Am. Gastroent. Assn., Med. Rsch. Coun. Can. (v.p. 1980-82). Home: 1496 Stoneybrook Crescent, London, ON Canada N5X 1C5 Office: U Western Ont. London, ON Canada N6A 5C1

VALBUENA-BRIONES, ANGEL JULIAN, language educator, author; b. Madrid, Jan. 11, 1928; naturalized, 1963; s. Angel Valbuena-Prat and Francisca Briones; m. Barbara Northrup Hobart, Nov. 9, 1957; children: Teresa, Vivian. Licenciado summa cum laude, Murcia (Spain) U., 1949; Ph.D. with honors, Madrid U., 1952. Prof. Ayudante Murcia U., 1949-51; lectr. Oxford (Eng.) U., 1953-55; prof. Ayudante Madrid U., 1955-56; vis. lectr. U. Wis., 1956-58; asst. prof. Yale U., 1958-60; Elias Ahuja prof. Spanish lit. U. Del., 1960—; lecture tour, S.Am., summer 1957; vis. prof. NYU, summers 1960, 61, U. Madrid, 1970-71, summers 1965, 77, U. Mex. at Aragon, summer 1979, Inst. Caro y Cuervo, Bogota, Colombia, summer 1980; mem. Fulbright-Hays nat. screening com., 1981-83, 89-90; mem. editl. com. for CD-ROM edit. Spanish Golden Age Theatre, Chadwyck-Healey/Spain and Consejo Superior Investigaciones Cientificas, 1995-97; bd. dirs. publs. U. Barcelona, Spain, Bull. Comediantes, U. Calif., Riverside, Hispanic Jour., Pa., Juan de la Cuesta Edits., Del.; profl. cons. NEH. Author: Neuva Poesia de Puerto Rico, 1952, Comedias de Capa y Espada de Calderon, 1954, Dramas de Honor de Calderon, 2 vols., 1956, Obras Completas de Calderon, vol. I, 1959, 3d reprinting, 1991, vol. II, 1956, 6th edit. 2 vols., 1988, Literatura Hispanoamericana, 1962, PErspectiva critica de los dramas de Calderon, 1965, Ideas y Palabras, 1968, El alcalde de Zalamea de Calderon, 1971, rev. 13th edit., 1995, Primera Parte de Comedias de Pedro Calderon de la Barca, Vol. 1, 1974, Vol. 2, 1981, 12th reprinting, 1995, Calderon y la comedia nueva, 1977, La vida es sueno. Antes que todo es mi dama. PEdro Calderon de la Barca, 1988, El mayor monstruo del mundo. de Calderon, 1995; contbr. articles to profl. jours., chpts. to books. Founder, pres. Valbuena Inst. Spanish Lit., Inc., 1986. Consejo Superior de Investigaciones Cientificas fellw, 1951, 70-71, Instituto de Cultura Hispánica fellow, 1951-52; recipient Excellence in Teaching award U. Del., 1988, Outstanding Scholar award Coll. Arts and Sci., 1996. Mam. MLA, AAUP, Am. Assn. Tchrs. Spanish and Portuguese, Inst. Iberoam. Lit., Internat. Fedn. Modern Langs. and Lits., Assn. Lit. Scholars and Critics, Internat. Assn. Hispanists, Am. Comparative Lit. Assn., Assn. for Hispanic Classic Theatre, Philol. Assn. Pacific Coast, Greenville Country Club, Sigma Delta Pi (hon.), Phi Kappa Phi. Home: 203 Nottingham Rd Newark DE 19711-7402

VALDÉS, MARIA, soil microbiology educator; b. Matamoros, Tamaulipas, Mexico, Nov. 1, 1938; d. Octavio Valdés and Consuelo Ramirez; children: Carlos and Daniel Hidalgo-Valdés. Degree in Biology, Nat. Univ., Mexico City, 1962; DS, U. de Caen, France, 1968. Prof. Nat. Polytech. Inst., Mexico City, 1968—; scientific adviser Nat. Inst. of Forest Rsch., Mexico, 1976-79; mem. sci. coun. State of Tamaulipas, Victoria, Mexico, 1990—; scientific reviewer Nat. Coun. of Sci. and Technology, Mexico, 1980—; scientific adviser Internat. Found. for Sci., Stockholm, 1985—; vis. scientist Tex. A&M Univ., College Station, 1983, Yale Univ., New Haven, 1988, UCLA, 1990, 91, 94; adj. prof. Mich. State U., East Lansing, 1986; stagier de recherche, ORSTOM-CIRAD, Forêt, Nogent-Sur-Marne, France, 1993. Author more than 50 scientific publs. on biological nitrogen fixation and on mycorrhizae; contbg. author: Tropical Mycorrhiza Research, 1980, Establecimiento de Pasturas, 1990, Better Management of Soil, Water and Nutrients in Tropical Plantations, 1995. Jury mem. Nat. Award Scis. & Arts, 1995. Grantee Internat. Found. for Sci., Sweden, 1974-82, Nat. Coun. for Sci. and Technology, Mexico, 1981-84, 90-92, 92-95, Nat. Acad. Scis./Bur. of Sci. and Tech. for Internat. Devel., 1987-91; recipient Nat. Rschr. award Dept. Pub. Edn., Mexico, 1984-96, Ecology medal Acad. of Scis., Mexico, 1986, Lazaro Cardenas Medal, Nat. Polytech. Inst., Mexico, 1992. Fellow Latin Am. Soc. on Rhizobium; mem. Am. Soc. Microbiology, Mexican Soc. for Mycology (pres. 1983-84), Mexican Soc. Nitrogen Fixation (pres. 1996—), Internat. Union of Forest Rsch. Orgn., Nat. Acad. Scis., Nat. Geographic Soc., The Smithsonian Instn. Avocations: movies, music, jogging. Office: Inst Politecnico Nacional ENCB, Biology Plan Ayala Y Carpio S/N, 11340 Mexico City Mexico

VALDES, MAXIMIANO, conductor. Student, Conservatory of Music, Santiago, Chile, Accademia Santa Cecilia, Rome. Asst. condr. Teatro Fenice, Venice, Italy, 1976; worked as conducting fellow with Leonard Bernstein and Seiji Ozawa, 1977; condr. Buffalo Philharm. Orch., 1989—. Operatic debut with La Traviata, Nice Opera, France; Paris Opera debut with Romeo and Juliet, 1986; London debut with English Chamber Orch., 1987; other opera appearances include The Barber of Seville in Lausanne, Le Nozze di Figaro and Werther in Barcelona, Agnese di Hohenstaufen and The Barber of Seville at Rome Opera, Eugene Onegin at Bonn Opera, Faust in Copenhagen; condr. orchs. of Spain, Denmark, Italy, S.Am.; leader London Philharm. Orch. on tour to Spain, Monte Carlo Philharm. on tour to Italy; prin. condr. Nat. Orch. of Spain, 1986-87; recs. with Monte Carlo Philharm., London Symphony, Nice Philharm., New Zealand Symphony; N.Am. debut with Buffalo Philharm., 1987; appointed music dir. Buffalo Philharm. Orch., 1989, asst. conductor at the Teatro Fenice in Venice, 1976. Recipient 2d prize Rupert Found. Conducting Competition, London, 1978, 1st prize Nicolai Malko Competition, Copenhagen, 1980, 1st prize Vittorio Gui Competition, Florence, Italy; awarded the Del Carlo Tanglewood fellowship, 1977. Office: Buffalo Philharm Orch 71 Symphony Circle PO Box 905 Buffalo NY 14213

VALDES-DAPENA, MARIE AGNES, pediatric pathologist, educator; b. Pottsville, Pa., July 14, 1921; d. Edgar Daniel and Marie Agnes (Rettig) Brown; m. Antonio M. Valdes-Dapena, Apr. 6, 1945 (div. Oct. 1980); children: Victoria Maria Valdes-Dapena Dead, Deborah Anne Valdes-Dapena Malle, Maria Cristina, Andres Antonio, Antonio Edgardo, Carlos Roberto, Marcos Antonio, Ricardo Daniel, Carmen Patricia Valdés-Dapena Fater, Catalina Inez Valdés-Dapena Amram, Pedro Pablo. BS, Immaculata Coll., 1941; MD, Temple U., 1944. Diplomate: Am. Bd. Pathology (spl. qualification-pediatric pathology 1990). Intern Phila. Gen. Hosp., 1944-45, resident in pathology, 1945-49; asst. pathologist Fitzgerald Mercy Hosp., Darby, Pa., 1949-51; dir. labs. Woman's Med. Coll. Pa., Phila., 1951-55; instr. pathology Woman's Med. Coll. Pa., 1947-51, asst. prof., 1951-55, assoc. prof., 1955-59; assoc. pathologist St. Christopher's Hosp. for Children, Phila., 1959-76; dir. sect. pediatric pathology U. Miami (Fla.)-Jackson Meml. Hosp., 1976-81, pediatric pathologist, dir. div. edn. in pathology, 1981-93, co.-dir. edn. in pathology, 1993—; cons., lectr. U.S. Naval Hosp., Phila., 1972-76; instr. pathology Sch. Medicine U. Pa., 1945-49; instr. Sch. Medicine U. Pa. (Sch. Dentistry), 1947, Sch. Medicine U. Pa. (Grad. Sch. Medicine), 1948-55, vis. lectr., 1960-62; asst. prof. Temple U. Med. Sch., 1959-63, assoc. prof., 1963-67, prof. pathology and pediatrics, 1967-76; prof. pathology and pediatrics U., Miami, 1976-93, prof. emeritus pathology and pediatrics, 1993—; cons. pediatric pathology div. med. examiner Dept. Pub. Health Phila., 1967-70; mem. perinatal biology and infant mortality research and tng. com. Nat. Inst. Child Health and Human Devel., NIH, 1971-73; mem. sci. adv. bd. Armed Forces Inst. Pathology, 1976-82; assoc. med. examiner, Dade County, Fla., 1976—; chmn. med. bd. Nat. Sudden Infant Death Syndrome Found., 1961-81, 87-91, pres., 1984-87, chmn. bd., 1985-88; mem. med. and sci. adv. coun. The SIDS Alliance, 1990—. Contbr. articles to profl. jours. NIH grantee. Mem. U.S. and Can. Acad. Pathology, Coll. Physicians Phila., Internat. Assn. Pediatric Pathology, Soc. for Pediatric Pathology (pres. 1980-81), Alpha Omega Alpha. Roman Catholic. Home: 179 Morningside Dr Miami FL 33166-5240 Office: Dept Pathology U Miami Sch Medicine PO Box 016960 Miami FL 33101-6960

VALDÉS-ZACKY, DOLORES, advertising executive; b. Mexico City, Sept. 22, 1947; came to U.S., 1976; d. German and Dolores (Menendez) Valdes; children: Lorena, Daphne. BA in Spanish and Latin Am. Studies, U. of the Ams., Mexico City, 1970; postgrad., Inst. Latin Am. Studies, London, 1970-71; MA in Spanish with distinction, UCLA, 1978. Producer McCann Erickson, Mexico City, 1971-72; copywriter Manin Display Internat., Mexico City, 1972-74; prof. lit. Colegio Columbia, Mexico City, 1974-76; account exec. Latmark Advt., Los Angeles, 1980-81; assoc. creative dir. Bermudez and Assocs., Los Angeles, 1981-82; v.p., creative dir. J. Walter Thompson/Hispania, Los Angeles, 1982-87; pres., creative dir. Valdes Zacky Assocs., Inc., Los Angeles, 1987—. Creative dir. (TV comms.) Nature, 1987 (Don Belding award), Te Quiero Mucho, 1987 (Don Belding award 1987); featured in the L.A. Times as one of So. Calif.'s Rising Stars, 1989. Recipient Se Habla Espanol awards, 1990; named one of 4 top women in advt. Adweek mag., 1986. Republican. Roman Catholic. Avocations: skiing, tennis, computers, music. Office: Valdes Zacky Assocs Inc 1925 Century Park E Fl 19 Los Angeles CA 90067-2701

VALDEZ, FELICIA M., special education educator; b. Washington, Feb. 24, 1948; d. Joseph Alvin and Bettye Mae (Weaver); children: Ronald Nathaniel Tabor II, Tracye Thomas. B, Antioch U., 1976, M, 1978; D, George Washington U., 1992. Tchr. Children's Inn, Washington, D.C., 1976-77; early childhood specialist Children's Hosp., Washington, D.C., 1977-86, coord. edn. svcs., 1986-92, dir. early intervention inst., 1992—; cons. Valdez & Assocs., Washington, 1993—, Mayor's Transition Team, Washington, 1990. Contbr. chpt. to book. Chair. Interagency Coordinating Coun., Washington, 1989-90; chairperson Devel. Disabilities Coun., Washington, 1990—; mem. President's Commn. Mental Retardation, 1991, state adv. panel Spl. Edn., Washington, 1988-89. Mem. Coun. for Exceptional Children, Am. Speech & Hearing Assn., Nat. Assn. Edn. Young Children, Assn. Supervision & Curriculum, Phi Beta Gamma, Phi Delta Kappa. Roman Catholic. Avocations: interior decorating, interior design, golfing, reading. Home: 312 Buchanan St NW Washington DC 20011-4726 Office: Children's Hosp 111 Michigan Ave NW Washington DC 20010-2970

VALDEZ, FRANCES VALDEZ, lawyer; b. San Antonio, Tex., Sept. 7, 1954; d. Juan Ortiz and Basilisa Flores Valdez; m. Joe Albert Gonzales, Sept. 26, 1981; children: Ana Lisa, Martin Esteban. BA, Yale U., 1977; JD, U. Tex., 1980. Bar: Tex. 1980, U.S. Dist. Ct. (no. dist.) Tex. 1981, U.S. Ct. Appeals (5th cir.) 1981, U.S. Ct. Appeals (10th cir.) 1981. Trial atty. office of the solicitor U.S. Dept. Labor, Dallas, 1980-84; briefing atty. no. dist. Tex. U.S. Bankruptcy Ct., Dallas, 1984-85; dir., shareholder, atty. Geary Glast & Middleton P.C., Dallas, 1985-92; regulatory/environ. atty. J.C. Penney Co. Inc., Plano, Tex., 1992—; mem. adv. panel The Bus. Forum, 1993—. Law vol. Cath. Charities, Dallas, 1992-95; mentor, spkr. Nike Club, Dallas, 1994—. Mem. Dallas Bar Assn. (spkr. com. mem. environ. sect. 1992—, internat. sec. 1991—), Mex.-Am. Bar Assn., Bankruptcy Bar Assn. (co-chair ct. liaison com., chair), Yale Club of Dallas, Hispanic C. of C. (planning com. chair, spkr. com. chair 1985—). Democrat. Roman Catholic. Avocations: cycling, basketball one on one, flower & wreath arranging, writing. Home: 9109 Livenshire Dr Dallas TX 75238 Office: JC Penney Co Inc Legal Dept 6501 Legacy Dr Plano TX 75024-3698

VALDIVIA, HECTOR H., medical educator; b. Loreto, Mex., Aug. 23, 1958; married. MD, Nat U. Mex., 1982, PhD, 1987. Teaching asst. Nat. U. Mex. Sch. Medicine, Mexico City, 1980-86; rsch. assoc. Baylor Coll. Medicine, Houston, 1986-89; assoc. scientist U. Wis. Sch. Medicine, Madison, 1989-92; rsch. asst. prof. U. Md. Med. Sch., Bapt., 1992-94; asst. prof. dept. physiology U. Wis. Med. Sch., Madison, 1994—; lectr. and researcher in field. Contbr. articles to profl. jours., chpts. to books. Cystic Fibrosis Found. fellow, 1989-91. Mem. Am. Heart Assn. (scintific coun. 1995—), Biophys. Soc. U.S.A. Office: U Wis Med Sch Dept Physiology 1300 University Ave Madison WI 53706

VALE, MARGO ROSE, physician; b. Balt., June 16, 1950; d. Henry and Pauline Esther (Koplow) Hausdorff; m. Michael Allen Vale, Aug. 22, 1971; children: Edward, Judith. BA magna cum laude, Brandeis U., 1971; MD, Albert Einstein Coll. Medicine, 1975. Diplomate Am. Bd. Dermatology. Resident in internal medicine and dermatology NYU, N.Y.C., 1975-79, Bellevue Hosp., N.Y.C., 1975-79, VA Hosp., N.Y.C., 1975-79; staff physician HIP Greater N.Y., Bay Shore, 1979-81; pvt. practice medicine Huntington, N.Y., 1981—; cons. in dermatology Huntington Hosp., 1981—, Gurwin Jewish Geriatric Ctr., Commack, N.Y., 1990—. Contbr. articles to profl. jours. Mem. Am. Acad. Dermatology, Med. Soc. State N.Y., Long Island Dermatology Soc., Suffolk County Med. Soc., Suffolk Dermatology Soc. (pres. 1990-92), Phi Beta Kappa. Avocations: cooking, photography, sketching, music. Office: 205 E Main St Huntington NY 11743-2923

VALE, NORMAN, advertising executive; b. N.Y.C., Jan. 19, 1930; s. Henry and Evelyn (Spaulder) F.; m. Irene Loebenson Vale, Dec. 22, 1957; children: Margaret, Jennifer. BBA, CCNY, 1952. Acctg. exec. Grey Advt., N.Y.C., 1954-60, SSCB Co., N.Y.C., 1960-62; sr. asst. to chief exec. officer Lennen & Newell, N.Y.C., 1962-67; dep. dir. internat. Needham Harper, N.Y.C., 1967-73; mng. dir. Grey Internat., N.Y.C., 1974-90; dir. gen. IAA, N.Y.C., 1990—. Chmn. Dunewood Fire Dist., Fire Island, N.Y. Cpl. U.S. Army, 1952-54. Mem. Internat. Advt. Assn. (world bd. 1986—), Am. Assn. Advt. Agys. (chmn. internat. com. 1987-89), Achilles Track Club. Avocations: triathlons, skiing, ballet, theater. Office: IAA 521 Fifth Ave Ste 1807 New York NY 10175

VALE, VICTOR JOHN EUGENE, II, lawyer; b. Heampstead, N.Y., Oct. 6, 1958; s. Victor E. and Caroline Katherine Frances V. BBA, Midd. Tenn. State U., 1990; JD, Marquet Univ., 1993. Bar: Fla., 1994, Wis., 1993; U.S. Dist. Ct. (ea. dist.) Wis., 1993. Law clk. Mingo & Yankala, Milw., 1991; appellate law clk. Mitchner & Mitchner, Milw., 1992-93; intern Pub. Def. 19th Jud. Cir., Ft. Pierce, Fla., 1992-94; pvt. practice Ft. Pierce, 1994—; vice-chmn. econ. devel. com., Port St. Lucie, Fla., 1994—; chmn. met. planning orgn. citizen's adv. com., St. Lucie County, Fla., 1994—. Contbg. author: Wisemen on Criminal Procedures, 1993; editor: Grenig on Civil Procedure, 1993. Parliamentarian Port St. Lucie Rep. Club, 1994—; treas. Young Reps., Murfreesboro, Tenn., 1989-90. Staff sgt. U.S. Army, 1976-86. Recipient Law Student award Bur. Nat. Affairs, Washington, 1993; cert. appreciation Comm. on Bicentennial of U.S. Constn., Washington, 1992, 93. Mem. Disabled Am. Vets., Federalist Soc. (pres. 1992-93), Omicron Delta Epsilon, Sigma Xi. Roman Catholic. Avocations: golf, tennis, sailing, skiing, chess. Office: 205 S 2nd St Fort Pierce FL 34950

VALEK, BERNARD MICHAEL, accounting executive; b. Joliet, Ill., Nov. 19, 1945; s. Peter Anthony and Ann Monica (Hertko) V.; m. Kathleen Mary Clarke, Aug. 16, 1969; 1 child, Emily Ann. BS, No. Ill. U., 1968, MBA, 1969. CPA, Calif., Ill. Asst. prof. Ferris State U., Big Rapids, Mich., 1969-72; staff mgr. Arthur Andersen & Co., Chgo., 1972-78; dir. Calif. CPA Fedn., Palo Alto, 1979-84; pres. Alliance of Practicing CPAs, Long Beach, Calif., 1985—; cons. ANA, L.A., 1984-86. Author: ANA Practice Management Manuals, 1985; pub. (newsletter) The CPAdvocate, 1990—. Bd. dirs. Am. Heart Assn., Long Beach, 1993-94; bd. dirs., treas. Cities in Schs. Long Beach, 1988—, Long Beach Phone Friend, 1988-93. Named One of 100 Most Influential People in Acctg., Acctg. Today newspaper, 1996. Mem. AICPA (bd. dirs. 1982-84), Calif. CPA Soc. (bd. dirs. 1979-84). Roman Catholic. Avocations: exercising, hiking, travel, health. Office: Alliance of Practicing CPAs 3909 California Ave Long Beach CA 90807-3511

VALENCIA, JAIME ALFONSO, chemical engineer; b. Arequipa, Peru, Apr. 2, 1952; came to the U.S., 1970; s. Luis A. and Julia (Chavez) V.; m. Cecelia Ann Ingram, Nov. 21, 1987; 1 child, Julia Nicole. BSChE, U. Md., 1974; DSc in Chem. Engring., MIT, 1978. Registered profl. engr., Tex. Mem. cons. staff Arthur D. Little, Inc., Cambridge, Mass., 1978-82; group leader Exxon Prodn. Rsch. Co., Houston, 1982-86; dir. tech. devel. Novatec, Inc., Houston, 1986-89; v.p. Novatec Prodn. Systems, Inc., Houston, 1988-91; dir. strategic tech. devel. Aspen Tech., Inc., Houston, 1995—; prin. NOVI Enterprises, Houston, 1986-95; cons. Exxon, Houston, 1990-95. Contbr.: Flue Gas Desulfurization, 1982; contbr. articles to Internat. Jour. Heat and Mass Transfer, Hydrocarbon Processing; author: AIChE Symposium Series, 1977. Mem. bd. advisors Entrepreneurial Devel. Ctr., Houston, 1993-95. Mem. AIChE, MIT Alumni Club South Tex. (bd. dirs. 1990—, pres. 1994-95). Roman Catholic. Achievements include patents for cryogenic processing; invention of CFZ process for cryogenic separations; development of Novatec process for cleaning oil contaminated cuttings from drilling operations; basic principles for Ryan-Holmes technology for processing natural gas. Home: 9830 Stableway Dr Houston TX 77065-4368 Office: Aspen Tech Inc PO Box 22807 Houston TX 77227-2807

VALENS, EVANS GLADSTONE, sculptor, printmaker, author, former television producer, director; b. State College, Pa., Apr. 17, 1920; s. Evans G. and Mabel (Grazier) V.; m. Winifred A. Crary, Oct. 11, 1941 (div. 1976); children: Thomas Crary, Marc John, Jo Anne, Dan Malcolm.; m. Anne Kent Curtis, Dec. 18, 1980 (div. 1987). BA, Amherst Coll., 1941; MFA, San Francisco Art Inst., 1990. Reporter El Paso Herald-Post, 1942-43; corr. UPI, Central Pacific, U.S. and Europe, 1943-48; bur. chief UPI, Munich, 1946-48; producer-dir. KQED, San Francisco, 1954-62, 70-71. Author: (non-fiction): (with others) Elements of the Universe, 1958 (Thomas Alva Edison award); The Number of Things, 1963, A Long Way Up, The Story of Jill Kinmont, 1966, (with others) Viruses and the Nature of Life, 1961, The Attractive Universe, 1969, (with others) People-reading, 1975; poetry includes Cybernaut, 1968; juvenile books include Me and Frumpet, 1957; Wingfin and Topple, 1962, Wildfire, 1963, Magnet, 1965, Motion, 1965, The Other Side of the Mountain, 1975; Part II, 1978; producer-writer numerous films and TV prodns.; sculpture commn. Napa (Calif.) Town Ctr., 1988. Decorated Purple Heart.

VALENSTEIN, SUZANNE GEBHART, art historian; b. Balt., July 17, 1928; d. Jerome J. and Lonnie Cooper Gebhart; m. Murray A. Valenstein, Mar. 31, 1951. With dept. Asian Art Met. Mus. Art, N.Y.C., 1965—; rsch. curator Asian Art. Author: Ming Porcelains: A Retrospective, 1970, A Handbook of Chinese Ceramics, 1975, rev. and enlarged, 1989, Highlights of Chinese Ceramics, 1975, (with others) Oriental Ceramics: The World's Great Collections: The Metropolitan Museum, 1977, rev., 1983, The Herzman Collection of Chinese Ceramics, 1992. Mem. Oriental Ceramic Soc. (London), Oriental Ceramic Soc. (Hong Kong). Office: Met Mus Art Dept Asian Art Fifth Ave at 82nd St New York NY 10028

VALENTA, JANET ANNE, substance abuse professional; b. Cleve., Sept. 22, 1948; d. Frank A. and Ann (Kogoy) Shenk; m. Mario Valenta, May 22, 1971. BA, Cleve. State U., 1970; postgrad., Rutgers U., 1973, U. Cin., 1976-84. Cert. prevention cons., Ohio. Purchasing clk./typist Restaurant div. Stouffer Foods Corp., Cleve., 1967-71; cmty. info. specialist Trumbull Warren Office of Econ. Opportunity, Warren, Ohio, 1972; edn. dir. Trumbull County Coun. on Alcoholism, Warren, 1973-78; rehab. counselor Trumbull County Bur. Vocat. Rehab., Niles, Ohio, 1979-80; owner, operator Ironsmith, Niles, 1978-79; cons., trainer Ohio Network Tng. and Assistance to Schs. and Cmty., Youngstown, Ohio, 1987—; prevention edn. coord. Cmty. Recovery Resource Ctr., Youngstown, 1979-94; prevention coord. Neil Kennedy Recovery Clinic, Youngstown, 1994—; Ohio tng. coord. Babesworld Home, Inc., Detroit, 1986—; nat. chair pub. health caucus Nat. Assn. Prevention Profls., Chgo., 1976-77. Publicity chair Trumbull Art Guild, Warren, 1974-76; bd. dirs. Ebony Life Support Group, Inc., Youngstown, 1992; mem. Policy coun. Youngstown Cmty. Action, Headstart, 1988-90. Named Woman of Yr., Warren Bus. and Profl. Women's Assn., 1978, Tribute in Health Woman of Yr., YWCA, Youngstown, 1987. Mem. Alcohol and Drug Abuse Prevention Assn. Ohio. Office: Neil Kennedy Recovery Clin 2151 Rush Blvd Youngstown OH 44507

VALENTA, ZDENEK, chemistry educator; b. Havlickuv Brod, Czechoslovakia, June 14, 1927; came to Can., 1950; s. Karel Valenta and Jindra (Komers) Valentova; m. Noreen Elizabeth Donahoe, July 29, 1957; children—Katherine Elizabeth, Richard Karel, Michael Francis. Dipl. Ing. Chem., E.T.H., Zurich, Switzerland, 1950; M.S., U. N.B., 1952, Ph.D., 1953. Spl. lectr. dept. chemistry U. N.B., Fredericton, Can., 1953-54, lectr., 1954-56, asst. prof., 1957-58, assoc. prof., 1958-63, prof., 1963-90; rsch. prof. U. N.B., Fredericton, 1990—; head chemistry dept. U. N.B., Fredericton, Can., 1963-72; cons. Delmar Chems., LaSalle, Que., Can., 1970—, Ayerst Research Labs., Montreal, Que., Can., 1980-85, Torcan Chem., Toronto, Ont., Can., 1980—. Contbr. articles to profl. jours. Recipient Excellence in Teaching award U. N.B., 1974, Sci. Teaching award Atlantic Provinces Coun. on Scis./Northern Telecom 1987, award for chem. edn. Union Carbide, 1989. Fellow Chem. Inst. Can. (Merck, Sharp and Dohme award 1967), Royal Soc. Can. Home: 872 Windsor St, Fredericton, NB Canada E3B 4G5 Office: U NB Dept Chemistry, Bag Service 45222, Fredericton, NB Canada E3B 6E2

VALENTE, LOUIS PATRICK (DAN VALENTE), business and financial consultant; b. Somerville, Mass., July 26, 1930; s. Luigi and Mary Constance (Fedele) V.; m. Jeanne Barbara Peters, Oct. 3, 1992; children: Louis, Marianne, Steven, Diane, Richard, Carol, Susan. Cert., Bentley Coll., Boston, 1955. Cost acct. Cambridge Corp., Lowell, Mass., 1953-55; sr. acct. Flaherty, Bliss & Co., CPAs, Boston, 1956-61; fin. analyst Sanders Assocs., Nashua, N.H., 1961-62; fin. cons. Burlington, Mass., 1961-68; contract audit adminstr. Dept. Def. Audit Agy., Boston, 1962-66, DOE, Las Vegas, 1966-68; asst. controller EG&G, Inc., Wellesley, Mass., 1968-71, asst. v.p., treas., 1971-74, dir. fin., 1974-79, officer, corp. treas., 1979-83, v.p. bus. devel., 1985-91, sr. v.p. mergers, acquisitons and investments, 1991-95; bus. and fin. cons., 1995—; bd. dirs. Meditech Inc., Westwood, Mass., Micrion Corp., Patient Care Tech., Atlanta, MKS Instruments, Inc., Andover, Mass. Selectman Town of Burlington, 1970-73, 76-79, chmn., 1972-79; trustee, mem. fin. com. Choate-Symmes Hosp., Woburn, Mass., 1972—; pres.'s adv. coun. Bentley Coll. With USAF, 1951-53. Mem. AICPA, Fin. Execs. Inst., Mass. Soc. CPAs, Bentley Coll. Alumni Assn., New Eng. Council. Roman Catholic. Lodge: K.C. Home: 44 Concord Rd Weston MA 02193-1223 *Creativeness and its benefit to the business world is important. Credit to, and exposure of the creator is trivial.*

VALENTE, PETER CHARLES, lawyer; b. N.Y.C., July 3, 1940; s. Francis Louis and Aurelia Emily (Cella) V.; m. Judith Kay Nemeroff, Feb. 19, 1966; children: Susan Lynn, David Marc. BA, Bowdoin Coll., 1962; LLB, Columbia U., 1966; LLM, N.Y.U., 1971. Bar: N.Y. 1967. Assoc. Tenzer Greenblatt, LLP, N.Y.C., 1967-73, ptnr., 1973—, ptnr. in charge trusts and estates dept., 1973—. Co-author column on wills, estates and surrogate's practice N.Y. Law Jour. Fellow Am. Coll. Trust and Estate Counsel; mem. ABA, N.Y. State Bar Assn. (lectr. on wills, trusts and estates), Assn. of Bar of City of N.Y., N.Y. County Lawyers' Assn. (former bd. dirs. and chmn. com. on surrogates' ct., lectr. on wills, trusts and estates), Phi Beta Kappa. Office: Tenzer Greenblatt LLP 405 Lexington Ave New York NY 10174

VALENTI, CARL M., newspaper publisher. Pres., pub.-info. svc. Wall St. Jour., N.Y.C.; also sr. v.p. Dow Jones & Co., N.Y.C. Office: The Wall Street Journal Dow Jones & Co Inc 200 Liberty St New York NY 10281-1003

VALENTI, JACK JOSEPH, motion picture executive; b. Houston, Sept. 5, 1921; m. Mary Margaret Wiley, June 1, 1962; children: Courtenay Lynda, John Lyndon, Alexandra Alice. BA, U. Houston, 1946; MBA, Harvard U., 1948. Co-founder, formerly exec. v.p. Weekley and Valenti, Inc. (advt.), 1952-63; spl. asst. to Pres. Johnson, 1963-66; pres., chief exec. officer Motion Picture Assn. Am., Inc., 1966—; chmn. Alliance Motion Picture and TV Producers, Inc., 1966—; chmn., chief exec. officer Motion Picture Export Assn. Am.; adj. prof. govt. and pub. adminstrn. Am. U., 1977; bd. dirs. Riggs Nat. Corp. Washington. Author: Bitter Taste of Glory, 1971, A Very Human President, 1976, Speak Up With Confidence: How To Prepare, Learn and Deliver an Effective Speech, 1982, Protect and Defend, 1992; contbr. articles to mags. Trustee, bd. dirs. Am. Film Inst. Served with USAAF, 1942-45. Decorated D.F.C., Air medal with five oak leaf clusters, Disting. Unit Citation with cluster, European Theater Ribbon with 4 battle stars, Chevalier de la Legion d'honneur (France). Address: Motion Picture Assoc 1600 I St NW Washington DC 20006-4010 also: MPAA 1133 Avenue Of The Americas New York NY 10036-6710

VALENTIN, JOHN WILLIAM, professional baseball player; b. Mineola, N.Y., Feb. 18, 1967. Ed., Seton Hall U. Shortstop Boston Red Sox, 1992—. Achievements include completion of unassisted triple play (10th player in MLB history to do so). Office: Boston Red Sox 4 Yawkey Way Boston MA 02215

VALENTINE, ALAN DARRELL, symphony orchestra executive; b. San Antonio, July 18, 1958; s. Lonnie Darrell Jr. and Marjorie (Childs) V.; m. Jari Ann Ruhl, Aug. 10, 1979 (div. 1987); children: Brandon Darrell, Chelsea Michelle; m. Karen Kay Bingham, Oct. 21, 1989; 1 child, Nathan Lee. MusB, U. Houston, 1981. Orch. mgr. U. Houston Symphony, 1977-81; gen. mgr. Mid-Columbia Symphony Soc., Richland, Wash., 1981-83, Greensboro (N.C.) Symphony Soc., 1983-85; orch. mgr. Symphony Soc. San Antonio, 1985-87; mng. dir. Chattanooga Symphony and Opera, 1987-88; exec. dir. Okla. Philharm. Soc., Oklahoma City, 1988-; mem. adj. faculty Arts Adminstrn., Oklahoma City U., 1992—. Bd. dirs. Classen Sch. for Artistically and Academically Gifted, Arts Festival Okla. Mem. Am. Symphony Orch. League (bd. dirs. Community and Urban Symphony Orch. divsn. 1981-83), Met. Orch. Mgrs. Assn. (cons.), Rotary, Phi Mu Alpha. Presbyterian. Avocations: computers, racquetball, reading. Office: Okla City Philharm 428 W California Ave Ste 210 Oklahoma City OK 73102-2454

VALENTINE, FOY DAN, clergyman; b. Edgewood, Tex., July 3, 1923; s. John Hardy and Josie (Johnson) V.; m. Mary Louise Valentine, May 6, 1947; children: Mary Jean, Carol Elizabeth, Susan Foy. BA, Baylor U., 1944, LLD (hon.), 1979; ThM, Southwestern Baptist Theol. Sem., 1947, ThD, 1949; DD, William Jewell Coll., 1966, Louisiana Coll., 1989. Ordained to ministry Bapt. Ch., 1942. Dir. Bapt. student activities colls. in Houston, 1949-50; pastor First Bapt. Ch., Gonzales, Tex., 1950-53; dir. Christian life commn. Bapt. Gen. Conv. Tex., 1953-60; exec. dir., treas. Christian life commn. So. Bapt. Conv., 1960-87, exec. officer for devel., 1987-88; chmn. So. Bapt. inter-agy. council, 1965-67; Willson lectr. applied Christianity Wayland Bapt. Coll., 1963; Christian ethics lectr. Bapt. Theol. Sem., Ruschlikon-Zurich, Switzerland, 1966; Layne lectr. New Orleans Bapt. Theol. Sem., 1974; Jones lectr. Union U., 1976; Staley Disting. Christian scholar/lectr. La. Coll., 1981; Simpson lectr. Acadia Divinity Coll., Nova Scotia, 1982; H.I. Hester lectr. on preaching Midwestern Bapt. Theol. Sem., 1984; Belote lectr. Christian ethics Hong Kong Bapt. Theol. Sem., 1990; co-chmn. commn. religious liberty and human rights Bapt. World Alliance, 1966-75, chmn. commn. Christian ethics, 1976-80, mem. gen. coun., 1976-80; mem. Nashville Met. Human Rels. Commn., 1966-78, Pres.'s Commn. for Nat. Agenda for the Eighties, 1980; guest columnist USA Today; lectr. on Christian ethics Bible Inst. for Evangelism and Missions, St. Petersburg, USSR, 1991; pres. Ctr. for Christian Ethics, 1990—. Author: Believe and Behave, 1964, Citizenship for Christians, 1965, The Cross in the Marketplace, 1966, Where the Action Is, 1969, An Historical Study of Southern Baptists and Race Relations 1917-1947, 1980, What Do You Say After You Say Amen?, 1980, Hebrews, James, 1 and 2 Peter: Layman's Bible Book Commentary, 1981; editor: Christian Faith in Action, 1956, Peace, Peace, 1967, Christian Ethics Today, 1995—; contbr. to numerous anthologies, articles to profl. jours. Pres. Ctr. for Christian Ethics, 1990—; trustee Interfaith Alliance, 1994—, Ams. United for Separation of Ch. and State, 1960-93, pres., 1989-93; bd. dirs. Bapt. Joint Com. Pub. Affairs, 1960-87, Chs. Ctr. Theology and Pub. Policy, 1976-87, T.B. Maston Found., Texans Against Gambling; mem. bd. fellows Interpreter's House, 1967-78, Ctr. for Dialogue and Devel., 1987—. Recipient Disting. Alumnus award Southwestern Bapt. Theol. Sem., 1970, Brooks Hays Meml. Christian Citizenship award, 1983, Disting. Alumni award Baylor U., 1987. Mem. Am. Soc. Christian Ethics. Democrat. Home and Office: 12527 Matisse Ln Dallas TX 75230-1741

VALENTINE, GORDON CARLTON, secondary education educator; b. Norwich, N.Y., Nov. 18, 1946; s. Carlton Everett and Helen Janet (Thompson) V.; m. Deborah Lee Preston, Oct. 15, 1977; children: Heather, Megan, Matthew. BA, SUNY, Cortland, 1968, MS in Edn., 1970. Cert. tchr., N.Y. Tchr. Sherburne-Earlville Ctrl. Sch., Sherburne, N.Y., 1968-70, Marathon (N.Y.) Ctrl. Sch., 1970-87; social welfare examiner Dept. Social Svcs., Cortland, 1988; tchr. Homer (N.Y.) Ctrl. Sch., 1989—; adj. instr. Tompkins-Cortland C.C., Dryden, N.Y., 1982—; mem. profl. staff devel. and supportive supervision model Homer Ctrl. Sch., 1989-92, asst. varsity cross country coach, jr. high track coach. Recipient Christa McAliffe Tchr.'s award, 1991. Mem. ASCD, Homer Tchrs. Assn., Challenger Ctr. of NASA, Ctrl. N.Y. State Coun. for Social Studies, SUNY Cortland Alumni Assn. (bd. dirs. 1993—, mem. admissions com., mem. mktg. com., mem. rsch. devel. com.). Democrat. Avocations: running, reading, volunteer coaching. Home: 31 James St Homer NY 13077-1312 Office: Homer Ctrl Sch Box 500 West Rd Homer NY 13077

VALENTINE, H. JEFFREY, legal association executive; b. Phila., Sept. 28, 1945; s. Joshua Morton and Olga W. (Wilson) V.; 1 child, Karyn. BS, St. Louis U., 1964, postgrad., 1966-68. Programmer, systems analyst Honeywell Electronic Data Processing, Wellesley Hills, Mass., 1964-66; account exec. Semiconductor div. Tex. Instruments, New Eng., 1966-68; New Eng. sales exec., Mid-Atlantic regional mgr. Electronic Instrumentation Co., 1968-70; pres. Nat. Free Lance Photographers Assn., Doylestown, Pa., 1970-89; pres., dir. Towne Print & Copy Ctrs. Inc.; v.p., exec. dir. Nat. Paralegal Assn., 1982—; pres. Paralegal Assocs., Inc., 1982—; chief operating officer Doylestown Parking Corp., 1977-88; bd. dirs. Law Enforcement Supply Co., Solebury, Valtronics Supply Co., Towne Print & Copy Centers Inc., Solebury, Doylestown Stationery and Office Supply, Energy Mktg. Assocs., Inc., Solebury, Paralegal Placement Network; pres. Paralegal Pub. Corp., 1983-90; pub. Paralegal Jour.; pres. Valco Enterprises Inc., 1986—, Paralegal Employment Sys., Inc., 1988, Solebury Press, Inc., 1989—; ptnr. J&S Gen. Contractors, 1993—, J&S Landscaping Tree Svc., 1993—; owner Specialized Computer Consulting, 1992—. Author: Photographers Bookkeeping System, 1973, rev. edit., 1978, Photographers Pricing Guides, 1971, 72, 74, 75, Available Markets Director's - 4 Vols., 1973-77, National Model Sources Directory, Nat. Paralegal Salary and Employment Survey, 1985-86, 88, 90-92, 93-94; also articles, bulls. and pamphlets. Exec. sec. Doylestown Bus. Assn., 1972-78, pres., 1979, 83, v.p., 1981. Recipient Internat. Men of Achievement award, 1988; named Personalities of the Am., 1988. Mem. London Coll. Applied Scis., Nat. Fedn. Paralegal Assns., Photog. Industry Coun., Nat. Assn. Legal Assts., Am. Soc Assn. Execs., Soc. Assn. Mgrs., Nat. Fedn. Ind. Business (mem. action coun. com.), Nat. Parking Assn., Nat. Office Products Assn., Graphic Arts Assn. Delaware Valley, Nat. Assn. Federally Licensed Firearms Dealers, Nat. Compostition Assn., Internat. Platform Assn. Office: PO Box 406 Solebury PA 18963-0406

VALENTINE, HERMAN EDWARD, computer company executive; b. Norfolk, Va., June 26, 1937; s. Frank and Alice Mae (Heigh) V.; m. Dorothy Jones, Nov. 27, 1958; children: Herman Edward, Bryce Thomas. BS in Bus. Adminstrn., Norfolk State Coll., 1967; postgrad., Am. U., 1968; grad. student, Coll. William and Mary. Asst. bus. mgr. grad. sch. Dept. Agr., 1967, exec. officer grad. sch., 1967-68; bus. mgr. Norfolk State Coll., 1968; chmn., pres. Systems Mgmt. Am. Corp., Norfolk, 1969—, chmn., CEO, 1995—; chmn. Century Capitol Holders, Inc. Bd. dirs. PUSH Internat. Trade Bur., Cooperating Hampton Roads Orgn. for Minorities in Engring., Operation Smile, Greater Norfolk Corp.; mem. president's coun. Old Dominion U.; mem. adv. bd. Tidewater Vets. Meml. Project; mem. adv. coun. Va. Stage Co. Named Entrepreneur of Yr. Dept. Commerce Minority Bus. Devel. Agy., 1984, one of 10 Top Minority Owned Fed. Govt. Contractors Govt. Computer News, 1988, Outstanding Business Person of Yr. Va. Black Pres.'s Roundtable Assn., 1987, Amb. City of Norfolk, Va., 1986, Citizen of Yr. William A. Hunton YMCA, 1986, Pres.'s Coun. Am. Inst. Mgmt.; recipient Cert. of Merit City of Chg., 1985, McDonald's Hampton Roads Black Achievement award United Negro Coll. Fund., 1986, Colgate Whitehead Darden award, U. Va., 1987, cert. recognition Lt. Gov. Commonwealth of Va., 1987, Class III Supplier of Yr. award Nat. Minority Supplier Devel. Coun., 1987, Regional Minority Mfr. of Yr. award Minority Bus. Devel. Agy., 1988, Patriotic Svc. award U.S. Treasury Dept., 1989, Black Diamond award Operation Push, 1989; recognized by Upscale Mag., 1993. Mem. Armed Forces Communications and Electronics Assn., Tidewater Regional Minority Purchasing Coun., Downtown Norfolk Devel. Corp., Air Traffic Control Assn., Soc. Logistics Engrs., U.S. Navy League, Hampton Roads C. of C. Office: Systems Mgmt Am Corp 5 Koger Ctr Ste 219 Norfolk VA 23502*

VALENTINE, JAMES WILLIAM, paleobiology, educator, author; b. Los Angeles, Nov. 10, 1926; s. Adelbert Cuthbert and Isabel (Davis) V.; m. Grace Evelyn Whysner, Dec. 21, 1957 (div. 1972); children—Anita, Ian; m. Cathryn Alice Campbell, Sept. 10, 1978 (div. 1986); 1 child, Geoffrey; m. Diane Mondragon, Mar. 16, 1987. B.A., Phillips U., 1951; M.A., UCLA, 1954, Ph.D., 1958. From asst. prof. to assoc. prof. U. Mo., Columbia, 1958-64; from assoc. prof. to prof. U. Calif., Davis, 1964-77; prof. geol. scis. U. Calif., Santa Barbara, 1977-90; prof. integrative biology U. Calif., Berkeley, 1990—. Author: Evolutionary Paleoecology of the Marine Biosphere, 1973; editor: Phanerozoic Diversity, 1985; co-author: Evolution, 1977, Evolving, 1979; also numerous articles, 1954—. Served with USNR, 1944-46; PTO. Fulbright research scholar, Australia, 1962-63; Guggenheim fellow Yale U., Oxford U., Eng., 1968-69; Rockefeller Found. scholar in residence, Bellagio, Italy, summer 1974; grantee NSF, NASA. Fellow Am. Acad. Arts and Scis., AAAS, Geol. Soc. Am.; mem. Nat. Acad. Scis., Paleontol. Soc. (pres. 1974-75). Avocation: collecting works of Charles Darwin. Home: 1351 Glendale Ave Berkeley CA 94708-2025 Office: U Calif Dept Integrative Biolo Berkeley CA 94720

VALENTINE, JOHN LESTER, state legislator, lawyer; b. Fullerton, Calif., Apr. 26, 1949; s. Robert Lester and Pauline C. (Glood) V.; m. Karen Marie Thorpe, June 1, 1972; children: John Robert, Jeremy Reid, Staci Marie, Jeffrey Mark., David Emerson, Patricia Ann. BS in Acctg. and Econs., Brigham Young U., 1973, JD, 1976. Bar: Utah 1976, U.S. Dist. Ct. Utah, U.S. Ct. Appeals (10th cir.), U.S. Tax Ct.; CPA. Atty. Howard, Lewis & Petersen, Provo, Utah, 1976—; mem. Utah Ho. Reps., 1988—; instr. probate and estates Utah Valley State Coll.; instr. fin. planning., adj. prof. law Brigham Young U.; mem. exec offices, cts., corrections and legis. appropriations subcom., 1988-90, capital facilities subcom., 1988-90, retirement com., 1988-90, judiciary com., 1988—, strategic planning steering com., 1988-90, interim appropriations com., 1988—, tax. review commn., 1988-92, ethics com., 1990-92, human svcs. and health appropriations subcom., 1990-92, revenue and taxation com., 1988—, vice chmn. 1990-92; vice chmn. exec. appropriations., 1990-92, chmn. 1992—; chmn. exec. appropriations com., 1992-94, chmn. rules com., 1994, higher edn. appropriations com. 1994; bd. dirs. Utah Corrections Industries. Mem. adv. bd. Internat. Sr. Games, 1988—; active Blue Ribbon Task Force on Local Govt. Funding, Utah League Cities and Towns, 1990-94, Criminal Sentencing Guidelines Task Force, Utah Judicial Coun., 1990-92, Access to Health Care Task Force, 1990-92, Utah County Sheriff Search and Rescue, Orem Met. Water Bd., Alpine Sch. Dist. Boundary Line Com., Boy Scouts Am.; bd. regents Legis. Adv. Com. UVCC.; mem. exec. bd. Utah Nat. Parks Coun.; mem. adv. coun. Orchard Elem. Sch., Mountainlands Com. an Aging; bd. trustees Utah Opera Co.; judge nat. and local competitions Moot Ct.; voting dist. chmn.; state, county del.; lt. incident command sys. Utah County Sheriff. Recipient Silver Beaver award Boy Scouts Am., Taxpayer Advocate award Utah Taxpayer Assn. Mem. ABA (tax sect.), Utah State Bar, CPA Com., Tax Sect. Specialization Com., Bicentennial Com. Republican. Mormon. Avocation: mountain climbing. Office: Howard Lewis & Petersen 120 E 300 N Provo UT 84606-2907

VALENTINE, MICHAEL JOHN, lawyer; b. Hackensack, N.J., Oct. 1, 1957; s. William Glen and Joan Lorenzetti V.; m. Jennifer A. Barnes, Sept. 3, 1983; children: Michael Beowulf, Zachary John. BS, U. Houston, 1981, JD, 1986. Bar: Tex. 1986, U.S. Dist. Ct. (so. dist.) Tex. 1989, U.S. Dist. Ct. (no., ea. and we. dists.) Tex. 1995, U.S. Ct. Appeals (5th cir.) 1995, U.S. Tax Ct. 1989, U.S. Supreme Ct. 1995. Sr. tax cons. Touche Ross & Co., Houston, 1986-88; assoc. atty. Urquhart & Hassel, Houston, 1989-94; gen. counsel Warren Elec. Co., Houston, 1994—. Charter mem. Hedonistic Halloween Soc., Houston, 1984; treas. Knights of Bula, Houston, 1993. Disting. Svc. award Faculty U. Houston Law Ctr., 1986. Mem. ABA, Tex. Bar Assn., Houston Bar Assn., Italian-Am. Lawyers Assn., Tau Kappa Epsilon (bd. dirs., chmn. 1994—). Roman Catholic. Office: Warren Electric Co PO Box 67 2929 McKinney Houston TX 77001

VALENTINE, RALPH SCHUYLER, chemical engineer, research director; b. Seattle, Nov. 3, 1932; s. John Campbell and Elizabeth Florence (Patterson) V.; m. Jeanne Marie Belanger, June 15, 1957; children: Susan Diana, Jacqueline Leigh, John Campbell. BSChemE, U. Wash., 1955, PhDChemE, 1963; MSChemE, U. Ill., 1956. Registered profl. engr., Calif., Va., Wash. Rsch. engr. Chevron Rsch. Corp., Richmond, Calif., 1956-61; instr. U. Wash., Seattle, 1961-63; mgr. fluid dynamics Aerojet-Gen., Sacramento, 1963-69; mgr. chem. tech. Atlantic Rsch. Corp., Alexandria, Va., 1969-79; mgr. rsch. United Techs. Chem. Systems, San Jose, Calif., 1979-91; lectr. U.S. Naval Postgrad. Sch., Monterrey, Calif., 1968, UCLA Modern Devels. in Propulsion, L.A., 1967-68, USAF Astronautics Labs., Lancaster, Calif., 1967, U.S. Army R & D Unit, Sacramento, 1966. Contbr. 23 tech. articles to profl. jours.; patentee in field. Recipient NASA commendation for Apollo work, Houston, 1969, 1st prize Ceramographic Exhbn. Am. Ceramics Soc., 1974. Mem. Am. Inst. Chem. Engrs. (life). Republican. Home: 7242 Via Mimosa San Jose CA 95135-1413

VALENTINE, STEVEN RICHARDS, lawyer; b. Memphis, Jan. 30, 1956; s. William Robert and Lenita Joanne (Nelms) V.; m. Susan Marie Burke, Jan. 14, 1984; children: Christina Michele, William Robert II, Steven Richards Jr., Thomas Burke. Student, Earlham Coll., 1974-77; BGS with distinction, Ind. U., 1979, JD, 1982. Bar: Ill. 1983, D.C. 1985, U.S. Ct. Appeals (D.C. cir.) 1986, U.S. Supreme Ct. 1986, U.S. Ct. Appeals (9th cir.) 1989. Chief investigator consumer protection div. Office Atty. Gen., State of Ind., 1980-82; exec. dir. Ams. United for Life Legal Def. Fund, Chgo., 1982-83; chief counsel subcom. on separation of powers U.S. Senate, Washington, 1983-85, chief counsel subcom. on cts., 1985, adminstrv. asst., 1985-86; dir. Office of Policy Deve. and Comms. Office Policy Devel. and Comm. Legal Svcs. Corp., 1986-87; counselor to asst. atty. gen. Civil div. U.S. Dept. Justice, 1987-88; dep. asst. atty. gen. Civil div. U.S. Justice Dept., 1988-93; gen. counsel U.S. Senator Robert C. Smith, 1993—; mem. exec. com., bd. dirs. Deluxe West, Inc.; sec. bd. dirs. Yokefellows Internat., Inc., D. Elton Trueblood Acad. Endowment, Inc. Author: Each Time A Man, 1978, All Shall Live, 1980, (with others) Abortion and the Constitution, 1987; contbr. articles to profl. jours. Recipient spl. commendation U.S. Atty. Gen., 1993; John C. Stennis Congl. staff fellow, 1995-96. Mem. ABA (vice chmn. com. on govtl. info. and right to privacy), SAR, Wider Quaker Fellowship, Capitol Hill Club. Republican. Roman Catholic. Avocations: history, baseball. Home: 6513 Old Coach Ct Alexandria VA 22315-5045 Office: 332 Dirksen Ofc Bldg Washington DC 20510-2903

VALENTINE, WILLIAM EDSON, architect; b. Winston-Salem, N.C., Sept. 3, 1937; s. Howard Leon and Sally (Cunningham) V.; m. Jane Dorward, Aug. 13, 1939; children: Anne, Karen, William. BArch, N.C. State U., 1960; MArch, Harvard U., 1962. Co-chmn. Hellmuth, Obata & Kassabaum Inc., San Francisco, 1962—; chmn. Hellmuth, Obata & Kassabaum Design Bd., also bd. dirs. Served to 1st lt. U.S. Army, 1960-61. Fellow AIA. Club: Harvard. Office: Hellmuth Obata & Kassabaum Inc 71 Stevenson St Ste 2200 San Francisco CA 94105-2934

VALENTINE, WILLIAM NEWTON, physician, educator; b. Kansas City, Mo., Sept. 29, 1917; s. Herbert S. and Mabel W. (Watson) V.; m. Martha Hickman Winfree; children: William, James, Edward. Student, U. Mich., Ann Arbor, 1934-36, U. Mo., Columbia, 1936-37; MD, Tulane U., New Orleans, 1942. Diplomate: Am. Bd. Internal Medicine. Intern Strong Meml. Hosp., Rochester, N.Y., 1942-43, asst. resident in medicine, 1943, chief resident in medicine, 1943-44; specialist, attending physician in internal medicine Wadsworth Hosp., L.A., 1949-88, VA Ctr., L.A., 1949-88; specialist, attending physician in internal medicine Ctr. Health Scis. UCLA, 1949—, prof. medicine, 1957-88, chmn. dept., 1963-71; prof. emeritus medicine UCLA, Los Angeles, 1988—. Contbr. articles to profl. jours. Served to capt. MC, AUS, 1944-47. Recipient Mayo Soley award for excellence in research Western Soc. Clin. Research, 1978; 53d Annual UCLA faculty research lectr., 1978; Henry Stratton lectr. Am. Soc. Hematology, 1978; John Phillips Meml. award for Disting. Achievements in Internal Medicine, ACP, 1979. Fellow Am. Soc. Hematology, Internat. Soc. Hematology (v.p. U.S. 1976-80); mem. Am. Bd. Internal Medicine, ACP (master), Am. Soc. Clin. Investigation (v.p. 1962), Assn. Am. Physicians, Nat. Acad. Scis., Western Assn. Physicians (pres. 1969-70), Western Soc. Clin. Research, Am. Acad. Arts and Scis. Republican.

VALENTINO (VALENTINO GARAVANI), fashion designer; b. Voghera, Italy, May 11, 1932. Student, Academia Dell'Arte, Paris, Ecole des Beaux-Arts, Paris. Asst. designer Fashion Ho. of Jean Dessès, 1950-55, Fashion Ho. of Guy Laroche, 1956-58; co-owner Valentino Fashion Ho., Rome, 1959; developer Valentino Più, 1973; owner various boutiques, Rome, Milan, other cities. Exhibited at Victoria and Albert Mus., London, 1971, La Jolla Mus. Art, Calif., 1982; costume designer (films) Wild and Wonderful, 1964, Hello-Goodbye, 1970. Founder (with Giancarlo Giamcarlo) L.I.F.E., 1990—. Recipient Neiman-Marcus award, 1967. Office: Piazza Mignanelli 22, 00187 Rome Italy also: 823-825 Madison Ave New York NY 10021

VALENTINO, F. WILLIAM, energy executive. Pres. N.Y. State Energy Rsch. and Devel., Albany. Office: NY State Energy Rsch 2 Empire State Plz Ste 1901 Albany NY 12223-1253*

VALENTINO, STEPHEN ERIC, production and entertainment company executive, actor, singer; b. N.Y.C., Apr. 2, 1954; s. Joseph and Ina Mae (Diamond) V. Student, Hofstra U., N.Y.C., 1972-74, San Francisco Conservatory Music, 1974-78, Am. Inst. Mus. Studies, Graz, Austria, 1982. Gen. dir., chmn. bd. Mastic Community Theatre, Mastic Beach, N.Y., 1971-74; dir. advt. Marin Opera Co., San Rafael, Calif., 1979-80, Marin Ctr., San Rafael, 1983-85; pres., chief exec. officer Valentino & Assocs., Novato, Calif., 1978—; pres., CEO, co-founder Celebrity Events Internat., 1992—. Food and wine critic, contbg. editor San Francisco Mag., 1995—; contbg. author: Come Barefoot Eating Sensuous Things, 1979; prodr. Miss Julie, San Francisco; appeared in Firestorm, 1992, La Boheme, Daughter of the Regiment, (world premier) Calisto and Melibea, U. Calif., Davis, La Cenerentola, La Nozze de Figaro, The Merry Widow, La Traviata, The Bartered Bride, The Twelfth Night, Barber of Seville, Carmen, Die Fledermaus, Gianni Schicchi, I Pagliacci, Hansel and Gretel, The Magic Flute, Old Maid and the Thief, The Mikado, The Merry Wives of Windsor, (comml.) Ind. Live Ins. Corp. Am., (play) Feuerbach, Mary Stewart as Earl of Leister, 1996. Celebrity coord. Kids Say No To Drugs, 1987, MADD, 1987, ARC, San Jose, Calif., 1989; entertainment coord. Earthquake Relief Fund, San Francisco, 1989, Christmas Tree Program for the Needy, San Francisco, 1986, San Francisco Grand Prix BMW Polo Classic, Marin Suicide Prevention Ctr., 1987, Calif. Health Rsch. Found., 1988, UNICEF San Francisco, 1985, Little Sisters of The Poor, 1985, San Francisco Child Abuse Coun., 1988, 92; fundraiser Easter Seals, Marin County, Calif., 1988, Toys for Tots, Bay Area, Calif., 1987—, Global Youth Resource Orgn., Sunnyvale, Calif., 1989-90; mem. Dem. Nat. Com., 1988-90; commr. Bus. Ins. Adv. Commn., 1989; dir. celebrity basketball game Special Olympics, 1992, celebrity basketball game Easter Seals Soc., 1993; entertainer Shelters for the Homeless of L.A. Earthquake, 1994. Recipient Cert. of Honor, Bd. Suprs., City and County San Francisco, 1986, Awards of Appreciation Easter Seals Soc., 1988, Spl. Olympics, 1992; named Right Honourable, 1995. Mem. AFTRA, SAG. Home and Office: Valentino and Assocs 20 Prestwick Ct Novato CA 94949

VALENZUELA, JULIO SAMUEL, sociologist, educator; b. Concepción, Chile, Mar. 30, 1948; came to U.S., 1970; s. Raimundo Arms and Dorothy Dueul (Bowie) V.; m. Erika Fresia Maza, Mar. 22, 1969. Licenciatura, Universidad de Concepcion, 1970; PhD, Columbia U., 1979. Asst. prof. Yale U., New Haven, 1977-80; asst. prof. Harvard U., Cambridge, Mass., 1980-85, assoc. prof., 1986; assoc. prof. U. Notre Dame, Ind., 1987-89, prof., dept. chairperson, 1989-92, fellow Kellogg Inst., 1987—; sr. assoc. fellow St. Antony's Coll., Oxford U., 1992-93, 96—. Author: Democratizacion via Reforma, 1986; co-editor: Chile: Politics And Society, 1976, Military Rule In Chile, 1986, Issues In Democratic Consolidation, 1992; contbr. chpts. to books, articles to profl. jours. Fellow NEH ind. scholarship rsch. 1983-84, conf. grant 1987; John Simon Guggenheim fellow, 1996. Mem. Am. Sociol. Assn., Internat. Sociol. Assn. (v.p. rsch. com. #44 1990—), Latin Am. Studies Assn. (nominating com. 1987-88); New Eng. Coun. Latin Am. Studies (pres. 1984-85). Methodist. Office: U Notre Dame Dept Sociology Notre Dame IN 46556

VALERIANI, RICHARD GERARD, news broadcaster; b. Camden, N.J., Aug. 29, 1932; s. Nicholas and Christine (Camerota) V.; m. Kathie Berlin, Apr. 20, 1980; 1 child, Kimberly. BA, Yale U., 1953; postgrad., U. Pavia, Italy, 1953-54, U. Barcelona, Spain, 1954. Reporter The Trentonian, Trenton, 1957; with AP, 1957-61; corr. AP, Havana, Cuba, 1959-61; with NBC-TV News, 1961—; corr. NBC-TV News, Washington, 1964-83; nat. corr. NBC-TV News, N.Y.C., 1983-88; free-lance journalist, 1988—; participant 2d Carter-Ford debate, 1976. Author: Travels With Henry, 1979; actor: (feature film) Crimson Tide, 1995. With AUS, 1955-56. Recipient Overseas Press Club award for best radio reporting, 1965. Mem. Elihu Soc., Yale Club (N.Y.C.). Home: 23 Island View Dr Sherman CT 06784-2036

VALERIO, JOSEPH M., architectural firm executive, educator; b. Dec. 26, 1947; m. Linda A. Searl; children: Joseph Jr., Anthony. BArch, U. Mich., 1970; MArch, UCLA, 1972. Registered architect, Wis., Ill., Ind., Mo., Calif., Tex., Ariz., Minn., Ala., Iowa, Ind.; cert. Nat. Coun. Archtl. Registration Bds. Pres. Chrysalis Corp. Architects, 1970-85; assoc. prof. U. Wis., 1973-86; design dir. Swanke Hayden Connell Architects, 1985-86; v.p. architecture A. Epstein and Sons, Inc., 1986-88; pres. Valerio-Assocs. Inc., 1988-94; prin. Valerio Dewalt Train Assocs., Inc., Chgo., 1994—; speaker Ariz. State U., UCLA, U. Ariz., U. Cin., others; cons. USG Interiors, Formica Corp., AAAS, NAS, NEA: vis. critic and lectr. in field. Prin. works include corp., retail, health and residential bldgs.; author: Movie Palaces, 1983; editor: Architectural Fabric Structures, 1985. Mem. exec. bd. men's coun. Mus. Contemporary Art, 1989-91; mem. exec. bd. Contemporary Arts Coun., 1994. Recipient Honor awards Wis. Soc. Architects, 1975, 81, 84, 85, Gov.'s Award for Design Excellence, State of Mich., 1979, Gold medal Inst. Bus. Designers, 1988, Design award Progressive Architecture, 1991, Disting. Interior award Inst. Bus. Designers, Chgo., 1993; honored by Emerging Voices series Archtl. League N.Y., Met. Home mag., Interiors mag. Fellow AIA (programs chmn. design com. Chgo. chpt. 1990, mem. long range planning com. 1992, vice chair nat. com. on design 1996, Nat. Honor award 1981, 93, 96, Interiors award Chgo. chpt. 1988, 90, 92, 95, Disting. Bldg. award 1991, 93, Nat. Interior award 1993), Chgo. Architecture Club (pres. 1994). Office: Valerio Dewalt Train Assocs 200 N La Salle St Ste 2400 Chicago IL 60601-1014

VALERIO, MICHAEL ANTHONY, financial executive; b. Detroit, Sept. 20, 1953; s. Anthony Rudolph and Victoria (Popoff) V.; m. Barbara Ann Nabozny, Oct. 8, 1983. BA, U. Mich, Dearborn, 1975. CPA, Mich. Jr. acct. Carabell, Bocknek CPA's, Southfield, Mich., 1975-76; sr. acct. Purdy, Donovan & Beal, CPA's, Detroit, 1976-77; mgr. Buctynck & Co., CPA's, Southfield, 1978-79; controller Transcontinental Travel, Harper Woods, Mich., 1979-80; exec. v.p. Holland Cons., Inc., Detroit, 1980-85; controller, CFO SLC Recycling Industries, Inc., Warren, Mich., 1985—; owner Pinnacle Fin. Consulting, 1994—. Mem. AICPA, Mich. Soc. CPAs, Acctg. Rsch. Found. Roman Catholic. Office: SLC Recycling Industries Inc 21000 Hoover Rd Warren MI 48089-3153

VALERO, RENÉ ARNOLD, clergyman; b. N.Y.C., Aug. 15, 1930; s. Caesar J. and Maria Luisa (Cordova) Valero; B.A. in Liberal Arts, Immaculate Conception-Cathedral Coll., 1952; M.S.W., Fordham U., 1962. Ordained to ministry Roman Cath. Ch., 1956; asso. pastor St. Michael-St. Edward, Bklyn., 1956-57, St. Agatha, Bklyn., 1957-60; dir. Bklyn. Cath. Charities Family Service, 1960-69; dir. Bklyn. Diocesan Office for Aging, 1969-74; coordinator Bklyn. Diocesan Hispanic Apostolate, 1974-79; pastor Blessed Sacrament, Jackson Heights, N.Y., 1979-82; aux. bishop Diocese of Bklyn., 1980—; vicar for immigrants and refugees Diocese of Bklyn., 1983-90; regional bishop Queens, 1990-94, Queens North, 1994—. Home: 34-43 93rd St Jackson Hts NY 11372-3743 Office: Immaculate Conception Ctr 7200 Douglaston Pky Flushing NY 11362-1941

VALESIO, PAOLO, Italian language and literature educator, writer; b. Bologna, Italy, Oct. 14, 1939; came to U.S., 1963; s. Germano and Maria (Galletti) V.; 1 child, Sara. Dottorato in Lettere, U. Bologna, 1961, Libera Docenza in Glottologia, 1969; MA (hon.), Yale U., 1976. Lectr. Istituto di Glottologia, U. Bologna, 1961-62, 67-68; teaching fellow dept. Romance langs. and lit. Harvard U., Cambridge, Mass., 1965-66, lectr., 1969-70, assoc. prof., 1970-73; assoc. prof. Italian, dir. grad. studies dept. French and Italian NYU, 1973-75; prof. Italian, chmn. dept. Yale U., New Haven, Conn., 1976-88, dir. grad. studies dept. Italian, 1989-94; chmn. dept. Italian Yale U., New Haven, 1995—. Author: Novantiqua, 1980, Ascoltare il Silenzio, 1986, Gabriele d'Annunzio: The Dark Flame, 1992, (novel) Il Regno Doloroso, 1983, (poems) La Rosa Verde, 1987, Le Isole del Lago, 1990, Analogia del Mondo, 1992, Nightchant, 1995, (stories) S'Incontrano Gli Amanti, 1993; co-editor: Vocabolario Zingarelli, Bologna, 1970; Am. corr. mag. Poesia, Milan, 1992—. Recipient first prize Nat. Poetry Competition San Vito, 1992, Lit. prize Am. Assn. Italian Studies, 1993; named Cavaliere Ufficiale, Order of Merit of The Republic of Italy, 1994. Roman Catholic. Office: Yale Univ Dept Italian PO Box 208311 New Haven CT 06520-8311

VALESKIE-HAMNER, GAIL YVONNE, information systems specialist; b. San Francisco, May 16, 1953; d. John Benjamin and Vera Caroline (Granstrand) Valeskie; m. David Bryan Hamner, May 21, 1983. Student, Music Conservatory, Valencia, Spain, 1973, U. Valencia, 1973; BA magna cum laude, Lone Mountain Coll., 1973, MA, 1976. Fgn. exchange broker trainee Fgn. Exchange Ltd., San Francisco, 1978-79; fgn. exchange remittance supr. Security Pacific Nat. Bank, San Francisco, 1979-81; exec. sec. Bank of Am., San Francisco, 1981-83, fgn. exchange ops. supr, 1983-84; word processing specialist Wolborg-Michelson, San Francisco, 1984-86; office mgr. U.S. Leasing Corp., San Francisco, 1986-88; cons. Valeskie Data/Word Processing, San Francisco, 1987-89, pres., 1989—. Soc. chmn., mem. mission edn. com. Luth. Women's Missionary League, Vallejo, Calif., 1986-94; vol. Luth. Braille Workers, Vallejo, 1987; organist Shepherd of Hills Luth. Ch., San

Francisco, 1988—. Mem. NAFE, Profl. Assn. Secretarial Svcs. (pres. 1993—), Am. Guild Organists, Am. Choral Dirs. Assn. Avocations: singing, ceramics, piano, needlework, writing.

VALETTE, REBECCA MARIANNE, Romance languages educator; b. N.Y.C., Dec. 21, 1938; d. Gerhard and Ruth Adelgunde (Bischoff) Loose; m. Jean-Paul Valette, Aug. 6, 1959; children: Jean-Michel, Nathalie, Pierre. BA, Mt. Holyoke Coll., 1959, LHD (hon.), 1974; PhD, U. Colo., 1963. Instr., examiner in French and German U. So. Fla., 1961-63; instr. NATO Def. Coll., Paris, 1963-64, Wellesley Coll., 1964-65; asst. prof. Romance Langs. Boston Coll., 1965-68, assoc., 1968-73, prof., 1973—; lectr., cons. fgn. lang. pedagogy; Fulbright sr. lectr., Germany, 1974; Am. Council on Edn. fellow in acad. adminstrn., 1976-77. Author: Modern Language Testing, 1967, rev. edit., 1977, French for Mastery, 1975, rev. edit., 1988, Contacts, 1976, rev. edit., 1993, C'est Comme Ça, 1978, rev. edit., 1986, Spanish for Mastery, 1980, rev. edit., 1989, 94, Album: Cuentos del Mundo Hispanico, 1984, rev. edit., 1992, French for Fluency, 1985, Situations, 1988, rev. edit., 1994, Discovering French, 1994, A votre tour, 1995; contbr. articles to fgn. lang. pedagogy and lit. publs. Decorated officer Palmes académiques (France). Mem. Modern Lang. Assn. (chmn. div. on teaching of lang. 1980-81), Am. Coun. on Teaching Fgn. Langs., Am. Assn. Tchrs. French (v.p. 1980-86, pres. 1992-94), Am. Assn. Tchrs. German, Phi Beta Kappa, Alpha Sigma Nu, Palmes Academiques. Home: 16 Mt Alvernia Rd Chestnut Hill MA 02167-1019 Office: Boston Coll Lyons 311 Chestnut Hill MA 02167

VALIANT, LESLIE GABRIEL, computer scientist; b. Mar. 28, 1949; s. Leslie and Eva Julia (Ujlaki) V.; m. Gayle Lynne Dyckoff, 1977; children—Paul A., Gregory J. MA, Kings Coll., Cambridge, U.K., 1970; DIC, Imperial Coll., London, 1973; PhD, U. Warwick, U.K., 1974. Vis. asst. prof. Carnegie-Mellon U., Pitts., 1973-74; lectr. U. Leeds, Eng., 1974-76; lectr., reader U. Edinburgh, Scotland, 1977-82; vis. prof. Harvard U., 1982, Gordon McKay prof. computer sci. and applied math., 1982—. Guggenheim fellow, 1985-86; recipient Nevanlinna prize Internat. Math. Union, 1986. Fellow Royal Soc., Am. Assn. for Artificial Intelligence. Office: Harvard U 33 Oxford St Cambridge MA 02138-2901

VALK, HENRY SNOWDEN, physicist, educator; b. Washington, Jan. 26, 1929; s. Henry Snowden and Dorothy (Blencowe) V.; m. Gillian Wedderburn, June 20, 1968; children—Alison, Diana, Robert, Richard. B.S., George Washington U., 1953, M.S. (Agnes and Eugene Meyer scholar), 1954; postgrad., Johns Hopkins, 1953-54; Ph.D. (Shell fellow), Washington U., St. Louis, 1957. Profl. asst. NSF, 1957, asst. program dir. physics, 1959-60; asst. prof. physics U. Oreg., 1957-59; mem. faculty U. Nebr., 1960-70, prof. physics, 1964-70, chmn. dept., 1966-70; prof. physics Coll. Scis. and Liberal Studies, Ga. Inst. Tech., Atlanta, 1970—, acting dir. physics, 1991—, dean, 1970-82; cons. physics sect. NSF, 1961-62, program dir. theoretical physics, 1965-66; chmn. Gordon Rsch. Conf. Photonuclear Reactions, 1969; vis. prof. U. Frankfurt/Main, Germany, 1970, Rensselaer Poly. Inst., 1982, 88, Cath. U. Am., 1982-83, 88-89; chmn. SE regional Marshall scholarship com., 1974-92. Author: (with M. Alonso) Quantum Mechanics: Principles and Applications, 1973; contbr. articles to profl. jours. Decorated Most Excellent Order Brit. Empire. Fellow Am. Phys. Soc.; mem. Am. Math. Soc., Am. Assn. Physics Tchrs., Math. Assn. Am., Cosmos Club (Washington), Phi Beta Kappa, Sigma Xi. Home: 3032 St Helena Dr Tucker GA 30084-2227

VALK, ROBERT EARL, automotive company executive; b. Muskegon, Mich., Aug. 21, 1914; s. Allen and Lulu (Schuler) V.; m. Ann Parker, August 9, 1941 (div. July 1959); children: James A., Sara C.; m. Alice Melick, Dec. 29, 1960; children: Marie, Susan. B.S. in Mech. Engring, U. Mich., 1938. With Nat. Supply Co., 1938-55; plant mgr. Nat. Supply Co., Houston, 1945-48; works mgr. Nat. Supply Co., Toledo, Houston and Gainesville, Tex., 1949-55; asst. v.p. prodn. Electric Auto-Lite Co., Toledo, 1956, v.p., group exec. gen. products, 1956-60; gen. mgr. mfg. automotive div. Essex Internat., Inc., 1960-66, v.p. corp., gen. mgr. automotive div., 1966-74; pres. ITT Automotive Elec. Products Div., 1974-80; v.p. ITT N.Am. Automotive Ops. Worldwide, 1980-86; chmn. Chamberlin, Davis, Rutan & Valk, 1986—; trustee Henry Ford Health Care Sys., Detroit. Bd. dirs. Ecumenical Theological Ctr. Mem. Am. Soc. Naval Engrs., Soc. Automotive Engrs., Am. Ordnance Assn., Am. Mgmt. Assn., Air Force Assn., Am. Mfrs. Assn., Wire Assn., Nat. Elec. Mfrs. Assn., Engring. Soc. Detroit. Republican. Episcopalian. Clubs: Country (Detroit), Renaissance Club, Yondotega, Economics (Detroit); Grosse Pointe, Bay View Yacht; Little Harbor (Harbor Springs, Mich., Question Club. Home: 80 Renaud Rd Grosse Pointe MI 48236-1742 Office: 21 Kercheval Ave Ste 270 Grosse Pointe MI 48236-3601

VALLANCE, JAMES, church administrator, religious publication editor. Dir. Master's Men Dept. of the Nat. Assn. of Free Will Baptists, Antioch, Tenn.; pub. Attack, A Magazine for Christian Men. Office: Natl Assn of Free Will Baptists PO Box 5002 Antioch TN 37011-5002

VALLBONA, CARLOS, physician; b. Granollers, Barcelona, Spain, July 29, 1927; came to U.S., 1953, naturalized, 1967; s. José and Dolores (Calbó) V.; m. Rima Gretel Rothe, Dec. 26, 1956; children—Rima Nuria, Carlos Fernando, María Teresa, Marisa. B.A., B.S., U. de Barcelona, 1944, M.D., 1950. Diplomate Am. Bd. Pediatrics. Child health physician Escuela de Puericultura, Barcelona, 1952, Stagier Etranger Hôpital des Enfants Malades, Paris, 1952-53; intern, resident U. Louisville, 1953-55; resident Baylor Coll. of Medicine, 1955-56; prof. rehab. medicine Baylor Coll. Medicine, 1967—; assoc. prof. physiology and pediatrics Baylor U. Coll. Medicine, 1962-69, prof., chmn. dept. community medicine, 1969—, prof. family medicine, 1980—; adj. prof. U. Tex. Sch. Pub. Health, U. Tex. Health Sci. Ctr., Houston; chief community medicine service Harris County Hosp. Dist.; staff gen. med. service Tex. Children's Hosp.; staff The Inst. Rehab. and Research; staff St. Luke's Episcopal Hosp., con. staff VA Med. Ctr., Houston; Fulbright vis. prof., 1967; cons. WHO, NIH, Nat. Center Health Stats. Pan Am. Health Orgn., Nat. Center Health Service Research; advisor Conseller Sanitat, Catalunya. Author numerous articles in field; editorial bd. several Sci. jours. French Ministry of Edn. fellow, 1952; Children's Internat. Center fellow, 1953; co-recipient Gold medal 6th Internat. Congress Phys. Medicine, 1972; Public Citizen of Yr. San Jacinto chpt. Nat. Assn. Social Workers, 1974; Outstanding Tchr. award Baylor Coll. Medicine Class of 1980, 83, 85, 87, 88; decorated officer Order of Civil Merit (Spain), Medalla Narcis Monturiol (Catalunya). Mem. Am. Acad. Family Physicians, Am. Coll. Med. Informatics (founding mem. 1984), Nat. Acad. Practice (disting. practitioner 1984), Soc. Pediatric Research (emeritus), AMA, Tex. Med. Assn., Am. Coll. Chest Physicians, Am. Pub. Health Assn. (chmn. elect med. care sect. 1989-90), Am. Coll. Preventive Medicine, U.S.-Mex. Border Health Assn., AAAS, Am. Congress Rehab. Medicine, Catalan Soc. Pediatrics (hon.), Argentinian Soc. Internal Medicine (hon. 1986), Argentinian Med. Soc. (hon. 1986), Spanish Acad. Pediatrics (ambulatory pediatrics sect. hon. 1987), Assn. Tchrs. Preventive Medicine, Spanish Profls. Am. (pres. 1988), Soc. Catalana Hipertensio (hon. pres.), Sigma Xi, Alpha Omega Alpha. Roman Catholic. Home: 2001 Holcombe Blvd Houston TX 77030-4222 Office: Baylor Coll Medicine One Baylor Pla Houston TX 77030

VALLBONA, RIMA-GRETEL ROTHE, foreign language educator, writer; b. San Jose, Costa Rica, Mar. 15, 1931; d. Ferdinand Hermann and Emilia (Strassburger) Rothe; m. Carlos Vallbona, Dec. 26, 1956; children: Rima-Nuri, Carlos-Fernando, Maria-Teresa, Maria-Luisa. BA/BS, Colegio Superior de Senoritas, San Jose, 1948; diploma, U. Paris, 1953; diploma in Spanish Philology, U. Salamanca, Spain, 1954; MA, U. Costa Rica, 1962; D in Modern Langs., Middlebury Coll., 1981. Tchr. Liceo J.J. Vargas Calvo, Costa Rica, 1955-56; faculty U. St. Thomas, Houston, 1964-95, prof. Spanish, 1978-95, Cullen Found. prof. Spanish, 1989, head dept. Spanish, 1966-71, chmn. dept. modern fgn. lang., 1978-80, prof. emeritus, 1995—; vis. prof. U. Houston, 1975-76, Rice U., 1980-83, U. St. Thomas, Argentina, 1972, vis. prof. U. St. Thomas Merida program, 1987-95; vis. prof. Rice U. program in Spain, 1974. Author: Noche en Vela, 1968, Yolanda Oreamuno, 1972, La Obra en Prosa de Eunice Odio, 1981, Baraja de Soledades, Las Sombras que Perseguimos, 1983, Polvo del Camino, 1972, La Salamandra Rosada, 1979, Mujeres y Agonias, 1982, Cosecha de Pecadores, 1988, El arcangel del perdon, 1990, Mundo, demonio y mujer, 1991, Los infiernos de la mujer y algo mas, 1992, Vida i sucesos de la Monja Alférez, critical edition, 1992, Flowering Inferno-Tales of Sinking Hearts, 1994; mem. editorial bd. Letras Femeninas, Alba de America, U.S.; co-dir. Foro Literario, Uruguay, 1987-89; contbg. editor The Americas Review, 1989—; contbr. numerous articles and short stories to lit. mags. Mem. scholarship com. Inst. Hispanic Culture, 1978-79, 88, 91, chmn., 1979, bd. dirs., 1974-76, 88-89, 91-92, chmn. cultural activities, 1979, 80, 85, 88-89; bd. dirs. Houston Pub. Libr., 1984-86; bd. dirs. Cultural Arts Coun. of Houston, 1991-92. Recipient Aquileo J. Echeverria Novel prize, 1968, Agripina Montes del Valle Novel prize, 1978, Jorge Luis Borges Short Story prize, Argentina, 1977, Lit. award S.W. Conf. Latin Am. Studies, 1982; Constantin Found. grantee for rsch. U. St. Thomas, 1981; Ancora Lit. award, Costa Rica, 1984, Civil Merit award King Juan Carlos I of Spain, 1989. Mem. MLA, Am. Assn. Tchrs. Spanish and Portuguese, Houston Area Tchrs. of Fgn. Langs., South Cen. MLA, S.W. conf. Orgn. Latin Am. Studies, Latin Am. Studies Assn., Inst. Internat. de Lit. Iberoam., Latin Am. Writers Assn. of Costa Rica, Inst. Hispanic Culture of Houston, Casa Argentina de Houston, Inst. Lit. y Cultural Hispanico, Phi Sigma Iota, Sigma Delta Pi (hon.), Nat. Writers Assn. Roman Catholic. Home: 3706 Lake St Houston TX 77098-5522 Office: 3800 Montrose Blvd Houston TX 77006-4626

VALLE, LAURENCE FRANCIS, lawyer; b. N.Y.C., Feb. 16, 1943; s. Mario John and Marian Josephine (Longinotti) V.; m. Joan Strachan, June 11, 1966; children: Christopher John, Stacia Lyn. BS, U. Miami, 1966, JD, 1969. Bar: Fla. 1969, U.S. Ct. Mil. Appeals 1970, U.S. Dist. Ct. (so. and mid. dists.) Fla. 1975, U.S. Ct. Appeals (D.C. cir.) 1975, U.S. Ct. Appeals (5th and 11th cirs.) 1981, U.S. Dist. Ct. (we. dist.) Tex. 1989. Assoc. Underwood, Gillis & Karcher PA, Miami, Fla., 1973-77; ptnr. Underwood, Gillis, Karcher & Valle PA, Miami, 1977-87, Dixon, Dixon, Nicklaus & Valle, Miami, 1987-90, Nicklaus, Valle, Craig & Wicks, Miami, 1990-95, Valle & Craig, P.A., Miami, 1995—; of counsel Greater Miami Marine Assn., 1983—. Contbr. articles to profl. jours. Served to capt. U.S. Army, 1970-74. Mem. ABA, Fla. Bar Assn. (chmn. grievance com., 1982-85), Assn. Trial Lawyers Am., SE Admiralty Law Inst., Maritime Law Assn. of U.S., Bankers Club Miami. Republican. Roman Catholic. Avocations: tennis, running, water skiing, snow skiing. Office: World Trade Ctr Ste 2520 80 SW 8th St Miami FL 33130

VALLEE, BERT LESTER, biochemist, physician, educator; b. Hemer, Westphalia, Germany, June 1, 1919; came to U.S., 1938, naturalized, 1948; s. Joseph and Rosa (Kronenberger) V.; m. Natalie T. Kugris, May 29, 1947. ScB, U. Berne, Switzerland, 1938; MD, NYU, 1943; AM (hon.), Harvard, 1960; MD (honoris causa), Karolinska Institutet, Stockholm, Sweden, 1987; prof. (hon.), Tsinghua U., Beijing, 1987; DSC honoris causa, Naples, Italy, 1991; PhD in Chemistry (honoris causa), Ludwig-Maximilians U., Munich, 1995. Rsch. fellow Harvard Med. Sch., Boston, 1946-49; rsch. assoc. Harvard Med. Sch., 1949-51, assoc., 1951-56, asst. prof. medicine, 1956-60, assoc. prof., 1960-64, prof. biol. chemistry, 1964-65, Paul C. Cabot prof. biol. chemistry, 1965-80, Paul C. Cabot prof. emeritus, biochem. scis., 1980—, Disting. Sr. prof. biochem. scis., 1989-90, Edgar M. Bronfman Disting. sr. prof., 1990—; rsch. assoc. dept. biology MIT, Cambridge, 1948—; physician Peter Bent Brigham Hosp., Boston, 1961-80; biochemist-in-chief Brigham & Women's Hosp., Boston, 1980-89, emeritus, 1989—; sci. dir. Biophysics Rsch. Lab., Harvard Med. Sch., Peter Bent Brigham Hosp., 1954-80; head Ctr. for Biochem. and Biophys. Scis. and Medicine, Harvard Med. Sch. and Brigham & Women's Hosp., 1980—; Messenger lectr. Cornell U., 1988. Author 9 books; contbr. articles and chpts. to sci. publs. Founder, trustee Boston Biophysics Research Found., 1957—; founder, pres. Endowment for Research in Human Biology, Inc., 1980—. Recipient Warner-Chilcott award, 1969, Buchman Meml. award Calif. Inst. Tech., 1976; Linderstøm-Lang award and gold medal, 1980; Willard Gibbs Medal award, 1981, William C. Rose award in biochemistry, 1982, Order Andres Bello First Class of Republic of Venezuela. Fellow NAS, AAAS, Am. Acad. Arts and Scis., N.Y. Acad. Scis.; mem. Am. Soc. Biol. Chemists, Am. Chem. Soc. (Willard Gibbs gold medal 1981), Optical Soc. Am., Biophys. Soc., Swiss Biochem. Soc. (hon. fgn. mem.), Royal Danish Acad. Scis. and Letters, Japan Soc. for Analytical Chemistry (hon.), Alpha Omega Alpha. Home: 56 Browne St Brookline MA 02146-3445

VALLEE, JUDITH DELANEY, environmentalist, fundraiser; b. N.Y.C., Mar. 14, 1948; d. Victor and Sally Hammer; m. John Delaney, Apr. 9, 1974 (div. 1978); m. Henry Richard Vallee, May 15, 1987. BA, CUNY, 1976. Exec. dir. Save the Manatee Club, Maitland, Fla., 1985—; mem. U.S. Manatee Recovery Plan Team, Jacksonville, Fla., 1988—, Fla. Manatee Tech. Adv. Coun., Tallahassee, 1989—, Save the Manatee Com., Orlando, Fla., 1985-92; advisor Save the Wildlife Inc., Chuluota, Fla., 1992-93; bd. dirs. Environ. Fund for Fla. Lobbyist Save the Manatee Club, 1989; vol. Broward County Audubon Soc., Ft. Lauderdale, 1983, 84, Wild Bird Care Ctr., Ft. Lauderdale, 1984. Recipient Refuge Support award Chassahowitzka Nat. Wildlife Refuge, 1989. Mem. Fla. Coalition for Peace and Justice, People for Ethical Treatment of Animals, Friends of the Wekiva River, World Conservation Union/Sirenia Specialist Group. Democrat. Avocations: creative writing, antiques, wildlife observation, canoeing. Office: Save the Manatee Club Inc 500 N Maitland Ave Maitland FL 32751-4482

VALLERAND, PHILIPPE GEORGES, sales executive; b. Montreal, Que., Can., June 12, 1954; came to U.S., 1982; s. Louis Philippe and Beatrice (Goupil) V.; m. Laura Jean Frombach, Sept. 25, 1979; children: Harmonie May, Jeremy Thomas, Emilie Rose. Student, U. Montreal, 1974, U. Sherbrooke, 1975, U. Que., 1976, White Mgmt. Sch., London, 1981. Dir. resort Club Mediterranee Inc., Bahamas, Switzerland,, Africa,, Guadelupe, West Indies, 1978-80; v.p. Franglo/Sunsaver Inc., London and Hyeres, France, 1980-82; v.p. sales Source Northwest, Inc., Woodinville, Wash., 1982-93; pres. Prime Resource Group, Prime Source, Inc. Sr. comdr. Royal Rangers Boys Club, Monroe, Wash., 1988—; bd. mem. Christian Faith Ctr., Monroe, 1988-94; mem. Rep. Nat. Com. Named to 500 Inc. Mag., 1983, 89; recipient Disting. Sales & Mktg. Exec. award Internat. Orgn. Sales & Mktg. Execs., 1993, 96. Mem. Am. Mktg. Assn. (new mem. adv. bd.). Avocations: skiing, archery.

VALLERY, JANET ALANE, industrial hygienist; b. Lincoln, Nebr., Apr. 4, 1948; d. Gerald William and Lois Florence (Robertson) V.; BS, U. Nebr., Lincoln, 1970; diploma Bryan Meml. Sch. Med. Tech., Lincoln, 1971. Med. technologist Lincoln Gen. Hosp., 1971-72; congressional sec., 1973; lab. scientist Nebr. Dept. Health, 1973-79; sr. indsl. hygienist Nebr. Dept. Labor, 1979-85; indsl. hygienist U.S. Dept. Labor OSHA, 1985-89; indsl. hygienist VA Med. Ctr., Omaha, Nebr., 1989—. Mem. Am. Conf. Govt. Indsl. Hygienists, Am. Soc. Clin. Pathologists (assoc.), Arabian Horse Assn. Nebr., Nebr. Dressage Assn., Am. Indsl. Hygiene Assn., Am. Legion Aux. Republican. Methodist. Home: 4900 S 30th St Lincoln NE 68516-1603 Office: VA Med Ctr 4101 Woolworth Ave Omaha NE 68105-1850

VALLETTA, AMBER, model; b. Tulsa, Feb. 9, 1973; m. Hervé Le Bihan. With Boss Models, N.Y.C. Office: Boss Models 317 W 13th St New York NY 10014-1251

VALLEY, GEORGE EDWARD, JR., physicist, educator; b. N.Y.C., Sept. 5, 1913; s. George Edward and Edith Ringgold (Cummins) V.; m. Louisa King Williams, July 19, 1941 (div. Dec. 1960); children: George Cummins, John Williams, Katharine; m. Alice Shea LaBronté, 1960. S.B., Mass. Inst. Tech., 1935; Ph.D., U. Rochester, 1939. Optical engr. with Bausch & Lomb Optical Co., 1935-36; teaching asst. U. Rochester, 1936-39; research asso. Harvard, 1939-41, NRC fellow nuclear physics, 1940-41; project supr., sr. staff Radiation Lab., Mass. Inst. Tech., 1941-45; editorial bd. Radiation Lab. Tech. Series, 1945; successively asst. prof., asso. prof. Mass. Inst. Tech., 1946-57, prof. physics, 1957-78; now prof. emeritus, assisted founding Lincoln Lab., 1949, asso. dir., 1953-57, undergrad. planning prof., 1965-68; mem. Air Force Sci. Adv. Bd., 1946-64; chmn. Air Def. Systems Engring. Com. for Chief Staff USAF, 1950-51, chief scientist, 1957-58. Author and editor books and monographs. Recipient U.S. Army certificate of appreciation; President's certificate of merit; Air Force Assn. Sci. award; exceptional civilian service medal USAF, 1956, 58, 64. Fellow Am. Phys. Soc., Inst. Elec. and Electronics Engrs.; mem. Sigma Xi. Address: 607 Main St Concord MA 01742-3303

VALLONE, JOHN CHARLES, motion picture production designer; b. Phila., June 23, 1953; s. Louis Phillip and Laura Ann (Gagilone) V.; divorced; children: Gabriella, Lilli. BFA, NYU, 1975. Prodn. designer: (feature films) Southern Comfort, 1981, 48 Hours, 1982, Brainstorm, 1983, Streets of Fire, 1984, Brewster's Millions, 1985, Commando, 1985, Predator, 1987, Red Heat, 1988, The Adventures of Ford Fairlane, 1990, Die Hard 2, 1990, Rambling Rose, 1991, Cliffhanger, 1993, Bad Boys, 1995, 3 Wishes, 1995, (TV pilots) Private Eye, 1987, Sweet Justice, 1994, (TV movies) Shannon's Deal, 1989, Angel City, 1990; art dir.: (film) Star Trek: The Motion Picture, 1979 (Academy award nomination best art direction 1979). Mem. AOPA, SMPTVAD, Acad. Motion Picture Arts and Scis. (Best Art Direction award nomination 1981). Republican. Avocations: restoration of wooden yacht, pilot, sailing, woodworking, skiing.

VALOIS, CHARLES, bishop; b. Montreal, Apr. 24, 1924. Ordained priest Roman Cath. Ch., 1950; ordained bishop St. Jerome, Que., Can., 1977—. Office: 355 St George St, Saint Jerome, PQ Canada J7Z 5V3

VALVO, BARBARA-ANN, lawyer, surgeon; b. Elizabeth, N.J., June 7, 1949; d. Robert Richad and Vera (Kovach) V. BA in Biology, Hofsta U., 1971; MD, Pa. State U., 1975; JD, Loyola Sch. Law, 1993. Diplomate Am. Bd. Surgery; Bar: La. 1993. Surg. intern Nassau County Med. Ctr., East Meadow, N.Y., 1975-76; resident gen. surgery Allentown-Sacred Heart Med. Ctr., Allentown, Pa., 1976-80; asst. chief surgery USPHS, New Orleans, 1980-81; pvt. practice gen. surgery New Orleans, 1981-89, pvt. practice law, 1995—. Upjohn scholar, 1975. Fellow ACS; mem. ABA, FBA, La. Bar Assn., La. Trial Lawyers Assn. Republican. Avocations: computers, raising animals. Home and Office: PO Box 640217 Kenner LA 70064-0217

VAMVAKETIS, CAROLE, health services administrator; b. Bklyn., Mar. 1, 1943; d. William and Helen (Calacanis) Vamvaketis; 1 child, William. AA, Packer Collegiate Inst., Bklyn., 1962; BS, Columbia U., 1964; MA, Columbia Tchrs. Coll., 1969; AAS in Nursing, Rockland C.C., Suffern, N.Y., 1981; BSN, Dominican Coll., 1991. Tchr. elem. sch. A. Fantis Parochial Sch., 1964-67; tchr. Adelphi Acad., 1967-72, girls dean, 1968-72; nurse Nyack (N.Y.) Hosp., 1981-91; nurse mgr. Kings Harbor Care Ctr., 1991-93; assoc. dir. nursing Port Chester Nursing Home, 1993-94; CQI/edn. coord. Highbridge Woodycrest Ctr., 1994-95; profl. svcs. cons. Multicare Cos., Inc., Nanuet, N.Y., 1995—, personal svcs. cons., 1995-96, divsn. dir. clin. svcs., 1996—. Home and Office: 102 Poplar St Nanuet NY 10954-2007

VAN, GEORGE PAUL, international money management consultant; b. Isle Maligne, Que., Can., Feb. 12, 1940; s. Raymond Murdoch and Germaine Marie (Brassard) V.; m. Janine Marie Irene Therese Yvette Boily, Sept. 15, 1962; children: John, Robert, Caroline. BA, McGill U., 1961; DHA, U. Toronto, 1963. Sr. cons. Agnew Peckham and Assos., Toronto, Ont., Can., 1963-65; chief exec. officer, exec. dir. Misericordia Corp., Edmonton, Alta., Can., 1965-68; chief operating officer, exec. v.p. Texpack, Ltd., Brantford, Ont., 1968-70, also bd. dirs.; group v.p. Will Ross, Inc., Milw., 1970-73; exec. v.p. Nortek, Inc., Cranston, R.I., 1973-77, also bd. dirs.; pres., chief operating officer Hosp. Affiliates Internat. Inc. subs. INA Corp., Nashville, 1977-80, also bd. dirs.; chmn., pres., chief exec. officer Health Group Inc., Nashville, 1980-84; chmn., chief exec. officer Columbia Corp. (formerly Franklin Corp.), Nashville, 1984-88; pres. Grinders Switch Farms, Grinders Switch Shooting Club, Centerville, Tenn., 1990—; chmn. Van Hedge Fund Advisors, Inc., Nashville, 1992—. Bd. dirs. Tulane U. Med. Ctr., 1977-80, Nashville Inst. for the Arts, 1987-88, Nashville Symphony, 1987-88, Fedn. Internat. de Tir aux Armes Sportives de Chasse, Paris, 1990-92; mem. Internat. Tech. Commn. for Sporting Clays, Paris, 1990; bd. overseers U. Pa. Sch. of Nursing, 1979-82, 84-88, assoc. trustee U. Pa., 1979-82, 84-88; chmn. internat. com. U.S. Sporting Clays Assn., 1989-92; active pres.'s coun. Andrew Jackson Inst., 1993—; adv. bd. Fin. Mktg. Rsch. Ctr. Vanderbilt U. Recipient several scholarships. Mem. Westside Club, Grinders Switch Club. Contbr. articles to profl. jours. Home and Office: 1608 Chickering Rd Nashville TN 37215-4906

VAN, PETER, lawyer; b. Boston, Sept. 7, 1936; s. Frank Lewis and Ruth (Spevack) V.; m. Faye Anne Zinck, 1991; children: Jami Lynne, Robert Charles. BA, Dartmouth, 1958; LLD, Boston Coll., 1961. Bar: Mass. 1962. Assoc. Brown, Rudnick, Freed and Gesmer, Boston, 1961-63; assoc. Fine and Ambrogne, Boston, 1963-65, ptnr., 1966-73, sr. ptnr., 1973—, mng. ptnr., chmn. exec. com., 1988-90; ptnr., mem. exec. com. Mintz, Levin, Cohn, Ferris, Glovsky and Popeo, P.C., Boston, 1990—. Mem. fin. com., trustee Beth Israel Hosp. Boston. Mem. Masons. Office: One Financial Ctr Boston MA 02111

VAN ACKEREN, MAURICE EDWARD, college administrator; b. Cedar Rapids, Nebr., Aug. 21, 1911; s. Edward M. and Frances (O'Leary) Van A. B.A. in Chemistry, Creighton U., 1932; M.A. in Edn., St. Louis U., 1946; LL.D. (hon.), Benedictine Coll., 1976. Ordained Jesuit priest Roman Cath. Ch., 1943. Tchr. Campion High Sch., Prairie du Chien, Wis., 1937-40; prin. St. Louis U. High Sch., 1946-51; pres. Rockhurst Coll., Kansas City, Mo., 1951-77, chancellor, 1977—. Recipient Knight of Holy Sepulchre award Catholic Ch., Chgo., 1968, Chancellor's medal U. Mo.-Kansas City, 1981, Mr. Kansas City award Greater Kansas City C. of C., 1983; named to Creighton U. Athletic Hall of Fame, Omaha, 1971; named Mktg. Exec. of Yr., Sales and Mktg. Club Kansas City, 1979. Mem. C. of C. of Greater Kansas City. Lodge: Rotary (Paul Harris fellow 1983). Avocations: fishing; golf; baseball; football. Home and Office: 1100 Rockhurst Rd Kansas City MO 64110-2508

VAN ALLEN, JAMES ALFRED, physicist, educator; b. Mt. Pleasant, Iowa, Sept. 7, 1914; s. Alfred Morris and Alma E. (Olney) Van A.; m. Abigail Fithian Halsey, Oct. 13, 1945; children: Cynthia Schaffner, Margot Cairns, Sarah Trimble, Thomas, Peter. BS, Iowa Wesleyan Coll., 1935; MS, U. Iowa, 1936, PhD, 1939; ScD (hon.), Iowa Wesleyan Coll., 1951, Grinnell Coll., 1957, Coe Coll., 1958, Cornell Coll., Mt. Vernon, Iowa, 1959, U. Dubuque, 1960, U. Mich., 1961, Northwestern U., 1961, Ill. Coll., 1963, Butler U., 1966, Boston Coll., 1966, Southampton Coll., 1967, Augustana Coll., 1969, St. Ambrose Coll., 1982, U. Bridgeport, 1987. Research fellow, physicist dept. terrestial magnetism Carnegie Instn., Washington, 1939-42; physicist, group and unit supr. applied physics lab. Johns Hopkins U., 1942, 46-50; organizer, leader sci. expdns. study cosmic radiation Peru, 1949, Gulf of Alaska, 1950, Arctic, 1952, 57, Antarctic, 1957; prof. physics, head dept. U. Iowa, Iowa City, 1951-85, Carver prof. physics, 1985-90, Regent disting. prof., 1990—; Regents fellow Smithsonian Instn., 1981; rsch. assoc. Princeton U., 1953-54; mem. devel. group radio proximity fuze Nat. Def. Rsch. Coun., OSRD; pioneer high attitude rsch. with rockets, satellites and space probes. Author: Origins of Magnetospheric Physics, 1983, First to Jupiter, Saturn and Beyond, 1981; 924 Elementary Problems and Answers in Solar System Astronomy, 1993; contbg. author: Physics and Medicine of Upper Atmosphere, 1952, Rocket Exploration of the Upper Atmosphere; editor: Scientific Uses of Earth Satellites, 1956, Cosmic Rays, the Sun, and Geomagnetism: The Works of Scott E. Forbush, 1993; acting editor Jour. Geophys. Rsch.-Space Physics, 1991-92; contbr. numerous articles to profl. jours. *. Lt. comdr. USNR, 1942-46, ordnance and gunnery specialist, combat observer. Recipient Physics award Washington Acad. Sci., 1949, Space Flight award Am. Astronautical Soc., 1958, Louis W. Hill Space Transp. award Inst. Aero. Scis., 1959, Elliot Cresson medal Franklin Inst., 1961, Golden Omega award Elec. Insulation Conf., 1963, Iowa Broadcasters Assn. award, 1964, Fellows award of merit Am. Cons. Engrs. Coun., 1978, Nat. Medal of Sci., 1987, Vannevar Bush award NSF, 1991, Gerard P. Kuiper prize Am. Astron. Soc. 1994; named comdr. Order du Merit Pour la Recherche et l'Invention, 1964; Guggenheim Found. rsch. fellow, 1951. Fellow Am. Rocket Soc. (C.N. Hickman medal devel. Aerobee rocket 1949), IEEE, Am. Phys. Soc., Am. Geophys. Union (pres. 1982-84, John A. Fleming award 1963, William Bowie medal 1977); mem. NAS, AAAS (Abelson prize 1986), Iowa Acad. Sci., Internat. Acad. Astronautics (founding), Am. Philos. Soc., Am. Astron. Soc., Royal Astron. Soc. U.K. (gold medal 1978), Royal Swedish Acad. Sci. (Crafoord prize 1989), Am. Acad. Arts and Scis., Cosmos Club, Sigma Xi (Procter prize 1987), Gamma Alpha. Presbyterian. Achievements include discovery of radiation belts around earth. Office: Univ Iowa 701 Van Allen Hall Iowa City IA 52242-1403*

VAN ALLEN, KATRINA FRANCES, painter; b. Phoenix, Ariz., Feb. 18, 1933; d. Benjamin Cecile Sherrill and Magdalen Mary (Thomas) Adams; m. Ray C. Bennett II, Dec. 31, 1950 (div. 1955); m. William Allen Van Allen, Mar. 15, 1963 (dec. Mar. 1971); m. Donovan Wyatt Jacobs, Apr. 22, 1972; children: Ray Crawford Bennett III, Sherri Lou Bennett Maraney. Student,

Stanford U., 1950, 51, 52, Torrance C.C., 1962, 63; MA, U. Tabriz, Iran, 1978; studied with Martin Lubner, Jerold Burchman, John Lepper, L.A.; student, Otis Art Inst., Immaculate Heart Coll.; studied with Russa Graeme. Office mgr. H.P. Adams Constrn. Co., Yuma, Ariz., 1952-59; nurse Moss-Hathaway Med. Clin., Torrance, Calif., 1962-63; interviewer for various assns. N.Y.C., 1964-70. Solo shows include Zella 9 Gallery, London, 1972, Hambleton Gallery, Maiden Newton, Eng., 1974, Intercontinental Gallery, Teheran, Iran, 1976, USIA Gallery, Teheran, 1977, 78, Coos Art Mus., Coos Bay, Oreg., 1993; exhibited in group shows at La Cienega Gallery, L.A., 1970, 80, 81, 82, Design Ctr. Gallery, Tucson, 1985, Coos Art Mus., 1992, 93, 94, 95, 96; represented in permanent collections at Bankers Trust Bd. Rm., London, Mfrs. Hanover Bank, London U. Iowa Med. Sch., Iowa City, Bank of Am., Leonard Blakesles Esq. Enterprises, L.A., numerous pvt. collections. Bd. dirs. Inst. for Cancer and Leukemia Rsch., 1966-67, 68. Recipient Five City Tour and Honorarium, Iran Am. Soc., 1977, Most Improved Player C.C.C. Ladies Golf Assn., 1995. Mem. Nat. Women in the Arts, L.A. Art Assn., Coos Bay Art Assn., Coos Bay Power Squadron, Lower Umpqu Flycasters. Avocations: fly-fishing, hiking, bridge, golf, the Arts. Home and Studio: 3693 Cape Arago Coos Bay OR 97420-9604

VAN ALLEN, WILLIAM KENT, lawyer; b. Albion, N.Y., July 30, 1914; s. Everett Kent and Georgia (Roberts) Van A.; m. Sally Schall, Nov. 11, 1944; children: William Kent, Jr., George Humphrey, Peter Cushing. A.B., Hamilton Coll., 1935; LL.B., Harvard U., 1938. Bar: N.Y. 1938, D.C. 1939, N.C. 1951, U.S. Dist. Ct. (we. dist.) N.C. 1951, U.S. Dist. Ct. (mid. dist.) N.C. 1953, U.S. Ct. Appeals (4th cir.) 1951, U.S. Ct. Claims 1946, U.S. Tax Ct. 1940, FCC 1939, ICC 1940, U.S. Supreme Ct. 1946. With Hanson, Lovett & Dale, Washington, 1938-41, 46-50; ptnr. Lassiter, Moore and Van Allen and Moore and Van Allen, Charlotte, N.C., 1951-87; of counsel Moore & Van Allen, Charlotte, 1988—; permanent mem. Jud. Conf. 4th Jud. Circuit. Vestryman Episc. Ch., 1957-60, 66-69; mem. Mecklenburg County Bd. Public Welfare, 1954-59, chmn. 1957-59; bd. dirs. N.C. Found. Commerce and Industry, 1965-73, Found. U. N.C. at Charlotte, 1979-89, Charlotte Symphony Orch., 1981-82, Mercy Health Svcs., 1983-88; chmn. Charlotte Area adv. coun. Am. Arbitration Assn., 1967-76; bd. dirs. United Community Svcs., 1972-77, v.p., 1972; bd. mgrs. Charlotte Country Day Sch., 1956-61, chmn., 1959-61, bd. visitors, 1978—, chmn., 1987-88; bd. advisers U. N.C.-Charlotte, 1983-84; trustee Spastics Hosp., 1951-60, Mint Mus. Art, 1976-79, Surtman Found., 1955-90, Mercy Hosp. Found., 1979-84; bd. visitors Johnson C. Smith U., 1978-89; pres. Charlotte Symphony League, 1980-81, Friends of U. N.C. at Charlotte, 1990-91. Served with USNR, 1941-45, commdg. officer destroyer escort ATO and PTO; released to inactive duty as lt. comdr. Mem. ABA, Charlotte C. of C. (bd. dirs. 1971-75, v.p. 1972-75). Mil. Order of Carabao, Charlotte Country Club, Charlotte City Club, Chevy Chase Club (Md.), Mullett Lake Country Club (Mich.), Phi Beta Kappa, Chi Psi. Office: Moore & Van Allen 4700 NationsBank Corp Ctr Charlotte NC 28202-4003

VAN ALLSBURG, CHRIS, author, artist; b. Grand Rapids, Mich., June 18, 1949; s. Richard Allen and Doris Marie (Christiansen) Van A.; m. Lisa Carol Morrison, Aug. 17, 1976. BFA, U. Mich., 1972; MFA, R.I. Sch. Design, 1975. Tchr. R.I. Sch. Design, Providence. Author, illustrator: The Garden of Abdul Gasazi, 1979 (Caldecott Honor Book 1980, Irma Simonton Black award Bank St. Coll. Edn. 1980, Boston Globe/Horn Book award 1980), Jumanji, 1981 (Caldecott medal 1982, Boston Globe/Horn Book award 1982, Children's Choice award Internat. Reading Assn. 1982, Am. Book award, 1982, Ky. Bluegrass award No. Ky. U. 1983, Buckeye Children's Book award Ohio State Libr. 1983, Wash. Children's Choice Picture Book award Wash. Libr. Media Assn. 1984, W. Va. Children's Book award 1985), Ben's Dream, 1982 (Parents Choice award for illustration Parents' Choice Found. 1982), Wreck of the Zephyr, 1983 (Silver medal Soc. Illustrators 1983), The Mysteries of Harris Burdick, 1984 (Parents Choice award for illustration Parents' Choice Found. 1984, Irma Simonton Black award Bank St. Coll. Edn. 1985, Boston Globe/Horn Book award 1985, World Fantasy award 1985), The Polar Express, 1985 (Parents Choice award for illustration Parents' Choice Found. 1985, Caldecott medal 1986, Boston Globe/Horn Book award 1986, Ky. Bluegrass award No. Ky. U. 1987), The Stranger, 1986 (Parents Choice award for illustration Parents' Choice Found. 1986), The Z Was Zapped: A Play in Twenty-Six Acts, 1987, Two Bad Ants, 1988, Just A Dream, 1990, The Wretched Stone, 1991, The Widow's Broom, 1992, The Sweetest Fig, 1993, The Two Figs, 1993, Bad Day at River Bend, 1995; illustrator: Swan Lake, 1989; exhibited works at Whitney Mus. Art, N.Y.C., Mus. Modern Art, N.Y.C., Alan Stone Gallery, N.Y.C., Grand Rapids (Mich.) Art Mus., Port Washington (N.Y.) Pub. Libr.; permanent collections include Kerlan Collection at U. Minn. Recipient Hans Christian Andersen award nomination, 1985. Jewish.

VAN ALMEN, KAREN, art educator; b. Lakewood, Ohio, Oct. 13, 1940; d. Richard Earl and Arla Marie (Northam) Van Al.; m. Ken Connell 1963 (div. 1981); children: Korby Matthew, Kathren Diane, Kevin Andrew; m. Ronald Sackett, Feb. 14, 1985. BA, Baldwin-Wallace Coll., 1962; MA, Ohio State U., 1977. Cert. tchr. art edn., social studies, K-12, Mich. Art tchr. jr. high Bay Village (Ohio) City Schs., 1962-63; art tchr. high sch. Westchester County Schs., Hamilton, Ohio, 1963-64; art tchr. elem. Whitehall City Schs., Columbus, Ohio, 1964-66; tchr. Pennfield City Schs., Battle Creek, Mich., 1984-95; work purchased by Mich. State U. Med. Sch., East Lansing, 1990; participant Summet Tchr. Inst. on Latino Art and Culture in U.S., at Nat. Mus. Am. Art-Smithsonian Instn., 1995. Art exhbns. include Traverse City (Mich.) Resort, 1987, Graven Image Art Gallery, Kalamazoo, 1987, Stouffer's Battle Creek MAEA Exhibit, 1988, Tecumseh (Mich.) Radison Resort, 1989, Downtown Gallery, Grand Rapids, 1990, Noble Schuler's Gallery, Albion, Mich., 1990, Internat. Art and Galleries, Grand Rapids, 1990, Western Mich. U. Adminstrn. Bldg. Exhibit, Kalamazoo, 1991, MAEA Exhibit, Battle Creek, 1991, Access Vision, Battle Creek, 1992, Fife Lake (Mich.) Gallery, 1994, Kalamazoo (Mich.) Area Show, 1996, Pub. Tea Ceremony, 1996, others; pub. Teen Tour...Chicago's Sculptures, 1995. Mem. Internat. Rels. com. of Battle Creek, 1990—; amb. to Japan-Tchr. Exch., 1991. Recipient Outstanding Educator award W.K. Kellogg Found., Battle Creek, 1992. Mem. Nat. Art Edn. Assn., Mich. Art Edn. Assn. (coun. mem. liaison 1995-96), Mich. Edn. Assn., NEA, Pennfield Edn. Assn. Avocations: canoeing to remote areas for photography and painting of wild life, creating art surrounding history of old towns in Mich. Home and Studio: Westlake Woods Studio 55 Hickory Nut Ln Battle Creek MI 49015-1325

VAN ALSTYNE, JUDITH STURGES, English language educator, writer; b. Columbus, Ohio, June 9, 1934; d. Rexford Leland and Wilma Irene (Styan) Van A.; m. Dan C. Duckham (div. 1964); children: Kenton Leland, Jeffrey Clarke. BA, Miami U., Oxford, Ohio, 1956; MEd, Fla. Atlantic U., 1967. Sr. prof. Broward C.C., Ft. Lauderdale, Fla., 1967-88; ret., 1988; spl. asst. for women's affairs Broward C.C., 1972-88, dir. cmty. svcs., 1973-74, dir. cultural affairs, 1974-75; spkr., cons. Malaysian Coll., 1984; ednl. travel group tour guide, 1992—; v.p., ptnr. Downtown Travel Ctr., Ft. Lauderdale, Fla., 1993—. Author: Write It Right, 1980, Professional and Technical Writing Strategies, 3d edit., 1992; freelance writer travel articles; contbr. articles and poetry to profl. jours. Bd. dirs. Broward C.C. Found., Inc., 1973-89, Broward Friends of the Libr., 1994—, Broward Friends of Miami City Ballet, 1994—; active Sister Cities/People to People, Ft. Lauderdale, 1988—; docent Ft. Lauderdale Mus. Art, 1988—; officer Friends of Mus., Ft. Lauderdale, 1992—. Recipient award of achievement Soc. for Tech. Comm., 1986, award of distinction Fla. Soc. for Tech. Comm., 1986. Mem. English-Speaking Union (bd. dirs. 1984-89). Democrat. Episcopalian. Avocations: writing, reading, travel. Home: 1688 S Ocean Ln # 265 Fort Lauderdale FL 33316-3346

VAN ALSTYNE, W. SCOTT, JR., lawyer, educator; b. East Syracuse, N.Y., Sept. 21, 1922; s. Walter Scott and Cecil Edna (Folmsbee) Van A.; m. Margaret Reed Hudson, June 23, 1949 (div.); children: Gretchen Anne, Hunter Scott; m. Marion Graham Walker, May 3, 1980. B.A., U. Buffalo, 1948; M.A., U. Wis., 1950, LL.B., 1953, S.J.D., 1954. Bar: Wis. 1953. Assoc. Shea & Hoyt, Milw., 1954-56; asst. prof. law U. Nebr., 1956-58; pvt. practice Madison, Wis., 1958-72; prof. law U. Fla., 1973-90, prof. emeritus, 1990—; lectr. law U. Wis., 1958-72; lectr. Cambridge-Warsaw Trade Program Cambridge U. (Eng.), 1976; vis. prof. law Cornell U., 1977, U. Leiden, The Netherlands, 1988, 91; spl. lectr. U. Utrecht, The Netherlands, 1991; spl. counsel Gov. of Wis., 1966-70; bd. dirs. non-resident divsn. State Bar Wis., 1981-96, pres., 1988-90, bd. govs. 1988-90. Prin. author: Goals and Missions of Law Schools, 1990; contbr. articles to profl. jours. Mem. Gov.'s Commn. on edn., Wis., 1969-71; cons. Wis. Commn. on Legal Edn., 1995-96. Served with AUS, 1942-45, 61-62; col. Res., ret. Decorated Legion of Merit. Mem. SR (N.Y.), Holland Soc. (N.Y.), Madison (Wis.) Club, Ft. Rennselaer (N.Y.) Club, Netherland Club (N.Y.C.), Order of Coif, Phi Beta Kappa, Omicron Delta Kappa, Phi Delta Phi. Republican. Presbyterian. Office: U Fla Holland Law Ctr Gainesville FL 32611

VAN ALSTYNE, WILLIAM WARNER, legal educator; b. Chico, Calif., Feb. 8, 1934; s. Richard Warner and Margaret (Ware) Van A.; BA, U. So. Calif., 1955; JD, Stanford U., 1958; certificate Hague Acad. Internat. Law, 1961; LLD, Wake Forest U., 1976, Coll. William and Mary, 1979. Bar: Calif. 1958. m. Carol Frances Engstrom, Sept. 18, 1955 (div. 1979); children: Marshall, Allyn, Lisa; m. Pamela Gann, Jan. 1980. Dep. atty. gen. Calif., 1958; atty. civil rights div. U.S. Dept. Justice, Washington, 1959; from asst. prof. to prof. Ohio State U. Law Sch., 1959-63; prof. Duke U. Law Sch., Durham, N.C., 1965-73, William R. Perkins prof. law, 1974—. Mem. nat. bd. dirs. ACLU, 1972-76; mem. adv. council Carnegie Found. for Advancement Teaching, 1974-76. With USAF, 1959. Mem. AAUP (nat. pres. 1974-76, gen. counsel 1988-90), AAAS. Author: Interpretations of the First Amendment, 1984, First Amendment Cases and Materials, 2nd edit., 1995, Freedom and Tenure in the Academy, 1993; contbr. articles to profl. jours. Office: Duke U Sch Law Rm 106 Durham NC 27706

VAN AMBURGH, ROBERT JOSEPH, school system administrator; b. Albany, N.Y., Apr. 23, 1947; s. Roy Francis and Evelyn (Houting) Van A.; m. Barbara Ann McAteer, June 28, 1970; children: Brian, Amy. BA, Providence Coll., 1969; MA, Coll. of St. Rose, 1973. Cert. adminstr., N.Y. Tchr. City Sch. Dist. of Albany, 1969-77, supr. social studies, 1977—, prin. Albany evening H.S., 1979-85, prin. Albany summer sch., 1986—; cons. N.Y. State Edn. Dept., Albany, 1983-86, Houghton Mifflin Pub., 1985. Mem. Albany Common Coun., 1983—, Albany County Dem. Com., 1973—, Capitalize Albany Commn., 1994—. Mem. Albany Pub. Schs. Adminstrs. Assn. (pres. 1989), N.Y. State Social Studies Supervisory Assn. (v.p. 1984-86, Supr. of Yr. 1994), Providence Coll. Alumni Assn. (pres. 1991-93, Disting. Svc. award 1994). Democrat. Roman Catholic. Avocations: basketball, politics, local history. Home: 34 Cambridge Rd Albany NY 12203-3002 Office: City Sch Dist of Albany 700 Washington Ave Albany NY 12203-1404

VAN AMRINGE, JOHN HOWARD, retired oil industry executive, geologist; b. L.A., Oct. 11, 1932; s. Edwin Verne and Viola (Hail) Van A.; m. Mary Jane Lothras, Jan. 29, 1955; children: Kathryn Jean Van Amringe Ball, Kenneth Edwin. AA, Pasadena City Coll., 1954; BA, UCLA, 1956, MA, 1957. Geologist Unocal Corp., Santa Maria, Calif., 1957-58, Santa Fe Springs, Calif., 1958-64, New Orleans, 1964-66; dist. geologist Unocal Corp., Lafayette, La., 1966-68, dist. exploration mgr., 1968-79; exploration mgr. western region Unocal Corp., Pasadena, Calif., 1979-88; v.p. exploration Unocal Corp., L.A., 1988-92. Editor: Typical Offshore Oil and Gas Fields, 1973; author profl. paper. Bd. dirs. Pasadena City Coll. Found., 1986—, treas., 1992-95; pres. Pasadena Cmty. Orch., 1990-94. With U.S. Army, 1949-52, Korea. Named Geologist of Yr., Lafayette chpt. Am. Inst. Profl. Geologists, 1972. Mem. Am. Assn. Petroleum Geologists (del. 1972-73), Pacific Sect. of Am. Assn. Petroleum Geologists (editor 1961-63), Lafayette Geol. Soc. (pres. 1971-72). Republican. Avocations: tennis, travel, sailing, collecting, photography. Home: 1455 Old House Rd Pasadena CA 91107-1518

VAN ANDEL, JAY, direct selling company executive; b. Grand Rapids, Mich., June 3, 1924; s. James and Nella (Vanderwoude) Van A.; m. Betty J. Hoekstra, Aug. 16, 1952; children: Nan, Stephen, David, Barbara. Student, Pratt Jr. Coll., 1945, Calvin Coll., 1942, 46, Yale, 1943-44; DBA (hon.), No. Mich. U., 1976, Western Mich. U., 1979, Grand Valley State U., 1992; LLD (hon.), Ferris State Coll., 1977. Co-founder, sr. chmn. Amway Corp., Ada, Mich.; U.S. amb., commr. gen. Genoa Expo '92, 1992 World's Fair marking 500th Anniversary of Columbus Journey to Am.; chmn. bd. Amway Internat., Amway Hotel Corp., Amway Environ. Found., Nutrilite Products, Inc.; chmn. Ja-Ri Corp., Ada, Mich.; mem. adv. coun. Am. Private Edn. Participant White Ho. Conf. Indsl. World Ahead, 1972; chmn. Mich. Rep. fin. com., 1975-81; Founding chmn. Right Place Com., Grand Rapids, Mich.; mem. adv. council Nat. 4H Found.; trustee Hillsdale (Mich.) Coll., Citizens Rsch. Coun. Mich., Hudson Inst., Indpls. and Washington; dir. Jamestown Found., Gerald R. Ford Found.; bd. dirs., trustee, treas. Washington, Heritage Found., Washington; pres. Van Andel Found.; co-chmn. Mich. Botanic Garden Capital Campaign; founding chmn. Citizen's Choice, Washington; former bd. dirs. BIPAC, Washington, former chmn. Netherlands-Am. Bicentennial Commn; former mem. bd. govs. USO World. Served to 1st lt. USAAF, 1943-46. Knighted Grand Officer of Orange-Nassau, The Netherlands; recipient Disting. Alumni award Calvin Coll., 1976, Golden Plate award Am. Acad. Achievement, Gt. Living Am. award and Bus. and Profl. Leader of the Yr. award Religious Heritage Am., George Washington medal of Honor Freedom Found., Gold medals Netherland Soc. of Phila. and N.Y.C., Disting. Citizen award Northwood Inst., Patron award Mich. Found. for Arts, 1982, Achievement award UN Environment Programme, 1989, UN Environment Programme Achievement award Amway, 1989, Adam Smith Free Enterprise award Am. Legis. Exchange Coun., 1993, Disting. Svc. award Rotary Grand Rapids, Gold Medal Netherlands Soc. N.Y., Edison Achievement award Am. Mktg. Assn., 1994; named Bus. Person Yr. Econ. Club Grand Rapids, 1990; named to Grand Rapids Bus. Hall of Fame; World fellow Duke of Edinburgh's award. Mem. Sales and Mktg. Execs. Internat. Acad. Achievement (charter), Direct Selling Assn. (bd. dirs., hall of fame), U.S. C. of C. (past chmn. bd.), Right Place Com. (founding chmn.), de Tocqueville Soc. (former chmn.), Nat. Chamber Found. (dir.), Mensa Soc. USA, Peninsular Club, Cascade Hills Country Club, Lotus Club, Capitol Hill Club (Washington), Macatawa Bay Yacht Club (Holland, Mich., Le Mirador Country Club (Switzerland), Econ. Club (Grand Rapids), Omicron Delta Kappa (hon.). Mem. Christian Reformed Ch. (elder). Home: 7186 Windy Hill Dr SE Grand Rapids MI 49546-9745 Office: Amway Corp Fulton St E Ada MI 49355

VAN ANDEL, STEVE, financial executive; b. Ada, Mich., Oct. 9, 1955. BLS in Econ. & Bus., Hillsdale Coll.; MBA in MKtg., Miami (Ohio) U. V.p. mktg. Amway Corp., Worldwide; chmn. exec. com. policy bd. Amway Corp., Ada; vice chmn. Amway Japan Ltd.; chmn. Amway Asia Pacific Ltd., Amway Corp., Ada; bd. dirs. Met. Hosp., Mich. Nat. Bank Corp.; mem. dean's adv. bd. Seidman Sch. of Bus. Bd. dirs. Grand Rapids John Ball Soc., Amway Environmental Found. Office: Amway Corp 7575 Fulton St East Ada MI 49355-0001

VAN ANTWERPEN, FRANKLIN STUART, federal judge; b. Passaic, N.J., Oct. 23, 1941; s. Franklin John and Dorothy (Hoedemaker) Van A.; m. Kathleen Veronica O'Brien, Sept. 12, 1970; children: Joy, Franklin W., Virginia. BS in Engring. Physics, U. Maine, 1964; JD, Temple U., 1967; postgrad., Nat. Jud. Coll., 1980. Bar: Pa. 1969, U.S. Dist. Ct. (ea. dist.) Pa. 1971, U.S. Ct. Appeals (3d cir.) 1971, U.S. Supreme Ct. 1972. Corp. counsel Hazeltine, Corp., N.Y.C., 1967-70; chief counsel Northampton County Legal Aid Soc., Easton, Pa., 1970-71; assoc. Hemstreet & Smith, Easton, 1971-73; ptnr. Hemstreet & VanAntwerpen, Easton, 1973-79; judge Ct. Common Pleas of Northampton County (Pa.), 1979-87, U.S. Dist. Ct. (ea. dist.) Pa., Phila., 1987—; appointed to U.S. Sentencing Commn. Judicial Working Group, 1992-93; trial judge U.S. vs. Scarfo, 1988-89; adj. prof. Northampton County Area Community Coll., 1976-81; solicitor Palmer Twp., 1971-79; gen. counsel Fairview Savs. and Loan Assn., Easton, 1973-79. Recipient Booster award Bus. Indsl. and Profl. Assn., 1979, George Palmer award Palmer Twp., 1980, Man of Yr. award, 1981, Law Enforcement Commendation medal Nat. Soc. SAR, 1990; named an Alumnus Who Has Made a Difference in the World, U. Maine, 1991. Mem. ABA (com. on jud. edn.), Fed. Bar Assn. (hon.), Pa. Bar Assn., Northampton County Bar Assn., Am. Judicature Soc., Fed. Judges Assn., Pomfret Club, Nat. Lawyers Club Washington, Union League Club, Pa. Soc. Club, Sigma Pi Sigma. Office: US Dist Ct Holmes Bldg 2nd and Ferry St Easton PA 18042

VAN ANTWERPEN, REGINA LANE, underwriter, insurance company executive; b. Milw., Aug. 16, 1939; d. Joseph F. Gagliano and Sophia B. (Johannik) Wolfe; widowed; children: Thomas II, Victoria. Student, U. Wis., Milw., 1954-57. Office mgr. Gardner Bender Inc., Milw., 1972-80; mfg. rep. Rosenbloom & Co., Chgo., 1980-81; spl. agt. Northwestern Mut. Life Equities Inc., Milw., 1981-88, registered rep., 1985-88; account rep. Fin. Instn. Mktg. Co., Milw., 1988-93; investment specialist Fimco Securities Group, Inc., Milw., 1993—; pres. Anvers Ltd., 1990—, 1990—. Author: (poetry) One More Time Its Christmas, 1978, True Friendship, 1979, Beautiful Brown Eyes, 1990 (award 1992). Mgr. Sch. Bd. Elections, Fox Point, 1969; v.p. Suburban Rep. Women's CLub, Milw., 1968-72; vol. tchr. St. Eugene Sch., Milw., 1968-72. Mem. AAUW, Milw. Life Underwriters, Women's Life Underwriters (v.p. 1982-83), Legis. Orgn. Life Underwriters, Nat. Assn. Securities Dealers (lic.), Investment Club (sec. 1989-90, pres. 1990—). Republican. Roman Catholic. Avocations: writing, service work, gardening. Office: Fin Instn Mktg Co 111 E Kilbourn Ave Ste 1850 Milwaukee WI 53202-6611

VAN ARK, JOAN, actress; d. Carroll and Dorothy Jean (Hemenway) Van A.; m. John Marshall, Feb. 1, 1966; 1 child, Vanessa Jeanne. Student, Yale Sch. Drama. Appeared at Tyrone Guthrie Theatre, Washington Arena Stage, in London, on Broadway; performances include: (stage) Barefoot in the Park, 1965, School for Wives, 1971, Rules of the Game, 1974, Cyrano de Bergerac, Ring Round the Moon, A Little Night Music, 1994, Three Tall Women, 1995; (TV series) Temperatures Rising, 1972-73, We've Got Each Other, 1977-78, Dallas, 1978-81, Knots Landing, 1979-92 (also dir. episodes Letting Go, Hints and Evasions); (TV movies) The Judge and Jake Wyler, 1972, Big Rose, 1974, Shell Game, 1975, The Last Dinosaur, 1977, Red Flag, 1981, Shakedown on the Sunset Strip, 1988, My First Love, 1989, Murder at the PTA, 1990, To Cast a Shadow, 1990, Always Remember I Love You, 1990, Grand Central Murders, 1992, Tainted Blood, 1992, Someone's Watching, 1993, When the Darkman Calls, 1994; (TV miniseries) Testimony of Two Men, 1978; dir., star ABC-TV Afterschool Spl. Boys Will Be Boys, 1993. Recipient Theatre World award, 1970-71, L.A. Drama Critics Circle award, 1973, Outstanding Actress award Soap Opera Digest, 1986, 89. Mem. AFTRA, SAG, Actors Equity Assn., San Fernando Valley Track Club. Address: care William Morris Agy Inc 151 S El Camino Dr Beverly Hills CA 90212-2704 also: 1325 Avenue Of The Americas New York NY 10019-4702*

VAN ARNEM, HAROLD LOUIS, marketing professional; b. Cin., Dec. 19, 1940; s. Harold Louis and Elizabeth (Smith) Van A.; m. Karen Schram, Aug. 31, 1963 (div. 1980); children: Aleise, Heidi, Heather, Harold Louis IV; m. Bridget Elizabeth Sahlin, Feb. 17, 1990; children: Adam, Maxwell, Brandon. BBA, U. Cin., 1964; postgrad., U. Detroit, 1968, 69, 71. With fin. and mktg. depts. GE Computers, Phoenix, 1964-67; chief exec. officer Acts Computing Corp., Southfield, Mich., 1967-74; contractor Illiac IV Arpa/DOD Arpanet, 1969-75; chief exec. officer Van Arnem, Birmingham, Mich., 1974—, Finalco Group, Inc., Boca Raton, Fla., 1988—; gen. ptnr. Finalco Ltd., Birmingham, 1988—, Gemini Equities Ltd., Boca Raton, 1989—; chmn., chief exec. officer Gemini Group, Inc., Boca Raton, 1989—; CEO Libra Technologies, Inc., Deerfield Beach, Fla., 1994—; gen. ptnr. Detroit Express, profl. soccer team, Pontiac, Mich., 1978-84; commr. Am. Soccer Leaague, Pontiac, 1980; chmn. Cybergate, Inc., Deerfield Beach. Co-producer feature film Love at First Bite, 1979; assoc. producer feature film Quick and the Dead, 1978. Co-chmn. Mich. Rep. Legis. Com., 1977-81. Mem. CEO Orgn., Young Pres. Orgn., World Bus. Coun., Oakland Hills Country Club (Birmingham), Adios Golf Club (Deerfield Beach), Ocean Reef Yacht Club (Key Largo, Fla.). Avocations: jump rope, aerobics, spear fishing, golf. Office: Libra Tech Svcs 1301 W Newport Center Dr Deerfield Beach FL 33442-7734

VAN ARSDALE, DICK, professional basketball team executive; b. Indpls., Feb. 22, 1943; m. Barbara V.; children: Jill, Jason. AB in economics, Indiana U., 1965. Player New York Knicks (Nat. Basketball Assn.), N.Y.C., 1965-68; with Phoenix Suns, Phoenix, Ariz., 1968-77; color commentator, TV broadcasts Phoenix Suns, from 1977, interim mgr., 1987, from v.p., player personnel. Named "Mr. Basketball" of Indiana during high school, NCAA All-American, Indiana U. Office: care Phoenix Suns 201 E Jefferson St Phoenix AZ 85004-2412*

VAN ARSDALE, THOMAS HAROLD, bank executive; b. Bklyn., June 20, 1937; s. Frank and Katharyn (Seele) van A.; m. Susette Costello, Jan. 18, 1986; children: James R., Kathryn E., Debra S., Thomas R. AS with honors, Raritan Valley C.C., 1982; AA with honors, Thomas A. Edison State Coll., 1982; grad. with honors, Nat. Sch. Banking. Pres., CEO, trustee Franklin First Savs. Bank, Wilkes-Barre, Pa.; mem. faculty Nat. Sch. Banking, Fairfield, Conn.; chair community banking coun. Fed. Res. Bank Phila.; bd. dirs. Ctr. for Fin. Studies, Fairfield; vice chair Drayton Ins. Co., Ltd. Chair Cmty. Devel. Corp., Wilkes-Barre; bd. dirs. Coll. Misericordia, Dallas, Pa., F.M. Kirby Ctr. for Performing Arts, Greater Wilkes-Barre Partnership for Econ. Growth, Pa. Economy League, United Way of Wyoming Valley, WVIA Pub. Radio and TV; past sr. warden Holy Cross Episcopal Ch., N.J.; pres. Am. Inst. Banking, N.J., 1969, Bank Adminstrn. Inst., N.J., 1979; state dir. Bank Adminstr. Inst., N.J., 1981; chair N.J. Coun. Savs. Instns., 1990. Mem. Am.'s Cmty. Bankers (bd. dirs.), Pa. Bankers' Assn. (bd. dirs.), Pa. Assn. Cmty. Bankers (bd. dirs.), Pa. Soc., Most Venerable Order of St. John (officer), Westmoreland Club, Phi Theta Kappa. Home: 910 Lantern Hill Rd Shavertown PA 18708-9588 Office: Franklin First Savs Bank 44 W Market St Wilkes Barre PA 18773-0449

VAN ARSDALL, ROBERT ARMES, engineer, retired air force officer; b. Omaha, Oct. 5, 1925; s. Samuel Peter and Althea (Armes) Van A.; m. Margaret Cooper Kiersted, June 9, 1948; children—Robert Armes, Janet Althea, Susan DeBaun, Kathryn Ann. BS, U.S. Mil. Acad., 1948; postgrad., U. Colo., spring 1961; MS, George Washington U., 1968. Commd. 2d lt. USAF, 1948, advanced through grades to col., 1968; grad. Randolph AFB, Tex., 1949; assigned 5th Air Rescue Group, Westover AFB, Mass., 1949-51; student USAF Squadron Officer Sch., Maxwell AFB, Ala., 1950; pilot, ops. officer 9th Air Rescue Group, Burton-Wood, Manston and Bushy Park, Eng., 1951-55; ops. officer Hdqrs. Air Rescue Service, Orlando AFB, Fla., 1955-57; plans officer Hdqrs. Air R & D Command, Balt., also Andrews AFB, Md., 1957-60; grad. USAF jet qualification course, Randolph AFB, 1959; tng.-with-industry Air Force Inst. Tech., Martin Co., Denver, 1960-61; chief plans div. Hdqrs. Space Systems Div., L.A., 1961-63; exec. officer Office Space Systems, Office Sec. Air Force, 1963-67; assoc. Air War Coll. program, Washington, 1964-66; student Naval War Coll., 1967-68; dep. dir. Dept. Def. Manned Space Flight Support Office, Patrick AFB, Fla., 1968-69; dir. range engring., 1969-70; dir. range ops. Air Force Eastern Test Range, 1970-72; comdr. USAF Satellite Test Ctr., Sunnyvale, Calif., 1972-73; vice comdr. USAF Satellite Control Facility, L.A., 1973-74; comdr. USAF Satellite Control Facility, 1974-76; staff engr. Pan Am. World Airways, Cocoa Beach, Fla., 1976-78; project dir. Pan Am. World Airways, 1978-79, program mgr., 1980-85, dir. internat. projects, 1985-88; program dir. Diego Garcia, 1989, ret., 1989. Decorated Air Force Commendation medal with two oak leaf clusters, Legion of Merit with oak leaf cluster. Life mem. Assn. Grads. U.S. Mil. Acad.; charter mem. Nat. Soujourners, USAF Acad. Athletic Assn. Republican. Methodist. Clubs: Mason, Burtonwood Air Force (gov.), Bushy Park Air Force (gov.), Orlando Air Force (gov.), Andrews Air Force (gov.), Space Systems Division Air Force (gov.). Home: 660 Cinnamon Ct Satellite Beach FL 32937-4391

VANARSDALL, ROBERT LEE, JR., orthodontist, educator; b. Crewe, Va., Feb. 7, 1940; s. Robert Lee Sr. and Margie Mae (Jenkins) V.; m. Sandra E. Hoffman, Aug. 11, 1962; children: Robert Lee III, Lesley, Ashley. BA in Econs., Coll. William and Mary, 1962; DDS, Med. Coll. Va., 1970; cert. Orthodontics and Periodontics, U. Pa., 1973. Diplomate Am. Acad. Periodontology, Am. Bd. Orthodontics. Staff Children's Hosp., Phila., 1973—; prof. orthodontics, chmn. dept. orthodontics U. Pa., Phila., 1981—; prof. dentistry, chmn. Med. Coll. Pa., Phila., 1989—; bd. dirs. Nat. Dental Ins. Co., Denver. Editor: Internat. Jour. Adult Orthodontics and Orthognathic Surgery, 1986—, Orthodontoics: Current Principles and Techniques, 2d edit., 1994; editorial bd. profl. jours.; contbr. articles to profl. jours. Bd. dirs. Phila. Soc. William and Mary Alumni Assn. Lt. USNR, 1962-65. Fellow Coll. Physicians of Phila. 1978, Am. Coll. Dentistry 1980. Mem. ADA, Am. Assn. Orthodontists, Stomatological Club Phila., Angle Soc. Orthodontists, Phila. Soc. Orthodontists (pres. 1989, chmn. sci. affairs coun. 1990—). Roman Catholic. Avocations: antiques, architecture. Home: 208 Ashwood Rd Villanova PA 19085-1504 Office: Sinkler Bldg 588 E Lancaster Ave Radnor PA 19087-5235

VAN ARTSDALEN, DONALD WEST, federal judge; b. Doylestown, Pa., Oct. 21, 1919; s. Isaac Jeans and May Mable (Danenhower) Van A.; m. Marie Catherine Auerbach, June 20, 1953. Student, Williams Coll., 1937-40; LL.B., U. Pa., 1948. Bar: Pa. 1948, U.S. Supreme Ct. 1956. Practiced in Doylestown, 1948-70; dist. atty. Bucks County (Pa.), 1954-58; judge U.S. Dist. Ct. Pa. (ea. dist.), Phila., from 1970, now sr. judge, 1987. Served with Canadian Army, 1940-42; Served with AUS, 1942-45. Mem. Order of the Coif. Office: US District Court 14614 US Courthouse Ind Mall W 601 Market St Philadelphia PA 19106-1510*

VAN ARTSDALEN, ERVIN ROBERT, physical chemist, educator; b. Doylestown, Pa., Nov. 13, 1913; s. Isaac J. and May M. (Danenhower) Van A.; m. Mary Louise Naylor, June 14, 1945. B.S. in Chemistry cum laude, Lafayette Coll., 1935; Internat. Exchange fellow U. Munich, Germany, 1935-36; A.M., Harvard, 1939, Ph.D. in Phys. Chemistry, 1941. Instr., then asst. prof. chemistry Lafayette Coll., 1941-45; on leave to Nat. Def. Research Com., Johns Hopkins Med. Sch., 1943-45; group leader Los Alamos Atomic Bomb Lab., 1945-46; asst. prof. chemistry Cornell U., 1946-51; adminstrv. group leader Oak Ridge Nat. Lab., 1951-56; asst. dir. research, basic lab. Union Carbide Corp., Cleve., 1956-63; John W. Mallet prof. chemistry, chmn. dept. U. Va., 1963-68; prof. chemistry U. Ala., 1968-84, prof. emeritus, 1984—, head dept., 1968-72; with Inst. Energy Analysis, Oak Ridge, 1975-76; cons. to govt. and industry; mem. chemistry adv. com. USAF Office Sci. Rsch., 1958-72, chmn., 1963-70; mem. Radiation Safety Bd. of Health, State of Ala., 1980—. Contbr. to profl. jours., govt. reports.; Mem. editorial bd.: Jour. Phys. Chemistry, 1958-62. Dir. High Sch. Students and Tchrs. Sci. Workshops and Seminars, Cleve., 1957-60; bd. dirs. Oak Ridge Sch. Music, 1953-56, Oak Ridge Asso. Univs., 1969-75; mem. 1st Presbyn. Ch., Tuscaloosa. Recipient Distinguished Alumni Sci. Tchr. citation Lafayette Coll., 1966. Fellow Am. Inst. Chemists; mem. AAAS, Am. Chem. Soc., Am. Phys. Soc., Va. Acad. Sci., Oak Ridge Country Club, Indian Hills Country Club (Tuscaloosa, Ala.), Exch. Club, Phi Beta Kappa, Alpha Chi Sigma, Gamma Alpha, Gamma Sigma Epsilon, Kappa Delta Rho. Clubs: Oak Ridge Country; Indian Hills Country (Tuscaloosa, Ala.). Spl. research reaction kinetics and photochemistry, thermodynamics, fused salts, nuclear energy, energy analysis. Home: 1512 Bellingrath Dr Reston Pl Tuscaloosa AL 35406

VANASKIE, THOMAS I., lawyer; b. Shamokin, Pa., Nov. 11, 1953; s. John Anthony and Delores (Wesoloski) V.; m. Dorothy Grace Williams, Aug. 12, 1978; children: Diane, Laura, Thomas. BA magna cum laude, Lycoming Coll., 1975; JD cum laude, Dickinson U., 1978. Law clk. to chief judge U.S. Dist. Ct. (mid. dist.) Pa., Scranton, 1978-80; assoc. Dilworth, Paxson, Kalish & Kauffman, Scranton, 1980-85, ptnr., 1986—; counsel Gov. Robert P. Casey Com., Harrisburg, Pa., 1987—. Contbr. articles to profl. jours. Mem. Scranton Waste Mgmt. Com., 1989. Recipient James A. Finnegan award Finnegan Found. Mem. ABA, Judicature, Assn. Trial Lawyers Am., Pa. Bar Assn., Pa. Trial Lawyers Assn. Democrat. Avocations: golf, reading. Office: US Dist Ct Fed Courthouse 4th Fl Washington Ave & Linden St Scranton PA 18501

VAN ASPEREN, MORRIS EARL, banker; b. Wessington, S.D., Oct. 5, 1943; s. Andrew and Alyce May (Flagg) Van A.; m. Anne Virginia Merritt, July 2, 1966; 1 child, David Eric. BS in Math., U. Okla., 1966; MBA, Pepperdine U., 1979. Mgr. western dist. Svc. Rev. Inc., Northbrook, Ill., 1970-77; v.p. Hooper Info. Systems Inc., Tustin, Calif., 1977-78; v.p., chief fin. officer ATE Assocs. Inc., Westlake Village, Calif., 1978-84; mgmt. cons. Thousand Oaks, Calif., 1984-94; sr. v.p. Nat. Bank Calif., L.A., 1986—; chmn. liaison com. region IX SBA, 1990-94. Nat. advocate fin. svcs. SBA, 1989. Lt. USN, 1966-70. Mem. Nat. Assn. Govt. Guaranteed Lenders (bd. dirs. 1990-93), Robert Morris Assocs., Nat. Assn. Credit Mgmt., Am. Legion (bd. dirs. Post 339 1995). Avocations: art, music. Office: Nat Bank Calif 145 S Fairfax Ave Los Angeles CA 90036-2166

VANATTA, BOB, athletic administrator; b. Columbia, Mo., July 7, 1918; s. Claude W. and Viola (Toler) V.; m. Lois A. Williams; children: Robert, Thomas, Timothy. BA, Ctrl. Meth. Coll., 1942; MEd, U. Mo., 1949. Tchr., coach Boonville (Mo.) High Sch., 1942-43, Kemper Mil. Sch., Boonville, 1943-44, Springfield (Mo.) High Sch., 1944-47; tchr., dir. athletics, coach Ctrl. Meth. Coll., Fayette, Mo., 1947-50, S.W. Mo. State U., Springfield, 1950-53; coach U.S. Mil. Acad., West Point, N.Y., 1953-54; dir. athletics, coach Bardley U., Peoria, Ill., 1954-56; tchr., coach Memphis State U., 1956-62, U. Mo., Columbia, 1962-68; bank mktg. officer Empire Bank, Springfield, 1968-71; profl. basketball exec. dir. Memphis Pros, 1971-72; tchr., coach Delta State U., Cleve., 1972-73; dir. athletics Oral Roberts U., Tulsa, 1973-77; commr. Ohio Valley Athletic Conf., Nashville, 1977-80, Trans Am. Athletic Conf., Shreveport, La., 1980-83; dir. athletics La. Tech. U., Rustin, 1983-86; commr. Sunshine State Athletic Conf., Jupiter, Fla., 1986-94; cons., speaker in field. Author: Coaching Pattern Play Basketball, 1959; contbr. articles to profl. jours. Chpt. mem. Nat. Football Found. Hall of Fame. Named to Ctrl. Meth. Coll. Hall of Fame, S.W. Mo. State U. Hall of Fame, Nat. Athletic Intercollegiate Assn. Hall of Fame, Greater Springfield Hall of Fame, John Q. Hammons Mo. Sports Hall of Fame. Mem. Nat. Assn. Basketball Coaches, Am. Football Coaches Assn., Nat. Assn. Collegiate Dirs. Athletics.

VANATTA, CHESTER B., business executive, educator; b. Bartlesville, Okla., Sept. 3, 1935; s. Benjamin Franklin and Iona Ruth (Hayes) V.; m. Patsy Lou Straub, May 29, 1958; children—Tracy Ann, Christopher B., John Scott. B.S. in Mktg., U. Kans., Lawrence, 1959, M.S. in Acctg., 1962; Advanced Mgmt. Program, Harvard U., Cambridge, 1972. Mem. staff Arthur Young & Co., Kansas City, Mo., 1962-69; regional dir, Arthur Young & Co., Dallas, 1969-72, ptnr., 1969-85; mng. ptnr. Arthur Young & Co., Chgo., 1972-76, dir., 1973-85; mng. ptnr., vice chmn. ops. Arthur Young & Co., N.Y.C., 1976-81; mng. ptnr., vice chmn. S.W. Region Arthur Young & Co., Dallas, 1981-85; pres. Exec. Cons. Group, Lawrence, Kans., 1985—; exec. in residence, Paul J. Adam Disting. lectr. U. Kans. Sch. Bus., Lawrence, 1985-90; bd. dirs. Atlantis Group Inc., Miami, Fla., Arcadian Corp., Memphis, Adams Bus. Forms, Topeka. Trustee, exec. com., fin. com. Kans. U. Endowment Fund, 1983—; bd. dirs. Kans. Alumni Assn., 1984-91, pres., 1986-87. Mem. Am. Inst. CPA's, Kans. Soc. CPA's (Gold Key 1962). Republican. Clubs: Alvamar Country (Lawrence), Tournament Players-Summerlin (Las Vegas), Elkhorn Country (Sun Valley, Idaho). Avocations: golf, travel, photography. Home: # 356 2251 N Rampart Blvd Las Vegas NV 89128-7640

VAN ATTA, DAVID MURRAY, lawyer; b. Berkeley, Calif., Oct. 20, 1944; s. Chester Murray and Rosalind (Eisenstein) Van A.; m. Jo Ann Masaoka; 1 child, Lauren Rachel. BA, U. Calif., Berkeley, 1966; JD, U. Calif., Hastings, 1969. Bar: Calif. 1970. Asst. gen. counsel Boise Cascade Corp., Palo Alto, Calif., 1970-73; ptnr. Miller, Starr & Regalia, San Francisco, 1973-87, Graham & James, San Francisco, 1987-93, Hanna & Van Atta, Palo Alto, 1993—; instr. Golden Gate U., San Francisco, 1984-85; U. Calif., Berkeley, 1976-84. Mem. ABA, Am. Coll. Real Estate Lawyers, Calif. Bar Assn. (vice chmn. exec. com. real property law sect. 1982-85, chmn. condominium and subdivsn. com. real property law sect. 1981-83), Cmty. Assn. Inst., Urban Land Inst., Lambda Alpha Internat. Soc. Avocations: skiing, tennis, painting. Office: Hanna & Van Atta 525 University Ave Ste 705 Palo Alto CA 94301-1921

VANATTA, JOHN CROTHERS, III, physiologist, physician, educator; b. Lafayette, Ind., Apr. 22, 1919; s. John Crothers and Ida Lahr (Raub) V.; m. Carol Lee Geisler, July 30, 1944; children: Lynn Ellen, Paul Richard. B.A., Ind. U., 1941, M.D., 1944. Intern Wayne County Gen. Hosp., Eloise, Mich., 1944-45, resident in internal medicine, 1946-47; fellow in physiology, pharmacology Southwestern Med. Coll., Dallas, 1947-48, fellow in exptl. and internal medicine, 1948-49; instr. physiology U. Tex. Southwestern Med. Sch., 1949-50, asst. prof., 1950-53, assoc. prof., 1953-57, prof. physiology, 1957—, Robert W. Lackey prof. physiology, 1987-89; prof. physiology So. Meth. U. Dallas, Dallas, 1969-80, Baylor Coll. Dentistry, Dallas, 1992-94; mem. staff Parkland Meml. Hosp., Dallas, 1953-57, VA Hosp., Dallas, McKinney, Tex., 1956-58; cons. div. nuclear edn. tng. AEC, 1964-67. Author: Oxygen Transport, Hypoxia and Cyanosis, 1974, Fluid Balance - A Clinical Manual, 1988; contbr. articles to profl. jours. Scouter, Circle 10 council Boy Scouts Am., Dallas, 1963-78; v.p. Luth. Health Care Council N. Tex., 1975-80, pres., 1980-81. Served as lt. (j.g.) M.C., USNR, 1945-46, PTO. Mem. AMA, AAAS, Am. Physiol. Soc., Soc. Exptl. Biology and Medicine, Phi Beta Pi, Sigma Xi, Delta Tau Delta. Lutheran (councilman 1951-91, v.p. 1974-75). Home: 10416 Remington Ln Dallas TX 75229-5262

VAN AUKEN, ROBERT DANFORTH, business administration educator, management consultant; b. Chgo., Oct. 31, 1915; s. Howard Robert and Mable (Hanlon) Van A.; student Guilford Coll., 1933-35, Gen. Motors Inst. Tech., 1936-38, U. Pitts., 1953-54; BS, U. Dayton, 1958; MA, U. Okla., 1967; m. Ruth Bowen Cutler, Nov. 24, 1939 (dec.); children: Robert Hanlon, Joseph Marshall, David Danforth, Howard Evans, Jonathan Lewis; m. Vernia Maurine Long, July 9, 1993. Commd. aviation cadet U.S. Air Force, 1938; advanced through grades to lt. col., 1961; fighter pilot, squadron comdr., ops. officer, 1939-45; asst. air attaché, Paris, 1946-49; staff officer, Pentagon 1950-53; procurement-prodn. staff officer Wright-Patterson AFB, 1954-58, Tinker AFB, 1958-60, Holloman AFB, 1960-61, ret., 1961; personnel officer U. Okla., Norman, 1962-65, mem. faculty, 1965—, asst. prof. mgmt., 1979-83, prof. emeritus bus. adminstrn., 1983—, dir. student programs and career devel. Coll. Bus. Adminstrn., 1975-79; cons. seminars mgmt. amd compensation, 1963—; adj. instr. Park Coll., 1991—; instr. Park Coll., 1991—; cattle rancher, 1970—; owner VA Farms. Mem. Oklahomans for Improvement in Nursing Care Homes; ombudsman vol. Okla. Areawide Aging Agy., 1992—. Decorated Silver Star, Purple Heart. Mem. DAV, NRA, Newcomen Soc. U.S., Oklahoma City Human Resources Assn., Acad. Mgmt., Internat. Platform Assn., Nat. Beef Assn., Okla. Cattlemans Assn., Okla. Alliance Aging, Air Force Assn., Am. Legion, Ret. Officers Assn., Mil. Order of World Wars, Order of Deadalians, 5th Air Force Meml. Found., 49th Fighter Group Assn., 31st Fighter Officers Assn., Disabled Am. Vets., Masons, Beta Gamma Sigma, Delta Sigma Pi. Republican. Contbr. monographs in field. Home: 420 S Highland Rd Oklahoma City OK 73110-2138 Office: U Okla 307 W Brooks St Norman OK 73069-8822 *A person's success in life is often measure by the accumulation of wealth or influence. But a better measure might be that person's progress toward predetermined personal goals, whatever they may be.*

VANAUKER, LANA LEE, recreational therapist, educator; b. Youngstown, Ohio, Sept. 19, 1949; d. William Marshall and Joanne Norma (Kimmel) Speece; m. Dwight Edward VanAuker, Mar. 16, 1969 (div. 1976); 1 child, Heidi. BS in Edn. cum laude, Kent (Ohio) State U., 1974; MS in Edn., Youngstown (Ohio) U., 1989. Cert. tchr., Ohio; nat. cert. activity cons. Phys. edn. instr. St. Joseph Sch., Campbell, Ohio, 1973-75; program dir. YWCA, Youngstown, 1975-85; exercise technician Youngstown State U., 1985-86; health educator Park Vista Retirement Ctr., Youngstown, 1986-87; sch. tchr. Salem (Ohio) City Sch., 1987-88; recreational therapist Trumbull Meml. Hosp., Warren, Ohio, 1988—; activity cons. Mahoning/Trumbull Nursing Homes, Warren, 1990-92; adv. bd. rep. Ohio State Bur. Health Promotion Phys. Fitness, 1996—; mem. adv. bd. Ohio State Executive Physical Fitness Dept. Health, 1996. Producer chair exercise sr. video Excercise is the Fountain of Youth, 1993; photographer, choreographer. Vol. Am. Cancer Soc., 1980—, Am. Heart Assn., 1986—, Dance for Heart, 1980-86; mem. State of Ohio Phys. Fitness Adv. Bd., 1996. Youngstown State U. scholar, 1986-89. Mem. AAHPERD, Youngstown Camera Club (social chair 1989-90, pres. 1993-95), Resident Activity Profl. Assn. (pres. 1994, 95, 96), Pa. Activity Profl. Assn., Kappa Delta Pi. Democrat. Presbyterian. Avocations: photography, international dance, volleyball, aerobics, travel. Home: 385 N Broad St Canfield OH 44406-1256 Office: Trumbull Meml Hosp 1350 E Market St Warren OH 44483-6608

VAN BEBBER, GEORGE THOMAS, federal judge; b. Troy, Kans., Oct. 21, 1931; s. Roy Vest and Anne (Wenner) V.; m. Alleen Sara Castellani. AB, U. Kans., 1953, LLB, 1955. Bar: Kans. 1955, U.S. Dist. Ct. Kans. 1955, U.S. Ct. Appeals (10th cir.) 1961. Pvt. practice, Troy, 1955-58, 1961-82; asst. U.S. atty. Topeka, Kansas City, Kans., 1958-61; county atty. Doniphan County, Troy, 1963-69; mem. Kans. House of Reps., 1973-75; chmn. Kans. Corp. Commn., Topeka, 1975-79; U.S. magistrate Topeka, 1982-89; judge U.S. Dist. Ct., Kansas City, Kan., 1989—, chief judge, 1995—. Mem. ABA, Kas. Bar Assn. Episcopalian. Home: 6701 W 66th Ter Shawnee Mission KS 66202-4146 Office: US Dist Ct 529 US Courthouse 500 State Ave Kansas City KS 66101-2403

VAN BEEK, GUS WILLARD, archaeologist; b. Tulsa, Mar. 21, 1922; s. Gus Willard and Dove Lucille (Crupper) Van B.; children: John Phillip, Christopher Hicks, Stephen Dart; m. Ora Braunstein, Sept. 25, 1972. BA with honors, U. Tulsa, 1943; BD, McCormick Theol. Sem., Chgo., 1945; PhD, Johns Hopkins U., 1953. Fellow Hebrew Union Coll., Cin., 1947-49, Am. Schs. Oriental Research, Jerusalem, 1952; research assoc. Johns Hopkins U., Balt., 1954-59; assoc. curator Smithsonian Instn., Washington, 1959-67, curator, 1967—; dir. archeol. expdn. Hadhramaut, Arabia, 1961-62, Nejran, Saudi Arabia, 1968, Tell Jemmeh, Israel, 1970—; trustee Am. Schs. Oriental Rsch., 1988-93, mem. adv. bd., 1993—. Author: Hajar Bin Humeid, 1969; editor: The Scholarship of William Foxwell Albright: An Appraisal, 1989; also 150 articles on archeology, history; producer/curator exhibits: Dead Sea Scrolls of Jordan, 1965, Arabia Felix, 1972. Recipient Disting. Alumnus award U. Tulsa Coll. Arts. Scis., 1971. Mem. Archeol. Inst. Am., Am. Inst. Yemeni Studies, Am. Schs. Oriental Rsch., Phi Beta Kappa. Democrat. Presbyterian. Office: Smithsonian Inst Mus Natural History Mrc Nhb # 112 Washington DC 20560

VANBIESBROUCK, JOHN, professional hockey player; b. Detroit, Sept. 4, 1963; m. Rosalinde V. With N.Y. Rangers, 1981-93, Vancouver Canucks, 1993, Florida Panthers, 1993—; mem. NHL All-Star team, 1985-86; player NHL All-Star game, 1994. Recipient Vezina Trophy (NHL outstanding goaltender), 1985, 86, (with Ron Scott) Terry Sawchuk trophy, 1983-89, (with Marc D'Amour) F.W. Dinty Moore trophy, (with D. Bruce Affleck) Tommy Ivan trophy, 1983-84; named NHL All-Star, 1985-86, Sporting News NHL All-Star, 1985-86, 93-94. Office: Florida Panthers 100 NE 3rd Ave Fl 10 Fort Lauderdale FL 33301-1176*

VAN BLARICUM, AMY JOAN, perioperative nurse; b. Englewood, N.J., Sept. 23, 1963; d. Julius Herbert Jr. and Mildred Doris Van Blaricum. BSN, Widener U., Chester, Pa., 1987. RN, Pa.; cert. in chemotherapy adminstrn., venipuncture, 1987. Nurse med.-surg. unit Mercy Cath. Med. Ctr., Darby, Pa., 1987, nurse oncology unit, 1988, nurse operating room, 1989. Mem. Assn. Oper. Rm. Nurses (cert. oper. rm. nurse, 1992).

VAN BOKKELEN, WILLIAM REQUA, health facility administrator; b. Indpls., Mar. 27, 1946; s. Robert William and Wilma Louise (Reynolds) Van B.; m. Cheryl Lyn Steiling, June 12, 1972; children: Audrey Leigh, Adriane Lisa. BA, DePauw U., 1968; MBA, Northwestern U., Evanston, Ill., 1973. Adminstrv. intern Lake Forest (Ill.) Hosp., 1972; student assoc. VA Lakeside Hosp., Chgo., 1973; asst. adminstr. St. Francis Hosp., Evanston, Ill., 1973-76, v.p. clin. svcs., 1976-79; v.p. adminstrn. Louis A. Weiss Meml. Hosp., Chgo., 1979-83; adminstr. Christian hosp. Northeast, St. Louis, 1983-86; exec. v.p. Christian Hosp. Northeast/Northwest, St. Louis, 1986-90, pres., 1990—; bd. dirs. Durable Med. Equipment Co., Maryland Hieghts, Mo., Citizens Bank Florissant, Mo., Midwest Stone Inst., St. Louis. Chairperson Friends of Scouting, St. Louis, 1989—. Am. Coll. Healthcare Execs. fellow, 1983. Mem. Res. Officers Am., Florissant Valley C. of C. (bd. dirs. 1990—), Marygrove (bd. dirs. 1990), Norwood Hills Country Club, Florissant Rotary (bd. dirs. 1990-91). Methodist. Avocations: running, snow skiing, golf, fishing. Office: Christian Hosp NE-NW 11133 Dunn Rd Saint Louis MO 63136-6119*

VANBRODE, DERRICK BRENT, IV, trade association administrator; b. Elgin, Ill., Sept. 3, 1940. Grad., N.Y. Inst. Criminology, 1963. Sr. v.p. Am. Fraternal Programmers, Inc., North Miami, Fla., 1977—; mgmt. cons. Am. Fedn. Police, Am. Law Enforcement Officers Assn., Nat. Assn. Chiefs of Police, Am. Police Acad. Editor: Who's Who in American Law Enforcement, 1976-93, Crime Watch mag, 1981—, Police Times/Command, 1975—. Pres. Greater Miami Assn. Licensed Beverage Owners, 1973—. Decorated Grand Cross Knights of St. Michael; comdr. Royal Knights of Justice. Mem. Greater North Port Fla. C. of C. (founder, pres.). Clubs: Miami Millionaires (founder, past pres.), Millionaires Internat. (pres. 1983—), Miami Shores Country, Racquet. Office: 3801 Biscayne Blvd Miami FL 33137-3732

VAN BRUNT, ALBERT DANIEL, advertising agency executive; b. N.Y.C., Nov. 13, 1920; s. Ernest Robert and Helen (Rothschild) Isaacs. B.S. in Mktg., NYU, 1942. Dir. advt. Air France, N.Y.C., 1947-50; v.p. Buchanan Advt. Agy., N.Y.C., 1951-57; pres. Van Brunt & Co., Advt.-Mktg., Inc., N.Y.C., 1958-88, chmn. bd., 1989-90; pres. IMAA, Inc., N.Y.C., 1965-70; sr. v.p. IMAA, Inc., 1970-89; exec. v.p. Van Brunt & Co., Chgo., Inc., 1969-76, Van Brunt/Schaeffer, 1979-89; v.p. HBC/Van Brunt, Chgo., 1976-77; pres., chief exec. officer WDB Advt., Inc., N.Y.C., 1990—. Trustee N.Y. chpt. Leukemia Soc. Am., 1979-80; bd. dirs. Leukemia program Coll. Physicians and Surgeons, Columbia U. Served to lt. USNR, 1942-46. Mem. Am. Assn. Advt. Agys. (dir. N.Y. council 1969-74), Internat. Advt. Assn., SAR. Clubs: Wings (N.Y.C.), Lotos (N.Y.C.) (dir. 1966-72, 76-87, dir. emeritus 1987—, sec. 1972-75, treas. 1975-76). Home: 315 E 68th St New York NY 10021-5692 also: Jason's Ln East Hampton NY 11937 Office: WDB Prodns Inc 419 E 57th St New York NY 10022-3060

VAN BRUNT, EDMUND EWING, physician; b. Oakland, Calif., Apr. 28, 1926; s. Adrian W. and Kathryn Anne (Shattuck) Van B.; m. Claire Monod, Feb. 28, 1949; children: Karin, Deryk, Jahn. BA in Biophysics, U. Calif., Berkeley, 1952; MD, U. Calif., San Francisco, 1959; ScD, U. Toulouse, France, 1978. Postdoctoral fellow NIH, 1961-63; rsch. assoc. U. Calif., San Francisco, 1963-67; staff physician Kaiser Permanente Med. Ctr., San Francisco, 1964-91; dir. div. rsch. Kaiser Permanente Med. Program, Oakland, Calif., 1979-91; assoc. dir. Kaiser Found. Rsch. Inst., Oakland, 1985-91, sr. cons., 1991—; adj. prof. U. Calif., San Francisco, 1975-92; chmn. instnl. rev. bd. Kaiser Found. Rsch. Inst., 1986—; pres. bd. trustees French Found. Med. Rsch. and Edn., San Francisco, 1992—. Contbr. articles to profl. books and jours. With U.S. Army, 1944-46. Fellow ACP, Am. Coll. Med. Informatics; mem. AAAS, Calif. Med. Assn., U. Calif. Emeritus Faculty Assn., Sigma Xi. Avocations: flying, photography, swimming. Office: 131 Tamalpais Rd Berkeley CA 94708

VAN BUREN, ABIGAIL (PAULINE FRIEDMAN PHILLIPS), columnist, author, writer, lecturer; b. Sioux City, Iowa, July 4, 1918; d. Abraham and Rebecca (Rushall) Friedman; m. Morton Phillips, July 2, 1939; children: Edward Jay, Jeanne. Student, Morningside Coll., Sioux City, 1936-39; Litt.D. (hon.), Morningside Coll., 1965; L.H.D. (hon.), U. Jacksonville, Fla., 1984. Vol. worker for causes of better mental health Nat. Found. Infantile Paralysis; tng. Gray Ladies, ARC, 1939-56; pres. Minn.-Wis. council B'nai B'rith Aux., 1945-49; columnist Dear Abby San Francisco Chronicle, 1956, McNaught Syndicate, 1956-74, Chgo. Tribune Syndicate, 1974-80, Universal Press Syndicate, 1980—; syndicated U.S., Brazil, Mex., Japan, Philippines, Fed. Republic Germany, India, Holland, Denmark, Can., Korea, Thailand, Italy, Hong Kong, Taiwan, Ireland, Saudi Arabia, Greece, France, Dominican Republic, P.R., Costa Rica, U.S. Virgin Islands, Bermuda, Guam; host radio program The Dear Abby Show, CBS, 1963-75; life-time cons. Group for Advancement Psychiatry, 1985—. Author: Dear Abby, 1957 (also translated into Japanese, Dutch, German, Spanish, Danish, Italian, Finnish), Dear Teen Ager, 1959, Dear Abby on Marriage, 1962, The Best of Dear Abby, 1981, reissued, 1989, Dear Abby on Planning Your Wedding, 1988, Where Were You When President Kennedy Was Shot?: Memories and Tributes to a Slain President as Told to Dear Abby, 1993. Mem. nat. adv. council on aging NIH, HEW, 1978-81; hon. chairwoman 1st Nat. Women's Conf. on Cancer, Am. Cancer Soc., Los Angeles, 1979; mem. public adv. council Center for Study Multiple Gestation, 1981; trustee, mem. adv. bd. Westside Community for Ind. Living, 1981; bd. dirs. Guthrie Theatre, Mpls., 1970-74; charter mem. Franz Alexander Research Found., Los Angeles; charter trustee Armand Hammer United World Coll. of Am. West; bd. dirs. Am. Fedn. for Aging Research Inc.; mem. nat. bd. Goodwill Industries, 1968-75; nat. chmn. Crippled Children Soc., 1962; founding mem. The Amazing Blue Ribbon 400; hon. chmn. Easter Seal campaign Nat. Soc. Crippled Children and Adults, Washington, 1963; del. to Democratic Nat. Conf. from Calif., 1964; Calif. del. White House Conf. on Children and Youth, 1974; non. life mem. Concern for Dying-Am. Ednl. Council; mem. White House Conf. on Physically Handicapped, 1976, NIH, 1976; mem. adv. council Suicide Prevention Ctr., Los Angeles, 1977; mem. com. on aging HHS, 1977-82; council sponsor Assn. Vol. Sterilization, 1981; mem. Women's Trusteeship, 1980; sponsor Mayo Found., Rochester, 1982; bd. dirs. Lupus Found. Am., 1983; mem. adv. com. Ams. for Substance Abuse Prevention, 1984; participant XIII Internat. Congress Gerontology, N.Y.C., 1985; mem. adv. bd. Young Writer's Contest Found., 1985; bd. dirs. Am. Found. for AIDS Research, 1985—; mem. adv. bd. Nat. Council for Children's Rights, Washington, 1988; mem. adv. bd. San Diego Hospice, 1990; mem. adv. bd. Rhonda Fleming Mann Clinic for Women's Comprehensive Care, 1991; mem. Scripps Rsch. Coun. Recipient Times Mother of Yr. award, Los Angeles, 1958; Golden Kidney award, Los Angeles, 1960; Sarah Coventry award, Miami, 1961; Woman of Yr. award Internat. Rotary Club, Rome, 1965; award NCCJ, St. Louis, 1968; award for disting. service to sightless Internat. Lions Club, Dallas, 1972; Disting. Service award Suicide Prevention Center, San Mateo, Calif., 1975; Good Samaritan award Salvation Army, San Francisco, 1970; Margaret Sanger award Nat. Planned Parenthood, 1974; award for outstanding services in mental health So. Psychiat. Assn., 1974; Robert T. Morse writer's award Am. Psychiat. Assn., 1977; Tex. Gov.'s award in recognition of exceptional service to youth of Am. for Ops. Peace of Mind, 1979; Humanitarian award Gay Acad. Union, Los Angeles, 1979, Braille Inst. So. Calif., 1981, Gay and Lesbian Community Services Ctr., 1984; pub. Awardness trophy for Living Will, Soc. for Right to Die, 1983; citation of commendation Simon Weisenthal Found., 1984; Internat. Image in Media award Gay Fathers Coalition, 1985; 1st ann. Woman of Yr. Humanitarian award Rainbow Guild of Amy Karen Children's Cancer Clinic, Cedars-Sinai Med. Ctr., Los Angeles, 1985; Pub. Service award Nat. Kidney Found., 1985, John Rock award Ctr. Population Options, 1986, Serve Am. award Ladies Auxiliary to the VFW, 1986, Genesis award Fund for Animals, 1986, Disting. Service award Inst. Studies Destructive Behavior and Suicide Prevention Ctr., 1986, Citizen of Yr. award Beverly Hills, Calif. C. of C., 1988, Humanitarian award Nat. Council on Alcoholism, 1988, Helen B. Taussig medal Internat. Socs. for the Right to Die with Dignity, 1988, Media award So. Psychiat. Soc., 1988; named Hon. Dir. Found. for Craniofacial Deformities, 1988; Disting. Achievement award Nat. Assn. to Advance Fat Acceptance, 1988, Hand to Hand award Episc. Charities San Francisco, 1989; Nat. Media award for print Nat. Down Syndrome Congress, 1991; Sec.'s award for excellence in communication HHS, 1992; Dove award Assn. Retarded Citizens, 1992. Mem. Women in Communications (hon.), Am. Coll. Psychiatrists (hon. life mem.), Nat. Council Jewish Women (hon. life mem.), Newspapers Features Council, Soc. Profl. Journalists, Nat. Orgn. Women, "Women For", Nat. Com. Preserve Social Security and Medicare, Korean War Vets. Assn. (hon.), Sigma Delta Chi. Office: Phillips-Van Buren Inc Ste 2710 1900 Avenue of the Stars Los Angeles CA 90067 *"If a man loves the labor of his trade, apart from any question of success of fame, the gods have called him." (Robert Louis Stevenson.) The same holds true for women and I am one of them.*

VAN BUREN, PHYLLIS EILEEN, Spanish and German language educator; b. Montevideo, Minn., June 4, 1947; d. Helge Thorfin and Alice Lillian (Johnsrud) Goulson; m. Barry Redmond Van Buren, Apr. 4, 1970; children: Priscila Victoria Princesa, Barry Redmond Barón. Student, Escuela de Bellas Artes, Guadalajara, Mex., 1968; BS, St. Cloud (Minn.) State U., 1969, MS, 1976; postgrad., Goethe Inst., Mannheim, West Germany, 1984, U. Costa Rica, 1989; PhD, The Union Inst., Cin., 1992. Instr. in Spanish Red Wing (Minn.) Pub. Schs., 1969-70; instr. in Spanish and German St. Cloud Pub. Schs., 1970-80; prof. foreign lang. edn., German and Spanish St. Cloud State U., 1975, 79—; advanced placement reader Ednl. Testing Svcs., Princeton, N.J., 1987—; translator in field; mem. Cen. State Adv. Bd. Contbr. articles to El Noticiero, Minn. Lang. Rev., Hispania; textbook reviewer. Coord. children's programs St. Cloud, 1970—; vol. ELS instr. St. Cloud Community, 1973—; reviewer St. Cloud Pub. Schs., 1985-89. Dept. Def. fellow, 1969, Goethe Inst. fellow, 1983; grantee N.W. Area Found., 1985-86, Bush Found., 1986, Fund for the Improvement of Postsecondary Edn./NEH, 1993—. Mem. AAUW (exec. bd. 1988-92, grantee Minn. Internat. AR 1992), ASCD, MLA, Am. Assn. Tchrs. Spanish and Portuguese, Am. Assn. Tchrs. German, Am. Coun. Tchg. Fgn. Langs. (tester 1989—), Minn. Coun. Tchg. Fgn. Langs. (exec. bd.), Phi Kappa Phi (pres.-elect 1991-92, pres. 1992-93), Sigma Delta Pi, Delta Kappa Gamma, Delta Phi Alpha. Republican. Lutheran. Avocations: family, camping, cross-country skiing, swimming, crafts. Home: 3001 County Rd # 146 Clearwater MN 55320-1405 Office: St Cloud State U 720 4th Ave S Saint Cloud MN 56301-4442

VAN BUREN, WILLIAM BENJAMIN, III, retired pharmaceutical company executive; b. Bklyn., Mar. 25, 1922; s. William Benjamin and Dorothy Marjorie (Way) Van B.; m. Joan Cottrell Whitford, Sept. 11, 1948; children—Susan (dec.), Patricia, William S., Richard W. B.A., Washington and Lee U., 1944; LL.B., Yale U., 1949. Bar: N.Y. 1950. V.p., sec. Merck & Co., Inc., 1976-86; pres. Merck & Co. Found., 1982-86. Served with USNR, 1943-46. Mem. Phi Beta Kappa. Home: 8 Point North Dr Salem SC 29676-4113

VANBUTSEL, MICHAEL R., real estate developer; b. Alma, Nebr., Dec. 7, 1952; s. Julius and Margaret (McCorkle) VanB.; m. Jené Hendley; children: Vanessa, Stephanie, Jamie. BArch, U. Nebr., 1975. Lic. real estate broker, Fla. Asst. to v.p. constrn. cen. adminstrn. U. Nebr., Lincoln, 1975-76; architect Consol. Architects Engrs., Omaha, 1976-77; archtl. project mgr. Dana, Larson, Roubal Architects, Phoenix, 1977-79; mktg. dir. Dick, Fritsche Architects, Phoenix, 1979-81; mktg. mgr. Lendrum Design Group, Phoenix, San Diego, 1982-85; owner Developers Mgmt. Group, Phoenix, 1985-86; contracts mgr. Turner Constrn., Phoenix, 1986-87; v.p. devel. The Bay Plaza Co., St. Petersburg, Fla., 1987-96; COO Internat. Care, St. Petersburg, 1996—; bd. dirs. Cen. Ariz. Health Systems Agy. Commr. Housing Commn., City of Phoenix; mem. Paradise Valley Planning Com.; pres. The Mariners for Senator John McCain, Ariz.; surrogate spkr. for Congressman Eldon Rudd; mem. Senate roundtable Senator Connie Mack, Fla.; bd. dirs. Am. Stage Theater; campus adv. bd. U. South Fla., St. Petersburg, chmn. facilities and strategic planning com.; bd. dirs. Pinellas Econ. Devel. Coun.; chmn. Environ. Com., Transp. Com.; bd. dirs. St. Petersburg C. of C.; mem. environ. adv. com. S.W. Fla. Water Mgmt. Dist.; mem. Pinellas adv. bd. ARC. Mem. Fla. Gulfcoast Comml. Assn. Realtors, Leadership Tampa Bay, Urban Land Inst., Valley Leadership (Phoenix). Republican. Avocations: gourmet cooking, body building, geo-political books.

VAN CAMP, BRIAN RALPH, lawyer; b. Halstead, Kans., Aug. 23, 1940; s. Ralph A. and Mary Margaret (Bragg) Van C.; m. Diane D. Miller, 1992; children: Megan M., Laurie E. AB, U. Calif., Berkeley, 1962, LLB, 1965. Bar: Calif. 1966. Dep. atty. gen. State Calif., 1965-67; agy. atty. Redevel. Agy., City of Sacramento, 1967-70; asst./acting sec. Bus. and Transp. Agy., State Calif., 1970-71; commr. of corps. State of Calif., Sacramento, 1971-74; partner firm Diepenbrock, Wulff, Plant & Hannegan, Sacramento, 1975-77, Van Camp & Johnson, Sacramento, 1978-90; sr. ptnr. Downey, Brand, Seymour & Rohwer, 1990—; lectr. Continuing Edn. Bar, Practicing Law Inst., Calif. CPA Soc., others; mem. adv. bd. UCLA Securities Law Inst., 1978. Contbr. articles to profl. jours. Mem. Rep. State Ctrl. Com. Calif., 1974-78; pres. Sacramento Area Commerce and Trade Orgn., 1986-87; mem. electoral coll. Presdl. Elector for State of Calif., 1976; mem. Calif. Health Facilities Fin. Authority, 1985-89; mem. Capital Area Devel. Authority, 1989—, chmn., 1990—; bd. dirs. Sacramento Symphony Assn., 1973-85, 92-94, Sacramento Symphony Found., 1993—, Rep. Assocs. Sacramento County, 1975-79, Sacramento Valley Venture Capital Forum, 1986-90, League to Save Lake Tahoe, 1988-95, Valley Vision, Inc., 1993—; elder Fremont Presbyn. Ch., 1967—. Recipient Sumner-Mering Meml. award Sacramento U. of Calif. Alumni Assn., 1962, Thos. Jefferson award Am. Inst. Pub. Svc., 1994; Paul Harris fellow, 1995; named Outstanding Young Man of Yr., Sacramento Jaycees, 1970, Internat. Young Man of Yr., Active 20-30 Club Internat., 1973. Mem. ABA, Calif. State Bar (mem.com. on corps. 1977-80, partnerships and unincorporated bus. assns. 1983-87), Sacramento County Bar Assn., Calif. C. of C. (chmn. statewide energy task force 1979-85, bd. dirs. 1982—, chmn. edn. com. 1988-90), Sacramento Met. C. of C. (co-chmn. econ. devel. com. 1979, bd. dirs. 1986-88), Boalt Hall Alumni Assn. (bd. dirs. 1991-94), Lincoln Club Sacramento Valley (bd. dirs., pres. 1984-86), U. Calif. Men's Club (pres. 1968), Sutter Club, Kanadhar Ski Club, Rotary Club Sacramento (pres. 1993-94, Paul Harris Fellow award 1995). Republican. Presbyterian. Office: 555 Capitol Mall 10th Fl Sacramento CA 95814

VAN CAMPEN, DARRELL ROBERT, chemist; b. Two Buttes, Colo., July 15, 1935; s. Robert Lewis and Pauline (Comer) Van C.; m. Orlene Crone, Sept. 8, 1958 (div. 1976); children: Anthony, Bryan; m. Judith Ann Gorsky, June 27, 1978; 1 child, John. BS, Colo. State U., 1957; MS, N.C. State U., 1960, PhD, 1962. Postdoctoral fellow Cornell U., Ithaca, N.Y., 1962-63; rsch. chemist USDA ARS, Ithaca, 1964-80, lab. dir., 1980—. Contbr. articles and revs. to profl. jours. and chpts. to books. NIH fellow, 1962. Mem. Sigma Xi, Alpha Zeta, Phi Kappa Phi. Avocations: golf, gardening, numismatics. Home: 117 Simsbury Dr Ithaca NY 14850-1728 Office: USDA ARS Plant Soil & Nutrition Lab Tower Road Ithaca NY 14853

VAN CASPEL, VENITA WALKER, retired financial planner; b. Sweetwater, Okla.; d. Leonard Rankin and Ella Belle (Jarnagin) Walker; m. Lyttleton T. Harris IV, Dec. 26, 1987. Student, Duke, 1944-46; B.A., U. Colo., 1948, postgrad., 1949-51; postgrad., N.Y. Inst. Fin., 1962. CFP. Stockbroker Rauscher Pierce & Co., Houston, 1962-65, A.G. Edwards & Sons, Houston, 1965-68; founder, pres., owner Van Caspel & Co., Inc., Houston, 1968—, Van Caspel Wealth Mgmt.; owner, mgr. Van Caspel Planning Service, Van Caspel Advt. Agy.; sr. v.p. investments Raymond James and Assocs., 1987-95; ret., 1995; owner Diamond V Ranch; moderator PBS TV show The Money Makers and Profiles of Success, 1980; 1st women mem. Pacific Stock Exchange. Author: Money Dynamics, 1978, Money Dynamics of the 1980's, 1980, The Power of Money Dynamics, Money Dynamics for the 1990's, 1988; editor: Money Dynamics Letter. Bd. dirs. Horatio Alger Assn., Robert Schuller Ministries. Recipient Matrix award Theta Sigma Phi, 1969, Horatio Alger award for Disting. Americans, 1982, Disting. Woman's medal, Northwood Univ., 1988, Georgia Norlin award U. Colo. Alumni Assn., 1987. Mem. Internat. Assn. Fin. Planners, Inst. Cert. Fin. Planners, Phi Gamma Mu, Phi Beta Kappa. Methodist. Home: 4 Saddlewood Estates Dr Houston TX 77024 Office: 6524 San Felipe Rd Ste 102 Houston TX 77057

VANCE, ANDREW PETER, lawyer; b. Detroit, Jan. 23, 1925; s. Peter Andrew and Anna (Maktos) V.; m. Olvia Cambourelis, Nov. 23, 1952; children: Peter, Cathy, Penny, Dorothy. BA, Harvard Coll., 1948; LLB, Harvard Law Sch., 1952. Trial atty. U.S. Dept. Justice, Washington, 1953-62; chief customs sect. U.S. Dept. Justice, N.Y.C., 1962-76; sr. ptnr. Barnes, Richardson & Colburn, N.Y.C., 1976-93, of counsel, 1994—; mem. adv. com. U.S. Ct. Appeals (fed. cir.), Washington, 1983—, chmn., 1992—; mem. adv. com. Ct. Internat. Trade, N.Y.C., 1987-93. Contbr. articles to profl. jours. Trustee Greenwood Union Cemetary, Rye, N.Y., 1984—, St. Photios Found., St. Augustine, Fla., 1990—, Juanita Coll., Huntingdon, Pa., 1990—. Recipient St. Paul's medal Greek Orthodox Archdiocese N. Am. and S. Am., 1976. Mem. ABA (chmn. Standing Com. on Customs Law 1991-93), Customs and Internat. Trade Bar Assn. (pres. 1990-92), Fed. Cir. Bar Assn. (pres. 1989-90), Order of St. Andrew. Greek Orthodox. Office: Barnes Richardson & Colburn 475 Park Ave S New York NY 10016-6901

VANCE, BERNARD WAYNE, lawyer, government official; b. Meridian, Miss., May 31, 1947; s. Jack Bernard and Marjorie Opal (Ezell) V. BBA, U. Miss., 1969, JD, 1975. Bar: Miss. 1975, D.C. 1975. Trial atty. admiralty sect. Dept. Justice, Washington, 1975-77, dep. asst. atty. gen., 1982-85; chief of staff Sec. Transp., Washington, 1985-87; general counsel Dept. of Transp., Washington, 1987-89; atty. pvt. practice Washington, 1989—. Editor-in-chief Miss. Law Jour., 1975, articles editor, 1974. Lt. USN, 1969-72. Mem. ABA, D.C. Bar Assn., Phi Delta Phi, Phi Delta Theta, Phi Kappa Phi, Omicron Delta Kappa. Republican. Episcopalian. Office: 1203 Essex Manor Ct Alexandria VA 22308-1000

VANCE, CAROL STONER, lawyer; b. Beaumont, Tex., July 26, 1933; s. Carol Stoner and Fanelle (Philp) V.; m. Carolyn Ruth Kongabel, Dec. 6, 1954; children: Lynnell, Carroll III, Karen, Harold, Cheryl. BBA, U. Tex., 1955, LLB, 1958. Bar: Tex. 1957, U.S. Dist. Ct. (so. dist.) Tex. 1960, U.S. Dist. Ct. (no. dist.) Tex. 1964, U.S. Ct. Appeals (5th cir.) 1964, U.S. Supreme Ct. 1964. Asst. dist. atty. Harris County Dist. Atty.'s Office, Houston, 1958-66, dist. atty., 1966-79; sr. ptnr. Bracewell & Patterson, Houston, 1979—; adj. prof. law U. Houston Sch. Law, 1972-79; chmn. Tex. Dept. Criminal Justice, 1992-95. Recipient Outstanding Young Man of Houston award Houston Jr. C. of C., 1967. Mem. ABA (spl. com. on criminal justice standards 1975-77, coun. sect. criminal justice 1972-79), Am. Coll. Trial Lawyers, Tex. Bar Assn. (chmn. criminal law sect. 1969-70), Houston Bar Assn. (appellate judiciary com.), Houston Bar Found., Nat. Coll. Dist. Attys. (bd. regents), Tex. Bar Found. (life), Tex. Assn. Def. Counsel, Tex. Young Lawyers Assn. (bd. dirs. 1963-66, Outstanding Young Lawyer of Tex. award 1970), Tex. Dist. Atty.'s Assn. (pres. 1969-70), Nat. Dist. Atty.'s Assn. (pres. 1972-73, Outstanding Dist. Atty. award 1972), Houston Young Lawyers' Assn. (pres. 1964), Nat. Coll. Dist. Attys. (chmn. bd. regents 1979-80, mem. bd. 1973—), Houston C. of C. (crime control com., chmn. legis. com.), Phi Alpha Delta. Avocations: tennis, golf. Office: Bracewell & Patterson South Tower Pennzoil Pl 711 Louisiana St Ste 2900 Houston TX 77002-2721

VANCE, CHARLES FOGLE, JR., lawyer; b. Winston-Salem, N.C., Oct. 4, 1924; s. Charles Fogle and Margaret (Vaughn) V.; m. Eleanor James, May 10, 1952; children: Lucy, Charles, Burton, Margaret. BA in Physics, U. N.C., 1946, JD, 1949. Bar: N.C. 1949, U.S. Dist. Ct. (mid. dist.) N.C. 1949, U.S. Ct. Appeals (4th cir.) 1949. Pvt. practice Winston-Salem, 1949-52; assoc. Womble Carlyle Sandridge & Rice, Winston-Salem, 1952-57, ptnr., 1957—; asst. solicitor Mcpl. Ct. Winston-Salem, 1951-52. Trustee Moravian Coll., Bethlehem, Pa., 1953-59, Salem Coll., Winston-Salem, 1974-80, chmn., 1977-80. With U.S. Army, 1944-45. Recipient Whitney North Seymour medal Am. Arbitration Assn., 1984. Fellow Am. Coll. Trial Lawyers; mem. ABA, Am. Bar Found., Am. Judiacture Soc., nat. Assn. R.R. Trial Counsel, N.C. Bar Assn., N.C. State Bar Coun. (councilor 1986-95), Forsyth County Bar Assn. (pres. 1966), 4th Cir. Jud. Conf. Democrat. Avocations: coastal fishing, piano. Office: Womble Carlyle Sandridge & Rice So Nat Fin Ctr PO Box 84 200 W 2d St Winston Salem NC 27102-0084

VANCE, CYNTHIA LYNN, psychology educator; b. Norwalk, Calif., Mar. 31, 1960; d. Dennis Keith and Donna Kay (Harryman) V. BS, U. Oreg., 1982; MS, U. Wis., Milw., 1987, PhD, 1991. Teaching asst. U. Wis., Milw., 1983-89; computer graphics mgr. Montgomery Media, Inc., Milw., 1987-92; asst. prof. Cardinal Stritch Coll., Milw., 1992-93, Piedmont Coll., Demorest, Ga., 1993—. Contbr. articles to profl. jours. Vol. Dunwoody (Ga.)-DeKalb Kiwanis Club, 1993—. Mem. AAUP, APA, Assn. Women in Psychology, S.E. Psychol. Assn., Am. Psychol. Soc., Am. Assn. Higher Edn. Office: Piedmont Coll PO Box 10 Demorest GA 30535-0010

VANCE, CYRUS ROBERTS, lawyer, former government official; b. Clarksburg, W.Va., Mar. 27, 1917; s. John Carl and Amy (Roberts) V.; m. Grace Elsie Sloane, Feb. 15, 1947; children: Elsie Nicoll, Amy Sloane, Grace, Camilla, Cyrus Roberts. Student, Kent Sch.; B.A., Yale U., 1939, LL.B., 1942, LL.D. (hon.), 1968; LL.D. (hon.), Marshall U., 1963, Trinity Coll., 1968, W.Va. U., 1969, Bowling Green U., 1969, Salem Coll., 1970, Brandeis U., 1971, Amherst Coll., 1974, W.Va. Wesleyan U., 1974, Harvard U., 1981, Colgate U., 1981, Gen. Theol. Sem., 1981, Williams Coll., 1981, Notre Dame U., 1982, Mt. Holyoke Coll., 1982, Brown U., Davidson Coll., U. Haifa, Fairfield U., NYU, Northwestern U. Bar: N.Y. State 1947, U.S. Supreme Ct. 1970. Asst. to pres. Mead Corp., 1946-47; assoc. Simpson Thacher & Bartlett, N.Y.C., 1947-56; ptnr. Simpson Thacher & Bartlett, 1956-61, 67-77, 80—; spl. counsel preparedness investigating subcom. Senate Armed Services Com., 1957-60; gen. counsel Dept. Def., 1961-62; sec. of army, 1962-63, dep. sec. def., 1964-67; spl. rep. of Pres. Johnson in Cyprus crisis, 1967, Korea, 1968; U.S. negotiator Paris Peace Conf. on Vietnam, 1968-69; sec. state, 1977-80, personal envoy UN Sec. Gen. on Yugoslavia crisis, 1991-92, personal envoy UN Sec. Gen. on South Africa and Nagorno-Karabakh, 1992; co-chmn. UN-EC Internat. Conf. on Former Yugoslavia, 1992-93; spl. envoy UN Sec.-Gen. Greece-FYROM Negotiations, 1993—; cons. counsel Spl. Com. on Space and Astronautics, U.S. Senate, 1958; chmn. com. on adjudication of claims Adminstrv. Conf. U.S.; mem. Com. To Investigate Alleged Police Corruption in N.Y.C., 1970-72; chmn. UN Devel. Corp., 1976; mem. Ind. Com. on Disarmament and Security Issues, N.Y. State Commn. on Govt. Integrity, N.Y. State Jud. Commn. on Minorities in the Ct.; bd. dirs. N.Y. Times; bd. dirs. Fed. Res. Bank of N.Y., 1989-93, chmn., 1989-91. Trustee Yale Corp., 1968-78, 80-87; trustee Rockefeller Found., 1970-77, 80-82, chmn., 1975-77; chmn. Am. Ditchley Found., 1981-94. Lt. USNR, 1942-46. Recipient Medal of Freedom, 1969, Grand Cordon of Order of Rising Sun Govt. of Japan, 1990, Legion of Honor French Rep., 1993; apptd. Hon. Knight Comdr. in Civil div. of Most Excellent Order of British Empire, 1994. Fellow Am. Coll. Trial Lawyers; mem. ABA, Assn. of Bar of City of N.Y. (pres. 1974-76), Council on Fgn. Relations (dir., vice chmn. 1985-87), Japan Soc. (chmn. 1985-93). Office: Simpson Thacher & Bartlett 425 Lexington Ave New York NY 10017-3954

VANCE, DENNIS EDWARD, biochemistry educator; b. St. Anthony, Idaho, July 14, 1942; s. Russell Ernest and Josephine (Renner) V.; m. Jean Stuart Eaton, June 10, 1967; children: Russell Eaton, Fiona Natalie. BS, Dickinson Coll., 1964; PhD, U. Pitts., 1968. Postdoctoral fellow U. Pitts., 1968-70; postdoctoral fellow Harvard U., Cambridge, Mass., 1970-72, U. Warwick, Coventry, Eng., 1972-73; asst. prof. biochemistry U. B.C., Vancouver, Can., 1973-77, assoc. prof., 1977-82, prof., 1982-86, assoc. dean medicine, 1978-81, head dept., 1982-86; prof. biochemistry U. Alta., Edmonton, 1986—, dir. Lipid/Lipoprotein Group, 1986—. Author: (with others) Principles of Biochemistry, 1995; editor: Phosphatidylcholine Metabolism, 1989, Biochemistry of Lipids, Lipoproteins and Membranes, 1991, 1996, Phospholipid Biosynthesis, 1992. Grantee Med. Rsch. Coun., 1973—, Heart and Stroke Found. Can., 1974—. Fellow Royal Soc. Can.; mem. Am. Soc. Biochem. and Molecular Biology, Can. Soc. Biochemistry, Molecular and Cellular Biology (Boeringer Mannheim Can. prize 1989), Biochem. Soc. U.K. (Heinrich Wieland prize, Munich, 1995). Avocations: fishing, skiing, golf. Office: Univ Alta Faculty of Medicine, Lipid/Lipoprotein Rsch Group, Edmonton, AB Canada T6G 2S2

VANCE, DON KELVIN, baking industry consultant; b. Detroit, Jan. 3, 1935; s. George Paul and Marie Jo (Nichols) V.; children—James Delano, Sarah Elizabeth, David Paul. B.B.A., U. Mich., 1957, M.B.A., 1958. Various positions ITT Continental Baking Co., 1958-72; v.p. ITT Continental Baking Co., Rye, N.Y., 1972-83; sr. v.p., div. pres. Am. Bakeries Co., N.Y.C., 1983-86; cons. to baking industry; pres., chief oper. officer Country Home Bakers, Bridgeport, Conn., 1991-94; COO Quality Bakers of Am., Greenwich, Conn., 1994—. Served with USAFR, 1958-64. Methodist. Club: Pensacola (Fla.) Country. Avocations: sailing; skiing; golfing. Office: Quality Bakers of Am 70 Riverdale Ave Greenwich CT 06831-5030

VANCE, ELBRIDGE PUTNAM, mathematics educator; b. Cin., Feb. 7, 1915; s. Selby Frame and Jeannie (Putnam) V.; m. Margaret Gertrude Stoffel, Aug. 5, 1939 (div. 1975); children: Susan (Mrs. Timothy Griffin), Peter Selby, Douglas Putnam, Emily (Mrs. Charles Harold Beynon III); m. Jean Haigh, Jan. 1975. Student, Haverford Coll., 1932-33; A.B., Coll. Wooster, 1936; M.A., U. Mich., 1937, Ph.D., 1939. Asst. U. Mich., 1937-39; instr. U. Nev., 1939-41, asst. prof., 1941-43; vis. lectr. Oberlin (Ohio) Coll., 1943-46, asst. prof., 1946-50, asso. prof., 1950-54, prof., 1954-83, prof. emeritus, 1983—, chmn. dept., 1948-77, acting dean Coll. Arts and Scis., 2d semester, 1965-66, 1st semester, 1970-71; chmn. advanced placement com. Coll. Entrance Exam. Bd., 1961-65, chief reader, 1956-61; chmn. com. examiners math. Comprehensive Coll. Tests, Ednl. Testing Service, 1965-67. Author: Trigonometry, 2d edit, 1969, Unified Algebra and Trigonometry, 1955, Fundamentals of Mathematics, 1960, Modern College Algebra, 3d edit, 1973, Modern Algebra and Trigonometry, 3d edit, 1973, An Introduction to Modern Mathematics, 2d edit, 1968, Mathematics 12, 1968, Solution Manual for Mathematics 12, 1968; Book review editor: Am. Math. Monthly, 1949-57; asso. editor, 1964-67. Mem. Oberlin Sch. Bd., 1952-60, pres., 1957-60. NSF Faculty fellow, 1960-61. Mem. Math. Assn. Am., Nat. Council Tchrs. of Math., Am. Math. Soc., Phi Beta Kappa, Sigma Xi, Phi Kappa Phi. Home: 315 Yorktown Pl # 4D Vermilion OH 44089-2104

VANCE, JOAN EMILY JACKSON (MRS. NORVAL E. VANCE), elementary school educator; b. Anderson, Ind., Feb. 25, 1925; d. Virgil S. and Hannah (Hall) Jackson; B.S., Ball State U., 1947, M.A., 1955; m. Norval E. Vance, Aug. 17, 1955; 1 son, Bill E. Tchr. art and phys. edn. Winchester (Ind.) High Sch., 1948-50, 50-52, Wheatfield (Ind.) Elem. Sch., Wheatfield High Sch., 1952-54; tchr. Eaton (Ind.) Elementary Sch. and High Sch., 1954-90; tchr. elem. art, Elwood, Ind., 1954-90, bilingual-bi-cultural migrant sch., summers 1969-90; exhibited in group shows at Erica's Gallery, John Herron. Anderson Fine Art Ctr., state shows, street fairs. Mem. council Hoosier Salon, Indpls. Mus. Art. Recipient First prize Anderson Fine Arts Center show, 1975, 77; vol. Anderson Community Concerts, Anderson Fine Arts Ctr., Historic Home and Gruenwald House living history tours. Mem. NEA, Nat. Art Edn. Assn., Western Art Edn. Assn., Ind Art Edn. Assn. (council), Ind. Art Tchrs. Assn. (mem. council), Anderson Art League (pres. 1967-68, 76—) Anderson Soc. Artists (v.p.), Ind. Weavers Guild, Elwood Art League (pres. 1960-70), Brown County Gallery, Brown County Guild, Ind. Artists and Craftsmen Assn., Anderson Artists Assn. (treas.), Ind. State Tchrs. Assn., Elwood Classroom Tchrs. Assn., Ind. Ret. Tchrs. Assn., Delta Kappa Gamma (v.p.), Delta Theta Tau. Home: 9348 N 625 W Frankton IN 46044-9458 Office: Elwood Community Sch State Rd 13 N Elwood IN 46036

VANCE, RALPH BROOKS, oncologist and educator; b. Jackson, Miss., Dec. 4, 1945; s. Brooks C. and Chrystine G. (Gober) V.; m. Mary Douglas Allen, June 18, 1979; children: Brooks, Barrett. BA in Biology and German, U. Miss., 1968, MD, 1972. Asst. prof. medicine U. Miss., Jackson, 1978-86, assoc. prof. medicine, 1986-93, prof. medicine, 1993—; chief of staff U. Miss. Hosp. and Clinics, Jackson, 1989-90; pres. faculty senate Univ. Med. Ctr., Jackson, 1986-87, univ. clin. assoc., pres., 1987-89. Author (with others) Development in Molecular Virology: Herpes Virus DNA, 1982; contbr. numerous articles and abstracts to profl. jours. Bd dirs. Am. Cancer Soc., Atlanta, nat. bd. dirs., exec. com.; bd. dirs. ARC, Jackson; med. adv. bd. Blue Cross/Blue Shield, Jackson, 1989-92. Named to Hall of Fame, U. Miss., 1968. Mem. Am. Assn. for Cancer Edn., Am. Fedn. for Clin. Rsch., Am. Soc. Clin. Oncology, Am. Assn. for Cancer Rsch., Miss. Acad. Scis., S.W. Oncology Group, Sigma Xi. Episcopalian. Office: Univ of Miss Sch Medicine 2500 N State St Jackson MS 39216-4515

VANCE, ROBERT MERCER, textile manufacturing company executive, banker; b. Clinton, S.C., July 9, 1916; s. Robert Berly and Mary Ellen (Bailey) V.; m. Virginia Sexton Gray, Dec. 27, 1949; children: Mary Bailey Vance Suitt, Robert Mercer, Russell Gray. BSBA, Davidson Coll., 1937; postgrad., Northwestern U., 1942; postgrad. Carolina Bankers Conf., U. N.C., 1948-57; HHD (hon.), Presbyn. Coll., 1968. Trainee Clinton Cotton Mills, summers, 1931-36; paymaster Lydia Cotton Mills, Clinton, 1937-41; dir., asst. treas. Clinton Cotton Mills Inc. and Lydia Cotton Mills, 1948-53, v.p., 1953-58, pres., treas., 1958-75; pres., treas. Clinton Mills, Inc. (now known as CMI, Industries, Inc.), 1975; chmn. bd. Clinton Mills, Inc. (merger Clinton Cotton Mills and Lydia Cotton Mills), 1975-86, chmn. emeritus, 1986—; with M.S. Bailey & Son, Bankers, Clinton, S.C., 1946—; pres. M.S. Bailey & Son, Bankers, Clinton, 1948, chmn. bd., 1975—; dir. Clinton Mills Sales Corp., N.Y.C., 1948, v.p., asst. treas., 1953, treas., 1958-86; bd. dirs. Palmetto Expo. Ctr., Greenville, S.C.; trustee J.E. Sirrine Textile Found., Inst. Textile Tech., 1959-93, mem., advisor nat. Cotton Coun., 1970—; mem. N.Y. Cotton Exch., 1965—. Mem. orgn. com., dir., treas Community Chest Greater Clinton, 1952-55, pres., 1958; former mem. nom. com. for S.C. Carolinas United Community Svcs.; trustee exec. com. Edn. Resources Found., 1965; sec. bd. trustees Thornwell Orphanage, Clinton, 1959-67; mem. state adv. com. Commn. on Higher Edn., Clinton, 1965-67; mem. S.C. Commn. on Higher Edn., 1967-71, chmn., 1968-71; trustee S.C. Found. Ind. Colls.; trustee Presbyn. Coll., Clinton, 1953-76, chmn., 56-67, 73-93; bd. visitors Davidson (N.C.) Coll., 1959-62, 77—; mem. S.C. Water Resources Commn., 1981-83; deacon, elder First Presbyn. Ch., Clinton, 1950—, treas., 1950-58, past pres. Men's Sunday Sch. Class, other coms. With U.S. Army, 1941; lt. USN, 1942-46; lt. comdr. USNR, 1946-54. Decorated 17 battle stars; Named Clinton Man of Yr. Lions Club, 1955, Textile Man of Yr. N.Y. Bd. Trade, 1978. Mem. S.C. Bankers Assn. (v.p. 1953-55, pres. 1963-64), S.C. Textile Mfrs. Assn. (dir., v.p. 1966-67, pres. 1967-68), S.C. C. of C. (dir. 1959-60), Laurens County C. of C. (dir. 1982-86), Am. Legion, Poinsett Club (Greenville, S.C.), Lakeside Club (Clinton), Litchfield Club (Pawleys Island, S.C.), Musgrove Mill Golf Club, Moose. Masons, Kiwanis (former dir., pres. 1955), Shriners, Kappa Alpha. Presbyterian. Home: 311 S Broad St Clinton SC 29325-2506 Office: MS Bailey & Son Bankers 211 N Broad St Clinton SC 29325-2303 also: Clinton Mills Inc 600 Academy St Clinton SC 29325

VANCE, ROBERT PATRICK, lawyer; b. Birmingham, Ala., Feb. 12, 1948; s. James Robert and Lucy Juanita (McMath) V.; m. Sarah Elizabeth Savoia, June 11, 1971; 1 son, Robert Patrick, Jr. B.A. with honors, La. State U., 1970, J.D., 1975. Bar: La. 1975, U.S. Dist. Ct. (ea. dist.) La. 1975, U.S. Dist. Ct. (mid. dist.) La. 1978, U.S. Dist. Ct. (we. dist.) La. 1979, U.S. Ct. Appeals (5th cir.) 1975, U.S. Ct. Appeals (11th cir.) 1981, U.S. Supreme Ct. 1981. Assoc. Jones, Walker, Waechter, Poitevent, Carrere & Denegre, New Orleans, 1975-80, ptnr., 1980—, exec. com. 1991-95, mng. ptnr., 1994-95. Contbr. La. Law Rev.; author, editor: Bankruptcy Rules: Parts I, II, VII, VIII and IX, 1983; Overview of the Bankruptcy Code and the Court, 1983. Co-author: Bankruptcy-Current Developments, 1983, Current Developments in Commercial Law, 1984, Basic Bankruptcy of Louisiana, 1989, Fundamentals of Bankruptcy Law & Procedure in La., 1993; contbr. articles to profl. jours. Fellow Am. Coll. Bankruptcy, Nat. Bankruptcy Conf.; mem. ABA (chair bankruptcy litigation com.), Am. Law Inst., Am. Bankruptcy Inst., Fed. Bar Assn. (mem. bankruptcy law com., polit. campaign and election law com., editorial bd. Bankruptcy Briefs), La. State Bar Assn. (pres. consumer and bankruptcy law sect., chmn. CLE com.), New Orleans Bar Assn., La. Bankers Assn. (chmn. bank counsel com. 1992-93), Pi Sigma Alpha, Phi Beta Kappa (Faculty Group award), Phi Kappa Phi. Democrat. Roman Catholic. Home: 1821 State St New Orleans LA 70118-6219 Office: Jones Walker Waechter Poitevent Carrere & Denegre 201 Saint Charles Ave New Orleans LA 70170-1000

VANCE, SARAH S., federal judge; b. 1950. BA, La. State Univ., 1971; JD, Tulane Univ., 1978. With Stone, Pigman, Walther, Wittmann & Hutchinson, New Orleans, 1978-94; dist. judge U.S. Dist. Ct. (La. ea. dist.), 5th cir., New Orleans, 1994—. Recipient Phi Beta Kappa Faculty Group award. Mem. ABA, Am. Law Inst., Fed. Judges Assn., Nat. Assn. Women Judges, La. State Bar Assn., Fed. Bar Assn., New Orleans Bar Assn., Bar Assn. of the Fed. Fifth Circuit, Order of Coif. Address: US Courthouse 500 Camp St Rm C-255 New Orleans LA 70130-3313

VANCE, STANLEY CHARLES, management educator; b. Minersville, Pa., May 5, 1915; s. Stanley and Margaret (Zelin) V.; m. Regina Dober, Mar. 4, 1946. A.B., St. Charles Sem., 1937; M.A., U. Pa., 1944, Ph.D., 1951. Instr. U. Pa., 1945-47; asst. prof. U. Conn., 1947-52; prof. U. Mass., 1952-56; dean Coll. Bus. Adminstrn., Kent State U., 1956-60; H.T. Miner prof. bus. adminstrn. U. Oreg., Eugene, 1960-75; head dept. personnel and indsl. mgmt. U. Oreg., 1963-71; also acting dean Coll. Bus. Adminstrn.; William B. Stokely prof. mgmt. U. Tenn., Knoxville, 1975—; Mem. nat. council Nat. Planning Assn.; bd. dirs., pres. Inst. Adminstrv. Research. Author: American Industries, 1955, Industrial Administration, 1959, Management Decision Simulation, 1960, Industrial Structure and Policy, 1961, Quantitative Techniques for Operations Management, 1962, Board of Directors Structure and Performance, 1964, The Corporate Director, 1968, Managers and Mergers, 1971, Corporate Leadership: Boards, Directors and Strategy, 1983; Editor book revs.; scanning editor: Dirs. and Bds. Fellow Nat. Acad. Mgmt. (dean of fellows, pres. Western div., editor Jour. 1966-70, newsletter, 1971—, pres. 1975—), Internat. Acad. Mgmt. (vice chancellor); mem. AIM, C. of C., Am. Soc. Personnel Adminstrn., N.Am. Simulation and Gaming Assn. (dir.), Assn. Bus. Simulation and Exptl. Learning (pres.), N.Am. Simulation and Gaming Assn. (gov.), Dirs. Coun. Corp. Bds., Nat. Assn. Corp. Dirs., N.Am. Mgmt. Coun. (pres.), Rotary. Home: 1701 Cherokee Blvd Knoxville TN 37919-8335

VANCE, TAMMY RENA, special education educator; b. Ogden, Utah, July 1, 1966; d. James Carl Andre and Virginia Nell (Betts) Camp; m. Steven Allen Vance Sr., June 24, 1983; children: Steven Allen Jr., Jennifer Lauren. AAS, East Ark. C.C., 1986; BS in Edn., Ark. State U., Jonesboro, 1988, postgrad., 1989. Cert. tchr. early childhood and elem. sch. tchr., cert. tchr. mid. sch. English, Ark. Tchr. 1st grade Lee Acad., Marianna, Ark., 1988-89, Wheatly (Ark.) Elem. Sch., 1989-90; substitute tchr. Wynne (Ark.) Pub. Schs., 1990-91, paraprofl. 1st grade, 1991-93; substitute tchr. Wynne Intermediate Sch., 1993, spl. edn. tchr. 3rd grade, 1994—; dir. day care facility Tiny Town, Wynne, 1990. Active Christian Coalition, 1992—; treas. Women's Missionary Union; tchr., pianist, children's dir. East Bapt. Ch., 1987—. Mem. Gamma Beta Phi. Republican. Avocations: church activities, playing piano, song writing, camping, activities with family and friends. Home: 702 N Terry St Wynne AR 72396-2244 Office: Wynne Intermediate Sch Bridges St Wynne AR 72396

VANCE, THOMAS CARTER, historic site director; b. Danville, Ill., Oct. 19, 1946; s. John DeWitt and Maxine Margaret (Sherman) V.; m. Susan Ellen Addams Vance, Feb. 25, 1972; 1 child, Erin Katherine. BS in Wildlife Biology, U. Ill., 1969, MS in Entomology, 1971; MA in Historical Administrn., Ea. Ill. U., 1979. Rsch. asst. Ill. Natural History Survey, Urbana, Ill., 1969-71; naturalist Kickapoo State Park, Oakwood, Ill., 1971-73, park ranger, 1973-74; historic site mgr. Lincoln Log Cabin State Hist., Lerna, Ill., 1974—. Author: (rsch. perdiodical) Ill. Nat. History Survey Bulletin, 1974; editor: (mag.) Midwest Open Air Mus. Mag., 1986-91. mem. bd. dirs. Charleston Tourism Com., 1989—; mem. adv. bd. Coles Together Econ. Devel. Corp. Coles Co., 1991—. Recipient GOS Grant award Inst. Mus. Svcs., 1983, 85; MAP Grant award Am. Assn. Mus., 1988. Mem. Midwest Open Air Mus. (past pres. 1982-83), Assn. Living Hist. Farms (mem. bd. dirs. 1984-87), Charleston Rotary Club. Mem. The Universal Ch. Avocations: guitar, banjo, American Indian, personal development, firewalking. Home and Office: Lincoln Log Cabin State Hist Site RR 1 Box 172A Lerna IL 62440-9757

VANCE, THOMAS RAY, engineer; b. Charleston, W.Va., Sept. 24, 1938; s. Bethel Raymond and Madolyn Elizabeth (Fisher) V.; m. Janice Lee Jordan, Dec. 23, 1958; children: Barbara Vance, Jeffrey Ross, Deborah. BSME, W.Va. U., 1960, MSTAM, 1966, PhD, 1968. Registered profl. engr., W.Va., Ohio. Devel. engr. The Babcock and Wilcox Co., Alliance, Ohio, 1960-63; staff engr. Los Alamos (N.Mex.) Scientific Lab., 1964-66; program mgr. Tech. divsn. IBM Corp., Hopewell Junction, N.Y., 1968-92; dir. W.Va. State Farm Mus., Point Pleasant, W.Va., 1994—; prin. Vance & Assocs., Point Pleasant, 1992—; instr. coll. engring. W.Va. U., Morgantown, 1966-68; instr. evening dirsn. Dutchess C.C., Poughkeepsie, N.Y., 1962-68; chmn. adv. com. Dept. Engring. Ohio State U., 1988-91; mem. Stevens Inst. of Tech., Alliance for Tech. Mgmt., Hoboken, N.J.. Contbr. articles to profl. jours. Vice chmn. Point Pleasant River Mus. Com., 1993-94; mem. Point Pleasant Hist. Dist. Com., 1993-94. Scholarship NASA. Mem. W.Va. Assn. of Profl. Engrs., Nat. Assn. of Profl. Engrs. Republican. Lutheran. Achievements include patent in repair of thin film lines. Home: 4 Main St Point Pleasant WV 25550-1026 Office: Vance and Assocs 329 Main St Point Pleasant WV 25550

VANCE, VERNE WIDNEY, JR., lawyer; b. Omaha, Mar. 10, 1932; s. Verne Widney and June Caroline (Henckler) V.; m. Anita Paine, June 27, 1970; children: Lisa Joy, Charles Hebard Paine, Virginia Caroline. A.B., Harvard U., 1954, J.D., 1957. Bar: D.C. 1957, Mass. 1964. Law clk. U.S. Dist. Judge, Mass., 1957-58; assoc. Covington & Burling, Washington, 1958-60; atty. adv. Devel. Loan Fund, Washington, 1960-61; legal counsel AID, Washington, 1961-63; assoc. Foley, Hoag & Eliot, Boston, 1963-67, ptnr., 1967—; lectr. law Boston U., 1964-66; corp. clk. S.S. Pierce Co., 1971-72. Pres. UN Assn. Greater Boston, 1964-66, 77-78, treas., 1974-77; mem. Mass. Adv. Council on Edn., 1969-75, chmn., 1975; mem. Democratic City Com., Newton, Mass., 1972—, Gov.'s Local Govt. Adv. Commn., 1986-90; alderman City of Newton, 1982-91; pres. Newton Bd. of Aldermen, 1988-91; mem. Newton Sch. Com., 1994—; trustee Judge Baker Children's Ctr., 1994—; trustee Mass. Bay Community Coll., 1987—, vice chmn., 1989-91, chmn. 1991—. Mem. Boston Bar Assn. (bd. of editors bar jour. 1986-90) bd. dir. Boston Archtl. Ctr., 1991-92. Unitarian. Club: Longwood Cricket (Chestnut Hill, Mass.). Editor Harvard Law Rev., 1955-57; bd. editors Boston Bar Jour., 1986-90; contbr. articles to profl. jours. Home: 101 Old Orchard Rd Chestnut Hill MA 02167-1202 Office: Foley Hoag & Eliot 1 Post Office Sq Boston MA 02109-2103

VANCE, ZINNA BARTH, artist, writer; b. Phila., Sept. 28, 1917; d. Carl Paul Rudolph Barth and Dorothy Ellice (Wilson) Hart; m. Nathan E. Curry (div. 1959); m. Samuel Therrel Vance, Dec. 2, 1960; children: Barry, Scott Hart. BS in Edn. summa cum laude, Southwestern U., Georgetown, Tex., 1965; MA in Communications, U. Tex., 1969. Cert. in teaching langs., Tex. Freelance writer various publs., 1946-56; assoc. editor, newspaper Canacao Clipper, Philippines, 1956-58; dir. Region One Tex. Fine Arts Assn., Austin, 1962-63; curricular cons. U. Tex. Curricular Conf., 1966; sec. Tex. Fgn. Langs. Assn., 1967; publicity dir. Burnet (Tex.) Creative Arts, 1983—; freelance portrait artist, Liberty Hill, Tex.; owner Gallery Zinna Portrait Studio, Liberty Hill, Tex., 1978—; artist registry Hill Country Arts Found., Ingram, Tex., 1984—; art columnist two newspapers Burnet, 1983—. Contbr. numerous articles to profl. jours.; exhibited in pvt. and corp. collections; illustrator children's books; numerous one-woman shows. Active Hill Country Arts Found., 1978—, Burnet Creative Arts, 1980—, Hill Country Council of Arts, 1986—. Named one of Tex. Emerging Artists, Hill Country Arts Found., 1985; featured as Cover Story Philippines Internat. mag., 1957, featured in book Artists of Texas, 1989, 94. Mem. Nat. Mus. Women in Arts (charter mem.), Nat. Portrait Inst., Alpha Chi, Phi Kappa Phi. Republican. Episcopalian. Avocations: ranching, figure skating, Chinese brush painting. Home: 937CR323 Liberty Hill TX 78642-9501

VANCE SIEBRASSE, KATHY ANN, newspaper publishing executive; b. Kansas City, Kans., Oct. 28, 1954; d. Donald Herbert Vance and Barbara June (Boris) Vance-Young; m. Charles Richard Siebrasse, Mar. 8, 1980; 1 stepson, Michael; 1 child, Bradley. BS in Journalism, No. Ill. U., 1976. Reporter Des Plaines (Ill.) Suburban Times and Park Ridge Herald, 1974-75, DeKalb (Ill.) Daily Chronicle, 1976-78; stringer Rockford (Ill.) Register Star, 1978; editor The MidWeek Newspaper, DeKalb, 1978-81, owner and pub., 1982—. Active No. Ill. U. Found., 1992—, mem. exec. bd., 1994—, chair bus. and industry for No. Ill. U. campaign, 1993-94; pres. DeKalb Athletic Barb Boosters, 1995—; chair Kishwaukee Hosp. Health Coun., 1984-92, DeKalb County Partnership for a Substance Abuse Free Environment, 1990—; bd. dirs. DeKalb Edn. Found., sec., 1987-89, pres., 1989-93, active, 1987-94; sponsor Big Bros./Big Sisters Bowl-a-Thon. Recipient Comty. Svc. award Nat. Assn. of Advt. Pubs., 1980, Athena award Oldsmobile, DeKalb C. of C., 1990, Bus. of Yr., 1994. Mem. Ill. Press Assn., No. Ill. Newspaper Assn., Ind. Free Papers Am. (Cmty. Svc. award 1992-93), Free Papers Am., DeKalb County Farm Bur., DeKalb and Sycamore C. of C. (editor Sycamore newsletter 1994-96, mem. DeKalb Athena award com., bd. dirs., v.p. DeKalb 1996). Avocations: photography, reading, swimming, skiing, sailing. Office: The MidWeek Newspaper 121 Industrial Dr De Kalb IL 60115-3931

VAN CITTERS, ROBERT LEE, medical educator, physician; b. Alton, Iowa, Jan. 20, 1926; s. Charles and Wilhemina (Heemstra) Van C.; m. Mary E. Barker, Apr. 9, 1949; children: Robert, Mary, David, Sara. A.B., U. Kans., 1949; M.D., U. Kans. Med. Ctr., Kansas City, 1953; Sc.D. hon., Northwestern Coll., Orange City, Iowa, 1977. Intern U. Kans. Med. Ctr., Kansas City, 1953-54, resident, 1955-57, fellow, 1957-58; research fellow Sch. Medicine, U. Wash., Seattle, 1958-61, asst. prof. physiology and biophysics, 1962-65, assoc. prof, 1965-70, prof., 1970—; prof. medicine Sch. Medicine, U. Wash., 1970—, assoc. dean Sch. Medicine, 1968-70, dean Sch. Medicine, 1970-81; mem. staff Scripps Clinic and Research Found., La Jolla, Calif., 1961-62; exchange scientist joint U.S.-U.S.S.R. Sci. Exchange, 1962; mem. Liason Commn. on Med. Edn., Washington, 1981-85; mem. various coms., nat. adv. research council NIH, Bethesda, Md., 1980-83; mem. Va. Spl. Med. Adv. Commn., 1974-78, chmn., 1976-78; chmn. working group on mech. circulatory support systems Nat. Heart, Lung and Blood Inst. NIH, 1985—, mem. adv. coun. clin. applications and prevention, 1985-89. Contbr. numerous articles to profl. jours. Served to 1st lt. U.S. Army, 1943-46, PTO; to capt. M.C., USAF, 1953-55. Recipient research career devel. USPHS. Fellow AAAS; mem. Assn. Am. Med. Colls. (adminstrv. bd. and exec. council 1972-78, Disting. Service mem.), Am. Coll. Cardiology (Cummings medal 1970), Nat. Acad. Sci. Inst. Medicine, Am. Heart Assn., Wash. State Med. Assn. (hon. life). Office: U Wash Sch Medicine Seattle WA 98195

VAN CLEAVE, WILLIAM ROBERT, international relations educator; b. Kansas City, Mo., Aug. 27, 1935; s. Earl Jr. and Georgiana (Offutt) Van C.; children: William Robert II, Cynthia Kay. B.A. in Polit. Sci. summa cum laude, Calif. State U., Long Beach, 1962; M.A. in Govt. and Internat. Relations, Claremont (Calif.) Grad. Sch., 1964, Ph.D., 1966. Mem. faculty U. So. Calif., 1967-87, prof. internat. rels., 1974-87, dir. def. and strategic studies ctr., 1971-87; prof., dept. head, dir. Ctr. for Def. and Strategic Studies Southwest Mo. State U., 1987—; sr. rsch. fellow Hoover Instn. Stanford U., 1981—; chmn. Strategic Alternatives Team, 1977-90; acting chmn. Pres.'s Gen. Adv. Com. on Arms Control, 1981-82; spl. asst. Office Sec. Def., mem. Strategic Arms Limitation Talks (SALT) delegation, 1969-71; mem. B team on Nat. Intelligence Estimates, 1976; mem. exec. panel, bd. dirs. Com. Present Danger, 1980-93; dir. transition team Dept. Def., 1980-81; sr. nat. security advisor to Ronald Reagan, 1979-80; mem. nat. security affairs adv. council Republican Nat. Com., 1979—; research council Fgn. Policy Research Inst., Inst. Fgn. Policy Analysis; co-dir. Ann. Internat. Security Summer Seminar, Fed. Republic Germany; trustee Am. com. Internat. Inst. Strategic Studies, 1980—; vis. prof. U.S. Army Advanced Russian Inst., Garmisch, Fed. Republic Germany, 1978-79; chmn. adv. bd. Internat. Security Coun., 1991—; cons. in field, mem. numerous govt. adv. coms. Co-author: Strategic Options for the Early Eighties: What Can Be Done?, 1979, Tactical Nuclear Weapons, 1978, Nuclear Weapons, Policies, and the Test Ban Issue, 1987; author: Fortress USSR, 1986; bd. editors: Global Affairs. Co-chmn. Scholars for Reagan, 1984; mem. exec. coun., dir. for NCAA rels. Haka Bowl, NCAA Postseason Football Bowl. Recipient Freedom Found. award, 1976, Outstanding Contbn. award Air War Coll., 1979, award teaching excellence U. So. Calif., 1980, 86; named Outstanding Prof. U. So. Calif., 1977, Disting. Alumnus Claremont Colls., 1978; Woodrow Wilson fellow, 1962, NDEA fellow, 1963-65. Mem. Internat. Inst. Strategic Studies (U.S. com.). Home: 8226 Panther Hollow Rogersville MO 65742-9126 Office: Ctr for Def and Strategic Studies Southwest Mo State U Springfield MO 65804-0095

VAN CLEVE, JOHN VICKREY, history educator, university official; b. Evanston, Ill., Apr. 8, 1947; s. John William and Mildred Madelane (Vickrey) Van C. Student, U. Ill., 1965-67; BA, Western State Coll. Colo., 1970; MA, PhD, U. Calif., Irvine, 1976. Instr. history Gallaudet U., Washington, 1976-77, asst. to assoc. prof. history, 1977-84, chmn. dept. history, 1983-95, prof. history, 1984—, asst. to v.p. for acad. affairs, 1995—. Author: (with Barry A. Crouch) A Place of Their Own: Creating the Deaf Community in America, 1989; chmn. editorial bd. Gallaudet U. Press, 1985—; editor in chief Gallaudet Encyclopedia of Deaf People and Deafness, 1987 (Pres.' award); editor Deaf History Unveiled: Selections from the new Scholarship, 1993; contbr. articles to profl. jours. Mem. Orgn. Am. Historians, Hist. of Edn. Soc., Conv. Am. Instrs. of Deaf. Office: Gallaudet Univ Dept of History 800 Florida Ave NE Washington DC 20002-3660

VAN CLEVE, RUTH GILL, retired lawyer, government official; b. Mpls., July 28, 1925; d. Raymond S. and Ruth (Sevon) Gill; m. Harry R. Van Cleve, Jr., May 16, 1952; children: John Gill, Elizabeth Webster, David Hamilton Livingston. Student, U. Minn., 1943; A.B. magna cum laude, Mt. Holyoke Coll., 1946, LL.D., 1976; LL.B., Yale, 1950. Bar: D.C. 1950, Minn. 1950. Intern Nat. Inst. Pub. Affairs, 1946-47; atty. Dept. Interior, 1950-54, asst. solicitor, 1954-64; dir. Office Territorial Affairs, 1964-69, 1977-80, dep. asst. sec., 1980-81, acting asst. sec., 1993; atty. Solicitor's Office, 1981-93; atty. FPC, 1969-75, asst. gen. counsel, 1975-77. Author: The Office of Territorial Affairs, 1974, The Application of Federal Laws to the Territories, 1993. Recipient Fed. Woman's award, 1966, Disting. Service award Dept. Interior, 1968, Presdl. Rank award, Pres. U.S., 1989. Mem. Phi Beta Kappa. Unitarian. Home: 4400 Emory St Alexandria VA 22312-1321

VAN CLEVE, WILLIAM MOORE, lawyer; b. Mar. 17, 1929; s. William T Van Cleve and Catherine (Baldwin) Moore Van Cleve; m. Georgia Hess Dunbar, June 27, 1953; children: Peter Dunbar, Robert Baldwin, Sarah Van Cleve Van Doren, Emory Basford. Grad., Phillips Acad., 1946; AB in Econs., Princeton U., 1950; JD, Washington U., St. Louis, 1953. Bar: Mo. 1953. Assoc. Dunbar and Gaddy, St. Louis, 1955-58; ptnr. Bryan Cave (and predecessor firm), St. Louis, 1958—, chmn., 1973-94; bd. dirs. Emerson Electric Co. Trustee Washington U., 1983—, vice chmn. bd. trustees, 1988-93, 95—, chmn., 1993-95, mem. exec. com., 1985—; pres. Eliot Soc., 1982-86; chmn. Law Sch. Nat. Coun., 1986-93; commr. St. Louis Sci. Ctr., 1993—; bd. dirs., v.p. Parents As Tchrs. Nat. Ctr., 1991—. Mem. ABA, Bar Assn. Met. St. Louis, Mound City Bar Assn., St. Louis County Bar Assn., Order of Coif (hon.). Democrat. Episcopalian. Clubs: Princeton (pres. 1974-75), Noonday (pres. 1985), St. Louis Country, Bogey (pres. 1990-91), Round Table (St. Louis). Home: 8 Dromara Rd Saint Louis MO 63124-1816 Office: Bryan Cave 211 N Broadway Fl 36 Saint Louis MO 63102-2733

VANCO, JOHN L., art museum director; b. Erie, Pa., Aug. 21, 1945; s. John Jr. and Alice (Crozier) V.; m. Kathleen Merski, 1971; children: John H., Jesse L. BA, Allegheny Coll., 1967. Dir. Erie (Pa.) Art Mus., 1968—; mem. adv. panels Pa. Coun. on the Arts, Harrisburg, 1974—, Mid Atlantic Arts Found., Balt., 1992. Photographer miscellaneous exhbns.; curator miscellaneous exhbns. including Teco: Art Pottery of the Prairie Sch. in Harmony with the Earth; author: A Roycroft Desktop: Musings on Elbert Hubbard and the Roycroft Shops, 1994. Chief adminstrv. officer Discovery Square, Erie, 1991-92. Office: Erie Art Mus 411 State St Erie PA 16501-1106

VAN CULIN, SAMUEL, religious organization administrator; b. Honolulu, Sept. 30, 1930; s. Samuel and Susie (Mossman) Van C. A.B., Princeton U., 1952; B.D., Va. Theol. Sem., 1955, D.D. (hon.), 1955. Curate St. Andrew's Cathedral, Honolulu, 1955-56; Canon precentor, rector Hawaiian Congregation, Honolulu, 1956-58; asst. rector St. John's Ch., Washington, 1958-60; gen. sec. Lyman Internat., Washington, 1960-61; asst. sec. overseas Exec. Council of Episcopal Ch., N.Y.C., 1962-68, sec. for Africa, Middle East, 1968-76; exec. for world mission Episcopal Ch. U.S.A., N.Y.C., 1976-83; sec. gen. Anglican Consultative Council Eng., London, 1983-95; asst. priest All Hallows Ch., London, 1995—. Named Hon. Canon Canterbury, 1983, Jerusalem, 1983, Ibadan, 1984, Ch. Province of So. Africa, 1989, St. Andrew's Cathedral, Honolulu, 1994. Clubs: Atheneum (London); Princeton (N.Y.). Avocations: Music; travelling. Home: 16a Burgate, Canterbury 2HG, England Office: All Hallows Ch, 43 Trinity Sq, London EC3N 4DJ, England

VAN CURA, JOYCE BENNETT, librarian; b. Madison, Wis., Mar. 25, 1944; d. Ralph Eugene and Florence Marie (Cramer) Bennett; m. E. Jay Van Cura, July 5, 1986. BA in Liberal Arts (scholar), Bradley U., 1966; MLS, U. Ill., 1971. Library asst. rsch. library Caterpillar Tractor Co., Peoria, Ill., 1966-67; reference librarian, instr. library tech. Ill. Central Coll., East Peoria, 1967-73; asst. prof. Sangamon State U. (U. Ill.-Springfield), Springfield, Ill., 1973-80, assoc. prof., 1980-86; head library ref. and info. svcs. dept. Ill. Inst. Tech., 1987-90; dir. Learning Resources Ctr. Morton Coll., 1990—; convenor Coun. II, Ill. Clearinghouse for Acad. Library Instrn., 1978; presentor 7th Ann. Conf. Acad. Library Instrn., 1977, Nat. Women's Studies Assn., 1983, others; participant Gt. Lakes Women's Studies Summer Inst., 1981. Dem. precinct Committeewoman, 1982-85 . Pres., Springfield chpt. NOW, 1978-79. Ill. state scholar, 1962-66; recipient Am. Legion citizenship award, 1962; cert. of recognition Ill. Bicentennial Commn., 1974; invited Susan B. Anthony luncheon, 1978, 79, vice-moderator Fourth Presbyn. Women, 1989-90; elder Riverside (Ill.) Presbyn. Ch., 1992—; mem. adv. bd. Suburban Libr. System, 1992-94, Nat. Commn. Learning Resources; v.p. membership Riverside chpt. Lyric Opera Chgo., 1994-96; active Riverside (Ill.) Arts Ctr. Mem. ALA, Assn. Coll. and Rsch. Librs., Libr. Adminstrn. and Mgmt. Assn. (mem. reference and adult svcs. divsn.), Libr. Info. and Tech. Assn., Nat. Assn. Women in C.C., Ill. Library Assn. (presentor 1984) Ill. Assn. Coll. and Rsch. Libraries (bibliog. instrn. com.), Spl. Libraries Assn., No. Ill. Learning Resources Consortium Bd., Am. Mgmt. Assn., Women in Mgmt., AAUW (chmn. standing com. on women Springfield br., mem. com. on women Ill. state divsn., bd. dirs. Riverside br., 1992-94), Nat. Women's Studies Assn. (presentor 1983, 84, 85), No. Ill. Learning Resources Coop. (del. 1990—), Springfield Art Assn., Nat. Trust Historic Preservation, Women in Mgmt., Beta Phi Mu. Reviewer Library Jour., Am. Reference Books Ann. Contbr. article in field to publ. Home: 181 Scottswood Rd Riverside IL 60546-2221 Office: Morton Coll Learning Resources Ctr 3801 S Central Ave Chicago IL 60650-4306

VANCURA, STEPHEN JOSEPH, radiologist; b. Norton, Kans., June 26, 1951; s. Cyril William J. and Clara Mae (Ruthstrom) V.; BA in Chemistry magna cum laude, Kans. State U., 1972; MD, Kans. U., 1976; m. Lydia Acker, Dec. 10, 1976. Intern in medicine Letterman Army Med. Center, San Francisco, 1976-77, resident in radiology, 1977-80; practice medicine specializing in radiology, 1980—; chief dept. radiology Darnall Army Hosp., Ft. Hood, Tex., 1980-82; pvt. practice diagnostic radiology, 1982—; chief of staff Metroplex Hosp., 1985-86, 88-90. Served to maj. M.C., U.S. Army, 1976-82 Recipient Ollie O. Mustala award in clin. pharmacology Kans. U. Med. Center, 1974; A. Morris Ginsberg award in phys. diagnosis Kans. U. Med. Center, 1975; Resident Tchr. of Yr. award Letterman Army Med. Center, 1979; Staff Tchr. of Yr. award Darnall Army Hosp., 1982. Trembly Meml. scholar, 1972. Diplomate Am. Bd. Radiology. Mem. Am. Coll. Radiology, Radiologic Soc. N. Am., AMA, Tex. Med. Assn., Tex. Radiol. Soc., Ind. Med. Practitioners Assn. Ctrl. Tex. (pres.), Clinical Magnetic Resonance Soc., Sigma Xi, Alpha Chi Sigma, Alpha Omega Alpha. Home: 3302 Walnut Cir Harker Heights TX 76542 Office: Metroplex Hosp Dept Radiology 2201 Clear Creek Rd Killeen TX 76542-4110

VAN DALEN, PIETER ADRIAAN, broadcast equipment executive; b. Sprang-Capelle, Netherlands, Mar. 12, 1942; arrived in Fed. Republic Germany, 1988; s. Rokus and Lucia Elisabeth (Rijkers) van D.; m. Hendrika Geertje Visscher, May 3, 1968; children: Rokus H.J., Karsten E., Elmer C. M Phys. Engring., Tech. U. Eindhoven, Netherlands, 1963; PhD in Tech. Scis., Tech. U. Eindhoven, 1966. Postdoctoral rsch. fellow Faculty Scis., U. Paris, 1966-67; researcher Philips Rsch. Labs., Eindhoven, 1967-72; product mgr. Philips Med. Systems Div., Eindhoven, 1972-73, 75-80; mktg. mgr. Philips Med. Systems, Best, Netherlands, 1980-81; systems cons., med. systems div. N.Am. Philips, N.Y.C., 1981-82; mktg. mgr., med. systems div. N.Am. Philips, Shelton, Conn., 1982-88; dir. S&I div., then mng. dir. I&E div. Philips, Eindhoven, 1982-88; pres., chief exec. officer Broadcast Television Systems GmbH, Darmstadt, Fed. Republic Germany, 1988—; mem. program com. for comml. tng. of univ.-educated engrs., Tech. U. Eindhoven. Mem. Dutch Phys. Soc. Avocations: reading, history, travel, sports, music. Home: Amselweg 18, 6240 Königstein Fed Republic Germany Office: Broadcast Television System 2300 S 2300 W Salt Lake City UT 84119-2048

VAN DAM, HEIMAN, psychoanalyst; b. Leiden, The Netherlands, Feb. 5, 1920; s. Machiel and Rika (Knorringa) van D.; m. Barbara C. Strona, Oct. 6, 1945; children: Machiel, Claire Ilena, Rika Rosemary. AB, U. So. Calif., 1942, MD, 1945. Fellowship child psychiatry Pasadena (Calif.) Child Guidance Clinic, 1950; gen. practice psychiatry and psychoanalysis L.A., 1951—; instr. L.A. Psychoanalytic Inst., 1959—, co-chmn. com. on child psychoanalysis, 1960-67, tng. and supervising psychoanalyst, 1972—; supr. child and adolescent psychoanalysis So. Calif. Psychoanalytic Inst., 1986—; cons. Reiss Davis Child Study Center, 1955-76, Neighborhood Youth Assn., Los Angeles, 1964-69; asso. clin. prof. psychiatry UCLA Sch. Medicine, 1960—, asso. clin. prof. pediatrics, 1980—; vis. supr. child psychoanalysis San Francisco Psychoanalytic Inst., 1969-79, Denver Psycholanalytic Inst., 1972-74; mem. adv. bd. Western State U. Coll. Law, Fullerton, Calif., 1965-83. Corr. editor Arbeits Hefte Kinderanalyse, 1985—; contbr. articles to profl. jours. Trustee, mem. edn. com. Center for Early Edn., 1964-92, v.p., 1978-79; bd. dirs. Child Devel. and Psychotherapy Tng. Program, Los Angeles, 1975-80, pres., 1975-77; bd. dirs. Los Angeles Child Devel. Center, 1977-86, treas., 1978-80; mem. cult clinic Jewish Family Service, Los Angeles, 1978-86; bd. dirs. Lake Arrowhead Crest Estates, 1990—. Served to capt. M.C. AUS, 1946-48. Mem. Am. Psychoanalytic Assn. (com. on ethics 1977-80), Assn. Child Psychoanalysis (councillor 1966-69, sec. 1972-74, mem. nominating com. 1978-84, membership com. 1988—, Marianne Kris lectr. 1995), Internat. Assn. Infant Psychiatry (co-chmn. program com. 1980-83), Internat. Soc. Adolescent Psychiatry (sci. adv. com. 1988—), Phi Beta Kappa. Office: 1100 Glendon Ave Ste 941 Los Angeles CA 90024-3513

VANDAMENT, WILLIAM EUGENE, academic administrator, educator; b. Hannibal, Mo., Sept. 6, 1931; s. Alva E. and Ruth Alice (Mahood) V.; m. Margery Vandament, Feb. 2, 1952; children: Jane Louise, Lisa Ann. BA, Quincy Coll., 1952; MS, So. Ill. U., 1953; MS in Psychology, U. Mass., 1963, PhD, 1964. Psychologist Bacon Clinic, Racine, Wis., 1954-61; NDEA fellow U. Mass., Amherst, 1961-64; asst. prof. SUNY, Binghamton, 1964-69, univ. examiner and dir. instl. research, 1969-73, asst. v.p. planning, instl. research, 1972-76; exec. asst. to pres., dir. budget and resources Ohio State U., Columbus, 1976-79, v.p. fin. and planning, 1979-81; sr. v.p. adminstrn. NYU, N.Y.C., 1981-83; provost, vice chancellor acad. affairs Calif. State U. System, Long Beach, 1983-87; Trustees prof. Calif. State U., Fullerton, 1987-92; pres. No. Mich. U., 1991—. Contbr. articles to psychol. jours. and books on higher edn. Home: 1440 Center St Marquette MI 49855-1625 Office: Northern Michigan U 1401 Presque Isle Ave Marquette MI 49855-5300

VAN DAMME, JEAN-CLAUDE (JEAN-CLAUDE VAN VARENBERG), actor; b. Brussels, 1961; m. Darcy LaPier, Feb. 3, 1994; children: Kristopher, Bianca. Former European karate champion. Performances include: (films) Rue Barbar, No Retreat, No Surrender, 1986, Predator, 1987, Bloodsport, 1988, Black Eagle, 1988, Cyborg, 1989, Kickboxer, 1989, Death Warrant, 1990, Lionheart, 1991, Double Impact, 1991, Universal Soldier, 1992, Hard Target, 1993, Time Cop, 1994, Street Fighter, 1994, The Quest, 1995, Sudden Death, 1995. Winner Middleweight Championship, European Karate Assn. Office: ICM 8942 Wilshire Blvd Beverly Hills CA 90211*

VAN DECKER, WILLIAM ARTHUR, cardiologist; b. Passaic, N.J., May 27, 1957; s. William and Louise Adelaide (Meli) Van D.; m. Generosa Grana; children: Stephanie, William, Christopher. BS in Biology summa cum laude, Fairfield (Conn.) U., 1979; MD, Georgetown U., 1983. Bd. cert. internal medicine, bd. cert. cardiovascular diseases. Intern Temple U. Hosp., Phila., 1983-84, resident internal medicine, 1984-86, cardiology fellow, 1986-88, non-invasive cardiology imaging tng./rsch. fellow, 1988-89; assoc. dir. Non-Invasive Imaging, dir. Cardiology Clinic Med. Coll. Pa., Phila., 1989-95, asst. prof. medicine and cardiology, 1989—, dir. Heart Sta., 1990—; mem. com. on radiation safety Med. Coll. Pa., Phila., 1990—, chmn. com. on radiation safety, 1993—, mem. pharmacy and therapeutics com., 1992—, chmn. pulmonary and therapeutics com. 1993—, mem. continuing med. edn. com., 1992—, vice-chmn. quality assurance com., 1993—, group leader freshman bioethics, 1992—, med. student advisor, 1992—; presenter in field. Manuscript Peer reviewer Annals of Internal Medicine, 1993—; contbr. articles to profl. jours. Fellow Am. Heart Assn., Am. Coll. Cardiology, Am. Coll. Chest Physicians; mem. AMA, ACP, Am. Soc. for Echocardiography, Am. Fedn. for Clin. Rsch., Pa. Med. Soc., Soc. Nuclear Medicine, Am. Assn. for Nuclear Cardiology (founding mem.), Am. Soc. Nuclear Cardiology (founding mem.), Philadelphia County Med. Soc. (standing com. 1992—), Alpha Epsilon Delta, Alpha Omega Alpha. Office: Med Coll Pa 3300 Henry Ave Philadelphia PA 19129-1121

VANDEGRIFT, JOHN RAYMOND, priest, librarian; b. Wilmington, Del., Apr. 27, 1928; s. Ira Ambers and Florence (Metzler) V. AB in Chemistry, Princeton U., 1949; STB, Dominican House, 1959, STL/STLr, 1962; MLS, Columbia U., 1975. Ordained priest, Roman Cath. Ch., 1960. Lab. asst. Merck & Co., Inc., Rahway, N.J., 1949-52; instr. in theology Xaverian Coll., Silver Spring, Md., 1961-62, Aquinas Coll., Grand Rapids, Mich., 1962-65, Mercy Cen. Nursing Sch., Grand Rapids, 1963-65, Albertus Magnus Coll., New Haven, 1968-70; instr. in theology and philosophy St. Catharine (Ky.) Coll., 1965-68; dir. Dominican Coll. Libr., Washington, 1970—; instr. theology Aquinas Inst. for Religion, Grand Rapids, summers 1963-70; mem. faculty John Paul II Inst. on Marriage and the Family, 1988—; spiritual moderator Dominican Laity Chpt., McLean, Va., 1989—; chaplain Team of Our Lady, Arlington, Va., 1984—; preacher Sunday Eucharist, Washington, 1970—; confessor Shrine of Immaculate Conception, Washington, 1980—. Mem. ALA, Assn. Coll. and Rsch. Librs., Assn. Libr. Collections and Tech. Svcs., D.C. Libr. Assn., Am. Theol. Libr. Assn., Washington Theol. Consortium (chmn. com. of librs. 1981), Cluster Periodical Ctr. (com. librs.). Avocations: mountain climbing, backpacking, hiking, jogging. Home: 487 Michigan Ave NE Washington DC 20017-1584 Office: Dominican Coll Libr 487 Michigan Ave NE Washington DC 20017-1584

VANDE HEY, JAMES MICHAEL, corporate executive, former air force officer; b. Maribel, Wis., Mar. 15, 1916; s. William Henry and Anna (Zimmerman) VandeH.; m. Jean Margretta Schilleman, June 23, 1944; children: James Todd, Dale Michael, Dean Clark. Student, U. Wis., 1947-49; BA, U. Philippines, 1955; postgrad., Air War Coll., Maxwell AFB, Montgomery, Ala., 1956-57. Commd. 2d lt. USAAF, 1941; advanced through grades to brig. gen. USAF, 1967; fighter pilot PTO, 1941-45; including Hawaii, Dec. 7, 1941; duty in command and USAF level including duty in Europe (NATO) and Philippines, 1945-69; dep. chief of staff Hdqrs. USMACV, Saigon, Vietnam, 1969-71; assigned Hdqrs. Tactical Air Command, 1971—; mem. faculty Air War Coll., 1957-59, dep. for acads., dean of faculty, 1959-61; ret., 1971; pres. Vanson Inc., 1971—, Vande Hey Inc., 1976—. Decorated D.S.M., Legion of Merit with two oak leaf cluster, D.F.C. with two oak leaf cluster, Bronze Star, Air medal with 7 oak leaf clusters, decorations from

Philippine, Vietnamese and Korean govts. Mem. USAF Hist. Found., Air Force Assn. Roman Catholic. Home: 3374 S El Dorado Austin TX 78734-5232

VAN DE KAMP, JOHN KALAR, lawyer; b. Pasadena, Calif., Feb. 7, 1936; s. Harry and Georgie (Kalar) Van de K.; m. Andrea Fisher, Mar. 11, 1978; 1 child, Diana. BA, Dartmouth Coll., 1956; JD, Stanford U., 1959. Bar: Calif. 1960. Asst. U.S. atty. L.A., 1960-66, U.S. atty., 1966-67; dep. dir. Exec. Office for U.S. Attys., Washington, 1967-68, dir., 1968-69; spl. asst. Pres.'s Commn. on Campus Unrest, 1970; fed. pub. defender L.A., 1971-75; dist. atty. Los Angeles County, 1975-83; atty. gen. State of Calif., 1983-91; pres. Jour. Dewy Bulletin, L.A., 1991—, Thoroughbred Owners, Calif., 1996—; bd. dirs. United Airlines. Mem. Calif. Dist. Attys. Assn. (pres. 1975-83), Nat. Dist. Attys. Assn. (v.p. 1975-83), Peace Officers Assn. L.A. County (past pres.), Nat. Assn. Attys. Gen. (exec. com. 1983-91), Conf. Western Attys. Gen. (pres. 1986). Office: Dewey Ballantine 333 S Hope St Ste 3000 Los Angeles CA 90071-3039

VANDE KROL, JERRY LEE, architect; b. Oskaloosa, Iowa, Oct. 5, 1949; s. Glen Vande Krol and Nola Fern (Monsma) Emmert; m. Constance Louise Wood, May 30, 1970; children: Sarah Lynn, Rachel Ann, Molly Jayne. BArch, Iowa State U., 1972. Registered architect, Iowa. Designer City of Akron, Ohio, 1972-76; architect Brooks Borg and Skiles, Des Moines, 1976-90; founder VOV Architecture and Design, P.C., Des Moines, 1990—. Recipient Merit Desigh award Ohio Chpt. Soc. Landscape Architects, 1977. Mem. AIA (Iowa chpt., Design award 1984, 90, regional chpt. Design award 1985, 91), Des Moines Architects Coun. Republican. Mem. Brethren Ch. Avocations: music, classical guitar, reading, golf. Office: Vov Architecture Design 108 3rd St Ste 200 Des Moines IA 50309-4758

VANDELL, DEBORAH LOWE, educational psychology educator; b. Bryan, Tex., June 5, 1949; d. Charles Ray and Janice (Durrett) Lowe; m. Kerry Dean Vandell, May 16, 1970; children: Colin Buckner, Ashley Elizabeth. AB, Rice U., 1971; EdM, Harvard U., 1972; PhD, Boston U., 1977. Tchr. Walpole (Mass.) Pub. Schs., 1972-73; rschr. Ralph Nader Congress Project, Washington, 1972; asst. prof. U. Tex., Dallas, 1976-81, assoc. prof., 1981-89; prof. ednl. psychology U. Wis., Madison, 1989—; vis. scholar MacArthur Rsch. Network, Cambridge, Mass., 1985-86, U. Calif., Berkeley, 1988-89; mem. steering com. NICHD Study of Early Child Care. Assoc. editor Child Devel., 1993-95; mem. editl. bd. Child Devel., 1980-93, Jour. Family Issues, 1983-89, Devel. Psychology, 1989-93; co-author books; contbr. articles to profl. jours. Bd. dirs. Infant Mental Helath Assn., 1988-89; bd. dirs. Cmty. Coord. Child Care, Madison, Wis., chair, 1991-93; mem. Day Care Adv. Bd., State of Wis.; mem. altar guild and vestry St. Andrew's Ch., 1992-95. Named Outstanding Young Scholar, Found. for Child Devel., 1982. Mem. Am. Psychol. Assn. (exec. com. div. 7 1985-88), Southwestern Soc. Rsch. in Human Devel. (pres. 1988-90), Am. Psychol. Soc., Soc. for Rsch. in Child Devel., Phi Beta Kappa. Episcopalian. Office: U Wis Dept Ednl Psychology 1025 W Johnson St Madison WI 53706-1706

VANDELL, KERRY DEAN, real estate and urban economics educator; b. Biloxi, Miss., Jan. 8, 1947; s. Benedict Sandy and Eleanor Ruby (Lenhart) V.; m. Deborah Ann Lowe, May 16, 1970; children: Colin Buckner, Ashley Elizabeth. BA, MME, Rice U., 1970; M City Planning, Harvard U., 1973; PhD, MIT, 1977. Assoc. engr. Exxon Co., USA, Houston, 1970-71; asst. prof. So. Meth. U., Dallas, 1976-80, assoc. prof., 1980-86, prof., chmn. dept., 1986-89; prof. real estate and urban land econs., chm. dept. U. Wis., Madison, 1989-93, dir. Ctr. for Urban Land Econs. rsch., 1989—, Tiefenthaler chairholder, 1996; vis. assoc. prof. Harvard U., Cambridge, Mass., 1985-86; vis. prof. U. Calif., Berkeley, 1988-89; bd. dirs. Park Bank, Madison, U. Rsch. Pk.; chmn. bd. dirs. Domus Equity Corp. Mem. editl. bd. Jour. Real Estate Fin. and Econs., 1989—, Land Econs., 1989—, Jour. Property Rsch., 1989-94; contbr. numerous articles on mortgage default risk, neighborhood dynamics, econs. of architecture, and appraisal theory to profl. jours. Fellow Homer Hoyt Advanced Studies Inst. (faculty 1989—, bd. dirs.), Urban Land Inst.; mem. Am. Real Estate and Urban Econs. Assn. 92d v.p. 1989, 1st v.p. 1990, pres. 1991, co-editor jour. 1991-96). Episcopalian. Home: 3301 Topping Rd Madison WI 53705-1436 Office: U Wis Sch Bus 975 University Ave Madison WI 53706-1323

VANDEMAN, GEORGE ALLEN, lawyer; b. Muncie, Ind., Jan. 16, 1940; s. George Edward and Nellie Florence (Johnson) V.; m. Judith Ellen Meyers, June 16, 1959 (div. 1976); m. Winifred Margaret Hayward, Jan. 15, 1977; children: Shelli, Bradley, Craig. AB, U. So. Calif., 1963, JD, 1966. Bar: Calif. 1966. Atty., ptnr. Amgen Inc., Thousand Oaks, Calif., 1966-95; sr. v.p., gen. counsel, sec. amgen Inc., 1995—. Mem. bd. councilors U. So. Calif. Sch. Law, 1988—. Mem. Calif. State Bar (com. on takeover and corp. govt. 1987—). Avocations: travel, water sports, skiing. Home: 1652 Aldercreek Pl Westlake Village CA 91362

VANDEMARK, ROBERT GOODYEAR, retired retail company executive; b. Youngstown, Ohio, Sept. 1, 1921; s. Arthur Glenn and Lola (Goodyear) V.; m. Jean Chapman, Sept. 19, 1943; children: Ann (Mrs. William K. Butler), Peggy Lynn (Mrs. Michael Murray). B.Sc., Ohio U., 1943. Dept. mgr. F. & R. Lazarus, Columbus, Ohio, 1947-54; asst. controller Boston Store, Milw., 1954-57; v.p., treas. Cleland Simpson Co., Scranton, Pa., 1957-65; asst. to exec. v.p. Bergdorf Goodman, N.Y.C., 1965-68; treas. Garfinckel, Brooks Bros., Miller & Rhoads, Inc., Washington, 1968-69; v.p. Garfinckel, Brooks Bros., Miller & Rhoads, Inc., 1969-73, exec. v.p., 1973-79, vice chmn., 1979-83; chmn., chief exec. officer Garfinckel's, 1983-87. Head dept. and specialty stores div. United Fund, Scranton, Pa., 1960-65; bd. dirs. Goodwill Industries, 1964-65; treas. Washington Nat. Cathedral. Served to 1st lt. AUS, 1943-46; col. Res. Decorated Bronze Star with V and cluster, Mil. Order of Wilheim. Mem. Fin. Execs. Inst., Nat. Retail Mchts. Assn. (sec., treas., 1st v.p., pres., dir., mem. exec. com. fin. exec. divsn.), Delta Tau Delta, City Club Washington, Washington Golf and Country Club, Army-Navy Club, Burning Tree Golf Club, Laurel Oak Country Club (Fla.), Masons (32d degree), Kiwanis (Fla.). Home: 670 Potomac River Rd Mc Lean VA 22102

VAN DEMARK, RUTH ELAINE, lawyer; b. Santa Fe, N. Mex., May 16, 1944; d. Robert Eugene and Bertha Marie (Thompson) Van D.; m. Leland Wilkinson, June 23, 1967; children: Anne Marie, Caroline Cook. AB, Vassar Coll., 1966; MTS, Harvard U., 1969; JD with honors, U. Conn., 1976. Bar: Conn. 1976, U.S. Dist. Ct. Conn. 1976, Ill. 1977, U.S. Dist. Ct. (no. dist.) Ill. 1977, U.S. Supreme Ct. 1983, U.S. Ct. Appeals (7th cir.) 1984. Instr. legal research and writing Loyola U. Sch. Law, Chgo., 1976-79; assoc. Wildman, Harrold, Allen & Dixon, Chgo., 1977-84, ptnr., 1985-94; prin. Law Offices of Ruth E. Van Demark, Chgo., 1995—; bd. dirs., sec. Systat, Inc., Evanston, Ill., 1984-94; mem. Ill. Supreme Ct. Rules com., 1996—. Assoc. editor Conn. Law Rev., 1975-76. Mem. adv. bd. Horizon Hospice, Chgo., 1978—; del.-at-large White House Conf. on Families, Los Angeles, 1980; mem. adv. bd. YWCA Battered Women's Shelter, Evanston, Ill., 1982-86; mem. alumni coun. Harvard Divinity Sch., 1988-91; vol. atty. Pro Bono Advocates, Chgo., 1982-92, bd. dirs. 1993—, chair devel. com., 1993; bd. dirs. Friends of Pro Bono Advocates Orgn., 1987-89, New Voice Prodns., 1984-86, Byrne Piven Theater Workshop, 1987-90; founder, bd. dirs. Friends of Battered Women and their Children, 1986-87; chair 175th Reunion Fund Harvard U. Div. Sch., 1992. Mem. ABA, Ill. Bar Assn., Conn. Bar Assn., Chgo. Bar Assn., Appellate Lawyers Assn. Ill. (bd. dirs. 1985-87, treas. 1989-90, sec. 1990-91, v.p. 1991-92, pres. 1992-93), Women's Bar Assn. Ill., Jr. League Evanston (chair State Pub. Affairs Com. 1987-88, Vol. of Yr. 1983-84). Clubs: Chgo. Vassar (pres. 1979-81), Cosmopolitan (N.Y.C.). Home: 1127 Asbury Ave Evanston IL 60202-1136

VANDENBERG, EDWIN JAMES, chemist, educator; b. Hawthorne, N.J., Sept. 13, 1918; s. Albert J. and Alida C. (Westerhoff) V.; m. Mildred Elizabeth Wright, Sept. 9, 1950; children: David James, Jean Elizabeth. M.E. with distinction, Stevens Inst. Tech., 1939, Dr.Engring. (hon.), 1965. Rsch. chemist Hercules Inc. Rsch. Ctr., Wilmington, Del., 1939-44, asst. shift supr. Sunflower Ordnance Works, Kans., 1944-45, rsch. chemist Research Ctr., Wilmington, 1945-57, sr. research chemist, 1958-64, rsch.assoc., 1965-77, sr. rsch. assoc., 1978-82; adj. prof. chemistry Ariz. State U., Tempe, 1983-91, rsch. prof. chemistry, 1992—. Author: Polyethers, 1975; Coordination Polymerization, 1983; Contemporary Topics in Polymer Science V, 1984, Catalysis in Polymer Synthesis, 1992. Patentee in field. Mem. adv. bd. Jour. Polymer Sci., 1967-93, Macromolecules, 1979-81; chmn. Gordon Rsch. Conf. on Polymers, 1978. Recipient Indsl. Rsch. 100 award, 1965, Internat. award Soc. Plastics Engrs., 1994. Mem. Am. Chem. Soc. (councillor Del. sect. 1974-81, chmn. 1976, chmn. div. polychemistry 1979, coord. indsl. sponsors 1982—, Del. sect. award 1965, 79, Polymer Chemistry award 1981, Exceptional Svc. award 1983, 95, Applied Polymer Sci. award 1991, Charles Goodyear medal, 1991, Herman F. Mark award 1992). Home: 16223 E Inca Ave Fountain Hls AZ 85268-4518 Office: Ariz State U Dept Chemistry and Biochemistry Tempe AZ 85287-1604

VANDENBERG, JOHN DONALD, entomologist; b. Benton Harbor, Mich., Jan. 24, 1954; s. Robert Landis and Madelaine Louise (Westendorf) V.; m. Alice C. L. Churchill, Oct. 8, 1983. B.S. with Honors, U. Mich., 1975; M.S., U. Maine, 1977; Ph.D., Oreg. State U., 1982. Grad. rsch. asst. U. Maine, Orono, 1975-77; grad. teaching asst. Oreg. State U., Corvallis, 1977-78, grad. rsch. asst., 1978-82; postdoctoral assoc. Boyce Thompson Inst., Ithaca, N.Y., 1982-83; rsch. entomologist Agrl. Rsch. Svc., U.S. Dept. Agr., Beltsville, Md., 1983-87, rsch. leader Agrl. Rsch. Svc., Logan, Utah, 1987-93; lead scientist Agrl. Rsch. Svc., Ithaca, N.Y., 1993—; acting asst. dir. Midwest area Agrl. Rsch Svc., Peoria, Ill., 1991; equal employment opportunity counsellor, 1985-87. Contbr. articles to profl. jours. Mem. AAAS, Soc. for Invertebrate Pathology (chair elect microbial control divsn. 1995—, sec./treas. 1993-95), Entomol. Soc. Am., Am. Soc. for Microbiology, Sigma Xi. Avocations: singing, guitar, softball, gardening. Office: USDA-ARS Plant Protection US Plant Soil & Nutrition Lab Tower Rd Ithaca NY 14853

VANDENBERG, SISTER PATRICIA CLASINA, health system executive; b. N.Y.C., Mar. 15, 1948; d. Paul John and Alice Margaret (Walter) V. BSN cum laude, CUNY, 1970; MHA, Duke U., 1979. Nurse critical care staff Roosevelt Hosp., N.Y.C., 1967-69, St. Vincent's Hosp., N.Y.C., 1970; nurse specialist, instr. Meth. Hosp. Bklyn., 1970-71; cons., instr. St. John's Hosp., Anderson, Ind., 1972; nurse critical care, ambulatory svcs. Mt. Carmel Med. Ctr., Columbus, Ohio, 1974-77; v.p. clin. svcs., apostolic devel. Holy Cross Hosp., Silver Springs, Md., 1979-83; pres., chief exec. officer St. Alphonsus Regional Med. Ctr., Boise, Idaho, 1983—; trustee St. Alphonsus Regional Med. Ctr., Boise, 1983-88; sr. v.p. Holy Cross Health System Corp., South Bend, Ind., 1988-89; pres., chief exec. officer Holy Cross Health System Corp., South Bend, 1989—; trustee Holy Cross Hosp., Blue Cross Idaho, Boise, 1986—. Mem. task force United Way, Boise, 1985; bd. dirs. ARC, Boise, 1984-85. Mem. Idaho Hosp. Assn. (trustee), Greater Boise C. of C. (bd. dirs. 1987), Sigma Theta Tau. Roman Catholic. Office: Holy Cross Health System Corp 3606 E Jefferson Blvd South Bend IN 46615-3036*

VANDENBERG, PETER RAY, magazine publisher; b. Geneva, Ill., Sept. 8, 1939; s. Don George and Isabel (Frank) V.; m. Kathryn Stock, June 1973 (div. Apr. 1977). BBA, Miami U., 1962. Creative adminstr. E.F. McDonald Incentive Co., Dayton, Ohio, 1966-73; mfrs.' rep. Denver, 1974-75; mgr. Homestake Condominiums, Vail, Colo., 1975-76; desk clk. Vail Run Resort, 1976-77; sales rep. Colo. West Advt., Vail, 1977-79, pres., 1980-83; pres. Colo. West Publ., Vail, 1983—. With U.S. Army, 1963-66. Mem. Sigma Chi. Avocations: sports, music, reading.

VAN DEN BERGH, SIDNEY, astronomer; b. Wassenaar, Netherlands, May 20, 1929; emigrated to U.S., 1948; s. Sidney J. and Mieke (van den Berg) vandenB.; m. Paulette Brown; children by previous marriage: Peter, Mieke, Sabine. Student, Leiden (The Netherlands) U., 1947-48; A.B., Princeton U., 1950; M.Sc., Ohio State U., 1952; Dr. rer. nat., Goettingen U., 1956, DSc (honoris causa), 1995. Asst. prof. Perkins Obs., Ohio State U., Columbus, 1956-58; research assoc. Mt. Wilson Obs., Palomar Obs., Pasadena, Calif., 1968-69; prof. astronomy David Dunlap Obs., U. Toronto, Ont., Can., 1958-77; dir. Dominion Astrophys. Obs., Victoria, B.C., 1977-86; prin. rsch. officer NRC Can., 1977—; adj. prof. U. Victoria, 1977—. Decorated officer Order of Can. Fellow Royal Soc. London, Royal Soc. Can.; mem. Am., Royal Astron. Soc. (assoc.), Canadian Astronomy Soc. (sr. v.p. 1988-90, pres. 1990-92). Home: 418 Lands End Rd, Sidney, BC Canada V8L 5L9

VAN DEN BERGHE, PIERRE LOUIS, sociologist, anthropologist; b. Lubumbashi, Zaire, Jan. 30, 1933; s. Louis and Denise (Caullery) van den B.; m. Irmgard C. Niehuis, Jan. 21, 1956; children—Eric, Oliver, Marc. B.A., Stanford U., 1952, M.A., 1953; Ph.D., Harvard U., 1960. Asst. prof. sociology Wesleyan U., Middletown, Conn., 1962-63; asso. prof. sociology SUNY, Buffalo, 1963-65; prof. sociology and anthropology U. Wash., Seattle, 1965—; vis. prof. U. Natal, South Africa, 1960-61, Sorbonne, Paris, 1962, U. Nairobi, Kenya, 1967-68, U. Ibadan, Nigeria, 1968-69, U. Haifa, Israel, 1976, U. New South Wales, Australia, 1982, U. Strasbourg, France, 1985, U. Tuebingen, Fed. Republic Germany, 1986, Tel Aviv U., 1988, U. Cape Town, South Africa, 1989; fellow Advanced Study in Behavioral Scis., Stanford, Calif., 1984-85. Author: 22 books including South Africa, A Study in Conflict, 1965, Race and Racism, 1967, Academic Gamesmanship, 1970, Man in Society, 1978, Human Family Systems, 1979, The Ethnic Phenomenon, 1981, Stranger in Their Midst, 1989, State Violence and Ethnicity, 1990, The Quest for the Other, 1994. Served with M.C. U.S. Army, 1954-56. Mem. Am. Sociol. Assn., Am. Anthrop. Assn., Sociol. Research Assn., Human Behavior and Evolution Soc. Home: 2006 19th Ave E Seattle WA 98112-2902 Office: U Wash Dept Sociology DK-40 Seattle WA 98195

VANDENBERGHE, RONALD GUSTAVE, accountant, real estate developer; b. Oakland, Calif., July 1, 1937; s. Anselm Henri and Margaret B. (Bygum) V.; B.A. with honors, San Jose State Coll., 1959; postgrad. U. Calif. at Berkeley Extension, 1959-60, Golden Gate Coll., 1961-63; CPA, Calif.; m. Patricia W. Dufour, Aug. 18, 1957; children: Camille, Mark, Matthew. Real estate investor, pres. VandenBerghe Fin. Corp., Pleasanton, Calif., 1964—. Instr. accounting U. Cal., Berkeley, 1963-70; CPA, Pleasanton, 1963—. Served with USAF. Mem. Calif. Soc. CPAs. Republican. Presbyterian. Mason (Shriner). Home: PO Box 803 Danville CA 94526-0803 Office: 20 Happy Valley Rd Pleasanton CA 94566

VANDENBOS, GARY ROGER, psychologist, publisher; b. Grand Rapids, Mich., Dec. 16, 1943; s. Paul Martin and Irene (Dorenbos) V.; m. Jane Annunziata, Dec. 16, 1983; 1 child, Bret. BS, Mich. State U., 1967, MA, 1969; PhD, U. Detroit, 1973. Dir. Howell (Mich.) Area Community Mental Health Ctr., 1973-77; dir. nat. policy studies Am. Psychol. Assn., Washington, 1977-82, exec. dir. for publs., 1984—; prof. U. Bergen, Norway, 1982-84; project cons. Rand Corp., Santa Monica, Calif., 1984-89; bd. dirs. Am. Biodyne Found., San Francisco; newspaper pub. APA Monitor, 1985—. Author: Psychotherapy with Schizophrenic, 1981; editor Pscyhology and National Health Insurance, 1979; assoc. editor Am. Psychologist Jour. Office: Am Psychol Assn 750 1st St NE Washington DC 20002-4241

VANDEN BOUT, PAUL ADRIAN, astronomer, physicist, educator; b. Grand Rapids, Mich., June 16, 1939; s. Adrian and Cornelia (Peterson) Vanden B.; m. Rachel Ann Eggebeen, Sept. 1, 1961; children—Thomas Adrian, David Anton. A.B., Calvin Coll., 1961; Ph.D., U. Calif.-Berkeley, 1966. Postdoctoral fellow U. Calif., Berkeley, 1966-67; postdoctoral fellow Columbia U., N.Y.C., 1967-68; instr. Columbia U., 1968-69, asst. prof., 1969-70; asst. prof. U. Tex., Austin, 1970-74; assoc. prof. U. Tex., 1974-79, prof., 1979-84; dir. Nat. Radio Astronomy Obs., Charlottesville, Va., 1985—; cons. NSF, NASA. Fellow Fulbright Found., Heidelberg, Fed. Republic Germany, 1961-62, Leiden, Netherlands, 1977. Fellow AAAS, Am. Phys. Soc.; mem. Am. Astron. Soc., Internat. Astron. Union, Internat. Radio Sci. Union. Office: Nat Radio Astronomy Obs 520 Edgemont Rd Charlottesville VA 22903-2475

VANDENBROUCKE, RUSSELL JAMES, theatre director; b. Chgo., Aug. 16, 1948; s. Arthur C. Sr. and Ardelle (Barker) V.; m. Mary Allison Dilg, Sept. 7, 1974; children: Aynsley Louise, Justin Arthur. BA, U. Ill., 1970; MA, U. Warwick, Coventry, Eng., 1975; MFA in Drama, Yale U., 1977, DFA in Drama, 1978. Asst. literary mgr. Yale Repertory Theatre, New Haven, 1977-78; lit. mgr., dramaturg Mark Taper Forum, Los Angeles, 1978-85; assoc. producing dir. Repertory Theatre St. Louis, 1985-87; artistic dir. Northlight Theatre, Evanston, Ill., 1987—; vis. prof. Yale U., 1978, La. State U., 1981, U. Calif.-San Diego, 1983, Middlebury Coll., 1985, Washington U., 1986; adj. assoc. prof. Northwestern U., 1987—; on site evaluator, peer panelist Nat. Endowment for Arts, Washington, 1981—. Author: Truths the Hand Can Tough: The Theatre of Athol Fugard, 1985; adapted play Eleanor: In Her Own Words (for TV), 1985 (Emmy award 1986) (dir. for stage 1990), Los Alamos Revisted (for stage and radio), 1984, 87, Holiday Memories (from Truman Capote), 1991, Atomic Bombers (radio), 1995; adapted, stage dir. Feiffer's America, 1988, Eleanor: In Her Own Words, 1990; adapted An Enemy of the People, 1991; stage dir. Lucky Lindy, Love Letters in Blue Paper, 84 Charing Cross Road, Three Women Talking (also radio), Smoke on the Mountain, The White Rose, Betrayal, My Other Heart, Later Life, Hedda Gabler, Bubbe Meuses, Valley Song; contbr. articles to mags. and newspapers. Recipient L.A. Drama Critics Cir. award, 1984, Spl. Actors Equity Assn. award, 1990; Fulbright sr. scholar, Australia, 1996. Avocation: basketball. Office: Northlight Theatre 600 Davis St Evanston IL 60201-4419

VAN DEN HENDE, FRED JOSEPH, human resources executive; b. Chgo., Sept. 28, 1953; s. Maurice Everett and Alice Helen (Davey) Van Den H.; m. Sharon Joyce Kucharski, Oct. 4, 1975; children: John Michael, Karen Michelle. BA, DePaul U., 1975; cert. of grad., U. Wash., 1981. Asst. v.p. human resources Land of Lincoln Savs. and Loan, Berwyn, Ill., 1977-84; v.p. human resources Uptown Fed. Bank FSB, Niles, Ill., 1984-88; dir. employee svcs. Archdiocese of Chgo., 1988—; mem. Savs. Assn. Pers. Adminstrn., Berwyn, 1977-84; part-time instr. Inst. Fin. Edn., Chgo., 1984—, Moraine Valley C.C., Palos Hills, Ill., 1984—. Sch. bd. treas. St. Rene Sch., Chgo., 1981; sch. bd. mem. St. Daniel the Prophet Sch., Chgo., 1986-88, 93-95, sch. bd. chmn., 1988-89; boy scout leader St. Daniel Parish, Chgo., 1987-94. Recipient Oustanding Achievement in the Field of Athletics award St. Rita H.S. Alumni Assn., Chgo., 1991; Athletic scholar DePaul U., Chgo., 1971-75. Mem. Nat. Assn. Ch. Pers. Adminstrs., Soc. for Human Resource Mgmt., Ill. State C. of C. (human resources com. 1979—). Roman Catholic. Avocations: camping, fishing, coaching youth sports teams. Home: 5130 S Mulligan Ave Chicago IL 60638 Office: Archdiocese of Chgo 155 E Superior Chicago IL 60611

VANDEN HEUVEL, KATRINA, magazine editor; b. N.Y.C., Oct. 7, 1959; d. William Jacobus and Jean Babette (Stein) Vanden H.; m. Stephen F. Cohen, Dec. 4, 1988; 1 child, Nicola Anna. BA summa cum laude in Politics, Princeton U., 1982. Prodn. assoc. ABC Closeup Documentaries, 1982-83; asst. editor The Nation, N.Y.C., 1984-89, editor-at-large, 1989-93, acting editor-in-chief, 1994-95, editor-in-chief, 1995—; vis. journalist Moscow News, 1989; Moscow coord. Conf. Investigative Journalism After the Cold War, 1992; co-founder, co-editor Vyi i Myi, 1990—. Editor: The Nation, 1865-1990: Selections from the Independent Magazine of Politics and Culture, 1990; co-editor: Voices of Glasnost: Interviews with Gorbachev's Reformers, 1989; contbr. articles to newspapers. Recipient Maggie award Planned Parenthood Fedn. Am., 1994. Mem. Correctional Assn. N.Y. (dir.), Coun. Fgn. Rels., Inst. Policy Studies (trustee), Network of East-West Women (bd. advisors), Franklin and Eleanor Roosevelt Inst. (trustee), Moscow Ctr. for Gender Studies (mem. adv. com.). Office: The Nation 72 Fifth Ave New York NY 10011

VAN-DEN-NOORT, STANLEY, physician, educator; b. Lynn, Mass., Sept. 8, 1930; s. Judokus and Hazel G. (Van Blarcom) van den N.; m. June Le Clere, Apr. 17, 1954; children: Susanne, Eric, Peter, Katherine, Elizabeth. A.B., Dartmouth, 1951; M.D., Harvard, 1954. Intern then resident Boston City Hosp., 1954-56, resident neurology, 1958-60; research fellow neurochemistry Harvard, 1960-62; instr. medicine Case Western Res. U., Cleve., 1962-66; asst. prof. Case Western Res. U., 1966-69, assoc. prof., 1969-70; prof. neurology U. Calif., Irvine, 1970—; chair dept. neurology U. Calif., 1970-72, 86—, assoc. dean coll. Medicine, 1972-73, dean, 1973-85; mem. cons. staff U. Calif., Irvine Med. Center; mem. Long Beach (Calif.) Meml. Hosp., Long Beach VA Hosp.; mem. com. of revision U.S. Pharmacopoeial Conv., 1990-95. Mem. med. adv. bds., Nat. Multiple Scierosis Soc./Myasthenia Gravis, 1971—, Orange County chpt. Nat. Multiple Scierosis Soc., 1971—, Orange County Health Planning Coun., 1971-85, Nat. Com. Rsch. in Neurol. Disease, 1982-87. Lt. M.C. USNR, 1956-58. Fellow ACP, Am. Acad. Neurol.; mem. AAUP, AMA, Am. Neurol. Assn., Orange County Med. assn., Calif. Med. Assn., Am. Heart Assn. Home: 17592 Orange Tree Ln Tustin CA 92680-2353 Office: U Calif Dept Neurology 100 Irvine Hall Irvine CA 92717-4275

VANDERBEKE, PATRICIA K., architect; b. Detroit, Apr. 3, 1963; d. B. H. and Dolores I. VanderBeke. BS in Architecture, U. Mich., 1985, MArch, 1987. Registered architect, Ill. Archtl. intern Hobbs & Black, Assocs., Ann Arbor, Mich., 1984-86, Fry Assocs., Ann Arbor, 1988; architect Decker & Kemp Architecture/Urban Design, Chgo., 1989-92; prin., founder P. K. VanderBeke, Architect, Chgo., 1992—. Contbr. photographs and articles to Inland Architect mag.; contbr. photographs to AIA calendar. Chair recycling com. Lake Point Tower Condo. Assn., Chgo., 1990T, chair. ops. com., 1993. George S. Booth travelling fellow, 1992. Mem. AIA (1st place photog. contest award 1992, hon. mention 1994), Chgo. Archtl. Club. Office: P K VanderBeke Architect 505 N Lake Shore Dr Apt 808 Chicago IL 60611-3402

VANDERBILT, HUGH BEDFORD, SR., mineral and chemical company executive; b. N.Y.C., Apr. 23, 1921; s. Robert Thurlow and Mildred (Bedford) V.; m. Claire Frances McKiernan, Apr. 27, 1946; children: Laura V. Ernst, Linda V. Allen, Hugh B. Jr. Student, Trinity Coll., Hartford, Conn., 1940-42. With News Syndicate Corp., N.Y.C., 1946-54; chmn. bd. R.T. Vanderbilt Co., Inc., Norwalk, Conn., 1954—. Hon. trustee Greenwich (Conn.) Hist. Soc., 1957—; trustee hist. Deerfield (Mass.) Inc., 1976-93. 1st lt. U.S. Army, 1942-46. Mem. Chem. Mfrs. Assn. (bd. dirs. 1975-79), Blind Brook Club, Greenwich Country Club, Lyford Country Club, Everglades Club, Round Hill Club. Republican. Avocations: golf, skiing. Office: R T Vanderbilt Co Inc 30 Winfield St Norwalk CT 06855-1316

VANDERBILT, KERMIT, English language educator; b. Decorah, Iowa, Sept. 1, 1925; s. Lester and Ella (Qualley) V.; m. Vivian Osmundson, Nov. 15, 1947; 1 dau., Karen Paige. B.A., Luther Coll., Decorah, 1947, Litt. D. (hon.), 1977; M.A., U. Minn., 1949, Ph.D., 1956. Instr. English U. Minn., 1954-57; instr. U. Wash., 1958-60, asst. prof. English, 1960-62; asst. prof. San Diego State U., 1962-65, assoc. prof., 1965-68, prof., 1968-90, prof. emeritus, 1990—; vis. prof. Am. lit. U. B.C., Can., Vancouver, summer 1963; vis. prof. U. Oreg., summer 1968. Author: Charles Eliot Norton: Apostle of Culture in a Democracy, 1959, The Achievement of William Dean Howells: A Reinterpretation, 1968, American Literature and the Academy: The Roots, Growth and Maturity of a Profession, 1986 (Choice award for outstanding acad. books), Theodore Roethke in A Literary History of the American West, 1987; editor: (with others) American Social Thought, 1972, April Hopes (W.D. Howells), 1975, The Rise of Silas Lapham, 1983, spl. issue Am. Literary Realism, winter 1989, La Litterature Americaine, 1991, 2nd edit., 1994; mem. edit. bd. U. Wash. Press, 1960-62, Twentieth Century Lit., 1969—; contbr. numerous articles to profl. jours. Served with USNR, 1943-46. Outstanding Prof. San Diego State U., 1976; Guggenheim fellow, 1978-79; Huntington Library fellow, 1980; Am. Philos. Soc. grantee, 1964, Am. Council Learned Socs. grantee, 1972, Nat. Endowment for Humanities grantee, 1986. Mem. Am. Studies Assn. (exec. council 1968-69), So. Calif. Am. Studies Assn. (pres. 1968-69), Philol. Assn. Pacific Coast (chmn. sect. Am. lit. 1968), MLA, Internat. Mark Twain Soc. (hon.), United Profs. of Calif. (Disting. prof. 1978). Home: 6937 Coleshill Dr San Diego CA 92119-1920

VANDERBILT, OLIVER DEGRAY, financier; b. N.Y.C., Oct. 25, 1914; s. Oliver Degray Jr. and Madelon (Weir) V.; m. Frances Philips, Nov. 11, 1939; children: Oliver Degray IV, Madelon V. Peck. AB, Princeton U., 1937. With Tenn. Coal Iron & R.R. Co., Birmingham, Ala., 1939-40; v.p. Weir Kilby Corp., Cin., 1940-49; exec. v.p. Taylor Wharton Iron & Steel Co., Cin., 1949; pres. Taylor Wharton Iron & Steel Co., 1950-54; v.p. Harrisburg Steel Corp., 1954; pres. Twisco Corp., 1954-55; v.p., dir. Baldwin-Lima-Hamilton Corp., 1955-56; exec. v.p., dir. Blair & Co. Inc., Phila., 1957-62; chmn. Blair & Co. Inc., 1963-70; founder, pres. Vanderbilt Corp., Phila., 1963-68, Capitol Mgmt. Corp., 1968—, Innovest Group Inc., 1970—; pres., chief exec. officer Ecolaire Inc., 1971-74; founder, pres. Dorsey Corp., 1959, Standard Computers Inc., 1965, Systems Capital Corp., 1967, Marina City Corp., 1968; founder, chmn. bd. Tierra Corp., San Francisco, 1977—, Vanderbilt Energy Corp., N.Y.C., 1978—; founder, chmn. Seaborad Savs. Bank, Stuart, Fla., 1983—. Maj. AUS, 1942-45, ETO, NATOUSA. Decorated Croix de

Guerre (France); Bronze Star (U.S.). Mem. Links, Commonwealth Club, Jupiter Island Club, Racquet and Tennis Club, Gulph Mills Golf Club, Ivy Club, Nassau Club, Seminole Club, Maidstone Club. Republican. Episcopalian. Avocation: golf. Home: 111 Gomez Rd Hobe Sound FL 33455-2427

VANDER CLUTE, NORMAN ROLAND, lawyer; b. N.Y.C., Nov. 14, 1932; s. Carl Frederick and Agnes (Hansen) Vander C.; m. Sandra Sheffey, Dec. 30, 1978; children: William Bowditch, Edward Carl, Jeffrey. BA, Amherst Coll., 1954; LLB, Harvard U., 1957. Bar: N.Y. 1958, D.C. 1967. Law clk. 1st Cir. Ct. Appeals, Boston, 1957-58; atty. Standard Vacuum Oil Co., Hartsdale, N.Y., 1958-60; sr. atty. Am. Airlines, Inc., N.Y.C., 1960-63; asst. gen. counsel Agy. for Internat. Devel., Washington, 1963-65, office dir., 1965-67; ptnr. Surrey & Morse, Washington, 1967-85, Jones, Day, Reavis & Pogue, Washington, 1986-93, Winston & Strawn, 1993—. Mem. ABA. Presbyterian. Avocations: boating. Office: Winston & Strawn 1400 L St NW Washington DC 20005-3509

VANDERET, ROBERT CHARLES, lawyer; b. Bklyn., Apr. 12, 1947; s. James Gustav and Bernadette Cecelia (Heaney) V.; m. Sharon Kay Brewster, Oct 3, 1970; children: Erin Anne Brewster, Aidan McKenzie Brewster. AB, UCLA, 1969; JD, Stanford U., 1973. Bar: Calif. 1973, U.S. Dist. Ct. (cen. and so. dists.) Calif. 1974, U.S. Ct. Appeals (9th cir.) 1976, N.Y. 1978, U.S. Supreme Ct. 1978, U.S. Dist. Ct. (no. dist.) Calif. 1980, U.S. Dist. Ct. (ea. dist.) Calif. 1981. Extern law clk. to Justice Tobriner Calif. Supreme Ct., 1972-73; assoc. O'Melveny & Myers, Los Angeles, 1973-80, ptnr., 1980—; transition aide Chief Justice Rose Bird, Calif. Supreme Ct., 1976. Del. Dem. Nat. Conv., 1968; bd. dirs. Legal Aid Found. L.A., 1978-90, Constn. Rights Found., 1990, Inner City Law Ctr., 1994—; trustee Lawyers Commn. for Civil Rights Under Law, 1993—. Mem. ABA (chair media law and defamation torts com. 1991-92), Calif. State Bar (vice chair, com. on adminstrn. of justice 1995-96), L.A. Bar Assn. (pro bono coun. chair 1993-96). Democrat. Home: 834 Greentree Rd Pacific Palisades CA 90272-3911 Office: O'Melveny & Myers 400 S Hope St Los Angeles CA 90071-2801 *Notable cases include: Galloway vs. CBS, 14 Media L. Rep. 1161, 1987, in which he represented Dan Rather and CBS in celebrated libel case; Martha Raye vs. David Letterman, 14 Media L. Rep. 2047, 1987, in which he represented David Letterman and NBC; Robert Mahev vs. CBS, 201 Calif. App. 3d 662, 1988, in which he represented CBS, Playboy and other pubs.; Crane vs. The Ariz. Republic, 729 F. Supp. 698 Ct. Dist. Calif., 1989, in which he represented The Ariz. Republic; Kruse vs. Bank of Am., 202 Calif. App. 3d 38, 1988, in which he represented Bank of Am. in successful appeal of leading lender liability case; CHH vs. The Limited, 587 F. Supp. 246, Ct. Dist. Calif., 1984, in which he represented Carter Hawley Hale Stores, Inc. in major takeover battle.*

VANDERGRIFF, CHRISTINA RAI, controller; b. Prineville, Oreg., Nov. 13, 1964; d. Marvin Ronald and Virginia Lucille (Warren) Craig; m. Kenneth Wayne Vandergriff, Aug. 23, 1987. Cert. legal adminstrn. with honors, Trend Coll., Eugene, Oreg., 1989; BA in Acctg., Morrison Coll., Reno, 1996; Assoc. Bus. Adminstrn. in Bus. Mgmt., B of Bus. Adminstr. in Acctg. Shipper, asst. loan processor Centennial Mortgage Co., Inc., Eugene, 1989-90; asst. acct. Kimwood Corp., Cottage Grove, Oreg., 1990-91; sec., asst. Bill Vollendorff Appraisal, Walla Walla, Wash., 1991-92; inventory supr., purchaser Sierra Office Concepts/Nev. Copy Systems, Reno, 1992-95, mem. employee adv. com., 1993-94; with Tahoe Office Sys. Nev. Copy Sys., Tahoe City, Calif., 1995-96; asst. adminstrn., asst. contr. Interstate Safety and Supply, Inc., Sparks, Nev., 1996—. Active Adopt-A-Sch. Program, Reno, 1992;-co-sponsor Nev. Women's Fund, Reno, 1993. Democrat. Baptist. Avocations: reading, baking, fishing, nature hikes. Office: Interstate Safety and Supply 901 Meredith Way Sparks NV 89431

VANDERGRIFF, JERRY DODSON, retired computer store executive; b. Ft. Leonard Wood, Mo., Nov. 6, 1943; s. Oliver Wyatt Vandergriff and Mary Ella (Perkins) Myers; m. Donna Jean Niehof, Aug. 14, 1976 (div. Nov. 1987); children: Robert Lee II, William Oliver. BS in Bus., Emporia State U., 1974. Customer svc. mgr. Pictures, Inc., Anchorage, 1975-83, v.p., gen. mgr., 1983-87; gen. mgr. Pictures-The Computer Store, Anchorage, 1987-96; ret., 1996. Bd. dirs. Community Schs. Coun., Anchorage, 1986-87; mem. Gov.'s Coun. on Edn., 1989-90; bd. dirs. Romig Jr. High Sch., 1989-90, pres. PTSA, 1990-92; mem. exec. bd. Alaska's Youth Ready for Work, 1989-92. Mem. VFW. Republican. Avocations: movies, reading, pool, fishing, scuba diving. Home: 3831 Balchen Dr Anchorage AK 99517-2446

VANDERHEYDEN, MIRNA-MAR, resort management and services executive; b. Freeport, Ill., Oct. 8, 1932; d. Orville Ray and Frances Elmira (Miller) Van Brocklin; m. Roger Eugene Vanderheyden, Dec. 23, 1950 (div. 1983); children: Romayne Lee, Adana Dawn, Grayling Dwayne, Willow B., Tiffany LaMarr. Cert., Brown's Bus. Coll., Freeport, Ill., 1949; BA, Milliken U., 1953. Paralegal various locations, 1953-93; pres. Carlin Bay Corp., Coeur d'Alene, Idaho, 1981—. Lobbyist PTA, Springfield, Ill., 1972. Avocations: painting, water sports, reading, gardening, skiing. Home: 609 W Apple Dr Delta CO 81416-3062 Office: Carlin Bay Svcs 609 W Apple Dr Delta CO 81416-3062

VANDERHOEF, LARRY NEIL, academic administrator; b. Perham, Minn., Mar. 20, 1941; s. Wilmar James and Ida Lucille (Wothe) V.; m. Rosalie Suzanne Slifka, Aug. 31, 1963; children: Susan Marie, Jonathan Lee. B.S., U. Wis., Milw., 1964, M.S., 1965; Ph.D., Purdue U., 1969. Postdoctorate U. Wis., Madison, 1969-70; research assoc. U. Wis., summers 1970-72; asst. prof. biology U. Ill., Urbana, 1970-74; assoc. prof. U. Ill., 1974-77, prof., 1977—, head dept. plant biology, 1977-80; provost Agrl. and Life Scis., U. Md., College Park, 1980-84; exec. vice chancellor U. Calif., Davis, 1984-91, exec. vice chancellor, provost, 1991-94; chancellor, 1994—; vis. investigator Carnegie Inst., 1976-77, Edinburgh (Scotland) U., 1978; cons. in field. NRC postdoctoral fellow, 1969-70, Eisenhower fellow, 1987; Dimond travel grantee, 1975, NSF grantee, 1972, 74, 76, 77, 78, 79, NATO grantee, 1980. Mem. AAAS, Am. Soc. Plant Physiology (bd. editors Plant Physiology 1977-82, trustee, mem. exec. com., treas. 1982-88, chmn. bd. trustees 1994—), Nat. Assn. State Univ. and Land Grant Colls. Home: 615 Francisco Pl Davis CA 95616-0210 Office: U Calif Davis Office Chancellor Davis CA 95616

VANDERHOOF, IRWIN THOMAS, life insurance company executive; b. Newark, Dec. 4, 1927; s. Irwin and Dora (Blanchard) V.; m. Ruth Elizabeth Green, Feb. 18, 1949; children: Thomas Arthur Irwin, Karen McNeill Brundage. B.S., Worcester (Mass.) Poly. Inst., 1948; PhD in Fin., NYU, 1987. C.L.U.; chartered fin. analyst. Asst. actuarial supr. Met. Life Ins. Co., 1951-55; assoc. actuary U.S. Life Ins. Co., 1955-59; exec. v.p., treas. Standard Security Life Ins. Co., 1959-73; sr. v.p. Equitable Life Assurance Soc. U.S., N.Y.C., 1973-87; pres. Actuarial Investment Cons. Inc., Towaco, N.J., 1987—; prof. Stern Sch. Bus., NYU; bd. dirs. Analytic Risk Mgmt., Louisville. Author papers in field. Pres. Montville (N.J.) Twp. Bd. Edn., 1962. Fellow Soc. Actuaries, Life Officer Mgmt. Inst.; assoc. Casualty Actuarial Soc., Inst. Actuaries; mem. N.Y. Soc. Security Analysts, Am. Acad. Actuaries. Republican. Episcopalian.

VANDER HORST, KATHLEEN PURCELL, nonprofit association administrator; b. Glen Rock, N.J., Jan. 15, 1945; d. Thomas Ralph and Elizabeth Jeanne (Burnett) Purcell; m. John Vander Horst Jr., Feb. 12, 1972 (div. Oct. 1993). Dir. devel. svcs. Johns Hopkins U., Balt., 1968-71; dir. devel. Union of Colls. of Art, Kansas City, Mo., 1971-72; dir. pub. rels. Md. Ballet and Ctr. Stage, Balt., 1973-76; dir. program devel. Joint Ctr. for Polit. and Econ. Studies, Washington, 1976-90, v.p. for program devel., 1990—. Dir., chmn. fin. com. Roland Park Community Found., Balt., 1990—. Office: Joint Ctr for Polit & Econ 1090 Vermont Ave NW Washington DC 20005-4905

VAN DER KROEF, JUSTUS MARIA, political science educator; b. Djakarta, Indonesia, Oct. 30, 1925; came to U.S., 1942, naturalized, 1952; s. Hendrikus Leonardus and Maria Wilhelmina (van Lokven) van der K.; m. Orell Joan Ellison, Mar. 25, 1955 (dec.); children: Adrian Hendrick, Sri Orell. B.A., Millsaps Coll., 1944; M.A., U. N.C., 1947; Ph.D., Columbia U., 1953. Asst. prof. fgn. studies Mich. State U., 1948-55; Charles Dana prof., coord. dept. polit. sci. and sociology U. Bridgeport, Conn., 1956-92, prof. emeritus, 1992—; vis. prof. Nanyang U., Singapore, U. Philippines, Quezon City, Vidyodaya U., Sri Lanka Colombo; dir. Am.-Asian Ednl. Exchange, 1969—; chmn. editorial bd. Communications Research Services, Inc., Greenwich, Conn., 1971-80; mem. internat. adv. bd. Union Trust Bank, Stamford, Conn., 1974-88, adv. bd., 1988-94; mem. nat. acad. adv. council Charles Edison Meml. Youth Fund; bd. dirs. WUBC-TV, Bridgeport, Conn., 1978-80. Author: Indonesia in the Modern World, 2 vols., 1954-56, Indonesian Social Evolution. Some Psychological Considerations, 1958, The Communist Party of Indonesia: Its History, Program and Tactics, 1965, Communism in Malaysia and Singapore, 1967, Indonesia Since Sukarno, 1971, The Lives of SEATO, 1976, Communism in Southeast Asia, 1980, Kampuchea: The Endless Tug of War, 1982, Aquino's Philippines. The Deepening Security Crisis, 1988, Territorial Claims in the South China Sea, 1992, The South China Sea Problem: Some Alternative Scenarios, 1994; mem. editorial bd. World Affairs, 1975—, Jour. Asian Affairs, 1975—, Asian Affairs, 1980—, Asian Profile, 1983—, Jour. of Govt. and Adminstrn., 1985—, Jour. of Econ. and Internat. Relations, 1987—, Asian Affairs Jour. (Karachi), 1992—; mng. editor: Asian Thought and Society, 1986—; book rev. editor: Asian Thought and Soc, 1976-85. Mem. City Charter Revision Com. City of Bridgeport, 1983-86, 90-92. Served with Royal Netherlands Marine Corps, 1944-45. Sr. fellow Research Inst. Communist Affairs, Columbia U., 1965-66, Rockefeller Found.; fellow U. Queensland, Brisbane, Australia, 1968-69; research fellow Inst. Strategic Studies, Islamabad, Pakistan, 1982—; research fellow Mellon Research Found., 1983, 90; research fellow Internat. Ctr. Asian Studies, Hong Kong, 1983—. Mem. Univ. Profs. Acad. Order (nat. pres. 1970-71), Pi Gamma Mu, Phi Alpha Theta, Lambda Chi Alpha, Alpha Sigma Lambda Phi Sigma Iota. Home: 165 Linden Ave Bridgeport CT 06604-5730

VANDER LAAN, MARK ALAN, lawyer; b. Akron, Ohio, Sept. 14, 1948; s. Robert H. and Isabel R. (Bishop) Vander L.; m. Barbara Ann Ryzenga, Aug. 25, 1970; children: Aaron, Matthew. AB, Hope Coll., 1970; JD, U. Mich., 1972. Bar: Ohio 1973, U.S. Dist. Ct. (so. dist.) Ohio 1973, U.S. Ct. Appeals (6th cir.) 1978, U.S. Supreme Ct. 1981. Assoc. Dinsmore, Shohl, Coates & Deupree, Cin., 1972-79; ptnr. Dinsmore & Shohl, Cin., 1979—; spl. counsel Ohio Atty. Gen.'s Office, 1983—; spl. prosecutor State of Ohio, 1985-94; city solicitor City of Blue Ash, Ohio, 1987—; trustee Cin. So. Railway, 1994—. Mme. Cin. Human Rels. Commn., 1980-86; mem. Leadership Cin. Class XIII, 1989-90; trustee Legal Aid Soc. of Cin., 1981-94, pres., 1988-90. Mem. ABA, Ohio Bar Assn., Cin. Bar Assn. (ethics com. 1983—), Sixth Cir. Jud. Conf. (life), Potter Stewart Inn of Ct. (master), Queen City Club. Office: Dinsmore & Shohl 1900 Chemed Ct 255 E 5th St Cincinnati OH 45202-4700

VANDERLAAN, RICHARD B., marketing company executive; b. Grand Rapids, Mich., Sept. 2, 1931; s. Sieger B. and Helen (Kerr) V.; cert. liberal arts Grand Rapids Jr. Coll., 1952; cert. mech. engring. U. Mich., 1955; cert. indsl. engring. Mich. State U., 1960; cert. Harvard Bus. Sch., 1970; m. Sally E. Conroy, Mar. 26, 1982; children: Sheryl Vanderlaan, Pamella Vanderlaan DeVos, Brenda Vanderlaan Thompson. Tool engr. Four Square Mfg. Co., Grand Rapids, 1950-60; sales engr. Ametek, Lansdale, Pa., 1960-63; br. mgr. J.N. Fauver Co., Grand Rapids, 1964-68; v.p. Fauver Co. subs. Sun Oil Co., Grand Rapids 1968-76, exec. v.p., 1976-80; pres. House of Printers, Inc., 1980-82, also dir.; pres. Richard Vanderlaan Assocs., 1982—. Named eagle scout Boy Scouts Am. Mem. Mfrs. Agts. Nat. Assn., Soc. Automotive Engrs. Republican. Clubs: Birmingham Country, Oakland Hills Country, Economic of Detroit, Detroit Athletic. Avocations: golf, tennis. Office: 22157 Metamora Ln Franklin MI 48025-3609

VANDERLEEST, DIRK, airport executive. Exec. dir. Jackson (Miss.) Mcpl. Airport Authority, Jackson Internat. Airport. Office: Jackson Internat Airport PO Box 98109 Jackson MS 39298-8109

VANDERLINDE, RAYMOND EDWARD, clinical chemist; b. Newark, N.Y., Feb. 28, 1924; s. Isaac Edward and Hazel Effie (Robinson) V.; m. Ruth Louise Hansen, June 19, 1948; children: Susan Kay, Jeanne, William Edward. AB magna cum laude, Syracuse U., 1944, MS, 1945, PhD in Med. Biochemistry, 1950. Diplomate: Am. Bd. Clin. Chemistry. Asst. prof. biochemistry U. Md. Sch. Medicine, 1950-53, assoc. prof., 1953-57; lab. dir., asst. prof. Syracuse Meml. Hosp.-Upstate Med. Center, Syracuse, 1957-62; clin. chemist Meml. Hosp., Cumberland, Md., 1962-65; dir. labs. for clin. chemistry N.Y. State Dept. Health, Albany, 1965-76; prof. pathology and lab. medicine Hahnemann U., Phila., 1977-90, prof. emeritus, 1990; mem. lab. tech. adv. com. Pa. Dept. Health, 1981-85; mem. Coun. Nat. Reference Sys. in Clin. Chemistry, 1978—, vice chair holder, 1987, 91-93, chair holder, 1988-90; mem. Commn. on Accreditation in Clin. Chemistry, 1980-93; mem. enzyme subcom. Commn. on World Standardization, World Assn. Socs. of Pathology, 1978-90. Editor: Selected Methods of Clinical Chemistry, 1977-83, Annals of Clinical and Laboratory Science, 1981-93, Clinical Chemistry, 1983-92. Chmn. council on ministries, lay del. to annl. conf. Berwyn United Methodist Ch., 1979-82. Nat. Inst. Arthritis, Metabolism and Digestive Diseases grantee, 1977-81; NIH Lab. Standardization Panel for Lipids, 1986-90. Fellow Am. Assn. for Clin. Chemistry (bd. dirs. 1979-81, Fisher award 1985, Rheinhold award 1992); mem. Am. Chem. Soc., Am. Soc. Clin. Pathologists (assoc.), Acad. Clin. Lab. Physicians and Scientists, Assn. of Clin. Scientists, Soc. Mayflower Descs. of Am., Masons, Rotary (past pres. Delmar, N.Y.), Phi Beta Kappa, Sigma Xi. Democrat. Methodist. Home: Brookside #636 719 Maiden Choice Ln Catonsville MD 21228-6117

VANDERLINDEN, CAMILLA DENICE DUNN, telecommunications industry manager; b. Dayton, July 21, 1950; d. Joseph Stanley and Virginia Danley (Martin) Dunn; m. David Henry VanderLinden; Oct. 10, 1980; 1 child, Michael Christopher. Student, U. de Valencia, Spain, 1969; BA in Spanish and Secondary Edn. cum laude, U. Utah, 1972, MS in Human Resource Econs., 1985. Asst. dir. Davis County Community Action Program, Farmington, Utah, 1973-76; dir. South County Community Action, Midvale, Utah, 1976-79; supr. customer service Ideal Nat. Life Ins. Co., Salt Lake City, 1979-80; mgr. customer service Utah Farm Bur. Mutual Ins., Salt Lake City, 1980-82; quality assurance analyst Am. Express Co., Salt Lake City, 1983-86, quality assurance and human resource specialist, 1986-88; mgr. quality assurance and engring. Am. Express Co., Denver, 1988-91; mgr. customer svc. Tel. Express Co., Colorado Springs, Colo., 1991—; mem. adj. faculty Westminster Coll., Salt Lake City, 1987-88. mem. adj. faculty, mem. quality adv. bd. Red Rocks Community Coll., 1990-91. Vol. translator Latin Am. community; vol. naturalist Roxborough State Park; internat. exch. coord. EF Fgn. Exch. Program. Christian. Avocations: swimming, hosting fgn. exchange students. Home: 10857 W Snow Cloud Trl Littleton CO 80125-9210

VANDERLIP, ELIN BREKKE, philanthropic executive; b. Oslo, Norway, June 7, 1919; came to the U.S., 1934; m. Kelvin Cox, Nov., 1946 (dec. 1956); children: Kelvin Jr., Narcissa, Henrik and Katrina (twins). With Norwegian Embassy, Washington, Norwegian Fgn. Ministry, London, 1941-44, Red Cross, Calcutta, India; pres. Friends of French Art, Portuguese Bend, Calif.; sponsor of charity art conservation fundraising events Friends of French Art; tour leader Ile de France, Anjou, Bordelais, Provence-Cote d'Azur, Alsace, Dordogne, Lyonnais-Isere, Brittany, Burgundy, Normandy, Languedoc, Loire, Gascony, Le Nord, Charente and Champagne, 1978-96. Decorated Comdr. Order of Arts and Letters (France). Home and Office: Villa Narcissa 100 Vanderlip Dr Rancho Palos Verdes CA 90275

VAN DER MARCK, JAN, art historian; b. Roermond, The Netherlands, Aug. 19, 1929; s. Everard and Anny (Finken) van der M.; m. Ingeborg Lachmann, Apr. 27, 1961 (dec. Dec. 1988); m. Sheila Stamell, May 24, 1990. BA, U. Nijmegen, The Netherlands, 1952, MA, 1954, PhD in Art History, 1956; postgrad., U. Utrecht, The Netherlands, 1956-57, Columbia U., 1957-59. Curator Gemeentemuseum, Arnhem, The Netherlands, 1959-61; asst. dir. fine arts Seattle World's Fair, 1961-62; curator Walker Art Center, Mpls., 1963-67; dir. Mus. Contemporary Art, Chgo., 1967-70; assoc. prof. art history U. Wash., 1972-74; dir. Dartmouth Coll. Mus. and Galleries, 1974-80, Center for Fine Arts, Miami, 1980-85; curator 20th century art, chief curator Detroit Inst. Arts, 1986-95. Author: Romantische Boekillustratie in Belgie, 1956, George Segal, 1975, Arman, 1984, Bernar Venet, 1988, Decorated Bindings, 1996; contbr. articles to art jours., essays to catalogues. Decorated chevalier Order Arts and Letters; Netherlands Orgn. Pure Rsch. fellow, 1954-55, Rockefeller Found. fellow, 1957-59, Aspen Inst. fellow, 1974, 94; vis. sr. fellow Ctr. for Advanced Study in Visual Arts, Washington, 1986. Mem. Internat. Art Critics Assn., Internat. Coun. Museums.

VANDER MEER, HARRY, church administrator. Fin. co-ordinator Christian Ref. Ch. in N. Am. Office: Chirstian Ref Ch in N Am 2850 Kalamazoo Ave SE Grand Rapids MI 49508-1433

VAN DER MERWE, NIKOLAAS JOHANNES, archaeologist; b. Riviersonderend, Republic of South Africa, Aug. 11, 1940; came to U.S., 1958; s. Johannes Abraham and Rachel Maria (Burger) van der M.; m. Julia Ann Feeny, Nov. 11, 1962 (div. 1969); 1 child, Kerstin; m. Karen Elaine Bardou, Feb. 19, 1973; 1 child, Nicolina Thandiwe. BA cum laude, Yale U., 1962, MA, 1965, PhD, 1966; MA (hon.), Harvard U., 1988; DSc (hon.), U. Port Elizabeth, 1995. Curatorial asst. Yale Peabody Mus., New Haven, 1962-64; rsch. asst. Yale Radiocarbon Lab., New Haven, 1963-66; asst. prof. anthropology SUNY, Binghamton, 1966-69, assoc. prof., 1969-74; prof. archaeology U. Cape Town, Republic of South Africa, 1974-88; Landon Clay prof. sci. archaeology, earth and planetary scis. Harvard U., Cambridge, Mass., 1988—; dir. Ctr. African Studies, U. Cape Town, 1976-80. Author: The Carbon 14 Dating of Iron, 1969; co-editor: (collection of essays) Perspectives on South Africa's Future, 1979, Iron Age in Southern Africa, 1979; contbr. numerous articles to profl. jours. Fellow U. Cape Town, 1986; Ford Found. Fgn. Area fellow, 1964-66. Fellow AAAS, Royal Soc. South Africa (John F.W. Herschel medal 1994),, Am. Anthrop. Assn., Explorers Club, Soc. Antiquaries (London); mem. South African Archaeol. Soc. (life), Soc. Am. Archaeology, Hist. Metallurgy Group, South African Assn. Archaeologists (founder), West African Assn. Archaeology (founder), Soc. Archaeol. Sci. (life), Owl Club (Cape Town), Concord (Mass.) Rod and Gun, Sigma Xi. Avocations: flying, diving, shooting, hiking, cooking. Home: 475 River Rd Carlisle MA 01741-1819 Office: Harvard Univ Peabody Mus/Dept Anthropology 11 Divinity Ave Cambridge MA 02138-2096

VAN DER MEULEN, JOSEPH PIERRE, neurologist; b. Boston, Aug. 22, 1929; s. Edward Lawrence and Sarah Jane (Robertson) VanDer M.; m. Ann Irene Yadeno, June 18, 1960; children—Elisabeth, Suzanne, Janet. A.B., Boston Coll., 1950; M.D., Boston U., 1954. Diplomate: Am. Bd. Psychiatry and Neurology. Intern Cornell Med. div. Bellevue Hosp., N.Y.C., 1954-55; resident Cornell Med. div. Bellevue Hosp., 1955-56; resident Harvard U., Boston City Hosp., 1958-60, instr., fellow, 1962-66; assoc. Case Western Res. U., Cleve., 1966-67; asst. prof. Case Western Res. U., 1967-69, assoc. prof. neurology and biomed. engring., 1969-71; prof. neurology U. So. Calif., L.A., 1971—; also dir. dept. neurology Los Angeles County/U. So. Calif. Med. Center; chmn. dept. U. So. Calif., 1971-78, v.p. for health affairs, 1977—, dean Sch. Medicine, 1985-86, 95—, vice dean med. affairs, 1995—; vis. prof. Autonomous U. Guadalajara, Mex., 1974; pres. Norris Cancer Hosp. and Research Inst., 1983—. Contbr. articles to profl. jours. Mem. med. adv. bd. Calif. chpt. Myasthenia Gravis Found., 1971-75, chmn., 1974-75, 77-78; med. adv. bd. Amyotrophic Lateral Sclerosis Found., Calif., 1973-75, chmn., 1974-75; mem. Com. to Combat Huntington's Disease, 1973—; bd. dirs. Calif. Hosp. Med. Ctr., Good Hope Med. Found., Doheny Eye Hosp., House Ear Inst., L.A. Hosp. Good Samaritan, Children's Hosp. of L.A., Barlow Respiratory Hosp., USC U. Hosp., chmn., 1991—; bd. govs. Thomas Aquinas Coll.; bd. dirs. Assn. Acad. Health Ctrs., chmn., 1991-92; pres. Scott Newman Ctr., 1987-89; pres., bd. dirs. Kenneth Norris Cancer Hosp & Rsch. Inst. Served to lt. M.C. USNR, 1956-58. Nobel Inst. fellow Karolinska Inst., Stockholm, 1960-62; NIH grantee, 1968-71. Mem. AMA, Am. Neurol. Assn., Am. Acad. Neurology, L.A. Soc. Neurology and Psychiatry (pres. 1977-78), L.A. Med. Assn., Mass. Med. Soc., Ohio Med. Soc., Calif. Med. Soc., L.A. Acad. Medicine, Alpha Omega Alpha (councillor 1992—), Phi Kappa Phi. Home: 39 Club View Ln Palos Verdes Peninsula CA 90274-4208 Office: U So Calif 1540 Alcazar St Los Angeles CA 90033-1058

VANDER MOLEN, THOMAS DALE, lawyer; b. Ann Arbor, Mich., Oct. 30, 1950; s. John and Eleanor Ruth (Driesens) Vander M.; m. Marlese Kay Alden, June 29, 1974; children: Laura, David, Eric. BA, Calvin Coll., 1972; JD magna cum laude, Harvard U., 1975. Bar: Minn. 1976, U.S. Dist. Ct. Minn. 1981, U.S. Claims Ct. 1983, U.S. Tax Ct. 1977, U.S. Ct. Appeals 1988. Law clk. to judge U.S. Ct. Appeals-First Cir., Boston, 1975-76; assoc. Dorsey & Whitney, Mpls., 1976-81; ptnr. Dorsey & Whitney LLP, Mpls., 1982—; gen. counsel Dorsey & Whitney, P.L.L.P., Mpls., 1993—. Mem. editorial bd. Harvard Law Rev., 1973-75. Presbyterian. Office: Dorsey & Whitney LLP 2100 Pillsbury Ctr S 220 S 6th St Minneapolis MN 55402-1498

VANDER MYDE, PAUL ARTHUR, engineering services executive; b. Estherville, Iowa, Feb. 9, 1937; s. Louis John and Anna Marie (Pals) Vander M.; m. Jeanne Elizabeth Russell, Sept. 8, 1973. BA, U. Minn., 1959; MA, U. Iowa, 1966. Staff asst. Nat. Security Agy., Ft. Meade, Md., 1962-68; congressional fellow U.S. Rep. George Bush/U.S. Senator Bob Packwood, Washington, 1968-69; legis. asst. U.S. Senator Bob Packwood, Washington, 1969-71; exec. asst. Office of Vice-Pres., White House, Washington, 1971-73; staff mem. domestic council White House, Washington, 1973; dep. asst. sec. for conservation, research and edn. U.S. Dept. Agr., Washington, 1973-77; minority staff dir. Sci. and Tech. Com., Ho. of Reps., 1977-81; asst. sec. for congressional and inter-govtl. affairs U.S. Dept. Commerce, Washington, 1981-87; v.p. corp. affairs VSE Corp., Alexandria, Va., 1987—; guest speaker numerous profl. confs. and seminars. Contbr. articles to profl. jours. Bd. dirs. Profl. Svcs. Coun., Washington, U.S. Naval Aviation Mus., Pensacola, Fla; vice chmn. Adminstrv. Conf. of U.S., Washington. With USN, 1959-61; capt. USNR (ret.). Decorated Meritorious Svc. medal. Mem. Naval Res. Assn., U.S. Navy League, Alexandria C. of C. (vice chmn.), Sovereign Mil. Order Knights Templar of Jerusalem, Belle Haven Country Club, Rotary Club Alexandria. Episcopalian. Office: VSE Corp 2550 Huntington Ave Alexandria VA 22303-1400

VANDERPLOEG, JAMES M., preventive medicine physician; b. Upland, Calif., Nov. 22, 1950. BA, U. Iowa, 1975. Intern U. Hosp./U. Calif., San Diego, 1975-76; resident in otolaryngoloty U. Iowa Hosps., Iowa City, 1978-79; resident in occupational medicine U. Tex. Sch. Pub. Health, Houston, 1980-82, assoc. prof. occupational health; mem. staff St. John Hosp., Nassau Bay, Tex.; pvt. practice, ptnr. group practice; part-time med. adminstr. Mem. Am. Coll. Occupational Medicine, ACPrM-AerosMA. Office: Ctr for Aerospace &Occupational Medicine 700 Gemimi Ave Ste 110 Houston TX 77068*

VANDERPOEL, JAMES ROBERT, lawyer; b. Harvey, Ill., Sept. 27, 1955; s. Waid Richard and Ruth (Silberman) V.; m. Deanne Czabaranek, May 1987; children: Jacqueline, Robert, Jennifer. BS in Fin., Ind. U., 1978; JD, Santa Clara U., 1982. Bar: Calif. 1982, U.S. Dist. Ct. (no. dist.) Calif. 1982. Group contracts mgr. Motorola Computer Group, Tempe, Ariz., 1984—. Avocations: basketball, hiking, golf, snorkeling, gardening. Office: Motorola Computer Group 2900 S Diablo Way Tempe AZ 85282

VANDERPOOL, WARD MELVIN, management and marketing consultant; b. Oakland, Mo., Jan. 20, 1919; s. Oscar B. and Clara (McGuire) V.; m. Lee Kendall, July 7, 1935. MEE, Tulane U. V.p. charge sales Van Lang Brokerage, Los Angeles, 1934-38; mgr. agrl. div. Dayton Rubber Co., Chgo., 1939-48; pres., gen. mgr. Vee Mac Co., Rockford, Ill., 1948—; pres., dir. Zipout, Inc., Rockford, 1951—, Wife Saver Products, Inc., 1959—; chmn. bd. Zipout Internat., Kenvan Inc., 1952—, Shevan Corp., 1951—, Atlas Internat. Corp.; pres. Global Enterprises Ltd., Global Assos. Ltd.; chmn. bd. dirs. Am. Atlas Corp., Atlas Chem. Corp., Merzat Industries Ltd.; trustee Ice Crafter Trust, 1949—; bd. dirs. Atlas Chem. Internat. Ltd., Kenlee Internat., Ltd., Shrimp Tool Internat. Ltd.; mem. Toronto Bd. Trade; chmn. bd. dirs. Am. Atlas Corp., Am. Packaging Corp. Mem. adv. bd. Nat. Security Council, congl. adv. com. Heritage Found.; mem. Rep. Nat. Com., Presdl. Task Force, Congrl. Adv. Com. Hon. mem. Internat. Swimming Hall of Fame. Mem. Nat. (dir. at large), Rock River (past pres.) sales execs., Sales and Mktg. Execs. Internat. (dir.), Am. Mgmt. Assn., Rockford Engring. Soc., Am. Tool Engrs., Internat. Acad. Aquatic Art (dir.), Am. Inst. Mgmt. (pres. council), Am. Ordnance Assn., Internat. Platform Assn., Heritage Found., Ill. C. of C. Clubs: Jesters, Elks, IAA Swim, Exec., Elmcrest Country, Pyramid, Dolphin, Marlin, Univ., Univ. Athletic, Oxford. Lodges: Masons (consistory), Shriners, Elks. Home: 374 Parkland Dr SE Cedar Rapids IA 52403-2031 also: 40 Richview Rd # 308, Toronto, ON Canada

M9A 5C1 also: 704 Park Center Dr Santa Ana CA 92705-3563 Office: PO Box 1972 Cedar Rapids IA 52406-1972 also: 111 Richmond St W Ste 318, Toronto, ON Canada M5H 1T1

VANDER PUTTEN, LEROY ANDREW, insurance company executive; b. Appleton, Wis., Aug. 20, 1934; s. Theo S. and Lorraine M. (Quella) Vander P.; m. Evon Marie Schumacher, July 3, 1956; children: Suzanna, Dale, Lisa, Carole, Kim. BS in Math. and Psychology, Wis. State U., 1961; Advanced Mgmt. Program, Harvard U., 1983-84. Asst. sec. EDP research Aetna Life & Casualty, Hartford, Conn., 1968-69, asst. cashier, 1969-74, dir. investment planning, 1974-79, asst. v.p. investment planning, 1979-81, v.p. investment planning, 1981-82, v.p. corp. fin., 1982-86, v.p. and deputy treas., 1986-87, chmn., pres., chief exec. officer Exec. Re Idemnity Inc., Simsbury, Conn., 1987-93; chmn., chief exec. officer Exec. Risk, Inc., Simsbury, Conn., 1994—, also bd. dirs., 1986—; adv. bd. Conn. Nat. Bank, 1988—; Chmn. South Windsor Econ. Devel. Com., Conn., 1977; trustee Talcott Mountain Sci. Ctr., Avon, Conn. Recipient Distinguished Alumni award U. Wis., 1987—. With USCG, 1952-56. Mem. AMP 91 Assocs. of Boston (treas. 1982—). Republican. Roman Catholic. Avocations: sailing, sports car restoration, canoeing. Office: Exec Risk Inc 82 Hopmeadow St PO Box 2002 Simsbury CT 06070

VANDERRYN, JACK, philanthropic foundation administrator; b. Groningen, The Netherlands, Apr. 14, 1930; came to U.S., 1939; s. Herman Gabriel and Henrietta S.E. (Hartog) V.; m. Margrit Wolfes, Mar. 18, 1956; children: David, Judith, Amy, Daniel. BA, Lehigh U., 1951, MS, 1952, PhD, 1955. Rsch. and grad. teaching asst. Lehigh U., Bethlehem, Pa., 1952-55; asst. prof. chemistry Va. Poly. Inst., Blacksburg, 1955-58; rsch. participant Oak Ridge (Tenn.) Nat. Lab., 1957; chemist AEC, Oak Ridge, 1958-62, tech. adviser to asst. gen. mgr. R & D, Washington, 1962-67, asst. to gen. mgr., 1971-72, tech. asst. to dir. div. applied tech., 1972-73, chief energy tech. br., div. applied tech., 1973-75; acting dir. div. energy storage Energy Rsch. and Devel. Adminstrn., Washington, 1975, dir. Office Internat. R & D Programs, 1975-77; dir. Office Internat. Programs Dept. Energy, Washington, 1977-82; dir. energy and natural resources AID, Washington, 1982-91; program dir. environment Moriah Fund, Chevy Chase, Md., 1991—; sr. sci. adviser U.S. Mission to Internat. Atomic Energy Agy., Dept. State, Vienna, Austria, 1967-71; lectr. Brookings Instn., 1965-66. Mem., dep. pres., exec. bd. Am. Internat. Sch., Vienna, 1968-71; v.p. Oak Ridge Civic Music Assn., 1959-60; pres. Washington Print Club, 1986-91. Fellow AAAS. Home: 8112 Whittier Blvd Bethesda MD 20817-3123 Office: Moriah Fund 35 Wisconsin Cir Chevy Chase MD 20815-7015

VANDERSALL, JOHN HENRY, dairy science educator; b. Helena, Ohio, July 20, 1928; s. Clarence C. and Ida M. (Barnhope) V.; m. Patricia L. King, May 11, 1963; children: Eric John, Karen Susan. B.S., Ohio State U., 1950, M.S., 1954, Ph.D., 1959. Farm researcher Ralston Purina Co., 1950; from research asst. to instr. Ohio State U. Agrl. Expt. Sta., 1953-59; mem. faculty U. Md., 1959—, prof. dairy sci., 1971-93, prof. emeritus, 1993—. Contbr. articles to profl. jours. Served with AUS, 1950-52. Mem. Am. Dairy Sci. Assn., Am. Soc. Animal Sci., AAAS, Sigma Xi. Home: 10906 Ashfield Rd Hyattsville MD 20783-1003 Office: Dept Animal Sci Univ Md College Park MD 20742

VANDERSLICE, JOSEPH THOMAS, chemist; b. Phila., Dec. 21, 1927; s. Joseph R. and Mae (Daly) V.; m. Patricia Mary Horstmann, Nov. 20, 1954; children—Sharon, Joseph, Julie, Peter, John, Polly, Jeffrey, Amy. BS in Chemistry magna cum laude, Boston Coll., 1949; Ph.D. in Phys. Chemistry (Allied Chem. and Dye fellow), Mass. Inst. Tech., 1953. Mem. faculty Cath. U. Am., 1952-56, asst. prof., 1955-56; mem. faculty U. Md., College Park, 1956-79, prof. emeritus, 1978—; prof. chem. physics U. Md., 1963-79; dir. U. Md. (Inst. Molecular Physics), 1967-69, chmn. chemistry dept., 1968-76; research chemist Nutrition Inst., U.S. Dept. Agr., Beltsville, Md., 1978-94. Author: (with Schamp and Mason) Thermodynamics, 1966; mem. editl. bd. Jour. Micronutrient Analysis, 1985-91, Food Chemistry, 1992, Food Rsch. Internat., 1992—, Jour. Food Composition, 1994—; contbr. articles to profl. jours. Inducted into Boston Latin Sch. Athletic Hall of Fame, 1992; recipient Outstanding Alumni award Boston Coll., 1979. Fellow Washington Acad. Scis., Am. Phys. Soc.; mem. AAAS, Am. Inst. Food Technologists, Cosmos Club, Sigma Xi (award for sci. achievement 1971). Home: PO Box 221 Cobb Island MD 20625-0221

VANDERSLICE, THOMAS AQUINAS, electronics executive; b. Phila., Jan. 8, 1932; s. Joseph R. and Mae (Daly) V.; m. Margaret Hurley, June 9, 1956; children: Thomas Aquinas, Paul Thomas Aquinas, John Thomas Aquinas, Peter Thomas Aquinas. BS in Chemistry and Philosophy, Boston Coll., 1953; PhD in Chemistry and Physics, Cath. U. Am., 1956. With GE, Fairfield, Conn., from 1956, gen. mgr. electronic components bus. div., 1970-72, v.p., 1970, group exec. spl. systems and products group, 1972-77, sr. v.p., sector exec. Power System Sector, 1977-79, exec. v.p., sector exec. Power System Sector, 1979-84; chief oper. officer, dir. Gen. Tel. & Electronics Corp., Stamford, Conn., 1979-83; chmn., CEO, Apollo Computer, Inc., Chelmsford, Mass., 1984-89, M/A COM, Inc., Lowell, Mass., 1989-95; bd. dirs. Texaco, Inc. Patentee low pressure gas measurements and analysis, gas surface interactions and elec. discharges; co-author: Ultra High Vacuum and Its Applications, 1963; reviser: Scientific Foundations of Vacuum Technique, 1960; contbr. to profl. jours. Trustee Boston Coll., past chmn., past trustee Comm. Econ. Devel. Recipient Bicentennial medal Boston Coll., 1976; Fulbright scholar, 1953-56. Mem. NAE, ASTM, Am. Vacuum Soc., Am. Chem. Soc., Am. Inst. Physics, Royal Poinciana Golf Club (Naples, Fla.), Oyster Harbors Club, Sigma Xi, Tau Beta Pi, Alpha Sigma Nu, Sigma Pi Sigma. Office: TAV Associates Ste 3001 Two International Pl Boston MA 02110

VAN DER SMISSEN, M. E. BETTY, physical education educator; b. Great Bend, Kans., Dec. 27, 1927; d. Theodor Alwin and Margaret (Dirks) van der S. AB, U. Kans., 1949, JD, 1952; MS, Ind. U., 1954, D. Recreation, 1955. cons. in sport law, personal injury and negligence. Asst. prof. U. Iowa, Iowa City, 1956-65; prof. Pa. State U., University Park, 1965-79; dir. sch. health physical edn./prof. recreation Bowling Green (Ohio) State U., 1979-90; prof., chmn. park, recreation and tourism resources Mich. State U., East Lansing, 1990—. Author: Legal Liability and Risk Management of Public & Private Entities, 1990. Mem. Nat. Commn. for Accreditation of Park and Recreation Agys., 1st chair, 1994—. Recipient Disting. Fellow award Soc. Park and Recreation Educators, 1974, W.W. Patty Disting. Alumni award Ind. U. Sch. Health, Phys. Edn. and Recreation, 1993. Fellow Acad. Leisure Scis. (founder); mem. AAHPERD (R. Tait McKenzie award 1991), Nat. Recreation and Park Assn. (trustee 1988-90), Am. Acad. Park and Recreation Adminstrn. (bd. dirs. 1990-93), Am. Assn. Leisure and Recreation (Jay B. Nash award 1987), Am. Camping Assn. (nat. pres. 1980-82), Assn. for Experiential Edn. (Kurt Hahn award 1987). Home: 1920 Opaline Dr Lansing MI 48917-8639 Office: Mich State U 131 Natural Resources East Lansing MI 48824-1222

VAN DER SPIEGEL, JAN, engineering educator; b. Aalst, Belgium, Apr. 12, 1951; came to U.S., 1980; s. Robert and Celestine Van der Spiegel. BSEE, U. Leuven, 1971, MSEE, 1974, PhD in Elec. Engring., 1979; M of Arts and Sci., U. Pa., 1988. 2d lt. Belgian Air Force, 1979-90; asst. prof. elec. engring. U. Pa., Phila., 1981-87, assoc. prof., 1987-95, prof. elec. engring., 1995—, dir. Ctr. Sensor Tech., 1989—; Sec., treas. Corticon, Inc., Phila., 1991—; faculty master Ware Coll. Ho., U. Pa., Phila., 1992—. Patentee integ. ambient sensing, radiation sens. retina sens., gen prupost neural comp., novel ferroelectric sensors; editor Sensors and Actuators, 1986—. Postdoctoral fellow U. Pa., 1980-81; named Presdl. Young Investigator The White House, 1984. Mem. IEEE (sr.), Neural Network Soc., Tau Beta Pi. Office: U Pa Ctr Sensor Techs Moore Sch 200 S 33d St Rm 308 Philadelphia PA 19104-6314

VANDERSTAPPEN, HARRIE ALBERT, Far Eastern art educator; b. Heesch, The Netherlands, Jan. 21, 1921; came to U.S., 1959; s. Johannes and Johanna (van de Poel) V. Student, Theol. Sch., Helvoirt and Teteringen, The Netherlands, 1939-45, Chinese Lang. Sch., Peking, People's Republic of China, 1946-48; Ph.D. in Far Eastern Art, U. Chgo., 1955. Ordained priest Roman Catholic Ch., 1945. Student lang., also tchr., writer Tokyo, 1955-57; tchr. Nansan U., Nagoya, Japan, 1957-59; prof. Far Eastern art U. Chgo., 1959-92, chmn. dept. art, 1964-69. Author: The T.L. Yuan Bibliography of Chinese Art and Archaeology, 1975; author, editor: Ritual and Reverence, 1989; assoc. editor Monumenta Serica, 1955—; contbr. articles to profl. jours. Recipient Teaching of Art History award Nat. Coll. Art Assn. Am., 1985. Mem. Asia Soc., Assn. Asian Arts. Home: 2147 Bennett Ave Evanston IL 60201-2158

VANDERSTAR, JOHN, lawyer; b. Jersey City, Sept. 17, 1933; s. John Vanderstar and Rosemarie (Torraco) Legette; m. Beth S. Vanderstar, Nov. 7, 1956 (div. Oct. 1984); children: Pippa, Alexandra, Thankful, Eliza; m. M. Elizabeth Culbreth, Mar. 16, 1985. BSE, Princeton U., 1954; LLB cum laude, Harvard U., 1961. Bar: D.C. 1961, U.S. Dist. Ct. (D.C. dist.) 1961, U.S. Dist. Ct. Md. 1985, U.S. Ct. Claims 1976, U.S. Ct. Appeals (8th cir.) 1966, U.S. Ct. Appeals (5th cir.) 1969, U.S. Ct. Appeals (1st cir.) 1971, U.S. Ct. Appeals (4th cir.) 1974, U.S. Ct. Appeals (3d cir.) 1979, U.S. Ct. Appeals 11th cir.) 1981, U.S. Ct. Appeals (Fed. cir.) 1983, U.S. Supreme Ct. 1966. Assoc. Covington & Burling, Washington, 1961-70, ptnr., 1970—. Pres. ACLU Nat. Capital Area, Washington, 1976-78, bd. dirs., 1971-78; bd. dirs. NOW Legal Def. and Edn. Fund, N.Y.C., 1979-94. Lt. USNR, 1954-58. Recipient Alan Barth award, ACLU Nat. Capital Area, 1984. Mem. ABA, D.C. Bar (bd. govs. 1985-88). Episcopalian. Home: 3642 N Monroe St Arlington VA 22207-5317 Office: Covington & Burling 1201 Pennsylvania Ave NW PO Box 7566 Washington DC 20044

VANDERVEEN, JOHN E., federal agency administrator; b. Prospect Park, N.J., May 13, 1934; m. Ernestine Neuhardt, June 3, 1967; children: Keith Bradley, Kimetha Leigh. BS, Rutgers U., 1956; PhD, U. N.H., 1961. Nutritionist USAF, 1961-75; dir. divsn. nutrition FDA, Washington, 1975-92, dir. office plant & dairy foods and beverages, 1992—. Served to 1st lt. USAF, 1961-64. Office: FDA Ctr Food Safety and Applied Nutrition 200 C St SW Washington DC 20204-0001

VANDERVEEN, PETER, wholesale grocery company executive; b. 1931; married. LLB, U. Fla., 1949. With Hood Chem. Co., 1955-62; sales mgr. Fox Grocery Co., 1962-72; asst. to pres. Super Rite Foods, Inc., Harrisburg, Pa., 1977-80, pres., dir., 1980—. Office: Super Rite Foods Inc 3900 Industrial Rd Harrisburg PA 17110-2945*

VAN DERVEER, TARA, university athletic coach; b. Niagara Falls, N.Y., 1954. Grad., Indiana U., 1975. Coach women's basketball Stanford U. Cardinals, 1985—, U.S. Nat. Women's Team, 1995—. Champions NCAA Divsn. 1 A, 1990, 92. Office: c/o Stanford Univ Stanford CA 94305*

VANDERVELD, JOHN, JR., waste disposal company executive; b. Chgo., Oct. 24, 1926; s. John J. and Rose (Renkema) V. Pres. Nat. Disposal Contractors, Barrington, Ill., 1952-71; sr. v.p., dir. Browning Ferris Industries, Houston, 1971-78; pres. Pioneer Equities, Inc., 1975-90, C.J.V. Corp., Dallas, 1990-92; sr. corp. advisor Vector Environmental Techs., Inc., 1993—; dir. Am. Far East, Inc., Dallas and Tokyo; adv. bd. Southwestern Legal Found. Bd. dirs., exec. com. Internat. Bible Soc. Mem. Nat. Solid Waste Mgmt. Assn. (former chmn. govt. industry coordinating council, mem. environ. research com.). Home: 7031 Brookshire Dr Dallas TX 75230-4248

VANDER VELDE, WALLACE EARL, aeronautical and astronautical educator; b. Jamestown, Mich., June 4, 1929; s. Peter Nelson and Janet (Keizer) Vander V.; m. Winifred Helen Bunai, Aug. 29, 1954; children—Susan Jane, Peter Russell. B.S. in Aero Engring, Purdue U., 1951; Sc.D., Mass. Inst. Tech., 1956. Dir. applications engring. GPS Instrument Co., Inc., Newton, Mass., 1956-57; mem. faculty Mass. Inst. Tech., 1957—, prof. aero. and astronautics, 1965—; Cons. to industry, 1958—. Author: Flight Vehicle Control Systems, Part VII of Space Navigation, Guidance and Control, 1966, (with Arthur Gelb) Multiple-Input Describing Functions, 1968; also papers. Served to 1st lt. USAF, 1951-53. Recipient Edn. award Am. Automatic Control Coun., 1988. Fellow AIAA; mem. IEEE. Home: 50 High St Winchester MA 01890-3314 Office: MIT Rm 9-321 Dept Aero and Astronautics Cambridge MA 02139

VANDERVER, TIMOTHY ARTHUR, JR., lawyer; b. Birmingham, Ala., Jan. 25, 1944; s. Timothy Arthur and Jeanette (Grimes) V.; m. Virginia Cassandra Nye, Oct. 1, 1966; children: Timothy A. III, Glenn Bruce, Benjamin Richard. BA, Washington and Lee U., 1965; BA in Law, Oxford (Eng.) U., 1967, MA, 1983; JD, Harvard U., 1969. Bar: D.C., U.S. Ct. Appeals (D.C. cir.) 1969, U.S. Ct. Appeals (5th cir.) 1984, U.S. Ct. Appeals (3d and 11th cirs.) 1989, U.S. Supreme Ct. 1978. Assoc. Covington & Burling, Washington, 1969-72, Dept. of Interior, Washington, 1972-76; ptnr. Patton Boggs L.L.P., Washington, 1976—. Editor: Clean Air Law and Regulation, 1992, Environmental Law Handbook, 1994. Capt. U.S. Army, 1970-71. Presbyterian. Home: 9000 Congressional Ct Potomac MD 20854-4608 Office: Patton Boggs LLP 2550 M St NW Washington DC 20037-1301

VAN DER VOO, ROB, geophysicist; b. Zeist, The Netherlands, Aug. 4, 1940; came to U.S., 1970; s. Maximiliaan and Johanna Hendrika (Baggerman) Van der V.; m. Tatiana M. C. Graafland, Mar. 26, 1966; children—Serge Nicholas, Bjorn Alexander. B.S., U. Utrecht, Netherlands, 1961, M.S., 1965, Ph.D., 1969. Research asst. U. Utrecht, 1964-65, research asso., 1965-69, sr. research asso., 1969-70; vis. asst. prof. U. Mich., Ann Arbor, 1970-72; asst. prof. U. Mich., 1972-75, asso. prof., 1975-79, prof. geophysics, 1979—, chmn., 1981-88, 91-95, Arthur F. Thurnau prof., 1994—; guest prof. ETH, Zurich, Switzerland, 1978, Kuwait U., 1979. Author: Paleomagnetism of the Atlantic, Tethys and Iapetus Oceans, 1993; contbr. articles to profl. jours. Recipient Russel award U. Mich., 1976, Disting. Faculty Achievement award U.Mich., 1990. Mem. Geol. Soc. Am., Am. Geophys. Union, Geologische Vereinigung (W.Ger.), Royal Dutch Geol. and Mining Soc., Royal Acad. Scis. (Netherlands), Sigma Xi, Phi Kappa Phi. Home: 2305 Devonshire Rd Ann Arbor MI 48104-2703 Office: U Mich 4528 CC Little Bldg Ann Arbor MI 48109

VANDER VOORT, DALE GILBERT, textile company executive; b. Paterson, N.J., Feb. 7, 1924; s. Gilbert H. and Lillian (Hatton) Vander V.; m. Florine E. Storey, Aug. 6, 1944; children: Lydia Ann, Dale Gilbert, Roy Lee. B.M.E., Clemson U., 1944. Gen. mgr., dir. Stevens Line Assos., Webster, Mass., 1954-56; gen. mgr. Montreal Cottons Ltd., Valleyfield, Que., Can., 1951-54; supt. Mill 4 Dan River Mills, Danville, Va., 1946-51; sr. v.p. United Merchants & Mfrs. Inc., N.Y.C., 1972-77; chmn. bd. Asso. Textiles Can. Ltd., 1969-77; pres., chief exec. officer Arnold Print Works, Inc., Adams, Mass., 1977-83, Alton Fabrics, Allentown, Pa., 1983-85; pres. Asheville Dye & Finishing, Swannanoa, N.C., 1985-87; pres., chief exec. officer River Dyeing and Finishing Co., Asheville, N.C., 1988—; dir. Northwestern Bank, Asheville, N.C., Western Carolina Industries Inc., Brit. Silk Dyeing Co., Valchem Australia, Profile Sports Corp., West Lebanon, N.H. Mem. coun. Luth. Ch., 1962—. Lt. AUS, 1943-46. Decorated Bronze Star, Purple Heart. Mem. ASME, Am. Assn. Textile Chemists and Colorists, Can. Textile Inst. (dir.), Soc. Advancement of Mgmt. (nat. gov. 1961-62), Can. Club (N.Y.), Asheville Country Club. Home: 214 Stratford Rd Asheville NC 28804-1440 also: 131 Riverside Dr Asheville NC 28801-3136

VANDERVOORT, PETER, lawyer; b. Paterson, N.J., Dec. 15, 1929; s. Vincent and Jeannette Barbara (Scott) V.; m. Elena Drake, June 26, 1971. BA, Williams Coll., 1951; LLB, U. Va., 1954. Bar: Va. 1953, N.J. 1958. Assoc. Evans Hand, Paterson, 1958-62; ptnr. Evans Hand, West Paterson, N.J., 1963—; asst. sec. Essex Chem. Corp., Clifton, N.J., 1963-83, sec., 1983-88. Trustee West Side Presbyn. Ch., Ridgewood, N.J., 1961-67, Family Counselling Service of Ridgewood, 1968-77, Soc. Valley Hosp., Ridgewood, 1976-88; vice chmn. Valley Care Corp., 1988—; bd. dirs. Paterson YMCA, 1959-76, pres. 1967-74, trustee 1978—, chmn. 1984-88. Fellow Am. Coll. Trust and Estate Counsel; mem. ABA, N.J. Bar Assn., Va. Bar Assn., Ridgewood Country Club, Williams Club (N.Y.C.), Union League Club (N.Y.C.), Order of Coif, Phi Beta Kappa. Home: 2 Grove St Bath ME 04530 Office: Evans Hand 8th Fl 1 Garret Mountain Plz West Paterson NJ 07424-3318

VANDER WEELE, RAY, religious organization administrator. Adminstr. Min. Pension Fund. Office: Christian reformed ch in N Am 2850 Kalamazoo Ave SE Grand Rapids MI 49508-1433

VANDER WEG, PHILLIP DALE, art educator, academic administrator, sculptor; b. Benton Harbor, Mich., Aug. 16, 1943; s. Sam Dirk and Trena (Poort) Vander W.; m. Judith Greville, Dec. 15, 1966; 1 child, Kara Sue. BS in Design, U. Mich., 1965, MFA, 1968. Art instr., prof. art Mid. Tenn. State U., Murfreesboro, 1968-89; acting head Mid. Tenn. State U., Mufreesboro, 1983-85, 88-89; chair dept. art, prof. art Western Mich. U., Kalamazoo, 1989—; cons., editl. reviewer Prentice-Hall Pubs., Englewood Cliffs, N.J., 1978-90; mem. region 5 adv. panel Mich. Artist Program, Detroit Inst. Art, 1990-92; mem. rev. panel Tenn. Art Commn. Visual Arts, Nashville, 1986-89. Prin. works include Columbia State U., 1979, Vanderbilt U., Nashville, 1987, Tenn. Arts Commn., 1988. Mem. Kalamazoo Pub. Art Commn., 1992—. Mem. Nat. Assn. Schs. of Art and Design, Nat. Coun. Art Adminstrs., Founds. in Art Theory and Edn. (founder, bd. dirs. 1976-84). Home: 6791 Penny Ln Kalamazoo MI 49009-8539 Office: Western Mich U Dept Art Oliver St Kalamazoo MI 49008

VANDER WEIDE, VERNON JAY, lawyer; b. East Grand Rapids, Mich., Apr. 3, 1940; s. Henry Thomas and Della (Van Zoeren) V.W.; m. Gretchen Laurie Clemmons, Sept. 11, 1965; children: Jennifer, Stephanie, Vanessa. AA, Grand Rapids Jr. Coll., 1960; BA, U. Mich., 1962, LLB, 1965; LLM, George Washington U., 1971. Bar: D.C. 1970, Mich. 1970, Minn. 1977, U.S. Dist. Ct. Minn. 1977. Staff asst. House Rep. Conf., Washington, 1965-66; staff atty. ICC, Washington, 1969-70; br. chief atty. SEC, Arlington, Va., 1970-76; shareholder Wiese & Cox, Mpls., 1970-76; shareholder, bd. dirs. Head, Seifert & Vander Weide, Mpls., 1982—; lectr. Continuing Legal Edn. Corp. Orgn., 1981, 87. Writer, analyst, columnist for neighborhood newspaper, Mpls., 1982-94. Mem. task force Supt.'s Blue Ribbon Commn., Mpls., 1982; bd. deacons Westminster Presbyn. Ch., Mpls., 1993-95. Capt. U.S. Army, 1966-69. Mem. Minn. Bar Assn., Hennepin County Bar Assn. Avocations: sailing, investments, reading, teaching, family. Office: Head Seifert & Vander Weide 1 Financial Plz Ste 2400 120 S 6th St Minneapolis MN 55402-1923

VANDERWEIL, RAIMUND GERHARD, JR., consulting firm executive, mechanical engineer; b. Neptune, N.J., Nov. 21, 1940; s. Raimund Gerhard and Janet Stelle (Letson) V.; m. Anne Stuart Hinshaw, Oct. 10, 1970; children: Alexander Raimund, Shelley McMillan, Stefan Gerhard. AB in Engring. and Applied Physics, Harvard U., 1961; MSME, MIT, 1963. Registered profl engr. 20 states. Research asst. MIT, Cambridge, Mass., 1961-63; engr. Lockheed MSC, Sunnyvale, Calif., 1963-65, Atomic Power Dept. Gen. Electric, San Jose, Calif., 1965-67; pres. R.G. Vanderweil, Engrs., Boston, 1967—. Mem. ASME, ASHRAE, Nat. Soc. Profl. Engrs., Mass. Soc. Profl. Engrs. (Young Engr. of Yr., 1976). Club: Harvard (Boston). Home: 500 Jerusalem Rd Cohasset MA 02025-1148 Office: R G Vanderweil Engrs Inc 274 Summer St Boston MA 02210-1112*

VANDERWERF, MARY ANN, elementary school educator, consultant; b. Buffalo, N.Y., Aug. 18, 1938; d. Richard and Petronella Gertruida (Hell) V.; m. Malcolm Donald Brutman, Apr. 30, 1989; 1 child, Susan Still. BS in Edn., SUNY, Buffalo, 1970, MA in English, 1971, PhD in Rsch. and Evaluation in Edn., 1981. Cert. tchr., N.Y. Legal sec. Hetzelt & Watson, Buffalo, 1957-64; exec. sec. Bell Aerospace Corp., Wheatfield, N.Y., 1964-69; tchr. Amherst (N.Y.) Ctrl. Schs., 1972-94; instr. SUNY, Buffalo, 1979, 85-86, children's lit. cons., 1980-92; pres., cons., facilitator The Synergy Advantage, Inc., Amherst, 1994—; collaborator U.S. Space and Rocket Ctr./U.S. Space Acad., Huntsville, Ala., 1995—; presenter Williamsville Ctrl. Schs., Internat. Reading Assn., Ireland, 1982, Anaheim, Calif., 1983, New Orleans, 1985, 89, Toronto, Ont., Can., 1988, N.Y. State English Coun., Amherst, 1984, St. Bonaventure U., 1984, Amherst Ctrl. Sch. Dist., 1986, 92, 94, Creative Problem Solving Inst., Buffalo, 1986—, Early Childhood Edn. Conf., 1988, Early Childhood Edn. Coun. Western N.Y., Buffalo, 1990, U. Nev., Las Vegas, 1991; book reviewer Harper Collins Children's Books, 1991. Author: (with others) Science and Technology in Fact and Fiction/Children's, 1989, Science and Technology in Fact and Fiction: Young Adult, 1990, Teacher to Teacher: Strategies for the Elementary Classroom, 1993; contbr. articles to profl. jours. Advisor child life dept. Children's Hosp., Buffalo, 1984-85. Mem. Am. Fedn. Tchrs., Internat. Reading Assn. (cons. Niagara Frontier Reading Coun.), Creative Edn. Found., N.Y. State Coun. Tchrs. English (presenter), Children's Lit. Assn., Hans Christian Andersen Soc., Pi Lambda Theta (Alpha Nu chpt.). Avocations: sailing, reading, grandparenting, traveling. Home: 1860 N Forest Rd Williamsville NY 14221-1321 Office: The Synergy Advantage Inc 2495 Kensington Ave Amherst NY 14226-4929

VANDER WIEL, KENNETH CARLTON, computer services company executive; b. Sheldon, Iowa, July 6, 1933; s. Sylvan Vander Wiel and Irene F. (Weekley) Taylor; m. Loretta Marie Smith, Aug. 28, 1969; children: Gretchen G., Alison June, Joseph W., Carol Ann, Andrea., Beth L., David. BA, Bowling Green U., 1955. With mgmt. devel. Dayton (Ohio) Power & Light, 1955-68; cons. G.W. Young & Assocs., Dayton, 1968-69; pres. Datamac Corp., Dayton, 1970-84, Carlton Leasing Co., 1975—, The Carlton Systems Group, Dayton, 1984-89, Carlton Computer Systems, Inc., Dayton, 1989-95; CEO Carlton Computer Systems, Inc., Tampa, Fla., 1993-95; pres. Interlogic Systems of Dayton, Inc., 1995—. Chmn. Montgomery County Data Processing Task Force, Dayton, 1982. With USN, 1955-57. Recipient Commendations, Montgomery County Commn., Dayton, 1982. Mem. Dayton Area C. of C. (nat. affairs com., state legis. com.), Nat. Assn. Mgf. (nat. affairs com.), Dayton Engrs. Club, Dayton Execs. Club (1st lifetime mem. honoree 1995, pres. 1986). Avocations: sailing, fishing, travel. Office: Interlogic Systems Inc 1887 Southtown Blvd Dayton OH 45439-1965

VANDER WILT, CARL EUGENE, banker; b. Ottumwa, Iowa, Aug. 17, 1942; s. John Adrian and Wilma (Hulsbos) V W.; m. Carol Anne Szymanski, Jan. 29, 1977; children—Dirk Francis, Neal Adrian. BS, Iowa State U., 1964, PhD, 1968; grad. Advanced Mgmt. Program, Harvard U., 1986. Research economist Fed. Res. Bank, Chgo., 1970-73, asst. v.p., 1973-74, v.p., 1974-79, sr. v.p., 1979-84, sr. v.p., chief fin. officer, 1984—. Chmn. bd. dirs. Goodwill Industries Met. Chgo. Served to capt. U.S. Army, 1968-70. Mem. Execs. Club Chgo. (dir., chmn. reception com.), Banker's Club Chgo., Econ. Club Chgo. Home: 656 Locust St Winnetka IL 60093-3911 Office: Fed Res Bank 230 S La Salle St Chicago IL 60604-1496

VANDEUSEN, BRUCE DUDLEY, company executive; b. Lorain, Ohio, Aug. 20, 1931; s. Clarence Elmer and Margaret (Richards) VanD.; m. Ann Marie Groves, Aug. 17, 1957; children: David Bruce, Elizabeth Ann. Janet Marie. B.A., Ohio Wesleyan U., 1952; M.S., U. Mich., 1958, Ph.D., 1971; M.A.E., Chrysler Inst. Engring., Highland Park, Mich., 1958. Registered profl. engr., Mich. Fellow Ohio State U., Columbus, 1953-54; student engr. Chrysler Corp., Highland Park, 1956-58, sr. research scientist, 1958-67; chief engr. Chrysler Def., Inc., Center Line, Mich., 1967-79, mgr. advanced devel., 1979-82; dir. advanced devel. Gen. Dynamics, Warren, Mich., 1982-87, program dir., 1987-93; pres. Edn. Svcs., Birmingham, Mich., 1994—. Contbr. numerous articles to profl. publs.; patentee electronic cirs. Trustee Birmingham Bd. Edn., Mich., 1976-88, pres., 1979-84, 87-88; trustee Birmingham Community House, 1981-87. Mem. Soc. Automotive Engrs. (chmn. sci. engring. activity 1967-69, Arch T. Colwell award 1968), Am. Def. Preparedness Assn., Assn. U.S. Army. Republican. Methodist. Home: 1492 W Lincoln St Birmingham MI 48009-1830 Office: Edn Svcs PO Box 170 Birmingham MI 48012-0170 *Accept, embrace and instigate change, not for the sake of change but for the sake of improvement.*

VANDEVELDE, AGNES ANN, tax preparer; b. Carleton, Mich., Feb. 1, 1931; d. August John and Lena Eliza (Rivard) Wickenheiser; m. Oscar Maurice Vandevelde, May 1, 1954; children: Irene M., Edward J., Amy T., Nancy C., Martin G., Dennis J., Charles A., William P. Student, various tax insts. Bookkeeping clk. Monroe (Mich.) Pub. Co., 1950-54, 78-87; tax vol. Monroe Sr. Citizens, 1988—; tax preparer in pvt. practice, Monroe, 1990—. Vol., Ret. Srs. Vol. Program. Monroe, 1987—. Mem. Belgian-Am. Club, Monroe Sr. Citizens (pres. 1989-90). Democrat. Roman Catholic. Avocations: swimming, sewing, ceramics, grapevine crafts, entertaining grandchildren. Home: 3293 N Otter Creek Rd Monroe MI 48161-9576

VANDEVENDER, BARBARA JEWELL, elementary education educator, farmer; b. Trenton, Mo., Dec. 4, 1929; d. Raleigh Leon and Rose Rea (Dryer) S.; m. Delbert Lyle Vandevender, Aug. 15, 1948; children: Lyle Gail, James R. BS, N.E. Mo. State U., 1971, MA, 1973. Elem. tchr. Williams Sch., Spickard, Mo., 1948-49; reading specialist Spikard R-2 Sch., 1971-74,

Princeton (Mo.) R-5 Sch., 1974-89; mem. ad hoc com. State Dept. Edn., Jefferson City, Mo., 1994-95; speaker in field. Pres. Spickard PTA, 1963-64, Women's Ext. Club, Galt, Mo.; foster mother Family Svcs., Trenton, Mi., 1972-79; mem. ad hoc com. State Dept. of Edn., Jefferson City, Mo., 1994-95. Pres. Spickard PTA, 1963-64, Women's Ext. Club, Galt, Mo.; foster mother Family Svcs., Trenton, Mo., 1972-79; mem. ad hoc com. State Dept. Edn., Jefferson City, Mo., 1994-95. Recipient Mo. State Conservation award Goodyear Tire Co., Akron, Ohio, 1972, Balanced Farming award Gulf Oil Co., N.Y.C., 1972, Mo. State Farming award Kansas City C. of C., 1974, FHA State Farming award, Jefferson City, Mo., 1974, Outstanding Leadership Mo. U., Columbia, 1976, Ednl. Leadership award MSTA, Columbia, 1984, Outstanding Contbn. to Internat. Reading Assn., Newark, Del., 1988. Mem. Internat. Reading Assn. (pres. North Ctrl. coun. 1985-86). Republican. Baptist.

VAN DEVENDER, J. PACE, physical scientist; b. Jackson, Miss., Sept. 12, 1947; m. Nancy Jane Manning, 1971; 3 children. BA in Physics, Vanderbilt U., 1969; MA in Physics, Dartmouth Coll., 1971; PhD in Physics, U. London, 1974. Physicist diagnostics devel. Lawrence Livermore Lab., 1969; mem. tech. staff pulsed power rsch. and devel. Sandia Nat. Labs., 1974-78, divsn. supr. pulsed power rsch. divsn., 1978-82, dept. mgr. fusion rsch., 1982-84; dir. pulsed power scis. Sandia Nat. Labs., Albuquerque, 1984-93, dir. corp. comm., 1993, dir. Nat. Indsl. Alliances Ctr., 1993-95; pres. Prosperity Inst., 1995—; mem. rev. bd. Adv. Photon Source Project, Argonne Nat. Lab. Mem. editorial bd. Laser and Particle Beams, 1987-90. Mem. bd. trust Vanderbilt U., 1969-73. With U.S. Army, 1969-71. Recipient Ernest Orlando Lawrence Meml. award U.S. Dept. Energy, 1991; named one of 100 Most Promising Scientists Under 40, Sci. Digest, 1984; Marshal scholar U. London, 1971-74. Fellow Am. Phys. Soc.; mem. NAS (mem. bd. naval studies 1990—), Phi Beta Kappa, Omicron Delta Kappa, Sigma Xi. Office: Prosperity Inst 7604 Lamplighter NE Albuquerque NM 87109

VAN DEVENTER, ARIE PIETER, agricultural engineer; b. Hardinxveld-Giessendam, The Netherlands, June 11, 1963; m. Corine Margreet Geljon, Aug. 25, 1989; 1 child, Raisa Céline. BS, MS in Soil and Water Engring., Agrl. U. Wageningen, The Netherlands, 1981-88; PhD in Agrl. Engring., Ohio State U., 1992. Rsch. assoc. Ohio State U., Columbus, 1989-92, postdoctoral rschr. dept. agrl. engring., 1992-93; cons. dept. remote sensing and digital photogrammetry Grontmij Geogroep, Roosendaal, The Netherlands, 1993-95, head dept. geodata, 1995-96, head geodata svcs., 1996—; chmn. Interest Group on Global Understanding, 1991-93; treas. Stichting Auto Reizen Indonesia, 1993—. Contbr. articles to profl. jours. Mem. Am. Soc. Agrl. Engrs. (Robert E. Stewart Engring. Humanities award 1993), Am. Soc. Photogrammetry and Remote Sensing, Gamma Sigma Delta, Alpha Epsilon, Phi Kappa Phi, Phi Beta Delta. Home: Zuivelstraat 35a, 4611 PE Bergen op Zoom The Netherlands Office: Grontmij Geogroep, Postbus 1747, 4700 BS Roosendaal The Netherlands

VANDEVER, WILLIAM DIRK, lawyer; b. Chgo., Aug. 1, 1949; s. Lester J. and Elizabeth J. V.; m. Kathi J. Zellmer, Aug. 26, 1983; children: Barton Dirk, Brooke Shelby. BS, U. Mo., Kansas City, 1971, JD with distinction, 1974. Bar: Mo. 1975, U.S. Dist. Ct. (we. dist.) Mo. 1975. Dir. Popham Law Firm, Kansas City, Mo., 1975—; lectr. medicine, engring. and multiple CLE various hosps. and colls., Kansas City Mo., 1979—. Issue editor U. Mo.-Kansas City Law Rev., 1974. Mem. ABA, Am. Trial Lawyers Assn., Mo. Assn. Trial Attys., Kansas City Met. Bar Assn. (treas., sec., pres., exec. com. 1986—, elected to 16th Jud. Commn. 1988—), Kansas City Bar Found. (treas. 1992, sec. 1994), Interest on Lawyer Trust Accts. of Mo. (bd. govs.), Kansas City Mem. Svcs. (pres. 1988—, commr. 16th jud. cir. selection com.), Phi Delta Phi, Beta Theta Pi. Avocations: tennis, skiing, running, reading. Home: 11380 W 121st Ter Shawnee Mission KS 66213-1978 Office: Popham Law Firm 1300 Commerce Trust Bldg Kansas City MO 64106

VAN DE VYVER, SISTER MARY FRANCILENE, academic administrator; b. Detroit, Sept. 6, 1941; d. Hector Joseph and Irene Cecilia (Zygailo) V. BA, Madonna Coll., 1965; MEd, Wayne State U., 1970, PhD, 1977. Joined Sisters of St. Felix of Cantalice, Roman Cath. Ch., 1967. Tchr. Ladywood High Sch., 1965-74; adminstrv. asst. to pres. Madonna Coll., Livonia, Mich., 1974-75, acad. dean, 1975-76; now pres. Madonna U., Livonia, Mich. Office: Madonna U Office of President 36600 Schoolcraft Rd Livonia MI 48150-1176

VAN DE WALLE, ETIENNE, demographer; b. Namur, Belgium, Apr. 29, 1932; came to U.S., 1961; s. Arnould and Yolande (Blommaert) Van De W.; m. Francine Robyns de Schneidauer, Aug. 24, 1955; children: Dominique, Nicolas, Jean-Francois, Patrice. Dr. in Law, U. Louvain, Belgium, 1956, MA in Econs., 1957, PhD in Demography, 1973. Researcher Irsac, Rwanda, Burundi, 1957-61; rsch. assoc. Princeton (N.J.) U., 1962-64, rsch. staff, 1964-67, rsch. demographer, 1967-72; vis. lectr. U. Calif., Berkeley, 1971-72; prof. U. Pa., Phila., 1972—; dir. Population Studies Ctr., U. Pa., 1976-82; sr. assoc. The Population Coun., Bamako, Mali, 1982. Author: The Female Population of France, 1974; co-author: The Demography of Tropical Africa, 1968. Fellowship Woodrow Wilson Ctr. for Scholars, 1976. Mem. Internat. Union for Scientific Study of Population, Population Assn. of Am. (pres. 1992). Home: 261 Sycamore Ave Merion Station PA 19066-1545 Office: Population Studies Ctr 3718 Locust Walk Philadelphia PA 19104-6209

VANDEWALLE, GERALD WAYNE, state supreme court chief justice; b. Noonan, N.D., Aug. 15, 1933; s. Jules C. and Blanche Marie (Gits) VandeW. B.Sc., U. N.D., 1955, J.D., 1958. Bar: N.D., U.S. Dist. Ct. N.D. 1959. Spl. asst. atty. gen. State of N.D., Bismarck, 1958-75, 1st asst. atty. gen., 1975-78; justice N.D. Supreme Ct., 1978-92, chief justice, 1993—; mem. faculty Bismarck Jr. Coll., 1972-76. Editor-in-chief N.D. Law Rev, 1957-58. Active Bismarck Meals on Wheels. Recipient Sioux award U. N.D., 1992, Ednl. Law award N.D. Coun. Sch. Attys., 1987, Love Without Fear award Abused Adult Resource Ctr., 1995. Mem. ABA (co-chair bar admissions com.), State Bar Assn. N.D., Burleigh County Bar Assn., Am. Contract Bridge League, Order of Coif, N.D. Jud. Conf. (exec. com.), Phi Eta Sigma, Beta Alpha Psi (Outstanding Alumnus award Zeta chpt. 1995), Beta Gamma Sigma, Phi Alpha Delta. Roman Catholic. Clubs: Elks, K.C. Office: ND Supreme Ct State Capitol 600 E Boulevard Ave Bismarck ND 58505-0660

VANDEWATER, DAVID, hospital administrator. With Clearlake Hospital, 1975-78, Hospital Affiliates Internat., 1978-82, Republic Health Corp., 1982-90; pres. Columbia Healthcare Corp, Louisville, 1992—; now also ceo Nashville, TN. Office: Columbia/HCA Healthcare Corp 1 Park Plzain St PO Box 740033 Nashville TN 37203*

VAN DE WETERING, JOHN E(DWARD), academic administrator; b. Bellingham, Wash., Jan. 20, 1927; s. John and Jessie Van De W.; m. Maxine Schorr, Mar. 7, 1961; 1 son, Josh. B.A. in History, U. Wash., 1950, M.A. in History, 1953, Ph.D. in History, 1959. Instr. U. Idaho, 1959; instr. U. Wash., 1959-61, vis. asst. prof. history, 1963; asst. prof. U. Mont., 1961-64, asso. prof., 1964-69, prof., chmn. dept. history, 1969-76; acting pres. Eastern Mont. Coll., 1976-77, pres., 1977-81; pres. SUNY, Coll. at Brockport, 1981—; mem. Mont. Com. for Humanities, 1972-74; Danforth asso. Author: (with Jack Bumsted) What Must I Do to Be Saved? : The Great Awakening in Colonial America, 1976; contbr. articles to profl. jours. Bd. dirs. Park Ridge Long Term Care Bd., Rochester, N.Y., George Eastman House Mus. Photography, Rochester, Rochester Area Ednl. TV Assn. With C.E. U.S. Army, 1955-57. Home: 230 Holley St Brockport NY 14420-2124 Office: SUNY Coll at Brockport Office of Pres Brockport NY 14420

VAN DINE, HAROLD FORSTER, JR., architect; b. New Haven, Aug. 28, 1930; s. Harold Forster and Marguerite Anna (Eichstedt) Van D.; m. Maureen Kallick, Mar. 1, 1983; children by previous marriage: Rebecca Van Dine, Stephanie Van Dine Natale, Gretchen Van Dine Natale. BA, Yale Coll., 1952; MArch, Yale U., 1958. Registered architect. Designer Minoru Yamasaki & Assocs., Detroit, 1958-60; chief designer Gunnar Birkerts & Assocs., Detroit, 1960-67; prin. Straub, Van Dine & Assocs., Troy, Mich., 1967-80; chief architecture and design officer Harley Ellington, Pierce, Yee & Assocs., Southfield, Mich., 1980-95; archtl. design cons. Birmingham, Mich., 1995—; v.p. Fields, Devereaux, HEPY, L.A., 1984-95. Prin. works include Mcpl. Libr., Troy, Mich., campuses for Oakland (Mich.) Community Coll., North Hills Ch., Troy, First Ctr. Office Plaza, chemistry bldgs at. U. Mich. and Ind. U., G.M.F. Robotics Hdqrs., Flint Ink Rsch. and Devel. Ctr., Comerica Bank Ops. Ctr., Christ the King Mausoleum, Chgo., Resurrection Mausoleum, Staten Island, Mich. Biotech Inst., Ford Sci. Rsch. Labs, Fetzer Inst. Hdqrs. and Retreat Ctr., Cen. Mich. U. Music Sch., Oakland U. Sci. Techs. Bldg., Mead Corp. Rsch. Ctr., Dayton, Ohio, Corning (N.Y.) Credit Union. Bd. dirs. Cultural Coun. Birmingham/Bloomfield, 1990—. Served to lt. (j.g.) USN, 1952-55. Recipient Book award AIA, 1958, Excellence in Architecture Silver medal AIA, 1958, Gold medal Detroit chpt. AIA, 1987, Mich. Soc. of Architects gold medal, 1991, over 50 major design awards; William Wirt Winchester travelling fellowship Yale U. Sch. Architecture, 1958; elect. to AIA Coll. Fellows, 1979. Mem. Pewabic Soc. (bd. dirs. 1983—). Home and Office: 544 S Bates St Birmingham MI 48009-1423

VAN DINE, PAUL EDWIN, clergyman; b. Bluffton, Ind., June 19, 1939; s. Charles W. and Nellie Ruth (Maupin) Van D.; m. Carolyn Ann Shimp, June 12, 1960; children: Vicki Linn, Mark David, Karen Joan. BA magna cum laude, U. Miami, 1960; MDiv cum laude, Drew U., 1964. Ordained to ministry Meth. Ch., 1961. Student pastor Stockholm (N.J.) Meth. Ch., 1961-64; pastor Sylvan Abbey Meth. Ch., Clearwater, Fla., 1964-67, Union Park United Meth. Ch., Orlando, Fla., 1967-69, Port Orange (Fla.) United Meth. Ch., 1969-75; sr. pastor Cypress Lake United Meth. Ch., Ft. Myers, Fla., 1980-92, First United Meth. Ch., Clearwater, Fla., 1992—; assoc. pastor Pasadena Community Ch., St. Petersburg, Fla., 1975-80; sec. bd. missions and ch. extension Fla. Conf. United Meth. Ch., 1972-75, chmn. com. on communications, 1980-84; chmn. St. Petersburg Dist. Council on Ministries, 1977-80; bd. dirs., mem. exec. com. United Meth. Reporter newspaper, 1980-86. Contbr. prayers and sermons to religious publs. Democrat. Home: 305 Eastleigh Dr Clearwater FL 34616-2503 Office: First United Meth Ch 411 Turner St Clearwater FL 34616

VAN DINE, VANCE, investment banker; b. San Francisco, July 2, 1925; s. Melvin Everett and Grace Winifred (Harris) Van D.; m. Isabel Erskine Brewster, Sept. 8, 1956; 1 dau., Rose M. (dec.). BA, Yale U., 1949; LLB, NYU, 1955. Assoc. Morgan Stanley & Co., N.Y.C., 1953-59, 61-63; ptnr. Morgan Stanley & Co., 1963-75; mng. dir. Morgan Stanley & Co., Inc., N.Y.C., 1970-83; adv. dir. Morgan Stanley & Co., N.Y.C., 1983—; cons. Internat. Bank for Reconstn. and Devel., 1959-61; chmn. Doane Western Co. Author: The Role of the Investment Banker in International Transactions, 1970, The U.S. Market After Controls, 1974. Bd. dirs. Yale U. Alumni Fund, Rec. for Blind, Inc., N.Y.C., 1979-89; trustee L.I. U., 1979-91, Cancer Rsch. Inst., N.Y.C., Nassau County Art Mus.; gov. dir. Fgn. Policy Assn., 1980-89. With USN, 1943-46. Recipient Yale Class of 1949 Disting. Service award, 1983. Mem. The Pilgrims of the U.S., Union Club, Piping Rock Club, N.Y. Yacht Club, Seawanhaka Corinthian Yacht Club, Church Club, Yale Club (N.Y.C.), Met. Opera Club. Republican. Episcopalian. Office: Morgan Stanley & Co 1251 Avenue Of The Americas New York NY 10020-1104

VANDIVER, FRANCES, principal. Prin. Coral Springs (Fla.) Mid. Sch. Recipient Blue Ribbon Sch. award, 1990-91. Office: Coral Springs Mid Sch 10300 Wiles Rd Coral Springs FL 33076-2003

VANDIVER, FRANK EVERSON, institute administrator, former university president, author, educator; b. Austin, Tex., Dec. 9, 1925; s. Harry Shultz and Maude Folmsbee (Everson) V.; m. Carol Sue Smith, Apr. 19, 1952 (dec. 1979); children: Nita, Nancy, Frank Alexander; m. Renée Aubry, Mar. 21, 1980. Rockefeller fellow in humanities, U. Tex., 1946-47, Rockefeller fellow in Am. Studies, 1947-48, MA, 1949; PhD, Tulane U., 1951; MA (by decree), Oxford (Eng.) U., 1963; HHD (hon.), Austin Coll., 1977; DHL (hon.), Lincoln Coll., 1989, BA (hon.), 1994. Apptd. historian Army Service Forces Depot, Civil Service, San Antonio, 1944-45, Air U., 1951; prof. history La. State U., summers 1953-57; asst. prof. history Washington U., St. Louis, 1952-55; asst. prof. history Rice U., Houston, 1955-56, assoc. prof., 1956-58, prof., 1958-65, Harris Masterson Jr. prof. history, 1965-79, chmn. dept. history and polit. sci., 1962-63, dept. history, 1968-69, acting pres., 1969-70, provost, 1970-79, v.p., 1975-79; pres., chancellor N. Tex. State U., Denton and Tex. Coll. Osteo. Medicine, 1979-81; pres. Tex. A&M U., College Station, 1981-88, pres. emeritus, disting. U. prof., 1988—; founding pres. Acad. Marshall Plan, 1992; Sara and John Lindsey chair in humanities, 1988; Harmsworth prof. Am. history Oxford U., 1963-64; vis. prof. history U. Ariz., summer 1961; master Margarett Root Brown Coll., Rice U., 1964-66; Harman lectr. Air Force Acad., 1963; Keese lectr. U. Chattanooga, 1967; Fortenbaugh lectr. Gettysburg Coll., 1974; Phi Beta Kappa assoc. lectr., 1970—; vis. prof. mil. history U.S. Mil. Acad., 1973-74; hon. pres. Occidental U., St. Louis, 1975-80; chmn. bd. Am. U. Cairo, 1992—. Editor: The Civil War Diary of General Josiah Gorgas, 1947, Confederate Blockade Running Through Bermuda, 1861-65: Letters and Cargo Manifests, 1947, Proceedings of First Confederate Congress, 4th Session, 1953, Proceedings of Second Confederate Congress, 1959, A Collection of Louisiana Confederate Letters; new edit., J.E. Johnston's Narrative of Military Operations; new edit., J.A. Early's Civil War Memoirs, The Idea of the South, 1964, Battlefields and Landmarks of the Civil War, 1996; author: Ploughshares Into Swords: Josiah Gorgas and Confederate Command System, 1956, Mighty Stonewall, 1957, Fields of Glory, (with W. H. Nelson), 1960, Jubal's Raid, 1960, Basic History of the Confederacy, 1962, Jefferson Davis and the Confederate State, 1964, Their Tattered Flags: The Epic of the Confederacy, 1970, The Southwest: South or West?, 1975, Black Jack: The Life and Times of John J. Pershing, 1977 (Nat. Book Award finalist 1978), (address) The Long Loom of Lincoln, 1986, Blood Brothers: A Short History of the Civil War, 1992; also hist. articles; mem. bd. editors: U.S. Grant Papers, 1973—. Mem. bd. trustees Am. U. in Cairo, 1988, chmn., 1992—. Recipient Laureate Lincoln Acad., Ill., 1973, Carr P. Collins prize Tex. Inst. Letters, 1958, Harry S. Truman award Kansas City Civil War Round Table, Jefferson Davis award Confederate Meml. Lit. Soc., 1970, Fletcher Pratt award N.Y. Civil War Round Table, 1970, Outstanding Civilian Svc. medal Dept. Army, 1974, Nevins-Freeman award Chgo. Civil War Round Table, 1982, T. Harry Williams Meml. award, 1985; named Hon. Knight San Jacinto, 1993, Hon. Mem. Sons of Republic of Tex., 1986; rsch. grantee Am. Philos. Soc., 1953, 54, 60, Huntington Libr. rsch. grantee, 1961; Guggenheim fellow, 1955-56. Fellow Tex. Hist. Assn.; mem. Am. Hist. Assn., So. Hist. Assn. (assoc. editor jour. 1959-62, pres. 1975-76), Tex. Inst. Letters (past pres.), Jefferson Davis Assn. (pres., chmn. adv. bd. editors of papers), Soc. Am. Historians (councillor), Tex. Philos. Soc. (pres. 1978), Civil War Round Table (Houston), Orgn. Am. Historians, Phi Beta Kappa, SAR of Tex. (hon., Knight San Jacinto 1993). Clubs: Cosmos, Army and Navy (Washington); Briarcrest Country (College Station). Office: Tex A&M U Mosher Inst Internat Policy Studies College Station TX 77843-2400

VANDIVIER, BLAIR ROBERT, lawyer; b. Rapid City, S.D., Dec. 24, 1955; s. Robert Eugene and Barbara Jean (Kidd) V.; m. Elizabeth Louise Watson, July 26, 1980; children: Jessica Elizabeth, Jennifer Louise. BS magna cum laude, Butler U., 1978; JD cum laude, Ind. U., 1981. Bar: Ind. 1981, U.S. Dist. Ct. (so. dist.) Ind. 1981, U.S. Tax Ct. 1985. Assoc. Henderson, Daily, Withrow, Johnson & Gross, Indpls., 1981-83; assoc., ptnr. Johnson, Gross, Densborn & Wright, Indpls., 1983-85, of counsel, 1985-87; v.p., sec. Benchmark Products, Inc. (formerly Benchmark Chem. Corp.), Indpls., 1985-91, pres., 1991—, also bd. dirs.; ptnr. Gross & Vandivier, Indpls., 1987-89; of counsel Riley, Bennett & Egloff, Indpls., 1990—; mgmt. rep. Pro Com, L.L.C., 1991—; v.p. Seleco Inc., Indpls., 1988-93, pres., 1993—. Mem. com. Conner Prairie Settlement Fund Dr., Indpls., 1983-85, Riley Run, 1987—; mem. regulatory study com. City of Indpls., 1993—. Mem. ABA, Ind. Bar Assn., Indpls. Bar Assn (bd. dirs. young lawyers divsn. 1982-85), Am. Electroplaters & Surface Finisher's Soc. (chmn. nat. law com. 1986—, pres. Indpls. br. 1989, tech conf. bd. 1991—, chmn. SUR/FIN annual tech. conf. and exhbn. 1994, chmn. SUR/FIN Four Group 1994—, Tech. Conf. Bd. Recognition award 1996), Metal Finishing Suppliers Assn. (spl. projects svcs. com., 1988-93, chmn. 1993—, chmn. hazardous materials br. 1991-93, trustee 1992-95, v.p. 1995—), Highland Golf Club, Highland Country Club (chmn. ins. com. 1989-94, golf. com. 1992-94, bd. dirs. 1995—, chmn. fin. com. 1996), Econ. Club Indpls., Delta Tau Delta (chmn. 1987—, bd. dirs. Beta Zeta Found. 1986, Outstanding Alumnus Beta Zeta chpt. 1986). Republican. Episcopalian. Avocations: golf, reading. Home: 8927 Woodacre Ln Indianapolis IN 46234-2848 Office: Benchmark Products Inc PO Box 68809 Indianapolis IN 46268-0809

VAN DOMELEN, JOHN FRANCIS, academic administrator; b. Havana, Cuba, Oct. 19, 1942; s. Floyd and Sara (Molina) Van D.; m. Naomi Ruth Kittlesen. BS in Applied Physics, Mich. Tech. U., 1964; MS in Water Res. Mgmt., U. Wis., Madison, 1972; PhD in Civil Engring., U. Wis., 1974. Commd. 2nd lt. USAF, 1964, advanced through grades to col., 1988; mgr. engring. Charmin Paper Products Co., Green Bay, Wis., 1969-70; asst. prof. Norwich U., Northfield, Vt., 1974-79, head engring. and tech. dept., 1979-83, head engring. and tech. div., 1983-85, v.p. acad. affairs, dean of faculty, 1985-90; pres. Wentworth Inst. Tech., Boston, 1990—; mem. Engring. Workforce Commn. Contbr. articles to profl. jours. Mem. MassPep, Boston, 1990—. Decorated Cross of Gallantry (Vietnam); recipient Centennial medal IEEE, 1984. Mem. ASCE, Am. Soc. Engring. Edn., Sci. Rsch. Soc. N.Am., New Eng. Assn. Schs. and Colls. (commr. for inst. higher edn. 1994—). Avocations: racquetball, golf, science fiction. Office: Wentworth Inst Tech 550 Huntington Ave Boston MA 02115-5901

VAN DOMMELEN, DAVID B., artist, educator; b. Grand Rapids, Mich., Aug. 21, 1929; s. Henry and Thelma (Brown) Van D.; m. Michal Bohnstedt; children: Erica, Dorn. Diploma in interior design, Harrington Inst., Chgo., 1951; BA, Mich. State U., 1956, MA, 1957. Art cons. Warren (Mich.) Schs., 1957-59; instr. home art Pa. State U., State College, 1959-62; assoc. prof. interiors Pa. State U., 1964-73, prof. art edn., 1973-87, prof. emeritus, 1987—; asst. prof. design, U. Maine, Orono, 1962-64; instr., Haystack Mountain Crafts Schs., Deer Isle, Maine, 1963, 64, 74, Arrowmont Arts and Crafts, Gatlinburg, Tenn., 1971-82; vis. prof., U. Iowa, Iowa City, 1967, 68, 70. Author: Decorative Wall Hangings: Art with Fabric, 1962, Walls: Enrichment & Ornamentation, 1965, Designing & Decorating Interiors, 1965, New Uses for Old Cannonballs, 1966, Doughboy Letters, 1977; contbr. articles to various publications; represented in numerous art exhbns. Cpl. U.S. Army, 1952-54. Grantee for craft rsch., Ford Found., 1972, OAS, 1976, Pa. State U., 1986; recipient Eleanor Fishborn award, Ednl. Press. Am., 1973. Mem. Am. Craft Coun., Am. Home Econs. Assn. (bd. dirs. 1966-71), Pa. Home Econs. Assn. (pres. 1970), Am.-Scandinavian Found., Internat. Fedn. Home Econs., Lions. Avocation: stamp collecting. Home: RR 1 Box 631 Petersburg PA 16669-9248 Office: Pa State U 207 Arts Coll University Park PA 16802

VAN DOREN, EMERSON BARCLAY, administrative judge; b. Rahway, N.J., Dec. 30, 1940; s. Emerson Maynard and Jaqueline Pendleton (Hicks) Van D.; m. Janet Elisabeth Bumbarger, Dec. 28, 1963; children: Pendleton Barclay, Virginia Cary. BA, Harvard U., 1962; JD, U. Mich., 1965; postgrad. degree (hon.), Air War Coll., Maxwell AF Base, Ala., 1985. Bar: Ky. 1965, N.H. 1971, U.S. Dist. Ct. (we. dist.) Ky. 1966, U.S. Dist. Ct. N.H. 1972. Assoc. Brown, Ardery, Todd & Dudley, Louisville, 1965-66; judge adv. USAF, 1966-71, 72-76; pvt. practice N. Conway, N.H., 1971-72; sr. procurement atty. U.S. Dept. Energy, Washington, 1976-81, dep. asst. gen. counsel for procurement, 1981-85; adminstrv. judge U.S. Energy Bd. Contract Appeals, Arlington, Va., 1985, chmn., chief adminstrv. judge, 1985—; judge U.S. Energy Fin. Assistance Appeals Bd., U.S. Energy Prevention Licensing Appeals Bd., U.S. Energy Patent Compensation Bd. Co-chair Randolph-Wacon Woman's Coll. Adv. Coun. Admissions. Capt. USAF, 1966-76, col. USAFR, command mobilization asst. to staff judge adv., 1988-90, ret., 1990. Decorated Meritorious Svc. medal with one oak leaf cluster, Commendation medal with one oak leaf cluster, Legion of Merit award; Leckie fellow, Resident fellow U. Mich.; named Outstanding Young Judge Adv., AF Systems Command, 1975. Mem. ABA, Sr. Execs. Assn. (chpt. pres. 1993—), Bd. Contract Appeals Judges Assn. (bd. govs.), Fed. Bar Assn., N.H. Bar Assn., Ky. Bar Assn. Avocation: surf and fly fishing. Office: Energy Contract Appeals Bd 4040 Fairfax Dr Arlington VA 22203-1613

VAN DOVER, KAREN, middle and elementary school educator, curriculum consultant, language arts specialist; b. Astoria, N.Y.; d. Frederick A. and Frances L. (Thomas) Van D. BA, CUNY; MALS, SUNY, Stony Brook; postgrad., St. John's U., Jamaica, N.Y., 1992. Cert. permanent N-6 tchr., art tchr. K-12, sch. admnstr., supr., N.Y. Tchr., sch. dist. admnstr. St. James (N.Y.) Elem. Sch.; tchr. Nesaquake Intermediate Sch., St. James, lead tchr. English, 1984-92; lead tchr. English Smithtown Mid Sch., St. James, 1992-93, curriculum specialist, 1993—; leader staff devel. and curriculum devel. workshops Smithtown Sch. Dist., 1984—, mem. supt.'s adv. com. for gifted and talented, mem. supt. adv. com. for lang. arts assessment, mem. textbook selection coms. site-based mgmt. team, 1994—; mem. master tchr. bd. Prentice Hall, Englewood Cliffs, N.J., 1990—. Contbg. author: Prentice Hall Literature Copper, 1991, 94. Corr. sec. Yaphank Taxpayers and Civic Assn., 1984-86, Nesaquake Sch. PTA, 1990-91, mem., 1977-92; mem. Smithtown Mid. Sch. PTA, 1992—. Mem. ASCD, Am. Ednl. Rsch. Assn., Nat. Assn. Secondary Sch. Prins., Nat. Coun. Tchrs. English, Internat. Reading Assn., Nat. Middle Schs. Assn., N.Y. State English Coun., Nat. Assn. of Elem. Sch. Prins., Phi Delta Kappa. Home: 8 Penn Commons Yaphank NY 11980-2025 Office: Smithtown Middle Sch 10 School St Saint James NY 11780-1833

VAN DOVER, ROBERT BRUCE, physicist; b. Eatontown, N.J., Apr. 30, 1952. BS, Princeton U., 1974; MS, Stanford U., 1975, PhD, 1980. Mem. tech. staff Bell Labs., Lucent Techs., Murray Hill, N.J., 1980—. Mem. IEEE, Am. Phys. Soc., Materials Rsch. Soc. Office: Bell Labs, Lucent Techs Rm 1t-106 700 Mountain Ave New Providence NJ 07974

VAN DRESER, MERTON LAWRENCE, ceramic engineer; b. Des Moines, June 5, 1929; s. Joseph Jerome and Victoria (Love) Van D.; m. Evelyn Lenore Manny, July 12, 1952; children: Peter, Jennifer Sue. BS in Ceramic Engring., Iowa State U., 1951. Tech. supt. Owens-Corning Fiberglas Corp., Kansas City, Mo., 1954-57; rsch. engr. Kaiser Aluminum & Chem. Corp., Milpitas, Calif., 1957-60, rsch. sect. head, 1960-63, lab. mgr., 1963-65, assoc. dir. rsch., 1965-69; dir. refractories rsch. Kaiser Aluminum & Chem. Corp., Pleasanton, Calif., 1969-72; dir. non-metallic materials rsch. Kaiser Aluminum & Chem. Corp., 1972-83; v.p., dir. rsch. Indsl. Chem. div. and Harshaw/Filtrol Partnership Kaiser Aluminum & Chem. Corp., Cleve., 1983-85; dir. bus. devel. Kaiser Aluminum & Chem. Corp., Pleasanton, 1985-88, cons., 1988—; mem. adv. bd. dept. ceramic engring. U. Ill., 1974-78; chmn. tech. adv. com. Refractories Inst., 1980-84; mem. nat. materials adv. bd. Nat. Acad. Sci.; mem. Indsl. Rsch. Inst. Contbr. articles to sci. jours. Sustaining membership chmn. local dist. Boy Scouts Am., 1980; pres. PTA, 1967-68; vol. exec. Pakistan Internat. Exec. Svc. Corps, 1990-91. Aviator C.E., U.S. Army, 1951-54. Recipient Profl. Achievement citation Iowa State U., 1978. Fellow Am. Ceramic Soc. (v.p. 1973-74); mem. ASTM (hon.; com.), Brit. Ceramic Soc., Nat. Inst. Ceramic Engrs., Keramos (pres. 1976-78, herald 1980-84, Greaves Walker Roll of Honor award), Metall. Soc., AIME. Lodges: Rotary (Paul Harris fellow), Masons. Patentee in field. Avocation: comml. pilot.

VANDROSS, LUTHER, singer; s. Mary Ida Vandross. Albums include The Best of Luther Vandross...The Best of Love, Busy Body, Forever, For Always, For Love, Give Me The Reason, 1986, Never Too Much, The Night I Fell In Love, Any Love, 1989, The Power of Love, 1991, Never Let Me Go, 1993 (Grammy nomination: Best Rhythym & Blues Male Vocal for "How Deep Is Your Love"), Luther, 1993.

VAN DUSEN, ALBERT CLARENCE, university official; b. Tampa, Fla., Aug. 30, 1915; s. Charles H. and Maude E. (Green) Van D.; m. Margaret Davis, Jan. 3, 1943; children: Margaret Anne (Mrs. Joseph J. Pysh), Jane Katherine , Sally Elizabeth (Mrs. Frank J. Matyskiela). BS, U. Fla., 1937, AM, 1938; PhD, Northwestern, 1942; LittD, U. Tampa, 1959; L.H.D., Duquesne U., 1967. Instr., asst. prof. dept. psychology U. Fla., 1938-41; asso. prof. psychology Northwestern U., 1946, dir. summer session, 1948-52, v.p. pub. relations, 1952-56; prof. psychology, bus. adminstrn. and edn. U. Pitts., 1956-85, asst. chancellor for planning and devel., 1956-59, vice chancellor the professions, 1959-67, vice chancellor program devel. and pub. affairs, 1967-71, vice chancellor, sec. univ., 1971-80, vice chancellor emeritus, spl. asst. for pub. affairs, 1980-85, vice chancellor emeritus, prof. emeritus psychology, bus. adminstrn. and edn., 1985—, ctr. assoc. univ. ctr. for internat. studies, 1986—; bd. dirs. Dollar Bank, Pitts. Editor: Proc. Am. Coll. Personnel Assn; contbr. articles to profl. jours. Bd. govs. Pinchot Inst. Conservation Studies; vice chmn., bd. dirs. The Buhl Found., World Affairs Coun. Pitts., vice chmn. bd. dirs. Duquesne U., acting chmn., 1987-88; bd. dirs. Pitts. YMCA, ACTION Housing, Inc., Assn. Am.'s Pub. TV Stas., QED Communications Inc., chmn. 1981-88; bd. dirs. Japan-Am. Soc. Pa.; mem. Pa. Pub. TV Network Commn.; chmn., bd. trustees Pitts. History and

Landmarks Found.; pres. bd. trustees H.C. Frick Ednl. Commn., United Way Pa.; dir. South Hills Child Guidance Ctr.; chmn. selfcare study Health Edn. Ctr., Pitts., 1979-80; mem. Walter Reed Hovey Fellowship com. Pitts. Found. Lt. USNR, 1942-46. Fulbright sr. scholar Australian-Am. Ednl. Found., 1980. Fellow Am. Psychol. Assn., Am. Psychol. Soc., Pa. Psychol. Assn., Internat. Found. Social Econ. Deve.; mem. Internat. Assn. Schs. Insts. Adminstrn., C. of C. (dir. 1953-55), Am. Coll. Pub. Rels. Assn. (v.p. 1956-58), Assn. Deans and Dirs. Summer Sessions (sec. 1950-51), Profl. Schs. and World Affairs Com. (chmn. edn. and world affairs 1965-67), Am. Pers. and Guidance Assn., Midwest Psychol. Assn., Ea. Psychol. Assn., Pitts. Psychol. Assn., Internat. Assn. Applied Psychology, Western Pa. Coun. Econ. Edn., Internat. Assn. Schs. and Insts. Adminstrn., Friends of Art for Pitts. Schs. (charter mem.), Phi Beta Kappa, Sigma Xi, Beta Theta Pi, Beta Gamma Sigma. Clubs: Univ. (Pitts.), Duquesne (Pitts.). Home: 108 Blue Spruce Cir Pittsburgh PA 15243-1026

VAN DUSEN, DONNA BAYNE, educator, communication consultant, researcher; b. Phila., Apr. 21, 1949; d. John Culbertson and Evelyn Gertrude (Godfrey) Bayne; m. David William Van Dusen, Nov. 30, 1968 (div. Dec. 1989); children: Heather, James. BA, Temple U., 1984, MA, 1986, PhD, 1993. Instr. Kutztown (Pa.) U., 1986-87, Ursinus Coll., Collegeville, Pa., 1987-96; cons., rschr. Comm. Rsch. Assoc., Valley Forge, Pa., 1993—; asst. prof. Beaver Coll., Glenside, Pa., 1995—; rschr. Fox Chase Cancer Ctr., Phila., 1985-86; adj. faculty Temple U. Law Sch., 1994—, LaSalle U., 1994-96, Wharton Sch., U. Pa., 1994-95. Mem. NOW, AAUP, Speech Comm. Assn., Ea. Comm. Assn. Avocations: oil painting, creative writing, sailing, gardening, reading. Home: 15 Shirley Rd Narberth PA 19072-2015

VAN DUYN, MONA JANE, poet; b. Waterloo, Iowa, May 9, 1921; d. Earl George and Lora G. (Kramer) Van D.; m. Jarvis A. Thurston, Aug. 31, 1943. B.A., U. No. Iowa, 1942; M.A., U. Iowa, 1943; D.Litt. (hon.), Washington U., St. Louis, 1971, Cornell Coll., Iowa, 1972, U. No. Iowa, 1991, U. of the South, Sewanee, Tenn., 1993, George Wash. U., 1993; LHD, Georgetown U., 1993. Instr. in English U. Iowa, Iowa City, 1943-46; instr. in English U. Louisville, 1946-50; lectr. English Univ. Coll., Washington U., 1950-67; poetry editor, co-pub. Perspective, A Quar. of Lit., 1947-67; lectr. Salzburg (Austria) Seminar Am. Studies, 1973; adj. prof. poetry workshop Washington U., Spring 1983; vis. Hurst prof., 1987; poet-in-residence Sewanee Writers Conf., 1990, Breadloaf Writing Conf., Mass., 1974. Author: Valentines to the Wide World, 1959, A Time of Bees, 1964, To See, To Take, 1970, Bedtime Stories, 1972, Merciful Disguises, 1973, Letters from a Father and Other Poems, 1983, Near Changes, 1990 (Pulitzer Prize for poetry 1991), Firefall, 1993, If It Be Not I, 1993. Recipient Eunice Tietjens award, 1956, Helen Bullis prize, 1964, 76, Harriet Monroe award, 1968, Hart Crane Meml. award, 1968, Borestone Mountains 1st prize, 1968, Bollingen prize, 1970, Nat. Book award, 1971, Sandburg prize Cornell Coll., 1982, Shelley Meml. prize Poetry Soc. Am., 1987, Lilly prize for poetry, 1989, Mo. Arts award, 1990, Golden Plate award Am. Acad. Achievement, 1992, Arts and Edn. Coun. St. Louis award, 1994; named U.S. Poet Laureate, 1992-93; grantee Nat. Coun. Arts, 1967, NEA, 1985; Guggenheim fellow, 1972. Fellow Acad. Am. Poets (chancellor 1985); mem. NAAS, Nat. Acad. Arts and Letters (Loines prize 1976).

VAN DUYNE, RICHARD PALMER, analytical chemistry and chemical physics educator; b. Orange, N.J., Oct. 28, 1945; s. John Palmer and Lorraine Montgomery (Stoller) Van D.; m. Jerilyn Elise Miripol. B.A., Rensselear Poly. Inst., 1967; Ph.D., U. N.C., 1971. Asst. prof. analytical chemistry and chem. physics Northwestern U., Evanston, Ill., 1971-76, assoc. prof., 1976-79, prof., 1979-87, Charles E. and Emma H. Morrison prof. chemistry, 1987—; cons. Beckman Instrument Co., Fullerton, Calif., 1982-86, Eastman Kodak Co., Rochester, N.Y., 1978-91; disting. vis. prof. U. Tex., Austin, 1979; chmn. Vibrational Spectroscopy Gordon Conf., 1982; Camille and Henry Dreyfus lectr. U. Colo., Boulder, 1981; Kilpatrick lectr. Ill. Inst. Tech., 1982; O.K. Rice lectr. U. N.C., 1984; Henry Werner lectr. U. Kans., 1986; Arthur A. Vernon lectr. Northeastern U., 1992. Mem. adv. bd. Jour. Phys. Chemistry, 1983-88; contbr. chpts. to books, articles to profl. jours. Recipient Coblentz award, 1980, Fresenius award, 1981, Excellence in Surface Sci. award, 1996; Sloan Found. fellow, 1974-78. Fellow AAAS, Am. Phys. Soc.; mem. Am. Chem. Soc. Home: 1520 Washington Ave Wilmette IL 60091-2417 Office: Northwestern Univ 2145 Sheridan Rd Evanston IL 60201-2926

VAN DYCK, NICHOLAS BOORAEM, minister, foundation official; b. Pasadena, Calif., Aug. 10, 1933; s. David Bevier and Anna Booraem (Richardson) van D.; m. Marcia Perera, June 14, 1958; children: Karen Rhoads, Jennifer Bevier, Sarah Paxson, Rebecca Booraem. BA, Rutgers U., 1959; BD, Union Theol. Sem., N.Y.C., 1962; PhD, U. St. Andrews, 1965. Ordained to ministry Presbyn. Ch., 1962. Pastor Palisades (N.Y.) Presbyn. Ch., 1964-68; tchr., adminstr. Princeton (N.J.) Theol. Sem., 1968-76; exec. dir. Action Research Corp., Princeton, 1976-77; exec. dir., founder Nat. Council for Children & TV, Princeton, N.Y.C. and Los Angeles, 1977-82; pres. Nat. Council for Families and TV, Princeton, N.Y.C. and Los Angeles, 1982-87; pres., chief exec. officer Religion In Am. Life, Princeton, Phila, N.Y.C., 1988—; chmn. bd. Action Research Corp., Princeton, 1987—; chmn. Assn. for Theol. Field Edn., U.S. and Can., 1975-76. Pub., editor TV and Families, 1982-87; contbr. articles to profl. jours. Bd. dirs. ARC, Princeton, 1984-89, Princeton Youth Fund, 1983-89, YMCA, Princeton, 1986-89, George H. Gallup Internat. Inst., 1990—. Lt. USNR, 1954-58. Scholar-in-residence Aspen (Colo.) Inst. for Humanistic Studies, 1985. Mem. Soc. for Psychol. Study Social Issues, Ind. Sector. Clubs: Princeton (N.Y.C.); Nassau (Princeton). Lodge: Rotary (pres. Princeton club 1981-82, bd. dirs. found. 1985—). Avocation: collecting antique autos.

VAN DYCK, WENDY, dancer; b. Tokyo. Student, San Francisco Ballet Sch. With San Francisco Ballet, 1979—, prin. dancer, 1987—. Performances include Forgotten Land, The Sons of Horus, The Wanderer Fantasy, Romeo and Juliet, The Sleeping Beauty, Swan Lake, Concerto in d: Poulenc, Handel-a Celebration, Menuetto, Intimate Voices, Hamlet and Ophelia pas de deux, Connotations, Sunset, Rodin, In the Night, The Dream: pas de deux, La Sylphide, Beauty and the Beast, Variations de Ballet, Nutcracker, The Comfort Zone, Dreams of Harmony, Rodeo, Duo Concertant, Who Cares; performed at Reykjavik Arts Festival, Iceland, 1990, The 88th Conf. of the Internat. Olympic Com., L.A., 1984, with Kozlov and Co. Concord Pavilion; guest artist performing role Swan Lake (Act II), San Antonio Ballet, 1985, Giselle, Shreveport Met. Ballet, 1994; featured in the TV broadcast of Suite by Smuin. Office: San Francisco Ballet 455 Franklin St San Francisco CA 94102-4438

VAN DYK, FREDERICK THEODORE, writer, consultant; b. Bellingham, Wash., Oct. 6, 1934; s. Ted and June Ellen (Williams) Van D.; m. Julia Jean Covacevich, Nov. 22, 1957; children: Theodore, Robert, Terry Jean, Sue Ellen. B.A., U. Wash., 1955; M.S., Columbia U., 1956. Reporter, editor Seattle Times, 1956-57; advt. public relations exec. Boston and N.Y.C., 1958-62; acting dir. European Community Info. Service, Washington, 1962-64; asst. to Hubert Humphrey, Vice Pres. of U.S., 1964-68; v.p. Columbia U., N.Y.C., 1968-69; pres. Van Dyk Assocs., Washington, 1969-76; asst. adminstr. AID, Washington, 1977; v.p. Weyerhaeuser Co., Tacoma, 1978-80; pres. Center for Nat. Policy, Washington, 1981-85, Van Dyk Assocs., 1985—. Contbr. essays on govt. and politics to gen. publs. including L.A. Times, N.Y. Times, Wall St. Jour., Washington Post. Bd. dirs. Com. for Study of Am. Electorate, Franklin and Eleanor Roosevelt Inst., Jean Monnet Coun.; mem. Coun. on Fgn. Rels., Presdl. Commn. on Fgn. Assistance. Served with M.I. AUS, 1957, 61-62. Mem. Delta Upsilon (nat. trustee). Clubs: Fed. City, Army Navy (Washington), Rainier (Seattle). Home: 7500 Masters Dr Potomac MD 20854-3854 Office: Van Dyk Assocs 1250-24th St NW Washington DC 20037

VAN DYKE, CLIFFORD CRAIG, retired banker; b. Ft. Madison, Iowa, June 23, 1929; s. Charles Clifford and Frances Mary (Butterwick) Van D.; m. Edith Ellicott Powers, Aug. 4, 1951 (dec. Oct. 1980); children: Carol Elizabeth, Deborah Ellicott, Jill Anne, Lisa Ellicott. BA, Knox Coll., 1951; MBA, Harvard U., 1955. Asst. v.p. Nat. Bank of Detroit, 1962-65, v.p., 1965-76; pres. Peoples Nat. Bank & Trust Co. of Bay City, Mich., 1976-78, chmn. bd., pres., 1979-86; chmn. bd., pres., chief exec. officer New Ctr. Bank Corp., Bay City, Mich., 1986; chmn. First of Am. Bank-Bay City, N.A., 1987-89; sr. v.p. First of Am. Bank-Mid Mich. N.A., 1990-94; ret., 1994. Trustee Kantzler Found., Bay City, 1979—; bd. dirs., pres. Bay County Growth Alliance, 1987—. 1st lt. U.S. Army, 1951-53, Korea. Mem. Bay City Country Club, Saginaw Valley Torch Club, Saginaw Bay Yacht Club, Rotary, Elks. Republican. Unitarian. Office: Bay County Growth Alliance PO Box 369 Bay City MI 48707-0369

VAN DYKE, CRAIG, psychiatrist; b. Detroit, Oct. 4, 1941; married; two children. BS, U. Wash., 1963, MD, 1967. Asst. prof. psychiatry Yale U., New Haven, Conn., 1974-78; from assoc. to prof. psychiatry U. Calif., San Francisco, 1979-86, prof., chmn. dept. psychiatry, 1994—. Mem. Am. Psychosom. Soc., Internat. Coll. Psychosom. Medicine, Soc. Neurosci., Internat. Neuropsychol. Soc. Office: U Cal San Francisco Langley Porter Psychiatric Inst 401 Parnassus Ave San Francisco CA 94143

VAN DYKE, DANIEL L., geneticist; b. Paterson, N.J., Mar. 1, 1947. PhD, Ind. U., 1976. Cert. med. genetics and clin. cytogenetics Am. Bd. Med. Genetics. Divsn. head genetics labs. Henry Ford Hosp., Detroit, 1975—; faculty U. Mich. Med. Sch., Detroit, 1978—, Case Western Res. U., Cleve., 1994—. Address: Henry Ford Hospital Cytogenetics Lab 2799 W Grand Blvd Detroit MI 48202-2608

VAN DYKE, DICK, actor, comedian; b. West Plains, Mo., Dec. 13, 1925; m. Marjorie Willett, Feb. 12, 1948; children: Christian, Barry, Stacey, Carrie Beth. Ed. high sch. With Wayne Williams, founded advt. agy. Danville, Ill., 1946; chmn. Nick at Nite, 1992—. Appeared school plays, civic theatre prodns.; appeared with Philip Erickson in pantomine act The Merry Mutes, Eric and Van, 1947-53; TV master ceremonies The Music Shop, Atlanta; TV variety show Dick Van Dyke Show, New Orleans; master ceremonies: Morning Show, CBS, 1955, Cartoon Show, 1956; guest appearances nat. TV shows, 1958; host Flair, weekly TV show, ABC, 1960; Broadway debut in The Girls Against the Boys, 1959; performed in Broadway musical Bye Bye Birdie, 1960-61 (also motion picture version); weekly comedy program Dick Van Dyke Show, CBS-TV, 1961-66; star weekly comedy program New Dick Van Dyke Show, 1971-74; performer weekly comedy program Carol Burnett Show; host weekly comedy program Van Dyke and Company, 1976, The Van Dyke Show, CBS, 1988; appeared in TV series Diagnosis Murder, 1993-94; numerous TV guest appearances; performed in motion pictures including What a Way To Go, 1964, Mary Poppins, 1965, Divorce American Style, 1967, Chitty, Chitty, Bang, Bang, 1968, The Comic, 1969, Some Kind of Nut, 1969, Cold Turkey, 1971, The Morning After, 1974, The Runner Stumbles, 1979, Drop-Out Father, 1982, Found Money, 1983, Dick Tracy, 1990; Author: Faith, Hope, and Hilarity, 1970. With USAAC, World War II. Recipient Theater World award 1960, Antoinette Perry award for best mus. comedy actor 1961, Emmy award for comedy Nat. Acad. TV Arts and Scis. 1962, 64, 65. Office: William Morris Agy Inc care Sol Leon 151 S El Camino Dr Beverly Hills CA 90212-2704*

VAN DYKE, JERRY, actor, comedian; b. Danville, Ill.. Stand-up comedian for years, performing in Las Vegas, Atlantic City, other major showrooms; TV work includes (series) The Judy Garland Show, My Mother The Car, 1964, Coach, ABC-TV, 1990— (Emmy nomination, Supporting Actor - Comedy Series, 1994); film work includes The Courtship of Eddie's Father, Palm Springs Weekend. With USAF, 1952-54. Office: Sutton Barth Vennari 145 S Fairfax Ave Ste 310 Universal City CA 90036*

VAN DYKE, JOSEPH GARY OWEN, computer consulting executive; b. N.Y.C., Dec. 21, 1939; s. Donald Wood and Gladys Ann (Tague) Van D.; m. Lynne Diane Lammers; June 25, 1966; children: Alison Baird, Jeremy Wood, Matthew Kerr. BA, Rutgers U., 1961; postgrad., R.I. Sch. of Design, 1962, Am. U., 1964-67. Computer programmer System Devel. Corp., Paramus, N.J., 1962-64; sect. head computer tech. div. System Devel. Corp., Falls Church, Va., 1964-67; project mgr. Informatics Inc., Bethesda, Md., 1967-70; dept. dir. Informatics Inc., Rockville, Md., 1970-74, v.p., gen. mgr., 1974-78; owner, pres. J G Van Dyke and Assoc., Inc., Bethesda, 1978—; chmn. bd., chief exec. officer The Outreach Group, Inc., 1987—. Bd. dirs. Westbrook Sch., Bethesda, 1981-82, St. Columba's Ch., Washington, 1980-84; founder Computer Edn. Workshop, Bethesda, 1981; coach MSI soccer, Bethesda, 1979-89. Mem. Inst. Elec. Engring. Democrat. Episcopalian. Avocations: coaching soccer, sailing, graphic designing. Home: 5117 Dalecarlia Dr Bethesda MD 20816-1801 Office: JG Van Dyke & Assocs Inc 6550 Rock Spring Dr Ste 360 Bethesda MD 20817-1132*

VAN DYKE, MILTON DENMAN, aeronautical engineering educator; b. Chgo., Aug. 1, 1922; s. James Richard and Ruth (Barr) Van D.; m. Sylvia Jean Agard Adams, June 16, 1962; children: Russell B., Eric J., Nina A., Brooke A. and Byron J. and Christopher M. (triplets). B.S., Harvard U., 1943; M.S., Calif. Inst. Tech., 1947, Ph.D., 1949. Research engr. NACA, 1943-46, 50-54, 55-58; vis. prof. U. Paris, France, 1958- 59; prof. aero. Stanford, 1959—; prof. emeritus, 1992—; pres. Parabolic Press. Author: Perturbation Methods in Fluid Mechanics, 1964, An Album of Fluid Motion, 1982; editor: Ann. Rev. Fluid Mechanics, 1969—. Trustee Soc. For Promotion of Sci. and Scholarship, Inc. Served with USNR, 1944-46. Guggenheim and Fulbright fellow, 1954-55. Mem. Am. Acad. Arts and Scis., Nat. Acad. Engring., Am. Phys. Soc., Phi Beta Kappa, Sigma Xi, Sierra Club. Office: Stanford U Div Applied Mechanics Stanford CA 94305-4040

VAN DYKE, THOMAS WESLEY, lawyer; b. Kansas City, Mo., May 12, 1938; s. Harold Thomas and Elizabeth Louise (Barritt) Van D.; m. Sharon Edgar, Jan. 30, 1960; children: Jennifer Van Dyke Winters, Jeffrey. BA, U. Kans., 1960; JD, U. Mich., 1963. Bar: Mo. 1963, Kans. 1983. Atty. SEC, Washington, 1963-64; legal asst. to commr. Hamer E. Budge, Washington, 1964-65; from assoc. to ptnr. Linde Thomson Langworthy Kohn & Van Dyke, P.C., Overland Park, Kans., 1965-91; co-chmn. ALI-ABA Tax and Bus. Planning Seminar, 1981-96; mem. securities adv. panel Sec. of State of Mo., 1984-89. Mem. ABA (fed. regulation securities com bus. law sect. 1982-95, negotatiated acquisitions com. 1989-95), Kans. Bar Assn., Mo. Bar Assn. (corp. banking and bus. law com., chmn. full com. 1983-84, past chmn. securities law subcom.), Carriage Club (bd. dirs. 1986-89). Republican. Avocations: tennis, reading. Office: Bryan Cave LLP Ste 1100 7500 College Blvd Overland Park KS 66210

VAN DYKE, WILLIAM GRANT, manufacturing company executive; b. Mpls., June 30, 1945; s. Russell Lawrence and Carolyn (Grant) Van D.; m. Karin Van Dyke; children: Carolyn Julie, Colin Grant, Alexander Grant, Stephanie Joyce. BA in Econs., U. Minn., 1967, MBA, 1972. V.p., CFO Northland Aluminum Co., Mpls., 1977-78; controller Donaldson Co., Inc., Mpls., 1978-80, v.p. controller, 1980-82, v.p., CFO, 1982-84, pres., COO, 1984—, also bd. dirs.; bd. dirs. Graco Inc. Served to lt. U.S. Army, 1968-70, Vietnam. Mem. Kappa Sigma Alumni Assn. Avocations: running; bicycling. Office: Donaldson Co Inc 1400 W 94th St Minneapolis MN 55431-2301

VAN DYKE-COOPER, ANNY MARION, financial company executive; b. Howard, Ont., Can., Sept. 30, 1928; d. Anthony and Anna (Koolen) Van D.; m. John Arnold Cooper, Apr. 9, 1983. BA, Concordia U., 1959. Chartered fin. analyst. Tchr. Lanoraie Sch. Bd., 1946-47; sec. Can. Nat. Rys., Montreal, Que., Can., 1947-51; sec. Sorel Industries Ltd., Sorel, Que., Can., 1952-53; with Bell Investment Mgmt. Corp. and BIMCOR, Inc. subs. Bell Canada, Montreal, 1953-83; portfolio mgr. U.S. Equities, 1971-83; chmn., dir. Cooper, Van Dyke Assocs. Inc., Bloomfield Hills, Mich., 1983—. Mem. Inst. Chartered Fin. Analysts (trustee 1979-80), Fin. Analysts Soc. Detroit, Montreal Soc. Fin. Analysts (program chmn., pres. 1974-75), Can. Coun. Fin. Analysts (vice-chmn. 1976-77), Assn. for Investment Mgmt. and RSch. (treas. 1977-78, vice chmn. 1978-79, chmn. 1979-80). Home: 1111 N Woodward Ave Apt C228 Birmingham MI 48009-5423 Office: 1100 Woodward Ave Ste 238 Bloomfield Hills MI 48304-3971

VANE, DENA, magazine editor-in-chief. Editor-in-chief First for Women, Englewood Cliffs, N.J. Office: First for Women Bauer Pub Co 270 Sylvan Ave Englewood NJ 07632

VANE, TERENCE G., JR., finance and insurance company executive, lawyer; b. Elgin, Ill., Jan. 17, 1942; s. Terence Gregory and Velma Mary (Mersman) V.; m. Patricia Bryant, Aug. 29, 1964; children: Terence Gregory III, Lourdene DeLynne, Christopher Theodore. BA, Ind. U., 1964, JD, 1967. Bar: Ind. 1967, Tex. 1977, N.C. 1992. Staff atty. Assocs. Discount Corp., South Bend, Ind., 1967-69; asst. gen. counsel Assocs. Mgmt. Corp., South Bend, 1969-74, Assocs. Comml. Corp., South Bend, 1974-76, Assocs. Ins. Group, Inc., Dallas, 1976-77; gen. counsel, v.p. ins. ops. Assocs. Corp. N.Am., Dallas, 1977-80, gen. counsel, sr. v.p. ins. ops., 1981-82, gen. counsel, sr. v.p. consumer fin. and ins. ops., 1982-86, gen. counsel, sr. v.p. diversified consumer fin. services and credit card ops., 1986-88; exec. v.p., gen. counsel, sec., dir. Barclays Am. Corp., Charlotte, N.C., 1988-91; pres. Vector Fin. Svcs., Inc., Charlotte, 1991-95; bd. dirs., v.p., assoc. gen. counsel EquiCredit Corp., Jacksonville, Fla., 1996—; v.p., assoc. gen. counsel Equicredit Corp., Jacksonville, Fla., 1996—. Chmn. bd. dirs., sec. Youth Concert Found. for Promotion Creative Arts, 1981—; bd. dirs. N.C. Bus. Com. Edn., 1988-91. Mem. ABA, Ind. Bar Assn., Tex. Bar Assn., N.C. Bar Assn., Mecklenburg County Bar Assn., Nat. Assn. Ind. Insurers (laws com. 1978-86), Consumer Credit Ins. Assn. (chmn. property ins. legis. com. 1979-85), Am. Fin. Svcs. Assn. (law com., chmn. environ. law subcom.), Conf. Consumer Fin. Law (gen. com.). Home: PO Box 53077 Jacksonville FL 32201-3077 Office: PO Box 53077 10401 Deerwood Pk Blvd Jacksonville FL 32201-3077 Office: 10401 Deerwood Park Blvd Jacksonville FL 32256

VANECKO, ROBERT MICHAEL, surgeon, educator; b. Chgo., Aug. 15, 1935; s. Michael and Raphael Regina (Burns) V.; m. Mary Carol Daley; children: Robert G., Mark G., Richard J., Mary Clare. BS, Georgetown U., 1957; MS, Northwestern U., 1960, MD, 1961. Diplomate Am. Bd. Surgery, Am. Bd. Thoracic Surgery. Intern Cook County Hosp., Chgo., 1961-62, resident in gen. surgery, 1962-66; instr. surgery U. Ill., 1964-66; resident in cardiothoracic surgery Cook County Hosp., Chgo., 1966-67, Hines (Ill.) VA Hosp., 1969-70; attending surgeon VA Rsch. Hosp., Chgo., 1970—; attending surgeon Cook County Hosp., Chgo., 1972—, chief sect. thoracic trauma, 1972-78; assoc. attending Northwestern Meml. Hosp., Chgo., 1970-77, attending, 1977—; assoc. in surgery Northwestern U. Med. Sch., Chgo., 1970-71, asst. prof. surgery, 1971-75, assoc. prof. surgery, 1975-88, prof. clin. surgery, 1988-93, prof. surgery, 1993—, asst. dean, then assoc. dean grad. med. edn., 1988—; mem. numerous hosp. coms. Creator, writer numerous surgical movies, 1963-84; contbr. articles to profl. jours. Bd. govs. Chgo. Heart Assn., 1980-86, 88—, mem. phys. fitness com., 1973-80, mem. pub. policy and govt. rels. com., 1980—; mem. alumni coun. Northwestern U. Med. Sch., mem. instl. rev. bd.; mem. adv. com. Ill. Dept. Pub. Health, 1990—; bd. gov. Chgo. Access Corp., 1984-90, Crescent County Med. Found., 1984-87. Mem. AAAS, ACS (mem. motion picture com. 1974-80, mem. credentials com. 1978-86, chmn. met. credentials com. 1986—), AMA (alt. del. to ho. of dels. 1984-86, del. to ho. of dels. 1986—, mem. sect. med. schs. 1987—), Am. Assn. Thoracic Surgery, Am. Coll. Chest Physicians (chmn. motion picture com. 1977-80, treas. 1980-85, pres. Ill.-Great Lakes chpt. 1981-82, dir. edn. found. 1985—), Am. Hosp. Assn. (mem. nat. congress hosp. gov. bd. 1984—, mem. coordinating com. med. edn. 1989—), Am. Med. Writers Assn., Am. Trauma Soc., Ctrl. Surg. Assn., Chgo. Med. Soc. (mem. health planning com., mem. health care delivery com. 1982-86, mem. health system agy. com. 1978-84, bd. trustees 1984-89, sec. 1984-86, pres. 1987-88, chmn. bd. trustees 1986-87), Chgo. Surg. Soc. (rep. to Ill. State Med. Soc. 1984-86), Ill. Med. Soc., Ill. Surg. Soc., Ill. Hosp. Assn. (bd. trustees 1986—), Inst. Medicine Chgo. (bd. govs. 1984—, mem. grad. and undergrad. med. edn. com. 1975-79, treas. 1986-89), Soc. Med. History Chgo., Soc. Thoracic Surgeons, Western Surg. Assn. Office: Northwestern Med Sch 303 E Chicago Ave Chicago IL 60611-3008

VANEGAS, JORGE ALBERTO, civil engineering educator; b. Bogota, Colombia, Oct. 17, 1956; came to U.S., 1983; s. Carlos Enrique and Cecilia (Pabon) V.; m. Adriana Martinez, Dec. 18, 1987 (div. Dec. 1992); m. Loretta Sanders, Dec. 22, 1992). BS in Architecture, U. de los Andes, Bogota, 1979; MSCE, Stanford U., 1985, PhD in Civil Engring., 1988. Rsch. and teaching asst. Stanford (Calif.) U., 1984-87, acting asst. prof., 1988; asst. prof. Purdue U., West Lafayette, Ind., 1988-93; assoc. profl. civil engring. Ga. Inst. Tech., Atlanta, 1993—; cons. U.S. and Colombia, 1982—. Mem. ASCE (assoc.), Am. Soc. Engrs. in Edn. (assoc.). Roman Catholic. Home: 4205 Newpond Trl Kennesaw GA 30144-1667 Office: Sch Civil Engring Dept Civil Engring Ga Inst Tech Atlanta GA 30332-0355

VAN EGMOND, CORALEE ANN, chiropractor, consultant; b. Grand Rapids, Mich., Jan. 30, 1955; d. Elmer Eugene and Margorie Grace (Steketee) Van E. BA, Smith Coll., 1977; D of Chiropractic, Palmer Coll., 1986. Cert. chiropractic examiner, Ky. Pub. info. coord., asst. editor Am. Running and Fitness Assn., Washington, 1978-81; crisis counselor Families and Children in Trouble (Parents Anonymous), Washington, 1978-80; editor-in-chief Beacon Alumni and Student Newspaper, Davenport, Iowa, 1984-85; rsch. work asst. diagnosis/pathology dept. Palmer Coll., Davenport, Iowa, 1984-86; faculty instr. Palmer Sch. Chiropractic Technicians, Davenport, Iowa, 1985-86; intern Strang Chiropractic Clinic, Davenport, Iowa, 1985-86; assoc. dr. Chiropractic Assocs. Ark., Little Rock, 1986-87, Darnall Chiropractic Offices, Stockton, Calif., 1987-88, Goben Chiropractic Offices, Louisville, 1989-93; staff dr. Sports and Performance Rehab. Facility, Louisville, 1993—; cons. to health ins. cos., Louisville, 1989—; bd. dirs. Ky. State Bd. of Chiropractic Examiners, 1994—. Author: Chiropractic in the Prevention and Management of Drug and Alcohol Abuse, 1993; contbr. rsch. papers to profl. confs. Pres. Kentuckiana Women's Network, Louisville, 199-94; bd. dirs., program com. chair S.W. YMCA, Louisville, 1993—. Named Hon. Order of Ky. Cols., 1994. Mem. Ky. Chiropractic Soc. (congrl. del. 1989-93, Pres.'s award 1991), Internat. Chiropractors Assn. (charter mem. pediatrics coun. 1992-93, exec. com. coun. sports and fitness health sci.), Am. Running and Fitness Coun. Clinic Advisors, Kiwanis Internat. (bd. dirs. 1989-93, pres. 1990-91), Delta Delta Alumni Assn. (v.p. 1991-93). Avocations: growing old garden roses and healing herbs, creative writing, aerobic sports, traditional musical instruments, songs and stories, needlework. Office: Breuer Sports & Perf Rehab 1810 Sils Ave Louisville KY 40205-2161

VANEK, JAROSLAV, economist, educator; b. Prague, Czechoslovakia, Apr. 20, 1930; came to U.S., 1955, naturalized, 1960; s. Josef and Jaroslava (Tucek) V.; m. Wilda M. Marraffino, Dec. 26, 1959; children: Joseph, Francis, Rosemarie, Steven, Teresa. Degree in stats., Sorbonne, Paris, 1951; license in econ., U. Geneva, 1954; Ph.D., MIT, 1957. Instr., then asst. prof. Harvard U., 1957-63; adviser AID, 1964; mem. faculty Cornell U., 1964-96, prof. econs., 1966-96, Carl Marks prof. internat. studies, 1969-96, dir. program comparative econ. devel., 1968-73, dir. program participation and labor-managed systems, 1969-96, prof. emeritus, 1996—; mem. nat. adv. bd. econs. NSF, 1969-70; founder, pres. S.T.E.V.E.N. Found. (Solar Tech. and Energy for Vital Econ. Needs), 1985—. Author: International Trade: Theory and Economic Policy, 1962, The Balance of Payments, Level of Economic Activity and the Value of Currency, 1962, The Natural Resource Content of United States Foreign Trade, 1870-1955, 1963, General Equilibrium of International Discrimination, 1965, Estimating Foreign Resource Needs for Economic Development, 1966, Maximal Economic Growth, 1968, The General Theory of Labor-Managed Market Economies, 1970, The Participatory Economy, 1971, Self-Management: Economic Liberation of Man, 1975, The Labor-Managed Economy, 1977, Crisis and Reform: East and West; Essays in Social Economy, 1989, Toward Full Democracy, Political and Economic, In Russia, 1993; also manuscripts on solar tech.; contbr. to Advances in the Economic Analysis of Participatory and Labor-Managed Firms, Vol. 2, 1987; inventor several solar tech. designs including solar steam engines, pumps, refrigerators, cookers; holder 1 patent. Roman Catholic. Home: 414 Triphammer Rd Ithaca NY 14850-2521 Office: Cornell U Econs Dept Uris Hall # 462 Ithaca NY 14853-7601

VAN EMBURGH, JOANNE, lawyer; b. Palmyra, N.J., Nov. 18, 1953; d. Earl Henry and Clare (Kemmerle) Van E.; m. Samuel Michael Surloff, July 6, 1993. BA summa cum laude, Catholic U., 1975; JD cum laude, Harvard Law Sch., 1978. Assoc. atty. Agnew Miller & Carlson, L.A., 1978-82; ptnr. Sachs & Phelps, L.A., 1982-91, Heller, Ehrman, White & McAuliffe, L.A., 1991-96; with Toyota Motor Sales, Torrance, 1996—. Mem. ABA, L.A. County Bar (exec. com., bus. and corp. law sect. 1993—). Avocations: reading, cooking, sports. Office: Toyota Motor Sales 1900 S Western Ave Torrance CA 90509*

VAN ES, RICHARD JOHN, JR., electronics executive; b. South Bend, Ind., Aug. 3, 1957; s. Richard John Sr. and Barbara Jean (Frick) Van E.; m.

Mary Elizabeth Sartini, June 6, 1982. BBA, U. Notre Dame, Ind., 1980. CPA, Ind. Staff acct. Price Waterhouse, South Bend, 1980-82; asst. controller St. Joseph Bank and Trust Co., South Bend, 1982-84; sr. acct. McGladrey, Hendrickson & Pullen, Elkhart, Ind., 1984-87; v.p. fin. and acctg. Am. Electronic Components, Elkhart, 1987—; now pres., ceo. Mem. Am. Inst. CPA's, Ind. Soc. CPA's. Avocations: tennis, music. Home: 1560 Durham Way W Granger IN 46530 Office: Am Electronic Components 1010 N Main St Elkhart IN 46514-3205*

VAN ESELTINE, WILLIAM PARKER, microbiologist, educator; b. Syracuse, N.Y., Aug. 21, 1924; s. Glen Parker and Florence Marie (Lamb) Van E.; m. Marian Louise Vanderburgh, Aug. 25, 1948; children—Kenneth Leslie, Karen Elaine. A.B., Oberlin Coll., 1944; M.S., Cornell U., 1947, Ph.D., 1949. Asst. in bacteriology N.Y. State Agrl. Expt. Sta., Geneva, 1944-45, summer 1946; Asst. in bacteriology N.Y. State Coll. Agr., Cornell U., Ithaca, 1946-48; asso. prof. bacteriology Clemson (S.C.) Agrl. Coll., 1948-52; asst. prof. vet. hygiene U. Ga., Athens, 1952-59, asso. prof. microbiology and preventive medicine, 1959-67, prof. med. microbiology, 1967-87, prof. emeritus, 1987—. Contbr. articles on microbiology to profl. jours. Mem. Am. Soc. Microbiology, N.Y. Acad. Sci., Ga. Acad. Sci., Am. Leptospirosis Research Conf. (pres. 1987), AAAS, Sigma Xi, Phi Kappa Phi. Home: 237 Woodlawn Ave Athens GA 30606-4353

VANESS, CAROL, soprano; b. L.A., July 27, 1952; d. William Anthony and Dorotha Jean (Whitsun) V. BA, Calif. Poly. U., 1974; MA, Calif. State U., Northridge, 1976; student, Merola and Affiliate Artist programs, San Francisco, 1976-78. Made debut N.Y.C. Opera as Vitellia in La Clemenza di Tito, 1979; prodns. include Don Giovanni, 1980, Merry Wives of Windsor, 1981, La Boheme, Rigoletto, Pearl Fishers, Traviata and Alcina, 1983; revivals San Francisco Opera Don Giovanni, 1981, Dialogues of the Carmelites, 1982, La Traviata, 1991, Don Carlo, 1992; European debut Clemenza, Bordeaux, France, 1981, Buffalo Philharm., Rossini Stabat Mater, 1981; debut Phila. Opera as Countess in Figaro, 1982, N.Y.C. Opera in Figaro, Covent Garden debut as Mimi in La Boheme, 1982, Glyndebourne Festival Don Giovanni, 1982, Idomeneo, 1983, Cosi, 1984, Boccanegra, 1986; Paris Opera debut as Nedda in Pagliacci, 1982, Idomeneo & Clemenza, 1986, Berlin, Munich and Vienna debut in Don Giovanni, Met. Opera debut as Armida in Rinaldo, 1984, Australian debut in a Masked Ball, 1985, Rome debut in Faust, 1987, Barcelona, Spain debut in Tito, 1988, Salzburg Festival debut as Vitellia, Austria, 1988, Tito, 1988-89, Donna Elvira, 1990, Lyric Opera of Chbo. debut, 1988, Don Giovanni, 1989, N.Y. Philharm. debut, 1991, La Scala (Milan) debut Idomeneo, 1990; Met. Opera Figaro, 1985, Samson, 1986, Faust, 1990, Don Giovanni, 1990; recital debut, Liberty, Mo., 1986, Carnegie Hall debut Strauss 4 Last Songs, 1987, Live from Lincoln Ctr. Pavarotti Plus, 1986, 90, numerous recs. with EMI; rec. complete Giovanni and Cosi with Glyndebourne/Haitink; N.Y. recital debut Alice Tully Hall, 1987, , Carol Vaness Mozart An'as, Don Giovanni-Muti Mozart Duets with Placido Domingo, Rossini Stabat Matev Tosca-Muti, Verdi Requiem Iphigenie en Tauride, 1992. Winner San Francisco Opera Audition, 1976. Office: IMG Artists Europe Medin House, 3 Burlington Lane, London W4 2TH, England

VAN ETTEN, EDYTHE AUGUSTA, retired occupational health nurse; b. Arthur, N.D., Oct. 13, 1921; d. Lacy Edward and Emma Erna (Mundt) Roach; m. Robert Scott Van Etten, Feb. 12, 1944; children: Ronald, Cynthia Czernysz, Martin, Roger, Randall, Janet K. Diploma, Mt. Sinai Hosp. Sch. Nursing, Chgo., 1945; AS, Waubonsee Community Coll., Sugar Grove, Ill., 1978; BSN, No. Ill. U., 1981. Cert. occupational health nurse; RN, Ill. Occupation health nurse Barber-Greene Co., Aurora, Ill., 1965-82; occupational health relief nurse No. Ill. Gas Co., Naperville, Ill., 1983-85; supr. or staff nurse Michealsen Health Ctr., Batavia, Ill., 1982-93; occupational health relief nurse The Dial Corp., Montgomery, Ill., 1982-94; occupational health nurse cons. AT&T Svc. Ctr., West Chicago, Ill., 1988-94. Mem. adminstrv. bd. Ch. of the Good Shepherd Meth., Oswego, Ill., 1988-94; active Fox Bend Ladies Golf League, United Meth. Women; mem. Lyric Opera of Chgo. Mem. Suburban Chgo. Assn. Occupational Health Nurses, Dist. 2 Ill. Nurses Assn. (del. state conv. 1985, Award for Excellence in Nursing Practice 1993), Sr. Svcs. Assn. Inc. (adv. 1983-87, Humanitarian award 1985), Oswegoland Women's Civic Club (bd. dirs. 1985—). Republican. Avocations: piano, baseball. Home: 427 S Madison St PO Box 1 Oswego IL 60543

VAN ETTEN, PETER WALBRIDGE, hospital administrator; b. Boston, May 10, 1946; s. Royal Cornelius Van Etten and Peggy June (Walbridge) Hutchins; m. Mary Peters French, Oct. 13, 1968; children: Molly, Clarissa, Ellen. BA, Columbia U., 1968; MBA, Harvard U., 1973. Br. mgr. BayBanks, Brookline, Mass., 1968-71; loan officer Bank of Boston, 1973-76; CFO Univ. Hosp., Boston, 1976-79; exec. v.p., CFO New Eng. Med. Ctr., Boston, 1979-89; pres., CEO Transitions Systems, Boston, 1986-89; dep. chancellor U. Mass. Med. Ctr., Worcester, 1989-91; CFO Stanford (Calif.) U., 1991-94; pres., CEO Stanford Univ. Hosp., 1994—. Bd. dirs. The Hosp. Fund, New Haven, 1989—. Office: Stanford Hosp Pasteur Dr Stanford CA 94305

VAN EXEL, MICKEY MAXWELL, professional basketball player; b. Kenosha, Wis., Nov. 27, 1971; s. Mickey Maxwell and Joyce Van Exel; 1 child, Mickey Maxwell III. Attended, Trinity Valley C.C., 1989-91, U. Cin., 1993. Profl. basketball player L.A. Lakers, 1993—. Named to NBA All-Rookie 2d team, 1994. Office: LA Lakers Great Western Forum PO Box 10 3900 W Manchester Inglewood CA 90306

VAN EYS, JAN, pediatrician, educator, administrator; b. Hilversum, The Netherlands, Jan. 25, 1929; came to U.S., 1951; s. Jan and Geertruida (Floor) van E.; m. Catherine Travis; children: Jan Peter, D. Catherine. PhD in Biochemistry, Vanderbilt U., 1955; MD, U. Wash., 1966. Diplomate Nat. Bd. Med. Examiners, Am. Bd. Pediatrics, Am. Bd. Pediatric Hematology/Oncology. Postdoctoral fellow McCollum Pratt Inst., Johns Hopkins U., Balt., 1955-57; asst. prof. biochemistry Vanderbilt U., Nashville, 1957-62, assoc. prof., 1962-71, prof., 1971-73; intern, resident in pediatrics Vanderbilt U. Hosps., Nashville, 1966-69; pediatrician M.D. Anderson Hosp. U. Tex., Houston, 1973-94, prof. pediatrics, 1973-94, Mosbacher prof. pediatrics, 1979-87, Mosbacher chair, 1988-90, chmn. dept., 1983-88, head div., 1983-90, chmn. dept. exptl. pediatrics, 1983-90; David R. Park prof. pediatrics U. Tex. Med. Sch., Houston, 1990-94, chmn. dept., 1987-94; clin. prof. pediat. Sch. Medicine, Vanderbilt U., Nashville, 1994—; cons. Cancer Info. Svcs. for Code Ethics and Pediatric Cancers, 1986-89. Author: (with T.S. Carter and C. Jordan) The Howell Kindred, 1979, Humanity and Personhood: Personal Reactions to a World in Which Children Can Die, 1981, (with M. Weiner) Nicotinic Acid, Drug, Nutrient and Cofactor, 1983; contbr. numerous articles, abstracts, papers, book chpts., and revs. to profl. publs.; editor: (with J.T. Truman and C. Pochedly) Human Values in Pediatric Hematology/Oncology, 1986, (with R.A. Dowell and D. Copeland) The Child With Cancer in the Community, 1988, Cancer in the Very Young, 1989; chief editor pediatric sect. Year Book of Cancer, 1978-87, cons. editor, 1974-78; assoc. editor Nutrition and Cancer, 1978—, Jour. Pediatric Hematology/Oncology, 1982-92, Houston Med. Jour., 1986-93, Cancer Prevention Internat., 1993—, The Pharos, 1994—; also editor/co-editor proc. of workshops, clin. and mental health confs., ann. symposiums, etc. Pres. bd. trustees Inst. Religion, Houston, 1989-94; mem. adminstrv. bd. Westbury United Meth. Ch., Houston, 1989-94. Fellow Am. Acad. Pediatrics, Am. Coll. Nutrition; mem. Am. Pediatric Soc., Am. Soc. Hematology, Am. Soc. Clin. Oncology, Am. Med. Writers Assn., Am. Soc. for Parental and Enteral Nutrition, So. Med. Assn., World Fedn. for Hemophilia, Tex. Pediatric Soc., Houston Pediatric Soc. (pres. 1981-82), Houston Acad. Medicine, Harris County Med. Assn., U. Tex. M.D. Anderson Cancer Ctr. Assocs., Sigma Xi, Alpha Omega Alpha. Home and Office: 3504 Ruland Pl Nashville TN 37215-1812

VAN FLEET, GEORGE ALLAN, lawyer; b. Monterey, Calif., Jan. 20, 1953; s. George Lawson and Wilma Ruth (Williams) Van F.; m. Laurie Elise Koch, July 20, 1975; children: Katia Elaine, Alexander Lawson. BA summa cum laude, Rice U., 1976; JD, Columbia U., 1977. Bar: Tex. 1978, U.S. Dist. Ct. (so. dist.) Tex. 1978, U.S. Dist. Ct. (we. dist.) Tex. 1987, U.S. Dist. Ct. (no. dist.) Tex, 1988, U.S. Dist. Ct. (ea. dist.) Tex. 1991, U.S. Tax Ct., 1984, U.S. Ct. Appeals (5th cir.) 1978, U.S. Ct. Appeals (11th cir.) 1981, U.S. Ct. Appeals (D.C. cir.) 1982, U.S. Ct. Appeals (fed. cir.) 1993, U.S. Supreme Ct. 1981. Law clk. U.S. Ct. Appeals (2d cir.), N.Y.C., 1977; assoc. Vinson & Elkins, Houston, 1977-84, ptnr., 1984—; mem. NAFTA Tri-Nat. Task Force. Editor: Compliance Manuals for the New Antitrust Era, 1989, quarterly rev. Litigation News, 1983-86; contbr. articles to profl. jour. Regional dir. Anti-Defamation League, 1990-94; bd. visitors Columbia U., 1992—; mem. City of Houston Ethics Com., 1992—, chmn. 1995—. Recipient Ordronaux prize Columbia U., 1977; James Kent scholar Columbia U., 1974-77. Fellow Tex. Bar Assn.; mem. ABA (com. chmn. 1987-95, mem. coun. 1996—), Houston Bar Assn. (sec. chair 1991-93), Tex.-Mex. Bar Assn. (vice chmn. 1996—), Phi Beta Kappa. Democrat. Jewish. Home: 4323 N Roseneath Dr Houston TX 77021-1623 Office: Vinson & Elkins 1001 Fannin St Ste 2500 Houston TX 77002-6709

VAN FLEET, WILLIAM MABRY, architect; b. Point Richmond, Calif., Jan. 22, 1915; s. Harvey Lorenz and Allie O'Dell (Taylor) Van F.; m. Colette Sims, Apr. 26, 1940; children: Christine, Ellen, Peter. AB, U. Calif., Berkeley, 1938. Pvt. practice architecture, Eureka, Calif., 1951—; lectr. design Humboldt (Calif.) State U., 1965-66; ptnr. William & Colette Van Fleet, 1954—. Prin. works include Del Norte County Courthouse and Library, Crescent City, Calif., 1957, Freshwater (Calif.) Elem. Sch., 1954, Lee residence, Sunnybrae, Calif., 1962, Zane Jr. H.S., Eureka, 1965, offices for Brooks-Scanlon Lumber Co., Bend, Oreg., 1967. Chmn., No. Humboldt Vocat. Coun., 1964-65, Humboldt County Scenic Resources Com., 1965; pres. Humboldt-Del Norte Mental Health Soc., 1970-71; mem. Humboldt County Cmty. Svcs. Ctr. 1970, Humboldt Arts Council, 1970, Humboldt County Energy Adv. Com., 1979; chmn. Eureka Beautification Com., 1969, Humboldt Sr. Retirement Homes Com., 1979—; bd. dirs. Humboldt County Assn. Retarded Children, 1960-68, Humboldt Family Svc. Ctr., 1970, Redwoods United Workshop, 1973, Open Door Clinic, 1973, Coordinating Coun. Human Svcs. Humboldt County, 1976, Calif.-Oreg. Cmty. Devel. Soc., 1980—; mem. Humboldt Energy Adv. Com., 1980—, Eureka City Housing Adv. Bd., 1982. Recipient Merit award HHFA, 1964, 1st Honor award Pub. Housing Adminstrn., 1964, Gov. Calif. Design award, 1966, Outstanding Svc. award Far West Indian Hist. Soc., 1973, Man of Yr. award Redwood region Nat. Audubon Soc., 1976, resolutions of commendation Calif. State Senate and Assembly, 1982, Gold medal for 10k cross-country run, 1989; Humboldt Unitarian Universalist fellow. Mem. AIA, Net Energy Assn. (bd. dir.), Humboldt Native Plant Soc., Redwood Art Assn. (pres. 1970), Sierra Club (bd. dir. 1972), Fifty-Plus Runners Assn. (1st place in age group Nat. Fifty-Plus Runners Meet 1981). Unitarian. Club: Six Rivers Running (bd. dirs., All-Am. awards 1987, Hall of Fame, 1992). Lodge: Kiwanis (pres. Eureka 1976-77, Disting. Svc. award 1968). Participant in various marathons and races, including Internat. Marathon, Sacramento, 1983 (1st in 65-69 age group), World Vet. Championships Marathon, Rome, Italy, 1984 (1st in U.S., 8th in World, 70-74 age group), Fifty-Plus 5 mile run, Stanford, Calif., 1985 (1st in 70-74 age group, 2d all-time nationally), course records (70-74 age group) 300-meters and 5-kilometer runs Masters Hayward Classic Track & Field Meet, Eugene, Oreg., 1988, others, course record and Calif. state record (70-74 age group) in Nike Half-Marathon, San Francisco, 1988, Gold medal for 10K cross-country as a member of the U.S. team (70-74 age group), 1989, World Vets. Championships, Eugene, Oreg. (1st in 70-74 age group), 1990, All-Am. certs. 2nd nationally in 800 and 1500 meter run Pacific Assn./TAC Championship, Los Gatos, Calif., 1st half marathon, Calif., 1990, Four Generation Half Marathon (Am. Cancer Soc. award), 1993. Home: 71 Old Forest Ln Eureka CA 95503-9554 Office: 818 3rd St Eureka CA 95501-0512

VAN FOSSAN, KATHRYN RUTH, library director; b. Elmhurst, Ill., Feb. 24, 1948; d. Norman Harvey and Ruth Marion (Shoger) Zurbrigg; m. Randy Eugene Van Fossan, Feb. 15, 1969; children: Karen Irene, David Bryan. BA in Music, U. Ill., 1969; MA in Musicology, Ill. State U., 1979; MLS, U. Ill., 1983. Interlibr. loan libr. Garrett Theol. Sem., Evanston, Ill., 1970-71; acquisitions asst. Olivet Nazarene U., Kankakee, Ill., 1978-80, cataloger, 1980-83, head tech. svcs., 1983-92, libr. dir., 1992—. Bd. dirs. Bur Oak Libr. Sys., Shorewood, Ill., 1990-93. Mem. ALA, Ill. Libr. Assn., Assn. Coll. and Rsch. Librs., Assn. Libr. Collections and Tech. Svcs. Avocations: church organist, choir director. Office: Olivet Nazarene U Benner Libr and Resource Ctr PO Box 592 Kankakee IL 60901

VANG, TIMOTHY TENG, church executive; b. Xieng Khouang, Laos, May 10, 1956; came to U.S., 1976; s. Nao Chai and Mai (Yang) V.; m. Chee Yang, Jan. 1, 1974 (dec. June 1975); m. Lydia Joua Vang, July 7, 1979; children: Jennifer P., Nathan K. BS in Missions, Cin. Bible Coll., 1984; MDiv in Ch. Ministries, Can. Theol. Sem., Regina, Sask., 1991; postgrad., Fuller Theol. Sem., Pasadena, Calif., 1993—. Ordained to ministry Ch. of Christ, 1984, Christian and Missionary Alliance, 1986. Machine operator Pellet Co., Green Bay, Wis., 1977-78; mental health worker Inst. Human Design, Oshkosh, Wis., 1978-80; ch. planter Ch. of Christ, Eau Claire, Wis., 1984-86; pastor Boulder (Colo.) Hmong Alliance Ch., 1986-87; dir. Christian edn. Hmong dist. Christian and Missionary Alliance, Brighton, Colo., 1986-87, dist. supt., 1991—; Mem. bd. mgrs. Christian and Missionary Alliance, 1994—; trustee Crown Coll., 1992—. Organizer Fox Valley Lao/Hmong Assn., Appleton, Wis., 1979. Lt. U.S./Hmong Allied Army, 1971-75. Avocations: reading, writing, walking. Office: Hmong Dist 108 W Walnut St Brighton CO 80601-2827

VAN GASSE, JANICE MARTHA, school counselor; b. N.Y.C., May 1, 1951; d. Walter Thomas and mary Rebecca (Brookes) Porter; m. Randall Mark Van Gasse, July 14, 1984; children: Kristen Anne, Michael Porter. AB, U. Mich., 1973; MA, Ea. Mich. U., 1979. Lic. profl. elem. and secondary counselor, Mich. Tchr. Clinton (Mich.) Community Schs., 1973-90, counselor, peer advisor, testing coord., teenage inst. advisor, 1986—. Contbr. articles to profl. jours. Parent rep. Parent Adv. Com. ofr Spl. Edn., Adrian, Mich., 1991—. Named Counselor of Yr., Lenawee County Counselors Assn., 1991, Peer Advisor of Yr., Mich. South Ctrl. Substance Abuse Commn., 1991. Mem. Am. Sch. Counselors Assn. (assembly rep. 1994), Mich. Sch. Counselors Assn. (ethics chair 1989—, Mich. Counselor of Year award 1992), Mich. Counseling Assn. (ethics chair 1993—), Phi Delta Kappa. Home: 2559 Wilmoth Hwy Adrian MI 49221 Office: Clinton Community Schs 341 E Michigan Ave Clinton MI 49236-9586

VANGER, MILTON ISADORE, history educator; b. N.Y.C., Apr. 11, 1925; s. Max Manuel and Rose (Rothstein) V.; m. Elsa M. Oribe, Sept. 10, 1956; children: John, Mark, Rachel. A.B., Princeton U., 1948; M.A., Harvard U., 1950, Ph.D., 1958. Teaching fellow history Harvard U., 1952-56; instr. Okla. State U., 1956-58; asst. prof. history Sacramento State Coll., 1958-62; mem. faculty Brandeis U., Waltham, Mass., 1962—; prof. history Brandeis U., 1973-84, prof. emeritus, 1984—; chmn. com. Latin Am. studies, 1971-81; invited lectr. 50th anniversary conf. commemorating death of Batlle y Ordoñez of Uruguay, 1979; invitee to inauguration of pres. Sanguinetti, Uruguay, 1985; Barnette Miller vis. prof. history, Wellesley Coll., 1990. Author: José Batlle y Ordoñez of Uruguay: The Creator of His Times, 1902-1907, 1963, 2d edit., 1980, Spanish transl., 1968, 2d edit., 1992, The Model Country: José Batlle y Ordoñez of Uruguay, 1907-1915, 1980, Spanish transl., 1983, 2d edit., 1991, Reforma o Revolución La Polémica Batlle-Mibelli, 1917, 1989; outside reviewer NEH, Radcliffe Inst.; contbr. articles to profl. jours. Juror for Lindahl Prize, Inst. Latin Am. Studies, Stockholm. With AUS, 1943-45. Doherty Found. fellow, 1950-52; grantee Am. Philos. Soc., 1966; recipient Hermes prize for best history pub. in Uruguay, 1983. Mem. New Eng. Council Latin Am. Studies (sec.-treas. 1970-72), Am. Hist. Assn., Conf. on Latin Am. History, Amnesty Internat., Phi Beta Kappa. Democrat. Jewish. Address: 931 Massachusetts Ave Ste 503 Cambridge MA 02139

VAN GESTEL, ALLAN, lawyer; b. Boston, Dec. 3, 1935. BA, Colby Coll., 1957; LLB, Boston U., 1961. Bar: Mass. 1961, U.S. Dist. Ct. Mass. 1963, U.S. Ct. Appeals (1st cir.) 1969, U.S. Supreme Ct. 1972, U.S. Ct. Claims 1979, U.S. Ct. Appeals (2d cir.) 1980, U.S. Dist. Ct. (no. dist.) N.Y. 1980, U.S. Ct. Appeals (3d cir.) 1993, U.S. Ct. Appeals (5th cir.) 1995. Assoc. firm Goodwin, Procter & Hoar, Boston, 1961-70; ptnr. Goodwin, Procter & Hoar, 1970—; spl. counsel Boston Fin. Commn., 1974; spl. counsel to Mass. Commn. on Jud. Conduct, 1986; mem. Scituate (Mass.) Bd. Zoning Appeals, 1970, Scituate Planning Bd., 1972; spl. counsel Gov. of N.Y. on Indian Land Claims, 1985—; spl. counsel to Gov. and Atty. Gen. of Vt. on Indian Claims, 1987-90; chmn. standing adv. com. Mass. Rules Civil Procedure, 1986-93 ; overseer Colby Coll. Contbr. numerous articles on Eastern Indian land claims, ct. adminstrn., capital punishment to profl. jours. Fellow Am. Coll. Trial Lawyers; mem. ABA, Mass. Bar Assn., Boston Bar Assn. (chmn., task force on drugs and the cts.), Supreme Jud. Ct. Hist. Soc. (chmn. bd. overseers 1993—), Mass. Hist. Soc. Office: Goodwin Procter & Hoar Exchange Pl Boston MA 02109-2808

VAN GILDER, BARBARA JANE DIXON, interior designer, consultant; b. South Bend, Ind., Dec. 6, 1938; d. Vincent Alan and Wanda Anita (Rapell) Dixon Van Gilder; student Mich. State U.; postgrad. St. Mary's Coll., N.Y. Sch. Design, 1956-58; m. Erwin Delton Van Gilder, May 25, 1959; children: Eric Dalton, Marc David. Factory color cons. Smith-Alsop Paint Co., Terre Haute, Ind.; archtl. design cons., Mishawaka, Ind., 1956-58; residential-comml. designer, South Bend, Chgo., 1958-63; designer industrialized housing industry, Ga., Fla., Ind., Mich., Calif., 1962—; speaker seminars on career mitivation; design cons. Skyline Corp., Ind., Calif., Pa., 1962-66; v.p. design Treasure Chest Corp., Sturgis, Mich., 1969, also dir.; pres., dir. Sandpiper Art, Inc.; v.p. T.C.I. Ltd.; design cons. C.O. Smith Ind. Peachtree Housing, Moultrie, Ga., Nobility Homes, Ocala, Fla.; head merchandising and design Sandpiper Originals, clothing boutique, 1978-87; pres., owner mktg. design firm, 1987—; placement dir. specialized design mktg. STS Corp., South Bend, 1989—; currently pub. relations ofcl. Am. Mktg. Assn., adj. tchr. Lakeshore Sch. System. also coordinator trade show displays; nat. advt. rep. Studebaker-Packard Corp., Mercedes Benz, Clark Equipment, 1959-63; writer series on decorating for 2 Mich. newspapers, 1961-63; participant TV show Know Your Decorator, Calif. and Maine, 1962, 77. Officer Shoreham Village (Mich.) Bd. Zoning, 1960-63; presenter sales mktg. seminars McBride Assocs.; pres. Design Mktg. Assocs., 1992—. cons. Internat. Housing and Internat. Univ. Exchange Program, London, Amsterdam, 1993-94. Named Woman of Yr., Profl. Model's Club; recipient 1st pl. furniture design hardwoods Nat. Hardwoods Assn., 1956; 1st pl. Best in Show award, Louisville, Atlanta, 1964-65, 66, 69, 70-74, 76; others. Mem. Design Council Industrialized Housing (award 1974), Nat. Soc. Interior Designers, Mich. State U. Alumni Assn., Internat. Platform Assn., Internat. Biog. Assn., Berrien Art Guild. Contbg. editor Skyliner mag., 1962-66; permanent guest editor, contbr. Today's Home mag., 1974—. Home: 3630 S Lakeshore Dr Saint Joseph MI 49085-9260 Office: PO Box 244 Stevensville MI 49127-0244 also: PO Box 1100 Dunedin FL 34697-1100

VAN GILDER, JOHN CORLEY, neurosurgeon, educator; b. Huntington, W.Va., Aug. 14, 1935; s. John Ray and Sarah Pool (Corley) Van G.; m. Kerstin Margarita Olesson, Mar., 1965; children: Sarah, John, Rachel, David. BA, W.Va. U., 1957, BS, 1959; MD, U. Pitts., 1961. Diplomate Am. Bd. Neurol. Surgery. (examiner 1976, 79, 84). Intern Pa. Hosp., Phila., 1961, asst. resident in surgery, 1964-65; asst. resident in surgery Wilkes-Barre (Pa.) Hosp., 1962; asst. resident neurosurgery Barnes Hosp., St. Louis, 1966-68, sr. resident, 1968-69; instr. neurosurgery Yale U. Sch. Medicine, New Haven, 1970, asst. prof., 1970-73, assoc. prof., 1973-76; prof. neurosurgery U. Iowa, Iowa City, 1976—, chmn. div. neurosurgery, 1976—, exec. com. dept. surgery, 1978-81; fellow neurosurgery Wash. U. Sch. Medicine, St. Louis, 1965 -66, instr., 1966; attending neurosurgeon VA Hosp., New Haven, 1970-73, cons. 1973-76; assoc. to attending neurosurgeon Yale-New Haven Med. Ctr., 1970-76; cons. VA Hosp., Iowa City, 1976—; mem. clin. coordinating com. U. Iowa Cancer Ctr., 1979—; presenter numerous papers at profl. meetings., confs., symposia; vis. prof. U. Tenn., 1984, Tufts U. Med. Ctr., Boston, 1986, U. Tex., San Antonio, 1987, U. Mich., Ann Arbor, 1988, People's Republic China at Hunan Med. Coll., Beijing Neurol. Inst., Tianjin Med. Coll. Hosp., Tiantan Xili, Xian Gen. Hosp., 2d Mil. Coll., Shanghai, Suzhou Med. Coll. Shanghai, 1985, USSR at Burdenk Inst., Kiev Neurol. Inst., Leningrad Neurol. Soc., 1989, Western Reserve U., Cleve., 1993, Yale U., New Haven, Conn., 1994. Author: (with others): Principles of Surgery, 2d edit., 1973, Brief Textbook of Surgery, 1976, Aneurysmal Subarachnoid Hemorrhage, 1981, Operative Neurosurgical Techniques, Indications, Methods, and Results, 1982, Sports Medicine, 1982, Neurosurgery, 1982, Clinical Neurosurgery, 1982, Operative Neurosurgical Technique, Vol. II, 1982, 88, Vol. III, 1995, Current Therapy in Neurosurgical Surgery, 1985, 2d edit. , 1987, Craniovertebral Junction Abnormalities, 1987, Decision Making in Neurological Surgery, 1987, Neurological Surgery, 3d edit., 1988, Anterior Cervical Spine Surgery, 1993, Brain Surgery: Complication Avoidance and Management, 1993, Neurosurgical Emergencies, 1994, Techniques of Spinal Fusion and Instrumation, 1995, Somatic Gene Therapy, 1995; contbr. numerous articles and abstracts to profl. jours.; co-author teaching films; mem. editorial bd. Neurosurgery jour., 1978-84. Capt. USAF, 1962-64. Grantee NIH, 1973-78, Nat. Cancer Inst., 1980-88. Fellow ACS (membership com. Iowa dist. #1 1983—); mem. AMA (Physicians Recogniton award), Am. Physiol. Soc., Congress Neurol. Surgeons (resident placement com. 1970), Am. Assn. Neurol. Surgeons (bd. dirs. 1986-90, awards com. 1986-87, chmn. 1987-88), Rsch. Soc. Neurol. Surgeons, Neurol. Soc. Am. (long range planning com. 1984—, v.p. 1985), Iowa Med. Soc., Johnson County Med. Soc. (program com. 1984-88, chmn. 1985-86), Iowa-Midwest Neurosurg. Soc. (pres. 1978-79), Soc. Neurol. Surgeons (chmn. membership com. 1986-87, treas. 1991—, pres. elect 1996), Midwest Surg. Assn., Am. Acad. Neurol. Surgery (v.p. 1995—), Ga. Neurosurg. Soc. (hon. life), Am. Bd. Neurol. Surgery (dir. 1992—, residency rev. com.-neurol. surgery 1995—), Sigma Xi. Home: 330 S Summit St Iowa City IA 52240-3220 Office: U Iowa Hosps & Clinics Dept Neurosurgery 200 Hawkins Dr Iowa City IA 52242

VAN GINKEL, BLANCHE LEMCO, architect, educator; b. London, Dec. 14, 1923; d. Myer and Claire Lemco; m. H. P. Daniel van Ginkel, 1956; children: Brenda Renee, Marc Ian. B.Arch., McGill U., 1945; M.C.P., Harvard U., 1950. Tech. asst. Nat. Film Bd. Can., 1943-44; mgr. City Planning Office, Regina, Sask., Can., 1946; architect Atelier Le Corbusier, Paris, 1948; asst. prof. architecture U. Pa., 1951-57; ptnr. van Ginkel Assocs., Montreal, Que., Can., also Toronto, Ont., Can., 1957—; prof. architecture U. Toronto, 1977—, dir. Sch. Architecture, 1977-80, dean faculty architecture and landscape architecture, 1980-82; vis. critic Harvard U., 1958, 70; vis. prof. Universite de Montreal, McGill U.; curator exhbns. RCA, U. Toronto, and others. Contbr. articles to profl. jours. Mem. adv. com. Nat. Capital Planning Com., Ottawa; mem. adv. com. Nat. Mus.'s Corp.; mem. Que. Provincial Planning Commn. Recipient Lt. Gov.'s medal McGill U., 1945, Internat. Fedn. Housing and Planning Grand Prix award, 1956, Massey medal, 1962, Mademoiselle Mag. award, 1957, Queen's Silver Jubilee medal, 1977, Citizenship citation Can. Govt., 1991, Alumni award U. Toronto, 1991. Fellow Royal Archtl. Inst. Can. (exec. com. 1971-74), AIA (hon.); mem. Can. Inst. Planners (bd. dirs. 1961-64), Assn. Collegiate Schs. Architecture (bd. dirs. 1981-84, v.p. 1985-86, pres. 1986-87, Disting. Prof. award 1989), Assn. Royal Inst. Brit. Archs. (assoc.), Royal Can. Acad. Art (bd. dirs. 1992—). Office: 38 Summerhill Gardens, Toronto, ON Canada M4T 1B4

VAN GORDER, JOHN FREDERIC, lawyer; b. Jacksonville, Fla., Mar. 22, 1943; s. Harold Burton and Charlotte Louise (Anderson) Van G.; grad. Dover (Eng.) Coll., 1961; AB, Dartmouth Coll., 1965; postgrad. Air Force Inst. Tech., 1967-68; MS in Adminstrn., George Washington U., 1973; postgrad. U. Va., Coll. William and Mary, Cath. U. Am., Northeastern U., Babson Coll., U. South; JD, Fordham U. Sch. Law, 1981. m. Sandra Joan Hagen, June 4, 1977 (div. June 1995); children: Alyssa Jane, Kathryn Ann; m. Ann Michele Brancato, Oct. 7, 1995. Bar: N.J. 1981, U.S. Dist. Ct. N.J. 1981, N.Y. 1983, U.S. Supreme Ct. 1989. Commd. 2d lt. USAF, 1965, advanced through grades to capt., 1968; weapons contr. Aerospace Def. Command, Ft. Lee, Va., 1965-67; buyer electronics sys. divsn. Air Force Sys. Command, Bedford, Mass., 1968-69; project mgr. rsch. and devel. Hdqrs. USAF, Washington, 1969-73, br. chief pers., 1973-74; Presdl. social aide The White House, Washington, 1971-74; assoc. Louis C. Kramp & Assoc's., Washington, 1975; program officer J.M. Found., N.Y.C., 1975-81; assoc. firm Winne, Banta & Rizzi Esqs., Hackensack, N.J., 1981-83; asst. sec., program adminstr. Glenmede Trust Co., Phila., 1983-86; exec. dir. Leon Lowenstein Found., 1986—; mem. Tabernacle Twp. Planning Bd., 1985-88, Tabernacle Bd. Edn., 1988-91, Tabernacle Rep. Club, 1983-93; atty. Rent Leveling Bd., Borough of Bergenfield (N.J.), 1983. Chmn. N.Y.C. steering com. Nat. Congress on Volunteerism and Citizenship, 1976; mem. exec. com. Mayor's Vol. Action Coun., 1977-78; bd. govs. N.Y. Jaycees Found., 1978-79; bd. govs., 4th v.p. First Assembly Dist. Rep. Club, 1977-82; vestryman All Saints Episc. Ch., Bergenfield, N.J., 1982-83; Jr. Warden, 1987-88, sr. warden, 1989-90, vestryman, lay reader St. Peter's Episc. Ch., Medford, N.J., 1985-93; program adv. com. Toshiba Am. Found., 1993—; trustee Support Ctr. of N.Y., N.Y.C., Robert A. Taft Inst. Govt., N.Y.C. Col. USAFR, ret. Named Outstanding Young Man of Va., 1975, USAF Res. Officer of Yr.,

1985. Mem. Internat. (senator; v.p. 1975; rep. to UN 1976), U.S. (nat. v.p. 1973-74), D.C. (pres. 1972-73) N.Y.C. (bd. govs. 1978-79) Jaycees, S.A.R., Soc. Mayflower Descs., ABA, N.J. Bar Assn., Student Bar Assn. (class pres. 1978-81), Alpha Delta Phi. Republican. Episcopalian. Clubs:Toastmasters (local pres. 1969-70, area gov. 1970-71); Lodges: Lions (pres. Medford Twp. club 1985-86, co-chmn. Charity Ball 1987), Masons. Address: FDR Station Box 6754 New York NY 10150-6754

VAN GORKOM, JEROME WILLIAM, financial executive; b. Denver, Aug. 6, 1917; s. A.G. and Elizabeth (Laux) Van G.; m. Betty Jean Alexander, June 27, 1942; children: Gayle, Lynne. BS, U. Ill., 1939, JD, 1941. Bar: Ill. 1941; C.P.A., 1950. Law assoc. Kix Miller, Baar & Morris, Chgo., 1945-47; accountant Arthur Andersen & Co., 1947-54, ptnr., 1954-56; treas., contr. Trans Union Corp., Chgo., 1956—; dir. Trans Union Corp., 1957—, v.p., 1958-60, exec. v.p., 1960-63, pres., 1963-78, chmn. bd., 1978-82; under sec. Dept. State, 1982-83; mng. dir. Chgo. Housing Authority, 1987-88. Chmn. bd. Lyric Opera of Chgo.; chmn. Chgo. Sch. Fin. Authority, 1980-89. With USNR, 1941-45. Clubs: Chicago, Mid America, Comml, Onwentsia, Old Elm, Pauma Valley Country. Home: 245 W Westminster Rd Lake Forest IL 60045-2126

VAN GRAAFEILAND, ELLSWORTH ALFRED, federal judge; b. Rochester, N.Y., May 11, 1915; s. Ivan and Elsie (Gohr) VanG.; m. Rosemary Vaeth, May 26, 1945; children—Gary, Suzanne, Joan, John, Anne. A.B., U. Rochester, 1937; LL.B., Cornell U., 1940. Bar: N.Y. 1940. Practiced in Rochester; now sr. judge U.S. Ct. Appeals for 2d Cir. Fellow Am. Bar Found., N.Y. Bar Found.; mem. ABA (ho. dels. 1973-75), N.Y. State Bar Assn. (v.p. 1972-73, pres. 1973-74, chmn. negligence compensation and ins. sect. 1968-69), Monroe County Bar Assn. (past pres.), Am. Coll. Trial Lawyers., Masons, Kent Club, Oak Hill Country Club. Home: 76 Ramsey Park Rochester NY 14610-1333 Office: Fed Bldg 100 State St Ste 423 Rochester NY 14614-1309

VAN GRAAFEILAND, GARY P., lawyer. BA, Union Coll., 1968; JD, Cornell U., 1972. Bar: N.Y. 1973. Asst. gen. counsel Eastman Kodak, Rochester, N.Y., 1989-92, sr. v.p., gen. counsel, sec., 1992—. Office: Eastman Kodak Co 343 State St Rochester NY 14650-0208*

VAN GUNDY, GREGORY FRANK, lawyer; b. Columbus, Ohio, Oct. 24, 1945; s. Paul Arden and Edna Marie (Sanders) Van G.; m. Lisa Tamara Langer. B.A., Ohio State U., Columbus, 1966, J.D., 1969. Bar: N.Y. bar 1971. Asso. atty. firm Willkie Farr & Gallagher, N.Y.C., 1970-74; v.p. legal, sec. Marsh & McLennan Cos., Inc., N.Y.C., 1974-79; v.p., sec., gen. counsel Marsh & McLennan Cos., Inc., 1979—. Mem. ABA, Phi Beta Kappa. Roman Catholic. Club: University (N.Y.C.). Home: 232 Fox Meadow Rd Scarsdale NY 10583-1640 Office: Marsh & McLennan Cos Inc 1166 Avenue Of The Americas New York NY 10036-2708

VAN GUNDY, JAMES JUSTIN, biology educator; b. Peoria, Ill., Jan. 29, 1939; s. George Christian and Beatrice (Baird) Van. G.; m. Judith V. Mobley, Sept. 5, 1964; children: Douglas, Susan. MS, Pa. State U., 1969; PhD, U. Utah, 1973. Prof. biology U. Bridgeport, Conn., 1972-75; prof. biology, environ. scis. Davis and Elkins (W.Va.) Coll., 1975—; cons. Gannet, Fleming, Inc., Harrisburg, Pa., 1980-81; dir. W.Va. Highlands Conservancy, Charleston, 1984-88, W.Va. Pub. Lands Corp., Charleston, 1989-96. With U.S. Army,. 1959-61, Korea. Recipient Appalachian Scholar award U. Ky., 1991. Mem. AAAS, Nat. Speleol. Soc., W.Va. Acad. Sci. Democrat. Home: 240 Boundary Ave Elkins WV 26241-3902 Office: Davis and Elkins Coll 100 Sycamore St Elkins WV 26241-3971

VAN GUNDY, JEFF, coach; b. Hernet, Calif., Jan. 19, 1962; married. Graduate cum laude, Nazareth Coll. Head coach McQuaid Jesuit H.S., Rochester, N.Y., 1985-86; grad. asst., asst. coach Providence Coll., 1986-88; asst. coach Rutgers U., N.J., 1988-89; asst. coach N.Y. Knicks, N.Y.C., 1989-96, head coach, 1996—. Office: care NY Knicks Two Pennsylvania Plz New York NY 10121*

VAN GUNDY, SEYMOUR DEAN, nematologist, plant pathologist, educator; b. Toledo, Feb. 24, 1931; s. Robert C. and Margaret (Holloway) Van G.; m. Wilma C. Fanning, June 12, 1954; children: Sue Ann, Richard L. BA, Bowling Green State U., 1953; PhD, U. Wis., 1957. Asst. nematologist U. Calif., Riverside, 1957-63, assoc. prof., 1963-68, prof. nematology and plant pathology, 1968-73, assoc. dean rsch., 1968-70, vice chancellor rsch., 1970-72, chmn. dept. nematology, 1972-84, prof. nematology and plant pathology, assoc. dean rsch. Coll. Natural and Agrl. Scis., 1985-88, acting dean, 1986, interim dean, 1988-90, dean, 1990-93, emeritus dean and prof, 1993—. Former mem. editorial bd. Rev. de Nematologie, Jour. Nematology and Plant Disease; contbr. numerous articles to profl. jours. NSF fellow, Australia, 1965-66; grantee Rockefeller Found., Cancer Res., NSF, USDA. Fellow AAAS, Am. Phytopathol. Soc., Soc. Nematologists (editor-in-chief 1968-72, v.p. 1972-73, pres. 1973-74). Home: 1188 Pastern Rd Riverside CA 92506-5619 Office: U Calif Dept Nematology Riverside CA 92521

VAN HALEN, EDDIE, guitarist, rock musician; b. Nijmegan, The Netherlands, Jan. 26, 1957; came to U.S., 1967; s. Jan and Eugenia Van Halen; m. Valerie Bertinelli, Apr. 1981. Student, Pasadena City Coll.; studied piano. Formed group Broken Combs, name later Mammoth, with bro. Alex.; leader group Van Halen, 1974—; albums include Van Halen, 1978, Van Halen II, 1979, Women and Children First, 1980, Fair Warning, 1981, Diver Down, 1982, 1984, (1984), 5150, 1986, OU812, 1988, For Unlawful Carnal Knowledge, 1991, Van Halen Live: Right Here Right Now, 1993, Balance, 1995. Office: care Premier Talent Agy 3 E 54th St New York NY 10022-3108*

VANHANDEL, RALPH ANTHONY, librarian; b. Appleton, Wis., Jan. 17, 1919; s. Frank Henry and Gertrude Mary (Schmidt) Van H.; m. Alice Catherine Hogan, Oct. 27, 1945; children: William Patrick, Karen Jean, Mary Jo. BA, U. Wis., 1946; AB in Libr. Sci., U. Mich., 1947. Head libr. Lawrence (Kans.) Free Pub. Libr., 1947-51, Hibbing (Minn.) Pub. Libr., 1951-54; libr. dir. Gary (Ind.) Pub. Libr., 1954-74; libr. dir. Wells Meml. Pub. Libr., Lafayette, Ind. (name now Tippecanoe County Pub. Libr.), 1974-84, libr. cons., 1963—; mem. Ind. Library Cert. Bd., 1969-84, Ind. State Library and Hist. Bldg. Expansion Commn., 1973-81. Named Ind. Librarian of Year, 1971, Sagamore of Wabash, 1984. Mem. ALA, KC, Anselm Forum (sec. 1964, v.p. 1965), Ind. Libr. Assn. (pres. 1963-64), Kans. Libr. Assn. (v.p. 1951). Home: 3624 Winter St Lafayette IN 47905-3838

VANHARN, GORDON LEE, college administrator and provost; b. Grand Rapids, Mich., Dec. 30, 1935; s. Henry and Edna (Riemersma) VanH.; m. Mary Kool, June 12, 1958; children—Pamela L., Mark L., Barbara A. B.A., Calvin Coll., 1957; M.S., U. Ill., 1959, Ph.D., 1961. Asst. prof. biology Calvin Coll., Grand Rapids, Mich. 1961-68, prof., 1970-82, acad. dean, 1982-85, provost, 1985-94, sr. v.p., provost, 1994—; assoc. prof. biology Oberlin Coll., Ohio, 1968-70; assoc. physiologist Blodgett Meml. Med. Ctr., Grand Rapids, 1970-76; research assoc. U. Va., Charlotteville, 1975-76. Contbr. articles to profl. jours. Mem. sci. adv. com. Gerald R. Ford, 1972-73, Blodgett Hosp. research and review com., 1978-84; pres. bd. Grand Rapids Christian Sch. Assn., 1982-85; v.p. Christian Schs. Internat., 1987-93. Grass Found. fellow, 1969. Mem. AAAS, Am. Assn. Higher Edn., Phi Kappa Phi. Mem. Christian Reformed Ch. Home: 1403 Cornell Dr SE Grand Rapids MI 49506-4103 Office: Calvin Coll Office of the Provost Grand Rapids MI 49546

VAN HASSEL, HENRY JOHN, dentist, educator, university dean; b. Paterson, N.J., May 2, 1933; s. William Cornelius and Ina (Sturr) Van H.; m. Ann Newell Wiley, Dec. 28, 1960. BA, Maryville Coll., Tenn., 1954; DDS, U. Md., 1963; MSD, U. Wash., 1967, PhD, 1969. Diplomate Am.Bd. Endodontics. Dental dir. USPHS, Seattle, 1965-81; prof., chmn. dept. endodontics U. Md., Balt., 1981-84; dean dental sch. Oreg. Health Scis. U., Portland, 1984—, v.p. instl. affairs, 1989-91. Recipient Schlack award Assn. Mil. Surgeons U.S., 1976, Borrish award Acad. Gen. Dentistry, 1989. Mem. Am. Assn. Endodontists (pres. 1981-82, Grossman Gold medal 1984), Oreg. Dental Assn. (pres. 1990). Office: Oreg Health Scis U Dental Sch 611 SW Campus Dr Portland OR 97201-3001*

VAN HAUER, ROBERT, former health care company executive; b. Chgo., June 9, 1910; s. Francis Anthony and Della Agnes (Mulhern) Van H.; m. Elaine Greenwood, July 24, 1944 (dec. Nov. 1961); children: Peter, Jan, Mary, Christopher, Gretchen, Juliana; m. Margaret Ann St. Pierre Viehman, May 4, 1968; stepchildren: Gayle, Edwin, Thomas, John, Michael, Daniel. B.A. in Econs; B.B.A. in Accounting (Reiman scholar), U. Mont., Missoula, 1938; M.A. in Econs, U. Minn., Mpls., 1940. Jr. Auditor Peat Marwick Mitchell, C.P.A.'s, Mpls., 1938-40; asst. sales mgr. North Star Woolen Mill, Mpls., 1940-42; dir. contracts Mpls. regional office VA, 1946-51; with Health Central, Inc., Mpls., 1951-78; exec. v.p. Health Central, Inc., 1965, pres., chief exec. officer, 1970-78; exec. dir. Health Found., Mpls., 1979-81. Mem. planning commn. Golden Valley, Minn., 1959-66; past trustee St. Margaret's Acad., Benilde-St. Margaret's High Sch. Served to maj. AUS, 1941-46. Decorated Commendation ribbon; Rieman fellow, 1938-40. Mem. Am. Hosp. Assn., Minn. Hosp. Assn. (trustee, com. chmn. 1974-79), War Meml. Blood Bank (pres., dir. 1967), Physicians Health Plan Mpls. (dir., exec. com.), Am. Legion. Republican. Roman Catholic. Clubs: Mpls. Athletic, Minn. Valley Country, Elks; Union Hills Country (Sun City, Ariz.). Home: 6837 Olson Memorial Hwy Golden Valley MN 55427-4951

VAN HENGEL, MAARTEN, banker; b. Amsterdam, The Netherlands, Mar. 29, 1927; came to U.S., 1950, naturalized, 1957; s. Adrianus J. and Helena (Gips) van H.; m. Drusilla Drake Riley, Dec. 1, 1951; children: Maarten, Virginia, Hugh, Drusilla. Student, Kennemer Lyceum, Bloemendaal, Holland, 1939-45. With tng. programs of Amsterdamsche Bank, N.V., Amsterdam, Lazard Bros. & Co. Ltd., London and Canadian Bank of Commerce, Montreal, Que., Can., 1945-49; with Brown Bros. Harriman & Co., 1950—, ptnr., 1968—; chmn. Brown Bros. Harriman Trust Co. Bd. dirs. Netherlands-Am. Found., Phelps Meml. Hosp. Served with AUS, 1951-53. Clubs: India House, Netherland (N.Y.C.); Fishers Island Country, Hay Harbor (Fishers Island); Sleepy Hollow Country (Scarborough, N.Y.). Home: 350 River Rd Briarcliff Manor NY 10510-2418 Office: Brown Bros Harriman & Co 59 Wall St New York NY 10005-2818

VAN HEYDE, J. STEPHEN, lawyer; b. Columbus, Ohio, May 22, 1943. BBA magna cum laude, U. Notre Dame, 1965; JD cum laude, Ohio State U., 1968. Bar: Ohio 1968. Ptnr. Baker & Hostetler, Columbus, Ohio. Mem. ABA, Columbus Bar Assn. (bd. govs. 1989-90), Beta Gamma Sigma, Beta Alpha Psi, Phi Delta Phi. Office: Baker & Hostetler Capital Sq 65 E State St Ste 2100 Columbus OH 43215-4213*

VAN HOESEN, BETH MARIE, artist, printmaker; b. Boise, Idaho, June 27, 1926; d. Enderse G. and Freda Marie (Soulen) Van H.; m. Mark Adams, Sept. 12, 1953. Student, Escuela Esmaralda, Mexico City, 1945, San Francisco Art Inst., 1946, 47, 51, 52, Fontainbleau (France) Ecole des Arts, Acad. Julian and Acad., 5Grande Chaumier, Paris, 1948-51; B.A., Stanford U., 1948; postgrad., San Francisco State U., 1957-58. One-Woman shows include, De Young Mus., San Francisco, 1959, Achenbach Found., Calif. Palace Legion of Honor, San Francisco, 1961, 74, Santa Barbara (Calif.) Mus., 1963, 74, 76, Oakland (Calif.) Mus., 1980, John Berggruen Gallery, San Francisco, 1981, 83, 85, 88, 91; traveling exhibit Am. Mus. Assn., 1983-85; group shows include, Calif. State Fair, Sacramento, 1951 (award), Library of Congress, Washington, 1956, 57, San Francisco Mus. Modern Art, 70 (award), Boston Mus. Fine Arts, 1959, 60, 62, Pa. Acad. Fine Arts, Phila., 1959, 61, 63, 65, Achenbach Found., 1961 (award), Bklyn. Mus., 1962, 66, 68, 77, Continuing Am. Graphics, Osaka, Japan, 1970, Hawaii Nat. Print. Exhbn., Honolulu, 1980 (award), Oakland Mus., 1975 (award); represented in permanent collections, including, Achenbach Found., San Francisco, Fine Arts Mus., Bklyn. Mus., Mus. Modern Art, N.Y.C., Oakland Mus., San Francisco Mus. Modern Art, Victoria and Albert Mus., (London), Chgo. Art Inst., Cin. Mus., Portland (Oreg.) Art Mus. (Recipient award of Honor, San Francisco Art Commn. 1981); author: Collection of Wonderful Things, 1972, Beth Van Hoesen Creatures, 1987, Beth Van Hoesen Works on Paper, 1995. Mem. Calif. Soc. Printmakers (award 1993), San Francisco Women Artists. Office: care John Berggruen 228 Grant Ave Fl 3D San Francisco CA 94108-4612

VAN HOFTEN, JAMES DOUGAL ADRIANUS, business executive, former astronaut; b. Fresno, Calif., June 11, 1944; s. Adriaan and Beverly (McCurdy) van H.; m. Vallarie Davis, May 31, 1975; children—Jennifer Lyn, Jamie Juliana, Victoria Jane. B.S., U. Calif.-Berkeley, 1966; M.S., Colo. State U., 1968, Ph.D., 1976. Asst. prof. U. Houston, 1976-78; astronaut NASA, Houston, 1978-86; sr. v.p., mgr. advanced systems line Bechtel Nat., Inc., San Francisco, 1986-93; project mgr. Hong Kong New Airport projects, 1993-96; sr. v.p., mgr. N.E. Asis, gen. mgr. Bechtel Civil Co., Hong Kong, 1996—. Served with USN, 1969-74; lt. col. Air N.G. 1984—. Recipient Disting. Service award Colo. State U., 1984; Disting. Citizen award Fresno Council Boy Scouts Am., 1984; Disting. Achievement award Pi Kappa Alpha, 1984. Assoc. fellow AIAA; mem. ASCE (Aerospace Sci. and Tech. Application award 1984). Republican. Home: 10B The Harborview, 11 Magazine Gap Rd, Hong Kong Hong Kong Office: Pacific Bechtel Corp, Li Po Chun Chambers, Hong Kong Hong Kong

VAN HOLDE, KENSAL EDWARD, biochemistry educator; b. Eau Claire, Wis., May 14, 1928; s. Leonard John and Nettie (Hart) Van H.; m. Barbara Jean Watson, Apr. 11, 1950; children: Patricia, Mary, Stephen, David. B.S., U. Wis., 1949, Ph.D., 1952. Research chemist E.I. du Pont de Nemours & Co., 1952-55; research assoc. U. Wis., 1955-56; asst. prof. U. Wis. at Milw., 1956-57; mem. faculty U. Ill., Urbana, 1957-67; prof. dept. biochemistry and biophysics Oreg. State U., Corvallis, 1967; Am. Cancer Soc. rsch. prof., 1977-93, disting. prof., 1988-93, disting. prof. emeritus, 1993—; instr.-in-charge physiology course Marine Biol. Lab., Woods Hole, Mass., 1977-80; mem. research staff Centre des Recherches sur les Macromolecules, Strasbourg, France, 1964-65; mem. study sect. USPHS, 1966-69, 91—; staff Weizmann Inst., Israel, 1981, Lab. Léon Brillouin, Saclay, France, 1989-90. Author: Physical Biochemistry, 1971, Chromatin, 1988; (with C. Mathews) Biochemistry, 1989, 2nd edit., 1995; editor: Biochmica Biophysica Acta, 1966-68; mem. editl. bd. jours. Biol. Chemistry, 1968-75, 81-87, 91-92, assoc. editor, 1992—, Biochemistry, 1973-76, 82-89; contbr. profl. jours. Trustee Marine Biol. Lab., Woods Hole, 1979-82, 84-92. NSF sr. postdoctoral fellow, 1964-65; Guggenheim fellow, 1973-74; European Molecular Biology Orgn. fellow, 1975. Mem. NAS, Am. Soc. Biochemistry and Molecular Biology, Biophys. Soc., Am. Acad. Arts and Scis. Home: 229 NW 32nd St Corvallis OR 97330-5020 Office: Oreg State U Dept Biochemistry Corvallis OR 97331

VANHOLE, WILLIAM REMI, lawyer; b. Denver, June 25, 1948; s. Joseph L. and Mildred M. VanHole; m. Gemma VanHole, Feb. 7, 1971; 3 children. BS, Colo. State U., 1970; JD, U. Idaho, 1976. Bar: Idaho 1976, U.S. Dist. Ct. Idaho 1976, U.S. Ct. Appeals (9th cir.) 1983. Law clk. to judge U.S. Dist. Ct. Idaho, Boise, 1976-78; assoc. Quane, Smith, Howard & Hull, Boise, 1978-81, Langroise, Sullivan & Smylie, Boise, 1981-83; asst. U.S. atty. U.S. Dept. of Justice, Boise, 1983-87; U.S. atty. Dist. of Idaho, 1984-85; assoc. gen. counsel Boise Cascade Corp., 1987—. Served with U.S. Army, 1970-72. Mem. ABA, Fed. Bar Assn., Idaho Bar Assn., Idaho Assn. Def. Counsel, Def. Rsch. Inst., Am. Corp. Counsel Assn. Republican. Avocations: skiing, fishing, tennis. Office: Boise Cascade Corp PO Box 50 Boise ID 83728

VAN HOOMISSEN, GEORGE ALBERT, state supreme court justice; b. Portland, Oreg., Mar. 7, 1930; s. Fred J. and Helen F. (Flanagan) Van H.; m. Ruth Madeleine Niedermeyer, June 4, 1960; children: Geroge T., Ruth Anne, Madeleine, Matthew. BBA, U. Portland, 1951; JD, Georgetown U., 1955, LLM in Labor Law, 1957; LLM in Jud. Adminstrn., U. Va., 1986. Bar: D.C. 1955, Oreg. 1956, Tex. 1971, U.S. Dist. Ct. Oreg. 1956, U.S. Ct. Mil. Appeals 1955, U.S. Ct. Customs and Patent Appeals 1955, U.S. Ct. Claims 1955, U.S. Ct. Appeals (9th cir.) 1956, U.S. Ct. Appeals (D.C. cir.) 1955, U.S. Supreme Ct. 1960. Law clk. for Chief Justice Harold J. Warner Oreg. Supreme Ct., 1955-56; Keigwin teaching fellow Georgetown Law Sch., 1956-57; dep. dist. atty. Multnomah County, Portland, 1957-59; pvt. practice Portland, 1959-62; dist. atty. Multnomah County, 1962-71; dean nat. coll. dist. attys. U. Houston, 1971-73; judge Cir. Ct., Portland, 1973-81, Oreg. Ct. Appeals, Salem, 1981-88; assoc. justice Oreg. Supreme Ct., Salem, 1988—. Mem. Oreg. Ho. of Reps., Salem, 1959-62, chmn. house jud. com. With USMC, 1951-53; col. USMCR (ret.). Recipient Disting. Alumnus award U. Portland, 1972. Mem. ABA, Oreg. State Bar, Tex. Bar Assn., Arlington Club, Multnomah Athletic Club, Univ. Club. Roman Catholic. Office: Oreg Supreme Ct 1163 State St Salem OR 97310-1331

VAN HORN, JOHN KENNETH, health physicist, consultant; b. St. Louis, June 22, 1948; s. Harold E. and Norma L. (Klobe) Van H.; m. Christine A. Lump, Oct. 20, 1995; children: Shawn R., Mark R., Janina. AB in Physics and Math. Edn., Drury Coll., 1971; MS in Instrnl. Tech., No. Ill. U., 1988. Physics, math. tchr. Perryville (Mo.) Pub. Schs., 1971-76; math. dept. head Alden-Hebron (Ill.) Community Schs., 1976-84; program developer prodn. tng. Commonwealth Edison, Braidwood, Ill., 1984-87, health physics instr. prodn. tng., 1987-91; health physicist LaSalle Nuclear Sta. Commonwealth Edison, Marseilles, Ill., 1991—; unit health physicist Commonwealth Edison, Marseilles, Ill., 1993; lead radiation protection instr. LaSalle Nuclear Sta. Commonwealth Edison, Marseilles, Ill., 1995-96, instr. devel. specialist, 1996—. Co-author: New 10CFR20 for HP Technicians, 1992. Mem. Zoning and Planning Bd., Mazon, Ill, 1990-95; First Aid instr. ARC, Morris, Ill., 1986—; merit badge counselor Boy Scouts Am., Morris, 1989—. Mem. Nat. Soc. Performance and Instrn., Health Physics Soc. (co-chmn. exam. group 1991—, bd. dirs. 1991—, pres.-elect Midwest chpt. 1993, pres. 1994, past pres. 1995, pub. info. com. 1996—), Kappa Delta Pi. Avocations: photography, chess, karate. Office: Commonwealth Edison Tng Dept RR1 Box 220 2601 N 21st Rd Marseilles IL 61341

VAN HORN, LECIA JOSEPH, newswriter; b. L.A., Jan. 19, 1963; d. McKinley Joe and Opal Geneva (Ivie) Joseph; m. Philip Dale Van Horn, Apr. 19, 1986; children: Kari Christine, Brandon Joseph. BA in Journalism, U. Southern Calif., 1984. News reporter Sta. KSCR Radio, L.A., 1983; consumer news researcher Sta. KCBS-TV, L.A., 1983, Sta. KABC-TV, L.A., 1983-84; newswriter Headline News, Atlanta, 1984-85; editorial asst., newswriter, field producer Sta. KNBC-TV, Burbank, Calif., 1985-86; newswriter, assoc. producer Sta. WYFF-TV, Greenville, S.C., 1986; freelance newswriter, assoc. producer Sta. WSB-TV, Atlanta, 1987-88; newswriter CNN, Atlanta, 1987-94; freelance newswriter, assoc. producer Sta. KSTP-TV, St. Paul, 1995-96; freelance newswriter Sta. KABC-TV, L.A., 1996—. Author: Thoughts and Inspirational Sayings, 1985; contbr. poetry and articles to newspapers. Mem. U. So. Calif. Alumni. Mem. Science of Mind. Avocations: reading, music, dancing, gymnastics (Class III Calif. State Champion 1977), Taekwondo.

VAN HORN, O. FRANK, counselor, consultant; b. Grand Junction, Colo., Apr. 16, 1926; s. Oertel F. and Alta Maude (Lynch) Van H.; m. Dixie Jeanne MacGregor, Feb. 1, 1947 (dec. Nov. 1994); children: Evelyn, Dorothy. AA, Mesa Coll., 1961; BA, Western State Coll., 1963; MEd, Oreg. State U., 1969. Counselor, mgr. State of Oreg.-Employment, Portland and St. Helens, 1964-88; pvt. practice counselor and cons. St. Helens, 1988—; chair Task Force on Aging, Columbia County, 1977-79; advisor Western Interstate Commn. on Higher Edn., Portland, 1971, Concentrated Employment and Tng., St. Helens, 1977, County Planning Bd., Columbia County, Oreg., 1977-80, City Planning Bd., St. Helens, 1978, Youth Employment Coun., St. Helens, 1978, Task Force on Disadvantaged Youth, St. Helens, 1980; counselor Career Mgmt. Specialists Internat.; instr. Portland C.C. Mem. ACA, Oreg. Counseling Assn., Internat. Assn. Pers. in Employment Svc. (Outstanding Achievement award 1975), Nat. Employment Counselors Assn. Democrat. Home: 1111 St Helens St Saint Helens OR 97051

VAN HORN, RICHARD LINLEY, academic administrator; b. Chgo., Nov. 2, 1932; s. Richard Linley and Mildred Dorothy (Wright) Van H.; m. Susan Householder, May 29, 1954 (dec.); children: Susan Elizabeth, Patricia Suzanne, Lynda Sue; m. Betty Pfefferbaum, May 29, 1988. BS with highest honors, Yale U., 1954; MS, MIT, 1956; PhD, Carnegie-Mellon U., 1976; D of Bus. (hon.), Reitsumeikan U., Kyoto, Japan, 1991. Asst. dir. Army EDP Project, MIT, Cambridge, 1956-57; research staff Rand Corp., Santa Monica, Calif., 1957-60; head mgmt. systems group Rand Corp., 1960-67; dir., prof. mgmt. systems European Inst. Advanced Studies in Mgmt., Brussels, Belgium, 1971-73; asso. dean Grad. Sch. Indsl. Adminstrn., Carnegie-Mellon U., Pitts., 1967-71, dir. budget and planning, 1973-74, v.p. for bus. affairs, 1974-77, v.p. for mgmt., 1977-80, provost and prof. mgmt., 1980-83; chancellor U. Houston, 1983-86, pres., 1986-89; pres. U. Okla., 1989-94; pres. emeritus and regent's prof. Coll. of Bus. U. Okla., Norman, 1994—; Clarence E. Page prof. aviation U. Okla., Norman, 1995—. Author: (with Robert H. Gregory) Automatic Data Processing Systems, 1960, 2nd edit. 1963, (with R.H. Gregory) Business Data Processing and Programming, 1963, (with C.H. Kriebel and J.T. Heames) Management Information Systems: Progress and Perspectives, 1971; contbr. articles to profl. jours.; asso. editor: Jour. Inst. Mgmt. Scis, 1964-78. Bd. dirs. Last Frontier coun. Boy Scouts Am., Kirkpatrick Ctr., Nelson-Atkins Art Mus., Truman Libr. Inst., State Fair Okla., Okla. Futures Commn., Okla. Health Scis. Ctr. Found., Inc., Okla. Ednl. TV Authority. Mem. Inst. Mgmt. Sci. (nat. council mem. 1963-65, sec.-treas. 1964), Assn. for Computing Machinery (nat. lectr. 1969-70), Council on Govt. Relations (bd. dirs. 1981-83). Avocation: commercial pilot. Home: 701 NW 14th St Oklahoma City OK 73103-2211 Office: U Okla Coll of Bus Norman OK 73019

VAN HORNE, JAMES CARTER, economist, educator; b. South Bend, Ind., Aug. 6, 1935; s. Ralph and Helen (McCarter) Van H.; m. Mary A. Roth, Aug. 27, 1960; children: Drew, Stuart, Stephen. AB, De Pauw U., 1957, DSc (hon.), 1986; MBA, Northwestern U., 1961, PhD, 1964. Comml. lending rep. Continental Ill. Nat. Bank, Chgo., 1958-62; prof. fin. Stanford U. Grad. Sch. Bus., 1965-75, A.P. Giannini prof. fin., 1976—, assoc. dean, 1973-75, 76-80; dep. asst. sec. Dept. Treasury, 1975-76; bd. dirs. Sanwa Bank Calif., BB&K Internat. Fund, BB&K Fund Group; chmn. Montgomery St. Income Securities; commr. workers compensation Rate Making Study Commn., State of Calif., 1990-92. Author: Function and Analysis of Capital Market Rates, 1970, Financial Market Rates and Flows, 1994, Financial Management and Policy, 1995; co-author: Fundamentals of Financial Management, 1995; assoc. editor Jour. fin. and Quantitative Analysis, 1969-85, Jour. Fin., 1971-73, Jour. Fixed Income, 1990—. Mem. bd. trustees DePauw U. With AUS, 1957. Mem. Am. Econ. Assn., Am. Fin. Assn. (past pres., dir.), Western Fin. Assn. (past pres., dir.), Fin. Mgmt. Assn. Home: 2000 Webster St Palo Alto CA 94301-4049 Office: Stanford U Grad Sch Bus Stanford CA 94305

VAN HORNE, R. RICHARD, oil company executive; b. Milw., June 7, 1931; s. Ralph Rupert and Edna (Benson) Van H.; m. Elizabeth Whitaker Dixon, July 3, 1954; children—Ann Van Horne Arms, R. Ross, Margaret Van Horne Shuya. B.B.A., U. Wis., 1953. Various positions Anaconda Am. Brass Co., Milw. and Kenosha, Wis., 1955-72; pres., chief exec. officer Anaconda Am. Brass Co., Waterbury, Conn., 1972-74, Anaconda Aluminum Co., Louisville, 1974-82; sr. v.p. pub. affairs Atlantic Richfield Co., Los Angeles, 1982-85; bd. dirs. Citizens Fidelity Corp. Bd. visitors Sch. Bus., U. Wis., Madison; mem. U. Wis. Found.; trustee Brooklawn, Louisville Community Found. Served to 1st lt. U.S. Army, 1953-55. Sr. fellow Bellarmine Coll. Mem. Mchts. and Mfrs. Assn. (bd. dirs. 1983-85), Am. Petroleum Inst., Nat. Planning Assn. (com. on new Am. realities 1982-84), Bascom Hill Soc., Minocqua Country Club. Republican. Episcopalian. Avocations: golf; reading; gardening. Home: 5520 Tecumseh Cir Louisville KY 40207 Office: Atlantic Richfield Co 515 S Flower St Los Angeles CA 90071-2201

VAN HOUSEN, THOMAS CORWIN, III, architect, designer, builder; b. Oak Park, Ill., Jan. 2, 1927; s. Thomas Corwin and Dorothea (Saunders) Van H.; children: Deborah, Victoria, Constance. BA, Lawrence U., 1951; BArch, U. Minn., Mpls., 1954; MArch in Urban Design, Harvard U., 1962. Registered architect, Minn., Wis. With Ellerbe Assocs., Inc., St. Paul, 1951-61; architect, prin. Progressive Design Assocs., Inc., St. Paul, 1961-71; architect, developer, v.p. Landmark Devel. Corp./Appletree Enterprises, Inc., Bloomington, Minn., 1971-85; architect, developer Mortenson Devel. Co., Mpls., 1985-88; architect, design, bldg. dir. D&B Collaborative, Inc., Mpls., 1989—. Bldg. official City of North Oaks, Minn., 1964-78; mem. Minn. League of Municipalities-Metro, St. Paul, 1970-72, Gov.'s Open Space Adv. Com., St. Paul, 1972-74. With U.S. Air Force, 1945-47, ETO. Recipient Outstanding House award St. Paul Jaycees, 1958, 62; named finalist (team mem.) Archtl. competition Boston City Hall, 1962. Fellow AIA (nat. bd. dirs. 1985-88, v.p., pres.-elect Minn. chpt. 1994-95, pres. 1995, spl. award 1981, Presdl. citation 1988, 90); mem. N.W. Racquet and Swim Club. Republican. Lutheran. Avocations: tennis, skiing, swimming, music. Home: 6322 45th Place N Minneapolis MN 55428-5152

VAN HOUTEN, FRANKLYN BOSWORTH, geologist, educator; b. N.Y.C., July 14, 1914; s. Charles Nicholas and Hessie Osborne (Bosworth) Van H.; m. Jean Oliver Sholes, Feb. 18, 1943; children: Jean S., F. Bosworth, David Gordon. B.S., Rutgers U., 1936; Ph.D., Princeton U., 1941. Instr. dept. geology Williams Coll., 1939-42; asst. prof. Princeton U., 1946-51, assoc. prof., 1951-55, prof., 1955-85, prof. emeritus, 1985—; vis. prof. geology UCLA, 1964, State U. N.Y. at Binghamton, 1971; geologist U.S. Geol. Survey, 1948-67; temporary geologist Geol. Survey Can., 1953, Yukon Expdn., geol. expdns. to Morocco, Tunisia, Libya, Egypt, Madagascar. Author reports and articles on geology. Served as lt. USN, 1942-46. Fellow Geol. Soc. Am.; mem. Am. Assn. Petroleum Geologists, Soc. Econ. Paleontologists and Mineralogists (hon. mem., Twenhofel medal), Internat. Assn. Sedimentologists, Colombia Geol. Soc. (hon.), Delta Upsilon. Home: 168 Fitzrandolph Rd Princeton NJ 08540-7224

VAN HOUTEN, STEPHEN H., manufacturing company executive; b. Toronto. BA Honours, U. Western Ont., 1974; LLB, U. Ottawa, 1977; LLM, Osgoode Hall, Toronto, 1984. Bar: Ont. 1979. Legal counsel Gen. Motors, Can., 1980-84, mgr. bus. planning, 1984-87, dir. govt. rels., trade policy, 1987-88, dir. pub. rels., 1988-89; pres. Automotive Parts Mfrs'. Assn., Can., 1989-91, Can. Mfrs'. Assn., 1991—; mem., bd. dirs. numerous mfg. assns. Contbr. numerous articles to profl. jours. V.p. Traffic Injury Rsch. Found. Can. Office: Can Mfrs Assn, Ste 400, 75 International Blvd, Toronto, ON Canada M9W 6L9

VAN HOUTTE, RAYMOND A., financial executive; b. Detroit, Aug. 1, 1924; s. Maurice and Gabrielle (Hoorelbeke) Van H.; m. Margaret Graves, June 17, 1950; children—Raymond C., Jonathan P., Nancy J. B.B.A., U. Mich., 1949; J.D., U. Conn., 1955. Bar: N.Y. 1963; CPA, Conn. Sole practice Hartford, Conn., 1955-58; mem. new product devel. staff Nestle Co., White Plains, N.Y., 1958-60; pres. Ithaca Gun Co., 1960-68; v.p. Tompkins County Trust Co., Ithaca, 1968-73, pres., chief exec. officer, 1973-89, pres. emeritus, counselor, 1990—; pres. Tompkins County Area Devel., Ithaca, 1985; trustee Mut. Funds for Bank Trust Depts., Boston; bd. dirs. Ithaco, Inc., Evaporated Metal Product, Inc. Author: Responsibilities of Bank Directors, 1974. Bd. dirs. Ithaca City Sch. Dist., 1965-66, Tompkins Comty. Hosp.; trustee Paleontol. Rsch. Instn., Kendal at Ithaca. With USAF, 1944-45. Mem. AICPA, N.Y. State Bankers Assn. (2d v.p. 1985-86, pres. 1987-88), Chi Phi (treas.). Lodge: Rotary (chmn.). Home: 1 Strawberry Ln Ithaca NY 14850-1413

VAN HOUWELING, DOUGLAS EDWARD, university administrator, educator; b. Kansas City, Mo., Sept. 20, 1943; s. Cornelius Donald and Roberta Irene (Olson) Van H.; m. Andrea Taylor Parks, Aug. 28, 1965; children: Robert Parks, Benjamin Parks. BS, Iowa State U., Ames, 1965; PhD, Ind. U., 1974. Asst. prof. Cornell U., Ithaca, N.Y., 1970-81; dir. acad. computing Cornell U., 1978-81; vice provost Carnegie-Mellon U., Pitts., 1981-84; adj. assoc. prof. Carnegie-Mellon U., 1981-84; vice provost, dean, adj. prof. U. Mich., Ann Arbor, 1984—; mem. research adv. com. Online Coll. Library Consortium, Dublin, Ohio, 1984-87; trustee EDUCOM, vice chmn. bd. dirs., 1987-91; Princeton, vice chmn., 1987, council chmn., 1986-87; co-founder Interuniv. Consortium for Ednl. Computing, 1984; chmn. bd. MERIT computer network, 1986-90, Advanced Network and Svcs., 1990—; state of Mich. del. Midwest Tech. Inst., 1986-87. Contbr. chpts. in books, articles to profl. publs. NSF fellow, 1968; Indiana U. fellow, 1969; CAUSE nat. leadership award, 1986. Mem. Simulation Symposiums (pres. 1971; grants chmn. 1972-75), N.Am. Simulation and Gaming Assn. Home: 920 Lincoln Ave Ann Arbor MI 48104-3508 Office: U Mich 503 Thompson St Ann Arbor MI 48109-1340

VAN HOWE, ANNETTE EVELYN, retired real estate agent; b. Chgo., Feb. 16, 1921; d. Frank and Susan (Linstra) Van Howe; m. Edward L. Nezelek, Apr. 3, 1961. BA in History magna cum laude, Hofstra U., 1952; MA in Am. History, SUNY-Binghamton, 1966. Editorial asst. Salute Mag., N.Y.C., 1946-48; assoc. editor Med. Econs., Oradell, N.J., 1952-56; nat. mag. publicist Nat. Mental Health Assn., N.Y.C., 1956-60; exec. dir. Diabetes Assn. So. Calif., L.A., 1960-61; corp. sec., v.p., editor, pub. rels. dir. Edward L. Nezelek, Inc., Johnson City, N.Y., 1961-82; realtor, broker, Ft. Lauderdale, 1980-96, ret., 1996; mgr. condominium, Fort Lauderdale, Fla., 1982-83; dir. Sky Harbour East Condo, 1983-88; substitute tchr. high schs., Binghamton, N.Y., 1961-63. Editor newsletters Mental Health Assn., 1965-68, Unitarian-Universalist Ch. Weekly Newsletter, 1967-71. Bd. dirs. Broome County Mental Health Assn., 1961-65, Fine Arts Soc., Roberson Ctr. for Arts and Scis., 1968-70, Found. Wilson Meml. Hosp., Johnson City, 1972-81, White-Willis Theatre, 1988—, Found. SUNY, Binghamton, mem., 1991-95; mem. Fla. Women's Alliance, 1989—; v.p. Fla. Women's Polit. Caucus, 1989-92; chair Women's History Coalition, Broward County, 1986—; pres. Fla. Women's Consortium, 1989-92; trustee Broome C.C., 1973-78; v.p. Broward County Commn. on Status of Women, 1982-93; bd. dirs. Ft. Lauderdale Women's Coun. of Realtors, 1986-88, Broward Arts Guild, 1986; grad. Leadership Broward Class III, 1985, Leadership Am., 1988; trustee Unitarian-Universalist Ch. of Ft. Lauderdale, 1982-89; mem. adv. bd. Planned Parenthood, 1991-93; pres. Broward Alliance of Planned Parenthood, 1993-94; sec. Nat. Women's Conf. Com., 1994-96; bd. dirs. Nat. Women's Party, 1987-93. Named Feminist of Yr., Broward County, 1987; Women's Hall of Fame, Broward County, 1992, Feminist Heroine Nat. Am. Humanist Assn., 1996. Mem. AAUW (legis. chair Fla. divsn. 1986-87, chair women's issues 1989-94, v.p. Ft. Lauderdale br. 1993—), NAFE, Am. Med. Writers Assn., LWV (bd. dir. Broome County 1969-70), Alumni Assn. SUNY Binghamton (bd. dir. 1970-73), Fla. Bar Assn. (grievance com. 1991-94), Am. Acad. Polit. and Social Sci. Broward Women's Alliance, Broward County Voice for Choice (pres. 1995—), Am. Heritage Soc., Nature Conservancy, Nat. Hist. Soc., Symphony Soc., Pacers, Zonta, Alpha Theta Beta, Phi Alpha Theta, Phi Gamma Mu, Binghamton Garden Club, Binghamton Monday Afternoon Club, Acacia Garden Club (pres.), 110 Tower Club, Tower Forum Club (bd. dirs. 1989—), Downtown Coun., Ft. Lauderdale Woman's Club. Home: 2100 S Ocean Dr Fort Lauderdale FL 33316-3806

VANÍČEK, PETR, geodesist; b. Sušice, Czechoslovakia, July 18, 1935; emigrated to Can., 1969, naturalized, 1975; s. Ivan and Irena (Blahovcová) V.; m. Valeria Vášáriová, 1991; children from previous marriage: Filip, Štěpán, Naninka. Degree in Engring., Czech Tech. U., Prague, 1959; PhD in Math. Physics, Czechoslovak Acad. Scis., Prague, 1968; DrSc in Math. and Physical Scis., Czech. Acad. Scis., 1993. Lic. prof. engr. Geodesist Inst. Surveying, Prague, 1959-63; computer cons. Czech Tech. U., 1963-67; Natural Environ. Research Council sr. research fellow Tidal Inst., U. Liverpool, Eng., 1967-68; sr. sci. officer Natural Environ. Research Council, U.K., 1968-69; NRC Can. postdoctoral fellow Fed. Govt., Ottawa, 1969-71; prof. geodesy U. N.B., Fredericton, 1971—; prof. geodesy Erindale Coll., U. Toronto, 1980-83, adj. prof., 1983-89; vis. prof. U. Parana, Brazil, summers 1975-76, 79, 87, U. Stuttgart, Germany, 1981, 82, U. São Paulo, Brazil, 1981, 84, 87; vis. scientist U.S. Geol. Survey, Menlo Park, Calif., 1977; sr. vis. scientist NAS, 1978; pres. Can. Geophys. Union, 1987-89; v.p. internat. adv. bd. tech. aspects law of sea, 1994—; v.p. IAG Commn. on Recent Crustal Movements, 1991—; sr. vis. scientist Royal Inst. Tech., Stockholm, 1986; sr. vis. fellow Council of Sci. and Indsl. Research, South Africa, 1986. Author: (with V. Pleskot and others) Základy Programování Pro Ural, vol. I, 1964, (with J. Čulík, T. Hrušková), vol. II, 1965, (with E.J. Krakiwsky) Geodesy: The Concepts, 1982, rev. edit., 1986, (with others) Guide to GPS Positioning, 1986; editor: Proc. Internat. Symposium on N.Am. Geodetic Networks, 1974, Proc. Can. Geophys. Union Symposium on Satellite Geodesy and Geodynamics, 1975, (with S. Cohen) Slow Deformation and Transmission of Stress in the Earth, 1989, (with N. Christou) Geoid and its Geophysical Interpretations, 1993; editor-in-chief Manuscripta Geodaetica, Bull. Geodesique; mem. internat. editl. bd. Studia Geofisica et Geodetica; contbr. articles to profl. jours. Recipient Humboldt sr. rsch. award Federal Republic of Germany; Am. Geophys. Union fellow. Fellow Geol. Assn. Can., Internat. Assn. Geodesy, Explorers Club; mem. Can. Geophys. Union (J. Tuzo Wilson medal 1996), Czechoslovak Soc. Arts and Scis. Am., Sigma Xi. Home: 667 Golf Club Rd, Fredericton, NB Canada E3B 4X4 *As one coming from communist central Europe, I cannot stop marveling at the opportunities this society offers to anyone willing to work earnestly. One must feel sorry for those who do not conduct their lives to take an advantage of this offer.*

VANIER, JACQUES, physicist; b. Dorion, Que., Can., Jan. 4, 1934; s. Henri and Emma (Boileau) V.; m. Lucie Beaudet, July 8, 1961; children: Lyne, Pierre. BA, U. Montreal, 1955, BSc, 1958; MSc, McGill U., 1960, PhD, 1963. Lectr. U. Montreal, 1961-63, McGill U., 1960-63; physicist Varian Assocs., Beverly, Mass., 1963-67, Hewlett Packard Co., Beverly, 1967; prof. elec. engring. U. Laval, Que., 1967-83; physicist Nat. Rsch. Coun., Ottawa, 1983-94, head elec. and time standards, 1984-86, dir. Lab. Basic Standards, 1986-90, dir. gen. Inst. for Nat. Measurement Standards, 1990-93; prof. physics U. de Montreal, 1995—; cons. Comm. Components Corp., Costa Mesa, Calif., 1974-76, EGG Co., Salem, Mass., 1979-82, Kernco, Danvers, Mass., 1995—; chmn. com. A URSI, 1990-93; chmn. exec. com. CPEM, 1990-94; mem. Internat. Com. Weights and Measures, 1992-96. Author: Basic Theory of Lasers and Masers, 1971, (with C. Audoin) The Quantum Physics of Atomic Frequency Standards, 1989; contbr. articles to profl. jours.; inventor nuclear quadrupole resonance thermometer. Recipient I.I. Rabi Prize, Am. Physical Soc., 1994. Fellow IEEE (Centennial medal 1984, Rabi award 1994), Royal Soc. Can., Am. Phys. Soc.

VANIER, KIERAN FRANCIS, business forms printing company executive; b. Alliance, Ohio, May 10, 1914; s. Joseph A. and Johanna Mary (McCarthy) V.; m. Marjory S. Kitchen, 1937 (dec.); children: Denis K., Annette Vanier Fritzenkotter; m. June Day, 1975 (dec. 1995). B.S., Loyola U., 1937. Salesman Moore Bus. Forms, to 1946; founder Vanier Graphics Corp., 1946, ret. chmn. bd.; ret. vice chmn. Am. Bus. Products, Inc., Atlanta; founder, chmn. Kieran Label Corp. Founder Amoyotrophic Lateral Sclerosis Found. San Diego; past chmn. San Diego chpt. Muscular Dystrophy; past pres. San Diego Employers Assn. Knight Order of Holy Sepulcher, Pope John Paul II. Mem. San Diego Yacht Club, San Diego Country Club, De Anza Country Club. Office: 8765 Olive Ln Santee CA 92071-4165

VAN INWAGEN, PETER JAN, philosophy educator; b. Rochester, N.Y., Sept. 21, 1942; s. George Butler and Mildred Gloria (Knudson) van I; m. Margery Bedford Naylor, Mar. 31, 1967 (div. Apr. 1988); 1 child, Elizabeth Core; m. Elisabeth Marie Bolduc, June 3, 1989. B.S., Rensselaer Poly. Inst., 1965; Ph.D., U. Rochester, 1969. Vis. asst. prof. U. Rochester, N.Y., 1971-72; asst. prof. Syracuse U., N.Y., 1972-74, assoc. prof., 1974-80, prof. philosophy, 1980-95; John Cardinal O'Hara prof. of philosophy U. Notre Dame, South Bend, Ind., 1995—; vis. prof. U. Ariz., Tucson, 1981. Author: An Essay on Free Will, 1983, Material Beings, 1990, Metaphysics, 1993, God, Knowledge and Mystery, 1995; editor: Time and Cause, 1980, Alvin Plantinga, 1985; mem. editl. bd. Jour. Faith and Philosophy, Philos. Perspectives, Nous, Philos. Studies; contbr. articles to profl. jours. Served to capt. U.S. Army, 1969-71. NEH grantee, 1983-84, 89-90. Mem. Am. Philos. Assn., Soc. Christian Philosophers. Democrat. Episcopalian. Home: 52145 Farmington Square Rd Granger IN 46530 Office: U Notre Dame Dept Philosophy South Bend IN 46556

VAN ITALLIE, JEAN-CLAUDE, playwright; b. Brussels, May 25, 1936; came to U.S., 1940; s. Hughes Ferdinand and Marthe Mathilde Caroline (Levy) van I. BA, Harvard U., 1958; PhD (hon.), Kent State U., 1977. Tchr. theater, playwriting New Sch. for Social Research, N.Y.C., 1966, Yale U. Sch. Drama, New Haven, 1969, 84, Naropa Inst., Boulder, Colo., 1976-83, 87-88, Princeton U., N.J., 1976-88, NYU, 1982-88, U. Colo., Boulder, 1985, 89, 91, Columbia U., 1986, Am. Repertory Theatre, Cambridge, Mass., 1990; vis. Mellon prof. Amherst Coll., Mass., fall 1976. Playwright for Open Theatre ensemble, N.Y.C., 1963-68; playwright War, 1963, Almost Like Being, 1965, I'm Really Here, 1965, America Hurrah, 1966 (Drama Desk award, Outer Cir. Critics award 1967), The Serpent, 1968 (Obie award 1969), A Fable, 1975, King of the United States, 1972, Mystery Play, 1973, Medea, 1979, Bag Lady, 1979, Tibetan Book of the Dead, 1983, Early Warnings, 1983, The Traveler, 1986, new English versions Chekhov's The Seagull, 1973, Cherry Orchard, 1977, Three Sisters, 1982, Uncle Vanya, 1983, Paradise Ghetto, 1981, Struck Dumb, (with Joseph Chaikin), 1987, Ancient Boys, 1989; transl. Genet's The Balcony, 1986, The Odyssey (mus.), 1991, Bulgahov's Master & Margarita, 1993, Tibetan Book of the Dean (opera libretto), 1996. Grantee Rockefeller Found., 1973, Ford Found., 1979, Creative Artists Pub. Service, 1975; recipient Playwrights award NEA, 1986, Creative Artists Pub. Service award, 1975; Guggenheim fellow, 1963, 83. Buddhist.

VANITALLIE, THEODORE BERTUS, physician; b. Hackensack, N.J., Nov. 8, 1919; s. Dorus Christian and Lucy M. (Pohle) VanI.; m. Barbara Cox, Sept. 25, 1948 (div. Mar. 1992); children: Lucy M., Theodore Bertus, Christina M., Elizabeth B., Katharine R.; m. Sallie Newton Calhoun, Mar. 11, 1992. B.S., Harvard U., 1941; M.D., Columbia U., 1945. Diplomate: Am. Bd. Internal Medicine. Intern in medicine St. Luke's Hosp., N.Y.C., 1945-46, asst. resident in internal medicine, 1948-49, resident, 1949-50, dir. nutrition and metabolism rsch. lab., 1952-55; assoc. Peter Bent Brigham Hosp., Boston, 1955-57; dir. medicine St. Luke's Hosp. Center, N.Y.C., 1957-75; dir. Obesity Rsch. Ctr., 1974-85, co-dir., 1986-88; asst. prof. Sch. Pub. Health, Harvard U., 1955-57; assoc. clin. prof. medicine Columbia, N.Y.C., 1957-65, clin. prof., 1965-71, prof., 1971-88, prof. emeritus, 1988—; vis. prof. internal medicine Am. U. Beirut, 1968-69, trustee, 1976-93; spl. advisor on human nutrition Surgeon Gen., 1980-81; mem. sci. adv. bd. Nutrition Found., 1967-71; pres. Am. Bd. Nutrition, 1968-71; mem. food and nutrition bd. NRC, 1970-76; med. adv. com. on cyclamates HEW, 1969-70; mem. gastrointestinal and nutrition tng. com. NIH, 1969-73, mem. adv. coun. Nat. Arthritis, Diabetes, Digestive and Kidney Diseases, NIH, 1978-81; mem. joint nutrition monitoring evaluation com. USDA and HHS, 1982-86; dir. Miles Labs., 1976-84; vis. physician Rockefeller U. Hosp., 1986-89; adj. prof. Rockefeller U., 1986-89; vis. prof. medicine in psychiatry, U. Pa., 1990-94. Mem. editorial bd.: Diabetes, 1960-71; editor-in-chief: Am. Jour. Clin. Nutrition, 1979-81. Mem. Englewood (N.J.) Bd. Edn., 1960-65, v.p., 1964-65; trustee St. Luke's-Roosevelt Hosp. Ctr., 1988-94. Lt. (j.g.) USNR, 1946-68. Recipient citation FDA, 1983. Fellow ACP (disting. physicians award 1987), AAAS, Am. Inst. Nutrition; mem. AMA (mem. coun. on foods and nutrition 1967-74, vice chmn. 1974, Joseph B. Goldberger award 1985), Am. Soc. Clin. Investigation, Soc. Exptl. Biology and Medicine, Am. Clin. and Climatol. Assn., Am. Soc. Clin. Nutrition (coun. 1970-73, pres. 1976-77, Elmer V. McCollum award 1985), Soc. Study of Ingestive Behavior (disting. sci. award 1994), Order of Malta (knight comdr. Quebec priory 1990—), Century Assn., Fla. Hist. Soc. (bd. dirs. 1995—). Research and contbr. numerous publs. on obesity, body composition, pancreatic hormone, glucagon, mechanism of energy balance regulation, treatment of pruritus and hypercholesteremia in biliary cirrhosis, physiology and clin. use of medium chain triglyceride. Address: PO Box 775 1678 Jose Gaspar Dr Boca Grande FL 33921

VAN KILSDONK, CECELIA ANN, retired nursing administrator, volunteer; b. Beaver Dam, Wis., Sept. 28, 1930; d. Walter and Pauline (Yagodzinski) Klapinski; (div.); children: Dan, Greg, Paula, Steve. Diploma, Mercy Hosp. Sch. Nursing, 1951; BS, Coll. of St. Frances, Peoria, Ill., 1983. Clin. nurse Divsn. of Ambulatory Care, Phoenix, 1965-70, clin. charge nurse, 1970-82, regional nursing supr., 1982-87, nurse adminstr., 1987-92; mgr. nursing svc. Maricopa County Health Dept. Svcs., Phoenix. Mem. Continuing Edn. review Com., 1989—; vol. Primary Care Ctr.; disaster nurse ARC. Mem. ANA, Ariz. Nurse's Assn., Nat. League for Nursing, Phi Theta Kappa. Home: 2502 E Minnezona Ave Phoenix AZ 85016-4927

VAN KIRK, JOHN ELLSWORTH, cardiologist; b. Dayton, Ohio, Jan. 13, 1942; s. Herman Corwin and Dorothy Louise (Shafer) Van K.; m. Patricia L. Davis, June 19, 1966 (div. Dec. 1982); 1 child, Linnea Gray. BA cum laude, DePauw U., Greencastle, Ind., 1963; BS, Northwestern U., Chgo., 1964, MD with distinction, 1967. Diplomate Am. Bd. Internal Medicine, Am. Bd. Internal Medicine subspecialty in cardiovascular disease; cert. Nat. Bd. Med. Examiners. Intern Evanston (Ill.) Hosp., 1967-68; staff assoc. Nat. Inst. of Allergy & Infectious Diseases, Bethesda, Md., 1968-70; resident internal medicine U. Mich. Med. Ctr., Ann Arbor, 1970-72, fellow in cardiology, 1972-74, instr. internal medicine, 1973-74; staff cardiologist Mills Meml. Hosp., San Mateo, Calif., 1974—, vice-chief medicine, 1977-78, dir. critical care, 1978—, critical care utilizaton rev., 1988—, dir. pacemaker clinic, 1976—; mem. active staff Peninsula Hosp. and Med. Ctr.; mem. courtesy staff Sequoia Hosp. Contbr. rsch. articles to profl. jours. Recipient 1st prize in landscaping Residential Estates, State of Calif., 1977, Physician's Recognition award AMA, 1968, 72, 75, 77, 80, 82, 85, 87, 89, 93. Fellow Am. Coll. Cardiology; mem. AMA, Calif. Med. Assn., San Mateo County Med. Soc., Am. Heart Assn., San Mateo County Heart Assn. (bd. dirs. 1975-78, bay area rsch. com. 1975-76, edn. com. 1975-77, pres. elect 1976-77, pres. 1977-79), Alpha Omega Alpha. Republican. United Brethren. Avocations: gardening, computer science, tennis, woodworking, electronics, ham radio. Office: Unified Med Clinics of Peninsula 50 S San Mateo Dr Ste 270 San Mateo CA 94401-3859

VAN KIRK, ROBERT JOHN, nursing case manager, educator; b. Jersey City, N.J., Sept. 18, 1944; s. Robert and Doris V.; m. Marjorie Ann Carroll, Mar. 23, 1968 (div. Nov. 30, 1993); children: Walter, Michael, Robert Jr., Peggy. BA cum laude, U. Conn., 1974; MEd, Kent State U., 1983; D of Nursing, Case Western Reserve U., 1986. RN. Sales mgr. Nutmeg Home Protection, Middlebury, Conn., 1972-74; theater mgr. SBC Mgmt. Corp., Boston, 1974; dist. supr. Selected Theatres Mgmt. Corp., Lyndhurst, Ohio, 1974-86; nat. sales mgr. ZBS Video, Inc., Lyndhurst, Ohio, 1981-82; staff nurse Cleve. Clinic Found., 1986-87, clin. instr., 1987-88, head nurse, 1988-93; case mgr., 1993—; asst. clin. prof. Case Western Reserve U., Frances Payne Bolton Sch. Nursing, Cleve., 1990—; case mgr. Cleve. Clin. Home Care, 1993—. Health officer Lake County (Ohio) Bd. Alcohol, Drug Addiction and Mental Health Svcs., 1991—; co-chmn. United Way, Cleve., 1991-93. Staff sgt. U.S. Army, 1964-71, Vietnam. Recipient Achievement award Greater Cleve. Nurses Assn., 1986. Mem. AACN, Am. Assn. Tchrs. German, Am. Assn. Tchrs. Portuguese and Spanish, Assn. Specialists in Aging, Frances Payne Bolton Sch. Nursing Alumni Assn. (pres. 1992-93), Kappa Delta Pi, Sigma Theta Tau. Avocations: pocket billards, furniture making. Home: 5011 Nob Hill Dr Apt 9C Chagrin Falls OH 44022 Office: Cleve Clinic Found 9555 Rockside Rd Valley View OH 44125

VAN KIRK, THOMAS L., lawyer; b. Pa., June 25, 1945; s. Theodore and Mary Jane (Young) Van K.; children: Thomas Jr., Christopher. BA, Bucknell U., 1967; JD cum laude, Dickinson U., 1970. Bar: Pa., U.S. Dist. Ct. (we. and ea. dists.) Pa. 1971, U.S. Ct. Appeals (3d cir.) 1972, U.S. Supreme Ct. 1976. Clk. Pa. Superior Ct., 1970-71; assoc. Buchanan Ingersoll, Pitts., 1971-77, ptnr., 1978—, chief oper. officer, 1985—; bd. dirs. Buchanan Ingersoll P.C., Civic Light Opera; v.p. State Pa. Economy League, Western Pa. Economy League. Chmn. Allegheny County Heart Assn. Walk, 1992, Pitts. Downtown Partnership; bd. dirs. Rivers Club of Pitts.; sec., treas., bd. dirs. Capital Divsn. Pa. Economy League. Mem. ABA, Allegheny County Bar Assn., Duquesne Club, Rivers Club, Racquet Club Phila., The Club at Nevillewood. Democrat. Lutheran. Home: 1010 Osage Rd Pittsburgh PA 15243-1014 Office: Buchanan Ingersoll PC 301 Grant St 20th Fl Pittsburgh PA 15219-1410

VAN LANDINGHAM, LEANDER SHELTON, JR., lawyer; b. Memphis, July 15, 1925; s. Leander Shelton and Bertha (Shumaker) Van L.; m. Henrietta Adena Stapf, July 5, 1959; children: Ann Henrietta, Leander Shelton III. BS in Chemistry, U. N.C., 1948, MA in Organic Chemistry, 1949; JD, Georgetown U., 1955. Bar: D.C. 1955, Md. 1963, Va. 1976. Patent adviser Dept. Navy, Washington, 1953-55; sole practice comml. law and patent, trademark and copyright law, Washington met. area, 1955—. Served to lt. USNR, 1943-46, 51-53. Mem. Am. Chem. Soc., Sci. Assn., Fed. Bar Assn., ABA, D.C. Bar Assn., Va. Bar Assn., Md. Bar Assn., Am. Intellectual Property Law Assn., Am. Judicature Soc., Sigma Xi, Phi Alpha Delta. Home: 10726 Stanmore Dr Potomac MD 20854-1518 Office: 2001 Jefferson Davis Hwy Arlington VA 22202-3603

VAN LARE, WENDELL JOHN, lawyer; b. Newark, N.Y., Mar. 1, 1945; s. Julian J. and Doris Elizabeth (Lacknor) Van L.; m. Sheila Gilbert, Aug. 20, 1967 (div. Apr. 1987); children: Jonathan S., Allison R.; m. L. Karen Stack, May 7, 1987. BS, SUNY, New Paltz, 1967; JD, Union U., 1972. Bar: N.Y. 1973, U.S. Supreme Ct., 1980. Assoc. Harter, Secrest & Emery, Rochester, N.Y., 1972-77; asst. dir. labor rels. Gannett Co., Inc., Rochester, 1977-80; dir. labor rels. Gannett Co., Inc., Rochester and Arlington, 1980-93; v.p., labor counsel Gannett Co., Inc., Arlington, 1993-94, v.p., sr. labor counsel, 1994—. Comments editor Albany Law Rev., 1971-72. Pres. Opera Theatre of Rochester, N.Y., 1983-85. Lt. (j.g.) USNR, 1968-70. Mem. ABA, N.Y. Bar Assn., River Bend Golf and Country Club. Avocation: genealogy. Office: Gannett Co Inc 1100 Wilson Blvd Arlington VA 22234

VAN LEBEN SELES, JAMES W., transportation executive; b. Oakland, Calif.. Dir. Caltrans; dir. transp. State of Calif., Sacramento, 1991—; vice chmn. Transp. Rsch. Bd. Bd. dirs. Assn. State Hwy. & Transp. Ofcls., U.S. Transp. Rsch. Bd., Intelligent Transp. Soc. Am. Office: 1120 N St Sacramento CA 95814*

VAN LEUVEN, ROBERT JOSEPH, lawyer; b. Detroit, Apr. 17, 1931; s. Joseph Francis and Olive (Stowell) Van L.; student Albion Coll., 1949-51; BA with distinction Wayne State U., 1953; JD, U. Mich., 1957; children: Joseph Michael, Douglas Robert, Julie Margaret. Bar: Mich. 1957. Since practiced in Muskegon, Mich.; ptnr. Hathaway, Latimer, Clink & Robb, 1957-68, ptnr. McCroskey, Libner & Van Leuven, 1968-81, ptnr. Libner, Van Leuven & Kortering, 1982—; past mem. council negligence law sect. State Bar Mich. Bd. dirs. Muskegon Children's Home, 1965-75. Served with AUS 1953-55. Fellow Mich. Bar Found., Mich. Trial Lawyers Assn., Am. Coll. Trial Lawyers; mem. Assn. Trial Lawyers Am., Delta Sigma Phi. Club: Muskegon Country. Home: 2397 Westwood Muskegon MI 49441 Office: Libner Van Leuven & Kortering Muskegon Mall 400 Comerica Muskegon MI 49443

VAN LINT, VICTOR ANTON JACOBUS, physicist; b. Samarinda, Indonesia, May 10, 1928; came to U.S., 1937; s. Victor J. and Margaret (DeJager) Van L.; m. M. June Woolhouse, June 10, 1950; children: Lawrence, Kenneth, Linda, Karen. BS, Calif. Inst. Tech., Pasadena, 1950, PhD, 1954. Instr. Princeton (N.J.) U., 1954-55; staff mem. Gen. Atomic, San Diego, 1957-74; physics cons. San Diego, 1974-75; staff mem. Mission Research Corp., San Diego, 1975-82, 83-91; cons., 1991—; spl. asst. to dep. dir. sci. and tech. Def. Nuclear Agy., Washington, 1982-83. Author, editor: Radiation Effects in Electronic Materials, 1976; contbr. articles to profl. jours. Served with U.S. Army, 1955-57. Recipient Pub. Service award NASA, 1981. Fellow IEEE. Republican. Mem. United Ch. of Christ. Home and Office: 1032 Skylark Dr La Jolla CA 92037-7733

VAN LOBEN SELS, JAMES W., transportation executive; b. Oakland, Calif.. BS, U.S. Mil. Acad.; MS in Space Physics, USAF Inst. Tech. Registered profl. engr. Va. Dir. Caltrans, Calif. Dept. Transp., Sacramento, 1991—; vice chmn. Transp. Rsch. Bd. Bd. dirs. Am. Assn. State Hwy. & Transp. Ofcls., U.S. Transp. Rsch. Bd., Intelligent Transp. Soc. Am. Office: 1120 N St Sacramento CA 95814*

VAN LOPIK, JACK RICHARD, geologist, educator; b. Holland, Mich., Feb. 25, 1929; s. Guy M. and Minnie (Grunst) Van L.; 1 son, Charles Robert (dec.). B.S., Mich. State U., 1950; M.S., La. State U., 1953, Ph.D., 1955. Geologist, sect. chief, asst. chief, chief geology br. U.S Army C.E., Waterways Expt. Sta., Vicksburg, Miss., 1954-61; chief engrs. environ. adv. bd. U.S. Army C.E., 1988-92; chief area evaluation sect., tech. dir., mgr. Space and Environ. Sci. Programs, tech. requirements dir. geosciences ops. Tex. Instruments, Inc., Dallas, 1961-68; chmn. dept. marine sci. La. State U., Baton Rouge, 1968-74; prof. dept. marine sci., dir. sea grant devel., dean Center for Wetland Resources, La. State U., Baton Rouge, 1968-91; prof. dept. oceanography and coastal scis. La. State U., Baton Rouge, 1991—; exec. dir. sea grant devel., La. State U., 1991—; chmn. Coastal Resources Directorate of U.S. Nat. Com. for Man and Biosphere, U.S. Nat. Commn. for UNESCO, 1975-82; dir. Gulf South Rsch. Inst., 1974-89; mem. Nat. Adv. Com. Oceans and Atmosphere, 1978-84; mem. Lower Miss. River Waterway Safety Com. USCG 8th dist., 1983-94; mem. adv. coun. Nat. Coastal Resources Rsch. and Devel. Inst., 1985—; ofcl. del. XX Congreso Internacional, Mexico City, 1956, XII Gen. Assembly Internat. Union Geodesy and Geophysics, Helsinki, 1960; chmn. panel on geography and land use Nat. Acad. Scis.-NRC, com. on remote sensing programs for earth resources surveys, 1969-77. Fellow Geol. Soc. Am., AAAS; mem. Am. Astronautical Soc. (dir. S.W. sect. 1967-68), Am. Soc. Photogrammetry (dir. 1969-72, chmn. photo interpretation com. 1960, 65, rep. earth scis. divsn. NRC 1968-71), Am. Geophys. Union, Am. Assn. Petroleum Geologists (acad. adv. com. 1973-78), Assn. Am. Geographers, Soc. Econ. Paleontologists and Mineralogists (rsch. com. 1962-65), Am. Mgmt. Assn., Soc. Rsch. Administrs., Marine Tech. Soc., Am. Water Resources Assn., Soc. Am. Mil. Engrs., Sea Grant Assn. (exec. bd. dirs. 1972-74, 80-82, 88-91, pres.-elect

1988-89, pres. 1989-90), Nat. Ocean Industries Assn. (adv. coun. 1973-83), Nat. Conf. Advancement Rsch. (exec. com. 1988-92), La. Partnership for Tech. and Innovation (bd. dirs. 1989—), Sigma Xi. Home: 9 Rue Sorbonne Baton Rouge LA 70808-4682 Office: La State U Office Sea Grant Devel Baton Rouge LA 70803

VAN LOUCKS, MARK LOUIS, venture capitalist, business advisor; b. Tampa, Fla., June 19, 1946; s. Charles Perry and Lenn (Bragg) Van L.; m. Eva Marianne Forsell, June 10, 1986; children: Brandon, Charlie. BA in Comm. and Pub. Policy, U. Calif., Berkeley, 1969. Sr. v.p. mktg., programming and corp. devel. United Cable TV Corp., Denver, Colo., 1970-81, advisor, 1983-89; sr. v.p., office of chmn. Rockefeller Ctr. TV Corp., N.Y.C., 1981-83; advisor United Artists Commun. Corp., Englewood, 1989-91; investor, business advisor in pvt. practice Englewood, 1983—; founder, prin. owner Glory Hole Saloon & Gaming Hall, Central City, Colo., 1990—, Harrah's Casino, Black Hawk, Colo., 1990—; chmn., CEO Bask Internat., Englewood, 1990—; bd. dirs. Wild West Devel. Corp., Denver; sr. v.p., bd. dirs. GSI Cable TV Assocs., Inc., San Francisco, 1984-90; guest lectr. on cable TV bus., 1985-91; cons. Telecommunications, Inc., Denver, 1989-93. Producer HBO spl. Green Chili Showdown, 1985; producer TV spl. 3 Days for Earth, 1987; producer, commd. artist nuclear war armament pieces; contbr. articles to profl. jours. Chmn. Cops in Crisis, Denver, 1990—; bd. dirs. The NOAH Found., Denver, 1976—; founding dir. Project for Responsible Advt., Denver, 1991-92; chmn. mayor's mktg. adv. bd., Central City, Colo. Named hon. capt. Denver Police Dept., 1991—, fin. advisor L. Rose Co., 1995—. Mem. Casino Owners Assn. (founding dir. 1989—), Colo. Gaming Assn. (dir. 1990—), recipient S'nnaeel Evol award, 1995), Glenmoor Country Club, The Village Club. Republican. Jewish. Avocations: music, woodworking, philanthropy, vintage autos. Office: MLVL Inc 333 W Hampden Ave Ste 1005 Englewood CO 80110-2340

VANMARCKE, ERIK HECTOR, civil engineering educator; b. Menen, Belgium, Aug. 6, 1941; came to U.S., 1965, naturalized, 1976; m. Louis Eugene and Rachel Louisa (van Hollebeke) V.; m. Margaret Maria Delesie, May 25, 1965; children: Lieven, Ann, Kristien. BS, U. Louvain, Belgium, 1965; MS, U. Del., 1967; PhD in Civil Engring, MIT, 1970. From instr. to prof. civil engring. MIT, Cambridge, 1969-85; Gilbert W. Winslow Career Devel. prof. MIT, 1974-77, dir. civil engring. systems group, 1976-80; prof. civil engring. and ops. rsch. Princeton U., 1985—, dir. grad. studies civil engring. and ops. rsch., 1990—; cons. Office Sci. and Tech. Policy, 1978-80; vis. scholar in engring. Harvard U., 1984-85; Shimizu Corp. vis. prof. Stanford U., 1991; cons. various govt. agys. and engring. firms; mem. exec. com. Princeton Materials Inst., 1991-93. Author: Random Fields: Analysis and Synthesis, 1983, Quantum Origins of Cosmic Structure, 1995; editor: Internat. Jour. Structural Safety, 1981-91. Recipient Sr. Scientist award for study in Japan, Japan Soc. for Promotion of Sci., 1991. Mem. ASCE (Raymond C. Reese rsch. award 1975, Walter L. Huber rsch. prize 1984, chair com. on safety and reliability in geotech. engring. 1993—), Am. Geophys. Union, Seismol. Soc. Am., Internat. Soc. Soil Mechanics and Found. Engring., Sigma Xi. Home: 50 Brooks Bnd Princeton NJ 08540-7530 Office: Room E311 Engring Quadrangle Princeton U Princeton NJ 08544

VAN MASON, RAYMOND, dancer, choreographer. Prin. dancer Ballet West, Salt Lake City. Dance performances include Swan Lake, Gisells, Sleeping Beauty, Romeo & Juliet, Anna Karenina, The Nutcracker, Carmina Burana, White Mourning, Ophelia; choreographer: Requiem: A Liturgical Ballet, 1990, A Pilgrimage: A Liturgical Ballet, 1992, Lady Guinevere, Chameleon, Carmina Burana, Symphony # 7, 1992, others. Office: Ballet West 50 W 200 S Salt Lake City UT 84101-1642

VAN MATRE, JOYCE DIANNE, rehabilitation nurse; b. Bklyn., June 1, 1943; d. Gerard Thibault and Helene Clara (Wright) Hair; m. Richard Givens Van Matre, Aug. 27, 1965; children: Kimberly, Karyn, Richard. Diploma in Nursing, Gordon Keller Sch. Nursing, 1964; BS in Health Arts, Coll. of St. Francis, 1990. Cert. ins. rehab. specialist; Fla. rehab. svc. provider; cert. case mgr. Case supr. rehab. Vocat. Placement Svcs., Tampa, Fla., 1980-81; RN mgr. Always Care Nursing Svc., Tampa, 1981-82; staff nurse Vis. Nurse's Assn., Tampa, 1983-84; rehab. coord. Underwriter's Adjusting Co., Tampa, 1984-85; pres. of corp., case mgr., supr., bus. owner Ind. Group Consultants, Inc., Brandon, Fla., 1985-90; case mgr. Sullivan Health & Rehab. Mgmt., Inc., St. Petersburg, Fla., 1991-92; rehab. nurse Liberty Mut. Ins. Co., Tampa, 1992—. Recipient Disting. Acad. Achievement award Coll. of St. Francis, 1991. Mem. Assn. Rehab. Nurses, West Coast Regional Case Mgr. Assn. Office: Liberty Mut Ins Co 3350 Buschwood Park Dr Tampa FL 33618-4314

VAN METER, ABRAM DEBOIS, lawyer, retired banker; b. Springfield, Ill., May 16, 1922; s. A.D. and Edith (Graham) Van M.; m. Margaret Schlipf, Dec. 1, 1956; children: Andy, Alice, Ann. BS, Kings Point Coll., 1946; JD, Northwestern U., 1948. Bar: Ill. 1949. Ptnr. Van Meter, Oxtoby & Funk, Springfield, 1949—; adminstrv. asst. to treas. State of Ill., Springfield, 1963; v.p. Ill. Nat. Bank, Springfield, 1964-65, pres., 1965-88, chmn. bd. dirs., 1988-90, also bd. dirs.; chmn. bd. dirs. First of Am.-Springfield, N.A., 1990-93, dir. emeritus, 1993—. Chmn. bd. dirs. Ill. Housing Devel. Authority, 1977—; chmn. bd. trustees So. Ill. U., 1989—; bd. dirs., mem. exec. com. Meml. Med. Ctr. (emeritus). Mem. ABA, Ill. Bar Assn., Sangamon Bar Assn., Chgo. Club, Chgo. Athletic Club, Sangamo Club, Island Bay Yacht Club,. Home: 6 Fair Oaks St Springfield IL 62704-3222 Office: First of Am Springfield NA 1 N Old State Capitol Plz Springfield IL 62701-1323

VAN METER, JOHN DAVID, lawyer; b. Owensboro, Ky., Oct. 30, 1951; s. Leslie Evan and Agnes Regina (Gropp) Van M.; m. Laura Ann Isbell, May 19, 1984; children: Katherine Leigh, Elizabeth Grace, Jennifer Marie. BA in Journalism, U. Ky., 1973, JD, 1978. Bar: Ky. 1978. Atty. Ashland (Ky.) Oil Inc., 1978-83, exec. asst. to chmn., 1983-88; adminstrv. v.p. Valvoline Oil Co. div. Ashland Oil, Inc., Lexington, Ky., 1988-90; pres. Ashland Internat. Ltd. subs. Ashland, Inc., London, 1990—. Bd. dirs. London City Ballet. Mem. ABA, Ky. Bar Assn., Boyd County Bar Assn., Fayette County Bar Assn., Am. C. of C. (bd. dirs.), Ends of the Earth Club (bd. dirs.), Carlton Club, Buck's Club, Pilgrim's Club. Republican. Roman Catholic. Home: 8 Reston Pl Hyde Park Gate, London SW7 5DY, England Office: 58 St James's St, London SW1A 1PR, England

VANMETER, VANDELIA L., library director; b. Seibert, Colo., July 17, 1934; d. G.W. and A. Pearl Klockenteger; m. Victor M. VanMeter, Jan. 21, 1954; children: Allison C., Kristopher C. BA, Kansas Wesleyan U., 1957; MLS, Emporia State U., 1970; PhD, Tex. Woman's U., 1986. Cert. libr. media specialist. Tchr. Ottawa County Rural Sch., Kans., 1954-55; social scis. tchr. McClave (Colo.) High Sch., 1957-58, Ellsworth (Kans.) Jr. High Sch., 1959-68; libr., media specialist Ellsworth (Kans.) High Sch., 1968-84; asst. prof. libr. sci. U. So. Miss., Hattiesburg, 1986-90; chair dept. libr./info. sci. Spalding U., Louisville, 1990-96, libr. dir., 1991—; cons. to sch., pub. and spl. librs., Kans., Miss., Ky., 1970—; mem. Ky. NCATE Bd. Examiners. Author: American History for Children and Young Adults, 1990, World History for Children and Young Adults, 1992; editor: Mississippi Library Media Specialist Staff Development Modules, 1988, Library Lane Newsletter, 1991—; contbr. chpts. to books; contbr. articles to profl. jours. Active City Coun., Ellsworth, Kans., 1975-79, Park Bd., Ellsworth, 1975-79; bd. dirs. Robbins Meml. Libr., 1977-79. Grantee Kans. Demonstration Sch. Libr., 1970-72, Miss. Power Found., 1989; named Women of Yr. Bus. and Profl. Women of Ellsworth, Kans., 1976. Mem. ALA, Am. Assn. Sch. Librs., Nat. Assn. State Edn. Media Profls., Assn. Coll. & Rsch. Librs., Ky. Libr. Assn., Ky. Sch. Media Assn., Ky. Assn. Tchr. Educators, Assn. for Libr. and Info. Sci. Educators. Office: Spalding U Libr 851 S 4th St Louisville KY 40203-2115

VAN METRE, MARGARET CHERYL, artistic director, dance educator; b. Maryville, Tenn., Nov. 24, 1938; d. Robert Fillers and Margaret Elizabeth (Goddard) Raulston; m. Mitchell Robert Van Metre II, Aug. 25, 1956; 1 child, Mitchell Robert. Elem., intermediate and advanced teaching certs. Dir. Van Metre Sch. of Dance, Maryville, 1958—; artistic dir. Appalachian Ballet Co., Maryville Coll., 1972—; chmn. dance panel Tenn. Arts Commn.; 1973-74; chmn. Bicentennial Ballet Project, Tenn., 1975-76. Choreographer ballets: DeLusion, 1965; Hill Heritage Suite, 1972; Dancing Princesses, 1983. Mem. Tenn. Assn. of Dance (pres. 1972). Democrat. Episcopalian. Home: 609 Kendrick Pl Knoxville TN 37902-2019 Office: Appalachian Ballet Co 215 W Broadway Ave Maryville TN 37801-4705

VAN METRE, THOMAS EARLE, physician, allergist; b. Newport, R.I., Jan. 11, 1923; s. Thomas Earle and Anne Heap (Gleaves) Van M.; m. Mary Rosalie Evans, Sept. 7, 1947 (dec. Jan., 1967); children: Rosalie Van Metre Baker, Anne Gleaves Van Metre Kibbe, Mary Evans Van Metre Chodroff, Elizabeth Bowyer Van Meter Domowski, Helen Jenkins Van Metre Weary; m. Adéla Bell Hurst Winand, June 29, 1968; stepchildren: William Thomas Winand III, Bruce Hurst Winand. BS cum laude, Harvard U., 1943; MD cum laude, Harvard Med. Sch., 1946. Diplomate Am. Bd. Internal Medicine, Am. Bd. Allergy. Intern in internal medicine Johns Hopkins Hosp., 1946-47, resident in internal medicine, 1947-48, 50, 1951-52, Am. Cancer Soc. fellow virology and bacteriology, 1952-53, physician diagnostic clin., asst. physician allergy clinic, 1954-56, physician, 1956—, physician OPD, allergy and infectious disease clinic, 1956—, pediatrician, 1957-66, physician-in-charge allergy clinic, 1966-84; pvt. practice in internal medicine and allergy Balt., 1954—; asst. in medicine Johns Hopkins U. Med. Sch., 1947-48, 51-52, 54-56, part-time instr. in medicine 1953-63, part time asst. prof. medicine 1963-70, part-time assoc. prof. medicine, 1970-94, part-time prof., 1994—; attending physician Balt. City Hosp. (now Johns Hopkins Bayview Med. Ctr.), 1954—; active staff The Union Meml. Hosp., 1959—; courtesy staff Church Home and Hosp., 1956-66. Contbr. numerous articles to profl. jours. John Harvard fellowship Harvard Med. Sch., 1945. Fellow ACP, Am. Acad. of Allergy and Immunology (pres. 1978-79, exec. com. 1973-81, other coms., Disting. Svc. award 1986, Disting. Clinician award 1994), Am. Acad. of Allergy; mem. Am. Assn. for Certified Allergists (co-chmn. allergen and immunotherapy com. 1973-77), Am. Bd. of Internal Medicine, Am. Clin. and Climatol. Assn., Am. Fedn. for Clin. Rsch., Am. Soc. of Internal Medicine, Asthma and Allergy Found. of Am. (coms.), Balt. City Med. Soc. (coms.), Joint Coun. of Allergy and Immunology (bd. dirs. 1975-84, tres. 1976-84), Md. Blue Cross and Blue Shield, Md. Found. for Health Care, Md. Soc. of Allergy (pres. 1973-74), Md. Soc. of Internal Medicine (pres. elect 1971-73, pres. 1973-75), So. Med. Assn., U.S. FDA (adv. com.), Sigma Xi. Achievements include contributions to understanding risk factors for pneumococcal pneumonia, longitudinal growth of children treated with corticosteroids, inflammatory diseases of eye, severe asthma and immunotherapy for hay fever and asthma. Home: 1902 A Indian Head Rd Baltimore MD 21204 Office: Ste 4 E 11 E Chase St Baltimore MD 21204

VAN MOL, LOUIS JOHN, JR., public relations executive; b. Knoxville, Tenn., Oct. 7, 1943; s. Louis John and Evelyn (Ramsay) Van M.; m. Deborah Ruth Boyd, Nov. 1, 1969; children: Derek, Millicent. BS, U. Tenn., 1966. Staff writer, editor AP, Knoxville and Nashville, 1963-66, 69; account exec. to exec. v.p. Holder, Kennedy & Co., Nashville, 1970-74, exec. v.p., 1978-79; dir. info. TVA, Knoxville, 1974-78; co-founder, ptnr. Dye, Van Mol & Lawrence, Nashville, 1980—; bd. dirs. Fogel & Assocs., Columbia, Tenn.; chmn. bd. Goodwill Industries Mid. Tenn., 1996—. Bd. dirs. East Tenn. Children's Hosp., Knoxville, 1977-78, Martha O'Bryan Ctr., Nashville, 1985-87, United Way Comm. Com., 1987-91, Am. Heart Assn. Mid. Tenn., Nashville, 1991-92, Leadership Nashville, 1992-93, Crime Stoppers Nashville, 1986-92, Alcohol and Drug Coun. Mid. Tenn., Nashville, 1991-93. Lt. U.S. Army, 1966-68. Decorated Bronze Star. Mem. Richland Country Club, Cumberland Club, Sigma Delta Chi. Presbyterian. Home: 712 Bowling Ave Nashville TN 37215-1049 Office: Dye Van Mol & Lawrence Pub Rels 209 7th Ave N Nashville TN 37219-1802

VAN MOLS, BRIAN, publishing executive; b. L.A., July 1, 1931; s. Pierre Matthias and Frieda Caryll (MacArthur) M.; m. Barbara Jane Rose, Oct. 1, 1953 (dec. 1968); children—Cynthia Lee, Matthew Howard, Brian; m. Nancy Joan Martell, June 11, 1977; children—Thomas Bentley, Cynthia Bentley, Kristi. A.B. in English, Miami U., Oxford, Ohio, 1953. Media supr. McCann-Erickson Inc., 1955-58; salesman Kelly Smith Co., 1959; with sales Million Market Newspaper Inc., 1959-63; sales mgr. Autoproducts Mag., 1964; sr. salesman True Mag., 1965-68, Look Mag., 1969-70; regional advt. dir. Petersen Pub. Co., Los Angeles, 1971-74; pub. Motor Trend, 1982-84; nat. automotive mktg. mgr. Playboy Enterprises, Inc., N.Y.C., 1984-85, nat. sales mgr., 1985—; western advt. dir. Playboy mag., 1985-86; assoc. pub., advt. dir. Cycle World CBS, Inc., Newport Beach, Calif., 1974-81, pub., 1981; v.p., advt. dir. Four Wheeler Mag., Canoga Pk., Calif., 1986-88; v.p., dir. advt. western div. Gen. Media, Inc., 1988-91; v.p., dir. new bus. devel. Paisano Pub., Inc., Agoura Hills, Calif., 1991-92; dir. mktg. Crown Publs., 1993-94; exec. v.p. Voice Mktg. Inc., Thousand Oaks, Calif., 1994, DMR The Reis Co., Thousand Oaks, Calif., 1995—. Served with U.S. Army, 1953-55. Mem. Los Angeles Advt. Club, Adcraft Club Detroit, Advt. Sportsmen of N.Y. Republican. Episcopalian. Home: 5 Odyssey Ct Newport Beach CA 92663

VANN, JOHN DANIEL, III, university dean, historian; b. Raleigh, N.C., July 14, 1935; s. John Daniel Jr. and Sybil Dean (Wilson) V.; m. Ellen Jane Rogers, June 21, 1969; children: John Daniel IV, Justin Fitz Patrick. BA with honors, U. N.C., 1957; MA, Yale U., 1959, PhD, 1965; M in Librarianship, Emory U., 1971; postgrad., Columbia U., 1962-63, Stanford U., 1977-78. Ordained deacon, elder Presbyn. Ch. Assoc. prof. history Campbell Coll., Buie's Creek, N.C., 1961-63; bibliographer European history and lit. Newberry Libr., Chgo., 1963-65, asst. reference librarian, 1963-65; prof. history Calif. Bapt. Coll., Riverside, 1965-66; dir. libr., prof. history Bapt. Coll. at Charleston, S.C., 1966-69; libr. Keuka Coll., Keuka Park, N.Y., 1969-71; chief libr., prof. libr., chmn. libr. dept. S.I. Community Coll. CUNY, 1971-76; prof. libr. Coll. S.I. CUNY, 1976-79; head libr. Lockwood Libr./SUNY, Buffalo, 1979-80; asst. dir. for planning, univ. librs. SUNY, Buffalo, 1980-81; exec. dir. librs. and learning resources, prof. U. Wis., Oshkosh, 1981-87; dir. libr. svcs. Bloomsburg U. Pa., 1987-89, dean libr. svcs., 1989—; resident planner, cons. on libr. bldgs. and collection devel.; bd. dirs. Coun. Wis. Librs., 1983-86, Susquehanna Libr. Coop., 1987—, sec./treas., 1993-95. Contbr. chpts. to books, articles to profl. jours. Trustee Maplewood (N.J.) Meml. Libr., 1977-79, v.p., 1979; bd. dirs. Coun. Wis. Librs., 1983-86, Midwest Rotary Multi-Dist. Short Term Internat. Youth Exch., 1987, Oshkosh (Wis.) Symphony Assn., 1986-87, United Cerebral Palsy of Winnebagoland, Oshkosh, 1986-87; active coms. Winnebago Presbytery, Presbyn. Ch., 1984-87; com. on min. Northumberland Prsbytery, Presbyn. Ch., 1992-96, com. on preparation for ministry, 1996—. Acad. Libr. Mgmt. intern Coun. on Libr. Resources Stanford U., 1977-78. Mem. ALA (com. mem.), Am. Hist. Assn., Archons of Colophon, Assn. for Libr. Collections and Tech. Svcs., Assn. Coll. and Rsch. Librs. (com. chmn., sec. chmn. 1977-78, editl. bd., bd. dirs. 1976-78), Bibliog. Soc. Am., Libr. Adminstrn. and Mgmt. Assn. (com. mem.), Libr. and Info. Tech. Assn., Medieval Acad. Am., Pa. Libr. Assn. (sect. dir.), Bloomsburg Rotary Club, Beta Phi Mu, Phi Alpha Theta. Republican. Home: 810 E 2nd St Bloomsburg PA 17815-2011 also: 1216 Rennie Ave Richmond VA 23227 Office: Bloomsburg U Pa Harvey A Andruss Libr Bloomsburg PA 17815

VANN, JOSEPH MCALPIN, nuclear engineer; b. Clinton, N.C., Dec. 30, 1937; s. Joseph Rose and Louise Myrtle (Beaver) V.; m. Edith Ausley, Apr. 1, 1961; 1 child, Natasha Vann Bottoms. BS in Math., N.C. State U., 1958; MEd in Math., U. N.C., Chapel Hill, 1961; M in Physics, East Carolina U., 1972; MS in Nuclear Engring., Va. Polytechnic Inst., 1973. Chmn. math. dept. Mt. Olive (N.C.) Coll., 1961-71; safety and licensing engr. Gen. Pub. Utility, Parsippany, N.J., 1973-76; nuclear engr. N.J. Dept. Environ. Protection, Trenton, 1976-81; sr. radiol. engr. Ebasco Co., N.Y.C., 1981-89; sr. engr. West Valley (N.Y.) Nuclear Svcs., 1990-92; emergency planner Princeton (N.J.) Plasma Physics Lab., 1992—; sr. scientist Gen. Physics Corp., Aiken, S.C., 1992. Contbr. articles to profl. jours. Mem. Am. Physical Soc., Sigma Xi, Sigma Pi Sigma, Pi Mu Epsilon. Home: 23 Hillview Ave Madison NJ 07940-1738 Office: Princeton Plasma Physics Lb Princeton NJ 08543

VAN NELSON, NICHOLAS LLOYD, business council executive; b. Milw., Feb. 28, 1942. BS, Jacksonville U., 1963, MA, 1967; MA, Am. U., Washington, 1970; postgrad., Harvard U. Kennedy Sch. Govt., 1980. Adminstrv. asst. to Congressman Charles E. Bennett Washington, 1967-74; dir. Owens Ill. Corp., Washington, 1974-77; v.p., gen. mgr. Am. Paper Inst., Washington, 1977-80; v.p. govt. Champion Internat. Corp., Washington, 1980-89; pres. U.S.-Korea Bus. Coun., 1990—; bd. dirs., mem. exec. com. Tysons Nat. Bank, 1990-92. State chmn. Fla. Jaycees, Jacksonville, 1966; scoutmaster Boy Scouts Am. Named Outstanding Civic Leader in Am., 1967; Jacksonville U. pres.'s scholar, 1961-63. Mem. Pub. Affairs Coun. (bd. dirs. 1982-85), Washington Golf and Country Club, Dem. Club, Georgetown Club. Democrat. Roman Catholic. Home: 1023 15th St NW Washington DC 20005-2602

VANNEMAN, EDGAR, JR., lawyer; b. El Paso, Ill., Aug. 24, 1919; s. Edgar and Fern (Huffington) V.; m. Shirli Thomas, Apr. 28, 1951 (dec.); children: Jill, Thomas. BS, BA, Northwestern U., 1941, J.D., 1947. Bar: Ill. 1947. Mem. firm Campbell, Clark & Miller, 1947-48; gen. atty. Chgo. and NorthWestern R.R. Co., 1949-62; gen. atty., asst. sec. Brunswick Corp., Skokie, Ill., 1962-89, ret.; sec. Sherwood Med. Industries, Inc., 1976-82. Pres. Northeastern Ill. Planning Commn., 1978-82; dir. Suburban Health Systems Agy., 1976-82; mayor City of Evanston (Ill.), 1970-77; alt. del. Republican Nat. Conv., 1952, 56. Served with USAF, 1942-46. Decorated Bronze Star. Mem. ABA, Ill. Bar Assn. (past bd. govs.), Chgo. Bar Assn., Soc. Trial Lawyers. Presbyterian. Club: Law (Chgo.). Home: 715 Monticello Pl Evanston IL 60201-1745

VAN NESS, JAMES EDWARD, electrical engineering educator; b. Omaha, June 24, 1926; s. Hubert James and Jean (Woodruff) Van N.; m. Mary Ellen Dolvin, Dec. 28, 1948; children: Rebecca Ellen, Barbara Jean, Margaret Ann, Julie Lynn. B.S., Iowa State U., 1949; M.S., Northwestern U., 1951, Ph.D., 1954. Faculty elec. engring. dept. Northwestern U., 1952—, now prof., chmn. dept., 1969-72; dir. Computer Center, 1962-65; vis. assoc. prof. U. Calif., Berkeley, 1958-59; vis. prof. MIT, 1973-74, Ariz. State U., winter 1984. Contbr. Articles to profl. jours. Served with USNR, 1944-46. Fellow IEEE; mem. AAUP. Home: 2601 Noyes St Evanston IL 60201-2170

VAN NESS, JOHN RALPH, university foundation administrator; b. Columbus, Ohio, Oct. 22, 1939; s. Ralph Taylor and Norma Gertrude (Thorp) Van N.; children: Heather Thorpe, Hilary Clark. BA, The Colo. Coll., Colo. Springs, 1965; MA, U. Pa., 1969, PhD, 1979. Instr. West Chester (Pa.) U., 1969-70, Knox Coll., Galesburg, Ill., 1970-73, Fort Lewis Coll., Durango, Colo., 1974-76; cons. fund raising pvt. practice Phila., 1977-79; capital campaign con. John F. Rich Co., Phila., 1979-84; v.p. for coll. relations, adjunct prof. Anthropology Ursinus Coll., Collegeville, Pa., 1984-89; exec. v.p., prof. Moore Coll. Art and Design, Phila., 1989-90, pres., 1990-92; pres. Mus. N.Mex. Found., Santa Fe, 1992-93, N.Mex. State U. Found., 1995—; bd. dirs. Ctr. for Land Grant Studies, Santa Fe, 1978-94; editl. bd. Jour. of the West, Manhattan, Kans., 1980-88. Co-author: Cañones: Values, Crisis and Survival in a Northern New Mexico Village, 1981; author: Hispanos in Northern New Mexico, 1991; co-editor: Spanish and Mexican Land Grants in New Mexico and Colorado, 1980, Land, Water and Culture, 1987; editor: New Mexico Land Grant Series, vols. 1-5, 1983, 84, 87, 89, 94. Recipient Teaching Fellowship U. Pa.; grantee Ford Found., Nat. Sci. Found. Mem. Am. Anthrop. Assn., Am. Assn. Museums, Coun. for Advance and Support Edn., Nat. Soc. Fund Raising Execs., Pi Gamma Mu. Democrat. Avocations: architecture, art, ballet, running, tennis.

VAN NESS, PATRICIA CATHELINE, composer, violinist; b. Seattle, June 25, 1951; d. C. Charles and Marjorie Mae (Dexter) Van N.; m. Adam Sherman, June 26, 1983. Student in music, Wheaton (Ill.) Coll., 1969-70; student, Gordon Coll., 1972. Composer: ballet score for Beth Soll, 1985, 87, 94, for Monica Levy, 1988, for Boston Ballet, 1988, 90, for Charleston Ballet Theatre, 1994; text and music for voices and early instruments with text translated into Latin for Evensong, 1991, Five Meditations, 1993, Cor Mei Cordis, 1994, Arcanae, 1995, Ego sum Custos Angels, 1995, Tu Risa, 1996, The Nine Orders of the Angels, 1996; various scores, 1985, 86, 87, 88; rec. violinist A&M Records, Private Lightning, 1996, Telarc Internat. Arcanae and Ego sum Custos Angela, 1996; composer-in-residence First Church in Cambridge (Mass.), Congregational, 1996—. Grantee Mass. Cultural Coun., 1993, 96, New Eng. Biolabs. Founds., 1989, Mass. Arts Lottery Coun., 1988; recipient Spl. Recognition award Barlow Internat. Composition for Evensong, 1993. Mem. ASCAP (Spl. award 1996), Chamber Music America, Am. Music Ctr., Alliance of Women in Music. Avocation: major league baseball.

VANNICE, M. ALBERT, chemical engineering educator, researcher; b. Broken Bow, Nebr., Jan. 11, 1943; s. Duane M. and Eugenia R. (Farmer) V.; m. Bette Ann Clark, Jan. 2, 1971. BSChemE, Mich. State Univ., 1964; MS, Stanford Univ., 1966, PhD, 1970. Engr. Dow Chemical Co., Midland, Mich., 1966, Sun Oil Co., Marcus Hook, Pa., 1970; sr. rsch. engr. Esso Rsch. & Engr. Co., Linden, N.J., 1971-76; assoc. prof. Pa. State Univ., State Coll., 1976-80, prof., 1980—, disting. prof., 1991—; M.R. Fenske prof. chem. engring., 1996—; cons. Eastman Chem. Co., Kingsport, Tenn., 1980—, DuPont Chem. Co., Wilmington, Del., 1993—; adv. bd. Adsorption Sci. & Tech., 1982-95. Mem. editorial bd. Jour. of Catalysis, 1988-94, assoc. editor, 1994—; contbr. articles to profl. jours. Recipient N.Y. Catalysis Soc. award, 1985, P.H. Emmett award, 1987, Pa.-Cleve. Catalysis Soc., 1988, Humboldt Rsch. award, 1990. Mem. AIChE (profl. Progress award 1986), Am. Chem. Soc., N.Am. Catalysis Soc. Achievements include 9 patents; effects of strong metal-support interactions on catalytic behavior; studies of CO hydrogenation, NOx reduction, catalyst characterization. Office: Pa State Univ 107 Fenske Lab University Park PA 16802-4400

VAN NIMAN, CYNTHIA MARIE, family physician, artist; b. Cin., Feb. 5, 1958; d. Kempton Charles and Colette Catherine (Ast) Van N.; m. Daniel John Wissel, July 27, 1980 (div. Oct. 1985); children: Catherine Marie, Stephanie Ann; m. David Alan Hart, May 20, 1995; 1 stepchild, Kyle Michael Hart; 1 child, Patrick Matthew. Diploma in German studies, U. Vienna, Ströbl, Austria, 1978; BA summa cum laude, Edgecliff Coll., Cin., 1980; MA in Art Therapy, Wright State U., 1983, MD, 1991. Diplomate Am. Bd. Med. Examiners, Am. Bd. Family Practice; cert. ACLS, PALS, ATR, neonatal resuscitation. Reservationist Gogo Tours, Cin., 1975-81; primary tchr. German, St. Agnes Sch., Cin., 1977-78; asst. counselor Living Arrangements for Developmentally Disabled, Cin., 1977-78; art therapist U. Cin. Med. Ctr., 1983-87, Millcreek Psychiat. Ctr. for Children, Cin., 1987; resident in family practice St. Elizabeth Med. Ctr., Dayton, Ohio, 1991-94, mem. staff, 1994-95; pvt. practice Beavercreek, Ohio, 1995—; pvt. practice Ohio Valley Family Physicians, Hillsboro, Ohio, Sabina, Ohio, 1994-95; keynote speaker Assn. for Edn. Young Children, Cin., 1987. One-woman show Emery Art Gallery, Cin., 1980. Judge Montgomery County Sci. Fair, 1988. Acad. presdl. and German studies scholar, 1976, activity scholar Edgecliff Coll., 1978, grad. scholar Wright State U., 1982, Cornaro scholar, 1990. Mem. Am. Acad. Family Practice, Ohio Med. Assn., Greene County Med. Soc., Chi Sigma Iota, Kappa Gamma Pi, Psi Chi. Roman Catholic. Avocations: choir, watercolor painting, drawing, piano. Office: Forest View Family Practice 1911 N Fairfield Rd Dayton OH 45432-2754

VAN NORMAN, WILLIS ROGER, computer systems researcher; b. Windom, Minn., June 17, 1938; s. Ralph Peter and Thelma Pearl (Bare) Van N.; m. Irene Anna Penner, Sept. 7, 1959; children: Eric Jon, Brian Mathew, Karin Ruth. AA, Worthington Jr. Coll., 1958; BS, Mankato State Coll., 1960; MS, St. Thomas U., 1991. Tchr. chemistry, St. Peter, Minn., 1961; tchr., Byron, Minn., 1962, spl. edn., Rochester, Minn., 1963-65; instr. pilots ground sch. Rochester Jr. Coll., 1968-69; with Mayo Clinic, Rochester, 1962-88 , developer biomed. computer systems, 1974—; staff analyst Analyst Internat., 1988—; instr. Gopher Aviation, 1968-71. Named Olmstead County Conservation Farmer of Yr., 1992. Treas., United Methodist Ch. Mem. Mankato State Alumni Assn. (dir.), Minn., Nat. ednl. assns., Internat. Flying Farmers (dir.), Minn Flying Farmers (v.p., pres.), Am. Radio Relay League (mgr. Minn. sect. traffic net), Rochester Amateur Radio Club (pres.). Founder, mgr. Van Norman's Flying V Ranch, 1972—, Van Norman Airport, St. Charles, 1977—. Home: 19230 26th St NE Saint Charles MN 55972-2016 Office: IBM Rochester MN 55901

VAN ORDEN, AMANDA KAY MITCHELL, insurance consultant; b. McAlester, Okla., Feb. 11, 1953; d. Fane LeRoy and Norma Evelyn (Magruder) Mitchell. BA magna cum laude, U. Utah, 1975. Registered health underwriter. V.p. Nirvana, Inc., Phoenix, 1978—. Vol. PHX Open, 1980—; vol. reader Sun Sounds, Phoenix, 1987-95; pledge dr. vol. PBS, Tempe, Ariz., 1988—; vol. Spl. Olympics, Phoenix, 1988—, Make a Wish Foundation, 1992—; co-leader Daisy coun. Girl Scouts U.S.A., 1993. Mem. Health Care Choice Coalition (membership dir. 1993, comm. chmn. 1993—), Women Life Underwriters, Greater Phoenix Assn. Health Underwriters, Greater Phoenix Assn. Life Underwriters, Jr. League of Phoenix, Christian

Bus. Women's Assn., Phoenix Art Mus., U. Utah Alumnae (founding mem.), Chi Omega (treas. 1985-92). Republican. Mem. ChristianCh. Avocations: tennis, golf, reading, travel, collecting teddy bears. Home: 10624 N 7th Pl Phoenix AZ 85020-5816 Office: Nirvana Inc 1240 E Missouri Ave Phoenix AZ 85014-2912

VAN ORDEN, PHYLLIS JEANNE, librarian, educator; b. Adrian, Mich., July 7, 1932; d. Warren Philip and Mabel A. Nancy (Russell) Van O. BS, Ea. Mich. U., 1954; AMLS, U. Mich., 1958; EdD, Wayne State U., 1970. Sch. librarian East Detroit (Mich.) Pub. Schs., 1954-57; librarian San Diego Pub. Library, 1958-60; media specialist Royal Oak (Mich.) Pub. Schs., 1960-64; librarian Oakland U., Rochester, Mich., 1964-66; instr. Wayne State U., Detroit, 1966-70; asst. prof. Rutgers U., New Brunswick, N.J., 1970-76; prof. library science Fla. State U., Tallahassee, 1977-91, assoc. dean for instrn., 1988-91; prof. libr. sci. program Wayne State U., Detroit, 1991-93; dir. Grad. Sch. of Libr. and Info. Sci. U. Wash., Seattle, 1993—. Editor: Elementary School Library Collection, 1974-77; author: Collection Program in Schools, 1995, Library Service to Children, 1992. Fla. State Libr. grantee, 1984, 86, 88; Lillian Bradshaw scholar Tex. Woman's U., 1993. Mem. Assn. Library Svc. to Children (past pres.), ALA (library resources and tech. svcs. div. Blackwell/N.Am. Scholarship award 1983), Assn. for Library and Info. Sci. Edn. (pres. 1990), Pi Lambda Theta. Avocations: music, knitting, physical fitness, cooking, travel. Office: U Wash Box 352930 133 Suzzallo Libr Seattle WA 98195-2930

VAN PATTEN, DICK VINCENT, actor; b. Kew Gardens, N.Y., Dec. 9, 1928; s. Richard Byron and Josephine (Acerno) Van P.; m. Patricia Poole, Apr. 25, 1954; children: Nels, Jimmy, Vince. Broadway debut in Tapestry in Gray, 1935; other stage appearances include Ah, Wilderness!, 1939, 40, Watch on the Rhine, 1942, The Skin of Our Teeth, 1942, Mister Roberts, 1948, 51, 53, The Tender Trap, 1955, Will Success Spoil Rock Hunter?, 1957, Don't Drink the Water, Next, 1969; films include Reg'lar Fellers, 1941, Charly, 1968, Making It, 1971, Joe Kidd, 1972, Dirty Little Billy, 1972, Snowball Express, 1972, Westworld, 1973, Soylent Green, 1973, Superdad, 1974, Freaky Friday, 1976, High Anxiety, 1977, Spaceballs, 1986, The New Adventures of Pippi Longstocking, 1988, Robin Hood: Men in Tights, 1993; radio series Young Widder Brown, 1941; also radio plays Kiss and Tell, 1947, State Fair, 1950, 53, Father of the Bride, 1951, Good Housekeeping, 1951; regular TV series Mama, 1949-58, Final Ingredient, 1959, The Partners, 1971-72, The New Dick Van Dyke Show, 1973-74, When Things Were Rotten, 1975, Eight is Enough, 1977-81, WIOU, 1990; TV spl. Grandpa Max, 1975; drama Ladies of the Corridor, 1975, A Memory of Two Mondays, 1971; TV movies Hec Ramsey, 1972, The Crooked Hearts, 1972, The Love Boat, 1976, With This Ring, 1978, Diary of a Hitchhiker, 1979, Eight is Enough: A Family Reunion, 1987, Going to the Chapel, 1988, An Eight is Enough Wedding, 1989, Jake Spanner: Private Eye, 1989. Mem. SAG, Actors Equity Assn. Office: care Artists Agy 10000 Santa Monica Blvd Ste 305 Los Angeles CA 90067*

VAN PATTEN, JAMES JEFFERS, education educator; b. North Rose, N.Y., Sept. 8, 1925; s. Earl F. and Dorothy (Jeffers) Van P.; married. BA, Syracuse U., 1949; ME, Tex. Western Coll., 1959; PhD, U. Tex., Austin, 1962. Asst. prof. philosophy and edn. Central Mo. State U., Warrensburg, 1962-64, assoc. prof., 1964-69; assoc. prof. vis. overseas U. Okla., Norman, 1969-71; prof. edn. U. Ark., Fayetteville, 1971—; visiting scholar, U. Mich., 1981, UCLA, 1987, U. Tex., Austin, 1987; vis. prof./scholar U. Fla., Gainesville, 1994. Served with inf., U.S. Army, 1944-45. Decorated Purple Heart. Mem. Am. Ednl. Studies Assn., Southern Future Soc., World Future Soc., Am. Philosophy Assn., Southwestern Philosophy of Edn. Soc. (pres. 1970), Am. Ednl. Rsch. Assn., Phi Delta Kappa (pres. chpt. U. Ark. 1976-77), NOLPE. Club: Kiwanis. Editor: Conflict, Permanency and Change in Education, 1976, Philosophy, Social Science and Education, 1989, College Teaching and Higher Education Leadership, 1990, Social-Cultural Foundations of Educational Policy in the U.S., 1991; Author: Academic Profiles In Higher Education, 1992, The Many Faces of the Culture of Higher Edn., 1993, (with John Pulliam) History of Education in America, 1995, The Culture of Higher Education: A Case Study Approach, 1996; contbr. articles to books, profl. jours.; founder Jour. of Thought. Home: 434 Hawthorne St Fayetteville AR 72701-1934

VAN PATTEN, JOYCE BENIGNIA, actress; b. Bklyn.; d. Richard Byron and Josephine (Acerno) Van P.; divorced; children: T. Casey King, Talia Balsam. Appeared in Broadway plays including Loves Old Sweet Song, 1941, Tomorrow the World, 1943, The Perfect Marriage, 1944, Wind is Ninety, 1945, Desk Set, 1956, Hole in the Head, 1957, Same Time Next Year, 1975, Murder at the Howard Johnson, 1978, The Supporting Cast, Rumors, Brighton Beach Memoirs, I Ought To Be In Pictures, Jake's Women (with daughter Talia Balsam), 1992, L.A. prodn., 1993, (off Broadway plays) Ivanov, The Seagull, All My Sons, A Fair Country; (films) Trust Me, Monkey Shines, St. Elmo's Fire, Falcon and the Snowman, Billy Galvin, Mame, Blind Date, Infinity (TV shows) The Haunted, Sirens, Under The Influence, Malice In Wonderland, First Lady of the World; (TV movie) Breathing Lessons, Jake's Women, Granpa's Funeral; (TV series) Unhappily Ever After; (short) Patricia Nixon Flying; writer (play) Donuts, (screenplay) Would You Show Us Your Legs Please?. Co-founder The Workshop Theatre West; fund raiser AIDS Project L.A., West Hollywood, 1989, 90. Mem. Am. Film Inst. Avocations: tennis, needlework, painting, writing.

VAN PELT, FRED RICHARD, lawyer; b. Joplin, Mo., June 26, 1958; s. Fred L. and Dorthy (Carlton) Van P.; m. Kay A. Willenbrink; children: Fred Ryan, Natalie Marie. BA, Pitts. State U., 1980; JD, U. Mo., 1983. Sole practice law Springfield, Mo., 1983-84; pres., shareholder Van Pelt and Van Pelt, Springfield, 1984—; pres. V.P./H. Motels Inc., Joplin, 1994—. v.p., bd. dirs. CASA of SW Mo., Springfield, 1988—; mem. Child Protection Team of DFS, Springfield, 1989-92. Fellow Am. Acad. Matrimonial Lawyers; mem. ATLA, Mo. Bar Assn., Mo. Assn. Trial Lawyers, Springfield Metro. Bar Assn. Office: U-100 1200 E Woodhurst Dr Springfield MO 65804

VAN PRAAG, ALAN, lawyer; b. Bklyn., Mar. 6, 1947; s. Leopold Marcus and Rose (Wexell) Van P.; divorced; 1 child, Melissa Rose; m. Lynne Diamond, Nov. 24, 1991. BA, Hunter Coll., 1968; JD, Bklyn. Law Sch., 1971. Bar: U.S. Dist. Ct. (ea. dist.) N.Y. 1972, U.S. Dist. Ct. (so. dist.) N.Y. 1974, U.S. Ct. Appeals (2d cir.) 1976, U.S. Ct. Appeals (3rd cir.) 1978, U.S. Ct. Appeals (4th cir.) 1980, U.S. Ct. Appeals (11th cir.) 1994. Atty. Dept. of Navy, Bklyn., 1971-74; assoc. Poles Tublin Patestides, N.Y.C., 1974-80, ptnr., 1980-88, Snow Becker Krauss P.C., 1988-93, ptnr., 1993—; dir., gen. counsel Egyptian Am. C. of C., N.Y.C., 1986-92. Contbr. articles to Bklyn. Law Rev., 1970-71, ABA Litigation Jour., 1986. Chmn. Vol. Com. Rusk Inst. Rehab., N.Y., 1976-88. Mem. Maritime Law Assn. (chmn. subcom. bankruptcy 1988—, vice chmn. com. practice and procedures 1984—, stevedoring com, 1994), ABA (mem. sect. internat. law 1974—), N.Y. Trial Lawyers Assn. Home: 355 S End Ave Apt 34L New York NY 10280-1024 Office: Snow Becker Krauss PC 605 3rd Ave New York NY 10158

VAN PRAAG, HERMAN MEIR, psychiatrist, educator, administrator; b. Schiedam, The Netherlands, Oct. 17, 1929; came to U.S., 1982; s. Marinus and Charlotte (Leverpoll) van P.; m. Cornelia Elkens, Nov. 17, 1956; children: Marinus, Gido, Charlotte, Bart. M.D., State U. Leiden, Netherlands, 1956; Ph.D., U. Utrecht, 1962. Resident Found. Advanced Clin. Teaching, Rotterdam, Netherlands, 1958-63; chief of staff dept. psychiatry Dijkzigt Hosp., Rotterdam, Netherlands, 1963-66; founder, head dept. biological psychiatry Psychiat. U. Clinic, Groningen, Netherlands, 1966-77; assoc. prof. State U. Groningen, Netherlands, 1968, prof., 1970-77; prof., head dept. psychiatry Acad. Hosp. State U. Utrecht, 1977-82; Silverman prof., chmn. dept. psychiatry Albert Einstein Coll. Medicine, Bronx, N.Y., 1982-92; chief psychiatrist Montefiore Med. Ctr., Bronx, N.Y., 1982-92; prof., head Acad. Psychiat. Ctr. U. Limburg, Maastricht, The Netherlands, 1992—; head WHO Collaborating Ctr. for Residency Tng., Utrecht, 1974; vis. prof. Hebrew U., Jerusalem, 1976-77. Editor in chief: (6 vols.) Handbook of Biological Psychiatry, 1975-81; mem. editorial bd. numerous jours.; contbr. numerous articles to profl. jours. Decorated knight, Queen Beatrix, The Netherlands, 1990; recipient Anna-Monika prize Anna-Monika Found., 1973, Cramer award Columbia U. Coll. Physicians and Surgeons, 1983, Reynier de Graaf award Dutch Soc. for Advancement Biol. and Med. Scis., 1983, Lily Ctrl. Nervous Sys. award, 1990, 1st Sylvia Best Hunter Disting. Svc. award 1991, Open Mind award Janssen Rsch. Coun., 1992, Albert Einstein award for rsch. in psychiatry and related disciplines, 1993, Lily award European Coll. Neuropsycho-Pharmacology, 1995. Mem. Royal Acad. Scis. of the Netherlands, Soc. Biol. Psychiatry, N.Y. Acad. Medicine, Psychiat. Rsch. Soc., Am. Coll. Neuropsychopharmacology, Internat. Group Study Affective Disorders, Internat. Assn. Suicide Prevention, Sierra Club. Home: Proost Willemsstraat 34, 6231CW Meerssen The Netherlands Office: Univ Limburg, PO Box 616, 6200MD Maastricht The Netherlands

VAN RAALTE, JOHN A., research and engineering management executive; b. Copenhagen, Apr. 10, 1938; came to U.S., 1955; s. John A. and Laura W.M. (Louwerier) van R.; m. Andrée Valentine Greene, Dec. 28, 1963; children: Kirsten A., James E. BSEE, MIT, 1960, MSEE, 1960, elec. engrs. degree, 1962, PhD, 1964. Rsch. asst. MIT, Cambridge, 1960-64; mem. tech. staff RCA David Sarnoff Rsch. Ctr., Princeton, N.J., 1964-70, head display rsch., 1970-79, head videodisc record and playback, 1979-83, dir. videodisc systems rsch., 1983-84, dir. display systems rsch., 1984-87; dir. materials and process tech. lab. David Sarnoff Rsch. Ctr. subs. SRI Internat., Princeton, N.J., 1987-90; mgr. CRT engring. Thomson Consumer Electronics N.Am. Tube Div., Lancaster, Pa., 1990-92; dir. electron optics lab. Thomson Tubes & Displays, Genlis, France; mem. steering com. Internat. Display Rsch. Conf., U.S., Europe, Japan, 1981-88. Author: (with others) Electronic Engineer's Reference Handbook, 4th and 5th edits. Chmn. ednl. coun. MIT, N.J., 1978-83. Fellow IEEE, Soc. for Info. Display (pres., v.p., treas., sec. 1981-88, chmn. and program chmn. Internat. Symposium 1973-78); mem. MIT Club of Princeton, Chevalier du Tastevin, Sigma Xi, Tau Beta Pi, Eta Kappa Nu (pres. Boston chpt. 1964). Home: 24 rue des Templiers, 21121 Fontaine les Dijon France Office: Thomson Tubes & Displays, Ave du Gen de Gaulle, 21110 Genlis France

VAN REENEN, JANE SMITH, speech-language pathologist; b. Baton Rouge, Sept. 16, 1949; d. William Robert and Mary Jane (Laidlaw) Smith; m. Dirk Andries van Reenen, Mar. 3, 1973; children: Andrea Lee, Erika Lynn. BS in Speech Pathology, La. State U., 1971; MEd in Speech Pathology, Ga. State U., 1984. Cert. clin. competence Am. Speech-Lang.-Hearing Assn.; lic. Ga.; cert. tchr. Ga. Speech-lang. pathologist Livingston Parish Schs., La., 1971-73, Gwinnett County (Ga.) Schs., 1973-75, 95—; pvt. practice speech-lang. pathology Norcross, Ga., 1975—; speech-lang. pathologist Nova Care, Atlanta, 1979—, Gwinnett County Schs., 1994—; grad. asst. Ga. State U., Atlanta, 1983-84, substitute clin. supr., 1988-90, interim clinic coord., 1991; speech-lang. pathologist Americana Nursing Home, Decatur, 1984; chairperson Atlanta (Ga.) Orofacial Myology Study Group, 1987-89; adv. com. Comm. Disorders Program, Atlanta, 1990-94; mem. Ga. Supervision Network, 1991—; mem. Cognitive Remediation Interest Group, Atlanta, 1993—. Mng. editor: Internat. Jour. Orofacial Myology, 1989-91; contbr. articles to profl. jours. Ruling elder Northminster Presbyn. Ch., Roswell, Ga., 1981; mem. local sch. adv. com. Pinckneyville Middle Sch., Norcross, 1987-92, co-founder sch. based drug/alchol abuse prevention program, 1988; v.p. Parent Tchr. Student Assn. Norcross High Sch., 1990-91; pres. River Valley Estates Homeowners Assn., Norcross, 1991; local sch. adv. com. Norcross High Sch., 1993—, AIDS rep. PTSA, 1993—, drug/alcohol abuse rep., 1993—, care team, 1993—. Recipient Positive Parenting awards Ga. State Supt. of Schs., Atlanta, 1987-88, 88-89; named Outstanding Sch. Vol., Gwinnet County Bd. Edn., Lawrenceville, Ga., 1989-90. Mem. Am. Speech-Lang.-Hearing Assn. (congl. action contact com. 1991—), Ga. Speech-Lang.-Hearing Assn. (honors and ethics com. 1989-91), Internat. Assn. Orofacial Myology (mng. editor 1989-91). Republican. Avocations: tennis, walking/running, yard work, cooking, working with youth. Home and Office: 3992 Gunnin Rd Norcross GA 30092-1953

VAN REES, CORNELIUS S., lawyer; b. N.Y.C., May 29, 1929; s. Cornelius Richard and Beatrice Martin (Shreve) Van R.; m. Virginia Vandewater, Mar. 15, 1953 (div. 1984); children: Pamela Millet Van Rees Lundquist, Claire Katherine; m. Alix McIvor, Jan. 2, 1985. BA, Denison U., 1951; JD, Columbia U., 1954. Bar: N.Y. 1956, U.S. Dist. Ct. (so. dist.) N.Y. 1956, Conn. 1994. Assoc. Thacher Proffitt & Wood, N.Y.C., 1956-62, ptnr., 1963-93, of counsel, 1994—; mem. exec. com., officer, bd. dirs. Graham Corp.; lectr. in field. Writer in field. Trustee, sec. Williston Northhampton Sch.; mem. senate, honors and prizes com. Columbia U. Harlem Fisk Stone scholar Columbia U., 1954. Mem. ABA (coms. on internat. fin. trans., export credits, maritime fin. and devel. in bus. fin.), Maritime Law Assn. (com. on underseas devel. and exploration), Alumni Fedn. Columbia U., Inc. (Alumni medal 1984, pres. 1979-81), N.Y. Yacht Club. Avocation: sailing. Home and Office: 35 Cove Side Ln Stonington CT 06378-2902

VAN REMMEN, ROGER, management consultant; b. Los Angeles, Sept. 30, 1950; s. Thomas J. and Elizabeth (Vincent) V.; B.S. in Bus., U. So. Calif., 1972. Account mgr. BBDO, Los Angeles, 1972-78; account mgr. Dailey & Assocs. Advt., L.A., 1978—, v.p., mgmt. supr., 1980-84, sr. v.p., 1985-90; dir. Aux. Aids Inc., Richstone Family Ctr; dir. mktg. communications, Teradata, 1990-91, ptnr. Brown, Bernardy, Van Remmen Exec. Search, L.A., 1991—. Chmn. adv. bd. El Segundo (Calif.) First Nat. Bank; bd. dirs. Advt. Emergency Relief Fund., Richstone Family Ctr. Mem. Univ. So. Calif. Alumni Assn., Advt. Club of Los Angeles. Roman Catholic. Home: 220 9th St Manhattan Beach CA 90266-5506 Office: Brown Bernardy Van Remmen 12100 Wilshire Blvd Ste 40M Los Angeles CA 90025-7120

VAN REMOORTERE, FRANCOIS PETRUS, chemical company research and development executive; b. Haasdonk, Belgium, Dec. 16, 1943; came to U.S., 1968; s. Jozef Frederik and Celine (van de Vyver) van R.; m. Jane Louise Evans; children: Kier, Pieter, David. BS in Chemistry, U. Louvain, Belgium, 1965, PhD in Phys. Chemistry, 1968. Rsch. chemist The Dow Chem. Co., Midland, Mich., 1968-74, group leader, 1974-77, rsch. mgr., 1977-79; dir. R & D planning Am. Can Co., Greenwich, Conn., 1979-83; v.p. tech. and planning W.R. Grace & Co., Columbia, Md., 1983-86, pres. rsch. div., 1986—; mem. adv. coun. Johns Hopkins U. Whiting Sch. Engring. Bd. visitors U. Md., College Park, 1988—; trustee Howard County Gen. Hosp., 1989-93, Howard County Hosp. Found., 1993-95. Mem. AAAS, Am. Chem. Soc., Coun. for Chem. Rsch., Indsl. Rsch. Inst., N.Y. Acad. Sci., Cosmos Club (Washington). Office: W R Grace & Co Rsch Divsn Washington Rsch 7500 Grace Dr Columbia MD 21044-4098

VAN RIPER, PAUL KENT, marine corps officer; b. Brownsville, Pa., July 5, 1938; s. James Frederic and Mary Katherine (Davis) Van R.; m. Lillie Catherine Alford, Jan. 27, 1968; children: Stephen Kent, Cynthia Leigh. BA in Edn., California (Pa.) State Coll., 1963. Enlisted USMCR, 1956; advanced through grades to lieut. gen. USMC, 1995, commd. 2d lt., 1963; instr. The Basic Sch., 1966-68; student Amphibious Warfare Sch., 1968; platoon comdr., co. exec. officer, asst. ops. officer 1st Bn. 8th Marines, Dominican Republic, 1965; Marine advisor Vietnamese Marine Corps, 1965-66; co. comdr., asst. ops. officer 3d bn. 7th Marines, 1st Marine Div., Vietnam, 1968-69; instr., staff officer JFK Inst. for Mil. Assistance, Ft. Bragg, N.C., 1969-71; spl. projects officer Office Chief of Staff, Hdqrs. Marine Corps, Washington, 1971-72; tng. specialist Tng. Div., Washington, 1972-74; ops. officer 3d bn. 8th Marines, Camp Lejeune, N.C., 1974-75, regt ops officer, 1975-76; exec. officer 1st bn. 8th Marines, 1976-77; student Naval War Coll., Newport, R.I., 1977-78; mil. observer U.S. Mil. Observer Group, UN Truce Supervision Orgn., Palestine, 1978-79; comdg. officer Marine Barracks, Naval Air Sta., Cecil Field, Fla., 1979-81; student Army War Coll., Carlisle, Pa., 1981-82; regtl. exec. officer 7th Marines, 1st Marine Div., Camp Pendleton, Calif., 1982-83, comdr. 2d bn., 1983-84; exercise, readiness and tng. officer I Marine Amphibious Force, Camp Pendleton, 1984-85; regtl. comdr. 4th Marines, 3d Marine Div., Okinawa, Japan, 1985-86; asst. chief of staff, then chief of staff 3d Marine Div., Okinawa, 1986-88; dir. Command and Staff Coll., Quantico, Va., 1988-89; pres. Marine Corps U., Quantico, 1989-90; dir. Marine Air-Ground Tng. and Edn. Ctr., Quantico, 1990-91; comdg. gen. 2d Marine Div., Camp LeJeuene, N.C., 1991-93; asst. chief of staff, dir. intelligence command control, comm. and computer HQMC, Washington, 1993-95; commanding general Marine Corps Combat Development Command, Quantico, 1995—. Contbr. numerous articles to profl. mil. jours. Tchr. Sunday sch. Mil. Chapels. Decorated Silver Star medal with gold star (2), Legion of Merit, Bronze Star meda with Combat V, Purple Heart, Meritorious Svc. medal, Joint Svc. Commendation medal, Army commendation medal, Navy Achievement medal, Combat Action Ribbon with gold star, Nat. Def. Svc. medal with one bronze star (2), Vietnam Svc. medal with one silver and one bronze star, others; UN medal; Gallantry Cross and Campaign medal (Republic of Vietnam); Southwest Asia Svc. meda., Kuwaiti Liberation medal. Presbyterian. Avocations: history, running, fishing. Address: USMC Quarters One MCB Quantico VA 22134

VAN RIPER, PAUL PRITCHARD, political science educator; b. Laporte, Ind., July 29, 1916; s. Paul and Margaret (Pritchard) Van R.; m. Dorothy Ann Dodd Samuelson, May 11, 1964; 1 child, Michael Scott Samuelson. A.B., DePauw U., 1938; Ph.D., U. Chgo., 1947. Instr. Northwestern U., 1947-49, asst. prof. polit. sci., 1949-51; mgmt. analyst Office Comptroller Dept. Army, 1951-52; mem. faculty Cornell U., 1952-70, prof., 1957-70; chmn. gov. bd., exec. com. Cornell Social Sci. Research Center, 1956-58; prof., head dept. polit. sci. Tex. A&M U., 1970-77, prof., 1977-81, prof. emeritus, 1981—, coordinator M.P.A. program, 1979-81; vis. prof. U. Chgo., 958, Ind. U., 1961, U. Strathclyde, Scotland, 1964, U. Mich., 1965, U. Okla., 1969—, U. Utah, 1979—. Author: History of the United States Civil Service, 1958, Some Educational and Social Aspects of Fraternity Life, 1961, (with others) The American Federal Executive, 1963, Handbook of Practical Politics, 3d edit., 1967; editor and co-author: the Wilson Influence on Public Administration, 1990. Mem. exec. com. Civil Svc. Reform Assn., N.Y., 1960-64, hist. adv. com. NASA, 1964-66; bd. dirs. Brazos Valley Cmty. Action Agy., 1975-79, Brazos County Hist. Commn., 1976—; charter mem. Brazos Heritage Soc., pres. 1977-79. Maj. AUS, 1942-46; lt. col. USAR ret. Decorated Croix de Guerre (France). Mem. Am. Polit. Sci. Assn., So. Polit. Sci. Assn., S.W. Polit. Sci. Assn. (exec.com. 1975-77), Am. Soc. Pub. Adminstrn. (nat adv. com. 1957-60, Dimock award 1984, Waldo award 1990), Internat. Personnel Mgmt. Assn., Rotary (pres. Bryan club 1991-92), Phi Beta Kappa, Beta Theta Pi (v.p. 1962, gen. sec. 1963-65), Pi Alpha Alpha, Pi Sigma Alpha, Phi Kappa Phi, Sigma Delta Chi. Republican. Baptist. Home: 713 E 30th St Bryan TX 77803-4789 Office: Tex A and M Univ Dept Polit Sci College Station TX 77843-4348

VAN ROOIJ, VINCENT A. M., university president. Pres. Bayamon (P.R.) Ctrl. U. Office: Bayamon Central U Office of President PO Box 1725 Bayamon PR 00960-1725

VAN ROOY, JEAN-PIERRE, international executive; b. Louvain, Belgium, Dec. 11, 1934; came to U.S., 1982; s. Félix C. and Betty H. (van Weelden) van R.; m. Marie Claire Duquesne, Oct. 8, 1960; children: Ann M., Eric M., Martine M. BA, Inst. Universitaire, St. Louis, Brussels, 1954; JD, Cath. U. of Louvain, 1958, M in Fin., 1960. Mng. dir. Otis Elevator Cy, Belgium, 1971-74, Italy, 1973-75; v.p. Otis Elevator Europe, Africa, Middle East, Paris, 1975-82; pres. Carrier Internat. Corp., Syracuse, N.Y., 1982-86; exec. v.p. Carrier Corp., Syracuse, 1986; sr. v.p. Otis Elevator ETO, Paris, 1987-89; pres. Otis N.Am. Ops., Farmington, Conn., 1989-90, Otis Elevator Co., Farmington, 1990—; bd. dirs. of numerous corps. worldwide. Served to lt. Belgium Navy, 1958-60. Republican. Roman Catholic. Club: Cercle Union Interalliée (Paris). Avocations: history, sailing. Office: Otis Elevator Co. 10 Farm Springs Rd Farmington CT 06032-2526

VAN RYSSELBERGE, CHARLES H., organization administrator; b. Evanston, Ill., Oct. 8, 1945; s. John F. Van Rysselberghe and Marguerite Irene (Van Witzenburg) Van Rysselberge-Yaple; m. Joan E. Roberts, June 22, 1968; children: Denise, Michelle. ABJ, U. Ga., 1968, MA, 1971, cert. in mgmt., 1977. Membership mgr. Shreveport (La.) C. of C., 1972-74, exec. v.p., 1986-88; group mgr. Chattanooga (Tenn.) C. of C., 1974-77, gen. mgr., 1979-81; exec. v.p. Monroe (La.) C. of C., 1977-79, Dalton-Whitfield (Ga.) C. of C., 1981-86, Atlanta C. of C., 1988-93; pres. Oklahoma City C. of C., 1993—. Communications mgr. Greenville (S.C.) C. of C., 1969-70. 1st lt. Signal Corps, U.S. Army, 1970-72, USAR, 1972-73. Mem. Am. C. of C. Execs. Assn., Ga. Assn. C. of C. Execs. (bd. dirs. 1983-86), So. Assn. C. of C. Execs. (bd. dirs. 1988-90), Century Club (chmn. 1984-86), Phi Kappa Tau. Mem. Reformed Ch. Am. Avocation: jogging. Home: 5017 Misty Glen Cir Oklahoma City OK 73142-5402 Office: C of C of Oklahoma City 123 Park Ave Oklahoma City OK 73102-9031

VAN SANT, GUS, JR., director, screenwriter; b. Louisville, 1952. BA in Filmmaking, RISD, 1975. Films include Mala Noche, 1985 (L.A. Film Critics award 1987), Drugstore Cowboy, 1989 (with Daniel Yost: Nat. Soc. Film Critics Best Dir. award 1990, Best Screenplay award 1990, N.Y. Film Criticcs Best Screenplay award 1990, L.A. Film Critics Best Screenplay award 1989), Internat. PEN Literary award for Screenplay Adaptation (with Daniel Yost 1989), My Own Private Idaho, 1991 (Best Screenplay 1992, Best Film 1992), Even Cowgirls Get the Blues, 1993, To Die For, 1995. Office: William Morris Agency Inc 151 S El Camino Dr Beverly Hills CA 90212-2704

VAN SANT, PETER RICHARD, news correspondent; b. Seattle, Feb. 21, 1953; s. Richard Murdock and Joy Marie Van Sant; m. children: Erik, Jeffrey, Stefani, Kristina; m. Sarma Anete Dindzans, Apr. 20, 1994. BS in Comm. cum laude, Washington State U., 1975. Reporter, anchor KMVT-TV, Twin Falls, Idaho, 1976; reporter KCRG-TV, Cedar Rapids, Iowa, 1976-77, KETV-TV, Omaha, 1977-78; anchor, reporter KOOL-TV, Phoenix, 1978-82; reporter WFAA-TV, Dallas, 1982-84; corr. CBS News, Atlanta, 1984-89, London, Eng., 1989-92, N.Y.C., 1992—. Recipient Emmy Investigative Reporting NATAS, 1987, Alfred I. Dupont award Columbia U., 1989-90. Avocations: hiking, fishing, travel. Office: CBS News/Street Stories 524 W 57th St New York NY 10019-2902

VAN SANT, ROBERT WILLIAM, manufacturing company executive; b. Iowa Falls, Aug. 19, 1938; s. Oscar and Muriel (Mullane) Van S.; m. Marilyn J. Noonan, May 31, 1981; children: William, Kathy, David, Susan, Jeffrey. BSMechE, U. Iowa, 1966, MSMechE, 1967. With Deere & Co., 1957-83; gen. mgr. Waterloo, Iowa, 1975-80; dir. Moline, Ill., 1980-81; v.p. Deere & Co., Moline, Ill., 1981-83; pres. Cessna Aircraft Co., Wichita, Kans., 1983-87, also bd. dirs.; pres., CEO Blount, Inc., Montgomery, Ala., 1987-91, also bd. dirs.; chmn. Lukens Steel Co., Coatsville, Pa., 1991—, also bd. dirs.; bd. dirs. NAM, Lukens Inc., Blount, Inc. Trustee Mfrs.'s Alliance for Productivity Innovation. Home: 1288 Farm Rd Berwyn PA 19312-2000*

VAN SCHAACK, ERIC, art historian, educator; b. Evanston, Ill., June 10, 1931; s. Cornelius Peter and Sigrid (Schold) Van S.; m. Carol Fryling, June 16, 1965; children—Elizabeth M., Leslie A. A.B., Dartmouth Coll., 1953; Ph.D., Columbia U., 1969. Lectr., rsch. asst. The Frick Collection, N.Y.C., 1960-62; asst. prof. fine arts, then full prof. visual arts Goucher Coll., Balt., 1964-77; prof. art and art history Colgate U., Hamilton, N.Y., 1977—, chmn. dept. art and art history, 1978-83; vis. prof. fine arts Md. Inst. Coll. Art Johns Hopkins U., Balt. Author: Master Drawings in Private Collections, 1962, Baroque Art in Italy, 1964; contbr. articles to profl. jours., encys. Served with U.S. Army, 1954-56. Grantee Fulbright/Italian Govt., 1962-63, Ford Found., 1972-73, Colgate U. faculty, 1979-80, 92-93, others. Mem. Coll. Art Assn., Am. Soc. Archtl. Historians, Nat. Trust Hist. Preservation. Club: Hamilton. Home: 28 W Pleasant St Hamilton NY 13346-1216 Office: Colgate U Dept Art & Art History Hamilton NY 13346-1398

VAN SCHOONENBERG, ROBERT G., corporate lawyer; b. Madison, Wis., Aug. 18, 1946; s. John W. and Ione (Henning) Schoonenberg. BA, Marquette U., 1968; MBA, U. Wis., 1972; JD, U. Mich., 1974. Bar: Calif. 1975, Fla. 1976. Atty. Gulf Oil Corp., Pitts., 1974-81; sr. v.p., gen. counsel, sec. Avery Dennison Corp., Pasadena, Calif., 1981—; judge pro tem Pasadena Mcpl. Ct., 1987-89. Dir., v.p. fin. adminstrn. Am. Cancer Soc., San Gabriel Vally Unit, 1987—; v.p., treas., dir., v.p. investments Pasadena Symphony Assn.; bd. dirs. Pasadena Recreation and Parks Found., 1983-84; mem. Pasadena Citizens Task Force on Crime Control, 1983-84. With U.S. Army, 1969-71. Mem. ABA, Am. Corp. Counsel Assn. (bd. dirs.), Am. Soc. Corp. Secs. (bd. dirs., pres. Southern Calif. chpt.), L.A. County Bar Assn. (past chair, corp. law dept. sect.), Corp. Counsel Inst. (bd. govs.), Jonathon Club, Flint Canyon Tennis Club, Pasadena Athletic Club, Wis. Union. Clubs: Athletic (Pasadena); Wis. Union. Office: Avery-Dennison Corp 150 N Orange Grove Blvd Pasadena CA 91103-3534

VANSELL, SHARON LEE, nursing administrator, nursing educator, researcher, obstetrical and psychiatric clinical nurse; b. Indpls., Feb. 7, 1944; d. Leo Roland and Mimadel (Klipsch) VanSell; m. Thomas Wayne Davidson, Apr. 10, 1967 (div. Nov. 1978); 1 child, Daniel Zane; m. Glenn

William Meintz, Mar. 17, 1982 (div. Mar. 1995). BSN, Murray State U., 1968; MEd in Health Edn., Memphis State U., 1971; MS in Nursing Administrn., U. Colo., 1985; EdD in Guidance Counseling, U. Denver, 1986. Sr. rsch. assoc. Planning and Human Systems, Inc., Washington, 1975-77; ob-gyn coord. Meml. Hosp., Colorado Springs, Colo., 1978-79; indsl. nurse Ramport Industries, Colorado Springs, 1979-80; psychiat. nurse N.E.E.D. Jr./Sr. High Sch., Colorado Springs, 1980-84; dir. rsch. Ireland Corp., Englewood, Colo., 1984; staff nurse perinatal float pool Univ. Hosp., Denver, 1985; dir. reproductive and pediatric nursing, asst. dir. patient care svcs. U. Calif. Med. Ctr., San Diego, 1986-90; relief charge nurse Charter Hosp., Las Vegas, 1990-94; assoc. prof. U. Nev., Las Vegas, 1990—; relief charge nurse Manti Vista Hosp., 1994-95; maternal child nurse Sunrise Med. Ctr., 1995—; nursing cons. Comprehensive Health Care Devel., Inc., Fairfax, 1974—, Bur. Quality Assurance and Profl. Svcs. Revises Orgn., DHEW, Rockville, Md., 1972-75; pres., ceo C.P.E., Colorado Springs, 1977-80; founder NURMETRICS and computational nursing, 1990—; pres. Omega Techs., Inc., Las Vegas, 1995—. Editor: PSRO: Utilization and Adult, 1976, Alcoholism and Health, 1980; sr. author: Nursing Care Evaluation: Concurrent and Retrospective, 1977, Obstetrical Nursing, 1980; co-author: PSRR: The Promise Perspective, 1981; mem. editl. bd. RN, Family and Cmty. Health Jour.; contbr. articles to profl. jours. 1dst lt. U.S. Army Nurse Corps, 1966-69. U. Colo. Gannett scholar for excellence in nursing, 1985-86; recipient March of Dimes So. Nev. Nurse of the Yr. award in Edn., 1992, Disting. Women of Nev. award, 1995, Future Vision Sci. award, 1995. Mem. Nev. Nurses Assn., Western Inst. Nursing (nominating com. 1988-90), Phi Kappa Delta, Sigma Theta Tau. Avocations: needlepoint, traveling. Home: 3678 Crest View Dr Las Vegas NV 89120-1202 Office: U Nev BHS 435 4505 S Maryland Pky Las Vegas NV 89154

VANSELOW, NEAL ARTHUR, university administrator, physician; b. Milw., Mar. 18, 1932; s. Arthur Frederick and Mildred (Hoffmann) V.; m. Mary Ellen McKenzie, June 20, 1958; children: Julie Ann, Richard Arthur. AB, U. Mich., 1954, MD, 1958, MS, 1963. Diplomate: Am. Bd. Internal Medicine, Am. Bd. Allergy and Immunology. Intern Mpls. Gen. Hosp., 1958-59; resident Univ. Hosp., Ann Arbor, Mich., 1959-63; instr. medicine U. Mich., 1963-64, asst. prof., 1964-68, assoc. prof., 1968-72, prof., chmn. dept. postgrad. medicine and health professions edn., 1972-74; dean Coll. Medicine U. Ariz., Tucson, 1974-77; chancellor med. ctr. U. Nebr., Omaha, 1977-82, v.p., 1977-82; v.p. health scis. U. Minn., 1982-89, prof. internal medicine, 1982-89; chancellor Tulane U. Med. Ctr., New Orleans, 1989-94; prof. internal medicine, adj. prof. health sys. mgmt. Tulane U., New Orleans, 1989—; chmn. Joint Bd. Osteo. and Med. Examiners Ariz., 1974-77; chmn. coun. on Grad. Med. Edn., Dept. Health and Human Svcs., 1986-91; mem. com. on educating dentists for future Inst. Medicine, NAS, 1993-95, chairperson com. on future of primary care, 1994-96, co-chairperson com. on the U.S. physician supply, 1995-96, scholar in residence, 1994-95. Bd. dirs. Devel. Authority for Tucson's Economy, 1975-77, Minn. Coalition for Health Care Costs, 1983-87, La. Health Care Authority, 1989-90, United Way Greater New Orleans Area, 1992—; mem. exec. com. United Way Midlands, 1980-82, vice chmn. 1981 campaign; bd. dirs., mem. exec. com. Health Planning Coun. Midlands, Omaha, 1978-82, v.p., 1981-82; bd. dirs. Minn. High Tech. Coun., 1983-86; mem. commn. on Health Professions Pew Charitable Trusts, 1990-92; mem. Gov.'s Pan Am. Commn., La., 1991-92; mem. mktg. mgmt. governing coun. U. Hosp. Consortium, 1993-95. Fellow ACP, Am. Acad. Allergy, Am. Coll. Physician Execs.; mem. Assn. Acad. Health Ctrs. (bd. dirs. 1983-89, chmn. bd. dirs. 1988), Soc. Med. Adminstrs., Phi Beta Kappa, Sigma Xi, Alpha Omega Alpha, Beta Theta Pi, Nu Sigma Nu. Home: 1828 Palmer Ave New Orleans LA 70118-6216 Office: Tulane U 1430 Tulane Ave New Orleans LA 70112-2699

VAN SETERS, JOHN, biblical literature educator; b. Hamilton, Ont., Can., May 2, 1935; s. Hugo and Anne (Hubert) Van S.; m. Elizabeth Marie Malmberg, June 11, 1960; children: Peter John, Deborah Elizabeth. B.A., U. Toronto, 1958; M.A., Yale U., 1959, Ph.D., 1965; B.D., Princeton Theol. Sem., 1962. Asst. prof. dept. Near Eastern studies Waterloo Luth. U., 1965-67; asso. prof. Old Testament Andover Newton Theol. Sch., 1967-70; asso. prof. dept. Near Eastern studies U. Toronto, 1970-76, prof., 1976-77; James A. Gray prof. Bibl. lit., dept. religion U. N.C., Chapel Hill, 1977—; chmn. dept. religious studies U. N.C., 1980-88, 93-95. Author: The Hyksos: A New Investigation, 1966, Abraham in History and Tradition, 1975, In Search of History, 1983, Der Jahwist als Historiker, 1987, Prologue to History, 1992, The Life of Moses, 1994. Recipient James Henry Breasted prize Am. Hist. Assn., 1985, Book award Am. Acad. Religion, 1986; Woodrow Wilson fellow, 1958; J.J. Obermann fellow, 1962-64; Guggenheim fellow, 1979-80; NEH fellow, 1985-86, Am. Coun. Learned Socs. fellow, 1991-92. Mem. AAUP, Soc. Bibl. Lit., Am. Schs. Oriental Rsch., Soc. Study of Egyptian Antiquities, Am. Oriental Soc., Soc. for Old Testament Study, Cath. Bibl. Assn. Home: 104 Mullin Ct Chapel Hill NC 27514-2646 Office: U NC 101 Saunders Hall CB # 3225 Chapel Hill NC 27599

VAN SICKLE, BRUCE MARION, federal judge; b. Minot, N.D., Feb. 13, 1917; s. Guy Robin and Hilda Alice (Rosenquist) Van S.; m. Dorothy Alfreda Hermann, May 26, 1943; children: Susan Van Sickle Cooper, John Allan, Craig Bruce, David Max. BSL, U. Minn., 1941, JD, 1941. Bar: Minn. 1941, N.D. 1946. Pvt. practice law, Minot, 1947-71; judge U.S. Dist. Ct. N.D., 1971-85, sr. judge, 1985—; mem. N.D. Ho. of Reps., 1957, 59. Served with USMCR, 1941-46. Mem. ABA, N.D. Bar Assn., N.W. Bar Assn., Ward County Bar Assn., Am. Trial Lawyers Assn., Am. Coll. Probate Counsel, Am. Judicature Soc., Bruce M. Van Sickle Inns of Ct., Masons, Shriners, Elks. Office: US Dist Ct 430 US Courthouse PO Box 670 Bismarck ND 58502-0670

VAN SICKLE, FREDERICK L., federal judge; b. 1943; m. Jane Bloomquist. BS, U. Wis., 1965; JD, U. Wash., 1968. Ptnr. Clark & Van Sickle, 1970-75; prosecuting atty. Douglas County, Waterville, Wash., 1971-75; judge State of Wash. Superior Ct., Grant and Douglas counties, 1975-79, Chelan and Douglas Counties, 1979-91; judge U.S. Dist. Ct. (ea. dist.) Wash., Spokane, 1991—; co-chair rural ct. com. Nat. Conf. State Trial Judges, 1987-91. 1st lt. U.S. Army, 1968-70. Mem. ABA (nat. conf. state trial judges jud. adminstrn.), Am. Adjudicature Soc., Wash. State Bar Assn., Masons (pres. badget mountain lodge 1982-83), Scottish Rite, Spokane Rotary. Office: US Dist Cts US Courthouse 920 W Riverside Ave Rm 914 Spokane WA 99201-1008

VAN SICKLE, PAUL BRUNTON, financial executive; b. Toronto, Ont., Can., Sept. 17, 1939; came to U.S., 1967; s. Percy Orton Van Sickle and Audrey Winefred (Dandie) Palmquist; m. Christine Cornfoot, Sept. 9, 1967 (div. July 1985); children: Giles, Kirsten; m. Jeanne Marie Wetta, May 6, 1989; children: Matthew, Lauren. Grad. advanced mgmt. program, Harvard U., 1986. Canadian chartered acct. V.p. Fin. Rexcel, Ludlow, Mass., 1973-76, Specialty Products Sector, LaGrange, Ga., 1976-77; v.p. Thompson Industries, Phoenix, 1977-79, exec. v.p., 1979-81; controller Home & comml. Products Group, Northbrook, Ill., 1981-82, Duracell, Inc., Danbury, Conn., 1982-83; sr. v.p. fin. Hobart Corp., Troy, Ohio, 1983-85; v.p., controller Dart & Kraft, Inc., Northbrook, Ill., 1986; v.p., controller Premark Internat., Deerfield, Ill., 1986-88, v.p. control and info. systems, 1988-89; v.p., chief fin. officer Tupperware, Orlando, Fla., 1989—. Avocations: golf, skiing, sailing. Office: Tupperware PO Box 2353 Orlando FL 32802

VANSINA, JAN MARIA JOZEF, historian, educator; b. Antwerp, Belgium, Sept. 14, 1929; came to the U.S., 1960; s. Dirk and Suzanne (Verellen) V.; m. Claudine Marie-Jeanne Herman, Mar. 26, 1933; 1 child, Bruno. PhD, Katolieke U. Leuven, 1957. Rsch. fellow Inst. for Scientific Rsch. Ctrl. Africa, 1952-60; prof. history and anthropology U. Wis., 1960—, Vilas rsch. prof., 1976—; J.D. MacArthur prof., 1987-93; prof. emeritus U. Wis., 1994—; prof. anthropology U. Leuven, 1973-75; vis. prof. numerous univs., 1963—. Author 19 books, including Paths in the Rainforest Towards a History of Political Tradition in Equatorial Africa, 1990, Living with Africa, 1994; mem. editl. bb. 14 jours. in African studies; contbr. articles to profl. jours. Sgt. Belgian Army, 1954-56. Recipient Herskovits prize in African studies, 1967, Belgian Nat. prize in history, 1967, A. Von Humboldt prize, 1983; Guggenheim grantee, 1980. Mem. U.S. Acad. Arts and Scis., UNESCO Com. Gen. History Africa, Belgian Acad. Overseas, Brit. Acad. Avocations: oral history, oral tradition, African history, anthropology, African art history. Home: 2810 Ridge Rd Madison WI 53705-5224

VAN SINDEREN, ALFRED WHITE, former telephone company executive; b. Bklyn., June 20, 1924; s. Adrian and Jean (White) Van S.; m. Suzanne Petersen, Apr. 21, 1962; children: Alexander, David Cabot, Sylvia Van Sinderen Abbate, Jean Van Sinderen Vashaw, Katherine Van Sinderen Tucker. B.A., Yale U., 1945; M.B.A., Harvard U., 1947. With So. New Eng. Telephone Co., New Haven, 1947-85; v.p. So. New Eng. Telephone Co. (No. area), Hartford, Conn., 1962-65; v.p. ops. So. New Eng. Telephone Co., 1965-67, pres., 1967-82, chmn., chief exec. officer, 1982-84, chmn. bd., 1984-85; William H. Donaldson disting. faculty fellow Yale U. Sch. Mgmt., 1985-89. Past mem. adv. bd. Yale-U.S. Sch. Orgn. and Mgmt.; mem. Yale Libr. Assocs.; past co-chmn. Gov. Conf. Human Rights, 1967; past bd. dirs. Conn. Econ. Devel. Corp., Hartford; bd. dirs., past chmn. Shirley Frank Found.; pres Found. for New Haven Green, Inc., 1986-91. With USNR, 1943-46. Recipient Charter Oak Leadership medal Hartford, 1965; Conn. Man of Yr. New Eng. Council, 1976; Human Relations award NCCJ, 1981. Mem. Quinnipiack Club (New Haven). Home: 12 Highview Dr Woodbridge CT 06525-1934

VAN SLYKE, ANDREW JAMES, professional baseball player; b. Utica, N.Y., Dec. 21, 1960; m. Lauri Van Slyke; children: Andrew, Jr., Scott, Jared. With St. Louis Cardinals, 1979-87; formerly with Pitts. Pirates, Balt. Orioles; now with Phila. Phillies; mem. Nat. League All-Star Team, 1988, 1992; Sporting News All-Star team, 1988, 92; recipient Gold Glove award, 1988-92, Silver Slugger award, 1988, 92, Sporting News Nat. League Player of the Yr. award, 1988. Office: Phila Phillies PO Box 7575 Philadelphia PA 19101

VAN STAVOREN, WILLIAM DAVID, management consultant, retired government official; b. Lunenburg, Va., Mar. 14, 1936; s. James Eugene and Marion Estelle (Boyer) Van S.; m. Rosa Kouyoundjian, Dec. 29, 1962; children: John, Christopher, Diane. B.S., Va. Poly. Inst., 1960, M.S., 1966. Budget analyst U.S. Treasury Dept., Washington, 1963-68; fin. mgr. AID, Washington, 1968-69; fin. mgr. U.S. Dept. Justice, Washington, 1969-74, dep. asst. atty. gen., 1977-84, dep. assoc. atty. gen., 1984-85; mgmt. cons., 1985—; mgmt. advisor Va. Commn. on State Govt. Mgmt., Richmond, 1974-76. Served with U.S. Army, 1954-56. Methodist. Office: 2526 E Meredith Dr Vienna VA 22181-4038

VANSTROM, MARILYN JUNE, retired elementary education educator; b. Mpls., June 10, 1924; d. Harry Clifford and Myrtle Agnes (Hagland) Christensen; m. Reginald Earl Vanstrom, Mar. 20, 1948; children: Gary Alan, Kathryn June Vanstrom Marinello. AA, U. Minn., 1943, BS, 1946. Cert. elem. tchr., N.Y., Ill. Tchr. Pub. Sch., St. Louis Park, Minn., 1946-47, Deephaven, Minn., 1947-50, Chicago Heights, Ill., 1950-52, Steger, Ill., 1964; substitute tchr. Pub. Sch., Dobbs Ferry, N.Y., 1965-72, Yonkers, N.Y., 1965-92. Mem. Ch. Women, Christ Meml. Luth. Ch. Named to Nat. Women's Hall of Fame, 1995-96. Mem. AAUW (life, pres. 1988-90, Ednl. Found. award 1990, Morning Book Club, Evening Book Club Met. West br.), Yonkers Fedn. Tchrs. Democrat. Avocations: painting, sketching, choir, piano, travel. Home: 12300 Marion Ln W Apt 2105 Minnetonka MN 55305-1317

VAN TAMELEN, EUGENE EARLE, chemist, educator; b. Zeeland, Mich., July 20, 1925; s. Gerrit and Henrietta (Vanden Bosch) van T.; m. Mary Ruth Houtman, June 16, 1951; children: Jane Elizabeth, Carey Catherine, Peter Gerrit. A.B., Hope Coll., 1947, D.Sc., 1970; M.S., Harvard, 1949, Ph.D., 1950; D.Sc., Bucknell U., 1970. Instr. U. Wis., 1950-52, from asst. to assoc. prof., 1952-59, prof., 1959-61, Homer Adkins prof. chemistry, 1961-62; prof. chemistry Stanford, 1962-87, prof. emeritus chemistry, 1987—, chmn. dept., 1974-78; Am.-Swiss Found. lectr., 1964. Mem. editorial adv. bd.: Chem. and Engring. News, 1968-70, Synthesis, 1969-91, Accounts of Chem. Research, 1970-73; editor: Bioorganic Chemistry, 1971-82. Recipient A.T. Godfrey award, 1947; G. Haight traveling fellow, 1957; Guggenheim fellow, 1965, 73; Leo Hendrik Baekeland award, 1965; Prof. Extraordinarius Netherlands, 1967-73. Mem. NAS, Am. Chem. Soc. (Pure Chemistry award 1961, Creative Work in Synthetic Organic Chemistry award 1970), Am. Acad. Arts and Scis., English-Speaking Union (patron 1990—), Rolls Royce Owners Club, Churchill Club (bd. dirs. 1990-92, vice chmn. 1991-92), Los Altos Tomorrow (bd. dirs. 1991—). Home: 23570 Camino Hermoso Los Altos CA 94024 also: Moorings, Box 101, Castries Castries/Saint Lucia West Indies

VAN TASSEL-BASKA, JOYCE LENORE, education educator; b. Toledo, July 28, 1944; d. Robert Rae and Eleanor Jane (Kenyon) Sloan; m. Thomas Harold Van Tassel, May 21, 1964 (div. 1975); m. Leland Karl Baska, July 25, 1980; 1 child, Ariel Sloan. BEd cum laude, U. Toledo, 1966, MA, MEd, 1969, EdD, 1981. Tchr. Toledo Pub. Schs., 1965-72, coord. gifted programs, 1973-76; dir. gifted program Ill. State Bd. Edn., Springfield, 1976-79; dir., area svc. ctr. Matteson (Ill.) Sch. Dist., 1979-82; dir. Ctr. for Talent Devel. Northwestern U., Evanston, Ill., 1982-87; Smith prof. edn. Coll. William and Mary, Williamsburg, Va., 1987—; dir. Ctr. for Gifted Edn. Coll. William and Mary, Williamsburg, 1988—; mem. Va. Adv. Bd. on Gifted and Talented, 1988—; mem. State Ohio Adv. Bd. Gifted and Talented, 1975-76; mem. edn. coun. Nat. Bus. Consortium, 1981-84. Mem. editorial bd. Roeper Rev., 1980-82; pub. Talent Devel. Quar., 1983-87; manuscript rev. editor Jour. Edn. of Gifted, 1981—; mem. editorial adv. bd. Critical Issues in Gifted Edn. series; mem. editorial bd. Gifted Child Quar., 1984—, Jour. Advanced Devel.; column editor Understanding the Gifted Newsletter author 8 books; contbr. chpts. and over 200 articles to profl. jours. Bd. trustees Lourdes High Sch., Chgo., 1985-86. Recipient Outstanding Faculty award State Coun. Higher Edn. Va., 1993; grantee U.S. Office Edn., 1977-78, 78-79, 89—, Ill. State Bd. Edn., 1979-82, 84-91, Richardson Found., 1986, 89, Fry Found., 1987-90, Va. State Coun. Higher Edn., 1987-89, 90-91, 93-95, Bur. Indian Affairs, 1989, Hughes Found., 1989-94, Va. State Libr., 1989-90, Va. State Dept. Edn., 1990-93, 93-95, Funding Agy. U.S. Dept. Edn., 1989—, 90-93, 93-95; eminent scholar Coll. William and Mary, 1987—, Nat. Ednl. policy fellow U.S. Office Edn., 1979-80, Paul Witty fellow in gifted edn., 1979, Outstanding Rsch. Paper award Mensa, 1995. Mem. ASCD, Nat. Assn. Gifted Children (bd. dirs. 1984-90), Coun. Exceptional Children, Assn. for Gifted (pres. 1980-81), World Coun. on Gifted, Am. Ednl. Rsch. Assn., Phi Beta Kappa, Phi Delta Kappa (pres. Northwestern chpt. 1986-87). Avocations: photography, tennis, writing. Home: 225 Richard Burbydge Williamsburg VA 23185-5115 Office: Coll William and Mary Jones Hall Williamsburg VA 23185

VAN'T HOF, WILLIAM KEITH, lawyer; b. N.Y.C., Feb. 18, 1930; s. William and Nell (DeValois) Van't H.; m. Barbara Marie Rogers, Oct. 6, 1961; children: Sarah Lynn, David Edward. BA, Hope Coll., 1951; LLB, U. Mich., 1954. Bar: Mich. 1954, Conn. 1955, U.S. Dist. Ct. (we. dist.) Mich. 1956, U.S. Ct. Appeals (6th cir.) 1956. Assoc. Gumbart, Corbin, Tyler & Cooper, New Haven, 1954-56; ptnr. McCobb, Heaney & Van't Hof, Grand Rapids, Mich., 1959-72, Schmidt, Howlett, Van't Hof, Smell & Vana, Grand Rapids, 1972-82, Varnum, Riddering, Schmidt & Howlett, Grand Rapids, 1983—; mem. faculty Inst. Continuing Legal Edn., Ann Arbor, Mich., 1974—. Chmn. Mich. Heart Assn., 1973-75; pres. United Way Kent County, 1979-80, hon. life mem., 1986—; chmn. Am. Heart Assn., Dallas, 1989-90. Mem. ABA, State Bar Mich. (grievance and arbitration panel 1970-91, 94—, chmn. com. on coops. and condos. 1982-86), Grand Rapids Bar Assn. (trustee 1965-67), West Mich. Hort. Soc. (pres. 1992-93), Cascade Hills Country Club, Univ. Club. Home: 3160 Hall St SE Grand Rapids MI 49506-3171 Office: Varnum Riddering Schmidt & Howlett 333 Bridge St NW Grand Rapids MI 49504-5356

VAN'T HOFF, WINFRIED C. J., retired diversified manufacturing executive; b. The Hague, The Netherlands, Feb. 20, 1928; s. Johannes Adrianus Wilhelmus and Anna Frieda (Naegelin) van't H.; m. Maria Jonanna Jacoba Popma, June 28, 1957; children: Ingeborg, Annelies, Caroline. BA in Bus. Law, U. Amsterdam, 1949, M of Law, 1952. Mktg. mgr. Philips Internat. B.V., Eindhoven, The Netherlands, 1955-60; mktg. mgr. Philips Chile, Santiago, 1960-62, pres., 1962-66; pres. Philips India, Bombay, 1966-70, Philips Internat. B.V., Eindhoven, 1970-83, Philips Norden AB, Stockholm, 1983-86; exec. v.p. N.Am. Philips Corp., N.Y.C., 1986-89, ret., 1989. Avocations: golf, sailing.

VAN TIL, WILLIAM, education educator, writer; b. Corona, N.Y., Jan. 8, 1911; s. William Joseph and Florence Alberta (MacLean) Van T.; m. Beatrice Barbara Blaha, Aug. 24, 1935; children: Jon, Barbara, Roy. B.A., Columbia, 1933; M.A., Tchrs. Coll., 1935; Ph.D., Ohio State U., 1946. Tchr. N.Y. State Tng. Sch. for Boys, 1933-34; instr. dept. univ. schs. Coll. Edn., Ohio State U., 1934-36, asst. prof., 1936-43, on leave, 1943-45; researchist, writer Consumer Edn. Study NEA, 1943-44; dir. learning materials Bur. Intercultural Edn., 1944-47; prof. edn. U. Ill., 1947-51; prof. edn., chmn. div. curriculum and teaching George Peabody Coll. Tchrs., Nashville, 1951-57; prof. edn., chmn. dept. secondary edn. N.Y. U., 1957-66, head div. secondary and higher edn., 1966-67; Coffman disting. prof. edn. Ind. State U., Terre Haute, 1967-77, prof. emeritus, 1977; dir. univ. workshops Writing for Profl. Publs., 1978—; founder Lake Lure Press, 1983. Author: The Danube Flows Through Fascism, Economic Roads for American Democracy, The Making of a Modern Educator, Modern Education for the Junior High School Years, The Year 2000: Teacher Education, One Way of Looking At It, Education: A Beginning, Another Way of Looking At It, Van Til on Education, Secondary Education: School and Community, Writing for Professinal Publication, rev., 1986; autobiography My Way of Looking At It, 1983; Sketches, 1989; editor: Forces Affecting American Education, Curriculum: Quest for Relevance, ASCD in Retrospect, 1986; co-editor: Democratic Human Relations, Intercultural Attitudes in the Making, Education in American Life; adv. editor Houghton Mifflin, 1964-70; interviewed in Social Education, 1989; contbr. to numerous other publs. including Saturday Rev., Woman's Day, Parents; author articles, reviews and editorials; columnist: Ednl. Leadership, Contemporary Edn., Kappan; adv. bd. Profl. Educator, 1984-95. Mem. Ill. Interracial Commn., 1949-51; moderator Nashville Sch. desegregation meetings, 1955-57; mem. adv. bd. Jour. Tchr. Edn., 1956-59; co-organizer Nashville Community Rels. Conf., 1956; cons. Phelps-Stokes Fund project, 1958-62; mem. staff P.R. Edn. Survey, 1958-59, Iran Tchr. Edn. Survey, 1962, V.I. Edn. Survey, 1964; lectr. abroad, 1974; mem. staff U. Ind. Phi Delta Kappa Inst., 1984-90; 1st Ann. Van Til lectr. Ind. State U., 1989. Recipient Centennial Achievement award, Ohio State U., 1970; awards N.J. Collegiate Press Assn., 1962; N.J. Assn. Tchrs. English, 1962; inducted into Edn. Hall of Fame, Ohio State U., 1989; Annual Van Til Lectr. Series, Ind. State U., est. 1989, est. Annual Van Til Writing award, 1989. Mem. John Dewey Soc. (v.p. 1957-60, acting pres. 1958-59, pres. 1964-66, award 1977, 86, Outstanding Achievement award 1991), Assn. Supervision and Curriculum Devel. (dir. 1951-54, 57-60, pres. 1961-62, chmn. rev. council 1972-73, resolutions com. 1982-85), United Educators (chmn. bd. educators 1969-77), Nat. Soc. Coll. Tchrs. Edn. (pres. 1967-68), Am. Edn. Studies Assn. (editorial bd. 1970-77), Asso. Orgn. Tchr. Edn. (adv. council 1967-73, chmn. issues tchr. edn. 1972-73), Nat. Soc. Study Edn. (editor Yearbook Issues in Secondary Edn. 1976), Kappa Delta Pi (laureate 1980—, chmn. book-of-yr. com. 1984-86). Home: 10200 E Spence Ave Terre Haute IN 47803-9712 Office: Ind State U IN State U Terre Haute IN 47809 *As an educator and writer, I believe that mankind's best hope is education which meets individual needs, illuminates social realities, fosters democratic values and utilizes relevant knowledge.*

VAN TILBURG, JOHANNES, architectural firm executive. Student, Coll. Arts and Architecture. Founder Johannes Van Tilburg & Ptnrs., Architects, Inc., 1971—; with Van Tilburg, Banvard & Soderbergh, Santa Monica, 1995—. Prin. works include Seacliff on the Greens, La Florentine, Renaissance La Jolla, San Diego Design Ctr., The 1993 New Am. Home for Nat. Assn. Home Builders, Crossroads Condominiums (Project of Yr. Nat. Assn. Home Builders and Bulder Mag. 1990), Venice Renaissance (Citation AIA 1991), Janss Ct., Santa Monica. Fellow AIA. Office: Van Tilburg Banvard & Soderbergh 225 Arizona Ave Santa Monica CA 90401-1203

VAN TOL, WILLIAM, religious organization administrator. Dir. Christian Ref. World Missions. Office: Christian Ref Ch in N Am 2850 Kalamazoo Ave SE Grand Rapids MI 49560-0200

VAN TREESE, JAMES BRYAN, book publishing and investment company executive; b. Dallaas, Dec. 23, 1946; s. James Braswell and Vivian Pauline (Bowdon) Van T.; m. Lynne Irma Erekson, Apr. 9, 1970; children: Jason Bryan, Annillicia, Madison Lynne. Sales mgr. Globe Life Ins. Co., Oklahoma City, 1972-74; owner, mgr. Van Treese Fin. Corp., Dallas, 1974-81, Rockwell One Inc., Dallas, 1979—, N.W. Pub. Inc., Salt Lake City, 1984—; designer, editor, pub. over 400 books, 1984—. Republican. Baptist. Office: Northwest Publishing 6906 Cottonwood St Midvale UT 84047-1049 Office: Northwest Pub Inc PO Box 57890 Salt Lake City UT 84157-0890

VAN TUYL, CECIL L., investment company executive. Chmn., pres., CEO VT Inc., Merriam, Kans. Office: V T Inc PO Box 795 Shawnee Mission KS 66201*

VAN TUYLE, GREGORY JAY, nuclear engineer; b. Chgo., Feb. 19, 1953; s. Willard D. and Mary E. (Kershner) Van T.; m. Frances A. Weinstein, Aug. 16, 1994; 1 child, William Steven. BSE magna cum laude, U. Mich., 1975, MSE, 1976, PhD of Nuclear Engring., 1978. From dep. divsn. head to program mgr. Brookhaven Nat. Lab., Upton, N.Y., 1978—. Contbr. articles to profl. jours. Mem. ASME, Am. Nuclear Soc. (Reactor Safety divsn. program com. sec. to vice-chmn. 1991—, chmn. 1996, past pres., v.p., treas. L.I. chpt. 1979-95), Am. Phys. Soc., Brookhaven Nat. Lab. Toastmasters (pres., v.p. 1990-95, awards 91, 92, 94). Republican. Achievements include performing computer simulation of Chernobyl-4 accident based on Soviet explanation prior to release of Soviet analyses, subsequently cross-comparing analyses, confirming similarities and evaluating differences. Office: Brookhaven Nat Lab Bldg 197 D Upton NY 11973-5000

VAN TYNE, ARTHUR MORRIS, geologist; b. Syracuse, N.Y., Aug. 12, 1925; s. Roy Hanford and Isabelle Marguerite (Hoag) Van T.; m. Patricia Wilson Boyd, July 13, 1946; children: Judith, Cynthia, Mark, Peter. AB, Syracuse U., 1951, MS, 1958. Cert. petroleum geologist; lic. geologist, Pa. Field asst. Syracuse U. Rsch. Inst., 1951-53; geologist Shell Oil Co., Rockies, Gulf Coast, 1953-57; sr. geologist-in-charge N.Y. State Geol. Survey-Oil and Gas Rsch. Office, Wellsville and Alfred, N.Y., 1958-81; geol. cons. Van Tyne Cons., Wellsville, N.Y.C., 1981—. Contbr. articles to profl. jours. Bd. dirs. Jones Meml. Hosp., Wellsville, 1974—, bd. chmn. 1986-95, dir. Wellsville United Way, 1968-80, pres. 1974-75; dep. mayor Village of Wellsville, 1992—; committeeman Rep. Party, 1962-77. Recipient Cert. of Appreciation Am. Petroleum Inst., 1975, 80, Award of Merit Internat. Oil Scouts Assn. and Appalachian Sect., 1961, 66, 88. Mem. N.Y. Acad. Scis., Am. Assn. Petroleum Geologists (sec., dir. 1989-91, Disting. Svc. award 1994, hon. mem. 1996, hon. mem. Ea. sect.), Russian Assn. Oil and Gas Geologists, N.Y. State Oil Producers Assn. (dir., exec. com. 1980, Svc. award 1981), Ind. Oil and Gas Assn. N.Y. (pres. 1985-88), No. Appalachian Geol. Soc. (pres. 1966-68), Geol. Soc. Am., Wellsville Rotary Club (pres. 1979-80, Paul Harris fellow 1994). Achievements include discoveries of gas production from queenston formation in N.Y., discovered Bass Islands thrust structure, a major oil and gas producer in N.Y. and Pa. Home: 24 Oak St Wellsville NY 14895 Office: Van Tyne Cons 159 1/2 N Main St Wellsville NY 14895

VAN UITERT, LEGRAND GERARD, retired chemist; b. Salt Lake City, May 6, 1922; s. Antone and Lambertha Maria (Groeneveld) Van U.; m. Marion Emma Woolley, June 8, 1945; children: Robert, Bonnie, Craig. B.S., George Washington U., 1949; M.S., Pa. State U., 1951, Ph.D., 1952. Union Carbide fellow Pa. State U., 1951-52; materials scientist Bell Telephone Labs., Murray Hill, N.J., 1952-89, ret., 1989. Served with USN, 1940-46. Co-recipient W.R.G. Baker award IEEE, 1971, recipient Quantum Electronics award, 1992; recipient H.N. Potts award Franklin Inst., 1975, George Wash. Alumni Assn. award, 1980, Indsl. Rsch. award for new materials, 1981, AT&T Patent award, 1993, R.W. Wood prize Optical Soc. Am., 1993. Mem. Nat. Acad. Engring., Am. Chem. Soc. (award for creative invention 1978), Sigma Xi. Research on microwave ferrites, lasers, bubble domain memory, electro, non-linear and acusto-optic materials, luminescence, optical fibers, crystal growth, passive displays, supercondr. dielectric films for processing and correlation of properties of matter. Home: 2 Terry Dr Morristown NJ 07960-4713

VAN UMMERSEN, CLAIRE A(NN), academic administrator, biologist, educator; b. Chelsea, Mass., July 28, 1935; d. George and Catherine (Courtovich); m. Frank Van Ummersen, June 7, 1958; children: Lynn, Scott. BS, Tufts U., 1957, MS, 1960, PhD, 1963; DSc (hon.), U. Mass., 1988, U. Maine, 1991. Rsch. asst. Tufts U., 1957-60, 60-67, grad. asst. in embryology, 1962, postdoctoral teaching asst., 1963-66, lectr. in biology, 1967-68; asst. prof. biology U. Mass., Boston, 1968-74; assoc. prof. U. Mass.,

1974-86, assoc. dean acad. affairs, 1975-76, assoc. vice chancellor acad. affairs, 1976-78, chancellor, 1978-79, dir. Environ. Sci. Ctr., 1980-82; assoc. vice chancellor acad. affairs Mass. Bd. Regents for Higher Edn., 1982-85, vice chancellor for mgmt. systems and telecommunications, 1985-86; chancellor Univ. System N.H., Durham, 1986-92; sr. fellow New Eng. Bd. Higher Edn., 1992-93; sr. fellow New Eng. Resource Ctr. Higher Edn. U. Mass., 1992-93; pres. Cleve. (Ohio) State U., 1993—; cons. Mass. Bd. Regents, 1981-82, AGB, 1992—, Kuwait U., 1992-93; asst. Lancaster Course in Ophthalmology, Mass. Eye. and Ear Infirmary, 1962-69, lectr., 1970-93, also coord.; reviewer HEW; mem. rsch. team which established safety stds. for exposure to microwave radiation, 1958-65; participant Leadership Am. program, 1992-93. Mem. N.H. Ct. Systems Rev. Task Force, 1989-90; mem. New Eng. Bd. Higher Edn., 1986-92, mem. exec. com., 1989-92, N.H. adv. coun., 1990-92; chair Rhodes Scholarship Selection Com., 1986-91; bd. dirs. N.H. Bus. and Industry Assn., 1987-90, 90-93; governing bd. N.H. Math. Coalition, 1991-92; exec. com. 21st Century Learning Community, 1992-93; state panelist N.H. Women in Higher Edn., 1986-93; bd. dirs. Urban League Greater Cleve., 1993—, mem. strategic planning com., chair edn. com., 1996—; bd. dirs. Great Lakes Sci. & Tech. Mus., 1993—, Sci. & Tech. Coun. Cleve. Tomorrow, Ohio Aerospace Inst., 1993—, Northeast Ohio Coun. Higher Edn., 1993—; mem. Leadership Am. Class '93, Leadership Cleve. Class '95. Recipient Disting. Svc. medal U. Mass., 1979, Am. Cancer Soc. grantee Tufts U., 1960. Mem. Am. Coun. on Edn. (com. on self-regulation 1987-91), State Higher Exec. Officers (fed. rels. com., cost accountability task force, exec. com. 1990-92), ACE (com. leadership devel.), Nat. Assn. Sys. Heads (exec. com. 1990-92), Nat. Ctr. for Edn. Stats. (network adv. com. 1989-92, chair accreditation teams 1988—), New Eng. Assn. Schs. and Colls. (commn. on higher edn. 1990-93), North Ctrl. Assn. Schs. and Colls. (evaluator 1993, 95, 96), Soc. Devel. Biology, Greater Cleve. Round Table (bd. dirs. 1993—), Cleve. Playhouse (trustee 1994—), United Way (bd. dirs. 1995—), Nat. Assn. State Univs. and Land Grant Colls. (exec. com. on urban agenda, state rep. AASCU), Phi Beta Kappa, Sigma Xi. Office: Cleve State Univ Rhodes Tower Euclid Ave at E 24th St Cleveland OH 44115

VAN VALEN, LEIGH MAIORANA, biologist, educator; b. Albany, N.Y., Aug. 12, 1935; s. A. Donald and Eleanor (Williams) Van V.; m. Phebe May Hoff, 1959; children: Katrina, Diana; m. Virginia C. Maiorana, 1974. B.A., Miami U., Ohio, 1956; M.A., Columbia U., 1957, Ph.D., 1961. Boese postdoctoral fellow Columbia U., N.Y.C., 1961-62; NATO and NIH fellow Univ. Coll. London, 1962-63; with Am. Mus. Natural History, N.Y.C., 1963-66; asst. prof. anatomy U. Chgo., 1967-71, assoc. prof. evolutionary biology & conceptual founds. sci., 1971-73, assoc. prof. biology & conceptual founds. of sci., 1973-76, prof. biology and conceptual founds. of sci., 1976-88, prof. ecology, evolution, conceptual founds. sci., 1988—; research assoc. dept. geology Field Mus., Chgo., 1971—. Author: Deltatheridia, A New Order of Mammals, 1966, Paleocene Dinosaurs or Cretaceous Ungulates in South America?, 1988, The Origin of the Plesiadapid Primates and the Nature of Purgatorius, 1994; editor: Evolutionary Theory, 1973—, Evolutionary Monographs, 1977—; mem. editl. bd. Jour. Molecular Evolution, 1970-76, Evolución Biológica, 1988—; mem. editl. bd. commentators Behavioral and Brain Scis., 1978—; assoc. editor Evolution, 1969-71. Mem. nat. adv. bd. Voice of Reason, N.Y., 1981—. NIH Research Career Devel. awardee, 1967-72; NSF grantee, 1963-71; others. Mem. AAUP (pres. U. Chgo. chpt.), Soc. Study Evolution (v.p. 1973, 80), Am. Soc. Naturalists (v.p. 1974-75), Paleontol. Soc. (councillor 1980-82), Internat. Soc. Cryptozoology (bd. dirs.), Ecol. Soc. Am. Office: Univ Chgo Dept Ecology and Evolution 1101 E 57th St Chicago IL 60637-1503

VAN VALIN, CLYDE EMORY, bishop; b. Windham, N.Y., Nov. 24, 1929; s. Ernest Clyde and Josephine Louise (Howard) Van V.; m. Beatrice Mae Roushey, Aug. 25, 1950; children: Carolyn, Wendell, Martha, Luella, Loretta. A.B., Roberts Wesleyan Coll., North Chili, N.Y., 1951; B.D., Asbury Theol. Sem., Wilmore, Ky., 1954, D.D. (hon.), 1972. Ordained deacon Free Meth. Ch. N.Am., 1954, elder, 1955, consecrated bishop, 1976. Pastor Free Meth. Ch., Allentown, Pa., 1954-58; Eastern regional dir. Free Meth. youth, Winona Lake, Ind., 1958-60; dir., chaplain John Wesley Sem. Found., Wilmore, 1960-74, asst. dir., 1974-76; pastor Wilmore Free Meth. Ch., 1961-76, 92-94; bishop Free Meth. Ch. N.Am., Winona Lake, 1976-91; internat. quizmaster Free Meth. Youth, 1958-60; chmn. bd. dirs. Nat. Coalition Against Pornography, 1988-91; pres., bd. dirs. Free Meth. Ch., 1985-91, pres. bd. adminstrn., 1985-89; pres. Free Meth. World Fellowship, 1985-89; chmn. constl. counsel Free Meth. Ch., 1985-91, pres. bd. adminstrn., 1985, 89; chmn. Free Meth. Bd. of Bishops, 1989-90; chmn. study commn. on doctrine, Free Meth. Ch., 1979-85, 90-91. Author: Transforming Grace and Tithing, God's Plan for the Church, 1990; editor: Pastor's Handbook Free Methodist Church of North America, 1982. Trustee Asbury Theol. Sem., 1982-91. Named Today's Young Leader, Roberts Wesleyan Coll., 1959; recipient Disting. Service award Asbury Theol. Sem., 1973. Mem. Christian Holiness Assn. (exec. com., bd. adminstrn. 1989-94), Theta Phi. Methodist. Republican. Club: Nicholasville Rotary (Ky.) (hon. life).

VAN VALKENBURG, EDGAR WALTER, lawyer; b. Seattle, Jan. 8, 1953; s. Edgar Walter and Margaret Catherine (McKenna) Van V.; m. Turid L. Owren, Sept. 29, 1990; children: Ingrid Catherine, Andrew Owren. BA, U. Wash., 1975; JD summa cum laude, Willamette Coll. of Law, 1978; LLM, Columbia U., 1984. Bar: Oreg. 1978, U.S. Dist. Ct. Oreg. 1979, U.S. Ct. Appeals (9th cir.) 1980. Law clk. to assoc. justice Oreg. Supreme Ct., Salem, 1978-79; assoc. Stoel, Rives, Boley, Fraser & Wyse, Portland, Oreg., 1979-82, 84-86; ptnr. Stoel Rives LLP, Portland, Oreg., 1986—; instr. Columbia U., N.Y.C., 1982-84. Editor-in-chief: Williamette Law Jour. 1977-78. Mem. ACLU (pres. Oreg. chpt. 1991-93), Oreg. State Bar (chmn. antitrust sect. 1989-90, mem. Ho. of Dels. 1996—). Office: Stoel Rives LLP 900 SW 5th Ave Portland OR 97204-1235

VAN VALKENBURG, MAC ELWYN, retired electrical engineering educator; b. Union, Utah, Oct. 5, 1921; s. Charles Mac and Nora (Walker) Van V.; m. Evelyn J. Pate, Aug. 27, 1943; children: Charles Mac II, JoLynne, Kaye, David R., Nancy J., Susan L. B.S. in Elec. Engring, U. Utah, 1943; M.S., Mass. Inst. Tech., 1946; Ph.D., Stanford, 1952. With Radiation Lab., Mass. Inst. Tech., 1943-45, Research Lab. Electronics, 1945-46; mem. faculty U. Utah, 1946-55, U. Ill., 1955-66; prof. elec. engring. Princeton, 1966-74, chmn. dept., 1966-72; prof. elec. engring. U. Ill., Urbana, 1974—, acting dean Coll. Engring., 1984-85, dean Coll. Engring., 1985-88, dean emeritus, 1988—; ret., 1988; vis. prof. Stanford, U. Colo., U. Calif., Berkeley, U. Hawaii, Manoa, 1978-79, U. Ariz., 1982-83. Author: Network Analysis, 3d edit, 1974, Introduction to Modern Network Synthesis, 1960, Introductory Signals and Circuits, 1967, Signals in Linear Circuits, 1974, Circuit Theory: Foundations and Classical Contributions, 1974, Linear Circuits, 1982, Analog Filter Design, 1982; editor-in-chief: IEEE Press, 1983-86. Recipient Disting. Alumni award U. Utah, 1991. Fellow IEEE (v.p., bd. dirs. 1969-73, editor transactions 1960-63, proc. 1966-69, Edn. medal 1972, Cirs. medal 1987), Am. Soc. Engring. Edn. (George Westinghouse award 1963, Benjamin Garver Lamme award 1978, Guillemin prize 1978, Hall of Fame 1993, Centennial Medallion 1993); mem. NAE, Sigma Xi, Tau Beta Pi, Phi Kappa Phi. Home: 2609 SW 64th Pl Portland OR 97225-3168

VAN VARENBERG, JEAN-CLAUDE See VAN DAMME, JEAN-CLAUDE

VAN VLEET, WILLIAM BENJAMIN, retired lawyer, life insurance company executive; b. Milw., Dec. 4, 1924; s. William Benjamin and Irene (Peppey) Van V.; m. Marilyn Nilles, Dec. 26, 1946; children: Terese Van Vleet Svetich, Susan Van Vleet Waldo, William Benjamin III, Monica Van Vleet McCarthy, Mark. Student, Marquette U., 1942-43, Lawrence Coll., Appleton, Wis., 1943-44; LLB, JD, Marquette U., 1948. Bar: Wis. 1948, Ill. 1950. Gen. counsel George Rogers Clark Mut. Casualty Co., Rockford, Ill., 1948-59; gen. counsel Pioneer Life Ins. Co. Ill., Rockford, 1950-68, 81-94, v.p., 1959-91, gen. counsel, 1968-91, exec. v.p., 1981-95, also bd. dirs.; exec. v.p., gen. counsel Pioneer Fin. Svcs., Inc., Rockford, 1985-95, gen. counsel emeritus, dir., 1995—; pres. Nat. Group Life Ins. Co., Rockford, 1992-93, exec. v.p., gen. counsel, 1993-94, also bd. dirs.; pres. Western Life Ins. Co. Am., Rockford, 1981-82, Health & Life Ins. Co. Am., Rockford, 1984-92, exec. v.p., gen. counsel, 1993-94; pres. Manhattan Nat. Life Ins. Co., Cin., 1990-92, exec. v.p., gen. counsel, 1993-94, also bd. dirs.; exec. v.p., gen. counsel Continental Life and Accident Co., Boise, Idano, 1993-94, also bd. dirs.; bd. dirs. Nat. Health Svcs. Milw. Mem. adminstrn. Boylan Ctrl. Cath. H.S., Rockford, 1965-72; pres. Diocesan Bd. Edn., Rockford, 1970-78; v.p., pres. Nat. Assn. Bds. Edn., 1972-78; v.p., pres. Nat. Assn. Bds. Edn., 1972-78; v.p., pres. Nat. Assn. Bds. Edn., 1972-78; mem. bd. advisors Marion Coll., 1976-79; mem. adv. bd. St. Anthony's Hosp., Rockford, 1978-91; bd. dirs. Crimestoppers, Rockford, 1982-90; co-chmn. United Cerebral Palsy Telethon, Rockford, 1985-95. Mem. ABA, Ill. Bar Assn., Winnebago County Bar Assn., Forest Hills Country Club, Masons. Office: Pioneer Fin Svcs Inc 303 N Main St Rockford IL 61101 *Credibility is one of the few things we leave behind us.*

VAN VLIET, CAROLYNE MARINA, physicist, educator; b. Dordrecht, Netherlands, Dec. 27, 1929; emigrated to U.S., 1960, naturalized, 1967; d. Marinus and Jacoba (de Lange) Van V. B.S., Free U. Amsterdam, Netherlands, 1949, M.A., 1953, Ph.D. in Physics, 1956. Research fellow Free U. Amsterdam, 1950-54, research assoc., 1954-56, asst. dir., 1958-60; postdoctoral fellow U. Minn., Mpls., 1956-57; mem. faculty U. Minn., 1957-58, 60-70, prof. elec. engring. and physics, 1965-70; prof. theory physics U. Montreal, Que., Can., 1969-95; sr. rschr. math. rsch. ctr. U. Montreal, Que., 1969—; vis. prof. U. Fla., 1974, 78-88 (4 months annually); prof. elec. and computer engring. Fla. Internat. U., 1992—. Contbg. author: Fluctuation Phenomena in Solids, 1965; editor Proc. 9th Internat. Conf. Noise in Physical Systems, 1987; author numerous articles. Research grantee NSF; Research grantee Air Force OSR; Research grantee Nat. Sci. and Engring. Research Council, Ottawa. Fellow IEEE; mem. Am. Phys. Soc., Can. Phys. Soc., European Phys. Soc., N.Y. Acad. Scis., Am. Acad. Mid. Ea. Dance. Home: 920 Van Dyck Ave, Brossard, Montreal, PQ Canada J4W 2E6 *The purpose of life is to honor God and to serve mankind.*

VAN VLIET, CLAIRE, artist; b. Ottawa, Ont., Can., Aug. 9, 1933; d. Wilbur Dennison and Audrey Ilene (Wallace) Van V. A.B., San Diego State Coll., 1952; M.F.A., Claremont Grad. Sch., 1954; DFA (hon.), U. of the Arts, Phila., 1993. Instr. printmaking Phila. Coll. Art, 1959-65; owner The Janus Press, 1954—; vis. lectr. printmaking U. Wis.-Madison, 1965-66; mem. bd. advisors Hand Papermaking. One-man exhbns. include Print Club Phila., 1963, 66, 73, 77, Wiggin Gallery, Boston Pub. Libr., 1977, Rutgers U. Art Gallery, 1978, AAA Gallery, Phila., 1980, Dolan/Maxwell Gallery, Phila., 1984, 91, Mary Ryan Gallery, N.Y.C., 1986, Mills Coll., 1986, U. of the Arts, Phila., 1989, Victoria and Albert Mus., London, 1994, Ottawa Sch. Art Gallery, Can., 1994, Bates Coll. Mus. of Art, Lewiston, Maine, 1994; group exhbns. include Bklyn. Nat., Phila. Arts Festival, Kunst zu Kafka, Germany, Paper as Medium, Smithsonian Instn., Washington, Paper Now, Cleve. Mus. Art, 1986, Boyle Arts Festival, Ireland, 1993; represented in permanent collections Nat. Gallery Art, Phila. Mus. Art, Boston Pub. Libr., Libr. of Congress, Cleve. Mus. Art, Montreal Mus. Fine Arts, Victoria and Albert Mus. London. NEA grantee, 1976-80, Ingram-Merrill Found. grantee, 1989; MacArthur fellow, 1989. Mem. Soc. Printers Boston, Nat. Acad. of Design. Address: RR 1 West Burke VT 05871-9801

VAN VUGT, ERIC J., lawyer; b. Grand Rapids, Mich., Sept. 17, 1951; s. Ernest and Phyllis N. (Van Someren) Van V.; m. Wendy S. Yonker, June 3, 1972; children: Erin L., Heather J., Timothy D. BA, Calvin Coll., 1973; JD, Marquette Univ., 1976. Bar: Wis. 1976, U.S. Dist. Ct. (ea. and we. dist.) Wis. 1976, U.S. Dist. Ct. (we. dist.) Mich. 1993, U.S. Ct. Appeals (7th cir.) 1976, U.S. Ct. Appeals (fed. cir.) 1990, U.S. Supreme Ct. 1994. Assoc. Kluwin, Dunphy & Hankin, Milw., 1976-80; ptnr. Kluwin, Dunphy, Hankin & McNulty, Milw., 1980-85, Minahan & Peterson, Milw., 1985-91, Quarles & Brady, Milw., 1991—. Mem. ABA, State Bar Wis. Avocations: aviation, golf. Home: 14910 Hushing Brae Ct Brookfield WI 53005-2682 Office: Quarles & Brady 411 E Wisconsin Ave Milwaukee WI 53202-4409

VAN WACHEM, LODEWIJK CHRISTIAAN, petroleum company executive; b. Pangkalan Brandan, Indonesia, July 31, 1931; m. Elisabeth G. Cristofoli, June 10, 1958; 3 children. Degree Mech. Engring., Delft U., Delft, The Netherlands., 1953. With Bataafsche Petroleum Maatschappij, The Hague, The Netherlands, 1953; pres. Royal Dutch Petroleum Co., The Hague, The Netherlands, 1982-92; chmn. com, mng. dir. Royal Dutch/Shell Group, The Hague, The Netherlands, 1985-92; chmn. supr. bd. Royal Dutch Petroleum Co., The Hague, The Netherlands, 1992—; head prodn. divsn. Shell Internat. Petroleum Maatschappij, The Hague, 1971-72, coord. exploration and prodn., 1976-79; mng. dir. Royal Dutch Petroleum Co., until 1982, pres. 1982-92; mem. presidium bd. dirs. Shell Petroleum Co., Ltd., 1977-92; chmn. bd. dirs. Shell Oil Co. USA, 1982-92, De Nederlandsche Bank N.V., 1987-92; non-exec. dir. IBM, Armonk, 1992—, Credit Suisse Holding, Zurich, 1992-96, Atco Ltd., Calgary, 1993—, Zurich Versicherungs Gesellschaft, 1993, AAB Brown Boveri Ltd., Zurich; mem. supr. bd. AKZO, Arnhem, 1992—, Philips Electronics, Eindhoven, 1993—, BMW, Munich, 1994—; chmn. suprervisory bd. Royal Dutch Petroleum Co., 1992—. Decorated C.B.E. (hon.), Knight Brit. Empire (hon.), Comdr. Order of Oranje Nassau, Knight Order Netherlands Lion. Office: Royal Dutch Petroleum Co, 30 Carel van Bylandtlaan, 2596 HR The Hague The Netherlands

VAN WAGONER, ROBERT LOUIS, lawyer; b. Lake Orion, Mich., June 4, 1936; s. Ray John and Gladys Elizabeth Van W.; m. Charlotte Robertson, June 10, 1968 (div. 1979); m. Mary Carlin Kaczor, Aug. 10, 1984. BS, Northwestern U., 1958; JD, Calif. We. U., 1966; cert., Nat. Jud. Coll., Reno, Nev., 1981. Bar: Nev. 1967, U.S. Dist. Ct. Nev. 1969, U.S. Supreme Ct. 1973. Commd. ensign USN, 1958; advanced through grades to lt., retired, 1963; asst. atty. City of Reno, 1967-69, city atty., 1971-78, 83-87; assoc. Law Offices Richard Fray, Reno, 1969-71; judge County of Washoe, Reno, 1979-82; pvt. practice Reno, 1987-88; adminstrv. atty. Pub. Svc. Commn. Nev., 1988—, adminstrv. law judge, 1989-95, judicial state leader Nat. Judicial Coll., 1992—. Author: Tort Liability for Firemen, 1986, (bulletin series) Reno Land Use Planning, 1983-87; editor: La Balanza Law Jour., 1963-66. Chmn. Dem. Com. County of Washoe, 1969-71; bd. dirs. Child Runaway Youth Svcs., Reno, 1987—, No. Nev. chpt. Multiple Sclerosis Soc., 1969— (citation of merit 1986); active on Nev. Crime Commn., Carson City, 1971-78; mem. Nat. Assn. of Transp. Practitioners, 1989—, Nat. Conf. State Trans. Specialists, 1990—, Nat. Assn. Administrv. Law Judges, 1992—, The Nat. Trust for Historic Preservation, 1994—; assoc. mem. Am. Mus. Nat. History, 1994—. Mem. ABA, Nev. Bar Assn., Am. Judicature Soc., U.S. Naval Inst., Elks, Masons, Prospectors, Jesters Reno Ct. (bd. dirs. 1984), Am. Legion, The Nat. Trust for Hist. Preservation, Am. Mus. of Nat. History, Nat. Assn. Transp. Practitioners, Nat. Jud. Coll. (state jud. leader 1992—), Nat. Assn. Adminstrv. Law Judges. Avocations: golf, fishing, home repair.

VAN WINKLE, EDGAR WALLING, electrical engineer, computer consultant; b. Rutherford, N.J., Oct. 12, 1913; s. Winant and Jessie Walcott (Mucklow) Van W.; m. Jessie Stetler, Apr. 23, 1938 (dec. 1992); children: Barbara Van Winkle Clifton, Catrina Van Winkle Poindexter, Cornelia Van Winkle Schloss; m. Martha Polyé, May 22, 1993. B.E.E., Rutgers U., 1936; M.S. in Indsl. Engring., Columbia U., 1943, P.E. in Indsl. Engring., 1966. Registered profl. engr., N.J. Elec. engr. A.B. Dumont Labs. Passaic, N.J., 1943-48; chief engr. Facsimile Electronics, Passaic, 1948-52; cons. Bur. Ships, Washington, 1952; asst. sr. staff scientist Bendix Corp., Teterboro, N.J., 1952-67; sr. staff scientist Conrac Corp., West Caldwell, N.J., 1967-78; pres. Empac, Inc., Rutherford, N.J., 1979—. Contbr. articles, papers to profl. jours; patentee in field. Ruling elder Presbyterian Ch., Rutherford, 1984-91, chmn. endowment com., 1984—. Mem. IEEE (life, treas. artificial intelligence sect. North N.J. Chpt. 1982-84), Bendix Mgmt. Club (life), North N.J. Automatic Control Group (chmn. 1967-68), Met. Engring. Mgmt. (chmn. 1966-67), Mensa, Holland Soc., Green Pond Yacht Club (past commodore), Delta Phi. Republican. Club: Upper Montclair Country. Current work: Artificial intelligence and robotics. Subspecialty: Mathematical software.

VAN WINKLE, WESLEY ANDREW, lawyer, educator; b. Kansas City, Mo., Sept. 22, 1952; s. Willard and Cleone Verlee (O'Dell) Van W.; m. Ruth Kay Shelby, Apr. 10, 1984. B, U. Nebr., 1972; JD, San Francisco Law Sch., 1987. Bar: Calif. 1987, U.S. Dist. Ct. (no. dist.) Calif. 1987, U.S. Supreme Ct. 1994. Atty. Bagetelos & Fadem, San Franicsco, 1987-91; pvt. practice Berkeley, Calif., 1991—; prof. law San Francisco Law Sch., 1990—. Editor (legal newspaper/rev.) Res Ipsa Loquitur, 1986. Mem. Calif. Attys. for Criminal Justice, Calif. Appellate Def. Counsel (v.p.), San Francisco Law Sch. Alumni Assn., Delta Theta Phi. Democrat. Office: PO Box 5216 Berkeley CA 94705-0216

VAN WINKLE, WILLIAM, financial planner; b. Englewood, N.J., July 3, 1934; s. Marshall Jr. and Helen (Wescott) V.; m. Beverly Elsie Peterson, Sept. 9, 1956; children: Stuart Wilson, Ainsley Ann, Carrie Lee. BS in Mech. Engring. and Bus. Adminstrn., Lehigh U., 1957. Cert. fin. planner, CLU. Ops. mgr., plant engr. Procter and Gamble, N.Y., Ga., Kans., Calif., Ohio, 1957-67; ops. mgr. Sheffield Chem. div. Kraftco, Union, N.J., 1967-71; dir. mfg. USA C.R. Bard, Inc., Murray Hill, N.J., 1971-74; v.p. Estey Corp., Eatontown, N.J., 1974-79; pres. Van Winkle Assocs., Tinton Falls, N.J., 1979—. Host, prodr. (cable TV program) Financial Matters, 1980—; contbr. articles to profl. jours. Bd. dirs. Vis. Nurse Assn. Ctrl. Jersey, Red. Bank, N.J., 1985—; trustee Greater Red Bank (N.J.) YMCA, 1986-94; past pres., trustee Brookdale C.C. Found., Lincroft, N.J. Mem. Inst. CFPs, Internat. Assn. Fin. Planning (bd. dirs. ctrl. N.J. chpt. 1986-91), NALU (nat. quality award 1983—), Monmouth Assn. Life Underwriters (pres. 1982-83), Ctrl. N.J. Estate Planning Coun., Million Dollar Round Table (divsnl. v.p. 1994-95), Navesink Country Club, Seabright Beach Club, Holland Soc. (pres. Jersey Shore br. 1994—), N.Y. Club. Republican. Episcopalian. Avocations: sailing, walking, reading. Home: 41 Breezy Pt Little Silver NJ 07739-1703 Office: Van Winkle Assocs 776 Shrewsbury Ave Eatontown NJ 07724-3006

VAN WYCK, GEORGE RICHARD, insurance company executive; b. Wilmington, Vt., Feb. 6, 1928; s. Harold Wait Van Wyck and Ruth Anna Learnard; m. Jeanne Mildred Anderson, Apr. 17, 1948; children: Diana Lee Van Wyck Jenkins, Beryl Jeanne. BS in Math. cum laude, St. Lawrence U., 1953. Actuarial clk. Aetna Life Ins. Co., Hartford, Conn., 1953-55; with Am. Bankers Ins. Group, Miami, Fla., 1955-91, sec., bd. dirs., 1983-89, ret., 1991. Bd. dirs. Jr. Achievement of Greater Miami, 1966-83, pres., 1975-76; bd. dirs., chmn. fin. com. Epworth Village Retirement Complex, Miami, 1966—; founding dir., pres. Brickel Children's Ctr., Miami, 1980-82; mem. pers. adv. bd., vice chmn. Dade County, Miami, 1987-89. With USAF, 1946-49. Fellow Life Office Mgmt. Inst.; mem. 1st United Meth. Ch. So. Miami, Phi Beta Kappa. Democrat. Methodist. Avocations: photography, golf, bridge. Home: 8455 SW 44th St Miami FL 33155-4126

VAN WYK, JUDSON JOHN, endocrinologist, pediatric educator; b. Maurice, Iowa, June 10, 1921; s. John Cornelius and Amelia Susan (Menning) Van W.; m. Persis Ruth Parker, June 8, 1944; children: Judith Parker, Persis Allen, Peter Menning, Judson John. AB, Hope Coll., 1943, ScD (hon.), 1979; postgrad. in biochemistry, St. Louis U., 1943-44; MD, Johns Hopkins U., 1948. Diplomate Am. Bd. Pediatrics. Intern Johns Hopkins Hosp., 1948-49, resident in pediatrics, 1949-50, fellow in pediatric endocrinology, 1953-55; resident in pediatrics Cin. Children's Hosp., 1951-52; asst. prof. pediatrics U. N.C. Sch. Medicine, 1955-59, assoc. prof., 1959-62, prof., 1962-91, prof. biology, 1987—, Kenan prof. pediatrics, 1975-91, prof. emeritus, 1992—, chief div. endocrinology, 1955-89, dir. tng. program in endocrinology and metabolism, 1962-89; mem. staff N.C. Meml. Hosp.; cons. Womack Army Hosp., Ft. Bragg, N.C., 1957-88; vis. scientist Karolinska Institutet, Stockholm, 1968-69; mem. div. cell biology Lineberger Cancer Rsch. Ctr., 1976—; vis. prof. basic med. scis. Mich. State U., 1984. Editor Progress in Growth Factor Research, 1988-94; mem. editl. bd. Jour. Clin. Endocrinology and Metabolism, 1956-71, editor, 1983-89; mem. editl. bd. Pediatrics, 1969-70; contbr. chpts. to books, articles to profl. jours. Mem. basic sci. adv. com. March Dimes, 1985-88. With USPHS, 1951-53. Recipient numerous fellowships and grants, Lauria honoris causa, U. Genoa, "To commemorate 500th Anniversary of Discovery of N. Am. by Christopher Columbus", 1992, O. Max Gardner award Bd. Govs. U. N.C., 1980. Fellow Am. Acad. Pediatrics; mem. NIH (endocrine study sect. 1968-720, Endocrine Soc. (mem. coun. 1975-79, awards com. 1991-96, publs. com. 1996—, Fred Conrad Koch medal 1989), Soc. Pediatric Rsch., Am. Pediatric Soc., So. Soc. Clin. Investigation, Am. Fedn. Clin. Rsch., So. Soc. Pediatric Rsch., Lawson Wilkins Pediatric Endocrine Soc. (prs. 1976-77), Internat. Endocrine Soc. (ctrl. com. 1988—), La Sociedad Peruana de Pediatria (hon.), Sociedad Pediatrica de Trujillo (hon.), European Soc. for Pediatric Endocrinology (corr.), Japanese Pediatric Endocrine Soc. (hon.). Presbyterian. Home: 1020 Highland Woods Rd Chapel Hill NC 27514-4410 Office: U NC Sch Medicine Dept Pediatrics CB 7220 509 Burnett-Womack Chapel Hill NC 27599-7220

VAN WYLEN, GORDON JOHN, former college president; b. Grant, Mich., Feb. 6, 1920; s. John and Effa (Bierema) Van W.; m. Margaret E. DeWitt, Dec. 29, 1951; children—Elizabeth Ann Van Wylen Rudenga, Stephen John, Ruth Margaret Van Wylen Jasperse, David Gordon, Emily Jane Van Wylen Overway. A.B., Calvin Coll., 1942; B.S.E., U. Mich., 1942, M.S., 1947; Sc.D., MIT, 1951. Indsl. engr. duPont Co., 1942-43; instr. mech. engring. Pa. State U., 1946-48; asst. prof. mech. engring. U. Mich., 1951-55, assoc. prof., 1955-57, prof., 1957-72, chmn. dept., 1958-65, dean Coll. Engring., 1965-72; pres. Hope Coll., Holland, Mich., 1972-87, pres. emeritus, 1987—. Author: Thermodynamics, 1959, (with R.E. Sonntag) Fundamentals of Classical Thermodynamics, 1965, 4th edit., 1994, Fundamentals of Statistical Thermodynamics, 1966, Introduction to Thermodynamics, 1971, 3d edit., 1991, Encounter at Dea, 1994; contbr. articles to profl. jours. Lt. USNR, 1943-46. Fellow ASME, AAAS; mem. Phi Beta Kappa (hon.), Sigma Xi, Tau Beta Pi, Phi Kappa Phi. Mem. Reform Ch. Am. Home: 817 Brook Village Dr Holland MI 49423-4641

VAN ZANTE, SHIRLEY M(AE), magazine editor; b. Elma, Iowa; d. Vernon E. and Georgene (Woodmansee) Borland; m. Dirk C. Van Zante. AA, Grandview Coll., 1950; BA, Drake U., 1952. Assoc. editor Mchts. Trade Jour., Des Moines, 1952-55; copywriter Meredith Pub. Co., Des Moines, 1955-60, book editor, 1960-67; home furnishings editor Better Homes and Gardens Spl. Interest Publs., Meredith Corp., 1967-74; home furnishing and design editor Better Homes and Gardens mag., 1974-89; writer, editl. cons., 1989—. Named Advt. Woman of Yr. in Des Moines, 1961; recipient Dorothy Dawe award, 1971, 73, 75, 76, 77, Dallas Market Ctr. award, 1983, So. Furniture Market Writer's award, 1984. Mem. Am. Soc. Interior Designers (press affiliate), Alpha Xi Delta. Address: 1905 74th St Des Moines IA 50322-5701

VAN ZANTEN, FRANK VELDHUYZEN, retired library system director; b. Heemstede, The Netherlands, Oct. 21, 1932; came to U.S., 1946, naturalized, 1953; s. Adrian V. and Cornelia (Van Eesteren) Van Z.; m. Lois Ruth Holkeboer, June 17, 1961; children—Kiki Maria, Lili Roxanne, Amy Suzanne. A.B., Calvin Coll., Mich., 1959; postgrad., U. Wash., 1960; M.A. in L.S, U. Mich., 1961. Cataloger, extension project asst. Mich. State Library, Lansing, 1961-62; dir. Dickinson County (Mich.) Library, 1962-65, Mid-Peninsula Library Fedn., Iron Mountain, Mich., 1963-65, St. Clair County (Mich.) Library, 1965-68, Tucson Pub. Library, 1968-73; library cons. Ill. State Library, Springfield, 1973-75; asso. dir. for library devel. Ill. State Library, 1975-78; dir. Mid-Hudson Library System, Poughkeepsie, N.Y., 1978-95. Served with AUS, 1953-55. Mem. ALA, N.Y. Libr. Assn. Home: 138 Wilbur Blvd Poughkeepsie NY 12603-4635

VAN ZELST, THEODORE WILLIAM, civil engineer, natural resource exploration company executive; b. Chgo., May 11, 1923; s. Theodore Walter and Wilhelmina (Oomens) Van Z.; m. Louann Hurter, Dec. 29, 1951; children: Anne, Jean, David. B.S., U. Calif., Berkeley, 1944; BS in Naval Sci., Northwestern U., 1944, B.A.S., 1945, M.S. in Civil Engring., 1948. Registered profl. engr., Ill. Pres., Soil Testing Services, Inc., Chgo., 1948-52; pres. Soiltest, Inc., Chgo., 1948-78; chmn. bd. Soiltest, Inc., 1978-80; sec., dir. Exploration Data Cons., Inc., 1980-82; exec. v.p. Cenco Inc., Chgo., 1962-77; vice chmn. Cenco Inc., 1975-77, also dir., 1962-77; bd. dirs. Minann, Inc., Testing Sci., Inc., 26th St. Venture, Lunarè Ltd., Rsch. Park, Inc., Northwestern U., 1992-95, chmn. bd. dirs. Envirotech Svcs., Inc.1983-85; sec., bd. dirs. Van Zelst, Inc. Wadsworth, Ill., 1983—; pres., bd. dirs. Geneva-Pacific Corp., 1969-83, Geneva Resources, Inc., 1983-91. Treas. Internat. Road Fedn., 1961-64, sec., 1964-79, dir., 1973-88, vice chmn., 1980-87; pres. Internat. Road Edn. Found., 1978-80, 87-88, hon. life bd. dirs., 1988—; bd. dirs. Chgo. Acad. Scis., 1983-86, v.p., 1985-86, hon. dir., 1986—; bd. dirs. Pres.'s Assn., Chgo., 1985-86; mem. adv. bd. Mitchell Indian Mus., Kendall Coll., 1977-94. Lt. (j.g.) USNR, 1942-45. Recipient Service award Northwestern U., 1970, Merit award, 1974, Alumni medal, 1989, Svc. award U. Wis., 1971, La Sallian award, 1975. Mem. ASCE (Chgo. Civil Engr. of

Yr., 1988), Nat. Soc. Profl. Engrs., Western Soc. Engrs., Evanston C. of C. (v.p. 1969-73), Ovid Esbach Soc. (pres. 1968-80), Northwestern U. Alumni Assn., Tau Beta Pi. Clubs: Economic, North Shore. Inventor engring. testing equipment for soil, rock concrete and asphalt. Home: 1213 Wagner Rd Glenview IL 60025-3219 Office: PO Box 126 Glenview IL 60025-0126

VARANASI, USHA, environmental scientist; b. Bassien, Burma. BS, U. Bombay, 1961; MS, Calif. Inst. Technology, 1964; PhD in Chemistry, U. Wash., 1968. Rsch. assoc. lipid biochemistry Oceanic Inst., Oahu, Hawaii, 1969-71, assoc. rsch. prof., 1971-75; supr. rsch. chemist and task mgr. Northwest Fisheries Ctr., 1975-87; dir. Environ. Conservation Divsn. Nat. Maring Fisheries Svc./Nat. Oceanic & Atmos. Adminstr., Seattle, 1987—; rsch. prof. chemistry Seattle U., 1975—; vis. scientist Pioneer Rsch. Unit, Northwest Fisheries Ctr., nat. Marine Fisheries Svc., nat. oceanic & Atmospheric Adminstrn., Wash., 1969-72, rsch. chemist, 1975-80; from affil. assoc. to affil. prof. chem. U. Wash., 1980-88. Mem. Am. Soc. Biol. Chemists, Am. Chem. Soc., Am. Assn. Cancer Rsch., Am. Soc. Tixocol. and Exptl. Therapeutics, Am. Women Sci. Office: Northwest Fisheries Sci Ctr 2725 Montlake Blvd E Seattle WA 98112*

VARAT, JONATHAN D., law educator; b. 1945. BA, U. Pa., Phila., 1967, JD, 1972. Law clk. to judge Walter Mansfield U.S. Ct. Appeals (2d cir.), N.Y.C., 1972-73; law clk. to justice Byron White U.S. Supreme Ct., Washington, 1973-74; assoc. O'Melveny & Myers, Los Angeles, 1974-76; acting prof. UCLA, 1976-81, prof., 1981—, assoc. dean, 1982-83, 91-92. Office: U Calif Sch Law 405 Hilgard Ave Los Angeles CA 90024-1301

VARCHMIN, THOMAS EDWARD, environmental health administrator; b. Chgo., Dec. 5, 1947; s. Arthur William and Laurie Eileen (Allen) V.; m. Beth Virginia Plank, Dec. 16, 1972; children: Jeffrey Thomas, Brian Arthur, Jennifer Beth, Matthew James. B.A., St. Mary's Coll., Winona, Minn., 1969; M.S., Western Ill. U., Macomb, 1977. Registered sanitarian, Wis. Virologist, microbiologist Chgo. Dept. Health, 1974-78; environ. health and safety mgr. Great Atlantic & Pacific Tea Co., Chgo., 1978-79; adminstr. occupational safety and environ. health Nat. Safety Council, Chgo., 1979-80; mgr. environ. health Lake County Health Dept., Waukegan, Ill., 1980-84, mgr. environ. health and pub. relations, 1984-87; mgr. environ. health Cook County Dept. Pub. Health, Oak Park, Ill., 1987-89, asst. dir. environ. health, mgr. intergovtl. rels., 1989—; environ. health cons. Editor: Food and Beverage Newsletter, Hospital and Health Care Newsletter, Trades and Services Newsletter, 1979-80. NSF grantee, 1968-69. Mem. Nat. Environ. Health Assn. (registered environ. health specialist), Ill. Environ. Health Assn. (registered environ. health practitioner), Nat. Safety Coun., Am. Soc. Microbiology, Anvil Club of Ill., Phi Mu Alpha, Delta Epsilon Sigma. Research on autumn food habits of game fish, behavioral and phys. devel. of barred owl nestlings in Ill. Office: Cook County Dept Pub Health 1010 Lake St Ste 300 Oak Park IL 60301-1133

VARDON, JAMES LEWES, bank executive; b. Aylesbury, Buckinghamshire, Eng., May 22, 1941; came to U.S., 1979; s. Sidney James and Veronica (Williams) V.; m. Gillian Spain, Sept. 9, 1965; children—Helen Antonia, Catherine Philippa, Emma Frances. M.A., Univ. Coll., Oxford, Eng., 1962. Chartered acct. Pub. acct., 1963-68; European treasury analyst Occidental Petroleum Corp., Geneva, Switzerland, 1969-71; controller European ops. Ashland Oil Inc., London, 1971-73; v.p. Marine Midland Bank, London, 1973-77; sr. v.p., controller Security Pacific Nat. Bank, Los Angeles, 1977-82; exec. v.p., chief fin. officer Southeast Banking Corp., Miami, Fla., 1982-84, First Empire State Corp., Buffalo, 1984—; dir. M & T Capital Corp., Buffalo, 1984—. Bd. dirs. Zool. Soc. Buffalo Inc., 1984, Studio Arena Theatre, 1990, Daemen Coll., 1991. Fellow Inst. Chartered Accts. Eng. and Wales; mem. Inst. Taxation (assoc.), Fin. Execs. Inst. Brit. Conservative. Episcopalian. Clubs: Oxford, Cambridge (London); Oxford Union (Oxford). Avocations: tennis; theatre; baroque music. Office: 1st Empire State Corp 1 Montana Ave Buffalo NY 14211-1638

VARELLAS, SANDRA MOTTE, judge; b. Anderson, S.C., Oct. 17, 1946; d. James E. and Helen Lucille (Gilliam) Motte; m. James John Varellas, July 3, 1971; children: James John III, David Todd. BA, Winthrop Coll., 1968; MA, U. Ky., 1970, JD, 1975. Bar: Ky. 1975, Fla. 1976, U.S. Dist. Ct. (ea. dist.) Ky. 1975, U.S. Ct. Appeals (6th cir.) 1976, U.S. Supreme Ct. 1978. Instr. Midway Coll., Ky., 1970-72; adj. prof. U. Ky. Coll. Law, Lexington, 1976-78; instr. dept. bus. adminstrn. U. Ky., Lexington, 1976-78; atty. Varellas, Pratt & Cooley, Lexington, 1975-93; atty. Varellas & Pratt, Lexington, 1993—; Fayette County judge exec., Ky., 1980—; hearing officer Ky. Natural Resources and Environ. Protection Cabinet, Frankfort, 1984-88. Committeewoman Ky. Young Dems., Frankfort, 1977-80; pres. Fayette County Young Dems., Lexington, 1977; bd. dirs. Ky. Dem. Women's Club, Frankfort, 1980-84; grad. Leadership Lexington, 1981; chairwoman Profl. Women's Forum, Lexington, Ky., 1985-86, bd. dirs., 1984-87, Aequum award com, 1989-92; mem. devel. coun. Midway Coll., 1990-92; co-chair Gift Club Com., 1992. Named Outstanding Young Dem. Woman, Ky. Young Dems., Frankfort, 1977, Outstanding Former Young Dem., Ky. Young Dems., 1983. Mem. Ky. Bar Assn. (treas. young lawyers div. 1978-79, long range planning com., 1988-89), Fla. Bar, Fayette County Bar Assn. (treas. 1977-78, bd. govs. 1978-80), LWV (nominating com 1984-85), Greater Lexington C. of C. (legis. affairs com. 1994-95, bd. dirs. coun. smaller enterprises 1992-95). Club: The Lexington Forum, Lexington Philharm. Guild (bd. dirs. 1979-81, 86—), Nat. Assn. Women Bus. Owners (chmn. community liaison/govtl. affairs com. 1992-93), Lexington Network (bd. dirs. and sec. 1994—). Office: Varellas & Pratt 167 W Main St Lexington KY 40507-1713

VARET, MICHAEL A., lawyer; b. N.Y.C., Mar. 9, 1942; s. Guster V. and Frances B. (Goldberg) V.; m. Elizabeth R. Varet, June 3, 1973; 3 children. BS in Econs., U. Pa., 1962; LLB, Yale U., 1965. Bar: N.Y. 1966, U.S. Supreme Ct. 1975, U.S. Dist. Ct. (ea. and so. dists.) N.Y. 1975, U.S. Tax Ct. 1975, U.S. Claims Ct. 1975, U.S. Ct. Appeals (2d cir.) 1975. Mem., chmn. Varet & Fink P.C. (formerly Milgrim Thomajan & Lee), N.Y.C., 1982-95; mem. firm Piper & Marbury LLP, N.Y.C., 1995—; dir. B. Rothschild Found. for the Advancement of Science in Israel, 1986—; dir., sec. Am. Found. for Basic Rsch. in Israel, 1990—. Trustee Montefiore Med. Ctr., Bronx, N.Y., 1980-92; bd. dirs. Sem. Libr. Corp. Jewish Theol. Sem., N.Y.C., 1983-87, United Jewish Appeal-Fedn. Jewish Philanthropies of Greater N.Y., Inc., 1979-86, Mosholu Preservation Corp., Bronx, 1982-88; bd. overseers Jewish Theol. Sem., 1982-90, Jewish Publ. Soc. of Am., 1986—, exec. com., 1989-94, 95—; mem. exec. com. Montefiore Med. Ctr., 1985-92, Yale Law Sch. Assn., 1990-93; mem. coun. of overseers United Jewish Appeal fedn. of Jewish Philanthropies of Greater N.Y., Inc., 1986-95. Mem. ABA, N.Y. State Bar Assn., Assn. of Bar of City of N.Y. (bd. dirs., exec. com. 1971-75), Internat. Fiscal Assn., Internat. Tax Planning Assn., Yale Club, (N.Y.C.), Lotos Club (N.Y.C.). Democrat. Office: Piper & Marbury LLP 1251 Avenue of the Americas New York NY 10020

VARGA, RICHARD STEVEN, mathematics educator; b. Cleve., Oct. 9, 1928; s. Steven and Ella (Krejcs) V.; m. Esther Marie Pfister, Sept. 22, 1951; 1 dau., Gretchen Marie. BS, Case Inst. Tech. (merged with Case Western Res. U.), 1950; AM, Harvard U., 1951, PhD, 1954; hon. doctorate, U. Karlsruhe, 1991, U. Lille, 1993. With Bettis Atomic Power Lab., Westinghouse Electric Co., 1954-60, adv. mathematician, 1959-60; full prof. math. Case Inst. Tech. (now Case We. Res. U.), 1960-69; univ. prof. Kent (Ohio) State U., 1969—, dir. rsch. Inst. for Computational Math.; Cons. to govt. and industry. Author: Matrix Iterative Analysis, 1962, Functional Analysis and Approximation Theory in Numerical Analysis, 1971, Topics in Polynomial and Rational Interpolation and Approximation, 1982, Zeros of Sections of Power Series, 1983, Scientific Computation on Mathematical Problems and Conjectures, 1990; editor: Numerical Solution of Field Problems in Continuum Physics, 1970, Padé and Rational Approximations: Theory and Applications, 1977, Rational Approximations and Interpolation, 1984, Computational Methods and Function Theory, 1990, Numerical Linear Algebra, 1993; editor-in-chief. Numerische Math., Electronic Transactions Numerical Analysis; mem. editl. bd. Linear Algebra and Applications, Constructive Approximation, Computational Mathematics (China), Utilities Mathematica, Revue Française d'Automatique, Informatique, Recherche Opérationelle, Numerical Algorithms, Analysis. Recipient Rsch. award Sigma Xi, 1965, von Humboldt prize, 1982, Pres.' medal Kent State U., 1981; Guggenheim fellow, 1963; Fairchild scholar, 1974. Home: 7065 Arcadia Dr Cleveland OH 44129-6065 Office: Kent State U Inst Computational Mat Kent OH 44242

VARGAS, PATTIE LEE, author, editor; b. Spencer, S.D., Feb. 4, 1941; d. Gilbert Helmuth and Carol Maxine (Winans) Bohlman; m. Richard D. Gulling Sr., July 17, 1960 (div. 1977); children: Richard D. Jr., David M., Toni C.; m. Allen H. Vargas, May 9, 1979 (dec. 1993). BS in Secondary Edn. cum laude, Miami U., 1969; MA in English, U. Dayton, 1972. Tchr. Kettering (Ohio) City Schs., 1972-83; editor Gurney's Gardening News, Yankton, S.D., 1984-88; dir. pub. relations Gurney Seed and Nursery Co., Yankton, 1985-89; creative supr. catalogs Dakota Advt. div. Gurney Seed and Nursery Co., Yankton, 1986-89; v.p. A.H. Vargas Assocs., Vermillion, S.D., 1987-93; editl. project mgr. Mazer Corp., Dayton, Ohio, 1993—; v.p. A.H. Vargas Assocs. Mktg. and Comm. Cons., Vermillion, S.D., 1987-93; pub. rels. cons. Cath. Conf. of Ohio, Columbus, 1975-76. Author: Country Wines, 1991, Stay Well Without Going Broke, 1993, Cordially Yours, 1996; writer: (movie) Planning Cath. Schs. Week, 1975, (multi-media show) Tribute to the Bicentennial, 1976. Mem. Miamisburg (Ohio) Sch. Bond Steering Com., 1980. Mem. Nat. Fedn. of Press Women (recipient Editorial Writing award, 1986, 87, 88), S.D. Press Women (recipient Sweepstakes award 1987, 1988, Catalog award 1988), Nat. Garden Writing Assn. Avocations: painting, boating, bicycling.

VARGAS-ALCARO, JUANA AMADA, elementary education educator; b. Tenares, Dominican Republic, Mar. 30, 1952; came to U.S., 1968; d. Jorge Ramon and Virginia (Rojas) Vargas; m. Sidney Feldman, Aug. 9, 1976 (div. 1979); m. Elizardo de Jesus Pérez, Apr. 7, 1982 (dec. Sept. 1992); children: Steven Louis Feldman, Sylvester Ely; m. Jack D. Alcaro, Feb. 14, 1994. BA in Fgn. Lang., Gordon Coll., Wenham, Mass., 1976; MEd in Adminstrn., U. Mass., Lowell, 1988; MEd and Computers, Lesley Coll., 1988; postgrad., Nova Southeastern U. Bilingual tchr. Lawrence (Mass.) Pub. Schs., 1976-77, bilingual and ESL tchr., 1982-85, tchr. computers, 1985-90; tchr. Spanish, Carol Morgan Sch. Santo Domingo, Dominican Republic, 1978-82; tchr. lit. Am. Sch. Santo Domingo, 1990-92; tchr. Spanish, Dade County Pub. Schs., Miami, Fla., 1992-93, tchr. computers, 1993—; mem. grant writing team Allapattah Elem. Sch., Miami, 1993—. Avocations: reading, computers, antiques, music, art. Home: PO Box 820225 Pembroke Pines FL 33082-0225 Office: Allapattah Elem Sch 4700 NW 12th Ave Miami FL 33127-2214

VARGO, RICHARD JOSEPH, accounting educator, writer. BS, Marietta Coll., 1963; MBA, Ohio U., 1965; PhD, U. Wash., 1969. CPA, Calif. Asst. prof. acctg. Sch. Bus. Adminstrn. U. So. Calif., 1968-71; assoc. prof. acctg., chair dept. acctg. Sch. Bus. Adminstrn. Coll. William and Mary, 1971-73; assoc. prof. Coll. Bus. Adminstrn. U. Tex., Arlington, 1973-74, assoc. dean for grad. studies Coll. Bus. Adminstrn., 1974-76, prof. acctg. Coll. Bus. Adminstrn., 1976-81; prof. acctg. Eberhardt Sch. Bus. U. of Pacific, 1981—; adj. prof. Family Practice and Cmty. Medicine, U. Tex. Southwestern Med. Sch., Dallas, 1977-81; adj. prof. acctg. McGeorge Sch. Law, U. of Pacific, 1982-93; spkr. in field. Author: Effective Church Accounting, 1989; co-author: (with Paul Dierks) Readings in Governmental and Nonprofit Accounting, 1982, (with Lanny Solomon and Larry Walther) Principles of Accounting, 1983, 4th edit., 1993, (with Lanny Solomon and Larry Walther) Financial Accounting, 1985, 3d edit., 1992; contbr. articles to profl. jours. Recipient grant U. Tex. Sys. Organized Rsch. Funds, 1973-74, 75-76, grant U. of Pacific and Kosciuszko Found., 1987, grant Kemper Found., 1989, grant U.S. Dept. Edn. and Rockefeller Bros. Found., 1991. Mem. Beta Alpha Psi (pres. Ohio U. chpt. 1964-65), Beta Gamma Sigma, Phi Kappa Phi. Office: Univ of Pacific Eberhardt School of Bus Stockton CA 95211

VARIAN, HAL RONALD, economics educator; b. Wooster, Ohio, Mar. 18, 1947; s. Max Ronald and Elaine Catherine (Shultzman) V.; m. Carol Johnston, Nov. 1986. S.B., MIT, 1969; M.A., U. Calif.-Berkeley, 1973, Ph.D. (NSF fellow), 1973. Asst. prof. econs. MIT, 1973-77; prof. U. Mich., 1977-95, prof. fin., 1983-95, Reuben Kempf prof. econs., 1984-95; prof. sch. bus., dean sch. info. mgmt. and sys. U. Calif., Berkeley, 1995—, Class of 1944 prof., 1996—; Siena chair in econs., U. Siena, Italy, 1990. Author: Microeconomic Analysis, 1978, Intermediate Microeconomics, 1987; co-editor Am. Econ. Rev., 1987-90. Guggenheim fellow, 1979-80; Fulbright scholar, 1990. Fellow AAAS, Econometric Soc.; mem. Am. Econ. Soc. Home: 1198 Estates Dr Lafayette CA 94549-2749 Office: U Calif SIMS 102 South Hall Berkeley CA 94720

VARIN, ROGER ROBERT, textile executive; b. Bern, Switzerland, Feb. 15, 1925; came to U.S., 1951; s. Robert Francois and Anna (Martz) V.; m. Annemarie Louis, May 24, 1951; children: Roger R.R., Edward C.H., Viviane A.H. BBA, Mcpl. Coll., Bern, 1944; PhD in Chemistry, U. Bern, 1951. Rsch. fellow Harvard U., Cambridge, Mass., 1951-52; rsch. assoc. E.I. DuPont De Nemours, Wilmington, Del., 1952-62; dir. rsch. Riegel Textile Corp., Ware Shoals, S.C., 1962-71; founder, chief exec. officer Varinit Corp., Greenville, S.C., 1971—; founder, chief exec. officer Varinit S.A., Geneva, 1974—. Pres. Greenville Sister City Internat., 1993. Mem. Am. Chem. Soc., Fiber Soc., Soc. Advanced Materials and Process Engring., Rotary (pres. Greenville chpt. 1979-80), Sigma Xi. Office: Varinit Corp PO Box 6602 Greenville SC 29606-6602

VARLACK, ADRIAN, church administrator. Adminstr. comm. mem. Ch. of God of Prphecy. Office: Ch God Prophecy Can PO Box 2910 Cleveland TN 37320-2910

VARLEY, HERBERT PAUL, Japanese language and cultural history educator; b. Paterson, N.J., Feb. 8, 1931; s. Herbert Paul and Katharine L. (Norcross) V.; m. Betty Jane Geiskopf, Dec. 24, 1960. B.S., Lehigh U., 1952; M.A., Columbia U., 1961, Ph.D., 1964; DHL (hon.), Lehigh U., 1988. Asst. prof. U. Hawaii, Honolulu, 1964-65; asst. prof. dept. East Asian Langs. and Cultures Columbia U., N.Y.C., 1965-69, assoc. prof., 1969-75, prof., 1975-94, chmn. dept. East Asian Langs. and Cultures, 1983-89; Sen Soshitsu XV prof. Japanese Cultural History U. Hawaii, spring 1991-93, 94—. Author: The Onin War, 1967, The Samurai, 1970, Imperial Restoration in Medieval Japan, 1971, Japanese Culture, 1973, A Chronicle of Gods and Sovereigns, 1980, Tea in Japan: Essays on the History of Chanoyu, 1989, Warriors of Japan, As Portrayed in the War Tales, 1994. Bd. govs. Japanese Cultural Ctr. of Hawaii. Served with U.S. Army, 1952-54, Japan. Mem. Assn. Asian Studies, Japan Soc., Soc. Am. Magicians (pres. local chpt. 1983-84). Avocations: sleight of hand magic; piano. Home: 38 S Judd St Apt 15B Honolulu HI 96817-2607 Office: U Hawaii History Dept Sakamaki Hall A 203 2530 Dole St Honolulu HI 96822-2303

VARMA, ARVIND, chemical engineering educator, researcher; b. Ferozabad, India, Oct. 13, 1947; s. Hans Raj and Vijay L. (Jhanjhee) V.; m. Karen K. Guse, Aug. 7, 1971; children: Anita, Sophia. BS ChemE, Panjab U., 1966; MS ChemE, U. N.B., Fredericton, Can., 1968; PhD ChemE, U. Minn., 1972. Asst. prof. U. Minn., Mpls., 1972-73; sr. research engr. Union Carbide Corp., Tarrytown, N.Y., 1973-75; asst. prof. chem. engring. U. Notre Dame, Ind., 1975-77, assoc. prof., 1977-80, prof., 1980-88, Arthur J. Schmitt prof., 1988—, chmn. dept., 1983-88; vis. prof. U. Wis., Madison, fall 1981; Chevron vis. prof. Calif. Inst. Tech., Pasadena, spring 1982; vis. prof. Ind. Inst. Tech.-Kanpur, spring 19899, U. Cagliari, Italy, summer, 1989, 92; vis. fellow Princeton U., spring 1996. Editor: (with others) The Mathematical Understanding of Chemical Engineering Sytstems, 1980, Chemical Reaction and Reactor Engineering, 1987; contbr. numerous articles to profl. jours. Recipient Tchr. of Yr. award Coll. Engring. U. Notre Dame, 1991, Spl. Presdl. award 1992, R.H. Wilhelm award AIChE, 1993; Fulbright scholar; Indo-Am. fellow, 1988-89. Home: 52121 N Lakeshore Dr Granger IN 46530-7848 Office: Dept Chem Engring U Notre Dame Notre Dame IN 46556

VARMA, BAIDYA NATH, sociologist, broadcaster, poet; m. Savitri Devi. PhD, Columbia U., 1958. Radio broadcaster to India UN; Asian News Moderator Nat. Edn. TV Network, N.Y.C.; prof. emeritus sociology CUNY; prodr. radio dramas Voice of Am.; wrote, narrated over 200 documentary films, News of the Day; lectr. numerous univs. U.S., Can., Eng., India; chair Plenary Sessions World Congress of Sociology, Internat. Congress Anthrop. and Enthnological Scis; cons. Nat. Endowment Humanities, Ctr. Migration Studies, Dept. Energy, Wenner-Gren Found. Anthrop. Rsch. in U.S., Can. Coun., Indian Law Inst.; chair faculty seminars Columbia U.; presided Centenary Celebrations Indian Writers, N.Y.C.; vis. prof. Columbia U., other U.S., Indian Univs.; chair panel on religions and sexuality Parliament of World's Religions, 1993. Author: The Sociology and Politics of Development: A Theoretical Study, 1980, Social Science and Indian Society, 1985, New Directions in Theory and Methodology, 1993, Contemporary India (cert. of merit German Govt.), Love Feast, 1995, Spring of Civilization, 1995; author, editor others; contbr. articles Ency. Americana, profl. jours.; edit. adv. nat., internat. sociol. jours. Assoc. trustee Wordsworth Trust; trustee Taraknath Das Found.; bd. scholars Buddhist Cultural Inst., U.S.; judge Permanent People's Tribunal Indsl. and Environ. Hazards and Human Rights, Rome; established Varma Found.; chmn. Sravi Found.; founding mems. Lincoln Ctr. for Performing Arts, N.Y.C.; chmn. bd. trustees Soc. for Restoration of Ancient Vidyadhams of India; trustee Internat. Found. for Vedic Edn., U.S., U.S. Capitol Hist. Soc. Sr. faculty fellow Am. Inst. Indian Studies, 1964-65, 84-85; elected to Am. Film Inst.; guest fellow Oxford U., The Sorbonne, Inst. Advanced Study; named Hon. Citizen, Colonial Williamsburg; recipient Cert. of Merit, City Coun. Pres. Yonkers. Mem. N.Y. Acad. Scis., South Asian Sociols. (1st pres.), Soc. Indian Acads. in Am. (exec. com.), Global Orgn. People of Indian Origin (life), U.S. Capitol Hist. Soc. (trustee). Home: 62 Belvedere Dr Yonkers NY 10705-2814

VARMUS, HAROLD ELIOT, government health institutes administrator, educator; b. Oceanside, N.Y., Dec. 18, 1939; s. Frank and Beatrice (Barasch) V.; m. Constance Louise Casey, Oct. 25, 1969; children: Jacob Carey, Christopher Isaac. AB, Amherst Coll., 1961, DSc (hon.), 1984; MA, Literature, Harvard U., 1962; MD, Columbia U. Med. Sch., 1966. Lic. physician, Calif. Intern, resident Presbyn. Hosp., N.Y.C., 1966-68; clin. assoc. NIH, Bethesda, Md., 1968-70; lectr. dept. microbiology U. Calif., San Francisco, 1970-72, asst. prof., depts. microbiology and immunology, biochemistry and biophysics, 1972-74, assoc. prof., 1974-79, prof., 1979-83, Am. Cancer Soc. research prof., 1984-93; dir. NIH, Bethesda, Md., 1993—; chmn. bd. on biology NRC. Editor: Molecular Biology of Tumor Viruses, 1982, 85; Readings in Tumor Virology, 1983; assoc. editor Genes and Development Jour., Cell Jour.; mem. editorial bd. Cancer Surveys. Named Calif. Acad. Sci. Scientist of Yr., 1982; co-recipient Lasker Found. award, 1982, Passano Found. award, 1983, Armand Hammer Cancer prize, 1984, GM Alfred Sloan award 1984, Shubitz Cancer prize, 1985, Nobel Prize in Physiology or Medicine, 1989. Mem. AAAS, NAS, Inst. Medicine of NAS, Am. Soc. Virology, Am. Soc. Microbiology, Am. Acad. Arts and Scis. Democrat. Research (with J. Michael Bishop) on the replication of retroviruses. Office: National Istitutes of Health Bldg 1 Rm 126 1 Center Dr MSC 0148 Bethesda MD 20892-0148*

VARNEDOE, JOHN KIRK TRAIN, museum curator; b. Savannah, Ga., Jan. 18, 1946; s. Samuel Lamartine and Lilla (Train) V.; m. Elyn Zimmerman. BA with honors, Williams Coll., 1967, DFA (hon.), 1994; MA, Stanford U., 1970, PhD, 1972. Asst. instr. art history Williams Coll., 1967-68; asst. prof. art history Stamford (Calif.) U., 1973-74; asst. prof. Columbia U., N.Y.C., 1974-80; assoc. prof. Inst. Fine Arts, NYU, N.Y.C., 1980-88; prof. fine arts Inst. Fine Arts, NYU, 1984-88; chief curator dept. painting and sculpture Mus. Modern Art, N.Y.C., 1989—; vis. lectr. in law Columbia U. Law Sch., 1980-81; adj. curator dept. painting and sculpture Mus. Modern Art, 1985-88; mem. adv. bd. J. Paul Getty Program for Art on Film, 1985-87, Ctr. for Advanced Study in Visual Arts, 1990-93; mem. selection panel J. Paul Getty Postdoctoral Fellowships, 1985-88, J. Paul Getty Sr. Fellowships, 1988-90; Slade prof. art history Oxford (Eng.) U., 1992; lectr. in field. Author: The Drawings of Auguste Rodin, 1971, Vienna 1900, 1986, Gustave Caillebotte, 1987, Northern Light, 1988 (Henry Allen Moe prize 1983), A Fine Disregard--What Makes Modern Art Modern, 1990, High and Low: Modern Art and Popular Culture, 1990, Cy Twombly: A Retrospective, 1994; mem. editl. bd. The Art Bull., 1985-90; contbr. articles and revs. to profl. jours. Decorated knight The Royal Order of Donnebroge (Denmark); David E. Finley fellow Nat. Gallery Art, 1970-73, NEH fellow, 1977-78, McArthur Found. fellow, 1984-89; Rsch. grantee Columbia U., 1975, Travel grantee Am. Coun. Learned Socs. Fellow Am. Acad. Arts & Scis., NYU Soc. Fellows. Office: Mus of Modern Art 11 W 53rd St New York NY 10019-5401

VARNER, BARTON DOUGLAS, lawyer; b. Ida Grove, Iowa, May 2, 1920; s. Charles R. and Mary E. (Whinery) V.; m. Frances Elaine Seaton, May 9, 1943; children: Charles R., John A. Student, U. Nebr., 1938-42; LL.B., U. Mo. at Kansas City, 1951. Bar: Mo. 1951. Since practiced in Kansas City and Lake Ozark, Mo., ret. 1985; of counsel Gage and Tucker (now Lathrop & Gage), Kansas City and Lake Ozark, 1985—; partner firm Gage and Tucker (and predecessors), 1955-85. Bd. mgrs. Kansas City YMCA, 1958-80, chmn., 1962; pres. Miller County Hist. Soc., 1991-92, 94-95. With USNR, 1942-45. Mem. ABA, Mo. Bar Assn., Nebr. U. Alumni Assn. Kansas City (pres. 1958-60, bd. dirs., counsel), Kansas City Club, Delta Sigma Pi, Delta Theta Phi. Methodist (steward 1964-66, trustee 1968-69). Home: 8 Maple Tree Cir Lake Ozark MO 65049-8672 Office: Mut Benefit Life Bldg Kansas City MO 64108 *Ralph Waldo Emerson best expressed the principle that has helped me the most in attaining what success that I have attained when he stated in his Essay on Self Reliance the following: "There is a time in every man's education when he arrives at the conviction that envy is ignorance; that imitation is suicide; that he must take himself for better or worse as his portion; that though the wide universe is full of good, no kernel of nourishing corn can come to him but through his toil bestowed on that plot of ground which is given him to till. The power which resides in him is new in nature and none but he knows what that is which he can do, nor does he know until he has tried."*

VARNER, CHARLEEN LAVERNE MCCLANAHAN (MRS. ROBERT B. VARNER), nutritionist, educator, administrator, dietitian; b. Alba, Mo., Aug. 28, 1931; d. Roy Calvin and Lela Ruhama (Smith) McClanahan; student Joplin (Mo.) Jr. Coll., 1949-51; BS in Edn., Kans. State Coll. Pittsburg, 1953; MS, U. Ark., 1958; PhD, Tex. Woman's U. 1966; postgrad. Mich. State U., summer, 1955, U. Mo., summer 1962; m. Robert Bernard Varner, July 4, 1953. Apprentice county home agt. U. Mo., summer 1952; tchr. Ferry Pass Sch., Escambia County, Fla., 1953-54; tchr. biology, home econs. Joplin Sr. H.S., 1954-59; instr. home econs. Kans. State Coll., Pittsburg, 1959-63; lectr. foods, nutrition Coll. Household Arts and Scis., Tex. Woman's U., 1963-64, rsch. asst. NASA grant, 1964-66; assoc. prof. home econs. Central Mo. State U., Warrensburg, 1966-70, adviser to Colhecon, 1966-70, adviser to Alpha Sigma Alpha, 1967-70, 72, mem. bd. advisers Honors Group, 1967-70; prof., head dept. home econs. Kans. State Tchrs. Coll., Emporia, 1970-73; prof., chmn. dept. home econs. Benedictine Coll., Atchison, Kans., 1973-74; prof., chmn. dept. home econs. Baker U., Baldwin City, Kans., 1974-75; owner, operator Diet-Con Dietary Cons. Enterprises, cons. dietitian, 1973—, Home-Con Cons. Enterprises. Mem. Joplin Little Theater, 1956-60. Mem. NEA, Mo., Kans. state tchrs. assns., AAUW, Am., Mo., Kans. dietetics assns., Am., Mo., Kans. home econs. assns., Am. Acad. Scis., AAUP, U. Ark. Alumni Assn., Alumni Assn. Kans. State Coll. of Pittsburg, Am. Vocat. Assn., Assn. Edn. Young Children, Sigma Xi, Beta Sigma Phi, Beta Beta Beta, Alpha Sigma Alpha, Delta Kappa Gamma, Kappa Kappa Iota, Phi Upsilon Omicron, Theta Alpha Pi, Kappa Phi. Methodist (organist). Home: PO Box 1009 Topeka KS 66601

VARNER, CHILTON DAVIS, lawyer; b. Opelika, Ala., Mar. 12, 1943; s. William Cole and Frances (Thornton) Davis; m. K. Morgan Varner III, June 19, 1965; 1 child, Ashley Elizabeth. AB with distinction, Smith Coll., 1965; JD with distinction, Emory U., 1976. Assoc. King & Spalding, Atlanta, 1976-83, ptnr., 1983—; trustee Emory U., Atlanta, 1995—. Author: Appellate Handbook for Georgia Lawyers, 1995. Mem. Leadership Atlanta, 1984-85; asst. clk., elder, bd. elders Trinity Presbyn. Ch., Atlanta, 1985-88; exec. com. Ate Arts Alliance, Atlanta, 1981-85; mem. Atlanta Symphony Chorus, 1970-74. Fellow Am. Coll. Trial Lawyers; mem. ABA, Ga. Bar Assn., Atlanta Bar Assn., Bleckley Inn of Ct. (master), Order of Coif, Phi Beta Kappa. Office: King & Spalding 191 Peachtree St NE Atlanta GA 30303-1740

VARNER, DAVID EUGENE, lawyer; b. Dallas, Oct. 9, 1937; s. E.C. and D. Evelyn (Bauguss) V.; m. Joan Paula Oransky, Aug. 13, 1962; children: Michael A., Kevin E., Cheryl L. B.A., So. Meth. U., Dallas, 1958, J.D., 1961. Bar: Tex. 1961, Fla. 1974, Okla., 1977, U.S. Supreme Ct. 1978. Assoc. Eldridge, Goggans, Davidson & Silverberg, Dallas, 1962-65; atty., asst. sec. Redman Industries, Inc., Dallas, 1965-66; assoc. gen. atty. Tex. Instruments, Inc., Dallas, 1966-73; sr. atty., asst. sec. Fla. Gas Co., Winter

Park, 1973-76; v.p., gen. counsel, sec. Facet Enterprises, Inc., Tulsa, 1976-78, Summa Corp., Las Vegas, Nev., 1978-82; sr. v.p., gen. counsel, sec. Transco Energy Co., Houston, 1982-95. Mng. editor Southwestern Law Jour., 1960-61. Mem. ABA, Houston Bar Assn., Tex. Bar, Okla. Bar, Fla. Bar, Am. Soc. Corp. Secs.

VARNER, JOYCE EHRHARDT, librarian; b. Quincy, Ill., Sept. 13, 1938; d. Wilbur John and Florence Elizabeth (Mast) Ehrhardt; m. Donald Giles Varner, Sept. 12, 1959; children: Amy, Janice, Christian, Matthew, Nadine. BA, Northeastern Okla. State U., 1980; MLS, U. Okla., 1984. Lab. analyst Gardner Denver Co., Quincy, 1956-60; sales rep. Morrisonville, Ill., 1963-69; libr. clk. U. Ill., Urbana, 1973-75; libr. tech. asst. Northeastern Okla. State U., Tahlequah, 1976-86; asst. reference libr. Muskogee (Okla.) Pub. Libr., 1986-90; libr. Jess Dunn Correctional Ctr., Taft, Okla., 1990—. Editor Indian Nations Audubon Nature Notes, 1977-81, 96—; contbr. articles to newspaper. Vol. Lake-Wood coun. Girl Scouts U.S.A., 1975—, bd. dirs. 1992—, pres., 1995—; sec.-treas. Cherokee County Rural Water Dist. 7, 1987—; edn. chmn. Indian Nations chpt. Nat. Audubon Soc., 1989—. Recipient Thanks Badge, Lake-Wood coun. Girl Scouts U.S.A., 1990. Mem. ALA, AAUW, Okla. Libr. Assn. (nominating com. 1989), Okla. Acad. Sci., Okla. Ornithol. Soc. (chmn. libr. com. 1978-88, Award of Merit 1990, pres.-elect 1994, pres. 1995—), Am. Correctional Assn., Okla. Correctional Assn., Alpha Chi, Beta Beta Beta, Phi Delta Kappa (Found. rep. 1984-86, historian 1992—). Avocations: nature study, needlework, square dancing, genealogy. Home: RR 1 Box 1 Welling OK 74471-9701 Office: Jess Dunn Correctional Ctr Leisure Libr PO Box 316 Taft OK 74463-0316

VARNER, ROBERT EDWARD, federal judge; b. Montgomery, Ala., June 11, 1921; s. William and Georgia (Thomas) V.; children: Robert Edward, Carolyn Stuart.; m. Jane Dennis Hannah, Feb. 27, 1982. BS, Auburn U., 1946; JD, U. Ala., 1949. Bar: Ala. 1949. Atty. City of Tuskegee, 1951; asst. U.S. atty. U.S. Dist. Ct. (mid. dist.) Ala., 1954-58; pvt. practice Montgomery, 1958-71; ptnr. Jones, Murray, Stewart & Varner, 1958-71; U.S. dist. judge Montgomery, 1971—; guest lectr. bus. law Huntingdon Coll. Pres. Montgomery Rotary Charity Found.; v.p., fin. chmn. Tukabatchee Area coun. Boy Scouts Am.; mem. Macon County Bd. Edn., 1950-54. With USNR, 1942-46. Recipient Silver Beaver award Boy Scouts Am. Mem. ABA, FBA, ATLA, Montgomery Bar Assn. (pres. 1971), Macon County Bar Assn., Jud. Conf. U.S. (mem. com. on operation of jury sys.), Rotary (pres. club 1961), Phi Alpha Delta (Outstanding Alumnus award 1996), Phi Delta Theta. Republican. Methodist. Office: US Dist Ct PO Box 2046 Montgomery AL 36102-2046

VARNER, STERLING VERL, retired oil company executive; b. Ranger, Tex., Dec. 20, 1919; s. George Virgle and Christina Ellen (Shafer) V.; m. Paula Jean Kennedy, Nov. 17, 1945; children: Jane Ann, Richard Alan. Student, Murray State Sch. Agr., 1940, Wichita State U., 1949. With Kerr-McGee, Inc., 1941-45; with Koch Industries, Inc., Wichita, Kans., 1945-90, pres., chief operating officer, 1974-86, vice chmn., 1987-90, chmn. bd. dirs., 1990, now bd. dirs.; ret.; owner Shadow Valley Ranch; bd. dirs. Koch Industries Inc. Trustee The Nature Conservancy; bd. dirs. YMCA, Maude Carpenter Children's Ctr. Mem. Wichita Country Club, Crestview Country Club. Mem. Ch. of Christ. Home: 1515 N Linden Ct Wichita KS 67206-3312 Office: Koch Industries Inc PO Box 2256 411 E 37th St N Wichita KS 67201-2256

VARNERIN, LAWRENCE JOHN, physicist, retired educator; b. Boston, July 10, 1923; s. Lawrence John and Josephine (Nangeroni) V.; m. Marie Elizabeth Hynes, Apr. 19, 1952; children: Melanie, Lawrence, Gregory, Sharon, Suzanne, Bruce, Carol, Jeffrey. SB in Physics, MIT, 1947, PhD in Physics, 1949. Supr. TR/ATR microwave tube, electronics divsn. Sylvania corp., Boston, 1949-52; acting mgr. physics dept. Westinghouse Rsch. Labs., Pitts., 1952-57; head heterojunction IC and materials dept. AT&T Bell Labs., Murray Hill, N.J., 1957-86; Chandler-Weaver prof. elec. engring., chmn. elec. engring. computer sci. dept. Lehigh U., Bethlehem, Pa., 1986-92, Chandler-Weaver prof. emeritus, 1992—. Assoc. editor Jour. Magnetism and Magnetic Materials, 1973-94. Served with U.S. Army, 1943-46. Fellow IEEE, Am. Phys. Soc.; mem. Magnetics Soc. Roman Catholic. Home: PO Box 1107 Wolfeboro NH 03894-1107

VARNEY, BERNARD KEITH, financial executive, consultant; b. Coos Bay, Oreg., Nov. 5, 1919; s. Earnest and Daisy Inez (Lattin) V.; m. Norma Betty Rosick, Aug. 31, 1945; children: Mark Keith, Michael Matthew. B of Econs. and Bus. cum laude, U. Wash., 1950. CPA, Wash. Acctg. mgr. Rainier Nat. Ins. Co., Seattle, 1950-55; v.p. fin. Calif. State Auto Assn. Inter-Ins. Bur., San Francisco, 1955-84; treas. Calif. State Auto Assn., San Francisco, 1955-84, investment and fin. cons., 1984-93; bd. dirs. Auto Club Ins. Co., Columbus, Ohio. 2d lt. U.S. Army, 1944-46. Decorated Army Commendation Medal, 1946. Mem. Ins. Acctg. and Statis. Assn. (pres.), Marin Country Club, Phi Beta Kappa, Beta Gamma Sigma, Beta Alpha Psi. Avocations: golf, travel. Home: 313 Fairway Dr Novato CA 94949-5832

VARNEY, CARLETON BATES, JR., interior designer, columnist, educator; b. Lynn, Mass., Jan. 23, 1937; s. Carleton Bates and Julia (Raczkowskos) V.; divorced; children: Nicholas, Seamus, Sebastian. BA, Oberlin Coll., 1958; student, U. Madrid, 1957; MA, NYU, 1969; LHD (hon.), U. Charleston, 1987. Sch. tchr., 1958-59; asst. to pres. Dorothy Draper & Co., Inc., 1959-63, exec. v.p., 1963-66, pres., 1966—; dean Carleton Varney Sch. of Art & Design, U. Charleston, W.Va. Designer: chairs, decorative fabrics, dinnerware and china, crystal glassware, table and bed linen, ready to wear resort collection Cruzanwear, 1987, mens' wear furnishings for Rawlinson & Marking, London, 1987; interior designer: Dromoland Castle, Ireland, 1963, 88, Westbury Hotel, Belgium, 1964, N.Y. World's Fair, 1965, Clare Inn, Ireland, 1968, Greenbrier Hotel, White Sulphur Springs, W.Va., 1968, Westbury Hotel, San Francisco, 1973, Copley Plaza Hotel, Boston, 1976, Amway Grand Plaza Hotel, Grand Rapids, Mich., 1980, The Grand Hotel, Mackinac Island, Mich., 1978, Equinox House, Manchester, Vt., 1984, Brazilian Ct. Hotel, Palm Beach, Fla., 1985, Waldorf Towers, N.Y.C., 1985, Dawn Beach Hotel, St. Maarten, 1985, Christian Broadcasting Conv. Ctr., 1986, Met. Opera House boutique, N.Y.C., 1985, (cruise ship) World Discoverer, 1984, Arrowwood Conv. Ctr., Purchase, N.Y., 1987, Boca Raton Hotel and Club, Fla., 1987, Speedway Club, Charlotte, N.C., 1987, Coccoloba Plantation, Anguilla, Brit. Virgin Islands, 1987, Villa Madeleine, St. Croix, V.I., 1987, Ashford Castle, Ireland, 1988, Adare Manor, Ireland, 1988, The Breakers, Palm Beach, Fla., 1989, Jackson Lake Lodge, Wyo., 1989, The Pub. Rms., V.P.'s Residence, Washington, 1989, Cormorant Cove, St. Croix, V.I., 1990, The Buccaneer Hotel, St. Croix, 1991, Dromoland Castle, Internat. Ctr., Ireland, 1991, West Village Golf Resort, Tokyo, 1993, Half Moon Bay Club, Jamaica, numerous others; designer: White House party for celebration Israel-Egypt Peace Treaty, 1979; Palm Beach Cares fashion benefit for Am. Found. for AIDS Research, 1988, log home for Pres. and Mrs. Carter, Ellijay, Ga., 1983; color cons. Carter Presdl. Library, 1986; trustee and curator: former presdl. yacht U.S.S. Sequoia, 1982; retail stores: Carleton Varney at the Greenbrier, White Sulphur Springs, W.Va., 1981, Carleton Varney at the Mill, Christiansted, St. Croix, 1988, Carleton Varney By-The Yard, Sarasota, Fla., 1990, Carleton Varney Rose Cottage, Newmarket-on-Fergus, Ireland, 1991; author: numerous books including You and Your Apartment, 1960, The Family Decorates a Home, 1962 Carleton Varney Decorates Windows, 1975, Be Your Own Decorator, 1979, There's No Place Like Home, 1980, Down Home, 1981, Carleton Varney's ABC's of Decorating, 1983, Staying in Shape: An Insider's Guide to the Great Spas, 1983, Room by Room Decorating, 1984, Color Magic, 1985, The Draper Touch, 1988, Kiss the Hibiscus Goodnight, 1992; syndicated columnist: Your Family Decorator, 1968—; contbg. editor Good Housekeeping Mag., 1993-95; style editor Men's Style mag. Recipient Shelby Williams award for design achievement, 1967, Tommy design award for Covington's Heraldry collection, 1989, Interior Design Hall of Fame award, 1990. Mem. Indsl. Designers Soc. Am., N.Y. State Bd. for Interior Design. Clubs: N.Y. Athletic; Shannon Rowing (Ireland); Millbrook Golf and Tennis (N.Y.). Office: Dorothy Draper & Co Inc 60 E 56th St New York NY 10022-3204 also: Rose Cottage, NewMarket-on-Fergus, County Clare Ireland *My success, I believe, is due to an ability to understand and use vibrant color appropriately, and to strive for perfection of detail in all my designs as details separate the excellent from the ordinary.*

VARNEY, CHRISTINE A., federal official. Honors degree in Politics, Philosophy and Econs., Trinity Coll., Dublin, Ireland, 1975; BA in Polit. Sci. and History magna cum laude, SUNY, Albany, 1977; MPA in Policy Analysis, Legislation and Rsch. magna cum laude, Syracuse U., 1978; JD cum laude, Georgetown U., 1986. Legis. asst. N.Y. Senate, Albany, 1977; econ. analyst GAO, Washington, 1978; econ. devel. dir. El Centro, Calif., 1979; dir. Neighborhood Outreach Program, San Diego, 1980-82; assoc. Surry & Morse, Washington, 1984-86, Pierson, Semmes & Finley, Washington, 1986-88; counsel Hogan & Hartson, Washington, 1990-92; chief counsel Clinton for Pres. Primary Campaign, 1992, Clinton-Gore Campaign, 1992; gen. counsel Dem. Nat. Com., 1992, Presdl. Inauguration Com., 1993; dep. asst. to President U.S., sec. to Cabinet The White House, Washington, 1993-94; commissioner FTC, Wasington, 1994—. Active Women's Legal Def. Fund. Mem. D.C. Bar Assn., N.Y. State Bar Assn., Nat. Lawyer's Coun. Office: FTC 6th & Pennsylvania Ave NWRm 326 Washington DC 20580*

VARNEY, RICHARD ALAN, medical office manager; b. Concord, N.H., July 8, 1950; s. John Berry and Hattie Elizabeth (Harrington) V.; m. Cheryl Suzanne Glaab, Dec. 31, 1983; stepchildren: Alysen Suzanne, Craig Judson. BS in Phys. Edn., U. N.H., 1972; MHA in Healthcare Adminstrn., Baylor U., 1984; diploma, Command and Gen. Staff Coll., 1986. Commd. 2d lt. U.S. Army, 1973, advanced through grades to lt. col., 1991; dep. asst. CEO Cutler Army Hosp., Ft. Devens, Mass., 1973-76; field med. asst. 38th ADA Bde., Osan Air Base, Korea, 1977-78; dep. asst. CEO 15th Med. Battalion, Ft. Hood, Tex., 1979-81; adminstrv. resident Ireland Army Hosp., Ft. Knox, Ky., 1982-83; COO, exec. officer U.S. Army Dental Activity, Ft. Knox, 1983-86; grad. instr. Army-Baylor Healthcare Program, San Antonio, 1986-90; project mgr. Office of the Army Surgeon Gen., Washington, 1990-93; ret. U.S. Army, 1993; office mgr. Aebi, Ginty, Romaker & Sprouse MD's, Inc., Lancaster, Ohio, 1993—; mem. Source Selection Evaluation Bd.-Champus Reform, Arlington, Va., 1987. Adult leader Boy Scouts Am., Tex., Va. and Ohio, 1988—; mem. Lancaster City Bd. of Health, 1996—. Decorated Legion of Merit, Order of Mil. Med. Merit award, Expert Field Med. badge; named to Hon. Order Ky. Cols., 1989, Outstanding Young Men of Am., 1982. Fellow Am. Coll. Healthcare Execs. (examiner oral portion mem. exam); mem. Ctrl. Ohio Health Adminstrs. Assn., Ohio Med. Group Mgmt. Assn., Mid-Ohio Med. Mgmt. Assn., Am. Assn. Procedural Coders, Lancaster Area Soc. for Human Resource Mgmt., Am. Hosp. Assn., Nat. Eagle Scout Assn., The Ret. Officers Assn., Am. Legion, Alpha Phi Omega. Avocations: home improvement, camping, hiking, music. Home: 1025 E 5th Ave Lancaster OH 43130-3276 Office: Aebi Ginty Romaker Sprouse 1800 Granville Pike Lancaster OH 43130

VARNUM, JAMES WILLIAM, hospital administrator; b. Grand Rapids, Mich., May 29, 1940; s. Robert Otto and Jeannette (Badger) V.; m. Lucinda Hotchkiss, June 6, 1964; children: Kenneth James, Susan Lucinda. A.B., Dartmouth Coll., 1962; M.Hosp. Adminstrn. with honors, U. Mich., 1964. Adminstrv. asst. U. Wis. Hosps., Madison, 1963-64; asst. supt. U. Wis. Hosps., 1964-68, asso. supt., 1968-69, supt., 1969-73; hosp. adminstr. U. Wash. Hosp., Seattle, 1973-78; pres. Mary Hitchcock Meml. Hosp., Lebanon, N.H., 1978—; prof. Med. Sch., Dartmouth Coll., 1978—. Mem. Am. Hosp. Assn. (bd. trustees 1994—), The Hitchcock Alliance (pres. 1983—). Home: 7 Woodcock Ln Etna NH 03750-4403 Office: Mary Hitchcock Meml Hosp 1 Medical Center Dr Lebanon NH 03756-0001

VARON, DAN, electrical engineer; b. Tel-Aviv, Israel, July 24, 1935; came to U.S., 1961; s. Reuven and Stephanie Varon; m. Judith Hilda Mansbach, Aug. 12, 1962; 2 children:. BSEE, The Technion, Haifa, Israel, 1957, Diplom Ingenieur, 1960; MSc, Polytechnic U., Bklyn., 1963; D of Engring. Sci., NYU, 1965. Engr. Israeli Air Force, Israel, 1957-61; rsch. fellow Polytechnic U., Bklyn., 1961-63; teaching asst. NYU, N.Y.C., 1963-65; mem. tech. staff Bell Telephone Labs., Whippany, N.J., 1965-69; mgr. Tymshare (Dial Data, Inc.), Newton, Mass., 1969-71; prin. engr. Raytheon Co., Marlborough, Mass., 1971—. Contbr. articles to Bell System Tech. Jour., IEEE, Radio Sci., Jour. Air Traffic Control Assn. Mem. IEEE (mem. tech. program com. 1970), N.Y. Acad. Scis., Assn. Computing Machinery.

VARRO, BARBARA JOAN, editor; b. East Chicago, Ind., Jan. 25, 1938; d. Alexander R. and Lottie R. (Bess) V. B.A., Duquesne U., 1959. Feature reporter, asst. fashion editor Chgo. Sun-Times, 1959-64, fashion editor, 1964-76, feature writer, 1976-84; v.p. pub. rels. Daniel J. Edelman Inc., Chgo., 1984-85; v.p. PRB/Needham Porter Novelli, Chgo., 1985-86; editor Am. Hosp. Assn. News, Chgo., 1987-94; asst. editor spl. sects. Chgo. Tribune, 1995—. Recipient awards for feature writing Ill. AP, 1978, 79, 80. Office: Chgo Tribune 435 N Michigan Ave Chicago IL 60611-4001

VARSBERGS, VILIS, minister, former religious organization administrator; b. Prauliena, Latvia, June 1, 1929; s. Viktors and Marta (Barbans) V.; m. Biruta Grinbergs, July 2, 1960; children: Anita Valda, Krista Maija, Victor Andrew. BA magna cum laude, Midland Coll., 1954; MDiv, Luth. Sch. Theology, Chgo., 1957. Ordained to ministry United Luth. Ch., 1957. Mission developer, pastor Grace Luth. Ch., Albion, Mich., 1957-63; pastor Messiah Luth. Ch., Constantine, Mich., 1963-69; adminstr., dir. Latvian Ctr. Garezers, Inc., Three Rivers, Mich., 1969-72; pastor Zion Latvian Luth. Ch., Chgo., 1973-94; pres. Latvian Evang. Luth. Ch. in Am., 1984-93; dean dept. of theology U. Latvia, Riga, 1994—; assembly del. Luth. World Fedn., Budapest, Hungary, 1984, Curitiba, Brazil, 1990. Sec. Helsinki Monitoring Com., Chgo., 1983-85; mem. adv. bd. Ill. Ethnic Cons., Chgo., 1986; bd. dirs. Luth. Immigration & Refugee Svc., N.Y.C., 1988-94. Office: U Latvia Raina Blvd 19 Chicago IL 60634

VARSHNI, YATENDRA PAL, physicist; b. Allahabad, India, May 21, 1932; emigrated to Can., 1960; s. Harpal and Bhagyawati V. B.Sc., U. Allahabad, 1950, M.Sc., 1952, Ph.D., 1956. Asst. prof. U. Allahabad, 1955-60; postdoctoral fellow NRC, Ottawa, Ont., Can., 1960-62; asst. prof. U. Ottawa, 1962-65, assoc. prof., 1965-69, prof., 1969—. Contbr. numerous articles to profl. jours. Fellow Am. Phys. Soc., Indian Phys. Soc., Royal Astron. Soc. (U.K.), Inst. Physics U.K.; mem. AAAS, Royal Soc. Chemistry (U.K., assoc.), Am. Astron. Soc., Astron. Soc. of Pacific, Can. Astron. Soc., Can. Assn. Physicists, Royal Astron. Soc. Can., Astron. Soc. India, Am. Assn. Physics Tchrs. Office: Dept Physics, U Ottawa, Ottawa, ON Canada K1N 6N5

VASHOLZ, LOTHAR ALFRED, retired insurance company executive; b. Milw., Feb. 20, 1930; s. Alfred and Charlotte Vasholz; m. Marji Cartwright, Dec. 26, 1954; children: Julie, Ann, Eric. BS, U. Colo., 1952; M (hon.), U. Rio Grande. ChFC. Sr. cons. Life Ins. Mktg. & Rsch., Hartford, Conn., 1966-70; v.p. N.Am. Life, Chgo., 1970-73; sr. v.p. Bankers Mut., Freeport, Ill., 1973-75; sales dir. Security Life of Denver, 1975-81; v.p. Union Cen. Life Ins. Co., Cin., 1981-85, sr. v.p., 1985-86; mgr. Union Cen. Life Ins. Co., Columbus, Ohio, 1986-87; sr. v.p., chief mktg. officer Union Cen. Life Ins. Co., Cin., 1987-91, exec. v.p., corp. mktg. officer, 1991-95; chmn. Carillon Investments, 1991-95; ret., 1995; cons., owner Transitions Unltd., Cin., 1995—; bd. dirs. Carillon Investments, Manhattan Life. Trustee U. Rio Grande, Ohio; elder Presbyn. Ch. Fellow Life Mgmt. Inst.; mem. Phi Delta Theta (past internat. pres.). Republican. Office: Transitions Unltd PO Box 42561 Cincinnati OH 45242-0561

VASIL, INDRA KUMAR, botanist; b. Basti, India, Aug. 31, 1932; arrived in U.S., 1962; s. Lal Chand and Pyshra Lata (Abrol) V.; married, 1959; children: Kavita, Charu. BS, Banaras Hindu U., 1952; MS in Botany, U. Delhi, 1954, PhD in Botany, 1958. Lectr. in botany U. Delhi, 1959-63; postdoctoral rsch. assoc. U. Ill., Champaign-Urbana, 1962-63, U. Wis., Madison, 1963-65; scientist Coun. Sci. and Indsl. Rsch., New Delhi, 1966, Dept. Sci. and Indsl. Rsch., Palmerston North, New Zealand, 1974; assoc. prof. to prof. U. Fla., Gainesville, 1967-79, grad. rsch. prof., 1979—; vis. scientific expert Cath. U., Nijmegen, Netherlands, 1970; vis. prof. U. Hohenheim/Giessen, West Germany, 1975, 76; chmn. Biotechnology Action Coun. UNESCO, Paris, 1990—; svc. many internat. coms.; dir. numerous internat. tng. courses and workshops. Editor (20 vols.) Plant Cell Culture and Somatic Cell Genetics and Cellular and Molecular Biology of Plants, 1980—; editorial bd. six major internat. scientific jours. Fulbright fellowship U.S. Ednl. Found., 1962, Climate Lab. fellowship Govt. of New Zealand, 1974; recipient Humboldt award Alexander von Humboldt Found. Mem. Internat. Soc. Plant Morphologists (pres. 1995—), Internat. Cell Rsch. Orgn. (convenor of panel on plant cell biology and biotech.). Avocations: travel, reading, stamps, gardening. Home: 4901 NW 19th Pl Gainesville FL 32605-3498 Office: U Fla 1143 Fifield Hall Gainesville FL 32611-2092

VASILACHI, GHEORGHE VASILE, priest, vicar; b. Idrici, Romania, Jan. 29, 1909; s. Gheorghe and Aglala (Nestian) V. ThD, Universiti Iassy, Romania, 1938. Dir. Mitropolia, Iasi, 1935-39; secretar patriarchy Bucharest, 1939-42, preacher patriarchy, 1942-44; abbott Monastery Antim, Bucharest, 1943-48; igumen Pocrov, Romania, 1949-59; priest for prisons, 1959-64; priest Bobâlna, 1965-69; priest Southbridge, Mass., 1969-79, Windsor, Can., 1979-84; priest St. Nicholas Parish, N.Y.C., 1984—; vicar Romanian Archdiocese Detroit, 1973. Author: Jesus Christ through the Ages, 1973, We Belong to Christ, 1980, Another World: Memories from Communist Prisons, 1987, The Supremacy of God--All in My Theology and Collection from the Word of Life, 1991; translator Holy Bible in Romanian lang.; pub. over 50 books in Romanian lang. Recipient Recognition award Commonwealth Mass., 1975. Republican. Office: The Romanian Orthodox Ch 45-03 48th Ave Flushing NY 11377-6553

VASILE, GENNARO JAMES, health care executive; b. Auburn, N.Y., Jan. 16, 1946; s. Louis Joseph and Regina Elena (Santaniello) V.; m. Mary Ellen Dwyer, Aug. 10, 1968; children: Kevin, Colleen, Brian. B.A., St. John Fisher Coll., 1967; M.B.A., Xavier U., 1969; Ph.D., U. Iowa, 1973. Asst. adminstr. St. Elizabeth Hosp., Utica, N.Y., 1971-74; sr. cons. Booz-Allen & Hamilton, Inc., N.Y.C., 1974-75; asst. provost adminstrn. Med. Coll. Va., Va. Commonwealth U., Richmond, 1975-78; dir. hosp. and health services mgmt. consulting Booz-Allen & Hamilton, Inc., Bethesda, Md., 1978-79; exec. dir. Strong Meml. Hosp. of U. Rochester, N.Y., 1979-84; pres. United Health Services Inc., Binghamton, N.Y., 1984-93; exec. v.p. Johns Hopkins Hosp., Balt., 1993-95; v.p. Gemini Cons. Am's. Healthcare Practice, 1996—; asst. prof. U. Rochester, Med. Coll. Va.; assoc. prof. Johns Hopkins U.; vis. prof. U. Rochester Med. Ctr.; dir., pres. Med. Ctr. Ins. Co.; cons. health-related agencies. Author: Comprehensive Health Planning, 1971, 74. Bd. dirs. Rochester Soc. Prevention of Cruelty to Children, 1980, asst. treas., 1981; bd. dirs. Pittsford Vince Lombardi Youth Football, 1980, v.p., 1981; bd. dirs. St. Ann's Home, Voluntary Hosps. Am. Inc., Broome County C. of C., 1985, United Way, 1985; trustee St. John Fisher Coll. Recipient Dean's award for contbns. to Sch. Medicine Med. Coll. Va., 1978, Outstanding Contbn. to Mankind, 1993, Exec. of Yr., 1985, Preceptor of Yr. Xavier U., 1992. Fellow Am. Coll. Health Care Execs., Am. Acad. Med. Care Adminstrs. (bd. dirs. 1988); mem. Am. Coll. Hosp. Adminstrs., Am. Hosp. Assn., Council Teaching Hosps., Assn. Am. Med. Colls. Roman Catholic. Home: 204 Lambeth Rd Baltimore MD 21218-1108 *The approach I have taken to my professional and personal life has been to seek out the world as it is, formulate a vision as to how it can be improved, and strive to bridge the resultant gaps. If I have been successful in bridging any gaps, it is only because of the substantial support I have received along the way.*

VASILOPOULOS, ATHANASIOS V., engineering educator; b. Mavranei, Grevena, Greece, May 25, 1937; came to U.S., 1955; s. Vasilios and Ekaterini Vasilopoulos; m. Paraskevi Tsiotas, Feb. 5, 1961; children: Basil John, Katherine, Pamela. BEE, NYU, 1962, MEE, 1965, PhD in Ops. Rsch., 1974. Computer technician Atomic Energy Commn., NYU, N.Y.C., 1957-59; asst. engr. Am. Electric Power Co., N.Y.C., 1959-62; staff engr. Grumman Aerospace, Bethpage, N.Y., 1962-78; assoc. prof. ops. rsch. St. John's U., Jamaica, N.Y., 1978—; adj. prof. math. SUNY at Farmingdale, 1974-78; vis. prof. U. Crete, Greece, 1980; cons. State of N.Y., Albany and Syracuse, summer 1982, AT&T, N.Y.C., summer 1985, Grumman Aerospace, 1980-91, Blue Bay Shipping, N.Y.C., 1983-84. Referee ASME Jour. Engring. for Industry, 1984, Jour. Collegiate Microcomputer, Terre Haute, Ind., 1984-87; contbr. articles to Jour. Quality Tech., Jour. Collegiate Microcomputer, Jour. Bus. Forecasting, others. Mem. coun. Boy Scouts Am., Commack, N.Y., 1970-75; soccer coach Huntington (N.Y.) Boys Club, 1974-75; v.p. St. Paraskevi Greek Orthodox Ch., Greenlawn, N.Y., 1976-78, chmn. edn. com., 1968-85. Recipient Patriarch Athenagoras medallion Greek Orthodox Archdiocese N.Y.C., 1981. Mem. IEEE (sr.), N.Y. Acad. Scis., Ops. Rsch. Soc. Am., Inst. of Mgmt. Scis. Achievements include development of method for analyzing generalized quality control data, method for generating correlated random variables for quality control applications, use of extended input-output methodology for forecasting purposes; proposal of methodology to use computer to generate density functions for sums of independent random variables; use of computer to demonstrate validity of central limit theorem and law of large numbers in statistics. Office: St John's Univ Grand Central And Utopia Pky Jamaica NY 11439-0002

VASILY, JOHN TIMOTHY, information systems executive, state government official; b. Everett, Mass., Feb. 5, 1961; s. Andrew and Catherine Agnes (Coyne) V. BA, U. Mass., 1983; MBA, Suffolk U., 1992. Data analyst Higher Edn. Coord. Coun., Boston, 1984-92; database architect, adminstr. Babson Coll., Babson Park, Mass., 1992-96; mgr. applications and multi-media devel. Dept. Youth Svcs., Boston, 1996—; adj. instr. Newbury Coll., Brookline, Mass., 1992-95. Co-author: Massachusetts Integrated Post Secondary Education Data System, 1990; author: 1986-87 Completions Supplement, 1989. Mem. Boston Computer Soc., Delta Mu Delta, Omicron Delta Epsilon. Avocations: bowling, fishing, hiking, golf.

VASLEF, IRENE, historian, librarian; b. Budapest, Hungary, Mar. 23, 1934; came to U.S., 1956, naturalized, 1960; d. Imre and Ilona (Selyebi-Kovats) Szabo; m. Nicholas P. Vaslef, Sept. 22, 1956; children—Suzanne, Steven. B.A., San Jose (Calif.) State U., 1960; M.S., Simmons Grad. Sch. Library Sci., Boston, 1963; postgrad., Columbia U., 1968, U. Colo., 1961-62, U. Munich, 1967-68; Ph.D., Catholic U. Am., 1984. Librarian Cambridge, Mass., 1962-64; librarian Colorado Springs (Colo.) Sch. System, 1964-67; head catalog librarian Colo. Coll., Colorado Springs, 1968-72; librarian Dumbarton Oaks Rsch. Libr., Trustees for Harvard U., 1972—. Editor/compiler Am. Byzantine Bibliography in Byzantine Studies/Etudes Byzantines, 1979—, Classica et Mediaevalia, 1986, Leyden: Brill, 1986; contbr. articles to profl. jours. Mem. Spl. Libraries Assn., Art Libraries Assn. N.Am., Phi Gamma Mu. Home: 4131 N River St Mc Lean VA 22101-2512 Office: Harvard U Dumbarton Oaks Rsch Libr 1703 32nd St NW Washington DC 20007-2934

VASQUEZ, WILLIAM LEROY, marketing professional, educator; b. Austin, Tex., Mar. 9, 1944; s. Eliseo M. and Janie (Garcia) V. BS with distinction, Nova U., 1983, MBA, 1985, DBA, 1992. Cert. Inst. Cert. Profl. Mgrs., 1990, Inst. Cert. Computing Profls., 1993. Svc. mgr. Data Gen. Corp., various, Latin Am., 1972-80; product mgr. Gould, Inc., Ft. Lauderdale, Fla., 1980-84, Tektronix Inc., Portland, Oreg., 1984-86, Racal-Milgo, Ft. Lauderdale, 1988-90, Citibank Internat., Ft. Lauderdale, 1990—; instr. City U., Portland campus, 1987-88, Maryhurst Coll., 1985-88, Nova Southeaastern U. (domestic and internat.), 1988—, St. Thomas U., 1989—, Fla. Atlantic U., 1993—, Barry U., 1995—; mem. adv. com. Art Inst. of Ft. Lauderdale; freelance writer DataPro divsn. McGraw-Hill, 1991—. Mem. mktg. com. Fla. Philharm. Orch., 1994. Served on USN nuclear submarines, 1962-70. Mem. IEEE, VFW, Am. Mktg. Assn. (pres.), Nat. Mgmt. Assn., Mensa. Republican. Presbyterian. Avocations: guitar, jogging, fine arts, poetry. Home: 4090 NW 110th Ave Coral Springs FL 33065-7718 Office: Citibank NA 6th Fl 899 W Cypress Creek Rd Fort Lauderdale FL 33309-2064

VASS, JOAN, fashion designer; b. N.Y.C., May 19, 1925; d. Max S. and Rose L.; children by previous marriage: Richard, Sara, Jason. Student Vassar Coll., 1941; BA, U. Wis., 1946. Pres. Joan Vass Inc., N.Y.C., 1977—, Vass-Ludacer, N.Y.C., 1993—. Recipient Prix de Cachet, Prince Machiabelli, 1980, Coty award, 1979, Disting. Woman in Fashion award Smithsonian Instn., 1980. Office: Joan Vass Inc 117 E 29th St New York NY 10016-8022 also: 485 7th Ave Ste 510 New York NY 10018-6804

VASSAR, WILLIAM GERALD, gifted and talented education educator; b. Springfield, Mass., Oct. 5, 1925; s. William Walter and Mary Ellen (Burns) V.; m. Barbara Ellen Benhard, June 21, 1952; children: William G., James P., Richard G., Carol A. Vassar Pettit. BA in History magna cum laude, Am. Internat. Coll., Springfield, 1950; MEd, Springfield Coll., 1951; cert. of advanced grad. study, U. Mass., 1967, postgrad., 1962-70. Elem. tchr. West Springfield (Mass.) Pub. Schs., 1950-53, jr. high tchr., 1953-55, secondary sch. prin., 1955-65, dir. program for gifted, 1955-65; sr. supr. academically talented Mass. State Dept. Edn., Boston, 1965-66; state dir. programs for gifted and talented Conn. State Dept. Edn., Hartford, 1966-86; coord. gifted edn., dept. spl. edn. Cen. Conn. State U., New Britain, 1968-86, asst. to dean Sch. Edn., 1986-88; spl. cons. advanced placement program The Coll. Bd., N.Y.C., 1986—; prodr. interactive satellite confs. on Advanced Placement, 1992—; coord. White House Task Force Gifted and Talented, Washington, 1967-68, U.S. Dept. Edn. Congl. Study Gifted and Talented, Washington, 1969-71, Capitol Region Edn. Coun. Info. and Resource Ctr., Windsor, Conn., 1992—; cons. gifted and talented U.S. Dept. Edn., 1967-85, Nat. Assn. State Bds. Edn., 1978-84, George Washington U. Edn. Policy Fellowship Program, 1978-84; spl. cons. gifted and talented legislation Staff of Senate subcom. on Edn., 1967-85; vis. lectr. U. Conn., 1966-83, So. Conn. State U., 1970-84, Sacred Heart U., 1986—, others. Contbg. editor The Gifted Child Quar., Jour. Talented and Gifted; author monographs; contbr. numerous articles to profl. jours. Mem. exec. bd. Mass. Commn. on Children and Youth, Boston, 1959-65, Nat. Commn. Orgn. and Children and Youth, Washington, 1964-68; mem. Conn. Commn. on Youth Svcs., Hartford, 1966-70; mem. Mass. Hwy. Safety Commn., Boston, 1957-63; baseball scout San Francisco Giants, 1957-70. With USN, 1943-46, PTO. Named Disting. Educator U.S. Dept. Edn. Office Gifted, Washington, 1974, Disting. Educator, Conn. State Legislature, Hartford, 1986; recipient Disting. Svc. award Mass. Commn. on Children and Youth, Boston, 1966. Mem. Internat. Coun. Exceptional Children (pres. Assn. Gifted div. 1970-71, chmn. regionals 1969-78, Disting. Svc. award 1976), Nat. Assn. Gifted Children (life, pres. 1965-68, bd. dirs. 1960-68, Disting. Svc. award 1970), Coun. State Dirs. Gifted (pres. 1977-80), Conn. Assn. Gifted, Conn. Assn. Pub. Sch. Supts., Nat. Football Hall of Fame Found., Eastern Assn. Intercollegiate Football Ofcls., Indian Hill Country Club, Eastern Coll. Athletic Conf., Phi Delta Kappa. Democrat. Roman Catholic. Avocations: reading, golf, football. Home: 47 Dowd St Newington CT 06111-2611

VASSELL, GREGORY S., electric utility consultant; b. Moscow, Dec. 24, 1921; came to U.S., 1951, naturalized, 1957; s. Gregory M. and Eugenia M. Wasiljeff; m. Martha Elizabeth Williams, Apr. 26, 1957; children: Laura Kay, Thomas Gregory. Dipl. Ing. in Elec. Engring, Tech. U. Berlin, 1951; MBA in Corp. Fin., NYU, 1954. With Am. Electric Power Svc. Corp., Columbus, Ohio, 1951-88; v.p. system planning Am. Electric Power Svc. Corp., 1973-76, dir., 1973-88, sr. v.p. system planning, 1976-88; electric utility cons. Upper Arlington, Ohio, 1988—; bd. dirs. Columbus & Southern Ohio Electric Co., 1981-88, Cardinal Operating Co.; mem. tech. adv. com. transmission FPC, 1968-70, FERC Task Force on Power Pooling, 1980-81; mem. U.S. com. World Energy Coun. Contbr. articles to profl. jours. Fellow IEEE (life); mem. NAE, Internat. Conf. Large High Voltage Electric Systems, Am. Arbitration Assn., The Surf Golf and Beach Club (North Myrtle Beach, S.C.). Home and Office: 2247 Pinebrook Rd Columbus OH 43220-4327

VASSIL, PAMELA, graphic designer; b. N.Y.C., Nov. 29, 1943; d. George Peter and Lenora (Zabludofsky) Vassilopoulos; 1 child, Sadye Lee. B.S. in Art Edn., Hofstra U., 1965; M.A. in Art Edn., NYU, 1968. Designer Columbia Records, N.Y.C., 1970-72; assoc. art dir. Harper's Bazaar, N.Y.C., 1972-74; designer, mech. artist Album Graphics Inc., N.Y.C., 1974-75; free-lance designer, mech. artist; prodn. dir. Push Pin Studios, N.Y.C., 1975-77; art dir. op. editorial page N.Y. Times, N.Y.C., 1977-79, art dir. arts and leisure sect., 1982-87, art dir. living sect., 1987; free-lance designer/art dir./mech. artist, 1979-82; instr. production, graphic design and illustration Parsons Sch. Design, N.Y.C., 1974—; instr. illustration Sch. Visual Arts, 1981; features art dir. The Daily News, N.Y.C., 1987; sr. art dir. Wells, Rich, Greene Inc., N.Y.C., 1987-88; free-lance graphic designer/art dir., 1988-89; design dir. Roger Black Inc., N.Y.C., 1989-90; design dir. McCall's mag., N.Y.C., 1990-91, freelance art dir., 1991-92; dir., Continuing Edn Parson's Sch. Design, 1992—. Assoc. editor and designer: (book) Images of Labor, 1981.

VATER, CHARLES J., lawyer; b. Pitts., Feb. 8, 1950; s. Joseph A. and Helen M. (Genellie) V.; m. Diane E. Vater, June 10, 1972; children: Allison D., Elizabeth A. BA, U. Notre Dame, 1971; JD, U. Pitts., 1975. Bar: Pa. 1975, U.S. Dist. Ct. (we. dist.) Pa. 1975, U.S. Ct. Appeals (3d cir.) 1979. Assoc. Tucker Arensberg, P.C., Pitts., 1975-80, ptnr., shareholder, 1980—, mng. shareholder. Contbr. articles to profl. jours. Mem. Allegheny County Bar Assn. (probate coun. 1988—), Estate Planning Coun. Pitts. (bd. dirs. 1988-90, 95—), Order of Coif, Phi Beta Kappa. Home: 1615 Trolist Dr Pittsburgh PA 15241-2650 Office: Tucker Arensberg 1500 One PPG Place Pittsburgh PA 15222

VATTER, PAUL AUGUST, business administration educator, dean; b. Boston, Sept. 14, 1924; s. August John and Elizabeth Emelia (Kunstler) V.; m. Josette Roman, July 23, 1966; children: Joel Paul, Katherine Alexandra. BA, Holy Cross Coll., 1944; MA, U. Pa., 1947, PhD, 1953; MA (hon.), Harvard U., 1970. Instr. U. Pa., Phila., 1945-53, asst. prof., 1953-58, vice dean of men, 1953-58; asst. dean Harvard U. Bus. Sch., Boston, 1958-62, assoc. prof. bus. adminstrn., 1962-70, prof., 1970-95, Lawrence E. Fouraker prof. bus. adminstrn., sr. assoc. dean, 1989-91, Lawrence E. Fouraken prof. bus. adminstrn. emeritus, 1995—; bd. dirs. Hartford (Conn.) Steam Boiler Inspection & Ins. Co., Sbarro, Inc., L.I., N.Y. Author: Quantitative Methods in Management, 1978, The Structure of Retail Trade by Size of Store, 1979, also video tapes. Home: 244 Clifton St Belmont MA 02178-2647 Office: Harvard U Bus Sch Soldiers Fld Boston MA 02163

VAUGHAN, ALDEN TRUE, history educator; b. Providence, Jan. 23, 1929; s. Dana Prescott and Muriel Louise (True) V.; m. Lauraine A. Freethy, June 1, 1956 (div. 1981); children: Jeffrey Alden, Lynn Elizabeth; m. Virginia Mason Carr, July 16, 1983. BA, Amherst Coll., 1950; MEd, Columbia U., 1956, MA in History, 1958, PhD, 1964. Tchr. Hackley Sch., Tarrytown, N.Y., 1950-51, A.B. Davis High Sch., Mt. Vernon, N.Y., 1956-60; From history instr. to prof. Columbia U., N.Y.C., 1961—, prof. emeritus, 1994; editor Polit. Sci. Quar., N.Y.C., 1970-71; gen. editor Early Am. Indian Documents, Univ. Pubs. of Am., 1977—; assoc. editor Ency. of the N.Am. Colonies, Scribners, N.Y., 1993; vis. adj. prof. CUNY, Lehman Coll., N.Y.C., 1971; vis. prof. Clark U., Worcester, Mass., 1987. Author: New England Frontier, 1965, rev. edit., 1979, 3d edit., 1995, American Genesis, 1975, Shakespeare's Caliban, 1991, Roots of American Racism, 1995; contbr. articles to Am. Heritage, Am. Hist. Rev., New Eng. Quar., others. Lt. (j.g.) USNR, 1951-55. Recipient fellowship Guggenheim Found., 1973, Sr. fellowship Folger Shakespeare Libr., 1977, 89, Sr. fellowship Am. Antiquarian Soc., 1983. Mem. Am. Antiquarian Soc. (sr. fellowship), Am. Hist. Assn., Soc. Am. Historians (exec. sec., treas. 1965-70), Orgn. Am. Historians (program chmn. 1976), Inst. Early Am. History and Culture (coun. mem. 1985-87), Colonial Soc. Mass. Home: 50 Howland Ter Worcester MA 01602-2631

VAUGHAN, EDWIN DARRACOTT, JR., urologist, surgeon; b. Richmond, Va., May 13, 1939; s. Edwin Darracott and Blanche V. (Bashaw) V.; m. Virginia Anne Lloyd, June 30, 1962; children: Edwin Darracott III, Barbara Anderson. BS, Washington and Lee U., 1961; MD, U. Va., 1965, MS, 1969; DSc, Washington and Lee U., 1982. Diplomate Am. Bd. Urology (trustee, v.p. 1988, pres. 1989). Intern Vanderbilt U., 1965-66, asst. resident, 1966-67; chief resident in urology U. Va., 1970-71, asst. prof. urology, 1973-75, assoc. prof., 1975-78, prof., 1978; clin. research fellow Columbia U., 1971-72, research assoc. dept. medicine, 1972-73; James J. Colt prof. urology, chmn. dept. urology Cornell U. Med. Coll., N.Y.C. and; attending urologist-in-chief N.Y. Hosp., N.Y.C., 1978—; sr. assoc. dean clin. affairs Cornell U. Med. Coll., N.Y.C., 1993—, chmn. dept. urology, 1993—; mem. sci. adv. bd. Nat. Kidney Found., 1977-81; sec.-treas. Urology Coun., 1977-80, chmn., 1980-81; mem. med. adv. bd. Coun. High Blood Pressure, 1977. Editor: Seminars in Urology, 1983-95; assoc. editor Investigative Urology, 1977-78, mem. editorial bd., 1978-94; editor Campbell's Urology; contbr. articles on obstructive uropathy, renal hemodynamics, hypertension to profl. jours. Recipient Research Career Devel. award NIH, 1976-78; NIH tng. grantee, 1967-68; USPHS grantee, 1971-73, 74-77; Am. Heart Assn. grantee, 1976-79. Mem. ACS, AAAS, N.Y. Acad. Scis., Soc. Univ. Urologists, Am. Urol. Assn. (chmn. rsch. com. 1980-91, treas. N.Y. sect. 1985, v.p. N.Y. sect. 1986, pres. N.Y. sect. 1987, Golden Cystoscope award 1981, bd. dirs. 1992-96, Disting. Contbn. award 1992), Urol. Soc. Australasia (hon.), Soc. Exptl. Biology and Medicine, Soc. Univ. Surgeons, Soc. Internat. Urology, Am. Found. Urol. Disease (pres. 1987-92), Nat. Kidney and Urol. Disease Adv. Bd. (dep. chmn.), Intersoc. for Kidney and Urol. Disease Rsch. (chmn. 1987), Am. Assn. Genito-Urinary Surgeons (Barringen medal 1993), Am. Surg. Assn., Sigma Xi, Alpha Omega Alpha (award 1976), Omicron Delta Kappa (award 1981). Home: 1165 Park Ave Apt 6A New York NY 10128-1210 Office: 525 E 68th St New York NY 10021-4873

VAUGHAN, EMMETT JOHN, academic dean, insurance educator; b. Omaha, Dec. 1, 1934; s. Leo William and Mary (Simones) V.; m. Lonne Kay Smith, July 2, 1955; children: Therese, Timothy, Mary, Joan, Thomas, Michael, Emmett (dec.). BA in Econs., Creighton U., 1960; MA in Econs. and Ins., U. Nebr., 1962, PhD in Econs. and Ins., 1964. Asst. prof. U. Iowa, Iowa City, 1963-65, assoc. prof., 1965-68, Partington Disting. prof. ins., 1968—, dean Div. Continuing Edn., 1986—. Author: Fundamentals of Risk and Insurance, 1972, 7th edit., 1996, Risk Management, 1996; contbr. numerous articles to profl. jours. Participated in assessment of war damages in Kuwait UN Commn. on Compensation, 1992. Capt. USAR, 1955-75. Mem. Japan Risk Mgmt. Soc. (hon.). Office: U Iowa 116 Internat Ctr Inst Ins Edn & Rsch Iowa City IA 52242

VAUGHAN, HERBERT WILEY, lawyer; b. Brookline, Mass., June 1, 1920; s. David D. and Elzie G. (Wiley) V.; m. Ann Graustein, June 28, 1941. Student, U. Chgo., 1937-38; SB cum laude, Harvard U., 1941, LLB, 1948. Bar: Mass. 1948. Assoc. Hale and Dorr, Boston, 1948-54, jr. ptnr., 1954-56, sr. ptnr., 1956-82, co-mng. ptnr., 1976-80; pres. Herbert W. Vaughan, P.C., sr. ptnr. Hale and Dorr, 1982-89, of counsel, 1990—. Sec. and mem. standing com., The Trustees of Reservations; mem. Com. of Fund for Preservation of Wildlife and Natural Areas; mem. bd. trustees, Am. Friends of New Coll. (Oxford Univ.); bd. dirs. Am. Friends Fund of Inst. of U.S. Studies of U. London. Fellow Am. Bar Found. (life); mem. ABA, Chesterton Soc. (internat. com.), Mass. Bar Assn., Boston Bar Assn., Internat. Bar Assn., Am. Law Inst., Am. Coll. Real Estate Lawyers, Bay Badminton and Tennis Club, Union Club (Boston), Boston Econ. Club, Longwood Cricket Club (Brookline, Mass.). Office: Hale & Dorr 60 State St Boston MA 02109-1803

VAUGHAN, JOHN CHARLES, III, horticultural products executive; b. N.Y.C., July 30, 1934; s. John Charles II and Lucille Grace (Dixon) V.; m. Ruth Darden MacLeod, Mar. 4, 1962; children: Elizabeth, John IV, George. AB in Econs., Cornell U., 1956; MBA, Northwestern U., 1962. Salesman Hall & Ellis, Chgo., 1959-62; br. mgr. Vaughan's Seed Co., Downers Grove, Ill., 1963-74, exec. v.p., 1974-76, pres., 1976-84, chmn. bd., 1985-93, ret., 1993; regional v.p. Am. Seed Trade Assn., Washington, 1985-88; pres. Atlantic Seedsmen's Assn., N.Y.C., 1968; dir. Nat. Seed Co., Ill. & N.J., Jacklin Seed Co., Post Falls, Idaho, V.J. Growers, Inc., Apopka, Fla. Bd. dirs. George Williams Coll., Downers Grove, 1982-92. 1st Lt. USMCR, 1956-59. Mem. Downers Grove C. of C. (chmn. 1989).

VAUGHAN, JOHN THOMAS, veterinarian, educator, university dean; b. Tuskegee, Ala., Feb. 6, 1932; s. Henry Asa and Mary (Howard) V.; m. Ethel Evelyn Sell, July 7, 1956; children: John Thomas, Faythe, Michael Sell. D.V.M., Auburn U., 1955, M.S., 1963. Clin. resident U. Pa. Sch. Vet. Medicine, Phila., 1958; instr. Auburn U. Coll. Vet. Medicine, Ala., 1955-57; asst. prof. Auburn U. Coll. Vet. Medicine, 1959-65, assoc. prof., 1965-70, prof., head dept. large animal surgery and medicine, 1974-77, dean, 1977-95; ret.; tenured prof. vet. surgery, dir. Large Animal Hosp. N.Y. State Vet. Coll., Cornell U., Ithaca, N.Y., 1970-74; bd. dirs. Compass Bank, Auburn. Co-author 2 textbooks; contbr. chpts. to books, articles to profl. jours. Chmn. ofcl. bd. Auburn Meth. Ch., 1968-69; pres. bd. dirs. United Fund, Auburn Meth. Ch., 1968-69, Hughston Orthopaedic Rsch. Found., 1985—, So. Heart and Lung Inst., 1988-90; bd. dirs., pres. exec. com. Diabetes Trust Fund, 1992; cons. U. San Carlos, Guatemala, 1989-90, Nat. Horse Show Commn., 1990—, Fed. U. of Goias, Brazil, 1996. Mem. AVMA, Am. Assn. Equine Practitioners (pres.), Am. Coll. Vet. Surgeons (pres., chmn. bd. regents), Assn. Am. Vet. Med. Colls. (coun. deans), Nat. Acads. Practice, Nat. Assn. State Univs. and Land Grant Colls. (chmn. bd. vet. medicine 1987, 91-94, chmn., bd. dirs. vet. medicine of commn. on food, environment and renewable resources 1991-94, exec. com. bd. on agriculture 1992-94), Ala. Vet. Med. Assn. (Vet. of Yr. 1985), Rotary. Office: Auburn U Coll Vet Medicine Auburn AL 36849 *Far from pursuing any manifest destiny, my efforts have been directed to the tasks at hand, some assigned, some assumed, whether great or small. This has been influenced by a lifestyle inclined to self-reliance with no requirements on extravagance. Aside from striving for a measure of competence in a specific field of endeavor, recognition and acceptance of one's principles and purposes depends much upon a positive attitude and the ability to associate agreeably with one's fellows.*

VAUGHAN, JOSEPH LEE, language educator; b. Lynchburg, Va., Jan. 26, 1905; s. Ellis Lee and Anna Margaret (Worley) V.; m. Ann Cleveland Doner, Aug. 3, 1938 (dec. Aug. 1992); children: Joseph Lee, Ann Sahlman. AB, U. Va., 1926, AM, 1927, PhD, 1940. Instr. English, U. Va., Charlottesville, 1930-32; instr. English dept. engring. U. Va., 1932-35, asst. prof., 1936-40, assoc. prof., 1940-45, prof., 1945—, Joseph L. Vaughan prof. humanities, chmn. dept., 1970—, provost, 1956-60, chancellor Community Colls., 1960-66, dir. studies Humanities Inst., 1968-70; lectr., cons. Inst. Textile Tech., Charlottesville, 1947-81, pres., 1951-53; assoc. dir. sch. for tchrs. of English in engring. colls. U. Mich., 1941; mem. info. coun. NSF; cons. Va.-Md. Bankers Assn., Fieldcrest Mills, State Farm Ins. Co., Va. Employment Commn. Author: (with W.O. Birk, H. Melvin, F. Holmes) Basic Principles of Writing, 1937, rev. edit., 1943; (sect.) 19th Century America; Good Reading, 1948, Oral Communications for the Layman, (with O.A. Gianniny Jr.) Thomas Jefferson's Rotunda Restored, 1981, Rotunda Tales, 1991; editor: English Notes sect. Jour. Engring. Edn., 1936-40; contbr. articles to jours., 1940—; assoc. editor: Report on Instruction in English in Engineering Colleges in the U.S., 1940; assoc. editor and contbr.: A Guide to Good Reading, 1942-48; contbr. to prof. publs. Recipient Significant Sig award, 1969, Raven award, 1970, Disting. Prof. award, 1971, Mac Wade award, 1975, Disting. Svc. award Va. Engring. Found., 1991, Vaughan House, U. Va. named in his honor, 1992. Mem. Albemarle Art Assn., Albemarle Hist. Assn., Va. Watercolor Soc., Ctrl. Va. Watercolor Guild, Phi Beta Kappa, Omicron Delta Kappa, Pi Delta Epsilon, Sigma Chi, Raven Soc. Presbyterian. Clubs: Colonnade, Farmington Country. Specialist in communication techniques. Home: The Colonnades 2600 Barracks Rd Charlottesville VA 22901-2100

VAUGHAN, JOSEPH LEE, JR., education educator, consultant; b. Charlottesville, Va., Dec. 31, 1942; s. Joseph Lee and Ann (Doner) V.; children: Leigh Ann, Kelley. BA, U. Va., 1964, MEd, 1968, EdD, 1974. Tchr. Madison (Va.) High Sch., 1965-67, Darlington Sch., Rome, Ga., 1967-69, Woodberry Forest (Va.) Sch., 1969-74; asst. prof. edn. U. Ariz., Tucson, 1974-80; prof. East Tex. State U., Commerce, 1980—, dir. programs in reading edn., 1980-86, 91-02; dir. programs in reading edn. East Tex. State U., 1980-86, 91-92; dir. Tex. Ctr. Learning Styles, 1989-95; bd. dirs. Nat. Learning Styles Network, 1991-95; exec. dir. Children's Inst. of Love and Discovery, Inc., 1995—. Co-author: Reading and Learning in Content Classrooms, 1978, 2d rev. edit., 1985, Reading and Reasoning Beyond The Primary Grades, 1986. Bd. govs. Sancta Sophia Sem., 1991—. Mem. ASCD, Nat. Reading Conf., Internat. Reading Assn., Internat. Inst. Integral Human Scis., Agni Yoga Soc. Universalist. Avocations: spiritual sci. studies, golf, travel, reading. Home: 3103 Bourbon St Rockwall TX 75087 Office: East Tex State U 2600 Motley Dr Mesquite TX 75150-3840 *I am most content when I find time every day to laugh, love, and learn.*

VAUGHAN, JOSEPH ROBERT, lawyer; b. Los Angeles, Jan. 28, 1916; s. Vincent B. and Lucile (Eichler) V.; m. Margaret Koetters, Jan. 20, 1940; children: Barbara (Sister Kieran, CSJ), Christine, Judith (Sister Judith Marie, CSJ). A.B., Loyola U., 1937, J.D., 1939. Bar: Calif. 1939. Mem. firm Vaughan, Brandlin, Robinson & Roemer, 1939-65; v.p. finance Knudsen Creamery Co. of Calif., Los Angeles, 1965; exec. v.p. Knudsen Creamery Co. of Calif., 1965-69; pres. Knudsen Corp., 1969-71, pres., chief exec. officer, 1971-77, chmn., pres., 1977-78, chmn. bd., 1979-80; bd. dirs. Dominguez Water Co., 1983-91, Fed. Res. Bank of San Francisco, 1973-84, chmn. L.A. br., 1974-77, Carson Estate Co., 1981-89. Bd. dirs. Los Angeles Beautiful, 1957-65, fin. chmn., 1980; trustee Pacific Legal Found., 1973-85; trustee Mt. St. Mary's Coll., 1979-83, regent, 1983—; bd. dirs. Daniel Freeman Hosp., 1955-65, sec., 1959-60, pres., 1963-65; bd. dirs. Nat. Dairy Coun., 1972-81, vice chmn., 1978-81; bd. visitors Loyola Law Sch., 1978-90, chmn., 1978-79; bd. regents Loyola Marymount U., 1973-79; bd. dirs. Tom and Valley Knudsen Found., 1954—, pres., 1971—; bd. dirs. Fritz B. Burns Found., 1986—, William H. Hannon Found., 1989—, Dominguez Hills Found., Calif. State U., 1990-94, Kirk Mayer, Inc., 1992-94. Mem. Calif. State Bar Assn., Inst. Corp. Counsel (gov. 1981-85), Los Angeles C. of C. (gov. 1971-73). Home: 404 Lorraine Blvd Los Angeles CA 90020-4730 Office: 1434 Omni Ctr 900 Wilshire Blvd Los Angeles CA 90017-4701

VAUGHAN, KIRK WILLIAM, banker; b. St. Louis, Oct. 16, 1943; s. William Edward and Daisy Lenore (Coates) V.; m. Barbara Jean Aaron, Mar. 7, 1986; children: William Aaron, Michael Bartlett. BA, Baker U., 1966. Field sales mgr. Ford Motor Co., Richmond, Va., 1967-73; exec. v.p. United Mo. Bank of Kansas City, 1973—. Editor: The Best of Bill Vaughan, 1979. Republican. Presbyterian. Home: 800 W 54th St Kansas City MO 64112-2330 Office: United Mo Bank Kansas City 1010 Grand Blvd Kansas City MO 64106-2225

VAUGHAN, LINDA, publishing executive. Pub. Soap Opera Digest, N.Y.C. *

VAUGHAN, MARTHA, biochemist; b. Dodgeville, Wis., Aug. 4, 1926; d. John Anthony and Luciel (Ellingen) V.; m. Jack Orloff, Aug. 4, 1951 (dec. Dec. 1988); children: Jonathan Michael, David Geoffrey, Gregory Joshua. Ph.B., U. Chgo., 1944; M.D., Yale U., 1949. Intern New Haven Hosp., Conn., 1950-51; research fellow U. Pa., Phila., 1951-52; research fellow Nat. Heart Inst., Bethesda, Md., 1952-54, mem. research staff, 1954-68; head metabolism sect. Nat. Heart and Lung Inst., Bethesda, 1968-74; acting chief molecular disease br. Nat. Heart, Lung and Blood Inst., Bethesda, 1974-76, chief cell metabolism lab., 1974-94; dep. chief pulmonary and critical care medicine br. Nat. Heart, Lung, and Blood Inst., Bethesda, 1994—; mem. metabolism study sect. NIH, 1965-68; mem. bd. sci. counselors Nat. Inst. Alcohol Abuse and Alcoholism, 1988-91. Mem. editl. bd. Jour. Biol. Chemistry, 1971-76, 80-83, 88-90, assoc. editor, 1992—; editl. adv. bd. Molecular Pharmacology, 1972-80, Biochemistry, 1989-94; editor: Biochemistry and Biophysics Rsch. Comms., 1990-91; contbr. articles to profl. jours., chpts. to books. Bd. dirs. Found. Advanced Edn. in Scis., Inc., Bethesda, 1979-92, exec. com., 1980-92, treas., 1984-86, v.p., 1986-88, pres., 1988-90; mem. Yale U. Coun. com. med. affairs, New Haven, 1974-80. Recipient Meritorious Svc. medal HEW, 1974, Disting. Svc. medal NEW, 1979, Commd. Officer award USPHS, 1982, Superior Svc. award USPHS, 1993. Mem. NAS, Am. Acad. Arts and Scis., Am. Soc. Biol. Chemists (chmn. pub. com. 1984-86), Assn. Am. Physicians, Am. Soc. Clin. Investigation. Home: 11608 W Hill Dr Rockville MD 20852-3751 Office: Nat Heart Lung & Blood Inst NIH Bldg 10 Rm 5N-307 Bethesda MD 20892

VAUGHAN, MARTHA LOUISE, agency administrator; b. Shreveport, La., Aug. 14, 1944; d. Thomas Worth and Martha Louise (Shepherd) V. BS in Edn., Centenary Coll., 1966; MA in Sociology, Stephen F. Austin State U., 1974. Cert. EMT. High sch. tchr. Airline High Sch., Bossier City, La., 1966-68; grad. asst. Stephen F. Austin State U., Nacogdoches, Tex., 1969; camp dir. YWCA of Greenville, S.C., 1970-74, exec. dir., 1974-83; asst. dir. Alston Wilkes Soc., 1985-86, facility dir., 1986—; therapist Holder and Assocs., 1991-92. Hospice vol. Greenville Hosp. System, 1992—; mem. coms. ARC, Greenville, 1970—; team mem. S.C. Crisis Response Team, 1987; vice chair Women's Task Force, 1993-94; safety officer River Falls Fire Dept., 1986—; mem. Nova Nat. Crisis Response Team, 1990—; sec./treas. Greenville Homeless Coalition, 1991-92. Recipient Clara Barton award Greenville chpt. ARC, 1989, Disting. Svc. award Greenville chpt. ARC, 1990, Parker Eualt award S.C. Assn. Community Residential Programs, 1988, Boss of Yr. award Am. Bus. Women's Assn., 1978. Mem. AID Upstate (pres. 1991-93), Nat. Fire Protection Assn. Democrat. Avocation: photography. Home: 2351 Farm Rd 134 Box 141 Jonesville TX 75659 Office: Alston Wilkes Soc 614 Pendleton St Greenville SC 29601-3320

VAUGHAN, MICHAEL RICHARD, lawyer; b. Chgo., Aug. 27, 1936; s. Michael Ambrose and Loretta M. (Parks) V.; m. Therese Marie Perri, Aug. 6, 1960; children—Charles Thomas, Susan Enger. Student U. Ill., 1954-59; LL.B., U. Wis., 1962. Bar: Wis. 1962. Chief atty. bill drafting sect. Wis. Legislature, 1962-68; dir. legis. attys., Wis., 1968-72; assoc. Murphy & Desmond, and predecessor, Madison, Wis., 1972-73, ptnr., 1974—; mem. Commn. Uniform State Laws, 1966-72; cons. Nat. Commn. on Marihuana and Drug Abuse, 1971-73; dir. State Bar Govtl. and Adminstrv. Law Sect., 1971-78, State Bar Interprofl. and Bus. Relations Com., 1976-89; lectr. continuing legal edn. seminars. Warden and vestryman St. Dunstan's Episcopal Ch., 1973-78, 80-87; mem. Wis. Episc. Conf., 1972-76. Mem. ABA, State Bar of Wis., Dane County Bar Assn., U. Wis. Law Sch. Bencher Soc., Delta Kappa Epsilon. Club: Madison. Contbr. articles to profl. jours. Home: 4714 Lafayette Dr Madison WI 53705-4865 Office: 2E E Mifflin St Madison WI 53701

VAUGHAN, ODIE FRANK, oil company executive; b. Camden, Ark., Feb. 3, 1936; s. Odie Frank and Bernece (May) V.; m. Sandra Beard, Sept. 8, 1962; children: Christopher Michael, Laura Elizabeth. Student, So. State U., 1954-55; BS in Acctg., La. Tech. U., 1959. Acct. Peat, Marwick, Mitchell & Co., Dallas, 1959-61; asst. v.p., dir. tax Murphy Oil Corp., El Dorado, Ark., 1962-72, treas., 1991—; v.p., treas. Ocean Drilling and Exploration Co., New Orleans, 1973-91. Mem. AICPA, Am. Petroleum Inst. (gen. tax com.), Fin. Execs. Inst., Tax Execs. Inst. Baptist. Home: 1700 N Calion Rd El Dorado AR 71730-3420 Office: Murphy Oil Corp 200 Peach St El Dorado AR 71730

VAUGHAN, PETER HUGH, theater critic; b. Oxford, Eng., Dec. 12, 1937; children: Rachel V., Thomas Hugh, Jeremy P. BA, Yale U., 1959; LLB, London U., 1963. With Mpls. Star Tribune, 1965—, theater critic, 1974—. Mem. French-Am. Theatrical Friendship Soc. Montrichard (founding), John Falstaff Eating and Drinking Ensemble of Otisville. Avocations: travel, reading, tennis, cooking, gun control. Office: Star Tribune 425 Portland Ave Minneapolis MN 55488-0001

VAUGHAN, ROLAND, church administrator. Dir. Ch. of God World Missions. Office: Ch of God World Missions PO Box 8016 Cleveland TN 37320-8016

VAUGHAN, SAMUEL SNELL, editor, author, publisher; b. Phila., Aug. 3, 1928; s. Joseph and Anna Catherine (Alexander) V.; m. Jo LoBiondo, Oct. 22, 1949; children: Jeffrey Marc, Leslie Jane, Dana Alexander, David Samuel. B.A., Pa. State U., 1951. Deskman King Features Syndicate, N.Y.C., 1951; asst. mgr. Doubleday Syndicate, 1952-54; advt. mgr. Doubleday & Co., Inc., N.Y.C., 1954-56; sales mgr., 1956-58, sr. editor, 1958-68; exec. editor Doubleday & Co., Inc., 1969-70, pub., pres. pub. div., 1970-82, v.p. parent co., 1970-86, editor in chief, 1982-86; sr. v.p., editor Random House, Inc., 1986-90; editor-at-large Random House, Inc., Wm. Morrow Co., 1990—; mem. faculty dept. English, Columbia U., 1978-88; lectr. Harvard U., Libr. Congress, U. Denver, Bowker meml. lectr. Author: (juvenile) Whoever Heard of Kangaroo Eggs? 1957, New Shoes, 1961, The Two-Thirty Bird, 1965, (history) The Little Church, 1969, Medium Rare: A Look at the Book and Its People, 1977, (humor) Little Red Hood, 1979; prin. author: The Accidental Profession, 1979, The Community of the Book, 1983, The State of the Heart, 1985; contbr. to N.Y. Times, Sunday Times of London, Daedalus, Am. Heritage, others. Served with USMC, 1946-48. Named Disting. Alumnus Pa. State U., 1977, Alumni fellow, 1981. Mem. Tenafly Tennis Club, Quantuck Beach Club (Westhampton, N.Y.), Century Assn. Episcopalian. Home: 23 Inness Rd Tenafly NJ 07670-2714 Office: c/o Random House 201 E 50th St New York NY 10022-7703

VAUGHAN, STEPHANIE RUTH, water aerobics business owner, consultant; b. Winchester, Va., Feb. 27, 1956; d. Robert Hall Sr. and Peggy (Owen) Hahn; m. Ward Pierman Vaughan, Nov. 29, 1980; children: Carol Owen, Eva Virginia, Robert Alexander. BS in Biology, Shenandoah U., 1983, MBA, 1985. Sales rep., cashier Best Products, Roanoke, Va., 1977-78; dir. Peg-Ell Sch. Modeling, Winchester, 1978-79; mgr. purchasing and metal fabrication materials Fabritek Co., Inc., Winchester, 1979-84, sec. bd. dirs., 1980—; CEO, owner Splash Internat., Winchester, 1991—; tennisinstr. Camp Camelot, Wilmington, N.C., summer 1978; cons. Fabritek Co., Inc., 1993-95; membership dir. Stonebrook Swim and Racquet Club, Winchester, 1992-93, corp. fitness dir., 1993; instr. Workout in Water class Crooked Run Fitness and Racquet Club, Front Royal, Va., 1992—, Winchester Parks and

Recreation Dept., 1991-92; instr., designer Children's Water Fitness Classes Winchester Country Club, Va., 1993, Stonebrook Country Club, 1994. Author: Water Exercises for Physicians, Physical Therapists and Water Fitness Instructors, 1994 (award); contbr. articles to profl. jours. Steering com. mem. Habitat for Humanity, 1995. Patentee for water fitness product. Mem. AAHPERD, NAFE, AAUW, AMA, Am. Coll. Sports Medicine, Va. Assn. Health, Phys. Recreation and Dance (conf. presenter, chair aquatic coun. 1994-95, v.p. recreation coun. 1996—), Va. Recreation and Parks Soc. (conf. presenter), U.S. Water Fitness Assn. (adv. bd., chair tech. com. 1993—, mem. nat. tech. com. 1992—, C. Carson Conrad Top Water Fitness Leader for Va. award 1993, Deep Water Running Champion 1993, BEMA Nat. Water Fitness Champion 1993, cert. pool coord., cert. instr., nat. conf. aquatic fashion show dir. 1992, 93, 94, conf. presenter, leader 1st Nat. Aquatic Summit, Washington, Team Water Aerobics champoin 1994, June Andrus Entrepreneur of Yr. award 1995, Champion Deep Water Instr. 1995), United Daus. of Confederacy, Aquatic Exercise Assn. (conf. presenter, regional rep. 1994-96), U.S. Synchronized Swimming, Shenandoah U. Alumni Assn. (bd. dirs.), Aquatic Alliance Internat. (mktg. dir. 1996—), Aquatic Edn. Assn. Avocations: water and snow skiing, flying, scuba diving, sewing, smocking. Home: 115 Old Forest Cir Winchester VA 22602

VAUGHAN, THOMAS JAMES GREGORY, historian; b. Seattle, Oct. 13, 1924; s. Daniel George and Kathryn Genevieve (Browne) V.; m. Elizabeth Ann Perpetua Crownhart, June 16, 1951; children: Meagan, Margot, Stephen, Cameron. BA, Yale U., 1948; MS, U. Wis., 1950, doctoral residence, 1951-53; LittD, Pacific U., 1969; LLD, Reed Coll., 1975. Exec. dir. Oreg. Hist. Soc., Portland, 1954-90; editor in chief Oreg. Hist. Quar., 1954-89; adj. prof. Portland State U., 1968—; chmn. bd. Salar Enterprises, Ltd.; bd. dirs. Am. Heritage Pub. Co., 1976-85; film producer, 1958-76; historian laureate State of Oreg., 1989. Author: A Century of Portland Architecture, 1967, Captain Cook, R.N, The Resolute Mariner: An International Record of Oceanic Discovery, 1974, Portland, A Historical Sketch and Guide, 1976, 2d edit., 1983, Voyage of Enlightenment: Malaspina on the Northwest Coast, 1977; editor: Space, Style and Structure: Building in Northwest America, 2 vols., 1974, The Western Shore, 1975, Ascent of the Athabasca Pass, 1978, Wheels of Fortune, High and Mighty, 1981, Soft Gold, 1982, 2d edit., 1990, To Siberia and Russian America, Vols. I, II and III, also others.; co-editor: Siberica, 1989; mem. adv. bd. Am. Heritage Mag., 1977-90; prodr. film The Crimean War, 1994. 1st chmn. Oreg. State Com. for Humanities, NEH, 1969—; 1st chmn. Gov.'s Adv. Com. on Historic Preservation Oreg., 1970-77; sec. Oreg. Geog. Names Bd., 1958-89; adviser 1000 Friends of Oreg., 1972—; lay mem. Oreg. State Bar Disciplinary Rev. Bd., 1975-82; vice chmn. adv. panel Nat. Endowment Arts, 1975—; mem. Nat. Hist. Publs. and Records Commn. Matrix, 1975-76; historian laureate State of Oreg., 1989. With USMC, 1942-45. Decorated comdr. Order Brit. Empire; recipient Aubrey Watzek award Lewis and Clark Coll., 1975;, Edith Knight Hill award, 1977, Disting. Svc. award U. Oreg.; grantee English Speaking Union, 1961; Columbia Maritime Mus. 1st rsch. fellow, 1992. Fellow Royal Geog. Soc.; mem. Am. Assn. State and Local History (bd. dirs. 1955-74, pres. 1976-78), Am. Assn. Mus. (coun., exec. com.), Nat. Trust Hist. Preservation (adv. coun.), Ctr. for Study Russian Am., Russian Acad. Scis., City Club (Portland, bd. govs.), Univ. Club (Portland, bd. govs.), The Arts Club (London). Home: 2135 SW Laurel St Portland OR 97201-2367

VAUGHAN, WILLIAM WALTON, atmospheric scientist; b. Clearwater, Fla., Sept. 7, 1930; s. William Walton and Ella Vermelle (Warr) V.; m. Wilma Geraldine Stapleton, Dec. 23, 1951; children: Stephen W., David A., William D., Robert T. BS with honors, U. Fla., 1951; grad. cert., USAF Inst. Tech./Fla. State U., 1952; PhD, U. Tenn., 1976. Sci. asst. Air Force Armament Center, Eglin AFB, Fla., 1955-58; Army Ballistic Missile Agy., Huntsville, Ala., 1958-60; chief aerospace environ. div. Marshall Space Flight Center, NASA, Huntsville, 1960-76; chief atmospheric scis. div. Marshall Space Flight Center, NASA, 1976-86; rsch. prof. atmospheric sci. U. Ala., Huntsville, 1986—, dir. Rsch. Inst., 1986-94; retired, 1994; cons. atmospheric sci.; mem. adv. com. NASA. Contbr. articles to profl. jours. Served to capt. USAF, 1951-55. Recipient Exceptional Service medal NASA, 1971. Assoc. fellow AIAA (Losey Atmospheric Scis. award 1980); fellow Am. Meterol. Soc.; mem. AAAS, Am. Geophys. Union, Sigma Xi. Office: Univ Ala Atmospheric Sci Dept Huntsville AL 35899

VAUGHAN, WORTH EDWARD, chemistry educator; b. N.Y.C., Feb. 1, 1936; s. Royal Worth and Sylvia Marie (Fernholz) V.; m. Diane Marilyn Mayer, Aug. 9, 1969; 1 child, Wayne John. B.A., Oberlin Coll., 1957; M.A., Princeton U., 1959, Ph.D., 1960. Asst. prof. chemistry U. Wis.-Madison, 1961-66, assoc. prof., 1967-76, prof., 1977—; mem. bd. advisors Am. Exchange Bank West Br., Madison, 1983-87. Author: Dielectric Properties and Molecular Behavior, 1969; editor: Digest of Literature on Dielectrics, 1974; translation editor: Dipole Moments of Organic Compounds, 1970; contbr. articles to profl. jours. Mem. Am. Chem. Soc. (pres. Wis. sect. 1968), Am. Phys. Soc., AAAS, Phi Beta Kappa, Sigma Xi, Alpha Chi Sigma. Avocations: canoeing, contract bridge. Home: 501 Ozark Trl Madison WI 53705-2538 Office: Univ Wis 1101 University Ave Madison WI 53706-1322

VAUGHN, GORDON E., bishop. Bishop of Western Pa. Ch. of God in Christ, Pitts. Office: Ch of God in Christ 6437 Stanton Ave Pittsburgh PA 15206-2248

VAUGHN, GREGORY LAMONT, professional baseball player; b. Sacramento, July 3, 1965. Student, Sacramento City Coll., Miami Coll. Player Milw. Brewers, 1986—; mem. Am. League All-Star Team, 1993. Named Midwest co-MVP, 1987, Am. Assn. MVP, 1989. Office: Milw Brewers Milw County Stadium PO Box 3099 Milwaukee WI 53215*

VAUGHN, JACKIE, III, state legislator. BA, Hillsdale (Mich.) Coll.; MA, Oberlin (Ohio) Coll.; LittB, Oxford U.; LLD (hon.), Marygrove Coll., Detroit, Shaw Coll., Detroit; HHD (hon.), Highland Park (Mich.) Community Coll. Tchr. U. Detroit, Wayne State U., Detroit, 1963-64; mem. Mich. Ho. of Reps., Lansing, 1966-78; mem. Mich. Senate, Lansing, 1978—, asst. pres. pro tem, 1978-82, pres. pro tem, 1982-86, assoc. pres. pro tem, 1986—. Past pres. Mich. Young Dems.; chmn. Mich. Dr. Martin Luther King Jr. Holiday commn.; exec. bd. dirs. Detroit NAACP. With USN. Fulbright fellow; recipient Frank J. Wieting Meml. Service award, 1977, Focus and Impact award Cotillion Club, 1980, Outstanding Achievement award Booker T. Washington Bus. Assn., Outstanding Community Service award Charles Stewart Mott Community Coll. and Urban Coalition of Greater Flint, Mich., 1981; named Outstanding State Senator of Yr., Detroit Urban League Guild, 1983, Most Outstanding Legislator of Yr., Washburn-Ilene Block Club, 1983, numerous others. Mem. Am. Oxonian Assn., Fulbright Alumni Assn. Baptist. Home: 19930 Roslyn Rd Detroit MI 48221-1853 Office: Mich Senate PO Box 30036 Lansing MI 48909-7536

VAUGHN, JAMES ENGLISH, JR., neurobiologist; b. Kansas City, Mo., Sept. 17, 1939; s. James English and Sue Katherine (Vaughn); m. Christine Singleton, June 18, 1961; children: Stephanie, Stacey. B.A., Westminster Coll., 1961; Ph.D., UCLA, 1965. Postdoctoral rsch. fellow in brain rsch. U. Edinburgh (Scotland), 1965-66; asst. prof. Boston U. Sch. Medicine, 1966-70; head sect. of molecular neuromorphology Beckman Rsch. Inst. of City of Hope, Duarte, Calif., 1970—, pres. rsch. staff, 1986, chmn. div. neuroscience, 1987—. Fellow Neuroscience Rsch. Program, 1969; Rsch. grantee NIH, 1969—, NSF, 1983-87. Mem. AAAS, Am. Soc. Cell Biology, Am. Assn. Anatomists, Soc. for Neuroscience (chmn. short course 1977), Internat. Brain Rsch. Orgn., N.Y. Acad. Scis., Sigma Xi. Achievements include original immunoelectron microscopic demonstration of a neurotransmitter synthesizing enzyme in brain synaptic terminals; original proposal and evidence of synaptotropic modulation of dendritic development in the central nervous system; discovered that genetically-associated changes in neuronal migration correlate with altered patterns of synaptic connectivity in the brain; discovered that all neurons of a major brain relay station use GABA as their neurotransmitter; discovered previously unknown cholinergic neurons in the brain and spinal cord; discovered unique migratory patterns of preganglionic sympathetic neurons in developing spinal cord; first immunocytochemical evidence of a role gamma aminobutyric acid (GABA) neurons in focal epilepsy; first demonstration of lesion-induced synaptic plasticity of GABA neurons; contbr. articles to profl. jours.; assoc. editor Jour. Neurocytology, 1978-86; mem. editorial bd. Synapse, 1986—; reviewer for Jour. Comparative Neurology, 1974—, Brain Research, 1976—. Office: Beckman Research Inst 1450 Duarte Rd Duarte CA 91010-3011

VAUGHN, JOHN CARROLL, minister, educator; b. Louisville, Sept. 22, 1948; s. Harold D. and Morel (Johnson) V.; m. Brenda Joyce Lyttle, June 17, 1968; children: Deborah, John, Rebecca, Daniel, Joseph. BA, Bob Jones U., 1977, MMin, 1991, DD, 1989. Ordained to ministry Bapt. Ch., 1978. Sr. pastor Faith Baptist Ch., Greenville, S.C., 1977—; founder/adminstr. Hidden Treasure Christian Sch., Greenville, S.C., 1980-84; founder Iglesia Bautista de la Fe, Greenville, S.C., 1981-93; founder/dir. Hidden Treasure Ministries, Greenville, 1985—; exec. bd. Associated Gospel Chs., Hopewell, Va., 1987-93; chaplain Greenville Police Dept., 1987—. Editor: (instrnl. video) Sufficient Grace, 1987; author: (textbook) Special Education: A Biblical Approach, 1991, (biography) More Precious Than Gold, 1994. Chmn. Greenville County Human Rels. Commn., 1986-89; lt. col., chaplain Greenville Composite Squadron CAP, 1985—; counselor Greenville County Crisis Response Team, 1987-91; co-chmn. Greenville County Sex Edn. Adv. Com., 1988-91; mem. exec. bd. dirs. Fundamental Bapt. Fellowship, 1988—, The Wilds, 1992—, Internat. Bapt. Missions, 1993—, Christians for Religious Freedom, 1993—. Mem. Internat. Conf. Police Chaplains, Am. Assn. Christian Schs. (exec. bd. dirs. 1992—), ACFT Owners and Pilots Assn., S.C. Law Enforcement Assn., S.C. Assn. Christian Schs. (pres. 1988—). Republican. Avocations: flying, golf, gardening, reading, history, writing. Home: 117 Frontline Dr Taylors SC 29687-2675 Office: Faith Bapt Ch 500 W Lee Rd Taylors SC 29687-2513

VAUGHN, JOHN ROLLAND, auditor; b. Iola, Kans., Aug. 4, 1938; s. Ralph H. and Alice (Dille) V.; m. Doris K. Black, Sept. 4, 1960; children: Lisa Ann, Brian Douglas. BS in Bus, Emporia State U., 1960. Sr. auditor Arthur Andersen & Co., Kansas City, Mo., 1961-66; gen. auditor First Nat. Bank Kansas City, 1966-69, Commerce Bancshares, Inc., 1969-73; sr. v.p. Adminstrv. Services div. Peoples Trust Bank, Ft. Wayne, Ind., 1973-77; dep. gen. auditor, v.p. Crocker Nat. Bank, San Francisco, 1978-79; v.p., gen. auditor S.W. Bancshares, Houston, 1980-83; sr. v.p., gen. auditor MCorp., Houston, 1984-87, mng. dir., 1988-89; audit dir. Banc One Corp., Dallas, 1990-92; v.p., gen. auditor St. Paul Cos., St. Paul, 1992—. Treas. Overland Park (Kans.) Jr. C. of C., 1965-66; outside dir. Overland Park Credit Union; controller Fort Wayne Bicentennial Commn., 1974-77. Mem. Mo. Air N.G., 1961-67. Mem. Inst. Internal Auditors (1st v.p. Kansas City 1969-70, pres. 1970-71, midwest regional v.p. 1971-72, Twin Cities chpt. gov. 1993—, pres. 1994-95, internat. profl. conf. com. 1995—), Fin. Execs. Inst. (dir. Ft. Wayne 1976-77), Risk and Ins. Mgmt. Soc., Hartsmen, Soc. Preservation and Encouragement Barber Shop Quartet Singing in Am., Vocal Majority Chorus, Gt. No. Union Chorus, Sigma Tau Gamma. Home: 8986 Hunters Trl Woodbury MN 55125-8667 Office: 385 Washington St Saint Paul MN 55102-1309

VAUGHN, JOHN VERNON, banker, industrialist; b. Grand Junction, Colo., June 24, 1909; s. John S. and Alice Ann (Baylis) V.; m. Dorothy May Pickrell, Oct. 12, 1934; children: Dorothy (Mrs. Richard H. Stone), John Spencer. AB, UCLA, 1932; LLD (hon.), Pepperdine U., 1974. Br. mgr. Nat. Lead Co., 1932-37; sales mgr. Sillers Paint & Varnish Co., 1937-46, pres., gen. mgr., dir., 1946-58; pres., chmn. Dartell Labs., Inc., 1959-70; vice chmn. bd. Crocker Nat. Bank and Crocker Nat. Corp., San Francisco, 1970-75; dir. Crocker Nat. Bank and Crocker Nat. Corp., 1969-85; hon. dir. Crocker Nat. Bank; cons. Coopers & Lybrand, 1975-85; chmn. bd. Recon Optical, Inc., 1979-90; bd. dirs. Trust Svcs. Am., Forest Lawn Corp., Am. Security & Fidelity Corp.; IT Corp. Chmn. San Marino Recreation Commn., 1956-58, La. Better Bus. Bur., 1959-61, Invest-in-Am., 1970-73; chmn. citizen's adv. Council Pub. Transp., 1965-67; commr. Los Angeles Coliseum Commn., 1971-74; trustee Calif. Mus. Found., 1968-79; bd. dirs. Orthopaedic Hosp., 1965-87, pres., 1974-78, chmn. bd., 1978-79; bd. dirs. YMCA, Los Angeles, 1965-77, Central City Assn., So. Calif. Visitors Council, 1970-76, NCCJ, Calif. Museum Sci. and Industry, United Way of Los Angeles, Am. Heart Assn.; mem. Los Angeles Adv. Bd., Friends of Claremont Coll., 1973-78, Los Angeles Beautiful, 1972-74; regent U. Calif., 1958-59; hon. trustee UCLA Found., 1967—, Forest Lawn Meml. Park, 1968—, Claremont Men's Coll., 1970-71, Pepperdine U., 1972—; regent, mem. bd. visitors Grad. Sch. Bus. Adminstrn. UCLA, 1971-85; mem. Chancellor's Assocs., Calif. State Univs. and Colls. Recipient Disting. Svc. award UCLA, 1965, Outstanding Community Svc. award UCLA, , 1970, Alumnus of Yr. UCLA award, 1971; Brotherhood award NCCJ, 1971; Los Angeles Jaycees award of merit, 1972; Most Disting. Citizen Los Angeles Realty Bd., 1972; other honors. Mem. Los Angeles Area C. of C. (bd. dirs. 1961, pres. 1969, chmn. 1970), World Affairs Coun. (chpt. v.p., treas. 1970-85, hon. dir. 1985—), Iranian-Am. Chamber Industry and Commerce (pres. 1971-79), Paint, Varnish and Lacquer Assn. (past nat. v.p., past chpt. pres.), Town Hall Calif. (dir. 1973-75), Young Pres.'s Orgn., Jonathan Club (pres. 1964), Los Angeles Country Club (bd. dirs. 1979-85), California Club, San Gabriel Country Club (bd. dirs. 1964-68), Valley Hunt Club, Pasadena Athletic Club, Bohemian Club of San Francisco, Internat. Order St. Hubertus, Masons, Beta Theta Pi (pres. 1960). Republican. Presbyterian. Avocations: fishing, hunting, golf. Home and Office: 454 S Orange Grove Blvd Pasadena CA 91105

VAUGHN, KAREN IVERSEN, economics educator; b. N.Y.C., July 21, 1944; d. Willy and Cecelia (Douglas) Iversen; m. Garrett Alan Vaughn, Sept. 7, 1968; 1 child, Jessica Susan. BA, Queens Coll. CUNY, 1966; MA, Duke U., 1969, PhD, 1971. Asst. prof. U. Tenn., Knoxville, 1969-75; assoc. prof. George Mason U., Fairfax, Va., 1978-84, chmn. dept. econs., 1982-89, prof. econs., 1984—; sr. rsch. asssoc. Ctr. for Study Market Processes, 1981-92; adj. scholar CATO Inst., Washington, 1982-90. Author: John Locke: Economist and Social Scientist, 1980, Austrian Economics in America: The Migration of a Tradition, 1994; editor: Perspectives on the History of Economic Thought, vol. 10, 1994; mem. editorial bd. History of Polit. Economy Jour., 1984-88, Jour. of History of Economic Thought, 1993—; editor: HES Bull., 1978-84; contbr. articles to profl. jours. NDEA fellow, 1966-69. Mem. So. Econs. Assn. (exec. com. 1978-80, v.p. 1986-87, pres.-elect 1993-94, pres. 1994-95), Am. Econs. Assn., History of Econs. Soc. (v.p. 1988-89, pres.-elect 1991-92, pres. 1992-93), Mont Pelerin Soc. Avocations: piano, voice. Office: George Mason U Dept Economics 4400 University Dr Fairfax VA 22030-4443

VAUGHN, LISA DAWN, family physician, educator; b. Ashland, Ky., May 10, 1961; d. Charles Clinton and Mildred Darlene (Cantrell) V. AS in Biology, U. Ky., 1981, BS in Zoology, 1983; DO, W.Va. Sch. Osteo. Medicine, 1988. Diplomate Nat. Osteo. Med. Bd. gen. intern Doctors Hosp. Inc., Massillon, Ohio, 1988-89; family practice resident Doctors Hosp. Inc., Massillon, 1989-91; emergency room physician Coastal Emergency Svcs., Snowpark, Ohio, 1989-90; urgent care physician Acute Care Specialists, Akron, Ohio, 1991; physician Portage Family Practice Clinic, North Canton, Ohio, 1991-95, First Care Family Health & Immediate Care Ctr., Canton, Ohio, 1995-95; dir. occupl. medicine First Care, Canton, 1996—; clin. asst. faculty Ohio U. Coll. Medicine, Athens, 1990-91, adj. clin. faculty, 1992—; asst. dir. family practice residency Ohio U. Coll. Medicine-Doctors Hosp. Inc., Massillon, 1992-95; urgent CARE physician First Care, Canton, Ohio, 1995—; med. dir. family home health svc. Doctors Hosp., 1992-94, chmn. dept. family medicine, 1994-95; med. advisor Boy Scouts Med. Explorers, Massillon, 1989-90; med. career advisor Girl Scouts Career Day, Canton, 1990; affiliate physician Cleve. Clinic, 1991—. Contbr. poems. Col. Ky. Cols. Assn., Ashland, 1989—; vol. United Way of Stark County, 1990-91. Mem. Cleve. Clinic Found. (affiliate physician), AMA, Am. Coll. Gen. Practitioners, Am. Osteo. Assn. (cert.), Ohio State Med. Assn., W.Va. Sch. Osteo. Medicine, Stark County Med. Soc., Sigma Sigma Phi (sec. 1985-86). Democrat. Avocations: writing poetry and children's stories, horseback riding, teaching med. students. Office: First Care 4612 Tuscarawas St W Canton OH 44708

VAUGHN, MAURICE SAMUEL (MO VAUGHN), professional baseball player; b. Norwalk, Conn., Dec. 15, 1967. Student, Seton Hall U., 1987-89. Infielder Boston Red Sox, 1989—. Active cmty. svc. with youth groups, Boston. Named MVP Baseball Writers' Assn., 1995; named to Sporting News Silver SLugger team, 1995, Am. League All-Star Team, 1995. Office: Boston Red Sox 4 Yawkey Way Boston MA 02215-3409*

VAUGHN, ROBERT (FRANCIS VAUGHN), actor; b. N.Y.C., Nov. 22, 1932; s. Walter and Marcella Vaughn; m. Linda Staab, 1974; children: Caitlin, Cassidy. BS in Theatre Arts, Los Angeles State Coll., MA in Theatre Arts, 1956; PhD in Communications, U. So. Calif., 1970. Appeared in local Calif. stage prodn. End as a Man, then small roles in several motion pictures; appeared as Napoleon Solo on TV series: The Man From U.N.C.L.E, 1964-67; star TV series Emerald Point NAS, 1983-84; appeared in motion pictures Hell's Crossroads, 1957, No Time to be Young, 1957, Unwed Mother, 1958, Good Day for a Hanging, 1959, The Young Philadelphians, 1959 (Acad. Motion Picture Arts and Scis. nomination 1960), The City Jungle, The Big Show, 1961, The Caretakers, 1963, To Trap a Spy, 1966, The Spy With My Face, 1966, One Spy Too Many, 1966, The Venetian Affair, 1967, How to Steal a Million, The Bridge at Remagen, 1969, If It's Tuesday, This Must Be Belgium, 1969, The Clay Pigeon, The Towering Inferno, 1974, Bullitt, 1968, The Mind of Mr. Soames, 1970, The Assassination of Julius Caesar, The Statue, 1971, The Magnificent 7, 1960, Brass Target, 1978, Battle Beyond the Stars, 1980, Virus, 1980, Cuba Crossing, 1980, Hangar 18, 1981, S.O.B., 1981, Superman III, 1983, The Delta Force, 1986, Black Moon Rising, 1986, Delta Force, 1986, Hour of the Assassin, 1987, River of Death, 1989, Nobody's Perfect, 1990, That's Adequate, 1990; appeared as Hamlet at Pasadena Playhouse, 1964; star one-man play F.D.R, 1978; portrayed Harry Truman in TV play: The Man From Independence, 1974; Woodrow Wilson in TV movie: Backstairs at the White House, 1979; appeared in TV mini-series Washington: Behind Closed Doors, 1977 (Emmy award), The Blue and the Gray, 1984, Evergreen, 1985, Centennial, 1978-79; TV movies include: The Greatest Heroes of the Bible, 1978, The Rebels, 1979, The Gossip Columnist, 1980, International Airport, 1985, Private Sessions, 1985; author: Only Victims, 1972. Former chmn. registration and Speaker's Bur., Calif. Democratic Com. Mem. Am. Acad. Polit. and Social Scis. Democrat. Roman Catholic. Address: care Agy for Performing Arts 9000 W Sunset Blvd Ste 1200 Los Angeles CA 90069-5812*

VAUGHN, ROBERT LOCKARD, aerospace and astronautics company executive; b. Rochester, N.Y., Sept. 19, 1922; s. Henry Clifford and Belva Blanche (Lockard) V.; m. Virginia Ethel Harness, June 19, 1943; children—Sandra Sue, Roberta Jean, Larry Lockard, Virginia Gail. B.S. in M.E, Iowa State U. Sci. and Tech., 1952; MS in Tech. Adminstrv. Mgmt., Calif. State U., Northridge, 1967. Registered profl. engr., Calif. Journeyman Washington Naval Gun Factory, 1940-49; lab. technician U.S. AEC, Ames (Iowa) Lab., 1949-52; with Lockheed Corp., 1953-88; corp. dir. productivity Lockheed Missiles & Space Co., Inc., Sunnyvale, Calif., 1977-88; pres. R.L. Vaughn & Assoc., Cons. Engrs., Ramona, Calif., 1988—. Contbr. over 140 articles to tech. jours. and other publications. With AUS, World War II, ETO. Recipient Calif. State Legis. Resolution award, 1982; various other awards. Fellow ASME, Soc. Mfg. Engrs. (Internat. Gold Medal award 1969), Inst. Advancement of Engring., Instn. Prodn. Engrs.; mem. San Fernando Valley Engrs. Coun. (past pres., dir.), Calif. Soc. Profl. Engrs. (past pres., dir. San Fernando Valley chpt., Oustanding Svc. award 1972, 73, 76), Nat. Mgmt. Assn., (Internat. award for mfg. excellence 1983, McGraw-Hill Am.), Am. Soc. Metals, Am. Assn. Engring. Socs. (bd. govs., dir.), Fedn. Materials Socs. (past trustee), Soc. Mfg. Engrs. (past pres., dir.). Patentee in field. Home: 23635 Barona Mesa Rd Ramona CA 92065

VAUGHN, RODNEY CORNELL, primary school educator; b. Washington, Dec. 3, 1965; s. Clearance and Ernestine Vaughn; m. July 30, 1993; 1 child, Raamah Cinque. BA in Fgn. Rels., Bowie (Md.) State U., 1989; MA in Edn. Adminstrn., Coll. of William & Mary, 1994. Social studies instr. Berkeley Middle Sch., Williamsburg, Va., 1989-90; intervention counselor Bacon St., Williamsburg, 1990-92; world cultures instr. Kenmore Middle Sch., Landover, Md., 1992—; head football coach Berkeley Middle Sch., Williamsburg; defensive coord. Northwestern H.S.; chmn. Sch. Based Mgmt. Team, Landover, 1990-93; counselor Violence Prevention Edn., Landover, 1992-93. Male mentor Youth Rites of Passage, Landover, 1992-94; dir. community svc., Landover, 1993-94. With USNR, 1985—. Mem. ASCD, Kappa Alpha Psi. Avocations: physical fitness, rottweillers training and coaching, football. Home: 8610 Fort Foote Rd Fort Washington MD 20744-6700

VAUGHN, ROGER, insurance company executive. Exec. v.p. Nations Bank of Ga., NA. Office: 123 N Wacker Dr Ste 1000 Chicago IL 60606

VAUGHN, RUFUS MAHLON, psychiatrist; b. Ensley, Ala., Oct. 31, 1924; s. Rufus Samuel and Anna Martina (Fink) V.; children: Stephen Andrew, Alexander. Student, U. Mich., 1942-43, 46-47; AB, Birmingham So. Coll., 1949; MD, Med. Coll. Ala., 1953. Diplomate Am. Bd. Psychiatry and Neurology, Am. Bd. Forensic Psychiatry. Intern USPHS Hosp., San Francisco, 1953-54; resident in psychiatry Ind. U. Hosp., Indpls., 1954-56, U. Calif. Hosp., L.A., 1956-57; dir. psychiatry Student Health Svc., U. Mass., Amherst, 1958-59; researcher Boston State Hosp., 1959-61; assoc. prof. psychiatry U. Fla., Gainesville, 1961-70; dir. Palm Beach County Mental Health Ctr., West Palm Beach, Fla., 1970-71; med. dir. Lake Hosp. and Clinic, Lake Worth, Fla., 1971-73; dir. tng., rsch. So. Fla. State Hosp., Hollywood, 1973-74, supt., 1974; chief Bur. Mental Hosp. Svcs., Fla. Div. Mental Health, Tallahassee, 1974-75; pvt. practice medicine specializing in forensic psychiatry West Palm Beach, 1975-87; sr. physician No. Fla. Evaluation and Treatment Ctr., Gainesville, 1982-89; clin. prof. psychiatry U. Miami, 1973-75; med. dir. USPHS Res., 1980—; clin. assoc. prof. psychiatry U. Fla., 1983—; med. dir. Mental Health Svcs. Inc., Gainesville, Fla., 1989-94, cons., 1994—. With USNR, 1943-46. Home: 1205 NW 35th Ave Gainesville FL 32609-2112 Office: 4300 SW 13th St Gainesville FL 32608-4006

VAUGHN, VICKI LYNN, education educator; b. New Castle, Ind., Nov. 10, 1947; d. Robert Allen and Geneva Aileen (Bishop) Fulton; m. Virgil Encil Vaughn, Jr., Aug. 26, 1967; children: Joshua Allen, Jordan Tanner. BS, Ball State U., Muncie, Ind., 1969, MA, 1973; PhD, Purdue U., 1991. Elem. tchr. New Castle (Ind.) Cmty. Sch. Corp., 1969-86; gifted/talented tchr. Marion (Ind.) Cmty. Sch. Corp., 1986-88, Lafayette (Ind.) Sch. Corp., 1988-93; prin./dept. chair/asst. prof. Ball State U., Muncie, 1993—; lectr. grad. courses Purdue U., West Lafayette, Ind., 1991—; assoc. Ctr. for Gifted Studies and Talent Devel., Muncie, 1993—, Ctr. for Creative Learning, Sarasota, Fla., 1994—; cons. Ind. schs., 1993—. Co-editor Nat. Assn. Labs. Schs. Jour.; reviewer articles Jour. Secondary Gifted Edn., Tchr. Educator, others; contbr. articles to profl. jours. Ind. Dept. Edn. learning grantee, 1993, 4Rs grantee, 1994. Mem. ASCD (assoc.), Nat. Assn. for Gifted Children, Nat. Assn. for Lab. Schs., Ind. Assn. for Gifted (rsch. com. 1988—), Phi Delta Kappa, Phi Kappa Phi. Avocations: reading, dancing, travel. Home: 1004 N Meadow Ln Muncie IN 47304-6714 Office: Burris Laboratory Sch 2000 W University Ave Muncie IN 47306-1022

VAUGHN, WILLIAM PRESTON, historian, educator; b. East Chicago, Ind., May 28, 1933; s. James Carl and Georgiana (Preston) V.; m. Virginia Lee Meyer, June 10, 1961; 1 child, Rhonda Louise. AB, U. Mo., Columbia, 1955; MA, Ohio State U., 1956, PhD, 1961. Instr. in history U. So. Calif., 1961-62; asst. prof. history U. N. Tex., Denton, 1962-65, assoc. prof., 1965-69, prof., 1969-91; instr. Tex. Project, Malaysia, 1986, 88. Author: Schools for All: The Blacks and Public Education in the South, 1865-77, 1974, The Antimasonic Party in the United States, 1826-43, 1983; editor Transactions Tex. Lodge of Rsch., 1988—; contbr. numerous articles on black edn. masonry and polit. antimasonry to profl. jours. With arty. U.S. Army, 1956-57. Mem. SAR, So. Hist. Assn. (life), Historians Early Am. Republic, Masons, Phi beta Kappa, Phi Alpha Theta (manuscript competition winner 1972), Phi Delta Kappa, Phi Delta Beta. Republican. Episcopalian. Home: 908 Hilton Pl Denton TX 76201-8606

VAUGHN, WILLIAM WEAVER, lawyer; b. Los Angeles, Aug. 29, 1930; s. William Weaver and Josephine (Sweigert) V.; m. Claire Louise M'Closkey, June 2, 1962; children: Robert, Gregory, Elizabeth, Anthony, Christina, James. B.A., Stanford U., 1952; LL.B., UCLA, 1955. Bar: Calif. 1956. Mem. O'Melveny & Myers, L.A., 1955-56, 57—, ptnr., 1964—; mem. adv. group U.S. Dist. Ct. (ctrl. dist.) Calif. 1991-93, L.A. Area alt. dispute resolution panel Ctr. for Pub. Resources, 1988—. Served with U.S. Army, 1956-57. Recipient Learned Hand award Am. Jewish Com., 1991. Fellow Am. Coll. Trial Lawyers (bd. regents 1992-95); mem. L.A. County Bar Assn. (trustee 1976-78, 80-82), L.A. County Bar Found. (bd. dirs. 1991-95), Assn. Bus. Trial Lawyers (bd. govs. 1980-82), Order of Coif. Clubs: California

(Los Angeles), Chancery (Los Angeles). Office: O'Melveny & Myers 400 S Hope St Los Angeles CA 90071-2801

VAUGHT, RICHARD LOREN, urologist; b. Ind., Oct. 28, 1933; s. Loren Judson and Bernice Rose (Bridges) V.; widowed, July 1987; children: Megan, Niles, Barbara, Mary; m. Nancy Lee Gusa, Aug. 1992. AB in Anatomy and Physiology, Ind. U., 1955; MD, Ind. U., Indpls., 1958. Diplomate Am. Bd. Urology. Intern, then resident in gen. surgery U.S. Naval Hosp., St. Albans, N.Y., 1958-60, resident in urology, 1960-63; spl. fellow Sloan Kettering Meml. Hosp. for Cancer and Allied Diseases, N.Y.C., 1962; pediatric urology observer Babies Hosp., Columbia-Presbyn. Med. Ctr., N.Y.C., 1962; head urology U.S. Naval Hosp., Beaufort, S.C., 1963-65; asst. chief urology, head pediatric urology U.S. Naval Hosp., San Diego, 1965-68; pvt. practice Plaza Urol., Sioux City; med. dir. dept. hyperbaric medicine St. Luke's Regional Med. Ctr., Sioux City, 1988-95; pres., chmn. bd. dirs. Care Choices of Siouxland, Sioux City, 1987-94; med. dir. Male Impotence Clinic, Marian Health Ctr., Sioux City, 1995—. Organizer telecommunications system for deaf, Siouxland, 1983. Lt. comdr. USN, 1958-68. Fellow ACS, Internat. Soc. Cryosurgery, Am. Acad. Pediat.; mem. Am. Urol. Assn., Soc. Pediatric Urology, European Soc. Pediatric Urology (corr.), Undersea and Hyperbaric Medicine Soc., Am. Coll. Hyperbaric Medicine, Am. Soc. Laser Medicine and Surgery, Am. Lithotripsy Soc., Am. Coll. Physician Execs. (assoc.), Woodbury County Med. Soc. (pres.), Am. Confedn. Urology, Sertoma (Sertoman of Yr. award 1983). Home: 10 Cottonwood Landing South Sioux City NE 68776 Office: Plaza Urol PC 2800 Pierce St Ste 308 Sioux City IA 51104-3759

VAUGHT, WILMA L., foundation executive, retired air force officer; b. Pontiac, Mich., Mar. 15, 1930; d. Willard L. and Margaret J. (Pierce) V. BS, U. Ill., 1952; MBA, U. Ala., 1968; postgrad., Indsl. Coll. Armed Forces, 1972-73; D Pub. Affairs (hon.), Columbia Coll., 1992. Cert. cost acct. Commd. 2d lt. USAF, 1957, advanced through grades to brig. gen., 1980; chief data services div. 306th Combat Support Group USAF, McCoy AFB, Fla., 1963-67; mgmt. analyst Office Dep. Chief of Staff, comptroller Mil. Assistance Command USAF, Saigon, Vietnam, 1968-69; chief advanced logistics systems plans and mgmt. group Air Force Logistics Command USAF, Wright-Patterson AFB, Ohio, 1969-72; chief cost factors br., chief security assistance br. USAF, Washington, 1973-75, Directorate Mgmt. Analysis, Office of Comptroller, 1973-75; dir. program and budget Office Dep. Chief of Staff, comptroller Hdqrs. Air Force Systems Command USAF, Andrews AFB, Md., 1980-82; comdr. U.S. Mil. Entrance Processing Command USAF, North Chicago, Ill., 1982-85; ret. USAF, 1985; pres. Women in Mil. Svc. Meml. Found., Arlington, Va., 1987—; pres. bd. dirs. Pentagon Fed. Credit Union, 1975-82; bd. regents Inst. Cost Analysis, 1979-83; Air Force sr. mil. rep. Def. Adv. Com. on Women in Services, 1982-85; chmn. Com. on Women in Armed Forces, NATO, Brussels, 1984-85. Bd. dirs. Air Force Retired Officer Community, 1986-90; mem. adv. bd. Jane Addams Conf.; mem. bd. trustees The Teller Found. Decorated Bronze Star medal, Def. Disting. Service medal, U.S. Air Force Disting. Service medal; recipient Ill. Achievement award U. Ill., 1983. Mem. Chgo. Network, Internat. Women's Forum. Methodist. Home: 6658 Van Winkle Dr Falls Church VA 22044-1010 Office: Women in Mil Svc Meml Found 5510 Columbia Pike Ste 302 Arlington VA 22204-3123

VAUSE, EDWIN HAMILTON, research foundation administrator; b. Chgo., Mar. 30, 1923; s. Harry Russell and Sylvia Clair (Webster) V.; m. Harriet Evelyn Oestmann, June 30, 1951; children—Karen L., Russell E., Kurt H., Dirk C., Luke E. B.S., U. Ill., 1947, M.S., 1948; M.B.A., U. Chgo., 1952; D.Sc. (hon.), U. Evansville, 1977. Registered profl. engr., Ill., Ind. Engr., research dept. Standard Oil Co., Ind., 1948-52; asst. gen. foreman mfg. dept. Standard Oil Co., 1952-57; dir. research adminstrn. Mead Johnson & Co., Evansville, Ind., 1957-60; v.p. Charles F. Kettering Found., Dayton, Ohio, 1960-66; v.p., adminstrn. dir. Charles F. Kettering Found., 1966-67, exec. v.p., 1967-71, v.p. for sci. and tech., 1971-88; trustee The Found. Center, 1967-73; mem. adv. com. Acad. Forum, Nat. Acad. Scis. Vice-pres. Washington Twp. Bd. Edn., 1963-67; mem. Centerville-Washington Twp. Joint Planning Commn., 1967-68; mem. adv. bd. Center for Students Rights, Dayton, 1966-70; active Boy Scouts Am. Mem. Am. Inst. Chem. Engrs. (past chmn. Chgo. sect.), N.Y. Acad. Scis., Agrl. Research Inst., Nat. Industry State Agrl. Research Council. Republican. Lutheran. Clubs: Elks, Kiwanis (past pres.), Masons. Home: 11834 Calle Parral San Diego CA 92128-4534

VAUX, DORA LOUISE, sperm bank official, consultant; b. White Pine, Mont., Aug. 8, 1922; d. Martin Tinus and Edna Ruth (Pyatt) Palmlund; m. Robert Glenn Vaux, Oct. 25, 1941; children: Jacqueline, Cheryl, Richard, Jeanette. Grad. high sch., Bothell, Wash. Photographer Busco-Nestor Studios, San Diego, 1961-68; owner, mgr. Vaux Floors & Interiors, San Diego, 1968-82; cons., mgr. Repository for Germinal Choice, Escondido, Calif., 1983-91; adminstr. Found. for the Continuity of Mankind, Spokane, 1991—. Republican. Home: 2727 S Skipworth Rd Spokane WA 99206 Office: Found Continuity of Mankind 1209 W 1st Ave Spokane WA 99204-0601 *Personal philosophy: It does not matter what our start in life has been, we can set goals and by our own hard work, achieve them. We must find our own answers to our problems and with this will come great pride and enjoyment.*

VAVALA, DOMENIC ANTHONY, medical scientist, educator, retired air force officer; b. Providence, Feb. 1, 1925; s. Salvatore and Maria (Grenci) V. BA, Brown U., 1947; MS, U. R.I., 1950; MA, Trinity U., San Antonio, 1954; PhD in Physiology, Accademia di Studi Superiori "Minerva", Italy, 1957; MEd, U. Houston, 1958; DSc (hon.), Nobile Accademia di Santa Teodora Imperatrice, Rome, 1966, DMS (hon.), 1970; DPH (hon.), Nobile Accademia di Santa Teodora Imperatrice, 1983; D Pedagogy (hon.), Studiorum Universitas Constantiniana of Sovrano Ordine Constantiniano di San Giorgio, Rome, 1966; DEd (hon.), Imperiale Accademia di San Cirillo, Pomezia, Italy, 1977; LittD, Univ. Internazionale Sveva "Frederick II", Bergamo, Italy, 1979; D Health Scis. (hon.), Johnson & Wales U., 1993. Research asst. tumor research U. R.I., also asst. entomol. research, 1950; research asst. pharmacology Boston U. Sch. Medicine, 1950-51; commd. 2d lt. med. service USAF, 1951, advanced through grades to lt. col., 1968; physiologist cold injury research team Army Med. Research Lab., Osaka (Japan) Army Hosp., 1951-52; research aviation physiologist USAF Sch. Aviation Medicine, Randolph AFB, Tex., 1952-54, 3605th USAF Hosp., Ellington AFB, Tex., 1955-57; chief physiol. tng. 3605th USAF Hosp., 1957; cons. aviation physiology, film prodn. dept. U. Houston, 1956; research aviation physiologist, head acad. sect. dept. physiol. tng. USAF Hosp., Lackland AFB, Tex., 1957-58; vis. prof. physiology Incarnate Word Coll., San Antonio, 1958; research aviation physiologist, chief physiol. tng. comdr. 832d Physiol. Tng. Flight, 832d Tactical Hosp., Cannon AFB, N.Mex., 1958-65; adj. faculty mem. Eastern N.Mex. U., Portales, 1959-64; instr. adult edn. div. Clovis (N.Mex.) mcpl. schs., 1960; research aviation physiologist, comdr. 15th Physiol. Tng. Flight, 824th USAF Dispensary, Kadena Air Base, Okinawa, 1965-66; research scientist, directorate fgn. tech., aerospace med. div. Brooks AFB, Tex., 1966-68; chief R & D support and interface div., dep. dir. for fgn. tech., 1968-70; adj. instr. Johnson & Wales U., Providence, 1973-74; instr. humanities Johnson and Wales U., Providence, 1974-75, asst. prof. humanities, 1975-77, prof. health scis. and nutrition, 1977-93, prof. emeritus, 1993—, coord. biomed. and behavioral scis. Day Coll. div., 1973-75, psychology coord. vets. div. Coll. Continuing Edn., 1974-76, assoc. dean adj. faculty, 1975, dean faculty, 1975-77, coord. acad. devel., 1977-78, dir. musical series, 1990—, curator Chapel Empress St. Theodora, 1992—; pres. corp., chmn. bd. Sovereign Constantinian Order of St. George, Inc., R.I., 1986—. Writer, producer: (TV Series) Your Body in Flight, Sta. KUHT, Houston, 1956; (TV series) Highway to Health, Okinawa, 1965; editor-in-chief: NADUS Jour., 1963-85; compiled and edited: Fifty Years of Progress of Soviet Medicine, 1917-67; abstractor: Am. Chem. Soc., 1963-74. Contbr. articles to profl. jours. Trustee, Gov. Ctr. Sch., Providence, 1979-85; mem. scholarship com. St. Sahag and St. Mesrob Armenian Apostolic Ch., Providence. Served with AUS, 1943-44. Recipient Disting. Svc. award Clovis (N.Mex.) Jaycees, 1959, Acad. Palms Gold medal Accademia di Studi Superior "Minerva", 1960, citation from chief chaplains USAF, 1970, chief biomed. scientist insignia, biomed. scis. corps USAF Med. Svc., 1970, spl. faculty citation Johnson and Wales U., 1981; academician divsn. scis. Accademia di Studi Superiori "Minerva", 1960; Min. Plenipotentiary for U.S. of Nobile Accademia di Santa Teodora Imperatrice, Rome, 1967, rector pro tempore, 1980, pres. R.I. Corp., chmn. bd., 1988; decorated knight grand officer Merit Class, Sovereign Constantinian Order St. George, Rome, 1969, Knight of Grand Cross with Constantinian neckchair, Justice Class, Sovereign Constantinian Order of St. George, 1969, Knight of Grand Cordon Justice Class, Order of Teutonic Knights, Sao Paulo, 1986, Knight of Grand Cross Justice Class, Mil. Order St. Gereon, Sao Paulo, 1986, Knight of Grand Cross Jus Class, Mil. and Hospitalier Order St Jean d'Acre and St. Thomas, Capua, Italy, 1987, Knight of Grand Cross Justice Class, Mil. and Hospitalier Order St. Mary of Bethlehem, Capua, 1987; named Magnificent Rector and Pres. of the Constantin U. (Studiorum Universitas Constantiniana), Italy, 1970. Fellow AAAS, Tex. Acad. Sci., Royal Soc. Health (London), Am. Inst. Chemists; mem. Assn. Mil. Surgeons U.S., Nat. Assn. Doctors U.S. (founder 1958, sec.-treas. 1958-85), Accademia di San Cirillo Italy (hon.), N.Y. Acad. Scis., Phi Sigma, Kappa Delta Pi, Phi Kappa Phi, Alpha Beta Kappa (charter mem., pres. R.I. Alpha chpt. Johnson & Wales U. 1984-92). Home: 30 Oaklawn Ave Apt 219 Cranston RI 02920-9319

VAWTER, NANCY VANDEGRIFF, environmental research administrator; b. Henning, Tenn., May 26, 1941; d. Wilmer Montell and Ruby May (Pittman) Vandergriff; m. Bartlett Chesterfield Durham III, Feb. 23, 1965 (div. Aug. 1976); children: Colin Sanford Durham, Blair Pierson Durham; m. William Franklin Vawter, Oct. 28, 1989. BS in Edn. magna cum laude, U. Tenn., Nashville, 1975; MS in Biology magna cum laude, Peabody/Vanderbilt U., 1976; postgrad., U. Calif., Berkeley, 1987. Tchr. sci. Hillwood H.S., Nashville, 1975-76, Bellevue H.S., Nashville, 1976-78; tchr., rschr. Pelham (Ala.) H.S., 1978-79; tchr.-in-residence Ala. Power Co., Birmingham, 1987-89; ednl. cons. in pvt. practice N. Vawter & Assocs., Montgomery, Ala., 1990-93; with Troy (Ala.) State U., 1989-90, project dir. Ctr. for Environ. Rsch. and Svc., 1993-95; assoc. dir. Ala. Sci. in Motion, chemistry trainer Ala. State U., 1996—; chmn. bd. ALA-NEED, Ala. Dept. Econ. and Cmty. Affairs, Montgomery, 1991-94; mem. team Global Environ. Conf./Washington Press Club, Washington. Grant writer; book reviewer. Advisor Ala. Power Co./So. Ctrl. Bell, statewide, 1989-94; trustee Gorgas Found., Birmingham, 1993-94. Mem. AAAS, NEA, ASCD, Ala. Acad. Sci., N.Y. Acad. Sci., Assn. for Presdl. Award Winers in Sci. Teaching (nat. dir.-at-large, pres.), Nat. Sci. Tchrs. Assn., Ala. Sci. Tchrs. Assn. (gen. chair 1988-90), Ala. Edn. Assn., Coalition for Better Edn., Montgomery C. of C. (chmn. task force 1992-93), Capitol City Club. Republican. Methodist. Avocations: writing poetry, reading, singing in church choir, gardening, hiking. Home: 532 Wakefield Dr Montgomery AL 36109-2318

VAYHINGER, JOHN MONROE, psychotherapist, minister; b. Upland, Ind., Jan. 27, 1916; s. Paul Johnson and Harriet Estelle (Palmer) V.; m. Ruth Imler, Spet. 17, 1939; children: John Earl, Karen Lynn Vayhinger Kuper Childs. AB, Taylor U., 1937; grad., Asbury Theol. Sem., Wilmore, Ky., 1937-39; BD, MA, Drew U., 1940, 51; MA, PhD, Columbia U., 1948, 56. Diplomate Am. Bd. Psychology; ordained Meth. Ch. as pastor. Pastor United Meth. Ch., Conn., Ind., N.Y., Colo., 1938-68, ret.68; assoc. prof., head dept. W.Va. Wesleyan U., Buckhannon, 1949-51; chief clin. psychologist Mental Health Clin., South Bend, Ind., 1951-58; lectr. Ind. U., South Bend, 1953-58; prof. psychology and pastoral counseling Garrett Theol. Sem. Northwestern U., Evanston, Ill., 1958-64; prof. psychology of religion and pastoral counseling Iliff Sch. Theology U. Denver, 1964-67; prof. psychology and pastoral counseling Anderson (Ind.) U. Sch. Theology, 1968-81, Asbury Theol. Sem., Wilmore, Ky., 1981-84, ret.84; pvt. practice Ky., Ind., Ill, Colo., 1958—, Colorado Springs, Colo., 1984—; dir. inst. ministries Ind. Coun. Chs., Indpls., 1968-81; chairperson Pastoral Counseling Inst., Atlanta, 1985—. Author: Before Divorce, 1972, (with Newman Cryer), Casebook of Pastoral Counseling, 1962; contbr. 12 chpts. edited books. Tchr. police schs., South Bend, Ind., Anderson, Ind., Denver. Capt. AUS, 1944-47, PTO. Fellow Am. Orthopsychiatric Assn., Am. Assn. Sci. Study of Religion, Christian Assn. Psychol. Studies, Am. Assn. Clin. Sexiologists, Am. Assn. Christian Counselors; mem. Am. Assn. Pastoral Counselors (diplomate), Soc. Psychol. in Pvt. Practice, Am. Psychol. Assn., AAUP, AAAS, Colo. Psychol. Assn., Ind. Psychol. Assn., Am. Assn. Marital and Family Therapists (clin.), Religious Rsch. Assn., Am. Assn. Sex Educators, Counselors and Therapists, Nat. Coun. Family Relations, Assn. Clin. Pastoral Edn., Nat. Congress Parents and Tchrs. (life), USN Inst., and more. Republican. Home: 119 Illini Dr Woodland Park CO 80863-8705 Office: 420 N Nevada Ave Colorado Springs CO 80903-1227

VAYO, DAVID JOSEPH, composer, music educator; b. New Haven, Mar. 28, 1957; s. Harold Edward and Joan Virginia (Cassidy) V.; m. Margot Ehrlich, May 16, 1981; children: Rebecca Lynne, Gordon Francis. MusB, Ind. U., 1980, MusM, 1982; D of Musical Arts, U. Mich., 1990. Prof. Nat. U., Heredia, Costa Rica, 1982-84, Nat. Symphony Youth Sch., San Jose, Costa Rica, 1982-84; asst. prof. music Conn. Coll., New London, 1988-91; asst. prof. music Ill. Wesleyan U. Sch. Music, Bloomington, 1991-95, assoc. prof., 1995—; resident artist Banff Ctr. for Arts, 1992, 94, Va. Ctr. for Creative Arts, 1994; participating composer Internat. Soc. Contemporary Music-World Music Days, Mexico City, 1993, Internat. Double Reed Festival, Rotterdam, The Netherlands, 1995. Composer chamber composition Poem, 1990 (winner Spectri Sonori Internat. Composition competition Tulane U. 1992), Symphony: Blossoms and Awakenings, 1990 (performer St. Louis Symphony, Leonard Slatkin condr. 1993), Wind Quintet, 1991 (winner Symposium Seven for New Woodwind Quintet Music, U. Ga. 1993), Eight Poems of William Carlos Williams for solo trombonist, 1994 (commd. by St. Louis Symphony); works pub. by MMB Music and A.M. Percussion Publs. Charles E. Ives scholar Am. Acad. and Inst. Arts and Letters, 1988. Mem. ASCAP (awards 1988—), Am. Music Ctr. (copying assistance grantee 1992), Coll. Music Soc. (presenter nat. conf. 1990-94), Soc. for Electro-Acoustic Music in U.S. (presenter nat. conf. 1989), Soc. Composers (membership chmn. 1990—, presenter nat. conf. 1990, 92, 95), Am. Composers Forum. Avocations: athletics, Latin American culture, traveling, reading. Office: Ill Wesleyan U Sch Music PO Box 2900 Bloomington IL 61702-2900

VAZIRI, NOSRATOLA DABIR, internist, nephrologist, educator; b. Tehran, Iran, Oct. 13, 1939; came to U.S., 1969, naturalized, 1977; s. Abbas and Tahera V. M.D., Tehran U., 1966. Diplomate: Am. Bd. Internal Medicine, Am. Bd. Nephrology. Intern Cook County Hosp., Chgo., 1969-70; resident Berkshire Med. Ctr., Pittsfield, Mass., 1970-71, Wadsworth VA Med. Ctr., 1971-72, UCLA Med. Ctr., 1972-74; prof. medicine U. Calif.-Irvine, 1979—, chief nephrology div., 1977—, dir. hemodialysis unit, 1977—, vice chmn. dept. medicine, 1982—; chmn. dept. medicine, 1994—; mem. sci. adv. council Nat. Kidney Found., 1977—. Contbr. numerous articles to med. jours. Recipient Golden Apple award, 1977; named outstanding tchr. U. Calif-Irvine, 1975, 78, 79, 80, 82. Fellow ACP; mem. Am. Soc. Nephrology, Am. Paraplegia Soc. (pres. 1992-94), Western Assn. Physicians, Assn. Profs. of Medicine, Alpha Omega Alpha. Home: 66 Balboa Cv Newport Beach CA 92663-3226 Office: U Calif Irvine Med Ctr Div Nephrology Dept Medicine 101 City Dr Orange CA 92668

VAZQUEZ, GILBERT FALCON, lawyer; b. Eagle Pass, Tex., Oct. 29, 1952; s. Catalina (Falcon) Vazquez. AB in Polit. Sci., Yale U., 1975; JD, Harvard U., 1978. Bar: Tex. 1978, U.S. Dist. Ct. (we. dist.) Tex. 1980, U.S. Ct. Appeals (5th and 11th cirs.) 1981. Ptnr. Matthews & Branscomb, San Antonio, Tex., 1978-85, Akin, Gump, Strauss, Hauer & Feld, L.L.P., San Antonio, 1985—. Co-chmn. issues com. H. Cisneros Mayoral Campaign, San Antonio, 1981; bd. dirs. Bexar County-San Antonio United Way, 1982-87, 91—, San Antonio World Affairs Coun., 1993—, San Antonio Mus. Assn., 1993-95; mem. exec. com. Mayor's Target 90 Commn., San Antonio, 1985-89, vice chmn., 1987-89; chmn. City of San Antonio Charter Rev. Com., 1991-93, State of Tex. Pension Rev. Bd., 1991—, vice-chmn., 1994, chair, 1995; bd. dirs. San Antonio Zool. Soc., 1988—, mem. exec. com. Named Outstanding Young San Antonian, U.S. Jaycees, 1985, Outstanding Vol., J.C. Penny Co., 1984. Mem. ABA (internat. law sect., assoc. editor newsletter 1985-87), Nat. Assn. Bond Lawyers, Tex. Bar Assn. (governing coun. internat. law sect. 1985-88), San Antonio Bar Assn., San Antonio Young Lawyers Assn. (Outstanding Young Lawyer 1987), Hispanic Nat. Bar Assn. (regional pres. 1987-88, nat. sec. 1988-89, v.p. 1989-90), San Antonio World Trade Assn. (bd. dirs. 1987-90), Mexican C. of C. (bd. dirs. 1984-85), Greater San Antonio C. of C. (bd. dirs. 1992-95), Yale Club South Tex. (pres. 1982-85). Democrat. Roman Catholic. Avocations: community redevelopment, music, reading. Office: Akin Gump Strauss Hauer & Feld LLP 300 Convent St Ste 1500 San Antonio TX 78205-3716

VAZQUEZ, MARTHA ALICIA, judge; b. Santa Barbara, Calif., Feb. 21, 1953; d. Remigio and Consuelo (Mendez) V.; m. Frank Mathew, Aug. 7, 1976; children: Cristina Vazquez Mathew, Nicholas Vazquez Matthew, Nathan Vazquez Matthew. BA in Govt., U. Notre Dame, 1975, JD, 1978. Bar: N.Mex. 1979, U.S. Dist. Ct. (we. dist.) N.Mex. 1979. Atty. Pub. Defender's Office, Santa Fe, 1979-81; ptnr. Jones, Snead, Wertheim, Rodriguez & Wentworth, Santa Fe, 1981-93; judge U.S. District Ct., 10th Circuit, Santa Fe, 1993—. Chmn. City Santa Fe Grievance Bd. Mem. N.Mex. Bar Assn. (fee arbitration com., chmn. trial practice sect. 1984-85, mem. task force on minority involvement in bar activities), Santa Fe Bar Assn. (jud. liasion com.), Nat. Assn. Criminal Def. Lawyers, Assn. Trial Lawyers Am., N.Mex. Trial Lawyers Assn. Democrat. Roman Catholic. Office: US Courthouse PO Box 2710 Santa Fe NM 87504-2710*

VEACH, ROBERT RAYMOND, JR., lawyer; b. Charleston, S.C., Nov. 28, 1950; s. Robert Raymond and Evelyn Ardell (Vegter) V.; m. Lori Sue Erickson, May 27, 1989. Student, St. Olaf Coll., 1968-70; BS in Acctg., Ariz. State U., 1972; JD, So. Meth. U., 1975. Bar: Tex. 1975, Nebr. 1975, U.S. Dist. Ct. Nebr. 1975, U.S. Dist. Ct. (no. dist.) Tex. 1975, Temporary Emergency Ct. Appeals 1975. Acctg. instr. Sch. Bus. So. Meth. U., Dallas, 1973-74; law clk. to Hon. Joe E. Estes U.S. Dist. Ct. No. Dist. Tex.-Temp. Emergency Ct. Appeals, Dallas, 1975-76; assoc. Locke Purnell Boren Laney & Neely, Dallas, 1976-80; v.p. The Lomas & Nettleton Co., Dallas, 1980-83, Rauscher Pierce Refsnes, Inc., Dallas, 1983-87; pres. RPR Mortgage Fin. Corp., Dallas, 1985-87; sr. shareholder Locke Purnell Rain Harrell, Dallas, 1987—; allied mem. N.Y. Stock Exch., 1985-87; lectr. securities and banking confs.; bd. dirs. pvt. corps. Author legal articles. Dir. North Tex. affiliate Am. Diabetes Assn., Dallas, 1978-81; mem. Gov.'s Task Force Wash. State Housing Commn., 1982-83. Mem. ABA, State Bar of Tex., Nebr. State Bar Assn., Fed. Bar Assn., Dallas Bar Assn. Republican. Methodist. Avocations: golf, antique Am. firearms. Home: 4223 Brookview Dr Dallas TX 75220-3801 Office: Locke Purnell Rain Harrell 2200 Ross Ave Ste 2200 Dallas TX 75201-6766

VEACO, KRISTINA, lawyer; b. Sacramento, Calif., Mar. 4, 1948; d. Robert Glenn and Lelia (McCain) V. BA, U. Calif., Davis, 1978; JD, Hastings Coll. of the Law, 1981. Legal adv. to commr. William T. Bagley Calif. Public Utilities Commn., San Francisco, Calif., 1981-86; sr. counsel Pacific Telesis Group, San Francisco, Calif., 1986-94; sr. counsel corp. and securities and pol. law Air Touch Comms., San Francisco, 1994—. Mem. ABA, Calif. Women Lawyers, San Francisco Bar Assn., Am. Soc. Corp. Secs., Phi Beta Kappa. Democrat. Episcopalian. Avocations: cooking, reading. Office: Air Touch Coms 1 California St Rm 2108 San Francisco CA 94111-5401

VEALE, TINKHAM, II, former chemical company executive, engineer; b. Topeka, Dec. 26, 1914; s. George W. and Grace Elizabeth (Walworth) V.; m. Harriett Alice Ernst, Sept. 6, 1941; children: Harriett Elizabeth Veale Leedy, Tinkham III, Helen Ernst Veale Gelbach. BS in Mech. Engring., Case Inst. Tech., 1937; LLD, Kenyon Coll., 1981. Registered profl. engr. With Gen. Motors Corp., 1937-38, Avery Engring. Co., 1939, Reliance Electric Co., 1940-41; asst. to pres. Ohio Crankshaft Co., 1942-46; gen. mgr. Tocco Co., 1947-51; pres. Ric Wil Corp., 1952-53; pres. Alco Chem. Corp., 1954-56, dir., 1954-86; spl. ptnr. Ball Burge & Kraus, investment bankers, 1957-60; chmn. bd. V. and V. Cos., Inc. and subs., Cleve., 1960-65, Alco Standard Corp. and subs., Valley Forge, Pa., 1965-86, Horsehead Industries, Inc. and subs., N.Y.C., 1981—, HTV Industries Inc. and subs., Cleve., 1978—; ptnr. Fair Elm Farm, 1948—, Kennedy Veale Stable, 1954—. Trustee V. and V. Charitable Found., 1966—. Recipient Silver Bowl award Case Inst. Tech., 1980; recipient Gold Medal Case Inst. Tech., 1982. Mem. Cleve. Engring. Soc., Nat. Soc. Registered Profl. Engrs., Newcomen Soc., Phi Kappa Psi. Home: Fair Elm Gate Mills OH 44040 Office: HTV Industries Inc PO Box 295 Gates Mills OH 44040-0295

VEASEL, WALTER, minister, educator; b. Balt., Apr. 11, 1925; s. William Edward Veasel and Mary Lula (Boyd-Veasel) Ebert; m. Helen Ilene Gank; children: William, Holly, Bradley, Heide. ThB, Holmes Coll. of the Bible, 1947; BS in Elem. Edn., Towson State U., 1970; M in Ministries, Zion Sem., 1986. Ordained to ministry Christian Ch., 1947; cert. tchr., Md. Tchr. Balt. City Schs., 1959-84; pastor Mid Atlantic Conf. Pentecostal Holiness Ch., 1948-54, St. Catherines and London, St. Catherines and London, ON, Can., 1955-59; tchr. Balt. City Schs., 1959-84; pastor Mid Atlantic Conf. Pentecostal Holiness Ch., Georgetown, D.C. and Daniels, Md., 1960-70; tchr. Balt. City Schs., 1959-84; founder, pastor Community Ch., 1970-90; pastor emeritus Woodbridge Valley Ch. of God, 1990-94; prin. Tabernacle Christian Sch., Balt., 1988-94; conf. Sunday sch. sec./treas.; conf. youth v.p.; conf. sec./treas. and bd. dirs., 1950-70; instr. Tabernacle Bible Inst., 1970-75, Faith Sch. Theology, 1993. Vol. nursing homes, reform schs. and prisons, 1948—. Recipient Vols. Cert., House of Correction, 1975-96. Mem. Ministerial Assn. Republican. Home: 5025 Montgomery Rd Ellicott City MD 21043-6750 also: 638 Clark Lohr Rd Swanton MD 21561

VEATCH, JEAN LOUISE CORTY, telemetry nurse; b. Farmer City, Ill., June 4, 1932; d. Eugene Louis and Mary Violette (Mounce) Corty; m. July 23, 1955 (div.); children: Irvin, Ronald, Steven, Julie, James, Jeffery. Diploma, Holy Cross Cen. Sch. Nursing, 1954; BS, Coll. St. Francis, 1984; student, Valparaiso U. Cert. ACLS, coronary, critical care trained IMCU, obstetrics. Obstetrics nurse Holy Family Hosp., LaPorte, Ind., 1954-64; office nurse Dr. McDonald, Gulfport, Miss.; office nurse Dr. Jack Cartwright, LaPorte, Ind., med./telemetry unit nurse, 1977-96; staff nurse level III LaPorte Hosp., 1987-96, charge nurse, preceptor, 1988—. Mem. Am. Heart Assn., 1979-96; mem. Square Dance Club (B&B of Valparaiso, Ind.); organizer yearly square dance Toys for Tots, 1981-89; den mother Cub Scouts, Valparaiso. Mem. Am. Assn. Diabetic Educators. Home: 4409 Campbell St Valparaiso IN 46383-1303

VEATCH, JOHN WILLIAM, speech pathologist; b. Mitchell, S.D., Dec. 9, 1923; s. William Homer and Helen Gwendolyn (Lowther) V.; m. Doris Lavelle Guthrie (dec. 1978); children: Dean, Joan; m. Winnifred Ann Sawin, 1982 (div. 1992); m. Joy Sullivan, Aug. 21, 1993. BA in Speech, Wash. State U., 1946, BEd, 1951; MA in Speech, U. Wash., 1950; EdD, U. Idaho, 1970. Pvt. practice speech pathology Spokane, Wash., 1950-79; pvt. practice speech pathology and ednl. cons. Tacoma, 1980—; dir. rsch., edn. & bus. Sullivan Ctr. & Phys. Therapy, Puyallup, Wash., 1993—; dir. rsch. edn. and bus. Sullivan Ctr. & Physical Therapy, Puyallup, Wash., 1993—; lectr. in speech pathology Gonzaga U., Spokane, Wash., 1963-70; adj. prof. Wash. State U., 1972-77, Applied Psychology, Eastern Wash. U., 1977; chief exec. officer and dir. rsch. Espial Inst., Tacoma, 1982-92; mem. home health adv. bd. Spokane County Health Dept., past. pres. Wash. State Health Dept. Crippled Children's Svc. Adv. Bd. Maxillofacial Defects; co-dir. Sullivan Ctr., 1992—; cons. in field; workshops and training in alternative medicine techniques; co-developer V.E.A.T.C.H. Technique. Author: (with D. Hughes) Teacher Qualities, 1947; (test profiles) Personal Stress Balance Profile, 1982, Info. Processing Style, 1984, The Deep Screening Profile of Tongue Thrusting Activity, 1985, The Tongue Thrust Screening Test, 1986, Learning Style Profile, 1986; writer, contbr. guides, workbooks, studies and films in field. Fellow Northwest Acad. Speech Pathology (pres. 1978-82, 86-91); mem. Am. Speech-Lang.-Hearing Assn. (life, pres. bd. Oakbridge U. 1989-90). Office: 2717 E Main Ave Puyallup WA 98372-3165

VEATCH, ROBERT MARLIN, philosophy educator, medical ethics researcher; b. Utica, N.Y., Jan. 22, 1939; s. Cecil Ross and Regina (Braddock) V.; m. Laurelyn Kay Lovett, June 17, 1961 (div. Oct. 1986); children: Paul Martin, Carlton Elliot; m. Ann Bender Pastore, May 23, 1987. BS, Purdue U., 1961; MS, U. Calif. at San Francisco, 1962; BD, Harvard U., 1964, MA, 1970, Ph.D., 1971. Teaching fellow Harvard U., 1968-70; research assoc. in medicine Coll. Physicians and Surgeons, Columbia U., 1971-72; assoc. for med. ethics Inst. of Society, Ethics and Life Scis., Hastings-on-Hudson, N.Y., 1970-75; sr. assoc. Inst. of Society, Ethics and Life Scis., 1975-79; prof. med. ethics Kennedy Inst. Ethics Georgetown U., 1979—, prof. philosophy, 1981—, dir., 1989—; assoc. prof. depts. community and family medicine and ob/gyn, 1984—; mem. vis. faculty various colls. and univs.; mem. gov. bd. Washington Regional Transplant Consortium, 1988—; bd. dirs. Hospice Care D.C., 1989-96, pres., 1993-95; active United Network Organ Sharing Ethics Com., 1989-95. Author: Value-Freedom in Science and Technology, 1976, Death, Dying and the Biological Revolution, 1976, rev. edit., 1989, Case Studies in Medical Ethics, 1977, A Theory of Medical

Ethics, 1981, The Foundations of Justice, 1987, The Patient as Partner, 1987; (with Sarah T. Fry) Case Studies in Nursing Ethics, 1987, The Patient-Physician Relationship: The Patient as Partner, Part 2, 1991; (with James T. Rule) Ethical Questions in Dentistry, 1993; editor or co-editor: Bibliography of Society, Ethics and the Life Sciences, 1973, rev. edit., 1978, The Teaching of Medical Ethics, 1973, Death Inside Out, 1975, Ethics and Health Policy, 1976, Teaching of Bioethics, 1976, Population Policy and Ethics, 1977, Life Span: Values and Life Extending Technologies, 1979, Cases in Bioethics From the Hastings Center Report, 1982, Medical Ethics, 1989, Cross Cultural Perspectives in Medical Ethics, 1989; (with Edmund D. Pellegrino and John P. Langan) Ethics, Trust, and the Professions, 1991; (with Tom L. Beauchamp) Ethical Issues in Death and Dying, 1996; assoc. editor Encyclopedia of Bioethics; editl. bd. Jour. AMA, 1976-86, Jour. Medicine and Philosophy, 1980—, Harvard Theol. Rev., 1975—, Jour. Religious Ethics, 1981—; editl. adv. bd. Forum on Medicine, 1977-81; contbg. editor Hosp. Physician, 1975-85, Am. Jour. Hosp. Pharmacy, 1989—; sr. editor Kennedy Inst. Ethics Jour., 1991—; contbr. articles to profl. jours. Mem. Soc. Christian Ethics. Home: 11200 Richland Grove Dr Great Falls VA 22066-1104 Office: Georgetown U Kennedy Inst Of Ethics Washington DC 20057

VEATCH, SHEILA WILLIAMSON, counselor; b. Fitchburg, Mass., Jan. 10, 1950; d. William Robert Barse Jr. and Joan Jessie (Tothill) Williamson; stepfather George P. Williamson; m. Michael Alan Veatch, July 3, 1993; children: Michael and Katie Pitts. BSEd, U. Ga., 1971; MEd in Counseling, West Ga. Coll., 1991, EdS in Counseling, 1992. Nat. bd. cert. counselor; lic. profl. counselor. Tchr. Cobb County Schs., Marietta, Ga., 1971-73, 86-91, counselor, 1991—; pvt. practice, 1996—; instr. Cobb Staff Devel., Marietta, 1992-93; workshop leader Kennesaw (Ga.) Student Educators, 1993; presenter Cobb Mega Conf., 1992. Co-author: Manners Mania, 1993 (rsch. grantee 1992). Rsch. grantee social skills program Cobb County, 1991-92, 92-93, anger/aggression reduction, 1993-94, parenting edn., 1994-95. Mem. ACA, Ga. Sch. Counselors Assn. (presenter), Am. Sch. Counseling Assn., Cobb Sch. Counselor Assn. (v.p. 1995-96, pres. 1996—), Atlanta Adlerian Soc., PTA (hon., life State of Ga. 1992). Avocations: antiques, interior decorating, Bridge, travel. Home: 3146 Due West Ct Dallas GA 30132-7300 Office: Cobb County Sch Sys Glover St Marietta GA 30060

VEAZEY, DORIS ANNE, field office administrator; b. Dawson Spring, Ky., Feb. 16, 1935; d. Bradley Basil and Lucy Mable (Hamby) Sisk; m. Herman Veazey Jr., Aug. 15, 1964 (dec. Sept. 1987); 1 child, Vickie Dianne Veazey Kicinski. Murray State U., 1952-54. Unemployment ins. examiner Dept. for Employment Svcs., Madisonville, Ky., 1954-73, unemployment ins. supr., 1973-85, field office mgr., 1985-95; bd. dirs., adv. bd. region II Vocat. Tech. Schs., Madisonville, 1988-92. Mem. Mayor's Work Force Devel. Com., 1993—, Ky. Indsl. Devel. Com., 1992—; dept. dir. Adult III Sunday Sch., 1994—, ch. choir, 1990—. Mem. Internat. Platform Assn., Internat. Assn. of Pers. in Employment Svcs., Southeastern Employment and Tng. Assn., Tenure, Order of Ky. Cols., Greater Madisonville C. of C. (dir. leadership 1988-93). Baptist. Avocations: reading, T.V., travel, photography. Office: Dept Employment Svcs 56 Federal St # 1226 Madisonville KY 42431-2043

VEBLEN, THOMAS CLAYTON, management consultant; b. Hallock, Minn., Dec. 17, 1929; s. Edgar R. and Hattie (Lundgren) V.; m. Susan Alma Beaver, Sept. 1, 1950 (div. 1971); children: Kari Christen, Erik Rodli, Mark Andrew, Sara Catherine; m. Linda Joyce Eaton, Aug. 30, 1975; 1 child, Kristen Kirby. Student, U. Calif., Santa Barbara, 1950-51; BS, Calif. Poly. U., 1953; MS, Oreg. State U., 1955. Corp. v.p. Cargill, Inc., Wayzata, Minn., 1955-75; spl. asst. Sec. Interior, Washington, 1965; dir. food and agr. SRI Internat., Menlo Park, Calif., 1975-80; pres. Food Sys. Assocs., Inc., Washington, 1980-94; also bd. dirs. Food System Assocs., Inc., Washington; chmn. Enterprise Cons., Inc., Washington, 1990—; dir. Georgetown Cons., Inc., 1993-95; convener The Superior Bus. Firm Roundtable, 1993—; dir. Georgetown Cons., Inc., 1993-95; mem. CMC Inst. Mgmt. Cons., 1988—, pres. Washington chpt., 1991-93. Author: The U.S. Food System, 1978; (with M. Abel) Creating a Superior National Food System, 1992; editor Food System Update, 1986-95. Treas., bd. dirs. White House Fellows Assn., Washington, 1985; trustee Freedom from Hunger Found., Davis, Calif., 1980—, chmn., 1986-89; bd. dirs. Patterson Sch., U. Ky., Lexington, Pax World Svc., Am. Near East Refugee Aid. Recipient Presdl. Appointment White House Fellows Commn., Washington, 1965. Mem. Coun. for Nat. Interest, Coun. on Fgn. Rels., Cosmos Club. Episcopalian. Avocations: canoeing, ice skating. Office: Enterprise Cons Inc 2806 36th Pl NW Washington DC 20007-1417

VECCHIO, ROBERT PETER, business management educator; b. Chgo., June 29, 1950; s. Dominick C. and Angeline V.; m. Betty Ann Vecchio; Aug. 21, 1974; children: Julie, Mark. BS summa cum laude, DePaul U., 1972; MA, U. Ill., 1974, PhD, 1976. Instr. U. Ill., Urbana, 1973-76; mem. faculty dept. mgmt. U. Notre Dame, 1976-86, dept. chmn., 1983-90, Franklin D. Schurz Prof. Mgmt., 1986—. Editor Jour. of Mgmt., 1995—. Mem. Acad. Mtm., Am. Psychol. Assn., Assn. Consumer Rsch., Am. Inst. Decision Scis., Midwest Acad. Mgmt., Midwest Psychol. Assn., Phi Kappa Phi, Delta Epsilon Sigma, Phi Eta Sigma, Psi Chi. Home: 16856 Hampton Dr Granger IN 46530-6907 Office: U Notre Dame Dept Mgmt Notre Dame IN 46556

VECCHIONE, FRANK JOSEPH, lawyer; b. Newark, June 11, 1935; s. Francesco and Philomena (DiDomenico) V.; m. Polly Plaisted, June 1, 1957; children: Amy, Carrie, Jennifer, Matthew. AB, Syracuse U., 1957; LLB, Seton Hall, 1964. Bar: N.J. 1965, U.S. Ct. Appeals (3d cir.) 1972. Ptnr. Crummy Del Deo Dolan Griffinger & Vecchione, Newark, 1965—; adj. prof. law Seton Hall U. Sch. Law, 1970—; lectr. Inst. Continuing Legal Edn.; del. 3d Cir. Jud. Conf., 1982-84, 86—. Contbr. articles to profl. jours. Trustee Bloomfield (N.J.) Coll., 1978-87. 1st lt. U.S. Army, 1957-59. Named Outstanding Alumnus Seton Hall Law Sch., 1992. Fellow Am. Coll. Bankruptcy, Am. Bar Found.; mem. N.J. State Bar Assn. (chmn. debtor/creditor sect. 1978-80). Office: Crummy Del Deo Dolan Griffinger & Vecchione 1 Riverfront Plz Newark NJ 07102-5401

VECCHIOTTI, ROBERT ANTHONY, management and organizational consultant; b. N.Y.C., May 21, 1941; s. R. Lucien and Louise Victoria V.; BS, St. Peter's Coll., 1962; MA, Fordham U., 1964; PhD, St. Louis U., 1973; m. Dorothea Irene Hoban, Oct. 12, 1963; children: John Robert, Rachel Irene, Sara Christine. Psychologist Testing and Advisement Ctr.NYU, Washington Sq. campus, 1964-65; group psychologist McDonnell Douglas, St. Louis, 1967-76, sr. bus. analyst, 1976-77, mgr. bus. systems planning, 1977-79; pres. Organizational Cons. Svcs., Inc., St. Louis, 1980—; adj. assoc. prof. mgmt. Maryville Coll., St. Louis, 1975-81. Bd. dirs. Cath. Charities of St. Louis, 1981-86, Cath. Family Svc., 1986—, Mental Health Assn. St. Louis, 1989—, Sta. KWMU-FM, 1989-94. With U.S. Army, 1965-67. Lic. psychologist, Mo. Mem. Am. Psychol. Assn., Strategic Leadership Forum, Inst. Mgmt. Cons., Human Factors Soc. Club: Mo. Athletic. Lodge: Rotary (past pres.). Office: Organizational Consulting Svcs Inc 230 S Bemiston Ave Ste 1107 Clayton MO 63105-1907

VECCI, RAYMOND JOSEPH, airline industry consultant; b. N.Y.C., Jan. 22, 1943; s. Romeo John and Mary (Fabretti) V.; m. Helen Cecelia Clampett, Sept. 3, 1967; children: Brian John, Damon Jay. BBA, CCNY, 1965; MBA, NYU, 1967. Adminstrv. asst. Internat. Air Transport Assn., N.Y.C., 1961-66; econ. analyst United Airlines, Chgo., 1967-74; asst. v.p. planning and regulatory affairs Alaska Airlines Inc., Seattle, 1975-76, staff v.p. planning and regulatory affairs, 1976-79, staff v.p. planning, 1979, v.p. planning, 1979-85, exec. v.p., chief operating officer, 1986-90, pres., chief exec. officer, 1990—; chmn., dir. Alaska Airlines Inc., 1991—; also chmn., pres., chief exec. officer, dir. Alaska Air Group Inc. Served with U.S. Army, 1968-69, Vietnam. Decorated Bronze Star. Roman Catholic. *

VECELLIO, LEO ARTHUR, JR., construction company executive; b. Beckley, W.Va., Oct. 26, 1946; s. Leo Arthur and Evelyn (Pais) V.; m. Kathryn Grace Cottrill, Nov. 29, 1975; children: Christopher Scott, Michael Andrew. BCE, Va. Poly. Inst. and State U., 1968; MCE, Ga. Inst. Tech., 1969; LLD (hon.), Northwood U. Sr. v.p. Vecellio & Grogan, Inc., Beckley, 1973-96, pres., CEO, chmn. bd. dirs., 1996—; pres. Vecellio Contracting Corp. and subs. (Ranger Constrn. Industries, West Palm Beach, PAVEX Corp., Deerfield Beach, White Rock Quarries, Miami), Fla., 1982—; mng. ptnr. Vecellio Realty Co., Deerfield Property Assocs.; bd. dirs. United Nat. Bank-South, Beckley, Barnett Bank of Palm Beach County; founder, past dir. Gulf Nat. Bank, Sophia, W.Va.; founder, past dir. Nat. Bankers Trust, Beckley. Chmn. bd. dirs. Econ. Coun. Palm Beach County, Fla., 1985—, chmn.-elect, 1987, chmn., 1989; gov. Northwood U., West Palm Beach, 1985—; organizer, trustee Beckley Area Found., 1985; v.p., trustee Vecellio Family Found., Beckley, 1972-96, pres., trustee, 1996—; active Mini-Grace Commn., Fla. Coun. 100, 1989—, vice-chmn., 1991—; commn. dir., v.p. Criminal Justice Commn.; chmn. Budget Rev. Task Force, Budget Oversight Task Force; bd. dirs. Gulfstream Coun. Boy Scouts Am., 1989-93, Palm Beach County Cultural Coun. and Art Sch. Task Force, Fla. Coun. 100, Floridians for Better Transp., exec. com.; corporator Schepens Eye Rsch. Inst./Harvard U., 1993—; engring. coun. 100 Va. Tech. Capt USAF, 1969-73. Recipient Free Enterprise medal Palm Beach Atlantic Coll., 1988. Mem. Flexible Pavements Assn. (found, bd. dirs. 1979—), Contractors Assn. W. (bd. dirs. 1975—). Republican. Roman Catholic. Clubs: Mayacoo Lakes Country (West Palm Beach), Adios Golf (Coconut Creek, Fla.), Jupiter Hills (Fla.), Lost Tree. Avocations: golf, boating, skiing. Home: 771 Village Rd No Palm Beach FL 33408-3331 Office: Vecellio Contracting Corp PO Box 15065 West Palm Beach FL 33416-5065

VECOLI, RUDOLPH JOHN, history educator; b. Wallingford, Conn., Mar. 2, 1927; s. Giovanni Battista and Settima Maria (Palmerini) V.; m. Jill Cherrington, June 27, 1959; children: Christopher, Lisa, Jeremy. BA, U. Conn., 1950; MA, U. Pa., 1951; PhD, U. Wis., 1963. Fgn. affairs officer Dept. State, 1951-54; instr. history Ohio State U., 1957-59, Pa. State U., 1960-61; asst. prof. Rutgers U., 1961-65; assoc. prof. U. Ill., Champaign, 1965-67; prof. history, dir. Immigration History Research Center, U. Minn., Mpls., 1967—; vis. prof. U. Uppsala, Sweden, 1970, U. Amsterdam, The Netherlands, 1988, Maria Curie-Sklodowsk U., Lublin, Poland, 1992. Author: The People of New Jersey, 1965, Foreword to Marie Hall Ets, Rosa: The Story of an Italian Immigrant, 1970, (with Joy Lintelman) A Century of American Immigration, 1884-1984, (with others) The Invention of Ethnicity, 1990; contbg. author: Encyclopedia of the United States in the Twentieth Century, (1996), The Cambridge Survey of World Migration, (1995); Gil italiani fuori d'Italia, 1983, They Chose Minnesota: A Survey of the State's Ethnic Groups, 1981, Pane e Lavoro: The Italian American Working Class, 1980, Perspectives in Italian Immigration and Ethnicity, 1977, Immigrants and Religion in Urban America, 1977, The State of American History, 1970, The Reinterpretation of American History and Culture, 1973, Failure of a Dream, Essays in the History of American Socialism, 1984, Italian Americans: New Perspectives, 1985, May Day Celebration, 1988, In the Shadow of the Statue of Liberty, 1988, From Melting Pot to Multiculturalism, 1990, Studi Sull' Emigrazione, 1991, The Lebanese in the World, 1992, Swedes in America: New Perspectives, 1993, The Statue of Liberty Revisited, 1994, La Riscoperta delle Americhe, 1994, The Encyclopedia of Twentieth Century America, 1995, The Cambridge Survey of World Migration, 1995; editor, contbg. author: The Other Catholics, 1978, Italian Immigrants in Rural and Small Town America, 1987, The Gale Encyclopedia of Multicultural America, 1994; mem. editl. bd. Jour. Am. Ethnic History, Studi Emigrazione, America: History and Life Mid-America, Internat. Migration Rev., Estudios Migratorios Latino Americanos, Altreitalle; co-editor (with Suzanne Sinke) A Century of European Migrations, 1830-1930, 1991; contbr. articles to profl. jours. Chair history com. Statue of Liberty-Ellis Island Centennial Commn., 1983-90. With USNR, 1945-46. Decorated Knight Officer, Order of Merit (Italy); recipient Am. Philos. Soc. grantee, 1970; Newberry Libr. fellow, 1964, Am.-Scandinavian Found. fellow, 1970, NEH fellow, 1985-86; Fulbright-Hays sr. rsch. scholar Italy, 1973-74; Am. Coun. Learned Soc. grantee, 1974, 86, U.S. Dept. State Travel grantee, 1977, Acad. Specialist, U.S. Info. Agy., Brazil, 1993. Mem. Am. Italian Hist. Assn. (pres., mem. exec. council), Am. Hist. Assn., Orgn. Am. Historians, AAUP, Immigration History Soc. (pres., exec. council). Home: 610 E 58th St Minneapolis MN 55417-2426

VECSEY, GEORGE SPENCER, sports columnist; b. Jamaica, N.Y., July 4, 1939; s. George Stephen and May (Spencer) V.; m. Marianne Graham; children: Laura, Corinna, David. BA in English, Hofstra Coll., 1960; LHD (hon.), Hofstra U., 1991. Sports reporter Newsday, Garden City, N.Y., 1960-68; sports reporter N.Y. Times, N.Y.C., 1968-70, nat. corr., 1970-73, met., religion reporter, 1973-80, sports reporter, 1980-82, sports columnist, 1982—. Author: (with others) Naked Came the Stranger, 1969, Joy in Mudville: Being a Complete Account of the Unparalleled History of the New York Mets, 1970, One Sunset a Week: The Story of a Coal Miner, 1974, (with Loretta Lynn) Coal Miner's Daughter, 1976, (with Jacques Lowe) Kentucky: A Celebration of American Life, 1979, (with George C. Dade) Getting Off the Ground: The Pioneers of Aviation Speak for Themselves, 1978, (with Leonore Fleischer) Sweet Dreams, 1985, (with Martina Navratilova) Martina, 1985, (with Bob Welch) Five O'Clock Comes Early: A Young Man's Battle with Alcoholism, 1982, A Year in the Sun, 1989, (with Barbara Mandrell) Get to the Heart, 1991; author 8 children's books; editor: The Way It Was: Great Sports Events from the Past, 1974. Recipient Disting. Writing award Am. Soc. Newspaper Editors, 1995; named N.Y. State Sportswriter of Yr. Nat. Sportscasters and Sportswriters Assn., 1985-95. Mem. Kentuckians (bd. dirs. 1988—). Avocations: running, swimming, music, travel, languages. Office: NY Times 229 W 43rd St New York NY 10036-3913

VEDDER, BYRON CHARLES, newspaper executive; b. Adrian, Mich., Feb. 9, 1910; s. Adelbert and Adah (Dibble) V.; m. Kathleen Fry, June 20, 1936 (dec. 1960); children: Richard Kent, Robert Allen; m. Helen Cochrane, Dec. 16, 1976. A.B., U. Mich., 1933. Grad. mgr. student publs. U. Mich., Ann Arbor, 1933-34; with Champaign-Urbana (Ill.) Courier, 1934-64, pub., 1960-64; v.p. ops. Lindsay-Schaub Newspapers, Inc., 1964-75, v.p. planning, 1975-79; v.p. Sun Coast Media Inc., 1979—; sec. Pasco Pub. Inc., 1981-86; bd. dirs. Comml. Savs. & Loan Assn., Urbana, v.p., 1975-76, chmn., 1977-83; bd. dirs. Mut. Home and Savs., 1983-86. Mem. Arrowhead council exec. bd. Boy Scouts Am., 1951—, pres., 1960-64; mem. Pres.'s Com. Traffic Safety, 1954-58. Recipient Silver Beaver award Boy Scouts Am., 1959; named Boss of Year Champaign-Urbana chpt. Nat. Secs. Assn., 1958; Disting. Service to Journalism award U. Minn., 1979, Disting. Svc. award Inland Press Assn., 1991; James E. West fellow Boy Scouts of Am. award, 1995. Mem. Inland Daily Press Assn. (bd. dirs. 1950-53, pres. 1954, chmn. 1955, Disting. Svc. award 1991), Cen. States Circulation Mfrs. Assn. (pres. 1944-46), Ill. Daily Newspaper Markets Assn. (pres. 1962-63, chmn. 1963-64), Am. Newspaper Pubs. Assn. (com. chmn.), Urban Assn. Commerce (v.p. 1946), Campus Bus. Men's Assn. (bd. dirs.), Champaign C. of C. (bd. dirs. 1955-57, Internat. Circulation Mfrs. Assn. (hon.), U. Ill. Quarterback Club (hon. life). Presbyterian (trustee). Club: Urbana Country, Champaign Country. Lodge: Kiwanis (lt. gov. 1951, dir., Kiwanian of Year 1971, pres. 1978). Home: 3 Stanford Pl Champaign IL 61820-7620

VEDDER, EDDIE, singer; b. Evanston, Ill., Dec. 23, 1965; m. Beth Liebling, June 3, 1994. lead singer (band) Pearl Jam, 1991—; albums include Ten, 1991, Vs., 1993, Vitalogy, 1994; contbr. vocals (album) Temple of the Dog, 1991, Mother Love Bone, 1992, Bob Dylan Thirtieth-Anniversary Tribute, 1993, Sweet Reliefe: A Tribute to Victoria Williams, 1993, Shame, 1993, Judgement Night Soundtrack, 1993; film appearances include Singles, 1992. Office: c/o Epic Records 550 Madison Ave New York NY 10022-3211*

VEDROS, NEYLAN ANTHONY, microbiologist; b. New Orleans, Oct. 6, 1929; s. Phillip John and Solange Agnes (Melancon) V.; m. Elizabeth Corbett, Apr. 9, 1955; children: Sally Ann, Philippa Jane. B.S. in Chemistry, La. State U., 1951, M.S. in Microbiology, 1957; Ph.D., U. Colo., 1960. Postdoctoral fellow Nat. Inst. Allergy and Infectious Diseases, U. Oreg., Portland, 1960-62; microbiologist Naval Med. Research Inst., Bethesda, Md., 1962-66; research microbiologist Naval Biosci. Lab., Oakland, Calif., 1966-67; assoc. prof. med. microbiology and immunology U. Calif., Berkeley, 1967-72; prof. U. Calif., 1972-91, prof. emeritus, 1991—; dir. Naval Biosci. Lab., 1968-81; mem. expert panel on bacteriology WHO, 1972-91. Bd. trustees Alameda (Calif.) Library, 1973-78. Served to comdr. M.S.C. USNR, 1952-55, 62-67. Mem. Am. Assn. Immunologists, Am. Soc. Microbiology, Internat. Assn. Human and Animal Mycology, Internat. Assn. Microbiol. Sci., Internat. Assn. Aquatic Animal Medicine, Assn. Mil. Surgeons. Home: 2610 Evelyn Ct Alameda CA 94501-6333 Office: 239 Warren Hall U Calif Berkeley CA 94725

VEEDER, PETER GREIG, lawyer; b. Pitts., Aug. 13, 1941. AB, Princeton U., 1963; JD, U. Pitts., 1966. Bar: Pa. 1966, D.C. 1976. Lawyer Thorp Reed & Armstrong, Pitts. Office: Thorp Reed & Armstrong One Riverfront Ctr Pittsburgh PA 15222

VEENKER, CLAUDE HAROLD, health education educator; b. George, Iowa, July 31, 1919; s. Ralph C. and Fannie (Casjens) V.; m. Elizabeth Louise Higgins, Jan. 1, 1944; children—Jo Lee, Vicki Susan. BA, U. No. Iowa, 1943; MA, U. No. Colo., 1953; D of Health and Safety, Ind. U., 1957. Tchr. Osage (Iowa) High Sch., 1946-47, Mason City (Iowa) Pub. Schs., 1947-55; teaching asst. Ind. U., 1955-56, vis. lectr., 1956-57; asst. prof. Purdue U., Lafayette, Ind., 1957-61, assoc. prof., 1961-66, prof., 1966-84, prof. emeritus, 1984—, chmn. health edn. sect., 1961-77; chmn. health edn. test project Ednl. Testing Svc., Princeton, 1965-74; cons. bur. rsch. coop. rsch. br. U.S. Office Edn., 1966-68; cons. healthful sch. environment AMA, NEA, Washington, 1969; mem. Ind. Coun. on Sch. Health, 1971-84, Ind. Adv. Com. on Drug Edn., 1969-74, Ind. Gov.'s Regional Com. on Mental Health, 1966-67. Editor, contbr. author: Synthesis of Research in Selected Areas of Health Instruction, 1963; mem. editorial bd.: Jour. Health, Phys. Edn. and Recreation, 1961-62, 64-66; Contbr. articles to profl. jours. Served to 1st lt. USMC, 1943-46. Decorated Purple Heart. Fellow Am. Sch. Health Assn., Am. Pub. Health Assn. (governing council 1974-76, mem. sch. health sect. council 1970-73); mem. Am. Alliance for Health, Phys. Edn. and Recreation (exec. council sch. health div. 1964-67, chmn. sch. health service sect. 1959-60), Mid-Am. Coll. Health Assn., Ind. Assn. Health Educators (pres. 1970), Phi Delta Kappa, Eta Sigma Gamma. Methodist. Club: Elks. Home: 224 Knox Dr West Lafayette IN 47906-2150 Office: Purdue U Lambert Bldg Lafayette IN 49707 *Life as a child during the Roaring 20's, as a young teen-ager during the Great Depression of the 30's, and as a young adult during World War II, was a great adventure. But the world is no easier now than it was then. It seems that living is a continual challenge: to seek, to find, to try, to conquer. To succeed, one must live with confidence and hope, fearing neither failure nor success. To live well is to live with self-discipline in the present, using the hard-learned lessons of the past to brighten one's prospects for the future.*

VEGA, BENJAMIN URBIZO, retired judge; b. La Ceiba, Honduras, Jan. 18, 1916; m. Janie Lou Smith, Oct. 12, 1989; AB, U. So. Calif., 1938, postgrad., 1939-40; LLB, Pacific Coast U. Law, 1941. Bar: Calif. 1947, U.S. Dist. Ct. (so. dist.) Calif. 1947, U.S. Supreme Ct. 1958. Assoc. Anderson, McPharlin & Connors, L.A., 1947-48, Newman & Newman, L.A., 1948-51; dep. dist. atty. County of L.A., 1951-66; judge L.A., County Mcpl. Ct., East L.A. Jud. Dist., 1966-86, retired, 1986; leader faculty seminar Calif. Jud. Coll. at Earl Warren Legal Inst., U. Calif-Berkeley, 1978. Mem. Calif. Gov.'s Adv. Com. on Children and Youth, 1968; del. Commn. of the Califs., 1978; bd. dirs. Los Angeles-Mexico City Sister City Com.; pres. Argentine Cultural Found., 1983. Recipient award for outstanding services from Mayor of L.A., 1973, City of Commerce, City of Montebello, Calif. Assembly, Southwestern Sch. Law, Disting. Pub. Service award Dist. Atty. L.A. Mem. Conf. Calif. Judges, Mcpl. Ct. Judges' Assn. (award for Outstanding Services), Beverly Hills Bar Assn., Navy League, L.A. County, Am. Judicature Soc., World Affairs Council, Pi Sigma Alpha. Home: 101 California Ave Apt 1207 Santa Monica CA 90403-3525

VEGA, FRANK J., newspaper publishing executive. Pres., CEO Detroit Newspapers. Office: 615 W Lafayette Blvd Detroit MI 48226-3124

VEGA, J. WILLIAM, aerospace engineering executive, consultant; b. Elizabeth, N.J., Jan. 30, 1931; s. John Charles and Margaret (Walker) V.; m. Carolyn Louise Burt, June 7, 1957 (div. 1976); children: Lynn Vega Membreño, Lore Vega Hynes, Susan; m. Pauline Anne Garner, Apr. 27, 1983. BSE, Princeton U., 1952, postgrad., 1955-56; MS, U.S. Internat. U., 1973. Sr. engr. Reaction Motors, Inc., Denville, N.J., 1956-58; sr. engr. Convair div. Gen. Dynamics, San Diego, 1958, project engr., sr. project engr., asst. chief engr., 1970-75, dir. advanced programs, 1975-83, v.p. advanced programs, 1983-88, v.p. rsch. and engring., 1988-90; cons. aerospace mgmt., 1991—. Pres. bd. dirs. Durango (Colo.) Art Ctr. Lt. USN, 1952-55. Fellow AIAA (assoc.); mem. Phi Beta Kappa. Avocations: skiing, sailing, hiking, camping.

VEGA, MARYLOIS PURDY, journalist; b. Chgo., Nov. 4, 1914; d. William Thomas and Mary Helene (Buggy) Purdy; m. Carlos Juan Vega, Sept. 4, 1965. B.A., U. Wis., Madison, 1935. With Time mag., N.Y.C., 1942-84; chief Letters to the Editor, 1951-67, chief editl. rsch., 1967-76, assoc. editor, 1976-84. Roman Catholic. Club: Overseas Press. Home: 140 West End Ave New York NY 10023-6131 also: PO Box 266 Gardiner NY 12525

VEGA, MATIAS ALFONSO, lawyer; b. Paris, Feb. 2, 1952; s. Matias Guillermo and Colette (Lafosse) V.; m. Carmella Margarita Kurczewski, Nov. 20, 1982; 1 child, Alexandra Lafosse. AB, Yale U., 1974; JD, Harvard U., 1977. Bar: N.Y. 1978, U.S. Dist. Ct. (so. and ea. dists.) N.Y. 1979, U.S. Supreme Ct. 1984, U.S. Ct. Appeals (6th and 9th cirs.) 1985, U.S. Dist. Ct. (no. dist.) Calif. 1985. Assoc. Curtis, Mallet-Prevost, Colt & Mosle, N.Y.C., 1977-85, ptnr., 1986—. Contbr. articles to profl. jours. Mem. ABA, Am. Assn. Internat. Law, N.Y. State Bar Assn. (chmn. com. Latin Am. law, internat. law and practice sect. 1987-90), Yale Club. Republican. Roman Catholic. Home: 809 Long Hill Rd W Briarcliff Manor NY 10510-2124 Office: Curtis Mallet-Prevost Colt 101 Park Ave New York NY 10178-0061

VEGHTE, ROBERT ILLINGWORTH, packaging company executive; b. Newark, Mar. 2, 1952; s. Robert D. and Bathsheba (Anderson) V.; m. Melissa Leib, May 23, 1975; 1 child, Robert H. BA with honors, U. Va., 1974. With sales and mktg. depts. Wheaton Glass Co., Millville, N.J., 1974-79; v.p., gen. mgr. Wheaton Injection Molding, Millville, 1979-86; exec. v.p. Wheaton Industries, Millville, 1987-90, pres., chief exec. officer, 1990—. Home: RR 1 Salem NJ 08079-9801 Office: Wheaton Industries 1101 Wheaton Ave Millville NJ 08332-2529*

VEIGEL, JON MICHAEL, science administrator; b. Mankato, Minn., Nov. 10, 1938; s. Walter Thomas and Thelma Geraldine (Lein) V.; m. Carol June Bradley, Aug. 10, 1962. BS, U. Washington, 1960; PhD, UCLA, 1965. Program mgr. Office of Tech. Assessment, U.S. Congress, Washington, 1974-75; div. mgr. Calif. Energy Commn., Sacramento, 1975-78; asst. dir. Solar Energy Rsch. Inst., Golden, Colo., 1978-81; pres. Alt. Energy Corp., Rsch. Triangle Park, N.C., 1981-88, Oak Ridge (Tenn.) Associated Univs., 1988—; bd. dirs. Am. Coun. Energy Efficient Economy, Washington, Pacific Internat. Ctr. for High Tech. Rsch., Honolulu. Contbr. articles to jours. Bd. dirs. Oak Ridge Community Found., also chmn.; trustee Maryville Coll., Mendeleyev U., Moscow, Russia. 1st lt. USAF, 1965-68. Mem. AAAS (com. on sci. and engring. pub. policy). Avocations: photography, flying. Office: Oak Ridge Assoc Univs PO Box 117 Oak Ridge TN 37831-0117

VEINOTT, CYRIL GEORGE, electrical engineer, consultant; b. Somerville, Mass., Feb. 15, 1905; s. Jason A. and I. Laura (Fales) V.; m. Dorothy Helen Bassett, Nov. 28, 1936 (dec. Sept. 1988); 1 child, Richard A.; m. June Urlwin, Jan. 6, 1990. BSEE cum laude, U. Vt., 1926; EE, 1939; D in Engring. (hon.), 1951. Mgr. induction motor sect. Westinghouse, Lima, Ohio, 1926-52; chief engring. analyst Reliance Elec. Co., Cleve., 1953-70; invited prof. Laval U., Quebec City, Can., 1970-72; vol. exec. Internat. Exec. Svc. Corps, N.Y.C., 1972-79; pvt. practice as consultant in computer-aided design of electric motors, Sarasota, Fla., 1970—. Author: Fractional HP Electric Motors, 1939, 4th edit. 1986; Theory and Design Small Motors, 1959; How to Design a 1-ph Motor on a Personal Computer, 1989; How to Design a Metric 1-ph Motor on a PC, 1991; Computer-Aided Design Electric Machines, 1972. Patentee in field. Recipient Merit award Rsch. Inst. Rotating Machines Czechoslovakia, 1968; named to Hall of Fame Small Motors Mfg. Assn., 1985. Fellow IEEE (chmn. standards com. 1962-63, Tesla medal 1977, Centennial medal 1984), AIEE (v.p. 1949-51, chmn. rotating machines com. 1951-53, chmn. standards com. 1961-62); mem. Navy League U.S., Phi Beta Kappa, Eta Kappa Nu, Tau Beta Pi. Republican. Presbyterian. Club: High Twelve. Lodges: Masons, Shriners, Honorable Order Ky. Cols. Avocations: devel. of computer-aided design software for induction machines, home computers. Home: 4197 Oakhurst Cir W Sarasota FL 34233-1443

VEIT, CLAIRICE GENE TIPTON, measurement psychologist; b. Monterey Park, Calif., Feb. 20, 1939; d. Albert Vern and Gene (Bunning) Tipton; children: Steven, Barbara, Laurette, Catherine. BA, UCLA, 1969, MA, 1970, PhD, 1974. Asst. prof. psychology Calif. State U., L.A., 1975-77, assoc. prof. psychology, 1977-80; rsch. psychologist The Rand Corp., Santa Monica, Calif., 1977—; rsch. cons. NATO Tech. Ctr., The Hague, The Netherlands, 1980-81; faculty Rand Grad Sch., Santa Monica, 1993—. Developer subjective transfer function (STF) method to complex sys. analysis. Mem. LWV, NOW, Mil. Ops. Rsch. Soc. Am., Inst. Mgmt. Sci., Soc. Med. Decision-Making, Soc. for Judgement and Decision-Making, L.A. World Affairs Coun., L.A. Opera League. Avocations: mountain climbing, playing piano, travel, music, theatre. Office: The Rand Corp 1700 Main St Santa Monica CA 90401-3208

VEIT, FRITZ, librarian; b. Emmendingen, Baden, Germany, Sept. 17, 1907; came to U.S., 1935, naturalized, 1940; s. Samuel W. and Helene (Geismar) V.; m. Lucille Stearns, June 11, 1939; children: Joanne Grace, Mary Catherine (dec.). Student, U. Berlin, 1927, Heidelberg U., 1928; J.U.D., U. Freiburg, 1932; B.S. in Library Sci, Peabody Library Sch., Nashville, 1936; Ph.D., U. Chgo. Grad. Library Sch., 1941. Research asst. Inst. History Law, U. Freiburg, Germany, 1932-33; librarian U. Chgo. Grad. Library Sch., 1937-42, Social Sci. Reading Room, 1942; acting librarian Law Sch., 1943; librarian Chgo. City Jr. Coll. (Englewood evening br.), 1941-48; law librarian U.S. R.R. Retirement Bd., Chgo., 1943-49; supr. library John Marshall Law Sch., 1949-57; vis. prof. library sci. Rosary Coll., River Forest, Ill., 1950-78, Western Mich. U., summer 1959, Ariz. State U., summer 1964, 65, 67, 68, Emporia State U., summer 1977, Grad. Library Sch. U. Chgo., summer 1975, 78, fall 1977; dir. libraries Chgo. State U., 1949-73, also Kennedy-King Coll., 1949-72; chmn. adv. com. library tech. program Chgo. City Colls., 1968-74; mem. adv. council librarians U. Ill. Grad. Sch. Library Sci., 1971-74. Author: The Community College Library, 1975, Presidential Libraries and Collections, 1987; mem. editorial bd. Internat. Jour. Revs. in Libr. and Info. Sci., 1984-89, Third World Librs., 1990—; contbr. articles to profl. jours. Mem. ALA (sec., chmn. tchr. edn. libraries sect. ACRL 1959-61, assoc. editor monographs 1952-60, local chmn. ACRL 1963 Conf), Ill. Library Assn., Chgo. Library Club (pres. 1964-65), Pi Gamma Mu. Home: 1716 E 55th St Chicago IL 60615-5914

VEITCH, STEPHEN WILLIAM, investment counselor; b. Albuquerque, Aug. 19, 1927; s. Kenneth Easton and Edna (Miller) V.; B.A., U. N.Mex., 1949; LL.B., Stanford, 1957; student U. Nacional, Mex., 1949; m. Nancy Baker, June 28, 1951; children—Christopher Oxnard, Julia Blair. Bar: Calif., 1958. Probate adminstr. Wells Fargo Bank, San Francisco, 1957-59; sr. v.p. Van Strum & Towne, Inc., San Francisco, 1959-76, sr. v.p., 1976-82, pres., 1982-91, vice chmn, 1991—. Mem. Guardsman, San Francisco, 1960—. With USNR, 1945-46; 1st lt. USAF, 1950-54. Mem. Am., San Francisco bar assns., Delta Theta Phi, Sigma Chi. Republican. Episcopalian. Clubs: Commonwealth, Pacific Union (San Francisco); Menlo Circus (Atherton, Calif.). Home: 33 Spencer Ln Atherton CA 94027-4038 Office: 505 Sansome St Ste 1001 San Francisco CA 94111-3134

VEITH, ILZA, historian of psychiatric and Oriental medicine; b. Ludwigshafen, Germany, May 13, 1915; came to U.S., 1937, naturalized, 1945; m. Hans von Valentini Veith, Oct. 20, 1935 (dec. Mar. 1991). Student med. schs., Geneva and Vienna, Austria, 1934-36; M.A., Johns Hopkins, 1944, Ph.D., 1947; Igaku hakase (M.D., D.M.S.), Sch. Medicine, Juntendo U., Tokyo, 1975. Cons. Oriental medicine Armed Forces Med. Library, Washington, 1947-57; lectr. in history medicine U. Chgo., 1949-51; editorial bd. U. Chgo. Press, 1951-53; asst. prof. history medicine U. Chgo., 1953-57, assoc. prof., 1957-63; cons. in History of Medicine Nat. Inst. Health, 1959-64; vis. prof. Menninger Sch. Psychiatry, 1963; prof. history medicine, vice chmn. dept. U. Calif. at San Francisco Med. Center, 1964-79, prof. history psychiatry, 1967-79, prof. emeritus, 1979—; D.J. Davies Meml. lectr. U. Ill. Sch. Medicine, 1958; Sloan vis. prof. Menninger Found., 1963, 66; John Shaw Billings lectr. U. Ind. Sch. Medicine, Indpls., 1970; George W. Corner lectr. history medicine U. Rochester, N.Y., 1970; Logan Clendenning lectr. history of medicine U. Kans. Sch. Medicine, 1971; spl. lectr. VI World Congress Psychiatry, 1977; Hideyo Noguchi lectr. Johns Hopkins U., 1977. Author: Leverkusen, 1961, Medizin in Tibet, 1962, Hysteria: The History of a Disease, 1965, 3d edit., 1993, Yellow Emperor's Classic of Internal Medicine, 1966, Englishman or Samurai? The Story of Will Adams, 1981, Can You Hear the Clapping of One Hand? Learning to Live With a Stroke, 1988; co-author: Great Ideas in the History of Surgery, 3d edit., 1961, Acupuncture Therapy: Current Chinese Practice, 1973, 2d rev. and enlarged edit., 1976, Histoire de l' hystérie, 1974, Nei-Ching: Canone di Medicina Interna dell' Imperatore Giallo, 1976, Ishimpo The Essentials of Medicine in Ancient China and Japan, 1986; mem. editorial. bd. Ency. Britannica; contbr. articles to profl. jours. Decorated officer's Cross of Merit Fed. Republic Germany, 1971; recipient Gold-Headed Cane award U. Kans. Sch. Medicine, 1976, Disting. Service award for sci. achievement Med. Alumni Assn. of U. Chgo., 1983. Hon. fellow Am. Psychiat. Assn. (Benjamin Rush Meml. lectr. 1987); mem. Am. Assn. History of Medicine (council mem. 1958-62, 73-77), AAAS, Soc. History of Medicine Chgo. (pres. 1954-64), Soc. History Med. Scis. Los Angeles (hon.), History Sci. Soc., AMA (asso.), Marin Med. Soc. (hon.), Spanish Soc. History of Medicine (hon., corr. mem.), Bay Area Med. History Soc. (v.p. 1972), Johns Hopkins Alumni Assn. (past pres. Ill.), Royal Soc. Medicine (London), Vishwa Inst. of Oriental Medicine, Sri Lanka (hon.), German Soc. History Medicine, Sci. and Tech. (hon.), Sigma Xi. Home: 2235 Centro St E Belvedere Tiburon CA 94920-1947 Office: U Calif Med Ctr San Francisco CA 94143 also: Med Ctr, PO Box 70, Abidi Village Anambra State, Nigeria *In a long and severely handicapped life I have had to live with chronic illness and pain. Thanks to my husband's endless patience and helpfulness, I have learned to accept what cannot be changed, and to change what can be altered. I have had a successful and highly satisfactory academic career in spite of endless obstacles that lie in the way of a woman scholar. In short, I have had a difficult but eminently happy life.*

VEITH, MARY ROTH, assistant dean; b. Middletown, Conn., Feb. 7, 1931; d. John Stephen and Margaret (Healey) Roth; children: Richard, Frank, Margaret, Katherine. BS, U. Conn., 1952; MBA, Iona Coll., 1975. Registered dietitian. Asst. head dietitian St. Francis Hosp., Hartford, Conn., 1954-55; dietitian Quality Control Lab A&P Corp., N.Y.C., 1955-56; head dietitian Cabrini Hosp., N.Y.C., 1956; homemaker, 1957-75; instr. mgmt. Coll. New Rochelle, N.Y., 1975; instr. mktg. Iona Coll., New Rochelle, N.Y., 1975-78, asst. prof., 1979—; asst. dean Hagan Sch. of Bus., Iona Coll., New Rochelle, N.Y., 1985—; treas. Advt. Club Westchester, N.Y. Mem. Am. Dietetic Assn., N.Y. Dietetic Assn., Am. Mktg. Assn., World Trade Club (Westchester). Avocations: tennis, skiing. Office: Hagan Sch Business Iona College 715 North Ave New Rochelle NY 10801-1830

VEIZER, JÁN, geology educator; b. Pobedim, Slovakia, June 22, 1941; came to Can., 1973; s. Viktor and Brigita (Brandstetter) V.; m. Elena Ondrus, July 30, 1966; children: Robert, Andrew Douglas. Prom. Geol., Comenius U., Bratislava, Slovakia, 1964; RNDr, Comenius U., Bratislava, Slovak Republic, 1968; CSc, Slovak Acad. Sci., Bratislava, Slovakia, 1968; PhD, Australian Nat. U., Canberra, 1971. Asst. lectr. Comenius U., 1963-66; research scientist Slovak Acad. Sci., 1966-71; vis. asst. prof. UCLA, Los Angeles, 1972; vis. research scientist U. Göttingen, Fed. Republic Germany, 1972-73; research scientist U. Tübingen, Fed. Republic Germany, 1973; from asst. prof. to full prof. U. Ottawa, Ont., Can., 1973—; prof. Ruhr U., Bochum, Germany, 1988—; cons. NASA, Houston, 1983-86; vis. prof. and scholar Northwestern U., Evanston, Ill., 1983-87; vis. fellow Australian Nat. U., 1979; vis. prof. U. Tübingen, 1974; Lady Davis professorship Hebrew U., Jerusalem, 1987. Contbr. articles to profl. jours., chpts. to books. Served to j.lt. Med., 1965-66, Czechoslovakia. Recipient W. Leibniz prize German Rsch. Found., 1992; named Rsch. Prof. of Yr., 1987; Humboldt fellow, 1980, Killam Rsch. fellow Can. Coun., 1986-88. Fellow Royal Soc. Can. (Willet G. Miller medal 1991), Geol. Soc. Can. (Past Pres. medal 1987, Logan medal 1995), Geol. Soc. Am.; mem. Geochem. Soc. Am., Ski Club. Roman Catholic. Avocations: reading, hiking, skiing, history. Office: U Ottawa Dept Geology, Derry/Rust Rsch Group, Ottawa, ON Canada K1N 6N5 also: Ruhr U Inst Geologie, Lehrstuhl Sedimentgeologie, 44780 Bochum Germany

VEJSICKY, CATHLEEN LYNN, management executive, educator; b. Columbus, Ohio, June 25, 1958; d. Eugene Joseph and Jane Ann (Thomas) V. BS, U. So. Calif., L.A., 1981, MBA, 1987, postgrad. Cert. tchr., bus. mgmt. and mktg. tchr., C.C. tchr., Calif., CLAD cert. Sr. product mgr. Dataproducts Corp., Woodland Hills, Calif., 1980-86; product mktg. mgr. Light Signatures, Century City, Calif., 1987-88; mgr., mgmt. cons. KPMG Peat Marwick, L.A., 1988-92; v.p. Stranberg & Assocs., Newport Beach, Calif., 1993—; substitute tchr. Long Beach (Calif.) Unified Sch. Dist., 1993-95; tchr. Anaheim (Calif.) City Sch. Dist., 1994—; guest mktg. lectr. U. So. Calif., 1986—; developer, leader U. So. Calif. Western Europe's Grad. Bus. Exch. Program, 1987. Polit. campaign vol., Long Beach, Calif., 1989—; mem. Patrick Henry Leadership Team, Anaheim Unified Sch. Dist. Ins. Com., P.Q.R. sci. Team; leader Anaheim Math. Republican. Presbyterian. Avocations: golf, reading, swimming, biking, kayaking. Home: 6016 Bixby Village Dr Long Beach CA 90803

VELA, FILEMON B., federal judge; b. Harlingen, Tex., May 1, 1935; s. Roberto and Maria Luisa Cardenas V.; m. Blanca Sanchez, Jan. 28, 1962; children: Filemon, Rafael Eduardo, Sylvia Adriana. Student, Tex. Southmost Coll., 1954-56, U. Tex., 1956-57; JD, St. Mary's U., San Antonio, 1962. Bar: Tex. 1962. Mem. Vela & Vela, 1962-63; atty. Mexican-Am. Legal Def. Fund, 1962-75; pvt. practice law Brownsville, 1963-75; judge dist. 107, Tex. Dist. Ct., 1975-80; judge U.S. Dist. Ct. (so. dist.) Tex., Brownsville, 1980—; instr. Law Enforcement Coll. City commr., Brownsville, 1971-73. Served with U.S. Army, 1957-59. Mem. State Bar Tex. Democrat. Office: US Courthouse PO Box 1072 Brownsville TX 78520*

VELARDO, JOSEPH THOMAS, molecular biology and endocrinology educator; b. Newark, Jan. 27, 1923; s. Michael Arthur and Antoinette (Iacullo) V.; m. Forresta M. Monica Power, Aug. 12, 1948 (dec. July 1976). AB, U. No. Colo., 1948; SM, Miami U., 1949; PhD, Harvard U., 1952. Rsch. fellow in biology and endocrinology Harvard U., Cambridge, Mass., 1952-53; rsch. assoc. in pathology, ob-gyn. and surgery Sch. Medicine Harvard U., Boston, 1953-55; asst. in surgery Peter Bent Brigham and Women's Hosp., Boston, 1954-55; asst. prof. anatomy and endocrinology Sch. Medicine, Yale U., New Haven, 1955-61; prof. anatomy, chmn. dept. N.Y. Med. Coll., N.Y.C., 1961-62; cons. N.Y. Fertility Inst., 1961-62; dir. Inst. for Study Human Reprodn., Cleve., 1962-67; prof. biology John Carroll U., Cleve., 1962-67; mem. rsch. and edn. divs. Saint Ann Obstetric and Gynecologic Hosp., Cleve., 1962-67; head dept. rsch. Saint Ann Hosp., Cleve., 1964-67; prof. anatomy Stritch Sch. Medicine Loyola U., Chgo., 1967-88, chmn. dept. anatomy Stritch Sch. of Medicine, 1967-73; pres. Internat. Basic and Biol.-Biomed. Curricula, Lombard, Ill., 1979—; course moderator laparoscopy Brazil-Israel Congress on Fertility and Sterility, and Brazil Soc. of Human Reproduction, Rio de Janeiro, 1973; organizer, chmn. symposia in field. Author, contbr.: (with others) Annual Reviews Physiology, Reproduction, 1961, Histochemistry of Enzymes in the Female Genital System, 1963, The Ovary, 1963, The Ureter, 1967, rev. edit., 1981; editor, contbr.: Endocrinology of Reproduction, 1958, The Essentials of Human reproduction, 1958; cons. editor, co-author: The Uterus, 1959; contbr. Progestational Substances, 1958, Trophoblast and Its Tumors, 1959, The Vagina, 1959, Hormonal Steroids, Biochemistry, Pharmacology and Therapeutics, 1964, Human Reproduction, 1973; co-editor, contbr.: Biology of Reproduction, Basic and Clinical Studies, 1973; contbr. articles to profl. jours.; live broadcasts on major radio and TV networks on subjects of bioscis., biomed. careers, biomed. subjects; co-author movie on human reprodn. The Soft Anvil. Apptd. U.S. del. to Vatican, 1964; charter mem. U.S. Rep. Presdl. Task Force, 1988—; rep. U.S. Senate Inner Circle, 1988—, U.S. Rep. Senatorial Commn., 1991—. With USAAF, 1943-45. Decorated Presdl. Unit citation, 2 Bronze Stars; recipient award Lederle Med. Faculty Awards Com., 1955-58; named hon. citizen City of Sao Paulo, Brazil, 1972; U.S. del. to Vatican, 1964. Fellow AAAS, N.Y. Acad. Scis. (co-organizer, chmn., consulting editor internat. symposium The Uterus), Gerontol. Soc., Pacific Coast Fertility Soc. (hon.); mem. Am. Assn. Anatomists, Am. Soc. Zoologists (organizer symposium The Uterus 1973), Am. Physiol. Soc. (vis. prof. 1962), Endocrine Soc., Soc. Endocrinology (Gt. Britain), Soc. Exptl. Biology and Medicine, Am. Soc. Study Sterility (Rubin award 1954), Internat. Fertility Assn., Pan Am. Assn. Anatomy (co-organizer symposium Reproduction 1972), Midwestern Soc. Anatomists (pres. 1973-74), Mexican Soc. Anatomy (hon.), Harvard Club, Sigma Xi, Kappa Delta Pi, Phi Sigma, Gamma Alpha, Alpha Epsilon Delta. Achievements include extensive original research and publications on the physiology and development of decidual tissue (experimental equivalent of the maternal portion of the placenta) in the rat; biological investigation of eighteen human adenhohypophyses (anterior lobes of the human pituitray glands); induction of ovulation utilizing highly purified adenohypophyseal gonadotropic hormones in mammals; the pacemaker action of ovarian sex steroid hormones in reproductive processes; and the interation of steroids in reproductive mechanisms. Office: 607 E Wilson Ave Lombard IL 60148-4062 *Personal philosophy: Success is best highlighted by the invincible instruments of truth, integrity, hard work, thinking, running the extra mile, leading or giving help where no other help seems forthcoming, recognizing the talents of our fellow man and lady, and above all, practicing of the Golden Rule.*

VELASQUEZ, ANA MARIA, languages educator; b. Callao, Lima, Peru, Nov. 18, 1947; came to U.S. 1980; d. Victor and Yolanda (Reinoso) V.; m. Scott Mathew Nakada, Mar. 19, 1981; 1 child, Victor Min Nakada. Bachelor's Degree, San Marcos U., Lima, 1969; student French Paris VI U., 1971-72, student English Prince George Coll., 1983-84, student Quechua Yachay Wasi Coll., Lima, 1986. Cert. tchr., Peru. Educator San Jose de Cluny, Lima, 1968-71; translator Aubert & Duval, Paris, 1972-76; linguistic coordinator Ser. de Maquinaria, Lima, 1977-80; educator, cons. INLINGUA, Washington, 1981-83, CACI, Inc., Arlington, Va., 1982-89; educator Diplomatic Lang. Svcs., Inc., Arlington, Va., 1990-94; dir. AKTA Internat., San Diego, 1984—. Author: Pronunciacion Basica Universal, 1974; South American Dialects, 1977; Abbreviated Telephone Communications System, 1984; Teaching Languages to Adults, 1985; Languages 365 Days, 1986. Coordinator literacy campaign, Puno, Peru, 1969. Mem. Am. Assn. Applied Linguistics, Mensa. Republican. Roman Catholic. Avocations: chess, skiing. Home and Office: 14858 Summerbreeze Way San Diego CA 92128-3733

VELASQUEZ, JORGE LUIS, JR., jockey; b. Panama, Dec. 28, 1946; s. Jorge Luis and Francisca V.; m. Margaria Knipping, Nov. 13, 1969; children: Jorge, Michele, Monique. Jockey; rider horses Pleasant Colony, Alydar, Fort Marcy; Devona Dale (Triple Crown Winner for fillies), 1974; rider horses Hawaii, Fort Maray, Late Bloomer, Our Mims, Before Dawn, others. Mem. Jockeys Guild. Nat. leader in wins, 1967, in money won, 1969; 6 times leading rider in N.Y.; winner Ky. Derby and Preakness riding Pleasant Colony; winner richest thoroughbred match riding Chris Evert, 1973; winner Fla. Derby and Breeders' Cup riding Proud Truth, 1985; set N.Y. record for 6 wins out of 6 mounts, July 1981. Office: Jockey's Guild 20 E 46th St Rm 901 New York NY 10017-2417*

VELAZQUEZ, ANABEL, sales executive; b. Havana, Cuba, July 26, 1958; came to U.S, 1966; d. Joel Velazquez and Elsa (Miranda) V.; m. Richard P. DiBacco; children: Alexandra Chloe, Richard Philip. BS in Nursing, Fla. Internat. U., 1987; AS, So. Coll., Collegedale, Tenn., 1979. RN, Fla.; CRRN, CEN; cert. ins. rehab. specialist; cert. case mgr. Staff nurse Hialeah (Fla.) Hosp., 1980-85; home care supr. Med. Pers. Pool, Miami, 1985-88; regional mgr. Peninsular Rehab. Assocs., Winter Park, Fla., 1988-89; med. sales specialist Bristol Myers-Squibb, Evansville, Ind., 1989-91; clin. sales specialist, sr. hosp. sales rep. Fujisawa Pharm. Co., Ill., 1990-92; pres. Workers Rehab. Inc., Winter Park, Fla., 1993—. Recipient award Am. Legion. Mem. Coun. on Future of Nurses, Assn. Rehab. Nurses, Case Mgr. Soc. Assn. Home: 229 Crooked Stick Ct Orlando FL 32828-8831 Office: Workers Rehab Inc PO Box 2464 Goldenrod FL 32733-2464

VELAZQUEZ, NYDIA M., congresswoman; b. Yabucoa, P.R.. Grad., U. P.R.; MA, NYU, 1976. Mem. 103rd-104th Congress from 12th N.Y. dist., Washington, D.C., 1992—. Office: US Ho of Reps 132 Cannon Bldg Washington DC 20515-3212

VELÁZQUEZ DE CANCEL, LOURDES, religious organization executive, educator, interpreter, translator, poet; b. Santurce, P.R., Jan. 28, 1941; d. Manuel Velázquez-Conde and Ramonita Torres-Marrero; m. Eduardo Cancel-Rodriguez, June 3, 1961; children: Lourdes Isabel, Eduardo Juan, Daniel Eduardo. Grad., Inst. Children's Lit., West Redding, Conn., 1993. Pres., founder Ralvec Ministries, Carolina, 1991—. Author: A Crisis of Faith, 1986, Does Anyone Care? 1991, My Secret Garden, 1991, On Love and Power, 1991, On a Daily Basis, 1991, A Question of Integrity, 1991, Amidst Deep Waters, 1991, No One is So Great or So Small, 1994, The Tree of Life, 1994, Erotika-Poems, Proverbs and Undiluted Thoughts, 1994, His Way, 1992, Tulip Woman, 1993, Erotika, 1994, It is not Enough to Beg, 1994, The Money Value of Man, 1994, Come Home, Mother Come Home, 1994, The Signet, The Shield, The Pair of Keys, 1994; author numerous hymns, psalms, poems and short stories; editor Resurrection Life Mag., 1991. Translator ARC, San Juan, P.R., 1989-90. Recipient Merit award Internat. Soc. Poets, 1992. Mem. Soc. Tech. Communicators. Office: Ralvec Ministries PO Box 9466 Plaza Carolina Sta Carolina PR 00628

VELDE, JOHN ERNEST, JR., business executive; b. Pekin, Ill., June 15, 1917; s. John Ernest and Alga (Anderson) V.; m. Shirley Margaret Walker, July 29, 1940 (dec. 1969); 1 dau., Drew; m. Gail Patrick, Sept. 28, 1974 (dec. July 1980); m. Gretchen Swanson Pullen, Nov. 7, 1981. A.B., U. Ill., 1938. Pres. Velde, Roelfs & Co., Pekin, 1955-60; dir. Herget Nat. Bank, 1948-75, Kroehler Mfg. Co., 1974-81; pres. Paisano Prodns., Inc., 1980-94, mng. ptnr., 1994—; mng. ptnr. The Gardner Partnership, 1994—. Trustee Pekin Pub. Library, 1948-69, Pekin Meml. Hosp., 1950-69, Everett McKinley Dirksen Rsch. Ctr., 1965-74, Am. Libr. Assn. Endowment, 1976-82, Joint Coun. Econ. Edn., 1977-83, Ctr. Am. Archeology, 1978-83, Western Heritage Mus., Omaha, 1994—; chmn. Am. Libr. Trustee Assn. Found., 1976; chmn. trustees, bd. dirs. Ctr. Ulcer Rsch. and Edn. Found., 1977-82; mem. bd. councilors Brain Rsch. Inst. UCLA, 1977-82; mem. Nat. Commn. on Libr. and Info. Sci., 1970-79; mem. adv. bd. on White House Conf. on Librs., 1976-80; bd. dirs. U. Ill. Found., 1977-83, Omaha Pub. Libr. Found., 1985-92, James Madison Coun. Libr. Congress, 1990—; vice chmn. U. Ill. Pres.' Coun., 1977-79, chmn., 1979-81, mem. fin. resources coun. steering com., 1976-78; mem. adv. coun. UCLA Grad. Sch. Libr. and Info. Sci., 1981-82; pres. Ill. Valley Library System, 1965-69; dir. Lakeview Ctr. for Arts and Scis., Peoria, Ill., 1962-73; mem. Nat. Book Com., 1969-74. Served as lt. (j.g.) USNR, World War II. Mem. Am. Libr. Trustee Assn. (regional v.p. 1970-72, chmn. internat. rels. com. 1973-76), Internat. Boy Scouts (Baden-Powell fellow 1987—), Kappa Sigma. Clubs: Chgo. Yacht, Internat. (Chgo.); California (Los Angeles); Outrigger Canoe (Honolulu); Thunderbird Country (Rancho Mirage, Calif.); Chaine des Rotisseurs, Chevaliers du Tastevin; Circumnavigators (N.Y.C.); Omaha, Omaha Country; Old Baldy (Saratoga, Wyo.), Eldorado Country (Indian Wells, Calif.). Home: 8405 Indian Hills Dr Omaha NE 68114-4048 also: 40-231 Club View Dr Rancho Mirage CA 92270-3527 also: 123 Arapahoe Dr Saratoga WY 82331

VÉLEZ-JUARBE, LUIS ANTONIO, industrial pharmacy educator; b. Utuado, P.R., June 9, 1947; s. Bonafacio and Luz E. (Juarbe) V.; m. Nayda I. Santiago, Mar. 4, 1988; children: Krystal, Luis M., Antonio L., Eileen, Luis A., Krystal A. BS in Pharmacy, U. Puerto Rico, 1971; PhD in Indsl. Pharmacy, Purdue U., 1977. Prof. U. Puerto Rico, San Juan, 1971-85; pharm. tech. mgr. Warner Lambert, Inc., Vega Baja, P.R., 1986-89; mfg. mgr. Parmax Divsn. Baxter, Aguada, P.R., 1989-92; tech. svc. mgr. Dade Diagnostics of P.R., Inc., Aguada, 1992—; indsl. cons. mfg., mktg., P.R., Mex., U.S., 1976-85; chairmn. adv. bd. Econ. Devel. Adminstrn., San Juan, 1977-86; v.p. Bioequivalence Bd., San Juan, 1982-86;. Editor P.R. Health Sci. Jour., 1982-86, P.R. Pharm. Assn. Jour., 1983-84 (award 1983). Mem. internal review bd. U. Puerto Rico, 1976-86, cons. on indsl. affairs, 1994—; evaluator PR2000 Indsl. Excellence, P.R., 1992—. Recipient cert. Puerto Rico Pharm. Assn., San Juan, 1982-83; named Rschr. of Yr., U. Puerto Rico, 1985. Mem. Am. Assn. Pharm. Scientists, Puerto Rico Mfg. Assn. (1st v.p.), Am. Chem. Soc., Am. Soc. Quality Control, Rho Chi, Rho Pi Phi. Roman Catholic. Achievements include development of bioadheside polymers /co-polymer for controlled release drug delivery system; project mgr. for technology transfer for Warner Lambert, Inc. and Paramax, division of Baxter; comparative study of Maxide and Diazide as consultant; establishment of industrial validation group for PRMA/FDA Organization 1976-95. Avocations: tennis, jogging, music, meditation, reading fin. aspects, weight lifting. Office: Dade Diagnostics of PR Inc Rd 115 Km 22.6 PO Box 865 Aguada PR 00602

VELIANOFF, GEORGE D., medical center administrator. Diploma, Bethesda Hosp. Sch. Nursing, Cin., 1979; BSN, Edgecliff Coll., 1981; PhD in Nursing Sci., Ind. U., Indpls., 1986. RN, Ohio, W.Va., Ind. Nurse Bethesda Hosp., Cin., 1979-81, chg. nurse emer. dept., 1981-82, nursing supr., 1982-85; asst. dir. med.-surg. nursing Univ. Hosps., Cleve., 1986-89; asst. adminstr. Heartland Hosps., St. Joseph, Mo., 1989-90; adminstr. for nursing Charleston (W.Va.) Area Med. Ctr., 1990-95; v.p. patient svcs. Upper Chesapeake Health Sys., Balt., 1995—; clin. nurse to plastic and reconstructive surgeon in pvt. practice, Cin., 1980-85; asst. clin. prof. Frances Payne Bolton Sch. Nursing, Case Western Res. U., Cleve., 1986-89; mem. affiliate faculty U. Mo. Sch. Nursing, Kansas City, 1989-91; lectr. to profl. orgns. and confs.; mem. adj. faculty Marshall U., 1991-95. Editor: NurseNet, 1991; contbr. articles to profl. pubs. Mem. ANA, AACN, Nat. League Nursing, Sigma Theta Tau. Home: 301 Cannery Ct Forest Hill MD 21050 Office: Upper Chesapeake Health Sys 200 Milton Ave Fallston MD 21047

VELICER, JANET SCHAFBUCH, elementary school educator; b. Cedar Rapids, Iowa, Aug. 27, 1941; d. Allan J. and Geraldine Frances (Stuart) Schafbuch; m. Leland Frank Velicer, Aug. 17, 1963; children: Mark Allan, Gregory Jon, Daniel James. BS, Iowa State U., 1963, MS, 1966; cert. Elem. Edn., Mich. State U., 1976. Tchr. chemistry Prendergast High Sch., Upper Darby, Pa., 1964-65; tchr. home econs. Cardinal O'Hara High Sch., Springfield, Pa., 1965-66; substitute tchr. Pa., Mich., 1967-76; elem. tchr. Winans Elem. Sch., Waverly, Mich., 1976-78, Wardcliff Elem. Sch., Okemos, Mich., 1978-94; tchr. gifted and talented alternative program grades 4 and 5 Hiawatha Elem. Sch., Okemos, 1994-95; tchr. grade 4 Wardcliff Elem. Sch., 1995—; computer coord., Great Books coord.; dist. com. mem. math, computer, substance abuse, cable TV, evaluation revision Okemos Pub. Schs., Instructional Coun. Author: (video) Wardcliff School Documentary, 1982, The Integrated Arts Program of the Okemos Elementary Schools, 1983. Citizens adv. com. to develop a five-yr. plan, 1982-83, Bldg. utilization adv. com., 1983-84, Community use of schs. adv. com., 1984-85, Strategic planning steering com., 1989-90, Taking our schs. into tomorrow com., 1990-91, Bonding election steering com., 1991; chmn. wellness com. Okemos Pub. Schs., 1993-95. Recipient Classrooms of Tomorrow Tchr. award Mich. Dept. Edn., 1990. Mem. NEA, NAFE, Mich. Edn. Assn., Inst. Noetic Scis., Okemos Edn. Assn., Phi Kappa Phi, Mich. Coun. Tchrs. Math., Omicron Nu, Iota Sigma Pi. Democrat. Avocations: swimming, reading, hiking, travelogs,cultural events. Home: 2678 Blue Haven Ct East Lansing MI 48823-3804 Office: Okemos Pub Schs 4406 Okemos Rd Okemos MI 48864-2553

VELICK, SIDNEY FREDERICK, research biochemist, educator; b. Detroit, May 3, 1913; s. Harry Alexander and Ella (Stocker) V.; m. Bernadette Stemler, Sept. 5, 1941; children: William Frederick, Martha Elizabeth. B.S., Wayne State U., 1935; Ph.D., U. Mich., 1938. Research fellow parasitology Johns Hopkins U., 1939-40; research asso. chemistry Yale U., 1941-45; mem. biol. chemistry dept. Washington U. Sch. Medicine, St. Louis, 1946-63; prof. biol. chemistry Washington U. Sch. Medicine, 1958-64; prof., head dept. biol. chemistry U. Utah Coll. Medicine, 1964-79, prof. emeritus, 1988—; mem. biochemistry study sect. NIH. Assoc. editor: Archives Biochemistry and Biophysics; editorial bd.: Jour. Biol. Chemistry; contbr. papers on enzyme chemistry to tech. lit. Co-founder, pres. Alliance for the Mentally Ill Utah, 1980-85. Mem. NAS, AAAS, Am. Soc. Biol. Chemists, Am. Chem. Soc., Sigma Xi. Home: 4183 Parkview Dr Salt Lake City UT 84124-3436

VELICK, STEPHEN H., medical facility administrator. BS, Wayne State U., 1970, MS, 1980. Mgr. billing Henry Ford Hosp., Detroit, 1970-72, 72-74, mgr. patient svcs., 1974-75, asst. dir. bus., 1975-76, dir. bus. office, 1976-78, assoc. adminstr., 1978-83, group v.p., COO, 1990—; exec. dir. Greenfield Health Sys. Corp., Detroit, 1983-86; chief adminstrv. officer Henry Ford Med. Group, Detroit, 1986-90; adv. bd., bd. dirs. various healthcare orgns. Active various cmty. orgns. Mem. Am. Coll. Healthcare Execs. (assoc.). Office: Henry Ford Hosp 2799 W Grand Blvd Detroit MI 48202*

VELIE, ASHLEY LIVINGSTON, television news bureau editor; b. Albany, N.Y., May 28, 1968; d. John Joseph and Sondra (Murray) V. BS in Broadcast Journalism cum laude, Syracuse U., 1990. Producer, segment writer WAMC-FM, Albany, 1990-91; freelancer Potomac TV, Washington, 1992; field producer TV Direct Conus Comm., Washington, 1992-93, custom producer, 1993-95, mng. editor Washington Bureau, 1995—. Vol. Emmaus/ Bread for the City, Washington, 1994—. Mem. Senate/House Radio-TV Gallery. Avocations: flute, softball, skiing, jazz dancing. Office: Conus Communications 1825 K St NW # 915 Washington DC 20006

VELIE, LESTER, journalist; b. Kiev, Ukraine, 1907; came to U.S., 1912, naturalized, 1922; s. Samuel and Sarah (Spector) V.; m. Frances Rockmore, Oct. 29, 1932; children: Alan R., Franklin Bell. BA, U. Wis., 1929. Reporter AP, N.Y., 1931-32; suburban editor Bklyn. Eagle, 1932-35; assoc. editor Jour. Commerce, N.Y.C., 1937-46; radio analyst Sta. WQXR, N.Y.C., 1941-45; assoc. editor Collier's, 1945-52; roving editor Reader's Digest, 1953-85. Author: Labor U.S.A, 1959, Labor U.S.A. Today, 1964, Countdown in the Holy Land, 1969, Desperate Bargain: Why Jimmy Hoffa had to Die, 1977, Murder Story: A Tragedy of Our Time, 1983; contbr. to Op Ed, N.Y. Times; ABC TV series Target the Corrupters based on mag. articles. Recipient Disting. Svc. award for mag. journalism Sigma Delta Chi, 1949, Sch. Bell award for mag. journalism NEA, 1966, Silver Gavel award ABA, 1973; Ford Found. grantee, 1981-82. Home and Office: 1022 Kings Rd Norman OK 73069

VELIOTES, NICHOLAS ALEXANDER, professional association executive, former ambassador and assistant secretary of state; b. Oakland, Calif., Oct. 28, 1928; s. Alexander and Irene (Kiskaskis) V.; m. Patricia Jane Nolan, July 17, 1953; children: Christopher, Michael. BA, U. Calif.-Berkeley, 1952, MA, 1954; postgrad., Princeton U., 1969-70. Teaching asst. U. Calif.-Berkeley, 1952-54; commd. officer U.S. Fgn. Service, 1955; held various Fgn. Service posts Italy, India, Laos, Israel, Jordan, Egypt; Asst. Sec. of State Near East/South Asia, 1981-83; ambassador to Jordan, 1978-81, ambassador to Egypt, 1983-86; pres. Assn. Am. Pubs., 1986—. Bd. dirs. Fund for Free Expression, Amer. Acad. Diplomacy, Com. on Pres., Access and Amideast. Served with U.S. Army, 1946-48. Recipient Sec. of State and Presdl. Disting. Service awards. Mem. Council on Fgn. Relations, VFW. Office: Assn Am Pub 1718 Connecticut Ave NW Washington DC 20009*

VELLENGA, KATHLEEN OSBORNE, former state legislator; b. Alliance, Nebr., Aug. 5, 1938; d. Howard Benson and Marjorie (Menke) Osborne; m. James Alan Vellenga, Aug. 9, 1959; children: Thomas, Charlotte Vellenga Landreau, Carolyn. BA, Macalester Coll., 1959. Tchr. St. Paul Pub. Schs., 1959-60, Children's Ctr. Montessori, St. Paul, 1973-74, Children's House Montessori, St. Paul, 1974-79; mem. Minn. Ho. of Reps., St. Paul, 1980-94, mem. tax. com. and rules com., 1991—, chmn. St. Paul del., 1985-89, chmn. criminal justice div., 1989-90, chmn. crime and family law div., 1987-88, mem. Dem. steering com., 1987-94; chmn. judiciary Minn. Ho. of Reps., 1991, 92, chmn. edn. fin., 1992-93, 93-94; mem. St. Paul Family Svcs. Bd., 1994-95; exec. dir. St. Paul/Ramsey County Children's Initiative, 1994—. Chmn. Healthstart, St. Paul, 1987-91; mem. Children, Youth and Families Consortium, 1995—, Macalester Coll. Bd. Alumni, 1995-96, Minn. Higher Edn. Svcs. Coun., 1995-96. Mem. LWV (v.p. St. Paul chpt. 1979), Minn. Women Elected Ofcls. (vice chair 1994). Democrat. Presbyterian. Office: A H Wilder 919 Lafond Ave Saint Paul MN 55104-2108

VELMANS, LOET ABRAHAM, retired public relations executive; b. Amsterdam, Netherlands, Mar. 18, 1923; s. Joseph and Anna (Cohen) V.; m. Pauline Edith Van Hessen, Mar. 29, 1949; children: Marianne and Hester (twins), Jessica. Grad., U. Amsterdam, 1947. Info. officer Dutch Govt. in, Singapore, 1945-47; with Hill & Knowlton, Inc., 1953-86; v.p. Hill Knowlton Internat., Geneva, 1959-69; pres. Hill Knowlton Internat., 1960-74; vice chmn. Hill Knowlton Internat., London, 1969-76; pres. Hill Knowlton Internat., N.Y.C., 1976-86; chmn. bd., chief exec. officer Hill Knowlton Internat., 1980-86. Contbr. articles on multinat. corps. to profl. jours. Bd. dirs. Lincoln Ctr. Inst., Netherland Am. Found., Global Pub. Affairs Inst. NYU. Decorated Grande Ufficiale Order of Merit, Italy, 1989. Club: Mid-Atlantic of N.Y. Inc. (pres.). Home: PO Box 178 Sheffield MA 01257-0178

VELZ, JOHN WILLIAM, literature educator; b. Englewood, N.J., Aug. 5, 1930; s. Clarence Joseph and Harriet Josephine (O'Brien) V.; m. Sarah Elizabeth Campbell, Oct. 18, 1967; children: Jody, Emily; 3 children from previous marriage. BA in English with high distinction and honors, U. Mich., 1953, MA in English and French, 1954; PhD in English and Classical Greek, U. Minn., 1963. Instr. Coll. St. Thomas, St. Paul, 1958-60; asst. prof. English Rice U., Houston, 1963-69; prof. U. Tex., Austin, 1969-96; vis. prof. U. Paul Valery, Montpelier, France, 1977-78, Julius Maximillians U., Wuerzburg, West Germany, 1981-82, 85-86; asst. dir., lit. adv. Odessa Shakespeare Festival, 1977; faculty mem. Oreg. Shakespeare Festival, 1979; lectr. tour Cen. and Ea. Europe univs., 1993; dir. acad. prodns. of Shakespeare and medieval drama; mem. Acad. Adv. Coun. Globe Theatre Ctr., 1981—; mem. U.S. Com. for Shakespeare's Globe, 1990—. Author: Shakespeare and the Classical Tradition, 1968 (ALA citation, Assn. Coll. and Rsch. Librs. citation); editor: Julius Caesar in MLA's New Variorum Shakespeare, 1966-95, (N.Am.) Cahiers Elisabethains, 1979-81; Shakespeare's English Histories: A Quest for Form and Genre, 1996; co-editor: Collected Papers of James G. McManaway, 1969, One Touch of Shakespeare: Letters of Joseph Crosby to Joseph Parker Norris 1875-1878, 1986; contbr. numerous scholarly, interpretive articles, mainly on Shakespeare and medieval drama, to profl. jours.; presenter numerous papers to learned socs., mem. editl. bd. Shakespeare Quar., 1975—, Classical and Modern Lit., 1981-85, Tex. Studies in Lit. and Lang., 1969-92, Shakespeare and the Classroom, 1993—; mem. editl. adv. bd. Complete Works of Shakespeare, 3d edit., 1980, 4th edit., 1992; cons. editor South Ctrl. Rev., 1989-92; mem. cons. com. Internat. Studies in Shakespeare and His Contemporaries, 1990—. Recipient Fulbright award, 1977-78, 81-82; recipient Oreon E. Scott award U. Mich., 1953; NEH fellow, 1967-68; Folger Library fellow, 1968. Mem. MLA, Assn. Lit. Scholars and Critics, Internat. Shakespeare Assn. (charter), Shakespeare Assn. Am., Malone Soc., Renaissance English Text Soc., Medieval and Renaissance Drama Soc., Marlowe Soc. of Am., Soc. for Textual Scholarship, H.W. Fowler Soc. (charter), Phi Beta Kappa, Phi Kappa Phi, Phi Eta Sigma. Home: 809 W 32nd St Austin TX 78705-2115 Office: U Tex Dept English Austin TX 78712 *Academic life is predicated on the obligation to teach as generously as we have been taught, to serve others as we have been served. This sense of mutuality has been a rationale for my professional life, though it would be impossible to pay all I owe.*

VELZY, CHARLES O., mechanical engineer; b. Oak Park, Ill., Mar. 17, 1930; s. Charles R and Ethel B. V.; m. Marilyn A. Gilman, Aug. 17, 1957; children: Charles Mark, Barbara Helen, Patricia Ethel. B.S.M.E., U. Ill., 1953, B.S. in Civil Engring., 1960, M.S. in San. Engring., 1959. Registered profl. engr., N.Y., 13 other states. Design engr., project engr. Nussbaumer, Clarke & Velzy, N.Y.C., 1959-66; sec.-treas., dir. Charles R Velzy Assos., Inc., Armonk, N.Y., 1966-76; pres. Charles R. Velzy Assoc., Inc., 1976-92; v.p. Roy F. Weston Inc., 1987-92; pres. Charles O. Velzy, P.E., Lyndonville, Vt., 1992—. Contbr. articles to profl. jours. Mem. White Plains (N.Y.) Bldg. Code Appeals Bd., 1970-92. With U.S. Army, 1954-56. Fellow ASME (chmn. solid waste processing divsn 1973-74, mem. policy bd. rsch. 1974-78, bd. govs. 1983-84, pres. 1989-90, Centennial medal 1980, medal of achievement 1981), Am. Cons. Engrs. Coun.; mem. ASTM, ASCE (life), NSPE, Am. Acad. Environ. Engrs. (trustee 1984-87, treas. 1993—), Am. Water Works Assn. (life), Water Environ. Fedn., Air Waste Mgmt. Assn. Methodist. *After deciding on what is needed in a specific situation, based on the facts, establish your objectives and goals and persist to a successful conclusion.*

VENA, DAVID HENRY, lawyer; b. Los Angeles, Dec. 21, 1938; s. David P. and Frances (Wilks) V.; m. Carolyn Willis, Jan. 20, 1961 (div. Dec. 1980); children: Gabrielle, Arianne; m. Carol A. Vena-Mondt, Sept. 30, 1984. AB, UCLA, 1961; LLB, Harvard U., 1964. Bar: Calif. 1965, U.S Dist. Ct. (so. dist.) Calif. 1965, U.S. Ct. Appeals (9th cir.) 1965. Assoc. Latham & Watkins, Los Angeles, ptnr.; legal cons. Concept Team Summa Corp., Marina del Ray, Calif., 1984—; bd. dirs. The Becket Group, Santa Monica, Calif. Founder Mus. Contemporary Art, Los Angeles; trustee Friends of Photography, Carmel, Calif., 1983—; bd. dirs. Otis/Parsons, Los Angeles, 1980—, Skystone Found. Inc., Flagstaff, Ariz., 1985—, UCLA Arts Council, 1986—. Mem. Los Angeles Bar Assn.,. Club: Los Angeles Country. Avocations: collecting contemporary art, golf. Home: 929 E 2nd St Ste 206 Los Angeles CA 90012-4337 Office: Latham & Watkins 633 W 5th St Ste 4000 Los Angeles CA 90071-2005*

VENDELA, model. With Ford Models, Inc., N.Y., 1986, Elizabeth Arden, 1988. appeared on cover of Sports Illustrated Swimsuit Edition, 1993. Office: Ford Models Inc 344 E 59th St New York NY 10022-1570

VENDLER, HELEN HENNESSY, literature educator, poetry critic; b. Boston, Mass., Apr. 30, 1933; d. George and Helen (Conway) Hennessy; 1 son, David. A.B., Emmanuel Coll., 1954; Ph.D., Harvard U., 1960; Ph.D. (hon.), U. Oslo; D.Litt. (hon.), Smith Coll., Kenyon Coll., U. Hartford, Union Coll.; Fitchburg State U.; D.Litt. (hon.), Columbia U., George Washington U., Marlboro Coll., St. Louis; DHL (hon.), Dartmouth Coll., U. Mass., Bates Coll., U. Toronto, Ont., Can., Trinity Coll., Dublin, Ireland, Fitchburg State U.; George Washington U. Instr. Cornell U., Ithaca, N.Y., 1960-63; lectr. Swarthmore (Pa.) Coll. and Haverford (Pa.) Coll., 1963-64; asst. prof. Smith Coll., Northampton, Mass., 1964-66; assoc. prof. Boston U., 1966-68, prof., 1968-85; Fulbright lectr. U. Bordeaux, France, 1968-69; vis. prof. Harvard U., 1981-85, Kenan prof., 1985—, Porter U. prof., 1990—, assoc. acad. dean, 1987-92, sr. fellow Harvard Soc. Fellows, 1981-93; poetry critic New Yorker, 1978—; mem. ednl. adv. bd. Guggenheim Found., 1991—, Pulitzer Prize Bd., 1991—. Author: Yeats's Vision and the Later Plays, 1963, On Extended Wings: Wallace Stevens' Longer Poems, 1969, The Poetry of George Herbert, 1975, Part of Nature, Part of Us, 1980, The Odes of John Keats, 1983, Wallace Stevens: Words Chosen Out of Desire, 1984; editor: Harvard Book of Contemporary American Poetry, 1985, Voices and Visions: The Poet in America, 1987, The Music of What Happens, 1988, Soul Says, 1995, The Given and the Made, 1995, The Breaking of Style, 1995, Poems, Poets, Poetry, 1995. Bd. dirs. Nat. Humanities Ctr., 1989-93. Recipient Lowell prize, 1969, Explicator prize, 1969, award Nat. Inst. Arts and Letters, 1975, Radcliffe Grad. Soc. medal, 1978, Nat. Book Critics award, 1980, Keats-Shelley Assn. award, 1994, Truman Capote award, 1996; Fulbright fellow, 1954, AAUW fellow, 1959, Guggenheim fellow, 1971-72, Am. Coun. Learned Socs. fellow, 1971-72, NEH fellow, 1980, 85, 94, Overseas fellow Churchill Coll., Cambridge, 1980, Charles Stewart Parnell fellow Magdalene Coll., Cambridge, 1996, hon. fellow, 1996—. Mem. MLA (exec. coun. 1972-75, pres. 1980), AAAL, English Inst. (trustee 1977-85), Am. Acad. Arts and Scis. (v.p. 1992-95), Norwegian Acad. Letters and Sci., Am. Philos. Soc., Phi Beta Kappa. Home: 54 Trowbridge St # 2 Cambridge MA 02138-4113 Office: Harvard U Dept English 8 Prescott St Cambridge MA 02138-3929

VENEGAS, ARTURO, JR., chief police; b. San Nicolas de Ibarra, Jalisco, Mexico, Dec. 22, 1948; m. Anna Marie Venegas; children: Angela, Adriana, Anthony, Andrew. BA, U. San Francisco, 1978; MS in Mgmt., Calif. Poly., Pomona, 1991. Police officer Fresno (Calif.) Police Dept., 1970-75, police specialist, 1975-79, sgt., field supr., 1979, 80-85, lt., 1985-90, lt., acting divsn. comdr. adminstrv. svcs., 1990-92, dep. chief police investigations divsn., 1992-93; chief program devel., program mgr. State Office Criminal Justice Planning, Sacramento, Calif., 1979-80; chief police Sacramento Police Dept., 1993—. Mem. Calif. Atty. Gen.'s Policy Coun. on Violence Prevention; bd. dirs. Safety Ctr.; mem. exec. bd. Sacramento Safe Sts.; mem. adv. bd. Cath. Social Svcs. With U.S. Army, 1966-68. Mem. Internat. Assn. Chiefs of Police, Calif. Assn. Chiefs of Police, Calif. Peace Officers Assn. (chair law and legis. com.), Police Exec. Rsch. Forum, Ctrl. Sierra Police Chiefs Assn., FBI Nat. Acad. Assocs., Latino Peace Officers Assn., Hispanic-Am. Command Officers Assn., Am. Legion, Footprinters Internat., KC. Office: Police Dept Hall of Justice 813 6th St Sacramento CA 95814-2403

VENEMAN, GERARD EARL, paper company executive; b. Wheeling, W.Va., June 30, 1920; s. F. Earl and Ethel Martha (Joyce) V.; m. Doris D. Alexander, Jan. 10, 1948; children: Stephanie Joyce, Dean Gerard, Leslie Ann, Nancy Ellen, Jill Edwards. Student, U. Detroit, Northwestern U. Sales mgr. Agar Packing Co., Chgo., 1945-49; with Nekoosa Papers Inc., Port Edwards, Wis., 1949-85; v.p., dir. sales Nekoosa Papers Inc., 1954-62, exec. v.p., dir. mktg., 1962-69, exec. v.p., 1969-70, pres., 1970-85; bd. dirs. Wood County Nat. Bank, Wisconsin Rapids, Wis., Franklin Electric, Bluffton, Ind., Sentry Ins. Co., Stevens Point, Wis. Pres., bd. dirs. Alexander Charitable Found.; bd. dirs., v.p. South Wood County YMCA, Port Edwards; bd. regents U. Wis. System, 1979-86. Served with AUS, World War II. Decorated Bronze Star. Mem. Sales Assn. Paper Industry (pres. 1960, gov. 1964—), Writing Paper Mfrs. Assn. (exec. and finance coms. 1954—, chmn. sulphite bond group 1960-62, v.p. 1960-62, pres. 1963-65), Printing and Writing Assn. (chmn. 1975), Am. Paper Inst. (rep. bd. govs. 1963-65). Home: PO Box 70 Port Edwards WI 54469-0070

VENERABLE, SHIRLEY MARIE, gifted education educator; b. Washington, Nov. 12, 1931; d. John Henry and Jessie Josephine (Young) Washington; m. Wendell Grant Venerable, Feb. 15, 1959; children: Angela Elizabeth Maria Venerable-Joyner, Wendell Mark. PhB, Northwestern U., 1963; MA, Roosevelt U., 1976, postgrad., 1985. Cert. in diagnostic and prescriptive reading, gifted edn., finger math., fine arts, Ill. Tchr. Lewis Champlin Sch., 1963-74, John Hay Acad., Chgo., 1975-87, Leslie Lewis Elem. Sch., Chgo., 1988—; sponsor Reading Marathon Club, Chgo., 1991—; co-creator Project SMART (Stimulating Math. and Reading Techniques) John Hay Acad., Chgo., 1987-90, curriculum coord., 1985-87; creative dance student, tchr. Kathryn Duham Sch., N.Y.C., 1955-56; creative dance tchr. Doris Patterson Dance Sch., Washington, 1953-55; recorder evening divsn. Northwestern U., Chgo., 1956-62; exch. student tchr. Conservatory Dance Movements, Chgo., 1958-59; art cons. Chgo. Pub. Sch., 1967. Author primary activities Let's Act and Chat, 1991-94, Teaching Black History Through Classroom Tours, 1989-90. Solicitor, vol. United Negro Coll. Fund, Chgo., 1994; sponsor 21st Ward Reading Assn., Chgo., 1991-94. Recipient Meritorious award United Negro Coll. Fund, 1990, 94, Recognition award Alderman Percy Giles, Chgo., 1993. Mem. ASCD (assoc., Recognition of Svcs. award 1989), Internat. Reading Assn., Eta Zi Sigma, Sigma Gamma Rho (Delta Sigma chpt. 1963-93, Sigma chpt. 1992), Phi Delta Kappa. Roman Catholic. Home: 1108 N Euclid Ave Oak Park IL 60302-1219

VENETSANOPOULOS, ANASTASIOS NICOLAOS, electrical engineer, educator; b. Athens, Greece, June 19, 1941; emigrated to Can., 1968; s. Nicolaos Anastasios and Elli (Papacondilis) V. Diploma, Athens Coll., 1960; diploma in elec. and mech. engring., Nat. Tech. U., Athens, 1965, hon. doctorate, 1994; MS, Yale U., 1966, MPhil, 1968. Registered profl. engr., Greece, Ont. Asst. in instrn. engring. and applied sci. Yale U., 1966-68, research asst., 1968-69; lectr. U. Toronto, Ont., Can., 1968-69; asst. prof. elec. engring. U. Toronto, 1970-73, assoc. prof., 1973-81, prof., 1981—, chmn. communications group dept. elec. engring., 1974-78, 81-86, assoc. chmn. elec. engring., 1978-79, mem. elec. engring. exec. com., 1974-78, 81-86, mem. elec. engring. curriculum com., 1972-79; acad. visitor Imperial Coll. Arts and Tech., U. London, 1979-80; vis. prof. Nat. Tech. U. Athens, spring 1979-80, Fed. U. of Technology of Lausanne, Switzerland, 1986-87, 93-94, U. Florence, Italy, summer 1987; cons. elec. engring. Consociates Ltd. Editor Can. Elec. Engring. Jour., 1981-83; contbr. over 500 articles to profl. jours. and to 25 books. Mem. allocations and agy. relations com. United Community Fund, Toronto, 1971-74; pres. Hellenic-Can. Cultural Soc., 1972-75; sec. gen. Greek Community Met. Toronto, 1973-75. Fulbright travel grantee in U.S., 1965; Def. Research Bd. Can. grantee, 1972-75, UN grantee; NSF grantee; J.P. Bickell Found. grantee; Natural Scis. and Engring. Research Council of Can. Fellow IEEE (fin. chmn. internat. symposium on circuit theory 1973, tech. program chmn. internat. conf. communications 1978, 86, vice-chmn. Toronto sect. 1976-77, chmn. 1977-79, assoc. editor transactions on circuits and systems 1985-87, guest editor spl. issue Transactions on Circuits and Systems in Image Processing 1987), Engring. Inst. Can.; mem. Assn. Profl. Engrs. Ont., Assn. Profl. Elec. Engrs. Greece, Assn. Profl. Mech. Engrs. Greece, Can. Soc. Elec. Engring. (chmn. Toronto sect. 1975-77, nat. dir. 1976-88, pres. 1983-86), Yale Sci. and Engring. Assn., N.Y. Acad. Scis., Tech. Chamber Greece, Am.-Hellenic Ednl. Progress Assn. (v.p. Toronto sect. 1973-75, pres. 1975-77), Intercultural Council (chmn. ednl. com. 1971-80, sr. v.p. 1977-80), Sigma Xi. Office: U Toronto, Dept Elec and Computer Engring, Toronto, ON Canada M5S 1A4

VENEZKY, RICHARD LAWRENCE, English educator; b. Pitts., Apr. 16, 1938; s. Bernard Jacob and Isabel (Zeisel) V.; m. Karen F. Gauz, Aug. 2, 1964; children: Dina Yael, Elie Michael. BEE, Cornell U., 1961, MA, 1962; postgrad., U. Calif.-Berkeley, 1962-63; PhD, Stanford U., 1965. Systems programmer, tech. writer Control Data Corp., Palo Alto, Calif., 1962-65; asst. prof. English and computer scis. U. Wis., Madison, 1965-69; asso. prof. computer scis. U. Wis., 1969-74, prof., 1974-77, chmn. dept., 1975-77; Unidel prof. ednl. studies, prof. computer and info. sci. U. Del., Newark, 1977—; Benton fellow in literacy U. Chgo., 1994-95; vis. rsch. assoc. Tel Aviv U., 1969-70, rsch. fellow, 1973; cons. Oxford English Dictionary Supplement; dir. computing Dictionary of Old English, 1971— co-dir. for R&D Nat. Ctr. on Adult Literacy, 1990—. Author: The Structure of English Orthography, 1970, Testing in Reading, 1974, Random House Spelling Across the Curriculum, 1988; co-author: A Microfiche Concordance to Old English, 1981, Letter and Word Perception, 1980, PRS-Pre-Reading Skills Program, 1985, The Subtle Danger, 1987, World of Reading, 1989, The Intelligent Design of Computer-Assisted Instruction, 1991; co-editor: Orthography, Reading and Dyslexia, 1980, Toward Defining Literacy, 1990; contbr. articles to profl. jours., chpts. to books. Chmn. edn. commn Madison Jewish Community Coun., 1973-77; v.p. Jewish Fedn. Del., 1986-89; regional chmn. Am. Profs. for Peace in Mid. East, 1968-73. Named to Reading Hall of Fame, 1991; grantee Office of Edn., 1964-66, NSF, 1966-74, Nat. Inst. Edn., 1973-77, NEH, 1978-89, Office of Ednl. Rsch. and Improvement, Dept. Edn., 1990—. Mem. Am. Psychol. Soc., Am. Edn. Rsch. Assn., Internat. Reading Assn., Assn. Computing Machinery. Democrat. Jewish. Home: 206 Hullihen Dr Newark DE 19711-3651

VENKATA, SUBRAHMANYAM SARASWATI, electrical engineering educator, electri energy and power researcher; b. Nellore, Andhra Pradesh, India, June 28, 1942; came to U.S., 1968; s. Ramiah Saraswati and Lakshmi (Alladi) V.; m. Padma Subrahmanyam Mahadevan, Sept. 3, 1971; children: Sridevi Saraswati, Harish Saraswati. BSEE, Andhra U., Waltair, India, 1963; MSEE, Indian Inst. Tech., Madras, 1965; PhD, U. S.C., 1971. Registered profl. engr., W.Va., Wash. Lectr. in elec. engring. Coimbatore (India) Inst. Tech., 1965-66; planning engr. S.C. Elec. & Gas Co., Columbia, 1969-70; postdoctoral fellow U. S.C., Columbia, 1971; instr. elec. engring. U. Mass., Lowell, 1971-72; asst. prof. W.Va. U., Morgantown, 1972-75, assoc. prof., 1975-79; prof. U. Wash., Seattle, 1979—; cons. Puget Sound Power & Light, Bellevue, Wash., 1980—, GEC/Alsthom, N.Y.C., 1991—; series editor, bd. dirs. PWS Pub. Co., 1991—. Author: Introduction of Electrical Energy Devices, 1987; patentee adaptive var compensator. Advisor Explorers Club, Morgantown, 1976-78; sec. Hindu Temple and Cultural Ctr. Pacific N.W., Seattle, 1990, chmn., 1991, 95. Recipient W.Va. U. Assocs. award W.Va. U. Found., 1974, 78. Fellow IEEE (best paper award 1985, 88, 91); mem. Conf. Internat. des Grands Reseaux Electriques, Sigma Xi, Tau Beta Pi, Eta Kappa Nu. Democrat. Avocations: photography, tennis, table tennis. Home: 14520 183rd Ave NE Woodinville WA 98072-9377 Office: Univ Wash Dept Elec Engring Box 352500 Seattle WA 98195

VENNAT, MICHEL, lawyer; b. Sept. 17, 1941; m. Marie-Anne Tawil; children: Catherine, Charles-Alexandre, Frédéric, Michèle Anne, Philippe-Olivier. B.A. magna cum laude, Coll. Jean-de-Brébeuf, Montreal, Que., Can., 1960; LL.L., U. Montreal, 1963; M.A., Oxford U., Eng., 1965. Bar: Que. 1966, Paris 1995; apptd. Queen's Counsel 1983, Office of the Orderof Can., 1995. Fgn. affairs officer Dept. External Affairs, Ottawa, Ont., Can., 1965; spl. asst. to Min. Fin., 1966-68; spl. asst. to Hon. Pierre E. Trudeau, Prime Min. of Can., 1968-70, spl. counsel, 1977; chmn. Can. Film Devel. Corp., Montreal, 1976-81; sr. ptnr. Stikeman, Elliott, Montreal, 1970-90; pres. Dumez Investments Inc., 1986-87, Westburne Internat. Industries Ltd., 1987; vice chmn. United Westburne Inc., 1990, vice chmn., CEO, 1991-93, chmn., CEO, 1993-94, also bd. dirs.; pres. Bastos du Canada Limitée, 1987—, also bd. dirs.; ptnr. Stikeman Elliot, Montreal, 1994—; lectr. in constl. law U. Montreal, 1970; bd. dirs. Nat. Bank of Greece (Can.), Meloche-Monnex Inc.; Hewlett-Packard (Can.) Ltd., Acklands Ltd., NAV Can.; pres. bd. Maxi-Krisp Can., Inc. Rhodes scholar, 1963-65. Mem. Barreau du Que., Barreau du Paris, Can. C. of C., French C. of C. (Can. bd. dirs.), Montreal Badminton and Squash Club, Mt. Bruno Country Club, Hillside Tennis Club, Mt. Royal Club, Hermitage Club. Avocations: squash, golf, tennis, skiing. Home: 22 Claude Champagne, Outremont, PQ Canada H2V 2X1 Office: Stikeman Elliott, 1155 René-Lévesque Blvd W, Montreal, PQ Canada H3B 3V2

VENNING, ROBERT STANLEY, lawyer; b. Boise, Idaho, July 24, 1943; s. William Lucas and Corey Elizabeth (Brown) V.; m. Sandra Macdonald, May 9, 1966 (div. 1976); 1 child, Rachel Elizabeth; m. Laura Siegel, Mar. 24, 1979; 1 child, Daniel Rockhill Siegel. AB, Harvard U., 1965; MA, U. Chgo., 1966; LLB, Yale U., 1970. Bar: Calif., U.S. Dist. Ct. (no. dist.) Calif., 1971, U.S. Dist. Ct. (cen. dist.) Calif. 1973, U.S. Ct. Appeals (9th cir.) 1977, U.S. Supreme Ct. 1977, U.S. Ct. Appeals (fed. cir.) 1986, U.S. Ct. Appeals (D.C. cir.) 1987. Assoc. Heller, Ehrman, White & McAuliffe, San Francisco, 1970-73, 73-76, ptnr., 1977—, mem. exec. com., 1991-94; vis. lectr. U. Wash., Seattle, 1973, Boalt Hall Sch. Law, U. Calif., Berkeley, 1982-85, 89, Sch. Bus., Stanford U., 1986-87. Editor Yale Law Jour., 1969-70. Early neutral evaluator U.S. Dist. Ct. (no. dist.) Calif., 1987—; mem. Natural Resources Def. Coun. Fellow Am. Bar Found.; mem. ABA, Am. Arbitration Assn. (mem. panel arbitrator), San Francisco Bar Assn. (past chair judiciary com.). Office: Heller White & McAuliffe 333 Bush St San Francisco CA 94104-2806

VENTO, BRUCE FRANK, congressman; b. St. Paul, Oct. 7, 1940; s. Frank A. and Ann (Sauer) V.; children: Michael, Peter, John. AA, U. Minn., 1961; BS, Wis. State U., River Falls, 1965. Tchr. sci., social studies Mpls. Pub. Schs.; mem. Minn. Ho. of Reps., 1971—; asst. majority leader 95th-103rd Congresses from 4th Minn. Dist., 1974-76; chmn. Ramsey County del., gen. legis. and vet. affairs com.; vice-chmn. jud. com.; chmn. natural resources subcom. on nat. parks, forests and pub. lands, 1985-94; mem. resource com. and subcoms; mem. banking and fin. svcs. com., ranking mem. subcom. on fin. instns. and consumer credit; mem. housing and devel. subcom.; chmn. speaker's task force on homelessness 103d Congress. Mem. legis. rev. com. Minn. Commn. on Future Del.; Democratic Farmer Labor party Central com., 1972; chmn. Ramsey County com., 1972. Recipient numerous awards including Ansel Adams award Wilderness Soc.; NSF scholar, 1966-70. Mem. Minn. Fedn. Tchrs., Beta Beta Beta, Kappa Delta Phi. Office: US House of Reps 2304 Rayburn Bldg Washington DC 20515-0005

VENTRE, FRANCIS THOMAS, environmental design and policy educator; b. Old Forge, Pa., Sept. 16, 1937; s. Thomas Anthony and Theresa Mary (Grippi) V.; m. Mary Alice Tibbals, Apr. 4, 1964; children—Antonina Alma, Emily Lucrezia. B.Arch., Pa. State U., 1961; M.C.P., U. Calif., Berkeley, 1966; Ph.D., M.I.T., 1973. City planner Louisville and Jefferson County (Ky.) Planning Commn., 1962-64; asst. prof. arch. and urban planning UCLA, 1966-68; research assoc. MIT-Harvard Joint Center Urban Studies, Cambridge, 1970-73; chief environ. design research div. Nat. Bur. Standards, Washington, 1973-83; prof. environ. design and policy, dir. Ctr. for Building Econs. and Industry Studies Va. Poly. Inst., Blacksburg, 1983-90, dir. Environ Systems Lab., 1983-87; prin. BuildingMeasure, cons. firm; mem. faculty U.Md., UCLA.; faculty mem. Va. Polytech. State U., 1983-93; faculty emeritus; mem. com. tech. advanced bldg. NAS, Nat. Acad. Engring., NRC, 1985-87; elected Consultative Coun. Nat. Inst. Bldg. Scis.; mem. Info. Com. co-founder, past assoc. editor, editorial adv. bd. Environ. and Behavior; mem. editorial bd. Jour. Archtl. and Planning Rsch., 1989-90; contbr. articles to profl. jours., chpts. to books. Mem. indsl. and profl. adv. coun. Pa. State Coll. Engring., 1979-84; del. State, Montgomery County, Va. Dem. Conv., 1989; libr. reader Nat. Gallery Art, 1989. With AUS, 1961-62. Mellon fellow in city planning, 1964-66; recipient award Pa. Soc. Architects, 1961; Stern Family Fund grantee, 1969; Catherine Bauer Wurster fellow, 1971-72; Nat. Endowment Arts grantee, 1984; NSF grantee, 1985, 87, Urban Land Inst. grantee, 1987. Mem. AIA (assoc.), Am. Inst. Cert. Planners, Am. Planning Assn., Environ. Design Rsch. Assn., ASTM, Internat. Facilities Mgmt. Assn., Archtl. Rsch. Ctrs. Consortium (founding sec., mem. panel on bldg. econs. and industry studies, 1984-90), AAUP (pres. Va. Poly. Inst. chpt.), Intelligent Bldgs. Inst. Found. (apptd. trustee), Va. Poly. Inst. Faculty Senate and Senate Cabinet, Montgomery County Stroke Club. Home: 4007 Rickover Rd Silver Spring MD 20902-2330

VENTURA, MANUEL MATEUS, biochemist, educator; b. Fortaleza, Brazil, June 17, 1921; s. Antonio Rodrigues and Maria Raymunda (Lima) V.; m. Aglaeda Facó; children: Rita-Maria, Sandro, Manuel, Maria Monica. BSc, Agrl. Sch. Ceara, Fortaleza, 1943. Asst. prof. Agrl. Sch. Ceara, Fortaleza, 1945-48, prof., 1949-68; prof. Inst. of Chemistry of Fed. U. Ceara, Fortaleza, 1969-75; prof. biochemistry Inst. Biology, U. Brasilia, Brazil, 1975-91, prof. emeritus, 1992—; dir. Inst. Chemistry of Fed. U. Ceara, 1958-68. Contbr. articles to profl. jours. Recipient Anisio Teizeira prize Ministry of Edn., Brazil, 1981, Sci. Merit medal Fed. U. Ceara, 1988, Nat. Scientific Merit Order Ministry of Sci. and Tech., 1995. Mem. Brazilian Acad. Sci., N.Y. Acad. Sci., Protein Soc. Avocations: classical music, photography. Home: SQN 107 BL H Apto 504, 70743 Brasilia Brazil Office: U Brasilia Lab Biofisica-CEL-IB, Campus Universitario, 70910 Brasilia Brazil

VENTURA, ROBIN MARK, professional baseball player; b. Santa Maria, Calif., July 14, 1967. Student, Oklahoma State U. Mem. U.S. Olympic Baseball Team, Seoul, South Korea, 1988; with Chgo. White Sox, 1988—. Recipient Golden Glove award, 1991-93, Golden Spikes award USA Baseball, 1988; named Sporting News Coll. Player of Yr., 1987-88, Third Basemen Sporting News All-Am. team, 1987-88; named to Am. League All-Star team, 1992. Office: Chgo White Sox 333 W 35th St Chicago IL 60616-3621*

VENTURI, ROBERT, architect; b. Phila., June 25, 1925; s. Robert C. and Vanna (Lanzetta) V.; m. Denise (Lakofski) Scott Brown, July 23, 1967; 1 child, James Charles. Grad., Episcopal Acad., 1943; A.B. summa cum laude, Princeton U., 1947, M.F.A., 1950, D.F.A. (hon.), 1983; D.F.A. (hon.), Oberlin Coll., 1977, Yale U., 1979, U. Pa., 1980, Phila. Coll. Art, 1985; LHD (hon.), N.J. Inst. Tech., 1984; Laurea Honoris Causa in Architecture, U. Rome "La Sapienza", 1994. Designer firms of Oskar Stonorov, Eero Saarinen and Assos., Louis I. Kahn, 1950-58; partner firm Venturi, Cope & Lippincott, Phila., 1958-61, Venturi and Short, Phila., 1961-64, Venturi and Rauch, Phila., 1964-80; ptnr. firm Venturi, Rauch & Scott Brown, Phila., 1980-89, Venturi, Scott, Brown and Assocs., Inc., 1989—; from asst. to assoc. prof. architecture U. Pa., 1957-65; Charlotte Shepherd Davenport prof. architecture Yale, 1966-70. Author: Complexity and Contradiction in Architecture, 1966, 2d edit., 1977, (with Denise Scott Brown and Steven Izenour) Learning from Las Vegas, 1972, 2d edit., 1977, (with Denise Scott Brown) A View from the Campidoglio, Selected Essays, 1953-84, Iconography and Electronics upon a Generic Architecture, 1996, others, also articles; prin. works include Vanna Venturi House, Phila., 1961, Guild House, Phila., 1961, Humanities Bldg., SUNY, 1972, Franklin Ct., Phila., 1972, addition to Allen Meml. Art Mus., Oberlin Coll., 1973, Inst. for Sci. Info. Corp. Hdqrts., Phila., 1978, Gordon Wu Hall, Princeton U., 1980, Seattle Art Mus., 1984, The Nat. Gallery, Sainsbury Wing, London, 1986, Fisher and Bendheim Halls, Princeton U., 1986, Gordon and Virginia MacDonald Med. Rsch. Labs. (with Payette Assocs.), UCLA, 1986, Charles P. Stevenson Jr. Libr., Bard Coll., 1989, Regional Govt. Bldg., Toulouse, France, 1992, Kirifuri Resort Facilities, Nikko, Japan, 1992. Trustee Am. Acad. Rome, 1966-71. Recipient Nat. Medal of Arts, 1992, Pritzker Architecture prize, 1991, Benjamin Franklin medal The Royal Soc. for Encouragement of Arts, Mfrs. and Commerce, 1993; Rome Prize fellow Am. Acad. in Rome, 1954-56. Fellow AIA (awards 1974, 77, 78), Am. Acad. in Rome, Am. Acad. of Arts and Letters, Am. Acad. Arts and Scis., Royal Inst. of Brit. Architects (hon.), Royal Incorp. Architects of Scotland (hon.), Accademia Nazionale di San Luca; mem. Phi Beta Kappa. Office: 4236 Main St Philadelphia PA 19127-1603

VENZA, JAC, broadcast executive, cultural and arts program administrator; b. Chgo., Dec. 23, 1926. Student, Goodman Sch. Theater and Design, Chgo. Producer, assoc. producer, designer, CBS, N.Y.C., 1950-64, exec. producer, NET Playhouse (Peabody award 1968, Emmy award 1969), for cultural programs, NET, N.Y.C., 1964-69 (recipient Prix D'Italia 1966), for drama, 1969-73; dir.: Performance Programs, PBS WNET/13, N.Y.C., 1981; exec. producer: Dance In America, Nureyev and the Joffrey Ballet in Tribute to Nijinsky (Emmy award nomination), Adams Chronicles (Emmy award nomination 1976, Peabody award 1977), WNET's Great Performances; series including Dance in America (Emmy awards 1979, 87), Theater in America (Peabody award 1974), Fine Music (Emmy award 1975); spls. (TV Critics Circle awards 1976-77), Fred Astaire: Change Partners and Dance, 1980; organizer, dir., Mus. Modern Art's TV USA-13 season, 1976; condr.: workshop Creating Dramas for TV, Tarrytown, N.Y., 1976; exec. producer: Am. Masters, Broadway's Dreamers (Emmy award). Recipient Emmy award for opera Nixon in China, 1988, Capezio award, 1987. Mem. Nat. Acad. TV Arts and Scis. Office: Sta WNET-TV 356 W 58th St New York NY 10019-1804

VENZKE, RAY FRANK, psychotherapist; b. Wood County, Wis., Sept. 7, 1933; s. Herman A. and Christina (Sojka) V.; m. Dawn Woltman, June 14, 1953 (div. Feb. 1972); 1 child, Diane W. Doersch; m. Joy Leadbetter, June 21, 1972 (div. Nov. 1985); m. DeMaris Hafner Unruh, May 31, 1986. BA in Ednl. Psychology, Wartburg Coll., 1955; MDiv, Trinity Sem., Columbus, Ohio, 1959; MA in Psychology, U. N.D., 1974. Lic. clin. profl. counselor, Mont. Pastor Bearlake Luth. Parish, Twin Lakes, Minn., 1959-63; missionary Thailand Luth. Mission, 1963-64; pastor First Luth. Parish, Washburn, N.D., 1965-67; addiction counselor Heartview Found., Mandan, N.D., 1971-74; therapist, program evaluator Badlands Human Svc. Ctr., Dickinson, N.D., 1975-85; psychotherapist Dickinson, N.D., 1985-87, Chrysalis Counseling Svcs., Helena, Mont., 1988—; cons. Lewis and Clark County Law Enforcement Chaplains, Helena, 1988-95. Narrator Mont. Libr. for the Blind, Helena, 1990—; chair task force CISM Mont. Dept. Disaster, 1994—; mem. Mont. Gov.'s Task Force on Mental Health Medicaid, Helena, 1993—. Mem. Am. Counselors Assn., Am. Mental Health Counselors, Mont. Clin. Mental Health Counselors (treas. 1992-94), Mont. Counselors Assn., Lions (Dist. Gov. 5NW award 1983), Am. Philatelic Soc. Avocations: stamp collecting, reading, photography. Home: 2019 Missoula Ave Helena MT 59601-3245 Office: Chrysalis Counseling Svc Apt 201 3117 Cooney Dr Helena MT 59601-0200

VÉR, ISTVÁN LÁSZLÓ, noise control consultant; b. Tápiószecsö, Hungary, Dec. 22, 1934; came to U.S., 1965; s. István and Erzsebet G. (Darázs) V.; m. Elisabeth H. Waltering, Dec. 6, 1961; 1 child, Kristina M. BSEE, Tech. U., Budapest, 1956; MSEE, Tech. U., Aachen, Germany, 1960; PhD in Acoustics, Tech. U., Munich, 1963. R&d engr. Rohde and Schwarz, Munich, 1960-65; prin. cons. Bolt Beranek & Newman Inc., Cambridge, Mass., 1965—. Author, editor: Noise & Vibration Engineering, 1992; holder patents. Recipient U.S. Sr. Scientist award Alexander von Humboldt Found., Germany, 1978, Best Paper award Am. Soc. Heating and Refrigeration Engring., 1979. Fellow Acoustical Soc. Am.; mem. Inst. Noise Control Engring. USA (dir. 1976-77), German Acoustical Soc. Avocations: literature, philosophy, travel, tennis. Office: Bolt Beranek and Newman Inc 10 Moulton St Cambridge MA 02138-1119

VERANO, ANTHONY FRANK, retired banker; b. West Harrison, N.Y., Jan. 4, 1931; s. Frank and Rose (Viscome) V.; m. Clara Cosentino, July 8, 1951; children—Rosemarie, Diana Lynn. Student, Am. Inst. Banking, 1956-60, Bank Adminstrn. Inst., U. Wis., 1962-64, RCA Programmers Sch., 1965, Burroughs Programmers Sch., 1965, N.J. Bankers Data Processing Sch., 1966-68, others. With County Trust Co., White Plains, N.Y., 1949-61; sr. auditor County Trust Co., 1960-61; with State Nat. Bank Conn., Bridgeport, 1961—; auditor State Nat. Bank Conn., 1962-79, exec. auditor, 1979—; exec. auditor Conn. Bank & Trust Co., 1983—; v.p., auditor Gateway Bank, Newtown, Conn., 1987, first v.p., auditor, 1988-94, sr. v.p., auditor, 1989-94, ret., 1994; tchr. bank auditing Am. Inst. Banking, 1976-78. Mem. adv. bd. Norwalk Community Coll., 1968—. Served with USN, 1951-52. Mem. Bank Adminstrn. Inst. (dir. Stamford chpt. 1967-68, sec. Western Conn. chpt. 1968-69, treas. 1969-70, v.p. 1970-71, pres. 1971-72), Am. Acctg. Assn., Inst. Internal Auditors (cert. bank auditor, cert. bank compliance officer). Home: 59 Bug Hill Rd Monroe CT 06468 *It is difficult to define the elements of success. There are those who say success is achieved through drive and ambition only. However, those who have achieved their goals in life using only these two principles have probably destroyed more than they have created. Success, I feel, is achieved when drive and ambition are tempered with honesty, fairness, and respect for others. An individual must have a sense of dedication not only to his work and for those with whom he works but, most importantly, for those who work for him. This has been my philosophy in achieving my success.*

VERBA, SIDNEY, political scientist, educator; b. Bklyn., May 26, 1932; s. Morris Harold and Recci (Salman) V.; m. E. Cynthia Winston, June 17, 1955; children—Margaret Lynn, Ericka Kim, Martina Claire. B.A., Harvard U., 1953; M.A., Princeton U., 1955, Ph.D., 1959. Asst. prof. polit. sci. Princeton U., 1960-63, asso. prof., 1963-64; prof. Stanford U., 1964-68, U. Chgo., 1968-72; prof. govt. Harvard U., 1972—, now Carl H. Pforzheimer prof., dir. univ. library, chmn. dept. govt., 1976-80, asso. dean Faculty Arts and Scis., 1981—; dir. Harvard U. Library; chmn. bd. dirs. Harvard U. Press, 1991—; chmn. policy com. Social Sci. Rsch. Coun., 1980-86; mem. Commn. on Behavioral and Social Scis., NRC, 1986-91; Commn. on Preservation and Access, chair com. on internat. conflict and cooperation, NRC, 1991-93; vis. com. MIT Polit. Sci. Dept., Stanford U. Libr. Author: Small Groups and Political Behavior, 1961, The Civic Culture, 1963, Caste, Race and Politics, 1969, Participation in America, 1972, Vietnam and the Silent Majority, 1972, The Changing American Voter, 1976, Participation and Political Equality, 1978, Injury to Insult, 1979, Introduction to American Government, 1983, Equality in America, 1985, Elites and the Idea of Equality, 1987, Designing Social Inquiry, 1994, Voice and Equality, 1995. Guggenheim fellow, 1980-81. Fellow Am. Acad. Arts and Scis.; mem. NAS, Am. Polit. Sci. Assn. (exec. coun. 1971-74, v.p. 1979-81, pres.-elect 1993-94, pres. 1994-95, Gladys Kammerer award 1972, Woodrow Wilson Found. award 1976, James Madison award 1993), Internat. Studies Assn. (v.p. 1971-72). Jewish. Home: 142 Summit Ave Brookline MA 02146-2358 Office: Harvard U Harvard Univ Library Director Cambridge MA 02138

VERBEELEN, DIERIK LEO, internist, researcher; b. Brugge, Belgium, Mar. 7, 1947; m. Anne Marie Claes, Oct. 26, 1976; children: Hendrik, Pieter. MD, Vrije Univ., Brussels, 1973, PhD, 1989. Cert. of specialist internal medicine. Tng. internal medicine and nephrology Brugmann Hosp., Brussels and Tenon Hosp., Paris, 1973-78; asst. prof. Vrije U., 1979-89; dir. divsn. nephrology Academisch Ziekenhuis, Brussels, 1989—; prof. medicine Vrije Univ., Brussels, 1989—; exec. bd. mem. Academisch Ziekenhuis, Brussels, 1987-94. Mem. Internat. Soc. Nephrology, Belgian Soc. Internal Medicine (sec.-treas.). Office: AZ-VUB Nephrology, Laarbeeklaan 101, B1090 Brussels Belgium

VERBEKE, FRANK GIRARD, JR., mechanical engineer; b. Detroit, Dec. 11, 1934; s. Frank Girard and Elizabeth Aurelia (Winter) V.; children: Kerri Lynn, Frank Girard III. BSME, U. Mich., 1958. Registered profl. engr., Calif. Devel. engr. Continental Aviation and Engring., Detroit, 1958-59, Curtiss Wright Corp., Santa Barbara, Calif., 1959-60; devel. engr. Solar divsn. Internat. Harvester Co., San Diego, 1960-68; v.p. King-Knight Co., Emeryville, Calif., 1968-70; pres. Alturdyne, Inc., Altur-Service, Altuair, Verbeke & Assocs., Engring. Reps. Co., San Diego, 1970—. Mem. ASME, IEEE, ASHRE, NSPE, Soc. Automotive Engrs., Exptl. Aircraft Assn., San Diego C. of C., Mission Bay Yacht Club. Republican. Episcopalian. Office: 8050 Armour St San Diego CA 92111-3720

VERBEKE, KAREN ANN, education educator; b. Clearfield, Pa., Mar. 31, 1948; d. Maurice George and Evelyn (Czarnecki) V. BA, Pa. State U., 1970; MEd, U. Md., 1971; postgrad., U. Colo., 1974; PhD, U. Md., 1982. Cert. elem. edn., spl. edn. Tchr. emotionally handicapped Dade County Pub. Schs., Miami, Fla., 1971-72; tchr. learning disabled, gifted, math. Howard County Pub. Schs., Ellicott City, Md., 1972-82; faculty rsch. assoc. U. Md., College Park, 1982-85; asst. prof. Beaver Coll., Glenside, Pa., 1985-90; assoc. prof., coord. of spl. edn., dept. edn. assoc. prof. dept. edn. and coord. spl. edn., Princess Anne, 1990—; faculty fellow Beaver Coll., Glenside, Pa., 1988-89; adj. instr. Va. Commonwealth U., Richmond, 1979-80; instr. The Cath. U. Am., Washington, 1983; lectr. Howard U., Washington, 1984-85; hearing officer Dept. Spl. Edn., Md. State Dept. Edn., Balt., 1983—; apptd. mem. Md. State Adv. Com. on Spl. Edn., 1994—; bd. dirs. Odyssey of the Mind, Inc., Glassboro, N.J., scholarship chmn., 1988-91. Editor: Md. Coun. for Tchrs. of Math. Jour., 1982-84; contbr. articles to profl. jours. Mem. appointed Md. state (adv. com. on spl. edn. 1994, task force on gifted edn. 1994-95, awarded Regional Staff Devel. Ctr. for Gifted/Talented grant Dept. of Edn. and Nat. Security Agency). Recipient Lindback award for Disting. Teaching, Christian and Mary Lindback Found., Beaver Coll., 1987, Sam Kirk Educator of Yr. in Learning Disabilities award, 1994-95, Pres.'s Tchr.-Scholar award UMES, 1994, Beaver Coll. Phi Delta Kappa Educator of the Yr., 1994; Retraining Tchrs. grantee Pa. Dept. Edn., Harrisburg, 1989; Md. Higher Edn Commn. grantee, 1991-92, Md. Dept. Edn./Nat. Security Agy. grantee for Regional Staff Devel. Ctr. for Gifted/Talented; Policy fellow Inst. Ednl. Leadership George Washington U., 1977-78; Eisenhower grantee. Mem. Rsch. Coun. for Diagnostic and Prescriptive Math. (mem. coord. 1987-93), Pa. Fedn. Coun. for Exceptional Children (pres. tchr. edn. divsn. 1988-90), Pa. State U. Alumni Assn., U. Md. Alumni Assn., Zonta Internat., Phila. Club (svc. chmn. 1988-90, v.p. 1990), Phi Delta Kappa (v.p. programs 1994-95, v.p. membership 1995—), Kappa Delta Pi (convocation com.). Home: 419 Rolling Rd Salisbury MD 21801-7114

VERBRIDGE, GERALD, religious organization administrator. Pres. Bd. of Dir. of the Reformed Church in America, N.Y.C. Office: Reformed Church in Am 475 Riverside Dr Ste 1811 New York NY 10115-0122

VERBURG, EDWIN ARNOLD, federal agency administrator; b. Lakehurst, N.J., Oct. 6, 1945; s. Edwin Donald Verburg and Dorothy (Orrell) Hoodless; m. Joyce Elaine Majack, Sept. 14, 1968; children: Adelle Kristine, Wendi Elizabeth. BS, Calif. Polytech. U., 1968; M in City Planning, U. Calif., Berkeley, 1970; D in Pub. Adminstrn., George Washington U., 1975. Asst. planner City of Inglewood (Calif.), 1970-71; planner City of Glendale (Calif.), 1971-72; grad. assoc. U.S. Army Corps Engrs., Washington, 1974-75; mgr. fiscal analysis Met. Washington Council Govts., 1975-77; sr. program analyst U.S. Fish and Wildlife Service, Washington, 1977-79, asst. div. chief, 1979-80, div. chief, 1980-82, asst. dir. planning and budget, 1982-86, dep. asst. dir. policy budget and adminstrn., 1986-87; dir. office of fin. U.S. Dept. Treas., Washington, 1987-88, dir. fin. svcs. directorate, 1988-91, dir. fin. svcs. directorate, dep. CFO, 1991-95; assoc. adminstr. adminstrn. FAA, 1995—. Author: Local State and Federal Fiscal Flows, 5 Vols., 1976; contbr. articles to fed. jours. Recipient Disting. Pub. Svc. award George Washington U., Sch. Bus. and Pub. Mgmt., 1994, Sec. of Treasury Disting Svc. award, 1995. Mem. Am. Inst. Cert. Planners, Am. Planning Assn. (cert. govt. fin. mgr., Merit award Calif. chpt. 1973, First award Nat. Capital area chpt. 1980, Peer award for pub. svc. Dept. of Treasury 1990, sec. of treas. cert. appreciation 1991, Pres.'s Meritorious Svc. award 1991). Home: 538 N Oakland St Arlington VA 22203-2219

VERBURG, KENNETH, political scientist, educator, writer; b. Feb. 13, 1933; s. Cornelius and Lucy VerB.; m. Esther Marie VerBurg, June 30, 1955; children: Kenneth M., Marilou, Craig Alan, Rachel Sue, Jeffrey R.C. AB in Pre-law, Calvin Coll., 1957; MA in Polit. Sci., Mich. State U., 1960. Asst. instr. inst. community devel. Mich. State U., East Lansing, 1957-59, community devel. specialist inst. community devel., 1959-60, from asst. to assoc. prof. inst. community devel., 1969-78, prof., 1978-83, prof. community devel. programs, 1985-90, prof. dept. resource devel., 1990—, acting assoc. dean lifelong edn. programs, 1983-85; exec. asst. Durabilt Homes Mfg., Inc., Kalamazoo, Mich., 1960-61; bus. mgr. Grand Valley State Coll., Allendale, Mich., 1961-67; supr. fiscal sect. bur. higher edn. Mich. Dept. Edn., 1967-69; com. counsel Senate labor com. Mich. State Senate, 1958-59; cons. Mich. Legislature, Mich. Mcpl. League, Mich. Twp. Assn., Mich. Assn. Counties, others. Author: (with others) Michigan Political Atlas, 1984, Guide To Michigan County Government, 2d edit., 1987, (with Gordon Thomas) Conducting Public Meetings, 2d edit., 1987, (with Charles Press) American Politicians and Journalists, 1988, (with William P. Browne) The Government and Politics of Michigan, 1991, numerous others. Chair, mem. Mich. State Boundary Commn., 1991—; v.p. River Ter. Christian Reformed Ch., 1992-94. Recipient Outstanding Contbn. award Mich. Twps. Assn., 1984, Spl. Recognition award United County Officers Assn., 1987, Spl. Appreciation award Mich. Assn. Assessors, 1988, Award for Innovation, Nat. Univ. Continuing Edn. Assn. and Am. Testing Svc., 1988. Office: Mich State U Dept Resource Devel 312A Natural Resources Bldg East Lansing MI 48824-1222

VERCAUTEREN, RICHARD FRANK, career officer; b. Manchester, N.H., Feb. 9, 1945; s. Louis P. and Janet (Beliveau) V.; m. Gail Anne Settoon, June 3, 1972. BA in Sociology, Providence Coll., 1967; MA in Bus. Mgmt., George Washington U., 1980; MA in Internat. Studies, Georgetown U., 1996. Commd. 2d lt. USMC, 1967, advanced through grades to brig. gen., 1993; platoon comdr. 2d bn., 9th Marines, Vietnam, 1968; comdg. officer Rifle Co., Hawaii, 1971-73; mil. observer UN, Egypt, Israel, Lebanon, 1976-78; comdg. officer Spl. Task Force, S.Am., 1982; aide de camp Marine Forces Atlanic, Norfolk, Va., 1982-84; bn. comdr. 3d bn., 2nd Marines, Camp Lejeune, N.C., 1985-87; regional comdr. Embassy Guards SubSahara Africa, Nairobi, Africa, 1987-90; dep. dir. plans Hdqs., USMC, Washington, 1990-92, dir. plans, 1990-92; comdg. officer 2nd Marine Regiment, Camp Lejeune, 1992-93; comdg. gen. 1st Marine Exped Brigade, Honolulu, 1993-95. Mem. exec. bd. Capitol dist. Boy Scouts Am., Washington, 1991-92; sr. counselor Seminar XXII, MIT, Washington, 1995-96. Decorated Silver Star medal, Legion of Merit; recipient Holland M. Smith award Navy League, 1982; MIT Ctr. Internat. Tech. Studies fellow in fgn. politics, 1991, fellow in nat. security studies Harvard U., 1995. Mem. Army-Navy Club (Washington), Muthaiga Club (Nairobi). Avocations: running, golfing, skiing, history, travel. Office: USMC Hdqs Office Dir Plans Washington DC 22001

VERCELLOTTI, JOHN RAYMOND, research chemist; b. Joliet, Ill., May 2, 1933; s. Joseph Francis and Mary Teresa (Walowski) V.; m. Sharon Cecile Vergez, Sept. 3, 1966; children: Ellen Theresa, Paul Auguste. BA, St. Bonaventure U., 1955; MS, Marquette U., 1960; PhD, Ohio State U., 1963. Lectr., rsch. assoc. Ohio State U., Columbus, 1963-64; asst. prof. Marquette U., Milw., 1964-67; assoc. prof. U. Tenn., Knoxville, 1967-70; prof. Va. Poly. Inst. & State U., Blacksburg, 1970-79; vis. prof. Inst. G. Ronzoni, Milan, Italy, 1977-78; sr. scientist Gulf South Res. Inst., New Orleans, 1980-85; rsch. chemist, rsch. leader so. regional rsch. ctr. USDA, New Orleans, 1985—; cons. chemist V-Labs Inc., Covington, La., 1980-85; adj. prof. food sci. La. State U., Baton Rouge, 1985—; adj. prof. chemistry and physics S.E. La. U., Hammond, 1986—. Contbr. over 160 articles to Elsevier & Am. Chem. Soc. Symposium Series; author, co-author numerous book chpts., 1960—; contbr. numerous articles to profl. jours. U. Tenn. minority colls. grantee, 1968-70, NSF grantee, 1964—. Mem. Am. Chem. Soc. (sec. 1968-90, Melville L. Wolfrom award 1994), Inst. Food Technologists; fellow Sigma Xi. Democrat. Roman Catholic. Achievements include research on food flavor quality and agricultural commodity utilization, origin of flavor from carbohydrates, lipid oxidation products, and peptides. Avocations: golfing, fishing, gardening, playing accordian. Home: 113 E 25th Ave Covington LA 70433 Office: USDA ARS So Regional Rsch Ctr 1100 Robert E Lee Blvd New Orleans LA 70124

VERDECCHIA, GUILLERMO LUIS, playwright; b. Buenos Aires, Dec. 7, 1962; arrived in Can., 1969.; m. Tamsin Kelsey; children: Anais Kelsey-Verdecchia, Theo Kelsey-Verdecchia. Author: (plays) Not Another Banana Republic, 1988, i.d., 1989 (Chalmers award Outstanding New Play 1990, Dora award Outstanding Prodn. 1990), Get Off the Stage, 1990, Final Decisions (WAR), 1991, (with Daniel Brooks) The Noam Chomsky Lectures, 1991 (Chalmers award Outstanding New Play 1992, Gov.-Gen.'s Literary award Shortlist), Fronteras Americanas, 1993 (Gov.-Gen.'s Literary award for drama 1993, Chalmers Can. Play award 1994), (with M. Youssef) A Line in the Sand, 1995; (screenplay) Crucero/Crossroads, 1993; (radio) Cancion en el Viento, Fronteras Americanas 1 & 2; (books) Fronteras Americanas, The Noam Chomsky Lectures, A Line in the Sand.

VERDEJA, SAM, newspaper publishing executive. V.p. cmty. rels./mktg. svcs., v.p. mktg. and promotions The Miami Herald, Fla. Office: The Miami Herald One Herald Plz Miami FL 33132-1693

VERDERBER, JOSEPH ANTHONY, capital equipment company executive; b. Cleve., Nov. 30, 1938; s. Joseph Arthur and Dorothy Louise (Buchta) V.; m. Anita Barto, Sept. 10, 1960; children: Joseph Anthony, Lisa C., Paul A. BS in Mech. Engring., MIT, 1960, MS in Mech. Engring., 1961. Registered profl. engr., Ohio. Mgr. rsch. AM Internat., Cleve., 1964-70; dir. engring. Varityper div., East Hanover, N.J., 1971-73, product mgr., 1973-77; v.p. advanced bus. devel. multigraphics div., Mt. Prospect, Ill., 1977-81, gen. mgr. imaging systems group, Bedford, Mass., Chgo., 1981, pres. Varityper div., East Hanover, N.J., 1982-88; corp. v.p. bus. devel. AM Internat., Inc., Chgo., 1988-89; pres. Am. Splty. Products, Dayton, Ohio, 1989-90; pres. Barco Graphics, Inc., Dayton, 1990; pres. Gen. Scanning, Laser Sys. Divsn., Somerville, Mass., 1991—; lectr. Cleve. State U., 1962-67. Recipient Karl Taylor Compton prize MIT, 1960; NSF fellow, 1961; named Inventor of Yr., AM Internat., Chgo., 1980. Mem. ASME, Nat. Printing Equipment and Supply Assn. (bd. dirs. 1986-88, chmn. SEMI New Eng. Forum 1994—). Office: TLSI 32 Cobble Hill Rd Somerville MA 02143-4412

VERDERY, DAVID NORWOOD, broadcast programming executive; b. Waco, Tex., Dec. 12, 1943; s. David Paul and Ruthe (McCawley) V.; m. Randy Lee Mahan, June 6, 1968 (div. 1970); 1 child, David Roderick. Student, Baylor U., 1961-64. Announcer KEFC, Waco, 1962-64; announcer, producer KHFI, Austin, Tex., 1964-65; announcer, prodn. dir. KIXL, Dallas, 1965-66; program dir. KVIL, Dallas, 1967, KABL, San Francisco, 1968-69; nat. program coord. The McLendon Co., Dallas, 1969-73; v.p. programming TM Programming, Dallas, 1973-80, Bonneville Broadcasting Sys., Northbrook, Ill., 1980-86; music dir. Bonneville Broadcasting Sys., Northbrook, 1985-95; asst. program dir., music dir. KBIG, L.A., 1995—. Mem. Project Angel Food, L.A., 1992-94; mem. Permanent Charities Com., L.A., 1995—. Named Adult Contemporary Music Dir. of Yr., The Gavin Report, 1992, 93. Avocations: gourmet cooking, theater, travel, musical composing and arranging. Office: KBIG Radio 7755 W Sunset Blvd Los Angeles CA 90046-3911

VERDI, DAVID JOSEPH, broadcast news executive; b. Newark, Apr. 4, 1956; s. Joseph Peter and Georgina Alice (Meing) V.; m. Bernadette Rubino, June 26, 1982; children: Andriana Rubino, David Rubino, Stephen Rubino. BA in Journalism, U. No. Colo., 1979. Desk asst. ABC News, N.Y.C., 1980-82, prodn. assoc. Nightline, 1982-84, assoc. prodr. World News Tonight, 1984-86; field prodr. ABC News, St. Louis, 1986-88; prodr. This Week with David Brinkley ABC News, Washington, 1988-90; exec. news dir. NBC News, N.Y.C., 1990—. Office: NBC News 30 Rockefeller Plz New York NY 10112

VERDI, ROBERT WILLIAM, sports columnist; b. Bklyn., Aug. 31, 1946. BA in English, Lake Forest Coll., Ill., 1967. Reporter L.I. Press, Queens, N.Y., summers 1964, 65; sports columnist Chgo. Tribune, 1967—. Named Sportswriter of Yr. for Ill., Nat. Sportscasters and Sportswriters Assn., 1975-78, 80-82, 84-87, 89-90. Mem. Baseball Writers Assn. Am., Football Writers Assn. Am., Golf Writers Assn.

VERDINE, GREGORY LAWRENCE, chemist, educator; b. Somers Point, N.J., June 10, 1959; s. Richard Daniel and Therese Mary (Delaney) V.; m. Kasumi Koseki, Dec. 1, 1987; children: Vanessa Kaori, Lauren Arika, Erika Rose. BS, St. Joseph's U., Phila., 1982; MA, Columbia U., 1983, PhD, 1986; AB (hon.), Harvard U., 1995. Postdoctoral fellow MIT, Cambridge, Mass., 1986, 87, Harvard Med. Sch., Boston, 1987, 8; asst. prof. chemistry Faculty Arts and Scis. Harvard U., Cambridge, 1988-92, Thomas D. Cabot assoc. prof. chemistry, 1992-94, prof., 1994—; mem. sci. adv. bd. Ariad Pharms., Cambridge, 1992—, La Jolla (Calif.) Pharms., 1990—; cons. Hoffmann-LaRoche, Nutley, N.J., 1991—. Assoc. editor Chemistry and Biology, 1994—; contbr. numerous articles to profl. jours. Recipient Excellence in Chemistry award Zeneca Pharms., 1994; DuPont Young Faculty fellow, 1988, Searle scholar, 1990, Eli Lilly grantee, 1990, Alfred P. Sloan fellow, 1991, NSF Presdl. Young Investigator award, 1991, others. Mem. AAAS, Am. Chem. Soc. (Arthur C. Cope Scholar award 1994). Achievements include research in chemical genetics: the propagation, preservation and expression of genetic information. Office: Harvard U Dept Chemistry 12 Oxford St Cambridge MA 02138-2902

VERDON, GWEN (GWYNETH EVELYN), actress, dancer, choreographer; b. L.A., Jan. 13, 1925; d. Joseph William and Gertrude (Standring) V.; m. James Henaghan, 1942 (div. June 1947); children: James O'Farrell; m. Robert Louis Fosse, Apr. 3, 1960; 1 child, Nicole. Ed. pub. schs., studied dance with E. Belcher, Carmelita Marrachi, Jack Cole. Bd. dirs. Postgrad. Center for Mental Health. Broadway debut in Alive and Kicking, 1950; appeared in musical plays including: Can Can (Tony award 1954), 1953-54, Damn Yankees (Tony award 1956), 1955-56, New Girl in Town (Tony award 1958), 1957, Red Head (Tony award 1959), 1959, Sweet Charity, 1966, (starring role) Chicago, 1975; staged 2d co.: musical Dancin; also acted as dance mistress; appeared in play Love Letters, L.A., 1990; motion pictures: On The Riviera, 1951, Meet Me After the Show, 1951, David and Bathsheba, 1952, Mississippi Gambler, 1953, Damn Yankees, 1958, Cotton Club, 1984, Cocoon, 1986, Nadine, 1987, Cocoon II, 1988, Alice, 1990; TV series appearances include: MASH, Fame, All is Forgiven, Trapper John M.D., The Equalizer, Magnum P.I. (Emmy award nominee), Webster, Dear John, HBO's Dream On (Emmy award nominee), Homicide (Emmy award nominee). Recipient Donaldson award for acting and dancing, Lambs Gambol award for acting, Grammy award, 1959, Silver Bowl award Dance Mag., 1961. Office: care Shapiro & Lobel 111 W 40th St New York NY 10018-2506

VERDON, JANE KATHRYN, lawyer; b. Manchester, N.C., 1943. BA, Newton Coll., 1964; JD, U. San Diego, 1991. Bar: N.C. 1992. Legal intern San Diego City Atty. - Criminal Divsn., 1991; law clk. criminal def. Cheshire, Parker, Hughes and Manning, Raleigh, N.C., 1991-92; pvt. practice Raleigh, 1992—; creative dir., corp. v.p., ptnr. Internat. Creative Sys.; account exec., publicity dir., TV spokesperson H. Richard Silver, Inc.; fashion, beauty editor, spokesperson for major consumer mags., newspapers, TV; cons. new product devel., advt. and promotion in all areas of health, beauty and fashion. Assoc. fashion editor, assoc. managing editor Seventeen Mag.; fashion dir. Woman's World Mag.; contbg. editor, writer for newspapers and consumer mags.; all-media program designer, newspaper, radio and TV features, brochures, scripts, promotional programs, mediation, negotiations; TV and comml. appearances. Mem. AFTRA, ABA, Am. Trial Lawyers Assn., N.C. Bar Assn., N.C. Trial Lawyers Assn., N.J. Foster Parents' Assn., Lawyers' Club, Phi Alpha Delta. Office: 514 Daniels St # 151 Raleigh NC 27605

VERDOORN, SID, food service executive; b. Albert Lea, Minn., Feb. 11, 1939; s. Cornelius Emery and Gwen (Pickell) V.; m. Carol Joyce Hoekstra, July 3, 1959; children: Jay Richard, Jeffrey Lee, James Dale. Student, Cen. Coll., Pella, Iowa. With sales C.H. Robinson Co., Mpls., 1963-66; mgr. C.H. Robinson Co., San Francisco, 1966-71; pers. dir. C.H. Robinson Co., Mpls., 1971-75, v.p., 1975-77, pres., chief exec. officer, 1977—; bd. dirs. Produce Mktg. Assocs., Newark, United Fruit and Produce, Washington. With U.S. Army, 1959-61. Republican. Avocations: hiking, water sports. Home: 28210 Woodside Rd Excelsior MN 55331-7950 Office: C H Robinson Co Inc 8100 Mitchell Rd Ste 200 Eden Prairie MN 55344-2231*

VERDOORN, TODD A., medical educator; b. Dec. 12, 1960. BA in Chemistry, Cen. Coll., Pella, Iowa, 1983; PhD in Neurobiology, U. N.C., 1988. Rsch. asst. Nat. Inst. Environ. Health Scis., Research Triangle Park, N.C., 1984; postdoctoral fellow Max-Planck-Inst., Heidelberg, Germany, 1988-91; asst. prof. dept. pharmacology Vanderbilt U., Nashville, 1991—; presented seminars in field; cons. NIMH, 1994, NIH, 1995, others. Editl. bd.: Molecular Pharmacology, 1995-97, Jour. Biol. Chemistry, 1996-98; contbr. articles to profl. jours. Recipient VerSteeg Sci. scholarship Cen. Coll., 1981-83, postdoctoral fellowships The Pharm. Mfrs. Assn. Found., 1987-88, Alexander von Humboldt Found., Bonn, Germany, 1988-90, The Max Planck Soc., Germany, 1990-91, others. Mem. N.Am. Soc. Neurosci. Office: 209 Lighthall Rd Nashville TN 37232

VERDORN, JERRY, actor; b. Sioux Falls, S.D.; married; children: Jacob, Peter. Student, Moorehead State U. Actor: (theatre) Black Elk Speaks, Are you Now or Have You Ever Been?, Man and Superman, The Star-Spangled Girl; (TV) Guiding Light, 1979—; (TV movie) The Cradle Will Fall, 1983. Recipient Best Supporting Actor Drama Series Daytime Emmy. Office: CBS Studio 222 E 44th St New York NY 10017*

VERDUIN, JACOB, botany educator; b. Orange City, Iowa, Nov. 19, 1913; s. Peter and Jennie (Lagestee) V.; m. Bethy Albertha Anderson, July 3, 1942; children: Lans, Jan, Charlotte (dec.), Leslie, Bethy. B.S., Iowa State Coll., 1939, M.S., 1941, Ph.D., 1947. Farmer, 1933-35; head botany dept. S.D. State U., 1946-48; asso. prof. hydrobiology F. T. Stone Lab., Ohio State U., 1948-54; head biology dept. Bowling Green State U., 1955-64; prof. botany So. Ill. U., Carbondale, 1964-84, prof. emeritus, 1984—; Cons. NIH, summer 1954; cons. water pollution control sect. TVA, summer 1957, Commonwealth Edison, 1972-86, EPA, 1975-79. Mem. editorial bd.: Ecology, 1954-57, Limnology and Oceanography, Ohio Jour. Sci, Trans. Am. Fisheries Soc. Served to ensign USNR, 1942-45. Fellow Ohio Acad. Sci. (exec. v.p. plant sci. sect. 1958), AAAS; mem. Am. Inst. Biol. Scis., Societas Internationalis Limnologiae, Ecol. Soc. Am., Am. Fisheries Soc., Am. Assn. Limnologists and Oceanographers, Sigma Xi, Phi Kappa Phi, Beta Beta Beta, Gamma Sigma Delta, Omicron Delta Kappa. Episcopalian. Home: 2999 Country Club Rd Carbondale IL 62901-7334 *As a scientist, I have always believed that objectivity and integrity were more important than prestige. As a teacher I have believed that understanding is the goal and memorization should never be a substitute for it. As a person I have believed that most misunderstandings result from inadequate communication.*

VERED, RUTH, art gallery director; b. Tel Aviv, Sept. 26, 1940; d. Abraham and Helen (Psisuska) Rosenblum; children: Sharon, Oren. BA in Art Hisotry with honors, Bezalel U., Jerusalem, 1964. Freelance art cons., Israel and N.Y.C., 1965-75; dir. Vered Gallery, East Hampton, N.Y., 1977—. Sgt. paratroops Israeli Army, 1958-60. Home: 891 Park Ave New York NY 10021-0326 Office: Vered Gallery East Hampton NY 11937

VER EECKE, WILFRIED CAMIEL, philosopher, educator; b. Tielt, Belgium, Aug. 22, 1938; came to U.S., 1966; s. Jerome and Maria (Declercq) Ver E.; license philosophy, Cath. U. Leuven (Belgium), 1962, PhD, 1966; postgrad. U. Freiburg, 1966, Harvard U., 1966-67; MA in Econs., Georgetown U., 1972; m. Josiane Berten, Sept. 4, 1967; children: Mieke, Stefaan, Renaat, Jan. H.S. tchr., Heule, Belgium, 1962-63, Kortrijk, 1963-65; NSF research fellow, Belgium, 1965-69; asst. prof. Georgetown U., Washington, 1967-72, assoc. prof., 1972-80, prof., 1980—, chmn. dept. philosophy, 1980-83. Alexander von Humboldt fellow, Ger., 1975-76, 78. Mem. Am. Philos. Assn., Am. Cath. Philos. Assn., Hegel Soc. Am., Soc. Phenomenology and Existential Philosophy, Public Choice, Washington Forum Psychiatry-Humanities. Roman Catholic. Author: Negativity and Subjectivity, 1977; translator: Schizophrenia (La psychose) (A. De Waelhens), 1978; Saying No, 1984; contbr. articles to profl. jours. Home: 4100 Nebraska Ave NW Washington DC 20016-2736 Office: Dept Philosophy Georgetown U Washington DC 20057

VEREEN, BEN, actor, singer, dancer; b. Miami, Fla., Oct. 10, 1946; m. Nancy Vereen; children: Benjamin, Malakia, Naja, Kabara, Karon. Student, High Sch. of Performing Arts; LHD (hon.), Emerson Coll., 1977. Debut off-Broadway in The Prodigal Son, 1965; played Brother Ben in Sweet Charity, N.Y.C., Las Vegas, San Francisco, 1966, Daddy Brubeck in Can. tour, 1968, in Los Angeles co. of Hair, 1968, joined Broadway cast, 1969; played role of Judas in Jesus Christ Superstar, 1971 (Theatre World award); leading role in Pippin', 1972 (Tony award, Drama Desk award); appeared in Grind, 1985, Jelly's Last Jam, 1993; numerous theatrical appearances, including I'm Not Rappaport, San Francisco, 1989; appeared in TV movie Louis Armstrong-Chicago Style, 1976; created role of Chicken George in TV miniseries Roots, 1977 (TV Critics award); other TV miniseries include Ellis Island, 1984, A.D., 1985; appeared in TV spl. Ben Vereen-His Roots, 1978, Uptown-A Tribute to the Apollo Theatre; film appearances: Funny Lady, 1975, All That Jazz, 1979, Buy and Cell, 1989, Once Upon a Forrest, 1993 (voice only); TV series include: Tenspeed and Brown Shoe, 1980, Webster, J.J. Starbuck, 1988; also nightclub appearances. Chmn. Dance for Heart campaign Am. Heart Assn.; internat. chmn. Sudden Infant Death Syndrome; established Naja Vereen Meml. Scholarship Fund, 1988; founder, pres. Celebrities for a Drug-Free Am. Recipient George M. Cohan award Am. Guild Variety Artists, 1976, Image award NAACP, 1978, 79, Israel's Cultural award, 1978, Israel's Humanitarian award, 1979, Eleanor Roosevelt Humanitarian award, 1983. Mem. Actor's Equity Assn., Am. Guild Variety Artists, AFTRA, SAG. *I am like the turtle--determined and will stick my neck out; turtles also teach me patience.*

VEREEN, ROBERT CHARLES, retired trade association executive; b. Stillwater, Minn., Sept. 8, 1924; s. George and Leona Lucille (Made) Wihren; m. Rose Catherine Blair, Nov. 5, 1945; children: Robin, Stacy, Kim. Grad. high sch. Mng. editor Comml. West Mag., Mpls., 1946-50, Bruce Pub. Co., St. Paul, 1950-53, Nat. Retail Hardware Assn., Indpls., 1953-59; mng. dir. Liberty Distbrs., Phila., 1959-63; editor Hardware Retailing, Indpls., 1963-80; assoc. pub., dir. communications Nat. Retail Hardware Assn., 1980-84, sr. v.p., 1984-87; Vereen & Assocs., Mgmt., Mktg. Cons., 1987—; lectr. mgmt. insts.; guest lectr. on distbn. pub.; co-founder U.S.A. Direct; co-founder, ptnr. Eurotrade Mktg., 1988—. Author: (with Paul M. Doane) Hunting for Profit, 1965, The Computer Age in Merchandising, 1968, Perpetuating the Family-Owned Business, 1970, The How-To of Merchandising, 1975, The How-To of Store Operations, 1976, A Guide to Financial Management, 1976, Productivity: A Crisis for Management, 1978, Hardlines Rep Report Newsletter, 1984—, Guidelines to Improve the Rep/Factory Relationships, 1992. Served with AUS, 1943-46. Mem. Am. Soc. Bus Press Editors (dir., v.p. 1966-70), Soc. Nat. Assn. Publs. (dir., pres. 1970-75, chmn. journalism edn. liaison com. 1976-79), Toastmasters (v.p., treas., sec. 1955-59), Am. Hardware Mfrs. Assn. (co-founder, sec.-treas. Young Execs. Club 1958-59, 63-65), Hardware-Housewares Packaging Expn. (founder 1960, chmn. com. packaging 1960-62, chmn. judging com. Hardware-Packaging Expn. 1975-78), Packaging Inst., Household Consumer Products Export Council (chmn. 1981-83), World-Wide DIY Council (exec. sec. 1981—). Home and Office: 4560 Lincoln Rd Indianapolis IN 46208-6706

VEREEN, WILLIAM JEROME, uniform manufacturing company executive; b. Moultrie, Ga., Sept. 7, 1940; s. William Coachman and Mary Elizabeth (Bunn) V.; m. Lula Evelyn King, June 9, 1963; children: Elizabeth King, William Coachman. BS in Indsl. Mgmt, Ga. Inst. Tech., 1963. With Riverside Mfg. Co., Moultrie, 1967—; v.p., then exec. v.p. Riverside Mfg. Co., 1970-77, pres., 1977-84, pres., treas., CEO, 1984—; also dir.; v.p., dir. Moultrie Cotton Mills, 1969—; exec. v.p. Riverside Industries, Inc., Moultrie, 1973-77; pres. Riverside Industries, Inc., 1977-84, CEO, 1984—, also dir.; v.p., bd. dirs. Riverside Uniform Rentals, Inc., Moultrie, 1971-80, pres., 1980-84, CEO, bd. dirs., 1984—; pres. Riverside Mfg. Co. (Ireland) Ltd., 1977—, Right Image Corp., Riverside Mfg. Co. GmbH, Germany, 1979—, also CEO, dir., 1984; pres., treas., CEO G.A. Rivers Corp., Riverside Mfg. Co. (U.K.) Ltd.; pres., treas. CEO, bd. dirs. Textile Clothing Tech. Corp.; chairholder Tyner eminent scholars, prof. coll. human scis. Fla. State U., 1993-94, mem. coll. human scis. devel. bd.; bd. dirs. Ga. Power Co., Gerber Sci., Inc., Blue Cross/Blue Shield Ga., Cerulean Cos., Inc.; mem. trilateral commn. apparel labeling NAFTA; so. regional dir. Nations Bank of Ga., N.A.; advisor textile and apparel tariffs and quotas U.S. Dept. State Bd.; active Gov. Devel. Coun. With Gov. Devel. Coun. State of Ga.; bd. dirs. Moultrie-Colquitt County (Ga.) Devel. Authority, 1973-77, Moultrie-Colquitt County United Givers, 1968-75, Moultrie YMCA, 1968-75, Colquitt County Cancer Soc., 1969-73; trustee Cmty. Welfare Assn. Moultrie, 1970—, Pineland Sch., Moultrie, 1971-75, Leadership Ga., 1972—, Ga. Coun. Econ. Edn.; trustee Am. Apparel Edn. Found.; adv. bd. Ga. Tech. sch. of textile and fiber engring.; elder 1st Presbyterian Ch.; exec. com. existing industry coun. State Ga. Capt. USMCR, 1963-67. Decorated Bronze Star, Purple Heart. Mem. Internat. Apparel Fedn. (2d v.p., 1st v.p., bd. dirs., exec. com., chmn. 1991-92), Am. Apparel Mfrs. Assn. (bd. dirs., exec. com., edn. found. com., 2d vice chmn., chmn. 1990-91), Nat. Assn. Uniform Mfrs. and Distbrs. (bd. dirs. 1988-91), Am. Apparel Edn. Found. (v.p., trustee), Capital City Club (Atlanta), Commerce Club (Atlanta), Sunset Country Club, Ga. C. of C. (vice chmn., bd. dirs., mem. exec. com., chmn. existing industry com.), Elks, Kiwanis, Sigma Alpha Epsilon. Home: 21 Dogwood Dr Moultrie GA 31768-6537 Office: PO Box 460 Moultrie GA 31776-0460

VERGAMINI, JUDITH SHARON ENGEL, counselor, educator; b. Milw., May 21, 1941; d. Max E. and Rose (Ladish) Engel; m. Jerome Carl Vergamini, May 1, 1965; children: Michael David, Beth Allison, Daniel Carl. BS, U. Wis., 1963, postgrad., 1964, 66-76; MS, U. Oreg., 1978, postgrad., 1980—. Nat. cert. counselor; lic. profl. counsellor, tchr., sch. counselor, marriage and family therapist. Elem. tchr. Crestwood Elem. Sch., Northbrook, Ill., 1963-64, Odana Elem. Sch., Madison, Wis., 1964-65, Fitzmorris Elem. Sch., Arvada, Colo., 1965-66; tchr. Headstart, Madison, Wis., 1966; coord., founder parent vols. program Alternate Sch., Eugene, Oreg., 1976-77; pvt. practice counselor Eugene, 1978—; instr. Lane C.C., Eugene, Oreg., 1978—; lectr. Addictions Treatment Hosp. Program, 1989-92; mental health specialist Headstart of Lane County, Oreg., 1993-94; resource counselor Newman Ctr. U. Oreg., Eugene, 1979—, adj. prof., 1994—; presenter in field. Recipient Appreciation award Eugene Edn. Assn., 1980, Svc. to Edn. award, Oreg. Edn. Assn., 1980, Dedication and Performance award Nat. Disting. Svc. Registry, 1990, Outstanding Merit award Nat. Bd. Cert. Counselors, 1991. Fellow Am. Orthopsychiatric Assn.; mem. AACD, Am. Assn. for Marriage and Family Therapy (clin.), Am. Mental Health Counselors Assn., Oreg. Counseling Assn. Avocations: art, theatre. Home: 1047 Brookside Dr Eugene OR 97405-4913 Office: 1508 Oak St Eugene OR 97401-4042

VERGANO, LYNN (MARILYNN BETTE VERGANO), artist; b. N.Y.C., Nov. 14; d. George and Sis Anagnostis (Helaine Haas); children: Scott, Stephen, Sandy, Sefton. Student, Pratt Inst., 1959-60; BA, NYU, Heights, 1963; MA, NYU, 1964. Lectr. art Morris County Coll., 1982; lectr. UN Pan Pacific and S.E. Asia Women's Assn., N.Y. chpt., 1996; lectr. in field; judge, art juror. Author/illustrator: (book) Paintings, 1980; one-woman shows include Papermill Playhouse, N.J., 1976, 79, 83, Fairleigh Dickinson U., N.J., 1977, Drew U., N.J., 1977, Rutgers U., N.J., 1978, 79, Hong Kong Arts Ctr., 1980, Am. Univ. Alumni, Bangkok, Thailand, 1980, Caldwell Coll., N.J., 1980, União Cultural Brasil-Estados Unidos, São Paulo, Brazil, 1982, Galleria Fenice, Venice, Italy, 1985, St. Sophia Mus., Istanbul, Turkey, 1988, Nat. Arts Club, N.Y.C., 1989, Centreplace, Hamilton, New Zealand, 1990; exhibited in group shows Monmouth Mus., Lincroft, N.J., 1976, 77, 82, Morris Mus., Morristown, N.J., 1977, 78, N.J. State Capital Mus., Trenton, 1979, Macculloch Hall Hist. Mus., N.J., Morristown, 1984, 87, 89, 92, 96, Nat. Audubon Artists, N.Y.C., 1981, Salmagundi Club, N.Y.C., 1981, World Trade Ctr., N.Y., 1981, Nat. Arts Club, N.Y.C., 1981-96, Bergen Mus., Paramus, N.J., 1983, Lincoln Ctr., N.Y.C., 1987, Bklyn. Botanic Gardens, N.Y., 1987, many others. Pres., chpt. charter mem., 1969-70, hon. mem. Welcome Wagon Club, Randolph, N.J., 1969—. Recipient UN 25th Anniversary Creative Writing award, 1970, John H. Miller award Morris County Coll., 1979, Grumbacher gold medallion, 1984, Torch award NYU, 1993. Mem. AAUW, Am. Watercolor Soc. (assoc.), UN Pan Pacific and S.E. Asia Women's Assn. Internat. (hon.), Am. Watercolor Soc. (assoc.), Nat. Arts Club (exhibiting), Nat. Soc. Arts and Letters (exec. bd. N.J. chpt. 1979—), Federated Art Assns. N.J. (trsutee 1982—, pres., chmn. bd. dirs. 1982-88, Heritage plaque 1989), Morris County Art Assn., Dover Art Assn. (hon.), Millburn-Short Hills Arts Ctr. Home: 80 Old Stonehouse Rd Bedminster NJ 07921 also: 229 Van Cortlandt Pk Ave Yonkers NY 10705-1520

VERGARA, SCOTT GREGORY, botanical garden director. Exec. dir. Rhododendron Species Botanical Garden, Federal Way, Wash. Office: Rhododendron Bot Garden PO Box 3798 Federal Way WA 98063*

VERGE, PIERRE, legal educator; b. Quebec City, Can., Jan. 9, 1936; s. Francis and Regina (Roy) V.; m. Colette Habel, June 29, 1963; children—Marc, Caroline, Louis. B.A., Laval U., 1956, LL.L., 1959, LL.D., 1971; M.A., McGill U., 1962, Cambridge U., 1977; LL.M., U. Toronto, 1968; 1971. Bar: Que. 1961, Queen's Counsel 1976. Pvt. practice law Quebec City, Can., 1961-66; mem. faculty Laval U. Faculty of Law, 1966—; dean Laval U. Faculty of Law (Faculty of Law), 1973-77. Commonwealth fellow St. John's Coll., Cambridge U., 1977-78. Mem. Assn. Can. Law Tchrs. (pres. 1972-73, chmn. conf. law deans 1975-76), Que. Bar, Canadian Bar, Royal Soc. Can. Home: 2542 de la Falaise, Sillery, PQ Canada G1T 1W3 Office: Cite Universitaire, Universite Laval, Quebec, PQ Canada

VERGER, MORRIS DAVID, architect, planner; b. Ft. Worth, Mar. 25, 1915; s. Joseph and Dora (Bunyan) V.; m. Florence Brown, June 21, 1939; children: Paul, Alice. B.Arch., U. Calif., Berkeley, 1943. Naval architect U.S. Navy Bur. Ships, San Pedro, Calif., 1943-45; draftsman various archtl. firms So. Calif., 1946-50; pvt. practice as architect and planner Los Angeles, 1951—; lectr. architecture UCLA Extension; vis. critic Calif. State U., San Luis Obispo; leader Seminar on Interactive Planning, San Francisco; cons. to legal profession, tech. witness. Works include program for City of Hope, Duarte, Calif., 1972, Terman Engring. Ctr., Stanford U., 1974, and design of Huntington Dr. Sch., L.A., 1975, Flax Artist Materials Bldg., L.A., 1976, Frank D. Lanterman H.S., L.A., 1978, exec. offices S.E. Rykoff & Co., L.A., 1982, condominiums, Stoneman Corp., L.A., 1988, 91; developed DiscoveryBased Planning, 1994. Recipient design awards Westwood C. of C., 1974, 75. Fellow AIA (pres. So. Calif. chpt. 1975, v.p. environ. affairs Calif. council 1976, v.p. Calif. council 1979-80, pres. Calif. council 1980). Inventor (with E.H. Porter) Interactive Planning, evolved to Connective Planning; developed method for computer design of Interstitial Space and computer-generated drawings for affordable housing using related dimensions and datum points to coordinate all trades. Home: 1362 Comstock Ave Los Angeles CA 90024-5315 Office: 10801 National Blvd Los Angeles CA 90064-4126

VERGHESE, ABRAHAM CHEERAN, internist, writer, educator; b. Addis Ababa, Ethiopia, May 30, 1955; came to U.S., 1980; s. George and Mary Verghese; children: Steven, Jacob. MD, Madras (India) U., 1979; intern Govt. Gen. Hosp., Madras Med. Coll., India, 1979-80; from. res. to chief res., E. Tenn. State U., Johnson City, 1980-83; MFA, U. Iowa, 1991. Diplomate Am. Bd. Internal Medicine, Am. Bd. Infectious Diseases, Geriat., and Pulmonary Medicine. Instr. in medicine E. Tenn. State U., Johnson City, 1982-83, asst. prof. medicine, 1985-88, assoc. prof. medicine, 1988-90; teaching asst. medicine Boston U., 1983-85; chief infectious diseases VA Med. Ctr., Johnson City, 1986-90, asst. chief medicine, 1988-90; vis. assoc. U. Iowa, Iowa City, 1990-91; prof. medicine Tex. Tech. U., El Paso, Tex., 1991—; chief infectious diseases Tex. Tech. Regional Acad. Health Ctr., El Paso, 1991—. Author: My Own Country: A Doctor's Story of a Town and Its People in the Age of AIDS, 1994, (with others) Infection in the Nursing Home, 1990. Named Tchr. of Yr. Internat. Medicine residents and Alpha Omega Alpha E. Tenn. State U., 1989; recipient James Michener fellowship to Writer's Workshop U. Iowa. Fellow ACP (publs. coms.), Royal Coll. Physicians Can., Infectious Diseases Soc. Am., Coll. Chest Physicians; mem. Am. Geriat. Soc., Am. Fedn. for Clin. Rsch., Am. Soc. Microbiology, Soc. for Exptl. Biology and Medicine. Office: Tex Tech U 4800 Alberta Ave El Paso TX 79905-2709

VERGILIS, JOSEPH SEMYON, mechanical engineering educator; b. Odessa, Ukraine, Aug. 14, 1934; came to U.S., 1988; s. Semyon E. and Zinaida I. (Gleizerman) V.; m. Zhanna S. Berenfeld, Apr. 30, 1963; children: Helen, Irene. BS in Mfg. Engring., Poly. Inst., Odessa, 1958; PhD in Mech. Engring., Exptl. R&D Inst. Machine Tools, Moscow, 1973. Mfg. engr. Factory of Machine Tools, Odessa, 1958-66; sr. scientist R&D Inst. ENIMS, Moscow, 1966-87; cons. Beltran Assn., Inc., Bklyn., 1988-90; prof. mech. engring. Murray (Ky.) State U., 1990-92; cons. Russtrad, Inc., Richmond, Mass., 1992-93; prof. mech. engring. U. Turabo, Gurabo, P.R., 1993-94, CCNY, 1994—. Author: Fine-Boring Heads, 1972, Spindle Heads for Precision Tools, 1975; contbr. articles to profl. jours. Mem. ASME, Soc. Mfg. Engrs. (sr. mem.), Am. Soc. Engring. Edn. Republican. Jewish. Achievements include patents for tool holders for machine tools. Home: 868 E 24 St Brooklyn NY 11210 Office: CCNY Convent Ave at 135 St New York NY 10031

VERHALEN, ROBERT DONALD, consultant; b. Chgo., July 6, 1935; s. William Joseph and Pearl Evelyn (Anderson) V.; m. Phyllis Scandridge, Jan. 11, 1958; children: Elizabeth L., David S. BA, U. Iowa, 1963; MPH, U. N.C., 1965, DrPH, 1972. Expediter Fansteel Metall. Corp., North Chicago, Ill., 1957-58; tech. writer Collins Radio Co., Cedar Rapids, Iowa, 1958-59; rsch. aide Dept. Physics and Astronomy, Iowa City, 1960-63; sanitarian Lake County Health Dept., Waukegan, Ill., 1963-64; cons. safety mgmt. Ga. Dept. Pub. Health, Atlanta, 1965-68; instr. U. N.C., Chapel Hill, 1968-70; chief task force Pres.'s Commn. on Product Safety, Washington, 1969-70; asst. dir. Bur. Product Safety FDA, Washington, 1970-73; assoc. dir. U.S. Consumer Product Safety Commn., Washington, 1973-95; pres. Verhalen & Assocs., McLean, Va., 1995—; guest lectr. Sch. Pub. Health U. N.C., Chapel Hill, 1975—, Walter Reed Army Med. Ctr., Washington, 1982—. Mem. editorial bd. Jour. Safety Rsch.; developer Nat. Electronic Injury Surveillance System; contbr. articles to profl. jours. Mem. Conservative Network, Washington, 1985—. Sgt. USMC, 1953-57. Mem. Am. Coll. Epidemiology, Soc. Epidemiologic Rsch., Am. Pub. Health Assn., Am. Statis. Assn., Sr. Exec.'s Assn., Sr. Exec. Svc. Lutheran. Avocation: sailing. Home: 7209 Matthew Mills Rd Mc Lean VA 22101 Office: Verhalen & Assocs Ste 115-134 1350 Beverly Rd Mc Lean VA 22101-3924

VERHEY, JOSEPH WILLIAM, psychiatrist, educator; b. Oakland, Calif., Sept. 28, 1928; s. Joseph Bernard and Anne (Hanken) V.; BS summa cum laude, Seattle U., 1954; MD, U. Wash., 1958; m. Darlene Helen Seiler, July 21, 1956. Intern, King County Hosp., Seattle, 1958-59; resident Payne Whitney Psychiatric Clinic, N.Y. Hosp., Cornell Med. Center, N.Y.C., 1959-62, U. Wash. Hosp., Seattle, 1962-63; pvt. practice, Seattle, 1963-78; mem. staff U. Providence Hosp., 1963-78, Fairfax Hosp., 1963-78, VA Med. Center, Tacoma, 1978-83, chief inpatient psychiatry sect., 1983—; clin. instr. psychiatry U. Wash. Med. Sch., 1963-68, clin. asst. prof. psychiatry, 1968-82, clin. assoc. prof., 1982—; cons. psychiatry U.S. Dept. Def., Wash. State Bur. Juvenile Rehab.; examiner Am. Bd. Psychiatry and Neurology. Diplomate Am. Bd. Psychiatry and Neurology. Fellow N. Pacific Soc. Psychiatry and Neurology, Am. Psychiat. Assn.; mem. AMA, Am. Fedn. Clin. Rsch., World Fedn. Mental Health, Soc. Mil. Surgeons of U.S., Wash. Athletic Club, Swedish Club (life). Home: 1100 University St Seattle WA 98101 Office: VA Med Ctr Tacoma WA 98493

VERHEYEN, EGON, art historian, educator; b. Duisburg, Germany, Apr. 13, 1936; came to U.S., 1966; s. Franz and Klara (Läufer) V.; children: Peter David, Gero, Esther. Student, U. Mainz, Germany, 1956-58; Ph.D., U. Würzburg, Fed. Republic Germany, 1962. With German Nat. Museum, Nuremberg, 1961; Herodotos mem. Inst. for Advanced Study, Princeton, N.J., 1962-63, mem., 1983; research fellow Bayerische Staatsgemäldesammlungen, Munich, Fed. Republic Germany, 1965-66; asst. prof. history of art U. Mass., Amherst, 1966; asst. prof. U. Mich., Ann Arbor, 1967-70; assoc. prof. U. Mich., 1970-72; prof. dept history of art Johns Hopkins, 1972-87, chmn. dept., 1972-76; Clarence J. Robinson prof. humanities George Mason U., 1987—; research fellow Bibliotheca Hertziana, Rome, Italy, 1963-65; bd. dirs. Univ. Press Va. Author: Minoritenkirche Duisburg, 1959, Goldene Evangelienbuch von Echternach, 1963, Studiolo of Isabella d'Este, 1971, Palazzo del Te in Mantua, 1977; bd. editors: Emblemata, Architectura. Max Planck Gesellschaft grantee, 1963-65; Horace H. Rackham Found. grantee, 1968, 70; NEH grantee, 1972, 76, 77, 85, 90; Fritz Thyssen Gesellschaft grantee, 1965-66; U. Mich. travel grantee, 1971-72; Office Rsch. Adminstrn. grantee, 1971. Mem. Soc. Archtl. Historians (v.p. Latrobe chpt. 1990-91), Am. Goethe Soc. (pres. Md. chpt. 1984-86), Coll. Art Assn., Soc. for Emblem Studies, Internat. Soc. Classical Tradition. Office: MS1D6 George Mason U Fairfax VA 22030-4444

VERHOEK, SUSAN ELIZABETH, botany educator; b. Columbus, Ohio, 1942; m. S.E. Williams; 1 child. Student, Carleton Coll., 1960-62; BA, Ohio Wesleyan U., 1964; MA, Ind. U., 1966; PhD, Cornell U., 1975. Herbarium supr. Mo. Bot. Garden, St. Louis, 1966-70; asst. prof. Lebanon Valley Coll., Annville, Pa., 1974-82, assoc. prof., 1982-85, prof., 1985—; vis. researcher Cornell U., Ithaca, N.Y., 1982-83; content cons. Merrill Pub. Co., 1987-89; vis. profl. Chgo. Bot. Garden, 1991. Author: How to Know the Spring Flowers, 1982; contbr. articles to profl. jours., newspapers, and bulls. Trustee Lebanon Valley Coll., Annville, 1979-82, 84-90, 92—; dir. Lebanon Valley Coll. Arboretum, 1996—. Mem. Soc. for Econ. Botany (pres. 1985-86), Bot. Soc. Am., Am. Soc. Plant Taxonomists, Am. Assn. Bot. Gardens and Arboreta. Office: Lebanon Valley Coll Dept Botany Annville PA 17003-0501

VERHOEVEN, PAUL, film director; b. Amsterdam, Netherlands, July 18, 1938. PhD in Maths., Physics, U. Leiden. Dir. (films) Wat Zien Ik?, 1971, Turkish Delight, 1973, Keetje Tippel, 1975, Spetters, 1981, The Fourth Man, 1983, Robocop, 1987, Total Recall, 1990, Basic Instinct, 1992, Showgirls, 1995, Starship Troopers, 1996, Crusade, 1996, (episode of TV series) Hitchhiker (TV series) Floris, 1969, (documentary with the Royal Netherlands Navy) Het Korps Mariniers, 1965; dir., co-screenwriter Soldier of Orange, 1979, Flesh and Blood, 1985. Office: care Marion Rosenberg 8428 Melrose Pl Ste C West Hollywood CA 90069-5308 also: Robert Brenner Brenner & Glassberg 2049 Century Park E Ste 950 Los Angeles CA 90067-3111*

VERING, JOHN ALBERT, lawyer; b. Marysville, Kans., Feb. 6, 1951; s. John Albert and Bernadine E. (Kieffer) V.; m. Ann E. Arman, June 28, 1980;

children: Julia Ann, Catherine Ann, Mary Ann. BA summa cum laude, Harvard U., 1973; JD, U. Va., 1976. Bar: Mo. 1976, U.S. Dist. Ct. (we. dist.) Mo. 1976, U.S. Ct. Appeals (10th cir.), 1980, U.S. Ct. Appeals (4th cir.) 1987, Kans. 1990, U.S. Dist. Ct. Kans. 1990; arbitrator, mediator, Mo., Kans. Assoc. Dietrich, Davis, Dicus, Rowlands, Schmitt & Gorman, Kansas City, Mo., 1976-81, ptnr., 1982—. Editor: U. Va. Law Rev., 1974-76. Bd. dirs. Greater Kansas City YMCA Southwest Dist., 1987. Mem. Harvard Club (schs. com. Kansas City 1977-96, v.p. 1981-82, 92-93, pres. 1994-96). Democrat. Roman Catholic. Home: 1210 W 68th Ter Kansas City MO 64113-1904 Office: Armstrong Teasdale Schlafy & Davis 1700 City Ctr S 2345 Grand Blvd Ste 2000 Kansas City MO 64108

VERINK, ELLIS DANIEL, JR., metallurgical engineering educator, consultant; b. Peking, China, Feb. 9, 1920; s. Ellis Daniel and Phoebe Elizabeth (Smith) V.; m. Martha Eulala Owens, July 4, 1942; children: Barbara Ann, Wendy Susan. B.S., Purdue U., 1941; M.S., Ohio State U., 1963, Ph.D., 1965. Registered profl. engr., Fla., Pa., Calif. Mgr. chem. sect., sales devel. div. Alcoa, New Kensington, Pa., 1946-59; mgr. chem. and petroleum indsl. sales Alcoa, Pitts., 1959-62; assoc. prof. metall. engring. U. Fla., Gainesville, 1965-68, prof. materials sci. and engring., 1968—; disting. service prof. U. Fla., 1984-91; prof. emeritus U. Fla., Gainesville, 1991—; pres. Materials Cons., Inc., 1970—; cons. Aluminum Assn., Washington, 1966-84; mem. U.S. nuclear waste tech. rev. bd., 1989—. Author: Corrosion Testing Made Easy, The Basics, 1993; editor: Methods of Materials Selections, 1968, Material Stability and Environmental Degradation, 1988; contbr. articles to profl. jours. Pres. Gainesville YMCA, 1977. Recipient Sam Tour award ASTM, 1979, Donald E. Marlowe award Am. Soc. Engring. Edn., 1991; recipient Disting. Alumnus award Ohio State U., 1982, Disting. Faculty award Fla. Blue Key, 1983; named Tchr.-Scholar of Year U. Fla., 1979. Fellow Metall. Soc. of AIME (pres. 1984, Educator of Yr. award 1988), Am. Soc. Materials Internat., Nat. Assn. Corrosion Engrs. Internat. (bd. dirs. 1984-87, Willis Rodney Whitney award; mem. Masons, Shriners, Kiwanis, Sigma Tau, Tau Beta Pi. Republican. Presbyterian. Home: 4401 NW 18th Pl Gainesville FL 32605-3423 Office: U Fla Dept Materials Sci Eng Gainesville FL 32611

VERITY, GEORGE LUTHER, lawyer; b. Oklahoma City, Jan. 3, 1914; s. George H. and Mae (Tibbals) V.; m. Ellen Van Hoesen, Mar. 18, 1939; children: George Luther II, Grover Steven, David Webster, Mark Sidney. LLB, Okla. U., 1937; M of Theol. Studies, So. Meth. U., 1989. Bar: Okla. 1937, Tex. 1939, N.Mex. 1957. Practice in Shawnee, Okla., 1937-39, Wichita Falls, Tex., 1939-40, 46-48, Oklahoma City, 1948-57, Farmington, N.Mex., 1957-64, Oklahoma City, 1964—; ptnr. Verity, Brown & Verity (and predecessor), 1964-77; of counsel Bay, Hamilton, Lee, Spears & Verity, 1978—; chmn. bd., dir. Big D Industries; pres., dir. Okla. Mgmt. Co., Okla. Ind. Exploration Co.; former chmn. bd., dir. Progress Life & Accident Ins. Co. Author: The Modern Oil and Gas Lease, From Bataan to Victory, An Agnostic Finds God in Jananese Prison Camp. Trustee Rocky Mountain Mineral Law Found. Capt. USAAF, 1941-46, PTO; prisoner of war. Decorated Purple Heart. Mem. ABA, Okla. Bar Assn., State Bar N.Mex. (chmn. mineral sect.), State Bar Tex., Assn. Trial Lawyers Am., Okla. Trial Lawyers Assn., Acacia. Lodges: Masons; Elks. Home: Villa 55 3101 Castle Rock Rd Oklahoma City OK 73120-1899 Office: 5620 SW 29th St Oklahoma City OK 73179-7603 *In a Japanese prison camp during World War II the love of God came into my life in a magnificent and dramatic way. The expression of this love has brought to my life, health, happiness, and success.*

VERKADE, JOHN GEORGE, inorganic/organic chemistry educator, researcher; b. Chgo., Jan. 15, 1935; widowed; 3 children. BS, U. Ill., 1956, PhD in Inorganic Chemistry, 1960; AM, Harvard U., 1957. Sloan fellow, 1966-68; instr. to assoc. prof. Iowa State U., Ames, 1960-70, prof. inorganic chemistry, 1970—. Grantee NSF, 1961—, Petroleum Rsch. Found., 1963-66, 89-96, NIH, 1972-78, DOE 1987-90, 92-97. Mem. Am. Chem. Soc., Sigma Xi. Office: Iowa State U Dept Chemistry 1275 Gilman Ames IA 50011-2010

VERLICH, JEAN ELAINE, writer, public relations consultant; b. McKeesport, Pa., July 5, 1950; d. Matthew Louis and Irene (Tomko) V.; m. S(tanley) Wayne Wright, Sept. 29, 1979 (div. June 1988). Student, Bucknell U., 1968-69; BA, U. Pitts., 1971. Press sec. Com. to Re-elect President, S.W. Pa., 1972; adminstrv. asst. Pa. Rep. James B. Kelly III, 1972-73; reporter Beaver (Pa.) County Times, 1973-74; proofreader Ketchum, MacLeod & Grove, Pitts., 1975-76; community rels. specialist, PPG Industries, Pitts., 1976-77, editor PPG News, 1977-79, sr. staff writer, 1979-84, comm. coord., 1984-85; pub. rels. assoc. Glass Group, 1986-87; mgr. pub. rels. Glass Group PPG Industries, 1987-92; account mgr. Maddigan Comm., Pitts., 1992-93; owner JV Comm., Pitts., 1993—. Mem. Internat. Assn. Bus. Communicators (bd. dir. Pitts. chpt. 1981, v.p. pub. rels. Pitts. chpt. 1982, v.p. programs Pitts. chpt. 1985, pres. Pitts. chpt. 1986), Travelers Aid Soc. Pitts. (bd. dirs. 1992-95, v.p. 1994-95), Phi Beta Kappa, Delta Zeta. Office: JV Comm 3 Gateway Ctr Ste 1526 Pittsburgh PA 15222

VERMA, GHASI RAM, mathematics educator; b. Sigari, Rajasthan, India, Aug. 1, 1927; came to U.S., 1958; s. Lachhu Ram and Jiwani Devi (Punia) V.; children: Om Prakash, Subhash, Anand. BA, Birla Coll., Pilani, 1950; MA, Banaras U., 1954; PhD, Rajasthan U., Jaipur, 1957. Postdoctoral fellow Courant Inst. Math. Scis., N.Y.C., 1958-59; asst. prof. Fordham U., N.Y.C., 1959-61; reader Birla Inst. Tech., Pilani, India, 1961-64; assoc. prof. U. R.I., Kingston, 1964-80, prof., 1980—. Contbr. articles to profl. jours. Home: 61 Paul Ave Wakefield RI 02879-1504 Office: U RI 214 Tyler Hall Kingston RI 02881

VERMA, SURJIT K., school system administrator; b. India, May 17, 1940; arrived in Canada 1966; s. Sohara Lal and Gian Devi V.; m. Raj Verma; 1 child, Soania. MEd, St. Francis Xavier U., N.S., 1975; postgrad., Dalhousie U., N.S., U. Ottawa, Ont., Can, 1979. Cert. tchr. Nova Scotia. Sci. dept. head Halifax County Bedford Dist. Sch. Bd., N.S., Canada, 1968-88, curriculum supr., 1988—; served on C.T.F. Project Overseas Can. Teams, W.I., Nigeria, 1976, 77; mem. provincial sci. task force, biology rev. com., elem. sci.; mem. Internat. Sci. Symposium, 1979; worksop presenter numerous sci. workshops. Contbr. to profl. jours. Chmn. First Metro Halifax Dartmouth Reg Sci. Fair, 1975; co-chmn. Canada Wide Sci Fair, 1984. Recipient Sci. Tchg. Achievement Recognition award U.S. Nat. Sci. Tchrs. Assn. and Am. Gas Assn., 1993, Profl. Devel. award N.S. Tchrs. Union, Tchg. Excellence in Sci., Tech. and Math. award Prime Min. Can., 1993, 94, Sci. on Display award NASCO, 1993-94, Outstanding Achievement in Sci. Edn. award Halifax County Sch. Bd., 1993; U. Ottawa fellow, 1979, Dalhousie U. grad. fellow, 1980, Math. Sci. Tech. Edn. fellow Royal Bank Queen's U., 1994; Dalhousie U. Rsch. Devel. grantee, 1979; N.S. Tchrs. Union scholar, 1979; Can./N.S. Tech. Devel. grantee, 1995; Surjit Verma award for tchg. excellence created in his honor Halifax County Bedford Dist. Sch. Bd., 1994. Mem. Nat. Sci. Tchrs. Assn., Nova Scotia Assn. Sci. Tchrs., Nova Scotia Assn. Curriculum Suprs., Assn. for Suprs. and Curriculum Devel. (provincial sci. 10 task force and rev. com.). Avocations: jogging, yoga. Home: 49 Rosewood Ave, Timberlea, NS Canada B3T 1C6

VERMEER, MAUREEN DOROTHY, sales executive; b. Bronxville, N.Y., Mar. 21, 1945; d. Albert Casey and Helen (Valentine Casey) Vermeer; m. John R. Fassnacht, Feb. 11, 1966 (div. 1975); m. George M. Dallas Peltz IV, Oct. 26, 1985. Grad., NYU Real Estate Inst., 1976. Lic. real estate broker, notary pub., N.Y. With Douglas Elliman, N.Y.C., 1965-74, mgmt. supr., 1974-78, v.p., 1978-83; real estate broker Rachmani Corp., N.Y.C., 1983-84; v.p. sales and mktg. Carol Mgmt. Corp., N.Y.C., 1984-90; v.p. mktg. The Sunshine Group, N.Y.C., 1990; v.p., sec., bd. dirs. H.J. Kalikow & Co., N.Y.C., 1991—. Mem. Real Estate Bd. N.Y. (bd. dirs., residential mgmt. com.), Assn. Real Estate Women (sec., bd. dirs.). Republican. Presbyterian. Avocations: skiing, scuba diving. Home: 111 Broadway Norwood NJ Office: H J Kalikow & Co 101 Park Ave New York NY 10178

VERMETTE, RAYMOND EDWARD, clinical laboratories administrator; b. Lewiston, Maine, June 30, 1942; s. Edward Louis and Anna Lucy (Raymond) V.; m. Ernestine Pero, Dec. 28, 1963; children: Tamara, Gregory. BS in Bacteriology, U. Maine, 1964; MS in Biochemistry, U. Wis., 1966; cert. personnel mgmt. Va. Dept. Edn., Fairfax, 1969; MBA, Temple U., 1973; master tchrs.' cert., Cath. Diocese of Boston, 1981. Supr. animal toxicology Hazleton Labs., Vienna, Va., 1967-71; personnel mgr. Damon Clin. Lab., Phila., 1971-73, ops. mgr., 1973-75, gen. mgr., Needham, Heights, Mass., 1975-90; v.p. ops. Damon Corp., Needham Hts., 1983-87, corp. v.p., 1987-89, sr. v.p., 1990-93; sr. v.p., gen. mgr. Corning/MetPath, Westwood, Mass., 1994-95; ret. 1995; vis. lectr fin. mgmt. and bus. adminstrn. Framingham State Coll., 1978-84; instr. mgmt. Newbury Jr. Coll., Boston, 1976-79. Author: (with B. Kliman and E. Kolowrat) What You Should Know About Medical Lab Tests, 1979. V.p. fin. com. Framingham, Mass., 1982-84; mem. capital budget com., Town of Framingham, 1987; mem.-elect, Town Meeting, 1987—; chmn. bd. religious edn. Cath. Ch., Framingham, 1981-84, co-chmn. Pre-Marriage Preparation Council, 1981—, organist, 1979—. Democrat. Home: 11 Willowbrook Dr Framingham MA 01701-5515

VERMEULE, CORNELIUS CLARKSON, III, museum curator; b. Orange, N.J., Aug. 10, 1925; s. Cornelius Clarkson, Jr. and Catherine Sayre (Comstock) V.; m. Emily Dickinson Townsend, Feb. 2, 1957; children—Emily D. Blake, Cornelius Adrian Comstock. Grad., Pomfret Sch., 1943; A.B., Harvard, 1949, M.A., 1951; Ph.D., U. London, Eng., 1953; DHL (hon.), Boston Coll., 1995. Instr. fine arts, then asst. prof. U. Mich., 1953-55; asst. prof. classical archaeology Bryn Mawr (Pa.) Coll., 1955-57; curator classical art Mus. Fine Arts, Boston, 1956-96, curator emeritus, 1996—; acting dir. Mus. Fine Arts, 1972-73; assoc. curator coins Mass. Hist. Soc., 1965-71, curator, 1971—; lectr. fine arts Smith Coll., 1960-64, Boston U., Harvard, Wellesley Coll.; vis. prof. Yale, 1969-70, 72-73; Thomas Spencer Jerome lectr. U. Mich., 1975-76; vis. prof. Boston Coll., 1978—; vis. prof. U. Aberdeen, Scotland, 1993; pres. Internat. Com. to Save Jewish Catabombs of Italy, 1980-84, chmn., 1984—. Author: (with N. Jacobs) Japanese Coinage, 1948, 2d edit., 1972, Bibliography of Applied Numismatics, 1956, The Goddess Roma, 1959, 2d edit., 1974, Dal Pozzo-Albani Drawings, 1960, European Art and the Classical Past, 1964, Drawings at Windsor Castle, 1966, Roman Imperial Art in Greece and Asia Minor, 1968, Polykleitos, 1969, Numismatic Art in America, 1971, (with M. Comstock) Greek Etruscan and Roman Bronzes, 1972, (with N. Neuerburg) Catalogue of the Ancient Art in the J. Paul Getty Museum, 1973, Greek and Roman Sculpture in Gold and Silver, 1974, Greek and Roman Cyprus, 1976, (with M. Comstock) Sculpture in Stone, 1976, Greek Sculpture and Roman Taste, 1977, Roman Art: Early Republic to Late Empire, 1978, (with A Herrmann) The Ernest Brummer Collections, Vol. II, 1979, Greek Art: Socrates to Sulla, 1980, The Jewish Experience in Roman Art, 1981, Masterpieces of Greek and Roman Sculpture in America, 1982, Greek Art: Prehistoric to Perikles, 1982, Numismatic Studies, 1983, Alexander the Great Conquers Rome, 1985, The Cult Images of Imperial Rome, 1986, Numismatic Art of the Greek Imperial World, 1987, Philatelic Art in America, 1987, (with M. Comstock) Sculpture in Stone and Bronze, 1988, (with A. Brauer) Stone Sculptures, The Greek, Roman and Etruscan Collections of the Harvard University Art Museums, 1990, (with others) Le Sport dans la Grèce Antique, 1992, Du Jeu à la Compétition, 1992, (with others) El Deporte en la Grecia Antigua, La génesis del olimpismo, 1992-93, (with others) Vase-Painting in Italy, 1993. Trustee Cardinal Spellman Philatelic Mus., 1980-93. Served to 1st lt. AUS, 1943-47. Recipient Bicentennial medal Boston Coll., 1976; Fulbright fellow, 1951-53; Guggenheim fellow, 1968. Fellow AAAS, Am. Numis. Soc. (life), Royal Numis. Soc., Soc. Antiquaries; mem. Coll. Art Assn. (life), Archaeol. Inst. Am. (life) German Archaeol. Inst., Holland Soc. N.Y., Colonial Lords of Manors in Am., Mass. Hist. Soc. (hon.). Republican. Episcopalian. Club: Tavern (medalist 1986) (Boston). Home: 47 Coolidge Hill Rd Cambridge MA 02138-5509 Office: Mus Fine Arts 465 Huntington Ave Boston MA 02115-5523 *To teach, collect and record the past, as exemplar for the present, as prologue to the future, can there be any better use of a historian's and archaeologist's professional life?.*

VERMEULE, EMILY TOWNSEND (MRS. CORNELIUS C. VERMEULE, III), classicist, educator; b. N.Y.C., Aug. 11, 1928; d. Clinton Blake and Eleanor (Meneely) Townsend; m. Cornelius C. Vermeule III, Feb. 2, 1957; children: Emily Dickinson Blake, Cornelius Adrian Comstock. AB, Bryn Mawr Coll., 1950; student, Am. Sch. Classical Studies, Athens, 1950-51, St. Anne's Coll., Oxford U., 1953; MA, Harvard, 1954; PhD, Bryn Mawr Coll., 1956; DLitt, Douglass Coll.; D. Litt., Rutgers U., 1968, Tufts U., 1980, U. Pitts., 1983, Bates Coll., 1983, U. Miami, Oxford, Ohio, 1986; LL.D., Regis Coll., 1971; D. Fine Arts, U. Mass, Amherst, 1971; D.Litt., Smith Coll., 1972, Wheaton Coll., 1973, Trinity Coll., 1974; LHD, Emmanuel Coll., 1980, Princeton U., 1989, Bard Coll., 1994. Instr. Greek lang. Bryn Mawr Coll., 1956-57; instr. Wellesley (Mass.) Coll., 1957-58, prof. art and Greek, 1965-70, chmn. dept. art, 1966-67; asst. prof. classics Boston U., 1958-61, assoc. prof. classics, 1961-65; fellow for research Boston Mus. Fine Arts, 1965—; James C. Loeb vis. prof. classical philology Harvard, 1969; dir. univ. Cyprus expdn. Harvard U., 1971—, Samuel and Doris Zemurray Stone-Radcliffe prof., 1970-94; prof. emerita and Sather prof. U. Calif., Berkeley, 1975; Geddes-Harrower prof. Greek art and archaeology U. Aberdeen, 1980-81; Bernhard vis. prof. Williams Coll., 1986; excavations in Greece, Turkey, Libya, Cyprus. Author: Euripides v. Electra, 1959, Greece in the Bronze Age, 1964, The Trojan War in Greek Art, 1964, Götterkult, 1974, Toumba tou Skourou, The Mound of Darkness, 1975, Death in Early Greek Art and Poetry, Mycenaean Pictorial Vase-Painting (with U. Karageorghis), 1982, Toumba tou Skourou, A Bronze Age Potters' Quarter on Morphou Bay in Cyprus (with F.Z. Wolsky), 1990; contbr. articles to scholarly publs. Judge Nat. Book Award, 1977; bd. dirs. Humanities Rsch. Inst., U. Calif., 1988-91, bd. govs., 1988-90; trustee Isabella Stewart Gardner Mus., 1988-96. Recipient Gold medal for disting. achievement Radcliffe Coll. Grad. Soc., 1968; Guggenheim fellow, 1964-65. Fellow Soc. Antiquaries, Brit. Acad. (corr.), German Archaeol. Inst. (corr.); mem. AAAS, Am. Inst. Archaeology, Am. Philos. Soc. (v.p. 1978-81), Am. Philol. Assn. (Charles J. Goodwin award 1980, pres. 1995), Smithsonian Coun. (bd. scholars 1983-89), Hellenic Soc.

VERMILYE, PETER HOAGLAND, banker; b. N.Y.C., Jan. 17, 1920; s. Herbert Noble and Elise Tace (Hillyer) V.; m. Lucy Shaw Mitchell, Oct. 14, 1950; children: Peter H., Dana R., Andrew R., Mary S. AB, Princeton U., 1940. V.p. pension investments J.P. Morgan & Co. and Morgan Guaranty Trust, 1940-64; ptnr. State St. Research & Mgmt., Boston, 1965-69; pres. Alliance Capital Mgmt., N.Y.C., 1970-77; sr. v.p., chief investment officer Citibank, N.Y.C., 1977-84; chmn. Baring Am. Asset Mgmt., Boston, 1984-89; sr. advisor Baring Asset Mgmt., 1990-95, Harbor Capital Mgmt., Boston, 1996—; chmn. bd. dirs. Huntington Theatre' bd. dirs. Baring Puma Fund, Fosterlane Mgmt. Trustee Boston U. Clubs: Brook, Somerset, Myopia. Home: 157 School St Manchester MA 01944-1236 also: 107 Chestnut St Boston MA 02108-1038 Office: Harbor Capital Mgmt 125 High St 26th Flr Boston MA 02110-2701

VERMYLEN, PAUL ANTHONY, JR., oil company executive; b. N.Y.C., Dec. 5, 1946; s. Paul Anthony and Nancy Primrose (Barr) V.; m. Robin S. Collins, Jan. 24, 1970; children: Robert T.C., Nancy Barr, Sarah Morgan, Paul Anthony III. AB, Georgetown U., 1968; MBA, Columbia U., 1971. V.p. Citibank N.A., N.Y.C., 1971-78; treas. Commonwealth Oil Refining Co., San Antonio, 1978-81; v.p. fin., chief fin. officer Commonwealth Oil Refining Co., 1981-82; v.p., chief fin. officer, dir. Meenan Oil Co., Inc., Syosset, N.Y., 1982-91, pres., 1992—; pres. Meenan Oil Co., L.P., 1992—; bd. dirs. Petroleum Industry Rsch. Found., 1992—. Bd. dirs. Huntington Arts Coun., N.Y., 1983-89, v.p., 1986-87, pres., 1987-89; bd. dirs. Cold Spring Harbor Whaling Mus., 1995—; bd. advisors Cold Spring Harbor Lab. DNA Learning Ctr., 1991—. Mem. Empire State Petroleum Assn. (bd. dirs. 1994—), Winter Club, Cold Spring Harbor Beach Club, Seawanhaka Corinthian Yacht Club, N.Y. Yacht Club. Office: 6900 Jericho Tpke Syosset NY 11791-4407

VERNBERG, FRANK JOHN, marine and biological sciences educator; b. Fenton, Mich., Nov. 6, 1925; s. Sigurd A. and Edna (Anderson) V.; m. Winona M. Bortz, Sept. 7, 1945; children—Marcia Lynn, Eric Morrison, Amy Louise. A.B., DePauw U., 1949, M.A., 1950; Ph.D., Purdue U., 1951. Prof. zoology Duke Marine Lab., Beaufort, N.C., 1951-69; Belle W. Baruch prof. marine ecology, dir. Bell W. Baruch Marine Biology and Coastal Rsch. Inst., Columbia, 1969—; interim dean Coll. Sci. and Math. Belle W. Baruch Coastal Research Inst., U. S.C., Columbia, 1993-94; dean Sch. of Environment U. S.C., Columbia, 1995—; vis. prof. U. Coll. West Indies, Jamaica, 1957-58, U. Sao Paulo, Brazil, 1965; program dir. exptl. analytical biogeography of sea Internat. Biol. Program, 1967-69; mem. com. manned orbital research lab. Am. Inst. Biol. Scis.-NASA, 1966-68; pres. Estuarine Research Fedn., 1975-77. Contbr. articles to profl. jours.; spl. editor: Am. Zoologist, 1963; mem. editorial bd.: Biol. Bull., 1977-80; editor: Jour. Exptl. Marine Biology and Ecology, 1978—. Served with USNR, 1944-46. Recipient W.S. Proctor award Sigma Xi, award Drug Sci. Found., 1987; Guggenheim fellow, 1957-58; Fulbright-Hayes fellow, 1965. Fellow AAAS, Am. Soc. Zoologists (sec.-treas. divsn. comparative physiologists 1959-61, sec.-treas. edn. com. 1960-62, mem. coun. 1965-67, pres. 1982), Southeastern Estuarine Rsch. Soc. (pres. 1974-76), So. Assn. Marine Labs. (pres. 1993), Estuarine Rsch. Fedn. (pres. 1975-77), S.C. Wildlife Fedn. (Conservationist of Yr. 1983). Office: U SC Belle W Baruch Coastal Rsch Inst Columbia SC 29208

VERNER, JAMES MELTON, lawyer; b. Selma, Ala., Sept. 19, 1915; s. Singleton Foster and Jennie (Harris) V.; m. Gretchen Gores, Aug. 12, 1939; children: Ann Verner Picardo, James Singleton, William Melton. Student, Biltmore Coll., 1932-34; A.B., U. N.C., 1936, LL.B., 1938. Bar: N.C. 1938, Tenn. 1947, D.C. 1950, Va., 1986. Assoc. firm Gover & Covington, Charlotte, N.C., 1938; law clk. atty. gen. N.C., 1938-40; atty. CAB, Washington, 1940-43; asst. gen. counsel Chgo. & So. Airlines, Memphis, 1946-47; atty. Air Transport Assn. Am., Washington, 1947-49; hearing examiner CAB, 1949-50, exec. asst. to chmn., 1950, exec. dir., 1950-53; atty. Turney & Turney, 1953-60, ptnr., 1954-60; ptnr. firm Verner, Liipfert, Bernhard, McPherson & Hand, Chartered (and predecessor firms), 1960-88, hon. mem. bd. dirs., 1988—; mem. policy adv. bd. Legal Counsel for the Elderly, Washington. Assoc. editor: N.C. Law Rev, 1937-38. Former mem., chmn. policy bd. Legal Counsel for Elderly, Washington. Served as lt. (j.g.) USNR, 1943-46; legal officer Naval Air Transport Svc., 1945-46. Mem. ABA, Order of Golden Fleece, Cosmos Club (Washington). Home: 3618 N Nelson St Arlington VA 22207-5319 Office: 901 15th St NW Washington DC 20005-2327 *My belief is that if you treat other people fairly and trust them, you will seldom be disappointed and will be the better for it.*

VERNER, LINDA HOGAN, manager cardiac surgery operating room; b. Washington, Aug. 24, 1945; d. Inman Curry and Julia Belk (Spratt) Hogan; m. David Howard Verner, Mar. 14, 1971 (div. Sept., 1976); children: Heather, Stacy. ASN, Ga. Southwestern Coll., 1966. RN, Ga. Staff nurse med. surg. unit St. Joseph's Hosp., Augusta, Ga., 1966-68; staff nurse operating room St. Joseph's Hosp., Atlanta, 1968-71, charge nurse neurosurgery, 1971-75, staff nurse cardiac surgery, 1976-79, mgr. cardiac surgery, 1979—; cons. Kimberly Clark Corp., Atlanta, 1992—, Goodroe and Assocs., Atlanta, 1994—. Producer (film) Introduction to the Cardiovascular Operating Room, Kimberly Clark, Atlanta, 1992; lectr. to hosps. and health oriented orgns. on cardiovascular operating procedures, 1984—. Coord. donations of supplies to third world countries St. Joseph's Hosp., Atlanta, 1988—, donations to Transplant Olympic Games, L.A., 1992; mem. cardiac surgery team to Hosp. Militar, San Salvador, El Salvador, 1995. Mem. AORN (tellers com. 1978—, chmn. 1981, bd. dirs. 1980, del. nat. congress 1979, 80), Cardiovascular Specialty Group AORN. Avocations: reading, gardening, walking, travel. Office: St Joseph's Hosp of Atlanta 5665 Peachtree Dunwoody Rd Atlanta GA 30342

VERNEY, JUDITH LA BAIE, health program administrator; b. Buffalo, Mar. 23, 1937; d. Arthur W. and Mary B. (Grant) La Baie; m. George R. Verney, Dec. 27, 1958; children: Michael, Timothy, Christopher. BSN, Russell Sage Coll., 1958; MS, Rutgers State U., Newark, 1977. Cert. clin. specialist, cmty. health nurse; cert. pub. mgr. State coord. provider svcs. Healthstart N.J. State Dept. Health, Trenton; dir. HealthStart, Trenton; coord. preventive and primary care svcs. N.J. State Dept. Health, 1993—; clin. instr. grad. nursing program Rutgers U.; clin. preceptor Grad. Nurse Program, Kean Coll. Mem. ANA, N.J. Pub. Health Assn., N.J. State Nurses Assn. (Cmty. Health Nurse of Yr. award 1986), Nat. Soc. Cert. Pub. Mgrs., N.J. Assn. Pub. Health Nurse Adminstrs., N.J. Nat. Svc. Corp. Commn.

VERNIER, RICHARD, educator, author; b. Clermont-Ferrand, France, Feb. 1, 1929; came to U.S., 1951; s. Marcel Eugene Vernier amd Marie José Font; m. Kathleen Manion, July 14, 1962; children: Matthew, John, Stephan. Student in pre-med., Université de Bordeaux, France, 1949; AB, U. Calif., Berkeley, 1958, PhD, 1965. Instr. Mills Coll., Oakland, Calif., 1961-62; lectr. CCNY, 1962-63; asst. prof. San Diego State Coll., 1963-66, U. Wash., Seattle, 1966-72; prof. French Wayne State U., Detroit, 1973-92, prof. emeritus, 1993—; cons. NEH, 1989. Author: Paul Eluard, 1971, Le Feu Parmi les Arbres, 1981, Yves Bonnefoy, 1985, La Patience, 1986, Parcours américain, 1991; Naufrage À Munising, 1995; mem. editorial bd. Swiss-French Studies, Wolfville, N.S., 1981-87. With U.S. Army, 1952-54, Korea. Decorated chevalier Palmes Académiques, Republic of France, 1981, officier, 1990. Avocations: long walks, ancient music. Home: 1326 Marion St Enumclaw WA 98022-2623

VERNIERO, PETER, state attorney general; married; 1 child. BA summa cum laude, Drew U., 1981; JD, Duke U., 1984. Law clk. to Justice Robert L. Clifford, 1984; with Pitney, Hardin, Kipp & Szuch, Morristown, N.J., 1985-87; dir. Herold & Haines P.A., Warren, N.J.; chief counsel, chief of staff Gov. Christine Whitman, Trenton, N.J.; atty. gen. State of N.J., Trenton, 1996—; adj. prof. bus. law County Coll. Morris, 1986. Exec. dir. Rep. State Com., 1989-90. Office: Office Atty Gen Justice Complex CN 080 Trenton NJ 08625*

VERNON, CARL ATLEE, JR., retired wholesale food distributor executive; b. Topeka, Aug. 15, 1926; s. Carl Atlee and Capitola May (Jarboe) V.; m. Marion Leila Colton, May 7, 1950; children—Mary Catherine, Matthew Fowler, Susan Elizabeth. B.S., Yale U., 1947. Merchandising mgr. Fleming Cos., Topeka, 1957-61, dir. merchandising, 1961-66, dir. info. services, 1966-72, v.p. info. services, 1972-74, v.p. regional systems, 1974-79; sr. v.p. mktg. services Fleming Cos., Oklahoma City, 1979-88. Chmn. Shawnee County chpt. ARC, Topeka, Kans., 1957-58. Served to ensign USNR, 1944-46. Republican. Episcopalian. Avocations: golf; gardening; travel.

VERNON, DAVID HARVEY, lawyer, educator; b. Boston, Aug. 9, 1925; s. Bernard Nathan and Ida E. (Cohen) V.; m. Rhoda Louise Sterman, June 1, 1947; children: Amy Lynne, Charles Adam. AB, Harvard U., 1949, LLB, 1952; LLM, NYU, 1953, JSD, 1960; DCL (hon.), U. Durham, Eng., 1988. Bar: Mass. 1952, Iowa 1966. Instr. NYU, 1953-54; asst. prof. law U. Houston, 1954-55; from asst. prof. to prof. law U. N.Mex., Albuquerque, 1955-64; assoc. dean, prof. law U. Wash., Seattle, 1964-66; prof. law U. Iowa, 1966—, dean Coll. Law, 1966-71, A.D. Vestal prof. law, 1986—, acad. v.p., 1988-90; vis. prof. Sch. Law, Washington U., St. Louis, 1974-75, U. Durham (Eng.), fall 1980, Victoria U. Wellington, New Zealand, 1986; vis. scholar Sch. Law, Washington and Lee U., Lexington, Va., spring 1991, So. Tex. Coll. Law, spring 1993. Editor: (with Depew) General State Food and Drug Law, Annotated, 1955, Title XIV of the American Law of Mining, 1960, Conflict of Laws: Cases, Problems and Essays, 1973, supplement, 1979, Contracts: Theory and Practice, 1980, 2d edit., 1991, Conflict of Law: Theory and Practice, 1982, 2d edit., 1991, (with Weinberg, Reynolds and Richmond) Conflict of Law: Cases, Materials and Problems, 1991. Bd. dirs. Wash. State affiliate ACLU, 1964-66, Iowa Civil Liberties Union, 1966-72. With USNR, 1943-46. Fulbright travel awardee, New Zealand, 1986. Mem. ABA (ho. of dels. 1986-91, trustee law sch. admission coun. 1985-86), Iowa Bar Assn., Assn. Am. Law Schs. (mem. exec. com. 1978-80, pres. 1983, editor Jour. Legal Edn. 1987-92). Home: 327 Koser Ave Iowa City IA 52246-3036 Office: U Iowa Coll Law Iowa City IA 52242

VERNON, LILLIAN, mail order company executive; b. Leipzig, Germany; d. Herman and Erna Menasche; children: Fred, David. DCS (hon.), Mercy Coll., Dobbs Ferry, N.Y., 1984, Coll. New Rochelle, DSc in Bus. Adminstrn. (hon.), Bryant Coll., LLD (hon.), Baruch Coll., LHD (hon), Old Dominion U., DCS (hon.) Mercy Coll., DCS (hon.) Coll. New Rochelle, D in Bus. Adminstrn. (hon.) Bryant Coll., LLD (hon.) Baruch Coll. CEOLillian Vernon, New Rochelle, N.Y., 1951—; lectr. in field. Contbr. articles to profl. jours. Bd. dirs. Westchester County Assn., N.Y., Mental Health Assn. Westchester County, Ctr. Preventive Psychiatry, Va. Opera, Children's Mus. Arts, Retinitis Pigmentosa Found.; trustee Coll. Human Svcs., Bryant Coll.; mem. adv. bd. Giraffe Project, Girl Scout Coun. Tidewater, Women's News; mem. bd. overseers Columbia U. Bus. Sch., NYU; mem. adv. com. Citizen Amb. Program; mem. bus. com. Met. Mus. Art; bd. govs. The Forum; mem. nat. com. The Kennedy Ctr. for Performing Arts, Washington; active The Ellis Island Reopening Com., Women's News Bd. Advisors; bd. govs. The Forum. Recipient Dist. Achievement award Lab. Inst. Merchandising, Entrepreneural award Women's Bus. Owners of N.Y., 1983, Bravo award YWCA, Woman of Achievement award Woman's News, Nat. Hero award Big Bros./Big Sisters, Legend in Leadership award Emory U., A Woman Who Has Made A Difference award Inter. Womens Forum, medal of honor Ellis Island, Bus. Leadership award Gannett Newspapers, Outstanding Bus. Leader award Northwood Inst., Congl. Record Commendation award, Crystal award Coll. Human Svcs., City of Peace award Bonds of Israel, Svc. award Sr. Placement Bur., Excellence award Westchester Assn. Women Bus. Owners, Commendation in Congl. Record, Magnificent Seven award Bus. and Profl. Women, Woman of Distinction award Birmingham So. Coll.; named Va. Press Women Newsmaker of Yr., Woman of Yr., Women's Direct Response Group and Westchester County Fedn. Women's Clubs, Hampton Roads Woman of Yr., So. New England Entrepreneur Yr., Bravo award YWCA; named to Acad. Women Achievers, YWCA, Direct Mktg. Assn. Hall of Fame. Mem. Am. Bus. Conf. (dir.), Am. Stock Exch. (listed co. adv. com.), Com. of 200, Women's Forum, Nat. Retail Fedn. (bd. dirs.), Lotos Club. Office: Lillian Vernon Corp 543 Main St New Rochelle NY 10801-7214*

VERNON, RAYMOND, economist, educator; b. N.Y.C., Sept. 1, 1913; s. Hyman and Lillian (Sonnenberg) V.; m. Josephine Stone, Aug. 9, 1935; children: Heidi, Susan Patricia. A.B. cum laude, CCNY, 1933; Ph.D., Columbia U., 1941; M.A. (hon.), Harvard, 1959. Statistician SEC, 1935-42, asst. dir. trading and exchange div., 1942-46; asst. chief internat. resources div. Dept. State, 1946-48; became adviser on comml. policy, 1948; dep. dir. Office of Econ. Def. and Trade Policy, 1951, acting dir., 1954; staff mem. joint Presdl. Congl. Commn. on Fgn. Econ. policy, 1953- 54; planning and control dir. Hawley and Hoops, Inc., 1954-56; dir. N.Y. Met. Region Study, 1956-59; prof. Harvard U. Bus. Sch., 1959-78, dir. Harvard Devel. Adv. Service, 1962-65, dir. Ctr. for Internat. Affairs, 1973-78, prof. internat. relations, 1978-83, prof. emeritus, 1983—; bd. dirs. Cambridge Energy Rsch. Assocs.; lectr. Am. U., 1946-48, Princeton U., 1954-55, Swarthmore Coll., 1955-56; adj. prof. Fletcher Sch. Law and Diplomacy., 1979-81; mem. Mission on Japanese Combines, Tokyo, 1946; mem. U.S. del. GATT, Geneva, 1950, Torquay, Eng., 1951, vice chmn. U.S. del., Geneva, 1952; spl. cons. to undersec. Dept. State, 1962, Dept. Treasury, 1978-79; participant UN Conf. on Regional Devel., Tokyo, 1958; vis. prof. World Bank, 1987. Author: Regulation of Stock Exchange Members, 1941, America's Trade Policy and GATT, 1954, Organizing for World Trade, 1956, (with Edgar M. Hoover) Anatomy of a Metropolis, 1959, Metropolis 1985, 1960, The Dilemma of Mexico's Development, 1963, Myth and Reality of Our Urban Problems, 1965, Manager in The International Economy, 1968, Sovereignty at Bay, 1971, Storm over the Multinationals, 1976, Two Hungry Giants, 1983, Exploring the Global Economy, 1985, (with D.L. Spar) Beyond Globalism, 1988; editor: Public Policy and Private Enterprise in Mexico, 1964, How Latin America Views the U.S. Investor, 1966, The Technology Factor in International Trade, 1970, Big Business and the State, 1974, The Oil Crisis, 1976, State-owned Enterprises in the Western Economies, 1980, The Promise of Privatization, 1988, (with D.L. Spar and Glenn Tobin) Iron Triangles and Revolving Doors, 1991, (with Ethan Kapstein) Defense and Dependence in a Global Economy, 1992; founding editor Jour. Policy Analysis and Mgmt., 1981-85; contbr. articles to profl. jours. Recipient Meritorious Svc. award Dept. State, 1951, Disting. Svc. award Harvard Bus. Sch., 1986; decorated Order of Rising Sun (Japan), 1986; named Eminent scholar Internat. Studies Assn., 1994. Fellow Am. Acad. Arts and Scis., Acad. Internat. Bus.; mem. Council on Fgn. Relations, U.S./UN Assn., Phi Beta Kappa. Home: 1 Dunstable Rd Cambridge MA 02138-3341 Office: Harvard U Kennedy Sch Govt 79 JFK St Cambridge MA 02138-5801

VERNON, SHIRLEY JANE, architect, educator; b. Mt. Kisco, N.Y., Dec. 9, 1930; d. J.H. and M.R. (Maher) V. B.Arch. cum laude, Pa. State U., 1953. Asso., coordinating architect for design, designer Vincent G. Kling and Assos., Phila., 1953-68; pvt. practice architecture Phila., 1968-74, 75—; mgr. archtl. design Ballinger Co., Phila., 1974-75; instr. architecture Drexel U., 1956-58, adj. asst. prof., 1959-64, adj. asso. prof., 1965-69, adj. prof., 1970-87; sr. advisor Phila. Coll. Art, 1980-81; prof. Moore Coll. Art and Design (formerly Moore Coll. Art), 1986—. Recipient 25 Yr. Service award Drexel U., 1982. Fellow AIA (chpt. dir. 1973, 79, chpt. v.p. 1975); mem. Art Alliance Phila., Assn. Collegiate Schs. Architecture, Print Club Phila., Tau Beta Pi. Office: 1704 Delancey St Philadelphia PA 19103-6715

VERNON, WESTON, III (WES VERNON), journalist; b. N.Y.C., Aug. 23, 1931; s. Weston, Jr. and Adelaide (Neilson) V.; m. Alida Steinvoort, Oct. 5, 1951; children: Rosanne, Weston IV, Diane, John Randall. Student, Utah State U., 1949-50, Brigham Young U., 1953-54. Reporter, producer KBUH, Brigham City, Utah, 1950-51, KVRS, Rock Springs, Wyo., 1952, KOVO, Provo, Utah, 1952-54, Intermountain Network, Salt Lake City, 1954, KLO, Ogden, Utah, 1954, KBMY, Billings, Mont., 1954-63; news dir.-polit. specialist KSL Radio-TV, Salt Lake City, 1963-68; bur. chief Bonneville Internat. Corp., Washington, 1968-72; corr. CBS Radio Stas. News Service, CBS Radio, Washington, 1972—; host CBS Crosstalk; bd. dirs. Am. Zephyr, Inc. Columnist The High Green, The Timetable; contbr. to Passenger Train jour., Railfan and Railroad. Bd. dirs. Winding-Orchard Citizens Assn., Wheaton-Glenmont, Md., 1974-77, 86—, pres., 1975-76. Served with AUS, 1951-52. Recipient Journalism awards Mont. A.P. Press Stas., 1960, Journalism awards Utah Bar Assn., 1965, Journalism awards Utah Broadcasters Assn., 1965-66. Mem. Radio-TV Corrs. Assn., Am. Legion (comdr. Yellowstone Post 4 1962-63), Railroad Enthusiasts (pres. Chesapeake divsn. 1992-94), Nat. Assn. Radio Talk Show Hosts. Office: CBS Radio Stas News Svc 2020 M St NW Washington DC 20036-3368

VERONIS, GEORGE, geophysics educator; b. New Brunswick, N.J., June 6, 1926; s. Nicholas Emmanuel and Angeliki (Efthimakis) V.; m. Anna Margareta Olsson, Nov. 8, 1963; m. Catherine Elizabeth, Jan. 29, 1949 (div. Nov. 1962); children—Melissa, Benjamin. A.B., Lafayette Coll., 1950; Ph.D., Brown U., 1954; M.A. (hon.), Yale U., 1966. Staff meteorologist Inst. Advanced Study, Princeton, 1953-56; staff mathematician Woods Hole Oceanographic Inst., Mass., 1956-64, mem. staff, dir. geophys. fluid dynamics summer program, 1959—, assoc. prof. MIT, Cambridge, 1961-64, research oceanographer, 1964-66; prof. geophysics and applied sci. Yale U., New Haven, 1966—, Henry Barnard Davis prof., 1985—, chmn. geology and geophysics, 1976-79, dir. applied math, 1979-93. Editor Jour. Marine Rsch., 1973—; contbr. articles to profl. jours. Served with USN, 1943-46. Fellow Am. Acad. Arts and Scis., Am. Geophys. Union; mem. NAS, Norwegian Acad. Scis. (Robert L. and Bettie P. Cody award 1989). Greek Orthodox.

VERONIS, PETER, publisher; b. New Brunswick, N.J., June 15, 1923; s. Nicholas M. and Angeliki (Efthemakis) V.; m. Dorothy E. White, Sept. 8, 1946; 1 dau., Judith Anne Veronis Rodgers. Student, Columbia U., 1951-54. Nat. advt. mgr. Springfield (Mass.) Newspapers, 1954-57; v.p., gen. sales mgr. Ridder Johns Co., N.Y.C., 1957-62; corp. exec. Curtis Pub. Co., N.Y.C., 1963-64; assoc. sales mgr. Look mag., 1964-68; v.p., advt. dir. Psychology Today mag., 1968-71; v.p. advt. Saturday Rev., N.Y.C., 1971-73; pub. Book Digest, N.Y.C., 1973-80; pres. PV Pub. Inc., N.Y.C., 1980-81, Conn., 1988—; v.p., dir. CBS Mag. Network, N.Y.C., 1981-85, pres., 1985-87; pres. Diamandis Mag. Network, 1987-88. Served with USN, 1941-51. Home: 42 Thornwood Rd Stamford CT 06903-2613

VERPLANCK, WILLIAM SAMUEL, psychologist, educator; b. Plainfield, N.J., Jan. 6, 1916; s. William Samuel and Kathryn (Tracy) V. B.S., U. Va., 1937, M.A., 1938; Ph.D., Brown U., 1941. Asst. prof. Ind. U., 1946-50; asst. prof. Harvard, 1950-55, acting asso. prof., 1955-56; research asso. Stanford U., 1956-57; asso. prof. Hunter Coll., 1957-59; prof. U. Md., 1958-62; prof. psychology U. Tenn., 1963-81, head dept., 1963-73; founder, chmn. Resource Assocs., Inc., 1980-82; bd. dirs. Cambridge Ctr. for Behavioral Sci. Author: (with others) Modern Learning Theory, 1953. Served to lt. USNR, 1943-46. Recipient travel grant Am. Philos. Assn., 1953. Fellow APA, Am. Psychol. Soc., Assn. Study Animal Behavior, AAAS; mem. Ea. Psychol. Assn., Psychonomic Soc. (founder, past sec.-treas., bd. govs.), Sigma Xi, Sigma Alpha Epsilon. *The history of psychology is largely constituted of a succession of fads overlying the continuity given by a few plausible technological methods which have been progressively misapplied, with little critical concern for their social, political or scientific consequences. Can any person, working over a period of fifty years, make a difference?.*

VERPLOEGEN, LORRAINE JEAN, elementary school educator; b. Havre, Mont., Mar. 15, 1950; d. Edwin Edgar and Donna Lee (Perry) Larson; m. Frank Edward Verploegen, Nov. 17, 1973; children: Eric James, Erin Jean. BS in Edn., Mont. State U., Billings, 1972; MEd, Mont. State U., Havre, 1991. Remedial reading tchr. Huntley Project, Worden, Mont., 1972; primary resource tchr. Havre Pub. Schs., 1972-75, 78-79, 1991-92, intermediate resource tchr., 1989-91, tchr. grades 1, 2 and 3, 1976-79, 79-80, reading recovery tchr. leader, 1992—; itinerant resource tchr. Bear Paw Coop, Chinook, Mont., 1988; primary resource tchr. Rocky Boy Elem. Sch., Box Elder, Mont., 1988; tchr. K-6 Cottonwood Country Sch., Havre, 1982-86. 4-H leader Hill County 4-H, Havre, 1984-94. Mont. State Reading Coun. Tchr. Project grantee, 1993-94. Mem. NEA, Tri-County Reading Coun. (pres., v.p.), Mont. State Reading Coun. (state chair 1982-92, Leadership award 1991), Havre Edn. Assn. (pres.), Internat. Reading Assn. Avocations: reading, cross-stitch, crocheting, music. Home: 3190 7th St E Havre MT 59501

VERRECCHIA, ALFRED J., toy company executive; b. 1943. Asst. controller Hasbro Inc., 1965-70, controller, 1970-74, treas., 1974—, v.p., 1980—, then sr. v.p. fin., then exec. v.p. fin. and adminstrn., pres. mfg. svcs. div., exec. v.p., 1989—, chief oper. officer, 1989—. Office: Hasbro Inc 1027 Newport Ave Pawtucket RI 02861-2539*

VERRECCHIA, ALFRED JOSEPH, consumer products company executive; b. Providence, Feb. 19, 1943; s. Alfred Augustus and Elda Lucy (Tortolani) V.; m. Geraldine Macari, June 11, 1964; children: Michael, Michele, Melisa, Lisa. BS, U. R.I., 1967, MBA in Fin., 1971; Doctorate (hon.), Johnson & Wales U., 1991. V.p. fin. Hasbro, Inc., Pawtucket, R.I., 1980-82; sr. v.p. fin., CFO Hasbro, Inc., Pawtucket, 1982-86, exec. v.p. fin., CFO, 1986-89, exec. v.p., 1989, pres. Hasbro mfg. svcs., 1989, co-COO, 1989, COO, 1990—. Chmn. Bradley Hosp., East Providence, R.I.; pres. R.I. Pub. Expenditure Coun., Providence; bd. mem. Bd. of Govs. for Higher Edn., Providence, U. R.I. Coll. Bus., Kingston, R.I. Mem. Toy Mfrs. Am. (bd. mem.). Office: Hasbro Inc 1027 Newport Ave Pawtucket RI 02862

VERRET, JOHN CYRIL, advertising executive; b. Burlington, Vt., Oct. 21, 1945; s. Albert A. and Barbara (Cote) V.; m. Margaret Simisky, Feb. 20, 1971; children: Michael John, Justin Thomas. BS in Econ., St. Michael's Coll., 1968. Account exec. Quinn and Johnson, Boston, 1969-75; account supr. Hill Holliday Connors Cosmopulus, Boston, 1975-76; v.p. account supr. Pearson and MacDonald, Boston, 1976-78; v.p. mgmt. supr. Ingalls Assoc., Boston, 1978-87; exec. v.p. Arnold and Co., Boston, 1987-88, pres., 1988-89; pres. New Eng. Broadcasting, 1988—; vice chmn. Arnold, Fortuna, Lawner & Cabot, 1990—; 1st v.p. New Eastland Broadcasting Assn., Boston, 1970—. Mem. Boston Ad Club (pres. 1990-91), Execs. Club. Roman Catholic,. Avocations: coaching, basketball, carpentry, reading, squashing.

VERRILL, CHARLES OWEN, JR., lawyer; b. Biddeford, Maine, Sept. 30, 1937; s. Charles Owen and Elizabeth (Handy) V.; m. Mary Ann Blanchard, Aug. 13, 1960 (dec.); children: Martha Anne, Edward Blanchard, Ethan Christopher, Elizabeth Handy, Matthew Lawton, Peter Goldthwait; m. Diana Baber, Dec. 11, 1993. AB, Tufts U., 1959; LLB, Duke U., 1962. Bar: D.C. 1962. Assoc. Weaver & Glassie, 1962-64; assoc. Barco, Cook, Patton & Blow, 1964-66, ptnr., 1967; ptnr. Patton, Boggs & Blow, 1967-84, Wiley, Rein & Fielding, Washington, 1984—; adj. prof. internat. trade law Georgetown U. Law Ctr., Washington, 1978—, Charles Fahy Disting. adj. prof., 1993; conf. chmn. The Future of Internat. Steel Industry, Bellagio, Italy, 1984, U.S. Agenda for Uruguay Round, Airlie House, Warrenton, Va., 1986, Polish Joint Venture Law, Cracow, Poland, 1987, Internat. Steel Industry II, Bellagio, 1987, Bulgaria and the GATT, Washington, 1977; lectr. Duke U. Law Sch., 1970-73; chair, spkr. Protection of Intellectual Property from Theft and Piracy Abroad Southwestern Legal Found. Fgn. Investment Symposium, 1995, chair, panel on NAFTA 2 1/2 Years Later, 1996. Local dir. Tufts U. Ann. Fund, 1965-69; mem. Duke Law Alumni Coun., 1972-75; trustee Internat. Law Inst., 1981—, chmn. bd. trustees, 1983-87; trustee Bulgarian Am. Friendship Soc., 1992—, Christ Ch., Dark Harbor, Maine; apptd. to roster of dispute settlement panelists World Trade Orgn., 1995. Mem. ABA, Internat. Bar Assn., D.C. Bar Assn., Order of Coif, Theta Delta Chi, Phi Delta Phi, Met. Club (Washington), Chevy Chase Club (Md.), Tarratine Club (Dark Harbor, Maine). Home: 3000 Q St NW Washington DC 20007-3080 Office: 1776 K St NW Washington DC 20006-2304

VERRILL, F. GLENN, advertising executive; b. N.Y.C., Dec. 17, 1923; s. Ralph Francis and Rose (Verner) V.; m. Jean Demar, Aug. 25, 1946; children: Gary, Joan. A.B., Adelphi Coll., 1949; A.M., Harvard U., 1950. With Batten, Barton, Durstine & Osborn, Inc., 1952—, v.p., 1964; creative dir. Batten, Barton, Durstine & Osborn, Inc. (Burke Dowling Adams div.), Atlanta, 1965-70, exec. v.p., gen. mgr., 1970-71, pres., 1971-88, chmn., 1988—, also dir. parent co. Author: Advertising Procedure, 1983, rev. edit., 1986, 88. Mem. adv. bd. U. Ga.; vice chmn. bd. overseers Coll. Bus. Adminstrn., Ga. State U.; bd. dirs. Atlanta Humane Soc., pres., 1980-81; chmn. Advanced Advt. Inst. Atlanta, 1981; mem. Peabody award com., 1984—; bd. dirs. Atlanta Coll. of Art, 1990. With USAAF, 1943-46. Mem. Am. Assn. Advt. Agys. (nat. dir. 1973—). Episcopalian. Clubs: Atlanta Athletic, Cherokee, Harvard (Atlanta). Home: 2600 W Wesley Rd NW Atlanta GA 30327-2036 Office: 3414 Peachtree Rd NE Atlanta GA 30326-1113

VERRILLO, RONALD THOMAS, neuroscience educator, researcher; b. Hartford, Conn., July 31, 1927; s. Francesco Paul and Angela (Forte) V.; m. Violet Silverstein, June 3, 1950; children—Erica, Dan, Thomas. B.A., Syracuse U., 1952; Ph.D., U. Rochester, 1958. Asst. prof. Syracuse U., 1957-62, research assoc., 1959-63, research fellow, 1963-67, assoc. prof., 1967-74, prof., 1974-94, prof. emeritus, 1995, assoc. dir. Inst. Sensory Research, 1980-84, dir., 1984-93, dir. grad. neurosci. program, 1984-93; advisor com. on hearing, bioacoustics and biomechanics NRC. Author: Adjustment to Visual Disability, 1961 (award 1962). Contbr. many chpts. to books, articles to profl. jours. Served with USN, 1945-46. Fellow Am. Found. for Blind, 1956, NATO, 1970; grantee NSF, 1969-72, 84-87, NIH, 1972—. Fellow Acoustical Soc. Am.; mem. Soc. for Neurosci. N.Y. Acad. Scis., Sigma Xi (research award 1982). Home: 312 Berkley Dr Syracuse NY 13210-3031 Office: Syracuse U Inst Sensory Rsch Merrill Ln Syracuse NY 13244

VERRONE, PATRIC MILLER, lawyer, writer; b. Glendale, N.Y.C., Sept. 29, 1959; s. Pat and Edna (Miller) V.; m. Margaret Maiya Williams, 1989; 1 child, Patric Carroll Williams. BA, Harvard U., 1981; JD, Boston Coll., 1984. Bar: Fla. 1984, Calif. 1988, U.S. Dist. Ct. (mid. dist.) Fla. 1984, U.S. Dist. Ct. (ctrl. dist.) Calif. 1995, U.S. Ct. Appeals (9th cir.) 1995. Assoc. Allen, Knudsen, Swartz, DeBoest, Rhoads & Edwards, Ft. Myers, Fla., 1984-86; writer The Tonight Show, Burbank, Calif., 1987-90; temp. judge L.A. Mcpl. Ct., 1995—. Dir., producer, writer The Civil War–The Lost Episode, 1991; writer The Larry Sanders Show, 1992-94, The Critic, 1993-95; producer, writer The Simpsons, 1994-95, Muppets Tonight!, 1995—; editor Harvard Lampoon, 1978-84, Boston Coll. Law Rev., 1983-84, Fla. Bar Jour., 1987-88, L.A. Lawyer, 1994—; contbr. articles to profl. jours. including Elysian Fields Quar., Baseball and the American Legal Mind. Bd. dirs. Calif. Confedn. of Arts, Mus. Contemporary Art. Mem. ABA (vice chair arts, entertainment and sports law com.), Calif. Bar, Calif. Lawyers for Arts, L.A. County Bar Assn. (sec. barristers exec. com., chair artists and the law com., steering com. homeless shelter project, intellectual property and entertainment law sect., legis. activity com.), Fla. Bar Assn., Writers Guild Am. West (contracts com. animation writers caucus), Harvard Club Lee County (v.p. 1985-86), Harvard Club So. Calif. Republican. Roman Catholic. Avocations: filmmaking, video, baseball. Home and Office: 6466 Odin St Los Angeles CA 90068-2730

VERSACE, GIANNI, fashion designer; b. Reggion Calabria, Italy, Dec. 2, 1946; s. Antonio and Francesca Versace. Student, pub. sch., Italy. Designer: Complice, Genny and Callaghan, Milan, Italy, 1972-78; 1st signature women's wear collection, Milan, Italy, 1978—, menswear collection, Versaci Signature exhbn., Berlin, 1995; founder 1st of 80 exclusive boutiques, Milan, 1979—; developer namesake fragrance, Italy, France, Switzerland, Austria and U.S.A., 1981—; costume desginer for ballets Leib und Leid, Josephlegende, Dyonisos, for opera Don Pasquale (La Scala), 1984; collaborator South Beach Stories, 1992; author: Designs, 1994. Recipient Golden Eye award for best fashion designer of women's wear for fall-winter, 1982-84, Cutty Sark award, 1983, International award, CFDA, 1992, VH1 Fashion and Music award, 1995. Home: Via Gesu 12, 20121 Milan Italy Office: Gianni Versace Boutique 816 Madison Ave New York NY 10021-4904

VERSCHOOR, CURTIS CARL, business educator, consultant; b. Grand Rapids, Mich., June 7, 1931; s. Peter and Leonene (Dahlstrom) V.; m. Marie Emilie Kritschgau, June 18, 1952; children—Katherine Anne, Carolyn Marie, John Peter, Carla Michelle. BBA with distinction, U. Mich., 1951, MBA, 1952; EdD, No. Ill. U., 1977. CPA; cert. mgmt. acctg., cert. fin. planner, cert. fraud examiner, cert. internal auditor; chartered fin. cons. Pub. accountant Touche, Ross, Bailey & Smart (C.P.A.'s), 1955-63; with Singer Co., 1963-68, asst. controller, 1965-68; controller Colgate-Palmolive Co., 1968-69; asst. controller bus. products group Xerox Corp., 1969-72; controller Baxter Internat., 1972-73; v.p. finance Altair Corp., Chgo., 1973-74; prof. DePaul U., Chgo., 1974-94, ledger and quill alumni rsch. prof., 1994—; pres. C.C. Verschoor & Assocs., Inc., 1981—; part-time instr. Wayne State U., 1955-60. Contbg. editor: Jour. Accountancy, 1961-62, Jour. Internal Auditing, 1985—. Served with AUS, 1953-55. Recipient Elijah Watts Sells award Am. Inst. C.P.A.'s, 1953. Mem. AICPA, Ill. Soc. CPAs, Fin. Execs. Inst., Am. Acctg. Assn., Inst. Mgmt. Accts., Inst. Internal Auditors, Nat. Assn. Corp. Dirs., Beta Gamma Sigma, Beta Alpha Psi, Delta Pi Epsilon, Phi Kappa Phi, Phi Eta Sigma. Home: 231 Wyngate Dr Barrington IL 60010-4840 Office: DePaul Univ One E Jackson Blvd Chicago IL 60604-2287

VERSCHOYLE, JULIA ANN, advocate, artist; b. San Antonio, July 17, 1954; d. Hubert Henry and Katherine Leota (Largent) V.; m. Herbert E. Jordan, Dec. 29, 1973; 3 children. Student, S.W. Tex. State U., 1972-73, 89. tchr. Carnegie Arts Ctr., Leavenworth, Kans., spring 1993, summer and fall, 1994; contractor as advocate, resource contact exceptional family mem. program (EFMP) Army Community Svcs. (ACS), 1993—; speaker Acad. Allergy and Immunology, Kansas City, Kans., 1994; various positions retail sales. Exhibited in San Antonio Area Art Shows, 1989, Kuntslerbund Cafe Art Guild Annual Show, Stuttgart, Germany, 1992, Gallery 93, Kansas City, Kans., 1993, Women Vision Art Show, Kansas City, Mo., 1993, Carnegie Arts Ctr., Leavenworth, 1990, 1995 Theme Show Muse Gallery, Kansas City, Corpus Christi Ctr. for the Arts, Demensions Art Show, 1995-96, Rockport Ctr. for the Arts, 1995-96, Rockport Tex. Vol. receptionist, newsletter editor/illustrator ACS, Ft. Bliss, Tex., 1981-83, parent rep. EFMP, Ft. Ord, Calif., 1983-84, Leavenworth 1992—; vol. Cystic Fibrosis Found., Tuscaloosa, Ala., 1984; coord. asthma support group, vol. EFMP office Brooke Army Med. Ctr., San Antonio, 1984-90; vol. parent speaker asthma seminars Am. Lung Assn., San Antoinio, 1984-90; den leader, treas., com. chmn. Boy Scouts Am., San Antonio, 1984-90, com. vol., Stuttgart, 1990-92; mayor U.S. mil. housing areas during Desert Storm, Stuttgart, 1990-92; facilitator med. care com. DA Family Symposium, Stuttgart, 1990-92; mem. DOD Families and Schs. Together, Stuttgart, 1990-92; bd. dirs. Army Cmty. Svcs., 6th Area Support Group, Robinson Barracks, Stuttgart, 1990-92; vol. Asthma & Allergy Found., Leavenworth, 1992-95; coord. Leavenworth Asthma Network, 1992—; mem. parents adv. coun. Leavenworth Special Edn. Coop., 1992-94; del. as advisor for handicapped Pioneers of Change handicapped, 1993, mem. pioneers of change state of Kansas; parent advocate Children with Spl. Needs, Leavenworth, 1993-94; com. mem. Levenworth County Spl. Edn. Coop. Transition Coun.; mem. Leavenworth Area Coordinating Coun. Early Childhood Devel.; vol. early childhood devel. program compliance reviews State of Kans. Recipient VII Corps Desert Shield/Storm Vol. award U.S. Army, 1992, Gahagen Svc. award. Home: Rt HC04 Box 104B Leavenworth KS 66048

VERSFELT, DAVID SCOTT, lawyer; b. Mineola, N.Y., Feb. 17, 1951; s. William H. and Ruth (Gerland) V.; m. Mary Deborah Garber, Aug. 31, 1974; children: Christopher L., William S., Kathryn H. AB, Princeton U., 1973; JD, Columbia U., 1976. Bar: N.Y. 1977, U.S. Dist. Ct. (so. and ea. dists.) N.Y. 1977, U.S. Ct. Appeals (D.C. cir.) 1979, U.S. Ct. Appeals (2d and 7th cirs.) 1980, U.S. Supreme Ct. 1980, U.S. Ct. Appeals (9th cir.) 1981, U.S. Ct. Appeals (3d cir.) 1982, Ct. Internat. Trade 1990, U.S. Ct. Appeals (fed. cir.) 1994. Mem. Coun. of Community Law Office; vol. div. Legal Aid Soc., N.Y.C., 1985-88; dir. Partnership for a Drug-Free Am., 1989—. Mem. ABA, Assn. Bar City N.Y. (com. on state legislation 1983-85), Phi Beta Kappa. Office: Donovan Leisure Newton & Irvine 30 Rockefeller Plz New York NY 10112

VERSIC, LINDA JOAN, nurse educator, research company executive; b. Grove City, Pa., Aug. 27, 1944; d. Robert and Kathryn I. (Fagird) Davies; m. Ronald James Versic, June 11, 1966; children: Kathryn Clara, Paul Joseph. RN, Johns Hopkins Sch. of Nursing, 1965; BS in Health Edn., Ctrl. State U., 1980. Asst. head nurse Johns Hopkins Hosp., Balt., 1965-67; staff Nurse Registry Miami Valley Hosp., Dayton, Ohio, 1973-90; instr. Miami Jacobs Jr. Coll. Bus., Dayton, 1977-79; pres. Ronald T. Dodge Co., Dayton, 1979-86, chmn. bd., 1987—; chmn. bd. dirs. A-1 Travel, Inc. instr. Warren County (Ohio) Career Ctr., 1980-84, coord. diversified health occupations, 1984—. Coord. youth activities, mem. steering com. Queen of Apostles Cmty. Recipient Excellence in Tchg. award, 1992, award for Project Excellence, 1992. Active Miami Valley Mil. Affairs Assn., Glen Helen, Friends of Dayton Ballet, Dayton Art Inst., Cin. Art Mus. Mem. Ohio Vocat. Assn., Am. Vocat. Assn., Vocat. Indsl. Clubs Am. (chpt. advisor 1982—). Roman Catholic. Club: Johns Hopkins, Yugoslav of Greater Dayton. Home: 1601 Shafor Blvd Dayton OH 45419-3103 Office: Ronald T Dodge Co PO Box 630 Dayton OH 45459-0630

VERSTANDIG, TONI GRANT, federal agency administrator; b. Pitts., Jan. 15, 1953; d. Louis A. and Ruth M. (O'Block) Grant; m. Lee L. Verstandig, Feb. 20, 1982; 1 stepchild, Scott B.; 1 child, Grant L. BA, Boston U., 1974; AD, Stephens Coll., 1972. Legis. asst. subcom. on agrl. labor House Com. on Edn. and Labor, 1976-77; staff dir. subcom. on accts. House Adminstrn. Com., 1977-78; mem. profl. staff subcom. on internat. security/sci. affairs House Com. on Fgn. Affairs, 1978-86; mem. profl. staff Com. on Fgn. Affairs, 1986-93; dep. asst. sec. of state Near Ea. affairs U.S. Dept. of State, Washington, 1993—; cons. to com. on fgn. affairs U.S. Ho. of Reps., 1978-93, staff dir. subcom. accts., com. on house adminstrn., prin. legis. asst. to Congressman John N. Dent. Vol. cons. on fgn. policy and nat. security Clinton-Gore Presdl. Campaign, 1992. Recipient Spl. Merit of Honor commendation Mayor Kevin White. Office: Dept of State Near Eastern Affairs 2201 C St NW Rm 6244 Washington DC 20520-0001

VER STEEG, CLARENCE LESTER, historian, educator; b. Orange City, Iowa, Dec. 28, 1922; s. John A. and Annie (Vischer) Ver S.; m. Dorothy Ann De Vries, Dec. 24, 1943; 1 child, John Charles. AB, Morningside Coll., Sioux City, Iowa, 1943; MA, Columbia U., 1946, PhD, 1950; LHD, Morningside Coll., 1988. Lectr., then instr. history Columbia U., N.Y.C., 1946-50; mem. faculty Northwestern U., Evanston, Ill., 1950—, prof. history, 1959—, dean grad. sch., 1975-86; vis. lectr. Harvard U., 1959-60; mem. council Inst. Early Am. History and Culture, Williamsburg, Va., 1961-64, 68-72, chmn. exec. com., 1970-72; vis. mem. Inst. Advanced Study, Princeton, N.J., 1967-68; chmn. faculty com. to recommend Master Plan Higher Edn. in Ill., 1962-64; mem. Grad. Record Exam. Bd., 1981-86, chmn., 1984-86; bd. dirs. Ctr. for Research Libraries, 1980-85, Council Grad. Schs. in U.S., 1983-87; pres. Assn. Grad. Schs., 1984-85; mem. steering com. Grad. Research Project, Consortium on Financing Higher Edn., 1981-85; mem. working group on talent Nat. Acad. Scis., 1984-87; mem. Higher Edn. Policy Adv. Com. to OCLC, Online Computer Library Ctr., 1984-87. Author: Robert Morris, Revolutionary Financier, 1954, A True and Historical Narraative of the Colony of Georgia, 1960, The American People: Their Historical, 1961, The Formative Years, 1607-1763, 1964 (Brit. edit.), 1965, The Story of Our Country, 1965, (with others) Investigating Man's World, 6 vols., 1970, A People and a Nation, 1971, The Origins of a Southern Mosaic: Studies of Early Carolina and Georgia, 1975, World Cultures, 1977, American Spirit, 1982, rev. edit., 1990; sr. author: Health Social Studies, 7 Vols., 1991, Planning at Northwestern University in the 1960s, 1993; editor: Great Issues in American History, From Settlement to Revolution 1584-1776, 1969; editl. cons.: Papers of Robert Morris, vols. I-VIII, 1973—; contbr. articles to profl. jours. Served with USAAF, 1942-45. Decorated Air medal with 3 oak leaf clusters; 5 Battle Stars; Social Sci. Research Council fellow, 1948-49, George A. and Eliza Gardner Howard Found. fellow, 1954-55, Huntington Library research fellow, 1955, Am. Council Learned Socs. sr.

fellow, 1958-59, Guggenheim fellow, 1964-65, NEH sr. fellow, 1973. Mem. AAUP, Am. Hist. Assn. (nominating com. 1965-68, chmn. 1967-68, Albert J. Beveridge prize 1952, hon. mention 1991 Eugene Asher Disting. Teaching award), Orgn. Am. Historians (editorial bd. Jour. Am. History 1968-72), So. Hist. Assn. (nominating com. 1970-72). Presbyterian. Home: 2619 Ridge Ave Evanston IL 60201-1717 Office: Northwestern Univ Dean Grad Sch Evanston IL 60208

VER STEEG, DONNA LORRAINE FRANK, nurse, sociologist, educator; b. Minot, N.D., Sept. 23, 1929; d. John Jonas and Pearl H. (Denlinger) Frank; m. Richard W. Ver Steeg, Nov. 22, 1950; children: Juliana, Anne, Richard B. BSN, Stanford, 1951; MSN, U. Calif., San Francisco, 1967; MA in Sociology, UCLA, 1969, PhD in Sociology, 1973. Clin. instr. U. N.D. Sch. Nursing, 1962-63; USPHS nurse rsch. fellow UCLA, 1969-72; spl. cons., adv. com. on physicians' assts. and nurse practitioner programs Calif. State Bd. Med. Examiners, 1972-73; asst. prof. UCLA Sch. Nursing, 1973-79, assoc. prof., 1979-94, asst. dean, 1981-83, chmn. primary ambulatory care, 1976-87, assoc. dean, 1983-86, prof. emeritus/recalled, 1994—, chair primary care, 1994—; co-prin. investigator PRIMEX Project, Family Nurse Practitioners, UCLA Extension, 1974-76; assoc. cons. Calif. Postsecondary Edn. Commn., 1975-76; spl. cons. Calif. Dept. Consumer Affairs, 1978; accredited visitor Western Assn. Schs. and Colls., 1985; mem. Calif. State Legis. Health Policy Forum, 1980-81; mem. nurse practitioner adv. com. Calif. Bd. RNs, 1995—. Contbr. chpts. to profl. books. Recipient Leadership award Calif. Area Health Edn. Ctr. System, 1989, Commendation award Calif. State Assembly, 1994; named Outstanding Faculty Mem. UCLA Sch. Nursing, 1982. Fellow Am. Acad. Nursing; mem. AAAS, ANA (chair Calif. intern 1995-96), Am. Soc. Law and Medicine, Nat. League Nursing, Calif. League Nursing, N.Am. Nursing Diagnosis Assn., Am. Assn. History Nursing, Assn. Health Svcs. Rsch., Stanford Nurses Club, Sigma Theta Tau (Gamma Tau chpt. Leadership award 1994), Sigma Xi. Home: 708 Swarthmore Ave Pacific Palisades CA 90272-4353 Office: UCLA Sch Nursing 700 Tiverton Ave Box 956919 Los Angeles CA 90095

VERTS, LITA JEANNE, university administrator; b. Jonesboro, Ark., Apr. 13, 1935; d. William Gus and Lolita Josephine (Peeler) Nash; m. B. J. Verts, Aug. 29, 1954 (div. 1975); 1 child, William Trigg. BA, Oreg. State U., 1973; MA in Lingustics, U. Oreg., 1974; postgrad., U. Hawaii, 1977. Librarian Forest Research Lab., Corvallis, Oreg., 1966-69; instr. English Lang. Inst., Corvallis, 1974-80; dir. spl. svcs. Oreg. State U., Corvallis, 1980—, faculty senator, 1988—. Editor ann. book: Trio Achievers, 1986, 87, 88; contbr. articles to profl. jours. Precinct com. Rep. Party, Corvallis, 1977-80; adminstrv. bd. 1st United Meth. Ch., Corvallis, 1987-89, mem. fin. com., 1987-93, tchr. Bible, 1978—; bd. dirs. Westminster Ho., United Campus Ministries, 1994-95; adv. coun. Disabilities Svc., Linn, Benton, Lincoln Counties, 1990—, vice-chmn., 1992-93, chmn. 1993-94. Mem. N.W. Assn. Spl. Programs (pres. 1985-86), Nat. Coun. Ednl. Opportunities Assn. (bd. dirs. 1984-87), Nat. Gardening Assn., Alpha Phi (mem. corp. bd. Beta Upsilon chpt. 1990-96). Republican. Methodist. Avocations: gardening, photography, golf. Home: 530 SE Mayberry Ave Corvallis OR 97333-1866 Office: Spl Svcs Project Waldo 337 OSU Corvallis OR 97331

VERU, THEODORE, advertising agency executive. Formerly exec. v.p., chief operating officer, then pres., chief operating officer Lois Pitts Gershon Pon/GGK (now Lois/GGK) Lois Pitts Gershon Pon/GGK (now Lois/USA Inc.), N.Y.C. Office: Lois/USA Inc 40 W 57th St New York NY 10019-4001

VERVILLE, ELIZABETH GIAVANI, federal official; b. N.Y.C., July 13, 1940; d. Joseph and Gertrude (Levy) Giavani. BA, Duke U., 1961; LLB, Columbia U., 1964. Bar: Mass. 1965, U.S. Supreme Ct. 1970, D.C. 1980. Assoc. Snow Motley & Holt, successor Gaston Snow & Ely Bartlett, Boston, 1965-67; asst. atty. gen. Commonwealth of Mass., Boston, 1967-69; atty. advisor for African affairs U.S. Dept. State, Washington, 1979-72, asst. legal adviser for East Asian and Pacific affairs, 1972-80, dep. legal adviser, 1980-89; dep. asst. sec. state Bur. Politico-Mil. Affairs Bur. Politico-Mil. Affairs, Washington, 1989-92; sr. coord. Bur. Politico-Mil. Affairs, 1992-95; dir. for global and multilateral affairs Nat. Security Coun., Washington, 1995—. Recipient presdl. rank of meritorious exec., 1985, 90, presdl. rank disting. exec., 1988. Mem. Am. Soc. Internat. Law, Coun. on Fgn. Rels. Home: 3012 Dumbarton Ave NW Washington DC 20007-3305 Office: Nat Security Coun The White House Washington DC 20504

VESCOVI, SELVI, pharmaceutical company executive; b. N.Y.C., June 14, 1930; s. Antonio and Desolina V.; BS, Coll. William and Mary, 1951; m. Elma Pasquinelli, Oct. 16, 1954; children: Mark, James, Anne. Salesman, Upjohn Co., N.Y.C., 1954-59, sales supr.,1959-62, product mgr. U.S. domestic pharm. dir., 1962-65, mgr. mktg. planning internat. div., 1965-71, v.p. Europe, 1971-74, group v.p. Europe, 1975-77, exec. v.p. Upjohn Internat., Inc., Kalamazoo, Mich., 1978-85, pres., gen. mgr., 1975-88, v.p. parent co., 1978-88; adj. prof. mgmt. Western Mich. U., Kalamazoo, 1988-92; chmn. bd. Carrington Labs; bd. dirs. Cytrx Pharms. Corp. 2d lt. M.C., U.S. Army, 1951-53. Mem. Internat. Pharm. Mfrs. Assn., NYAC (N.Y.). Republican. Roman Catholic. Office: Upjon Internat Co 7000 Portage Rd Kalamazoo MI 49001-0102

VESELL, ELLIOT SAUL, pharmacologist, educator; b. N.Y.C., Dec. 24, 1933; s. Harry and Evelyn (Jaffe) V.; m. Kristen Paige Peery, Mar. 24, 1968; children: Liane Clark, Hilary Peery. AB, Harvard U., 1955, MD, 1959; DSc (hon.), Phila. Coll. Pharmacy & Sci., 1988; PhD, Philipps U., Marburg, Germany, 1991. Intern, children's med. svc. Mass. Gen. Hosp., Boston, 1959-60; rsch. assoc. Rockefeller U., N.Y.C., 1960-62; resident in medicine Peter Bent Brigham Hosp., Boston, 1962-63; clin. assoc. Nat. Inst. Arthritis and Metabolic Diseases, NIH, Bethesda, Md., 1963-65; head sect. pharmacogenetics Nat. Heart Inst., NIH, Bethesda, 1965-68; Evan Pugh prof. pharmacology, chmn. dept. Pa. State U., Hershey, 1968—, asst. dean grad. edn., 1973—; Frohlich vis. prof. Royal Soc. Medicine, 1985, Pfizer vis. prof., Burroughs Wellcome vis. prof. Editor: The Life and Works of Thomas Cole, 1964, Progress in Basic and Clinical Pharmacology, 1990, numerous others; contbr. numerous articles to profl. jours. Recipient Von Humboldt award, 1988. Fellow AAAS, Royal Soc. of Medicine; mem. Assn. Am. Physicians, Am. Soc. for Clin. Investigation, Am. Soc. Pharmacology and Exptl. Therapeutics (sec.-treas. 1995-98, Exptl. Therapeutics award 1971, Harry Gold award in clin. pharmacology, 1985), Am. Coll. Clin. Pharmacology (pres. 1980-82), Am. Soc. Clin. Pharmacology and Therapeutics (Oscar B. Hunter Meml. award 1991). Office: Pa State U Coll Medicine Dept Pharmacology PO Box 850 Hershey PA 17033-0850

VESELY, ALEXANDER, civil engineer; b. Ladmovce, Czechoslovakia, Dec. 7, 1926; came to U.S., 1949; s. Joseph and Margaret (Lefkovitz) V.; m. Harriet Lee Roth, Aug. 11, 1957; 1 child, David Seth. BSCE, Carnegie Mellon U., 1952; postgrad. John Marshall Law Sch., 1955; MSCE, Ill. Inst. Tech., 1957. Registered profl. engr., Ind., Mass.; registered land surveyor, Ind. Staff engr., Amoco Oil Co., Whiting, Ind., 1952-62; mgr. engring. Borg Warner Chem. Co., Washington, W.Va., 1962-77; assoc. engr. Mobil Rsch. & Devel. Corp., Princeton, N.J., 1977-83; cons. engr. D.G. Peterson & Assocs. Inc., Greenfield, Mass., 1983-87; prin. Alexander Vesely & Assocs., 1987—; assoc. prof. Community Coll., Parkersburg, W.Va., 1965-67; chmn. Engrs. Week Com., Parkersburg, 1973. Pres. B'nai Israel Congregation, Parkersburg, 1976; bd. dirs. Bros. of Israel Congregation, Trenton, N.J., 1978-83. Served with U.S. Army, 1952-54. Carnegie Mellon U. scholar, 1950-52. Mem. Nat. Soc. Profl. Engrs. (pres. Parkersburg chpt. 1973-74), Am. Inst. Plant Engrs., ASCE, Scrabble Club, Chess Club, Bridge Club, Tau Beta Pi (life). Republican. Jewish. Avocations: ping-pong, tennis, swimming. Home and Office: 48 Hillcrest Dr Northampton MA 01060-1362

VESPA, NED ANGELO, photographer; b. Streator, Ill., May 31, 1942; s. Ned James and Evelyn Blanche (Flanigan) V.; m. Carol DeMasters, Sept. 11, 1976; 1 child, Nicole Marie; 1 son by previous marriage, James Paul. B.S., So. Ill. U., 1965. Photographer Milw. Jour. Co., 1965-95, Milw. Sentinel, 1965-95; ret., 1995, freelance, 1995—. Mem. Nat. Press Photographers Assn., Wis. News Photographers Assn. (past pres.), Milw. Press Photographers. Home: 38309 Genesee Lake Rd Oconomowoc WI 53066-8614

VESPER, CAROLYN F., newspaper publishing executive. Sr. v.p. and assoc. publisher USA TODAY, Arlington, Va. Office: USA Today 1000 Wilson Blvd Arlington VA 22209-3901

VESPER, KARL HAMPTON, business and mechanical engineering educator; b. San Marino, Calif., Aug. 12, 1932; s. Karl Conrad and Roxie (Armstrong) V.; m. Joan Frantz, June, 1964; children—Karen, Linda, Holly, Nancy. B.S. in Mech. Engring, Stanford U., 1955; M.S. in Mech. Engring, 1965, Ph.D., 1969; M.B.A., Harvard U., 1960. Casewriter Harvard Bus. Sch., 1960-61; bus. mgr., mech. engr. Marine Advisers, 1961-62; cons. Dept. State, summer, 1963; dir. Hosmer Machine Co., Contoock, N.H., 1966-67; dir. summer insts. Stanford U., 1966, 67, dir. case devel., research asso., lectr. mech. engring., 1963-69, research asso., NASA faculty fellow in air pollution research design project, summer 1970; editor mech. engring. series McGraw Hill Book Co., N.Y.C., 1966-74; prof. bus. adminstrn., mech. engring. and marine studies U. Wash., Seattle, 1969—; Paul T. Babson prof. Babson Coll., 1980-81. Author: How To Write Engineering Cases, 1966, 73, Engineers at Work, 1975, The Entrepreneurial Function, 1977, Entrepreneurship Education, 1985, New Venture Strategies, 1980, rev. edit., 1990, Frontiers of Entrepreneurship Research, 1981-91, Entrepreneurship and National Policy, 1983, New Venture Mechanics, 1993, (with Paul Larson) Washington Entrepreneur's Guide, 1993, New Venture Experience, 1993, rev. edit., 1996; contbr. chpts. to books and articles to profl. jours. Served with USAF, 1955-57. Mem. Am. Inst. for Decision Scis., Acad. Mgmt., Sigma Xi. Home: 3721 47th Pl NE Seattle WA 98105-5224 Office: U Wash Sch Business Adminstrn Seattle WA 98195

VESSEL, ROBERT LESLIE, lawyer; b. Chgo., Mar. 21, 1942; s. Louis Frank and Margaret Ruth (Barber) V.; m. Diane White, Oct. 12, 1966; m. Lise Vessel, Dec. 19, 1992. BA, U. Ill., 1964; JD, Seton Hall U., 1973; LLM in Taxation, U. Miami, Coral Gables, Fla., 1980. Bar: N.J. 1973, Fla. 1981, U.S. Dist. Ct. (so. and mid. dists.) Fla. 1981, U.S. Ct. Appeals (11th cir.) 1981; bd. cert. civil trial, Fla. Assoc. Bennett & Bennett P.A., East Orange, N.J., 1973-76; ptnr. Kantor & Vessel, P.A., Wayne, N.J., 1976-81; assoc. Haddad Josephs & Jack, P.A., Coral Gables, Fla., 1981-85; ptnr. Mitchell Alley Rywant & Vessel, Tampa, 1985-89, Moffitt & Vessel, P.A., Tampa, 1989-94, Vessel & Morales, P.A., Tampa, 1994—. With USNR, 1964-66. Mem. Assn. Trial Lawyers Am., Nat. Inst. Trial Advocacy, Acad. Fla. Trial Lawyers, Hillsboro County Bar Assn. Avocation: sailing. Office: Vessel & Morales PA 5401 W Kennedy Blvd Tampa FL 33609

VESSEY, JOHN WILLIAM, JR., army officer; b. Mpls., June 29, 1922; s. John William and Emily (Roche) V.; m. Avis Claire Funk, July 18, 1945; children: John William, David, Sarah. BS, U. Md., 1963; MS, George Washington U., 1967; LLD, Concordia Coll., St. Paul, 1978, U. Md., 1983, Concordia Sem., St. Louis, 1983; DMS (hon.), Norwich U., Northfield, Vt., 1985; grad., Command and Gen. Staff Coll., 1958, Indsl. Coll. Armed Forces, 1966. Commd. 2nd lt. U.S. Army, 1939, advanced through grades to gen., 1976; comdr. U.S. Army Support Command Thailand, 1970-71; chief Mil. Assistance Adv. Group Laos, 1972-73; dir. ops. Dept. Army Washington, 1973-74; comdr. 4th Inf. Div. Ft. Carson, Colo., 1974-75; dep. chief of staff-ops. Dept. Army Washington, 1975-76; comdr.-in-chief UN Command/U.S. Forces in Korea Seoul, 1976-79; comdr.-in-chief Republic of Korea/U.S. Combined Forces Command, 1978-79; vice chief of staff U.S. Army Washington, 1979-82, chmn. Joint Chiefs of Staff, 1982-85; ret. U.S. Army, 1985; presdl. emissary to Hanoi for POW/MIA matters, 1987-93. Bd. dirs. Youth Svcs., Inc., Nat. Flag Day Com.; with Mission Svcs. Luth. Ch., Mo.; chair bd. vistors U. Mo.; chmn. bd. Ctr. Preventive Action Def. Sci. Bd. Decorated D.S.C., Def. D.S.M., D.S.M., AF D.S.M., Navy D.S.M., Legion of Merit, Bronze Star, Air medal, Joint Svcs. Commendation medal, Army Commendation medal, Purple Heart (U.S.), Presdl. Medal of Freedom, decorated by govts. of Austria, Chile, Colombia, Fed. Republic Germany, France, Greece, Honduras, Korea, Luxembourg, Norway, Pakistan, Saudi Arabia, Spain, Thailand, Uruguay, Fed. Republic of Germany; recipient State of Minn. Disting. Svc. medal, Excellence in Diplomacy award Am. Acad. of Diplomacy, Alumni Achievement award and Disting. Pub. Svc. award George Washington U., Disting. Alumnus award U. Md., Golden Plate award Am. Acad. Achievement, Adm. John M. Will award N.Y. Coun. Navy League, hon. award Nat. League Families, Excellence in Diplomacy award Am. Acad. Diplomacy. Mem. VFW (Eisenhower medal), Assn. U.S. Army (George Marshall medal), Army Aviation Assn., U.S. Armor Assn., Coun. Fgn. Rels. (chair bd. dirs. ctr. for prevention action), Phi Kappa Phi. Lutheran.

VESSOT, ROBERT FREDERICK CHARLES, physicist; b. Montreal, Que., Can., Apr. 16, 1930; s. Robert Charles Ulysses and Marguerite Yvonne (Giauque) V.; m. Norma Newman Wight, Apr. 18, 1959; children: Judith Norma, Margaret Anne, Nancy Elizabeth. B.A., McGill U., 1951, B.Sc., 1954, Ph.D., 1956. Mem. research staff MIT, 1956-60; mgr. Maser Research and Devel., Varian Assos., Hewlett Packard, Beverly, Mass., 1960-69; sr. physicist Harvard-Smithsonian Center for Astrophysics, Cambridge, Mass., 1969—. Contbr. articles to profl. jours. Served with RCAF, 1951-53. Recipient medal for outstanding sci. achievement NASA, 1978, I.I. Rabi award IEEE, 1993. Fellow Am. Phys. Soc.; mem. Eastern Yacht Club. Patentee in field. Office: 60 Garden St Cambridge MA 02138-1516

VEST, CHARLES MARSTILLER, academic administrator; b. Morgantown, W.Va., Sept. 9, 1941; s. Marvin Lewis and Winifred Louise (Buzzard) V.; m. Rebecca Ann McCue, June 8, 1963; children: Ann Kemper, John Andrew. BSME, W.Va. U., 1963; MSME, U. Mich., 1964, PhD, 1967; DEng (hon.), Mich. Tech. U., 1992, W.Va. U., 1994. Asst. prof., then assoc. prof. U. Mich., Ann Arbor, 1968-77, prof. mech. engring., 1977-90, assoc. dean acad. affairs Coll. Engring., 1981-86, dean Coll. Engring., 1986-89, provost, v.p. acad. affairs, 1989-90; pres. MIT, Cambridge, 1990—; bd. dirs. E.I. du Pont de Nemours and Co., IBM; vis. assoc. prof. Stanford (Calif.) U., 1974-75. Author: Holographic Interferometry, 1979; assoc. editor Jour. Optical Soc. Am., 1982-83; contbr. articles to profl. jours. Trustee Wellesley Coll., Woods Hole Oceanographic Inst., New Eng. Aquarium, WGBH Ednl. Found.; adv. trustee Environ. Rsch. Inst. Mich. Recipient Excellence in Rsch. award U. Mich., 1980, Disting. Svc. award, 1972, Disting. Visitor award U. La Plata, Argentina, 1979, Centennial medal Am Soc. Engring. Edn., 1993. Fellow AAAS, Am. Acad. Arts and Scis., Optical Soc. Am.; mem. ASME, NAE, Sigma Xi, Tau Beta Pi, Pi Tau Sigma. Presbyterian. Office: MIT 77 Massachusetts Ave Cambridge MA 02139-4307

VEST, FRANK HARRIS, JR., bishop; b. Salem, Va., Jan. 5, 1936; s. Frank Harris and Viola Gray (Woodson) V.; m. Ann Jarvis, June 14, 1961; children: Nina Woodson, Frank Harris III, Robert Alexander. BA, Roanoke Coll., 1959; MDiv, Va. Theol. Sem., 1962, DD, 1985; DD (hon.), U. of South, 1987; LHD (hon.), St. Paul's Coll., 1991. Ordained to ministry Episcopal Ch. as deacon, 1962, as priest 1963. Curate St. John's Episcopal Ch., Roanoke, Va., 1962-64; rector Grace Episcopal Ch., Radford, Va., 1964-68; rector Christ Episcopal Ch., Roanoke, 1968-73, Charlotte, N.C., 1973-85; suffragan bishop Diocese of N.C., Raleigh, 1985-89; bishop coadjutor Diocese of So. Va., Norfolk, 1989-91, bishop, 1991—. Chmn. exec. com. Thompsons Children's Home, Charlotte, 1976-79; pres. Crisis Assistance Ministry, Charlotte, 1983-85; trustee Va. Theol. Sem., Alexandria, 1968-73, 91—, U. of South, Sewanee, Tenn., 1985-89, Episc. Radio TV Found., Atlanta, 1986-82; chair Dispatch of Bus., House of Bishops, 1988—. Democrat. Avocations: tennis, reading, walking, golf, fly-fishing. Office: Diocese of So Va 600 Talbot Hall Rd Norfolk VA 23505-4361

VEST, GAYLE SOUTHWORTH, obstetrician and gynecologist; b. Duluth, Minn., Apr. 7, 1948; d. Russell Eugene and Brandon (Young) Southworth; m. Steven Lee Vest, Nov. 27, 1971; 1 child, Matthew Steven. BS, U. Mich., 1970. Diplomate Am. Bd. Ob-Gyn. Intern in ob-gyn. Milw. County Gen. Hosp., 1974-75, So. Ill. U. Sch. Medicine, 1975-78; pvt. practice Chapel Hill (N.C.) Ob-Gyn., 1978-80; asst. attending physician dept. ob-gyn. U. N.C. Sch. Medicine, Chapel Hill, 1978-80; clin. assoc. dept. ob-gyn. Duke U. Med. Ctr., Durham, N.C., 1978-80; pvt. practice Big Stone Gap (Va.) Clinic, 1980-88, Norwise Ob-Gyn. Assocs., Norton, Va., 1988—. Fellow Am. Coll. Obstetricians and Gynegologists; mem. Am. Soc. Reproductive Medicine, Va. Ob-Gyn. Soc., Va. Perinatal Assn., Med. Soc. Va., Wise County Med. Soc. Avocations: skiing, kayaking, travel. Office: Norwise Ob-Gyn Assocs Med Arts Bldg 3 102 15th St NW Norton VA 24273-1618

VEST, GEORGE SOUTHALL, diplomat; b. Columbia, Va., Dec. 25, 1918; s. George Southall and Nancy Margaret (Robertson) V.; m. Emily Barber Clemons, June 21, 1947; children—Jeannie, George, Henry. B.A., U. Va., 1941, M.A., 1947. Fgn. service duty SHAPE and NATO, Quito, Ottawa, Paris; dir. bur. polit. mil. affairs Dept. State; asst. sec. of state for European affairs Dept. State, Washington, 1977-81; ambassador to European Communities Brussels, 1981-85; dir. gen. Fgn. Svc. Dept. State, Washington, 1985-89; career amb. Dept. State, 1987-89, ret., 1989; cons. Akin, Gump, Strauss, Hauer and Feld, Washington, 1989—. Served to capt. U.S. Army, 1941-46, ETO. Mem. Phi Beta Kappa. Episcopalian. Avocations: bicycling; hiking; gardening. Home: 5307 Iroquois Rd Bethesda MD 20816-3104

VEST, HYRUM GRANT, JR., horticultural sciences educator; b. Salt Lake City, Sept. 23, 1935; s. Hyrum and Josephine Gwendolyn (Lund) V.; m. Gayle Pixton, Sept. 18, 1958; children: Kelly, Lani, Kari, Kamille, Kyle. B.S., Utah State U., 1960, M.S., 1964; Ph.D., U. Minn., 1967. Pathologist, agronomist U.S. Dept. Agr., Beltsville, Md., 1967-70; vegetable breeder Mich. State U., East Lansing, 1970-76; dept. head dept. hort. and landscape architecture Okla. State U., Stillwater, 1976-83; head dept. hort. scis. Tex A & M U., College Station, 1983-89; head dept. plants, soils and biometeorology Utah State U., Logan, 1989-95, assoc. dir. Utah Agrl. Experiment Sta., 1995—; mem. Nat. Plant Genetics Resource Bd., Washington, 1982-88. Served to 1st lt. U.S. Army, 1960-63. Univ. research fellow Utah State U., 1963-64. Fellow Am. Soc. Hort. Sci. Republican. Ch. Jesus Christ of Latter-day Saints. Lodge: Rotary. Home: 368 Spring Creek Rd Providence UT 84332-9432 Office: Utah State U Utah Agrl Experiment Sta Logan UT 84322-4810

VEST, JAMES MURRAY, educator; b. Roanoke, Va., Mar. 27, 1947; s. Eddie Lewis and Irene (Cannaday) V.; m. Nancy Foltz, June 6, 1970; 1 child, Cecelia. BA, Davidson (N.C.) Coll., 1969; MA, Duke U., 1971, PhD, 1973. From asst. to assoc. prof. Rhodes Coll., Memphis, 1973-91, prof., 1991—; adminstr. Rhodes in Paris Program, France, 1978-87; organizer faculty teaching seminars, 1988—. Author: The French Face of Ophelia, 1989, The Poetic Works of Maurice de Guérin, 1991; contbr. articles to profl. jours. Chmn. Urban Outreach Commn., Memphis, 1978-81; leader youth groups, 1983—. Capt. U.S. Army Res., 1973—. Recipient campus svc. award Sears-Roebuck, 1990, outstanding tchg. award Clarence Day Found., Memphis, 1984, Am. Assn. Higher Edn., 1988; Woodrow Wilson fellow, 1971, NDEA Title IV fellow, 1969. Mem. MLA, So. Atlantic Modern Lang. Assn., Am. Assn. of Tchrs. of French. Avocations: cinema, hiking. Office: 2000 N Pkwy Rhodes C Memphis TN 38112

VEST, MARVIN LEWIS, mathematical educator; b. Elkins, W.Va., May 17, 1906; s. Marvin Johnson and Margaret (Kley) V.; m. Winifred Louise Buzzerd, Aug. 3, 1930; children: Marvin Lewis, Charles Marstiller. BS, Davis and Elkins Coll., 1927, ScD (hon.), 1970; MS, W.Va. U., 1932; AM, U. Mich., 1942, PhD in Math., 1948. Prin. Franklin (W.Va.) High Sch., 1927-28; instr. Elkins High Sch., 1928-31, 33-35; assoc. prof. math. Davis and Elkins Coll., 1935-38; mem. faculty W.Va. U., Morgantown, 1931-33, 38—, prof. math., 1955-73, emeritus, 1973—; cons. U.S. Bur. Mines, 1952-57. Mem. Am. Math. Soc., Math. Assn. Am., W.Va. Acad. Scis. (sec. 1934-37, pres. 1950-51), Sigma Xi, Pi Mu Epsilon. Republican. Presbyterian (elder). Lodge: Mason. Home: 417 Elm St Morgantown WV 26505-6507

VEST, R. LAMAR, church administrator. Dir. Ch. of God Media Ministries. Office: Ch of God PO Box 2430 Cleveland TN 37320-2430

VESTA, RICHARD V., meat packing company executive. CEO Packerland Packaging, Green Bay, Wis. Office: Packerland Packaging PO Box 23000 Green Bay WI 54305

VESTAL, LUCIAN LAROE, financier; b. Whitewright, Tex., Aug. 10, 1925; s. Rolla C. and Lora A. (Robinson) V.; m. Gretalee Kranz Banzhaf, Nov. 8, 1994; 1 child, Denise Vestal Cline. Student, Baylor U., 1942-43; B.S., U. Pitts., 1947; postgrad., N.Y.U., 1948-50, Ill. Inst. Tech., 1960. Security analyst Lionel D. Edie & Co., N.Y.C., 1947-54; asst. dir. finance Champion Papers, Inc., Hamilton, Ohio, 1954-55; dir. research Rotan, Mosle & Co., Houston, 1955-58; dir. planning Pure Oil Co., Palatine, Ill., 1958-63; dir. planning and fin. services Weyerhaeuser Co., Tacoma, 1963-65; treas. Sunray DX Oil Co., Tulsa, 1965-68; asst. treas. Sun Oil Co., Phila., 1968-69; group v.p. Tesoro Petroleum Corp., San Antonio, 1969-72; sr. v.p. affiliate banking Palmer Bank Corp., Sarasota, Fla., 1973-75; trustee Citizens Growth Properties, 1969-78; chmn., dir. Palmer banks of Siesta Key, Village Plaza, N.A., Gulf Gate, Sarasota, Palmer Bank of Bradenton (N.A.), Fla., Palmer Bank & Trust Co. Naples (N.A.), Fla., Palmer Bank & Trust Co. Ft. Myers (N.A.), Fla.; pres., dir. Point Palma Sola, Inc., 1975-78, Cortez Yachts, Inc., 1975-78, So. Yachts, Inc., 1978-90; ceo, chmn., dir. Advantage Nat. Charge System, Sarasota, 1990; pres. Gen. Securities Transfer, 1995—; dir. Seaman Corp., Ohio; chmn. Trident Environ. Sys., Inc., Citizens Growth Properties, Omni Films Internat., Inc. Served to 1st lt., inf. USMCR, 1943-45, 50-51. Decorated Navy Cross, Purple Heart. Mem. N.Y. Soc. Security Analysts, Retired Officers Club, U.S. Power Squadron, Sarasota Yacht Club (mem., dir.), Delta Tau Delta. Republican. Baptist. Home: 1648 Pine Harrier Cir Sarasota FL 34231

VESTAL, THELMA SHAW, history educator; b. Spring Hill, Tenn., Apr. 19, 1946; d. Ester Lena McKissack; m. Danny Vestal, June 28, 1976; children: Danny La'Brian, Felecia De'Lece. BS, Tenn. State U., 1969, MS, 1972. Sec. Tenn. State U., Nashville, 1969-72, counselor, 1972-76; substitute tchr. Metro Pub. Schs., Nashville, 1977-85; U.S. history tchr. Dupont-Tyler Mid. Sch., Hermitage, Tenn., 1985—; Mem. Operation C.A.N., Nashville, 1985—. Active ARC, Nashville, 1988—. Named Educator of Yr., Nashville Mid. Sch. Assn., 1992-93; recipient Outstanding Christian award Schrader Lane Ch. of Christ, Nashville, 1989-90. Mem. Nat. Geographic Soc., Metro Nashville Coun. for Social Studies, Tenn. Edn. Assn., NEA, Nat. Coun. for Social Studies. Democrat. Ch. of Christ. Avocations: reading, bowling, music, dancing.

VESTAL, TOMMY RAY, lawyer; b. Shreveport, La., Sept. 19, 1939; s. Louie Wallace and Margaret (Golden) V.; m. Patricia Marie Blackwell, Jan. 24, 1981; children: Virginia Ann Hollingsworth, John Wallace Vestal, Douglas William Yancy. BSME, U. Houston, 1967, JD, 1970. Bar: Tex. 1970, U.S. Patent Office 1972, U.S. Ct. Appeals (D.C. cir.) 1975. Patent atty. Am. Enka Corp., Asheville, N.C., 1970-71, Akzona Inc., Asheville, 1971-84, Akzo Am., Inc., Asheville, 1985-86; sr. patent atty. Fibers div. BASF Corp., Enka, N.C., 1986-87, div. patent counsel, 1987-89, sr. patent counsel, 1989-90; pvt. practice law, 1990-91; dir. Geary Glast & Middleton, Dallas, 1992; ptnr. Falk, Vestal & Fish, Dallas, 1992—. Mem. ABA, State Bar Tex., Am. Intellectual Property Law Assn., Carolina Patent, Trademark and Copyright Law Assn. (bd. dirs. 1983-85, 2d v.p. 1985-86, 1st v.p. 1986-87, pres. 1987-88), Dallas Bar Assn. (mem. com. law in schs. and comm., schs. and the community bd.), DFW Patent Law Assn., Asheville C. of C. (chmn. legal affairs com.), Phi Alpha Delta. Republican. Lutheran. Lodge: Kiwanis (pres. 1982). Avocations: golf, fishing, hiking. Home: 3109 Squireswood Dr Carrollton TX 75006-5218 Office: 700 N Pearl St Dallas TX 75201-7424

VESTNER, ELIOT N., JR., bank executive; b. Bronxville, N.Y., Aug. 4, 1935; s. Eliot N. and Priscilla Alden (Fuller) V.; m. Elizabeth Gwin, Jan. 1, 1966 (div. 1992); children: Alice-Lee, Charles Fuller; m. Louise R. Cutler, Aug. 11, 1995. B.A., Amherst Coll., 1957; M.A., U. Mich., 1958; LL.B., Columbia U., 1962. Bar: N.Y. 1963. Assoc. Debevoise, Plimpton, Lyons & Gates, N.Y.C., 1962-68; spl. counsel N.Y. State Bank Dept., 1968-70; spl. asst. to Gov. Nelson A. Rockefeller, 1970-72; 1st dep. supt. N.Y. State, 1972-75, supt. banking, 1974-75; sr. v.p., gen. counsel Irving Trust Co., 1975-82, exec. v.p., 1982-87; exec. counsel Bank of Boston, 1987—; dir. Boston-AIG Co., 1994—. Republican. Episcopalian. Home: Devonshire Pl # 2605 Boston MA 02109 Office: Bank of Boston PO Box 2016 Boston MA 02106-2016

VETERE, LAURA ANN, school system administrator, educator; b. Elizabeth, N.J., Nov. 17, 1958; d. Robert and Pearl V. BS magne cum laude, East Stroudsburg U., 1980; M in edn. adminstrn., Kean Coll., 1994. Cert. elem. edn. tchr., secondary edn. tchr. Tchr. Elizabeth (N.J.) H.S.,

1980-88, Colonia (N.J.) H.S., 1988-94; v.p. Newbury Sch., Howell, N.J., 1994—; registered Holistic scorer Hunterdon County Edn. Svcs. commn., Flemington, N.J., 1990—. Recipient Commendation award Kean-Comprehensive Examiners, 1994. Mem. Phi Delta Kappa. Avocations: reading, body shaping. Office: 179 Newbury Rd Howell NJ 07731

VETOG, EDWIN JOSEPH, retired gas utility executive; b. N.Y.C., Apr. 7, 1921; s. Lester and Lucy V.; m. Elizabeth Ann Long, July 18, 1942; children: Judith Ann Vetog Ciafone, Victoria Ann Vetog Thode. B.B.A., CCNY, 1949; M.B.A., NYU, 1953. With Bklyn. Union Gas Co., 1941-86, various positions, 1941-67, comptroller, 1967-69, v.p., 1969-75, sr. v.p., chief fin. officer, 1975-81, adminstrv. v.p., chief fin. officer, 1981-84, exec. v.p., chief fin. officer, 1984-86; trustee Ridgewood Savs. Bank, L.I., 1980—; adv. bd. Mfrs. Hanover Trust Co., Bklyn., 1979-86 ; chmn. Delaware Valley Propane Co., Moorestown, N.J., 1981-86. Pres. Indsl. Home for the Blind, L.I., 1976-85. Served to capt. C.E., U.S. Army, 1942-46. Decorated Bronze Star; decorated medal of Metz (France). Mem. Am. Gas Assn., Fin. Execs. Inst. Lutheran. Club: Brooklyn. Home: 5 View Rd Setauket NY 11733-3040

VETTER, HERBERT, physician, educator; b. Vienna, Austria, Aug. 24, 1920; m. Eleonore von Hacklaender, July 6, 1946 (div. 1969); 1 child, Barbara Weber; m. Brigitte Frei, Dec. 20, 1973 (div. 1993). M.D., U. Vienna, 1948. Physician, Allgemeines Krankenhaus, Vienna, Austria, 1948-60; Brit. Council research fellow, 1951; research fellow Sloan-Kettering Inst. Cancer Research, N.Y.C., 1954; head radioisotopes lab. 2d Med. Univ. Clinic, Vienna, 1951-60; asso. prof. medicine U. Vienna, 1959-67, prof., 1967—; sr. officer IAEA, 1958-81; chmn. sci. adv. council Austrian Soc. Energy Affairs, 1979—; v.p. Austrian Nuclear Tech. Soc., 1980—; bd. dirs. Austrian sect. Internat. Physicians for Prevention of Nuclear War, 1983-86; chmn. planning bd. IB, Internat. Commn. Radiation Units and Measurements, 1962-69, cons., 1969-89. Author: (with N. Veall) Radioisotope Techniques in Clinical Research and Diagnosis, 1958, Zwickmnühle Zwentendorf, 1983; editor: Radioaktive Isotope in Klinik und Forschung, Vols. I-III, 1955-58, (with E.H. Belcher) Radioisotopes in Medical Diagnosis, 1971, Jour. Nuclear Medicine, 1959-95, Internat. Jour. Biomed. Engring., 1971-89. Recipient prize for art and sci. Republic of Austria, 1956, award of distinction Philippine Soc. Nuclear Medicine; Paul Harris fellow, 1983. Affiliate Royal Soc. Medicine; mem. Gesellschaft der Aerzte, Gesellschaft für Innere Medizin, Österreichische Roentgengesellschaft, Österreichische Gesellschaft für Nuklearmedizin (hon.). Club: Rotarian (pres. Vienna 1975-76). Home: Am Hausberg 1, 2344 Maria Enzersdorf Austria

VETTER, JAMES GEORGE, JR., lawyer; b. Omaha, Apr. 8, 1934; s. James George and Helen Louise (Adams) V.; m. Mary Ellen Froelich, June 25, 1960; 1 child, James G. III. BS, Georgetown U., 1954; JD, Creighton U., 1960. Bar: Nebr. 1960, Tex. 1967. Counsel IRS, Washington, 1960-64, Dallas, 1964-67; practiced in Dallas, 1967—; sr. ptnr. Vetter, Bates, Tibbals, Lee & DeBusk P.C., 1979-89; mem. Godwin & Carlton P.C., 1989—, mng. dir., 1994—; lectr. taxation seminars; bd. dirs. Pilgrim's Pride Corp., AFV Energy, Inc., VLSI Packaging Corp. Contbr. articles to profl. jours. Asst. sgt.-at-arms Tex. Dem. Conv., 1968; advisor selection com. Georgetown U., 1970-85; scoutmaster Boy Scouts Am., 1974-75. With USAF, 1954-57; capt. USAFR, ret. Mem. Nebr. Bar Assn., State Bar Tex. (cert. tax law 1983—), Coll. State Bar Tex., Dallas Bar Assn. (chmn. fee disputes com. 1985, chmn. publs. com. 1988, chmn. pictoral directory com. 1993), Real Estate Fin. Execs. Assn. (pres. 1982-83), Cash Alliance (pres. 1987-88), Creighton U. Alumni Assn. (pres. Dallas-Ft. Worth 1969-70), Ctrl. Dallas Assn. (bd. dirs. 1994—), Park Cities Club, City Club, Delta Theta Phi. Roman Catholic. Home: 11023 Rosser Rd Dallas TX 75229-3915 Office: Godwin & Carlton 2500 Nations Bank Plz Dallas TX 75202

VETTER, JAMES LOUIS, food research association administrator; b. St. Louis, Jan. 26, 1933; s. Charles W. and Dorothy (Smith) V.; m. Rose Marie Gentille, Aug. 21, 1954; children: Douglas John, Debra Dianne. AB, Washington U., St. Louis, 1954; MS, U. Ill., 1955, PhD, 1958. Food technologist Monsanto Co., St. Louis, 1958-63; dir. rsch. Keebler Co., Elmhurst, Ill., 1963-72; v.p. tech. dir. div. Standard Brands, Fraklin Park, Ill., 1972-75; pres. West Tex. Milling, Amarillo, 1975-77; v.p. Am. Inst. Baking, Manhattan, Kans., 1977—; adj. prof. Kans. State U., Manhattan, 1977—; tech. cons. Author: Food Labeling-Requirements for FDA Regulated Products, 1992; editor: Adding Nutrients to Foods, 1982; Dairy Products for Cereal Processing, 1984. Contbr. articles to profl. jours. Patentee in field. Bd. dirs., pres. Wharton Manor Nursing Home, Inc., Manhattan, 1980-81. Fellow Inst. Food Technologists; mem. Am. Assn. Cereal Chemists (sec. 1983-85, pres. 1986-87), Kiwanis (bd. dirs.). Avocations: photography; golf. Home: 1947 Bluestem Ter Manhattan KS 66502-4530 Office: Am Inst Baking 1213 Bakers Way Manhattan KS 66502-4555

VETTRUS, RICHARD JAMES, minister; b. Superior, Wis., Oct. 23, 1938; s. Ole K. and Clara (Olson) V. BA, Pasadena Coll., 1964; MDiv, Luth. Brethren Sem., 1967; MS in Edn., Wagner Coll., 1975. Ordained to ministry Luth. Ch., 1971. Youth worker 59th St. Luth. Brethren Ch., Bklyn., 1958-60; nat. pres. Luth. Brethren Youth Fellowship, Fergus Falls, Minn., 1965-69; pastor Elim Luth. Ch., Floral Park, N.Y., 1967-69, Nanuet (N.Y.) Luth. Brethren Ch., 1971-74, 59th St Luth. Brethren Ch., Bklyn., 1975-79, Immanuel Luth. Ch., Pasadena, Calif., 1979-82, Bethany Luth. Ch., West Union, Iowa, 1982—; youth page editor Luth. Brethren Youth, Fergus Falls, 1958-60; studnet coun. rep. Fuller Theol. Sem., Pasadena, 1964-66; tour dir. to Israel, Jordan and Greece, Bklyn., 1979, to Israel, Jordan, Egypt and Greece, Pasadena, 1981. Dist. pres. Ch. Luth. Brethren, Ea. Dist., 1978-79, synodical sec., 1986—; bd. dirs. Tuscarora Inn Conf. Ctr., Mt. Bethel, Pa., 1978-79. Luth. Brotherhood scholar, Mpls., 1967. Republican. Avocations: photography, travel, antique cars, reading. Home: 707 Crestview Dr West Union IA 52175-1004 Office: Church The Lutheran Brethren Am 707 Crestview Dr West Union IA 52175

VEYSEY, ARTHUR ERNEST, reporter, administrator, biographer; b. Boulder, Colo., Sept. 28, 1914; s. Ernest Charles and Lillian (Larson) V.; m. Florence Jones, 1937 (dec. 1940); 1 dau., Priscilla Joan; m. Gwendolyn Morgan, 1946. B.A., U. Colo., 1935; L.H.D., Ill. Benedictine Coll., 1986. Reporter Denver Post, 1935-37, Scottsbluff (Neb.) Star-Herald, 1937-41, Omaha World-Herald, 1941-43; war corr. Southwest Pacific, Chgo. Tribune, 1943- 45, fgn. corr., 1946-50, chief London bur., 1950-75; gen. mgr. Cantigny Trust, 1975-86. Author: Death in the Jungle, 1966, (with Gwen Morgan) Halas by Halas, 1979, (with Gwen Morgan) Poor Little Rich Boy, Biography of Col. R.R. McCormick. Bd. dirs. The Forest Found. Recipient Norlin award U. Colo., 1986, Margaret Landon award, 1986. Address: 3 Cobham Ct, PO Box 232, Kerikeri Bay of Islands New Zealand

VEZIROGLU, TURHAN NEJAT, mechanical engineering educator, energy researcher; b. Istanbul, Turkey, Jan. 24, 1924; came to U.S., 1962; s. Abdul Kadir and Ferruh (Bürün) V.; m. Bengi Isikli, Mar. 17, 1961; children: Emre Alp, Oya Sureyya. A.C.G.I., City and Guilds Coll., London, 1946; B.Sc. with honors, U. London, 1947; D.I.C., Imperial Coll., London, 1948; Ph.D., U. London, 1951. Engring. apprentice Alfred Herbert Ltd., Coventry, U.K., 1945; project engr. Office of Soil Products, Ankara, Turkey, 1953-56; tech. dir. M.K.V. Constrn. Co, Istanbul, 1957-61; assoc. prof. mech. engring. U. Miami, Coral Gables, Fla., 1962-65; prof. U. Miami, Coral Fables, Fla., 1966—; dir. grad. studies mech. engring. U. Miami, Coral Gables, Fla., 1965-71, chmn. dept. mech. engring., 1971-75, assoc. dean research Coll. Engring., 1975-79, dir. Clean Energy Research Inst., 1974—; UNESCO cons., Paris; vis. prof. Middle East Tech. U., Ankara, 1969. Editor-in-chief: Internat. Jour. Hydrogen Energy, 1976—. Pres. Learning Disabilities Found., Miami, 1972-73, advisor, 1974-80. Recipient Turkish Presdl. sci. award Turkish Sci. and Tech. Research Found., 1975; named hon. prof. Xian Jiaotong U., China, 1982. Fellow AAAS, ASME, Instn. Mech. Engrs.; mem. Internat. Assn. Hydrogen Energy (pres. 1975), AIAA, Assn. Energy Engrs., Am. Nuclear Soc., Am. Soc. Engring. Edn., AAUP, Internat. Soc. Solar Energy, Systems Engring. Soc., Sigma Xi. Home: 4910 Biltmore Dr Miami FL 33146-1724 Office: U Miami Clean Energy Rsch Inst PO Box 248294 Miami FL 33124-8294 *Hydrogen energy system will provide the world with clean and abundant energy, while doing away with pollution, acid rains and the greenhouse effect. It is a noble and worthwhile goal to strive for.*

VIADERO, ROGER C., government official; b. N.Y.C.. BBA in Pub. Acctg., Pace U., MBA in Mgmt. Acctg. Former police officer and homicide investigator N.Y.C. Police Dept.; various positions FBI, 1979-94, chief internal auditor N.Y. div.; chief audit unit FBI, Washington; prof. FBI Nat. Acad., Quantico, Va.; insp. gen. USDA, Washington, 1994—. Contbr. numerous articles on law enforcement and mgmt. to profl. publs. Office: USDA Office Insp Gen Adminstrn Bldg Washington DC 20250

VIALL, J(OHN) THOMAS, non-profit organization executive, fundraiser; b. Ft. Hood, Tex., Aug. 15, 1948; s. Otis DePry and Margaret Helen (Cowie) V.; m. Susan Jane Bright, Aug. 25, 1973 (div. Dec. 1980); m. Barbra Jill Baken, Oct. 17, 1982; children: Larissa Rachel, Alessandra Lauren. BA, Fairleigh Dickinson U., 1970, MA magna cum laude, 1972; postgrad., Columbia U., 1972-74; Tchg. Cert., Montclair State Coll., 1975. Tutor ED/LD Bd. of Edn., Bogota and Ridgefield Par, N.J., 1975-77; dir. devel. The Vail-Deane Sch., Elizabeth, N.J., 1977-83; dir. corp. devel. Save the Children, Westport, Conn., 1983-86, Thirteen/WNET, N.Y.C., 1986-87; exec. dir. Sister City Program of City of N.Y., Office of Mayor, 1987-91; dir. devel. Sister Cities Internat., Alexandria, Va., 1991-93; exec. dir. Internat. Coll. Surgeons, Chgo., 1993-96, Orton Dyslexia Soc., 1996—; editor: N.Y.-Beijing Directory, 1987; project coord.: Hard Choices-Portraits of Poverty and Hunger in America, 1983. Recipient Key to City, Mayorof Owensboro, Ky., 1992. Mem. U.S. Golf Assn. Achievements include negotiation of loan of 2 giant pandas from Beijing Zoo to N.Y. Zool. Soc. Avocations: golf, tennis, computer technology. Home: 2905 Keystone Rd Northbrook IL 60062 Office: Chester Bldg # 382 8600 LaSalle Rd Baltimore MD 21286-2044

VIANDS, DONALD REX, plant breeder and educator; b. Riverdale, Md., Apr. 1, 1952; s. Walter Leroy and Lydia (Zeh) V.; m. Janice Ann Ruppelt, Aug. 7, 1976; children: Jamie Christopher, April Suzanne. BS in Agronomy, U. Md., 1974; MS in Plant Breeding, U. Minn., 1977, PhD in Plant Breeding, 1979. Undergrad. rsch. asst. U. Md., College Park, 1969-74; grad. rsch. asst. U. Minn., St. Paul, 1974-79; asst. prof. Cornell U., Ithaca, N.Y., 1979-85, assoc. prof., 1985-92, prof., 1992—, assoc. dir. acad. programs, 1995—; mem. adv. com. biotech. sci. adv. com. EPA, Washington, 1987-95; mem. steering com. N.Y. State North Country Devel. Program, 1990—; adv. N.Y. State Forage and Grassland Coun., 1984-90, Alfalfa Crop Adv. Com., 1984-92. Contbr. articles to profl. jours., chpts. to books. Sunday sch. tchr. People's Bapt. Ch., Newfield, N.Y., 1988—, deacon, 1988-90, 93—, Awana comdr., 1993—. Named Most Influential Faculty Mem. for Merrill Presdl. Scholar, Cornell U., 1991. Mem. Am. Soc. Agronomy, Crop Sci. Soc. Am., Am. Seed Trade Assn. (mem. minimum distance com. 1988-94), N.Am. Alfalfa Improvement Conf. (sec. 1984-86, v.p. 1986-88, pres. 1988-90), Ea. Forage Improvement Conf., Am. Forage and Grassland Coun., N.Y. State Forage and Grasslands Coun. Republican. Achievements include development of 11 alfalfa varieties. Office: Cornell Univ Office Acad Programs 155 Roberts Hall Ithaca NY 14853

VIANI, JAMES L., lawyer; b. Kincaid, Ill., Dec. 24, 1932; s. Frank Jerome and Alfonsina V.; m. Virginia Lee Wilson, Dec. 27, 1958; children: Theresa, Diana, Deborah. BS, Millikin U., 1954; LLB, Wash. U., St. Louis, 1957. Bar: Ill. 1957, Mo. 1957. Assoc. Blackmar, Swanson, Midgley, Jones & Eager, Kansas City, Mo., 1958-59, Stinson, Mag & Fizzell, Kansas City, 1960-62; ptnr. Stinson, Mag & Fizzel, Kansas City, 1962-87, chmn. corp. dept., 1979-87, cons. ptnr., 1988-92. Br. bd. chmn. YMCA, Kansas City, 1979-81. With U.S. Army, 1957-63. Mem. ABA, Phi Kappa Phi, Order of the Coif. Republican. Avocations: hiking, reading, farming. Home: 11106 Belleview Ave Kansas City MO 64114-5115 Office: Stinson Mag & Fizzell PO box 419251 1201 Walnut St Kansas City MO 64141-6251

VIANO, DAVID CHARLES, automotive safety research scientist; b. San Mateo, Calif., May 7, 1946; s. James Louis and Dorothy Marie (Clark) V.; m. Sharon Lynne Henderson, Dec. 7, 1975. BSEE, U. Santa Clara, 1968; MS in Applied Mechanics, Calif. Inst. Tech., 1969, PhD in Applied Mechanics, 1972; postdoctoral degree in biomed. sci., Swiss Inst. Tech., Zurich, 1974. Sr. rsch. engr. biomed. scis. dept., GM Rsch. Labs., Warren, Mich., 1974-76, staff rsch. engr., 1976-78, asst. dept. head, 1978-87, prin. rsch. scientist, leader safety rsch. program, 1987-92; mgr. global R&D programs, 1992—; tech. sec. med. com. for automotive safety biomed. scis. dept., GM Rsch. Labs., Warren, Mich., 1984—, mem. accident avoidance tech. com., 1989-93; adj. asst. prof. dept. mech. engring. Wayne State U., Detroit, 1981-86, adj. assoc. prof., 1986-89, adj. prof., 1989—; vis. prof. Chalmers U., Sweden, 1992—; chmn. indsl. adv. com. Bioengring. Ctr., Wayne State U., 1984—; mem. injury rsch. grant rev. com. CDC, HHS, Atlanta, 1986-88, mem. adv. com. for injury prevention and control, 1989-92; mem. indsl. adv. com. bioengring. divsn. U. Pa., Phila., 1988-95; mem. com. on fed. trauma rsch., NRC, NAS, 1984-85; mem. com. sch. bus. safety, 1987-89, com. on occupant restraint rsch. needs, 1988-92; mem. Transp. Rsch. Bd., NRC; com. to rev. CDC injury control program progress, NRC, 1988; mem. engring. directorate rev. panel bioengring. NSF, 1987. Assoc. editor Jour. Biomech. Engring., 1982-88, Accident Analysis and Prevention, 1988—; editl. cons. Jour. Trauma, 1988-92, emeritus, 1992—; tech. reviewer Handbook of Bioengineering, 1985, Protecting Your Bank From Injury, 1985. Mem. property tax assessment bd. rev. City of Bloomfield Hills, Mich., 1986—; bd. dirs., mem.-at-large Mich. Head Injury Alliance chpt. Nat. Head Injury Found., 1987-89, exec. com., bd. dirs. nat. orgn., Southborough, Mass., 1987-91, treas., chmn. fin. com., 1988-91; trustee Del. Harder Rehab. Fund Bd., 1987-89, pres., 1989, Rehab. Inst. Found., Detroit; bd. trustees Detroit Med. Ctr., clin. svcs. adv. bd. rehab. and post-acute svcs., 1989—. Recipient Safety Engring. Excellence award Nat. Hwy. Traffic Safety Adminstrn., Dept. Transp., 1989, Best Paper award 30th Stapp Car Crash Conf., 1988, Bertil Aldman award IRCOBI, 1992. Fellow ASME (mem. transp. safety com. 1982-92, bioengring. honors com. 1982—, govt. rels. contact bioengring. div. 1980-92, program chmn. editor symposium, 1981), Soc. Automotive Engrs. (chmn. Stapp car crash adv. com., 1976-90, passenger protection com. 1980—, safety adv. com. 1985—, Ralph Isbrandt automotive safety engring. awards bd. 1987-89, organizer, editor 18 symposia 1982-86, mem. other coms., Isbrandt medals 1981, 85, 86, Forest R. McFarland Ouststanding Svc. award 1982, Arch T. Colwell awards 1982, (3) 1988, (2) 1989), Assn. Advancement Automotive Medicine (chmn. ad hoc com. for impairment scaling, 1985—, mem. exec. bd. 1986-91, pres.-elect 1988, pres. 1989); mem. Am. Trauma Soc. (bd. dirs. 1989—), Motor Vehicle Mfrs. Assn. (mem. biomechanics task group 1976-84), U.S. Nat. Com. on Biomechanics (Soc. Automotive Engrs. del. 1982-89), Internat. Standards Orgn. (impact safety group 1976—), Am. Soc. Biomechanics, ACS (com. on truama and burns conjoint coun. surg. rsch. 1986—), Biomed. Engring. Soc. (sr.), AAAS. Republican. Home: 265 Warrington Rd Bloomfield Hills MI 48304 Office: Gen Motors Rsch and Devel Ctr Warren MI 48090-9055

VIAULT, BIRDSALL SCRYMSER, history educator; b. Mineola, N.Y., Sept. 20, 1932; s. Joseph Choate and Helen Lee (Scrymser) V.; m. Sarah Reed Underhill, May 9, 1970. BS, Adelphi U., 1955, MA, 1956; MA, Duke U., 1957, PhD, 1963. Instr. history Adelphi U., Garden City, N.Y., 1959-63, asst. prof. history, 1963-68; assoc. prof. history Winthrop U., Rock Hill, S.C., 1968-72, prof. history, 1972—, chmn. dept. history, 1979-89; vis. assoc. prof. Duke U., Durham, N.C., 1970. Author: World History in the 20th Century, 1969, American History Since 1865, 1989, rev. edit., 1993, Western Civilization Since 1600, 1990, Modern European History, 1990, English History, 1992; author weekly column, 1979-87; contbr. articles and revs. to profl. jours. Mem. Nassau County (N.Y.) Dem. Com., 1961-68, S.C. Commn. for Archives and History, 1979-89, S.C. Bd. Rev. for Nat. Register of Hist. Places, 1988—; del. S.C. State Dem. Conv., 1972, 74, 94, 96; leader ann. tours to Europe, 1977—. Ford Found. Coop. Program for Humanities Postdoctoral fellow U. N.C., Duke U., 1969-70. Mem. So. Hist. Assn., Am. Cath. Hist. Assn., Soc. Historians of Am. Fgn. Rels., S.C. Hist. Assn., Kiwanis Club Rock Hill, Phi Kappa Phi, Phi Alpha Theta, Zeta Beta Tau. Roman Catholic. Avocations: travel, photography, cooking. Home: 2186 Wentworth Dr Rock Hill SC 29732-1242 Office: Winthrop U Dept History Rock Hill SC 29733

VIAULT, SARAH UNDERHILL, civic volunteer; b. Richmond, Va., Aug. 6, 1938; d. Gary Madison and Sarah Jane (Reed) Underhill; m. David Ashmun Dobbins, Aug. 12, 1961 (div. 1969); m. Birdsall Scrymser Viault, May 9, 1970. BA in Liberal Arts, Sweet Briar Coll., 1960; BS in Elem. Edn., U. Minn., 1962. Exec. sec. Harper & Row Pub., N.Y.C., 1960-61; tchr. Efland (N.C.) Elem. Sch., 1963-65; adminstrv. sec. to chief of neurology Duke U. Med. Ctr., Durham, N.C., 1967-70; dir. med./social svc., newsletter editor York Gen. Hosp., Rock Hill, S.C., 1971-72; exec. sec. Kelly Svcs., Charlotte, N.C., 1973; med. transcriptionist Charlotte Meml. Hosp., 1973-74; Uniforce temp. exec. sec. Spring Industries, Rock Hill, 1979-82; ind. proofreader Rock Hill, 1988—. Bd. dirs. Carolina Community Action, Rock Hill, 1974-76; bd. dirs., officer Fine Arts Assn. Rock Hill, 1975-79; phone bank organizer local Dem. campaigns, 1982; vol. Am. Cancer Soc. Support Group, 1982-92, past circle chmn., sec. Women of Oakland Ave. Presbyn. Ch.; charter officer, sec. York County Dem. Forum, 1991-93; pres. Ebinport precinct York County Dem. Party, 1994; del. to state S.C. Dem. Party Conv., 1994. Named Disting. Vol., Boys Club Mpls., 1962; recipient Cert. of Honor, York County Hospice, 1987, Outstanding York County Dem. Vols., S.C. Dem. Party, 1993. Mem. AAUW (bd. dirs., chmn. drama group 1990-92), Amelia Pride Book Club (pres. 1990-92), Town and Country Garden Club (sec.), Sierra Club, Swan Meadows Garden Club (pres. 1994). Avocations: piano, singing, writing poetry, flower arranging, travel. Home: 2186 Wentworth Dr Rock Hill SC 29732-1242

VICCARO, JAMES RICHARD, marketing executive; b. Sewickley, Pa., Dec. 12, 1945; s. James Edward and Frances (Mastro) V.; m. Linda Schutte, May 14, 1966; children: James Richard Jr., Christy, Gina. BS, Indiana U. Pa., 1967; MBA, U. Phoenix, 1986. Vice pres. mktg. and sales Lee Pharms., South El Monte, Calif., 1973-78; pres., cons. Corp. Mktg. Dynamics, Huntington Beach, Calif., 1977—; dir. sales and mktg. chem. packaging div. Ga.-Pacific Co., Newport Beach, Calif., 1980-83; pres., chief operating officer Arnco Mktg., Ltd., Irvine, Calif., 1987-91; pres., owner Poly-Tak, Huntington Beach, Calif., 1992—. Mem. Am. Mktg. Assn., U. Phoenix Network for Profl. Devel., Tau Kappa Epsilon. Home: 6891 Loyola Dr Huntington Beach CA 92647-4053

VICCELLIO, HENRY, JR., career military officer. BS, USAF Acad., 1962; MA in Latin Am. Studies, Am. U., 1969; grad., Armed Forces Staff Coll., 1973. Commd. 2d lt. USAF, 1962, advanced through grades to gen., 1992, various mil. positions, 1962-83; comdr. 1st Tactical Fighter Wing, Langley AFB, Va., 1983-85; vice comdr. San Antonio Air Logistics Ctr., Kelly AFB, Tex., 1985-86; dep. chief of staff for logistics Hdqrs. Tactical Air Command, Langley AFB, Va., 1986-89; dep. chief of staff for logistics and engring. Hdqrs. USAF, Washington, 1989-91; dir. The Joint Staff, Washington, 1991-92; comdr. Air Edn. and Tng. Command, Randolph AFB, Tex., 1992-95, Air Force Materiel Command, Wright-Patterson AFB, Ohio, 1995—. Decorated Def. Disting. Svc. medal, Disting. Svc. medal, Lion of Merit with oak leaf cluster, DFC with oak leaf cluster, Air medal with 11 oak leaf clusters, Republic of Vietnam Gallantry Cross with Palm. Office: HQ AFMC/PAC 4375 Chidlaw Rd Ste 6 Dayton OH 45433-5006

VICE, JON EARL, hospital executive; b. Fairfield, Ala., July 1, 1947; s. Jon Walker Vice and Martha Ann (Lee) Cain; m. Sara Rose Romano Marino, July 26, 1967 (div. Feb. 1975); children: Jon E. Jr., Lisa Ann; m. Joanne Katherine Richter, June 28, 1975 (div. Mar. 1992); children: Jeffrey Walker, Jessica Lynn. BS, U. Ala., Tuscaloosa, 1970; MS, U. Ala., Birmingham, 1974. Asst. to adminstr. Children's Hosp. Ala., Birmingham, 1971-72, adminstr., chief operating officer, 1977-79; assoc. adminstr. Children's Hosp. Med. Ctr., Cin., 1972-76; exec. v.p., chief operating officer Children's Hosp. Wis., Milw., 1979-84, pres., chief exec. officer, 1984—; chmn., bd. dirs. Milw. Regional Med. Ctr., 1985—, Child Health Corp. Am., Kansas City, Mo.; pres., bd. dirs. Total Care Health Plan (HMO), Milw., 1985-87; mem. Greater Milw. Com.; bd. dirs. Milw. Ednl. Trust. Named Outstandng Alumnus Grad. Program in Health Adminstrn., U. Ala.-Birmingham Alumni Assn., 1987. Mem. Am. Coll. Healthcare Execs., Nat. Assn. Childrens Hosps. (exec. coun., bd. dirs. 1986—, chmn. 1989—), Westmoore Country Club (v.p. bd.), Univ. Club. Presbyterian. Avocations: golf, skiing. Office: Children's Hosp Wis PO Box 1997 Milwaukee WI 53201-1997

VICE, LAVONNA LEE, lawyer; b. Lexington, Ky., May 27, 1952; d. Keith Romould and Helen (Singer) V. BA summa cum laude, U. Balt., 1980, JD, 1983. Bar: Md. 1983, U.S. Ct. Appeals (4th cir.) 1987, U.S. Dist. Ct. Md. 1988, D.C. 1989, U.S. Supreme Ct. 1989. Trial atty. Ellin & Baker, Balt., 1983—; lectr., writer, rschr. med., surg. and hosp. standards of care. Mem. ABA, ATLA, Md. State Bar Assn., D.C. Bar Assn., Balt. City. Bar Assn. Office: Ellin & Baker 1101 Saint Paul St Baltimore MD 21202-2662

VICENTE, ESTEBAN, artist; b. Turegano, Segovia, Spain, Jan. 20, 1903; came to U.S. 1941; s. Toribio Y Ruiz and Sofia Perez Y (Albarez); m. Harriet Godfrey, Dec. 1963. Art cert., Artes De San Fernando, Madrid, 1921-24; hon. PhD, Parsons Sch. Design, N.Y.C., 1984, Long Island U., South Hampton, N.Y., 1993. Faculty mem. art dept. various univs., 1949-74; tchr., artist-in-residence Vermont Studio Ctr., Johnson, Vt., 1985, Parsons Sch. Design, N.Y.C., 1991-93; founding mem., artist-in-residence N.Y. Studio Sch. Drawing, Painting & Sculpture, N.Y.C., 1964—. Recipient Lifetime Achievement in the Arts award Guild Hall Mus., East Hampton, N.Y., 1993, Gold Medal for fine arts Spanish Coun. of Ministers, Govt. of Spain, 1991. Mem. Am. Acad. Arts & Letters, Nat. Acad. of Design. Home: 1 W 67th St New York NY 10023

VICK, COLUMBUS EDWIN, JR., civil engineering design firm executive; b. Jacksonville, Fla., Nov. 8, 1934; s. Columbus Edwin Sr. and Lucretia (Dean) V.; m. Laura Anne McGowan, Mar. 20, 1964; children: Jennifer, Carolyn, Elizabeth. BSCE, N.C. State U., 1956, MSCE, 1960. Registered profl. engr., 15 states. Research asst. N.C. State Civil Engring. Dept., Raleigh, 1958-60; transp. planning engr. Harland Bartholomew & Assocs., Memphis, 1960-64; office and project mgr. Harland Bartholomew & Assocs., Raleigh, 1964-67; prin., co-founder Kimley-Horn and Assocs. Inc., Raleigh, 1967-72, pres., 1972-92; chmn., 1992—. Co-author: North Carolina Atlas; contbr. numerous research and tech. publs. in fields of transp. engring. planning and traffic engring. Past pres., bd. dirs. N.C. State U. Engring. Found., Kenan Inst. for Engring., Tech. and Sci.; past pres. bd. assocs. Meredith Coll.; past dir. N.C. State U. Alumni Assn.; past 2d v.p. Bapt. State Conv. of N.C.; bd. dirs. Assoc. Bapt. Press, Bibl. Recorder. Named Disting. Engring. alumnus N.C. State U. Engring. Found., 1991. Fellow ASCE (Outstanding Young Engr. award ea. br. N.C. sect. 1966), Inst. Transp. Engrs. (Oustanding Individual Activity award so. sect. 1978, Disting. Svc. award so. sect. 1981, Lifetime Svc. award N.C. sect. 1994); mem. NSPE, Am. Con. Engrs. Coun., Am. Inst. Cert. Planners (PSMA Coll. of Fellows), Phi Kappa Phi (Outstanding Engring. Achievement award N.C. sect. 1992). Baptist. Home: 2205 Nancy Ann Dr Raleigh NC 27607-3318 Office: Kimley-Horn and Assocs Inc 3001 Weston Pky Cary NC 27513-2301

VICK, EDWARD HOGE, JR., advertising executive; b. N.Y.C., Feb. 27, 1944; s. Edward Hoge and Margaret Jane (Sprankle) V.; m. Nancy Jane Newcomer; 1 son, Joshua D. A.B., U. N.C., 1966; M.S., Northwestern U., 1971. With Benton & Bowles, Inc., N.Y.C., 1971-75, Ogilvy & Mather, Inc., N.Y.C., 1975-83; exec. v.p., dir. account service Ammirati & Puris Inc., N.Y.C., 1983-85; pres., chief operating officer Ammirati & Puris Inc., 1985-90; pres., chief exec. officer Levine, Huntley, Vick & Beaver, N.Y.C., 1990—. Author: An Examination of the Creative Process, 1971. Served to lt. U.S. Navy, 1966-69. Decorated Bronze Star (2). Mem. St. Andrew's Soc. Republican. Presbyterian. Office: Landor Assocs 1001 Front St San Francisco CA 94111-1424

VICK, FRANCES BRANNEN, publishing executive; b. Trinity, Tex., Aug. 14, 1935; d. Carl Andrew and Bess (courtney) B.; m. Ross William Vick Jr., June 23, 1956; children: Karen Lynn, Ross William III, Patrick Brannen. BA, U. Tex., 1958; MA, Stephen F. Austin State U., 1968. Teaching fellow Stephen F. Austin State U., Nacogdoches, Tex., 1966-68, lectr., 1968-69; lectr. Angelina Coll., Lufkin, Tex., 1969-71, Baylor U., Waco, Tex., 1974-75, 77-78; vice prin. Vanguard Sch., Waco, 1975-77; pres. E-Heart Press, Inc., Dallas, 1979—; co-dir. UNT Press U. North Tex., Denton, 1987-89, dir., 1989—. Publisher 120 books; editor 40 books. Leadership coun. Ann Richards Com., Austin, 1990-94; amb. Inst. Texan Cultures; mem. Tex. Commn. on Arts, Lit., 1991. Mem. AAUW, Book Pubs. Tex. (v.p. 1990-96, pres. 1996), Tex. Folklore Soc. (councillor 1991-93), Tex. Humanities Resource Ctr. (bd. dirs. 1990-91), Conf. Coll. Tchrs. English, Western Lit. Assn., Western Writers Am., Philos. Soc. Tex., Pen Ctr. U.S.A. West, Tex. State Hist. Assn. (life), East Tex. Hist. Assn., Western Writers Am., Western Lit. Assn., Soc. Scholarly Pub., Women in Scholarly Pub., Rocky Mountain Book Pubs. Assn., Leadership Tex., Leadership Am., Tex. Humanities Alliance, UNT League Profl. Women. Democrat. Episcopalian. Home: 3700 Mockingbird Ln Dallas TX 75205-2125 Office: U North Tex PO Box 13856 Denton TX 76203-6856

VICK, JAMES ALBERT, publishing executive, consultant; b. Norwalk, Conn., Feb. 5, 1945; s. James Albert and Madeline (Mayhew) V.; m. Deborah M. Ashley, Dec. 23, 1964 (div. Oct. 1974); children: James Ashley, Guy Robert; m. Susan Jane Collins, May 14, 1977; 1 child, Jonathan Scott. BS, Boston U., 1967. Dist. mgr. McGraw Hill Pub. Co., N.Y.C., 1969-75, Cahners Pub. Co., N.Y.C., 1975-79; mgr. advt. ASCE, N.Y.C., 1979-82; v.p. mktg. Bill Communications, N.Y.C., 1982-87; pub. Thomas Pub. Co., N.Y.C., 1987-95; v.p. Web Property Devel. Poppe Tyson, 1995—; cons. Carvajal, Calle, Columbia, 1984, McLarens, London, 1987. Capt. USAR, 1967-70, Vietnam. Mem. Bus. Mktg. Assn. (cert. bus. communicator), Am. Bus. Press (pubs. com.), Soc. Plastics Engrs., Pharm Ad Club, Instrument Soc. Am., Indsl. Computing Soc., Princeton Club, Beacon Hill Country Club, Port Royal Golf Club, Elks. Episcopalian. Avocations: golf, sailing, antique restoration. Home: 17 Sailers Way Rumson NJ 07760-1242 Office: Poppe Tyson 40 W 23rd St New York NY 10010-5201

VICK, MARIE, retired health science educator; b. Saltillo, Tex., Jan. 22, 1922; d. Alphy Edgar and Mollie (Cowser) Pitts; m. Joe Edward Vick, Apr. 5, 1942; children: Mona Marie, Rex Edward. BS, Tex. Woman's U., Denton, 1942, MA, 1949. Tchr. Coahoma (Tex.) High Sch., 1942-43, Santa Rita Elem. Sch., San Angelo, Tex., 1943-45, Crozier Tech. High Sch., Dallas, 1946-47, Monroe Jr. High Sch., Omaha, 1947-48; instr. Tex. Woman's U., Denton, 1948-50; tchr. San Angelo (Tex.) Jr. High Sch., 1957-58, San Angelo (Tex.) Sr. High Sch., 1957-58, Harlingen Bonham Elem. Sch., 1958-59, Harlingen (Tex.) High Sch., 1959-62; prof. health sci. Coll. Edn. U. Houston, 1962-80. Author: A Collection of Dances for Children, 1970; Health Science in the Elementary School, 1979; contbr. articles to profl. jours.; artist in oil, watercolor and acrylic. Mem. exec. bd. Health Care Task Force of Walker County. Recipient Cert. of Achievement, Tex. Commn. Intercollegiate Athletics for Women, 1972, Research Service award Tex. Cancer Control Program, 1978-79, Plaudit award Nat. Dance Assn., 1982, Disting. Service award Pan Am. U., 1983, Service citation Am. Cancer Soc., Cert. of Appreciation, Tex. div. Am. Cancer Soc., 1980; Favorite Prof. honoree Cap and Gown Mortar Bd., U. Houston, 1974. Mem. AAHPERD (dance editor 1971-74), NEA, AARP (chmn. legis. com. Huntsville chpt. 1988-90, bd. dirs., liaison person Walker County commrs. 1989-90, chmn. cmty. svc. project Walker County Unpaved Rd. Survey, 1989, mem. exec. bd. 1992—), Am. Sch. Health Assn., So. Assn. Health, Phys. Edn. Coll. Women (sec. dance sect. 1970-73), Tex. State Tchrs. Assn. (sect. chmn. 1964-65), Tex. Assn Health, Phys. Edn. and Recreation (chmn. dance sect. 1968-69), Tex. Assn. Coll. Tchrs., Nat. Ret. Tchrs. Assn. (legis. chmn. 1988-89), Tex. Assn. Ret. Tchrs., Property Owners Assn. (organizer, 1st pres.), U. Houston Assn. Ret. Profs., Tex. Women's U. Nat. Alumnae Assn. (life), Tex. Women's Pioneer Club, U. Houston 20 Yr. Club. Democrat. Methodist. Home: RR 15 Box 345 Huntsville TX 77340-0980

VICK, NICHOLAS A., neurologist; b. Chgo., Oct. 3, 1939. MD, U. Chgo., 1965. Diplomate Am. Bd. Neurology. Intern U. Chgo. Hosps., 1965, resident in neurology, 1966-68; fellow in neurology NIH, Bethesda, Md., 1968-70; staff Evanston (Ill.) Hosp., 1975—; prof. neurology Northwestern U. Med. Sch., Evanston, Ill., 1978—. Office: Evanston Hosp Div Neurology 2650 Ridge Ave Evanston IL 60201-1718

VICK, SUSAN, playwright, educator; b. Raleigh, N.C., Nov. 4, 1945; d. Thomas B. Jr. and Merle (Hayes) V. MFA, Southern Meth. U., 1969; PhD, U. Ill., 1979. Prof. drama/theatre Worcester (Mass.) Poly. Inst., 1981—, dir. theatre programs; dir. theatre tech., playwright Excuse Me For Living Prodns., Cambridge, Mass., 1989—; playwright Ensemble Studio Theatre, Glasgow, Scotland and London, 1993-94; founder WPI Ann. New Voices Festival of Original Plays, 1992. Editor: (2 vols.) Playwrights Press, Amherst, 1988—; playwright plays including When I Was Your Age, 1982, Ord-Way Ames-Gay, 1982, Investments, 1985, Half Naked, 1989, Quandary, 1983, Meat Selection, 1984, Give My Love to Everyone But, 1989; appeared in plays including Rip Van Winkle, 1979, Why I Live at The P.O., 1982, The Play Group, 1984-85, Present Stage, 1985, Sister Mary Ignatius Explain It All, 1986, Wipeout, 1988, Bogus Joan, 1992, 93; dir. play Give My Love to Everyone But, 1990 (Edinburgh Festival); theatre editor: Sojourner The Women's Forum, 1995—. Dir., Women's Community Theatre, Amherst, 1981-84, Upstart, Wis., 1994. Faculty fellow U. Ill., 1976-77. Mem. Drama League, Dramatists Guild (assoc.), Soc. Stage Dirs. and Choreographers (assoc.), Alpha Psi Omega (Svc. to Students award 1996). Avocations: puppets, frogs. Office: Worcester Poly Tech Inst 100 Institute Rd Worcester MA 01609-2247

VICKER, RAY, writer; b. Wis., Aug. 27, 1917; s. Joseph John and Mary (Young) V.; m. Margaret Ella Leach, Feb. 23, 1944. Student, Wis. State U., Stevens Point, 1934, Los Angeles City Coll., 1940-41, U.S. Mcht. Marine Officers' Sch., 1944, Northwestern U., 1947-49. With Chgo. Jour. Commerce, 1946-50, automobile editor, 1947-50; mem. staff Wall St. Jour., 1950-83; European editor Wall St. Jour., London, Eng., 1960-75. Author: How an Election Was Won, 1962, Those Swiss Money Men, 1973, Kingdom of Oil, 1974, Realms of Gold, 1975, This Hungry World, 1976, Dow Jones Guide to Retirement Planning, 1985, The Informed Investor, 1990; also numerous articles. Served with U.S. Merchant Marine, 1942-46. Recipient Outstanding Reporting Abroad award Chgo. Newspaper Guild, 1959; Best Bus. Reporting Abroad award E. W. Fairchild, 1963, 67; hon. mention, 1965; Bob Considine award, 1979; ICMA Journalism award, 1983. Mem. Soc. Profl. Journalists, Authors Guild. Roman Catholic. Clubs: Overseas Press (Reporting award 1963, 67) (N.Y.C.); Press (Chgo.). Home and Office: 4131 E Pontatoc Canyon Dr Tucson AZ 85718-5227

VICKERS, JAMES HUDSON, veterinarian, research pathologist; b. Columbus, Ohio, Apr. 21, 1930; s. Carl James and Olga Elizabeth (Schaer) V.; m. Valerie Janet May, Apr. 5, 1964; 1 child, Dana Carlton. BS, Ohio State U., 1952, DVM, 1958; MS, U. Conn., 1966. Diplomate Am. Coll. Vet. Pathologists. Veterinarian Columbus Mcpl. Zoo, 1958-60; dir. pathology dept. Lederle Labs., Pearl River, N.Y., 1960-70; v.p., dir. rsch. Primelabs. Inc., Farmingdale, N.J., 1970-72; dir. spl. studies Johnson & Johnson, Washington Crossing, N.J., 1972-73; dir. pathology and primatology br. FDA, Bethesda, Md., 1973-92, dir. div. vet. svcs., 1992-95; pres. PathPro Assocs., Ijamsville, Md., 1995—; rep. interagy. rsch. animal commn. FDA, Bethesda, 1974-89; cons. Gov. Arab Republic Egypt, Cairo, 1976-84, Paul Erlich Inst., Frankfurt, Fed. Republic Germany, 1977-78; chmn. com. on animalcare Ctr. for Biologics, Bethesda. Contbr. chpts. to books. Spokesman Urbana (Md.) Civic Assn., 1987. Capt. U.S. Army, 1952-54. Recipient Presdl. citation Pres. James Carter, 1980, Alumni Svc. award Ohio State Coll. Vet. Medicine, 1987, FDA Commr.'s spl. citation, 1988; FDA Commr.'s Disting. Career Svc. award, 1995. Mem. Am. Vet. Med. Assn., Soc. Toxicology, Interant. Acad. Pathology, Ohio State Vet. Med. Assn., Zane Grey's West Soc. (rpes. 1987-95), Westerners Internat. Avocations: fine arts, books. Office: PathPro Assocs 2324 Oak Dr Ijamsville MD 21754

VICKERS, ROGER SPENCER, physicist, program director; b. Hitchin, Hertfordshire, Eng., Nov. 13, 1937; came to U.S., 1963, naturalized, 1974; s. John Hector and Corona (McCarthy) V.; m. Solvi Loken, May 18, 1968; children—Michelle, Jacqueline, Kevin. B.Sc. with honors, Southampton U., Eng., 1959, Ph.D., 1963. Physicist Ill. Inst. Tech. Research Inst., Chgo., 1963-66; research asso. Stanford U., 1966-68; v.p. sci. and applications E.R.A., Inc., Houston, 1969-70; asso. prof. elec. engring. Colo. State U., 1970-73; dir. advanced radar program SRI Internat., Menlo Park, Calif., 1973—; cons. NSF. Mem. Soc. Exploration Geophysicists, IEEE. Home: 1143 Los Altos Ave Los Altos CA 94022-1021 Office: SRI Internat Bldg G Menlo Park CA 94025

VICKERY, ANN MORGAN, lawyer; b. Anderson, S.C., June 25, 1944; d. Joseph Harold and Doris (Rogers) Morgan; m. Raymond Ezekiel Vickery, Jr., June 23, 1979; children: Raymond Morgan, Philip Dickens. AB History, Mary Baldwin Coll., 1965; JD, Georgetown U., 1978. Bar: D.C. 1978. Elem. sch. tchr. Chesterfield County, Va., 1965-66; legal publs. specialist Nat. Archives and Record Svc., Washington, 1966-69; speech writing staff to Pres., rsch. asst., chief rschr., staff asst. The White House, Washington, 1969-74; summer clerk Graham & James, Washington, 1975; various positions Dept. Treasury, Washington, 1975-78; atty. Hogan & Hartson, Washington, 1978—; health group dir. Hogan and Hartson, Washington, 1991—, exec. com., 1992-95, 96—; gen. counsel Nat. Hospice Orgn., 1982— (named Woman of the Yr. 1986); spkr. in field. Contbr. articles to profl. jours. Dir. Hospice No. Va., Arlington, 1987-93; trustee Nat. Hospice Found., 1996—. Mem. ABA, Nat. Health Lawyers Assn., D.C. Bar, Health on Wednesday, Phi Alpha Theta. Office: Hogan & Hartson Columbia Square 555 13th St NW Washington DC 20004-1109

VICKERY, RAYMOND EZCKIEL, JR., government official; b. Brookhaven, Miss., Apr. 30, 1942; s. Raymond Ezckiel and Clarene Helen (Dickens) V.; m. Raymond Claur Brown, Dec. 23, 1967 (div. June 1976); m. Ann Morgan, June 25, 1979; children: Raymond Morgan, Philip Dickens. AB, Duke U., 1964; postgrad., U. Sri Lanka, 1964-65; LLB, Harvard U., 1968. Assoc. Hogan & Hartman, Washington, 1968-77; ptnr. Johnson & Vickery, Vienna, Va., 1977-81, Reed Smith Shaw & McClay, McLean, Va., 1981-85, Hogan & HArtman, McLean, Va., 1985-93; asst. sec. for trade devel. U.S. Dept. Commerce, Washington, 1993—. Contbr. articles to profl. jours. Del. Va. Gen. Assembly, Richmond, 1974-80; mem. Dem. Com., Farifax County, Va., 1971-93; Dem. nominee for Congress, Va., 1992; mem. State Contra Com., Va., 1993; mem. Libt. Bd., Fairfax County, 1972-74. Fulbright scholar, 1964. Mem. ABA, Va. Bar Assn., D.C. Bar Assn., City Club, Phi Beta Kappa, Omicron Delta Kappa. Baptist. Avocations: fishing, horseback riding. Home: 2733 Willow Dr Vienna VA 22181 Office: US Dept Commerce 14th & Constitution Ave NW Washington DC 20230

VICKERY, TRAMMELL EUGENE, lawyer; b. Dalton, Ga., Sept. 6, 1932; s. James Edmond and Eva Mae (Houston) V.; m. Mae Gohley, Feb. 11, 1955; children—Trammell Eugene, David Ray, Alan Scott. B.A., Emory U., 1953, LL.B., 1956. Bar: Ga. 1955. Assoc. Jones, Bird & Howell, Atlanta, 1955-75; assoc. Hansell & Post, Atlanta, 1975-89; ptnr. Troutman Sanders, Atlanta, 1989—; chmn. NCBE, Chgo., 1977-78; chmn. State Bd. Bar Examiners Ga., 1971-74; faculty mem. Emory U. Sch. of Law, Atlanta, 1968-70; lectr. Legal Edn. Ga. Contbr. articles to Bus. Law jours., Ency. Ga. Law. Mem. ABA, Atlanta Bar Assn., Am. Coll. Trial Lawyers. Office: Troutman Sanders 5200 Nationsbank Plz 600 Peachtree St NE Atlanta GA 30308-2220

VICKREY, WILLIAM SPENCER, economist, emeritus educator; b. Victoria, B.C., Can., June 21, 1914; came to U.S., 1914; s. Charles Vernon and Ada Eliza (Spencer) V.; m. Cecile Montez Thompson, July 21, 1951. B.A. in Math. with high honors (scholar), Yale, 1935; M.A., Columbia, 1937, Ph.D., 1947; D.H.L., U. Chgo., 1979; Social Sci. Research Council predoctoral field fellow, 1938-39. Jr. economist Nat. Resources Com., Washington, 1937-38; research asst. 20th Century Fund, 1939-40; economist OPA, 1940-41; sr. economist, div. tax research Treasury Dept., 1941-43; civilian pub. service assignee, 1943- 46, tax cons. to gov. P.R., 1946; mem. faculty Columbia U., N.Y.C., 1946-81; prof. econs. Columbia U., 1958-81; chmn. dept. Columbia, 1964-67, McVickar prof. polit. economy, 1971-81, prof. emeritus, 1981—; Cons. to govt. and industry, 1949—; participant numerous confs., seminars; Ford research prof. Columbia, 1958-59; instr. IBM Systems Research Inst., 1964; vis. lectr. Monash U., Melbourne, Australia, 1971; inter-regional adviser UN, 1974-75. Author: Agenda for Progressive Taxation, 1947, Microstatics: Metastatics and Macroeconomics, 1964, Public Economics, 1994. Clk. Scarsdale (N.Y.) Friends Meeting, 1959-62. Fellow Inst. Advanced Study Behavioral Scis., Stanford, 1967-68. Fellow Am. Econ. Assn. (pres. 1992), Econometric Soc.; mem. Met. Econ. Assn., Am. Statis. Assn., Royal Econ. Soc., Ea. Econ. Assn., Atlantic Econ. Soc. (pres. 1992-93). Home: 162 Warburton Ave Hastings Hdsn NY 10706-3706 Office: Econ Dept Columbia Univ New York NY 10027 *Having been born with considerable talent in an environment that encouraged its development and provided a modicum of recognition for its exercise, I can claim no special virtue for what this has enabled me to achieve. Indeed I have left undone many things that I ought to have done and can only hope that there is enough health left in me to make good some of the deficiency.*

VICTOR, A. PAUL, lawyer; b. N.Y.C., Nov. 6, 1938; s. Samuel L. and Sophie (Ostrow) V.; m. Ellen Grabois, Aug. 30, 1959; children: Stephanie, Rebecca, Diana. BBA, U. Mich., 1960, JD with distinction, 1963. Bar: N.Y. 1964, D.C. 1964. Atty. antitrust div. U.S. Dept. Justice, Washington, 1963-66; assoc. Kirkland, Ellis & Rowe, Washington, 1966-68; assoc. Weil, Gotshal & Manges, N.Y.C., 1968-72, ptnr., 1972—; adj. prof. law Fordham U., N.Y.C., 1983—; mem. adv. bd. Southwestern Legal Found., Dallas, 1984—; bd. dirs. Toray Industries (Am.) Inc., N.Y.C., 1987—. Contbr. numerous articles to law revs., other legal publs. regarding U.S. internat. antitrust and trade law. Mem. visitors com. U. Mich. Law Sch., 1980—; trustee Mass. Sch. of Law, Andover, 1989—; mem. pub. affairs adv. com. Japan Soc., N.Y.C., 1987-89. Mem. ABA (vice-chair 1994-95, coun. mem. sect. on antitrust law 1983-86, 91-94, chmn. internat. antitrust com. 1982-85, 87-90), Internat. Bar Assn., N.Y. State Bar Assn. Jewish. Avocations: golf, travel, swimming. Office: Weil Gotshal & Manges 767 5th Ave New York NY 10153

VICTOR, LORRAINE CAROL, critical care nurse; b. Duluth, Minn., June 14, 1953; d. George E. and Phyllis M. (Pierce) Drimel; m. Robert G. Victor. BA in Nursing, Coll. St. Scholastica, 1975; MS in Nursing, U. Minn., 1984. Cert. regional trainer for neonatal resuscitation program. Staff nurse St. Mary's Hosp., Rochester, Minn., 1975-79, 80-81, U. Wis. Hosp., Madison, 1979-80, U. Minn. Hosps., Mpls., 1981-84, 85-86; clin. instr. neonatal ICU, Children's Hosp. Inc., St. Paul, 1984-86; clin. nurse specialist neonatal ICU, Orlando (Fla.) Regional Med. Ctr., 1986-88, Children's Hosp. St. Paul, 1988—. Mem. AACN (Critical Care Nurse of Yr. award Greater Twin Cities chpt. 1992), Nat. Cert. Corp. (cert. in neonatal intensive care nursing), Nat. Assn. Neonatal Nurses, Sigma Theta Tau. Office: Children's Health Care St Paul Birth Ctr 345 N Smith Ave Saint Paul MN 55102-2392

VICTOR, MICHAEL GARY, lawyer, physician; b. Detroit, Sept. 20, 1945; s. Simon H. and Helen (Litsky) V.; m. Karen Sue Hutson, July 20, 1975; children: Elise Nicole, Sara Lisabeth. Bars: Ill. 1980, U.S. Dist. Ct. (no. dist.) Ill. 1980, U.S. Ct. Appeals (7th cir.) 1981; diplomate Am. Bd. Legal Medicine. Pres., Advocate Adv. Assocs., Chgo., 1982—; asst. prof. medicine Northwestern U. Med. Sch., Chgo., 1982—; pvt. practice law, Barrington, Ill., 1982—; dir. emergency medicine Loretto Hosp., Chgo., 1980-85 , chief sect. of emergency medicine St. Josephs Hosp., Chgo., 1985-87; v.p. Med. Emergency Svcs. Assocs., Buffalo Grove, Ill., 1989; v.p. MESA Mgmt. Corp.; of counsel Bollinger, Ruberry & Garvey, Chgo. Author: Informed Consent, 1980; Brain Death, 1980; (with others) Due Process for Physicians, 1984, A Physicians Guide to the Illinois Living Will Act, The Choice is Ours!, 1989. Recipient Service awards Am. Coll. Emergency Medicine, 1973-83. Fellow Am. Coll. Legal Medicine (bd. govs. 1996—, alt. del. to AMA House of Dels. 1996—), Chgo. Acad. Legal Medicine; mem. Am. Coll. Emergency Physicians (pres. Ill. chpt. 1980, med.-legal-ins. council 1980-81, 83-84), ABA, Ill. State Bar Assn., Am. Soc. Law and Medicine, Chgo. Bar Assn. (med.-legal council 1981-83), AMA, Ill. State Med. Soc. (med.-legal council 1980-86, 88), Chgo. Med. Soc. Jewish. Home and Office: 1609 Guthrie Cir Barrington IL 60010-5721

VICTOR, ROBERT EUGENE, real estate corporation executive, lawyer; b. N.Y.C., Dec. 17, 1929; s. Louis and Rebecca (Teitelbaum) V.; m. Dorothy Saffir, Oct. 14, 1951; children—Priscilla Saffir Victor Faubel, Pandora Saffir. LL.B., St. John's U., 1953, J.D., 1968. Bar: N.Y. bar 1953, Calif. bar 1965. With firm Szold and Brandwen, N.Y.C., 1953-54; atty. Dept. Army, Phila., 1955-56; with Hughes Aircraft Co., Culver City, Calif., 1956-62; v.p., gen. counsel Packard Bell Electronics Corp., Los Angeles, 1962-70; sr. v.p., gen. counsel Cordon Internat. Corp., Los Angeles, 1970-78; also dir.; gen. counsel Am. Harp Soc., 1969-85; pres. Vanowen Realty Corp., 1978-93, also dir. Mem. Los Angeles County Bar Assn. Club: Masons. Office: 722 Walden Dr Beverly Hills CA 90210-3125

VICTOR, WILLIAM WEIR, retired telephone company executive, consultant; b. Marshall, Ill., Apr. 16, 1924; s. Sturges L. and Esther (Weir) V.; m. Patricia Kelly, Sept. 7, 1946; children: William K., Jill Victor Buelsing, D. Gregory. Student, U. Okla., 1943-44; E.E., U. Cin., 1948, U. Ill., 1949. Various positions Cin. Bell Telephone, Ohio, 1947-69, v.p., 1972-85, sr. v.p., 1986-87; v.p. 195 Corp., N.Y., 1969-72; bd. dirs. Skidmore Sales and Distbn. Co. Trustee Goodwill Industries, Cin., 1973-91, WCET Ednl. TV Found., Cin., 1972-86, Bethesda Hosp., Cin., 1978, Herman Schneider Found., Cin., 1983, Armstrong Chapel Found., 1992; trustee, v.p. Millcreek Valley Conservancy Dist., 1990—. Sgt. USAR, 1943-45, ETO, lt. col. USAR, ret. Mem. IEEE, Engring. Soc. Cin., Cin. Country Club. Home: 5440 Windridge Ct Cincinnati OH 45243-2967

VICTORIN, HIS EMINENCE THE MOST REVEREND ARCHBISHOP See URSACHE, VICTORIN

VICTORINO, LOUIS D., lawyer; b. Lemoore, Calif., May 27, 1945; s. Louis and Mayme (Garcia) V.; m. Kathleen Gilman Berl, June 7, 1975. BA, Stanford U., 1967; JD, UCLA, 1970. Assoc./ptnr. Pettit & Martin, San Francisco, L.A., 1970-84; ptnr. Seyfarth, Shaw, Fairweather & Geraldson, L.A., 1984-88, Pillsbury & Madison, L.A., 1988-93, Fried, Frank, Harris, Shriver & Jacobson, L.A., 1993—; adv. bd. Govt. Contractor, Washington, 1990—; legal advisor Commn. Govt. Procurement, 1971. Co-author: Proving & Pricing Construction Claims, 1990, Government Contractor Briefing Papers Collection, 1987-95. Mem. ABA (pub. contract law sect., reg. pres. 1975, editl. bd. Pub. Contract Law Jour. 1992-95), Fed. Bar Assn. (reg. v.p.), Ct. Fed. Claims Bar Assn., Bd. Contract Appeals Bar Assn. Office: Fried Frank Harris Shrive & Jacobson 725 S Figueroa St Ste 1200 Los Angeles CA 90017

VIDAL, ALEJANDRO LEGASPI, architect; b. Kawit, Cavite, The Philippines, May 3, 1934; came to U.S. 1954; s. Antonio and Patrocinia Santonil (Legaspi) V.; m. Fe Del Rosario, Aug. 16, 1962; 1 child, Alex Anthony. BS in Architecture, Mapua Inst. Tech., 1962. Registered arch., The Philippines. Prin. A.L. Vidal Arch., Manila, The Philippines, 1962-63; staff arch. Vinnell Wall & Green, Agana, Guam, 1963-64; project engr. Dillingham Corp. of Nevada, Hawaii and Guam, 1964-74; sr. project mgr., preconstrn. svc. mgr. Fletcher-Pacific Constrn. Co. Ltd., Honolulu, 1974—. Designer, builder first application of integrated aluminum forming sys. for high rise concrete construction; co-inventor building sys. Active Rep. Presdl. Task Force, Washington, 1980-88, Rep. Senatorial Com., Washington, 1980-88. With USN, 1954-58, Korea. Mem. Am. Concrete Inst., Am. Mgmt. Assn., Soc. Am. Mil. Engrs., Am. Legion, U. Hawaii Found., Chancellor's Club, Disabled Am. Vets., Comdrs. Club, Oxford Club. Roman Catholic. Avocations: golf, swimming, volunteer work. Home: 1051 Kaluanui Rd Honolulu HI 96825-1321

VIDAL, GORE, writer; b. West Point, N.Y., Oct. 3, 1925; s. Eugene L. and Nina (Gore) V. Grad., Phillips Exeter Acad., 1943. Author, 1946—. Author: (novels) Williwaw, 1946, In a Yellow Wood, 1947, The City and the Pillar, 1948, The Season of Comfort, 1949, A Search for the King, 1950, Dark Green, Bright Red, 1950, The Judgment of Paris, 1952, Messiah, 1954, , Julian, 1964, Washington, D.C, 1967, Myra Breckinridge, 1968, Two Sisters, 1970, Burr, 1973, Myron, 1974, Kalki, 1978, Creation, 1981 (Prix Deauville 1983), Duluth, 1983, Lincoln, 1984, Empire, 1987, Hollywood/Live From Golgotha, 1990, (under name Edgar Box) Death in the Fifth Position, 1952, Death Before Bedtime, 1953, Death Likes It Hot, 1954, (short stories) A Thirsty Evil, 1956; (play) Visit to a Small Planet, 1957, (TV and Broadway prodns.) The Best Man, 1960, Romulus, 1962, Weekend, 1968, An Evening with Richard Nixon, 1972, (essays) Rocking the Boat, 1962, Sex, Death, and Money, 1968, Reflections upon a Sinking Ship, 1969, Homage to Daniel Shays, 1973, Matters of Fact and of Fiction, 1977, The Second American Revolution, 1982 (Nat. Book Critics Circle award for criticism 1982), Armageddon?, 1987 (London), United States: Essays 1952-1992, 1993 (Nat. Book award for nonfiction 1993), Live from Golgotha: The Gospel According to Gore Vidal, 1993; (films) The Catered Affair, 1956, I Accuse, 1958, The Left-Handed Gun, 1958, The Scapegoat, 1959, Suddenly Last Summer, 1959, The Best Man, 1964 (Cannes Critics prize 1964), Is Paris Burning?, 1966, The Last of the Mobile Hotshots, 1970; (teleplays) Barn Burning, 1954, Dark Possession, 1954, Smoke, 1954, Visit to a Small Planet, 1955, Dr. Jekyll and Mr. Hyde, 1955, A Sense of Justice, 1955, Summer Pavilion, 1955, The Turn of the Screw, 1955, Stage Door, 1955, A Farewell to Arms, 1955, The Death of Billy the Kid, 1955, Honor, 1956, The Indestructible Mr. Gore, 1959, Dear Arthur, 1960, Dress Gray, 1986, Billy the Kid, 1989; actor: Fellini Roma, 1978, Bob Roberts, 1992, With Honors, 1994, (memoire) Screening History, 1992. Mem. Pres.'s Adv. Com. on Arts, 1961-63. Dem.-Liberal candidate for U.S. Congress, 1960, candidate for Dem. nomination from Calif., 1982; co-chmn. The New Party, 1970-71. Served with AUS, 1943-46. Recipient Edgar Allan Poe award TV drama Mystery Writers of Am., 1955; named hon. citizen Ravello, Italy, 1983. *

VIDALE, JOHN EMILIO, geologist; b. Phila., Mar. 15, 1959; s. Guido Levi and Rosemary (Jacobson) V; 1 child, Laura. BS, Yale U., 1981; PhD, Calif. Inst. Tech., 1986. Scientist U. Calif., Santa Cruz, 1987-90, U.S. Geol. Survey, Menlo Park, Calif., 1991-95; assoc. prof. UCLA, 1995—. Editor Bulletin Seismology Soc. Am., 1988-93; contbr. articles to profl. jours. Gilbert fellow U.S. Geol. survey, 1994-95; Co-Recipient James B. Macelwane YoungInvestigator medal Am. Geophysical Union, 1994. Fellow Am. Geophys. Union (Macelwane medal 1994). Home: 10421 Colina Way Los Angeles CA 90077 Office: Dept Earth and Space Sci UCLA Los Angeles CA 90024

VIDAS, VINCENT GEORGE, engineering executive; b. Phila., May 25, 1931; s. Joseph and Blanche (Misch) V.; m. Judith Weber, Oct. 15 1955; children: Lisa Louise, Jeffrey Vincent, Kristen Judith. BSEE, Drexel U., 1959, MSEE, 1964. Systems engr. RCA, Moorestown, N.J., 1959-65, Sci. Mgmt. Assn., Haddonfield, N.J., 1965-67; chief exec. officer, owner SEMCOR, Inc., Mt. Laurel, N.J., 1967—; also bd. dirs.; chmn., owner, bd. dirs. Edn. Mgmt. Corp., Cherry Hill, N.J., 1991-93. Staff Sgt. USAF, 1949-53. Mem. IEEE. Avocations: chess, tennis, photography, music. Office: SEMCOR Inc 815 E Gate Dr Mount Laurel NJ 08054-1240

VIDELL, JARED STEVEN, cardiologist; b. Phila., Apr. 9, 1947; s. Harry and Rose (Malken) V.; m. Cyla Trocki, Dec. 27, 1969; children: Haviv Elana, Mikhael Alon, Samara Pilar. AA, Miami-Dade Jr. Coll., Opalocka, Fla., 1966; BEd, U. Miami, 1969; DO, Phila. Coll. Osteo. Medicine, 1976. Resident and chief resident in internal medicine Atlantic City (N.J.) Med. Ctr., 1976-79; fellow in cardiovascular diseases Albert Einstein Med. Ctr., Phila., 1979-81; rsch. fellow in nuclear cardiology Deborah Heart and Lung Ctr., Browns Mills, N.J., 1981-82; dir. employee health svcs. Deborah Heart and Lung Ctr., Browns Mills, 1982-84; asst. dir. cardiology Pritikin Longevity Ctr., Downington, Pa., 1984-87; cardiologist, dir. clin. lab. Physician Care, P.C., Towanda, Pa., 1987-90; from co-chmn. intensive care to dir. cardiac stress lab. Meml. Hosp., Towanda, 1987-90; dir. house staff, intensive/cardiac care Lower Bucks Hosp., Bristol, Pa., 1992-94; dir. house staff ICU-Critical Care Unit North Phila. Health Systems, 1994—; med. dir. Am. Cancer Soc. chpt., 1989-90; mem. state peer rev. KEPRO, 1989-90. Contbr. rsch. articles to profl. jours. Fellow Am. Coll. Angiology; mem. AMA, Am. Coll. Chest Physicians, Am. Soc. Internal Medicine, Internat. Soc. Internal Medicine, Internat. Soc. Endovascular Surgery, Internat. Platform Assn., Pa. Med. Soc., Phila. County Med. Soc., Alumni Assn. Phila. Coll. Osteo. Medicine. Jewish. Avocations: squash, cycling, cross country skiing, traveling, fishing.

VIDRICKSEN, BEN EUGENE, food service executive, state legislator; b. Salina, Kans., June 11, 1927; s. Henry and Ruby Mae Vidricksen; m. Lola Mae Nienke, Jan. 20, 1950; children: Nancy, Janice, Ben, Penelope, Jeffery. AB, Kans. Wesleyan U., 1951. Field supt. Harding Creamery div. Nat. Dairy Products, Kearney, Kans., 1951-52; plant mgr. Kraft divsn. Nat. Dairy Products, O'Neill, Nebr., 1952-59; owner Vidricksen's Food Service, Salina, 1959—; cons. in field; mem. Kansas Senate, 1979—, asst. majority leader; chmn. joint bldg. constrn. com., legis. and congressional apportionment com., legis. post audit,econ. devel., transp. and utilities, pub. health and welfare, fed. and state affairs, govtl. orgn., spl. interim com. on efficiency in state govt., 1983; del. White House Conf. Small Bus., 1995, White House Conf. on Tourism and Travel, 1995; mem. Hennessy/USAF Worldwide Food Service Evaluation Team, 1978, 79. Mem. Salina Airport Authority, 1972-84, chmn., 1976-77; chmn. Republican Central Com., County of Saline, Kans., 1974-79; adv. council SBA, 1982—, chmn. adv. coun. small bus. devel. ctr.; mem. adv. bd. Salvation Army; past chmn. Salina Convention and Tourism Bur.; vice chmn. Kans. Turnpike Authority, 1995—. Served with USN, 1945-46. Recipient Salut au Restaurateur award Fla. State U., 1974, Gov.'s Spl. award Kans. Assn. Broadcasters, Guardian award Nat.

Fedn. Indep. Bus., 1989, Promotion of Tourism and Travel award Travel Ind. Assn. Kans., 1989, Support of Kans. Nat. Guard award Kans. Adjutant Gen., 1990, Good Citizenship award Kans. Engring. Soc., 1991, 92, Freedom award NRA, 1994; named Nat. Rep. Legislator of Yr., Nat. Rep. Legislators Assn., 1991, Assoc. of Yr., Am. Womens Bus. Assn., 1992. Mem. USAF Assn., Assn. U.S. Army, Nat. Rep. Legislators Assn., Am. Legis Exch. Coun., Pan Am. Hwy. Assn. (Internat. Achievement award 1992, Road Builders award 1995), North Salina Bus. Assn. (past pres.), Internat. Bridge, Tunnel and Tpke. Assn., Kans. Restaurant Assn. (past pres., Restaurateur of Yr. 1973), Kans. Tourism and Travel Commn., Kans. Film Commn., Nat. Restaurant Assn. (dir. 1977—), Travel Industry Assn. Kans. (dir.) VFW (life), Salina C. of C. (past bd. dirs.), Am. Legion, Optimists, North Salina Lions Club, Elks, Moose, Eagles, Masons (knight commdr. Scottish rite, 1994), Shriners. Office: State Senate State Capitol Topeka KS 66612

VIE, RICHARD CARL, insurance company executive; b. St. Louis, Sept. 26, 1937; s. George William and Geraldine (Bell) V.; m. Joan Kay Wilschetz, June 4, 1960; children: Laura, Mark, Todd, Amy, Paul, Sarah. Student, St. Louis U., U. Mo. With Reliable Life Ins. Co., St. Louis, 1962-79; pres. Commonwealth Life Ins. Co., St. Louis, 1979-82; pres., chmn. bd. dirs. United Ins. Co. Am., Chgo., 1983—; sr. v.p., bd. dirs. Unitrin, Inc., 1990-92, pres., CEO, 1992—; chmn. Life Insurers Conf., 1994; trustee Life Underwriters Tng. Coun., 1990-94; mem. exec. com. (home svc.) Life Ins. Mktg. and Rsch. Assn., 1990-92. Bd. dirs. Concordia U. Found., 1985-94, Valparaiso U., 1995—; trustee Luth. Assn. Higher Edn., St. Louis, 1979-82. Lt. USN, 1958-62. Mem. The Racquet Club St. Louis. Office: Unitrin Inc 1 E Wacker Dr Chicago IL 60601

VIELE, GEORGE BROOKINS, library executive; b. Flint, Mich., Apr. 20, 1932; s. Roy Millard and Mable Anna (Brookins) V.; m. Shirley Louise Larzelere, Aug. 29, 1955; 1 child, Sara (dec.). B.S., Central Mich. U., 1960, M.A., 1965; M.S.L.S., U. N.C., 1969; postgrad. Wayne State U. Cert. pub. librarian; cert. adminstrv. mgr. Asst. dir. Wake County Pub. Library, Raleigh, N.C., 1968-71; dir. Greensboro Pub. Library, N.C., 1971—; instr. library sch. U. N.C.-Greensboro, 1977-79. Contbr. articles to profl. jours. Bd. dirs. Lawndale Community Club, Greensboro, 1976-78, Guilford County Pub. Sch. Student Enrichment Found., 1992—; councilman Twining Town Council, Mich., 1963-65; mem. fin. com., chmn. edn. com. Fellowship Presbyn. Ch., Greensboro, 1978-80, elder, 1989-92; mem. Habitat for Humanity. Served to cpl. U.S. Army, 1953-55. Mem. N.C. Library Assn. (stats. com. Pub. Library sect., chmn. 1977-79, devel. com. 1977-79), Triad Management Assn. (pres. 1992-94). Republican. Lodges: Torch, Lions, Rotary. Avocations: bridge, photography, gardening. Office: Greensboro Pub Libr 201 N Greene St Greensboro NC 27401-2410

VIEMEISTER, TUCKER L., industrial designer; b. Dayton, Ohio, Aug. 14, 1948; s. Read and Beverly (Lipsett) V. B Indsl. Design, Pratt Inst., 1974. Jr. designer Vie Design Studios, Yellow Springs, Ohio, 1969; owner, mgr. Ohio Silver, Yellow Springs, 1971-73; designer Wyman & Cannon, N.Y.C., 1974-77; ptnr. Ted Muehling, N.Y.C., 1977-79; v.p. Smart Design Inc., N.Y.C., 1979—; juror Ann. ID Design Rev., Archtl. Record, Pew Found., 1991 IDEA awards, design e7e 89, Nagoya, Japan; lectr. Form One Conf., 1986, Pratt Inst., 1985, 86, RISD, 1986, Cranbrook Acad. Art, 1986, Axis in Tokyo, 1989; faculty Parsons Sch. Design, 1986; sr. critic Yale U., 1996; del. Internat. coun. Socs. Indsl. Design Congress, Amsterdam, 1987; workshop condr. Contbr. articles to profl. publs. and confs.; represented in permanent collections Cooper-Hewitt Mus., Smithsonian Instn., N.Y.C., Staatliches Mus. fur Angewandte Kunst, Munich-Mus. Modern Art, N.Y.C.; work reviewed in numerous publs. Trustee Rowena Reed Kostellow Fund, Pratt Inst., 1989—. Recipient Presdl. Design Achievement award, 1984, best symbol award Archtl. League, 1986, award Neste, Finland, 1988, also others. Mem. Indsl. Designer Soc. Am. (co-chmn. N.Y. chpt. 1986-87, dir.-at-large 1991-92, nat. conf. chair 1995), Am. Inst. Graphic Designers, Am. Ctr. for Design. Office: Smart Design Inc 137 Varicle St New York NY 10013

VIENER, JOHN D., lawyer; b. Richmond, Va., Oct. 18, 1939; s. Reuben and Thelma (Kurtz) V.; m. Karin Erika Bauer, Apr. 7, 1969; children: John D. Jr., Katherine Bauer. BA, Yale U., 1961; JD, Harvard U., 1964. Bar: N.Y. State 1965, U.S. Supreme Ct. 1970, U.S. Dist. Ct. (so. dist.) N.Y. 1974, U.S. Tax Ct. 1975. Assoc. Satterlee, Warfield & Stephens, N.Y.C., 1964-69; sole practice N.Y.C., 1969-76; founder, bd. dirs., gen. counsel Foxfire Fund Inc., 1968-88; sr. ptnr. Christy & Viener, N.Y.C., 1976—; gen. counsel, bd. dirs. Landmark Communities, Inc., 1970—, NF&M Internat., Inc., 1976—, Singer Fund, Inc., 1979—; gen. counsel Nat. Cancer Found. Cancer Care, 1982-85, Am. Continental Properties Group, 1978—, Troster, Singer & Co., 1970-77; bd. dirs. Gen. Financiere Immob. et Commer. S.A., 1985-89; spl. counsel fin. instns., investment banking and securities concerns; real estate and tax advisor. Mem. Meeker Brook Sporting Assn., Fairfield County Hounds, Manursing Island Club, Washington Club. Home: 45 E 62nd St New York NY 10021-8025 also: Washington CT 06793 Office: Christy & Viener 620 5th Ave New York NY 10020-2402

VIENNE, DOROTHY TITUS, school principal; b. Buffalo, May 8, 1939; d. Robert Paul and Bertha (Wissman) Titus; m. Richard Paul Vienne, Aug. 27, 1960; children: Richard Paul Jr., Kerstina Elaine. BS in Elem. Edn., SUNY, Brockport, 1960; MS in Elem. Edn., SUNY, Buffalo, 1964; postgrad., U. Buffalo, 1968-76, Canisius Coll., 1978. Cert. elem. tchr., N.Y. Elem. tchr. Lancaster (N.Y.) Cen. Schs., 1960-62, reading tchr., 1962-68, reading specialist, 1968-76; program supr. Kenmore-Town of Tonawanda, Kenmore, N.Y., 1976-79, 81-86; coordinator pupil personnel services Assn. for Retarded Children, Buffalo, 1980-81; prin. Thomas Edison Sch., Kenmore-Tonawanda Union Free Sch. Dist., Kenmore, 1986—; adj. prof. ednl. adminstrn. SUNY, Buffalo; apkr. Summer Inst. for Prins., 1987—, 1st Internat. Forum on Total Quality, Brazil, 1993; trainer 4MAT learning styles; author, presenter on total quality mgmt. in schs.; ednl. cons. U.S. Info. Svcs., Brazil, 1994. Named N.Y. State Disting. Elem. Prin., 1991. Mem. ASCD, Sch. Adminstrs. N.Y. State, Western N.Y. Women in Adminstrn. (bd. dirs., Woman Adminstr. of Yr. award 1990), Phi Delta Kappa (officer). Republican. Methodist. Avocations: skiing, travel, bridge. Home: 50 Gaylord Ct Elma NY 14059-9450 Office: Thomas Edison Elem Sch 236 Grayton Rd Tonawanda NY 14150-8620

VIERA, JAMES JOSEPH, financial executive; b. Erie, Pa., June 14, 1940; s. Joseph C. and Margaret (Kelly) V.; m. Cheryl Batchelder, Dec. 9, 1967; children: Robert, James Jay. BS, Rensselaer Poly. Inst., 1962; MBA, Columbia U., 1970. Fin. analyst Ford Motor Co., Dearborn, Mich., 1970-75; asst. compt. Pullman, Inc., Chgo., 1975-76; div. compt. The Pillsbury Co., Mpls., 1976-80; pres., chief fin. officer Jefferson Co., Mpls., 1980-87; chief fin. officer Cowles Media Co., Mpls., 1987—. Bd. dirs. Edina (Minn.) Hockey Assn., 1985-87, Edina Baseball Assn., 1985-87, Glenwood-Lyndale Cmty. Ctr., Sci. Mus. of Minn., 1990—. Mem. Mpls. C. of C. (bd. dirs. 1992—). Avocations: jogging, skiing. Home: 7131 Gleason Rd Minneapolis MN 55439-1610 Office: Cowles Media Co 329 Portland Ave Minneapolis MN 55415-1112

VIERE, GORDON, accounting company executive. Exec. ptnr.-in-charge Larson, Allen Weishair & Co., LLP, Mpls. Office: Larson Allen Weishair & Co 220 S 6th St Minneapolis MN 55402-4502*

VIERECK, PETER, poet, historian, educator; b. N.Y.C., Aug. 5, 1916; s. George S. and Margaret (Hein) V.; m. Anya de Markov, June 1945 (div. May 1970); children: John-Alexis, Valerie Edwina (Mrs. John Gibbs); m. Betty Martin Falkenberg, Aug. 30, 1972. B.S. summa cum laude, Harvard, 1937, M.A., 1939, Ph.D., 1942; Henry fellow, Christ Ch., Oxford U., Eng., 1937-38; L.H.D. (hon.), Olivet Coll., 1959. Teaching asst. Harvard, 1941-42, instr. German lit., tutor history and lit. dept., 1946-47; instr. history U.S. Army U., Florence, Italy, 1945; asst. prof. history Smith Coll., 1947-48, vis. lectr. Russian history, 1948-49; assoc. prof. Modern European, Russian history Mt. Holyoke Coll., 1948-55, prof., 1955—; vis. lectr. Am. Culture Oxford U., 1953; Whittal lectr. in poetry Library of Congress, 1954, 63, 79; Fulbright prof. Am. poetry and civilization U. Florence, Italy, 1954-56; Elliston chair poetry lectr. U. Cin., 1956; vis. lectr. U. Calif. at, Berkeley, 1957; Disting. William R. Kenan prof. Mt. Holyoke Coll., 1979—; Charter mem. Council Basic Edn.; vis. poet Russian-Am. cultural exchange program Dept. State, USSR, 1961; vis. research scholar 20th Century Fund, USSR, 1962-63; vis. scholar Rockefeller Study Center at Bellagio, Italy, 1977; vis. artist and scholar Am. Acad. in, Rome, 1949-50, 78; dir. poetry workshop N.Y. Writers Conf., 1965-67; research fellow Huntington Library, San Marino, Calif., 1978. Author: Metapolitics—From the Romantics to Hitler, 1941 (Swedish edit., 1942, Italian, 1948), Terror and Decorum, poems, 1948, reprinted, 1972, Who Killed the Universe, novelette included in anthology New Directions Ten, 1948, Conservatism Revisited-The Revolt Against Revolt 1815-1949, 1949 (English edit, 1950), Strike Through the Mask, New Lyrical Poems, 1950, reprinted, 1972, The First Morning: New Poems, 1952, reprinted, 1972, Shame and Glory of the Intellectuals, 1953, rev. edit., 1965, reprinted 1978, Dream and Responsibility, The Tension Between Poetry and Society, 1953, The Unadjusted Man; a New Hero for Americans, 1956, reprinted, 1973, Conservatism: From John Adams to Churchill, 1956, reprinted, 1978, The Persimmon Tree, poems, 1956, Inner Liberty, The Stubborn Grit in the Machine, 1957, The Tree Witch: A Verse Drama, 1961, reprinted, 1973, Meta-politics, The Roots of the Nazi Mind, 1961, rev. expanded edit. 1965, Conservatism Revisited and The New Conservatives: What Went Wrong; rev. paperback edits., 1962, 65, reprinted hardcover, 1978, New and Selected Poems, 1932-67, 1967, Archer in the Marrow: The Applewood Poetry Cycles of 1967-87, 1987, Tide & Continuities: Last & First Poems, 1995; also author of selections in symposium books Towards a World Community, 1950, Midcentury American Poets, 1950, Arts in Renewal, 1951, The New American Right, 1955, Education in a Free Society, 1958, The Radical Right, 1962, Soviet Policy Making, 1967, Outside Looking In, 1972, A Question of Quality, 1976, The Southern California Anthology, 1987, rev. edits., 1987, 89, Decade: New Letters Anthology of the 80s, 1990; contbr. essays, poems to popular mags., and profl. jours., monograph on Conservatism in Ency. Brit., 1974. Sgt. U.S. Army, 1943-45, Africa and Italy. Decorated 2 battle stars; awarded Tietjens prize for poetry, 1948, Pulitzer prize for poetry, 1949; recipient Most Disting. Alumnus award Horace Mann School for Boys, 1958, Poetry Translation award Translation Center, Columbia U., 1978, Sadin poetry prize N.Y. Quar., 1977, Golden Rose award New Eng. Poetry Club, 1981, Varoujan prize, 1983; Guggenheim fellow Rome, 1949-50; Rockefeller Found. researcher in history Germany, summer 1958; NEH sr. rsch. fellow USSR, 1969; Mass. Artists Found. fellow, 1978. Mem. Am. Hist. Assn., Oxford Soc., Poetry Soc. Am., P.E.N., Phi Beta Kappa. Clubs: Harvard (N.Y.C. and London); Bryce (Oxford, Eng.). Home: 12 Silver St South Hadley MA 01075-1616 *After 79 years of books, scars, and sugar plums, my rock-bottom thought on life is a line of Vachel Lindsay: "Courage and sleep are the principal things."*

VIEREGG, ROBERT TODD, lawyer; b. Woodstock, Ill., Oct. 3, 1934; s. Robert and Mae (Todd) V.; m. Darla Jean Ax, Dec. 12, 1959 (div. Oct. 1983); children: Dorian Jean Griffin, Robert Todd II; m. Carilane Newman Awalt, May 25, 1985. Student, U. Ill., 1952-53; BA, Mich. State U., 1955; postgrad., U. Chgo., 1968-69; JD cum laude, Northwestern u., 1970. Bar: Ill. 1970, U.S. Dist. Ct. (no. dist.) Ill. 1970. From assoc. to ptnr. Sidley & Austin, Chgo., 1970—. With USN, 1956-59. Mem. ABA, Ill. Bar Assn., Chgo. Bar Assn., Law Club Chgo., Union League (bd. dirs. 1987-88), Glen View Country Club. Republican. Office: Sidley & Austin 1 First Nat Plz Chicago IL 60603

VIERHELLER, TODD, software engineering consultant; b. Winter Park, Fla., June 22, 1958; s. Irvin Theodore and Jeanne Marie (Zeller) V.; m. Susan Lindhe Watts, Dec. 22, 1984; children: Renate Jeanne, Clark, Lindhe Marie, Kent. BS in Computer Sci., U. Mo., Rolla, 1980; MA in Bibl. Studies, Multnomah Sch. Bible, Portland, Oreg., 1986. Tech. writer, software engr. Tektronix, Beaverton, Oreg., 1981-86, software engring. mgr., 1988-89; software engr., supr. Intel Corp., Hillsboro, Oreg., 1986-88; software engring. mgr. Summation, 1989-90; software cons. Quality First, Lynnwood, Wash., 1990—; software engring. cons. Digital Equipment Corp., Bellevue, Wash., 1990-91, GTE, Bothell, Wash., 1990-91, Frank Russell Co., Tacoma, Wash., 1992-93, InterConnections, Inc., Bellevue, 1993, Novell, San Jose, Calif., 1993; software engring. mgmt. cons. Weyerhauser, Federal Way, Wash., 1991-92, Frank Russell, Tacoma, Wash., 1994, ConnectSoft, Inc., Bellevue, 1994, Microsoft, Redmond, Wash., 1995. Mem. IEEE, Washington Software Assn., Upsilon Pi Epsilon, Kappa Mu Epsilon. Republican. Mem. Evang. Christian Ch. Avocations: camping, bicycling, shooting sports, kung fu. Home: 22810 25th Ave W Lynnwood WA 98036-8303 Office: Quality First PO Box 6212 Lynnwood WA 98036-0212

VIERMETZ, KURT F., banker; b. Augsburg, Bavaria, Germany, Apr. 27, 1939; came to U.S., 1985; s. Alfons and Claire (Bruck) V.; m. Felicitas Kempe, May, 1966; 1 child, Maximilian. Grad., Heilig Kreuz Coll., Germany, 1957. With Morgan Guaranty Trust Co. of N.Y., Frankfurt, Fed. Republic Germany, 1966-69; asst. v.p. Morgan Guaranty Trust Co. of N.Y., Frankfurt, 1969-71; v.p. Morgan Guaranty Trust Co. of N.Y., Paris, 1971-82; sr. v.p. for Central Europe Morgan Guaranty Trust Co. of N.Y., N.Y.C., 1982-85; vice chmn. Morgan Guaranty Trust Co. N.Y., 1990—; also bd. dirs. Morgan Guaranty Trust Co. of N.Y., N.Y.C.; vice chmn. J.P. Morgan & Co., Inc., 1990—; gen. mgr. Saudi Internat. Bank, London, 1975-77. Author books and articles on internat. fin. to profl. publs. Mem. Am. C. of C. in Germany. Roman Catholic. Home: 30 Island Dr Rye NY 10580-4306 Office: Morgan Guaranty Trust Co NY 60 Wall St New York NY 10260*

VIERTEL, JACK, theatrical producer, writer; b. Stamford, Conn., Feb. 7, 1949; s. Joseph Maurice and Janet (Man) V.; m. Linda Gilmore, July 31, 1973; children: Joshua Louis, Anna Daisy. AB, Harvard Coll., 1971. Theater critic L.A. Reader, 1977-80; theater critic L.A. Herald Examiner, 1980-85, arts editor, 1984-85; dramaturg Mark Taper Forum Theater, L.A., 1986-87; creative dir. Jujamcyn Theaters, N.Y.C., 1987—. Co-author: (nonfiction) Becoming Parents, 1978; adaptor (play) Ghetto, 1986. Cert. judge Memphis-in-May Barbecue Contest Circuit, 1992—. Mem. League Am. Theaters and Producers. Democrat. Jewish. Avocation: guitar. Office: Jujamcyn Theatres 246 W 44th St New York NY 10036-3910

VIESSMAN, WARREN, JR., academic dean, civil engineering educator, researcher; b. Balt., Nov. 9, 1930; s. Warren and Helen Adair (Berlinckee) V.; m. Gloria Marie Scheiner, May 11, 1953 (div. Apr. 1975); children: Wendy, Stephen, Suzanne, Michael, Thomas, Sandra; m. Elizabeth Gertrude Rothe, Aug. 8, 1980; children: Heather, Joshua. B in Engring., Johns Hopkins U., 1952, MS in Engring., 1958, DEng, 1961. Registered profl. engr., Md. Engr. W. H. Primrose & Assocs., Towson, Md., 1955-57; project engr. Johns Hopkins U., Balt., 1957-61; from asst. to assoc. prof. N.Mex. State U., Las Cruces, 1961-66; prof. U. Maine, Orono, 1966-68, U. Nebr., Lincoln, 1968-75; sr. specialist Libr. Congress, Washington, 1975-83; prof., chmn. U. Fla., Gainesville, 1983-90, assoc. dean for rsch. and grad. study, 1990-91, assoc. dean for acad. programs, 1991—; vis. scientist Am. Geophys. Union, 1970-71; Maurice Kremer lectr. U. Nebr., 1985; lectr. Harvard U. Water Policy Seminar, 1988; Wayne S. Nichols Meml. Fund lectr. Ohio State U., 1990; mem. steering com. on groundwater and energy U.S. Dept. Energy, 1979-80; mem. task group on fed. water rsch. U.S. Geol. Survey, 1985-87; mem. com. of water sci. and tech. bd. NAS, 1986-90; mem. water resources working group Nat. Coun. on Pub. Works Improvement, 1987; chmn., chief of engrs. Environ. Adv. Bd., Washington, 1991-93; chmn. solid and hazardous waste mgmt. adv. bd. State U. Sys. Fla. Co-author: Water Supply and Pollution Control, 1993, Water Management: Technology and Institutions, 1984, Introduction to Hyrdology, 1996; contbr. over 145 articles to profl. jours. Mem. Water Mgmt. Com., Gainesville, 1983-88, Fla. Environ. Efficiency Study Commn., 1986-88. 1st lt. U.S. Army C.E., 1952-54, Korea. Fellow ASCE (Julian Hinds award 1989), Am. Water Resources Assn. (nat. pres. 1990, Icko Iben award 1983), Univs. Coun. on Water Resources (pres. 1987, Warren A. Hall medal 1994), Sigma Xi, Tau Beta Pi. Avocations: scuba diving, woodworking. Office: U Fla Coll Engring PO Box 116550 Gainesville FL 32611-6550

VIEST, IVAN M(IROSLAV), consulting structural engineer; b. Bratislava, Slovakia, Czechoslovakia, Oct. 10, 1922; came to U.S., 1947, naturalized, 1955; s. Ivan and Maria (Zacharova) V.; m. Barbara K. Stevenson, May 23, 1953. Ing., Slovak Tech. U., Bratislava, 1946; M.S., Ga. Inst. Tech., 1948; Ph.D., U. Ill., 1951. Registered profl. engr., Pa. Research asst. U. Ill., Urbana, 1948-50; research assoc. U. Ill., 1950-51, research asst. prof., 1951-55, research assoc. prof., 1955-57; bridge research engr. Am. Assn. State Hwy. Ofcls.; rd. test Nat. Acad. Scis., Ottawa, Ill., 1957-61; structural engr. Bethlehem Steel Corp., Pa., 1961-67; sr. structural cons. Bethlehem Steel Corp., 1967-70, asst. mgr. sales engring. div., 1970-82; pvt. cons. structural engr. IMV Cons., 1983—; lectr. in field. Author: Composite Construction, 1958, History of Engineering Foundation, 1991, Composite Construction--Design for Buildings, 1996. Recipient Constrn. award Engring. News Record, 1972. Fellow AAAS, Am. Concrete Inst. (Wason Rsch. medal 1956); mem. NAE, ASCE (hon., v.p. 1973-75, Rsch. prize, Ernest E. Howard award 1991), Internat. Assn. Bridge and Structural Engring., Transp. Rsch. Bd., Czechoslovak Soc. Arts and Scis. (exec. v.p. 1992-93), Earthquake Engring. Rsch. Inst., Saucon Valley Country Club (Bethlehem). Research, numerous publs. on various steel and concrete structures, especially bridges and bldgs., to profl. jours. Office: PO Box 1428 Bethlehem PA 18016-1428

VIETH, G. DUANE, lawyer; b. Omaha, Sept. 20, 1923; s. Walter E. and Irene E. (Horn) V.; m. Jane G. Richardson, Feb. 16, 1952; children: Peter D., Robert R., Jane G. BA, U. Iowa, 1947, JD, 1949. Bar: Iowa 1949, D.C. 1949, U.S. Dist. Ct. Iowa 1953, U.S. Dist. Ct. Md. 1955, U.S. Ct. Claims 1958, U.S. Ct. Appeals (3d cir.) 1960, U.S. Dist. Ct. (ea. dist.) Wis. 1965, U.S. Supreme Ct. 1966, U.S. Ct. Appeals (2d cir.) 1970, U.S. Ct. Appeals (7th cir.) 1971. Ptnr. Arnold & Porter, Washington, 1949—; mem. D.C. Commn. on Budget and Financial Priorities, 1989-90. Trustee Iowa Law Sch. Found., Iowa City, 1971-88, Fed. City Council, Washington, 1972—. With USAAF, 1942-45, ETO. Mem. ABA, D.C. Bar Assn., Iowa State Bar Assn., Columbia Country Club, Burning Tree Club, Met. Club. Lutheran. Avocation: golf. Home: 3717 Cardiff Rd Bethesda MD 20815-5943 Office: Arnold & Porter Ste 955 555 12th St NW Washington DC 20004-1202

VIETH, WOLF RANDOLPH, chemical engineering educator; b. St. Louis, May 5, 1934; s. Hans W. and Hedy (Fahrig) V.; m. Peggy Schira, July 6, 1957; children—Jane, Linda, Christopher, Mark. S.B. in Chem. Engring, Mass. Inst. Tech., 1956, Sc.D., 1961; M. Sc., Ohio State U., 1958. Registered profl. engr., N.J. From asst. prof. to assoc. prof. chem. engring. MIT, Cambridge, 1961-68, dir. Sch. Chem. Engring. Practice, 1965-68; prof. chem. and biochem. engring. Rutgers U., New Brunswick, N.J., 1968—, chmn. dept., 1968-78; cons. to govt. and industry; chmn. Gordon Research Conf. on Separation and Purification, 1975, Engring. Conf. on Biochem. Engring., 1978. Mem. econ. study subcom., planning bd. Montgomery (N.J.) Twp., 1970—. Served to 1st lt. AUS, 1961. Recipient DuPont Co. Invention award, 1960, St. Albert the Great medal for sci. Aquinas Coll., 1952; Vis. Fgn. Scientist award Japan Soc. for Promotion Sci., 1975; Ford postdoctoral fellow, 1961. Fellow Am. Inst. Chemists, N.Y. Acad. Scis.; mem. Am. Inst. Chem. Engrs., Am. Chem. Soc., Am. Soc. Engring. Edn., Sigma Xi, Phi Lambda Upsilon. Research on applied molecular biology, semipermeable membranes, polymers. Office: Chem Dept Heights Campus Rutgers Univ New Brunswick NJ 08903

VIETOR, HAROLD DUANE, federal judge; b. Parkersburg, Iowa, Dec. 29, 1931; s. Harold Howard and Alma Johanna (Kreimeyer) V.; m. Dalia Artemisa Zamarripa Cadena, Mar. 24, 1973; children: Christine Elizabeth, John Richard, Greta Maria. BA, U. Iowa, 1955, JD, 1958. Bar: Iowa 1958. Law clk. U.S. Ct. Appeals 8th Circuit, 1958-59; ptnr. Bleakley Law Offices, Cedar Rapids, Iowa, 1959-65; judge Iowa Dist. Ct., Cedar Rapids, 1965-79, chief judge, 1970-79; U.S. dist. judge So. Dist. Iowa, Des Moines, 1979—, chief judge, 1985-92; lectr. at law schs., legal seminars U.S. and Japan. Contbr. articles to profl. jours. in U.S. and Japan. Served with USN, 1952-54. Mem. ABA, Iowa Bar Assn. (pres. jr. sect. 1966-67), Iowa Judges Assn. (pres. 1975-76), 8th Cir. Dist. Judges Assn. (pres. 1986-88). Office: US Dist Ct 221 US Courthouse 123 E Walnut St Des Moines IA 50309-2038

VIETS, HERMANN, college president, consultant; b. Quedlinburg, Fed. Republic Germany, Jan. 28, 1943; came to U.S., 1949, naturalized, 1961; s. Hans and Herta (Heik) V.; m. Pamela Deane, June 30, 1968; children: Danielle, Deane, Hans, Hillary. BS, Polytech. U., 1965, MS, 1966, PhD, 1970. Postdoctoral fellow von Karman Inst., Brussels, 1969-70; group leader Wright-Patterson AFB, Dayton, Ohio, 1970-76; prof. Wright State U., Dayton, Ohio, 1976-81; assoc. dean W.Va. U., Morgantown, 1981-83; dean U. R.I., Kingston, 1983-91; pres. Milw. Sch. Engring., 1991—; chmn. bd. dirs. Precision Stampings, Inc., Beaumont, Calif., 1977—; bd. dirs. Astro Med, Inc., West Warwick, R.I.; cons. USAF Aero Propulsion Lab., Dayton, 1976-80, Covington & Burling, Washington, 1976-77; cons. several cos. and govt. agys. Patentee in aero. field; contbr. numerous articles to tech. publs. Mem. Greater Milw. Com.; dir. Greater Milw. Edn. Trust, Competitive Wis., Gov. Regional H.S. Excellence Co., 1994, Gov.'s Export Strategy Commn., 1994; trustee Pub. Policy Forum. Recipient Tech. Achievement award USAF, 1974, Sci. Achievement award, 1975, Gov.'s Sci. and Tech. award State of R.I., 1987, Goodrich Pub. Svc. award, 1990, Citation R.I. Legislature, 1987, 90, 91, Outstanding Alumnus award aerospace engring. dept. Poly. U., 1994; Disting. Alumnus Poly. U., 1995; postdoctoral fellow NATO, 1969-70, NASA, 1965-69. Fellow AIAA (assoc., Best Tech. Paper award Allegheny-Pitts. sect. 1982); mem. Deutsche Gesellschaft fur Luft und Raumfahrt, Am. Soc. Engring. Edn., Japsn-Am. Soc. (bd. dirs. 1994), Soc. Mfg. Engrs., Rotary, Sigma Xi, Phi Kappa Phi, Tau Beta Pi, Sigma Gamma Tau. Avocations: antique automobiles; beer steins. Home: 4216 N Lake Dr Shorewood WI 53211-1722 Office: Milw Sch Engring 1025 N Broadway Milwaukee WI 53202-3109

VIETS, ROBERT O., utilities executive; b. Girard, Kans., Dec. 8, 1943; s. Willard O. and Caroline L. (Bollwinkel) V.; m. Karen M. Kreiter, June 13, 1980. BA in Econs., Washburn U., 1965; JD, Washington U., 1969. Bar: Kans. 1966, Mo. 1969, Ill. 1975; CPA, Kans. Auditor Arthur Andersen & Co., St. Louis, 1969-73; mgr. spl. studies Cen. Ill. Light Co., Peoria, 1973-76, mgr. rates and regulatory affairs, 1976-80, asst. v.p., regulatory affairs, 1980-81, v.p. fin. services, 1981-83, v.p. fin. group, 1983-86, sr. v.p., 1988—; sr. v.p. Cilcorp, Inc., Peoria, 1986-88; pres., chief exec. officer, chmn. bd. Cilcorp, Inc and Cen. Ill. Light Co., Peoria, 1988—; bd. dirs. First of Am. Bank, N.A., Ill., Lincoln Office Supply, Inc., RLI Corp., Environ. Sci. and Engring., Inc., Peoria. Bd. dirs. Meth. Health Svcs., Inc.; trustee Bradley U. Mem. ABA, Ill. Bar Assn., Peoria County Bar Assn., AICPA, Ill. Soc. CPAs. Republican. Lutheran. Lodge: Rotary (bd. dirs. 1985—, pres. 1986-87). Avocation: golf. Home: 11305 N Pawnee Rd Peoria IL 61615-9796 Office: Cilcorp Inc Hamilton Blvd Peoria IL 61602

VIG, VERNON EDWARD, lawyer; b. St. Cloud, Minn., June 19, 1937; s. Edward Enoch and Salley Johanna (Johnson) V.; m. Susan Jane Rosenow, June 10, 1961; 1 child, Elizabeth Karen. BA, Carleton Coll., 1959; LLB, NYU, 1962, LLM, 1963; postdoctoral Université de Paris, Faculté de Droit, 1964. Bar: N.Y. 1962, Avocat (France) 1992. Assoc. Cleary, Gottlieb, Steen & Hamilton, Paris, 1964-65; assoc. Donovan, Leisure, Newton & Irvine, N.Y.C. and Paris, 1965-72, ptnr., 1972-86; ptnr. LeBoeuf, Lamb, Greene & MacRae, N.Y.C., 1986—. Sr. warden Grace Ch., Bklyn., 1986—. George F. Baker scholar, Fullbright scholar, 1963-64, Ford Found. scholar, 1963-64. Mem. ABA (internat. trade com.), N.Y. State Bar Assn. (chmn. antitrust 1987-88), Assn. of Bar of City of N.Y., Internat. Bar Assn., Union Internationale des Avocats. Episcopalian. Clubs: Heights Casino (Bklyn.); Merriewold (Forestburgh, N.Y., bd. dirs. 1985-91). Office: LeBoeuf Lamb Greene & MacRae 125 W 55th St New York NY 10019-5369

VIGIER, FRANÇOIS CLAUDE DENIS, city planning educator; b. Geneva, Oct. 14, 1931; s. Eugene Henri Rene and Françoise (Dupuy) V. BArch, MIT, 1955; M in City Planning, Harvard U., 1959, PhD, 1967. Architect UN Relief and Works Agy., Jordan, 1955-57; designer Town Planning Cons., Cambridge, Mass., 1957-58; mem. faculty Harvard Grad. Sch. Design, Cambridge, 1960—, prof. city planning and urban design, 1968-85, Charles Dyer Norton prof. regional planning, 1985—, dir. unit for housing and urbanization, 1987—, chmn. spl. programs, 1982-86; chmn. dept. urban planning and design, 1992—; vis. lectr. art Dartmouth Coll., 1962, 64; vis. critic urban design U. N.C., 1963; cons. Ford Found. Latin Am. program, 1964-65, Ednl. Svcs., Inc., 1966; dir. Harvard Ctr. Environ. Design Studies, 1967-69; pres. Nash-Vigier Inc., Cambridge, 1965-91. Author: Change and Apathy: Liverpool and Manchester During the Industrial Revolution, 1970, Housing in Tunis, 1987; contbr. articles to various periodicals. Decorated Knight, Order of Merit, France, 1995. Mem. Am. Inst. Cert. Planners, Am. Planning Assn. Home: 27 Fayerweather St Cambridge MA 02138-3329

VIGIL, CHARLES S., lawyer; b. Trinidad, Colo., June 9, 1912; s. J.U. and Andreita (Maes) V.; m. Kathleen A. Liebert, Jan. 2, 1943; children: David Charles Edward, Marcia Kathleen. LL.B., U. Colo., 1936. Bar: Colo. 1936.

Dep. dist. atty. 3d Jud. Dist. Colo., 1937-42, asst. dist. atty., 1946-51; U.S. atty. Dist. Colo., 1951-53; pvt. practice law Denver.; Dir., sec. Las Animas Co. (Colo); ARC. Author: Saga of Casimiro Barela. Bd. dirs. Family and Children's Svc. Denver, Colo. Humane Soc., Animal Rescue Soc., Auraria Community Ctr.; mem. Bishop's com. on housing; Dem. candidate for U.S. Congress, 1988. Lt. USCG, 1942-46. Recipient award of civil merit Spain, 1960, award of civil merit Colo. Centennial Expn. Bd., 1976; award Colo. Chicano Bar Assn., 1979. Mem. Internat. Law Assn., ABA, Fed. Bar Assn., Colo. Bar Assn. (bd. govs.), So. Colo. Bar Assn., Hispanic Bar Colo. (bd. dirs.), Am. Judicature Soc., Internat. Bar Assn., Inter-Am. Bar, V.F.W. (comdr.), Am. Legion (comdr.), Nat. Assn. Def. Lawyers, Assn. Trial Lawyers Am., Lambda Chi Alpha, Elks, Eagles, Cootie. Home: 1085 Sherman St Denver CO 80203-2880 Office: 1715 Colo State Bank 1600 Broadway Denver CO 80202-4927 *Desire to serve and achieve in all matters related to public good as promoted and espoused by thoughts of father and mother-and family-brothers and sisters.*

VIGILANTE, JOSEPH LOUIS, social worker, social policy educator; b. Phila., June 21, 1925; m. Florence W. Vigilante; children: Amy, Grace, Theodore. A.B., Temple U., 1950; M.S., Columbia U., 1951, D.S.W., 1968. Cert. social worker, N.Y. Child welfare worker Div. Children and Youth Wis. Dept. Welfare, 1951-53; caseworker, student supr. VA Hosp., Northport, N.Y., 1953-55; part-time caseworker, case supr., chief social worker Mid-Nassau Community Guidance Clinic, Hicksville, N.Y., 1955-60; dir. field work, asst. prof. Sch. Social Work, Adelphi U., Garden City, N.Y., 1955-60, asst. prof., asst. dean, 1960-62, assoc. prof., acting dean, 1962, prof., dean, 1962-87, univ. prof. social policy, 1987—, exec. v.p. Inst. for Child Mental Health, 1976-89; prof. part-time New Sch. for Social Rsch., N.Y.C., 1972-75, Florence Hollis prof. Social Policy, summer 1988, Smith Coll., Northampton, Mass., 1987—; vis. prof. Rutgers U., 1987, Yeshiva U., 1988; cons. South Oaks Hosp., L.I., 1987-92, ICMH, N.Y., 1989—, cons. to Office Sec. Health, Edn, and Welfare, Washington, 1965; team leader, Social Welfare Mission, Agy. Internat. Devel., Egypt, 1974; rep. Nat Coun. Aging, UN NGO Com. Aging, 1994—; ptnr. Balaban Assocs.; performer, dir. Adelphi Film Co.; speaker in field. Editor: (with others) Social Service Delivery Systems: An International Annual; Sophie Moses Robison; Twentieth Century Women, 1982; editor in chief Ency. of Social Work; mem. editorial bd.: Smith Coll. Studies in Social Work, 1989—; contbr. articles to profl. jours. Bd. dirs. Nassau County Health and Welfare Coun., Huntington Hosp., N.Y., 1982, Cmty. Advs., Great Neck, N.Y., Cmty. Coun. of Greater N.Y., Young Adult Inst., 1982-95; chair Joint Task Force on Labor Force Needs, NASW/Coun. Social Work Edn. Mem. NASW, AAUP, N.Y. State Assn. Deans of Schs. Social Work (pres. 1975), Acad. Cert. Social Workers, Acad. Polit. Sci., Coun. Social Work Edn., Phi Gamma Mu. Office: Adelphi U Earle Hall Rm 106 Garden City NY 11530

VIGNELLI, MASSIMO, architecture and design executive; b. Milan, Italy, Jan. 10, 1931; came to U.S., 1965; s. Ettore and Noemi (Guazzoni) V.; m. Lella Elena Valle, Sept. 15, 1957; children: Luca, Valentina. Student, Brera Acad. Art, Milan, 1948-50, Politecnico di Milano, 1950-53, U. Venice, 1953-57; DFA (hon.), Parsons Sch. Design, 1983, Pratt Inst., 1987, R.I. Sch. Design, 1988, Istituto Universitario di Architettura, Venice, 1994, Corcoran Sch. Art, 1994. Prin. Lella & Massimo Vignelli Office Design and Architecture, Milan, 1960-64; dir., sr. v.p. design Unimark Internat., Milan and N.Y.C., 1965-71; pres. Vignelli Assocs., N.Y.C., 1971—; chmn. Vignelli Designs, Inc., N.Y.C., 1978—. Retrospective shows include: Parsons Sch. Design, N.Y.C., 1980, Padiglione d'Arte Moderna, Milan, 1980, Acad. of Art USSR, Moscow and Leningrad, 1989, Helsinki, 1989, London, 1990, Budapest, Barcelona, 1991, Copenhagen, Munich, 1992, Prague, Paris, 1992-93; represented in permanent collections Mus. Modern Art, N.Y.C., Cooper-Hewitt Mus., N.Y., Met. Mus. Art, N.Y., Bklyn. Mus., Die Neue Sammlung, Munich, Musée des Arts Décoratifs, Montreal, Tel Aviv Mus. Modern Art; designer: (dinnerware) Heller, 1964, (glass bakeware) 1975, (furniture), Sunar, 1979, Rosenthal, 1980, Knoll, 1985, Poltrona Frau, 1988, (tableware) Sasaki Crystal, 1985, (glassware) Steuben, 1993; interiors St. Peters Ch., Citicorp Ctr., N.Y.C., 1975, Inst. Fine Arts., Mpls., 1974; corp. image Knoll Internat., 1966, Lancia, 1978, Ciga Hotels, 1979, Solomon R. Guggenheim Mus., 1992—, Am. Ctr. in Paris, 1994, COSMIT, Milan, 1994, Bayerische Ruck, Munich, 1994—, Benetton Worldwide, 1995—, graphics Am. Airlines, 1967, Bloomingdales, 1972, books for Rizzoli Internat., 1980—; author: Knoll Design, 1981 (Am. Inst. Graphic Arts award). Recipient Indsl. Arts medal AIA, 1973, Presdl. Design award, 1985, Gold medal for design Nat. Arts Club, 1991, Fellowship of Excellence Interior Product Designers, 1992, Lifetime Achievement award Bklyn. Mus., 1995; named to Hall of Fame N.Y. Art Dirs. Club, 1982, Compasso d'Oro, 1964, Interior Design Hall of Fame, 1988. Mem. Am. Inst. Graphic Arts (pres. 1976-77 Gold medal 1983), Indsl. Designers Soc. Am., Alliance Graphique Internationale (past pres.), Archtl. League N.Y. (v.p.). Office: Vignelli Assocs 475 10th Ave New York NY 10018-1120

VIGNERON, ALLEN HENRY, theology educator, rector; b. Mt. Clemens, Mich., Oct. 21, 1948; s. Elwin E. and Bernadine K. (Kott) V. AB in Philosophy, Sacred Heart Sem., Detroit, 1970; STL in Fundamental Theology, Pontifical Gregorian U., 1977; PhD in Philosophy, Cath. U. Am., 1987. Ordained deacon Roman Cath. Ch., 1973, ordained priest, 1975. Assoc. pastor Our Lady Queen of Peace Ch., Harper Woods, Mich., 1975-79; asst. prof. philosophy and theology Sacred Heart Major Sem., Detroit, 1985—; addetto of the secretariat of his Holiness the Pope The Holy See, Vatican City, 1991-94; rector, pres. Sacred Heart Major Sem., Detroit, 1994—; adj. prof. theology Pontifical Gregorian U., Rome, 1992-94. Office: Sacred Heart Major Sem 2701 Chicago Blvd Detroit MI 48206

VIGNIERI, CHARLES JOSEPH, meat packing co. exec.; b. Chgo., Oct. 7, 1924; s. Frank and Rosario (Saporito) V.; student pub. schs., Kenosha, Wis.; m. Lorraine Vander Warn, June 29, 1946; children—Allan, Susan, Dennis, Richard, Patricia, Joseph, Thomas, Daniel, Mark. With Frank Vignieri & Sons, Kenosha, 1936-54; with Kenosha Packing Co., 1954—, pres., 1960—; pres. Birchwood Meat & Provision, Inc., Kenosha, 1960—; dir. Kenosha Savs. & Loan Assn.; sec. Milw. Meat Council, 1965-67; guest lectr. Carthage Coll., Kenosha, 1970-75, bd. assos., 1970—. Co-chmn. March of Dimes Campaign, Kenosha, 1964; chmn. Paris-Kenosha County Plan Commn., 1965; co-founder, chmn. Kenosha Youth, Inc., 1968-70; bd. dirs. United Way, Kenosha, 1966-68, 72-75, campaign gen. chmn., 1972, pres., 1973-74; mem. adv. bd. Dominican Sisters of Bethany, Kenosha, 1963-71. Served with AUS, 1943-46; PTO. Mem. Kenosha C. of C. (dir. 1965-68), Nat. Meat Assn. (dir. 1965-77, v.p. central div. 1974-77, 1st v.p. 1978, chmn. 1980-82). Roman Catholic (trustee, treas. 1952-66, parish chmn. archibishops fund appeal 1952-66). Clubs: Elks, Rotary (dir. 1965-70, pres. 1967-68). Contbr. articles to profl. jours. Home: 4001 5th Pl Kenosha WI 53144-1032 Office: Kenosha Beef Internat Ltd 3111 152nd Ave Kenosha WI 53144-7630*

VIGNOLO, BIAGIO NICKOLAS, JR., chemical company executive; b. New Brunswick, N.J., June 15, 1947; s. Biagio and Helen (Carleo) V.; m. Olga Tkachuk, Mar. 23, 1974; children: Adam, John. BS in Acctg., Rider Coll., 1970. Mgr. acctg. staff Peat, Marwick & Mitchell Co., Trenton, N.J., 1969-77; controller Revlon Inc., N.Y.C., 1977-83; v.p., controller Am. Bakeries Co., N.Y.C., 1983-88; sr. v.p. fin. Sun Chem. Corp., Ft. Lee, N.J., 1989—. Fellow Am. Inst. CPA's, N.J. Soc. CPA's. Republican. Roman Catholic. Office: Sun Chem Corp 222 Brg Plz S Fort Lee NJ 07024

VIGTEL, GUDMUND, museum director emeritus; b. Jerusalem, July 9, 1925; came to U.S., 1948, naturalized, 1966; s. Arne Jonsen and Elisabeth (Petri) V.; m. Solveig Lund, 1951 (div. 1964); 1 child, Elisabeth; m. Carolyn Gates Smith, July 18, 1964; 1 child, Catherine Higdon. BFA, U. Ga., 1952, MFA, 1953; DFA (hon.), Atlanta Coll. Art, 1991. Adminstrv. asst. Corcoran Gallery Art, Washington, 1954-61, asst. dir., 1961-63; dir. High Mus. Art, Atlanta, 1963-91, dir. emeritus, 1991—. Contbr. articles and essays to profl. publs. Served with Royal Norwegian Air Force, 1944-45. Decorated Chevalier des Arts et Lettres, Minister of Culture (France); recipient Order of Merit First Class Fed. Republic Germany, 1989. Home: 2082 Golf View Dr NW Atlanta GA 30309-1210

VIJH, ASHOK KUMAR, chemistry educator, researcher; b. Multan, India (now Pakistan), Mar. 15, 1938; s. Bishamber Nath and Prem Lata (Bahl) V.; m. Danielle Blais (div.); 1 child, Aldous Ian. BSc with honors, Panjab U., India, 1960, MSc with honors, 1961; PhD, Ottawa U., 1966; LLD (hon.), Concordia U., 1988; DSc (hon.), Waterloo U., 1993. Group leader Inst. Research Hydro-Quebec, 1969-74, program leader, 1975-81, maitre-de-research, 1973—; vis. prof., thesis dir. INRS-Energie, U. Que., 1970—; Xerox lectr. U. Montreal, 1991. Author: Electrochemistry of Metals and Semiconductors, 1973; editor: Oxides and Oxide Films; mem. editorial bd. Applied Physics Communications, Internat. Jour. Hydrogen Energy, Materials Chemistry and Physics, also several other jours.; contbr. over 250 articles to profl. jours. Decorated officer Order of Can.; chevalier de Ordre Nationale de Quebec; knight Order o Malta; recipient Urgel Archambault medal Assn. Candienne pour Advancement Scis., 1984, Commemorative medal 125th Anniversary Confedn. Can., 1992, le Prix de l'excellence, Govt. Québec, 1994, Compagnon de LaVoisier, Order of Chemists of Québec, 1995. Fellow IEEE, Royal Soc. Chemistry, Chem. Inst. Can. (Noranda lectr. 1979, Palladium medal 1990), Inst. Physics (U.K.), Royal Soc. Can. (dir. applied scis. and engring. divsn. 1990, elected dir. math. and phys. scis. divsn. Acad. Sci. 1994—, Thomas W. Eadie medal 1989), Am. Phys. Soc., Third World Acad. Scis., Nat. Acad. Scis. India, Acad. Francophone d'Ingenieus (France; founding fellow 1993), Indian Nat. Sci. Acad. (fgn.); mem. European Acad. Arts, Scis. and Humanities (academician), Electrochem. Soc. (Lash Miller award 1973), Can. Com. Scientists and Scholars (exec. 1994, v.p. 1995), Can. Coun. (mem. KILLAM awards selection com. 1994, Izaak Walton Killam Meml. prize 1987), Materials Rsch. Soc. India (hon.). Office: Hydro-Quebec Research Inst, 1800 Montee Ste Julie, Varennes, PQ Canada J3X 1S1

VIKAN, GARY KENT, art museum administrator; b. Fosston, Minn., Nov. 30, 1946; s. Franklin and Wilma (Johnson) V.; m. Elana Klausner, Sept. 12, 1971; children: Nicole, Sonia. BA, Carleton Coll., 1967; MA, Princeton U., 1970, PhD, 1976. Art mus. adminstr., curator Byzantine art Dumbarton Oaks, Washington, 1975-84, Harvard U., 1985—; dir. Walters Art Gallery, 1994—. Woodrow Wilson Found. fellow, 1967-68. mem. Byzantine Studies Counf. (governing bd. 1989—), U.S. Nat. Com. for Byzantine Studies (exec. com., 1988-92.

VIKEN, LINDA LEA MARGARET, lawyer; b. Sioux Falls, S.D., Oct. 27, 1945; d. Carl Thomas and Eleanor Bertha (Zehnpfennig) Crampton; m. Jerry Lee Miller, June 10, 1967 (div. 1975); m. Jeffrey Lynn Viken, Feb. 2, 1980. BS in Bus. Edn., U. S.D., 1967, JD in Law, 1977. Bar: S.D. 1978, U.S. Dist. Ct. S.D. 1978, U.S. Ct. Appeals (8th cir.) 1981. Tchr. Yankton (S.D.) High Sch., 1967-69, Edison Jr. High Sch., Sioux Falls, 1969-75; pvt. practice law Sioux Falls, 1978; ptnr. Finch, Viken, Viken, & Pechota, Rapid City, S.D., 1978-92, Viken, Viken, Pechota, Leach & Dewell, Rapid City, 1992—; part-time instr. Nat. Coll., Rapid City, 1978-80; magistrate judge Seventh Jud. Cir., Rapid City, 1983-84; chair S.D. Commn. on Child Support, 1985, 88; mem. S.D. Bd. of Bar Examiners, 1987-88. Contbr. articles to profl. jours. State rep. S.D. Legislature Minnehaha County, 1973-76, Pennington County, 1988-92; state party vice chair S.D. Dem. party, 1978-80, 92-94; chair Pennington County Dem. Party, Rapid City, 1985-87. Named Woman Atty. of Yr. Law Sch. Women, 1987. Fellow Am. Acad. Matrimonial Lawyers; mem. ABA, S.D. Bar, S.D. Trial Lawyers Assn. Democrat. Roman Catholic. Avocations: poetry, skiing. Home: 4760 Trout Ct Rapid City SD 57702-4751 Office: Viken Viken Pechota Leach and Dewell 1617 Sheridan Lake Rd Rapid City SD 57702-3423

VIKIS-FREIBERGS, VAIRA, psychologist, educator; b. Riga, Latvia, Dec. 1, 1937; d. Karlis and Annemarie (Rankis) V.; m. Imants F. Freibergs, July 16, 1960; children: Karlis Roberts, Indra Karoline. B.A., U. Toronto, 1958, M.A., 1960; Ph.D., McGill U., 1965; LLD, Queen's U., 1991. Clin. psychologist Toronto (Ont.) Psychiat. Hosp., 1960-61; asst. prof. dept. psychology U. Montreal, Que., Can., 1965-72; asso. prof. U. Montreal, 1972-77, prof., 1977—; pres. Social Sci. Fedn. Can., 1980; chmn. NATO (spl. program panel on human factors), 1980; dir. Latvian Youth Ethnic Heritage Seminars Divreizdivi, 1979; mem. Sci. Council Can., 1980-89, vice chmn., 1984-89. Author: La Frèquence Lexicale au Quebec, 1974, The Amber Mountain, 1989, Against the Current, 1993; co-author: Latvian Sun Songs, 1988; editor: Linguistics and Poetics of Latvian Folk Songs, 1989; contbr. articles to profl. jours. Recipient Prof. A. Abele Meml. prize, 1979, Disting. Contbn. prize World Assn. Free Latvians, 1989, Order of the Three Stars, Republic of Latvia, 1995; Can. Coun. leave fellow, 1974-75; Killam Rsch. fellow Can. Coun., 1993-95. Fellow Can. Psychol. Assn. (pres. 1980), Royal Soc. Can. (Pierre Chauveau medal for disting. wk. in the humanities 1995); mem. Acad. Sci. Latvia (fgn.), Assn. Advancement Baltic Studies (pres. 1984-86), Assn. Canadienne Francaise pour l'Avancement des Scis. (Marcel-Vincent prize and medal 1992), Sigma Xi. Lutheran. Home: 444 Grenfell Ave, Town of Mount Royal, PQ Canada H3R 1G5 Office: U Montreal Dept Psych CP 6128, Succursale Centre-ville, Montreal, PQ Canada H3C 3J7

VIKLUND, WILLIAM EDWIN, banker; b. Bklyn., June 12, 1940; s. Edwin Oscar and Anna Ingegard (Kvarnstrom) V.; m. Joyce Eleanor Larson, Apr. 14, 1962; children—Mark William, David Andrew, Andrea Lynn. B.A., L.I. U., Bklyn., 1960. Vice-pres. Anchor Savs. Bank, Bklyn., 1966-72; sr. v.p. Bankers Trust Co., N.Y.C., 1972-80; pres. L.I. Bancorp., Melville, N.Y., 1980—. Contbr. articles to profl. jours. Trustee L.I. U., 1995; mem. bd. overseers Tilles Ctr. for Performing Arts, 1987. Mem. Westhampton Country Club. Lutheran. Office: The Long Island Savs Bank 201 Old Country Rd Melville NY 11747-2725

VILA, ADIS MARIA, corporate executive, former government official, lawyer; b. Cuba, Aug. 1, 1953; came to U.S., 1962; d. Calixto Vila and Adis C. Fernandez. BA with distinction, Rollins Coll., 1974; JD with honors, U. Fla., 1978; LLM with high honors, Institut Universitaire de Hautes Estudes Internationales, Geneva, 1981. Bar: Fla. 1979, D.C. 1984. Assoc. Paul & Thomson, 1979-82; White House fellow Office Pub. Liaison, Washington, 1982-83; spl. asst. to sec. state for inter-Am. affairs Dept. State, Washington, 1983-86; dir. Office of Mex. and Caribbean Basin, Dept. Commerce, Washington, 1986-87; sec. Dept. Adminstrn., State of Fla., 1987-89; asst. sec. for adminstrn. USDA, Washington, 1989-91; vis. asst., prof. Fla. Internat. U., 1993-94; vis. fellow Nat. Def. U., Washington, 1992-93; v.p. internat. devel. The Vigoro Corp., Chgo., 1994—; trustee So. Ctr. for Internat. Studies, 1987—. Bd. dirs. Rollings Coll. Alumni Coun., Winter Park, Fla., 1979—. Named one of 100 Most Influential Hispanics, 1988, Paul Harris fellow Rotary Internat., 1983, U.S.-Japan Leadership fellow, 1991-92, Eisenhower Exch. fellow, Beca Fiore, Argentina, 1992. Mem. Dade County Bar Assn. (bd. dirs. young and lawyers sect. 1979-87), Coun. Fgn. Rels (term mem. 1987-92), Am. Coun. Young Polit. Leaders (bd. dirs. 1984—), Women Execs. in State Govt. (bd. dirs. 1987—). Republican. Roman Catholic. Avocations: tennis, skiing, golf, theater, arts.

VILA, ROBERT JOSEPH, television host, designer, real estate developer; b. Miami, Fla., June 20, 1946; s. Roberto and Esperanza (Robles) V.; m. Diana Barrett, Oct. 3, 1975; children: Christopher, Monica, Susannah. BA in Architecture, Miami Dade Jr. Coll., 1966; BS in Journalism, U. Fla., 1969. Editor English Lang. Cons., Stuttgart, Fed. Republic of Germany, 1971; stagehand Wurttemburg State Theatre, Stuttgart, 1972; project mgr. Barrett Assocs., Boston, 1973-74; pres. R.J. Vila, Inc., Boston, 1975-85; host This Old House Sta. WGBH-TV, Boston, 1978-89; host Bob Vila's Home Again, Cape Cod and Chgo., 1990; host Plymouth, Mass., Naples, Fla., 1991—; host Martha's Vineyard and Malibu, Calif., 1991-92. Author: This Old House, 1980, Bob Vila's This Old House, 1982, Guide to Building Materials, 1986, Guide to Buying Your Dream House, 1990, Bob Vila's Tool Box, 1993, Bob Vila's Guide to Historic Homes of New England, 1993, Bob Vila's Guide to Historic Homes of the South, 1993, Bob Vila's Guide to Historic Homes of the Mid-Atlantic, 1993, Bob Vila's Workshop, 1994. Bd. dirs. Plimouth Plantation, Plymouth, Mass., Nat. Alliance to End Homelessness, Washington. Emmy award New England Region, 1979, Nat., 1985. Mem. Am. Fedn. TV Radio Artists, Screen Actors Guild, Oyster Harbors Club (Osterville, Mass.), Friars Club (N.Y.C.). Roman Catholic. Avocations: sailing, fishing, cycling, gardening, woodworking. Home: PO Box 749 Marstons Mills MA 02648-0749 Office: BVTV PO Box 749 Marstons Mills MA 02648-0749

VILARDEBO, ANGIE MARIE, management consultant, parochial school educator; b. Tampa, Fla., July 15, 1938; d. Vincent and Antonina (Fazio) Noto; m. Charles Kenneth Vilardebo, June 26, 1960; children: Charles, Kenneth, Michele, Melanie. BA, Notre Dame Md., 1960; postgrad., Rollins Coll., 1980. Cert. tchr., Fla. Tchr. Sea Park Elem. Sch., Satellite Beach, Fla., 1960-61; office mgr. Computer Systems Enterprises, Satellite Beach, 1973-76; artist Satellite Beach, 1976-79; employment counselor Career Cons., Melbourne, Fla., 1979-80; tchr. Our Lady of Lourdes Parochial Sch., Melbourne, 1980-89; pres. Consol. Ventures, Inc., Satellite Beach, 1989—, Versatile Suppliers, Inc., Satellite Beach, 1989—; prin. search com. Diocese of Orlando, Fla., 1989-90. Patentee personal grading machine. V.p. Jaycees, Satellite Beach, 1976-77, pres., 1977-78. Recipient 1st Place Art award Fla. Fedn. Woman's Clubs, 1978, 2nd Place Art award, 1979, Honorable Mention, 1980. Mem. Satellite Beach Woman's Club, Paper Chaser's Investment Club, Brevard Arts Ctr. & Mus., Space Coast Art League (social chmn. 1987—). Roman Catholic. Avocations: bridge, writing, reading, oil painting, entrepreneurship. Home: 606 Barcelona Ct Melbourne FL 32937

VILCEK, JAN TOMAS, medical educator; b. Bratislava, Czechoslovakia, June 17, 1933; came to U.S., 1965, naturalized, 1970.; s. Julius and Friderika (Fischer) V.; m. Marica F. Gerhath, July 28, 1962. MD, Comenius U., Bratislava, 1957; CSc (PhD), Czechoslovak Acad. Sci., Bratislava, 1962. Fellow Inst. Virology, Bratislava, 1957-62, head of lab., 1962-64; asst. prof. microbiology NYU Med. Ctr., N.Y.C., 1965-68, assoc. prof., 1968-73, prof., 1973—, head biol. response modifiers, 1983—; lectr. Chinese Acad. Med. Sci., Beijing, 1981, 83, Osaka U., 1987-88; chmn. nomenclature com. WHO, 1981-86, cons. biol. standardization com., 1982-88; mem. adv. com. Cancer Soc., 1981-87, chmn., 1983; expert French Ministry Health, 1983-88; mem. sci. adv. bd. Max Planck Inst., Munich, 1987-95. Author: Interferon, 1969; editor in chief Jour. Archives of Virology, 1975-86, Cytokine and Growth Factor Revs., 1995—; editor: Interferons and the Immune Systems, 1984, Tumor Necrosis Factor: Structure, Function and Mechanism of Action, 1991; mem. editl. bd. Virology, 1979-81, Archives of Virology, 1986-92, Infection and Immunity, 1983-85, Antiviral Rsch., 1984-88, Jour. Interferon Rsch., 1988—, Jour. Immunological Methods, 1986—, Natural Immunity and Cell Growth Regulation, 1986-92, Jour. Immunology, 1987-89, Lymphokine Rsch., 1987-94, Jour. Biol. Chemistry, 1988-90, ISI Atlas Sci., Immunology, 1988-89, Jour. Cellular Physiology, 1988—, Cytokine, 1989—, Biologicals, 1989-95, Acta Virologica, 1991—, Internat. Archives of Allergy and Immunology, 1992—, Folia Biologica, 1993—, Cellular Immunology, 1993, Jour. of Inflammation, 1994—; contbr. articles to profl. jours. Mem. rev. panel Israel Cancer Rsch. Fund, 1993—; mem. fellowship rev. com. Am. Heart Assn., 1992-94. Recipient Rsch. Career Devel. award USPHS, 1968-73, Recognition award Japanese Inflammation Soc., 1989, Outstanding Investigator award Nat. Cancer Inst., NIH, 1991—; grantee USPHS, numerous other orgns. Mem. AAAS, Soc. Gen. Microbiology, Am. Soc. Microbiology, Am. Assn. Immunologists, Internat. Soc. Interferon Rsch., Czech Immunology Soc., Internat. Cytokine Soc. (councillor), Czechoslovak Soc. for Microbiology. Office: NYU Med Ctr 550 1st Ave New York NY 10016-6481

VILELLA, FRANCISCO JOSÉ, wildlife research biologist; b. Arecibo, P.R., Sept. 25, 1955; s. Juan José and Olga Maria (Janeiro) V.; m. Ana B. Arnizaut, Sept. 24, 1988; 1 child, Isabela Beatriz. BS, U. P.R., Mayaguez, 1978; MA, Hofstra U., 1983; PhD, La. State U., 1989. NSF rsch. fellow Water Resources Rsch. Inst., U. P.R., Mayaguez, 1978-79; teaching asst. biology dept. Hofstra U., Hempstead, N.Y., 1981-83; rsch. asst. Wild Fish Dept. La. State U., Baton Rouge, 1984-89; fish and wildlife biologist USFWS-Caribbean Field Office, Boqueron, P.R., 1989-90, FWS-P.R. Parrot Field Office, Luquillo, P.R., 1990-94; asst. unit leader Miss. Coop. F&W Rsch. Unit Miss. State U., Mississippi State, 1994—; v.p. La. State U. chpt. of The Wildlife Soc., 1984-85. Contbr. articles to profl. jours. Recipient Outstanding Performance award U.S. Fish & Wildlife Svc., 1992-94. Mem. Soc. Caribbean Ornithology (bd. governors 1993-94), Am. Ornithologists Union, Soc. Conservation Biology, Am. Mus. Natural History. Democrat. Roman Catholic. Achievements include implementation of results from molecular genetics rsch. into conservation programs for endangered species; sponsorship of scientists from Latin America including Cuba for tng. in wildlife conservation; design of new field techniques for managing Amazon parrot species. Home: 1101 Robin Dr Starkville MS 00759 Office: Mississippi State U Dept of Wildlife & Fishery PO Drawer BX Mississippi State MS 00762

VILIM, NANCY CATHERINE, advertising agency executive; b. Quincy, Mass., Jan. 15, 1952; d. John Robert and Rosemary (Malpede) V.; m. Geoffrey S. Horner, Feb. 16, 1992; children: Matthew Edward Cajda, Megan Catherine Cajda, Margaret Horner. Student, Miami U., Oxford, Ohio, 1970-72. Media asst. Draper Daniels, Inc., Chgo., 1972-74; asst. buyer Campbell Mithun, Chgo., 1974-75; buyer Tatham, Laird & Kudner, Chgo., 1975-77; media buyer Adcom, Inc. div. Quaker Oats Corp., Chgo., 1977-79; media supr. G.M. Feldman, Chgo., 1979-81; v.p. media dir. Media Mgmt., 1981-83; v.p. broadcast dir. Bozell, Jacobs, Kenyon & Eckhardt, Chgo., 1983-88; v.p., media mgr. McCann-Erickson, Inc., 1989—; judge 27th Internat. Broadcast Awards, Chgo., 1987. Co-pres. Immaculate Conception Religious Edn. Parents Club, 1995-96. Recipient Media All Star awards Sound Mgmt. Mag., N.Y.C., 1987. Mem. Broadcast Advt. Club Chgo., Mus. Broadcast Communications, NAFE. Office: McCann-Erickson Inc 625 N Michigan Ave Chicago IL 60611-3110

VILLA, JACQUELINE IRENE, newspaper editor; b. N.Y.C., Oct. 30, 1917; d. Thomas Charles and Ada Louise (Clementi) V. BA, Hofstra U. Reporter Newsday, Hempstead, N.Y., 1942, editor, 1942-47; editor L.I. Press, Jamaica, N.Y., 1951-58, night city editor, 1958-67, entertainment editor, 1967-77; travel and food editor The Ariz. Daily Star, Tucson, 1977-95, copy editor, 1995—. Mem. Ariz. Press Women (bd. dirs., sec., chairwoman So. chpt.). Office: The Ariz Daily Star PO Box 26807 4850 S Park Ave Tucson AZ 85726-6807

VILLABLANCA, JAIME ROLANDO, medical scientist, educator; b. Chillán, Chile, Feb. 29, 1929; came to U.S., 1971; naturalized, 1985; s. Ernesto and Teresa (Hernàndez) V.; m. Guillermina Nieto, Dec. 3, 1955; children: Amparo C., Jaime G., Pablo J., Francis X., Claudio I. Bachelor in Biology, Nat. Inst. Chile, 1946; licentiate medicine, U. Chile, 1953, MD, 1954. Cert. neurophysiology. Rockefeller Found. postdoctoral fellow in physiology John Hopkins and Harvard Med. Schs., 1959-61; Fogarty internat. rsch. fellow in anatomy UCLA, 1966-68, assoc. research anatomist and psychiatrist, 1971-72; assoc. prof. psychiatry and biobehavioral scis. UCLA Sch. Medicine, 1972-76; prof. psychiatry and biobehavioral scis. UCLA, 1976—, prof. anatomy and cell biology, 1977-95, prof. Sch. Medicine, 1995—; mem. faculty U. Chile Sch. Medicine, 1954-71, prof. exptl. medicine, 1970-71; vis. prof. neurobiology Cath. U. Chile Sch. Medicine, 1974; cons. in field. Author over 200 rsch. papers, book chpts., abstracts; chief regional editor Developmental Brain Dysfunction, 1988—. Decorated Order Francisco de Miranda (Venezuela); recipient Premio Reina Sofia, Madrid, 1990, Fgn. Scientist Traveling grant Tokyo (Japan) Met. Govt., 1995; fellow Rockefeller Found., 1959-61, Fogarty Internat. Rsch. fellow NIH, 1966-68; grantee USAF Office Sci. Rsch., 1962-65, Found. Fund Rsch. Psychiatry, 1969-72, USPHS-Nat. Inst. Child Human Devel., 1972—, USPHS-Nat. Inst. Drug Abuse, 1981-85, USPHS-Nat. Inst. Neurol. Disorders and Stroke, 1988-92. Mem. AAAS, AAUP, Am. Assn. Anatomists, Mental Retardation Rsch. Ctr., Brain Rsch. Inst., Internat. Brain Rsch. Orgn., Am. Physiol. Soc., Soc. for Neurosci., Assn. Venezolana Padres de Niños Excepcionales, Sci. Coun. Internat. Inst. Rsch. and Advice in Mental Deficiency (Madrid), Soc. Child and Adolescent Psychiatry and Neurology (Chile) (hon.), Sigma Xi. Home: 200 Surfview Dr Pacific Palisades CA 90272-2911 Office: UCLA Dept Psychiatry & Biobehavioral Scis Los Angeles CA 90024

VILLAFRANCA, JOSEPH J., pharmaceutical executive, chemistry educator; b. Silver Creek, N.Y., Mar. 23, 1944; s. Joseph Nicholas and Mildred (Dolce) C.; children: Jennifer, June. BS, SUNY, Fredonia, 1965; PhD, Purdue U., 1969. From asst. prof. to prof. Pa. State U., University Park, 1971-76, Evan Pugh prof. chemistry, 1986—; cons. Monsanto Corp., St. Louis, 1985-89, Eastman Kodak Co., Rochester, N.Y., 1985-87. Author over 170 sci. publs. Mem. Am. Chem. Soc. (councilor 1986-89), Am. Soc. for Biochemistry and Molecular Biology, Biophys. Soc., Protein Soc. Avocation: skiing. Office: Bristol-Myers Squibb Pharm Res Inst PO Box 4000 Princeton NJ 08543

VILLAGONZALO, AMPARO DE LA CERNA, management analyst; b. Cebu, Philippines, Oct. 30, 1939; came to U.S.A., 1970; d. Ignacio Carangue and Josefa (De La Cerna) V.; adopted children: Victor, Emerald. AA, U. Visayas, 1956, LLB magna cum laude, 1960; postgrad., U. Philippines, 1966-67. Bar: Philippines, 1961. Atty. Villagonzalo Law Offices, Cebu City, Philippines, 1960-62; mgmt. analyst Presdl. Com. on Adminstrn. Performance Efficiency, Manila, Philippines, 1962-65; mgmt. analyst II Commn. on Elections, Manila, Philippines, 1965-70; spl. correspondent Bankers Life Ins. Co., Chgo., 1970-74; from transit mgmt. analyst to assoc. mgmt. analyst N.Y.C. Transit Authority, 1974-80, mgr., materials mgmt. dept., 1980—. Scholar U. Visayas, 1954-60, U. Philippines, 1966-67. Roman Catholic. Avocations: collecting plates, dolls. Home: 15811 86th St Jamaica NY 11414-3002

VILLALBA, MARY KAYE, school nurse; b. Scott City, Kans., Oct. 18, 1939; d. Andrew Michael and Anne (Eder) Kershen; m. Pete S. Villalba, Apr. 2, 1977; children: John Glenn, Margarita Ann. RN, St. Anthony's Sch. Nursing, Amarillo, Tex., 1960; BSN, Incarnate Word Coll., 1962; MSN, Tex. Tech. U., 1990. Cert. sch. nurse. Staff nurse Ft. Sam Houston, San Antonio, Tex., 1962-68; staff/surg. office nurse Assoc. Physicians, Clovis, N.Mex., 1968-80; staff nurse Dr. Nick Rowley, Clovis, 1980-83, U. Med. Ctr., Lubbock, Tex., 1983-84; sch. nurse Lubbock Ind. Sch. Dist., 1984-90; faculty mem. Meth. Sch. Nursing, Lubbock, 1990-91; sch. nurse specialist Slaton (Tex.) Ind. Sch. Dist., 1991—; relief charge nurse Meth. Hosp., Lubbock, 1991—; chairperson profl. bd. March of Dimes, Lubbock, 1988-91; mem. health adv. bd. Edn. Svc. Ctr., Lubbock. Contbr. articles to profl. jours. Pres. Woman's Orgn., Lubbock, 1986; parent advisor 4-H Club, Rosevelt, Tex., 1987-90; tchr. Cath. Youth Study Group, Slaton, 1989-92. Mem. Tex. Assn. Sch. Nurses (pres. 1994-95, exec. bd. 1990—), Nat. Assn. Sch. Nurses, Sigma Theta Tau. Avocations: walking, step aerobics, reading. Home: 96 E Canyonview Dr Ransom Canyon TX 79366-2309 Office: Slaton Ind Sch Dist 300 S 9th St Slaton TX 79364-4110

VILLALOBOS, REYNALDO, cinematographers. Cinematographer: (films) Nine to Five, 1980, Urban Cowboy, 1980, The Ballad of Gregorio Cortez, 1983, Mike's Murder, 1984, Windy City, 1984, Blame It on Rio, 1984, Grandview, U.S.A., 1984, Saving Grace, 1986, Band of the Hand, 1986, Desert Bloom, 1986, Lucas, 1986, Punchline, 1988, Major League, 1989, Sibling Rivalry, 1990, Coupe de Ville, 1990, American Me, 1992, A Bronx Tale, 1992, PCU, 1993; dir.: (TV movies) Louis L'Amour's Conagher, 1991. Office: Am Soc of Cinematographers PO Box 2230 Los Angeles CA 90078-2230

VILLALOBOS PADILLA, FRANCISCO, bishop; b. Guadalajara, Mexico, Feb. 1, 1921. Ordained priest Roman Cath. Ch., 1949; named titular bishop of Colonnata, 1971; now bishop of Saltillo Mexico, 1975—. Office: Bishop's Residence, Obispado Apartado 25, Saltillo Coahuila, Mexico also: Hidalgo Sur 166, Apartado 25 CP25000, Saltillo Mexico Coahuila

VILLAR-PALASI, CARLOS, pharmacology educator; b. Valencia, Spain, Mar. 3, 1928; came to U.S., 1963; s. Vicente Villar Bolinaga and Teresa (Palasi-Pinazo); m. Amparo Gosalvez-Sobrino, Aug. 17, 1957 (dec. July 1978); children: Victor, Carlos, Juan Jose, Maria Amparo. MS in Chemistry, U. Valencia, Spain, 1951; PhD in Biochemistry, U. Madrid, Spain, 1955; MS in Pharmacy, U. Barcelona, Spain, 1962. Rsch. fellow med. sch. U. Hamburg, Fed. Republic of Germany, 1953-54, Spanish Rsch. Coun., Madrid, 1954-57, Case Western Res. U., Cleve., 1960-63; rsch. assoc. Spanish Rsch. Coun., Madrid, 1960-63, Case Western Res. U., Cleve., 1963-64; rsch. assoc. U. Minn., Mpls., 1964-65, asst. prof., 1965-69; assoc. prof. U. Va., Charlottesville, 1969-72, prof., 1972—; invited speaker Fedn. European Biochem. Soc., 1969. March Found. fellow, 1957; recipient Rsch. award Cleve. Diabetes Found., 1960, NIH, 1967-69. Mem. AAAS (Rsch. award 1960-62), Am. Soc. Pharmacology, Am. Soc. Biol. Chemistry. Roman Catholic. Avocations: horse riding, camping. Home: PO Box 101 Ivy VA 22945-0101 Office: U Va Med Sch Dept Pharmacology 1300 Jefferson Park Ave Charlottesville VA 22903-3363

VILLARREAL, CARLOS CASTANEDA, engineering executive; b. Brownsville, Tex., Nov. 9, 1924; s. Jesus Jose and Elisa L. (Castaneda) V.; m. Doris Ann Akers, Sept. 10, 1948; children: Timothy Hill, David Akers. BA, U.S. Naval Acad., 1948; MS, U.S. Navy Postgrad. Sch., 1950; LLD (hon.), St. Mary's U., 1972. Registered profl. engr. Commd. ensign U.S. Navy, 1948, advanced through grades to lt., 1956; comdg. officer U.S.S. Rhea, 1951, U.S.S. Osprey, 1952; comdr. Mine Div. 31, 1953; resigned, 1956; mgr. marine and indsl. operation Gen. Electric Co., 1956-66; v.p. mktg. and adminstrn. Marquardt Corp., 1966-69; head Urban Mass Transit Adminstrn., Dept. Transp., Washington, 1969-73; commr. Postal Rate Commn., 1973-79, vice chmn., 1975-79; v.p. Washington ops. Wilbur Smith and Assocs., 1979-84, sr. v.p., 1984-86, exec. v.p., 1987—, also bd. dirs.; lectr. in field; mem. industry sector adv. com. Dept. Commerce; mem. sect. 13 adv. com. Dept. Transp., 1983-86. Contbr. to profl. jours. Mem. devel. com. Wolftrap Farm Park for the Performing Arts, 1973-78; mem. council St. Elizabeth Ch., 1982-86, chmn. fin. com.; mem. bd. edn. St. Elizabeth Sch.; bd. dirs. Assoc. Catholic Charities, 1983-86; mem. fin. com. Cath. Charities, U.S.A. Decorated knight Sovereign Mil. Hospitaller Order St. John of Jerusalem of Rhodes and Malta, 1981, Knight Equestrian Order of the Holy Sepulchre of Jerusalem; recipient award outstanding achievement Dept. Transp. Fellow ASCE, Am. Cons. Engrs. Coun. (vice chmn. internat. com.); mem. IEEE, NSPE (pres. D.C. soc. 1986-87, bd. dirs. 1988-91), Am. Pub. Transit Assn., Soc. Naval Architects and Marine Engrs., Soc. Am. Mil. Engrs., Am. Rds. and Transp. Builders Assn. (chmn. pub. transp. adv. coun.), Transp. Rsch. Bd., Washington Soc. Engrs., Internat. Bridge, Tunnel and Turnpike Assn., Inst. Traffic Engrs., Intelligent Transp. Soc. Am. (chmn. fin. com., bd. dirs.), Univ. Club, Army-Navy Club. Republican. Roman Catholic. Office: Wilbur Smith Assocs 2921 Telestar Ct Falls Church VA 22042-1205

VILLARREAL, HOMERO ATENÓGENES, human resources executive; b. McAllen, Tex., June 13, 1946; s. Atenógenes Alejandro and Estella Marie (Lopez) V.; m. Lynne Carol Kastrup, Sept. 20, 1980; children: Alissa Lynne, Ashley Cameron, Ana Victoria. BBA, U. Houston, 1969. Asst. mgr. manpower internat. div. Mobil Corp., N.Y.C., 1974-77; dir. adminstrn. CBS Inc., N.Y.C., 1977-80; mgr. internat. human resources AT&T Inc., Basking Ridge, N.J., 1981-89; v.p. HR Cadbury-Schweppes Inc., Stamford, Conn., 1989—; v.p. AIESEC-Houston, 1967-69. Served with U.S. Army, 1969-72. Mem. Am. Compensation Assn., Soc. Human Resources Mgmt. Republican. Presbyterian. Office: Cadbury-Schweppes Inc 6 High Ridge Park Stamford CT 06905-1327

VILLARREAL, JESUS MORÓN, newswriter, publisher, poet, artist; b. Key West, Fla., Dec. 7, 1952; s. Gonzalo and Clariza (Villarreal) M.; m. Maria Marroquin Guerra (div.); children: Nancy, Ruby, Xochitl Linda; m. Maria de Jesus Hernandez; 1 child, Mario de Jesus. Course in black and white photography, Martinez Studios, Coahuila, Mexico, 1967; course in photo retouching, coloring, restoration, lighting techniques, Jesus Trejo Labs., Monterrey, Mexico, 1969; course in chromegacolor processor, color print finishing and negative processing, Wabash Photo Labs., Chgo., 1973; cert., Photo Lab. Tech., 1988; course in videography and cinematography, Martinez Photography Studios, Houston, 1989. Journalist, photographer El Sol Newspaper, Houston, 1978-90; v.p. La Prensa News, Houston, 1978-79, El Torniquete, Monterrey, Mex., 1980; journalist, photographer Mas Noticias, Houston, 1981; subdirector Diario de Houston, 1982; art critic Critica Magazine, Houston, 1983-85; pub., editor Gaceta de Texas News, Houston, 1992—; lectr. U. Houston, 1978; artist Machtilli Gallery, 1978-93; photographer Gaceta de Tex. News, 1993-94; writer Machtilli Publs., 1992; historian Universidad Autonoma de Nuevo Leon, Monterey, Mex., 1992. Solo exhbns. include Mayors of Zuazua Photo Exhbn. Mus. Casa de Cultura, Imagenes C.R.O.C. Fedn. Gallery, 1981; group exhbns. at Art and Photography Festival Buckingham Found., 1975, Bilingual Bicultural Ctr. R. Salazar Gallery, 1976, S.S.C.C. Phot Contest South Side Camera Ctr., 1978, S.W. Chgo. Arts Ctr., Houston, 1978, The Glassell Sch. Art, Mus. Fine Arts, Houston, 1982, Fala Mems. Exbhn. Fala Midtown Art Gallery, 1983, Ceestem Gallery, Mexico City, 1983, O'Kane Gallery, Houston, 1983, Leopoldo Carpinteyro Gallery, Mex., 1986; permanent exhbn. Hacienda San Pedro, Zuazua, Mex.; author: (book) How to Write Poems, Como Declamar y Escribir Poesia, 1992, Manual de Pintura Nahuatl, 1995, Gutierrez and Magee Tex-Mex Heroes, 1995. union rep. Cesar Chavez United Farmworkers, 1968-69. Recipient 3d Place in Painting award Mus. Sci. and Industry, 1975, 1st Place in Photography award South Side Camera, 1980, Painting award Mus. Casa de Cultura, 1981, 4th Pl. in Painting award Vitro Art Mus., 1980, Editors Choice award Nat. Libr. of Poetry, 1994. Mem. Houston Arts Coun., Seventh Flower Artists, Bar of Artists and Critics Assn., Croc Syndicate of Photographers, Internat. Soc. Poets (life mem.). Democrat. Avocations: poetry, music, visual arts, history. Office: Gaceta de Tex Pub Co PO Box 87236 Houston TX 77287-7236

VILLARREAL, SHARON MARIE, elementary education educator; b. Ventura, Calif., Mar. 26, 1961; d. José G. and Sharon N. (Kay) V.; 1 child, Elizabeth Maribel. BA in Spanish, U. Calif., Davis, 1985; bilingual cert. competence in Spanish, Calif. State U., Dominguez Hills, 1988, multiple subject tchg. credential, 1993. Cert. multiple subject tchr. with bilingual emphasis, Calif. Tchr. Nevin Avenue Elem. Sch., L.A. Unified Sch. Dist., 1985—, bilingual coord., 1989-93, mem. sch. leadership coun., 1991. Mem. Booster Club, St. Andrew Sch., Pasadena, Calif., 1993—; tchr. religious edn. St. Andrew Parish, 1994—. Mem. NEA, Am. Fedn. Tchrs., Union Tchrs. L.A., Calif. Aggie Alumni Assn. Democrat. Avocations: camping, basketball, Spanish literature, volleyball, poetry. Office: Nevin Avenue Elem Sch 1569 E 32nd St Los Angeles CA 90011-2213

VILLARS, FELIX MARC HERMANN, physicist, educator; b. Biel, Switzerland, Jan. 6, 1921; came to U.S., 1949, naturalized, 1955; s. Jean Felix and Alma (Engel) V.; m. Jacqueline Dubois, June 25, 1949; children: J. Frederic, Cecile, Monique, Philippe. Diplome, Swiss Fed. Inst. Tech., Zurich, 1945, D.Sc.Nat., 1946. Research asst. Swiss Fed. Inst. Tech., 1946-49; vis. mem. Inst. Advanced Study at Princeton, 1949-50; research asso. MIT, 1950-52, asst. prof. physics, 1952-55, assoc. prof., 1955-60, prof., 1960-91, prof. emeritus, sr. lectr., 1991—; lectr. biophysics Harvard Med. Sch., 1974—. Served with Swiss Army, 1940-45. Fellow Am. Acad. Arts and Scis., AAAS; mem. Am. Phys. Soc., N.Y. Acad. Sci. Home: 55 Orchard St Belmont MA 02178-3008 Office: Ctr for Theoretical Physics MIT 77 Massachusetts Ave Cambridge MA 02139-4301

VILLAVASO, STEPHEN DONALD, urban planner, lawyer; b. New Orleans, July 12, 1949; s. Donald Philip and Jacklyn (Tully) V.; m. Regina Smith, Apr. 17, 1971; children: Christine Regina, Stephen Warner. BS in Econs., U. New Orleans, 1971, M in Urban and Regional Planning, 1976; JD, Loyola U., New Orleans, 1981. Bar: La. 1982; recognized ct. expert in land use, planning and zoning. Urban and regional planner Barnard & Thomas, New Orleans, 1976-78; dir. analysis and planning City of New Orleans, 1978-81, counsel for planning and devel., 1983-84; dir. planning and environ. affairs Tecon Realty, New Orleans, 1981-83; v.p. for planning and project mgmt. Morphy, Makofsky, Mumphrey & Masson, New Orleans, 1984-89; bus. devel. mgr. Waste Mgmt., Inc., New Orleans, 1989—; bd. dirs. Regional Loan Corp.; guest lectr., adj. prof. Coll. of Urban and Pub. Affairs, U. New Orleans, 1976—; spl. instr. grad. studies in urban planning So. U. New Orleans, 1987—. Bd. dirs. New Orleans Traffic and Transp. Bur., 1981-86, Riverfront Awareness, New Orleans, 1984-86; bd. dirs. Vols. Am. Greater New Orleans, 1987—, vice chmn., 1990, chmn. bd., 1992-95. With USN, 1971-74. Named one of Outstanding Young Men of Am., 1980, 82. Mem. ABA, Am. Inst. of Cert. Planners, Am. Planning Assn. (pres. La. div. 1980-84, disting. svc. award 1985), Urban Land Inst., La. Bar Assn., U. New Orleans Alumni Assn. (bd. dirs. 1990—), Phi Kappa Phi, Delta Sigma Pi (pres. 1971), Omicron Delta Kappa. Democrat. Roman Catholic. Avocations: philately, camping, travel, road racing. Home: 6304 Beauregard Ave New Orleans LA 70124-4502

VILLECCO, JUDY DIANA, substance abuse, mental health counselor, director; b. Knoxville, Tenn., Jan. 19, 1948; d. William Arthur and Louise (Reagan) Chamberlain; m. Tucker, June 10, 1965 (div. 1974); children: Linda Louise (Tucker) Smith, Constance Christine; m. Roger Anthony Villecco, May 3, 1979. BA in Psychology, U. West Fla., 1988, MA in Psychology, 1992. Lic. mental health counselor, Fla.; cert. addiction profl., Fla.; internat. cert. alcohol and drug counselor. Counselor Gulf Coast Hosp., Ft. Walton Beach, Fla., 1986-87; peer counselor U. West Fla., Ft. Walton Beach, 1987-89; family and prevention counselor Okaloosa Guidance Clinic, Ft. Walton Beach, 1988-89; family svc. dir. Anon Anew of Tampa (Fla.), Inc., 1989-91; dir. Renew Counseling Ctr., Ft. Walton Beach, 1990-92; substance abuse dept. dir. Avalon Ctr., Milton, Fla., 1992-93; adult coord. Partial & Rivendell, Ft. Walton Beach, 1994-95; pvt. practice Emerald Coast Psychiat. Care, P.A., Fort Walton Beach, 1994-95, Associated Psychotherapists, Ft. Walton Beach, 1995—; internat. substance abuse counselor, dir. and presenter in field. Author: Co-dependency Treatment Manual, 1992; creator Effective Treatment for Codependants, 1992. Named Outstanding Mental Health Profl. of Yr., Nat. Mental Health Assn., 1994. Mem. ACA, Phi Theta Kappa, Alpha Phi Sigma. Avocations: crafts, grandchildren, travel. Office: 348 Miracle Strip Pky Ste 38 Fort Walton Beach FL 32548

VILLEE, CLAUDE ALVIN, JR., biochemistry educator; b. Lancaster, Pa., Feb. 9, 1917; s. Claude Alvin and Mary Elizabeth (Nestel) V.; m. Dorothy Theresa Balzer, Jan. 21, 1952; children: Claude Alvin III, Stephen Eric Fortney, Suzanne Villee, Charles Andrew. BS, Franklin and Marshall Coll., 1937; PhD, U. Calif.-Berkeley, 1941; AM (hon.), Harvard U., 1957; ScD (hon.), Franklin and Marshall Coll., 1991. Research fellow U. Calif. at Berkeley, 1941-42; asst. prof. U. N.C., 1942-45; mem. faculty Harvard, 1946—, prof. biol. chemistry, 1962-63, Andelot prof. biol. chemistry, 1964—; fellow Winthrop House, 1957—; tech. aide Nat. Acad. Scis., 1946-47; research assoc. Boston Lying in Hosp., 1950-66; dir. lab. reproductive biology Boston Hosp., 1966—; disting. vis. prof. U. Belgrade, Yugoslavia, 1974, 77; vis. prof. Mahidol U., Bangkok, Thailand, 1974; cons. NSF, Ford Found., Nat. Found./March of Dimes; mem. nat. adv. child health and human devel. council NIH; pres. Internat. Symposium Foeto-Placental unit, Milan, 1968. Author: Biology, 10th edit, 1993, General Zoology, 6th edit, 1984, Fallout from the Population Explosion, 1986, Metabolism, 1985, Introduction to Animal Biology, 1979, Control of Ovulation, 1961, Mechanism of Action of Steroid Hormones, 1960, The Placenta and Fetal Membranes, 1960, Gestation, Vols. 2-5, 1955-58, Respiratory Distress Syndrome, 1973, Biological Principles and Processes, 1976, The Placenta: A Neglected Experimental Animal, 1979, Human Reproduction, 1981, PDQ Biochemistry, 1986; mem. editorial bd. Paragon House Pus., 1984—; contbr. articles to profl. jours. Trustee Forsythe Dental Center, Boston, Winsor Sch.; trustee, v.p. Internat. Found. for Biochem. Endocrinology, 1980—; bd. dirs. Moors Assn., Falmouth, Mass. Lalor fellow, 1946-47; Guggenheim fellow, 1949-50; recipient Ciba award, 1956, Rubin award, 1957. Fellow Am. Acad. Arts and Scis., Am. Gynecol. Soc. (hon.), Am. Coll. Obstetrics and Gynecology (hon.), Soc. for Gynecol. Investigation (hon.), Serbian Acad. Arts and Scis. (hon.); mem. Moors Assn. Falmouth (pres.), Am. Soc. Biol. Chemists, Endocrine Soc. Am., Biochem. Soc. (Eng.), Am. Chem. Soc., Soc. Devel. Biology, Marine Biol. Lab. (Woods Hole, Mass). Home: 485 Elm Rd Falmouth MA 02540-2414 Office: 25 Shattuck St Boston MA 02115-6027

VILLELLA, EDWARD JOSEPH, ballet dancer, educator, choreographer, artistic director; b. L.I., N.Y., Oct. 1, 1936; s. Joseph and Mildred (DeGiovanni) V.; m. Janet Greschler (div. Nov. 1980); 1 child, Roddy; m. Linda Carbonetta, Apr. 1981; children: Christa Francesca, Lauren. BS in Marine Transp., N.Y. State Maritime Coll., 1957; LHD (hon.), Boston Conservatory, 1985; hon. degree, Skidmore Coll., Fordham U., Nazareth Coll., Siena Coll., Union Coll., Schenectady, N.Y., 1991; DHL (hon.), St. Thomas U., Miami, Fla. Mem. N.Y.C. Ballet, 1957, soloist, 1958-60, prin. soloist, 1960-83; artistic dir. Ballet Okla., Oklahoma City, 1983-86; founding artistic dir. Miami (Fla.) City Ballet, 1985—; vis. artist U.S. Mil. Acad., West Point, 1981-82; vis. prof. dance U. Iowa, 1981; resident Heritage chair arts and cultural criticism George Mason U.; lectr. in field. Performed dances in Symphony C, Scotch Symphony, Western Symphony, Donizetti Variations, Swan Lake, La Source, The Nutcracker, Agon, Stars and Stripes, The Prodigal Son; premiered in Balanchine works including The Figure in the Carpet, 1960, Electronics, 1961, A Midsummer Night's Dream, 1962, Bugaku, 1963, Tarantella, 1964, Harlequinade, 1965, The Brahms-Schoenberg Quartet, 1966, Jewels, 1967, Symphony in Three Movements, 1972, Schéhérazade, 1975; choreography includes Narkissas, 1966, Shostakovitch Ballet Suite, 1972, Shenandoah, 1972, Gayane Pas de Deux, 1972, Salute to Cole, 1973, Sea Chanties, 1974, Prelude, Riffs and Fugues, 1980; TV appearances include The Ed Sullivan Show, Bell Telephone Hour, Mike Douglas Show, (TV spl.) Harlequin, 1975 (Emmy award), summer theaters, festivals, U.S. and abroad, 1957—; co-author: (autobiography) Prodigal Son, 1991. Mem. Nat. Coun. of Arts, 1968-74; chmn. Commn. for Cultural Affairs City N.Y., 1978; bd. visitors N.C. Sch. for the Arts; mem. dance adv. panel Nat. Endowment for Arts; trustee Wolf Trap Found. for the Arts. Recipient Dance Mag. award, 1964, Lions of the Performing Arts award N.Y. Pub. Libr., 1987, Capezio Dance award, 1989, Gold medal Nat. Soc. Arts and Letters, 1990, William G. Anderson merit award AAHPERD, 1991; named Miamian of Yr., UNICO Nat., 1993.

VILLENEUVE, DONALD AVILA, biology educator; b. Ventura, Calif., Oct. 25, 1930; s. Victor Fredrick V.; and Florence Ann (Pelletier) Goodin; m. Marylyn Yvonne Peoples, Jan. 7, 1950; children: Debra Lynn, Theresa Dianne, Karen Elaine, Kathryn Anne. BS, U. Idaho, 1958; MS, Univ. of Pacific, 1960; MA, U. Colo., 1967; PhD, UCLA, 1976. Cert. tchr., Calif., cert. community coll. tchr., adminstr. Biology tchr. Glendora (Calif.) High Sch., 1960-61; prof. biology and environ. sci. Ventura Coll., 1961-76; dir. div. math. and sci. Moorpark (Calif.) Coll., 1976-78; asst. prof. biol. sci. Calif. Poly. U., San Luis Obispo, Calif., 1978; prof. biology and environ. sci. Ventura Coll., 1978-92 (ret.); pres. acad. senate Ventura Coll., 1985-87; bd. dirs. Calif. Acad. Partnership Program, Long Beach, 1985-88; curriculum cons. Calif. State Dept. Edn., Sacramento, 1986-87; mem. sci. tchr. preparatory panel Calif. Comm. on Tchr. Credentialing, Sacramento, 1988-93. Mem. City Coun. City of San Buenaventura, Ventura, 1987-91; mem. Calif. Coastal Commn., Santa Barbara, 1977-81; mem. planning commn. City of San Buenaventura, 1975-77, parks and recreation commn., 1974-75; v.p. Ventura County Symphony Assn., 1969-71; bd. dirs. Beach Erosion Authority, 1987-91, League for Coastal Protection, 1985—, League Calif. Cities, 1987-91; mem. Ventura County Ctr. Planned Parenthood Adv. Coun., 1991-94; treas. Cambria Dem. Club; mem. San Luis Obispo County Dem. Ctrl. Com.; v.p. Cambria Friends of the Ranchland; mem. North Coast Adv. com., land use subcom. Sgt. U.S. Army, 1950-53. NIMH grantee, 1971-72. Mem. Faculty Assn. Calif. Community Colls., Calif. Fedn. Tchrs. (bd. dirs. 1985-87). Avocations: fishing, camping, hiking, boating. Home: 394 Orlando Dr Cambria CA 93428-4406

VILLENEUVE, JEAN-PIERRE, science association director, educator; b. Roberval, Que., Can., May 19, 1938; s. Pascal and Simone (Duval) V.; m. Céline Laroche, Feb. 9, 1962 (div.); children: Isabelle, Elise; m. Christiane Marcoux, Oct. 9, 1979. BScA in Civil Engring., U. Laval, Que., 1963; DES in Hydrodynamics, U. Toulouse, France, 1964, PhD in Hydraulics, 1966. Project engr. Natural Resources Can., Que., 1967; jr. lectr. U. Sherbrooke, Can., 1968-69, U. Que. è Chicoutimi, 1969-70; prof. U. Laval, 1966-70; prof. INRS-Eau, Ste. Foy, Que., 1970—, dir., 1990; pres. bd. dirs. Revue des Scis. de l'Eau, Que. and France, 1995, sci. dir., 1988-94. Contbr. numerous articles to profl. publs. Recipient prize for sci. excellence SNC Lavallin-AQTE, 1994. Mem. Am. Geophys. Union (mem. network design com. 1976-87), Club Tennis Montcalm (pres. 1984—). Achievements include development of software in field. Office: INRS-Eau, 2800 rue Einstein Ste 020, Quebec, PQ Canada G1X 4N8

VILLERS, PHILIPPE, mechanical engineer; b. Paris, June 20, 1935; came to U.S., 1940, naturalized, 1946; s. Raymond and Garda (Schmidt) V.; m. Annie Louise Young, July 13, 1957 (div. 1973); children: Jocelyn Anne (dec.), Renata Jane; m. Katherine Stephan, 1973; children: Noel Stephan, Carolyn Grace. AB in Applied Scis. cum laude, Harvard U., 1955; SM in Mech. Engring, Mass. Inst. Tech., 1960. Mem. mfg. tng. program Gen. Electric Co., 1955-58; project engr. Perkin-Elmer Corp., Wilton, Conn., 1959-62; project engr. Apollo Antenna pointings sensor Barnes Engring. Co., Stamford, Conn., 1962-65; project mgr. Advanced Products Center, Link Group, Gen. Precision, Inc., Binghamton, N.Y., 1965-67; mgr. advanced products Concord Control, Inc., Boston, 1967-69; co-founder, sr. v.p., dir. Computervision Corp., Bedford, Mass., 1969-80; founder, pres., dir. Automatix, Inc., Billerica, Mass., 1980-84; chmn. bd. Automatix Inc., Billerica, Mass., 1984-86; founder, pres., dir. Cognition Inc., 1985-88; bd. dirs. Xyvision, Inc., Wakefield, Mass., chair 1992-94; bd. dirs. Conflict Mgmt. Group, Cambridge, Mass., Energia Global, Wakefield, Lifesource Inc., Newport, R.I., Grainpro Inc., Boston. Patentee process welding aluminum liners to steel surfaces, horizon sensor for visible wavelength, infrared roughness testing instrument, improved thermopile constrn. thermal die marker; pioneer design and feasibility solar sail applications for interplanetary probe propulsion and stblzn. Mem. Dem. Town Com., Wilton, Conn., 1963, Concord, Mass., 1978—, chmn., 1984-96; mem. Harvard Com. on Univ. Resources, 1981-92; mem. various vis. coms. MIT, 1981-91; mem. vis. com. Nat. Bur. Standards, 1981-84; trustee U. Lowell, 1985-91; founder, pres. Families U.S.A. Founds. (formerly Villers Found.), Washington, 1981—, Bay State Retiree Vol. Coun., Concord, 1989-92; del. Dem. Nat. Conv., 1988, 92. NSF grad. fellow, 1959-60. Mem. IEEE, ASME, Amnesty Internat. (bd. dirs. 1990-96, ombudsman 1992-96, exec. com. 1994—), Soc. Mfg. Engrs., ACLU (pres. com. 1981—, bd. dirs. Physicians for Human Rights 1991-94), Unitarian-Universalist Assn. (pres. coun. 1982-86), Sigma Xi. Home: 20 Whits End Rd Concord MA 01742-5411 Office: 97 Lowell Rd Ste 11-4 Concord MA 01742-1700

VILLFORTH, JOHN CARL, health physicist; b. Reading, Pa., Dec. 28, 1930; s. Carl and Grace L. (Fichthorn) V.; m. Joanne E. Heine, Sept. 12, 1953; children: Mary Jane Smith, Elaine, Jennifer. B.S. in San. Engring., Pa. State U., 1952, M.S., 1954; M.S. in Physics, Vanderbilt U., 1958. Cert. Am. Bd. Health Physics. With USPHS, 1961-90; dir. Ctr. for Devices and Radiol. Health, 1969-90, asst. surgeon gen., 1972-90, chief engr., 1985-89; pres. Food and Drug Law Inst., Washington, 1990—. Served to capt. USAF, 1954-61. Recipient Meritorious Svc. medal USPHS, 1974, D.S.M., 1980, 84, Outstanding Svc. medal, 1986. Mem. Health Physics Soc. (pres. 1976-77, Elda Anderson award 1970), Am. Soc. Quality Control, AAAS, Internat. Radiation Protection Assn., Regulatory Affairs Profl. Soc., Commd. Officers Assn. Office: 1000 Vermont Ave NW Washington DC 20005-4903 *Understand the problem! Too much energy is wasted and too many relationships arestrained because we fail to understand the underlying problem before we embark on a solution.*

VILLINSKI, PAUL STEPHEN, artist; b. York, Maine, May 28, 1960; s. Paul Bernard and Jacqueline L. (Whalen) V. Student, Mass. Coll. Art, 1980-82; BFA, Cooper Union, 1984. adj. lectr. art history LaGuardia C.C., CUNY, L.I. City, 1990-93. Solo exhbns. include St. Peter's Ch. at Citicorp Ctr., N.Y.C., 1987, Midtown Payson Galleries, N.Y.C., 1989, Queens Mus. Art at Bulova Corp. Ctr., Jackson Heights, N.Y., 1990; group shows include Ridge St. Gallery, N.Y.C., 1986-87, Queens Mus. Art, Flushing, N.Y., 1987, Studio K Gallery, L.I., N.Y., 1987, 88, Midtown Payson Galleries, 1988, 89, The Barn Gallery, Ogunquit, Maine, 1990, PS Gallery Ogunquit, 1991, 92, DMB&B, N.Y.C., 1991, Cooper Union, N.Y.C., 1992, Nat. Acad. Design, N.Y.C., 1992, Paine Webber Art Gallery, N.Y.C., 1992, Fuel Gallery, Seattle, 1992, Herron Test-Site, Bklyn., 1992, Jamaica (N.Y.) Arts Ctr., 1992, 80 Washington Square Galleries, N.Y.C., NYU, 1993, Bklyn. Union Gas Co. Cmty. Galleries, 1993, PDG Gallery, 1993, Flushing Coun. on Culture and Arts Town Hall, 1994, Ronald Feldman Gallery, N.Y.C., 1995, The Cooper Union, N.Y.C., 1996; represented in permanent collections. Resident Millay Colony for Arts, Austerlitz, N.Y., 1987; grantee Nat. Endowment Arts, 1987; Agnes Bourne fellow in painting Djerassi Found., Woodside, Calif., 1988, fellow Montalvo Ctr. for the Arts, Saratoga, Calif., 1991, fellow Ucross Found., 1992. Home: 9-01 44th Dr Long Island City NY 11101-7012

VILLOCH, KELLY CARNEY, art director; b. Kyoto, Japan, July 22, 1950; d. William Riley and stepdaughter Hazel Fowler Carney; m. Joe D. Villoch, Aug. 9, 1969; children: Jonathan Christopher, Jennifer. A in Fine Arts, Dade C.C., Miami, Fla., 1971; student, Metro Fine Arts, 1973-74, Fla. Internat. U., 1985-88. Design asst. Lanvin, Miami, 1971—, Fieldcrest, Miami, 1974-77; art dir. Advercolor, Miami, 1977-78; art dir. copywriter ABC, Miami, 1978-89; writer Armed Forces Radio & TV Network; multimedia dir. ADVITEC, 1989-91; art dir. writer Miami Write, 1979—; owner Beach Point Prodns., 1992—; lectr. Miami Dade C.C., cons. Studio Masters, North Miami, 1979-89. Prin. works include mixed media, 1974 (Best of Show 1974), pen and ink drawing, 1988 (Best Poster 1988); writer, dir., editor, prodr. (video film): Bif, 1988, Drink + Drive = Die, 1994; writer, dir., prodr. (pub. svc. announcement) Reading is the Real Adventure, 1990; film editor Talent Times Mag.; author: Winds of Freedom, 1994; art dir., exec. com. Miami Hispanic Media Conf., 1992, 93, 94; editor-in-chief, film editor: In Grove Miami Mag., 1994-96; webmaster, web content provider, website design cons., writer, graphic artist Guru Comms., 1996. State of Fla.

grantee LimeLite Studios, Inc., 1990, William Douglas Pawley Found. grantee, Frances Wolfson scholar, Cultural Consortium grantee, 1993. Mem. Am. Film Inst., Phi Beta Kappa. Avocations: pen and ink drawing, printmaking, skin diving, boating, painting.

VILTER, RICHARD WILLIAM, physician, educator; b. Cin., Mar. 21, 1911; s. William Frederick and Clara (Bieler) V.; m. Sue Potter, Aug. 17, 1935; 1 son, Richard William. A.B., Harvard U., 1933, M.D., 1937. Diplomate: Am. Bd. Internal Medicine. Intern, resident internal medicine Cin. Gen. Hosp., 1937-42, founding dir. divsn. hematology/oncology, 1945-56, asst. dir. dept. internal medicine, 1953-56, dir., 1956-78; assoc. prof. medicine U. Cin. Coll. Medicine, 1948-56, Gordon and Helen Hughes Taylor prof., 1956-78, prof. medicine on spl. assignment, 1978-81, prof. medicine emeritus, 1981—, asst. dean, 1945-51; cons. VA, 1947—; cons. hematology Good Samaritan Hosp., Cin.; cons. physician Christ, Drake hosps., Cin.; mem. sci adv. bd. Nat. Vitamin Found., 1953-56; spl. cons. nutrition and anemias in Egypt WHO, 1954; cons. Pan Am. Sanitary Bur. Anemias of Kashiorkor in Guatemala and Panama, 1955; mem. Am. Cancer Soc. Com. on Investigation and Therapy of Cancer, 1960-64, chmn. 1964; chmn. hematology sect. NIH, 1965-69, nat. adv. com. anemia malnutrition Rsch. Ctr. Chiengmai, Thailand, 1967-75. Assoc. editor Jour. Clin. Investigation, 1951-52; contbr. to profl. publs. Recipient Joseph Goldberger award AMA, 1960, Daniel Drake medal U. Cin., 1985, Golden Apple award U. Cin., 1985, award for excelence U. Cin., 1990, Daniel Drake Humanitarian award Acad. Medicine, Cin., 1991, 1st recipient U. Cin. Coll. Medicine Lifetime Tchg. award, 1995. Master ACP (past gov. Ohio bd. regents, sec. gen. 1973-78, pres.-elect 1978-79, pres. 1979-80, pres. emeritus 1984); mem. Federated Coun. for Internal Medicine (chmn. 1979-80), Clin. and Climatol. Assn. (v.p. 1982-83), Assn. Am. Physicians, Am. Soc. Clin. Nutrition (pres. 1960-61), Am. Soc. Clin. Investigation, Ctrl. Soc. Clin. Rsch. (coun. mem. 1957-60), Am. Soc. Hematology, Am. Bd. Nutrition, Internat. Soc. Hematology, Cin. Lit. Club (pres. 1990-91), Phi Beta Kappa, Alpha Omega Alpha, Nu Sigma Nu. Home: 5 Annwood Ln Cincinnati OH 45206-1419 Office: U Cin Med Center Cincinnati OH 45267-0562

VINAY, PATRICK, academic dean. Dean Faculty Medicine Univ. Montreal, Quebec, Can. Office: Univ Montreal, PO Box 6128 Sta A, Montreal, PQ Canada H3C 3J7

VINCE, CLINTON ANDREW, lawyer; b. Bklyn., May 31, 1949; s. Tibor Andrew and Priscilla (Ward) V.; m. Pamela Anne McHale, May 17, 1980; children: Matthew McHale, Jennifer Anne. AB, Trinity Coll., 1971; JD, Georgetown U., 1974. Bar: N.Y. 1975, U.S. Dist. Ct. (so. and ea. dists.) N.Y. 1975, U.S. Ct. Appeals (2nd cir.) 1975, D.C. 1976, U.S. Dist. Ct. D.C. 1976, U.S. Ct. Appeals (D.C. and 8th cirs.) 1976, U.S. Supreme Ct. 1979, U.S. Ct. Appeals (4th and 11th cirs.) 1984, U.S. Ct. Appeals (5th cir.) 1985, U.S. Ct. Appeals (10th cir.) 1988. Ptnr. Verner, Liipfert, Bernhard, McPherson & Hand, Washington, 1984—, also bd. dirs., exec. com.; chief energy cons. City of New Orleans, 1983—; gen. counsel Southeastern Power Resources Com., Tucker, Ga., 1986—. Contbr. articles to profl. jours. Bd. dirs. The McLean Sch. Md., Inc., Fed. City Coun., Keystone Energy Trustees; treas. The Writers Ctr., One Voice. Mem. ABA, ATLA, Fed. Energy Bar Assn. (chmn. bd. dirs., chair Fed. Energy Law Jour. Found.), D.C. Bar Assn., Econ. Club Washington, City Tavern Club. Avocations: sailing, skiing, tennis, literature, writing. Office: Verner Liipfert Bernhard McPherson & Hand 901 15th St NW Washington DC 20005-2327

VINCENT, CHARLES EAGAR, JR., sports columnist; b. Beaumont, Tex., Mar. 24, 1940; s. Charles Eagar and Hazel Ruth (Balston) V.; m. Mary Jacquelyn Bertman, Aug. 8, 1959 (div. Jan. 1969); children: Lisa Marie, Dixie Ann, Charles Joseph, John Patrick; m. Patricia Helene Skinner, Mar. 28, 1970 (div. Apr. 1985); 1 child, Susanna Lee; m. Karen Judith Peterson, Aug. 17, 1985. Student, Victoria Coll., 1958-59. Reporter Victoria (Tex.) Mirror, 1958-59, Taylor (Tex.) Daily Press, 1959-60; sports writer Beaumont (Tex.) Jour., 1960-62; sports editor Galveston (Tex.) Tribune, 1962-63; sports writer San Antonio Express-News, 1963-69, Sandusky (Ohio) Register, 1969-70; sports writer Detroit Free Press, 1970-85, sports columnist, 1985—. Author: Welcome to My World, 1994. Recipient 4th Pl. award Nat. AP Sports Editors, 1981, 5th Pl., 1989, 92, Sister Mary Leila Meml. award, 1991, Mich. Columnist of Yr. award, 1991; Afro-Am. Night honoree, 1991. Mem. Baseball Writers Assn. Am. Avocations: traveling, cooking, genealogy. Office: Detroit Free Press 321 W Lafayette Blvd Detroit MI 48226-2705

VINCENT, DAVID RIDGELY, management consulting executive; b. Detroit, Aug. 9, 1941; s. Charles Ridgely and Charlotte Jane (McCarroll) V.; m. Margaret Helen Anderson, Aug. 25, 1962 (div. 1973); children: Sandra Lee, Cheryl Ann; m. Judith Ann Gomez, July 2, 1978; 1 child, Amber; stepchildren: Michael Jr., Jesse Joseph Flores. BS, BA, Calif. State U.-Sacramento, 1964; MBA, Calif. State U.-Hayward, 1971; PhD Somerset U, 1991. Cert. Mgmt. Cons. 1994. Sr. ops. analyst Aerojet Gen. Corp., Sacramento, 1960-66; contr. Hexcel Corp., Dublin, Calif., 1966-70; mng. dir. Memorex, Austria, 1970-74; sales mgr. Ampex World Ops., Switzerland, 1974-76; dir. product mgmt. NCR, Sunnyvale, Calif., 1976-79; v.p. Boole & Babbage Inc., gen. mgr. Inst. Info. Mgmt., Sunnyvale, Calif., 1979-85; pres. The Info. Group, Inc., Santa Clara, Calif., 1985—. Deacon Union Ch., Cupertino, Calif.; USSF soccer referee. Author: Perspectives in Information Management, Information Economics, 1983, Handbook of Information Resource Management, 1987, The Information-Based Corporation: stakeholder economics and the technology investment, 1990, Reengineering Fundamentals: Business Processes and the Global Economy, 1994; contbr. monographs and papers to profl. jours. Home: 2803 Kalliam Dr Santa Clara CA 95051-6838 Office: PO Box Q Santa Clara CA 95055-3756

VINCENT, EDWARD See BRACKEN, EDDIE

VINCENT, FREDERICK MICHAEL, neurologist, educational administrator; b. Detroit, Nov. 19, 1948; s. George S. and Alyce M. (Borkowski) V.; m. Patricia Lucille Cordes, Oct. 7, 1972; children: Frederick Michael, Joshua Peter, Melissa Anne. BS in Biology, Aquinas Coll., 1970; MD, Mich. State U., 1973. Diplomate Am. Bd. Psychiatry and Neurology, Am. Bd. Electrodiagnostic Medicine, Nat. Bd. Med. Examiners, Am. Bd. Forensic Examiners, Am. Bd. Forensic Medicine. Intern St. Luke's Hosp., Duluth, Minn., 1974-75; resident in neurology Dartmouth Med. Sch., Hanover, N.H., 1975-77, instr. dept. medicine, chief resident neurology, 1977-78; chief, neurology sect. Munson Med. Ctr., Traverse City, Mich., 1978-84; asst. clin. prof. medicine and pathology Mich. State U., East Lansing, 1978-84, chief sect. neurology Coll. Human Medicine, 1984-87; clin. prof. psychiatry and internal medicine Mich. State U., 1989—; clin. prof. medicine, 1990—; pvt. practice Neurology, Neuro-oncology and Electrodiagnostic Medicine, Lansing, Mich., 1987—; clin. and research fellow neuro-oncology Mass. Gen. Hosp., Boston, 1985; clin. Fellow in neurology Harvard Med. Sch., Boston, 1985; cons. med. asst. program Northwestern Mich. Coll., Traverse City, 1983-84; neurology cons. radio call-in show Sta. WKAR, East Lansing, 1984—, Sta. WCMU TV, 1987, 1993—. Author: Neurology: Problems in Primary Care, 1987, 2d edit., 1993; contbr. articles to profl. jours. Fellow NSF, 1969, Nat. Multiple Sclerosis Soc., 1971. Fellow ACP, Am. Acad. Neurology (mem. program accreditation and devel. subcom. 1993—), Am. Assn. Electrodianostic Medicine (mem. computer and electronics com. 1995—); mem. Am. Coll. Legal Medicine, Am. Acad. Clin. Neurophysiology, Am. Heart Assn., Am. Soc. Clin. Oncology, Am. EEG Soc., Am. Fedn. Clin. Rsch., Am. Soc. Neurol. Investigation, Am. Sleep Disorders Assn., Am. Epilepsy Soc., Soc. for NeuroSci., N.Y. Acad. Scis., Am. Bd. of Forensic Examiners, Am. Soc. for Neuro-Rehab., Movement Disorders Soc., Univ. Club, Alpha Omega Alpha. Roman Catholic. Office: 1515 Lake Lansing Rd Ste C1 Lansing MI 48912-3703

VINCENT, HAL WELLMAN, marine corps officer, investor; b. Pontiac, Mich., Sept. 27, 1927; s. Harold and Glenda (Wellman) V.; m. Virginia Bayler, June 9, 1951; children: David B., Dale W., Deborah K. Vincent Minder. Student, Navy V-5 program Western Mich. Coll./Colgate U., 1945; BS, U.S. Naval Acad., 1950; postgrad., Marine Officers Basic Sch., 1950, Flight Sch., 1952, Test Pilot Sch., 1955, Navy Fleet Air Gunnery Sch., 1958, Air Force Fighter Weapons Sch., 1959, Marine Corps Command and Staff Coll., 1964, Indsl. Coll., 1969, Marine Air Weapons Tng. Unit, 1972. Cert. flight and instrument instr. Commd. 2d lt. U.S. Marine Corps, 1950, advanced through grades to maj. gen., 1974; rifle and machinegun platoon comdr. Camp Lejeune, N.C., 1951; fighter pilot El Toro, Calif. and, Korea, 1953-54; test pilot Flight Test Div., Patuxent River, Md., 1955-57; ops. officer, squadron asst. and fighter pilot El Toro, 1958-59; conventional weapons project test pilot Naval Air Weapons Test Ctr., China Lake, Calif., 1960-62; squadron ops. and exec. officer El Toro and Japan, 1962-64; aviation specialist Marine Corps amphibious warfare presentation team and staff officer Quantico, Va., 1965-66; comdg. officer 2d Marine Aircraft Wing fighter-attack squadron, Beaufort, S.C., 1967-68; exec. officer Marine Aircraft Group, Vietnam, 1969; logistics staff officer Fleet Marine Force Pacific, Hawaii, 1970-72; comdg. officer Marine Aircraft Group, Yuma, Ariz., 1972-73; chief of staff 3d Marine Aircraft Wing, El Toro, 1973-76; dep. chief. of staff plans and policy to Comdr. in Chief Atlantic, Norfolk, Va., 1976-78; comdg. gen. 2d Marine Aircraft Wing, Cherry Point, N.C., 1978-80; dep. comdg. gen. Fleet Marine Force Atlantic, Norfolk, 1980-81; ret., 1981, pvt. investor, 1981—; flight test pilot; preliminary pilot, evaluator new mil. aircraft. Contbr. numerous articles on tactics and conventional weapons delivery, flight test stability and control to various mil. publs. Decorated Legion of Merit with 2 gold stars, D.F.C., Bronze Star with combat V, Air medal with star and numeral 14, Joint Svcs. Commendation medal U.S.; Honor medal 1st class; Cross of Gallantry with gold star (Republic of Vietnam). Mem. SAR, Soc. Exptl. Test Pilots, Marine Corps Assn., Early Pioneer Naval Aviators, Marine Corps Aviation Assn., Mach 2 Club, Marbella Country Club. Invented Triple Ejector Rack for delivery of conventional bombs, 1961; devel. fighter tactics in F8 and F4 aircraft, 1958-69; flew 165 models of fgn. and U.S. mil. aircraft; flew 8 models of fixed wing and helicopters on 242 combat missions; first Marine to fly MACH-2. *In all 36 years in the service I am convinced that war is bad, and little is accomplished in the long term by warfare. However when National policy dictates a war, then we must not limit what can be done. We must win! My thought then remains: "Winning isn't everything, it's the only thing!" When I must go to battle I want to be allowed to "fight to win."*

VINCENT, JAMES LOUIS, biotechnology company executive; b. Johnstown, Pa., Dec. 15, 1939; s. Robert Clyde and Marietta Lucille (Kennedy) V.; m. Elizabeth M. Matthews, Aug. 19, 1961; children: Aimee Archelle, Christopher James. BSME, Duke U., 1961; MBA in Indsl. Mgmt., U. Pa., 1963. Mgr. Far East div. Tex. Instruments, Inc., Tokyo, 1970-72; pres. Tex. Instrument Asia, Ltd., Tokyo, 1970-72; v.p. diagnostic ops., pres. diagnostics div. Abbott Labs., North Chgo., Ill., 1972-74, group v.p., bd. dirs., 1974-81, exec. v.p., COO, bd. dirs., 1979-81; corp. group v.p., pres. Allied Health and Sci. Products Co. Allied Corp., Morristown, N.J., 1982-85; CEO Biogen, Inc., 1985—; also bd. dirs. Bd. trustees Duke U.; bd. dirs. Found. for the Nat. Tech.; bd. overseers Wharton Grad. Bus. Sch. U. Pa. Recipient Young Exec. Achievement Young Execs. Club, Chgo., 1976, Disting. Alumni award Duke U., 1988. Mem. Biotech. Industry Orgn. (bd. dirs.), Econ. Club Chgo., Shoreacres Country Club, Algonquin Club, Boston Club, Chgo. Club, The Links (N.Y.C.). Republican. Presbyterian. Office: Biogen Inc 14 Cambridge Ctr Cambridge MA 02142-1401

VINCENT, JEFFREY ROBERT, labor studies educator; b. Regensberg, Germany, Mar. 18, 1956; came to U.S., 1956; s. John J. and Norma J. (Trindle) V.; m. Patti Ann E. Knoff, Aug. 18, 1978; children: Natalie and Nicole (twins). BS in Ednl. Studies, U. Wis., Milw., 1978, MS in Indsl. Rels., 1984. Rsch. dir. Ind. U., Bloomington, 1985—; tchr., unions and labor mgmt. coms., Colo., Fla., Ill., Ind., Mich., Ohio and Tenn. Contbr. articles to profl. jours. Bd. dirs. Unitarian Universalist Ch. of Bloomington, Ind. Mem. AFL-CIO, Workers Edn. Local 189, Univ. and Coll. Labor Edn. Assn., Indsl. Rels. Rsch. Assn. Home: 3261 E Carowind Ct Bloomington IN 47401-9589 Office: Ind Univ Divsn Labor Studies Poplars 628 Bloomington IN 47405

VINCENT, JON STEPHEN, foreign language educator; b. Denver, Feb. 28, 1938; s. Joseph William and Lillian (Diamond) V.; m. Maria Louise Girard, June 13, 1962; children—Sean David, Tanya Maria. B.A., U. N.Mex., 1961, Ph.D., 1970. Instr., U. N.Mex., Albuquerque, 1963-64; asst. prof. U. Kans., Lawrence, 1967-74, assoc. prof., 1974-79, prof., 1979—, assoc. chmn. dept. Spanish, 1974-78, chmn., 1978-82; vis. prof. U. Costa Rica, San Jose, 1972; co-dir. Latin Am. Studies, 1987-89, dir., 1989-92. Author: Joao Guimaraes Rosa, 1978; assoc. editor Hispania, 1984-90, Brasil/Brazil, 1989—; asst. editor Latin Am. Theatre Rev., 1969—; mem. rev. staff World Lit. Today, 1983—. Served with U.S. Army, 1953-56. Mem. MLA (chmn. Luso-Brazilian div. 1982), Am. Assn. Tchrs. Spanish and Portuguese, Latin Am. Studies Assn., Fulbright Am. Republics, Kans. Fgn. Lang. Assn., Am. Republics Adv. Com. Democrat. Avocations: Fishing; hunting. Home: 1104 Centennial Dr Lawrence KS 66049-2700 Office: U Kans Dept Spanish And Portuguese Lawrence KS 66045

VINCENT, NORMAN FULLER, broadcasting executive; b. Boston, Oct. 5, 1930; s. Norman Harrison and Marian Bernice (Fuller) V.; m. Karen Ann Walter, June 21, 1969. B.A., Denison U., 1953. Sales mgr. Sta. WMBR, Jacksonville, Fla., 1956-62; gen. mgr. Sta. WZOK, Jacksonville, 1962-66; owner, pres. Norm Vincent Sound Recording Studios, Inc., Jacksonville, 1966-75; dir. radio ops. Sta. WJCT, Jacksonville, 1975-91; announcer, narrator radio, TV film and video, talking books, 1991—. Producer, host (radio): Swing Time with Norm Vincent, 1992—. Served with USN, 1953-56; to comdr. USNR, 1958-80. Mem. Navy League, Advt. Fedn. Am., Jacksonville C. of C. (armed services com.), Exchange Club. Republican. Episcopalian. Home: 2110 The Woods Dr Jacksonville FL 32246-1016

VINCENT, NORMAN L., retired insurance company executive; b. Milw., July 21, 1933; s. Victor V. Vincent and Hilda I. (Boedecker) Vincent Patlow; m. Arlene Page, Jan. 31, 1953 (div. 1978); children: J. Todd, Meg; m. Donna Jean Doll, Aug. 8, 1980. B.S., U. Wis., 1957; M.S., Purdue U., 1958, Ph.D., 1960. Diplomate Am. Bd. Profl. Psychology; registered psychologist., Ill., C.P.C.U., C.L.U. Supr. agy. research State Farm Ins. Cos., Bloomington, Ill., 1960-63, dir. agy. research., 1963-66, asst. v.p. agy., 1966-69, asst. v.p. exec., 1969-70, v.p. data processing, 1970-94; systems v.p., 1994-95. Pres. Bloomington Bd. Edn., 1974-77; bd. dirs. YMCA, Bloomington, 1971-85. Served with M.I. U.S. Army, 1953-55. Mem. AAAS. Home: W332 N 5861 Meadowlark Ct Nashotah WI 53058

VINCENT, THOMAS JAMES, retired manufacturing company executive; b. Balt., Mar. 17, 1934; s. Thomas Alonzo and Helen Geraldine (Cloman) V.; divorced; children: Wayne S., Robin K. MS, MIT, 1968. Div. gen. mgr. Fairchild Industries, St. Augustine, Fla., 1969-72; pres. T.J. Vincent Properties Ltd., St. Augustine, 1972-75, Pacific Concrete & Rock Co., Honolulu, 1975-77, Ramsey Engring. Co., St. Paul, 1977-80, Kobe Inc., Los Angeles, 1980-84, Milchem Inc., Houston, 1984-85; pres. York (Pa.) Internat. Corp., 1985-88, also bd. dirs., cons.; chmn., CEO Hawaii Seafood Growers, Inc., Kahuku, 1990-92. Author: Fairplan, 1962. Founder, pres. Thomas J. Vincent Found. Inc., Casselberry, Fla., 1990—; founder, v.p., treas. Winter Park (Fla.) Family Health Ctr., Inc., 1995—. Named one of Outstanding Young Men in Am., Jaycees, 1965; Alfred P. Sloan fellow MIT, 1967; recipient Research for Progress Achievement award, 1972. Avocations: deep sea fishing, orchid growing. Home and Office: 225 Overbrook Dr Casselberry FL 32707-4343

VINCENTI, WALTER GUIDO, aeronautical engineer, emeritus educator; b. Balt., Apr. 20, 1917; s. Guido A. and Agnes (Nicolini) V.; m. Joyce H. Weaver, Sept. 6, 1947; children—Margaret Anna, Marc Guido. A.B., Stanford U., 1938, Aero. Engr., 1940. Aero. research scientist NACA, 1940-57; prof. aero. and astronautics and history of tech. Stanford U., 1957-83, prof. emeritus, 1983—; cons to industry, 1957—; mem. adv. panel engring. sec. NSF, 1960-63. Author: (with Charles H. Kruger, Jr.) Introduction to Physical Gas Dynamics, 1965, (with Nathan Rosenberg) The Britannia Bridge, 1978, What Engineers Know and How They Know It, 1990; also papers.; co-editor (with Milton Van Dyke) Annual Review of Fluid Mechanics, 1970-76. Served with USN, 1945-46. Recipient Gold medal Pi Tau Sigma, 1948; Rockefeller Pub. Service award, 1956; Guggenheim fellow, 1963. Fellow AIAA; mem. Internat. Acad. Astronautics (corr.), History of Sci. Soc., Soc. History Tech. (Usher prize 1984), Nat. Acad. Engring., Newcomen Soc., Phi Beta Kappa, Sigma Xi, Tau Beta Pi. Home: 13200 E Sunset Dr Los Altos CA 94022-3427 Office: Stanford U Stanford CA 94305

VINCENTI-BROWN, CRISPIN RUFUS WILLIAM, engineering executive; b. Epsom, Surrey, England, Sept. 20, 1951; came to U.S., 1989; s. Douglas Hector and Joan Margaret Patricia (Lowe) Brown; m. Terry Doreen Bennett, May 20, 1978 (dec. Oct. 1992); children: Genevieve Louise, Juliette Alexandra; m. Margaret Anna Vincenti, Feb. 13, 1993. BSc in Engring. Prodn., U. Birmingham, 1974. Mgr. Soc. M.O.M, Grans, France, 1975; prin. cons. Ingersoll Engrs. Inc., Rugby, England, 1975-79; pres., dir. Ingersoll Engrs. SA, Annecy, France, 1979-89; sr. ptnr. Ingersoll Engrs. Inc., Los Altos, Calif., 1989—; v.p. Groupe de Tailores, Geneva, 1987-89; bd. dirs. Ops. Mgmt. Assn., Waco, Tex. Fellow Inst. Elec. Engrs. (chartered engr.). Avocation: fixed wing and helicopter pilot. Home: 1098 Eastwood Ct Los Altos CA 94024-5015 Office: Ingersoll Engrs 5100 E State St Ste 4 Rockford IL 61108-2398

VINCI, JOHN NICHOLAS, architect, educator; b. Chgo., Feb. 6, 1937; s. Nicholas and Nicolina (Camiola) V. B.Arch., Ill. Inst. Tech., 1960. Registered architect, Ill., Mich. Draftsman Skidmore, Owings, Merrill, Chgo., 1960-61; with City of Chgo., 1961; stencil restorer Crombie Taylor, Chgo., 1961-62; designer Brenner, Danforth, Rockwell, Chgo., 1962-68; architect Vinci, Inc., Chgo., 1977-95; ptnr. Vinci/Hamp, Architects, Inc., Chgo., 1995—; lectr. Roosevelt U., Chgo., 1969-72, Ill. Inst. Tech., Chgo., 1972-90. Author: (booklet) Trading Room-Art Inst. Chgo., 1977; contbr. articles to profl. jours. Bd. dirs. Music of Baroque, Chgo., 1976-87, Campbell Ctr. Found.; mem. adv. com. Commn. on Chgo. Archtl. and Hist. Landmarks, 1971-83; exec. sec. Richard Nickel Com, Chgo., 1972—; chmn. Howard Van Doren Shaw Soc., 1994—; vice chmn. Van Allen Found., Clinton, Iowa, 1993—; internat. arts adv. coun. Wexner Ctr. for the Arts, 1994—. Fellow AIA; mem. Soc. Archtl. Historians, Frank Lloyd Wright Home and Studio Found., Art Inst. Chgo., The Corp. of YADDO, Chgo. Hist. Soc., Arts Club of Chgo. Roman Catholic. Home: 3152 N Cambridge Ave Chicago IL 60657-4613 Office: Vinci/Hamp Architects Inc 1147 W Ohio St Chicago IL 60622-5874

VINCIGUERRA, SALVATORE JOSEPH, scientific instrument company executive; b. Methuen, Mass., Jan. 21, 1938; s. Joseph Frederick and Erminia (Bonnacorsi) V.; m. Grace Stevens, Apr. 20, 1963; children: Elizabeth, Catherine, Joseph, Suzanne. BSE, Princeton U., 1959; MBA, Harvard U., 1968. Systems analyst GE, Phoenix, 1962-63; cons. Arthur D. Little, Inc., Cambridge, Mass., 1964-66; with Instron Corp., 1968—; contr. Canton, Mass., 1968-71; treas. Canton, 1971-76; gen. mgr. Asia/Pacific Ops. Toyko, 1976-81; v.p., gen. mgr. Western Hemisphere Ops. Canton, 1981-85, pres., 1985—; pres. Serro Fluidics, Inc., Nashua, N.H., 1995—; dir. Lytron Inc., Woburn, Mass. Dir. Japan Soc. Boston, 1986—; corp. mem. Children's Mus. Boston, 1984—. Mem. High Tech. Council, Internat. Bus. Ctr. Clubs: Harvard (Boston); Harvard of Japan (Toyko) (treas. 1978-81). Office: Serro Fluidics 40 Simon St Nashua NH 03061*

VINCIGUERRA, THOMAS MICHAEL, chemical engineer; b. Beaver Falls, Pa., Apr. 22, 1953; s. Stephen H. and Gloria I. (Casiato) V.; m. Joan Knueven, Sept. 13, 1980; children: Lisa, Janna. BSChemE summa cum laude, U. Cin., 1976. Project engr. Merrell Nat. Labs., Cin., 1976-78, asst. dir. prodn., 1978-80; prodn. mgr. Merrell Dow Pharms., Inc., Cin., 1980-84, environ. engr., 1984-89; supr. environ. svcs. Marion Merrell Dow, Inc., Cin., 1989-91, mgr. environ. svcs. and indsl. hygiene, 1991-92, mgr. dry products mfg., 1992—; mem. Reading Schs. and Merrell Ptnrship. in Edn. Daycare Com., Cin., 1988-91; mem. steering com., 1991-93, head steering com., 1993—. Counselor Jr. Achievement, Cin., 1988; coach Youth Soccer, Cin., 1988—; mem. Hamilton County (Ohio) Emergency Planning Com., 1989-92. Recipient special recognition New Richmond (Ohio) High Sch., 1990. Mem. Am. Inst. Chem. Engrs. Avocation: photography. Office: Marion Merrell Dow Inc 2110 E Galbraith Rd Cincinnati OH 45237-1625

VINEBURGH, JAMES HOLLANDER, banking executive; b. Hartford, Conn., July 17, 1943; s. Lawrence Harold and Dorothy Helen (Brandvein) V.; m. Nancy Cynthia Taylor; children: James Hollander Jr., Philip Lawrence Taylor. AB, Tufts U., 1966. CLU. From mgmt. trainee to sr. v.p. Conn. Gen. Life Ins. Co./CIGNA Corp., 1967-88; exec. v.p. Conn. Bank and Trust Co., N.A., Hartford, 1989-91; chmn., dir. Bank of New Eng. Trust Co., 1989-91; exec. v.p. Fleet Bank, N.A., Hartford, Conn., 1991-93; sr. v.p. The Pvt. Bank, Bank of Boston, 1994—. Class sec. The Hill Sch., Pottstown, Pa., 1986—; bd. dirs. Big Bros. Assn. Greater Boston, Boston Olympics Organizing Com.; trustee, pres. parent's com. Middlesex Sch., Concord, Mass., 19956; past chmn. bd. dirs. Child and Family Svcs., Hartford, 1983-93; past pres., bd. dirs. West Hartford Youth Baseball League, 1981-90; bd. dirs., exec. com. Riverfront Recapture, Hartford, 1986-94; adv. bd. WALKS Found., Simsbury, Conn., 1983-94; trustee Bushnell Meml. Hall, Hartford, 1992-94. Mem. Leadership Greater Hartford. Avocations: golf, politics, squash. Office: Bank of Boston 100 Federal St Boston MA 02110-1802

VINECOUR, ONEIDA AGNES, nurse; b. Port Arthur, Tex., Oct. 15, 1917; d. Ernest Eugene and Gertrude Mary (Wooldridge) Thorn; m. Seymour Vinecour, Jan. 14, 1943 (dec. 1976); children: Seymour Jacob, Rebecca Leah. Diploma, St. Mary's Hosp. Sch. Nursing, Port Arthur, 1939; postgrad., cert. Surg. Tech., Anesthesia, Cook County Hosp., 1939-40; postgrad. U. Chgo., 1939-40, Tex. Coll. Mines, 1943, U. Tex. Health Ctr. R.N., cert. occupational audiometric technician, occupl. spirometric technician. Operating room supr., instr. Schumpert Meml. Hosp., Shreveport, La., 1940-41; anesthetist St. Joseph Hosp., Albuquerque, 1941-42; operating room supr., instr. Lynn City Hosp. (Mass.), 1946-48; staff anesthetist St. Mary's Hosp., Port Arthur, Tex., 1951-53, in service dir., 1971-73; staff nurse Tyler County Hosp., Woodville, Tex., 1964-65; dept. head, supr. Park Pl. Hosp., Port Arthur, 1965-71; operating room supr. Mid-County Hosp., Nederland, Tex., 1973-81; staff nurse Baptist Meml. Hosp., Beaumont, Tex., 1973-81; part time staff Health Care Svcs., Port Arthur, 1983—; indsl. nurse Synpol Inc., 1984-86; staff nurse Texaco Chem. Plant, Port Arthur, 1986-92, Olsten Health Care Svcs., 1992—. Served as officer U.S. Army Nurse Corps, 1942-46. Mem. Am. Nurses Assn., Mass. Nurses Assn., Tex. State Nurses Assn., Assn. Occupational Health Nurses. Republican. Methodist. Home: 2502 Glenwood Dr Port Arthur TX 77642-2639

VINES, CHARLES JERRY, minister; b. Carroll County, Ga., Sept. 22, 1937; s. Charles Clarence and Ruby Johnson V.; m. Janet Denney, Dec. 17, 1960; children: Joy Vines Williams, Jim, Jodi, Jon. BA, Mercer U., 1959; BD, New Orleans Bapt. Sem., 1966; ThD, Luther Rice Sem., Jacksonville, Fla., 1974; DD (hon.), Criswell Coll., 1991, Liberty U., 1991. Pastor West Rome Bapt. Ch., Rome, Ga., 1968-74, 79-81, Dauphin Way Bapt. Ch., Moblie, Ala., 1974-79, 1st Bapt. ch., Jacksonville, Fla., 1981—. Author: Practical Guide to Sermon Preparation, An Effective Guide to Sermon Delivery, Great Events in the Life of Christ, I Shall Return - Jesus, Family Fellowship, Great Interviews of Jesus, God Speaks Today, Exploring the Epistles of John, Exploring Daniel, Exploring Mark, Wanted: Soul Winners, Wanted: Church Growers, Basic Sermons on the Ten Commandments. Pres. So. Bapt. Conv., 1988-89. Office: First Bapt Ch 124 W Ashley St Jacksonville FL 32202-3104

VINET, LUC, physicist; b. Montreal, Apr. 16, 1953; s. Jean and Françoise (Ouellette) V.; m. Letitia Muresan, May 19, 1989; children: Jean-François, Laurent. BSc, U. Montreal, 1973, MSc, 1974, PhD, 1980; D. U. P.& M. Curie, Paris, 1979. Rsch. assoc. MIT, Cambridge, 1980-82; rsch. fellow, asst. prof., assoc. prof. U. Montreal, Can., 1982-92; prof. physics U. Montreal, 1992—; invited prof. U. Cath. de Louvain, 1980-81; vis. scholar MIT, Cambridge, 1987; vis. prof. UCLA, 1989-90; dir. Ctr. Rsch. Math., Montreal, 1993—. Editor: Particle Physics and Quantum Field Theory, 1995, Symmetry and Integrability of Difference and Equations, 1995, Quantum Groups Integrable Models and Statistical Systems, 1993, Group Theoretical Methods in Physics, 1989. Grantee FCAR, 1984—, NSERC, 1982—, rsch. fellow, 1982-92. Mem. APS, AMS, SIAM, CAP, CMS. Achievements include contributions in theoretical physics and mathematics - symmetry studies of difference equations; algebraic interpretation of q-special functions using quantum groups; applications of Berry potentials in the nuclear collective model; identification of Lie superalgebras as dynamical algebras in quantum mechanics; development of dimensional reduction in Yang Mills theories.

VINH, BINH, architect; b. Hue, Vietnam, Oct. 23, 1945; came to U.S., 1975; s. Tri and Chinh H. (Nguyen) Buu; m. Hang T. Nguyen, Jan. 22, 1975; 1 child, Michael. MArch and Urban Planning, U. Saigon, 1973; MArch, U.

Pa., 1977; postgrad., Harvard U., 1991. Registered arch., Pa., N.J., N.C., S.C., Ala., Tenn., N.Y., Ark., Md., Tex., Ariz., Fla. Prin. BV Architects, Saigon, 1974-75; designer Berger Assocs., Harrisburg, Pa., 1975-77; project architect, designer Kling Partnership, Phila., 1977-89; ptnr., design prin. Kling Lindquist Partnership, Phila., 1989—; assoc. prof. Thu Duc (Vietnam) Poly. Inst., 1974-75; vis. critic U. Pa.; speaker and presenter in field. Prin. works include Ethyl Corp. Hdqs., Richmond, Va., Chester County Libr., Exton, Pa., C.C. Phila. (First Place Silver medal AIA Phila. chpt. 1982), Radnor/Plymouth Meeting (Pa.) Exec. Campus, SOHIO Corp. Rsch. Ctr., Cleve., Prudential Ins. Co., Roseland, N.J., Greyhound Terminal, Phila., E.I. du Pont de Nemours & Co., Inc. Life Scis. Complex, Wilmington, Del., Boehringer Ingelheim, Ltd., Danbury and Ridgefield, Conn., NIH Bldg 29B, Bethesda, Md., Kennametal, Inc. Corp. Tech. Ctr., Latrobe, Pa. (Best Bld. in Westmorland County, Latrobe C. of C.), Ethyl Corp. Hdqs., Richmond, Va., Am. Cyanamid Co. Greenhouse Support Facility, Princeton, N.J., Ciba-Geigy Corp. Prodn. Facility, Suffern, N.Y., FAA Continuous Airworthiness Rsch. Facility, Jet Propulsion Testing and Fuels Rsch. Lab., Atlantic City (N.J.) Internat. Airport, Nat. Cancer Inst. Monoclonal Antibodies and Recombinant Protein Facility, Frederick, Md., Allied-Signal Corp. Charles W. Nichols, Jr. Tech. Ctr., Morristown, N.J. (Lab of Yr.'s High Honors award Rsch. and Devel. Mag.), Glaxo Inc. Rsch. and Devel. Facilities, Rsch. Triangle Park, N.C. (Triangle Devel. award 1992, Design Excellence award Archtl. Precast Assn. 1993, Best Mixed Use Project award Precast/ Prestressed Concrete Inst. 1993), Miles, Inc. Pharm. Rsch. and Devel. Hdqs., West Haven, Conn., Glaxo Group Rsch. Ltd. Rsch. and Devel. Hdqs., Stevenage, Hertfordshire, Eng., Glaxo Wellcome Medicine Rsch. Ctr., FDA office Regulatory Affairs, Jefferson, Ark., Rohm & Haas Polymer & Resin Rsch. Facility, Spring House, Pa., Pfizer Hdqs. Health Group, West Chester, Pa., Wyeth Ayerst Pham. Sci. Bldg., Pearl River, N.Y.; contbr. articles to, works featured in numerous profl. and popular jours. Bd. dirs. Harrisburg chpt. ARC; active Phila. Fellowship Commn. Mem. AIA (regional liaison Pa., coms. on design, environ. and internat. practice), Precast/Prestressed Concrete Inst., Union Internat. Archs., Fedn. Pan Am. Assn. Archs., L'Ordre Archs. D'Ile de France, Pa. Soc. Archs., Phila. Solar Energy Assn., Phila. Philos. Consortium. Avocations: tennis, golf, music, travel, painting. Office: Kling-Lindquist Partnership 2301 Chestnut St Philadelphia PA 19103-3035

VINH, NGUYEN XUAN, aerospace engineering educator; b. Yen Bay, Vietnam, Jan. 3, 1930; came to U.S., 1962; s. Nguyen X. and Thao (Do) Nhien; m. Joan Cung, Aug. 15, 1955; children: Alphonse, Phuong, Phoenix, John. PhD in Aerospace Engring., U. Colo., 1965. Asst. prof. aerospace engring. U. Colo., Boulder, 1965-68; assoc. prof. aerospace engring. U. Mich., Ann Arbor, 1968-72, prof. aerospace engring., 1972—; vis. lectr. U. Calif., Berkeley, 1967; vis. prof. ecol. nat. sup. aero., France, 1974; chair prof. Nat Tsing Hua U., Taiwan, 1982. Co-author: Hypersonic and Planetary Entry Flight Mechanics, 1980; author: Optimal Trajectories in Atmospheric Flight, 1981, Flight Mechanics of High Performance Aircraft, 1993. Chief of staff Vietnam Air Force, 1957-62. Recipient Mechanics and Control of Flight award AIAA, 1994. Mem. Internat. Acad. Astronautics, Nat. Acad. Air and Space (France). Research in ordinary differential equations; astrodynamics and optimization of space flight trajectories; theory of nonlinear oscillations. Office: U Mich Dept Aerospace Engring 3001 FXB Bldg Ann Arbor MI 48109-2118

VINIK, H(YMIE) RONALD, anesthesiologist, physician; b. Johannesburg, Transvaal, Republic of South Africa, Aug. 27, 1932; came to U.S., 1976, naturalized, 1986; s. Joseph and Fanny (Shain) V.; m. Sandra Lois Kirkel, Mar. 26, 1967; children—Dion, Grant, Russell. Nat. Sr. Cert., Regis Coll., Johannesburg, 1955; M.B., U. Witwatersrand, Johannesburg, 1961. Resident Coll. of Medicine, South Africa, 1972-75; prin. anesthesiologist Baragwanath Hosp., Johannesburg, South Africa, 1975-76; assoc. prof. anesthesiology U. Ala., Birmingham, 1977-89, prof., 1989—; dir. pain ctr. U. Ala., 1977—; dir. anesthesia svcs. Eye Found. Hosp., Birmingham, 1989—; mem. faculty Merck, Sharp & Dohme, Phila., 1982—. Mem. editorial bd. Ala. Jour. Med. Scis., Birmingham, 1985; contbr. articles on pain and anesthesia to profl. jours. Merit scholar U. Witwatersrand. Mem. AMA, Internat. Assn. for Study of Pain, Am. Soc. Anesthesiology (chmn. com. for pain therapy 1986). Avocations: golf; sailing. Home: 3128 Warrington Rd Birmingham AL 35223-2754 Office: U Ala 1920 7th Ave S Birmingham AL 35233-2006

VINING, GLEN W., JR., insurance company executive. With Farmers New World Life Ins., Mercer Island, Washington, 1961, now pres. Office: Farmers New World Life Ins 3003 77th Ave SE Mercer Island WA 98040-2837*

VINING, (GEORGE) JOSEPH, law educator; b. Fulton, Mo., Mar. 3, 1938; s. D. Rutledge and Margaret (McClanahan) V.; m. Alice Marshall Williams, Sept. 18, 1965; children: George Joseph IV, Spencer Carter. BA, Yale U., 1959, Cambridge U., 1961; MA, Cambridge U., 1970; JD, Harvard U., 1964. Bar: D.C. 1965. Atty. Office Dep. Atty. Gen., Dept. Justice, Washington, 1965; asst. to exec. dir. Nat. Crime Commn., 1966; assoc. Covington and Burling, Washington, 1966-69; asst. prof. law U. Mich., 1969-72, assoc. prof., 1972-74, prof., 1974-85, Hutchins prof., 1985—. Author: Legal Identity, 1978, The Authoritative and the Authoritarian, 1986, From Newton's Sleep, 1995. Bd. dirs. Am. Friends of Cambridge U. NEH sr. fellow, 1982-83. Fellow Am. Acad. Arts and Scis.; mem. ABA, D.C. Bar Assn. Am. Law Inst., Century Assn. Office: U Mich 432 Hutchins Hall Ann Arbor MI 48109-1215

VINING, ROBERT LUKE, JR., federal judge; b. Chatsworth, Ga., Mar. 30, 1931; m. Martha Sue Cates; 1 child, Laura Orr. BA, JD, U. Ga., 1959. With Mitchell & Mitchell, 1958-60; ptnr. McCamy, Miner & Vining, Dalton, 1960-69; solicitor gen. Conasauga Judicial Cir., 1963-68; judge Whitfield County Superior Ct., Dalton, 1969-79; judge U.S. Dist. Ct. (no. dist.) Ga., 1979-95, chief judge, 1995—. Served to staff sgt. USAF, 1951-59. Office: US Dist Ct PO Box 6226 600 E 1st St Rm 345 Rome GA 30162*

VINKEN, PIERRE JACQUES, publishing executive, neurosurgeon; b. Heerlen, The Netherlands, Nov. 25, 1927; M.D., U. Utrecht, 1955, postgrad. in psychiatry, neurology and neurosurgery, U. Amsterdam, 1957-63; hon. Dr., U. Paris, 1981. Staff neurosurgeon Univ. Clinic, Amsterdam, 1964-69; pres., chief editor Excerpta Medica Found., Amsterdam and Princeton, N.J., 1962-88; mng. dir. Elsevier Pub. Co., Amsterdam, 1972-78; chmn. Elsevier Pub. Co., Amsterdam, 1979-95; chmn. bd. dirs. Reed Elsevier, London, 1993-95, Reed Internat., Londonk 1993-95; chmn. supervising bd. Elsevier, Amsterdam; bd. dirs. Wereldhave Investment Co., The Hague, Mees Pierson (chmn.), Amsterdam, Logica, London, Halder Holdings (chmn.), The Hague, Aalberts Industries, Driebergen; chmn. Hiscom, Leyden; chmn. Port O' Call, Amsterdam, Blue Horse Prodns., Hilversam; dep. chmn. European Pubs. Coun.; prof. med. database informatics U. Leyden, 1975-93; mem. Nat. Sci. Policy Council, The Hague, 1983-90; chmn. Netherlands del. Intergovtl. Unisist Conf., Paris, 1970; mem. Netherlands Unisist Commn., 1971-79. Chmn. Netherlands Commn. Bibliography and Documentation, 1972-81; pres. Internat. Congress Patient Counselling, 1976-79; chmn. The Lancet, London, 1991-95; bd. dirs. Pearson, London, 1988-91, The Economist, London, 1989-92. Mem. European Info. Providers Assn. (pres. 1980-83), Neurol. Soc. India (hon.), French Neurol. Soc. (hon.), Amsterdam Neurol. Soc. (hon.), Peruvian Soc. Psychiat. Neurology and Neurosurgey (hon.). Founder, editor-in-chief: Handbook of Clinical Neurology, 77 vols.; editor sci. books; contbr. articles to profl. jours. Home: 142 Bentveldsweg, 2111 EE Aerdenhout The Netherlands

VINOCUR, M. RICHARD, publisher; b. Columbus, Ohio, Nov. 16, 1934; s. Louis O. and Edith (Solomon) V.; m. Carol S. Lennard, Oct. 26, 1957; children: Michael Drew, Lesle Jane. B.A. in Journalism, Ohio State U., 1956. Asso. editor R.H. Donnelley, 1956-59; v.p., pub. Vance Pub., N.Y.C., 1959-79; pub. Graphic Arts Monthly, N.Y.C., 1979-87, group pub. Fire Engring.; pres. Footprint Communications, Inc., N.Y.C., 1987—; pub. Footprints (twice monthly newsletter for printing industry execs.), Vue/Point:The Hard Copy Mag., Web Offset: The Hard Copy; columnist Am. Printer Mag., 1988—; organizing mgr., founder Vue/Point 90, 1990—; lectr. N.Y. U.; cons. CSV Found. Author: How to Win Occasionally, 1980. Pres. Greentree Assn.; sec. S. Harris Fund. Named Pub. of Yr., Hopkins Found., 1980, Internat. Assn. Printers and Craftsmen; recipient citizenship award Newcomb Club, 1979, Gutenberg media award Printing Industries, 1995, 96. Mem. Graphic Arts Tech. Found., Sigma Delta Chi. Republican. Jewish. Club: Bonat BG. Home: 9 Greentree Ter Tenafly NJ 07670-2405 Office: Footprint Communications Inc PO Box 255 Tenafly NJ 07670-0255 also: Footprint Communications Inc 2400 Lemoine Ave Fort Lee NJ 07024-6204

VINROOT, RICHARD ALLEN, lawyer, mayor; b. Charlotte, N.C., Apr. 14, 1941; s. Gustav Edgar and Vera Frances (Pickett) V.; m. Judith Lee Allen, Dec. 29, 1964; children: Richard A., Laura Tabor, Kathryn Pickett. BS in BA, U. N.C., 1963, JD, 1966. Bar: N.C. 1966, U.S. Dist. Ct. (ea., mid. and we. dists.) N.C. 1969, U.S. Ct. Appeals (4th cir.) 1969. Ptnr. Robinson, Bradshaw & Hinson, P.A., Charlotte, 1969—; mayor City of Charlotte, N.C., 1991-95. Mem. Charlotte City Coun., 1983-91. Mem. ABA, N.C. Bar Assn., Mecklenburg County Bar Assn. (sec. 1976). Republican. Presbyterian.

VINSON, C. ROGER, federal judge; b. Cadiz, Ky., Feb. 19, 1940; m. Ellen Watson; children: Matt, Todd, Cate, Patrick, Joey. BS, U.S. Naval Acad., 1962; JD, Vanderbilt U., 1971. Commd. ensign USN, 1962, advanced through grades to lt., 1963, naval aviator, until 1968, resigned, 1968; assoc. to ptnr. Beggs & Lane, Pensacola, Fla., 1971-83; judge U.S. Dist. Ct. (no. dist.) Fla., Pensacola, 1983—; mem. Jud. Conf. Adv. Com. on Civil Rules, 1993—; mem. 11th Cir. Pattern Instrn. Com. Office: US Courthouse 100 N Palafox St Pensacola FL 32501-4858

VINSON, JAMES SPANGLER, academic administrator; b. Chambersburg, Pa., May 17, 1941; s. Wilbur S. and Anna M. (Spangler) V.; m. Susan Alexander, Apr. 8, 1967; children: Suzannah, Elizabeth. B.A., Gettysburg Coll., 1963; M.S., U. Va., 1965, Ph.D., 1967. Asst. prof. physics MacMurray Coll., Jacksonville, Ill., 1967-71; asso. prof. physics U. N.C., Asheville, 1971-78; prof. physics U. N.C., 1974-78, chmn. dept. physics, dir. acad. computing, 1974-78; prof. physics, dean Coll. Arts and Scis. U. Hartford (Conn.), 1978-83; v.p. acad. affairs Trinity U., San Antonio, 1983-87; pres. U. Evansville, Ind., 1987—; computer cons. Contbr. articles to profl. jours. Mem. Am. Phys. Soc., World Future Soc., AAAS, Am. Assn. for Advancement of Humanities, Am. Assn. for Higher Edn., Am. Assn. Physics Tchrs., Phi Beta Kappa, Sigma Xi, Phi Sigma Kappa. Methodist. Office: U Evansville 1800 Lincoln Ave Evansville IN 47722-0001

VINSON, LAURENCE DUNCAN, JR., lawyer; b. Gadsden, Ala., Mar. 17, 1947. BS with hons., U. Ala., Tuscaloosa, 1969; JD, U. Ala., 1973. Bar: Ala., U.S. Dist. Ct. (no., mid. and so. dists.) Ala., U.S. Ct. Appeals (11th cir.), U.S. Supreme Ct. Assoc. Bradley, Arant, Rose & White, Birmingham, Ala., 1973-79; ptnr. Bradley, Arant, Rose & White, 1979—; Bar: Ala. 1973, U.S. Dist. Ct. (no. dist.) Ala. 1973, U.S. Supreme Ct. 1977, U.S. Ct. Appeals (11th cir.) 1981, U.S. Dist. Ct. (so. dist.) Ala. 1989, U.S. Dist. Ct. (mid. dist.) Ala. 1991. Chmn. Ala. Uniform Comml. Code Revisions Coms., Arts 3, 4, and 4A. Mem. ABA, Birmingham Bar Assn., Ala. State Bar, Ala. Law Inst., Order of Coif, Phi Beta Kappa, Omicron Delta Kappa. Office: Bradley Arant Rose & White PO Box 830709 2001 Park Pl Ste 1400 Birmingham AL 35283-0709

VINSON, MARK ALAN, English language and literature educator; b. Murray, Ky., July 14, 1958; s. C.D. Jr. and Betty Sue (Outland) V.; m. Lisa Carole Fennell, July 16, 1994. Student, Murray State U., 1976-79; BA, BSE, Memphis State U., 1981, MA, 1983; Specialist of Arts in English, U. Miss., 1987. Ordained to ministry Bapt. Ch. as deacon, 1989. Teaching asst. Memphis (Tenn.) State U., 1982-83; instr. English Memphis State U., 1987-90; teaching asst. U. Miss., Oxford, 1984; instr. English N.W. Miss. Jr. Coll., Oxford, 1984-87, Shelby State C.C., Memphis, 1989, State Tech. Inst., Memphis, 1989; asst. prof. English Union U., Memphis, 1990-95, Crichton Coll., Memphis, 1995—. Named one of Outstanding Young Men of Am., 1988, 92. Mem. Am. Cut Glass Assn. (life), Conf. on Christianity and Lit., Sigma Tau Delta (charter mem., program chmn. 1981-83), Modern Lang. Assn. Republican. Southern Baptist. Avocations: collecting American brilliant cut glass, fossils, William Faulkner memorabilia. Home: 191 Perkins Extd Memphis TN 38117 Office: Crichton Coll 999 Monroe Ave Memphis TN 38104-3141

VINSON, VICTORIA DEAN, middle school educator; b. Cedartown, Ga., June 19, 1952; d. BennieDean Vinson and Katherine Louise (Green) Easterwood; m. Richard E. Wright, July 23, 1994. BSEd, U. Ga., 1975; postgrad., Valdosta State U., 1976-78, Berry Coll., 1980-81, U. Maryland, Lakenheath, Eng., 1982-84, W. Ga. Coll., 1991. Cert. K-12 gifted tchr., Ga. Tchr. Tift County High Sch., Tifton, Ga., 1976-79; tchr. Elm St. Mid. Sch., Rockmart, Ga., 1980-81, 85-89, tchr. of gifted, 1991—; tchr. RAF Feltwell (Eng.)-Lakenheath Mid. Sch., 1981-84; instr. aerobics Floyd Med. Ctr., Rome, Ga., 1985-89; tchr./asst. Baird Ballet Co., Rome, 1984-88; tchr., choreographer Rome City Ballet, 198991, Acad. Performing Arts, Cedartown, 1992-93. Mem. ASCD, NEA, Ga. Edn. Assn., Polk Edn. Assn., Nat. Coun. Tchrs. English, Ga. Supporters for Gifted, Profl. Dance Tchrs. Assn., Nat. Dance Exercise Inst. Tng. Assn., Beta Sigma Phi. Republican. Home: 99 Seab Green Rd Cedartown GA 30125-4637 Office: Elm St Mid Sch 100 Morgan Valley Rd Rockmart GA 30153-1610

VINZ, FRANK LOUIS, electrical engineer; b. Laredo, Tex., Jan. 5, 1932; s. Louis and Margaret Reeves (Schaer) V.; m. Mary Marguerite Harlow, June 24, 1956; children: Laura Lee, Susan Elizabeth, Bradley Louis. BSEE, Tex. A&M U., 1953; MSEE, USAF Inst. Tech., 1963; postgrad. in Elec. Engring., U. Tenn., 1967. Cert. FAA flight instr. Officer USAF, 1953-58; project officer Air Force Armament Ctr., 1955-58; electronic engr. Army Ballistic Missile Agy., Redstone Arsenal, Ala., 1958-60; engring. supr. Marshall Space Flight Ctr. NASA, Huntsville, Ala., 1960-89; prin. engr. BDM Internat., Inc., Huntsville, 1989-91; sr. engr. Loral AeroSys divsn., Huntsville, 1991-94; ret., 1994; participant Apollo/Saturn, space shuttle, space sta. programs NASA. Contbr. articles to Jour. Inst. Navigation, SPIE Symposium on Intelligent Robots. Trustee, chmn. Presbyn. Ch., Huntsville, 1974-76, elder, 1959-63, 78-81, 83-85. Grad. sch. scholarship NASA-MSFC, U. Tenn., 1966-67. Mem. AIAA (com. for flight simulation), Huntsville Assn. Tech. Socs. (pres. 1995-96), U.S. Power Squadrons (squadron comdr. 1984-86), Tau Beta Pi. Home: 1006 San Ramon Ave SE Huntsville AL 35802-2659

VIOLA, BILL, artist, writer; b. N.Y.C., Jan. 25, 1951; s. William John and Wynne Viola; m. Kira Perov; children: Blake Perov, Andrei. BFA, Syracuse U., 1973, DFA, 1995. Tech. dir. Art/Tapes/22 Video Studio, Florence, Italy, 1974-76; artist-in-residence Sta. WNET, N.Y.C., 1976-83, Sony Corp., Atsugi Labs., Japan, 1980-81, San Diego Zoo, 1984; instr. Calif. Inst. of Arts, Valencia, 1983; represented by Anthony d'Offay Gallery, London. Solo exhbns. include The Kitchen Ctr., N.Y., 1974, Everson Mus. Art, Syracuse, N.Y., 1975, Mus. Modern Art, N.Y.C., 1979, 87, Whitney Mus. Art, N.Y.C., 1982, Musée d'Art Moderne, Paris, 1983, Mus. Contemporary Art, L.A., 1985, Fukui Prefectural Mus. Art, Fukui City, Japan, 1989, Staditsche Kunsthalle Düsseldorf, 1992, Moderna Museet, Stockholm, 1993, Museo Nacional Centro de Arte Reina Sofia, Madrid, Spain, 1993, Musée Cantonal des Beaux-Arts, Lausanne, Switzerland, 1993, Whitechapel Art Gallery, London, 1993, Tel Aviv Mus. Art, 1994, Musée d'Art Contemporain, Montreal, Que., Can., 1993, Centro Cultural/Banco de Brazil, Rio de Janeiro, 1994, 46th Venice Biennale, 1995; group exhbns. include De Saisset Art Gallery and Mus., Santa Clara, Calif., 1972, Whitney Mus. Am. Art, 1975-87, 89, 93, Stedelijk Mus., Amsterdam, The Netherlands, 1984, Carnegie Mus. Art, Pitts., 1988, Kölnischer Kunstverein, Cologne, Germany, 1989, Israel Mus., Jerusalem, 1990, Musée Nat. d'Art Moderne, Ctr. Georges Pompidou, Paris, 1990, Martin Gropius Bau, Berlin, 1991, Mus. Moderne Kunst, Frankfurt, Germany, 1991, Royal Acad., London, 1993, Denver Art Mus., Columbus (Ohio) Art Mus., 1994, Anthony d'Offay Gallery, London, 1995, Mus. Modern Art, N.Y.C., 1995, Tate Gallery, London, 1995; spl. screening film: Déserts, Vienna, Austria, 1994; commns. include The Stopping Mind, Mus. Moderne Kunst, Frankfurt, 1991, Nantes Triptych, Délegation aux Arts Plastiques, Nantes, France, 1992, Slowly Turning Narrative, Inst. Contemporary Art, Phila., Va. Mus. Fine Art, Richmond, 1992, Tiny Deaths, Biennale d'Art Contemporain de Lyon, France, 1993, Déserts, Konzerthause, Vienna, 1994; composer: (album) David Tudor-Rainforest IV, 1981; (video) Bill Viola: Selected Works, 1986, I Do Not Know What It Is I Am Like, 1986, The Passing, 1991. Japan/U.S. Creative Arts fellow NEA, 1980, Rockefeller Found. Video Artist fellow, 1982, Visual Artist fellow NEA, 1983-89, Guggenheim Meml. Found. fellow, 1985, Intercultural Film/Video fellow Rockefeller Found., 1991; recipient Jury prize U.S. Film and Video Festival, 1982, Grand prize, 1983, Jury prize Video Culture/Can., 1983, Grand prize for video art, 1984, First prize for video art Athens (Ohio) Film/Video Festival, 1984, Maya Deren award Am. Film Inst., 1987, First prize Festival Internat. d'Art Video et des Nouvelles Images Electroniques de Locarno, 1987, John D. and Catherine T. MacArthur Found. award, 1989, Skowhegan medal, 1993, First prize Festival Internat. de Video, Cidade de Vigo, Spain, 1993, Medienkunstpreis, Siemens Kulturprogramm and Zentrum fur Kunst und Medientechnologie, Germany, 1993. Subject numerous books. Home: 282 Granada Ave Long Beach CA 90803

VIOLA, FRANK JOHN, JR., professional baseball player; b. East Meadow, N.Y., Apr. 19, 1960; m. Kathy Daltas; children: Frank III, Brittany Ann, Kaley Marie. Student, St. John's U. Pitcher Minnesota Twins, Mpls., 1981-89, N.Y. Mets, 1989-92, Boston Red Sox, 1992-94, Toronto Blue Jays, 1994—; mem. Am. League All-Star Team, 1988; mem. Nat. League All-Star Team, 1990-91; World Series champions, 1987; Nat. League Innings Pitched Leader, 1990. Recipient Am. League Cy Young award, 1988; named to Sporting News All-Star Team, 1988, Sporting News Nat. League All-Star Team, 1990; named Sporting News Am. League Pitcher of Yr., 1988. Office: Toronto Blue Jays, One Blue Jay Way Ste 3200, Toronto, ON Canada M5V 1J1

VIOLA, HERMAN JOSEPH, museum director; b. Chgo., Feb. 24, 1938; s. Joseph and Mary (Incollingo) V.; m. Susan Patricia Bennett, June 13, 1964; children—Joseph, Paul, Peter. B.A., Marquette U., 1960, M.A., 1964; Ph.D., Ind. U., 1970. Founding editor Prologue: Jour. of Nat. Archives, 1969-72; dir. Nat. Anthrop. Archives, 1972-86; dir. quincentenary programs Mus. Natural History Smithsonian Inst., Washington, 1986-94; curator emeritus Smithsonian Instn., Washington, 1994—. Author: Thomas L. McKenney, Architect of America's Early Indian Policy, 1816-1830, 1974, The Indian Legacy of Charles Bird King, 1976, Diplomats in Buckskins: A History of Indian Delegations in Washington City, 1981, The National Archives of the United States, 1984, Magnificent Voyagers: The U.S. Exploring Expedition, 1938-42, 1985, Exploring the West: A Smithsonian Book, 1987, After Columbus: America's Indians Since 1492, 1990, Seeds of Change: Five Hundred Years Since Columbus, 1991, Ben Nighthorse Campbell: An American Warrior, 1993, Memoirs of Charles Henry Veil, 1994. Served with USNR, 1960-62. Mem. Orgn. Am. Historians, Western History Assn., Am. Hist. Assn., Soc. Am. Archivists (program chmn. 1972). Home: 7307 Pinewood St Falls Church VA 22046-2725 Office: Mus Natural History Smithsonian Instn Washington DC 20560

VIOLENUS, AGNES A., school system administrator; b. N.Y.C., May 17, 1931; d. Antonio and Constance Violenus. BA, Hunter Coll., 1952; MA, Columbia U., 1958; EdD, Nova U., 1990. Tchr. N.Y. State Day Care, N.Y.C., 1952-53, N.Y.C. Bd. Edn., 1953-66; asst. prin. N.Y.C. Elem. and Jr. High Sch., 1966-91; adj. instr. computer dept. continuing edn. divsn. York Coll., N.Y.C., 1985-88; adj. instr. tchr. mentor program grad. edn. divsn. CCNY, 1990-91; reviewer ednl. and instrnl. films; judge news and documentary Emmy awards NATAS, 1995. Co-author: LOGO: K-12, 1980; contbr. articles to profl. jours. Mem. mid-Manhattan br. NAACP, mem. com. on Afro-Am. acad., cultural, and tech. olympics; life mem. Girl Scouts U.S., N.Y.C.; bd. visitors Manhattan Psychiat. Ctr., 1995; vol. advisor math., sci., computers Workshop Ctr., CCNY, 1995. Recipient Dedicated Svc. award Coun. Suprs. and Adminstrs., Appreciation award Aerospace Edn. Assn., 1985, Significant Contbn. award Am. Soc. for Aerospace Edn., 1985. Mem. ASCE, Am. Ednl. Rsch. Assn., Assn. for Advancement of Computing in Edn., Assn. for Computers in Math. and Sci. Tchg., Soc. for Info., Tech., and Tchr. Edn., Assn. for Women in Sci., N.Y. Acad. Scis. (scientists in schs. program 1995), Nat. Assn. Negro Bus. and Profl. Women's Clubs (scholarship com. 1989—, family math. com. 1995), Nat. Black Child Devel. Inst. (bd. dirs. 1991—, sci. exhibit com. 1995, pub. policy com. 1991—), Pub. Edn. Assn. (mem. good schs. exch. com.), Schomburg Ctr. Rsch. in Black Culture (bd. trustee, co-chair corp. task force on African-Am. in math., sci., and tech. 1992—, pres. 1995), Doctorate Assn. N.Y. Educators, N.Y. Alliance Black Sch. Educators, Hunter Coll. Alumni Assn. (bd. dirs. 1993—), Bank St. Alumni Coun. Greater N.Y. (asst. sect. 1991—), Wistarians Alumni Hunter Coll. (exec. com. 1990—, pres. 1990-94). Democrat. Roman Catholic. Avocations: aeronautics and space science, music, collecting black education memorabilia, instructing survival strategies and techniques for women and children. Office: Farley Bldg PO Box 699 New York NY 10116

VIORST, JUDITH STAHL, author; b. Newark, Feb. 2, 1931; d. Martin Leonard and Ruth June (Ehrenkranz) Stahl; m. Milton Viorst, Jan. 30, 1960; children: Anthony Jacob, Nicholas Nathan, Alexander Noah. BA, Rutgers U., 1952; grad., Washington Psychoanalytic Inst., 1981. Author: (children's books) Sunday Morning, 1968, I'll Fix Anthony, 1969, Try It Again Sam, 1970, The Tenth Good Thing About Barney, 1971 (Silver Pencil award 1973), Alexander and the Terrible Horrible No Good Very Bad Day, 1972, My Mama Says There Aren't Any Zombies, Ghosts, Vampires, Creatures, Demons, Monsters, Fiends, Goblins or Things, 1973, Rosie and Michael, 1974, Alexander, Who Used to Be Rich Last Sunday, 1978, The Good-Bye Book, 1988, Earrings!, 1990, The Alphabet from Z to A (with Much Confusion on the Way, 1994, Alexander, Who's Not (Do You Hear Me? I Mean It!) Going to Move, 1995; (poetry) The Village Square, 1965-66, It's Hard to Be Hip Over Thirty and Other Tragedies of Married Life, 1968, People and Other Aggravations, 1971, How Did I Get to Be Forty and Other Atrocities, 1976, If I Were in Charge of the World and Other Worries, 1981, When Did I Stop Being Twenty and Other Injustices, 1987, Forever Fifty and Other Negotiations, 1989, Sad Underwear and Other Complications, 1995; (with Milton Viorst) The Washington Underground Gourmet, 1970, Yes Married, 1972, A Visit From St. Nicholas (To a Liberated Household), 1977, Love and Guild and the Meaning of Life, Etc., 1979, Necessary Losses, 1986, Murdering Mr. Monti, 1994; columnist Redbook mag. (Penney-Mo. award 1974, Am. Acad. Pediatrics award 1977, AAUW 1980). Jewish. Home: 3432 Ashley Ter NW Washington DC 20008-3238

VIORST, MILTON, writer; b. Paterson, N.J., Feb. 18, 1930; s. Louis and Betty (LeVine) V.; m. Judith Stahl, Jan. 30, 1960; children—Anthony, Nicholas, Alexander. B.A. summa cum laude, Rutgers U., 1951; student (Fulbright scholar), U. Lyon, France, 1952; M.A., Harvard U., 1955; M.S., Columbia U., 1956. Reporter Bergen (N.J.) Record, 1955-56, Newark StarLedger, 1956-57, Washington Post, 1957-61; Washington corr. N.Y. Post, 1961-64; syndicated columnist Washington Evening Star, 1971-75; staff writer The New Yorker, N.Y.C., 1987-93; Ferris prof. journalism Princeton (N.J.) U., 1995-96; lectr. in field. Author: Hostile Allies: FDR and deGaulle, 1965, Great Documents of Western Civilization, 1965, Fall from Grace: The Republican Party and the Puritan Ethic, 1968, Hustlers and Heroes, 1971, Fire in the Streets: America in the 1960's, 1980, Making a Difference: The Peace Corps at Twenty-five, 1986, Sands of Sorrow: Israel's Journey from Independence, 1987, Reaching for the Olive Branch: UNRWA and Peace in the Middle East, 1990, Sandcastles: The Arabs in Search of the Modern World, 1994; also articles.; contbg. editor Tikkun. Chmn. Fund for Investigative Journalism, 1969-78; bd. dirs. Georgetown Day Sch., 1977-80. Served as officer USAF, 1952-54. Recipient Columbia Journalism Alumni award, 1992; Woodrow Wilson sr. fellow, 1973-79, Alicia Patterson fellow, 1979; Middle East Inst. sr. scholar. Mem. PEN, Soc. Profl. Journalists, Author's Guild, Coun. on Fgn. Rels., Am. Peace Now (bd. dirs.), Phi Beta Kappa.

VIRGO, JOHN MICHAEL, economist, researcher, educator; b. Pressburry, Eng., Mar. 11, 1943; s. John Joseph and Muriel Agnes (Franks) V.; m. Katherine Sue Ulmrich, Sept. 6, 1980 (div. 1979); 1 child, Debra Marie. BA, Calif. State U., Fullerton, 1967, MA, 1969; MA, Claremont Grad. Sch., 1971, PhD, 1972. Instr. econs. Whittier (Calif.) Coll., 1970-71, Calif. State U., Fullerton and Long Beach, 1971-72, Claremont (Calif.) Grad. Sch., 1971-72; asst. prof. econs. Va. Commonwealth U., Richmond, 1972-74; assoc. prof. mgmt. So. Ill. U., Edwardsville, 1975-83, prof., 1984—; bd. dirs., founder Internat. Health Econ. & Mgmt. Inst., Edwardsville, 1983-87. Author: Legal & Illegal California Farmworkers, 1974; author, editor: Health Care: An International Perspective, 1984, Exploring New Vistas in Health Care, 1985, Restructuring Health Policy, 1986; founder, editor-in-chief Internat. Advances in Econ. Rsch. Served with USN, 1965-68. Mem. Internat. Hosp. Fedn., Am. Econ. Assn., Am. Hosp. Assn., Am. Soc. Assn. Execs., Royal Econ. Soc., Atlantic Econ. Soc. (founder, exec. v.p., mng.

editor jour. 1973—), Allied Social Scis. Assn. (chmn. exec. confs. 1982-84), AMA, So. Econs. Assn., Sunset Hills Club (Edwardsville). Democrat. Roman Catholic. Avocations: tennis, skiing. Home: 5277 Lindell Blvd Saint Louis MO 63108-1223 Office: So Ill U Atlantic Econ Soc PO Box 1101 Edwardsville IL 62026

VIRGO, JULIE ANNE CARROLL, management consultant; b. Adelaide, South Australia, Australia, June 14, 1944; came to U.S., 1966; d. Archibald Henry and Norma Mae (Gillett) Noolan; m. Daniel Thuering Carroll, Aug. 20, 1977. M.A., U. Chgo., 1968, Ph.D., 1974, Exec. M.B.A., 1983. With State Library of South Australia, 1962-63, Repatriation Dept. South Australia, 1962-66; asst. librarian U. Chgo. Libraries, 1966-68; dir. edn. Med. Library Assn., Chgo., 1972-77; exec. dir. Assn. Coll. and Research Libraries, Chgo., 1977-84; exec. v.p., COO COO Carroll Group, Inc., Chgo., 1984-95, pres., 1995—; mem. faculty U. Chgo., 1968-89. Author: Libraries and Accreditation in Higher Education; contbr. articles to jours. U. Chgo. fellow, 1967-68, Higher Edn. Act fellow, 1969-72; Nat. Library of Medicine grantee, 1967-69; named Outstanding Young U.S. Leader 1985 Coun. on the U.S.,.. Mem. ALA, Am. Soc. Assn. Execs., Am. Mgmt. Assn., Spol. Librs. Assn., Am. Soc. for Info. Scis. (past pres., doctoral award, Watson Davis award), ASTD, Nat. Tng. Labs. (bd. dirs. 1990-94), Orgn. Devel. Network, Internat. Assn. Neuro-Linguistic Programming (bd.dirs. 1990-93), Internat. Plant Genetic Resources Inst. (Rome, bd. dirs. 1991—), Internat. Ctr. Agrl. Rsch. in Dry Areas (Syris, bd. dirs. 1992—), Planning Forum, Beta Phi Mu.

VIRKHAUS, TAAVO, symphony orchestra conductor; b. Tartu, Estonia, June 29, 1934; came to U.S., 1949; s. Adalbert August and Helene Marie (Sild) V.; m. Nancy Ellen Herman, Mar. 29, 1969. MusB U. Miami, 1955; MusM Eastman Sch. of Music, Rochester, 1957, DMA, 1967. Dir. music U. Rochester (N.Y.), also assoc. prof. Eastman Sch., Rochester, 1967-77; music dir., condr. Duluth (Minn.) Superior Symphony Orch., 1977-94; guest condr. Rochester Philharm., Minn. Orch., Balt. Symphony, Vancouver Symphony and others, 1972—; music dir., condr. Hunstville (Ala.) Symphony Orch., 1989—; guest condr. at Tallinn, Estonia, 1978, 88, 90, 92, 93, 94; lectr. U. Minn.-Duluth, U. of Wis.-Superior. With U.S. Army, 1957-58, USAR, 1957-61. Recipient Howard Hanson Composition award, 1966, Am. Heritage award JFK Libr. for Minorities, 1974; Fulbright scholar, Musickhochschule, Cologne, 1963. Mem. Am. Symphony Orch. League, Condrs. Guild, Am. Fedn. of Musicians. Composer: Violin Concerto, 1966, Symphony No. 1, 1976, Symphony No. 2, 1979, Symphony No. 3, 1984, Symphony No. 4, 1989, Symphony No. 5, 1994. Republican. Lutheran.

VIRKLER, DENNIS M., film editor. Editor: (films) Burnt Offerings, 1976, Xanadu, 1980, Continental Divide, 1981, Airplane II: The Sequel, 1982, Gorky Park, 1983, Independence Day, 1983, The River Rat, 1984, Secret Admirer, 1985, Nobody's Fool, 1986, (with William M. Anderson and Sheldon Kahn) Big Shots, 1987, Distant Thunder, 1988, (with John Wright) The Hunt for Red October, 1990 (Academy award nomination best film editing 1990), (with Don Brochu, Robert A. Ferretti, and Dov Hoenig) Under Siege, 1992, (with David Finfer) The Fugitive, 1993 (Academy award nomination best film editing 1993), Batman Forever, 1995.

VISCHER, HAROLD HARRY, manufacturing company executive; b. Toledo, Oct. 17, 1914; s. Harry Philip and Hazel May (Patterson) V.; m. DeNell Meyers, Feb. 18, 1938; children: Harold Harry, Robert P., Michael L. B.B.A., U. Toledo, 1937. With Ohio Bell Telephone Co., 1937-38; with Firestone Tire & Rubber Co., Toledo, 1948-61; nat. passenger tire sales mgr. Firestone Tire & Rubber Co., 1953-57, dist. mgr., 1957-61; with Bandag Inc., Muscatine, Iowa, 1961-80; exec. v.p., pres. Bandag Inc. (Rubber and Equipment Sales group), 1975-80; also dir.; pres., gen. mgr. Hardline Internat., Inc., Jackson, Mich., 1980-82; chmn. Tred-X Corp., 1982—. Mem. City Council, Muscatine, 1964-76; chmn., mem. Dist. Export Council Iowa, 1964-81; chmn. Muscatine United Way, 1969-70; mem. adv. bd. Engring. Coll. Iowa State U., 1970-81; mem. Muscatine Light & Water Bd., 1979-80. Elected to Nat. Tire Dealers and Retreaders Assn. Hall of Fame, 1988, to Internat. Tire Retreading and Repairing Hall of Fame, 1990. Mem. Nat. Tire and Retreaders Suppliers Group Assn. (chmn. 1979-80, exec. com. 1977-80), Tire Retread Info. Bur. (exec. com. 1974-81), Am. Retreading Assn. (adv. bd. 1970-72), Retreading Industry Assn., Industry Man of Yr. 1979), Christian Business men's Com., Gideons, Rotary. Republican. Baptist. Home: 13500 Vischer Rd Brooklyn MI 49230-9022 Office: 116 Frost St Jackson MI 49202-2371

VISCLOSKY, PETER JOHN, congressman, lawyer; b. Gary, Ind., Aug. 13, 1949; s. John and Helen (Kauzlaric) V. B.S. in Acctg., Ind. U.-Indpls., 1970; J.D., U. Notre Dame, 1973; LL.M. in Internat. and Comparative Law, Georgetown U., 1983. Bar: Ind., D.C., U.S. Supreme Court. Legal asst. Dist. Atty.'s Office, N.Y.C., 1972; assoc. Benjamin, Greco & Gouveia, Merrillville, Ind., 1973-76, Greco, Gouveia, Miller, Pera & Bishop, Merrillville, Ind., 1982-84; assoc. staff appropriations com. U.S. Ho. of Reps., Washington, 1976-80, assoc. staff budget com., 1980-82; mem. 99th-104th Congresses from 1st dist. Ind., 1985—; mem. Appropriations com., subcoms. treasury, postal svc., gen. govt. and military constrn. Democrat. Roman Catholic. Office: US House of Reps 2464 Rayburn Bldg Washington DC 20515-1401*

VISCOVICH, ANDREW JOHN, educational management consultant; b. Oakland, Calif., Sept. 25, 1925; s. Peter Andrew and Lucy Pauline (Razovich) V.; m. Roen Shirley Mulvana, Apr. 19, 1952 (div. Feb. 1985); children: Randal Peter, Andra Clair; m. Elena Beth Wong, Apr. 28, 1993; 1 child, Alison Wong. BA, U. Calif., Berkeley, 1949; MA, San Francisco State U., 1960; EdD, U. Calif., Berkeley, 1973; cert. labor dispute resolution, Golden Gate U., 1976. Supt. Palm Springs (Calif.) Unified Sch. Dist., 1976-79, Garvey Sch. Dist., Rosemead, Calif., 1979-88, Berkeley Unified Sch. Dist., 1988-900; pres. Ctr. for Ednl. Rsch. in Adminstrn., Stockton, Calif., 1990—; state adminstr. Coachella Unified Sch. Dist., Sacramento, Calif., 1992; adj. prof. U. Calif., Berkeley, 1965-67, Calif. State U., Hayward, 1970-76, L.A., 1971-88; exec. dir. Marcus Foster Edn. Found., Oakland, 1975-76; cons. Spanish Ministry Edn., 1987—, Republic of China Ministry Edn., Taipei, Taiwan, 1986-89, Croatian Ministry Edn., Zagreb, 1993—, Marriott Sch. Svcs, 1992—, CSHQH, Idaho; pre-sch. dir. Oakland Unified Sch. Dist., 1974-76; asst. dir. Bay Area Bilingual Edn. League, 1971-75; dir. Bay Area Tchr. Ctr., 1974, asst. dir. Far West Edl. Lab., 1974; adj. assoc. prof. Calif. State U. at L.A.and Hayward, U. South Fla., U. Oreg., Coll. of Holy Names; exec. dir. ANRO Cons., Inc., 1973-82. Author: Language Programs for the Disadvantaged, 1965, R.E.S. Plus, 1978; contbr. The School Principal, 1978. Chair United Way, Pasadena, Calif., 1985; pres. Croatian Scholarship Found., San Ramon, Calif., 1993-94. Served to ens. USNR, 1959-64. Recipient award for innovations in alternative schools Behavioral Rsch. Lab., San Francisco, 1973; named Knight of Civil Order of Merit King Juan Carlos of Spain, 1990. Mem. Am. Mgmt. Assn., Am. Assn. Sch. Adminstrs., Assn. Calif. Sch. Adminstrs., Calif. City Sch. Supts., Calif. Tchrs. Assn. (John Swett award 1978). Avocations: golf, reading, travel. ultralite flying. Home: 3754 Fort Donelson Dr Stockton CA 95219

VISEK, ALBERT JAMES, computer engineer; b. Phila., July 7, 1934; s. Albert John and Rose (Schlacta) V.; m. Patricia Ann Mullen, Aug. 25, 1962; children: Patrick Albert, Kelly Ann. BS in Physics and Electronics, LaSalle Coll., 1968; MBA, Temple U., 1978. Project engring. mgr., test dir. spl. projects GE Co., Phila., 1961-73; mgr. EMI/EMC Group Sperry Corp. Hdqtrs., Blue Bell, Pa., 1973-86; program coord. Tempest Def. Systems Div., Great Valley, Pa., 1986-87; mgr. product engring. and environ. support Info. Systems Group, Exton, Pa., 1987-89; OEM product quality staff engr. Personal Workstation Div., Flemington, N.J., 1990-92; staff engr. Power Supply Engring. Group Computer Systems Group, Tredyffrin, Pa., 1992—; with Unisys Corp., Blue Bell, 1973—; co-founder, dir. engring., cons. Computer Room Specialists, Bethlehem, Pa., 1989-92; co. rep., vice-chmn. CBEMA trade assn.; presenter tech. papers in field, seminars and confs. in field. With USN, 1957-59. Mem. IEEE (presenter paper symposium 1986), Nat. Assn. Radio and Telecomm. Engrs. (cert. electromagnetic compatibility engr.). Roman Catholic. Avocations: fishing, boating, travel, cooking, reading. Home: 1306 Hartranft Ave Fort Washington PA 19034-1604 Office: Unisys 2476 Swedesford Rd Paoli PA 19301

VISEK, WILLARD JAMES, nutritionist, animal scientist, physician, educator; b. Sargent, Nebr., Sept. 19, 1922; s. James and Anna S. (Dworak) V.; m. Priscilla Flagg, Dec. 28, 1949; children: Dianna, Madeleine, Clayton Paul. B.Sc. with honors (Carl R. Gray scholar), U. Nebr., 1947; MSc (Smith fellow in agr.), Cornell U., 1949, Ph.D., 1951; M.D. (Peter Yost Fund scholar), U. Chgo., 1957; DSc (hon.), U. Nebr., 1980. Diplomate Nat. Bd. Med. Examiners, 1960. Grad. asst., lab. animal nutrition Cornell U., 1947-51; AEC postdoctoral fellow Oak Ridge, 1951-52; research assoc., 1952-53; research asst. pharmacology U. Chgo., 1953-57, asst. prof., 1957-61, assoc. prof., 1961-64; rotating med. intern U. Chgo. Clinics, 1957-58, 58-59, 59; prof. nutrition and comparative metabolism, dept. animal sci. Cornell U., Ithaca, N.Y., 1964-75; prof. clin. sci. (nutrition and metabolism) Coll. Medicine and dept. food sci. U. Ill. Coll. Agr., Urbana-Champaign, 1975—; prof. dept. internal medicine U. Ill. Coll. Medicine, Urbana-Champaign, 1986-93, prof. emeritus, 1993—; bd. dirs. Coun. Agriculture, Sci. and Tech., 1994—; bd. sci. advisors Coun. Sci. and Health, 1994—; Brittingham vis. prof. U. Wis. Madison, 1982-83; Hogan meml. lectr. U. Mo., 1987; mem. subcom. dog nutrition com. animal nutrition NRC-Nat. Acad. Sci., 1965-71; adv. coun. Inst. Lab. Animal Resources, NRC-Nat. Acad. Sci., 1966-69; subcom. animal care faciltities Survey Inst. Lab. Animal Resources, 1967-70; cons., lectr. in field; mem. sci. adv. com. diet and nutrition cancer program Nat. Cancer Inst., 1976-81; mem. nutrition study sect. NIH, 1980-84; chmn. membership com. Am. Inst. Nutrition-Am. Soc. Clin. Nutrition, 1978-79, 80-83, 85; cons. VA, NSF, indsl. orgns.; Wellcome vis. prof. in basic med. scis. Oreg. State U., 1991-92; bd. sci. counselors USDA, 1989—. Mem. editorial bd. Jour. Nutrition, 1980-84, editor, 1990—; contbr. articles to profl. jours. Bd. dirs. Coun. for Agrl. Sci. and Tech., 1994—; active local Boy Scouts Am. Served with AUS, 1943-46. Recipient alumni award Nebr. 4-H, 1967, Osborne and Mendel award, 1985, faculty merit award U. Ill. Coll. Medicine, 1988, Conrad Elvehjem award, 1996; Nat. Cancer Inst. spl. fellow MIT, rsch. fellow Mass. Gen. Hosp., 1970-71; sr. scholar U. Ill., 1988. Fellow AAAS, Am. Inst. Nutrition, Am. Soc. Animal Sci. (chmn. subcom. antimicrobials, mem. regulatory agency com. 1973-78); mem. Soc. Pharmacology and Exptl. Therapeutics, Am. Inst. Nutrition (council 1980-83, 85-86), Soc. Exptl. Biology and Medicine, Am. Soc. Clin. Nutrition, Am. Therapeutic Soc., Am. Gastroenterol. Assn., Am. Bd. Clin. Nutrition, Innocents Soc., Fedn. Am. Socs. Exptl. Biology (sci. steering group life scis. rsch. office, adv. com. 1986-92), Am. Bd. Nutrition (bd. dirs.), Nat. Dairy Coun. (rsch. adv. com. 1987-91, vis. prof. nutrition program 1981-92), Gamma Alpha (pres. 1948-49), Phi Kappa Phi (pres. 1981-82), Alpha Gamma Rho (pres. 1946-47), Gamma Sigma Delta. Presbyterian (elder). Home: 1405 W William St Champaign IL 61821-4406 Office: U Ill 190 Med Sci Bldg 506 S Mathews Ave Urbana IL 61801-3618

VISHNEVSKAYA, GALINA PAVLOVNA, soprano, opera company director; b. Leningrad, USSR, Oct. 25, 1926; m. Mstislav Rostropovich; children: Olga, Elena. Soprano, Bolshoi Opera, Moscow, to 1974; appeared throughout Europe, U.S., S.Am., including Covent Garden, Paris Opera, Met. Opera; appeared as Tatiana in Eugene Onegin, Paris 1982, Leonora in Fidelio, Aida, Kupava in Snow Maiden, Lisa in Queen of Spades, Chio-Chio-San in Madame Butterfly, Margaret in Faust, Natasha in War and Peace, Cherubino in Marriage of Figaro. Author: Galina (autobiography), 1985. Decorated officier Legion of Honor (France); recipient People's Artist of USSR prize, Lenin prize. Mem. Sigma Alpha Iota. Russian Orthodox. Office: care Victor Hochhauser, 4 Holland Park Ave, London W11 3QU, England

VISHWANATH, PALAMADI SUBRAMANYAN, technology company executive, consultant. BTech in Engring., Indian Inst. Tech., Bombay, India, 1980; MS in Engring., Cleve. State U., 1981. Registered profl. engr., Ohio, 1986. Program mgr. A.G.A. Labs., Independence, Ohio, 1981-87; dir. product and industry devel. Smart House, L.P., Upper Marlboro, Md., 1987-92; prin. V-Tech, Inc., Annapolis, Md., 1992—; cons. tech. and product devel. Innotech Corp., IdeaScope, CyberMedia Group; presenter in field. Patentee in field; contbr. articles to profl. jours. Office: V-Tech Inc 125 Maple Dr Ste B100 Annapolis MD 21403-3925

VISKANTA, RAYMOND, mechanical engineering educator; b. Lithuania, July 16, 1931; came to U.S., 1949, naturalized, 1955; s. Vincas and Genovaite (Vinickas) V.; m. Birute Barbara Barpsys, Oct. 13, 1956; children: Renata, Vitas, Tadas. BSME, U. Ill., 1955; MSME, Purdue U., 1956, PhD, 1960; DEng (hon.), Tech. U. Munich, 1994. Registered profl. engr., Ill. Asst. mech. engr. Argonne (Ill.) Nat. Lab., 1956-59, student rsch. assoc., 1959-60, assoc. mech. engr., 1960-62; assoc. prof. mech. engring. Purdue U., West Lafayette, Ind., 1962-66, prof. mech. engring., 1966-86, Gross disting. prof. engring., 1986—; guest prof. Tech. U. Munich, Germany, 1976-77, U. Karlsruhe, Germany, 1987; vis. prof. Tokyo Inst. Tech., 1983. Contbr. over 400 tech. articles to profl. jours. Recipient Sr. U.S. Scientist award Alexander von Humboldt Found., 1975, Sr. Rsch. award Am. Soc. Engring. Edn., 1984, Nusselt-Reynolds prize, 1991, Thermal Engring. award for Internat. Activity, Japan Soc. Mech. Engrs., 1994; Japan Soc. for Promotion of Sci. fellow, 1983. Fellow ASME (Heat Transfer Meml. award 1976, Max Jakob Meml. award 1986, Melville medal 1988), AIAA (Thermophysics award 1979); mem. AAUP, AAAS, NAE, Acad. Engring. Scis. Russian Fedn. (fgn.), Sigma Xi, Pi Tau Sigma, Tau Beta Pi. Home: 3631 Chancellor Way West Lafayette IN 47906-8809 Office: Purdue Univ 1288 Mechanical Engring Bui West Lafayette IN 47907

VISOCKI, NANCY GAYLE, data processing consultant; b. Dumont, N.J., May 13, 1952; d. Thomas and Gloria (Valle) V. BA in Maths., Manhattanville Coll., 1974; MS in Ops. Rsch. and Stats., Rensselaer Poly. Inst., 1977. Rsch. asst. Coll. Physicians and Surgeons Columbia U., N.Y.C., 1974-75; programmer analyst R. Shriver Assocs., Parsippany, N.J., 1977-79; sr. tech. rep. GE Info. Svcs. Co., East Orange, N.J., 1979-81; mgr. project office GE Info. Svcs. Co., Morristown, N.J., 1981-83, tech. dir., 1983-87, tech. mgr., 1988-89; area mgr. system devel. and consulting GE Info. Svcs. Co., Parsippany, N.J., 1989-92; area tech. mgr. system devel. and cons., Fin. Info. Systems GE Info. Svcs. Co., Parsippany, N.J., 1992-93, sr. cons. electronic commerce info. svcs., 1993—. Active Western Hills Christian Ch., Tranquility, N.J., 1986—; vol. Women's Ctr., Hackettstown, N.J., 1989-93; class fundraising and gift chmn. Rensselaer Poly. Inst., 1991-95; vol. Elfun Soc. Manhattanville Coll. grantee, Purchase, N.Y., 1970-71; tuition fellow Rensselaer Poly. Inst., Troy, N.Y., 1975-77. Mem. NAFE, Women of Accomplishment. Avocations: skiing, needlepoint, walking, bicycling, reading. Home: 140 E Linden Ave Dumont NJ 07628-1916 Office: GE Info Svcs Co Ste 302 20 Waterview Blvd Parsippany NJ 07054-1219 *Many people in business think that it takes time and costs money to be thoughtful and kind to others. It doesn't take time or money, but only a little effort to nurture a sincere concern and love for those around you. I guarantee the return on your efforts will astound you.*

VISSER, JOHN EVERT, university president emeritus, historian; b. Orange City, Iowa, Apr. 24, 1920; s. Arthur J. and Frances (TePaske) V.; m. Virginia Jean Schuyler, May 29, 1946; children: Betty Jean, Mary Frances, Nancy Ann, Martha Ellen. BA, Hope Coll., 1942, LittD (hon.), 1995; MA, U. Iowa, 1947, PhD, 1957; D honoris causa, Indsl. U. Santander, Bucaramanga, Colombia, 1968. Asst. prof. history Hope Coll., Holland, Mich., 1949-56; asst. registrar Western Mich. U., 1956-57; asst. dean Ball State U., 1957-58, exec. asst. to pres., prof. history, 1962-67; dean Grand Rapids (Mich.) Jr. Coll., 1958- 62; pres. Emporia (Kans.) State U., 1967-84; cons. U. Alaska, 1985-86; interim chancellor U. Alaska, Juneau, 1986-87; interim vice chancellor, U. Wis., Green Bay, 1987-88. Served to capt. inf. AUS, 1942-46. Inducted into Infantry OCS Hall of Fame, 1982. Mem. Nat. Assn. Intercollegiate Athletics (pres., mem. exec. com.), Am. Assn. State Colls. and Univs. (treas. 1971-75), Kans. Assn. Colls. and Univs. (pres. 1972-73), Blue Key, Phi Delta Kappa, Phi Alpha Theta. Presbyn. Club: Rotarian. Home: RR 1 Box 52 Vassar KS 66543-9716

VISSER, VALYA ELIZABETH, physician; b. Chgo., Oct. 2, 1947; d. Roy Warren and Tania Eugenia (Morozoff) Nelson; children: Kira Elizabeth Visser, Michael Philip Visser. BS, Iowa State U., 1968; MD, U. Iowa, 1973. Diplomate Am. Bd. Pediatrics, Sub-Bd. Neonatal-Perinatal Medicine. Resident pediatrics U. Iowa Hosps. and Clinics, Iowa City, 1976; fellow neonatology Children's Mercy Hosp., Kansas City, 1978; asst. prof. pediatrics U. Kans. Sch. Medicine, Kansas City, 1978-81; staff pediatrician U.S. Army Med. Corps., Ft. Bragg, N.C., 1981-83; attending neonatologist Carolinas Med. Ctr., Charlotte, 1983—; acting chair dept. pediatrics Carolinas Med. Ctr., Charlotte, 1991-94; conf. chair Extracorporeal Life Support Orgn., Ann Arbor, Mich., 1993-95. Major Med. Corps., 1981-83. Fellow Am. Acad. Pediatrics; mem. Soc. for Critical Care Medicine. Mem. Unitarian-Universalist Ch. Avocations: parenting, music. Office: Carolinas Med Ctr Dept Pediatrics PO Box 32861 Charlotte NC 28232-2861

VISTICA, JERROLD FRANCIS, publishing executive; b. Stockton, Calif., Jan. 16, 1925; s. Louis and Mary Theresa (McCarty) V.; m. Lorraine Louise Miller, May 3, 1957 (dec. Nov. 1961); children: Victoria Vistica Palmieri, Mary Theresa II. AA, Yuba Coll., 1951; postgrad., U. Calif., Berkeley, 1952; BS, U. San Francisco, 1963; postgrad., Golden Gate U., 1983-84. Lic. real estate broker Calif. Ranch mgr. L. Vistica & Son Ranch, Live Oak, Calif., 1953; pres. Louis Vistica Nurseries, Yuba City, Calif., 1954-59; real estate sales Trevor & Co., San Francisco, 1960, Andre F. Bosc, San Francisco, 1961; real estate broker pvt. practice, San Francisco, 1962-89; mng. dir., auctioneer Asset Disposal Svcs., San Francisco, 1989-93; mng. editor The Common Good Press, San Francisco, 1994—; environ. cons. O.E. Griffin & Assocs., San Francisco, 1971-80; security cons., San Francisco, 1980-89. Author: Common Sense Self Protection Primer, 1993; editor: (newsletter) Self Protection Letter, 1994. Pres. Bella Vita Soc., San Francisco, 1974; mem. Fine Arts Mus., 1960—. Mem. Calif. Acad. Scis. (life), Mechanics Inst., Commonwealth Club Calif., Calif. Alumni Assn., U. San Francisco Alumni Assn., Alpha Gamma Sigma. Avocations: fgn. travel, classical music, walking, reading, martial arts. Office: The Common Good Press PO Box 193002 San Francisco CA 94119-3002

VITALE, ALBERTO ALDO, publishing company executive; b. Vercelli, Italy, Dec. 22, 1933; came to U.S., 1960; s. Sergio and Elena (Segre) V.; m. Gemma G. Calori, Oct. 11, 1961; children—Raffaele Robert, Alessandro David. Dr. Econs. and Bus. Adminstrn., U. Turin, Italy, 1956, postgrad., 1956-57; postgrad. (Fulbright scholar), Wharton Sch. Finance, U. Pa., 1957-58. With Olivetti Corp. Am., 1959-72; dir. corp. planning Olivetti Corp. Am., N.Y.C., 1965-69; v.p. adminstrn. Olivetti Corp. Am., 1969-70; v.p. adminstrn., treas. Olivetti Corp. Am., N.Y.C., 1970-72; prin. officer IFI, Torino, 1972-75; exec. v.p., chief operating officer, dir. Bantam Books, Inc., N.Y.C., 1975-85, pres., 1985-87, co-chief exec. officer, 1985-86, chief exec. officer, 1986-87; pres., chief exec. officer Bantam, Doubleday, Dell Publishing Group, from 1987; now chmn. bd., pres., chief exec. officer Random House, N.Y.C.; bd. dirs. Transworld Pubs. Ltd. Mem. Assn. Am. Pubs. (dir. 1979, 86). Home: 505 Alda Rd Mamaroneck NY 10543-4002 Office: Random House Inc 201 E 50th St New York NY 10022-7703*

VITALE, DICK, color commentator, sports writer; b. Garfield, N.J.; m. Lorraine Vitale; children: Terri, Sherri. Basketball coach East Rutherford (N.J.) High Sch., 1965-71; asst. basketball coach Rutgers U., New Brunswick, N.J., 1972; coll. basketball coach U. Detroit, 1973-77, athletic dir., 1978; pro basketball coach Detroit Pistons, Auburn Hills, Mich., 1978-79; TV color commentator ESPN Sports, 1979—, ABC Sports, 1987—; sports radio commentator ABC Radio Network, 1987—; sports columnist Basketball Times, 1979—, Ea. Basketball, 1979—; radio commentator The J. P. McCarthy Show, Detroit; guest spkr., lectr. Co-author: (with Curay Kirk Patrick) Vitale: Just Your Average, Bald, One-Eyed Basketball Wacko Who Beat the Ziggy and Became a PTP'er, 1989, (with Dick Weiss) Time Out, Baby!, 1992, (with Mike Douchant) Tourney Time, It's Awesome Baby, 1994; co-author various computer games; appeared in TV commls. for Adidas, Taco Bell. Named Sports Personality of Yr., Am. Sportscasters Assn., 1989. Roman Catholic. Earned 5 sectional and 2 consecutive state championships as high sch. basketball coach. Office: IMG Peter Goldberg 22 E 71st St New York NY 10021-4911

VITALE, FRANCIS M., preschool director; b. Bronx, N.Y., Dec. 26, 1937; d. Peter Robert and Vitina (Incandella) DiPaola; m. Anthony Joseph Vitale, Apr. 26, 1970; children: Stephanie Maria, Jeffrey Anthony. BA, Coll. of New Rochelle, 1991. Founder, dir. The Caring Place, Inc., New Rochelle, N.Y. Mem. Westchester Assn. for Edn. of Young Children, Child Care Coun. Westchester, New Rochelle C. of C. Home: 36 Robins Rd New Rochelle NY 10801-1115

VITALIANO, CHARLES J(OSEPH), geologist, educator; b. N.Y.C., Apr. 2, 1910; s. Joseph and Catherine (deBarberi) V.; m. Dorothy A. Brauneck, Oct. 19, 1940; children: Judith E., Peter W. B.S., CCNY, 1936; A.M., Columbia U., 1938, Ph.D. (James Furman Kemp fellow), 1944. Instr. extension div. Columbia U., 1938-40; instr. ceramics dept. Rutgers U., 1940-42; geologist U.S. Geol. Survey, 1942-47; asso. prof. geology Ind. U., Bloomington, 1947-57; prof. Ind. U., 1957-80, prof. emeritus, 1980—; prof. field geology Ind. U. Field Sta. in Mont., summers 1948-50, 58-74; mem. sci. adv. com. Ind. U., 1979-81; chmn. Ind. U. Credit Union, 1967-68, bd. dirs., 1966-84; prof. field geology U.S. Geol. Survey, Nev. and N.Mex., summers 1950-58; cons. Earth Resources Tech. Satellite project, U. Mont., summer 1973; geol. cons. archaeol. projects, Greece, summers, 1971, 74, 78, 79. Contbr. articles to profl. jours. Fulbright sr. research fellow N.Z., 1954-55; Fulbright lectr. Australia, 1955; NSF grantee, 1957-61, 66-72; recipient Outstanding Teaching award Ind. U., 1982. Fellow Geol. Soc. Am. (chmn. archaeol. geology div. 1985—), AAAS, Mineral. Soc. Am.; mem. Geochem. Soc., Soc. Econ. Geologists. Unitarian. Office: Indiana U Dept Geology Bloomington IN 47405

VITALIANO, ERIC NICHOLAS, state legislator, lawyer; b. S.I., N.Y., Feb. 27, 1948; m. Helen M. Fleming, Sept. 9, 1983; children: Michael, Emma, Abigail. AB, Fordham Coll., 1968; JD cum laude, NYU, 1971; postgrad., U. Colo., 1977. Bar: N.Y. 1971. Law clk. to Mark A Costantino, U.S. Dist. Ct. for Ea. Dist. N.Y., N.Y.C., 1971-72; assoc. Simpson Thacher & Bartlett, N.Y.C., 1972-79; chief staff to Congressman John M. Murphy U.S. Ho. of Reps., N.Y.C., 1979-80; mem. Russo, Silverman & Vitaliano, N.Y.C., 1982-86, N.Y. Assembly, Albany, 1982—; counsel Behrins & Behrins, N.Y.C., 1995—; counsel to Behrins & Behrins, P.C., Staten Island, 1995—. Rsch. editor NYU Law Rev., 1970-71. Co-founder Citizens Against Bus Exhaust; co-founder Bodine Creek Civic Assn.; former parish chmn. Cardinal's Archdiocesan Appeal; mem. Dem. Com. Richmond County, N.Y.; past pres. N.Y. Conf. Italian-Am. State Legislators; past adv. Assumption Coun., K.C. Recipient Stella Falletta Meml. award Clifton Homeowners and Tenants Assn., S.I., 1986, Aldo R. Benedetto Outstanding Citizen award Am. Legion, 1994; named Dem. of Yr., Young Dems. Richmond County, 1980, Friend of Edn., Susan E. Wagner H.S., S.I., 1983, Legislator of Yr., N.Y. State Clks. Assn., 1987, Friend of Italian-Am. Inst. Inst., CUNY, 1990, Man of Yr., Italian Club S.I., 1991, Man of the Yr., Met. Police Conf. of N.Y. State, 1995. Mem. ABA, KC (past advisor Assumption coun. S.I.), Order of Coif. Home: 130 Chapin Ave Staten Island NY 10304-2927 Office: NY State Assembly 839 Legislative Office Bldg Albany NY 12248

VITEK, VACLAV, materials scientist; b. Olomouc, Czechoslovakia, Sept. 10, 1940; came to U.S., 1978; s. Josef and Ruzena V.; m. Ludovita Stankovicova, Aug. 5, 1972; children: Adrian Joseph, Clementine Mary. BSc in Physics, Charles U., Prague, 1962; PhD in Physics, Czechoslovakian Acad. Scis., Prague, 1966. Research assoc. dept. metall. materials sci. and research fellow Wolfson Coll., Oxford (Eng.) U., 1967-75; research officer Central Elec. Research Labs., Central Elec. Generating Bd., Leatherhead, Eng., 1975-78; prof. materials sci. and engring. U. Pa., 1978—; vis. prf. U. Groningen, The Netherlands, 1985-86. Recipient Humboldt award for sr. scientists, Germany, 1992-93, Acta metallurgica Gold medal, 1996. Fellow Inst. Physics (London), Am. Soc. Metals Internat.; mem. Am. Phys. Soc., Materials Rsch. Soc. Research on atomistic models of lattice defects, interfaces and amorphous structures, fracture processes and mechanisms, plastic deformation, intermetallic compounds. Office: U Pa Dept Materials Sci and Engring 3231 Walnut St Philadelphia PA 19104-6202

VITERBI, ANDREW JAMES, electrical engineering and computer science educator, business executive; b. Bergamo, Italy, Mar. 9, 1935; came to U.S., 1939, naturalized, 1945; s. Achille and Maria (Luria) V.; m. Erna Finci, June 15, 1958; children: Audrey, Alan, Alexander. SB, MIT, 1957, SM, 1957; PhD, U. So. Calif., 1962; DEng (honoris causa), U. Waterloo, 1990. Research group supr. C.I.T. Jet Propulsion Lab., 1957-63; mem. faculty Sch. Engring. and Applied Sci., UCLA, 1963-73, assoc. prof., 1965-69, prof., 1969-73; exec. v.p. Linkabit Corp., 1973-82; pres. M/A-Com Linkabit, Inc., 1982-84; chief scientist, sr. v.p. M/A-Com. Inc., 1985; prof. elec. engring. and computer sci. U. Calif., San Diego, 1985-94; vice chmn., chief tech.

officer Qualcomm Inc., 1985—; chmn. U.S. Commn. C, URSI, 1982-85; vis. com. dept. elec. engring. and computer sci. MIT, 1984—. Author: Principles of Coherent Communication, 1966, CDMA: Principles of Spread Spectrum Communications, 1995, (with J. K. Omura) Principles of Digital Communication and Coding, 1979; bd. editors: Information and Control, 1967, Transactions on Info. Theory, 1972-75. Recipient award for valuable contbns. to telemetry, space electonics and telemetry group IRE, 1962, best original paper award Nat. Electronics Conf., 1963, outstanding papers award, info. theory group IEEE, 1968, Christopher Columbus Internat. Comms. award, 1975, Aerospace Comm. award AIAA, 1980, Outstanding Engring. Grad. award U. So. Calif., 1986; co-recipient NEC Corp. C and C Found. award, 1992, S.O. Rice award, 1994, Edward Rhein Found. award, 1994; Marconi Internat. fellow, 1990. Fellow IEEE (Alexander Graham Bell medal 1984, Shannon lectr. internat. symposium on info. theory 1991); mem. NAE. Office: Qualcomm Inc 6455 Lusk Blvd San Diego CA 92121-2779

VITIELLO, JUSTIN, language educator; b. N.Y., Feb. 14, 1941; s. Michael and Ruth (Weishaupt) V.; 1 child, Domenic. BA in English and Spanish, Brown U., 1963; MA in Spanish, U. Mich., 1966, PhD in Comparative Lit., 1970. Asst. prof. comparative lit. U. Mich., Ann Arbor, 1970-73; asst. prof., assoc. Italian Temple U., Phila., 1974-91, prof. Italian, 1991—. Author: Confessions of a Joe Rock, 1992, Poetics and Literature of the Sicilian Diaspora, 1993, (essays) Sicily Within, 1991, (poems) Vanzetti's Fish Cart, 1991, Subway Home, 1994. Grantee Fulbright, 1963-64. Mem. Modern Lang. Assn., Arba Sicula (editl. bd.), Indsl. Workers World (Phila. chpt.). Avocation: woodworking. Office: Temple U Dept French/Italian Philadelphia PA 19122

VITITOE, JAMES WILSON, lawyer; b. Oklahoma City, Mar. 14, 1947; s. Theodore Curtis Vititoe and Eula Mae (Cope) Seboth; m. Karen Dutcher, May 29, 1984; children: Justin Ryan, Travis James. BA in Psychology, Coll. William & Mary, 1971; JD, Southwestern U., 1976. Bar: Iowa 1977, Calif. 1977. Atty. Law Office of Edward Masry, L.A., 1977-84; ptnr. Masry & Vititoe, Studio City, Calif., 1985—. Named Outstanding Lawyer Yr. Congressman Mervin Dymally, 1992, 93. Mem. ATLA, Consumers Atty. Assn. L.A., Calif. Trial Lawyers Assn., Calif. Applicants Assn., Toastmasters (L.A.), Jonathan Club. Avocations: jogging, travel, theater, movies. Office: Masry & Vititoe 10850 Riverside Dr Ste 605 Toluca Lake CA 91602-2238

VITKOWSKY, VINCENT JOSEPH, lawyer; b. Newark, Oct. 3, 1955; s. Boniface and Rosemary (Ofack) V.; m. Mary Gunzburg, May 16, 1981; children: Vincent Jr., Victoria. BA, Northwestern U., 1977; JD, Cornell U., 1980. Bar: N.Y. 1981. Assoc. Hart and Hume, N.Y.C., 1980-84, Kroll & Tract, N.Y.C., 1984-87; of counsel Nixon, Hargrave, Devans & Doyle, N.Y.C., 1988-89; ptnr. Buchalter, Nemer, Fields & Younger, N.Y.C., 1990-95, Edwards & Angell, N.Y.C., 1996—; lectr. industry and bar groups. Contbr. articles to profl. jours. Mem. ABA (com. chmn.), Am. Arbitration Assn., Internat. Bar Assn. (com. officer), Assn. Bar City of N.Y. Home: 16 Weed St New Canaan CT 06840-6111 Office: Edwards & Angell 750 Lexington Ave New York NY 10022

VITOUSEK, PETER M., botany educator, research ecologist; b. Honolulu, Jan. 24, 1949. BA, Amherst Coll., 1971; PhD in Biol. Scis., Dartmouth Coll., 1975. Asst. prof. biology Ind. U., Bloomington, 1975-79; assoc. prof. botany U. N.C., Chapel Hill, 1980—. Mem. AAAS, Nat. Acad. Sci., Soil Sci. Soc. Am., Ecol. Soc. Am. Office: Stanford U Dept of Biological Sciences Stanford CA 94305*

VITT, DAVID AARON, medical manufacturing company executive; b. Phila., Aug. 3, 1938; s. Nathan and Flora B.; m. Renee Lee Salkever, Oct. 20, 1963; children: Nadine Lori, Jeffrey Richard. BS, Temple U., 1961. Sales engr. Picker X-Ray Corp., Phila., 1961-65; sales engr. Midwest Am., Chgo., 1965-67, product mgr., 1967-68, product mgr. regional sales, 1968-70; dir. mktg. Valtronic & Living Wills, Bronx, N.Y., 1970-74; v.p. Siemens Med. Systems Inc., gen. mgr. dental div., Iselin, N.J., 1974-86, past corp. v.p.; CEO, pres. Pelton & Crane, Charlotte, N.C., 1986-89; v.p. govt. sales Siemens Med. Systems Corp. Officers, ret., 1994; founder, pres., CEO D.A.V., Inc., 1995—; industry rep. to Am. Nat. Standards Inst.; co. rep. U.S.-USSR Trade and Econ. Coun.; mem. exec. com. Jr. Achievement, Charlotte. Bd. dirs. Am. Fund for Dental Health; apptd. mem. Charlotte Mecklenburg Community Relations Com.; mem. bd. visitors, bd. vis. U. N.C., Charlotte; Jr. Achievement exec com. mem., officer. Served in USAR, 1961-68. Mem. Am. Mgmt. Assn. (bd. dirs. N.J. chpt.), Am. Mktg. Assn., Am. Dental Trade Assn. (bd. dirs.), Dental Mfrs. Am. (past pres.), Am. Acad. Dental Radiology, Charlotte C. of C. (bd. advisors), Acad. Gen. Dentists (bd. mem. found.), Masons (32 deg.), Shriners. Republican.

VITT, SAMUEL BRADSHAW, communications media services executive; b. Greensboro, N.C., Oct. 23, 1926; s. Bruno Caesar and Gray (Bradshaw) V.; m. Marie Foster, Oct. 30, 1955; children: Joanne Louise, Michael Bradshaw, Mark Thomas. A.B., Dartmouth Coll., 1950. Exec. asst. TV film CBS, N.Y.C., 1950-52; broadcast media buyer Benton & Bowles, Inc., N.Y.C., 1952-54; broadcast media buyer Biow Co., N.Y.C., 1954-55, assoc. account exec., 1955-56; advt. dir. Banking Law Jour., 1955-69; broadcast media buyer Doherty, Clifford, Steers & Shenfield, Inc., N.Y.C., 1956-57, media supr., 1958-59, v.p., media supr., 1960, v.p., assoc. media dir., 1960, v.p., media dir., 1960-63, v.p. in charge media and broadcast programming, 1963-64; v.p., exec. dir. media-program dept. Ted Bates & Co., Inc., N.Y.C., 1964-66, sr. v.p., exec. dir. media-program dept., 1966-69; dir. Advt. Info. Services, Inc., 1964-65; founder, pres. Vitt Media Internat., Inc., N.Y.C., 1969-81, chmn., CEO, 1982-91, chmn. emeritus, 1991—; lectr. in field, 1967—; lectr. advt. media NYU, 1973, 74, Am. Mgmt. Assn., 1974, 75, Assn. Nat. Advertisers, 1967, 69, 70, Advt. Age Media Workshop, 1975. Media columnist Madison Ave, 1963-68; editorial cons. Media/Scope, 1968-69; contbr. Advertising Procedure, 1969, rev. edit., 1973, 5th, 6th, 7th edits., 1977, Exploring Advertising, 1970; contbg. editor Handbook of Advertising Management, 1970; contbg. editor Nation's Bus., Broadcasting, Variety, Anny, TV/Radio Age, Sponsor, Printer's Ink; producer rec. album The Body in the Seine; cover story guest editor Media Decisions, 1967. Chmn. radio-TV reps. divsn. Greater N.Y. Fund, 1962, chmn. consumer pub. divsn., 1963; mem. Nat. UN Day Com., 1973, vice chmn., 1974, assoc. chmn. 1975, co-chmn., 1976-77; bd. dirs. UN Assn. Am., 1977; bd. dirs., chmn. Rsch. Inst. Hearing and Balance Disorders Ltd., 1979—; mem. advt. adv. com. The Acting Com., 1984; mem. Pres. Reagan's Joint Presdl. Congl. Steering Com., 1982, Bush Presdl. Roundtable, 1990—. Served to Lt. (j.g.) USN, 1944-46. Recipient Media awards Sta. WRAP, Norfolk, Va., 1962, award of Merit Greater N.Y. Fund, 1963, Gold Key Advt. Leadership award Sta. Reps. Assn., 1967, ann. honors Ad Daily, 1967, Cert. Merit Media/Scope, 1967, 69, Creative Pub. Statement Concerning Advt. award, Cert. of Appreciation, U.S. Congress, 1993, Rep. Congl. Order Liberty, Nat. Rep. Congl. Com., 1993, Order of Merit, Nat. Rep. Senatorial Com., 1994, Rep. Presdl. award Pres. Ronald Reagan and Rep. Senate Leadership, 1994, (with wife) Rep. Senatorial Medal of Freedom, 1994; named one of 10 Best Dressed Men in Advt. Cmty., Gentlemen's Quar., 1979; honoree (with wife) New Rochelle Hosp. Med. Ctr. Centennial Waldorf-Astoria Gala, 1992. Mem. Am. Assn. Advt. Agys. (broadcast media com. dir. corr. 1958-63, media operating com. on consumer mags. 1964-65), Internat. Radio and TV Soc. (time-buying and selling seminar com. dir. 1961-62), Internat. Radio and TV Found. (faculty seminar 1974), Nat. Acad. Arts Sci. (mem. com. dir.), Media Dirs. Coun., Sigma Alpha Epsilon, Manor Park Beach Club, N.Y. Athletic Club, Roxbury Run Club (N.Y., Denver). Presbyterian. Avocations: tennis, skiing, golf, swimming, chess. Home: 3 Roosevelt Ave Larchmont NY 10538-2912

VITTADINI, ADRIENNE, fashion designer; b. Gyor, Hungary; came to U.S., 1957; d. Alexander and Aranka (Langhiel) Toth; m. Gian Luigi Maria Vittadini, 1972; 1 stepchild, Emanuele. Ed., Moore Coll. Art, Phila. Designer Rosanna-Warneco, N.Y.C., 1970-76; v.p. for design Kimberly Knitwear-Gen. Mills, N.Y.C., 1976-78; chmn. bd. Adrienne Vittadini Inc., N.Y.C., 1979—. Recipient Design award Retail Fashion Authorities Am., 1979, Outstanding Phila. Fashion Designer award Council for Labor and Industry, Phila., 1984, Coty Am. Fashion Critics award, 1984. Avocations: tennis; skiing; sailing; swimming. Office: Adrienne Vittadini Inc 575 7th Ave Fl 29 New York NY 10018-1805

VITTER, JEFFREY SCOTT, computer science educator, consultant; b. New Orleans, Nov. 13, 1955; s. Albert Leopold Jr. and Audrey Malvina (St. Raymond) V.; m. Sharon Louise Weaver, Aug. 14, 1982; children: Jillian St. Raymond, J. Scott Jr., Audrey Louise. BS in Math. with highest honors, U. Notre Dame, 1977; PhD in Computer Sci., Stanford U., 1980; AM (hon.), Brown U., 1986. Teaching fellow Stanford (Calif). U., 1979; asst. prof. Brown U., Providence, 1980-85, assoc. prof., 1985-88, prof., 1988-93; Gilbert, Louis and Edward Lehrman prof. computer sci. Duke U., Durham, N.C., 1993—, chmn. dept., 1993—; cons. IBM, 1981-86, Inst. for Def. Analyses, 1986, Ctr. for Computing Scis., 1992—; mem. rsch. staff Math. Scis. Rsch. Inst., Berkeley, 1986, Inst. Recherche en Informatique et en Automatique, Roquencourt, France, 1986-87; vis. prof. Ecole Normale Superieure, Paris, 1986-89; vis. and adj. prof. Tulane U., 1990—; lectr. Asian Sch. on Computer Sci., Bangkok, 1987; assoc. mem. Ctr. Excellence in Space Data and Info. Scis. Author: The Design and Analysis of Coalesced Hashing, 1987; editor Algorithmica, 1988, 94—, guest editor, 1994; editor Math. Sys. Theory: Internat. Jour. on Math. Computing Theory, 1991—, Soc. for Indsl. and Applied Math. Jour. on Computing, 1989—; contbr. articles to profl. jours.; patentee in field. Recipient Faculty Devel. award IBM, 1984, NSF Presdl. Young Investigator award, 1985; NSF grad. fellow, 1977-80; Guggenheim fellow, N.Y.C., 1986-87. Fellow IEEE (editor Trans. on Computers 1985, 87-91), Assn. for Computing Machinery (editor Comms. 1988-95, mem.-at-large spl. interest group on automata and computability theory 1987-91, vice chair spl. interest group on algorithms and computation theory 1991—), Phi Beta Kappa, Sigma Xi. Avocations: reading, golf, basketball, baseball, football. Office: Duke U Dept Computer Sci Durham NC 27708-0129

VITTETOE, MARIE CLARE, retired medical technology educator; b. Keota, Iowa, May 19, 1927; d. Edward Daniel and Marcella Matilda Vittetoe. BS, Marycrest Coll., 1950; MS, W.Va. U., 1971, EdD, 1973. Staff technician St. Joseph Hosp., Ottumwa, Iowa, 1950-70; instr. Ottumwa Hosp. Sch. Med. Tech., 1957-70, St. Joseph Hosp. Sch. Nursing, Ottumwa, 1950-70; asst. prof. U. Ill., Champaign-Urbana, 1973-78; prof. clin. lab. scis. U. Ky., Lexington, 1978-94. Contbr. articles to profl. jours. Recipient Kingston award for Creative Teaching; Recognition award for svc. to edn. Commonwealth of Ky. Coun. on Higher Edn.; named Ky. Col. Mem. Am. Soc. for Med. Tech. (chmn. 1986-89, Profl. Achievement award 1991, Ky. Mem. of Yr. award 1994), Am. Soc. Clin. Lab. Scis., Am. Soc. Clin. Pathologists (assoc.), Alpha Mu Tau, Phi Delta Kappa, Alpha Eta. Avocation: bicycling.

VITTORIA, JOSEPH V., car rental company executive; b. 1935; married; 4 children. B.S., Yale U., 1957; M.B.A., Columbia U., 1959. With Hertz Corp., 1960-65, 77-82, former pres., chief exec. officer; with Avis Inc., Garden City, N.Y., 1965-77, 82—, regional mgr., 1965-69, mng. dir. Avis Italy, 1969-71, v.p., gen. mgr. Avis Europe, 1971-73, sr. v.p., gen. mgr. Avis Europe, 1973-77, exec. v.p. sales and mktg., 1982-83, exec. v.p., 1983-87, pres., CEO, 1987—, also chmn., CEO; bd. dirs. UAL Corp. Bd. visitors Georgetown U.; mem. devel. bd. Yale U., bd. dirs. Columbia U. Grad. Sch. of Bus.; adv. dir. Nat. Crime Prevention Coun.; bd. govs. Nat. Ctr. for Disability Svcs.; bd. overseers Columbia U. Bus. Sch., N.Y.C. Mem. Georgetown U. Alumni Assn., Columbia U. Bus. Sch. Alumni Assn. Office: Avis Inc 900 Old Country Rd Garden City NY 11530-2128

VITTORINI, CARLO, publishing company executive; b. Phila., Feb. 28, 1929; s. Domenico and Helen (Whitney) V.; m. Alice Hellerman, Oct. 10, 1953 (div. Dec. 1993); children: Carolyn, Stephen Whitney; m. Nancy Braddock, Dec. 19, 1993. B.A., U. Pa., 1950. Promotion assoc. Chilton Co., Phila., 1950-51; merchandising mgr. Farm-Jour., Inc., Phila., 1951-53; advt. sales rep. Saturday Evening Post, Phila., 1953-61; assoc. advt. mgr. Look Mag., N.Y.C., 1961-65; publisher Redbook Mag., N.Y.C., 1965-75; pres. Charter Publishing, N.Y.C., 1975-78, Harlequin Publishing, N.Y.C., 1978—; chmn. pub., chief exec. officer Parade Publications subs. Advance Pubs. Inc., N.Y.C., 1979—. Trustee The Jackson Lab., Bar Harbor, Maine, 1973—; former mem. vestry St. Matthew's Ch., Bedford, N.Y. Served with USAR, 1950-57. Judge Advt. Hall of Fame, Am. Advt. Fedn. Mem. Advt. Coun. N.Y.C. (dir.-at-large 1974—), Mag. Pubs. Assn. (bd. dirs. 1970-79), Am. Advt. Fedn. (chmn. 1992-93), The Sky Club. Avocations: outdoor activities; tennis. Home: 40 Dusenberry Rd Bronxville NY 10708-2421 Office: Parade Publications 711 3d Ave New York NY 10017-4014

VITTUM, DANIEL WEEKS, JR., lawyer; b. Lynch, Ky., Feb. 10, 1939; s. Daniel W. and Kathryn Margaret (Jones) V.; m. Stephanie Ann Empkie, Aug. 18, 1962 (div. July 1987); children: Daniel W., III, Stephen F.; m. Christine L. Jacobek, Nov. 17, 1990. BS, U. Ill., 1961; JD, U. Mich., 1964. Bar: Ill. 1964, U.S. Dist. Ct. (no. dist.) Ill. 1965, U.S. Supreme Ct. 1977, U.S. Ct. Appeals (7th cir.) 1976, U.S. Ct. Appeals (4th cir.) 1982, U.S. Ct. Appeals (9th cir.) 1978, U.S. Ct. Appeals (Fed. cir.) 1982, U.S. Ct. Appeals (6th cir.) 1992. Assoc. Kirkland & Ellis, Chgo., 1964-69, ptnr., 1970—. Bd. dirs., pres. Northwestern U. Settlement Assn.; mem. vis. com. U. Mich. Law Sch. Mem. ABA, Am. Intellectual Property Assn., Intellectual Property Law Assn. Chgo., Order of Coif, Phi Beta Kappa. Clubs: Mid-Am., East Bank (Chgo.), Chgo. Yacht Club. Office: Kirkland & Ellis 200 E Randolph St Chicago IL 60601-6436

VITULLI, CLARK JOSEPH, auto manufacturing company executive; b. Bklyn., Apr. 2, 1946; s. William and Rosaria (Stallone) V. B.S., U. Fla., 1968. With Chrysler Corp., various locations, 1969—, zone mgr., Los Angeles, 1980-84, nat. mdse. mgr. Dodge div., Detroit, 1984-86, regional mgr., Anaheim, Calif., 1986—; mem. dealer licensing div. Fla. Dept. Motor Vehicles, 1978-79. Mem. Am. Mgmt. Assn., Sales and Mktg. Execs. Los Angeles, Adcraft Club of Detroit, Internat. Platform Assn., Mensa, Beta Theta Pi.

VITUNAC, ANN E., judge; b. 1949. BS, Univ. of Fla., 1970; JD, Stetson Coll. of Law, 1972. Chief trial atty. Fla. State Attorney's Office, West Palm Beach, 1973-85; magistrate judge U.S. Dist. Ct. (Fla. so. dist.), 11th circuit, West Palm Beach, 1985—. Recipient Moot Court award Stetson Coll. of Law, 1972, Robert Sykes award Stetson Coll. of Law, 1973. Mem. Phi Delta Phi Legal Frat., Palm Beach County Bar Assn. Office: US Courthouse 701 Clematis St Rm 423 West Palm Beach FL 33401-5112

VITZ, PAUL CLAYTON, psychologist, educator; b. Toledo, Aug. 27, 1935; m. Evelyn Birge; 6 children. BA high honors in Psychology, U. Mich., 1953; PhD, Stanford U., 1962. Instr. psychology Pomona (Calif.) Coll., 1962-64; asst. prof. NYU, 1965-70, assoc. prof., 1970-85, dir. psychology dept. undergrad. program, 1973-79, prof., 1985—, acting dir. master's program, 1988-89, 90-91, acting dir. grad. program, 1989-90; adj. prof. John Paul II Inst. on Marriage and Family, Washington, 1990—, Internat. Acad. Philosophy, 1994—; lectr. in field. Author: Psychology as Religion: The Cult of Self-Worship, 1977, 2d edit., 1994, (with A.B. Glimcher) Modern Art and Modern Science: The Parallel Analysis of Vision, 1984, Censorship: Evidence of Bias in Our Children's Textbooks, 1986, Sigmund Freud's Christian Unconscious, 1988; contbr. articles to profl. jours., chpts. to books. Rsch. grantee Nat. Inst. Mental Health, 1963-64, 64-66, 66-67, Nat. Inst. Neurol. Diseases and Blindness grantee, 1970-73, 73-74, Shalom Found. grantee, 1974-78, Nat. Inst. Edn. grantee, 1983, 84-85, Dept. Edn. grantee, 1986-87. Office: NYU Dept Psychology New York NY 10003

VIVIAN, JOHNSON EDWARD, retired chemical engineering educator; b. Montreal, Que., Can., July 6, 1913; came to U.S., 1936, naturalized, 1942; s. Edgar John and Mary Meade (McMahon) V.; m. Florence Evelyn Frye, Feb. 10, 1940; children: John Edward, David James, Ann. B. Chem. Engring., McGill U., 1936; S.M., Mass. Inst. Tech., 1939, Sc.D., 1945. Research engr. Canadian Pulp and Paper Assn., 1936; teaching asst. MIT, Cambridge, 1937-38; asst. dir. Bangor chem. engring. practice sch. MIT, 1938-41, dir. Buffalo chem. engring. practice sch. sta., 1941-43, research engr. govt. project, 1943-46, assoc. prof. chem. engring., 1946-56, prof., 1956-80, sr. lectr., 1980-85, prof. emeritus, 1980—, dir. chem. engring. practice sch., 1946-57, 72-80, dir. Oak Ridge E.P.S., 1948-57; Cons. chem. engring., 1946—; vis. prof. Birla Inst. Tech. and Sci., Pilani, Rajasthan, India, 1972—; exec. officer dept. chem. engring., 1974-79. Fellow Am. Inst. Chem. Engrs. (Colburn award 1948); mem. TAPPI, Am. Chem. Soc., AAAS, Am. Soc. Engring. Edn., Sigma Xi. Home: Ledgewood E #203 80 Austin Dr Burlington VT 05401-5448 Office: Mass Inst Tech Dept Chem Engring Cambridge MA 02139

VIVIANO, SAM JOSEPH, illustrator; b. Detroit, Mar. 13, 1953; s. Thomas John Viviano and Prudy Katherine (DiGiuseppe) LaMendola; m. Diane E. Bloomfield, Sept. 3, 1988; 1 child, Alicia Catherine Viviano. BFA, U. Mich., 1975. Textile designer Manes Fabric Co., N.Y.C., 1976-77; freelance illustrator N.Y.C., 1976—; art instr. Sch. Visual Arts, N.Y.C., 1981-93, Pratt Manhattan Sch. Art, 1992—. Mem. Graphic Artists Guild (chmn. N.Y.C. chpt. 1981-87, treas. 1987-89). Office: 25 W 13th St New York NY 10011-7955

VIVONA, JOSEPH F., federal agency administrator; b. Bklyn., Mar. 18, 1951; m. Barbara Baird; children: Christopher, Jonathan. BA, St. John's U., 1972; MA, NYU, 1974. Various positions including asst. commr. for mgmt. & budget N.J. Dept. Human Svcs., 1977-83; dep. vice chancellor CUNY, 1983-85, vice chancellor, 1985-90; dep. state budget dir., dep. state contr. Office of Mgmt. and Budget, State of N.J., 1990-94; CFO U.S. Dept. Energy, Washington, 1994—. Office: Dept of Energy Chief Financial Officer 1000 Independence Ave SW Washington DC 20585

VIZARD, FRANK JOSEPH, journalist; b. N.Y.C., July 7, 1955; s. Matthew Joseph and Anne (Tierney) V.; m. Mary McAleer, Apr. 28, 1984. BA, NYU, 1977. News editor Paper Trade Jour., N.Y.C., 1977-78; mng. editor Paperboard Packaging, N.Y.C., 1978-80; editor Autosound & Communications, N.Y.C., 1980-84; freelance writer N.Y.C., 1984-90; electronics and photography editor Popular Mechanics mag., N.Y.C., 1990—. Avocations: basketball, Irish affairs, sports science. Office: Popular Mechanics Mag 224 W 57th St New York NY 10019-3212

VIZCAINO, JOSE LUIS PIMENTAL, professional baseball player; b. San Cristobal, Dominican Rep., Mar. 26, 1995. Grad. high sch., Dominican Rep. With L.A. Dodgers, 1989-90, Chgo. Cubs, 1991-93; infielder N.Y. Mets, 1994—. Office: NY Mets Roosevelt Ave and 126th St Flushing NY 11368*

VIZQUEL, OMAR ENRIQUE, professional baseball player; b. Caracus, Venezuela, Apr. 24, 1967. Grad. high sch., Caracus. With Seattle Mariners, 1989-93; shortstop Cleve. Indians, 1993—. Recipient Winner Am. League Golden Glove, 1993-94. Office: Cleve Indians 2401 Ontario St Cleveland OH 44115*

VIZZA, ROBERT FRANCIS, hospital executive, former university administrator, marketing educator; b. N.Y.C., Apr. 2, 1933; s. Saverio and Agatha (Costanzo) V.; m. Joan Kilday, Dec. 11, 1954; children: Lorraine, Mary, Cathy, Robert. BBA, Pace Coll., 1954; MBA, CUNY, 1959; PhD, NYU, 1967; LLD (hon.), LaSalle Coll., 1978. Account exec. Diebold Inc., N.Y.C., 1954-61; asst. prof. mktg. St. John's U., 1962-66; assoc. prof. mktg., chmn. dept. bus. adminstrn. C.W. Post Coll., 1966-67; dean Sch. Bus., prof. mktg. Manhattan Coll., 1967-85; pres., CEO St. Francis Hosp., Roslyn, N.Y., 1985-95, vice chmn., 1995—; pres., CEO, St. Francis Corp., 1985—, St. Francis Hosp. Found., Ind., 1985—, St. Francis Rsch. and Ednl. Corp., 1985—; cons. to industry; bd. dirs. Emery Air Freight Corp., Am. Assembly Collegiate Schs. Bus., The Green Point Savs. Bank, Phoenix Home Life, Ins., Green Point Fins., Holding Co., Greater N.Y. Hosp. Assn. Author: Improving Salesmen's Use of Time, 1962, Measuring the Value of the Field Sales Force, Training and Developing the Field Sales Manager, 1965, Basic Facts in Marketing, 1966, Adoption of the Marketing Concept, 1967, New Handbook of Sales Training, 1967, Time and Territory Management, 1972, Time and Territorial Management-A Programmed Learning Course, 1975, 2d edit., 1979; contbr. articles to profl. jours. Pres. bd. St. Mary's Sch.; bd. dirs. Pace U., Sch. of the Holy Child. Ford Found. fellow; recipient Jerome Levy Found. award. Fellow Internat. Acad. Mgmt.; mem. Middle Atlantic Assn. Colls. of Bus., Adminstrn. (v.p. 1970-71, pres. 1972-73, exec. com. 1969—), Sales Execs. Club N.Y. (bd. dirs.), Am. Mktg. Assn., Delta Sigma Pi, Delta Mu Delta, Pi Sigma Epsilon. Home: 3 Maria Ln Old Brookville NY 11545-2507 Office: St Francis Hosp 100 Port Washington Blvd Roslyn NY 11576-1353

VLACH, JIRI, electrical engineering educator, researcher; b. Prague, Czechoslovakia, Oct. 5, 1922; emigrated to Can., 1969; s. Frantisek and Bozena (Papouskova) V.; m. Dagmar Gutova, Oct. 22, 1949; 1 son, Martin. Dipl.eng., Tech. U. Prague, 1947, C.Sc., 1957. With Research Inst. for Radio Communications, Prague, 1948-67; head math. dept. Research Inst. for Radio Communications, until 1967; vis. prof. U. Ill., Urbana, 1967-69; prof. elec. engring. U. Waterloo (Ont., Can.), 1969—. Author: Computerized Approximation and Synthesis of Linear Networks, 1969, (with others) Computer Methods for Circuit Analysis and Design, 1983, 2nd edit., 1994, Basic Network Theory with Computer Applications, 1992; assoc. editor IEEE Trans. on Circuits and Systems, 1979-80. Fellow IEEE; mem. Eta Kappa Nu. Home: 355 Craigleith Dr, Waterloo, ON Canada N2L 5B5 Office: University Waterloo, 200 University Ave West, Waterloo, ON Canada N2L 3G1

VLADECK, BRUCE CHARNEY, charitable organization executive; b. N.Y.C., Sept. 13, 1949; s. Stephen Charney and Judith (Pomarlen) V.; m. Fredda Wellin, Aug. 5, 1973; children—Elizabeth Charney, Stephen Isaiah, Abigail Sarah. B.A., Harvard U., 1970; M.A., U. Mich, 1972, Ph.D. in Polit. Sci., 1973. Assoc. social scientist N.Y.C.-Rand Inst., 1973-74; asst. prof. Columbia U., N.Y.C., 1974-78; assoc. prof. Columbia U., 1978-79; asst. commr. health planning and resources devel. N.J. Dept. Health, Trenton, 1979-82; asst. v.p. Robert Wood Johnson Found., Princeton, N.J., 1982-83; pres. United Hosp. Fund, N.Y.C., 1983—; now adminstr. Dept. Health & Human Services, Washington; adj. prof. pub. adminstrn. NYU, 1984—; cons. U.S. Gen. Acctg. Office, other agys., Washington, 1984—; mem. N.Y. State Coun. on Health Care Financing, Albany, 1978—; mem. com. on nursing home regulation Inst. Medicine, Washington, 1983-85, chmn. com. on health care for homeless people, 1986-88, mem. prospective payment assessment com., 1986—. Author: Unloving Care: The Nursing Home Tragedy, 1981. Contbr. numerous articles to profl. pubs. Fellow N.Y. Acad. Medicine; mem. Inst. Medicine, Nat. Acad. Scis., Phi Beta Kappa. Home: 161 W 15th St New York NY 10011-6720 Office: Dept of Health & Human Services Healthcare Financing Admin 200 Independence Ave SW Washington DC 20201-0004*

VLADEM, PAUL JAY, investment advisor, broker; b. Chgo., Apr. 5, 1952; s. Arthur I. and Elaine A. (Ascher) V.; m. Sondra Joyce Berman, Dec. 27, 1981; children: Ashley Sherree, Evan David. BSBA with honors and high distinction, U. Ill., Chgo., 1974. Lic. brokerage securities, Fla., Ill., Ariz., Conn., Ga., Ind., N.C., Colo., Md., Nev., N.Y., Ohio, Calif., Utah; registered investment advisor; lic. ins. agt., Fla., Ill., Ind., Utah, Conn.; CPA, Fla., Ill.; lic. real estate agt., Fla. In charge acct. Peat Marwick, Fort Lauderdale, Fla., 1974-76; mgr. McGladrey & Pullen, CPA, Fort Lauderdale, 1976-85; sr. v.p. fin. Integrated Resources formerly Easter Kramer, Boca Raton, Fla., 1985-89; pres. Associated Investor Svcs., Fort Lauderdale, 1989—. Bd. dirs. Israel Bonds, Ft. Lauderdale, 1994, Jewish Family Svc., Ft. Lauderdale, 1993; chmn. CPA Com. on Israel Bonds, Ft. Lauderdale, 1994; co-chmn. investment com. Jewish Fedn. Found., Hollywood, Fla., 1994—, mem. prof. adv. com., 1992—. Named One of Top Ten Brokers of Yr. Registered Rep. Mag., 1994. Mem. AICPA (personal planning divsn.), Fla. Inst. CPAs (mem. personal fin. planning com., 1985), Internat. Platform Assn. Democrat. Jewish. Avocations: tennis, basketball, attending sporting events. Home: 11157 NW 18th Ct Coral Springs FL 33071 Office: Associated Investor Svcs 2699 Stirling Rd # 100 Fort Lauderdale FL 33312-6517

VLASIC, ROBERT JOSEPH, food company executive; b. Detroit, Mar. 9, 1926; m. Nancy Rita Reuter; children: James, William, Richard, Michael, Paul. BS, U. Mich., 1949. Chmn. Vlasic Foods, Inc., West Bloomfield, Mich., 1963-88, chmn. emeritus, 1988—; chmn. Campbell Soup Co., Camden, N.J., 1988-93, chmn. emeritus, 1993—; bd. dirs. Reynolds Metals Co., Richmond, Va. Vice chmn. bd. trustees Henry Ford Health System, Detroit, 1977; vice chmn. bd. trustees Cranbrook Ednl. Community, Bloomfield Hills, 1979. Home: 1910 Rathmor Rd Bloomfield Hills MI 48304-2149 Office: 710 North Woodward Bloomfield Hills MI 48304-2851*

VLAZNY, JOHN GEORGE, bishop; b. Chgo., Feb. 22, 1937; s. John George and Marie Hattie (Brezina) V. BA, St. Mary of the Lake Coll., Mundelein, Ill., 1958; STL, Pontifical Gregorian U., Rome, 1962; MA in

Classics, U. Mich., 1967; MEd, Loyola U., 1972. Ordained priest Roman Catholic Church, 1961, consecrated bishop, 1983. Assoc. pastor St. Paul of the Cross Ch., Park Ridge, Ill., 1962-63; assoc. pastor St. Clement Ch., Chgo., 1963-68; assoc. pastor St. Aloysius Ch., Chgo., 1968-72, pastor, 1979-81; assoc. pastor St. Sylvester Ch., Chgo., 1972-74, Precious Blood Ch., Chgo., 1974-79; faculty Quigley Prep., North Chgo., 1963-79; dean of studies Quigley Prep., 1969-79; rector Niles Coll., Chgo., 1981-83; aux. bishop Archdiocese of Chgo., 1983-87; Episcopal vicar Vicariate I, Chgo., 1983-87; bishop Episc. Ch., Winona, Minn., 1987—; pres. Presbyteral Senate, Chgo., 1976-77; mem. Diocesan Clergy Personnel Bd., Chgo., 1981-84, chmn., 1983-84. Bd. dirs. NED, Latino Tng. Ctr., Chgo., 1980-81, Sacred Heart Sch. Theology, Hales Corners, Wis., 1986—, St. Mary's Coll., Winona, 1987—. Mem. Nat. Communications Found. (bd. dirs. 1990—), Nat. Conf. Cath. Bishops (various coms. 1983—). Roman Catholic. Avocations: music; running. Office: Chancery Office PO Box 588 55 W Sanborn Winona MN 55987-0588*

VLCEK, DONALD JOSEPH, JR., food distribution company executive, consultant; b. Chgo., Oct. 30, 1949; s. Donald Joseph and Rosemarie (Krizek) V.; m. Claudia Germain Meyer, July 22, 1978 (div. 1983); 1 child, Suzanne Mae; m. Valeria Olive Russell, Nov. 11, 1989; children: James Donald, Victoria Rose. BBA, U. Mich., 1971. Gen. mgr. Popps, Inc., Hamtramck, Mich., 1969-76; pres. Domino's Pizza Distbn. Corp., Ann Arbor, Mich., 1978-93, chmn., 1993-94, also bd. dirs.; pres. Don Vlcek & Assocs., Ltd., Plymouth, Mich., 1994—; trustee Domino's Pizza Ptnrs. Found.; bd. dirs. RPM Pizza Inc., Gulfport, Miss., Dimango Corp., South Lyon, Mich.; sr. v.p. distbn. and tech. Domino's Ohio Commissary, Zanesville; pres. Morel Mountain Corp.; judge 1994 Duck Stamp contest U.S. Dept. Interior, Jr. Fed. Duck Stamp Contest, 1995. Author: The Domino Effect, 1991 (Best of Bus. award ALA 1992, Soundview's Top 30 Business books of 1993); contbr. articles to profl. jours. Bd. dirs. Men's Hockey League of Oak Park, Mich., 1973-78. Named Person of Yr. Bd. Franchises, Boston, 1981; recipient Teal award Ducks Unltd., 1992, State Major Gifts Chmn. award, 1992, 93, State Chmn.'s award, 1992, State Major Gifts award, 1994. Mem. Mich. Steelheaders Assn. (life), Ducks Unltd. (life, Domino's Pizza chpt. treas., sponsor, chmn. 1988—, Mich. state bd. dirs., life sponsor, chmn. 1989, 91-92, state trustee 1992—, chmn. exec. com. 1992-94, major gifts chmn. 1993—, chmn. strategic devel. com. 1994, sponsor in perpetuity Grand Slam Life), Mich. United Conservation Club (life), Whitetails Unltd. (life), Pheasants Forever (life), Midstates Masters Bowling Assn. (bd. dirs. 1976-85), Barton Hills Country Club (golf com., capt. dist. team), U. Mich. Alumni Assn. (life), Domino's Lodge/Drummond Island Wildlife Habitat Found. (pres., chmn. bd.), Vlcek Family Wildlife Found. (pres., chmn. bd.), Elks (life), Die Hard Cubs Fan Club. Republican. Roman Catholic. Avocations: hunting, fishing, hockey, collecting wildlife art, coins, and sports cards and memorabilia. Home: 9251 Beck Rd N Plymouth MI 48170-3336 Office: Don Vlcek & Assoc Ltd PO Box 701353 Plymouth MI 48170-0963

VLIET, GARY CLARK, mechanical engineering educator; b. Bassano, Alta., Can., June 3, 1933. B.Sc. in Chem. Engring, U. Alta., 1955; M.S. in Mech. Engring, Stanford U., 1957, Ph.D., 1962. With Lockheed Research Labs., Palo Alto, Calif., 1961-71; mem. faculty U. Tex., Austin, 1971—; prof. mech. engring. U. Tex., 1979—, W. R. Woolrich prof. engring., 1985—. Contbr. articles to profl. jours. Mem. Austin Renewable Energy Commn., 1979-83. Recipient awards and fellowships. Fellow ASME (Best Heat Transfer Paper award 1970); mem. ASHRAE, Am. Solar Energy Soc., Tex. Solar Energy Soc. (founder, bd. dirs. 1976—, pres. 1980, 94). Research areas include heat and mass transfer, solar energy. Office: U Tex Dept Mech Engr ETC 5.160 Austin TX 78712

VOEDISCH, LYNN ANDREA, reporter; b. Evanston, Ill., June 20, 1954; d. Robert William and Elaine Theresa (Strand) V.; m. Kent Van Meter, June 21, 1981 (div. 1987); 1 child, Erik Kyle. BA, Grinnell Coll., 1976. Reporter Pioneer Press, Wilmette, Ill., 1977-79, Los Angeles Times, 1979, Chgo. Sun-Times, 1980—. Recipient Stick O'Type award Chgo. Newspaper Guild, 1984. Democrat. Episcopalian. Avocations: singing, theater, baroque music, sewing. Office: Chgo Sun-Times 401 N Wabash Ave Chicago IL 60611-3532

VOEGELI, VICTOR JACQUE, history educator, dean; b. Jackson, Tenn., Dec. 21, 1934; s. Victor Jacque and Winnie Lou (Lassiter) V.; m. Anna Jean King, Oct. 14, 1956; children: Victor Jacque, Charles Lassiter. B.S., Murray State Coll., 1956; M.A., Tulane U., 1961, Ph.D., 1965. Instr. history Tulane U., 1963-65, asst. prof., 1965-67; asst. prof. history Vanderbilt U., 1967-69, assoc. prof., 1969-73, prof. history, 1973—, chmn. history dept., 1973-76, dean Coll. Arts and Sci., 1976-92. Author: Free But Not Equal: The Midwest and the Negro During the Civil War, 1967. Served with U.S. Army, 1956-58. Nat. Endowment Humanities grantee, 1969-70, 72. Mem. So. Hist. Assn. Presbyterian. Home: 3704D Estes Rd Nashville TN 37215-1729 Office: Vanderbilt U Nashville TN 37240

VOELKER, CHARLES ROBERT, archbishop, academic dean; b. Cleve., June 12, 1944; s. Charles Christ and Bertha Elizabeth (Zak) V. BA, Nat. Coll. Edn., 1968; MS, TCU, 1974; STL, Holy Trinity Sem., 1989; PhD, Internat. Sem., 1989. Ordained to ministry Orthodox Ch. as priest, 1974, as bishop, 1984. Parish priest Am. Orthodox Ch., Cleve., 1974-84; bishop Am. Orthodox Ch., Deltona, Fla., 1984—; tchr., adminstr. Ashtubula County Schs., 1971-76; acad. dean Internat. Sem., Plymouth, Fla., 1990—; pres., rector Holy Trinity Sem., Deltona, 1985—; dir. human svcs. New London (Ohio) Hosp., 1981-84; pres. Eagles Fitness Ctr., Middleburg Heights, Ohio, 1977-84; tchr. Polaris Vocat. Ctr., Middleburg Heights, 1981-83. Chaplain maj. Air Force Aux., CPA, 1993—. Mem. Order of St. Gregory the Illuminator (comdr. 1989—), Order of St. George (comdr. 1989—), Order St. John of Jerusalem. Home: 1088 Eastbrook Ave Deltona FL 32738-6925 Office: Internat Sem PO Box 1208 Plymouth FL 32768-1208 *To feed God's people you must first feed yourself.*

VOELKER, MARGARET IRENE (MEG VOELKER), gerontology, medical, surgical nurse; b. Bitburg, Germany, Dec. 31, 1955; d. Lewis R. and Patricia Irene (Schaffner) Miller; 1 child, Christopher Douglas. Diploma, Clover Park Vocat.-Tech., Tacoma, 1975, diploma in practical nursing, 1984; ASN, Tacoma (Wash.) C.C., 1988; postgrad., U. Washington Tacoma, Tacoma, 1992-95; student nurse practitioner program, U. of Wash., 1995—. Cert. ACLS. Nursing asst. Jackson County Hosp., Altus, Okla., 1976-77; receptionist Western Clinic, Tacoma, 1983; LPN, Tacoma Gen. Hosp., 1984-88, clin. geriatric nurse, 1988-90, clin. nurse post anesthesia care unit peri-operative svcs., 1990—; pre-admit clinic nurse, 1995—; mem. staff nurse coun. Tacoma Gen. Hosp., 1990-91. Recipient G. Corydon Wagner endowment fund scholarship. Mem. PostAnesthesia Nurses Assn., Phi Theta Kappa, Sigma Theta Tau.

VOELL, RICHARD ALLEN, private investor; b. Chgo., Dec. 29, 1933; s. John Herman and Esther Frances (Anderson) V.; m. Virginia Charlotte Broderick, Dec. 20, 1958; children: David Broderick, Gregory Jon, Jeffrey Scott. B.A., U. Ill., 1956; M.B.A., U. Hawaii, 1960. With Beatrice Foods Co., Chgo., 1958-79, group mgr. recreational products group, 1971-73, corp. v.p., 1973-75, vice chmn., 1975-79; pres., chief operating officer Penn Central Corp., Greenwich, Conn., 1979-81, chief exec. officer, 1981; pres., chief exec. officer The Rockefeller Group, N.Y.C., 1982-95; chmn. Harbor Rock Corp.; mem. adv. bds. Fiat and Club Med; mem. bds. SPA Exor and Con Edison; vice chmn. N.Y.C. Partnerships. Chair nominating com. Wildlife Conservation Soc.; chmn. Bus. Coun. for UN; mem. bd. Mcpl. Art Soc., N.Y.C. 1st lt. AUS, 1956-58. Mem. Chief Execs. Orgn., Coun. on Fgn. Rels., Econ. Club N.Y. (past chmn.), Rockefeller Ctr. Club, Greenwich (Conn.) Country Club, Riverside (Conn.) Yacht Club, Chgo. Club, U. Ill. Founders Club. Home: 25 Pilot Rock Ln Riverside CT 06878-2615 Office: Rockefeller Group 1230 Avenue Of The Americas New York NY 10020-1513

VOET, PAUL C., specialty chemical company executive; b. Cin., July 7, 1946; s. Leo C. and Claire G. (Burdick) V.; m. Judy A. Gates, Aug. 24, 1968; children—Jeffrey, Jeannette, Jamie, Jodie. B.A., U. Cin., 1968; M.B.A., U. Pa., 1970. Asst. to pres. KDI Corp., Cin., 1970; asst. to pres. Chemed Corp., 1970-72; v.p. Vestal Labs. div. Chemed, St. Louis, 1972-74, exec. v.p., 1974-76, pres., 1976-80; exec. v.p., chief operating officer Chemed Corp., Cin., 1986-88, exec. v.p., 1988—; pres., CEO Nat. Sanitary Supply Co. Mem. Pres.'s adv. council St. Louis U., 1979. Mem. Am. Mgmt. Assn. (president's coun.), Young Pres. Assn., Phi Beta Kappa, Beta Gamma Sigma (dir.'s table), Omicron Delta Epsilon, Phi Alpha Theta, Phi Eta Sigma. Avocations: scuba diving, photography, personal computers. Home: 8180 Graves Rd Cincinnati OH 45243-3631 Office: Chemed Corp 2900 Chemed Ctr 255 E 5th St Cincinnati OH 45202-4700 Also: Nat San Supply Co 255 E 5th St Cincinnati OH 45202-4700

VOGEL, ARTHUR ANTON, clergyman; b. Milw., Feb. 24, 1924; s. Arthur Louis and Gladys Eirene (Larson) V.; m. Katharine Louise Nunn, Dec. 29, 1947; children: John Nunn, Arthur Anton, Katharine Ann. Student, U. of South, 1942-43, Carroll Coll., 1943-44; B.D., Nashotah House Theol. Sem., 1946; M.A., U. Chgo., 1948; Ph.D., Harvard, 1952; S.T.D., Gen. Theol. Sem., 1969; D.C.L., Nashotah House, 1969; D.D., U. of South, 1971. Ordained deacon Episcopal Ch., 1946, priest, 1948; teaching asst. philosophy Harvard, Cambridge, Mass., 1949-50; instr. Trinity Coll., Hartford, Conn., 1950-52; mem. faculty Nashotah House Theol. Sem., Nashotah, Wis., 1952-71; asso. prof. Nashotah House Theol. Sem., 1954-56, William Adams prof. philosophical and systematic theology, 1956-71, sub-dean Sem., 1964-71; bishop coadjutor Diocese of West Mo., Kansas City, 1971-72; bishop Diocese of West Mo., 1972-89; rector Ch. St. John Chrysostom, Delafield, Wis., 1952-56; dir. Anglican Theol. Rev., Evanston, Ill., 1964-69; mem. Internat. Anglican-Roman Cath. Consultation, 1970-90; mem. Nat. Anglican-Roman Catholic Consultation, 1965-84, Anglican chmn., 1973-84; mem. Standing Commn. on Ecumenical Relations of Episcopal Ch., 1957-79; mem. gen. bd. examining chaplains Episcopal Ch., 1971-72; del. Episcopal Ch., 4th Assembly World Council Chruches, Uppsala, Sweden, 1968, and others. Author: Reality, Reason and Religion, 1957, The Gift of Grace, 1958, The Christian Person, 1963, The Next Christian Epoch, 1966, Is the Last Supper Finished?, 1968, Body Theology, 1973, The Power of His Resurrection, 1976, Proclamation 2: Easter, 1980, The Jesus Prayer for Today, 1982, I Know God Better Than I Know Myself, 1989, Christ in His Time and Ours, 1982, God, Prayer and Healing, 1995, Radical Christianity and the Flesh of Jesus, 1995; editor: Theology in Anglicanism, 1985; contbr. articles to profl. jours. Vice chmn. bd. dirs. St. Luke's Hosp., Kansas City, Mo., 1971, chmn., 1973-89. Research fellow Harvard, 1950. Mem. Am. Philos. Assn., Metaphys. Soc. Am., Soc. Existential and Phenomenological Philosophy, Catholic Theol. Soc. Am. Home: 524 W 119th Ter Kansas City MO 64145-1043

VOGEL, BERNARD HENRY, lawyer; b. N.Y.C., May 23, 1941; s. Harold and Bertha (Steinberg) V.; m. Alyce Vogel, June 13, 1965; children: Jennifer Lyn, Jonathan Harlan. BA, Queens Coll., 1963; LLB, Bklyn. Law Sch., 1966, JD, 1967. Bar: N.Y. 1967, U. S. Dist. Ct. (so. and ea. dists.) N.Y. 1974. Assoc. Seavey Gallet & Fingerit, N.Y.C., 1968-72; ptnr. Seavey Fingerit & Vogel, N.Y.C., 1972-80; mng. ptnr. Seavey Fingerit Vogel & Oziel, N.Y.C., 1980—; lectr. coop. orgns., N.Y.C., 1980—; lectr., author articles Fedn. N.Y. Housing Coops., N.Y.C., 1984—; arbitrator Am. Arbitration Assn., N.Y.C., 1980—; adv. bd., bd. dirs. various corps., N.Y.C., 1968—. Mem. Queens County Bar. Home: 27 Hummingbird Dr Roslyn NY 11576 Office: Seavey Fingerit Vogel & Oziel 60 E 86th St New York NY 10028-1009

VOGEL, CARL-WILHELM ERNST, immunologist, biochemistry educator; b. Hamburg, Fed. Republic Germany, Mar. 9, 1951; came to U.S., 1979; s. Erich Hermann Walter and Lisbeth Klara (Barbulla) V; m. Candice G. McMullan-Vogel, 1989. MD, U. Hamburg, 1976, diploma in biology, 1980, PhD in Biochemistry, 1986. cert. lab. medicine (Germany). Predoctoral rsch. fellow Tropical Inst., Hamburg, 1973-75; intern Univ. Hosps., Hamburg and Kiel, Fed. Republic Germany, 1976-78; postdoctoral rsch. fellow Rsch. Inst. Scripps Clin., La Jolla, Calif., 1979-82, asst. prof. biochemistry and medicine Georgetown U., Washington, 1982-87, resident medicine, pathology, allergy/immunology, 1984-86, 88-89, assoc. prof. 1987-91, adj. prof., 1991—; mem. Vincent T. Lombardi Cancer Rsch. Ctr., Washington, 1982-92; mem. Internat. Ctr. for Interdisciplinary Studies of Immunology, Washington, 1982-94, sci. dir., 1987-91; prof., chmn. dept. biochemistry and molecular biology U. Hamburg, Germany, 1990—; vis. prof. pathology and lab. medicine Ind. U.-Purdue U. Med. Ctr., Indpls., 1996—. Mem. editorial bd. Jour. Devel. and Comparative Immunology, 1984—; mem. and examiner Bd. Lab. Medicine (Germany); cons. to biomed. corps. Overseas research fellow Studienstiftung des Deutschen Volkes (Fed. Republic Germany), 1978-79; U.S.A. research fellow Deutsche Forschungsgemeinschaft (Fed. Republic Germany), 1980-92; NIH rsch. grantee, 1983-94; NCI/NIH Rsch. Career Devel. award. Mem. AMA, AAAS, Gesellschaft für Biologische Chemie, Am. Soc. Microbiology, Am. Assn. Immunologists, Am. Soc. Biochemistry and Molecular Biology, Am. Assn. Cancer Rsch., Am. Soc. Tropical Medicine and Hygiene, AAUP, Internat. Soc. Devel. and Comparative Immunology, Am. Fedn. of Clin. Rsch. Gesellschaft für Immunologie, Gesellschaft Deutsche Chemiker, Am. Soc. Clin. Investigation, German Soc. Cell Biology, German Soc. Lab. Medicine, Japanese Biochem. Soc., Sigma Xi. Office: U Hamburg-Dept Biochem & Mol Biology, Martin Luther King Pl 6, 20146 Hamburg Germany

VOGEL, CHARLES STIMMEL, lawyer; b. L.A., Aug. 26, 1932; s. Charles Paul and Thurza Mae V.; m. Miriam Friedfeld, May 11, 1979; children by previous marriage: Steven, Beverly. B.A., Pomona Coll., 1955; LL.B., UCLA, 1959. Bar: Calif. 1959, U.S. Dist. Ct. (so. dist.) Calif. 1959. Partner firm Allard, Shelton & O'Connor, Pomona, Calif., 1959-69; judge Mcpl. Ct., Pomona Jud. Dist., 1969-70, Los Angeles Superior Ct., 1970-77; partner firm Nossaman, Krueger & Marsh, Los Angeles, 1977-81, Sidley & Austin, Los Angeles, 1981-93; assoc. justice Calif. Ct. Appeals (2d dist., divsn. 4), L.A., 1993-95, presiding justice, 1995—. Served with USN, 1955-56. Fellow Am. Bar Found., Am. Coll. Trial Lawyers; mem. Los Angeles County Bar Assn. (trustee 1980-82, pres. 1985-86), UCLA Law Alumni Assn. (pres. 1977), Assn. Bus. Trial Lawyers (pres. 1984-85), State Bar Calif. (bd. govs. 1987—, pres. 1990-91). Office: Calif Ct Appeals 300 S Spring St Los Angeles CA 90013-1230

VOGEL, DIANE OSCHERWITZ, primary education educator; b. Cin., Nov. 1, 1951; d. Louis and Florence (Small) Oscherwitz; m. Edward Herschel Vogel, Nov. 30, 1975; children: Steven, Ross. BS in Edn., Miami U., Oxford, Ohio, 1973; MEd, Ga. State U., 1975. Cert. tchr., Ga. Tchr. spl. edn. DeKalb County Schs., Decatur, Ga., 1973-82; primary tchr. Hebrew Acad., Atlanta, 1982-85, Bibb County Bd. Edn., Macon, Ga., 1986—. Sundy sch. prin. Congregation Sherah Israel, Macon, 1989-94; host family Ga. Jr. Miss State Program, Macon, 1989—. Mem. Profl. Assn. Ga. Educators, Mid. Ga. Reading Coun., Hadassah (life). Avocation: Prodigy computer network. Home: 527 Commanche Dr Macon GA 31210-4204 Office: Redding Elem Sch 8062 Eisenhower Pky Lizella GA 31052-1066

VOGEL, DONALD STANLEY, gallery executive, artist; b. Milw., Oct. 20, 1917; s. Walter Frederick and Francis Osborne (Talmadge) V.; m. Margaret Katherine Mayer, Oct. 14, 1947 (dec. June 1974); children—Eric Stefan, Kevin Eliot, Katherine Barley; m. Erika Kjar Farkac, Oct. 4, 1980. Student Chgo. Art Inst., 1936. With WPA Easel Project, Chgo., 1940; tech. dir. Dallas Little Theatre, 1942-43; dir. Betty McLean Gallery, Dallas, 1951-54; dir., owner Valley House Gallery, Dallas, 1954—; dir., ptnr. Main Place Gallery, Dallas, 1968-70. Author: (with Margaret Mayer) Aunt Clara: The Paintings of Clara McDonald Williamson, 1966, Charcoal and Cadmium Red, 1989, Not for Revenge, 1991, King of the Hill, 1991, Transcendent Collector, 1992, Drawing for Paintings, 1992, The Untold Studio Secret, A Fantasy, 1992, The Boardinghouse, 1995, Prime Targets, 1996, Seeking the Intangible, 1996; also essays and catalogues. Mem. Art Dealers Assn. Am. Inc. Avocations: travel; swimming. Office: Valley House Gallery 6616 Spring Valley Rd Dallas TX 75240-8635

VOGEL, EUGENE L., lawyer; b. Balt., May 2, 1931; s. Phillip and Dorothy (Shor) V.; m. Sara Altman, Aug. 22, 1958; children—Jennifer L., Amanda J. B.S., U. Md., 1953; J.D. magna cum laude, Harvard U., 1958. C.P.A., Md. Bar: N.Y. Assoc. atty. Rosenman and Colin, N.Y.C., 1958-67, tax ptnr., 1967-77, sr. tax ptnr., 1977—; adj. prof. law NYU, 1977-88. Coauthor: (with Ness): Taxation of the Closely-Held Corp., 5th edit. 1991; contbr. articles to profl. jours. Bd. dirs. The Appleseed Found., Washington; bd. dirs., treas. N.Y. Lawyers For Pub. Interest, N.Y.C., 1984-87; lectr. Practicing Law Inst. Served to 1st Lt. USAF, 1953-55. Mem. ABA, N.Y. State Bar Assn. (exec. com. tax sect.), Assn. of Bar of City of N.Y. (chmn. com. on personal income taxation 1991-94, coun. on taxation 1990—). Home: 245 E 50th St New York NY 10022-7752 Office: Rosenman & Colin 575 Madison Ave New York NY 10022-2511

VOGEL, EZRA F., sociology educator; b. Delaware, Ohio, July 11, 1930; s. Joseph H. and Edith (Nachman) V.; m. Suzanne Hall, July 5, 1953 (div.); children: David, Steven, Eva; m. Charlotte Ikels, Nov. 3, 1979. BA, Ohio Wesleyan U., 1950; MA, Bowling Green State U., 1951; PhD, Harvard U., 1958; LittD (hon.), Kwansai Gakuin, 1980, Wittenberg Coll., 1981, Bowling Green State U., 1982, U. Md., 1983, Albion Coll., 1988, Chinese U., Hong Kong, 1992; Ohio Wesleyan, 1996, U. Mass., Lowell, 1996. Research fellow Harvard (for work in Japan), 1958-60; asst. prof. Yale U., 1960-61; research assoc., lectr. Harvard U., 1961-67, prof., 1967—, Henry Ford II prof. social scis., 1990—, assoc. dir. East Asian Research Ctr., 1967-73, dir., 1973-77, chmn. council East Asian studies, 1977-80, dir. program on U.S.-Japan relations, 1980-87, hon. chmn. program on U.S.-Japan rels., 1988—, mem. faculty council, 1981-84; nat. intelligence officer for East Asia Nat. Intelligence Coun., 1993-95, dir. Fairbank Ctr. East Asian Studies, 1995—; Mem. Joint Com. on Contemporary China, 1968-75, Com. on Scholarly Communication with Peoples Republic China, 1973-75, Joint Com. Japanese Studies, 1977-79. Author: Japan's New Middle Class, 1963, Canton Under Communism, 1969, Japan As Number One, 1979, Comeback, 1985, The Impact of Japan on a Changing World, 1987, One Step Ahead in China, 1989, The Four Little Dragons, 1991; editor: (with Norman W. Bell) A Modern Introduction to the Family, 1960, Modern Japanese Organization and Decision-Making, 1975, (with George Lodge) Ideology and National Competitiveness. Trustee Ohio Wesleyan U., 1970-75, 80-94. Served with AUS, 1951-53. Recipient Harvard faculty prize for book of year, 1970; Guggenheim fellow, 1972. Mem. Assn. Asian Studies (bd. dirs. 1970-72), Am. Sociol. Assn., Am. Acad. Arts and Scis. Home: 14 Sumner Rd Cambridge MA 02138-3018

VOGEL, FREDERICK JOHN, diplomat; b. Annapolis, Md., July 11, 1943; s. Raymond William Vogel and Clair Patricia (O'Neill) Foley; m. Donsiri Kamak, Dec. 26, 1983; children: Chantharaphon M., Jenchira Erin, Thinarom Clair. BS in Engring., US Naval Acad., 1965; postgrad, Purdue U., 1961; cert. in Lao lang., Def. Lang. Inst., 1970; postgrad., U.S. Army War Coll., 1995—; cert. in Thai lang., Union Lang. Sch., Bangkok, 1975; cert. Korean lang., Fgn. Svc. Inst., 1979. Lic. pvt. pilot, lic. tae kwon do instr., 2d Dan, lic. D parachutist, lic. 2d class diver. Commd. 2nd lt. USMC, 1965, advanced through grades to col., 1986; fgn. svc. officer on assignment to Pentagon Bangkok, London,, Washington, 1972-88; dept. of state rep. to conf. on disarmament Geneva, 1988-90; dep. chief of mission Am. Embassy, Vientiane, Laos, 1991-93, charge d' affaires, 1993; asst. dir. of fgn. mil. rights affairs, office of the Sec. of Def. The Pentagon, 1994—; embassy rep. Thai-Am. Edn. Found., Bangkok, 1976-78; sec. martial arts com. Royal Bangkok Sports Club, 1984-86; chmn. Vientiane Internat. Sch. Bd., 1991-93. Active Am. Community Supprt Assn., Bangkok, 1984-85. Mem. Am. Fgn. Svc. Assn., Marine Corps Assn., U.S. Naval Acad. Alumni Assn., Force Recon Assn. Roman Catholic. Avocations: martial arts, parachuting, private flying, traveling, languages. Home: 1332 Cassia St Herndon VA 22070-2500

VOGEL, H. VICTORIA, psychotherapist, educator. BA, U. Md., 1968; MA, NYU, 1970, 1975; MEd, Columbia U., 1982, postgrad., 1982—; cert., Am. Projective Drawing Inst., 1983. Art Therapist Childville, Bklyn., 1962-64; tchr., Montgomery County (Md.) Jr. H.S., 1968-69; with H.S. div. N.Y.C. Bd. Edn., 1970—, guidance counselor, instructor, psychotherapist in pvt. practice; clinical counseling cons. psychodiagnosis and devel. studies, art/play therapy, The Modern School, 1984—; art/play therapist Hosp. Ctr. for Neuromuscular Disease and Devel. Disorders, 1987—; employment counselor-adminstr. N.Y. State Dept. Labor Concentrated Employment Program, 1971-72; intern psychotherapy and psychoanalysis psychiat. divsn. Cen. Islip Hosp., 1973-75; with Calif. Grad. Inst., L.A.; Columbia U. Tchrs. Coll., N.Y. intern psychol. counseling and rehab. N.J. Coll. Medicine, Newark, 1979. Mem. com. for spl. events NYU, 1989; participant clin. and artistic perspectives Am. Acad. Psychoanalysis Conf., 1990, participant clin. postmodernism and psychoanalysis, 1996; auxilary police officer N.Y. Police Dept. Precinct 19, N.Y.C., 1994—; chair bylaws com. Columbia U., 1995—. Mem. APA, AAAS, Am. Psychol. Soc., Am. Orthopsychiat. Assn., Am. Soc. Group Psychotherapy & Psychodrama (publs. com. 1984—), Am. Counseling Assn., N.Y.C. Art Tchrs. Assn., Art/Play Therapy, Assn. Humanistic Psychology (exec. sec. 1981), Tchrs. Coll. Adminstrv. Women in Edn., Phi Delta Kappa (editor chpt. newsletter 1981-84, exec. sec. Columbia U. chpt. 1984—, chmn. nominating com. for chpt. officers 1986—, nominating com. 1991, pub. rels. exec. bd. dirs. 1991, rsch. rep. 1986—), Phi Delta Kappa (v.p. programs NYU chpt. 1994—). Author: The Never Ending Story of Alcohol, Drugs and Other Substance Abuse, 1992, Variant Sexual Behavior and the Aesthetic Modern Nudes, 1992, Psychological Science of School Behavior Intervention, 1993, Joycean Conceptual Modernism: Relationships and Deviant Sexuality, 1995, Electronic Evil Eyes, 1995.

VOGEL, HENRY ELLIOTT, retired university dean and physics educator; b. Greenville, S.C., Sept. 16, 1925; s. Henry Lamprecht and Alice (Cousins) V.; m. Barbara Argyle Gladden, Aug. 16, 1953; children: Alisabeth, Henry L. II, Barbara Alice, Susan Marie. BS, Furman U., 1948; MS, U. N.C., 1950, PhD, 1962. Instr. dept. physics Clemson (S.C.) U., 1950-52, asst. prof. physics, 1952-59, assoc. prof., 1959-65, prof., 1965-67, prof., head physics dept., 1967-71; prof., dean Clemson (S.C.) U. Coll. Scis., 1971-87, prof. physics, 1987-90, dean emeritus, prof. emeritus dept. physics and astronomy, 1990—; mem. S.C. ad hoc com. for NSF exptl. program to stimulate competitive research, 1978-87; mem. tech. adv. bd. S.C. Research Authority, 1984-87. Served with AUS, 1943-45. Decorated Purple Heart. Mem. Am. Phys. Soc., Am. Assn. Physics Tchrs., Sigma Xi, Sigma Pi, Alpha Epsilon Delta. Address: 222 Wyatt Ave Clemson SC 29631-3003

VOGEL, HOWARD H., lawyer; b. Paris, Tenn., Sept. 4, 1949; s. Herman Lentz and Caroline Powell (Carothers) V.; m. Kathryn Lynn Massey, Sept. 14, 1974; children: Caroline Carothers, Patrick Alexander, Anna Kathryn. BA, Vanderbilt U., 1971; JD, U. Tenn., 1974. Assoc. atty. O'Neil, Parker & Williamson, Knoxville, Tenn., 1976-77; ptnr. O'Neil, Parker & Williamson, 1977—. Pres. Dogwood Arts festival Inc., Knoxville, 1990-92. Fellow Tenn. Bar Found., Am. Bar Found.; mem. ABA (bd. govs. 1985-88, chmn. standing com. on meetings and travel 1990-92, chair 1993-94), Tenn. Young Lawyers Conf. (pres. 1980-81), Knoxville Bar Assn. (pres.-elect 1990-92, pres. 1993), Tenn. Bar Assn. (v.p. 1993-94, pres.-elect 1994—). Office: PO Box 217 Knoxville TN 37901-0217 also: O'Neil, Parker & Williamson 416 Cumberland Ave Knoxville TN 37902-2301*

VOGEL, HOWARD STANLEY, lawyer; b. N.Y.C., Jan. 21, 1934; s. Moe and Sylvia (Miller) V.; m. Judith Anne Gelb, June 30, 1962; 1 son, Michael S. B.A., Bklyn. Coll., 1954; J.D., Columbia U., 1957; LL.M. in Corp. Law, NYU, 1969. Bar: N.Y. 1957, U.S. Supreme Ct. 1964. Assoc. Whitman & Ransom, N.Y.C., 1961-66; with Texaco Inc., 1966—, gen. atty., 1970-73, assoc. gen. counsel, 1973-81, gen. counsel Texaco Philanthropic Found. Inc., 1979-82, gen. counsel Jefferson Chem. Co., Texaco Chems. Can. Inc., 1973-82, assoc. gen. tax counsel, gen. mgr. adminstrn., White Plains, N.Y., 1981—; gen. tax counsel Texaco Found. Inc., 1995—. Pres., dir. 169 E. 69th Corp., 1981—. Served to 1st lt. JAGC, U.S. Army, 1958-60. Mem. ABA, Assn. Bar City N.Y., Fed. Bar Council, Assn. Ex-Mems. of Squadron A (N.Y.C.). Club: Princeton (N.Y.C.). Home: 169 E 69th St Apt 9D New York NY 10021-5163 Office: 2000 Westchester Ave White Plains NY 10650-0001

VOGEL, JULIUS, consulting actuary, former insurance company executive; b. N.Y.C., Jan. 22, 1924; s. Max and Bertha V.; m. Corinne Iskowitz, Mar. 11, 1947; children: Robert, Charles. B.A., Bklyn. Coll., 1943. With Prudential Ins. Co. Am., Newark, 1946-82; sr. v.p., chief actuary Prudential Ins. Co. Am., 1977-82; chmn. Pruco Services Inc., 1979-82, Prudential's Gibraltar Fund, 1980-82. Served with U.S. Army, 1944-46. Recipient Disting. Public Service award Dept. Navy, 1976. Fellow Soc. Actuaries (pres. 1979-80); mem. Am. Acad. Actuaries. Office: 72 Colt Rd Summit NJ 07901-3041

VOGEL, MICHAEL N., journalist, writer, historian; b. Buffalo, May 26, 1947; s. Ralph John and Florence Helen (Pohlmann) V.; m. Stasia Zoladz, Aug. 28, 1971; children: Charity Ann, Rebecca Marie, Alex Christian. BA in English, Canisius Coll., 1969; MA in English, So. Ill. U., 1970. Journalist

Buffalo News, 1970—; assoc. prof. journalism Buffalo State U. Coll., 1979-80. Author: Maritime Buffalo, 1990, Echoes in the Mist, 1991, America's Crossroads, 1993. Pres. Buffalo Lighthouse Assn., Inc., 1985—; co-founder St. Michael's Sch. at Greycliff, Derby, N.Y., 1987; pres. Buffalo Newspaper Guild, 1994-96; bd. dirs. Landmark Soc. Niagara Frontier, 1990-91, Western N.Y. Heritage Inst., 1994—, Friends of N.Y. State Newspaper Project, 1996—; mem. Erie County Local Emergency Planning Com. 1st lt. U.S. Army, 1971-73. Recipient numerous awards including One to One Media award, 1978, 79, Newspaper Editorial Workshop award, 1979-80, N.Y. State AP award, 1982-90, Am. Planning Assn. award, 1987. Mem. AAAS, U.S. Lighthouse Soc., Nat. Assn. Sci. Writers, Gt. Lakes Hist. Soc., Buffalo & Erie County Hist. Soc. (Augspurger award 1989, Niederlander award 1990), Buffalo Mus. Sci. Roman Catholic. Avocations: sailing, photography, reading. Home: 6540 Lake Shore Rd Derby NY 14047-9755 Office: Buffalo News PO Box 100 1 News Plz Buffalo NY 14240

VOGEL, NELSON J., JR., lawyer; b. South Bend, Ind., Oct. 13, 1946; s. Nelson J. and Carolyn B. (Drzewiecki) V.; m. Sandra L. Cudney, May 17, 1969; children: Ryan C., Justin M., Nathan J., Lindsey M. BS cum laude, Miami U., Oxford, Ohio, 1968; JD cum laude, U. Notre Dame, 1971. Bar: Ind. 1971, Mich. 1971, U.S. Dist. Ct. (no. dist.) Ind. 1971, Fla. 1972, U.S. Tax Ct. 1972, U.S. Ct. Appeals (5th cir.) 1975, U.S. Ct. Claims 1980. Acct. Coopers & Lybrand, South Bend, 1969-71; assoc. Barnes & Thornburg, South Bend, 1971-76, ptnr., 1977—; lectr. U. Notre Dame, South Bend, 1971, 74-80; instr. Ind. U., South Bend, 1971-74; mem. bd. advisors Goshen Coll. Family Bus. Program. Pres. Big Bros., Big Sisters, South Bend, 1978-79; bd. pres. South Bend Regional Mus. Art, 1984-86; mem. ethics com. Meml. Hosp., South Bend, 1986-94. Mem. Nat. Employee Stock Ownership Plan Assn. (sec.-treas. Ind. chpt. 1993-95), Am. Assn. Atty.-CPAs, Nat. Assn. State Bar Tax Sec. (exec. com. 1982-84), Ind. State Bar Assn. (chmn. taxation sect. 1981-82, Citation of Merit 1979), Mich. Bar Assn. (tax sect.), Fla. Bar Assn., Michiana World Affairs Coun. (bd. dirs. 1992-96), Michiana World Trade club (bd. dirs. 1992—). Home: 1146 Dunrobbin Ln South Bend IN 46614-2150 Office: Barnes & Thornburg 600 1st Source Bank 100 N Michigan St South Bend IN 46601-1630

VOGEL, RAYMOND JOHN, federal government executive; b. Wheeling, W.Va., Aug. 9, 1940; s. Richard Edward and Eleanor Rose (Byrne) V.; m. Georgia Ann Faris, June 19, 1965; children: Raymond John Jr., Matthew Edward, Anne Marie. BA in Polit. Sci., Wheeling Jesuit Coll., 1962; MS in Govtl. Adminstrn., George Washington U., 1975. Mgmt. intern U.S. Steel Corp. (now USX), Pitts., 1965-67; agt. Conn. Gen. Life Ins. Co., Pitts., 1967-68; adjudicator Vets. Benefit Office Dept. Vets. Affairs, Washington, 1968-73; cons. VA Cen. Office, Washington, 1973-75; adjudication officer VA Regional Office, Portland, Oreg., 1975-77, dir., 1979-83; adjudication officer VA Regional Office, Washington, 1977-79; dir. VA Regional Office and Ins. Ctr., Phila., 1983-85; chief benefits dir. VA Cen. Office, Washington, 1985-90; dir. Bay Pines, Fla. VA Med. Ctr., 1990-93, dep. under sec., 1993-94, under sec. for benefits, 1994—; chmn. Fed. Exec. Bd., Portland, 1982-83, mem. bd., Phila., 1983-85; bd. dirs. Ded. Quality Inst., Washington, 1988—. With U.S. Army, 1963-65. Mem. DAV, Am. Legion, AMVETS, Am. Coll. Healthcare Execs., Non-commd. Officers Assn., Sr. Execs. Assn., Fed. Exec. Assn. (pres. 1990-92). Roman Catholic. Avocations: golf, fishing. Home: 21611 Goshen Oaks Rd Gaithersburg MD 20882 Office: Dept Vets Affairs Vets Benefits 810 Vermont Ave NW Washington DC 20420

VOGEL, ROBERT, lawyer, educator; b. Coleharbor, N.D., Dec. 6, 1918; s. Frank A. and Louella (Larsen) V.; m. Elsa Mork, May 29, 1942; children: Mary Lou, Sarah May, Frank, Robert. B.S., U. N.D., 1939; LL.B., Mpls. Coll. Law, 1942. Bar: N.D. 1943. Practiced in Garrison, 1943-54; state's atty. McLean County, 1948-54; U.S. atty. Fargo, 1954-61; mem. Vogel, Bair & Brown, Mandan, N.D., 1961-73; judge N.D. Supreme Ct., 1973-78; prof. U. N.D. Law Sch., Grand Forks, 1978-95. Democratic candidate for U.S. Ho. of Reps., 2d Dist. N.D., 1962; mem., sec. Nonpartisan League State Exec. Com., 1952; mem. N.D. Parole Bd., 1966-73. Fellow Am. Bar Found.; mem. Am. Coll. Trial Lawyers, Am. Law Inst. Home: 524 Harvard St Grand Forks ND 58203-2845 Office: 108 N 3rd St Grand Forks ND 58203-3716

VOGEL, ROBERT LEE, college administrator, clergyman; b. Phillipsburg, Kans., Sept. 27, 1934; s. Howard and Marie V.; m. Sally M. Johnson, June 3, 1956; children—Susan, Kirk. B.A., Wartburg Coll., 1956; B.D., M.Div., Wartburg Theol. Sem., 1960, D.D. (hon.), 1976. Ordained to ministry Am. Lutheran Ch., 1960. Organizing pastor Faith Luth. Ch., Golden, Colo., 1960-65; regional dir. div. youth activity Am. Luth. Ch., Chgo., 1965-67; dir. parish resources, div. youth activity Am. Luth. Ch., Mpls., 1967-69; sr. pastor Our Savior's Luth. Ch., Denver, 1969-73; exec. asst. to pres. Am. Luth. Ch., Mpls., 1973-80; pres. Wartburg Coll., Waverly, Iowa, 1980—; v.p. Internat. Luther League, Am. Luth. Ch., 1953-58, pres., 1958-60; ofcl. observer Luth. World Fedn. Assembly, 1957; mem. com. on laity Am. Luth. Ch., 1964-67. Recipient Alumni citation Wartburg Coll., 1978. Mem. Coun. Ind. Colls., Iowa Assn. Ind. Colls. and Univs. (chmn. bd. 1987-88), Luth. Ednl. Conf. N. Am. (pres. 1988-89), Nat. Assn. Ind. Colls. and Univs. (commn. mem.). Lodge: Rotary. Office: Wartburg Coll 222 9th St NW Waverly IA 50677-2215

VOGEL, RONALD BRUCE, food products executive; b. Vancouver, Wash., Feb. 16, 1934; s. Joseph John and Thelma Mae (Karker) V.; m. Carol Vandecar, Mar. 16, 1958; children: Joseph S., Rhonda L., Theresa J., Denise R.; m. Donita Dawn Schneider, Aug. 8, 1970 (dec. June 1974); 1 child, Cynthia Dawn; m. Karen Cracknel, Feb. 14, 1992. BS in Chemistry, U. Wash., 1959. Glass maker Penberthy Instrument Co., Seattle, 1959-60; lab. technician Gt. Western Malting Co., Vancouver, 1960-62, chief chemist, 1962-67, mgr. corp. quality control, 1967-72, mgr. customer svcs., 1972-77, v.p. customer svcs., 1977-79, v.p. sales, 1979-84, gen. mgr., 1984-89, pres., CEO, 1989-95; ret. Chmn. bd. dirs. Columbia Empire Jr. Achievement, Portland, Oreg., 1991-92. With U.S. Army, 1954-56. Recipient numerous awards. Mem. Master Brewers Assn. Am. (pres. 1996), Am. Malting Barley Assn. (chmn. 1984-86, 89-91), Vancouver C. of C. (chmn. 1991-93), Applied Phytologics, Inc. (bd. dirs.). Home: 11500 NE 76th St # A3-151 Vancouver WA 98662

VOGEL, SARAH, state agency administrator, lawyer; b. Bismarck, N.D., May 3, 1946; d. Robert and Elsa Marie (Mork) V.; 1 child, Andrew. BA, U. N.D., 1967; JD, NYU, 1970. Bar: N.Y. 1970, N.D. 1982. Commr. N.D. Agrl. Dept., Bismarck, N.D. Office: ND Agrl Dept 600 E Boulevard Ave Bismarck ND 58505-0660

VOGEL, SUSAN MULLIN, museum director. BS in French and English Literature, Georgetown U., 1964; MA, NYU, 1971, cert. mus. tng., 1977, PhD in Art History, 1977. Libr. asst. USIS Libr., Abidjan, 1964-65; libr. asst. Mus. Primitive Art, N.Y.C., 1966-67, asst. registrar, 1967-70, asst. curator, 1971-74; assoc. curator Met. Mus. Art, N.Y.C., 1975-82, sr. cons. African Art, 1982-84; exec. dir. The Ctr. for African Art, N.Y.C., 1982-1994; dir. Yale U Art Gallery, 1995—; lectr. in field. Arranged exhbns. including The Art of Black Africa: Nigeria and Cameroon, Met. Mus. Art, 1971, The Sculpture of Black Africa: Upper Volta, Mus. Primitive Art, 1972, Faces (Africa only), Mus. Primitive Art, 1973, Gods of Fortune: The Cult of the Hand in Nigeria, Mus. Primitive Art, 1974, Rapacious Birds and Severed Heads: Early Bronze Rings from Nigeria, Art Inst. Chgo., 1979, The Buli Master: An African Artist of the 19th Century, Met. Mus. Art, 1980, For Spirits and Kings: African Art from the Paul and Ruth Tishman Collection, Met. Mus. Art, 1981, Michael C. Rockefeller Meml. Wing permanent installation of African art, Met. Mus. Art, 1982, African Masterpieces from the Musee de l'Homme Paris, Ctr. for African Art, 1984, African Aesthetics: The Carlo Monzino Collection, Ctr. for African Art, 1986, African Masterpieces from the Staatliches Mus. fur Volkerkunde Munich, Ctr. for African Art, 1987, Perspectives: Angles on African Art, Ctr. for African Art, 1987, Art/Artifact, Ctr. for African Art, 1988, The Art of Collecting African Art, Ctr. for African Art, 1988, Closeup: Lessons in the Art of Seeing African Art, Ctr. for African Art, 1990, Africa Explores: 20th Century African Art, Ctr. for African Art and New Mus. Contemporary Art, 1991, Home and the World: Archtl. Sculpture of two contemporary African Art, 1993, Fusion: West African Artist and the Venice Bienniale, Italy Mus. for African Art, 1993, Exhibition-ism: Mus. and African Art, Mus. for African Art, 1994; author exhbn. catalogues Ctr. for African Art: African Masterpieces from the Musee de l'Homme, 1985, African Aesthetics: The Carlo Monzino Collection, 1986, Africa Explores: 20th Century African Art, 1991, Closeup: Lessons in the Art of Seeing African Art, 1990; editor For Spirits and Kings, Met. Mus. Art, 1981; editor chpts. of books; contbr. articles to profl. jours. and many books in field. Office: Yale U Art Gallery PO Box 208271 New Haven CT 06520-8271

VOGEL, WILLIAM CHARLES, advertising executive; b. New York, N.Y., Aug. 16, 1941; s. Samuel and Pearl (Lefkowitz) V.; m. Nicole Lund, Sept. 30, 1968; children: David Roswell, Peter Samuel, (div. 1977); m. Joan Baeder, May 19, 1985. BA, NYU, 1964. Asst. account exec. Doyle Dane Bernbach, New York, 1965-68; account exec. McCann-Erickson, San Francisco, 1968-70; account dir. Foote, Cone and Belding, L.A., 1970-77; sr. v.p. Hall and Levine Advt., L.A., 1977-79; sr. v.p., gen. mgr. Cunningham and Walsh, L.A., 1979-85; prin. Liebowitz, Olshever, Vogel and Baruch, 1985-86; exec. v.p., mng. ptnr. Abert, Newhoff and Burr, L.A., 1986-87; pres. The Vogel Communications Group, Los Angeles, 1987-92; sr. v.p. DDB Needham Worldwide, 1992-94; mktg. cons. Vogel Internat. Mktg., 1994—; v.p. Western States Advt. Agencies Assoc., Los Angeles, 1977-78. Mem. Citizens Adv. Commn., L.A. Olympic Orgn. Com., 1983-84, bd. dir. L.A. Art Fair. With M.I. U.S. Army, 1964-65. Recipient, Dare award, City Long Beach, Calif., 1987, Recognition award, L.A.Olympic Orgn. Commn., 1984, Dallas Advt. League, 1985, Diplome D' Excellence, UTA French Airlines, Paris, 1981. Mem. L.A. Advt. Club, The Aero Club, Riviera Tennis Club, St. James Club. Avocations: art collecting, horticulture, tennis. Home: 2187 Mcnell Rd Ojai CA 93023-9318 Office: Vogel Internat Mktg The Queen Mary 1126 Queens Hwy Long Beach CA 90802-6331

VOGELEY, CLYDE EICHER, JR., engineering educator, artist, consultant; b. Pitts., Oct. 19, 1917; s. Clyde Eicher and Eva May (Reynolds) V.; m. Blanche Wormington Peters, Dec. 15, 1947; children: Eva Anne, Susan Elizabeth Steele. BFA in Art Edn., Carnegie Mellon U., 1940; BS in Engring. Physics, U. Pitts., 1944, PhD in Math., 1949. Art supr. Pub. Sch. System, Spingdale, Pa., 1940-41; rsch. engr. Westinghouse Rsch. Labs., East Pitts., Pa., 1944-54; adj. prof. math. U. Pitts., 1954-64; sr. scientist Bettis Atomic Power Lab., W. Mifflin, Pa., 1956-59; supr. tech. tng. Bettis Atomic Power Lab., W. Mifflin, 1959-71; mgr. Bettis Reactor Engring. Sch., W. Mifflin, 1971-77, dir., 1977-92; cons. U.S. Dept. Energy, Washington, 1992-95; cons. Bettis Atomic Power Lab., W. Mifflin, 1954-56; U.S. Navy Nuclear Power Schs., Mare Island, Calif., Bainbridge, Md., 1959-69. Author: (grad. sch. course) Non-linear Differential Equations, 1954; (rev. text) Ordinary Differential Equations, Rev. edit. 5, Shock and Vibration Problems, Rev. Edit. 6, 1991; rsch. report distributed to Brit., Can. and U.S. Govts. for use in design of airborne radar systems, 1944; oil painting represented in permanent Latrobe collection; acrylics, water colors and Christmas card designs in several pvt. collections. Pres., trustee Whitehall (Pa.) Pub. Libr., 1985. Recipient USN commendation, Naval Reactors Br., 1992. Mem. IEEE (life), Am. Phys. Soc., Associated Artists of Pitts. (hon.), Pitts. Watercolor Soc., Sigma Pi Sigma, Sigma Tau, Sigma Xi. Presbyterian. Achievements include patents for Automatic Continuous Wave Radar Tracking System, Modulating Signals Passing Along Ridged Waveguides, Ridged Waveguide Matching Device, Method for Joining Several Ridged Waveguides, Antenna Feed Modulation Unit, others. Home: 185 Peach Dr Pittsburgh PA 15236-2145 *My life as an artist, scientist, and teacher has been a wonderful journey - made richer by my family, teachers, friends, colleagues, and students. It has never seemed like work.*

VOGELGESANG, SANDRA LOUISE, federal government official; b. Canton, Ohio, July 27, 1942; d. Glenn Wesley and Louise (Forry) Vogelgesang; m. Geoffrey Ernest Wolfe, July 4, 1982. BA, Cornell U., 1964; MA, Tufts U., 1965, MA in Law and Diplomacy, 1966, PhD, 1971. With Dept. State, Washington, 1975—, policy planner for sec. state and European Bur., 1975-80, dir. Econ Analysis Office, Orgn. Econ. Coop. and Devel., 1981-82, econ. minister U.S. Embassy, Ottawa, Can., 1982-86, dep. asst. sec. Internat. Orgn. Affairs Bur., 1986-89; dep. asst. adminstr. Office Internat. Activities Environ. Protection Agy., Washington, 1989-92; with Dept. State, Washington, 1992; sr. policy advisor Agy. for Internat. Devel., 1993; U.S. amb. to Nepal Dept. State, Washington, 1994—; bd. dirs. Edward R. Murrow Ctr. for Pub. Diplomacy, Fletcher Sch., Medford, Mass., 1978-81; bd. advisors Am.'s Soc., N.Y.C., 1986-89. Author: Long Dark Night of the Soul, The American Intellectual Left and the Vietnam War, 1974, American Dream-Global Nightmare: The Dilemma of U.S. Human Rights Policy, 1980. Recipient Meritorious Service awards, 1973, 74, 82, 83, 86, Disting. Honor award, 1976 Dept. State, Pres.' Disting. Service award, 1985. Mem. Council on Fgn. Relations. Office: US Embassy Kathmandu Dept of State Washington DC 20521-6190

VOGELMAN, JOSEPH HERBERT, scientific engineering company executive; b. N.Y.C., Aug. 18, 1920; s. Jacob and Sabina (Weingarten) V.; m. Norma Schneider, Dec. 8, 1946; children: Jeffrey Allan, Leslie Sue, Linda Leigh. B.S., CCNY, 1940; M.E.E., Poly. Inst. Bklyn., 1948, D.Elec. Engring., 1957. Registered profl. engr., N.Y., N.J. Project engr. Signal Corps Engr. Labs., Belmar, N.J., 1943-45; chief devel. br. Watson Labs., Eatontown, N.J., 1945-50; chief scientist Rome Air Devel. Center, Griffiss AFB, N.Y., 1951-52; chief electronic warfare lab. Rome Air Devel. Center, 1953-56, dir. communications, 1956-59; v.p., dir. Capehart Corp., N.Y.C., 1959-64; dir. electronics Chromalloy Am. Corp., N.Y.C., 1964-67; gen. mgr. pocket fone div. Chromalloy Am. Corp., 1966-67, v.p., 1967-73; v.p., dir. Cro-Med Bionics Corp., 1968-73; vice chmn. bd., dir. Laser Link Corp., 1968-73; chief scientist, dir. Orentreich Found. for Advancement Sci., 1973—; pres. Vogelman Devel. Corp., 1973—; chmn. tech. adv. com. Compupix, Inc., 1984-86. Contbr. articles to profl. jours. and encys.; patentee in field. Served with AUS, 1942-43. Recipient Outstanding Performance award USAF, 1957. Fellow AAAS, IEEE; mem. Titulaire, Societe Francaise de Electroniciens et des Radio Electriciens, N.Y. Acad. Scis., Sigma Xi, Eta Kappa Nu. Home: 48 Green Dr Roslyn NY 11576-3221 Office: 910 5th Ave New York NY 10021-4155

VOGELSTEIN, BERT, oncology educator. BS, U. Pa., 1970; MD, Johns Hopkins U. Rsch. assoc. Nat. Cancer Inst., 1976-78; prof. dept. oncology Johns Hopkins U. Sch. Medicine, Balt., 1978—; advisor Nat. Insts. Health Scientific Review Groups, Nat. Cancer Inst. Assoc. editor Genes, Chromosomes and Cancer; mem bd. reviewing editors Science Magazine; contbr. article to profl. jours. Recipient Anne & Jason Farber Lecture award Am. Acad. Neurology, 1991, Gairdner Found. Internat. award Gairdner Found., 1992, Medal of Honor Am. Cancer Soc., 1992, Richard Lounsbery award Nat. Acad. Scis., 1993, Baxter Rsch. award Assn. Am. Med. Coll., 1994, G.H.A. Clowes Meml. award Am. Assn. Cancer Rsch. 1995; laureates Passano Found., 1994. Mem. NAS, Am. Acad. Arts Scis. Achievements include revolutionizing our understanding of complex genetic mutations that occur when an normal bowel epithelial cell is transformed into a malignant cell. Office: Johns Hopkins U Sch Med Dept Oncology 720 Rutland Ave Baltimore MD 21205-2109*

VOGET, JANE J., city official, lawyer; b. Montréal, Que., Can., Jan. 2, 1949; d. Frederick Wilhelm and Mary Kay (Mee) V.; m. Frederick Walton Hyde, Oct. 9, 1988. BA in German and Anthropology, So. Ill. U., 1971, MS in Planning and Cmty. Devel., 1977; JD, Lewis and Clark Coll., 1990. Bar: Wash. 1991. Program mgr. Ill. Dept. Local Govt. Affairs, Springfield, 1975-78, U.S. Dept. Housing and Urban Devel., Washington, 1978; mem. staff The White House, Office Asst. to Pres. for Intergovtl. Affairs, Washington, 1979-80; exec. dir. Ctr. for Collaborative Problem Solving, San Francisco, 1981-83; hotel asst. mgr. Hyatt Regency Waikiki, Honolulu, 1983-85; housing project mgr. Multnomah County, Portland, Oreg., 1985-88; sr. project mgr. City of Seattle, 1989—; pvt. practice, Seattle, 1991—. Co-author govtl. publs. Mem. admissions com. United Way Bay Area, 1983; vol. lawyer West Seattle Legal Clinic, 1994-95; active Cascade Animal Protection Soc., Seattle, 1993-95, 11th Dist. Dems., Seattle, 1993-95, Halau Hula O'Napualandi, Seattle, 1995. Mem. ABA (mem. affordable housing fin. com. 1991-95), Wash. State Bar Assn., Wash. State Trial Lawyers Assn., Wash. Assn. Criminal Def. Lawyers, King County Bar Assn. (mem. legis. com., govt. ops. subcom. 1995, legal aid com.). Avocations: swimming, Hawaiian music and dance, animal rights advocate. Home: 5946 39th Ave SW Seattle WA 98136 Office: City of Seattle 618 Second Ave Seattle WA 98104

VOGL, OTTO, polymer science and engineering educator; b. Traiskirchen, Austria, Nov. 6, 1927; came to U.S., 1953, naturalized, 1959; s. Franz and Leopoldine (Scholz) V.; m. Jane Cunningham, June 10, 1955; children: Eric, Yvonne. Ph.D., U. Vienna, 1950; Dr. rer. nat. h.c., U. Jena, 1983; Dr h.c., Poly. Inst., Iasi, Romania, 1992. Instr. U. Vienna, 1948-55; research asso. U. Mich., 1953-55, Princeton U., 1955-56; scientist E.I. Du Pont de Nemours & Co., Wilmington, Del., 1956-70; prof. polymer sci. and engring. U. Mass., 1970-83, prof. emeritus, 1983—; Herman F. Mark prof. polymer sci. Poly. U., Bklyn., 1983—; guest prof. Kyoto U., 1968, 80, Osaka U., 1968, Royal Inst. Stockholm, 1971, 87, U. Freiburg, Germany, 1973, U. Berlin, 1977, Strasbourg U., 1976, Tech. U. Dresden, 1982; guest Soviet Acad. Sci., 1973, Polish Acad. Sci., 1973, 75, Acad. Sci. Rumania, 1974, 76; cons. in field. Chmn. com. on macromolecular chemistry Nat. Acad. Sci. Author: Polyaldehydes, 1967, (with Furukawa) Polymerization of Heterocyclics, 1973, Ionic Polymerization, 1976, (with Simionescu) Radical Co and Graftpolymerization, 1978, (with Donaruma) Polymeric Drugs, 1978, (with Donaruma and Ottenbrite) Polymers in Biology and Medicine, 1980, (with Goldberg and Donaruma) Targeted Drugs, 1983, (with Immergut) Polymer Science in the Next Decade, 1987; contbr. articles to profl. jours. Recipient Fulbright award, 1976, Humboldt prize, 1977, Chemistry Pioneer award, 1985, Gold medal City of Vienna, Austria, 1986, Exner medal, 1987, Mark medal, 1989, Honor Ring, City of Traiskirchen, 1989; Japan Soc. Promotion of Sci. sr. fellow, 1980. Mem. AAAS, Am. Chem. Soc. (chmn. div. polymer chemistry 1974, chmn. Conn. Valley sect. 1974, award applied polymer chemistry 1990), Am. Inst. Chemistry, Austrian Chem. Soc., Japanese Soc. Polymer Sci. (award 1991), N.Y. Acad. Sci., Austrian Acad. Sci., Royal Swedish Acad. Sci., Pacific Polymer Fedn. (pres.), Slovak Chem. Soc. (hon. mem.), Croatian Chem. Soc. (hon. mem.), Soc. Polymer Sci. Japan (life), Sigma Xi. Home: 12 Canterbury Ln Amherst MA 01002 Office: U Mass Dept Polymer Sci/Engring Amherst MA 01003

VOGLER, FREDERICK WRIGHT, French language educator; b. Burlington, Vt., May 27, 1931; s. Curtis Linville and Marion (Wright) V.; m. Mary Frances Angle, Aug. 27, 1965; 1 child, Robert. BA, U. N.C., 1953, MA, 1955, PhD, 1961; postgrad, U. Strasbourg, France, 1953-54. Instr. U. N.C., Chapel Hill, 1961-62, asst. prof., 1963-66, assoc. prof., 1966-78, prof. French, 1978—, assoc. dean arts and scis., 1976-87, dir. undergrad. studies French and Italian, 1989-95; asst. prof. U. Iowa, Iowa City, 1962-63; cons. Ednl. Testing Service, Princeton, N.J., 1967-70. Author: Vital d'Audiguier and the Early 17th Century French Novel, 1964; editor: Moliere Mocked: Three Contemporary Hostile Comedies, 1973; contbr. articles on French lit. and cultural history to profl. jours. Served to 1st lt. U.S. Army, 1955-65. Fulbright Commn. scholar, Washington, Paris, 1953; So. Fellowship Bd. fellow, Chapel Hill, 1955. Mem. Am. Assn. Tchrs. French, Swiss Am. Hist. Soc. Episcopalian. Home: 1010 Dawes St Chapel Hill NC 27516-3010

VOGLER, JAMES R., lawyer; b. St. Louis, Oct. 4, 1952. BA magna cum laude, Harvard U., 1974; JD, So. Ill. U., 1977. Bar: Ill. 1977, U.S. Dist. Ct. (no. dist.) Ill. 1977, U.S. Ct. Appeals (7th cir.) Ill. 1979, U.S. Dist. Ct. (no. dist. trial bar) Ill. 1983, U.S. Supreme Ct. 1984. Ptnr. Winston & Strawn, Chgo.; now ptnr. Foley & Hardner. Mem. Ill. State Bar Assn., Chgo. Bar Assn. (mem. com. evaluation of jud. candidates 1980-83). Office: Foley & Hardner 330 N Wabash Ave Ste 3300 Chicago IL 60611*

VOGT, ERICH WOLFGANG, physicist, academic administrator; b. Steinbach, Man., Can., Nov. 12, 1929; s. Peter Andrew and Susanna (Reimer) V.; m. Barbara Mary Greenfield, Aug. 27, 1952; children: Edith Susan, Elizabeth Mary, David Eric, Jonathan Michael, Robert Jeremy. B.S., U. Man., 1951, M.S., 1952; Ph.D., Princeton U., 1955; D.Sc. (hon.), U. Man., 1982, Queen's U., 1984, Carleton U., 1988; LL.D. (hon.), U. Regina, 1986. Rsch. officer Chalk River (Ont.) Nuclear Labs., 1956-65; prof. physics U. B.C., Vancouver, 1965-95, prof. emeritus, 1995—, assoc. dir. TRIUMF Project, 1968-73, dir. TRIUMF Project, 1981-94, v.p. univ., 1975-81; chmn. Sci. Council B.C., 1978-80. Co-editor: Advances in Nuclear Physics, 1968—; Contbr. articles to profl. jours. Decorated officer Order of Can.; recipient Centennial medal of Can., 1967. Fellow Royal Soc. Can., Am. Phys. Soc.; mem. Can. Assn. Physicists (past pres., gold medal for achievement in physics 1988). Office: Triumf, 4004 Wesbrook Mall, Vancouver, BC Canada V6T 2A3

VOGT, EVON ZARTMAN, JR., anthropologist; b. Gallup, N.Mex., Aug. 20, 1918; s. Evon and Shirley (Bergman) V.; m. Catherine Christine Hiller, Sept. 4, 1941; children—Shirley Naneen (Mrs. Geza Teleki), Evon Zartman III, Eric Edwards, Charles Anthony. A.B., U. Chgo., 1941, M.A., 1946, Ph.D., 1948. Instr. Harvard U., 1948-50, asst. prof., 1950-55, assoc. prof., 1955-59, prof. anthropology, 1959-89, prof. emeritus, 1989—, dir. Harvard Chiapas project, 1957—, chmn. dept. anthropology, 1969-73, master Kirkland House, 1974-82; asst. curator Am. ethnology Harvard (Peabody Mus.), 1950-59, curator Middle Am. ethnology, 1960-89, hon. curator Middle Am. ethnology, 1990—; vis. prof. U. Hawaii, 1972; Mem. div. anthropology and psychology NRC, 1955-57. Author: Navaho Veterans, 1951, Modern Homesteaders, 1955, (with W.A. Lessa) Reader in Comparative Religion, 1958, (with Ray Hyman) Water Witching U.S.A., 1959, 2nd edit., 1970, Zinacantan: A Maya Community in The Highlands of Chiapas, 1969 (Harvard Press Faculty prize Sahagun prize 1969), The Zinacantecos of Mexico: A Modern Maya Way of Life, 1970, 2d edit. 1990, Tortillas for the Gods: A Symbolic Analysis of Zinacanteco Rituals, 1976, 2d edit., 1993, Fieldwork Among the Maya: Reflections on The Harvard Chiapas Project, 1994; editor: Desarrollo Cultural de Los Mayas, 1964, Los Zinacantecos, 1966, People of Rimrock, 1966, Handbook of Middle American Indians, vols. 7 and 8, 1969, Aerial Photography in Anthropological Field Research, 1974, (with Richard M. Leventhal) Prehistoric Settlement Patterns, 1983. Served from ensign to lt. USNR, 1942-46. Decorated Order Aztec Eagle Mexico; fellow Center for Advanced Study in Behavioral Sci., 1956-57. Fellow Am. Acad. Arts and Scis. (councilor 1974-78), Am. Anthrop. Assn. (exec. bd. 1958-60); mem. NAS (chmn. anthropology sect. 1981-84, class V behavioral and social scis. 1986-89), Soc. Am. Archaeology, Royal Anthrop. Inst. Gt. Britain and Ireland, Am. Ethnological Soc., Harvard Club, Tavern Club. Home: 14 Chauncy St Cambridge MA 02138-2528

VOGT, JOHN HENRY, corporate executive; b. Ft. Madison, Iowa, Dec. 31, 1918; s. John Andrew and Edith Elizabeth (Cramer) V.; m. Jean Hilleary, Aug. 4, 1942; children: John Hilleary, Linda Jean, Lisa Louise. B.S.C., Iowa U., 1940. Retail exec. trainee Sears Roebuck & Co., 1940-41; mgmt. trainee, then chief standards engr. Nat. Pressure Cooker Co., Eau Claire, Wis., 1946; sr. indsl. engr. Continental Can Co., 1950-51; with aircraft engine div. Ford Motor Co., Chgo., 1951-57; asst. to gen. mgr. Ford Motor Co., 1956-57; exec. adminstr. Lions Internat., Chgo., 1957-71; exec. v.p. Dairy and Food Industries Supply Assn., Washington, 1971-73; pres. Nat. Eye Research Found., Chgo., 1973-79; exec. dir. North Bus. and Indsl. Council Chgo., 1979-80; exec. dir. Nat. Assn. Corp. Real Estate Execs., West Palm Beach, Fla., 1980-85, sr. mgmt. advisor, 1985-90. Mem. at large nat. coun. Boy Scouts Am.; bd. dirs. Nat. Eye Rsch. Found., 1973-79. Capt. USAAF, 1941-46. Mem. Am. Soc. Assn. Execs. (life), Internat. Assn. Attys. and Execs. in Corp. Real Estate (founder, exec. v.p. 1990—), Toastmasters (past pres. Chgo. chpt.), Lions, Execs. Club Chgo. Home and Office: 18421 Lakeview Circle E Tinley Park IL 60477

VOGT, ROCHUS EUGEN, physicist, educator; b. Neckarelz, Germany, Dec. 21, 1929; came to U.S., 1953; s. Heinrich and Paula (Schaefer) V.; m. Micheline Alice Yvonne Bauduin, Sept. 6, 1958; children: Michele, Nicole. Student, U. Karlsruhe, Germany, 1950-52, U. Heidelberg, Germany, 1952-53; SM, U. Chgo., 1957, PhD, 1961. Asst. prof. physics Calif. Inst. Tech., Pasadena, 1962-65, assoc. prof., 1965-70, prof., 1970—, R. Stanton Avery Disting. Service prof., 1982—, chmn. faculty, 1975-77, chief scientist Jet Propulsion Lab., 1977-78, chmn. div. physics, math. and astronomy, 1978-83; acting dir. Owens Valley Radio Obs., 1980-81; v.p. and provost Calif. Inst. Tech., Pasadena, 1983-87; vis. prof. physics MIT, 1988-94; dir. Caltech/MIT Laser Interferometer Gravitational Wave Observatory Project, 1987-94. Author: Cosmic Rays (in World Book Ency.), 1978, (with R.B. Leighton) Exercises in Introductory Physics, 1969; contbr. articles to profl. jours. Fulbright fellow, 1953-54; recipient Exceptional Sci. Achievement medal NASA, 1981, Profl. Achievement award U. Chgo. Alumni Assn., 1981. Fellow AAAS, A. Phys. Soc. Achievements include research in astrophysics and gravitation. Office: Calif Inst Tech # 51-33 Pasadena CA 91125

VOHAR, BRUCE ALEXANDER, chemical engineer; b. Sewickley, Pa., Nov. 2, 1954; s. Stephen and Agnes (Dubensky) V.; m. Carol Ann Karpa, July 2, 1977 (div. 1990); 1 child, Alexander; m. Maria Rosalda Martins, May 24, 1990; children: Simone, Maryann, Christopher Feld. BSChE, Pa. State U., 1976; MSChE, U. Pitts., 1981. Registered profl. engr., Pa. Field petroleum engr. Texaco Inc., New Iberia, La., 1976-77; plant process engr. Witco Corp., Petrolia, Pa., 1977-79, hydrogenation dept. engr., 1979-82, prodn. supr., 1982-86, process engr. supr., 1986-89, plant engring. supt., 1989-92, plant gen. supt., 1992—; cons. Brasilco, Inc., Butler, Pa., 1990—; judge Pa. Jr. Acad. Sci., 1981, 82, 84. Speaker Rotary Club Butler, 1993. Mem. AIChE, Pa. Soc. Profl. Engrs. Republican. Roman Catholic. Achievements include start-up and design in hydrogenation. Home: 102 Aubrey Dr Butler PA 16001-1830 Office: Witco Corp 100 Witco Ln Petrolia PA 16050-0336

VOHRA, RANBIR, political scientist, educator; b. Lyallpur, Punjab, Pakistan, Mar. 5, 1928; came to U.S., 1964; s. Dualatram and Gurandevi V.; m. Meena Vincent, Jan. 14, 1954. B.A. with honours, Govt. Coll., Lahore, 1946; diploma in Chinese, Peking (China) U., 1959; M.A. (Ford Found. fellow 1964-68, teaching fellow 1965-67, 68-69), Harvard U., 1965, Ph.D., 1969. Program exec. All India Radio, 1947-64, head Chinese unit external services, 1959-64; instr., then lectr. history Harvard U., 1969-71; asso. prof. U. Calgary, Alta., Can., 1971-73; mem. faculty Trinity Coll., Hartford, Conn., 1973—; Charles A. Dana prof. polit. sci. Trinity Coll., 1975—, chmn. dept., 1973-85, 93-96; tutor Dudley House, Harvard U., 1966-71, vis. prof., summer 1972; vis. prof. Amherst Coll., spring 1974; vis. scholar Harvard Ctr. for East Asian Rsch., 1989-90. Author: Lao She and the Chinese Revolution, 1974, China's Path to Modernization, 1987, 2d edit., 1992, China: The Search for Social Justice and Democracy, 1990; editor: The Chinese Revolution 1900-1950, 1974. Mem. Assn. Asian Studies, Internat. Polit. Sci. Assn., India Internat. Center. Home: 4 Shepard Rd Hartford CT 06110-2021 Office: Trinity Coll Hartford CT 06106

VOHS, JAMES ARTHUR, health care program executive; b. Idaho Falls, Idaho, Sept. 26, 1928; s. John Dale and Cliff Lucille (Packer) V.; m. Janice Hughes, Sept. 19, 1953; children: Lorraine, Carol, Nancy, Sharla. B.A., U. Calif., Berkeley, 1952; postgrad., Harvard Sch. Bus., 1966. Employed by various Kaiser affiliated orgns., 1952-92; chmn., pres., CEO Kaiser Found. Hosps. and Kaiser Found. Health Plan, INc., Oakland, Calif., 1975-92, chmn. emeritus; chmn. bd. dirs. Holy Names Coll., 1981-92; chmn. Marcus Foster Inst., 1981—; bd. dirs. Clorox Co.; dep. chmn. Fed. Res. Bank San Francisco, chmn., 1991-94. Bd. dirs. Oakland-Alameda County Coliseum Complex, Bay Area Coun., 1985-94, chmn., 1991-92; mem. Oakland Bd. Port Commrs. With AUS, 1946-48. Mem. NAS, Inst. Medicine. Office: Kaiser Center Ordway Bldg Oakland CA 94612

VOIGHT, ELIZABETH ANNE, lawyer; b. Sapulpa, Okla., Aug. 6, 1944; d. Robert Guy and Garnetta Ruth (Bell) Voight; m. Bodo Barske, Feb. 22, 1985; children: Anne Katharine, Ruth Caroline. BA, U. Ark.-Fayetteville, 1967, MA, 1969; postgrad. U. Hamburg (W.Ger.), 1966-67; J.D., Georgetown U., 1978. Bar: N.Y. 1979. Lectr. German, Oral Roberts U., Tulsa, 1968-69; tchr. German, D.C. pub. schs., 1971-73; instr. German, Georgetown U., Washington, 1973-74, adminstrv. asst. to dean Sch. Fgn. Svc., 1974-77; law clk. Cole & Corette, Washington, 1977-78; atty. Walter, Conston, Alexander & Green, P.C., N.Y.C., 1978-88, Munich, 1990—. Translator articles for profl. jours. Chmn. regional screening Am. Field Svc., N.Y.C., 1981-86. German Acad. Exchange Program fellow, 1966-67. Mem. Assn. Bar City N.Y., ABA, Internat. Fiscal Assn., Internat. Bar Assn., Am. C. of C. in Germany, Phi Beta Kappa, Kappa Kappa Gamma.

VOIGHT, JON, actor; b. Yonkers, N.Y., Dec. 29, 1938; s. Elmer and Barbara (Camp) V.; m. Lauri Peters, 1962 (div. 1967); m. Marcheline Bertrand, Dec. 12, 1971 (div.); children: James Haven, Angelina Jolie. BFA, Cath. U., 1960; studied with, Sanford Meisner and Samantha Harper, N.Y.C. Stage appearances include O Oysters Revue, 1961, The Sound of Music, 1961, A View from the Bridge, 1965, Romeo and Juliet, 1966, The Tempest, 1966, Two Gentlemen of Verona, 1966, That Summer-That Fall, 1967 (Theatre World award 1967), A Streetcar Named Desire, 1973, The Hashish Club, 1975, Hamlet, 1976, The Seagull, 1992; TV appearances include Cimarron Strip, Gunsmoke; films include Fearless Frank, 1967, Hour of the Gun, 1967, Out of It, 1969, Midnight Cowboy, 1969 (Best Actor Acad. award nominee 1969, N.Y. Critics Circle award 1969, L.A. Film Critics Best Actor award 1969, Brit. Acad. Most Promising Newcomer to Leading Film Role award 1969), Catch-22, 1970, The Revolutionary, 1970, Deliverance, 1972, The All American Boy, 1973, Conrack, 1974, The Odessa File, 1974, End of the Game, 1976, Coming Home, 1978 (Best Actor Acad. award 1978, Golden Globe award 1978, Cannes Internat. Film festival award 1978, N.Y. Film Critics Best Actor award 1978, L.A. Film Critics Best Actor award 1978), The Champ, 1979 (Golden Globe award 1979), Runaway Train, 1985 (Acad. award nominee 1986, London Film Critics award nominee 1986), Desert Bloom, 1986, Eternity, 1990; TV films include Chernobyl: The Final Warning, 1991, The Last of His Tribe, 1992; actor, prodr., co-writer film Lookin' To Get Out, 1982; actor, prodr. film Table for Five, 1983. Winner Best Actor awards for Midnight Cowboy and Coming Home, Cannes Internat. Film Festival, Golden Globe award for Best Actor, Coming Home and The Champ, Acad. award for Best Actor, Coming Home 1979, N.Y. Film Critics award, Los Angeles Film Critics award for Best Actor, Midnight Cowboy, Coming Home. Office: care CAA 9830 Wilshire Blvd Beverly Hills CA 90212*

VOIGT, CYNTHIA, author; b. Boston, Feb. 25, 1942; d. Frederick C. and Elise (Keeney) Irving; married, 1964 (div. 1972); m. Walter Voigt, Aug. 30, 1974; children: Jessica, Peter. BA, Smith Coll., 1963. High sch. tchr. English Glen Burnie, Md., 1965-67; tchr. English Key Sch., Annapolis, Md., 1968-69, dept. chmn., 1971-79, tchr., dept. chmn., 1981-88. Author: Homecoming, 1981, Tell Me If the Lovers Are Losers, 1982, Dicey's Song, 1982 (John Newbery medal 1983), The Callender Papers, 1983 (Edgar award 1984), A Solitary Blue, 1983, Building Blocks, 1984, Jackeroo, 1985, The Runner, 1985 (Silver Pencil award 1988, Deutscher Jugend Literator Preis 1989, ALAN award 1989), Come a Stranger, 1986, Izzy, Willy Nilly, 1986 (Calif. Young Reader's award 1990), Stories About Rosie, 1986, Sons From Afar, 1987, Tree by Leaf, 1988, Seventeen Against the Dealer, 1989, On Fortune's Wheel, 1990, The Vandemark Mummy, 1991, Orfe, 1992, Glass Mountain, 1991, David and Jonathan, 1992, The Wings of a Falcon, 1993, When She Hollers, 1994. *

VOIGT, PAUL WARREN, research geneticist; b. Ann Arbor, Mich., Mar. 20, 1940; s. Melvin John and Susie (Warkentin) V.; m. Josephine Bergeret, Aug. 24, 1963; children: Valorie Christine, Suzanna Jo, Peter Charles. BS, Iowa State U., 1962; MS, U. Wis., 1964, PhD, 1967. Rsch. geneticist Agrl. Rsch. Svc., USDA, Woodward, Okla., 1967-74, Temple, Tex., 1974-78; rsch. geneticist, rsch. leader Grassland Soil & Water Rsch. Lab., Temple, Tex., 1978-93; rsch. geneticist Appalachian Soil and Water Conservation Rsch. Lab., 1993—; v.p. Grass Breeder's Work Planning Conf., 1971-73, pres., 1973-75; mem. Nat. Cert. Grass Variety Rev. Bd., 1976-78, 84-87, Grass Crop Adv. Com., 1982-93. Author: (with others) The Science of Grassland Agriculture, 1985, Forages Vol. 1: An Introduction to Grassland Agriculture, 1995; contbr. numerous articles to profl. jours. Mem. Temple Civic Chorus, 1979-90. Fellow Am. Soc. Agronomy, Crop Sci. Soc. Am. (assoc. editor jour. 1980-82, tech. editor 1985-87); mem. Am. Forage and Grassland Coun., Soc. for Range Mgmt., Sigma Xi. Avocations: music, gardening, swimming, camping, photography. Office: Appalachian Soil & Water Conservation Rsch Lab PO Box 867 Beckley WV 25802-0867

VOIGT, RICHARD, lawyer; b. Oskaloosa, Iowa, Jan. 20, 1946; s. Franz Otto Wilhelm and Minni (Heilbrunn) V.; m. Annemarie H. Riemer, Oct. 2, 1976; children: Samuel, Nicholas. BA, Conn. Wesleyan U., 1968; JD, U. Va., 1974. Bar: Va. 1974, U.S. Dist. Ct. (ea. dist.) Va. 1979, Conn. 1981, U.S. Dist. Ct. Conn. 1982, U.S. Ct. Claims 1982, U.S. Ct. Appeals (4th cir.) 1982. Assoc. counsel regional litigation Solicitor's Office Osha Div., 1978-80; staff atty. U.S. Dept. Labor, Washington, 1974-78; prin. Siegel, O'Connor, Schiff, Zangari & Kainen, P.C., 1981-88, 87-88; ptnr. Cummings & Lockwood, Hartford, 1988—. Contbg. author: ABA Treatise on Occupational Safety and Health Law, 1988; contbr. articles to profl. jours. Bd. dirs. Urban League Greater Hartford, 1984-88, Isnt. for Non-Profit Tng. and Devel., 1991—, Hartford Proud and Beautiful, 1995—. Mem. ABA (labor and employment law sect., OSHA com., litigation sect.), Conn. Bar Assn. (labor employment law sect., employment discrimination com., com. on alternative dispute resolution). Avocations: acrylic design, history, sports. Office: 36th Floor Cityplace I Hartford CT 06103

VOIGT, ROBERT GARY, numerical analyst; b. Olney, Ill., Dec. 21, 1939; s. Donald E. and Jean C. (Fishel) V.; m. Susan J. Strand, Aug. 25, 1962; children: Christine, Jennifer. BA, Wabash Coll., 1961; MS, Purdue U., 1963; PhD, U. Md., 1969. Mathematician Naval Ship R & D Ctr., Washington, 1962-69, 71-72; vis. prof. U. Md., College Park, 1969-71; asst. dir. Inst. for Computer Application in Sci. and Engring., Hampton, Va., 1973-83, assoc. dir., 1983-86, dir., 1986-91; program dir. NSF, Arlington, Va., 1992-94; high performance computing and comm. coord. NSF, Arlington, 1994—; mem. tech. adv. bd. NSF, NASA, Dept. of Energy, and others. Co-author: Solution of Partial Differential Equations on Parallel and Vector Computers, 1985; co-editor 7 books; editor numerous jours.; contbr. 21 articles to profl. jours. Recipient Pub. Svc. award NASA, 1989. Mem. IEEE, Am. Math. Soc., Assn. for Computing Machinery, Soc. for Indsl. and Applied Math. (sec. 1987-91). Office: NSF Rm 1105 4201 Wilson Blvd Arlington VA 22230

VOINOVICH, GEORGE V., governor; b. Cleve., July 15, 1936; m. Janet Voinovich; 3 children. B.A., Ohio U., 1958; J.D., Ohio State U., 1961; LL.D. (hon.), Ohio U., 1981. Bar: Ohio 1961, U.S. Supreme Ct. 1968. Asst. atty. gen. State of Ohio, 1963-64; mem. Ohio Ho. of Reps., 1967-71; auditor Cuyahoga County, Ohio, 1971-76; commr., 1976-78; lt. gov. State of Ohio, 1979; mayor City of Cleve., 1979-90; gov. State of Ohio, 1991—; 1st v.p. Nat. League Cities, 1984-85, pres., 1985; trustee U.S. Conf. Mayors; chmn. Midwestern Govs. Conf., 1991-92, Coun. Gt. Lakes Govs., 1992-94. Recipient cert. of Merit award Ohio U., Humanitarian award NCCJ, 1986; named one of Outstanding Young Men in Ohio Ohio Jaycees, 1970; one of Outstanding Young Men in Greater Cleve. Cleve. Jaycees; Disting. Urban Mayor award Nat. Urban Coalition, 1987; named to All-Pro City Mgmt. team City & State Mag., 1987. Mem. Rep. Govs. Assn. (vice chmn. 1991-92, chmn. 1992-93), Nat. Govs. Assn. (chmn. edn. action team on sch. readiness 1991, chmn. child support enforcement work group 1991-92, mem. strategic planning task force 1991-92, mem. human resources com. 1991—, co-chmn. task force on edn. 1992-93, mem. exec. com. 1993—, co-lead gov. on fed. mandates 1993—), Omicron Delta Kappa, Phi Alpha Theta, Phi Delta Phi. Republican. Office: Office of Governor 77 S High St 30th fl Columbus OH 43266-0601*

VOITLE, ROBERT ALLEN, college dean, physiologist; b. Parkersburg, W.Va., May 12, 1938; s. Ray Christian and Ruby Virginia (Hannaman) V.; m. Linda Ellen Loveday, Dec. 5, 1975; children: Robert Allen, Elizabeth Anne, Christian Blair, Vanessa Virginia. BS, W.Va. U., 1962; M.S., W.Va., 1965; Ph.D., U. Tenn., 1969. Asst. in poultry U. Tenn., Knoxville, 1965-69; asst. prof. physiology U. Fla., Gainesville, 1969-75, assoc. prof., 1975-79; prof., head dept. poultry Calif. Poly. State U., San Luis Obispo, 1979-81; assoc. dean Coll. Agr., Auburn U., Ala., 1981—; cons. Columbia Bank for Coops., S.C., 1972. Contbr. articles to sci. jours. Pres., other offices Alachua County Fair Assn., Gainesville, 1969-79. Recipient Pub. Service award Alachua County Commn., 1975; recipient Tchr. of Yr. award U. Fla., 1977, Golden Feather award Calif. Poly. Inst., 1982. Mem. Poultry Sci. Assn., So. Poultry Sci. Assn., Gainesville Jaycees (JCI senatorship), Sigma Xi, Gamma Sigma Delta. Episcopalian. Club: Elks. Home: 2247 Longwood Dr Auburn AL 36830-7105 Office: Auburn U Coll Agr Auburn AL 36849

VOKETAITIS, ARNOLD MATHEW, bass-baritone, educator; b. East Haven, Conn., May 11, 1930; s. Mathew Joseph and Agnes Mary (Pilvelis) V.; m. Marion Lee Dever, June 1959 (div. 1967); children: Arnold Mathew Jr., Paul Stanley; m. Nijole Lipciute, Sept. 6, 1968. B.S. in Bus. Adminstrn, Quinnipiac Coll., 1954; postgrad., Yale U. Dir. opera program De Paul U., Chgo., 1987-89; lectr. on singing, acting Northwestern U., Evanston, Ill., 1986; mem. adv. panels in music and ethnic affairs Ill. Arts Coun.; mem. panel for opera and mus. theatre NEA; faculty mem. Brevard (N.C.) Summer Music Ctr., 1987, 88; artist-in-residence for opera Auburn U., Ala., 1990-93. Condr. master classes in singing; Operatic Debut with, N.Y.C. Opera, 1958, European debut at, Liceo, Barcelona, Spain, 1968; mem., Met. Opera Nat. Co., appeared with maj. operatic and symphonic orgns. in U.S., Can., Mex., Cen. Am., S.Am., Lyric Opera of Chgo., 1966-84, 89, rec. artist for, Desto, Vox, Columbia, RCA, Turnabout; recitalist appearances on Pay-TV; classical soloist, U.S. Army Band, Washington. Served as sgt. U.S. Army, 1954-56. Recipient 1st place award Conn. Opera Assn. auditions, 1957, Rockefeller Found. award, 1964, Lithuanian Man of Yr. award, 1990, Disting. Alumni award Quinnipiac Coll., 1991. Mem. AFTRA, Am. Guild Mus. Artists (life), Actors Equity. Avocations: golfing, fishing, theater. *I have felt very strongly over the years that opera was written to be enjoyed, not revered, and that it cried out to be acted as well as sung. With television's influence on the viewer, necessity became reality and my hopes are being realized.*

VOLAN, WENDY TYSON, marketing professional; b. Phila., July 21, 1953; d. James Robert and Caroline Helen (Macintyre) Tyson; m. Gregory D. Volan, Jan. 21, 1978. Student, U. Colo., 1971-75. Customer svc. mgr. Pallas Photo Labs, Inc., Denver, 1976-79; prin., dir. grafic design Volan Design Assocs., Boulder, Colo., 1979—. Mem. mktg. com. Boulder County United Way. Mem. Am. Ctr. Design, Inst. Packaging Profls., Rock Mountain Writers Guild. Avocations: sports cars, photography, bicycling. Office: Volan Design Assocs 1800 38th St Boulder CO 80301-2622

VOLBERG, HERMAN WILLIAM, electronics engineer, consultant; b. Hilo, Hawaii, Apr. 6, 1925; s. Fred Joseph and Kathryn Thelma (Ludloff) V.; m. Louise Ethel Potter, Apr. 26, 1968; children: Michael, Lori. BSEE, U. Calif., Berkeley, 1949. Project engr. Naval Electronics Lab., San Diego, 1950-56; head solid state rsch. S.C. div. Gen. Dynamics, San Diego, 1956-60; founder Solidyne Solid State Instruments, La Jolla, Calif., 1958-60; founder, v.p. electronics divsn. Ametek/Straza, El Cajon, Calif., 1960-66; founder, cons. H.V. Cons., San Diego, 1966-69; sr. scientist Naval Ocean Systems Ctr., Oahu, Hawaii, 1970-77; chief scientist Integrated Scis. Corp., Santa Monica, Calif., 1978-80; founder, pres. Acoustic Sys. Inc., Goleta, Calif., 1980-84; founder, pres. Invotron, Inc., Lafayette, Calif., Murray, Utah, 1984—; tech. dir. Reson, Inc., Santa Barbara, Calif., 1992—; cons. U. Utah Ctr. for Engring. Design, 1991; cons. on autonomous underwater vehicle sonar systems Mitsui/U. Tokyo, 1992; lectr. solid state course UCLA and IBM, 1956-62; instr. Applied Tech. Inst., Columbia, Md., 1988—; contbr. to undersea acoustical rsch. and devel. programs European Union, 1990—. Contbr. articles to IRE Bull., IEEE Ocean Electronics Symposium. Mem. adv. panels for advanced sonar systems and for high resolution sonars, USN, 1970-77. 1st lt. U.S. Army, 1944-47, ETO. Recipient award of merit Dept. Navy, 1973, 94. Mem. IEEE, AAAS, NRA, Acoustical Soc. Am., Mine Warfare Assn., N.Y. Acad. Scis., Marine Tech. Soc., U.S. Naval Inst., Planetary Assn., Old Crows, Masons, Elks. Achievements include patents for device for detecting and displaying the response of tissue to stimuli, high rate neutralizer (HIRAN), crane high-voltage sensing system. Home and Office: 41 W 6830 S Murray UT 84107-7124

VOLCKER, PAUL A., economist; b. Cape May, N.J., Sept. 5, 1927; s. Paul A. and Alma Louise (Klippel) V.; m. Barbara Marie Bahnson, Sept. 11, 1954; children: Janice, James. AB summa cum laude, Princeton U., 1949, LLD (hon.), 1982; MA, Harvard U., 1951, LLD (hon.), 1985. Economist Fed. Res. Bank N.Y., 1952-57; pres. Fed. Res. Bank of N.Y., 1975-79; economist Chase Manhattan Bank, N.Y.C., 1957-61, v.p., dir. planning, 1965-68; with Dept. Treasury, Washington, 1961-65, 69-74, dep. under sec. monetary affairs, 1963-65, under sec., 1969-74; chmn. bd. govs. Fed. Res. Bd., Washington, 1979-87; chmn. Wolfensohn & Co., Inc., N.Y.C., 1988—; prof. internat. econ. policy Princeton U., 1988; chmn. Nat. Commn. on Pub. Svc., 1987-90, Trilateral Commn., Group of Thirty. Sr. fellow Woodrow Wilson Sch. Pub. and Internat. Affairs, 1974-75.

VOLCKHAUSEN, WILLIAM ALEXANDER, lawyer, banker; b. N.Y.C., Mar. 13, 1937; s. William Louis and Jessie (Rankin) V.; m. Grace Lyu, Aug. 2, 1968; children: Sharon, Alexander. AB, Princeton U., 1959; AM, U. Calif., Berkeley, 1963; JD, Harvard U., 1966. Bar: N.Y. 1967. Program officer Asia Found., N.Y.C. and San Francisco, 1966-69; mng. atty. Moblzn. for Youth Legal Services, N.Y., 1969-73; dep. supt., gen. counsel N.Y. State Banking Dept., N.Y.C., 1973-79; spl. counsel Hughes Hubbard & Reed, N.Y.C., 1979-80; exec. v.p., counsel, sec. The Dime Savs. Bank of N.Y. Fed. Savs. Bank, N.Y.C., 1980-89, sr. counsel, pub. affairs exec., 1989—; adj. prof. Cardozo Sch. Law Yeshiva U., N.Y.C., 1980-95. Bd. dirs. N.Y.C. Tech. Coll., Asian-Am. Fedn. of N.Y., 100 Yr. Assn., Circle in the Square Theatre, Bklyn. Legal Svcs.-Corp. A, Princeton-in-Asia. Bd. dirs. N.Y. Tech. Coll., Asian-Am. Fedn. of N.Y., 100 Yr. Assn., Circle in the Square Theatre, Bklyn. Legal Svcs.-Corp. A. Mem. ABA, Assn. of Bar of City of N.Y., Princeton Club (N.Y.C.). Democrat. Avocations: swimming, skiing, gardening, reading, travel. Home: 262 President St Brooklyn NY 11231-4346 Office: Dime Savs Bank 589 5th Ave Fl 2 New York NY 10017-1923

VOLGY, THOMAS JOHN, political science educator, organization official; b. Budapest, Hungary, Mar. 19, 1946; m. Susan Dubow, Feb. 1987. BA magna cum laude, Oakland U., 1967; MA, U. Minn., 1969, PhD, 1972. Prof. polit. sci. U. Ariz., Tucson; dir. Univ. Teaching Ctr.; mayor City of Tucson, 1987-91; exec. dir. Internat. Studies Assn., 1995—; chmn. telecom. com. U. Conf. Mayors, 1988—; cons. H.S. curriculum project Ind. U.; bd. dirs. Nat. League of Cities, 1989-91. Co-author: The Forgotten Americans, 1992; editor: Exploring Relationships Between Mass Media and Political Culture: The Impact of Television and Music on American Society, 1976; contbr. numerous articles to profl. jours.; producer two TV documentaries for PBS affiliate. Mem. Nat. Women's Polit. Caucus Conv., 1983, U.S. Senate Fin. Com., 1985, U.S. Ho. of Reps. Telecommunications Com., 1988—, Polit. Sci. Adminstrn. Com., 1986, Gov.'s Task Force on Women and Poverty, 1986, United Way, 1985-87; bd. dirs. Honors Program, 1981—, U. Teaching Ctr., 1988—, Tucson Urban League, 1981, Ododo Theatre, 1984, So. Ariz. Mental Health Care Ctr., 1987, Nat. Fedn. Local Cable TV Programmers; chmn. Internat. Rels. Caucus, 1981, 86—, Transp. and Telecommunications Com. Nat. League Cities, 1986, 88, 89-91. Recipient NDEA scholarship, 1964-76, NDEA fellowship, 1967-70, Oasis award for oustanding prodn. of local affairs TV programming; named Outstanding Young Am., 1981, Outstanding Naturalized Citizen of Yr., 1980; faculty research grantee U. Ariz., 1972-73, 73-74, 74-75, 77-78. Mem. Pima Assn. Govts., Nat. Fedn. Local Cable Programmers. Democrat. Jewish. Office: U Ariz Polit Dept Sci Tucson AZ 85721

VOLK, HARRY J., banker; b. Trenton, N.J., July 20, 1905; s. Michael T. and Susan (Harkins) V.; m. Marion E. Waters, Oct. 12, 1931 (dec. 1972); children: Robert H., Richard R., Carolyn E. Volk Jacques (dec. 1987); m. Marjorie L. Hale, Aug. 14, 1976. A.B., Rutgers U., 1927, LL.B., 1930, L.H.D., 1958; L.H.D., Hebrew Union Coll., 1992; LL.D., Pepperdine U., 1982. With Prudential Ins. Co., 1927-57; v.p. in charge Western ops. Prudential Ins. Co., Los Angeles, 1947-57; pres. Union Bank of Los Angeles, 1957-69, dir., 1957-80, chmn., 1969-80; chmn., dir. Union Bancorp, Inc., 1969-79; dir. Standard Chartered Bancorp, 1978-80; chmn., chief exec. officer Weingart Found., 1980-93. Trustee Rutgers U., 1942-47, Calif. Inst. Tech., 1950-80, Hosp. of Good Samaritan, 1970-80; pres. Nat. Alumni Assn., Rutgers U., 1940-45. Served as div. chief U.S. Strategic Bombing Survey, 1945. Recipient Milliken medal Calif. Inst. Tech., 1980. Mem. Los Angeles C. of C. (dir. 1949-52), USC Assocs., Pepperdine Assocs., Los Angeles County Mus. Art, Assocs. Calif. Inst. Tech. Clubs: The Founders (Calif.), Bohemian, Los Angeles Country, Calif. Office: Union Bank 1900 Avenue Of The Stars Los Angeles CA 90067-4301

VOLK, JAN, professional sports team executive; b. Davenport, Iowa; m. Lissa Volk; children: Shari, Matthew. Grad., Colby Coll., Maine, 1968; J.D., Columbia U., 1971. With Boston Celtics, 1971—, dir. ticket sales, mgr. equipment purchases, travel arrangements, bus. mgr., legal counsel, 1974-76, v.p., 1976-83, gen. mgr., 1983—, now also v.p. Office: Boston Celtics 151 Merrimac St Boston MA 02114-4714*

VOLK, KENNETH HOHNE, lawyer; b. Hackensack, N.J., Nov. 8, 1922; s. Henry L. and Constance (Brady) V.; m. Joyce Geary, May 11, 1954; children: Christopher H., Cynthia. BS, U.S. Naval Acad., 1946; LLB, Yale U., 1953. Ptnr. Burlingham, Underwood, N.Y.C., 1955-92; of counsel McLane, Graf, Raulerson & Middleton, Portsmouth, N.H., 1992—; speaker various symposia and confs. on maritime law. Contbr. articles to profl. jours. Pres. Maritime Assocs., N.Y.C., 1967-68; chmn. bd. dirs. Seamen's House YMCA, N.Y.C., 1971-76; sec., bd. dirs. Seamen's Ch. Inst., N.Y.C., 1977-92; bd. dirs. Strawbery Banke Mus., Portsmouth, N.H.; mem. adv. bd. Tulane Admiralty Law Inst.. Fellow Am. Bar Found., Am. Coll. Trial Lawyers; mem. ABA, Assn. Bar of City of N.Y., Maritime Law Assn. U.S. (exec. com. 1977-80, pres. 1990-92), Comite Maritime Internat. (titulary mem.), Quaker Hill Country Club (pres. 1976-78). Republican. Espicopalian. Avocations: reading, hiking, swimming. Office: McLane Graf Raulerson 30 Penhallow St Portsmouth NH 03801-4017

VOLK, NORMAN HANS, financial executive; b. N.Y.C., Jan. 10, 1935; s. Hans and Mary (Zurl) V.; m. Karlyn Schram, Aug. 17, 1959; children: Kari, Heidi, Jenny. BA, Valparaiso (Ind.) U., 1957; MA, Marquette U., Milw., 1959. Dir. pub. rels. Wagner Coll., N.Y.C., 1961-62; asst. to owner Alan M. Wood, N.Y.C., 1962-72; sr. v.p. Bessemer Trust Co., N.Y.C., 1972-85; pres. Chamberlain & Steward, N.Y.C., 1985—. Trustee John Hartford Found., N.Y.C., 1979—. With U.S. Army, 1959-61. Mem. Univ. Club, Univ. Glee Club of N.Y.C., Doubles Club. Lutheran. Home: 445 Walton Rd Maplewood NJ 07040-1119 Office: 400 Park Ave New York NY 10022-4406

VOLK, ROBERT HARKINS, aviations company executive; b. East Orange, N.J., Nov. 27, 1932; s. Harry Joseph and Marion (Waters) V.; m. Barbara June Klint, Sept. 10, 1954; children: Christopher G., William W., Laura L., Elisabeth M. BA, Stanford U., 1954, LLB, 1958. Bar: Calif. 1959. Assoc. Adams Duque & Hazeltine, L.A., 1959-62; ptnr. Adams Duque & Hazelyine, L.A., 1962-67; commr. of corps. State of Calif., Sacramento, 1967-69; pres. Union Bancorp, L.A., 1969-73; pres., chmn. Union Am., L.A., 1973-79; owner, chief exec. officer Martin Aviation Inc., Santa Ana, Calif., 1980-90, Media Aviation L.P. Burbank, 1984—. Sgt. USAF, 1955-57. Mem. Calif. Bar Assn. Republican. Episcopalian. Avocations: skiing, golf, tennis. Home: 332 Conway Ave Los Angeles CA 90024-2604 Office: Media Aviation LP 3000 N Clybourn Ave Burbank CA 91505-1012

VOLK, STEPHEN RICHARD, lawyer; b. Boston, Apr. 22, 1936; s. Ralph and Miriam (Rose) V.; m. Veronica J. Brown, June 19, 1959 (dec. Feb. 1989); children: Jeffrey A., Andrew M., Michael J.; m. Diane Kemelman, Apr. 22, 1990; 1 child, Anne. Student, Dartmouth Coll., 1957; JD, Harvard U., 1960. Bar: N.Y. 1961. Assoc. Sherman & Sterling, N.Y.C., 1960-68, ptnr., 1968—, dep. sr. ptnr., 1988-91, sr. ptnr., 1991—. Trustee St. Luke's/Roosevelt Hosp., N.Y.C., 1990; ptnr. N.Y.C. Partnership, 1991. Mem. ABA (com. on securities regulation 1974), Am. Law Inst., Assn. Bar City N.Y., Coun. on Fgn. Rels., Univ. Club, Phi Beta Kappa. Office: 599 Lexington Ave New York NY 10022-6030

VOLKER, DALE MARTIN, state senator, lawyer; b. Lancaster, N.Y., Aug. 2, 1940; s. Julius J. and Loretta (O'Neill) V.; m. Carol A. Suchyna, Nov. 28, 1970; children: Martin Andrew, Mark Dale, Meredith Ann. BA, Canisius Coll., 1963; JD, SUNY-Buffalo, 1966. Bar: N.Y. 1967. Police officer Village of Depew, N.Y., 1966-72; assemblyman State Assembly, Albany, N.Y., 1972-74; mem. N.Y. State Senate, Albany, 1975—; sole practice law, Lancaster. Mem. Erie County Bar Assn., Elks, Moose, Eagles. Republican. Roman Catholic. Home: 92 Center Dr Depew NY 14043-1706 Office: 708 Legislative Office Bldg Albany NY 12247

VOLKHARDT, JOHN MALCOLM, food company executive; b. Chester, Pa., Apr. 13, 1917; s. George Thomas and Evelyn (Mitchell) V.; m. Linda J. Volkhardt; children—Jacqueline, Janet, Dana. A.B. cum laude, Brown U., 1939. Product mgr. Vick Chem. Co., N.Y.C., 1939-48; gen. mgr. Northam Warren Co., Stamford, Conn., 1948-56, Rit div. Best Foods Co., N.Y.C., 1956-58; with Best Foods div. CPC Internat. Inc., Englewood Cliffs, N.J., 1958-78, exec. v.p., 1968-71, pres., 1971-78; pres. North Am. div. CPC Internat. and exec. v.p. CPC Internat., 1978-82, group v.p., 1979; v.p. CPC, 1971-78, dir., 1977-82; pres., chmn. Full Circle Corp., Moss Creek, 1985-91; pres. Water Oak Utility, 1985-91. Chmn. bd. Keep Am. Beautiful, Inc., 1979-82, chmn. bd. trustees, 1982. Recipient Herbert Hoover award Nat.

Assn. Wholesale Grocers Am.; honoree Nat. Jewish Hosp., 1976. Mem. Phi Beta Kappa.

VOLKMANN, DANIEL GEORGE, JR., architect; b. San Francisco, June 3, 1924; s. Daniel George and Beatrice (Simpson) V.; m. Marvin Johnson, Sept. 1, 1949 (dec. 1991); children: Daniel G., William R., David R., Wendy. BA, Yale U., 1945, U. Calif., Berkeley, 1950; MA, U. Calif., Berkeley, 1951. Practice architecture San Francisco, 1952—; prin. emeritus Bull, Volkmann, Stockwell, Architects, 1969-91; ltd. ptnr. Dean Witter & Co., San Francisco, 1967-69; bd. dirs. St. Francis Hosp Found., Gleeson Libr. Assoc., San Francisco Libr. Found. Mem. coun. Friends Bancroft Libr. U. Calif., Berkeley, 1976-82; trustee San Francisco Mus. Art, 1970-81, Marin Country Day Sch., 1972-77, San Francisco Conservatory Music, 1982-90, Cypress Lawn Cemetery, 1979—; pres., bd. dirs. Cypress Lawn Cemetery, 1993—; mem. Art Commn. City and County San Francisco, 1975—; bd. dirs. Pacific Enterprises, 1967-93. With USNR, 1944-46. Mem. AIA (numerous awards in design), San Francisco Planning and Urban Renewal Assn., Cow Hollow Improvement Assn. (bd. dirs., pres. 1970), Bohemian Club, Olympic Club, McCloud Fly Fishing Club, Pacific Union (San Francisco), Grolier Club (N.Y.C.). Home: 2616 Union St San Francisco CA 94123-3817

VOLKMANN, FRANCES COOPER, psychologist, educator; b. Harlingen, Tex., May 4, 1935; d. Edward O. and Elizabeth (Bass) C.; m. John Volkmann, Nov. 1, 1958 (dec.); children: Stephen Edward, Thomas Frederick. A.B. magna cum laude, Mt. Holyoke Coll., 1957; M.A., Brown U., 1959, Ph.D., 1961; DSci., Mt. Holyoke Coll., 1987. Research assoc. Mt. Holyoke Coll., South Hadley, Mass., 1964-65; lectr. U. Mass., Amherst, 1964-65, Smith Coll., Northampton, Mass., 1966-67; asst. prof. Smith Coll., 1967-72, assoc. prof., 1972-78, prof. psychology, 1978—, dean faculty, 1983-88, Harold E. Israel and Elsa M. Siipola prof. psychology, 1988—, acting pres., 1991; vis. assoc. prof. Brown U., Providence, 1974, vis. prof., 1978-82; vis. scholar U. Wash., Seattle, summer 1977. Contbr. articles to profl. jours. Trustee Chatham Coll., 1987—. USPHS fellow, 1961-62; NSF grantee, 1974-78; Nat. Eye Inst. grantee, 1978-82. Fellow APA, AAAS, Optical Soc. Am.; mem. Ea. Psychol. Assn., Soc. Neurosci. Psychonomic Soc., Assn. Rsch. in Vision and Ophthalmology, New Eng. Assn. Schs. and Colls. (vice chair commn. instns. higher edn. 1991-93, chair 1993-95). Home: 40 Arlington St Northampton MA 01060-2003 Office: Smith Coll Northampton MA 01063

VOLKMER, HAROLD L., congressman; b. Jefferson City, Mo., Apr. 4, 1931; m. Shirley Ruth Braskett; children: Jerry Wayne, John Paul, Elizabeth Ann. Student, Jefferson City Jr. Coll., 1949-51, St. Louis U. Sch. Commerce and Finance, 1951-52; LL.B., U. Mo., 1955. Bar: Mo. 1955. Individual practice law Hannibal, 1958—; asst. atty. gen. Mo., 1955; pros. atty. Marion County, 1960-66; mem. Mo. Ho. of Reps., 1966-76; chmn. judiciary com., mem. revenue and econs. com.; mem. 95th-104th Congresses from 9th Mo. Dist., 1977—; ranking minority mem. agr. subcom. livestock, dairy, & poultry. Served with U.S. Army, 1955-57. Recipient award for meritorious pub. service in Gen. Assembly St. Louis Globe-Democrat, 1972-74. Mem. Mo., 10th Jud. Circuit bar assns. Roman Catholic. Clubs: KC, Hannibal Lions. Office: US House of Reps 2409 Rayburn House Bldg Washington DC 20515*

VOLKOFF, GEORGE MICHAEL, educational administator, former physics educator; b. Moscow, Feb. 23, 1914; came to Can., 1924; s. Mikhail Mikhailovich and Elizabeth Pavlovna (Titova) V., m. Olga Okulitch, June 22, 1940; children—Elizabeth Volkoff Bell, Alexandra, Olga Volkoff Richardson. B.A., U. B.C., Vancouver, Can., 1934, M.A., 1936, D.Sc. (hon.), 1945; Ph.D., U. Calif.-Berkeley, 1940. Asst. prof. physics U. B.C., Vancouver, 1940-46, prof., 1946-79, head dept. physics, 1961-71, dean Faculty of Sci., 1972-79, prof. emeritus, 1979—; research physicist NRC, Montreal, 1943-45; head theoretical physics br. div. atomic energy NRC, Chalk River, Ont., 1945-46; vis. lectr. McGill U., spring 1946, Purdue U., spring 1948, U. Wash., spring 1949, UCLA, summer 1950, 51, 52, U. Calif.-Berkeley; cons. in field. Translator 2 books, author numerous articles. Mem. Univ. Hill Sch. Bd., Vancouver, 1959-61; trustee Vancouver Gen. Hosp., 1980-86, chmn. bd. trustees, 1984-85. Decorated mem. Order Brit.Empire, officer Order of Can.; recipient Centennial medal Govt. of Can., 1967. Fellow Royal Soc. Can., Am. Phys. Soc., AAAS; mem. Can. Assn. Physicists (pres. 1962-63). Club: Round Table (Vancouver). Avocations: hiking; listening to music. Home: 1776 Western Pkwy, Vancouver, BC Canada V6T 1V3

VOLL, JOHN OBERT, history educator; b. Hudson, Wis., Apr. 20, 1936; s. Obert Frank and Ruth Olivia (Seaberg) V.; m. Sarah Lynne Potts, June 12, 1965; children: Sarah Layla, Michael Obert. A.B. summa cum laude, Dartmouth Coll., 1958, Ph.D. (Ford Found. fellow), 1969; A.M. (Danforth fellow), Harvard U., 1960. Instr. history U. N.H., Durham, 1965-69, asst. prof., 1969-74, assoc. prof., 1974-82, prof., 1982-95, chair dept., 1988-91; prof. Georgetown U., Washington, 1995—; mem. history and social scis. adv. com. Coll. Bd. 1983-86, chmn. European history and world cultures achievement test com., 1985-88; teaching fellow Harvard U., 1969; del. Am. Coun. Learned Socs., 1989—, also del. exec. com., 1989-92. Author: Historical Dictionary of the Sudan, 1978, 2d edit., 1992, Islam Continuity and Change in the Modern World, 2d edit., 1994; (with others) The Sudan: Unity and Diversity, 1985, Eighteenth Century Renewal and Reform in Islam, 1987, Sudan: State and Society in Crisis, 1991, Islam and Democracy, 1996; contbr. articles to profl. jours. Mem. bd. Ecumenical Ministry U. N.H., 1974-78, pres., 1975-77; chmn. social action Durham Community Ch., 1974-75, mem. ch. council, 1977-78, deacon, 1986—. Sheldon traveling fellow, 1960-61, U. N.H. summer fellow, 1969, 89, NEH fellow, 1971-72, Fulbright faculty rsch. abroad fellow, 1978-79, Inst. Advanced Studies fellow Hebrew U., 1984-85; recipient Egyptian Presdl. medal, 1991. Mem. Am. Coun. Learned Socs. (del. exec. com. 1989-92, bd. dirs. 1990-92), New Eng. Hist. Assn. (sec. 1975-78, v.p. 1981, pres. 1982), Sudan Studies Assn. (bd. dirs. 1981-82, co-exec. dir. 1990-94), N.H. Coun. on World Affairs (bd. dirs. 1978-95), Am. Hist. Assn., Mid. East Studies Assn. (bd. dirs. 1987-89, pres. 1992-93), Am. Coun. for Study of Islamic Socs. (bd. dirs. 1989—, v.p. 1989-91), N.H. Humanities Coun. (bd. dirs. 1991-95). Mem. United Ch. of Christ. Home: 4 Croghan Ln Durham NH 03824-3027 Office: Ctr Muslim Christian Understanding Georgetown U Washington DC 20057

VOLLBRECHT, EDWARD ALAN, school superintendent; b. Freeport, N.Y., July 22, 1941; s. Edward Chester and Lillian Elizabeth (Heinecke) V.; m. Catherine Ann Salgado, Dec. 2, 1977; 1 child, Matthew Grayson. BS, SUNY, New Paltz, 1963; MS, Hofstra U., 1968; PhD, Walden U., Naples, Fla., 1973. Adminstrv. asst. Pearl River (N.Y.) Sch. Dist., 1968-70, asst. prin., 1970-71; prin. Mark Twain Mid. Sch., Yonkers, N.Y., 1971-73; asst. dir. mid. schs. Yonkers Pub. Schs., 1973-74, dir. secondary edn., 1974-75; asst. supt. Bethlehem (Pa.) Area Sch. Dist., 1975-78; supt. schs. South Williamsport (Pa.) Area Sch. Dist., 1978-84, N.W. Area Sch. Dist., Shickshinny, Pa., 1984-88, Everett (Pa.) Area Sch. Dist., 1988—; cons. New Eng. Sch. Devel. Coun., Boston, 1973-75; adj. prof. Manhattan Coll., N.Y.C., 1975-76, Lehigh U., Bethlehem, 1978-79. Mem. Everett Area Indsl. Devel. Corp., 1988—, Wet Providence Indsl. Devel. Authority, Bedford County Devel. Authority, Bedford County Devel. Assn., Bedford County Planning Commn. Recipient Jenkins Meml. award Yonkers PTA, 1974, Svc. for Youth award YMCA, Yonkers, 1975. Mem. ASCD, Am. Assn. Sch. Adminstrs., Pa. Assn. Sch. Adminstrs., Pa. Sch. Bds. Assn., Bedford County Edni. Found., Allegany C.C. Found., Lions, Rotary, Naurashank, Phi Delta Kappa. Republican. Roman Catholic. Home: 415 Locust Ct Dr Everett PA 15537 Office: Everett Area Sch Dist 15 South St Extension Everett PA 15537

VOLLEN, ROBERT JAY, lawyer; b. Chgo., Jan. 23, 1940; s. Ben N. and Rose (Belonsky) V.; m. Judith Paula Spector, Aug. 12, 1961; children: Steven, Neil, Jennifer. A.B., U. Mich., 1961; J.D., U. Chgo., 1964. Bar: Ill. 1964, D.C. 1965, U.S. Supreme Ct. 1975. Atty. appellate sect. Civil Div., U.S. Dept. Justice, Washington, 1964-65; asso. firm Schiff Hardin & Waite, Chgo., 1965-70; partner firm Schiff Hardin & Waite, 1971-72; gen. counsel BPI (Bus. and Profl. People for Pub. Interest), Chgo., 1972-83; ptnr. Schwartz & Freeman, Chgo., 1983-87. Mem. vis. com. U. Chgo. Law Sch., 1978-81. Mem. Chgo. Council Lawyers (gov. 1972-76, 79-81), ABA (ho. of dels. 1974-76). Home: 2 Kingswood Ln Deerfield IL 60015-1912

VOLLHARDT, KURT PETER CHRISTIAN, chemistry educator; b. Madrid, Mar. 7, 1946; came to U.S., 1972; Vordiplom, U. Munich, 1967; PhD, U. Coll., London, 1972. Postdoctoral fellow Calif. Inst. Tech., Pasadena, 1972-74; asst. prof. chemistry U. Calif., Berkeley, 1974-78, assoc. prof., 1978-82, prof., 1982—; prin. investigator Lawrence Berkeley Lab., 1975—; cons. Monsanto Corp., St. Louis, Exxon Corp., Annandale, N.J., Maruzen Corp., Tokyo; vis. prof. U. Paris-Orsay, 1979, U. Bordeaux, 1985, U. Lyon, 1987, U. Rennes, 1991, U. Paris VI, 1992, Tech. U. Munich, 1992. Author: Organic Chemistry, 1987, 2d edit., 1994; co-author: Aromatizität, 1972; assoc. editor: Synthesis, 1984-89; editor Synlett, 1989; contbr. articles to profl. jours.; patentee in field. Sloan fellow, 1976-90; Camille and Henry Dreyfus scholar, 1978-83; recipient Adolf Windaus medal, 1983, Humboldt Sr. Scientist award, 1985, 92, Otto Bayer prize, 1990, A.C. Cope scholar award, 1991, Japan Soc. for Promotion of Sci. award, 1995, German Sci. Book award, 1996; named one of Am.'s 100 Brightest Scientists Under 40, Sci. Digest, 1984. Mem. Am. Chem. Soc. (Organometallic Chemistry award 1987), German Chem. Soc., Chem. Soc. of London, Internat. Union Pure & Applied Chemistry (organic chemistry div. com.). Office: U Calif Berkeley Dept of Chemistry Berkeley CA 94720

VOLLMANN, JOHN JACOB, JR., cosmetic packaging executive; b. Elizabeth, N.J., Apr. 10, 1938; s. John Jacob and Marie Louise (Sirois) V.; m. Marian Ethel Snetsinger, May 29, 1976; children: Andrea Leah, John Jacob III. BA, Queen's U., Kingston, Ont., 1973, BA with honor, 1976; postgrad., Rutgers U., 1977; PhD, Walden U., Naples, Fla., 1991. Cert. hypnotherapist; criminal justice instr., Fla. V.p. No. Trading Co., Inc., Madawaska, Maine, 1976—, also chmn., bd. dirs., 1996—; instr. Sch. of Justice and Safety Adminstrn., Miami-Dade Community Coll., 1978—; bd. dirs. Edward Sagarin Inst. for Study of Deviance and Social Issues. Contbr. articles to profl. jours. Vice chmn. Police & Fire Pension Bd., Dania, Fla., 1984; chmn. Unsafe Structures Bd., Dania, 1984; code Enforcement Bd., Dania, 1984; adv. dep. Broward County Sheriff, Ft. Lauderdale, Fla., 1986-92; maj. Fla. Sheriff's Adv. Coun., 1992—. Recipient Richard A. McGhee award Am. Justice Inst., 1992. Mem. NRA, Am. Correctional Assn., Am. Soc. Criminology (life), Acad. Criminal Justice Scis. (life), Am. Jail Assn., Am. Probation and Parole Assn., Northeastern Criminal Justice Assn. (life), Fla. Criminal Justice Educators (pres. 1984-88), So. Assn. Criminal Justice (bd. dirs. 1981-90), Internat. Assn. for Study Organized Crime, N.Am. Assn. Wardens and Supts., Optimists (lt. gov. South Fla. dist. 1993—, lt. gov. New Eng. 1995-96). Avocations: hunting, fishing. Home: 411 SE 3rd Pl Dania FL 33004-4703 Office: No Trading Co Inc 190-202 E Main St Madawaska ME 04756-1510

VOLLMAR, JOHN RAYMOND, electrical engineer; b. Phila., Nov. 8, 1929; s. William Gustav and Pauline Marie (Jesanker) V.; m. Sara Lois Jacob, Feb. 1, 1964; children—Paul Gary, Virginia Ann, Pamela Jean, Barbara Gayle, Thomas Edward, Timothy Morris. B.E.E., Drexel U., Phila., 1952. Registered profl. engr., Pa. Sales and application engr. Gen. Electric Co., Erie, Pa., 1955-59; rail transit and equipment engr. Louis T. Klauder & Assocs., Phila., 1959-65; ptnr. in charge r.r. and transit equipment engring. Louis T. Klauder & Assocs., 1965-84; v.p. LTK Engring. Svcs., Phila., 1985-92, sr. v.p., 1993-94; cons. emeritus, 1995—. Served with C.E. AUS, 1952-54. Decorated Army Commendation ribbon. Mem. Nat., Pa. socs. profl. engrs., IEEE, Am. Pub. Transit Assn. Methodist. Clubs: Union League (Phila.). Home: 727 Gregory Dr Horsham PA 19044-1123 Office: 2 Valley Sq Ste 300 Blue Bell PA 19422-2717

VOLLMER, JAMES E., consulting company executive; b. Phila., Apr. 19, 1924; s. Edward L. and Elizabeth (MacMichael) V.; m. Mary Campolieto, Nov. 16, 1946 (dec. July 1992); children: Jamie, Kurt, Kimarie; m. Avalon E. Kolar, Jan. 27, 1994. B.S., Union Coll., Schenectady, 1945; M.A., Temple U., Phila., 1951, Ph.D., 1956; grad., Advanced Mgmt. Program, Harvard U. Bus. Sch., 1971. Instr. physics Temple U., 1946-51; research supr. Honeywell Corp., Phila., 1952-59; with RCA, 1959—, dir. Advanced Tech. Labs., Camden, N.J., 1959-72; div. v.p., gen. mgr. Govt. Systems Group, RCA, Moorestown, N.J., 1972-79; corp. group v.p. Govt. Systems Div., Comml. Communications Div. and Picture Tube Div. RCA, Cherry Hill, N.J., 1979-83; corp. sr. v.p. RCA, Princeton, N.J., 1983-84; pres. James Vollmer Assocs. Inc., Jupiter Inlet Colony, Fla., 1984-89; disting. lectr. Am. Soc. Engring. Edn., 1972. Author; patentee in field. Vice pres. Palm Beach County (Fla.) United Way, 1974-75; exec. adv. council Fla. Atlantic U., Boca Raton, Fla., 1974-75; vice chmn. campaign Camden County (N.J.) United Way, 1980; bd. dirs. W. Jersey Hosp., Camden, 1980; bd. govs. Franklin Inst., Phila., 1980; chmn. bd. Bartol Rsch. Found., 1980-87. With USNR, 1943-45. Fellow IEEE, AAAS; mem. Am. Phys. Soc., Nat. Security Indsl. Assn. (nat. trustee, past pres. Phila. chpt.), World Affairs Coun. Phila. (bd. dirs. 1982-85), Navy League (life), S. Jersey C. of C. (dir. 1975-77), Northland C. of C., Tequesta Country Club, Phi Beta Kappa, Sigma Xi, Sigma Pi Sigma, Eta Kappa Nu. Home: 212 Turtle Creek Dr Tequesta FL 33469-1545 *Management is the process of making decisions in the presence of uncertainty. Success comes to those who recognize this and correctly evaluate their uncertainty, tolerance, and work to maximize it.*

VOLLMER, RICHARD WADE, federal judge; b. St. Louis, Mar. 7, 1926; s. Richard W. and Beatrice (Burke) V.; m. Marilyn S. Stikes, Sept. 17, 1949. Student, Springhill Coll., 1946-49; LLB, U. Ala., 1953. Bar: Ala. 1953, U.S. Dist. Ct. (so. dist.) Ala. 1956, U.S. Ct. Appeals (5th cir.) 1963, U.S. Ct. Appeals (11th cir.) 1983. Judge U.S. Dist. Ct. (so. dist.) Ala., 1990—. Mem. Mobile Bar Assn. (pres. 1990), Rotary (Paul Harris fellow 1988). Roman Catholic.

VOLLUM, ROBERT BOONE, management consultant; b. Abington, Pa., Sept. 13, 1933; s. Charles Milton and Marion (Yocum) V.; m. Gayle Lorraine Timmerman, July 8, 1956; children: Robert Boone III, Jeffrey Charles. BS in Engring. and Sci., U.S. Naval Acad., 1955. Sr. cons., group leader Stevenson, Jordan & Harrison, Inc., N.Y.C., 1959-65; asst. to pres., plant supt., sales engr. W.L. Gore & Assocs., Inc., Newark, Del., 1965-69; gen. mgr. Philmont Pressed Steel subs. Gulf & Western Industries, Inc., Bethayres, Pa., 1969-72, Air Shields div. Narco Sci. Industries, Inc., Hatboro, Pa., 1972-75; pres. Advanced Airflow Tech., Inc., Warminster, Pa., 1975-76, R.B. Vollum & Assocs., Huntingdon Valley, Pa., 1986—, RBV Mktg. Inc., Willow Grove, Pa., 1992—; chmn. bd. dirs., CEO SFM Technologies, Willow Grove, 1994—; prin. mfg. cons. Sperry Corp., Blue Bell, Pa., 1976-84; dir. cons. Creative Output, Inc., Milford, Conn., 1984-86; spkr. in field. Contbr. articles to profl. jours. Bd. dirs. Upper Moreland Little League, 1965-76. Served to lt. USN, 1955-59. Fellow Am. Prodn. and Inventory Control Soc. (chpt. pres. 1984-85); mem. soc. Mfg. Engrs (sr. mem.), Computer and Automated Systems Assn. (sr. mem.). Republican. Episcopalian. Home: 525 Overlook Ave Willow Grove PA 19090-2818 Office: PO Box 206 Huntingdon Valley PA 19006-0206

VOLMAN, DAVID HERSCHEL, chemistry educator; b. Los Angeles, July 10, 1916; s. Carl Herman and Blanche (Taylor) V.; m. Ruth Clare Jackson, Sept. 15, 1944; children: Thomas Peter, Susan Frances, Daniel Henry. B.A., UCLA, 1937; M.S., 1938; Ph.D. (Standard Oil Co. fellow), Stanford U., 1940. Mem. faculty U. Calif.-Davis, 1940-41, 46—, prof. chemistry, 1956-87, emeritus prof. chemistry, 1987—, chmn. dept., 1974-81, chmn. Acad. Senate, 1971-72; research chemist OSRD, 1941-46; research fellow Harvard U., 1949-50; Vis. prof. U. Wash. 1958. Editor: Advances in Photochemistry, 1983; mem. editorial bd. Jour. Photochemistry and Photobiology, 1972; contbr. articles to profl. jours. Grantee Research Corp. Am.; Grantee NIH; Grantee U.S. Army Research Office; Grantee NSF; Guggenheim fellow, 1949-50. Mem. Am. Chem. Soc., AAUP, Inter-Am. Photochem. Soc., Assn. Harvard Chemists, Sigma Xi. Office: U Calif-Davis Dept Chemistry Davis CA 95616

VOLPE, ANGELO ANTHONY, university administrator, chemistry educator; b. N.Y.C., Nov. 8, 1938; s. Bernard Charles and Serafina (Martorana) V.; m. Jennette Murray, May 15, 1965. B.S., Bklyn. Coll., 1959; M.S., U. Md., 1962, Ph.D., 1966; M.Engring. (hons.), Stevens Inst. Tech., 1975. Rsch. chemist USN Ordnance Lab., Silver Spring, Md., 1961-66; asst. prof. to prof. chemistry Stevens Inst. Tech., Hoboken, N.J., 1966-77; chmn. dept. chemistry East Carolina U., Greenville, N.C., 1977-80, dean. coll. arts and scis., 1980-83, vice chancellor for acad. affairs, 1983-87; pres. Tenn. Tech. U., 1987—; adj. prof. textile chem. N.C. State U., Raleigh, 1978-82; guest lect. Plastics Inst. Am., Hoboken, 1967-82. Contbr. articles to profl. jours. Recipient Ednl. Svc. award Plastics Inst. Am., 1973; named Freygang Outstanding Tchr., Stevens Inst. Tech., 1975. Mem. Am. Chem. Soc., Tenn. Acad. of Scis., Sigma Xi, Phi Kappa Phi. Democrat. Roman Catholic. Avocations: golf; reading. Home: Tenn Tech U Walton House Box 5007 Cookeville TN 38505 Office: Tenn Tech U Office of Pres Cookeville TN 38505

VOLPE, EDMOND L(ORIS), college president; b. New Haven, Nov. 16, 1922; s. Joseph D. and Rose (Maisano) V.; m. Rose Conte, May 20, 1950; children: Rosalind, Lisa. A.B., U. Mich., 1943; M.A., Columbia U., 1947, Ph.D., 1954. Instr. N.Y. U., 1949-54; mem. faculty City Coll. N.Y., 1954-74, prof. English, 1968-74, chmn. dept., 1964-70; pres. Richmond Coll., 1974-76, Coll. S.I., 1976-94; Fulbright prof. Am. lit., France, 1960-61. Author: A Reader's Guide to William Faulkner, 1964; also anthologies and coll. text books.; Co-editor: Eleven Modern Short Novels. Bd. dirs. Staten Island United Way, 1975—, S.I. council Boy Scouts Am., 1977-84, S.I. Doctors Hosp., 1977-78, Snug Harbor Cultural Ctr., 1978-83, St. Vincent's Hosp., 1979—; mem. N.Y.C. Mayor's Commn. on Bias, 1986-88. With AUS, 1943-46. Recipient Commendatore Order of Merit, Republic of Italy, Cmty. Svc. award Italian Club S.I., Humanitarian award S.I. Jewish Found. Sch., Mills G. Skinner award S.I. br. N.Y. Urban League, Christopher Columbus award Columbian Assn. Bd. Edn., Disting. Cmty. Svc. award YMCA, Cmty. Svc. award S.I. Women's divsn. Am. Com. on Italian Migration, Outstanding Achievement award Guiseppe Mazzini Lodge of Sons of Italy; named Educator of Yr. Am. Legion Richmond County. Mem. MLA, Am. Studies Assn., Assn. Dept. English (exec. com. 1969-71), Am. Assn. State Colls. and Univs. (task force ednl. opportunites for the aging, research and liason com., com. internat. programs, health affairs com.), Am. Assn. Higher Edn., Am. Assn. Colls. for Tchr. Edn., Am. Assn. Univ. Profs., Am. Council Edn., Am. Studies Assn., Assn. Colls. and Univs. N.Y., Assn. Depts. of English (nat. exec. com.), Coll. English Assn. (nat. bd. dirs.), Consortium Internat. Programs, Inst. Internat. Edn., Inc., Middle States Assn. Colls. and Schs. Club: Andiron N.Y. (pres. 1972-75).

VOLPE, EILEEN RAE, special education educator; b. Fort Morgan, Colo., Aug. 23, 1942; d. Earl Lester and Ellen Ada (Hearting) Moore; m. David P. Volpe, July 28, 1965 (div. 1980); children: David P. Jr., Christina Marie. BA, U. No. Colo., 1964, MA, 1978. Cert. fine art tchr., learning handicapped specialist, resource specialist. 5th grade tchr. Meml. Elem. Sch., Milford, Mass., 1967-68; fine arts jr./sr. high tchr. Nipmuc Regional Jr. Sr. H.S., Mendon, Mass., 1968-69; spl. edn. tchr. Saugus (Calif.) High Sch., 1979—; publicity dir. Sacred Heart Ch. Sch., Milford, Mass., 1974-75, float coord. bicentennial parade, 1975. Author: (poetry) Seasons to Come, 1994. Mem. Calif. Tchr. Assn., Coun. for Exceptional Children, DAR, Phi Delta Kappa, Kappa Delta Pi. Republican. Avocations: arts and crafts, photography, travel, doll collecting and creation. Office: Saugus High Sch 219000 W Centurion Way Saugus CA 91350

VOLPE, ERMINIO PETER, biologist, educator; b. N.Y.C., Apr. 7, 1927; s. Rocco and Rose (Ciano) V.; m. 1991; children: Laura Elizabeth, Lisa Lawton, John Peter. B.S., City Coll. N.Y., 1948; M.A., Columbia, 1949, Ph.D. (Newberry award 1952), 1952. Asst. zoologist Columbia U., N.Y.C., 1948-51; instr. biology CCNY, N.Y.C., 1951-52; asst. prof. zoology Newcomb Coll., Tulane Uu., 1952-81, chmn. dept. zoology, 1954-64, 64-66, 69-79; W.R. Irby disting. prof. biology Tulane U., 1979-81, asso dean grad. sch., 1967-69; prof. basic med. scis. (genetics) Mercer U. Sch. Medicine, Macon, Ga., 1981—; cons. Nat. Commn. Undergrad. Edn. in Biol. Scis., 1964-71; mem. steering com. Biol. Scis. Curriculum Study, 1966-70; panelist NRC, 1967-70; mem. U.S. Nat. Commn. for UNESCO, 1968-72; regional lectr. Sigma Xi, 1970-72; lectr. Elderhostel, 1988—; chmn. Advanced Placement Test in Biology, Ednl. Testing Service, 1975-80. Author: (textbook) Understanding Evolution, 1985, Human Heredity and Birth Defects, 1971, Patterns and Experiments in Developmental Biology, 1973, Man, Nature, and Society, 1975, The Amphibian Embryo in Transplantation Immunity, 1980, Biology and Human Concerns, 1993, Patient in the Womb, 1984, Test-Tube Conception: A Blend of Love and Science, 1987; mem. editorial bd. jour. Copeia, 1962-63; asso. editor Jour. Exptl. Zoology, 1968-76, 84-85; editor (jour.) Am. Zoologist, 1975-80; contbr. articles to profl. jours. Served with USNR, 1945-46. Fellow AAAS; mem. Genetics Soc. Am., Am. Soc. Zoologists (pres. 1981), Am. Soc. Naturalists, Soc. Devel. Biology, Soc. Study Evolution, Am. Soc. for Cell Biology, Am. Soc. Human Genetics, Phi Beta Kappa (v.p. Tulane U. chpt. 1962), Sigma Xi (pres. Tulane U. chpt. 1964, faculty award 1972.). Office: Mercer Univ Sch Medicine PO Box 134 Macon GA 31207-0002

VOLPE, JOSEPH, opera company administrator. Gen. mgr. Met. Opera Assn., N.Y.C.

VOLPE, JOSEPH JOHN, pediatric neurologist, educator; b. Salem, Mass., Dec. 17, 1938; s. John Rosario and Anne Eleanor (Femino) V.; m. Sara Lee Solov, June 2, 1980; children from previous marriage: Joanna Marie, Joseph Anthony, John Matthew. BA, Bowdoin Coll., 1960; MD, Harvard U., 1964. Diplomate Am. Bd. Pediatrics, Am. Bd. Neurology and Psychiatry with spl. competence in child neurology. Pediatric intern Mass. Gen. Hosp., Boston, 1964-65, pediatric resident, 1965-66, neurology and pediatric resident, 1968-71; rsch. assoc. Nat. Inst. Child Health and Human Devel., Bethesda, Md., 1966-68; asst. prof. pediatrics and neurology Washington U. Med. Sch., St. Louis, 1971-76, assoc. prof. pediatrics and neurology, 1976-79, prof. pediatrics and neurology, 1979—, prof. biol. chemistry, 1980-90, dir. div. pediatric neurology, 1984-90; Bronson Crothers prof. neurology Harvard Med. Sch., Boston, 1990—; neurologist in chief Children's Hosp., Boston, 1990—. Author: Neurology of the Newborn, 1981, 2d edit., 1987, 3d edit., 1995; contbr. over 240 articles to profl. jours. Capt. USPHS, 1966-68. Recipient Weinstein-Goldensohn award United Cerebral Palsy Assn., 1985; rsch. grantee NIH, 1973—, March of Dimes Nat. Found., 1985-87. Office: Children's Hosp 300 Longwood Ave Boston MA 02115-5724

VOLPE, PETER ANTHONY, surgeon; b. Columbus, Ohio, Dec. 17, 1936; s. Peter Anthony and Jeanette Katherine (Volz) V.; m. Suzanne Stephens, Sept. 5, 1959 (div. 1977); children: John David, Michael Charles; m. Kathleen Ann Townsend, Mar. 28, 1978; 1 child, Mark Christopher. BA cum laude, Ohio State U., 1958, MD summa cum laude, 1961. Diplomate Am. Bd. Surgery, Am. Bd. Colon and Rectal Surgery (pres. 1988). Pvt. practice San Francisco, 1969-86; sr. ptnr. Volpe, Russell, Chiu, Abel, MD's, San Francisco, 1987—; clin. prof. surgery U. Calif., San Francisco, 1995—; asst. clin. prof. surgery U. Calif., San Francisco, 1972-95, clin. prof., 1995—; chmn. dept. surgery St. Mary's Hosp. and Med. Ctr., San Francisco, 1978-90. Contbr. articles to profl. jours. Lt. USN, 1962-64. Fellow ACS (bd. govs. 1988-94), Am. Soc. Colon and Rectal Surgeons (treas. 1985-89, pres. 1990); mem. San Francisco Surg. Soc., San Francisco Med. Soc. Republican. Roman Catholic. Office: Volpe Russell Chiu Abel 3838 California St San Francisco CA 94118-1522

VOLPE, RALPH PASQUALE, insurance company executive; b. Souderton, Pa., Sept. 20, 1936; s. Pasquale S. and Katie M. (Hartzell) V.; m. Marie F. Romano, Feb. 6, 1965; children: William, Anthony, Lynda. BA in Polit. Sci., Pa. State U., University Park, 1963. Claim cons. Aetna Life & Casualty Co., King of Prussia, 1964—. Mem. Upper Merion Twp. Bd. Suprs., 1974-79, 82-87, 94—, chmn., 1984, 86, 87, 96, vice chmn., 1985, 95, 2d. v.p. Montgomery County Assn. Twp. Ofcls., 1995—; mem. exec. bd. Greater Valley Forge Transp. Mgmt. Assn., 1994—; mem. Upper Merion Govt. Study Commn., 1974, Rte 202 Exec. Com., 1994—; chmn. Upper Merion Dems., 1980-81; chmn. Montgomery County Dem. Campaign, 1975. With U.S. Army, 1259-61. Recipient Good Govt. award Upper Merion Jaycees, 1977. Mem. Chapel Four Chaplains, Legion Hon. Mem., Optimists, Valley Forge Order Sons of Italy in Am. #1776. Republican. Roman Catholic. Home: 240 Strawberry Ln King Of Prussia PA 19406

VOLPÉ, ROBERT, endocrinologist; b. Toronto, Mar. 6, 1926; s. Aaron G. and Esther (Shulman) V.; m. Ruth Vera Pullan, Sept. 5, 1949; children: Catherine, Elizabeth, Peter, Edward, Rose Ellen. MD, U. Toronto, 1950. Intern U. Toronto, 1950-51, resident in medicine, 1951-52, 53-55, fellow in endocrinology, 1952-53, Nat. Rsch. Coun. fellow, 1955-57, sr. rsch. fellow dept. medicine, 1957-62, McPhedran fellow, 1957-65, asst. prof., 1962-68, assoc. prof., 1968-72, prof., 1972-92, prof. emeritus, 1992—, dir. div. endocrinology and metabolism, 1987-92, chmn. Centennial Com., 1987-88; attending staff St. Joseph's Hosp., Toronto, 1957-66; active staff Wellesley Hosp., Toronto, 1966—; dir. endocrinology rsch. lab. Wellesley Hosp., 1968—, physician-in-chief, 1974-87; trans-Atlantic vis. prof. Caledonia Endocrine Soc., 1985; Hashimoto Meml. lectr. Kyushu U., Fukuoka, Japan, 1992; K.J.R. Wightman vis. prof. Royal Coll. Physicians, Can., 1994; celebratory lectr. commemorating 200th anniversary of birth of Robert Graves, Dublin, Ireland, 1996. Author: Systematic Endocrinology, 1973, 2d edit., 1979, Thyrotoxicosis, 1978, Auto-immunity in the Endocrine System, 1981, Auto-immunity and Endocrine Disease, 1985, Thyroid Function and Disease, 1987, Autoimmunity in Endocrine Disease, 1990; also over 300 rsch. articles mostly on immunology of thyroid disease; past editl. bd. Jour. Clin. Endocrinology and Metabolism, Clin. Medicine, Clin. Endocrinology, Annals Internal Medicine, Endocrine Pathology; editl. bd.: Am. Jour. Physiology, Opinions in Endocrinolgy Metabolism, Thyroid. Served with Royal Can. Naval Vol. Res., 1943-45. Recipient Goldie medal for med. rsch. U. Toronto, 1971, Novo-Nordisk prize Irish Endocrine Soc., 1990; Med. Rsch. Coun. Can. grantee, 1960—. Fellow Royal Coll. Physicians Can. (coun. 1988—, chmn. ann. meetings com. 1988-94, sci. program com. 1988-94, chmn. rsch. com. 1994—, v.p. medicine 1994—), Royal Coll. Physicians Edinburgh and London, Royal Soc. Medicine, ACO (gov. for Ont. 1978-83); mem. AAAS, Can. Soc. Endocrinology and Metabolism (past pres., Sandoz prize lectr. 1985, disting. svc. award 1990), Toronto Soc. Clin. Rsch. (Baxter prize lectr. 1984), Can. Soc. Clin. Investigation, Am. Thyroid Assn. (pres. 1980-81, disting. scientist award 1991), Assn. Am. Physicians, Endocrine Soc., Am. Fedn. Clin. Rsch., Can. Soc. Nuclear Medicine (Jamieson prize lectr. 1980), Can. Inst. Acad. MEdicine, N.Y. Acad. Sci., European Thyroid Assn. (corr.), Latin Am. Thyroid Assn. (corr.), Soc. Endocrinology and Metabolism of Chile (hon.), Caledonia Soc. Endocrinology (hon.), Japan Endocrine Soc. (hon., gold medal 1986), F+Donalda Club, Alpine Ski Club (bd. dirs. 1987-89), U. Toronto Faculty Club. Home: 3 Daleberry Pl, Don Mills, ON Canada M3B 2A5 Office: Wellesley Hosp, Toronto, ON Canada M4Y 1J3 *Rigid adherence to high standards and integrity is essential. Do what is worth doing now, not tomorrow.*

VOLPE, THOMAS J., advertising executive; b. Bklyn., Dec. 22, 1935; s. John G. and Josephine (Fontana) V.; m. Anita Mazzei, Nov. 24, 1957; children: Lisa, Lori, John. BS in Econs., Bklyn. Coll., 1957; MBA, CCNY, 1965. Mgr. Deloitte Haskins & Sells, N.Y.C., 1957-70; v.p., treas. Colgate Palmolive Co., N.Y.C., 1970-85; sr. v.p., fin. ops. Interpublic Group of Cos., N.Y.C., 1986—. Trustee St. Francis Coll., Bklyn., 1971—; bd. dirs., treas. Multiple Sclerosis Soc., N.Y.C. chpt., 1979—. Mem. Fin. Execs. Inst. (com. chmn.), N.Y. State Soc. of CPA's (com. chmn.). Office: The Interpub Group Cos Inc 1271 Avenue Of The Americas New York NY 10020

VOLPERT, RICHARD SIDNEY, lawyer; b. Cambridge, Mass., Feb. 16, 1935; s. Samuel Abbot and Julia (Fogel) V.; m. Marcia Flaster, June 11, 1958; children: Barry, Sandy, Linda, Nancy. B.A., Amherst Coll., 1956; LL.B. (Stone scholar), Columbia U., 1959. Bar: Calif. bar 1960. Atty. firm O'Melveny & Myers, Los Angeles, 1959-86; ptnr. O'Melveny & Myers, L.A., 1967-86, Skadden, Arps, Slate, Meagher & Flom, L.A., 1986-95, Munger, Tolles & Olson, L.A., 1995—; pub. Jewish Jour. of Los Angeles, 1985-87 . Editor, chmn.: Los Angeles Bar Jour, 1965, 66, 67, Calif. State Bar Jour, 1972-73. Chmn. community relations com. Jewish Fedn.-Council Los Angeles, 1977-80; bd. dirs. Jewish Fedn.-Council Greater Los Angeles, 1976—, v.p., 1978-81; pres. Los Angeles County Natural History Mus. Found., 1978-84, trustee, 1974—, chair bd. dirs., 1992—; chmn. bd. councilors U. So. Calif. Law Center, 1979-85; vice chmn. Nat. Jewish Community Relations Adv. Council, 1981-84, mem. exec. com., 1978-85; bd. dirs. U. Judaism, 1973-89, bd. govs., 1973-89; bd. dirs. Valley Beth Shalom, Encino, Calif., 1964-88; mem. capital program major gifts com. Amherst Coll., 1978-86; bd. dirs., mem. exec. com. Los Angeles Wholesale Produce Market Devel. Corp., 1978-95, v.p., 1981-93, pres. 1993-96; mem. exec. bd. Los Angeles chpt. Am. Jewish Com., 1967—; vice-chmn. Los Angeles County Econ. Devel. Council, 1978-81; bd. dirs. Jewish Community Found., 1981—, Brandeis-Bardin Inst., 1995—; mem. Pacific S.W. regional bd. Anti Defamation League B'nai B'rith, 1964—. Named Man of Year, 1978. Fellow Am. Bar Found.; mem. ABA, Urban Land Inst., Los Angeles County Bar Assn. (trustee 1968-70, chmn. real property sect. 1974-75), Los Angeles County Bar Found. (trustee 1977-80), Calif. Bar Assn. (com. on adminstrn. justice 1973-76), Am. Coll. Real Estate Lawyers, Anglo-Am. Real Property Inst., Amherst Club of So. Calif. (dir. 1968-85, pres. 1972-73), City Club (L.A.). Jewish. Home: 4001 Stansbury Ave Sherman Oaks CA 91423-4619 Office: Munger Tolles & Olson 355 S Grand AVe Los Angeles CA 90071-1560

VOLPICELLI, STEPHEN L., lawyer; b. Norristown, Pa., Jan. 5, 1945; s. Dominic Joseph and Mary (Lesinicchia) V.; m. Margaret M. Pipala, Dec. 4, 1971; 1 child, Regina A. BA, Albright Coll., Reading, Pa., 1966; JD, Dickinson Sch. Law, 1969. Bar: Pa. 1970, U.S. Dist. Ct. (ea. dist.) Pa. 1970, U.S. Ct. Appeals (3d cir.) 1970, U.S. Supreme Ct. 1976, N.Y. 1986. Asst. counsel Fidelity Mut. Life Ins. Co., Phila., 1971-72; ptnr. Garfinkel & Volpicelli, Phila., 1972-86, Mesirov, Gelman, Jaffe, Cramer & Jamieson, Phila., 1986-88, Dechert, Price & Rhoads, Phila., 1988-94, Montgomery, McCracken & Rhoades, 1994—; lectr. grad. legal div. Temple U., Phila., 1976—, Pa. Bar Inst., 1988—; lectr., course planner Nat. Bus. Inst., Phila., 1992—. Mem. ABA, Pa. Bar Assn., Phila. Bar Assn. Roman Catholic. Office: Montgomery, McCracken & Rhoades 123 S Broad St Philadelphia PA 19103*

VOLTZ, JEANNE APPLETON, author b. Collinsville, Ala.; d. James Lamar and Marie (Sewell) Appleton; m. Luther Manship Voltz, July 31, 1943 (dec. Aug. 1977); children: Luther Manship, Jeanne Marie; m. Frank B. MacKnight, Aug. 6, 1988 (div. Sept. 1994). AB, U. Montevallo, Ala., 1942. Corr., The Birmingham (Ala.) News, 1939-42; reporter The Press-Register, Mobile, Ala., 1942-45; reporter, feature writer The Miami Herald, 1947-53, food editor, 1953-60; food editor Los Angeles Times, 1960-73, Woman's Day, N.Y.C., 1973-84; free-lance writer, food cons., N.Y.C., 1984-88, Chapel Hill, N.C., 1988—; instr. wine and food in civilization UCLA, 1972-73; expert witness Senate Com. on Nutrition and Health, Ft. Lauderdale, Fla., 1980; adj. prof. Dept. Nutrition Hotel Mgmt. NYU, 1986—, Home Econs. Hotel Mgmt., 1987—; judge Hardee's Willow Creek Rib Cook-Off, Raleigh, N.C., 1993-96; Blue Ridge Barbecue and Rib Festival, Tryon, N.C., 1994-96. Author: The California Cookbook, 1970 (Tastemaker award 1970), The Los Angeles Times Natural Foods Cookbook, 1974, The Flavor of the South, 1976 (Tastemaker award 1976), An Apple A Day, 1983, Barbecued Ribs and Other Great Feeds, 1985 (Tastemaker award 1985), Community Suppers, 1987, Barbecued Ribs, Smoked Butts and Other Great Feeds, 1991; author: (with Burks Hamner) The L.A. Gourmet, 1971, (with Elayne Kleeman) How to Turn a Passion for Food into Profit, 1979, (with Caroline Stuart) The Florida Cookbook, 1993. Mem. N.C. Mus. Art, Raleigh. Mem. adv. bd. James Beard Found., N.Y. Recipient Vesta award Am. Meat Inst., 1962-72; Alumna of Yr. award U. Montevallo, 1981. Mem. Les Dames d'Escoffier (dir. 1976, pres. 1985-86, internat. pres. 1986-87), Inst. Food Technologists, Women in Communications, Soc. Women Geographers, Internat. Assn. Culinary Profls., The Authors' Guild N.Y., Am. Inst. Wine and Food (chairperson Piedmont chpt.), Culinary Historians N.Y., Phi Tau Sigma. Democrat. Methodist.

VOLTZ, CHARLES HARVIE, JR., lawyer; b. Richmond, Va., Sept. 15, 1925; s. Charles Harvie and Mary V. (Mallory) V.; m. Constance A. Lewis, July 30, 1976; children: Charles Harvie III, Judith C. BS, U. Ala., 1950, JD, 1951. Bar: Ala. 1951. Spl. agt. FBI, 1951; claim mgr. Allstate Ins. Co., 1952-54; claims atty. State Farm Ins. Co., 1954-57; sole practice, 1954-59; ptnr. Roberts, Orme & Volz, 1959-61; sole practice Montgomery, 1961-63; asst. dir. Dept. Indsl. Relations, State of Ala., 1959-62; ptnr. Volz, Capouano, Wampold & Prestwood, 1963-84, Volz & Volz, 1984-95, Volz, Prestwood & Hanan, 1995—. Note editor Ala. Law Rev, 1950-51. Campaign dir. March of Dimes, 1958, Am. Cancer Soc., 1967; exec. sec. Gov.'s Com. on Employment Physically Handicapped, 1959-62; mem. Pres.'s Com. on Employment Physically Handicapped, 1959-62; pres., bd. dirs. Montgomery chpt. Am. Cancer Soc. Served to 2d lt. USAAF, 1943-45. Recipient Outstanding Service award Am. Cancer Soc., 1967. Mem. Am. Arbitration Assn. (mem. nat. panel), ABA, Ala. Bar Assn., Assn. Trial Lawyers Am. (state committeeman 1973-75), Ala. Trial Lawyers Assn. (bd. govs.), Phi Alpha Delta. Methodist. Lodges: Masons, Kiwanis. Home: 1638 Cobblestone Ct Montgomery AL 36117-1713 Office: 350 Adams Ave Montgomery AL 36104

VOLZ, MARLIN MILTON, legal educator; b. Cecil, Wis., Sept. 3, 1917; s. Edward A. and Mae C. (Winter) V.; m. Esther R. Krug, Aug. 23, 1941; children: Marlin M., Karen D., Thomas A. BA, U. Wis., 1938, JD, 1940, SJD, 1945; LLD (hon.), San Juan (P.R.) Law Sch., 1957. Bar: Wis. 1940, Mo. 1951, Ky. 1958. Asst. prof. law sch. faculty U. Wis., 1946-50; prof., dean sch. law U. Kansas City (now U. Mo. in Kansas City), 1950-58; dean sch. law U. Louisville, 1958-65, prof. sch. law, 1965-87, ret., 1987; county judge pro tem, probate judge Jefferson County, Ky., 1970-74; chmn. Ky. Pub. Svc. Commn., Frankfort, 1981-82; mem. panel labor arbitrators Fed. Mediation and Conciliation Svc., Am. Arbitration Assn.; reporter on legal draftsmanship Am. Law Inst.; adviser San Juan (P.R.) Sch. Law; mem. Nat. Coun. Legal Clinics, Chgo., 1960-67; mem. Louisville Labor Mgmt. Com. Co-author: Drafting Partnership Agreements, 7th edit., 1984, 86, Wisconsin Practice Methods, 1949, Missouri Practice Methods, 1953, Iowa Practice Methods, 1954, Kansas Practice Methods, 1957; co-author, gen. editor rev. edit. West's Federal practice Manual; co-author, gen. editor Kentucky Legal Forms, vol. 3 and 4, 1965, co-author, vol. 5 and 6, gen. editor revision, 1985; co-author, gen. editor Caldwell's Kentucky Form Book; editor: Cases and Materials, Civil Procedure, 1975, 83. Chmn. Ky. Com. Correctonal Rsch., Frankfort, 1962-65, Louisville Human Rels. Commn., 1962-65; candidate for mayor, Louisville, 1965. Sgt. U.S. Army, 1943-46. Recipient Teaching and Major Svc. awards. Mem. ABA (co-chair arbitration com. 1986-89), Fed. Bar Assn., Ky. Bar Assn., Wis. Bar Assn., Am. Judicature Soc. (bd. dir. 1976-80), Nat. Orgn. Legal Problems Edn. (nat. pres. 1963), Nat. Acad. Arbitrators (com. chmn. 1987-88, bd. govs. 1989-92), Rotary. Democrat. Methodist. Home: 1819 Woodfill Way Louisville KY 40205-2433 Office: U Louisville Sch Law Louisville KY 40292

VOLZ, WILLIAM HARRY, law educator, administrator; b. Sandusky, Mich., Dec. 28, 1946; s. Harry Bender and Belva Geneva (Riehl) V. B.A., Mich. State U., 1968; A.M., U. Mich., 1972; J.D., Wayne State U., 1975; M.B.A., Harvard U., 1978. Bar: Mich. 1975. Sole practice, Detroit, 1975-77; mgmt. analyst Office of Gen. Counsel, HEW, Woodlawn, Md., 1977; asst., then assoc. prof. bus. law Wayne State U., Detroit, 1978-85, interim dean sch. Bus. Adminstrn., 1985, now prof. bus law, dean; cons. Merrill, Lynch, Pierce, Fenner & Smith, N.Y.C., 1980—, City of Detroit law dept., 1982, Mich. Supreme Ct., Detroit, 1981; ptnr. Mich. C.P.A. Rev., Southfield, 1983-85. Author: Managing a Trial, 1982; contbr. articles to legal jours.; editorial bds. of bus. and law jours, AACSB visitation com.; internat. adv. bd., Inst. of Mgmt., Univ. of L'viv, Ukraine, Legal counsel Free Legal Aid Clinic, Inc., Detroit, 1976—, Shared Ministries, Detroit, 1981, Sino-Am. Tech. Exchange Council, People's Republic of China, 1982; chair advt. rev. panel Better Bus. Bur. Detroit, 1988-90; pres. Mich. Acad. Sci., Arts and Letters; bd. dirs. Greater Detroit Alliance Bus., Olde Custodian Fund. Recipient Disting. Faculty award Wayne State Sch. Bus. Adminstrn., 1982. Mem. ABA, Am. Bus. Law Assn., Amateur Mendicant Soc. (commissionaire 1981-85), Players, Golden Key, Alpha Kappa Psi, Beta Alpha Psi. Mem. Reorganized Ch. Latter Day Saints. Clubs: Detroit Athletic Club, Econ. of Detroit, Harvard Bus. Sch. of Detroit. Home: 3846 Wedgewood Dr Bloomfield Hills MI 48301-3949 Office: Wayne State U Sch Bus Adminstrn Cass Ave Detroit MI 48202

VOM BAUR, FRANCIS TROWBRIDGE, retired lawyer; b. Riverton, N.J., Sept. 17, 1908; s. Carl H. and Edith V. (Trowbridge) vom B.; m. Carolyn Bartlett Laskey, June 6, 1934 (dec. Aug. 1988); children: Nerissa Trowbridge, Daphne de Blois. BA, Amherst Coll., 1929; LLB, Harvard U., 1932. Bar: N.Y. 1934, D.C. 1948, Ill. 1952. Assoc. firm Milbank, Tweed & Hope, N.Y.C., 1933-42; spl. agt. War Dept., 1942; regional counsel Office Coordinator Inter-Am. Affairs (C.A.), Haiti, Panama, 1942-46; practiced law Washington, also Chgo., 1947-53; gen. counsel Dept. of Navy, Washington, 1953-60; mem. firm Hensel and vom Baur, 1960-62; sr. ptnr. vom Baur, Coburn, Simmons & Turtle (and successor firm Gage, Tucker & vom Baur), 1963-83; gen. counsel Naval Undersea Mus. Found., Washington, 1980-90; lectr. on govt. contracts, 1961-80. Author: Federal Administrative Law, 2 vols, 1942, Standards of Admission for Practice before Federal Administrative Agencies, a Report for the Survey of the Legal Profession, 1953, The Practical Lawyer's Manual on Memoranda of Law, 35th Anniversary, 1991; editor: Navy Contract Law, 2d edit, 1959; contbr. articles to profl. jours. Chmn. Republican finance com. D.C., 1975-77; mem. nat. fin. com. Mem. ABA (mem. ho. of dels. 1957, chmn. post conv. com. to visit Germany 1957, chmn. standing com. on unauthorized practice law 1958-62, chmn. sect. pub. contract law 1970-71, chmn. coordinating com. model procurement code 1972-83, chmn. emeritus 1983—, Extraordinary Service award 1979), Fed. Bar Assn. (pres. D.C. chpt. 1954-55, award for exceptionally disting. service 1972), Assn. of Bar of City of N.Y., Bar Assn. of D.C., Amherst Alumni Assn. (pres. Washington chpt. 1969-70, nat. v.p. 1971-80), Beta Theta Pi, Delta Sigma Rho. Clubs: Cosmos (Washington), City Tavern Assn. (Washington), Kennebunk River (Kennebunkport), Arundel Beach (Kennebunkport). Home: RR 1 Box 341 Warrenton VA 22186-9603

VON ARX, DOLPH WILLIAM, food products executive; b. St. Louis, Aug. 30, 1934; s. Adolph William and Margaret Louise (Linderer) von A.; m. Sharon Joy Landolt, Dec. 21, 1957; children: Vanessa von Arx Gilvarg, Eric S., Valerie L. BSBA, Washington U., St. Louis, 1961; LHD, St. Augustine Coll., 1988. Account exec. Compton Advt., N.Y.C., 1961-64; v.p. mktg. Ralston Purina Co., St. Louis, 1964-69; exec. v.p. mktg. Gillette Personal Care Div., Chgo., 1969-72; exec. v.p. gen. mgmt. group T.J. Lipton Inc., Englewood Cliffs, N.J., 1973-87; pres., chief exec. officer R.J. Reynold Tobacco Co., Winston-Salem, N.C., 1987-88; chmn., chief exec. officer Planters LifeSavers Co., Winston-Salem, 1988-91; bd. dirs. Carolina Medicorp, Winston-Salem, Wachovia Bank & Trust Co., Winston Salem, 1988-92, Cree Rsch. Inc., Durham, N.C.; chmn. Morrison's F.C. Mobile, Ala. Bd. visitors U. N.C., 1988-92; chmn. bd. trustees Wake Forest U. Grad. Sch. Mgmt., 1988—; pres. bd. trustees N.C. Dance Theater, Winston-Salem, 1989-90; bd. dirs. Forsyth Meml. Hosp., 1988-92, Naples Conservancy, Naples Philharmonic Ctr. for Arts, Wheeling Thunderbirds Hockey, Inc., Reynolds Mus. Am. Art, Naples Cmty. Hosp., chmn., 1994—. Mem. Belle Haven Club (Greenwich) (bd. dirs. 1983-87), Naples Yacht Club, Univ. Club (N.Y.C.), Linville Ridge Country Club (Linville, N.C.), Collier Res. Club (Naples, Fla.). Avocation: tennis. Home: 4951 Gulf Shore Blvd N Apt 1402 Naples FL 33940-2692

VON BERG, HORST RÜDIGER, computer company executive; b. Gotenhafen, Germany, Nov. 20, 1941; came to U.S., 1988; s. Alexander Nicolai and Kira (Tahv) von B.; m. Montserrat R. Torres, May 9, 1968 (div. Sept. 1987); children: Nathalie, Alexandre; m. Micheline T. Verhaegen, Mar. 19, 1988. Lic. in linguistics, U. Antwerp, 1967; postgrad., Inst. Catholique Hautes Études Commerciales, Brussels, 1970. Freelance translator Brussels, 1967-69; with Redirack, Nivelles, Belgium, 1969-70; sales mgr. Desmed & Meynaert, Brussels, 1970-71, Metal Profil, Liege, Belgium, 1972-73; br. mgr. Applicon Inc., Brussels and Paris, 1973-81; mktg. exec. Computervision Corp., Hayes, Eng., 1981-83; mng. dir. Computervision Corp., Brussels, 1983-87; v.p. internat. sales Prime Computer Corp. div. Computervision Corp., Bedford, Mass., 1988-89, v.p. European ops., 1989-93; v.p. internat Formtek (Lockheed), Sunnyvale, Calif., 1993-94; v.p., co-founder Integration Ptnrs., Inc., San Diego, 1994—. Mem. Am. Mgmt. Assn., Mgmt. Ctr. Europe. Avocations: classical music, reading. Office: 5120 Shoreham Pl Ste 200 San Diego CA 92122

VON BERGEN WESSELS, PENNIE LEA, state legislator; b. Sterling, Ill., Mar. 19, 1949; d. Donald LeRoy and Mary Lou (Hammerle) von Bergen; m. Michael J. Wessels, Aug. 23, 1969. AA, Sauk Valley Coll., 1969; BSEd in English and Theater, No. Ill. U., 1971; postgrad., So. Ill. U., 1972-73; JD magna cum laude, U. Ill., 1983. Bar: Ill., 1983; cert. tchr., Ill. English and theater tchr. various schs., Ill., 1971-80; pvt. practice law Morrison, Ill., 1984-85; mem. Whiteside County Bd., Morrison, 1984-88, Ill. Gen. Assembly, Springfield, 1993-95. Bd. dirs. Ill. Citizens Utility Bd., 1989-92, Equip for Equality, 1994—, Ill. Alliance for Arts Edn., 1994—; del. candidate Dem. Nat. Convention, 1980, 92. Named Outstanding Working Woman of Ill. Ill. Bus. and Profl. Women, 1988; recipient Mounders Pride award Mt. Morris Sch. Dist., 1993, Friend of Agr. award Farm Bus. Activator Com., 1994, Outstanding Freshman Legislator award Ill. Edn. Assn., 1994. Unitarian. Avocation: theater. Home: 1300 Sinnissippi Park Rd Sterling IL 61081-4127

VON BERNUTH, CARL W., diversified corporation executive, lawyer. BA, Yale U., 1966, LLB, 1969. Bar: N.Y. 1970, Pa. 1990. Corp. atty. White & Case, 1969-80; assoc. gen. counsel Union Pacific Corp., Bethlehem, Pa., 1980-83, dep. gen. counsel fin. and adminstrn., 1984-88, v.p., gen. counsel, 1988-91, sr. v.p., gen. counsel, 1991—. Office: Union Pacific Corp 8th & Eaton Aves Bethlehem PA 18018

VON BERNUTH, ROBERT DEAN, agricultural engineering educator, consultant; b. Del Norte, Colo., Apr. 14, 1946; s. John Daniel and Bernice H. (Dunlap) von B.; m. Judy M. Wehrman, Dec. 27, 1969; children: Jeanie, Suzie. BSE, Colo. State U., 1968; MS, U. Idaho, 1970; MBA, Claremont (Calif.) Grad. Sch., 1980; PhD in Engring., U. Nebr., 1982. Registered profl. engr., Calif., Nebr. Agrl. product mgr. Rain Bird Sprinkler Mfg., Glendora, Calif., 1974-80; instr. agrl. engring. U. Nebr., Lincoln, 1980-82; from assoc. prof. to prof. U. Tenn., Knoxville, 1982-90; prof., chmn. Mich. State U., East Lansing, 1990—; v.p. Von-Sol Cons., Lincoln, 1980-82; prin. Von Bernuth Agrl. cons., Knoxville, East Lansing, 1982—. Patentee in field. With USNR, 1970-95, Vietnam. Decorated DFC (2); recipient Disting. Naval Grad. award USN Flight Program, Pensacola, Fla., 1970. Mem. ASCE, Am. Soc. Agrl. Engrs., Irrigation Assn. (Person of Yr. 1994), Naval Res. Assn. Avocations: flying, skiing, antique tractors. Office: Mich State U Dept Agrl Engring 215 Farrall Hall East Lansing MI 48824

VON BRANDENSTEIN, PATRIZIA, production designer. Prodn. designer films including Girlfriends, 1978, Heartland, 1979, Breaking Away, 1979, Ragtime, 1981 (Academy Award nomination best art direction 1981), Silkwood, 1983, Amadeus, 1984 (Academy Award best art direction 1984), Beat Street, 1984, A Chorus Line, 1985, The Money Pit, 1986, No Mercy, 1987, The Untouchables, 1987 (Academy Award nomination best art direction 1987), Betrayed, 1988, Working Girl, 1988, The Lemon Sisters, 1990, Postcards From the Edge, 1990, State of Grace, 1990, Billy Bathgate, 1992, Sneakers, 1992, Leap of Faith, 1993, Six Degrees of Separation, 1993, The Quick and the Dead, 1995, Just Cause, 1995; costume designer films including Between the Lines, 1977, Saturday Night Fever, 1977, A Little Sex, 1982. Address: 161 W 15th St Apt 7B New York NY 10011-6768 Office: care Lawrence Mirisch The Mirisch Agency 10100 Santa Monica Blvd Ste 700 Los Angeles CA 90067-4011

VON BUEDINGEN, RICHARD PAUL, urologist; b. Rochester, N.Y., Sept. 14, 1938; s. Wilmer Edward and Clara Elma von B.; BS, U. Wis., 1960, MA in Philosophy, 1961, MD, 1965; m. Bari Luwe Solesky, Nov. 26, 1966 (dec. 1992); children: Kirsten Karla, Christian Karl. Commd. ensign U.S. Navy, 1964, advanced through grades to capt., 1975, intern, U.S. Naval Hosp., St. Albans, N.Y., 1965-66, resident in internal medicine, in plastic and thoracic surgery, in urology affiliate programs Naval Regional Med. Ctr., Oakland, Calif., and U.S. Hosp., Oakland, U. Calif. San Francisco, Stanford U., 1969-73, fellow in pediatric urology, 1973, scientist astronaut trainee Naval Aerospace Med. Inst., Pensacola, Fla., 1966-67, group flight surgeon Marine Corp Air Sta., Beaufort, S.C., 1967-69, chief urology Naval Regional Med. Ctr., Long Beach, Calif., 1973-75, asst. clin. prof. urology, U. Calif., Irvine, 1973-75, resigned, 1975; pvt. practice urology, Aiken, S.C., 1975-80; bd. trustees, chief of surgery HCA Aiken Regional Med. Ctrs., 1985-91. Fellow Internat. Coll. Surgeons, ACS; mem. AMA, Am. Urol. Assn., S.C. Med. Assn. (com. on continuing edn. 1981-83), S.C. Urol. Assn., So. Med. Assn., Soc. Govt. Urologists, Aiken County Med. Soc., Am. Cancer Soc. (chmn. com. profl. edn. in S.C. 1980-82, nat. award for contbns. to profl. edn. 1982), Am. Diabetes Assn. (state bd. dirs., med. edn. com.), Am. Fertility Soc., Am. Lithotripsy Soc. Club: Edisto River Hounds (Master of Foxhounds). Contbr. articles to profl. publs. Home: 1500 Huntsman Dr Aiken SC 29803-5236 Office: 210 University Pky Ste 2300 Aiken SC 29801-6808

VON DER HAAR, THOMAS H., meteorology educator; b. Quincy, Ill., Dec. 28, 1942; m. Dee M. Clark, 1980; children: Kim, Kurt, Nicholas, Krista, Matthew. BS, St. Louis U., 1963; MS, U. Wis., 1964, PhD in Meteorology, 1968. Assoc. scientist meteorology Space Sci. & Engring. Ctr. U. Wis., Madison, 1968-70; assoc. prof. meteorology Colo. State U., Ft. Collins, 1970-77, head dept. atmospheric sci., 1974—, prof. atmospheric sci., 1977—; cons. U.S. Army, McDonnell-Douglas Corp., Ball Bros. & Rsch. Corp., 1969—; acting dean coll. English Colo. State U., Ft. Collins, 1982. Mem. Am. Meteorol. Soc., Sigma Xi. Home: Coop Inst Rsch in Atmosphere Colo State U 515 S Howes St Fort Collins CO 80521*

VON DER HEYDEN, KARL INGOLF MUELLER, manufacturing company executive; b. Berlin, July 18, 1936; came to U.S., 1957, naturalized, 1967; s. Werner and Erika (Mueller) von der H.; m. Mary Ellen Terrell, Aug. 17, 1963; children: Ellen, Eric. Student, Free U., Berlin, 1959-61; B.A., Duke, 1962; M.B.A., Wharton Sch. U. Pa., 1964. C.P.A., Pa. Mgmt. trainee Berliner Bank, Berlin, 1955-57; sr. staff accountant Coopers & Lybrand, Phila., 1963-66; asst. comptroller, corporate comptroller Pitney-Bowes, Inc., Stamford, Conn., 1966-74; v.p., controller PepsiCo., Inc., Purchase, N.Y., 1974-77; v.p. finance Pepsi-Cola Co., 1977-79, v.p. mfg., 1979-80; v.p. fin., treas. H.J. Heinz Co., Pitts., 1980-83, sr. v.p. fin., chief fin. officer; also bd. dirs., 1983-89; exec. v.p., chief fin. officer RJR Nabisco Inc., N.Y.C., 1989-93, co-chmn., CEO, 1993; pres., CEO Metallgesellschaft Corp., N.Y.C., 1993-94; sr. advisor The Clipper Group, 1994—; bd. dirs. Federated Dept. Stores, Inc., Trizec Corp. Ltd., Cadbury Schweppes Plc., BT Office Products Internat., Inc., The Country Baskets Indek Fund, Inc; chmn. Fin. Acctg. Stds. Adv. Coun., 1995—. Bd. trustees Duke U.; vice chmn. YMCA Greater N.Y. Mem. AICPA, Univ. Club (N.Y.C.), Field Club (Greenwich, Conn.). Home: 15 Khakum Wood Rd Greenwich CT 06831-3728 Office: The Clipper Group 12 E 49th St Fl 30 New York NY 10017-1028

VON DER HEYDT, JAMES ARNOLD, federal judge, lawyer; b. Miles City, Mont., July 15, 1919; s. Harry Karl and Alice S. (Arnold) von der H.; m. Verna E. Johnson, May 21, 1952. A.B., Albion (Mich.) Coll., 1942; J.D., Northwestern, 1951. Bar: Alaska 1951. Pvt. law practice Nome, 1953-59; judge superior ct. Juneau, Alaska, 1959-66; U.S. dist. judge Alaska, 1966—; U.S. commr. Nome, Alaska, 1951—; U.S. atty. div. 2 Dist. Alaska, 1951-53; mem. Alaska Ho. of Reps., 1957-59. Pres. Anchorage Fine Arts Mus. Assn. Mem. Alaska Bar Assn. (mem. bd. govs. 1955-59, pres. 1959-60), Wilson Ornithologists Soc., Am. Judicature Soc., Sigma Nu, Phi Delta Phi. Club: Mason (32 deg.), Shriner. Avocation: researching Arctic bird life. Office: US Dist Ct 222 W 7th Ave Box 40 Anchorage AK 99513

VONDRACEK, BETTY SUE, interior designer, remodeling contractor, real estate agent; b. Tulsa, Aug. 27, 1938; d. John Carson and Susan Elizabeth (Nall) Bumgarner; m. Rudy J. Vondracek, Feb. 4, 1961 (dec. Sept. 1990); children: Richard, John (dec.), Vikki. BFA, U. Kans., 1960. Lic. interior designer; lic. real estate agt. Comml. artist Hall & Floyd Advt., Tulsa, 1960-62; freelance artist El Dorado, Ark., 1962-67, Chgo., 1967-69; interior designer Jeanette Interiors, Dallas, 1974-76; owner, designer, contractor Bee Vee Studio, Dallas, 1976—; real estate agt. Mahoney Realty Svcs., Dallas, 1992—; mem. grievance com. Greater Dallas Bd. Realtors, 1992—; mem. Dallas Supts. Adv. Com. Designer Scottish Rite Hosp. Parade of Homes, 1984, March of Dimes Holiday Tour of Homes, 1985-86, Christmas at DeGolyer, 1988-90, Dallas Symphony Showhouse, 1985, 87, 89, 92. Elected ofcl. Dallas Ind. Sch. Dist., 1986-92; pres. West-Lake Rep. Women, Dallas, 1975-77, 92-94; chmn. bd. dirs. Am. Heart Assn., Dallas, 1990-91, Tex. chpt. bd. dirs., 1990—, chmn. bd. Tex. affiliate, 1996—, chmn. capital campaign, chmn. pub. affairs; mem. edn. com. Women's Coun. Dallas County. Recipient Dwight D. Eisenhower award Am. Heart Assn., 1993, Douglas S. Perry Vol. of Yr., Am. Heart Assn., 1990, Key Communicator award Tex. Sch. Pub. Rels., 1984, Disting. Svc. award Nat. Com. for Citizens in Edn., 1984. Mem. Am. Soc. Interior Designers. Roman Catholic. Avocations: painting, gardening, cooking, skiing. Office: Bee Vee Studio 6215 Chesley Ln Dallas TX 75214-2118

VON DREHLE, DAVID JAMES, journalist; b. Denver, Feb. 6, 1961; s. Richard Reynolds and Dorothy Ann (Love) Von D.; m. Karen Janene Ball, Oct. 7, 1995. BA, U. Denver, 1983; M Letters, Oxford (Eng.) U., 1985. Sports aide Denver Post, 1978-83; staff writer Miami (Fla.) Herald, 1985-89; nat. corr. Miami (Fla.) Herald, N.Y.C., 1989-91; N.Y. bur. chief Washington Post, N.Y.C., 1991-93; nat. politics writer Washington Post, 1993-94, arts editor, 1994-95, asst. mng. editor, 1995—. Author: Among the Lowest of the Dead, 1995; co-author: Best Newspaper Writing, 1990, Best American

Sportswriting, 1992, Best Newspaper Writing, 1995. Recipient Silver Gavel award ABA, 1989, Livingston award Mollie Parris Livingston Found., 1989, Deadline Writing award Am. Soc. Newspaper Editors, 1990; Marshall Aid Commemoration Commn. scholar, 1983. Episcopalian. Office: Washington Post 1150 15th St NW Washington DC 20071

VON DREHLE, RAMON ARNOLD, lawyer; b. St. Louis, Mar. 12, 1930; s. Arnold Henry and Sylvia E. (Ahrens) Von D.; m. Gillian Margaret Turner, Sept. 13, 1980; children by previous marriage: Carin L., Lisa A., Courtney A. BS, Washington U., St. Louis, 1952; JD, U. Tex., Austin, 1957; postgrad, Parker Sch. Internat. Law, Columbia U., 1965. Bar: Tex. 1956, Mich. 1957, U.S. Supreme Ct. 1981. Sr. atty. Ford Motor Co., Dearborn, Mich., 1957-67; assoc., asst. gen. counsel Ford of Europe, Inc., Brentwood, Essex, Eng., 1967-75; v.p., gen. counsel Ford of Europe, Inc., 1975-79; v.p. legal Ford Motor Credit Co., Dearborn, 1979-87; v.p., gen. counsel Am. Road Ins. Co., Dearborn, 1979-87; exec. dir. legal affairs Ford Fin. Services Group, Dearborn, 1987-91; leader in residence Walsh Coll., Mich., 1992; panelist large complex case program Am. Arbitration Assn., 1993—; advisor to Czech Republic Ministry of Privatization, Prague, 1993-94; leader Russian Def. Conversion Project, 1995; lectr. in Ea. Europe, 1995; pres. Focus Internat. LLC, 1995—. Article editor: Tex. Law Rev, 1956-57. Trustee Birmingham Unitarian Ch., 1966-67. Served to 1st lt. AUS, 1952-54, Korea. Mem. ABA, Mich. Bar Assn., Tex. Bar Assn., Internat. Bar Assn., Am. Fin. Svcs. Assn. (chmn. 1990-91, bd. dirs. 1981-91), Fin. Svcs. Coun. (bd. dirs. 1987-91), Washington U. Alumni Club Detroit (past pres.), Order of Coif, Renaissance Club (Detroit), Tower Club (Tysons, Va.), Les Ambassadeur (London), Confrèrie des Chevilier du Tastevin (France), Capitol Hill Club (Washington), Royal Automobile Club (London), Tau Beta Pi, Omicron Delta Kappa. Mem. Christ Ch. Home and Office: 519 Princess St Alexandria VA 22314

VON ESCHEN, ROBERT LEROY, electrical engineer, consultant; b. Glasgow, Mont., Oct. 3, 1936; s. Leroy and Lillian Victoria (Eliason) Von E.; m. Carolyn Kay Frampton, Dec. 14, 1965; children: Eric Leroy, Marc Alfred. BSEE, Mont. State U., 1961; postgrad., U. Liberia, Lakeland C.C., Glendale C.C. Registered profl. engr., Pa. Hydro constrn. engr. U.S. Army Corps of Engrs., Mont. and S.D., 1961-62; hdqrs. chief engr. Eagle Constrn. Co., Colo., 1962; resident elec. engr. transmission and distbn. divs. Stanley Cons., Inc., West Africa, 1962-63; fosil power plant constrn. engr. Stanley Cons., Inc., Ky. and Colo., 1963-65; constrn. startup/hydro engr. Stanley Cons., Inc., West Africa, 1965-66; cons. engr. fossil div. Gilbert Assocs., Inc., 1968-72, cons. engr. nuclear div., 1972-74, 77-84, project site mgr., 1974-77; cons. engr. nuclear div. United Energy Svcs. Corp., 1984-86; safety sustems functional insp. nuclear div. United Energy Svcs. Corp., Marietta, Ga., 1986-91, mgmt. assessment, 1992-93; mgr. maintenance planning Mason & Hanger-Silas Mason Co., Inc., Amarillo, Tex., 1993-94, condition assessment survey mgr., 1994—; tech. cons. World Bank, Monrovia, 1963; engring. cons. USN, Manila, 1967. Founder, dir. Madison (Ohio) Computer Soc., 1983-85; v.p., bd. dirs. N.E. coun. Boy Scouts Am., Painesville, 1983-85. Recipient Silver Beaver award Boy Scouts Am., 1981, 84. Mem. IEEE, NRA, NPSE, ANPA, Nat. Assn. Ret. Persons, Soc. Am. Mil. Engrs., Ohio Profl. Engrs. Soc., Tex. Profl. Engrs. Soc., Masons (life), Scottish Rite (life), Shriners. Avocations: target and skeet shooting, constrn. design, computers, electronics. Home: 3445 Gladstone Ln Amarillo TX 79121-1525 Office: Mason & Hanger-Silas Mason Co Inc PO Box 30020 Amarillo TX 79177-0001

VON FRAUNHOFER-KOSINSKI, KATHERINA, bank executive; b. N.Y.C.; m. Jerzy Kosinski, Feb. 15, 1987 (dec. May 3, 1991). Student, St. Joseph's Convent, London, Clark's Coll., London. Various positions Robert W. Orr & Assocs., N.Y.C., 1954-55; with traffic dept. Compton Advt., Inc., N.Y.C., 1956-63; acct. exec. J. Walter Thompson Co., N.Y.C., 1963-69; product mgr. Natural Wonder line Revlon Co., N.Y., 1969-71; pres. Scientia Factum, Inc., N.Y.C., 1971—; co-founder Polish Am. Resources Corp., N.Y.C., 1988—, pres., CEO, 1992—; founder, CEO, pres. Polish Am. Techs., L.P., N.Y.C., 1992—; chmn. bd. dirs. AmerBank, Warsaw, 1991—. Co-founder Westchester Sports Club. Avocations: skiing, horse/polo, swimming, photography. Home: 60 W 57th St New York NY 10019-3911

VON FURSTENBERG, BETSY, actress, writer; b. Neiheim Heusen, Germany, Aug. 16, 1931; d. Count Franz-Egon and Elizabeth (Johnson) von F.; m. Guy Vincent de la Maisoneuve (div.); 2 children.; m. John J. Reynolds, Mar. 26, 1984. Attended Miss Hewitt's Classes, N.Y. Tutoring Sch.; prepared for stage with Sanford Meisner at Neighborhood Playhouse. Made Broadway stage debut in Second Threshold, N.Y., 1951; appeared in Dear Barbarians, 1952, Oh Men Oh Women, 1954, The Chalk Garden, 1955, Child of Fortune, 1956, Nature's Way, 1957, Much Ado About Nothing, 1959, Mary Mary, 1965, Paisley Convertible, 1967, Avanti, 1968, The Gingerbread Lady, 1970 (toured 1971), Absurd Person Singular, 1976; off Broadway appearances include For Love or Money, 1951; toured in Petrified Forest, Jason and Second Man, 1952; appeared in Josephine, 1953; subsequently toured, 1955; What Every Woman Knows, 1955, The Making of Moo, 1958 (toured 1958), Say Darling, 1959, Wonderful Town, 1959, Season of Choice, 1959, Beyond Desire, 1967, Private Lives, 1968, Does Anyone Here Do the Peabody, 1976; appeared in Along Came a Spider, Theatre in the Park, N.Y.C., 1985; appeared in film Women Without Names, 1950; TV appearances include Robert Montgomery Show, Ed Sullivan Show, Alfred Hitchcock Presents, One Step Beyond, The Mike Wallace Show, Johnny Carson Show, Omnibus, Theatre of the Week, The Secret Storm, As the World Turns, Movie of the Week, Your Money or Your Wife, Another World; writer syndicated column More Than Beauty; contbr. articles to newspapers and mags. including N.Y. Times Sunday Arts and Leisure, Saturday Rev. of Literature, People, Good Housekeeping, Art News, Pan Am Travel; co-author: (novel) Mirror, Mirror, 1988. Avocations: tennis, painting, photography. Office: care Don Buchwald 10 E 44th St New York NY 10017-3601

VON FURSTENBERG, DIANE SIMONE MICHELLE, fashion designer; b. Brussels, Belgium, Dec. 31, 1946; came to U.S., 1969; d. Leon L. and Liliane L. (Nahmias) Halfin; m. Eduard Egon von Furstenberg, July 16, 1969 (div.); children: Alexandre, Tatiana. Student, U. Madrid, 1965-66, U. Geneva, 1966-68. Founder, pres. Diane von Furstenberg Studio, N.Y.C., 1970—; pres. Diane Von Furstenberg Ltd., N.Y.C. Author: Diane Von Furstenberg's Book of Beauty and Beds, The Bath; contbg. editor Vanity Fair. Recipient Ellis Island Medal of Honor, 1986. Office: Diane Von Furstenberg Studio 745 5th Ave Fl 24 New York NY 10151-0002 *Honesty in all ways—honest products, honest and straight approach to needs.**

VON FURSTENBERG, GEORGE MICHAEL, economics educator, researcher; b. Germany, Dec. 3, 1941; came to U.S., 1961; s. Kaspar Freiherr and Elisabeth Freifrau (von Boeselager) von F.; m. Gabrielle M. Freiin Koblitz von Willmburg, June 9, 1967; 1 child, Philip G. Ph.D., Princeton U., 1967. Asst. prof. econs. Cornell U., Ithaca, N.Y., 1966-70; assoc. prof. econs. Ind. U., Bloomington, 1970-73, prof., 1976-78, Rudy prof. econs., 1983—; sr. staff economist Council Econ. Advisors, Washington, 1973-76; div. chief research dept. IMF, Washington, 1978-83; project dir. Am. Coun. Life Ins., Washington, 1976-78; sr. advisor Brookings Instn., Washington, 1978-90; vis. sr. economist planning and analysis staff Dept. State, Washington 1989-90; Bissell-Fulbright vis. prof. Can.-Am. rels. U. Toronto, 1994-95. Contbg. author, editor: The Government and Capital Formation, 1980, Capital, Efficiency and Growth, 1980, Acting Under Uncertainty: Multidisciplinary Conceptions, 1990; editor: International Money and Credit: The Policy Roles, 1983; assoc. editor Rev. of Econs. and Stats., 1987-92; contbr. articles to profl. jours. Fulbright grantee to Poland, 1991-92. Mem. Am. Econ. Assn., Am. Fin. Assn. Roman Catholic. Avocations: tennis; sailing. Office: Ind U Dept Econs Bloomington IN 47405

VON GIERKE, HENNING EDGAR, biomedical science educator, former government official, researcher; b. Karlsruhe, Germany, May 22, 1917; came to U.S., 1947, naturalized, 1977; s. Edgar and Julie (Braun) Von G.; married; 2 children. Dipl. Ing., Karlsruhe Tech., 1943, Dr. Engr., 1944. Asst. in acoustics Karlsruhe Tech., 1944-47, lectr., 1946; cons. Aerospace Med. Research Labs, Wright-Patterson AFB, Ohio, 1947-54; chief bioacoustics br. Aerospace Med. Research Labs, 1954-63, dir. biodynamics and bionics div., 1963-88; assoc. prof. Ohio State U., 1963-88; clin. prof. Wright State U., 1980—; mem. com. hearing bioacoustics and biomechanics NRC, 1953-93, chmn. 1990-93, bio-astronaut com., 1959-61; mem. adv. com., flight medicine and biology NASA, 1960-61. Author over 160 tech. publs., book chpts.; patentee in field. Recipient Dept. Def. Disting. Civilian Svc. award, 1963, Hubertus Strughold medal, 1980, Meritorious and Disting. Exec. Presdl. rank Pres. of U.S., 1980, 81, H.R. Lissner award ASME, 1983, Lord Rayleigh medal, 1988. Fellow Acoustical Soc. Am. (pres. 1979-80, Silver medal 1981), Aerospace Med. Assn. (v.p. 1966-67, E. Liljenkrantz award 1966, A.D. Tuttle award 1974), Inst. Environ. Scis. (hon.), Internat. Acad. Aviation and Space Medicine; mem. NAE, Inst. Noise Control Engring., Biomed. Engring. Soc., Internat. Acad. Astronautics. Researcher in bioacoustics, acoustics, biomechanics and bioengring. Home: 1325 Meadow Ln Yellow Springs OH 45387-1219 Office: Armstrong Aerospace Med Rsch Lab Dayton OH 45433

VON GLAHN, KEITH G., lawyer; b. Passaic, N.J., May 4, 1952. BA, St. Peter's Coll., 1974; JD, Vermont Law Sch., 1977. Bar: N.J. 1978, U.S. Tax Ct. 1982, U.S. Dist. Ct. N.J., U.S. Supreme Ct. 1983, N.Y. 1988, U.S. Dist. Ct. N.Y. Law clk. to Hon.William Arnold, 1977-78; asst. prosecutor Paterson, N.J., 1987-81; ptnr. Wilson, Elser, Moskowitz, Edelman and Dicker, Newark, N.J., 1983—. Mem. ABA, N.J. Bar Assn., Essex County Bar Assn., William Brennan Inn of Ct. (master). Office: Wilson Elser Moskowitz Edelman & Dicker Gateway II Ste 1200 Newark NJ 07102

VON GUNTEN, J. DAVID, church administrator. Dir., contr. Missionary Church, Fort Wayne, Ind. Office: The Missionary Church PO Box 9127 3811 Vanguard Dr Fort Wayne IN 46899-9127

VON HAKE, MARGARET JOAN, librarian; b. Santa Monica, Calif., Oct. 27, 1933; d. Carl August and Inez Garnet (Johnson) von Hake;. BA, La Sierra U., 1955; MS in Library Sci., U. So. Calif., 1963. Tchr. Newbury Park (Calif.) Acad., 1955-60, librarian, 1957-60; librarian Columbia Union Coll., Takoma Park, Md., 1962-67, library dir., 1967—. Mem. ALA, Md. Libr. Assn., Congress of Acad. Libr. Dirs. of Md., Md. Ind. Coll.and Univ. Assn. Libr. Dirs. Roundtable, Assn. Seventh Day Adventist Librs. (newsletter editor 1982, 83, pres. 1989-90), Paul Hill Chorale, Sligo Federated Music Club (pres. 1988-89). Republican. Office: Columbia Union Coll 7600 Flower Ave Silver Spring MD 20912-7796

VON HERZEN, RICHARD PIERRE, research scientist, consultant; b. L.A., May 21, 1930; s. Constantine Pierre Von Herzen and Elizabeth Martha (Hevener) Hough; m. Janice Elaine Rutter, Mar. 8, 1958; children—Brian P., Carol E. B.S., Calif. Inst. Tech., 1952; M.A., Harvard U., 1956; Ph.D., UCLA, 1960. Asst. researcher Scripps Inst. Oceanography, LaJolla, Calif., 1960-64, vis. investigator, lectr., 1974-75; dep. dir. office oceanography UNESCO, Paris, 1964-66; assoc. to sr. scientist Woods Hole Oceanog. Inst., Mass., 1966—, chmn. dept. geology and geophysics, 1982-85. Author/co-author numerous peer-reviewed articles. Served with U.S. Army, 1953-55. Fellow Am. Geophys. Union (pres. Tectonics sect. 1986-88, assoc. editor Jour. Geophys. Research 1969-71). Avocations: sports; sailing; biking. Home: P O Box 271 Woods Hole MA 02543 Office: Woods Hole Oceanog Inst Woods Hole MA 02543

VON HIPPEL, FRANK NIELS, public and international affairs educator; b. Cambridge, Mass., Dec. 26, 1937; s. Arthur Robert and Dagmar (Franck) von H.; m. Patricia Bardi, June, 1987; 1 child from previous marriage, Paul Thomas. S.B., MIT, 1959; Ph.D., Oxford U., 1962. Rsch. assoc. U. Chgo., 1962-64, Cornell U., Ithaca, N.Y., 1964-66; asst. prof. Stanford U., Calif., 1966-69; assoc. physicist Argonne Nat. Lab., Ill., 1970-73; research physicist Princeton U., N.J., 1974-83, prof. pub. and internat. affairs, 1983-93, 95—; asst. dir. for nat. security Pres.'s Office of Sci. and Tech. Policy, Washington, 1993-94; bd. dirs. Bull. of Atomic Scientists, Chgo., 1983-86, mem. editl. bd., 1996—, chmn. editl. bd., 1991-93. Author: Advice and Dissent, 1974, Citizen Scientist, 1991; chmn. editl. bd. Sci. and Global Security, 1989—; contbr. articles to profl. jours. Rhodes scholar, 1959-62; McArthur Found. Prize fellow, 1993-98. Fellow AAAS (bd. dirs. 1987-88, Hilliard Roderick prize in Sci., Arms Control and Internat. Security 1994); mem. Fedn. Am. Scientists (chmn. 1979-84, Pub. Svc. award 1989), Fedn. Am. Scientists Fund (chmn. 1986-93, 96—). Home: 3 University Way Princeton Junction NJ 08550-1617 Office: Princeton Univ Ctr for Energy & Environ Studies Princeton NJ 08544

VON HIPPEL, PETER HANS, chemistry educator; b. Goettingen, Germany, Mar. 13, 1931; came to U.S., 1937, naturalized, 1942; s. Arthur Robert and Dagmar (franck) von H.; m. Josephine Baron Raskind, June 20, 1954; children: David F., James A., Benjamin J. B.S., MIT, 1952, M.S., 1953, Ph.D., 1955. Phys. biochemist Naval Med. Research Inst., Bethesda, Md., 1956-59; from asst. prof. to assoc. prof. biochemistry Dartmouth Coll., 1959-67; prof. chemistry, mem. Inst. Molecular Biology U. Oreg., 1967-79, dir. Inst. Moledular Biology, 1969-80, chmn. dept. chemistry, 1980-87; rsch. prof. chemistry Am. Cancer Soc., 1989—; chmn. biopolymers Gordon Conf., 1968; mem. trustees vis. com. biology dept. MIR, 1973-76; mem. bd. sci. counsellors Nat. Inst. Arthritis, Metabolic and Digestive Diseases, NIH, 1974-78, mem. coun. Nat. Inst. Gen. Med. Scis., 1982-86, mem. dir.'s adv. com., 1987-92; mem. sci. and tech. ctrs. adv. com. NSF, 1987-89; bd. dirs. Fedn. Am. Socs. for Exptl. Biology, 1994—. Mem. editl. bd. Jour. Biol. Chemistry, 1967-73, 76-82, Biochem. Biophys. Acta, 1965-70, Physiol. Revs., 1972-77, Biochemistry, 1977-80, Trends in Biochem. Soc., 1987—, Protein Sci., 1990-95; editor Jour. Molecular Biology, 1986-94; contbr. articles to profl. jours., chpts. to books. Lt. M.S.C. USNR, 1956-59. NSF predoctoral fellow, 1953-55; NIH postdoctoral fellow, 1955-56; NIH sr. fellow, 1959-67; Guggenheim fellow, 1973-74. Fellow Am. Acad. Arts and Scis.; mem. AAAS, Am. Chem. Soc., Am. Soc. Biol. Chemists, Biophys. Soc. (mem. council 1970-73, pres. 1973-74), Nat. Acad. Scis., Fedn. Am. Scientists, Sigma Xi. Home: 1900 Crest Dr Eugene OR 97405-1753

VON HOFFMAN, NICHOLAS, writer, former journalist; b. N.Y.C., Oct. 16, 1929; s. Carl and Anna (Bruenn) von H.; m. Ann Byrne, 1950 (div.); children: Alexander, Aristodemos, Constantine; m. Patricia Bennett, 1979 (div.). Grad., Fordham Prep. Sch., 1948. Assoc. dir. Indsl. Area Found., Chgo., 1954-63; mem. staff Chgo. Daily News, 1963-66, Washington Post, 1966-76. Author: Mississippi Notebook, 1964, Multiversity, 1966, We Are The People Our Parents Warned Us Against, 1968, Two, Three, Many More, 1969, Left at The Post, 1970, (with Garry Trudeau) Fireside Watergate, 1973, Tales From the Margaret Mead Taproom, 1976, Make-Believe Presidents: Illusions of Power from McKinley to Carter, 1978, Organized Crimes, 1984, Citizen Cohn, 1988, Capitalist Fools, 1992; also articles.

VON HOLDEN, MARTIN HARVEY, psychologist; b. Bronx, N.Y., May 29, 1942; s. Leon and Gertrude (Fishbein) Von H.; m. Virginia T. Brown, Dec. 17, 1971; 1 child, Mark Walter; children by previous marriage: Sandi Gwen Bitton, David Lawrence; 1 stepchild, Theresa Ann Brilli-Rogers. B.A., NYU, 1964; M.A., U. Toledo, 1965; D.P.A., NYU, 1981. Sr. psychologist N.Y. State Dept. Mental Hygiene, Rockland State Hosp., Orangeberg, 1966-67, team leader, 1970-71, dir. interdisciplinary tng. team, 1971-73; chief of service Metro Unit Harlem Valley Psychiat. Ctr., Wingdale, N.Y., 1973-74, dep. dir. programs, 1974-75; dep. dir. treatment services Pilgrim Psychiat. Ctr., West Brentwood, N.Y., 1975-76; dir. Matteawan State Hosp., Beacon, N.Y., 1977, Central N.Y. Psychiat. Ctr., Marcy, N.Y., 1977-82; exec. dir. Rochester Psychiat. Ctr., Rochester, N.Y., 1982—; assoc. dir. Inst. for Motivation Rsch., Croton-on-Hudson, N.Y., 1965-73; dir. Martin H. Von Holden Assocs., motivation rsch., Fairlawn, N.J., 1970-74; cons. psychologist, group therapist Green Haven Correctional Facility, Stormville, N.Y., 1970-77; cons. psychologist, group therapist Auburn Correctional Facility, N.Y., 1977-94, Butler Correctional Facility, 1994—; clin. assoc. prof. dept. psychiatry Sch. Medicine, U. Rochester, 1983—; speaker nat. and internat. profl. confs. including 2d World Congress on Prison Health Care, 1983. Contbr. articles to profl. jours. Mem. adv. coun. N.Y. State Commn. Quality Care to Mentally Disabled, 1989—. Capt. MSC, U.S. Army, 1967-70. Recipient James Gordon Bennett prize NYU, 1964, Outstanding Achievement award United Way of N.Y. State, 1994. Fellow Am. Assn. Mental Health Adminstrs. (cert. mental health adminstr.); mem. Am. Psychol. Assn., Am. Correctional Assn., Am. Assn. Correctional Psychologists, Assn. Facility Dirs. N.Y. State Office Mental Health (pres. 1984-85), Order of Arrow, Psi Chi. Jewish. Home: 15 Waterbury Ln Rochester NY 14625-1361

VONK, HANS, conductor; b. Amsterdam, The Netherlands, June 18, 1942; s. Frans Vonk; m. Jessie Folkerts. Degree in Music, Ignatius Coll., Amsterdam; Degree in Law, City U., Amsterdam, 1964; trained with Franco Ferrara, 1964-66. Condr. Nat. Ballet, Amsterdam, 1966-69; asst. condr. Concertgebouw Orch., Amsterdam, 1969-73; condr. Radio Philharm. Orch., Hilversom, The Netherlands, 1973-79; chief condr. Netherlands Opera, Amsterdam, 1976-85, Residentie Orkestra, Ben Haag, 1980-91, Staatskapelle, Dresden, Germany, 1985-90, Radio Symphonie Orch., Cologne, Germany, 1991—; assoc. condr. Royal Philharmonie, London, 1976-79; music dir., condr. St. Louis Symphony, 1996—; prin. guest condr. Netherlands Radio Philharm.; guest condr. l'Orchestre Nat. de France, Oslo Philharmonic, London Symphony, Norddeutsche Rendfunk, London Philharmonic, English Chamber Orch., Phila. Orch., Minn. Orch., Nat. Symphony Orch., Detroit Orch., Montreal Orch., Dallas Orch., Seattle Orch., Cleve. Orch., Boston Symphony Orch., Pitts. Orch., San Francisco Orch., Houston Orch., Balt. Orch., Mostly Mozart Festival Orch.; opera condr. La Scala, Rome, 1980, 88, Netherlands Opera, Dresden State Opera. Recs.: (with Christian Zacharias) 5 Beethoven piano concertos, Mozart overtures, The Nutcracker (Tchaikovsky), Der Rosenkavalier, Schumann symphonies and concertos, Bruckner Symphonies 4 and 6. Office: St Louis Symphony Orch Powell Symphony Hall 718 N Grand Blvd Saint Louis MO 63103-1011

VON KALINOWSKI, JULIAN ONESIME, lawyer; b. St. Louis, May 19, 1916; s. Walter E. and Maybelle (Michaud) von K.; m. Penelope Jayne Dyer, June 29, 1980; children by previous marriage: Julian Onesime, Wendy Jean von Kalinowski. BA, Miss. Coll., 1937; JD with honors, U. Va., 1940. Bar: Va. 1940, Calif. 1946. Assoc. Gibson, Dunn and Crutcher, L.A., 1946-52, ptnr., 1953-62, mem. exec. com., 1962-82, adv. ptnr., 1985—; CEO, chmn. Litigation Scis., Inc., Culver City, Calif., 1991-94, chmn. emeritus, 1994—; bd. dirs., mem. exec. com. W.M. Keck Found.; mem. faculty Practising Law Inst., 1971, 76, 78, 79, 80; instr. in spl. course on antitrust litigation Columbia U. Law Sch., N.Y.C., 1981; mem. lawyers dels. com. to 9th Cir. Jud. Conf., 1953-73; UN expert Mission to People's Republic China, 1982. Contbr. articles to legal jours.; author: Antitrust Laws and Trade Regulation, 1969, desk edit., 1981; gen. editor: World Law of Competition, 1978, Antitrust Counseling and Litigation Techniques, 1984. With USN, 1941-46, capt. Res. ret. Fellow Am. Bar Found., Am. Coll. Trial Lawyers (chmn. complex litigation com. 1984-87); mem. ABA (ho. of dels. 1970, chmn. antitrust law sect. 1972-73), State Bar Calif., L.A. Bar Assn., U. Va. Law Sch. Alumni Assn., Calif. Club, L.A. Country Club, La Jolla Beach and Tennis Club, N.Y. Athletic Club, The Sky Club (N.Y.C.), Phi Kappa Psi, Phi Alpha Delta. Republican. Episcopalian. Home: 12320 Ridge Cir Los Angeles CA 90049-1151 Office: Litigation Scis Inc 200 Corporate Pointe Ste 300 Culver City CA 90230-7633

VON KANN, CLIFTON FERDINAND, aviation and space executive, software executive; b. Boston, Oct. 14, 1915; s. Alfred and Lyllian (Kaufman) von K.; m. Sallie Emery Flint, Oct. 6, 1938 (div. May 1965); children: Curtis Emery, Lisa Christine; m. Kathryn Heyne, July 18, 1965. AB cum laude, Harvard U., 1937, MBA, 1948, D in Aero. Sc. (hon.), 1984; grad., Arty. Sch., 1942, Command and Gen. Staff Sch., 1945, Armed Forces Staff Coll., 1954, Nat. War Coll., 1957. Commd. 2d lt., F.A. U.S. Army, 1938, advanced through grades to maj. gen., 1962; various assignments, North Africa, Sicily and Italy, 1937-45; mem. War Dept. gen. staff, 1945-46, with Office Comptr., Dept. of Army, 1948-51, with CIA, 1951-53, comdg. officer 7th Inf. Div. Arty., 8th Army, 1954; with Korean Mil. Adv. Group Korea, 1954-55; with Hdqrs. Army Forces Far East and 8th Army, Japan, 1955-56; asst. div. comdr. 82d Airborne Div. Ft. Bragg, N.C., 1957-59; dir. army aviation Dept. Army, 1959-61; J-3 U.S. Strike Command, Tampa, Fla., 1961-62; comdg. gen. 1st cavalry div. Korea, 1962-63; comdg. gen. U.S. Army Aviation Ctr. Ft. Rucker, Ala., 1963-65; ret., 1965; v.p. ops. and engring. Air Transport Assn. Am., 1965-70, sr. v.p. ops. and airports, 1970-80; pres. Nat. Aeron. Assn., 1980-89; chmn. bd. Nat. Aeronautic Assn., 1989-90, chmn. emeritus, 1992—; bd. dirs. the AVEMCO Corp., Frederick, Md.; chmn. bd. dirs. Traverse Techs., Inc., 1994-95. Decorated Silver Star, Legion of Merit; Cross of Mil. Valor (Italy); recipient Charles Edwin Webb Meml. medal Pa. Mil. Coll., 1964, mil. rev. award Command and Gen. Staff Coll., 1964, Clifford W. Henderson award for achievement, 1990, Dept. Transp./FAA award for disting. svc., 1990. Mem. Am. Helicopter Soc. (chmn. bd. 1962-63, pres. 1961-62), World Aerospace Edn. Assn. (bd. dirs. 1987-93, pres. 1990-910, Fedn. Aeronautique Internat. (v.p. 1980-88, pres. 1988-90), Black Tie Club (Washington; pres. 1978-79), Aero Club (Washington; pres. 1969), Harvard Varsity Club (Cambridge), Met. Club, Nat. Aviation Club (pres. 1974-75). Clubs: Harvard Varsity (Cambridge); Metropolitan, Nat. Aviation (pres. 1974-75). Home and Office: 4311 Torchlight Cir Bethesda MD 20816-1846

VON KAPPELHOFF, DORIS See DAY, DORIS

VON KLEMPERER, KLEMENS, historian, educator; b. Berlin, Nov. 2, 1916; came to U.S., 1938; s. Herbert O. and Frieda (Kuffner) Von K.; m. Elizabeth Lee Gallaher, Dec. 19, 1953; children—Catharine Lee, James Alfred. Abitur, Französisches Gymnasium, Berlin, 1934; MA, Harvard U., 1940, Ph.D., 1949; MA, Cambridge U., 1974. Vis. prof. Stanford U., Palo Alto, Calif., 1960; prof. history Bonn U., Fed. Republic Germany, 1963-64; L. Clark Seelye prof. history Smith Coll., Northampton, Mass., 1960-87, prof. emeritus, 1987—; vis. prof. Amherst (Mass.) Coll., 1989, 91, 96; vis. fellow Trinity Coll., Oxford, Eng., 1982. Author: Germany's New Conservatism, 1957, Mandate for Resistance, 1969, Ignaz Seipel: Christian Statesman, 1972, German Resistance Against Hitler: The Search for Allied Abroad 1938-1945, 1992; editor: A Noble Combat. The Letters of Shiela Grant Duff and Adam von Trott, 1988, "Für Deutschland" Die Männer des 20 Juli, 1994; contbr. articles to profl. jours. Served with AUS, 1943-46, ETO. Guggenheim Found. fellow, 1957-58; Fulbright fellow, 1957-58, 63-64; Overseas fellow Churchill Coll., Cambridge, Eng., 1973-74; Inst. for Advanced Study fellow, Berlin, 1986; Am. Philos. Soc. grantee, 1977-78, Am. Council of Learned Socs. grantee, 1978-79. Mem. Am. Hist. Soc. (chmn. conf. group for central European history 1982-83). Club: Century (N.Y.C.). Avocations: playing recorder; mountaineering; hiking. Home: 23 Washington Ave Northampton MA 01060-2822 Office: Smith Coll Northampton MA 01063

VON KNORRING, HENRIK JOHAN, publisher; b. Lisbon, Portugal, Dec. 20, 1943; came to U.S., 1978; s. Helge and Denise (Halla) von K.; m. Robin Ellis Evans, Oct. 1966; children: Katharina Elizabeth, Helena Alexandra. MA, Oxford U., Eng., 1963. Joint mng. dir. Chapman and Hall Ltd., London, 1973-78; group mktg. dir. Associated Book Pub. Ltd., London, 1977-78; pres. Routledge Inc., N.Y.C., 1978—. Office: Routledge 29 W 35th St New York NY 10001-2299

VON KUTZLEBEN, BERND EBERHARD, nuclear engineer; b. N.Y.C., May 23, 1950; s. Siegfried Edwin and Ursula Herta (Klotz) von K.; m. Susan Eileen Thrane, Feb. 12, 1983 (div. 1991); children: John Hays Morgan, Alexander Joachim, Eric Raymond; m. Carolyn Alice Hays, Dec. 5, 1991. BS in Physics, U. Hamburg, 1974; BS in Physics Engring., Fachhochschule Wedel, 1976, MS, 1979. Nuclear test engr. Combustion Engring., Windsor, Conn., 1979-82, sr. nuclear test engr., 1982-85, nuclear test cons., 1985-90, nuclear test mgr., 1991-92, resident nuclear engring. mgr., 1992—; v.p. Treetop Water Corp., Fort Worth, 1990—. Mem. U.S. Nuclear Soc. Republican. Avocations: cooking, travel, foreign cultures and customs. Home: 35 Anvil Dr Avon CT 06001

VON LAUE, THEODORE HERMAN, historian, educator; b. Frankfurt Main, Germany, June 22, 1916; came to U.S., 1937, naturalized, 1945; s. Max Felix and Magda (Milkau) Von L.; m. Hildegarde Hunt, Oct. 23, 1943 (div. 1976); children: Christopher (dec.), Madeleine, Esther; m. Angela Turner, Nov. 13, 1976. A.B., Princeton U., 1939, Ph.D., 1944; cert. Russian Inst., Columbia U., 1948. Asst. prof. history U. Pa., Phila., 1948-49, Swarthmore Coll., (Pa.), 1949-51; lectr. Bryn Mawr Coll. and Swarthmore Coll., 1952-54; asst. prof. history U. Calif.-Riverside, 1955-59, assoc. prof., 1959-60, prof., 1960-64; prof. Washington U., St. Louis, 1964-70; Frances and Jacob Hiatt prof. history Clark U., 1970-82, Frances and Jacob Hiatt prof. history emeritus, 1983—; fgn. expert Shaanxi Tchrs. U., Xian, People's Republic of China, 1989-90. Author: Leopold Ranke, The Formative Years, 1950, Sergei Witte and the Industrialization of Russia, 1963, Why Lennin? Whi Stalin?, 1964, The GLobal City, 1969, The World Revolution of Westernization: The Twentieth Century in Global Perspective, 1987, Why Lenin? Why Stalin? Shy Gorbechev?, 1993, Faces of a Nation, 1996. Columbia U. Russian Inst. sr. fellow, 1951-52; Fulbright research fellow Finland, 1954-55; Guggenheim fellow, 1961-62, 74-75; Social Sci. Research Council grantee, 1951-52,58. Mem. Am. Hist. Assn., Am. Assn. Advancement Slavic Studies (dir. 1968-71), World History Assn. (coun. 1991-94, pres. New Eng. affiliate 1993-95). Quaker. Office: Clark U Dept History Worcester MA 01610

VON MANDEL, MICHAEL JACQUES, lawyer; b. Yokohama, Japan, Oct. 20, 1941; came to the U.S., 1946; s. Michael Maximillan and Suzanne (Jacques) V.M.; m. Mary Denise Bienvenue, Dec. 22, 1984; 1 child, Michelle Denise. BA in Econs., Georgetown U., 1964; JD, Cath. U., 1968; LLM in Taxation, NYU, 1970. Bar: Washington 1969, Conn. 1969, Ill. 1976, U.S. Dist. Ct. (no. dist.) Ill. 1976, Fla. 1977, U.S. Ct. Appeals (7th cir.) 1976. Trial atty. FTC, Washington, 1968-69; trial atty. tax divsn. U.S. Dept. Justice, Washington, 1970-76; pvt. practice Chgo., 1976-93; ptnr. Von Mandel & Von Mandel, Chgo., 1994—; adj. prof. grad. tax program DePaul U., Chgo., 1980-83. Contbr. chpts. to books. Mem. ABA (tax and litigation sects. 1976—), Chgo. Bar Assn. (fed. tax com. 1976—), Fed. Bar Assn. (bd. dirs. 1981-93), Bar Assn. 7th Fed. Cir., Union League Club. Roman Catholic. Office: Ste 2216 135 S LaSalle St Chicago IL 60603

VON MEHREN, ARTHUR TAYLOR, lawyer, educator; b. Albert Lea, Minn., Aug. 10, 1922; s. Sigurd Anders and Eulalia Marion (Anderson) von M.; m. Joan Elizabeth Moore, Oct. 11, 1947; children—George Moore, Peter Anders, Philip Taylor. S.B., Harvard U., 1942, LL.B., 1945, Ph.D., 1946; Faculty of Law, U. Zurich, 1946-47; Faculte de Droit, U. Paris, 1948-49; Doctor iuris (h.c.), Katholeke U., Leuven, 1985. Bar: Mass. 1950, U.S. Dist. Ct. Mass. 1980. Law clk. U.S. Ct. Appeals (1st cir.), 1945-46; asst. prof. law Harvard U., 1946-53, prof., 1953-76, Story prof., 1976-93, prof. emeritus, 1993—, dir. East Asian legal studies program, 1981-83; acting chief legislation br., legal div. Occupation Mil. Govt. U.S.,Germany, 1947-48, cons. legal div., 1949; tchr. Salzburg Seminar in Am. Studies, summers 1953, 54; Fulbright research prof. U. Tokyo, Japan, 1956-57, Rome, Italy, 1968-69; cons. legal studies Ford Found., New Delhi, 1962-63; vis. prof. U. Frankfurt, summer 1967, City Univ. Hong Kong, 1995; Ford vis. prof. Inst. Advanced Legal Studies, U. London, 1976; assoc. prof. U. Paris, 1977; Goodhart prof. legal sci. U. Cambridge, 1983-84, fellow Downing Coll., 1983-84, hon. fellow, 1984—; fellow Wissenschaftskolleg zu Berlin, 1990-91. Author: The Civil Law System, 1957, 2d edit. (with J. Gordley), 1977, Law in the United States: A General and Comparative View, 1988; co-author: The Law of Multistate Problems, 1965; bd. editors Am. Jour. Comparative Law, 1952-86; contbr. articles to profl. jours.; editor: Law in Japan-The Legal Order in a Changing Soc., 1963; mem. editorial com. Internat. Ency. Comparative Law, 1969—; mem. adv. bd. Internat. Ctr. for Settlement of Investment Disputes Rev.-Fgn. Investment Law Jour., 1985—. Mem. U.S. Del. Hague Conf. pvt. internat. law, 1966, 68, 76, 80, 85, 93. Named to Order of the Rising Sun, golden rays Japanese Govt., 1989; Guggenheim fellow, 1968-69; inst. fellow Sackler Inst. Advanced Studies, 1986-87. Mem. ABA, Am. Acad. Arts and Scis., Am. Fgn. Law Assn., Internat. Acad. Comparative Law, Institut de Droit Internat., Japanese Am. Soc. Legal Studies, Am. Arbitration Assn. (comml. panel), Am. Soc. Comparative Law (bd. dirs., pres.), Am. Soc. Polit. and Legal Philosophy, Internat. C. of C., Inst. Internat. Bus. Law and Practice (acad. coun.), Institut Grand-Duchal (corr.), Phi Beta Kappa. Office: Harvard Law Sch Cambridge MA 02138

VON MEHREN, GEORGE M., lawyer; b. Boston, Nov. 2, 1950; s. Arthur Taylor and Joan Elizabeth (Moore) von M.; m. Laurie Beth Markworth, July 25, 1987; children: Paige Elizabeth, Reed Carl. AB, Harvard U., 1972, JD, 1977; BA, Cambridge U., Eng., 1974, MA, 1985. Bar: Ohio 1977. Assoc. Squire, Sanders & Dempsey, Cleve., 1977-86, ptnr., 1986—, mem. mgmt. com., 1990-93, chmn. creditors rights litig. practice group, 1992—; mem. adv. com. U.S. Dist. Ct. (no. dist.) Ohio, 1991-95. Editor: Harvard Law Rev., 1975-77. Mem. ABA, Fed. Bar Assn., Ohio State Bar Assn., Cleve. Bar Assn. Office: Squire Sanders & Dempsey 127 Public Sq Cleveland OH 44114-1216

VON MEHREN, JANE, editor; b. N.Y.C., Feb. 12, 1963; d. Robert Brandt and Mary Katharine (Kelly) von M. BA, Vassar Coll., 1985. Editorial asst. Crown Publs., Inc., N.Y.C., 1984-85, asst. editor, 1985-87, assoc. editor, 1987-89, editor, 1989-90; sr. editor Ticknor & Fields, N.Y.C., 1990-93; exec. editor Viking Penguin Books, N.Y.C., 1994—; adj. lectr. NYU Sch. Continuing Edn., N.Y.C., 1990-94. Author: Editors on Editing, 1993, My First Year in Publishing, 1994. Mem. alumnae bd. Nightingale Bamford Sch., N.Y.C., 1984-86. Editl. fellow Jerusalem Internat. Bookfair, N.Y., 1993; Tony Godwin Meml. award, 1989. Mem. Women's Media Group)programming com. 1995—), Women in Publ. (treas. 1988-90), PEN. Office: Viking Penguin 375 Hudson St New York NY 10014-3658

VON MEHREN, ROBERT BRANDT, lawyer, retired; b. Albert Lea, Minn., Aug. 10, 1922; s. Sigurd Anders and Eulalia Marion (Anderson) von M.; m. Mary Katharine Kelly, June 26, 1948 (dec. Mar. 1985); children: Carl S., John M., Katharine, Jane, Margaret; m. Susan Heller Anderson, Apr. 2, 1988. BA summa cum laude with philosophical oration, Yale U., 1943; LLB magna cum laude, Harvard U., 1946. Bar: N.Y. 1946, U.S. Supreme Ct. 1954. Law clk. to Judge Learned Hand U.S. Ct. Appeals (2d cir.), 1946-47; law clk. to Assoc. Justice Stanley Reed U.S. Supreme Ct., 1947-48; assoc. Debevoise & Plimpton, N.Y.C., 1946, 48-57; ptnr. Debevoise & Plimpton, 1957-93, of counsel, 1994-95, ret., 1995; cons., arbitrator; sr. lectr. in law Wharton Sch. U. Pa., Phila., 1985-86; legal counsel Prep. Commn. for Internat. Atomic Energy Agy., N.Y.C., 1956-57; trustee Practising Law Inst., N.Y.C., 1972-96, emeritus, 1996, pres., 1979-86, chmn. bd., 1986-96. Bd. editors Harvard Law Rev., 1944-46, Am. Jour. Internat. Law, 1981-89, hon. editor, 1990—; contbr. articles to profl. jours. Trustee Axe Houghton Found., N.Y.C., 1965—; bd. dirs. Legal Aid Soc., N.Y.C., 1966-70; pres. Harvard Law Sch. Assn. N.Y., 1982-83. Mem. Assn. Bar City N.Y., Internat. Law Assn. (vice chmn. 1989—, pres. Am. br. 1978-86, chmn. exec. com. 1986-92), Coun. on Fgn. Rels., Univ. Club, Century Assn. N.Y.C. Home: 925 Park Ave New York NY 10028-0210 Office: Debevoise & Plimpton 875 3rd Ave New York NY 10022-6225

VON MERING, OTTO OSWALD, anthropology educator; b. Berlin, Germany, Oct. 21, 1922; came to Switzerland, 1933, to U.S., 1939, naturalized, 1954; s. Otto O. and Henriette (Troeger) von M.; m. Shirley Ruth Brook, Sept. 11, 1954; children: Gretchen, Karin, Gregory. Grad., Belmont Hill Sch., 1940; BA in History, Williams Coll., 1944; PhD in Social Anthropology, Harvard U., 1956. Instr. Belmont Hill Sch., Belmont, Mass., 1945-47, Boston U., 1947-48, Cambridge Jr. Coll., 1948-49; rsch. asst. lab. social rels. Harvard U., 1950-51, Boston Psychopathic Hosp., 1951-53; Russell Sage Found. fellow N.Y.C., 1953-55; asst. prof. social anthropology U. Pitts. Coll. Medicine, 1955-60, assoc. prof., 1960-65, prof. social anthropology, 1965-71; prof. child devel. and child care U. Pitts. Coll. Allied Health Professions, 1969-71; prof. anthropology and family medicine U. Fla., 1971-76, prof. anthropology in ob-gyn, 1979-84, prof. anthropology and gerontology, 1986—, joint prof. dept. medicine, coll. medicine, 1994—; lectr. Sigmund Freud Inst., Frankfurt, Germany, 1962-64, Pitts. Psychoanalytical Inst., 1960--71, Interuniv. Forum, 1967-71; tech. adviser Maurice Falk Med. Fund; Fulbright vis. lectr., 1962-63; Richard-Merton guest prof. Heidelberg U., Germany, 1962-63; vis. prof. Dartmouth, 1970-71; vis. lectr. continuing edn. Med. Coll. Pa., 1990-92, vis. lectr. U. Sheffield, Eng., Fall, 1995; bd. dirs. Tech. Assistance Resource Assocs., U. Fla., 1979-84; supr. grad. study program Ctr. Gerontologic Studies, U. Fla., 1983-85, assoc. dir. 1985-86, dir. 1986-95; mem. coordinating com. Geriatric Edn. Ctr., Coll. of Medicine, U. Fla.; mem. nat. tech. expert panel on long-term care Health Care Financing Adminstrn., Washington; chair, mem. adv. bd. Internat. Exchange Ctr. on Gerontology State U. System of Fla., 1987-92; adv. bd. Second Season Broadcasting Network, Palm Beach, Fla., 1989-92, Fla. Policy Exch. Ctr. on Aging, State U. System Fla., 1991-95, Assoc. Health Industries of Fla., Inc., Nat. Shared Housing Resource Ctr., Balt.; cons. mental hosps. Author: Remotivating the Mental Patient, 1957, A Grammar of Human Values, 1961, (with Mitscherlich and Brocher) Der Kranke in der Modernen Gesellschaft, 1967, (with Kasdan) Anthropology in the Behavioral and Health Sciences, 1970, (with R. Binstock and L. Cluff) The Future of Long Term Care, 1996; also articles; commentary editor: Human Organization, 1974-76; corr. editor Jour. Geriatric Psychiatry; mem. editl. bd. Med. Anthropology, 1976-84, Ednl. Gerontology, 1990—, Australasian Leisure for Pleasure Jour., 1995—. Mem. nat. adv. bd. Nat. Shared Housing Resource Ctr., 1994-95; pres. Dedicated Alt. Resources for the Elderly, 1996—. Recipient Fulbright-Hayes Travel award, 1962-63; grantee Wenner-Gren Found., N.Y., 1962-63, Am. Philos. Soc., 1962-63, Maurice Falk Med. Fund, 1970-71, HHS, 1979-83, Walter Reed Army Inst. Rsch., 1987-91. US-ADA/FLDOEA, 1993-94; spl. fellow NIMH, 1971-72. Fellow AAAS, Am. Anthrop. Assn. (mem. James Mooney award com. 1978-81, vis. lectr. 1961,-62, 71-74, 91-92), Am. Gerontol. Soc., Royal Soc. Health, Acad. Psychosomatic Medicine, Am. Ethnological Soc., Soc. Applied Anthropology, Royal Anthrop. Inst.; mem. Assn. Am. Med. Colls., Assn. Anthrop. Gerontol. (pres.-elect 1991-92, pres. 1992-93), Am. Fedn. Clin. Research, Am. Public Health Assn., Canadian Assn. Gerontology, British Soc. Gerontology, Med. Group Mgmt. Assn., World Fedn. Mental Health, Internat. Assn. Social Psychiatry (regional counselor), Internat. Hosp. Fedn., Help Age Internat. (London). Home: 818 NW 21st St Gainesville FL 32603-1027 Office: U Fla Ctr for Gerontol Studies 3355 Turlington Hall Gainesville FL 32611 *Three guides to conduct I value most: always search for the best fit of fact, argument, and experience. Every first remedy must be amended quickly. When the past disturbs the present, more work on the future is needed.*

VON MINCKWITZ, BERNHARD, publishing company executive; b. Göttingen, Germany, Aug. 11, 1944; s. Erasmus and Mary (von Lilienfeld) von M.; m. Cornelia Böhning; children: Alexis, Vanessa, Nicolas. Diploma, U. Berlin, 1971. Bd. dirs. Bertelsmann AG, Gütersloh, Fed. Republic Germany, Verband Bayerische Zeitschriftenverlage. Office: Bertelsmann Fachinformation, Neumarkter Strasse 18 PF 802020, 81673 Munich Germany also: Bertelsmann Profl Info 1540 Broadway New York NY 10036-4039

VONNEGUT, KURT, JR., writer; b. Indpls., Nov. 11, 1922; s. Kurt and Edith Sophia (Lieber) V.; m. Jane Marie Cox, Sept. 1, 1945 (div. 1979); children: Mark, Edith, Nanette; adopted nephews: James, Steven and Kurt Adams; m. Jill Krementz, 1979, 1 child, Lily. Student, Cornell U., 1940-42, U. Chgo., 1945-47; MA in Anthropology, U. Chgo., 1971. Reporter Chgo. City News Bur., 1946; pub. relations with Gen. Electric Co., 1947-50; free-lance writer N.Y.C., 1950-65, 74—; lectr. writers workshop U. Iowa, Iowa City, 1965-67; lectr. in English Harvard U., Cambridge, Mass., 1970; disting. prof. CCNY, 1973-74. Author: (novels) Player Piano, 1951, Sirens of Titan, 1959, Mother Night, 1961, Cat's Cradle, 1963, God Bless You, Mr. Rosewater, 1964, Slaughterhouse-Five, 1969, Breakfast of Champions, 1973, Slapstick, or Lonesome No More, 1976, Jailbird, 1979, Deadeye Dick, 1982, Galápagos, 1985, Bluebeard, 1987, Hocus Pocus, 1990, (collected stories) Welcome to the Monkey House, 1968; (play) Happy Birthday, Wanda June, 1970; (TV Script) Between Time and Timbuktu or Prometheus-5, 1972; (essays) Wampeters, Foma and Granfalloons, 1974; (Christmas Story with illustrations by Ivan Chermayeff) Sun Moon Star, 1980; (autobiographical collage) Palm Sunday, 1981, (collection of speeches and essays) Fates Worse Than Death, 1991; also short stories, articles, revs. Served with inf. AUS, 1942-45. Guggenheim fellow, 1967-68. Mem. Nat. Inst. Arts and Letters (recipient Lit. award 1970). Office: care Donald C Farber 150 E 58th St New York NY 10155

VON OHAIN, HANS JOACHIM P., aerospace scientist; b. Dessau, Germany, Dec. 14, 1911; came to U.S., 1947; s. Wolf and Katherine L. (Nagel) von O.; m. Hanny Lemke, Nov. 26, 1949; children: Stephen, Christopher, Catherine, Stephanie. PhD in physics and aerodyn., U. Goettingen, Fed. Republic of Germany, 1935; DSc (hon.), U. W.Va., 1982. Head jet proplusion devel. div. Heinkel Aircraft Corp., Rostock, Fed. Republic of Germany, 1935-45; cons. U.S. Navy, Stuttgart, Fed. Republic of Germany, 1945-46; chief scientist USAF, Dayton, Ohio, 1947-79, with Aerospace Research Lab., 1963-75, with Propulsion Lab., 1975-79; now aerospace research cons. U. Dayton Research Inst. Multiple patents in field; contbr. article to profl. jours. Recipient R. Tom Sawyer award ASME, 1990, Godfrey L. Cabot award Aero Club New Eng., 1993. Fellow AIAA (hon., Goddard prize 1966, Daniel Guggenheim Medal award 1991); mem. NAE (Charles Stark Draper prize 1991). Club: Wings (N.Y.C.). Home and office: 3305 Nan Pablo Dr Melbourne FL 32934-8392

VON PASSENHEIM, JOHN B., lawyer; b. Calif., Nov. 25, 1964; s. Burr Charles and Kathryn E. (Kirkland) Passenheim. BA in English with honors, U. Calif.-Santa Barbara, 1986; JD, U. Calif., Hastings, 1989. Bar: Calif. 1989, U.S. Dist. Ct. (so. dist.) Calif. 1991. Pvt. practice Law Office J. B. Von Passenheim, San Diego, 1990—; organizer Rock The Vote, San Diego, 1992; primary atty. Calif. Lawyers for the Arts, San Diego; panelist Ind. Music Seminar, 1992, 93, 94; mem. Surfrider Found. Nat. Adv. Bd., 1995; gen. counsel Greyboy Records, Poptones Records, STV. Contbg. staff DICTA mag., 1990-94; editor (legal column) It's the Law, 1990-93. Exec. counsel San Diego chpt. Surfrider Found., 1991-95; vol. atty. San Diego Vol. Lawyer Program, 1990-93. Office: 4425 Bayard St Ste 240 San Diego CA 92109

VON PRINCE, KILULU MAGDALENA, occupational therapist, sculptor; b. Bumbuli, Lushoto, Tanzania, Jan. 9, 1929; came to U.S., 1949; d. Tom Adalbert and Juliane (Martini) Von P. BA in Occupational Therapy, San Jose State U., 1958, MS in Occupational Therapy, 1972; EdD, U. So. Calif., 1980. Registered occupational therapist; cert. work evaluator, work adjustment specialist. Commd. 2d lt. U.S. Army, 1959, advanced through grades to lt. col.; staff asst. U.S. Army, Denver, 1959-62; hand rehab. asst., hand therapy Walter Reed Army Med. Ctr., 1962-65; hand rehab. asst. occupational therapist 97th Gen. Hosp., U.S. Army, Frankfurt, Fed. Republic Germany, 1965-68; occupational therapist Inst. Surg. Rsch. U.S. Army, Ft. Sam Houston, Tex., 1967-70; occupational therapy dir., cons. U.S. Army, Honolulu, 1972-75; adminstr. occupational therapy clinic, cons. LAMC U.S. Army, Presido, Calif., 1975; asst. evening coll. program San Jose (Calif.) C.C., 1976-77; postdoctoral fellow allied health adminstrn. SUNY, Buffalo, 1978, Commonwealth U., Richmond, Va., 1978-79; project dir. Ctr. of Design, Palo Alto, 1980; part-time staff project developing pre-retirement program older adults De Anza Coll., Cupertino, Calif., 1980-81; part-time instr. Stroke Activity Ctr. Cabrillo Coll., Santa Cruz, Calif., 1981; dir. occupl. therapy Presbyn. Med. Ctr., 1981-86; ptnr., mgr. retail store, 1986-89; dir. rehab. therapy Merrithew Meml. Hosp. Contra Costa Med. Ctr., Martinez, Calif., 1990-93; sculptor, 1993—; part-time activity program coord. Calif. Women's Detention Facility, Chowchilla, Calif., 1994—; researcher, presenter workshops and seminars in field. Co-author: Splinting of Burned Patients, 1974; producer videos: Elbow Splinting of the Burned Patient, 1970, Self-Instruction Unit: Principles of Elbow Splinting, 1971; contbr. articles to profl. jours. Decorated Legion of Merit; recipient Disting. Alumni Honors award San Jose State U., 1982; grad. scholar U.S. Surgeon Gen.; Kellogg Found. postdoctoral fellow, 1979. Mem. Am. Occupational Therapy Assn., Occupational Therapy Assn. Calif. (award of excellence 1986, v.p. 1981-84, state chair pers. 1981-84, state chair continuing edn. 1984-86, Lifetime Achievement award 1994), Am. Soc. Hand Therapists (hon., life). Avocations: stone sculpture, gardening, kayaking, RV travel, fossil hunting. Home: 36141 Manon Ave Madera CA 93638-8613 Office: Calif Women's Detention Facility Chowchilla CA 93610-1501

VON RAFFLER-ENGEL, WALBURGA (WALBURGA ENGEL), linguist, lecturer, writer; b. Munich, Germany, Sept. 25, 1920; came to U.S., 1949, naturalized, 1955; d. Friedrich J. and Gertrud E. (Kiefer) von R.; m. A. Ferdinand Engel, June 2, 1957; children: Lea Maxine, Eric Robert von Raffler. DLitt, U. Turin, Italy, 1947; MS, Columbia U., 1951; PhD, Ind. U., 1953. Free-lance journalist, 1949-58; mem. faculty Bennett Coll., Greensboro, N.C., 1953-55, U. Charleston (formerly Morris Harvey Coll.), W.Va., 1955-57, Adelphi U., CUNY, 1957-58, NYU, 1958-59, U. Florence, Italy, 1959-60, Istituto Postuniversitario Organizzazione Aziendale, Turin, 1960-61, Bologna Center of Johns Hopkins U., 1964; assoc. prof. linguistics Vanderbilt U., Nashville, 1965-77, prof. linguistics, 1977-85, prof. emerita, sr. rsch. assoc. Inst. Pub. Policy Studies, 1985—; dir. linguistics program Vanderbilt U., 1978-86; chmn. com. on linguistics Nashville U. Ctr., 1974-79; Italian NSF prof. Psychol. Inst. U. Florence, Italy, 1986-87; prof. NATO Advanced Study Inst., Cortona, Italy, 1988; pres. Kinesics Internat., 1988—; vis. prof. linguistics Shanxi U., Peoples Republic China, 1985; vis. prof. U. Ottawa, Ont., Can., 1971-72, Lang. Scis. Inst., Internat. Christian U., Tokyo, 1976; grant evaluator NEH, NSF, Can. Coun.; manuscript reader Ind. U. Press, U. Ill. Press, Prentice-Hall; advisor Trinity U., Simon Frazer U.; pres. Kinesics Internat., 1988—; lectr. in field. Author: Il prelinguaggio infantile, 1964, The Perception of Nonverbal Behavior in the Career Interview, 1983, The Perception of the Unborn Across the Cultures of the World, Japanese edit., 1993, English edit., 1994 (transl. into Chinese); co-author: Language Intervention Programs, 1960-74, 75; editor, co-editor 12 books; author films and videotape; contbr. over 300 articles to scholarly jours., over 200 to profl. and popular publs. in various countries. Grantee Am. Coun. Learned Socs., NSF, Can. Coun., Ford Found., Kenan Venture Fund, Japanese Ministry Edn., NATO, UNESCO, Finnish Acad., Meharry Med. Coll., Internat. Sociol. Assn., Internat. Coun. Linguists, Tex. A&M U., Vanderbilt U., others. Mem. AAUP, Internat. Linguistic Assn., Linguistic Soc. Am. (chmn. Golden Anniversary film com. 1974, emerita 1985—), Linguistic Assn. Can. and the U.S., Internat. Assn. for Applied Linguistics (com. on discourse analyses, sessions chmn. 1978), Lang. Origins Soc. (exec. com. 1985—, chmn. internat. congress, 1987), Internat. Sociol. Assn. (rsch. com. for sociolinguistics, session co-chmn. internat. conf. 1983, session chmn. profl. conf. 1983), Internat. Assn. for Study of Child Lang. (v.p. 1975-78, chmn. internat. conf. 1972), Inst. for Nonverbal Communication Research (workshop leader 1981), Southeastern Conf. on Linguistics, 1980— (hon. mem. 1985—), Semiotic Soc. Am. (organizing com. Internat. Semiotics Inst. 1981), Sietar Internat., Nat. Assn. Scholars. Home and Office: 116 Brighton Close Nashville TN 37205-2501 *In the social sciences theories come and theories go. Carefully collected and objectively analyzed data are useful for generations and the cleanest research design in the lab does not equal a moderately neat design in the naturalistic setting.*

VON RECUM, ANDREAS F., bioengineer; b. Dillingen, Bavaria, Germany, July 5, 1939; came to U.S., 1971; s. Bogdan Freiherr and Ilse Freifrau (von Rosenberg) von R.; m. Grudrun F. Bredenbröker-Hardt, Oct. 2, 1965; children: Derik F., Vera F., Uta F., Horst F., Thomas F., Elsa F. BS, U. Giessen, 1965; DVM, Free U. Berlin, 1968, PhD, 1969; PhD in Vet. Surgery, Colo. State U., 1974. Practitioner farm animal medicine and surgery Meitingen, Germany, 1968-69; clin. staff small animal clinic Free U. Berlin (Germany), Coll. Vet. Medicine, 1969-72; rsch. asst. surg. lab. Colo. State U., Coll. Vet. Medicine, Ft. Collins, 1972-74; dir. surg. rsch. lab. Sinai Hosp. Detroit, 1975-77; prof. dept. bioengring. Clemson (S.C.) U., 1978-93, head dept. bioengring., 1982-93; chmn. bioengring. alliance S.C. Coll. Engring., Clemson U., 1984-88; scientific staff Shriners Hosp., Greenville, S.C., 1989—; prof. Hunter endowed chair bioengring. Clemson U. Coll. Engring., 1993—; adj. assoc. prof. comparative surgery Wayne State U. Sch. Medicine, Dept. Comparative Medicine, 1975-77; adj. prof. surgery U. S.C. Sch. Medicine, 1984—, Med. U. S.C., 1987—; adj. prof. biomaterials Coll. Dentistry U. Nijmegen, 1993—; cons. in field. Editor Jour. Investigative Surg.; patentee in field. Recipient Fulbright Scientist award, 1990-91, Alexander von Humboldt Sr. Scientist award, 1990-91; nat. and internat. fellow Biomaterials Sci. and Engring., 1996. Mem. AVMA, Am. Soc. Lab. Animal Practitioners (governing body), Coll. Vet. Medicine (elected), Blue Ridge Vet. Med. Assn. (pres. 1984), Soc. Biomaterials (asst. editor 1986—, editl. bd. 1983, program chmn. 1990, sec.-treas. 1990-92, pres. 1993-94), Internat. Soc. Artificial Internal Organs, Am. Soc. Artificial Organs, Am. Heart Assn., Acad. Surg. Rsch. (founder 1982, pres. 1982-83, newsletter editor 1982-85), Biomed. Engring. Soc., Am. Soc. Engring. Edn., Assn. Advancement Med. Instrumentation. Presbyterian. Office: Clemson Univ Dept of Bioengineering Clemson SC 29631

VON REIS CORNELL, SONJA MARGARETHA, artist; b. Gothenburg, Sweden, Nov. 19, 1925; came to the U.S., 1948; d. James Adolf Helmer and Iris Margaretha (Malmstrom) von R.; m. Lorain Dale Cornell, Oct. 29, 1949 (dec. Dec. 1988); children: Charles Peter, Susan Christina, Sonja Elizabeth. BA, Mich. State U., 1969, MA, 1970, MFA, 1975. Interpreter Gen. Motors Overseas, Detroit, 1948-49; tchr. art and humanities Dewitt (Mich.) Pub. Schs., 1970-88; instr. evening coll. Mich. State U., East Lansing, 1975-76; mem. Art Scholarships, Lansing, 1985-90; jurying Lansing Art Guild, Mich., 1990—, East Lansing Arts Orgn., 1991—. One person shows include Prints Ancient and Modern, East Lansing, Okemos (Mich.) Community Ch., Jacobsons', East Lansing, Creative Arts Gallery, Mt. Pleasant, Mich., Lansing Art Gallery, others; group shows include Art Now, Goteborg, Sweden, Katharine Rich Perlow Gallery, N.Y.C., Foster/White Gallery, Seattle, others; collections include Wharton Ctr., East Lansing, Phillips Petroleum Corp., Bartlesville, Okla., Ceco Corp., Chgo., Mich. Edn. Assn., East Lansing, others. Mem. Friend of Kresge Art Mus., East Lansing, 1975—. Mem. NEA, Swedish Internat. Edn. Assn., Mich. Edn. Assn., Detroit Swedish Coun., Jenny Lind Club Mich., Zonta Mich. Avocations: travel, opera, books.

VON REYN, C. FORDHAM, infectious disease physician; b. Montour Falls, N.Y., Sept. 24, 1945; m. Janet Elizabeth Goldberger, June 18, 1967; children: Leah Edana, Adam Daniel, Charles Alexander. AB, Dartmouth Coll., 1967, BMS, 1969; MD cum laude, Harvard U., 1971. Diplomate Am. Bd. Internal Medicine, Am. Bd. Infectious Diseases. Intern in medicine Beth Israel Hosp., Boston, 1971-72, jr. resident in medicine, 1972-73, sr. asst. resident in medicine, 1975-76; clin. fellow in infectious disease Beth Israel Hosp., Children's Hosp. Med. Ctr., Dana-Farber Cancer Ctr., Boston, 1976-77; clin. assoc. in medicine U. N.Mex. Sch. Medicine, Albuquerque, 1973-75, clin. assoc. in family & cmty. medicine, 1974-75, outpatient attending dept. medicine, 1976-77, inpatient attending dept. medicine, 1978-79; instr. epidemiology sch. medicine Tufts U., Boston, 1974, 76; adj. asst. prof. clin. medicine Dartmouth Med. Sch., Hanover, N.H., 1978-85, lectr. microbiology, 1978—, adj. assoc. prof. clin. medicine, 1986-87, assoc. prof. clin. medicine, 1988-91; attending physician infectious disease svc. dept. medicine, co-dir. infectious disease block scientific basis of medicine Dartmouth Med. Sch., 1988—; assoc. prof. medicine Dartmouth Med. Sch., Hanover, N.H., 1991-94, prof. medicine, 1994—; dir. microbiology, hosp. epidemiologist infectious disease dept. Concord (N.H.) Hosp., 1977-88; cons. staff Mary Hitchcock Meml. Hosp., Hanover, 1977-88, clin. staff, 1988—; hosp. epidemiologist, chief infectious disease section Dartmouth-Hitchcock Med. Ctr., Hanover, 1988—; cons. physician infectious diseases Vets. Adminstrn. Hosp., White River Junction, Vt., 1990—; asst. physician Harvard U. Health Svcs., Cambridge, 1975-77; pres. Concord Clinic Inc., 1984-85; section chief internal medicine Concord divsn. Hitchcock Clinic, 1985-88; cons. global program on AIDS World Health Orgn., 1987. Mem. editl. bd. Current Issues in Public Health, 1993—; mem. internat. editl. adv. bd. AIDS and Society, 1989—; contbr. articles to profl. jours. and chpts. in books. Pres. Frontiers of Knowledge Found., Concord, N.H., 1982-83; v.p. Concord Cmty. Music Sch., 1984-85, pres., 1986-88; trustee Am. Red Cross, Concord, 1986-88, N.H. AIDS Found., Manchester, 1989—; chmn. N.Mex. Task Force on Rabies, 1974, U.S. del. Congress of the Internat. Physicians for the Prevention of Nuclear War, Helsinki, 1984; mem. N.H. AIDS Adv. Com., 1985-87; mem. Commr.'s Task Force on HIV/AIDS Divsn. of Pub. Health Svcs., N.H., 1990— and numerous others. Med. officer USPHS, 1973-75. Recipient Gov.'s Spl. award for Pub. Svc., Santa Fe, N.Mex., 1975. Fellow Infectious Disease Soc. Am.; mem. Am. Soc. Microbiology, Internat. Immunocomprised Host Soc., Internat. AIDS Soc., Northern New England Infectious Disease Soc. (v.p. 1990-92, pres. 1992-94), Physicians for Social Responsibility, Soc. for Hosp. Epidemiology Am., Alpha Omega Alpha. Home: 44 Waterman Hill Rd Norwich VT 05055 Office: Dartmouth-Hitchcock Med Ctr Infectious Disease Sect One Medical Ctr Dr Lebanon NH 03756

VON RHEIN, JOHN RICHARD, music critic, editor; b. Pasadena, Calif., Sept. 10, 1945; s. Hans Walter and Elsa Maryon (Brossmann) von R. AA, Pasadena City Coll., 1965; BA in Eng., UCLA, 1967; BA in Music, Calif. State U., Los Angeles, 1970. Music reviewer Hollywood (Calif.) Citizen-News, 1968-70; music editor and critic, dance critic Akron (Ohio) Beacon Jour., 1971-77; music critic Chgo. Tribune, 1977—; prof. music appreciation Rio Hondo Jr. Coll., Calif., 1970-71; lectr., TV host, rec. annotator. Author: (with Andrew Porter) Bravi; contbr. revs. and articles to World Book Ency., 1994 Yr. Book, 1995 Yr. Book, Opera News, High Fidelity/Mus. Am., Ovation, L.A. Times, Boston Globe, Vanity Fair, Fanfare, Am. Record Guild, others. Music Critics Assn.-Kennedy Center for Performing Arts fellow, 1972, 75. Mem. Music Critics Assn. (edn. com., dir. 1988), Ravinia Critics Inst. (dir. 1988). Office: Chgo Tribune Co PO Box 25340 Chicago IL 60625-0340

VON RINGELHEIM, PAUL HELMUT, sculptor; b. Vienna; s. Henry and Rosita (Altschuler) Von R. BS, Bklyn. Coll., 1956; MA, Fairleigh Dickinson U., 1958; postgrad., Art Students League, N.Y.C., 1958-59, Acad. Fine Arts, Munich, 1960-61. Tchr. printmaking Bklyn. Mus. Sch., 1957-58; prof.

sculpture Sch. Visual Arts, N.Y.C., 1967-71. One-man shows include Niveau Art Gallery, N.Y.C., 1958, Am. House, Berlin, Munich and Hamburg, 1960-61, Rose Fried Gallery, N.Y.C., 1964, 67, Fairleigh Dickinson U., 1964, New Vision Galleries, London, 1964, N.Y. Cultural Center, 1975, O.K. Harris Gallery, N.Y.C., 1971-73, 76, 78, 80, 82, Mitzi Landau Gallery, Los Angeles, 1974, Amarillo Mus. of Art, 1987, Amarillo Art Ctr., Tex., 1987, Robert Berman Gallery, Los Angeles, 1988, Obelisk Gallery, 1992, 94; exhibited in group shows at Bklyn. Mus., 1958, Whitney Mus., 1963, 65, 68, 78, 82, 87, Mus. Modern Art, N.Y.C., 1964, 67, 69, 85, O.K. Harris Gallery, Providence, 1964, Ben Uri Gallery, London, 1965, Jewish Mus., N.Y.C., 1966, 68, 70, 74, Cleve. Mus., 1966, Obelisk Gallery, Boston, 1967, 69, Albright-Knox Gallery, Buffalo, 1967, Rose Art Mus., Brandeis U., 1967, Am. Embassy, Brussels, 1967, Meml. Hall, Boston, 1968, Finch Coll., N.Y.C., 1968, Frick Mus., Pitts., 1968, also in Rotterdam and Daensstadt, Cooper Hewitt, 1983, Internat. Airport Gallery, 1995, and numerous other galleries and museums; represented in permanent collections at Welton Becket Assos., Broadway Maintenance Corp., CBS, N.Y.C., Fairleigh Dickinson U., Martin Found., Mus. Modern Art, N.Y.C., Mus. Modern Art, Tel Aviv, Mus. Modern Art, Tokyo, Whitney Mus. Am. Art, Time and Life collections, N.Y.C., Smithsonian Instn., Internat. Sculpture Show, Hollycroft, Conn., others; archtl. commns. include World Peace Monument, U.S. Pavilion, World's Fair, 1964; Tangential 32 at Park Ave. and 55th St., N.Y.C., 1969; Variance inflatable at Internat. Sculpture Festival, Govt. Center, Boston, 1971; Fulcrum at Westinghouse Nuc. Ctr., Pitts., 1972; Vortex in Red for Main St. Ann. Art Festival, Houston, 1975, Nebr. Interstate 80 Bicentennial Sculpture Project, Houston Center, Tex. Eastern Corp.; also sculptures Columbia (N.C.) Mall, Taubman Corp., Century City, L.A., Diamond Shamrock, Dallas, Exec. Hdqrs. Becket Group, L.A.; also Endless Force for former Pres. Gerald R. Ford, Equinox for Diamond Shamrock Corp., fountain Exec. Hdqrs. Becket Group, L.A., Freeflight Lincoln Properties Co., San Jose, Calif., Perth, Australia, 1995, Edmonton, Can., 1995, Jakarta, Java, 1996. Recipient Outstanding Young Man of Yr. award N.Y. World's Fair, 1964; Fulbright scholar, 1974-75. Mem. Archtl. League City N.Y., Lambs Club (hon.), Explorers Club. Home: 9 Great Jones St New York NY 10012-1128

VON RYDINGSVARD, URSULA KAROLISZYN, sculptor; b. Deensen, Germany, July 26, 1942; cmae to U.S., 1950; d. Ignacy and Konegunda (Sternal) Karoliszyn; m. Pual Greengard. BA, MA, U. Miami, Coral Gables, Fla., 1965; postgrad., U. Calif., Berkeley, 1969-70; MFA, Columbia U., 1975; PhD (hon.), Md. Inst. Art, 1991. Instr. Sch. Visual Arts, N.Y.C., 1981-82; asst. prof. Pratt Inst., Bklyn., 1978-82, Fordham U., Bronx, N.Y., 1980-82; assoc. prof. Yale U., New Haven, 1982-86; prof. grad. divsn. Sch. Visual Arts, N.Y.C., 1986—. One-woman shows include Rosa Esman Gallery, 1981, 82, Studio Bassanese, Trieste, 1985, Laumeier Sculpture Gallery, St. Louis, 1988, Capp St. Project San Francisco, 1990, Lorence-Monk Gallery, N.Y.C., 1990-91, Zamek Ujazdowski Contemporary Art Ctr., Warsaw, Poland, 1992, Storm King Art Ctr., Mountainville, N.Y., 1992-94, Galerie Lelong, N.Y.C., 1994, Mus. Art R.I. Sch. Design, Providence, 1996; exhibited in group shows at Lowe Art Mus., Coral Gables, Fla., 1975, Aldrich Mus. Contemporary Art, Ridgefield, Conn., 1976, 55 Mercer Gallery, N.Y.C., 1983, Pratt Inst., Bklyn., 1985, Contemporary Arts Ctr., Cin., 1987, Krygier/Landau Contemporary Art Gallery, Santa Monica, Calif., 1989, Damon Brandt Gallery, N.Y.C., 1989, Met. Mus. Art, N.Y.C., 1989-93, Whitney Mus. Contemporary Art, 1990, Cultural Ctr., Chgo., 1991, Ctrl. Bur. Art Exhbns., Warsaw and Krakow, Poland, 1991, The Cultural Space/Exit Art, N.Y.C., 1992, Galerie Lelong, N.Y.C., 1993, Denver Art Mus. and Columbus Art Mus., 1994—, others; outdoor exhbns include Pelham Bay Park, Bronx, N.Y., 1978, Neuberger Mus., Purchase, N.Y., 1979, Artpark, Lewiston, N.Y., 1979, Laumeier Sculpture Park, St. Louis, 1989-94, Walker Art Ctr., Mpls., 1990-93, Oliver Ranch, Geyserville, Calif., Storm King Art Ctr., Mountainville, N.Y., 1992-93; contbr. articles to profl. jours. Fulbright Hays travel grantee, 1975; grantee N.Y. State Coun. Arts, Am. the Beautiful Fund, Nat. Endowment for Arts, Creative Artists Program Svc.; Griswald traveling grantee Yale U., 1985; Guggenheim fellow, 1983-84; Nat. Endowment for Arts individual artists grantee, 1986-87; recipient Alfred Turzykowski Found. Fine Arts award, 1996. Studio: 429 S 5th St Brooklyn NY 11211-7425

VON SCHACK, WESLEY W., energy services company executive; b. N.Y., 1944; married. AB, Fordham U., 1965; MBA, St. John's U., Jamaica, N.Y., 1971; doctorate, Pace U., 1990. V.p. fin. Duquesne Light Co., Pitts., 1984-86, pres., CEO, 1986—, chmn., CEO, 1987—; chmn., CEO, pres. Duquesne Light Co., 1989—; chmn., CEO DQE, 1989; also bd. dirs. Duquesne Light Co., Pitts.; bd. dirs. DQE, Mellon Bank Corp., Mellon Bank, N.A., RMI Titanium Co., Pitts. br. Fed. Res. Bank Cleve., Pitts. br. Chmn. Pitts. Cultural Trust. Office: DQE 301 Grant St Pittsburgh PA 15279-0001

VON STADE, FREDERICA, mezzo-soprano; b. Somerville, N.J., June 1, 1945; m. Peter Elkus, 1973 (div.); children: Jennie, Lisa; m. Michael G. Gorman, Jan. 1991. Student, Mannes Coll. Music, N.Y.C., Ecole Mozart, Paris; DMus (hon.), Yale U., 1985. Former nanny, salesgirl; sec. Am. Shakespeare Festival. Debut in Die Zauberfloete with Met. Opera, 1970, later resident mem., Covent Garden debut, 1975; appeared with opera cos. including Paris Opera, San Francisco Opera, Salzburg Festival, London Royal Opera, Spoleto Festival, Boston Opera Co., Santa Fe Opera, Houston Grand Opera, La Scala; recital artist, soloist with symphony orchs.; appeared in operas The Marriage of Figaro, Faust, The Magic Flute, Don Giovanni, Tales of Hoffman, Rigoletto, Der Rosenkavalier, The Seagull, Werther, The Barber of Seville, The Dangerous Liasons, Le Nozze di Figaro; albums Frederica Von Stade Sings Mozart-Rossini Opera Arias, French Opera Arias, Pelleas and Melisande, Idomeneo, La Sonnambula, Simple Gifts with Mormon Tabernacle Choir, Songs of the Cat with Garrison Keillor; created roles of Nina in the Seagull (Pastieri), 1974, Tina in the Aspern Papers (Arganto), 1988; starred in Dominick Argento's Casa Guidi, 1985, Carnegie Hall, N.Y.C.; rec. artist EMI. Mem. Am. Guild Mus. Artists. Roman Catholic. Avocations: tennis, skiing, dancing. Office: Columbia Artists Mgt Inc Arbib/Treuhaft Div 167 W 57th St New York NY 10019-2201

VON SYDOW, MAX (CARL ADOLF VON SYDOW), actor; b. Lund, Sweden, Apr. 10, 1929; s. Carl Wilhelm and Greta (Rappe) von S.; m. Christina Olin, Aug. 1, 1951; children: Clas Wilhelm, Per Henrik. Student, Royal Dramatic Theatre Acad. Stockholm, 1948-51. Appearances with Mcpl. Theatre of Norrköping-Linköping, 1951-53, Mcpl. Theatre of Hälsingborg, 1953-55, Mcpl. Theatre of Malmö, 1955-60, Royal Dramatic Theatre Stockholm, 1960-74, 1988; appeared in plays including: Peer Gynt, Henry IV, The Tempest, Le misanthrope, Faust, Ett Dromspel, La valse des toreadors, Les sequestres d'Altona, After the Fall, The Wild Duck, The Night of the Tribades, 1977, Duet for One, 1981, The Tempest, 1988; films include: Bara en mor, 1949, Miss Julie, 1950, Det sjunde inseglet, 1957, Ansiktet (The Face), 1958, The Seventh Seal, 1956, The Magician, 1958, The Virgin Spring, 1959, The Wedding Day, 1960, Through a Glass Darkly, 1961, The Mistress, 1962, The Wonderful Adventures of Nils, 1962, Winter Light, 1963, 4 X 4, 1965, The Hour of the Wolf, 1968, The Shame, 1969, A Passion, 1968, The Greatest Story Ever Told, 1963, Hawaii, 1965, The Reward, 1965, The Quiller Memorandum, 1966, The Kremlin Letter, 1971, Night Visitor, 1971, The Emigrants, 1972, The Exorcist, 1973, The New Land, 1973, Steppenwolf, 1973, Heart of a Dog, 1975, Three Days of the Condor, 1975, Cadaveri Eccelenti, 1976, Voyage of the Damned, 1976, The Desert of the Tartars, 1976, Flash Gordon, 1980, Death Watch, 1980, Victory, 1980, The Flight of the Eagle, 1981, Conan the Barbarian, 1982, She Dances Alone, 1982, Le Cercle des Passions, 1982, Never Say Never Again, 1983, Dune, 1984, Dreamscape, 1984, Emerald, 1985, Hannah and her Sisters, 1986, The Second Victory, 1986, Oviri, 1986, Duet for One, 1986, Pelle the Conqueror, 1987 (Acad. award for Best Fgn. Film 1989), The Wolf at the Door, 1987, The Second Victory, Dr. Grassler, Awakenings, Until the End of the World, A Kiss Before Dying, The Bachelor, 1991, Needful Things, 1993, Judge Dredd, 1995; TV appearances include: Diary of Anne Frank, 1967, The Last Civilian, 1983, Samson and Delilah, 1984, The Belarus File, 1984, Christopher Columbus, 1985, The Last Place on Earth, 1985, The Wisdom and the Dream, 1989, Citizen X, 1995; dir. Katinka, 1988. Served with Swedish Quartermaster Corps, 1947-48. Recipient Royal Found. Cultural award, 1954. Office: UTA 9560 Wilshire Blvd 5th Fl Beverly Hills CA 90212*

VON TAAFFE-ROSSMANN, COSIMA T., physician, writer, inventor; b. Kuklov, Slovakia, Czechoslovakia, Nov. 21, 1944; came to U.S., 1988; d. Theophil and Marianna Hajossy; m. Charles Boris Rossmann, Oct. 19, 1979; children: Nathalie Nissa Cora, Nadine Nicole. MD, Purkyne U., Brno, Czechoslovakia, 1967. Intern Valtice (Czechoslovakia) Gen. Hosp., 1967-68, resident ob-gyn, 1968-69; med. researcher Kidney Disease Inst., Albany, N.Y., 1970-71; resident internal medicine Valtice Gen. Hosp., 1972-73; gen. practice Nat. Health System, Czechoslovakia, 1973-74; pvt. practice West Germany, 1974-80; med. officer Baragwanath Hosp., Johannesburg, South Africa, 1984-85, Edendale Hosp., Pietermaritzburg, South Africa, 1985-86; pvt. practice Huntingburg, Ind., 1988-90, Valdosta, Ga., 1990—; med. researcher, 1966—. Contbr. articles on medicine to profl. jours.; inventor, patentee in field. Office: 2301 N Ashley St Valdosta GA 31602-2620

VON TERSCH, LAWRENCE WAYNE, electrical engineering educator, university dean; b. Waverly, Iowa, Mar. 17, 1923; s. Alfred and Martha (Emerson) Von T.; m. LaValle Sills, Dec. 17, 1948; 1 son, Richard George. B.S., Iowa State U., 1943, M.S., 1948, Ph.D., 1953. From instr. to prof. elec. engring. Iowa State U., 1946-56; dir. computer lab. Mich. State U., 1956-83, prof. elec. engring., chmn. dept., 1958-65, assoc. dean engring., 1965-68, dean, 1968-89, dean emeritus, 1989—. Author: (with A. W. Swago) Recurrent Electrical Transients, 1953. Mem. IEEE; mem. Sigma Xi, Tau Beta Pi, Eta Kappa Nu, Phi Kappa Phi, Pi Mu Epsilon. Home: 4282 Tacoma Blvd Okemos MI 48864-2734 Office: Michigan State U Coll Engring East Lansing MI 48823

VON TUNGELN, GEORGE ROBERT, retired university administrator, economics consultant; b. Golconda, Ill., July 18, 1931; s. Cecil Ernest and Rachel Elizabeth (Wright) von T.; m. Marilyn Ruth Burris, Nov. 6, 1955; children—Stuart, Cheryl, Brenda, Sonya, Eric. B.S., So. Ill. U., 1951, M.S., 1956; Ph.D., U. Ga., 1974. Asst. mgr. exptl. farms So. Ill. U., Carbondale, 1951-52; instr., research asst. Pa. State U., 1955-58; asst. prof. to prof. agrl. sci. Clemson (S.C.) U., 1958-85, asst. to dean internat. programs, 1977-85; cons. econs. and internat. econ. devel. El Paso, 1985—; Pres. P.T.O., 1973. Contbr. articles to profl. jours. Served with AUS, 1952-54. Mem. Assn. U.S. Univ. Dirs. Internat. Agrl. Programs, Partners of Americas, West Tex. Football Officials Assn., Phi Kappa Phi, Gamma Sigma Delta. Republican. Baptist. Clubs: S.C. Football Ofcls. Assn, Sertoma (chmn. bd. 1972). Home and Office: 547 Cocula Ave El Paso TX 79932-2731

VON WODTKE, HENRY, insurance executive. Asst. sec. Buck Cons. Office: 2 Penn Pla Fl 23 New York NY 10121

VON ZERNECK, FRANK ERNEST, television producer; b. N.Y.C, Nov. 3, 1940; s. Peter and Beatrice (Francis) von Z.; m. Julie Hawthorne Mannix, Jan. 15, 1965; children: Danielle, Frank. BA in Speech and Drama, Hofstra Coll., 1962. Gen. mgr. JuJamcyn Theatres, N.Y.C., 1965-70, Ctr. Theatre Group, Los Angeles, 1970-74; ptnr. Moonlight Prodns., Hollywood, Calif., 1974-84; prin. Frank von Zerneck Films, Studio City, Calif., 1984—; cons. Found. for the Extension and Devel. of Am. Profl. Theatre, N.Y.C., 1970-77; v.p. League of Resident Theatres, N.Y.C., 1970-75; sec. Portrait of A Bookstore, North Hollywood, 1985—. Prodr. numerous movies including: The Desperate Miles, 1975, 21 Hour at Munich, 1976, Sharon: Portrait of a Mistress, 1977, Portrait of a Stripper, 1979, Texas Rangers, 1980, Love Canal, 1982, Policewoman Centerfold, 1983, Summer Fantasy, 1984, Hostage Flight, 1985: (TV miniseries) Dress Gray, 1985, Queenie, 1987, To Heal a Nation, 1988, Billy the Kid, 1989, The Great Los Angeles Earthquake, 1990, Survive the Savage Sea, 1991, Too Young To Die, 1992, Jackie Collins' Lady Boss, 1992, The Broken Chain, 1994, Robin Cook's Mortal Fear, 1994, Take Me Home Again, 1994, The West Side Waltz, 1995, God's Lonely Man, 1996. Bd. dirs. Oakhill Sch., Los Angeles, 1984—. Recipient award of merit Nat. Cath. Broadcasters, N.Y.C., 1982, silver gavel award ABA, Washington, 1983, TV Prodr. of Yr. AFI, 1994. Mem. Caucus of Writers, Producers and Dirs., Producers Guild Am., League N.Y. Theatres and Prodns., Calif. Theatre Coun. (chmn. 1973-74), League Resident Theatres (v.p. 1972-73), ACI (bd. dirs. 1990-95). Home: 4355 Forman Ave Toluca Lake CA 91602-2909 Office: Frank von Zerneck Films 12001 Ventura Pl Ste 400 Studio City CA 91604-2629

VOOGT, JAMES LEONARD, medical educator; b. Grand Rapids, Mich., Feb. 8, 1944; married; 3 children. Student, Calvin Coll., 1962-64; BS in Biological Sci., Mich. Tech. Univ., 1966; MS in Physiology, Mich. State Univ., 1968, PhD in Physiology, 1970. Postdoc. fellow, lectr. dept. physiology U. Calif., San Francisco, 1970-71; asst. prof. dept. physiology and biophysics U. Louisville Sch. Medicine, 1971-77, assoc. prof. dept. physiology and biophysics, 1977; assoc. prof. dept. physiology U. Kans. Sch. Medicine, 1977-82, prof. dept. physiology, 1982—; assoc. in psychology, assoc. in oncology U. Louisville, 1973-77; assoc. dean rsch. U. Kans. Sch. Medicine, 1982-84, acting chmn. dept. physiology, 1987, chmn. dept. physiology, 1993—; vis. prof. Erasmus U., 1985. Mem. editl. bd. Endocrinology, 1984-86, 89-92, Am. Jour. Physiology, 1984-88, Doody's Jour., 1995—; ad hoc reviewer Neuroendocrinology, Sci., Biology of Reproduction, Life Scis., Jour. Endocrinology, Molecular Cellular Neuroscis., PSEBM, biochm. endocrinology study sect. NIH, 1992—, reproductive endocrinology study sect., 1994—; reviewer grants NSF; editor scientific proceedings Research Week, 1982, 83; contbr. over 120 articles to prof. publs., 4 chpts. to books. Grantee NIH, 1972-80, 80-81, 82-85, 88—, 90-93, 94—, NSF, 1985-86, 91-94, Ctr. on Aging, 1988, Nat. Inst. Drug Abuse, 1991-93; fellow Japan Soc. Promotion of Sci., 1993; recipient Outstanding Young Alumni award Mich. Tech. Univ., 1974, Honors in Edn., Med. Student Voice, 1990. Mem. AAAS, Endocrine Soc., Internat. Soc. Neuroendocrinology (charter mem.), Am. Physiol. Soc. (pub. affairs adv. com. 1983-87) Soc. Neuroscis., Phi Kappa Phi, Sigma Xi. Office: Dept Physiology U Kans Med Ctr 3901 Rainbow Blvd Kansas City KS 66160-7401*

VOOK, FREDERICK LUDWIG, physicist, consultant; b. Milw., Jan. 17, 1931; s. Fred Ludwig and Hedwig Anna (Werner) V.; m. Frederica Jean Sandin, Aug. 16, 1958; children: Eric Robert, Dietrich Werner. BA with honors, U. Chgo., 1951, BS, 1952; MS, U. Ill., 1954, PhD in Physics, 1958. With Sandia Labs., Kirtland AFB East, N.Mex., 1958-94; div. supr., 1962-71, mgr. dept. research, 1971-78, dir. research, 1978-94; pvt. cons. Albuquerque, 1994—. Editor: Radiation Effects in Semiconductors, 1968; coeditor: Applications of Ion Beams to Metals, 1974. Mem. coll. engring. adv. bd. U. Ill.; mem. policy bd. Nat. Nanofabrication Facility Cornell U.; mem. basic engring. sci. adv. com. Panel on Value of Basic Rsch. U. Chgo. and U. Ill. scholar and fellow. Fellow Am. Phys. Soc.; mem. IEEE (sr. mem.), Böhmische Physikalische Gesellschaft, Phi Beta Kappa, Sigma Xi.

VOOK, RICHARD WERNER, physics educator; b. Milw., Aug. 2, 1929; s. Fred Ludwig and Hedwig Anna (Werner) V.; m. Julia Deskins, Sept. 7, 1957; children: Katherine, Elizabeth, Richard S., Frederick W. BA, Carleton Coll., 1951; MS, U. Ill., 1952, PhD, 1957. Staff physicist IBM Rsch. Lab., Yorktown Heights, N.Y., 1957-61; sr. rsch. physicist Franklin Inst. Rsch. Labs., Phila., 1961-65; assoc. prof. of metallurgy Syracuse (N.Y.) U., 1965-70, prof. of materials sci., 1970-84, prof. of physics, 1984-93, prof. emeritus, 1993—, dir. solid state sci. and tech., 1984-87, 90-91; physicist/chemist U. Calif., Lawrence Livermore Nat. Lab., summers 1977-81; summer faculty mem. Sandia Nat. Lab., Albuquerque, 1983, 84; bd. editors Thin Solid Films, 1985—. Contbr. articles to profl. publs., chpts. to books. Recipient L. B. Pfeil medal and prize Metals Soc. of Great Britain, 1983. Mem. Am. Vacuum Soc., Electron Microscope Soc. Am., Materials Rsch. Soc., Phi Beta Kappa, Sigma Xi, Pi Mu Epsilon. Lutheran. Achievements include discovery of Auger R-factor characterization of thin film growth; development of theory of substrate-induced differential thermal expansion strains in thin films; first observation of Stranski-Krastanov growth mode in vapor deposited thin films, first use of flash evaporation to form high Tc superconducting thin films. Office: Syracuse Univ 201 Physics Bldg Syracuse NY 13244-1130

VOORHEES, JAMES DAYTON, JR., lawyer; b. Haverford, Pa., Nov. 14, 1917; s. James Dayton Voorhees and Elsa Denison Jameson; m. Mary Margaret Fuller, Sept. 5, 1942 (dec. Apr. 1991); children: J. Dayton III, Susan F. Voorhees-Maxfield, Jane Voorhees Kiss. BA, Yale U., 1940; JD, Harvard U., 1943. Bar: N.H. 1947, Colo. 1948, U.S. Dist. Ct. Colo. 1948, U.S. Ct. Appeals (10th cir.) 1949, U.S. Ct. Appeals (5th cir.) 1956, U.S. Supreme Ct. 1960. Assoc. Johnson & Robertson, Denver, 1947-50; atty. Conoco Inc., Denver, 1950-56; ptnr. Moran, Reidy & Voorhees, Denver, 1956-78, Kutak, Rock & Huie, Denver, 1978-80; ptnr., counsel Davis, Graham & Stubbs, Denver, 1980—; bd. dirs. Japex (U.S.) Corp., Houston, Mercury Internat. Techs., Tulsa. Mem. Denver Bd. Edn., 1965-71, pres. 1967-69. Lt. comdr. USNR, 1941-46, ATO, PTO. Mem. ABA, Colo. Bar Assn., Denver Bar Assn., Fed. Energy Bar Assn., Denver Country Club, University Club. Republican. Avocations: golf, skiing.

VOORHEES, JOHN LLOYD, columnist; b. DeWitt, Iowa, Aug. 30, 1925; s. Lloyd William and Elsie Irene (Bousselot) V. BA in History, U. Iowa, 1951; BA in Journalism, U. Wash., 1953. Tchr. Oelwein (Iowa) High Sch., 1951-52; columnist Seattle Post-Intelligencer, 1953-71; columnist, critic Seattle Times, 1971—. With U.S. Army, 1946-48. Democrat. Office: The Seattle Times Fairview Ave N & John St Seattle WA 98111

VOORHEES, RICHARD LESLEY, chief federal judge; b. Syracuse, N.Y., June 5, 1941; s. Henry Austin and Catherine Adeline (Fait) V.; m. Barbara Holway Humphries, 1968; children: Martha Northrop, Steven Coerte. BA, Davidson Coll., 1963; JD, U. N.C., Chapel Hill, 1968. Bar: N.C. 1968, U.S. Dist. Ct. (we. dist.) N.C. 1969, U.S. Tax Ct. 1969, U.S. Ct. Appeals (4th cir.) 1978, U.S. Dist. Ct. (mid. dist.) N.C. 1981. Mem., ptnr. Garland, Alala, Bradley & Gray, Gastonia, N.C., 1968-80; pvt. practice Gastonia, N.C., 1980-88; judge U.S. Dist. Ct., Charlotte, N.C., 1988—, chief judge, 1991—. Mem. N.C. State Rep. Exec. Com., Gaston County Rep. Com., chmn., 1979-83, U.S. Jud. Conf. Com., 1993—, case mgmt. and ct. adminstrn. com., 4th Cir. Ct. Appeals Jud. Coun., 1992-93; chmn. Gaston County Bd. Elections, Gastonia, 1985-86; alt. del. Rep. Nat. Conv., Kansas City, Kans., 1976. 1st lt. U.S. Army, 1963-65. Mem. N.C. Bar Assn., Fed. Judges Assn., Dist. Judges Assn. Avocation: boating. Office: US Dist Ct WDNC 195 CR Jonas Fed Bldg 401 W Trade St Charlotte NC 28202

VOORSANGER, BARTHOLOMEW, architect; b. Detroit, Mar. 23, 1937; s. Jacob H. and Ethel A. (Arnstein) V.; m. Lisa Livingston, 1964; m. Catherine Hoover, Sept. 10, 1983; children—Roxanna Virginia (dec.), Matthew Ansley. A.B. cum laude, Princeton U., 1960; diplome, Fontainebleau, 1960; M.Arch., Harvard U., 1964. Assoc. Vincent Ponte, Montreal, Que., Can., 1964-67, I.M. Pei & Ptnrs., 1968-78; dir. I.M. Pei & Ptnrs., Iran, 1975-78; co-chmn. Voorsanger & Mills (Architects), N.Y.C., 1978-90; founder, prin. Voorsanger & Assocs., Architects, N.Y.C., 1990—; founder Taylor/Voorsanger Urban Designers, 1991; lectr. Bennington (Vt.) Coll., U. Pa., Columbia U., Harvard U.; guest critic, lectr. Yale U., Pratt Inst., CUNY, R.I. Sch. Design, U. Cin., Syracuse U., U. Tex., Arlington; mem. adv. bd. Parson Sch. Architecture; mem. archtl. rev. panel Port Authority of N.Y. & N.J.; advisor to Samsung Corp., Korea. Exhbns. include: NYU, Archtl. Assn., London, Harvard Grad. Sch. Design, Vacant Lots Housing Study, N.Y., Deutsches Architeckur Mus., Frankfurt, Mus. Finnish Architecture, Avery Lib.Centennial Exhbn. Columbia Univ., Helsinki, Bklyn. Mus.; major projects include: Le Cygne Restaurant, Neiman houseboat, NYU Midtown Ctr., NYU Bus. Sch. Library, La Grandeur housing, NYU dormitories, Hostos Community Coll., N.Y.; finalist Bklyn. Mus. masterplan internat. competition, expansion and master plan Pierpont Morgan Libr., R. Krasnow Apt., N.Y.C.; fellow J. Pierpont Morgan Libr., N.Y. Mem. vis. com. R.I. Sch. Design, U. Tex., Arlington; mem. N.Y. Hist. Soc., also mem. archtl. cir. steering com.; chmn. bd. advisors Temple Hoyne Buell Ctr., Study Am. Architecture, Columbia U., N.Y.C., 1989—; mem. adv. bd. Parsons Sch. Architecture; chair archtl. rev. panel Port Authority N.Y. and N.J.; bd. dirs. Worldesign Found. 1st lt. U.S. Army, 1960-61. Recipient awards N.Y.C. chpt. AIA, AIA/Better Homes, Bard City Club, Interiors mag., Stone Inst., AIA/Libr., Lumen, Pratt Inst., NYU, N.Y.C. Art Commn. Fellow AIA (bd. dirs. N.Y.C. chpt. 1979-81, v.p. 1987, chmn. Brunner award com. 1978-80, Bard award pres.-elect N.Y.C. chpt. 1984, Nat. Honor award, N.Y. State award); mem. Archtl. League N.Y.C. (bd. dirs.), Sir John Soane Mus. Found., N.Y. Found. for Arch. (bd. dirs.), Century Assn., River Club, Thursday Evening Club, Wadawanuck Club, Alumni Coun. Grad. Sch. Design Harvard. Home: 350 E 52nd St Apt 9G New York NY 10022-6739 Office: 246 W 38th St Fl 14 New York NY 10018-5805 Home: 83 Main St Stonington CT 06378-1221

VOOS, PAULA BETH, economics educator; b. Everett, Wash., Apr. 15, 1949; d. Paul Allen and Loualta (Peterson) Vogel; m. Keith Frederick Voos, May 30, 1970; children: Johanna, Michaela. AB in English, Whitman Coll., 1971; MA in Econs., Portland (Oreg.) State U., 1976; PhD in Econs., Harvard U., 1982. Instr. U. Mass., Boston, 1978-81; asst. prof. U. Wis., Madison, 1981-87, assoc. prof. econs., 1987-92, prof., 1992—; Mem. Commn. on the Future of Worker-Mgmt. Rels., 1993-94; pres. Inst. Wis.'s Future, 1995—. Contbr. articles to profl. jours. Mem. Am. Econs. Assn., Indsl. Rels. Rsch. Assn. (exec. bd. 1988-90, editor 1993—). Democrat. Home: 2710 Willard Ave Madison WI 53704-5755 Office: U Wis Industrial Relations Rsch Inst 4226 Social Science Bldg Madison WI 53706-1320

VORA, ASHOK, financial economist; b. Bombay, India, July 19, 1947; came to U.S., 1970; s. Kevalchand and Laxmi (Mehta) V.; m. Rama Kata, Dec. 12, 1982; children: Anjali Serena, Amit Raunak. B.Sc., U. Bombay, 1967; M.B.A., Indian Inst. Mgmt., 1970; Ph.D., Northwestern U., 1973. Asst. to chmn. Vora Automotives Ltd., Bombay, 1963-67, dir., 1967-70; asst. prof. fin. CUNY, 1973-80; vis. asst. prof. fin. U. Wis., Madison, 1977; vis. assoc. prof. fin. Northwestern U., Evanston, Ill., 1979-80; assoc. prof. fin. CUNY, 1980-84, prof. fin., 1984—; dir. fin. rsch. Fed. Home Loan Mortgage Corp., Reston, Va., 1987-88; vis. prof. fin. Hofstra U., Hempstead, N.Y., 1990-91; cons. in field. Contbr. articles to profl. jours. Mem. Am. Econ. Assn., Am. Fin. Assn., Fin. Mgmt. Assn., So. Fin. Assn., S.W. Fin. Assn., Western Fin. Assn., Mensa, Nat. Wildlife Fedn., Beta Gamma Sigma. Office: CUNY Box E0621 17 Lexington Ave New York NY 10010-5585

VORA, MANU KISHANDAS, chemical engineer, quality consultant; b. Bombay, India, Oct. 31, 1945; s. Kishandas Narandas and Shantaben K. (Valia) V., m. Nila Narotamdas Kothari, June 16, 1974; children: Ashish, Anand. BSChemE, Banaras (India) Hindu U., 1968; MSChemE, Ill. Inst. Tech., Chgo., 1970, PhD in ChemE, 1975; MBA, Keller Grad. Sch. Mgmt., Chgo., 1985. Grad. asst. Ill. Inst. Tech., 1969-74; rsch. assoc. Inst. Gas Tech., Chgo., 1976-77, chem. engr., 1977-79, engring. supr., 1979-82; mem. tech. staff AT&T Bell Labs. (now Lucent Techs.), Holmdel, N.J., 1983-84, Naperville, Ill., 1984—; mgr. customer safisfaction AT&T Bell Labs. (now Lucent Techs.), Naperville and Milw., 1990—; mem. faculty Ill. Inst. Tech., Chgo., part-time, 1993—; spkr. in field. Invited editor Internat. Petroleum Encyclopedia, 1980. Chmn. Save the Children Holiday Fund Drive, 1986—; trustee Avery Coonley Sch., Downers Grove, Ill., 1987-91; pres., dir. Blind Found. for India, Naperville, 1989—; dir. Nat. Ednl. Quality Initiatives, Inc., Milw., 1991—, fellow, 1992. Recipient Non-Supervisory AA award Affirmative Actions Adv. Com., 1987, 92, Outstanding Contbn. award Asian Am. for Affirmative Actions, 1989, Disting. Svc. award Save the Children, 1990. Fellow Am. Soc. Quality Control (standing rev. bd. 1988—, editl. re. bd. 1989, tech. media com. 1989, mixed media rev. bd. 1994, nat. quality month regional planning com. 1989-94, nat. cert. com. 1989-94, chmn. cert. process improvements subcom. 1990-94, testimonial awards 1996, exec. bd. Chgo. sect., vice chmn. sect. affairs 1993-94, sect. chmn. 1994-95, spl. award 1991, Century Club award 1992, Founders' award 1993, Joe Lisy Quality award 1994); mem. Chgo. Assn. Tech. Socs. (ann. merit award 1992), Ill. Team Excellence (chief judge 1993—, steering com. 1993—, award). Hindu. Avocations: reading, photography, travel, philanthropic activities. Home: 1256 Hamilton Ln Naperville IL 60540-8373 Office: Lucent Techs 2000 N Naperville Rd Naperville IL 60566-7033

VORAN, JAMES F., principal. Prin. Sealey Elem. Sch. Recipient Elem. Sch. Recognition award U.S. Dept. Edn., 1989-90. Office: Sealey Elem Sch 2815 Allen Rd Tallahassee FL 32312-2614

VORBACH, JOAN BOUTON, physical educator educator; b. N.Y.C., Feb. 12, 1934; d. Paul and Elizabeth (Feher) Bouton; m. Joseph Robert Vorbach, Aug. 13, 1955 (div. 1981); children: Robert Joseph, Gail Elizabeth, Barry Charles. BS, SUNY, Cortland, 1955; MS, SUNY, New Paltz. Phys. edn./health tchr. Liverpool (N.Y.) High Sch., 1955-56, Katonah-Lewisboro C.S.D., Cross River, N.Y., 1956-57; phys. edn. tchr. Port Jervis (N.Y.) City Sch. Dist., 1969-72, Warwick (N.Y.) Valley C.S.D., 1973—; coach 7th and 8th grades cross country and track Warwick Valley C.S.D., 1985-90, mem. supts. liaison com., 1993-94, tchr., chaperone 6th grade outdoor edn. at Ashokan, N.Y., 1995, union bldg. rep., 1984-92. Vol. Reps.-Orange County, Middletown, N.Y., 1990; active Our Lady of Mt. Carmel Ch., Middletown,

Nature Conservancy, Amnesty Internat. Mem. AAHPERD, Local Tchrs. Assn. and NYSUT, N.Y. State AAHPERD, Sierra Club, Audubon Soc., Nat. Historic Preservation, Nat. Parks and Conservation Assn., Volksport Walking Club of West Point. Roman Catholic. Avocations: bird watching, doll collecting, auctions, historic trips, golf.

VORBRICH, LYNN KARL, lawyer, utility executive; b. Iowa City, Feb. 12, 1939; s. William August and Anna Margaretha (Seibert) V.; m. Jody Nolan; children: Sally, Andrew, Peter, David, Peter, Jill, Jason. BS Indsl. Adminstrn., Iowa State U., 1960; JD, U. Iowa, 1962. Bar: Iowa 1962, Ill. 1962. Assoc. Seyfarth, Shaw, Fairweather & Geraldson, Chgo., 1962-64; assoc., ptnr. Dickinson, Throckmorton, Parker, et al, Des Moines, 1964-69; asst. counsel The Bankers Life Co., Des Moines, 1969-73; assoc. counsel Iowa Power, Des Moines, 1973-76, assoc. gen. counsel, 1976-78, sec., assoc. gen. counsel, 1978-79, sr. v.p., 1985, exec. v.p., 1986-89, pres., 1989-92; exec. v.p. Midwest Power Systems, Inc., Des Moines, 1992-95; pres. electric divsn. Mid-American Energy Co., 1995—; bd. dirs. Bankers Trust Co., Des Moines, 1986-95, Preferred Risk Ins. Group, 1993—, Norwest Bank of Davenport. Trustee Davenport Mus. of Art; dir. Putnam Mus. of Natural History, Quad-City Econ. Devel. Group, Downtown Davenport Devel. Assn., Quad Cities United Way; mem. adv. com. Iowa State Boys Tng. Sch., Eldora, Iowa, 1987-95, legis. study com. on juvenile justice, 1989-90; dean's adv. coun. Iowa State U. Coll. Bus. Adminstrn., Ames, 1987-90; pres. bd. Polk County Legal Aid Soc., 1970, Iowa Children's and Family Svcs., 1970, 78, Planned Parenthood of Mid-Iowa, 1983, Des Moines Area C.C. Found., 1986-87; chmn. Des Moines Human Rights Commn., 1970; bd. dirs. Golden Circle Incubator bd., Golden Circle Labor-Mgmt. Commn., Ankeny, Iowa, 1988-95, Civic Music Assn., Des Moines, 1986-87; mem. Bur. Econ. Devel. Coun. of the Greater Des Moines C. of C., 1989-95. Named Outstanding Young Alumnus Iowa State U., 1973. Mem. ABA, Iowa Bar Assn., Des Moines Club (trustee 1982-88), rock Island Arsenal Golf Club, Davenport Country Club. United Church of Christ. Office: Mid-American Energy Co PO Box 4350 Davenport IA 52801

VORENBERG, JAMES, lawyer, educator, university dean; b. Boston, Jan. 10, 1928; s. F. Frank and Ida (Muhlfelder) V.; m. Dorothy Greeley, Oct. 25, 1952; children: Jill, Amy, Eliza; m. Elizabeth Weiner Troubh, June 20, 1970. A.B., Harvard U., 1948, LL.B., 1951. Law clk. to Justice Frankfurter, 1953-54; with firm Ropes & Gray, 1954-62, partner, 1960-62; prof. law Harvard U., Cambridge, Mass., 1962—, Roscoe Pound prof. law, 1981—; dean Law Sch. Harvard U., 1981-89; dir. Office of Criminal Justice, 1964-65; exec. dir. Pres.'s Commn. on Law Enforcement and Adminstrn Justice, 1965-67; asso. spl. prosecutor Watergate Spl. Prosecution Force, 1973-75. Trustee Legal Def. Fund, NAACP; chmn. Mass. Ethics Commn., 1978-83. With USAF, 1951-53. Home: 9 Willard St Cambridge MA 02138-4836 Office: Harvard U Law Sch Cambridge MA 02138

VORHIES, MAHLON WESLEY, veterinary pathologist, educator; b. Fairfield, Iowa, June 26, 1937; s. Harold Wesley and Edith Mae (Bender) V.; m. Ilene Lanore Hoffman, Aug. 29, 1959; children—Susan Rae, Robert Wesley. D.V.M., Iowa State U., 1962; M.S., Mich. State U., 1967. Veterinarian in pvt. practice Riverside, Iowa, 1962-64; clin. instr. Mich. State U., East Lansing, 1964-67; vet. pathologist Iowa State U., Ames, 1962-72; vet. pathologist, dir., dept. head S.D. State U., Brookings, 1972-86; dir., dept. head Kans. State U. Coll. Vet. Medicine, Manhattan, 1986-95, dept. head, diagonostic medicine patho biology, 1995—; cons. NIH, Commonwealth Pa., Winrock Internat. Hdqrs., U.S. Dept. Agr., FAO-Fundagro/MIAC, LIFE, Quito, Ecuador, 1991. Contbr. articles to profl. jours. Trustee Brookings United Presbyn. Ch., 1975-78, elder, 1981-84; mem. adv. com. Pipestone Area Vocat. Tech. Inst., 1984. Mem. AVMA, Assn. Am. Vet. Med. Colls., S.D. Vet. Med. Assn. (Vet. of Yr. award 1979), Kans. Vet. Med. Assn., Am. Assn. Avian Pathologists, U.S. Animal Health Assn., Am. Assn. Vet. Lab. Diagnosticians (E.P. Pope award 1984, pres. 1977), North Central Conf. Vet. Lab. Diagnosticians (chmn. 1984, 94), Commn. Vet Medicine, Phi Zeta, Gamma Sigma Delta. Clubs: Brookings Country (dir. 1983-86). Lodge: Shrine (chmn. 1984-85). Home: 2035 Rockhill Cir Manhattan KS 66502-3952 Office: Coll Vet Medicine Kans State U Manhattan KS 66506

VORHOLT, JEFFREY JOSEPH, lawyer, software company executive; b. Cin., Feb. 20, 1953; s. Edward C. and Rita L. (Kinross) V.; m. Marcia Anne Meyer, Apr. 30, 1976; children: Kimberly Anne, Gregory Michael, Karen Michelle. BBA cum laude, U. Cin., 1976; MBA, Xavier U., Cin., 1978; JD, Chase Law Sch., 1983. Bar: Ohio, 1983; CPA, Ohio. Sec., treas. Cin. Bell Info. Systems, Inc., 1983-84, v.p., chief fin. officer, 1984-88, also bd. dirs.; v.p., controller Cin. Bell, Inc., 1988-89; sr. v.p. Cin. Bell Info. Systems, Inc., 1989-91, Cin. Bell Telephone Co., 1991-93; CFO Structural Dynamics Rsch. Corp., Milford, Ohio, 1994—. Voting mem. Cin. Playhouse, 1986—; mem. fin. planning com. ARC, Cin., 1986-89; trustee U. Health Maintenance Orgn., Inc., 1990-93, St. Joseph Infant and Maternity Home, Inc. Mem. ABA, AICPAs, Ohio Bar Assn., Aircraft Owners and Pilots Assn., Cin. Hist. Soc., Bankers Club of Cin. (bd. govs. 1990—). Avocations: golf, tennis, hiking, photography. Office: Structural Dynamics Rsch Corp 2000 Eastman Dr Milford OH 45150-2712

VORIS, WILLIAM, educational administrator; b. Neoga, Ill., Mar. 20, 1924; s. Louis K. and Faye (Hancock) V.; m. Mavis Marie Myre, Mar. 20, 1949; children: Charles William II, Michael K. BS, U. So. Calif., 1947, MBA, 1948; PhD, Ohio State U., 1951; LLD, Sung Kyun Kwan U. (Korea), 1972, Eastern Ill. U., 1976. Teaching asst. Ohio State U., Columbus, 1948-50; prof. mgmt. Wash. State U., Pullman, 1950-52; prof., head dept. mgmt. Los Angeles State Coll., 1952-58, 60-63; dean Coll. Bus. and Pub. Adminstrn., U. Ariz., Tucson, 1963-71; pres. Am. Grad. Sch. Internat. Mgmt., Glendale, Ariz., 1971-89, pres. emeritus, 1989—, adj. prof., 1994—. Ford Found. research grantee Los Angeles State Coll., 1956; prof. U. Tehran (Iran), 1958-59; Ford Found. fellow Carnegie Inst. Tech., Pitts., 1961; prof. Am. U., Beirut, Lebanon, 1961, 62; cons. Hughes Aircraft Co., Los Angeles, Rheem Mfg. Co., Los Angeles, Northrop Aircraft Co., Palmdale, Calif., Harwood Co., Alhambra, Calif., ICA, Govt. Iran. Served with USNR, 1942-45. Fellow Acad. Mgmt.; mem. Ariz. Acad., Beta Gamma Sigma, Alpha Kappa Psi, Phi Delta Theta. Author: Production Control, Text and Cases, 1956, 3d edit., 1966; Management of Production, 1960. Research in indsl. future of Iran, mgmt. devel. in Middle East. Home: Thunderbird Campus Glendale AZ 85306

VOROUS, MARGARET ESTELLE, secondary, primary school educator; b. Charles Town, W.Va., Feb. 14, 1947; d. Benjamin Welton and Helen Virginia (Owens) Vorous. AA in Pre-Edn. (Laureate Scholar), Potomac State Coll., W.Va. U., 1967; BS in Elem. Edn., James Madison U., 1970, MS in Edn., 1975, postgrad., spring 1978, fall 1979, summer 1979, 81; postgrad. U. Va., summers 1977, 78, fall 1978, 89, 91, James Madison U., fall 1981-82, summer 1979, 81-82; MEd in Media Svcs., East Tenn. State U., 1988, 89. Cert. library sci., cert. adminstrn./supervisory. Tchr. 3d-4th grade Highview Sch., Frederick County, Va., 1968-69, 3d grade Kernstown Elem. Sch., Frederick County, 1970-71, E. Wilson Morrison Elem. Sch., Front Royal, Va., 1971-72, Stonewall Elem. Sch., Frederick County, 1972-78; tchr. 4th grade South Jefferson Elem. Sch., Jefferson County (W.Va.) Schs., 1978-79, Emergency Sch. Aid Act reading tchr./reading specialist, 1980-82, reading tchr./specialist Page Jackson Solar Elem. Sch., 1983-87; adult basic edn. tchr. Dowell J. Howard Vocat. Ctr., Winchester, Va., 1984-87, G.E.D. tchr., coordinator, 1985-87; libr., media specialist Powell Valley Middle Sch., 1988-91; ABE/GED/ESL tchr. for JOBS program Berkeley County Schs., 1992-94; libr., media specialist Northwestern Elem., 1994-95, first grade tchr., 1995—; tchr. 4th grade Ranson (W.Va.) Elem. Sch., 1979; reading tutor; reading tutor, trainer Laubach Literacy Internat., 1989; art rep. Creative Arts Festival at Kernstown, 1971, Stonewall elem. schs., 1973-77; mem. cultural task force Frederick County Sch., 1974-75, music task force, 1973-74, textbook adoption com. for reading, writing, 1976-77. Founder, editor: The Reading Gazette, The Reading Tribune, Emergency Sch. Aid Act Reading Program, South Jefferson Elem. Sch., 1980-81, Shepherdstown Elem. Sch., 1981-82; creator numerous reading games, activities. Vol. fundraiser Am. Cancer Soc., Frederick County, Va., 1981; vol. blood donor Am. Red Cross, 1978—; mem. Frederick County Polit. Action Com., Jefferson County Polit. Action Com.; del. 103-109th Ann. Diocesan Convs., Episc. Ch., registrar of vestry Grace Episc. Ch., Middleway, W.Va., 1980-87, lic. lay reader, 1980-90, lic. chalice bearer, 1983-90; lic. lay reader, lay eucharistic min. St. Paul's Episc. Ch.-on-the-Hill, Winchester, Va., 1996—; committeeperson Lebanon Dems., 1988-89; commd. mem. Order of Jerusalem, 1985—; VEMA leadership participant, 1989-91, 95; facilitator VEMA Conf., 1994; participant Seven Habits program Covey Leadership Ctr., 1993; lay reader and lay eucharistic minister St. Paul's on-the-Hill Episcopal Ch., Winchester, Va., 1996—. Recipient various awards, including being named Miss Alpine Princess, award for Excellence in Adult Basic Edn. Dept. Edn., Charleston, W.Va., 1994, RIF Site Coord. for Honorable mention, 1995, RIF Nat. Poster contest Storyteller for Chpt. I workshop and Ctrl. Elementary, 1994-95, Sigma Phi Omega, 1967. Mem. Internat. Reading Assn., NEA, Va. Reading Assn., Shenandoah Valley Reading Council, Assn. Supervision and Curriculum Devel., W.Va. Edn. Assn., NEA. Jefferson County Edn. Assn. (faculty rep.), Fauquier County Edn. Assn., Va. Edn. Assn., W.Va. Adult Edn. Assn., Va. Edn. Media Assn., South Jefferson PTA, Potomac State Coll. Alumni Assn., James Madison U. Alumni Assn., Frederick County Dem. Women, Kappa Delta Pi, Phi Delta Kappa, Phi Kappa Phi.

VOROUS, PATRICIA ANN MARIE, elementary school educator; b. Cleve., Sept. 12, 1951; d. Leon Jr. and Margaret (Cotter) V. BS Edn. in Elem. Edn., St. John Coll., Cleve., 1973; postgrad., Notre Dame Coll., Cleve., 1988, Baldwin-Wallace Coll., Berea, Ohio, summer 1979, 91; Ashland Coll., 1995. Cert. tchr., Ohio. Intermediate tchr. lang. arts, social studies St. Mel Sch., Cleve., 1973-74; grade 6 tchr. lang. arts, social studies and religion St. James Sch., Lakewood, Ohio, 1975-80; tchr. grades 5 and 6 Our Lady of the Angels Schs., Cleve., 1980—; supervisory tchr. for elem. edn. students Cleve. State U.; from asst. dir. to dir. Lakewood Recreation Dept. Summer Play Ctr., 1973-94, summer 1995; safety patrol coord. Our Lady of Angels, Cleve., 1985—. Craftsman animals, dolls, 3-D scenes for fall festivals and gifts. Roman Catholic. Avocations: travel, swimming, raising showing and training my Arabian gelding, basketball.

VORSANGER, FRED S., university administrator; b. Calumet City, Ill., Apr. 20, 1928; s. Fred and Hannah (Steifel) V.; m. Doreen D. Carter, Apr. 24, 1965; children: Diana, Bruce, Bob;. B.S. in Bus. Adminstrn., Ind. U., 1951; M.B.A., George Washington U., 1970; postgrad., U. Ark., 1971. Acct. Ernst & Ernst, Chgo., 1951-53; internal auditor Purdue U., Lafayette, Ind., 1953-59; treas., bus. mgr. Am. Council on Edn., Washington, 1959-68; v.p. U. Ark., Fayetteville, 1968—; mgr. Walton Arena U. Ark.; exec. dir. U. Ark. Found., Inc., 1985-88, v.p. emeritus, 1988—; lectr. U. Ky. Mgmt. Inst., 1976—, U. Calif. Mgmt. Inst., 1976-85; adj. prof. Coll. Bus. Adminstrn., 1985—; trustee Common Fund, N.Y.C., chmn., 1982-85; bd. dirs. Tyson Foods, Inc., United Educators Ins. Risk Retention Co., McIlroy Bank and Trust,Ozark Guidance Ctr.; spl. cons. Meridian House Found., Washington, 1960-68; examiner North Central Commn. on Accrediting, 1971—. Author: (with Julian H. Levi) Patterns of Giving to Higher Education, 1968; contbr. articles to profl. jours.; mem. editorial adv. bd. Commerce Clearing House, Inc, 1963-68; mem. editorial adv. com. Coll. and Univ. Bus. Mag. Pres. Washington County unit Am. Cancer Soc., 1971-72; bd. dirs. Nationwide Edn. Conf. Centers, N.W. Ark. Regional Planning Commn., Ark. Regional Med. Program, U. Ark. Found., Fayetteville Community Concert Assn., Northwest Ark. Film Commn., 1983—; city dir. N.W. Ark. Econ. Devel. Dist., alderman, 1993—, mayor, 1991, Fayetteville, Ark. Served with U.S. Army, 1945-47. Mem. Nat. Assn. Land Grant Colls. and State Univs. (dir.), Nat. Assn. Ednl. Buyers (treas., dir.), Nat. Assn. Coll. and Univ. Bus. Officers (dir., pres. 1984-85, Disting. Bus. Officer award 1991), So. Assn. Coll. and Univ. Bus. Officers (pres.), Am. Coun. Edn., Fayetteville C. of C. (dir., 2d v.p.), Blue Key, Fayetteville Country Club, Capitol Club, Rotary Internat. (dist. gov.), Delta Sigma Pi, Sigma Phi Epsilon. Home: 1315 E Ridgeway Dr Fayetteville AR 72701-2616 *From standing in a public welfare relief line to being listed in Who's Who; Thank God for America.*

VORWERK, E(TTA) CHARLSIE, artist; b. Tennga, Ga., Jan. 28, 1934; d. James A. and Hester L. (Davis) Pritchett. A.B., Ga. State Coll. for Women, 1955; m. Norman T. Vorwerk, Feb. 9, 1956; children: Karl, Lauren, Michael. Billboard design artist Vanesco Poster, Chattanooga, 1955; cartographic draftsman TVA, Chattanooga, 1955; fashion illustrator Loveman's, Chattanooga, 1956; freelance comml. artist, 1957—; pvt. art instr. children and adults, all media, 1966—; art instr. continuing edn. Bapt. Coll. Charleston, S.C., 1979-82. Mem. Bd. Archtl. Rev., Summerville, 1976—; chmn. YMCA Flowertown Festival Art Exhibit, 1972—; mem. women's bd. St. Paul's Episcopal Ch. 1968-84; active Boy Scouts Am., Girl Scouts U.S.; vol. Mental Health Clinic, 1972-74, others; coord. Washington Park Picolo-Spoleto Art Exhibit, 1983—, also exhibit chmn. for low country artists. Recipient 1st Pl. award Rice Festival, 1994. Mem. Ga. Miniature Art Soc., Charleston Artists Guild, League of Charleston Artists, Minature Art Soc. Fla., Am. Art Soc., Italian Art Acad. Illustrator: Tales and Taradidales; St. Paul's Epitahs; Captain Tom, others. Address: 315 W Carolina Ave Summerville SC 29483-4358

VORYS, ARTHUR ISAIAH, lawyer; b. Columbus, Ohio, June 16, 1923; s. Webb Isaiah and Adeline (Werner) V.; m. Lucia Rogers, July 16, 1949 (div. 1980); children: Caroline S., Adeline Vorys Cranson, Lucy Vorys Noll, Webb I.; m. Ann Harris, Dec. 13, 1980. BA, Williams Coll., 1945; LLB, JD, Ohio State U., 1949. Bar: Ohio 1949. From assoc. to ptnr. Vorys, Sater, Seymour & Pease, Columbus, 1949-82, sr. ptnr., 1982-93, of counsel, 1993—; supt. ins. State of Ohio, 1957-59; bd. dirs Vorys Bros., Inc., others. Trustee, past Children's Hosp., Greenlawn Cemetery Found.; trustee, former chmn. Ohio State U. Hosps.; regent Capital U.; del. Rep. Nat. Conv., 1968, 72. Lt. USMCR, World War II. Decorated Purple Heart. Fellow Ohio State Bar, Columbus Bar Assn.; mem. ABA, Am. Judicature Soc., Rocky Fork Headley Hunt Club, Rocky Fork Hunt and Country Club, Capital Club, Phi Delta Phi, Chi Psi. Home: 5826 Havens Corners Rd Columbus OH 43230-3142 Office: Vorys Sater Seymour & Pease PO Box 1008 52 E Gay St Columbus OH 43215-3161

VOS, FRANK, advertising and marketing executive; b. N.Y.C., Dec. 1, 1919; s. George W. and Anna (Lewis) V.; m. Mary C. Dempsey, June 24, 1951; children: George Andrew, Julia Elizabeth. Student, MIT, 1936-37; BA magna cum laude, Columbia U., 1982, MA, 1984, M of Philosophy, 1989. Copywriter firm Schwab & Beatty, N.Y.C., 1941-42, 46-48; sales promotion mgr. Doubleday & Co., N.Y.C., 1948-52; group head Kleppner Co., N.Y.C., 1952-57; founder, chmn. Vos & Co., N.Y.C., 1957, Vos & Co. (became Vos & Reichberg, 1965), Altman, Vos & Reichberg, Inc., 1970-76, Vos & White, Inc., 1976-79, Frank Vos Co. Inc., 1979-85; vis. lectr. NYU, 1961, 73, 75; chmn. Direct Mktg. Day, N.Y., 1972; spl. cons. dean Columbia U., 1983; instr. U. Conn., Stamford, 1986. Mem. adv. bd. The Ency. of N.Y.C. Bd. dirs. Stamford (Conn.) Symphony Soc., 1981-89. 1st lt. inf. AUS, World War II, ETO. Decorated Bronze Star U.S.; Knight's Cross Crown of Italy; recipient Silver Apple award N.Y.C. Direct Mktg. Club, 1985. Mem. Am. Hist. Assn., Orgn. Am. Historians, Urban History Soc., Lotos Club of N.Y.C. (chmn. lit. com. 1965-73, dir. 1971-79, admissions com. 1985—, Medal of Merit 1993), Stamford (Conn.) Yacht Club, Silvermine Golf Club (Conn.), Phi Beta Kappa. Home: 49 Whitmore Stamford CT 06902

VOS, GAIL ANN, talented and gifted educator; b. Dearborn, Mich., Feb. 27, 1956; d. Donald Parker and Marion I. (Brush) Mitchell; m. Bruce Everett Vos, June 26, 1977; children: Bryan Parker Vos, Justin Daniel Vos. BS, Ea. Mich. U., 1977; MEd, Wayne State U., 1995. Middle sch. tchr. Trenton (Mich.) Pub. Schs., 1977-79, 2nd grade tchr., 1979-80, learning disabilities resource tchr., 1980-89, sch. dist. tchr. cons., 1989-93, gifted tchr., 1993—; sch. dist. rep. Wayne County Parent Adv. Bd., Romulas, Mich., 1987-90. Cub scout com., chairperson, leader Boy Scouts Am., Trenton, 1988-94; elder, Christian edn. chairperson Presbyn. Ch., Allen Park, Mich., 1980-85. Grantee Wayne County Intermediate Sch. Dist., 1989, 92, 94, Electronic Data Sys., 1992; named Outstanding Educator Trenton Jaycees, 1989-90. Mem. ASCD, Mich. Assn. of Learning Disabilities Educators. Avocations: needlework, reading, travel camping, swimming. Office: Anderson Elem 2600 Harrison Trenton MI 48183

VOS, HUBERT DANIEL, private investor; b. Paris, Aug. 2, 1933; s. Marius and Aline (Porge) V.; m. Susan Hill, Apr. 18, 1958; children: Wendy, James. BA, Institut d'Etudes Politiques, U. Paris, 1954; M in Pub. Adminstrn., Princeton U., 1956. Internal auditor Internat. Packers Ltd., 1957-61, dir. fin., 1962-64; asst. to contr. Monsanto Co., 1964-66, contr. internat. div., 1966-69; v.p. planning and fin. Smith Kline Corp., 1969-72; sr. v.p. fin. Comml. Credit Co., Balt., 1972-74; sr. v.p. fin. and adminstrn., dir. Norton Simon Inc., N.Y.C., 1974-79; sr. v.p. fin., dir. Becton Dickinson and Co., Paramus, N.J., 1979-83; pres. Stonington Capital Corp., Santa Barbara, Calif., 1984—; bd. dirs. Rowe Price New Era Fund Inc., New Horizons Fund Inc., Equity Income Fund Inc., Capital Appreciation Fund, Inc., Sci. and Tech. Fund, Inc., Small Capital Appreciation Fund, Inc., Balanced Fund, Inc., Monarch Health Systems Inc. Bd. dirs. Surg. Eye Expdns. Internat. Mem. Am. Mgmt. Assn. (gen. mgmt. coun.), La Cumbre Golf and Country Club. Home: 800 Via Hierba Santa Barbara CA 93110-2222 Office: 1114 State St Ste 247 Santa Barbara CA 93101-2716

VOS, MORRIS, foreign languages educator, language services consultant; b. Mahaska County, Iowa, Dec. 10, 1944; s. Peter G. and Edith (De Vries) V.; m. Mary Elizabeth Posthuma, Aug. 16, 1966; children: Jeremy, Allison. AB in English and German, Calvin Coll., Grand Rapids, Mich., 1962-66; MA in German, Ind. U., 1968, PhD in German, 1975. Cert. oral proficiency tester in German. Assoc. instr. Ind. U., Bloomington, 1970-71; asst. prof. Western Ill. U., Macomb, 1971-79, assoc. prof., 1979-91, prof. German, 1991—; cons. Ill. State Bd. Edn., Springfield, 1984-87; mem. adv. coun. Cen. States Conf. on Teaching Fgn. Langs., 1980—. Editor: Essays in Literature, 1986-93; contbr. articles to profl. jours. Adult leader Boy Scouts Am., Macomb, 1985-87. Grantee NEH, DAAD, Goethe Inst.; recipient Lt. Gov.'s award State of Ill. for enhancement of profession, 1993. Mem. Am. Assn. Tchrs. German, Am. Coun. on the Tchg. of Fgn. Langs. (charter), Ill. Coun. on the Tchg. of Fgn. Langs., Presbyn. No. Ill. (treas. 1985—). Presbyterian. Avocation: aerobic fitness activities. Home: 456 S Edwards St Macomb IL 61455-3015 Office: Western Ill U Fgn Langs and Lits 1 University Circle Macomb IL 61455-1390

VOSBECK, ROBERT RANDALL, architect; b. Mankato, Minn., May 18, 1930; s. William Frederick and Gladys (Anderson) V.; m. Phoebe Macklin, June 21, 1953; children: Gretchen, Randy, Heidi, Macklin. BArch, U. Minn., 1954. Various archtl. positions, 1956-62; ptnr. Vosbeck-Vosbeck & Assocs., Alexandria, Va., 1962-66, VVKR Partnership, Alexandria, 1966-79; exec. v.p. VVKR Inc., 1979-82, pres., 1982-88; prin. Vosbeck/DMJM, Washington and Alexandria, Va., 1989-94; archtl. cons., 1994—; mem. Nat. Capital Planning Commn., 1976-81, U.S./USSR Joint Group on Bldg. Design and Constrn., 1974-79; mem. Nat. Park System Adv. Bd., 1983-88. Archtl. works include Pub. Safety Ctr., Alexandria, Va., 1987, Yorktown (Va.) Visitors Ctr, 1976, Frank Reeves Mcpl. Office Bldg., Washington, 1986, Fed. Bldg., NOrfolk, Va., 1979, Jeff Davis Assocs. Office Complex, Arlington, Va., 1991, Westminster Continued Care Retirement Community, Lake Ridge, Va., 1993. Served as engr. officer USMC, 1954-56. Recipient Plaque of Honor Fedn. Colegios Architects (Republic of Mexico); named Acadamecian, Internt. Acad. Architecture, hon. fellow Royal Architects of Can., Soc. Architects of Mexico; recipient hons. Collegios Architects Spain, Union Bulgarian Architects. Fellow AIA (bd. dirs. 1976-78, v.p. 1979-80, pres. 1981); mem. Internat. Union Architects (coun. 1981-87), Nat. Trust Hist. Preservation, Alexandria C. of C. (pres. 1974-75). Presbyterian. Home and Office: Unit A 770 Potato Patch Dr Vail CO 81657-4441

VOSBURG, BRUCE DAVID, lawyer; b. Omaha, June 17, 1943; s. Noble Perrin and Dena V. (Ferrari) V.; m. Susan Simpson, May 27, 1972; children—Margaret Amy, Wendy Christine, Bruce David. B.A., U. Notre Dame, 1965, B.S.M.E., 1966; J.D., Harvard U., 1969. Bar: Nebr. 1969, Ill. 1970, U.S. Supreme Ct. 1974. Law clk. U.S. Dist. Ct. Nebr., 1969-70; assoc. Kirkland & Ellis, Chgo., 1970-72; ptnr. Fitzgerald & Schorr, Omaha, 1972—. Pres. Children's Crisis Ctr., 1984-85, bd. dirs., 1981-85; pres. Child Sav. Inst., 1986-88; pres. Omaha Tennis Assn., 1975-76, bd. dirs., 1973-84; pres. Nebr. Tennis Assn., 1976-77; chmn. grievance com. Missouri Valley Tennis Assn., 1978—, mem. exec. com., 1976—; mem. Leadership Omaha, 1979; chmn. bd. dirs. City of Omaha Parks and Recreation, 1985-92; founding dir. Friends of the Parks, 1988—. Fellow Nebr. Bar Found.; mem. ABA, Nebr. Bar Assn. (chmn. securities com.), Omaha Bar Assn. (exec. council 1983-86), Nat. Assn. Bond Attys., Rotary (dir. 1993—), Tau Beta Pi. Republican. Roman Catholic. Author: Financing Small Businesses, 1981, Securities Law Practice, 1987, Securities Law-Going Public, 1989, Trade Secret Protection, 1994. Office: 1000 Woodmen Towers Omaha NE 68102

VOSBURG, NOBLE E., fur company executive; b. Omaha, Aug. 5, 1941; s. N.P. and Dena Vosburg; m. Susan E. Vosburg, Jan. 2, 1965; children—Victoria, Sally, Lindsay. B.S., Iowa State U., 1963; M.A., U. Nebr., 1965. Vice pres. U.S. Nat. Bank, Omaha, 1967-77; sr. v.p. Norwest Bank Great Falls, Mont., 1977-78, dir., 1983—; pres. Pacific Hide & Fur Depot, Great Falls, 1978—; dir. Hardrock Oil Co., Great Falls. Bd. dirs. Mont. Internat. Trade Commn., Helena, 1982—, Deaconess Hosp., Great Falls, 1981-83; ambassador State of Mont., Helena, 1984. Served to 1st lt. U.S. Army, 1963-65; Korea. Mem. Mont. C. of C. (bd. dirs. 1984—). Lodge: Rotary.*

VOSBURGH, FREDERICK GEORGE, writer, editor; b. Johnstown, N.Y., Sept. 16, 1904; s. John Ross and Alice (Baker) V.; m. Doris Kennedy, Jan. 2, 1929 (div. 1948); children: Richard Kennedy, Alan Frederick; m. Valerie Paterson, May 28, 1949. A.B., Syracuse U., 1925; postgrad., George Washington U., 1938-39. Reporter, Syracuse (N.Y.) Jour., 1922-24; Reporter Syracuse Post-Standard, 1925-26, AP, N.Y.C. and Washington, 1927-33; joined editorial staff Nat. Geog. Mag., 1933, asst. editor, 1951-56, sr. asst. editor, 1956, asso. editor, 1957-67, editor, 1967-70. Author numerous articles in various fields. Served to lt. col. USAAF, 1942-45, overseas. Recipient Bronze Star, Air Medal. Mem. Nat. Geog. Soc. (v.p. 1958-70, trustee 1962-79, trustee emeritus 1979—), Phi Beta Kappa. Club: Nat. Press. Home: 8500 W Howell Rd Bethesda MD 20817-6827

VOSBURGH, MARGARET MURPHY, hospital administrator; b. Aug. 29, 1948; d. John Joseph and Rita (Ryan) Murphy. Diploma, St. Clare's Hosp., 1971; BSN, Mount Saint Mary Coll., 1976; MS in Nursing, Russell Sage Coll., 1979; MBA, U. So. Calif., 1989. Dir. nursing Albany (N.Y.) Med. Ctr. Hosp., 1976-86; dir. nursing svc. Cedars-Sinai Med. Ctr., L.A., 1986-89; v.p. nursing svcs. Hoag Meml. Hosp., Newport Beach, Calif., 1989-92; v.p. patient care svcs. Hosp. of Good Samaritan, L.A., 1992-93; assoc. exec. dir. Swedish Health Sys., Seattle, 1993—. Wharton Fellow, 1983; recipient Fed. Traineeship award for Grad. Studies in Nursing. Mem. ANA, Am. Orgn. Nurse Execs., Orgn. Nurse Execs. Calif., Sigma Theta Tau.

VOSE, ROBERT CHURCHILL, JR., former art gallery executive; b. Boston, Mar. 30, 1911; s. Robert Churchill and Sarah Helen (Williams) V.; m. Ann Peterson, Mar. 8, 1941; children: Robert Churchill III, Abbot Williams. Student, Harvard, 1930-32. With Vose Galleries of Boston, Inc., 1932-85, treas., 1953-85, pres., 1976-80, chmn., 1980-85; ret., 1985; mem. Friends of Art, Boston U., 1957-59, Friends of Art, Colby Coll., 1959-89. Contbr. articles to profl. jours. Chmn. Community Fund drive, Dedham, Mass., 1952. Fellow Pilgrim Soc. (life); mem. Copley Soc. (dir. 1950-53, Copley medal 1987), Back Bay Assn. (v.p. 1958, dir. 1964-66), New Eng. Hist. Geneal. Soc. (coun. 1958-77, pres. 1971-74, trustee emeritus 1985—), Dedham Hist. Soc. (corr. sec. 1958), Boston Mus. Fine Arts, Bostonian Soc. (life), Albany Inst. History and Art, Conn. Hist. Soc., Duxbury Rural and Hist. Soc. (exec. com.), N.Y. State Hist. Assn., Mass. Hist. Soc. (chmn. house com., chmn. art com.), Colonial Soc. Mass., Back Bay Coun., Pilgrim Soc. (trustee 1992—), Neighbourhood Assn. Back Bay (dir. 1964-66), Plimouth Plantation, Harvard Club (Boston), Algonquin Club (Boston), Somerset Club (Boston). Republican. Unitarian (chmn. parish com. 1941). Address: 394 King Caesar Rd Duxbury MA 02332-3919

VOSKOGLOU, MICHAEL GREGORY, mathematical sciences educator; b. Mytilene, Greece, May 12, 1949; s. Gregory Michael and Xanthi George (Kambadellis) V.; m. Angela Loukas Kakoliris, Aug. 26, 1973; children: Gregory, Xanthi. Degree, U. Salonica, Greece, 1972; MSc, U. Leeds, United Kingdom, 1978; PhD, U. Patras, Greece, 1982. Tchr. math. Ministry of Edn., Patras, Greece, 1972-87, tchrs. educator, 1983-90; prof. math. Technol. Ednl. Inst., Patras, 1983-88; prof. math. scis. Technol. Ednl. Inst., Mesolongi, Greece, 1987—; dir. high sch. Ministry of Edn., Patras, 1983-87; v.p. rsch. com. Technol. Ednl. Inst., Mesolongi, 1990-95, dir. Sch. Adminstrn. and Econs., 1995—. Author: Mathematics for Administration and Economics, 1995; contbr. articles to profl. jours. Recipient Student's scholarship Greek Ministry of Edn., 1969-72; Rsch. fellow NATO, 1977-80. Mem. Greek Math. Soc. (adminstrn. com. 1982-84, gen. sec. 1996—), Assn. Teaching Staff Technol. Ednl. Inst., Prof's. Assn. Technol. Ednl. Inst.

Christian Orthodox. Avocations: jogging, weight lifting, swimming, football (soccer), chess. Home: Ag Saranda 6-8, 262 22 Patras Greece Office: Technol Ednl Inst, Nea Ktiria, 30 200 Mesolongi Greece

VOSS, BARRY VAUGHAN, lawyer; b. St. Paul, July 25, 1952; s. James Lee and Stella Marie (Stewart) V.; m. Marilyn Williams, Jan. 25, 1980; children: Rori, Tiffini, Aaron. BA, U. Minn., 1975; JD, Hamline U., 1978. Bar: Minn. 1978, U.S. Dist. Ct. Minn. 1980, U.S. Ct. Appeals (8th cir.) 1982. Pres. Voss, Goetz & Hickman, P.A., Mpls., 1978—; seminar speaker on drug induced robbery Bloomington, Minn. Police Dept., 1990. Bd. dirs. Ramsey County Corrections Adv. Bd., St. Paul, 1977-79. Recipient Most Well-Prepared award Minn. Lawyers Judges' Choice, 1991. Mem. Am. Trial Lawyers Assn., Minn. Assn. Criminal Def. Attys. (bd. dirs. 1992—), Minn. Trial Lawyers Assn., Minn. State Bar Assn. (civil litigation sect.), Hennepin County Bar Assn. Democrat. Lutheran. Avocations: public speaking, sports, reading. Office: Voss Goetz & Hickman PA 527 Marquette Ave S Ste 840 Minneapolis MN 55402-1301

VOSS, EDWARD WILLIAM, JR., immunologist, educator; b. Chgo., Dec. 2, 1933; s. Edward William and Lois Wilma (Graham) V.; m. Virginia Hellman, June 15, 1974; children: Cathleen, Valerie. A.B., Cornell Coll., Iowa, 1955; M.S., Ind. U., 1964, Ph.D., 1966. Asst. prof. microbiology U. Ill., Urbana, 1967-71; assoc. prof. U. Ill., 1971-74, prof., 1974—, dir. cell sci. ctr., 1988-94, LAS Jubilee prof., 1990; mem. rev. panel USDA on molecular biology-gene structure, Washington, 1985, 86, U.S. Dept. of Energy Rsch., 1994; panel mem. in biol. scis. NSF Minority Grad. Fellowships, Washington, 1986, 87, 88; mem. sci. adv. bd. Biotech. Rsch. and Devel. Corp., 1989—; mem. Peer Review Com. AHA, 1993-96. Author, editor: Fluorescein Hapten: An Immunological Probe, 1984, Anti-DNA Antibodies in SLE, 1988; adv. editor: Immunochemistry, 1975-78, Molecular Immunology, 1980—; mem. editorial bd.: Applied and Environ. Microbiology, 1979—; contbr. articles to profl. jours. Apptd. to pres.'s coun. U. Ill. Found., 1995. Served with U.S. Army, 1956-58. NIH fellow, 1966-67, NSF fellow, 1975-77; NIH grantee, 1967—, NSF grantee, 1967—; recipient Disting. Lectr. award U. Ill., 1983; named 1st James R. Martin Univ. scholar, 1994. Fellow Am. Inst. Chemists; mem. AAAS, Fedn. Am. Scientists, Am. Assn. Immunologists, Am. Assn. Biol. Chemists, Reticuloendothelial Soc., Am. Lupus Soc. (hon. bd. dirs. Cen. Ill. chpt. 1986—, named to Nat. Lupus Hall of Fame 1988), N.Y. Acad. Scis., U.S. Pharmacopeial Conv., Inc., Nat. Geog. Soc., Am. Chem. Soc. (tour speaker 1984-87), Protein Soc., Sigma Xi. Home: 2207 Boudreau Cir Urbana IL 61801-6601 Office: U Ill Dept Microbiology 131 Burrill Hall Urbana IL 61801 *Perserverance, determination and sacrifice only when coupled to appropriate goals in basic research and teaching yield results that justify the effort and commitment.*

VOSS, JACK DONALD, international business consultant, lawyer; b. Stoughton, Wis., Sept. 24, 1921; s. George C. and Grace (Tusler) V.; m. Mary Josephine Edgarton, May 7, 1955; children: Julia, Jennifer, Andrew, Charles. Ph.B., U. Wis., 1943; J.D., Harvard U., 1948. Bar: Ill. 1949, Ohio 1963. From assoc. to ptnr. Sidney & Austin predecessor firm, Chgo., 1948-62; gen. counsel Anchor Hocking Corp., Lancaster, Ohio, 1962-67, v.p., gen. counsel, 1967-72, gen. mgr. internat., 1970-86; pres. Anchor Hocking Internat. Corp., Lancaster, 1972-86; mng. ptnr. Voss Internat., Lancaster, 1986—; chmn. Internat. Coun. Conf. bd., 1985-87. Mem. Fairfield County Rep. Ctrl. and Exec. Com.; pres. Fairfield Heritage Assn., 1966-69; v.p. Lancaster Community Concert Assn., 1965-73; trustee, chmn. Ohio Info. Com. With USNR, 1943-46, ATO, MTO, PTO. Mem. ABA (internat. law & practice and bus. law sects.), Ohio Bar Assn. (chmn. corp. counsel sect. 1966), Columbus Bar Assn., Chgo. Bar Assn., Fairfield County Bar Assn., Licensing Execs. Soc., Am. Arbitration Assn. (panel mem.), Ctr. for Internat. Comml. Arbitration (panel mem.), Harvard Law Sch. Assn., Ohio Mfrs. Assn. (trustee, v.p. 1970-72), Symposiarch, Alpha Chi Rho. Lutheran. Clubs: Rotary (pres. Lancaster 1968), Racquet (Chgo.); Landsdowne (London). Home: 3375 Cincinnati-Zane Rd Lancaster OH 43130 Office: Voss Internat 212 S Broad St Lancaster OH 43130-4305

VOSS, JAMES FREDERICK, psychologist, educator; b. Chgo., Dec. 5, 1930; s. Leo Carl and Lydia (Isreal) V.; m. Marilyn Lydia Timm, June 20, 1953 (dec. Oct. 1982); children: Barbara Lynn, Katherine Ann, Mark Frederick, Carol Jean, David James; m. Deborah Jane Steinbach, Oct. 8, 1988; 1 child, Regina Lynn. B.A., Valparaiso (Ind.) U., 1952; M.S., U. Wis., 1954, Ph.D., 1956. Instr., asst. prof. Wis. State Coll., Eau Claire, 1956-58; asst. prof., assoc. prof. Coll. of Wooster, Ohio, 1958-63; asso. prof. U. Pitts., 1963-66, prof., 1966—, chmn. dept. psychology, 1968-70, assoc. dir. Learning Rsch. and Devel. Ctr., 1985-92; prin. investigator Nat. Inst. Child Health and Human Devel., 1956-58, 59-70; Fulbright Disting. prof., lectr., USSR, 1979; NSF fellow Ind. U., 1960; vis. prof. U. Wis., 1964; vis. prof., NIMH spl. fellow U. Calif., Irvine, 1970—; vis. prof. Mershon Ctr., Ohio State U., 1989. Author: Psychology as a Behavioral Science, 1974; editor: Approaches to Thought, 1969, Topics in Human Performance, 1972, Informal Reasoning and Education, 1990; cons. editor: Jour. Exptl. Psychology, 1975-80, Jour. Verbal Learning and Verbal Behavior, 1981-87. Recipient Disting. Alumni award Valparaiso U., 1979. Fellow Am. Psychol. Assn., AAAS; mem. Midwestern, Eastern psychol. assns., AAAS, N.Y. Acad. Sci., Psychonomic Soc. (sec.-treas. 1978-80), Am. Diabetes Assn. (chmn. bd. Western Pa. affiliate 1974-77, 173-75), Internat. Soc. Political Psychology, Sigma Xi. Home: 115 Glen David Dr Pittsburgh PA 15238-1513

VOSS, JAMES LEO, veterinarian; b. Grand Junction, Colo., Apr. 17, 1934; s. Edward John and Ruth I. (Michele) V.; m. Kathleen Alice Claxton, Dec. 19, 1954; children: Edward Duane, William David, Laura Jean. DVM, Colo. State U., 1958, MS, 1965. Instr. Colo. State U., Ft. Collins, 1958-60, asst. prof., 1960-66, assoc. prof., 1966-72, prof., 1972—, dept. head of clin. scis., 1974-86, dean coll. vet. medicine, biomedical scis., 1986—; cons. various horse breeding farms nationally and internationally, 1958—. Mem. AVMA (ho. of dels. 1986-89), Am. Assn. Equine Practioner (v.p. 1987, pres. 1989), Colo. Vet. Med. Assn. (pres. 1971), Nat. Swine Repopulation Assn. (bd. dirs. 1983-87), Am. Soc. Animal Sci. (editorial bd. 1983-87). Republican. Avocations: hunting, fishing. Home: 15240 West Co Rd 74E Livermore CO 80536 Office: Colo State U Coll Vet Med & Biomed Scis Office of the Dean Fort Collins CO 80523

VOSS, JERROLD RICHARD, city planner, educator, university official; b. Chgo., Nov. 4, 1932; s. Peter Walter and Annis Lorraine (Hayes) V.; m. Jean Evelyn Peterson, Aug. 21, 1954; children—Cynthia Jean, Tania Hayes. B.Arch., Cornell U., 1955; M. City Planning, Harvard U., 1959; Ph.D. (Bus. History fellow, Univ. fellow, IBM fellow), 1971. Asst. prof. U. Calif., 1960-61; asst. prof., asso. prof. U. Ill., 1961-69; asso. prof. Harvard U., 1969-71; prof. city and regional planning Ohio State U., Columbus, 1971—; chmn. dept. city and regional planning Ohio State U., 1971-79; dir. Ohio State U. (Knowlton Sch. Architecture), 1981—; UN advisor to Govt. Indonesia, 1964-65; social affairs officer UN Secretariat, 1970-71; project mgr. UN Task Force on Human Environment, Thailand, 1975-76; dir. rsch. and devel. UN Ctr. for Human Settlements (Habitat), 1979-81; cons. Ill. Dept. Devel., J.S. Bolles & Assocs., UN Office Tech. Cooperation, UN Devel. Program, AID, Bechtel Nat. Inc., other pvt. and pub. orgns.; mem. external examiners team United Arab U., 1992—. Author: Human Settlements: Problems and Priorities; Contbr. articles to profl. jours. Mem. pub. policy com. Smithsonian Instn., 1970-73; bd. dirs. Champaign County United Community Council, 1965-69, Columbus Theatre Ballet Assn., 1972-75. Served to 1st lt. U.S. Army, 1955-57. Mem. Acad. for Contemporary Problems (asso.), Am. Am. Inst. Planners, Am. Soc. Engring. Edn., Internat. Center for Urban Land Policy (London). Office: 190 W 17th Ave Columbus OH 43210-1320

VOSS, KATHERINE EVELYN, international management consultant; b. Cleve., Sept. 2, 1957; d. Wendell Grant and Ann Terry (Miller) Voss; m. James Everett Mathias, Oct. 6, 1984 (div. Dec. 1988). BS, Bowling Green State U., 1979, MBA, 1981. Sci. systems analyst Eli Lilly & Co., Indpls., 1981-83, systems tng. cons., 1983-84; customer liaison mgr. Ind. U., Bloomington, 1985; prodn. ops. mgr. Ind. U., Indpls., 1985-86; prin. systems cons. Wang Labs., Inc., Carmel, Ind., 1986-93; mgmt. cons. AMT-Sybex (I) Ltd., Dublin, 1994—; cons. Ind. Univ., Bloomington, 1984-85, Allied Irish Bank, Dublin, Ireland, 1990-91. Contbr. (book) Introduction to Business, 1980, Introduction to Accounting, 1981, Computers and Data Processing, 1981. Presidental advisor Jr. Achievement, Indpls., 1982-83; pres. PEO Chpt. AM, Indpls., 1987-89, Irish rep., 1995—. Mem. Assn. for Image and Info. Mgmt., Irish Computer Soc., Beta Beta Beta. Republican. Presbyterian. Avocations: scuba diving, photography, biking, crafts. Home: Hill Cottage, Brennanstown Rd Cabinteely, Dublin 18, Ireland Office: AMT-Sybex (I) Ltd, Elm House, Leopardstown Office Park, Foxrock Dublin 18, Ireland

VOSS, OMER GERALD, truck company executive; b. Downs, Kans., Sept. 14, 1916; s. John and Grace (Bohlen) V.; m. Annabelle Katherine Lutz, June 20, 1940; children—Jerrol Ann, Omer Gerald. A.B., Ft. Hays (Kans.) State Coll., 1937; J.D., U. Kans., 1939. Bar: Kans. bar 1939. With Internat. Harvester Co., 1936-79, v.p. farm equipment div., 1962-66, exec. v.p., dir., 1966—, vice chmn., 1977-79. Served with USAAF, 1943-46. Clubs: Chicago, Commercial, Westmoreland Country.

VOSS, REGIS DALE, agronomist, educator; b. Cedar Rapids, Iowa, Jan. 4, 1931; s. Francis Joseph and Mary Valeria (Womichil) V.; m. Margaret Anne Mitchell, Nov. 24, 1956; children: Lori Anne, John Patrick, David James. BS, Iowa State U., 1952, PhD, 1962. cert. profl. agronomist. Agriculturist Tenn. Valley Authority, Muscle Shoals, Ala., 1962-64; prof. Iowa State U., Ames, 1964--; bd. dirs. fertilizer adv. Farmland Industries, Kansas City, Mo. Co-author: (chpt.) Sulfur in Agriculture, 1986, Organic Farming, 1984; assoc. editor Jour. Prodn. Agr., 1988-92. Pres. FarmHouse Frat. Alumni Assn. Bd., Ames, 1990. 1st lt. USAF, 1952-56, Korea. Recipient Agronomic Extension Edn. award Am. Soc. Agronomy, 1984, Agronomic Achievement award Am. Soc. Agronomy, 1989, Werner L. Nelson award Am. Soc. Agronomy, 1992, Burlington No. Found. award Iowa State U., 1990, Faculty Citation Iowa State U., 1992. Fellow AAAS, Am. Soc. Agronomy (bd. dirs. 1976-78), Soil Sci. Soc. Am. (bd. dirs. 1980-83). Republican. Roman Catholic. Achievements include development of field laboratory for training of crop advisors on diagnosis of crop problems; research on effects of soil amendments on chemical indices and crop yields and economic analysis of crop yield response to soil amendments. Office: Iowa State Univ Agronomy Hall Ames IA 50011

VOSS, WILLIAM CHARLES, retired oil company executive; b. Buffalo, Sept. 22, 1937; s. William T. and Dorathea S. (Grotke) V.; m. Marilyn Erickson, Sept. 6, 1958; children: William, John, Douglas. AB with honors, Harvard U., 1959, MBA with honors, 1961. With Northwestern Refining Co., St. Paul Park, 1961-70; v.p. adminstrn. Northwestern Refining Co., 1969-71; with Ashland Oil Inc., Ky., 1971-89, v.p., 1973-79, adminstrv. v.p., 1979-80, sr. v.p., group operating officer, 1980-89; pres. Ashland-Warren Inc., 1979-83, APAC, Inc., 1980-82, 83-86. Mem. Am. Chem. Soc. Republican. Home: 2660 Peachtree Rd NW Atlanta GA 30305-3673

VOTAW, JOHN FREDERICK, educational foundation executive, educator; b. Richmond, Va., May 9, 1939; s. Frederick Lee and Katherine (B.) V.; m. Joyce Marie Miller, June 8, 1961; children: Laura, Cynthia, Mary, John Jr. BS, U.S. Mil. Acad., 1961; MA in History, U. Calif., Davis, 1969; grad., U.S. Army Colls., 1970, 85; PhD in History, Temple U., 1991. Commd. 2d lt. U.S. Army, 1961, advanced through grades to lt. col., 1976; comdr. Company C 1st bn. 69th Armor U.S. Army, Hawaii, 1964-65; comdr. Troop A 1st Squadron 11th ACR U.S. Army, South Vietnam, 1966-67; comdr. C&C Squadron 11th ACR U.S. Army, Fulda, Germany, 1975-77; asst. prof. history U.S. Mil. Acad., West Point, N.Y., 1970-73, asst. dean for plans and programs, 1980-81, asst. prof., 1981-82; dep. dir. U.S. Army Mil. History Inst., Carlisle Barracks, Pa., 1983-86; ret. U.S. Army, 1986; dir. First Divsn. Mus., Wheaton, 1986—; exec. dir. Cantigny First Divsn. Found., Wheaton, 1991—; adj. asst. prof. history Rosary Coll., River Forest, Ill., 1991—; dir. Col. Robt. R. McCormick Rsch. Ctr., Wheaton, 1991—; series editor Cantigny Mil. History Series. Contbg. author: The D-Day Ency., 1993, The Ency. of Am. Wars - The First World War, 1994, The European Powers in the First World War: An Ency., 1996, A Guide to the Study and Use of Military History, 1979; contbr. articles to profl. jours. Decorated Legion of Merit, Bronze Star with "V" device, Purple Heart (3 awards) and others. Mem. Am. Hist. Assn., Orgn. Am. Historians, Soc. for Mil. History, Am. Assn. Mus., U.S. Naval Inst. (life), U.S. Army War Coll. Alumni Assn. (life), Ret. Officers Assn. (life), Assn. Grads. U.S. Mil. Acad., U. Calif. Davis Alumni Assn. (life), Kiwanis (Wheaton club 1986—, pres. 1991-92), Phi Alpha Theta, Phi Kappa Phi (life). Avocations: reading, writing, classical music, golf. Office: First Divsn Mus at Cantigny 1 S 151 Winfield Rd Wheaton IL 60187-6097

VOTH, DOUGLAS W., academic dean. Exec. dean U. Okla. Coll. Medicine, Oklahoma City. Office: U Okla Coll Medicine PO Box 26901 Rm 357-BMSB Oklahoma City OK 73190

VOTOLATO, ARTHUR NICHOLAS, JR., judge; b. Providence, Aug. 20, 1930; s. Arthur N. and Mary (Tavani) V.; children: Dacia Lorraine, Hera Lisbeth; m. Janice Greene. BA, U. R.I., 1953; LLB, Boston U., 1956. Bar: R.I. 1956, U.S. Dist. Ct. R.I. 1956. Ptnr. Votolato & Votolato, Providence, 1956-62; chief spl. counsel R.I. Dept. Pub. Works, Providence, 1962-68; judge U.S. Bankruptcy Ct., Dist. R.I., Providence, 1968—; chief judge First Cir. Bankruptcy Appellate Panel, Mass. Panel; mem. Adv. Com. to Adminstrv. Office of U.S. Cts., 1988—; mem. faculty Roger Williams Coll., N.E. Bankruptcy Law Inst.; program speaker Bankruptcy Litigation and Practice Seminar. Republican candidate for R.I. Atty. Gen., 1962; bd. dirs. Urban League R.I., 1975-80, Ocean State Marathon Com., 1979-83; trustee U. R.I. Found., 1984-92. With USAF, 1951-52. Fellow Am. Coll. Bankruptcy; mem. R.I. Bar Assn., Fed. Bar Assn., Nat. Conf. Bankruptcy Judges (liason com., fed. cts. study com, gov. 1st cir.), Boston U. Alumni Assn., Aircraft Owners and Pilots Assn. Digest editor Am. Bankruptcy Law Jour., 1977-83, mem. editorial adv. bd., 1977-89; digest editor Bankruptcy Law Jour. Office: US Bankruptcy Ct 380 Westminster Mall The Federal Ctr Rm 619 Providence RI 02903

VOWELL, JACK C., former state legislator, investor; b. May 9, 1927; s. Jack C. and Daurice (McDaniel) V.; m. Mary Johnson, Apr. 19, 1957; 1 child, Janice Vowell Alexander. BS in Fgn. Svc., Georgetown U., 1948, MS in Fgn. Svc., 1952; MA in History, Tex. Western Coll., 1952; postgrad., Harvard U., 1953-55. Mem. faculty Sch. Fgn. Svcs. Georgetown U., Washington, 1948-49, U. Tex., El Paso, 1955-60; exec. v.p. Vowell Constrn. Co., El Paso, 1962-69, pres., chmn. bd., 1969-73; rep. Tex. Ho. of Reps., Austin, 1980-95, mem. numerous coms. 68th to 73rd legis., 1980-95; personal investor, 1973—; chmn. Tex. sunset commn., 1987-89. Pres. Yucca Coun., Boy Scouts Am., 1972-74, mem. adv. bd., 1987-92, adv. bd. we. region, 1993—; bd. dirs. South Ctrl. region, 1973-86, mem. adv. bd., 1987—, nat. coun., 1971-87; mem. adv. bd. Hotel Dieu Hosp., 1974-87; adv. dir. Tex. Art Alliance, 1981-83; bd. dirs. Goodwill Industries of El Paso, 1973-77, El Paso Indsl. Devel. Corp., 1962-82; pres. El Paso Hist. Soc., 1957-59, assoc. editor Password, 1962-64; chmn. pers. com. El Paso Pub. Libr. Sys., 1969-74, bd. dirs., 1969-74; adminstrv. adv. bd. City of El Paso, 1973-74; coun. state policy and planning agencies, 1989-92; adv. comm., 1985-89; Tex. coun. on disabilities, 1984-85; state coun. on child abuse, 1984-85. With U.S. Army, 1946-47. Recipient City of El Paso Conquistador award, 1967, 73, Goodwill Industries of El Paso Outstanding Svc. award to Handicapped Workers, 1972, Disting. Eagle award Boy Scouts Am., 1972, Silver Beaver award, 1973, Silver Antelope award, 1983, Tex. Assn. for Marriage and Family Therapy Recognition cert., 1982, U. Tex. El Paso Coll of Edn. Clin. Programs Assistance award, 1985, award for Commitment to Reshaping and Improvement of Svcs. MHMR, 1985, Texans for Children Support for Needy Children, 1985, U. Tex. El Paso Spl. Edn. commendation for Spl. Achievement Autism Program, 1985, Coalition of Texas with Disabilities Pub. Servant of Yr. award, 1985, Anti-Defamation League of El Paso Torch of Liberty award, 1985, Tex. Network of Youth Svcs. Outstanding Youth award, 1987, Nat. Coun. of State Human Svcs. Adminstrs. Nat. commendation, 1987, Disting. Svc. Award Tex. Assn. Deaf, 1987, Am. Public Welfare Assn. Nat. Recognition of Statesmanship in Tex. Ho. Reps., 1987, Better Life award Tex. Health Care Assn., 1987, Legis. Excellence award Tex. Health Care Assn., 1987, United Way of El Paso vol. of the year award, 1988, Am. Coll. of Health Care Adminstrs. Tex. chpt. award, 1988, award for contbn. developmentally delayed and at risk infants, 1988, 94, Tex. Head Injury Legislative award, 1991, Legis. award Tex. Rehab. Assn., 1991, Rio Grande Coun. Govt. Legislative Leadership in Human Svcs. award, 1992, Helen Farabee Leadership award Tex. Perinatal Assn., 1992, Friend of Child award Tex. Coalition Juvenile Justice, 1993, Alviane NO-AD, Public Svc. award, 1993, Unite El Paso Appreciation award, 1993, Gran Paseño award U. Tex. El Paso, 1994, Good Hands award Tex. Dept. Transp., 1994. Mem. El Paso C. of C. (bd. dirs. 1962-69), Rotary (bd. dirs. 1967-68, pres. 1968, Disting. Svc. award 1988). Republican. Episcopalian.

VOWLES, RICHARD BECKMAN, literature educator; b. Fargo, N.D., Oct. 5, 1917; s. Guy Richard and Ella (Beckman) V.; m. Ellen Noah Hudson, Aug. 1, 1942 (div. 1969); children: Elizabeth Ellen, Richard Hudson. B.S., Davidson Coll., 1938; postgrad., U. N.C., 1938-39, U. Stockholm, 1939-40; M.A., Yale U., 1942, Ph.D., 1950. Engr. Hercules Powder Co., Wilmington, Chattanooga, 1941-43; chemist Rohm & Haas, Knoxville, Tenn., 1943-44; econ. cons. War Dept., 1944; Am. vice consul Gothenburg, Sweden, 1945-46; asst. prof. English Southwestern U., Memphis, 1948-50, Queens U., N.Y.C., 1950-51; asso. prof. English U. Fla., 1951-60; prof. Scandinavian and comparative lit. U. Wis., Madison, 1960-85; prof. emeritus U. Wis., 1985—, chmn. comparative lit., 1962-63, 64-67, 71-72, chmn. Scandinavian studies, 1977-80; Am. specialist in Scandinavia Dept. State, summer 1963; vis. prof. N.Y.U., summer 1964, U. Helsinki, Finland, spring 1968, Stockholm, 1969; lectr., Sydney, Australia, 1975, Paris, 1975; master ceremonies Santa Fe Scandinavian Film Festival, 1984. Editor: Eternal Smile, 1954, Dramatic Theory, 1956, Comparatists at Work, 1968; Adv. editor: Nordic Council Series, 1965-70, Herder Ency. of World Lit; contbr. articles to profl. jours. Am.-Scandinavian Found. fellow Stockholm, 1939-40, Lassen fellow Am. Scandinavian Found., 1986; Fulbright fellow Copenhagen, 1955-56; Strindberg fellow Stockholm, 1973; Swedish govt. research award, 1978; Norwegian Govt. fellow, summer 1978. Mem. Modern Lang. Assn., Soc. Advancement Scandinavian Study (mem. exec. com.), Internat. Comparative Lit. Assn., Am. Comparative Lit. Assn. (adv. bd.), Strindberg Soc., Phi Beta Kappa. Home: 1115 Oak Way Madison WI 53705-1420

VOYLES, BARBARA JEAN, social worker, consultant; b. Desloge, Mo., Aug. 14, 1938; d. Walter Edward and Glena Mae (Moyer) V. AA, Flat River Jr. Coll., 1959; BS, Mo. Valley Coll., 1968; MSW, Washington U., 1980. Cert. tchr., Mo.; lic. clin. social worker, Mo. Social worker Family Svcs. Div. State of Mo., St. Genevieve, 1960-66; nurse Mo. Valley Health Svcs., Marshall, Mo., 1966-68, Fitzgibbon Hosp., Marshall, 1966-68; tchr. sci. Farmington (Mo.) Sch. Dist., 1968-72; tchr., sch. nurse, counselor R 14 Sch. Dist., Lonedell, Mo., 1972-75; social worker, clinician Family Svcs. Div. State of Mo., St. Louis, 1975-93; dir. social svcs. Mineral ARea Regional Med. Ctr., Farmington, Mo., 1993—; pvt. practice therapy, St. Louis, 1975—; cons. juvenile ct., St. Louis, 1980—, State of Mo. Licensing Bd., 1994; social worker home health, 1995. Contbr. articles to profl. jours., books. Mem. NASW, Acad. Cert. Social Workers, Mo. Assn. Social Workers, Mo. Assn. Prevention Adult Abuse, St. Louis County Juvenile Justice Assn., Washington U. alumni Assn., Order Ea. Star. Avocations: reading, drawing, painting, photography, sewing. Home: 309 Sycamore Desloge MO 63601 Office: Mineral Area Regional Med Ctr 1212 Weber Rd Farmington MO 63640-3309

VRABLE, JOHN BERNARD, oil and natural gas corrosion engineer, consultant; b. Greensburg, Pa., Sept. 24, 1929; s. John Joseph and Elizabeth Dorothy (Zubach) V.; m. Marjorie Ann Peters, Jan. 29, 1950 (div. 1990); children: John, Kathleen, Elizabeth, Michael, David; m. Rose Marie Wilkins, Aug. 16, 1990. BS in Petroleum Engring., U. Pitts., 1957. Engr. N.Y. State Natural Gas Co., Pitts., 1951-61; regional engr. Cathodic Protection Svc., Houston, 1961-63; rsch. cons. U.S. Steel Corp., Monroeville, Pa., 1963-86; sr. cons. engr. Harco Corp., Medina, Ohio, 1986-87; mgr. standards, quality assurance CNG Transmission Corp., Clarksburg, W.Va., 1987-94; ret., 1994; prin. investigator Nat. Coop. Hwy. Rsch. Program, Monroeville, 1977-80; adv. bridge corr. Fed. Hwy. Adminstrn., Washington, 1978-80; cons. USS Engrs. and Cons., Pitts., 1980-86; mem. pipeline rsch. com. Am. Gas Assn., Washington, 1989-94. 3 patents in field; contbr. articles to profl. jours. and chpts. to books. Recipient Rsch. Achievement award U.S. Steel Rsch., 1972, Spl. Recognition award Steel Tank Inst., Chgo., 1980, Appalachian Underground Corrosion Short Course Col. George C. Cox Outstanding award, 1995. Mem. Elks, Am. Assn. Ret. Persons. Republican. Roman Catholic. Home: 14031 W Horizon Dr Sun City West AZ 85375-2098

VRABLIK, EDWARD ROBERT, import/export company executive; b. Chgo., June 8, 1932; s. Steven Martin and Meri (Korbel) V.; m. Bernice G. Germer, Jan. 25, 1958; children: Edward Robert, II, Scott S. B.S. in Chem. Engring, Northwestern U., 1956; M.B.A., U. Chgo., 1961; postgrad., MIT, 1970. Registered profl. engr., Ill. Dir. indsl. mktg. Eimco Corp., 1956-61; dir. indsl. mktg. and planning Swift & Co., Chgo., 1961-68; v.p., gen. mgr. Swift Chem. Co., Chgo., 1968-73; pres., chief exec. officer Estech Gen. Chems. Corp., Chgo., 1973-86; pres. Kare Internat. Inc., Chgo., 1986—; pres. Julius and Assocs., Inc., Kare Internat., Inc.; bd dirs. Potash Phosphate Inst., Consol. Fertilizers, Ltd.; mem. mgmt. com. Esmark Inc., Korbel, Inc., Mister Lawn Care, Inc. Author. Bd. dirs., v.p. Northwestern U. Tech. Inst.; trustee Future Farmers Am. Mem. Internat. Superphosphate Mfrs. Assn. (dir.), Am. Inst. Chem. Engrs., Fertilizer Inst. (dir.). Lutheran. Clubs: Butler Nat. (Oak Brook, Ill.). Patentee in field. Home: 631 Thompsons Way Palatine IL 60067-4653 Office: 141 W Jackson Blvd Chicago IL 60604-2904

VRADENBURG, GEORGE, III, lawyer. AB cum laude, Oberlin Coll., 1964; LLB cum laude, Harvard U., 1967. Bar: N.Y., 1968. Sr. v.p., gen. counsel, sec. CBS Inc., N.Y.C., 1980-91; exec. v.p. Fox, Inc., L.A., 1991-95; ptnr., co-head entertainment, sports & media industry practice group Latham & Watkins, L.A., 1995—. Mem. Phi Beta Kappa.

VRANA, VERLON KENNETH, professional society administrator, conservationist; b. Seward, Nebr., June 25, 1925; s. Anton and Florence (Walker) V.; m. Elaine Janet Flowerday, June 5, 1949; children: Verlon Rodney, Timothy James, Carolyn Elaine, Jon David. Student, U. Nebr., 1959-62; BBA, George Washington U., 1967, MBA, 1970; mgmt. course, Harvard U., 1979. Field technician Soil Conservation Svc., USDA, Seward, 1948-58; watershed planner, cons. Soil Conservation Svc., USDA, Lincoln, Nebr., 1958-62; mem. pers. staff Soil Conservation Svc., USDA, Washington, 1962-72, dir. pers. div., 1972-76, asst. adminstr. for mgmt., 1976-79, assoc. dep. chief for adminstrn., 1979-80; chief planning div. Nebr. Natural Resources Com., Lincoln, 1980-88; owner-farmer Blue Ridge Farm, Seward, 1980-89; exec. v.p. Soil and Water Conservation Soc., Ankeny, Iowa, 1989-91; pres. Vrana Assocs., Seward, Nebr., 1992—; bd. dirs., sec. N.E. Natural Resources Dist., York, Nebr., 1988-89; bd. dirs. Watershed Coalition, Denver, Groundwater Policy Edn. Project, Mpls., Cattle Nat. Bank, Seward; alt. dir. Renewable Natural Resources Foun., Washington, 1989-91. Contbr. articles to jours. in field. Mem. Com. on Ministry Presbyn. Ch. U.S.A., 1986-89, elder, 1970—; vice moderator Homestead Presbytery, 1989; treas. Nebr. Soil and Water Conservation Found., 1992—. Recipient N.E. Centennial Grass Seeding award N.E. Centennial Commn., Lincoln, 1967, N.E. Soil Steward award N.E. Natural Resources Commn., Lincoln, 1986. Fellow Soil and Water Conservation Soc. (pres. N.E. Coun. 1986, Presdl. citation 1989), Isaac Walton League (dir. Seward chpt. 1984-89), Nat. Wildlife Fedn. (soil conservationist of yr. award 1987), Seward Grange (officer 1984-89, 92—), Shriner. Home and Office: Vrana Assocs 131 N 1st St Seward NE 68434-2130

VRANCKEN, ROBERT DANLOY, facilities planner,designer and educator; b. Charleston, W.Va., June 28, 1936; s. Roger Joseph and Kathryn Elizabeth (Toben) V.; children: Robert, Brett, Paige, Mark. BFA, U. Notre Dame, 1958, MBA, 1984; PhD in Facilities Mgmt., Union Inst., 1992. Cert. facilities mgr. Designer Stone & Thomas, Wheeling, W.Va., 1962-63; pvt. practice in designing Wheeling, W.Va., 1962-63; asst. to pres. Lederman Elevator Co., Detroit, 1963-66; mgr. facilities planning and design Sperry Univac, Blue Bell, Pa., 1966-82; assoc. prof. mgmt. Grand Valley State U., Grand Rapids, Mich., 1982—; cons. space planning facilities design and mgmt., W.Va., Mich., Pa., 1963—; active Ops. Mgmt. Edn. Rsch. Found. Mem. Internat. Facilities Mgmt. Assn. (Educator of Yr. 1986), Nat. Assn. Corp. Real Estate Execs., Work Place Environment Group, Indsl. Devel. Rsch. Coun., Notre Dame Club. Roman Catholic. Avocations: sailing, carpentry, tennis, singing. Office: Grand Valley State U 301 W Fulton St Grand Rapids MI 49504-6430

VRANICAR, MICHAEL GREGORY, lawyer; b. Hammond, Ind., Mar. 11, 1961; s. Melvin G. and Maryann R. (Szarek) V.; m. Marianna C. Livas, May

28, 1994. BSEE, U. Ill., 1983; JD, U. San Diego, 1987. Bar: Calif. 1987, Ill. 1988. Engr. Gen. Dynamics, San Diego, 1983-88; judge advocate USMC, Okinawa, Japan, 1988-91; assoc. Stellato & Schwartz, Chgo., 1992-94; ptnr. Plesha & Vranicar, Chgo., 1995—; arbitrator Cook County Arbitration Bd., Chgo., 1994—; judge retirement competition Nat. Moot Ct., Chgo., 1992. Mem. Ill. State Bar Assn., Chgo. Bar Assn., Okinawa Bench & Bar Assn., Am. Legion. Republican. Roman Catholic. Office: Ste 103 10540 S Western Ave Chicago IL 60643

VRATIL, KATHRYN HOEFER, federal judge; b. Manhattan, Kans., Apr. 21, 1949; d. John J. and Kathryn Ruth (Fryer) Hoefer; children: Alison K., John A., Ashley A. BA, U. Kans., 1971, JD, 1975; postgrad., Exeter U., 1971-72. Bar: Kans. 1975, Mo. 1978, U.S. Dist. Ct. Kans. 1975, U.S. Dist. Ct. (we. dist.) Mo. 1978, U.S. Dist. Ct. (ea. dist.) Mo. 1985, U.S. Ct. Appeals (8th cir.) 1978, U.S. Ct. Appeals (10th cir.) 1980, U.S. Ct. Appeals (11th dist.) 1983, U.S. Supreme Ct., 1995. Law clk. U.S. Dist. Ct., Kansas City, Kans., 1975-78; assoc. Lathrop Koontz & Norquist, Kansas City, Mo., 1978-83; ptnr. Lathrop & Norquist, Kansas City, 1984-92; judge City of Prairie Village, Kans., 1991-92; bd. dirs. Kans. Legal Svcs. Bd. editors Kans. Law Rev., 1974-75, Jour. Kans. Bar Assn., 1992—. Mem. Kansas City Tomorrow (XIV); bd. trustees, shepherd-deacon Village Presbyn. Ch.; nat. adv. bd. U. Kans. Ctr. for Environ. Edn. and Tng., 1993-95. Fellow Kans. Bar Found., Am. Bar Found.; mem. ABA, Am. Judicature Soc., Nat. Assn. Judges, Fed. Judges Assn., Kans. Bar Assn., Mo. Bar Assn., Kansas City Met. Area Bar Assn., Wyandotte County Bar Assn., Johnson County Bar Assn., Assn. Women Lawyers, Lawyers Assn. Kansas City, Supreme Ct. Hist. Soc., Kans. State Hist. Soc., U. Kans. Law Soc. (bd. govs. 1978-81), Kans. U. Alumni Assn. (mem. devel. com. 1985—, mem. Kansas City chpt. alumni bd. 1990-92, nat. bd. dirs. 1991—, bd. govs. Adams alumni ctr. 1992—, pres. 1985-86, membership chair 1983-84, mem. learned club 1992—, mem. chancellor's club 1993—, mem. Williams ednl. fund 1993—, mem. Jayhawks for higher edn. 1993—), Homestead Country Club Prairie Village (pres.), Sons and Daus. of Kans. (life), Rotary, Jr. League Wyandotte and Johnson Countie, Kans. State Hist. Soc., Supreme Ct. Hist. Soc., Order of Coif, Kans. Inn of Ct. (master 1993—), Overland Park Rotary, Univ. Club, Phi Kappa Phi. Republican. Presbyterian. Avocations: cycling, sailing. Office: US Courthouse 511 500 State Ave Kansas City KS 66101-2403

VREDENBURG, DWIGHT CHARLES, retired supermarket chain executive; b. Lamoni, Iowa, Jan. 17, 1914; s. David Milton and Kate Emelyn (Putnam) V.; m. Ruth Irene Taylor, Apr. 25, 1937; children: John, Martha Vredenburg Kraklow, Charles. Student, Graceland Coll., 1931-34, LLD, 1988; BS in Commerce, U. Iowa, 1935. Store mgr. Hy-Vee Food Stores Inc., Chariton, Iowa, 1935-38, pres., from 1938, chief exec. officer, 1978-89; chmn. Hy- Vee Food Stores Inc., Chariton, Iowa, 1978-89; pres. Chariton Storage Co.; pres., dir. Iamo Realty Co. Served with USCGR, 1942-44. Named Citizen of Yr., 1965-66. Mem. Masons, Shriners, Des Moines Club. Home: 1105 Mallory Dr Chariton IA 50049-9804

VREDEVOE, DONNA LOU, research immunologist, microbiologist, educator; b. Ann Arbor, Mich., Jan. 11, 1938; d. Lawrence E. and Verna (Brower) V.; m. John Porter, Aug. 22, 1962; 1 child, Verna. B.A. in Bacteriology, UCLA, 1959, Ph.D. in Microbiology (Univ. fellow, USPHS fellow), 1963. USPHS postdoctoral fellow Stanford U., 1963-64; instr. bacteriology UCLA, 1963, postgrad. research immunologist dept. surgery Center Health Scis., 1964-65, asst. research immunologist dept. surgery Center Health Scis., 1964-67; asst. prof. Sch. Nursing, Center Health Scis., 1967-70, asso. prof., 1970-76, prof., 1976—, asso. dean Sch. Nursing, 1976-78, acting assoc. dean Sch. Nursing, 1985-86, asst. dir. space planning Cancer Center, 1976-78, dir. space planning, 1978-90, cons. to lab. nuclear medicine and radiation biology, 1967-80; acting dean Sch. Nursing Center Health Scis., 1995—. Contbr. articles to profl. publs. Postdoctoral fellow USPHS, 1963-64; Mabel Wilson Richards scholar UCLA, 1960-61; research grantee including Am. Cancer Soc.; Calif. Inst. Cancer Research; Calif. div. Am. Cancer Soc.; USPHS; Am. Nurses Found.; Cancer Research Coordinating Com. U. Calif.; Dept. Energy. Mem Am. Soc. Microbiology, Am. Assn. Immunologists, Am. Assn. Cancer Research, Nat. League Nursing (2d v.p. 1979-81), Sigma Xi, Alpha Gamma Sigma, Sigma Theta Tau (nat. hon. mem.). Home: 355 21st Pl Santa Monica CA 90402-2503 Office: U Calif Sch Nursing Los Angeles CA 90024-6918

VREE, ROGER ALLEN, lawyer; b. Chgo., Oct. 2, 1943; s. Louis Gerard and Ruby June (Boersma) V.; m. Lauren Trumbull Gartside, Mar. 29, 1969; children: Jonathan Todd, Matthew David. BA, Wheaton Coll., 1965; MA, Stanford U., 1966, JD, 1969. Bar: Ill. 1969, U.S. Dist. Ct. (no. dist.) Ill. 1969. Assoc. Sidley & Austin, Chgo., 1969-75, ptnr., 1975—. Mem. ABA, Ill. Bar Assn., Chgo. Bar Assn., Law Club, Legal Club. Club: Caxton Club (Chgo.), University (Chgo.). Office: Sidley & Austin 1 First Nat Plz Chicago IL 60603

VROOM, VICTOR HAROLD, management consultant, educator; b. Montreal, Que., Can., Aug. 9, 1932; s. Harold Heard and Avice May (Brown) V.; m. Ann Louise Workman, June 12, 1956 (div. Jan. 1989); children: Derek Alan, Jeffrey James; m. Julia Ann Francis, Dec. 27, 1989; children: Tristan Alexander. B.Sc., McGill U., Montreal, 1953, M.Sc., 1955; Ph.D., U. Mich., 1958; M.A. (hon.), Yale, 1972. Lectr., study dir. U. Mich., Ann Arbor, 1958-60; asst. prof. psychology U. Pa., Phila., 1960-63; asso. prof. psychology and indsl. adminstrn. Carnegie-Mellon U., Pitts., 1963-66; prof. Carnegie-Mellon U., 1966-72; John G. Searle prof. orgn. and mgmt. Yale U., 1972—. Author: Work and Motivation, 1964, rev. edit. 1995, Leadership and Decision-Making, 1973, The New Leadership, 1988. Recipient Ford Found. Doctoral Dissertation award, 1958-59; McKinsey Found. research design award, 1967; Fulbright lectr. U.K., 1967-68. Fellow APA (James McKeen Cattell award 1970), APS Acad. Mgmt. Office: Yale U PO Box 1A New Haven CT 06520-0001

VUCANOVICH, BARBARA FARRELL, congresswoman; b. Fort Dix, N.J., June 22, 1921; d. Thomas F. and Ynez (White) Farrell; m. Ken Dillon, Mar. 8, 1950 (div. 1964); children: Patty Dillon Cafferata, Mike, Ken, Tom, Susan Dillon Stoddard; m. George Vucanovich, June 19, 1965. Student, Manhattanville Coll. of Sacred Heart, 1938-39. Owner, operator Welcome Aboard Travel, Reno, 1968-74; Nev. rep. for Senator Paul Laxalt, 1974-82; mem. 98th-104th Congresses from 2d Nev. dist., 1983—; chmn. appropriations subcom. on military construction. Pres. Nev. Fedn. Republican Women, Reno, 1955-56; former pres. St. Mary's Hosp. Guild, Lawyer's Wives. Roman Catholic. Club: Hidden Valley Country (Reno). Office: US Ho of Reps 2202 Rayburn Washington DC 20515*

VUCKOVICH, DRAGOMIR MICHAEL, neurologist, educator; b. Bileca, Herzegovina, Yugoslavia, Oct. 27, 1927; came to U.S., 1957; s. Alexander John and Anka Mia (Ivanisevich) V.; m. Brenda Mary Luther, Aug. 23, 1958; children: John, Nicholas, Adrian. M.D., U. Birmingham, Eng., 1953. Diplomate Am. Bd. Psychiatry and Neurology, Am. Bd. Pediatrics. Intern United Birmingham Hosps., Eng., 1953-54, resident in pediatrics, 1954-55; resident med. officer Princess Beatrice Hosp., London, 1955; sr. resident Hosp. for Sick Children, London, 1955; sr. resident in neurology Atkinson Morley br. St. George's Hosp., London, 1955-56; resident in neurology Nat. Hosp. Queens Sq., London, 1956-57, VA Hosp., Chgo., 1958-59; resident in psychiatry Wesley Meml. Hosp., Chgo., 1959-60; fellow in neurology Northwestern U. Med. Sch., Chgo., 1960; resident in pediatrics Children's Meml. Hosp., Chgo., 1961; asst. prof. neurology, psychiatry and pediatrics Northwestern U. Med. Ctr., Chgo., 1967-70; assoc. clin. prof. neurology and pediatrics Stritch Sch. Medicine, Chgo., 1970-77, clin. prof. neurology and pediatrics, 1977-93; chmn. Columbus Hosp., Chgo., 1981-88; chief of neurology svc. N. Chgo. VAMC, 1992-94; prof. neurology and pediatrics Finch U. Health Sch. Chgo. Med. Sch., 1994—; prof. clin. psychiatry Chgo. Med. Sch., 1995—; dir. EEG Lab. Columbus Hosp., Chgo., 1969-89, chief neurology and psychiatry, 1971-81; chief of child neurology Loyola U., Maywood, Ill., 1970-79; cons. Trinity House, 1988-92; acting chmn. neurology FUHS/CMS, 1993—; program dir. neurology residency program FUHS/CMS affiliated hosp., 1993—. Co-author: Psychoanalysis and the Two Cerebral Hemispheres, 1983; contbr., co-contbr. articles in field to profl. jours. Lt. col. MC, USAR, 1983-87. Decorated Army Achievement medal, Army Commendation medal, 1986; recipient Physician Recognition award AMA, 1971; named Best Attending Physician Med. House Staff, Columbus Hosp., 1979. Fellow Am. Acad. Pediatrics, Am. Acad. Neurology, Royal Soc. Health Eng.; mem. Am. Med. Electroencephalographic Assn., Profs. of Child Neurology, Cen. Neuropsychiat. Assn. Republican. Serbian Orthodox. Clubs: Beefeaters (N.Y.C.); Les Gourmet's (Chgo.). Avocations: music, reading, writing, tennis, swimming. Office: Neurosci Ctr 825 S Waukegan Rd Ste C8 Lake Forest IL 60045-2665

VUCUREVICH, CONSTANCE LANE, investment executive; b. Lynchburg, Va., Nov. 9, 1946; d. Landon Bell and Frances Nelson (Mathews) Lane; m. James Wilson Stanfield, Feb. 2, 1968 (div. July 1980); children: James Wilson Stanfield III, Amanda Page Stanfield; m. John Thomas Vucurevich, Oct. 1, 1988. Student, Sweet Briar Coll., 1965-68; BSBA in Mktg./Mgmt., Nat. Coll., Rapid City, S.D., 1984. Registered securities broker. Investment exec. Piper Jaffray & Hopwood, Rapid City, 1984-87; investment executive Wheat First Securities, Richmond, Va., 1987-88; asst. v.p. Piper Jaffray, Inc., Rapid City, 1988—. Founder, dir., v.p., sec. L.B. Lane Family Found., Hickory, N.C., 1988—; bd. dirs. John T. Vucurevich Found., Rapid City, 1991—, Rapid City Boys Club, 1991—, Rapid City YMCA, 1994—, Rapid City Regional Hosp., 1994—; grad. Leadership Rapid City, 1985; mem. Mayor's Econ. Devel. Com., Rapid City, 1990; mem. choir Emmanuel Episc. Ch., 1982—. Recipient Philanthropist of Yr. award Gov. of S.D., Pierre, 1992. Mem. Womens Network. Republican. Episcopalian. Avocations: swimming, hiking, entertaining, singing, hot air ballooning. Home: 1416 Flormann St Rapid City SD 57701-4438 Office: Piper Jaffray Inc 726 St Joe St Rapid City SD 57701

VUILLEUMIER, FRANCOIS, curator; b. Berne, Switzerland, Nov. 26, 1938; came to U.S., 1961; s. Willy Georges and Denise Geneviève (Privat) V.; m. Bonita Rae Johnson, 1972 (div. 1981); children: Alexis Brendan, Claire Anne; m. Rebecca Branch Finnell, Feb. 26, 1983; 1 child, Isabelle Finnell. Licence es sciences, U. Geneva, Switzerland, 1961; PhD, Harvard U., 1967. Instr. U. Mass., Boston, 1966-67, asst. prof., 1967-70, assoc. prof., 1971; prof. U. Lausanne, Switzerland, 1971-72; sr. researcher Marine Biol. Sta., Roscoff, France, 1972-73; assoc. curator Am. Mus. Natural History, N.Y.C., 1974-79, curator, 1979—; dir. Inst. Animal Ecology, U. Lausanne, 1971-72; vis. prof. U. Paris, 1973-74, U. of the Andes, Mérida, Venezuela, 1981; chmn. Dept. Ornithology, Chapman Fund, Am. Mus. Natural History, 1987-92. Author: High Altitude Tropical Biogeography, 1986; contbr. 196 articles to jours. in field. Chapman fellow Am. Mus., 1967-68. Fellow Am. Ornithologists Union; mem. French Ornithol. Soc. (hon.), Soc. for Study of Evolution. Avocations: painting, reading, foreign languages, cooking. Office: Am Mus Natural History Central Pk West At 79T St W New York NY 10024

VULGAMORE, MELVIN L., college president; b. Springfield, Ohio, July 19, 1935; s. Leo Beeman and Della Marie (McCoy) V.; m. Ethelanne Oyer, Feb. 17, 1957; children: Allison Beth, Sarah Faith Vulgamore Evans. B.A. with honors, Ohio Wesleyan U., 1957; B.D., Harvard U., 1960; Ph.D., Boston U., 1963. Chmn., prof. religion Ohio Wesleyan U., Delaware, 1962-78, assoc. dean faculty, 1972-73, dean acad. affairs, 1973-78; v.p., provost U. Richmond, Va., 1978-83; pres. Albion Coll., Mich., 1983—; vis. prof. Am. U. Beirut, 1971-72; dir. Chem. Bank; vis. scholar Harvard U., 1995. Contbr. articles to profl. jours. Trustee Howe Mil. Sch., Ind., 1984—; mem. Mich. Coun. for Humanities, 1985-89, 96-97. Mem. Am. Acad. Religion, Tillich Soc. N.Am., Univ. Club N.Y., Detroit Athletic's Club, Rotary, Univ. Club. N.Y., Phi Beta Kappa, Omicron Delta Kappa, Delta Sigma Rho, Pi Sigma Alpha. Lodge: Rotary. Club: Univ. Club. N.Y. Avocations: bicycling, tennis, classical music, antique collecting and refinishing. Home: 1620 Van Wert Rd Albion MI 49224-9743 Office: Albion Coll Office of Pres Albion MI 49224

VULIS, DIMITRI LVOVICH, computer consultancy executive; b. Leningrad, Russia, Dec. 29, 1964; came to U.S., 1979; s. Lev Klyukvin and Inna Vulis; m. Maryam Inzel, Mar. 30, 1988; children: Daniel Benjamin, Lawrence Michael. BA in Math. cum laude, CUNY, 1985, MA in Math., 1989, PhD in Math, 1995. Pres. D&M Consulting Svcs., Inc., Forest Hills, N.Y., 1989—; cons. Cornerstone Asset Mgmt., N.Y.C., 1989-93, Possev-USA, N.Y.C., 1990—, Goldman Sachs Asset Mgmt., 1994—; adj. prof. Fordham U., 1989-94, Touro Coll., 1994—. Author: (computer program) Russian TeX, 1989. Mem. Am. Math. Soc., TeX Users' Group. Republican. Avocations: cryptography, golf. Office: D&M Cons Svc Inc 67-67 Burns St Forest Hills NY 11375-3555

VYAS, CHAND BHAOURBHAI, coal company executive; b. Bombay, India, Oct. 2, 1944; s. Bhanubbhai and Dolar (Bhatt) V.; m. Debra Elaine Dellget, Apr. 6, 1974; children: Aaron, Christin. B of Commerce, Bombay U., 1966; MBA in Fin., Atlanta U., 1969. Div. contr. Consolidation Coal Co., 1974-75, regional contr., 1976-81; treas. Zeigler Coal Co., Des Plaines, Ill., 1982-84; sr. v.p. fin., adminstrn. Zeigler Coal Co., Fairview Heights, Ill., 1985—, sr. v.p., 1988—; bd. dirs. Zeigler Coal Holding Co., Fairview Heights, 1985—, Zeigler Coal Co., Fairview Heights, 1985—, Jefferson Oil and Gas Co., Fairview Heights, Ill.,1985—;mem. exec. com. Zeigler Coal Co., Fairview Heights, 1985—. Contbr. articles to profl. jours. Mem. Ill. Coal Assn. (tax com.), Nat. Coal Assn., Nat. Assn. of Accts., Ind. Exec. Program (dir. adv. bd.). Avocations: golf, gardening, tennis. Office: Zeigler Coal Co 50 Jerome Ln Fairview Heights IL 62208*

VYAS, GIRISH NARMADASHANKAR, virologist, immunohematologist; b. Aglod, India, June 11, 1933; came to U.S., 1965, naturalized, 1973; s. Narmadashankar P. and Rukshmani A. (Joshi) V.; m. Devi Ratilal Trivedi, Apr. 3, 1962; children: Jay, Shrikrishna. B.Sc., U. Bombay, 1954, M.Sc., 1956, Ph.D., 1964. Postdoctoral fellow Western Res. U., 1965-66; mem. faculty U. Calif., San Francisco, 1967—, chief blood bank, 1969-88; prof. lab. medicine U. Calif., 1977—; dir. transfusion rsch. program, 1985—; WHO cons., S.E. Asia, 1980; cons. in field; mem. com. viral hepatitis NRC, 1974-76; mem. task force blood processing Nat. Heart and Lung Inst., 1972-73; sci. program com. Am. Assn. Blood Banks, 1971-76; com. immunoglobulin allotypes WHO, 1974—; mem. U.S. del. immunologists to Romania and Hungary, 1980; mem. FDA com. on blood and blood products, 1987-92; cons. to VA on med. rsch., 1985, UN Devel. Program in India, 1986; and others; chmn. Transmed Biotech Inc., South San Francisco, 1989-95. Author: Hepatitis and Blood Transfusion, 1972, Laboratory Diagnosis of Immunological Disorders, 1975, Membrane Structure and Function of Human Blood Cells, 1976, Viral Hepatitis, 1978, Viral Hepatitis and Liver Disease, 1984, Use and Standardization of Chemically Defined Antigens, 1986; also research papers. Recipient Julliard prize Internat. Soc. Blood Transfusion, 1969; named Outstanding Immigrant in Bay Area Communities Mayor of Oakland, Calif., 1969; Fulbright scholar France, 1980. Mem. AAAS, Am. Soc. Hematology (chmn. com. on transfusion medicine 1989-90), Am. Assn. Immunologists, Am. Soc. Clin. Pathologists, Internat. Assn. for Biol. Standarization (coun. 1992—). Democrat. Hindu. Office: U Calif Lab Med S-555 San Francisco CA 94143-0134 *Truth alone wins. Truth in our actions manifests beauty in character. Beauty in character brings harmony into the home. Harmony in the home produces order in our society. Order in our society leads to peace in the nation. And peace in the nation can win for us universal prosperity and happiness for mankind, only if individuals practice truth in their actions.*

VYKUKAL, EUGENE LAWRENCE, wholesale drug company executive; b. Caldwell, Tex., June 26, 1929; s. Henry J. and Anna P. (Polansky) V.; m. Judith Anderson, Jan. 1, 1977; children—Anna K., Mark Roman, Laura Roman, Geni. B.S. in Pharmacy, U. Tex., Austin, 1952. Pharmacist Scarborough's Pharmacy, Baytown, Tex., 1952-53; pharmacist Gene Vykukal's Pharmacy, Clifton, Tex., 1953-57; with Southwestern Drug Corp. (name now Bergen Brunswig Drug Co.), 1957-86; gen. sales mgr. Southwestern Drug Corp., Dallas, 1966-67; v.p., dir. sales Southwestern Drug Corp., 1967-75, exec. v.p., dir. sales, 1975-81, exec. v.p., 1980-81, pres., chief exec. officer, 1981-86, vice chmn., 1985-86, dir., 1966-86; asst. dean for devel., lectr. Coll. Pharmacy U. Tex., Austin, 1991—, mem. adv. coun. Pharm. Found., chmn., 1978—; sr. v.p. profl. affairs Bergen Brunswig Corp., Bergen Brunswig Drug Co., 1986—. Mem. centennial endowment com. U. Tex., 1980—; bd. dirs. Baylor U. Med. Center Found., Dallas; mem. indsl. adv. coun. Coll. Pharmacy, U. Ky., 1990—. Recipient Disting. Alumni award U. Tex. Coll. Pharmacy, 1979, William J. Sheffield Disting. Alumni award U. Tex. at Austin Coll. Pharmacy, 1987. Mem. Nat. Wholesale Druggists Assn. (chmn. sales mgmt. com. 1972-73, dir. 1980—, chmn. bd. 1985-86, 1st vice chmn. 1983—, chmn. exec. com. 1987—, Timothy Barry award 1990), Am. Pharm. Assn., Tex. Pharm. Assn. (long range planning com. 1983—), Wholesale Druggist Assn. Tex. (pres. 1978-79), Drug Travelers Assn. Tex. (pres. 1977-78), Sales and Mktg. Execs. Dallas (dir. 1971-72). Roman Catholic. Office: U Tex Coll Pharmacy Pharmacy Bldg Austin TX 78712-1074 *The quality of life in our great country has been enhanced by the tremendous strides made in our health care delivery system over the past three decades. To have served in the pharmaceutical segment has been very rewarding.*

WAALAND, IRVING THEODORE, retired aerospace design executive; b. Bklyn., July 2, 1927; s. Trygve and Marie Waaland; m. Helen Rita Katz, Apr. 7, 1961; children: Theodore, Neil, Elizabeth, Scott, Diane. B of Aero. Engrng. magna cum laude, NYU, 1953. Project engr. Grumman Corp., Bethpage, N.Y., 1953-74; v.p., B-2 Chief Designer Northrop Corp., Pico Rivera, Calif., 1974-93. Patentee in field. With USAF, 1946-48. Fellow AIAA (Aircraft Design award 1989, Aircraft Design cert. merit 1989, Wright Bros. lectr. in Aeronautics 1991); mem. NAE, Am. Def. Preparedness Assn. (Leslie E Simon award 1990), SAE (Aerospace Engrng. Leadership award 1993). Home: 65 Rollingwood Dr Palos Verdes Peninsula CA 90274-2425

WABLER, ROBERT CHARLES, II, retail and distribution executive; b. Dayton, Ohio, Dec. 14, 1948; s. Robert Charles Sr. and Eileen Marie (Langen) W.; m. Linda Adele Rayburn; 1 child, Robert Charles III. BS in Acctg. cum laude, U. Dayton, 1971; MS in Acctg. magna cum laude, U. Ga., 1976. Sr. auditor Touche Ross and Co., Dayton, 1971-73; internal auditor So. Company Services, Atlanta, 1974-75; acctg. mgr. Rich's div. Federated Dept. Stores, Atlanta, 1976-77; dir. auditing Munford, Inc., Atlanta, 1977-81, v.p., controller, 1982-83, v.p. fin. analyses, 1983-86; v.p. adminstrn. World Bazaar div. Munford, Inc., Atlanta, 1981-82, sr. v.p. fin., 1986-89; sr. v.p. fin. and administrn., sec. The Athlete's Foot Group, Inc., Atlanta, 1989-93; exec. v.p., CFO, treas. Just for Feet Inc., Birmingham, Ala., 1993—. Author: The Minimum Expenses Needed Technique, 1985. Mem. AICPA, Ga. Soc. CPAs, Inst. Internal Auditors, Assn. Systems Mgmt., EDP Auditor Assn. (bd. dirs. 1978-79). Home: 1541 Fairway View Dr Hoover AL 35244-1316 Office: Just For Feet Inc 153 Cahaba Valley Pkwy N Pelham AL 35124

WACHAL, ROBERT STANLEY, linguistics educator, consultant; b. Omaha, Mar. 13, 1929; s. Stanley William and Marie Frances (Rokusek) W.; m. Jane McCune, Sept. 15, 1968. B.A., U. Minn., 1952; M.S., U. Wis., 1959, Ph.D., 1966. Tchr. Mound Sch. Dist., Minn., 1955-59; faculty mem. U. Iowa, Iowa City, 1964—, prof. linguistics, 1975—, chmn. dept., 1975-81; cons. Am. Coll. Testing Program, Iowa City, 1981-95, Ednl. Testing Svc., Princeton, N.J., 1996—, NSF, Washington, 1975-90, Can. Council, Ottawa, Ont., 1975-80, Nat. Endowment for Humanities, N.Y.C., 1978, 93; mem. editl. adv. com. Am. Speech, 1988-93. Fulbright prof. Athens, Greece, 1966-67; research grantee U.S. Office Naval Research, 1969-72, Can. Med. Research Council Victoria, B.C., 1967-74. Fellow Acad. Aphasia; mem. Linguistics Soc. Am., Am. Dialect Soc., Dictionary Soc. N.Am. Home: 8 Woodland Hts NE Iowa City IA 52240-9136 Office: U Iowa Linguistics Dept Iowa City IA 52242

WACHENDORF, MILES BENTON, naval officer; b. Munich, Sept. 21, 1952; (parents Am. citizens); s. Miles Lowell and Sara Elizabeth (Goff) W.; m. Kathryn Breen, June 12, 1976; children: Patrick Lowell, Elizabeth Teague, Maria Theresa. BS, U.S. Naval Acad., 1974; postgrad., U. Zurich, Switzerland, 1979-81, Harvard U., 1994; grad., Naval War Coll., Newport, R.I., 1984; MS in Engrng., Cath. U. Am., 1995. Commd. ensign USN, 1974, advanced through grades to capt., 1994; comdg. officer USS Parche (SSN683), Mare Island, Calif., 1988-93; head undersea surveillance Office Chief Naval Ops., Washington, 1993—. Decorated D.S.M., Legion of Merit; Olmsted scholar U. Zurich, 1979-81. Home: 7909 Scott Ct Springfield VA 22153 Office: Office Chief Naval Ops 2000 Navy Pentagon Rm N874 Washington DC 20350

WACHENFELD, WILLIAM THOMAS, lawyer, foundation executive; b. Orange, N.J., Feb. 9, 1926; s. William A. and Ann (Weir) W.; children: William S., Robin A., John C. A.B., Tufts U., 1947; LL.B., Duke U., 1950. Bar: N.J. 1949. Since practiced in Newark; mem. firm Lum, Biunno & Tompkins, 1957-58; pres. Charles Hayden Found., N.Y.C., 1968—; prof. law Jersey City divsn. Jersey City div. Rutgers U., 1954-56; v.p., assoc. gen. counsel Prudential Ins. Co. Am., 1965-84; of counsel Tompkins, McGuire & Wachenfeld, Newark, 1984—. Pres. Essex County Park Commn., 1960-65, Newark Acad., 1972-80; commr. pub. affairs, Orange, 1956-58; mem. N.J. Econ. Devel. Coun., 1980-88, 91-94; bd. govs. N.J. Hist. Soc., 1981-83; mem. adv. bd. N.Y. Zool. Soc., 1983-93; trustee Liberty Sci. Ctr., 1988-93. Fellow Am. Bar Found.; mem. ABA, N.J. Bar Assn., Essex County Bar Assn., N.Y. Regional Assn. Grantmakers (bd. dirs. 1992—), Eastward Ho Country Club, HC Yacht Club (commodore 1992—). Home: 40 Windsor Pl Essex Fells NJ 07021-1711 Office: Tompkins McGuire & Wachenfeld 4 Gateway Ctr 100 Mulberry St Newark NJ 07102-4004

WACHMAN, MARVIN, university chancellor; b. Milw., Mar. 24, 1917; s. Alex and Ida (Epstein) W.; m. Adeline Lillian Schpok, Apr. 12, 1942; children: Kathleen M., Lynn A. B.S., Northwestern U., 1939, M.A., 1940; Ph.D., U. Ill., 1942; LLD (hon.), U. Pa., 1964, Lincoln (Pa.) U., 1970, Del. Valley Coll. Sci. and Agr., 1973, Med. Coll. Pa., 1982, Bloomfield Coll., 1987, Albright Coll., 1991; DHL (hon.), Gratz Coll., 1973; LittD (hon.), Jewish Theol. Sem. Am., 1973, Drexel U., 1980; LHD (hon.), Colgate U., 1975, Widener U., 1976; DSc (hon.), Thomas Jefferson U., 1980. Asst. in history U. Ill., 1940-42; instr. Biarritz Am. U., Biarritz, France, 1945-46; vis. asst. prof. San Diego State Coll., summer 1948, U. Minn., 1950; assoc. prof. history U. Md. in Europe, 1952-53; from instr. to prof. Colgate U., 1946-61, dir. upper class core program, 1956-61; pres. Lincoln (Pa.) U., 1961-70; v.p. acad. affairs Temple U., 1970-73, pres., 1973-82, chancellor, 1982—, Dir. Salzburg Seminar in Am. Studies, 1958-60, pres. Fgn. Policy Rsch. Inst., 1983-89; acting exec. dir. Pa. Higher Edn. Assistance Agy., 1989; acting pres. Phila. Coll. Textiles & Sci., 1991; pres. Albright Coll., 1991-92; past chmn. Nat. Ctr. for Higher Edn. Mgmt. Sys.; specialist in Africa for State Dept., 1965, 68; mem. adv. coun. World Learning, Inc.; mem. Colgate Nat. Coun., Phila. Com. Fgn. Rels.; dir., chair Tech. Specialists; dir. emeritus Germantown Ins. Co. Author: History of Social-Democratic Party of Milwaukee, 1897-1910, 1945; contbr. articles to profl. jours. and newspapers, also chpts. in books. Mem. bd. overseers Coll. V.I.; hon. trustee Albright Coll.; hon. life trustee Temple U.; trustee Cheyney U.; trustee, chmn. Phila. Coll. Textiles and Sci.; vice chair Fgn. Policy Rsch. Inst.; trustee emeritus Balch Inst. Ethnic Studies; mem. adv. coun. Greater Phila. Urban Affairs Coalition, World Affairs Coun.; mem. bd. mgrs. Phila. Found.; bd. dirs., treas. Fund for Open Soc., Operation Understanding; hon. dir. Phila. Contributionship; alumni regent Phila. area Northwestern U. With AUS, 1942-46. Mem. NAACP, Am. Studies Assn. (past mem. exec. com.), AAUP (past pres. Colgate U. chpt.), Am. Hist. Assn., ACLU, Pa. Assn. Colls. and Univs. (past chmn., pres. 1993), Phi Beta Kappa. Office: Temple U Philadelphia PA 19122

WACHNER, LINDA JOY, apparel marketing and manufacturing executive; b. N.Y.C., Feb. 3, 1946; d. Herman and Shirley W.; m. Seymour Applebaum, Dec. 21, 1973 (dec., 1983). BS in Econs. and Bus., U. Buffalo, 1966. Buyer Foley's Federated Dept. Store, Houston, 1968-69; sr. buyer R.H. Macy's, N.Y.C., 1969-74; v.p. Warner divsn. Warnaco, Bridgeport, Conn., 1974-77; v.p. corp. mktg. Caron Internat., N.Y.C., 1977-79; chief exec. officer U.S. divsn. Max Factor & Co., Hollywood, Calif., 1979-82, pres., chief exec. officer, 1982-83; pres., chief exec. officer Max Factor & Co. Worldwide, 1983-84; mng. dir. Adler & Shaykin, N.Y.C., 1985-86; pres., CEO, chmn. Warnaco Inc., N.Y.C., 1986—; chmn., CEO Authentic Fitness Corp., 1991—; bd. dirs. The Travellers, Inc. Presdl. appointee Adv. Com. for Trade, Policy, Negotiations; trustee U. Buffalo Found., Carnegie Hall, Aspen Inst., Thirteen/WNET; bd. overseers Meml. Sloan-Kettering Cancer Ctr. Recipient Silver Achievement award L.A. YWCA; named Outstanding Woman in Bus. Women's Equity Action League, 1980, Woman of Yr., MS. Mag., 1986, one of the Yr.'s Most Fascinating Bus. People, Fortune Mag., 1986, one of 10 Most Powerful Women in Corp. Am., Savvy Woman Mag., 1989, 90, Am.'s Most Successful Bus. Woman, Fortune Mag., 1992, Queen of Cash Flow, Chief Exec. Mag., 1994. Mem. Am. Mgmt. Assn., Am. Apparel Mktg. Assn. (bd. dirs.), Bus. Roundtable, Coun. on Fgn. Rels. Republican.

Jewish. Office: Warnaco Inc/Authentic Fitness Corp 90 Park Ave New York NY 10016

WACHS, DAVID V., retired apparel executive; b. Phila.. Attended, U Penn Wharton, 1948. With Charming Shoppes Inc., 1950-95, C.E.O., 1988-95. Office: Charming Shoppes Inc 450 Winks Ln Bensalem PA 19020-5919

WACHS, MARTIN, urban planning educator, author, consultant; b. N.Y.C., June 8, 1941; s. Robert and Doris (Margolis) W.; m. Helen Pollner, Aug. 18, 1963; children: Faye Linda, Steven Brett. B.C.E., CUNY, 1963; M.S., Northwestern U., 1965, Ph.D., 1967. Asst. prof. U. Ill.-Chgo., 1967-69, Northwestern U., Evanston, Ill., 1969-71; assoc. prof. urban planning UCLA, 1971-76, prof., 1976—; dir. UCLA Inst. Tranp. Studies, 1993—; vis. disting. prof. Rutgers U., New Brunswick, N.J., 1983-84; mem. exec. com. Transp. Rsch. Bd., 1995—. Author: Transportation for the Elderly: Changing Lifestyles, Changing Needs, 1979, The Clean Air Act in Court: New Demands on Transportation Planning, 1996; also numerous articles; editor: Ethics in Planning, 1984, The Car and the City, 1992. Mem. steering com. Los Angeles Parking Mgmt. Study, 1976-78; bd. dirs. Los Angeles Commuter Computer, 1978-94, mem. Calif. Commn. on Transp. Investment, 1995. Served to capt. Ordnance Corps, U.S. Army, 1967-69. Recipient Pike Johnson award Transp. Research Bd., 1976, Disting. Teaching award UCLA Alumni Assn., 1986, Disting. Planning Educator award Calif. Planners Found., 1986, vis. fellow Oxford U. (Eng.), 1976-77; Guggenheim fellow, 1977; Rockefeller Found. humanities fellow, 1980. Fellow Am. Coun. Edn.; mem. Am. Planning Assn., Am. Inst. Cert. Planners, Architects, Designers, Planners for Social Responsibility. Jewish. Home: 1088 N Kenter Ave Los Angeles CA 90049-1336 Office: UCLA Dept Urban Planning Sch Pub Policy & Social Rsch Los Angeles CA 90095-1656

WACHSMAN, HARVEY FREDERICK, lawyer, neurosurgeon; b. Bklyn., June 13, 1936; s. Ben and Mollie (Kugel) W.; m. Kathryn M. D'Agostino, Jan. 31, 1976; children: Dara Nicole, David Winston, Jacqueline Victoria, Lauren Elizabeth, Derek Charles, Ashley Max, Marea Lane, Melissa Roseanne. B.A., Tulane U., 1958; M.D., Chgo. Med. Sch., 1962; J.D., Bklyn. Law Sch., 1976. Bar: Conn. 1976, N.Y. 1977, Fla. 1977, D.C. 1978, U.S. Supreme Ct. 1980, Pa. 1984, Md. 1986, Tex. 1987. Diplomate Nat. Bd. Med. Examiners; cert. Am. Bd. Legal Medicine, Am. Bd. Profl. Liability Attys. (pres.); cert. civil trial advocate Nat. Bd. Trial Advocacy (trustee). Intern surgery Kings County Hosp. Ctr., Bklyn., 1962-63; resident in surgery Kingsbrook Med. Ctr., Bklyn., 1964-65; resident in neurol. surgery Emory U. Hosp., Atlanta, 1965-69; practice medicine specializing in neurosurgery Bridgeport, Conn., 1972-74; ptnr. firm Wachsman & Wachsman, Great Neck, 1976—, Pegalis & Wachsman, Great Neck, N.Y., 1977—; adj. prof. neurosurgery SUNY, Stony Brook; adj. prof. law St. John's U. Sch. Law, U. South Fla. Coll. Medicine. Author: American Law of Medical Malpractice, Vol. I, 1980, 2d edit., 1992, American Law of Medical Malpractice, Vol. II, 1981, 2d edit., 1993, American Law of Medical Malpractice, Vol. III, 1982, 2d edit., 1994, Cumulative Supplement to American Law of Medical Malpractice, 1981, 82, 83, 84, 85, American Law of Medical Malpractice, 2d edit., Vols. I, II and II, Lethal Medicine, 1993; mem. editl. bd. Legal Aspects of Med. Practice, 1978-82. Bd. trustees SUNY. Fellow Am. Coll. Legal Medicine (mem. bd. govs. 1986, chmn. edn. com. 1983—, chmn. 1985 nat. meeting, New Orleans, chmn. 1988 nat. meeting, Va., bd. dirs. ACLM Found.), Am. Acad. Forensic Scis., Royal Soc. Medicine, Royal Soc. Arts (London), Royal Soc. Medicine (London), Roscoe Pound Found. of Assn. Trial Lawyers Am.; mem. ABA, Am. Soc. Law and Medicine, Congress Neurol. Surgeons, Assn. Trial Lawyers Am., Soc. Med. Jurisprudence (trustee), N.Y. Bar Assn., Conn. Bar Assn., Fla. Bar Assn., D.C. Bar Assn., N.Y. Acad. Scis., Assn. Trial Lawyers Am. (bd. govs.), N.Y. Trial Lawyers Assn., Conn. Trial Lawyers Assn., Fla. Acad. Trial Lawyers, Md. Trial Lawyers Assn., Tex. Trial Lawyers Assn., Pa. Trial Lawyers Assn., Nat. Bar Assn. (mem. com. on South Africa), Nassau County Bar Assn., Fairfield County Med. Soc., Nassau-Suffolk Trial Lawyers Assn. Club: Cosmos (Washington). Home: 55 Mill River Rd Oyster Bay NY 11771-2711 Office: 175 E Shore Rd Great Neck NY 11023-2430 *In my pursuit of knowledge and excellence in the fields of neurosurgery and the law, I Have found that arming oneself with the power of knowledge is truly the key to helping others. Let one's goal in life be to help others, and he shall always find fulfillment, challenge and hope.*

WACHSMANN, ELIZABETH RIDEOUT, reading specialist; b. Richmond, Va., Apr. 28, 1945; d. John Nelson and Lily Smith (Garter) Rideout; m. Marvin Rudolph Wachsmann, Aug. 14, 1966; children: Rebecca W. Campbell, Richard Nelson. BS, James Madison Univ., 1966; MEd in Adminstrn. and Supervision, Va. State U., 1989, MEd in Diagnosit and Remedial Reading, 1994. 1st grade tchr. Sussex (Va.) Pub. Schs., 1966-70; 6th grade tchr. Tidewater Acad., Wakefield, Va., 1978-89; 1st grade tchr. Surry (Va.) County Pub. Schs., 1989-92, reading specialist, 1992—. Named Tchr. of Yr. Daily Press/Newport News Shipbuilders, 1992. Mem. ASCD, Internat. Reading Assn., Richmond Area Reading Assn., Va. Br. ORton Dyslexic Soc., Assn. for Childhood Edn. Internat., Nat. Coun. Tchrs. of English, Va. Br. Orton Dyslexic Soc., Phi Delta Kappa, Kappa Delta Pi. United Methodist. Avocations: reading, handwork, cooking, gardening. Home: 13019 Robinson Rd Stony Creek VA 23882-3737 Office: Surry County Pub Schs PO Box 317 Surry VA 23883-0317

WACHSTETER, GEORGE, illustrator; b. Hartford, Conn., Mar. 12, 1911; s. Josef and Therese (Weiss) W.; m. Thelma Altshuler, July 29, 1939 (dec. 1991). Ed. pub. schs., Hartford. Illustrator Major Advt. Agys, Theatre and Motion Picture Prodns., 1936—, CBS, NBC, ABC Radio and TV Networks, 1937—; weekly illustrator and caricature to drama pages N.Y. Herald Tribune, 1941-50; contbr. illustration and caricature to drama and polit. pages N.Y. Times, 1938-50; caricaturist Theatre Guild On The Air, U.S. Steel, 1945-63; artist TV section N.Y. Times, 1950-51; featured drama artist N.Y. Jour. Am., 1956-63, artist TV mag. covers, 1958-63; artist TV mag. covers Hearst Syndicate, 1963-65; drama artist N.Y. World Telegram, 1964-66; syndicated feature illustrator Hallmark TV Drama Series, 1964-69. Illustrator, caricaturist (book) NBC Book of Stars, 1957; portrait Taft Meml. Fund Campaign, 1956; numerous work in pub. and pvt. collections. Jewish. Home: 85-05 Elmhurst Ave Elmhurst NY 11373-3357

WACHTEL, NORMAN JAY, lawyer; b. N.Y.C., June 1, 1941; s. A. Allen and Lillian (Rolnik) W.; m. C. Robin Fixler, June 12, 1969; children: Jonathan, Charles. AB, U. Pa., 1963, LLB, 1966; LLM, Boston U., 1967. Bar: N.Y. 1967. Assoc. Demov, Morris & Hammerling, N.Y.C., 1968-78, ptnr., 1978-87; ptnr. Rogers & Wells, N.Y.C., 1987—; bd. advisors 1st Am. Title Ins. Co. N.Y., 1982—. Author: (chpt.) Real Estate Titles, 1984. Office: Rogers & Wells 200 Park Ave Ste 5200 New York NY 10166-0005

WACHTLER, SOL, retired judge, arbitration corporation executive, writer; b. N.Y.C., Apr. 29, 1930; s. Philip Henry and Fay (Sobel) W.; m. Joan Wolosoff, Feb. 23, 1952; children: Lauren Jane, Marjorie Dru, Alison Toni, Philip Henry. BA, Washington and Lee U., 1951, LLB, 1952, postgrad., 1980, LLD (hon.), 1981; LLD (hon.), New Eng. Sch. Law, 1978, Bklyn. Law Sch., 1978, Hofstra U., 1980, SUNY, 1981, Syracuse U., Dowling Coll., 1990, Thomas M. Cooley Law Sch., 1990, New. Eng. Law Sch.; LHD (hon.), LIU, Coll. of St. Rose. Bar: N.Y. 1956. Justice N.Y. State Supreme Ct., 1968-72; judge N.Y. State Ct. Appeals, Albany, 1972-84; chief judge State of N.Y., Albany, 1985-93; guest lectr. Bklyn. Law Sch., Hofstra Law Sch., Yale U. Sch. Law, Albany Law Sch., St. John's Law Sch., 1968-77, USIA, Munich, Germany, 1973, Stuttgart, Germany, 1977, U. Leyden, Amsterdam, Stockholm, 1988, Madrid, 1989; chmn. N.Y. State Fair Trial/Free Press Conf., N.Y. State Commn. on Bicentennial of U.S. Constitution.; bd. dirs. Confs. Cief Justices; mem. Nat Jud. Coun. Contbr. articles to legal jours. Councilman Town of North Hempstead, N.Y., 1963-65, chief exec., 1965-67; mem. Nassau County Bd. Suprs., 1965-67, chmn. com. pub. safety, 1965-67; trustee L.I. Jewish-Hillside Med. Ctr., 1970—, L.I. U.; bd. overseers Nelson A. Rockefeller Inst. Govt.; dist. chmn. Boy Scouts Am., 1968-69; trustee Cerebral Palsy Assn., Assn. for Help of Retarded Children, 1966-67. Mem. Am. Law Inst., Assn. N.Y. State Supreme Ct. Justices, ABA, N.Y. State Bar Assn., Nassau County Bar Assn., Order of Coif, Phi Delta Phi. Jewish. Home: 58 Fairway Dr Manhasset NY 11030-3906 *As a people, we are fond of the observation that ours is a nation of laws and not of men. It too, like the words of our great laws, seems to lend security, a sense of certainty, and a predictability to the paths we travel. In the law particularly, the thought that past generations have separated right from wrong and good from evil can be comforting. Yet, here again, if we will just scratch the surface, we will find that the greatest responsibility for our national welfare does not rest with statutes carved in stone but with the principles, conscience, and morality of the individuals who constitute this generation.*

WACHTMEISTER, COUNT WILHELM H. F., diplomat; b. Vanas, Sweden, Apr. 29, 1923; s. Gustaf and Margaretha (Trolle) W.; m. Ulla Leuhusen, 1947; children: Anna, Erik. LLD, U. Stockholm, Sweden, 1946. Attache Swedish Ministry for Fgn. Affairs, 1946-47; attache Swedish Embassy, Vienna, Madrid and Lisbon, 1947-50; 2d sec. Swedish Ministry Fgn. Affairs, Stockholm, Sweden, 1950-55; 1st sec. Swedish Embassy, Moscow, 1955-58; personal asst. to UN Sec. Gen., 1958-61; head UN sect. Fgn. Ministry, Stockholm, 1962-65, dep. under-sec. polit. affairs, 1965-66; ambassador to Algeria Swedish Embassy, 1966-67; under-sec. for polit. affairs Swedish Ministry Fgn. Affairs, Stockholm, 1968-74; Swedish ambassador to U.S. Swedish Embassy, Washington, 1974-89; dean diplomatic corps in Washington, 1986-89; sr. advisor to chmn. AB Volvo, 1989-94. Mem. Soc. Cin. (France), New World Found. (chmn.), Swedish-Am. C. of C. (chmn. 1993-95), Met. Club of Washington. Avocation: tennis. Home: 4202 48th Pl NW Washington DC 20016-2338

WACKENHUT, RICHARD RUSSELL, security company executive; b. Balt., Nov. 11, 1947; s. George Russell and Ruth Johann (Bell) W.; m. Mariane Hutson Ball, Mar. 13, 1971; children: Jennifer Anne, Lisa Renee, Ashley Elizabeth, Lauren Hutson. BA in Polit. Sci., The Citadel Mil. Coll., 1969; grad. bus. sch. advanced mgmt. program, Harvard U., 1987. With Wackenhut Corp., Coral Gables and Palm Beach Gardens, Fla. and Columbia, S.C., 1973—; v.p. ops. Wackenhut Corp., Coral Gables, 1981-82, sr. v.p. domestic ops., 1982-83, sr. v.p. ops., 1983-86, pres., chief operating officer, 1986—, also bd. dirs. various subs.; bd. trustees St. Thomas U., Miami, Fla.; dir. Assoc. Industries of Fla. Mem. Internat. Assn. Chiefs Police, Internat. Security Mgmt. Assn., Am. Soc. Indsl. Security, Ocean Reef Club, Seabrook Island Club, Biltmore Club. Republican. Christian Scientist. Avocations: racquetball, jogging, boating. Office: Wackenhut Corp 4200 Wackenhut Dr #100 Palm Beach Gardens FL 33410-4243

WACKER, FREDERICK GLADE, JR., manufacturing company executive; b. Chgo., July 10, 1918; s. Frederick Glade Wacker and Grace Cook Jennings; m. Ursula Comandatore, Apr. 26, 1958; children: Frederick Glade III, Wendy, Joseph Comandatore. BA, Yale U., 1940; student, Gen. Motors Inst. Tech., 1940-42; LLD (hon.), Northwood U., 1989, GMI Engring. and Mgmt. Inst., 1996. Efficiency engr. AC Spark Plug divsn. Gen. Motors Corp., 1940-43; with Ammco Tools, Inc., North Chicago, Ill., 1947-87, pres., 1948-87, chmn. bd., 1948-87; founder, pres. Liquid Controls Corp., North Chicago, 1954-87, chmn. bd., 1954—; chmn. bd. Liquid Controls Europe, Zurich, Switzerland, 1985-87; ltd. ptnr. Francis I. DuPont & Co., N.Y.C., 1954-70; mem. exec. coun. Conf. Bd., 1971-92, chmn., 1977. Condr. Freddie Wacker and His Orch., 1955-69, orch. has appeared on TV and radio, recs. for Dolphin and Cadet records. Bd. govs. United Rep. Fund Ill., Art Inst. Chgo., 1984—; trustee Lake Forest Acad., 1956-71, life trustee, 1992—; trustee Warren Wilson Coll., 1973-81, Chgo. chpt. Multiple Sclerosis Soc.; bd. govs. Lyric Opera Chgo., 1963-66; bd. advisers Nat. Schs. Com., 1966-88; adv. coun. Trinity Evang. Div. Sch., 1977-87; adv. bd. Internat. Coun. Biblical Inerrancy, 1981-88; bd. dirs., vice chmn. Rockford Inst., 1983-91; bd. govs. GMI Engring. and Mgmt. Inst., 1983-91; bd. regents Milw. Sch. Engring., 1981-91; mem. pres.'s coun. Ligonier Ministries, 1989—. Lt. (j.g.) USNR, 1943-45, PTO. Recipient Outstanding Bus. Leader award, Northwood, 1994; named to Hall of Fame Lake Forest Acad., 1987. Mem. Chief Execs. Forum, Young Pres. Orgn. (chmn. Chgo. chpt. 1965-66), Sports Car Club Am. (founder Chgo. region 1949, pres. 1952-53), Ill. Mfrs. Assn. (bd. dirs. 1966-91, chmn. bd. 1975), Chgo. Pres. Orgn. (pres. 1972-73), Automotive Hall of Fame (life, bd. dirs. 1976-88, v.p. 1980-81, sec. 1981-88, Disting. Svc. Citation 1989, Chief Exec. Forum 1967-89), Soc. Automotive Engrs., World Bus. Coun., Waukegan C. of C. (bd. dirs. 1965-68), Art Inst. Chgo. (gov.), Chgo. Fedn. Musicians (life), Am. Motorcycle Assn. (life), Living Desert (life), Racquet Club (pres. 1960-61), Shoreacres Club, Onwentsia Club, Vintage Club, Conway Farms Golf Club, The Quarry. Presbyterian. Home: 1600 Green Bay Rd Lake Bluff IL 60044-2306 Office: Liquid Controls Corp 105 Albrecht Dr Lake Bluff IL 60044-2252

WACKER, WARREN ERNEST CLYDE, physician, educator; b. Bklyn., Feb. 29, 1924; s. John Frederick and Kitty Dora (Morrissey) W.; m. Ann Romeyn MacMillan, May 22, 1948; children: Margaret Morrissey, John Frederick. Student, Georgetown U., 1946-47; M.D., George Washington U., 1951; M.A. (hon.), Harvard, 1968. Intern George Washington U. Hosp., 1951-52, resident, 1952-53; resident Peter Bent Brigham Hosp., Boston, 1953-55; Nat. Found. Infantile Paralysis fellow, 1955-57; investigator Howard Hughes Med. Inst., Boston, 1957-68; mem. faculty Harvard Med. Sch., Boston, 1955—; assoc. prof. medicine Harvard Med. Sch., 1968-71, Henry K. Oliver prof. hygiene, 1971-89, prof. hygiene, 1989-95, dir. univ. health services, 1971-89; Henry K. Oliver prof. hygiene emeritus, 1995; acting master Mather House Harvard Med. Sch., 1974-75, acting master Kirkland House, 1975-76, master Cabot House, 1978-84; sr. med. cons. Risk Mgmt. Found. of the Harvard Med. Instns., Cambridge, 1992—; vis. scholar St. Mary's Hosp. Med. Sch., 1964; vis. prof. U. Tel Aviv, 1987; chmn. bd. Applied mgmt. Sys., Burlington, Mass., Millipore Corp., Bedford, Mass., 1971-94; mem. editorial adv. bd. Toxilogical and Environ. Chemistry. Author: Magnesium and Man, 1981; sec., editorial adv. bd.: Biochemistry, 1962-76; assoc. editor: Magnesium; contbr. articles to med. and sci. jours. Vestryman St. Paul's Episc. Ch., Brookline, Mass., 1965-68, 76-79, 91-94; bd. dirs. Harvard Cmty. Health Plan, Boston, 1973-84, mem. fin. com., 1984-86, mem. corp., 1986—; bd. dirs. Bishop Rhinelander Found., Cambridge, 1973-76, 78-84, Controlled Risk Ins. Co., 1976-78; pres. bd. overseers Peter Bent Brigham Hosp., Boston, 1979-84; trustee Brigham and Women's Hosp., Boston, 1984-89,Risk Mgmt. Found., 1979-92; mem. mgmt. bd., med. bd. MIT, 1985-95; mem. corp. Mt. Auburn Hosp., Cambridge, 1986—; mem. adv. bd. hospitality program Episc. Diocese Mass., 1989—. 1st lt. USAAF, 1942-45. Decorated Air medal, D.F.C., Liberation medal (Greece); named Disting. Alumnus, George Washington U., 1963; recipient Cert. of Merit, Soc. Magnesium Research, 1985. Mem. AMA, Am. Chem. Soc., Am. Soc. Biol. Chemistry, Am. Soc. Clin. Investigation, Mass. Med. Soc., A.C.P., Am. Coll. Health Assn. (pres. 1981, Boynton award 1986), Biochemistry Soc. (London), Am. Coll. Nutrition, Sigma Xi, Alpha Omega Alpha, Harvard Club (Boston). Home: 91 Glen Rd Brookline MA 02146-7764 Office: Risk Mgmt Found 840 Memorial Dr Cambridge MA 02139-3771

WACKERLE, FREDERICK WILLIAM, management consultant; b. Chgo., June 25, 1939; s. Fred and Babette (Buck) W.; m. Elaine Gately, Apr. 28, 1962 (div.); children: Jennifer, Ruth; m. Barbara L. Provus, Mar. 29, 1985. BA, Monmouth (Ill.) Coll., 1961. Prin. A.T. Kearney & Co., Chgo., 1964-66; v.p. Berry Henderson & Aberlin, Chgo., 1966-68, R.M. Schmitz & Co., Chgo., 1968-70; ptnr. McFeely-Wackerle-Shulman, Chgo., 1970—; dir. Rehab. Inst. Chgo. Trustee Monmouth Coll. Served with USAF, 1957-62. Mem. Assn. Exec. Search Cons. (bd. dirs., exec. v.p.), Tau Kappa Epsilon. Home: 3750 N Lake Shore Dr Apt 17F Chicago IL 60613-4234 Office: McFeely-Wackerle-Shulman 20 N Wacker Dr Ste 3110 Chicago IL 60606-3101

WADA, HARRY NOBUYOSHI, training company executive; b. North Platte, Nebr., Nov. 29, 1919; s. Gosaku and Hina (Arakawa) W.; m. Carol Tanaka, July 30, 1950; children: Sharon, Leslie, Gregg. B.S., Ill. Inst. Tech., 1954, M.S., 1956. Owner Palace Cafe, North Platte, 1946-50; mgr. purchases IIT Research Inst., Chgo., 1954-65; materials mgr. IIT Research Inst., 1965-76; dir. continuing edn. Nat. Assn. Purchasing Mgmt., 1976-83; pres. H. N. Wada & Assocs., 1983—; instr. Ill. Inst. Tech., Roosevelt U. Editor chpt. from George Aljians Handbook, 1973; contbr. articles to profl. jours. Mem. Bd. Standardization Cook County, Health and Hosps. Governing Commn. Served with AUS, 1942-46. Recipient J. Shipman Gold medal, 1976. Mem. Purchasing Mgmt. Assn. Chgo. (pres. 1969), Nat. Assn. Purchasing Mgmt. (chmn. dist. III profl. devel. 1970-71, program chmn. Internat. Conf. 1971, pres. 1974—, Brueggemann award 1974), Ill. C. of C., Ill. Inst. Tech. Alumni (bd. dirs.), Phi Eta Sigma, Sigma Iota Epsilon. Home and Office: 3128 Tarpon Dr #104 Las Vegas NV 89120

WADA, YUTAKA, electronics executive; b. Sapporo, Hokkaido, Japan, Feb. 2, 1932; s. Hiroshi and Toki (Hirano) W.; m. Makiko Hirate, Apr. 15, 1940; children: Takeshi, Kaori. BA, Tokyo U., 1953; Grad., London Sch. Economics, 1963. Cert. Nat. Civil Svc. With Ministry of Internat. Trade and Industry, Tokyo, 1953-64; dir. policy review and assessment sec. Small and Medium Enterprise Agy. MITI, Tokyo, 1968-70; counselor Japanese permanent delegation Internat. Orgn., Geneva, 1973-78; dir. gen. multilateral trade dept. MITI, Tokyo, 1975-76; dir. gen. first examination dept. Patent Office, Tokyo, 1978-79, dir. gen., adminstrn. dept., 1979-80; dir. gen. Bur. of Equipment, Defense Agency, Tokyo, 1980-82; exec. dir., bd. dir. The Overseas Economic Cooperation Fund, Tokyo, 1982-84; with Sharp Corp., Osaka, 1984—, exec. dir., bd. dir., 1985—, group gen. mgr. internat. bus. group, 1986-89, sr. exec., dir., mem. of exec. com., 1989-91, sr. exec., v.p. for internat. bus., mem. exec. com., 1991-95, sr. exec. v.p., and gen. mgr. Tokyo br., mem. exec. com., 1995—; interviewed by CNN Worldwide, 1994. Bimonthly articles contbr. (under Yasuhiko Hiromi) Keizai-kai Bus. Jour., 1978-80; contbr. articles Nippon Keizai Shinbun, 1994, The Nikkei Weekly, 1994, The Asian Wall Street Journal, 1994. Mem. Kansai Economic Fedn. (spl. com. on internat. bus. mgmt., 1993-94), The Osaka Indsl. Assn. (internat. community rels. com. 1993—), Osaka Fgn. Trade Assn. (dir. 1994—), Japan-China Investment Promotion Orgn. (dir. 1993—). Avocations: golf, swimming, skiing, go, reading. Office: Sharp Corp, 1-9-2 Nakase Mihama-Ku, Chiba-shi Chiba-Shi Chiba 261, Japan

WADDELL, HARRY LEE, editor, publisher; b. Monarch, Wyo., June 19, 1912; s. Edward Lee and Naomi (Epstein) W.; m. Eleanor Hazeltine, 1937 (dec.); children: Nancy, Caroline, Jessica; m. Helene Jamieson, Apr., 6, 1968 (dec.). A.B., Ohio U., 1933. Reporter, fin. editor, asst. city editor, news editor Buffalo Evening News, 1933-46; asst. mng. editor Bus. Week, McGraw-Hill, N.Y.C., 1946-49; editor Factory, 1949-53, pub. oil industry group, 1953-57, sr. v.p. mag. div., 1957-59, corp. exec. v.p., dir., 1959-65; gen. exec. Doubleday & Co., N.Y.C., 1966-69; with Simmons-Boardman Pub. Corp., N.Y.C., 1969—; chief editor Am. Bankers Assn. Banking Jour., 1971-82, editor emeritus, 1982—, chmn. bd., 1972-82, vice chmn., 1982—; lectr. Am. Press Inst., Columbia U., 1946-59; Mem. Ednl. Adv. Bd., Garden City, N.Y., 1955-58, chmn., 1957-58. Trustee Orange County Citizens Found., 1983—, v.p. 1987-93. Mem. Am. Bus. Press (dir. 1977-83), Phi Beta Kappa, Sigma Delta Chi, Beta Theta Pi. Republican. Presbyterian. Office: 345 Hudson St New York NY 10014-4502

WADDELL, JOHN COMER, electronics distribution company executive; b. Bridgeport, Conn., Sept. 10, 1937; s. John and Dorothy Margot (Comer) W. B.A., Yale U., 1959; M.B.A., Harvard U., 1965. Assoc. R.W. Pressprich & Co., N.Y.C., 1965-68; ptnr. Glenn, Green & Waddell, N.Y.C., 1968-80; exec. v.p. Arrow Electronics, Inc., Melville, N.Y., 1969-80; chmn. bd. Arrow Electronics, Inc., 1980—. Served with U.S. Navy, 1960-63. *

WADDELL, R. EUGENE, minister; b. Wayne County, N.C., Feb. 7, 1932; s. Robert Lee and Rena (Holland) W.; m. Elva Leah Nichols, July 22, 1954 (dec. Apr. 1962); children: Rhonda Waddell Sagraves, Robert, Paul, Marcia Waddell Thompson; m. Genevieve Johnson, July 4, 1963; children: Michael, John. BA, Free Will Bapt. Bible Coll., Nashville, 1954; MA, Columbia (S.C.) Bibl. Sem., 1966. Ordained to ministry Free Will Bapt. Ch., 1952. Pastor Bay Branch Free Will Bapt. Ch., Timmonsville, S.C., 1954-56, 1st Free Will Bapt. Ch., Portsmouth, Va., 1956-60, Garner (N.C.) Free Will Bapt. Ch., 1960-64, Cofer's Chapel Free Will Bapt. Ch., Nashville, 1964-81; assoc. dir. Free Will Bapt. Fgn. Missions Dept., Nashville, 1981-86, gen. dir., 1986—; bd. dirs. Free Will Bapt. Fgn. Missions, Nashville, 1959-78, bd. sec., 1971-78; founder, editor Free Will Bapt. Witness, Garner, 1962-63. Office: Free Will Bapt Fgn Missions 5233 Mount View Rd Antioch TN 37013-2306

WADDELL, THEODORE, painter; b. Billings, Mont., Jan. 6, 1941. Student, Bklyn. Mus. Art Sch., 1962; BS, Ea. Mont. Coll., 1966; MFA, Wayne State U., 1968. One-man shows include U. Calif., San Diego, 1984, Cheney Cowles Meml. Mus., Spokane, Wash., 1985, The New West, Colorado Springs, 1986, Bernice Stein Baum Gallery, N.Y., 1992; exhibited in group shows 38th Corcoran Biennial, Corcoran Gallery, Washington, 1983; represented in permanent collections Ea. Mont. Coll., Yellowstone Art Ctr., Billings, Sheldon Meml. Art Gallery, U. Nebr., Lincoln, City of Great Falls, Mont., Dallas Mus. Art, San Jose (Calif.) Mus. Office: c/o Stremmel Gallery 1400 S Virginia St Reno NV 89502

WADDELL, WILLIAM JOSEPH, pharmacologist, toxicologist; b. Commerce, Ga., Mar. 16, 1929; s. John Daniel and Lillian Marie (Vollrath) W.; m. Grace Carolyn Marlowe, Oct. 19, 1974; children: William Joseph, James Glenn, Martin Christie, Amy Alison. A.B. in Chemistry, U. N.C., 1951, M.D., 1955. Postdoctoral research fellow U. N.C. Sch. Medicine, 1955-58, asst. prof. pharmacology, 1958-62, asso. prof., 1962-72; asso. prof. oral biology U. N.C. Sch. Medicine (Dental Research Center), 1967-69, prof., 1969-72, asso. dir., 1968-72; prof. pharmacology U. Ky. Coll. Medicine, Lexington, 1972-77; prof., chmn. dept. pharmacology and toxicology U. Louisville, 1977—; Centennial Alumni Disting. vis. prof. U. N.C. Sch. Medicine, 1979. Contbr. articles to profl. jours. Fellow Acad. Toxicological Scis.; mem. Am. Soc. for Pharmacology and Exptl. Therapeutics, Am. Physiol. Soc., Am. Teratology Soc., Internat. Soc. for Study Xenobiotics, Soc. for Exptl. Biology and Medicine, Soc. Toxicology, Sigma Xi. Home: 14300 Rose Wycombe Rd Prospect KY 40059-9024 Office: U Louisville Dept Pharmacology Louisville KY 40292

WADDEN, RICHARD ALBERT, environmental engineer, educator, consultant, research director; b. Sioux City, Iowa, Oct. 3, 1936; s. Sylvester Francis and Hermina Lillian (Costello) W.; m. Angela Louise Trabert, Aug. 9, 1975; children—Angela Terese, Noah Albert, Nuiko Clare. Student, St. John's U., Collegeville, Minn., 1954-56; B.S. in Chem. Engring., Iowa State U., 1959; M.S. in Chem. Engring, N.C. State U., 1962; Ph.D. in Chem. and Environ. Engring., Northwestern U., 1972. Registered profl. engr., Ill.; cert. indsl. hygienist. Engr. Linde Co., Tonnawanda, N.Y., 1959-60, Humble Oil Co., Houston, 1962-65; instr. engring. Pahlavi U. Peace Corps, Shiraz, Iran, 1965-67; tech. adviser Ill. Pollution Control Bd., Chgo., 1971-72; asst. dir. Environ. Health Resource Ctr. Ill., Chgo., 1972-74; asst. prof. environ. and occupational health scis. Sch. Pub. Health U. Ill.-Chgo., 1972-75, assoc. prof., 1975-79, prof., 1979—, dir., 1984-86, 88-92; dir. Office Tech. Transfer U. Ill. Ctr. for Solid Waste Mgmt. and Resch., 1987-92; dir. indsl. hygiene and hazardous waste tng. programs Occupl. Safety and Health Ctr., U. Ill.-Chgo., Chgo.; vis. scientist Nat. Inst. Environ. Studies, Japan, 1978-79, invited scientist, 1983, 84, 88; cons. air pollution control, health implications of energy devel., indoor air pollution. Author: Energy Utilization and Environmental Health, 1978, (with P.A. Scheff) Indoor Air Pollution, 1983, Engineering Design for Control of Workplace Hazards, 1987; contbr. numerous articles to profl. publs. Sr. Internat. fellow Fogarty Internat. Ctr.-NIH, 1978-79, 83; WHO fellow, 1984. Mem. AIChE, Am. Chem. Soc., Am. Acad. Environ. Engrs. (diplomate), Am. Acad. Indsl. Hygiene (diplomate), Air and Waste Mgmt. Assn., Am. Indsl. Hygiene Assn., Am. Conf. Govtl. Indsl. Hygienists. Office: U Ill m/c 922 2121 W Taylor St Chicago IL 60612-7260

WADDEN, THOMAS ANTONY, psychologist, educator; b. Richmond, Va., Sept. 3, 1952; s. Thomas Antony Jr. and Mary Lloyd (Cradock) W.; m. Jan Robin Linowitz, Nov. 11, 1984; children: David Joseph, Michael James, Steven Zachary. AB magna cum laude, Brown U., 1975; PhD, U. N.C., 1981. Psychology intern Boston VA Med. Ctr., 1980-81; instr. in psychology U. Pa. Sch. Medicine, Phila., 1981-82, asst. prof. psychology, 1982-87, assoc. prof. psychology, 1987-91, prof. psychology, 1994—; prof. psychology, dir. clin. tng. Syracuse (N.Y.) U., 1992-93; clin. dir. Obesity Rsch. Group, U. Pa., Phila., 1983-91, dir. Weight and Eating Disorders Program, 1994—; dir. Ctr. for Health and Behavior, Syracuse U., 1992-93. Assoc. editor Annals of Behavioral Medicine, 1990-93; mem. editl. bd. Behavior Theraphy, Jour. Consulting and Clin. Psychology Obesity Rsch.; editor: (with T.B. VanItallie) Treatment of the Seriously Obese Patient, 1992, (with A.J. Stunkard) Obesity: Theory and Therapy, 1993; contbr. chpts. in books; writer numerous sci. papers. Recipient Nat. Rsch. Svc. award NIMH, 1983-85, Rsch. Scientist Devel. award, 1987-91, 94—. Mem. APA, Soc. Behavioral Medicine (bd. dirs. 1987-90), Assn. for Advancement of Behavior Therapy (New Rschr. award 1986), Acad. Behavioral Medicine, Phi Beta Kappa, Sigma Xi. Democrat. Avocations: tennis, squash, symphonic music, guitar.

Home: 433 Bolsover Rd Wynnewood PA 19096-1301 Office: U Pa 3600 Market St Fl 738 Philadelphia PA 19104-2611

WADDILL, VAN HULEN, entomology educator; b. Brady, Tex., Aug. 24, 1947. BS, Tex. A&M U., 1970, MS, 1971; PhD, Clemson U., 1974. From asst. prof. to prof. entomology Inst. Food & Agrl. Sci. U. Fla., West Palm Beach, 1975—; mem. Coun. Agrl. Sci. & Tech. Mem. Entomol. Soc. Am. Office: U Fla Everglades Rsch Edn Ctr PO Box 8003 Belle Glade FL 33430-8003

WADDINGHAM, JOHN ALFRED, artist, journalist; b. London, Eng., July 9, 1915; came to U.S., 1927, naturalized, 1943; s. Charles Alfred and Mary Elizabeth (Coles) W.; m. Joan Lee Larson, May 3, 1952; children: Mary Kathryn, Thomas Richard. Student, Coronado (Calif.) Sch. Fine Arts, 1953-54, Portland Art Mus., 1940-65, U. Portland, 1946-47; pupil, Rex Brandt, Eliot Ohara, George Post. Promotion art dir. Oreg. Jour., Portland, 1946-59; with The Oregonian, Portland, 1959-81; editorial art dir. The Oregonian, 1959-81; tchr. watercolor Ore. Soc. Artists, 1954-56; tchr. art Oreg. Sch. Arts and Crafts, 1981—, Portland Community Coll.; represented by several galleries, Oreg. and Wash. One man show includes Art in the Gov.'s Office Ore State Capitol, 1991; rep. mus. rental collections, Portland Art Mus., Bush House, Salem, Ore., U. Oreg. Mus., Vincent Price collection, Ford Times collection, also, Am. Watercolor Soc. Travelling Show; judge art events, 1946—, over 50 one-man shows; ofcl. artist, Kiwanis Internat. Conv., 1966; designed, dir. constrn. cast: concrete mural Genesis, St. Barnabas Episcopal Ch., Portland, 1960; spl. work drawings old Portland landmarks and houses; propr. John Waddingham Hand Prints, fine arts serigraphs and silk screen drawings, 1965—; featured artist: Am. Artist mag., May 1967, June 1990, published in numerous mags. Served with USAAF, 1942-46. Recipient gold medal Salone Internazionale dell' Umorismo, Italy, 1974, 76, 80; honored with a 45 yr. retrospective Assignment: The Artist as Journalist Oreg. Hist. Soc., 1991. Artist mem. Portland Art Mus.; mem. Portland Art Dirs. Club (past pres.), N.W. Watercolor Soc., Watercolor Soc. Oreg., Oreg. Soc. Artists (watercolor tchr.), Multnomah Athletic Club, Jewish Community Ctr., Univ. Oreg. Med. Sch., Art in the Mounts., Oreg. Old Time Fiddlers, Clan Macleay Bagpipe Band. Home and Studio: 955 SW Westwood Dr Portland OR 97201-2744

WADDINGTON, RAYMOND BRUCE, JR., English language educator; b. Santa Barbara, Calif., Sept. 27, 1935; s. Raymond Bruce and Marjorie Gladys (Waddell) W.; m. Linda Gayle Jones, Sept. 7, 1957 (div.); children: Raymond Bruce, Edward Jackson; m. Kathleen Martha Ward, Oct. 11, 1985. B.A., Stanford U., 1957; Ph.D., Rice U., 1963; postdoctoral (Univ. fellow in Humanities), Johns Hopkins U., 1965-66. Instr. English U. Houston, 1961-62; instr. U. Kans., 1962-63; asst. prof., 1963-65; asst. prof. English lit. U. Wis., Madison, 1966-68; asso. prof. U. Wis., 1968-74, prof., 1974-82; prof. English lit. U. Calif., Davis, 1982—. Author: The Mind's Empire, 1974; co-editor: The Rhetoric of Renaissance Poetry, 1974, The Age of Milton, 1980, The Expulsion of the Jews, 1994; mem. editl. bd. The Medal, 1991; sr. editor: Sixteenth Century Jour.; editor: Garland Studies in the Renaissance. Huntington Library fellow, 1967, 75; Inst. Research in Humanities fellow, 1971-72; Guggenheim fellow, 1972-73; NEH fellow, 1977, 83; Newberry Library fellow, 1978; Am. Philos. Soc. grantee, 1965. Mem. Renaissance Soc. Am., Milton Soc. Am., Am. Numismatic Soc., 16th Century Studies Conf. (pres. 1985), Logos Club. Home: 39 Pershing Ave Woodland CA 95695-2845 Office: U Calif Dept English Davis CA 95616

WADDLE, JOHN FREDERICK, former retail chain executive; b. Somerset, Ky., July 1, 1927; s. Lewis Everett and Anna Hail (Prather) W.; m. Catherine Joan Osborn, June 3, 1977; children: Lewis Victor, Joan Catherine, John Frederick. B.S., U. Ky., 1949; M.S., NYU, 1952. With Sears, Roebuck and Co., Chgo., 1949-85; nat. mgr. toys Sears, Roebuck and Co., 1969-72, asst. to sr. exec. v.p. merchandising, 1972-76, group nat. merchandising mgr., 1977-78, v.p. children's apparel, 1978-82; mng. dir., exec. v.p. Sears World Trade, Inc., Chgo., 1982-85. Served with USN, 1945-46. Republican. Presbyterian.

WADE, BEN FRANK, college administrator; b. Roanoke, Va., July 20, 1935; s. Frank Hart and Clyde Temple (Weaver) W.; m. Janice Marie Wine, June 14, 1958; children—Andrea Marie, Laurel Faye. B.A., Bridgewater Coll., 1957; M.Div. cum laude, United Theol. Sem., 1960; S.T.M., Boston U., 1961; M.S., Columbia U., 1966; Ph.D., Hartford Sem. Found., 1966. Prof. Shenandoah Coll., Winchester, Va., 1963-65, United Theol. Sem., Dayton, Ohio, 1965-69, James Madison U., Harrisonburg, Va., 1969-71; acad. dean Brevard Coll., N.C., 1971-73, Fla. So. Coll., Lakeland, Fla., 1973-77; pres. Westmar Coll., LeMars, Iowa, 1977-79; provost Bridgewater Coll., Va., 1979-85; v.p., acad. dean Fla. So. Coll., Lakeland, Fla., 1985-96; retired, 1996; mem., chmn. accreditation visit teams So. Assn. Colls. and Schs., State Council Higher Edn. Va.; vis. lectr. Div. chmn. YMCA Capital Funds Campaign, Lakeland, Fla., 1975. Named Disting. Alumnus, Bridgewater Coll., 1994; Hartzler fellow Hartford Sem. Found., 1961-62, 62-63. Mem. AAUP, Theta Chi Beta, Phi Eta Sigma, Omicron Delta Kappa. Mem. Ch. of Brethren. Avocations: breadmaking; saddle horses; music. Home: 3733 Highland Fairways Blvd Lakeland FL 33809

WADE, BENNY BERNAR, educational administrator; b. Crisp County, Ga., Oct. 3, 1939; s. Julius D. and Eleanor Eugenia (Boulware) W.; m. Merle Bailey Wade, Nov. 11, 1957; children: Noel, Tara. BS in Edn., Ga. So. Coll., 1964; MEd, U. Ga., 1968, Specialist Edn., 1973, EdD, 1977. Lic. reading specialist gifted, adminstrn. and supervision. Tchr., coach Turner County Bd. Edn., Ashburn, Ga., 1964-67; acad. skills coord. Ga. Southwestern Coll., Americus, 1968-71, asst. prof., 1978; curriculum dir. Dooly County Bd. Edn., Vienna, Ga., 1971-78; dir. edn. svcs. agy. Heart of Ga. Coop. Ednl. Svcs. Agy./Regional Ednl. Svcs. Agy., Eastman, 1979-94; exec. dir. RANREB Learning Enhancement Svcs., Inc., Eastman, Ga., 1994—; cons. parent edn., Eastman, 1977—; mem. Regional Ednl. Svcs. Agy. stds. task force Ga. Dept. Edn., Atlanta, 1988-91; mentor, coach So. Regional Ednl. Bd., 1993-94. Author: Benny's Book of Peruvian Proverbs, 1983; editor newsletter Ga. RESA Dirs., 1992. Organizer Four Dimensional Wellness Club, Eastman, 1991; activist Environ. Concers Agy., Eastman, 1989—. Exp. tchr. fellow U. Ga., Athens, 1967; recipient Alumni award for ednl. leadership Ga. Southwestern Coll., Americus, 1980. Mem. Internat. Reading Assn. (local leadership chairperson 1992-93), Ga. Regional Ednl. Svcs. Agy. Dirs. (pres. 1984-85), Ga. Assn. Ednl. Leaders, Eastman Rotary (pres. 1985-86), Phi Delta Kappa. Democrat. Methodist. Avocations: reading, writing, running, ruminating, renewing. Home: PO Box 334 Cordele GA 31010 Office: RANREB Learning Enhancement Svcs Inc PO Box 334 Cordele GA 31015-0334

WADE, BILL, airport executive. Gen. mgr. Met. Oakland (Calif.) Internat. Airport. Office: Met Oakland Internat Airport Box 45 1 Airport Dr Oakland CA 94621*

WADE, CHERYL H., church official. Counselor, tchr. Latin Sch. of Chgo.; assoc. pastor North Shore Bapt. Ch., Chgo., 1980-83; mem. staff Ministers and Missionaries Benefit Bd., 1984—, asst. treas., 1987-90, treas., 1990-92; assoc. gen. secs., treas. Am Bapt. Chs., Valley Forge, Pa., 1993—. Office: Am Bapt Chs in USA PO Box 851 Valley Forge PA 19482-0851

WADE, EDGAR L., church administrator. Sec. Christian Meth. Episcopal Ch. Annual Conf., Memphis.

WADE, EDWIN LEE, writer, lawyer; b. Yonkers, N.Y., Jan. 26, 1932; s. James and Helen Pierce (Kinne) W.; m. Nancy Lou Sells, Mar. 23, 1957; children: James Lee, Jeffrey K. BS, Columbia U., 1954; MA, U. Chgo., 1956; JD, Georgetown U., 1965. Bar: Ill. 1965; fgn. svc. officer U.S. Dept. State, 1956-57; mktg. analyst Chrysler Internat., S.A., Switzerland, 1957-61; intelligence officer CIA, 1961-63; industry analyst U.S. Internat. Trade Commn., 1963-65; gen. atty. Universal Oil Products Co., Des Plaines, Ill., 1965-72; atty. Amsted Industries, Inc., Chgo., 1972-73; chief counsel dept. gen. svcs. State of Ill., Springfield, 1973-75; sr. atty. U.S. Gypsum Co., Chgo., 1975-84; gen. atty., USG Corp., 1985, corp. counsel, 1986, asst. gen. counsel, 1987, corp. sec., 1987-90, corp. sec., asst. gen. counsel, 1990-93; prin. Edwin L. Wade, 1993-95. Author: (book) Constitution 2000: A Federalist Proposal for the Next Century, 1995; editor, pub. Let's Talk Sense, A Public Affairs Newsletter, 1994—. Fellow Chgo. Bar Assn. (life); mem. ABA, Ill. Bar Assn., Union League Club Chgo., Am. Philatelic Soc., Royal Philatelic Soc. Can., Toastmasters Internat. Home: 434 Mary Ln Crystal Lake IL 60014-7257 Office: Let's Talk Sense PO Box 6716 Chicago IL 60680-6716

WADE, GEORGE JOSEPH, lawyer; b. N.Y.C., Mar. 3, 1938; s. George J. and Catherine V. (Sweeney) W.; m. Gwendolen Belmont Livermore, June 27, 1964; children: Barbara Caroline, George J. A.B., Fordham Coll., 1959; LL.B., Harvard U., 1962. Bar: N.Y. 1963, U.S. Supreme Ct., U.S. Dist. Ct. (so. and ea. dists.) N.Y., U.S. Dist. Ct. (we. and no. dists.) Tex., U.S. Ct. Appeals (2d, 3d, 5th, 6th, 11th cir.). Assoc. Cravath, Swaine & Moore, N.Y.C., 1963-70; assoc. Shearman & Sterling, N.Y.C., 1970-72, ptnr., 1972—. Vestryman St. James Episcopal Ch., N.Y.C., 1984-90; chancellor Episcopal Diocese of N.Y., 1992—; bd. dirs. The Big Apple Circus, Ltd., 1977-94, pres., 1987-90; bd. dirs. Lamb's Theatre Co., N.Y.C., 1984-87. Mem. ABA, N.Y. State Bar Assn., Assn. of Bar of City of N.Y., Union Club, West Side Tennis (gov. 1982-92). Democrat. Office: Shearman & Sterling 599 Lexington Ave Fl 2C New York NY 10022-6030

WADE, GLEN, electrical engineer, educator; b. Ogden, Utah, Mar. 19, 1921; s. Lester Andrew and Nellie (Vanderwerff) W.; m. LaRee Bailey, Mar. 20, 1945; children: Kathleen Ann, RaLee, Lisa Jean, Mary Sue. B.S. in Elec. Engring, U. Utah, 1948, M.S., 1949; Ph.D., Stanford U., 1954. Research group leader, asso. prof. elec. engring. Stanford U., 1955-60; asso. dir. engring., microwave and power tube div. Raytheon Co., 1960-61, asst gen. mgr. research div., 1961-63; dir. Sch. Elec. Engring., Cornell U., 1963-66, J.P. Levis prof. engring., 1963-66; prof. elec. engring. U. Calif. at Santa Barbara, 1966—; indsl. advisor U. R.I., 1961-63; vis. lectr. Harvard, 1963; cons. to industry, 1956—; vis. prof. Tokyo U., 1971; Fulbright-Hays lectr., Spain, 1972-73; cons. me. Dept. Def. Adv. Group Electron Devices, 1966-73; Spl. Chair prof. Nat. Taiwan U., 1980-81; UN vis. prof. Nanjing Inst. Tech., 1986; internationally renowned fgn. scholar lectureship Nat. Taiwan U., 1988, UN vis. prof. S.E. U., People's Republic of China, 1989, Comité Naacional de Ciencia y Tecnologia vis. prof. U. de Guanajuato, Mex., 1994-95; elected mem. The Electromagnetics Acad., 1990. Editor: Transactions on Electron Devices, 1961-71, IEEE Jour. Quantum Electronics, 1965-68; series editor: Harcourt Brace Jovanovich, 1964—; contbr. articles to profl. jours. U.S. del. Tech. Cooperation Program internat. meeting, 1970. Served with USNR, 1944-46. Recipient ann. award Nat. Electronics Conf., 1959, Outstanding Teaching award Acad. Senate, U. Calif., Santa Barbara, 1977, Prof. of Yr. award U. Calif. at Santa Barbara Mortar Bd. Sr. Honor Soc., 1988, Hon. Chairmanship award Twentieth Acoustical Imaging, 1992. Fellow IEEE (life) (mem. adminstrv. com. profl. group election devices 1960-71, mem. publs. bd., chmn. info. processing com., mem. exec. com. 1971-72, dir. 1971-72, chmn. ednl. activities bd. 1971-72, editor proc. 1977-80, Centennial award 1984); mem. Am. Phys. Soc., Phi Kappa Phi, Tau Beta Pi, Sigma Xi, Eta Kappa Nu (Outstanding Young Elec. Engr. award 1955). Home: 1098 Golf Rd Santa Barbara CA 93108-2411

WADE, JAMES O'SHEA, publisher; b. Atlanta, June 17, 1940; s. Richard J. and Mary Clare (O'Shea) W.; m. Linda Norman, June 19, 1971; 1 child, Christopher Scott. AB magna cum laude, Harvard U., 1962. Editor Blaisdell Pub. Co., N.Y.C., 1963-65; asst. to pres., sr. editor Macmillan Co., 1966-69; editor-in-chief World Pub. Co., 1969-71; v.p., editorial dir. David McKay Co., 1971-74; founder, pres. Wade Pub. Co., Inc., N.Y.C., 1975-78; exec. v.p. Rawson, Wade Pubs., Inc., N.Y.C., 1978-82; sr. editor Crown Pubs., Inc., N.Y.C., 1982-85, exec. editor, 1985-95, v.p., 1988-95; with Ind. Editors Group, 1996—. Mem. Century Club (N.Y.C.), Iroquois/D.U. Club (Harvard), Hasty-Pudding Inst. 1770 (Harvard U.). Democrat. Home and Office: 1565 Baptist Church Rd Yorktown Heights NY 10598-5812

WADE, NICHOLAS MICHAEL LANDON, journalist; b. Aylesbury, Buckinghamshire, U.K., May 17, 1942; came to U.S., 1971; s. Michael Rubens and Laurien (Beesley) W.; m. Mary Veronica Scallan; children: Jessica, Alexander. Student, Eton (Eng.) Coll., 1955-59; BA, Cambridge (Eng.) U., 1960, MA, 1963. Journalist Nature mag., London, 1967-71, Science mag., Washington, 1972-82; editorial writer N.Y. Times, 1982-90, editor sci. sect., 1990—. Author: The Ultimate Experiment, 1977, The Nobel Duel, 1981, A World Beyond Healing, 1987; co-author: Betrayers of the Truth, 1983. Office: New York Times 229 W 43rd St New York NY 10036-3913

WADE, REBECCA HAYGOOD, education professional; b. Manila, Nov. 27, 1946; d. Wilbon Benfield and Gloria (Atencio) Haygood; m. William Edward Wade, Dec. 6, 1968; 1 child, William Edward, Jr. BA, U. Philippines, Manila, 1972; MA, Ball State U., 1979. Lic. profl. counselor, Nebr.; cert. profl. counselor, Nebr., Tex. Instr. U. Philippines, Clark AFB, 1972-73; testing specialist Zweibruecken AFB, Fed. Republic Germany, 1978-79; guidance counselor Untalan H.S., Barrigada, Guam, 1979-84; social svc. worker ARC, Andersen AFB, Guam, 1982-83, Family Support Ctr., Offutt AFB, Nebr., 1985-86; edn. counselor Edn. Ctr., Offutt AFB, 1986-90, edn. svcs. officer, 1990—; adj. prof. Met. C.C., Omaha, 1991—. Editor: AF Nathan Althsuler, 1989. Vol. USAF Wives Clubs, Clark AFB, Philippines, Bucks Harbor Air Force Sta., Maine, 1974-77; mem. Altrusa Internat. Club, Bellevue, Nebr., 1987—. Mem. Am. Counseling Assn., Assn. for Counselors and Educators in Govt., Nebr. Counseling Assn., Assn. for Multicultural Counseling and Devel., Nebr. Mental State Bd. (bd. dirs.), Nebr. Counseling and Devel. (bd. dirs. 1990-91, Counselor of Yr. 1990), Nebr. Commn. on Status of Women (Women of Yr. award 1992), Nebr. Assn. Multicultural Counseling and Devel. (pres. 1989-90). Avocations: sports, reading, traveling. Office: 55 Mission Support Squadron Offutt A F B NE 68113

WADE, ROBERT GLENN, engineering executive; b. Sturgeon, Mo., Nov. 21, 1933; s. Robert Clifford and Mildred Guinn (Bartee) W.; m. Geraldine Harris, Dec. 27, 1959; 1 child, Carolyn Ruth. BSCE, U. Mo., 1955. Registered profl. engr., Mo., Kans. Structural engr. Carter-Waters Corp., Kansas City, Mo., 1958-62; project mgr. Pfuhl & Stevson, Kansas City, 1962-76; prin. Stevson-Hall & Wade, Inc., Kansas City, 1976-82; pres. Structural Engring. Assocs., Inc., Kansas City, 1982-85, chmn., chief exec. officer, 1985—; mem. Mo. Bd. Architects, Engrs. and Land Surveyors, 1992—; mem. Midwest Concrete Industry Bd., pres., 1975-76. Contbg. author: Quality Assurance for Consulting Engineers, 1986. Com. mem. Downtown Coun., Kansas City, 1990. 1st lt. USAF, 1956-58. Recipient 1st merit award Midwest Concrete Industry Bd., 1976, award of excellence Am. Inst. Steel Constrn., 1982, Excellence in Design award Prestressed Concrete Inst., 1988. Fellow ASCE (pres. Kansas City sect. 1986-87, Leadership award 1987); mem. Am. Cons. Engrs. Coun. (firm rep., bd. dirs. 1987-88), Cons. Engrs. Coun. Mo. (firm rep., pres. 1986-87, Svc. award 1987). Avocation: golf. Office: Structural Engring Assocs 101 W 11th St Kansas City MO 64105-1803

WADE, ROBERT HIRSCH BEARD, international consultant, former government and educational association official; b. Tamaqua, Pa., Oct. 5, 1916; s. Edgar Gerber and Florence Annabelle (Hirsch) W.; m. Eleanor Marguerite Borden, Sept. 14, 1946; 1 son, Gregory Borden. A.B. magna cum laude, Lafayette Coll., 1937; diplome d'etudes universitaires, Bordeaux U., 1938; Ph.D., Yale U., 1942. Instr. French Yale U., 1939-42; chief Far Eastern analyst Office Naval Intelligence, 1946-54; asst. Office Nat. Security Coun. Affairs, Dept. Def., Washington, 1954-56, dir., 1956-61; spl. asst. to asst. sec. state for ednl. and cultural affairs, 1962; dir. multilateral and spl. activities Bur. Ednl. and Cultural Affairs, Dept. State, 1962-64; U.S. permanent rep. to UNESCO, with rank of minister, 1964-69; asst. dir. U.S. Arms Control & Disarmament Agy., Washington, 1969-73; exec. dir. Fgn. Student Service Council, Washington, 1974-77; dir. Washington office Am. Assembly Collegiate Schs. Bus., 1977-85; internat. cons., 1986—; Mem. U.S. del. to UNESCO Gen. Confs., 1962, 1964, 1966, 68; dep. U.S. mem. exec. bd. UNESCO, 1964-69; mem. U.S. Nat. Commn. for UNESCO, 1977-83, vice chmn., 1978-79. Author, editor: Management for XXI Century, 1982. Trustee Am. Coll. in Paris, 1967-78, chmn. bd., 1967-69. Served to lt. USNR, 1942-46, PTO. Recipient Merit Citation award Nat. Civil Service League. Fellow Acad. Internat. Bus.; mem. Am. Fgn. Svc. Assn., Friends of Vieilles Maisons Francaises, Phi Beta Kappa, Kappa Delta Rho (Ordo Honorium 1991). Republican. Christian Scientist. Clubs: Union Interallee (Paris), Racing (Paris); Chevy Chase (Washington). Avocations: tennis, swimming, piano. Home and Office: 3049 W Lane Ky NW Washington DC 20007-3057

WADE, ROBERT PAUL, lawyer; b. Atlantic City, Aug. 22, 1936; s. John Joseph and Irene Madeline (Saxon) W.; m. Jeanne Krohn, Aug. 5, 1979; children: Elliott Saxon, Kellyn Deirdre. AB, George Washington U., 1963, JD, 1968. Bar: D.C. 1968, Md. 1990. Assoc. Denning and Wohlstetter, Washington, 1968-69; atty. Office Compt. Gen. U.S., Washington, 1969-72; gen. counsel Nat. Endowment for the Arts, Washington, 1972-83; ptnr. Lowe, Bressler & Wade, Washington, 1983-86, Silverberg and Wade, Washington, 1986-94, Duncan & Wade Assocs., 1994—; vis. lectr. in intellectual property and employment law Stanford U., NYU, George Washington U. With U.S. Army, 1955-58. Mem. Phi Sigma Tau, Nat. Honor Soc. (philosophy). Home: RR 1 Box 467 Bluemont VA 22012-9510 Office: Ste 600 1625 Massachusetts Ave NW Washington DC 20036-2212

WADE, RODGER GRANT, financial systems analyst; b. Littlefield, Tex., June 25, 1945; s. George and Jimmie Frank (Grant) W.; m. Karla Kay Morrison, Dec. 18, 1966 (div. 1974); children: Eric Shawn, Shannon Annelle, Shelby Elaine; m. Carol Ruth Manning, Mar. 28, 1981. BA in Sociology, Tex. Tech. U., 1971. Programmer First Nat. Bank, Lubbock, Tex., 1971-73, Nat. Sharedata Corp., Odessa, Tex., 1973; asst. dir. computing ctr. Odessa Community Coll., 1973-74; programmer/analyst Med. Sci. Ctr., Tex. Tech U., Lubbock, 1974-76; sys. mgr. Hosp. Info. Sys., Addison, Tex., 1976-78; programmer, analyst Harris Corp., Grapevine, Tex., 1978-80, Joy Petroleum, Waxahachie, Tex., 1980-82; owner R&C Bus. Sys./Requerdos de Santa Fe, N.Mex., 1982-84; fin. sys. analyst Los Alamos (N.Mex.) Tech. Assocs., 1984-95; sr. cons. Unidata Corp., Denver, 1995—; owner El Rancho Herbs, Santa Fe, 1988-91, Wade Gallery, Santa Fe, 1990-91, Wade Systems, Santa Fe, 1992—. Vol. programmer Los Alamos Arts Coun., 1987-88; mem. regulations task force N.Mex. Gov.'s Health Policy Adv. Com.; vol. systems support Amigos Unidos of Taos, 1990—. Republican. Avocation: photography. Home: 7160 Berthoud St Westminster CO 80030 Office: Unidata Corp 1099 18th St Ste 2500 Denver CO 80202

WADE, THOMAS EDWARD, electrical engineering educator, university research administrator; b. Jacksonville, Fla., Sept. 14, 1943; s. Wilton Fred and Alice Lucyle (Hedge) W.; m. Ann Elizabeth Chitty, Aug. 6, 1966; children: Amy Renee, Nathan Thomas, Laura Ann. BSEE, U. Fla.-Gainesville, 1966, MSEE, 1968, PhD, 1974. Cert. Rsch. Adminstr., 1992—. Interim asst. prof. U. Fla.-Gainesville, 1974-76; prof. elec. engring. Miss. State U., Starkville, 1976-85, state-wide dir. microelectronics rsch. lab., Miss., 1978-85, assoc. dean., prof. electrical engring. U. South Fla., Tampa, 1985—, dir. Engring. Indsl. Experiment Sta., 1986-93, exec. dir. Ctrs. for Engring. Devel. and Rsch., 1985-90, mem. presdl. faculty adv. com. for rsch. and tech. devel., 1986-88, mem. fed. demonstration project com. for contracts and grants, 1986-88; mem. adv. bd. USF Exec. Fellows Program, 1987-91; chmn. evaluation task force applied rsch. grants program High Tech. and Industry Coun. State of Fla., 1988-90, vice chmn. microelectronics and materials subcom. 1987-93, mem. telecom. subcom., 1988-89, chmn. legis. report com. FHTIC, 1989-90; vice chmn. subcom. on microelectronics and materials Enterprise Fla. Innovation Partnership, 1993-94; mem. Tampa Bay Internat. Super Task Force, 1986-92, vice chmn. edn. com. 1988; dir. Fla. Ctr. for Microelectronics Design and Test, 1986-88; bd. dirs. NASA Ctr. Comml. Devel. of Space Comm. Ctr., Fla., 1990-93; rev. panel govt.-univ.-industry rsch. round table for fed. demonstration project, NAS, 1988; solid state circuit specialist Applied Micro-Circuits Corp., San Diego, 1981-82; sr. scientist NASA Marshall Space Flight Ctr., Huntsville, Ala., 1983; scientist Trilogy Semiconductor Corp., Santa Clara, Calif., 1984; organizer, chmn. Very Large Scale Integrated/Ultra Large Scale Integrated Multilevel Interconnection Conf., Seminar and Exhbn., editor proceedings, 1991—; organizer, gen. chmn. Dielectrics for Ultra Large Scale Integrated Multilevel Interconnection Conf., 1995—, Chem.-Mech.-Polish Planarization for Ultra Large Scale Integrated Multilevel Interconnection Conf., 1996—; cons. in field. Author: Polyimides for Very Large Scale Integrated Applications, 1984, (U.S. Army handbook) Modern Very Large Scale Integrated Circuit Fabrication Processess, 1984, Photosensitive Polyimides for Very Large Scale Integrated Applications, 1986, Very Large Scale Multilevel Interconnection Tutorial, 1987—, Very Large Scale Multilevel Interconnection State-of-the-Art Seminar, 1989—; contbr. to encys.; contbr. 120 articles to profl. jours. Treas. Tampa Palms Civic Assn., 1994-95; vol., United Fund, Miss. State U., 1983-85. Recipient Outstanding Engring. Teaching award Coll. Engring. U. Fla., 1976, Cert. of Recognition NASA (5 times), 1981-88, Outstanding Rsch. award Sigma Xi, 1984, Outstanding Contbn. to Sci. and Tech. award Fla. Gov., 1989, 90. Mem. AAAS, NSPE, IEEE (sr. mem., guest editor periodical 1982, gen. chmn. Internat. Very Large Scale Integrated Multilevel Interconnection Conf. annually 1984-90, editor conf. proceedings 1984-90, chmn. acad. affairs com. CHMT Soc. 1984-86, gen. chmn. univ./govt./industry microelectronics symposium, 1981, tech. program commn., 1991, bd. dirs. workshop on tungsten and other refractory metals 1987-90), Am. Soc. Engring. Edn. (gen. chmn. engring. research counc. ann. meeting 1987, chmn. engring. rsch. coun. adminstrv. com. 1987-90, chmn. coun., 1990-92, session chmn. ann. meeting 1990, 92, bd. dirs. 1990-92, mem. Nominations Com. 1992-94, mem. Long Range Planning Com. 1992-95, recipient ASEE Centennial Cert. 1992, 2d Century Cert. 1993), World Future Soc., Internat. Soc. Hybrid Microelectronics, Assn. U.S. Army (bd. dirs. Suncoast chpt. 1991-93), Soc. Photo Optical Instrumentation Engring., Univ. Faculty Senate Assn. of Miss. (organizer 1985), Am. Vacuum Soc., Am. Phys. Soc., Am. Electronics Assn., Am. Inst. Physics, Nat. Coun. Univ. Rsch. Adminstrn., Soc. Rsch. Adminstrs. (external rels. com. for SRA 1988-91), Fla. Engoc. (v.p. edn. com. 1987-92, pres. 1989-90, bd. dirs. 1989-90, Fla. engring. found. trustee 1989-90, ann. meeting steering com. 1989-90, Outstanding Svc. to the Profession award 1992), Soc. Am. Mil. Engring., Order of Engrs., 1991, Sigma Xi (v.p. 1985), Tau Beta Pi (Fla. Alpha chpt. pres. 1969, 71, nat. outstanding chpt. award 1969, 71, faculty advisor Miss. Alpha chpt. 1977-85, faculty advisor Fla. Gamma chpt. 1986—, recipient outstanding hon. soc. advisor award, 1994), Eta Kappa Nu (pres. 1968), Sigma Tau, Omicron Delta Kappa, Soc. Am. Inventors, Fla. Blue Key (v.p. 1972, sec, 1971), Epsilon Lambda Chi (founder 1970, pres. 1971). Club: Downtown Tampa Rotary (Paul Harris Fellow 1987, perfect attendance award 1986—, chmn. com. on environ. issues 1990), Rotary Club New Tampa (organizer, charter mem., pres. 1995-96, v.p. 1996—). Active First Bapt. Ch., Temple Terrace, Fla., vice-chmn. bd. deacons 1989-90, chmn. bd. deacons, 1990-91, 93-94, chmn. pastor search com. 1990-91, vice chmn. long range plannning com., 1989-91, vice chmn. pastor search com., 1994-95, dir. adult coed III Sunday sch. dept. 1993-94; ch. coun. 1994-95. Avocations: collecting antique furniture, carpentry, restoring antique sports cars, basketball. Home: 5316 Witham Ct E Tampa FL 33647-1026

WADKINS, LANNY, professional golfer; b. Richmond, Va., Dec. 5, 1949; s. Jerry Lanston and Francis Ann (Burnett) W.; m. Rachel Irene Strong, Jan. 2, 1971; 1 child, Jessica. Student, Wake Forest U. Winner Sahara Invitational, 1972, PGA, 1977, World Series of Golf, 1977, Can. PGA, 1978, Tournament Players' Championship, 1979, 82, 83, Los Angeles Open, 1979, Phoenix Open, 1982, Greater Greensboro, 1983, Bob Hope Desert Classic, 1985, Doral Ryder, 1987, Hawaiian Open, 1988, Colonial Open, 1988, Anheuser Busch Classic, 1990, Hawaiian Open, 1991, Greater Hartford Open, 1992; mem. Ryder Cup Team, 1993. Office: care PGA Tour 112 Tpc Blvd Ponte Vedra Beach FL 32082-3046*

WADLER, ARNOLD L., lawyer; b. Bklyn., Aug. 15, 1943; s. Samuel and Anne (Lowenthal) W.; m. Elissa I. Devor, Sept. 17, 1967; children: Craig A., Todd J. BA, Bklyn. Coll., 1964; JD, NYU, 1967. Bar: N.Y. 1968, N.J. 1974. Asst. gen. counsel Metromedia, Inc., N.Y.C., 1968-82, assoc. gen. counsel, Los Angeles, 1982-85, v.p., gen. counsel, Secaucus, N.J., 1985-86; sr. v.p., sec. and gen. counsel Metromedia Co., East Rutherford, 1986—; pres., S&A Restaurant Corp., East Rutherford, 1992; sr. v.p., gen. counsel Metromedia Internat. Group, Inc., 1995, also bd. dirs. Mem. Zoning Bd. Adjustment, Marlboro Twp., N.J., 1980-82; exec. v.p. Marlboro Jewish Ctr., 1980-82. Mem. ABA, N.Y. Bar Assn. Lodge: KP (asst. sec. 1961-63). Office: Metromedia Co Met Exec Towers 1 Meadowlands Plz Fl 6 East Rutherford NJ 07073-2137

WADLEY, M. RICHARD, consumer products executive; b. Lehi, Utah; s. Merlyn R. and Verna Ann (Ball) W.; m. Nancy Zwiers; children: Lisa Kathleen, Staci Lin, Eric Richard, Nicole Marie. BS, Brigham Young U., 1967; MBA, Northwestern U., 1968. Brand asst. packaged soap and detergent div. Procter & Gamble Co., Cin., 1968-69, asst. brand mgr. packaged soap and detergent div., 1970-71, brand mgr. Dawn detergent, 1972-73, copy supr. packaged soap and detergent div., 1974-75, brand mgr. Tide detergent, 1975-77, assoc. advt. mgr. packaged soap and detergent div., 1977-81; corp. product dir. Hallmark Cards, Inc., Kansas City, Mo., 1982-83, corp. product dir. Ambassador Cards div., 1983-85; v.p., gen. mgr. feminine protection div. Tambrands Inc., Lake Success, N.Y., 1986-88; sr. v.p. Bongrain, Inc., N.Y.C., 1988-89; pres., CEO Alta-Dena Inc., Divsn. of Bongrain, Inc., 1989-91; pres. The Summit Group, 1991—; chmn., CEO T-Chem Products Inc., 1993—; bd. dirs. T-Chem Products, Educarp Interactive. Bd. dirs. Long Beach Opera, 1991-95, L.I. Friends of the Arts, 1986-88; mem. adv. bd. Bus. Sch. Calif. State U., Long Beach, 1991-93. Avocations: Civil War history, tennis, travel.

WADLEY, SUSAN SNOW, anthropologist; b. Balt., Nov. 18, 1943; d. Chester Page and Ellen Snow (Foster) W.; m. Bruce Woods Derr, Dec. 28, 1971 (div. July 1989); children: Shona Snow, Laura Woods; m. Richard Olanoff, July 4, 1992. BA, Carleton Coll., Northfield, 1965; MA, U. Chgo., 1967, PhD, 1973. Instr. Syracuse U., 1970-73, asst. prof., 1973-76, dir. fgn. and comparative studies program, 1978-83, prof., 1982, dir. So. Asia Ctr., 1985—, Ford-Maxwell prof. South Asian Studies, 1996—, chair anthropology dept., 1990-95; trustee Am. Inst. Indian Studies, Chgo., 1984—, exec. com., 1991-94; mem. joint com. South Asia Social Sci. Rsch. Coun., 1982-89. Author: Shakti: Power in the Conceptual Struture of Krimpur Women, 1975, Women in India: Two Perspectives, 1978, revised, 1989, 95, Struggling with Destiny in Karimpur, 1925-84, 1994; editor: Power of Tamil Women, 1980, Oral Epics in India, 1989, Media and the Transformation of Religion in South Asia, 1995. Pres. Edward Smith Parent Tchr. Orgn., Syracuse, 1988-89. Grantee NSF, 1967-69, U.S. Dept. Edn., 1983-84, Smithsonian Instn., 1983-84, Am. Inst. Indian Studies, 1989, Social Scis. Rsch. Coun., 1989, NEH, 1995. Mem. Am. Anthropological Soc., Am. Folklore Soc., Soc. for Ethnomusicology, Assn. for Asian Studies. Home: 302 Carlton Dr Syracuse NY 13214-1906 Office: Syracuse U Maxwell Sch Syracuse NY 13244

WADLINGTON, WALTER JAMES, law educator; b. Biloxi, Miss., Jan. 17, 1931; s. Walter and Bernice (Taylor) W.; m. Ruth Miller Hardie, Aug. 20, 1955; children: Claire Hardie, Charlotte Taylor Griffith, Susan Miller, Derek Alan. AB, Duke U., 1951; LLB, Tulane U., 1954. Bar: La. 1954, Va. 1965. Pvt. practice New Orleans, 1954-55, 58-59; asst. prof. Tulane U., 1960-62; mem. faculty U. Va., 1962—, prof law, 1964—, James Madison prof., 1970—; prof. legal medicine U. Va. Med. Sch., 1979—; Harrison Found. rsch. prof. U. Va., 1990-92; tutor civil law U. Edinburgh, Scotland, 1959-60; vis. Tazewell Taylor prof. law Coll. William and mary, spring 1986; program dir. Robert Wood Johnson Med. Malpractice Program, 1985-91; mem.a dv. bd. clin. scholars program, 1989—; chmn. nat. adv. bd. Improving Malpractice Precention and Compensation Sys., 1994—; Disting. Health Law Tchr. Am. Soc. Law, Medicine and Ethics. Author: Cases and Materials on Domestic Relations, 1970, 3d edit., 1995; (with Waltz and Dworkin) Cases and Materials on Law and Medicine, 1980; (with Whitebread and Davis) Children in the Legal System, 1983; editor-in-chief Tulane U. Law Rev., 1953-54. Fulbright scholar U. Edinburg. Mem. Va. Bar Assn., Am. Law Inst., Inst. Medicine of NAS, Order of Coif. Home: 1620 Keith Valley Rd Charlottesville VA 22901-3018 Office: U Va Sch Law Charlottesville VA 22903

WADLINGTON, WARWICK PAUL, English language educator; b. New Orleans, May 2, 1938; s. Robert Lee and Della Frances (Guerin) W.; m. Elizabeth Bernard, Dec. 26, 1963 (div. 1988); children: Laura, Mark, Paul; m. Elizabeth H. Harris, Feb. 18, 1995. BS, U.S. Mil. Acad., 1961; MA, Tulane U., 1966, PhD, 1967. Asst. prof. English U. Tex., Austin, 1967-72, assoc. prof., 1972-78, prof., 1978—, Joan Negley Kelleher Centennial prof., 1987—. Author: The Confidence Game in American Literature, 1975, Reading Faulknerian Tragedy, 1987, As I Lay Dying: Stories Out of Stories, 1992; contbr. articles to profl. jours. With U.S. Army, 1961-64. Decorated Air medal. Mem. MLA, Faulkner Soc., Am. Studies Assn. Office: U Tex Dept English Austin TX 78712

WADLOW, JOAN KRUEGER, academic administrator; b. LeMars, Iowa, Aug. 21, 1932; d. R. John and Norma I. (IhLe) Krueger; m. Richard R. Wadlow, July 27, 1958; children: Dawn, Kit. B.A., U. Nebr., Lincoln, 1953; M.A. (Seacrest Journalism fellow 1953-54), Fletcher Sch. Law and Diplomacy, 1956; Ph.D. (Rotary fellow 1956-57), U. Nebr., Lincoln, 1963; cert., Grad. Inst. Internat. Studies, Geneva, 1957. Mem. faculty U. Nebr., Lincoln, 1966-79; prof. polit. scis. U. Nebr., 1964-79, assoc. dean Coll. Arts and Scis., 1972-79; prof. polit. scis., dean Coll. Arts and Scis., U. Wyo., Laramie, 1979-84, v.p. acad. affairs, 1984-86; prof. polit. sci., provost U. Okla., Norman, 1986-91; chancellor U. Alaska, Fairbanks, 1991—; cons. on fed. grants; bd. dirs. Key Bank Alaska; mem. Commn. Colls. N.W. Assn. Author articles in field. Bd. dirs. Nat. Merit Scholarship Corp., Lincoln United Way, 1976-77, Bryan Hosp., Lincoln, 1978-79, Washington Ctr., 1986—, Key Bank of Alaska; v.p., exec. commr. North Cen. Assn., pres., 1991; pres. adv. bd. Lincoln YWCA, 1970-71; mem. def. adv. com. Women in the Svcs., 1987-89; mem. community adv. bd. Alaska Airlines. Recipient Mortar Board Teaching award, 1976, Disting. Teaching award U. Nebr., Lincoln, 1979; fellow Conf. Coop. Man, Lund, Sweden, 1956. Mem. Internat. Studies Assn. (co-editor Internat. Studies Notes 1978-91), Nat. Assn. State Univs. and Land-Grant Colls. (exec. com. coun. acad. affairs 1989-91), Western Assn. Africanists (pres. 1980-82), Assn. Western Univs. (pres.-elect 1993—), Coun. Colls. Arts and Scis. (pres. 1983-84), Greater Fairbanks C. of C., Gamma Phi Beta. Republican. Congregationalist. Office: U Alaska Fairbanks Singers Hall Ste 320 Fairbanks AK 99775

WADLOW, R. CLARK, lawyer; b. Providence, Nov. 30, 1946. AB, Dartmouth Coll., 1968; JD, Harvard U., 1971. Bar: Alaska 1971, D.C. 1972, U.S. Supreme Ct. 1974. Law clk. to Hon. George F. Boney Alaska Supreme Ct., 1971-72; ptnr. Sidley & Austin, Washington; adj. prof. law Cath. U. Am., Washington, 1982-87. Mem. ABA (bd. govs. 1978-81, chmn. forum com. on comm. law 1987-89, chmn. standing com. on forum coms. 1990-92, chmn. standing com. on continuing edn. of the bar 1993—, chmn. com. on scope and correlation of work 1993-94), Fed. Bar Assn. (mem. exec. com. 1989-92). Office: Sidley & Austin 1722 I St NW Fl 4 Washington DC 20006-3705

WADMAN, WILLIAM WOOD, III, educational director, technical research executive, consulting company executive; b. Oakland, Calif., Nov. 13, 1936; s. William Wood, Jr., and Lula Fay (Raisner) W.; children: Roxanne Alyce Wadman Hubbling, Raymond Alan (dec.), Theresa Hope Wadman Boudreaux; m. Barbara Jean Wadman; stepchildren: Denise Ellen Varine Skrypkar, Brian Ronald Varine. M.A., U. Calif., Irvine, 1978. Cert. program mgr. tng. Radiation safety specialist, accelerator health physicist U. Calif. Lawrence Berkeley Lab., 1957-68; campus radiation safety officer U. Calif., Irvine, 1968-79; dir. ops., radiation safety officer Radiation Sterilizers, Inc., Tustin, Calif., 1979-80; prin., pres. Wm. Wadman & Assocs. Inc., 1980—; mem. operational review team Princeton U. Rsch. Campus TOKOMAK Fusion Test Facility, 1993-94; technical project mgr. for upgrades projects Los Alamos Nat. Lab. 1994-96, tech. project mgr. for 3 projects, 1995—; mem. team No. 1, health physics appraisal program NRC, 1980—, operational readiness review team to Princeton U. Rsch. Campus TOKOMAK Fusion Test Facility, 1993-94; cons. health physicist to industry; lectr. sch. social ecology, 1974-79, dept. community and environ. medicine U. Calif., Irvine, 1979-80, instr. in environ. health and safety, 1968-79, Orange Coast Coll., in radiation exposure reduction design engring. Iowa Electric Light & Power; trainer Mason & Hanger-Silas Mason Co., Los Alamos Nat. Lab.; instr. in medium energy cyclotron radiation safety UCLBL, lectr. in accelerator health physics, 1966, 67; curriculum developer in field; subject matter expert Los Alamos Nat. Lab., Earth and Environ. Scis., Tech. Support Office. Active Cub Scouts; chief umpire Mission Viejo Little League, 1973. Served with USNR, 1955-63. Recipient award for profl. achievement U. Calif. Alumni Assn., 1972, Outstanding Performance award U. Calif., Irvine, 1973. Mem. Health Physics Soc. (treas. 1979-81, editor proc. 11th symposium, pres. So. Calif. chpt. 1977, Professionalism award 1975), Internat. Radiation Protection Assn. (U.S. del. 4th Congress 1977, 8th Congress 1992), Am. Nuclear Soc., Am. Public Health Assn. (chmn. program 1978, chmn. radiol. health sect. 1979-80), Campus Radiation Safety Officers (chmn. 1975, editor proc. 5th conf. 1975), ASTM, Project Mgmt. Inst. Club: UCI Univ. (dir. 1976, sec. 1977, treas. 1978). Contbr. articles to tech. jours. Achievements include research in radiation protection and environmental sciences; Avocations: sailing, Tae Kwon Do, wood working, numesmantics. Home: 3687 Red Cedar Way Lake Oswego OR 97035-3525 Office: 675 Fairview Dr Ste 246 Carson City NV 89701-5468 *Personal philosophy: The continuous practice of patience, openmindedness, and open communication provide the essential ingredients for a full, satisfying personal and professional life. The timing of major decisions is not a matter of heart, but the culmination of the effective use of the practices above.*

WADSWORTH, CHARLES WILLIAM, pianist; b. Barnesville, Ga., May 21, 1929; s. Charles and Ethel (Capps) W.; m. Susan Popkin, June 5, 1966; 1 dau., Rebecca; children from previous marriage—David, Beryl. Student, U. Ga., 1946-48; BS, Juilliard Sch. Music, 1951, MS, 1952. Founder, artistic dir. Chamber Music Concerts of Spoleto (Italy) Festival, 1960-77; founder Chamber Music Concerts of the Spoleto Festival, Charlesston, S.C., 1977; founder, artistic dir., pianist Chamber Music Soc. of Lincoln Ctr., N.Y.C., 1969-89; artistic dir. chamber music Spoleto/USA, Charleston, 1994—, 1996 Olympic Arts Festival, Atlanta; pianist in recitals with Beverly Sills, Hermann Prey, Jennie Tourel, Shirley Verrett, Pinchas Zukerman, Dietrich Fischer-Dieskau. Decorated Cavaliere Ufficiale nel Ordine di Merito dalla Reppublica Italiana, 1975, Chevalier in the Order of Arts and Letters, France, 1986; recipient Mayors award for excellence in the arts N.Y.C., 1979, Handel medallion of City of N.Y. Mayor Edward Koch, 1989. Office: Chamber Music Soc of Lincoln Ctr 70 Lincoln Center Plz New York NY 10023

WADSWORTH, DYER SEYMOUR, lawyer; b. N.Y.C., June 16, 1936; s. Seymour and Phoebe Armistead (Helmer) W.; m. Beverley Allen Dunn Barringer, Feb. 2, 1963; children: Sophia, Jennifer. B.A., Yale U., 1959; J.D., Harvard U., 1962. Bar: N.Y. 1963, Pa. 1979. Assoc. Humes, Andrews & Botzow, N.Y.C., 1962-64; with Inco Ltd. and subs., N.Y.C., 1964-96; asst. gen. counsel Inco Ltd., N.Y.C.; pres. Inco U.S., Inc., N.Y.C., 1993-96; v.p., gen. coun., bd. dirs. Barringer Crater Co., Flagstaff, Ariz.; pres., treas., dir. Cass County Iron Co., Atlanta, Tex. Gen. counsel The Sailors Snug Harbor, Sea Level, N.C., 1987—; pres., bd. dirs. Amsterdam Nursing Home Corp., N.Y.C., 1986—; trustee Isaac Tuttle Fund for the Aged, N.Y.C., 1968-96; bd. dirs. N.Y. Health Care Network, Inc., N.Y.C. Named Trustee of Yr. N.Y. Assn. Homes and Svcs. for the Aging, 1995. Mem. Assn. of Bar of City of N.y., Meteoritical Soc. Clubs: Down Town Assn., Union, Pilgrims (N.Y.C.). Home: 215 E 48th St New York NY 10017-1538

WADSWORTH, FRANK WHITTEMORE, foundation executive, literature educator; b. N.Y.C., June 14, 1919; s. Prescott Kingsley and Elizabeth (Whittemore) W.; m. Roxalene Harriet Nevin, Oct. 22, 1943 (dec. 1979); Susan, Roxalene; m. Deborah Yohalem, Dec. 22, 1980. A.B., Princeton U., 1946, Ph.D., 1951. Instr. English Princeton (N.J.) U., 1949-50; instr. to assoc. prof. English UCLA, 1950-61; prof. English, dean div. humanities U. Pitts., 1962-67; acad. v.p. SUNY-Purchase, 1967-78, prof. lit., 1967-89, emeritus, 1989—; nat. rep. Woodrow Wilson Nat. Fellowship Found., 1958-61, trustee, 1973—; vice-chmn. bd. trustees, 1992—; trustee Wenner-Gren Found., N.Y.C., 1970—, chmn. bd. trustees, 1977-87. Author: The Poacher from Stratford, 1958; contbr. articles to publs. Trustee Rye Country Day Sch., N.Y. Served to lt. (j.g.) USNR, 1942-45. Woodrow Wilson fellow, 1946-47; Scribner fellow, 1948-49; Folger Shakespeare Library fellow, 1961; Guggenheim fellow, 1961-62. Mem. MLA, Am. Soc. Theatre Research, Malone Soc., Phi Beta Kappa. Clubs: Princeton; Conanicut Yacht (R.I.). Home: 430 Sterling Rd Harrison NY 10528-1404

WADSWORTH, HAROLD WAYNE, lawyer; b. Logan, Utah, Oct. 12, 1930; s. Harold Maughan and Nellie Grace (Grosjean) W.; m. Laila Anita Ingebrigtsen, Dec. 27, 1957; children: Warren, Kenneth, Jeffrey, Theresa, Erik. BS, Utah State U., 1952; JD with honor, George Washington U., 1959. Bar: D.C. 1959, Utah 1961, U.S. Dist. Ct. Utah 1961, U.S. Ct. Appeals (10th cir.) 1962, U.S. Ct. Appeals (9th cir.) 1978, U.S. Supreme Ct. 1972. Spl. agt. FBI, Atlanta and Macon, 1959-60; assoc. atty., ptnr. Hanson, Wadsworth & Russon, Salt Lake City, 1961-77; ptnr. Watkiss & Campbell, Salt Lake City, 1978-89, Watkiss & Saperstein, Salt Lake City, 1990-91, Ballard, Spahr, Andrews & Ingersoll, Salt Lake City, 1992-95, Jones Waldo Hollbrook & McDonough, Salt Lake City, Utah, 1996—. 1st lt. U.S. Army, 1952-54. Republican. Mem. LDS Ch. Avocations: horsemanship, hunting, fishing, opera, Shakespeare. Office: Jones Waldo Holbrook & McDonough 1500 1st Intersate Plz 170 S Main St Salt Lake City UT 84101

WADSWORTH, JACQUELINE DORÈT, private investor; b. San Diego, June 15, 1928; d. Benjamin H. Dilley and Georgia E. (Elliott) Dilley Waters; m. Charles Desmond Wadsworth Jr., June 16, 1954 (dec. 1963); 1 child, Georgia Duncan Wadsworth Barber. BS, U. Oreg., 1946-50; MA, San Diego State U., 1950-52. Cert. tchr. Calif., Oreg. Dir. Jr. Red Cross, San Diego County chpt. ARC, 1952-59; asst. dir. leadership ctrs. for 8 western states ARC, Calif., 1954-59; pvt. investor, comml. real estate and property devel., 1974—; interior designer J. Wadsworth Interiors, La Jolla, Calif., 1990—. Vol. chairperson nat. conv. ARC, San Diego, 1966; vol., fundraiser San Diego Symphony Orch. Orgn., 1974-83; mem. Gold Ribbon Patron com. San Diego Symphony, 1995—; friends mem., vol. San Diego Mus. Art, 1958—, Asian Arts Com., 1996—; mem. Scripps Found. for Medicine and Sci., 1990—; life mem., bd. programs Mercy Hosp. Aux., 1965—; life mem., chairperson, bd. dirs. Social Svc. Aux., 1968—. Recipient Svc. awards Mercy Hosp. Aux., 1967-70. Mem. Caridad Internat., Globe Gilders Theatre Aux. (activity chairperson 1966-85), San Diego Zool. Soc. (curator 1976—), Country Friends Charities La Jolla Group, Mus. Contemporary Art San Diego. Republican.

WADSWORTH, MICHAEL A., athletic director, former ambassador; b. Toronto, ON, Canada, 1943. Professional football player Toronto Argonauts, CFL, 1966-70; lawyer, 1971-81; ambassador to Ireland Canadian Foreign Min., 1989-94; athletic dir. U. Notre Dame, 1995—. Office: U Notre Dame Dept of Athletics Notre Dame IN 46556

WADSWORTH, ROBERT DAVID, advertising agency executive; b. Prestbury, Cheshire, Eng., May 20, 1942; came to U.S., 1978; s. Eric and Irene (Thorpe) W.; m. Kathleen O'Meara, Dec. 13, 1968; children: Tracey, Charles Robert. B.A., U. Natal, S. Africa, 1963. With Lever Bros. S. Africa, 1960-66, sr. brand mgr., 1964-66; sr. brand mgr. Gen. Foods S. Africa, 1967; account exec. London Press Exch., S. Africa, 1968, Grant Advt., S. Africa, 1969; dir., then mng. dir. Cen. Advt., Johannesburg, S. Africa, 1970-73; dir. new bus. coord. McCann-Erickson, South Africa, 1973-78; sr. v.p., mng. rep., new bus. coord. McCann-Erickson, Inc., N.Y.C., 1978-82; client dir., exec. v.p. Lintas, N.Y.C., 1983-90; dir. corp. strategy, regional dir. So. Africa Lintas Worldwide, N.Y.C., 1991—. Home: 20 Hobson St Stamford CT 06902-8114 Office: Lintas Worldwide 1 Dag Hammarskjold Plz New York NY 10017-2201

WAECHTER, ARTHUR JOSEPH, JR., lawyer; b. New Orleans, Nov. 20, 1913; s. Arthur Joseph and Elinor (Reckner) W.; m. Peggy Weaver, Feb. 20, 1939; children: Susan Porter Waechter McClellan, Sally Ann Waechter McGehee, Robert. AB, Tulane U., 1934, LLB, 1936. Bar: La. 1936. Since practiced in New Orleans; ptnr. Jones, Walker, Waechter, Poitevent, Carrere & Denegre, 1942—; prof. law Sch. Law Tulane U., 1947-68, prof. emeritus, 1968—; bd. dirs. Canal Barge Co., Inc. Bd. visitors Tulane U., 1959-64; bd. advisers to editors Tulane Law Rev. Assn., 1960—; bd. adminstrs. Tulane Ednl. Fund, 1968-83, emeritus bd. adminstrs., 1983—. Served to lt. (j.g.) USNR, 1943-46. Mem. ABA, La. Bar Assn. (gov. 1968-70), New Orleans Bar Assn. (pres. 1961-62), Internat. Assn. Def. Counsel, Tulane U. Alumni Assn. (pres. 1962-63), Maritime Law Assn. U.S., Am. Law Inst., Am. Judicature Soc., Am. Coll. Real Estate Lawyers (gov. 1983-86), Order of Coif, Pickwick Club, Boston Club, Stratford Club, La. Club, So. Yacht Club, The Plimsol (New Orleans), Phi Kappa Sigma, Phi Delta Phi. Home: 1210 Webster St New Orleans LA 70118-6031 Office: Jones Walker Waechter Poitevent Carrere & Denegre 201 Saint Charles Ave New Orleans LA 70170-1000

WAETJEN, WALTER BERNHARD, academic administrator emeritus; b. Phila., Oct. 16, 1920; s. Walter E. and Marguerite D. (Dettmann) W.; m. Betty Walls, Sept. 28, 1945; children: Walter Bernhard, Kristi Waetjen Jenkins, Daniel G. BS, U. Pa., Millersville, 1942; MS, U. Pa., 1947; EdD, U. Md., 1951; LittD (hon.), Hanyang U., Seoul, Korea, 1980; LLD (hon.), Gama Filho U., Brazil, 1980; LHD (hon.), Cleveland State U., 1992, Ashland U., 1993. Profl. football player Detroit Lions and Phila. Eagles 1942-45; tchr. Sch. Dist. Phila., 1945-48; rsch. fellow U. Md., 1948-50, mem. faculty, 1950-73, prof. ednl. psychology, 1957-65; dir. Bur. Ednl. Rsch. and Field Svcs., 1962-65; gen. dir. Interprofl. Rsch. Commn. Pupil Pers. Svcs., 1963-65, v.p. adminstrv. affairs, 1965-70, v.p. gen. adminstrn., 1970-73; pres. Cleve. State U., 1973-88; vis. prof. Cambridge U., 1988-89; sr. fellow Internat. Tech. Edn. Assn., 1989; interim pres. Ashland (Ohio) U., 1992-93; vis. rsch. fellow U. Edinburgh, Scotland, 1991; Patty Hill Smith Meml. lectr. U. Louisville, 1964; psychol. cons. to sch. systems, 1951—; bd. dirs. Overseas Capital Corp.; mem. governing bd. St. Vincent Quadrangle, Inc.; chmn., bd. dirs. Talbot Philanthropies, Inc., 1994; mem. pres.'s commn. NCAA, 1984-88; chmn. Internat. Tech. Edn. Adc. Coun.; Nat. Coun. on Sci. and Tech., 1991—. Co-author in field.; contbr. articles to ednl. jours. Trustee Woodruff Found.; mem. governing bd. St. Vincent Charity Hosp. and Health Ctr. Corp. Recipient Disting. Alumni award Pa. State Coll., 1972, Commdr's. Cross of Order of Merit award, Fed. Republic Germany, 1986, Order Yugoslav Flag Govt. of Yugoslavia, 1988. Mem. ASCD, AAAS (mem. nat. coun. on sci. and tech. edn. 1990—), Assn. Mid-Continent Univs. (pres. 1983), Soc. Rsch. Child Devel., Assn. Urban Univs. (chmn. 1984—), Am. Edn. Rsch. Assn., Aesculapian Soc., Blue Key, Iota Lambda Sigma, Phi Delta Kappa, Phi Kappa Phi, 50 Club, Union Club, Masons. Home and Office: 4790 Sailors Retreat Rd Oxford MD 21654-1739

WAGEMAN, LYNETTE MENA, librarian; b. Trinidad, West Indies, Aug. 18, 1934; came to U.S., 1955.; d. Hubert and Alma (Sampath) Jagbandhansingh. BA in Modern Fgn. Langs., Park Coll., Parkville, Mo., 1959; MLS, U. Hawaii, 1966, MA in Asian Studies, 1976. Serials asst. East-West Ctr. Libr., Honolulu, 1962-66; catalog libr. U. Hawaii, Honolulu, 1966-71, South Asia specialist, 1971-93, acting head Asia collection, 1991-93, head, 1993—, collection devel. mgr. Asia collection, pub. svc. head rep., 1991—; exec. com. Ctr. South Asian Studies, 1973-75, 77-79, 81-83, 85-86, 87-90, acting dir., 1988, 90, 92. Mem. Hawaii Libr. Assn. (mem. bd. 1990-92, co-editor newsletter 1990-92), Assn. Asian Studies (exec. bd. com. on South Asian Librs. and Documentation 1983-85, 90—, chairperson 1992—, exec. com. Asian Libr. Liaison com. 1991—, adv. com. Bibliography Asian Studies 1992—), Internat. Assn. Orientalist Librs., South Asian Lit. Assn., Com. on Women in Asian Studies. Avocation: cultivating Bromeliads and other exotic plants. Office: U Hawaii Asia Collection Hamilton Libr 2550 The Mall Honolulu HI 96822-2233 Office: Hamilton Libr Asia Collection 2550 The Mall Honolulu HI 96822-2233

WAGEMAN, VIRGINIA FARLEY, editor; b. Jersey City, N.J., Feb. 18, 1941; d. James Christopher and Charlotte Carter (Stebbins) Farley; m. Steven Lipson, Dec. 26, 1962 (div. 1964); 1 child, Melissa; m. James Carter Wageman, Apr. 22, 1968; children: Robinson Michael, Sarah Carter. BA, Bard Coll., 1964. Book editor, prodn. asst. AICPA, N.Y.C., 1964-67; prodn. mgr. U. Hawaii Press, 1967-68; asst. dir. office univ. rels. U. Md., Balt., 1968-70; dir. publs. art mus. Princeton U., 1971-81; writer, editor Hirshhorn Mus. and Sculpture Garden, Washington, 1982-86; freelance editor, 1986—; sr. editor Hudson Hills (N.Y.) Press, 1988-89; mgr. publs. Coll. Art Assn., N.Y.C., 1989—. Recipient Smithsonian Commendation for Exceptional Svc. Mem. Art Table, Assn. Freelance Art Editors (pres. 1984-86), Princeton Rsch. Forum. Home: 360 Ridgeview Rd Princeton NJ 08540-7667 Office: Coll Art Assn 275 7th Ave New York NY 10001-6708

WAGENER, HOBART D., retired architect; b. Sioux Falls, S.D., May 10, 1921; s. Frank Samuel and Beatrice (Hobart) W.; m. Violet LaVaughn, Dec. 16, 1944; children: Diane Kay Wagener Welch, Jeffrey Scott, Shaw Bradley. BArch, U. Mich., 1944. Registered architect, Colo. Draftsman Eggers & Higgins, Architects, N.Y.C., 1946-47, Pietro Belluschi, Architect, Portland, Oreg., 1947-50; designer James Hunter, Architect, Boulder, Colo., 1950-53; prin. Hobart D. Wagener Assocs., Boulder, 1953-77; prin. ptnr. Wagener VanderVorste, Architects, Boulder, 1977-86; ret., 1986; mem. selection com. Colo. Supreme Ct., Denver, 1968-72. Co-author: The School Library, 1962; work pub. in Archtl. Record, Sunset mag., N.Y. Times, House Beautiful, 25 Years of Record Houses. Chmn. Boulder Planning Commn., 1966; pres. Boulder C. of C., 1971. Lt. (j.g.) USN, 1944-46, PTO. Named Outstanding Designer for past 50 yrs. Hist. Boulder, 1983; also numerous nat. and regional design awards. Fellow AIA (pres. Colo. 1973, Colo. Architect of Yr. award 1985), Lions (pres. Boulder 1965). Avocations: travel, golf. Address: 1730 Avenida Del Mundo Apt 1607 Coronado CA 92118-3028

WAGENER, JAMES WILBUR, social science educator; b. Edgewood, Tex., Mar. 18, 1930; s. James W. and Ima (Crump) W.; m. Ruth Elaine Hoffman, May 31, 1952; children: LuAnn Wagener Powers, Laurie Kay Wagener Ulman. BA, So. Methodist U., 1951, BD, 1954; MA, U. Tex., Austin, 1967, PhD (Ellis fellow 1967-68), 1968. Instr. edn. U. Tex., Austin, 1967-68, asst. prof., 1970-74; asst. prof. U. Tenn., Knoxville, 1968-70; asst. to chancellor acad. affairs U. Tex. System, 1974; assoc. prof. U. Tex., San Antonio, 1974-78, acting pres., 1978, pres., 1978-89, prof. div. edn. Coll. Social and Behavioral Scis., 1978—; asst. to pres., then exec. asst. to pres. U. Tex. Health Sci. Center, San Antonio, 1974-78, acting dean Dental Sch., 1976-78. Author articles, book revs. in field. Bd. govs. Southwest Found. Research and Edn., San Antonio, 1978-89; bd. dirs., trustee Southwest Research Inst., 1978-89. Office: Dept Social Behavioral Scis U Tex at San Antonio San Antonio TX 78249-0654

WAGENER, ROBERT JOHN, bioethicist, mediator; b. Buffalo, N.Y., Mar. 6, 1946; s. Philip John and June Augusta (Bartels) W. BA, SUNY, Buffalo; MDiv, McCormick Theol. Sem., Chgo.; MA, Canisius Coll. Founder, pres. Ctr. for Med. Ethics and Mediation, San Diego, 1992—; mediation coord. Am. Arbitration Assn., 1993—; cons. U. Calif. San Diego Ethics Consultation Svc., 1985—; lectr., mediator, mentor, trainer in field. Contbr. articles to profl. jours. Bd. dirs. Hospice Buffalo, Victim Offender Reconciliation Program, San Diego, UCSD Med. Ctr. Ethics Com.; cons. San Diego Hospice Chaplaincy Project; vice chair Hotel Dieu Hosp. Hospice, New Orleans; v.p. Sudden Infant Death Found. Western N.Y. Mem. ABA (dispute resolution sect.), Am. Soc. Law, Medicine and Ethics, Soc. Profls. in Dispute Resolution, So. Calif. Mediation Assn., Internat. Bioethics Inst., Hastings Ctr. for Bioethics. Avocations: racquetball, skiing, antiques. Office: Ctr for Med Ethics & Mediation 1081 Camino del Rio S Ste 217 San Diego CA 92108

WAGENKNECHT, EDWARD, author; b. Chgo., Mar. 28, 1900; s. Henry E. and Mary (Erichsen) W.; m. Dorothy Arnold, Aug. 3, 1932; children: Robert Edward, David Arnold, Walter Chappell. PhB, U. Chgo., 1923, MA, 1924; PhD, U. Wash., 1932. Prof. of English Boston U., 1947-65, prof. emeritus, 1965—; editor Boston U. Studies in English, 1954-57; Lowell lectr., 1958. Author: many critical and biog. works, including The Man Charles Dickens, 1929, rev. edit., 1966, Mark Twain, The Man and His Work, 1935, rev., 1961, 67, Cavalcade of the English Novel, 1943, rev. edit., 1954, Cavalcade of the American Novel, 1952, A Preface to Literature, 1954, Longfellow, A Full Length Portrait, 1955, The Seven Worlds of Theodore Roosevelt, 1958, Nathaniel Hawthorne, Man and Writer, 1961, Washington Irving: Moderation Displayed, 1962, The Movies in the Age of Innocence, 1962, Edgar Allan Poe: The Man Behind the Legend, 1963, Chicago, 1964, Seven Daughters of the Theater, 1964, Harriet Beecher Stowe, The Known and The Unknown, 1965, Dickens and the Scandalmongers, 1965, Merely Players, 1966, Henry Wadsworth Longfellow: Portrait of an American Humanist, 1966, John Greenleaf Whittier: A Portrait in Paradox, 1967, The Personality of Chaucer, 1968, As Far As Yesterday: Memories and Reflections, 1968, William Dean Howells: The Friendly Eye, 1969, The Personality of Milton, 1970, James Russell Lowell: Portrait of a Many-Sided Man, 1971, Ambassadors for Christ: Seven American Preachers, 1972, The Personality of Shakespeare, 1972, Ralph Waldo Emerson: Portrait of a Balanced Soul, 1974; Nine Before Fotheringhay: A Novel about Mary Queen of Scots (under pseud. Julian Forrest), 1966, The Glory of The Lilies, A Novel about Joan of Arc (under pseud. Julian Forrest), 1969; (with Anthony Slide) The Films of D.W. Griffith, 1975, A Pictorial History of New England, 1976, Eve and Henry James: Portraits of Women and Girls in His Fiction, 1978; (with Anthony Slide) Fifty Great American Silent Films, 1912-20, 1980, Henry David Thoreau: What Manner of Man?, 1981, American Profile, 1900-1909, 1982, Gamaliel Bradford, 1982, The Novels of Henry James, 1983, Daughters of the Covenant, 1983, The Tales of Henry James, 1984, Henry Wadsworth Longfellow: His Poetry and Prose, 1986, Stars of the Silents,

1987, Nathaniel Hawthorne, The Man, His Tales and Romances, 1989, Sir Walter Scott, 1991, Seven Masters of Supernatural Fiction, 1991, Willa Cather, 1994; editor: Mrs. Longfellow: Selected Letters and Journals, 1956, The Supernaturalism of New England (John Greenleaf Whittier), 1969, The Letters of James Branch Cabell, 1974; also numerous anthologies including The Fireside Book of Christmas Stories, 1945, The Collected Tales of Walter de la Mare, 1950, An Introduction to Dickens, 1952, Chaucer: Modern Essays in Criticism, 1959, Stories of Christ and Christmas, 1963, The Stories and Fables of Ambrose Bierce, 1977, Washington Irving's Tales of the Supernatural, 1982. Home: 177 Leo Dr Gardner MA 01440-1213

WAGER, BARBARA, headmaster. Prin. James P.B. Duffy Sch. No. 12, Rochester, N.Y.; headmaster Boston Renaissance Pub. Charter Sch. Recipient Elem. Sch. Recognition award U.S. Dept. Edn., 1989-90. Office: James P B Duffy Sch No 12 999 South Ave Rochester NY 14620-2746

WAGER, DEBORAH MILLER, researcher, consultant; b. Phila., Sept. 5, 1938; d. Albert S. and Pauline (Goldberg) Miller; m. Robert J. Wager, July 3, 1966; 1 child, James M. BA, Skidmore Coll., 1960; MAT, Cornell U., 1963. Editor Toy Quality and Safety Report, Washington, 1972-88; cons. Wager Rsch., Washington, 1989—; devel. rschr. Sidwell Friends Sch., Washington, 1988-89, 92-93; trustee Sheridan Sch., Washington, 1978-84. Author: Good Toys, 1986. Mem. Assn. Profl. Rschrs. Advancement. Office: Wager Rsch Consulting 4545 29th St NW Washington DC 20008-2144

WAGER, DOUGLAS CHARLES, artistic director; b. Gloversville, N.Y., June 11, 1949; s. George Robert and Jane Margaret (Upright) W.; m. Cary Anne Spear, June 20, 1981 (div. Nov. 23, 1993). BA in English Lit. and Theater, SUNY, Albany, 1971; MFA in Directing, Boston U., 1974. Intern Arena Stage, Washington, 1974, asst. stage mgr., 1974-75, stage mgr., 1975-76, asst. prodn. coord., 1976-77, lit. mgr., 1977-80, assoc. dir., 1980-83, assoc. producing dir., 1983-91, artistic dir., 1991—; assoc. prof. drama Colo. Coll., Colorado Springs, 1981, 84, guest artist summer theatre inst., 1985, 86. Dir. (stage prodns.) Madmen, 1975, Singers, Scooping, 1976, Gemini Trappers, 1977, The Curse of the Starving Class, 1978, The Past, 1978, Conjuring an Event, 1978, You Can't Take It With You, 1979, The Man Who Came to Dinner, 1980, 89, The Child, 1980, A Lesson from Aloes, 1981, Tomfoolery, 1981, 83, Animal Crackers, 1981, On the Razzle, 1982, Candide, 1982, As You Like It, 1983, Accidental Death of an Anarchist, 1983, 84, Man and Superman, 1984, Execution of Justice, 1984 (Helen Hayes awards for Outstanding Direction and Outstanding Resident Prodn.), Women and Water, 1985, The Philadelphia Story, 1985, The Taming of the Shrew, 1985, Measure for Measure, 1986, Glengary Glen Ross, 1986, Don Pasquale, 1986, All the King's Men, 1987, The Rivers and Ravines, 1987, The Cocoanuts, 1987 (Helen Hayes award for Outstanding Resident Musical), L'Amico Fritz, 1987, A Lie of the Mind, 1988, On the Town, 1988, Merrily We Roll Along, 1989, Our Town, 1990, Pygmalion, 1990, The Seagull, 1990, A Wonderful Life, 1991, The Father, 1991, The Visit, 1991, Of Thee I Sing, 1992, The Skin of Our Teeth, 1992, Twelfth Night, 1993, The Revengers' Comedies, 1994, The Odyssey, 1994, Long Day's Journey Into Night, 1995, The Matchmaker, 1995, Candide, 1996. Recipient Creative Achievement in Theatre award Boston U. Sch. Arts Alumni Assn., 1989. Avocations: wine collection, tennis, hiking, biking. Office: Arena Stage 6th And Maine Ave SW Washington DC 20024

WAGER, PAULA JEAN, artist; b. Lansing, Mich., Dec. 19, 1929; d. Mervin Elihu and Cora Della (Raymer) Fowler; m. William Douglas Wager, May 4, 1952; children: Pamela Ann, Scott Alan. Student, Mich. State U., 1949-52. Music tchr. Toledo, Ohio, 1968-72, Union Lake, Mich., 1972-76; tchr. art, artist Paula Wager's Art Studio, Commerce Twp., Mich., 1984—; hostess Artistic Touch with Paula, Cable Comcast channel 44, Waterford, Mich., TCI West Oakland, Walled Lake, Mich., Channel 10, 1991-94. Exhibited in group shows including Village Art Supplies, 1982-88, Pontiac Oakland Soc. Artists, 1983—, Pontiac Galleria, 1983, Oakland C.C., Commerce Twp., 1985, Red Piano Gallery, Hilton Head, S.C., 1985-89, Mich. State U., East Lansing, 1986, Silver Pencil Gallery, Pontiac, 1987-89, Wooden Sleight, Vestaburg, Mich., 1988-93, Art Pad, Keego Harbor, Mich., 1990-93, Local Color Gallery, Union Pier, Mich., 1992-94, Mich. Assn. Artists, Southfield Civ. Ctr. Mich. 1995; Waterford Public Lib., Solo Exhibit, 1996; Swann Gallery, Detroit, 1995—, Millers Artist Supplies, Ferndale, Mich., 1996; one-woman shows include Waterford (Mich.) Pub. Libr., 1996; represented in pvt. collections. Recipient Outstanding Achievement award in instructional programming Comcast Cable TV, Waterford, 1992, 1st place, Waterford Friends of the Arts Art Show, 1988, Pontiac Oakland Soc. Artists Cmty. Rm., 1990, Am. Biog. Inst. Woman of Yr. Commemorative medal, 1995; Waterford Cable Commn. grantee, 1991, 93, Charter Twp. of Waterford grantee, 1991-94. Mem. Nat. Assn. Female Exec. Pontiac Oakland Soc. Artists, Waterford Friends of the Arts, Mich. Watercolor Soc., Birmingham Bloomfield Art Assn., Colored Pencil Soc. Am., Colored Pencil Soc. Detroit, Village Fine Arts Assn. Avocations: music, art. Home and Studio: 3316 Greenlawn Ave Commerce Township MI 48382-4629

WAGER, WALTER HERMAN, author, communications director; b. N.Y.C., Sept. 4, 1924; s. Max Louis and Jessie (Smith) W.; m. Sylvia Liebowitz Leonard, May 6, 1951 (div. May 1975); 1 child, Lisa Wendy; m. Winifred McIvor, June 4, 1975. BA, Columbia U., 1943; LLB, Harvard U., 1946; LLM, Northwestern U., 1949. Bar: N.Y. 1946. Spl. asst. to Israel dir. Civil Aviation, 1951-52; freelance writer N.Y.C., 1952-54; sr. editor UN, N.Y.C., 1954-56; freelance TV and mag. writer N.Y.C., 1956-63; editor-in-chief Playbill mag., N.Y.C., 1963-66; editor Show mag., N.Y.C., 1965; cons. pub. rels. and editorial dept. ASCAP, N.Y.C., 1966-72, dir. pub. relations, 1972-78; cons. pub. relations Nat. Music Pub. Assn., N.Y.C., 1978-84; dir. communications Juilliard Sch., N.Y.C., 1985-86; counsel pub. relations Mann Music Ctr., Phila., 1986-87, Eugene O'Neill Theater Ctr., N.Y.C., 1987-89; dir. pub. info. U. Bridgeport, 1991-93; tchr. Northwestern U., 1949, Columbia U., 1955-56; spl. asst. to atty. gen. N.Y. State investigation hate lit. in elections, 1962; bd. dirs. Jazz Hall of Fame, 1975-77. Author: Death Hits the Jackpot, 1954, Operation Intrigue, 1956, I Spy, 1965, Masterstroke, 1966, Superkill, 1966, Wipeout, 1967, Countertrap, 1967, Death Twist, 1968, The Girl Who Split, 1969, Sledgehammer, 1970, Viper Three, 1971 (filmed as Twilights's Last Gleaming 1977), Swap, 1972, Telefon, 1975 (filmed in 1977), My Side-By King Kong, 1976, Time of Reckoning, 1977, Blue Leader, 1979, Blue Moon, 1980, Blue Murder, 1981, Designated Hitter, 1982, Otto's Boy, 1984, 58 Minutes, 1987 (filmed as Die Hard 2, 1990); (non-fiction) Camp Century, 1962, Playwrights Speak, 1967, (with Mel Tillis) Stutterin' Boy, 1984. Pres. Columbia Coll., class 1944. Fulbright fellow Sorbonne, Paris, 1949-50, Northwestern U. Law Sch. fellow, 1948-49. Mem. Writers Guild Am., Mystery Writers Am. (bd. dirs. 1988-94), Authors League, Nat. Acad. Popular Music (bd. dirs. 1975-92). Democrat. Jewish. Avocation: traveling. Home and Office: 200 W 79th St New York NY 10024-6212

WAGGENER, RONALD EDGAR, radiologist; b. Green River, Wyo., Oct. 6, 1926; s. Edgar Fleetwood and Mary Harlene (Hutton) W.; m. Everina Ann Stalker, Aug. 1, 1948; children: Marta, Nancy, Paul, Daphne. Student, Colo. A&M U., 1944; student, Oreg. State U., 1945; BS, U. Nebr., 1949, MS, 1952, PhD, 1957, MD cum laude, 1954, postgrad., 1955-58; postgrad., St. Bartholomew's, London, 1956-57. Diplomate Am. Bd. Radiology. Intern U. Nebr. Hosp., 1954-55, resident, 1955-56, 57-58; radiation therapist Nebr. Meth. Hosp., Omaha, 1965-70, chmn. cancer com., 1964-89, dir. cancer and radiation therapy, 1964-89, chr. dept. radiology, 1970-89, dir. cancer fellowship program, 1977-89; instr. radiology U. Nebr., Omaha, 1958, asst. prof., 1959-61, radiation therapist, 1959-65, assoc. prof., 1962-80, clin. assoc. prof., 1981—; pres. Highland Assocs. Ltd., Omaha, 1977-89; mem. cancer com. Children's Meml. Hosp., Omaha, 1970-89. Contbr. articles to profl. jours. With C.E., U.S. Army, 1944-46. Fellow AEC, 1952-53, Am. Cancer Soc., 1956-57. Fellow Am. Coll. Radiologists; mem. Nebr. Radiology Soc. (pres. 1963-64), Sigma Xi, Alpha Omega Alpha, Phi Nu. Home: 1227 S 109th St Omaha NE 68144-1813 Office: 13304 W Center Rd Omaha NE 68144-3453

WAGGENER, SUSAN LEE, lawyer; b. Riverside, Calif., Oct. 21, 1951; d. Lee Richard and Alice Lillian (Fritch) W.; m. Steven Carl McCracken, July 29, 1979; children: Casey James McCracken, Scott Kevin McCracken. BA magna cum laude, U. So. Calif., 1973; JD magna cum laude, U. San Diego, 1976. Bar: Calif. 1977, Hawaii 1977. Law clk. to hon. Samuel P. King, Jr. U.S. Dist. Ct. Hawaii, Honolulu, 1976-77; assoc. Gibson, Dunn & Crutcher, Newport Beach, Calif., 1978-86; ptnr. Gibson, Dunn & Crutcher, Newport Beach, 1986—. Exec. editor U. San Diego Law Rev., 1975-76. V.p. 552 Club Hoag Hosp., Newport Beach, 1982-85. Mem. ABA, Orange County Bar Assn. Avocations: hiking, tennis, skiing, real estate law. Office: Gibson Dunn & Crutcher Jamboree Ctr 4 Park Plz Irvine CA 92714-8560*

WAGGONER, JAMES CLYDE, lawyer; b. Nashville, May 7, 1946; s. Charles Franklin and Alpha (Noah) W.; m. Diane Dusenbery, Aug. 17, 1968; children: Benjamin, Elizabeth. BA, Reed Coll., 1968; JD, U. Oreg., 1974. Bar: Oreg. 1974, U.S. Dist. Ct. Oreg. 1975, U.S. Ct. Appeals (9th cir.) 1980, U.S. Tax Ct. 1979, U.S. Supreme Ct. 1979. Clerk to presiding justice Oreg. Supreme Ct., Salem, 1974-75; assoc. Martin, Bischoff & Templeton, Salem, 1975-78; ptnr. Martin, Bischoff & Templeton, Portland, 1978-82, Waggoner, Farleigh, Wada, Georgeff & Witt, Portland, 1982-89, Davis Wright Tremaine, Portland, 1990—. Contbr. articles to profl. jours. Fulbright scholar U. London, 1968-69. Mem. ABA, Oreg. Bar Assn., Multnomah Bar Assn., Reed Coll. Alumni Assn. (v.p. 1988, pres. 1989, bd. mgmt.) Alzheimers Assn. of Columbia-Willamette (v.p. 1992, pres. 1993), Order Coif, Phi Beta Kappa. Democrat. Avocations: wood turning, calligraphy. Office: Davis Wright Tremaine 1300 SW 5th Ave Ste 2300 Portland OR 97201-5630

WAGGONER, JAMES VIRGIL, chemicals company executive; b. Judsonia, Ark., Oct. 29, 1927; s. Loren Dye and Vera (Meacham) W.; m. M.E. June Howell; children: Liz Waggoner Quisenberry, Jay. BS in Chemistry and Math., Ouachita Bapt. U., 1948, DSc (hon.), 1990; MS in Organic Chemistry and Math., U. Tex., 1950. Successively rsch. chemist, sales asst., asst. sales mgr., sales mgr. Monsanto, Texas City, Tex., 1950-57; dir. sales Monsanto, Springfield, Mass., 1957-59; product adminstr. Monsanto, St. Louis, 1959-61, dir. sales, 1961-63, dir. mktg., 1963-67, bus. dir., 1967-68, gen. mgr. petrochems. div., 1972-76, gen. mgr. cycle-safe div., 1976, corp. v.p., mng. dir. Plastics & Resins Co., 1977, group v.p., 1978-80; pres. petrochem. and plastics unit El Paso Co., Odessa, Tex., 1980-83; cons. to petrochem. industry Houston, 1984-85; pres., chief exec. officer Sterling Chems., Inc., Houston, 1986—; mem. adv. bd. 1st Comml. Bank, N.A., Little Rock; bd. dirs. Kirby Corp., Houston, Mail-Well Holdings, Inc., Englewood, Colo. Chmn. adv. coun. Coll. Natural Scis., U. Tex., Austin; mem. devel. coun. Ouachita Bapt. U.; bd. dirs. Tex. Rsch. League; bd. dirs., chmn. Good Samaritan Found., 1993-94; supporter, patron Star of Hope Mission; corp. leader, contbr. United Way, Texas City, LaMarque Area, Houston; mem. chmn.'s adv. bd. Rep. Nat. Conv. Mem. Nat. Petroleum Refiners Assn. (v.p., bd. dirs., exec. com.), Tex. Assn. Taxpayers (bd. dirs.). Avocations: golf, art collecting. Home: 11 Shadder Way Houston TX 77019-1415 Office: 1200 Smith St Ste 1900 Houston TX 77002-4312 *In my opinion, the greatest single character trait that separates those who excel and achieve from those who don't is their constant committment to excellence and to strive for continuing improvement.**

WAGGONER, LAWRENCE WILLIAM, legal educator; b. Sidney, Ohio, July 2, 1937; s. William J. and Gladys L. Waggoner; m. Lynne S. Applebaum, Aug. 27, 1963; children: Ellen, Diane. BBA, U. Cin., 1960; JD, U. Mich., 1963; PhD, Oxford U. (England), 1966. Assoc. Cravath, Swaine & Moore, N.Y.C., 1963; prof. law U. Ill., Champaign, 1968-72; prof. law U. Va., Charlottesville, 1972-74; prof. law U. Mich., Ann Arbor, 1974-84, James V. Campbell prof. law, 1984-87; Lewis M. Simes prof. law, 1987—; dir. rsch., chief reporter joint editorial bd. for Uniform Probate Code, 1986-94, dir. rsch., 1994—; adviser restatement (2d) of property, 1987-90; reporter restatement (3d) of property, 1990—. Served to capt. U.S. Army, 1966-68. Fulbright scholar Oxford U., 1963-65. Mem. Am. Law Inst., Am. Coll. Trust and Estates Counsel, Internat. Acad. Estate and Trust Law. Author: Estates in Land and Future Interests in a Nutshell, 1981, 2nd edit., 1993, Federal Taxation of Gifts, Trusts, and Estates (2d edit.), 1982, Family Property Law: Wills, Trusts, and Future Interests, 1991. Office: U Mich Law Sch 625 S State St Ann Arbor MI 48109-1215

WAGGONER, PAUL EDWARD, agricultural scientist; b. Appanoose County, Iowa, Mar. 29, 1923; s. Walter Loyal and Kathryn (Maring) W.; m. Barbara Ann Lockerbie, Nov. 3, 1945; children—Von Lockerbie, Daniel Maring. S.B., U. Chgo., 1946; M.S., Iowa State Coll., 1949, Ph.D., 1951. From asst. to chief scientist Conn. Agrl. Expt. Sta., New Haven, 1951-71; vice dir. Conn. Agrl. Expt. Sta., 1969-71, dir., 1972-87, disting. scientist, 1987—; lectr. Yale Forestry Sch., New Haven, 1962—; mem. panels on policy implications of global warming NAS, 1989-91. Contbr. articles to profl. jours. Served to capt. USAAF, 1943-46. Guggenheim fellow, 1963. Fellow AAAS (chmn. climate changes and water resources com. 1986-89), Am. Phytopath. Soc.; mem. NAS, Am. Meteorol. Soc. (Outstanding Achievement in Biometeorology award 1967), Conn. Acad. Sci. and Engring., Grads Club. Achievements include mathematical simulation of plant disease epidemics; hydrologic role of foliar pores; impact of climate change on agriculture and water resources; how much ten billion can spare for nature. Home: 314 Vineyard Point Rd Guilford CT 06437-3255 Office: Conn Agrl Expt Sta PO Box 1106 New Haven CT 06504-1106

WAGLE, SUSAN, state legislator, small business owner; b. Allentown, Pa., Sept. 27, 1953; m. John Thomas Wagle, Apr. 3, 1980; children: Julia Marie, Andrea Elizabeth, John Timothy, Paul Thomas. BA in Elem. Edn. cum laude, Wichita State U., 1979, post grad., 1979-82. Tchr. Chisholm Trail Elem., Kans., 1979-80; tchr. emotionally disturbed, special edn. Price Elem., Kans., 1980-82; real estate investor Kans., 1980—; prin. Wichita Bus. Inc., Kans., 1983—; mem. Kansas Ho. Reps., 1990, 92, 94—, speaker pro tem, 1994—. Mem. Am. Legis. Exchange Coun. (Outstanding Legis. of the Yr. 1994), Farm Bur., Nat. Fedn. Ind. Bus., Nat. Restaurant Assn., Wichita Ind. Bus. Assn. Home: 14 N Sandalwood St Wichita KS 67230-6612 Office: Kans Ho of Reps Rm 330 N State Capitol Topeka KS 66612-1504

WAGMAN, FREDERICK HERBERT, librarian, educator; b. Springfield, Mass., Oct. 12, 1912; s. Robert and Rebecca (Gaberman) W.; m. Ruth Jeannette Wagman, Nov. 21, 1941; children: Elizabeth L. Gaidos, William G. A.B. summa cum laude, Amherst Coll., 1933; A.M., Columbia U., 1934, Ph.D., 1942; L.H.D., Amherst Coll., 1958; LL.D. (hon.), Alderson Broaddus Coll., 1967; Litt.D., Luther Coll., 1969. Instr., Columbia Extension, 1933-35; Ottendorfer Meml. fellow NYU, 1935-36; teaching fellow Amherst Coll., 1936-37; instr. U. Minn., 1937-42; head planning unit postal div. U.S. Office Censorship, Washington, 1942-43; head regulations and trg. sect. postal div. U.S. Office Censorship, 1943-45, regulations officer, 1945; successively acting dir. personnel and acting dir. adminstrv. services Library of Congress, 1945-46, asst. dir. reference dept., 1946-47, dir. processing dept., 1947-51, dep. chief asst. librarian, 1951- 52, dir. adminstrn., 1952-53; dir. U. Mich. Library, Ann Arbor, 1953-78; prof. library sci. U. Mich. library, 1953-82; librarian Mich. Acad. Arts, Sci. and Letters, 1953-78; vice chmn. com. mgmt. Wm. L. Clements Library, 1953-78; exec. com. Mich. Hist. Collections, 1953-78; cons. UN Library, 1959-62, Hebrew U. Jerusalem, 1969, various other univs.; mem. exec. com. Nat. Book Com., 1963-64; vice chmn. Nat. Commn. Obscenity and Pornography, 1968-70; pres. Midwest Region Library Network, 1975-76; bd. dirs. Council Library Resources, 1956-91; bd. regents Nat. Library of Medicine, 1967-71. Author: Magic and Natural Science in German Baroque Literature, 1942. Named Hon. Alumnus, U. Mich. Sch. Library Sci. Mem. ALA (pres. 1963-64), Mich. Library Assn. (pres. 1960, hon. mem. 1978), Phi Beta Kappa, Phi Kappa Phi. Democrat. Home: 3840 Wynnstone Dr Ann Arbor MI 48105-2879 *Died Mar. 19, 1994.*

WAGMAN, GERALD HOWARD, retired biochemist; b. Newark, Mar. 4, 1926; s. David and Sophie (Milinsky) W.; B.S., Lehigh U., 1946; M.S., Va. Poly. Inst. and State U., 1947; m. Rhoda Kirschner, Dec. 9, 1948; children: Jan Donald, Neil Mark. Tech. research asst. Squibb Inst. for Med. Research, New Brunswick, N.J., 1947-49, research asst., 1954-57; mgr. Yankee Radio Corp., N.Y.C., 1950-54; assoc. biochemist Schering Corp. (now Schering-Plough Rsch. Inst.), Kenilworth, N.J., 1957-58, biochemist, 1958-65, sr. biochemist, 1966-68, sect. leader, 1969-70, mgr. antibiotics dept., 1970-74, assoc. dir. microbiol. scis.-antibiotics, 1974-76, assoc. dir. microbiol. scis. and head screening lab., 1977-78, dir. microbiol. strain lab., 1979-84, antibiotics isolation, 1984-85, microbial products chem. screening, 1985-87, prin. scientist, 1987-89, mgr. libr. info. ctr., 1989-93; ret., 1993; freelance tech. writing, editor, cons. 1993—; mem. adv. bd. Nat. Cert. Commn. in Chemistry and Chem. Engring., 1985-88. Coun. mem. Troop 23 Boy Scouts Am., 1964-66; communications officer East Brunswick Civil Def. and Disaster Control, 1966-71; mem. sci. adv. com. East Brunswick Bd. Edn., 1960-68; bd. dirs. Tamarack N. Homeowners Assn., 1983-84, 89—, pres., 1989-93, treas. 1994—. Recipient Public Svc. award Am. Radio Relay League, 1965. Chartered chemist, Gt. Britain. Fellow Am. Inst. Chemists; mem. AAAS, ALA, Spl. Librs. Assn., Am. Chem. Soc., Am. Soc. Microbiology, Am. Inst. Biol. Scis., Soc. Indsl. Microbiology, Soc. Applied Bacteriology (Gt. Britain), Royal Soc. Chemistry, Sigma Xi, Tau Delta Phi. Author: Chromatography of Antibiotics, 1973, rev. edit., 1984; mem. editorial bd. Antimicrobial Agents and Chemotherapy, 1971-74; co-editor: Isolation, Separation and Purification of Antibiotics, 1978, Natural Products Isolation, 1989; contbr. articles to profl. jours. and books. Patentee in field. Home and Office: 17 Crommelin Ct East Brunswick NJ 08816-2406 *Serendipity often plays a big part in research. One may discover something entirely different from the object of the research, but you must have an open mind and a wide angle of observation.*

WAGMAN, LAWRENCE D., surgical oncologist, educator; b. Bklyn., May 11, 1952; m. Michele Altman Wagman; children: Jennifer Lauren, Ashley Samantha, Brittany Hannah. BA in Biology magna cum laude, SUNY, Buffalo, 1974; MD, Columbia U., 1978. Diplomate Am. Bd. Surgery. Intern Med. Coll. of Va., 1978-79, resident, 1979-80, 82-84, chief resident, 1984-85; staff surgeon dept. of gen. oncologic surgery City of Hope Nat. Med. Ctr., Duarte, Calif., 1985-87, sr. surgeon dept. of gen. oncologic surgery, 1987—, assoc. rsch. scientist dept. metabolism and endocrinology, 1986—, coord. clin. elective in surg. oncology, 1986—; asst. clin. prof. dept. of surgery U. Calif., San Diego, 1989—; acting chmn. divsn. surgery City of Hope Nat. Med. Ctr., 1991-94, program dir. surg. oncology fellowship program, 1991—, dir. dept. of gen. oncologic surgery, 1992—, med. dir. ambulatory care svcs., 1993—, chmn. divsn. of surgery, 1994—; chmn. ambulatory care com. City of Hope Nat. Med. Ctr., 1986—, med. exec. com., 1991—, clin. cancer com., 1991—, many others; adv. coun. Calif. Dept. of Health Svcs. Breast and Cervical Cancer, 1994—; state chmn. Commn. on Cancer Liaison Program for the State of Calif., 1994-97; presenter in field. Contbr. numerous articles to profl. jours. Recipient many grants. Fellow ACS (commn. on cancer, nat. cancer data base clin. trials working group 1990-91, cancer liaison physician commn. on cancer 1992—); mem. Humera Surg. Soc., Assn. for Acad. Surgery, Soc. of Enteral and Parenteral Nutrition, Nat. Surg. Adjuvant Project for Breast and Bowel Cancers, S.W. Oncology Group (exec. com. of the surgery com. 1990—), Soc. of Surg. Oncology (examination com. 1993-96), L.A. Surg. Soc., Soc. of Head and Neck Surgeons. Home: 2611 King Way Claremont CA 91711-1722

WAGMAN, MICHAEL MARK, gifted and talented educator; b. Phila., Mar. 10, 1964; s. Marvin Morton and Elaine Judith (Kaplan) W.; m. Janice Ilene Heyderman, Aug. 5, 1990; 1 child, Aaron Seth. BS in Edn., Social Studies, West Chester U., 1986; MS in Tech. in Edn., Chestnut Hill Coll., 1993. Cert. instr. level II, social studies, lifetime, Pa. Asst. dir. Cherokee Day Camp, Bensalem, Pa., 1987-94 summers; tchr. social studies and gifted support Sch. Dist. of Springfield Twp., Oreland, Pa., 1987—; adj. prof. ednl. tech. Chestnut Hill Coll., Phila., 1993—; faculty advisor Model Orgn. Am. States, Washington, 1987—, World Affairs Coun. of Phila., 1988—, Tchg. in a Nuclear Age, Phila., 1989—; sec., bd. dirs. Global Edn. Motivators, Phila., 1992—; presenter ednl. tech. confs., Pa., 1991—. Prodr. of student local history videos for cmty. cable, 1993—. campus coord. Commonwealth Assn. of Students, West Chester, Pa., 1982-83; The Friar Soc. Svc. Soc., West Chester Chpt., 1985-86; sch. coord. blood drive ARC, 1989—, faculty advisor Springfield Twp. H.S. Student Coun., Erdenheim, Pa., 1989—; co-chair strategic planning Sch. Dist. Springfield Twp., Oreland, Pa., 1993-94. Mem. ASCD, NEA, Pa. Edn. Assn., Internat. Soc. for Tech. in Edn., Coun. for Exceptional Children, World Future Soc. Avocations: computers, sci. fiction, current events, reading. Office: Sch Dist of Springfield Twp 1901 Paper Mill Rd Oreland PA 19075-2418

WAGMAN, ROBERT JOHN, journalist, author; b. Chgo., Nov. 11, 1942; s. Albert Alan and Rosamond (Horner) W.; m. Carol Ann Mueller, Jan. 30, 1965; children: Jennifer, Robert, Patricia, Marilyn. A.B., St. Louis U., 1966, M.A., 1968, J.D., 1971. Analyst Dun & Bradstreet, 1965-67; with CBS News, 1967-71, 74-77; asst. to dean St. Louis U. Sch. Law, 1971-74; Washington bur. chief N.Am. Newspaper Alliance, 1977-80, Ind. News Alliance, 1980-82; columnist Newspaper Enterprise Assn., 1980-95; pub. Fed. Real Estate Letter, 1995—. Author, co-author: Hubert Humphrey, The Man and His Dream, 1978, Citizens Guide to the Tax Revolt, 1979, Asbestos: The Silent Killer, 1982, Lord's Justice, 1985, Instant Millionaires, 1986, The Nazi Hunters, 1988, The First Amendment Book, 1991, 2d edit., 1996, World Almanac Guide to the Supreme Court, 1993, Blood Oath, 1994; editor: World Almanac of U.S. Politics, 1988—. Recipient Thomas Stokes award in journalism.

WAGNER, ALAN BURTON, entrepreneur; b. Balt., June 8, 1938; s. Robert Ellsworth and Anna Margaret (Schnitzlein) W.; B.Engring. Sci. (scholastic leadership award) Johns Hopkins, 1960; M.M.E., Case-Western Res. U., 1962, Ph.D. in Bus. Mgmt., 1965; m. Lynn Felton Wynant, June 26, 1964; children: Brian Alan, David Scott, Elizabeth Lynn. Mgr. orgn. planning and devel. Internat. Minerals & Chem. Corp., Libertyville, Ill., 1964-67, dir., 1967-70, dir., v.p., 1970-73, corp. v.p., 1973-78; pres., dir. Taylor Tot Products, Inc., Frankfort, Ky., 1979-80, Fed. Mining Co., 1980-82, Wagner Mgmt. Corp., 1982—; prin., pres. Hilliard-Lyons, Wagner Assoc., 1982-92, Ky. Metals, Inc., Carolina Metal, Inc., Fla. Metals, Inc., Tex. Almet, Inc., Control Machine, Inc., FM Properties; lectr. in field. Trustee, Union Coll., Furman U. Fellow Alfred P. Sloan Nat. Found.; mem. Chgo. Assn. Commerce and Industry, Chem. Industries Council of Midwest, ASME, Am. Mgmt. Assn., ASHRAE, (Homer Addams award), AAAS, Ky. Coal Assn. (dir.), Sigma Xi, Omicron Delta Kappa. Clubs: Knollwood (Lake Forest, Ill); Greenbrier, Lafayette (Lexington). Home: 1523 Lakewood Ct Lexington KY 40502-2567 Office: 651 Perimeter Dr Ste 600 Lexington KY 40517-4139

WAGNER, ALAN CYRIL, television and film producer; b. N.Y.C., Oct. 1, 1931; s. Joseph and Isabelle (Chanson) W.; m. Martha Celia Dreyfus, Mar. 11, 1956; children: David Mark, Susan Jill, Elizabeth Celia. BA, Columbia U., 1951, MA in English, 1952. Mgr. network programs Benton & Bowles, Inc., N.Y.C., 1957-61; dir. program devel. CBS, N.Y.C., 1961-68; v.p. program devel. CBS, Hollywood, Calif., 1968-73; v.p. program planning and devel. CBS, N.Y.C., 1973-75, v.p. nighttime programs, 1975-78, v.p. programs, 1978-82; pres., chief exec. officer The Disney Channel, N.Y.C., 1982-83, Alan Wagner Prodns., Inc., N.Y.C., 1983—; exec. v.p. feature and TV devel. and prodn. Grosso-Jacobson Entertainment Corp., N.Y.C., 1985-90; pres. Boardwalk Entertainment, N.Y.C., 1990—; adj. assoc. prof. visual arts NYU, 1993—. Prodr., dir., host program Living Opera, Stas. WNYC-WNYC-FM, N.Y.C., 1958-68; host radio broadcasts N.Y.C. Opera Co., 1978-80; panelist Met. Opera broadcast Quiz, 1996—; exec. prodr. film Reunion at Fairborough, 1985; prodr. TV pilot We're Puttin' on the Ritz, 1986; author: Prima Donnas and other Wild Beasts, 1961; exec. com. The Gunfighters, Diamonds; supervising prodr. Cop Talk: Behind the Shield, 1988, 89, True Blue, TV movie and series, 1989, A Family for Joe, TV movie and series, 1989-90, TV series Counterstrike, 1990-93, Top Cops, 1989-94; exec. prodr. TV movies Spenser: Ceremony, Spenser: Pale Kings and Princes, 1993, Spenser: The Judas Goat, Spenser: A Savage Place, 1994, Wounded Heart, 1995, Hearts Adrift, Love's Young Dream, 1996, TV series The Marriage Counselor, 1994. Lt. (j.g.) USNR, 1953-57. Recipient Evelyn Burkey Meml. award Writers Guild Am., 1983. Mem. NATAS, Internat. Radio and TV Soc., Acad. Cable Programming, Columbia U. Alumni Assn. Avocations: opera, other music, sound reproduction, baseball, other sports. Office: Boardwalk Entertainment 210 E 39th St New York NY 10016-0911 *A decent and abiding respect for the opinions and talents of the creative community on one hand, and the consuming community on the other, has always served as the necessary framework for any decision making in both my professional and personal life. The doers and the thinkers are crucially important, but no more so than those for whom they do and think. If I can serve as an effective middle man, a good part of my life's objective is realizable.*

WAGNER, ALLAN RAY, psychology educator, experimental psychologist; b. Springfield, Ill., Jan. 6, 1934; s. Raymond August and Grace (Johnson) W.; m. Barbara Rae Meland, Nov. 21, 1959, (dec. Nov. 1994); children: Krystn Rae, Kathryn Rae. B.A., U. Iowa, 1956, M.A., 1958, Ph.D., 1959; M.A. hon., Yale U., 1970. Asst. prof. psychology Yale U., New Haven,

1959-64, assoc. prof., 1964-69, prof., 1970-89, chmn. psychology dept., 1983-89, James Rowland Angell prof. psychology, 1990—, chmn. philosophy dept., 1991-93, dir., divsn. of the soc. sci., 1992—; cons. NIMH, 1968-71; mem. Pres. Biomed. Research Panel, 1975-76; adv. bd. Cambridge Ctr. Behavioral Studies, 1982—; mem. psychobiology panel NSF, 1984-85, com. on basic research in behavioral and social scis. NRC, 1984-87. Author: Reward and Punishment, 1965; assoc. editor: Learning and Motivation, 1969-74, Animal Learning and Behavior, 1972-74; editor: Jour. Exptl. Psychology, 1974-81, Quantitative Analyses of Behavior, Vol. 3, 1982, Vol. 4, 1983, Vol. 7, 1988. Fellow NSF, 1958 (grantee 1960—), NIMH, 1963. Fellow APA, AAAS (mem. coun. 1988-91), Soc. Exptl. Psychologists (Howard Crosby Warren medal 1991), Am. Psychol. Soc.; mem. NAS, Psychonomic Soc., So. Quantitative Analysis of Behavior (sec. 1983-92), Ea. Psychol. Assn. (bd. dirs. 1985-88), Sigma Xi, New Haven Law Club. Home: 1405 Ridge Rd North Haven CT 06473-3051 Office: Yale U Dept Psychology PO Box 208205 New Haven CT 06520-8205

WAGNER, ALVIN LOUIS, JR., real estate appraiser, consultant; b. Chgo., Dec. 19, 1939; s. Alvin Louis and Esther Jane (Wheeler) W.; m. Susan Carole Fahey, Aug. 14, 1965; children: Alvin Louis III, Robert Percy. Student, U. Ill., 1958-59; BA, Drake U., 1962; postgrad., Real Estate Inst., Chgo., 1960-65. Asst. appraiser Oak Park (Ill.) Fed. Savings & Loan Co., 1955-60; v.p. real estate sales A. L. Wagner & Co., Flossmoor, Ill., 1961-63; real estate loan officer, chief appraiser Beverly Bank, Chgo., 1963-67; assoc. real estate appraiser C. A. Bruckner & Assocs., 1967-70; founder, profl. real estate appraiser, cons. A. L. Wagner & Co., Flossmoor, 1970—; mem. faculty Am. Inst. Real Estate Appraisers, Chgo., 1974—; instr. real estate appraising Prairie State Coll., Chicago Heights, Ill., 1970—; mem. adv. com. Real Estate Sch., 1972—; community prof. Gov.'s State U., 1977—. Author: The Relocation Appraisal Guide Book; mem. editorial bd. Appraisal Jour., 1975—; contbr. articles to real estate jours., also Mobility mag., Mcpl. Econ. Devel. Founding mem. real estate adv. bd. Gov.'s State U.; mem. Rich Township (Ill.) Personal Svcs. Commn., 1973—; v.p., drive chmn. Flossmoor Community Chest, Crusade of Mercy, 1974-75, pres., 1975-76; auditor Rich Township, 1973-77; mem. governing bd. Glenwood (Ill.) Sch. for Boys, 1973—; chmn. bus. edn. occupational adv. com. Homewood-Flossmoor High Sch., 1977; pres. South Suburban Focus Coun.; mem. South Suburban Mayors and Mgrs. Bus. and Industry Adv. Coun., Flossmoor Econ. Devel. Commn.; bd. dirs. Prairie State Coll. Found., 1985—; treas. U.S. Dept. Housing & Urban Devel. South Suburban Community Housing Resources Bd., 1981—; assoc. mem. Employee Relocation Coun. Recipient Profl. Recognition award, 1989, 92, Pres.'s award, 1989. Mem. Relocation Appraisers Consortium (founder, v.p. 1991), Am. Inst. Real Estate Appraisers (mem. governing coun. 1974-75, Profl. Recognition award 1977), Soc. Real Estate Appraisers (nat. pub. rels. com., vice chmn. 1985—), Real Estate Educators Assn., South Suburban Assn. Commerce and Industry, Chgo. Assn. Commerce and Industry, Chgo. Real Estate Bd., Homewood-Flossmoor Real Estate Bd., Nat. Assn. Realtors, Ill. Assn. Realtors, Appraisal Inst., Homewood-Flossmoor Jaycees, Flossmoor Country Club, Variety Club, Rotary, Masons, Phi Delta Theta (pres. chpt. 1960), Chgo. Phi Delta Theta Alumni Club (pres.), Omega Tau Rho, Lambda Alpha. Home: 927 Park Dr Flossmoor IL 60422-1122 Office: 2709 Flossmoor Rd Flossmoor IL 60422-1141

WAGNER, ARTHUR WARD, JR., lawyer; b. Birmingham, Ala., Aug. 13, 1930; s. Arthur Ward and Lucille (Lockheart) W.; m. Ruth Shingler, May 11, 1957; children: Celia Wagner Minter, Julia Wagner Dolce, Helen Wagner McAfee. BSBA, U. Fla., 1954, JD, 1957. Bar: Fla. 1957, U.S. Dist. Ct. (so. dist.) Fla. 1957, U.S. Dist. Ct. (mid. dist.) Fla. 1975. Ptnr. Wagner, Nugent, Johnson, & McAfee, P.A., West Palm Beach, Fla., 1959—; lectr. in field. Author: Art of Advocacy: Jury Selection, 1981; co-author: Anatomy of Personal Injury Lawsuit I & II, 1968 and 1981. Mem. 15th Jud. Nominating Com., Palm Beach City, 1979-82, 4th Dist. Nominating Commn., Palm Beach City, 1982-86; mem. pres.'s coun. U. Fla.; vestry, chancellor Holy Trinity Parish. Fellow Internat. Acad. Trial Lawyers, Am. Coll. Trial Lawyers, Internat. Soc. Barristers, Am. Bd. Trial Advs.; mem. Assn. Trial Lawyers Am. (pres. 1975-76, hon. life trustee Roscoe Pound Found.), So. Trial Lawyers Assn. (pres. 1991), U. Fla. Law Coll. Alumni (mem. bd. govs.). Democrat. Episcopalian. Office: Wagner Nugent Johnson & McAfee PA 1818 S Australian Ave West Palm Beach FL 33409-6487

WAGNER, BRUCE STANLEY, marketing communications executive; b. San Diego, Aug. 1, 1943; s. Robert Sheldon and Janet (Lowther) W.; m. Elizabeth Pearsall Winslow, Oct. 4, 1975; children: Sage Elizabeth, Alexander Winslow. BA, Dartmouth Coll., 1965; MBA, U. Pa., 1984. Sr. v.p. Grey Advt., Inc., N.Y.C., 1967-81; exec. v.p., chief operating officer Campaign '76 Media Communications, Inc., Washington, 1975-76; exec. v.p., bd. dirs. Ross Roy, Inc., Bloomfield Hills, Mich., 1981-91, Ross Roy Group, Inc., Bloomfield Hills, Mich., 1991-94; v.p. comm. ITT Automotive Inc., Auburn Hills, Mich., 1995—. Mem. Am. Assn. Advt. Agys. (bd. govs. ctrl. region 1988-94, chmn., bd. govs. Mich. coun. 1985-86), Wharton Alumni Assn. (chmn. 1983-85), Wharton Club of Mich. (bd. dirs. 1985—), Detroit Athletic Club, Orchard Lake Country Club, Birmingham Athletic Club. Home: 975 Arlington Rd Birmingham MI 48009-1684 Office: ITT Automotive Inc 3000 University Dr Auburn Hills MI 48326-2356

WAGNER, BURTON ALLAN, lawyer; b. Milw., June 13, 1941; s. Irwin and Jennie (Oxman) W.; m. Georgia Olchoff, Aug. 29, 1964; children: Andrew, Laura. B.B.A. in Acctg, U. Wis., 1963, J.D., 1966, M.A. in Health Services Adminstrn, 1976. Bar: Wis. 1966. Assoc. legal counsel U. Wis., 1968-74; asst. to vice chancellor, legal counselor U. Wis. Hosps., 1974-77; asst. sec. Wis. Dept. Health and Social Services, 1977-83, adminstr. div. community services, 1979-83; clin. assoc. prof. health adminstrn. U. Wis.; ptnr. Thomas Harnisch & Wagner, Madison, 1983-85, Whyte & Hirschboeck, Madison, 1985-90; ptnr. (of counsel) Katten Muchin and Zavis, Madison, 1990-93; ptnr. Reinhart Boerner Van Deuren Norris & Rieselbach, Madison, 1993—. Chmn. personnel com. Dane County chpt. ARC, 1977-90. Served with USAR, 1966-68, Vietnam. Decorated Bronze Star. Mem. Soc. Law and Medicine, Wis. Bar Assn., Dane County Bar Assn. Jewish. Office: PO Box 2020 Madison WI 53701-2020

WAGNER, CAROLYN ANN, adult and gerontological nurse practitioner; b. Harrisburg, Pa., Nov. 9, 1944; d. Robert E. and Thelma (Eshenour) Sheaffer; m. William F. Wagner, Aug. 10, 1963; children: William J., Elizabeth M. Diploma, Reading Hosp. Sch. Nursing, West Reading, Pa., 1967; AS, No. Va. C.C., Manassas, 1982; BSN, George Mason U., 1991, MSN, 1993. RN, Pa., Va., W.Va.; cert. adult nurse practitioner; cert. BLS; cert. gerontol. nurse practitioner; cert. ACLS. Staff nurse Cmty. Nursing Svc. of Delaware County, Lansdowne, Pa., 1970-73; insvc. dir., asst. dir. nurses Manassas Manor, 1973-79; staff nurse Fairfax (Va.) Nursing Ctr., 1975-77, 86-87, nursing supr., 1977-78, dir. ctrl. supply/insvc.dir., 1978-79, dir. purchasing, dir. ctrl. supply, 1979-86; patient care coord. Commonwealth Care Ctr., Fairfax, 1987-93; adult nurse practitioner Valley Health Sys., Winchester, Va., 1993—; adj. faculty Shenandoah U., Winchester, Va., 1995—; affiliate faculty George Mason U., Fairfax, Va., 1996—; mem. Gov.'s Conf. on Aging, Richmond, Va., 1993; chair adv. bd. Health Depot, Winchester, 1993—. Mem. Parish Nurse Caring Com., Winchester, 1993—. Mem. No. Va. Coun. Nurse Practitioners, Va. Coalition for the Aging, Va. Nurses Assn., ANA. Roman Catholic. Avocations: reading, camping, travel. Home: 116 Bell Haven Circle Stephens City VA 22655-9802 Office: Health Depot Valley Health Sys 333 W Cork St Winchester VA 22601-3862

WAGNER, CARRUTH JOHN, physician; b. Omaha, Sept. 4, 1916; s. Emil Conrad and Mabel May (Knapp) W. A.B., Omaha U., 1938; B.Sc., U. Nebr., 1938, M.D., 1941, D.Sc., 1966. Diplomate: Am. Bd. Sugery, Am. Bd. Orthopaedic Surgery. Intern U.S. Marine Hosp., Seattle, 1941-42; resident gen. surgery and orthopaedic surgery USPHS hosps., Shriners Hosp., Phila., 1943-46; med. dir. USPHS, 1952-62; chief orthopaedic service USPHS Hosp., San Francisco, 1946-51, S.I., N.Y., 1951-55; health mblzn. USPHS Hosp., 1959-62; asst. surgeon gen. dep. chief div. hosps. UPHS, 1957-59; chief div. USPHS, 1962-65, USPHS (Indian Health), 1962-65; dir. Bur. Health Services, 1965-68; Washington rep. AMA, 1968-72; health services cons., 1972-79; dept. health services State of Calif., 1979—. Contbr. articles to med. jours. Served with USCGR, World War II. Recipient Pfizer award, 1962; Meritorious award Am. Acad. Gen. Practice, 1965; Disting. Svc. medal, 1968, Calif. Dept. Health Svcs. Pub. Health Recognition award, 1995. Fellow A.C.S. (bd. govs.), Am. Soc. Surgery Hand, Am. Assn. Surgery Trauma, Am. Geriatrics Soc., Am. Acad. Orthopaedic Surgeons; mem. Nat. Assn. Sanitarians, Am. Pub. Health Assn. Sanitarians, Am. Pub. Health Assn., Washington Orthopaedic Club, Am. Legion, Alpha Omega Alpha. Lutheran. Club: Mason (Shriner). Home: 6234 Silverton Way Carmichael CA 95608-0757 Office: PO Box 638 Carmichael CA 95609-0638 *My success can best be summarized as the result of efforts of other people. First my family, particularly my mother, then my teachers and preceptors, and finally my associates. Throughout my life there has been a key individual who created an environment where I could exercise my maximum capabilities. Later in life when it became possible for me to provide similar opportunities for associates I found the benefits I derived far exceeded anything I could have achieved on my own. In summary, success means getting things done, getting planned things done, and getting planned things done largely through other people.*

WAGNER, CHARLENE BROOK, middle school educator, consultant; b. L.A.; d. Edward J. and Eva (Anderson) Brook; m. Gordon Boswell Jr. (div.); children: Gordon, Brook, John. BS, Tex. Christian U., 1952; MEd, Sam Houston U., 1973; postgrad., U. Tex., Austin, 1975, Tex. A&M U., 1977. Sci. educator Spring Branch Ind. Sch. Dist., Houston, 1970—; cons. Scott Foresman Pub. Co., 1982-83; owner Sci. Instrnl. Sys. Co., 1988—; Representative-World Class Network. Mem. Houston Opera Guild, Houston Symphony League, 1992, Mus. Fine Arts, Mus. of Art of Am. West, Houston, 1989, Women's Christian Home, Houston, 1991; social chmn. Encore, 1988; mem. Magic Circle Rep. Women's Club. Mem. NEA, NAFE, AAUW, Tex. State Tchrs. Assn., Spring Branch Edn. Assn., Internat. Platform Assn., Wellington Soc. for Arts (Houston chpt.), Shepherd Soc., Watercolor Arts Soc., Art League Houston, Clan Anderson Soc., Heather and Thistle Soc., Houston Highland Games Assn. Episcopalian. Avocations: painting, watercolor media. Home: B54 2670 Marilee Ln Houston TX 77057-4264 Office: Spring Oaks Mid Sch 2150 Shadowdale Dr Houston TX 77043-2608

WAGNER, CHARLES LEONARD, electrical engineer, consultant; b. Pitts., Nov. 23, 1925; s. Charles Fredrick and Ada Sophia (Hanna) W.; m. Rachel Mae Arbogast, Nov. 15, 1952 (dec. Mar. 1978); children: Charles John, Virginia Ann, Robert Alan. BSEE, Bucknell U., 1945; MSEE, U. Pitts., 1949. Registered profl. engr., Pa. Engr. Westinghouse Elec. Corp., Pitts., 1946-50, sponsor engr., 1950-67, mgr. transmission engring., 1967-76, cons. engr., 1976-85; pvt. cons. Export, Pa., 1985—; adj. instr. U. Pitts., Carnegie-Mellon U., 1952-85. Contbr. articles to profl. jours. Lt. (j.g.) USN, 1943-46. Fellow IEEE (C.P. Steinmetz award, Standards medallion, Centennial medal, Switchgear Com. Dist. Svc. award 1982, Relay Com. Dist. Svc. award 1985, Tech. Coun. Meritorious Svc. award 1990); mem. Internat. Conf. Large High Voltage Electric Systems (Attwood Assoc. award), Power Engring. Soc. of IEEE (chmn. tech. coun. 19771-81, v.p. 1981-83, pres. 1984-85, Meritorious Svc. award 1989, Paper prizes 1970, 90), Tau Beta Pi, Pi Mu Sigma. Presbyterian. Avocations: golf, woodworking, computing. Home and Office: 4933 Simmons Dr Export PA 15632-9330

WAGNER, CHRISTIAN NIKOLAUS JOHANN, materials engineering educator; b. Saarbrucken-Dudweiler, Germany, Mar. 6, 1927; came to U.S., 1959, naturalized, 1969; s. Christian Jakob and Regina (Bungert) W.; m. Rosemarie Anna Mayer, Apr. 5, 1952; children—Thomas Martin, Karla Regine, Petra Susanne. Student, U. Poitiers, France, 1948-49; Licence es Sci., U. Saar, Ger., 1951, Diplom-Ingenieur, 1954, Dr.rer.nat., 1957. Research asst. Inst. fur Metallforschung, Saarbrucken, 1953-54; vis. fellow M.I.T., 1955-56; research asso. Inst. fur Metallforschung, 1957-58; teaching, research asst. U. Saarbrucken, 1959; asst. prof. Yale U., New Haven, Conn., 1959-62; assoc. prof. Yale U., 1962-70; prof. dept. materials engring. UCLA, 1970-91, prof. emeritus, 1991—, chmn. dept., 1974-79, asst. dean undergrad. studies Sch. Engring. and Applied Sci., 1982-85, acting chmn., 1990-91; vis. prof. Tech. U., Berlin, 1969, U. Saarbrücken, 1979-80. Contbr. articles to profl. jours. Recipient U.S. Sci. Humboldt award U. Saarbrucken, 1989-90, 92. Fellow Am. Soc. Metals Internat.; mem. Am. Phys. Soc., Am. Crystallographic Assn., Minerals, Metals and Materials Soc. Home: 37621 Golden Pebble Ave Palm Desert CA 92211-1430 Office: UCLA 6532 Boelter Hall Los Angeles CA 90095-1595

WAGNER, CURTIS LEE, JR., judge; b. Kingsport, Tenn., Nov. 8, 1928; m. Jeanne E. Allen (dec.); children: Curtis L. III, Rex A. Student Tenn. Poly. Inst., 1947-49; LLB, U. Tenn., 1951. Bar: Tenn. 1952. Assoc. Kramer, Dye, McNabb and Greenwood, Knoxville, Tenn., 1951-54; atty.-adv. gen. crimes and fraud sect. Criminal Div., Dept. Justice, Washington, 1954-56, trial atty. Dept. Justice, 1954-60, assigned to Ct. of Claims sect. Civil Div., 1956-60; spl. asst. to JAG for communications, transp. and utilities, Office JAG, Dept. Army, Washington, 1960-64, chief Regulatory Law Div., 1964-74, mem. civilian lawyer career com., 1960-74, chmn. JAG incentive awards com. 1960-74, mem. Army Staff Awards Bd., 1964-74, mem. Army Environ. Policy Council, 1972-74. Adminstrv. law judge FERC, Washington, 1974-79, chief adminstrv. law judge, 1979—. Dist. commr. Nat. Capital Area council Boy Scouts Am., 1967-69. Decorated Meritorious Civilian Service award, Exceptional Civilian Service award; recipient citation for outstanding performance Dept. Army, 1961-74; Scouter's Tng. award Boy Scouts Am., 1965, Scoutmaster's Key, 1966, Commr.'s Key, 1968, Commr.'s Arrowhead Honor, 1966, Silver Beaver award, 1969. Mem. Order of Arrow. Methodist. Clubs: Annapolis Yacht (parliamentarian). Office: Fed Energy Regulatory Commn 888 First St NE Washington DC 20426

WAGNER, CYNTHIA GAIL, editor, writer; b. Bethesda, Md., Oct. 3, 1956; d. Robert Cheney and Marjory Jane (Kletzing) W. BA in English, Grinnell Coll., 1978; MA in Comms., Syracuse U., 1981. Editorial asst. The Futurist/World Future Soc., Bethesda, Md., 1981-82, staff editor, 1982-85, asst. editor, 1985-91, sr. editor, 1991-92, mng. editor, 1992—. Author: (plays) Discriminating Dining, 1993, Limited Engagement, 1993; columnist 3-2-1 Contact, 1994; contbr. Encyclopedia of the Future, 1995. Mem. Theatre Comm. Group, Soc. Profl. Journalists. Avocation: theater. Office: The Futurist World Future Soc 7910 Woodmont Ave Ste 450 Bethesda MD 20814-3015

WAGNER, D. WILLIAM, lawyer; b. Dixon, Ill., Jan. 14, 1943; s. Earl L. and Lois Mae (Schrock) W.; children: Peter Alan, Nicholas William. BA, Northwestern U., 1965, JD, 1968. Bar: Ill. 1968, U.S. Dist. Ct. (no. dist.) Ill. 1969, U.S. Ct. Appeals (7th cir.) 1971, Calif. 1982. Ptnr. firm Sidley & Austin, Chgo. and L.A., 1969—. Dir. Housing Options for People to Excell, Inc., 1992-95. Co-author: Illinois Municipal Law: Subdivisions and Subdivisions in Controls, 1978, 81. Mem. L.A. County Bar Assn., ABA, Ill. State Bar Assn., Chgo. Bar Assn. (chmn. real property land use com. 1980-81), Beverly Hills Bar Assn. (chmn. real estate sect. 1986-87). Presbyterian. Clubs: Legal (Chgo.); Beach (Santa Monica). Home: 20 Ocean Park Blvd Apt 25 Santa Monica CA 90405-3557 Office: Sidley & Austin 555 W 5th St Ste 4000 Los Angeles CA 90013-3000

WAGNER, DANIEL A., social services administrator; b. Chgo., July 18, 1946; married; 2 children. BS in Ops. Rsch. Engring., Cornell U., 1968; MA in Exptl. Psychology, U. Mich., 1971, PhD in Developmental Psychology, 1976. Vis. postdoctoral fellow lab. of human devel. Harvard U., Cambridge, Mass., 1979-81; prof. human devel. Grad. Sch. Edn. U. Pa., Phila., dir. Internat. Literacy Inst., dir. Literacy Rsch. Ctr.; dir. Nat. Ctr. on Adult Literacy, U.S. Dept. Edn., 1990-95. Contbr. articles to profl. publs. Recipient Nat. Rsch. Svc. award NIMH, 1980-81; grantee Nat. Inst. Child Health and Human Devel., 1981-84, NSF, 1990-93, UNESCO, USAID, 1991-96. Fellow APA. Office: U Pennsylvania Nat Ctr on Adult Literacy 3910 Chestnut St Philadelphia PA 19104-3111

WAGNER, DAVID J., art center director; b. Fort Knox, Ky., Mar. 4, 1952; s. Walter W. and Elsie G. (Zillner) W.; m. Kaye M. Kronenburg, June 21, 1975. BMA, U. Wis., Stevens Point, 1974; MA, Ind. U., 1976; PhD, U. Minn., 1992. Grad. asst. Univ. Mus., Bloomington, Ind., 1975-76; intern Children's Mus., Indpls., 1976; dir. Leigh Yawkey Woodson Art Mus., Wausau, Wis., 1977-87; exec. dir. Colorado Springs (Colo.) Fine Arts Ctr., 1987—; scholar-in-residence Sitka Ctr. Art and Ecology, Newskowin Found., Otis, Oreg., 1990; mem. adv. bd. Nat. Park Art Acad., Jackson Hole, Wyo., 1988-90; assoc. bd. Nat. Art Mus. of Sport, Indpls.; bd. dirs. Arts Commn. Pikes Peak Region, Colorado Springs; mem. adv. com. U. Colo., Colorado Springs, 1987—. Contbr.: (exhbn. catalogs) Americans in Glass, 1984, Rembrandt's Etchings, 1985, Wildlife in Art, 1987, Pikes Peak Vision: The Broadmoor Art Academy, 1919-1945; contbr. Wis. Acad. Rev., 1986, Arts for the Parks, 1988-90, Images of Penance, Images of Mercy, 1991. Chmn. non-profit orgn. com. United Way, Wausau, 1981, 84; bd. dirs. Wis. Citizens for the Arts, Madison, 1984-86; negotiator Budapest Mus. Old Masters Am. Tour, 1986, Birds in Art China Exhbn. Tour, 1987; bd. dirs. Wis. Humanities Com., Madison, 1984-87; treas. Persons for Arts and Scis., Colorado Springs, Colo., 1991-92. Winterthur Summer Ins. scholar, 1979, Victorian Soc. scholar, 1981, Inst. European Studies scholar, 1982; U. Minn. fellow, 1987, 90; postdoctoral fellow Robert S. and Grayce B. Kerr Found., 1994. Mem. Am. Assn. Mus., Am. Studies Assn., Assn. Art Mus. Dirs. Avocations: traveling, skiing, tennis. Office: Colo Springs Fine Arts Ctr 30 W Dale St Colorado Springs CO 80903-3210

WAGNER, DAVID JAMES, banker; b. Cin., Mar. 15, 1954; s. George A. and Mary (Tyssowski) W.; m. Kay A. Ambrosius, Dec. 27, 1975. BA, Ind. U., 1975, MBA, 1976. Credit analyst Old Kent Bank, Grand Haven, Mich., 1977, corp. banking officer, 1977-79, asst. v.p. to v.p. corp. banking, 1979-82; v.p., mgr. br. adminstrn. Old Kent Bank of Grand Haven, Mich., 1982-84, CEO, 1984-85; exec. v.p., retail mgr. Old Kent Bank, Grand Rapids, Mich., 1985, pres., 1986-89, CEO, 1989-91; exec. v.p. Old Kent Fin. Corp., Grand Rapids, Mich., 1991-94, pres., 1994-95, CEO, 1995—, chmn., 1995—. Office: Old Kent Fin Corp 1 Vandenberg Pl SE Grand Rapids MI 49506

WAGNER, DIANE M(ARGARET), theology educator; b. Hancock, Mich., Apr. 22, 1943; d. Benjamin Philip and Eunice Rose (La Mothe) W. BA, Alverno Coll., Milw., 1965; MA, Mundelein Coll., Chgo., 1972; student, Clin. Pastoral Edn., Milw., 1979-80. Cert. advanced standing chaplain, 1982. Tchr. grade 1 St. Peter Sch., Skokie, Ill., 1964-65; tchr. grades 1 and 2 St. Cecelia Sch., Hubbell, Mich., 1965-67; tchr. grades 1, 2, 4-6 St. Joseph Sch., Wilmette, Ill., 1967-71; tchr. grade 5, middle grade coord. St. Mary Sch., Buffalo Grove, Ill., 1971-73; tchr. grade 5 St. Alphonsus Sch., Greendale, Wis., 1973-74; recruiter Sch. Sisters of St. Francis, Milw., 1974-79; chaplain, dir. pastoral care Tau Home Health Care Agy., Milw., 1980-88, dir. vols., 1981-88; chaplain, dir. pastoral care St. Mary's Hill Hosp., Milw., 1988-92; tchr. theology, asoc. chaplain Divine Savior Holy Angels High Sch., Milw., 1993—; mem. Chaplain Adv. Bd., Milw., 1982-88, pres., 1985-88. Author: (tape) College of Chaplains, 1986. Vice pres bd. dirs. Clare Towers, Inc., Milw., 1981-87. Recipient Cert. Appreciation, Clare Towers, Inc., 1987. Mem. Nat. Assn. Cath. Chaplains (sec. regional bd. dirs. 1986-88), Milw. Area Dirs. Pastroal Care Assn. (pres. 1987-88). Democrat. Roman Catholic. Avocations: reading, camping, golfing. Home: 2619 N 39th St Milwaukee WI 53210-2503 Office: Divine Savior Holy Angels High Sch 4257 N 100th St Milwaukee WI 53222-1313

WAGNER, DONALD BERT, health care consultant; b. York, Pa., July 27, 1930; s. Bert Daniel and Mary Elizabeth (Roelke) W.; m. Janet Louise Bankert, July 12, 1952; children: Kimberly, Susan, David, John. Student, Franklin & Marshall, 1948-50; BS in Phys. Therapy, Columbia U., 1952; MHA, Baylor U., 1960. Commd. 2d lt. USAF, 1952, advanced through grades to brig. gen., 1981; physical therapist Randolph AFB, San Antonio, 1952-55; asst. adminstr. USAF/RAF S. Ruislip, London; adminstr. USAF/RAF Bentwaters, Ipswich, Eng., 1955-58; various adminstrv. roles USAF Hosps. and Commands, Europe and U.S., 1958-73; dep. comdr. USAF Sch. Health Care Sci., Wichita Falls, Tex., 1973-75; adminstr. Wilford Hall Med. Ctr., San Antonio, 1975-79; chief med. svc. corps Office Surgeon Gen. USAF, San Antonio, 1979-82; dep. surgeon gen. USAF Med. Svc. Ctr., San Antonio, 1981-82, ret., 1982; adminstr., assoc. v.p. M. D. Anderson/U. Tex. Cancer Ctr., Houston, 1982-85; chief exec. officer Meml. Southwest Hosp., Houston, 1985-91; v.p. Meml. Hosp. System, Houston, 1985-91, cons., 1992—; dir. residency edn., grad. program in healthcare adminstrn. U. Houston, Clear Lake; adj. prof. Baylor and Trinity U., San Antonio, 1975-82; assoc. prof. U. Houston, St. Louis U., 1982-88. Bd. dirs. Hospice at the Med. Ctr., Child Advocates, Houston, 1985-89, Kidney Found., Houston, 1985-88, Westland YMCA, Houston, 1985-88, 90-94, Greater Houston Hosp. Coun., 1983-87, Sam Houston area Alzheimer's Assn. 1990-94; chmn. external adv. bd. Sch. Allied Health, U. Tex. Med. Br. Named Disting. Alumnus Baylor U. Program in Healthcare Adminstrn., 1993. Fellow Am. Coll. Healthcare Execs. (edn. com.), Royal Soc. Health; mem. Am. Hosp. Assn. (bd. dirs. hosp. rsch. and edn. found. 1990—), Tex. Hosp. Assn., Assn. Mil. Surgeons U.S. (Ray E. Brown award 1982, Outstanding Sr. Level Healthcare Exec. Ache Regents award 1991), Am. Mgmt. Soc. Republican. Methodist. Avocation: music. Home: 1746 Carriage Way Sugar Land TX 77478-4201 Office: Meml Healthcare System 7737 Southwest Fwy Houston TX 77074-1815

WAGNER, DOUGLAS WALKER ELLYSON, journal editor; b. Orange, N.J., Nov. 5, 1938; s. Norman Raphael and Virginia (Taylor) W. B.A., Yale U., 1960. Editorial coordinator Med. World News, N.Y.C., 1965-69, assoc. editor, 1969-70; writer, assoc. editor Emergency Medicine, N.Y.C., 1970-76, sr. editor, 1976-81, editor-in-chief, 1981-87; editor, pub. Pediatric Primary Care (formerly Pediatric Therapeutics and Toxicology, Jersey City, 1987—; editor, publ. Pediatric Emergency and Critical Care (formerly Pediatric Trauma and Acute Care), 1988—; editor-in-chief Transition: Medicine and the Aging Process, N.Y.C., 1983. Mem. Nat. Assn. Sci. Writers, Am. Med. Writers Assn., Soc. for Acad. Emergency Medicine (assoc.), Soc. Pediatric Emergency Medicine, Am. Acad. Clin. Toxicology. Home: PO Box 23 72 Sussex St PO Box 23 Jersey City NJ 07303-0023 Office: Riverpress Inc PO Box 23 Jersey City NJ 07303-0023

WAGNER, DURRETT, former publisher, picture service executive; b. El Paso, Tex., Feb. 27, 1929; s. Francis and Florence (Durrett) W.; m. Betty Jane Brown, June 7, 1951; children—Gordon, Velma, Kendra. B.A., Baylor U., 1950; M.Div., Yale, 1954; postgrad., U. Chgo., 1954-59. Chmn. social sci. div. Kendall Coll., Evanston, Ill., 1959-63; dean Kendall Coll., 1963-67; partner v.p.; Swallow Press Inc., Chgo., 1967-92; owner, partner, pres. Hist. Pictures Service, Inc., Chgo., 1975-92; now pres. Bookworks, Inc., Chgo. Home and Office: 614 Ingleside Pl Evanston IL 60201-1742

WAGNER, EDWARD FREDERICK, JR., investment management company executive; b. Columbus, Ohio, Nov. 26, 1938; s. Edward Frederick and Margaret Ann (List) W.; m. Diana Beth Pietraszweski, Jan. 14, 1989; children: Edward Frederick III, John Patrick, James Francis, Caroline Elizabeth. BS, Xavier U., Cin., 1960; MBA, Miami U., Oxford, Ohio, 1965. Registered prin. and ops. rep. N.Y. Stock Exch., Am. Stock Exch.; registered rep. Nat. Assn. Securities Dealers. Investment analyst The Equitable Life Assurance Soc. U.S., N.Y.C., 1965-68; security analyst H.C. Wainwright & Co., N.Y.C., 1968-71; v.p. William D. Witter, Inc., N.Y.C., 1971-76, Wainwright Securities, Inc., N.Y.C., 1976-78, Blyth Eastman Dillon & Co., Inc., N.Y.C., 1978-79, Salomon Bros., Inc., N.Y.C., 1979-81, Lehman Bros., Kuhn Loeb & Co., Inc., N.Y.C., 1981-84; sr. v.p. Gabelli & Co., Inc., Rye, N.Y., 1984—, GAMCO Investors, Inc., Rye, 1984—. 1st lt. U.S. Army, 1961-63. Mem. N.Y. Soc. Security Analysts Inc., Assn. for Investment Mgrs. and Rsch., Racquet and Tennis Club (N.Y.C.), The Leash (N.Y.C.), The Rockaway Hunting Club (Cedarhurst, N.Y.), Southampton (N.Y.) Club, The Brook Club (N.Y.C.). Avocations: squash racquets, golf, billiards, gun dogs, ornithology. Home: 225 E 73rd St New York NY 10021-3654 Office: Gamco Investors Inc Corp Ctr at Rye Rye NY 10580-1430

WAGNER, EDWARD KURT, publishing company executive; b. N.Y.C., Sept. 29, 1936; s. Kurt Henry and Julia Marie (Selesky) W.; m. Ann Marie Philbin, Jan. 31, 1959; children: Denise, Steven, Kenneth, Jeanne. B.B.A., St. Francis Coll., 1961. With Pitman Pub. Corp., N.Y.C., 1952-75, v.p., treas., 1968-71, exec. v.p., 1971-75; financial mgr. Dun-Donnelley Pub. Corp., N.Y.C., 1975-76, contr. gen. book div., 1976-77; sr. mgr. contr.'s dept. Dun & Bradstreet, Inc., N.Y.C., 1977-78, asst. contr., 1978-83, contr., 1983-88, v.p., contr., 1989-96; ret., 1996—. Home: 1660 Goldspire Rd Toms River NJ 08755-0891

WAGNER, FLORENCE ZELEZNIK, telecommunications executive; b. McKeesport, Pa., Sept. 23, 1926; d. George and Sophia (Petros) Zeleznik; BA magna cum laude, U. Pitts., 1977, MPA, 1981; m. Francis Xavier Wagner, June 18, 1946; children: Deborah Elaine Wagner Franke, Rebecca Susan Wagner Schroettinger, Melissa Catherine Wagner Good, Francis Xavier, Robert Francis. Sec. to pres. Tube City Iron & Metal Co., Glassport,

Pa., 1944-50; cons. Raw Materials, Inc., Pitts., 1955; gen. mgr. Carson Compressed Steel Products, Pitts., 1967-69; ptnr. Universal Steel Products, Pitts., 1970-71; gen. mgr. Josh Steel Co., Braddock, Pa., 1971-78; owner Wagner's Candy Box, Mt. Lebanon, Pa., 1979-80; borough sec./treas. Borough of Pennsbury Village, Allegheny County, Pa., 1980-88; ptnr. Tele-Communications of Am., Burgettstown, Pa., 1984-86; trustee Profit-Sharing trust, Pension trust Josh Steel Co., 1986—, Consol, Inc., Upper St. Clair, Pa., 1989—; mem. Foster Parents, Jefferson Twp. Planning Commn., Washington County, Pa.; mem. sch. bd. St. Bernard Cath. Elem. Sch., Mt. Lebanon, Pa., sec., 1995—. Mem. AAUW, Pitts. Symphony Soc., Pitts. Ballet Theater Guild. Mem. Soc. Pub. Adminstrn. (founder U. Pitts. br.), Acad. Polit. Sci., U.S. Strategic Inst., Southwestern Pa. Sec. Assn., Alpha Sigma Lambda (past treas., sec., pres.). Republican. Home: 1611 Upper St Clair Dr Pittsburgh PA 15241

WAGNER, FREDERICK BALTHAS, JR., historian, retired surgery educator; b. Phila., Jan. 18, 1916; s. Frederick Balthas and Gertrude Louise (Mattes) W.; m. Jean Lockwood, June 30, 1945; children: Frederick B. III, Theodore Walter. AB, U. Pa., 1937; MD, Thomas Jefferson U., 1941. Diplomate: Am. Bd. Surgery. Clin. prof. surgery Jefferson Med. Coll. Thomas Jefferson U., Phila., 1954-78, Grace Revere Osler prof. surgery, 1978-84, historian, 1984—. Author: Twilight Years of Lady Osler, 1985; editor: Thomas Jefferson University: Tradition and Heritage, 1989. Recipient Alumni Achievement award Jefferson Med. Coll., 1987. Fellow Phila. Acad. Surgery (pres. 1985-86), Coll. Physicians Phila.; mem. Meigs Med. Assn. (pres. 1989-91), Jefferson Alumni Assn. (pres. 1975), Union League Phila. Republican. Methodist. Home: 800 Chauncey Rd Narberth PA 19072-1304

WAGNER, FREDERICK REESE, language professional; b. Phila., Apr. 15, 1928; s. Fred Reese and Mildred Wagner; m. Barbara Alexander Brady, May 9, 1959 (div. 1968); 1 child, Christopher A. BA summa cum laude, Duke U., 1948, MA, 1949, PhD, 1971. Advt mgr. Prentice-Hall, Inc., N.Y.C., 1955-57; promotion mgr. Harper & Row, N.Y.C., 1957-65; instr. English Duke U., Durham, N.C., 1967-69; asst. prof. Hamilton Coll, Clinton, N.Y., 1969-73, assoc. prof., 1973-78, prof. English, chmn. dept., 1978-90; prof. English Hamilton Coll, Clinton, 1990-95. Author: Famous Underwater Adventurers, 1962; Submarine Fighter of the American Revolution, 1963; Patriot's Choice: The Story of John Hancock, 1964; Robert Morris, Audacious Patriot, 1976. Mem. Thoreau Soc. (pres. 1984-86), Hawthorne Soc., MLA, Phi Beta Kappa. Home: 28 Dwight Ave Clinton NY 13323-1630

WAGNER, FREDERICK WILLIAM (BILL WAGNER), lawyer; b. Daytona Beach, Fla., Apr. 13, 1933; s. Adam A. and Nella (Schroeder) W.; m. Ruth Whetstone; children: Alan Frederick, Darryl William, Thomas Adam. BA, U. Fla., 1955, LLB with honors, 1960. Bar: Fla. 1960, U.S. Supreme Ct. 1967, D.C. 1989. Pvt. practice law Miami, Fla., 1960-63, Orlando, Fla., 1963-65, Tampa, Fla., 1965—; ptnr. law firm Nichols, Gaither, Beckham, Colson, Spence & Hicks, Tampa, Fla., 1965-67; partner law firm Wagner, Vaughan & McLaughlin (P.A. and predecessor names), 1967-87; mem. Gov.'s Judicial Nominations Commn., 1971-72, Constnl. Judicial Nominations Commn., 1972-75; mem. Fla. Bd. Bar Examiners, 1974-77; chmn. Civil Procedure Rules Com. Fla. Bar, 1977-78; bd. govs. Fla. Bar, 1978-83; trustee Roscoe Pound Found, 1984—. Contbr. articles to profl. jours. Capt. USAF, 1955-57. Fellow Am. Bar Found., Am. Coll. Trial Lawyers, Internat. Acad. Trial Lawyers; mem. Assn. Trial Lawyers Am. (bd. govs. 1973-80, 84-89, chmn. pub. affairs dept. 1984-89, treas. 1982-84, v.p. 1986-87, pres.-elect 1987-88, pres. 1988-89), Acad. Fla. Trial Lawyers (bd. dirs. 1965—, pres. 1972-73), Bay Area Trial Lawyers Assn. (v.p. 1966-68), Am. Law Inst. (coun. 1993—), Lawyer-Pilots Bar Assn., Fla. Bar Found., U. Fla. Alumni Assn., Nat. Bd. Trial Advocacy (cert. civil). Democrat. Methodist. Home: 78 Martinique Ave Tampa FL 33606-4053 Office: Wagner Vaughan & McLaughlin 601 Bayshore Blvd Ste 910 Tampa FL 33606-2761

WAGNER, GARY TED, lawyer; b. N.Y.C., Apr. 2, 1960; s. Adolph and Ruth (Heiferman) W. BA, Queens Coll., N.Y., 1982; JD, Temple U., Phila., 1985. Bar: Pa. 1985, N.J. 1985, N.Y. 1988. Assoc. Blank Rome Comisky & McCauley, Phila., 1985-87, Parker Chapin Flattau & Klimpl, N.Y.C., 1987-88; assoc. gen. counsel Robert Martin Co., Elmsford, N.Y., 1989—. Mem. Midnight Run, Dobbs Ferry, N.Y., 1994—, UJA Fedn., Westchester County, 1990—, Bronx H.S. Sci. Alumni Assn., 1985—. Mem. Westchester-Fairfield County Corp. Counsel Assn., The Corporate Bar. Avocations: tennis, hiking. Office: Robert Martin Co 100 Clearbrook Rd Elmsford NY 10523

WAGNER, GEORGE FRANCIS ADOLF, naval officer; b. S.I., N.Y., Mar. 24, 1941; s. George and Cornelia F. (Cosmen) W.; m. Sarah Elizabeth Lilly, June 6, 1962; children: Kristine, Gregory, Karin. BS, U.S. Naval Acad., 1962; MS, MIT, 1968, Naval Engr., 1968. Commd. ensign USN, 1962, advanced through grades to rear adm., 1991; staff fleet introduction officer Naval Sea Systems Command, Washington, 1977-79; instr. Sr. Officer Materiel Readiness Course, Idaho Falls, Idaho, 1979-81; comdg. officer USS John Rodgers (DD-983), Charleston, S.c., 1981-83; program mgr. Cruise Missiles Project, Washington, 1983-87; dep. and asst. Chief of Naval Rsch., Washington, 1987-89; mem. pers. policy staff Bur. Naval Pers., Washington, 1989-90; warfare system engr. Space and Naval Warfare System Command, Washington, 1990-91; program exec. officer cruise missiles projects and unmanned aerial vehicle joint project Washington, 1991-95; comdr. Space and Naval Warfare Sys. Command, Washington, 1995—. Decorated Def. Superior Svc. medal, Legion of Merit with oak leaf cluster. Episcopalian. Office: Comspawarsyscom 2451 Crystal Dr Arlington VA 22202-4804

WAGNER, HAROLD A., industrial gas and chemical company executive; b. Oakland, Calif., Nov. 12, 1935; s. Harold A. and Lurline Frances (Madsen) W.; m. Marcia Kenaston, July 14, 1956; children: Sandra Wagner Boyce, Kristi Wagner, Schwiering, Tracey, Erik. BS in Mech. Engring., Stanford U., 1958, SEP, 1982; MBA, Harvard U., 1963. Regional sales mgr. ind. gases U.S. Air Products & Chems., Allentown, Pa., 1963-70; mgr. GM ind. gases U.K.Air Products & Chems., 1970-76; regional sales mgr. GM Ind. Gases Continental Europe, 1976-80, GM Ind. Gases U.S., 1980-81; v.p. sales ind. gases div. FM, 1981-82; v.p. corp. planning Air Products & Chems., 1982-87, v.p. bus. div. chems., 1987-88; pres. AP Europe, 1988-90, exec. v.p., 1990-91, pres., COO, 1991-92, past chmn. pres., CEO; now chmn., pres., CEO, dir. Air Products and Chems. 1st Lt. USAF, 1958-61. Avocations: squash, photography. Home: 1306 Prospect Ave Bethlehem PA 18018-4917 Office: Air Prods & Chems Inc 7201 Hamilton Blvd Allentown PA 18195-1526*

WAGNER, HARVEY ALAN, finance executive; b. Detroit, Feb. 11, 1941; s. Max and Anne (Levine) W.; m. Arlene F. Tasman, Jan. 26, 1963 (dec. June 1988); children: Brooke D., Jennifer D; m. Arlene L. Rittenberg-Gelb, June, 1992. BBA in Acctg., U. Miami, 1963. Sr. acct. Hoch, Frey and Zugman, Ft. Lauderdale, Fla., 1963-67; contr. Canaveral Internat. Corp., Miami, Fla., 1967-68, Systems Engring. Lab., Ft. Lauderdale, 1968-70; dir. fin. and adminstrn., western area Arcata Comms., Inc., Menlo Park, Calif., 1971-73; sec., treas., contr. Commodore Bus. Machines Inc., Palo Alto, Calif., 1973-75; group contr. Fairchild Camera and Instrument Corp., Mountainview, Calif., 1975-83; v.p. contr. internat. GTE Corp., Phoenix, 1983-86; v.p. fin., sec., CFO Am. Microsystems, Inc., Santa Clara, Calif., 1986-89; v.p. fin., CFO Datapoint Corp., San Antonio, 1989, Computervision Corp., Bedford, Mass., 1989-94; v.p. fin., CFO, treas. Scientific-Atlanta, Inc., 1994—. Chmn. bd. Tech. Fed. Credit Union, San Jose, Calif., 1980-82, chmn. supervisory com., 1986-88, 78-80; v.p., founding dir. The Wellness Cmty., Atlanta; mem. pres.'s adv. bd. U. Miami, 1995—; mem. Wharton Exec. Edn. Adv. Bd., 1995—. With USAR, 1959-67. Mem. Inst. Mgmt. Accts., Fin. Exec. Inst. (bd. dirs.), Assn. for Corp. Growth, Buckhead Club (bd. govs. 1995). Republican. Jewish. Avocations: golf, travel, art collecting. Office: Scientific-Atlanta Inc 1 Technology Pky S Norcross GA 30092

WAGNER, HARVEY ARTHUR, nuclear engineer; b. Ann Arbor, Mich., Jan. 2, 1905; s. Emanuel M. and Emma (Kiebler) W.; m. Eleanor Mary Bond, July 6, 1929. B.S. in Mech. Engring., U. Mich., 1927; D.Eng., Lawrence Inst. Tech., 1969. With Proctor & Gamble Co., 1927-28; with Detroit Edison Co., 1928-70, exec. v.p., 1969-70; cons. engr., 1970—; chmn., dir. Overseas Adv. Assocs., Inc., 1974—; Mem. Detroit Bd. Water Commrs., 1952-60; Trustee Nat. Sanitation Found., 1965-82. Author papers in field. Recipient Disting. Alumnus award U. Mich. Coll. Engring., 1953, Outstanding Alumni Achievement award, 1989; Sesquincentennial award as outstanding exec. and nuclear power cons. U. Mich., 1967; cert. pub. service Fed. Power Commn., 1964. Fellow ASME, Am. Nuclear Soc. (Cisler Award, 1994), Engring. Soc. Detroit (pres. 1968-69); mem. Nat. Acad. Engring., Tau Beta Pi, Phi Kappa Phi. Home: 932 Trombley Rd Grosse Pointe MI 48230-1860 Office: 3000 Book Bldg Detroit MI 48226

WAGNER, HENRY NICHOLAS, JR., physician; b. Balt., May 12, 1927; s. Henry N. and Gertrude Loane W.; m. Anne Barrett Wagner, Feb., 1951; children—Henry N., Mary Randall, John Mark, Anne Elizabeth. A.B., Johns Hopkins U., 1948, M.D., 1952; D.Sc. (hon.), Washington Coll., Chestertown, Md., 1972, Free U., Brussels, 1985; M.D. (hon.), U. Gottingen, 1988. Chief med. resident Osler Med. Service, Johns Hopkins Hosp., Balt., 1958-59; asst. prof. medicine, radiology Johns Hopkins Med. Instns., 1959-64, asso. prof., 1964-65, prof., dir. divs. nuclear medicine and radiation health sci., 1965—. Author numerous books in field.; contbr. articles to med. jours. Served with USPHS, 1955-57. Recipient Georg von Hevesey medal, 1976. Fellow ACP; mem. Inst. Medicine of NAS, AMA (coun. sci. affairs, Sci. Achievement award 1991), Balt. City Med. Soc. (past pres.), World Fedn. Nuclear Medicine and Biology (past pres.), Am. Bd. Nuclear Medicine (founding mem.), Soc. Nuclear Medicine (past pres.), Am. Fedn. Clin. Research (past pres.), Research Socs. Council (past pres.), Assn. Am. Physicians, Am. Soc. Clin. Investigation, Phi Beta Kappa. Home: 5607 Wildwood Ln Baltimore MD 21209-4520 Office: 615 N Wolfe St Baltimore MD 21205-2103*

WAGNER, JAMES WARREN, engineering educator; b. Washington, July 12, 1953; s. Robert Earl and Bernice (Bittner) W.; m. Debbie Kelley, July 31, 1976; children: Kimberly Renee, Christine Kelley. BSEE, U. Del., 1975; MS, Johns Hopkins U., 1978, PhD, 1984. Electronics engr. U.S. FDA, Washington, 1975-84; asst. prof. Johns Hopkins U., Balt., 1984-88, assoc. prof., 1988-93, prof., 1993—, chmn. dept. materials scis. and engring., 1993—. Contbr. articles to profl. jours. Regional v.p. Chesapeake Bay Yacht Racing Assn., Annapolis, Md., 1982; elder Presbyterian Ch. U.S.A. Mem. IEEE, Optical Soc. Am., Materials Rsch. Soc., Laser & Electro-Optics Soc., Biomed. Engring., Am. Soc. for Nondestructive Evaluation, Soc. Exptl. Mechanics (Peterson award 1988), Nat. Materials Adv. Bd. Presbyterian. Achievements include contributions to the field of optical metrology applied to materials characterization, especially advanced holographic and laser-based ultrasonic methods. Office: Johns Hopkins Univ Materials Sci & Engring 3400 N Charles St 102 MD Baltimore MD 21218

WAGNER, JEANETTE SARKISIAN, cosmetics company executive; m. Paul A. Wagner. BS cum laude, Northwestern U.; MBA, Harvard U. Former editor-in-chief internat. editions, dir. new ventures Hearst Corp.; former editor Saturday Evening Post; with Estee Lauder Cos., 1975—, from v.p., dir. mktg. internat. divsn. to sr. v.p. Estee Lauder and Prescriptives Internat., past corp. sr. v.p., now pres. Estee Lauder Internat., Inc.; chmn. bd. dirs. Fragrance Found.; bd. dirs. White House Adv. Com. on Trade Policy Negotiations; bd. dirs., mem. audit and compensation coms. Am. Greetings.; bd. dirs., audit and nominating coms. Stride Rite Corp.; v.p. bd. dirs. Bus. Coun. for Econ. Understanding. Bd. dirs. Breastcancer Rsch. Found. Mem. Fashion Group Internat. (past pres. and chmn.), Cosmetic Exec. Women, Econ. Club, Harvard Bus. Sch. Club Greater N.Y. (past v.p., honor roll), Harvard Bus. Sch. Network Women Alumni, Womens Forum N.Y. (bd. dirs., exec. com.), Northwestern Coun. 100, Com. 200 (bd. dirs., chair long range planning), Asia Soc., China Inst., Japan Soc., Korean Soc., Fgn. Policy Assn., Women's Econ. Roundtable. Office: Estee Lauder Cos 767 5th Ave New York NY 10153

WAGNER, JOHN GARNET, pharmacy educator; b. Weston, Ont., Can., Mar. 28, 1921; came to U.S., 1949; naturalized, 1993; s. Herbert William and Coral (Cates) W.; m. Eunice Winona Kelsey, July 4, 1946; children: Wendie Lynn, Linda Beth. Pharm.B., U. Toronto, Ont., 1947; B.S. in Pharmacy, U. Sask., Can., 1948, B.A., 1949; Ph.D., Ohio State U., 1952, D.Sc. (hon.), 1980. Asst. prof. pharm. chemistry Ohio State U., 1952-53; with Upjohn Co., Kalamazoo, 1953-68; head pharmacy research sect. Upjohn Co., 1956-63, sr. research scientist med. research div., 1963-68; prof. pharmacy Coll. Pharmacy U. Mich., Ann Arbor, 1968-81, Albert B. Prescott prof. pharmaceutics, 1982-86, John G. Searle prof. pharmaceutics, 1986-91, John G. Searle prof. emeritus, 1991—, prof. pharmacology sch. medicine, 1986-91, prof. pharmacology emeritus, 1991—; asst. dir. R. and D. Pharmacy Service, Univ. Hosp., 1968-72; mem. staff Upjohn Center for Clin. Pharmacology, 1973-91; cons. Bur. of Drugs, FDA, Washington, 1971-73, Upjohn Co., 1968-90, Key Pharms., Miami, Fla., 1980-91, Warner-Lambert, Ann Arbor, Mich., 1983-84. Author: Biopharmaceutics and Relevant Pharmacokinetics, 1971, Fundamentals of Clinical Pharmacokinetics, 1975, Pharmacokinetics for the Pharmaceutical Scientist, 1993; also numerous articles.; mem. editorial bd.: Internat. Jour. Clin. Pharmacology, 1967-91, Clin. Pharmacol. Therapeutics, 1973-91, Biopharmceutics and Drug Disposition; cons. editor: Jour. Pharmacokinetics and Biopharmaceutics. Served with RCAF, 1941-45. Recipient L. George R. Parke Meml. scholarship and silver medal, 1946, John Roberts Gold medal for pharmacy and chemistry U. Toronto, 1947, Dr. William E. Upjohn award, 1960, Centennial Achievement award Ohio State U., 1970, Høst Madsen medal Fédération Internationale Pharmaceutique, 1972, Volwiler award Am. Assn. Colls. of Pharmacy, 1983, Rsch. Achievement award in pharmacokinetics, pharmacodynamics, drug metabolism, 1992; fellow Am. Found. Pharm. Edn., 1949-51; FDA grantee, 1969-76, Am. Assn. Pharm. Sci. fellow, 1986. Fellow AAAS, Am. Coll. Clin. Pharmacology and Chemotherapy, Acad. Pharm. Sci. (Stimulation of Rsch. award 1983, Pharmaceutics award 1984, Rsch. Achievement award 1984); mem. Am. Soc. Clin. Pharmacology and Therapeutics (bd. regents 1968-72, v.p. 1972, vice chmn. sect. on pharmacokinetics 1970-74), Am. Pharm. Assn. (Ebet prize 1961, rsch. award 1983, 84, Takeru Higuchi prize 1992), N.Y. Acad. Scis., Sigma Xi, Phi Lambda Upsilon, Rho Chi. Home: 908 Ivanhoe Dr Florence SC 29505-3614

WAGNER, JOHN LEO, federal judge, lawyer; b. Ithaca, N.Y., Mar. 12, 1954; s. Paul Francis and Doris Elizabeth (Hoffschneider) W.; m. Marilyn Modin, June 18, 1987. Student, U. Nebr., 1973-74; BA, U. Okla., 1976, JD, 1979. Bar: Okla. 1980, U.S. Dist. Ct. (we. dist.) Okla. 1980, U.S. Dist. Ct. (no. and ea. dists.) Okla. 1981, U.S. Ct. Appeals (10th cir.) 1982. Assoc. Franklin, Harmon & Satterfield Inc., Oklahoma City, 1980-82; ptnr. Franklin, Harmon & Satterfield, Inc., Oklahoma City, 1982; assoc. Kornfeld, Franklin & Phillips, Oklahoma City, 1982-85, ptnr., 1985; magistrate judge U.S. Dist. Ct. for No. Dist. Okla., Tulsa, 1985—. Pres. U. Okla. Coll. Law Assn., 1991-92. Mem. ABA, Fed. Magistrate Judge's Assn. (dir. 10th cir. 1987-89), 10th Cir. Edn. Com., Okla. Bar Assn., Council Oak Am. Inn of Cts. (pres. 1992-93), Jud. Conf. U.S. (com. ct. adminstrn. and case mgmt. 1992—). Republican. Office: US Magistrate Judge 333 W 4th St Rm 3355 Tulsa OK 74103-3819

WAGNER, JOSEPH CRIDER, retired university administrator; b. North Manchester, Ind., Feb. 19, 1907; s. Arthur Augustus and Grace (Crider) W.; A.B., Manchester Coll., 1929, LL.D., 1961; M.A. in Econs., U. Mich., 1936; postgrad. U. Wis., 1930, U. Chgo., 1931-32, Columbia, 1935; m. Geraldine B. Garber, June 30, 1933; 1 dau., Joene Henning. Tchr. Hartford City (Ind.) High Schs., 1929-35, prin., 1936-37, supt. schs., 1937-45; supt. schs., Crawfordsville, Ind., 1946; bus. mgr., treas. Ball State U., Muncie, Ind., 1946-61, v.p. for bus. affairs, 1961-73, v.p. emeritus, 1973—, treas., prof., gen. bus. adminstrn.; nat. chmn., 1976 Annual Fund. Drive; lectr. Mem. Ind. Common Sch. Bldg. Commn., 1960—. Active United Fund of Delaware County. Trustee Ind. Heart Found., Manchester Coll.; mem. ins. trust of Am. Assn. Ret. Persons and Nat. Ret. Tchrs. Assn.; bd. dirs. Muncie YMCA, Ind. State Tchrs. Retirement Fund. Mem. gen. bd. edn., nat. cons. in fin. Methodist Ch. in U.S. Paul Harris fellow Rotary; named Sagamore of the Wabash State of Ind. Gov's. Bowen and Orr, 1976, 88; recipient Friend of Journalism award, Friend of Music Citation, Retiree Recognition award Ball State U., 1992. Mem. Ind. Schoolmen's Club (pres. 1949), Ind. State Tchrs. Retirement Fund (bd. trustees 1975, pres. 1987-88), Retired Sch. Supt. Assn. Ind., Internat. Platform Assn., Am. Assn. Ret. Persons (ins. trust, Retiree Recognition award), Tau Kappa Alpha, Delta Pi Epsilon, Phi Delta Kappa (Cert. of Recognition), Sigma Alpha Epsilon. Mason, Rotarian (past pres.). Contbr. articles to profl. and religious jours. Home: 629 N Forest Ave Muncie IN 47304-3818

WAGNER, JOSEPH EDWARD, veterinarian, educator; b. Dubuque, Iowa, July 29, 1938; s. Jacob Edward and Leona (Callahan) W.; m. Kay Rose (div. Apr. 1983); children: Lucinda, Pamela, Jennifer, Douglas. DVM, Iowa State U., 1963; MPH, Tulane U., 1964; PhD, U. Ill., 1967. Asst. prof. U. Kans. Med. Ctr., Kansas City, 1967-69; assoc. prof. U. Mo. Coll. Vet. Medicine, Columbia, 1969-72, prof. vet. medicine, 1972—, Curator's prof., 1989—; cons. Harlan Sprague Dawley, Indpls., 1984—. Author: The Biology and Medicine of Rabbits and Rodents, 1989, 4th edit., 1995. Recipient award of excellence in lab. animal medicine Charles River Found., Wilmington, Mass., 1986. Mem. AMVA, Am. Coll. Lab. Animal Medicine (pres. 1985-86), Am. Assn. Lab. Animal Scis. (pres. 1980-81). Office: U Mo-Coll of Veterinary Medicine Dept of Vet Pathobiology 1600 E Rollins Rd Columbia MO 65211-1756

WAGNER, JOSEPH M., church administrator. Exec dir. Division for Ministry of the Evangelical Lutheran Church in America, Chgo. Office: Evangelical Lutheran Church Am 8765 W Higgins Rd Chicago IL 60631-4101

WAGNER, JUDITH BUCK, investment firm executive; b. Altoona, Pa. Sept. 25, 1943; d. Harry Bud and Mary Elizabeth (Rhodes) B.; m. Joseph E. Wagner, Mar. 15, 1980; 1 child, Elizabeth. BA in History, U. Wash., 1965; grad. N.Y. Inst. Fin., 1968. Registered Am. Stock Exch., N.Y. Stock Exch., investment advisor. Security analyst Morgan, Olmstead, Kennedy & Gardner, L.A., 1968-71; security analyst Boettcher & Co., Denver, 1972-75; pres. Wagner Investment Mgmt., Denver, 1975—; chmn., bd. dirs. The Women's Bank, N.A., Denver, 1977-94, organizational group pres., 1975-77; chmn. Equitable Bankshares Colo., Inc., Denver, 1980-94; bd. dirs. Equitable Bank of Littleton, 1983-88, pres., 1985; bd. dirs. Colo. Growth Capital, 1979-82; lectr. Denver U., Metro State, 1975-80. Author: Woman and Money series Colo. Woman Mag., 1976; moderator 'Catch 2' Sta. KWGN-TV, 1978-79. Pres. Big Sisters Colo., Denver, 1977-82, bd. dirs., 1973-83; bd. fellows U. Denver, 1985-90; bd. dirs. Red Cross, 1980, Assn. Children's Hosp., 1985, Colo. Health Facilities Authority, 1978-84, Jr. League Community Adv. Com., 1979-92, Brother's Redevel., Inc., 1979-80; mem. agy. rels. com. Mile High United Way, 1978-81, chmn. United Way Venture Grant com., 1980-81; bd. dirs. Downtown Denver Inc., 1988-95; bd. dirs., v.p., treas. The Women's Found. Colo., 1987-91; treas., trustee, v.p., Graland Country Day Sch., 1990—, pres. 1994—; trustee Denver Rotary Found., 1990-95; trustee Hunt Alternatives Fund, 1992—. Recipient Making It award Cosmopolitan Mag., 1977, Women on the Go award, Savvy mag., 1983, Minouri Yasoui award, 1986, Salute Spl. Honoree award, Big Sisters, 1987; named one of the Outstanding Young Women in Am., 1979; recipient Woman Who Makes A Difference award Internat. Women's Forum, 1987. Fellow Assn. Investment Mgmt. and Rsch.; mem. Women's Forum of Colo. (pres. 1979), Women's Found. Colo., Inc. (bd. dirs. 1986-91), Denver Soc. Security Analysts (bd. dirs. 1976-83, v.p. 1980-81, pres. 1981-82), Colo. Investment Advisors Assn., Rotary (treas. Denver chpt. found., pres. 1993-94), Leadership Denver (Outstanding Alumna award 1987), Pi Beta Phi (pres. U. Wash. chpt. 1964-65). Office: Wagner Investment Mgmt Inc 3200 Cherry Creek S Dr Ste 240 Denver CO 80209

WAGNER, JULIA A(NNE), retired editor; b. Alexandria, Va., Feb. 15, 1924; d. Luigi and Domenica (Di Giammarino) Coppa; Widowed. B.A., George Washington U., 1948, M.A., 1950. With U.S. Govt., Washington, 1941-55, publs. editor, 1951-55; editorial asst. Dell Pub. Co., N.Y.C., 1956-59, mng. editor, 1959-72, editor-in-chief, 1973-87. Mem. Am. Fedn. Astrologers. Democrat. Roman Catholic.

WAGNER, LAWRENCE M., diversified financial services company executive. Exec. v.p., chief oper. offices The Hillman Co., Pitts. Office: The Hillman Company 1900 Grant Bldg Pittsburgh PA 15219*

WAGNER, LINDSAY J., actress; b. L.A., June 22, 1949; d. Bill Nowels and Marilyn Louise (Thrasher) W.; m. Alan Rider (div.); m. Michael Brandon, Dec. 1976 (div.); m. Henry Kingi, 1981 (div.); m. Lawrence Mortorff, 1990; children: Dorian Henry, Alex Nathan. Student, U. Oreg., 1967. Tchr. acting children Founders Sch. Los Angeles, 1975. Actress numerous TV shows Universal Studios, Universal City, Calif., 1971-74; motion picture picture appearances include: Two People, 1972, The Paper Chase, 1973, Second Wind, 1976, Nighthawks, 1981, Martin's Day, 1984, Ricochet, 1991; TV series include The Bionic Woman, 1976-78, Jessie, 1984, Peaceable Kingdom, 1989; appeared in TV miniseries Scruples, 1980, Princess Daisy, 1983, The Dead of the Night, 1989, Voices of the Heart, 1990, To Be the Best, 1991; TV films include: The Two Worlds of Jennie Logan, 1979, The Incredible Journey of Dr. Meg Laurel, 1979, I Want to Live, 1983, Two Kinds of Love, 1983, Callie and Son, 1983, Passion, 1984, This Child is Mine, 1985, The Other Lover, 1985, Nightmare at Bitter Creek, 1988, The Taking of Flight 847, 1988, Shattered Dreams, 1990, Babies, 1990, A Message from Holly, 1992, Once in a Lifetime, 1994; author video film: (with others) Lindsay Wagner's New Beauty: The Acupressure Facelift. Office: care Jim Wyatt Internat Creative Mgmt 8942 Wilshire Blvd Beverly Hills CA 90211-1934*

WAGNER, LOUIS CARSON, JR., retired army officer; b. Jackson, Mo., Jan. 24, 1932; s. Louis Carson and Margaret Marie (Macke) W.; m. Judith Gifford, Sept. 24, 1955; children: Susan, Amy. B.S., U.S. Mil. Acad., 1954; M.S. in Applied Mechanics, U. Ill., 1961; grad., U.S. Naval War Coll., 1971. Commd. 2d lt. U.S. Army, 1954, advanced through grades to gen., 1987; served in Vietnam, Germany, Alaska; dep. dir. material plans and programs Office Dept. Chief Staff Research, Devel. and Acquisition, Washington, 1976-78, dir. combat support systems, 1978-80; comdg. gen. Armor Ctr., Ft. Knox, 1980-83; asst. dep. chief of staff for ops. and plans ODCSOPS, USA, Washington, 1983-84, dep. chief of staff for research, devel. and acquisition, 1984-87; comdg. gen. U.S. Army Materiel Command, Alexandria, Va., 1987-89; ret., 1989; fellow Inst. of Land Warfare Assn. of U.S. Army, Arlington, Va., 1990—. Decorated D.S.C., D.S.M. with oak leaf cluster, Silver Star, Legion of Merit with oak leaf cluster, Bronze Star, Air medal with oak leaf cluster, Purple Heart, Meritorious Service medal, Army Commendation medal with 2 clusters, Combat Inf. badge. Mem. Assn. Grads. U.S. Mil. Acad., Armor Assn., Assn. U.S. Army, Ret. Officers Assn. (chmn. bd. dirs.), Am. Def. Preparedness Assn., Army Aviation Assn. Am., Nat. Eagle Scout Assn. (bd. regents), S.C. Rsch. Authority (bd. advisors). Office: 6309 Chaucer Ln Alexandria VA 22304-3537

WAGNER, MARY ANN, human resources executive; b. St. Louis, May 24, 1947; d. John Gerard and Carmela Lucy (Cozza) Blethroad; 1 child, John Patrick. BA, Webster U., St. Louis, 1979, MA, 1982. Tchr. Our Lady of Fatima, St. Louis, Wetterau, St. Louis; personnel mgr. Venture, St. Louis, 1979-81; customer svc. coord. Venture, O'Fallon, Mo., 1981-84, personnel mgr., 1984-86; regional personnel mgr., 1986-88, dir. tng. and devel., 1988-92; divsn. v.p. dir. of assoc. rels. May Merchandising, St. Louis, 1995—; adj. prof. Webster U., 1990-95, divisional v.p. tng. and devel., 1992—. Chmn. United Way, O'Fallon, 1985, bd. dirs. Mem. AAIM Mgmt. Assn., Am. Soc. Tng. and Devel., Am. Mgmt. Assn. Roman Catholic. Avocations: antiques, music, sports. Home: 15525 Debridge Way Florissant MO 63034-3456

WAGNER, MARY KATHRYN, sociology educator, former state legislator; b. Madison, S.D., June 19, 1932; d. Irving Macaulay and Mary Browning (Wines) Mumford; m. Robert Todd Wagner, June 23, 1954; children: Christopher John, Andrea Browning. BA, U. S.D., 1954; MEd, S.D. State U., 1974, PhD, 1978. Sec. R.A. Burleigh & Assocs., Evanston, Ill., 1954-57; dir. resource ctr. Watertown (S.D.) Sr. High Sch., 1969-71, Brookings (S.D.) High Sch., 1971-74; asst. dir. S.D. Com. on the Humanities, Brookings, 1976-90; asst. prof. rural sociology S.D. State U., 1990—; mem. S.D. Ho. of Reps., 1981-88, S.D. Senate, 1988-92. Mem., pres. Brookings Sch. Bd., 1975-81; chair fund dr. Brookings United Way, 1985; bd. dirs. Brookings Chamber music Soc., 1981—, Advance and Career Learning Ctr. Named Woman of Yr., Bus. and Profl. Women, 1981, Legislator Conservationist of Yr., Nat. and S.D. Wildlife Fedn., 1988. Mem. Population Assn. Am., Midwest Sociol. Soc., Rural Sociol. Soc., Brookings C. of C. (mem. indsl. devel. com. 1988—), PEO, Rotary. Republican. Episcopalian. Avocations:

reading, gardening, music, golf, bridge. Home: 929 Harvey Dunn St Brookings SD 57006-1347

WAGNER, MARY MARGARET, library and information science educator; b. Mpls., Feb. 4, 1946; d. Harvey F.J. and Yvonne M. (Brettner) W.; m. William Moore, June 16, 1988; children: Lebohang Y.C., Nora M. BA, Coll. St. Catherine, St. Paul, 1969; MLS, U. Wash., 1973. Asst. libr. St. Margarets Acad., Mpls., 1969-70; libr. Derham Hall High Sch., St. Paul, 1970-71; youth worker The Bridge for Runaways, Mpls., 1971-72; libr. Guthrie Theater Reference and Rsch. Libr., Mpls., 1973-75; asst. br. libr. St. Paul Pub. Libr., 1975; assoc. prof. dept. info. mgmt. Coll. St. Catherine, St. Paul, 1975—; del. Minn. Gov.'s Pre-White House Conf. on Librs. and Info. Svcs., 1990; mem. Minn. Pre-White House Program Com., 1989-90, Continuing Libr. Info. and Media Edn. Com. Minn. Dept. Edn., Libr. Devel. and Svcs., 1980-83, 87—; mem. cmty. faculty Met. State U., St. Paul, 1980—; mem. core revision com. Coll. St. Catherine, 1992-93, faculty budget adv. com., 1992-95, faculty pers. com., 1989-92, acad. computing com. 1991-96; chair curriculum subcom. Minn. Vol. Cert. Com., 1993—. Contbr. articles to profl. jours. Bd. dirs. Christian Sharing Fund, 1976-80, chair, 1977-78. Grantee: U.S. Embassy, Maseru, Lesotho, Africa, Brit. Consulate, Maseru, various founds.; Upper Midwest Assn. for Intercultural Edn. travel grantee Assoc. Colls. Twin Cities. Mem ALA (libr. book fellows program 1990-91), Am. Soc. Info. Sci., Am. Soc. Indexers, Spl. Libr. Assn., Minn. Libr. Assn. (pres. 1981-82, chair continuing edn. com. 1987-90, steering com. Readers Adv. Roundtable, 1989-91), Minn. Ednl. Media Orgn., Twin Cities Women in Computing. Office: Coll St Catherine Dept Info Mgmt 2004 Randolph Ave Saint Paul MN 55105-1750

WAGNER, MICHAEL DICKMAN, state representative; b. Omaha, Sept. 24, 1957; s. Loyd R. and Donna (Dickman) W.; m. Paula Spriggs, Oct. 11, 1975; children: Jeremiah, Stephanie, Joshua. AAS in Bus. Mgmt., Kilian C.C., Sioux Falls, S.D., 1984, cert. computer programming, 1984; postgrad., Harvard U., 1995—. From mouldings worker to inventory database coord. Jordan Millwork Co., 1975-84; from dir. ops. info. systems to mgr. Austad's, 1984-93; owner grocery store, entertainment arcade, cons. svc., 1993-94; mayor Baltic, S.D., 1986-92; state rep. State of S.D., Pierre, 1988—, asst. majority leader, 1993-94, mem. legis. exec. bd., 1994—; instr. Kilian C.C., Sioux Falls, 1984-86. Del. leader Am. Coun. Young Polit. Leaders 1992 Exch. to China, del. 1990 Exch. to Japan; exec. dir. Habitat for Humanity, 1994-95; Bus. Leadership fellow, 1995. Bus. Leadership fellow, 1995. Mem. Nat. League of Cities (small cities coun., comty. and econ. devel. policy com. 1989-92), S.D. Mcpl. League (1st and 2d v.p. 1987-89, state exec. bd. trustee 1984-87, dist. chmn. S.E. S.D. 1984, legis. policy com., chmn. mcpl. computerization task force), Nat. Conf. State Legislature (vice chair fiscal oversight and intergovtl. affairs com.), S.E. Coun. Govts. (exec. bd.), Rotary Internat., Minnehaha County Rural Mayors Assn., Minnehaha County Centennial Commn., Baltic Area Cub Scouts (past chmn.), Baltic Area Jaycees, Baltic Comty. Club, Baltic Athletic Assn. Home: PO Box 308 Baltic SD 57003-0308

WAGNER, MURIEL GINSBERG, nutrition therapist; b. N.Y.C., Apr. 6, 1926; d. Irving A. and Anna Ginsberg; divorced; 1 child, Emily Lucinda Faith. BA, Wayne State U., 1948, MS, 1951; PhD, U. Mich., 1982. Registered dietitian. Nutritionist Merrill-Palmer Inst., Detroit, 1951-74; pvt. practice, nutritional therapist Southfield, Mich., 1976—; cons. select com. on nutrition U.S. Senate, 1973-74, Ford Motor Co., Dearborn, Mich., 1975-78, Detroit Dept. Consumer Affairs, 1979—; adj. faculty mem. Wayne State U., Detroit, 1970-80, U. Mich., Dearborn, 1974-79. Author: (cookbook) Tun...ahhh, 1993; contbr. articles to profl. publs. Vol. Am. Heart Assn. of Mich.; also various local and nat. govtl. groups. Recipient Outstanding Cmty. Svc. award Am. Heart Assn., 1990; named Outstanding Profl., Mich. Dietetic Assn., 1974. Fellow Am. Dietetic Assn. (organizer Dial-A-Dietitian); mem. Soc. Nutrition Edn., Am. Diabetes Assn. Avocations: cooking, recipe development, gardening. Office: 4400 Town Ctr Ste 275 Southfield MI 48075

WAGNER, NORMAN ERNEST, former energy company executive, former university president; b. Edenwold, Sask., Can., Mar. 29, 1935; s. Robert Eric and Gertrude Margaret (Brandt) W.; m. Catherine Hack, May 16, 1957; children: Marjorie Dianne, Richard Roger, Janet Marie. BA, U. Sask., 1958, MDiv, 1958; MA, U. Toronto, 1960, PhD in Near Eastern Studies, 1965; LLD, Wilfrid Laurier U., 1984. Asst. prof. Near Eastern studies Wilfrid Laurier U., Waterloo, Ont., 1962-65, assoc. prof., 1965-69, prof., 1970-78, dean grad. studies and rsch., 1974-78; pres. U. Calgary, Alta., Can., 1978-88; chmn. bd. Alta. Natural Gas Co., Ltd., 1988—; pres. emeritus U. Calgary, Can., 1988-95; chmn. Knowledge at Work Found., 1995—; chmn. audit com. Province of Alta.; bd. dirs., chmn. Terry fox Humanitarian Award Program; pres. Corp. Higher Edn. Forum, 1996—. Author: (with others) The Moyer Site: A Prehistoric Village in Waterloo County, 1974. Mem. Adv. Coun. on Adjustment, OCO '88, Alta. Heritage Found. for Med. Rsch., Nat. Adv. Bd. Sci. and Tech., Internat. Trade Adv. Com. Decorated officer Order of Can. Mem. Can. Soc. Bibl. Studies. Lutheran. Home: Box 5 Site 33 RR # 12, Calgary, AB Canada T3E 6W3 Office: Alta Natural Gas Co Ltd, 2900 240 Fourth Ave SW, Calgary, AB Canada T2P 4L7

WAGNER, PATRICIA HAMM, lawyer; b. Gastonia, N.C., Feb. 1, 1936; d. Luther Boyd and Mildred Ruth (Wheeler) Hamm; married; children: David Marion, Michael Marion, Laura Marion. AB magna cum laude, Wittenberg U., 1958; JD with distinction, Duke U., 1974. Bar: N.C. 1974, Wash. 1984. Asst. univ. counsel Duke U., Durham, N.C., 1974-75, assoc. univ. counsel health affairs, 1977-80; atty. N.C. Meml. Hosp., 1975-77; assoc. N.C. Atty. Gen. Office, 1975-77; assoc. Powe, Porter & Alphin, Durham, 1980-81, prin., 1981-83; assoc. Williams, Kastner & Gibbs, 1984-86, Wickwire, Goldmark & Schorr, 1986-88; spl. counsel Heller, Ehrman, White & McAuliffe, 1988-90, ptnr., 1990—; arbitrator Am. Arbitration Assn., 1978—; arbitrator, pro tem judge King County Superior Ct., 1986—; tchr. in field. Mem. bd. vis. Law Sch. Duke U., 1992—; bd. dirs. Seattle Edn. Ctr., 1990-91, Metroctr. YMCA, 1991-94, Cmty. Psychiat. Clinic, Seattle, 1984-86; bd. dirs., sec.-treas. N.C. Found. Alternative Health Programs, Inc., 1982-84; bd. dirs., sec.-treas. N.C. Ctr. Pub. Policy Rsch., 1976-83, vice-chmn., 1977-80; mem. task force on commitment law N.C. Dept. Human Resources, 1978; active Def. Rsch. Inst. 1982-84; bd. dirs. Law Fund, 1992—, v.p., 1993—. Fellow Am. Bar Found.; mem. ABA (mem. ho. dels. Seattle-King County Bar Assn. 1991-94, mem. litigation sect.), Am. Soc. Hosp. Attys., Wash. State Bar Assn. (mem. domestic rels. task force 1991-93), Seattle-King Bar Assn. (mem. bd. trustees 1990-93, sec. bd. 1989-90, chair judiciary and cts. com. 1987-89, mem. King County Superior Ct. delay reduction task force 1987-89, mem. gender bias com. 1990-94, chair 1990-91), Wash. Def. Trial Lawyers (chmn. ct. rules and procedures com. 1987, co-editor newsletter 1985-86), Wash. State Soc. Hosp. Attys., Wash. Women Lawyers (treas. 1986, 87). Office: Heller Ehrman White & McAuliffe 6100 Columbia Ctr 701 5th Ave Seattle WA 98104-7016

WAGNER, PAUL ANTHONY, JR., education educator; b. Pitts., Aug. 28, 1947; s. Paul A. and Mary K. Wagner; m. Nancy C. Wright; children: Nicole S., Eric P., Jason G. BS, N.E. Mo. State U., 1969; MEd, U. Mo., 1972; MA in Philosophy, 1976, PhD in Philosophy of Edn., 1978. Internal expeditor electromotive div. GM, La Grange, Ill., 1970-71; instr. Moberly (Mo.) Jr. Coll., 1972-73; instr. U. Mo., Columbia, 1973-78, dir. univ. self-study, acting dir. instl. rsch. and planning, 1990-92; instr. Mo. Mil. Acad., 1978-79; prof. edn. and philosophy U. Houston-Clear Lake, 1979—, Atrium Cir. Disting. Rsch. Prof., 1980, Chancellor's Disting. Svc. Prof., 1985; dir. Inst. Logical and Cognitive Studies, 1980—; dir. Project in Profl. Ethics Project in Profl. Ethics, 1992—; chmn. dept. edn. U. Houston-Clear Lake, 1989-92; adj. prof. bus. mgmt. U. Houston-Victoria, 1995—; pres. Wagner & Assocs. Ednl. Consulting, 1988-93; dir. Tex. Ctr. for Study Profl. Ethics in Tchg., 1988—; rsch. assoc. Ctr. for Moral Devel., Harvard U., 1985-86; vis. scholar Stanford U., Palo Alto, Calif., 1981; cons. to various sch. dists., 1979—; cons. in total quality mgmt. Golden Gate U., 1992-93, M.D. Anderson Cancer Ctr. & Hosp., 1992-93, U. Houston-Victoria, 1993; chair So. Accreditation of Colls. and Schs. steering com., U. Houston-Clear Lake, 1990-93; chair univ. planning com., 1993-94; mem. faculty Senate exec. com., 1993-95; mem. bd. dirs., chair planning and budgeting com. Houston Tenneco Marathon, 1992—; mem. steering com. Trilateral Conf. and Supershow Greater Human Partnership, 1994-95; cons. and ethics trainer Am. Leadership Forum, 1995—. Author: (with F. Kierstead) The Ethical Legal and Multicultural Founds. of Teaching, 1992; contbr. articles on sci. edn. and philosophy of edn. to profl. jours. Mem. editorial bd. Jour. of Thought, 1981—, Focus on Learning, 1982-85; editorial cons. Instrnl. Scis., 1981-83; editorial assoc. Brain and Behavioral Scis., 1986—. Mem. Human Rights Commn., Columbia, Mo., 1976-79, vice chmn., 1978-79; Sunday sch. tchr. Mary Queen Cath. Ch., Friendswood, Tex., 1979—; founding bd. mem. Bay Area Symphony Soc., 1983-85; capital campaign com. Soc. Prevention Cruelty to Animals, 1989-91; publicity com. Am. Cancer Soc., Houston chpt., 1989-92; mem. Houston-Tenneco Marathon bd., 1989—, chair steering com. for strategic planning, 1993, chair planning and budgeting com., 1993—; cons. in strategic planning to M.D. Anderson Cancer Ctr. vol. divsn. Sgt. Mo. N.G., 1970-76; mem. steering com. City of Houston Emerging Bus. Conf., 1994-95, Trilateral Conf., Greater Houston Partnership, 1994-95, active Houston Bus. Promise, 1995—. Recipient Cert. of Appreciation, City of Columbia, 1978; K.E. Graessle scholar, 1968, Mo. Peace Studies Inst. grantee, 1971. Mem. Assn. Applied and Profl. Ethics, Am. Assn. Pub. Adminstrs. (ethics com.), Am. Philos. Assn., Assn. Philosophers in Edn. (exec. bd., v.p.), Philosophy of Edn. Soc. (exec. sec.-treas., hospitality chair 1995—), Am. Ednl. Studies Assn., Brit. Soc. for Philosophy Sci., Philosophy Sci. Assn., S.W. Philosophy Edn. Soc., Tex. Network for Tchr. Tng. in Philosophy for Children (bd. dirs. 1983-90), Tex. Ctr. for Ethics in Edn. (bd. dirs. 1988—), Tex. Ednl. Found. Soc. (pres. 1986—), Tex. Assn. Coll. Tchrs., So. Assn. Colls. Coord., Houston Bar Assn. (mem. steering com. NAFTA Conf. 1993-94), Informal Logic Assn., Leadership Houston, Friends Hermann Pk., Clearlake Cir. (chair 1979-85), Phi Delta Kappa, Kappa Delta Pi. Roman Catholic. Avocations: running, racquetball, reading, opera, ballet. Address: RR 4 Box 217 Navasota TX 77868 Office: U Houston 2700 Bay Area Blvd # 338 Houston TX 77058-1098

WAGNER, PETER EWING, physics and electrical engineering educator; b. Ann Arbor, Mich., July 4, 1929; s. Paul Clark and Charlotta Josephine (Ewing) W.; m. Caryl Jean Veon, June 23, 1951; children: Ann Frances, Stephen Charles. Student, Occidental Coll., 1946-48; AB with honors, U. Calif., Berkeley, 1950, PhD, 1956. Teaching rsch. asst. U. Calif., 1950-56; rsch. physicist Westinghouse Rsch. Labs., Pitts., 1956-59; assoc. prof. elec. engring. Johns Hopkins, 1960-65, prof., 1965-73; dir. Ctr. for Environ. and Estuarine Studies U. Md., 1973-80, prof., 1973-81; vis. prof. physics U. Ala., Huntsville, 1980-81, prof., 1981; vice chancellor for acad. affairs, prof. physics U. Miss., 1981-84; provost, prof. physics and elec. engring. Utah State U., 1984-89; v.p. acad. affars and provost SUNY, Binghamton, 1989-92, prof. physics and elec. engring., 1989—; spl. projects engr. State of Md., 1971-72; mem. Gov.'s Sci. Adv. Coun., 1973-77, Md. Power Plant Siting Adv. Com., 1972-80; cons. in field. Contbr. articles to profl. jours.; patentee in field. Trustee Chesapeake Rsch. Consortium, 1974-80, chmn. bd. trustees, 1979-80. Guggenheim fellow Oxford U., 1966-67. Mem. Nat. Assn. State Univs. and Land Grant Colls. (mem. coun. acad. affairs, mem. affirmative action com. 1986-89, chmn. nominating com. 1988-89, chmn. libr. commn. 1989-92), Ctr. Rsch. Librs. (bd. dirs. 1991—, mem. budget and fin. com. 1991-93, vice chairperson 1992-93, chairperson 1993-94, chair nominating com. 1994-95), Blue Key, Gold Key, Phi Beta Kappa, Phi Beta Kappa Assocs. (life, bd. dirs. 1995—), Sigma Xi (life), Phi Kappa Phi. Home: 2748 Grandview Pl Endwell NY 13760-7043

WAGNER, RICHARD, business executive, former baseball team executive; b. Central City, Nebr., Oct. 19, 1927; s. John Howard and Esther Marie (Wolken) W.; m. Gloria Jean Larsen, May 10, 1950; children—Randolph G., Cynthia Kaye. Student, pub. schs., Central City. Gen. mgr. Lincoln (Nebr.) Baseball Club, 1955-58; mgr. Pershing Mcpl. Auditorium, Lincoln, 1958-61; exec. staff Ice Capades, Inc., Hollywood, Calif., 1961-63; gen. mgr. Sta. KSAL, Salina, Kans., 1963-65; dir. promotion and sales St. Louis Nat. Baseball Club, 1965-66; gen. mgr. Forum, Inglewood, Calif., 1966-67; asst. to exec. v.p. Cin. Reds, 1967-70, asst. to pres., 1970-74, v.p. adminstrn., 1975, exec. v.p., 1975-78, gen. mgr., 1977-83, pres., 1978-83; pres. Houston Astros Baseball Club, 1985-87; spl. asst. Office of Baseball Commr., 1988-93; asst. to chmn. Major League Exec. Coun., 1993-94; pres. RGW Enterprises, Inc., Phoenix, 1978—. Served with USNR, 1945-47, 50-52. Named Exec. of Yr., Minor League Baseball, Sporting News, 1958. Mem. Internat. Assn. Auditorium Mgrs. Republican. Methodist.

WAGNER, ROBERT, actor; b. Detroit, Feb. 10, 1930; m. Natalie Wood, 1957 (div. 1962); m. Marion Marshall Donen; 1 child, Kate; remarried Natalie Wood, 1972 (dec. 1981); 1 child, Courtney. Films include: Halls of Montezuma, The Frogmen, Let's Make It Legal, With a Song in My Heart, What Price Glory?, Stars and Stripes Forever, The Silver Whip, Titanic, Star of Tomorrow, Beneath the 12-Mile Reef, Prince Valiant, Broken Lance, White Feather, A Kiss Before Dying, The Mountain, The True Story of Jesse James, Stopover Tokyo, In Love and War, Say One For Me, Between Heaven and Hell, The Hunters, All the Fine Young Cannibals, Sail a Crooked Ship, The Longest Day, The War Lover, The Condemned of Altona, Harper, Banning, The Biggest Bundle of Them All, The Pink Panther, The Curse of the Pink Panther, Winning, The Affair, The Towering Inferno, Critical List, Dragon: The Bruce Lee Story; starred in TV series It Takes a Thief, Switch!, Hart to Hart, Lime St.; produced, starred in TV series Madame Sin; formed Robert Wagner Prodns.; other TV appearances include: Streets of San Francisco, The Ox-Bow Incident, Gun In His Hand, And Man Created Vanity, The Enemy on the Beach, Runaway Bay, How I Spent My Summer Vacation, Name of the Game, City Beneath the Sea, Cable Car Mystery, To Catch a King, Cat on a Hot Tin Roof, Indiscreet, 1988; Movies of the Week There Must Be a Pony, Love Amongst Thieves, This Gun for Hire. Address: care William Morris Agy 151 S El Camino Dr Beverly Hills CA 90212-2704*

WAGNER, ROBERT EARL, agronomist; b. Garden City, Kans., Mar. 6, 1921; s. Fay Arthur and Margaret (Longbottom) W.; m. Bernice Bittner, Aug. 7, 1948; children—Robert Earl, James Warren, Douglas Alan. B.S., Kans. State Coll., 1942; M.S., U. Wis., 1943, Ph.D., 1950. Forage crops specialist Ft. Hays Expt. Sta., Hays, Kans., 1943-45; asso. agronomist Plant Industry Sta., U.S. Dept. Agr., Beltsville, Md., 1945-48; research agronomist, asst. project leader pasture and range project Plant Industry Sta., U.S. Dept. Agr., 1951-54, research agronomist, project leader western pasture and range project, 1954-56; prof., head dept. agronomy U. Md., 1956-59; regional dir. American Potash Inst., 1959-66, also Found. for Internat. Potash Research, v.p. both orgns., 1966-67; dir. Coop. Extension Service, U. Md., 1967-75; pres., bd. dirs. Potash Inst., 1975-77; pres., bd. dirs. Potash and Phosphate Inst., 1977-88, pres. emeritus, 1988—; chmn., bd. dirs. Potash & Phosphate Inst. Can., 1975-88; pres., bd. dirs. Found. for Agronomic Rsch., 1980-87; owner Wagner Performance Cattle, Stone Mountain, Ga., 1985—; bd. dirs., mem. exec. com. Internat. Fertilizer Devel. Ctr., 1975—; bd. dirs. African Ctr. for Fertilizer Devel., 1988—; chmn. Nat. Ext. Com. on Orgn. and Policy; mem. U.S. del. 7th Internat. Grassland Congress, New Zealand. Author tech., popular publs.; Editor: Proc. Sixth Internat. Grassland Congress. Recipient Medallion award Am. Forage and Grassland Coun., Disting. Grasslander award, 1994; award Md. Farm Bur.; Disting. Svc. award in agr. Kansas State U., 1985, Disting. Alumnus award, 1990; Cert. of Disting. Citizenship, State of Md.; Robert E. Wagner Efficient Agr. award established in his honor; Disting. Grasslander award Am. Forages Md. Grassland Coun., 1994. Fellow AAAS, Am. Soc. Agronomy (chmn. grassland com., mem. exec. com., bd. dirs., pres. N.E. br.), Crops Sci. Soc. Am., Soil Sci. Soc. Am.; mem. Grassland Coun. (pres.), Am. Soc. Range Mgmt., Cosmos Club (Washington), Atlanta Athletic Club, Sigma Xi, Alpha Zeta, Gamma Sigma Delta, Phi Kappa Phi. Presbyterian. Home: 1934 Mountain Creek Dr Stone Mountain GA 30087-1016 Office: 655 Engineering Dr Norcross GA 30092-2821

WAGNER, ROBERT RODERICK, microbiologist, oncology educator; b. N.Y.C., Jan. 5, 1923; s. Nathan and Mary (Mendelsohn) W.; m. Mary Elizabeth Burke, Mar. 23, 1967. A.B., Columbia U., 1943; M.D., Yale U., 1946. Intern, asst. resident physician Yale-New Haven Med. Center, 1946-47, 49-50; research fellow Nat. Inst. Med. Research, London, Eng., 1950-51; instr., then asst. prof. medicine Yale U., 1951-55; asst., then assoc. prof. medicine Johns Hopkins U., Balt., 1956-59, assoc. prof. microbiology, 1959-64, asst., then assoc. dean med. faculty, 1957-63, prof. microbiology, 1964-67; vis. fellow, mem. Common Room All Souls Coll. Oxford U., 1967, 76; prof. microbiology U. Va., 1967—; chmn. dept. microbiology, 1967-94; Marion McNulty Weaver and Malvin C. Weaver prof. oncology U. Va., 1984—, dir. Cancer Ctr., 1984-94; vis. scientist Chinese Acad. Med. Scis., 1982; vis. prof. Univs. Giessen and Wuerzburg (W. Ger.), 1983; Cons. Am. Cancer Soc. Mem. coms.; USPHS, NSF, Assn. Am. Med. Colls., AMA, Nat. Bd. Med. Examiners.; bd. dirs. W. Alton Jones Cell Sci. Center, Lake Placid, N.Y., 1982—. Editor-in-chief: Jour. Virology, 1966-82. Served to lt. USNR, 1947-49. Rockefeller Found. resident scholar Villa Serbelloni, Bellagio, Italy, 1976; Macy Found. Faculty scholar Oxford U., 1976; recipient Disting. U.S. Scientist award Alexander von Humboldt Found., 1983. Fellow AAAS (councillor); mem. Assn. Am. Physicians, Am. Soc. Clin. Investigation, Am. Soc. Biol. Chemists, Am. Assn. Immunologists, Am. Soc. for Microbiology (councillor), Assn. Med. Sch. Microbiology Chmn. (pres. 1974), Am. Soc. Virology (pres. 1984). Office: Univ of Va Dept Microbiology Box 441 Charlottesville VA 22908

WAGNER, ROBERT TODD, university president, sociology educator; b. Sioux Falls, S.D., Oct. 30, 1932; s. Hans Herman and Helen Emilie (Castle) W.; m. Mary Kathryn Mumford, June 23, 1954; children: Christopher, Andrea. BA, Augustana Coll., Sioux Falls, 1954; MDiv, Seabury Western Theol. Sem., 1957, STM, 1970; PhD, S.D. State U., 1972; DHL, Augustana Coll., 1994. Ordained to ministry Episc. Ch., 1957. Staff analyst AMA, Chgo., 1954-57; vicar Ch. of Holy Apostles, Sioux Falls, 1957-64; chaplain All Saints Sch., Sioux Falls, 1962-64; rector Trinity Episcopal Ch., Watertown, S.D., 1964-69; prof. sociology S.D. State U., Brookings, 1971—, acting head dept. sociology, 1978, asst. to v.p. for acad. affairs, 1980-84, pres., 1985—; v.p. Dakota State U., Madison, S.D., 1984-85; cons. sociologist Devel. Planning and Research, Manhattan, Kans., 1976-85; bd. dirs. Deuel County Nat. Bank, Clear Lake, S.D., Found. Seed Stock. Bd. dirs. Karl Mundt Found., Prairie Repertory Theatre, REACH, S.D. 4-H Found., S.D. State U. Found., SA Found., Griffith Charitable Trust, F.O. Butler Found., Christian Edn. Camp and Conf. of Episcopal Dioceses of S.D. Arthur Vinning Davis Found. fellow, 1969-70, Episcopal Ch. Found. fellow, 1969-71, Augustana Coll. fellow, 1977. Mem. Nat. Assn. State Univs. and Land Grant Colls., Brookings C. of C., Phi Kappa Phi, Phi Kappa Delta, Pi Gamma Mu, Alpha Kappa Delta, Alpha Lambda Delta, Sigma Gamma Delta. Republican. Lodges: Elks, Rotary. Avocations: railroading, gardening, cooking. Home: 929 Harvey Dunn St Brookings SD 57006-1347 Office: SD State U Adminstrn Bldg 222 Office of Pres Brookings SD 57007-2298

WAGNER, ROBERT WALTER, photography, cinema and communications educator, media producer, consultant; b. Newport News, Va., Nov. 16, 1918; s. Walter George and Barbara Anna W.; m. Betty Jane Wiles, Nov. 21, 1948; children—Jonathan R., Jeffrey A., Jennifer J. B.Sc., Ohio State U., 1940, M.A., 1941, Ph.D., 1953. Motion picture writer-dir. Office War Info., N.Y.C. and Washington, 1942-43; writer-dir. Office Coordinator Interam. Affairs for South and Central Am., 1943-44; chief info. Div. Mental Hygiene, Ohio Dept. Pub. Welfare, 1944-46; dir. div. motion pictures Ohio State U., 1946-58, prof. communications, photography and cinema, 1960—; pres. Univ. Film Found., 1979-85; writer, dir. James Thurber's Columbus Town, 1990, Images of the Depression, 1990; internat. cons. communications; bd. dirs. Am. Film Inst., 1974-81; mem. faculty U. So. Calif., 1958-59, U. P.R., 1961, 66, 68, San Jose State U., 1967, Ariz. State U., 1971, Concordia U., Montreal, Que., Can., 1980, 81, Danish Nat. Film Sch., 1983, 84, Emerson Coll., Boston, 1987. Ency. Brit. fellow, 1953; Sr. Fulbright fellow, Peru, 1976; recipient Disting. Service award Columbus Community Film Council, 1986, Disting. Svc. award Ohio State U., 1988. Fellow Soc. Motion Picture and TV Engrs. (Eastman Gold Medal award 1981); mem. Acad. TV Arts and Scis. (Ohioana Pegasus award 1985), Univ. Film/Video Assn. (bd. editors jour. 1975-85, editor jour. 1956-75), Internat. Congress Schs. Cinema and TV (v.p. 1964-82), Assn. Ednl. Communication and Tech. (bd. editors jour. 1976—). Club: Torch (Columbus, Ohio). Author film series: Series of Motion Picture Documents on Communication Theory and New Educational Media, 1966; editor: Education of Film Maker, 1975. Home: 1353 Zollinger Rd Columbus OH 43221-2939 Office: Ohio State U 156 W 19th Ave Columbus OH 43210-1110

WAGNER, ROBIN SAMUEL ANTON, stage and set designer; b. San Francisco, Aug. 31, 1933; s. Jens Otto and Phyllis Edna (Smith-Spurgeon) W.; children: Kurt, Leslie, Christie. Student, Calif. Sch. Fine Arts, 1953-54. Pres. Scarab Prodns., Inc., 1975—; prof. theatre arts Columbia U., 1988—; sr. v.p. The Design Edge, 1989—. Designer on Broadway including Big, Death Defying Acts, Victor/Victoria, Angels in America, Millenium Approaches Perestroika, Crazy for You, Jelly's Last Jam, City of Angels, Jerome Robbins's Broadway, Teddy and Alice, Chess, Song and Dance, Merlin, Dreamgirls, 42nd Street, A Chorus Line, One the Twentieth Century, Ballroom, Mack and Mabel, Seesaw, Sugar, Jesus Christ Superstar, The Great White Hope, Promises, Promises, Lenny, Inner City, Hair; designer off Broadway, including: Putting It Together, Hamlet 90, In White America, View from the Bridge, Mahogony, The Prodigal, Between Two Thieves, Cages; designer regional theatres including Joseph Papp Pub. Theatre, Arena State, Washington, Actor's Workshop, San Francisco, Met Opera, San Francisco Balet, Am. Ballet Theatre, Am. Shakespeare Festival, Eliot Feld Ballet, N.Y. Shakespeare Festival, Ensemble Studio Theatre, N.Y.C. Ballet, Vienna State Opera, Hamburg State Opera, Malmo Music Theatre, Sweden, Royal Opera at Covent Garden, Rolling Stones Tour of Ams., 1975, (London prodns.), Gothenberg Opera, 1996, Crazy For You, City of Angels, Chess, 42d Street, A Chorus Line, Promises, Promises, Hair, (Tokyo prodns.), A Chorus Line, Dream Girls, 42nd St., City of Angels, Crazy For You. Mem. adv. bd. Nat. Corp. Theatre Fund, Theatre Adv. Coun. for City of N.Y.; mem. art adv. com. N.Y. Internat. Festival of the Arts; bd. trustees N.Y. Shakespeare Festival. Recipient Tony award for On the Twentieth Century, 1978, City of Angels, 1990, also numerous nominations; Drama Desk award, 1971, 78, 82, 90, Theatre World award, 1975, Outer Circle Critics award, 1978, 90, 92, Maharam award, 1973, 75, 82, Lumen award, 1975, Dramalogue award, 1980, Boston Critics award, 1974, 92, award for excellence in theatre Ensemble Studio Theatre, 1990, Dora award, 1995. Mem. United Scenic Artists. Office: Robin Wagner Studio 890 Broadway New York NY 10003-1211

WAGNER, ROD, library director; b. Oakland, Nebr., Sept. 14, 1948; s. Francis Lynn and Doris Jean (Egbers) W.; m. M. Diane Kennedy, June 14, 1969; children: Jennifer, Brian, James. BA Social Sci. Edn., Wayne (Nebr.) State Coll., 1970; MA Polit. Sci., U. Nebr. Lincoln, 1971; MA Libr. Sci., U. Mo., 1981. Rsch. coord. Nebr. Libr. Commn., Lincoln, 1972, planning, evaluation, rsch. coord., 1972-73, adminstrv. asst., 1973-74, dep. dir., 1974-87, dir., 1988—; bd. dirs. Nebr. Ctr. for the Book, Nebr. Devel. Network. With U.S. Army Nat. Guard, 1970-77. Mem. ALA (contbr. yearbook 1981-84), Nat. Mgmt. Assn., Mountain Plains Libr. Assn., Nebr. Libr. Assn. (pres.-elect 1993-94, pres. 1994-95), Chief Officers State Libr. Agencies, Western Coun. State Librs. (pres. 1992-93). Presbyterian. Home: 3205 W Pershing Rd Lincoln NE 68502-4844 Office: NE Libr Commn 1200 N St Ste 120 Lincoln NE 68508-2020

WAGNER, ROGER PHILIP, hotel executive; b. Billings, Mont., July 13, 1947; s. Joseph Philip and Rosa Wilhelmena (Eisenman) W.; m. Patricia Ann Dively, Dec. 29, 1973 (div. Mar. 1979); m. Catherine Jean Brooks, Nov. 28, 1980; children: Michelle, Jeffrey, Joseph. Student, U. Idaho; BS in Hotel Adminstrn., U. Nev., Las Vegas. Asst. hotel mgr. Sands Hotel & Casino, Las Vegas, 1970-73, asst. gen. mgr., 1976-77, exec. v.p., 1978-81; hotel mgr. Dunes Hotel & Casino, Las Vegas, 1973-74, Frontier Hotel & Casino, Las Vegas, 1974-76; exec. v.p. MGM Grand Hotel, Reno, Nev., 1977-78; v.p., gen. mgr. Edgewater Hotel & Casino, Laughlin, Nev., 1981-83; pres. Claridge Hotel & Casino Corp., Atlantic City, N.J., 1983—, also bd. dirs.; now coo Trump's Castle. Campaign dir. Atlantic County chpt. United Way, Atlantic City, 1986-87; hon. trustee So. Jersey Regional Theater, Sommers Point, N.J., 1986-87; trustee So. Jersey Conf. Christians and Jews, Atlantic City, 1987—. Mem. Hotel Sales and Mgmt. Assn., MGM Employees Credit Union (founder, v.p. 1977-78), SYMMA Employees Credit Union (founder, v.p., sec. 1975-77), Elks. Republican. Methodist. Avocations: water skiing, tennis. Office: Claridge Hotel & Casino Boardwalk At Park Pl Atlantic City NJ 08401 also: Trump's Castle Assoc Huron Ave Brigantine Blvd Atlantic City NJ 08401*

WAGNER, RONALD DEAN, petroleum engineer; b. Findlay, Ohio, Apr. 6, 1958; s. Richard Dean and Betty Lou (Jones) W.; m. Vicki Marie James, Aug. 16, 1980; children: Ronald Dean Jr., Lara Marie. AS, Casper (Wyo.) Coll., 1978; BS in Petroleum Engring., U. Wyo., 1981. Registered profl. engr., Wyo. Petroleum engr. I Oxy USA, Inc., Gillette, Wyo., 1981-82, petroleum engr. II, 1982-85, staff petroleum engr., 1985-86; sr. petroleum engr. Oxy USA, Inc., Gillette and Midland, Tex., 1986-91; profl. petroleum engr. Amerada Hess Corp., Williston, N.D., 1991-93; v.p. prodn. Pathfinder Energy, Inc., Gillette, Wyo., 1993—. Mem. Soc. Petroleum Engrs. (profl. regulatory com. 1994—), Masons. Republican. Methodist. Achievements include research in reduced paraffin treating of 15,000 bopd from $1,000,000 per year to $250,000 by use of chemical treating versus hot oil treating. Office: Pathfinder Energy Inc PO Box 187 Gillette WY 92717

WAGNER, ROY, anthropology educator, researcher; b. Cleve., Oct. 2, 1938; s. Richard Robert and Florence Helen (Mueller) W.; m. Brenda Sue Geilhausen, June 14, 1968 (div. Dec. 1994); children: Erika Susan, Jonathan Richard. AB, Harvard U., 1961; AM, U. Chgo., 1962, PhD, 1966. Asst. prof. anthropology So. Ill. U., Carbondale, 1966-68; assoc. prof. Northwestern U., Evanston, Ill., 1969-74; prof. U. Va., Charlottesville, 1974—, chmn. dept., 1974-79; mem. cultural anthropology panel NSF, Washington, 1981-82. Author: Habu, 1972, The Invention of Culture, 1975, Lethal Speech, 1978, Symbols That Stand for Themselves, 1986. Social Sci. Research Council faculty research grantee, 1968; NSF postdoctoral research grantee, 1979. Fellow Am. Anthropol. Assn. Avocation: student hot-air balloon pilot. Home: 726 Cargil Ln Charlottesville VA 22902-4302 Office: U Va Dept Anthropology University Station Charlottesville VA 22906

WAGNER, SAMUEL, V, secondary school English language educator; b. West Chester, Pa., Dec. 28, 1965; s. Samuel and Mary Ann (Baker) W.; m. Allison Lee Lewis, May 25, 1991; 1 child, Samuel Jackson. BS in English Lit., Haverford Coll., 1988; MEd, U. New Orleans, 1995. Intern in English, asst. coach Westtown (Pa.) Sch., spring 1989; tchr. upper sch. English Metairie (La.) Pk. Country Day Sch., 1989—; asst. varsity soccer coach Metairie Pk. Country Day Sch., 1989-94; advisor to student senate Metairie Country Sch., 1990-95 chairperson/headmaster adv. com., 1994—, coll. counselor, 1995—; presenter ann. conf. Ind. Sch. Assn. of the South, New Orleans, 1992, 96. Mem. NASAA, NASSP, SACAD, NACAC, Nat. Coun. Tchrs. English, La. Coun. Tchrs. English, Alpha Theta Epsilon, Phi Delta Kappa, Kappa Delta Pi. Republican. Mem. Soc. of Friends. Home: 416 Severn Ave Metairie LA 70001-5145 Office: Metairie Pk Country Day Sch 300 Park Rd Metairie LA 70005-4142

WAGNER, SIGURD, electrical engineering educator, researcher; came to U.S., 1968; naturalized in 1990; s. Richard A. and Pauli (Steiner) W.; m. Erika Freiberger, 1968; children: Matthias, Wolfgang. PhD, U. Vienna, Austria, 1968. Univ. postdoctoral fellow Ohio State U., 1969-70; mem. tech. staff Bell Labs., Murray Hill, N.J., 1970-73, Holmdel, N.J., 1973-78; chief photovoltaic research br. Solar Energy Research Inst., Golden, Colo., 1978-80; prof. elec. engring. Princeton U., N.J., 1980—. Contbr. articles on electronic materials and devices to profl. jours.; assoc. editorial bd. Materials Letters, 1982—; patentee electronic materials and devices. Fellow Am. Phys. Soc.; mem. IEEE, Electrochem. Soc., Am. Chem. Soc., Materials Rsch. Soc.

WAGNER, SUE ELLEN, state official; b. Portland, Maine, Jan. 6, 1940; d. Raymond A. and Kathryn (Hooper) Pooler; m. Peter B. Wagner, 1964 (dec.); children: Kirk, Kristina. B.A. in Polit. Sci., U. Ariz., 1962; M.A. in History, Northwestern U., 1964. Asst. dean women Ohio State U., 1963-64; tchr. history and Am. govt. Catalina High Sch., Tucson, 1964-65; reporter Tucson Daily Citizen, 1965-68; mem. Nev. Assembly, 1975-83; mem. Nev. Senate from 3d dist.; elected lt. gov. of Nev., 1990-94. Author: Diary of a Candidate, On People and Things, 1974. Mem. Reno Mayor's Adv. Com., 1973-84; chmn. Blue Ribbon Task Force on Housing, 1974-75; mem. Washoe County Republican Central Com., 1974-84, Nev. State Rep. Central Com., 1975-84; mem. Nev. Legis. Commn., 1976-77; del. social service com. Council State Govts.; v.p. Am. Field Service, 1973, family liaison, 1974, mem.-at-large, 1975. Kappa Alpha Theta Nat. Grad. scholar, also Phelps-Dodge postgrad. fellow, 1962; named Outstanding Legislator, Nev. Young Republicans, 1976. Mem. AAUW (legis. chmn. 1974), Bus. and Profl. Women, Kappa Alpha Theta. Episcopalian. Home: 845 Tamarack Dr Reno NV 89509-3640*

WAGNER, TERESA LEE, training and organization consultant; b. Reading, Pa., Jan. 24, 1954; d. Fred LeRoy and Emily (Wiest) W. BA in Psychology magna cum laude, Alvernia Coll., 1977; postgrad., U. Nottingham, Eng., 1978; MS in Counseling and Human Rels., Villanova U., 1981; postgrad., Columbia U., 1985-86. Trainer Juvenile Justice Ctr. Nat. Tng. Inst., Phila., 1977-80; sr. indsl. rels. rep. missile and surface radar RCA, Moorestown, N.J., 1980-81; mgr. orgnl. devel. govt. systems divsn. RCA, Cherry Hill, N.J., 1981-84; mgr. orgn. planning and devel. RCA Global Comms., Inc., N.Y.C., 1984-88; pres. T. L. Wagner Assocs., Monterey, Calif., 1988—; bd. dirs. Intersea Rsch. Author: (tng. manuals) Recovering from Grief, 1990, Managing Job Loss, 1991, Grief Support Skills, 1993, (self-assessment instrument) Grief Support Skills Assessment Profile, 1990. Docent Point Lobos State Res., Carmel, Calif., 1990—; mem. beach and seal watch, Am. Cetacean Soc., Monterey, 1990—; bd. dirs. Friends of Monterey County Wildlife, 1993—, Horse Power Internat., Monterey, 1990—, Assisi Animal Inst., 1994—. Mem. ASTD, Orgn. Devel. Network, Assn. for Death Edn. and Counseling. Avocations: rose gardening, hiking, nature and wildlife observation and preservation. Home and Office: T L Wagner Assocs PO Box 522 Monterey CA 93942-0522

WAGNER, THOMAS JOSEPH, lawyer, insurance company executive; b. Jackson, Mich., June 29, 1939; s. O. Walter and Dorothy Ann (Hollinger) W.; m. Judith Louise Bogardus, Jan. 15, 1961; children—Ann Louise, Mark Robert, Rachel Miriam. B.A., Earlham Coll., 1957; J.D., U. Chgo., 1965. Bar: Ill. 1968, U.S. Supreme Ct. 1975. Asst. to gov. State of Ill., Springfield, 1966-67, legal counsel, adminstrv. asst. to treas., 1967-70; adminstrv. asst. to U.S. senator Adlai E. Stevenson, Washington, 1970-77; sr. v.p. govt. affairs div. Am. Ins. Assn., Washington, 1977-80; staff v.p. Ina Corp., 1980-82; v.p., chief counsel Property Casualty Group, CIGNA Corp., Phila., 1982-86, v.p., assoc. gen. counsel, 1986-88, sr. v.p., corp. sec., 1988-91, exec. v.p., gen. counsel, 1992—; trustee Eisenhower Exchange Fellowships, Inc.; bd. dirs. Inst. Law and Econs., U. Penn. Past chmn. Phila. Crime Commn. Africa-Asia Pub. Svc. fellow Syracuse U., 1965-66. Mem. ABA (bus. law com.), Am. Corp. Counsel Assn. Office: Cigna Corp PO Box 7716 1 Liberty Place 55th Fl Philadelphia PA 19192-1550

WAGNER, WARREN HERBERT, JR., botanist, educator; b. Washington, Aug. 29, 1920; s. Warren Herbert and Harriet Lavinia (Claflin) W.; m. Florence Signaigo, July 16, 1948; children: Warren Charles, Margaret Frances. A.B., U. Pa., 1942; Ph.D., U. Calif. at Berkeley, 1950; spl. student, Harvard, 1950-51. Instr. Harvard, summer 1951; vis. prof., 1991; faculty U. Mich. at Ann Arbor, 1951—, prof. botany, 1962-91, prof. emeritus, 1991—, curator pteridophytes, 1961—, dir. Bot. Gardens, 1966-71, chmn. dept. botany, 1975-77; spl. rsch. higher plants, origin and evolution ferns, groundplan/divergence methods accurate deduction phylogenetic relationships fossil and living plants, pteridophytes of Hawaii, 1962-65; prin. investigator project evolutionary characters ferns NSF, 1960—, monograph grapeferns, 1980—, pteridophytes of Hawaii, 1991—; chmn. Mich. Natural Areas Coun., 1958-59; mem. Smithsonian Coun., 1967-72, hon. mem., 1972—; cons. mem. Survival Svc. Commn., Internat. Union for Conservation of Nature and Natural Resources, 1971—; mem. nat. hist. bd. Nat. Mus., 1989—. Trustee Cranbrook Inst. Scis. Recipient Distinguished Faculty Achievement award U. Mich., 1975, Amoco Outstanding Tchr. award, 1980, Disting. Sr. Lectr. award U. Mich., 1986. Fellow AAAS (sec. sect. bot. scis., v.p. sect. 1968), Am. Acad. Arts and Scis.; mem. NAS, Am. Fern Soc. (sec. 1952-54, curator, libr. 1957-77, pres. 1970, 71, hon.), Am. Soc. Plant Taxonomists (coun. 1958-65, pres. 1966, Asa Gray award 1990), Soc. for Study Evolution (v.p. 1965-66, coun. 1967-69, pres. 1972), Am. Soc. Naturalists, Internat. Assn. Pteridologists (v.p. 1981-87, pres. 1987-93), Bot. Soc. Am. (pres. 1977, Merit award 1978), Mich. Bot. Club (pres. 1967-71), Torrey Bot. Club, New Eng. Bot. Club, Internat. Soc. Plant Morphologists, Internat. Assn. Plant Taxonomy, Sigma Xi, Phi Beta Kappa, Phi Kappa Tau. Home: 2111 Melrose Ave Ann Arbor MI 48104-4067

WAGNER, WILLIAM BRADLEY, lawyer; b. Memphis, Dec. 30, 1949; s. William G. and Wilmeth (Norman) W. BS in Econs., U. Fla., 1971; JD, U. Va., 1974. Bar: U.S. Ct. Appeals (5th and 11th cirs.) 1981, Tex. 1989, U.S. Dist. Ct. (ea., fed. and so. dists.) Tex. 1989, U.S. Tax Ct. Ptnr. Fulbright & Jaworski, Austin, Tex., 1974—. Contbg. author: (handbook) Natural Gas Regulation. Home: 1600 Westlake Dr Austin TX 78746-3740 Office: Fulbright & Jaworski 600 Congress Ave Ste 2400 Austin TX 78701-3248

WAGNER, WILLIAM BURDETTE, business educator; b. Oswego, N.Y., Apr. 27, 1941; s. Guy Wesley and Gladys M. (Redlinger) W.; divorced; 1 child, Geoffrey D. BA with highest honors, Mich. State U., 1963; MBA, Ohio State U., 1965, PhD, 1967. Research and teaching asst. Ohio State U., Columbus, 1966-68; prof. mktg. and logistics U. Mo., Columbia, 1969—; guest prof. mktg. U. Nanjing, Peoples Republic of China, 1985-87, Prince of Songla U., Hat Yai, Thailand, 1990, 92; expert witness petroleum industry, 1989—; adv. dir. Mo. State Bank, St. Louis, 1981-93. Contbr. articles to profl. jours. Univ. coordinator book procurement program for minorities McDonnell Douglas, St. Louis, 1972—; mem. St. Louis-Nanjing Sister City Com., 1985—; faculty ambassador U. Mo. Alumni Assn., 1987—; mem. speakers bur., high sch. liaison team U. Mo., 1987—; Mizzou Outreach prof., 1987—; bd. dirs. Cen. Mo. Sheltered Enterprises for Handicapped, Columbia, 1985-92. Recipient Civic Svc. award McDonnell Douglas, 1977, Educator of Yr. award Jr. C. of C., 1983, Prof. of Yr. award Coll. of Bus. and Pub. Adminstrn., 1987, Golden Key Honor Soc. Faculty Mem. of Yr. award, 1987, Faculty Mem. of Yr. award Beta Theta Pi, 1990, Prof. of Yr. award Kans. City Alumni Assn., 1990; named Mktg. Prof. of Yr., U. Mo., 1987-88, 89-91; rsch. grantee SBC, Econ. Devel. Adminstrn., U. Mo.; NDEA fellow Ohi State U., 1963-66, William T. Kemper Teaching fellow, 1991, Wakonse Teaching fellow, 1995; Fulbright scholar, Korea, 1992. Mem. Nat. Assn. Purchasing Mgmt., St. Louis Purchasing Mgmt. Assn., Coun. Logistics Mgmt., Nat. Fulbright Assn., Nat. Eagle Scout Assn., Am. Soc. Transp. and Logistics (pres. Mo. chpt. 1974-75, bd. govs. 1970-74, 75-82), Delta Sigma Pi, Beta Gamma Simga, Omicron Delta Epsilon, Rotary Internat. Methodist. Clubs: Mo. Athletic (St. Louis); Country of Mo. (Columbia). Avocations: stamp and coin collecting, bridge, golf, swimming, jogging. Home: 2401 Bluff Blvd Columbia MO 65201-8613 Office: Univ Mo 324 Middlebush Hall Columbia MO 65211

WAGNER, WILLIAM CHARLES, veterinarian; b. Elma, N.Y., Nov. 12, 1932; s. Frederick George and Doris Edna (Newton) W.; m. Donna Ann McNeill, Aug. 14, 1954 (div. May 1993); children: William Charles, Elizabeth Ann, Victoria Mary, Kathryn Farrington; m. Victoria Sandberg Eggleton, Oct. 21, 1995. D.V.M., Cornell U., 1956, Ph.D., 1968. Gen. practice vet. medicine Interlaken, N.Y., 1956-57; research veterinarian Cornell U., 1957-65, NIH postdoctoral fellow dept. animal sci., 1965-68; asst. prof. vet. medicine Vet. Med. Research Inst., Iowa State U., Ames, 1968-69; assoc. prof. Vet. Med. Research Inst., Iowa State U., 1969-74, prof., 1974-77; prof. physiology, head dept. vet. bioscis. U. Ill., Urbana, 1977-90, assoc. dean for rsch. and grad. studies Coll. Vet. Medicine, 1990-93; prin. vet. scientist USDA Coop. State Rsch. Edn. & Extension Svc., 1993—; gen. sec. Internat. Congress on Animal Reprodn., urbana, 1984, pres. standing com., 1988—; v.p. Conf. Rsch. Workers in Animal Disease, 1987-88, pres., 1988-89; prin. vet. scientist USDA-Coop. State Rsch. Svcs., Washington, 1990-91. Pres. Ames Community Theater, 1972-73, 76-77. Recipient Alexander von Humboldt U.S. Scientist award Humboldt Stiftung, Freising-Weihenstephan, W. Ger., 1973-74; Fulbright prof., W. Ger., 1984-85. Mem. Am. Coll. Theriogenologists (diplomate; Bartlett award and lectr. 1995), AVMA (mem. coun. on edn. 1987-93), Nat. Acad. of Practice Vet. Medicine, Physiol. Soc., Am. Soc. Animal Sci., Soc. Study Reprodn., Soc. Study Fertility, N.Y. Acad. Scis., Sigma Xi, Phi Kappa Phi, Phi Zeta, Gamma Sigma Delta, Alpha Zeta. Lutheran. Home: 20676 Cutwater Pl Sterling VA 20165-5830 Office: USDA CSREES Ag Box 2230 901 D St SW Washington DC 20250-2230 *I believe that it is important to be friendly to others, to try to understand the other person's position or feelings and deal with colleagues and subordinates in an impartial and fair manner. One should always remember that talents are a gift to be used wisely and to the fullest extent possible.*

WAGNER, WILLIAM GERARD, university dean, physicist, consultant, information scientist, investment manager; b. St. Cloud, Minn., Aug. 22, 1936; s. Gerard C. and Mary V. (Cloone) W.; m. Janet Agatha Rowe, Jan. 30, 1968 (div. 1978); children: Mary, Robert, David, Anne; m. Christiane LeGuen, Feb. 21, 1985 (div. 1989); m. Yvonne Naomi Moussette, Dec. 4, 1995; children: Mark, David, Paul, Jonathan. B.S., Calif. Inst. Tech., 1958, Ph.D. (NSF fellow, Howard Hughes fellow), 1962. Cons. Rand Corp., Santa Monica, Calif., 1960-65; sr. staff physicist Hughes Research Lab., Malibu, Calif., 1960-69; lectr. physics Calif. Inst. Tech., Pasadena, 1963-65; asst. prof. physics U. Calif. at Irvine, 1965-66; assoc. prof. physics and elec. engring. U. So. Calif., L.A., 1966-69, prof. depts. physics and elec. engring., 1969—, dean div. natural scis. and math. Coll. Letters, Arts and Scis., 1973-87, dean interdisciplinary studies and developmental activities, 1987-89, spl. asst. automated record services, 1975-81; founder program in neural, informational & behavioral scis., 1982—; chmn. bd. Malibu Securities Corp., L.A., 1971—; cons. Janus Mgmt. Corp., L.A., 1970-71, Croesus Capital Corp., L.A., 1971-74, Fin. Horizons Inc., Beverly Hills, Calif., 1974—; allied mem. Pacific Stock Exch., 1974-82; fin. and computer cons. Hollywood Reporter, 1979-81; mem. adv. coun. for emerging engring. techs. NSF, 1987—. Contbr. articles on physics to sci. publs. Richard Chase Tolman postdoctoral fellow, 1962-65. Mem. Am. Phys. Soc., Nat. Assn. Security Dealers, Sigma Xi. Home: 2828 Patricia Ave Los Angeles CA 90064-4425 Office: U So Calif Hedco Neurosci Bldg Los Angeles CA 90089

WAGNER-SERWIN, DOROTHY ELIZABETH, elementary education educator; b. Wauzeka, Wis., Nov. 19; d. Albert Magnus and Evelyn Cecelia (Degnan) Doll; m. Melvin Herman Wagner, June 30, 1941 (div. July 1981); m. Robert Carl Serwin, Dec. 26, 1987; children: Diana, Jeannie, Lori, Richard. BA, Dominican Coll., 1974. Tchr. grades 2-4 St. Joseph's Sch., Racine, Wis., 1960-68, 69; tchr. grade 1 St. Lucy's Sch., Racine, 1969; tchr. Learning Ctr. St. John Nepomuk Sch., Racine, 1969-71, tchr. grades 1 and 2, 1971-91, ret., 1991. Mem. AAUW (chmn. publicity com. 1975-94), Assn. Early Childhood Edn. (sec. 1970-92), Am. Legion Aux., KC, Shoop Park Golf Club (asst. chmn. 1994-95). Avocations: golf, tennis, skiing, skating, swimming.

WAGNESS, LORRAINE MELVA, gifted education educator; b. Bellingham, Wash., June 11, 1933; d. William Barkley and Laura Iola (Starr) Nattrass; m. Lee Wagness, Aug. 24, 1969; 1 child, Kathryn Lorraine. BA, Western Wash. State U., 1955; MA, City U., Seattle, Wash., 1993. Cert. tchr. grades kindergarten through 12, Wash. Tchr. Bellingham Sch. Dist., 1955-57, Eugene (Oreg.) Sch. Dist., 1957-59; tchr. talented and gifted, libr., arts specialist Seattle Pub. Schs., 1959—; chmn. Science Fair, 1995, 96, Art Show, 1995, 96. Photographer various publs., 1984-90; exhibited batik/paintings area shows (1st pl. Wash. Arts Contest 1990). Vol., demonstrator weaving and spinning Woodland Pk. Zoo Guild, Seattle, 1984—; pres. Sigma Kappa Mothers' Club, U. Wash., 1982-84. Sci. scholar Wash. State Garden Clubs, Seattle, 1960; partnership grantee Lafayette Sch. PTA, Seattle, 1994, 95. Mem. NEA (bldg. rep. 1980-90), Wash. Edn. Assn. (bldg. rep. 1980-90), Seattle Tchrs. Assn. (bldg. rep. 1980-90), AAUW (Outstanding Sr. award 1955), Internat. Reading Assn. (mem. coms. 1990-96), Associated Women Students (pres. 1955), Gen. Fedn. Women's Clubs (sec., treas. 1988-92, Club Woman of Yr. 1986, 90), Evergreen Garden Club (treas., sec. 1985—), Delta Kappa Gamma (v.p. Beta Beta chpt. 1991-96), Pi Lambda Theta (mem. coms. Seattle area chpt. 1988—). Presbyterian. Avocations: international travel, arts and crafts, gardening, reading, photography. Home: 17040 Sylvester Rd SW Seattle WA 98166

WAGNON, JOAN, former state legislator, association executive; b. Texarkana, Ark., Oct. 17, 1940; d. Jack and Louise (Lucas) D.; m. William O. Wagnon Jr., June 4, 1964; children: Jack, William O. III. BA in Biology, Hendrix Coll., Conway, Ark., 1962; MEd in Guidance and Counseling, U. Mo., 1968. Sr. research technician U. Ark. Med. Sch., Little Rock, 1962-64; sr. research asst. U. Ark. Med. Sch., Columbia, Mo., 1964-68; tchr. No. Hills Jr. High Sch., Topeka, 1968-69, J.S. Kendall Sch., Boston, 1970-71; counselor Neighborhood Youth Corps, Topeka, 1973-74; exec. dir. Topeka YWCA, 1977-93; mem. Kans. Legislature, 1983-94. Mem. Health Planning Rev. Commn., Topeka, 1984-85. Recipient Service to Edn. award, Topeka NEA, 1979, Outstanding Achievement award, Kans. Home Econs. Assn., 1985; named Woman of Yr. Mayors Council Status of Women, 1983; named one of Top Ten Legislators Kans. Mag., Wichita, 1986. Mem. Topeka Assn. Human Svc. Execs. (pres. 1981-83), Topekans for Ednl. Involvement (pres. 1979-82), Women's Polit. Caucus (state chair). Democrat. Methodist. Lodge: Rotary. Avocations: music, swimming, boating. Home: 1606 SW Boswell Ave Topeka KS 66604-2729 Office: Kans Families for Kids 2209 SW 29th St Topeka KS 66611-1908

WAGONER, DAVID EVERETT, lawyer; b. Pottstown, Pa., May 16, 1928; s. Claude Brower and Mary Kathryn (Groff) W.; children: Paul R., Colin H., Elon D., Peter B.; m. Jean Morton Saunders; children: Dana F., Constance A., Jennifer L., Melissa J. B.A., Yale U., 1950; LL.B., U. Pa., 1953. Bar: D.C. 1953, Pa. 1953, Wash. 1953. Law clk. U.S. Ct. Appeals (3d cir.), Pa., 1955-56; law clk. U.S. Supreme Ct., Washington, 1956-57; ptnr. Perkins & Coie, Seattle, 1957—; panel me. of arbitration forum worldwide including Republic of China, British Columbia Internat. Comml. Arbitration Ctr., Hong Kong Internat. Arbitration Centre, Asian/Pacific Ctr. for Resolution of Internat. Bus. Disputes and the Ctr. for Internat. Dispute Resolution for Asian/Pacific Region. Mem. sch. com. Mcpl. League Seattle and King County, 1958—, chmn., 1962-65; mem. Seattle schs. citizens coms. on equal ednl. opportunity and adult vocat. edn., 1963-64; mem. Nat. Com. Support Pub. Schs.; mem. adv. com. on community colls., to 1965, legislature interim com. on edn., 1964-65; mem. community coll. adv. com. to state supt. pub. instrn., 1965; chmn. edn. com. Forward Thrust, 1968; mem. Univ. Congl. Ch. Council Seattle, 1968-70; bd. dirs. Met. YMCA Seattle, 1968; bd. dirs. Seattle Pub. Schs., 1965-73, v.p., 1966-67, 72-73, pres., 1968, 73; trustee Evergreen State Coll. Found., chmn. 1986-87, capitol campaign planning chmn.; trustee Pacific NW Ballet, v.p. 1986. Served to 1st lt. M.C., AUS, 1953-55. Fellow Am. Coll. Trial Lawyers (mem. ethics com., legal ethics com.), Chartered Inst. Arbitrators, Singapore Inst. Arbitrators; mem. ABA (mem. standing com. fed. jud. imprisonment, chmn. appellate advocacy com.), Wash. State Bar Assn., Seattle-King County Bar Assn., Brit. Acad. Experts, Swiss Arbitration Assn., Comml. Bar Assn. London, Nat. Sch. Bds. Assn. (bd. dirs., chmn. coun. Big City bds. edn. 1971-72), English-Speaking Union (v.p. Seattle chpt. 1961-62), Chi Phi. Office: Perkins Coie 1201 3rd Ave Fl 40 Seattle WA 98101-3000

WAGONER, DAVID RUSSELL, author, educator; b. Massillon, Ohio, June 5, 1926; s. Walter Siffert and Ruth (Banyard) W.; m. Patricia Lee Parrott, July 8, 1961 (div. June 1982); m. Robin Heather Seyfried, July 24, 1982; children: Alexandra Dawn, Adrienne Campbell. B.A. in English, Pa. State U., 1947; M.A. in English, Ind. U., 1949. Instr. English DePauw U., 1949-50; instr. Pa. State U., 1950-53; asst. prof. U. Wash., 1954-57, assoc. prof., 1958-66, prof., 1966—; Elliston lectr. U. Cin., 1968; editor Poetry NW, 1966—; poetry editor Princeton U. Press, 1977-81, Mo. Press, 1983—. Author: (poetry books) Dry Sun, Dry Wind, 1953, A Place to Stand, 1958, The Nesting Ground, 1963, Staying Alive, 1966, New and Selected Poems, 1969, Working Against Time, 1970, Riverbed, 1972, Sleeping in the Woods, 1974, Collected Poems, 1976, Who Shall Be the Sun?, 1978, In Broken Country, 1979, Landfall, 1981, First Light, 1983, Through the Forest, 1987, Walt Whitman Bathing, 1996, (novels) The Man in the Middle, 1954, Money, Money, Money, 1955, Rock, 1958, The Escape Artist (also film 1982), 1965, Baby, Come on Inside, 1968, Where is My Wandering Boy Tonight?, 1970, The Road to Many a Wonder, 1974, Tracker, 1975, Whole Hog, 1976, The Hanging Garden, 1980; editor: Straw for the Fire: From the Notebooks of Theodore Roethke, 1943-63, 1972. Recipient Morton Dauwen Zabel prize Poetry mag., 1967, Blumenthal-Leviton-Blonder prize, 1974, 2 Fels prizes Coordinating Coun. Lit. Mags., 1975, Tietjens prize, 1977, English-Speaking Union prize, 1980, Sherwood Anderson award, 1980, Ruth Lilly Poetry prize, 1991, Levinson prize, 1994; Guggenheim fellow, 1956, Ford fellow, 1964, Nat. Inst. Arts and Letters grantee, 1967, Nat. Endowment for Arts grantee, 1969. Mem. Acad. Am. Poets (chancellor 1978—), Soc. Am. Magicians, Nat. Assn. Blackfeet Indians (asso.). Home: 5416 154th Pl SW Edmonds WA 98026-4348 Office: U Wash 4045 Brooklyn Ave NE Seattle WA 98105-6210

WAGONER, GERALDINE VANDER POL, music educator; b. Kankakee, Ill., Sept. 16, 1931; d. Ralph and Josie (Mieras) VanderPol; BA, Central U. of Iowa, 1954; MA, Montclair State Coll., 1968; postgrad. Juilliard Sch. Music, 1955, 56, 66, 67, NYU, Royal Conservatory, Toronto, 1971, Mozarteum, Salzburg, Austria, 1972; children: Joel Timothy, Stephanie Anne. Music coach, piano pedagog, cons. Bd. Edn., Edison, N.J., Englewood and Ridgewood, N.J., 1954-74; music specialist, Ridgewood, 1975-95; cons. NYU spl. project; cons. Project Impact. Trustee, Hudson Symphony Orch., 1965-71; mem. Met. Mus. of Art. Teaching fellow NYU, 1990-91; adj. prof. music William Patterson Coll., Wayne, N.J. Mem. Profl. Music Tchrs. Guild (cert. for highest goals and achievements 1966), Nat. Music Tchrs. Assn., N.J. Music Tchrs. Assn., Am. Orff Schulwerk Assn., NEA, Music Educators Assn., Bergen County Music Educators Assn., Choristers Guild, Theater Devel. Found., Met. Opera Guild, Netherland-American Found., Vis. Nurses of N.Y.C., Collegiate Chorale. Clubs: Knickerbocher Rep., Netherland, Overseas Yacht Club, Les Amis du Vin. Composer creative tonal and rhythm curriculum for children and assessing beginning instrumental music instructional strategies.

WAGONER, JENNINGS LEE, JR., history educator; b. Winston-Salem, N.C., July 26, 1938; s. Jennings Lee and Carolyn Nelme (Phifer) W.; m. Shirley Canady, Aug. 12, 1962; children: David Carroll, Brian Jennings. BA, Wake Forest U., 1960; MATeaching, Duke U., 1961; PhD, Ohio State U., 1968. Tchr. High Point Pub. Schs., N.C., 1960-62; instr. Wake Forest U., 1962-65; teaching assoc. Ohio State U., 1965-68; from asst. prof. to prof. history of edn. U. Va., Charlottesville, 1968—, dir. Ctr. for Study Higher Edn., 1975-85, chmn. leadership and policy studies, 1985-87, disting. prof. Curry Sch. Edn. U. Va., 1987, William C. Parrish Jr. Endowed prof., 1994—; vis. research scholar Harvard U., 1972, U. Calif., Berkeley, 1984; vis. prof. Monash U., Melbourne, Australia, 1992. Author: Thomas Jefferson and the Education of a New Nation, 1976; co-author: American Education: A History, 1996; contbr. articles to profl. jours.; co-editor: Changing Politics of Education, 1978; editorial bd. History of Edn. Quar., Ednl. Studies jour. Sesquicentennial fellow U. Va., 1972, 84, 90. Mem. History of Edn. Soc. (pres. 1983-85, bd. dirs. 1979-81), Am. Ednl. Research Assn. (v.p. div. F 1981-83), Orgn. Am. Historians, Am. Ednl. Studies Assn. (bd. dirs.), Assn. Study Higher Edn., Raven Soc., Sierra Club, Outward Bound, Kappa Delta Pi, Phi Delta Kappa, Omicron Delta Kappa (faculty advisor), Golden Key Nat. Honor Soc. Avocations: hiking, fishing, canoeing. Home: 468 Dry Bridge Rd Charlottesville VA 22903-7456 Office: U Va 405 Emmet St Charlottesville VA 22903-2495

WAGONER, PORTER, country music singer, composer; b. nr. West Plains, Mo., Aug. 12, 1927; s. Charles and Bertha W.; children: Richard, Denise, Debra. Former clerk, butcher. Singer, composer, radio and TV personality, 1950—, rec. artist, RCA Record Co., MCA/DOT Records, 1986—, radio and TV appearances include radio, KWPM, West Plains, Mo., 1950, KWTO, Springfield, Mo., 1951, Jubilee, U.S.A, ABC-TV, 1955, radio, WSM Grand Ole Opry, Nashville, Tenn., 1957—, Porter Wagoner TV Show; Records include A Satisfied Mind, Heartwarming Songs, Porter Wagoner Today, Best of Porter Wagoner, Porter & Dolly, Two of a Kind; composer songs including (with Gary Walker) Trade Mark, 1953, (with Michael Pearson) Bottom of the Fifth, 1982. Recipient (with Dolly Parton) Vocal Group of Yr. award, Vocal Duo of Yr. award Country Music Assn., 1970, 71. Address: PO BOx 290785 Nashville TN 37229

WAGONER, RALPH HOWARD, academic administrator, educator; b. Pitts., May 30, 1938; s. Richard Henry and Charlotte (Stevenson) W.; m. Wilma Jo Staup, Dec. 21, 1961; children: Amanda Jane, Joseph Ryan. AB in Biology, Gettysburg Coll., 1960; MS in Ednl. Adminstrn., Westminster Coll., 1963; PhD, Kent State U., 1967; postgrad., MIT, 1973, Dartmouth Coll., 1979. Prin., tchr., coach Williamsfield (Ohio) Elem. and Jr. High Sch., 1960-62; dir. elem. edn. Pymatuning Valley (Ohio) Local Schs., 1962-64, asst. supt. instrn., 1964-65; acad. counselor, asst. to dean coll. edn. Kent (Ohio) State U., 1965-66, instr. edn., 1966-67; asst. prof. Drake U., Des Moines, Iowa, 1967-70, assoc. prof., 1970-71, chmn. dept. elem. edn., 1968-70, chmn. dept. tchr. edn., 1970-71, acad. adminstrn. intern Am. Council Edn., Office of Pres., 1971-72, asst. to pres., 1972-77, dir. devel., 1975-77; v.p. pub. affairs and devel., prof. Western Ill. U., Macomb, 1977-87, pres., 1987-93; pres. Augustana Coll., Sioux Falls, S.D., 1993—; adj. prof. San Francisco Theol. Sem., 1971; mem. senate Drake U., 1968-77; sponsor interhall council Western Ill. U., 197893, mem. BOG/UPI task force on incentives for faculty excellence, co-chmn., faculty mentor, 1985-93; cons. in field. Co-author: (with L. Wayne Bryan) Societal Crises and Educational Response: A Book of

Readings, 1969, (with Robert L. Evans) The Emerging Teacher, 1970, (with William R. Abell) The Instructional Module Package System, 1971, Writing Behavioral Objectives or How Do I Know When He Knows, 1971; contbr. articles to profl. jours. Chmn. Mid-Ill. Computer Consortium, 1980, 85, Western Ill. Corridor of Opportunity, 1987-93; mem. Pres.' Regional Adv. Coun., 1977-87; mem. investments com. McDonough County YMCA; mem. exec. com. Macomb Area Indsl. Corp.; trustee Robert Morris Coll., 1983-88, Chgo. and Carthage, Ill., 1983-88; bd. dirs. Ill. Coun. Econ. Edn., 1987-93, McDonough County United Way Dr., 1980-82; bd. trustees The Cornerstone Found. LSS of Ill., 1990-96; mem. Sioux Falls Tomorrow Task Force, 1993-94; bd. dirs. S.D. Symphony, 1993—, Edn. Telecomms. State of S.D., 1993—, Sioux Falls Devel. Found., 1993—, Children's Inn, 1993—, Sioux Valley Physicians Alliance, 1995—, LECNA, 1996—; life trustee Lutheran Social Svcs., 1996—. Recipient Man of Yr. award Andover Rotary Club, 1964, Quax Honor award, 1969-70, Disting. Alumni award Gettysburg (Pa.) Coll., 1991; named McDonough County Citizen of Yr., Elks, 1982. Fellow Am. Coun. Edn. (cons. fund raising 1984-87); mem. Am. Assn. State Colls. and Univs. (com. econ. devel. 1988, com. on athletics 1987), Ednl. Computing Network (chmn. policy bd. 1985-87), Assn. Midcontinent Univs. (coun. dels. 1987-93), Gateway Conf. (coun. dels. 1987-93), Coun. for Advancement and Support of Edn. (discussion leader, speaker, 1975, 77, 80, 84, 86, 91, 92, 93, 94, Citation award 1981, 83, Grand award 1982, Bronze award 1985, Silver award 1986), Macomb C. of C. (exec. com., bd. dirs.), Ill. Chamber Econ. Devel. Policy Task Force, Blue Key (hon.), Omicron Delta Kappa, Phi Eta Sigma (hon.), Phi Mu Alpha. Lutheran. Lodge: Rotary. Home: 2817 S Grange Ave Sioux Falls SD 57105-4616 Office: Augustana Coll 29th and Summit Sioux Falls SD 57197

WAGONER, ROBERT HALL, engineering educator, researcher; b. Columbus, Ohio, Jan. 8, 1952; s. Robert H. and Leorra (Schmucker) W.; m. Robyn K. O'Donnell, Aug. 30, 1980; children: Erin A. Wagoner Hansgen, Amy J. BS, Ohio State U., 1974, MS, 1975, PhD, 1976. NSF postdoctoral rschr. U. Oxford, Eng., 1976-77; staff rsch. scientist GM Rsch. Labs., Warren, Mich., 1977-83; assoc. prof. material sci. engring. Ohio State U., Columbus, 1983-86, prof., 1986—, chmn. dept., 1992—; maitre de recherche Ecole des Mines de Paris, Sophia Antipolis, France, 1990-91; dir. Ohio State U. Rsch. Found., 1991-94, Ctr. Advt. Materials Mfg. Auto Components, 1994—; trustee Orton Found., 1992—. Co-author: Fundamentals of Metal Forming, 1996; editor: Novel Techniques in Metal Deformation, 1983, Forming Limit Diagrams, 1989. Recipient Raymond Meml. award AIME, 1981, 83; Disting. Scholar award Ohio State U., 1990, Harrison award for tchg. excellence, 1988; Presdl. Young Investigator award NSF, 1984; NSF postdoctoral fellow Oxford (Eng.) U., 1976. Fellow ASM Internat.; mem. Nat. Acad. Engring., Minerals, Metals and Materials Soc. (founding mem., dir. 1991-95, Mathewson Gold medal 1988, Hardy Gold medal 1981, v.p. 1996—). Developed SHEET-3 and SHEET-S, sheet forming simulation programs for indsl. use; introduced first quantitative test for plane-strain work hardening; invented formability test and friction test. Office: Ohio State U Dept Material Sci Engring 2041 College Rd Columbus OH 43210-1179

WAGONER, ROBERT VERNON, astrophysicist, educator; b. Teaneck, N.J., Aug. 6, 1938; s. Robert Vernon and Marie Theresa (Clifford) W.; m. Lynne Ray Moses, Sept. 2, 1963 (div. Feb. 1986); children: Alexa Frances, Shannon Stephanie; m. Stephanie Nightingale, June 27, 1987. B.M.E., Cornell U., 1961; M.S., Stanford U., 1962, Ph.D., 1965. Research fellow in physics Calif. Inst. Tech., 1965-68, Sherman Fairchild Disting. scholar, 1976; asst. prof. astronomy Cornell U., 1968-71, asso. prof., 1971-73; asso. prof. physics Stanford U., 1973-77, prof., 1977—; George Ellery Hale disting. vis. prof. U. Chgo., 1978; mem. Com. on Space Astronomy and Astrophysics, 1979-82, theory study panel Space Sci. Bd., 1980-82, physics survey com. NRC, 1983-84; grant selection com. NSERC (Can.), 1990-93. Contbr. articles on theoretical astrophysics and gravitation to profl. publs., mags.; co-author Cosmic Horizons. Sloan Found. rsch. fellow, 1969-71; Guggenheim Meml. fellow, 1979; grantee NSF, 1973-90, NASA, 1982—. Fellow Am. Phys. Soc.; mem. Am. Astron. Soc., Internat. Astron. Union, Tau Beta Pi, Phi Kappa Phi. Patentee. Office: Stanford U Dept Physics Stanford CA 94305-4060

WAGONER, WILLIAM HAMPTON, university chancellor; b. Washington, N.C., May 12, 1927; s. William Gotha and Lossie Bell (Barrington) W.; June 3, 1952; children: William Michael, David Robin, Mark Hampton. BS cum laude, Wake Forest U., 1949, LLD, 1981; MA, East Carolina U., 1953; PhD in Ednl. Adminstrn. and Polit. Sci, U. N.C., Chapel Hill, 1958. Tchr. Washington (N.C.) High Sch., 1950-53; asst. prin. Elizabeth City (N.C.) High Sch., 1953-55; prin. Hattie Harney Elementary Sch., Elizabeth City, 1956; instr. U. N.C., 1957; asso. exec. sec. N.C. State Sch. Bds. Assn., 1958-59; supt. Elizabeth City Schs., 1959-61, Wilmington-New Hanover County Schs., 1961-68; pres. Wilmington Coll., 1968; chancellor U. N.C., Wilmington, 1969-90, chancellor emeritus, 1990—; Speaker before various profl. groups at confs., convs. Pres. N.C. Div. Supts., 1967-68; chmn. bd. govs. N.C. Advancement Sch., 1967; mem. Gov.'s Tech. Coordinating Com. for Marine Sci. Council; pres. N.C. Assn. Colls. and Univs., 1981. Trustee Cape Fear Meml. Hosp. With USNR, 1945-46. Recipient East Carolina Alumni award as Univ.'s Outstanding Alumni Award Winner, 1968. Mem. N.E.A. (life). Democrat. Episcopalian. Home: 2202 Marlwood Dr Wilmington NC 28403-6030 Office: U NC Wilmington 601 S College Rd Wilmington NC 28403-3201

WAGONSELLER, JAMES MYRL, real estate executive; b. Zanesville, Ohio, July 29, 1920; s. Myrl H. and Florence L. (Pfeiffer) W.; m. Mary J. McCauley, Nov. 16, 1943; children—Thomas James, John Myrl, Anne Elizabeth Wagonseller Bauswein. Grad. high sch. Draftsman apprentice machinist Hermann Mfg. Co., Lancaster, Ohio, 1945-47; advt. sales Lancaster (Ohio) Eagle-Gazette, 1947-50, classified mgr., 1950-52, dir. advt. sales, 1952-54; real estate salesman Larkin Durdin (Realtor), Lancaster, 1954-60; ptnr. Lancaster Realty Co., 1960-65, Simons & Wagonseller (Realtors), Lancaster, 1965-77; prin. James M. Wagonseller, Appraiser; Pres. Lancaster Bd. Realtors, 1965; mem. bd. Zoning Appeals Lancaster, 1972-74. Pres. Community Service Council, 1944, United Appeal, 1968; Mem. central, exec. coms. Fairfield County Democratic Com., 1960-70, mem. exec. com., 1976—. Served with USAF, 1941-45. Decorated D.F.C., Air medal with 3 clusters. Mem. Lancaster C. of C. (pres. 1970), Nat. Assn. Real Estate Brokers, Ohio Assn. Real Estate Brokers, Am. Assn. Cert. Appraisers, Am. Legion (nat. comdr. 1974-75). Democrat. Roman Catholic. Lodges: Kiwanis (pres.), Elk (Ann. Citizen award 1975). Home and Office: 1973 Coldspring Dr Lancaster OH 43130-1458

WAGSTAFF, ROBERT HALL, lawyer; b. Kansas City, Mo., Nov. 5, 1941; s. Robert Wilson and Katherine Motter (Hall) W. A.B., Dartmouth Coll., 1963; J.D., U. Kans., 1966. Bar: Kans., Alaska, U.S. Ct. Appeals (9th cir.), U.S. Supreme Ct. Asst. atty. gen. State of Kans., 1966-67; asst. dist. atty. Fairbanks (Alaska), 1967-69; ptnr. Boyko & Walton, Anchorage, 1969-70; sr. ptnr. Wagstaff et. al., Anchorage, 1970—. Pres. U.S. Aerobatic Found., Oshkosh, Wis., 1986—. Mem. Alaska Bar Assn. (bd. govs. 1985-88, pres. 1987-88), Lawyer-Pilots Bar Assn. (regional v.p.), ACLU (nat. bd. dirs. 1972-78), Nat. Transp. Safety Bd. Assn. Office: 425 G St Ste 610 Anchorage AK 99501-2137

WAHBA, GRACE, statistician, educator; b. Washington; d. Harry and Anne Goldsmith; 1 child, Jeffrey A. BA, Cornell U.; MA, U. Md.; PhD, Stanford U. Prof. statistics U. Wis., Madison, 1967-87, Bascom prof., 1987—; fellow Weizmann Inst., Israel, St. Cross Coll., Oxford (Eng.) U.; Lady Davis fellow Technion, Israel, Australian Nat. U., Canberra; Clare Booth Luce vis. prof. Yale U.; cons. to industry and govt. Author: Spline Models for Observational Data, 1990; assoc. editor; SIAM Jour. Sci. Computing, 1985—; adv. bd. Jour. Computational Graphical Stats., 1990—. Recipient Emanuel and Carol Parzen prize for Statis. Innovation, 1994, NSF Creativity award, 1994. Fellow AAAS, Inst. Math. Statis. (Neyman lectr. nat. meeting 1994), Am. Statis. Assn., Internat. Statis. Inst.; mem. Soc. Indsl. and Applied Math. (plenary speaker nat. meeting 1994), Bernoulli Soc., Am. Math. Soc., Am. Meteorol. Soc. Achievements include development of new methods of curve and surface smoothing, of new statistical methods in biology and meteorology, of new methods for multivariate response function estimation, of analysis of variance in function spaces, of approximate solution of ill posed explicit and implicit inverse problems with noisy data, and of the assimilation of data from heterogenous sources. Office: U Wis Dept Stats 1210 W Dayton St Madison WI 53706-1613

WAHL, ARTHUR CHARLES, retired chemistry educator; b. Des Moines, Sept. 8, 1917; s. Arthur C. and Mabel (Mussetter) W.; m. Mary Elizabeth McCauley, Dec. 1, 1943; 1 child, Nancy Wahl Miegel. BS, Iowa State Coll., 1939; PhD, U. Calif., Berkeley, 1942. Group leader Los Alamos (N.Mex.) Nat. Lab., 1943-46; assoc. prof. chemistry Washington U., St. Louis, 1946-53, Farr prof. of radiochemistry, 1953-83, prof. emeritus, 1983—; cons. Los Alamos Nat. Lab., 1950—. Author, editor: Radioactivity Applied to Chemistry, 1951; contbr. articles to profl. jours. NSF fellow, 1967; recipient Sr. Vis. Scientist Humboldt award Humboldt Found., 1977. Mem. Am. Chem. Soc. Office: Los Alamos Nat Lab MS # 514 Los Alamos NM 87545

WAHL, FLOYD MICHAEL, geologist; b. Hebron, Ind., July 7, 1931; s. Floyd Milford and Ann Pearl (DeCook) W.; m. Dorothy W. Daniel, July 4, 1953; children: Timothy, David, Jeffrey, Kathryn. A.B., DePauw U., 1953; M.S., U. Ill., 1957, Ph.D., 1958. Cert. profl. geologist. Prof. geology U. Fla., Gainesville, 1969-82, assoc. dean Grad. Sch., 1974-80, acting dean, 1980-81; exec. dir. Geol Soc Am., Boulder, Colo., 1982-94; ret., 1994. Contbr. articles to profl. jours. Served to cpl. U.S. Army, 1953-55. Recipient Outstanding Tchr. award U. Ill., 1967. Fellow Geol. Soc. Am.; mem. Mineral Soc. Am., Am. Inst. Profl. Geologists (chpt. pres.), Sigma Xi.

WAHL, HOWARD WAYNE, retired construction company executive, engineer; b. Hitterdal, Minn., Jan. 17, 1935; s. Milo Ormenzo and Esther Marie (Sorenson) W.; m. Carroll May Pollock, Aug. 16, 1958; children: Jeffrey David, Michael Edward, Nancy Elizabeth. BCE, U. Washington, 1957. Registered engr., Calif., N.Y., Mich., Ohio, Md. Structural engr. Bechtel Corp., San Francisco, 1956-69; project engr. Bechtel Corp., Gaithersburg, Md., 1969-72; chief civil engr. Bechter Power Corp., San Francisco, 1972-74; mgr. engring. and constrn. Bechter Power Corp., 1975-78; v.p., mgr. Ann Arbor Power Div.-Bechtel, Mich., 1978-84; dir. Bechtel Group, Inc., 1982-92; pres. Bechtel Ea. Power Corp., Gaithersburg, 1984-88; mng. dir. Bechtel Power Corp., San Francisco, 1988-89; pres. European region Bechtel Corp., Paris, 1989-91; ret., 1991; dir. Ann Arbor Bank-1st Am., 1978-84. Contbr. articles to profl. jours. Campaign chmn. Washtenaw County United Way, Ann Arbor, 1982; chmn. Turkish-U.S. Bus. Coun., Washington, 1988-90; mem. exec. coun. Boy Scouts Am., Ann Arbor, 1978-84; mem. devel. coun. U Wash. Coll. Engring.; trustee Desert Rsch. Inst. U. Nev., Reno. Mem. ASCE, Am. Concrete Inst., U. Mich. Pres. Club and Victors Club, U. Washington Pres. Club, Olympic Club (San Francisco). Republican. Presbyterian. Avocations: woodworking, gardening, cooking, boating, hiking. Home: PO Box 7601 Incline Village NV 89452-7601

WAHL, STEVEN ALAN, podiatric physician and surgeon; b. Jersey City, Mar. 27, 1953; s. Harold Irving and Libby Rose (Stiskin) W.; m. Jordanna Kyle Lenter, Feb. 2, 1990. BS in Biology, Upsala Coll., 1975, Ill. Coll. Podiatric Medicine, 1979; D Podiatric Medicine, Ill. Coll. Podiatric Medicine, 1979. Diplomate Nat. Bd. Podiatry Examiners; lic. podiatrist, N.J., Pa. With Ill. Coll. Podiatric Medicine Clinic, Chgo., 1976-78, 78; podiatrist Mt. Sinai Hosp., Englewood Health Ctr., Henrotin Hosp., Chgo., 1978—; asst. chief resident dept. surgery div. podiatry Coney Island Hosp., Bklyn., 1979-80; pvt. practice, Paterson, N.J., 1980-81, Englewood, N.J., 1980-81, Millburn, N.J., 1981—; clin. instr., attending podiatry staff, asst. chief dept. St. Michael's Med. Ctr., Newark, 1987—; mem. adj. clin. faculty Pa. Coll. Podiatric Medicine, Phila.; mem. exec. com. div. podiatry West Essex Gen. Hosp., Livingston, N.J., 1983-88; attending podiatry staff Roseland (N.J.) Surg. Ctr.; former attending Irvington Gen., South Bergen, No. Community, Bergen Pines, Barnet hosps.; former editorial cons. Current Podiatry; former cons. Wood Crest Ctr. Nursing Home, Camp Nejeda. Podiatric screener Health Fair, Millburn and Maplewood Twps., 1981—. Fellow Am. Soc. Podiatric Medicine, Am. Acad. Podiatric Microsurgery (charter), Am. Assn. Hosp. Podiatrists; mem. APHA, Am. Podiatric Med. Assn., Am. Coll. Podopediatrics (assoc.), Am. Acad. Podiatric Sports Medicine (assoc.), N.J. Podiatric Med. Soc. (ho. of dels. ea. div. 1982-85, pres. 1984-85), N.J. Pub. Health Assn., Am. Physicians Fellowship for Medicine in Israel, N.Y. Acad. Scis., Ill. Coll. Podiatric Medicine Alumni Assn., Upsala Coll. Alumni Assn., Nat. Honor Soc., Beta Beta Beta. Avocations: ballroom dancing, racquetball. Office: 120 Millburn Ave Ste 205 Millburn NJ 07041-1935

WAHLBERG, PHILIP LAWRENCE, former bishop, legislative liaison; b. Houston, Jan. 18, 1924; s. Philip Lawrence and Ella Alieda (Swenson) W.; m. Rachel Conrad, June 1, 1946; children: David, Christopher, Pauli, Sharon. AA, Tex. Luth. Coll., 1942, DD (hon.), 1963; BA, Lenoir Rhyne Coll., Hickory, N.C., 1944; MDiv, Luth. Theol. Sem., Columbia, S.C., 1946. Ordained to ministry United Luth. Ch. in Am., 1946. Pastor St. Luke Luth. Ch., Thunderbolt, Ga., 1946-50, Redeemer Luth. Ch., Wilmington Island, Ga., 1946-50, St. Mark Luth. Ch., Corpus Christi, Tex., 1950-59; pres. Tex.-La. Synod, United Luth. Ch. Am., Austin, Tex., 1959-62; bishop Tex.-La. Synod, Luth. Ch. Am., Austin, 1963-87; acting dir. devel. Lutheran Outdoor and Retreat Ministries Southwest, 1987-88; legis. liaison Tex. Impact, Austin, 1989-91; interim coord. Regional Ctr. for Mission Evang. Luth. Ch. in Am., Dallas, 1991-92; acting dir. devel. Luth. Sem. Program of Southwest, 1992—; mem. com. on appeals, also chmn. Evang. Luth. Ch. in Am., 1988-95, hearing officer, 1995—; also mem. exec. coun. Luth. Ch. in Am., N.Y.C., 1980-87, chmn. com. on legal matters, 1984-87; mem. mgmt. com. Div. for Mission in N.Am., N.Y.C., 1972-80, chmn., 1972-76; bd. dirs. Bd. Am. Missions, N.Y.C., 1963-72, chmn., 1968-72; bd. dirs. Luth. Sch. Theology, Chgo., 1967-87. Author articles in religious jours., sermons; author theol. cassette, 1973. Named Disting. churchman Tex. Luth. Coll., 1978; Disting. Alumnus, Lenoir Rhyne Coll., 1962; named Man of Year, Thunderbolt, Ga. C. of C., 1950. Mem. Interfaith Impact. Democrat. Avocations: winemaking, golf, choral singing. Office: 5804 Cary Dr Austin TX 78757-3108

WAHLEN, EDWIN ALFRED, lawyer; b. Gary, Ind., Mar. 12, 1919; s. Alfred and Ethel (Pearson) W.; m. Alice Elizabeth Condit, Apr. 24, 1943 (div. 1983); children: Edwin Alfred, Virginia Elizabeth, Martha Anne; m. Elizabeth L. Corey, Nov. 23, 1984. Student, U. Ala., 1936-38; A.B., U. Chgo., 1942, J.D., 1948. Bar: Ill. 1948. Practiced in Chgo., 1948—; mem. firm Haight, Goldstein & Haight, 1948-55; ptnr. Goldstein & Wahlen, 1956-59, Arvey, Hodes, Costello & Burman (and predecessor), 1959-91, Wildman, Harrold, Allen & Dixon, 1992—. Author: Soldiers and Sailors Wills: A Proposal For Federal Legislation, 1948. Served to 2d lt. AUS, 1942-46. Decorated Silver Star medal, Bronze Star medal. Mem. ABA, Ill. Bar Assn., Chgo. Bar Assn., Order of Coif, Phi Beta Kappa, Phi Alpha Delta. Home: 3750 N Lake Shore Dr Chicago IL 60613-4238 Office: 225 E Wacker Dr Chicago IL 60601-5103

WAHLEN, EDWIN ALFRED, JR., venture capitalist; b. Gary, Ind., Nov. 17, 1947; s. Edwin Alfred and Alice Elizabeth (Condit) W.; m. Catherine Frances Willard, Jan. 7, 1978. BS in Indsl. Mgmt., Ga. Inst. Tech., 1970; MBA, U. N.C., Chapel Hill, 1972. CFA. Assoc. investment banking Interstate Securities Corp., Charlotte, N.C., 1972-73; loan officer First Nat. Bank Chgo., Atlanta, 1973-77; sr. v.p. investment banking Dean Witter Reynolds, Inc., Atlanta, 1977-85; mng. ptnr. Cravey, Green & Wahlen Inc., Atlanta, 1985—; mng. dir. CGW S.W. Ptnrs., Atlanta, 1991—; bd. dirs. CGW Holdings, Inc., Atlanta, Intelimedia Corp., Atlanta, Ashley Aluminum, Inc., Tampa, Fla., Summit Cons., Inc., Lakeland, Fla., Sovitec Holdings, Inc.; chmn. bd. dirs. Rehrig Internat., Inc., Richmond, Va., Visionworks Holdings, Inc., Clearwater, Fla., Medaes Inc., Norcross, Ga. Chmn. bd. dirs. Met. Atlanta chpt. Am. Diabetes Assn., 1990, sec. bd. dirs. Ga. affiliate. Fellow Soc. Internat. Bus. Fellows; mem. Atlanta Venture Forum, U. N.C. Bus. Sch. Club Atlanta (pres. 1982-83), Ravinia Club, Burge Plantation Hunting Club, Lake Toxaway Country Club, Smoke Rise Field Club.

WAHLERT, ROBERT HENRY, food company executive; b. Dubuque, Iowa, Jan. 19, 1939; s. Robert Charles and Celeste Joan (Canepa) W.; m. Donna Jane Allendorf, June 3, 1961; children: Robert C., Amy, Kathleen, Marni, Mark. B.Sc., U. Iowa, 1963. Sales trainee Dubuque Packing Co., 1961-63, advt. mgr., 1963-65, gen. sales mgr., 1965-69, v.p. sales, 1969-73, exec. v.p., 1973-77, chmn. bd., chief exec. officer, 1977-82; founder, pres., chief exec. officer FDL Foods, Inc., Dubuque, 1982; dir., founder Key City Bank, Dubuque; dir. Rigid-Pak Corp., San Juan, P.R., Edelcar Corp., San Juan, Hawkeye Bank of Dubuque, Hawkeye Banks (parent co.); v.p. Dubuque Symphony Orch., 1967-74. Bd. dirs., pres., treas. Wahlert Found.; v.p. Dubuque Symphony Orch., 1967-74. Republican. Roman Catholic. Club: Dubuque Golf and Country (past pres.). Home: 600 Sunset Rdg Dubuque IA 52003-7763 Office: FDL Foods Inc 701 E 16th St Dubuque IA 52001-4948*

WAHLKE, JOHN CHARLES, political science educator; b. Cin., Oct. 29, 1917; s. Albert B.C. and Clara J. (Ernst) W.; m. Virginia Joan Higgins, Dec. 1, 1943; children: Janet Parmely, Dale. A.B., Harvard U., 1939, M.A., 1947, Ph.D., 1952. Instr., asst. prof. polit. sci. Amherst (Mass.) Coll., 1949-53; assoc. prof. polit. sci. Vanderbilt U., Nashville, Tenn., 1953-63; prof. polit. sci. SUNY, Buffalo, 1963-66, U. Iowa, 1966-71, SUNY, Stony Brook, 1971-72, U. Iowa, Iowa City, 1972-79; prof. polit. sci. U. Ariz., Tucson, 1979-87, prof. emeritus, 1987—. Author: (with others) The Legislative System, 1962, Government and Politics, 1966, The Politics of Representation, 1978; editor: Causes of the American Revolution, 1950, Loyalty in a Democratic State, 1952; co-editor: Legislative Behavior, 1959, The American Political System, 1967, Comparative Legislative Behavior, 1973. Served to capt., F.A. AUS, 1942-46. Decorated Air medal with 2 oak leaf clusters. Mem. AAAS, Am. Polit. Sci. Assn. (past pres.), Internat. Polit. Sci. Assn., So. Polit. Sci. Assn., Midwest Polit. Sci. Assn. (past pres.), Western Polit. Sci. Assn., Southwestern Polit. Sci. Assn., Assn. Politics and the Life Scis. Home: 5462 N Entrada Catorce Tucson AZ 85718-4851 Office: U Ariz Dept Polit Sci Tucson AZ 85721

WAHOSKE, MICHAEL JAMES, lawyer; b. Ripon, Wis., June 4, 1953; m. Marcia Wilson; children: Jennifer, John. BA with highest honors, U. Notre Dame, 1975, JD summa cum laude, 1978. Bar: Minn. 1978, U.S. Dist. Ct. Minn. 1979, U.S. Ct. Appeals (7th cir.) 1979, U.S. Ct. Appeals (8th and 9th cirs.) 1980, U.S. Ct. Appeals (10th cir.) 1982, U.S. Supreme Ct. 1982, U.S. Ct. Appeals (6th cir.) 1988, U.S. Ct. Appeals (fed. cir.) 1989, U.S. Ct. Appeals (D.C. cir.) 1992, U.S. Ct. Appeals (4th cir.) 1994. Law clk. to judge Luther M. Swygert U.S. Ct. Appeals (7th cir.), Chgo., 1978-79; law clk. to chief justice Warren E. Burger U.S. Supreme Ct., Washington, 1979-80; assoc. Dorsey & Whitney, Mpls., 1980-85, ptnr., 1986—; adj. prof. law U. Minn., Mpls., 1981-83. Exec. editor U. Notre Dame Law Rev., 1977-78; co-editor: Freedom & Education: Pierce v. Society of Sisters Reconsidered, 1978. Recipient Vol. Recognition award Nat. Assn. Attys. Gen., 1993, Supreme Ct. Reception hons. State and Local Legal Ctr., 1991, 92, 93, 95. Mem. ABA, Fed. Bar Assn., Minn. Bar Assn., Hennepin County Bar Assn., Phi Beta Kappa. Office: Dorsey & Whitney LLP 220 S 6th St Minneapolis MN 55402-1498

WAILAND, GEORGE, lawyer; b. Munich, Fed. Republic Germany, Mar. 14, 1947; came to U.S., 1951; s. Max and Bella (Grylak) W.; m. Adele M. Rosen, Aug. 20, 1972; children: J. Zachary, William J. BS, NYU, 1969, JD, 1972. Bar: N.Y. 1973, U.S. Supreme Ct. 1976, U.S. Dist. Ct. (so., ea. dists.) N.Y. 1973, U.S. Dist. Ct. (no. dist.) N.Y. 1981, U.S. Claims Ct. 1979, U.S. Tax Ct., 1979, U.S. Ct. Appeals (2d cir.) 1973, U.S. Ct. Appeals (fed. cir.) 1982, U.S. Ct. Appeals (4th cir. and 9th cir.) 1986, U.S. Ct. Appeals (7th cir.) 1987. Assoc. Cahill Gordon & Reindel, N.Y.C., 1972-80, ptnr., 1980—. John Norton Pomeroy scholar NYU, 1970. Mem. ABA, Fed. Bar Council. Home: 1050 Park Ave New York NY 10028-1031 Office: Cahill Gordon & Reindel 80 Pine St New York NY 10005-1702

WAIN, CHRISTOPHER HENRY FAIRFAX MORESBY, actuary, insurance and investment consultant; b. Toronto, Ont., Can., Nov. 21, 1918; came to U.S., 1923; s. Andrew Martin and Eve Margaret (Fairbain) W.; m. Jeane Crawford Thomas, June 26, 1948; children: Christopher H. Jr., Margot Crawford. BA, UCLA, 1940. Actuarial student Occidental Life of Calif., L.A., 1946-48; various positions including v.p., actuary Prudential Ins. Co. Am., Newark and L.A., 1948-83; ins. and investment cons. L.A., 1984—; mem. various coms. Am. Coun. Life Ins., Washington, 1965-83. Capt. U.S. Army, 1941-45. Regents scholar UCLA, 1938-39. Fellow Soc. Actuaries; mem. Am. Acad. Actuaries. Home: 3338 Red Rose Dr Encino CA 91436-4212

WAINBERG, ALAN, footwear company executive; b. Zelechow, Poland, June 25, 1937; came to U.S., 1949; s. Jaime M. and Pearl (Boruchowicz) W.; m. Karen Sue Schneider, July 31, 1966; children: David, Laura, Daniel. BS in Indsl. Engring., U. Miami, 1964; MS in Ops. Rsch., NYU, 1965. Indsl. engr. U.S. Naval Propellant Plant, Indian Head, Md., 1964; sr. cons., mgr. Arthur Andersen & Co., N.Y.C., 1965-70; sr. cons. Alexander Grant & Co., Miami, 1970-71; sr. v.p., sec., treas., dir. Suave Shoe Corp., Miami, 1971-75, 78-84; group v.p. G.H. Bass & Co., Falmouth, Maine, 1984-86, pres., 1986-88; pres. Alan Wainberg & Assocs., Cumberland Center, Maine, 1988; v.p. Internat. New Balance Athletic Shoes Inc., Boston, 1991-95; v.p. sourcing strategic devel. Stride Rite Corp., Lexington, Mass., 1995—; owner, cons., pres. Mgmt. Cons. Services, Miami, 1975-77; dir., pres. Damaron Investment Services, Miami, 1975-78; vis. com. Coll. Engring. U. Miami. Mem. Footwear Industries Am. (mem. tech. steering com., chmn. new tech. com., 1981, bd. dirs. 1986—), U. Miami Coll. Engring. Alumni Assn. (bd. dirs., officer). Office: Stride Rite Corp 191 Spring St Lexington MA 02173-9191

WAINERDI, RICHARD ELLIOTT, medical center executive; b. N.Y.C., Nov. 27, 1931; s. Harold Roule and Margaret (Greenhut) W.; m. Angela Lampone, June 2, 1956; children: Thomas Joseph, James Cooper. B.S. in Petroleum Engring, Okla. U., 1952; M.S., Pa. State U., 1955, Ph.D., 1958. Registered profl. engr., Tex. Research asst., fellow petroleum engring. Pa. State U., 1953-55; mem. faculty Tex. A. and M. U., College Station, 1957-77; prof. chem. engring. Tex. A. and M. U., 1961-77, assoc. v.p. acad. affairs, 1974-77, also founder, head activation analysis lab., 1957-77; sr. v.p. 3D/Internat., Houston, 1977-82; coord. nuclear activities Dresser Industries Inc., Dallas, 1956-57; head Nuclear Sci. Ctr. Tex. Engring. Expt. Sta., 1957-59; pres. Gulf Research & Devel. Co. div. Gulf Oil Corp., Houston, 1982-84; pres., chief exec. officer Tex. Med. Ctr., Houston, 1984—. Author: Modern Methods of Geochemical Analysis, 1971; regional editor: Internat. Jour. Radioanalytical Chemistry; contbg. editor: Producers Monthly, 1957-69; assoc. editor: Radiochemical and Radioanalystical Letters; mem. editorial adv. bd. Talanta jour., 1969; contbr. to profl. jours. Served with USAF, 1952-53. Recipient 1st pl. presentation award Am. Inst. Chem. Engrs. and Chem. Inst. Can., 1961, faculty disting. rsch. award Tex. A. and M. U., 1962, George Hevesy medal, 1977, others. Mem. Am. Nuclear Soc. (chmn. isotopes and radiation divsn. 1964), Internat. Union Pure and Aplied Chemistry (chmn. com. on analytical radiochemistry), Am. Chem.. Soc., River Oaks Country Club, Ramada Club, Sigma Xi, Tau Beta Pi, Phi Kappa Phi, Sigma Tau, Pi Epsilon Tau, Phi Eta Sigma. Office: Tex Med Ctr 406 Jesse H Jones Libr Bldg Houston TX 77030

WAINESS, MARCIA WATSON, legal management consultant; b. Bklyn., Dec. 17, 1949; d. Stanley and Seena (Klein) Watson; m. Steven Richard Wainess, Aug. 7, 1975. Student, UCLA, 1967-71, 80-81, Grad. Sch. Mgmt. Exec. Program, 1987-88, grad. Grad. Sch. Mgmt. Exec. Program, 1988. Office mgr., paralegal Lewis, Marenstein & Kadar, L.A., 1977-81; office mgr. Rosenfeld, Meyer & Susman, Beverly Hills, Calif., 1981-83; adminstr. Rudin, Richman & Appel, Beverly Hills, 1983; dir. adminstrn. Kadison, Pfaelzer, L.A., 1983-87; exec. dir. Richards, Watson and Gershon, L.A., 1987-93; legal mgmt. cons. Wainess & Co., L.A., 1993—; faculty mem. UCLA Legal Mgmt. & Adminstrn. Program, 1983, U. So. Calif. Paralegal Program, L.A., 1985; mem. adv. bd. atty. asst. tng. program, UCLA, 1984-88. Mem. ABA (chair Displaywrite Users Group 1986, legal tech. adv. coun. litig. support working group 1986-87), L.A. County Bar Assn., San Fernando Valley Bar Assn., Profl. Liability Underwriting Soc., Assn. Legal Adminstrs. (bd. dirs. 1990-92, asst. regional v.p. Calif. 1987-88, regional v.p. 1988-89, pres. Beverly Hills chpt. 1985-86, membership chair 1984-85, chair new adminstrn. sect. 1982-84, mktg. mgmt. sect. com. 1989-90, internat. conf. com.), Beverly Hills Bar Assn., Internat. Platform Assn., Cons. Roundtable of So. Calif. Avocations: historic preservation, antiques, interior design. Office: 415 N Camden Dr Beverly Hills CA 90210

WAINTROOB, ANDREA RUTH, lawyer; b. Chgo., Dec. 23, 1952; d. David Samuel and Lees (Carson) W. AB, Brown U., 1975; JD, U. Chgo., 1978. Bar: Ill. 1978, U.S. Dist. Ct. (no. dist.) Ill. 1978, U.S. Dist. Ct. (cen. dist.) Ill. 1996, U.S. Ct. Appeals (7th cir.) 1982, U.S. Supreme Ct. 1989.

Assoc. Vedder, Price, Kaufman and Kammholz, Chgo., 1978-84; ptnr. Vedder, Price, Kaufman, Chgo., 1984-94, Franczek, Sullivan, Mann, Crement, Hein, Relias, P.C., Chgo., 1994—; lectr. indsl. relations Grad. Sch. Bus. U. Chgo. Mem. Chgo. Bar Assn., Nat. Coun. Sch. Attys. Home: 1345 E 54th St Chicago IL 60615-5318 Office: Franczek Sullivan et al 300 S Wacker Dr Ste 3400 Chicago IL 60606-6703

WAINWRIGHT, CARROLL LIVINGSTON, JR., lawyer; b. N.Y.C., Dec. 28, 1925; s. Carroll Livingston and Edith Katherine (Gould) W.; m. Nina Walker, July 2, 1948; children: Delos Walker, Mark Livingston. A.B., Yale U., 1949; LL.B., Harvard U., 1952. Bar: N.Y. 1953. With Milbank, Tweed, Hadley & McCloy (and predecessor), N.Y.C., 1952-58, 60-62, ptnr., 1963—; asst. counsel Gov. N.Y., 1959-60; mem. State Commn. Jud. Conduct, 1974-83; dir. U.S. Trust Corp.; trustee U.S. Trust Co. N.Y.; adj. prof. law Washington and Lee U. Sch. Law, 1991—; mem. governing bd. N.Y. Community Trust, 1991—. Trustee Am. Mus. Natural History, Edward John Noble Found., Boys' Club N.Y., 1966—, pres., 1986-94; vice-chmn. Cooper Union Advancement Sci. and Art, 1988-95; also trustee; trustee Ch. Pension Fund and Affiliates, 1974-91, treas. 1974-78; mem. univ. coun. Yale U., 1978-81; mem. vestry Trinity Ch., N.Y.C., 1983-90. Served with USMCR, 1943-46. Mem. ABA, N.Y. State Bar Assn., Assn. Bar City N.Y. (treas. 1970-73, v.p. 1975-76), Union Club, Down Town Assn. (pres. 1985-92), Maidstone Club (pres. 1970-73). Home: 825 5th Ave New York NY 10021-7268 Office: Milbank Tweed Hadley & McCloy 1 Chase Manhattan Plz New York NY 10005-1401

WAINWRIGHT, DAVID STANLEY, intellectual property professional; b. New Haven, May 23, 1955; s. Stanley Dunstan and Lillian (Karelitz) W.;m. Catherine Demetra Kefalas, Aug. 11, 1984; children: Maxwell Stanley Hector, Eric George Alexander. BSc with 1st class honors in Physics, Dalhousie U., Halifax, N.S., 1976; MSc in Physics, U. B.C., Vancouver, 1979. Registered patent agt., U.S., Can. Model plant supr., scientist, technician Moli Energy Ltd., Maple Ridge, B.C., Can., 1978-84, project leader cell devel., 1984-88, cell devel. mgr., 1988-90; cell devel. mgr. Moli Energy (1990) Ltd., Maple Ridge, 1990-92, mgr. intellectual property, 1992—. Contbr. articles to profl. jours. Mem. Patent and Trademark Inst. Can. Home: 2585 W 1st Ave, Vancouver, BC Canada V6K 1G8 Office: Moli Energy Ltd Maple Ridge, 20000 Stewart Crescent, Maple Ridge, BC Canada V2X 9E7

WAINWRIGHT, PAUL EDWARD BLECH, construction company executive; b. Annapolis, Md., Jan. 28, 1917; s. Richard and Alice Sorrel (Blech) W.; m. Helen Mae Rogers, July 10, 1941; children—Richard, Paul Edward Blech, John. B.S. in Civil Engring, Va. Mil. Inst., 1938. Cost engr. Turner Constrn. Co., N.Y.C., 1938-40; cost engr., asst. supt. Turner Constrn. Co., 1945-46; cost. engr. for contractors Pacific Naval Air Bases, Honolulu, 1940-42; with Dillingham Corp., Honolulu, 1946-82; asst. v.p., then v.p. Dillingham Corp., 1961-69, group v.p. constrn., 1969-82; cons. constrn. Honolulu, 1982—. Bd. dirs. Hawaii Visitors Bur., 1967, Goodwill Industries Hawaii, 1965-70; pres. Citizens Adminstrn. of Justice Found., 1968, Hawaii Epilepsy Soc., 1975. Served with AUS, 1942-45. Decorated Legion of Merit, Bronze Star, Air medal. Mem. Am. Soc. Mil. Engrs., Beavers, Gen. Contractors Assn. Hawaii (pres. 1966), Hawaii C. of C. (dir. 1964-65). Republican. Episcopalian. Clubs: Waikiki Yacht, Outrigger Canoe. Home: 4301 Providence Point Pl SE Issaquah WA 98029

WAISANEN, CHRISTINE M., lawyer, writer; b. Hancock, Mich., May 27, 1949; d. Frederick B. and Helen M. (Hill) W.; m. Robert John Katzenstein, Apr. 21, 1979; children: Jeffrey Hunt, Erick Hill. BA with honors, U. Mich., 1971; JD, U. Denver, 1975. Bar: Colo. 1975, D.C. 1978. Labor rels. atty. U.S. C. of C., Washington, 1976-79; govt. rels. specialist ICI Americas, Inc., Wilmington, Del., 1979-87; dir. cultural affairs City of Wilmington, 1987; founder, chief writer Hill, Katzenstein & Waisanen, 1988—. Chmn. Delaware State Coastal Zone Indsl. Control Bd., 1993—. Mem. Fed. Bar Assn., Jr. League of Wilmington (v.p. 1985-86), Women's Rep. Club of Wilmington (bd. dirs. 1988-93). Republican. Presbyterian. Home: 1609 Mt Salem Ln Wilmington DE 19806-1134

WAIT, CAROL GRACE COX, organization administrator; b. L.A., Dec. 20, 1942; d. Earl George Atkinson Sr. and Virginia Rose (Clanton) Boggs; m. David L. Edwards (div. 1974); children: Nicole Rose Smith, Alexandra Edwards; m. Gary G. Cox, Jan. 25, 1975 (div. 1982); m. Robert Atwood Wait, July 4, 1991. AA in Pre Law, Cerritos Coll., 1966; AB in History, Whittier Coll., 1969. Probation counselor Los Angeles County Probation Dept., Downey, Calif., 1967-69; corp. sec., mgr. Dennis and Dennis Personnel, Santa Ana, Calif., 1969-71; owner, pres. Cox Edwards & Assocs., Santa Ana, 1971-73; adminstrv. services officer County of Santa Cruz (Calif.), 1973-74; cons. State of Calif., Sacramento, 1974-75; project dir. Nat. Assn. Counties, Washington, 1975-77; legis. dir. U.S. Senate Com. on the Budget, Washington, 1977-81; pres. Com. for a Responsible Budget, Washington, 1981—, Carol Cox & Assocs., Washington, 1984—; bd. dirs. Cigna Corp.; cons. to bus. and other orgns. on the fed. budget, the budget process and other econ. issues; writer and speaker on the budget and budget process. Am. participant USIS/Brazilian Senate Symposium on Budget Process, Brazilia, Brazil, 1985—, Ampart speaker on 1990 budget agreement France, Ger., 1990. Named one of 150 Who Make a Difference Nat. Jour., 1986; recipient Nat. Disting. Svc. award Am. Assn. Budget and Program Analysis. Mem. Washington Women's Forum, Internat. Women's Forum (pres.). Republican. Episcopalian. Avocations: party bridge, wing shooting, tennis. Office: Com Responsible Fed Budget 220 1/2 E St NE Washington DC 20002-4923

WAIT, JAMES RICHARD, electrical engineering educator, scientist; b. Ottawa, Ont., Can., Jan. 23, 1924; came to U.S., 1955, naturalized, 1960; s. George Enoch and Doris Lillian (Browne) W.; m. Gertrude Laura Harriet, June 16, 1951; children: Laura, George. BASc, U. Toronto, Ont., 1948, MASc, 1949, PhD, 1951. Research engr. Newmont Exploration, Ltd., Jerome, Ariz., 1949-52; sect. leader Def. Research Telecommunications Establishment, Ottawa, 1952-55; scientist U.S. Dept. Commerce Labs., Boulder, Colo., 1955-80; adj. prof. elec. engring. U. Colo., Boulder, 1961-80; prof. elec. engring., geosci. U. Ariz., Tucson, 1980-88, Regents prof., 1988-90, emeritus Regents prof., 1990—; prin. Geo-Em Cons., Tucson, 1990—; fellow Coop. Inst. Rsch. Environ. Scis., 1968-80; sr. scientist Office of Dir. Environ. Rsch. Labs., Boulder, 1967-70, 72-80; vis. rsch. fellow lab. electromagnetic theory U. Denmark, Copenhagen, 1961; vis. prof. Harvard, 1966-67, Catholic U., Rio de Janeiro, 1971; vis. prof. elec. engring. U. B.C., Vancouver, Can., 1987; mem.-at-large U.S. nat. com. Internat. Sci. Radio Union, 1963-65, 69-72, del. gen. assemblies, Boulder, 1957, London, 1690, Tokyo, 1963, Ottawa, 1969, Warsaw, Poland, 1972, Lima, Peru, 1975, Helsinki, Finland, 1978; sec. U.S. nat. com., 1976-78; Lansdowne lectr. U. Victoria, B.C., Can., 1992; adj. prof. in mining and geol. engring. U. Ariz., Tucson, 1995—. Founder Jour. Radio Sci, 1959, editor, 1959-68; assoc. editor: Pure and Applied Geophysics, 1964-75, Geoexploration, Ludea, Sweden, 1983-91; co-editor internat. series monographs on electromagnetic waves Pergamon Press, 1961-73, Instn. Elec. Engrs, London, 1974—. Served with Canadian Army, 1942-45. Recipient Gold medal Dept. Commerce, 1958; Samuel Wesley Stratton award Nat. Bur. Standards, 1962; Arthur S. Flemming award Washington C. of C., 1964; Outstanding Publ. award Office Telecommunications, Washington, 1972; Rsch. and Achievement award Nat. Oceanic and Atmospheric Adminstrn., 1973; Van der Pol gold medal, 1978; Evans fellow Otago U., New Zealand, 1990. Fellow IEEE (adminstrv. com. on antennas and propagation 1966-73, Harry Diamond award 1964, Centennial medal 1984, Disting. Achievement award geosci. and remote sensing 1985, Disting. Achievement award antennas and propagation soc. 1990, Heinrich Hertz medal 1992), AAAS, Sci. Rsch. Soc. Am. (Boulder Scientist award 1960); mem. Soc. Exploration Geophysicists (hon.), Internat. Union Radio Sci. (mem. editl. adv. bd. Radio Sci. Bull. 1995—). Home and Office: 2210 E Waverly St Tucson AZ 85719-3848

WAIT, SAMUEL CHARLES, JR., academic administrator, educator; b. Albany, N.Y., Jan. 26, 1932; s. Samuel C. and Isabel M. (Cassedy) W.; m. Carol D. Petrie, June 6, 1957; children: Robert J., Alison R. BS in Chemistry, Rensselaer Polytechnic Inst., 1953, MS in Physical Chemistry, 1955, PhD in Physical Chemistry, 1956. Postdoc. teaching fellow U. Minn., 1958-59; visiting asst. prof. Carnegie Inst. Tech., 1959-60; rsch. sci. Nat. Bur. Standards, 1960-61; from asst. prof. to prof. of chemistry Rensselaer Poly. Inst., Troy, N.Y., 1961—, from asst. dean of sci. to assoc. dean of sci., 1974—, acting dean of sci., 1978-80, 88-89; dir. Cooperative Coll. Sci. Improvement Program, Troy, 1972-73, Rsch. Participation for High Sch. Tchrs., Troy, 1962-67; asst. dir., prof. M of Sci. in Natural Scis. Program, Troy, 1962-74. Author: Scattering of Laser Radiation, 1971; contbr. articles to profl. jours. Pres. dist. 2 Niskayuna (N.Y.) Fire Co., 1970-72; mem. Niskayuna Bd. Fire Commrs., 1978-83; v.p., trustee Dudley Obs., 1990-91, pres., 1991—; mem. math., sci. and tech. adv. com. Schenectady County C.C., 1976—, chmn., 1977-78; vice chmn. Schenectady County Fire Adv. Bd., 1978-79; mem. Schenectady County Hazardous Materials Team, 1991—. Recipient Disting Faculty award Rensselaer Alumni Assn., 1988, Alumni Key award, 1994, Rensselaer Alumni Admission award of excellence, 1993; named fellow Rsch. Corp., 1954-55, Eastman Kodak Co., 1955-56; Fulbright scholar, 1956-58. Mem. Am. Chem. Soc., Optical Soc. Am., Coblentz Soc., Rensselaer Premed. Soc., Sigma Xi, Alpha Epsilon Delta, Phi Theta Kappa. Office: Rensselaer Poly Inst 1C 05 Sci Ctr Troy NY 12180-3590

WAITE, CHARLES MORRISON, food company executive; b. Chgo., Oct. 1, 1932; s. Norman and Lavinia M. (Fyke) W.; m. Barbara Chowning Wham, Aug. 21, 1954; children: Susan R., Charles M., John B., David T. B.A., Yale, 1954; M.B.A., Harvard, 1958. Mgr. planning and analysis Standard Fruit & Steamship Co., New Orleans, 1958-62; v.p., exec. v.p. Standard Fruit & Steamship Co., 1969-72, dir., 1972-76; div. mgr. Standard Fruit Co., La Ceiba, Honduras, 1962-69; dir. Standard Fruit Tropical Charities, Inc., 1970-76; sr. v.p. Castle & Cooke, Inc., Honolulu, 1972-76; exec. v.p. Castle & Cooke Foods, San Francisco, 1974-76; pres. United Fruit Co., Boston, 1976-77; sr. v.p. United Brands Co., Boston, 1976-77; pres. Genoa Packing Co., Boston, 1977-78, Catelli Foods, Inc., 1979-90; pres. Howard Foods Inc., Danvers, Mass., 1990—, also bd. dirs.; bd. dirs. Rock of Ages Corp., Barre, Vt., Swenson Granite Co., Concord, N.H. Served to 1st lt. USAF, 1955-57. Mem. Zeta Psi. Republican. Episcopalian. Club: Harvard (Boston). Home: 520 Cherry Valley Rd Gilford NH 03246-7841 Office: Howard Foods Inc 5 Ray St Danvers MA 01923-3531

WAITE, DANIEL ELMER, retired oral surgeon; b. Grand Rapids, Mich., Feb. 19, 1926; s. Charles Austin and Phoebe Isabel (Smith) W.; m. Alice Darlene Carlile, June 20, 1948; children—Christine Ann, Thomas Charles, Peter Daniel, Julie Marilyn, Stuart David. AA, Graceland Coll., 1948; DDS, State U. Ia., 1953, MS Grad. Coll., 1955. Diplomate: Am. Bd. Oral Surgery. Resident oral surgery State U. Ia. Hosps., 1953-55; instr. oral surgery State U. Ia. Coll. Dentistry, 1955-56, asst. prof., 1956-57, asso. prof., acting head dept. oral surgery, 1957-59, prof. head dept., 1959-63; mem. staff Mayo Clinic, Mayo Grad. Sch. Medicine, Rochester, Minn., 1963-68; prof., also chmn. div. oral surgery U. Minn., 1968-84; chmn. dept. oral and maxillofacial surgery, asst. dean for hosp. affairs Baylor Coll. Dentistry, Dallas, 1984-90, prof. emeritus, 1990—, asst. dean emeritus, 1990—; clin. prof. U. Mo. Dental Sch., Kans. City, 1993—; vis. prof. U. Adelaide, Australia, 1980, U. Jinan, Guangzhou, China, 1987, U. Costa Rica, 1988; mem. Health Mission Team, Bolivia, 1991, Honduras, 1992. Author: Textbook of Practical Oral Surgery, 1972, 3d edit., 1986; contbr. over 100 articles to sci. jours., author of 7 book chpts. Active People to People Found.; with Project HOPE, Peru, 1962, Sri Lanka, 1969, Egypt, 1975; trustee Graceland Coll., Lamoni, Iowa, 1960-78, Park Coll., Parkville, Mo., 1972-78, 90—, Outreach Internat., 1990—; bd. dirs. Hennepin County unit Am. Cancer Soc., 1970-73; evangelist Reorganized LDS Ch.; pres. med. and dental assn. health missions, Bolivia, 1990, Honduras, 1991, 92, 93. With USAAF, 1944-46; sr. dental surgeon USPHS Res. Recipient Novice award Internat. Assn. Dental Rsch., 1955, Disting. Alumni award Graceland Coll., 1989; named Man of Yr. U. Minn. Sch. Dentistry Century Club, 1980, Hon. Fellow Sch. Dentistry, U. Minn., 1990; Daniel E. Waite Lectureship established in his honor U. Minn., 1991—. Fellow Am. Coll. Dentists, Am. Soc. Oral Surgeons; mem. Christian Med. Soc., Midwestern Soc. Oral Surgeons, Ia. Soc. Oral Surgeons (sec. 1958-61, pres. 1962), Minn. Soc. Oral Surgeons (pres. 1974), Am. Dental Assn., Internat. Assn. Dental Research (sec. Ia. sect. 1957-62), Tex. Soc. of Oral & Maxillofacial Surgeons, Southwestern Soc. of Oral and Maxillofacial Surgeons, Kans. City Soc. of Oral and Maxillofacial Surgeons, Sigma Xi, Omicron Kappa Upsilon. Home: 319 NW Blue Beech Pt Lees Summit MO 64064-1813

WAITE, DENNIS VERNON, investor relations consultant; b. Chgo., Aug. 26, 1938; s. Vernon George and Marie G. Waite; m. Christine Rene Hibbs; 1 child, Kip Anthony. BA, U. Ill., 1968; MS in Journalism, Northwestern U., 1969. Fin. reporter, columnist Chgo. Sun-Times, Chgo., 1969-76; asst. prof. Northwestern U., Evanston, Ill., 1978-79; assoc. prof. Mich. State U., East Lansing, 1979-82; ptnr. Fin. Rels. Bd., Inc., Chgo., 1982-90, sr. ptnr., 1991—; reporter, producer econ. affairs Sta. WTTW-TV, Sta. WBBM-TV, Chgo., 1973-76. Mem. editorial adv. bd. alumni relations U. Ill., Chgo., 1980-84, 90-94. With USAF, 1956-60, PTO. Rutgers U. fellow, 1972. Mem. Medill Alumni Assn. (bd. dirs. 1989-92). Avocations: reading, tennis, fishing. Office: Financial Relations Bd John Hancock Ctr 875 N Michigan Ave Chicago IL 60611-1803

WAITE, ELLEN JANE, vice presidentof academic services; b. Oshkosh, Wis., Feb. 17, 1951; d. Earl Vincent and Margaret (Luft) W.; m. Thomas H. Dollar, Aug. 19, 1977 (div. July 1984); m. Kent Hendrickson, Mar. 26, 1994 (div. Dec. 1995). BA, U. Wis., Oshkosh, 1973; MLS, U. Wis., Milw., 1977. Head of cataloging Marquette U., Milw., 1977-82; head catalog librarian U. Ariz., Tucson, 1983-85; assoc. dir. libraries Loyola U., Chgo., 1985-86, acting dir. libraries, 1986-87, dir. libraries, 1987-94, v.p. acad. svcs., 1994—; cons. Loyola U., Chgo., 1984, Boston Coll., 1986, U. San Francisco, 1989; bd. trustees Online Computer Lib. Ctr., Dublin, Ohio, 1994—. Contbg. author: Research Libraries and Their Implementation of AACR2, 1985; author: (with others) Women in LC's Terms: A Thesaurus of Subject Headings Related to Women, 1988. Mem. ALA. Avocation: photography. Office: Loyola U 25 E Pearson St Chicago IL 60611-2001

WAITE, HELEN ELEANOR, funeral director; b. Richmond, Va., Aug. 7, 1947; d. Julia F. (Braxton) Candia; m. Malcolm L. Waite, July 24, 1982. AB, Va. State U., 1968, MA, 1977; degree in funeral svc., Northampton C.C., Bethlehem, Pa., 1994. Cert. tchr., Pa., N.J. Tchr. Westmoreland County Schs., Montross, Va.; tchr. English Rittenhouse Acad., Phila.; funeral dir. T.W. Waite Funeral Home, Phila. Mem. Nat. Coun. Tchrs. English, Pa. Coun. Tchrs. English, Nat. Funeral Dirs. Assn., Pa. Funeral Dirs. Assn. Home: 820 N 65th St Philadelphia PA 19151-3303

WAITE, NORMAN, JR., lawyer; b. Chgo., Mar. 16, 1936; s. Norman and Lavinia (Fyke) W.; m. Jaqueline A. Hurlbutt; children: Leslie Catherine, Lindsay H., Norman III. BA, Yale U., 1958; LLB, Harvard U., 1963. Bar: Ill. 1963. Assoc. Winston & Strawn, Chgo., 1963-69, ptnr., 1969-78, capital ptnr., 1978—, exec. com., 1978-95, vice chmn., 1989—. Bd. dirs. Met. Family Svcs., Jr. Achievement, Chgo., Steadman/Hawkins Sports Medicine Found. Lt. (j.g.) USN, 1958-60. Mem. ABA, Chgo. Bar Assn., Univ. Club Chgo., The Tavern Club Chgo., Indian Hill Club (Winnetka, Ill.), Econ. Club, Eagle Springs Club (Vail, Colo.). Republican. Home: 1710 N Burling St Chicago IL 60614-5102 Office: Winston & Strawn 35 W Wacker Dr Chicago IL 60601-1614

WAITE, PETER ARTHUR, literacy educator, educational consultant; b. San Mateo, Calif., Jan. 8, 1951; s. James Bishop and Beverly Jane (Petrich) W.; m. Lauren Chapman Singer, Sept. 10, 1977; children: Hillary, Christopher, Hannah. BA, U. Vt., 1973, MEd, 1976; EdD, Seattle U., 1986. Cert. tchr. Tchr. Winooski (Vt.) High Sch., 1972-73; program developer NEA, Washington, 1973-74; coord. Ctr. for Svc. Learning, Burlington, Vt., 1974-76; instr. Champlain Coll., Burlington, 1975-76; exec. dir. Winooski Youth Commn., 1976-79, Wash. Literacy, Inc., Seattle, 1979-82, Laubach Literacy Action, Syracuse, N.Y., 1982—; sr. policy advisor Bus. Coun. for Effective Literacy, N.Y.C., 1982—; bd. dirs. Literacy Network, Mpls., 1987—; mem. exec. com. Nat. Coalition for Literacy, Chgo., 1989—. Author: Handbook for Industry-Literacy, 1986. Del. Seattle Dem. Com., 198l; bd. dirs. Friends of VISTA, Washington, 1986—; founder Concerned Citizens Skaneateles (N.Y.), 1987—. Named Ky. col. State of Ky., 1985, hon. citizen City of Memphis, 1986, San Diego County, 1988; recipient state achievement award State of Okla., 1988. Mem. Assn. for Adult and Continuing Edn., Am. Literacy Assn., Community Edn. Assn., Ind. Sector. Democrat. Episcopalian. Avocations: running, skiing, sailing, mountain climbing, book collecting. Office: Laubach Literacy Internat 1320 Jamesville Ave Syracuse NY 13210

WAITE, RALPH, actor; b. White Plains, N.Y., June 22, 1929; s. Ralph H. and Esther (Mitchell) W.; m. Kerry Shear, 1972 (div. 1980); children: Kathleen, Suzanne, Liam; m. Linda East, 1982. B.A., Bucknell U.; B.D., Yale U. Social worker Westchester County, N.Y.; Presbyterian minister Garden City, N.Y.; publicity dir. and asst. religious books editor Harper & Row Pub. Co., N.Y.C.; founder Los Angeles Actors Theatre, 1975, artistic dir., from 1975. Stage appearances include Hogan's Goat, 1965, Watering Place, 1969, The Trial of Lee Harvey Oswald, 1967, Blues for Mr. Charlie, The Father, 1981, The Balcony, 1981, Buried Child, South Coast Repertory, Costa Mesa, Calif., 1986, All My Sons, Long Wharf Theatre, New Haven, Conn., 1986-87 season, Half Deserted Streets, off Broadway, 1988, Bunker Reveries, Roundabout Theatre, N.Y.C., 1987; films include A Lovely Way to Die, 1968, Five Easy Pieces, 1970, Lawman, 1971, The Grissom Gang, 1971, The Sporting Club, 1971, The Stone Killer, 1973, On the Nickel, 1980, The Bodyguard, 1992, Cliffhanger, 1993; regular TV series The Waltons, 1972-80, The Mississippi, 1983, also appeared in TV movies A Wedding on Waltons Mountain, 1982, Mother's Day on Waltons Mountain, 1982, A Day for Thanks on Waltons Mountain; on ltd. dramatic series Roots, 1977; TV films include The Secret Life of John Chapman, Red Alert, Ohms, Angel City, The Gentleman Bandit, A Good Sport. Office: Care Andy Freedman 20 Ironsides St Apt 18 Marina Del Rey CA 90292

WAITE, RIC, cinematographer; b. Sheboygan, Wis., July 10, 1933; s. Howard Pierce and Bertha Ann (Pippert) W.; m. Judy Lescher, Apr. 24, 1965; children: Richard R., Burgandy B. Student, U. Colo. Cinematographer: (films) Adventures in Babysitting, 1988, Cobra, 1988, Great Outdoors, 1989, Marked for Death, 1990, Price of Our Blood, 1990, 48 Hours, Uncommon Valor, Rep Dawn, Long Riders, The Border, Tex, Class, Volunteers, On Deadly Ground. 1st lt. USAF, 1951-56. Recipient Emmy award, 1976. Mem. Am. Soc. Cinematographers. Avocations: sailing, flying. Home: PO Box 1322 Friday Harbor WA 98250-1322 Office: 1216 Roulac Ln Friday Harbor WA 98250-9572 also: The Gersh Agency 232 N Canon Dr Beverly Hills CA 90210-5302

WAITE, ROBERT GEORGE LEESON, history educator; b. Cartwright, Manitoba, Can., Feb. 18, 1919; came to U.S., 1929, naturalized, 1943; s. George Lloyd and Alice (Carter) W.; m. Anne Barnett, Sept. 8, 1943; children: Geoffrey, Peter. AB, Macalester Coll., 1941; MA, U. Minn., 1946, Harvard U., 1947; PhD, Harvard U., 1949; postgrad., U. Munich, 1953-54. Teaching asst. Macalester Coll., 1941; Emerton fellow history Harvard U., Cambridge, Mass., 1947, teaching fellow, 1947-49; asst. prof. history Williams Coll., 1949-53, assoc. prof., 1953-58, prof., 1958-88, Brown prof., 1960-88, chmn. dept., 1967-72; dir. History Insts., 1968, 69; vis. prof. U. Minn., summer 1957, U. Tex., Austin, 1974; sr. assoc. mem. St. Antony's Coll. Oxford U., 1978, 82; sr. fellow Inst. Humanities, Williams Coll., 1989-91. Author: Vanguard of Nazism: The Free Corps Movement in Postwar Germany, 1918-23, 1952, 69, The Psychopathic God: Adolf Hitler, 1977, rev. 1993; Editor, contbr. Hitler and Nazi Germany, 1965, 69; mem. editorial bd. Jour. Modern History, 1957-60; contbr. World Book, 1958, Collier's Ency, 1961, Afterword to the Mind of Adolf Hitler, 1972, Human Responses to the Holocaust, 1981, Genocide and the Modern Age, 1987, War: The Psychological Dimension, 1990; co-translator: (Erich Eyck) A History of the Weimar Republic, 2 vols., 1962, 70; cons. History of Third Reich Time-Life Mag., 1989-91. Guggenheim fellow, 1953-54; sr. Fulbright research fellow Germany, 1953-54; Am. Council Learned Socs. grantee, 1967, 82; grantee Social Sci. Research Council, 1967. Mem. Am. Hist. Assn., Central European Study Group (sec.-treas. 1970-72). Conglist. (bd. deacons). Home: PO Box 451 Williamstown MA 01267-0451

WAITE, STEPHEN HOLDEN, lawyer; b. Rochester, N.Y., Dec. 5, 1936; s. Richard Holden and Judith H. (Lapp) W.; m. Sarah T. Caswell, Aug. 20, 1960; children: Sarah T., Richard H. B.A., Amherst Coll., 1958; J.D., Yale U., 1961. Bar: N.Y. 1961. Mem. firm Nixon, Hargrave, Devans & Doyle, Rochester, N.Y., 1961-69; v.p., counsel Lincoln First Banks Inc., Rochester, 1969-73, sr. v.p., 1973-77, exec. v.p., 1978-81; chief fin. officer Lincoln First Banks Inc., 1973-81; sr. v.p. Schlegel Corp., 1981-82; mem. firm Harris, Beach, Wilcox, Rubin & Levey, Rochester, 1982-88, Underberg & Kessler, Rochester, 1988—; bd. dirs. Inst. for Rsch. and Reform in Edn., Inc. Past chmn. Rochester Area Hosp. Assn.; past bd. dirs. Highland Hosp., Monroe County Long Term Care, Inc., Rochester Regional Rsch. Libr. Coun., Hosp. Assn. N.Y. State, Health Futures for Rochester, Harley Sch., Hearing and Speech Ctr. Rochester; mem. strategic planning commn. Monroe Cmty. Hosp.; bd. dirs., treas. Hosp. Trustees N.Y. State; bd. dirs., past chmn. Ctr. for Govtl. Rsch. With U.S. Army, 1962. Mem. ABA, N.Y. State Bar Assn., Monroe County Bar Assn., Country Club Rochester. Home: 115 Pelham Rd Rochester NY 14610-2522 Office: 1800 Lincoln First Sq Rochester NY 14604

WAITER, SERGE-ALBERT, retired civil engineer; b. Paris, Feb. 8, 1930; came to the U.S., 1959; s. Bernard and Anny (Suskind) W.; 1 child, Thomas Bernard. DSc, Sorbonne-Paris U., 1954. Registered civil engr., France. Engr. Onera, Chatillon, France, 1949-51; flight test engr. Fouga, Aire S/ Adour, France, 1951-53; mgr. prototype Sud Aviation, Courvevoie, France, 1953-59; rsch. scientist USC/EC, L.A., 1959-62; sr. specialist Rockwell Internat., Downey, Calif., 1962-88; sr. cons. Dassault Aviation, St. Cloud, France, 1988-92; attaché scientifique avions. Contbr. articles to profl. jours. Fellow (assoc.) AIAA; mem. Ingenieurs Scientifiques de France. Achievements include work on Apollo, Shuttle, and HERMES programs. Home: 801 Crest Vista Dr Monterey Park CA 91754-3749

WAITES, CANDY YAGHJIAN, former state official; b. N.Y.C., Feb. 21, 1943; d. Edmund Kirken and Dorothy Joanne (Candy) Yaghjian; children: Jennifer Lisa, Robin Shelley. B.A., Wheaton Coll., Mass., 1965. Elected county councilwoman Richland County, S.C., 1976-88, mem. S.C. Ho., 1988-94; dir. external programs The Leadership Inst., Columbia Coll., 1993—; vice chmn. Adv. Commn. on Intergovtl. Relations, S.C., 1977-87; bd. dirs. Interagy. Council on Pub. Transp., S.C., 1977-85, Central Midlands Regional Planning Council, Columbia, S.C., 1977-84; dir. Wachovia Bank. Vice pres. bd. dirs. United Way of Midlands, 1977-89; trustee Columbia Mus. Art, 1982-88; bd. dirs. Rape Crisis Network, 1984-87; chmn. County Coun. Coalition; mem. C. of C. Leadership Forum, S.C. Fedn. of the Blind; mem. adv. bd. U. S.C. Hunanities and Social Scis. Coll., Family Shelter, Nurturing Ctr.; pres Trinity Housing Corp.; found. bd. Richland Meml. Hosp., 1995. Named Outstanding Young Career Woman, Columbia YWCA, 1980, YWCA Hall of Fame, 1993, Outstanding Young Woman of Yr., Columbia Jaycees, 1975, Pub. Citizen of Yr. Nat. Assn. Social Workers, hon. mem. Mortar Bd. Soc., 1994; recipient Ann. Legis. award Common Cause S.C., 1990, 91, Legis. Yr. award by S.C. Assn. Counties, 1992. Mem. S.C. Women in Govt. (vice chmn. 1984-86), S.C. Assn. Counties (bd. dirs. 1982-88 , Pres's award 1983), Network Female Execs., LWV (pres. 1973-76), Omicron Delta Kappa. Democrat. Episcopalian. Club: Univ. Assocs. (Columbia). Avocations: exercising, drawing, gardening, walking. Home: 3419 Duncan St Columbia SC 29205-2705 Office: Columbia Coll Leadership Inst 1301 Cola Coll Dr Columbia SC 29203

WAITS, JOHN A., lawyer; b. Greenville, Miss., June 6, 1947. BA summa cum laude, U. Miss., 1969; MA with honors, U. Va., 1973; JD, NYU, 1977. Bar: N.Y. 1978, U.S. Dist. Ct. (ea. and so. dists.) N.Y. 1978, D.C. 1988. Counsel to Ho. Agrl. Subcom. U.S. Ho. of Reps., Washington, 1979-80, asst. to Congressman David R. Bowen, 1980-82; ptnr. Winston & Strawn, Washington. Fulbright scholar. Mem. Assn. Bar City N.Y. Office: Winston & Strawn 1400 L St NW Washington DC 20005-3509

WAITS, PATRICIA DIANE, oncological nurse; b. Oklahoma City, July 23, 1945; d. John Aaron and Joyce Maxine (White) Flynn; m. Delbert Wayne Waits, Apr. 5, 1963; children: Kristin, Joseph, Michael. ADN, Tulsa (Okla.) Jr. Coll., 1989. Cert. oncological nurse. Staff nurse bone marrow unit St. Francis Hosp., Tulsa, 1990—, mem. coms., 1991—. Vol. Tulsa County Health Dept., 1990—, ARC, 1992—. Mem. Oncology Nursing Soc. Republican. Mem. Assembly of God Ch. Avocations: cooking, cross-stitch. Home: 6937 E 73rd St Tulsa OK 74133-2734

WAITS, THOMAS ALAN, composer, actor, singer; b. Pomona, Calif., Dec. 7, 1949; s. Frank W. and Alma (Johnson) McMurray; m. Kathleen Patricia Brennan, Aug. 10, 1980; children: Kellesimone Wylder, Casey Xavier, Sullivan Blake. Composer 14 albums including Closing Time, 1973, The Heart of Saturday Nite, 1974, Nighthawks at the Diner, 1975, Small Change, 1976, Foreign Affairs, 1978, Heartattack and Vine, 1980, Swordfishtrombones, 1983, Rain Dogs, 1985, Anthology, 1985, Frank's Wild Years, 1987, Big Time, 1988, Bone Machine, 1992, The Black Rider, 1993; composer (film scores) One from the Heart, 1983, Streetwise, 1985, Night on Earth, 1991; co-author music and songs (with Kathleen Brennan) for Night on Earth, 1991, film American Heart; composer songs and music for The Black Rider opera, Hamburg, Germany, 1990, Alice in Wonderland opera, Hamburg, 1992; actor (musical) Frank's Wild Years, 1986, (stage play) Demon Wine, 1989; appeared in films Paradise Alley, 1978, The Outsiders, 1983, Rumble Fish, 1983, The Cotton Club, 1984, Down by Law, 1986, Ironweed, 1987, Candy Mountain, 1987, Big Time, 1988, Cold Feet, 1989, The Bearskin, 1991, Queen's Logic, 1991, At Play in the Fields of the Lord, 1991, Bram Stoker's Dracula, 1992, Short Cuts, 1993. Recipient Acad. Award nomination Best Song Score for One from the Heart, 1983; Grammy award for best alternative album Bone Machine, 1992. Mem. ASCAP, Musicians Union Local 47, SAG, AFTRA, Motion Picture Acad. Office: care Howard Grossman 10960 Wilshire Blvd Ste 2210 Los Angeles CA 90024-3808

WAITT, TED W., computer company executive. CEO Gateway 2000, 1992—, chmn., pres. Office: Gateway 2000 610 Gateway Dr North Sioux City SD 57049*

WAITZKIN, HOWARD BRUCE, physician, sociologist, educator; b. Akron, Ohio, Sept. 6, 1945; s. Edward and Dorothy (Lederman) W.; m. Stephany Borges, Mar. 13, 1983; 1 stepchild, Daren; 1 child, Sofia. BA summa cum laude, Harvard U., 1966, MA, 1969, MD, PhD, 1972. Diplomate Am. Bd. Internal Medicine, Am. Bd. Geriatric Medicine. Resident in medicine Stanford (Calif.) U. Med. Ctr., 1972-75, Robert Wood Johnson clin. scholar depts. sociology-medicine, 1973-75; sr. resident in medicine Mass. Gen. Hosp., Boston, 1977-78; assoc. prof. sociology, clin. asst. prof. medicine U. Vt., Burlington, 1975-77; vis. assoc. prof. health and med. scis. U. Calif., Berkeley, 1978-82; clin. asst. prof. medicine U. Calif., San Francisco, 1978-82; internist La Clínica de la Raza, Oakland, Calif., 1978-82; prof. medicine and social scis. U. Calif., Irvine, 1982—, chief div. gen. internal medicine and primary care, 1982-90; med. dir. U. Calif.-Irvine-North Orange County Community Clinic, Anaheim, 1982-90; regional rep., nat. sec. bd. dirs. Physicians for Nat. Health Program, Cambridge, Mass., 1989-91; cons. documentary Health Care Across the Border, Nat. Pub. TV, N.Y.C., 1989-90, documentary on U.S. health care system Nat. TV Austria, 1991; cons. BBC, 1992, Pew Health Professions Commn., 1992-94, Assn. Am. Med. Colls., 1992-93, Robert Wood Johnson Found., 1992, Rsch. and Tng. Group in Social Medicine, Santiago, Chile, 1990—, Eisenhower Rural Health Ctrs., Idyllwild, Calif., 1995—; lectr. med. sociology U. Amsterdam, The Netherlands, 1977; vis. prof. Northwestern U., 1994, U. Ill., Chgo., 1994, U. Wash., 1996, U. N.Mex., 1996, U. Ky., 1996. Co-author: The Exploitation of Illness in Capitalist Society, 1974; author: The Second Sickness: Contradictions of Capitalist Health Care, 1983, paperback edit., 1986, The Politics of Medical Encounters: How Patients and Doctors Deal with Social Problems, 1991, paperback edit., 1993. Cons. on health policy Jesse Jackson Presdl. Campaign, 1988; bd. dirs., mem. com. on litigation Orange County Pub. Law Ctr., 1990—. Fellow in ind. study & rsch. NEH, 1984-85, Fulbright fellow, 1983, 88-90, 93-94, sr. fellow NIA, 1989-91, Fogarty Internat. Ctr., NIH, 1994—. Fellow ACP, Am. Acad. Physician and Patient; mem. APHA, Am. Sociol. Assn. (nat. coun.-at-large med. sociology sect. 1989-92, coord. resolution process concerning nat. health program 1990-91), Soc. Gen. Internal Medicine, Phi Beta Kappa. Avocations: music, athletics, gardening, mountain hiking. Office: U Calif at Irvine Health Policy and Rsch 320 Berkeley Pl Irvine CA 92717

WAIXEL, VIVIAN, journalist; b. Norfolk, Va., July 22, 1946; d. Julius and Julia (Heimann) W.; m. Steven E. Scharbach, Aug. 24, 1969. BS in Communication, Simmons Coll., 1967; MA in Communication, U. Wis., 1971. Teaching asst. U. Wis., Madison, 1967-69; reporter Wis. State Jour., Madison, 1969-72, The Record, Hackensack, N.J., 1972-74; bus. editor The Record, Hackensack, 1974-76, assignment editor, 1976-86, sports editor, 1986-88, chief news editor, 1988-92, mng. editor, 1992—. Recipient Tribute to Women and Industry award, YWCA, 1976. Avocations: snorkeling, fitness walking, music, reading. Office: The Record 150 River St Hackensack NJ 07601-7110

WAJENBERG, ARNOLD SHERMAN, retired librarian, educator; b. Indpls., Apr. 11, 1929; s. Henry and Hazel L. (Johnson) W.; m. Joyce E. Dunham, Sept. 6, 1952; 1 child, Earl S. B.A., Butler U., Indpls., 1951, M.A., 1953; M.A., U. Chgo., 1955. Cataloger U. Chgo. Library, 1953-69; catalog librarian U. Ill., Chgo., 1969-74; asst. catalog librarian U. Ill., Champaign-Urbana, 1974-78, prin. cataloguer, 1979-94; retired, 1994; prof. library adminstrn. U. Ill., Champaign-Urbana; prin. educator, Ill. Tng. Program for Implementation of Anglo-Am. Cataloguing Rules, 2d edit., 1979-80; mem. editorial policy com. Dewey Decimal, 1981-92; Ill. rep. cataloging adv. com., Online Computer Libr. Ctr. 1979-82, cataloging and database svcs. adv. com., 1989-92. Author: FLC FEDLINK AACR 2 Cataloging Manual for Federal Libraries, 1981; contbr. articles to profl. jours. Mem. ALA (com. on cataloging: description and access 1981-86, mem.-at-large exec. com. cataloging and classification sect. 1982-86). Avocations: walking, science fiction. Home: 1702 Sheridan Rd Champaign IL 61821-4811

WAJER, RONALD EDWARD, management consultant; b. Chgo., Aug. 31, 1943; s. Edward Joseph and Gertrude Catherine (Rytelny) W.; m. Mary Earlene Hagan, July 5, 1969; children: Catherine, Michael. BSIE, Northwestern U., 1966; MBA, Loyola U., Chgo., 1970. Cert. mgmt. cons. Project engring. mgr. Procter & Gamble, Chgo., 1966-67; indsl. engring. mgr. Johnson & Johnson, Bedford Park, Ill., 1967-71; project mgr. Jewel Cos., Franklin Park, Ill., 1971-73; div. engring. mgr. Abbott Labs., North Chicago, Ill., 1973-79; pres. Bus. Engring. div. R.E. Wajer & Assocs., Northbrook, Ill., 1979—. Contbr. articles to profl. jours. Sec. Downtown Redevel. Commn., Mt. Prospect, Ill., 1977-78; fundraising vol. Maryville Acad., Des Plaines, 1985—; bd. dirs. Lattof YMCA, Des Plaines, 1984-95; profl. advisor Sch. for New Learning, DePaul U., 1994—. Recipient Cmty. Svc. award Chgo. Lighthouse for the Blind, 1989, Cert. of Merit, Village of Mt. Prospect, 1978. Mem. Inst. Indsl. Engrs. (community svc. chmn. 1984), Inst. Mgmt. Cons. (exec. v.p., bd. dirs. 1987-94), Assn. Mgmt. Cons. (ctrl. regional v.p. 1985-87), Midwest Soc. Profl. Cons., Northwestern Club Chgo. Roman Catholic. Office: Bus Engring 5 Revere Dr Ste 200 Northbrook IL 60062-8000

WAJNERT, THOMAS C., leasing company executive; b. Evergreen Park, Ill., May 9, 1943; s. Chester J. and Gabriella M. (Postanowicz) W.; m. Marianne Amanda Kienly, Sept. 9, 1967 (dec. 1981); m. Theresa Irene Altmix, Jan. 2. 1982; children—Melissa, Rachel, Sophia, Drew. B.S., Ill. Inst. Tech., Chgo., 1965; M.B.A., So. Methodist U., Dallas, 1966. Exec. v.p. U.S. Leasing Corp., San Francisco, 1968-81; pres. U.S. Portfolio Leasing, San Francisco, 1981-83, U.S. Instrument & Rentals, San Mateo, Calif., 1983-84; pres., chief exec. officer AT&T Credit Corp., Whippany, N.J., 1984-89; pres., chmn., CEO AT&T Capital Corp., Morristown, N.J., 1990—. Home: Young Rd Bernardsville NJ 07924 Office: AT&T Capital Corp 44 Whippany Rd Morristown NJ 07960-4558

WAKE, DAVID BURTON, biology educator; b. Webster, S.D., June 8, 1936; s. Thomas B. and Ina H. (Solem) W.; m. Marvalee Hendricks, June 23, 1962; 1 child, Thomas Andrew. BA, Pacific Luth. U., 1958; MS, U. So. Calif., 1960, PhD, 1964. Instr. anatomy and biology U. Chgo., 1964-66, asst. prof. anatomy and biology, 1966-69; assoc. prof. zoology U. Calif., Berkeley, 1969-72, prof., 1972-89, prof. integrative biology, 1989-91, John and Margaret Gompertz prof., 1991—; dir. Mus. Vertebrate Zoology U. Calif., Berkeley, 1971—. Author: Biology, 1979; co-editor: Functional Vertebrate Morphology, 1985, Complex Organismal Functions: Integration and Evolution in the Vertebrates, 1989. Mem. nat. bd. Nat. Mus. Natural History. Recipient Quantrell Teaching award U. Chgo., 1967, Outstanding Alumnus award Pacific Luth. U., 1979; grantee NSF, 1965—; Guggenheim fellow, 1982. Fellow AAAS, NRC (bd. biology 1986-92); mem. Internat. Union for Conservation of Nature and Natural Resources (chair task force on declining amphibian populations 1990-92), Am. Soc. Zoologists (pres. 1992), Am. Soc. Naturalists (pres. 1989), Am. Soc. Ichthyologists and Herpetologists (bd. govs.), Soc. Study Evolution (pres. 1983, editor 1979-81), Soc. Systematic Biology (coun. 1980-84), Herpetologist's League (Disting. Herpetologist 1984). Home: 999 Middlefield Rd Berkeley CA 94708-1509

WAKE, MARVALEE HENDRICKS, biology educator; b. Orange, Calif., July 31, 1939; d. Marvin Carlton and Velvalee (Borter) H.; m. David B. Wake, June 23, 1962; 1 child, Thomas A. BA, U. So. Calif., 1961, MS, 1964, PhD, 1968. Teaching asst./instr. U. Ill., Chgo., 1964-68, asst. prof., 1968-69; lectr. U. Calif., Berkeley, 1969-73, asst. prof., 1973-76, assoc. prof., 1976-80, prof. zoology, 1980-89, chmn. dept. zoology, 1985-89, chmn. dept. integrative biology, 1989-91, assoc. dean Coll. Letters and Sci., 1975-78, prof. integrative biology, 1989—; mem. NAS/NRC Bd. on Sustainable Devel., 1995—. Editor, co-author: Hyman's Comparative Vertebrate Anatomy, 1979; co-author: Biology, 1978; contbr. articles to profl. jours. NSF grantee, 1978—; Guggenheim fellow, 1988-89. Fellow AAAS, Calif. Acad. Sci. (trustee 1992—); mem. Am. Soc. Ichthyologists and Herpetologists (pres. 1984, bd. govs. 1978—), Internat. Union Biol. Scis. (U.S. nat. com. 1986-95, chair 1992-95; sec.-gen. 1994—), World Congress of Herpetology (sec.-gen. 1994—). Home: 999 Middlefield Rd Berkeley CA 94708-1509 Office: U Calif Dept Integrative Biology Berkeley CA 94720

WAKE, RICHARD W., food products executive; b. 1953. With Aurora (Ill.) Eby-Brown Co., Inc., 1975—; co-pres. Aurora (Ill.) Eby-Brown Co., Inc., Naperville, Ill. Office: Aurora Eby-Brown 280 Shuman Blvd Ste 280 Naperville IL 60566*

WAKE, THOMAS G., food products executive. Co-pres. Eby-Brown Co., Naperville, Ill. Office: Eby Brown Co 280 Shuman Blvd Ste 280 Naperville IL 60563*

WAKE, WILLIAM S., wholesale distribution executive; b. 1926. MBA, U. Mich., 1948. With Aurora (Ill.) EBy-Brown Co., Inc., 1948-56, chmn. bd., CEO, 1956. With USN, 1944-46. Office: Eby-Brown Co 280 Shuman Blvd Ste 280 Naperville IL 60563*

WAKEFIELD, BENTON MCMILLIN, JR., banker; b. Monroe, La., Apr. 8, 1920; s. Benton McMillin and Adele (Rhodes) W.; m. Cindy Walton, May 19, 1951; children: Benton McMillin, III, Will Walton. BS in Commerce summa cum laude, Washington and Lee U., 1941; postgrad., Grad. Sch. Banking, U. Wis., 1949-51. Asst. v.p. First Nat. Bank Memphis, 1946-52; v.p. Ouachita Nat. Bank, Monroe, La., 1952-63; pres., CEO, bd. dirs. Merc. Nat. Bank Ind., Hammond, 1963-72; pres., CEO 1st Bank and Trust Co., South Bend, Ind., 1972-79, FBT Bancorp., 1972-79; chmn., CEO First Nat. Bank of Jefferson Parish, 1979-84; chmn., pres., CEO First Fin. Bank, New Orleans, 1984-88; prin. Bank and Thrift Cons. Group, New Orleans, 1988—; dir. Eureka Homestead Soc., New Orleans, 1995—; cons., including trial expert testimony Fin. Litigation Support, 1988; bd. dirs. 10 banks, Mich. and Ind., 1972-79, Carpetland U.S.A., Chgo.; vice chmn. Jefferson Steering Com. on Edn.; mem. fin. adv. coun. Fed. Res. Bank Atlanta; mem. visitors com. Loyola U. Bus. Sch.; Chpt. 11 bankruptcy trustee Kirk Mfg. Inc. Bd. dirs. Econ. Devel. Com. New Orleans, Bur. Govt. Research, United Way. Served to lt. comdr. USNR, 1941-46. Mem. Am. Bankers Assn. (econ. policy com.), U.S. C. of C. (fin. com.), New Orleans Country Club, Bienville Club, Phi Beta Kappa, Sigma Alpha Epsilon, Omicron Delta Kappa, Beta Gamma Sigma, Rotary, Royal Soc. St. George, Huguenot Soc. Methodist. Home: 5301 Marcia Ave New Orleans LA 70124-1050 Office: 5301 Marcia Ave New Orleans LA 70124

WAKEFIELD, DAN, author, screenwriter; b. Indpls., May 21, 1932; s. Benjamin H. and Brucie (Ridge) W. B.A., Columbia U., 1955; Nieman fellow, Harvard U., 1963-64. News editor Princeton (N.J.) Packet, 1955; staff writer Nation mag., 1956-59; free lance writer, 1959—; contbg. editor The Atlantic Monthly, 1968-80; staff Bread Loaf Writers Conf., 1964, 66, 68, 70, 86; contbn. writer GQ mag., 1992—; vis. lectr. U. Mass., Boston, 1965-66; vis. lectr. journalism U. Ill., 1968; writer-in-residence Emerson Coll., 1989-92; Disting. vis. writer Fla. Internat. U., 1995—. Creator, story cons. TV show James at 15, 1977-78, Heartbeat, 1988; author: Island in the City: The World of Spanish Harlem, 1959, Revolt in the South, 1961, Ananthology, 1963, Between the Lines, 1966, Supernation at Peace and War, 1968, Going All the Way, 1970 (Nat. Book Award nomination), Starting Over, 1973, All Her Children, 1976, Home Free, 1977, Under the Apple Tree, 1982, Selling Out, 1985, Returning: A Spiritual Journey, 1988, The Story of Your Life: Writing a Spiritual Autobiography, 1990, New York in the Fifties, 1992, Expect a Miracle, 1995, Creating from the Spirit, 1996; editor: The Addict: An Anthology, 1963; (teleplay) The Innocents Abroad (Mark Twain) for PBS, 1983; writer, co-prodr. TV movie The Seduction of Miss Leona, 1980; contbg. editor: Atlantic Monthly, 1969-80. Bernard DeVoto fellow Bread Loaf Writers Conf., 1957, Rockefeller Grant in Creative Writing, 1968; short story prize, Nat. Council of Arts, 1968. Mem. Authors Guild Am., Writers Guild Am., Nat. Writers Union, Vestry of King's Chapel. Address: c/o Janklow & Nesbit 598 Madison Ave New York NY 10022

WAKEFIELD, RICHARD ALAN, energy consulting firm executive; b. Exeter, N.H., June 22, 1947; s. Frederick Irving and Helen (Smith) W.; m. Priscilla Jean Warnock, Aug. 16, 1969; 1 child, Laura Katherine. BSEE magna cum laude, U. N.H., 1969; MSEE, U. Ill., 1970; PhD in Elec. Engring., U. Wash., 1975. Project engr. Air Force Avionics Lab., Wright-Patterson AFB, Ohio, 1973-77; sr. engr., project mgr. Mathtec, Inc., Arlington, Va., 1977-81; v.p. CSA Energy Cons., Arlington, 1981-88, sr. v.p., 1988-90, pres., 1991—. Bd. drs. Arlington Cmty. Residences, Inc., 1983-88, chmn., 1988-89; bd. dirs. Arlington Cmty. Svcs., 1989-95. Capt. USAF, 1973-77. Recipient Nat. Capital award D.C. Coun. Engring. and Archtl. Socs., Washington, 1982, Perske award Assn. for Mentally Retarded, Arlington, 1983. Mem. IEEE (sr., mem. demand-side mgmt. subcom. Power Engring. Soc. 1983-90, mem. sys. planning subcom. Power Engring. Soc. 1985—, mem. energy policy com. 1992—), AAAS, Conf. Internat. Grands Réseaux Electriques a Haute Tension (Cigré). Democrat. Roman Catholic. Avocations: tennis, fly fishing. Office: CSA Energy Cons 1901 Fort Myer Dr Ste 503 Arlington VA 22209-1604

WAKEFIELD, STEPHEN ALAN, lawyer; b. Olney, Ill., Oct. 18, 1940; s. George William and Blanche Lucille (Sheesley) W.; children from previous marriage: Melissa Cox, Tracy Lenz, Stephen Alan Jr.; m. Patricia Ann McGuire, Nov. 29, 1980; 1 child, Mark. LLB, U. Tex., Austin, 1965. Bar: Tex. 1965. Assoc. Baker & Botts, Houston, 1965-70, ptnr., 1974-84, sr. ptnr., chmn. energy dept., 1986-89; atty. Federal Power Commn., Washington, 1970-72; dep. asst. sec. energy programs Dept. Interior, Washington, 1972-73, asst. sec. energy and minerals, 1973-74; asst. adminstr. Fed. Energy Office, Washington, 1973-74; vice chmn., gen. counsel United Energy Resources, Inc., Houston, 1985-86; pres. United Gas Pipe Line Co., Houston, 1985-86; exec. v.p. MidCon Corp., 1985-86; gen. coun. Dept. Energy, Washington, 1989-91; ptnr. Akin, Gump, Strauss, Hauer & Feld, L.L.P., 1991—. Bd. dirs. Houston Advanced Rsch. Ctr.; bd. visitors M.D. Anderson Cancer Ctr. Mem. ABA, Tex. Bar Assn., Fed. Energy Bar Assn. Clubs: River Oaks Country, Coronado (Houston). Home: 16 West Ln Houston TX 77019-1008 Office: Akin Gump Strauss Et Al 711 Louisiana St Ste 1900 Houston TX 77002-2720

WAKEFIELD, WESLEY HALPENNY, church official; b. Vancouver, B.C., Can., Aug. 22, 1929; s. William James Elijah and Jane Mitchell (Halpenny) W.; m. Mildred June Shouldice, Oct. 24,1959. Ed. pub. schs., 1936-45, student tech. inst., 1945-47, student theology, 1947-51. Ordained to ministry The Bible Holiness Movement, 1951. Pastor Penticton, B.C., 1949-56; itinerant evangelist, 1956-59; internat. leader, bishop-gen. The Bible Holiness Movement, Vancouver, 1949—; mission to native Indians in Alta., Can., 1960-65, to Nigeria and Liberia, 1966, to drug culture youth in Pacific N.W., 1969—, among alcoholics, 1956-59, 64-66, 73; guest speaker, dir. Bible Broadcast, 1952-56, Freedom Broadcast, 1984-85; sec.-treas. Penticton Ministerial Assn., 1956; mgr. Evang. Book Svc., 1964—, Liberty Press, 1964—; presented opening prayer Fall legis. session, B.C., 1972; lectr. in field. Author: Bible Doctrine, 1951, Bible Basis of Christian Security, 1956, Jesus Is Lord, 1976, How to Incorporate a Nonprofit Society, 1976, Foundations of Freedom, 1978, Fire from Heaven, 1987, Bringing Back the Ark, 1987, John Wesley: The Burning Heart, 1988, Like Lightning, 1990, Antinomianism: The Curse of the Ages, 1990; legis. rsch. submissions: Effects of Marijuana and Youth, 1969, Labour Legislation Clauses, 1973, Religious Liberty in the Constitution, 1978, Alternatives to Electro-shock Therapy, 1988, 90, Present Day Slavery, 1973, 90; editor Hallelujah mag. (formerly Truth on Fire!), 1949—, Christian Social Vanguard, 196-61, Canadian Church and State, 1977-90, Hallelujah Songbook, 1981-83, Wesleyan Annotated Edition of the Bible, 1980—, Miniature Railways (quar.), 1988—. Chmn. Christians Concerned for Racial Equality, 1975—; v.p. Can. United for Separation of Ch. and State, 1977-90; chmn. Religious Freedom Coun. of Christian Minorities, 1978—; rsch. dir. United Citizens for Integrity, 1979—; v.p. Can. Coun. Japan Evang. Band, 1988—; chmn. Religious Info. Ctr., 1978—; Western Can. rep. Can. for the Protection of Religious Liberty, 1979—. Recipient Internat. Community Svc. award Gt. Britain, 1976, 79, Religious Liberty Advocacy award Religious Freedom Crusade, 1986, 87. Mem. NAACP, Anti-Slavery Soc., Can. Bible Soc., Bible Sci. Assn., Christian Holiness Assn. (com. mem.), Nat. Black Evang. Assn. (denomination rep. 1980-86), Wesley Study Bible (reference com. 1988-90), Evangs. for Social Action, Internat. Platform Assn., Salvation Army Hist. Soc. Avocation: miniature railways. Office: Bible Holiness Movement, PO Box 223 Postal Sta A, Vancouver, BC Canada V6C 2M3 *The real Christian is one who has exchanged the love of life for a life of love and desires the whole will of God—nothing else, nothing less, and nothing more. This consistency of service is the jewel of life and holiness its crowning glory.*

WAKEHAM, HELMUT RICHARD RAE, chemist, consulting company executive; b. Hamburg, Germany, Apr. 15, 1916; s. Rae G. and Augusta (Beiss) W.; m. Kathleen Ferguson, June 22, 1939; children: Stuart, Susan, Rosemary. B.A., U. Nebr., 1936, MA, 1937; PhD, U. Calif.-Berkeley, 1939. Research chemist Standard Oil Co. Calif., 1939-41, So. Regional Research Lab., U.S. Dept. Agr., 1941-47; research assoc. Inst. Textile Tech., Charlottesville, Va., 1947-49; project head chem.-physics sect. Textile Research Inst., also research dir., 1949-56; dir. Ahmedabad (India) Textile Industries Research Assn., 1956-58; staff asst. for research to v.p. Philip Morris, Inc., 1958-59, dir. research and devel., 1959-61, v.p., dir. research and devel., 1961-65, v.p. corporate research and devel., 1965-75, v.p. sci. and tech., 1975-80, v.p. world tobacco tech. group, 1980-82; pres. HRW Tech. Assocs. Inc., 1982-93; chmn. MEGG Assocs., Inc., 1984—; pres. Vigor Corp., 1985-87; mem. Sci. Commn. of CORESTA (internat. tobacco research orgn.), 1966-72; gen. chmn. CORESTA/TCRC Conf., Williamsburg, Va., 1972; chmn. Nat. Conf. Adminstrn. Research, 1970; mem. gen. adv. com. Textile Research Inst., 1961-65; mem. tobacco working group Nat. Cancer Inst., 1967-76; session chmn. Nat. Cancer Plan Workshop, 1971. Pres. Robert E. Lee council Boy Scouts Am., 1972-75; pres. Sci. Mus. of Va. Found., 1974-77, Va. Ctr. for Performing Arts, 1980-85; chmn. Carpenter Ct. for Performing Arts; exec. v.p. Richmond Symphony, 1976-79, pres., 1979-81, chmn., 1981-83. Cultural Laureate in sci. and tech. State of Va., 1977; Angel award Internat. Soc. Performing Arts Adminstrs., 1985. Fellow Am. Inst. Chemists, Textile Inst. (Great Britain), Va. Acad. Sci., AAAS; mem. Am. Chem. Soc. (chmn. local program sect. 1943-45, Disting. Chemist award Va. sect. 1982), Fiber Soc. (program chmn., councilor 1950-55), Am. Inst. Physics. Home: 8905 Norwick Rd Richmond VA 23229-7715 Office: 2716 Enterprise Pky Richmond VA 23294-6334

WAKEMAN, FREDERIC EVANS, JR., historian educator; b. Kansas City, Kans., Dec. 12, 1937; s. Frederic Evans and Margaret Ruth (Keyes) W.; divorced; children: Frederic Evans III, Matthew Clark, Sarah Elizabeth. B.A., Harvard Coll., 1959; postgrad., Institut d'Etudes Politiques, U. Paris, 1959-60; M.A., U. Calif.-, Berkeley, 1962, Ph.D., 1965. Asst. prof. history U. Calif., Berkeley, 1965-67, assoc. prof., 1968-70, prof., 1970-89, Haas prof. Asian Studies, 1989—, dir. Ctr. Chinese Studies, 1972-79; humanities research prof., vis. scholar Corpus Christi Coll., U. Cambridge, Eng., 1976-77, Beijing U., 1980-81, 85; acad. adviser U.S. Ednl. Del. for Study in China; chmn. Joint Com. Chinese Studies Am. Coun. Learned Socs./Social Sci. Rsch. Coun.; sr. adviser Beijing office NAS; pres. Social Sci. Rsch. Coun., 1986-89, chmn. com. on scholarly comm. with China, 1995—; dir. Inst. East Asian Studies, Berkeley, 1990—. Author: Strangers at the Gate, 1966, History and Will, 1973, The Fall of Imperial China, 1975, Conflict and Control in Late Imperial China, 1976, Ming and Qing Historical Studies in the People's Republic of China, 1981, The Great Enterprise, 1986, Shanghai Sojourners, 1992, Policing Shanghai, 1995. Harvard Nat. scholar, 1955-59; Tower fellow, 1959-60; Fgn. Area fellow, 1963-65; Am. Coun. Learned Socs. fellow, 1967-68; Guggenheim fellow, 1973-74; NRC fellow, 1985. Mem. Am. Acad. Arts and Scis., Coun. on Fgn. Rels., Am. Hist. Assn. (pres.). Home: 702 Gonzalez Dr San Francisco CA 94132-2234 Office: University of California Inst East Asian Studies Berkeley CA 94720

WAKEMAN, RICK, musician, composer; b. Middlesex, Eng., May 18, 1949; s. Cyril and Mildred W.; m. Nina Carter, 1983; children: Jemma, Oscar; children from previous marriages: Oliver, Adam, Benjamin. Educated, Royal Coll. Music, London. Keyboard and composition tng. Royal Coll. Music, 1968. Performed with group Strawbs, 1970-71; with Yes, 1971-72, 77-79, 91; with Anderson Bruford Wakeman Howe, 1989; formed own group, 1973—; rec. artist A & M Records, 1971-80, Charisma Records, from 1980, others; composed film score based on works of Liszt for film Lisztomania, 1975; original film scores White Rock, 1976, The Burning, 1982, G'Olé, 1983, Crimes of Passion, 1984; albums include Journey to the Centre of the Earth, 1974, Six Wives of Henry VIII, 1974, Myths and Legends of King Arthur, 1975, No Earthly Connection, 1976, Criminal Record, 1977, Best Known Works, 1978, 81, 84, Rhapsodies, 1979, Silent Nights, 1985, Live at Hammersmith, 1985, The Family Album, 1987, (with Tony Fernandez) Zodiaque, 1988, A Suite of Gods, 1988, Time Machine, 1988, Black Knights in the Court of Ferdinand IV, 1990, Phantom Power, 1990, Aspirant Sunset, 1990, Aspirant Sunrise, 1990, Softsword, King John & the Magna Carta, 1991, Greater Hits, 1994, numerous others; toured U.S. with Nat. Philharm. Orch. and Chorus, 1974, with own group, 1975, with Yes, 1977, 78, 79, 91, with Anderson Bruford Wakeman Howe, 1989. Address: Bajonor Ltd, Bajonor House, 2 Bridge St, Peel Isle of Man

WAKIL, SALIH JAWAD, biochemistry educator; b. Kerballa, Iraq, Aug. 16, 1927; s. Jawad and Milook (Attraqchi) W.; m. Fawzia Bahrani, Nov. 30, 1952; children: Sonya, Aida, Adil, Youssef. B.Sc., Am. U., Beirut, 1948; Ph.D., U. Wash., 1952. Research fellow U. Wash., 1949-52; research fellow U. Wis., Madison, 1952-56, asst. prof., 1956-59; asst. prof. Duke U., 1959-60, assoc. prof., 1960-65, prof., 1965-71; prof. biochemistry, chmn. dept. Baylor Coll. Medicine, Houston, 1971—, Lodwick T. Bolin prof., chmn. dept. biochemistry, 1984—, prof. biotechnology, 1986-95, Disting. Svc. prof., 1990—. Recipient Paul Lewis award in enzyme chemistry Am. Chem. Soc., 1967, Disting. Duke Med. Alumnus award 1973, Chilton award U. Tex. Southwestern Med. Ctr., Dallas, 1985, Kuwait prize Kuwait Found. Advancement Sci., 1988, Disting. Svc. award Arab Am. Med. Assn., 1990, Supelco Rsch. award Am. Oil Chemists Soc., 1993; John Simon Guggenheim fellow, 1968-69. Fellow Am. Acad. Microbiology; mem. NAS, Assn. Med. and Grad. Depts. Biochemistry (pres. 1988-89). Office: Baylor Coll Medicine Biochemistry Dept 1 Baylor Plz Houston TX 77030-3411

WAKIM, FAHD GEORGE, physicist, educator; b. Mieh-Mieh, Lebanon, Aug. 6, 1933; s. George Hanna and Marriam (Semaan) W.; m. Bertha Villarreal. BSc in Physics, Am. U. Beirut, 1956; MA in Solid State Physics, U. Tex., 1960, PhD in Solid State Physics, 1964. Rsch. physicist Itek Corp., Lexington, Mass., 1965-70; investigator Tex. Christian U., Ft. Worth, 1970-71; assoc. prof. Am. U. Cairo, 1971-73; prof. physics Kuwait U., Kuwait, 1973-84; assoc. prof. dept. elec. engring U. Mass., Lowell, 1984—; Presenter numerous seminars. Patentee process for producing images with photosensitive materials and their products; contbr. articles to profl. jours. Grantee Kuwait Inst. for Sci. Rsch., 1978, 79, 91, Kuwait U., 1979. Mem. IEEE, Am. Phys. Soc., Materials Rsch. Soc. Office: U Mass-Lowell 1 University Ave Lowell MA 01854-2881

WAKLEY, JAMES TURNER, manufacturing company executive; b. Springfield, Ohio, Feb. 17, 1921; s. James Henry and Edith Lynn (Welsh) W.; m. Mary Pennell, May 18, 1945; children: Ruth Nadine, Gary James, Martin Pennell. Student, pub. schs., Springfield. Regional sales mgr. Nat. Supply Co., 1947-54; exec. v.p. Kanawha Sand Co., 1956-60; pres. Ohio River Sand & Gravel Co., Parkersburg, W.Va., 1960-77; v.p., bd. dirs.

McDonough Co., Parkersburg, 1960-81; pres. McDonough Found., 1981—; chmn. bd. dirs. Marmac Corp., Parkersburg, 1981-95. Chmn. Parkersburg Urban Renewal Authority, 1968-75; trustee Ohio Valley Improvement Assn., Marietta Coll., W.Va. Found. Ind. Colls. Decorated DFC, Air medal. Mem. Nat. Sand and Gravel Assn. (bd. dirs. 1976-79). Lutheran. Home: 1906 Washington Ave Parkersburg WV 26101-3608 Office: PO Box 1825 Parkersburg WV 26102-1825

WAKOSKI, DIANE, poet; b. Whittier, Calif., Aug. 3, 1937; d. John Joseph and Marie Elvira (Mengel) W. BA in English, U. Calif., Berkeley, 1960. Writer-in-residence Mich. State U., East Lansing, 1976—, Univ. Disting. prof., 1990—; vis. writer Calif. Inst. Tech., 1972, U. Va., 1972-73, Wilamette U., 1973, Lake Forest Coll., 1974, Colo. Coll., 1974, U. Calif., Irvine, 1974, Macalester Coll., 1975, U. Wis., 1975, Hollins Coll., 1974, U. Wash., 1978, Whitman Coll., 1976, Emory U., 1980-81, U. Hawaii, 1978. Author: books Coins and Coffins, 1962, Discrepancies and Apparitions, 1966, Inside The Blood Factory, 1968, The George Washington Poems, 1967, The Magellanic Clouds, 1969, The Motorcycle Betrayal Poems, 1971, Smudging, 1972, Dancing On The Grave of A Son Of A Bitch, 1973, Trilogy, 1974, Virtuoso Literature For Two and Four Hands, 1976, Waiting For the King of Spain, 1977, The Man Who Shook Hands, 1978, Cap of Darkness, 1980, The Magician's Feastletters, 1982, The Collected Greed: Parts I-XIII, 1984, The Rings of Saturn, 1986, Emerald Ice: Selected Poems 1962-87, 1988 (William Carlos Williams prize 1989), Medea The Sorceress, 1991, Jason the Sailor, 1993, The Emerald City of Las Vegas, 1995. Cassandra Found. grantee, 1970; N.Y. State Cultural Council grantee, 1971-72; Nat. Endowment for Arts grantee, 1973-74; Guggenheim grantee, 1972-73; Fulbright grantee, 1984; Mich. Arts Coun. grantee, 1988; recipient Mich. Arts Found. award, 1989, Disting. Faculty award Mich. State U., 1989, Univ. Disting. Prof., 1990. Office: Mich State U 207 Morrill Hall East Lansing MI 48824-1036

WAKS, JAY WARREN, lawyer; b. Newark, Dec. 6, 1946; s. Isadore and Miriam Waks; m. Harriet S. Siedman, July 27, 1969; children: Jonathan Warren, Allison Lindsay. BS, Cornell U., 1968, JD, 1971. Bar: N.Y. 1972, U.S. Ct. Appeals (2d cir.) 1972, U.S. Dist. Ct. (no. dist.) N.Y. 1972, U.S. Dist. Ct. (so. & ea. dists.) N.Y. 1973, U.S. Ct. Appeals (3d cir.) 1983, U.S. Dist. Ct. D.C. 1985, U.S. Supreme Ct. 1991. Law clk. to Hon. Inzer B. Wyatt U.S. Dist. Ct. So. Dist. N.Y., 1971-72; assoc. Kaye, Scholer, Fierman, Hays & Handler, N.Y.C., 1972-80, ptnr., 1981—, co-chmn. labor and employment law dept., chmn. health care law practice group and ADR practice group; gen. counsel, sec. to bd. dirs. Work in Am. Inst., Inc., Scarsdale, N.Y., 1989—, exec. com., 1995—; mem., chair faculty numerous employment and labor law confs., 1982—; chair Ann. Employment Law and Litigation Conf., 1992—; participant NYU 40th Nat. Conf. on Labor, 1987, 43d Nat. Conf. on Labor, 1990; spkr. Nat. Law Jours. Gen. Coun. Conf., 1988—, Am. Employment Law Coun. Bus. watch columnist Nat. Law Jour., 1990—; contbg. author numerous articles to profl. jours. Mem. emplyment disputes com. CPR Inst. for Dispute Resolution, 1988—, chair, 1991—; chmn. 20th and 25th reunion campaigns Cornell Law Sch., Ithaca, N.Y., 1991; mem. and chair designate dean's spl. leadership commn., 1996. Named among nation's best litigators in employment law, The Nat. Law Jour., 1992; named among best lawyers in N.Y. and among 7 best corporate side labor/employment lawyers, N.Y. Mag., 1995. Mem. ABA, State Bar Calif., N.Y. State Bar Assn. (co-chair employment alternative dispute resolution com., labor and employment law sect.), Assn. Bar of City of N.Y. (chmn. labor and employment law com. 1990-93), N.Y. C. of C. and Industry (chmn. adv. panel on employment litigation 1986—). Avocations: swimming, tennis, skiing, bicycling, rollerblading. Home: 44 Eton Rd Larchmont NY 10538-1424 Office: Kaye Scholer Fierman Hays & Handler LLP 425 Park Ave New York NY 10022-3506

WAKS, STEPHEN HARVEY, lawyer; b. Decatur, Ill., Apr. 9, 1947; s. Paul and Regina (Geisler) W. BA, U. Wis., 1969; JD, U. Calif., San Francisco, 1974. Bar: Calif. 1974, U.S. Ct. Appeals (9th cir.) 1977, U.S. Tax Ct. 1977. Assoc. Wohl, Cinnamon, Hagedorn, Dunbar & Johnson, Sacramento, 1978-79; mem. Waks Law Corp., Sacramento, 1979—; instr. U. Calif.-Davis, 1982—, Golden Gate U., 1983—. Co-author: Real Estate Taxation, 1983. bd. dirs. Am. River Bank, Sacramento. Mem. ABA, Calif. Bar Assn., Sacramento County Bar Assn., Phi Delta Phi. Office: 555 Capitol Mall Ste 450 Sacramento CA 95814-4503

WAKSBERG, JOSEPH, statistical company executive, researcher; b. Kielce, Poland, Sept. 20, 1915; s. Harry and Anna (Kalichstein) W.; m. Roslyn Karr, Dec. 25, 1941; children: Arlene, Mark. BS, CCNY, 1936; postgrad., NYU, 1936-37, Am. U., 1941-43. Project dir. WPA, Phila., 1938-40; assoc. dir. stats. U.S. Bur. Census, Washington, 1940-73; chmn. bd. dirs. Westat, Inc., Rockville, Md., 1973—; tchr. U. Mich., Ann Arbor, 1968-75; statis. cons. CBS, N.Y.C., 1967-90, UN, 1975-81, Voter News Svc., N.Y.C., 1992—. Editor: Telephone Survey Methodology, 1988; assoc. editor Survey Methodology, 1992—; contbr. articles to profl. jours. Mem. tech. adv. com. Coun. Jewish Fedns., N.Y.C., 1978—. Recipient Gold medal U.S. Dept. Commerce, 1965. Fellow Am. Statis. Assn. (bd. dirs., chair several sects.); mem. Internat. Statis. Inst., Internat. Assn. Survey Statisticians (mem. coun. 1975-77). Office: Westat Inc 1650 Research Blvd Rockville MD 20850

WAKSMAN, BYRON HALSTED, neuroimmunologist, experimental pathologist, educator, medical association administrator; b. N.Y.C., Sept. 15, 1919; s. Selman A. and Bertha (Mitnik) W.; m. Joyce Ann Robertroy, Aug. 11, 1944; children: Nan, Peter. BS, Swarthmore Coll., 1940; MD, U. Pa., 1943. Intern Michael Reese Hosp., Chgo., 1944; fellow Mayo Found., 1946-48; NIH fellow Columbia U. Med. Sch., 1948-49; assoc., then asst. prof. bacteriology and immunology Harvard Med. Sch., 1949-63; research fellow, then assoc. bacteriologist (neurology) Mass. Gen. Hosp., 1949-63; prof. microbiology Yale U., 1963-74, prof. pathology, 1974-78, chmn. dept., 1964-70, 72-74, prof. pathology and biology, 1979-89; v.p. rsch. programs Nat. Multiple Sclerosis Soc., N.Y.C., 1979-87; v.p. research and med. programs Nat. Multiple Sclerosis Soc., N.Y.C., 1987-89; adj. prof. pathology NYU, 1979—; vis. scientist in neurology Harvard U., 1990—; mem. expert panel immunology WHO, 1963-83; microbiology fellowships panel and study sect. mem. NIH, 1961-69; bd. trustees Found. for Microbiology, 1968—, pres., 1970—; bd. trustees Biosis, 1988-91; dir. sci. writing fellowships program Marine Biol. Lab., Woods Hole, Mass., 1990-95; Humboldt prof. Max Planck Inst., Munich, 1991-92; dir. European Initiative for Communicators Sci., 1992-95. Author numerous articles on thymus, cell-mediated immunity, tolerance, lymphokines, lymphocyte stimulation mechanisms, autoimmunity; editor: Progress in Allergy/Chemical Immunology, 1962—; mem. editl. adv. bd. Cellular Immunology, 1970—, Immunol. Comms., 1972—, Annales d'Immunologie, 1970-78, Pathologie et Biologie, 1975-89, Inflammation, 1975—; assoc. editor: Bacteriol. Revs., 1963-67, Jour. Immunology, 1962-66, Internat. Archives Allergy and Applied Immunology, 1962—. Served as psychiatrist AUS, 1944-46. Mem. Am. Assn. Immunologists (councillor 1965-70, pres. 1970-71), British Soc. Immunology, Am. Soc. Microbiology (councillor 1967-69). Home: 300 E 54th St New York NY 10022-5018 Office: NYU Med Ctr Dept Pathology 550 1st Ave New York NY 10016-6481

WAKSMAN, TED STEWART, lawyer; b. N.Y.C., July 4, 1949; s. Alfred and Helen (Greenberger) W.; m. Lois J. Lichter, Dec. 26, 1970; children: Scott, Michael. BS, Cornell U., 1970; JD, NYU, 1973. Bar: N.Y. 1974. Ptnr. Weil, Gotshal & Manges, N.Y.C., 1973—. Mem., assoc. editor NYU Law Rev., 1971-73. Mem. ABA (comml. fin. services com.), N.Y. State Bar Assn. Office: Weil Gotshal & Manges 767 5th Ave New York NY 10153

WAKUMOTO, YOSHIHIKO, electronics company executive; b. Bunkyo-Ku, Tokyo, June 4, 1931; s. Yoshitaro and Fumie (Oka) W.; m. Reiko Tanaka, Mar. 28, 1959; children: Yoshiaki, Yoshiyuki. BA, Tokyo U., 1955; postgrad., Columbia U., 1960-61. Dep. mgr. license negotiation Toshiba Corp., Tokyo, 1964-67, mgr. overseas mfg. ops., 1967-72, mgr. fin. div., 1972-74, gen. mgr. internat. fin. div., 1974-81, gen. mgr. internat. affairs div., 1981-88, v.p., dep. group exec.-internat. staff group, 1988-91, exec. v.p. for corp. planning, info. sys. and group cos., 1991-95, also bd. dirs., exec. v.p. for internat. rels., 1995—. Co-author: Foreign Exchange Risk and International Financial Strategy, 1973, The Run-up of 21st Century, 1991; translator: Management By Exception, 1968. Mem. Internat. House of Japan, Am.-Japan Soc., Fgn. Corr. Club Japan (assoc.), Bus. Rsch. Inst., Inc. (trustee). Home: 3-43-18 Hongo Bunkyo-ku, Tokyo 113, Japan Office: Toshiba Corp, 1-1-1 Shibaura Minato-Ku, Tokyo 105, Japan

WALASH, EILEEN ROBIN, theater promotions and public relations specialist; b. Bklyn., Jan. 30, 1964; d. Myron and Marilyn Estelle (Rosner) W. BA, Miami U., Oxford, Ohio, 1986. Asst. editor Gralla Publs., N.Y.C., 1986-88; market editor Women's Wear Daily, N.Y.C., 1988-89; account supr. The Rowland Co., N.Y.C., 1989-92; pub. rels. and promotions coord., freelance writer N.Y.C., 1992-94; pub. rels. and promotions cons. Radio City Music Hall, N.Y.C., 1994-95; ind. promotions cons., 1994-95; promotions mgr. Radio City Music Hall, N.Y.C., 1994—. Vol. N.Y. Cares, N.Y.C., 1993—, Gay Men's Health Crisis, 1995—. Mem. NAFE, Pub. Rels. Soc. Am., Publicity Club of N.Y., N.Y. Alumni Assn. Miami U. (steering com.). Democrat.

WALASZEK, EDWARD JOSEPH, pharmacology educator; b. Chgo., July 4, 1927; married; two children. BS, U. Ill., 1949; PhD in Pharmacology, U. Chgo., 1953; MD honoris causa, U. Helsinki, 1990. Rsch. fellow U. Edinburgh, 1953-55; asst. prof. neurophysiology and biochemistry U. Ill., 1955-56; asst. prof. pharmacology U. Kans. Sch. Medicine, Kansas City, 1957-59; assoc. prof. U. Kans. Sch. Medicine, 1959-62, prof., 1962—, chmn. dept., 1964-92; USPHS spl. rsch. fellow, 1956-61; mem. health study sect. med. chemistry NIH, 1962-66, mem. health study sect. on rsch. career devel. award, 1966-70, mem. health study sect. on pharmacology-toxicology, 1974-78, rsch. career award, 1963; mem. com. tchg. of sci. Internat. Coun. Sci. Unions; mem. adv. coun. Internat. Union Pharmacology, 1972-81, chmn. sect. teaching, 1975-85; chmn. bd. Computer Assisted Teaching Systems Consortium. Editorial bd.: Med. Biology, 1974-84, Arch. int. Pharmacodyn, 1977. Recipient vice-chancellor's award U. Kans., 1974, Rector's medal U. Helsinki, 1975, Recognition medal Vanderbilt U., 1991, Arstiteaduskond medal Tartu U., Estonia, 1993. Fellow Am. Coll. Clin. Pharmacologists, AAAS, Am. Chem. Soc., Soc. Pharmacology, Soc. Neurosci.; mem. Finnish Acad. Sci. and Letters (fgn.), Finnish Pharm. Soc. (hon.), Hungarian Pharm. Soc. (hon.), Sigma Xi, Alpha Omega Alpha, Rho Chi. Office: U Kans Sch Medicine Dept Pharmacology Kansas City KS 66160

WALBERG, HERBERT JOHN, psychologist, educator, consultant; b. Chgo., Dec. 27, 1937; s. Herbert J. and Helen (Bauer) W.; m. Madoka Bessho, Aug. 20, 1965; 1 child, Herbert J. III. BE in Edn. and Psychology, Chgo. State U., 1959; ME in Counseling, U. Ill., 1960; PhD in Ednl. Psychology, U. Chgo., 1964. Instr. psychology Chgo. State U., 1962-63, asst. prof., 1964-65; lectr. edn. Rutgers U., New Brunswick, N.J., 1965-66; asst. prof. edn. Harvard U., Cambridge, Mass., 1966-69; assoc. prof. edn. U. Ill., Chgo., 1970-71, prof., 1971-84, rsch. prof., 1984—, external examiner, 1981; external examiner, 1981; ednl. cons. numerous orgns.; external examiner Monash U., 1974, 76, Australian Nat. U., 1977; speaker in field; former coord. worldwide radio broadcasts on Am. Edn. Voice of Am., USIA, Office Pres. U.S., cons. Ctr. for Disease Control U.S. Pub. Health Svcs., 1985-90. Author, editor 49 books; chmn. editl. bd. Internat. Jour. Ednl. Rsch., 1985—; contbr. over 350 articles to profl. jours., chpts. to books. Mem. Chgo. United Edn. Com., also other civic groups, 1971-86; bd. dirs. Family Study Inst., 1987; chmn. bd. dirs. Heartland Inst., 1995. Nat. Inst. Edn. rsch. grantee, 1973, NSF rsch. grantee, 1974, March of Dimes rsch. grantee, 1976, numerous others. Fellow AAAS, Am. Psychol. Assn., Royal Statis. Soc.; mem. Internat. Acad. Edn. (founding), Am. Ednl. Rsch. Assn., Assn. for Supervision and Curriculum Devel., Brit. Ednl. Rsch. Assn., Nat. Soc. for Study Edn., Evaluation Rsch. Soc., Internat. Acad. Scis., Phi Delta Kappa (Disting. Rsch. award U. Chgo. chpt. 1971, cert. of recognition 1985), Phi Kappa Phi (hon.). Lutheran. Avocation: travel. Home: 522 N Euclid Ave Oak Park IL 60302-1618 Office: U Ill PO Box 4348 Chicago IL 60680-4348

WALBORSKY, HARRY M., chemistry educator, consultant; b. Lodz, Poland, Dec. 15, 1923; came to U.S., 1929; s. Israel and Sarah (Miedowicz) Wolborski; m. Paula Levitt, Nov. 28, 1970; children: Edwin, Eric, Lisa, Irene. BS, CCNY, 1945; PhD, Ohio State U., 1949. Rsch. assoc. Calif. Inst. Tech., Pasadena, 1948; rsch. assoc. UCLA Med. Sch., 1949-50, rsch. assoc. chemistry dept. UCLA, 1950; instr. Fla. State U., Tallahassee, 1950-51, asst. prof. chemistry, 1951-54, assoc. prof., 1954-59, prof., 1959—, Disting. prof., 1980—; cons. Dow Chem. Co., Midland, Mich., 1956-72. Contbr. over 150 articles to profl. jours., 1949—. Recipient Sr. Scientist award von Humboldt Soc., Federal Republic of Germany, 1987; USPH fellow, 1951, Japanese Soc. for Promotion Sci. fellow, 1977. Mem. Am. Chem. Soc. (award Fla. chpt. 1978), N.Y. Acad. Sci., Chem. Soc. London, Sigma Xi, Phi Lambda Upsilon. Avocations: tennis, bridge. Office: Fla State U Dept Chemistry Tallahassee FL 32306

WALBRIDGE, WILLARD EUGENE, broadcasting executive; b. Republic, Pa., Mar. 11, 1913; s. Peter D. and Anna (Higbee) W.; m. Marietta H. Arner, Nov. 15, 1941; 1 child, Peter F. A.B., U. Mich., 1936. Salesman, Sta. WWJ, Detroit, 1939-43; mgr. Sta. WWJ-TV, Detroit, 1946-53; exec. v.p., gen. mgr. Sta. WJIM AM-TV, Lansing, Mich., 1953-54, Sta. KTRK-TV, Houston, 1954-70; sr. v.p. corp. affairs Capital Cities Communications, Inc., 1970-78, cons., 1978-81; dir. Houston Lighting & Power Co., Houston Industries, Inc., 1975-83, Internat. Systems & Controls, Inc., Tex. Commerce Med. Bank. Pres., Greater Houston Community Found.; bd. dirs. Salvation Army, Houston Area council Boy Scouts Am., Houston Grand Opera Assn.; mem. nat. bd. govs. ARC, 1974-80, also bd. dirs. Houston chpt., 1965-83, chmn. Houston chpt., 1972-75; chmn. bd. TV Info. Office, N.Y.C., 1965-70; trustee Mus. Broadcasting, 1978-82. Served from ensign to lt. USNR, 1943-46. Decorated Silver Star. Mem. Maximum Service Telecasters (dir. 1971-81), Houston Assn. Community TV (dir. 1972-82), Internat. Radio and TV Fedn. (dir. 1969-76), Nat. Assn. Broadcasters (dir. 1965-70, chmn. bd. 1970-71), U.S. C. of C. (dir. 1975-81), Houston C. of C. (dir. 1971-83, chmn. bd. 1975-76), Houston Council Fgn. Relations (chmn. 1977-78). Home: 2828 Bammel Ln Apt 1203 Houston TX 77098-1132 Office: 1 E Greenway Plz Ste 716 Houston TX 77046-0103 also: Hill & Knowlton Innc 1415 Louisiana Ste 2601 Houston TX 77002-2546

WALBURN, JOHN CLIFFORD, mental health services professional; b. Marion, Ind., Apr. 6, 1945; s. Rex Raymond and Norma Jane (Clifford) W.; m. Linda Sue Spall, Sept. 21, 1968 (div. Dec. 1987); 1 child, Geoffrey Jacob; m. Mitzi Lynn Johnson, June 20, 1992; 1 child, Abigail Rae. BS, Ball State U., 1969, MA, 1975; JD, I.U., Indpls., 1991. Bar: Ind. 1992. Planner Metro. Planning Commn., Muncie, Ind., 1970-72; dir. adult svcs. Del. County Assn. for Retarded, Muncie, Ind., 1972-76; exec. dir. Fayette-Union Assn. for Retarded, Connersville, Ind., 1976-83; cons. Ind. Protection and Advocacy, Indpls., 1984-86; case mgr. Ind. Dept. Mental Health, Indpls., 1986-87; v.p. Cardinal Svc. Mgmt., New Castle, Ind., 1987—; ofcl. Ind. Spl. Olympics, 1973—; chmn. Ind. Residential Mgmt. Com., 1991—; cons. DLG Cons. and Mktg. Svc., Ind., 1992. Co-author: Feldman/Walburn Habilitation System, 1988; photo, drawing artist, 1978—. With USN, 1965-67. Named Ky. Col., Commonwealth of Ky., 1978. Mem. Am. Assn. Mental Retardation (bd. dirs. 1991—). Avocations: sports, playing/listening to music, movies, art, reading fiction. Home: 1121 Indiana Ave New Castle IN 47362-4620 Office: Cardinal Svc Mgmt Inc PO Box 505 New Castle IN 47362-0505

WALBY, SANDRA LEE, principal; b. Detroit, Aug. 10, 1950; d. Glenn Bernard and Laura (Dolan) Titus; m. Brian Richard Walby Sr., Aug. 19, 1978; children: Brian Richard, Michelle Laurén. BS, Eastern Mich. U., 1972, MA, 1977; EdS, Oakland U., Rochester, Mich., 1993. Cert. tchr., adminstr., Mich. Reading tchr. Our Lady Star of the Sea Sch., Grosse Pointe Woods, Mich., 1973-77; reading specialist Allegan (Mich.) Pub. Schs., 1977-78, Anchor Bay Schs., New Baltimore, Mich., 1978-79; chpt. 1 of gifted program Forest Hills Schs., Grand Rapids, Mich., 1979-80, 1st grade tchr., 1981-82, kindergarten tchr., 1979-84; adult edn. tchr. Chippewa Valley Schs., Clinton Twp., Mich., 1984-87, lang. arts. cons., chpt. I dir., 1987-90; at risk coord., cons. Avondale Schs., Auburn Hills, Mich., 1990-95; prin. Plumbrook Elem., Utica Schs., Sterling Heights, Mich., 1995—; speaker in field. Author: Mentor/Business Partnership, 1991, Implementing and Evaluation a Peer Tutor Program, 1991, Whole Group Instruction, Meeting Individual Needs, 1992. Recipient Leadership award Dow Chem. Co., 1971; Rochester Hills C. of C. grantee, 1991, 95. Mem. ASCD, Mich. Reading Assn., Learning Disabilities Assn., Internat. Reading Assn. Avocations: reading, tennis, dancing, painting, writing. Home: 2671 Munster Rd Rochester Hills MI 48309 Office: Plumbrook Elem 39660 Spalding Sterling Heights MI 48313

WALCH, PETER SANBORN, museum director, publisher; b. Portland, Maine, Oct. 10, 1940; s. J. Weston and Ruth Dyer (Sanborn) W.; m. Margaret S. Segal, June 29, 1962 (div. 1983); children: Maximilian F.S., Abigail M.; m. Linda P. Tyler, Aug. 3, 1990. BA, Swarthmore Coll., 1962; MFA, Princeton U., 1964, PhD, 1968. Asst. prof. fine arts Pomona Coll., Claremont, Calif., 1966-68, Vassar Coll., Poughkeepsie, N.Y., 1968-69, Yale U., New Haven, 1969-71; assoc. prof. U. N.Mex., Albuquerque, 1971-85, dir. Art Mus., 1985—; chmn., bd. dirs. J. Weston Walch, Pub., Portland, 1990—. Author: (exhbn. catalog) French Eighteenth-Century Oil Sketches, 1980, French Oil Sketches and the Academic Tradition, 1994; editor N.Mex. Studies in the Fine Arts jour., 1978-86. Mem. Contemporary Art Soc., Cogawesco Club. Home: 1520 Columbia Dr NE Albuquerque NM 87106-2635 Office: Univ NMex Art Mus Fine Arts Ctr Albuquerque NM 87131

WALCH, TIMOTHY GEORGE, library administrator; b. Detroit, Dec. 6, 1947; s. George Louis Walch and Margaret Mary (Shields) DeSchryver; m. Victoria Irons, June 24, 1978; children: Thomas Emmet, Brian Edward. BA, U. Notre Dame, 1970; PhD, Northwestern U., 1975. Assoc. dir. Soc. Am. Archivists, Chgo., 1975-79; grants analyst Nat. Hist. Publ. Commn., Washington, 1979-81; budget analyst Nat. Archives, Washington, 1981-82, editor Prologue, 1982-88; asst. dir. Hoover Presdl. Libr., West Branch, Iowa, 1988-93, dir., 1993—. Author: Catholicism in America, 1989, Pope John Paul II, 1989, Parish School, 1996, others; editor: Farewell to the Chief, 1990, Herbert Hoover & Harry S Truman, 1992, Immigrant America, 1994, and others; assoc. editor: U.S. Cath. Historian, 1983—; mem. editl. bd. Soc. Am. Archivists, 1982-86; series editor: Garland Pub. Co., 1988-92; contbr. articles to profl. jours. Recipient Achievement and Svc. awards Nat. Archives, 1980, 83, 87, 89, 93, Journalism awards U.S. Cath. Press Assn., 1986-91, 1st place publ. award Nat. Assn. Govt. Communicators, 1988. Mem. Soc. Am. Archivists, Orgn. Am. Historians, U.S. Cath. Hist. Soc., Rotary Internat. Home: 65 N Westminster St Iowa City IA 52245-3833 Office: Hoover Presdl Libr PO Box 488 West Branch IA 52358-0488

WALCHER, ALAN ERNEST, lawyer; b. Chgo., Oct. 2, 1949; s. Chester R. and Dorothy E. (Kullgren) W.; m. Penny Marie Walcher; children: Dustin Alan, Michael Alan, Christopher Ray; 1 stepchild, Ronald Edwin Culver. BS, U. Utah, 1971, cert. in internat. rels., 1971, JD, 1974. Bar: Utah 1974, U.S. Dist. Ct. Utah 1974, U.S. Ct. Appeals (10th cir.) 1977, Calif. 1979, U.S. Dist. Ct. (cen. dist.) Calif. 1979, U.S. Ct. Appeals (9th cir.) 1983, U.S. Dist. Ct. (ea., no., and so. dists.) Calif. 1994. Sole practice, Salt Lake City, 1974-79; ptnr. Costello & Walcher, L.A., 1979-85, Walcher & Scheuer, 1985-88, Ford & Harrison, 1988-91, Epstein Becker & Green, 1991—; judge pro tem Los Angeles Mcpl. Ct., 1986-91; dir. Citronia, Inc., Los Angeles, 1979-81. Trial counsel Utah chpt. Common Cause, Salt Lake City, 1978-79. Robert Mukai scholar U. Utah, 1971. Mem. Soc. Bar and Gavel (v.p. 1975-77), ABA, Fed. Bar Assn., Los Angeles County Bar Assn., Century City Bar Assn., Assn. Bus. Trial Lawyers, Phi Delta Phi, Owl and Key. Club: Woodland Hills Country (Los Angeles). Home: 17933 Sunburst St Northridge CA 91325-2848 Office: Epstein Becker & Green 1875 Century Park E Ste 500 Los Angeles CA 90067-2506

WALCOTT, CHARLES, neurobiology and behavior educator; b. Boston, July 19, 1934; s. Charles Folsom and Susan (Cabot) W.; m. Jane Clayton Taylor, Aug. 14, 1976; children: Thomas Stewart, Samuel Cabot. AB, Harvard U., 1956; PhD, Cornell U., 1959. Asst. prof. div. engring. and applied physics Harvard U., Cambridge, Mass., 1961-65; asst. prof. biology Tufts U., Medford, Mass., 1965-67; assoc. prof. dept. biology SUNY, Stony Brook, 1967-74, prof. dept. biology, 1974-81; prof., exec. dir. Cornell Lab. of Ornithology, Ithaca, N.Y., 1981-93, Louis Agassiz Fuertes dir., 1992-95; prof. neurobiology and behavior Cornell U., 1995—; cons., dir. Elem. Sci. Study, Watertown, Mass., 1961-67; dir. 3-2-1- Contact, Children's TV Workshop, N.Y.C., 1978—; dir. L.A. Fuertes. Contbr. many rsch. papers to sci. jours. Dir. sci. TV, Mass. Audubon, Lincoln, 1959-61. Avocations: gardening, sailing, photography. Home: 84 Besemer Hill Rd Ithaca NY 14850-9636 Office: Cornell U Sect Neurobiology Behavior W255 Seeley Mudd Hall Ithaca NY 14853

WALCOTT, DEREK ALTON, poet, playwright; b. Castries, St. Lucia, Jan. 23, 1930; s. Warwick and Alix W.; m. Fay Moston, 1954 (div. 1959); 1 son; m. Margaret Ruth Maillard, 1962 (div.); 2 daus.; m. Norline Metivier (div.). BA, U. West Indies, Kingston, Jamaica, 1953, DLitt, 1972. Former tchr. St. Lucia, Grenada, Jamaica; poet-in-residence Hollins Coll., Roanoke, VA, 1980; prof. English Boston U.; founding dir. Trinidad Theatre Workshop, 1959—; lectr. Rutgers U., Yale U.; vis. prof. Columbia U., 1981, Harvard U., 1982, Boston U., 1985. Author: (poetry) Twenty-Five Poems, 1948, Epitath for the Young: A Poem in XII Cantos, 1949, Poems, 1953, In A Green Night: Poems, 1948-1960, 1962, Selected Poems, 1964, The Castaway and Other Poems, 1965 (Heinemann award Royal Soc. Lit. 1966), The Gulf and Other Poems, 1969 (Cholmondeley award 1969), Another Life, 1973 (Jock Campbell/New Statesman prize 1974), Sea Grapes, 1976, Selected Verse, 1976, The Star-Apple Kingdom, 1979, The Fortunate Traveller, 1981 (Heinemann award Royal Soc. Lit. 1983), Selected Poetry, 1981, Midsummer, 1984, Collected Poems, 1948-1984, 1986 (L.A. Times Book Rev. prize 1986), The Arkansas Testament, 1987, Omeros, 1990 (W.H. Smith Literary award 1991), Selected Poetry, 1993, Antiles: Fragments of Epic Memory, 1993; (plays) Henry Christophe: A Chronicle in Seven Scenes, 1950, Henry Dernier, 1951, Wine of the Country, 1953, The Sea at Dauphin: A Play in One Act, 1953, Ione: A Play with Music, 1957, Drums and Colours: An Epic Drama, 1958 (Jamaica Drama Festival prize 1958), Ti-Jean and His Brothers, 1958, Malcochon; or, Six in the Rain, 1959, Dream on Monkey Mountain, 1967 (Obie award 1971), In a Fine Castle, 1970, The Joker of Seville, 1974, The Charlatan, 1974, O Babylon!, 1976, Remembrance, 1977, Pantomime, 1978, The Isle Is Full of Noises, 1982, The Last Carnival, 1986, Beef, No Chicken, 1986, A Branch of the Blue Nile, 1986, The Odyssey, 1992. Recipient Guinness award, 1961, Nat. Writer's Coun. prize Welsh Arts Coun., 1979, Queen Elizabeth II Gold Medal for poetry, 1988, Nobel Prize for Lit., 1992; Rockefeller Found. fellow, 1957, 58; Eugene O'Neill Found.-Wesleyan U. fellow, 1969; MacArthur Found. grantee, 1981; decorated Order of the Hummingbird, Trinidad and Tobago, 1969. Founded Trinidad Theater workshop. Home: 71 St Mary's St Boston MA 02215 Office: Playwright's Theatre 949 Commonwealth Ave Boston MA 02215 also: care Farrar Straus & Giroux 19 Union Sq W New York NY 10003-3307*

WALCOTT, JOHN L., journalist; b. Paterson, N.J., Aug. 29, 1949; s. Henry Richards Jr. and Katharine McCauley (Fearing) W.; m. Nancy Bittles, Aug. 11, 1973; children: Jennifer James, Allison Tierney, Elizabeth Bittles. BA, Williams Coll., Williamstown, Mass., 1971. Reporter The Ridgewood (N.J.) News, 1972, The Bergen Record, Hackensack, N.J., 1972-75; Washington correspondent The Bergen Record, Washington, 1975-77; Washington correspondent Newsweek Mag., Washington, 1977-81, chief diplomatic correspondent, 1981-86; nat. security correspondent The Wall Street Journal, Washington, 1986-89; fgn. editor U.S. News & World Report, Washington, 1989-94, nat. editor, 1994—; U.S. Rep. U.N. Conf. on Media, Igls, Austria, 1983; mem. Georgetown U. Sch. Fgn. Svc. Leadership Seminar, Washington, 1985. Co-author: (with David C. Martin) Best Laid Plans: The Inside Story of America's War Against Terrorism, 1988. Named Disting. Friend, Georgetown U. Sch. Fgn. Svc., 1985—; recipient Edward Weintal prize Georgetown U., 1988, Edwin M. Hood award Nat. Press Club, 1983, Freedom of the Press award, 1995, Overseas Press Club award, 1983, 84, Newspaper Guild of N.Y. award, 1985. Mem. Overseas Writers Club (pres. 1986-88), White House Correspondents Assn., Sigma Delta Chi. Presbyterian. Office: US News & World Report 2400 N St NW Washington DC 20037-1153

WALCOTT, ROBERT, healthcare executive, priest; b. Boston, July 31, 1942; s. Robert and Rosamond (Pratt) W.; m. Diane Palmer, Sept. 1, 1966; 1 child, Sara. BA, Coll. of Wooster, 1964; MDiv, Ch. Div. Sch., Berkeley, Calif., 1967; M Healthcare Adminstrn., Ohio State U., 1972. Ordained Episc. priest, 1968. Planning specialist Health Planning and Devel. Coun., Wooster, Ohio, 1972-73, asst. dir., 1974-75; asst. dir. St. Joseph Hosp., Lorain, Ohio, 1975-78, assoc. dir., 1978-81; CEO, Lakeside Meml. Hosp., Brockport, N.Y., 1981-85; adminstr. Dent Neurologic Inst., Buffalo, 1986-

87, Oak Hills Nursing Ctr., Lorain, 1994; pastor Ch. of Transfiguration, Buffalo, 1988-91, St. Michael and All Angels Ch., Uniontown, Ohio, 1991-93; adminstr.-in-tng. Chapel Hill Cmty., Canal Fulton, Ohio, 1993; interim adminstr. Regina Health Ctr., Richfield, Ohio, 1994-95; adminstr. Ohio Pythian Sisters Home, Sophia Huntington Parker Home, Medina, 1995—. Mem. planning com. Tremont Devel. Corp., Cleve., 1994—; mem. steering com. Habitat for Humanity, Cleve., 1994—. Fellow Am. Coll. Healthcare Execs.; mem. Am. Coll. Health Care Adminstrs. Democrat. Avocations: travel, reading. Home: 2672 W 14th St Cleveland OH 44113 Office: Ohio Pythian Sisters Homes 550 Miner Dr Medina OH 44256

WALCZAK, JOANNE CAROL, accountant; b. Buffalo, Feb. 8, 1959; d. Joseph Charles and Carol Dolores (Nicklas) Moorhouse; m. John T. Walczak, Aug. 2, 1980; 1 child, Bryan. BS in Acctg., SUNY, Geneseo, 1986; MBA in Fin. and Corp. Acctg., U. Rochester, 1991. CPA, N.Y. Staff acct. Genesee C.C., Batavia, N.Y., 1986-87; sr. acct. Strong Meml. Hosp., Rochester, N.Y., 1987-88; ptnr. J&L Assocs., Batavia, 1988-93, Landers & Walczak, Batavia, 1993—; adj. faculty Genesee C.C., 1988—. Bd. dirs. YWCA Genesee County, Inc., Batavia, 1989-90; mem. bus. devel. com. Genesee County C. of C., 1992—; v.p. Zonta Club of Batavia-Genesee, 1994-95, pres. 1996-97. Mem. N.Y. State Soc. CPAs. Roman Catholic. Avocations: golf, tennis, bowling, reading, crafts. Home: 16 Linwood Ave Batavia NY 14020-3714 Office: Landers & Walczak 12 Center St Batavia NY 14020-3204

WALD, BERNARD JOSEPH, lawyer; b. Bklyn., Sept. 14, 1932; s. Max and Ruth (Mencher) W.; m. Francine Joy Weintraub, Feb. 2, 1964; children—David Evan, Kevin Mitchell. B.B.A. magna cum laude, CCNY; J.D. cum laude, NYU, 1955. Bar: N.Y. 1955, U.S. Dist. Ct. (so. dist.) N.Y. 1960, U.S. Dist. Ct. (ea. dist.) N.Y. 1960, U.S. Ct. Appeals (2d cir.) 1960, U.S. Supreme Ct. 1971. Mem. Herzfeld & Rubin, P.C. and predecessor firms, N.Y.C., 1955—. Mem. ABA, N.Y. State Bar Assn., Assn. Bar City N.Y., N.Y. County Lawyers Assn. Office: Herzfeld & Rubin PC 40 Wall StSte 5400 New York NY 10005

WALD, DONNA GENE, advertising executive, media specialist; b. Peekskill, N.Y., July 24, 1947; d. David and Blossom (Karlin) W. BA, Rider Coll., 1969; MA, Hunter Coll., 1974. Broadcast traffic rep. SSC&B Inc., N.Y.C., 1969-74; broadcast buyer J. Walter Thompson, N.Y.C., 1974-78, regional broadcast supr., v.p., Dallas, 1978-81; v.p., regional broadcast supr., Los Angeles, 1981-85; prof. UCLA, 1984; sr. v.p., account dir. Western Internat. Media, Calif., 1985-95, exec. v.p., regional dir. account svcs., 1995—. Mem. Advt. Industry Emergency Fund, Hollywood Radio and TV Soc., Assn. Broadcast Execs. of Tex. (bd. dirs. 1979-80, sec. 1980-81). Home: 14844 Dickens St Apt 106 Sherman Oaks CA 91403-3655 Office: Western Internat Media Corp 8544 W Sunset Blvd West Hollywood CA 90069-2310

WALD, FRANCINE JOY WEINTRAUB (MRS. BERNARD J. WALD), physicist, academic administrator; b. Bklyn., Jan. 13, 1938; d. Irving and Minnie (Reisig) Weintraub; student Bklyn. Coll., 1955-57; BEE, CCNY, 1960; MS, Poly. Inst. Bklyn., 1962, PhD, 1969; m. Bernard J. Wald, Feb. 2, 1964; children: David Evan, Kevin Mitchell. Engr., Remington Rand Univac div. Sperry Rand Corp., Phila., 1960; instr. Poly. Inst. Bklyn., 1962-64, adj. research asso., 1969-70; lectr. N.Y. C.C., Bklyn., 1969, 70; instr. sci. Friends Sem., N.Y.C., 1975-76, chmn. dept. sci., 1976-94; instr. sci., chmn. dept. sci. Nightingale-Bamford Sch., N.Y.C., 1994—. NDEA fellow, 1962-64. Mem. Am. Phys. Soc., Am. Assn. Physics Tchrs., Assn. Tchrs. in Ind. Schs., N.Y. Acad. Scis., Nat. Sci. Tchrs. Assn., AAAS, Sigma Xi, Tau Beta Pi, Eta Kappa Nu.

WALD, GEORGE, biochemist, educator; b. N.Y.C., N.Y., Nov. 18, 1906; s. Isaac and Ernestine (Rosenmann) W.; m. Frances Kingsley, May 15, 1931 (div.); children: Michael, David; m. Ruth Hubbard, 1958; children: Elijah, Deborah. B.S., NYU, 1927, D.Sc. (hon.), 1965; M.A., Columbia U., 1928, Ph.D., 1932; M.D. (hon.), U. Berne, 1957, U. Leon, Nicaragua, 1984; D.Sc. (hon.), Yale U., 1958, Wesleyan U., 1962, McGill U., 1966, Amherst Coll., 1968, U. Rennes, 1970, U. Utah, 1971, Gustavus Adolphus U., 1972, Hamline U., 1977, Columbia U., 1990; D.H.L. (hon.), Kalamazoo Coll., 1984. NRC fellow at Kaiser Wilhelm Inst. Berlin and Heidelberg, U. Zurich, U. Chgo., 1932-34; tutor biochem. scis. Harvard U., 1934-35, instr. biology, 1935-39, faculty instr., 1939-44, assoc. prof. biology, 1944-48, prof., 1948-77, Higgins prof. biology, 1968-77, prof. emeritus, 1977—; vis. prof. biochemistry U. Calif., Berkeley, summer 1956; Nat. Sigma Xi lectr., 1952; chmn. divisional com. biology and med. scis. NSF, 1954-56; Guggenheim fellow, 1963-64; Overseas fellow Churchill Coll., Cambridge U., 1963-64; participant U.S.-Japan Eminent Scholar Exchange, 1973; guest China Assn. Friendship with Fgn. Peoples, 1972; v.p. Permanent Peoples' Tribunal, Rome, 1980—. Co-author: General Education in a Free Society, 1945, Twenty Six Afternoons of Biology, 1962, 66, also sci. papers on vision and biochem. evolution. Recipient Eli Lilly prize Am. Chem. Soc., 1939, Lasker award Am. Pub. Health Assn., 1953, Proctor medal Assn. Rsch. in Opthalmology, 1955, Rumford medal Am. Acad. Arts and Scis., 1959, Ives medal Optical Soc. Am., 1966, Paul Karrer medal in chemistry U. Zurich, 1967, T. Duckett Jones award Helen Hay Whitney Found., 1967, Bradford Washburn medal Boston Mus. Sci., 1968, Max Berg award, 1969, Priestley medal Dickinson Coll., 1970, Columbia U. award for Disting. Achievement, 1991; co-recipient Nobel prize for physiology or medicine, 1967. Fellow NAS, Am. Acad. Arts and Scis., Am. Philos. Soc.; mem. Optical Soc. Am. (hon.). Home: 21 Lakeview Ave Cambridge MA 02138-3325 Office: Harvard U Dept Biology Cambridge MA 02138 *"A scientist lives with all reality. There is nothing better. To know reality is to accept it, and eventually to love it. A scientist is in a sense a learned child. There is something of the scientist in every child. Others must outgrow it. Scientists can stay that way all their lives." (Remarks on receiving the Nobel Prize, Stockholm, 1967).*

WALD, NIEL, medical educator; b. N.Y.C., Oct. 1, 1925; s. Albert and Rose (Fischel) W.; m. Lucienne Hill, May 24, 1953; children: David, Phillip. A.B., Columbia U., 1945; M.D., NYU, 1948. Sr. hematologist Atomic Bomb Casualty Commn., Hiroshima, Japan, 1954-57; head biologist health physics div. Oak Ridge Nat. Lab., 1957-58; med. rsch. and teaching specializing in radiation medicine and cytogenetics Pitts., 1958—; mem. faculty U. Pitts. Grad. Sch. Pub. Health and Med. Sch., 1958—, prof. radiation health, 1962-91, prof. environ. and occupational health, 1991—, prof. radiology, 1965—; prof. human genetics U. Pitts., 1991—; chmn. dept. radiation health U. Pitts. Grad. Sch. Pub. Health and Med. Sch., 1969-76, 77-89, chmn. dept. occupational health, 1975-76, chmn. dept. indsl. environ. health scis., 1976-77; dir. radiation medicine dept. Presbyn.-Univ. Hosp., 1966—; med. dir. Cllin. Cytogenetics Lab., U. Pitts., 1982—; cons. U.S. Nuclear Regulatory Commn. Office of Nuclear Materials Safety and Safeguards, mem. adv. panel for decontamination of Three Mile Island Nuclear Power Sta. Unit 2, 1981-93, cons. adv. com. on reactor safeguards, 1989-94; mem. U.S. working group on health effects, U.S.-USSR Joint Coordinating Com. for Civilian Nuclear Reactor Safety, 1989-92; cons. USN, nuclear industries and utilities; chmn. radiol. health study sect. USPHS, 1967-71; mem. Nat. Coun. Radiation Protection and Measurements, 1969-81, consociate mem., 1981—; mem. Gov. Pa. Adv. Com. Atomic Energy Devel. and Radiation Control, 1966-84, chmn., 1974-76; mem. Pa. Dept. Environ. Protection adv. com. on low level radioactive waste disposal, 1985—. Contbr. numerous articles to sci. and med. publs. Served to capt. M.C. USAF, 1952-54. Recipient Health Physics Faculty Rsch. award U.S. Dept. Energy, 1992-95. Mem. Health Physics Soc. (pres. 1973-74), Am. Pub. Health Assn. (governing council 1971-73, program devel. bd. 1973-74), Radiation Rsch. Soc. (assoc. editor jour. 1965-68), Soc. Nuclear Medicine (assoc. editor jour. 1959-69), Am. Soc. Human Genetics, Am. Coll. Occupational & Environ Medicine, AAAS, AMA, Internat. Soc. Hematology. Achievements include research in the diagnosis and treatment of accidental human radiation injury, in human radiation dosimetry by automatic image analysis of radiation-induced chromosome aberrations, and in the cytogenetics of murine radiation induced leukemia. Office: U Pitts Grad Sch Pub Health A-744 Crabtree Hall Pittsburgh PA 15261

WALD, PATRICIA MCGOWAN, federal judge; b. Torrington, Conn., Sept. 16, 1928; d. Joseph F. and Margaret (O'Keefe) McGowan; m. Robert L. Wald, June 22, 1952; children—Sarah, Douglas, Johanna, Frederica, Thomas. BA, Conn. Coll., 1948; LLB, Yale U., 1951; HHD (hon.), Mt. Vernon Jr. Coll., 1980; LLD (hon.), George Washington Law Sch., 1983, CUNY, 1984, Notre Dame U., John Jay Sch. Criminal Justice, Mt. Holyoke Coll., 1985, Georgetown U., 1987, Villanova U. Law Sch., Amherst Coll., N.Y. Law Sch., 1988, Colgate U., 1989, Hofstra Law Sch., 1991, New Eng. Coll., 1991, Hoffstra U., 1991, Vermont Law Sch., 1995. Bar: D.C. 1952. Clk. to judge Jerome Frank U.S. Ct. Appeals, 1951-52; asso. firm Arnold, Fortas & Porter, Washington, 1952-53; mem. D.C. Crime Commn., 1964-65; atty. Office of Criminal Justice, 1967-68, Neighborhood Legal Svc., Washington, 1968-70; co-dir. Ford Found. Project on Drug Abuse, 1970, Ctr. for Law and Social Policy, 1971-72, Mental Health Law Project, 1972-77; asst. atty. gen. for legis. affairs U.S. Dept. Justice, Washington, 1977-79; judge U.S. Ct. Appeals (D.C. cir.), 1979—, chief judge, 1986-91. Author: Law and Poverty, 1965; co-author: Bail in the United States, 1964, Dealing with Drug Abuse, 1973; contbr. articles on legal topics. Trustee Ford Found., 1972-77, Phillips Exeter Acad., 1975-77, Agnes Meyer Found., 1976-77, Conn. Coll., 1976-77; mem. Carnegie Council on Children, 1972-77. Mem. ABA (exec. bd. 1994—, bd. editors ABA Jour. 1978-86), Am. Law Inst. (coun. 1979—, exec. com. 1985—, 2d v.p. 1988-93, 1st v.p. 1993—), Inst. Medicine, Am. Acad. Arts and Scis., Phi Beta Kappa. Office: US Ct Appeals US Courthouse 3rd & Constitution Ave NW Washington DC 20001

WALD, RICHARD CHARLES, broadcasting executive; b. N.Y.C.; s. Joseph S. and Lily (Forstate) W.; m. Edith May Leslie; children: Matthew Leslie, Elizabeth Tole, Jonathan Simon. BA, Columbia U., MA; AB, Clare Coll., Cambridge. From reporter to mng. editor N.Y. Herald Tribune, 1955-66; asst. mng. editor Washington Post, 1967; exec. v.p. Whitney Communications Corp., N.Y.C., 1968; pres. NBC News, 1968-77; sr. v.p. ABC News, 1978; dir. Worldwide TV News; chmn. bd. Columbia Daily Spectator. Annotator: (with James Bellows) The World of Jimmy Breslin, 1967. Office: ABC News 47 W 66th St New York NY 10023-6201

WALD, SYLVIA, artist; b. Phila., Oct. 30, 1915. Ed., Moore Inst. Art, Sci. and Industry. One-woman shows include U. Louisville, 1945, 49, Kent State Coll., 1945, Nat. Serigraph Soc., 1946, Grand Central Moderns, N.Y.C., 1957, Devorah Sherman Gallery, Chgo., 1960, New Sch., 1967, Book Gallery, White Plains, N.Y., 1968, Benson Gallery, Bridgehampton, L.I., 1977, Knoll Internat., Munich, Germany, 1979, Amerika Havs, Munich, 1979, Aaron Berman Gallery, N.Y.C., 1981, Hirschltadler Gallery, 1994, New Britain (Conn.) Mus., 1994, Dongah Art Gallery, Seoul, Korea, 1995, Hanlim Art Gallery, Daejun, 1995-96, Kwanju City art Mus, Pusanm Korea; group shows include Nat. Sculpture Soc., 1940, Sculpture Internat., Phila., 1940, Chgo. Art Inst., 1941, Bklyn. Mus., 1975, Library of Congress, 1943, 52, 58, Smithsonian Instn., 1954, Internat. Print Exhbn., Salzburg and Vienna, 1952, 2d Sao Paulo Biennial, 1953, N.Y. Cultural Center, 1973, Mus. Modern Art, N.Y.C., 1975, Benson Gallery, Bridgehampton, L.I., 1982, Dumon-Landis Gallery, New Brunswick, N.J., 1982-83, Suzuki Gallery, N.Y.C., 1982, Sid Deutch Gallery, N.Y.C., 1983, Aaron Berman Gallery, N.Y.C., 1983, Full House Gallery, Kingston, N.J., 1984, Worcester Mus., 1991, Boston Mus. Fine Arts, 1991, Hirschl & Adler Gallery, N.Y.C., 1993, others; represented in permanent collections Aetna Oil Co., Am. Assn. U. Women, Ball State Tchrs. Coll., Bibliotheque Nationale, Paris, Bklyn. Mus., Howard U., State U. Iowa, Library of Congress, U. Louisville, Nat. Gallery, Mus. Modern Art, Phila. Mus., N.C. Mus., Rose Mus. Art at Brandeis U., Whitney Mus., N.Y.C., Finch Coll. Mus., N.Y.C., U. Nebr., Ohio U., U. Okla., Princeton, Victoria and Albert Mus., Walker Gallery, Worcester (Mass.) Art Mus., Guggenheim Mus., N.Y.C., Grunewald Mus., U.Calif. Los Angeles, Rutgers Mus., N.J., Aschenbach Collection Mus., San Francisco, Grunewald Coll. Mus. UCLA; Contbr. to profl. publs. Address: 417 Lafayette St New York NY 10003-7005

WALDBAUER, GILBERT PETER, entomologist, educator; b. Bridgeport, Conn., Apr. 18, 1928; s. George Henry and Hedwig Martha (Gribisch) W.; m. Stephanie Margot Stiefel, Jan. 2, 1955; children: Gwen Ruth, Susan Martha. Student, U. Conn., 1949-50; BS, U. Mass., 1953; MS, U. Ill., Urbana, 1956, PhD, 1960. Instr. entomology U. Ill., Urbana, 1958-60, asst. prof., 1960-65, assoc. prof., 1965-71, prof., 1971—, prof. agrl. entomology Coll. Agr., 1971—, prof. emeritus, 1995—; sr. scientist Ill. Natural History Survey; vis. scientist ICA, Palmira, Colombia, 1971; vis. sr. scientist Internat. Rice Rsch. Inst., 1978-79; cons. AID, 1985; vis. prof. U. Philippines, 1978-79. Author: Insects Through the Seasons, 1996; contbg. author: Insect and Mite Nutrition, 1972, Introduction to Insect Pest Management, 1975, Evolution of Insect Migration and Diapause, 1978, Sampling Methods in Soubean Entomology, 1980, Evolutionary Process, 1988, Ann. Rev. Entomology, 1991; contbr. numerous articles to profl. jours. Served with AUS, 1946-47, PTO. Grantee Agrl. Rsch. Svc. USDA, 1966-71, 83-90, Nat. Geog. Soc., 1972-74, NSF, 1976-79, 82-90. Mem. AAAS, Entomol. Soc. Am., Entomol. Soc. Washington, Soc. for Study of Evolution, Mich. Entomol. Soc., Sigma Xi, Phi Kappa Phi. Home: 807A Ramblewood Ct Savoy IL 61874-9568 Office: U Ill Dept Entomology 320 Morrill Hall Urbana IL 61801

WALDECK, JOHN WALTER, JR., lawyer; b. Cleve., Sept. 10, 1949; s. John Walter Sr. and Marjorie Ruth (Palenschat) W.; m. Cheryl Gene Cutter, Sept. 10, 1977; children: John III, Matthew, Rebecca. BS, John Carroll U., 1973; JD, Cleve. State U., 1977. Bar: Ohio 1977. Product applications chemist Synthetic Products Co., Cleve., 1969-76; assoc. Arter & Hadden, Cleve., 1977-85, ptnr., 1986-88; ptnr. Porter, Wright, Morris and Arthur, Cleve., 1988-90, ptnr. in charge, 1990-96; ptnr. Walter & Haverfield, Cleve., 1996—. Chmn. Bainbridge Twp. Bd. Zoning Appeals, Chagrin Falls, Ohio, 1981-94; trustee Greater Cleve. chpt. Lupus Found. Am., 1978-91, sec., 1979-86; trustee LeBlond Housing Corp., Cleve., 1990—, sec., 1996—, Univ. Circle, Inc., 1993—, Fairmount Ctr. for Performing and Fine Arts, Novelty, Ohio, 1993—, sect., 1994—; bd. dirs. Geauga County Mental Health Alcohol and Drug Addiction Svc. Bd., Chardon, Ohio, 1988—, treas., 1991-93, vice chmn., 1993-95, chmn., 1995—; mem. bd. advisors Palliative Care Svcs., Cleve. Clinic Cancer Ctr., 1989-91. Mem. ABA (real property sect.), Ohio State Bar Assn. (real property sect. bd. govs. 1992), Greater Cleve. Bar Assn. (real property, corp. banking sect., co-chair real estate law inst. 1990, 95, 96), The Union Club, Chagrin Valley Athletic Club. Democrat. Roman Catholic. Avocations: beekeeping, gardening, jogging. Home: 18814 Rivers Edge Dr W Chagrin Falls OH 44023-4968 Office: Walter & Haverfield 1300 Terminal Tower 50 Public Sq Cleveland OH 44113

WALDEN, DANIEL, humanities and social sciences educator; b. Phila., Aug. 1, 1922; s. Benjamin and Reba (Freedman) Weinroth; m. Beatrice Schulman, Oct. 12, 1957; children: Moss Carl, Ruth E. Walden Turek. BA, CCNY, 1959; MA, Columbia U., 1961; PhD, NYU, 1964. Lectr. Queens Coll., N.Y.C., 1960-63; asst. prof. Mich. State U., East Lansing, 1963-66; prof. Pa. State U., University Park, 1966—. Co-editor: On Being Black, 1970, W.E.B. DuBois, The Crisis Writings, 1972, On Being Jewish, 1974, Twentieth Century American Jewish Fiction Writers, 1984, The World of Chaim Potok, 1985, The World of Cynthia Ozick, 1987, Bernard Malamud: in Memoriam, 1988, American Jewish Poets: The Roots and the Stems, 1990, Herbert Gold and Beyond, 1991, Jewish Identity: From Midrash to Modernity, 1991, American Jewish Women Writers, 1992, The Changing Mosaic: Cahan to Malamud and Ozick, 1993, New Voices in an Old Tradition, 1994, Bernard Malamud's Literary Imagination: A New Look, 1995. Mem. ALA, MLA (MELUS pres. 1977-78, Disting. MELUS award 1993), N.E. MLA (pres. 1991-92), Soc. Am. Jewish Lit. (pres. 1991-92, Disting. Svc. award 1992), Am. Studies Assn., Am. Culture Assn., Soc. for Utopian Studies. Democrat. Jewish. Avocations: reading, music, photography. Office: Dept English/Am Studies Pa State U University Park PA 16802

WALDEN, JAMES WILLIAM, accountant, educator; b. Jellico, Tenn., Mar. 5, 1936; s. William Evert and Bertha L. (Faulkner) W.; m. Eva June Selvia, Jan. 16, 1957 (dec. Aug. 1988); 1 child, James William; m. Hattie Nan Lamb, Jan. 6, 1990 (div. June 1992); m. Janet Faulkner, Aug. 12, 1993. BS, Miami U., Oxford, Ohio, 1963; MBA, Xavier U., Cin., 1966. CPA, Ohio. Tchr. math. Middletown (Ohio) City Sch. Dist., 1963-67, Fairfield (Ohio) High Sch., 1967-69; instr. accounting Sinclair Community Coll., Dayton, Ohio, 1969-72, asst. prof., 1972-75, assoc. prof., 1975-78, prof., 1978-89, prof. emeritus, 1991—; cons., public acct. Group comdr. Ohio Wing, CAP. Served with USAF, 1954-59. Mem. Butler County Torch Club, Pub. Accts. Soc. Ohio (pres. S.W. chpt. 1985-86), Inst. Mgmt. Accts., Nat. Soc. Pub. Accts., Greater Hamilton Estate Planning Coun., Ohio Soc. CPAs, Beta Alpha Psi. Home: PO Box 469 Springboro OH 45066-0469 Office: Sinclair C C 444 W 3rd St Dayton OH 45402-1421

WALDEN, LINDA L., lawyer; b. Dallas, Aug. 16, 1951; d. Leslie LaFayette Jr. and Neva Irene (McBee) W.; m. David Lee Finney, June 9, 1984. BA, Tex. Women's U., 1972; JD, St. Mary's U., 1975. Asst. city atty. City of Amarillo, Tex., 1976-77; asst. dist. atty. 84th Jud. Dist., Borger, Tex., 1977-79; asst. atty. gen. Office Atty. Gen. Tex., Austin, 1979-84; litigation atty. Friedman & Ginsberg, Dallas, 1984-86, Bradford & Snyder, Dallas, 1986-88; corp. counsel Occidental Chem. Co., Dallas, 1988—. Home: 2209 Greenview Dr Carrollton TX 75010-4110 Office: Occidental Chem Corp 5005 Lyndon B Johnson Fwy Dallas TX 75244-6119

WALDEN, PHILIP MICHAEL, recording company executive, publishing company executive; b. Greenville, S.C., Jan. 11, 1940; s. Clemiel Barton and Carolyn Hayes (McClendon) W.; m. Peggy Hackett, Sept. 13, 1969; children: Philip Michael, Amantha Starr. A.B. in Econs., Mercer U., 1962. Pres. Phil Walden & Assocs., 1961, Capricorn Records, Inc., 1969—. Campaign chmn. Macon Muscular Dystrophy Assn., 1975; chmn. Macon Heritage Found.; mem. In-Town Macon Neighborhood Assn.; Mem. nat. finance com. Jimmy Carter for Pres.; mem. Com. for Preservation of the White House; mem. nat. adv. bd. NORML; bd. dirs. Brandywine Conservancy; mem. Presdl. Inaugural Com., 1977; trustee Ga. Trust for Historic Preservation.; founder Otis Redding Scholarship Fund, Mercer U., Phil Walden scholarship. Served to 1st lt. Adj. Gen. Corps AUS, 1963-65. Recipient Gold and Platinum Record awards, pub. awards; Big Bear award Mercer U., 1975; Martin Luther King, Jr. Humanitarian award, 1977; Human Relations award Am. Jewish Com., 1978. Mem. Common Cause, Middle Ga. Hist. Soc., Nat. Assn. Rec. Arts and Scis., Rec. Industry Assn. Am. (dir.), Nat. Assn. Rec. Merchandisers, Phi Delta Theta Alumni Assn. Home: 3925 Woodlawn Dr Nashville TN 37205-1933

WALDEN, ROBERT THOMAS, physicist educator, consultant; b. Paducah, Ky., Mar. 25, 1939; s. Charles Robert and Anna Catherine (Robertson) W.; m. Nellie Sue Clayton, June 9, 1962; children: Clayton Thomas, Alan Keith. BS, Murray State U., 1961, MS, 1968; PhD, Miss. State U., 1973. Tchr. math. Dongola (Ill.) High Sch., 1962-63; instr. physics Paducah C.C., 1963-68; asst. prof. Ky. Wesleyan Coll., Owensboro, 1968-70; chair sci. Miss. Gulf Coast C.C., Perkinston, 1973-87; staff scientist Nat. Ctr. Phys. Acoustics, U. Miss., University, 1987-91; prof. physics, dean gen. edn. Mid-Continent Coll., Mayfield, Ky., 1990-96; cons. Walden Assocs., Paducah, 1990—; vis. prof. U. Miss., University, 1986-87; cons. Paducah Gaseous Diffusion Plant, 1992—; organizer, chair 1st nat. symposium on agroacoustics; organizer, chair Miss. Alliance Sci. Advancement. Contbr. articles to Jour. Molecular Spectroscopy, Jour. Miss. Acad. Sci. Dir., founder Stone County Jr. Basketball League, Wiggins, Miss., 1979-82; vice-chmn. Stone Coutny Hosp. Bd., Wiggins, 1983-85. Mem. Acoustical Soc. Am., Rotary (Rotarian of Yr. Wiggins unit 1981), Sigma Pi Sigma, Phi Kappa Phi. Baptist. Achievements include initiation of acoustic remote sensing of bark beetles. Home: 420 Hutchinson Ave Paducah KY 42003-5726 Office: Walden Assocs 453 Hutchinson Ave Paducah KY 42003-5725

WALDEN, STANLEY EUGENE, composer, clarinetist; b. Bklyn., 1932. BA in Music with honors, Queens Coll.; studied composition with Ben Weber, clarinet with David Weber. Faculty C.W. Post Coll.; guest lectr. U. Wis., Yale Drama Sch.; mem. dance faculty (music) Juilliard Sch., N.Y.C., 1965-71; faculty Sarah Lawrence Coll., 1973-75, SUNY, Purchase, 1973-78; prof., chmn. musical/show dept. H.D.K. Berlin, 1990. Guest composer: So. Meth. U., 1984, Eastman Sch., 1985; pianist for Martha Graham, Anna Sokolow; music dir. Tamaris-Nagrin Dance Co., Horseman, Pass By, 1967, Am. Dance Festival, 1984; solo clarinetist Contemporary Chamber Ensemble, Bennington Composers Conf., Penn Contemporary Players; guest artist N.Y. Woodwind Quintet.; commns. include Dance Sonata for Daniel Nagrin, Stretti for Group for Contemporary Music Columbia, Image for Harkness Ballet, (with Anna Sokolow) Manhattan Festival Ballet, Invisible Cities for Phila. Orch., 1985, 3 Ladies for Jan De Gaetani and Gilbert Kalish, Songs and Dances for Joel Krosnick and Gilbert Kalish, 1986; composer incidental music Off-Broadway prodn. Scuba Duba, 1967; mem. Open Theater (The Serpent, Mutation Show) 1968-72; music for Pinkville, Am. Place Theater, 1970, The Kid, 1972, Sigmunds Freude, Bremen Stadt Theater, 1975, Weewis for Joffrey Ballet, 1971; film The Crazy American Girl, Paris, 1975, Desperado City, 1980 (winner Camera d'Or at Cannes 1981), Frohes Fest (winner 1st Prize Mannheim Festival), The Open Window Trio; solo recitals, albums for Vanguard, Three Views; commd. and recorded (as mem.) Louisville Orch., 1969; music and lyrics Oh! Calcutta!, 1969; new score The Caucasian Chalk Circle, Arena Theater, Washington, 1978, musical Back Country, 1978, Shylock, 1978, My Mother's Courage, 1979, Untergang der Titanic, 1980, Hamlet, 1980; dir. We Each Got a Reason for Being Here Tonight, Vienna Festival, 1981, Der Voyeur; actor Berlin Festival, 1982, Jubiläum for Bochum Schauspielhaus, 1983, opera Doctor Faustus Lights the Lights (G. Stein), Cologne Schauspielhaus, 1983, Peepshow (G. Tabori), Bochum, 1984, The Beggars Opera, Renaissance Theater, Berlin, 1984, Claire, Bochum, 1985, U Ber Die Städte, Burg Theater, Vienna, 1986, Mein Kampf (G. Tabori) Burg Theater, 1987; co-dir. Der Tod Dankt Ab, 1987, Sigmunds Freude, 1987; Pour La Seconde Fois (J.C. Carrière) actor/composer-Der Kreis, Vienna, 1988; musical Bahn Frei! for Hochschule der Künste, Berlin, 1989, Lear's Schatten, Bregenz Festival, 1989, Othello-Burg Theater, 1990, Miami Lights-Coconut Grove Playhouse, 1990, Faust-Bad Hersfeld Festspiele, 1990, Endangered Species, 1990, BAM Nextwave Fest, Babylon Blues, 1991, Goldberg Variationen at Burg Theater, Vienna, 1991, Miami Lights at Theater Works, Palo Alto, Calif., 1991, Kasimir and Karoline, Schloss Park Theater, Berlin, 1991, Abendwind and Mrozek, Schlosspark Theater, Berlin, 1992, Der Grossinquisitor (Tabori), Seville, 1992, Munich Residenz Theater, Potsdam; condr. Cividale Mittelfest, 1992, Pottsdam, 1993, Requiem Fur Einen Spion (Tabori) Burg Theatre, 1993, Memini Mortuarum, Eastman and Potsdam, 1993, Brandenburg Philharmonic, 1993, Die 25te Stunde (Tabori), Burg Theater, 1994; recitals with Hanna Schygulla, Hebbel Theater, Berlin, 1994., Delirium (Enzensberger) Thalia Theatre, Hamburg, 1994, Die Massenmörderin (Tabori) Akademie Theater, Vienna, 1995, Ballade von Wiener Schnitzel (Tabori), 1996, Liebster Vater, Chamber Opera after Kafka, Stadttheatre, Bremen. Address: 60 Miller Hill Rd Hopewell Junction NY 12533-6829

WALDERA, WAYNE EUGENE, crisis management specialist; b. Cayuga, N.D., Mar. 23, 1930; s. Bernard Cyril and Eleanor Nee (Kugler) W.; m. Eva Jenzene Personius, Jan. 13, 1958; children: Anthony, Lori, Mia, Shauna. BSBA, N.D. State U., 1952. With Gamble-Skogmo, 1954-88; pres. Gamble div. Gamble-Skogmo, Mpls., 1972-88; pres., CEO Retail Resource Co., Mpls., 1988-89; pres., CEO Amdura Corp., Denver, 1989-92, also bd. dirs.; chmn. Sullivan Waldera, Inc., Mpls., 1992-93; prin., CEO Waldera & Co. Inc., Mpls., 1993—. 1st lt. USAF, 1952-54. Home: 12125 62nd St Waconia MN 55387-9411 Office: Waldera & Co Inc 15500 Wayzata Blvd Ste 604-208 Wayzata MN 55391-1435

WALDFOGEL, MORTON SUMNER, prefabricated housing/plywood company executive; b. Somerville, Mass., Nov. 5, 1922; s. Benjamin and Gertrude (Levins) W.; m. Lillian Thelma Gouse, June 16, 1949; children: Peter Douglas, Jane Leslie. AB, Harvard U., 1944; MBA, Boston U., 1948. Assoc. prof. math. econs. Boston U., 1947-48; mgr. Roddis Plywood Co., Cambridge, Mass., 1948-51; partner East Coast Mill Sales, 1951—; chmn. bd., chief exec. officer Allied Industries Inc., Charlestown, Mass., 1954-89; chmn., chief exec. officer Gilwal Industries, Charlestown, Mass., 1982—; pres. United Internat. Inc., Boston, 1990—. Served with USNR, 1942-47. Decorated Letter of Commendation. Jewish. Home: 16 Brown Rd Swampscott MA 01907-1608 Office: Gilwal Industries PO Box 580 Charlestown MA 02129-0001

WALDHAUSEN, JOHN ANTON, surgeon, educator; b. N.Y.C., May 22, 1929; s. Max. H. and Agnes H. (Stettner) W.; m. Marian Trescher, June 4, 1957; children: John H., Robert Rodney, Anthony Gordon Scarlett. B.S. magna cum laude, Coll. Great Falls, 1950; M.D., St. Louis U., 1954. Diplomate Am. Bd. Surgery (bd. dirs. 1985-88), Am. Bd. Thoracic Surgery (bd. dirs. 1989—). Intern Johns Hopkins Hosp., 1954-55, resident, 1955-57; clin. asst. Nat. Heart and Lung Inst., NIH, 1957-59; resident Hosp. U. Pa., 1959, Ind. U. Med. Center, 1960-62; practice medicine specializing in cardiothoracic surgery Indpls., 1962-66, Phila., 1966-70; mem. staff Milton S. Hershey (Pa.) Med. Ctr., 1969—, Milton S. Hershey Med. Ctr., Hershey, Pa., 1969—; from instr. to asst. prof. Ind. U. Med. Ctr., 1962-66; assoc. prof. surgery U. Pa., Phila., 1966-70; prof. surgery Pa. State U. Coll. Medicine/

Milton S. Hershey Med. Ctr., Hershey, 1966-83, 94—, J.W. Oswald prof., 1983-94, assoc. dean and dir. Univ. Physicians, 1993—, sr. mem. grad. faculty, 1970—, chmn. dept. surgery, 1969-94, vice chmn. med. policy bd., 1971-72, interim provost, dean, 1972-73, assoc. dean health care, 1973-75. Mem. editl. bd. Jour. Cardiovascular Surgery, 1985-93, Jour. Pediatric Surgery, 1972-78, Jour. Thoracic and Cardiovascular Surgery, 1982, editor, 1994; cons. editor Archives of Surgery, 1972-74; contbr. chpts. to books and articles to med. jours. Served with USPHS, 1957-59. Recipient Career Devel. award USPHS, 1964. Mem. AMA, AAAS, ACS (chpt. pres. 1974-75, gov. 1979-85, chmn. adv. coun. Conn. surgery 1992—), Am. Acad. Pediatrics, Am. Assn. Surgery of Trauma, Am. Coll. Cardiology (sec. 1981-82, trustee 1984-89, mem. editorial bd. jour. 1983, assoc. editor 1986-89), Am. Fedn. Clin. Rsch., Am. Heart Assn., Am. Physiol. Soc., Am. Soc. Artificial Internal Organs, Am. Assn. Thoracic Surgery (1st v.p. 1990-91, pres., 1991-92), Am. Surg. Assn. (1st v.p. 1984-85), Central Surg. Assn., Internat. Cardiovascular Soc. (chpt. recorder 1969-74), Pa. Assn. Thoracic Surgery (pres. 1977-78), Thoracic Surgery Dirs. Assn. (pres. 1977-79), Societe Internationale de Chirurgie (membership chmn. 1987-92, treas. 1992-94), Soc. Clin. Surgery (treas. 1971-80, v.p. 1981-82, Pres. 1982-83), Soc. Surg. Chairmen, Soc. Thoracic Surgeons, Soc. Univ. Surgeons, Soc. Vascular Surgery, So. Surg. Assn., Sigma Xi, Alpha Omega Alpha. Home: RR 1 Box 158G Annville PA 17003-9704 Office: Pa State U Coll Med MS Hershey Med Ctr PO Box 850 Hershey PA 17033-0850

WALDHOF, SHARKA EVA, lawyer; b. Prague, Czech Republic, Aug. 8, 1962; came to U.S., 1966; d. Martin and Libuse Kral; m. Kenneth James Waldhof; children: Kevin, Brian. BA, L.I.U., 1985; JD, St. John's U., 1988. Bar: N.Y. 1989, Conn. 1989. Atty. European Am. Bank, Uniondale, N.Y., 1989-90, asst. counsel, 1990-92, sr. atty., 1992—; bd. dirs. First Class at EAB, Inc., Uniondale. Active First Class Child Care Parent Adv. Coun., Uniondale, 1992—. Mem. ABA, N.Y. State Bar Assn., Nassau County Bar Assn. Avocations: skiing, swimming. Office: European Am Bank 1 EAB Plz Uniondale NY 11555-0001

WALDMAN, ANNE LESLEY, poet, performer, editor, publisher, educational administrator; b. Millville, N.J., Apr. 2, 1945; d. John Marvin and Frances (Le Fevre) W.; m. Reed Eyre Bye; 1 son, Ambrose. B.A., Bennington Coll., 1966. Dir. The Poetry Project, St. Marks Ch. In-the-Bowery, N.Y.C., 1968-78; co-dir. Jack Kerouac Sch. of Disembodied Poetics at Naropa Inst., Boulder, Colo., 1974—; adj. faculty Inst. Am. Indian Arts, Santa Fe; bd. dirs. Com. for Internat. Poetry, Eye and Ear Theatre, N.Y.C.; poet-in-residence with Bob Dylan's Rolling Thunder Rev. Author: (poetry) On the Wing, 1968, O My Life, 1969, Baby Breakdown, 1970, Giant Night, 1970, No Hassles, 1971, Life Notes, 1973, Fast Speaking Woman, 1975, Journals and Dreams, 1976, Shaman, 1977, Countries, 1980, Cabin, 1981, First Baby Poems, 1982, Makeup on Empty Space, 1983, Invention, 1986, Skin Meat Bones, 1986, The Romance Thing, 1987, Blue Mosque, 1988, Helping the Dreamer: New and Selected Poems, 1989, Not a Male Pseudonym, 1990, Lokapala, 1991, Troubairitz, 1993, Iovis: All is Full of Jove, 1993, Kill or Cure, 1994; editor: Nice To See You: Homage to Ted Berrigan, 1991, The Beat Book, 1996, (anthologies) The World Anthology, 1969, Another World, 1972, Talking Poetics From Naropa Institute vol. 1, 1978, vol. 2, 1979, Out of This World, 1991, (with Andrew Schelling) Disembodied Poetics: Annals of the Jack Kerowac School, 1994; translator (with Andrew Schelling) Sons & Daughters of the Buddha, 1996; publisher: anthologies Angel Hair Books, N.Y.C., Full Ct. Press, N.Y.C.; recordings: The Dial-a-Poem Poets Disconnected, Anne Waldman/John Giorno, Fast Speaking Woman, The Nova Convention, Big Ego, Uh-oh Plutonium!, 1982, Crack in My World, 1986, Assorted Singles, 1990; performance videos include Eyes in All Heads, 1990, Live at Naropa, 1991, Battle of the Bards, 1991; featured on nat. pub. radio show All Things Considered, also featured in the poetry documentary Poetry In Motion. Dir. summer writing program Naropa; organizer Surrealist, Objectivist, Feminist, Pan Am. Ecology, Performance Confs., and The Robert Creeley Symposium. Recipient Dylan Thomas Meml. award New Sch., N.Y.C., 1967, Blue Ribbon Am. Film Festival, Nat. Literary Anthology award, 1970; named Heavyweight Champion Poet, 1989, 90; Cultural Artists Program grantee, 1976-77; Nat. Endowment for Arts grantee, 1979-80. Mem. PEN Club, Amnesty Internat. Office: care Naropa Inst 2130 Arapahoe Ave Boulder CO 80302-6602

WALDMAN, DIANE, museum deputy director; b. N.Y.C., Feb. 24, 1936; m. Paul Waldman, 1957. B.F.A., Hunter Coll., 1956; M.A., Inst. Fine Arts, NYU, 1965, postgrad. With Solomon R. Guggenheim Mus., N.Y.C., 1965—, asst. curator, 1967-69, assoc. curator, 1969-71, curator exhbns., 1971-81, dir. exhbns., 1981-82, dep. dir., sr. curator, 1982—; Mem. adv. bd. Skowhegan Sch. Painting and Sculpture. Author: (monographs) Roy Lichtenstein, 1971, 93, Mark Rothko, 1994; (books) Ellsworth Kelly: Drawings, Collages and Prints, 1971, Joseph Cornell, 1977, Anthony Caro, 1982, Willem de Kooning, 1988, Collage, Assemblage and the Found Object in Twentieth-Century Art, 1992; contbr. articles to profl. jours. Am. commr. to Biennale Sydney, 1988; mem. adv. bd. Ctr. Internat. Am. Relations, Am. Soc.; mem. com. internat. Musee d'Art Moderne; mem. N.Y. State Gov.'s Task Force on Asbestos, 1987—. Mem. Am. Assn. Mus. (mus. accreditation com.), Internat. Council Mus., Internat. Com. for Mus. and Collections Modern Art, Internat. Adv. Bd. ROSC, Ireland, Louis Comfort Tiffany Found. (trustee), Am. Soc. Safety Engrs. Office: Solomon R Guggenheim Mus 1071 5th Ave New York NY 10128-0112

WALDMAN, JAY CARL, judge; b. Pitts., Nov. 16, 1944; s. Milton and Dorothy (Florence) W.; m. Roberta Tex Landy, Aug. 28, 1969. B.S., U. Wis., 1966; J.D., U. Pa., 1969. Bar: Pa. 1970, D.C. 1976, U.S. Supreme Ct. 1976. Assoc., Rose, Schmidt, Dixon & Hasley, Pitts., 1970-71; asst. U.S. atty. western dist. Pa., Pitts., 1971-75; dep. asst. U.S. Atty. Gen., Washington, 1975-77; counsel Gov. of Pa., Harrisburg, 1978-86; sr. ptnr., Dilworth, Paxson, Kalish & Kauffman, Phila., 1986-88; judge U.S. Dist. Ct. (ea. dist.) Pa., 1988—. Dir. Thornburgh for Gov. campaign., Pa., 1977-78; commr. Pa. Convention Ctr. Authority, 1986-88. Fellow Am. Bar Found.; mem. ABA, Fed. Bar Assn., Union League Phila. Republican. Office: US Dist Ct Pa 9613 US Courthouse 601 Market St Philadelphia PA 19106-1510

WALDMAN, PAUL, artist; b. Erie, Pa., 1936. Student, Bklyn. Mus. Art Sch., 1955, Pratt Inst., 1956. Instr. painting Sch. Visual Arts, N.Y.C., 1966—; vis. prof. U. Calif., Davis, 1966; vis. artist Ohio State U., 1966; artists-in-residence, The Clamworks Studio Workshop, N.Y., 1982; instr. painting Sch. Visual Arts, N.Y.C., 1966—, Bklyn. Mus. Art Sch., N.Y., 1966-67, N.Y. C.C., 1963-64, Greenwich (Conn.) Art Ctr., 1963. One man shows include Allan Stone Gallery, N.Y., 1963, 65, Albright Gallery of Art, Hax Art Ctr., St. Joseph, Mo., 1966, Leo Castelli Gallery, N.Y.C., 1973, 75, 78, 81, 84, 88, 91, Blum-Helman Gallery, N.Y.C., 1978, Kunsthalle Tranegarden, Copenhagen, 1981, Norblyllands Kunstmuseum, Aalborg, Denmark, 1981, Castelli Graphics, N.Y.C., 1984, Fariden Cadot Gallery, Paris, 1987, 88, 91, Phyllis Kind Gallery, Chgo., 1988, Leo Castelli Gallery, N.Y.C., 1991; exhibited in group shows include Allan Stone Gallery, 1961, Louis Alexander Gallery, N.Y.C., 1962, Gallery of Modern Art, Washingotn, 1963, 64, Wadworth Atheneum, Hartford, Conn., 1964, Rutgers U., New Brunswick, N.J., 1964, Knoedler Gallery, 1965, Visual Arts Gallery, The Sch. of Visual Arts, N.Y.C., 1965, 68, 83, Art Mus., U. of Ind., Bloomington, 1965, Richard Feigen Gallery, Chgo., 1965, Ark. Arts Ctr., Little Rock, 1966, Ithaca Coll. Mus. Art, N.Y., 1967, Smithsonian Inst., 1967-68, Kansas City Art Inst., Mo., 1967, Newark Mus., 1968, Leo Castelli Gallery, 1973, 75, 78, 81, 84, 88, Castelli Graphics, 1976, 82, 84, Phila. Coll. Art., 1976, Guggenheim Mus., 1977, 79, 84, La Jolla Mus. Art, 1982, Jan van Eyck Acad., Maastricht, Germany, 1985, Cooper-Hewitt Mus., N.Y.C., 1987, Williams Coll. Mus. Art, 1990, Thread Waxing Space, 1993, Lennon Weinberg, N.Y.C., 1993; represented in permanent collections Mus. Modern Art, Newark Mus., Bklyn. Mus., L.A. County Mus. Art, NYU, Hirshhorn Mus. and Sculpture Garden, Smithsonian Inst., Des Moines Mus., Guggenheim Mus., Mus. Fine Arts, Houston, Balt. Mus. Art, Carnegie Mus., Dallas Mus. Fine Arts, DeCordova Mus., Norbyllands Kunstmuseum, Aalborg, Denmark, Denver Art Mus., Allen Meml. Art Mus., Oberlin Coll., Dartmouth Coll., Solomon R. Guggenheim Mus., Russell Sage Collection, Storm King Art Ctr., Rose Art Mus., Brandeis U., Smithsonian Inst., Palace Legion Honor Achenbach Found., MIT, L.A. County Mus. Art, U. Mass., Fairleigh Dickinson U., others. Grantee Ford Found., 1965.

WALDMANN, THOMAS ALEXANDER, medical research scientist, physician; b. N.Y.C., Sept. 21, 1930; s. Charles Elizabeth (Sipos) W.; m. Katharine Emory Spreng, Mar. 29, 1958; children—Richard Allen, Robert James, Carol Ann. A.B., U. Chgo., 1951; M.D., Harvard U., 1955; PhD (hon.), U. Med. Sch., Debrecin, Hungary, 1991. Diplomate Am. Bd. Allergy and Immunology. Intern Mass. Gen. Hosp., Boston, 1955-56; clin. assoc. Nat. Cancer Inst. NIH, Bethesda, Md., 1956-58, sr. investigator, 1958-68, head immunophysiology sect., 1968-73, chief metabolism br., 1971—; cons. WHO, 1975, 78; bd. dirs., v.p. Found. for Advanced Edn. in Scis., Bethesda, 1980—, treas., 1988-90, v.p., 1990-92; William Dameshek vis. prof. U. Calif., Irvine, 1984; mem. med. adv. bd. Howard Hughes Med. Inst., 1987-93; vis. com. mem. Harvard Med. Sch., Boston, 1988-94; mem. sci. adv. com., chmn. Mass. Gen. Hosp., 1992-96; cons. HealthCare Investment Corp., Edison, N.J., 1986—. Author: Plasma Protein Metabolism, 1970; contbr. over 570 articles to profl. jours. With USPHS, 1956-58, 59-63, 75-94. Recipient Henry M. Stratton medal Am. Hemotology Soc., 1977; named Man of Yr. Am. Leukemia Soc., 1980; recipient G. Burroughs Mider award NIH, 1980; Disting. Service medal Dept. Health and Human Services, 1983. Fellow Am. Acad. Allergy (Bela Schick award 1974, John M. Shelton award 1984, Lila Gruber prize 1986, Simon Shubitz prize 1987, CIBA-GEIGY Drew award 1987, Milken Family Med. Found. Disting. Basic Scientist prize, Artois Latour Internat. Rsch. prize 1991, Bristol-Myers Cancer prize 1992); mem. NAS (chmn. 1985—), Am. Acad. Arts and Scis., Inst. Medicine, Nat. Acad. Scis., Assn. Am. Physicians, Am. Soc. Clin. Investigation (mem. editorial bd. 1978-80, 83-88), Clin. Immunology Soc. (pres. 1988). Achievements include the defining of structure of multisubunit IL-2 receptor; identifying novel cytokine IL-15; introduction of different forms of IL-2R-directed therapy using alpha- and beta-emitting radionuclide chelate versions of humanized monoclonal antibodies for treatment of cancer; introduction of analysis of immunoglobulin gene rearrangements to define clonality and classifying human lymphoid neoplasia; discovered intestinal lymphagesctasia and allergic gastroenteropathy. Office: Nat Inst Health 9000 Rockville Pike Bethesda MD 20892-0001

WALDMEIR, PETER NIELSEN, journalist; b. Detroit, Jan. 16, 1931; s. Joseph John and Helen Sarah (Nielsen) W.; m. Marilyn C. Choma; children—Peter William, Patti Ann, Lindsey Marilyn, Christopher Norman. Student, Wayne State U., 1949-58. With Detroit News, 1949—, sports columnist, 1962-72, gen. columnist, 1972—. Trustee, Cleary Coll., Ypsilanti, Mich., 1985—; pres. Old Newsboys Goodfellow Fund, Detroit, 1988. Served with USMC, 1951-53. Recipient Headliners award Nat. Headliners Club, 1971; named Mich. Sports Writer of Yr., Nat. Sportscasters and Sportswriters, 1967, 69, 71; Heart award Variety Club Internat., 1985. Mem. Sigma Delta Chi. Roman Catholic. Office: Detroit News 615 W Lafayette Blvd Detroit MI 48226-3124

WALDMEIR, PETER WILLIAM, lawyer; b. Bethlehem, Pa., Sept. 18, 1953; s. Pete and Dorothy Grace (Bastianelli) W.; m. Renee Zamboni, Feb. 28, 1986; children: Sara Grace, Charlotte. BA summa cum laude, U. Mich., 1975; JD, George Washington U., 1978. Bar: D.C. 1979, Mich. 1987, U.S. Dist. Ct. (ea. dist.) Mich., U.S. Ct. Appeals (6th cir.). Law clk. President's Commn. on Rev. Nat. Policy toward Gambling, Washington, 1975-76, Duncan, Allen & Mitchell, Washington, 1976-77, Vinson & Elkins, Washington, 1977-78; jud. clk. to chief judge 6th Jud. Ct., Detroit, 1977; jud. clk. to assoc. justice Mich. Supreme Ct., Detroit, 1978-80; trial atty. civil div. fed. programs br. U.S. Dept. Justice, Washington, 1980-84; assoc. Miller, Canfield, Paddock and Stone, Detroit, 1984-87, sr. ptnr., 1987—; bd. dirs. Grosse Point Cable; instr. legal rsch. writing Detroit Coll. Law, 1978-80. Councilman-elect Grosse Pointe City Coun., 1989-93. Mem. ABA, Mich. Bar Assn., D.C. Bar Assn., Fed. Bar Assn., Goodfellows. Roman Catholic. Office: Miller Canfield Paddock & Stone 150 W Jefferson Ave Ste 2500 Detroit MI 48226-4415*

WALDO, BURTON CORLETT, lawyer; b. Seattle, Aug. 11, 1920; s. William Earl and Ruth Ernestine (Corlett) W.; m. Margaret Jane Hoar, Aug. 24, 1946; children: James Chandler, Bruce Corlett. BA, U. Wash., 1941, JD, 1948. Bar: Wash. 1949. Assoc. Vedova, Horswill & Yeomans, Seattle, 1949-50, Kahin, Carmody & Horswill, Seattle, 1950-54; ptnr. Keller Rohrback & predecessor firms, Seattle, 1954-86; mng. ptnr. Keller Rohrback & predecessor firms, 1978-83, sr. ptnr., 1983-86, of counsel, 1986—. Mem. Seattle Bd. Theater Suprs., 1958-61, Mcpl. League of Seattle/King County. Capt. U.S. Army, 1942-46, ETO. Mem. ABA, Internat. Assn. Def. Counsel, Fedn. Ins. and Corp. Counsel, Wash. Bar Assn., Wash. Def. Trial Lawyers Assn., Seattle-King County Bar Assn. (trustee 1965-68), Fedn. Fly Fishers (life), S.R., Puget Sound Civil War Roundtable, Rainier Club, Wash. Athletic Club, The Steamboaters, Flyfishers Club Oreg., Hope Island King-50 Club, Delta Tau Delta, Phi Delta Phi, Alpha Kappa Psi. Avocation: fly fishing.

WALDO, CATHERINE RUTH, private school educator; b. Erie, Pa., Nov. 5, 1946; d. James Allen and Ruth Catherine (Rubner) Babcock; m. James Robert Waldo, June, 1968; children; Robert, Ruth Ann. BA in History magna cum laude, Duke U., 1968. Cert. tchr., Okla. Tchr. Shawnee (Okla.) Pub. Schs., 1968-70; tchr., team leader Norman (Okla.) Pub. Schs., 1971-73; tchr., social studies chmn. Westminster Sch., Oklahoma City, Okla., 1990—. Mem. edn. commn. Westminster Presbyn. Ch., Oklahoma City, 1980-93, deacon, 1981-84, coord. early childhood programs, 1988-90, elder, 1990-93; mem. coun. Ward 2 City of Nichols Hills, Okla., 1989-93; bd. dirs. Assn. Ctrl. Okla. Govts., Oklahoma City, 1989-93; vol., planning com. World Neighbors. Recipient Colonial Williamsburg Summer Inst., Okla. Found. for Excellence, 1994. Mem. Nat. Coun. Tchrs. English, Nat. Coun. for Social Studies, Okla. Coun. for Social Studies, Okla. Coun. Tchrs. English. Presbyterian. Avocations: reading, hiking, Odyssey of the Mind, local political issues. Home: 1100 Tedford Way Oklahoma City OK 73116-6007 Office: Westminster Sch 612 NW 44th St Oklahoma City OK 73118-6627

WALDO, (CLIFFORD) DWIGHT, political science educator; b. DeWitt, Nebr., Sept. 28, 1913; s. Cliff Ford and Grace Gertrude (Lindley) W.; m. Gwendolyn Payne, Sept. 17, 1937; children: Mary Grace, Martha Gwen, Margret Ann. B.A., Nebr. State Tchrs. Coll., Peru, 1935; M.A., U. Nebr., 1937; Ph.D., Yale U., 1942. Instr. polit. sci. Yale U., 1941-42; price analyst OPA, 1942-44; adminstrv. analyst Exec. Office Pres., 1944-46; mem. faculty U. Calif. at Berkeley, 1946-67, prof. polit. sci., 1953-67, dir. Inst. Govt. Studies, 1958-67; Albert Schweitzer prof. humanities Syracuse U., 1967-79, emeritus prof., 1979—; Carl Hatch prof. law and pub. adminstrn. U. N.Mex., 1984-85; vis. disting. prof. Fla. Internat. U., 1989; resident fellow Woodrow Wilson Internat. Center for Scholars, Smithsonian Instn., Washington, 1979-81. Author: The Administrative State, 1948, The Study of Public Administration, 1955, Perspectives on Administration, 1956, Political Science in the U.S.A, 1956; Editor: Public Administration in a Time of Turbulence, 1972, others; editor-in-chief: Pub. Adminstrn. Rev, 1966-77. Mem. Am. Polit. Sci. Assn. (v.p. 1961-62), Am. Soc. Pub. Adminstrn., (v.p. 1985-86), Internat. City Mgmt. Assn. (hon. life), Nat. Assn. Schs. Pub. Affairs and Adminstrn. (v.p. 1976-77, pres. 1977-78), Nat. Acad. Pub. Adminstrn. Home: Apt 1411W 3713 S George Mason Dr Falls Church VA 22041-3738

WALDO, KATITA, ballet dancer; b. Madrid. Student, Escuela de Danza Classica, San Francisco Ballet Sch. Apprentice San Francisco Ballet, 1987-88, mem. Corps de Ballet, 1988-90, soloist, 1990-94, prin. dancer, 1994—; tchr. summer programs Ithaca (N.Y.) Ballet, Modesto Ballet, 1993. Appeared in ballets The Sleeping Beauty, Swan Lake, Concerto in d: Poulenc, Ballet d'Isoline, Guiliani: Variations on a Theme, Beads of Memory, Aurora Polaris, Handel- a Celebration, Menuetto, Bugaku, The Four Temperaments, Who Cares?, Theme and Variations, Stars and Stripes, Agon, Ballo della Regina, Serenade, La Pavane Rouge, Calcium Light Night, The Concert, Interplay, Rodin, Dark Elegies, Tagore, Nutcracker, Romeo and Juliet, La Sylphide, In the middle, somewhat elevated, Pulcinella, In Perpetuum, Job, The Sons of Horus, The "Wanderer" Fantasy, Dreams of Harmony, The Comfort Zone, Scarlatti Portfolio, Vivaldi Concerto Grosso, Variations de Ballet, La Fill mal gardee. Office: San Francisco Ballet 455 Franklin St San Francisco CA 94102-4438

WALDO, ROBERT LELAND, retired insurance company executive; b. Pittsville, Wis., Sept. 1, 1923; s. Elmer Harley and Edith Viola (Senter) W.; m. Elaine Anne Jossie, June 4, 1947; children: Daniel Robert, Thomas Parker, Susan Jeanne. BA, U. Wis., 1949, JD, 1951. Assoc. atty. Foley & Lardner, Milw., 1951-59; asst. sec., asst. gen. counsel Wis. Gas Co., Milw., 1959-69; v.p., gen. counsel Verex Corp. and Subss., Madison, Wis., 1969-72; exec. v.p., sec. Verex Corp. and subs., Madison, Wis., 1972-78, pres., chief operating officer, 1978-82, pres., chief exec. officer, 1982-85, chmn., chief exec. officer, 1985-86. Served as sgt. U.S. Army, 1943-46, ETO. Mem. Wis. Bar Assn., Dane County Bar Assn., Mortgage Ins. Co.'s Am. (pres. 1980-82), Maple Bluff Country Club. Republican. Methodist. Avocations: travel, golf. Home: 818 Charing Cross Rd Madison WI 53704-6010

WALDRON, ELLIS LEIGH, retired political science educator; b. Denver, Feb. 21, 1915; s. Grover C. and Maud M. (Dolbeer) W.; m. Phyllis Schwoegler, May 16, 1941; 1 child, Jean Madelene. BA, Ohio State U., 1936; MA, U. Wis., 1939, PhD, 1952; student, Duke, 1939-40. Staff polit. corr. U.P., Columbus, Ohio, 1941-44; instr. polit. sci. extension div. U. Wis., 1946-49, fellow polit. sci., 1949-50; faculty dept. polit. sci. U. Mont., 1950—, prof. polit. sci., 1957—; dean U. Mont. (Grad. Sch.), 1957-61, emeritus, 1980—; fellow law and polit. sci. Harvard Law Sch., 1963-64. Author: Montana Legislators 1864-1979: Profiles and Biographical Directory, Mont. Politics Since 1864, An Atlas of Elections, 1958; (with Paul B. Wilson) Atlas of Montana Elections 1889-1976, 1978, Social and Economic Dimensions of Popular Vote on 110 State Ballot Issues in Montana, 1926-86, 1990-91. Mem. Mont. Constl. Conv. Commn., 1971-72. Served with AUS, 1944-46. Mem. Am. Polit. Sci. Assn. (coun. 1969-71), Phi Beta Kappa, Kappa Sigma, Phi Kappa Phi. Home: 53 Oak Creek Trl Madison WI 53717-1509

WALDRON, JEREMY JAMES, law educator; b. Invercargill, Southland, New Zealand, Oct. 13, 1953; s. Francis Herbert and Joyce Annette (Ainge) W.; m. Helen McGimpsey, Jan. 26, 1974 (div. Oct. 1989); 1 child, Samuel James. BA with honors, U. Otago, New Zealand, 1974, LLB with honors, 1978; DPhil, Oxford U., 1986. Bar: New Zealand 1978. Asst. lectr. philosophy U. Otago, 1975-78; fellow in polit. theory Lincoln Coll., Oxford, Eng., 1980-82; lectr. in polit. theory U. Edinburgh, Scotland, 1982-87; prof. law U. Calif., Berkeley, 1987—. Editor: collection of essays Theories of Rights, 1984, Nonsense Upon Stilts, 1987; author: (textbook) The Law, 1990, (monograph) The Right to Private Property, 1988; contbr. articles to profl. jours. Avocations: romance, music, travel. Home: 1061 Keith Ave Berkeley CA 94708-1604 Office: U Calif Sch Law Boalt Hall Berkeley CA 94720*

WALDRON, KENNETH JOHN, mechanical engineering educator, researcher; b. Sydney, NSW, Australia, Feb. 11, 1943; came to U.S., 1965; s. Edward Walter and Maurine Florence (Barrett) W.; m. Manjula Bhushan, July 3, 1968; children: Andrew, Lalitha, Paul. BEngring., U. Sydney, 1964, M Engring. Sci., 1965; PhD, Stanford U., 1969. Registered profl. engr., Tex. Acting asst. prof. Stanford (Calif.) U., 1968-69; lectr., sr. lectr. U. NSW, Sydney, 1969-74; assoc. prof. U. Houston, 1974-79; assoc. prof. mech. engring. Ohio State U., Columbus, 1979-81, prof., 1981—, Nordholt prof., 1984—, chmn. dept. mech. engring., 1993—. Co-author: Machines That Walk, 1988; editor: Advanced Robotics, 1989; contbr. over 215 articles to profl. jours. and conf. procs. Recipient, Machine Ądesign award Am. Soc. of Mechanical Enginners, 1994. Fellow ASME (tech. editor Trans. Jour. Mech. Design 1988-92, Leonardo da Vinci award 1988, Mechanisms award 1990, Machine Design award 1994); mem. Soc. Automotive Engrs. (Ralph R. Teetor award 1977), Am. Soc. for Engring. Edn. Achievements include work on adaptive suspension vehicle project. Office: Ohio State U 206 W 18th Ave Columbus OH 43210-1189

WALDRON, ROBERT LEROY, II, physician; b. Carbondale, Ill., Feb. 6, 1936; s. Robert Leroy and Violet Mae (Thompson) W.; m. Sandra Sellers; children: Richard, Robert Leroy III, Ryan, Burton Johnson. AB, Princeton U., 1958; MD, Harvard U., 1962. Diplomate Am. Bd. Radiology; cert. added qualifications in neuroradiology. Intern, Mass. Gen. Hosp., Boston, 1962-63; resident in radiology Columbia-Presbyn. Med. Center, N.Y.C., 1965-68; instr. radiology Coll. Physicians and Surgeons, Columbia U. and spl. fellow in neuroradiology Neurol. Inst., N.Y.C., 1968-69; clin. asst. in radiology Harvard Med. Sch., asst. radiologist Mt. Auburn Hosp. and MIT, Cambridge, 1969-71; assoc. prof. clin. radiology Coll. Physicians and Surgeons, 1971-73; dir. radiology French Hosp. and French Med. Clinic, San Luis Obispo, 1973-80, v.p., dir., 1976-77; assoc. clin. prof. radiology Loma Linda U. Sch. Medicine, 1977-80; dir. radiology Richland Meml. Hosp., Columbia, S.C., 1980-90; chief radiology svcs. Richland Meml. Hosp., 1982-90, trustee, 1990—; prof. radiology U. S.C. Sch. Medicine, Columbia, 1985—; mng. ptnr. Richland Radiol. Assn., Columbia, 1988-90; founder Chilean N.Am. Hosp. Corp., 1989; pres. MedBill; Bd. dirs. Am. Cancer Soc., San Luis Obispo. With USPHS, 1963-65. Recipient grants James Picker Found., Am. Cancer Soc., NRC, Nat. Acad. Scis., Nat. Cancer Inst. Fellow Am. Coll. Radiology, Soc. Internat. Med. Sci. Cooperation; mem. AMA, Am. Roentgen Ray Soc., Radiol. Soc. N.Am., Am. Soc. Neuroradiology, Western Neuroradiol. Soc., Southeastern Neuroradiol. Soc., S.C. Med. Assn., San Luis Obispo County Med. Soc. (pres. 1979), Columbia Med. Soc., Sierra-Cascade Trauma Soc. (pres. 1983-84), S.C. Radiol. Soc. (pres. 1992-93). Republican. Methodist. Clubs: Ivy of Princeton; Wildewood, Capital City (Columbia). Contbr. articles to profl. jours. Home: 1420 Adger Rd Columbia SC 29205-1406 Office: 1814 Bull St Columbia SC 29201-2506

WALDROP, BERNARD KEITH, English educator; b. Emporia, Kans., Dec. 11, 1932; s. Arthur and Opal Irene (Mohler) W.; m. Rosmarie Sebald, Jan. 22, 1959. B.A., Kans. State Tchrs. Coll., Emporia, 1955; M.A., U. Mich., Ann Arbor, 1958, Ph.D., 1964. Mem. faculty Brown U., Providence, 1968, prof. English, 1980—; editor Burning Deck Press, Providence, 1961—. Author: (poems) A Windmill Near Calvary, 1968, The Garden of Effort, 1977, The Ruins of Providence, 1984, A Ceremony Somewhere Else, 1984, Selected Poems, 1990, Shipwreck in Haven, 1992, The Locality Principle, 1995; (prose) Hegel's Family, 1989, Light While There is Light, 1993. Served with U.S. Army, 1953-55. Mem. PEN Am. Ctr. Home: 71 Elmgrove Ave Providence RI 02906-4132 Office: Brown U English Dept 79 Waterman St Providence RI 02912-9079

WALDROP, FRANCIS NEIL, physician; b. Asheville, N.C., Oct. 5, 1926; s. Troy Lester and Emma Louise (Ballard) W.; m. Eleanor Dorothy Wickes, June 10, 1950; children—Mark Lester, Barbara Louise. A.B., U. Minn., 1946; M.D., George Washington U., 1950. Intern George Washington U. Hosp., Washington, 1950-51; resident St. Elizabeth's Hosp., Washington, 1951-54; med. officer St. Elizabeth's Hosp., 1951-71; dir. manpower and tng. programs NIMH, Rockville, Md., 1972-75; dep. adminstr. Alcohol, Drug Abuse and Mental Health Adminstrn., HEW, Rockville, 1975-79; ret., 1979; clin. prof. psychiatry George Washington U. Recipient Superior Service award HEW, 1962, Disting. Service award, 1964. Fellow Am. Psychiat. Assn. (Vestermark award 1980). Research, publs. in field. Home: 1775 Elton Rd Silver Spring MD 20903-1726

WALDROP, GIDEON WILLIAM, composer, conductor, former president music school; b. Haskell County, Tex., Sept. 2, 1919; s. Gideon William and Margaret (Pierson) W. MusB, Baylor U., 1940; Mus M, U. Rochester, 1941, PhD, 1952. Asso. prof. music Baylor U., Waco, Tex., 1946-51; condr. Waco-Baylor Symphony Orch., 1946-51; editor Rev. Recorded Music, N.Y.C., 1952-54, Musical Courier, N.Y.C., 1953-58; cons. div. arts and humanities Ford Found., N.Y.C., 1958-61; asst. to pres. Juilliard Sch. Music, N.Y.C., 1961-63, dean, 1963-86, acting pres., 1983-84; pres. Manhattan Sch. Music, N.Y.C., 1986-89; mem. adv. com. Toscanini Archives; cons. to Minister Edn., Israel, summers 1972-74, Portugal, summer 1979, Fundacion Isaac Albeniz, Madrid, Spain, 1989—. Condr. Shreveport Symphony, 1941-42; composer (symphony overture) Prelude and Fugue for Orchestra, chamber music, choral works and songs.; commd. by, San Antonio Symphony Soc., 1958, 63. Served to maj. USAAF, 1942-46, ETO. Decorated Bronze Star. Mem. ASCAP, Phi Beta Kappa, Phi Mu Alpha. Democrat. Clubs: Players, Bohemians, N.Y. Athletic, Century (N.Y.C.).

WALDROP, LINDA M., medical administrator; b. Jefferson County, Ala., Oct. 24, 1942; d. Luther Grady Jr. and Anna Katherine (Gray) McGill; m. Bennie Lee Waldrop Jr., Mar. 14, 1961; children: Tracy L., Terry L. AS, Jefferson State Jr. Coll., 1971; BSN, Samford U., 1985; MA, U. Ala., Birmingham, 1989. Head nurse open heart ICU Bapt. Med. Ctr.-Montclair, Birmingham, 1976-82, head nurse telemetry unit, 1985-87, head nurse med. unit, 1983-85, head nurse oncology unit, 1987-90, edn. coord.; internal auditor Bapt. Med. Ctr.-Montclair, 1991; dir. med.-surg. telemetry nursing Shelby Med. Ctr., Alabaster, Ala., 1991—, dir. gastroenterol. svcs., 1993—, dir. women's svcs., nursing internal auditor, 1993—. Mem. ANA (cert. nursing adminstrn.), AACN, Oncology Nursing Soc., Nat. Mgmt. Assn., Ala. Orgn. Nurse Execs., Birmingham Regional Orgn. Nurse Execs.

WALDROP, WILLIAM THOMAS, executive; b. Jackson, Tenn., Dec. 1, 1929; s. Homer Hampton and Nelle (Hundley) W.; m. Doris Ebersole, Nov. 8, 1957; children: Robert Buxton, John Winfield. BS, U.S. Mil. Acad., 1952; M of Theol. Studies, Gordon-Conwell Theol. Sem., 1974. Ordained to ministry, Bapt. Ch. Commd. 2d lt. USAF, 1952, advanced through grades to lt. col., retired, 1972; sr. pastor Grace Evang. Ch., Atlanta, 1975-85; min.-at-large Advancing Chs. in Mission Commitment, Atlanta, 1985-88; pres. ACMC, Inc., Carol Stream, Ill., 1988-95. Contbr. articles to profl. jours. Decorated Air medal, Disting. Flying Cross, Meriterious Svc. medal. Avocations: reading, hiking, bird-watching. Office: ACMC Inc 135 E St Charles Carol Stream IL 60188

WALDSTEIN, SHELDON SAUL, physician, educator; b. Chgo., June 23, 1924; s. Herman S. and Sophia (Klapper) W.; m. Jacqueline Sheila Denbo, Apr. 2, 1952; children: Sara Jean, Peter Denbo, David John. Student, Harvard U., 1941-43; M.D., Northwestern U., 1947. Diplomate: Am. Bd. Internal Medicine. Intern Cook County Hosp., 1947-48, resident in internal medicine, 1948-51; chief Northwestern Med. Service, 1954-62, exec. dir. dept. medicine, 1962-64, chmn. dept. medicine, 1964-69; exec. dir. North Suburban Assn. Health Resources, 1969-72; mem. faculty Northwestern U. Med. Sch., 1954-61, assoc. prof. medicine, 1961-66, prof. medicine, 1966—, assoc. dean health services, dir. Northwestern U. Med. Assos., 1974-77; exec. v.p. Nat. Ctr. for Advanced Med. Edn., Chgo., 1977-91; pres. Nat. Ctr. Advanced Med. Edn., Chgo., 1991—. Contbr. articles to med. jours. Trustee Nat. Ctr. Advanced Med. Edn., Chgo., 1961—. Served to capt. M.C., AUS, 1952-54. Fellow Am. Coll. Physicians, Am. Coll. Endocrinology; mem. AMA, Chgo. Med. Soc., Cen. Soc. Clin. Rsch., Endocrine Soc., Am. Assn. Clin. Endocrinology, Am. Fedn. Clin. Rsch., Chgo. Soc. Internal Medicine, Alpha Omega Alpha. Home: 813 Moseley Rd Highland Park IL 60035-4635 Office: 541 N Fairbanks Ct Chicago IL 60611-3319

WALEN, HARRY LEONARD, historian, lecturer, author; b. Winchester, Mass., June 26, 1915; s. Harry Leonard and Alice (Garland) W.; m. Elizabeth Rowe Benson, June 26, 1939; children: Harry Benson, Kimball Frederick, Robert Leonard. AB cum laude, Harvard U., 1937, AM, 1942. Tchr. Los Alamos (N.M.) Ranch Sch., 1937-42, head English dept., 1939-42; tchr. English Groton (Mass.) Sch., 1942-46; instr. English, faculty marshal Newton Jr. Coll., 1946-51; tchr. English and journalism Newton High Sch., Newtonville, Mass., 1946-51, adminstr., 1951-55; directing editor secondary sch. English textbooks Ginn and Co., Boston, 1955-61; prin. Needham (Mass.) High Sch., 1961-72, career and post secondary guidance counselor, 1972-79; Mem. Regional Interviewing Com. for Overseas Grants and Fellowships, 1961-84; mem. planning com. Task Force on High Sch. Graduation Requirements, Mass Dept. Edn., 1976-80. Author: (books) The Family Travel-Camper, 1955, (with E. Gordon and others) Types of Literature, American Literature, English Literature, 1964, The Memory Book of the New England Association of Teachers of English, 1981, The Sons of the American Revolution 1962-82: An Historical Anthology, 1984; (monographs) English Learning Environments, 1972, History of the Order of Founders and Patriots of America, 1982, Centennial History, 1996; co-author Alluring Rockport, rev. edit. 1986; editor The English Leaflet, 1947-54; cons. editor on career edn. New Voices Series, 1978; contbr. chpts., articles, poems to books, profl. jours. and periodicals. Alderman City of Newton, Mass., 1961-72; corp. mem. USS Mass. Meml. Com., Inc., 1972—, bd. dirs., 1984-91, honorary dir., 1995—; chmn. edn. com. N.E. Conf. NCCJ, 1972-82, mem. study mission to Israel, 1974; vice chmn. New Eng. Conf. on Quality of Life, Boston, 1973; mem. Newton Regional Adv. Manpower Planning Bd., 1973-77; pres. counseling svcs. YMCA, Greater Boston, 1976-7; chmn. Newton Highlands Bd. Christian Edn., 1974-75; pres. bd. trustees weekday ch. sch. 1st Congl. Ch., Rockport, Mass., ch. historian, 1982—; del. Mass. Conf. United Ch. Christ, 1989-96. John Hay fellow, 1965, Mass. Dept. Edn. Commonwealth fellow, 1971; recipient citation U.S. Commr. Edn., 1971, citation New Eng. Assn. Schs. and Colls., 1984, cert. of Appreciation, City of Newton, 1971, Service award, YMCA, 1978. Mem. Nat. Council Tchrs. English (assoc. chmn. nat. conv. 1965, chmn., co-founder Emeritus Assembly 1979-83, various other coms. and offices, Citation 1969), Nat. Assn. Secondary Sch. Prins., Headmasters Assn. (life), New Eng. Assn. Tchrs. English (life, past pres., chmn. ann. C. S. Thomas award com. 1975—, historian 1978—, Thomas award 1978), Mass. Secondary Sch. Prins. Assn. (diploma standards com. 1973-78, Bronze plaque 1974), Mass. Council Tchrs. English (co-founder), Mass. Schoolmasters Club (past pres., hon. life), Mensa, Friends of Jackson Homestead, Newton Hist. Soc. (life, past pres.), Los Alamos (N.Mex.) Hist. Soc. (life), Sandy Bay Hist. Soc. (pres. 1983-86), Essex County Geneal. Soc., Greater Boston Guidance Club (hon.), Nat. Gavel Soc., New Eng. Hist. and Geneal. Soc., SAR (pres. state 1979-81, nat. trustee 1981-83, historian gen. 1983-86, sec. Mus. Bd. 1982-88, Minuteman award 1985), Gen. Soc. Mayflower Descs. (mem. nat. exec. com. 1990-93), Mass. Soc. Mayflower Descs. (gov. 1985-88, dep. gov. gen. 1988-93), Pilgrim John Howland Soc. (pres. 1987—, led pilgrimage to Eng., 1989), Mass. Huguenot Soc. (pres. 1990-92, nat. del. 1983-92), Descs. Colonial Clergy, Soc. Colonial Wars, Navy League U.S. (life), Sons and Daus. of 1st Settlers of Newbury (pres. 1982-84), Piscataqua Pioneers (pres. 1990-91), Order of Crown of Charlemagne, Order Founders and Patriots (nat. treas. 1978-81, dep. gov. gen. 1981-84, exec. com. 1992—, councillor gen. Mass. 1984—, N.H., 1987-90, 93—, gov. 1992-95, councillor gen. 1993—), Boston Athenaeum, Harvard Club, Boston Authors Club (pres. 1995—), English Lunch Club (pres. 1975-82), Friday Evening Club (most 979-86), Sandy Bay Yacht Club, Masons (32d degree, 50-Yr. award). Home: Penzance Rd Rockport MA 01966

WALES, GWYNNE HUNTINGTON, lawyer; b. Evanston, Ill., Apr. 18, 1933; s. Robert Willett and Solace (Huntington) W.; m. Janet McCobb, Feb. 8, 1957; children—Thomas Gwynne, Catherine Anne, Louise Carrie. A.B., Princeton U., 1954; J.D., Harvard U., 1961. Bar: N.Y. 1962. Asso. White & Case, N.Y.C., 1961-69; partner White & Case, 1969—; resident partner White & Case, Brussels, 1969-75. Served with USN, 1954-58. Mem. ABA, N.Y. State Bar Assn., Am. Law Inst., Union Internat. des Avocats. Club: Round Hill (Greenwich, Conn.). Home: 16 Oakwood Ln Greenwich CT 06830-3909 Office: White & Case 1155 Ave Of The Americas New York NY 10036-2711

WALES, HAROLD WEBSTER, lawyer; b. Seattle, June 23, 1928; s. John Harold and Clara (Webster) W.; m. Dorothy C. Kotthoff, July 15, 1955; children—Elizabeth Marie, Mary Celine. B.C.S. cum laude, Seattle U., 1950; J.D., U. San Francisco, 1958. Bar: Calif. 1959, Ariz. 1959. Pvt. practice, Phoenix, 1959—; pres. Central Ariz. Estate Planning Council, 1964-65; lectr. Tax Inst., Ariz. State U., 1962, 64, Nat. Automobile Dealers Assn., 1975-76; lectr., income tax Scottsdale (Ariz.) Community Coll., 1971—. Pres. Cath. Social Svc., Phoenix, 1964; Ariz. chmn. Nat. Found. March of Dimes, 1969; bd. dirs. Camelback Hosp., 1984-90, ARC, Maricopa County, Cath. Family and Cmty. Svcs., 1960-86; mem. exec. com. Friends of Orphans, 1990. With USAF, 1950-54. Mem. ABA, Maricopa County bar assns., State Bar Calif., State Bar Ariz. (chmn. taxation sect. 1966-67), Am. Coll. Trust and Estate Counsel, Ariz. Acad., Order of Malta, We. Assn., Alpha Sigma Nu. Republican. Club: Serra of Phoenix (pres. 1964-65, 86-87). Lodge: Rotary of Scottsdale. Home: 3106 E Vermont Ave Phoenix AZ 85016-3717 Office: 3101 N Central Ave Ste 1500 Phoenix AZ 85012-2644

WALES, PATRICE, school system administrator; b. Washington, Sept. 9, 1935; d. Robert Corning and Bernadette Mary (Dyer) W. BA, Dunbarton Coll. of Holy Cross, 1957; MTS, Cath. U. Am., 1978; PhD, U. Md., 1993. Cert. tchr., supt., Md. Tchr. mid. sch. St. Marys, Laurel, Md., 1960-61; tchr. high sch. St. Vincent Pallotti High Sch., Laurel, Md., 1962-65; instr. nursing sch. St. Mary's Sch. Nursing, Huntington, W.Va., 1965-66; tchr. St. Vincent Pallotti High Sch., Laurel, 1967-76, adminstr., 1976—, chair sci. dept., 1962-80, dean students, 1976-87, sponsorship dir., 1988—; bd. dirs. St. Vincent Pallotti H.S., Laurel, 1988—; trustee St. Joseph's Hosp., Backhannon, W.Va., 1990—; dir. German Exch. Program, Laurel, Ahlen, Germany, 1976—. Senator Sisters Senate Archdiocese of Washington, 1993—. NSF grantee, 1967, 69, 71. Mem. ASCD, Nat. Cath. Edn. Assn. Roman Catholic. Avocations: walking, hiking, biking. Home: 404 8th St Laurel MD 20707-4032 Office: St Vincent Pallotti High Sch 113 8th St Laurel MD 20707-4025

WALES, ROSS ELLIOT, lawyer; b. Youngstown, Ohio, Oct. 17, 1947; s. Craig C. and Beverly (Bromley) W.; m. Juliana Fraser, Sept. 16, 1972; children: Dod Elliot, James Craig. AB, Princeton U., 1969; JD, U. Va., 1974. Bar: Ohio 1974, U.S. Dist. Ct. (so. dist.) Ohio 1974, U.S. Ct. Appeals (5th cir.) 1979. Assoc. Taft, Stettinius & Hollister, Cin., 1974-81, ptnr., 1981—; pres. U.S. Swimming, Inc., Colorado Springs, 1979-84, U.S. Aquatic Sports, Inc., Colorado Springs, 1984-88, 94—. Pres. Cin. Active to Support Edn., 1987-88; chmn. sch. tax levy campaign, Cin., 1987; trustee The Childrens Home Cin., 1987—, v.p., 1995—; bd. sec. Cin. State Tech. and C.C., 1995—. Mem. ABA, Ohio Bar Assn., Cin. Bar Assn., Internat. Swimming Fedn. of Lausanne, Switzerland (sec. 1988-92, v.p. 1992—). Presbyterian. Office: 1800 Star Bank Ctr 425 Walnut St Cincinnati OH 45202-3957

WALES, WALTER D., physicist, educator; b. Oneonta, N.Y., Aug. 2, 1933; s. Walter D. and Anna Laura (Brockway) W.; m. Margaret Irene Keiter, June 19, 1955; children: Stephen Dirk, Carolyn Sue. B.A., Carleton Coll., 1954; M.S., Calif. Inst. Tech., 1955, Ph.D., 1960. Instr. physics U. Pa., Phila., 1959-62, asst. prof., 1962-64, assoc. prof., 1964-72, prof., 1972—, chmn. dept. physics, 1973-82, assoc. dean, 1982-87, acting dean, 1987-88; assoc. dean U. Pa., 1988-92, dep. provost, 1992-95; assoc. dir. Princeton-Pa. Accelerator, Princeton, N.J., 1968-71; staff physicist AEC, 1972-73. Fellow Am. Phys. Soc.; mem. Am. Assn. Physics Tchrs. Research in exptl. particle physics. Home: 404 Drew Ave Swarthmore PA 19081-2406 Office: 209 S 33rd St Philadelphia PA 19104

WALGREEN, CHARLES RUDOLPH, III, retail store executive; b. Chgo., Nov. 11, 1935; s. Charles Rudolph and Mary Ann (Leslie) W.; m. Kathleen Bonsignore Allen, Jan. 23, 1977; children: Charles Richard, Tad Alexander, Kevin Patrick, Leslie Ray, Chris Patrick; stepchildren—Carleton A. Allen Jr., Jorie L. Allen Grassie. B.S. in Pharmacy, U. Mich., 1958. With Walgreen Co., Chgo., 1952—, adminstrv. asst. to v.p. store ops., 1963-65, 65-66, dist. mgr., 1966-69, regional dir., 1968-69, v.p., pres., 1969-71, pres., chief exec. officer, 1971-76, chmn., chief exec. officer, 1976—, also bd. dirs. Mem. bus. adv. coun. Chgo. Urban League.; bd. dirs. Jr. Achievement Chgo. Mem. Nat. Assn. Chain Drug Stores (bd. dirs.), Ill. Retail Mchts. Assn. (bd. dirs. 1966—), Am. Pharm. Assn., Ill. Pharm. Assn., Comml. Club of Chgo., Great Lakes Cruising Club, Exmoor Country Club (Highland Park, Ill.), Key Largo (Fla.) Anglers Club, Sailfish Point Club (Stuart, Fla.), Conway Farms Golf Club (Lake Forest, Ill.), Delta Sigma Phi. Office: Walgreen Co 200 Wilmot Rd Deerfield IL 60015-4620

WALI, MOHAN KISHEN, environmental science and natural resources educator; b. Kashmir, India, Mar. 1, 1937; came to U.S., 1969, naturalized, 1975; s. Jagan Nath and Somavati (Wattal) W.; m. Sarla Safaya, Sept. 25, 1960; children: Pamela, Promod. BS, U. Jammu and Kashmir, 1957; MS, U. Allahabad, India, 1960; PhD, U. B.C., Can., 1970. Lectr. S.P. Coll., Srinagar, Kashmir, 1963-65; rsch. fellow U. Copenhagen, 1965-66; grad. fellow U. B.C., 1967-69; asst. prof. biology U. N.D., Grand Forks, 1969-73, assoc. prof., 1973-79, prof., 1979-83, Hill rsch. prof., 1973, dir. Forest River Biology Area Field Sta., 1970-79, Project Reclamation, 1975-83, spl. asst. to univ. pres., 1977-82; staff ecologist Grand Forks Energy Rsch. Lab., U.S. Dept. Interior, 1974-75; prof. Coll. Environ. Sci. and Forestry, SUNY, Syracuse, 1983-89, dir. grad. program environ. sci., 1983-85; prof. Sch. Natural Resources, 1990—; dir., Sch. Nat. Resources, assoc. dean, Coll. Agr., 1990-93; vice chmn. N.D. Air Pollution Adv. Council, 1981-83; co-chair IV Internat. Congress on Ecology, 1986. Editor: Some Environmental Aspects of Strip-Mining in North Dakota, 1973, Prairie: A Multiple View, 1975, Practices and Problems of Land Reclamation in Western North America, 1975, Ecology and Coal Resource Development, 1979, Ecosystem Rehabilitation-Preamble to Sustainable Development, 1992; co-editor Agriculture and the Environment, 1993; sr. editor Reclamation Rev., 1976-80, chief editor, 1980-81; chief editor Reclamation and Revegetation Rsch., 1982-87; contbr. articles to profl. jours. Recipient B.C. Gamble Disting. Teaching and Svc. award, 1977. Fellow AAAS, Nat. Acad. of Scis. India; mem. Ecol. Soc. Am. (chmn. sect. internat. activities 1980-84), Brit. Ecol. Soc., Can. Bot. Assn. (dir. ecology sect. 1976-79, v.p. 1982-83), Ohio Acad. Sci., Torrey Bot. Club, Am. Soc. Agronomy, Am. Inst. Biol. Sci. (gen. chmn. 34th ann. meeting), Internat. Assn. Ecology (co-chmn. IV Internat. Congress Ecology), Internat. Soc. Soil Sci., N.D. Acad. Sci. (chmn. editorial com. 1979-81), Sigma Xi (nat. lectr. 1983-85, pres. Ohio State chpt. 1993-94, pres. Syracuse chpt. 1984-85, Outstanding Rsch. award U. N.D. chpt. 1975). Office: Ohio State U Sch Natural Resources 2021 Coffey Rd Columbus OH 43210-1043

WALICKI, ANDRZEJ STANISLAW, history of ideas educator; b. Warsaw, Poland, May 15, 1930; came to U.S., 1986, naturalized 1993.; s. Michal Walicki and Anna (Szlachcinska) Chmielewska; m. Janina Derks, Mar. 10, 1953 (div. June 1970); m. Maria Wodzynska, June 17, 1972 (div. May 1985); children: Malgorzata, Adam; m. Marzena Balicka, July 27, 1985. MA, Warsaw U., 1953; PhD, Polish Acad. Scis., 1957. Asst. prof. Warsaw U., 1958-60; asst. prof. Polish Acad. Scis., Warsaw, 1960-64, assoc. prof., 1964-72, prof., head dept. Inst. Philosophy, 1972-81; sr. rsch. fellow Australian Nat. U., Canberra, 1981-86; O'Neill prof. history U. Notre Dame, Ind., 1986—; vis. Kratter prof. history Stanford U. Author: The Slavophile Controversy, 1975, A History of Russian Thought, 1979, Philosophy and Romantic Nationalism, 1982, Legal Philosophies of Russian Liberalism, 1987, Marxism and the Leap to the Kingdom of Freedom: The Rise and Fall of the Communist Utopia, 1995; also 13 others. Recipient award A. Jurzykowski Found., N.Y.C., 1983; Rsch. grantee Ford Found., N.Y.C., 1960, vis. fellow All Souls Coll., U. Oxford, 1966-67, 73, Guggenheim fellow J.S. Guggenheim Meml. Found., 1991. Mem. Am. Hist. Assn., Am. Assn. for Advancement Slavic Studies, Polish Acad. Scis. Roman Catholic. Office: U Notre Dame Dept History Notre Dame IN 46556

WALINSKY, LOUIS JOSEPH, economic consultant, writer; b. London, Apr. 19, 1908; came to U.S., 1912; s. Ossip Joseph and Rose (Newman) W.; m. Michele Benson, 1936 (div. 1947); 1 child, Adam; m. Dorothy Monie; children—Marian, Louisa. B.A. in Econs. with honors, Cornell U., 1929; postgrad., U. Berlin, CCNY, New Sch. Social Research. Tchr. econs. N.Y.C. Bd. Edn., 1930-43; econ. cons. War Prodn. Bd., Washington, 1943-47; fin. dir., dir. Germany-Austria ops., sec.-gen. World ORT Union, N.Y.C., 1947-49; v.p. Robert Nathan Assocs., Washington, 1950-63; econ. cons. Washington and Cohasset, Mass., 1963—; exec. sec. combined pulp and paper com. Combined Raw Materials Bd., 1944-45; dir. office of econ. rev. and analysis Civilian Prodn. Adminstrn., 1946-47; mem. and/or leader econ. missions to Korea, Afghanistan, El Salvador, Brazil, East Africa, Israel, Iran, India, Bolivia, Venezuela, Newfoundland, Papua-New Guinea and P.R.; chief resident econ. adviser Govt. Burma, Rangoon, 1953-58; spl. advisor Asia Dept. World Bank, 1971-72; cons. OECD, 1978. Author: Heil Hitler!, 1936, (dramatization) Brave New World, 1939, Economic Development in Burma, 1962, Planning and Execution of Economic Development, 1963, (wth others) Planning Economic Development, 1963, Work, Youth and Unemployment, 1968, Man, State and Society in Contemporary Southeast Asia, 1969, Issues Facing World Jewry, 1981, Coherent Defense Strategy, 1982; editor: Unfinished Business of Land Reform, 1977; contbr. articles to profl. jours. Mem. nat. bd. Ams. for Dem. Action, Washington, 1950-51; dir. internat. commn. World Jewish Congress, N.Y.C., 1979-80; vice chmn. Am. Friends Democracy in Burma, 1991—. Avocations: golf; music; reading. Home and Office: 4000 Massachusetts Ave NW Washington DC 20016-5105

WALK, RICHARD DAVID, retired psychology educator; b. Camp Dix, N.J., Sept. 25, 1920; s. Arthur Richard and Elsie (Roberts) W.; m. Lois MacDonald, Apr. 1, 1950; children: Joan MacDonald Scharf, Elizabeth Walk Robbins, Richard David Jr. AB, Princeton U., 1942; MA, U. Iowa, 1947; PhD, Harvard U., 1951. Research assoc. Human Resource Research Office, George Washington U., Washington, 1952-53, from assoc. prof. to prof., 1959-91; asst. prof. Cornell U., Ithaca, N.Y., 1953-59, prof. emeritus, 1991—; vis. prof. MIT, Cambridge, 1965-66, London Sch. Econs., U. London, 1981. Author: Perceptual Development, 1981; editor: (with H.L. Pick Jr.) Perception and Experience, 1978, Chinese edit., 1987, Intersensory Perception and Sensory Integration, 1981; contbr. articles to profl. jours., chpts. to books. Served to 1st lt. U.S. Army, 1942-45, ETO, 1951-52. Fellow AAAS, Am. Psychol. Soc.; mem. Am. Psychol. Assn., Soc. for Rsch. in Child Devel., Psychonomic Soc., Brit. Psychol. Assn. (fgn. assoc.), Sigma Xi, Vet. OSS. Democrat. Episcopalian. Club: Princeton Terrace (N.J.); Princeton, Harvard (Washington). Home: 7100 Oakridge Ave Chevy Chase MD 20815-5170

WALKE, DAVID MICHAEL, public relations executive; b. Mt. Vernon, N.Y., Dec. 30, 1954; s. Charles Philip and Elinor Mae (Denner) W.; m. Linda Susan Berkover, Nov. 26, 1978; children: Evan Matthew, Hilary Rose. BS in Acctg., Syracuse U., 1976. Account exec. Ecom Cons., Inc., N.Y.C., 1976-79, Anametrics, Inc., N.Y.C., 1979-81, Ruder, Finn & Rotman, Inc., N.Y.C., 1981-82; prin. Morgen-Walke Assocs., Inc., N.Y.C., 1982—, ptnr. Mem. Nat. Investor Rels. Inst. Office: Morgen-Walke Assocs Inc Ste 5100 380 Lexington Ave New York NY 10168-0002*

WALKEN, CHRISTOPHER, actor; b. Astoria, N.Y., Mar. 31, 1943; s. Paul W. Attended Hofstra U., studied with Wynn Handman, Actors Studio. Stage appearances include Broadway, off-Broadway and regional theatres throughout U.S. and Can.; Broadway debut in J.B, 1959; other stage appearances include Best Foot Forward, West Side Story, Macbeth, The Lion in Winter (Clarence Derwent award 1966), Hamlet, The Rose Tatoo (Theatre World's Most Promising Personality 1966-67), Romeo and Juliet, The Seagull, The Night Thoreau Spent in Jail (Joseph Jefferson award 1970-71), Kid Champion (Obie award 1975), Miss Julie, Sweet Bird of Youth, Hurlyburly, 1984, Cinders, 1984, A Bill of Divorcement, 1985, Coriolanus, 1988, Othello, 1992, (also playwright) Him, 1995; films include The Anderson Tapes, 1971, Next Stop Greenwich Village, The Sentinel, 1977, Roseland, 1977, Annie Hall, 1977, The Deer Hunter, 1978 (N.Y. Film Critics Best Supporting Actor award 1978, Acad. award best supporting actor 1979), Last Embrace, 1979, Dogs of War, 1981, Heavens Gate, 1980, Pennies From Heaven, 1981, The Happiness Cage, 1982, The Dead Zone, 1983, Brainstorm, 1983, A View to a Kill, 1984, At Close Range, 1986, Deadline, 1987, Puss in Boots, 1988, The Milagro Beanfield War, 1988, Biloxi Blues, 1988, Communion, 1989, King of New York, 1990, Homeboy, 1991, The Comfort of Strangers, 1991, McBain, 1991, All American Murder, 1992, Batman Returns, 1992, True Romance, 1993, A Business Affair, 1994, Wayne's World II, 1994, Pulp Fiction, 1994, Search and Destroy, 1995; TV films include Sarah, Plain and Tall, 1991, Skylark, 1993, Scam, 1993. Office: William Morris Agy 151 S El Camino Dr Beverly Hills CA 90212-2704*

WALKER, A. HARRIS, lawyer, manufacturing executive; b. Lincoln, Ill., Feb. 7, 1935; s. Arthur M. and Margaret (Harris) W.; m. Ann Pontious, Aug. 27, 1960; children: Christine, Stuart, Melinda. BA, Northwestern U., 1956; JD, U. Mich., 1963; MBA, U. Chgo., 1969. Bar: Ill. 1963, U.S. Dist. Ct. (no. dist.) Ill. 1964, U.S. Ct. Appeals (7th cir.) 1963. Assoc. Peterson, Lowry, Rall, Barber & Ross, Chgo., 1963-66; atty. Am. Hosp. Supply Co., Evanston, Ill., 1966-71; sr. atty. A.B. Dick Co., Chgo., 1971-74, asst. gen. counsel, 1974-86, v.p., gen. counsel, sec., 1986—, also bd. dirs., officer of various subs. Presbyterian. Office: AB Dick Co 5700 W Touhy Ave Niles IL 60714-4628

WALKER, ALICE MALSENIOR, author; b. Eatonton, Ga., Feb. 9, 1944; d. Willie Lee and Minnie (Grant) W.; m. Melvyn R. Leventhal, Mar. 17, 1967 (div. 1976); 1 dau., Rebecca Walker Leventhal. BA, Sarah Lawrence Coll., 1966; PhD (hon.), Russell Sage U., 1972; DHL (hon.), U. Mass., 1983. Co-founder, pub. Wild Trees Pr., Navarro, Calif., 1984-88; writer in residence, tchr. black studies Jackson State Coll., 1968-69, Tougaloo Coll., 1970-71; lectr. literature Wellesley Coll., 1972-73, U. Mass., Boston, 1972-73; disting. writer Afro-American studies dept. U. Calif., Berkeley, 1982; Fannie Hurst Prof. of Literature Brandeis U., Waltham, Mass., 1982; cons. Friends of the Children of Miss., 1967. Author: Once, 1968, The Third Life of Grange Copeland, 1970, Five Poems, 1972, Revolutionary Petunias and Other Poems, 1973 (Nat. Book award nomination 1973, Lillian Smith award So. Regional Coun. 1973), In Love and Trouble, 1973 (Richard and Hinda Rosenthal Found. award Am. Acad. and Inst. of Arts and Letters 1974) Langston Hughes: American Poet, 1973, Meridian, 1976, Goodnight, Willie Lee, I'll See You in the Morning, 1979, You Can't Keep a Good Woman Down, 1981, The Color Purple, 1982 (Nat. Book Critics Circle award nomination 1982, Pulitzer Prize for fiction 1983, Am. Book award 1983), In Search of Our Mothers' Gardens, 1983, Horses Make a Landscape Look More Beautiful, 1984, To Hell With Dying, 1988, Living By the Word: Selected Writings, 1973-1987, 1988, The Temple of My Familiar, 1989, Her Blue Body Everything We Know: Earthling Poems, 1965-1990, 1991, Finding the Green Stone, 1991, Possessing the Secret of Joy, 1992, (with Pratibha Parmar) Warrior Marks, 1993, (with others) Double Stitch: Black Women Write About Mothers & Daughters, 1993, Everyday Use, 1994; editor: I Love Myself When I'm Laughing... And Then Again When I'm Looking Mean and Impressive, 1979. Recipient first prize Am. Scholar essay contest, 1967, O. Henry award for "Kindred Spirits", 1986, Nora Astorga Leadership award, 1989, Fred Cody award for lifetime achievement Bay Area Book Reviewers Assn., 1990, Freedom to Write award PEN Ctr. USA West, 1990; Bread Loaf Writer's Conf. scholar, 1966; Merrill writing fellowship, 1967; McDowell Colony fellowship, 1967, 77-78; National Endowment for the Arts grantee, 1969, 77; Radcliffe Inst. fellowship, 1971-73; Guggenheim fellow, 1977-78.

WALKER, ANNETTE, counseling administrator; b. Birmingham, Ala., Sept. 20, 1953; d. Jesse and Luegene (Wright) W. BS in Edn., Huntingdon Coll., 1976; MS in Adminstrn. and Supervision, Troy State U., 1977, 78, MS in Sch. Counseling, 1990, AA in Sch. Adminstrn., 1992; diploma, World Travel Sch., 1990; diploma in Cosmetology, John Patterson Coll., 1992; MEd in higher Edn. Adminstrn., Auburn (Ala.) U., 1995. Cert. tchr., adminstr., Ala.; lic. cosmetologist, Ala. Tchr. Montgomery (Ala.) Pub. Sch. System, 1976-89, sch. counselor, 1989—; gymnastics tchr. Cleveland Ave. YMCA, 1971-76; girls coach Montgomery Parks and Recreation, 1973-76; summer sch. sci. tchr. grades 7-9, 1977-88; chmn. dept. sci. Bellingrath Sch., 1987-90, courtesy com., 1987-88, sch. discipline com., 1977-84; recreation asst. Gunter AFB, Ala., 1981-83; calligraphy tchr. Gunter Youth Ctr., 1982; program dir. Maxwell AFB, Ala., 1983-89, vol. tchr. Internat. Officer Sch., 1985—, Ala. Goodwill Amb., 1985—, day camp dir., 1987, calligraphy tchr., 1988; trainer internat. law for sec. students, Ala., 1995—; leader of workshops in field; evening computer tchr. high sch. diploma program, 1995—; sales rep. Ala. World Travel, 1990—; behavior aid Brantwood Children's Home, 1996—. Mem. CAP; tchr. Sunday sch. Beulah Bapt. Ch., Montgomery; vol. zoo activities Tech. Scholarship Program for Ala. Tchrs. Computer Courses, Montgomery, Ala.; bd. dirs. Cleveland Ave. YMCA, 1976-80; sponsor Bell-Howe chpt. Young Astronauts, 1986-90, Pate Howe chpt. Young Astronauts, 1991-92; judge Montgomery County Children Festival Elem. Sci. Fair, 1988-90; bd. dirs. Troy State U. Drug Free Schs., 1992—; chmn. Maxwell AFB Red Cross-Youth, 1986-88; goodwill amb. sponsor to various families (award 1989, 95); State of Ala. rep. P.A.T.C.H.-Internat. Law Inst., 1995. Recipient Outstanding High Sch. Sci./Math. Tchr. award Sigma Xi, 1989, Most Outstanding Youth Coun. Leader award Maxwell AFB Youth Ctr., 1987, Outstanding Ala. Goodwill Amb. award, 1989, 95; named Tchr. of the Week, WCOV-TV, 1992, Ala. Tchr. in Space Program, summer 1989, Local Coord. Young Astronaut Program, 1988. Mem. NEA, Internat. Platform Assn., Nat. Sci. Tchrs. Assn., Ala. Sch. Counselors, Montgomery Sch. Counselors Assn., Montgomery County Ednl. Assn., Space Camp Amb., Huntingdon Alumni Assn. (sec.-treas.), Ala. Goodwill Amb., Montgomery Capital City Club, Young Astronauts, Ea. Star, Zeta Phi Beta, Chi Delta Phi, Kappa Pi. Avocations: international travel, calligraphy, international food, cruising. Home: 2501 Westwood Dr Montgomery AL 36108-4448 Office: Paterson Sch 1015 E Jefferson St Montgomery AL 36104-2712

WALKER, ARTHUR LONZO, religious organization administrator; b. Birmingham, Ala., Apr. 10, 1926; s. Arthur Lonzo and Nannie Agnes (Bynum) W.; m. Gladys Evelyn Walker, Aug. 4, 1949; children: Marcia Lea Hamby, Gregory Arthur. BA, Samford U., 1949; MDiv, So. Bapt. Theol. Sem., 1952; ThD, New Orleans Bapt. Theol. Sem., 1956; LHD (hon.), Campbell U., 1984; HHD (hon.), Houston Bapt. U., 1985. Prof. theology Samford U., Birmingham, 1956-76, v.p. student affairs, 1965-68, v.p. adminstrv. affairs, 1968-73; v.p. student affairs So. Bapt. Theol. Sem., Louisville, 1976-78; exec. dir. edn. commn. So. Bapt. Conv., Nashville, 1978—; sec.-treas. So. Bapt. Commn. Am. Bapt. Theol. Sem., Nashville, 1978—;

mem. adv. bd. Ctr. for Constl. Studies, Macon, Ga., 1978-90; mem. nat. adv. coun. J.M. Dawson Inst. of Ch. State Studies, Waco, Tex., 1990—. Author: By Their Fruits, 1982; editor: Educating For Christian Missions, 1981, Directory of Southern Baptist Colleges, 1986; (jour.) The Southern Baptist Educator, 1978—. Pres. Birmingham Council of Christian Edn., 1970-71. Served as sgt. U.S. Army, 1944-46, PTO. Mem. Nat. Assn. Ind. Colls. and Univs. (bd. dirs. 1987-91). Office: Assn So Baptist Colls 901 Commerce St Ste 750 Nashville TN 37203-3629

WALKER, BAILUS, JR., environmental scientist, dean, health facility administrator. MPH, U. Mich., 1959, PhD in Occupl. and Environ. Health, 1975. Environ. health scientist, adminstr. Environ. Health Svc., Washington, 1972-79; dir. occupl. health standard U.S. Dept. Labor, 1979-81; commr. pub. health Commonwealth Mass., 1983-87; toxicologist Sch. Pub. Health SUNY, Albany, 1987-90; prof. dept. occupl. and environ. health, dean coll. pub. health U. Okla. Health Sci. Ctr., 1990—; now prof. Howard U Sch. Pub. Health-cancer ctr.; head U.S. Exch. Mission to Japan, collaborator U.S.-Japanese efforts in occupl. medicine, 1980; mem Physicians Human Rights Mission, South Korea, 1987, Mozambique Health Assessment Mission, 1988, Sec.'s Coun. Health Prom & Dis Prev U.S. Dept. Health & Human Svc., Commn. Study Future Pub. Health U.S. NAS. Fellow Royal Soc. Health; mem. Inst. Medicine NAS. Research in physical, chemical, and biological hazards in macroenvironments. Office: School of Public Health Howard University 2400 6th St NW Washington DC 20059

WALKER, BETSY ELLEN, computer products and services company executive; b. Atlanta, Sept. 14, 1953; d. John Franklin and Betty Louise (Brown) W.; 1 child, William Franklin. BA summa cum laude, Duke U., 1974; MBA, Harvard U., 1978. Mgmt. trainee, First Atlanta, 1974, officer, 1975-76; analyst Coca Cola, Atlanta, 1977; bus. analyst Am. Mgmt. Systems Inc., N.Y.C., 1978-80, prin., 1981, v.p., 1982—, dir. fin. svcs. group, 1982-90, IBM Svcs. sector group, 1990-92, fin. strategic initiatives group, 1993, dir. fin. industry Strategic Alliance Group, 1994—; mem. mgmt. policy com. Am. Mgmt. Systems, 1988—, mem. corporate operating group, 1994—. J. Spenser Love fellow Harvard U., 1976-78. Mem. Alexandria North Ridge Citizens Assn. (exec. bd.), Phi Beta Kappa, Pi Mu Epsilon (bd. mgrs. Madison Green 1990-91, treas.), Harvard Bus. Sch. Club, Downtown Athletic Club (N.Y.C.). Office: Am Mgmt Systems Inc 4050 Legato Rd Fairfax VA 22033-4003

WALKER, BILLY KENNETH, computer science educator, academic administrator; b. Canyon, Tex., June 17, 1946; m. Anita Marie Ransdell, Mar. 8, 1980. BS in Math., West Tex. State U., 1968, postgrad., 1974, 77; postgrad., U. Utah, 1969; MS in Math., Tex. Tech U., 1970, PhD in Math., 1974. Teaching fellow in math. U. Utah, Salt Lake City, 1968-69; teaching asst. in math. Tex. Tech U., Lubbock, 1969-70, part-time instr. math., 1970-74, adj. prof. elec. engring., 1979-83; instr. sci., physics and math. Carver Learning Ctr., Amarillo, Tex., 1974-76; instr. computer info. systems West Tex. State U., Canyon, 1976-77, acting head dept. computer info. system, 1977; asst. prof. computer info. system Amarillo Coll., 1977-79; asst. prof. elec. engring. and computer sci. U. Okla., Norman, 1979-83; assoc. prof. computer sci. East Okla. State U., Ada, 1983-87; prof. and chmn. dept. computer sci. East Cen. U., Ada, 1983—; mem. engring. computer network user's com. computer sci. U. Okla., Ada, chmn. convocation com. Coll. Engring.; cons. Amstar Corp., Dimmit, Tex., Silverman and Silverman, Attys. at Law, Hutchinson County Mus., City of Amarillo, City of Cushing, Okla., Southwestern Bell Telephone Co., U.S. Armu Corps Engrs.; researcher in field. Author: A Structured Approach to Pascal, 1983, Essentials of Pascal, 1984, Modula-2 Programming with Data Structures, 1986; editorial reviewer Math. Revs., Ann ARbor, Mich., Apple Edn. Found., Cupertino, Calif., Dept. Army; contbr. numerous articles to profl. jours. NSF fellow U. Utah, 1969. Mem. IEEE (sr.), Am. Math. Soc., Assn. for Computing Machinery, Math. Assn. Am., Am. Indian Sci. and Engring. Soc., Okla. Acad. Sci. (vice-chmn. computer sci. section 1987, 89, chmn. computer sci. section 1988, mem. exec. com. 1987-89), Am. Radio Relay League, Comanche War Dance Soc., Comanche Gourd Clan, Lone Star War Dance Soc., Masons, Order Eastern Star, Pi Mu Epsilon, Kappa Mu Epsilon, Alpha Chi. Home: PO Box 2107 Ada OK 74821-2107 Office: East Cen U Dept Computer Sci Ada OK 74820

WALKER, BRENDA JUNE, secondary school educator; b. McAlester, Okla., Aug. 26, 1955; d. Johnie H. and Theresa (Wilson) W. BS in Biology, Chemistry, Northeastern State U., Tahlequah, Okla., 1977; MA in Counseling, Northeastern State U., 1980. Physical sci. tchr. Tahlequah Pub. Schs., 1977—; tchr. gifted and talented Explorations in Creativity, Okla. City, 1990; curriculma adviser Holt, Rinehart and Winston, Orlando, Fla., 1993. Mem. Sequoyah High Sch. Bd., Tahlequah, 1988-94, Cherokee Nation Edn. Core Com., Tahlequah, 1993-94, Gifted and Talented Com., 1993-94, Miss Cherokee Adv. Bd., 1992-94. Named Sertoma Tchr. of Month, 1987, 88. Mem. AAUW, NEA, Okla. Edn. Assn., Tahlequah Edn. Assn., Okla. Acad. Sci. Democrat. Home: PO Box 72 Tahlequah OK 74465-0072

WALKER, BRUCE EDWARD, anatomy educator; b. Montreal, Que., Can., June 17, 1926; s. Robinson Clarence and Dorothea Winston (Brown) W.; m. Lois Catherine McCuaig, June 26, 1948; children—Brian Ross, Dianne Heather, Donald Robert, Susan Lois. B.S., McGill U., 1947, M.S., 1952, Ph.D., 1954; M.D., U. Tex. at Galveston, 1966. Instr. anatomy McGill U., 1955-57; asst. prof. anatomy U. Tex. Med. Br., 1957-61, assoc. prof. anatomy, 1961-67; prof. Mich. State U., East Lansing, 1967—, chmn. dept., 1967-75. Contbr. articles to profl. jours. Mem. Am. Assn. Anatomists, Teratology Soc., Am. Assn. for Cancer Research. Office: Mich State U Anatomy Dept East Lansing MI 48824

WALKER, CAROLYN PEYTON, English language educator; b. Charlottesville, Va., Sept. 15, 1942; d. Clay M. and Ruth Peyton. BA in Am. History and Lit., Sweet Briar Coll., 1965; cert. in French, Alliance Francaise, Paris, 1966; EdM, Tufts U., 1970; MA in English and Am. Lit., Stanford U., 1974, PhD in English Edn., Stanford U., 1977. Tchr. Elem. and jr. high schs. in Switzerland, 1967-69; tchr. elem. grades Boston Sch. System, 1966-67, 69-70; Newark (Calif.) Unified Sch. System, 1970-72; instr. div. humanities Canada Coll., Redwood City, Calif., 1973, 76-78; instr. Sch. Bus., U. San Francisco, 1973-74; evaluation cons. Inst. Profl. Devel., San Jose, Calif., 1975-76; asst. dir. Learning Assistance Ctr., Stanford U., Calif., 1972-77, dir., 1977-84, lectr. Sch. Edn., 1975-84, dept. English, 1977-84, supr. counselors, tutors and tchrs., 1972-84; assoc. prof. dept. English, San Jose State U., Calif., 1984-93; dir. English dept. Writing Ctr., 1986-93, Steinbeck Rsch. Ctr., 1986-87; mem. faculty U. Calif., Berkeley and Santa Cruz, 1995—; corp. trainer, 1993—; pres. Waverley Edn., Inc., Ednl. Cons., 1983-91, tchr. writing and Am. culture for fgn. profls., U. Calif. at Berkeley, 1995—, pvt. prac. corp. trng., 1983—; head cons. to pres. to evaluate coll.'s writing program, San Jose City Coll., 1985-87; cons. U. Tex., Dallas, 1984, Stanford U., 1984, 1977-78, CCNY, 1979, U. Wis., 1980, numerous testing programs; cons. to pres. San Diego State U., 1982, Ednl. Testing Svc., 1985-88, also to numerous univs. and colls.; condr. reading and writing workshops, 1972—; reviewer Random House Books, 1978—, Rsch. in the Teaching of English, 1983—, Course Tech., Inc., 1990—; cons. Basic Skills Task Force, U.S. Office Edn., 1977-79, Right to Read, Calif. State Dept. Edn., 1977-82, Program for Gifted and Talented, Fremont (Calif.) Unified Sch. Dist., 1981-82; bd. dirs. high tech. sci. ctr., San Jose, 1983-84; speaker numerous profl. confs. Author: (with Patricia Killen) Handbook for Teaching Assistants at Stanford University, 1977, Learning Center Courses for Faculty and Staff: Reading, Writing, and Time Management, 1981, How to Succeed as a New Teacher: A Handbook for Teaching Assistants, 1978, ESL Courses for Faculty & Staff: An Additional Opportunity to Serve the Campus Community, 1983, (with Karen Wilson) Tutor Handbook for the Writing Center at San Jose State University, 1989, (with others) Academic Tutoring at the Learning Assistance Center, 1980, Writing Conference Talk: Factors Associated with High and Low Rated Writing Conferences, 1987, Lifeline Mac: A Handbook for Instructors in the Macintosh Computer Classrooms, 1989, Communications with the Faculty: Vital Links for the Success of Writing Centers, 1991, Coming to America, 1993, Teacher Dominance in the Writing Conference, 1992, Instant Curriculum: Just Add Tutors and Students, 1993; contbr. chpts. to Black American Literature Forum, 1991; contbr. articles to profl. jours. Vol. fundraiser Peninsula Ctr. for the Blind, Palo Alto, Calif., 1982—, The Resource Ctr. for Women, Palo Alto, 1975-76. Recipient Award for Outstanding Contbns., U.S. HEW, 1979, award ASPIRE (federally funded program), 1985, two awards Student Affirmative Action, 1986, award Western Coll. Reading & Learning Assn., 1984; numerous other awards and grants. Mem. MLA, Coll. Reading & Learning Assn. (treas. 1982-84, bd. dirs. 1982-84), Nat. Coun. Tchrs. English, No. Calif. Coll. Reading Assn. (sec.-treas. 1976-78), Am. Assn. U. Profs., Jr. League Palo Alto (bd. dirs. 1977-78, 83-84). Home: 2350 Waverley St Palo Alto CA 94301-4143

WALKER, CHARLES ALLEN, chemical engineer, educator; b. Wise County, Tex., June 18, 1914; s. Jackson Lamar and Eula (Hamilton) W.; m. Bernice Rolf, Dec. 24, 1942; children: Allen Rolf, John Lamar, Laurence Gordon. BS, U. Tex., 1938, MS, 1940; DEng, Yale U., 1948. Mem. faculty Yale U., New Haven, 1942-84, prof. chem. engring., 1956-84, master Berkeley Coll., 1959-69, chmn. dept. engring. and applied sci., 1974-76, Raymond John Wean prof., 1979-84, prof. emeritus, 1984—, chmn. dept. chem. engring., 1981-84; mem. staff Yale Instn. for Social and Policy Studies, 1970-84; cons. chem. engr., 1942—. Bd. dirs. Conn. Fund for the Environ., 1978-86. Fellow AAAS; mem. AICE, Sci. Rsch. Soc. Am. (past nat. dir., treas. 1968-73), Am. Chem. Soc. (petroleum rsch. fund adv. bd. 1970-81, chmn. 1972-81), Am. Soc. Engring. Edn., Conn. Acad. Sci. and Engring., Conn. Acad. Arts and Scis., Yale Club, Phi Beta Kappa (hon.), Sigma Xi (bd. dirs. 1976-78), Tau Beta Pi, Phi Lambda Upsilon. Home: 1155 Whitney Ave Hamden CT 06517-3434

WALKER, CHARLES B., chemicals company executive; b. 1939. Attended, Univ. of Richmond, Richmond, VA, 1961. With Southern States Co-Op, Inc., 1961-64, Albemarle Paper Mfg. Co., 1965-68; pres. Spotless Stores, Richmond, Va., 1969-74; with State Comp. State of Va., 1974-81, sec. adminstrn. and fin., 1978; v.p. Ethyl Corp., Richmond, 1981—; now CFO, vice chmn., tng. dir. Ethyl Corp, Richmond. Office: Ethyl Corp 330 S 4th St Richmond VA 23219-4304*

WALKER, CHARLES DODSLEY, conductor, organist; b. N.Y.C., Mar. 16, 1920; s. Marshall Starr and Maude Graham (Marriott) W.; m. Janet Elizabeth Hayes, May 30, 1949; children: Peter Hayes, Susan Starr. BS, Trinity Coll., 1940; AM, Harvard U., 1947. Organist, choirmaster Am. Cathedral, Paris, 1948-50, Ch. of the Heavenly Rest, N.Y.C., 1951-88; music dir. Blue Hill Troupe, Ltd., N.Y.C., 1955-90, The Chapin Sch., N.Y.C., 1961-85; mem. organ faculty Union Theol. Sem., N.Y.C., 1962-73, NYU, 1968-80; dean, music dir. Berkshire Choral Inst., Sheffield, Mass., 1982-91; organist, choirmaster Trinity Episcopal Ch., Southport, Conn., 1988—. Contbr. articles to profl. jours. Lt. comdr. USNR, 1942-46. Recipient Disting. Alumnus award Cathedral Choir Sch., 1988. Fellow Am. Guild of Organists (nat. pres. 1971-75); mem. Am. Fedn. of Musicians, Canterbury Choral Soc. (founder, conductor 1952—), Saint Wilfrid Club, The Bohemians. Avocations: travel, photography. Home: 160 W 96th St Apt 15N New York NY 10025-9212 Office: Trinity Episcopal Ch 651 Pequot Ave Southport CT 06490-1416

WALKER, CHARLES MONTGOMERY, lawyer; b. St. Louis, Sept. 30, 1915; s. Charles J. and Gertrude (Zoll) W.; m. Gertrude E. Acton, Apr. 30, 1943. A.B., U. Mo., 1937, LL.B., 1939. Bar: Mo. 1939, Calif. 1941, D.C. 1977. Practiced law Los Angeles, 1941—; mem. Brady, Nossaman & Walker, 1941-62; partner Paul, Hastings, Janofsky & Walker, 1962-75, 77-81, counsel, 1981—; asst. sec. treasury for tax policy Washington, 1975-77. Served with AUS, 1942-46. Decorated Bronze Star. Fellow Am. Bar Found., Am. Coll. Tax Counsel (bd. regents 1987-93), Am. Bar Retirement Assn. (bd. dirs.,pres. 1986), Am. Tax Policy Inst. (trustee, pres. 1990-93); mem. ABA (chmn. taxation sect. 1979-80, coms.), L.A. Bar Assn., Am. Law Inst., Am. Judicature Soc., State Bar Calif., Order of Coif, L.A. Country Club, Chevy Chase Club, Metropolitan Club, Sigma Chi. Home: 9255 Doheny Rd West Hollywood CA 90069-3201 Office: 1299 Ocean Ave Santa Monica CA 90401-1004

WALKER, CHARLES NORMAN, retired insurance company executive; b. Buchanan, Mich., Mar. 8, 1923; s. Leland Seymour and Beatrice (Fairchild) W.; m. Rosemary McElwee, Aug. 21, 1919 (dec.); children: James Charles, Christopher Hugh. Student, Western Mich. U., 1939-41; B.S., U. Mich., 1945, M.A., 1947. With Lincoln Nat. Life Ins. Co., Ft. Wayne, Ind., 1947-75; asst. v.p., mgr. accident and sickness Lincoln Nat. Life Ins. Co., 1957-60, 2d v.p., 1960-64, v.p., 1964-75; v.p. selection and issue New Eng. Mut. Life Ins. Co., Boston, 1975-83. Served to 1st lt. USAF, 1943-46. Fellow Soc. Actuaries; mem. Am. Acad. Actuaries. Episcopalian. Home: 506 Mill Rd Woodstock VA 22664-2308

WALKER, CHARLES THOMAS, physicist, educator; b. Chgo., Sept. 5, 1932; s. Charles William and Velma Rose (Reich) W.; m. Alice Ann Pawlak, Dec. 26, 1953 (div. 1973); children: David John, Valerie Anne, Carolyn Marie; m. Carrie Anna Ramsey, Sept. 14, 1973. A.B. in Math., U. Louisville, 1956, M.S. in Physics, 1958; PH.D. in Physics, Brown U., 1961. Research assoc Cornell U., Ithaca, N.Y., 1961-63; asst. prof. Northwestern U., Evanston, Ill., 1963-67, assoc. prof., 1967-71; prof. physics Ariz. State U., Tempe, 1971-85, chmn. dept., 1981-85; corp. scientist 3M Co./Photonics Rsch. Lab., St. Paul, 1985—; cons. U.S. Dept. Def., Washington, 1966-71, Coronet Films, Chgo., 1969-71, Motorola, Inc., Phoenix, 1974-78. Contbr. articles to profl. jours. Served to sgt. U.S. Army, 1953-55. Guggenheim Found. fellow, 1967-68; Alexander von Humboldt Found. sr. U.S. scientist, 1978-79. Fellow Am. Phys. Soc.; mem. AAAS, Optical Soc. Am. Home: 163 Riverview Acres Rd Hudson WI 54016-6753 Office: 3M Co/Photonics Rsch Lab Corp Rsch Lab 3M Center 201-2S-05 Saint Paul MN 55144-1000

WALKER, CHARLES URMSTON, retired university president; b. Bolivar, Pa., June 20, 1931; s. Charles William and Frances May (Urmston) W.; m. Cherie Hall Duckworth, Aug. 7, 1959; children: Douglas Leland, Christy Lynn. BA, U. Pitts., 1953; MA, Columbia U., 1958; PhD, Stanford U., 1964; LLD (hon.), Kanto Gakuin U., 1979; LHD (hon.), Linfield Coll., 1992. Asst. prof. English Rockford (Ill.) Coll., 1958-61; dept. head, residence dir. Menlo Coll., Menlo Park, Calif., 1961-64; v.p., dean Hamline U., St. Paul, 1964-70; pres. Russell Sage Coll., Troy, N.Y., 1970-75; pres. Linfield Coll., McMinnville, Oreg., 1975-92, pres. emeritus, 1992—; ednl. cons., 1992—; dir. Ford scholar program Ford Family Found., Roseburg, Oreg., 1994—; chmn. bd. dirs. 1st Fed. Savs. & Loan, McMinnville; bd. dirs. Wespro Ins. Co., Oreg. Mut. Ins. Co.; mem. Univ. Pres. Initiative, IIE/USIA/NATO, Brussels, 1991. Mem. bd. dirs., pres. Hillside Manor, McMinnville, 1990; bd. dirs. South Tillamook County Libr., 1994, McMinnville Indsl. Promotions, 1993, Oreg. Bapt. Found., Portland, v.p.; bd. dirs. Coll. and Univ. Partnership Program, Memphis; pres. Newkowin (Oreg.) Chamber Music; chmn. long range planning First Bapt. Ch., McMinnville; dir. Oreg. Coun. Humanities. Warg scholar U. Pitts., 1949-51; Univ. fellow Stanford U., 1963-64; Hill Found. grantee, St. Paul, 1970; Paul Harris fellow Rotary Internat., 1987; recipient Community Svc. award Troy, N.Y. Troy C. of C., 1975, First Citizen award McMinnville, Oreg., 1989; named Man of Yr., Troy C. of C., 1975. Mem. Univ. Club (Portland), Rotary (past pres. McMinnville). Home: 1324 Gilorr St McMinnville OR 97128-6617

WALKER, CHARLS EDWARD, economist, consultant; b. Graham, Tex., Dec. 24, 1923; s. Pinkney Clay and Sammye D. (McCombs) W.; m. Harmolyn Hart, June 24, 1949; children: Carolyn, Charls Edward. BBA, U. Tex., 1947, MBA, 1948; PhD in Econs., U. Pa., 1955. Instr. fin. U. Tex., 1947-48, asst. prof., then assoc. prof., 1950-54; instr. fin. U. Pa. Wharton Sch., 1948-50; fin. economist Fed. Res. Bank Phila., 1953; with Fed. Res. Bank Dallas, 1954-61, v.p., econ. adviser, 1958-61; economist Republic Nat. Bank Dallas, 1955-56; asst. to sec. treasury, 1959-61; exec. v.p. Am. Bankers Assn., N.Y.C., 1961-69; under sec. treasury, 1969-72, dep. sec., 1972-73; adj. prof. fin. and pub. affairs U. Tex., Austin, 1986—; bd. dirs. Enron Corp., Washington Campus. Co-editor: The Bankers Handbook, New Directions in Federal Tax Policy, The Consumption Tax: A Better Alternative, 1987, Intellectual Property Rights and Capital Formation, 1988, The U.S. Savings Challenge, 1990; contbr. articles to profl. jours. and newspapers, chpts. to books. Founder, chmn. Am. Coun. for Capital Formation; co-founder Com. on the Present Danger, chmn. Pres.'s adv. coun. on minority enterprise, 1973-75; co-chmn. Presdl. Debates, 1976; co-founder, co-chmn. Bretton Woods Com.; chmn. Ronald Reagan's Task Force on Tax Policy, 1980; sr. advisor Nat. Issues Conv., U. Tex., 1996. Recipient Alexander Hamilton award U.S. Dept. Treasury, Urban League award, Baker award for Exemplary Svc. to Econ. Edn.; named Disting. Alumnus, U. Tex., 1994. Mem. Coun. Fgn. Rels., Burning Tree Club, Congressional Club (Bethesda, Md.), The Hills of Lakeway Club (Austin, Tex.). Home: 10120 Chapel Rd Potomac MD 20854-4143 *What's good for the public interest ultimately is good for every person, business, or other group in the nation. This, combined with modern application of the Golden Rule, about sums it up.*

WALKER, CLARENCE EUGENE, psychology educator; b. Monongahela, Pa., Jan. 8, 1939; s. Lewis G. Walker and Olga T. Brioli; divorced; children: Chad Eugene, Kyle Lewis, Cass Emanuel. BS in Psychology summa cum laude, Geneva Coll., 1960; MS in Clin. Psychology, Purdue U., 1963, PhD in Clin. Psychology, 1965. Lic. psychologist, Okla. Asst. prof. Westmont Coll., 1964-68; from asst. prof. to assoc. prof. Baylor U., 1968-74; pvt. practice clin. psychology Waco, Tex., 1970-74; assoc. prof. med. sch. U. Okla., Oklahoma City, 1974-80; chief pediatric psychology svc. Okla. Children's Meml. Hosp., 1974-80, dir. out-patient pediatric psychology clinic, 1974-80; prof. med. sch., dir. pediatric psychology tng. program U. Okla., Oklahoma City, 1980—; assoc. chief mental health svcs. Children's Hosp. Okla., 1980—; intern in clin. psychology Riley Children's Hosp., West 10th St. VA Hosp., Indpls., 1963-64; psychology trainee West 10th St. VA Hosp., Indpls., 1963; cons. Head Start Program, Waco, 1968-70, VA Hosp, Waco, 1969-74, VA Ctr., Temple, Tex., 1969-74, Region XII Ednl. Svc. Ctr., Waco, 1971-74, Rusk (Tex.) State Hosp., 1972-74, Bapt. Children's Home, Oklahoma City, 1975-79; rsch. cons. Los Alamos (N.Mex.) Pub. Schs., 1975-79; chmn. div. edn. and psychology Westmont Coll., 1966-68. Author: Learn to Relax, 1975, 2nd edit., 1991, (with P. Clement, A. Hedberg and L. Wright) Clinical Procedures for Behavior Therapy, 1981, (with B.L. Bonner and K. Kaufman) The Physically and Sexually Abused Child, 1988, others; editor: The History of Clinical Psychology in Autobiography, Vol. I, 1992, Vol. II, 1993, (with M.C. Roberts) Handbook of Clinical Child Psychology, 1992; contbr. articles to profl. jours. Fellow APA; mem. AAAS, Southwestern Psychol. Assn. (pres. 1977), Okla. Psychol. Assn. (pres. 1983), Soc. Pediat. Psychology (pres. 1986), Ctrl. Tex. Psychol. Assn. (pres. 1973), Sigma Xi. Avocations: reading, wine tasting, travel. Office: U Okla Med Sch Po Box 26901 920 S L Young Blvd Oklahoma City OK 73190

WALKER, CLARENCE WESLEY, lawyer; b. Durham, N.C., July 19, 1931; s. Ernie Franklin and Mollie Elizabeth (Cole) W.; m. Ann-Heath Harris, June 5, 1954; children: Clare Ann, Wesley Gregg. A.B., Duke U., 1953, LL.B., 1955. Bar: N.C. 1955. Assoc. Mudge Stern Baldwin & Todd, 1955-59; ptnr. Kennedy, Covington, Loddell & Hickman, Charlotte, N.C., 1959—; bd. dirs. Lawyers Mut. Liability Ins. Co., Legal Services Corp. N.C., Oakwood Home Corp. Glendale Hosiery Co.; lectr. N.C. Bar Found. Continuing Legal Edn. Insts., N.C. Jud. Planning Com., 1978-79; pres. Pvt. Adjudication Found. Chmn. bd. mgrs. Charlotte Meml. Hosp. and Med. Ctr., 1981-87; trustee N.C. Ctrl. U., 1979-83; vice-chmn. Charlotte-Mecklenburg Hosp. Authority; adv. bd. Ctrl. Piedmont Paralegal Sch.; pres. Charlotte-Mecklenburg Hosp. Found.; trustee Charlotte Country Day Sch., 1977-81; state chmn. Nat. Found. March of Dimes, 1968-70; chmn. Charlotte Park and Recreation Commn., 1970-73; bd. dirs. Charlotte Symphony, 1965-71, Bethlehem Ctr., 1975-77, N.C. Recreators Found., 1973-75; adv. bd. Charlotte Children's Theatre, 1972; bd. dirs. Charlotte C. of C., 1970-72; bd. visitors Duke U. Law Sch.; dir., gen. campaign chmn. United Way Ctrl. Carolinas, 1985. Fellow Am. Bar Found.; mem. N.C. Bar Assn. (pres. 1978-79, gov. 1971-75), ABA (state del. 1980-89, assembly del.) 26th Jud. Dist. Bar Assn., Mecklenburg Bar Found. (trustee), Am. Law Inst., Order of Coif, Phi Eta Sigma, Phi Beta Kappa. Democrat. Methodist. Home: 1047 Ardsley Rd Charlotte NC 28207-1815 Office: Kennedy Covington Lobdell & Hickman NationsBank Ctr 100 N Tryon St Ste 4200 Charlotte NC 28202-4000

WALKER, CRAIG MICHAEL, lawyer; b. Vt., 1947; m. Patricia A. Magruder; two children. BA, Williams Coll., 1969; JD, Cornell U., 1972. Bar: N.Y. 1973, U.S. Dist. Ct. (so. dist.) N.Y. 1975, U.S. Ct. Appeals (2d cir) 1975, U.S. Supreme Ct 1976. Assoc. Alexander & Green, N.Y.C., 1972-80, ptnr., 1980-86, chmn. litigation dept., 1985-86; ptnr. Walter, Conston, Alexander & Green P.C., N.Y.C., 1987-89, Rogers & Wells, N.Y.C., 1990—. Contbr. author: New York Forms of Jury Instruction, 1992; contbr. articles to profl. jours. Fellow Am. Bar Found.; mem. ABA, N.Y. State Bar Assn., Def. Rsch. Inst., Fed. Bar Coun. Democrat.

WALKER, DALE RUSH, financial company executive; b. High Point, N.C., Jan. 14, 1943; s. Raymond Lowe and Virginia (Rush) W.; m. Linda Gates, 1990; children by previous marriage: Virginia Ashley, Whitney Beaumont. BS in Math., Wake Forest U., 1965; MBA, U. N.C., 1967. Asst. cashier Citibank, N.Y.C., 1967-70; sr. v.p. Union Bank, San Francisco, 1970-75, regional v.p., 1975-78; regional v.p. Union Bank, Oakland, Calif., 1978-80; chief mktg. officer Wells Fargo Leasing, San Francisco, 1980-81, chmn. bd., CEO, 1986-89; exec. v.p. and group head real estate group Wells Fargo Bank, San Francisco, 1981-92; exec. v.p. chief credit officer ITT Fin. Corp., St. Louis, 1993-95; chmn., pres., CEO ITT Lyndon Ins. Cos., St. Louis, 1993-95; pres. AIG Consumer Fin. Group, N.Y.C., 1995—. Chmn. Pacific Vision Found., 1989-93. Democrat. Presbyterian. Avocations: skiing, piano, golf. Office: AIG Consumer Fin Group 125 Maiden Ln New York NY 10038

WALKER, DAVID A(LAN), finance educator; b. York, Pa., Jan. 5, 1941; s. Arthur Benjamin and Alva (Strasbougher) W. BA, Pa. State U., 1962; MS, Iowa State U., 1964, PhD, 1968. Asst. prof. Pa. State U., 1968-70; economist FDIC, 1970-76, 78-80; vis. assoc. prof. Northwestern U., 1976-77; dir. rsch. Office Compt. Currency, 1977-78; assoc. prof. fin. Georgetown U., 1980-82, prof., 1982-92, assoc. dean, 1985-87, John A. Largay Scholar, 1992—; dir. Ctr. for Bus. and Govt. Rels., 1989—; advisor U.S. Dept. Treas., U.S. SBA; cons. in field. Co-author textbooks; editor Jour. Fin. Rsch., 1981-87; co-editor Jour. Small Bus. Fin., 1992-95; mem. editl. bd. Jour. Fin. Rsch., Fin. Mgmt., J.F.Q.A., Fin. Rev., Quarterly Rev. Econs. and Fin., Jour. Small Bus. Fin.; contbr. articles to profl. jours. NDEA fellow, 1962-64. Mem. Am. Econ. Assn., So. Fin. Assn. (bd. dirs.), Ea. Fin. Assn. (bd. dirs.), Fin. Mgmt. Assn. (v.p. 1990-91, pres.-elect 1993-94, pres. 1994-95, bd. trustees 1995—). Republican. Home: 4845 Loughboro Rd NW Washington DC 20016-3454 Office: Georgetown U Sch Bus Washington DC 20057

WALKER, DAVID BRADSTREET, political science educator; b. Salem, Mass., May 7, 1927; s. George Lincoln and Mildred (Bradstreet) W.; m. Jeanne Hallahan, Sept. 1955; children: Melissa J., Stephen B., Justin D. BA, Boston U., 1949, MA, 1950; PhD, Brown U., 1956. Instr. in govt. Bowdoin Coll., Brunswick, Maine, 1956-57; asst prof. in govt. Bowdoin Coll., 1957-63; staff dir. subcom. on intergovt. relations U.S. Senate, Washington, 1963-66; asst. dir. for govt. structure & function Adv. Commn. on Intergovt. Relations, Washington, 1966-84; prof. polit. sci. U. Conn., Storrs, 1984—; dir. Inst. Pub. & Urban Affairs, U. Conn., Storrs, 1986-90; publ. and urban affairs keynote speaker ann. meetings of nat. orgns.; speaker at polit. sci. and govtl. orgns.; Fulbright prof. U. Göttingen, Germany, 1990-91. Author: Toward a Functioning Federalism, 1981, (with others) Managing Public Programs, 1989, (with others) The Great Society and its Legacy, 1986, The Rebirth of Federalism, 1995; contbr. articles to profl. jours. Citizen mem. Conn. Adv. Commn. on Intergovt. Rels., Hartford, 1985, chmn., 1986-90; bd. dirs. Nat. Civic League, Denver. With U.S. Army, 1945-47. Recipient Disting. Citizen award Nat. Mcpl. League, 1986, Donald C. Stone award for Significant Contbn. to Intergovt. Mgmt. in Acad./Rsch. Areas Membership, NAt. Acad. Pub. Adminstrn., Bosworth Meml. award Conn. chpt. Mem. Am. Soc. Pub. Adminstrn., Am. Polit. Sci. Assn. (spl. achievement award 1995), Phi Alpha Alpha, Phi Beta Kappa. Democrat. Episcopalian. Avocations: swimming, gardening, white water rafting, fishing. Home: 31 Edgewood Lane Ext Mansfield Center CT 06250-1210 Office: Inst Pub and Urban Affairs U 106 / U Conn 421 Whitney Rd Storrs CT 06268

WALKER, DAVID ELLIS, JR., dean, educator, minister, consultant; b. Richmond, Va., Oct. 5, 1938; s. David Ellis and Laura Eloise (Vaughan) W.; m. Sandra Suzanne Barnes, Feb. 3, 1964; children: David Ellis III, Virginia Suzanne Walker Frizzell, Cindy Poole Key, Michelle Poole. BA, David Lipscomb U., 1960; MA, U. Fla., 1961, PhD, 1969. Ordained to ministry Ch. Christ, 1954. Instr. Jacksonville (Fla.) U., 1963-65; min. Ch. of Christ, 1954—; prof. Middle Tenn. State U., Murfreesboro, 1965—; dean Theol. U. of Am., Cedar Rapids, Iowa, 1989—; cons. 1981—; acting chmn. dept. speech Middle Tenn. State U., summer 1984, fall 1990, dir. debate, 1965-70, pres. faculty senate, 1983-84. Author: Aletheia, 1991; editor Jour. of Non-Traditional Education, 1992—; contbr. articles to profl. jours. and Ency. of

U.S.A. Grad. fellow U. Fla., 1961-63; grantee Mid. Tenn. State U., 1967, 72, 77, 78, 88, 89, 90, 92, 93, 94, David Walker scholarship Mid. Tenn. State U., 1993—. Mem. Tenn. State Comm. Assn. (v.p. 1973-74, pres. 1974-75, editor Jour. Tenn. Speech Comm. Assn. 1977-85), Tenn. Intercollegiate Forensic Assn. (pres. 1966-67, exec. sec. 1967-68), Popular Culture Assn., Popular Culture Assn. of South, So. Speech Comm. Assn., Fla. Comm. Assn., Pi Kappa Delta (gov. province of S.E. 1966-68), Phi Kappa Phi (chpt. treas. 1989-90). Democrat. Avocations: reading, walking. Home: 2644 E Compton Rd Murfreesboro TN 37130-6848 Office: Dept of Theol Mid Tenn State U Murfreesboro TN 37132

WALKER, DAVID MICHAEL, compensation and benefits consultant, accountant; b. Birmingham, Ala., Oct. 2, 1951; s. David Sellers and Dorothy Ann (West) W.; m. Mary Carmel Etheredge, June 12, 1971; children: Carol Marie, James Andrew. BS in Acctg., Jacksonville U., 1973; Sr. Exec. Govt. Cert., Harvard U., 1986. CPA, Fla., Tex., Ga. Sr. auditor Price Waterhouse & Co. and Coopers & Lybrand, Jacksonville, Fla., 1973-76; dir. personnel Coopers & Lybrand, Atlanta and Houston, 1976-79; Ea. regional mgr. Source Services Corp., Washington, 1979-83; acting exec. dir. and dep. exec. dir. Pension Benefit Guaranty Corp., Washington, 1983-85; dep. asst. sec. U.S. Dept. of Labor, Washington, 1985-87, asst. sec., 1987-89; worldwide mng. ptnr. human capital svcs. practice Arthur Andersen LLP, Atlanta, 1989—; speaker in field. Contbr. articles, editorial adv. bd. several profl. jours. Asst. Pvt. Pension and Welfare Plans; dir., former chmn. Investment and Acctg. Issues Com.; former vice-chmn. chair legis. affairs com. So. Employee Benefits Inst.; sec. of labor Erisa Adv. Coun.; former trustee Social Security and Medicare Trust Funds. Recipient numerous industry and achievement awards for outstanding svc. and contbns. Mem. AICPA (chmn. employee benefit plans com.), Fla. Inst. CPAs, Ga. Soc. CPAs, Nat. Acad. Social Ins., ESOP Assn. and Internat. Found. of Employee Benefit Plans. Republican. Methodist. Home: 997 Peachtree Battle Ave NW Atlanta GA 30327-1315 Office: Arthur Andersen & Co 133 Peachtree St Atlanta GA 30303

WALKER, DECKER FANNIN, education educator; b. Catlettsburg, Ky., Jan. 14, 1942; s. Robert Farrel Walker and Ruby Opal (Cyrus) Stotts; m. Joanne Edith Bakunas, 1962 (div. 1975); children: Glenn, David; m. Mary Ellen Bock, June 12, 1981; 1 child, Decker Jr. BS in Physics, Carnegie-Mellon U., 1963, MA in Natural Sci., 1966; PhD, Stanford U., 1971. Sci. tchr. Taylor Anderdice High Sch., Pitts., 1963-67; asst. prof. Sch. Edn. Stanford U., Palo Alto, Calif., 1971—; assoc. prof. U. Ill., Urbana, 1973-74; program officer NSF, Washington, 1988-89. Author: Fundamentals of Curriculum, 1990; co-author: Curriculum and Aims, 1991. Recipient Young Scholar award Spencer Found., 1975. Mem. Am. Ednl. Rsch. Assn. (v.p. div. B 1975), Assn. for Supervision and Curriculum Devel., Computer Using Educators.

WALKER, DEWARD EDGAR, JR., anthropologist, educator; b. Johnson City, Tenn., Aug. 3, 1935; s. Deward Edgar and Matilda Jane (Clark) W.; m. Candace A. Walker; children: Alice, Deward Edgar III, Mary Jane, Sarah, Daniel, Joseph Benjamin. Student, Ea. Oreg. Coll., 1953-54, 56-58, Mexico City Coll., 1958; BA in Anthropology with honors, U. Oreg., 1960-61, PhD in Anthropology, 1964; postgrad., Wash. State U., 1962. Asst. prof. anthropology George Washington U., Washington, 1964-65; asst. prof. anthropology Wash. State U., Pullman, 1965-67, research collaborator, 1967-69; assoc. prof., chmn. dept. Sociology/Anthropology, lab. dir. U. Idaho, Moscow, 1967-69; prof. U. Colo., Boulder, 1969—, research assoc. in population processes program of inst. behavioral sci., 1969-73, assoc. dean Grad. Sch., 1973-76; affiliate faculty U. Idaho, 1971—. Founder, co-editor Northwest Anthropol. Rsch. Notes, 1966—; editor, Plateau Vol.: Handbook of North American Indians, 1971; author, co-author 135 books, reports, articles and papers. Mem. Tech. Steering Panel Hartford Environ. Dose Reconstruction Project, Hanford, 1988-95, Basalt Waste Isolation Project, Hanford, 1986-88; advisor on Native Am. affairs. With U.S. Army, 1954-62. Fellow NSF, 1961, NDEA, 1961-64. Fellow Am. Anthropol. Assn. (assoc. editor Am. Anthropologist 1973-74), Soc. Applied Anthropology (hon. life, exec. com. 1970-79, treas. 1976-79, chmn. 1980-95, cons., expert witness tribes of N.W., editor Human Orgn. 1970-76, rsch. over 65 projects with 135 monographs, articles, reports, and papers); mem. AAAS, Am. Acad. Polit. and Social Scis., N.W. Anthropol. Conf. Avocations: geology, mining. Home: PO Box 4147 Boulder CO 80306-4147 Office: U Colo PO Box 233 Boulder CO 80309-0233 *I have been both lucky and happy to have had the opportunities to do so many wonderful things in my life as an anthropologist.*

WALKER, DONALD ANTHONY, economist, educator; b. Mar. 6, 1934; s. Timothy Anthony and Helen (Walker) W.; m. Patricia Ann McKeage, Feb. 14, 1961; 1 dau., Valerie Alana. A.B., S.W. Tex. State U., 1952; M.A., U. Tex., 1956; Ph.D., Harvard U., 1961. Asst. prof. econs. Miami U., Oxford, Ohio, 1961-67; assoc. prof. econs. Miami U., 1967-69; prof. econs. Indiana U. Pa., 1969-88, chmn. dept., 1969—, Univ. prof., 1988—. Author: Walras's Market Models, 1996; editor: William Jaffé's Essays on Walras, 1983, Money and Markets: Essays by Robert W. Clower, 1984, Perspectives on the History of Economic Thought, 1989, Welfare Economics and the Theory of Economic Policy, 1995, Jour. of the History of Econ. Thought; contbr. articles to profl. jours. Recipient Commonwealth of Pa. Distinguished Acad. Service award, 1974, Ind. U.-Pa. Disting. Research Award, 1984; Harvard fellow, 1956-57, 57-58; Henry Lee Meml. fellow, 1957-58. Mem. History of Econs. Soc. (pres. 1987-88). Home: 48 Shady Dr Indiana PA 15701-3245 Office: Indiana U of Pennsylvania Dept Econs Keith Hall Indiana PA 15705-1087

WALKER, DONALD EDWIN, educator; b. Hammond, Ind., Feb. 6, 1941; s. Carl Thurston and Verla Irene (Cutler) W.; m. Julie Ann Woerpel, Dec. 20, 1960; children: Theodore R., Susan J. Walker. BA, Ind. U., 1963; MA, U. S.D., 1964; postgrad., U. Wyo., 1964-65; PhD, Mich. State U., 1982. Asst. prof. Olivet (Mich.) Coll., 1965-74, assoc. prof., 1974-82, prof., 1982—; cons. Score Cards, Westport, Conn., 1991. Co-author: Baseball and American Culture, 1995; contbr. articles to profl. jours. City coun. mem. Olivet City Coun., 1977—; police commr. Olivet Police Dept., 1984—; mayor pro tempore City of Olivet, 1983—. Mem. Orgn. of Am. Historians, Western History Assn., Phi Alpha Theta, Phi Kappa Phi, Omicron Delta Kappa, Phi Mu Alpha. Methodist. Avocations: gardening, music, reading, traveling, walking. Home: PO 516 407 Washington Olivet MI 49076 Office: Olivet Coll Dept Ed Mott Building Olivet MI 49076

WALKER, DONALD EZZELL, retired academic administrator; b. Springfield, Mo., July 13, 1921; s. Edward Everett and Cecilia (Ezzell) W.; m. Ann Lathrop, Dec. 17, 1943; 1 son, Craig Lathrop. A.B., U. So. Calif., 1943, M.Th., 1947; Ph.D., Stanford U., 1954; L.H.D. (hon.), Southeastern Mass. U., 1973. Recreational dir. club work All Nations Found., Los Angeles, 1941-42, Wilshire Meth. Ch., Los Angeles, 1942-43; asst. minister Vincent Meth. Ch., Los Angeles, 1943-44; minister Encinitas Meth. Ch., 1945-47; teaching asst. Stanford U., 1947-49; instr. sociology San Diego State Coll., 1949-51, asst. prof. sociology, 1951-54, assoc. dean students, counseling, 1954-56, dean counseling, 1956-58, v.p. acad. affairs, 1968-71, acting pres., 1971-72; dean of students San Fernando Valley State Coll., Northridge, Calif., 1958-60; pres. Idaho State U., 1960-64; dean of students Sonoma State Coll., Rohnert Park, Calif., 1964-66; vice chancellor student affairs U. Calif., Irvine, 1966-68, sr. lectr. Grad. Sch. Administrn., 1967-68, fellow Univ. Coll., 1967-68; pres. Southeastern Mass. State U., N. Dartmouth, 1972-83; chancellor Grossmont-Cuyamaca Community Coll. Dist., El Cajon, Calif., 1983-92; ret., 1992. Author: (with others) Readings in American Public Opinion; The Effective Administrator: A Practical Approach to Problem-Solving, Decision-Making, and Campus Leadership, 1979; contbr. (with others) articles to profl. jours. Home: 8661 Lake Murray Blvd Apt 19 San Diego CA 92119-2837

WALKER, DOUGLAS, computer developement company executive. Graduate, Vanderbilt U., 1976. With Western Data Corp., Seattle, 1976-80; with Walker, Richer & Quinn, Inc., Seattle, 1980—, now pres., 1989—. Office: Walker Richer & Quinn Inc 1500 Dexter Ave N Seattle WA 98109-3051*

WALKER, DOUGLAS CRAIG, publishing company executive; b. Kansas City, Mo., May 7, 1944; s. Garnet Cleveland Walker and Mary Frances (Schuette) Bivins. BS, U. Mo., 1966, MA, 1968. Editorial mgr. Hallmark Cards, Kansas City, Mo., 1974-81; editorial dir. Hippocrene/Lee Publs. Group, N.Y.C., 1981-82; book club dir. Scholastic Inc., N.Y.C., 1984-91; pub., v.p. Putnam/Grosset & Dunlap, N.Y.C., 1991-94; editl. dir. Scholastic paperbacks Scholastic Inc., N.Y.C., 1994—. Editor, creator children's sci. book series The Magic Schoolbus, 1990— (Boston Globe Hornbook award for nonfiction 1990). With U.S. Army, 1968-70. Democrat. Lutheran. Home: 175 E 96th St New York NY 10128-6200 Office: Scholastic Inc 555 Broadway New York NY 10012-3919

WALKER, DUARD LEE, medical educator; b. Bishop, Calif., June 2, 1921; s. Fred H. and Anna Lee (Shumate) W.; m. Dorothea Virginia McHenry, Aug. 11, 1945; children: Douglas Keith, Donna Judith, David Cameron, Diane Susan. A.B., U. Calif. - Berkeley, 1943, M.A., 1947; M.D., U. Calif. - San Francisco, 1945. Diplomate Am. Bd. Microbiology. Intern, U.S. Naval Hosp., Shoemaker, Cal., 1945-46; asst. resident internal medicine Stanford U. Service San Francisco Hosp., 1950-52; asso. prof. med. microbiology and preventive medicine U. Wis., Madison, 1952-59; prof. med. microbiology U. Wis., 1959-88, prof., chmn. med. microbiology, 1970-76, 81-88, Paul F. Clark prof. med. microbiology, 1977-88, prof. emeritus, 1988—; cons. Naval Med. Rsch. Unit., Gt. Lakes, Ill., 1958-74; mem. microbiology tng. com. Nat. Inst. Gen. Med. Scis., 1966-70; mem. nat. adv. Allergy and Infectious Diseases Coun., 1970-74; mem. adv. com. on blood program rsch. ARC, 1978-79; mem. study group on papovaviridae Internat. Com. on Taxonomy of Viruses, 1976-90; mem. vaccines and related biol. products adv. com. FDA, 1985-89. Mem. editorial bd. Infection and Immunity, 1975-83, Archives of Virology, 1981-83, Microbial Pathogenesis, 1985-90. Served to lt. comdr. USNR, 1943-46, 53-55. NRC postdoctoral fellow virology Rockefeller Inst. Med. Research, N.Y.C., 1947-49; USPHS fellow immunology George Williams Hooper Found., U. Calif. - San Francisco, 1949-50. Fellow Am. Pub. Health Assn., Am. Acad. Microbiology, Infectious Diseases Soc. Am.; mem. NAS, Am. Assn. Immunologists, Am. Soc. Microbiology, AAAS, Soc. Exptl. Biology and Medicine (editorial bd. Procs.), Reticuloendothelial Soc. AAUP, Am. Soc. Virology, Wis. Acad. Scis., Arts and Letters. Home: 618 Odell St Madison WI 53711-1435 Office: U Wis Med Sch 1300 University Ave Madison WI 53706-1510

WALKER, EARL E., manufacturing executive; b. St. Louis, Mo., Feb. 12, 1921; s. Thomas T. and Ella Mary (Steggerman) W.; m. Myrtle Agnew, Sept. 27, 1942; children: Mary, Tom, Nancy, Peggy. Grad., Ranken Tech. Sch., 1941. Welder Curtis-Wright Aircraft Co., St. Louis, 1941-49; welder McDonnell-Douglas Aircraft Co., St. Louis, 1949-51, foreman, 1951-53; pres. S.N.W. Welding, St. Louis, 1952-53, Coeur Lane Mfg. Co., St. Louis, 1953-55, Carr Lane Mfg. Co., St. Louis, 1955—; bd. dirs. All Am. Products Co., Los Angeles, Am. Assn. Indsl. Mgmt. Chmn. Coop. Edn. Program, Scottish Rite Clinic for Childhood Lang. Disorders, U. Tex. Sch. Nursing; sec. of interior, Jefferson Nat. Meml. Commn., 1986—. Named Subcontractor of Yr. Small Bus. Adminstrn., Midwest Region VII, 1987; recipient Silver Platter award, Scottish Rite, Mo. Valley. Mem. Soc. Mfg. Engrs. (internat. dir., chmn. nat. exposition com., Nat. Businessman of Yr. 1975, Mgmt. Achievement award, Eli Whitney award 1991, Edn. Found. award for individual achievement 1991, Fellows award 1993), Masons (33 degree). Avocation: golf. Office: Carr Lane Mgf Co 4200 Carr Lane Ct Saint Louis MO 63119-2129*

WALKER, EDWARD KEITH, JR., business executive, retired naval officer; b. Annapolis, Md., Jan. 23, 1933; s. Edward Keith and Miriam (Whitmore) W.; m. Carol Ann Turner, June 12, 1954; children: Lynn Walker Streett, Wendy Louise. BS, U.S. Naval Acad., 1954; postgrad., Armed Forces Staff Coll., 1966; MBA in Fin. Mgmt., George Washington U., 1970. Commd. ensign U.S. Navy, 1954, advanced through grades to rear admiral, 1981; force supply officer COMSUBLANT Norfolk, Va., 1975-78; exec. officer SPCC Mechanicsburg, Pa., 1978-80; comdr. Naval Supply Ctr., Puget Sound, Bremerton, Wash., 1980-81; Atlantic Fleet supply officer CINCLANTFLT Norfolk, 1981-83; asst. comptroller Navy Dept., Washington, 1983-84; comdr. Naval Supply Systems Command and 35th chief supply corps Washington, 1984-88; v.p. adminstrn. and corp. strategy Resource Cons. Inc., Vienna, Va., 1989—. Decorated D.S.M., Legion of Merit (3 awards); recipient Def. Superior Service medal, 1983. Mem. Vinson Hall Corp. (bd. dirs.), Naval Acad. Found. (trustee), U.S. Navy Meml. Found. (bd. dirs., treas.), Supply Corps Found. (past pres.), Supply Corps Assn. (past pres.), Am. Soc. Mil. Comptrs., U.S. Naval Inst., Am. Soc. Naval Engrs., Soc. Logistics Engrs., Nat. Security Indsl. Assn., Naval Submarine League, Naval Order U.S., Navy League U.S., Am. Def. Preparedness Assn., N.Y. Yacht Club, Chesapeake Yacht Club. Republican. Episcopalian. Home: 3520 Saylor Pl Alexandria VA 22304-1831 Office: Resource Cons Inc 1960 Gallows Rd Vienna VA 22182-3824 *There is no greater satisfaction than to see your people succeed, and then to insure they get the credit.*

WALKER, EDWARD S., JR., diplomat; b. Abington, Pa., June 13, 1940; s. Edward Stanley and Rosabel Dunlop (Gould) W.; m. Wendy Jane Griffiths, Apr. 7, 1973; Kathryn Erica, Christopher James. BA, Hamilton Coll., 1963; MA, Boston U., 1965. Joined Fgn. Svc., Dept. State, Washington, 1967; polit. officer Am. Embassy, Tel Aviv, 1969-73; staff asst. Nr. Ea. affairs Fgn. Svc., Dept. State, Washington, 1974-75; Arabic lang. trainee Fgn. Svc. Inst., Lebanon, Tunis, Egypt, 1975-77; polit. officer Am. Embassy, Damascus, Syria, 1977-79; spl. asst. Pres.'s personal rep., Washington, 1980-82; exec. dir. Office of Dep. Sec. State, Washington, 1982-84; mem. Royal Coll. Def. Studies, London, 1984-85; dep. chief of mission Am. Embassy, Riyadh, Saudi Arabia, 1985-88; dep. asst. sec. Dept. State, 1988-89; U.S. amb. to United Arab Emirates Abu Dhabi, 1989-92; dept. permanent rep. to UN, N.Y.C., 1993-94; U.S. amb. to Egypt Cairo, 1994—. With U.S. Army, 1962-65. Recipient Superior Honor award Dept. State, 1975, Meritorious Honor award, 1976, Abu Dhabi, Order of Independence, 1992. Mem. Internat. Inst. Strategic Studies. Episcopalian. Office: US Embassy AMB Unit 64900 Box 1 APO AE 09839-4900

WALKER, ELJANA M. DU VALL, civic worker; b. France, Jan. 18, 1924; came to U.S., 1948; naturalized, 1954; student Med. Inst., U. Paris, 1942-47; m. John S. Walker, Jr., Dec. 31, 1947; children: John, Peter, Barbara. Pres., Loyola Sch. PTA, 1958-59; bd. dirs. Santa Claus shop, 1959-73; treas. Archdiocese Denver Catholic Women, 1962-64; rep. Cath. Parent-Tchr League, 1962-65; pres. Aux. Denver Gen. Hosp., 1966-69; precinct committeewoman Arapahoe County Republican Women's Com., 1973-74; mem. re-election com. Arapahoe County Rep. Party, 1973-78, Reagan election com., 1980; block worker Arapahoe County March of Dimes, Heart Assn., Hemophilia Drive, Muscular Dystrophy and Multiple Sclerosis Drive, 1978-81; cen. city asst. Guild Debutante Charities, Inc. Recipient Distinguished Service award Am.-by-choice, 1966; named to Honor Roll, ARC, 1971. Mem. Cherry Hills Symphony, Lyric Opera Guild, Alliance Franciase (life mem.), ARC, Civic Ballet Guild (life mem.), Needlework Guild Am. (v.p. 1980-82), Kidney Found. (life), Denver Art Mus., U. Denver Art and Conservation Assns. (chmn. 1980-82), U. Denver Women's Library Assn., Chancellors Soc, Passage Inc., Friends of the Fine Arts Found. (life), CHildren's Diabetes Found. (life). Roman Catholic. Clubs: Union (Chgo.); Denver Athletic, 26 (Denver); Welcome to Colo. Internat. Address: 2301 Green Oaks Dr Greenwood Village CO 80121

WALKER, ELVA MAE DAWSON, health consultant; b. Everett, Mass., June 29, 1914; d. Charles Edward and Mary Elizabeth (Livingston) Dawson; m. John J. Spillane Jr. R.N., Peter Bent Brigham Hosp., Boston, 1937; student Simmons Coll., 1935, U. Minn., 1945-48; m. Walter Willard Walker, Dec. 16, 1939 (div. 1969). Supr. nursery Wesson Maternity Hosp., Springfield, Mass., 1937-38; asst. supr. out-patient dept. Peter Bent Brigham Hosp., Boston, 1938-40; supr. surgery and out-patient dept. Univ. Hosps., Mpls., 1945. Chmn. Gov.'s Citizens Coun. on Aging, Minn., 1960-68, acting dir., 1962-66, Econ. Opportunity Com. Hennepin County, 1964-69; v.p., treas. Nat. Purity Soap & Chem. Co., 1968-69, pres., 1969-76, chmn. bd., 1976—, co. exec. officer, 1993—; cons. on aging to Minn. Dept. Pub. Welfare, 1962-67; mem. nat. adv. Coun. for Nurse Tng. Act, 1965-69, Com. Status on Women in Armed Svcs., 1967-70; dir. Nat. Coun. on the Aging, 1963-67, sec., 1965-67, 1986-88, chairperson, 1988-91; chmn. Minn. Bd. on Aging, 1982-91, Nat. Retiree Vol. Ctr., 1982-89; dir. Planning Agy. for Hosps. of Met. Mpls., 1963-67, United Hosp. Fund of Hennepin County, 1955-60, Nat. Coun. Social Work Edn., 1966-68; vice chmn. Hennepin County Gen. Hosp. Adv. Bd., 1965-68; sec. Hennepin County Health Coalition, 1973; chmn. bd. dirs. Am. Rehab. Found, 1962-68, vice chmn., 1968-70, chmn. Minn. Bd. On Aging, 1988-91, Sr. Resources, 1985-87, Older Persons Vision Coun., United Way, 1995—; pres. bd. trustees Northwestern Hosp., 1956-59, Children's Hosp. Mpls., 1961-65; dir. Twin Cities Internat. Program for Youth Leaders and Social Workers, Inc., 1965-67; mem. community adv. coun. United Cmty. Funds and Coun. Am., Inc., 1968, Nat. Assembly Social Policy and Devel., Inc., 1968-74, Minn. Action for Children Commn., 1989—, mem., 1991—; mem. priorities determination com. United Fund Mpls., 1971; vice chmn. govt. specifications com. Soap and Detergent Assn., 1972-76, vice-chmn. indsl. and instn. com., 1974-76, chmn., 1976-78, bd. dirs., 1974—; candidate for Congress, 3d Minn. Dist., 1966; trustee Macalester Coll., Archie D. and Bertha H. Walker Found.; chmn. St. Mary's Jr. Coll. Bd., 1970-74, 78-80, Older Persons vis. com. coun. United Way, 1996—; pres. U. Minn. Sch. Nursing Found., 1958-70; pres. Minn. Gerontological Soc., 1994-95; sec. Metro Area Agy. Aging Minn., 1995—. Mem. Am. Pub. Welfare Assn., Minn. Gerontol. Soc. (pres. 1994—), Mpls. Med. Research Found., Minn. League Nursing (pres. 1971-73), Jr. League Mpls. Democrat. Presbyterian. Home: 3655 Northome Rd Wayzata MN 55391-3020 Office: Nat Purity Soap & Chem Co 434 Lakeside Ave Minneapolis MN 55405-1529

WALKER, EVELYN, retired educational television executive; b. Birmingham, Ala.; d. Preston Lucas and Mattie (Williams) W.; AB, Huntingdon Coll., 1927; student Cornell U., 1927-28; MA, U. Ala., 1963; LHD, Huntingdon Coll., 1974. Speech instr. Phillips High Sch., Birmingham, 1930-34; head speech dept. Ramsay High Sch., Birmingham, 1934-52; chmn. radio and TV, Birmingham Pub. Schs., 1944-75, head instructional TV programming svcs., 1969-75; mem. summer faculty extension div. U. Va., 1965, 66, 67; former regional cons. ednl. TV broadcasting; Miss Ann, broadcaster children's daily radio program, Birmingham, 1946-57; prodr. Our Am. Heritage radio series, 1944-54; TV staff prodr. programs shown daily Ala. Pub. TV Network, 1954-75; past cons. Gov.'s Ednl. TV Legis. Study Com., 1953; nat. del. Asian-Am. Women Broadcasters Conf., 1966; former regional cons. Ednl. TV Broadcasting. Mem. emerita Nat. Def. Adv. Com. on Women in Svcs.; past TV-radio co-chmn. Gov.'s Adv. Bd. Safety Com.; past chmn. creative TV-radio writing competition Festival of Arts; past audio-visual chmn. Ala. Congress, also past mem. Birmingham coun. PTA; media chmn. Gov.'s Commn. on Yr. of the Child; bd. dirs. Women's Army Corps Mus., Fort MiClellen, 1960-93. Recipient Alumnae Achievement award Huntingdon Coll., 1958; Tops in Our Town award Birmingham News, 1957; Air Force Recruiting plaque, 1961; Spl. Bowl award for promoting arts through Ednl. TV. Birmingham Festival of Arts, 1962; citation 4th Army Corps., 1962; cert. of appreciation Ala. Multiple Sclerosis Soc., 1962; Freedoms Found. at Valley Forge Educator's medal award, 1963; Top TV award ARC, 1964; Ala. Woman of Achievement award, 1964; Bronze plaque Ala. Dist. Exch. Clubs, 1969; cert. of appreciation Birmingham Bd. Edn., 1975; Obelisk award Children's Theatre, 1976; 20-Yr. Svc. award Ala. Ednl. TV Commn.; key to city of Birmingham, 1966; named Woman of Yr., Birmingham, 1965; named Ala. Woman of Yr., Progressive Farmer mag., 1966; hon. col. Ala. Militia. Mem. Am. Assn. Ret. Persons, Ala. Assn. Ret. Tchrs., Huntingdon Coll. Alumnae Assn. (former internat. pres.), Former Am. Women in Radio and TV, Arlington Hist. Assn. (dir., pres. 1981-83), Magna Charta Dames (past state sec.-treas.), DAR (former pub. rels. com. Ala., TV chmn., state program chmn. 1979-85, state chmn. Seimes Microfilm com. 1985-88, state chmn. Motion Picture, Radio TV com. 1988-94, tricom. chmn. 1988-94), Colonial Dames 17th Century, U.S. Daus. 1812 (past state TV chmn.), Daus. Am. Colonists (past 2d v.p. local chpt., past state TV and radio chmn.), Ams. Royal Descent, Royal Order Garter, Plantagenets Soc. Am., Salvation Army Women's Aux., Symphony Aux., Humane Soc. Aux., Eagle Forum, Nat. League Am. Pen Women, Womens's Com. 100 for Birmingham (bd. dirs.), Royal Order Crown, Women in Communications (past local pres., nat. headliner 1965), Internat. Platform Assn., Birmingham-Jefferson Hist. Soc., Delta Delta Delta (mem. Golden Circle), Ladies Golf Assn., Birmingham Country Club, The Club. Methodist. Home: Mountain Brook 744 Euclid Ave Birmingham AL 35213-2538

WALKER, FLOYD LEE, lawyer; b. Kiefer, Okla., Mar. 27, 1919; s. Willis and Sarah Josephine (McFarl) W.; children by previous marriage: Mary Lea Walker Byrd, Cheryl Sue Walker Newman, James M.; m. Virginia Gifford Raines, Oct. 8, 1971. LLB, Tulsa U., 1949. Bar: Okla. 1949. Claims atty. Standard Ins. Co., Tulsa, 1949-53; pvt. practice Tulsa, 1953—. 1st lt. USAAF, 1942-45. Decorated DFC, Air medal with 3 oak leaf clusters. Fellow Am. Coll. Trial Lawyers; mem. ABA, ATLA, Okla. Bar Assn. (bd. govs. 1979-82), Tulsa County Bar Assn. (pres. 1973), Okla. Trial Lawyers Assn. Home: 1502 S Boulder Ave Apt 7B Tulsa OK 74119-4022 Office: 900 Oneok Plz Tulsa OK 74103

WALKER, FRANCIS JOSEPH, lawyer; b. Tacoma, Aug. 5, 1922; s. John McSweeney and Sarah Veronica (Meechan) W.; m. Julia Corinne O'Brien, Jan. 27, 1951; children: Vincent Paul, Monica Irene Hylton, Jill Marie Nudell, John Michael, Michael Joseph, Thomas More. B.A., St. Martin's Coll., 1947; J.D., U. Wash., 1950. Bar: Wash. asst. atty. gen. State of Wash., 1950-51; pvt. practice law, Olympia, Wash., 1951—; gen. counsel Wash. Cath. Conf., 1967-76. Lt. (j.g.) USNR, 1943-46; PTO. Home and Office: 2723 Hillside Dr SE Olympia WA 98501-3460

WALKER, FRANK BANGHART, pathologist; b. Detroit, June 14, 1931; s. Roger Venning and Helen Frances (Reade) W.; m. Phyllis Childs; children: Nancy Anne, David Carl, Roger Osborne, Mark Andrew. BS, Union Coll., N.Y., 1951; MD, Wayne State U., 1955, MS, 1962. Diplomate Am. Bd. Pathology (trustee 1982-94, treas. 1984-91, v.p. 1991-92, pres. 1993-94). Intern Detroit Meml. Hosp., 1955-56; resident Wayne State U. and affiliated hosps., Detroit, 1958-62; pathologist, 1962-93; dir. labs. Detroit Meml. Hosp., 1984-87, Cottage Hosp., Grosse Pointe, Mich., 1984-93; pathologist, dir. labs. Macomb Hosp Ctr. (formerly South Macomb Hosp.), Warren, Mich., 1966-93, Jennings Meml. Hosp., Detroit, 1971-79, Alexander Blain Hosp., Detroit, 1971-85; ptnr. Langston, Walker & Assocs., P.C., Grosse Pointe, 1968-93; instr. pathology Wayne State U. Med. Sch., Detroit, 1962-72, asst. clin. prof., 1972-94, assoc. clin. prof., 1994—. Pres. Mich. Assn. Blood Banks, 1969-70; mem. med. adv. com. ARC, 1972-83; mem. Mich. Higher Edn. Assistance Authority, 1975-77; trustee Alexander Blain Meml. Hosp., Detroit, 1974-83, Detroit-Macomb Hosp. Corp., 1974-93, 95—; bd. dirs. Wayne State Fund, 1971-83. Capt. M.C., U.S. Army, 1956-58. Recipient Disting. Svc. award Wayne State U. Med. Sch., 1990. Fellow Detroit Acad. Medicine (pres.-elect 1995-96); mem. AMA (coun. on long-range planning and devel. 1982-88, vice chmn. 1985-87, chmn. 1987-88, trustee 1988—), Coll. Am. Pathologists (Disting. Svc. award 1989), Am. Soc. Clin. Pathologists (sec. 1971-77, pres. 1979-80, Disting. Svc. award 1989), Mich. Soc. Pathologists (pres. 1980-81), Wayne County Med. Soc. (pres. 1984-85, trustee 1986-91, chmn. 1990-91), Mich. Med. Soc. (bd. dirs. 1981-90, vice chmn. 1985-88, chmn. 1988-90), Am. Assn. Blood Banks, Mich. Assn. Blood Banks, Wayne State U. Alumni Assn. (bd. govs. 1968-71), Wayne State U. Med. Alumni Assn. (pres. 1969, trustee 1970-85, Disting. Alumni award 1974), Econ. Club Detroit, Detroit Athletic Club, Lochmoor Club, Mid-Am. Club, Alpha Omega Alpha, Phi Gamma Delta, Nu Sigma Nu. Republican. Episcopalian. Home and Office: 14004 Harbor Place Dr Saint Clair Shores MI 48080-1528

WALKER, FRANK DILLING, market research executive; b. Indpls., Dec. 31, 1934; s. Frank D. and Dorothy Mae (Cole) W.; m. Jane Tatman, Aug. 25, 1979; children—Steven F., Leah R. B.A., DePauw U., 1957. Chmn., chief exec. officer Walker Group, Indpls., 1960-95, Walker Clin. Evaluations, Inc., Indpls., 1986-95; chmn. Walker Info., 1995—; bd. dirs. Am. United Life Ins. Co., NBD Ind. Nat. Bank, State Life Ins. Co.; frequent speaker on market rsch. to various groups. Contbr. articles trade publs. Past mem. Indpls. Hist. Preservation Commn.; bd. dirs. Ind. Repertory Theatre, Meth. Hosp., United Way of Greater Indpls.; adv. council Indpls. Mus. Art, Buchanan Counseling Center; former chmn. Central Ind. Better Bus. Bur.; former chmn. Indpls. Econ. Devel. Corp.; trustee Children's Mus. Indpls., Univ. Indpls.; former bd. dirs. Jr. Achievement Central Ind., mem. adv. council; trustee The Children's Mus., YMCA Found.; bd. dirs. Citizens Gas and Coke Utility. With USAF, 1958-60. Mem. Council Am. Survey Research Orgns. (past chmn. bd.), Am. Mktg. Assn. (past pres. Ind. chpt.), Indpls. Sales and Mktg. Execs. Assn. (past pres.), Indpls. C. of C. (past chmn.), Mktg. Rsch. Assn. (hon. life), Sigma Chi. Republican. Methodist. Office: Walker Info 3939 Priority Way South Dr Indianapolis IN 46240-1496

WALKER, FRED ELMER, broadcasting executive; b. Trenton, N.J., May 31, 1931; s. Elmer and Adele F. (Decker) W.; m. Catharine Middleton Sullivan, Nov. 26, 1952; children: Catharine Walker Bergstrom, Elizabeth Walker Phillips, Frederick Christopher. Student, Trenton State Coll., 1952, NYU, 1953. Dir. pub. relations Sta. WPTZ-TV, Phila., 1953; v.p., gen. mgr. Sta. WTTM-AM, Trenton, 1956-59; gen. sales mgr. Sta. KYW-AM, Cleve., 1959-62; v.p., gen. mgr. Sta. KDKA-AM, Pitts., 1962-65, Sta. KYW-TV, Phila., 1965-67, Sta. KPIX-TV, San Francisco, 1967-69, Sta. WLWT-TV, Cin., 1969-71; pres. Broad St. Communications Corp., New Haven, 1971-85; v.p. radio group Westinghouse Broadcasting, N.Y.C., 1985-88; exec. v.p. Broad St. Ventures, N.Y.C., 1988—; pres. Broad St. TV Corp., 1988—, Broad. St. Mgmt. Corp., 1988—; bd. dirs. Broadcast Music, Inc., 1984-87, Call for Action, Washington, 1993—. Bd. dirs. Long Wharf Theatre, New Haven; chmn. Long Wharf Theatre Future Fund campaign, 1983-85, chmn. devel., 1986-90, chmn. and pres., 1990—; mem. Pres.'s Coun. Albertus Magnus Coll.; trustee Hamden Hall Country Day Sch., chmn. devel. com.; chmn. 250th fund dr. United Ch. Christ, 1987—; chmn. Call For Action, Washington, 1994—. Recipient Alfred P. Sloan award, 1954, Ohio State Ednl. award, 1953; fellow Berkeley Coll. Yale U., 1976. Mem. Radio Advt. Bur. (dir.), TV Bur. Advt., Nat. Assn. Broadcasters, New Haven C. of C. (vice chmn.), New Haven Lawn Club, Quinnipiac Club. Republican. Office: Sturbridge Commons North Haven CT 06473 also: Long Wharf Theatre 222 Sargent Dr New Haven CT 06511-5919

WALKER, GARY CLINTON, lawyer; b. Belleville, Ill., July 4, 1944; s. Delbert Clayton and Olive Imogene (McGough) W.; m. Joan Wolosenka; children: Lisa, Honorée, Byron. BA, U. Kans., 1966; LLB, Yale U. Law Sch., 1969. Assoc. Cravath, Swaine & Moore, N.Y.C., 1969; program developer Vera Inst. of Justice, N.Y.C., 1970; pres. Pioneer Diversified Services, N.Y.C., 1971-72; personnel officer Wildcat Service Corp., N.Y.C., 1973-74; sr. v.p. MDRC, Inc., N.Y.C., 1975-82; ptnr. Grinker, Walker & Assocs., Inc., N.Y.C., 1983-85; exec. v.p. Pub.-Pvt. Ventures, Inc., Phila., 1986—; cons. U.S. Gen. Acctg. Office, Washington, 1983—, Council on Founds., Washington, 1984, The Ford Found., N.Y.C., 1983-84, The Rockefeller Found., N.Y.C., 1987-88. Author: An Independent Sector Assessment of the Federal Job Training Partnership Act, 3 vols., 1984-86. Avocation: fiction writing. Home: 851 Plymouth Rd Norristown PA 19401-2525 Office: Pub-Pvt Ventures Inc 2005 Market St Philadelphia PA 19103

WALKER, GEORGE KONTZ, law educator; b. Tuscaloosa, Ala., July 8, 1938; s. Joseph Henry and Catherine Louise (Indorf) W.; m. Phyllis Ann Sherman, July 30, 1966; children: Charles Edward, Mary Neel. BA, U. Ala., 1959; LLB, Vanderbilt U., 1966; AM, Duke U., 1968; LLM, U. Va., 1972; postgrad. (Sterling fellow), Law Sch. Yale U., 1975-76. Bar: Va. 1967, N.C. 1976. Law clk. U.S. Dist. Ct., Richmond, Va., 1966-67; assoc. Hunton, Williams, Gay, Powell & Gibson, Richmond, 1967-70; pvt. practice Charlottesville, Va., 1970-71; asst. prof. Law Sch. Wake Forest U., Winston-Salem, N.C., 1972-73, assoc. prof. Law Sch., 1974-77, prof. Law Sch., 1977—; mem. bd. advisors Divinity Sch. Wake Forest U., 1991-94; Charles H. Stockton prof. internat. law U.S. Naval War Coll., 1992-93; vis. prof. Marshall-Wythe Sch. Law, Coll. William and Mary, Williamsburg, Va., 1979-80, U. Ala. Law Sch., 1985; cons. Naval War Coll., 1976—, Nat. Def. Exec. Res., 1991—, Naval War Coll., Operational Law Adv. Bd., 1993—. Author: International Law for the Naval Commander, 1985; contbr. articles to profl. jours. With USN, 1959-62, capt. USNR, ret. Woodrow Wilson fellow, 1962-63; recipient Joseph Branch Alumni Svc. award, Wake Forest, 1988; named Hon. Atty. Gen. N.C., 1986. Mem. ABA, Va. Bar Assn., N.C. Bar Assn. (chair internat. law & practice sect. 1995-96), Am. Soc. Internat. Law (exec. coun. 1988-91), Internat. Law Assn., Am. Judicature Soc., Am. Law Inst., Maritime Law Assn., Order of Barristers, Piedmont Club, Phi Beta Kappa, Sigma Alpha Epsilon, Phi Delta Phi. Democrat. Episcopalian. Home: 3321 Pennington Ln Winston Salem NC 27106-5439 Office: Wake Forest U Sch Law PO Box 7206 # U Winston Salem NC 27109

WALKER, GEORGE THEOPHILUS, JR., composer, pianist, music educator; b. Washington, June 27, 1922; s. George Theophilus Sr. and Rosa (King) W.; children: Gregory, Ian. MusB, Oberlin Coll., 1941; student of, Rudolf Serkin, Rosario Scalero; Artist Diploma, Curtis Inst. music, 1945; student, Nadia Boulanger; D of Mus. Arts, U. Rochester, 1957; DFA (hon.), Lafayette Coll., 1982; MusD (hon.), Oberlin Coll., 1983; student of, Nadia Boulanger. Instr. Dillard U., New Orleans, 1953-54; instr. Dalcroze Sch. Music, N.Y.C., 1960-61, New Sch. Social Research, N.Y.C., 1961; instr. to assoc. prof. Smith Coll., Northampton, Mass., 1961-68; assoc. prof. U. Colo., Boulder, 1968-69; disting. prof. Rutgers U., Newark, 1976-92, prof. emeritus, 1992; concert pianist Nat. Concert Artists, N.Y.C., 1950-53, Columbia Artists, N.Y.C., 1959-60; adj. prof. Peabody Inst. Johns Hopkins U., Balt., 1973-76; disting. prof. U. Del., Newark, 1975-76. Composer: Sonata for 2 Pianos (Harvey Gaul prize 1963), numerous sonatas, cantatas and concertos, Concerto for Cello and Orch., 1982, Sinfonias for Orch. Bd. dirs. Am. Bach Found., 1988. Recipient award Am. Acad. and Inst. Arts and Letter, 1982, Koussevitsky award, 1988, Pulitzer prize, 1996; grantee Smith Coll., U. Colo., Rutger U. Rsch. Coun., NEA, N.J. State Coun. for Arts; Fulbright fellow, 1957, John Hay Whitney fellow, 1958, Guggenheim fellow, 1969, 88, Rockefeller fellowship, 1971-74; commd. N.Y. Philharm., Cleve. Orch., Boston Symphony. Mem. ASCAP, Am. Bach Found. (bd. dirs. 1988), Am. Symphony League. Democrat. Avocations: tennis, photography, audio. Home: 323 Grove St Montclair NJ 07042-4223

WALKER, GEORGE W., bishop. Bishop, treas. Bd. Bishops AME Zion Ch., flossmoor, Il. Office: AME Zion Church 3654 Poplar Rd Flossmoor IL 60422-2239

WALKER, GORDON DAVIES, former government official, writer, lecturer, consultant; b. Logan, Utah, July 10, 1944; s. Rudger Harper and Fawn Lucile (Davies) W.; m. Carlene Martin, June 5, 1968; children—Kimberly Anne, Kelly Anne, Gordon Davies Jr., Bradford Martin. A.B., Brigham Young U., 1968; M.B.A., Harvard U., 1971. Project dir. Becker Research Co., Boston, 1969-71; dir. mktg. Am. Nat. Enterprises, Salt Lake City, 1971-72; v.p., dir. Sweetwater Properties, Salt Lake City, 1972-76; gen. ptnr. Covecrest Properties, Salt Lake City, 1976—; spl. asst. to sec. HUD, Washington, 1981-82; dep. under sec. HUD, 1983-86; cons. real estate, fin. Commerce Cons., Washington, 1986-87; pres., chief exec. officer Deseret Fed. Savs. and Loan, Salt Lake City, 1987-88; pres. U.S. Resources, Inc., Phoenix, 1988-92, also bd. dirs.; pres. Energy Lock Inc., Salt Lake City, 1992—. Author: Finance Your Own Way to Success, 1980; Develop Your Way to Success, 1981; Hottest New Ideas of the 1980's, 1982. Rep. state del., Salt Lake City, 1974; del. Rep. Nat. Conv., 1988. Mem. Nat. Assn. Realtors. Mem. LDS Ch.

WALKER, GORDON T., lawyer; b. June 12, 1942; M. Nancy Geary; children: Angus, Gwendolyn. AB, Tufts U., 1964; LLB, Harvard U., 1967. Bar: Mass. 1968, U.S. Dist. Ct. Mass., U.S. Ct. Appeals (1st cir.), U.S. Supreme Ct. Assoc., then ptnr. Hale and Dorr, Boston, 1968-82; ptnr. Finnegan, Stanzler, Nadeau & Walker, Boston, 1982-84; ptnr., head litigation dept. McDermott, Will & Emery, Boston, 1984—. Mem. ABA (co-chmn. litigation sect. alternative dispute resolution com. 1986-91, vice chmn. 1993-94), Am. Arbitration Assn., Boston Bar Assn. (chair com. internat. dispute resolution 1992-94). Office: McDermott Will & Emery 75 State St Ste 1700 Boston MA 02109-1807

WALKER, H. LAWSON, lawyer; b. Cin., Feb. 10, 1949; s. H. Lawson and Lucille (Kerr) W.; m. Peggy L. Walker, June 1, 1974; children: Erin, Jonathan. BBA, U. Coll. of Bus., Cin., 1972; JD, U. Cin. Coll. of Law, Cin., 1975. Bar: 6th cir. 1975, U.S. Dist. Ct. (Ohio dist.) 1975, ED Ky. 1975, Ohio 1975, Ky. 1976. Assoc. Riggs & Riggs, Erlanger, Ky., 1975-80; ptnr. Riggs, Riggs & Walker, Erlanger, Ky., 1980-87, Dinsmore & Shohl, Florence, Ky., 1987-92, Brown, Todd & Heyburn, Covington, Ky., 1992—; dir. Liberty Nat. Bank of No. Ky. State rep. Ky. Legislature, Frankfort, 1987; chmn. Rep. Party, Fenton County, Ky., 1980, 85; chmn. No. Ky. Legis. Caucus, 1991-93; dist. chmn. Powderhorn dist. Boy Scouts Am., 1995—; bd. dirs. No. Ky. Easter Seals, Covington, 1982—, Sanitation Dist. of Kenton, Campbell and Boone Counties; deacon Lakeside Christian Ch., Ft. Mitchell, Ky., 1983—. Recipient Leadership award, Ky. C. of C., Frankfort, 1988. Mem. Ohio Bar Assn., Ky. Bar Assn., No. Ky. Bar Assn., Ky. Sch. Bd. Atty. Assn., Ky. Acad. Trial Attys., U. Cin. Alumni Assn. (bd. dirs. 1988-95). Republican. Christian. Home: 28A Linden Hill Dr Covington KY 41017-1308 Office: Brown Todd & Heyburn 50 E Rivercenter Blvd Covington KY 41011

WALKER, HAROLD BLAKE, minister; b. Denver, May 7, 1904; s. Herbert R. and Ethel G. (Blake) W.; m. Mary Alice Corder, Feb. 1, 1930; children—Herbert Elwood, Howard Deane, Timothy Blake. AB, U. Denver, 1925, DD, 1952; AM, Boston U., 1927; BD, McCormick Theol. Sem., 1932; postgrad., U. Chgo., 1933-34; DD, Emporia Coll., 1944, Hamilton Coll., 1949, U. Denver, 1952, Rocky Mountain Coll., 1971; LHD, Lake Forest U., 1959, Nat. Coll. Edn., 1970; STD, Northwestern U., 1970. Editor, writer A.P., Kansas City, 1927-30; ordained to ministry Presbyn. Ch., 1932; minister Fullerton-Covenant Ch., Chgo., 1932-36; minister First Ch., Utica, N.Y., 1936-42, Oklahoma City, 1942-47; minister 1st Presbyn. Ch., Evanston, Ill., 1947-69; columnist Splty. Salesman mag., 1954-67, Chgo. Tribune-N.Y. News syndicated columnist, 1954-81; lectr. homiletics McCormick Theol. Sem.; lectr., bd. dirs. Harold Blake Walker chair pastoral theology; cons. W. Clement Stone Enterprises, 1970-74; sem. v.p. Bd. Fgn. Missions Presbyn. Ch. U.S.A.; Nat. Commn. Evangelism, 1946-47; dir. Presbyn. Tribune, 1943-55; mem. Presbyn. Commn. on Consolidation, 1957-58, Commn. on Ecumenical Mission Relations, 1958-61. Author: Going God's Way, 1946, Ladder of Light, 1951, Upper Room on Main Street, 1954, Power to Manage Yourself, 1955, (with wife) Venture of Faith, 1959, Heart of the Christian Year, 1962, Faith for Times of Tension, 1963, Thoughts to Live By, 1965, To Conquer Loneliness, 1966, Prayers to Live By, 1966, Memories to Live By, 1968, Inspirational Thoughts for Everyday, 1970, Days Demanding Courage, 1978, History of St. John's of Red Cross of Constantine, 1985, Caring Community, 1986; contbr. to religious publs. Bd. dirs. Nat. Presbyn. Ch. and Ctr., Washington; bd. dirs. McCormick Theol. Sem., pres., 1953-55, 57-71; bd. dirs. Ill. Masonic Med. Center, Chgo., Lake Forest Coll.; trustee Maryville Coll. Recipient DeMolay Legion of Honor; Freedoms Found. sermon prize, 1950, 55, 77; citations Protestant Fund. Greater Chgo., 1970; Chgo. Inst. Medicine Citizens fellow, 1987; citations Chgo. Friends of Lit., 1971, 79; Disting. Alumnus award McCormick Theol. Sem., 1979. Mem. Utica Council Chs. (pres. 1940), Am. Theol. Soc. Chgo. Cleric, Pi Kappa Alpha. Clubs: Univ. (Chgo.). Lodge: Masons (Chgo., Evanston) (Shriner, 33 deg., grand chaplain N.Y. 1940-41). Home: 422 Davis St Evanston IL 60201-4610

WALKER, H(ERBERT) LESLIE, JR., architect; b. Wilmington, N.C., July 6, 1918; s. Herbert Leslie and May Bell (Sellers) W.; m. Elnita Frances Sellers, June 18, 1939 (dec.); children: Judy S., Robert L.; m. Ernie Katherine Watson, July 20, 1973. Student, N.C. State Coll., Raleigh, 1939-40, Duke U., 1948-49. Apprentice architect H. Raymond Weeks, architect, Durham, N.C., 1946-56; ptnr. Walker & Jackson, architects and engrs., Tampa, Fla., 1959-61; prin. H. Leslie Walker & Assocs., architects, Tampa, 1961-65, 66-71; ptnr. Walker & Weilage, Tampa, 1965-66, Walker & McLane, Architects, Engrs. & Planners Inc., Tampa, 1972-75; pres. H. Leslie Walker, Architect Inc., Tampa, 1975—. Fellow AIA (dir. Fla. region 1973-75, chmn. govtl. affairs commn. 1975, chmn. architect-engr. com. fedn. constrn. 1975, chmn. fed. agencies com. 1976-77, pres. Fla. Cen. chpt. 1962-63; Pullara Meml. award Fla. Cen. chpt. 1973, medal of honor 1974, pres. Fla. assn. 1969; Design Competition Honor award Fla. assn. 1965, Design Competition award merit 1966). Democrat. Clubs: Palma Ceia Golf and Country, Tampa Commerce (pres. 1964). Lodges: Masons (32 degree), Shriners. Home: 4645 Bay Crest Dr Tampa FL 33615-4901 Office: H Leslie Walker Architect Inc PO Box 260355 6105 Memorial Hwy Ste A Tampa FL 33685

WALKER, HERSCHEL, professional football player; b. Wrightsville, Ga., Mar. 3, 1962; m. Cindi Di Angelis. BS in Criminal Justice, U. Ga., 1984. Football player N.J. Generals, 1983-85, Dallas Cowboys, 1986-89, Minn. Vikings, 1989-91, Phila. Eagles, 1992-95, N.Y. Giants, 1995—. Named to Sporting News coll. All-Am. team, 1980-82, United States Football League All-Star team, 1983, 85, Pro Bowl, 1987, 88; recipient Heisman trophy, 1982; named Sporting News Coll. Football Player of Yr., 1982, Sporting News United States Football League Player of Yr., 1985. Office: NY Giants Giants Stadium East Rutherford NJ 07073

WALKER, HILL M., educator. Recipient Rsch. award Coun. for Exceptional Children, 1993. Office: U Oregon Ctr Ctr Human Devel 901 E 18th Ave Eugene OR 97403-1354

WALKER, HOWARD ERNEST, lawyer; b. Mobile, Ala., Mar. 3, 1944; s. Ernest W. and Denise (Kearney) W.; m. Michelle Ann Pinsonneault, June 20, 1992. BA, U. Ill., 1966; JD, Boston U., 1974. Bar: R.I. 1974. Assoc. Hinckley, Allen & Snyder, Providence, R.I., 1974-80, ptnr., 1980—. Trustee Providence Pub. Libr., 1978—, pres., 1988-92; trustee R.I. Wild Plant Soc., 1995—; trustee R.I. Civic Chorale & Orchestra, 1988-95. Lt. USNR, 1967-71. Mem. ABA, R.I. Bar Assn. (chmn. superior ct. bench/bar com. 1990-93, 94-95), Maritime Law Assn. of U.S., Nat. Assn. R.R. Trial Counsel, Def. Rsch. Inst., Phi Kappa Phi, Phi Beta Kappa. Avocations: Western Americana, nat. hist. Home: 39A Berrien Ln PO Box 118 Rockville RI 02873-0118 Office: Hinckley Allen & Snyder 1500 Fleet Ctr Providence RI 02903

WALKER, IRVING EDWARD, lawyer; b. Balt., Jan. 31, 1952; s. Bertram and Mildred (Shapiro) W.; m. Laura Sachs, May 21, 1978; children: Brandon Harris, Aaron Seth, Emily Celeste. BA, Duke U., 1973; JD, U. Md., 1978. Bar: Md. 1978, U.S. Dist. Ct. Md. 1978, U.S. Ct. Appeals (4th cir.) 1980, U.S. Supreme Ct. 1995. Assoc. Frank, Bernstein, Conaway & Goldman, Balt., 1978-85, ptnr., 1986-91; ptnr. Miles & Stockbridge, Balt., 1991—; chair Bankruptcy & Creditors Rights Group, 1991—. Contbg. author: Bankruptcy Deskbook, 1986. Legal advisor Balt. chpt. The Holiday Project, San Francisco, 1982—; bd. dirs. Jewish Community Ctr. Greater Balt., 1986-88. Mem. ABA (mem. chpt. 11 subcom. 1993, co-chairperson task force 3rd, 4th and D.C. cirs.), Md. Bar Assn., Bar Assn. Balt. City (chmn. bankruptcy and bus. law com. 1989-90), Am. Bankruptcy Inst., Bankruptcy Assn. Dist. Md. (pres. 1992-93, chmn. Balt. chpt. 1989-91), Order of Coif. Avocation: sports. Office: Miles & Stockbridge 10 Light St Baltimore MD 21202-1435

WALKER, JAMES ELLIOT CABOT, physician; b. Bryn Mawr, Pa., Sept. 28, 1926; s. Arthur Meeker and Sylvia (Cabot) W.; m. Audrey Crowder Wakeman, July 11, 1965; children—Holly Barnwell, James Elliot Cabot. B.A., Williams Coll., 1949; M.D., U. Pa., 1953; M.S. in Hygiene, Harvard U., 1966. Intern and resident in medicine U. Wis., 1953, U. Mich., 1954-55, Peter Bent Brigham Hosp., 1958-60; assoc. dir., sr. assoc. dept. medicine Peter Bent Brigham Hosp., Boston; also research asst., lectr. Harvard U. Med. Sch., 1959-65; chmn. dept. community medicine U. Conn. Med. Sch., Farmington, 1966-86, prof. medicine, 1966—; vis. prof. St. Thomas' Hosp., London, 1975-76, Harvard Med. Sch., Cambridge, Mass., 1986-87; pres. Northeast Can./Am. Health Coun., 1978-87; dir. Ctr. for Internat. Cmty. Health Studies, 1981-86; assoc. dir. Traveler's Ctr. on Aging, 1987—; chmn. Alzheimers Coalition of Conn., 1992-94; med. dir. Avery Heights Retirement Cmty., 1992—. Author articles, monograph in field. Served with Am. Field Service, 1945; to capt. M.C. U.S. Army, 1955-58. Fellow ACP, AGS. Home: 111 Westmont St West Hartford CT 06117-2929 Office: U Conn Health Center Farmington CT 06032

WALKER, JAMES KENNETH, judge; b. Decatur, Tex., Jan. 10, 1936; s. James Bluford and Elmer Vernice (Clark) W.; m. Mary Frank Garrett, July 9, 1960 (dec. Nov. 1976); children—James Garrett, Steven Wade; m. Jo Beth Robertson, July 28, 1978; 1 child, Ann Elizabeth. LLB, Baylor U., 1960. Bar: Tex. 1960. Practice law Lubbock, Tex., 1960-63, Morton, Tex., 1963-84; judge 286th Dist. Ct., 1984-91; Cochran County atty., 1965-73, 79-84. Bd. dirs. Morton Indsl. Found. Mem. ABA, Tex. Bar Assn. Methodist. Club: Lion. Home: 218 Sandalwood Ln Levelland TX 79336-6816

WALKER, JAMES ROY, microbiologist; b. Chestnut, La., Nov. 8, 1937; s. Clint Cortez and Annie Mae (Holland) W.; m. Barbara Ann Fess, Aug. 8, 1959; children: James Bryan, Melinda Lee. BS, Northwestern State U., 1960; PhD, U. Tex., 1963. Asst. prof. U. Tex., Austin, 1967-71, assoc. prof., 1971-78, prof., 1978—, chmn. dept. microbiology, 1981-93; mem. sci. adv. com. U. Tex. Health Science Ctr., Science Park Cancer Ctr., 1984-88. Contbr. articles to profl. jours. Served to capt. U.S. Army, 1963-65. Fellow NIH, 1965-67, Rosalie B. Hite U. Tex., 1960-63; grantee NIH, 1967-91, NSF, 1978-84, 91-95, Am. Cancer Soc., 1976-91, The Welch Found., 1982-91, Tex. Adv. Rsch. Program, 1992-93, Am. Heart Assn., 1995, Coun. for Tobacco Rsch., 1996—. Mem. Am. Soc. Microbiology (vis. professorship at Fed. U. Rio de Janeiro 1977). Home: 8504 Greenflint Ln Austin TX 78759-8131 Office: U Tex Dept Microbiology Austin TX 78712-1095

WALKER, JAMES SILAS, college president; b. LaFollette, Tenn., Aug. 21, 1933; s. John Charles and Ruth Constance (Yeagle) W.; m. Nadine Leas Mortenson, May 28, 1954; children: Steven J., David K., Bradley P., Scott C. BA, U. Ariz., 1954; BDiv, McCormick Theol. Sem., 1956; postgrad. U. Basel, Switzerland, 1956-57; PhD, Claremont Coll., 1963. Ordained to ministry Presbyn. Ch., 1956. Asst. pastor Central Presbyn. Ch., Denver, 1957-60; prof. Huron Coll., S.D., 1963-66; prof. Hastings (Nebr.) Coll., 1966-75, dir. devel., 1975-79, dean, 1979-83; pres. Jamestown Coll., N.D., 1983—; adj. faculty mem. Luther Northwestern Theol. Sem., St. Paul, 1984—. Author: Theology of Karl Barth, 1963. Bd. dirs. Salvation Army. Rotary Internat. Found. fellow, 1956-57; Nat. Def. Title IV grantee, 1960-63. Mem. Assn. Presbyn. Colls. and Univs., Presbytery of No. Plains (coun.), Rotary (dist. 563 gov. 1978-79). Republican. Avocations: travel, hunting, photography. Office: Jamestown Coll Office of Pres # 6080 Jamestown ND 58405

WALKER, JAMES WILLIAM, JR., lawyer; b. Birmingham, Ala., Aug. 19, 1927; s. James William and Eva Victoria (Harris) W.; m. Eileen Newton, Apr. 30, 1949; children: James William III, Michael, Lee, Helen, Caroline. AB, Birmingham So. Coll., 1949; JD, Emory U., 1953. Bar: Ga. 1954, D.C. 1966. With Merrill Lynch, Fenner & Smith, N.Y.C., 1954-67; exec. v.p. Am. Stock Exchange, N.Y.C., 1968-74, Securities Industry Assn., Washington, 1974-77; exec. v.p., gen. counsel INA Corp., Phila., 1977-82; exec. v.p., gen. counsel CIGNA Corp., Phila., 1982-92, ret., 1992. Mem. Emory U. Law Sch. Coun., pres. Inst. Gen. Counsel Studies; trustee Phila. Mus. Art. Capt. U.S. Army, 1946-48, Res. 1948-57. Mem. ABA, Am. Law Inst., Union League Phila.

WALKER, JERALD CARTER, university administrator, minister; b. Bixby, Okla., May 22, 1938; s. Joseph Carter and Trula Tosh (Jackson) W.; m. Virginia Canfield, Apr. 14, 1963; children: Elisabeth Katherine, Anne Carter. BA in Sociology, Oklahoma City U., 1960; BD, U. Chgo., 1964; D of Religion, Sch. Theology at Claremont, 1966. Ordained to ministry Meth. Ch., 1964. Dir., campus minister Campus Christian Assn., Chgo., 1961-64; minister of outreach Temple Meth. Ch., San Francisco, 1965-66; chaplain, asst. prof. religion Nebr. Wesleyan U., Lincoln, 1966-69; pres. John J. Pershing Coll., Beatrice, Nebr., 1969-70; v.p. univ. rels., assoc. prof. Southwestern U., Georgetown, Tex., 1970-74; pres. Baker U., Baldwin, Kans., 1974-79, Oklahoma City U., 1979—; ednl. adv. to bd. dirs. Tianjin U. Commerce, People's Republic of China; participant Okla. Ann. Conf. of United Meth. Ch. Co-author: The State of Sequoyah: An Impressionistic View of Eastern Oklahoma, 1985; contbr. chpt. book, articles to profl. jours. Bd. dirs., past chmn. Okla. Ind. Coll. Found. Recipient Alumni Recognition award Nebr. 4H Club, 1970, Okla. 4H Club, Disting. Alumnus award Oklahoma City U., 1974, Outstanding Citizen award Dist. 575 Rotary Internat., 1990, Award for Excellence Asia Soc. Okla., 1990, Humanitarian award for Okla/Ark. region NCCJ, 1992, Nat. Police Adminstrn. award for promotion or peace and order Rep. of China, 1992, Francis Asbury award for fostering United Meth. Ministries in Higher Edn., 1994. Mem. Nat. Assn. Schs. and Colls. of United Meth. Ch. (past pres.), Nat. Assn. Colls. and Univs. (bd. dirs.). Office: Oklahoma City U 2501 N Blackwelder Ave Oklahoma City OK 73106-1402

WALKER, JOAN H., public relations executive. With N.J. State Govt., 1973-80; pres. Richmann & Ptnrs. Ltd., 1980-88; exec. v.p. office chmn. Saatchi & Saatchi Worldwide, 1988-89; mng. dir. mktg. comm. Nynex, 1990-92; pres. Bozell Pub. Rels., N.Y.C., 1993—. Office: Bozell Pub Rels 75 Rockefeller Plz New York NY 10019-6908*

WALKER, JOHN DENLEY, foundation director, former government official; b. Petersburg, Va., July 15, 1921; s. John Otey and Evelyn Mildred (Denley) W.; m. Diana Taylor, Apr. 30, 1949 (div. 1980); children—Walker Diana, John Denley, Joseph Warren; m. Helen Hoogerwerff, Mar. 15, 1984; step children—Saskia Roskam, Hugo, Frederick. B.A., U. N.C.-Chapel Hill, 1944; postgrad., U. Pa., 1950-51. Superintendant N.J. Bell, 1946-48; asst. dir. labor div. ECA, Paris, France, 1948-50; mgmt. cons., 1951-53; fgn. service res. officer U.S. Govt., Paris, Malta, Israel, Australia, 1953-77; exec. dir. English Speaking Union of U.S., N.Y.C., 1978-87. Contbr. articles to profl. jours. Bd. dirs. Am. Student Ctr., Paris, 1953-57; v.p. Ctr. for Security Studies, 1988—. Lt. USN, 1942-45. Episcopalian. Clubs: Pilgrims, Standrews (N.Y.C.); Univ. (Washington); Chevy Chase (Md.). Lodges: Legion of Valor, Soc. Cin., Order of St. Johns of Jerusalem. Home: 3271 P St NW Washington DC 20007-2756

WALKER, JOHN LOCKWOOD, lawyer; b. Atlanta, Sept. 3, 1952; s. James William and Doris (Camp) W.; m. Caroline Asher Walker, Jan. 16, 1952; children: Ann Caroline, John Lockwood Jr., Elizabeth Davis, Lindsay Eleise. BA, Duke U., 1974, JD, 1977. Atty. legal div. bd. govs. FRS, Washington, 1977-79; assoc. Simpson Thacher & Bartlett, N.Y.C., 1979-84; ptnr. Simpson, Thacher & Bartlett, N.Y.C., 1984—. Mem. Fin. Svcs. Vol. Corps (dir., pres.), Coun. on Fgn. Rels., Met. Club of Washington, Univ. Club (N.Y.C.), Chevy Chase (Md.) Club, Bedford (N.Y.) Golf and Tennis Club. Democrat. Episcopalian. Office: Simpson Thacher & Bartlett 425 Lexington Ave New York NY 10017-3903*

WALKER, JOHN MERCER, JR., federal judge; b. N.Y.C., Dec. 26, 1940; s. John Mercer and Louise (Mead) W.; m. Cristy West, June 20, 1980 (div. Apr. 1983); m. Katharine Kirkland, Feb. 14, 1987. BA, Yale U., 1962; JD, U. Mich., 1966. Bar: N.Y. 1969, U.S. Dist. Ct. (so. dist.) N.Y. 1971, U.S. Ct. Appeals (2d cir.) 1972, U.S. Supreme Ct. 1977, U.S. Ct. Appeals (D.C. cir.) 1982. Maxwell Sch. Pub. Adminstrn. fellow, state counsel Republic of Botswana, Africa, 1966-68; assoc. Davis, Polk and Warwell, N.Y.C., 1969-70; asst. U.S. atty. U.S. Dist. Ct. (so. dist.) N.Y., N.Y.C., 1971-75; assoc. to ptnr. Carter, Ledyard and Milburn, N.Y.C., 1975-81; asst. sec. enforcement ops. Dept. Treasury, Washington, 1981-85; judge U.S. Dist. Ct. (so. dist.) N.Y., 1985-89, U.S. Ct. Appeals (2nd cir.), 1989—; adj. prof. NYU Law Sch., 1995—; gen. counsel Nat. Coun. on Crime and Deliquency, N.Y.C., 1977-81; chmn. Fed. Law Enforcement Tng. Ctr., Washington, 1981-85; spl. counsel Adminstrv. Conf. U.S., Washington, 1986-92; mem. budget com. jud. conf. Inst. Jud. Adminstrn., 1992—, dir., 1992—. Del. Rep. Nat. Conv., Detroit, 1980. With USMCR, 1963-67. Recipient Alexander Hamilton award Sec. of Treas., Washington, 1985, Secret Service Honor award, 1985. Mem. ABA, D.C. Bar Assn., Assn. Bar City of N.Y., Fed. Judges Assn. (pres. 1993-95). Republican. Episcopalian. Office: US Cir Ct US Courthouse FOLEY SQUARE New York NY 10007

WALKER, JOHN PATRICK, theater producer, actor; b. Elgin, Ill., Apr. 21, 1956; s. John Patrick and Ruth Ellen (Borror) W.; m. Pamela Jean Gay, Dec. 5, 1981; children: Miranda, Caitlin. BA, Notre Dame U., 1978; cert., Am. Conservatory Theatre, San Francisco, 1980. Actor Peninsula Players, Door County, Wis., 1978-84, gen. mgr., 1984-86; house mgr. Civic Ctr. Performing Arts, Chgo., 1984-86; gen. mgr. Royal George Theater, Chgo., 1986-89, Cullen, Henaghan, Platt, Chgo., 1989-91; mng. dir. Victory Gardens Theater, Chgo., 1991—; pres. League of Chgo. Theaters. Avocations: fly fishing, skiing. Office: Victory Gardens Theater 2257 N Lincoln Ave Chicago IL 60614-3717

WALKER, JOHN SUMPTER, JR., lawyer; b. Richmond, Ark., Oct. 13, 1921; s. John Sumpter, Martha (Wilson) W.; m. Eljana M. duVall, Dec. 31, 1947; children: John Stephen, Barbara Monika Ann, Peter Mark Gregory. BA, Tulane U., 1942; MS, U. Denver, 1952, JD, 1960; diploma Nat. Def. U., 1981. Bar: Colo. 1960, U.S. Dist. Ct. Colo. 1960, U.S. Supreme Ct., 1968, U.S. Ct. Appeals (10th cir.) 1960, U.S. Tax. Ct., 1981. With Denver & Rio Grande Western R.R. Co., 1951-61, gen. solicitor, 1961-89 ; pres. Denver Union Terminal Ry. Co. Apptd. gen. counsel Moffat Tunnel Commn., 1991; life mem. Children's Diabetes Found. With U.S. Army, 1942-46. Decorated Bronze Star. Mem. Colo. Bar Assn., Arapahoe County Bar Assn., Alliance Francaise (life), Order of St. Ives, U. Denver Chancellors' Soc., Cath. Lawyers Guild. Republican. Roman Catholic. Club: Denver Athletic.

WALKER, JOSEPH, retired research executive; b. Rockford, Ill., Dec. 28, 1922; s. Joseph H. and Elizabeth (McEachran) W.; m. June Farley Enerson, Jan. 22, 1944; children—Joseph A., Amy E., Richard H., Jeanne A. B.S. with high honors, Beloit Coll., 1943; M.S., U. Wis., 1948, Ph.D., 1950. Sr. research chemist Pure Oil Co. Research Center, Crystal Lake, Ill., 1950-51; project technologist Pure Oil Co. Research Center, 1952-54, sect. supr., 1954-58, div. dir. analytical research and service div., 1958-64, research coordinator, 1964, dir. research, 1965; assoc. dir. research Union Oil Co. of Calif., Research Center, Brea, Calif., 1966-78; v.p. chem. research Union Oil Co. of Calif., Research Center, 1979-85. Pres. Sch. Bd., Crystal Lake, 1963-65. Served to lt. (j.g.) USNR, 1943-46. Mem. Am. Chem. Soc., Am. Petroleum Inst., Phi Beta Kappa, Sigma Xi, Phi Lambda Upsilon, Sigma Alpha Epsilon. Home: 406A Pasadena Ct San Clemente CA 92672-5477

WALKER, K. GRAHAME, manufacturing company executive; b. West Bridgford, Nottinghamshire, Eng., June 19, 1937; came to U.S., 1979; s. John P. and Lilian (Wright) W.; m. Robina Mairy Bendell, Aug. 20, 1959 (div. 1979); children: Belinda Sharon, Victoria Jane; m. Shirley Dean Allison, Dec. 6, 1980. Student, Merchant Taylors' Sch., 1948-55; grad., Britannia Royal Naval Coll., 1955-57, Royal Naval Engring. Coll., 1959-62. Mktg. exec. Rank Orgn., Eng., 1962-65; mng. dir. Hysol Sterling Ltd., Eng., 1965-74, Dexter GmbH, Fed. Republic Germany, 1974-79; pres. Hysol div. The Dexter Corp., Industry, Calif., 1979-85; pres. specialty chems. and services group The Dexter Corp., Windsor Locks, Conn., 1985-88; pres., chief operating officer Dexter Corp., Windsor Locks, Conn., 1988-89, pres., chief exec. officer, dir., 1989-93; chmn., pres., CEO The Dexter Corp., Windsor Locks, Conn., 1993—, also bd. dirs.; bd. dirs. Life Techs., Inc. (subs. Dexter Corp.). Bd. dirs. Greater Hartford chpt. ARC, 1986-89, chmn., 1990-92; bd. dirs. Barnes Group Inc., Bristol, 1988—, New Eng. Air Mus., Windsor Locks, 1988—; trustee Hartford U., 1992—; corporator St. Francis Hosp., 1994—, Hartford Hosp., 1990. Lt. Royal Navy, 1955-62. Mem. Conn. Bus. and Industry Assn. (bd. dirs. 1990, chmn. 1994), Hartford Club. Avocations: skiing, gardening, literature. Office: The Dexter Corp 1 Elm St Windsor Locks CT 06096-2334

WALKER, KENNETH DALE, automotive parts company executive; b. Ft. Worth, Feb. 25, 1948; s. Billy Glenn and Jo Ann (Prestridge) W.; m. Cheri Lee Propp, Feb. 28, 1969 (div. Aug. 1980); children: Joel Glenn, Corbett Dale; m. Vickie Lynn Franklin, Sept. 27, 1980. BBA, U. Tex., 1970. CPA, Tex. Mgr. Arthur Young & Co., Ft. Worth, 1970-76; controller, v.p. fin. Big 4 Automotive, Ft. Worth, 1976-80, v.p. ops West Tex., 1980-82, v.p. retail, 1982-84; chief fin. officer southwest region AI Automotive Corp., Ft. Worth, 1984-86, v.p. ops., chief operating officer southwest region, 1986-88; owner Kenneth D. Walker Consulting Turn Around Mgmt. Projects, 1988; pres., CEO Cardis Corp., Buena Park, Calif., 1989-92, Parts Industry Corp., Memphis, 1992-96, Meineke Discount Muffler Shops, Inc., 1996—. Instr. project bus. Jr. Achievement, Ft. Worth, 1981; bd. dirs. All Pro Program, Inc., Andolusia, Ala., 1978-84. Bumper to Bumper Program, Ft. Worth, 1987—. Recipient Automotive Replacement Edn. award Northwood Inst., 1987. Mem. Inst. Internal Auditors (v.p. 1975-76, pres. 1976), Automotive Warehouse Distbr. Assn. (chmn. fin. stats. com. 1984-87, chmn. univ. faculty 1986-87, bd. govs. 1986—, Pursuit of Excellence award 1986), TPC-Southwind Club. Methodist. Avocations: golf, skiing. Office: Meineke Discount Muffler Ste 900 128 S Tryon St Charlotte NC 28202

WALKER, KENNETH HENRY, architect; b. N.Y.C., June 11, 1940; s. Matthew and Lillian (Goldfarb) W. B.A., Brown U., 1962; M.Arch., Harvard U., 1966. Founder, pres. Walker Grad, 1973-76; founder, pres. Walker Group, N.Y.C., 1976-85, WalkerGroup/CNI, N.Y.C., 1985-93; pres. Retail Options, Inc., N.Y.C., 1993—; lectr. on design. Prin. works include Isetan Dept. Store, Tokyo, Saks 5th Ave., N.Y.C., John Wanamaker, Phila., Bloomingdales, Boca Raton, Fla., FAO Schwarz, N.Y.C., Citibank (nationally), Galeries Lafayette, France; contbr. articles to Time mag., Fortune, Interior Design, Archtl. Record, others; exhibited indsl. designs at Whitney Mus. Past pres. Art Adv. Com., Brown U., Providence, 1979-83; mem. architecture and design commn. Mus. Modern Art, N.Y.C., 1976-93; trustee Village of Dering Harbor, Shelter Island, N.Y., 1982-87; pres. alumni coun. Harvard U. Grad. Sch. Design, 1985-88. Named to Interior Design Hall of Fame, Interior Design mag., 1985. Fellow AIA (over 20 design awards); mem. Young Pres.'s Orgn., Inst. Store Planners, Harvard U. Alumni Assn. Office: Retail Options Inc 15 E 26th St New York NY 10010-1505

WALKER, KENT, lawyer; b. Geneva, Ill., Oct. 4, 1944; s. Robert and Jean (McCullough) W.; m. Helene Feinberg, Sept. 14, 1984; children: Forrest, Lowell, Molly. BA, Wheaton Coll., 1966; JD, Northwestern U., Evanston, Ill., 1969. Bar: Ill. 1969, Del. 1970, Pa. 1984; U.S. Dist. Ct. Del. 1971, U.S. Dist. Ct. D.C. 1973, U.S. Dist. Ct. (ea. dist.) Pa. 1984; U.S. Ct. Appeals (3rd cir.) 1972, U.S. Ct. Appeals D.C. 1972; U.S. Tax Ct. 1975. Dep. atty. gen. Del. Dept. Justice, Wilmington, 1971-72, state solicitor and chief civil divsn., 1972-74; acting U.S. atty. U.S. Dept. Justice, Wilmington, 1977, 1st asst. U.S. atty., 1975-78; assoc. Garfinkel & Volpicelli, Phila., 1984-86; assoc., ptnr. Mesirov, Gelman, Jaffe, Cramer & Jamieson, Phila., 1986-89; ptnr. Ballard, Spahr, Andrews & Ingersoll, Phila., 1989-95; shareholder Buchanan Ingersoll, Phila., 1995—. Mem. ABA, Pa. Bar Assn., Phila. Bar Assn., Del. State Bar Assn. Republican. Episcopalian. Office: Buchanan Ingersoll Two Logan Sq 12th Fl Philadelphia PA 19103

WALKER, L. T., bishop. Bishop of Ark. ch. of God in Christ, Little Rock. Office: Ch of God in Christ 2315 S Chester St Little Rock AR 72206-2021

WALKER, LANNON, foreign service officer; b. Los Angeles, Jan. 17, 1936; s. James Orville and Esther W.; m. Arlette Daguet, July 14, 1954; children: Rachelle, Anne. B.S., Georgetown U., 1961. Fgn. service officer Dept. State, 71961; polit. officer Dept. State, Rabat, Morocco, 1962-64; prin. officer Dept. State, Constantine, Algeria, 1964-66; assigned Exec. Secretariat Dept. State, 1966-69; econ. counselor Dept. State, Tripoli, Libya, 1969-70; dep. chief mission Dept. State, Yaounde, Cameroon, 1971-73; adminstrv. counselor Dept. State, Saigon, Viet Nam, 1973-74; dep. chief mission Dept. State, Kinshasa, Zaire, 1974-77; dep. asst. sec. African Affairs Dept. State, Washington, 1977-82; spl. adviser African affairs Dept. State, 1983-84, dep. insp. gen., 1984-85, ambassador to Senegal, 1985-88, amb. to Nigeria, 1989-92; mem. Policy Planning Coun. Dept. of State, Washington, 1993-95; ambassador to Cote d'Ivoire Abidjan, 1995—; employed in pvt. sector, 1982-83; sr. assoc. Carnegie Endowment, 1988-89. Served with USAF, 1953-58. Mem. Am. Fgn. Service Assn. (chmn. 1966-69). Roman Catholic.

WALKER, LARRY KENNETH ROBERT, professional baseball player; b. Maple Ridge, B.C., Dec. 1, 1966. Grad. high sch., B.C., Can. With Montreal Expos, 1989-94; outfielder Colo. Rockies, 1995—. Named "The Sporting News" Nat. League All-Star Team, 1992, "The Sporting News" NAt. League Silver Slugger Team, 1992; recipient Gold Glove as outfielder, 1992-93. Office: Colo Rockies 2001 Blake St Denver CO 80205-2010

WALKER, LELAND JASPER, civil engineer; b. Fallon, Nev., Apr. 18, 1923; s. Albert Willard and Grayce (Wilkinson) W.; m. Margaret Frances Noble, Jan. 21, 1946; children: Thomas, Margaret, Timothy. B.S. in Civil Engring, Iowa State U., 1944; D. Eng. (hon.), Mont. State U., 1983. Engr. with various govtl. depts., 1946-51, 53-55; v.p. Wenzel & Co. (cons. engrs.), Great Falls, Mont., 1955-58; pres., chmn. bd. No. Engring. and Testing, Inc., Great Falls, 1958-88; pres. Ind. Labs. Assurance Co., 1977-79; bd. dirs. Mont. Power Co., Entech Inc., 1982-92, Lewis and Clark Biologicals, Inc., 1989-92, Applied Tech., Inc. Pres., trustee Endowment and Rsch. Found. Mont. State U., 1969-82, Mont. Deaconess Hosp., Great Falls, 1959-67. McLaughlin Rsch. Inst. Biol. Scis., 1989-92, Mont. Sch. Deaf and Blind Found., 1984—; trustee Rocky Mountain Coll., 1977-80, Dufresne Found., 1979-87; chmn., bd. dirs. Mont. Tech. Svcs. Adv. Coun. adv. coun. Engring. Coll. Mont. State U.; bd. dirs. Mont. State Fair, Engring. Socs. Commn. on Energy, 1977-79, Mont. Bd. Sci. and Tech., 1983-88, Great Falls Chamber Found., 1989-91, trustee Great Falls Public Libr. Found., 1995—. Fellow ASCE (pres. 1976-77), AAAS, Cons. Engrs. Coun. (pres. Mont. 1971), Accrediting Bd. Engring. and Tech. (v.p. 1978-79, pres. 1980-83); mem. Nat. Acad. Engring., Am. Coun. Ind. Labs. (hon. sec. 1973-76), Meadowlark Country Club, Pachyderm Club (bd. dirs., v.p. 1992-94), Chi Epsilon (nat. hon.), Tau Beta Pi (hon.). Republican. Methodist. Home: 1200 32nd St S # 9 Great Falls MT 59405 Office: PO Box 7425 Great Falls MT 59406-7425

WALKER, LEROY, Olympic official; b. 1918. BS, Benedict Coll.; MS, Columbia U., PhD. Former athletic coach N.C. Ctrl., former chancellor; former coach Olympic teams for Israel, Jamaica, Kenya and Ethiopia; coach U.S. Olympic Team, 1976; pres. The Athletic Congress; treas. U.S. Olympic Com.; pres. U.S. Olympic Com., Colorado Springs, Colo., 1992—. Office: US Olympic Com 2525 Meridan Pkwy Ste 230 Durham NC 27713*

WALKER, LEROY TASHREAU, university chancellor, coach; b. Atlanta, June 14, 1918; s. Willie and Mary Elizabeth (Thomas) W.; m. Katherine McDowell, Dec. 31, 1938 (dec.); children—LeRoy, Carolyn. BS, Benedict Coll., 1940, PhD (hon.); MA, Columbia U., 1941; PhD, NYU, 1957; PhD (hon.), Defiance Coll.; D of Sports Sci., U.S. Sports Acad.; LLD (hon.), Ea. Ky. U. and N.C. Cen. U., Wake Forest U., 1993, Morehouse U., 1993; DHL (hon.), Tuskegee U., 1993, Duke U., 1995; LHD (hon.), U. N.C., 1995, Queens Coll., 1995; Dr.Humanities, Princeton U., 1996. Chmn. dept. phys. edn., coach basketball, football, track and field Benedict Coll., Columbia, S.C., 1941-42; chmn. dept. phys. edn., coach basketball, football, track and field Bishop Coll., Marshall, Tex., 1942-43, Prairie View State U., 1943-45; chmn. dept. phys. edn. and recreation, coach basketball, football, track and field N.C. Cen. U., Durham, 1945-73; vice-chancellor for univ. relations N.C. Cen. U., 1974-83, chancellor, 1983-86, chancellor emeritus, 1986—; ednl. specialist Cultural Exchange Program, Dept. State, 1959, 60, 62,; dir. program, planning and tng. Peace Corps, Africa, 1966-68; coach Ethiopian and Israeli teams Olympic Games, Rome, 1960; adviser track and field teams throughout world; mem. U.S. Collegiate Sports Coun., 1971; chmn. Coll. Commrs. Assn., 1971-74; chmn. track and field com. Athletic Union U.S.A., 1973-75; head coach U.S. track and field team Olympic Games, Montreal, 1976; chmn. bd. U.S. Olympic Festival, 1987—; mem. exec. bd., treas. U.S. Olympic Com., pres., 1992—; chef de mission for 1992 Barcelona Olympic Games, 1991—; sr. v.p. sports Atlanta Com. for the Olympic Games 1996, 1991—. Author: Manual of Adapted Physical Education, 1960; Physical Education for the Exceptional Student, 1965; Championship Techniques in Track and Field, 1969, Track and Field for Boys and Girls, 1983; also articles. Bd. dirs. U.S.A.-China Rels. Com.; bd. trustees U.S. Olympic Com.; pres. Athletic Congress, U.S. Olympic Com., 1992—. Recipient James E. Shepard Outstanding Tchr. award Hamilton Watch Co., 1964, U. N.C. Systems Bd. Govs. award, 1989; Achievement award Cen. Intercollegiate Athletic Assn., 1967; Disting. Alumnus award Benedict Coll., 1968, Disting. Service award Kiwanis Internat., 1971, City of Durham, 1971, Durham C. of C., 1973, Gov.'s Ambassador of Goodwill award, 1974; O. Max Gardner award, 1976; N.C. Disting. Citizen award, 1977; Achievement in Life award Ency. Brit., 1977, Achievement award Sertoma; Heritage award YMCA, 1988, Robert Giegengack award The Athletics Congress, 1990, Amb. award Pres.' Coun. on Phys. Fitness and Sports, 1991, Disting. Alumni award NYU, 1993, Jim Corbett award Nat. Assn. Coll. Athletic Dirs., 1993; named to N.C. Hall of Fame, 1975, S.C. Hall of Fame, 1977, Nat. Assn. Sport and Phys. Edn. Hall of Fame, 1977, N.C. Cen. U. Hall of Fame, 1984, U.S. Olympic Hall of Fame, 1987, Ga. Hall of Fame, 1988, Benedict Coll. Hall of Fame, N.C. Soc. award The Olympic Order by Internat. Olympic cCom., 1995. Mem. Am. Alliance Health, Phys. Edn., Recreation, and Dance (nat. pres.; Honor award 1972, Gulick award), NEA, U.S. Track Coaches Assn. (Nat. Track Coach of Yr. 1972), N.C. Assn. Health, Phys. Edn., Recreation and Dance (Honor award 1971; v.p. div., dir.), Internat. Assn. Athletic Fedns. (U.S. rep. 1976—), Sigma Delta Psi, Alpha Phi Omega, Omega Psi Phi. Episcopalian.

WALKER, LESLEY, film editor. Editor: (films) Portrait of an Artist as a Young Man, 1979, The Tempest, 1980, Eagle's Wing, 1980, Richard's Things, 1981, Ill Fares the Land, 1982, Meantime, 1983, Winter's Flight, 1984, Letter to Brezhnev, 1985, Mona Lisa, 1986, Cry Freedom, 1987, Buster, 1988, Shirley Valentine, 1989, The Fisher King, 1991, Waterland, 1992, Born Yesterday, 1993, Shadowlands, 1993, (TV movies) Winston Churchill: The Wilderness Years, 1983, The Secret Life of Ian Fleming, 1990. Office: Sandra Marsh Mgt 9150 Wilshire Blvd Ste 220 Beverly Hills CA 90212-3429

WALKER, LOREN HAINES, electrical engineer; b. Bartow, Fla., Sept. 25, 1936; s. Robert Ellsworth and Vera May (Williams) W.; m. Barbara Gray Doss, Aug. 26, 1961; children: Linda Gray, Katherine Leigh, Virginia Kent. BEE, U. Fla., 1958; SM, MIT, 1961. Registered profl. engr., Va. Program engr. GE Corp., 1958-59; sr. design engr. specialty control dept. GE Corp., Waynesboro, Va., 1959-70; elec. engr. R & D GE Corp., Schenectady, N.Y., 1972-76; cons. engr. drive systems GE Corp., Salem, Va., 1976—; sr. devel. engr. Exide Power Systems div. ESB, Raleigh, N.C., 1970-72. Inventor 53 patents in field. Active Presbyn. Ch. Recipient IR-100 award Indsl. Rsch., 1974. Fellow IEEE (1st prize conf. papers 1979, 2d prize 1989). Office: GE Drive Systems 1501 Roanoke Blvd Salem VA 24153-6422

WALKER, LORENZO GILES, surgeon, educator; b. Phila., June 29, 1957; s. Manuel Lorenzo and Romaine Yvonne (Smith) W.; m. Anne Marie Gazzo, Aug. 13, 1990; children: Zachary Giles, Benjamin Lee. BA cum laude, U. Pa., 1978; MD, Harvard U., 1982. Diplomate Am. Bd. Orthopaedic Surgery, Nat. Bd. Med. Examiners; lic. surgeon, Mass., Calif.; cert. added qualification hand surgery, 1993. Intern in surgery New England Deaconess-Harvard Surg. Svc., Boston, 1982-83, asst. resident in surgery, 1983-84; resident in orthopaedic surgery Harvard U., Boston, 1985-88; fellow in hand surgery UCLA, 1988-89, asst. clin. prof. orthopaedic surgery, 1988—; ptnr. Ventura (Calif.) Orthopaedic Hand and Sprots Med. Group, 1994—; staff physician St. John's Plasant Valley Hosp., Camarillo, Calif., St. John's Regional Med. Ctr., Oxnard, Calif., Cmty. Meml. Hosp., Ventura, Calif.; attending physician, cons. Sepulveda (Calif.) VA Hosp.; presenter in field. Cons. reviewer Clin. Orthopaedics and related Rsch., 1990-92; contbr. numerous articles to profl. jours. Vol. Spl. Olympics, Ventura, 1994—, Direct Relief Internat., Santa Barbara, Calif., 1994—. Recipient Cert. of Appreciation, Am. Heart Assn., 1994; UCLA faculty fellow, 1988-89. Mem. Am. Soc. for Surgery of the Hand, Am. Assn. for Hand Surgery, AMA, Calif. Med. Assn., Calif. Orthopaedic Assn., Venture County Med. Soc., Internat. Soc. Aquatic Medicine, Western Orthopaedic Assn., Orthopaedic Overseas, UCLA Hand Club, Arthroscopy Assn. N.Am., Alpha Epsilon Delta. Avocations: photography, scuba diving, sports. Home: Ventura Orthopaedic Hand & Sports Med Group 11090 E Las Posas Rd Camarillo CA 93012 Office: 2100 Solar Dr Oxnard CA 93030-2661

WALKER, MACK, historian, educator; b. Springfield, Mass., June 6, 1929; s. Gilbert Creighton and Lavinia Pillsbury (Mack) W.; m. Irma Julianne Wiesinger, 1954; children: Barbara B., Gilbert C., Benjamin F. AB, Bowdoin Coll., 1950; PhD, Harvard U., 1959. Instr. R.I. Sch. of Design, Providence, 1957-59; instr., asst. prof. Harvard U., Cambridge, Mass., 1959-66; assoc. prof., prof. Cornell U., Ithaca, N.Y., 1966-74; prof. Johns Hopkins U., Balt., 1974—, dept. chmn., 1979-82. Author: Germany and the Emigration, 1964, German Home Towns, 1971, Johann Jakob Moser, 1981, The Salzburg Transaction, 1993; editor: Metternich's Europe, 1968, Plombières, 1968. Sgt. U.S. Army, 1951-53. Fellow Inst. for Advanced Study, Princeton, 1977, Wissenschaftskolleg zu Berlin, 1982-83, Max-Planck-Inst. für Geschichte, Göttingen, 1987-88; recipient Forschungspreis Alexander von Humboldt Found., 1989. Fellow Am. Acad. Arts and Scis. Office: Johns Hopkins U Dept of History Baltimore MD 21218

WALKER, MALLORY, real estate executive; b. Washington, Apr. 13, 1939; s. Oliver Mallory and Elizabeth Powell (Dunlop) W.; m. Diana Hardin Walker; children—Taylor Scott Walker, William Mallory. Ed., U. Va., 1958-63. Joined Walker & Dunlop, 1963, v.p., 1968-71, dir., 1969—, exec. v.p., 1971-76, pres., 1976—; cons. and lectr. in field; bd. dirs. Atlantic Trust Co., 1993-94, Charles E. Smith Residential Realty Inc., 1994—, Fed. Nat. Mortgage Assn., 1981-94, Fannie Mae Found.; trustee Group Hospitalization and Med. Svcs., Inc., 1989-93. Trustee Fed. City Coun., 1977—, Greater Washington Rsch. Ctr., 1977—, Eugene and Agnes E. Meyer Found., 1977-89, vice chmn. 1981-83, chmn. 1983-89. Mem. Am. Soc. Real Estate Counselors, Urban Land Inst., Mortgage Bankers Assn. Am. (bd. govs. 1986-90, exec. com. 1986-87). Office: Walker & Dunlop 7500 Old Georgetown Rd Ste 800 Bethesda MD 20814-6133

WALKER, MALLORY ELTON, tenor; b. New Orleans, May 22, 1935; s. James Hugh and Edith Mamie (Gilmore) W.; m. Carolyn Pryor, Dec. 21, 1956; children: Maria Vanessa, Anthony Hugh, Jamie Eugene. BA, Occidental Coll., 1957. Vocal instr. Boston Conservatory of Music, 1974-77. Prin. artist Met. Opera, N.Y.C., 1978-89; appeared with Dallas Opera, Cologne Opera, Stuttgart Opera, Miami Opera, L.A. Music Ctr. Opera; soloist Robert Shaw Chorale, 1960, also with L.A. Philharm., Cleve. Symphony, Boston Symphony, Phila. Orch., Chgo. Symphony. With U.S. Army Chorus, 1957-60. Rockefeller Found. grantee, 1962-63; Ford Found. grantee, 1963. Mem. Am. Guild Mus. Artists, AFTRA, SAG. Home: 1400 S Citrus Ave Apt 4 Fullerton CA 92633-4750

WALKER, MARGARET SMITH, real estate company executive; b. Lancashire, Eng., Oct. 14, 1943; came to U.S., 1964; d. Arthur Edward and Doris Audrey (Dawson) Smith; m. James E. Walker, Feb. 6, 1992. Lic. real estate agt., Hawaii. Broker Lawson-Worrall Inc. (now Worrall-McCarter), Honolulu, 1974-81; pres. Maggie Parkes & Assocs., Inc., Honolulu, 1981—. Bd. dirs. Hawaii Combined Tng. Assn., Honolulu, 1985—; dist. commr. Lio Lii Pony Club, Honolulu, 1980; com. chmn. Hist. Hawaii Found., Honolulu, 1990. Mem. Am. Horse Shows Assn., Hawaii Horse Shows Assn., Outrigger Canoe Club. Episcopalian. Avocations: dressage riding, horse show management. Office: PO Box 25083 Honolulu HI 96825-0083

WALKER, MARIE FULLER, elementary education educator; d. Gladys Fuller; m. Frederick T. Walker; children: Frederick T. Jr., Nicole Marie. BA in History, U. Philippines, 1969; MEd, West Chester U., 1992. Cert. elem. tchr., Calif., Pa., N.C., Okla., Ala.; cert. elem. adminstr., prin., Pa. Tchr. ESL Royal Thai Army Sch. Nursing, Bangkok, Thailand, 1975; tchr. 2d grade Ruam Rudee Internat. Sch., Bangkok, Thailand, 1975-76; tchr. 3d grade St. Adelaide Sch., Highland, Calif., 1976-77; tchr. Midwest City (Okla.) Sch., 1980-82; tchr. 4th grade Rainbow Elem. Sch., Coatesville, Pa., 1989—. Administered vol. programs ARC, Ft. Bragg and Pope AFB, recruited and trained vols., official community spokesperson, nat. cons., Washington, vol. cons., 1984 (Vol. of Yr. award N.C., 1983, Achievements awards 1983, 84, 85, Clara Barton award 1984). Recipient N.C. Outstanding Vol. Adminstr./Coord., Gov., 1984, Gift of Time award Family Inst., 1992, Dir. Edn. Excellence award IST PDE, 1994; grantee Arts Spl. Edn., 1995, grantee Arts in Edn., 1995, grantee Math. Lab., 1996. Mem. NEA, NAESP, PTA, Pa. Assn. Elem. Sch. Prins., Phi Delta Kappa. Avocations: reading, walking, gardening, travel. Home: 17 Willow Pond Rd Malvern PA 19355-2888 Office: Rainbow Elem Sch 50 Country Club Rd Coatesville PA 19320-1813

WALKER, MARK A., lawyer; b. N.Y.C., June 24, 1941; s. Joseph and Eleanor (Junger) W.; m. Tania Khodjamirian; children: Marie, Andrew. BA, Stanford U., 1963; LLB, Yale U., 1966. Bar: N.Y. 1967, U.S. Dist. Ct. (so. dist.) N.Y. 1977. Assoc. Cleary, Gottlieb, Steen & Hamilton, Paris, Brussels and N.Y., 1966-75; ptnr. Cleary, Gottlieb, Steen & Hamilton, N.Y.C., 1975—. Mem. Assn. Bar City N.Y.

WALKER, MARTIN DEAN, specialty chemical company executive; b. 1932; married. BS, GM Inst.; MBA, Mich. State U. With GM, Detroit, 1954-70; v.p. Am. Motors Corp., Detroit, 1970-72; exec. v.p. Rockwell Internat. Corp., Pitts., 1972-86; chmn., chief exec. officer M.A. Hanna Co., Cleve., 1986—. Office: M A Hanna Co 200 Public Sq Ste 36-5000 Cleveland OH 44114-2304*

WALKER, MARY L., lawyer; b. Dayton, Ohio, Dec. 1, 1948; d. William Willard and Lady D. Walker; 1 child, Winston Samuel. Student, U. Calif., Irvine, 1966-68; BA in Biology/Ecology, U. Calif., Berkeley, 1970; postgrad., UCLA, 1972-73; JD, Boston U., 1973. Bar: Calif. 1973, U.S. Supreme Ct. 1979. Atty. So. Pacific Co., San Francisco, 1973-76; from assoc. to ptnr. Richards, Watson, & Gershon, L.A., 1976-82; dep. asst. atty. gen. lands div. U.S. Dept. Justice, Washington, 1982-84; dep. solicitor U.S. Dept. Interior, Washington, 1984-85; asst. sec. for environment, safety and health U.S. Dept. Energy, Washington, 1985-88; spl. cons. to chmn. bd. Law Engring., Atlanta, 1988-89; v.p., West Coast and the Pacific Law Environ., Inc., San Francisco, 1989; ptnr., head environ. law dept. Richards, Watson & Gershon, San Francisco, 1989-91; ptnr. Luce, Forward, Hamilton & Scripps, San Diego, 1991-94; ptnr. and head San Diego Environ. Practice Group Brobeck, Phleger & Harrison, San Diego, 1994—; U.S. commr. InterAm. Tropical Tuna Commn., 1989-95. Bd. dirs. Endowment for Comty. Leadership, 1987—. Mem. Calif. Bar Assn., San Diego Bar Assn., San Diego BioCommerce Assn. (bd. dirs. 1991-96, pres. 1994), Profl. Women's Fellowship-San Diego (co-founder, pres. 1996—), World Affairs Coun., Renaissance Women. Republican.

WALKER, MICHAEL CHARLES, SR., retirement services executive; b. Rochester, N.Y., Mar. 4, 1940; s. Charles Boyle and Evelyn Esther (Young) W.; m. Patricia Ann Camelio, Feb. 2, 1963; children: Michael Charles Jr., Lyn, Lea, Matthew. BA, U. Colo., 1962; MBA, Columbia Pacific U., 1982, DBA, 1984. Adminstrv. trainee Lincoln Rochester (N.Y.) Trust Co., 1962-64, mktg. officer, 1964-68; asst. v.p. Lincoln First Bank of Rochester, 1968-72, v.p., 1972-77; pres. M.C. Walker Co., Inc., Spencerport, N.Y., 1977-80; exec. dir. The Valley Manor, Rochester, 1980-85; pres., chief exec. officer Presbyn. Residence Ctr. Corp., Rochester, 1985—; lectr. SUNY, Brockport, 1982-89; v.p., dir. Kilian and Caroline Schmitt Found., Rochester, 1985—; mem. adv. bd. Chase Lincoln 1st Bank, Rochester, 1989-92; trustee Rochester Hearing and Speech Ctr., 1989-95, chmn., 1993-94; bd. dirs. Genesee Region Home Care Assn., Rochester, 1990—, chmn., 1995—; trustee Greater Rochester Metro C. of C., 1981-89. Author: Introduction to Bank Marketing Research, 1969, rev. edit., 1972, Practical Handbook of Marketing Definitions, 1970; contbr. articles to profl. jours. Leader task force Spencerport Ctrl. Schs. Bd. Edn., 1977, 80-81, 85; chmn. Monroe County Svs. Bond Com., Rochester, 1972—; mem. United Way Evaluation Team, 1990-94; mem. bus. adv. bd. SUNY, Brockport, 1993—; mem. N.Y. State Bd. Profl. Med. Conduct, 1993—; mem. profl. adv. com. Self Help for Hard of Hearing, 1994—. Recipient Pres.'s Geneseekers award Rochester Area C. of C., 1979, Innovation of Yr. award NYAHSA, 1989. Mem. Am. Assn. Homes for Aging (various coms.), Am. Mktg. Assn. (pres. Rochester chpt. 1969-70), N.Y. State Bankers Assn. (pres. residential mortgage com. 1975-76), N.Y. Assn. Homes and Svcs. for Aging (various coms.), Ridgemont Country Club, Rochester Rotary. Episcopalian. Avocations: golf, reading, travel, physical fitness. Home: Spencerport NY 14559 Office: Presbyn Residence Ctr Corp 1570 East Ave Rochester NY 14610-1610

WALKER, MICHAEL CLAUDE, finance educator; b. Sherman, Tex., June 8, 1940; s. Andrew Jackson and Alice Lorene (Curry) W.; m. Martha Ellen Hindman, Sept. 10, 1966; children: Stephanie Elizabeth, Rebecca Elaine, Priscilla Eileen. BA, Austin Coll., 1965; MA, Ohio State U., 1966; PhD, U. Houston, 1971. Instr. U. Houston, 1969-70; asst. prof. Ga. State U., Atlanta, 1971-75; assoc. prof. U. Okla., Norman, 1975-78; prof., head dept. fin., ins. and real estate North Tex. State U., Denton, 1978-85; prof. U. Cin., 1985-88, dept. head, 1985—, Virgil M. Schwarm prof. fin. and investments, 1988—. Co-editor: Cases in Financial Institutions, 1979; contbr. articles to profl. jours. Served with AUS, 1958-61. Recipient Leonard P. Ayers fellowship award, 1973. Mem. Am. Fin. Assn., Fin. Execs. Inst., Fin. Mgmt. Assn., So. Fin. Assn. (bd. dirs. 1983-85, sec.-treas. 1986-88, v.p. 1988-89, pres. 1989-90), Southwestern Fin. Assn. (bd. dirs. 1986-88), Ea. Fin. Assn., Midwest Fin. Assn., Beta Gamma Sigma, Omicron Delta Epsilon. Methodist. Office: U Cin Fin Dept Mail Location 195 Cincinnati OH 45221-0195

WALKER, MICHAEL LEON, education educator; b. Cin., May 17, 1942; s. Degree and Annie (Wynn) W. BA, Wayne State U., 1970, EdD, 1991; MA, U. Detroit, 1978. Asst. prof. La. State U., Shreveport, 1991-92, U. Nebr., Lincoln, 1992-94, SUNY, Plattsburgh, 1994-95, Ea. Mich. U., 1995—. Mem. Martin Luther King Club, Plattsburgh, 1994. Recipient award for Svc. to Children, Salvation Army, Lincoln, 1993, 1994. Mem. Nat. Coun. Tchrs. of English, Internat. Reading Assn., Nat. Reading Conf., Phi Delta Kappa. Democrat. Baptist. Avocations: reading, organ, piano. Office: EMU 714 Pray Harold Ypsilanti MI 48197

WALKER, MICHAEL RONALD, chemist, researcher; b. Chgo., July 7, 1953; s. Jerry Richard Walker and Margaret Elizabeth (Erickson) Aceto; m. Linda Marie Rickard, July 7, 1972; children: Matthew Robert, Mason Rickard. Assoc. Degree, Joliet (Ill.) Jr. Coll., 1978; BA in Chemistry, Govs. State U., 1985; cert. completion, Quality Mgmt. Sys., Clearwater, Fla., 1990, Design of Experments, Madison, Wis., 1993; mgmt. tng., Dale Carnegie, St.

Petersburg, Fla., 1994. Chem. operator Insta Foam, Inc., Joliet, Ill., 1978-79; pilot plant chemist Stepan Chem. Co., Elwood, Ill., 1979-85; quality control chemist Unit Dose Pharm., Largo, Fla., 1985-86; tech. asst. Silor Optical, St. Petersburg, Fla., 1986-88; process engr. Silor Optical, St. Petersburg, 1988-90; lead engr. Essilor of Am., St. Petersburg, 1990-95, R&D chemist, 1995—; chem. off-shore tech. support profl. Essilor P.R., Ponce, 1989-93, Essilor Thailand, Bangkok, 1993-94, Essilor Philippines, Battan, 1993-95. Baseball coach Pony League, Pinellas Park, Fla., 1990-94; asst. den leader Cub Scouts, St. Petersburg, 1992-94; asst. soccer coach, St. Petersburg, 1992-94. Sgt. USAF, 1971-75. Mem. AAAS, Am. Chem. Soc. Lutheran. Achievements include work on a variety of opthalmic lens coating materials and lens coating processes. Avocations: sports, music, travel, art, literature. Home: 6573 71st St Pinellas Park FL 34665-4836 Office: Essilor of Am 4900 Park St N Saint Petersburg FL 33709-2228

WALKER, MOIRA KAYE, sales executive; b. Riverside, Calif., Aug. 2, 1940; d. Frank Leroy and Arline Rufina (Roach) Porter; m. Timothy P. Walker, Aug. 30, 1958 (div. 1964); children: Brian A., Benjamin D., Blair K., Beth E. Student, Riverside City Coll., 1973. With Bank of Am., Riverside, 1965-68, Abitibi Corp., Cucamonga, Calif., 1968-70; with Lily div. Owens-Illinois, Riverside, 1970-73; salesperson Lily div. Owens-Illinois, Houston, 1973-77; salesperson Kent H. Landsberg div. Sunclipse, Montebello, Calif., 1977-83, sales mgr., 1983-85; v.p., sales mgr. Kent H. Landsberg div. Sunclipse, Riverside, 1985—. Mem. NAFE, Women in Paper (treas. 1978-84), Kent H. Landsberg President's Club (1st female to make club, 1994, 95. Lutheran. Office: Kent H Landsberg Div Sunclipse 1180 W Spring St Riverside CA 92507-1327

WALKER, MORT, cartoonist; b. El Dorado, Kans., Sept. 3, 1923; s. Robin A. and Carolyn (Richards) W.; m. Catherine Prentice, Aug. 24, 1985; children: Greg, Brian, Polly, Morgan, Marjorie, Neal, Roger, Whitney, Cathy, Jr., Priscilla. Student, Kansas City Jr. Coll., 1941-42, Washington U., St. Louis, 1943-44; B.A., U. Mo., 1948; LL.D., William Penn Coll., 1981. Designer Hallmark Greeting Cards, 1941; editor Dell Pub. Co., 1948-49; free lance cartoonist Saturday Evening Post, other popular mags., 1948-50; scholar in residence Mo. U., 1992. Comic strip artist King Features, 1950—; creator Beetle Bailey, 1950, Hi and Lois, 1954, Sam's Strip, 1961, Boner's Ark, 1968, Sam and Silo, 1977, The Evermores, 1982, Betty Boop and Felix, 1984, (for United Features) Gamin and Patches, 1987; author: Most, 1971, Land of Lost Things, 1973, Backstage at the Strips, 1975, The Lexicon of Comicana, 1981, The Best of Beetle Bailey, 1984; contbr. to numerous anthologies and textbooks. Mem. Pres.'s Com. to Hire Handicapped, People to People Com. Exhbn. touring group show Met. Mus. Art, N.Y.C., 1951; chmn. Internat. Mus. Cartoon Art. Served to 1st lt. AUS, 1943-46, ETO. Recipient Outstanding Cartoonist award The Banshees, 1955, Il Secolo XIX award (Italy), 1972, Adamson award (Sweden), 1975, 88, Segar award, 1977, 4th Estate award Am. Legion, The Jester, 1979, Fourth Estate award, 1978, Power of Printing, 1977; named Man of Yr. NCCJ, 1988. Mem. Nat. Cartoonists Soc. (pres. 1959-60, Reuben award 1953, award for best humor strip of 1966, 69, Mus. Cartoon Art Hall of Fame 1989), Artists and Writers, Newspaper Features Coun. Authors Guild, Soc. Illustrators, Nat. Press Club, Gov.'s Club, Silvermine Club (Norwalk, Conn.), Greenwich Country Club, Quechee Club (Vt.), Boca Raton Resort and Club (Fla.), Kappa Sigma (Man of Yr. 1988). Office: care King Features Syndicate 235 E 45th St New York NY 10017-3305 *If I enjoy my own life that's one life enjoyed. But if I can help others enjoy their lives more, many lives are made more enjoyable.*

WALKER, OLENE S., lieutenant governor; b. Ogden, Utah, Nov. 15, 1930; d. Thomas Ole and Nina Hadley (Smith) W.; m. J. Myron Walker, 1957; children: Stephen Brett, David Walden, Bryan Jesse, Lori, Mylene, Nina, Thomas Myron. BA, Brigham Young U., 1954; MA, Stanford U., 1954; PhD, U. Utah, 1986. V.p. Country Crisp Foods; mem. Utah Ho. of Reps. Dist. 24; lt. gov. State of Utah, 1993—. Mem. Salt Lake Edn. Found. bd. dirs. 1983-90; dir. community econ. devel.; mem. Ballet West, Sch. Vol., United Way, Commn. on Youth, Girls Village, Salt Lake Conv. and Tourism Bd. Mormon. Office: Lieutenant Governor 203 State Capitol Building Salt Lake City UT 84114-1202*

WALKER, ORRIS G., JR., health facilities adminstrator. Pres. Episcopal Health Svcs. Inc., Uniondale, N.Y. Office: Episcopal Health Svcs Inc 333 Earle Ovington Blvd Uniondale NY 11553-3645*

WALKER, PHILIP CHAMBERLAIN, II, health care executive; b. Big Spring, Tex., July 7, 1944; s. Philip Chamberlain and Mary Catherine (St. John) W.; m. Linda Jane Holsclaw, Jan. 21, 1978; children: Shannon M., Meghan M. BA, Cen. Wash. State Coll., 1970; MS, U. Idaho, 1971. Exec. dir. Multnomah Found. for Med. Care, Portland, Oreg., 1972-81; chief exec. officer Peer Rev. Orgn. for Wash. State, Seattle, 1981-84; dir. Preferred Provider Orgn. devel. Provident Life and Accident, Chattanooga, 1984-88; v.p. Maxicare Health Plans, L.A., 1988-91; v.p., gen. mgr. Maxicare Health Plans Midwest, Chgo., 1991-92; pres. Health Plus, Peoria, Ill., 1992—; CEO, chmn. bd. Kepple & Co., Peoria, 1992—; v.p. Health Care Horizons, Albuquerque, 1992—; bd. dirs. RMR Group; cons. to numerous orgns. Contbr. articles to profl. jours. With USAF, 1961-66, Vietnam. Office: 209 W 5th St Peoria IL 61605-2502

WALKER, PHILLIP R., agricultural products supplier. Pres. Tenn. Farmers Coop., La Vergne, Tenn., Dyer Lauderdale Farmers, Inc., Dyersburg, Tenn. Office: Tenn Farmers Coop PO Box 3003 200 Waldron Rd La Vergne TN 37086 also: Dyer Lauderdale Farmers Inc Dyersburg TN 38024*

WALKER, RALPH CLIFFORD, lawyer; b. Bradenton, Fla., Apr. 30, 1938; s. Julius Clifford and Dorothy (Hefner) W.; m. Sarah Mildred Walker, Sept. 9, 1959 (div. Sept. 1971), 1 child, Laura Elizabeth; m. Katherine Marie Christensen, Oct. 10, 1971; children: Mark Clifford, Tyler Lanier. BA cum laude, Vanderbilt U., 1959; LLB, U. Calif., Berkeley, 1965. Bar: Calif. Ptnr. Orrick Herrington & Sutcliffe, San Francisco, 1965—. Town councilman Town of Ross, Calif., 1970-72.Lt. (j.g.) USN, 1959-62. Mem. ABA, State Bar Calif., San Francisco Bar Assn., University Club (San Francisco, dir. 1986-88, counsel 1983—), Meadow Club (Fairfax, Calif.), Order of Coif. Republican. Presbyterian. Avocations: golf, wine, youth sports. Office: Orrick Herrington & Sutcliffe 400 Sansome St San Francisco CA 94111-3308

WALKER, RANDALL WAYNE, lawyer; b. Pampa, Tex., Mar. 13, 1956; s. Jimmy Wayne and Dorothy Evelyn (Mercer) W.; m. Patricia Gale Vernon Walker, Dec. 12, 1992; children: Alissa Gail Walker Warner, Angie Marie Walker, Cory Walker, Nicholas Russell Rattan Walker. AA, Clarendon (Tex.) Coll., 1980; BS, West Tex. State U., Canyon, 1984; JD, Tex. Tech. U., Lubbock, 1986. Bar: Tex., 1987. Pvt. practice Clarendon, Tex., 1987-91; asst. atty. gen. Tex. Atty. Gen. Office, Wichita Falls, Tex., 1991—. Cubmaster Boy Scouts Am., Clarendon, 1988-89. Mem. Lions (v.p. Clarendon 1989). Avocations: fishing, camping, woodworking. Office: Attorney General Office 813 8th St Wichita Falls TX 76307

WALKER, RICHARD, diversified financial service company executive. Sr. v.p.-ops. Med. Mgmt. Info. Systems, Inc., Lewiston, Maine. Office: Med Mgmt Info Systems Inc PO Box 4800 19 Mollison Way Lewiston ME 04243-4800*

WALKER, RICHARD, JR., nephrologist, internist; b. Dayton, Ohio, Sept. 1, 1948; m. Madeleine Ann Walker. BS cum laude, Ohio State U., 1970, MD, 1973. Diplomate Nat. Bd. Med. Examiners, internal medicine, nephrology, critical care medicine Am. Bd. Internal Medicine. Intern medicine U. Tex. Southwestern, Dallas, 1973-74, resident internal medicine, 1974-76, fellow nephrology, 1976-78; staff nephrologist and internist Bay Med. Ctr., Panama City, Fla., 1978—, HCA Gulf Coast Hosp., Panama City, 1978—; pres., med. dir., CEO Panama City Artificial Kidney Ctr., 1978—, North Fla. Artificial Kidney Ctr., 1993—. Mem. AMA, ACP, Soc. Critical Care Medicine, Fla. Physicians Assn., The Bays Med. Soc., Fla. Med. Assn., Am. Soc. Nephrology, Internat. Soc. Nephrology, Fla. Soc. Nephrology, Renal Physicians Assn., Am. Soc. Internal Medicine, Fla. Soc. Internal Medicine, Nat. Kidney Found., Alpha Omega Alpha. Home: 320 Bunkers Cove Rd Panama City FL 32401-3912 Office: Nephrology Assocs PA 504 N Macarthur Ave Panama City FL 32401-3636

WALKER, RICHARD BRIAN, chemistry educator; b. Quincy, Mass., May 14, 1948; s. George Edgar and Eva Mary (Taylor) W. BS in Biochemistry, U. So. Calif., 1970; PhD in Pharm. Chemistry, U. Calif., San Francisco, 1975. Rsch. assoc. Oreg. State U., Corvallis, 1975-76, U. Wash., Seattle, 1976-78; lectr. U.S. Internat. U., San Diego, 1978-81, Hamdard Sch. Pharmacy, New Delhi, India, 1981-82; rsch. scientist Biophysica Found., San Diego, 1982-83; assoc. prof. Chemistry U. Ozarks, Clarksville, Ark., 1983-84; asst. prof. Chemistry U. Ark., Pine Bluff, 1984-89, assoc. prof. Chemistry, 1989—; prin. investigator minority biomed. rsch. support program NIH, Bethesda, Md., 1986—; project dir. Ark. Systemic Sci. Initiative. Contbr. articles to profl. jours. Coord. home Bible fellowship The Way Internat., Pine Bluff, 1984—; judge Ctrl. Ark. Sci. Fair, Little Rock, 1986—. NIH rsch. grantee, 1986, 89, 93. Mem. Am. Chem. Soc., Ark. Acad. Scis., Coun. on Undergrad. Rsch., Sigma Xi. Avocations: fishing, golf, skiing. Home: 301 W 33d Ave Pine Bluff AR 71603 Office: U Ark Dept Chemistry 1200 University Dr Pine Bluff AR 71601-2799

WALKER, RICHARD HAROLD, pathologist, educator; b. Cleve., Dec. 2, 1928; s. Harold Deford and Bernice Margaret (Wright) W.; m. Carolyn Franklin, Sept. 28, 1954; children: Bruce, Lynn, Cara, Leah. BS, Emory U., 1950, MD, 1953. Intern City Memphis Hosps., 1953-54; resident in pathology U. Tenn. Coll. Medicine, Memphis, 1954-55, 57-59; Am. Cancer Soc. clin. fellow U. Tenn. Coll. Medicine, 1957-59; med. dir. blood bank and transfusion service City of Memphis Hosps., 1961-70; prof. pathology Coll. Medicine, U. Tenn., Memphis, 1966-70; chief of blood bank and transfusion service William Beaumont Hosp., Royal Oak, Mich., 1970-95; med. dir. Sch. Med. Tech. William Beaumont Hosp., 1970-91; clin. prof. pathology Wayne State U. Sch. Medicine, Detroit, 1982-95. Contbr. articles on blood transfusion, blood group genetics and transfusion medicine to med. jours. With USNR, 1955-76. Recipient Murray Thelin Humanitarian award Memphis chpt. Nat. Hemophilia Found., 1968. Mem. AMA, Coll. Am. Pathologists, Am. Soc. Clin. Pathologists (Disting. Svc. award 1977, Ward Burdick award 1992), Am. Assn. Blood Banks (pres. 1976-77, John Elliott Meml. award 1986), Tenn. Assn. Blood Banks (L.W. Diggs award 1986), Internat. Soc. Blood Transfusion, Am. Soc. for Histocompatibility and Immunogenetics. Republican. Presbyterian. Home: 22301 Nottingham Dr Beverly Hills MI 48025-3518

WALKER, RICHARD K., lawyer; b. Knoxville, Tenn., Oct. 21, 1948. BA with honors, U. Kans., 1970, JD, 1975; student, U. Bonn, Germany. Bar: Ariz. 1975, D.C. 1977, U.S. Supreme Ct. 1977. Asst. prof. law U. S.C., 1977-81, assoc. prof. law, 1981-82; ptnr. Bishop, Cook, Purcell & Reynolds, Washington, 1981-90, Winston & Strawn, Washington, 1990-93; dir. Streich Lang, Phoenix, 1993—. Bd. trustees Ariz. Theatre Co., 1995—. Fulbright scholar. Mem. ABA (mem. equal employment opportunity law com. 1979—). Office: Streich Lang Renaissance One 2 N Central Ave Phoenix AZ 85004-2322

WALKER, RICHARD LOUIS, former ambassador, educator, author; b. Bellefonte, Pa., Apr. 13, 1922; s. Robert Shortlidge and Genevieve (Bible) W.; m. Celeno Claypole Kenly, Mar. 29, 1945; children: Geoffrey Kenly, Dorothy Anne, Stephen Bradley. BA, Drew U., 1944; cert. Chinese lang. and area, U. Pa., 1944; MA, Yale U., 1947, PhD, 1950; LLD (hon.), Coll. of Charleston, 1985, Drew U., 1986, The Citadel, 1990; D of Polit. Sci. (hon.), Seoul Nat. U., 1982; D. Pub. Svc., U. S.C., 1991. Asst. prof. history Yale U., 1950-57; prof. internat. studies U. S.C., 1957—, James F. Byrnes prof. internat. relations, 1959—, prof. emeritus, 1992—; U.S. amb. to Republic of Korea, 1981-86; amb.-in-residence U. S.C., 1986—; vis. assoc. prof. Nat. Taiwan U., Taipei, China, 1954-55; vis. prof. U. Wash., 1959, 65; prof. polit. affairs Nat. War Coll., 1960-61; spl. rsch. internat. rels., Far East; lectr., cons. U.S. Govt., 1953—, Dept. Def., 1969—; rep. U.S. Dept. State, USIS, 1973-74; lectr. numerous confs., major U.S. govt. svc. schs. and univs. in Asia, Australia and Europe. Author: Western Language Periodicals on China, 1949, Multi-State System of Ancient China, 1953, China Under Communism, 1955, China and the West, 1956, The Continuing Struggle, 1958, Democracy Confronts Communism in World Affairs, 1965, Edward R. Stettmius, Jr., 1965, The China Danger, 1966, Ancient China, 1969, Prospects in the Pacific, 1972, Asia in Perspective, 1974, Ancient Japan, 1975; contbr. articles to various symposium vols., learned jours. Bd. dirs. Nat. Com. U.S.-China Rels., 1968-94, U.S. Strategic Inst., 1977—, U. S.C. Ednl. Found., 1958—, Conf. on European Problems, 1967—. With AUS, 1942-46, PTO. Recipient Alumni Achievement award in arts Drew U., 1958; Disting. Service award Air U., 1970; Fgn. Service Inst. award, 1971; Armed Forces Staff Coll. award, 1978; Fulbright-Social Sci. Research Council research scholar Academia Sinica Republic China, 1965-66. Mem. Assn. Asian Studies, Am. Assn. for China Studies (pres. 1994-95, nat. pres. 1995-97), Aurelian Honor Soc., Forest Lake Club, Torch Club, Pi Gamma Mu, Omicron Delta Kappa. Episcopalian. Home: 700 Spring Lake Rd Columbia SC 29206-2111

WALKER, ROBERT DIXON, III, surgeon, urologist, educator; b. Rochester, N.Y., July 22, 1936; s. Robert Dixon, Jr. and Virginia (Weir) W.; m. Joyce Ann Copeland, June 23, 1961; children—Sherri Lynn, Lisa Marie, Jeffrey Alan. B.A., B.S., Carson-Newman Coll., 1959; M.D., U. Miami, Fla., 1963. Intern Wake Forest U., 1964; resident in surgery U. Fla., 1968, asst. prof., 1970-74, assoc. prof., 1974-76, prof. surgery, 1976—, dir. admissions Coll. Medicine, 1976-79; instr. U. Tenn., 1969-70; chief of staff Shands Teaching Hosp., 1976. Assoc. editor: Jour. Urology. Served to comdr. USNR, 1968-70. Fellow ACS (gov.); mem. Assn. Univ. Urologists, Am. Urol. Assn. (editorial bd. Update Series), Am. Assn. Genitourinary Surgeons, Soc. Pediatric Rsch., Soc. Pediatric Urology (exec. com., sec., pres.), Am. Acad. Pediatrics (sec., chmn. urology sect.), Fla. Urologic Soc. (sec., pres.). Home: 6322 SW 37th Way Gainesville FL 32608-5105 Office: Div of Urology Box J 247 JHM Health Center Gainesville FL 32610

WALKER, ROBERT HARRIS, historian, author, editor; b. Cin., Mar. 15, 1924; m. Grace Burtt; children: Amy, Rachel, Matthew. BS, Northwestern U., 1945; MA, Columbia U., 1950; PhD, U. Pa., 1955. Edn. specialist U.S. Mil. Govt., Japan, 1946-47; instr. Carnegie Inst. Tech., 1950-51, U. Pa., 1953-54; asst. prof., dir. Am. studies U. Wyo., 1955-59; assoc. prof. George Washington U., 1959-63, prof. Am. civilization, 1963-94, dir. Am. studies program, 1959-66, 68-70; first dir. edn. and pub. programs NEH, 1966-68; fellow Woodrow Wilson Internat. Ctr., 1972-73, Rockefeller Rsch. Ctr., 1979, Hoover Instn., Huntington Libr., 1980; specialist grants to Japan, Germany, Thailand, Iran, Greece, Israel, Brazil, China, People's Republic of Korea, Hong Kong, 1964-91; Fulbright lectr., Australia, New Zealand, Philippines, 1971, Sweden, France, West Germany, Norway, all 1987; Am. Coun. Learned Socs. alt. del. UNESCO Gen. Info. Program, 1978—; co-founder Algonquin Books, 1982. Author: Poet and Gilded Age, 1963, Life in the Age of Enterprise, 1967, American Society, 1981, 2d edit., 1995, Reform in America (nominated for Pulitzer prize in history), 1985, (with R.H. Gabriel) Course of American Democratic Thought, 3d edit., 1986, Cincinnati and the Big Red Machine, 1988, Everyday Life in Victorian America, 1994; editor, compiler: American Studies in the U.S., 1958, American Studies Abroad, 1975, Reform Spirit in America, 1976, 85, American Studies: Topics and Sources, 1976; editor: Am. Quar., 1953-54; sr. editor: Am. Studies Internat., 1970-80, Am. studies series for Greenwood Press, 1972—. Founding mem. Japan-U.S. Friendship Commn., 1977-80; pres. Friends of Raoul Wallenberg Found., 1989—. With USNR, 1943-46, 50. Mem. Am. Studies Assn. (nat. pres. 1970-71), Cosmos Club, Phi Beta Kappa. Office: 915 26th St NW Washington DC 20037-2029

WALKER, ROBERT MIKE, federal agency administrator; m. Romy Patterson. Student, U. Tenn. Page Washington; asst., budget analyst U.S. Rep. Joe L. Evins, 1969-76, nat. security & appropriations advisor U.S. Sen. Jim Sasser, 1977-94; mem. staff Senate's Com. on Appropriations, Washington, 1979-81, mem. staff Subcom. on Mil. Constrn., 1981-87, staff dir. Subcom. on Mil. Constrn., 1987-94; asst. sec. Army for Installations, Logistics and Environment, 1994—; head Senate Task Forces on Persian Gulf and Cen. Am.; mil. affairs advisor Senate dels. to former Yugoslavia, Ea. Europe, Somalia, Korea, and Antarctica. With Tenn. and D.C. Army N.G., 1969-75. Office: Dept of the Army Installations Logistics The Pentagon Washington DC 20310-0103

WALKER, ROBERT MOWBRAY, physicist, educator; b. Phila., Feb. 6, 1929; s. Robert and Margaret (Seivwright) W.; m. Alice J. Agedal, Sept. 2, 1951 (div. 1973); children: Eric, Mark; m. Ghislaine Crozaz, Aug. 24, 1973. B.S. in Physics, Union Coll., 1950, D.Sc., 1967; M.S., Yale U., 1951, Ph.D., 1954; Dr honoris causa, Université de Clermont-Ferrand, 1975. Physicist Gen. Electric Research Lab., Schenectady, 1954-62, 63-66; McDonnell prof. physics Washington U., St. Louis, 1966—; dir. McDonnell Center for Space Scis., 1975—; vis. prof. U. Paris, 1962-63; adj. prof. metallurgy Rensselaer Poly. Inst., 1958, adj. prof. physics, 1965-66; vis. prof. physics and geology Calif. Inst. Tech., 1972, Phys. Research Lab., Ahmedabad, India, 1981, Institut d'Astrophysique, Paris, 1981; nat. lectr. Sigma Xi, 1984-85; pres. Vols. for Internat. Tech. Assistance, 1960-62, 65-66, founder, 1960, bd. dirs., 1961—; mem. Lunar Sample Analysis Planning Team, 1968-70, Lunar Sample Rev. Bd., 1970-72; adv. com. Lunar Sci. Inst., 1972-75; mem. temporary nominating group in planetary scis. Nat. Acad. Scis., 1973-75, bd. on sci. and tech. for internat. devel., 1974-76, com. planetary and lunar exploration, 1977-80, mem. space sci. bd., 1979-82; bd. dirs. Univs. Space Research Assn., 1969-71; mem. organizing com. Com. on Space Research-Internat. Astron. Union, Marseille, France, 1984; mem. task force on sci. uses of space sta. Solar System Exploration Com., 1985-86; mem. Antarctic Meteorite Working Group, 1985-92; mem. NASA Planetary Geosci. Strategy Com., 1986-88; mem. European Sci. Found. Sci. Orgn. Com., Workshop on Analysis of Samples from Solar System Bodies, 1990; chmn. Antarctic Meteorite Working Group, 1990-92. Decorated officer de l'Ordre des Palmes Academiques (France); recipient Disting. Svc. award Am. Nuclear Soc., 1964, Yale Engring. Assn. award for contbn. to basic and applied sci., 1966, Indsl. Rsch. awards, 1964, 65; Exceptional Sci. Achievement award NASA, 1970; E.O. Lawrence award AEC, 1971; Antarctic Svc. medal NSF, 1985; NSF fellow, 1962-63. Fellow AAAS, Am. Phys. Soc., Meteoritical Soc. (Leonard medal 1993), Am. Geophys. Union; mem. NAS (mem. polar rsch. bd. com. 1995, J. Lawrence Smith medal 1991), Am. Astron. Soc. Achievements include research and publs. on cosmic rays, nuclear physics, geophysics, radiation effects in solids, particularly devel. solid state track detectors and their application to geophysics and nuclear physics problems; discovery of fossil particle tracks in terrestrial and extra-terrestrial materials and fission track method of dating; application of phys. scis. to art and archaeology; lab. studies of interplanetary dust and interstellar grains in primitive meteorites. Home: 3 Romany Park Ln Saint Louis MO 63132-4211

WALKER, ROBERT SMITH, congressman; b. Bradford, Pa., Dec. 23, 1942; s. Joseph Eddman and Rachael Viola (Smith) W.; m. Sue Ellen Albertson, Apr. 13, 1968. BS, Millersville (Pa.) U., 1964; MA in Polit. Sci, U. Del., 1968. Tchr. Penn Manor High Sch., Lancaster, Pa., 1964-67; legis. asst. to Congressman Edwin D. Eshleman, 1967-74, adminstrv. asst., 1974-76; mem. 95th-104th Congresses from 16th Pa. dist., Washington, D.C., 1977—; chmn. House Com. Sci. Co-author: Congress-The Pennsylvania Dutch Representatives, 1774-1974. Can You Afford This House, 1978, House of Ill Repute, 1987; contbr. articles to profl. jours. Served with Pa. NG, 1967-73. Republican. Office: US House of Reps 2369 Rayburn House Office Bldg Washington DC 20515 *When you decide to seek public office, you accept a trust. The responsibilities of that trust involve not only your talents, your wisdom and your energies, but also your integrity, your character and your commitment to a better tomorrow.**

WALKER, ROBERTA SMYTH, school system administrator; b. Tacoma, June 18, 1943; d. Robert Middleton and Maxine (Hartl) Smyth; m. Ronald E. Walker, Apr. 1962 (div. Mar. 1965); 1 child, David M.; m. James R. Hawkins, July 19, 1985 (dec. Sept. 1991). BA, Evergreen State Coll., Olympia, Wash., 1982; MS, Seattle Pacific U., 1989. Pers. analyst Seattle Sch. Dist., 1977-83, dir. staff rels., 1983-86; exec. dir. employee rels. Renton (Wash.) Sch. Dist., 1986—; adj. faculty Seattle Pacific U., 1989—, Western Wash. U., 1995—. Vol. Crisis Clinic, Seattle, 1993—. Recipient Angel in Seattle award AT&T Wireless and Intiman Theatre, 1995. Mem. Wash. Assn. Sch. Adminstrs., Employee Rels. and Negotiations Network (pres. 1991-92), Sno-King Negotiators. Office: Renton Sch Dist 435 Main Ave S Renton WA 98055-2711

WALKER, ROGER GEOFFREY, geology educator, consultant; b. London, Mar. 26, 1939; s. Reginald Noel and Edith Annie (Wells) W.; m. Gay Parsons, Sept. 18, 1965; children—David John, Susan Elizabeth. B.A., Oxford U., Eng., 1961; D.Phil., Oxford U., 1964. NATO postdoctoral fellow Johns Hopkins U., Balt., 1964-66; geology faculty McMaster U., Hamilton, Ont., Can., 1966—; prof. McMaster U., 1973—; vis. scientist Marathon Oil Research Ctr., Littleton, Colo., 1973-74, Amoco Can., Calgary, Alta., 1982; vis. prof. Australian Nat. U., Canberra, 1981; tchr. 80 profl. short courses on various aspects of oil exploration in clastic reservoirs, Can., U.S., Brazil, Australia, Japan; mem. grant selection com. earth scis. sect. Nat. Scis. and Engring. Rsch. Coun. Can., 1981-84. Editor: Facies Models, 1979, 3d edit., 1992; contbr. over 125 articles to profl. jours. Recipient operating and strategic grants Nat. Scis. and Engring. Rsch. Coun. Can., 1966—. Fellow Royal Soc. Can.; mem. Geol. Assn. Can. (assoc. editor 1977-80, Past President's medal 1975, Disting. Svc. award 1994), Can. Soc. Petroleum Geologists (Link award 1983, R.J.W. Douglas Meml. medal 1990), Am. Assn. Petroleum Geologists (Disting. lectr. 1979-80), Soc. Econ. Paleontologists and Mineralogists (pres. eastern sect. 1975-76, coun. for mineralogy 1979-80, hon. mem. 1991, assoc. editor 1970-78), Can. Assn. Univ. Tchrs., Internat. Assn. Sedimentologists. Avocations: skiing, classical music, photography, model railroading. Home: 71 Robin Hood Dr, Dundas, ON Canada L9H 4G2 Office: McMaster U Dept Geology, 1280 Main St W, Hamilton, ON Canada L8S 4M1

WALKER, RONALD C., oil company executive. BSc in Engring., Queen's U., Kingston, Ont., Can., 1964; LLB, McGill U., Montreal, Que., Can., 1973. V.p., gen. counsel Imperial Oil Ltd., Toronto, Ont. Office: Imperial Oil Ltd, 111 St Clair Ave W, Toronto, ON Canada M5W 1K3

WALKER, RONALD C., magazine publisher; m. Lou Ann Walker; two children. BA, U. Nebr. Market rsch. mgr. Lane Pub., Menlo Park, Calif., 1967-69, marketing dir., 1969-74, v.p., circulation dir., 1974-84, v.p., gen. mgr. Sunset mag., 1984-90; pub. Smithsonian mag., D.C., 1991—, Air & Space/Smithsonian mag., D.C., 1991—. Office: Smithsonian Mag 900 Jefferson Dr SW Washington DC 20560

WALKER, RONALD EDWARD, psychologist, educator; b. East St. Louis, Ill., Jan. 23, 1935; s. George Edward and Marnella (Altmeyer) W.; m. Aldona M. Mogenis, Oct. 4, 1958; children: Regina, Mark, Paula, Alexis. B.S., St. Louis U., 1957; M.A., Northwestern U., 1959, Ph.D., 1961. Lectr. psychology Northwestern U., 1959-61; faculty dept. psychology Loyola U., Chgo., 1961—; asst., then assoc. prof. Loyola U., 1961-68, prof., chmn. dept., 1965—; acting dean Loyola U. (Coll. Arts and Scis.), 1973-74, dean, 1974-80, academic v.p., 1980-81, sr. v.p., dean faculties, 1981-89, exec. v.p., 1989—; Cons. VA, Chgo., 1965-74; Am. Psychol. Assn.-NIMH; vis. cons., 1969; vis. scientist Am. Psychol. Assn. NSF, 1968; Cook County (Ill.) rep. from Ill. Psychol. Assn., 1969-72; cons.-evaluator North Cen. Assn., 1986—. Contbr. articles to profl. jours. Trustee St. Francis Hosp., Evanston, Ill., 1986-92, Chgo. Archdiocesan Sems., 1985—, Loyola Acad., Wilmette, Ill., 1987-93, St. Louis U., 1988—. Mem. Am. Psychol. Assn. (council rep. 1970-72), Ill. Psychol. Assn. (chmn. student devel. com. 1965-67, chmn. acad. sec. 1966-67, disting. psychologist of yr. award 1986), AAAS, Sigma Xi, Psi Chi. Home: 2712 Park Pl Evanston IL 60201-1337 Office: 820 N Michigan Ave Chicago IL 60611-2103

WALKER, RONALD F., corporate executive; b. Cin., Apr. 9, 1938; married. BBA, U. Cin., 1961. V.p. Kroger Co., Cin., 1962-72; with Am. Fin. Corp., Cin., 1972—, exec. v.p., 1978-84, pres., COO, bd. dirs., 1984-95; exec. v.p. Gt. Am. Ins., Cin., 1972-80, pres., 1980-87, vice chmn., 1987—; pres., COO Penn Cen. Corp., 1987-92, COO, 1987-92; pres., CEO Gen. Cable Corp., 1992-94; also bd. dirs.; bd. dirs. Chiquita Brands Internat., Cin., Am. Fin. Enterprises, Cin., Am. Annuity Gruop, Inc., Tejas Gas Corp. Office: Gt Am Ins Co 580 Walnut St Cincinnati OH 45202-3110 also: Am Fin Corp 1 E 4th St Cincinnati OH 45202-3717

WALKER, RONALD HUGH, executive search company executive; b. Bryan, Tex., July 25, 1937; s. Walter Hugh and Maxine (Tarver) W.; m. Anne Lucille Collins, Aug. 8, 1959; children: Lisa, Marjorie, Lynne. BA, U. Ariz., 1960. With Allstate Ins. Co., Pasadena, Calif., 1964-67, Hudson Co., 1967-69; asst. to sec. interior, 1969-70; founder, 1st dir., staff asst. to Pres.

U.S. White House Advance Office, 1970-72; spl. asst. to Pres., 1972-73; dir. Nat. Park Service, Washington, 1973-75; cons. Saudi Arabia, 1975; assoc. dir. World Championship Tennis, 1975-77; pres. Ron Walker & Assocs., Inc., Dallas, 1977-79; sr. officer, mng. dir. Korn/Ferry Internat., Washington, 1979—; bd. dirs. Guest Svcs. Inc., NOVAFAX. vol. Nixon/Agnew Campaign, 1968, transition and inauguration, 1969; founder, chmn. emeritus Order of Raft, 1972; mem. spl. presdl. del. to Prime Min. Indira Gandhi's funeral, New Delhi, 1984, Games of XXIV Olympiad, Seoul, 1988; trustee Nat. Outdoor Leadership Sch., Nat. Fitness Found., Pres.'s Coun. on Phys. Fitness and Sports, 1981-85; vice chmn., mem. Pres.'s Commn. on Bicentennial U.S. Constn., 1985—; mem. U.S. Olympic Com., 1989-93; bd. dirs., mem. exec. com. NCAA Found.; bd. dirs. Meridian Internat.; mem. Ctr. for Study of Presidency, 1988—, Coun. for Excellence in Govt., 1988—; chmn. Freedom Found. at Valley Forge, 1989—; trustee Ford's Theater, Washington; men's chair Project Hope Ann. Ball, 1989, 90, 91; chmn. ann. dinner Boys and Girls Clubs Am., 1993; chmn. 50th Presdl. Inauguration, Dedication Richard Nixon Libr., Birthplace, 1990, bd. dirs., 1990—; mgr. 1984 Rep. Nat. Conv.; sr. advisor Rep. Nat. Conv., 1988, 92, Bush/Quayle Presdl. Campaign, 1988; nat. chair Celebrities & Sports for Bush/Quayle; mem. oversite com. U.S. Rowing, 1993; active Commn. for Preservation of White House, 1973-75, Nat. Park adv. bd., 1973-75, Nat. Park Found., 1973-75, John F. Kennedy Ctr. for Performing Arts, 1973-75, Friends of Nancy Hanks Ctr., Meridian House Internat. Bd. Trustees, 1992—, USA Gymnasium Found., 1993—. Capt. U.S. Army, 1961-64. Recipient Disting. Citizen award U. Ariz., 1973, Outstanding Svc. award Dept. Interior, 1975, Centennial Medallion award U. Ariz., 1989, Ellis Island Congl. medal of honor, 1992. Mem. NCAA (bd. dirs. 1992—, exec. com. 1992—), Econs. Club of Washington, Met. Club of Washington, Congl. Country Club, Georgetown Club, City Club of Washington, Univ. Club. of N.Y., Burning Tree Club, Phi Delta Theta (named to Hall of Fame, 1991). Republican. Methodist. Office: Presidential Pla 900 19th St NW Washington DC 20006-2105

WALKER, RONALD R., writer, newspaper editor, educator; b. Newport News, Va., Sept. 2, 1934; s. William R. and Jean Marie (King) W.; m. O. Diane Mawson, Apr. 16, 1961; children: Mark Jonathan, Steven Christopher. BS, Pa. State U., 1956; postgrad. (Nieman fellow) Harvard U., 1970-71. Reporter, news editor, sr. editor, editorial page editor, mng. editor San Juan Star (P.R.), 1962-73, Washington columnist, 1982-84, city editor, 1984-87; instr. journalism Pa. State U., State College, 1973-74; asst. prof. Columbia U. Grad. Sch. Journalism, N.Y.C., 1974-76; editor The Daily News, V.I., 1976-77; press sec. Gov. V.I., 1978-79; special asst., chief of staff Rep. James H. Scheuer, U.S. Congress, 1980-82, special asst., chief of staff, Resident Commr. Jaime B. Fuster, U.S. Congress, 1987-92, spl. asst., press sec. Resident Commr. Antonio J. Colorado, 1992-93; independent profl. writer, weekly columnist editl. page San Juan Star, 1993—. Contbr. articles to nat. mags. and jours. Served with U.S. Army, 1957-59. Mem. Soc. Nieman Fellows., Harvard Club of Washington, Leica Hist. Soc. Am. Address: PO Box 599 Saint John VI 00831-0599 also: 5500 Friendship Blvd Apt 1522N Bethesda MD 20815-7208

WALKER, RUTH ANN, journalist; b. Elmhurst, Ill., June 22, 1954; d. Robert F. and Jeanne (Carsman) W. AB, Oberlin (Ohio) Coll., 1976. Staff reporter Aiken (S.C.) Standard, 1977-78; various editing and writing positions Christian Sci. Monitor, Boston, 1978-83, bus. corr., 1983-85, editorial writer, 1985-88, asst. editor editorial page, 1988, asst. mng. editor, 1988-90, dep. editor, 1990-94, assoc. editor, 1994-95, sr. correspondent Europe, 1995—. Recipient Exceptional Merit Media award Nat. Women's Polit. Caucus, 1987. Christian Scientist. Home and Office: Muensterstr 20, D53111 Bonn Germany

WALKER, SALLY BARBARA, retired glass company executive; b. Bellerose, N.Y., Nov. 21, 1921; d. Lambert Roger and Edith Demerest (Parkhouse) W. Diploma Cathedral Sch. St. Mary, 1939; AA, Finch Jr. Coll., 1941. Tchr. interior design Finch Coll., 1941-42; draftsman AT&T, 1942-43; with Steuben Glass Co., N.Y.C., 1943—, exec. v.p., 1959-62, exec. v.p. ops., 1962-78, exec. v.p. ops. and sales, 1978-83, exec. v.p., 1983-88, ret. 1988. Pres. 116 E. 66th St. Corp. Mem. Fifth Ave. Assn. Republican. Episcopalian. Clubs: Rockaway Hunting, Lawrence Beach, U.S. Lawn Tennis, Colony, English-Speaking Union. Home: 116 E 66th St New York NY 10021-6547

WALKER, SAMMIE LEE, retired elementary education educator; b. Elkhart, Tex., July 10, 1927; d. Samuel and Mary (Pigford) Nathaniel; m. R.L. Walker, Oct. 12, 1952 (dec. 1994); children: Winfred, Frederick, Mary, Pearlene, Gladys, Robert, Ethel. BS, Tex. Coll., 1951; MEd, Tex. So. U., 1979. Cert. tchr., home econs. educator, elem. educator. Seamstress Madonna Guild Factory, Houston, 1958-60; presch. tchr. Project Head Start, Houston, 1961-64; tchr. Houston Ind. Schs., 1964-86; tchr. Harris County Youth Authority, Clear Lake, Tex., 1985; costume maker CETA program Houston Ind. Sch. Dist., 1984. Tchr. Trinity Garden Ch. of Christ, 1956—; phys. fitness coord. Kashmere Garden Sr. Citizen Club, Houston, 1986-92; home care provider Tex. Home Health Care, Houston, 1988-93. Recipient Friendship award Houston Christian Inst., 1993. Mem. NEA. Avocations: sewing, cooking, travel, volunteer work for local charities and school districts. Home: 7911 Shotwell St Houston TX 77016-6548

WALKER, SANDRA, mezzo-soprano; b. Richmond, Va., Oct. 1, 1946; d. Phillip Loth and Mary Jane W.; m. Melvin Brown, May 17, 1975; 1 child, Noel Christian Brown. MusB, U. N.C., 1969; postgrad., Manhattan Sch. Music, 1971-72. Artist-in-residence Ky. Opera Assn., 1980. Recorded Ned Rorem's song cycle King Midas on Desto Records, 1974; debut San Francisco Opera, 1972, re-engaged 1986, Chgo. Lyric Opera, 1973, 88, re-engaged 1988, Washington Opera Soc., 1973, Phila. Lyric Opera, 1973, Teatro Communale, Florence, Italy, 1985, Met. Opera, N.Y.C., 1986, re-engaged 1989, Opernhaus Zurich, 1987, Stadt Theater Wiesbaden, 1987, Rigoletto, Eugene-Onegin, Met. Opera. 1989, Netherlands Opera, 1989, Orlands Furioso, San Francisco Opera, 1989, Ring Cycle, 1990; leading mezzo soprano N.Y.C. Opera, 1974—, Stadt Theater, Würzburg, Germany, 1980-82, Stadt Theater Gelsenkirchen, Fed. Republic Germany, 1983-85, Stadt Theater Essen, Fed. Republic Germany, 1984, Frankfurt Opera, Fed. Republic Germany, 1985; soloist Orchestra Santa Cecilia Academia, Rome, 1987, New Orch. Paris, 1988; singer in major U.S. and European music festivals Tanglewood, Caramoor, Spoleto-U.S.A. and Spoleto Festival of Two Worlds in, Italy; soloist, Am. Symphony, San Francisco Symphony, 1980; appeared in: PBS nat. telecasts Manon, The Ballad of Baby Doe, Saint of Bleeker Street, 1981, on Great Performances: in The Consul and Eugene Onegin, 1986; Met. Opera nat. broadcast Samson, 1986, Eugene Onegin, 1989; orchestral appearances with Nat. Symphony, Washington, St. Louis Symphony, Chgo. Symphony, Richmond (Va.) Symphony, Houston Symphony, San Francisco Symphony, Charlotte Symphony, Cleve. Orch.; comml. video prodns. Eugene Onegin, Manon, Orlando Furioso; opera appearances include Falstaff, Calgary Opera, 1991, Mephistofiles, Chgo. Lyric Opera, 1991, Barber of Seville, Phila. Lyric Opera, 1991, Theatre De Capitole Toulouse France, 1992, Paris Opera, 1993, Blossom Festival Clev. Opera, 1993, Met. Opera, 1994, Met. Opera, 1995, Recording Die Walkuere with Cleve. Orch. Recipient Nat. Endowment for Arts Affiliate Artist grant sponsored by Va. Opera Assn. and Sears Roebuck Co., 1978. Office: care Columbia Artists Mgmt Inc 165 W 57th St New York NY 10019-2201

WALKER, SHARON LOUISE, gifted education educator; b. St. Paul, Mar. 26, 1944; d. John Franklin and Catherine G. (Keiffer) Corkill; m. David Glenn Smith, June 11, 1964 (div. Feb. 1980); 1 child, Carina Ann Smith; m. William Laurens Walker III, Nov. 10, 1981. BS in Edn., U. Md., 1971; M in Adminstrn. and Supervision, U. Va., 1990. Cert. elem. sch. prin., K-12 tchr. of gifted, 1-7 classroom tchr., K-12 tchr. art, Va. Tchr. 3rd and 4th grades Seat Pleasant (Md.) Elem. Sch., 1971-75; tchr. 4th grade Venable Elem. Sch., Charlottesville, Va., 1975-79; tchr. 3rd and 4th grade gifted edn. Quest program Charlottesville City Schs., 1979—; coord. acad. summer sch. Summer Discovery grades kindergarten through 4 Charlottesville City Schs., 1988-94, mem. various curriculum, staff devel., award coms., 1990—; seminar leader summer enrichment program U. Va., Charlottesville, 1986-89. Mem., chairperson placement com. Jr. League, Charlottesville, 1977—; mem. edn. com. Bayly Art Mus., Charlottesville, 1984-89; bd. dirs., devel. chairperson Charlottesville Albemarle Youth Orch., 1991-93; bd. dirs., mem. program com. Madison Ho., U. Va., 1994—, bd. dirs., co-chair, 1996—. Mem. Charlottesville Edn. Assn., Phi Delta Kappa (U. Va. chpt.), Delta Kappa Gamma (v.p. 1993-95). Home: 1180 Old Garth Rd Charlottesville VA 22901-1916 Office: Quest Ctr 406 14th St NW Charlottesville VA 22903-2305

WALKER, STANLEY P., publishing executive; b. Arkham, Mass., May 23, 1955; s. Gerald Jeffrey and Rebecca (Chamberlain) W.; m. Faith Darwin, Aug. 17, 1977; children: Erin, Emily, Amy. BA in English, Oberlin Coll., 1977; MFA in Creative Writing, Western Mich. U., 1979; MA in English Lit., Columbia U., 1982, PhD in English Lit., 1983. Sr. editor Farrar Straus Giroux, N.Y.C., 1980-83; assoc. prof. creative writing, early English lit. Columbia U., N.Y.C., 1983-87; pres., editor-in-chief Walker Press, N.Y.C., 1987-90; pres. Walker/Sturgeon Publs., Inc., New Providence, N.J., 1990—; vis. assoc. prof. Grinnell (Iowa) Coll., 1985-86; adj. prof. CUNY, 1987-90; cons. Farrar Straus Giroux, N.Y.C., 1990—. Author: (short story collections) The Rudeness of Youth, 1989, Life in the Sour Patch, 1991; co-author: (with L.Q. Sturgeon) Succeeding in Small-Scale Publishing, 1991; book reviewer numerous publs., N.Y.C., 1987—; contbr. articles to profl. jours. Trustee Grinnell Coll., 1990—; soccer coach, referee Am. Youth Soccer League, New Providence, 1990—. Mem. Writers Guild, Mensa, Ragnarok Lumberjacks, Phi Beta Kappa. Avocations: Old and Middle English writings, linguistics, music criticism, soccer, poker. *

WALKER, TENNYSON A., corporation executive; b. Moncton, N.B., Can., July 22, 1927; s. Trueman H. and Viola (Graves) W.; m. Hilda Hoar Thorne; 1 child, William T. Graduate, Success Bus. Coll., 1945. With Lounsbury Co. Ltd., Moncton, 1945-94, v.p. fin., 1976-79, pres., 1979-94, now shareholder and bd. dirs. Mem. Gideons Internat., Rotary. Mem. Conservative Party. Baptist. Office: Lounsbury Co Ltd, 1655 Mountain Rd, Moncton, NB Canada E1C 8H7

WALKER, THOMAS H., federal agency administrator; b. Hattiesburg, Miss., Nov. 11, 1950; s. Thomas Ray and Mary Ella (Bennett) W.; m. Cynthia Kay Sherer, June 5, 1993; children: Ty, Kelly, Rachel, Stacey. BS in Engring., Miss. State U., 1972; MBA, U. West Fla., 1982; postgrad., Nat. Def. U., 1987-88, Harvard U., 1990, Fed. Exec. Inst., 1992. Registered profl. engr., Va. Indsl. engr. Navy Pub. Works Ctr., Norfolk, Va., 1973-75, Atlantic Divsn. Naval Facility Engring. Commn., Norfolk, Va., 1975-76; supervisory gen. engr. Naval Comm. Sta., Exmouth, Australia, 1976-78; indsl. engr. Western Divsn. Naval Facility Engring. Commn., San Bruno, Calif., 1978-79; head facilities mgmt. Navy Pub. Works Ctr., Pensacola, Fla., 1979-82, Subic Bay, The Philippines, 1982-85; dep. dir. facilities mgmt. USMC, Washington, 1985-89; asst. commr. GSA, Washington, 1989-92, dep. asst. regional adminstr., 1992-93; asst. regional adminstr. pub. bldgs. GSA, Kansas City, Mo., 1993—; bd. dirs. Kansas City BOMA. Coach Little League Baseball, Fairfax, Va., 1986-92, Girls Softball Team, Lees Summit, Va., 1995. cub scout den father Boy Scouts Am., Fairfax, 1987-88. Miss. State U. Disting. Engring. fellow, 1992; recipient Arthur S. Fleming award Washington Jaycees, 1989. Mem. NSPE, Va. Soc. Profl. Engrs., Bldg. Owners and Mgrs. Assn. (mem. govt. bldgs. com. 1991—, chmn. 1993—, mem. corp. facilities com. 1991—, nat. adv. coun. 1995—), Internat. Facilities Mgmt. Assn. (mem. pub. sector com. 1991—, Golden Cir. award 1994), Sr. Execs. Assn., Phi Kappa Phi, Alpha Pi Mu, Gamma Beta Phi. Methodist. Avocation: golf. Home: 328 NE Sunderland Ct Lees Summit MO 64064-1610 Office: GSA 1500 E Bannister Rd Kansas City MO 64131-3009

WALKER, TIMOTHY BLAKE, lawyer, educator; b. Utica, N.Y., May 21, 1940; s. Harold Blake and Mary Alice (Corder) W.; m. Sandra Blake; children: Kimberlee Corder, Tyler Blake, Kelley Loren. AB magna cum laude, Princeton U., 1962; JD magna cum laude, U. Denver, 1967, MA in Sociology, 1969. Bar: Colo. 1968, Calif. 1969, Ind. 1971. Asst. prof. law U. Pacific, 1968-69; vis. assoc. prof. U. Toledo, 1969-70; assoc. prof. Indpls. Law Sch., Ind. U., 1970-71; assoc. prof. U. Denver, 1971-75, prof., 1975—, dir. adminstrn. of justice program, 1971-78; sole practice law Denver, 1972-79; of counsel Robert T. Hinds, Jr. & Assocs. (P.C.), Littleton, Colo., 1980-85; ptnr., of counsel Cox, Mustain-Wood & Walker, Littleton, 1985—; cons. in field; rsch. on lay representation in adminstrv. agys., Colo., 1975-76. Contbr. articles to profl. publs.; lectr., symposium editor: Denver Law Jour., 1966-67; editor-in-chief: Family Law Quar., 1983-92. Mem. Ind. Child Support Commn., 1970-71; pres. Shawnee (Colo.) Water Consumers Assn., 1975-84, 93-95; del. Colo. Rep. Conv., 1978. Colo. Bar Assn. grantee, 1975-76. Fellow Am. Sociol. Assn., Am. Acad. Matrimonial Lawyers, Internat. Acad. Matrimonial Lawyers; mem. ABA (vice chmn. child custody subcom., sec. sect. family law 1992-93, vice-chairperson, sec. family 1993-94, chairperson-elect sect. family law 1994-95, chairperson sect. family law 1995-96, mem. child custody task force, chmn. alimony maintenance and support com.), Calif. Bar Assn., Colo. Bar Assn., Ind. Bar Assn., Colo. Trial Lawyers Assn. (cons.). Presbyterian. Home: 7329 Rochester Ct Castle Rock CO 80104-9281 Office: 1900 Olive St Denver CO 80220-1857 also: 6601 S University Blvd Littleton CO 80121-2913 *Law and justice require the combination of intellectual self-discipline and an awareness of human dignity. The path of the law is often twisted and circuitous, and my goal has been to leave the trail better than I found it.*

WALKER, VAUGHN R., federal judge; b. Watseka, Ill., Feb. 27, 1944; s. Vaughn Rosenworth and Catharine (Miles) W. AB, U. Mich., 1966; JD, Stanford U., 1970. Intern economist SEC, Washington, 1966, 68; law clk. to the Hon. Robert J. Kelleher U.S. Dist. Ct. Calif., L.A., 1971-72; assoc. atty. Pillsbury Madison & Sutro, San Francisco, 1972-77, ptnr., 1978-90; judge U.S. Dist. Ct. (no. dist.) Calif., San Francisco, 1990—; mem. Calif. Law Revision Commn., Palo Alto, 1986-89. Dir. Jr. Achievement of Bay Area, San Francisco, 1979-83, St. Francis Found., San Francisco, 1991—. Woodrow Wilson Found. fellow U. Calif., Berkeley, 1966-67. Fellow Am. Bar Found.; mem. ABA (jud. rep., antitrust sect. 1991-95), Lawyers' Club of San Francisco (pres. 1985-86), Assn. Bus. Trial Lawyers (dir. 1996—), Am. Law Inst., Am. Saddlebred Horse Assn., San Francisco Mus. Modern Art, Bohemian Club, Olympic Club, City Club. Office: US Dist Ct 450 Golden Gate Ave San Francisco CA 94102

WALKER, VIRGINIA BOYD, elementary school educator; b. Tuskegee, Ala.; d. Johnnie Lee and Lucy (Bryant) Boyd; m. Johnny Bee Walker, Apr. 18, 1978; children: Carolyn Annette Walker Stone, Kevin Cordell, Kenneth Boyd. BS in Elem. Edn., Tuskegee U., 1975; MS in Reading Edn., Ala. State U., Montgomery, 1979; cert. K-12 sch. counseling, Troy State U., Montgomery, Ala., 1980. Chpt I reading tchr. Tuskegee (Ala.) Sch. System, 1976-81, chpt. I reading lab. tchr., 1983, classroom tchr., 1984—; mem. sch. adv. com., Tuskegee, 1986, 92-93, coord. social studies subject area, 1992-93, grade level chair, 1985-86, mem. prin.'s adv. coun., 1990-91, student coun. sponsor, 1990-95, advisor, 1993-94. Mem. Tuskegee Dem. Club, 1983—, Ala. Dem. Orgn., 1988—. Mem. NEA, Ala. Edn. Assn., Macon County Edn. Assn., Am. Legion, VFW Ladies Aux., Elks, Phi Delta Kappa. Home: PO Box 81 Tuskegee AL 36083-0081

WALKER, VIRGINIA L., art educator; b. Elkridge, W.Va., June 29, 1926; d. William Frank and Margaret Elizabeth (Scott) Birchfield; m. Onyx Robbley Walker, Mar. 13, 1946; 1 child, Elaine Helene Walker Evans. BS, Morris Harvey Coll., 1954; MA, W.Va. U., 1967. Cert. art tchr., K-12, elem. tchr., W.Va. Tchr. Fayette County Bd. Edn., Elkridge, W.Va., Beards Fork, W.Va.; tchr. Oak Hill and Greenbrier Sch., Crighton, W.Va.; tchr. art 7-12 Kanawha County Schs., Cedar Grove, W.Va.; county art supr. Kanawna County Schs., Charleston, W.Va.; curriculum devel. specialist W.Va. Dept. Edn., Charleston; mem. adj. faculty W.Va. State Coll. Artist: (watercolor/acrylic) Through the Glass Darkly (award 1968), Spring (reviewed in Art Rev. jour. 1967), Mama! Mama! the Bridge (Appalachian Corridors 1968); contbr. articles to profl. jours.; exhibitor numerous shows. Past chmn. W.Va. Arts for Handicapped, W.Va. Alliance for Arts Edn. Mem. Nat. Art Edn. Assn., NEA, W.Va. Art Edn. Assn. (pres. 1976-78). Home: 2123 Ronda Granada Apt A Laguna Hills CA 92653

WALKER, WALDO SYLVESTER, academic administrator; b. Fayette, Iowa, June 12, 1931; s. Waldo S. and Mildred (Littelle) W.; m. Marie J. Olsen, July 27, 1952 (div.); children: Martha Lynn, Gayle Ann; m. Rita K. White, June 16, 1984. BS cum laude, Upper Iowa U., Fayette, 1953; MS, U. Iowa, 1957, PhD, 1959. Mem. faculty Grinnell (Iowa) Coll., 1958, assoc. dean coll., 1963-65, chmn. div. Natural Scis., 1968-69, dean of adminstrn., 1969-73, exec. v.p., 1973-77, dean coll., 1973-80, provost, 1977-80, exec. v.p., 1980-90, exec. v.p. and treas., 1988-90, v.p. for coll. svcs., 1990-95, prof. biology, 1968—; research assoc. U. B.C. Dept. of Botany, 1966-67. Author articles on plant physiology, ultrastructural cytology. Served with U.S. Army, 1953-55. Fellow NSF Sci. Faculty, 1966-67; recipient NSF research grants, 1960-63, 68. Mem. Am. Assn. Colls., Am. Conf. Acad. Deans (nat. chmn. 1977-78), Am. Assn. Higher Edn., Sigma Xi. Home: 1920 Country Club Dr Grinnell IA 50112-1130 Office: Grinnell Coll PO Box 805 Grinnell IA 50112-0805

WALKER, WALTER FREDERICK, professional basketball team executive; b. Bradford, Pa., July 18, 1954; m. Linda Walker. Diploma, U. Va.; MBA, Stanford U., 1987; BA, U. Va., 1976. Chartered Fin. Analyst. Player Portland (Oreg.) Trail Blazers, 1976-77; player Seattle SuperSonics, 1977-82, pres., gen. mgr., 1994—; player Houston Rockets, 1982-84; with Goldman Sachs and Co., San Francisco, 1987-94; prin. Walker Capital, Inc., San Francisco, 1994; mem. USA gold medal World Univ. Games basketball team, 1973; broadcaster basketball Raycom Network, 1989-94; cons. Seattle SuperSonics, 1994. Vice chmn. Capital Campaign; bd. dirs. Red Hook Ale Brewery; bd. dirs. Interpoint Corp., Gargoyles Performance Eyeware. Named 1st team Acad. All-Am. U. Va.; named to Pa. State Sports Hall of Fame. Office: Seattle SuperSonics Ste 200 190 Queen Anne Ave N Seattle WA 98109-9711

WALKER, WANDA GAIL, special education educator; b. Montgomery, Ala., June 7, 1946; d. Carter Warren Gamaliel and Ruth Jones (Carter) Walker. BS in Elem. Edn., Campbell U., 1968; MA in Christian Edn., Scarritt Coll., 1970; cert. in tchg. of learning disabled, Pembroke U., 1994. Cert. tchr. class A, N.C. Dir. Christian edn. United Meth. Ch., Roxboro, N.C., 1970-76; diaconal min. United Meth. Ch., Hamlet, N.C., 1976-77, Rockingham, N.C., 1977-85; head teller Montgomery Savs. and Loan, Rockingham, 1985-87; loan officer-credit R.W. Goodman Co., Rockingham, 1987-89; tchr. spl. edn. Richmond County Schs., Hamlet, 1989—; active Richmond County Reading Coun., Hamlet, 1989—. Bd. dirs. Sandhill Manor Group Home, Hamlet, 1977—; mem. Woman's Club Hamlet, 1989-94, treas., 1989-91, 1st v.p., 1992-94. Eisenhower grantee U. N.C., 1994; recipient Mission award United Meth. Women, N.C. Conf., 1990; named Best Working Mem., Women's Club Hamlet, 1991. Democrat. Avocations: church activities, reading, volunteer work. Home: 344 Raleigh St Hamlet NC 28345-2750 Office: Richmond County Schs Hamlet Ave Hamlet NC 28345

WALKER, WARREN STANLEY, English educator; b. Bklyn., Mar. 19, 1921; s. Harold Stanley and Althea (Luscher) W.; m. Barbara Jeanne Kerlin, Dec. 9, 1943; children—Brian, Theresa. BA, SUNY-Albany, 1947, MA, 1948; PhD, Cornell U., 1951; LittD (hon.), Selcuk U., 1989. Prof., chmn. dept. English Blackburn Coll., Carlinville, Ill., 1951-59; prof., dean arts and scis. Parsons Coll., Fairfield, Iowa, 1959-64; Fulbright lectr. Am. lit. Ankara (Turkey) U., 1961-62; prof. English Tex. Tech U., Lubbock, 1964-86; Horn prof. Tex. Tech U., 1972-86; dir. Archive Turkish Oral Narrative, 1971; adv. council Tex. Cultural Alliance, 1975. Author: Nigerian Folktales, 1961, Twentieth-Century Short Story Explication, 14 vols., 1961-93, James Fenimore Cooper, 1962, Leatherstocking and the Critics, 1965, Tales Alive in Turkey, 1966, Archive of Turkish Oral Narrative: Catalogue 1, 1975, Plots and Characters in the Fiction of J.F. Cooper, 1978, A Bibliography of American Scholarship on Turkish Folklore and Ethnography, 1982, Turkish Games for Health and Recreation, 1983, Archive of Turkish Oral Narrative: Catalogue 2, 1988, Catalogue 3, 1994, The Book of Dede Korkut-A Turkish Epic, 1991, More Tales Alive in Turkey, 1992; mem. editorial bd. Definitive Edit. Works of James Fenimore Cooper, 1968; bibliographer Studies in Short Fiction, 1973. Served with USAAF, 1943-45. Recipient Tex. Writers award, 1967; citation Turkish Ministry Edn., 1967, Turkish Ministry State, 1973; research grantee Am. Council Learned Socs., 1973, 79; Am. Philos. Soc., 1974, Tex. Tech U., 1971-74, 76, 83, Republic of Turkey, 1983, Inst. Turkish Studies, 1984. Mem. MLA, Am. Folklore Soc., Nat. Coun. Tchrs. English, Internat. Soc. Folk Narrative Rsch., Middle East Studies Assn., Tex. Assn. Middle East Scholars (exec. coun.), Turkish Studies Assn., Atatürk Supreme Coun. on Turkish Culture (hon.). Home: 3703 66th St Lubbock TX 79413-5325 Office: Tex Tech U Archive Turkish Oral N Lubbock TX 79409

WALKER, WESLEY M., lawyer; b. Union, S.C., Jan. 28, 1915; s. John Frost and Cornelia (Greer) W.; m. Martha Bratton, Nov. 8, 1941; children—Martha Bratton, Wesley M., Nancy F. A.B., U. S.C., 1936, LL.B., 1938. Bar: S.C. 1938. Now partner firm Leatherwood, Walker, Todd & Mann, Greenville, S.C.; city atty. Greenville, 1949-51; spl. circuit judge York County, 6th Jud. Circuit, 1962. Served to lt. USNR, 1941-45. Fellow Am. Bar Found. (50 Yr. award 1994); mem. ABA (ho. of dels. 1952-54, 72-86, mem. com. law lists 1955-68, chmn. 1965-68, bd. govs. 1976-79), S.C. Bar Assn. (state del. 1973-77), Greenville Bar Assn. (pres. 1973), Am. Law Inst., Am. Coll. Trust and Estate Counsel, Phi Delta Phi. Home: 233 Camille Ave Greenville SC 29605-1703 Office: 100 E Coffee St Greenville SC 29601-2707

WALKER, WILBUR GORDON, physician, educator; b. Lena, La., Sept. 18, 1926; s. Daniel Clark and Ettie (Hodnett) W.; m. Betty Couch, Aug. 23, 1947; children: Wilbur Gordon, Martha Jane, Joseph Marshall, Carla Frances. Student, La. State U., 1942-44, 46-47, La. Coll., 1947; M.D., Tulane U., 1951. Intern Johns Hopkins Hosp., Balt., 1951-52; asst. resident Johns Hopkins Hosp., 1953-54, fellow in medicine, 1954-56, resident physician, 1956-57, physician, 1957—, dir. Clin. Research Center, 1960-88; resident Charity Hosp., New Orleans, 1952-53; faculty Johns Hopkins U. Sch. Medicine, 1956—, prof. medicine, 1968—, prof. internat. health, 1990—, chmn. com. on clin. investigation, 1964-71; prof. internat. health Johns Hopkins U. Sch. Med., 1990—; ednl. policy com. Johns Hopkins U. Sch. Medicine, 1976-80; exec. com., dept. med., 1973-79; admissions com. Johns Hopkins U. Sch. Med., 1988-92; dir. renal div. Johns Hopkins U. Sch. Medicine, 1958—, admissions com., 1988-92; attending physician Balt. City Hosp., 1960—; established investigator Am. Heart Assn., 1957-60; dir. dept. rsch. medicine Good Samaritan Hosp., Balt., 1968—; chmn. med. bd., 1972-74; vis. prof. Guys Hosp. Med. Sch., London, 1980; clin., rsch. ctrs. com. NIH, 1970-76, renal disease and urology grants com., 1968-76; chmn. clin. rsch. ctrs. com., 1975-76; McIlrath prof., hon. cons. physician Royal Prince Alfred Hosp., Sydney, Australia, 1968—; chmn. Coun. on Rsch. Md. Heart Assn., 1963-64; chmn. med. adv. bd. Md. Kidney Found., 1966-68; mem. Md. Gov.'s Commn. on Kidney Disease, 1970-80, 83-88; chmn. Md. Kidney Commn., 1975-80; chmn. computer com. div. rsch. resources NIH, 1973-75, hypertension and chronic renal failure working group, 1988-90. Editl. adv. bd. Am. Jour. Medicine, 1975-85; editl. bd. Kidney Internat., 1978-82; sec. editor: Principles and Practices of Medicine, 17th-21st edits.; co-editor: Potassium in Cardiovascular and Renal Medicine; contbr. articles to profl. jours. Trustee Md. Heart Assn. Served with USNR, 1944-45. Fellow ACP; mem. Am. Physiol. Soc. Am. Fdn. Clin. Research, Am. Soc. Clin. Investigation, Am. Soc. Nephrology, Council High Blood Pressure Research, Am. Clin. and Climatol. Assn., Interurban Clin. Club (sec. 1977-81, pres. 1981-82). Club: Peripatetic. Home: 3812 Fenchurch Rd Baltimore MD 21218-1824

WALKER, WILLARD BREWER, anthropology educator, linguist; b. Boston, July 29, 1926; s. William Henry Clowes and Helen (Brewer) W.; m. C. Pearline Large, Oct. 18, 1952; children: Christopher William, Andrew Francis. AB, Harvard U., 1950; MA, U. Ariz., 1953; PhD, Cornell U., 1964. Teaching fellow dept. modern langs. Cornell U., Ithaca, N.Y., 1960-61; rsch. asst. comparative study codes and models Cornell U., Nat. Inst. Mental Health, Ithaca, N.Y., 1963; rsch. assoc. dept. anthropology U. Chicago, Tahlequah, Okla., 1964-66; asst. prof. anthropology Wesleyan U., Middletown, Conn., 1966-70, assoc. prof., 1970-77, prof., 1977-89, prof. emeritus, 1989—, chmn. anthropology dept., 1971, 74-77, chmn. linguistics program, 1986-89. Author: Cherokee Primer, 1965; co-author: Cherokee Stories, 1966, A History of World's End, 1973, 1984; co-editor: Hopis, Tewas, & the American Road, 1983, 1986; contbr. numerous articles to profl. jours. Fellow Am. Anthrop. Assn.; mem. Am. Ethnological Soc., Linguistic Soc. Am., Am. Soc. Ethnohistory, Soc. for the Study of Indigenous Langs. of the Americas. Democrat. Avocation: forestry. Address: RR 2 Box 3310 Canaan ME 04924-9714

WALKER, WILLIAM BOND, painter, retired librarian; b. Brownsville, Tenn., Apr. 15, 1930; s. Marshall Francis and Mary Louise (Taylor) W. B.A., State U. Iowa, 1953; M.L.S., Rutgers U., 1958. Librarian-trainee

Donnell br. N.Y. Public Library, N.Y.C., 1955-57; reference librarian/cataloger Met. Mus. Art, N.Y.C., 1957-59; chief librarian Bklyn. Mus., 1959-64; supervisory librarian Library of Nat. Collection Fine Arts and Nat. Portrait Gallery, Smithsonian Instn., Washington, 1964-80; Arthur K. Watson chief librarian Thomas J. Watson Library, Met. Mus. Art, N.Y.C., 1980-94; ret., 1994; adj. lectr. Columbia U. Sch. Library Service, 1987-88. Author: annotated bibliography American Sculpture, 18th-20th Century, 1979. Mem. ALA, Art Librs. Soc. N.Am (pres. 1975, Disting. Svc. award), Geneal. and Biog. Soc. (corr.), Phi Beta Kappa. Home: 54 Queechy Lake Dr PO Box 237 Canaan NY 12029

WALKER, WILLIAM EASTON, surgeon, educator, lawyer; b. Glasgow, Scotland, Aug. 7, 1945; came to U.S., 1969; s. William Telfer and Josephine Blair (Easton) W.; m. Mary Fraley Cooley, June 23, 1973; children—Sarah Cooley, Blair Easton, Denton Arthur Cooley, William Easton, II. M.D., Glasgow U., Scotland, 1968; Ph.D., Johns Hopkins U., 1975; JD, South Tex. Coll Law, 1993. Diplomate Am. Bd. Surgery, Am. Bd. Thoracic Surgery, Am. Bd. Vascular Surgery. Intern, resident Johns Hopkins U., Balt., 1969-75; resident Vanderbilt U., Nashville, 1976-79; assoc. prof., dir. div. thoracic and cardiovascular surgery U. Tex. Med. Sch., Houston, 1979—; cons. M.D. Anderson Hosp., Houston, 1979—. Recipient Harwell Wilson award Vanderbilt U., Nashville, 1979. Fellow ACS, So. Surg. Assn., Royal Coll. Surgeons, Am. Coll. Cardiology; mem. Am. Assn. Thoracic Surgery, Coun. Fgn. Rels., Confrèrie de la Chaine de Rôtisseurs, Houston Country Club, Belle Meade Country Club, Cosmos Club (Washington), Krewe of Endymion (New Orleans), Phi Beta Kappa, Sigma Xi. Republican. Presbyterian. Avocations: law, golf, flying, backgammon, bridge. Home and office: 2831 Sackett St Houston TX 77098-1125

WALKER, WILLIAM OLIVER, JR., religion educator; b. Sweetwater, Tex., Dec. 6, 1930; s. William Oliver and Frances Baker (White) W.; m. Mary Scott Daugherty, Dec. 22, 1955 (div. Dec. 1978); children: William Scott, Mary Evan, Michael Neal. BA, Austin Coll., 1953; MDiv, Austin Presbyterian Sem., 1957; MA, U. Tex., 1958; PhD, Duke U., 1962. Instr. religion Austin Coll., Sherman, Tex., 1954-55, Duke U., 1960-62; from asst. to prof. religion Trinity U., San Antonio, 1962—, chair dept., 1980-88, acting dean div. Humanities and Arts, 1988-89, dean, 1989—. Contbr. articles and book reviews to profl. jours. Editor: The Relationships, 1978, The Harper Collins Bible Pronunciation Guide, 1994; assoc. editor Harper's Bible Dictionary, 1985. Mem. Studiorum Novi Testamenti Soc., Soc. Bibl. Lit. (regional sec.-treas. 1980-86), Am. Acad. Religion (regional pres. 1966-67), Soc. Sci. Study Religion, Cath. Bibl. Assn. Am., Coll. Theology Soc. Democrat. Presbyterian. Avocations: tennis, traveling, photography. Home: 315 Cloverleaf Ave San Antonio TX 78209-3822 Office: Trinity U Office Dean Humanities & Arts 715 Stadium Dr San Antonio TX 78212-7200

WALKER, WILLIAM R., manufacturing executive, light; b. 1941. BS in Econs., U. Wis.; MBA, U. Md. CPA. With Exxon Corp., N.Y.C., 1964-84, Zilog, Inc., Campbell, Calif., 1984—; now sr. v.p. fin. and admnistrn., CFO Zilog, Inc., Campbell. Office: Zilog Inc 210 E Hacienda Ave Campbell CA 95008-6600*

WALKER, WILLIAM ROSS, accountant; b. Winnipeg, Man., Can., Apr. 15, 1934; s. Edwin and Mary Margaret (MacCharles) W.; m. Audrey Erickson, Nov. 20, 1959; children—Jayne, Karen, Graham, Douglas. B.Comm., U. Alta., 1956. With KPMG, Toronto, Ont., Can., 1956-93, ptnr., 1964, mng. ptnr., 1972-84, sr. ptnr., chief exec., 1984-89; chmn., chief exec. KPMG Peat Marwick Thorne, Toronto, Ont., Can., 1989-93, internat. exec. com. and bd., 1989—; international. exec. ptnr. KPMG, Amsterdam, Netherlands, 1993—; past mem. panel sr. advisors to auditor gen. of Can.; past vice-chmn., bd. dirs. Can. Comprehensive Auditing Found.; past chmn. U. Waterloo Acctg. Adv. Coun. Past chmn. bd. trustees Clarke Inst. Psychiatry; past. chmn. Ottawa Gen. Hosp. Decorated Queen's Jubilee medal. Fellow Inst. Chartered Accts. Ont., Alta. (coun. 1982-89, pres. 1988-89); mem. National, York, Rosedale Golf and Toronto Clubs. Clubs: National; York; Rosedale Golf; Toronto. Avocations: skiing, travel. Office: KPMG Internat Headquarters, PO Box 74111, 1070 BC Amsterdam The Netherlands

WALKER, WILLIAM TIDD, JR., investment banker; b. Detroit, Sept. 5, 1931; s. William Tidd and Irene (Rhode) W.; m. Patricia Louise Frazier, Sept. 10, 1953; children—Donna Louise, Carol Ann, Sally Lynn, Alyssa Jane. Student, Stanford, 1950. Rep. William R. Staats & Co., Los Angeles, 1952-57; sales mgr. William R. Staats & Co., 1957-58, syndicate partner, 1958-65; sr. v.p. Glore Forgan, William R. Staats Inc., N.Y.C., 1965-68; partner, exec. com. Lester, Ryons & Co., Los Angeles, 1968; exec. v.p. Bateman Eichler, Hill Richards Inc., Los Angeles, 1969-85; past pres., bd. dirs. Delhi Co., L.A.; pres., CEO, WTW Inc.; chmn., CEO Walker Assocs., bd. dirs. Go-Video, Inc., Elevision, Inc., Fortune Petroleum Corp., Eagle Lifestyle Nutrition, Inc.; adv. mem. Am. Stock Exch., 1981—. With USAF, 1949-52. Mem. Securities Industry Assn. (dir. nat. syndicate com., chmn. Calif. Dist. 10), Pacific Coast Stock Exch. (bd. govs. 1971-72), Investment Bankers Assn. (nat. pub. rels. com. 1966—), Bond Club L.A. (pres. 1973—), Calif. Yacht Club, Newport Harbor Yacht Club. Office: Walker Assocs PO Box 10684 Beverly Hills CA 90213-3684

WALKER, WILLIAM W, III, wholesale distribution executive. Chmn. Walker Drug Co., Pelham, Ala. Office: Walker Drug Co 172 Cahaba Valley Pky Pelham AL 35124-1143*

WALKER, ZOE ANN, special education educator; b. Bethpage, N.Y., Dec. 20, 1956; d. Douglas Alan and Elinor June (Mills) Deeds; 1 child, Stephanie. AAS, SUNY, Farmingdale, 1977; BS in Elem. Edn., SUNY, Geneseo, 1979; MA in Spl. Edn., Hofstra U., Uniondale, N.Y., 1981; PD in Sch. Adminstrn., L.I. U., 1992. Cert. sch. administr., elem., spl. and hearing impaired educator. Evaluator/tchr. Helen Keller Nat. Ctr., Sandspoint, N.Y., 1979-82; spl. edn. tchr. Nassau Ctr. for Developmentally Disabled, Woodbury, N.Y., 1982-85; asst. prin. Lake Grove (N.Y.) Sch., 1985-92; chairperson spl. edn. Lindenhurst (N.Y.) Pub. Schs., 1992—; adj. prof./tchr. Adelphi U., Garden City, N.Y., 1987-94; cons. amd lectr. in field. Com. mem. L.I. Resource Com., 1989, Newsday, Lake Grove, 1987; leader Career Awareness, Boy Scouts Am., Lake Grove, 1987-92; trainer East Farmingdale Fire Dept., 1992. Mem. Coun. Exceptional Children, L.I. Assn. Supervision and Curriculum Devel., Spl. Edn. Parent Assn. (scholarship chair 1992—). Mem. Council for Exceptional Children, L.I. Assn. Supervision and Curriculum Devel., Spl. Edn. Parent Assn. (scholarship chair 1992—). Avocations: skiing, painting, gardening. Avocations: skiing, painting, gardening. Office: Lindenhurst High Sch 350 Charles St Lindenhurst NY 11757-3902

WALKLET, JOHN JAMES, JR., publishing executive; b. Trenton, N.J., June 14, 1922; s. John James and Katherine Helen (Slamin) W.; m. Gretchen Crowell, Aug. 21, 1948; children: John III, Philip, Deborah, Preston, Richard, Colin, Keith, Christopher, Megan. BL in Journalism, Rutgers U., 1943. Reporter Montclair (N.J.) Times, 1943; prodn. editor Macmillan Pub. Co., N.Y.C., 1946-52, dir. mfg. sch. div., 1969-88, asst. v.p., 1982, v.p., 1983-88, cons., 1989, ret.; tech. writer Shell Chem. Corp., N.Y.C., 1952-54; dir. publs. Colonial Williamsburg, Williamsburg, Va., 1954-69; cons. book prodn. U. Press of Va., Charlottesville, 1963-69. Author, designer: Adventure in Williamsburg, 1960 (So. Books Competition award), A Window on Williamsburg, 1966 (So. Books Competition award); designer: The Journal of John Harrower, 1963 (One of 50 Books of Yr. award Am. Inst. Graphic Arts). Pres. Kiwanis Club of Williamsburg, 1969; cons. Va. Travel Coun., Richmond, 1960-69. Sgt. U.S. Army, 1943-46. Mem. Assn. Am. Pubs. (mfg. com. rep. Adv. Commn. Textbook Specifications 1980-84, vice chmn. mfg. com. 1984-86, chmn. mfg. com. 1986-88), Williamsburg Stirrup Club (bd. dirs. 1965-69), James Iredell Assn. (bd. dirs. Edenton soc. 1989—). Republican. Roman Catholic. Avocations: reading, piano and organ, golf, fishing, spectator sports. Home: 1222 Sound Shore Dr Edenton NC 27932-8916 *In one's career, success is augmented by the willingness of dedicated professionals to share their knowledge and experience and teach those individuals whose desire to learn and contribute is beyond measure.*

WALKOWIAK, VINCENT STEVEN, lawyer, educator; b. Chgo., Apr. 22, 1946; s. Vincent Albert and Elizabeth (Modla) W.; m. Linda Kae Schweigert, Aug., 1968; children—Jenifer, Steven. B.A., U. Ill., 1968, J.D., 1971. Bar: Ill. 1971, Tex. 1981, U.S. Ct. Appeals (8th cir.) 1971, U.S. Ct. Appeals (5th cir.) 1982, U.S. Dist. Ct. (so. and no. dists. Tex.) 1982. Assoc., Dorsey, Marquart, Windhorst, West & Halladay, Mpls., 1971-74; ptnr. Fulbright & Jaworski, Houston, 1982—; prof. Fla. State U., Tallahassee, 1974-76, So. Meth. U., Dallas, 1976-84. Editor: Uniform Product Liability Act, 1980; Trial of a Product Liability Case, vol. 1, 1981, vol. 2, 1982; Preparation and Presentation of Product Liability, 1983. Office: Fulbright & Jaworski 2200 Ross Ave Ste 2800 Dallas TX 75201-6773

WALKOWITZ, DANIEL J., historian, filmmaker, educator; b. Paterson, N.J., Nov. 25, 1942; s. Sol and Selda (Margel) W.; m. Judith Rosenberg, Dec. 26, 1965; 1 child, Rebecca Lara. AB, U. Rochester, 1964, PhD, 1972; postgrad., U. Grenoble, France, 1965. Lectr. in history U. Rochester, N.Y., 1967-69; instr. history Renssalaer Poly. Inst., Troy, N.Y., 1969-71; asst. prof. history Rutgers U., New Brunswick, N.J., 1971-78, NYU, N.Y.C., 1978-81; assoc. prof. NYU, 1981-88, co-dir. pub. history program, 1981-89, prof., 1988—, dir. met. studies, 1989—; ptnr., film producer PastTimes Prodns., N.Y.C., 1982—; vis. prof. Johns Hopkins U., 1991-92, U. Calif. Irvine, 1982; editorial sec. Radical History Rev., N.Y.C., 1985-89; bd. dirs. N.Y. Marxist Sch., 1987-90. Author: Worker City, Company Town, 1978; co-author: Workers of the Donbass Speak, 1995; film project dir. The Molders of Troy, 1980; co-editor: Workers in the Industrial Revolution, 1974, Working-Class America, 1984; video dir., co-prodr., dir., writer: Perestroika From Below, 1990; co-prodr., writer Public History Today. Grantee, Nat. Endowment Humanities, 1976, 78, 82. Mem. Nat. Coun. Pub. History (bd. dirs. 1986-89), Am. Hist. Assn., Orgn. Am. Historians, Oral History Assn. Avocation: international folk dance. Office: Dept of Met History Study Program NYU New York NY 10003

WALL, ARTHUR EDWARD PATRICK, editor; b. Jamestown, N.Y., Mar. 12, 1925; s. George Herbert and Doris (Olmstead) W.; student pub. schs., LLD (hon.) Rosary Coll., 1979; m. Marcella Joan Petrine, Nov. 5, 1954; children: John Wright, Marie Ann, David Arthur Edward. Copy editor Worcester (Mass.) Telegram, 1958; Sunday editor Hawaii Island Corr., Honolulu Star-Bull., 1958-60; editor Hilo (Hawaii) Tribune-Herald, 1960-63; Sunday editor Honolulu Advertiser, 1963-65, mng. editor, 1971-72; mng. editor Cath. Rev., 1965-66, editor, 1966-71; editor-in-chief Nat. Cath. News Service, Washington, 1972-76; editor, gen. mgr. The New World (name changed to Chgo. Catholic 1977), Chgo., 1976-86, pres., 1979-86; pres. New World Pub. Co., 1977-86; comm. officer Diocese of Cen. Fla., Orlando, 1988—; editor Cen. Fla. Episcopalian, Orlando, 1989—; dir. Noll Printing Co., Inc., Huntington, Ind. Dir. bur. info. Archdiocese Balt., 1965-66; mem. fin. com. Archdiocese Chgo., 1979-82; mem. council Internat. Cath. Union of Press, Geneva, 1972-84, v.p., 1974-77. Chmn., Gov.'s Com. Ednl. TV, Honolulu, 1964-65; regent Chaminade Coll., Honolulu, 1959-65, chmn., 1963-65; trustee St. Mary's Sem. and Univ., Balt., 1975-76; bd. dirs. Cath. Journalism Scholarship Fund, 1976-84, Our Sunday Visitor, Inc., Huntington, Ind., 1977-87, dir. emeritus, 1987—; mem. spiritual renewal and devel. com. 41st Internat. Eucharistic Congress, Phila., 1975-76; bd. dirs. Bible Reading Fellowship, 1996—. Named Young Man of Year, Hilo, Hawaii, 1960, Fla. Writer of Yr., 1988; recipient St. Francis de Sales award Cath. Press Assn., 1977; Father of Year, Honolulu C. of C., 1964; Spl. award U.S. Cath. Conf., 1980. Mem. Internat. Fedn. Cath. Press Agys. (pres. 1974-77), Internat. Fedn. Cath. Journalists (pres. 1977-80, v.p. 1981-83), Chgo. Acad. Sci., Cath. Press Assn. U.S. and Can. (bd. dirs. 1978-86), Fla. Cath. Exec. Bd., Sigma Delta Chi (past chpt. pres.), Internat. Order St. Luke the Physician (religious pub. rels. coun.). Episcopalian. Clubs: Nat. Press (Washington); Overseas Press (N.Y.C.). Author: The Big Wave, 1960, The Spirit of Cardinal Bernardin, 1983, If I Were Pope, 1989; contbr. articles to periodicals including The Orlando Sentinel, The Living Ch.; editor: Origins and Catholic Trends, 1972-76. Office: Diocese Cen Fla 1017 E Robinson St Orlando FL 32801-2023 *Most of my life has consciously involved words; almost everyone is a captive of words (fatso, nigger, turncoat, byu-now-pay-later, stupid, I love you) that trigger moods and actions almost in themselves. I guess it is the power of words, and especially the power of what most Christians call the Word, that has influenced me since a fortunate childhood in a literate household. I learned from my grandfather that a loud word limps (although I forget that once in a while), that decibel doesn't equal impact. I sometimes forget something else he taught me, that kinky four-letter words are weak and express a weakness inside. There are stronger words of the same size, such as soul and love, life and holy, good and idea, hear and talk. One who listens for those words hears something special; or to put it in a different vocabulary, God guides, and following that Guide leads to the only success there is.*

WALL, BARBARA WARTELLE, lawyer; b. New Orleans, Sept. 30, 1954; d. Richard Cole and Ruth Druhan (Power) W.; m. Christopher Read Wall, June 21, 1980; children: Christopher, Louisa. BA, U. Va., 1976, JD, 1979. Bar: N.Y. 1980, U.S. Dist. Ct. (so. and ea. dists.) N.Y. 1980. Assoc. Satterlee & Stephens, N.Y.C., 1979-85; asst. gen. counsel Gannett Co., Inc., Arlington, Va., 1985-90, sr. legal counsel, 1990-93, v.p., sr. legal counsel, 1993—. Mem. ABA (co-chair first amendment and media litigation com. of sect. litigation, chair forum on comm. law), N.Y. State Bar Assn., Assn. of Bar of City of N.Y. Republican. Roman Catholic. Home: 5026 Tilden St NW Washington DC 20016-2334 Office: Gannett Co Inc 1100 Wilson Blvd Arlington VA 22209-2297

WALL, BENNETT HARRISON, history educator; b. Raleigh, N.C., Dec. 7, 1914; s. Bennett Louis and Evie David (Harrison) W.; m. Neva White Armstrong, Sept. 7, 1968; children by previous marriage: Maie (Mrs. John E. Clark) (dec.), Diana (Mrs. John Freckman), Ann Bennett. AB, Wake Forest Coll., 1933; MA, U. N.C., 1941, PhD, 1947. Instr. N.C. State U., 1942-43; instr. U. N.C., 1943-44; instr. U. Ky., 1944-46, asst. prof., 1946-52, assoc. prof., 1952-64; prof. history dept. Tulane U., New Orleans, 1965-80; head dept. Tulane U., 1968-73; dir. Tulane Center Bus. History Studies, 1974-79; lectr. U. Ga., 1980-85. Author: Growth in a Changing Environment: History of Standard Oil Company New Jersey, 1950-1972, Exxon Corporation 1972-75, 1988; co-author Teagle of Jersey Standard, 1974; contbr. numerous articles to profl. jours. Fellow La. History Assn. (pres. 1974-75, McGinty award 1991); mem. Orgn. Am. Historians, Agrl. History Soc., Bus. History Soc., Econ. History Soc., So. History Assn. (sec., treas. 1952-85, v.p. 1986-87, pres. 1987-88), N.C. History Assn., S.C. Hist. Soc., Ga. History Soc., Omicron Delta Kappa, Phi Alpha Theta. Home: 150 Ashton Dr Athens GA 30606-1618

WALL, BRIAN ARTHUR, sculptor; b. London, Sept. 5, 1931; s. Arthur Francis and Dorothy (Seymour) W.; m. Sylvia Brown, Oct. 27, 1973; children—Nathaniel, Gideon. Student, Luton (Eng.) Coll. Art, 1951. First asst. to Dame Barbara Hepworth, St. Ives, Cornwall, Eng., 1954-59; instr. Ealing Coll. Art, Middlesex, Eng., 1961-62; prin. lectr. Central Sch. Art and Design, London, 1962-72; head dept. sculpture Central Sch. Art and Design, 1962-72; vis. lectr. U. Calif., Berkeley, 1969-73; lectr. U. Calif., 1973-75, asst. prof., 1975-77, asso. prof. art, 1977-81, prof., 1981-93; prof. emeritus, 1993—. One-man shows U. Nev., Las Vegas, 1976, Braunstein Gallery, San Francisco, 1974, 76, 78, Sculpture Now, N.Y.C., 1977, 78, Max Hutchinson Gallery, Houston, 1979, May Hutchinson Gallery, N.Y.C., 1981, Seattle Art Mus., 1982, San Francisco Mus. Modern Art, 1983, John Berggruen Gallery, San Francisco, 1983, Lowinsky Gallery, N.Y.C., 1987, Francis Graham-Dixon Gallery, London, 1992, Jernigan Wicker Fine Arts, 1995, Sheldon Meml. Art Gallery, U. Nebr., 1995; exhibited in group shows, including Mus. Modern Art, Paris, 1961, U. Tex., Dallas, 1976, Crocker Art Mus., Sacramento, 1979, Tate Gallery, London, 1985; works represented in permanent collections Tate Gallery, Mus. Art, Dublin, Art Gallery NSW, Australia, Univ. Art Mus., Berkeley, U. Houston, Sheldon Meml. Art Gallery, Seattle Art Mus., Towson State U., Balt., Oakland Mus.; works include Thornaby, 1968, Alai, 1978. Mem. Arts Council Gt. Brit., 1969-72; trustee San Francisco Art Inst., 1974-77; mem. San Francisco Twin Bicentennial Arts Com., 1975-76. Served with RAF, 1950-52. U. Calif. at Berkeley Humanities Rsch. Fellowship Program grantee, 1978-79; recipient prize BART Sculpture Competition, 1975. Subject of numerous profl. articles. Home: 306 Lombard St San Francisco CA 94133-2415

WALL, CLARENCE VINSON, state legislator; b. Athens, Ga., Oct. 17, 1947; s. Clarence Jacob and Fannie Lucile (Clark) W.; m. Linda Gail Mason, Dec. 6, 1969 (div. 1980); 1 child, Jeffrey Vinson. Grad. high sch., Lawrenceville, Ga., 1965. Rep. Ga. Ho. of Reps., Lawrenceville, 1973-82, 85—. Staff sgt. Ga. ANG, 1967-73. Republican. Baptist. Home: 164 E Oak St Lawrenceville GA 30245-4900

WALL, DONALD ARTHUR, lawyer; b. Lafayette, Ind., Mar. 17, 1946; s. Dwight Arthur and Myra Virgina (Peavey) W.; m. Cheryn Lynn Heinen, Aug. 29, 1970; children: Sarah Lynn, Michael Donald. BA, Butler U., 1968; JD, Northwestern U., 1971. Bar: Ohio 1971, U.S. Dist. Ct. (no. dist.) Ohio 1973, U.S. Ct. Appeals (6th cir.) 1982, U.S. Supreme Ct. 1980, Ariz. 1982, U.S. Dist. Ct. (no. dist.) W.Va. 1982, U.S. Dist. Ct. Ariz. 1983, U.S. Ct. Appeals (9th and 10th cir.) 1984, U.S. Ct. Appeals (5th cir.) 1988. Assoc. Squire, Sanders & Dempsey, Cleve., 1971-80, ptnr., 1980-82, Phoenix, 1983—; speaker at profl. meetings; program moderator. Contbr. articles to profl. jours. Mem. adminstrv. bd. Ch. of Saviour, Cleve. Heights, Ohio, 1980-83; trustee Ch. of the Saviour Day Center, Cleve. Heights, 1979-82; fin. com. Paradise Valley (Ariz.) United Meth. Ch., 1986-87; bd. dirs., div. commr. North Scottsdale (Ariz.) Little League, 1983-92; bd. dirs. Epilepsy Found. N.E. Ohio, 1976-82, pres., 1981-82, N.E. Cmty. Basketball Assn., 1993-95. Mem. ABA (torts and ins. practice and litigation sect., past chmn. r.r. law com., litigation sect.), Def. Research Inst., Ariz. Bar Assn. (labor and trial practice sects.), Maricopa County Bar Assn., Am. Judicature Soc., Ariz. Assn Def. Counsel. Methodist. Office: Squire Sanders & Dempsey 40 N Central Ave Phoenix AZ 85004-4424

WALL, FRED WILLARD, agricultural products supplier; b. 1923. With Porterville (Calif.) Drug Co., 1946-49; with Walco Internat. Inc., 1950—, now pres., chmn. bd., CEO. With USN., 1946. Office: Walco Internat Inc 15 W Putnam Ave Fl 2 Porterville CA 93257-3627*

WALL, FREDERICK THEODORE, retired chemistry educator; b. Chisholm, Minn., Dec. 14, 1912; s. Peter and Fanny Maria (Rauhala) W.; m. Clara Elizabeth Vivian, June 5, 1940; children: Elizabeth Wall Ralston, Jane Vivian Wall-Meinike. B.Chemistry, U. Minn., 1933, Ph.D., 1937. Mem. faculty chemistry dept. U. Ill., 1937-64, dean grad. coll., 1955-63; prof., chmn. dept. chemistry U. Calif., Santa Barbara, 1964-66, vice chancellor rsch., 1965-66; vice chancellor grad. studies and research, prof. chemistry U. Calif. at San Diego, 1966-69; exec. dir. Am. Chem. Soc., Washington, 1969-72; prof. chemistry Rice U., Houston, 1972-78; Pres. Assn. Grad. Schs., 1961; trustee Inst. Def. Analyses, 1962-64; mem. governing bd. Nat. Acad. Scis.-NRC, 1963- 67. Author: Chemical Thermodynamics, 1958; editor Jour. Phys. Chemistry, 1965-69. Mem. Am. Chem. Soc. (Pure Chemistry award 1945, dir. 1962-64), Finnish Chem. Soc. (corr.), Am. Acad. Arts and Scis., Nat. Acad. Scis. Achievements include early work on Monte Carlo computer simulation of macromolecular configurations and of basic reaction probabilities. Home: 2468 Via Viesta La Jolla CA 92037-3935

WALL, JAMES EDWARD, telecommunications, petroleum and pharmaceutical executive; b. Santa Barbara, Calif., Nov. 24, 1947; s. Charles Caswell II and Lydia (Sinn) W.; m. Judith Ann Hochman, Aug. 1, 1976. AA, Bakersfield Coll., 1967; BS, Calif. State U., Los Angeles, 1969; MBA, UCLA, 1970; D of Profl. Studies, Pace U., 1985; PMD, Harvard U. Sch. Bus., 1987. CPA, Calif. Agt. IRS, Los Angeles, 1971-74; agt. service office internat. ops. IRS, Washington, 1974-76; mgr. fin. forecasts Am. Ultramar, Ltd., Mt. Kisco, N.Y., 1976-80, treas., 1980-85, v.p., treas., 1985-91; exec. dir. fin. and adminstrn. Ultramar Exploration, London, 1991; v.p., treas. Ultramar Corp., Greenwich, Conn., 1992-94; v.p., corp. treas. ICN Pharms., Costa Mesa, Calif., 1994-95; treas. AirTouch Comms., Inc., San Francisco, 1995—; chief fin. officer Enstar Corp., Indonesia; mem. bd. mgmt. Unimar Co., 1985-91. Recipient award in acctg. UCLA, 1972, award in gen. bus. mgmt., 1973. Mem. AICPA, Fin. Execs. Inst., Nat. Assn. Corp. Treas., UCLA Grad. Sch. Alumni Assn., Harvard U. Bus. Sch. Alumni Assn. Office: AirTouch Comms Inc 9th Fl One California St San Francisco CA 94111

WALL, JOHN W., trust company executive; b. Providence, Conn., 1924. With Bank of Boston Corp., 1949-89, retired, 1989-90; chmn., pres. Rhode Island Hosp. Tr. Nat. Bank, Providence, 1990-92; vice chmn. Rhode Island Hosp. Tr. Nat. Bank, 1992—. Office: Rhode Island Hosp Tr Nat Bk 1 Hosp Trust Plz Providence RI 02903

WALL, LEONARD J., bishop; b. Windsor, Ont., Can., Sept. 27, 1924; Ordained Roman Catholic priest, June 11, 1949; ordained titular bishop of Leptiminus and aux. bishop of Toronto, 1979-92; archbishop of Winnipeg Archdiocese of Winnipeg, 1992—. Office: Archdiocese of Winnipeg, 1495 Pembina Hwy, Winnipeg, MB Canada R3T 2C6

WALL, M. DANNY, financial services consultant, real estate company. BArch, N.D. State U., 1963. Exec. dir. Urban Renewal Agy., Fargo, N.D., 1964-71, Salt Lake City Redevel. Agy., 1971-75; dir. legis. Office U.S. Senator Jake Garn, Washington, 1975-78; minority staff dir. Senate Com. for Banking, Housing and Urban Affairs, Washington, 1979-80, staff dir., 1980-86, Rep. staff dir., 1987; chmn. Fed. Home Loan Bank Bd./Fed. Home Loan Mortgage Corp., Washington, 1987-89; dir. Office Thrift Supervision (formerly Fed. Home Loan Bank Bd.), 1989-90; pres. Realty World Holding Corp., Salt Lake City.

WALL, ROBERT ANTHONY, JR., lawyer; b. Hartford, Conn., Mar. 3, 1945; s. Robert Anthony and Eileen (Fitzgerald) W.; divorced; children: Andrea, Melanie, Victoria, Robert, Natalie. BA, Georgetown U., Washington, 1968; JD, Am. U., Washington, 1973. Bar: Conn. 1974, U.S. Ct. Appeals (D.C. cir.) 1974, U.S. Dist. Ct. Conn. 1974, U.S. Supreme Ct. 1977. Ptnr. Wall, Wall & Frauenhofer, Torrington, Conn., 1974-87; pvt. practice Torrington, 1987—. Mem. State of Conn. Rep. Ctrl. Com., 1976-79. Mem. Conn. Trial Lawyers Assn. (bd. govs. 1984-86), Ct. Washington #67 Foresters of Am. (trustee 1988—). Roman Catholic. Home: 55 Quail Run Torrington CT 06790-2550 Office: 8 Church St Torrington CT 06790-5247

WALL, ROBERT EMMET, educational administrator, novelist; b. N.Y.C., Apr. 29, 1937; s. Robert Emmet and Sabina (Daly) W.; m. Regina Palasek, Aug. 1, 1959; children—Elizabeth, Nina, Amy, Christopher, Craig. BA, Holy Cross Coll., 1960; MA, Yale U., 1961, PhD, 1965. Asst. in instrn. Yale U., New Haven, 1963; instr. history Duke U., Durham, N.C., 1963-65; asst. prof. Mich. State U., East Lansing, 1965-69, asso. prof. history, 1970; asso. prof. Concordia U. (Sir George Williams U.), Montreal, Que., Can., 1971-72, prof., 1972-80, chmn. dept., 1972-77, dean, 1977-80; provost, acting v.p. Fairleigh Dickinson U., Rutherford, N.J., 1980-85; v.p. academic affairs Gannon U., Erie, Pa., 1986-92; acad. v.p. Fairfield (Conn.) U., 1992—. Author: Massachusetts Bay, The Crucial Decade, 1640-1650, 1972, The Canadians, Vol. I (Blackrobe), 1981, Vol. II (Bloodbrothers), 1981, Vol. III (Birthright), 1982, Vol. IV (The Patriots), 1982, Vol. V (The Inherators), 1983, Vol. VI (Dominion), 1984, Vol. VII (Brotherhood), 1985, The Acadians, 1984, Sierre Gold, 1987, The Massachusetts Bay General Court, 1630-1686, 1990, The Cat and The Rat, 1991. Home: 1232 Windward Rd Milford CT 06460-1744

WALL, ROBERT F., lawyer; b. Chgo., Jan. 7, 1952. BA with distinction, Northwestern U., 1973; JD summa cum laude, U. Santa Clara, 1977. Bar: Ill. 1977, U.S. Dist. Ct. (no. dist.) Ill. 1977. Ptnr. Winston & Strawn, Chgo. Mem. editorial bd. M&A and Corp. Control Law Reporter, 1988—. Mem. ABA. Office: Winston & Strawn 35 W Wacker Dr Chicago IL 60601-1614

WALL, ROBERT THOMPSON, secondary school educator; b. Luray, Va., May 31, 1943; s. Robert Alexander and Mary Ann (Coffman) W.; m. Sarah S. Wall, Aug. 19, 1967; children: Melissa Coffman, Jennifer Grey. BA, Va. Poly. Inst. and State U., 1966; MA, Radford (Va.) U., 1971; postgrad., U. Fla., 1978. Tchr. instrumental and choral music Halifax County Schs., Halifax, Va.; tchr. instrumental music Montgomery County Schs., Christiansburg, Va.; chmn. fine arts dept. Christiansburg Middle Sch., 1991—; judge, clinician for marching and concert bands; curriculum and instrn. clin. affiliate Va. Poly. Inst. and State U., Blacksburg; clinician, guest condr. for mid-Atlantic band camps Ferrum Coll., Va.; guest condr. all-dist. bands in Va., N.C., S.C. Composer: Published Windsor Portrait, 1990, Adagio for horn and piano, 1982, Nocturne for flute and piano, 1987, Royal Brigade, 1988, Prelude and tarantelle, 1991, An American Tattoo, 1994; compositions commd. by Va. State Symphony Orch., Charlotte (N.C.) Mecklenburg County Schs., Rural Retreat (Va.) H.S.; music performed at Va. Music Educators Conf., 1990, Midwest Band Conv., Chgo., 1990, Finland Radio,

1993, Great Britain, 1993, 94. Recipient Young composers award Va. Music Clubs, 1960, Va. Govs. Sch. Presdl. citation, 1990, 92, Teaching award Halifax County Schs., 1972. Mem. ASCAP, Music Educators Nat. Conf., Nat. Band Assn., Va. Music Educators Assn. (exec. bd.), Va. Band and Orch. Dirs. Assn. (instrumental chmn. dist. VI), Modern Music Masters (life, past adv. coun., exec. bd.), Phi Beta Mu, Phi Delta Kappa. Home: 2810 Mt Vernon Ln Blacksburg VA 24060-8121

WALL, ROBERT WILSON, JR., former utility executive; b. Monticello, Ark., June 11, 1916; s. Robert Wilson and Thursa (Cotham) W.; m. Joyce Esther Hoffman, Sept. 27, 1943; children: Mary Lynn Wall Sykes, Kathy Ann Wall Theros. B.A., U. Miss., 1938, J.D., 1940; grad. exec. program bus. adminstrn., Columbia U., 1974. Bar: Miss. bar 1940. With FBI, 1940-41, 47-53, spl. agt. in charge Miami (Fla.) office, 1951-53; with U.S. Fgn. Service, 1941-46; legal attache embassy U.S. Fgn. Service, Mexico City, 1944-46; personnel dir. Phillips Petroleum Co., Caracas, Venezuela, 1946-47; with Fla. Power & Light Co., Miami, 1953-81; v.p. Fla. Power & Light Co., 1963-73, sr. v.p., 1973-81; asst. chmn. Nat. Alliance Businessmen, 1966-70; bd. dirs. Southeastern Legal Found.; adv. bd. U. Miami Sch. Bus. Adminstrn. Div. chmn. United Fund Dade County, 1964-67; bd. dirs. Miami Better Bus. Bur., 1955-62, Goodwill Industries Miami, 1964-66, Miami council Girl Scouts Am., 1971-72. Mem. Am. Bar Assn., Am. Soc. Corp. Secs., Am. Arbitration Assn. (panel 1987), Soc. Former Spl. Agts. FBI, Miss. Bar Assn., Greater Miami C. of C. (dir. 1963, exec. com. 1964), Blue Key, Phi Delta Theta, Phi Delta Phi, Omicron Delta Kappa. Republican. Home: 16 Kituhwa Trl Brevard NC 28712-9438

WALL, SONJA ELOISE, nurse administrator; b. Santa Cruz, Calif., Mar. 28, 1938; d. Ray Theothornton and Reva Mattie (Wingo) W.; m. Edward Gleason Holmes, Aug. 1959 (div. Jan. 1968); children: Deborah Lynn, Lance Edward; m. John Aspesi, Sept. 1969 (div. 1977); children: Sabrina Jean, Daniel John; m. Kenneth Talbot LaBoube, Nov. 1, 1978 (div. 1989); 1 child, Tiffany Amber. BA, San Jose Jr. Coll., 1959; BS, Madonna Coll., 1967; student, U. Mich., 1968-70; postgrad., Wayne State U. RN, Calif., Mich., Colo. Staff nurse Santa Clara Valley Med. Ctr., San Jose, Calif., 1959-67, U. Mich. Hosp., Ann Arbor, 1967-73, Porter and Swedish Med. Hosp., Denver, 1973-77, Laurel Grove Hosp., Castro Valley, Calif., 1977-79, Advent Hosp., Ukiah, Calif., 1984-86; motel owner LaBoube Enterprises, Fairfield, Point Arena, Willits, Calif., 1979—; staff nurse Northridge Hosp., L.A., 1986-87, Folsom State Prison, Calif., 1987; co-owner, mgr. nursing registry Around the Clock Nursing Svc., Ukiah, 1985—; critical care staff nurse Kaiser Permanente Hosp., Sacramento, 1986-89; nurse Snowline Hospice, Sacramento, 1989-92; carepoint home care and travel nurse Hosp. Staffing Svcs. Inc., Placerville, Calif., 1992-94, interim home health nurse, 1994-95; owner Sunshire Manor Resdl. Care Home, Placerville, Calif., 1995—; owner Royal Plantation Petites Miniature Horse Farm. Contbr. articles to various publs. Leader Coloma 4-H, 1987-91; mem. mounted divsn. El Dorado County Search and Rescue, 1991-93; docent Calif. Marshall Gold Discovery State Hist. Park, Coloma, Calif. Mem. AACN, NAFE, Soc. Critical Care Medicine, Am. Heart Assn. (CPR trainer, recipient awards), Calif. Bd. RNs, Calif. Nursing Rev., Calif. Critical Care Nurses, Soc. Critical Care Nurses, Am. Motel Assn. (beautification and remodeling award 1985), Nat. Hospice Nurses Assn., Soroptimist Internat. Calif., Am. Miniature Horse Assn. (winner nat. grand championship 1981-82, 83, 85, 89), DAR (Jobs Daus. hon. mem.), Cameron Park Country Club. Republican. Episcopalian. Avocations: pinto, paint, Thoroughbred and miniature horses, real estate devel., swimming. Home and Office: Around the Clock Nursing Svc PO Box 559 Coloma CA 95613-0559

WALL, TERESA LAURINE, nursing and healthcare administrator; b. Redmond, Oreg., May 22, 1951; d. Monroe James and Arlene (Manuel) W.; 1 child, Richard James. BSN, Ariz. State U., 1981; MPH in Health Adminstrn., U. Okla. Health Scis. Ctr., 1990. Pub. health nurse trainee Gila River Indian Community, Sacaton, Ariz., 1982, pub. health nurse, 1985-88; clin. nurse USPHS Indian Health Svc., Sacaton, 1982-85; pub. health nurse USPHS Indian Health Svc., Watonga, Okla., 1988-90; exec. dir. Gila River Indian Community Dept. Health Svcs., 1990—; bd. dirs. Gila River Care Ctr., treas., 1992—; alt. mem. Indian Health Svc., Phoenix Indian Med. Ctr. Instnl. Rev. Bd., 1993—; commn. mem. Ariz. Area Health Edn. Ctr., 1993—. Lt. USPHS, 1983-86. Mem. APHA, Am. Coll. Healthcare Execs. (assoc.), Okla. Coll. Pub. Health Alumni Assn., Arizonans for Prevention. Democrat. Avocations: reading, beauty consultant. Home: 1762 W Mariposa Ct Chandler AZ 85224-6605

WALL, WILLIAM E., lawyer, former utility executive; b. 1928. BS, U. Wash., 1951, LLB, 1954. Asst. atty. gen. State of Wash., 1956-59; chief examiner Pub. Svc. Commn., 1959; sec., house counsel Cascade Natural Gas Corp., 1959-64; pres. United Cities Gas Co., 1964-65; exec. v.p. Cascade Natural Gas Corp., 1965-67; spl. asst. to chmn. bd. Consol. Edison Co., N.Y.C., 1967-68, v.p., 1968-70, sr. v.p. gas ops., 1970-71, exec. v.p. div. ops., 1971-73; gen. mgr. pub. affairs Standard Oil Co., 1973-74; exec. v.p. Kans. Power and Light Co., Topeka, 1974-75, pres., 1975-85, chief exec. officer, 1976-88, chmn., 1979-88; of counsel Siderius, Lonergan & Crowley, Seattle, 1988—. Served with AUS, 1954-56. Office: Siderius Lonergan & Crowley 500 Union St 847 Logan Bldg Seattle WA 98101*

WALLACE, ALICEANNE, civic worker; b. Chgo., Sept. 28, 1925; d. Alexander and Mary (Zurek) Zalac; m. Henry Clay Wallace, Jr., Apr. 10, 1948; children: Laura Lillian Wallace Bergin, Christine Claire Wallace Stockwell. Student, St. Teresa Coll., Winona, Minn., 1944-45, DePaul U., 1946-48, North Tex. State U., 1971, 72. City sec. City of Southlake, Tex., 1969-77; pres. AZW, Inc., real estate sales, Roanoke, Tex., 1977-84. Mem. Trinity Valley Mental Health-Mental Retardation, Ft. Worth, 1971-72; chmn. ways and means Tex. Silver-Haired Legis., Austin, 1986-90, parliamentarian, 1991-94; treas. TSHL Found., 1990-92, pres., 1992-96; sec., bd. dirs. Sr. Citizens Activities, Inc., Temple, Tex., 1989-90; sec. CTCOG Area Agy. on Aging, Citizens Adv. Coun. Bd., Belton, Tex., 1991; bd. dirs. Tex. Dept. on Aging, Austin, 1991—; congl. sr. intern U.S. Ho. of Reps., Washington, 1991; pres. Tri-County Tex. Dem. Women, 1990-94; elected State Dem. Exec. Com. Senatorial Dist. #24, 1994—. Mem. Am. Assn. Ret. Persons (legis. chmn. Temple chpt. 1990-94, regional coord. VOTE 1991-96, assoc. state coord. 1996—), Tex. Fedn. Women's Clubs (state legis. chmn. 1990-92, resolutions chmn. 1992-94, parliamentarian Capitol dist. 1990-92), North Ctrl. Tex. Secy. Assn. (pres. 19760, City Fedn. Women's Clubs (corr. sec. 1991-92, records custodian 1991—), Triangle Forum (pres. 1992-94), Daus. Republic Tex. (assoc.), Internat. Inst. Mcpl. Clks. (state cert.), Epsilon Eta Phi. Home: RR 2 Box 2585 Belton TX 76513-9611

WALLACE, ANDREW GROVER, physician, educator; b. Columbus, Ohio, Mar. 22, 1935; s. Richard Homes and Eleanor Bradley (Grover) W.; m. Kathleen Barrick Altvater, June 22, 1957; children: Stephen Andrew, Michael Bradley, Kathleen Claude. BS, Duke, 1958, MD, 1959. Diplomate Am. Bd. Internal Medicine. Intern medicine Duke U., Durham, N.C., 1959-60, asst. resident, 1960-61; fellow NIH, 1961-63; chief resident medicine Duke U., Durham, 1963-64, asst. prof., 1965-67, assoc. prof., 1967-71, chief, div. cardiology, 1970, prof. medicine, 1971, Walter Kempner prof. medicine, 1973; vice chancellor health affairs, chief exec. officer Duke U. Hosp., Durham, 1981; v.p. Duke U., 1987; dean Dartmouth Med. Sch., Hanover, N.H., 1990—; v.p. for health affairs Dartmouth Coll., 1990; cons. program project com., cardiology adv. com. and pharmacology study sect. Nat. Heart and Lung Inst., cardiovascular merit rev. bd. VA. Mem. editorial bd. Am. Jour. of Physiology, 1965-70, Jour. of Pharmacology and Exptl. Therapeutics, 1966-71, Jour. of Molecular and Cellular Cardiology, 1970-75, Jour. of Clin. Investigation, 1973-78. Pres. Durham YMCA Swim Assn., 1975-77. Markle scholar, 1965-70. Mem. AAMC, COD, Am. Fedn. for Clin. Rsch., Am. Soc. Clin. Investigation, Am. Heart Assn. (coun. on clin. cardiology), Am. Physiol. Soc., Biomed. Engring. Soc., Assn. U. Cardiologists, Am. Assn. Physicians, Soc. Med. Administrs., VA Spl. Med. Adv. Group (chair). Home: 62 Oak Ridge Rd West Lebanon NH 03784-3113 Office: Dartmouth Coll Med Sch Office of Dean Hanover NH 03755-3833

WALLACE, ANTHONY FRANCIS CLARKE, anthropologist, educator; b. Toronto, Ont., Can., Apr. 15, 1923; s. Paul A.W. and Dorothy Eleanor (Clarke) W.; m. Betty Louise Shillott, Dec. 1, 1942; children: Anthony, Daniel, Sun Ai, Samuel, Cheryl, Joseph. B.A., U. Pa., 1948, M.A., 1949, Ph.D., 1950; L.H.D. (hon.), U. Chgo., 1983. Instr. anthropology Bryn Mawr Coll., 1948-50; asst. instr. anthropology U. Pa., research sec. Behavioral Research Council, 1951-55; research asst. prof. U. Pa., 1952-55, vis. assoc. prof., 1955-61, prof., 1961—, chmn. dept., 1961-71, Geraldine R. Segal prof. Am. social thought, 1980-83, Univ. prof. anthropology, 1983-88, prof. emeritus, 1988—; sr. research assoc. anthropology Eastern Pa. Psychiat. Inst., 1955-60, dir. clin. research, 1960-61, med. research scientist, III, 1961-80; mem. tech. adv. com. N.J. Psychiat. Inst., 1958; cons. disaster studies NRC, 1956-57; cons. Phila. Housing Authority, 1952; mem. research adv. com. Commonwealth Mental Health Research Found., 1960-61, U.S. Office Edn., 1965-68; mem. behavioral scis. study sect. NIMH, 1964-68; mem. NRC, 1963-66; mem. various adv. coms. NIMH, 1962—; mem. social sci. adv. council NSF, 1969-72. Author: King of the Delawares: Teedyuscung, 1700-1763, 1949, Culture and Personality, 1961, rev. edit., 1970, Religion: An Anthropological View, 1966, Death and Rebirth of the Seneca, 1970, Rockdale: The Growth of an American Village in the Early Industrial Revolution, 1978, Social Context of Innovation, 1983, St. Clair, 1987, The Long, Bitter Trail, 1993. Bd. mgrs. Founds. Fund for Research in Psychiatry, 1969-71. Served AUS, 1942-45. Recipient Bancroft prize in Am. History, 1979, Dexter prize in History of Technology, 1989; Guggenheim fellow, 1978-79. Fellow Am. Anthrop. Assn. (pres. 1971-72),; mem. Nat. Acad. Scis., Am. Philos. Soc., Am. Acad. Arts and Scis. Office: Univ PA Dept Anthropology 33rd and Spruce Sts Philadelphia PA 19174

WALLACE, ARTHUR, JR., college dean; b. Muskogee, Okla., June 12, 1939; s. Arthur and Edna (Collins) W.; m. Claudina Young, Oct. 4, 1969; children: Dwayne, Jon, Charles. BS, Langston U., 1960; MS, Okla. State U., Stillwater, 1962, PhD, 1964. Dir. commodity rsch. Gen. Foods Corp., White Plains, N.Y., 1964-67; v.p., sr. economist Merrill Lynch & Lionel D. Edie & Co., N.Y.C., 1968-71; econ. cons. Wall St. fin. instns. Group IV Econs., N.Y.C., 1972-76; mgr. U.S. and Can. econs. Internat. Paper Co., N.Y.C., 1976-78, chief economist, 1978-82, dir. corp. affairs and policy analysis, 1982-83; corp. sec. Internat. Paper Co., Purchase, N.Y., 1983-87; v.p., corp. sec. Internat. Paper Co., 1987-93; pres. Internat. Paper Co. Found., 1983-93; dean coll. bus. San Francisco State U., 1993—. Home: 1085 Greenwich St Apt 1 San Francisco CA 94133-2545 Office: San Francisco State U School of Business 1600 Holloway Ave San Francisco CA 94132-1722

WALLACE, BARBARA BROOKS, writer; b. Soochow, China, Dec. 3, 1922; came to U.S., 1938; d. Otis Frank and Nicia Brooks; m. James Wallace Jr., Feb. 27, 1954; 1 child, James V. BA, UCLA, 1945. Script sec. Foote, Cone & Belding, Hollywood, Calif., 1946-49; tchr. Wright MacMahon Secretarial Sch., Beverly Hills, Calif., 1949-50; head fund drive Commerce and Industry Divsn. ARC, San Francisco, 1950-52. Author: Claudia, 1969 (Nat. League of Am. Pen Women Juvenile Book award 1970), Andrew the Big Deal, 1970, The Trouble with Miss Switch, 1971, Victoria, 1973, Can Do, Missy Charlie, 1974, The Secret Summer of L.E.B. (Nat. League of Am. Pen Women Juvenile Book award 1974), Julia and the Third Bad Thing, 1975, Palmer Patch, 1976, Hawkins, 1977, Peppermints in the Parlor, 1980 (William Allen White award 1983), The Contest Kid Strikes Again, 1980, Hawkins and the Soccer Solution, 1981, Miss Switch to the Rescue, 1981, Hello, Claudia, 1982, Claudia and Duffy, 1982, The Barrel in the Basement, 1985, Argyle, 1987, 92, Perfect Acres, Inc., 1988, The Twin in the Tavern, 1993 (Edgar award Mystery Writers Am. 1994), Cousins in the Castle, 1996. Mem. Children's Book Guild of Washington, Alpha Phi. Episcopalian. Home and Office: 2708 George Mason Pl Alexandria VA 22305-1620

WALLACE, CHRISTOPHER, broadcast television correspondent; b. Chgo., Oct. 12, 1947; s. Mike and Norma (Kaphan) W.; m. Elizabeth Farrell, May 12, 1973; children: Peter Farrell, Margaret Coleman, Andrew Farrell, Catherine Farrell. BA, Harvard U., 1969. Nat. reporter Boston Globe, 1969-73; polit. reporter Sta. WBBM-TV, Chgo., 1973-75; investigative reporter Sta. WNBC-TV, N.Y.C., 1975-78; polit. reporter NBC News, Washington, 1978-81; anchor Today Show, 1981-82; corr. White House, 1982-89, Prime Time Live, ABC-TV, 1989—; anchor Meet The Press, 1987-88. Reporter, writer: documentaries NBC The Migrants, 1980, Protection For Sale: The Insurance Industry, 1981, Nancy Reagan, The First Lady, 1985. Recipient Peabody award U. Ga., 1978, Emmy award NATAS, 1981, 90, award Overseas Press Club, 1981, Humanitas Found. award, 1981, Investigative Reporters and Editors award U. Mo. Sch. Journalism, 1990, 95, George Polk award, 1992. Office: PrimeTime Live 1717 Desales St NW Washington DC 20036-4401

WALLACE, DAVID DUNSMORE, architect, planner, urban designer; b. Haverhill, Mass., Oct. 26, 1928; s. Henry Arthur and Doris Stanley (Conley) W.; m. June A. Feuer, June 7, 1953; children—Susan, Andrew, Gordon. B.A., Middlebury Coll., 1950; B.Arch., M.I.T., 1952, M. Arch., 1956. Registered architect, Mass., Tex., N.H., Nat. Council Archtl. Registration Bds. Prin. architect Geometrics, Inc., Cambridge, Mass., 1961-70, Wallace, Floyd, Ellenzweig, Moore, Inc., Cambridge, 1970-81, Wallace, Floyd, Assocs. Inc., Boston, 1981—. Prin. archtl. works include univ. bldgs., pub. housing renovation, mass transit and train stations, also Boston's Ctrl. Artery/Tunnel Project. Trustee Schwamb Mill Preservation Trust, Arlington, 1970—; mem. town Meeting, Arlington, 1965-72, Conservation Commn., Arlington, 1967-72; incorporator Cambridge Sch. of Weston, Mass., 1979-85. Voorhis, Walker, Smith & Smith research fellow MIT, 1955-56; Fulbright research grantee, 1960. Fellow AIA; mem. Am. Planning Assn., Am. Water Works Assn. Avocations: watercolor painting; photography; tennis. Office: Wallace Floyd Assocs Inc 286 Congress St Boston MA 02210-1038

WALLACE, DON, JR., law educator; b. Vienna, Austria, Apr. 23, 1932; s. Don and Julie (Baer) W. (parents Am. citizens); m. Daphne Mary Wickham, 1963; children: Alexandra Jane, Sarah Anne, Benjamin James. B.A. with high honors, Yale U., 1953; LL.B. cum laude, Harvard U., 1957. Bar: N.Y. 1957, D.C. 1978. Assoc. Fleischmann, Jaeckle, Stokes and Hitchcock, N.Y.C., 1959-60, Paul, Weiss, Rifkind, Wharton and Garrison, N.Y.C., 1957-58, 60-62; rsch. asst. to faculty mem. Harvard Law Sch., Cambridge, Mass., 1958-59; regional legal adv. Middle East AID, Dept. State, 1963-65, dep. asst. gen. counsel, 1965-66; assoc. prof. law Georgetown U. Law Ctr., Washington, 1966-71, prof., 1971—; chmn. Internat. Law Inst., Washington, 1969—; cons. AID, 1966-70, UN Centre on Transnat. Corps., 1977-78; counsel Wald, Harkrader & Ross, Washington, 1978-86, Arnold & Porter, 1986-89, Shearman & Sterling, 1989—; legal advisor State of Qatar, 1979-82; chmn. adv. com. on tech. and world trade Office of Tech. Assessment, U.S. Congress, 1976-79; mem. Sec. of State's Adv. Com. on Pvt. Internat. Law, 1979—; mem. U.S. del. UN Conf. on State Succession in Respect of Treaties, Vienna, 1978; mem. U.S. del. new internat. econ. order working group UN Commn. Internat. Trade Law, Vienna, 1981—. Co-author: Internat. Business and Economics: Law and Policy; author: International Regulation of Multinational Corporations, 1976, Dear Mr. President: The Needed Turnaround in America's International Economic Affairs, 1984; editor: A Lawyer's Guide to International Business Transactions, 1977-87; contbr. numerous articles on internat. trade and law to profl. jours., books revs. on law and bus. to profl. jours. Coord. Anne Arundel County (Md.) Dem. Nat. Com., 1972-79; sec. Chesapeake Found., 1972-73; nat. chmn. Law Profs. for Bush and Quayle, 1988, 92. Fulbright fellow, 1967, Eisenhower Exch. fellow, 1976. Mem. ABA (chmn. sect. internat. law 1978-79), Ho. of Dels. 1982-84), Am. Law Inst., Internat. Law Assn., Shaybani Soc. of Internat. Law (v.p.), Ctrl. and Ea. European Law Initiative (mem. adv. bd.), Cosmos Club, Met. Club. Home: 2800 35th St NW Washington DC 20007-1411 Office: Georgetown U Law Ctr 600 New Jersey Ave NW Washington DC 20001-2075

WALLACE, DOROTHY ALENE, special education administrator; b. Wright County, Mo., Sept. 11, 1942; d. Stephen Foster and Lois Alene (Breman) Dudley; widowed; children: Michael Dean Huckaby, David Lee. BS in Edn., Drury Coll., 1975, MS in Edn., 1978; Specialist in Ednl. Adminstrn., Southwest Mo. State U., 1988. Cert. tchr. and adminstr., Mo. Tchr. 3rd grade Mansfield (Mo.) R-IV Schs., 1975-78, tchr. 1st grade, 1978-85, tchr. learning disabled, 1985-89, adminstr. spl. edn., 1989-92, adminstr. spl. svcs., 1992—; active sch. coms. on curriculum and nutrition Mansfield R-IV Schs., mem. sch./cmty. adv. coun., 1992—. Mem. Am. Salers Assn., Mo. State Tchrs. Assn., Mo. Coun. Adminstrs. of Spl. Edn., Coun. for Exceptional Children, Coun. Adminstrs. of Spl. Edn., Local Adminstrs. of Spl. Edn., Cmty. Tchrs. Assn. Avocations: raising beef cattle, writing, collecting antiques. Home: 3489 Jerico Rd Seymour MO 65746

WALLACE, FRANKLIN SHERWOOD, lawyer; b. Bklyn., Nov. 24, 1927; s. Abraham Charles and Jennie (Etkin) Wolowitz; student U. Wis., 1943-45; BS cum laude, U.S. Mcht. Marine Acad., 1950; LLB, JD, U. Mich., 1953; m. Eleanor Ruth Pope, Aug. 23, 1953; children: Julia Diane, Charles Andrew. Bar: 1954. Practiced in Rock Island; ptnr. firm Winstein, Kavensky & Wallace; asst. state's atty. Rock Island County, 1967-68; local counsel UAW at John Deere-J.I. Case Plants. Former bd. dirs. Tri City Jewish Ctr.; former trustee United Jewish Charities of Quad Cities; bd. dirs. Blackhawk Coll. Found. Mem. ABA, Ill. Bar Assn. (chmn. jud. adv. polls com. 1979-84), Rock Island County Bar Assn., Am. Trial Lawyers Assn., Ill. Trial Lawyers Assn., Nat. Assn. Criminal Def. Lawyers, Ill. Appellate Lawyers Assn., Am. Orthopsychiat. Assn., Am. Judicature Soc., Blackhawk Coll. Found. Democrat. Jewish. Home: 3405 20th Street Ct Rock Island IL 61201-6201 Office: Rock Island Bank Bldg Rock Island IL 61201

WALLACE, G. DAVID, magazine editor; b. New Castle, Pa., Jan. 4, 1941; s. Glenn Wright and Luise (McAfee) W.; m. Ann Byrne Bransfield, June 23, 1972; children: Kevin, Colin, Shannon. BA, Coll. Wooster, Ohio, 1962. Gen. assignment reporter Titusville (Pa.) Herald, 1962-63; reporter Associated Press, Washington, 1966-77; correspondent Reuters, Washington, 1977-80, Bus. Week, Washington, 1980-83; editor Bus. Week, N.Y., 1983-91, asst. mng. editor, 1992—. Author: (book) Money Basics, 1984. Recipient John Hancock Financial Journalism award Fordham U. Journalism Sch., 1992. Mem. Am. Soc. Mag. Editors, Nat. Assn. Science Writers. Office: Business Week 1221 6th Ave 39th Flr New York NY 10020

WALLACE, GLADYS BALDWIN, librarian; b. Macon, Ga., June 5, 1923; d. Carter Shepherd and Dorothy (Richard) Baldwin; m. Hugh Loring Wallace, Jr., Oct. 14, 1941 (div. Sept. 1968); children: Dorothy, Hugh Loring III. BS in Edn., Oglethorpe U., 1961; MLS, Emory U., 1966; EdS, Ga. State U., 1980. Libr. pub. elem. schs., Atlanta, 1956-66; libr. Northside High Sch., Atlanta, 1966-87, Episc. Cathedral St. Philip. Author: The Time of My Life, 1994. Mem. High Mus. Art, Madison-Morgan Cultural Ctr. Ga. Dept. Edn. grantee, 1950, NDEA grantee, 1963, 65. Mem. AAUW, Atlanta Bonsai Soc., Inc., Nat. Audubon Soc., The Cousteau Soc., Atlanta Bot. Garden, Am. Assn. Ret. Persons, Ga. Conservancy, Ga. Geneal. Soc., Oglethorpe U. Nat. Alumni Assn., Emory U. Alumni Assn., Ga. State U. Alumni Assn., Atlanta Hist. Soc., Ga. Trust for Historic Preservation, Piedmont Health and Fitness Club. Home: NC 6 136 Peachtree Memorial Dr NW Atlanta GA 30309-1030

WALLACE, HAROLD JAMES, JR., physician; b. South Hadley Falls, Mass., Aug. 15, 1930; s. Harold James and Evelyn (Mason) W.; m. Dorothy Ann Green, July 4, 1959; children—Harold James III, Elizabeth Marie, John Hill. BA, U. Vt., 1954, MD cum laude, 1958. Intern Mary Fletcher Hosp., Burlington, Vt., 1958-59; resident Mary Fletcher Hosp., 1959-62; practice medicine specializing in oncology Buffalo, 1970-79, Rutland, Vt., 1979—; assoc. chief dept. medicine Roswell Pk. Meml. Inst., Buffalo, 1970-75; dir. Cancer Control Rehab. and Adolescent Program, 1976-79; oncologist Rutland Hosp., 1979—; dir. Cmty. Cancer Ctr., Rutland Regional Med. Ctr., 1989-93; rsch. prof. medicine Darmouth Med. Sch.; exec. officer Cancer and Leukemia Group B, 1992-95. Mem. Am. Cancer Soc. (pres. Vt. div. 1983-84, Nat. div. award 1969), Am. Assn. for Cancer Research, Am. Soc. Clin. Oncology, Green Mountain Oncology Group (chmn. 1983—), Alpha Omega Alpha. Congregationalist. Office: Comm Cancer Ctr Rutland Reg Med Ctr 160 Allen St Rutland VT 05701-4560

WALLACE, HAROLD LEW, historian, educator; b. Montgomery, Ind., Nov. 9, 1932; s. Lewis Alfred and Winifred Maria (Summers) W.; m. Janice June Inman, June 22, 1957; children: Stefanie Ann, Stacy Elizabeth, Jason Lew. A.B., Ind. U., 1961, M.A. (Univ. grantee), 1964, Ph.D., 1970. Tchr. history and English Mooreseville (Ind.) High Sch., 1961-63; teaching asst. Ind. U., 1963-64, univ. fellow, 1964-65; asst. prof., then assoc. prof. history Murray (Ky.) State U., 1965-71; prof. history, head social sci. div. No. Ky. U., Highland Heights, Ky., 1971—, dir. oral history program, 1980—; mem. continuing seminar community edn. Ball State U. and Mott Found., 1973—; mem. adv. bd. Ky. Oral History Commn., 1981—; vis. prof. Ky. Inst. for European Studies, Bregenz, Austria, summer 1987, Andhra U., Visakhapatnam, India, spring 1989. Author: Coal in Kentucky, 1975; Contbr. articles to profl. jours.; Editorial bd.: U. Ky. Press, 1971—; cons., reviewer: Oceana Press, Inc, 1973—. Mem. advisory com. pub. documents, State of Ky.; Bd. dirs. Coll. Programs for No. Ky. Sr. Citizens; faculty regent No. Ky. Bd. Regents, 1985-91, pres. Ky. Conf. State AAUP, 1991—. Served with USNR, 1952-56. Recipient Svc. award State of Ind., 1957, Univ. Teaching award Andhra Univ., India, 1992; Eli Lilly fellow, 1962, 63, Smithsonian fellow, 1982; Harry S. Truman Rsch. scholar, 1965, 71; Murray State U. grantee, 1967, 71, No. Ky. State U. grantee, 1973, 76, 78, 90, Ky. Humanities Coun. grantee, 1988, 90, Ky. Oral History Commn. grantee, 1988; Fulbright grant lectr. Andhra U., India, 1992; Art Coll. Gold medal Andhra Univ., India, 1992. Mem. AAUP (pres. Ky. chpt. 1991—, Disting. Svc. award 1992), Am., So. hist. assns., Orgn. Am. Historians, Polit. Sci. Acad., AAUP, Center Study Democratic Instrn., Mensa, Intertel, Sierra Club, Alpha Epsilon Delta, Phi Delta Kappa, Phi Alpha Theta. Home: 22 Orchard Ter Newport KY 41076-1532 Office: Dept of Ed No Ky State U Highland Heights KY 41076

WALLACE, HARRY LELAND, lawyer; b. San Francisco, June 26, 1927; s. Leon Harry and Anna Ruth (Haworth) W.; 1 child, Mary Ann Wallace Frantz. A.B. in Govt.; B.S. in Bus, Ind. U., 1949; J.D., Harvard U., 1952. Bar: Wis. 1953. Law clk. U.S. Supreme Ct. Justice Sherman Minton, Washington, 1952-53; assoc. firm Foley & Lardner, Milw., 1953-61; partner Foley & Lardner, 1961-96, retired, 1996; officer and/or dir. various corps. treas. Mequon-Thiensville Sch. Bds., 1966-67, 71-73, pres., 1965-66, 67-71, 73-75; bd. dirs. Milw. County Assn. for Mental Health, 1970-76, Milw. Mental Health Found., 1983-94; chmn. financing policies com. Gov.'s Commn. on Edn., 1969-70; mem. Gov.'s Task Force on Sch. Financing and Property Tax Reform, 1972-73; chmn. Gov.'s Commn. on State-Local Rels. and Fin. Policies, 1975-76; trustee Pub. Policy Forum, 1976-92, sec., 1984-86, pres., 1986-88. Served with USN, 1945-46. With USN, 1945-46. Mem. Am., Wis., Milw. bar assns., Am. Law Inst., Phi Beta Kappa, Beta Gamma Sigma, Delta Tau Delta. Methodist. Club: Milwaukee. Home: 1913 Somerset Ln Northbrook IL 60062

WALLACE, HELEN MARIE, secondary school educator, coach; b. Chgo., Mar. 4, 1939; d. James and Birdie (Burdett) W. BS in Health and Phys. Edn., George Williams Coll., 1963, MS in Counseling Psychology, 1973, MS in Adminstrn., 1973. Cert. tchr. and adminstr., Ill. Girls and boys track, volleyball, and swimming coach Chgo. Pub. H.S.; adminstrv. asst. Chgo. Commn. on Urban Opportunity, summers 1965-68; phys. instr. Chgo. Park Dist., 1958-64; phys. edn. tchr. Chgo. Pub. Sch. Sys., 1963—, athletic dir. Harrison H.S., 1967-87, phys. edn. tchr. Lincoln Park H.S., 1987—, mem. citywide objectives for phys. edn. com., 1993-94, mem. health edn. curriculum com., 1992-94, mem. co-chair girls track com., 1983—; phys. edn. tchr., dept. chair Lincoln Park H.S.; mem. state track com. Ill. H.S.; co-author health edn. curriculum Chgo. Pub. H.S.'s; cons. for devel. of health and phys. edn. programs, adminstrv. guidelines, inter-intra-mural sport programs. Jr. ch. organist, celestial choir dir., organist dir. and orgnaist for women's chorus Original Providence Bapt. Ch.; soprano soloist numerous functions. Mem. AAHPERD, Am. Choral Dirs. Assn., Gospel Music Workshop Am. Office: Lincoln Park HS 2001 N Orchard St Chicago IL 60614-4415

WALLACE, HERBERT WILLIAM, physician, surgery educator, researcher; b. Bklyn., Dec. 11, 1930; s. Philip and Jean (Brand) W.; m. Rosalie Sandra Becker, Dec. 18, 1954; children: Ira, Ellen, Lisa. AB, Harvard U., 1952; MD, Tufts U., 1956, MS, 1960; MBA, U. Pa., 1981, MA (hon.), 1973. Diplomate Am. Bd. Surgery, Am. Bd. Thoracic Surgery. Resident in gen. surgery Tufts U.-New Eng. Med. Ctr., Boston, 1956-61; thoracic and cardiovascular surg. resident Mt. Sinai Hosp., N.Y.C., 1963-65; assoc. in surgery and physiology U. Pa., Phila., 1966-70, asst. prof. surgery, 1970-72, assoc. prof. surgery, physiology and bioengring., 1972-76, prof., 1976—; chief div. thoracic and cardiovascular surgery Grad. Hosp. U. Pa., 1976-79; assoc. in univ. seminar on biomaterials Columbia U., N.Y.C., 1972—. Contbr. over 100 articles to profl. jours. Rsch. grantee NIH, 1965—. Fellow Am. Coll. Surgeons, Am. Heart Assn.; mem. Am. Assn. Cancer Rsch., Am. Assn. Thoracic Surgery, Am. Thoracic Soc., Biomedical

Engring. Soc., Soc. Thoracic Surgeons, others. Avocations: computers, squash, sailing, skiing. Home: 255 Harrogate Rd Wynnewood PA 19096-3131 Office: U Pa Dept Surgery One Graduate Pla Philadelphia PA 19146

WALLACE, J. CLIFFORD, federal judge; b. San Diego, Dec. 11, 1928; s. John Franklin and Lillie Isabel (Overing) W.; m. Elaine J. Baenes, Apr. 8, 1996; 9 children. B.A., San Diego State U., 1952; LL.B., U. Calif., Berkeley, 1955. Bar: Calif. 1955. With firm Gray, Cary, Ames & Frye, San Diego, 1955-70; judge U.S. Dist. Ct. (so. dist.) Calif., 1970-72; judge U.S. Ct. Appeals (9th cir.), 1972-91, chief judge, 1991-96. Contrbr. articles to profl. jours. Served with USN, 1946-49. Mem. Am. Bd. Trial Advocates, Inst. Jud. Adminstrn. Mem. LDS Ch. (stake pres. San Diego East 1962-67, regional rep. 1967-74, 77-79). Office: US Ct Appeals 9th Cir 940 Front St Ste 4192 San Diego CA 92101-8918 *My principles, ideals and goals and my standard of conduct are embodied in the Gospel of Jesus Christ. They come to fruition in family life, service, industry and integrity and in an attempt, in some small way, to make my community a better place within which to live.*

WALLACE, JACK HAROLD, employee development specialist, educator; b. Pleasant Ridge, Mich., Dec. 3, 1950; s. Jack Alfred and Mary Hilda (Hemming) W.; m. Laura Jeannine Placer, May 20, 1978. AA, Oakland Community Coll., 1972; BA, Oakland U., 1974; postgrad., Cen. Mich. U., 1984; MeD, Wayne State U., 1986, postgrad., 1988—. Cert. secondary tchr., Mich. Supply systems analyst TACOM, Warren, Mich., 1979-84; employee devel. specialist Army Tank Automotive Command, Tng. and Dev. Div., Warren, 1985—; site coord. TA COM long distance learning program Nat. Tech. U., Warren, 1993—; v.p. acad. affairs Virtual U., Bloomfield Hills, Mich., 1994—; instr. Ferndale (Mich.) Bd. of Edn., 1976-86; instr., cons. Jordan Coll., Detroit, 1986—, Detroit Coll. Bus., Dearborn, Mich., 1986—; trainer, instr. govt. agys. Co-author: (book) Balancing the Scales of Justice, 1986, (cable TV prodn.) A Course in Law and Application in Everyday Living, 1989. Mem. Am. Soc. for Tng. and Devel., Assn. for Ednl. Comm. and Tech., Fed. Mgrs. Assn., Mich. Soc. Instructional Tech., Phi Delta Kappa. Lutheran. Avocations: reading, camping, fishing, public speaking, travel. Home: 3005 Kenmore Rd Berkley MI 48072-1684 Office: TACOM Amsta-PD Warren MI 48397-5000

WALLACE, JAMES HAROLD, JR., lawyer; b. Atlanta, Feb. 8, 1941; s. James Harold Sr. and Ruth (Cocking) W. BSEE, U. S.C., 1963; JD, Georgetown U., 1966. Bar: D.C. 1967. Patent examiner U.S. Patent & Trademark Office, Washington, 1966-67; trial atty. antitrust div. U.S. Dept. Justice, Washington, 1967-70; from assoc. to ptnr. Kirkland & Ellis, Washington, 1970-83; ptnr. Wiley, Rein & Fielding, Washington, 1983—; mem. adv. bd. BNA Patent, Trademark & Copyright Jour., Washington, 1971—. Contbr. articles to profl. jours. Mem. ABA. Home: 3029 Cambridge Pl NW Washington DC 20007-2914 Office: Wiley Rein & Fielding 1776 K St NW Washington DC 20006-2304

WALLACE, JANE HOUSE, geologist; b. Ft. Worth, Aug. 12, 1926; d. Fred Leroy and Helen Gould (Kixmiller) Wallace; A.B., Smith Coll., 1947, M.A., 1949; postgrad. Bryn Mawr Coll., 1949-52. Geologist, U.S. Geol. Survey, 1952—, chief Pub. Inquiries Offices, Washington, 1964-72, spl. asst. to dir., 1974—, dep. bur. ethics counselor, 1975—, Washington liaison Office of Dir., 1978—. Recipient Meritorious Service award Dept. Interior, 1971, Disting. Svc. award, 1976, Sec.'s Commendation, 1988, Smith Coll. medal, 1992. Fellow Geol. Socs. Am., Washington (treas. 1963-67); mem. Sigma Xi (asso.). Home: 3003 Van Ness St NW Washington DC 20008-4701 Office: Interior Bldg 19th and C Sts NW Washington DC 20240 also: US Geol Survey 103 National Ctr Reston VA 22092

WALLACE, JANE YOUNG (MRS. DONALD H. WALLACE), editor; b. Geneseo, Ill., Feb. 17, 1933; d. Worling R. and Margaret C. (McBroom) Young; m. Donald H. Wallace, Aug. 24, 1959; children: Robert, Julia. BS in Journalism, Northwestern U., 1955, MS in Journalism, 1956; LittD (hon.), Johnson and Wales U., 1990. Diplomate Nat. Restaurant Assn. Edn. Found., 1991. Editor house organ Libby McNeill & Libby, Chgo., 1956-58; prodn. editor Instns. Mag., Chgo., 1958-61; food editor Instns. Mag., 1961-65, mng. editor, 1965-68, editor-in-chief, 1968-85; editor Restaurants and Instns., 1970-85, editorial dir., 1985-89, assoc. pub., 1985-89, pub., 1989-94; pub. R & I Market Pl., 1989-94, v.p., editor/pub. emeritus, 1994—; editorial dir. Hotels and Restaurants Internat. Mag., 1971-89; v.p., editor/pub. emeritus Restaurants and Instns., 1994—; editorial dir. Foodservice Equipment Specialist Mag., 1975-89; v.p. Cahners Pub. Co. (Reed USA), 1982; mem. editorial quality audit bd. Reed USA, 1993—; cons. Nat. Restaurant Assn., dir., 1977-82; cons. Nat. Inst. for Food Svc. Industry; vis. lectr. Fla. Internat. U., 1980. Editor: The Professional Chef, 1962, The Professional Chef's Book of Buffets, 1965, Culinary Olympics Cookbook, 1980, 3d edit., 1988, Academy of American Culinary Foundation Cookbook, 1985, American Dietetic Associaton Foundation Cookbook, 1986; contbr. restaurant chpt. World Book Ency., 1975, 94, Food Service Trends, American Quantity Cooking, 1976. Mem. com. investigation vocat. needs for food svc. tng. U.S. Dept. Edn., 1969; mem. Inst. Food Editors' Conf., 1959-88, pres., 1967; mem. hospitality industry edn. adv. bd. Ill. Dept. Edn., 1976, mem. adv. bd. Ill. sch. foodsvc., 1978; mem. corp. adv. bd. Am. Dietetic Assn. Found., 1981-92, bd. dirs., 1996—; trustee Presbyn. Ch., Barrington, Ill., 1983-85; bd. trustees Culinary Inst. Am., 1987—. Recipient Jesse H. Neal award for best bus. press editorial, 1969, 70, 73, 76, 77, 79, 82, 87, Diplomate award Nat. Restaurant Assn. Edn. Found., 1991; named Outstanding Woman Northwood Inst., 1983. Fellow Soc. for Advancement Foodservice Rsch. (dir. 1975-77, sec. 1980); mem. Internat. Foodservice Mfrs. Assn. (Spark Plug award 1979), Nat. Assn. Foodservice Equipment Mfrs., Am. Bus. Press Assn. (chmn. editl. com. 1978), Am. Inst. Interior Designers (assoc.), Women in Comms. (v.p. Chgo. 1957-58), Ivy Soc. Restauranteurs of Distinction (co-founder 1970—), Am. Dietetic Assn. (hon., bd. dirs. 1996—), Roundtable for Women in Food Service (bd. dirs. 1980-84; Foodservice Woman of Yr. 1988, Lifetime Recognition award 1994), Les Dames d'Escoffier (charter mem.), Culinary Inst. of Am. (ambassador 1986, trustee 1987—), Brotherhood of Knights of Vine (Gentlelady award 1980, 81), Disting. Restaurateurs of N.Am. (Hall of Fame award 1994), Internat. Assn. Cooking Profls., Gamma Phi Beta, Kappa Tau Alpha. Home: 186 Signal Hill Rd Barrington IL 60010-1929 Office: Cahners Publishing PO Box 5080 1350 E Touhy Ave Des Plaines IL 60018-3303

WALLACE, JEANNETTE OWENS, state legislator; b. Scottsdale, Ariz., Jan. 16, 1934; d. Albert and Velma (Whinery) Owens; m. Terry Charles Wallace Sr., May 21, 1955; children: Terry C. Jr., Randall J., Timothy A., Sheryl L., Janice M. BS, Ariz. State U., 1955. Mem. Los Alamos (N.Mex.) County Coun., 1981-82; cons. County of Los Alamos, 1983-84; chmn., vice chmn. Los Alamos County Coun., 1985-88; cons. County of Los Alamos, Los Alamos Schs., 1989-90; rep. N.Mex. State Legislature, 1991—; mem. appropriations and fin. govt. and urban affairs, N.Mex., 1991—, legis. fin. com., Indian affairs, radioactive and hazardous materials, co-chmn. Los Alamos County's dept. energy negotiating com., 1987-88; mem. legis. policy com. Mcpl. League, N.Mex., 1986-88. Bd. dirs. Tri-Area Econ. Devel., 1988-94, 96—, Crime Stoppers, Los Alamos, 1988-92, Los Alamos Citizens Against Substance Abuse, 1989-94; mem. N.Mex. First, Albuquerque, 1989-96; legis. chmn. LWV, 1990; mem. Los Alamos Rep. Women, pres., 1989-90. Mem. Los Alamos Bus. & Profl. Women (legis. chmn. 1990), Los Alamos C. of C., Mana del Norte, Kiwamis. Methodist. Avocations: tennis, needlework, reading. Home: 146 Monte Rey Dr S Los Alamos NM 87544-3826

WALLACE, JESSE WYATT, pharmaceutical company executive; b. Canton, Ga., Jan. 24, 1925; s. Jesse Washington and Lula (Wyatt) W.; m. Myra Brown, Jan. 2, 1949; children: Karin, Kimberly, Stephen, David. BBA magna cum laude, U. Ga., 1954; MS, Ga. Inst. Tech., 1960. Chmn. svc. groups Ga. Tech, Atlanta, 1953-57; adminstrv. mgr. Am. Viscose Corp., Marcus Hook, Pa., 1957-61; various exec. positions FMC Corp., Phila., 1961-85; pres. Wallco Internat. Corp., Wilmington, Del., 1985-89; v.p., sec. Pharm. Svc. and Tech., Inc., Woodbury, N.J., 1989—, also bd. dirs.; bd. dirs. Wallco Internat. Corp., Artist Alive, Inc., Pharm. Svc. and Tech., Inc.; adv. bd. Pharm. Tech. Conf., 1986—. Editor: Controlled Release Systems, 1988; contbr. Encyclopedia, 1989; contbr. articles to profl. jours; author (manual) Problem Solver, 1980. Vice chmn. Ch. Deacons, Wilmington; v.p., pres. Wilmington Gideons, 1969-71; v.p. ACA Acad., 1971-73; vice chmn. Del. Family Found., 1990—. Lt. USN, 1943-46, 50-53. Recipient Publ. award Pharm. Technology, 1989. Fellow Acad. Pharm. Scis., Am. Assn. of Pharm. Scientists; mem. Internat. Platform Assn., Controlled Release Soc., La. Fedn. Internat. Pharm., Am. Assn. Pharm. Scientists, Mensa, Delta Sigma Pi (life), Delta Mu Delta. Republican. Avocations: reading, golf, racquet ball, travel, family. Home: 1106 Grinnell Rd Wilmington DE 19803-5126 Office: Pharm Svc and Tech Inc 15 E Centre St Ste 201 Woodbury NJ 08096-2415

WALLACE, JOAN SCOTT, psychologist, social worker, international consultant; b. Chgo., Nov. 8, 1930; d. William Edouard and Esther (Fulks) Scott; m. John Wallace, June 12, 1954 (div. Mar. 1976); children—Mark, Eric, Victor; m. Maurice A. Dawkins, Oct. 14, 1979. A.B., Bradley U., 1952; M.S.W., Columbia U., 1954; postgrad., U. Chgo., 1965; Ph.D., Northwestern U., 1973; H.H.D. (hon.), U. Md., 1979; L.H.D. (hon.), Bowie State Coll., 1981; LLD (hon.), Ala. A&M U., 1990. Lic. social psychologist, social worker. Asst. prof., then assoc. prof. U. Ill.-Chgo., 1967-73; assoc. dean, prof. Howard U., Washington, 1973-76; v.p.-programs Nat. Urban League, N.Y.C., 1975-76; v.p. adminstrn. Morgan State U., Balt., 1976-77; asst. sec. adminstrn. USDA, Washington, 1977-81, adminstr. Office Internat. Cooperation and Devel., 1981-89; rep. to Trinidad and Tobago Inter Am. Inst. for Cooperation in Agr., USDA, 1989; internat. cons. U.S. Partnerships Internat., Ft. Lauderdale, 1993—; speaker in field. Contbr. articles, chpts. to profl. publs. Chair Binat. Agrl. Research and Devel. Fund, 1987. Recipient Disting. Alumni award Bradley U., 1978, Meritorious award Delta Sigma Theta, 1978, award for leadership Lambda Kappa Mu, 1978, award for outstanding achievement and svc. to nation Capital Hill Kiwanis Club, 1978, Links Achievement award, 1979, Presdl. Rank for Meritorious Exec., 1980, NAFEO award, 1989, Community Svc. award Alpha Phi Alpha, 1987, Pres.' award for outstanding pub. svc. Fla. A&M U., 1990. Mem. APA, NASW, AAAS, Am. Consortium for Internat. Pub. Adminstrn. (exec. com., governing bd. 1987), Soc. Internat. Devel. (Washington chpt.), Sr. Exec. Assn., Soc. for Internat. Devel., White House Com. on Internat. Sci., Engring. and Tech., Internat. Sci. and Edn. Coun. (chmn. 1981-89), Am. Evaluation Assn., Consortium Internat. Higher Edn. (adv. com.), Caribbean Studies Soc., Caribbean Assn. of Agriculture Economists, Assn. Polit. Psychologists, Pi Gamma Mu. Presbyterian. Avocations: crafts, painting, collecting international art. Home: 6010 S Falls Circle Dr Fort Lauderdale FL 33319-6900 Office: Joan Wallace and Assocs 5557 W Oakland Park Blvd Fort Lauderdale FL 33313-1411 also: Ams for Democracy in Africa 11921 Freedom Dr # 505 Reston VA 22090

WALLACE, JOHN EDWIN, retired meteorologist, consultant; b. Holton, Kans., Dec. 22, 1913; s. Verne P. Wallace and Clara E. Lott; m. Elizabeth Ann Johnson, June 24, 1944; 1 son, David A. BSME, Rice U., 1937; MS in Meteorology, Calif. Inst. Tech., 1942. Indsl. salesman Gulf Oil Corp., Houston, 1937-39; rsch. cons. MIT, Cambridge, 1946-47; pres., founder, chief exec. officer Weather Svcs. Corp., Lexington, Mass., 1947-93; pres. Coun. Indsl. Meteorologists, Denver, also bd. dirs. Contbr. articles on meteorology to various trade jours. Major AC, U.S. Army, 1939-45, PTO. Recipient Outstanding Svc. award N.J. Turnpike Authority, 1986. Fellow Am. Meteorol. Soc. (award for pioneering pvt. meteorology 1974), Belmont Hill Club (bd. dirs. 1972-74). Avocations: fishing, tennis, travel, golf. Home: 8 Glen Rd Lexington MA 02173-3614

WALLACE, JOHN LOYS, aviation services executive; b. Decatur, Tex., July 31, 1941; s. John K. and Flora Viola (Lumsden) Montgomery W.; m. Linda M. Jackson, May 18, 1962; children—John, Amy Lynn, Katherine Lea, Elizabeth D'Ann. Student, U. Tex.-Arlington, 1961-65, North Tex. State U., Denton, 1960-61. V.p. acctg. svcs. Cooper Airmotive, Dallas, 1975-77, v.p. fin., 1977-80, exec. v.p., gen. mgr. Gen. Aviation div., 1980-82; exec. v.p. fin., adminstrn. Aviall, Dallas, 1982-85; exec. v.p., chief oper. officer Aviall Inc., Dallas, 1985-89, pres. Gen. Aviation Svcs. div., 1989-93; pres. Ryder Aviall Inc., ret. 1993. Mem. Fin. Execs. Inst., N. Dallas C. of C., U.S./Mex. C. of C. (bd. dirs.), Chief Exec.'s Round Table, Delta Sigma Phi. Republican. Presbyterian. Clubs: Univ., Cotton Creek Club. Avocation: gardening, fishing, golf. Home: 3651 Pinehurst Cir Gulf Shores AL 36542-9052

WALLACE, JOHN ROBERT, county administrator; b. Princeton, Ind., Mar. 24, 1939; s. Robert Floyd and Marjorie Eloise (Steele) W.; m. Karen Sue Katilius, June 18, 1967 (div. Mar. 1985). BS in Engring. with honors, USCG Acad., 1961; BS in Civil Engring. with honors, U. Ill., 1967. Commd. ensign USCG, 1961, advanced through grades to capt., 1982; facilities engr. Coast Guard Res. Tng. Ctr., Yorktown, Va., 1975-77; chief engr. Coast Guard Activities Europe, Am. Embassy, London, 1977-80; mem. planning/plans evaluation staff USCG Chief of Staff, Washington, 1980-82; dep. chief civil engring. USCG Office Engring., Washington, 1982-83; chief, dep. chief office USCG Office Rsch. and Devel., Washington, 1983-86; commanding officer, sr. engr. USCG Facilities Design and Constrn. Ctr., Norfolk, Va., 1986-89; asst. county adminstr. planning and community devel. Pittsylvania County, Chatham, Va.; county adminstr. County of Amelia, Va., 1992—. Recipient Man of Yr. award Optimists, 1982, Spl. award Kennedy Found., 1984, Haskel Small USO Vol. awards, Washington, 1985, 86. Fellow Soc. Am. Mil. Engrs.; mem. VFW, NRA (life), Am. Def. Preparedness Assn., U.S. Lighthouse Soc., Naval Airship Assn., Royal Nat. Lifeboat Instn. Eng., Scottish Soc. Tidewater, St. Andrews Soc. Tidewater, Clan Wallace Soc., Scottish-Am. Mil. Soc., Am. Legion, Retired Officers Assn., Am. Planning Assn., Va. Citizen's Planning Assn., Va. Econ. Developers Assn., Va. Assn. County Ofcls., Coast Guard Combat Vets. Assn., Va.-Carolina Scottish Soc., Lions. Office: County of Amelia PO Box A Amelia Court House VA 23002-0066

WALLACE, JOYCE IRENE MALAKOFF, internist; b. Phila., Nov. 25, 1940; d. Samuel Leonard and Henrietta (Hameroff) Malakoff; A.B., Queens Coll., City U. N.Y., 1961; postgrad. Columbia U., 1962-64; M.D. State U. N.Y., 1968; m. Lance Arthur Wallace, Aug. 30, 1964 (div. 1974); 1 dau., Julia Ruth; m. Arthur H. Kahn, Oct. 7, 1979 (div. 1986); 1 son, Aryeh N. Kahn. Intern, St. Vincent's Hosp. Med. Center, N.Y.C., 1968-70; resident Manhattan VA Hosp., N.Y.C. and Nassau County Med. Center, East Meadow, N.Y., 1972-73; practice medicine, N.Y.C., 1970-71, North Conway, N.H., 1974-75; practice medicine specializing in internal medicine, N.Y.C., 1976—; mem. attending staff Nassau County Med. Center, 1974, St. Vincent's Hosp. and Med. Center, N.Y.C., 1976—; asst. prof. medicine Mt. Sinai Med. Sch., N.Y.C.; pres. Found. for Research on Sexually Transmitted Diseases, Inc., 1986-89, exec. and med. dir., 1989—. Diplomate Am. Bd. Internal Medicine. Fellow ACP, N.Y. Acad. Medicine; mem. Am. Med. Women's Assn., N.Y. County, N.Y. State med. socs. Office: 369 8th Ave New York NY 10001-4852

WALLACE, JULIA DIANE, newspaper editor; b. Davenport, Iowa, Dec. 3, 1956; d. Franklin Sherwood and Eleanor Ruth (Pope) W.; m. Doniver Dean Campbell, Aug. 23, 1986; children: Emmaline Livingston Campbell, Eden Jennifer Campbell. BS in Journalism, Northwestern U., 1978. Reporter Norfolk (Va.) Ledger-Star, 1978-80, Dallas Times Herald, 1980-82; reporter, editor News sect. USA Today, Arlington, Va., 1982-89, mng. editor spl. projects, 1989-92; mng. editor Chgo. Sun-Times, 1992—. Mem. Am. Soc. Newspaper Editors. Office: Chgo Sun-Times 401 N Wabash Ave Chicago IL 60611-3532

WALLACE, KEN, magazine publisher. BBA, St. John's U. With Reader's Digest mag., 1967-1981; v.p. advt. Sylvia Porter's Personal Finance mag.; v.p., advt. dir. Parade mag.; now pub. Prevention mag., Emmaus, Pa. Office: Prevention 733 Third Ave 15th Fl New York NY 10017 also: Prevention 33 East Minor St Emmaus PA 18098*

WALLACE, KENNETH ALAN, investor; b. Gallup, N.Mex., Feb. 23, 1938; s. Charles Garrett and Elizabeth Eleanor (Jones) W. A.B. in Philosophy, Cornell U., 1960; postgrad. U. N.Mex., 1960-61; m. Rebecca Marie Odell, July 11, 1980; children: Andrew McMillan, Aaron Blue, Susanna Garrett, Megan Elizabeth, Glen Eric. Comml. loan officer Bank of N.Mex., Albuquerque, 1961-64; asst. cashier Ariz. Bank, Phoenix, 1964-67; comml. loan officer Valley Nat. Bank, Phoenix, 1967-70; pres. WWW, Inc., Houston, 1970-72; v.p. fin. Hometels of Am., Phoenix, 1972-77, Precision Mech. Co., Inc., 1972-77; ptnr. Schroeder-Wallace, 1977-93; chmn. Shalako Corp., Phoenix; mng. ptnr., pres. Blackhawk, Inc., Phoenix, 1977—, also, bd. dirs.; pres., chmn. bd. AlphaSat Corp., Phoenix, 1990—; pres. chmn. bd. dirs. Black Diamond Cable Co., LLC, Park City, Utah; gen. ptnr. Wallco Enterprises, Ltd., Mobile, Ala., Am. Entertainment Network, LLC, Phoenix; mng. gen. ptnr. The Village at University Heights, Flagstaff. Loaned exec. Phoenix United Way, 1966, Tucson United Way, 1967; mem. Valley Big Bros., 1970—; bd. dirs. Phoenix Big Sisters, 1985-87; mem. Alhambra Village Planning Com.; fin. dir. Ret. Sr. Vol. Program, 1973-76; mem. Phoenix Men's Arts Coun., 1968—, dir., 1974-75; mem. Phoenix Symphony Coun. Campaign committeeman Rep. gubernatorial race, N.Mex., 1964; treas. Phoenix Young Reps., 1966; bd. dirs. Devel. Authority for Tucson, 1967. Mem. Soaring Soc. Am. (Silver badge), Am. Rifle Assn. (life), Nat. Mktg. Assn. (Mktg. Performance of Year award 1966), Nat. Assn. Skin Diving Schs., Pima County Jr. C. of C. (bd. dir. 1967), Phoenix Little Theatre, Phoenix Musical Theatre, S.W. Ensemble Theatre (bd. dir.), Wheelmen of Am., Masons, Shriners, Kona Kai Club (San Diego), Paradise Valley Country Club, Alpha Tau Omega. Office: The Wallace Group of Cos PO Box 7703 Phoenix AZ 85011-7703

WALLACE, KENNETH DONALD, lawyer; b. Spokane, Wash., Oct. 2, 1918; s. Donald and Adillah (Mason) W.; m. Ida H. Harvey, June 6, 1946 (div. 1965); children: Ann H., Jane B.; m. Betty Casey Major, July 31, 1965. AB summa cum laude, Wash. State U., 1940; LLB, Columbia U., 1946. Bar: N.Y. 1947, Conn. 1971. Pvt. practice law N.Y.C. and Conn., 1947—; with Cahill, Gordon, Reindel & Ohl, 1946-60; gen. counsel, sec. Bigelow-Sanford, Inc., 1960-70; v.p., dir. Oconee Realty Corp.; dir. JAI Press, Inc., 1984—; of counsel Philip E. Silberberg, N.Y.C.; gen. counsel Johnson Assocs., JAI Press, Inc., Alpen Pantry, Inc. Editor: Columbia Law Review, 1946. Trustee Bigelow-Charitable Trust. Served to 1st lt. USAAF, 1942-46. Decorated D.F.C. with oak leaf cluster, Air medal with oak leaf cluster; recipient Presdl. citation, medal, pilot's wings, Republic of China. Mem. ABA, Am. Acad. Polit. Sci. (life), Fed. Bar Coun., N.Y. State Bar Assn., Conn. Bar Assn., Assn. Bar City N.Y., Stamford/Darien Bar Assn., Am. Soc. Corp. Secs., Hump Pilor's Assn. (life), Phi Beta Kappa, Phi Sigma Kappa. Home and Office: PO Box 843 947 Ridge Rd New Canaan CT 06840-0843

WALLACE, LINDA SUZAN, journalist; b. Chgo., Dec. 1, 1954; d. Henry Bronlow and Adelaide (Hawkins) W.; m. Karanja Ajanaku, Jan., 1978. B in Journalism, U. Mo., 1976. Reporter St. Louis Post-Dispatch, 1976-77; edn. reporter Memphis Comml. Appeal, 1977-85, Dallas Times-Herald, 1985-87; bus. reporter Phila. Inquirer, 1987-89; nat. corr. Phila. Inquirer, Houston, 1989-92; copy editor Phila. Inquirer, 1992, real estate editor, 1992—; instr. Am. Press Inst., Washington, 1988, 89; organizer journalism workship for high sch. students, Memphis, 1984. Active Big Sisters, Phila., 1992—; dist. organizer Girl Scouts, Memphis, 1984-85. Fellow Inst. for Ednl. Leadership, 1984, Multicultural Edn. Seminar U. Mo., 1988. Mem. Phila. Assn. Black Journalists. Avocations: reading, exercise. Office: Phila Inquirer 400 N Broad St Philadelphia PA 19130

WALLACE, MARILYN JEAN, academic director; b. Oak Park, Ill., Feb. 11, 1950; d. Jay Emmons and Libbie (Novak) Phillips; m. David Stuart Wallace, Sept. 11, 1971; children: David, Douglas. BA, Principia Coll., 1972. Cert. music and edn. elem. and secondary grade levels. Music tchr. Granneman Elem., Hazelwood, Mo., 1972-73, Chicago Jr. Sch., Elgin, Ill., 1973-74, Sch. Dist. 30, Northbrook, Ill., 1974-77; 2nd grade tchr. Sch. Dist. 27, Northbrook, 1978-79; 5th grade tchr. Sch. Dist. 30, Northbrook, 1979-83, 2nd grade tchr., 1984-86; middle sch. social studies tchr. Creative Children's Acad., Mt. Prospect, Ill., 1991-92; acad. dean Creative Children's Acad., Mt. Prospect, 1992-93; acad. dir. Creative Children's Acad., Palatine, Ill., 1993—; mem. adv. bd. Joyful Parenting, Oconomowoc, Wis., 1994—, Understanding Our Gifted, Boulder, Colo., 1994—, Nat. Louis U., Evanston, Ill., 1995—; presenter in field. Named Educator of Yr., Phi Delta Kappa, Evanston, 1993. Mem. Nat. Assn. for Gifted Children, Ill. Assn. for Gifted Children. Avocations: quilting, golfing, cooking. Home: 502 Brockway Palatine IL 60067 Office: Creative Childrens Acad 500 N Benton Palatine IL 60067

WALLACE, MARK ALLEN, hospital executive; b. Oklahoma City, Apr. 24, 1953; s. William Howell and Mollie Marie (Godsy) W.; children: Emily, Benjamin. BS, Okla. Bapt. U., 1975; MS, Washington U., St. Louis, 1978. Adminstrv. asst. Bapt. Med. Ctr., Oklahoma City, 1975-77; administrv. resident Meth. Hosp., Houston, 1977-78; asst. v.p. Tex. Meth. Hosp., Houston, 1978-80, v.p., 1980-83, sr. v.p., 1983-89; exec. dir., chief exec. officer Tex. Children's Hosp., Houston, 1989—; adj. instr. Washington U., 1984—; adj. asst. prof. Tex. Womans U., Houston, 1983—; bd. dirs., chmn. fin. com., treas. Greater Houston Hosp. Svc. Corp., 1986-90. Contbr. articles to profl. jours. Chmn. campaign drives United Way, Houston, 1984, 86; class chmn. alumni vision for excellence and growth for future campaigns Okla. Bapt. U., 1982; bd. dirs. Tex. Gulf Coast chpt. March of Dimes Birth Defects Found., 1985-91. Recipient Emerging Leaders in Health Care award Healthcare Forum Mag. and Korn/Ferry Internat., 1987, Robert S. Hudgens Meml. award, 1992. Fellow Am. Coll. Healthcare Execs. (com. on membership, subcom. on recruitment 1990—, Young Healthcare Exec. of Yr.), mem. Am. Heart Assn. (med. adv. com. 1990-91), Healthcare Forum (pres. emerging leaders alumni group 1988-91), Am. Hosp. Assn., Tex. Hosp. Assn. (bd. dirs., bd. dirs. polit. action com. 1988—), Greater Houston Hosp. Coun. (bd. dirs. 1991—), Houston Area Health Care Coalition, Childrens Hosp. Assn. Tex. (pres. 1992—), Tex. Gulf Coast Arthritis Found. (bd. dirs. 1990-91). Republican. Baptist. Office: Tex Children's Hosp PO Box 300630 Houston TX 77230-0630

WALLACE, MARY ELAINE, opera director, author; m. Robert House. BFA cum laude, U. Nebr., Kearney, 1940; MusM, U. Ill., 1954; postgrad., Music Acad. West, Santa Barbara, Calif., 1955, Eastman Sch. Music, 1960, Fla. State U., 1962. Prof. voice, dir. opera La. Tech. U., Ruston, 1954-62, SUNY-Fredonia, 1962-69, So. Ill. U.-Carbondale, 1969-79; dir. Marjorie Lawrence Opera Theatre, Opera on Wheels; adminstrv. adviser Summer Playhouse, Carbondale; stage mgr. Chautauqua Opera Co., N.Y., 1963; asst. mus. dir., condr. Asolo Festival, Sarasota, Fla., 1961; music editor, critic The Chautauquan Daily; adjudicator Met. Opera auditions; exec. sec. Nat. Opera Assn., 1981-91. Co-author: Opera Scenes for Class and Stage, 1979, (with Robert Wallace) More Operas Scenes for Class and Stage, 1990, Upstage Downstage, 1992. Mem. Nat. Opera Assn. (pres. 1974, 75), Music Tchrs. Nat. Assn., Nat. Assn. Tchrs. Singing, AAUP, AAUW, Met. Opera Guild, Mortar Bd., Sigma Tau Delta, Pi Kappa Lambda, Phi Beta, Alpha Psi Omega, Delta Kappa Gamma. Address: 3106 Lakeside Dr Rockwall TX 75087-5319

WALLACE, MARY MONAHAN, elementary and secondary schools educator; b. Teaneck, N.J., Nov. 22, 1943; d. Thomas Gabriel and Louise Grace (Monaco) Monahan; m. James Anthony Wallace, Nov. 22, 1978; (dec. May, 1992); 1 child, Meg. BS, Fordham U., 1967; MA, 1971; postgrad. in Supervision, Montclair U., 1978; postgrad. in Edn., various colls. Cert. tchr. language arts, supr., N.Y. 1st and 4th grades tchr. Holy Rosary Sch., Harlem, N.Y., 1963-65; 7th grade tchr. Immaculate Conception Sch., Bronx, N.Y., 1965-66; 8th grade tchr. St. Finbar Sch., Bklyn., 1966-68, St. Patrick Mil. Acad., Harriman, N.Y., 1968-69; English tchr. St. Stephen H.S., Bklyn., N.Y., 1969-70, Holy Rosary Acad., Union City, N.J., 1970-71, Harriman (N.Y.) Coll., 1971-72, Montclair (N.J.) Coll., 1981-82; English tchr. elem. and secondary schs. Fairlawn (N.J.) Schs., 1972—; advisor Fair Lawn H.S. Yearbook, 1977-80, Nat. Lang. Arts Olympiad, Fair Lawn, 1987-89; mem. Mid. Sch. Task Force Fair Lawn Schs., 1991-93, dist. wide steering com. Edn. Recognition Day, Fair Lawn, 1992, 93, mem. steering com. Fair Lawn Mid. Schs., 1994—. Editor (newsletter) Concern, 1970-72; mem. editorial staff (newsletter) Flea Bytes, 1988, 89, 90. Participant Summer in the City U.S. Antipoverty Program, Staten Island, N.Y., 1965. Named Meml. Sch. Tchr. of Yr. N.J. Gov.'s Recognition Program, 1993. Mem. NEA, N.J. Edn. Assn., N.J. Middle Sch. Assn., Nat. Coun. Tchrs. of English, Fair Lawn Edn. Assn. (treas. 1990-93, pres. 1993—). Roman Catholic. Avocations: reading, swimming, boating, travel. Home: 20-18 Saddle River Rd Fair Lawn NJ 07410-5933 Office: Fair Lawn Edn. Assn. 3-13 4th St Fair Lawn NJ 07410

WALLACE, MIKE, television interviewer and reporter; b. Brookline, Mass., May 9, 1918; s. Frank and Zina (Sharfman) W.; m. Lorraine Perigord (dec.); children: Peter (dec.), Christopher, Pauline; m. Mary Yates, June 28, 1986. AB, U. Mich., 1935-39, hon. degree, 1987; hon. degree, U. Mass., 1978, U. Pa., 1989. Associated with radio, 1939—, TV, 1946—; commentator, CBS-TV, 1951-54, TV interviewer, reporter, 1951—, CBS news corr., 1963—; co-editor: 60 Minutes, CBS; Author: Mike Wallace Asks, 1958, Close Encounters, 1984. Recipient Robert Sherwood award, 18 ATVAS Emmy awards, George Foster Peabody awards, 1963-71, DuPont Columbia Journalism award, 1972, 83, Carr Van Anda award, 1977, Thomas Hart Benton award, 1978. Mem. Century Assocs., Sigma Delta Chi. Office: CBS News 60 Minutes 555 W 57th St New York NY 10019-2925

WALLACE, PEGGY MARIE, state commissioner; b. Barbourville, Ky., Jan. 3, 1950; d. Chester and Katherine (White) W. BS, Union Coll., 1971; MSSW, U. Louisville, 1977. Eligibility worker Dept. Econ. Security, State of Ky., Barbourville, 1972-74; social worker Dept. Social Svcs., Barbourville, 1974-76; social svcs. trainer, cons. Dept. Social Svcs., Frankfort, 1977-78, budget analyst, 1978-80, adminstrv. asst., 1980-81, adminstrv. supr., 1981, exec. asst., 1981-85, prin. asst., 1985-88, dep. commr., 1988-92, commr., 1992—; mem. Ky. Atty. Gen.'s Task Force on Child Sexual Abuse, Ky. Child Labor Task Force, Ky. Multi-Disciplinary Commn. on Child Sexual Abuse, Ky. Crime Commn. (mem. juvenile justice adv. com.), Ky. Children's Justice Act Task Force, Ky. Family Resource and Youth Svcs. Ctr. Task Force, Ky. Child Care Policy Coun., Ky. Adv. Coun. on the Homeless, Ky. Early Intervention System Interagy. Coord. Coun., Ky. Gender Fairness Standing Com. (mem. subcom. on domestic violence), Ky. Birth Surveillance Adv. Com., Ky. Long Range Juvenile Detention Planning Com., Ky. State Interagy. Coun. for Children and Youth; chair Am. Pub. Welfare Assn's. Children, Families and Adult Svcs. Com. Mem. NASW (mem. bluegrass chpt.), Nat. Forum for Black Pub. Adminstrs. Baptist. Avocations: antiques, reading, old movies. Office: Social Svcs Dept 275 E Main St Frankfort KY 40601-2321

WALLACE, PHILIP RUSSELL, retired physics educator; b. Toronto, Ont., Can., Apr. 19, 1915; s. George Russell and Mildred (Stillwaugh) W.; m. Jean Elizabeth Young, Aug. 15, 1940; children—Michael David, Kathryn Joan, Robert Philip. B.A., U. Toronto, 1937, M.A., 1938, Ph.D., 1940. Lectr. U. Cin., 1940-42; lectr. MIT, Cambridge, 1942; assoc. research physicist Atomic Energy of Can., Montreal and Chalk River, Que., 1943-46; assoc. prof. dept. math. McGill U., Montreal, Que., 1946-50, prof. math., 1950-60, prof. physics, 1961-81, MacDonald prof., 1972-81, prof. emeritus, 1981—; prin. Sci. Coll. Concordia U., Montreal, 1984-87; vis. prof. U. Paul Sabatier, Toulouse, France, 1972-73, 81-82. Author: Mathematical Analysis of Physical Problems, 1972-84, Physics: Imagination and Reality, 1991, Paradox Lost: Images of the Quantum, 1996; contbr. over 90 sci. articles on relativity, nuc. physics, radar meterology, solid state physics, intense magnetic field effects; editor: Superconductivity, 1968, New Developments in Semiconductors, 1972, Can. Jour. Physics, 1972-80. Fellow Royal Soc. Can., Nat. Acad. Sci. (hon., India); mem. Am. Phys. Soc., Can. Assn. Physicists (pres. theoretical physics div. 1957-58), Am. Assn. Physics Tchrs. Club: McGill Faculty (pres. 1960-61). Avocations: medieval history, art and architecture. Home: 104-1039 Linden Ave, Victoria, BC Canada V8V 4H3 Office: McGill University Dept Physics, 3600 University St, Montreal, PQ Canada H3A 2T8

WALLACE, R. BYRON, lawyer; b. Seattle, Dec. 19, 1945. AB, Harvard U., 1968; JD, Case Western Reserve U., 1974. Bar: Ohio 1974. Ptnr. Baker & Hostetler, Cleve. Office: Baker & Hostetler 3200 Nat City Ctr 1900 E 9th St Cleveland OH 44114-3401*

WALLACE, RALPH, superintendent; b. Halifax, Nova Scotia; s. Ralph and Alberta (Warren) W.; m. Haunani Wallace, Aug. 1, 1980; children: Lianne, Travis. BEd, U. British Columbia, 1968, MEd, 1976; postgrad., U. Conn., 1986; CAGS, Boston U., 1987, EdD, 1992. Cert. supt., int. adminstr., Conn. Asst. supt. West Vancouver (B.C.) Bd. Edn., 1967-83; prin. Farmington (Conn.) Bd. Edn., 1983-85; prin. Granby (Conn.) Bd. Edn., 1985-88, supt., 1988-92; supt. Cheshire (Conn.) Bd. Edn., 1992—; apptd. Pres. Nat. Excellence Panel. Contbr. articles to profl. jours. Dir. Gov.'s Sch., Conn. State U.; mem. Conn. Tech. Commn. Recipient Nat. Excellence award U.S. Dept. Edn.; named Conn. Supt. of Yr., 1992. Mem. ASCD, SDE (Conn. tech. com.), PDK, Am. Assn. Sch. Adminstrn., Conn. Assn. Pub. Sch. Supts. (legis), Am. Edn. Rsch. Assn., Edn. Rsch. Svc., Conn. Transp. Commn. (hon.), Conn. Tech. Commn. Home: 40 Dorset Ln Farmington CT 06032-2330 Office: Cheshire Pub Schs 29 Main St Cheshire CT 06410-2405

WALLACE, RICHARD, editor, writer; b. Bronxville, N.Y., May 25, 1947; m. Elisabeth Wallace; 1 child, Eric B. BA, Columbia U., 1974. Reporter, editor, contbr. varius industry and bus. pubs., Electronic News, EE Times, 1976-92; editor-in-chief Electronic Engring Times, Manhasset, N.Y., 1992—. Mem. Internat. Platform Assn. Democrat. Avocations: running, writing, reading, orchardist. Office: CMP Pubs Inc Electronic Engring Times 600 Community Dr Manhasset NY 11030-3847

WALLACE, RICHARD CHRISTOPHER, JR., school system administrator, educator; b. Haverhill, Mass., Jan. 3, 1931; s. Richard C. and Anna Catharine (Rogan) W.; m. Rita Wallace, June 18, 1957; children: Monica, Margaret, Mona. BS in Edn., Gorham State Coll., Maine, 1953; MEd, Boston Coll., 1960, EdD, 1966; postgrad., Stanford U., 1968-69. Dir. Eastern Regional Inst. Edn., Syracuse, N.Y., 1969-70, 1970-71; deputy dir. program planning and evaluation U. Tex., Austin, 1971-73; supt. Fitchburg (Mass.) Pub. Schs., 1973-80, Pitts. Pub. Schs., 1980-92; prof. U. Pitts., 1993—; chmn. nat. adv. panel ctr. sch. restructuring U. Wis., 1990—; rsch. assoc. Learning Rsch. and Devel. Ctr. U. Pitts., 1983—; chmn. nat. adv. panel Ctr. Effective Secondary Schs., U. Wis., Madison, 1986-90, mem. Coun. of Great City Schs. Exec. Com., 1980-92, Coun. of Great City Schs. Bylaws and Personnel Policies Com., 1986-87. Contbr. articles to profl. jours. Trustee Chatham Coll., 1984—; bd. dirs. Urban League Pitts, 1985-92, Sta. WQED-TV, Pitts., 1987, Carnegie Found. for Advancement of Teaching, 1990. Named Man of Yr. Edn. Vectors, Pitts., 1981; recipient Shaw medal Boston Coll., Chestnut Hill, Mass., 1985, Leadership for Learning award Am. Assn. Sch. Adminstrs., Washington, 1987, Harold W. McGraw Jr. prize, 1990. Mem. Am. Assn. Sch. Adminstrs., Am. Ednl. Research Assn., Assn. Supervision Curriculum Devel. Democrat. Roman Catholic. Lodge: Rotary (chnm. youth com. 1980) (Pitts.). Office: U Pitts 5034 Forbes Quad Pittsburgh PA 15260

WALLACE, ROBERT BRUCE, surgeon; b. Washington, Apr. 12, 1931; s. William B. and Anne E. W.; m. Betty Jean Newel, Aug. 28, 1955; children: Robert B., Anne E., Barbara N. B.A., Columbia U., 1953, M.D., 1957. Diplomate: Am. Bd. Surgery, Am. Bd. Thoracic Surgery. Chmn., prof. dept. surgery Mayo Clinic and Mayo Med. Sch., Rochester, Minn.; bd. govs. Mayo Clinic, 1968-79; prof. dept. surgery Georgetown U. Sch. Medicine, 1980—, chmn. dept. surgery, 1980-95, surgeon and chief univ. hosp., 1980-95. Trustee Mayo Found., 1970-78. Mem. ACS (bd. govs. 1975-79), Am. Surg. Assn., Soc. Clin. Surgery, Am. Assn. Thoracic Surgery (pres. 1994-95), Internat. Cardiovascular Soc., Soc. Vascular Surgery. Home: 1322 Darnall Dr Mc Lean VA 22101-3009 Office: Dept Surgery Georgetown U Hosp 3800 Reservoir Rd NW Washington DC 20007-2196

WALLACE, ROBERT EARL, geologist; b. N.Y.C., July 16, 1916; s. Clarence Earl and Harriet (Wheeler) W.; m. Gertrude Kivela, Mar. 19, 1945; 1 child: Alan R. BS, Northwestern U., 1938; MS, Calif. Inst. Tech., 1940, PhD, 1946. Registered geologist, Calif., engring. geologist, Calif. Geologist U.S. Geol. Survey, various locations, 1942—; regional geologist U.S. Geol. Survey, Menlo Park, Calif., 1970-74; chief scientist Office of Earthquakes, Volcanoes and Engring. U.S. Geol. Survey, Menlo Park, 1974-87, emeritus, 1987—; asst. and assoc. prof. Wash. State Coll., Pullman, 1946-51; mem. adv. panel Nat. Earthquake Prediction Evaluation Coun., 1980-90, Stanford U. Sch. Earth Sci., 1972-82; mem. engring. criteria rev. bd. San Francisco Bay Conservation and Devel. Commn., chmn. 1981-92. Contbr. articles to profl. jours. Recipient Alfred E. Alquist award Calif. Earthquake Safety Found., 1995. Fellow AAAS, Geol. Soc. Am. (chair cordillidan sect. 1967-68), Earthquake Engring. Rsch. Inst., Calif. Acad. Scis. (hon. 1991); mem. Seismol. Soc. Am. (medalist 1989). Avocations: bird watching, ham radio, water color painting. Office: US Geol Survey MS-977 345 Middlefield Rd Menlo Park CA 94025-3561

WALLACE, ROBERT GEORGE, retired construction company executive, civil engineer; b. Flagstaff, Ariz., Apr. 30, 1928; s. William Robert Francis and Maeclaire (Wright) W.; m. Gloria Mae Reid, Oct. 29, 1960. B.S.C.E., U. Ariz., Tucson, 1953. Registered profl. civil engr. Pres. Wallace & Royden Equipment Co., Phoenix, 1956-67; v.p. Royden Constrn. Co., Phoenix, 1953-67; v.p. The Tanner Cos., Phoenix, 1967-81, exec. v.p., 1971-82, pres., 1982-88, also dir.; nat. bd. dirs. Scripps Rsch. Inst., Kasler Holding Co., The Fenton Cos. Bd. dirs. Assn. Gen. Contractors, 1973-80, The Road Information Rrogram 1978-82, The Beavers, 1982-88, Western Force, 1972-78. Served with USN, 1946-48; PTO. Recipient award of Disting. Service Ariz. Assoc. Gen. Contractors, 1967; Disting. Citizen award U. Ariz. Engring. Coll., 1983. Mem. La Jolla Country Club, La Jolla Beach and Tennis Club, Masons (32d degree). Republican. Episcopalian. Home: 1001 Genter St Apt 8F La Jolla CA 92037-5526

WALLACE, ROBERT JAMES, mathematics and science educator; b. Chgo., Sept. 1, 1942; s. James H. and Maryella (Wilder) W.; m. Amy S. Briskin, Nov. 10, 1991; children: Lisa, Brenda. BS, No. Ill. U., 1964, MA, 1970; MA, Princeton U., PhD, 1975. Geologist CUNY, Bklyn., 1972-80; v.p. Audio Vistas, Inc., N.Y.C., 1980-85; computer cons. N.Y.C. Bd. Edn., 1984-86; computing chair St. Ann's Sch., Bklyn., 1985-93; cons. sci., math. The Harbor Acad. for Math./Sci., N.Y.C., 1985—; cons. Packer Collegiate Inst., Bklyn., 1987-93; cons. educator Metrotech, Bklyn., 1988-90. Author: Geology Lab Manual, 1980, New York City-Wide Test Results, 1986. Adventure facilitator Harbor for Girls and Boys, N.Y.C., 1990—. Mem. AAAS, Nat. Sci. Tchrs. Assn., Sigma Xi. Avocations: tennis, bicycling, roller-skating. Office: Harbor for Girls and Boys 1 E 104th St New York NY 10029-4402

WALLACE, RUSTY, race car driver; b. St. Louis, Aug. 14, 1956; m. Patti Wallace; children: Greg, Katie, Stephen. Stock race car driver, 1980—; mem. Miller Genuine Draft team. Winner NASCAR Winston Cup, 1989; has finished 1st 39 times; 1st place finishes include Goodwrench 500, Budweiser 500, Hanes 500, UAW-GM Teamwork 500, Miller Genuine Draft 400, Goody's 500 (twice), SplitFire Spark Plug 500 (all 1994); 2d place finishes Pontiac Excitement 400, First Union 400, Coca-Cola 600, Charlotte, N.C. (all 1994), winner Hanes 500, 1995, Miller Genuine Draft 400, 1995. Office: NASCAR PO Box 2875 Daytona Beach FL 32120-2875*

WALLACE, SPENCER MILLER, JR., hotel executive; b. Portland, Maine, Aug. 17, 1923; s. Spencer M. and Caroline (Clark) W.; m. Margaret Keeler, May 12, 1956; 1 son, Daniel Walker. With Hotels Statler, 1944-54, Hilton Hotels Corp., 1954-57, Hilton Hotels, Internat., 1957-61; exec. v.p., dir. Hotel Syracuse Corp., N.Y., 1961-80; chmn. Onondaga County Tourism and Conv. Com.; mem. N.Y. State Tourism Adv. Council. Trustee Milton J. Rubenstein Mus. Sci. and Tech. Mem. N.Y. State Hotel Assn., Am. Hotel and Motel Assn. (past dir.), N.Y. State Hotel and Motel Assn. (past pres.), Am. Diabetes Assn. (bd. dirs. N.Y. state affiliate), N.Y. Srs. Golf Assn. (past pres.), Ea. Srs. Golf Assn., Rotary (Syracuse Club), Masons (Shriner, Jester). Episcopalian. Clubs: Mason (Shriner, Jester), Onondaga Golf and Country (bd. dirs.). Home: 11 Wheeler Ave Fayetteville NY 13066-2530 Office: 6875 E Genesee St Fayetteville NY 13066-1026

WALLACE, THOMAS C(HRISTOPHER), editor, literary agent; b. Vienna, Austria, Dec. 13, 1933; came to U.S., 1938; s. Don and Julia (Baer) W.; m. Lois Kahn, July 19, 1962; 1 son, George Baer. Grad., Peddie Sch., 1951; BA, Yale U., 1955, MA in History, 1957. Editor G.P. Putnam Sons, N.Y.C., 1959-63; with Holt, Rinehart & Winston, N.Y.C., 1963-81, editor-in-chief gen. books div., 1968-81; v.p., sr. editor Simon and Schuster, N.Y.C., 1981; editor W.W. Norton, N.Y.C., 1982-87; v.p. Wallace Lit. Agy., N.Y.C., 1987—; bd. dirs. Roger Klein Found. Mem. PEN, Yale Club, Century Assn. (N.Y.C.), Pound Ridge (N.Y.) Tennis Club. Home: 45 E 82nd St New York NY 10028-0326 Office: Wallace Lit Agy 177 E 70th St New York NY 10021-5109

WALLACE, THOMAS J., magazine editor-in-chief. Editor-in-chief Conde Nast Traveler, N.Y.C. Office: Conde Nast Traveler 360 Madison Ave New York NY 10017-3136

WALLACE, THOMAS PATRICK, university administrator; b. Washington, Apr. 11, 1935; 4 children. BS, SUNY, Potsdam, 1958; MS, Syracuse U., 1961, St. Lawrence U., 1964; PhD in Physical Chemistry, Clarkson U., 1968. Asst. prof. chemistry SUNY, Potsdam, 1961-67; Mellon Inst. fellow Carnegie-Mellon Inst., 1967-68; mem. faculty Rochester (N.Y.) Inst. Tech., 1968-78, assoc. prof., 1970-78, head dept. chemistry, 1970-72, assoc. dean, 1972-73, dean, 1973-78; prof. chem. scis. Old Dominion U., Norfolk, Va., 1978-86, dean sci. and health professions, 1978-83, v.p. acad. affairs, 1983-86; chancellor Ind. U.-Purdue U., Ft. Wayne, 1986-88; pres. Ill. State U., Normal, 1988—. Contbr. articles to profl. jours. Mem. Am. Chem. Soc. Office: Ill State U Office of Pres Normal IL 61761

WALLACE, VICTOR L., II, lawyer; b. Shawnee, Okla., Jan. 14, 1938. BS, U. Okla., 1961, JD, 1967. Bar: Colo. 1967, Tex. 1991. Ptnr. Baker & Hostetler, Denver. Capt. USMC, 1961-64. Fellow Am. Coll. Mortgage Attys. (bd. regents 1984—, pres., 1989-90), Am. Coll. Real Estate Lawyers; mem. ABA, Colo. Bar Assn., Denver Bar Assn., State Bar Tex., Phi Delta Phi. Office: Baker & Hostetler 303 E 17th Ave Ste 1100 Denver CO 80203-1264*

WALLACE, WALTER C., lawyer, government official; b. N.Y.C., Mar. 25, 1924; m. Frances Helm, Apr. 5, 1963; 1 dau., Laura. BA magna cum laude, St. John's U., Hillsdale, N.Y., 1948; LLB with distinction, Cornell U., 1951. Bar: N.Y. 1952, Calif. 1954, D.C. 1975, U.S. Dist. Ct. (no. dist.) Calif. 1954, U.S. Ct. Appeals (9th cir.) 1954, D.C. 1975, U.S. Dist. Ct. D.C. 1975, U.S. Ct. Appeals (D.C. cir.) 1975. Assoc. Cahill, Gordan & Reindel, N.Y.C., 1951-54; exec. asst. sec. of labor Dept. of Labor, Washington, 1955-60, asst. sec. of labor, 1960-61; gen. counsel Presdl. R.R. Commn., Washington, 1961; v.p. labor rels. Hudson Pulp & Paper Corp., N.Y.C., 1963-73; pres. Bituminous Coal Operators Assoc., Washington, 1974-75; ptnr. Ables & Wallace, Washington, 1977-80; prin. Law Offices Walter C. Wallace, N.Y.C., 1981-82; mem. Nat. Mediation Bd., Washington, 1982—, chmn., 1983, 85, 88; U.S. del. Internat. Labor Orgn. Conf. on Labor Rels. in Timber Industry, Geneva, 1958. Mem. bd. editors Cornell Law Quar., 1950-51. Bd. dirs. Nat. Safety Coun., Washington, 1974-75; asst. to chmn. United Givers Fund, Washington, 1956, mem. admission and allocations com., 1957-58. Staff sgt. U.S. Army, 1943-45, ETO. Decorated Bronze Star; recipient Presdl. commendation Pres. Eisenhower, Washington, 1961, Disting. Svc. award United Givers Fund, 1956. Mem. Calif. Bar Assn., N.Y. State Bar Assn., D.C. Bar Assn., Order of Coif. Republican. Roman Catholic. Home: 55 Central Park W New York NY 10023-6003

WALLACE, WALTER L., sociologist, educator; b. Washington, Aug. 21, 1927; s. Walter L. and Rosa Belle (Boisseau) W.; children: Jeffrey Richard, Robin Claire, Jennifer Rose. B.A., Columbia U., 1954; M.A., Atlanta U., 1955; Ph.D., U. Chgo., 1963. Instr. Spelman Coll., Atlanta U., 1955-57; from lectr. to prof. sociology Northwestern U., Evanston, Ill., 1963-71; prof. sociology Princeton, 1971—; staff sociologist Russell Sage Found., N.Y.C., 1969-77, vis. scholar, 1968; fellow Ctr. for Advanced Study in Behavioral Scis., Stanford, Calif., 1974-75. Author: Student Culture, 1966, Logic of Science in Sociology, 1971, (with James E. Conyers) Black Elected Officials, 1975, Principles of Scientific Sociology, 1983, A Weberian Theory of Human Society, 1994; editor, author: Sociological Theory, 1969; mem. social scis. adv. com. World Book, 1977-94, editorial bd. Social Forces, 1984-87, The Am. Sociologist, 1988-91, Sociol. Quar., 1989-92. Mem. exec. com. Assembly of Behavioral and Social Scis. Nat. Rsch. Coun., 1974-77. With AUS, 1950-52. Mem. Am. Sociol. Assn. (council 1971-74, theory sect. 1988—), Sociol. Rsch. Assn. Office: Princeton U Dept Sociology Princeton NJ 08544

WALLACE, WILLIAM, III, engineering executive; b. Bklyn., June 7, 1926; s. William and Ruth (Fitch) W.; m. Dorothy Ann Reimann, Aug. 2, 1969 (dec.); 1 child, Andrew William. B.E.E., Union Coll., 1947. Registered prof. engr., 22 states. Test engr. Gen. Electric Co., Schenectady, 1947; engr. Ebasco Services Inc., N.Y.C., 1948-67, chief elec. engr., 1967-70, mgr. projects, 1970-73; v.p. Atlanta office Ebasco Services Inc., Norcross, Ga., 1973-76; exec. v.p. Ebasco Services Inc., N.Y.C., 1976-80, dir., pres., chief exec. officer, 1980-82, chmn., chief exec. officer, 1982-86, also bd. dirs.; cons., 1986—; bd. dirs. McNab Corp. Chmn. bd. advisors Sch. engring., N.C. State U., 1986-89; mem. adv. bd. trustees Union Coll.; trustee Poly. Prep. Country Day Sch.; v.p. Saddle River Day Sch.; deacon West Side Presbyn. Ch., Ridgewood, N.J., 1988-90, elder, 1990-93. Mem. IEEE (sr.), NSPE, N.J. State Soc. Profl. Engrs., World Rehab. Fund (bd. dirs.), N.Y.C. C. of C. and Industry (bd. dirs. 1980-88), Delta Upsilon (vice chmn. Ednl. Found.). Republican. Home and Office: 84 Buckhaven Hl Upper Saddle River NJ 07458

WALLACE, WILLIAM AUGUSTINE, philosophy and history educator; b. N.Y.C., May 11, 1918; s. William Augustine and Louise Cecilia (Teufel) W. BEE, Manhattan Coll., 1940, LHD (hon.), 1975; MS in Physics, Cath. U. Am., 1952; PhD in Philosophy, U. Freiburg, Switzerland, 1959, STD, 1962; Lector of Sacred Theology, Dominican House of Studies, Washington, 1954, M of Sacred Theology, 1967; DSc (hon.), Providence Coll., 1973; DLitt (hon.), Molloy Coll., 1974; LHD (hon.), Fairfield U., 1986. Entered Dominican Order, 1946; ordained priest Roman Cath. Ch., 1953. Elec. engr. Consol. Edison, N.Y.C., 1940-41; rsch. engr. Naval Ordnance Lab., Washington, 1941-43; lector philosophy Dominican House of Philosophy, Dover, Mass., 1954-62; philosophy editor New Cath. Ency., Washington, 1962-65; rsch. assoc. Harvard U., Cambridge, Mass., 1965-67; regent of studies Dominican House of Studies, Washington, 1967-70; prof. philosophy and history Cath. U. Am., Washington, 1970-88, prof. emeritus, 1988—; prof. philosophy U. Md., College Park, 1988—; mem. Inst. for Advanced Study, Princeton, 1976-77; fellow Woodrow Wilson Ctr. for Scholars, Washington, 1983-84; dir. gen. Leonine Commn., Washington, 1976-87. Author: The Scientific Methodology of Theodoric of Freiberg, 1959, The Role of Demonstration in Moral Theology, 1963, Causality and Scientific Explanation, vol. 1, 1972, vol. 2, 1974, The Elements of Philosophy, 1977, From a Realist Point of View, 1979 2d edit. 1983, Prelude to Galileo, 1981, Galileo and His Sources, 1984, Galileo, the Jesuits, and the Medieval Aristotle, 1991, Galileo's Logic of Discovery and Proof, 1992, The Modeling of Nature, 1996; editor, translator: Thomas Aquinas: Cosmogony, 1967, Galileo's Early Notebooks: the Physical Questions, 1977, Galileo's Logical Treatises, 1992; editor: Reinterpreting Galileo, 1986, Albertus Magnus, 1996; co-editor: Galileo Galilei: De praecognitionibus and De demonstratione, 1988; mem. editorial bd. Rev. of Metaphysics, The Thomist; contbr. over 325 articles to jours., encys. and books. Lt. Comdr. USN, 1941-46, PTO. Decorated Legion of Merit; recipient Alumni Achievement award Manhattan Coll., 1967, Alumni Achievement award Cath. U. Am., 1986; grantee NSF, 1965-84, NEH, 1981-89. Mem. Am. Cath. Philos. Assn. (pres. 1969-70, Aquinas medal 1983), History of Sci. Soc. (mem. coun. 1974-77, 88-91), Philosophy of Sci. Assn., Phi Beta Kappa, Sigma Xi. Democrat.

WALLACE, WILLIAM C., airline executive; b. Pittsburg, Tex., July 12, 1941; m. Joyce Johnson, Apr. 22, 1978; children: Kristin, Kari, Michael. BBA, U. Tex., Arlington, 1965. Various positions Am. Airlines, Dallas, Ft. Worth, 1967-79, mgr. passenger svcs., 1979-82; div. mgr. reservations Am. Airlines, L.A., 1982-84; mgr. airport terminal svcs. Am. Airlines, Dallas, Ft. Worth, 1984-85, dir. idea systems, 1985-87; regional mgr. Am. Airlines, Nashville, 1987-88, v.p. field svc., 1990—; exec. v.p. Nashville Eagle (Am. Eagle), 1988-89, pres., 1989-90. Exec. bd. Nashville Symphony, 1990-93; adv. bd. Girl Scouts Am., Nashville, 1990-93; bd. dirs. Mid. Tenn. coun. Boy Scouts Am., 1991-93. Capt. U.S. Army, 1965-70. Mem. Nashville C. of C. (bd. govs. 1991-93). Republican. Episcopalian. Avocations: photography, gardening. Office: Am Airlines Inc PO Box MD 1110 619616 Dallas TX 75261

WALLACE, WILLIAM EDWARD, engineering educator,scientist; b. Fayette, Miss., Mar. 11, 1917; s. James D. and Mattie (Rogers) W.; m. Helen Meyer, June 21, 1947; children: Richard Glen, Donald Alan, Marcia Louise. BS, Miss. Coll., 1936; PhD, U. Pitts., 1940. Teaching asst. U. Pitts., 1936-40, rsch. assoc. chemistry, 1941-45, mem. faculty, 1945-83, prof. chemistry, chmn. dept., 1963-77, prof. materials and metall. engring., 1973-83, prof. chem. engring., 1977-83; prof. applied sci. and engring. Carnegie-Mellon U., Pitts., 1983—; rsch. assoc. manhattan project Ohio State U., 1945; cons. Wright-Patterson AFB, 1962—, Du Pont, 1977—, Gen. Motors, 1974—, Amoco, 1977—; Union Oil Co., 1979—; mem. Pa. Gov.'s Sci. Com., Pa. Sci. and Engring. Found.; fellow Carnegie Instn., Washington, 1940-42; pres. Advanced Materials Corp., 1986-93. Recipient Frank Spedding award 1978, Morley award, 1983; Buhl fellow, 1942-44; Guggenheim fellow, 1954-55. Fellow AAAS; mem. Am. Chem. Soc., Phi Beta Kappa (hon.), Sigma Xi, Phi Lambda Upsilon. Research on metals and intermetallics, hydrogen as a fuel, magnetic materials. Home: 201 Pinecrest Dr Pittsburgh PA 15237-3652

WALLACE, WILLIAM FRANKLIN, management consultant; b. St. Petersburg, Fla., Jan. 19, 1955; s. William Powell and Sara Laughlin (Collins) W.; m. Anne Borden Evans, Apr. 24, 1982; children: William, Sara. AB, Harvard U., 1977, MBA, 1980. Assoc. Harcomm, Cambridge, Mass., 1977-78, The MAC Group, Cambridge and Washington, 1980-83; sr. assoc. The MAC Group, Washington, 1983-89; v.p. The MAC Group (now named Gemini Consulting), McLean, Va., 1989-91; sr. v.p. Gemini Consulting, McLean, 1991-94; COO Gemini Consulting, Morristown, N.J., 1994—. Presbyterian. Office: Gemini Consulting Inc 2535 Airport Rd Morristown NJ 07960

WALLACE, WILLIAM HALL, economic and financial consultant; b. Senatobia, Miss., Aug. 8, 1933; s. Woodard Harvey and Cellie (Carter) W.; m. Margaret Jaeger, Mar. 7, 1964 (dec. 1978); children—Amy Margaret, William Douglas, John Richard Bruce; m. Virginia Wilson, Aug. 25, 1979. B.B.A., U. Miss., 1955, M.B.A., 1956; Ph.D., U. Ill., 1962. Asst. prof. econs. Duke U., Durham, N.C., 1962-67; v.p. Fed. Res. Bank Richmond, Va., 1967-73; prof. econs. N.C. State U., Raleigh, 1973-74; staff dir. Fed. Res. Bd., Washington, 1974-80; 1st v.p., chief oper. officer Fed. Res. Bank Dallas, 1981-91; prof. fin., dean Coll. Bus. and Pub. Adminstrn. Old Dominion U., Norfolk, Va., 1991-94; ret., 1994; pres. Wallace Cons., Inc., 1994—; co-dir. Eurasia Found. Program in Banking & Fin. Markets for Russia and CIS, 1994-95. Trustee Dallas Hist. Soc.; mem. Dallas Com. Fgn. Rels. Served to 1st lt. U.S. Army, 1956-58. Mem. Am. Econs. Assn., Am. Statis. Assn., Cen. Dallas Assn. (exec. com.), Greater Dallas C. of C. (edn. com. 1984-88, chmn. edn. com. 1989-90), Rotary. Methodist. Home: 6 Mansilla Way Hot Springs National Park AR 71909-4312 Office: Wallace Consultants Inc Hot Springs National Park AR 71909

WALLACE, WILLIAM RAY, fabricated steel manufacturing company executive; b. Shreveport, La., Mar. 25, 1923; s. Jason Mohoney and Mattie Evelyn (Adair) W.; m. Minyone Milligan Rose, Oct. 5, 1966; children: Jayne Cecile Rose McDearman, Susan Rose O'Brien, H. Robert Rose; children by previous marriage: Patrick Scott, Michael B., Timothy R., Shelly W. Taetz. BS in Engring., La. Tech., 1944. Field engr. Austin Bridge Co., Dallas, 1944-45; core analyst Core Labs., Bakersfield, Calif., 1945-46; chief engr., then sec.-treas., exec. v.p. Trinity Industries, Inc., Dallas, 1946-58, pres., CEO, 1958—, also bd. dirs.; bd. dirs. Lomas Fin. Corp., Trinity Industries, ENSERCH Corp. Trustee Dallas Meth. Hosps. Found. Methodist. Office: Trinity Industries Inc 2525 N Stemmons Fwy Dallas TX 75207-2401*

WALLACH, ALAN, art historian, educator; b. Bklyn., June 8, 1942; s. Israel and Vivian (Esner) W.; m. Phyllis Rosenzweig, Jan. 3, 1988. BA, Columbia U., 1963, MA, 1965, PhD, 1973. Assoc. prof. Kean Coll., Union, N.J., 1974-89; Ralph H. Wark prof. art and art history Coll. William and Mary, Williamsburg, Va., 1989—; vis. prof. UCLA, 1982-83, Stanford (Calif.) U., 1987, CUNY, 1988, U. Mich., 1989; co-curator Nat. Mus. Am. Art, Washington, 1991-94. Author: (with William Truettner) Thomas Cole: Landscape into History, 1994; contbr. articles to profl. jours. Sr. Postdoctorate Rsch. award Smithsonian Inst., 1985-86. Mem. Am. Studies Assn., Coll. Art Assn. (bd. dirs. 1996-2000), Assn. Art Historians. Home: 2009 Belmont Rd NW Washington DC 20009-5449 Office: Coll William and Mary Dept Art and Art History Williamsburg VA 23187-8795

WALLACH, ALLAN HENRY, former senior critic; b. N.Y.C., Oct. 23, 1927; s. Julius and Beatrice (Markowitz) W.; m. Shirley Meyrowitz, Nov. 26, 1953; children: Jonathan, Mark, Paul. B.A. magna cum laude, Syracuse U.,

1951. Tech. writer H.L. Yoh Co., Phila., 1951-53; reporter Patchogue (N.Y.) Advance, 1953-54; reporter, copy editor New Haven Register, 1954-56; successively reporter, copy editor, asst. night city editor, news feature editor, entertainment editor Newsday, Melville, N.Y., 1957-71; chief drama critic Newsday, 1972-88; sr. critic N.Y. Newsday, N.Y.C., 1988-92. Served with USNR, 1946-47. Mem. Drama Desk, N.Y. Drama Critics Circle (past pres.). Home: 315 W 70th St Apt 4J New York NY 10023-3507

WALLACH, ANNE JACKSON See JACKSON, ANNE

WALLACH, EDWARD ELIOT, physician, educator; b. N.Y.C., Oct. 8, 1933; s. David Abraham and Madeleine (Spiro) W.; m. Joanne Levey, June 24, 1956; children: Paul, Julie. BA, Swarthmore Coll., 1954; MD, Cornell U., 1958; MA (hon.), U. Pa., 1970. Diplomate Am. Bd. Ob-gyn. (bd. dirs. 1989—, dir. divsn. reproductive endocrinology 1989—), subcert. in reproductive endocrinology. Intern 2d med. div. Bellevue Hosp., N.Y.C., 1958-59; resident obstetrics and gynecology Kings County Hosp., Bklyn., 1959-63; asst. instr. State U. N.Y. Downstate Med. Center, Bklyn., 1962-63; mem. faculty U. Pa. Sch. Medicine, 1965-84, prof. obstetrics and gynecology, 1971-84, chief endocrinology sect., div. human reprodn., dept. obstetrics and gynecology, 1968-71, mem. admissions com., 1970-73, mem. community health com., 1966-71, mem. student adv. com., 1966-84, mem. com. for appointments and promotions, 1972-77, chmn., 1974-77; dir. dept. obstetrics and gynecology Pa. Hosp., 1971-84, sec., treas. profl. staff, 1972-75; prof., chmn. dept. ob-gyn. Johns Hopkins U. Sch. Medicine, 1984-94, chmn. med. staff, 1991-94, prof., 1984-94; vis. prof. ob-gyn. U. Kyoto Sch. Medicine, 1981; vis. prof. Keio U. Sch. Medicine, 1987; mem. fertility and maternal health drugs adv. com. FDA, 1992-96. Assoc. editor: Fertility and Sterility, 1974—; co-editor: Modern Trends in Infertility and Conception Control; editor-in-chief Postgrad. Obstetrics and Gynecology, 1980—; mem. editorial bd. Fertility and Sterility, 1970—, Obstetrics and Gynecology, 1976-79, Contemporary Obstetrics and Gynecology, 1976—, Biology of Reproduction, 1978-84; editor-in-chief Current Opinion in Obstetrics and Gynecology, 1989-93; contbr. to med. jours. Trustee Marriage Council Phila., 1970-78; chmn. finance com. Phila. Coordinating Council for Family Planning, 1972-73, chmn. med. adv. com., 1973-76; trustee Balt. Chamber Orch., 1989—. Served as surgeon USPHS, 1963-65. Trainee NIH, 1961-62; recipient Lindback Found. Disting. Teaching award U. Pa., 1971. Fellow Am. Coll. Ob-Gyn., Am. Fertility Soc. (dir. 1977-81, pres. 1985-86); mem. AAAS, Am. Gynecol. and Obstet. Soc. (v.p. 1983-84), Endocrine Soc., Soc.Gynecol. Investigation (pres. 1986-87), Am. Bd. Ob-Gyn. (bd. dirs. 1989—, dir. divsn. reproductive endocrinology 1989—), Phila. Endocrine Soc., Obstet. Soc. Phila. (program chmn. 1969-70, 70-71, 71-72, mem. coun. 1972-83, v.p. 1976-77, pres. 1979-80), Soc. Study Reprodn., Inst. Medicine/NAS, Alpha Omega Alpha. Office: Johns Hopkins Med Instn Houck Bldg Rm 201 600 N Wolfe St Dept Gyne-Ob Baltimore MD 21287-1201

WALLACH, ELI, actor; b. Bklyn., Dec. 7, 1915; s. Abraham and Bertha (Schorr) W.; m. Anne Jackson, Mar. 5, 1948; children: Peter Douglas, Roberta Lee, Katherine Beatrice. AB, U. Tex., 1936; MS in Edn, CCNY, 1938; student, Neighborhood Playhouse Sch. of Theatre, 1940; hon. doctorate, Emerson Coll., Boston, Sch. for Visual Arts, 1991. Corp. mem., dir. Neighborhood Playhouse Sch. Theatre. Actor, 1945—; Broadway plays include Antony and Cleopatra, 1948, Mr. Roberts, 1949-50, Rose Tatoo, 1950-52, Camino Real, 1953, Mademoiselle Colombe, 1953, Teahouse of the August Moon, 1954-55, London prodn., 1954, Twice Around the Park, 1983, Major Barbara, 1956, Rhinoceros, 1961, Luv, 1964, Promenade All, 1972, Opera Comique, Kennedy Ctr. Performing Arts, 1987, The Flowering Peach, Fla., 1987, Broadway, 1994, Cafe Crown, 1989; appeared off-Broadway prodn. Typists and the Tiger, 1962-63, London prodn., 1964, Saturday, Sunday, Monday, 1974, (with wife and 2 daus.) Diary of Anne Frank, 1977-78; appeared in: nat. tour co. Waltz of the Toreadors, 1973-74; appeared in TV film Murder By Reason of Insanity, 1985, TV series Our Family Honor, 1985, TV miniseries Christopher Columbus, 1985, Executioner's Song, 1986; motion pictures include Baby Doll, 1955, The Misfits, 1960, The Victors, 1962, Lord Jim, 1964, How To Steal a Million, The Good, the Bad and the Ugly, The Tiger Makes Out, Band of Gold, Zig-Zag, Cinderella Liberty, 1973, Crazy Joe, 1973, Movie, Movie, 1976, Sam's Son, 1985, Tough Guys, 1986, Rocket to the Moon,1986, Nuts, 1987, The Impossible Spy, 1987, Godfather III, 1990, The Two Jakes, 1990, Article 99, Mistress, 1991, Night and the City, 1991, Honey, Sweet Love, 1993, Two Much Film, 1995. Served to capt. Med. Adminstrn. Corps AUS, World War II. Recipient Donaldson, Theatre World, Variety, Antoinette Perry, Drama League awards, Brit. Film Acad. award, 1956, Disting. Alumnus award U. Tex., 1989. Original mem. Actors Studio.

WALLACH, ERIC JEAN, lawyer; b. N.Y.C., June 11, 1947; s. Milton Harold and Jacqueline (Goldschmidt) W.; m. Miriam Grunberger, Mar. 21, 1976; children: Katherine, Emily, Peter. BA, Harvard Coll., 1968, JD, 1972. Bar: N.Y. 1973, U.S. Dist. Ct. (so. and ea. dists.) N.Y. 1973, U.S. Dist. Ct. (no. dist.) N.Y. 1989, U.S. Ct. Appeals (2nd cir.) 1973, U.S. Tax Ct. 1976. Assoc. Webster & Sheffield, N.Y.C., 1972-77; assoc. Rosenman & Colin, N.Y.C., 1977-80, ptnr., 1981—, mem. mgmt. com., 1993—, chmn. employment practice group, 1985—. Mem. editl. bd. You and the Law, 1992-96; contbr. articles to profl. jours. Sec., treas. Art Dealers Assn. Am., Inc., N.Y.C., 1985—; trustee C.G. Jung Found. for Analytical Psychology; trustee Am. Jewish World Svc., Inc., N.Y.C., 1989—, chmn., 1995—. Mem. Harvard Club N.Y.C. (admissions com. 1992-94), Sunningdale Country Club, Poughkeepsie Tennis Club. Democrat. Avocations: sports, travel, reading. Home: 20 W 64th St New York NY 10023-7129 Office: Rosenman & Colin 575 Madison Ave New York NY 10022-2511 Home: 16 Buttonwood Ln Rhinebeck NY 12572-2402

WALLACH, IRA DAVID, lawyer, business executive; b. N.Y.C., June 3, 1909; s. Joseph and Della (Kahn) W.; m. Miriam Gottesman, Dec. 25, 1938. AB, Columbia U., 1929, JD, 1931, LLD (hon.), 1983; LLD (hon.), U. Maine, 1983. Bar: N.Y. 1932. Practiced in N.Y.C., 1932-45; exec. v.p. Gottesman & Co., Inc. (name changed to Central Nat.-Gottesman Inc. 1984), N.Y.C., 1952-56; pres., CEO Gottesman & Co., Inc. (name changed to Central Nat.-Gottesman Inc. 1984), 1956-74, chmn., CEO, 1974-79, chmn., 1979—, dir., 1947—; exec. v.p. Ctrl. Nat. Corp., N.Y.C., 1952-56, pres., CEO, 1956-74, chmn., CEO, 1974-79, chmn., 1979—, dir., 1948—; exec. v.p. Eastern Corp., Bangor, Maine, 1951-52, dir., 1947-58; dir., pres. Sejak Corp., N.Y.C., dir., exec. v.p. Cenro Corp., N.Y.C.; bd. dirs. Stora Kopparberg Sales Co., Inc., N.Y.C. Pres. D. S. and R. H. Gottesman Found., 1956—, bd. dirs., 1941—; chmn., dir. Miriam and Ira D. Wallach Found., 1956—; bd. dirs. Internat. Peace Acad., People for the Am. Way. Lt. USNR, 1943-46. Mem. Am. Bar Assn., Assn. of Bar of City of N.Y., N.Y. Co. Lawyers Assn. Home: 5 Sherbrooke Rd Scarsdale NY 10583-4429 Office: 3 Manhattanville Rd Purchase NY 10577-2116

WALLACH, JOHN PAUL, foundation administrator, author; b. N.Y.C., Jan. 18, 1943; s. Paul and Edith (Putzel) W.; m. Janet Lee Weil, June 9, 1974; children: David, Michael. BA, Middlebury Coll., 1964; MA, New Sch. for Social Research, 1966. Corr. state dept. Hearst Newspapers, Washington, 1968-74, corr. white house, 1974-76, fgn. editor, 1976-95; founding editor WE, Russian-Am. newspaper, 1992-94; founder, pres. Seeds Peace Found., 1993—; exec. dir. Elie Wiesel Found. for Humanity, N.Y.C., 1995—. Author: Arafat: In the Eyes of the Beholder, 1990, The New Palestinians, 1993; co-author: (with Janet Wallach) Still Small Voices: The Human Story Behind the Intifada, 1989; contbg. editor Washingtonian mag., 1984-89. Founder, dir. Chautauqua (N.Y.) Conf. U.S.-Soviet Rels., 1983-87; founder Seeds of Peace Found., 1993—; mem. nat. adv. bd. Am. U., Washington. Recipient Raymond Clapper award Standing Com. Corrs., 1979, Edward Weintal prize Georgetown U., 1980, Overseas Press Club award, 1980, 83, Edwin Hood award Nat. Press Club, 1989, Washingtonian of Yr. award Washingtonian mag. 1993, Alumni award Middlebury Coll., 1996; named Adj. Prof. of Yr. Am. U., 1985. Mem. Overseas Writers Club (pres. 1991-92). Office: Elie Wiesel Found Humanity 1177 Ave of Americas New York NY 10036

WALLACH, JOHN S(IDNEY), library administrator; b. Toronto, Ohio, Jan. 6, 1939; s. Arthur M. and Alice I. (Smith) W.; children: John Michael, Wendy Anne, Bethany Lynne, Kristen Michele; m. Joyce Bapst. B.S. in Edn, Kent State U., 1963; M.L.S., U. R.I., 1968; M.P.A., U. Dayton, 1977. Dir. Mercer County (Ohio) Library, 1968-70, Greene County (Ohio) Library, 1970-77; asso. dir. Dayton and Montgomery County (Ohio) Library, 1978, dir., 1979—. Bd. dirs. Dayton Mus. Natrual History, Family Svc. Assn., Dayton, Technology Resource Ctr. Served with USN, 1963-68, capt. ret. Mem. ALA, Ohio Libr. Assn. Office: Dayton & Montgomery County Pub Libr 215 E 3rd St Dayton OH 45402-2103

WALLACH, LESLIE ROTHAUS, architect; b. Pitts., Feb. 4, 1944; s. Albert and Sara F. (Rothaus) W.; m. Susan Rose Berger, June 15, 1969; 1 child, Aaron. BS in Mining Engring., U. Ariz., 1967, BArch, 1974. Registered architect, Ariz.; registered contractor, Ariz. Prin. Line and Space, Tucson, 1978—. Representative projects include Ariz. Sonora Desert Mus. Restaurant Complex, Tucson, Elgin Elem. Sch., Ariz., Hillel Student Ctr. U. Ariz., Tucson, Boyce Thompson Southwestern Arborteum Vis. Ctr., Superior, Ariz., San Pedro Riparian Ctr., Sierra Vista, Ariz., Nat. Hist. Trails Ctr., Casper, Wyo., 1996; contbr. Sunset Mag., Architecture Mag. and Fine Homebuilding; exhibited at U. Ariz., AIA Nat. Conv., Washington. Bd. dirs Tucson Regional Plan, Inc. Recipient Roy P. Drachman Design award, 1982, 85, 93, Electric League Ariz. Design award, 1987, 88, Gov. Solar Energy award, 1989, Desert Living awards citation, 1991, Ariz. Architect's medal, 1989, also 25 additional design awards, including 4 received in 1995. Fellow AIA (Ariz. Honor award 1989, 92, AIA/ACSA Nat. Design award 1991, Western Mountain region Design award 1992, CA AIA/Phoenix Homes and Gardens Home of the Yr. Honor award 1992, 96); mem. SAC AIA (past pres., Design award 1985, 88, 90). Office: Line and Space 627 E Speedway Blvd Tucson AZ 85705-7433

WALLACH, MARK IRWIN, lawyer; b. Cleve., May 19, 1949; s. Ivan A. and Janice (Grossman) W.; m. Harriet Kinney, Aug. 11, 1974; children: Kerry Melissa, Philip Alexander. BA magna cum laude, Wesleyan U., 1971; JD cum laude, Harvard U., 1974. Bar: Ohio 1974, U.S. dist. ct. (no. dist.) Ohio 1974, U.S. Ct. Appeals (6th cir.) 1985, U.S. Supreme Ct. 1985. Law clk. U.S. Dist. Ct., Cleve., 1974-75; assoc. Baker & Hostetler, Cleve., 1975-79; chief trial counsel City of Cleve., 1979-81; assoc. Calfee, Halter & Griswold, Cleve., 1981-82, ptnr., 1982—; mem. fed. ct. adv. com. U.S. Dist. Ct. (no. dist.) Ohio, 1991-95. Author: Christopher Morley, 1976. Chmn. bd. trustees Ohio Group Against Smoking Pollution, 1986-90; trustee Cleve. chpt. Am. Jewish Com., 1986—, sec. 1989-91, v.p., 1991-95, pres., 1995—; bd. trustees Citizens League of Greater Cleve., 1978-79, 87-92; pres. Wesleyan Alumni Club Cleve., 1983-87, 1992—; trustee Lyric Opera, Cleve., 1995—, treas., 1996—, Ratner Schs., 1994—. Mem. ABA, Ohio Bar Assn., Fed. Bar Assn., Cuyahoga County Law Dirs. Assn., Greater Cleve. Bar Assn., The Club at Soc. Ctr. Republican. Avocations: reading, bicycling, space exploration, politics. Home: 15700 Van Aken Blvd # 24 Shaker Heights OH 44120 Office: Calfee Halter & Griswold 1400 McDonald Investment Ctr 800 Superior Ave E Cleveland OH 44114-2601

WALLACH, PHILIP C(HARLES), financial, public relations consultant; b. N.Y.C., Nov. 17, 1912; s. Edgar Smith and Rix Wallach; m. Magdalena Charlotta Falkenberg, Mar. 5, 1950. Student, NYU, 1930-33. Editor, writer Hearst Publs., N.Y.C., 1935-42; editor Shell Oil Co., N.Y.C., 1943-46; editor, dir. pub. relations W.R. Grace & Co., N.Y.C., 1946-54; dir. pub. relations and advt. H.K. Porter & Co., N.Y.C., 1954-58; pres. Wallach Assocs., Inc., N.Y.C., 1958-85; officer and v.p. investor rels. Occidental Petroleum Co., L.A., 1985-91; v.p. Occidental Internat. Corp., N.Y.C., 1987-91, cons., 1991-92. Pres. St. Paul Guild, N.Y.C., 1959-68, bd. dirs., 1964-72; pres. Cath. Inst. Press, N.Y.C., 1959-75; co-founder Air Force Assn., Washington, 1946; nat. committeeman Rep. Party, N.Y., 1945-60; mem. Rep. Nat. Com., Greenwich, Conn., 1982-91; bd. dirs., mem. exec. com. U.S. Pakistan Econ. Coun. With USAF, 1942-43. Mem. Overseas Press Club. Home: 126 W Lyon Farm Dr Greenwich CT 06831-4352

WALLACH, STANLEY, medical educator, consultant, administrator; b. Bklyn., Dec. 10, 1928; s. Abraham and Ida Helen (Pevin) W.; m. Pearl Small, 1973; children: Sara Lynn, Rhonda, Peter, Francine, Shellie, Allen, Corinne, Mara. AB, Cornell U., 1948; MA in Phys. Chemistry, Columbia U., 1949; MD, SUNY Downstate Med. Ctr., 1953. Diplomate Am. Bd. Internal Medicine, Am. Bd. Endocrinology and Metabolism. Intern Kings County Hosp., Bklyn., 1953-54; resident in internal medicine VA Hosp./Salt Lake Gen. Hosp., Salt Lake City, 1954-56; fellow in endocrinology and metabolism Mass. Gen. Hosp., Boston, 1956-57; attending physician Kings County Hosp., Bklyn., 1957-73, SUNY Hosp., Bklyn., 1966-73, Albany (N.Y.) Med. Ctr., 1973-83; chief of med. svc. VA Med. Ctr., Albany, 1973-83, Bay Pines, Fla., 1983-90; cons. VA Med. Ctr., Tampa, Fla., 1991-92; attending physician Tampa Gen. Hosp., 1991—, Moffitt Cancer Ctr., 1991-92; dir. med. edn. Cath. Med. Ctr., Jamaica, N.Y., 1992-93; dir. endocrinology and osteoporosis ctr. Hosp. for Joint Diseases, N.Y.C., 1993—; instr. in medicine SUNY Downstate Med. Ctr., 1957-58, from asst. prof. to assoc. prof., 1960-71, prof., 1971-73; prof., asst. chmn. dept. medicine Albany Med. Coll., 1973-77, prof., assoc. chmn. dept. medicine, 1977-83; prof. internal medicine Coll. Medicine U. South Fla., 1983-92, assoc. chmn. dept. internal medicine, 1988-92; exec. dir. Am. Coll. Nutrition, 1993—; clin. prof. medicine NYU Sch. Medicine, N.Y.C., 1995—; pres. Certification Bd. for Nutrition Specialists, 1992—; career scientist Health Rsch. Coun., City of N.Y., 1967-71; program dir. USPHS Clin. Rsch. Ctr., SUNY Downstate Med. Ctr., 1966-73; rsch. collaborator Brookhaven Nat. Lab., Upton, N.Y., 1970-82; vice-chmn. Gordon Rsch. Conf. on Magnesium in Biochem. Processes and Medicine, 1987, chmn., 1990; cons. NIH, NSF, USDA, Nat. Osteoporosis Found., Nat. Arthritis Found., U.S. Pharmacopeial Conf. Mem. editl. bd. Jour. Am. Coll. of Nutrition, 1981—, Magnesium and Trace Elements, 1982—, Jour. Trace Elements in Exptl. Medicine, 1987—; reviewer Am. Jour. Medicine, Annals of Internal Medicine, Archives of Internal Medicine, Jour. Clin. Endocrinology and Metabolism, Endocrinology, Metabolism, Calcified Tissue Internat., Jour. Bone and Mineral Rsch., Osteoporosis Internat., Procs. of Soc. Exptl. Biology and Medicine, Jour. Nutritional Biochemistry; contbr. numerous articles to profl. jours. Capt. USNR, 1957-88. Co-recipient Hektoen Silver award AMA Conv., 1959, John B. Johnson award Paget's Disease Found., 1989. Fellow ACP (emeritus), Am. Coll. Clin. Pharmacology, Am. Coll. Endocrinology, Am. Coll. Nutrition (bd. dirs. 1982—, v.p. 1983-85, pres.-elect 1985-87, pres. 1987-89, sec., treas. 1991-93); mem. Assn. Am. Physicians, Am. Soc. for Clin. Investigation (emeritus), Am. Fedn. Clin. Rsch. (emeritus), Am. Soc. for Magnesium Rsch., Am. Soc. Bone and Mineral Rsch., Am. Soc. for Clin. Nutrition, Am. Inst. of Nutrition, Am. Assn. Clin. Endocrinology, Endocrine Soc., Confedn. of Nutrition Socs., European Calcified Tissue Soc., Paget's Disease Found. (bd. dirs. med. adv. panel), Internat. Conf. on Calcium Regulating Hormones, Internat. Soc. Trace Element Rsch. in Humans, Nat. Orgn. Rare Disorders, Harvey Soc. (emeritus), Sigma Xi. Office: Hosp for Joint Diseases 301 E 17th St New York NY 10003-3804

WALLACH, WENDEE ESTHER, secondary school educator; b. N.Y.C., Dec. 29, 1948; d. Leonard Morris and Annette (Cohen) W.; divorced; 1 child, Nanette René. BS in Edn., SUNY, Cortland, 1970; MA in Teaching, N.Mex. State U., 1975. Cert. tchr., N.Mex. Tchr. phys. edn. Las Cruces (N.Mex.) Pub. Schs., 1970-96; mem. Shoemaker-Levy Observing Team, 1996—; intramural and athletic coord. White Sands Sch., 1970-93; instr. swimming N.Mex. State U. Weekend Coll., Las Cruces, 1986-96; dir., coord. learn to swim program ARC, Las Cruces, 1973-96; instr. phys. edn., coach volleyball and track, athletic coord. Sierra Mid. Sch., 1993-96. Instr. trainer water safety ARC, 1973—, CPR, 1974—; instr. life guard, trainer, health and safety specialist, 1988-96, instr., trainer standard first aid, 1991—; chair com. health and safety svcs. Don Ana County Red Cross. Named Water Safety Instr. of Yr. ARC, Las Cruces, 1986, 89, 25 Yr. Svc. award, 1992. Mem. AAHPERD, N.Mex. Alliance Health, Phys. Edn. Recreation and Dance (spkr. 1988, 92, 93, aquatic chmn. 1990-92), Nat. Intramural-Recreational Sports Assn., N.Mex. H.S. Athletic Dirs. Assn. Democrat. Jewish. Avocations: skywatching, swimming, needlework, square dancing. Home and Office: 2500 E Wetstones Rd Vail AZ 85641

WALLANCE, GREGORY J., lawyer; b. Washington, Oct. 24, 1948; s. Donald Aaron Wallance and Shula Cohen; m. Elizabeth Van Veen, Jan. 4, 1981; children: Daniel, Carina, Lisanne. BA, Grinnell Coll., 1970; JD, Bklyn. Law Sch., 1976. Bar: N.Y. 1977, U.S. Dist. Ct. (ea. dist.) N.Y. 1977, U.S. Dist. Ct. (so. dist.) N.Y. 1978, U.S. Ct. Appeals (2d cir.) 1980, U.S. Dist. Ct. (no. dist.) 1989. Clk. to Hon. Jacob Mishler N.Y.C., 1976-77; assoc. Paul, Weiss, Rifkind, Wharton & Garrison, N.Y.C., 1977-79; asst. U.S. atty., U.S. Atty's. Office, N.Y.C., 1979-85; assoc. Kaye Scholer Fierman Hays & Handler, N.Y.C., 1985-88; ptnr. Kaye, Scholer, Fierman, Hays & Handler, 1988—. Author: Papa's Game, 1981; assoc. prodr. (HBO) Sakharov, 1981; columnist Nat. Law Jour., 1993—; contbr. articles to profl. jours. Vol. VISTA, N.Y.C., 1970-72. Mem. ABA, Assn. for Bar of City of N.Y. Office: Kaye Scholer Fierman Hays & Handler 425 Park Ave New York NY 10022-3506

WALLCRAFT, MARY JANE LOUISE, religious organization executive, songwriter, author; b. Deloraine, Man., Can., Nov. 2, 1933; d. Norman Zephaniah and Mary Jane (McKinney) Sexton; m. James Orval Wallcraft, Oct. 13, 1956; children: Angela Mae, Ronald Clarke. Assoc. in piano, Royal Conservatory Toronto, Brandon, Man., 1952; AA, Victor Valley Coll., 1973. Tchr. piano Souris, Man., 1963-67; church organist St. George's Anglican, Brandon, 1960-63, St. Lukes Anglican, Souris, Man., 1963-67, Victorville (Calif.) United Meth. Ch., 1970-74; tchr. piano Hines House of Music, Victorville, 1969-72; ch. sec. Fredericksburg (Va.) United Meth. Ch., 1977-79; med. transcriptionist Mary Washington Hosp., Fredericksburg, 1985-87, Shady Grove Adventist, Rockville, Md., 1987-89; founder, pres. Make Me a Blessing Ministries, Inc., Zellwood, Fla., 1992—; Author: Make Me a Blessing, 1991, Sing Your Way to Victory, "Reflections," 1994, A Modern Day Psalter, Shadows, Symbols and Strategies, 1994; songwriter albums Make Me a Blessing, 1992, Grandkid's Praise, 1993, Grandma Jean's Unity Rap, 1993, A Word of Encouragement from Make Me a Blessin, 1995. Author: Make Me a Blessing, 1991, Sing Your Way to Victory, "Reflections", 1994, A Modern Day Psalter, Shadows, Symbols, and Strategies, 1994; songwriter albums Make Me a Blessing, 1992, Grandkid's Praise, 1993, Grandma Jane's Unity Rap, 1993, A Word of Encouragement From Make Me a Blessing, 1995; completion of 5-yr. investigation of Benny Hinn; choir accompanist New Hope Presbyn. Ch., 1995, 96; recommenced ministry to Care Homes, 1996. Choir accompanist, alt. pianist New Hope Presbyn. Ch., Eustis, Fla., 1995—. Republican. Avocations: writing and compiling daily devotional book and putting the scriptures to music, playing piano and organ, cooking, walking. Home and Office: 4162 Greenbluff Ct Zellwood FL 32798-9005

WALLEIGH, ROBERT SHULER, consultant; b. Washington, Mar. 31, 1915; s. Charles Henry and Martha (McDaniel) W.; m. Catherine Richarde Coulon, Feb. 22, 1938; children—Margaret Coulon (Mrs. Shaffer), Catherine Richarde (Mrs. Carnevale). B.S. in Elec. Engring, George Washington U., 1936. Test engr. Gen. Electric Co., 1936-38; rating examiner Civil Service Commn., 1938-39; adminstrv. asst. Pub. Roads Adminstrn., Washington, 1939-42; elec. engr. to dep. asst. dir. for adminstrn. Nat. Bur. Standards, 1943-53, asso. dir for adminstrn., 1955-75, acting dep. dir., 1975-79, sr. adv. internat. affairs, 1978-79; asst. for adminstrn. Diamond Ordnance Fuze labs. Dept. Army, 1953-55; cons. IEEE, Washington, 1979—. Recipient Naval Ordnance Devel. award, 1945; Exceptional Service award with gold medal Dept. Commerce, 1967; Engr. Alumni Achievement award George Washington U., 1975; others. Methodist. Home: 5701 Springfield Dr Bethesda MD 20816-1237

WALLEN, LINA HAMBALI, educator, consultant; b. Garut, West Java, Indonesia, Mar. 24, 1952; came to U.S., 1986; d. Mulyadi and Indra (Hudiyana) Hambali; m. Norman E. Wallen, Apr. 16, 1986. BA, IKIP, Bandung, Indonesia, 1975, DRA, 1984; PhD in Psychology, Columbia Pacific U., San Rafael, Calif., 1990; MA in Economics, San Francisco State U., 1993. Cert. tchr. Clk. PT Radio Frequency Communication, Bandung, 1972-74; adminstrv. mgr. CV Electronics Engring., Jakarta, Indonesia, 1974-76; exec. sec. PT Tanabe Abadi, Bandung, 1977-81; br. mgr. PT Ama Forta, Bandung, 1982-84; tchr. SMA Pembangunan, Bandung, 1976-83, Patuha Coll., Bandung, 1980-84.

WALLENBORN, JANICE RAE, retired elementary education educator; b. Chgo., Jan. 22, 1938; d. Ramon Joseph and Anne Joan (Seaquist) W. BEd, Beloit Coll., 1960; MEd, The George Washington U., 1966; postgrad., George Mason U., 1987-88, U. Va., 1965-85; Degree in Theol. Edn., U. of South, 1989. Cert. tchr. Va. Tchr. Quantico (Va.) Marine Base, 1960-62; elem. tchr. Pearl Harbor Elem. Sch., Honolulu, 1962-64; elem. tchr. Quantico Dependents Sch. System, 1964-95, ret., 1995. Counselor Diet Ctr., Springfield, Va., 1979-89. Mem. NEA (life), Quantico Edn. Assn. (treas. 1968-72), Va. Edn. Assn., Pi Lambda Theta (life), Kappa Alpha Theta (treas. 1979-81, pres. North Va. chpt. 1981-85, alumni dist. pres. 1989-95). Republican. Episcopalian. Avocations: sewing, crafts, cooking, yardwork, lay Eucharistic minister. Home: 8576 Gwynedd Way Springfield VA 22153-3422 also: PO Box 427 Cobbs Creek VA 23035

WALLENDER, MICHAEL TODD, lawyer; b. Schenectady, N.Y., Apr. 8, 1950; s. Kenneth Clark and Martha Lee (Getty) W.; m. Joyce Ann Mushaw, June 3, 1978; children: Kristina Lee, Michael David. BA, Colgate U., 1972; JD, Harvard U., 1975. Law asst. N.Y. State Supreme Ct. Appellate Div., Albany, 1975-76; assoc. DeGraff, Foy, Conway, Holt-Harris & Mealey, Albany, 1976-80, ptnr., 1981-90; counsel N.Y. State Assn. Realtors, Albany, 1981—, Albany County Bd. Realtors, 1985-92, Capital Regional Multiple Listing Svc., Albany, 1986—, Greater Capitol Assn. Realtors, 1992—. Author: Realtors and the Law of Agency, 1988. counsel Tercentenary Fund, Schenectady, 1978, Step 6 Citizens Against Child Sexual Abuse, Schenectady, 1985. Mem. Am. Trial Lawyers Assn., ABA, N.Y. State Bar Assn., Albany County Bar Assn., Ft. Orange Club, Mohawk Golf Club, Colgate Club (capital dist. chpt., Albany), Saratoga Reading Rm. Avocation: thoroughbred horse racing. Home: 28 Cheshire Pl Niskayuna NY 12309-4939 Office: Ste 1501 90 State Street Albany NY 12207

WALLENSTEIN, JAMES HARRY, lawyer; b. N.Y.C., Oct. 28, 1942; s. Ira Jerome and Jane Irene (Hoffman) W.; m. Marcia Faye Michaelson, July 9, 1967; children: Julie, Debbie. BA cum laude, Washington and Lee U., 1964; LLB cum laude, So. Meth. U., 1967. Bar: Tex. 1967, U.S. Ct. Appeals (5th cir.) 1967. Law clk. to justice U.S. Ct. Appeals (5th cir.), Dallas, 1967-68; assoc. Johnson, Bromberg & Leeds, Dallas, 1970-73; pvt. practice law Dallas, 1973-78; ptnr. Wallenstein & St. Claire, Dallas, 1978-81, Jenkens & Gilchrist, Dallas, 1981-88, Jenkens & Gilchrist, P.C., Dallas, 1988—; adj. prof. So. Meth. U. Law Sch., 1978-91; lectr. numerous orgns. including U. Tex., So. Meth. U. Law Sch., State Bar Tex., N.W. Ctr. for Profl. Edn., 1974—. Editor in chief S.W. Law Jour., 1966-67; contbr. articles to profl. jours. Capt. U.S. Army, 1969-70, Vietnam. Mem. ABA (lectr., chair opinion letter com. real property, probate and trust law sect. 1985-89), Tex. Bar Assn. (lectr., coun. sect. on real estate, probate and trust law 1976-84, 86-89, chair sect. 1988-89, chair opinion letter com. 1983—, chair subcom. legal fees paid by title cos. 1985-89, editor newsletter 1981-84), Dallas Bar Assn. (lectr., chair real property sect. 1980-81), Am. Coll. Real Estate Lawyers (lectr.), Dallas Area Real Estate Lawyers' Discussion Group (founder, chair 1976—), Order of Coif, Barristers. Democrat. Jewish. Avocations: reading, swimming. Office: Jenkens & Gilchrist PC 1445 Ross Ave Ste 3200 Dallas TX 75202-2770

WALLENTINE, MARY KATHRYN, secondary educator; b. Moscow, Idaho, Dec. 27, 1943; d. Elwood Vernon and Mary Berenice (Hillard) White; m. William Edward Wallentine, Dec. 29, 1977; 1 child, Vicki. BA, Whitman Coll., 1966. Tchr. math. and art Mt. Rainier High Sch., Des Moines, Wash., 1966-85; pres. Highline Edn. Assn., Seattle, 1985-88; tchr. math., dept. head Tyee High Sch., SeaTac, Wash., 1988—; tchr. leadership cadre Highline Sch. Dist., 1988-92, co-chair dist. site-based decision making com., 1989-92; tchr. leadership cadre Tyee H.S., SeaTac, 1995—, sr. class advisor, graduation advisor, 1994-96. Precinct committeeperson Dem. Cen. Com., King County, Wash., 1980-92, state committeewoman, 1982-88, del. nat. conv., 1980. Mem. NEA (PULSE dir. 1992—, resolutions com. 1987-92, nat. del. 1980-96), Nat. Coun. Tchrs. Math. (spkr.), Wash. Edn. Assn., Highline Edn. Assn. (pres. 1986-89). Episcopalian. Avocations: gardening, politics, visual arts, community service. Home: 860 100th Ave NE Apt 34 Bellevue WA 98004-4132

WALLER, AARON BRET, III, museum director; b. Liberal, Kans., Dec. 7, 1935; s. Aaron Bret and Juanita M. (Slawson) W.; m. Mary Lou Dooley, Sept. 3, 1959; children: Bret, Mary Elizabeth. BFA, Kansas City Art Inst., 1957; MFA, U. Kans., 1958, postgrad., 1964-67; postgrad. (Fulbright grantee), U. Oslo, 1963-64. Grad. asst. U. Kans., 1957-58; dir. The Citadel Mus., Mil. Coll. S.C., 1957-58, Mus. Art, U. Kans., 1964-71; dept. head public edn. and higher edn. Met. Mus. Art, N.Y.C., 1971-73; dir. Museum Art, U. Mich., Ann Arbor, 1973-80, Meml. Art Gallery, U. Rochester, N.Y.,

1980-85; adj. assoc. prof. fine arts dept. Meml. Art Gallery, U. Rochester, 1980-85; assoc. dir. for edn. and pub. affairs J. Paul Getty Mus., Malibu, Calif., 1985-90; dir. Indpls. Mus. Art, 1990—; assoc. prof. U. Mich., 1973-80; coordinator museum studies program Inst. Fine Arts, NYU, 1971-73; tchr. City Coll. N.Y., 1971-73. Mem. Assn. Art Mus. Dirs. (treas. 1980-81, trustee 1992-94), Intermuseum Conservation Assn. (pres. 1977-78), Am. Assn. Museums (nat. com. on mus. tng. 1976-78, counselor-at-large 1986-89, treas. standing com. on edn. 1990-92), Coll. Art Assn. Office: Indpls Mus Art 1200 W 38th St Indianapolis IN 46208-4101

WALLER, EPHRAIM EVERETT, retired professional association executive; b. Sioux City, Iowa, Aug. 10, 1928; s. Everett and Ruth Emma (Little) W.; m. Virginia Louise Harper, Oct. 3, 1959. BA, U. Iowa, 1951, MA, 1959; grad. with honors, Comd. and Gen. Staff Coll., 1966, State Dept. Fgn. Svc. Inst., 1967, Turkish Lang. Sch., 1968; EdD, U. S.D., 1981. Cert. fgn. area specialist, cryptologist. Commd. 2d lt. U.S. Army, 1951, advanced through grades to lt. col., 1967, retired, 1979; exec. dir. Midwest Agrl. Chems. Assn., Sioux City, Iowa, 1981-95; cons., 1996—; mem. sci. and regulatory oversight coun. Am. Crop Protection Assn., Washington, 1990-95; mem. interregional coord. coun. Joint Body U.S. Regional Agrl. Assns., Dawson, Ga., 1991-95. Contbr. numerous articles to profl. jours. Mem. coms. 1st Congrl. Ch., Sioux City, 1937—. Decorated Bronze Star, Cross of Gallantry with Silver Star, Legion of Merit with Oak Leaf Cluster, Chinese and Vietnamese Honor medals. Mem. Retired Officers Assn., Siouxland C. of C. (com. mem. 1981-95), Scottish Rite, Masons, Phi Delta Kappa, Delta Sigma Rho. Avocations: swimming, hiking, travel, stamp collecting, writing.

WALLER, GARY FREDRIC, English language educator, poet; b. Auckland, N.Z., Jan. 3, 1944; came to U.S., 1983; s. Fred and Joan Elsie (Smythe) W.; m. Jennifer Robyn Denham, July 2, 1966 (div. 1980); children: Michael, Andrew; m. Kathleen Ann McCormick, Nov. 12, 1988; one child, Philip. BA, U. Auckland, 1965, MA, 1966; PhD, Cambridge U., Eng., 1970. Assoc. prof. English U. Auckland, New Zealand, 1969-72, Delhousie U., Nova Scotia, Can., 1972-78; head, prof. English Wilfrid Lawrie U., Waterloo, Can., 1978-83; head, prof. lit. and cultural studies Carnegie Mellon U., Pitts., 1983-92; dean arts and scis., prof. lit. and cultural studies U. Hartford, Wittenford, Conn., 1992-95; Donaldson Bye fellow Magdalene Coll., Cambridge, 1967-69; assoc. prof. English Dalhousie U., Purchase, 1972-78; prof., head English dept. Wilfrid Laurier U., Can., 1978-83; prof. lit. and cultural studies, head English dept. Carnegie Mellon U., 1983-92; prof. English and interdisciplinary studies, dean arts/scis. U. Hartford, Conn., 1992-95; v.p. acad. affairs, prof. lit. and cultural studies Purchase (N.Y.) Coll., 1995—. Author: The Strong Necessity of Time, 1976, The Triumph of Death, 1977, Pamphilia to Amphilanthus, 1977, Dreaming America, 1979, Mary Sidney Countess of Pembroke, 1979, Sir Philip Sidney and the Interpretation of Renaissance Culture, 1984, Sixteenth Century Poetry, 1986, 2d edit., 1993, Reading Texts, 1986, Lexington Introduction to Literature, 1987, Shakespeare's Comedies, 1991, Reading Mary Wroth, 1991, The Sidney Family Romance, 1993, Edmund Spenser: A Literary Life, 1994; (poems) Other Flights, Always, 1991, Impossible Futures Indelible Pasts, 1983.

WALLER, GEORGE MACGREGOR, historian, educator; b. Detroit, June 7, 1919; s. George and Marguerite (Rowl) W.; m. Martha Huntington Stifler, Oct. 16, 1943; children: Susan, Marguerite, Elizabeth, Donald, Richard. Grad., Deerfield Acad., 1937; AB, Amherst Coll., 1941; MA, Columbia U., 1947, PhD, 1953. Comml. rep. Detroit Edison Co., 1941-42; lectr. Hunter Coll., 1946-47; instr. Amherst Coll., 1948-52; chief Am. history research center Wis. Hist. Soc., 1952-54; prof., head dept. history and polit. sci. Butler U., Indpls., 1954-84, McGregor prof. history, 1987-89, McGregor prof. history emeritus, 1989—; Fulbright sr. scholar U. Southampton, Eng., 1961-62; vis. prof. Ind. U., 1967-69. Author: Samuel Vetch. Colonial Enterpriser, 1960, The American Revolution in the West, 1976; editor: Puritanism in Early America, 1950, rev., 1973, Pearl Harbor, Roosevelt and the Coming War, 1953, 65, 3d edit., 1976; contbr. to: Ency. So. History, World Book Ency., Dictionary of Can. Biography, Vol. I., Ency. of Indpls. Mem. Ind. Am. Revolution Bicentennial Commn., 1971-82. Served to lt. comdr. USNR, 1943-46. Recipient Holcomb award, 1960, Daus. of Founders and Patriots of Am. award, 1977, Disting. Hoosier award, 1989, Sagamore of the Wabash award, 1990. Mem. Ind. Acad. Social Scis. (pres. 1983), Ind. Mus. Soc. (past pres.), Internat. Platform Assn., Phi Beta Kappa (past pres. Ind. chpt.), Phi Kappa Phi, Phi Alpha Theta. Home: 740 Broad Ave S Naples FL 34102-7330

WALLER, HAROLD MYRON, political science educator; b. Detroit, Oct. 12, 1940; s. Allan L. and Lillian R. (LeVine) W.; m. Diane Carol Goodman, June 28, 1966; children: Sharon, Dahvi, Jeffrey. SB, MIT, 1962; MS, Northwestern U., 1966; PhD, Georgetown U., 1968. Asst. prof. McGill U., Montreal, 1967-71, assoc. prof., 1971-93, prof., 1993—, chmn. polit. sci. dept., 1969-74, 89-90, acting chmn., 1980-81, 86-87, assoc. dean (acad.) faculty arts, 1991-94, acting dean faculty arts, 1994-95; pres. McGill Assn. Univ. Tchrs., Montreal, 1978-79; fellow Jerusalem Ctr. Pub. Affairs, 1980—; dir. Can. Ctr. Jewish Community Studies, Montreal, 1980—. Co-author: Maintaining Consensus: The Canadian Jewish Polity in the Postwar World, 1990; co-editor: Canadian Federalism: From Crisis to Constitution; contbg. editor: Middle East Focus; mem. editorial bd. Jewish Political Studies, Patterns of Prejudice; chmn. editorial bd. Viewpoints; contbr. numerous articles to profl. jours. and books in field. Com. chmn. Can. Jewish Congress, Montreal, 1971-74; chair, nat. exec. Can. Profs. for Peace in Middle East, Toronto, 1975-85; pres. Akiva Sch., Montreal, 1984-85; com. chmn. Jewish Edn. Council, Montreal, 1986-88. Recipient Nat. Jewish Book award Jewish Book Coun., N.Y.C., 1991; Grad. fellowship NSF, Washington, 1965-66; leave fellowship Social Sci. Humanities Rsch. Council, Ottawa, 1981-82. Mem. Am. Polit. Sci. Assn., Can. Polit. Sci. Assn., Assn. Jewish Studies, Assn. Sociol. Study of Jewry, Assn. Israel Studies, Sigma Xi, Pi Sigma Alpha. Jewish. Club: MIT Hillel (Cambridge, Mass.) (pres. 1961-62). Avocations: travel, athletics, reading, politics. Office: McGill U Dept Polit Sci, 855 Sherbrooke St W, Montreal, PQ Canada H3A 2T7

WALLER, JIM D., holding company executive. CEO Ithaca Holdings, Wilkesboro, N.C. Office: Ithaca Industries Inc Hwy 268 Wilkesboro NC 28697*

WALLER, JOEL N., consumer products executive; b. 1939. Pvt. practice L.A., 1963-75; with Bermans Leather Experts, Mpls., 1975-83; with Wilsons House of Suede, Mpls., 1983—, officer, 1983—, pres., 1984—. Served U.S. Army, 1962-63. Office: Rosedale Wilsons Inc 400 Highway 169 S Ste 600 Minneapolis MN 55426-1114*

WALLER, JOHN LOUIS, anesthesiology educator; b. Loma Linda, Calif., Dec. 1, 1944; s. Louis Clinton and Sue (Bruce) W.; m. Jo Lynn Marie Haas, Aug. 4, 1968; children: Kristina, Karla, David. BA, So. Coll., Collegedale, Tenn., 1967; MD, Loma Linda U., 1971. Diplomate Am. Bd. Anesthesiology. Intern Hartford (Conn.) Hosp., 1971-72; resident in anesthesiology Harvard U. Med. Sch.-Mass. Gen. Hosp., Boston, 1972-74, fellow, 1974-75; asst. prof. anesthesiology Emory U. Sch. Medicine, Atlanta, 1977-80, assoc. prof., 1980-86, prof., chmn. dept., 1986—; svc. chief anesthesiology Emory Univ. Hosp., Atlanta, 1986-94, med. dir., 1993-95; assoc. v.p. for info. svcs., Woodruff Health Scis. Ctr. Emory U. Sch. Medicine, 1995—; chief info. officer Emory U. Sys. Healthcare, 1995—; cons. Arrow Internat., Inc., Reading, Pa., 1988—; bd. dirs. Clifton Casualty Co., Colo.; mem. adv. com. on anesthetic and life support drugs FDA, Washington, 1986-92; numerous vis. professorships and lectures. Contbr. articles to med. jours. Maj. M.C., USAF, 1975-77. Recipient cert. of appreciation Office Sec. Def., 1983. Fellow Am. Coll. Anesthesiologists, Am. Coll. Chest Physicians; mem. AMA, Am. Soc. Anesthesiologists, Soc. Cardiovascular Anesthesiologists (pres. 1991-93), Internat. Anesthesia Rsch. Soc. (trustee 1984—, sec. 1993—), Assn. Univ. Anesthetists, Soc. Acad. Anesthesia Chairmen (councillor 1989—), Assn. Cardiac Anesthesiologists. Avocations: tennis, sailing, swimming. Office: Emory U Hosp Dept Anes 1364 Clifton Rd NE Atlanta GA 30322-1059

WALLER, JOHN OSCAR, English language educator; b. L.A., Oct. 29, 1916; s. David Oscar and Susan Veva (Williams) W.; m. Elaine Louise Johnson, Jan. 6, 1946. B.A., San Diego State Coll., 1941; M.A., U. So. Calif., 1949; Ph.D., 1954. Instr. San Diego State Coll., 1946-48; dir. publs. Oxnard (Calif.) Union High Sch., 1951-52; mem. faculty Walla Walla Coll., College Place, Wash., 1952-60; prof. English Andrews U., Berrien Springs, Mich., 1960-88, chmn. dept., 1963-79. Author: A Circle of Friends: The Tennysons and the Lushingtons of Park House; author articles on lit. history; mem. editl. bd. Abstracts of English Studies, 1967-80; contbr. articles to profl. jours., 1988-95. Served with USNR, 1941-45. Mem. Seventh Day Adventist Ch. Home: 8886 George Ave Berrien Springs MI 49103-1406

WALLER, MARY BELLIS, education educator, consultant; b. Milw., May 18, 1940; d. Ernest Anthony and Hazel Mary (Addie) Bellis; m. Michael I. Waller, May 9, 1987; children: Eric B. Griswold, Andrew D. Griswold, Megan E. Griswold Simone. BS, U. Wis., Milw., 1969, MS, 1971, PhD, 1992. Coord. Wis. Coalition for Ednl. Reform, Milw., 1971-74; instr. U. Wis., Milw., 1974-77; exec. dir. Worker Rights Inst., Milw., 1977-87; adj. prof. Nat. Coll. Edn., Evanston, Ill., 1981-96; preceptor, clin. program coord. U. Wis.-Parkside, Kenosha, 1987-96; Wis. lead cons. Emprise Designs, 1993—; cons. on drug-affected children; ctr. scientist Ctr. for Addiction and Behavioral Health Rsch., 1996—, pres. program devel. and evaluation, 1993—. Author: Crack-Affected Children: A Teacher's Guide, 1993; contbr. numerous articles on drug-affected children. Mem. ASCD, Am. Ednl. Rsch. Assn., Assn. Tchr. Educators, Wis. Improvement Project, Phi Delta Kappa (Disting. Svc. award 1992). Home: 8316 N Regent Rd Milwaukee WI 53217-2736

WALLER, MITZI DUNCAN, special education educator; b. Nathalie, Va., Dec. 22, 1955; d. Richard Edward Sr. and Barbara Gayle (Brown) Duncan; m. Ronnie Lee Waller, Mar. 3, 1979; children: Blair Marie, Blake Edward. BS in Therapeutic Recreation, Longwood Coll., 1979, MS in Edn., 1994. Edn. students with learning disabilities Halifax (Va.) County/South Boston City Pub. Schs., 1991—; chmn. sch. renewal com. Volens Elem., Nathalie, Va., 1994—. Sunday sch. pianist Mulberry Bapt. Ch., Nathalie, 1980-94, Sunday sch. tchr., 1980-95; pres. North Halifax Ladies' Aux., Nathalie, 1982-84; parent Lucky Leaf 4-H Club, Nathalie, 1990—. Mem. NEA, Va. Edn. Assn. Baptist. Avocations: youth sports, reading, swimming. Home: Rt 3 Box 418 Nathalie VA 24577 Office: Volens Elem Sch Rt 3 Box 157 Nathalie VA 24577

WALLER, PATRICIA FOSSUM, transportation executive, researcher, psychologist; b. Winnipeg, Man., Can., Oct. 12, 1932; d. Magnus Samuel and Diana Isabel (Briggs) Fossum; m. Marcus Bishop Waller, Feb. 27, 1957; children: Anna Estelle, Justin Magnus, Martha Wilkinson, Benjamin Earl. AB in Psychology cum laude, U. Miami, Coral Gables, 1953, MS in Psychology, 1955; PhD in Psychology, U. N.C., 1959. Lic. psychologist, N.C. Psychology intern VA Hosp., Salem, Va., 1956; psychology instr. Med. Sch. U. N.C., Chapel Hill, 1957; USPHS postdoctoral fellow R.B. Jackson Lab., Bar Harbor, Maine, 1958-60; psychologist VA Hosp., Brockton, Mass., 1961-62; psychology lectr. U. N.C., Chapel Hill, Greensboro, 1962-67; assoc. dir. driver studies Hwy. Safety Rsch. Ctr. U. N.C., Chapel Hill, 1967-89, dir. Injury Prevention Rsch. Ctr., 1987-89; dir. Transp. Rsch. Inst. U. Mich., Ann Arbor, 1989—; bd. dirs. Intelligent Transp. Soc. Am., Washington, 1991—, Traffic Safety Assn. Mich., Lansing, 1991—; bd. advisors Eno Transp. Found., Inc., Landsdowne, Va., 1994—; chair group 5 coun. Transp. Rsch. Bd. of NRC, Washington, 1992-95, chmn. Task Force Operator Regulations, 1974-76, mem. study com. devel. ranking rail safety R&D projects, 1980-82, chmn. group 3 coun. operation, safety and maintenance transp. facilities, 1980-83, mem. IVHS-IDEA tech. rev. panel, 1993—, chair workshop human factors rsch. in hwy. safety, 1992, chair ad hoc com. environ. activies, 1992, mem. task force on elderly drivers, 1990-93, mem. com. vehicle user characteristics, 1983-86, mem. com. planning and adminstrn. of transp. safety, 1986-92, mem. com. alcohol, other drugs and transp., 1986—, numerous other coms., mem. spl. coms. including Inst. Medicine Dana Award com., 1986-90, com. of 55MPH nat. maximum speed limit, 1983-84; mem. motor vehicle safety rsch. adv. com. Dept. Transp., Washington, 1991—; reviewer JAMA, Jour. Studies on Alcohol, Jour. of Gerontology, Am. Jour. Pub. Health; apptd. Pres. Coun. Spinal Cord Injury, 1981; apptd. advisor Nat. Hwy. Safety Adv. Com. to Sec. U.S. Dept. Transp., 1979-80, 80-83; author numerous reports on transp. to govtl. coms. and univs. Author: (with Paul G. Shinkman) Instructor's Manual for Mogan and King: Introduction to Psychology, 1971; author: (with others) Psychological Concepts in the Classroom, 1974, Drinking: Alcohol in American Society—Issues and Current Research, 1978, The American Handbook of Alcoholism, 1982, The Role of the Civil Engineer in Highway Safety, 1983, Aging and Public Health, 1985, Young Driver Accidents: In Search of Solutions, 1985, Alcohol, Accidents and Injuries, 1986, Transportation in an Aging Society: Improving the Mobility and Safety for Older Persons, 1988, Young Drivers Impaired by Alcohol and Drugs, 1988; mem. editorial bd. Jour. Safety Rsch., 1979—; assoc. guest editor Health Edn. Quar., 1989; assoc. editor Accident, Analysis, and Prevention, 1978-84, mem. editorial bd., 1976-87; contbr. articles to profl. jours. Grantee HHS, 1982, 92, 93, NIH; named Widmark laureate Internat. Coun. Alcohol, Drugs and Traffic Safety, 1995. Mem. AAAS, APA (Harold M. Hildreth award 1993), APHA (injury control and emergency health svcs. sect., Disting. Career award 1994, transp. rsch. bd., Roy W. Crum award for rsch. contbns. 1995), Assn. for the Advancement of Automotive Medicine (chmn. human factors sect. 1978-80, bd. dirs. 1979-82, pres. 1981-82), Coun. Univ. Transp. Ctrs. (exec. com. 1991—), Transp. Rsch. Bd., Ea. Psychol. Assn., Sigma Xi. Democrat. Avocations: gardening, reading. Office: U Mich Transp Rsch Inst 2901 Baxter Rd Ann Arbor MI 48109-2150

WALLER, ROBERT JAMES, writer; b. Aug. 1, 1939; s. Robert Sr. and Ruth W.; m. Georgia Ann Wiedemeier; 1 child, Rachael. Student, U. Iowa, 1957-58, U. No. Iowa, 1958; PhD, Ind. U., 1968. Prof. mgmt. U. No. Iowa, Cedar Falls, 1968-91, dean bus. sch., 1979-85. Author: Just Beyond the Firelight: Stories & Essays, 1988, One Good Road is Enough: Essays, 1990, The Bridges of Madison County, 1992, Slow Waltz in Cedar Bend, 1993, Old Songs in a New Cafe: Selected Essays, 1994, Border Music, 1995; recorded album The Ballads of Madison County, 1993. Recipient Literary Lion award New York Public Library, 1993. Office: care Aaron Priest Literary Agy 708 3rd Ave 23rd Fl New York NY 10017

WALLER, ROBERT REX, ophthalmologist, educator, foundation executive; b. N.Y.C., Feb. 19, 1937; s. Madison Rex and Sally Elizabeth (Pearce) W.; m. Sarah Elizabeth Pickens, Dec. 27, 1963; children: Elizabeth, Katherine, Robert Jr. BA, Duke U., 1958; MD, U. Tenn., 1963. Diplomate Am. Bd. Ophthalmology (dir. 1982—, vice chmn. 1988-89, chmn. 1989—). Intern City of Memphis Hosps., 1963-64; resident internal medicine Mayo Grad. Sch. Medicine, Rochester, Minn., 1966-67, resident in ophthalmology, 1967-70, mem. faculty, 1970—; assoc. prof. ophthalmology Mayo Clinic, Rochester, Minn., 1974-78, prof., 1978—; chmn. dept. ophthalmology Mayo Med. Sch., Rochester, Minn., 1974-84, cons., 1970—, mem. bd. govs., 1978-93, chmn., 1988-93; trustee Mayo Found., Rochester, 1978—, pres., chief exec. officer, 1988—. Contbr. chpts. to books, articles to profl. jours. Elder 1st Presbyn. Ch., Rochester, 1975-78; mem. Rochester Task Force on Pub. Assembly Facilities, 1983-84. Sr. asst. surgeon USPHS, 1964-66. Ocuplastic surgery fellow U. Calif. San Francisco, 1973. Mem. AMA, Minn. State Med. Assn., Zumbro Valley Med. Assn., Am. Acad. Ophthalmology, Am. Ophthalmol. Soc., Am. Soc. Plastic and Reconstructive Surgery, Orbital Soc., Am. Soc. Ophthalmic Plastic and Reconstructive Surgery, Minn. Acad. Ophthalmology and Otolaryngology, Rochester Golf and Country Club, Augusta Nat. Golf Club, Alpha Omega Alpha, Delta Tau Delta. Presbyterian. Avocations: golf, travel, photography, dogs. Home: 800 12th Ave SW Rochester MN 55902-2071

WALLER, STEPHEN, air transportation executive; b. 1949. Student, New Zealand U., 1970-74. Courier, country mgr., european mktg. mgr. DHL Airways, Inc., London, 1975-80, Tehran, Iran, 1975-80; sr. v.p. DHL Airways, Inc., Redwood City, Calif., 1981—. Office: DHL Airways Inc 333 Twin Dolphin Dr Redwood City CA 94065-1401

WALLER, WILHELMINE KIRBY (MRS. THOMAS MERCER WALLER), civic worker, organization official; b. N.Y.C., Jan. 19, 1914; d. Gustavus Town and Wilhelmine (Claflin) Kirby; m. Thomas Mercer Waller, Apr. 7, 1942. Ed., Chapin Sch., N.Y.C. Conservation chmn. Garden Club Am., 1959-61, pres., 1965-68, chmn. nat. affairs, 1968-74, dir., 1969-71; mem. adv. com. N.Y. State Conservation Commn., 1959-70; mem. Nat. Adv. Com. Hwy. Beautification, 1965-68; trustee Mianus River Gorge Conservation Com. of Nature Conservancy, 1955—, Arthur W. Butler Meml. Sanctuary, 1955-79; dir. Westchester County Soil and Water Conservation Dist., 1967-74; adviser N.Y. Gov.'s Study Commn. Future of Adirondacks, 1968-70; adv. com. N.Y. State Parks and Recreation Commn., 1971-72; adv. com. to sec. state UN Conf. Human Environment, 1971-72; mem. Pres.'s Citizens Adv. Com. on Environ. Quality, 1974-78. Mem. planning bd., Bedford, 1953-57; mem. Conservation adv. coun., Bedford, N.Y., 1968-70, Westchester County Planning Bd., 1970-88; bd. govs. Nature Conservancy, 1970-78; Mem. Lyndhurst council Nat. Trust for Historic Preservation, 1965-74; bd. dirs. Scenic Hudson, Inc., 1985-88. Recipient Frances K. Hutchinson medal Garden Club Am., 1971, Holiday mag. award for beautiful Am., 1971, Conservation award Am. Motors Corp., 1975, Oak Leaf award Nature Conservancy, 1988. Mem. Nat. Soc. Colonial Dames, Huguenot Soc. Am., Daus. of Cincinnati. Address: Tanrackin Farm Bedford Hills NY 10507

WALLER, WILLIAM KENNETH, health physicist; b. Yazoo City, Miss., May 28, 1954; s. William Thomas and ruth Inez (Gary) W.; m. Gail Paige Knott, Aug. 11, 1979; children: Enid Michelle, William Charles. AA, Holmes C.C., Goodman, Miss., 1974; BS, Delta State U., Cleveland, Miss., 1976; Cert., Oak Ridge Assoc. U., 1977. Chief radioactive materials sect. Divsn. Radiol. Health, Miss. State Bd. Health, Jackson, 1976-80; from project mgr. to dir. waste mgmt. US Ecology, Inc., Louisville, 1980-90; sr. scientist Battelle Pacific NW Lab., Richland, Wash., 1990-91; tech. dir. environ. restoration and radiation svcs. Law Engrng. and Environ. Svcs., Inc., Kennesaw, Ga., 1991—. Co-author: Guidance Manual of REviewing RCRA and CERCLA Documentation, 1989, Comparative Review of U.S. DOE CERCLA Federal Facility Agreements, 1989; contbr. articles to profl. jours. Chmn. ops. stewards Summit Bapt. Ch., Kennesaw, 1994, 95; chmn. pers. stewards Towne View Bapt. Ch., Kennesaw, 1992. Mem. Am. Nuclear Soc., Am. Mgmt. Assn., Health Physics Soc., Internat. Soc. for Decontaimination/Decommissioning Profls. Avocations: golf, fishing, woodworking basketball. Home: 1073 Bostwick Rdg Woodstock GA 30189 Office: Law Engrng Environ Svcs 114 Townpark Dr Kennesaw GA 30144-5561

WALLERSTEIN, GEORGE, astronomy educator; b. N.Y.C., Jan. 13, 1930; s. Leo and Dorothy (Calman) W. B.A., Brown U., 1951; M.S., Calif. Inst. Tech., 1954, Ph.D., 1958. Research asso. Calif. Inst. Tech., Pasadena, 1957-58; instr. U. Calif., Berkeley, 1958-60; asst. prof. U. Calif., 1960-64, asso. prof., 1964-65; prof., chmn. astronomy U. Wash., Seattle, 1965-80; prof. astronomy U. Wash., 1980—. Trustee Brown U., Providence, 1975-80. Served with U.S. Navy, 1951-53. Mem. Am. Astron. Soc., Astron. Soc. Pacific, AAAS, Arctic Inst. N. Am. Home: 2309 NE 77th St Seattle WA 98115 Office: U Wash Astronomy Seattle WA 98195 *It is not sufficient "to follow knowledge like a sinking star, beyond the utmost bounds of human thought." One must endeavor to create knowledge, and beyond that to create understanding.*

WALLERSTEIN, MITCHEL BRUCE, government official; b. N.Y.C., Mar. 8, 1949; s. Melvin Julian and Rita Helen (Nomburg) W.; m. Susan Elyse Perlik, June 29, 1974; children: Matthew, Leah. AB, Dartmouth Coll., 1971; MPA, Syracuse U., 1972; MS, MIT, 1977, PhD, 1978. Assoc. dir. Internat. Food Policy Program MIT, Cambridge, Mass., 1978-83, lectr. dept. polit. sci., 1978-83; asst. prof. dept. polit. sci. Holy Cross Coll., Worcester, Mass., 1979-81; exec. dir. Office Internat. Affairs NAS, Washington, 1983-89; dep. exec. officer NAS, Washington, 1989-93; dep. asst. sec. for counter-proliferation policy U.S. Dept. Def., Washington, 1993—; adj. prof. Sch. Advanced Internat. Studies, Johns Hopkins U., Washington, 1992—; adj. prof. Sch. Fgn. Svc., Georgetown U., Washington, 1989-93. Author: Food for War - Food for Peace: The Politics of U.S. Food Aid, 1979; author, dir. reports in field including multiple NAS reports on tech. transfer and nat. security. Mem. AAAS, Internat. Inst. Strategic Studies, Coun. Fgn. Rels. Democrat. Office: US Dept Def Rm 4B 856 The Pentagon Washington DC 20301-2600

WALLERSTEIN, RALPH OLIVER, physician; b. Dusseldorf, Germany, Mar. 7, 1922; came to U.S., 1938, naturalized, 1944; s. Otto R. and Ilse (Hollander) W.; m. Betty Ane Christensen, June 21, 1952; children: Ralph Jr., Richard, Ann. A.B., U. Calif., Berkeley, 1943; M.D., U. Calif., San Francisco, 1945. Diplomate: Am. Bd. Internal Medicine. Intern San Francisco Hosp., 1945-46, resident, 1948-49; resident U. Calif. Hosp., San Francisco, 1949-50; research fellow Thorndike Meml. Lab., Boston City Hosp., 1950-52; chief clin. hematology San Francisco Gen. Hosp., 1953-87; faculty U. Calif., San Francisco, 1952—; clin. prof. medicine U. Calif., 1969—. Served to capt. M.C. AUS, 1946-48. Mem. AMA, ACP (gov. 1977-87, chmn. bd. govs. 1980-81, regent 1981-87, pres. 1988-89), Am. Soc. Hematology (pres. 1978), San Francisco Med. Soc., Am. Clin. and Climatol. Assn., Am. Fedn. Clin. Rsch., Am. Soc. Internal Medicine, Am. Bd. Internal Medicine (bd. govs. 1975-83, chmn. 1982-83), Am. Assn. Blood Banks, Inst. Medicine, Calif. Acad. Medicine, Internat. Soc. Hematology, Western Soc. Clin. Rsch., Western Assn. Physicians, Gold Headed Cane Soc. Republican. Home: 3447 Clay St San Francisco CA 94118-2008 Office: 3838 California St Rm 707 San Francisco CA 94118-1509

WALLERSTEIN, ROBERT SOLOMON, psychiatrist; b. Berlin, Jan. 28, 1921; s. Lazar and Sarah (Guensberg) W.; m. Judith Hannah Saretsky, Jan. 26, 1947; children—Michael Jonathan, Nina Beth, Amy Lisa. B.A., Columbia, 1941, M.D., 1944; postgrad., Topeka Inst. Psychoanalysis, 1951-58. Assoc. dir., then dir. rsch. Menninger Found., Topeka, 1954-66; chief psychiatry Mt. Zion Hosp., San Francisco, 1966-78; tng. and supervising analyst San Francisco Psychoanalytic Inst., 1966—; clin. prof. U. Calif. Sch. Medicine, Langley-Porter Neuropsychiat. Inst., 1967-75, prof., chmn. dept. psychiatry, also dir. inst., 1975-85, prof. dept. psychiatry, 1985-91, prof. emeritus, 1991—; vis. prof. psychiatry La. State U. Sch. Medicine, also New Orleans Psychoanalytic Inst., 1972-73, Pahlavi U., Shiraz, Iran, 1977, Fed. U. Rio Grande do Sul, Porto Alegre, Brasil, 1980; mem., chmn. rsch. scientist career devel. com. NIMH, 1966-70; fellow Ctr. Advanced Study Behavioral Scis., Stanford, Calif., 1964-65, 81-82, Rockefeller Found. Study Ctr., Bellagio, Italy, 1992. Author 14 books and monographs; mem. editl. bd. 19 profl. jours; contbr. over 230 articles to profl. jours. Served with AUS, 1946-48. Recipient Heinz Hartmann award N.Y. Psychoanalytic Inst., 1968, Disting. Alumnus award Menninger Sch. Psychiatry, 1972, J. Elliott Royer award U. Calif., San Francisco, 1973, Outstanding Achievement award No. Calif. Psychiat. Soc., 1987, Mt. Airy gold medal, 1990, Mary Singleton Sigourney award, 1991. Fellow ACP, Am. Psychiat. Assn., Am. Orthopsychiat. Assn.; mem. Am. Psychoanlytic Assn. (pres. 1971-72), Internat. Psychoanalytic Assn. (v.p. 1977-85, pres. 1985-89), Group for Advancement Psychiatry, Brit. Psycho-Analytical Soc. (hon.), Phi Beta Kappa, Alpha Omega Alpha. Home: 290 Beach Rd Belvedere CA 94920-2472 Office: 655 Redwood Hwy Ste 261 Mill Valley CA 94941-3011

WALLESTAD, PHILIP WESTON, retired business owner; b. Madison, Wis., May 14, 1922; s. John Oscar and Dorothy Francis (White) W.; BA, U. Wis., 1947, MD, 1954; m. Edith Stolle, Jan. 15, 1949 (div. Mar. 1967); children: Kristin Eve, Ingrid Birgitta, Erika Ann; m. 2d, Muriel Annette Moen, June 22, 1968; children: Thomas John, Scott Philip. Intern, Calif. Luth. Hosp., L.A., 1954, resident in surgery, 1955-56; pvt. practice medicine, Fredonia and Port Washington Wis., 1957-72, Libby, Mont., 1972-74; staff physician VA Hosp., Fort Harrison, Mont., 1974-77, Tomah, Wis., 1977-78, VA Hosp., Iron Mountain, Mich., 1978-88, ret., 1989; owner Wallestad's Arms, mil. antique collectables store, Sturgeon Bay, Wis., 1989-95, ret., 1995. Mem. Conservative Caucus. Served with AUS, 1943-46; ETO; lt. col. USAF Res., 1979-82. Mem. NRA, DAV, VFW, Am. Legion, Air Force Assn., Conservative Caucus, Res. Officers Assn., Sons of Norway, Coun. for Inter-Am. Security, U. Wis. Alumni Assn., Nat. W Club, Rotary. Republican. Presbyterian Ch. (elder). Home: 443 N 12th Ave Sturgeon Bay WI 54235-1313

WALLEY, ANNE, federal official. Dep. asst. to pres., co-dir. scheduling & advance Exec. Office of Pres., 1995—. Office: Presdl Scheduling & Advance 1600 Pennsylvania Ave NW Washington DC 20500*

WALLEY, BYRON See CARD, ORSON SCOTT

WALLFESH, HENRY MAURICE, business communications company executive, editor, writer; b. N.Y.C., June 15, 1937; s. David Shibe and Rose (Silk) W.; m. Suzanne Krakowitch, Dec. 26, 1960; children: Saundra Kay, Gerald Bruce. Grad. indsl. and labor rels., Cornell U., 1958. Editor, co-pub. Indsl. Rels. News, N.Y.C. and Stamford, Conn., 1960-67; pres., chief exec. officer RAI div. Hearst Bus. Communications, N.Y.C., 1968-91, sr. v.p., editor at large, 1991; pres. Whale Communications, Inc., Stamford, Conn., 1992—; pres. Indsl. Rels. Inst., Stamford, 1964-67; founder, bd. dirs. Internat. Soc. Pre-Retirement Planners, 1975-88; bd. dirs. VSOP Mktg., Boston. Author: Implications of the Age Discrimination in Employment, 1977, When a CEO Retires, 1978. Bd. dirs. Aging in Am., N.Y.C., 1985-90, N.Y.C. Anti-Defamation League, 1987-89; mem. alumni bd. dirs. Cornell Inst. Labor Rels., 1995—. Capt. inf. USAR, 19658-67. Recipient Corp. Achievement award Nat. Assn. for Sr. Living Industries, 1990; inducted into Internat. Soc. Pre-Retirement Planners Hall of Fame, 1988. Mem. Roxbury Swim and Tennis Club (bd. dirs. 1975-78), Cornell Club. Jewish. Avocations: tennis, theatre, writing. Home and Office: 1616 Long Ridge Rd Stamford CT 06903-3902

WALLIN, FRANKLIN WHITTELSEY, educational consultant, former college president; b. Grand Rapids, Mich., Jan. 22, 1925; s. Franklin Whittelsey and Agnes (Sarles) W.; m. Florence Gilbert Evans, Feb. 21, 1948; children: Susan Q. (Mrs. Ray Michael Hively), Thomas E., Elizabeth W. (Mme. Henri Sirot), Franklin B. B.S., U. Wis., 1948; M.A., U. Calif. at Berkeley, 1950, Ph.D., 1953; DHL (hon.), Haverford Coll., 1983, Earlham Coll., 1987. From instr. to assoc. prof. history Wayne State U., 1953-68, asst. to pres., 1958-60; provost, dean faculty Colgate U., 1968-73, acting pres., 1969; pres. Inst. for World Order (now World Policy Inst.), 1973-74, bd. dirs., 1972-90; pres. Earlham Coll., Richmond, Ind., 1974-83; resident scholar Inter-Univ. Centre, Dubrovnik, Yugoslavia, 1983-84; pres. Asheville (N.C.) Art Mus., 1993—; planning cons. Franklin Coll., Lugano, Switzerland, 1985; co-dir. Nat. Commn. Global Edn., 1986-87; vis. prof. Earlham Coll., 1987; prof. Coll. for Srs., adj. prof. dept. humanities U. N.C., Asheville. Bd. dirs. Friends Sch., Detroit, 1962-68, chmn., 1962-64, 67-68; bd. dirs. Global Perspectives in Edn. (now Am. Forum), 1976—, Joyce Mertz-Gilmore Found., 1982—, Asheville Art Mus., 1992—, Community Arts Coun., Asheville, 1990—. With USN, 1942-46. Mem. Am. Coun. on Edn. (dir. 1978-81), Nat. Assn. Ind. Colls. and Univs. (dir. 1981-83). Home: 1 Ladyslipper Rd Weaverville NC 28787-9780 Office: Asheville Art Mus 2 S Pack Sq Asheville NC 28801

WALLIN, JACK ROBB, research plant pathology educator; b. Omaha, Nov. 21, 1915; s. Carl O.A. (Wallin) and Elizabeth Josephine (Smith) W.; m. Janet Mary Melhus, Sept. 25, 1937; children: Jack I.M., Robb M. B.S., Iowa State U., 1939, Ph.D., 1944. Rsch. asst. prof. Iowa State U., Ames, 1944-47; rsch. prof., rsch. plant pathologist Agr. Rsch. Svc. USDA/Iowa State U., 1947-75; prof. plant pathology, researcher Agrl. Rsch. Svc. USDA/ U. Mo., Columbia, 1975-87; ret., 1986; disaster assistance employee region 7 Fed. Emergency Mgmt. Agy., Kansas City, 1989—; U.S. rep. World Meteorol. Orgn., Geneva, 1959-61; mem. aeriobiology com. Nat. Acad. Sci., NRC, Washington, 1976-80. Patentee (in field). Recipient 1st Peterson award Internat. Soc. Biometeorology, 1966. Mem. Internat. Assn. Aerobiology, Am. Phytopathol. Soc. (sec. treas. N. Central div. 1964-65), Internat. Soc. Plant Pathology, Mo. Acad. Sci. (chmn. agrl. div. 1976-81). Republican. Presbyterian. Lodge: Rotary. Home: 4036 Fletcher Blvd Ames IA 50010 *My genetic constitution must be basically responsible for those talents and abilities that have been expressed in any success that I have attained. Along with reasonable intelligence, I have been endowed with determination, tenacity and loyalty in the desire to achieve set goals. A sense of humor has enabled me to survive mistakes and failures. An agricultural scientist father-in-law inspired me to make a useful contribution to mankind. A supportive wife provided encouragement along the way. Always remember to dedicate your life to helping others less fortunate, we pass this way but once!.*

WALLIN, LELAND DEAN, artist, educator; b. Sioux Falls, S.D., Oct. 14, 1942; s. Clarence Forrest and Leona Mae (McInnis) W.; m. Meredith Maria Hawkins, Mar. 26, 1977; 1 child, Jessica Hawkins. Student, Columbus Coll. Art and Design, 1961-62; BFA in Painting, Kansas City (Mo.) Art Inst., 1965; MFA in Painting, U. Cin. and Cin. Art Acad., 1967. Prof., coord. drawing St. Cloud (Minn.) State U., 1967-86; prof. Queens Coll., CUNY, Flushing, 1983-84; prof., coord. MFA painting Marywood Coll., Scranton, Pa., 1985-90; assoc. prof. painting and drawing East Carolina U., Greenville, N.C., 1993—; lectr. Carnegie-Mellon U., Pitts., 1988; juror Belin Arts Grant Com., Waverly, Pa., 1989; curator Philip Pearlstein Retrospective Exhibit, Scranton, 1988; vis. prof. painting East Carolina U., Greenville, N.C., 1992-93; judge/juror No. Nat. Art Competition, 1993. One man shows include Mpls. Coll. Art and Design, 1978, Harold Reed Gallery, 1983, Gallery Henoch, N.Y.C., 1991, others; group shows at The Bklyn. Mus., 1979, Greenville County Mus. of Art, 1983, The Mus. of Modern Art, 1993, Huntsville Mus. Art, 1994, Sacramento Fine Arts Ctr. Internat., 1995, Salon Internat., 1994, San Bernardino County Mus. Internat., Calif., 1995; represented in permanent collections N.Y.C. Gallery, Gallery Henoch, 1986—; contbr. articles to profl. jours. Named Outstanding Tchr., East Carolina U., 1994, 95; recipient numerous rsch. awards East Carolina U., 1992—. Mem. Coll. Art Assn. Am., Pa. Soc. Watercolor Painters. Home and Studio: 218 York Rd Greenville NC 27858

WALLIN, WINSTON ROGER, manufacturing company executive; b. Mpls., Mar. 6, 1926; s. Carl A. and Theresa (Hegge) W.; m. Maxine Houghton, Sept. 10, 1949; children: Rebecca, Brooks, Lance, Bradford. BBA, U. Minn., 1948. With Pillsbury Co., Mpls., 1948-85, v.p. commodity ops., 1971-76, exec. v.p., 1976, pres., chief oper. officer, 1977-84, vice chmn. bd., 1984-85; with Medtronic, Inc., Mpls., 1985-91, chmn. bd., CEO, chmn. bd., 1991—; bd. dirs. Bemis Co., McGlynn Bakeries, SuperValu, Cargill, Inc. Chmn. bd. trustees Carleton Coll.; bd. overseers U. Minn. Bus. Sch.; chmn. Caux (Switzerland) Round Table. With USN, 1944-46. Mem. Mpls. Club, Minikahda Club, Interlachen Club. Home: 7022 Tupa Cir Minneapolis MN 55439-1640 Office: Medtronic Inc 7000 Central Ave NE Minneapolis MN 55432-3568

WALLING, CHEVES THOMSON, chemistry educator; b. Evanston, Ill., Feb. 28, 1916; s. Willoughby George and Frederika Christina (Haskell) W.; m. Jane Ann Wilson, Sept. 17, 1940; children—Hazel, Rosalind, Cheves, Janie, Barbara. A.B., Harvard, 1937; Ph.D., U. Chgo., 1939. Rsch. chemist E.I. duPont de Nemours, 1939-43, U.S. Rubber Co., 1943-49; tech. aide Office Sci. Research, Washington, 1945; sr. rsch. assoc. Lever Bros. Co., 1949-52; prof. chemistry Columbia U., N.Y.C., 1952-69; Disting. prof. chemistry U. Utah, Salt Lake City, 1970-91, prof. chemistry emeritus, 1991—. Author: Free Radicals in Solution, 1957, Fifty Years of Free Radicals, 1995; also numerous articles. Fellow AAAS; mem. Nat. Acad. Scis., Am. Acad. Arts and Scis., Am. Chem. Soc. (editor jour. 1975-81, James Flack Norris award 1970, Lubrizol award 1984). Home: PO Box 537 Jaffrey NH 03452-0537

WALLINGFORD, DANA R(IO), financial consultant; b. Long Beach, Calif., Jan. 19, 1948; s. Richard Keller and Faith (Gribell) W.; m. Susan C. Kollmar, Oct. 21, 1978; children: Sidney Miller, Melissa Miller. BA in Bus. Adminstrn., U. Wash., 1971. Cert. fin. mgr., 1988, comml. underwater diver. Comml. underwater diver Seattle, 1975-76; asst. mgr. loss prevention Seattle Stevedore Co., Seattle, 1976-78; asst. mgr. loading ops. Sea Star Stevedore Co., Anchorage, 1978-80; asst. v.p. pvt. client group Merrill Lynch, Anchorage, 1981-87; v.p. pvt. client group Merrill Lynch, Phoenix, Ariz., 1987—; charter mem. Master Network, Merrill Lynch, Phoenix, 1990—, mem. Chmn.'s Club, 1992, 93, 94; charter founding mem. Phoenix Forum, 1994—. Com. mem. Fiesta Bowl, Tempe, Ariz., 1987-94; charter mem. Anchorage Sr. Ctr. Endowment, 1985-86; mem. Sheriff's Posse, Maricopa County, Ariz., 1994—. Capt. U.S. Army, 1971-75. Mem. Mason (Master, Phonecia # 58, sgt. at arms 1992-93), El Zaribah Temple (Shrine Noble 1992—), U. Wash. Alumni Assn. (geographic coord. Ariz. chpt., chmn. 1992—), Rotary Internat. (Paul Harris fellow 1986). Republican. Avocations: horseback riding, scuba diving, classic car collecting, hiking, traveling. Office: Merrill Lynch # 300 2525 E Camelback Rd Ste 300 Phoenix AZ 85016-4225

WALLINGFORD, JOHN RUFUS, lawyer; b. Artesia, N.Y., Apr. 6, 1940; s. Joseph Keevil and Ellen (Williams) W.; m. Katharine Tapers, July 22, 1966; children: Halley Martha, John Beckett. BA, U. of the South, 1962; LLB, So. Meth. U., 1965. Bar: Tex. 1965. Sr. ptnr. Fulbright & Jaworski, Houston, 1967-93; sr. v.p., gen. counsel Browning Ferris Industries, Houston, 1994—. Bd. dirs. St. Luke's Episcopal Hosp., Houston, 1986—, The Children's Mus., Houston, 1994—. Fellow Am. Coll. Trial Lawyers; mem. Internat. Soc. of Barristers, Am. Bd. Trial Advocates. Office: Browning Ferris Industries 757 N Eldridge Pky Houston TX 77079-4435*

WALLIS, CARLTON LAMAR, librarian; b. Blue Springs, Miss., Oct. 15, 1915; s. William Ralph and Tellie (Jones) W.; m. Mary Elizabeth Cooper, Feb. 22, 1944; 1 child, Carlton Lamar. B.A. with spl. distinction, Miss. Coll., 1936; M.A., Tulane U., 1946; B.L.S., U. Chgo., 1947; L.H.D., Rhodes Coll., Memphis, 1980. English tchr., coach Miss. Pub. Schs., 1936-41; teaching fellow Miss. Coll. and Tulane U., 1941-42; chief librarian Rosenberg Library, Galveston, Tex., 1947-55; city librarian Richmond, Va., 1955-58; dir. Memphis Pub. Library, 1958-80, ret., 1980. Author: Libraries in the Golden Triangle, 1966; contbr. articles to library jours. Trustee Belhaven Coll., 1978-82, Nat. Ornamental Metal Mus., 1989—. Served as chief warrant officer AUS, 1942-46. Decorated Bronze Star. Mem. ALA (chmn. library mgmt. sect. 1969-71), Pub. Library Assn. (dir. 1973-77), Tex. Library Assn. (pres. 1952-53), Va. Library Assn., Southwestern Library Assn. (exec. bd. 1950-55), Southeastern Library Assn. (chmn. pub. library sect. 1960-62), Tenn. Library Assn. (pres. 1969-70, Distinguished Service award 1979). Presbyterian (elder). Club: Egyptian (pres. 1973-74). Home: 365 Kenilworth Pl Memphis TN 38112-5405

WALLIS, DIANA LYNN, artistic director; b. Windsor, Eng., Dec. 11, 1946; d. Dennis Blackwell and Joan Williamson (Gatcombe) W. Grad., Royal Ballet Sch., Eng., 1962-65. Dancer Royal Ballet Touring Co., London, 1965-68; ballet mistress Royal Ballet Sch., London, 1969-81, dep. ballet prin., 1981-84; artistic coord. Nat. Ballet of Can., Toronto, 1984-86, assoc. artistic dir., 1986-87, co-artistic dir., 1987-89; free-lance prod., tchr. London; dep. artistic dir. English Nat. Ballet, London, 1990-94; artistic dir. Royal Acad. Dancing, 1994—. Fellow Imperial Soc. Tchrs. Dancing. Home: 41 Musard Rd, London W68NR, England

WALLIS, DONALD WILLS, lawyer; b. Wilkes-Barre, Pa., Aug. 22, 1950; s. Donald and Hazel (Jansen) W.; m. Kathryn Macon Waggoner, Aug. 28, 1971; children: Neill Jansen, Kathryn Spencer. AB, Duke U., 1971, JD, 1974. Bar: Fla. 1974, U.S. Tax Ct. 1975, U.S. Dist. Ct. (mid. dist.) Fla. 1977, U.S. Ct. Appeals (5th cir.) 1978, U.S. Claims Ct. 1978, U.S. Supreme Ct. 1979. Assoc. Mahoney, Hadlow, Chambers & Adams, Jacksonville, Fla., 1974-78; mem. firm Fisher, Tousey & Wallis, P.A., Jacksonville, Fla., 1978-89; ptnr. Holland & Knight, Jacksonville, Fla., 1989—. Co-author: Bank Holding Companies: A Practical Guide to Bank Acquisitions and mergers, 1978; tax notes editor: The Florida Probate System, 1977; contbg. editor Jour. Partnership Taxation, 1989-95. Chmn. Duke U. Alumni Admissions Adv. Com., Jacksonville, 1986—; chmn. Beaches Fine Arts Series, Inc., Jacksonville Beach, Fla., 1990—. Mem. ABA (taxation sect.), Fla. Bar (tax sect., bd. cert. tax atty.), Jacksonville Bar Assn. (tax sect.), Duke U. Alumni assn. (admissions com. 1986—), Selva Marina Country Club, Inc. (bd. govs. 1987-89). Episcopalian. Avocations: Jacksonville symphony chorus, sailing, scuba diving, backpacking, cycling. Office: Holland & Knight 50 N Laura St Ste 3900 Jacksonville FL 32202-3622

WALLIS, GRAHAM BLAIR, engineer, educator; b. Rugby, Warwickshire, Eng., Apr. 1, 1936; came to U.S., 1957; s. Alfred Stanley and Dora (Fleming) W.; m. Suzanne Harriet White, Sept. 12, 1959; children: Iain, Tasha, Peter, Jeremy. B.A., Cambridge U., Eng., 1957; Ph.D., Cambrige U., Eng., 1961; M.S., MIT, 1959. Registered profl. engr., N.H. Asst. prof. Dartmouth Coll., Hanover, N.H., 1962-65, assoc. prof., 1966-72, prof., 1972—, assoc. dean, 1989-93; prof. engring. Sherman Fairchild, 1991—; interim dean engring., 1994-95; cons. Creare Inc., Hanover, 1964—. Author: One-Dimensional Two-Phase Flow, 1959. Recipient Inst. Mech. Engring. Ludwig Mond prize, 1962, Fluids Engineering awardAm. Soc. of Mechanical Engineers, 1994. Mem. ASME (Moody award 1971, Centennial award and medal 1980, Fluids Engring. award 1994). Home: Blood Rd Norwich VT 05055 Office: Dartmouth Coll Thayer Dept of Engring Sch Hanover NH 03755

WALLIS, JOHN JAMES (JIMMY WALLIS), entertainer, ventriloquist, video production executive; b. Searcy, Ark., Mar. 21, 1939; s. Prentiss Bascom and Maxine (James) W.; children: Lori Diana Wallis Waterman, Shauna Kathleen. Grad., Okla. U., 1960. advisor Am. Acad. for Entertainment at U.S. Vets. Hosps., N.Y.C., 1988—. Nat. TV debut Art Linkletter's Hollywood Talent Scouts, 1966; entertained troops in S.E. Asia, 1967-70; performed with Ann Murray, Lou Rawls, Lola Falana, Ben Vereen, Al Hirt, Debbie Reynolds, Rip Taylor, Suzanne Somers, others; performed in numerous clubs including Tropicana, Las Vegas, The Sahara, Las Vegas, The Flamingo, Las Vegas, Chauteau Champlain, Montreal, The Cave, Vancouver, The Paradise Island Casino, The Bahamas, The Superstar Theater, Atlantic City, Riviera, Las Vegas, Harrah's, Reno, The Reno Hilton, Las Vegas Hilton, Flamingo Hilton; featured in Royal Caribbean Cruise Lines, Premier's Disney Theme Cruises, Norwegian Cruise Lines, Holland Am. and Celebrity Cruise Lines. Named Okla.'s Top Comedian, Okla. Ho. of Reps.; recipient Am. Legion medal. Mem. Internat. Platform Assn., Nat. Park and Conservation Assn., Planetary Soc., Nat. Space Soc., Smithsonian Assocs. Presbyterian. Avocations: photography, scuba diving, computers, tennis, target shooting. Office: PO Box 276100 Boca Raton FL 33427-6100

WALLIS, RICHARD FISHER, physicist, educator; b. Washington, May 14, 1924; s. William F. and Alberta (Sigelen) W.; m. Mary Camilla Williams, Aug. 20, 1955; children: Maria Fisher, Sylvia Camilla. BS, George Washington U., 1945, MS, 1948; PhD, Cath. U. Am., 1952. Postdoctoral fellow (U. Md.), College Park, 1951-53; chemist Applied Physics Lab. Johns Hopkins U., Silver Spring, Md., 1953-56; physicist Naval Rsch. Lab., Washington, 1956-66, 67-69, head semiconductors br., 1958-66, 67-69; prof. physics U. Calif., Irvine, 1966-67, 69—; prof. emeritus, 1993—; chmn. dept. physics U. Calif., Irvine, 1972-75, 80-83; cons. Gen. Motors, Naval Rsch. Lab.; vis. prof. U. Paris, 1975-76, 79, 85. Author: (with Maradudin and Dobrzynski) Handbook of Surfaces and Interfaces, 1980, (with Balkanski) Many-Body Aspects of Solid State Spectroscopy, 1986; editor: Lattice Dynamics, 1965, Localized Excitations in Solids, 1968 (with Stegeman) Electromagnetic Surface Excitations, 1986, (with Birman and Sebenne) Elementary Excitations in Solids, 1992; contbr. articles to profl. jours. Served with U.S. Army, 1945-46. Recipient Pure Sci. award Naval Rsch. Lab., 1964, Disting. Alumni Achievement award George Washington U., 1991. Fellow Am. Phys. Soc., AAAS; mem. Philos. Soc. Washington, Phi Beta Kappa, Sigma Xi. Home: 2635 Alta Vista Dr Newport Beach CA 92660-4102 Office: U Calif Dept Physics Irvine CA 92717

WALLIS, RICHARD JAMES, lawyer; b. Hagerstown, Md., June 24, 1954; s. O. Lee and Teresa Marie (Rigley) W.; m. Leslie Wallis; children: Rory Evan, Rebecca Erin, Ryan Christopher. BA magna cum laude, Duquesne U., 1976; JD magna cum laude, U. Pitts., 1979. Bar: Wash. 1979, U.S. Dist. Ct. (we. dist.) Wash. 1979, U.S. Ct. Appeals (9th cir.) 1982, U.S. Supreme Ct. 1985. Assoc. Bogle & Gates, P.L.L.C., Seattle, 1979-86, mem., 1987—; CEO Bogle & Gates, P.L.L.C., 1993—. Author: (with others) Antitrust Counselling and Litigation Techniques, 1984; editor Washington Antitrust Law Developments, 1985 and Washington Antitrust Law Developments, 2d edit. 1988. Mem. ABA (antitrust sect. coun. 1995—, chair pvt. lit. com. 1992-95), Fed. Bar Assn. of Western Dist. Wash. (pres. 1990-91), Wash. State Bar Assn. (exec. com. 1987—, chmn. antitrust sect. 1989-90, disciplinary bd. mem. 1994—, vice chmn. 1995—). Democrat. Roman Catholic. Clubs: Tyee (Knight Inlet, B.C.), Sahalee Golf and Country, Columbia Tower (Seattle), Washington Athletic. Avocations: hiking, climbing, fly fishing, golf. Office: Bogle & Gates Two Union Sq 601 Union St Seattle WA 98101-2327

WALLIS, ROBERT RAY, psychologist, entrepreneur; b. Hardwood, Okla., Sept. 1, 1927; s. Walter William and Osie Oma (Luckett) W.; m. Joan Elaine Martino, Sept. 10, 1955; children: Rosalie, Glenn, Damon, Gina, Darren. Student, Southwestern Inst. Tech., 1945; B.A., U. Okla., 1951, Ed.M., 1960, Ph.D., 1963. Lic. psychologist, Pa., N.J. From psychology intern to dir. div. psychology Greater Kansas City Mental Health Found., 1962-71; from fellow to chief psychologist Western Mo. Mental Health Center, Kansas City, 1965-71; from program dir. to exec. dir. Horizon House Inc., Phila., 1971-79; chief exec. officer Ancora Psychiat. Hosp., Hammonton, N.J., 1979-81; individual practice clin. and cons. psychology, Medford, N.J., 1981—; propr. Wallis Printing Ctr., Phila., 1984-91; clin. supr. Alcoholism and Psychotherapy Assocs., Medford, N.J., 1985—, Middlesex Counseling Assocs., Cranbury, N.J., 1985-89; from asst. prof. to chmn. div. psychology dept. psychiatry, U. Mo., Kansas City Sch. Medicine, 1965-71. Contbr. articles to profl. jours. Served with USNR, 1945-46. Mem. Am. Psychol. Assn. Home and Office: 32 Schoolhouse Dr Medford NJ 08055-9209 *Treat each person with respect and dignity, without regard to rank or power.*

WALLIS, W(ILSON) ALLEN, economist, educator, statistician; b. Phila., Nov. 5, 1912; s. Wilson Dallam and Grace Steele (Allen) W.; m. Anne Armstrong, Oct. 5, 1935 (dec. Oct. 1994); children: Nancy Wallis Ingling, Virginia Wallis Cates. AB, U. Minn., 1932, postgrad., 1932-33; postgrad. fellow, U. Chgo., 1933-35, Columbia U., 1935-36; DSc, Hobart and William Smith Colls., 1973; LLD, Roberts Wesleyan Coll., 1973, U. Rochester, 1984; LHD, Grove City Coll., 1975; D of Social Scis., Francisco Marroquin U., Guatemala, 1992. Economist Nat. Resources Com., 1935-37; instr. econs. Yale U., 1937-38; asst. to assoc. prof. econs. Stanford U., 1938-46; Carnegie rsch. assoc. Nat. Bur. Econ. Rsch., 1939-40, 41; dir. war rsch. Statis. Rsch. Group Columbia U., 1942-46; prof. stats. and econs. U. Chgo., 1946-62, chmn. dept. stats., 1949-57, dean Grad. Sch. Bus., 1956-62; pres. (title later chancellor) U. Rochester, N.Y., 1962-82; under sec. for econ. affairs U.S. Dept. State, Washington, 1982-89; resident scholar Am. Enterprise Inst., Washington, 1989—; staff Ford Found., 1953-54; fellow Ctr. for Advanced Study in Behavioral Scis., 1956-57. mem. math. div. NRC, 1958-60; bd. dir. Nat. Bur. Econ. Rsch., 1953-74; spl. asst. Pres. Eisenhower, 1959-61; pres. Nat. Commn. Study of Nursing and Nursing Edn., 1967-70; chmn. Commn. Presdl. Scholars, 1969-78; mem. Pres.'s Commn. on All-Vol. Armed Force, 1969-70; chmn. Pres.'s Commn. Fed. Stats., 1970-71; mem. Nat. Coun. Ednl. Rsch., 1973-75; chmn. Adv. Coun. Social Security, 1974-75; bd. dirs. Corp. Pub. Broadcasting, 1975-78, chmn., 1977-78. Author: (with others) Consumer Expenditures in the United States, 1939, A Significance Test for Time Series and Other Ordered Observations, 1941, Sequential Analysis of Statistical Data: Applications, 1945, Techniques of Statistical Analysis, 1947, Sampling Inspection, 1948, Acceptance Sampling, 1950, Statistics: A New Approach, 1956, The Nature of Statistics, 1962, Welfare Programs: An Economic Appraisal, 1968; An Overgoverned Society, 1976; co-compiler: The Ethics of Competition and Other Essays by Frank H. Knight, 1935; chmn. editorial adv. bd.: Internat. Ency. Social Scis., 1960-68; contbr. articles to profl. jours. Trustee Tax Found., 1961-82, chmn. bd., 1972-75, chmn. exec. com., 1975-78; bd. overseers Hoover Instn. War, Revolution and Peace, 1972-78; trustee Eisenhower Coll., 1969-79, Nat. Opinion Rsch. Ctr., 1957-62, 64-68, Com. Econ. Devel., 1965-71, Colgate Rochester Div. Sch., 1963-82, Ctr. Govtl. Rsch., Inc., 1962-82, Internat. Mus. Photography at George Eastman House, 1963-82, Robert A. Taft Inst. Govt., 1973-77, Ethics and Pub. Policy Ctr., 1980-82, 89—; mem. Com. on the Present Danger, 1980-82, 1989-92; chmn. bd. overseers Ctr. Naval Analyses, 1967-82. Recipient Sec.'s Disting. Svc. award Dept. of State, Washington, 1988. Fellow Am. Soc. Quality Control, Inst. Math. Stats., Am. Statis. Assn. (editor Jour. 1950-59, pres. 1965, Wilks medal 1980), Am. Acad. Arts and Scis.; mem. Am. Econ. Assn. (exec. com. 1962-64), Rochester C. of C. (trustee 1963-68, 70-75), Mont Pelerin Soc. (treas. 1949-54), Washington Inst. Fgn. Affairs, Cosmos Club (Washington), Bohemian Club (San Francisco), Phi Beta Kappa, Chi Phi, Beta Gamma Sigma. Office: Am Enterprise Inst 1150 17th St NW Washington DC 20036-4603

WALLISON, FRIEDA K., lawyer; b. N.Y.C., Jan. 15, 1943; d. Ruvin H. and Edith (Landes) Koslow; m. Peter J. Wallison, Nov. 24, 1966; children: Ethan S., Jeremy L., Rebecca K. AB, Smith Coll., 1963; LLB, Harvard U., 1966. Bar: N.Y. 1967, DC 1982. Assoc. Carter, Ledyard & Milburn, N.Y.C., 1966-75; spl. counsel, div. market regulation Securities & Exchange Commn., Washington, 1975; exec. dir., gen. counsel Mcpl. Securities Rulemaking Bd., Washington, 1975-78; ptnr. Rogers & Wells, N.Y.C. and Washington, 1978-83; ptnr. Jones, Day, Reavis & Pogue, N.Y.C., and Washington, 1983—; mem. Govtl. Acctg. Standards Adv. Council, Washington, 1984-90, Nat. Council on Pub. Works Improvement, Washington, 1985-88; mem. environ. fin. adv. bd. EPA. Fellow Am. Bar Found.; mem. Nat. Assn. Bond Lawyers, N.Y.C. Bar Assn. Contbr. articles to profl. jours. Office: Jones Day Reavis & Pogue 1450 G St NW Ste 600 Washington DC 20005-2088

WALLMAN, CHARLES JAMES, historian; b. Kiel, Wis., Feb. 19, 1924; s. Charles A. and Mary Ann (Loftus) W.; m. Charline Marie Moore, June 14, 1952; children: Stephen, Jeffrey, Susan, Patricia, Andrew. Student Marquette U., 1942-43, Tex. Coll. Mines, 1943-44; BBA, U. Wis., 1949. Sales promotion mgr. Brandt, Inc., Watertown, Wis., 1949-65, v.p., 1960-70, exec. v.p., 1970-80, v.p. corp. devel., 1980-83, past dir.; written formal paper to the inst. "The 48ers of Watertown", presented orally at Symposium U. Wis.-Madison (Inst. for German-Am. Studies), 1986, written formal paper "Business, Industry and the German Press in Early Watertown, Wis., 1853-65", presented orally at symposium U. Wis.-Madison Inst. for German-Am. Studies, 1987; guest speaker dept. German, U. Wis.-Madison, 1987; dir., sec. The Friends of the Max Kade Inst. for German Am. Studies U. Wis.-Madison. Author: Edward J. Brandt, Inventor, 1984, Pioneer Memoirs of Early Watertown, 1986, The Joe Davies Scholars, 1988, The German-Speaking Forty-Eighters: Builders of Watertown, Wisconsin, 1990, Built on Irish Faith, 150 Years at St. Bernard's, 1994, (with others) The Prisoners of War of the 12th Armored Division, 1988. Former mem. exec. bd. Potawatomi council Boy Scouts Am., also former v.p. council; former bd. dirs., former pres. Earl and Eugenia Quirk Found., Inc. Trustee, mem. Joe Davies Scholarship Found.; former bd. dirs., former exec. com. mem. Watertown Meml. Hosp., dir. emeritus. Served with armored inf. AUS, 1943-45; ETO. Decorated Bronze Star; recipient Local History Award of Merit, State Hist. Soc. Wis., 1994. Mem. Am. Legion, E. Central Golf Assn. (past pres.), Wis. Alumni Assn. (local pres. 1950-52, 89-91, bd. dirs. nat. orgn. 1989-91), 12th Armored Div. Assn., Watertown Hist. Soc. (bd. dirs.), Am. Ex-Prisoners of War, Inc., Phi Delta Theta. Republican. Roman Catholic. Club: Watertown County (past dir.). Lodges: Rotary (past pres., former bd. dirs., Paul Harris fellow), Elks (past officer). Home: 604 Votech Dr Watertown WI 53098-1124

WALLMAN, GEORGE, hospital and food services administrator; b. N.Y.C., Apr. 10, 1917; s. Joseph and Celia (Kascawal) W.; m. Benita B. Kaufman, June 11, 1941. Student public schs., N.Y.C. Dir. food and banquet services Normandy Hotel, Hollywood, Calif., 1945-47; dir. food services Med. Center, N.Y.C., 1947-64; menucologist and cons. to hosps., 1964-67; dir. food services Montefiore Hosp., Pitts., 1967—; cons. public schs., homes and hosps. for aged, 1947—, cons. new food products various cos., 1967—; mem. Cancer Rehab. Project, U. Pitts., 1973—; lectr. on food to various profl. orgns., 1947—. Lectr.: program Exercise is Not Enough, Sta. NBC-TV, 1976; narrator, CBS Evening News; show Hosp. Gourmet, 1974; Contbg. editor, feature writer: Today's Chef, 1978—. Mem. Nat. Restaurant Assn., Am. Hosp. Assn., Am. Fedn. Musicians. Home: 1420 Centre Ave Pittsburgh PA 15219-3517 Office: Montefiore Hosp Fifth Ave Pittsburgh PA 15213 *My goals are to continue to maintain the ultimate in high level quality food service enhanced with the very best of culinary skill. Ten years ago I wrote an article in a national food trade magazine titled 'The Great Captive Audience in White'. I stated that hospitals should serve a beautiful orchestrated food tray to romanticize the pleasure of fine food, rather than the usual adequate meal that is merely nutritionally sufficient. It would mean so much to the patients. Let each dinner be serendipity, each dinner a dining event not just eating.*

WALLMAN, STEVEN MARK HARTE, lawyer; b. N.Y.C., Nov. 14, 1953; s. Eugene and Doris (Lee) W.; m. Kathleen M. Harte, May 5, 1985. BS, MIT, 1975, MS, 1976; postgrad., Harvard U., 1976-77; JD, Columbia U., 1978. Bar: D.C. 1978, Va. 1986. Assoc. Covington & Burling, Washington, 1978-86, ptnr., 1986-94; commr. SEC, Washington, 1994—. Home: 9332 Ramey Ln Great Falls VA 22066-2025 Office: SEC 450 5th St NW Washington DC 20549-0002

WALLMANN, JEFFREY MINER, author; b. Seattle, Dec. 5, 1941; s. George Rudolph and Elizabeth (Biggs) W.; BS, Portland State U., 1962; PhD, U. Nev., 1996. Pvt. investigator Dale Systems, N.Y.C., 1962-63; asst. buyer, mgr. pub. money bidder Dohrmann Co., San Francisco, 1964-66; mfrs. rep. electronics industry, San Francisco, 1966-69; dir. pub. rels. London Films, Cinelux-Universal and Trans-European Publs., 1970-75; editor-in-chief Riviera Life mag., 1975-77; cons. Mktg. Svcs. Internat., 1978—; instr. U. Nev., Reno, 1990—; books include: The Spiral Web, 1969, Judas Cross, 1974, Clean Sweep, 1976, Jamaica, 1977, Deathtrek, 1980,

Blood and Passion, 1980; Brand of the Damned, 1981; The Manipulator, 1982; Return to Conta Lupe, 1983; The Celluloid Kid, 1984; Business Basic for Bunglers, 1984, Guide to Applications Basic, 1984; (under pseudonym Leon DaSilva) Green Hell, 1976, Breakout in Angola, 1977; (pseudonym Nick Carter) Hour of the Wolf, 1973, Ice Trap Terror, 1974; (pseudonym Margaret Maitland) The Trial, 1974, Come Slowly, Eden, 1974, How Deep My Cup, 1975; (pseudonym Amanda Hart Douglass) First Rapture, 1972, Jamacia!, 1978; (pseudonym Grant Roberts) The Reluctant Couple, 1969, Wayward Wives, 1970; (pseudonym Gregory St. Germain) Resistance #1: Night and Fog, 1982, Resistance #2: Maygar Massacre, 1983; (pseudonym Wesley Ellis) Lonestar on the Treachery Trail, 1982, numerous others in the Lonestar series; (pseudonym Tabor Evans) Longarm and the Lonestar Showdown, 1986; (psyeudonym Jon Sharpe) Trailsman 58: Slaughter Express, 1986, numerous others in Trailsman series; also many other pseudonyms and titles; contbr. articles and short stories to Argosy, Ellery Queen's Mystery Mag., Alfred Hitchcock's Mystery Mag., Mike Shayne's Mystery Mag., Zane Grey Western, Venture, Oui, TV Guide; also (under pseudonym William Jeffrey in collaboration with Bill Pronzini) Dual at Gold Buttes, 1980, Border Fever, 1982, Day of the Moon, 1983. Mem. Mystery Writers of Am., Sci. Fiction Writers Am., Western Writers Am., Nat. Coun. Tchrs. English, Crime Writers Assn., Nev. State Coun. Tchrs. English, Esperanto League N.Am., Western Literature Assn., Internacia Societo De Amikeco Kaj Bonvolo, Science Fiction Rsch. Assn., Internat. Assn. of the Fantastic in the Arts, Nat. Assn. Sci. Tech. & Sci., Soc. Internat. d'Amitié et Bonne Volonté, Nat. Coun. Tchrs. English, Western Lit. Assn. Office: Jabberwocky Lit Agy 41-16 47th Ave # 2D Sunnyside NY 11104-3040

WALLOT, JEAN-PIERRE, archivist, historian; b. Valleyfield, Que., Can., May 22, 1935; s. Albert and Adrienne (Thibodeau) W.; m. Denyse Caron; children: Normand, Robert, Sylvie. B.A., Coll. Valleyfield, 1954; lic. es lettres, U. Montreal, 1957, M.A. in History, 1957, Ph.D. in History, 1965; D (hon.), U. Rennes, France, 1987. Reporter Le Progres de Valleyfield, 1954-61; lectr. U. Montreal, 1961-65, asst. prof., 1965-66, prof. dept. history, 1973-85, chmn. dept., 1973-75, vice dean studies faculty arts and scis., 1975-78, vice dean research Faculty Arts and Scis, 1979-82, academic v.p., 1982-85; nat. archivist, Can., 1985—; historian Nat. Mus. Man, Ottawa, Ont., 1966-69, assoc. prof. U. Toronto, 1969-71; prof. Concordia U., Montreal, Que., 1971-73; dir. Etude Associé Ecole Pratique des Hautes Etudes en Sciences Sociales, Paris, 1975, 79, 81, 83, 85, 87, 89, 94. Author: Intrigues françaises et americaines au Canada, 1965, (with John Hare) Les Imprimés dans le Bas-Canada, 1967, Confrontations, 1971, (with G. Paquet) Patronage et Pouvoir dans le Bas-Canada, 1973, Un Quebec qui bougeait, 1973; Editor: (with R. Girard) Memoires de J.E. McComber, bourgeois de Montréal, 1981; (with J. Goy) Evolution et eclatement du monde rural, 1986. Pres. internat. adv. com. on memory of the world, UNESCO. Decorated officer Order Arts et Lettres (France), 1987; officer Order of Can., 1991; recipient Marie Tremaine medal, 1973, Tyrrell medal, 1982, Royal Soc. Centenary medal, 1994. Fellow Royal Soc. Can. (sect. pres. 1985-87); mem. Am. Antiquarian Soc., Acad. des Lettres du Quebec, Inst. d'Histoire l'Amerique Francaise (pres. 1973-77), Can. Hist. Assn. (pres. 1982), Assn. Can.-Francaise l'Avancement Scis. (pres. 1981-83), Assn. Archivists Que., Assn. Can. Archivists, Internat. Coun. on Archives (v.p. 1988-92, pres. 1992—). Roman Catholic. Office: Nat Archives, 395 Wellington St, Ottawa, ON Canada K1A 0N3

WALLRAFF, BARBARA JEAN, magazine editor, writer; b. Tucson, Mar. 1, 1953; d. Charles Frederick and Evelyn Pauline (Bartels) W.; m. Julian Hart Fisher, Apr. 25, 1992. BA in Polit. Sci. and Philosophy, Antioch Coll., 1972. Sect. editor Boston Phoenix, 1979-83; assoc. editor The Atlantic Monthly, Boston, 1983-89, sr. editor, 1989—; freelance writer, 1978—. Columnist Word Court, 1995—. Office: Atlantic Monthly 77 N Washington St Boston MA 02114

WALLS, CARL EDWARD, JR., communications company official; b. Magnolia, Ark., Sept. 9, 1948; s. Carl E. and Melba Rene (Garrard) W.; m. Doris Duhart, Aug. 1, 1970; children: Carl Edward, Forrest Allen. Student San Antonio Coll., 1966-68. Div. mgr. Sears Roebuck & Co., San Antonio, 1967-73, area sales mgr., 1973-78; service cons. Southwestern Bell, 1978-79, account exec., 1979-82; account exec., industry cons. AT&T Info. Systems, 1983-88, account mgr., 1988-89; gen. mgr. Tex. State Govt., 1989—. Mem. citizens advisory com. Tex. Senate, 1975-81; legis. aide Tex. Ho. of Reps., 1981-85; commr. Alamo Area council Boy Scouts Am., 1970-79, Capitol Area council, 1980—, nat. jamboree staff, 1973, 77, 81, 85, 89, 93; mem. Republican Nat. Com., 1980—, Rep. Presdl. Task Force, 1980—, Rep. Senatorial Club, 1981—. Recipient Patriotic Service award U.S. Treasury Dept., 1975-76; Scouters Key and Commrs. award Boy Scout Am., Dist. Merit award Boy Scouts Am., 1978. Mem. Scouting Collectors Assn. (pres. South Central region 1979-80, v.p. region 1980-81, sec. 1983-86), U. Ark. Alumni Assn. (life), Am. Legion. Baptist. Home: 11712 D K Ranch Rd Austin TX 78759-3770 Office: 1624 Headway Ct Austin TX 78754

WALLS, CARMAGE, newspaper publishing executive; b. Crisp County, Ga., Oct. 28, 1908; s. Benjamin Gaff and Anna (Byrd) W.; m. Odessa Dobbs (div.); children: Carmage Lee, Ronald Eugene (dec.), Mark Thomas (dec.), Dinah Jean Garcich; m. Martha Ann Williams, Jan. 2, 1954; children: Byrd Cooper, Lissa Walls Vahldiek. Ed. pub. schs., Fla. Bus. mgr. Orlando (Fla.) Newspaper, Inc., 1934-40; pub. Macon (Ga.) Telegraph News, 1940-47; pres. Gen. Newspapers, Inc., Gadsden, Ala., 1945-59, So. Newspapers, Inc., Montgomery, Ala., 1951-69; also dir.; pub. Montgomery (Ala.) Advt.-Jour., 1963-69; chmn. bd., dir. Galveston Newspapers, Inc., Tex.; owner Walls Investment Co., Houston.; bd. dirs. Tex. City Newspapers, Inc. Pres. Macon Area Devel. Commn., 1943-44, Macon C. of C., 1945; trustee Birmingham-So. Coll., 1971-7. Mem. So. Newspaper Pubs. Assn., Soc. Profl. Journalists, The Houstonian. Episcopalian. Home: 623 Shartle Cir Houston TX 77024-5521 Office: 1050 Wilcrest Dr Houston TX 77042-1608

WALLS, HERBERT LEROY, school system administrator; b. Springfield, Ohio, July 12, 1944; s. James Edward and Hattie Beatrice (Jackson) W.; m. Vonzile Green, Feb. 4, 1967 (div. 1975); children: Herbert Le Roy Jr., Jomica Yvette. BA in English, Calif. State U., L.A., 1972; MA in Spl. Edn., Calif. State U., Dominguez Hills, 1982; MEd, U. LaVerne, 1992; HHD (hon.), Mt. Zion Bible Sem., 1991. Cert. English tchr., spl. edn. tchr., adminstr., Calif. Tchr. Golden Day Schs., L.A., 1971-72; English tchr. M.L. King Jr. Middle Sch., Boston, 1972-74; spl. edn. tchr. Arnold RE-ED West, Carmichael, Calif., 1974-75; adminstr., tchr. Golden Day/Univ. Alternative Sch., L.A., 1975-79; dir. spl. edn. Dorothy Brown Sch., L.A., 1979-84; prin., tchr. Westside Acad., L.A., 1984-86; tchr. spl. edn. Sacramento City (Calif.) Unified Sch. Dist., 1987-93, prin., 1993—; dean Christ Temple Bible Inst., Sacramento, 1991-93; ednl. cons. Little Citizen Schs., L.A., 1994. Contbr. poetry to anthologies. Sgt. USMC, 1962-66, Vietnam. Mem. Mt. Zion Sem. Alumni Fellowship, Phi Delta Kappa. Mem. Apostolic Ch. Avocations: watercolor impressionist painting, piano, drama, singing gospel and classical music. Home: 2600 Cadjew Ave Sacramento CA 95832-1424

WALLS, MARTHA ANN WILLIAMS (MRS. B. CARMAGE WALLS), newspaper executive; b. Gadsden, Ala., Apr. 21, 1927; d. Aubrey Joseph and Inez (Cooper) Williams; m. B. Carmage Walls, Jan. 2, 1954; children: Byrd Cooper, Lissa Walls Vahldiek. Student pub. schs., Gadsden. Pres., dir. Walls Newspapers, Inc., 1969-70; sec., treas., dir. Summer Camps, Inc., Guntersville, Ala., 1954-69; CEO, pres., dir. So. Newspapers, Inc., Houston, 1970—; v.p., dir. Scottsboro (Ala.) Newspapers, Angleton (Tex.) Times, Ft. Payne (Ala.) Newspapers, Inc.; sec.-treas., dir. Portales (N.M.) News Tribune Publ. Co., Quay County Sun Newspaper, Inc., Tucumcari, N.M.; v.p., dir. Bay City (Tex.) Newspapers, Inc.; bd. dirs. Liberal (Kans.) Newspapers, Inc., Monroe (Ga.) Newspapers, Inc., Moore Newspapers, Inc., Dumas, Tex., Jefferson Pilot Corp., Greensboro, N.C., Jefferson-Pilot Life Ins. Co., Jefferson Pilot Communications. Bd. dirs. Montgomery Acad., 1970-74. Mem. Soc. Profl. Journalists, The Houstonian. Episcopalian. Office: So Newspapers Inc 1050 Wilcrest Dr Houston TX 77042-1608

WALLS, THOMAS FRANCIS, management consultant; b. Phila., June 4, 1947; s. Thomas Francis and Margaret Mary (Whalen) W.; m. Kathleen Cecilia Lyons, Dec. 7, 1968; children: Thomas, James, Eleanor. ABA in Econs., U. Pa., 1974, BBA in Mgmt., 1977. Cert. practitioner inventory mgmt. Programmer Gen. Elec. Re-entry Systems, King of Prussia, Pa., 1965-69; mgr. Keane Assocs., Paoli, Pa., 1969-73, Alco Standard Corp., Valley Forge, Pa., 1973-80, Comserv Corp., Mendota Heights, Minn., 1980-88; mgr. Andersen Cons., Chgo., 1988-89, Phila., 1989-95; with Andersen Cons., St. Charles, Ill., 1995—. Contbg. author: APICS Dictionary. With USNR, 1967-68, Vietnam. Mem. Am. Prodn. and Inventory Control Soc. Roman Catholic. Avocations: family, rowing, soccer, reading. Office: Andersen Cons 1405 N Fifth Ave Saint Charles IL 60174

WALLS, WILLIAM HAMILTON, judge; b. Atlantic City, Nov. 28, 1932; s. Clifford Hamilton and Nannette Verneice (Anderson) W.; married, Aug. 6, 1960 (div. 1985); children: Claire Alexia, Peter Graves. AB, Dartmouth Coll., 1954; LLB, Yale U., 1957. Bar: N.J. 1959, U.S. Ct. Appeals (3d cir.) 1966. Asst. corp. counsel City of Newark, 1966-68; judge Mcpl. Ct., City of Newark, 1968-70; corp. counsel City of Newark, 1970-73, bus. adminstr., 1974-77; judge County of Essex, Newark, 1977-79, N.J. Superior Ct., Newark, 1979—. Mem. Yale Law Alumni N.J. (Achievement award 1978), Phi Beta Kappa. Avocations: photography, hiking, travel. Office: NJ Superior Ct 318 Hall of Records 465 Dr Martin L King Blvd Newark NJ 07102

WALLS, WILLIAM WALTON, JR., consultant; b. Phila., Oct. 3, 1932; s. William Walton and Mary Crown (Elliott) W.; m. Nina Catherine deAngeli, July 1, 1961; 1 child, Deborah. BSME, Swarthmore Coll., 1959. With Boeing Helicopters, Phila., 1959-96, v.p. light helicopter joint venture, 1988-91, v.p. devel. programs, 1991-92, v.p. rsch. and engring., 1992-96; small high-tech. bus. cons. Ridley Park, Pa., 1996—; cons. in field. Chmn. aerospace adv. coun. Pa. State Coll., 1974-79; mem. NATO Indsl. Advisors Group, 1988-93; mem. bd. advisors Rotocraft Ctr. Excellence, Rensselaer Polytech. Inst., 1982-84. Mem. Am. Helicopter Soc. (pres. 1988-89, chmn. 1989-90). Republican. Avocations: skiing, jogging, personal computer applications. Home: 502 Harrison St Ridley Park PA 19078-3208

WALLWORK, WILLIAM WILSON, III, automobile executive; b. Fargo, N.D., Mar. 8, 1961; s. William Wilson Jr.; m. Shannon Brodshaug, July 12, 1991. AA in Automotive Mktg., Northwood Inst., 1981; student, San Diego State U., Moorhead State U. Lease rep. Wallwork Lease and Rental, 1984-86; sales mgr. W.W. Wallwork, Inc., Fargo, N.D., 1986-87, v.p., 1987-91, pres., 1991—; v.p. Valley Imports Inc., Fargo, N.D., 1986-91; pres. Valley Imports Inc., Fargo, N.D., 1991—; vice chmn. Kenworth 20 Group, 1992-93, chmn., 1994-95; mem. Rockwell Internat. Dealer Adv. Bd., 1995—. Mem. Fargo-Moorhead Automobile Dealers Assn. (v.p. 1986-88, pres. 1988-90). Avocation: skiing. Office: W W Wallwork Inc 4001 Main Ave Fargo ND 58103-1145

WALMAN, JEROME, psychotherapist, publisher, consultant, critic; b. Charleston, W.Va., June 19, 1937; s. Joe and Madeline Minnie (Levy) W.; m. Mary Joan Granara, Sept. 5, 1960. Student, U. W.Va.; student, Boston U., Berkley Sch. Music, Boston. Producer, composer, writer mus. compositions Carnegie Hall, Broadway Theatre, 1962, 63; pvt. practice psychotherapy in spl. hypnosis and music therapy, 1964—; designer Jerome Walman Systems Applied Hypnosis, 1969; travel-restaurant-wine-entertainment critic Sta. WNCN-FM Radio; critic travel, food, wine Sta. WNCN-FM Radio, Fodor's N.Y. restaurant sect.; marriage and family counselor; lectr. dir. tng. programs in memory improvement and speed reading; cons. personal image, wine and food Dept. Def., NYU; cons., dir. Cooking for Relaxation and Wieght Control; restaurant publicist; condr. courses in wine appreciation and food; restaurant, wine and food critic Sta. WCNC-GAF Radio; host travel, restaurant and wine show Sta. WEVD Radio. Dir., producer syndicated TV show Enterprises Unltd., 1978—; producer, composer I Murdered Mary, N.Y.C., 1976, Last Call, N.Y.C., 1977, TV Mag., 1978; lectr. East-West Ctr., N.Y.C., 1978, Actors Tng. and Acting Therapy Ctr. Am., Westwinds Learning Ctr., The Learning Exchange, 1986; editor Punch In Internat. Electronic Travel, Wine and Restaurant mag.; pub. Wine On Line mag., The Computer User's Survival Newsletter and Syndicated Column; originator facimile news svc. Fax It To Me; author papers on hypnosis, psychic phenomena and memory, music therapy, biofeedback and meditation application; featured in various publs. including Fortune, Gentleman's Quar., Cosmopolitan, Leaders mag., Mademoiselle; editor Punch in Internat. Wine, Restaurant and Travel Electronic mag.; syndicated columnist travel and wine Cab Mag.; reviewer Wine-on-Line Internat. Wire Svc., The Computer User's Survival Newsletter; contbg. writer Chocolatier Mag., Troika Mag.; contbr. The Official Airline Guides Electronic Edition, Fodor's N.Y. Sunday in N.Y. and Pocket N.Y. Travel Guide. Mem. Music Therapy Internat., Meditation and Mental Devel. Ctr. N.Y., Memory Improvement and Concentration Ctr. Am., Delphi-Gen. Videotex Svc.-Nynex Info-Logic, Internat. Foods, Wine & Travel Writers Assn. Office: Punch In Syndicate 400 E 59th St Apt 9F New York NY 10022-2344

WALMER, EDWIN FITCH, lawyer; b. Chgo., Mar. 24, 1930; s. Hillard Wentz and Anna C. (Fitch) W.; m. Florence Poling, June 17, 1952; children: Linda Diane Walmer Dennis, Fred Fitch. BS with distinction, Ind. U., 1952, JD with high distinction, 1957. Bar: Wis. 1957, U.S. Dist. Ct. (ea. dist.) Wis. 1957. Assoc. Foley & Lardner, Milw., 1957-65, ptnr., 1965-90, ret., 1990. Served to 1st lt. U.S. Army, 1952-54. Recipient Cal. C. Chambers award Culver (Ind.) Mil. Acad., 1948. Fellow Am. Coll. Trust and Estate Counsel; mem. Order of Coif, Dairymen's Country Club (Boulder Junction, Wis.), Vineyards Country Club (Naples, Fla.), Phi Eta Sigma, Beta Gamma Sigma. Republican. Congregationalist. Avocations: golf, fishing. Office: Foley & Lardner 777 E Wisconsin Ave Milwaukee WI 53202-5302

WALMSLEY, ARTHUR EDWARD, bishop; b. New Bedford, Mass., May 4, 1928; s. Harry Barlow and Elizabeth Doris (Clegg) W.; m. Roberta Brownell Chapin, Dec. 29, 1954; children: Elizabeth Trent, John Barlow. B.A., Trinity Coll., Hartford, Conn., 1948; D.D. (hon.), Trinity Coll., 1982; M.Div., Episcopal Theol. Sch., Cambridge, Mass., 1951; Hum.D. (hon.), New Eng. Sch. Law, Boston, 1970; D.D. (hon.), Berkeley Div. Sch., New Haven, 1980. Ordained to ministry Episcopal Ch., 1952, consecrated bishop, 1979. Asst., then rector Ch. of Holy Apostles, St. Louis, 1951-53; rector Trinity Ch., St. Louis, 1953-58; staff office exec. council Episcopal Ch., N.Y.C., 1958-68; dir. Mass. Council Chs., Boston, 1969-72; dep. to rector Trinity Ch., N.Y.C., 1972-73; rector St. Paul's Ch., New Haven, 1974-79; bishop Diocese of Conn., Hartford, 1979-93. Editor: The Church in a Society of Abundance, 1963. Trustee Berkeley Divsn. Sch., 1979-92, Trinity Coll., 1982-92. Sr. fellow Am. Leadership Forum; mem. Phi Beta Kappa, Pi Gamma Mu. Home: RR 1 Box 224 Hillsboro NH 03244-9333

WALNER, ROBERT JOEL, lawyer; b. Chgo., Dec. 22, 1946; s. Wallace and Elsie W.; m. Charlene Walner; children: Marci, Lisa. BA, U. Ill., 1968; JD, De Paul U., 1972; M in Mgmt. with distinction, Northwestern U., 1991. Bar: Ill. 1972, U.S. Dist. Ct. (no. dist.) Ill. 1972, U.S. Ct. Appeals (7th cir.) 1972, Fla. 1973. Atty. SEC, Chgo., 1972-73; pvt. practice Chgo., 1973—; adminstrv. law judge Ill. Commerce Commn., Chgo., 1973-76; atty. Allied Van Lines, Inc., Broadview, Ill., 1976-79; sr. v.p., gen. counsel, sec. The Balcor Co., Skokie, Ill., 1979-92; prin. fin. ops. Balcor Securities divsn. The Balcor Co., Skokie, 1984-92, pres., 1989-92; of counsel Lawrence, Walner & Assocs., Ltd., Chgo., 1992-93; sr. v.p., gen. counsel, sec. Grubb & Ellis Co., San Francisco, 1994—; mem. securities adv. com. to Ill. Sec. of State, 1984-94; mem. editl. bd. Real Estate Securities Jour., Real Estate Securities and Capital Markets; program chmn. Regulators and You seminar. Contbr. chpts. to books, articles on real estate and securities law to profl. jours.; assoc. editor De Paul U. Law Rev. Mem. Kellogg Career Devel. Com., 1992—, Kellogg Bus. Adv. Com., 1992—; mem. enterprise forum MIT, 1992—, mem. exec. com., 1993-94. With USAR, 1968-73. Mem. ABA, Ill. Bar Assn., Chgo. Bar Assn., Am. Real Estate Com. (pres. com. 1985-90), Real Estate Syndication Com. (chmn. 1982-85), Ill. Inst. Continuing Legal Edn., N.Am. Securities Adminstrs. Assn. Inc. (industry adv. com. to real estate com., 1987-89), Real Estate Securities and Syndication Inst. of Nat. Assn. Realtors (chmn. regulatory and legis. com., 1984, 87, specialist, real estate investment, group v.p., 1987, exec. com. 1987-90), Nat. Real Estate Investment Forum (chmn. 1985, 88), Real Estate Investment Assn. (founder, exec. com. 1990-92), Beta Gamma Sigma.

WALPIN, GERALD, lawyer; b. N.Y.C., Sept. 1, 1931; s. Michael and Mary (Gordon) W.; m. Sheila Kainer, Apr. 13, 1957; children: Amanda Eve, Edward Andrew, Jennifer Hope. BA, CCNY, 1952; LLB cum laude, Yale Law Sch., 1955. Bar: N.Y. 1955, U.S. Supreme Ct. 1965, U.S. Ct. Appeals (2d cir.) 1960, (6th cir.) 1969, (3d cir.) 1976, (8th cir.) 1982, (9th cir.) 1983, (llth cir.) 1983, (7th cir.) 1984, U.S. Ct. Claims 1984. Law clk. to Hon. Justice E.J. Dimock U.S. Dist. Ct. (so. dist.) N.Y., N.Y.C.; law clk. to hon. F.P. Bryan U.S. Dist. Judge (so. dist.) N.Y., N.Y.C., 1955-57; asst. U.S. atty., chief spl. prosecutions U.S. Atty. Office, N.Y.C., 1960-65; sr. ptnr. Rosenman & Colin and predecessor firm, N.Y.C., 1965—, chmn. litigation dept., 1985—; mem. adv. com. Fed. Ct. So. Dist. N.Y., 1991—; co-chmn. Lawyers div. Anti-Defamation League, N.Y., 1994—. Editor Yale Law Jour., 1953-54, mng. editor, 1954-55; contbr. articles to profl. jours. Pres., trustee Parker Jewish Geriatric Inst., New Hyde Park, N.Y., 1979-87, chmn., trustee, 1987—; bd. dirs. Fund for Modern Cts., N.Y.C., 1985-91; mem. law com. Am. Jewish Com., 1980—; mem. Com. for Free World, N.Y.C., 1983-91; trustee, mem. exec. com. United Jewish Appeal-Fedn. Jewish Philanthropies, N.Y.C., 1984—; mem. Nassau County Crime Commn., 1970; pres. Kensington Civic Orgn., Gt. Neck, N.Y., 1972-73. Recipient Quality of Life award United Jewish Appeal Fedn., 1978, Human Rels. award Am. Jewish Com., 1982, Gift of Life award Jewish Inst. Geriatric Care, 1987, Learned Hand award Am. Jewish Com., 1990. Mem. ABA, Assn. Bar City N.Y., Fed. Bar Coun. (chmn. modern cts. com. 1989, v.p. 1991-95, chmn. bench and bar liaison com. 1994-95, vice chmn. 1995—), Federalist Soc. (chmn. litigation sect. 1996—), Univ. Club, Yale Club. Republican. Jewish. Home: 875 Park Ave New York NY 10021-0341 Office: Rosenman & Colin 575 Madison Ave New York NY 10022-2511 *My life should be an appropriate response to God and this country for providing me with the opportunities I have had: Contribution to our society and strengthening of our country's steadfast opposition to discrimination for or against anyone based on race, religion or sex.*

WALPOLE, ROBERT, heavy manufacturing executive. BA, Principia Coll., 1962; MBA, Washington U., 1964. Distbn. sales office, planning and distbn. mgr. Ford Motor Co., Atlanta, 1964-70; officer Walbro Corp., Cass City, Mich., 1970—; now v.p. Walbro Corp., Cass City; pres. Walbro Engine Mgmt. Corp., 1991—. Office: Walbro Corp 6242 Garfield Ave Cass City MI 48726-1342*

WALRATH, HARRY RIENZI, minister; b. Alameda, Calif., Mar. 7, 1926; s. Frank Rienzi and Cathren (Michlar) W.; AA, City Coll. San Francisco, 1950; BA, U. Calif. at Berkeley, 1952; MDiv, Ch. Div. Sch. of Pacific, 1959; m. Dorothy M. Baxter, June 24, 1961; 1 son, Gregory Rienzi. Dist. exec. San Mateo area council Boy Scouts Am., 1952-55; ordained deacon Episcopal Ch., 1959, priest, 1960; curate All Souls Parish, Berkeley, Calif., 1959-61; vicar St. Luke's, Atascadero, Calif., 1961-63, St. Andrew's, Garberville, Calif., 1963-64; asso. rector St. Luke's Ch., Los Gatos, 1964-65, Holy Spirit Parish, Missoula, Mont., 1965-67; vicar St. Peter's Ch., also headmaster St. Peter's Schs., Litchfield Park, Ariz., 1967-69; chaplain U. Mont., 1965-67; asst. rector Trinity Parish, Reno, 1969-72; coordinator counciling svcs. Washoe County Council Alcoholism, Reno, 1972-74; adminstr. Cons. Assistance Svcs., Inc., Reno, 1974-76; pastoral counselor, contract chaplain Nev. Mental Health Inst., 1976-78; contract mental health chaplain VA Hosp., Reno, 1976-78; mental health chaplain VA Med. Ctr., 1978-83, staff chaplain, 1983-85, chief, chaplain service, 1985-91, also triage coord. for mental health, ret., 1991; per diem chaplain Washoe Med. Ctr., Reno, 1993; assoc. priest Trinity Episcopal Ch., Reno, 1995; dir. youth Paso Robles Presbytery; chmn. Diocesan Commn. on Alcoholism; cons. teen-age problems Berkeley Presbytery; mem. clergy team Episcopal Marriage Encounter, 1979-85, also Episc. Engaged Encounter. Author: God Rides the Rails-Chapel Cars on American Railroads at the Turn of the Century, 1994. Mem. at large Washoe dist. Nev. area council Boy Scouts Am., scoutmaster troop 73, 1976, troop 585, 1979-82, asst. scoutmaster troop 35, 1982-92, assoc. adviser area 3 Western region, 1987-89, regional com. Western Region, 1989-90; lodge adviser Tannu Lodge 346, Order of Arrow, 1982-87; docent coun. Nev. Hist. Soc., 1992; South Humboldt County chmn. Am. Cancer Soc. Trustee Community Youth Ctr., Reno. Served with USNR, 1944-46. Decorated Pacific Theater medal with star, Am. Theater medal, Victory medal, Fleet Unit Commendation medal; recipient dist. award of merit Boy Scouts Am., St. George award Episc. Ch.-Boy Scouts Am., Silver Beaver award Boy Scouts Am., 1986, Founders' award Order of the Arrow, Boy Scouts Am., 1985; performance awards VA-VA Med. Ctr., 1983, 84; named Arrowman of Yr., Order of Arrow, Boy Scouts Am. Cert. substance abuse counselor, Nev. Mem. Ch. Hist. Soc., U. Calif. Alumni Assn., Nat. Model R.R. Assn. (life), Sierra Club Calif., Missoula Council Chs. (pres.), Alpha Phi Omega. Democrat. Club: Rotary. Home: 580 E Huffaker Ln Reno NV 89511-1203 *The study of history has taught me one thing: that human nature has not changed, only the means of its execution. This same study has also taught me that human nature reveals the glory of God in our quest for our future.*

WALRATH, PATRICIA A., state legislator; b. Brainerd, Minn., Aug. 11, 1941; d. Joseph James and Pansy Patricia (Drake) McCarvill; m. Robert Eugene Walrath, Sept. 1, 1961; children: Karen, Susan, David, Julie. BS, Bemidji State U., 1962; MS, SUNY, Oswego, 1975. Cert. secondary math. tchr., N.Y., Mass. Programmer analyst Control Data Corp., Mpls., 1962-65; crewleader dept. commerce U.S. Census, Middlesex County, Mass., 1979-80; selectman Town of Stow, Mass., 1980-85; tchr. math. Hale Jr. High Sch., Stow, 1981-82; instr. math. Johnson & Wale Coll. Hanscom AFB, Bedford, Mass., 1983-84; test examiner Hanscom AFB, Bedford, 1983-84; state rep. 3d Middlesex dist. State of Mass., Boston, 1985—; mem. House Ways and Means com., 1987-92, joint coms. on local affairs, 1993-95, pub. svc., 1993—, election law, 1995—, sci. and tech. com., 1995—. Chmn. Mass. Indoor Air Pollution Commn., Boston, 1987-88; mem. Stow Dem. Com., 1988—; merit badge counselor Boy Scouts Am., Stow and Hudson, Mass., 1990—; bd. dirs. Hudson Arts Alliance, 1991—. Recipient Disting. Svc. award Auburn N.Y. Jaycees, 1976. Mem. LWV (pres. 1973-76, dir. fin. 1977-78), Am. Legis. Exch. Coun., Mass. Legislators' Assn., Mass. Dem. Leadership Coun. (v.p. 1991-92, co-chmn. 1993-94, treas. 1995-96), Mass. Women's Legis. Caucus (chair 1986). Roman Catholic. Avocations: gardening, stamp collecting, travel. Home: 20 Middlemost Way Stow MA 01775-1363 Office: State Capital RM 275 Boston MA 02133

WALRAVEN, JOSEPH WILLIAM (BILL WALRAVEN), writer, publisher; b. Dallas, July 1, 1925; s. Orange Daniel Sr. and Valerie (Garrison) W.; m. Marjorie Kathryn Yeager, May 28, 1950; children: Valerie Ruth, Wilson Frederick, Joseph William Jr. BA, Tex. A&I U., 1950; postgrad. sch. profl. writing, U. Okla., 1950-51. Copy editor San Antonio Light, 1951-52; reporter Corpus Christi (Tex.) Caller-Times, 1952-68, daily columnist, 1968-89; pub. Sandcrab Press, Corpus Christi, 1983—, Javelina Press, Corpus Christi, 1989—; freelance writer Corpus Christi, 1989—. Author, pub.; Real Texans Don't Drink Scotch in Their Dr Pepper, 1983; author: Corpus Christi, History of a Texas Seaport, 1983, Walraven's World or Star Boarder (and other) Wars, 1985, El Rincon, A History of Corpus Christi Beach, 1990, (with Marjorie Kathryn Walraven) The Magnificent Barbarians, Little-Told Tales of The Texas Revolution, 1993, All I Know Is What's On TV, 1995. V.p. South Tex. Hist. Soc., 1978; active Tex. State Hist. Assn. With USN, 1943-45, PTO. Recipient 1st pl. gen. interest column Harte-Hanks Newspapers, 1979, 2nd prize, 1987; recipient 2nd pl. news story Tex. AP, 1954, 1st pl. features, 1958; recipient 2nd prize series Animal Def. League Tex., 1987; award recipient Corpus Christi Police Officers Assn., 1967, ARC, 1970, Tex. Hist. Commn. and Tex. Hist. Found., 1980, 81, Corpus Christi Landmark Commn., 1987, Nueces County Hist. Commn., 1989; named Civic Salesman of Yr., Sales and Mktg. Execs. Corpus Christi, 1984. Mem. Nat. Soc. Newspaper Columnists, Corpus Christi Press Club (v.p. 1964, pres. 1965, many awards). Democrat. Methodist. Avocations: reading, travel, flounder fishing. Home: 4609 Wilma Dr Corpus Christi TX 78412-2357 Office: Sandcrab Press PO Box 1479 Corpus Christi TX 78403-1479

WALROD, DAVID JAMES, retail grocery chain executive; b. Toledo, Dec. 9, 1946; s. Maynard Elmer and Isabella (Soldwish) W.; m. Judith Kay Stevens, Aug. 17, 1968; children—David, Bryant, Marc. Student, Michael Owens Coll.; student in food distbn. mgmt. mktg., Toledo U., 1968. With Seaway Food Town, Inc., Maumee, Ohio, 1963—, grocery merchandiser, 1971-74, v.p. supermarket ops., 1974-77, corp. v.p. ops., 1977-80, sr. v.p. ops., 1980-88, exec. v.p., chief oper. officer, 1988—; bd. dirs. Ohio Grocers Assn. Bd. dirs. Toledo Mud Hens, Riverside Hosp., St. Francis Desales H.S., Toledo, Corp. for Effective Govt., Junior Achievement, Toledo City Parks Commn., Labor Mgmt. Coun., Bishop's Edn. Coun. Cath. Diocese of Toledo. Mem. Brandywine Country Club. Office: Seaway Food Town Inc 1020 Ford St Maumee OH 43537-1820

WALSER, MACKENZIE, physician, educator; b. N.Y.C., Sept. 19, 1924; s. Kenneth Eastwood and Jean (Mackenzie) W.; m. Elizabeth C. Gearon, Sept. 17, 1988; children from previous marriage: Karen D., Jennifer McK., Cameron M., Eric H. Grad., Phillips Exeter Acad., 1941; A.B., Yale, 1944; M.D., Columbia, 1948. Diplomate: Am. Bd. Internal Medicine. Intern Mass. Gen. Hosp., Boston, 1948-49; asst. resident in medicine Mass. Gen. Hosp., 1949-50; resident Parkland Hosp., Dallas, 1950-52; staff mem. Johns Hopkins Hosp., Balt., 1957—; instr. U. Tex. at Dallas, 1950-51, asst. prof., 1951-52; investigator Nat. Heart Inst., Bethesda, Md., 1954-57; asst. prof. pharmacology Johns Hopkins Med. Sch., 1957-61, assoc. prof., 1961-70, prof., 1970—, asst. prof. medicine, 1957-64, assoc. prof., 1964-74, prof., 1974—; Med. dir. USPHS, 1970—, pharmacology study sect., 1968-72. Co-author: Mineral Metabolism, 2d edit., 1969, Handbook of Physiology, 1973, The Kidney, 1976, 5th edit., 1996, also articles; co-editor: Branched-Chain Amino and Ketoacids, 1981, Nutritional Management, 1984. Served with USNR, 1942-45; to lt. M.C. USNR, 1952-54. Recipient Research Career Devel. award USPHS, 1959-69. Mem. AAAS, AAUP (pres. Johns Hopkins 1970), Am. Soc. Clin. Investigation, Assn. Am. Physicians, Am. Fedn. Clin. Rsch., Am. Physiol. Soc., Biophys. Soc., Am. Soc. Pharmacology and Exptl. Therapeutics (Exptl. Therapeutics award 1975), Am. Soc. Nephrology, Am. Inst. Nutrition, Am. Soc. Clin. Nutrition (Hermann award 1988), Internat. Soc. Nutrition and Metabolism in Renal Disease (Addis award 1994), Century Assn. Club. Home: 7513 Club Rd Baltimore MD 21204-6418 Office: Johns Hopkins U Sch Medicine Baltimore MD 21205

WALSH, ANNMARIE HAUCK, research firm executive; b. N.Y.C., May 5, 1938; d. James Smith and Ann-Marie (Kennedy) Hauck; m. John F. Walsh, Jr., Aug. 20, 1960; children: Peter Hauck, John David. BA, Barnard Coll., 1961; MA, Columbia U., 1969, PhD, 1971. Sr. staff mem. Inst. Pub. Adminstrn., N.Y.C., 1961-72, pres., 1982-89, trustee, Gulick scholar, 1989—, dir. programs in Ctrl. Europe and NIS, 1991—; dir. Ctr. for Urban and Policy Studies, CUNY Grad. Ctr., N.Y.C., 1972-79, Govs.' Task Force on Regional Planning, N.Y., Conn., N.J., 1979-81; disting. vis. prof. Bklyn. Coll., 1991-93; cons. pub. enterprise, civil svc., urban and regional mgmt., tng., pub. fin. UN, China, Indonesia, Bangladesh, Czech Republic and Slovakia, Poland, state and local govts., U.S. Postal Svc., U.S. Dept. Transp. Author: Urban Government for Zagreb, Yugoslavia, 1968, Urban Government for Lagos, Nigeria, 1968, Urban Government for the Paris Region, 1968, The Urban Challenge to Government: An International Comparisons of Thirteen Cities, 1969, The Public's Business: Politics and Practices of Government Corporations, 1978, 2d edit., 1980, Designing and Managing the Procurement Process, 1989, Privatization-Implications for Public Management, 1996; editor: Agenda for a City, 1970. Project dir. 20th Century Fund, Pub. Enterprise, 1972-76, pub.-pvt. partnerships, 1989—; bd. dirs. Ralph Bunche Inst., UN, 1978-82, Regional Plan Assn., 1987-91. Herbert Lehmann fellow, 1966-69. Fellow, Nat. Acad. Pub. Adminstrn. (ADP mgmt. deregulation in govt., civil svc. reform, NASA reorgn., nominating com.); mem. Regional Plan Assn., Phi Beta Kappa. Office: Inst Pub Admistrn 55 W 44th St New York NY 10036-6609

WALSH, CHARLES RICHARD, banker; b. Bklyn., Jan. 30, 1939; s. Charles John and Anna Ellen Walsh; m. Marie Anne Goulden, June 24, 1961; children: Kevin C., Brian R., Gregory M. BS, Fordham U., 1960; MBA, St. John's U., 1966, D of Comml. Scis. (hon.), 1985. V.p. Mfrs. Hanover Trust Co., Hicksville, N.Y., 1974-80, sr. v.p., 1980-86, exec. v.p., 1986-90, group exec., mem. mgmt. com., 1990-92; exec. v.p., group exec. Chem. Banking Corp., Hicksville, N.Y., 1992-95, The Chase Manhattan Corp., 1995—; bd. dirs. Mastercard Internat.; bd. dirs., former chmn. Eastern States Monetary Svcs., Lake Success, N.Y., 1978-88; former pres., CEO, bd. dirs. The Bankcard Assn., Hicksville, 1988-91. Sustaining mem. Rep. Nat. Com., 1978—; vice chmn. adv. bd. St. John's U., 1982—. With USAR, 1960, 61-62. Mem. N.Y. State Bankers Assn. (former bd. dirs., mem. gov. coun., chmn. consumer banking divsn.), Am. Bankers Assn. (mem. govt. rels. coun., chmn. bank card divsn., mem. exec. com., former mem. comms. coun. and chmn. edn. com.), Am. Mgmt. Assn., N.Y. Credit and Fin. Mgmt. Assn., Soc. Cert. Consumer Credit Execs. (cert.), Beta Gamma Sigma, Omicron Delta Epsilon, North Hempstead Country Club, Gov.'s Club Kiawah Island (S.C.). Republican. Home: 9 Blueberry Ln Oyster Bay NY 11771-3901 also: 121 Turnberry Dr Johns Island SC 29455-5726 Office: 100 Duffy Ave Hicksville NY 11801-3639

WALSH, CHRISTOPHER ANDREW, neuroscientist, neurologist, educator; b. Plainfield, N.J., July 26, 1957; s. James Joseph and Arleen W.; m. Ming Hui Chen, June 8, 1991; 1 child, Jennifer Ming. BS in Chemistry, Bucknell U., 1978; PhD in Neurobiology, U. Chgo., 1983, MD, 1985. Diplomate Nat. Bd. Med. Examiners, Am. Bd. Psychiatry and Neurology. Intern in medicine Mass. Gen. Hosp., Boston, 1985-86, resident in neurology, 1986-89, chief resident in neurology, 1988-89; fellow in neurology and genetics Mass. Gen. Hosp. and Harvard Med. Sch., Boston, 1989-92; asst. prof. neurology Harvard Med. Sch., 1993—; assoc. in neurology Beth Israel Hosp., Boston, 1993—; Deutscher Akademischer Austanschdienst fellow Max-Planck-Inst. für Hirnforschung, Frankfurt, Germany, 1982-83. Contbr. over 40 articles to profl. publs. Neurosci. fellow Dana Found., 1989-91. Mem. Am. Acad. Neurology, Am. Epilepsy Soc., Soc. for Neurosci., Phi Beta Kappa, Alpha Chi Sigma. Home: 11 Arlington Rd Chestnut Hill MA 02167-2612 Office: Beth Israel Hosp Dept Neurology 330 Brookline Ave Boston MA 02215

WALSH, CORNELIUS STEPHEN, leasing company executive; b. N.Y.C., Dec. 27, 1907; s. William Francis and Frances (Murphy) W.; m. Edwyna Lois Senter, May 1, 1930; children: Jane Linda (Mrs. Walsh Weed), Richard Stephen, Suzanne Patricia. Student, Eastman-Gaines Sch., 1924-25. Assoc. with Dyson Shipping Co., Inc., 1925-27, Interocean Steamship Corp., 1928-30; sec. States Marine Corp., 1931-38, v.p., 1938-53, pres., 1953-65, dir., 1950-65; pres., dir. States Marine Corp. Del., 1946-65; chmn. Waterman Steamship Corp., N.Y.C., 1965-89, Waterman Industries Corp., 1965-89, Hammond Leasing Corp., 1967—; dir. Oliver Corp. Mem. Far East-Am. Coun. Commerce and Industry (bd. dirs.), Soc. Naval Architects and Marine Engrs. (assoc.), Soc. of Four Arts (Palm Beach, Fla.), Japan Soc. (hon. bd. dirs.), Am. Bur. Shipping, Yacht Club (N.Y.C.), Seawanhaka Corinthian Yacht Club (Oyster Bay, L.I., N.Y.), N.Am. Sta. Royal Scandinavian Yacht Club, Pine Valley Golf Club (Clementon, N.J.), Everglades Club (Palm Beach), Bath and Tennis Club (Palm Beach), Sailfish of Fla. Club (Palm Beach). Home: 220 El Bravo Way Palm Beach FL 33480-4722

WALSH, DANIEL FRANCIS, bishop; b. San Francisco, Oct. 2, 1937. Grad., St. Joseph Sem., St. Patrick Sem., Catholic U. Am. Ordained priest, Roman Catholic Ch., 1963. Ordained titular bishop of Tigia, 1981; aux. bishop of San Francisco, 1981-87, bishop of Reno-Las Vegas, 1987—. Home: 2809 Cameo Cir Las Vegas NV 89107-3213 Office: Diocese of Reno-Las Vegas Office of Bishop PO Box 18316 Las Vegas NV 89114-8316*

WALSH, DAVID GRAVES, lawyer; b. Madison, Wis., Jan. 7, 1943; s. John J. and Audrey B. Walsh; married; children: Michael, Katherine, Molly, John. BBA, U. Wis., 1965; JD, Harvard U., 1970. Bar: Wis. Law clk. Wis. Supreme Ct., Madison, 1970-71; ptnr. Walsh, Walsh, Sweeney & Whitney, Madison, 1971-86; ptnr.-in-charge Foley & Lardner, Madison, 1986—; bd. dirs. Nat. Guardian Life, Madison, 1981—; lectr. U. Wis., Madison, 1974-75, 77-78. Chmn. State of Wis. Elections Bd., Madison, 1978. Lt. USN, 1965-67, Vietnam. Maple Bluff Country Club (Madison) (pres. 1987). Roman Catholic. Avocations: tennis, golf, fishing. Home: 41 Fuller Dr Madison WI 53704-5962 Office: Foley & Lardner 150 E Gilman PO Box 1497 Madison WI 53701-1497

WALSH, DENNY JAY, reporter; b. Omaha, Nov. 23, 1935; s. Gerald Jerome and Muriel (Morton) W.; m. Peggy Marie Moore, Feb. 12, 1966; children by previous marriage—Catherine Camille, Colleen Cecile; 1 son, Sean Joseph. B.J., U. Mo., 1962. Staff writer St. Louis Globe-Democrat, 1961-68; asst. editor Life mag., N.Y.C., 1968-70; assoc. editor Life mag., 1970-73; reporter N.Y. Times, 1973-74, Sacramento Bee, 1974—. Served with USMC, 1954-58. Recipient Con Lee Kelliher award St. Louis chpt. Sigma Delta Chi, 1962; award Am. Polit. Sci. Assn., 1963; award Sigma Delta Chi, 1968; Pulitzer prize spl. local reporting, 1969; 1st prize San Francisco Press Club, 1977. Office: Sacramento Bee 21st and Q Sts Sacramento CA 95813

WALSH, DIANA CHAPMAN, academic administrator, social and behavioral sciences educator; b. Phila., July 30, 1944; d. Robert Francis and Gwen (Jenkins) Chapman; m. Christopher Thomas Walsh, June 18, 1966; 1 child, Allison Chapman Walsh. BA, Wellesley Coll., 1966; MS, Boston U. Sch. of Pub. Comm., 1971; PhD, Boston U., 1983; LHD (hon.), Boston U, 1994, Amer. Coll. of Greece, Athens, 1995. Mgr. spl. events Barnard Coll., N.Y.C., 1967-70; dir. info., edn. Planned Parenthood League, Newton, Mass., 1971-74; sr. program assoc. Dept Pub. Health, Boston, 1974-76; assoc. dir. Boston U. Health Policy Inst., 1985-90; prof. Sch. Pub. Health, Sch. Medicine, Boston U., 1987-90, prof., 1988-90, adj. prof. pub. health, 1990—; adj. prof. Harvard Sch. Pub. Health, 1993—; pres. Wellesley Coll., 1993—. Author: (book) Corporate Physicians, 1987; editor: Women, Work, and Health: Challenges to Corporate Policy, 1980, (book series) Industry and Health Care, 1977-80; contbr. articles to profl. jours. Bd. dirs. Planned Parenthood League of Mass., 1974-79, 1981-85, bd. of overseers 1993-94; trustee Occupational Physicians Scholarship Fund, 1987-94; trustee WGBH Educational Found., 1993—. Kellogg Nat. fellow, 1987-90. Mem. AAAS. Intersts include: gender and health, leadership studies, social policy, the craft of writing, skiing. Office: Wellesley Coll Office of the Pres Wellesley MA 02181

WALSH, DON, marine consultant, executive; b. Berkeley, Calif., Nov. 2, 1931; s. J. Don and Marguerite Grace (Van Auker) W.; m. Joan A. Betzmer, Aug. 18, 1962; children—Kelly Drennan, Elizabeth McDonough. BS, U.S. Naval Acad., 1954; MS, Tex. A&M U., 1967, PhD, 1968; MA, San Diego State Coll., 1968. Commd. ensign USN, 1954, advanced through grades to capt., 1974; officer-in-charge Bathyscaph Trieste USN, Trieste, 1959-62; comdr. in USS Bashaw USN, 1968-69; dir. Inst. Marine and Coastal Studies, prof. ocean engring. U. So. Calif., Los Angeles, 1975-83; pres., chief exec. officer Internat. Maritime, Inc., Los Angeles, 1976—; mng. dir. Deep Ocean Engring., Inc., 1990—, also bd. dirs.; dir. Ctr. for Marine Transp. Studies, U. So. Calif., 1980-83, Coastal Resources Ctr., 1990-94; trustee USN Mus. Found., 1989—; mem. Nat. Adv. Com. on Oceans and Atmosphere, 1979-85; bd. govs. Calif. Maritime Acad., 1985-95; pres. Parker Diving, 1989-94. Author: Law of the Sea: Issues in Ocean Resource Management, 1977, Energy and Resources Development of Continental Margins, 1980, Energy and Sea Power: Challenge for the Decade, 1981, Waste Disposal in the Oceans: Minimizing Impact, Maximizing Benefits, 1983; editor Jour. Marine Tech. Soc., 1975-80; mem. editorial bd. U.S. Naval Inst., 1974-75. Decorated Legion of Merit (2), Meritorious Service medal (2); Woodrow Wilson Internat. Ctr. for Scholars fellow, 1973-74. Fellow Marine Tech. Soc. (hon. life), Acad. Underwater Arts and Scis., Explorers Club (hon. life, bd. dirs. 1994—); mem. AAAS, Soc. Naval Archs. and Marine Engrs., Am. Soc. Naval Engrs., Navy League, Navy Inst., Adventurers Club (hon. life). Office: Internat Maritime Inc HC-86 Box 101 Myrtle Point OR 97458-9726

WALSH, DONNIE, sports club executive; married; 5 children. Grad., U. N.C.; attended, N.C. Law Sch. Bar: 1977. Assoc. head coach U. N.C.; staff coach Denver Nuggets, head coach, 1979-81; asst. coach Ind. Pacers, 1984-86, exec. v.p., gen. mgr., 1986-92, pres., 1992—. Office: Ind Pacers Market Sq Arena 300 E Market St Indianapolis IN 46204-2603*

WALSH, EDWARD JOSEPH, toiletries and food company executive; b. Mt. Vernon, N.Y., Mar. 18, 1932; s. Edward Aloysius and Charlotte Cecilia (Borup) W.; m. Patricia Ann Farrell, Sept. 16, 1961; children: Edward Joseph, Megan Simpson, John, Robert. BBA, Iona Coll., 1953; MBA, NYU, 1958. Sales rep. M & R Dietetic Labs., Columbus, Ohio, 1955-60; with Armour & Co., 1961-71, Greyhound Corp., 1971-87; v.p. toiletries div. Armour Dial Co., Phoenix, 1973-74; exec. v.p. Armour Dial Co., 1975-77; pres. Armour Internat. Co., Phoenix, 1978-84; pres. The Dial Corp. (formerly Armour-Dial Co.), Phoenix, 1984-87, chief exec. officer, 1984-87; pres., chief exec. officer Purex Corp., 1985; chmn., chief exec. officer The Sparta Group Ltd., Scottsdale, Ariz., 1988—; bd. dirs. Guest Supply Inc., New Brunswick, N.J., WD-40 Co., San Diego, Nortrust Ariz. Holding Corp., Phoenix, No. Trust Bank of Ariz., N.A., Exec. Svcs. Corps. of Ariz., Inc. Bd. trustees Scottsdale Meml. Health Found.; pres. Mt. Vernon Fire Dept. Mems. Assn., 1960-61. Served with U.S. Army, 1953-55, Germany. Mem. Am. Mgmt. Assn., Nat. Meat Canner Assn. (pres. 1971-72), Cosmetic, Toiletries and Fragrance Assn. (bd. dirs. 1985—), Nat. Food Processors Assn. (bd. dirs.). Republican. Roman Catholic. Office: The Sparta Group Ltd 6623 N Scottsdale Rd Scottsdale AZ 85250-4421

WALSH, EDWARD PATRICK, federal agency administrator; b. N.Y.C., Nov. 21, 1937; s. Edward P. and Marion B. (Burnich) W.; m. Kathleen F. Ringrose, Nov. 25, 1967; children: Megan, Brendan. BS in Econs., Villanova U., 1959. Patrol inspector U.S. Border Patrol Immigration and Naturalization Svc., Harlingen, Tex., 1962-65; spl. agt. U.S. Secret Svc., 1965-86; dep. asst. dir. U.S. Secret Svc., Washington, 1986; dir. Bur. Investigations FMC, Washington, 1986, mng. dir., 1986—. Trustee, assoc. Villanova U., 1990—. With U.S. Army, 1959-61, Korea. Recipient Presdl. Rank award, 1989. Mem. Internat. Assn. Chiefs of Police, Assn. Former Secret Svc. Agts., Fed. Exec. Inst. Alumni Assn., Sr. Exec. Assn.

WALSH, ERIC, food products executive. Pres. Klondike Ice Cream Inc., Green Bay. Office: Good Humor Corp 909 Packerland Dr Green Bay WI 54303-4827*

WALSH, F. HOWARD, oil producer, rancher; b. Waco, Tex., Feb. 7, 1913; s. P. Frank and Maude (Gage) W.; m. Mary D. Fleming, Mar. 13, 1937; children: Richard F., F. Howard, D'Ann E. Walsh Bonnell, Maudi Walsh Roe, William Lloyd. BBA, Tex. Christian U., 1933, LLD (hon.), 1979. Self employed oil producer, rancher, 1942—; pres. Walsh & Watts, Inc. Mem. Tex. Jud. Qualifications Commn., 1970-74; pres. Walsh Found.; v.p. Fleming Found.; hon. trustee Tex. Christian U.; guarantor Ft. Worth Arts Council (also hon. bd. mem.), Schola Cantorum, Ft. Worth Ballet, Tex. Boys' Choir, Ft. Worth Theatre, Ft. Worth Opera; bd. dirs. Southwestern Expdn. and Fat Stock Show, Ft. Worth. Named Valuable Alumnus, Tex. Chriatisn U., 1967, Patron of Arts in Ft. Worth, 1970, 91, Edna Gladney Internat. Grandparents, 1972, PAtron of Yr. Live Theater League Tarrant County, 1996; recipient spl. recognition for support Univ. Ranch Tng. Program, Royal Purple (with wife) Tex. Christian U., 1979, Disting. Svc. award So. Bapt. Radio and TV Commn., 1972, tng. Commn., 1976, Brotherhood citation NCCJ, 1978, Friends of Tex. Boys' Choir, 1981, donor Walsh Med. Bldg., Southwestern Bapt. Theol. Sem., land and bldgs. to Tex. Boys Choir, 1971, Wurlitzer Organ of Cana Manana, 1972, appreciation award an citation Southwestern Bapt. Theol. Sem., 1981, B.H. Carroll Founders Southwestern Bapt. Theol. Sem., 1982, (with wife) St. Citizen award, 1985, Silver Spur award, 1990, Horizon award Fine Arts Dept. Tex. Christian U., 1995, Disting. Philanthropist award, 1995; Tarrant County Jr. Coll. Libr. dedicated in his honor, 1978, ballet season dedicated in his honor by Ft. Worth Ballet Assn., 1978-79, TCU Athletic Complex dedicated in his honor, 1994, benefactor ann. prodn. Littlest Wiseman, Christmas Gift to City of Ft. Worth. Mem. Tex.-Mid-Continent Oil and Gas Assn., West Central Tex. Oil and Gas Assn., North Tex. Oil and Gas Assn., Ind. Petroleum Assn., Tex. Ind. Producers and Royalty Owners, Am.-Internat. Charolais Assn., Tex. Christian U. Ex-Letterman's Assn. Baptist bd. sr. deacons. Clubs: Garden of Gods; Colorado Springs Country (Colorado Springs); Steeplechase, Fort Worth, Ridglea, Frog, Colonial Country, Shady Oaks Country, Century II, Petroleum, City, River Crest Country. Home: 2425 Stadium Dr Fort Worth TX 76109-1055 Office: Walsh & Watts Inc 1007 InterFirst Ft Worth Bldg Fort Worth TX 76102 also: 1801 Culebra Colorado Springs CO 80907

WALSH, GARY L., consumer products company executive; b. 1942. Sr. mgmt. Sara Lee Corp. and Sysco Foods, 1966-77; CEO Miller Cascade Foodsvc. of Am., 1977-1990; chmn., pres., CEO Core-Mark Internat., Inc., South San Francisco, 1990—. Office: Core-Mark International Inc 395 Oyster Point Blvd South San Francisco CA 94080-1928 also: Core Mark Interrlated Cos 311 Reed Cir Corona CA 91719-1349*

WALSH, GEORGE WILLIAM, publishing company executive, editor; b. N.Y.C., Jan. 16, 1931; s. William Francis and Madeline (Maass) W.; m. Joan Mary Dunn, May 20, 1961; children—Grail, Simon. B.S., Fordham U., 1952; M.S., Columbia U. Sch. Journalism, 1953. Copy editor, reporter Cape Cod Standard-Times, Hyannis, Mass., 1955; communications specialist IBM, N.Y.C., 1955-58; editorial trainee Time, Inc., 1958-59; writer-reporter Sports Illus., N.Y.C., 1959-62; book editor Cosmopolitan, N.Y.C., 1962-65; mng. editor Cosmopolitan, 1965-74; editor-in-chief, v.p. Ballantine Books div. Random House, N.Y.C., 1974-79, Macmillan Pub. Co., N.Y.C., 1979-85; pub. cons., 1985—. Author: Gentleman Jimmy Walker, 1974, Public Enemies, 1980. Served with AUS, 1953-55. Mem. Assn. Am. Pubs. Roman Catholic. Clubs: Univ. (N.Y.C.); Pamet Harbor Yacht and Tennis (Truro, Mass.). Home: 35 Prospect Park W Brooklyn NY 11215-2370

WALSH, GEORGE WILLIAM, engineering executive; b. Teton County, Idaho, Mar. 22, 1923; s. Raymond Eugene and Maude Ethel (Brack) W.; m. Catherine Mary Yunker, July 1, 1950; children: Dwight, Maureen, John. BSEE, U. Idaho, 1947; MEE, Rensselaer Poly. Inst., 1960. Registered profl. engr., N.Y. With GE, 1947-94; test engr. GE, Cleve. and Schenectady, N.Y., 1947-49; design engr. GE, Pittsfield, Mass., 1949-50; power system engr. GE, Schenectady, 1950-66, mgr. power system engring., 1966-85, mgr. power system cons. engring., 1985-93, cons., 1993-94; profl. cons. engr., 1994—. Contbr. numerous papers and articles relating to electric power system engring. to profl. publs. Recipient GE Power Systems Engring. awards for Outstanding Tech. Contbn., 1986, and Outstanding Profl. and Social Svcs., 1991. Fellow IEEE (life, Centennial medal 1984, Richard Harold Kaufmann field award for outstanding contbn. to indsl. engring. 1993); mem. IEEE Industry Applications Soc. (pres., mem. exec. bd., adminstrv. and tech. coms., Power Systems Achievement award 1980, Outstanding Achievement award 1990), IEEE Power Engring. Soc. Home and Office: 26 St Stephens Ln E Schenectady NY 12302-4221

WALSH, GERALDINE FRANCES, nursing administrator; b. Phila., July 3, 1946; d. Raymond S. and Marie Ruth (Lipsett) Lore; m. Harry G. Walsh, Jan. 29, 1966; children: Michael, Gregory. AA, No. Va. Community Coll., 1979; BS, St. Joseph's Coll., Windham, Maine, 1987, postgrad. Cert. in nursing adminstrn.; cert. instr. basic life support; cert. dir. nursing adminstrn. long term care. Charge nurse, asst. head nurse Parkview Hosp., Phila., 1968-73; staff nurse JFK Med. Ctr., Edison, 1973-76; clin. nursing supr., charge nurse med.-surg. Loudoun Hosp. Ctr., Leesburg, Va., 1976-88; asst. dir. nursing Loudoun Long Term Care Ctr., Leesburg, 1988-95; dir. nursing Cameron Glen Care Ctr., Reston, Va., 1995—. Recipient Nursing Achievement award. Mem. ANA, NAFE, Nat. League Nursing, Va. League Nursing, Va. Nurses Assn., Am. Coll. Healthcare Execs. (student assoc. mem.), Nat. Assn. for Healthcare Quality, Assn. Healthcare Adminstrs. of Nat. Capitol Area. Address: 20380 Harmony Ct Ashburn VA 22011-3300

WALSH, JAMES HAMILTON, lawyer; b. Astoria, N.Y., May 20, 1947; s. Edward James and Helen Smith (Hamilton) W.; m. Janice Ausherman, Aug. 3, 1968; children: Tracy, Courtney, Eric. B.A. in Psychology, Bridgewater Coll., 1968; J.D., U. Va., 1975. Bar: Va. 1975, U.S. Dist. Ct. (ea. and we. dists.) Va. 1975, U.S. Ct. Appeals (4th cir.) 1976, U.S. Supreme Ct. 1982. Assoc. McGuire, Woods, Battle & Boothe (and predecessor firms), Richmond, Va., 1975-82, ptnr., 1982—; instr. Nat. Inst. Trial Adv.; adj. prof. U. Richmond, 1992, 93; spl. prosecutor U.S. Dist. Ct. (ea. dist.) Va., 1979, 84. Mem. bd. trustees Bridgewater (Va.) Coll., mem. exec. com.; mem. staff Va. Law Rev. With U.S. Army, 1969-72. Mem. ABA (mem. antitrust sect. health care com., litigation sect.), Va. State Bar (bd. govs. antitrust sect. 1984-90, chmn. 1986), Va. Bar Assn. (vice chmn. criminal law sect.), Richmond Bar Assn., Order Coif, Phi Delta Phi. Episcopalian. Clubs: Willow Oaks. Contbr. articles to profl. jours. Home: 113 Adingham Ct Richmond VA 23229-7761 Office: McGuire Woods Battle & Boothe 1 James Ctr 910 E Cary St Richmond VA 23219-4004

WALSH, JAMES JEROME, philosophy educator; b. Seattle, May 23, 1924; s. John Jerome and Agnes (Counihan) W.; m. Carol Jean Paton, Sept. 16, 1946; children—John Jerome II, James Paton. B.A., Reed Coll., 1949, Oxford (Eng.) U., 1951; M.A., Oxford (Eng.) U., 1956; Ph.D., Columbia U., 1960. Mem. faculty Columbia U., 1954-90, prof. philosophy, 1966-90, prof. emeritus, 1990—, dir. grad. studies philosophy dept., 1963-66, 73-88, chmn. dept., 1967-73, acting chmn. dept., 1982-83; vis. instr. U. Calif.-Berkeley, 1958; cons. TV series G.E. Coll. Bowl, 1965-70. Author: Aristotle's Conception of Moral Weakness, 1963, Philosophy in the Middle Ages, 1967, 2d edit., 1983; Editor Jour. Philosophy, 1965-90. Mem. Rockland County Democratic Com., 1960-63. Served with AUS, 1943-45. Decorated Purple Heart.; Rhodes scholar, 1949; Ford Found. fellow, 1958; Am. Coun. Learned Socs. fellow, 1962; Guggenheim fellow, 1966. Mem. Soc. Medieval and Renaissance Philosophy. Home: 300 Haverstraw Rd Suffern NY 10901-3137

WALSH, JAMES JOSEPH, lawyer; b. Kansas City, Mo., Nov. 11, 1930; s. James J. and Kathryn J. (Pierce) W.; m. Lavern Snellen, Oct. 4, 1952; children: Michelle, Kelley. BJ, U. Mo., Columbia, 1951; LLB, U. Mo., Kansas City, 1961. Bar: Calif. 1963. Atty. Dept. Justice, Washington, 1961-62; assoc. Pillsbury, Madison & Suto, San Francisco, 1962-71, ptnr., 1971—. With USN, 1953-55. Mem. ABA, Calif. Bar Assn., Bar Assn. San Francisco. Home: 60 Rowley Cir Belvedere Tiburon CA 94920-1427 Office: Pillsbury Madison & Sutro 235 Montgomery St San Francisco CA 94104-4207

WALSH, JAMES PATRICK, lawyer; b. North Bend, Oreg., Dec. 28, 1944; s. William P. And Ethel A. (Smith) W.; m. Cynthia J. Raffel, Aug. 3, 1968; children: Nicholas, Faye, Robinson. AB, Stanford U., 1967; JD, U. Wash., 1970, LLM, 1971. Bar: Wash. 1970, D.C. 1976. Asst. atty. gen. State of Wash., Olympia, 1971-72; staff counsel com. on commerce U.S. Senate, Washington, 1972-76, gen. counsel, 1977-78; dep. adminstr. NOAA, Washington, 1978-81; of counsel Davis Wright Jones, Washington, 1983-84; ptnr. Davis Wright Tremaine, Washington, 1985—. Lt. USAR, 1970-76. Home: 4403 Klingle St NW Washington DC 20016-3578 Office: Davis Wright Tremaine 1155 Connecticut Ave NW Ste 700 Washington DC 20036-4306

WALSH, JAMES THOMAS, congressman; b. Syracuse, N.Y., June 19, 1947. BA, St. Bonaventure U., 1970. Agrl. extension agt. Peace Corps, 1970-72; mktg. exec. telecommunications co., 1974-88; exec.-in-residence telecommunications inst. Coll. Tech. SUNY, Utica, Rome, N.Y., 1986-87; common councilor City of Syracuse, 1977-85, pres. common coun., 1986-88; mem. 101st-present Congresses from 27th (now 25th) N.Y. dist., Washington, D.C., 1989—. Republican. Office: US House of Reps 1330 Longworth House Washington DC 20515 also: 1269 Federal Bldg 45 Church St Cortland NY 13045-2743 also: One Lincoln St Auburn NY 13021

WALSH, JOHN, museum director; b. Mason City, Wash., Dec. 9, 1937; s. John J. and Eleanor (Wilson) W.; m. Virginia Alys Galston, Feb. 17, 1962; children: Peter Wilson, Anne Galston, Frederick Matthiessen. B.A., Yale U., 1961; postgrad., U. Leyden, Netherlands, 1965-66; MA, Columbia U., 1965, PhD, 1971. Lectr., rsch. asst. Frick Collection, N.Y.C., 1966-68; assoc. higher edn. Met. Mus. Art, N.Y.C., 1968-71; assoc. curator European paintings Met. Mus. Art, 1970-72, curator dept. European paintings, 1972-74, vice-chmn., 1974-75; adj. asso. prof. art history Columbia U., N.Y.C., 1969-72; adj. prof. Columbia U., 1972-75; prof. art history Barnard Coll., Columbia U., N.Y.C., 1975-77; Mrs. Russell W. Baker curator paintings Mus. Fine Arts, Boston, 1977-83; dir. J. Paul Getty Mus., Malibu, Calif., 1983—; vis. prof. fine arts Harvard U., 1979; mem. governing bd. Yale U. Art Gallery, 1975—, Smithsonian Coun., 1990—. Contbr. articles to profl. jours. Mem. Dem. County Com., N.Y.C., 1968-71; mem. vis. com. Fogg Mus., Harvard U., 1982-87; bd. fellows Claremont U. Ctr. and Grad. Sch., 1988—. With USNR, 1957-63. Fulbright grad. fellow The Netherlands, 1965-66. Mem. Coll. Art Assn., Am. Assn. Mus., Archaeol. Inst. Am., Am. Antiquarian Soc., Assn. Art Mus. Dirs. (trustee 1986—, pres. 1989-90), Century Assn. N.Y.C. Office: J Paul Getty Museum PO Box 2112 Santa Monica CA 90407

WALSH, JOHN BREFFNI, aerospace consultant; b. Bklyn., Aug. 20, 1927; s. George and Margaret Mary (Rigney) W.; m. Marie Louise Leclerc, June 18, 1955; children: George Breffni, John Leclerc, Darina Louise. B.E.E., Manhattan Coll., 1948; M.S., Columbia U., 1950; postgrad., NYU, 1954-62. Asst., instr. Columbia U., N.Y.C., 1948-51, asst. prof., asst. dir. Electronics Research Labs., 1953-66; various positions through tech. dir. Intelligence and Reconnaissance Div., Rome Air Devel. Center, N.Y., 1951-53; dep. for research to asst. sec. Air Force, 1966-71; sr. staff mem. Nat. Security Council, 1971-72, asst. to Pres.'s sci. advisor, 1971-72; dep. dir. Def. Research and Engring., 1972-77; asst. sec. gen. for def. support NATO, 1977-80; holder chair in systems acquisition mgmt., dean exec. inst. Def. Systems Mgmt. Coll., Ft. Belvoir, Va., 1981-82; prof. emeritus Def. Systems Mgmt. Coll., Ft. Belvoir, 1982—; v.p., chief scientist Boeing Mil. Airplane

Co., Wichita, Kans., 1982-89; v.p. rsch. and engring. programs Boeing Aerospace and Electronics div., Seattle, 1990-92; v.p. strategic analysis Boeing Defense and Space Group, Seattle, 1992-93; prin. John B. Walsh Assocs., 1993—; mem. aeros. adv. com. NASA; mem. Congl. Adv. Com. on Aeros., 1984-85; assoc. Def. Sci. Bd.; mem. indsl. adv. bd. Wichita State U. Coll. Engring., adj. prof. elec. engring., 1989-90; chmn. tech. working group Def. Trade Adv. Group Dept. State, 1992-95. Author: Electromagnetic Theory and Engineering Applications, 1960, (with K.S. Miller) Introductory Electric Circuits, 1960, Elementary and Advanced Trigonometry, 1977; contbr. tech. papers to publs.; patentee in field. Mem. planning bd., Cresskill, N.J., 1964-66; commr. Kans. Advanced Tech. Commn., 1985-86; bd. dirs. Kans. Inc., 1986-90; mem. math. scis. edn. bd. NRC, 1989-92. Served with U.S. Army, 1946-47. Recipient Air Force Exceptional Civilian Service award, 1969; recipient Dept. Def. Meritorious Civilian Service award, 1971, Disting. Civilian Service award, 1977, Air Force Assn. citation of honor as outstanding Air Force civilian employee of year, 1971, Theodore von Karman award Air Force Assn., 1977. Fellow IEEE (life), AIAA (v.p. tech. 1987-89); mem. N.Y. Acad. Scis., GPS Internat. Assn., Electromagnetics Acad., Sigma Xi, Eta Kappa Nu. Roman Catholic.

WALSH, J(OHN) B(RONSON), lawyer; b. Buffalo, Feb. 20, 1927; s. John A. and Alice (Condon) W.; m. Barbara Ashford, May 20, 1966; 1 child, Martha. AB, Canisius Coll., 1950; JD, Georgetown U., 1952. Bar: N.Y. 1953, U.S. Supreme Ct. 1958, U.S. Ct. Internat. Trade 1969, U.S. Ct. Customs and Patent Appeals 1973. Trial atty. Garvey & Conway, N.Y.C., 1953-54; vol. atty. Nativity Mission, N.Y.C., 1953-54; ptnr. Jaeckle, Fleischmann, Kelly, Swart & Augspurger, Buffalo, 1955-60; pvt. practice Buffalo, 1961-75; ptnr. Jaeckle, Fleischmann & Mugel, Buffalo, 1976-80; with Walsh & Cleary, P.C., Buffalo, 1980-84; pvt. practice, 1984—; spl. counsel Ecology and Environment, Inc., Lancaster, N.Y., 1989—; trial counsel antitrust div. Dept. Justice, Washington, 1960-61; spl. counsel on disciplinary procedures N.Y. Supreme Ct., 1960-76; appointee legal disciplinary coordinating com. State of N.Y., 1971; legis. counsel, spl. counsel to mayor Buffalo, 1995—; counsel to sheriff Erie County, 1969-72; legis counsel Niagara Frontier Transp. Authority; cons. Norfolk So. R.R., Ecology and Environment on Govtl. Affairs; guest lectr. univs. and profl. groups. Author: (TV series) The Law and You (Freedom Found. award, ABA award, Internat. Police Assn. award). Past pres. Ashford Hollow Found. Visual and Performing Arts; past trustee Dollar Bills, Inc.; past co-producer Grand Island Playhouse and Players. With U.S. Army, 1945-46. Recipient Gold Key Buffalo Jr. C. of C., 1962, award Freedom Found., 1966. Fellow Am. Bar Found.; mem. ABA (del. internat. conf. Brussels 1963, Mexico City 1964, Lausanne, Switzerland 1964, Award of Merit com. 1961-70, sec., vice chair, chmn. sect. bar activities 1965-69, mem. ho. of dels. 1969-70, mem. crime prevention and control com. 1968-70, vice chair sr. lawyers divsn., com. legislation and adminstrn. regulations 1992—, vice chair sr. lawyers divsn. membership com. 1993-94), N.Y. Trial Lawyers Assn., Am. Immigration Lawyers Assn., Am. Judicature Soc., N.Y. State Bar Assn. (past exec. sec.), Erie County Bar Assn., Buffalo Bar Assn., Nat. Pub. Employer Labor Relations Assn., Capital Hill Club of Buffalo, Am. Assn. Airport Execs., N.Y. State Bus. Coun. (environ. law subcom., chmn. subcom.), Buffalo Irish Club (bd. dirs.), Buffalo Athletic Club (past bd. dirs., past v.p.), Buffalo Canoe Club, Buffalo Club, Ft. Orange of Albany Club, KC, Knights of Equity, Leoknights, Phi Delta Phi. Roman Catholic. Home: 95 North Dr Eggertsville NY 14226-4158 Office: 368 Pleasant View Dr Lancaster NY 14086-1316 also: 210 Ellicott Sq Bldg Buffalo NY 14203

WALSH, JOHN CHARLES, metallurgical company executive; b. Indpls., Sept. 8, 1924; s. John Charles and Nell (O'Neil) W.; m. Mary Louise Dreiss, Feb. 5, 1949; children: Michael S., Carolyn Ann, Anne D. B.S., Notre Dame U., 1949. Auditor Herdrich Boggs & Co., Indpls., 1949-50; with P.R. Mallory & Co., Inc., 1949-80; pres. Walgang Co. Inc., Indpls., 1980—; v.p., treas. P.R. Mallory & Co., 1971. Served with USMCR, 1943-45. Mem. Fin. Execs. Inst., Indpls. C. of C., Ind. Hist. Soc., Econ. Club, Notre Dame Club, Rotary. Home: 7365 Huntington Rd Indianapolis IN 46240-3657 Office: 6100 N Keystone Ave Indianapolis IN 46220-2452

WALSH, JOHN E., JR., business educator, consultant; b. St. Louis, Apr. 28, 1927; s. John E. and Ann M. (Narkewicz) W. B.S., U.S. Naval Acad., 1950; M.B.A., Washington U., St. Louis, 1957; D.B.A., Harvard U., 1960. Asst. prof. Washington U., St. Louis, 1959-60; assoc. prof. Washington U., 1960-68, prof., 1968—; vis. assoc. prof. Stanford U., 1964-65; vis. prof. INSEAD, Fontainebleau, France, 1970. Author: Preparing Feasibility Studies in Asia, 1971, Guidelines for Management Consultants in Asia, 1973, Planning New Ventures in International Business, 1976, (with others) Strategies in Business, 1978, Management Tactics, 1980, International Business Case Studies: For the Multicultural Market Place, 1994. Served to 1st lt. USAF, 1950-54. Zurn Found. fellow, 1958. Mem. St. Louis Com. on Fgn. Rels., Harvard Club N.Y.C. Home: 5471 Charglow Dr Saint Louis MO 63129-3564 Office: Washington U Grad Sch Bus PO Box 1133 1 Brookings Dr Saint Louis MO 63130-4889

WALSH, JOHN HARLEY, medical educator; b. Jackson, Miss., Aug. 22, 1938; s. John Howard and Aimee Nugent (Shands) W.; m. Courtney Kathleen McFadden, June 12, 1963 (div. 1979); children: Courtney Shands (Mrs. Peter Phleger), John Harley Jr.; m. Mary Carol Territo, Feb. 4, 1989. BA, Vanderbilt U., 1959, MD, 1963. Diplomate Am. Bd. Internal Medicine, Am. Bd. Gastroenterology. Intern N.Y. Hosp., N.Y.C., 1963-64; resident N.Y. Hosp. Cornell Med. Ctr., N.Y.C., 1964-67; rsch. assoc. Bronx VA Hosp., N.Y., 1969-70; fellow gastroenterology Wadsworth, Va., LA, 1970-71; clin. investigator Wadsworth VA Hosp., L.A., 1971-73; asst. to assoc. prof. UCLA, 1970-78, prof. medicine, 1978—, dir. Integrated Gastroenterology Tng. Program, 1983-89, dir. Div. Gastroenterology, 1988-93, Dorothy and Leonard Straus prof., 1989—; rsch. dir. CURE Digestive Diseases Rsch. Ctr., L.A., 1993—; dep. dir. Ctr. Ulcer Rsch. and Edn., L.A., 1974-80, assoc. dir., 1980-87, dir. 1987—, CURE Digestive Diseases Rsch. Ctr., 1995—; adv. coun. mem. NIH, Bethesda, Md., 1982-85; mem. Nat. Digestive Disease Adv. Bd., 1987-91. Assoc. editor: Gastroenterology Jour., 1976-86; mem. editorial bd. Am. Jour. Physiology, Jour. Clin. Endocrinology and Metabolism, Peptides Jour.; contbr. articles to profl. jours. Served with USPHS, 1967-69. Recipient AGA Fiterman/Kirsner Clinical Rsch. award, 1993, Rorer award So. Calif. Soc. Gastroenterology, 1972, Western Gastroent. Rsch. prize Western Gut Club, 1983, Merit award NIH, 1987. Mem. Am. Gastroent. Assn. (v.p., 1992-93, pres.-elect 1993-94, pres. 1994-95), Am. Soc. Clin. Investigation, Assn. Am. Physicians, Endocrine Soc., Western Soc. Clin. Investigation (counselor 1978-81). Episcopalian. Avocations: tennis, golf, ballet, modern fiction. Home: 247 S Carmelina Ave Los Angeles CA 90049 Office: CURE Digestive Diseases Rsch Ctr 11301 Wilshire Blvd Los Angeles CA 90073-1792

WALSH, JOHN JOSEPH, medical school administrator, physician; b. N.Y.C., July 31, 1924; s. Patrick Joseph and Elizabeth (Lawless) W.; m. Gloria Paolini (dec. 1971); children: Maureen Walsh Garland, John Joseph Jr., Kathleen Walsh Saer; m. Dorothy B. Ray, 1989. Student, Fordham U., 1941-43, Cornell U., 1943-44; MD, L.I. Coll. Medicine, 1948; postdoctoral, Tulane U., 1957-58; ScD (hon.), SUNY, 1989. Diplomate Am. Bd. Internal Medicine. Commd. USPHS, 1948, advanced through grades to rear admiral, 1966; intern USPHS Hosp., Staten Island, N.Y., 1948-49; resident USPHS Hosp., Seattle, 1951-54; asst. chief medicine USPHS Hosp., New Orleans, 1954-56, dep. chief, 1956-57, chief research activites, 1958-64, chief med. service, 1963-64, med. dir., med. officer in charge, 1964-66; asst. surgeon gen., dir. div. direct health services USPHS, 1966-68, ret., 1968; instr. Tulane U. Sch. Medicine, New Orleans, 1957-58, asst. prof., 1958-60, assoc. prof., 1960-67, prof., 1967-89, prof. medicine emeritus, 1989—, dean, 1968-69; dean, coordinator health sci. and programs Tulane U. Med. Ctr., New Orleans, 1968-69, v.p. health affairs, 1969-78, chancellor, 1973-89; chancellor emeritus Tulane U. Med. Ctr., 1989—; acting dean sch. pub. health and tropical medicine Tulane U. Med. Ctr., New Orleans, 1974, Jack R. Aron prof. in adminstrv. medicine, 1978-89; adj. prof. Tulane U. Sch. Pub. Health and Tropical Medicine, 1978-89; pres., CEO Mahorner Clinic, Kenner, La., 1989-92; cons. VA Hosp., New Orleans, 1969-89, VA Hosp., Alexandria, La., 1969-89, USPHS Hosp., New Orleans, 1968-89; vis. physician Charity Hosp., New Orleans, 1957-66, sr. vis. physician, 1966-89, chief service Tulane div., 1968-69, acting chief service Tulane div., 1972; instr. La. State U. Sch. Medicine, New Orleans, 1956-57; mem. bd. cons. to comdr. Naval Med. Command Dept. Navy, Washington, 1983-86; mem. adv. com. to dir. NIH, 1983-85. Contbr. articles to profl. jours. Mem. planning com. Touro Infirmary, New Orleans; bd. dirs., mem. exec. com. Am. Cancer Soc., Internat. House, 1978-82, 83-84; mem. New Orleans Area Health Planning Council, 1968-70, task force in health manpower; trustee La. Sci. Ctr., 1983-85, La. Regional Med. Programs, 1969; bd. dirs. Friends of Charity Inc., 1986-89, Blue Cross, Washington, 1966-68, New Orleans Area/Bayou-River Health Systems Agy., 1978-82, Tuberculosis Assn. Greater New Orleans, 1968—, Flint-Goodridge Hosp., New Orleans, 1978-82. Fellow Tulane U. Sch. Medicine, 1957-58; recipient Outstanding Alumni award Downstate Med. Ctr., 1973. Fellow ACP, Am. Coll. Cardiology, Am. Coll. Chest Physicians, Am. Coll. Clin. Pharmacology and Chemotherapy; mem. AMA (com. on emergency health service), Am. Thoracic Soc. (councilor), La. Thoracic Soc. (pres. 1964), Nat. Adv. Rsch. Resources Coun. (mem. health care tech. study sect. 1970-74, chmn. 1972-74), Am. Lung Assn. La. (hon. life.), Delta Omega, Kappa Delta Phi, Alpha Epsilon Delta, Omicron Delta Kappa, Alpha Omega Alpha. Roman Catholic. Office: Tulane Univ Office Chancellor New Orleans LA 70118

WALSH, JOSEPH A., JR., lawyer; b. Teaneck, N.J., July 19, 1949. BA magna cum laude, Ind. U., 1971, JD magna cum laude, 1974. Bar: Ill. 1974, Fla. 1988, U.S. Dist. Ct. (no. dist. Ill.) 1988. Ptnr. Winston & Strawn, Chgo. Mem. ABA, Fla. Bar. Office: Winston & Strawn 35 W Wacker Dr Chicago IL 60601-1614*

WALSH, JOSEPH MICHAEL, magazine distribution executive; b. N.Y.C., Jan. 19, 1943; s. John Redmond and Bridget Judith (Donovan) W.; m. Theresa Rose Vericker, Oct. 3, 1964; children—Joseph, Matthew, Teresa Ann, John, James. B.B.A. in Acctg., Iona Coll., 1964. With Peat, Marwick, Mitchell & Co., C.P.A.s, N.Y.C., 1964-70, audit supr., until 1970; asst. to chmn. bd. and pres. Cadence Industries Corp., West Caldwell, N.J., 1970-71, v.p., 1971-74, exec. v.p., 1974-87; pres. subs. Curtis Circulation Co., 1972-74, chmn., chief exec. officer, 1982—; pres. Data Services for Health, 1976-77, U.S. Pencil and Stationery Co., 1977-79, Perfect Subscription Co. (merger Perfect Sch. Plans, Perfect Telephone Plan, Moore Cottrell and Keystone Readers Service), 1980-83. Mem. AICPA, N.Y. State Soc. CPAs, K.C. Home: 9 Pond Rd Washington Township NJ 07675 Office: Curtis Circulation Co 9 Pond Rd Washington Township NJ 07675

WALSH, JOSEPH THOMAS, state supreme court justice; b. Wilmington, Del., May 18, 1930; s. Joseph Patrick and Mary Agnes (Bolton) W.; m. Madeline Maria Lamb, Oct. 6, 1955; children: Kevin, Lois, Patrick, Daniel, Thomas, Nancy. BA, LaSalle Coll., 1952; LLB, Georgetown U., 1955. Bar: D.C. 1955, Del. 1955. Atty. Ho. of Reps., Dover, Del., 1961-62; chief counsel Pub. Svc. Commn., Dover, 1964-72; judge Del. Superior Ct., Wilmington, 1972-84; vice chancellor Ct. of Chancery, Wilmington, 1984-85; justice Del. Supreme Ct., Wilmington, 1985—. Capt. U.S. Army, 1955-58. Democrat. Roman Catholic. Office: Del Supreme Ct PO Box 1997 Wilmington DE 19899-1997*

WALSH, KENNETH ALBERT, chemist; b. Yankton, S.D., May 23, 1922; s. Albert Lawrence and Edna (Slear) W.; m. Dorothy Jeanne Thompson, Dec. 22, 1944; children: Jeanne K., Kenneth Albert, David Bruce, Rhonda Jean, Leslie Gay. BA, Yankton Coll., 1942; PhD, Iowa State U., 1950. Asst. prof. chemistry Iowa State U., Ames, 1950-51; staff mem. Los Alamos Sci. Lab., 1951-57; supr. Internat. Minerals & Chem. Corp., Mulberry, Fla., 1957-60; mgr. Brush Beryllium Co., Elmore, Ohio, 1960-72; assoc. dir. tech. Brush Wellman Inc., Elmore, 1972-86; cons., patentee in field. Democratic precinct chmn., Los Alamos, 1956, Fremont, Ohio, 1980. Mem. AIME, Am. Chem. Soc. (sect. treas. 1956), ASM Internat., Toastmasters Internat., Theta Xi, Phi Lambda Upsilon. Methodist.

WALSH, KENNETH ANDREW, biochemist; b. Sherbrooke, Que., Can., Aug. 7, 1931; s. George Stanley and Dorothy Maud (Sangster) W.; m. Deirdre Anne Clarke, Aug. 22, 1953; children: Andrew, Michael, Erin. BSc in Agr., McGill U., 1951; MS, Purdue U., 1953; PhD, U. Toronto, 1959. Postdoctoral fellow U. Wash., Seattle, 1959-62, from asst. prof. to assoc. prof. Biochemistry, 1962-69, prof. Biochemistry, 1969—, chair, 1990—. Author (book) Methods in Protein Sequence Analysis, 1986. Mem. The Protein Soc. (sec.-treas. 1987-90), Am. So. Biochemistry/Molecular Biology. Office: U Wash Dept Biochem Box 357350 Seattle WA 98195

WALSH, LAWRENCE EDWARD, lawyer; b. Port Maitland, N.S., Can., Jan. 8, 1912; came to U.S., 1914, naturalized, 1922; s. Cornelius Edward and Lila May (Sanders) W.; m. Mary Alma Porter; children: Barbara Marie, Janet Maxine (Mrs. Alan Larson), Sara Porter, Dale Edward, Elizabeth Porter (Mrs. Joseph Wells). A.B., Columbia, 1932, LL.B., 1935; LL.D., Union U., 1959, St. John's U., 1975, Suffolk U., 1975, Waynesburg Coll., 1976, Vt. Law Sch., 1976. Bar: N.Y. 1936, D.C. 1981, Okla. 1981, U.S. Supreme Ct. 1951. Spl. asst. atty. gen. Drukman Investigation, 1936-38; dep. asst. dist. atty. N.Y. County, 1938-41; assoc. Davis Polk Wardwell Sunderland & Kiendl, 1941-43; asst. counsel to gov. N.Y., 1943-49, counsel to gov., 1950-51; counsel Pub. Service Commn., 1951-53; gen. counsel, exec. dir. Waterfront Commn. of N.Y. Harbor, 1953-54; U.S. judge So. Dist. N.Y., 1954-57; U.S. dep. atty. gen., 1957-60; partner firm Davis, Polk & Wardwell, 1961-81; counsel firm Crowe & Dunlevy, Oklahoma City, 1981—; ind. counsel Iran/Contra investigation, 1986-93; chmn. N.Y. State Moreland Commn. Alcoholic Beverage Control Law, 1963-64; pres. Columbia Alumni Fedn., 1968-69; dep. head with rank of amb. U.S. del. meetings on Vietnam, Paris, 1969; counsel to N.Y. State Ct. on Judiciary, 1971-72; 2d crct. mem. U.S. Crct. Judge Nominating Commn., 1978-80. Trustee emeritus Columbia U., Mut. Life Ins. Co., N.Y.; trustee William Nelson Cromwell Found. Recipient medal for excellence Columbia U., 1959, Law Sch., Columbia U., 1980, John Jay award Columbia Coll., 1989. Fellow Am. Bar Found., Am. Coll. Trial Lawyers; mem. Am. Law Inst. (coun.), ABA (pres. 1975-76), N.Y. State Bar Assn. (pres. 1966-67), Oklahoma County Bar Assn., Okla. State Bar Assn., Internat. Bar Assn., Assn. of Bar of City of New York, N.Y. County Lawyers Assn., Fed. Bar Coun.; hon. mem. Law Soc. Eng. and Wales, Can. Bar Assn., Mexican Bar Assn., Beta Theta Pi. Presbyterian. Clubs: N.Y. India House, The Century, Oklahoma City Golf and Country; Petroleum (Oklahoma City), Beacon (Oklahoma City). Home: 1902 Bedford Dr Oklahoma City OK 73116-5306 Office: 1800 Mid Am Towers Oklahoma City OK 73102

WALSH, MARIE LECLERC, nurse; b. Providence, Sept. 11, 1928; d. Walter Normand and Anna Mary (Ryan) Leclerc; m. John Breffni Walsh, June 18, 1955; children: George Breffni, John Leclerc, Darina Louise. Grad., Waterbury Hosp. Sch. Nursing, Conn., 1951; BS, Columbia U., 1954, MA, 1955. Team leader Hartford (Conn.) Hosp., 1951-53; pvt. duty nurse St. Luke's Hosp., N.Y.C., 1953-57; sch. nurse tchr. Agnes Russel Ctr., Tchrs. Coll. Columbia U., N.Y.C., 1955-56; clin. nursing instr. St. Luke's Hosp., N.Y.C., 1957-58; chmn. disaster nursing ARC Fairfax County, Va., 1975; course coord. occupational health nursing U. Va. Sch. Continuing Edn., Falls Church, 1975-77; mem. disaster steering com. No. Va. C.C., Annandale, 1976; adj. faculty U. Va. Sch. Continuing Edn., Falls Church, 1981; disaster svcs. nurse ARC, Wichita, Kans., 1985-90; disaster svcs. nurse Seattle-King County chpt. ARC, Seattle, 1990-96; rsch. and statis. analyst U. Va. Sch. Continuing Edn. Nursing, Falls Church, 1975; rsch. libr. Olive Garvey Ctr. for Improvement Human Functioning, Inc., Wichita, 1985. Sec. Dem. party, Cresskill, N.J., 1964-66; county committeewoman, Bergen County, N.J., 1965-66; pres., v.p., Internat. Staff Wives, NATO, Brussels, Belgium, 1978-80; election officer, supr. Election Bd., Wichita, 1987, 88. Mem. AAAS, AAUW, N.Y. Acad. Sci., Pi Lambda Theta, Sigma Theta Tau. Avocation: travel, gardening. Home: 8800 Prestwould Pl Mc Lean VA 22102

WALSH, MARY D. FLEMING, civic worker; b. Whitewright, Tex., Oct. 29, 1913; d. William Fleming and Anna Maud (Lewis) Fleming; B.A., So. Meth. U., 1934; LL.D. (hon.), Tex. Christian U., 1979; m. F. Howard Walsh, Mar. 13, 1937; children: Richard, Howard, D'Ann Walsh Bonnell, Maudi Walsh Roe, William Lloyd. Pres. Fleming Found.; v.p. Walsh Found.; partner Walsh Co.; charter mem. Lloyd Shaw Found., Colorado Springs; mem. Big Bros. Tarrant County; guarantor Fort Worth Arts Council, Scholar Cantorum. Fort Worth Opera, Fort Worth Ballet, Fort Worth Theater, Tex. Boys Choir; hon. mem. bd. dirs. Van Cliburn Internat. Piano Competition; co-founder Am. Field Service in Ft. Worth; mem. Tex. Commn. for Arts and Humanities, 1968-72, mem. adv. council, 1972-84; bd. dirs. Wm. Edrington Scott Theatre, 1977-83, Colorado Springs Day Nursery, Colorado Springs Symphony, Ft. Worth Symphony, 1974-81; hon. chmn. Opera Ball, 1975, Opera Guild Internat. Conf., 1976; co-presenter (with husband) through Walsh Found., Tex. Boys Choir and Dorothy Shaw Bell Choir ann. presentation of The Littlest Wiseman to City of Ft. Worth; granted with husband land and bldgs. to Tex. Boys Choir for permanent home, 1971, Walsh-Wurlitzer organ to Casa Manana, 1972. Sem. Recipient numerous awards, including Altrusa Civic award as 1st Lady of Ft. Worth, 1968; (with husband) Disting. Service award So. Bapt. Radio and Television Commn., 1972; Opera award Girl Scouts, 1977-79; award Streams and Valleys, 1976-80; named (with husband) Patron of Arts in Ft. Worth, 1970, 91, Edna Gladney Internat. Grandparents of 1972, (with husband) Sr. Citizens of Yr, 1985; Mary D. and Howard Walsh Meml. Organ dedicated by Bapt. Radio and TV Commn., 1967, tng. ctr. named for the Walshes, 1976; Mary D. and Howard Walsh Med. Bldg., Southwestern Bapt. Theol. Sem.; library at Tarrant County Jr. Coll. N.W. Campus dedicated to her and husband, 1978; Brotherhood citation Tarrant County chpt. NCCJ, 1978; Spl. Recognition award Ft. Worth Ballet Assn.; Royal Purple award Tex. Christian U., 1979; Friends of Tex. Boys Choir award, 1981; appreciation award Southwestern Bapt. Theol. Sem., 1981, B. H. Carroll Founders award, 1982, (with husband) Patrons of the Arts award, 1991; Outstanding Women of Fort Worth award City of Fort Worth, 1994, numerous other award for civic activities. Mem. Ft. Worth Boys Club, Ft. Worth Children's Hosp., Jewel Charity Ball, Ft. Worth Pan Hellenic (pres. 1940), Opera Guild, Fine Arts Found. Guild of Tex. Christian U., Girl's Service League (hon. life, hon. chmn. Fine Arts Guild Spring Ballet, 1985), AAUW, Goodwill Industries Aux., Child Study Center, Tarrant County Aux. of Edna Gladney Home, YWCA (life), Ft. Worth Art Assn., Ft. Worth Ballet Assn., Tex. Boys Choir Aux., Friends of Tex. Boys Choir, Round Table, Colorado Springs Fine Art Center, Am. Automobile Assn., Nat. Assn. Cowbelles, Ft. Worth Arts Council (hon. bd. mem.), Am. Guild Organists (hon., Ft. Worth chpt.), Rae Reimers Bible Study Class (pres. 1968), Tex. League Composers (hon. life), Children's Hosp. Woman's Bd. (hon. 1991), Chi Omega (pres. 1935-36, hon. chmn. 1986), others. Baptist. Clubs: The Woman's (Club Fidelite), Colorado Springs Country, Garden of Gods, Colonial Country, Ridglea Country, Shady Oaks Country, Chi Omega Mothers, Chi Omega Carousel, TCU Woman's. Home: 2425 Stadium Dr Fort Worth TX 76109-1055 also: 1801 Culebra Ave Colorado Springs CO 80907-7328

WALSH, MASON, retired newspaperman; b. Dallas, Nov. 27, 1912; s. Herbert C. and Margaret (Hayes) W.; m. Margaret Anne Calhoun, Mar. 7, 1947; children: Margaret Anne (Mrs. James G. Dunn), Timothy Mason, Kevin Calhoun. B.A. in Polit. Sci., So. Meth. U., 1934. Staff Dallas Evening Jour., 1929-37; staff Dallas Dispatch-Jour. (later Dallas Jour.), 1938-42; editor Austin (Tex.) Tribune, 1942; dir. employee relations N.Am. Aviation, Dallas, 1942-45; with Dallas Times-Herald, 1945-60, mng. editor, 1952-60; mng. editor Phoenix Gazette, 1960-66; gen. mgr. Phoenix Newspapers, Inc., 1966-75, asst. pub., 1975-78; pub. Ariz. Republic and Phoenix Gazette, 1978-80, pub. emeritus, 1980—. Profl. musician, 1929-35. Chmn. Ariz. Dept. Econ. Planning and Devel. Bd., 1968-71; bd. dirs., v.p. Goodwill Industries Central Ariz., 1978-84, v.p., 1982-83; bd. dirs. Western Newspaper Found., 1974-81; trustee Desert Found., Scottsdale, 1982-85; mem. Nat. Def. Exec. Res., 1964-80. Mem. A.P. Mng. Editors Assn. (dir. 1956-63, pres. 1963), A.P. Assn. Calif., Ariz., Hawaii and Nev. (pres. 1976-77), Ariz. Acad. (dir. 1973-81, v.p. 1980-81), Valley Forward Assn. (dir. 1970-87), Newcomen Soc., Phoenix 40, Sigma Delta Chi. Episcopalian. Clubs: University, Arizona. Home: 4102 N 64th Pl Scottsdale AZ 85251-3110

WALSH, MICHAEL FRANCIS, advertising executive; b. Pitts., June 22, 1956; s. Peter Paul and Joan Brooks (Murdoch) W.; m. Lisa Ann Ruscillo, May 14, 1983; children: Megan, Allison. BA, Duquesne U., 1978; MBA, U. Pitts., 1990. Asst. media planner Ketchum Advt./Pitts., 1978-79, media planner, 1979-82, media supr., 1982-84, v.p., assoc. media dir., 1984-86, dir. media ops., 1986-87, media dir., 1987-88, sr. v.p., media dir., 1988-92, dir. ops. and fin., 1993—; part-time mem. faculty U. Pitts., 1990—; adj. faculty Point Park Coll., 1992—. Contbr. articles to advt. jours. Mem. Pitts. Radio and TV Club (bd. dirs. 1988-91), Info. Tech. Media Adv. Coun. (pres. 1995—), Bus. and Profl. Advt. Internat., Inc. (bd. dirs., exec. com. 1991—), U. Pitts. Alumni Assn. (pres.). Office: Ketchum Communications Inc 6 PPG Pl Pittsburgh PA 15222-5406

WALSH, MICHAEL J., lawyer; b. Portland, Oreg., Sept. 4, 1932; s. Frank M.J. and Elisemary (Derbes) W.; m. June Griffin, Nov. 28, 1959; children: Molly, Erin, Kathryn (dec.), Anne. BA, U. Portland, 1954; JD, Georgetown U., 1959. Bar: D.C. 1959, Oreg. 1959, U.S. Ct. Appeals (fed. and 9th cirs.) 1959, U.S. Tax Ct. 1959, U.S. Supreme Ct. 1968. Law ck. to presiding justice Oreg. Supreme Ct., Salem, 1959-60; mng. ptnr. Rankin, Walsh, Ragen and Roberts, Portland, 1960-75; sole practice Portland, 1976-81; ptnr. Walsh and Conolly, Portland, 1982-83; of counsel McEwen, Hanna, Gisvold and Rankin, Portland, 1983-85, Bullivant, Houser, Bailey, Pendergrass, & Hoffman, Washington, 1985—; chmn. Employees Compensation Appeals Bd. U.S. Dept. Labor, Washington, 1985—; legal counsel to Reagan-Bush '84, Nat. Hdqtrs., Washington, 1983-84. Chmn. legal dev. March of Dimes, 1967; chmn. admissions Georgetown U., Oreg., 1972-83; trustee Christie Sch., 1974-78; trustee Cath. Charities Oreg., 1966-72, pres. 1971; trustee Parry Ctr. for Children, 1967-73, v.p. 1970-71; trustee Portland Tennis Ctr. Assn., 1972-83, pres. 1976-82; bd. dirs. Portland Traffic Safety Commn., 1981-83. Served with JAGC, USAF, capt. res. Mem. Am. Judicature Soc., Am. Trial Lawyers Assn., Nat. Assn. Coll. and Uiv. Attys., Am. Arbitration Assn., D.C. Bar Assn., Oreg. Bar Assn. (mem. various coms.), Multnomah County Bar Assn., Portland C. of C. (bd. dirs. 1975-78, chmn. legis. coun. 1975). Club: Georgetown Univ. (Oreg.) (pres. 1966). Home: 3273 Sutton Pl NW # B Washington DC 20016-3537

WALSH, NICOLAS EUGENE, rehabilitation medicine physician, educator; b. Mpls., July 1, 1947; s. Leonard Cyril and June Alice (Otte) W.; m. Wendy Sarah Allnutt, June 1, 1973; children: Meghan, Rorey, Katlin, Alaine. BS, USAF Acad., 1969; MS, Marquette U., 1974; MD, U. Colo., 1979. Asst. prof. naval sci. Marquette U., Milw., 1972-74; from asst. prof. to assoc. prof. rehab. medicine U. Tex. Health Sci. Ctr., San Antonio, 1982-89, prof., chmn. rehab. medicine, 1989—; med. dir. U. Health Sys., San Antonio, 1992—, mem. devel. bd., 1991—; dir. Am. Bd. Phys. Medicine and Rehab., Rochester, Minn., 1994—. Author: (book chpts.) CIBA Collection of Medical Illustrations, 1993, Management of Cancer Pain, 1993, Low Back Pain, 1994; editor: Rehabilitation of Chronic Pain, 1991; editor-in-chief Archives of Physical Medicine and Rehabilitation, Chgo., 1994—. Bd. dirs. Goodwill Industries, San Antonio, 1991—; mem. prof. adv. com. Our Lady of the Lake U., San Antonio, 1992—; mem. devel. bd. Incarnate Word Coll., San Antonio, 1991-93. Recipient Excellence in Rsch. award Am. Jour. Phys. Medicine & Rehab., 1991; named Health Care Profl. of Yr., Gov.'s Com. for Disabled Persons, 1989. Fellow Am. Bd. Pain Medicine (v.p. 1993-94, sec. 1994—), Am. Acad. Phys. Medicine and Rehab. (Richard and Hinda Rosenthal Found. award 1991); mem. Assn. Acad. Physiatrists (v.p. 1993—), Phys. Medicine and Rehab. Edn. and Rsch. Found. (pres. 1993—, Excellence in Rsch. award 1991). Office: Rehab Medicine Dept UTHSC-SA 7703 Floyd Curl Dr San Antonio TX 78284-6200

WALSH, PATRICK CRAIG, urologist; b. Akron, Ohio, Feb. 13, 1938; s. Raymond Michael and Catherine N. (Rodden) W.; m. Margaret Campbell, May 23, 1964; children—Christopher, Jonathan, Alexander. A.B., Case Western Res. U., 1960, M.D., 1964. Intern in surgery Peter Bent Brigham Hosp., Boston, 1964-65; asst. resident in surgery Peter Bent Brigham Hosp., 1965-66; asst. resident in pediatric surgery Children's Hosp. Med. Center, Boston, 1966-67; resident in urology U. Calif.-Los Angeles Med. Center, 1967-71; dir. Brady Urol. Inst., urologist-in-chief Johns Hopkins Hosp., Balt., 1974—; prof., dir. dept. urology Johns Hopkins U. Sch. Medicine, 1974—. Contbr. articles to med. jours. Served to comdr. M.C. USN, 1971-73. mem. Soc. Univ. Surgeons, Am. Assn. Genitourinary Surgeons, Clin. Soc. Genitourinary Surgeons, Am. Urol. Assn., Endocrine Soc., Am. Surg. Assn. Inst. Medicine of NAS, Alpha Omega Alpha. Roman Catholic. Office: Johns Hopkins Med Insts 600 N Wolfe St Baltimore MD 21205-2110

WALSH, PAUL S., food products executive. CEO Pillsbury Co., Mpls. Office: Pillsbury Co 200 S 6th St Minneapolis MN 55402

WALSH, PETER JOSEPH, physics educator; b. N.Y.C., Aug. 21, 1929; s. Peter and Mary Ellen (Kelly) W.; m. Rosemarie Imundo, May 13, 1952;

children: Kathleen, Mary Ellen, Susan, Carole, Karen. B.S., Fordham U., 1951; M.S., N.Y.U., 1953, Ph.D., 1960. Research physicist Westinghouse Elec. Co., Bloomfield, N.J., 1951-60; supervisory physicist Am. Standard, Piscattaway, N.J., 1960-62; prof. Fairleigh Dickinson U., 1962-93; prof. emeritus, 1993—; vis. rsch. scientist MIT, 1977; vis. prof. electronics and elec. engring. U. Sheffield, 1978-79; NASA fellow U. Santa Clara, 1980; Am. Soc. Engring. Edn. Navy fellow Naval Rsch. Labs., 1981, 82, 86, NASA Langley, 1987, Air Force fellow Hanscom AFB, 1988, Kirtland AFB, 1990; vis. prof. U. Genoa, 1984; vis. scholar Stanford U., 1984-85, cons. physics to 20 labs., 1963—; chmn. bd. trustees EMS Ednl. Corp., 1982—. Author: Dark Side of Knowledge, articles in field. Mem. Am. Phys. Soc., AAAS, N.J. Acad. Sci., Sigma Xi (sec. 1969). Patentee in field. Home: 40 St Josephs Dr Stirling NJ 07980-1224 Office: Fairleigh Dickinson U Dept of Ed Teaneck NJ 07666

WALSH, PHILIP CORNELIUS, mining consultant; b. Harrison, N.J., May 23, 1921; s. Philip Cornelius and Frances Walsh (Prendergast) W.; m. Alexandra Somerville Tuck, May 19, 1945 (dec. Sept. 1993); children: Eugenie Philbin Flaherty, Philip C.C., Frances Cornelia Cummings, Alexander Tuck, Nicholas Holladay, Elizabeth Lovering. BA, Yale U., 1943; member of the Class of 1944. With W.R. Grace & Co., Lima, Peru and N.Y.C., 1946-71; v.p. parent co., chief operating officer Latin Am. group, 1961-71, group exec. corp. adminstrv. group, 1970-71; v.p. Cerro Corp., 1972-74, Newmont Mining Corp., 1974-80; chmn. bd. Foote Mineral Co., Exton, Pa., 1979-80; vice chmn. St. Joe Minerals Corp., 1980-85; chmn. bd. Chilean Lithium Co. Ltd., 1980-94; dir. Cyprus Minerals Co., 1985-93, Piedmont Mining Co., 1985-94; bd. dirs. T. Rowe Price Assocs., Inc.; mem. Nat. Strategic Minerals and Metals Program Adv. Commn. Mem. Harding Twp. Bd. Edn., N.J., 1960-66; mem. Harding Twp. Com., 1966-72, police commr., 1966-72; trustee Morristown Meml. Hosp., 1969-79; vis. com. Colo. Sch. Mines, Global Systems and Cultures. 1st lt. F.A., U.S. Army, 1943-46. Decorated Silver Star, Purple Heart. Mem. AIME (Saunders gold medal 1992, Disting. Mem. award 1993), Pan Am. Soc. U.S. (past vice chmn.), Am. Soc. (hon. dir.), Am. Assn. Order of Malta (chancellor, bd. councillors), Racquet and Tennis Club, Edgartown Yacht Club (commodore), Edgartown Golf Club, Phi Beta Kappa, Sigma Xi. Republican. Roman Catholic. Home: Caleb Pond Rd Edgartown MA 02539

WALSH, RAYMOND JOHN, medical educator; b. Dec. 13, 1947; married; 2 children. BS in Zoology, U. Mass., 1969; PhD in Anatomy, Tufts U., 1976. Rsch. asst. dept. comparative pathology New Eng. Regional Primate Rsch. Ctr., 1969-72; postdoctoral rsch. fellow dept. ob-gyn. Royal Victoria Hosp., McGill U., Montreal, 1976-78; asst. prof. anatomy George Washington U., Washington, 1978-82, assoc. prof., 1982-91, interim chmn. anatomy, 1990-95, prof. and chmn. anatomy, 1995—; participant numerous ednl. confs.; lectr. in field; sponsor Ednl. Commn. for Fgn. Med. Grads., Quaid-i-Azam Med. Coll. Bahawalpur, Pakistan, 1992-93; external examiner dept. anatomy Kuwait U., 1993, 94. Contbr. numerous articles and abstracts to profl. jours. Chmn. anatomical bd. Dept. Human Svcs., D.C. Govt., 1992—. Grantee Biomed. Rsch. Support, 1978-79, 85-86, 90-91, NINCDS, 1979-83, 83-85, NSF, 1986-90, Souers Fund, 1994-95. Mem. Am. Assn. Anatomists (local organizing com. ann. meeting 1987), Soc. Neurosci., Internat. Brain Rsch. Orgn., Soc. for Applied Learning Tech., Am. Assn. Neurol. Surgeons (local organizer workshop 1994), Washington Soc. for Electron Microscopy (chmn. sponsor site orgn. com. 1980). Office: George Washington Univ Dept Anatomy 2300 I St NW Washington DC 20037

WALSH, RICHARD GEORGE, agricultural economist; b. Seward, Nebr., Aug. 16, 1930; s. Thomas George and Francis Kathryn (Pape) W.; m. Patricia Burke Bard, 1976; children by previous marriage: Cathryn M., Susan E., Thomas R., Robert J. B.S., U. Nebr., 1952, M.A., 1955; Ph.D., U. Wis., 1961. From asst. prof. to prof. agrl. econs. U. Nebr., 1958-68; prof. dept. agrl. and resource econs. Colo. State U., Ft. Collins, 1968—; intergovt. exchange EPA, 1973-74; cons. FTC, 1965-66, 72, 78-79, U. P.R., 1967, Justice Dept., 1971, U.S. Forest Service, 1972, 82, 86, Bur. Land Mgmt., 1973, 85, Nat. Park Service, 1975-79; vis. prof. U. Md., 1965, Stanford Research Inst., 1971, U. Newcastle upon Tyne, 1991. Author: Economics of the Baking Industry, 1963, Market Structure of the Agricultural Industries, 1966, The Structure of Food Manufacturing, 1966, Organization and Competition in Food Retailing, 1966, Economic Benefits of Improved Water Quality, 1982, Wilderness Resource Economics, 1982, Wild and Scenic River Economics, 1985, Recreation Economic Decisions: Comparing Benefits and Costs, 1986, Long-Run Forecasts of Participation in Fishing, Hunting and Nonconsumptive Wildlife Recreation, 1987, Economic Demand Studies with Nonmarket Benefit Estimates, 1988, Recreation Value of Ranch Open Space, 1994, Benefits of Ranch Open Space to Local Residents, 1996; contbr. articles to profl. jours. Bd. dirs. North Ft. Collins Sanitation Dist., 1971-73. Served to lt. (j.g.) USNR, 1952-54. Mem. Am. Agrl. Econs. Assn. (Outstanding Published Research award 1964), Assn. Environ. & Resource Econs., Western Agrl. Econs. Assn., European Assn. Environ. & Resource Econs., Internat. Soc. Ecological Economics. Office: Colo State U Dept Agrl Resource Eco Fort Collins CO 80523

WALSH, ROBERT, publishing executive. Pres. Directoriesamerica, Inc., Shawnee Mission, Kas., 1989—. Office: Directoriesamerica Inc 7015 College Blvd Ste 400 Shawnee Mission KS 66211-1535*

WALSH, RODGER JOHN, lawyer; b. Kansas City, Mo., Apr. 20, 1924; s. John Joseph and Margaret Mary (Halloran) W.; m. Patricia Ann O'Brien, Nov. 18, 1950; children—Regina, Martin, Eileen, Daniel, Veronica, Bernard, Kathleen. B.S., Rockhurst Coll., 1947; J.D., Georgetown U., 1950. Bar: Mo. 1950, D.C. 1950, U.S. Ct. Appeals (8th cir.) 1955, U.S. Supreme Ct. 1960. Spl. agt. FBI, Washington, 1950-53; ptnr. Linde-Thomson Van Dyke Fairchild, Kansas City, Mo., 1953-63, Biersmith & Walsh, 1963-69; v.p., asst. gen. counsel Riss Internat., 1969-83, exec. v.p., gen. counsel, 1983-87; pvt. practice law Independence, Mo., 1987—; chmn., mem. Mo. State Pers. Adv. Bd., Jefferson City, 1979-84; mem. Mo. State Environ. Improvement Authority, 1977-83. Bd. dirs. Mo. Bus and Truck Assn., Jefferson City, 1983-87, Democracy Inc., Kansas City, Mo., 1960—; hon. dir. Rockhurst Coll., 1960—. With U.S. Army, 1942-45; ETO. Decorated Air Medal with 5 oak leaf clusters. Mem. Mo. Bar Assn., Fed. Bar Assn., Kansas City Bar Assn., Am. Legion, Soc. Former FBI Agts. Democrat. Roman Catholic. Home: 10512 Mersington Ave Kansas City MO 64137-1626 Office: 115 W Lexington Independence MO 64050-3705

WALSH, SEMMES GUEST, retired insurance company executive; b. Annapolis, Md., June 15, 1926; m. Annette Hunt Cromwell, Aug. 23, 1952; children: Semmes. G. Jr., Annette T., Marion H., Jacquelyn C. BE, Yale U., 1946; MBA, Harvard U., 1950. Gen. ptnr. Baker, Watts & Co., Balt., 1962-74, mng. ptnr., 1974-80; exec. v.p., chief fin. officer Monumental Corp., Balt., 1980-89, ret., 1989. Bd. dirs. Wm. G. Baker Meml. Fund, Jas. L. Kernan Hosp. Found. Lt. (j.g.) USNR, 1943-46. Republican. Episcopalian. Avocations: tennis, golf. Home: 230 Hopkins Ln Owings Mills MD 21117-4327

WALSH, THOMAS A., production designer. Prodn. designer: (IMAX films) Flyers, 1980, Speed, 1984, The Discoverers, 1993, (TV movies) Miss Lonely Hearts, 1981, A Gathering of Old Men, 1986 (Emmy award nomination outstanding art direction 1987), Eugene O'Neill, 1986, War Story: Vietnam, 1988, Without Warning: The James Brady Story, 1990 (Emmy award nomination outstanding art direction 1991), Blindspot, 1992, In Search of Dr. Seuss, 1994, (documentaries) John Huston, 1988, MGM: When the Lion Roars, 1992 (Emmy award outstanding art direction 1993), (feature films) The Handmaid's Tale, 1990, Prayer of the Rollerboys, 1990. Office: Doug Apatow Agency 10559 Blythe Ave Los Angeles CA 90064-3338

WALSH, THOMAS CHARLES, lawyer; b. Mpls., July 6, 1940; s. William G. and Kathryne M. Walsh; m. Joyce Williams, Sept. 7, 1968; children: Brian Christopher, Timothy Daniel, Laura Elizabeth. BS in Commerce magna cum laude, St. Louis U., 1962, LLB cum laude, 1964. Bar: Mo. 1964, U.S. Supreme Ct. 1971, U.S. Dist. Ct. (ea. dist.) Mo. 1964, U.S. Ct. Appeals (8th cir.) 1968, U.S. Ct. Appeals (6th cir.) 1972, U.S. Ct. Appeals (5th cir.) 1974, U.S. Ct. Appeals (D.C. cir.) 1980, U.S. Ct. Appeals (7th cir.) 1982, U.S. Ct. Appeals (9th cir.) 1987, U.S. Ct. Appeals (4th cir.) 1989, U.S. Ct. Appeals (11th and Fed. cirs.) 1992, U.S. Ct. Appeals (2d and 10th cirs.) 1993. Jr. ptnr. Bryan, Cave, McPheeters & McRoberts, St. Louis, 1964-73, ptnr. Bryan Cave, LLP, 1974—, mem. exec. com., 1980—; mem. 8th Cir. Adv. Com., 1983-86. Bd. dirs. St. Louis Symphony Soc., 1983-95. Served with U.S. Army, 1965-66, to lt. USNR, 1966-71. Fellow Am. Coll. Trial Lawyers, Am. Acad. Appellate Lawyers; mem. ABA, Mo. Bar, St. Louis Bar Assn., Am. Law Inst., Mo. Athletic Club, Noonday Club, Bellerive Country Club. Roman Catholic. Office: Bryan Cave LLP 1 Metropolitan Sq 211 N Broadway Saint Louis MO 63102-2750

WALSH, THOMAS GEORGE, information services industry executive; b. Carroll, Iowa, Aug. 28, 1945; s. Raphael Edward and Helen Esther (Lawler) W.; m. Barbara Ellen Stoffel, Aug. 16, 1969; children: Meghan M., Molly A., Michaela E., Thomas P., Timothy R., Mary Colleen, Michael F., Brighid C., Daniel X., Emily M. BSBA, Creighton U., 1967. Customer svc. mgr. Mid-Am. Bankcard Assn., Omaha, Nebr., 1969-71; customer svc. dir. First Data Resources, Omaha, 1971-74; customer svc. dir. SE region First Data Resources, Atlanta, 1975-77; v.p. mktg. First Data Resources, Omaha, 1978-88; v.p. client svcs. Am. Express Integrated Payment Sys., Englewood, Colo., 1989-91, sr. v.p. mktg., 1991-92; exec. v.p. integrated svcs. divsn. First Data Corp., Englewood, 1992—; mem. exec. com. FDC Colo. Open Golf Tournament, Englewood, 1992—. Sec., treas., bd. dirs. Travis Hukil Fund, Englewood, 1989—; mem. Boys Hope-Denver, St. Louis, 1994—; pres. bd. dirs. Boys Town Booster Club, 1984-92; trustee Am. Irish Youth Found., 1995—. With U.S. Army, 1967-68. Mem. KC (Family of Yr. award 1988), Ducks Unltd., N.Am. Fishing Club (life), Douglas County Soccer Assn. (bd. dirs. 1991-93), Am. Legion. Roman Catholic. Avocations: kids activities, golf, fishing, hunting, boating. Office: First Data Corp 6200 S Quebec St Englewood CO 80111-4750

WALSH, THOMAS GERARD, actuary; b. N.Y.C., Jan. 14, 1942; s. Martin Joseph and Margaret Ellen (Moyles) W.; children: Brian, Kristen, Meghan, Jacqueline. B.S., Manhattan Coll. Exec. v.p. Tchr. Ins. & Annuity Am./ CREF, N.Y.C. Fellow Soc. Actuaries. Office: Tchrs Ins & Annuity Assn Am 730 3rd Ave New York NY 10017-3206

WALSH, THOMAS JAMES, state senator; b. Chgo., July 4, 1960; s. William Dowdle and Barbara Ann (Kennedy) W. BBA, Loras Coll., 1982. Lic. real estate salesperson. From sales rep. to pub. rels. mgr. Binks Mfg. Co., Franklin Park, Ill., 1982—; state rep. State of Ill., Springfield, 1992—; state senator, 1994—. Commr. Met. Water Reclamation Dist. of Greater Chgo., 1988-90, chmn. Engring. com., Health and Pub. Welfare com.; active LaGrange Park Caucus, LaGrange Park Libr., St. Francis Xavier Ch., LaGrange. Mem. Irish Fellowship Club Chgo., Phoenix Soc. of Community Family Svc. and Mental Health Assn., LaGrange Kiwanis, Loras Coll. Alumni Club Chgo. Office: State of Ill 10544 W Cermak Rd Westchester IL 60154-5202

WALSH, THOMAS JOHN, oncologist, scientist; b. Hartford, Conn., May 5, 1952; s. John Thomas and Frances (Zeneski) W.; m. Sherril Ross, Apr. 8, 1989; 1 child, Laura. BA in Biology/Chemistry, Assumption Coll., Worcester, Mass., 1974; MD, The Johns Hopkins U., 1978. Diplomate Am. Bd. Internal Medicine, Am. Bd. Infectious Diseases, Am. Bd. Med. Oncology. Resident in medicine Michael Reese Hosp., U. Chgo., 1978-82; fellow pathology Johns Hopkins Hosp. and Univ., Balt., 1979-80; fellow infectious diseases U. Md., Balt., 1982-85, fellow med. oncology, 1985-86; fellow med. oncology Nat. Cancer Ctr., Bethesda, Md., 1986-87, sr. staff fellow, 1987-88, med. officer, 1988-93, sr. investigator, 1993—, head mycology unit, 1993—, head immunocompromised host sect., 1996—; assoc. prof. U. Md. Sch. Medicine, Balt., 1992—; lectr. The Johns Hopkins U. Sch. Medicine, Balt., 1985—; adj. assoc. prof. Loyola Coll., Balt., 1990—. Contbr. chpts. to Management of Infections in Patients with Cancer, 1985, Critical Problems in Trauma Care, Vol. II Medical Management, Current Therapy in Hematology/Oncology, 1987, Tenth Congress of the International Society for Human and Animal Mycology-ISHAM Proceedings, 1988, Diagnosis and Therapy of Systemic Mycoses, 1989, Respiratory Diseases in the Immunosuppressed Host, 1990, Hematology: Basic Principles and Practice, 1991, Medical Microbiology, 3d edit., 1991, Pediatric AIDS, 1990, Current Therapy in Critical Care Medicine, 1990, Emerging Targets in Antibacterial and Antifungal Chemotherapy, 1991, The Principles and Practice of Medical Intensive Care, 1993, Aspergillus: The Biology and Industrial Applications, 1991, New Strategies in Fungal Disease, 1992, Oral Fungal Infections in Immunocompromised Patients, 1991, Current Therapy in Pediatric Infectious Diseases, 3rd edit., 1993, Hematopoietic Growth Factors and Mononuclear Phagocytes, 1993, Fungal Diseases of the Lung, 2d edit., 1993, Manual of Clinical Microbiology, 6th edit., 1994, Hematology: Basic Principles and Practice, 2d edit., 1995, Infectious Complications of Cancer, 1995; contbr. more than 200 publications to profl. jours. and 146 rsch. abstracts. Comdr. USPHS, 1991—, NIH. Recipient Med. Mycology Fellow award Nat. Found. for Infectious Diseases, 1984, Young Investigator award ICAAC and Am. Soc. Microbiology, USPHS Commendation medal, 1993. Fellow ACP, Am. Acad. Microbiology, Infectious Diseases Soc. Am., Am. Coll. Chest Physicians. Achievements include development of exptl. and clin. found. for new approaches to diagnosis, treatment and prevention of invasive candidiasis and aspergillosis in immunocompromised patients; devel. of new understanding of pathogenesis, diagnosis, and treatment of emerging mycoses; devel. new approaches to augmentation of host defenses in neutropenic hosts against invasive mycoses. Office: NIH Bldg 10 Rm 13 N 240 Bethesda MD 20892

WALSH, THOMAS JOSEPH, neuro-ophthalmologist; b. N.Y.C., Sept. 18, 1931; s. Thomas Joseph and Virginia (Hughes) W.; m. Sally Ann Maust, June 21, 1958; children—Thomas Raymond, Sara Ann, Mary Kelly, Kathleen Meghan. BA, Coll. Fordham, 1954; MD, Bowman Gray Med. Sch., 1958. Intern St. Vincent's Hosp., N.Y.C., 1958-59; resident ophthalmology Bowman Gray Med. Sch., Winston-Salem, N.C., 1961-64; fellow neuro-ophthalmology Bascom Palmer Eye Inst., Miami, Fla., 1964-65; practice medicine specializing in neuro-ophthalmology Stamford, Conn., 1965—; dir. neuro-ophthalmology service, asst. prof. ophthalmology and neurology Yale Sch. Medicine, New Haven, 1965-74; assoc. prof. Yale Sch. Medicine, 1974-79, prof., 1979—, also bd. permanent officers; dir. ophthalmology Stamford Hosp., 1978-83; mem. staff St. Joseph Hosp., Yale New Haven Hosp.; cons. to surgeon gen. army in neuro-ophthalmology Walter Reed Hosp., Washington, 1966—, VA Hosp., West Haven, 1965—, Silver Hill Found., New Canaan, Conn., 1974—; frequent lectr. various univs. Contbr. articles to various publs. Mem. adv. bd. Stamford Salvation Army, 1972-92; mem. med. bd. Darien Nurses Assn., Conn., 1972—; surgeon Darien Fire Dept., 1969—. With AUS, 1959-61. Decorated Knight of Malta, 1983; Centennial fellow Johns Hopkins, 1976. Mem. AMA, Conn., Fairfield County med. socs., Acad. Ophthalmology, Oxford Ophthal. Congress, Acad. Neurology, Am. Assn. Neurol. Surgeons, Internat. Neuro-Ophthalmology Soc., Soc. Med. Cons. to Armed Forces, Cosmos Club (Washington), Darien County Club, Yale Club (N.Y.C), Lions, Army-Navy Club. Office: 1100 Bedford St Stamford CT 06905-5301

WALSH, W. TERENCE, lawyer; b. Toledo, Ohio, Nov. 18, 1943; s. Walter James and Ann (Gifford) W.; m. Patricia Jane Walker, Dec. 17, 1966; children: Christopher O'Brien, Ryan Kerrick, Ann Elisabeth. AB, Brown U., 1965; JD, Emory U., 1970. Bar: Ga., 1971, U.S. Dist. Ct. (no. dist.) Ga., 1971, U.S. Ct. Appeals (11th cir.), 1971. Assoc. Alston, Miller & Gaines, Atlanta, 1970-76, ptnr., 1976-83; ptnr. Alston & Bird, Atlanta, 1983—; lectr. various seminars on appellate procedure, juvenile law, ethics, and professionalism. Contbr. articles to profl. jours. Bd. dirs. Georgians for Children, 1993—, The Bridge, 1992—, Ga. Justice Project, 1987—; bd. dirs. Atlanta Legal Aid Soc., Inc., 1976—, pres., 1987; bd. dirs. Capital Area Mosaic, chmn., 1994-95; chmn. sch. bd. Christ the King Sch., 1982-84; alumni trustee Brown U., 1994—; chmn. KIND, Inc., 1993—. Fellow Ga. Bar Found.; mem. ABA, State Bar Ga. (bd. govs. 1979—, pres. young lawyers sect. 1980-81, H. Sol Clark award 1987), Atlanta Bar Assn. (bd. dirs. 1987-93, pres. 1991-92, Charles E. Watkins award 1994), Gate City Bar Assn., Emory Law Alumni Assn. (exec. com. 1990—). Avocations: sports, gardening, reading. Office: Alston & Bird 1201 W Peachtree St NW Atlanta GA 30309-3400

WALSH, WILLIAM, former football coach; b. Los Angeles, Nov. 30, 1931. Student, San Mateo Jr. Coll.; BA, San Jose State U., 1954, MA in Edn., 1959. Asst. coach Monterey Peninsula Coll., 1955, San Jose State U., 1956; head coach Washington Union High Sch., Fremont, Calif., 1957-59; asst. coach U. Calif., Berkeley, 1960-62, Stanford U., 1963-65, Oakland Raiders, Am. Football League, 1966-67, Cin. Bengals, 1968-75, San Diego Chargers, Nat. Football League, 1976; head coach Stanford U., 1977-78; head coach, gen. mgr. San Francisco 49ers, NFL, 1979-89, exec. v.p., 1989; broadcaster NBC Sports, 1989-91; head coach Stanford U., 1992-95. Named NFL Coach of Yr., Sporting News, 1981; coached Stanford U. winning team Sun Bowl, 1977, Bluebonnet Bowl, 1978, Blockbuster Bowl, 1993, San Francisco 49ers to Super Bowl championships, 1981, 84, 88; elected to Pro Football Hall of Fame, 1993. Office: c/o Stanford U Gary Migdol Sports Info Office Dept Athletics Stanford CA 94305-1684*

WALSH, WILLIAM ALBERT, management consultant, former naval officer; b. Gilman, Ill., Aug. 15, 1933; s. Lawrence Eugene and Myrtle R. (Mulder) W.; m. Joan Elizabeth Kennedy, Dec. 28, 1957; children: Kathryn, Michael, Julie. B.S. in Commerce, U. Notre Dame, 1955; M.S. in Mgmt. with distinction, U.S. Naval Postgrad. Sch., Monterey, Calif., 1962; M.S. in Internat. Affairs with honors, George Washington U., 1972. Commd. ensign U.S. Navy, 1955, advanced through grades to rear adm., 1981; exec. asst. to dep. chief naval ops. (Surface Warfare), Washington, 1974-76; comdg. officer USS Juneau, San Diego, 1976-78; comdr. Amphibious Squadron Three, San Diego, 1978-79; head plans and policy div., comdr. rapid deployment naval forces Comdr. in Chief U.S. Pacific Fleet, Honolulu, 1979-81; comdr. Amphibious Group Eastern Pacific, San Diego, 1981-82; dir. surface warfare div. Office Chief Naval Ops., Pentagon, Washington, 1983-85; ret., 1985; pres. Air/Space Am., San Diego, 1986-89, W.A. Walsh Enterprises, 1990—. Decorated Legion of Merit with 2 gold stars, Bronze Star, Navy Commendation medal U.S.; Disting. Service Order 2d Class Vietnam.

WALSH, WILLIAM ARTHUR, JR., lawyer; b. Washington, Mar. 17, 1949; children: Jesse Creighton, Patrick McKay. BS in Econs. and Fin., U. Md., 1972; JD, U. Richmond, 1977. Bar: Va. Ptnr. Hunton & Williams, Richmond, Va.; mem. adv. bd. for law rev. U. Richmond. Mem. adv. bd. Boys' and Girls' Club Richmond chpt. Salvation Army, 1993. Mem. ABA, Va. Bar Assn. (chmn. real estate legal opinions com.), Richmond Bar Assn., Ctrl. Richmond Assn. (mem. bd. dirs.), Omicron Delta Kappa. Home: 4705 Leonard Pky Richmond VA 23226-1337 Office: Hunton & Williams Riverfront Pla East Tower 951 E Byrd St Richmond VA 23219-4040

WALSH, WILLIAM DESMOND, investor; b. N.Y.C., Aug. 4, 1930; s. William J. and Catherine Grace (Desmond) W.; m. Mary Jane Gordon, Apr. 5, 1951; children: Deborah, Caroline, Michael, Suzanne, Tara Jane, Peter. BA, Fordham U., 1951; JD, Harvard U., 1955. Bar: N.Y. State bar 1955. Asst. U.S. atty. So. dist. N.Y., N.Y.C., 1955-58; counsel N.Y. Commn. Investigation, N.Y.C., 1958-61; mgmt. cons. McKinsey & Co., N.Y.C., 1961-67; sr. v.p. Arcata Corp., Menlo Park, Calif., 1967-82; gen. ptnr. Sequoia Assocs., 1982—; pres., chief exec. officer Atacra Liquidating Trust, 1982-88; chmn. bd. dirs. Deanco, Inc., Ithaca, N.Y., Newell Indsl. Corp., Lowell, Mich., Champion Rd. Machinery Ltd., Goderick, Ont.; bd. dirs. URS Inc., San Francisco, Newcourt Credit Group, Inc., Toronto, Can., Basic Vegetable Products, King City, Calif., Consolidated Freightways, Inc., Palo Alto, Calif., Nat. Edn. Crop. of Irvine, Calif. Mem. bd. visitors Sch. Bus. U. So. Calif., Harvard Law Sch.; mem. com. on univ. resources Harvard U. Mem. N.Y. State Bar Assn., Harvard Club (N.Y.C. and San Francisco), Knights of Malta. Home: 279 Park Ln Menlo Park CA 94027-5448 Office: 3000 Sand Hill Rd Bldg 2 Ste 140 Menlo Park CA 94025-7116

WALSH, WILLIAM EGAN, JR., electronics executive; b. Springfield, Mass., Dec. 2, 1948; s. William Egan and Veronica (Maroney) W.; m. Terese Anne Sullivan, Oct. 25, 1952; children: Brian, Kathleen, John, Kevin. BA in Physics, Holy Cross, 1970; MS in Physical Oceanography, U.S. Naval Sch., Monterey, Calif., 1971; MBA, U. North Fla., 1975. Oceanographer Sippican, Inc., Marion, Mass., 1975-77, mktg. mgr., 1977-80, from v.p. to sr. v.p., 1980-90, pres., 1990—, also bd. dirs.; bd. dirs. Phys. Scis., Inc., Andover, Mass. Lt. USN, 1970-75, lt. comdr. USNR, 1976-80. Mem. Marine Tech. Soc. Roman Catholic. Avocations: boating, jogging, racquetball, photography. Office: Sippican Inc 7 Barnabas Rd Marion MA 02738-1421

WALSH, WILLIAM JOHN, educational administrator; b. Natrona Heights, Pa., Mar. 29, 1941; s. William Henry and Helen Constance W.; BA in Sociology, Duquesne U., 1969; MEd in Ednl. Adminstrn., Pa. State U., 1971; JD, LaSalle U., 1993; m. Carol Jean Miller, Sept. 3, 1966; children: Keirsten, Shannon. Classification analyst Pa. State U., University Park, 1969-73; asst. pers. dir. W.Va. U., Morgantown, 1973-78; exec. asst. to pres., 1977; dir. pers. adminstrn., dir. purchasing audit W.Va. Bd. of Regents, Charleston, 1978-86; dir. salary adminstrn. and benefits Pa. State U., 1986-92; dir. employee benefits and retirement U. Miami, 1992—; cons. in field. Served with USMC, 1962-66; Vietnam. Mem. Coll. and Univ. Personnel Assn. Republican. Roman Catholic. Home: 2126 Harbor Way Fort Lauderdale FL 33326-2345

WALSKE, M(AX) CARL, JR., physicist; b. Seattle, June 2, 1922; s. Max Carl and Margaret Ella (Fowler) W.; m. Elsa Marjorie Nelson, Dec. 28, 1946; children: C. Susan, Steven C., Carol A. BS in Math. cum laude, U. Wash., 1944; PhD in Theoretical Physics, Cornell U., 1951. Staff mem., asst. theoretical divsn. leader Los Alamos Sci. Lab., 1951-56; dep. rsch. dir. Atomics Internat., Canoga Park, Calif., 1956-59; sci. rep. AEC in U.K., London, 1961-62; theoretical physicist RAND Corp., 1962-63; sci. attache U.S. missions to NATO and OECD, Paris, 1963-65; staff mem. Los Alamos Sci. Lab., 1965-66; asst. to sec. def. (atomic energy), 1966-73; pres., chief operating officer Atomic Indsl. Forum, Inc., Washington, 1973-87; chmn. Dept. Def. Mil. Liaison Com. to U.S. AEC, 1966-73; mem. U.S. del. Conf. Suspension Nuclear Tests, Geneva, 1959-61; chair reunion com. U. Wash., 1994-95; mem. fin. com. Ctrl. Kitsap Sch. Dist., 1994-96. Chair Upper Hood Canal Watershed Mgmt. Com., 1994—. Lt. (J.G.) USNR, 1973-46. Recipient Disting. Civilian Service medal Dept. Def. Fellow Explorers Club, Am. Phys. Soc.; mem. Am. Nuclear Soc., U.S. Power Squadrons (comdr. Agate Pass squadron 1995-96), Poulsbo Yacht Club, Phi Beta Kappa, Sigma Xi. Home: PO Box 370 Silverdale WA 98383-0370 *To seek out positions which appeared the most challenging and personally satisfying; to gain my reward through self-respect rather than public recognition; to expend extra effort as an offset to my limitations.*

WALSKE, STEVEN C., computer software company executive; b. 1952. Grad., Harvard U., 1978. With venture capital divsn. Paine Webber, Boston, 1978-83; pres., CEO Multiplication Software, Cambridge, Mass., 1983-85; CFO Computer Corp. of Am., Cambridge, 1985-86; pres., CEO Parametric Tech. Corp., Waltham, Mass., 1986—. Office: Parametric Technology Corp 128 Technology Dr Waltham MA 02154-8902*

WALSTON, RAY, actor; b. Laurel, Miss., Nov. 2, 1924; s. Harry Norman and Mittie (Kimbrell) W.; m. Ruth Calvert, Nov. 3, 1943; 1 dau., Katharine Ann. Grad. high sch., New Orleans. Appeared at Margo Jones Theatre, Houston, 1938-43, Cleve. Playhouse, 1943-45; Broadway appearances include GI Hamlet, 1945, Front Page, 1946, The Survivors, 1947, The Insect Comedy, 1948, Richard III, 1949, Summer and Smoke, 1949 (Clarence Derwent award 1949), The Rat Race, 1949, South Pacific, 1950, Me and Juliet, 1953, House of Flowers, 1954, Damn Yankees, 1955 (Tony award 1955); films include Kiss Them for Me, 1957, South Pacific, 1957, Damn Yankees, 1958, Tall Story, 1958, The Apartment, 1959, Portrait in Black, 1960, Wives & Lovers, 1963, Kiss Me Stupid, 1964, Paint Your Wagon, 1968, Who's Minding the Store, Caprice, The Sting, 1973, The Silver Streak, 1976, Popeye, 1980, Fast Times at Ridgemont High, 1982, Johnny Dangerously, 1984, From the Hip, 1986, Fine Gold, 1987, A Man of Passion, 1988, Popcorn, 1989, Ski Patrol, 1989, Of Mice and Men, 1991; dir.: Broadway musical Damn Yankees, 1974; TV series My Favorite Martian, 1963-66, Picket Fences, 1993— (Emmy award, Supporting Actor - Drama Series, 1995); TV movies include: The Stand, 1994. Mem. Actors Studio, Players Club. *Regarding success in any field, two of the most important words in the English language, or any language for that matter, are persistence and determination. They are all-powerful; nothing can match them.*

WALSTON, RODERICK EUGENE, state government official; b. Gooding, Idaho, Dec. 15, 1935; s. Loren R. and Iva M. (Boyer) W.; m. Margaret D. Grandey; children: Gregory Scott W., Valerie Lynne W. A.A., Boise Jr. Coll., 1956; B.A. cum laude, Columbia Coll., 1958; LL.B. scholar, Stanford U., 1961. Bar: Calif. 1961, U.S. Supreme Ct. 1973. Law clk to judge U.S. Ct. Appeals 9th Cir., 1961-62; dep. atty. gen State of Calif., San Francisco,

1963-91, head natural resources sect, 1969-91, chief asst. atty. gen. pub. rights div., 1991—; spl. dep counsel Kings County, Calif., 1975-76; mem. environ. and natural resources adv. coun. Stanford (Calif.) Law Sch. Contbr. articles to profl. jours.; bd. editors: Stanford Law Rev., 1959-61, Western Natural Resources Litigation Digest, Calif. Water Law and Policy Reporter; spl. editor Jour. of the West. Co-chmn. Idaho campaign against Right-to-Work initiative, 1958; Calif. rep. Western States Water Coun., 1986—; environ. and natural resources adv. coun., Stanford Law Sch. Nat. Essay Contest winner Nat. Assn. Internat. Rels. Clubs, 1956, Stanford Law Rev. prize, 1961; Astor Found. scholar, 1956-58. Mem. ABA (chmn. water resources com. 1988-90, vice chmn. and conf. chmn. 1985-88, 90—), Contra Costa County Bar Assn., U.S. Supreme Ct., Hist. Soc., Federalist Soc., World Affairs Coun. No. Calif. Office: Calif Atty Gen's Office 1300 I St Ste 1720 Sacramento CA 95814-4017

WALT, HAROLD RICHARD, rancher; b. Berkeley, Calif., Jan. 30, 1923; s. Ralph Sidney and Frances Kathryn (Leahy) W.; m. Kathleen Dorothy O'Connell, Dec. 20, 1947; children: Michael Lowney, Timothy Gordon, Kimberly Ann, Patrick Randolph, Jennifer Joan, Carolyn Marie. B.S. in Forestry, U. Calif.-Berkeley, 1948, B.S. in Bus. Adminstrn., 1950, M.B.A. in Corp. Fin., 1953. Vice chancellor fin., lectr. bus. adminstrn. U. Calif., Berkeley, 1948-60; asst. budget dir. Kaiser Industries Corp., Oakland, Calif., 1961-64; dep. dir. fin. State of Calif., 1965-66; dir. civil systems Aerojet-Gen. Corp., El Monte, Calif., 1967-68; exec. v.p. SysteMed Corp., Newport Beach, Calif., 1969-71; pres. William L. Pereira Assos., Los Angeles, 1972-74; dean Coll. Bus. Adminstrn., U. San Francisco, 1978-89, prof. mgmt., 1989; rancher, co-owner, mgt. Box D Ranch, Ashland, Oreg., 1989—; vis. prof. fin. San Francisco State U., 1978; chmn. bd. Fidelity Savs. & Loan Assn., 1982; bd. dirs. Homestead Savs.vis. scholar, 1981; bd. dirs. Eureka Savs. & Loan; adv. com. Fed. Home Loan Mortgage Corp., Washington, 1980-83; vis. scholar Coll. Natural Resources, U. Calif., 1984; S.J. Hall lectr. in indsl. forestry U. Calif., Berkeley, 1986; vis. prof. forest policy U. Calif., 1987, 88. Contbr. over 50 articles related to bus. and forestry. Mem. Calif. Gov.'s Commn. Ocean Resources, 1965-66, Gov.'s Com. Econ. Devel., 1965-66; chmn. Calif. State Bd. Forestry, 1983-90; chmn. bd. Children's Hosp., Stanford, Calif., 1974-80; bd. dirs. Calif. Dept. Forestry, 1990-91, Nat. Forest Found., 1992-94. Served with USMCR, 1942-47. Fellow Fund Adult Edn., 1958; named Calif. Forester of Yr., Calif. Assn. Resource Conservation Dists., 1986. Mem. Soc. Am. Foresters, Am. Forestry Assn. (bd. dirs.), Fin. Execs. Inst., Bay Area Pub. Affairs Council, Acad. Mgmt., Security Analysts Soc., Town Hall of Calif. (bd. dirs. 1972-74), Beta Gamma Sigma, Pi Sigma Alpha, Alpha Zeta, Xi Sigma Pi, Theta Delta Chi, Delta Sigma Pi, Beta Alpha Psi. Republican. Roman Catholic. Clubs: Bohemian (San Francisco); Sutter (Sacramento). Home: PO Box 1267 Ashland OR 97520-0043

WALT, MARTIN, physicist, consulting educator; b. West Plains, Mo., June 1, 1926; s. Martin and Dorothy (Mantz) W.; m. Mary Estelle Thompson, Aug. 16, 1950; children: Susan Mary, Stephen Martin, Anne Elizabeth, Patricia Ruth. B.S., Calif. Inst. Tech., 1950; M.S., U. Wis., 1951, Ph.D., 1953. Staff mem. Los Alamos Sci. Lab., 1953-56; research scientist, mgr. physics Lockheed Missiles and Space Co., Palo Alto (Calif.) Rsch. Lab., 1956-71, dir. phys. scis., 1971-86, dir. research, 1986-93; cons. prof. Stanford U., 1986—; mem. adv. com. NRC, NASA, Dept. Def., U. Calif. Lawrence Berkeley Lab. Contbr. articles to sci. jours. Served with USNR, 1944-46. Wis. Research Found. fellow, 1950-51; AEC fellow, 1951-53. Fellow Am. Geophys. Union, Am. Phys. Soc.; mem. Am. Inst. Physics (bd. govs.), Bd. Overseers for Superconducting Supercollider, Fremont Hills Country Club. Home: 12650 Viscaino Ct Los Altos CA 94022-2517 Office: Stanford U Starlab Durand 317 Stanford CA 94305

WALTER, ALAN STUART, crop insurance consulting company executive; b. Ottawa, Ill., May 21, 1945; s. Arthur L. and Edna L. (Schobert) W.; m. M. Kathleen Yednock, Aug. 26, 1967; children: Aaron, Bryce. BS in Agrl. Econs., U. Ill., 1967; MS in Agrl. Econs., Cornell U., 1969; PhD in Agrl. Econs., Wash. State U., 1974. Agrl. economist Econ. Rsch. Svc., Washington, 1974-77; br. chief Structures br. Econ. Rsch. Svc., Washington, 1978-79; staff economist Fed. Crop Ins. Corp., Kansas City, Mo., 1980-81, dir. reins., 1981-84; dir. multiple peril svcs. Crop Hail Ins. Actuarial Assn., Overland Park, Kans., 1984-87, v.p. actuarial svcs., 1987-89; pres. Nat. Crop Ins. Svcs., Overland Park, Kans., 1990-93; prin. Walter Agrl. Cons., 1993-95; pres. Agrl. Risk Mgmt. N.Am., 1995—; adv. com. Midwest Climate Ctr., Champaign, Ill., 1989—. Cubmaster Boy Scouts Am., Overland Park, 1987; bd. dirs., umpire Little League Baseball, Overland Park, 1985-90; Sunday sch. tchr., 1989—. With U.S. Army, 1969-71. Decorated Bronze Star. Mem. Am. Agrl. Econ. Assn. (Disting. Policy Contbn. 1978). Avocations: reading, travel.

WALTER, DONALD ELLSWORTH, federal judge; b. Jennings, La., Mar. 15, 1936; s. Robert R. and Ada (Lafleur) D'Aquin; m. Charlotte Sevier Donald, Jan. 5, 1942; children: Laura Ney, Robert Ellsworth, Susannah Brooks. BA, La. State U., 1961, JD, 1964. Bar: La. 1964, U.S. Supreme Ct. 1969. Assoc. Cavanaugh, Brame, Holt & Woodley, 1964-66, Holt & Woodley, Lake Charles, La., 1966-69; U.S. atty. U.S. Dept. Justice, Shreveport, La., 1969-77; lawyer Hargrove, Guyton, Ramey & Barlow, Shreveport, La., 1977-85; judge U.S. Dist. Ct. (west. dist.) La., Monroe, 1985-92, Shreveport, La., 1993—. Served with AUS, 1957-58. Office: US Dist Ct 300 Fannin St Rm 4200 Shreveport LA 71101-3121*

WALTER, DOUGLAS HANSON, lawyer; b. Chgo., Sept. 13, 1941; m. Priscilla Ann McConnell, Sept. 6, 1964; children: Kristin L., Nicholas D. BA magna cum laude, Harvard U., 1963, JD, 1966. Bar: Ill. 1966. Office: Jones Day Reavis & Pogue 77 W Wacker Dr Chicago IL 60601-1629*

WALTER, ELDON G., diversified financial services company executive; b. 1942. Mng. ptnr. Mayer, Hoffman & McCann, Kansas City, Mo. Office: Mayer Hoffmann & McCann 420 Nichols Rd Kansas City MO 64112

WALTER, FRANK SHERMAN, retired health care corporation executive; b. Denver, June 23, 1926; s. Frank J. and Nancy (Sherman) W.; m. Carolyn May Cox, July 29, 1949; children: Douglas, Steven, Nancy. Student, U. Colo., 1944; B.S., U. Ore., 1950; M.B.A., U. Chgo., 1951. Adminstrv. resident Grad. Hosp. U. Pa., 1950-51, adminstrv. asst., 1951-52, asst. dir., 1952-55; adminstr. Meth. Hosp., Phila., 1955-63, St. Barnabas Hosp., Mpls., 1963-70; pres. Met. Med. Center, Mpls., 1970-83; exec. v.p. Health One Corp., 1983-85; clin. preceptor U. Minn., 1965-85; trustee Blue Cross/Blue Shield of Minn., 1977-85. Bd. dirs. Mpls. War Meml. Blood Bank, 1964-70, Health Manpower Mgmt., 1972-77; vestryman Episc. Ch., Mpls., 1966-69. With USAAF, 1944-46. Fellow Am. Coll. Hosp. Adminstrs.; mem. Twin City Hosp. Assn. (dir., pres. 1970-71), Minn. Hosp. Assn. (trustee 1970-77, treas. 1973-74, pres. 1975-76), Am. Hosp. Assn., Upper Midwest Hosp. Conf. (dir. 1977-85), Downtown Council (dir. 1977-85). Home: 6809 Dovre Dr Minneapolis MN 55436-1714

WALTER, INGO, economics educator; b. Kiel, Fed. Republic of Germany, Apr. 11, 1940; s. Hellmuth and Ingeborg (Moeller) W.; m. Jutta Ragnhild Dobernecker, June 24, 1963; children: Carsten Erik, Inga Maria. AB summa cum laude, Lehigh U., 1962, MS, 1963; PhD, NYU, 1966. Asst. prof. econs. U. Mo., St. Louis, 1965-67, assoc. prof., chmn. dept., 1967-70; prof. econs. and fin. Stern Sch. Bus. Adminstrn. NYU, N.Y.C., 1970—, assoc. dean academic affairs, 1970-79, chmn. internat. bus. and fin. depts., 1980-85, Dean Abraham L. Gitlow chair, 1987-90; Charles Simon chair, dir. NYU Salomon Ctr., 1990—; Swiss Bank Corp. prof. internat. mgmt. (joint appointment) INSEAD, Fontainebleau, France, 1985—; cons. in field. Author. editor 22 books including Secret Money, 1985, 2d edit., 1989, Global Financial Services, 1990, Universal Banking in the United States, 1994; contbr. articles to profl. jours. Recipient Bernhard Harms medal, 1992; Ford Found. fellow, 1974-76, Rockefeller Found. fellow, 1977-78. Mem. Am. Econ. Assn., Am. Fin. Assn., Acad. Internat. Bus., Royal Econ. Soc., So. Econ. Assn., Phi Beta Kappa, Beta Gamma Sigma, Omicron Delta Epsilon. Home: 77 Club Rd Montclair NJ 07043-2528 Office: NYU Stern Sch Bus 44 W 4th St New York NY 10012-1126

WALTER, J. JACKSON, foundation executive, consultant; b. Abington, Pa., Nov. 6, 1940; s. Joseph Horace and Edith Wilson (Jackson) W.; m. Susan Draude, Feb. 3, 1978; 1 child, Allison K. Mabe. A.B., Amherst Coll., Mass., 1962; LL.B., Yale U., New Haven, 1966. Sec. Fla. Dept. Bus. Regulation, Tallahassee, 1976-79; dir. U.S. Office Govt. Ethics, Washington, 1979-82; pres. Nat. Acad. Pub. Adminstrn., Washington, 1982-84, Nat. Trust Historic Preservation, Washington, 1984-92; exec. dir. Waterford (Va.) Found.; cons. in field. Co-author: America's Unelected Government, 1983. Contbr. articles to profl. jours. Bd. dirs. Sabre Found., Boston, 1983—, Am. Alliance for Rights and Responsibilities, Washington. Mem. Nat. Acad. Pub. Adminstrn., ABA, Yale (N.Y.C.) Club, Met. (Washington) Club.

WALTER, JOHN, newspaper editor. Mng. editor Atlanta Jour. and Constn. Office: Journal-Constitution PO Box 4689 72 Marietta St NW Atlanta GA 30303-2804

WALTER, JOHN ROBERT, printing company executive; b. Pitts., Jan. 20, 1947; s. Jack and Helen (Sech) W.; m. Carol Ann Kost, Sept. 6, 1969; children: Lindsay, Ashley. BBA, Miami U., Oxford, Ohio, 1969. With R.R. Donnelley & Sons Co., Chgo., 1969—, various sales positions, 1969-77, v.p. sales, 1977-81, sr. v.p. sales, 1981-83, dir. mfg. div., 1983-85, group pres., 1985-86, exec. v.p., 1986-87, pres., 1987-89, pres., chmn., CEO, 1989, chmn., CEO, 1990—; bd. dirs. Abbott Labs., Deere & Co., Dayton Hudson Corp., NAM; mem. bus. adv. com. Miami U., 1987—. Trustee Chgo. Symphony Orch.; mem. univ. assocs. bd. Northwestern U.; CEO bd. advisors U. So. Calif.; bd. dirs. Evanston (Ill.) Hosp., Steppenwolf Theatre Co. Mem. Am. Soc. Corp. Execs., Internat. Adv. Coun. of Singapore Econ. Devel. Bd., Bus. Coun., Bus. Round Table (policy com.), Comml. Club Chgo., Chgo. Commonwealth Club, Exec. Club (bd. dirs.), Links Club (N.Y.), River Club (N.Y.), Chgo. Club, Econ. Club Chgo., Historic Georgetown Club. Republican. Lutheran. Avocations: golfing, tennis, sailing.

WALTER, JUDITH ANNE, government executive; b. Ames, Iowa, Feb. 13, 1941; d. Gordon Escher and Eileen Anna (Womeldorff) Walter; m. Irvin B. Nathan; stepchildren: Daniel Nathan, Jonathan Nathan. BA, U. Wis., 1964; MA, U. Calif., Berkeley, 1968, MBA, 1976. Intelligence analyst Nat. Security Agy., Ft. Meade, Md., 1964-66; asst. v.p. internat. Wells Fargo Bank, San Francisco, 1969-75; spl. asst. to under sec. State Dept., Washington, 1975-76; exec. asst. to pres. Am. U., Washington, 1976-77; v.p. corp. banking Wells Fargo Bank, San Francisco, 1977-79; dep. dir. strategic analysis Office of the Comptroller of the Currency, Washington, 1979-82, dir. strategic planning, 1982-85, dep. comptroller ops., 1985-86, sr. dep. comptroller adminstrn., 1986—. Bd. dirs., chmn. governance com. Girl Scout Coun. of Nation's Capital, Washington; bd. govs. The Shakespeare Theatre Guild, Washington. Mem. White House Fellows Assn. (pres.), Women in Housing and Fin. Office: Office of the Comptroller of the Currency 250 E St SW Washington DC 20024-3208

WALTER, KENNETH LUVERNE, agricultural facility director; b. Buffalo Lake, Minn., June 20, 1936; s. Clarence Andrew and Ruth (Schafer) W.; m. Nancy Lee Woolard, Jan. 30, 1959; children: Katrina Lynn, Matthew Thomas (dec.), Janelle Mae. BS in Agr., U. Minn., St. Paul, 1963. Sales and tech. rep. Midland Coops. Inc., Mpls., 1963-68; asst. to supt. Agr. Experiment Sta. U. Minn., Rosemount, 1968-90, acting supt. Agr. Experiment Sta., 1990-93, dir. ops. Agr. Experiment Sta., 1993—. With USN, 1955-59. Mem. Am. Soc. Agrl. Engrs. Office: U Minn Agrl Experiment Sta 1605 160th St W Rosemount MN 55068-6053

WALTER, PAUL HERMANN LAWRENCE, chemistry educator; b. Jersey City, N.Y., Sept. 22, 1934; s. Helmuth Justus and Adelaide C. J. (Twardy) W.; m. Grace Louise Carpenter, Aug. 25, 1956; children: Katherine Elizabeth Walter Bousquet, Marjorie Allison Walter Moran. BS, MIT, 1956; PhD, U. Kans., 1960. Rsch. scientist DuPont Cen. Rsch. Dept., Wilmington, Del., 1960-67; prof. chem. Skidmore Coll., Saratoga Springs, N.Y., 1967—, chair chemistry and physics, 1975-85. Translator: (book) Foundations of Crystal Chemistry, 1968; contbr. articles to sci. publs. Fellow Chem. Inst. Can.; mem. AAAS, AAUP (pres. 1984-86), Am. Chem. Soc. (bd. dirs. 1991—, chmn. 1993-95), Sociedad Quimica de Mexico (hon.). Democrat. Presbyterian. Achievements include patents in field. Home: 9 Walter Dr Saratoga Springs NY 12866-9233 Office: Skidmore Coll Dept Chemistry and Physics N Broadway Saratoga Springs NY 12866-1632

WALTER, PRISCILLA ANNE, lawyer; b. Chgo., Feb. 9, 1943; d. William M. and Anne (Rogers) McConnell; m. Douglas H. Walter, Sept. 6, 1964; children: Kristin Lynn, Nicholas D. BA, Wellesley Coll., 1965; MSc, London Sch. Econ., 1967; JD magna cum laude, Northwestern U., 1978. Bar: Chgo. 1978. Law clk. to presiding justice 7th Cir. Ct. Appeals, Chgo., 1978-79; ptnr. Gardner, Carton & Douglas, Chgo., 1979—. Pres. bd. trustees The Latin Sch., Chgo., 1988-90; bd. govs. Met. Planning Coun.; co-chair Field Mus. of Natural History Founder's Coun. Elected one of the 100 Top Women in Computing, Open Computing mag., 1995. Mem. ABA, Info. Industry Assn. (proprietary rights com.), Chgo. Bar Assn., Computer Law Assn., Am. Bar Found. Office: Gardner Carton & Douglas 321 N Clark St Ste 3400 Chicago IL 60610-4714

WALTER, RICHARD LAWRENCE, physicist, educator; b. Chgo., Nov. 1, 1933; s. Lawrence Barnabas and Marie Ann (Boehmer) W.; m. Carol Elizabeth Goethals, Dec. 27, 1958; children—Timothy, Susan, Matthew. B.S., St. Procopius Coll., 1955; Ph.D., Notre Dame U., 1960. Teaching asst., research asst. Notre Dame U., 1955-59; research asso. dept. physics U. Wis., 1960-61, instr., 1961-62; asst. prof. physics Duke U., Durham, N.C., 1962-67; asso. prof. Duke U., 1967-74, prof., 1974—; vis. staff mem. Los Alamos Sci. Lab., 1964, 70, 75; vis. prof. Max Planck Inst. fur Kernphysik, Heidelberg, Germany, 1970-71, Fudan U., Shanghai and Tsinghua U., Beijing, People's Republic of China, 1985, 88, 91, 94, 95, 96; staff mem. Triangle Univs. Nuclear Lab., 1970—. Contbr. articles to profl. jours. Fulbright scholar, 1970-71. Mem. Am. Phys. Soc., Environ. Metals Group (council 1973-76), Sigma Xi, Sigma Pi Sigma (nat. council 1964-68). Home: 2818 McDowell Rd Durham NC 27705-5621 Office: Duke Univ Dept Physics PO Box 90305 Durham NC 27708-0305

WALTER, ROBERT D., wholesale pharmaceutical distribution executive; b. 1945. BMechE, Ohio U., 1967; MBA, Harvard U., 1970. With Cardinal Foods Inc. (acquired by Roundy's Inc. 1988), Dublin, Ohio, 1971-88; CEO, chmn. bd. Cardinal Health, Inc., Dublin, 1979—. Office: Cardinal Health Inc 655 Metro Pl S Dublin OH 43017-3313*

WALTER, ROBERT IRVING, chemistry educator, chemist; b. Johnstown, Pa., Mar. 12, 1920; s. Charles Weller and Frances (Riethmiller) W.; m. Farideh Asghari, Oct. 17, 1973. AB, Swarthmore Coll., 1941; MA, Johns Hopkins U., 1942; PhD, U. Chgo., 1949. Instr. U. Colo., 1949-51, U. Conn., 1953-55; rsch. assoc. Rutgers U., 1951-53; assoc. physicist Brookhaven Nat. Lab., 1955-56; mem. faculty Haverford Coll., 1956-68, prof. chemistry, 1963-68; prof. U. Ill., Chgo., 1968—, prof. emeritus, 1990—; vis. lectr. Stanford (Calif.) U., winter 1967; acad. guest U. Zurich, 1976; U.S. NAS exch. visitor to Romania, 1982, 88. Mem. Adv. Council Coll. Chemistry, 1966-70. Served with USNR, 1944-46. Grantee U.S. Army Signal Research and Devel. Lab., NIH, NSF, Dept. Energy; NSF fellow, 1960-61. Fellow AAAS; mem. Am. Chem. Soc. (vis. scientist div. chem. edn. 1964-73), Sigma Xi. Achievments include special research preparation, proof of structure, chemical and physical properties of stable aromatic free radicals, Cl reactions and mechanisms in heterogeneous catalysis, reactions of porphyrin bases. Home: 987 Inverleith Rd Lake Forest IL 60045-1607

WALTER, VIRGINIA LEE, psychologist, educator; b. Temple, Tex., Oct. 30, 1937; d. Luther Patterson and Virginia Lafayette (Wilkins) W.; m. Glen Ellis, 1958 (div.); children: Glen Edward, David Walter; m. Robert Reinehr, 1963 (div.); 1 son, Charles Allen; m. Robert Bruininks, 1975 (div.). B.S., U. Tex.-Austin, 1959, M.Edn., 1967; postgrad. internship program in spl. Edn. Adminstrn., 1970; Ed.D., U. Houston, 1973. Tchr. elem. sch. Austin Ind. Sch. Dist., 1959-60, Houston Ind. Sch. Dist, 1965; teaching asst. and research asst. dept. ednl. psychology U. Tex.-Austin, 1965-66; intern Austin State Hosp., 1967; curriculum specialist Spl. Ednl. Instructional Materials Ctr. U. Tex., 1967-68; dir. field activities Edn. Personnel Devel., Austin, 1969-70; parent trainer-communication coordinator Edn. Service Ctr., Austin, 1970-71; grad. asst. U. Houston, 1971-72, teaching fellow, summer 1972, evaluator lab. experiences Tchrs. Inst. Program, 1972-73, grad. asst., advisor in curriculum and instrn. student services ctr., 1972-73, teaching fellow dept. curriculum and instrn., 1973; prof. ednl. psychology dept. ednl. psychology U. Minn., Mpls., 1973-85; pres. Sch. Resource Ctr., Austin, Tex., 1985-90; tchr. Llano Pub. Schs., 1988—; chmn. State Adv. Council for Inservice Tng. Regular Classroom Tchrs., 1977-79; cons. spl. ednl. various sch. dists., state depts. and agys.;. Editorial cons.: Jour. Ednl. Psychology, 1979, Reading Research Quar., 1982; assoc. editor: Exceptional Children, 1979-84; assoc. editor Teaching Exceptional Children, 1985-89; contbr. articles to profl. jours., papers to profl. confs. Named Minn. Spl. Educator of Yr., 1978; recipient Service award Internat. Council Exceptional Children, 1978; HEW Office of Human Devel. Services grantee, 1976-80; Dept. Edn. contractee, 1980-83. Mem. Council for Exceptional Children, Nat. Assn. Children with Learning Disabilities (dir. Minn. chpt. 1978-80), Nat. Assn. Retarded Citizens, AAUP, Assn. Supervision and Curriculum Devel. Home and Office: PO Box 493 Llano TX 78643-0493

WALTER, WILLIAM ARNOLD, JR., physician; b. Pitts., May 17, 1922; s. William Arnold and Theresa Elizabeth (Schank) W.; m. Carol Patricia Turner, June 22, 1946; children—Kathleen Ann, Elizabeth Louise. A.B., Ind. U., 1943, M.D., 1945; M.P.H., Johns Hopkins U., 1951. Intern St. Ann's Hosp., Chgo., 1945-46; med. officer in charge Ky. Treatment Centers, Ky. Bd. Health, Louisville, 1948-50; dir. div. venereal disease control Fla. State Bd. Health, Jacksonville, 1951-53; asso. dir. Bur. Preventable Diseases, 1953-55; mem. staff epidemiology sect. Nat. Cancer Inst., 1955-57; med. officer in charge Houston Pulmonary Cytology Project, U. Tex.; M.D. Anderson Hosp. and Tumor Inst., 1957-59; med. officer in charge Phila. Cytology Project, Women's Med. Coll. Pa., 1959-60; program dir. research grants br. Nat. Cancer Inst., Bethesda, Md., 1960-65; dep. dir. extramural activities Nat. Cancer Inst., 1969-72, dep. dir. div. cancer grants, 1972-74, dep. dir. div. cancer research resources and centers, 1974-80, acting dir. centers and treatment program, 1976-77, acting dir. div. extramural activities, 1980—, assoc. dir. rev. activities, 1983—; pvt. cons. med. research and rev., 1984—. Served to capt AUS, 1946-48. Recipient Commendation medal USPHS, 1969, 74. Mem. Am. Venereal Disease Assn., Am. Social Hygiene Assn., Soc. Epidemiologic Research, Assn. Mil. Surgeons U.S., Am. Public Health Assn., AMA, Commd. Officers Assn. USPHS. Roman Catholic. Office: 6310 Wilson Ln Bethesda MD 20817-5534

WALTERS, ARTHUR SCOTT, neurologist, educator, clinical research scientist; b. Balt., Feb. 20, 1943; s. Charles Henry and Jean Vivian (Scott) W.; m. Bokyun Kim, May 18, 1985 (div. Oct. 1992); m. Lesley J. Gill, Dec. 19, 1992. BA, Kalamazoo Coll., 1965; MS, Northwestern U., 1967; MD, Wayne State U., 1972. Diplomate Am. Bd. Psychiatry and Neurology; diplomate Am. Bd. Sleep Medicine. Intern Oakwood Hosp., Dearborn, Mich., 1972-73; resident in neurology SUNY Downstate Med. Ctr., Bklyn., 1976-79; movement disorder fellow Neurol. Inst., N.Y.C., 1982-84; asst. prof. neurology Robert Wood Johnson Med. Sch., U. Medicine & Dentistry N.J., New Brunswick, 1984-91, assoc. prof. neurology, 1991—; asst. chief divsn. neurology Lyons (N.J.) VA Med. ctr., 1985-89, neurology cons., 1984—; nat. chmn. med. adv. bd. Restless Legs Syndrome Found., 1992—; organizer Internat. Restless Legs Study Group, 1992—; head Restless Legs Syndrome and Periodic Limb Movement Coun. for the Nat. Sleep Found., 1994—; neurology cons. Coney Island Hosp., Bklyn., Bklyn. Jewish Hosp., 1980-81; presenter in field. Contbr. articles, abstracts, to profl. publs., chpts. to books, organizer symposia. Grantee UMDNJ, 1984-86, VA RAG, 1985-86, Sandoz Corp., 1985-88, VA Merit Rev., 1989—, Clemente Found., 1994-95. Fellow Am. Acad. Neurology, Am. Sleep Disorders Assn.; mem. AAAS, Sleep Rsch. Soc., Movement Disorder Soc., N.Y. Acad. Scis., N.J. Sleep Soc. (sec. 1995—). Home: 207 S Adelaide Ave Highland Park NJ 08904-1605 Office: UMDNJ-Robert Wood Johnson Med Sch Dept Neurology CN19 1 Robert Wood Johnson Pl New Brunswick NJ 08903-0019

WALTERS, BARBARA, television journalist; b. Sept. 25, 1931; d. Lou and Dena (Selett) W.; 1 child, Jacqueline. Grad., Sarah Lawrence Coll., 1953; LHD (hon.), Ohio State U., Marymount Coll., Tarrytown, N.Y., 1975, Wheaton Coll., 1983. Former writer-producer WNBC-TV; then with Stas. WPIX and CBS-TV; joined Today Show, 1961, regular panel mem., 1964-74, co-host, 1974-76; moderator syndicated program Not For Women Only, 1974-76; newscaster ABC Evening News (now ABC World News Tonight), 1976-78; host The Barbara Walters Spls., 1976—; co-host ABC TV news show 20/20, 1979—. Contbr. to ABC programs Issues and Answers. Author: How To Talk With Practically Anybody About Practically Anything, 1970; contbr. to Reader's Digest, Good Housekeeping, Family Weekly. Recipient award of yr. Nat. Assn. TV Program Execs., 1975, Emmy award Nat. Acad. TV Arts and Scis., 1975, Mass Media award Am. Jewish Com. Inst. Human Relations, 1975, Hubert H. Humphrey Freedom prize Anti-Defamation League-B'nai B'rith, 1978, Matrix award N.Y. Women in Communications, 1977, Barbara Walters' Coll. Scholarship in Broadcast Journalism established in her honor Ill. Broadcasters Assn., 1975, Pres.'s award Overseas Press Club, 1988, Lowell Thomas award Marist Coll., 1990, Lifetime Achievement award Internat. Women's Media Found., 1992; named to 100 Women Accomplishment Harper's Bazaar, 1967, 71, One of Am.'s 75 Most Important Women Ladies' Home Jour., 1970, One of 10 Women of Decade Ladies' Home Jour., 1979, One of Am.'s 100 Most Important Women Ladies' Home Jour., 1983, Woman of Year in Communications, 1974, Woman of Year Theta Sigma Phi, Broadcaster of Yr. Internat. Radio and TV Soc., 1975, One of 200 Leaders of Future Time Mag., 1974, One of Most Important Women of 1979 Roper Report, One of Women Most Admired by Am. People Gallup Poll, 1982, 84, to Hall of Fame Acad. TV Arts and Scis., 1990. Office: 20/20 147 Columbus Ave Fl 10 New York NY 10023-5900 also: Barbwall Productions The Barbara Walters Specials 825 7th Ave Fl 3 New York NY 10019-6014*

WALTERS, BILL, state senator, lawyer; b. Paris, Ark., Apr. 17, 1943; s. Peter Louis and Elizabeth Cecelia (Wilhelm) W.; m. Joyce Leslie Garrett Moore, Jan. 9, 1964 (div. 1970); children: Jamie, Sherry Ann; m. Shirley Ann Dixon, Aug. 20, 1971; 1 child, Sandra. BS, U. Ark., 1966, JD, 1971. Bar: Ark. 1971, U.S. Dist. Ct. Ark. 1971. Asst. prosecuting atty. 12th Jud. Dist. Ark., Ft. Smith, 1971-74; pvt. practice Greenwood, Ark., 1975—; mem. Ark. Senate, Little Rock, 1982—; bd. dirs. 1st Ark. Title Co., Pine Bluff; bd. dirs., sec.-treas. Mineral Owners Collective Assn. Inc., Greenwood; v.p., bd. dirs. Sebastian County Abstract & Title Ins. Co., Greenwood; mem. Ark. Real Estate Comm., Ark. Abstract and Title Commn. Committeeman Rep. Ctrl. Com. Ark., Ft. Smith, 1980; search pilot CAP, Ft. Smith. Decorated Silver Medal of Valor; recipient Cert. of Honor Justice for Crime's Victims, 1983. Mem. Ark. Bar Assn., South Sebastian County Bar Assn. (pres. 1991-94), Profl. Landmen's Assn. Roman Catholic. Home: PO Box 280 Greenwood AR 72936-0280 Office: 44 Town Square St Greenwood AR 72936-4019

WALTERS, CHRISTOPHER KENT, lawyer; b. Bryn Mawr, Pa., Oct. 10, 1942; s. Lester K. and Margaret (Becker) W.; m. Teri R. Simon, Nov. 23, 1980. AB, Princeton U., 1964; JD, U. Mich., 1967. Bar: Pa. 1967, U.S. Supreme Ct. 1980. Ptnr. Reed Smith Shaw & McClay, Phila., 1980—. Capt. U.S. Army, 1968-70, Vietnam. Office: Reed Smith Shaw & McClay 2500 One Liberty Pl Philadelphia PA 19103

WALTERS, DANIEL RAYMOND, political columnist; b. Hutchinson, Kans., Oct. 10, 1943; s. Howard Duke and Glenna Lucille (Hesse) W.; m. Doris K. Winter, June 16, 1995; children: Danielle, Staci. Mng. editor Hanford (Calif.) Sentinel, 1966-69, Herald News, Klamath Falls, Oreg., 1969-71, Times-Standard, Eureka, Calif., 1971-73; polit. writer and columnist Sacramento (Calif.) Union, 1973-84; polit. columnist Sacramento Bee, 1984—. Author: The New California: Facing the 21st Century, 1986; founding editor Calif. Polit. Almanac, 1989. Office: The Sacramento Bee 925 L St Ste 1404 Sacramento CA 95814-3704

WALTERS, DAVID MCLEAN, lawyer; b. Cleve., Apr. 4, 1917; s. William L. and Marguerite (McLean) W.; m. Betty J. Latimer, Mar. 25, 1939 (dec. 1983); 1 child, Susan Patricia (Mrs. James Edward Smith); m. Rebecca Brewer, Feb. 14, 1991. BA, Baldwin-Wallace Coll., 1938; LHD (hon.); LLB, Cleve. Sch. Law, 1943; JD, U. Miami, 1950; LHD (hon.), St. Thomas of Villanova U. Bar: D.C. 1950, Fla. 1950, Fed. 1950. Judge adminstrv. practices U.S. Dept. Justice, Washington, 1940-50; sr. law ptnr. firm Walters & Costanzo, Miami, Fla., 1950-80; of counsel firm Walters, Costanzo, Russell, Zyne, 1980-85; amb. to Vatican, 1976-78; fellow internat. medicine, bd. advisors Med. Sch., Boston U., 1985. Chmn. Fla. Harbor Pilot Commn., 1952-54, City of Miami Seaport Commn., 1953-54, Nat. Leukemia Soc., 1965-66, Archbishops Charities Dr., 1975-76; spl. bond counsel Dade

County, 1957-58; gen. counsel Dade County Port Authority, 1957-58; vice-chmn. Nat. Dem. Fin. Coun., 1960-77; mem. Gov.'s Adv. Bd. on Health and Rehabilitative Svc., 1976-77; sec.-treas. Inter-Am. Ctr. Authority, 1960-74; bd. advisor St. Thomas Law Sch., 1985-88; personal rep. Pres. Reagan F.D.R. Meml. Commn., 1985; bd. dirs. Barry U.; chmn. bd. trustees Variety Children's Hosp.; pres. Miami Children's Hosp. Found., 1980—; trustee Gregorian Inst. Found., Rome. Served with Counter Intelligence Corps., U.S. Army, 1943-46. Decorated Bronze Star medal., Knight St. Gregory the Great; recipient Silver medallion NCCJ, Resolution of Commendation award for civic contbn. Fla. Legislature, 1988. Mem. Am., Fla., Fed., D.C., Interam. bar assns., Am. Assn. Knights of Malta (v.p.), Serra Club, Sovereign Mil. Order Malta (master knight 1975—, exec. com. papal visit to U.S. 1987), Omicron Delta Kappa, Lambda Chi Alpha. Democrat. Roman Catholic. Home: 9202 SW 78th Pl Miami FL 33156-7590 Home (summer): 5 St Helens, Marine Parade Sandycove, Dublin Ireland Office: 3000 SW 62nd Ave Miami FL 33155-3065

WALTERS, DORIS LAVONNE, pastoral counselor; b. Peachland, N.C., Feb. 24, 1931; d. H. Lloyd and Mary Lou (Helms) W. BA cum laude, Carson-Newman Coll., 1961; MRE, Southwestern Bapt. Theol. Sem., 1963; MA in Pastoral Counseling, Wake Forest U., 1982; DMin in Pastoral Counseling, Southeastern Bapt. Theol. Sem., 1988. Min. of edn. and youth First Bapt. Ch., Orange, Tex., 1963-66; assoc. prof. Seinan Jo Gakuin Jr. Coll., Japan, 1968-72; dir. Fukuoka (Japan) Friendship House, 1972-88, pastoral counselor, chaplain, 1983-86; Tokyo lifeline referral counselor (in English) Hiroshima-South, Fukuoka, 1983-86; supr. Japanese and Am. staff Fukuoka Friendship House, 1972-86; with chaplaincy Med. Coll. Va., Richmond, 1976; resident chaplain N.C. Bapt. Hosp., Winston-Salem, 1981-82, counselor-in-tng. pastoral care dept., 1986-88; dir. missionary counseling and support svcs. Pastoral Care Found. N.C. Bapt. Hosp., Winston-Salem, 1989-93; dir. Missionary Family Counseling Svcs., Inc., Winston-Salem, 1993—; mem. Japan Bapt. Mission Exec. Com., Tokyo, 1973-76. Author: An Assessment of the Reentry Issues of the Children of Missionaries, 1991; translator: The Story of the Craft Dogs, 1983. J.M. Price scholar Southwestern Bapt. Theol. Sem., 1962; First Bapt. Ch. Blackwell grantee Southeastern Sem., 1986-88. Mem. Assn. for Clin. Pastoral Counselors (assoc.), Am. Assn. Pastoral Counselors (pastoral affiliate). Democrat. Avocations: photography, travel, reading, classical music, concerts. Home: 208 Oakwood Sq Winston Salem NC 27103-1914 Office: Missionary Family Counseling Svcs Inc 514 S Stratford Rd Winston Salem NC 27103-1823

WALTERS, EVERETT, retired university official, author; b. Bethlehem, Pa., Apr. 4, 1915; s. Raymond and Elsie (Rosenberg) W.; m. Jane C. Schrader, Apr. 23, 1938; children: Diane Colley (Mrs. Patrick B. Hearne), Everett Garrison. A.B., U. Cin., 1936; M.A., Columbia U., 1940, Ph.D., 1947. Instr. Finch Jr. Coll., 1940-43; rep. U.S. Civil Service Commn., 1943-44; instr. history Ohio State U., 1946-48, asst. prof., 1948-54, assoc. prof., 1954-63, asst. dean Grad. Sch., 1954-55, acting dean Grad. Sch., 1956-57, dean Grad. Sch., 1957-63, chmn. editorial bd. Ohio State U. Press; Vis. prof. Whittier Coll., summer 1950; dir. grad. fellowship program U.S. Office Edn., 1962-63; v.p. acad. affairs Boston U., 1963-69, sr. v.p., dean faculties, 1969-71; dean faculties U. Mo.-St. Louis, 1971-75, vice chancellor community affairs, 1975-79, prof., 1979-80, interim chancellor, 1972-73; Chmn. Grad. Conf. on Grad. Study and Research, 1961-62. Author: Joseph Benson Foraker; An Uncompromising Republican, 1948; Editor, contbr: Graduate Education Today, 1965; Contbr. articles to hist., ednl. jours. Bd. dirs. Sta. KETC-TV, St. Louis, 1973-80, chmn., 1979-80; chmn. bd. dirs. St. Louis Bach Soc., 1977-78. Served as lt. USNR, 1944-46; Naval Officers Candidate Sch. 1950-52, Newport, R.I. Recipient Centennial Achievement award Ohio State U., 1970. Mem. Am. Hist. Assn., Ohio Hist. Soc. (trustee 1961-63, 82-87), Ohio Hist. Found. (trustee, sec. 1987-91), Assn. Grad. Schs. (sec.-treas. 1960-61, editor Procs. Jour. 1959-63), St. Louis Council World Affairs (chmn. bd.), Columbus Met. Club, University Club (Columbus), Phi Delta Theta. Episcopalian. Home: 2872 Pickwick Dr Columbus OH 43221-2920

WALTERS, FARAH M., hospital administrator; b. Feb. 10, 1945. BS, Ohio State U., 1968; MS, Case Western Res. U., 1975, MBA, 1984. Sr. v.p., gen. mgr. Univs. Hosps., Cleve., 1987-89, exec. v.p., 1989-91, exec. dir., 1991-92, pres., CEO, 1992—. Office: Univ Hosps Cleve 11100 Euclid Ave Cleveland OH 44106*

WALTERS, GEOFFREY KING, physicist, educator; b. Baton Rouge, Aug. 23, 1931; s. Robert King and Harriett (Fuller) W.; m. Jeanette Long, June 17, 1954; children—Terry, Jeffrey, Gina. B.A., Rice U., 1953; Ph.D., Duke, 1956. Research asso. Duke, 1956-57; mem. tech. staff Tex. Instruments, Inc., Dallas, 1957-62; corporate research asso. Tex. Instruments, Inc., 1962-63; prof. physics and space sci. Rice U., Houston, 1963—, Worden prof., 1994—; chmn. physics dept. Rice U., 1973-77, dean natural scis., 1980-87; acting chief fire tech. divsn. Nat. Bur. Standards, Gaithersburg, Md., 1971-72; dir. Rsch. Corp., 1977—, Rsch. Corp. Techs., 1987—; Guggenheim fellow Stanford U., 1977-78; vis. prof. Collège de France, Paris, 1987; vis. com. Nat. Bur. Standards, 1980-82, 92-94, chmn. vis. com., 1982. Contbr. articles on low temperature, solid state, atomic collision, nuclear physics, solar-terrestrial relationships, radio astronomy to profl. jours. Recipient Disting. Alumnus award Rice U., 1990. Fellow AAAS, Am. Phys. Soc. (chmn. div. electron and atomic physics 1972-73, councillor 1974-79, 89, chmn. Nominating Com. 1989); mem. Am. Geophys. Union. Home: 5102 Jackwood St Houston TX 77096-1416 Office: Rice University PO Box 1892 6100 South Main Houston TX 77251

WALTERS, GEORGE JOHN, oral and maxillofacial surgeon; b. Balt., June 16, 1956; s. George John Sr. and Henrietta Jean (Parker) W.; m. Melanie Ann Goodreau, June 23, 1989. BS, Loyola Coll., 1978; DDS, U. Md., 1983; postgrad., John Hopkins, 1991, U. Pa., 1992, U. Pa., 1993. Cert. argon laser. Rsch. asst. dept. otolaryngology The Johns Hopkins Sch. Medicine, Balt., 1978-79; ind. learning ctr. technician Balt. Coll. Dental Surgery, Dental Sch., U. Md., 1980-81; audio-visual technician U. Md. Law Sch., Balt., 1981-82, res. material circulation asst., 1982-83; resident gen. practice residency York (Pa.) Hosp., 1983-84; resident dept. anesthesia The Med. Coll. of Pa. and Hosp., Phila., 1984-85; resident dept. dentistry div. oral and maxillofacial surgery U. Md. Med. System, Balt., 1985-89, chief adminstrv. resident dept. dentistry, 1988-89; assoc. in oral and maxillofacial surgery Miller Oral Surgery and Pa. Jaw Treatment Ctr., Harrisburg, Pa., 1989-91; ptnr. Oral and Maxillofacial Surgery, Panama City, Fla., 1991-95; individual practice oral and maxillofacial surgery Panama City, Fla., 1995—; explorer advisor for health career explorer post Balt. Coll. Dental Surgery, Dental Sch., U. Md., 1981, dental rsch. student com., 1982, vol. for recruitment of minority students, 1983; testifier Sen. House Com. on Medicaid Funding, State House, Annapolis, Md., 1987-88; lectr. Gulf Coast C.C., 1991—. Copntbr. to profl. jours. Health vol. overseas Nepal Mission for Cleft Lip and Palate, 1989; vol. Guatemala Med. Mission Cleft Lip and Palate, 1994. John Hopkins fellow 1989. Mem. ADA, Am. Assn. Oral and Maxillofacial Surgery, Mid. Atlantic Soc. Oral and Maxillofacial Surgery, Bay County Dental Soc., Fla. Dental Soc., N.W. Dental Soc. Fla., Fla. Soc. Oral and Maxillofacial Surgery, Gorgas Odontological Soc., Rotary, Bay County Civil War Roundtable, Gamma Pi Delta. Roman Catholic. Avocations: golf, boating, baseball, travel, reading. Home: PO Box 27473 1702 Wahoo Cir Panama City FL 32411-7230 Office: 2202 State Ave Ste 200 Panama City FL 32405

WALTERS, GLEN ROBERT, banker; b. Mpls., Sept. 11, 1943; s. Sterling Thomas and Mildred Eunice (Parkinson) W.; m. Gail Elvira Engelsen, June 11, 1966; children—Nicole Marie, Brent Aaron, Hillary Renee. B.A., U. Minn., Mpls., 1965, postgrad., 1965-67; banking degree, Stonier Grad. Sch. Banking, Rutgers U., New Brunswick, N.J., 1982. Comml. banker 1st Nat. Bank, Mpls., 1967-83, sr. v.p. human resources, 1983-90; sr. v.p. Firstar Bank Minn., Mpls., 1990—. Served to sgt. USNG, 1967-73. Republican. Presbyterian. Office: Firstar Bank 1550 E 79th St Minneapolis MN 55425-1139

WALTERS, GWENDOLYN MAE (WALLACE), nursing educator, clinical specialist; b. Northville, Mich., Feb. 15, 1943; d. Leo William and Marian Ruth (Lamb) Wallace; m. John Patrick Walters, Aug. 3, 1968; children: Daniel, Debra, David, Douglas. BSN, Mercy Coll. Detroit, 1971; MSN, Madonna U., 1992. RN, Mich., Ohio. Practical nurse New Grace Hosp., Detroit, 1970-71, RN, 1971; RN in-house contingent staff St. Mary Hosp., Livonia, 1972-73; primary care nurse critical care unit Met. West Hosp., Westland, Mich., 1974-79, newspaper reporter, chairperson nursing care rev., peer rev. and coronary care coms., 1975-81, pharmacy nurse IV ad mixture and acute care, 1979-80, team leader Outpatient Clinic, 1980-81; contingent staffing SRT Med-Staff Internat., 1981-83; staff nurse, team leader, charge nurse critical care div. Saratoga Hosp., Detroit, 1981-83; staff nurse critical care div. Providence Hosp., 1983-84; nursing faculty ADN program Henry Ford Community Coll., Dearborn, Mich., 1984-91; RN in-house contingent staffing and med./surg. units U. Mich. Med. Ctr., 1988-90; nurse Favorite Nurses, Southfield, Mich., 1990-91, Nurses, Inc., Southfield, Mich., 1990-92, STAT Health Svcs., Inc., Southfield, Mich., 1992—; nursing instr. staff devel. VA Med. Ctr., Allen Park, Mich., 1992-93; nursing faculty Med. Coll. Ohio Sch. Nursing, Toledo, 1994—. Vol. adult leader Sr. Assistance Program, Detroit, 1986—, Appalachia Svc. Project, Johnson City, Tenn., 1986—; vol. leader Care for the Homeless, Detroit, 1984—; vol. med. staff nurse UAW Black Lake Camp and Conference Ctr., Detroit, 1977-81;vol. Focus Hope-Assistance to the Elderly, Pontiac, 1980—; mem. Am. Heart Assn.; mentor nursing career Girl Scouts U.S., Livonia, 1990—. Mem. ANA (cert. continuing edn. and staff devel., del. conv. Houston chpt. 1980), AACN, Acad. Med.-Surg. Nurses, Mich. Nurses Assn., Detroit Dist. Nurses Assn. (bd. dirs. 1978, 79, med./surg. membership com.), Mich. League for Nursing (nurse practice com.), Sigma Theta Tau (Kappa Iota and Zeta Theta chpts.). Mem. United Methodist Ch. Avocations: reading, baking, camping, cycling, creative handicrafts. Home: 34415 Wallace Ct Livonia MI 48150-2692 Office: Med Coll Ohio Sch Nursing 3355 Glendale Ave Toledo OH 43699

WALTERS, JANE, state agency administrator. MusB, Rhodes Coll., BA in Music History; MA in Counseling, U. Memphis; PhD in Sch. Adminstrn., Duke U. Tchr., counselor Messick H.S., Memphis, asst. prin.; asst. dir. computer svcs. Memphis City Schs.; prin. Craigmont Jr. H.S., 1974-79, Craigmont Jr. and Sr. H.S., 1979-95; 21st commr. edn. State Dept. Edn., Nashville, 1995—; adv. com. edn. depts. Rhodes Coll, Christian Brothers Com., Tenn. Arts Acad.; cons. College Bd. advanced placement program. Grant reader NEA; mem. Goals for Memphis Edn. Com.; bd. dirs. World Affairs Coun, Nat. Coun. Christians and Jews, Memphis Coun. Internat. Visitors, Memphis Youth Symphony, Am. Cancer Soc., Memphis chpt. Office: Tenn State Dept Edn 6th Fl Gateway Plz 710 James Robertson Pkwy Nashville TN 37243-0375

WALTERS, JEFFERSON BROOKS, musician, retired real estate broker; b. Dayton, Ohio, Jan. 20, 1922; s. Jefferson Brooks and Mildred Frances (Smith) W.; m. Mary Elizabeth Espey, Apr. 6, 1963 (dec. July 22, 1983); children: Dinah Christine Basson, Jefferson Brooks; m. Carol Elaine Clayton Gillette, Feb. 19, 1984. Student, U. Dayton, 1947. Composer, cornetist Dayton, 1934—, real estate broker, 1948-88; ret., 1988. Condr., composer choral, solo voice settings of psalms and poetry Alfred Lord Tennyson; composer Crossing the Bar (meml. performances U.S. Navy band), 1961; composer The Yorktown Grand March (Good Citizenship medal SAR, 1988). Founder Am. Psalm Choir, 1965; apptd. deferred giving officer Kettering (Ohio) Med. Ctr., 1982-85. Served with USCGR, 1942-45, PTO, ETO. Mem. SAR, Greater Dayton Antique Study Club (past pres.), Dayton Art Inst., Montgomery County Hist. Soc., Masons (32d deg.). Brethren Ch. Home: 4113 Roman Dr Dayton OH 45415-2423

WALTERS, JOEL W., lawyer; b. Kansas City, Mo., Sept. 12, 1960; s. Harry and Margaret Ruth (Armstrong) W.; m. Gail Susan Einstein, Mar. 2, 1992; children: Evan Daniel, Stephanie Lianne. BSBA, U. Mo., Columbia, 1981; JD with distinction, U. Mo., Kansas City, 1984. Bar: Mo. 1984, Fla. 1986, U.S. Dist. Ct. (we. dist.) Mo. 1986, U.S. Dist. Ct. (mid. dist.) Fla. 1986, U.S. Dist. Ct. (so. dist.) Fla. 1988, U.S. Ct. Appeals (8th and 11th cirs.) 1986. Law clk. to Hon. Robert T. Donnelly Supreme Ct. of Mo., Jefferson City, 1984-86; assoc. Abel, Band, Brown, Russell & Collier, Chartered, Sarasota, Fla., 1986-91; founding shareholder, ptnr. Brown Clark & Walters, Sarasota, 1991—; cert. mediator Supreme Ct. of Fla., 1992—; arbitrator nat. panel Am. Arbitration Assn., Miami, Fla., 1994—; spkr. in field. Bd. dirs., pres. Police Athletic League, Sarasota, 1990—; bd. dirs. Longboat Key (Fla.) Recreation Ctr., 1994—; mem. adv. bd. dirs. Sunnyland coun. Boy Scouts Am., 1991-92. Mem. Sarasota County Bar Assn., Acad. Fla. Trial Lawyers, Charlotte County Bar Assn. Avocations: boating, tennis, fishing, diving, skiing. Home: 584 Cutter Ln Longboat Key FL 34228 Office: Brown Clark & Walters PA 1819 Main St Ste 1100 Sarasota FL 34236

WALTERS, JOHN LINTON, electronics engineer, consultant; b. Washington, Mar. 8, 1924; s. Francis Marion Jr. and Roma (Crow) W.; m. Grace Elizabeth Piper, June 19, 1948; children: Richard Miller, Gretchen Elizabeth, Christopher Linton, John Michael, Kim Anne. BS, U.S. Naval Acad., 1944; SM, Harvard U., 1949; DrEng, Johns Hopkins U., 1959. Staff mem. Los Alamos (N.Mex.) Sci. Lab., 1949-52; rsch. assoc. Johns Hopkins U., Balt., 1952-59; assoc. elec. engr. Brookhaven Nat. Lab., Upton, N.Y., 1959-62; rsch. scientist Johns Hopkins U., Balt., 1962-70; electronics engr. Naval Rsch. Lab., Washington, 1970—; sci. advisor Comdr. 6th Fleet, Gaeta, Italy, 1979-80; lectr. dept. elec. engring. Johns Hopkins U., 1964-65. Lt. (j.g.) USN, 1944-47, PTO. Recipient commendation Dir. of Navy Labs., 1979. Mem. IEEE, Sigma Xi. Achievements include research on electronic countermeasures, refinements to measurement techniques used in particle accelerators, analysis of radar and jamming phenomena, measurement and analysis of anomalous propagation in atmosphere. Home: 212 Beach Dr Annapolis MD 21401-5856 Office: Radar Divsn Naval Rsch Lab Washington DC 20375

WALTERS, JOHN SHERWOOD, retired newspaperman; b. Junction City, Ark., May 15, 1917; s. John Thomas and Cora (McBride) W.; m. Claire Dailey, June 1, 1941; children: Elizabeth Claire, Mary Dailey (dec.). B.A., La. Tech. Inst., 1939; M.A., La. State U., 1941. Editor Ruston (La.) Daily Leader, 1940; reporter Baton Rouge Morning Adv., 1941; rating examiner Jacksonville Naval Air Sta., 1941-42; reporter Fla. Times-Union, Jacksonville, 1943, 44-53; city editor Fla. Times-Union, 1953-60; exec. editor Times-Union and Jacksonville Jour., 1960-78, asso. pub., 1978-82, ret., 1982; asst. prof. journalism La. Tech. Inst., 1943-44; mem. jud. Nominating Commn., 1st Dist. Ct. Appeals of Fla. Bd. dirs. Duval County chpt. A.R.C., chmn., 1966-67; charter trustee U. North Fla. Found., Inc., pres., 1973-75; chmn. council advisers U. North Fla., 1975; bd. dirs. Health Planning Council, N.E. Fla. Cancer Program, Jacksonville Blood Bank. Mem. Am. Soc. Newspaper Editors, Fla. Soc. Newspaper Editors (pres. 1971-72), Alpha Lambda Tau, Sigma Delta Chi. Democrat. Methodist. Clubs: Rotarian (Jacksonville) (sec. 1970-71, pres. 1971-72); Timuquana Country, River. Home: 1750 Dogwood Pl Jacksonville FL 32210-2202

WALTERS, JOHNNIE MCKEIVER, lawyer; b. nr. Hartsville, S.C., Dec. 20, 1919; s. Tommie Ellis and Lizzie Lee (Grantham) W.; m. Donna Lucile Hall, Sept. 1, 1947; children: Donna Dianne Walters Gent, Lizbeth Kathern Walters Kukorowski, Hilton Horace, John Roy. AB, Furman U., 1942, LLD, 1973; LLB, U. Mich., 1948. Bar: Mich. 1948, N.Y. 1955, S.C. 1961, D.C. 1973. Atty. office chief counsel IRS, Washington, 1949-53; asst. mgr. tax div. law dept. Texaco, Inc., N.Y.C., 1953-61; ptnr. firm Geer, Walters, & Demo, Greenville, S.C., 1961-69; asst. atty. gen. tax div. Dept. Justice, Washington, 1969-71; commr. IRS, 1971-73; ptnr. firm Hunton & Williams, Washington, 1973-79, Leatherwood Walker Todd & Mann, P.C., Greenville, 1979-94; exec. v.p., gen. counsel Colonial Trust Co., 1996—; bd. dirs. Textile Hall Corp., Greenville, Santee Cooper, Moncks Corner, S.C. Mem. S.C. Coun. on Competitiveness, 1987-91; bd. dirs. Greenville Hosp. System Found., S.C. State Mus. Found. With USAAF, 1942-45. Fellow Am. Coll. Tax Counsel (founding regent), Am. Coll. Trust and Estate Counsel, Am. Bar Found., S.C. Bar Found. (bd. dirs. 1988-92); mem. ABA (taxation sect.), S.C. Bar (chmn. taxation sect. 1983-84), Rotary (pres. local club 1968-69). Republican. Baptist. Home: PO Box 2817 1804 N Main St Greenville SC 29609-4729 Office: PO Box 2817 Greenville SC 29602-2817

WALTERS, JUDITH RICHMOND, neuropharmacologist; b. Concord, N.H., June 20, 1944; d. Samuel Smith and Hazel Albertina (Stewart) Richmond; m. James Wilson Walters, Aug. 23, 1969 (div. 1992); children: James Richmond, Gregory Stewart, Douglas Powers. BA, Mt. Holyoke Coll., 1966; PhD, Yale U., 1972. Postdoctoral fellow dept. psychiatry Yale U. Med. Sch., New Haven, rsch. assoc. dept. pharmacology, asst. prof. dept. psychiatry; unit chief neurophysiol. pharmacology sect. exptl. therapeutics br. Nat. Inst. Neurol. Disease and Stroke, Bethesda, Md., 1976-81, sect. chief physiol. neuropharmacology sect. exptl. therapeutics br.; mem. sci. adv. bd. Hereditary Disease Found., L.A., 1977-80, 82-86, Tourette Syndrome Assn., 1992—; mem. bd. sci. counselors Nat. Inst. on Alcohol Abuse and Alcoholism, 1992-95; mem. Inst. of Medicine Com. to Raise the Profile of Rsch. on Substance Abuse, 1995-96. Sect. editor Neuroscience.net, 1996—; contbr. over 100 articles on neuropharmacology and neurophysiology to profl. jours. Recipient NIH Dir.'s award, 1994. Mem. Am. Soc. Pharmacology and Exptl. Therapeutics, Soc. for Neurosci. (mem. com. 1995-98). Home: 3615 Littledale Rd Kensington MD 20895-3435 Office: NIH Bldg 10 Rm 5C106 Bethesda MD 20892

WALTERS, MILTON JAMES, investment banker; b. Hornell, N.Y., May 21, 1942; s. James Henry and Frances Eleanor (Simmons) W.; m. Caroline Houck, May 24, 1963; children: Melissa Ann, Gregory Thomas, Timothy Allen. BA, Hamilton Coll., 1964. Trainee Mfrs. Hanover, 1964-65; with A.G. Becker Paribas Inc., N.Y.C., 1965-84, v.p., 1969-78, mng. dir., 1978-84; sr. v.p. corp. fin., mng. dir. Smith Barney, N.Y.C., 1984-88; pres. Tri-River Capital Group, 1988—; trustee Hamilton Coll., Clinton, N.Y., 1983-88, Friends Acad., Locust Valley, N.Y., 1981-91. Mem. Econ. Club N.Y., Mill River Club. Republican. Presbyterian. Office: Tri River Capital Group Inc 689 5th Ave New York NY 10022-3133

WALTERS, NORMAN EDWARD, hospital administrator, chief financial officer; b. Williamsburg, Ky., Nov. 21, 1941; s. Winford and Dorothy Florence (Clifford) W.; m. Elizabeth Lou Custer, Sept. 7, 1963; children: Pamela Denise, Scot Edward. BS, Southeastern U., 1969; MS, St. Joseph's U., Windham, Maine, 1991. Br. mgr. GEICO, Chevy Chase, Md., 1965-68; asst. dept. head, internal audit mgr., dir. of fin. Commonwealth of Va., Alexandria and Richmond, 1968-77; asst. contr. Cumberland County Hosp. System, Fayetteville, N.C., 1978-81; contr., asst. adminstr. Hosp. Mgmt. Assoc., Williamson, W.Va., 1981; asst. adminstr. Advanced Health System, Inc., Marlow and Elk City, Okla., 1981-87; asst. adminstr., CFO Taylor County Hosp., Campbellsville, Ky., 1987—; v.p. Pikeville (Ky.) Meth. Hosp., 1991—; govt. cons. healthcare com. Health Care Fin. Mgmt. Assn., Campbellsville, 1991. Contbr. articles to profl. jours. Member Christian Profl. Bus. Men, Alexandria, 1970-80, Lions, Marlow and Elk City, 1981, 83Gov. Jim Hunt's Health Care Task Force, Raleigh, N.C., 1980; ; treas. Rotary, Campbellsville, 1987. Capt. USAF, 1959-65. Decorated Hon. Order of Ky. Cols. Mem. Am. Mgmt. Assn. (chmn. 1968-75, 88-89), Health Care Fin. Mgmt. Assn. (nat. matrix 1978—, health care task force com. Charleston, W.Va. chpt. 1981-82, program chmn. N.C. chpt. 1980-81, health care reform task force Ky. chpt. 1991-92, mem. adv. com. health care task force nat. com., Leffer Plaque 1981), Health Law Mgmt. Assn. (assoc. chmn. Ky. chpt. 1988-89, Leffer Plaque 1989, 90). Democrat. Baptist. Avocations: reading, fishing, hunting, softball, basketball. Home: 224 College St Apt 2A Pikeville KY 41501-1771

WALTERS, PHILIP RAYMOND, real estate executive; b. Frankfort, Ind., Jan. 26, 1938; s. Raymond and Ruth Edna (Grimes) W.; m. Sharon Pearl Wilfong, May 31, 1958 (div. Nov. 1992); children: Raymond (dec.), Robert, Sharon Ruth; m. Candace Gina Oden, Jan. 29, 1994. BSBA, Olivet Nazarene Coll., 1959; JD, Ind. U., Indpls., 1969; postgrad., NYU, 1969-70. Bar: Ind. 1969, U.S. Dist. Ct. (so. dist.) Ind. 1969; real estate broker, Fla., Ind.; lic. in life, health and variable annuities, Fla., N.C., gen. securities prin. Co-corp. counsel Ind. Farm Bur. Ins., Indpls., 1975-79; dir. gift & estate planning Orlando (Fla.) Regional Healthcare Found., 1991-96; pres. House Investments, Inc., Longwood, Fla.; dep. atty. gen. State of Ind., Indpls.; planned giving officer Wheaton (Ill.) Coll.; campaign dir. Ketchum, Inc., Pitts.,; dir. planned giving Presbyn. Sch. Christian Edn., Richmond, Va.; presenter in field. Contbr. articles to profl. jours. Mem. Wekiva Presbyn. Ch., Longwood. Mem. Nat. Soc. Fundraising Execs, Nat. Assn. Realtors, Ind. State Bar Assn., Fla. Assn. Realtors, Ctrl. Fla. Estate Planning Coun., Mid-Fla. Regional MLS, Greater Orlando Realtors, Employee Relocation Coun., Citrus Club. Republican. Avocation: running. Home: 897 Cutler Rd Longwood FL 32779-3525

WALTERS, PHYLLIS SANDRA, chemical dependency nurse; b. Washington, Apr. 14, 1946; d. Dale Edward and Amelia Maud (Johnston) Wolber; m. Franklin Britt (div. 1973); m. Robert Dean Walters, Sept. 22, 1984; children: Ellen, Christina, Kathleen (dec.). ADN, DSM Area Community Coll., 1977; BS in Health Adminstrn., Coll. St. Francis, Joliet, Ill., 1992, postgrad. RN, Iowa, Va., Md. Staff nurse CCU Des Moines Gen. Hosp., 1977-80; staff nurse ICU Hampton (Va.) Gen. Hosp., 1980-83; staff nurse emergency rm. Mary Immaculate Hosp., Newport News, Va., 1980-82; staff nurse MIEMS, 1983; unit nurse mgr. Mercy Hosp. Med. Ctr., Des Moines, 1983-86, staff nurse, 1986-87, staff nurse alcohol and drug recovery program, 1987-91; staff nurse Harold Hughes Recovery, Des Moines Gen. Hosp., 1991—. Iowa state and dist. Dem. del., Des Moines, 1987. Mem. Nat. Nurses Soc. Addictions (cert. addictions nurse), Iowa Nurses Soc. Addictions (chair bylaws com. 1991-94, bd. dirs. 1991-94, hearing com. 1991-94). Roman Catholic.

WALTERS, RAYMOND, JR., newspaper editor, author; b. Bethlehem, Pa., Aug. 23, 1912; s. Raymond and Elsie (Rosenberg) W. A.B., Swarthmore Coll., 1933; postgrad., Princeton U., 1933-35; M.A., Columbia U., 1937, Ph.D., 1942. Editorial staff Current History mag., 1937-39; editorial staff Saturday Rev., 1946-58, book rev. editor, 1948-58; editor Encore mag., 1946-48; editor, columnist N.Y. Times Book Rev., 1958—; Mem. fiction jury Pulitzer Prize adv. bd., 1968. Author: Alexander James Dallas: Lawyer, Politician, Financier, 1943, Albert Gallatin: Jeffersonian Financier and Diplomat, 1957 (named One of Notable Books of Year, ALA), The Virginia Dynasty, 1965, Paperback Talk, 1985; Contbr. articles to profl. jours. Served with USAAF, 1942-46; hist. office hdqrs. USAAF, 1943-46. Mem. Am. Hist. Assn., Soc. Am. Historians (v.p.), P.E.N., Authors Guild. Episcopalian. Home: 315 E 68th St New York NY 10021-5692

WALTERS, ROBERT ANCIL, II, protective services coordinator; b. Washington, Sept. 21, 1945; s. Robert Ancil and Etha Jane (McKinley) W.; m. Sandra Faye Roy, June 30, 1969; children: Anthony Wayne, Byron Edward. Student, Western Ky. U., 1964-65, Internat. Acad., 1965-66, U. Md., 1969-70. Cert. fire tng instr., Ky., emergency med. technician, Ky., profl. emergency mgr., Md. Computer operator U.S. Naval Weapons Lab., Dahlgren, Va., 1969-70; instr. computer programming Brentwood Acad., Lexington, Ky., 1970-71; data control supr. Dept. Child Welfare, State of Ky., Frankfort, 1971-74; military personnel supr. Ky. Army Nat. Guard, Frankfort, 1974-77; area coord. Ky. Disaster and Emergency Svcs., Somerset, Ky., 1977—. Chmn. bd. dirs. Somerset-Pulaski County Rescue Squad, Ky., 1982-86, active mem., 1978-89; bd. dirs. Nancy Fire Dept., 1986-87, active mem., 1979-95; bd. dirs., disaster chmn. Lake Cumberland (Ky.) chpt. ARC, 1982-86, instr. CPR and first aid, 1979-88; mem. prospect listing and evaluation com. Ptnrs. in Progress, Somerset C.C., 1994. Sgt. U.S. Army, 1968-69, Vietnam. Recipient Ky. Commendation medal, 1975, 77, 79, Ky. Merit citation, 1976, 80, 892, Ky. Humanitarian citation, 1974, 77, Ky. Achievement medal, 1978, 82, 93. Mem. Ky. Disaster and Emergency Svcs Assn., Ky. Emergency Mgmt. Assn., Nat. Emergency Mgrs. Assn., Order of Kentucky Colonels, Somerset Colonel, Adair County General. Democrat. Baptist. Home: 1063 Prather Dr Nancy KY 42544-8722

WALTERS, RONALD OGDEN, finance company executive; b. Holcombe, Wis., July 13, 1939; s. Ogden Eugene and Josephine Ann (Hennekens) W.; m. Margaret Ellen Weisheipl, July 14, 1962; children—Laurie, Cheryl, Michael, Patrick. Student, U. Wis. Mgr. Thorp Fin., LaCrosse, Wis., 1962-65; regional mgr. Thorp Fin., Milw., 1965-69, ITT Consumer Fin. Corp., Milw., 1969-74; sr. v.p. ITT Consumer Fin. Corp., Brookfield, Wis., 1974—, exec. v.p. adminstrn., 1991-93; CEO Ideal Fin. Corp., 1994—. Mem. Wis. Fin. Services Assn. (pres. 1980). Republican. Roman Catholic. Avocations: boating; fishing; hunting. Home: N62w15763 Skyline Dr Menomonee Falls WI 53051-5748

WALTERS, VICTOR, holding company executive. Treas. One UP Enterprises Inc., Falls Church, Va. Office: One UP Enterprises Inc 7777 Leesburg Pike Ste 406N Falls Church VA 22043-2403*

WALTERS, WILLIAM LEROY, physics educator; b. Racine, Wis., Mar. 30, 1932; s. Robert N. and Elsie (Ahrens) W.; m. Darlene A. Kessenich, Feb. 5, 1955; children: Judy, Sandra, Robert, James. BS, U. Wis., 1954, MS, 1958, PhD, 1961. Assoc. dean scis. Coll. Letters and Sci. U. Wis., Milw., 1965-67, spl. asst. to chancellor, 1967-68, exec. asst. chancellor, 1968-69, asst. chancellor, acting dean Coll. Applied Sci. and Engring., 1969-70, vice chancellor univ., 1971-81, prof. physics, 1981-95, emeritus prof. physics, 1996—; sci. edn. grant adminstr., cons. Contbr. articles to physics jours. With U.S. Army, 1954-56. Mem. AAAS, Am. Assn. Physics Tchrs., Am. Phys. Soc., Nat. Assn. State Univs. and Land Grant Colls. (mem., chmn. exec. com. coun. acad. affairs 1978), Physics Club Milw. (dir. 1964-67, 82-92). Home: 2100 E Jarvis St Milwaukee WI 53211-2003

WALTHALL, DAVID N., advertising executive; b. 1945. Grad., U. Kans., 1967; MBA, Drake U., 1971. With Iowa Des Moines Nat. Bank, 1969-74, Hawkeye Capital Bank & Trust, Des Moines, 1974-85; officer Heritage Comm., Inc., Des Moines, 1985-87; pres., CEO Heritage Media Corp., Dallas, 1987—; bd. dirs. Equitable Bank, Equitable Bankshares. Office: Heritage Media Corp 13355 Noel Rd Dallas TX 75240-6602*

WALTHALL, LEE WADE, artistic director, dancer; b. Houston, Nov. 12, 1953; s. L.W. and Martha Virginia (Tacker) W. Student, Sch. of Am. Ballet, N.Y.C., 1973-75; BA cum laude, U. Wash., 1994. Prin. dancer Dutch Nat. Ballet, Amsterdam, 1975-82, Pacific N.W. Ballet, Seattle, 1982-90; dancer, ballet master Ballet Austin, Tex., 1990-91; artistic dir. Eastside Dance Theatre, Seattle, 1993-94, The Evergreen City Ballet, 1994—; dir. Evergreen City Ballet Acad., 1995—; artist in residence Hong Kong Ballet, 1991; guest artist Nureyev Internat. Ballet Festival, Kazan, Russia, 1994. Guest appearances throughout Europe and U.S.; starring role in Nutcracker-The Movie, 1986. Study grantee U. Wash. Dept. Dance, 1991-94.

WALTHER, JOSEPH EDWARD, health facility administrator, retired physician; b. Indpls., Nov. 24, 1912; s. Joseph Edward and Winona (McCampbell) W.; m. Mary Margaret Ruddell, July 11, 1945 (dec. July 1983); children: Mary Ann Margolis, Karl, Joanne Landman, Suzanne Conran, Diane Paczesny, Kurt. BS, Ind. U., 1936, MD, 1936; postgrad., U. Chgo., Harvard U., U. Minn., 1945-47. Diplomate Nat. Bd. Med. Examiners, Am. Bd. Internal Medicine, Am. Bd. Gastroenterology. Intern Meth. Hosp. and St. Vincent Hosp. of Indpls., 1936-37; physician, surgeon U.S. Engrs./Pan Am. Airways, Midway Islands, 1937-38; chief resident, med. dir. Wilcox Meml. Hosp., Lihue, Kauai, 1938-40; internist, gastroenterologist Meml. Clinic Indpls., 1947-83, med. dir., pres., chief exec. officer, 1947—; founder, pres. Doctors' Offices Inc., Indpls., 1947—; founder, pres., chief exec. officer Winona Meml. Found. and Hosp. (now Walther Cancer Inst.), Indpls., 1956—; clinical asst. prof. medicine Ind. U. Sch. Medicine, Indpls., 1948-93, clin. asst. prof. emeritus, 1993—. Author: (with others) Current Therapy, 1965; mem. edit. rsch. bd. Postgrad. Medicine, 1982-83; contbr. articles to profl. jours. Bd. dirs. March of Dimes, Marion County div., 1962-66, Am. Cancer Soc., Ind. div., 1986—. Col. USAAF, 1941-47, PTO. Decorated Bronze Star, Silver Star, Air medal; recipient Clevenger award Ind. U. 1989;, Disting. Alumnus award Ind. U. Sch. Med., 1990, Sagamore of Wabash award State of Ind., 1995; Dr. Joseph E. Walther Disting. Physician's award named in honor Winona Meml. Hosp., 1995. Master Am. Coll. Gastroenterology (pres. 1970-71, Weiss award 1988); mem. AMA (del. 1970-86), Soc. Cons. to Armed Forces, Ind. Med. Assn., Marion County Med. Assn., Ind. U. Alumni Assn. (life), Hoosier Hundred (charter), Highland Golf and Country Club (hon.), Waikoloa Golf and Country Club (Hawaii), Indpls. Athletic Club, 702 Club. Republican. Home: 4266 N Pennsylvania St Indianapolis IN 46205-2613 Office: Walther Cancer Inst 3202 N Meridian St Indianapolis IN 46208-4646

WALTHER, ROBERT R., physician, educator; b. Bayshore, N.Y., Aug. 19, 1947; s. Raymond Edward and Adeline Ann (Haas) W.; m. Virgina Anne Newland, Sept. 15, 1973; 1 child, Robert John. AB in Chemistry, Cornell U., 1969; MD, U. N.C., 1973. Diplomate Am. Bd. Internal Medicine, Am. Bd. Dermatology, Am. Bd. Med. Examiners; lic. physician, N.Y., Fla. Intern U. Miami Affiliated Hosp., 1973-74, resident in medicine, 1974-75; resident in dermatology Columbia Presbyn. Med. Ctr., N.Y.C., 1975-77; rsch. fellow dept. metabolism and pharmacology Rockefeller U. Hosp., N.Y.C., 1978; from asst. prof. to assoc. prof. dermatology Columbia U., N.Y.C., 1978-89, clin. prof., 1989—, vice chair dept. dermatology, 1994—; attending dermatologist Presbyn. Hosp., N.Y.C., 1989—, dir. clin. svcs., 1994—. Contbr. numerous articles to med. jours. USPHS vis. fellow to Yugoslavia, 1972. Fellow ACP, N.Y. Acad. Medicine (chmn. sect. on dermatology 1993-94); mem. AMA, Soc. for Investigative Dermatology, N.Y. County Med. Soc., Internat. Soc. Tropical Dermatology, Dermatology Found., Assn. Profs. Dermatology, Dermatologic Soc. Greater N.Y. Episcopalian. Home: 1070 Park Ave Apt 14D New York NY 10128 Office: Columbia Presbyn Med Ctr Col of Physicians & Surgeons New York NY 10032

WALTI, RANDAL FRED, management consultant; b. Chgo., Apr. 10, 1939; s. Fred Henry and Alice Ann (Steger) W.; m. Judith Ann Hodson, Jan. 31, 1960; children: Lee, Rod, Lynn. BSME, Purdue U., 1961. Program mgr. Aerojet Gen., El Monte, Calif., 1961-66; applications mgr. TRW Systems, Redondo Beach, Calif., 1966-70; br. mgr. A.B. Dick Co., Long Beach, Calif., 1970-71; pres. Randal Data Systems, Inc., Torrance, Calif., 1971-79, The Oaktree Consulting Group, Torrance, Calif., 1980—; founder, bd. dirs. Software Coun. So. Calif., Torrance; bd. dirs. Silver Cloud Travel, Inc., Torrance; chmn. The Exec. Com., La Jolla, Calif., 1986-88. Author: The Internet MArketing Report, 1995, 10 CEO Guides to Prosperity, 1996. Chmn. So. Calif. Leadership Coun., Christian Businessmen's Com., Santa Ana, Calif., 1991—; co-chmn. VentureNet Conf. on Venture Capital for Internet Cos., 1996. Republican. Mem. Covenant Ch. Home: 1806 Mount Shasta Dr San Pedro CA 90732-1527 Office: Oaktree Consulting Group 21041 S Western Ave Ste 160 Torrance CA 90501-1727

WALTNER, JOHN RANDOLPH, banker; b. San Diego, Dec. 11, 1938; s. Glenn H. and Pauline B. (Hoffman) W.; m. Janice L. McNamara, Nov. 23, 1963; children: Mary E., Ann L. BSBA, U. S.D., 1961, MBA, 1989. Trainee 1st Nat. Bank, Freeman, S.D., 1961-62, v.p., cashier and bd. dirs., 1968-87, pres., CEO and bd. dirs., 1988—; ops. officer Wells Fargo Bank, Monterey, Calif., 1964-67; bd. dirs. S.D. Blue Shield; mem. faculty U. S.D., Vermillion, 1990—, bus. adv. coun. Sch. of Bus., 1985—, chmn., 1992; mem. S.D. Investment Coun., 1994—, S.D. Lottery Commn., 1996—. Mem. S.D. Lottery Commn., 1996—; mem. Freeman Cmty. Devel. Corp., 1967—, past pres.; pres. Freeman Sch. Bd., 1981-84; treas. City of Freeman, 1961-62. With U.S. Army, 1962-64. Mem. Am. Bankers Assn. (govt. rels. coun. 1995—), S.D. Bankers Assn. (bd. dirs., v.p. 1991, pres.-elect 1992, pres. 1993-94), Freeman C. of C. (past sec.-treas.), Beta Gamma Sigma. Republican. Mennonite. Avocations: pub. speaking, community theater, amateur radio, astronomy, chess. Home: 541 S Poplar St PO Box 566 Freeman SD 57029 Office: 1st National Bank PO Box H Freeman SD 57029

WALTON, ALAN GEORGE, venture capitalist; b. Birmingham, Eng., Apr. 3, 1936; s. Thomas George and Hilda (Glover) W.; m. Jasmin Yvonne Christensen, Sept. 1, 1958 (dec. Nov. 1970); children: Kimm A., Keir D.A.; m. Elenor Jean McElliott, Aug. 6, 1977; children: Kristin M., Sherri L. Ph.D., U. Nottingham, Eng., 1960, D.Sc., 1973. Research assoc. Ind. U., Bloomington, 1960-62; asst. prof. chemistry Case Western Res. U., Cleve., 1962-66, assoc. prof., 1966-69, assoc. prof. macromolecular sci., 1969-71, prof., 1971-81, dir. Lab. for Biol. Macromolecules, 1972-81; pres., chief exec. officer Univ. Genetics Co., 1981-86, chmn., 1986-87; ptnr. Oxford Ptnrs., Stamford, Conn., 1987—; chmn. Oxford Biosci. Corp., 1992—; vis. lectr. biol. chemistry Harvard Med. Sch., 1971; mem. Pres. Carter's Task Force on Sci. and Tech.; U.S. project officer Rudjer Boskovic Inst., Zagreb, Yugoslavia, 1967-75; bd. dirs. Human Genome Sci. Inc., Collaborative Clin. Rsch. INc.; chmn. AVID Corp., Gene Logic Inc.; chmn. CEO Senatics Corps; bd. govs. Nat. Ctr. Genome Resources. Author: Formation and Properties of Precipitates, 1967, Biopolymers, 1973, Structure and Properties of Amorphous Polymers, 1980, Polypeptide and Protein Structure, 1981, Recombinant DNA, 1981, Yearbook of Genetic Engineering and Biotechnology, 1983, 85, 88. Recipient Israel State medal, 1972, Case Inst. Centennial Scholar medal, 1981. Mem. Nat. Venture Capital Assn., Conn. Venture Group, Sigma Xi (Research award 1973), Pi Kappa Alpha. Home: 17 Walnut Ln Weston CT 06883-1417 Office: Oxford Venture Biosci Corp 215 Post Rd W Westport CT 06880-4603

WALTON, ALICE L., bank executive; b. Newport, Ark., Oct. 7, 1949; d. Sam and Helen (Robson) W. BBA, Trinity U., 1971; D. of Bus. Adminstrn. (hon.), S.W. Bapt. U., 1988. Investment analyst First Commerce Corp., New Orleans, 1972-75; dir., v.p. investments Walton Enterprises, Bentonville, Ark., 1975—; retail & investment broker E.F. Hutton Co., New Orleans, 1975-79; vice chair, investment dir. Walton Bank Group, Bentonville, Ark., 1982-88; pres., chair, CEO Llama Co./Llama Asset Mgmt. Co., Fayetteville, Ark., 1988—; dean's adv. coun. U. Ark. Coll. Bus. Adminstrn., Fayetteville, 1989-90; internat. judge Students in Free Enterprise, Springfield, Mo., 1990; bd. trustees The Asia Soc., N.Y.C., 1991. Chairperson N.W. Ark. Coun., Fayetteville, 1990—; bd. dirs. Pillar's Club-United Way, Easter Seals Soc.-Arkansan of Yr., Walton Arts Ctr. Coun., Fayetteville, Ark. Named Disting. Bus. Lectr. Cen. State U., Edmond, Okla., 1989. Office: Llama Company One McIlroy Pla Fayetteville AR 72701

WALTON, ANGELA DESHAE, management consultant; b. Duluth, Ga., Nov. 19, 1957; d. Jessie I. and Lorraine Hopson W. BA, Brandeis U., 1980. Sales rep. ITT, Atlanta, 1980-82, Allnet Comm., Atlanta, 1982-84; ter. mgr. Cook-Wave Labs., Atlanta, 1984-86; major accounts mgr. Minolta Corp., Atlanta, 1986-87; sr. account exec. Friden Alcate 1, Atlanta, 1987-88; pres. ADW & Assocs., Atlanta, 1988-95; mgmt. cons. Fred Pryor Resources, Kansas City, Kans., 1995—. Mem. resource devel. bd. Apex Mus., Atlanta, 1991; active Ga. Rep. Found., Atlanta, 1992—, United Way of Atlanta. Martin Luther King scholar Brandeis U., 1976; named Outstanding Vol., NAACP, 1994. Mem. ASTD, Sales and Mktg. Exexs. of Atlanta, V.I.P. Initiative, Alpha Kappa Alpha. Avocations: golf, tennis, downhill skiing.

WALTON, ANTHONY JOHN (TONY WALTON), theater and film designer, book illustrator; b. Walton on Thames, Eng., Oct. 24, 1934; s. Lancelot Henry Frederick and Hilda Betty (Drew) W.; m. Julie Andrews, May 10, 1959 (div. 1968); 1 child, Emma Kate; m. Genevieve LeRoy, Sept. 12, 1991; 1 stepchild, Bridget. Student, Oxford Sch. Tech. Art and Commerce, 1949-52, Slade Sch. Fine Art, London, 1954-55. Designer settings, costumes for theater prodns., London, off-Broadway, 1957-60, Broadway, 1961—; Broadway prodns. include Pippin, 1972 (Tony award 1972-73, Drama Desk award 1972-73), Shelter, 1973 (Drama Desk award 1972-73), Sophisticated Ladies, 1981, The Real Thing, 1984, Hurlyburly, 1984, I'm Not Rappaport, 1985, House of Blue Leaves, 1986 (Tony award 1985-86), Drama Desk award 1985-86), Front Page, 1986, Social Security, 1986 (Drama Desk award 1985-86), Anything Goes, 1987, Grand Hotel, 1989, Six Degrees of Separation, 1990, The Will Rogers Follies, 1991, Death and the Maiden, 1992, Conversations with My Father, 1992, Four Baboons Adoring the Sun, 1992, Guys and Dolls, 1992 (Tony award 1991-92, Drama Desk award 1991-92), Tommy Tune Tonight, 1992, She Loves Me, 1993, A Grand Night for Singing, 1993, Laughter on the 23rd Floor, 1993, Picnic, 1994, A Christmas Carol, N.Y.C., 1994, Company, 1995, Moonlight, 1995, A Fair Country, 1996, A Funny Thing Happened on the Way to the Forum, 1996; ballets, principally San Francisco Ballet Co., Am. Ballet Theatre; films include Mary Poppins, A Funny Thing Happened on the Way to the Forum, Murder on the Orient Express, The Wiz, All That Jazz (Acad. award with Philip Rosenberg 1980), Prince of the City, Star 80, The Glass Menagerie, 1987, Regarding Henry, 1991; operas in London, 1963-68, Spoleto, Italy, 1965, Santa Fe, 1975, San Francisco, 1992, Chgo., 1993; author: Adeile Penguin in Wonders, 1981; illustrator Wonders, 1981, The Importance of Being Earnest, 1973, Lady Windemere's Fan, 1973, Popcorn, 1972, God Is a Good friend, 1969, Witches Holiday, 1971, others. Served with RAF, 1952-54. Recipient Emmy award Death of a Salesman, 1986; named to Theatre Hall of Fame, 1991; elected to Interior Design Hall of Fame, 1993. Mem. United Scenic Artists, Costume Designers Guild Calif., Acad. Motion Picture Arts and Scis. Office: care Martino ICM 40 W 57th St New York NY 10019-4001

WALTON, BILL (WILLIAM THEODORE WALTON, III), sportscaster, former professional basketball player; b. La Mesa, Calif., Nov. 5, 1952; s. Theodore and Gloria W.; m. Susan Walton; children: Adam, Nathan, Luke. Grad., UCLA, 1974. Team center Portland Trail Blazers, 1974-79, capt., 1976-77; with Los Angeles Clippers (formerly San Diego Clippers), 1979-85, Boston Celtics, 1985-87; sportscaster NBC Sports, 1993—; mem. NCAA Divisional Championship Team, 1972-73, NBA Championship Teams, 1977, 86. Recipient James E. Sullivan Meml. award, 1974, James Naismith award, 1972, 73, 74, Adolph Rupp trophy, 1972, 73, 74, NBA Sixth Man award, 1986; named NBA Most Valuable Player, 1978. Office: care Boston Celtics Boston Garden Boston MA 02114-1310

WALTON, BRIAN, labor union administrator; b. London, Dec. 24, 1947; came to U.S., 1966; s. Frank William and Irene Mary (Thornton) W.; (div.); children: Robert, Sarah; m. Deborah R. Baron. BA with honors, Brigham Young U., 1969, MA in Polit. Sci., 1971; JD, U. Utah, 1974. Bar: Calif. 1974, U.S. Dist. Ct. (ctrl., so. and no. dists.) Calif. 1974. Law clk. to Hon. J. Allan Crockett Utah Supreme Ct., 1974; assoc. Reavis & McGrath and predecessor firms, L.A., 1974-82; ptnr. Selvin and Weiner, L.A., 1982-85; exec. dir. Writers Guild Am., West, Inc., L.A., 1985—; teaching asst. Coll. Law, Utah U., 1973, asst. to v.p. of spl. projects, 1971-73, rsch. asst. Coll. Law, 1972-74, tchr., dir. legal skills seminar Coll. Law, 1974. Contbr. articles to law jours. Edwin S. Hinckley scholar. Mem. ABA (antitrust sect.), L.A. County Bar Assn. (antitrust sect., intellectual property and unfair competition sect.), Assn. Bus. Trial Lawyers, Internation Assn. des Avocats du Droit d'Auteur. Office: 7000 W 3d St Los Angeles CA 90036

WALTON, CAROLE LORRAINE, clinical social worker; b. Harrison, Ark., Oct. 20, 1949; d. Leo Woodrow Walton and Arlette Alegra (Cohen) Armstrong. BA, Lambuth Coll., Jackson, Tenn., 1971; MA, U. Chgo., 1974. Diplomate Clin. Social Work, Acad. Cert. Social Workers; bd. cert. diplomate; lic. clin. social worker. Social worker Community Mental Health, Flint, Mich., 1971-72; clin. social worker Community Mental Health, Westchester, Ill., 1974-76; dir. self-travel program Chgo. Assn. Retarded Citizens, 1973; coord. family svcs. Inner Harbors Psych. Hosp., Douglasville, Ga., 1976-83; sr. mental health clinician Northside Mental Health Ctr., Atlanta, 1983—. Mem. NASW, Ga. Soc. for Clin. Work (pres. 1981-82, pres. 1993-95). Avocation: tennis. Office: Northside Mental Health Ctr 5825 Glenridge Dr NE Bldg 4 Atlanta GA 30328-5387

WALTON, CHARLES MICHAEL, civil engineering educator; b. Hickory, N.C., July 28, 1941; s. Charles O. and Virginia Ruth (Hart) W.; m. Betty Grey Hughes; children: Susan, Camila, Michael, Gantt. BS, Va. Mil. Inst., 1963; MCE, N.C. State U., 1969, PhD, 1971. Research asst. N.C. State U., Raleigh, 1967-71; transp. planning engr. N.C. Hwy. Commn., Raleigh, 1970-71; asst. prof. civil engring. U. Tex., Austin, 1971-76, assoc. prof., 1976-83, prof., 1983—, Bess Harris Jones Centennial prof. natural resource policy studies, 1987-91, Paul D. and Betty Robertson Meek Centennial prof. engring., 1991-93, Ernest H. Cockrell Centennial chair engring., 1993—, chmn. dept. civil engring., 1988—; transp. cons., 1970—; assoc. dir. Ctr. for Transp. Rsch. U. Tex., 1980-88; chmn., exec. com. Transp. Rsch. Bd., NRC, 1991, Disting. Lectr., 1994. Contbr. articles to profl. jours. Past chmn. Urban Transp. Commn., Austin. Recipient Disting. Engring. award N.C. State U., 1995, Joe J. King Profl. Engring. Achievement award U. Tex. at Austin, 1995-96. Fellow ASCE (Harland Bartholomew urban planning award 1987, Frank M. Masters transp. engring. award 1987, James Laurie prize 1992), Inst. Transp. Engrs.; mem. NSPE, NAE, Intelligent Transp. Soc. Am. (vice chair tech. coord. coun., immediate past chair tech. com. on comml. vehicle ops.), Soc. Automotive Engrs., Urban Land Inst., Inst. for Ops. Rsch. and Mgmt. Scis., Soc. Am. Mil. Engrs., Internat. Rd. Fedn. (bd. dirs.), Internat. Rd. Ednl. Found. (bd. dirs.), Austin C. of C. (Leadership Austin program). Democrat. Methodist. Home: 3404 River Rd Austin TX 78703-1031 Office: U Tex Dept Civil Engring Dept Civil Engring ECJ Hall Ste 4.2 Austin TX 78712

WALTON, CLARENCE, political science and history educator; b. Scranton, Pa., June 22, 1915; s. Leo and Mary (Southard) W.; m. Elizabeth Kennedy, June 1, 1946; children: Thomas Michael, Mary Elizabeth. BA, U. Scranton, 1937; MA, Syracuse U., 1938; PhD, Cath. U., 1951. Social sci. instr. Duquesne U., 1940-42; prof., chmn. dept. history and polit. sci. U. Scranton, 1946-53; dean Duquesne U. (Sch. Bus. Adminstrn.), 1953-58; assoc. dean, prof. Grad. Sch. Bus. Columbia U., 1958-64, dean Sch. Gen. Studies, 1964-69, prof. Grad. Sch. Bus., 1978-80; pres. Cath. U. Am., 1969-78; Charles Lamont Post disting. prof. Am. Coll., 1980-85, now prof. emeritus, 1985—; Penfield fellow Inst. Advanced Internat. Studies, Geneva, Switzerland, 1951-52; vis. prof. U. Helsinki, Finland, summer 1959, U. Buenos Aires, summer 1961, U. Calif., Berkeley, 1963-64, Oreg. State U., 1969, Villanova U., 1984-93, Santa Clara U., 1986-87; Kukin Disting. vis. prof. Yeshiva U., 1993. Author: Corporate Social Responsibilities, Big Government and Big Business, 1968, Ethos and the Executive, 1969; editor: Ethics of Corporate Conduct, 1977, Inflation and National Survival, 1979, (with others) Disorder in Higher Education, 1979, Management's Rights and Prerogatives, 1986, The Moral Manager, 1988, Enriching Business Ethics, 1990, Corporate Encounters: Ethics and Law in the Business Environment, 1992; contbr. articles to profl. jours. Mem. Scranton Sch. Bd., 1948-52; chmn. Gov.'s Commn. on Pa. Housing, 1956-57, Pres.'s Panel on Non-Pub. Edn., 1975-76; bd. dirs. emeritus Am. Assembly; trustee emeritus Rosemont Coll. Lt. USNR, 1942-46. Home: 1336 Montgomery Ave Bryn Mawr PA 19010-1629

WALTON, GERALD WAYNE, English educator, university officiala; b. Union, Miss., Sept. 11, 1934; s. Willie Jay and Ruby Elizabeth (Williamson) W.; m. Juliet Katherine Hart, Aug. 26, 1960; children: Katherine Hart, Dorothy Elizabeth, Margaret Stevens. A.A., East Central Jr. Coll., 1954; B.S., U. So. Miss., 1956; M.A., U. Miss., 1959, Ph.D., 1967. Tchr. asst. U. Miss., 1956-59, instr. English, 1959-62, asst. prof., 1962-67, assoc. prof., 1967-70, prof., 1970—, assoc. dean Coll. Liberal Arts, 1970-76, dean, 1976-82, assoc. vice chancellor for acad. affairs, 1982-94, interim vice chancellor for acad. affairs, 1994-96, provost, 1996—. Contbr. articles to profl. jours. Vice-pres. Oxford Human Rels. Coun., 1968; mem. adminstrv. bd. Oxford U. Meth. Ch., chmn. bd. trustees, 1971-72; bd. dirs. Yoknapatawpha Arts Coun., 1980-81; sec.-treas. So. Lit. Festival, 1965. Tri-Univ. fellow in linguistics U. Nebr., 1969-70. Mem. MLA, Am. Dialect Soc., Miss. Folklore Soc., Friends of Arts in Miss., Miss. Assn. English Tchrs. (sec. 1968), Miss. Inst. Arts and Letters (sec. 1979-80), Nat. Coun. Tchrs. English, William Faulkner Soc., Miss. Hist. Soc., Rotary, Golden Key, Phi Kappa Phi, Sigma Tau Delta, Omicron Delta Kappa. Home: 106 Ole Miss Dr Oxford MS 38655-2615 Office: U Miss Vice Chancellor Acad Affairs University MS 38677

WALTON, HAROLD VINCENT, former agricultural engineering educator, academic administrator; b. Christiana, Pa., June 17, 1921; s. Howard King and Alice Lauretta (Kirk) W.; m. Velma Purvis Braun, June 24, 1946; children: H. Richard, Marilyn J. Walton Friedersdorf, Carol A. B.S. in Agrl. Engring., Pa. State U., 1942, M.S. in Agrl. Engring., 1950; Ph.D. in Agrl. Engring., Purdue U., 1961. Test engr. Gen. Electric Co., Schenectady, 1943-45; instr. Pa. State U., 1947-50, asst. prof. agrl. engring., 1950-52, assoc. prof., 1952-61, prof., 1961, 76-85, head dept. agrl. engring., 1976-85, ret., 1985; prof., chmn. dept. agrl. engring. U. Mo.-Columbia, 1962-69; chief of party U. Mo.-Columbia, Bhubaneswar, India, 1969-71; prof. U. Mo.-Columbia, 1971-76; cons. OAS, Trinidad and Tobago, 1980, Ptnrs. of Ams., Brazil, 1984. Served with U.S. Army, 1945-46. Fulbright scholar, Cyprus, 1989-90. Fellow Am. Soc. Agrl. Engrs. (bd. dirs. 1967-69, 85-87). Republican.

WALTON, JAMES M., investment company executive; b. Pitts., Dec. 18, 1930; m. Ellen Carroll; 4 children. B.A., Yale U.; M.B.A., Harvard U. With Gulf Oil Corp., Phila., Houston, Pitts., Tokyo, Rome, 1958-67; pres. Carnegie Inst., Pitts., 1968-84, Carnegie Mus. Natural History and Mus. of Art, Pitts., 1968-84, Carnegie Library, Pitts., 1968-84; life trustee, pres. emeritus Carnegie Inst. and Carnegie Library, Pitts., 1984—; vice chmn. bd. dirs. MMC Group Inc.; bd. dirs. Irish Investment Fund, Inc. Mem. sponsoring com. Penn's Southwest Assn.; life trustee Carnegie-Mellon U.; treas. Carnegie Hero Fund Commn.; dir. World Affairs Coun. of Pitts., One Hundred Friends of Pitts. Art; trustee Sarah Scaife Found. Inc., Scaife Family Found., Matthew T. Mellon Found.; chmn. Vira I. Heinz Endowment; mem. Cultural Dist. Devel. Com. Lt. U.S. Army, 1954-56. Office: 525 William Penn Pl Rm 3902 Pittsburgh PA 15219-1707

WALTON, JOAN See FROHOCK, JOAN

WALTON, KATHLEEN ENDRES, librarian; b. Columbus, Ohio, Mar. 24, 1961; d. Kenneth Raymond and Mary Margaret (Brown) Endres; m. Thomas Walton, Dec. 7, 1985; children: Tristan James, Arden Siobhan. BA, U. Md., 1982; MLS, Cath. U. Am., 1985. Head engrng./architecture/math libr. Cath. U. Am. Libr., Washington, 1985-87; libr. Congl. Quarterly Inc., Washington, 1987-90, head libr., 1991-92, libr. dir., 1992—. Mem. ALA, Am. Assn. Law Librs., D.C. Libr. Assn., Spl. Librs. Assn. Roman Catholic. Office: Congl Quarterly Inc 1414 22nd St NW Washington DC 20037-1003

WALTON, MATT SAVAGE, retired geologist, educator; b. Lexington, Ky., Sept. 16, 1915; m. Kathryn Ralston, Dec. 6, 1940 (div.); m. Nalda Robinson, May 22, 1969 (dec.); m. Kay Ann Thorson, June 21, 1970; children: Matt Savage III, Kate Johns, Lisa Baar, Anne Elizabeth, Owen Hardwick. B.A., U. Chgo., 1936; M.A. (James Furman Kemp fellow), Columbia U., 1947, Ph.D., 1951. Geologist U.S. Geol. Survey, 1942-46; asso. prof. Yale U., New Haven, 1948-65; geologist N.Y. State Geol. Survey, summers, 1947-57; cons. geologist, 1947-73; regents lectr. environ. sci. and engring. UCLA, 1970-71; dir. Minn. Geol. Survey, U. Minn., 1973-86, prof. geology and geophysics, 1973-86, prof. emeritus, 1986—; cons. on geologic conditions affecting excavation and undergroung constrn., 1995—; dir. Deep Observation and Sampling of the Earth's Continental Crust, Inc., 1984-86; mem. exec. com. Great Lakes Internat. Project. Contbr. articles on engring. geology to sci. jours. Pres. Old Town Restorations, Inc., St. Paul, 1974-79; bd. dirs. Summit Hill Assn., 1974-79. Fellow Geol. Soc. Am.; mem. Assn. Am. State Geologists. Avocations: writing, consulting. Home: 30 Crocus Pl Saint Paul MN 55102-2810

WALTON, MORGAN LAUCK, III, lawyer; b. Woodstock, Va., July 30, 1932; s. Morgan Lauck Jr. and Frances (Allen) W.; m. Jeannette Freeman Minor, Mar. 4, 1961; children: Morgan Lauck IV, Charles Lancelot Minor, Christopher Allen, Laura Cathlyn. BA, Randolph-Macon Coll., 1953; LLB, U. Va., 1959. Bar: Va. 1959, N.Y. 1959, U.S. Ct. Appeals (2d cir.) 1959, U.S. Dist. Ct. (ea. and so. dists.) N.Y. 1960, U.S. Dist. Ct. (we. dist.) Va. 1988. Assoc. Donovan Leisure Newton & Irvine, N.Y.C., 1959-68; ptnr. Donovan, Leisure, Newton & Irvine, N.Y.C., 1968-84; counsel FDIC, Washington, 1989-90, asst. gen. counsel, 1990—. Contbr. articles to legal jours. Trustee Randolph-Macon Acad., Front Royal, Va., 1987-92, Unitarian Ch. Shenandoah Valley, Stephens City, Va., 1987—; mem. coun. Law Sch. U. Va., 1989-92; treas. Shenandoah Valley Music Festival, Woodstock, 1986-87; chmn. bd. All Souls Ch., N.Y.C., 1974-76. With U.S. Army, 1953-56. Mem. ABA (co-chmn. long term planning com. govt. lawyers divsn. 1993-94, chmn. Clayton Act com. antitrust sect. 1976-78), Assn. of Bar of City of N.Y., Univ. Club, Collectors Club, Order of Coif, Phi Beta Kappa. Democrat. Home: 908 Kern Springs Rd Woodstock VA 22664-3216 Office: FDIC 550 17th St NW H6018 Washington DC 20429-0001

WALTON, ORTIZ MONTAIGNE, musician, sociologist; b. Chgo.; m. Kara Dozier. Student, Hartt Sch. Music, 1951-54, Mannes Sch. Music, 1954-55; BS in Psychol., Roosevelt U., 1966; MA in Sociol., U. Calif., Berkeley, 1970, PhD in Socio., 1973. Musician Hartford, New Haven, Springfield, Bridgeport Symphony Orchestras, 1951-54, Buffalo Philharmonic Orchestra, 1954-57, Boston Symphony Orchestra, 1957-63; program coord. Chgo. Assn. Retarded Children, 1964-66; musician Cairo (Egypt) Symphony, 1963-64; prin. investigator Soc. Survey of Alcohol and Drug Use among Adolescents and Young Adults Nat. Inst. Alcohol Abuse and Alcoholism, 1977-79; asst. dir. Chgo. Fedn. Settlement Houses, 1964-66; instr. Dept. African-Am. Studies U. Calif. Berkeley, 1974-76; faculty Wright Inst. of Berkeley Grad. Sch., 1974-75; mem. bd. of studies in sociology U. Calif. Santa Cruz, 1975; career and guidance counseling Opportunities Industrialization, Oakland, Calif., 1967-68; cons. alcohol, drugs and youth criminal justics Merritt Coll., Oakland, 1979, curriculum devel., 1973; program devel., talent recruitment Today's Artists, Berkeley, 1979. Solo recitals (contrabass) include U. Buffalo, 1956, Merkin Concert Hall, N.Y.C., 1987, Weil Recital Hall at Carnegie Hall, N.Y.C., 1987, Bklyn. Acad. Music, 1988, YMCA Harlem Branch, 1988, Rutgers U., New Brunswick, N.J., 1989, Lehman Coll., N.Y.C., 1989, Cheyney, U. Pa., 1990, Chgo. State U., 1993; composer: Fantasy to Duke Ellington for solo contrabass, 1968, Scale Method for contrabass, 1981, Resonance for contrabass and piano, 1983, Sonata for contrabass and piano, 1985; recordings: (with Ishmael Reed) Black Box, Nat. Philharmonic Orchestra, The Walton Statement for Contrabass and Orch. (by Arthur Cunningham), 1987, Art of the Bass Viol: Music of the Baroque Era, 1991; author: Music: Black, White and Blue, 1972, others. Active mayoral campaign Harold Washington, Chgo., 1983. U. Calif. Berkeley Grad. fellow, 1968-72; Nat. Inst. Mental Health fellow, 1968-72; Ford Found. dissertation grant 1970-71; Inst. Community and Race Relations grant U. Calif. Berkeley, 1970-71. Mem. Am. Sociol. Assn., Internat. Soc. Bassists, Chamber Music Am. Home: 1129 Bancroft Way Berkeley CA 94702-1849 Home: 1129 Bancroft Way Berkeley CA 94702-1849

WALTON, PAUL TALMAGE, petroleum geologist; b. Salt Lake City, Feb. 4, 1914; s. Paul and Margaret Lenore (Watts) W.; m. Dorothy Woolley, May 29, 1942 (div. Nov. 1943); 1 child, Holly Lenore; m. Helen Elizabeth Baer, July 3, 1944; children: Paul Talmage Jr., Ann Elizabeth. BS in Geol. Engring., U. Utah, 1935, MS in Geology, 1940; PhD in Geology, MIT, 1942. Cert. petroleum geologist. Engr. soil conservation svc. S.C.S. U.S. Dept. Agr., Price, Utah, 1935-38; geophysicist St. Oil Calif., Dahran, Saudi Arabia, 1938-39; geologist Texaco, Denver, 1942-44, Getty Oil Interest, Casper, Wyo., 1944-49; geologist, ptnr. Morgan Walton Oils, Salt Lake City, 1949-54, Walton Kearns, Salt Lake City, 1954-69, Paul T. Walton & Assocs., Salt Lake City, 1970—; pres. Am. Geol. Enterprises, Salt Lake City, 1972—. Author: Prospect to Prosperity, 1994. Mem. AAPG, AIPG. Republican. Avocations: polo, skiing. Home: Box 325 Star Rt Jackson WY 83001 Office: Paul T Walton & Assoc 175 S Main St Salt Lake City UT 84111-1916

WALTON, RALPH GERALD, psychiatrist, educator; b. Darlington, Eng., Aug. 18, 1942; came to U.S., 1950; s. Kenneth and Paula (Weissman) W.; m. Ellen Paula Liebling, Feb. 15, 1970 (div. 1980); children: Deborah, Rachel; m. Mary Elaine Hultburg, Sept. 27, 1981; children: Lisa, Jonathan. AB, U. Rochester, 1963; MD, SUNY, Syracuse, 1967. Diplomate Am. Bd. Psychiatry and Neurology. Intern Strong Meml. Hosp., Rochester, N.Y., 1967-68, resident in psychiatry, 1968-71; asst. prof. psychiatry Sch. Medicine U. Rochester, N.Y., 1973-76; chief psychiatry Jamestown (N.Y.) Gen. Hosp., 1976-88; commr. mental health Chautauqua County, Jamestown, 1985-88; chmn. dept. psychiatry Western Res. Care System, Youngstown, Ohio, 1988—; prof. psychiatry N.E. Ohio Univs. Coll. of Medicine, Rootstown, Ohio, 1988—; med. dir. Profl. Recovery Plus Alcoholic Clinic, Youngstown, 1992—. Contbr. chpt. to: Dietary Phenylalanine and Brain Function, 1988; contbr. foreword to: Katherine It's Time, 1989; contbr. articles to profl. jours., 1972—. Maj. U.S. Army, 1971-73, Panama. Fellow Am. Psychiat. Assn. Jewish. Office: 725 Boardman Canfield Rd Youngstown OH 44512-4380

WALTON, RICHARD EUGENE, business educator; b. Pulaski, Iowa, Apr. 15, 1931; s. Lee Richard and Florence (King) W.; m. Sharon Claire Doty, Apr. 13, 1952; children—John, Elizabeth, Margaret, Andrew. B.S., Purdue U., 1953, M.S., 1954; postgrad., Victoria U., New Zealand, 1953; D.B.A., Harvard, 1959. Faculty Harvard Bus. Sch., 1968—, Edsel Bryant Ford prof. bus., 1970-76, dir. rsch. div., 1970-76, now Wallace Brett Donham prof. bus.; cons. various indsl. firms, govt. agys. including Dept. State; bd. dirs. Champion Internat. Corp. Author: A Behavioral Theory of Labor Negotiations: An Analysis of a Social Interaction System, 1965, (with R.B. McKersie) The Impact of the Professional Engineering Union, 1961, (with M. Beer and others) Human Assets, 1984, (with P. Lawrence) Human Resource Management Trends and Challenges, 1985, Managing Conflict, 1987, Innovating to Compete, 1987, Up and Running, 1989, (with Joel Cutcher-Gershenfeld and Robert B. McKersie) Strategic Negotiations: A Theory of Change in Labor-Management Relations, 1994, (with Joel Cutcher-Gershenfeld and Robert B. McKersie) Pathways to Change: Case Studies of Strategic Negotiations, 1995. Served with AUS, 1954-56. Ford Found. faculty grantee U. Mich., 1962-63. Home: 109 Beaver Rd Weston MA 02193-1035 Office: Harvard Bus Sch Dept of Bus Boston MA 02163

WALTON, ROBERT LEE, JR., plastic surgeon; b. Lawrence, Kans., May 30, 1946; s. Robert L. and Thelma B. (Morgan) W.; m. Laura Lake, May 1, 1971; children: Marc, Morgan, Lindsey. BA, U. Kans., 1968; MD, U. Kans., Kansas City, 1972. Diplomate Am. Bd. Surgery, Am. Bd. Plastic Surgery. Resident in surgery Johns Hopkins Hosp., Balt., 1972-74, Yale-New Haven (Conn.) Hosp., 1974-78; chief of plastic surgery San Francisco Gen. Hosp., 1979-83; prof. and chmn. dept. plastic surgery U. Mass. Med. Ctr., Worcester, 1983—. Contbr. articles to profl. jours. Founder Federico Trilla Hosp. Found. for Handicapped Children, Carolina, P.R., 1990. Mem. Am. Assn. Plastic Surgery, Am. Coll. Surgeons, Am. Soc. Plastic and Reconstructive Surgery, Am. Soc. Surgery of the Hand, Alpha Omega Alpha. Office: U Mass Med Ctr 55 Lake Ave N # 54-751 Worcester MA 01655-0002

WALTON, RODNEY EARL, lawyer; b. Corvallis, Oreg., Apr. 28, 1947; s. Ray Daniel Jr. and Carolyn Jane (Smith) W. BA, Coll. of Wooster, 1969; JD, Cornell U., 1976. Bar: Fla. 1976, U.S. Dist. Ct. (so. dist.) Fla. 1976, U.S. Dist. Ct. (mid. dist.) Fla. 1977, U.S. Supreme Ct. 1980, U.S. Ct. Appeals (11th cir.) 1981. Assoc. to jr. ptnr. Smathers & Thompson, Miami, Fla., 1976-87; ptnr. Kelley, Drye and Warren, Miami, 1987-93; of counsel Heinrich Gordon Hargrove Weihe & James, P.A., Ft. Lauderdale, 1994—. Sec. bd. dirs. Kings Creek Condominium Assn., Miami, 1984-89, treas., 1984, pres., 1990-91. 1st lt. U.S. Army, 1969-73, Vietnam. Decorated Bronze Star. Mem. ABA, Fla. Bar, Broward County Bar Assn., Maritime Law Assn. Republican. Methodist. Avocations: travel, reading, sports. Home: 2331 NW 33rd St Apt 301 Fort Lauderdale FL 33309-6444 Office: Heinrich Gordon PA 500 E Broward Blvd Ste 1000 Fort Lauderdale FL 33394

WALTON, ROGER ALAN, public relations executive, mediator, writer; b. Denver, June 25, 1941; s. Lyle R. and Velda V. (Nicholson) W.; m. Helen Anderson. Attended, U. Colo., 1960-63. Govt. rep. Continental Airlines, Denver, 1964-72; dir. pub. affairs Regional Transp. Dist., Denver, 1972-77; pub. affairs cons. Denver, 1977—; res. pub. info. officer Fed. Emergency Mgmt. Agy., 1995-96; pres. Colo. Times Pub. Co.; res. pub. info. officer FEMA, 1995. Author: Colorado-A Practical Guide to its Government and Politics, 1973, 6th rev. edit., 1990, Colorado Gambling - A Guide, 1991; columnist The Denver Post newspaper, 1983—, The Rocky Mountain Jour., 1977-81. Mem. U.S. Presdl. Electoral Coll., Washington, 1968; commr. U.S. Bicentennial Revolution Commn., Colo., 1972-76, U.S. Commn. on the Bicentennial of U.S. Constn., Denver, 1985-90, pres.; trustee Arapahoe County (Colo.) Libr. Bd., 1982-86; chmn. lobbyist ethics com. Colo. Gen. Assembly, 1990-91. Republican. Avocations: reading, fishing, photography. Home and Office: 12550 W 2nd Dr Lakewood CO 80228-5012

WALTON, RUSSELL SPAREY, foundation administrator; b. Trenton, N.J., Nov. 28, 1921; s. Lewis Kirk and Edna Russell (Sparey) W.; m. Ila E. Lappe, Aug. 23, 1969. Student, King's Coll., 1938-39, DHL (hon.), 1991; student, Temple U., 1940-41. Mgr. publs. and pub. rels. Rexall Drug Co., L.A., 1946-49; mgr. advt. and pub. rels. Gladding McBean & Co., Glendale, Calif., 1949-51; editor, pub. San Bruno (Calif.) Herald, 1951-52; dir. pub. affairs West Divsn. Nat. Assn. Mfgrs., Palo Alto, Calif., 1952-62; exec. dir. United Rep. Calif., Los Altos, 1962-66; sec. program devel. Gov. Calif., Sacramento, 1967-71; columnist, radio commentator newspapers in Calif. and Midwest, 1971-74; mng. editor Third Century Pub., Washington, 1974-76; exec. dir. Plymouth Rock Found., Marlborough, N.H., 1976—. Author: One Nation Under God, 1978, Fundamentals for American Christians, 1979, Biblical Solutions to Contemporary Problems, 1984. Capt. U.S. Army Air Corps, 1941-46. Baptist. Office: Plymouth Rock Found Fisk Mill on Water St Marlborough NH 03455

WALTON, S. ROBSON, discount department store chain executive; b. 1945; s. Sam Moore W.; married. Grad., Columbia U., 1969. Formerly with Conner, Winters, Ballaine, Barry & McGowen; with Wal-Mart Stores Inc., Bentonville, Ark., 1969—, sr. v.p., 1978-82, also bd. dirs., vice chmn. bd., 1982-92, chmn., 1992—. Office: Wal-Mart Stores Inc 702 SW 8th St Bentonville AR 72716-0001*

WALTON, STANLEY ANTHONY, III, lawyer; b. Chgo., Dec. 10, 1939; s. Stanley Anthony and Emily Ann (Pouzar) W.; m. Karen Kayser, Aug. 10, 1963; children: Katherine, Anne, Alex. BA, Washington and Lee U., 1962, LLB, 1965. Bar: Ill. 1965, U.S. Dist. Ct. (no. dist.) Ill. 1966, U.S. Ct. Appeals (7th cir.) 1966. With Winston & Strawn, Chgo., 1965-89; ptnr. Sayfarth Shaw Fairweather, Chgo. Trustee Village of Hinsdale (Ill.), 1985-89; bd. dirs. Washington and Lee Law Sch., Lexington, Va., 1975-78, bd. dirs. univ. alumni, 1983-87, pres. 1986-87; bd. dirs. UNICEF, Chgo., 1983; pres. Hinsdale Hist. Soc., 1979-81, St. Isaac Jogues PTA, 1980 . Mem. ABA, Phi Alpha Delta. Republican. Roman Catholic. Club: Hinsdale Golf. Home: 6679 Snug Harbor Dr Willowbrook IL 60514 Office: Sayfarth Shaw Fairweather 55 E Monroe St Fl 42 Chicago IL 60603-5702

WALTON, THOMAS E., research scientist, director; b. McKeesport, Pa., Dec. 2, 1940; s. Thomas E. and Matilda S. Walton; m. Mary Louise Monahan, Apr. 10, 1987; children: Anne L., Leigh E., Thomas A. DVM, Purdue U., 1964; PhD, Cornell U., 1968. Diplomate Am. Coll. Vet. Microbiologists. Vet. med. officer Mid. Am. Rsch. Unit, Ancon, Panama Canal Zone, 1968-72, Animal Diseases Rsch. Lab., Denver, 1972-74; rsch. leader USDA, Denver, 1974-85, Laramie, Wyo., 1985-92; nat. program leader USDA, Beltsville, Md., 1992-95; dir., supervisory vet. med. officer Nat. Animal Disease Ctr., Ames, Iowa, 1995—; affiliate faculty mem. Colo. State U., Fort Collins, 1974—; adj. prof. vet. sci. U. Wyo., Laramie, 1986—; tech. adv. assignments, sci. field studies, or cons. in Australia, Austria, Belice, Colombia, Costa Rica, Egypt, El Salvador, England, France, Greece, Guadeloupe, Guatemala, Honduras, Israel, Mexico, Netherlands, Nicaragua, Panama, Poland, Puerto Rico, Spain, Switzerland, Venezuela. Presenter in field; contbr. numerous articles to profl. jours. Mem. Soc. for Tropical Vet. Medicine (treas. 1991—). Address: USDA-ARS-NPS 2906 Ridgetop Rd Ames IA 50014*

WALTRIP, DARRELL LEE, professional stock car driver; b. Owensboro, Ky., Feb. 5, 1947; s. Leroy and Margaret Jean (Evans) W.; m. Stephanie Hamilton Rader, Aug. 15, 1969; 1 child, Jessica Leigh. Student, Ky. Wesleyan Coll. Driver for Junior Johnson & Assocs., Rick Hendrick Motor Sports. Named Driver of Yr., Nat. Motorsports Press Assn., 1977, Olsonite Driver of Yr., 1979; winner Winston Cup, 1982, Nat. Assn. Stock Car Auto Racing Championship, 1985, Winston Cup Championship, 1981, 82, 85, numerous auto races including Coca Cola 600, 1985, 88, 89, Wrangler 500, 1985, Busch 500, 1986, Budweiser 400, 1986, Holly Farms 400, 1986, Goody's 500, 1987, 88, 89, Motorcraft 500, 1989, Daytona 500, 1989, Champion Spark Plug 500, 1991. Mem. Nat. Assn. Stock Car Auto Racing. Republican. Presbyterian. Top Motor Sport money winner worldwide with more than 7.5 million dollars.

WALTZ, JON RICHARD, lawyer, educator, author; b. Napoleon, Ohio, Oct. 11, 1929; s. Richard R. and Lenore (Tharp) W. B.A. with honors in Polit. Sci, Coll. Wooster, 1951; J.D., Yale U., 1954. Bar: Ohio 1954, Ill. 1965. Assoc. Squire, Sanders & Dempsey, Cleve., 1954-64; chief prosecutor City of Willowick (Ohio), 1958-64; assoc. prof. law Northwestern U. Sch. Law, Chgo., 1964-65; prof. law Northwestern U. Sch. Law, 1965-78, Edna B. and Ednyfed H. Williams prof. law emeritus; instr. med. jurisprudence Northwestern Med. Sch., 1969—; book critic Washington Post, Chgo. Tribune, others; Disting. vis. prof. law Ill. Inst. Tech.-Chgo.-Kent Coll. Law, 1974; lectr. Author: The Federal Rules of Evidence—An Analysis, 1973, Criminal Evidence, 1975, Chinese lang. ed., 1994, Evidence: A Summary Analysis, 1976, Introduction to Criminal Evidence, 1991, Chinese lang. edit., 1993; co-author: The Trial of Jack Ruby, 1965, Cases and Materials on Evidence, 1968, Principles of Evidence and Proof, 1968, Medical Jurisprudence, 1971, Cases and Materials on Law and Medicine, 1980, Evidence: Making the Record, 1981, Criminal Prosecution in the People's Republic of China and the United States of America: A Comparative Study, 1995; note and comment editor Yale Law Jour., 1953-54; mem. editorial adv. bd. Harcourt Brace Law Group,. 1978—; contbr. numerous articles to profl. jours. Mem. Ill. adv. com. U.S. Commn. on Civil Rights, 1971-74; mem. Ill. Criminal Justice System Policy and Planning Com., 1973-74, Ill. Jud. Inquiry Bd., 1980-88; mem. com. med. edn. AMA, 1982-83; mem. Gov.'s Task Force on Med. Malpractice, 1985; Rep. candidate Ill. Appellate Ct., 1978. Capt. AUS, 1955-58. Decorated Commendation medal; recipient Disting. Svc. award Soc. Midland Authors, 1972, Disting. Alumni award Coll. Wooster, 1987. Mem. Assn. Am. Law Schs., Judge Advs. Assn., Soc. Am. Law Tchrs., Order of Coif, Phi Alpha Delta, Pi Sigma Alpha. Presbyterian. Home: 421 W Melrose St Chicago IL 60657-3848 also: 4005 Lakeridge Dr Holland MI 49424-2263 Office: Northwestern U Sch Law 357 E Chicago Ave Chicago IL 60611-3008

WALTZ, JOSEPH MCKENDREE, neurosurgeon, educator; b. Detroit, July 23, 1931; s. Ralph McKinley and Bertha (Seelye) W.; m. Janet Maureen Journey, June 26, 1954; children: Jeffrey McKinley, Mary Elaine, David Seelye, Stephen McKendree; m. Marilyn Liska, June 5, 1967; 1 child, Tristana McKendree. Student, U. Mich., 1950; B.S., U. Oreg., 1954, M.D., 1956. Diplomate Am. Bd. Neurol. Surgery. Surg. intern U. Mich. Hosp., 1956-57, gen. surg. resident, 1957-58, clin. instr. neurosurgery, 1960-63; neurosurg. assoc. St. Barnabas Hosp., N.Y.C., 1963—; assoc. dir. Inst. Neurosci., 1974—, dir. dept. neurol. surgery, 1977—; assoc. cons. in neurosurgery Englewood (N.J.) Hosp., 1964—; assoc. prof. neurosurgery NYU Med. Str., 1974—; asst. prof. dept. surgery (neurosurgery) N.Y. Coll. Osteo. Medicine, 1989—; bd. dirs. Neurol. Surgery Rsch. Found., 1978; mem. alumni bd. U. Mich. Med. Ctr., 1995. Author papers on functional neurosurg. treatment of abnormal movement disorders cerebral palsy, others; cryothalamectomy-cryopulvinectomy and implantation brain pacemakers; chpt. in book on cryogenic surgery; contbr. chpts. to Cryogenic Surgery, Neurology, 1982, Advances in Neurology, 1983. Patentee 4-electrode quadrapolar computerized spinal cord stimulator. Mem. sci. adv. bd. Dystonia Med. Research Found., 1980—; trustee St. Barnabas Hosp., 1980—. Served to capt. M.C. AUS, 1958-60. Recipient Bronze award Am. Congress Rehab. Medicine, 1967, World Cmty. Svc. award Rotary, Disting. Trustee award United Hosp. Fund, 1995. Mem. AMA, Am. Paralysis Assn., World Soc. Stereotactic and Functional Neurosurgery, Congress Neurol. Surgeons, Math. Assn. Am., Internat. Neural Network Soc., Soc. for Cryobiology, N.Y. State Med. Soc., Bronx County Med. Soc., N.Y. State Neurosurg Soc., Nat. Ski Patrol, Phi Beta Pi. Achievements include spl. rsch. on neurophysiology and treatment of epilepsy, basal ganglia disorders, abnormal movement disorders, cerebral palsy, also neurosurg. application stereotactic thalamic surgery and spinal cord stimulation. Home: Four B Island South 720 Milton Rd Rye NY 10580-3258 Office: St Barnabas Hosp Dept Neurosurgery New York NY 10457

WALTZ, KENNETH NEAL, political science educator; b. Ann Arbor, Mich., June 8, 1924; s. Christian Benjamin and Luella (Braun) W.; m. Helen Elizabeth Lindsley, June 4, 1949; children: Kenneth L., Thomas E. (dec.), Daniel E. AB, Oberlin Coll., 1948; MA, Columbia U., 1950, PhD, 1954; D honoris causa, Copenhagen U., 1995. Instr., then asst. prof. Columbia U., 1953-57; from assoc. prof. to prof. politics Swarthmore Coll., 1957-66; research assoc. Center Internat. Affairs, Harvard, 1963-64, 68-69, 72; prof. politics Brandeis U., Waltham, Mass., 1966-71, Adlai E. Stevenson prof. internat. politics, 1967-71; Ford prof. polit. sci. U. Calif., Berkeley, 1971-94, Ford prof. emeritus, 1994—; vis. sr. research assoc. King's Coll., U. London, 1986-87; cons. govt. agys.; vis. scholar philosophy London Sch. Econs., 1976-77; vis. scholar Rsch. Sch. Pacific Studies, Australian Nat. U., 1978; vis. scholar dept. internat. politics Beijing U., 1982, 91, Fudan U., Shanghai, 1991, USAF Acad., 1991-92. Author: Man, The State and War, 1959, Foreign Policy and Democratic Politics, 1967, Theory of International Politics, 1979, The Spread of Nuclear Weapons, 1981; co-author: The Spread of Nuclear Weapons: A Debate, 1995: co-author, co-editor: Conflict in World Politics, 1971, The Use of Force, 1971, 4th edit., 1993; mem. edtl. bd. Jour. Strategic Studies, ABC Polit. Sci. Served to 1st lt. AUS, 1944-46, 51-52. NSF grantee, 1968-71; Guggenheim fellow, 1976-77; fellow Woodrow Wilson Center, Internat. Center for Scholars, 1979-80; Heinz Eulau award for best article in the Am. Polit. Sci. Rev., 1990. Fellow Am. Acad. Arts and Scis.; mem. Am. Polit. Sci. Assn. (sec. 1966-67, pres. 1987-88), Internat. Studies Assn. (pres. New Eng. sect. 1966-67), Coun. Fgn. Rels., Am. Acad. Arts and Scis., Phi Beta Kappa. Office: U Calif at Berkeley Polit Sci Dept 210 Barrows Hall Berkeley CA 94720-1950

WALVOORD, JOHN FLIPSE, academic administrator, theologian; b. Sheboygan, Wis., May 1, 1910; s. John Garrett and Mary (Flipse) W.; m. Geraldine Lundgren, June 28, 1939; children: John Edward, James Randall, Timothy, Paul. A.B., Wheaton Coll., 1931, D.D., 1960; B.Th., Dallas Theol. Sem., 1934, M.Th., 1934, D.Th., 1936; A.M., Tex. Christian U., 1945; D.Litt. (hon.), Liberty Bapt. Sem. Registrar Dallas Theol. Sem., 1935-45, prof. systematic theology, 1936-52, prof., 1952-85, regent, 1940-86, asst. to pres., 1945-52, pres., 1952-86, chancellor, 1986—; editor Sem. Bull., 1940-53; pastor Ft. Worth, 1935-50; editor Bibliotheca Sacra, 1952-85. Author: The Doctrine of the Holy Spirit, 1943, The Holy Spirit, 1954, The Return of the Lord, 1955, The Thessalonian Epistles, 1956, The Rapture Question, 1957, The Millennial Kingdom, 1959, To Live Is Christ, 1961, Israel in Prophecy, 1962, The Church in Prophecy, 1964, The Revelation of Jesus Christ, 1966, The Nations in Prophecy, 1967, Jesus Christ Our Lord, 1969, Philippians, 1971, Daniel, 1971, The Holy Spirit at Work Today, 1973, Major Bible Themes, 1974, Armageddon, Oil and the Middle East Crisis, 1974, 2d edit., 1990, Matthew: Thy Kingdom Come, 1975, The Blessed Hope and the Tribulation, 1976, Prophecy Knowledge Handbook, 1990, What We Believe: Discovering the Truths of Scripture, 1990, Major Bible Prophecies, 1991; contbr. to: Four Views of Hell, 1992, Prophecy: 14 Essential Keys to Understanding the Final Drama, 1993; editor: Inspiration and Interpretation, 1957, Truth for Today, 1963; co-editor: The Bib Sac Reader, 1983, The Bible Knowledge Commentary, N.T. edit., 1983, Old Testament edit., 1985; editor: Lewis Sperry Chafer Systematic Theology, abridged edit., 1988. Named Alumnus of Yr. Wheaton Coll., 1981. Mem. Evang. Theol. Soc., Wheaton Coll. Scholastic Honor Soc. Home: 1302 El Patio Dr Dallas TX 75218-3209

WALWER, FRANK KURT, dean, legal educator; b. 1930; s. Kurt and Beatrice (Ahlert) W.; m. Maryann Pancake, Apr. 15, 1961; 1 child, Gregory F. AB, Columbia U., 1952, LLB, 1956. Bar: N.Y. 1959. Assoc. dean Columbia U., 1972-80; dean, prof. U. Tulsa, 1980-91, trustee's prof. law, 1991-94, dean, prof. Tex. Wesleyan U. Law Sch., 1994—, chmn. Grad. and Profl. Sch. Fin. Aid Svc., 1976-78, pres. Law Sch. Admission Coun. , 1983-84; bd. dirs. The Coun. on Postsecondary Accreditation, 1989-92. Mem. Assn. Am. Law Schs. (chmn. sect. econs. of legal edn. 1974-76), ABA (accreditation com. 1988-94, chair legal edn. and bar admissions sect. 1986-87, lawyer competency com. 1986-92, standards rev. com. 1986-94, AALS/ABA commn. on financing), Am. Bar Fellows, Am. Inns of Court. Office: 2535 E Grauwyler Rd Irving TX 75061-3410

WALWORTH, ARTHUR, author; b. Newton, Mass., July 9, 1903; s. Arthur Clarence and Ruth Richardson (Lippincott) W. Grad., Phillips Andover Acad., 1921; B.A., Yale U., 1925. Ednl. dept. Houghton Mifflin Co., 1927-43; staff OWI, 1943; Staff Medomak Camp, Washington, Maine, summers 1943-63. Author: School Histories at War, 1938, Black Ships Off Japan, 1946, Cape Breton, 1948, The Medomak Way, 1953, Woodrow Wilson, 2 vols, 1958, 1 vol., 1967, 78, America's Moment: 1918, 1977, Wilson and his Peacemakers, 1986. Recipient Pulitzer prize in biography, 1958. Clubs: Cosmos; Graduates (New Haven). Home: North Hill 865 Central Ave Apt C201 Needham MA 02192-1338

WALZ, BRUCE JAMES, radiation oncologist; b. Waterloo, Ill., Sept. 18, 1940; s. George Frederick and Alberta Emma (Heyl) W.; m. Renata T. Jaeger, Mar. 8, 1970; children: Jennifer Mara Walz Kuhn, Rachel Elizabeth. A.B., Washington U., 1962, M.D., 1966. Diplomate Am. Bd. Radiology Therapy. Intern, St. Luke's Hosp., St. Louis, 1966-67; resident Washington U. St. Louis, 1969-72; instr. Harvard Med. Sch., Boston, 1972-74; asst. prof. Washington U., 1974-82, assoc. prof., 1982-86, clin. assoc. prof., 1986—; dir. radiation therapy St. Anthony's Med. Ctr., St. Louis. 1986—. Contbr. articles to profl. jours. Active med. adv. com. Medicare, 1992—. Served to lt. comdr. USNR, 1967-69, Vietnam. Harvard Med. Sch. fellow, 1972-73. Fellow Am. Coll. Radiology; mem. AMA, Am. Cancer Soc. (bd. dirs. Mo. divsn. 1992-96), Mo. Med. Soc. (ho. of dels. 1975—), Mo. State Radiol. Soc. (bd. dirs. 1982-87, sec.-treas. 1987-90, v.p. 1990-91, pres. 1991-92, ACR counselor 1995—), St. Louis Metro Med. Assn. (councilor 1987-89), Greater St. Louis Soc. Radiologists (chair therapy sect. 1985, sec.-treas. 1988-89, pres. elect 1989-90, pres. 1990-91), Am. Soc. Therapeutic Radiologists and Oncologists, Am. Coll. Radiology, Am. Soc. Clin. Oncologists, Arab-Am. Med. Soc. Presbyterian. Clubs: Whittemore House (Clayton, Mo.). Avocations: gardening, travelling, scuba diving. Office: St Anthony's Med Ctr Div Radiation Therapy Saint Louis MO 63128

WALZ, JACK, advertising executive; b. 1938. Grad., Ga. Inst. Tech., 1960. With IBM, 1960; various positions BBDO, Atlanta, 1963—, now exec. v.p., worldwide account dir. With USAF, 1961-63. Office: BBDO Atlanta 3414 Peachtree Rd NE Atlanta GA 30326-1113*

WALZER, MICHAEL LABAN, political science educator; b. N.Y.C., Mar. 3, 1935; s. Joseph P. and Sally (Hochman) W.; m. Judith Borodovko, June 17, 1956; children: Sarah, Rebecca. B.A., Brandeis U., 1956; Ph.D., Harvard U., 1961. Fulbright fellow Cambridge (Eng.) U., 1956-57; asst. prof. Princeton U., 1962-66; faculty Harvard U., 1966-80, prof. govt., 1968-80; prof. Sch. Social Scis., Inst. Advanced Study, Princeton, N.J., 1980—. Author: The Revolution of the Saints, 1965, Obligations: Essays on Disobedience, War and Citizenship, 1970, Political Action, 1971, Regicide and Revolution, 1974, Just and Unjust Wars, 1977, Radical Principles: Reflections of an Unreconstructed Democrat, 1980, Spheres of Justice: A Defense of Pluralism and Equality, 1983, Exodus and Revolution, 1985, Interpretation and Social Criticism, 1987, The Company of Critics: Social Criticism and Political Commitment in the Twentieth Century, 1988, What It Means To Be an American, 1993, Thick and Thin: Moral Argument at Home and Abroad, 1994, (with David Miller) Pluralism, Justice, and Equality, 1995; mem. editl. bd. Dissent mag., 1960—; contbg. editor New Republic, 1976—. Bd. govs. Hebrew U., Jerusalem, 1975—; trustee Brandeis U., 1983-88 ; chmn. faculty adv. cabinet United Jewish Appeal, 1977-81. Home: 103 Linwood Cir Princeton NJ 08540-3625

WALZER, NORMAN CHARLES, economics educator; b. Mendota, Ill., Mar. 17, 1943; s. Elmer J. and Anna L. (Johnston) W.; m. Dona Lee Maurer, Aug. 22, 1970; children: Steven, Mark. BS, Ill. State U., Normal, 1966; MA, U. Ill., 1969, PhD, 1970. Rsch. dir. Cities and Villages Mcpl. Problems Com., Springfield, Ill., 1974-84; vis. prof. U. Ill., Urbana, 1977-78; prof. econs. Western Ill. U., Macomb, 1978—, chmn. dept. econs., 1980-89, dir. Ill. Inst. Rural Affairs, 1988—, interim dean coll. bus. and tech., 1993-95. Author: Cities, Suburbs and Property Tax, 1981; Government Structure and Public Finance, 1984; editor: Financing State and Local Governments, 1981, Rural Community Economic Development, 1991; co-editor: Financing Local Infrastructure in Non Metro Areas, 1986, Financing Economic Development in The 1980s, 1986, Financing Rural Health Care, 1988, Rural Health Care, 1992, Rural Community Economic Development, 1992, Local Economic Development: International Trends and Issues, 1995, Community Visioning Programs: Practice and Principles, 1996. Mem. Am. Econs. Assn., Ill. Econs. Assn. (pres. 1979-80), Mid-Continent Regional Sci. Assn. (pres. 1985-86). Lodge: K.C. Home: 727 Auburn Dr Macomb IL 61455-3002 Office: Western Ill U Ill Inst Rural Affairs 518 Stipes Hall Macomb IL 61455

WALZOG, NANCY LEE, film and television executive; b. Balt., Feb. 12, 1963; d. William Richard and Barbara Jane (Lombardi) W. BFA, NYU, 1983; MBA, Pace U., 1991. Dir. TV sales and mktg. Internat. Film Exch., N.Y.C., 1984-86; producer ABC Entertainment, N.Y.C., 1984; comml. producer Nancy Walzog Film and TV, Ltd., N.Y.C., 1982-84; v.p. Tapestry Internat., Ltd., N.Y.C., 1986-94, pres., 1994—. Recipient Emmy award, Acad. TV Arts and Scis., N.Y.C., 1987, Emmy nominiation, 1990, ACE award, Nat. Acad. Cable TV Programming, Washington, 1987, Gold award San Francisco Internat. Film Festival, 1987, Hugo award Chgo. Internat. Film Festival, 1988. Office: Tapestry Internat 920 Broadway Fl 16 New York NY 10010-6004

WAMBAUGH, JOSEPH, author; b. Pitts., Jan. 22, 1937; s. Joseph Aloysius and Anne (Malloy) W.; m. Dee Allsup, Nov. 26, 1955; children: Mark (dec.), David, Jeannette. BA, Calif. State Coll., L.A., 1960; MA, Calif. State Coll., Los Angeles, 1968. Police officer, L.A., 1960-74. Author: The New Centurions, 1971, The Blue Knight, 1972, The Onion Field, 1973 (Edgar Allan Poe award Mystery Writers Am. 1974), The Choirboys, 1975, The Black Marble, 1978, The Glitter Dome, 1981, The Delta Star, 1983, Lines and Shadows, 1984 (Rodolfo Walsh prize Internat. Assn. Crime Writers 1989), The Secrets of Harry Bright, 1985, Echoes in the Darkness, 1987, The Blooding, 1989, The Golden Orange, 1990, Fugitive Nights, 1992, Finnegan's Week, 1993, Floaters, 1996;. Served with USMC, 1954-57.

WAMBOLD, JUDSON J., lawyer; b. Columbus, Ohio, 1952. BS magna cum laude, U. Pa., 1974; JD, Cornell U., 1978. Bar: Pa. 1978. Ptnr. Dechert Price & Rhoads, Phila.; now corp. mgmt. dir. Julian J. Studley Corp. Office: Dechert Price & Rhoads 4000 Bell Atlantic 1717 Arch St Philadelphia PA 19103-2713 Office: Julian J Studley Corp 1650 Market St Ste 2775 Philadelphia PA 19103*

WAMBOLT, RONALD RALPH, electronics company executive; b. Halifax, N.S., Can., Aug. 15, 1934; came to U.S., 1974; s. Howard H. and Mildred M. (Slaunwhite) W.; m. Shirley Marie Burgess, June 22, 1957; children: Cathy, David, Robert, Ronald, Deborah. Grad. high sch., Halifax, 1952. Field service engr. Sperry Gyroscope Can. Ltd., 1960-65; field engr. Tektronix, Inc., Can., 1965-69, advt. program mgr., 1969-71; internat. sales mgr. Tektronix, Inc., Beaverton, Oreg., 1974-77, gen. mgr. Americas/Pacific, 1977-79; asst. sales mgr. Tektronix Can. Ltd., 1971-72, v.p., gen. mgr., 1972-74; mgr. internat. ops. John Fluke Mfg. Co., Inc., Everett, Wash., 1979-82, dir. internat. ops., 1982-84, v.p., dir. internat. ops., 1984-87, sr. v.p., dir. worldwide sales, 1987-91, sr. v.p., dir. worldwide sales and svc., 1991—; mem. adv. bd. World Trade Council, Seattle, 1984-87, Wash. export council internat. trade, Dept. Commerce, Seattle, 1986—; trustee Wash. State Taiwan Trade Assn., Seattle, 1987; bd. dirs. Wash. Coun. on Internat. Trade, 1991—. Adv. bd. Global Reach Consortium, 1986-87. Served with RCAF, 1952-55. Mem. Machinery and Allied Products Inst. Roman Catholic. Office: John Fluke Mfg Co Inc 6920 Seaway Blvd PO Box 9090 Everett WA 98206*

WAMP, ZACH P., congressman; b. Ft. Benning, Ga., Oct. 28, 1957; m. Kim Wamp; 2 children. Student, U. N.C., U. Tenn. Chmn. Hamilton County Rep. Party, 1987; regional dir. Tenn. Rep. Party, 1989; v.p. Charter Real Estate Corp., 1989-92; real estate broker Fletcher Bright Co., 1992-94; mem. 104th Congress from 3d Tenn. dist., 1995—. Office: US House Reps 423 Cannon House Office Bldg Washington DC 20515-4203

WAMPLER, BARBARA BEDFORD, entrepreneur; b. New Bedford, Mass., July 23, 1932; d. William and Mary (Fitzpatrick) Bedford; m. John H. Wampler, Oct. 21, 1950; children: John H. Jr., William C., James B., Robert T. AS, Tunxis C.C., 1975; MEd, Cambridge Coll., 1996. Lic. real estate agt., Mass., 1986-95. Counselor Wampler Rehab. Counseling Svcs., Farmington, Conn., 1975-85; owner, mgr. Wampler Mktg., Farmington, 1980-84, Earth Campgrounds I and II, Otis, Mass., 1984—; pres., mgr. Earth Works (name now Earth Enterprises), Otis, Mass., 1984—; founder, pres. Advt. Matters, Otis, 1989—; v.p. Mastery Books, Otis, 1989—; mem., clk. Zoning Bd. Appeals, Otis, Mass., 1988-92; notar pub., 1988—; aft. Primerica Fin. Svcs., 1992-94. Author: Do It Yourself Empowerment, 1996; contbr. articles to profl. jours. Dir. music First Congl. Ch., Otis, 1984—, trustee, 1994—; family counselor Berkshire Coun. Alcoholism and Addictions, 1994-96, Berkshire Mediation Option Plus, 1994—. Faculty scholar U. Hartford, 1976. Mem. Acad. Family Mediators, Am. Assn. Christian Counselors, Bus. Mgrs. Assn., Kiwanis. Avocations: vocal soloist, organist, choir director. Home and Office: Earth Enterprises 1856 S Main Rd Box 690 Otis MA 01253

WAMPLER, LLOYD CHARLES, retired lawyer; b. Spencer, Ind., Nov. 4, 1920; s. Charles and Vivian (Hawkins) W.; m. Joyce Ann Hoppenrath, Sept. 28, 1950 (dec. 1954); 1 child, Natalie Gay (dec.); m. Mary E. Shumaker, Sept. 16, 1982. AB, Ind. U., 1942, JD, 1947. Bar: Ind. 1947, U.S. Supreme Ct. 1971. Instr. bus. law U. Kans., 1947-49; dep. atty. gen. Ind., 1949-50; mem. legal com. Interstate Oil Compact Commn., 1950; asst. pub. counselor Ind., 1950-53; mem. Stevens, Wampler, Travis & Fortin, Plymouth, 1953-83; claim counsel Am. Family Ins. Group, Indpls., 1983-88; ret., 1988. Mem. Ind. Rehab. Services Bd., 1978-86; Dem. nominee for judge Ind. Supreme Ct., 1956. With USNR, 1942-46. Mem. ABA, Am. Judicature Soc., Ind. Bar Assn. (bd. mgrs. 1975-77), Indpls. Bar Assn., Ind. Acad. Sci., Ind. Def. Lawyers Assn. (bd. dirs. 1967-72, v.p. 1970, pres. 1971-72), Ind. Hist. Soc., Marshall County Hist. Soc. (bd. dirs. 1969-75), Sagamore of the Wabash, Am. Legion, Phi Delta Phi. Home: 4000 N Meridian St Indianapolis IN 46208-4034

WAMSLEY, JAMES LAWRENCE, III, lawyer; b. Cleve., June 18, 1950; s. James Lawrence Jr. and Dorothy Mae (Auberger) W.; m. Christine Lou Anderson, July 29, 1972; children: Bryan Douglas, Katherine Anne. BS in Electrical Engring., U. Va., 1972; JD, U. Mich., 1975. Bar: Ohio 1975, U.S. Patent and Trademark Office 1984, U.S. Ct. Appeals (6th cir.) 1976, U.S. Ct. Appeals (Fed. cir.) 1984. Assoc. Jones, Day, Reavis & Pogue, Cleve., 1975-84, ptnr., 1985—. Mem. Am. Intellectual Property Law Assn., Cleve. Intellectual Property Law Assn. Avocations: reading, theater, golf, skiing. Office: Jones Day Reavis & Pogue 901 Lakeside Ave E Cleveland OH 44114-1116*

WAN, FREDERIC YUI-MING, mathematician, educator; b. Shanghai, Jan. 7, 1936; arrived in U.S., 1947; s. Wai-Nam and Olga Pearl (Jung) W.; m. Julia Y.S. Chang, Sept. 10, 1960. SB, MIT, 1959, SM, 1963, PhD, 1965. Mem. staff MIT Lincoln Lab., Lexington, 1959-65; instr. math. MIT, Cambridge, 1965-67, asst. prof., 1967-69, assoc. prof., 1969-74; prof. math., dir. Inst. Applied Math. and Stats. U. B.C., Vancouver, 1974-83; prof. applied math. and math. U. Wash., Seattle, 1983-95, chmn. Dept. Applied Math., 1984-88, assoc. dean scis. coll. arts and scis., 1988-92; prof. math., prof. mech. and aero. engring. U. Calif., Irvine, 1995—, vice chancellor rsch., dean grad. studies, 1995—; program dir. Divsn. Math. Sci. NSF, 1986-87, divsn. dir., 1993-94; cons. indsl. firms and govt. agys.; mem. MIT Ednl. Coun. for B.C. Area of Can., 1974-83. Assoc. editor Jour. Applied Mechancs, 1991-95, Can. Applied Math. Quar., Studies in Applied Math., Jour. Dyn. Discrete, Continuous and Impulsive Sys.; contbr. articles to profl. jours. Sloan Found. award, 1973, Killam sr. fellow, 1979. Fellow AAAS, ASME, Am. Acad. Mechanics (sec. fellows 1984-90, pres.-elect 1992-93, pres. 1993-94), Soc. Indsl. and Applied Math., Can. Applied Math. Soc. (coun. 1980-83, pres. 1983-85, Arthur Beaumont Disting. Svc. award 1991), Am. Math. Soc., Math. Assn. Am., Sigma Xi. Home: 22 Urey Ct Irvine CA 92715 Office: U Calif Irvine Office Rsch & Grad Studies 155 Administration Irvine CA 92717-3175

WANAMAKER, ROBERT JOSEPH, advertising company executive; b. Oak Park, Ill., Nov. 24, 1924; s. Daniel John and Mabel (Maloney) W.; m. Carol Anne George, Apr. 20, 1968; children: Stacey Lynne, Bethanne. Ed., Northwestern U., 1949. Vice pres., copy dir. Edward H. Weiss & Co., Chgo., 1957-62; sr. v.p., U.S. creative dir. Clinton E. Frank, Inc., Chgo., 1962-72; sr. v.p., creative dir. Grey-North, Inc., Chgo., 1972-76; sr. v.p., dir. creative services Y & R/Buchen, Reincke, Chgo., 1976-79; v.p., dir. creative services Pollenex, Chgo., 1979-86; pres. Robert Wanamaker "Getting Thru" Mktg. Comms., River Forest, Ill., 1987—. Served with AUS, 1943. Named one of 100 top advt. creative people in U.S.A. Ad Daily U.S.A., 1975. Home and Office: 7225 Division St River Forest IL 60305-1267 *One of the biggest problems with success in worldly things is keeping your sense of values in proper perspective. Affluence can dull your sensitivity to the needs and aspirations of those less fortunate. You can become obsessed with building your own financial assets. The misguided fear of losing your status, your luxuries, your comforts can be abnormally painful. Every once in awhile you have to chasten your thinking and remind yourself that the only three riches in life are love, health, and being at peace with yourself and your God.*

WANBAUGH, REBECCA BOWDEN HERRICK, history educator; b. Sargentville, Maine, Apr. 12, 1923; d. Chandler Hale and Lilla Estelle (McIntyre) Bowden; BA, U. Maine, Orono, 1945, MA, 1964, PhD, 1980; student (merit scholar) Andover-Newton Theol. Sch., 1957-58. Personnel/tng. supr. Sibley, Lindsay & Curr Co., Rochester, N.Y., 1946-49; vocat. rehab. counselor N.Y. State Dept. Edn., Rochester, 1958-59; instr. sociology U. Maine, Orono, 1959-62; dean of women U. Maine, Presque Isle, 1963-74, instr. social sci., 1963-71, asst. prof. sociology and history, 1971-74, asso. prof. sociology and history, 1974-82, prof. history, 1982—, faculty rep. to bd. trustees, 1979-81, bd. trustees acad. planning com. on student life, 1979-80; social sci. cons. State Dept. Ednl. and Cultural Svcs., 1987-92; mem. Women's Studies Consortium U. Main, 1989-92. Exec. council Alcohol Info. and Referral Services, 1976-82; bd. dirs. N.E. chpt. Audubon Soc., 1991—; active Central Aroostook Assn. Retarded Citizens, 1965—. Faculty Devel. grantee U. Maine, 1978-79, Women and Women's Issues in Victorian Eng. fed. grantee, 1983; Alumni Grad. scholar U. Maine, 1980. Mem. AAUW, NEA, Am. Sociol. Assn., Am. Hist. Assn., Phi Eta Sigma, Pi Beta Phi. Baptist. Home: 6 Haven Ct Presque Isle ME 04769-3113 Office: U Maine 181 Main St Presque Isle ME 04769-2888

WAND, PATRICIA ANN, librarian; b. Portland, Oreg., Mar. 28, 1942; d. Ignatius Bernard and Alice Ruth (Suhr) W.; m. Francis Dean Silvernail, Dec. 20, 1966 (div. Jan. 19, 1986); children: Marjorie Lynn Silvernail, Kirk Dean Silvernail. BA, Seattle U., 1963; MAT, Antioch Grad. Sch., 1967; AMLS, U. Mich., 1972. Vol. Peace Corps, Colombia, S.Am., 1963-65; secondary tchr. Langley Jr. High Sch., Washington, 1965-66; asst. libr. Wittenberg U. Libr., Springfield, Ohio, 1967-69; secondary tchr. Caro (Mich.) High Sch., 1969-70; assoc. libr. Coll. of S.I. (N.Y.) Libr., 1972-77; head, access svcs. Columbia U. Librs., N.Y.C., 1977-82; asst. univ. libr. U. Oreg., Eugene, 1982-89; univ. libr. The Am. U., Washington, 1989—; cons. Bloomsburg (Pa.) U. Libr., 1990. Contbr. articles to profl. jours. Pres. West Cascade Returned Peace Corps Vols., Eugene, 1985-88; v.p. Friends of Colombia, Washington, 1990—; speaker on Peace Corps, 1965—, libr. and info. svcs., 1979—. Honors Program scholarship Seattle U., 1960-62, Peace Corps scholarship Antioch U., 1965-66; recipient Beyond War award, 1987, Fulbright Sr. Lectr. award Fulbright, 1989, Disting. Alumnus award Sch. of Info. and Libr. Studies, U. Mich., 1992. Mem. ALA, Assn. Coll. and Rsch. Librs. (chair budge and fin. bd. dirs. 1987-89, chair WHCLIS task force 1989-92), On-line Computer Librs. Ctr. (adv. com. on coll. and univ. librs. 1991), D.C. Libr. Assn. (bd. dirs. 1993—, pres. 1996—). Home: 4854 Bayard Blvd Bethesda MD 20816-1785 Office: Am Univ Libr 4400 Massachusetts Ave NW Washington DC 20016-8001

WAND, RICHARD WALTON, paper company executive; b. Shelbyville, Ind., Sept. 20, 1939; s. J. Harold and Josephine Katharine (Harvey) W.; m. Sharon Brierly, June 21, 1964; children: Brian James, Katharine. BS in Mech. Engring., Purdue U., 1961; MBA, Ind. U., 1964. Project engr. Combustion Engring., Inc., 1961-63; mgr. tech. ops. Aerospace Research Applications Ctr., Ind. U., 1963-65; with Bergstrom Paper Co., Neenah, Wis., 1965-80, adminstrv. v.p., 1972-79, exec. v.p. ops., 1979-80; v.p. adminstrn. P.H. Glatfelter Co., Spring Grove, Pa., 1980—; retired, 1995—; bd. dirs. Ecusta Australia Ltd. Contbg. editor: Infosystems Mag., 1972-73. Bd. dirs. Jr. Achievement York County, Pa., York Found., Strand Capitol Performing Arts Ctr.; mem. Citizens Adv. Coun. to Pa. Dept. Environ. Resources. Mem. Am. Paper Inst. (dir. pulp consumers bd.), Syracuse Pulp and Paper Found. (dir., pres.), Beta Theta Pi. Republican. Presbyterian. Home: 391 Tri-Hill Rd York PA 17403-3854 Office: PH Glatfelter Co 228 S Main St Spring Grove PA 17362-1000

WANDER, HERBERT STANTON, lawyer; b. Cin., Mar. 17, 1935; s. Louis Marvin and Pauline (Schuster) W.; m. Ruth Cele Fell, Aug. 7, 1960; children: Daniel Jerome, Susan Gail, Lois Marlene. AB, U. Mich., 1957; LLB, Yale U., 1960. Bar: Ohio 1960, Ill. 1960. Law clk. to judge U.S. Dist. Ct. (no. dist.) Ill., 1960-61; ptnr. Pope Ballard Shepard & Fowle, Chgo., 1961-78, Katten Muchin & Zavis, Chgo., 1978—; trustee Michael Reese Found., 1991—; bd. dirs. Tel. & Data Systems, Chgo., 1968—, Advance Ross Corp., 1991—; mem. legal adv. com. to the bd. govs. N.Y. Stock Exch., 1989-92; mem. legal adv. bd. Nat. Assn. Securities Dealers, Inc., 1996—. Contbr. numerous articles to profl. jours. Bd. dirs. Jewish Fedn. Met. Chgo., 1972—, pres., 1981-83; bd. dirs. Jewish United Fund, 1972—, pres., 1981-83, chmn. pub. affairs com., 1984-87, gen. campaign chmn., 1993; former regional chmn. nat. young leadership cabinet United Jewish Appeal; vice chmn. large city budgeting conf. Council Jewish Fedns., 1979-82, bd. dirs., 1980—, exec. com., 1983-84. Editor (jour.) Bus. Law Today, 1992-93; editor-in-chief (jour.) The Bus. Lawyer, 1993-94. Mem. ABA (sec. bus. law sect. 1992-93, vice-chair 1993-94, chair-elect 1994-95, chair 1995—), Chgo. Bar Assn., Ill. State Bar Assn., Yale Law Sch. Assn. (exec. com. 1982-86), Phi Beta Kappa. Clubs: Standard, Econ. (Chgo.); Northmoor Country (Highland Park, Ill.). Home: 70 Prospect Highland Park IL 60035-2513 Office: Katten Muchin & Zavis 525 W Monroe St Ste 1600 Chicago IL 60661-3629

WANDERS, HANS WALTER, banker; b. Aachen, Germany, Apr. 3, 1925; came to U.S., 1929, naturalized, 1943; s. Herbert and Anna Maria (Kusters) W.; m. Elizabeth Knox Kimball, Apr. 2, 1949; children: Crayton Kimball, David Gillette. BS, Yale U., 1947; postgrad. Grad. Sch. Banking, Rutgers U., 1961-64. With GE, 1947-48, Libbey-Owens-Ford Glass Co., 1948-53, Allied Chem. Co., 1953-55, McKinsey & Co., Inc., 1955-57; from asst. cashier to v.p. No. Trust Co., Chgo., 1957-65; v.p. Nat. Blvd. Bank, Chgo., 1965-66, pres., 1966-70; exec. v.p. Wachovia Bank & Trust Co., N.A., Winston-Salem, N.C., 1970-74, chmn., 1977-85, vice chmn., 1985-88, also bd. dirs.; pres. Wachovia Corp., Winston-Salem, 1974-76, 85-87, chmn., 1977-85, vice chmn., 1987-88, also bd. dirs.; pres., chief exec. officer 1st Wachovia Corp. Services, Inc., Winston-Salem, 1986-88, ret., 1988; dir. Exxon Supply Co., 1989-94, Goody's Pharmaceuticals, 1989-94; dir. Gulf USA, Inc., 1989-92. Chmn. Winston-Salem Found. Com., 1981-82; bd. dirs. N.C. Textile Found., N.C. Engring. Found., Inc., 1971-88; trustee, mem. exec. com. Salem Coll. and Acad., 1986-91, Tax Found., 1982—, vice chmn., 1984-86, chmn., 1986-88, chmn. exec. com., 1989; mem. bd. visitors Fuqua Sch. Bus., Duke U., 1978-89; mem. nat. corps. com. United Negro Coll. Fund; mem., chmn. N.C. Bd. Econ. Devel., 1989-93; corporator Belmont Hill Sch., 1996—. Lt. USNR, 1943-46, 51-53. Mem. Am. Bankers Assn. (chmn. mktg. divsn. 1979-80, dir. 1971-73), Assn. Res. City Bankers, Conf. Bd. (So. regional adv. coun.), Assn. Bank Holding Cos. (bd. dirs., exec. com. 1981-83), Chgo. Club, Commonwealth Club Chgo., Piedmont Club, Old Town Club Winston-Salem, Roaring Gap Club N.C. Home: 10 Graylyn Pl Winston Salem NC 27106 Office: Wachovia Corp 420A W 4th St Winston Salem NC 27101

WANDLING, MARILYN ELIZABETH BRANSON, artist, art educator; b. Alton, Ill., May 16, 1932; d. Ralph Marion and Mary Mildred (Branson) W.; children: Jeffrey, Douglas, Pamela. Student, Monticello Coll., Godfrey, Ill, 1950-51, U. Ill. U-C Sch. Fine Arts, 1951-53; BA in Art, Webster U., St. Louis, 1968; MA Edn. in Art Edn., Washington U., St. Louis, 1975. Cert. tchr. art Kindergarten-Grade 12, Mo. 4th grade tchr. Alton (Ill.) Pub. Schs., 1961-62; art. buuying dept. Gardner Advt. Co. Inc., St. Louis, 1962-63; art tchr. mid. sch. Lindbergh Sch. Dist., St. Louis, 1968-75; cons., designer V.P. Fair, Inc., St. Louis, 1982; adminstrv. asst. to headmaster, coll. counseling dept. John Burroughs Sch., St. Louis, 1979-82; dir. pub. rels. and advt. Dance St. Louis, 1983-85; freelance art and design St. Louis, 1970—; art tchr. mid. sch. St. Louis Pub. Schs., 1987-90, art tchr. Elem. Magnet Sch. for Visual & Performing Arts, 1990—; tchr. drawing and painting Summer Arts Inst., St. Louis Pub. Schs., 1992, graphic arts designer, cons. comty. affairs divsn., 1985—, sch. vol. divsn., 1990-92, Webster Groves (Mo.) Sch. Dist., 1989-90, Pub. Sch. Retirement Sys., St. Louis, 1991; implementer classroom multi-cultural art edn. projects, 1987—; summer participant Improving Visual Arts Edn., Getty Ctr. for Edn. in Arts, 1990; book illustrator-McGraw Hill Inter-Americana de Mexico, Mexico City, 1994-95. Designer Centennial Logo for St. Louis Pub. Schs. Sesquicentennial, 1988; painter, designer murals for Ctrl. Presbyn. Ch. Nursery, 1978-79, St. Nicholas Greek Orthodox Ch., 1980; designer two outdoor villages VP Fair, Arch Grounds, St. Louis, 1982. Recipient merit and honor awards Nat. Sch. Pub. Rels. Assn., 1990, 91, 92, 93, Mo. Sch. Pub. Rels. Assn., 1989-90, 91, 92, 93. Mem. Nat. Art Edn. Assn., St. Louis Art Mus., PEO Sisterhood, Nat. Soc. DAR, Chi Omega Alumnae. Avocations: Native American arts and culture, paintings, drawings, portraits. Office: Ames Visual & Performing Arts Center Admin Office 2900 Hadley St Saint Louis MO 63107-3911

WANDYCZ, PIOTR STEFAN, history educator; b. Krakow, Poland, Sept. 20, 1923; s. Damian Stanislaw and Stefania (Dunikowska) W.; m. Maria Teresa Chrzaszcz, Aug. 13, 1963; children: Anna, Joanna, Antoni. B.A., Cambridge U., 1948, M.A., 1952; Ph.D., London U., 1951; M.A. (hon.), Yale U., 1968; PhD (hon.), Wroclaw U., Poland, 1993. Instr. to assoc. prof. history Ind. U., 1954-66; fellow Harvard's Russian Research Center, 1963-65; assoc. prof. history Yale U., 1966-68, prof., 1968-89, chmn. Russian and East European council, 1974-76, 81-83, Bradford Durfee prof., 1989—; vis. prof. history Columbia U., 1967, 69, 74. Author: Czechoslovak-Polish Confederation and Great Powers, 1956, France and Her Eastern Allies, 1962, Soviet-Polish Relations, 1969, The Lands of Partitioned Poland, 1974, United States and Poland, 1980, August Zaleski, 1980, Polska i Zagranica, 1986, The Twilight of French Eastern Alliances, 1988, Z Dziejow dyplomacji, 1988, Polish Diplomacy 1914-1945, 1988, The Price of Freedom, 1992, Die Freiheit und ihr Preis, 1993, Pod zaborami, 1994, Cena wolnosci, 1995; contbr. articles to profl. jours.; mem. editl. bd. Slavic Rev., Internat. History Rev., Polish Rev., Polin., East European Politics and Soc. Served as 2d lt. Polish Army, 1942-45. Decorated Comdr.'s Cross of Polonia Restituta; recipient Alfred Jurzykowski Found. award in history, 1977; fellow Guggenheim Found., Ford Found., Rockefeller Found., Am. Philos. Soc., Am. Coun. Learned Socs., Social Sci. Rsch. Coun., Internat. Rsch. and Exchs. Bd. Mem. AAAS (Wayne Vucinich prize 1989), Am. Hist. Assn. (George Louis Beer prize 1962, 89), Polish Hist. Assn. (hon.), Polish Acad. Arts and Scis., Polish Acad. Scis., Polish Inst. Arts and Scis. Abroad (A. Lenkszewicz prize 1991), Czechoslovak Acad. of Scis. (Hlavka medal 1992), Czechoslovak Soc. Arts and Scis. Home: 27 Spring Gardens St Hamden CT 06517-1913 Office: Yale U Dept History New Haven CT 06520

WANEK, RONALD G., manufacturing executive; b. 1941. With Winona (Minn.) Industries, Inc., 1961-63, Red Wing (Minn.) Industries, Inc., 1963-70; chmn. bd., CEO Ashley Furniture Industries, Arcadia, Wis., 1970—. Office: Ashley Furniture Industries 1 Ashley Way Arcadia WI 54612-1218*

WANEK, STEPHEN J., electronics executive. V.p. ops. divsn. Rosemount Inc., Hopkins, Minn., 1973-90; exec. v.p. Interactive Tech., Inc., Saint Paul, Minn., 1990—. Office: Interactive Tech Inc 2266 2nd St N Saint Paul MN 55109-2914*

WANEK, WILLIAM CHARLES, public relations executive; b. Ridgewood, N.Y., Oct. 21, 1932; s. William John and Anna (Benes) W.; m. Robbie Gene Fairbanks, Feb. 14, 1974; children: William Robert, Jennifer Leigh. BA in English, CCNY, 1954; MA in Psychology, The New Sch. Social Rsch., N.Y.C., 1982. Asst. editor Soap Chem. Spltys. Mag., N.Y.C., 1956-58; editor in chief Maintenance Supplies Mag., N.Y.C., 1958-60; acct. exec. O.S. Tyson & Co. Inc., N.Y.C., 1960-62; dir. advt. and pub. rels. Pa. Glass Sand Corp., N.Y.C., 1962-64; sr. acct. exec. McCann-Erickson Inc., N.Y.C., 1964-66; acct. supr. Burson-Marsteller Assocs., N.Y.C., 1966-71; exec. v.p. Gibbs & Soell Inc., N.Y.C., 1971—. With U.S. Army, 1954-56. Mem. Am. Agrl. Editors Assn., Nat. Agri-Mktg. Assn. (bd. dirs. ea. chpt. 1974-76), Nat. Assn. Farm Broadcasters. Presbyterian. Avocations: horticulture, classical music, theater, reading, swimming. Office: Gibbs & Soell Inc 600 3rd Ave New York NY 10016-1901

WANG, ALBERT JAMES, violinist, educator; b. Ann Arbor, Mich., Nov. 19, 1958; s. James and Lydia (Ebenhoch) W.; m. Bridget Renee Becker, June 30, 1987; children: Ona Lenore, Kevin Lewis. BM, Ind. U., 1979; MM, U. Mich., 1981; DMA, Am. Conservatory, 1993. Prin. second violin Baton Rouge Symphony Orch., 1981-82; first violin Valcour String Quartet, Baton Rouge, 1981-82, Loyola String Quartet, 1982-83; mem. Lyric Opera Chgo. Orch., 1982—; mem. Orch. Ill., Chgo., 1982-88; prin. 2d violin Internat. Symphony Orch., Port Huron, Mich., 1984; 1st violin Internat. String Quartet, Port Huron, 1984; concertmaster, soloist Chgo. Chamber Orch., 1985-88, Chgo. Philharm., 1985—; mem. Grant Park Symphony Orch., Chgo., 1986-87; concertmaster, soloist Birch Creek Music Festival, Wis., Woodstock (Ill.) Mozart Festival Orch., 1988-90; concertmaster Rockford (Ill.) Symphony Orch., 1990-91, Northwestern Music Festival Orch., 1990—; soloist, concertmaster Pro Musica Orch. of Mauritius, 1992-93; soloist, concertmaster China tour Classical Symphony Orch., 1994, 95; soloist, concertmaster Midweset Symphony Orch., 1995—; music dir. Baroque Masterplayers, 1994—; concertmaster Midwest Symphony Orch., 1995—; artist-in-residence St. Clair Coll., Port Huron, 1984, Elgin C.C., 1994—; lectr. Am. Conservatory Music, Chgo., 1989-92; Fulbright lectr. Francois Mitterand Conservatory of Music, Quatre Bornes, Mauritius, 1992-93; asst. prof. violin Roosevelt U., 1993—. Numerous solo, recital and chamber music appearances and master classes throughout U.S., Can., Mauritius and China; recs. and broadcasts by Mauritian Nat. Radio and WFMT Chgo. Fine Arts Sta., PBS, Nat. Pub. Radio, and Chinese Nat. Radio & TV; numerous world premiers; adjudicator for state and nat. music competitions; contbr. articles and revs. to profl. jours. Vol. ARC, Literacy Vols. Am., Chgo. Pub. Librs., United Way; bd. advisors Prism Music Festival, 1984—, Am. Chamber Symphony, 1985, Symphony II, 1993-94. Fulbright grantee, 1992-93; recipient 1st prize Ann Arbor (Mich.) Symphony Competition, 1976, Soc. Am. Musicians Competition, Chgo., 1984, Internat. Concerts Atlantique Competition, N.Y.C., 1989, Chgo. Park Dist. Competition, 1991, 2nd prize Biennial Adult Artist Competition, 1992; selected to Arts Am. Touring Artist Roster, 1993; finalist Lilly Fellows Program in Humanities and the Arts, Valparaiso U., 1994; recipient Leo Sowerby medal, 1994. Mem. Am. Fedn. Musicians, Am. String Tchrs. Assn., Coll. Music Soc., Chamber Music Am., Am. Music Ctr., Music Tchrs. Nat. Assn. Avocations: powerlifting, fishing, travel, woodworking. Office: Roosevelt U 430 S Michigan Ave Chicago IL 60605-1301 also: Lyric Opera Chgo 20 N Wacker Dr Chicago IL 60606-2806 also: Elgin CC 1700 Spartan Dr Elgin IL 60123-7189 also: Baroque Masterplayers 5528 S Hyde Park Blvd Ste 1002 Chicago IL 60637-1938

WANG, ALLAN ZUWU, cell biologist, pharmacologist; b. Shanghai, China, June 1, 1939; came to U.S., 1982; m. Qin-Yu Chen, Mar. 30, 1968; 1 child, George Qi. MD, Shanghai Med. U., 1962; PhD, Chinese Acad. Scis., 1966. Rsch. assoc. Chinese Acad. Sci., Shanghai, 1966-80; postdoctoral rsch. fellow Imperial Cancer Rsch. Fund, London, 1980-82; assoc. rsch. scientist U. Tex. System Cancer Ctr., Houston, 1982-83; assoc. prof. Chinese Acad. Scis., 1983-85; Stanley Reimann rsch. scientist Fox Chase Cancer Ctr., Phila., 1987-90; acting scientific dir. Western Pa. Hosp. Found. Rsch. Inst., Pitts., 1990-91, dir. rsch. dept. medicine, sr. faculty scientist, 1990—; faculty collaborator NSF Sci. and Tech. Ctr. Carnegie Mellon U., 1990—; vis. assoc. prof. Med. Coll. Pa., 1986-87; mem. rsch. bd. advisors Am. Biophys. Inst., N.C., 1989—, Internat. Biophys. Ctr., Cambridge, Eng., 1989—; com. mem. Instnl. Animal Care and Use Com., Western Pa. Found., 1990—. Contbr. articles to 115 profl. jours. Mem. AAAS, Am. Coll. Rheumatology, Inflammation Assn., Am. Soc. Cell Biology, Am. Assn. Cancer Rsch., Brit. Soc. Cell Biology, Brit. Assn. Cancer Rsch., Inflammation Rsch. Assn. Achievements include research in mechanisms of cell adhesion, migration, and interactions between cells to cells and cells to extracellular matrix, pharmacological study of anti-cancer drug Methoxyl Sarcolysin; application of image processing in SEM investigation of experimental tumor matastasis, synoviocyte chemotaxis migration and invasion, renal epithelial membrane polarity and electrolyte transport. Office: Western Pa Hosp Found 4800 Friendship Ave Pittsburgh PA 15224-1722

WANG, ARTHUR CHING-LI, law educator, lawyer; b. Boston, Feb. 4, 1949; s. Kung Shou and Lucy (Chow) W.; m. Wendy F. Hamai, May 22, 1976 (div. 1981); m. Nancy J. Norton, Sept. 1, 1985; children: Alexander Xinglin, Sierra Xinan. BA, Franconia Coll., 1970; JD, U. Puget Sound, 1984. Bar: Wash. 1984. Printer Carmel Valley (Calif.) Outlook, 1970-73; project coord. Tacoma (Wash.) Community House, 1973-76; rsch. analyst Wash. Ho. of Reps., Olympia, Wash., 1977-80, mem., 1981-94; of counsel Davies Pearson, P.C., Tacoma, 1984-94; adj. prof. U. Puget Sound Law Sch., Tacoma, 1987-93, Seattle U. Law Sch., Tacoma, 1995—; chmn House Capital Budget Com., 1993-94, Revenue Com., 1989-92, Commerce and Labor Com., 1985-88; mem. Wash. Pers. Appeals Bd., Olympia, 1994—. Assoc. editor U. Puget Sound Law Review, 1983-84. Vista vol. Tacoma Urban League, 1973-74; del. Dem. Nat. Conv., 1976. Named Chinese Am. Man of Yr., Seattle Chinese Post, 1991, Legislator of Yr., Wash. Health Care Assn., 1992. Democrat. Avocation: birding. Home: 3319 N Union Ave Tacoma WA 98407-6043 Office: Wash Pers Appeals Bd PO Box 40911 Olympia WA 98504

WANG, ARTHUR WOODS, publisher; b. Port Chester, N.Y., Oct. 7, 1918; s. Israel and Madolin (Woods) W.; m. Mary Ellen Mackay, Aug. 13, 1955; 1 son, Michael Anthony. B.S., Bowdoin Coll., 1940; postgrad., Columbia U., 1949-51. Advt. research McCann-Erickson, Inc., 1940-41; editor Doubleday & Co., 1942-43, Alfred A. Knopf, Inc., 1943, T.Y. Crowell (Pub.), 1943-47; with E.M. Hale & Co., Eau Claire, Wis., 1947-52; editor A.A. Wyn, Inc., 1952-56; co-founder, pres., editor-in-chief Hill & Wang, Inc., 1956-71; pub., editor-in-chief Hill & Wang div. Farrar, Straus & Giroux, Inc., N.Y.C., 1971-87; sr. editor Hill and Wang div. Farrar, Straus & Giroux, Inc., 1988—; also v.p. Hill & Wang div. Farrar, Straus & Giroux, Inc.. Mem. Am. Book Pubs. Coun. (bd. dirs. 1968-70). Home: 150 E 69th St New York NY 10021-5704 Office: Hill & Wang 19 Union Sq W New York NY 10003-3307

WANG, CHAO-CHENG, mathematician, engineer; b. Peoples Republic of China, July 20, 1938; came to U.S., 1961; s. N.S. and V.T. Wang; m. Sophia C.L. Wang; children: Ferdinand, Edward. BS, Nat. Taiwan U., 1959; PhD, Johns Hopkins U., 1965. Registered profl. engr., Tex. Asst. prof. Johns Hopkins U., Balt., 1966-68, assoc. prof., 1968-69; prof. Rice U., Houston, 1968-79, Noah Harding prof., 1979—, chmn. math. sci. dept.,, 1983-89, chmn. mech. engring. and materials sci., 1991-94. Author numerous books in field; contbr. articles to profl. jours. Named Disting. Young Scientist Md. Acad. Sci., 1968. Mem. ASME, Soc. Natural Philosophy (treas. 1985-86), Am. Acad. Mechs. Office: Rice Univ Dept Mech Engring Materials Sci Houston TX 77251

WANG, CHARLES B., computer software company executive; b. Shanghai, Rep. China, Aug. 19, 1944. BS, Queens Coll., 1967. Chmn., CEO Computer Assocs., Islandia, N.Y., 1976—. Office: Computer Assocs Internat Inc 1 Computer Assocs Plz Islandia NY 11788-7000

WANG, CHEN CHI, electronics company executive, real estate executive, finance company executive, investments services executive, international trade executive; b. Taipei, Taiwan, Aug. 10, 1932; came to U.S., 1959, naturalized, 1970; s. Chin-Ting and Chen-Kim Wang; m. Victoria Rebisoff, Mar. 5, 1965; children: Katherine Kim, Gregory Chen, John Christopher, Michael Edward. B.A. in Econs., Nat. Taiwan U., 1955; B.S.E.E., San Jose State U., 1965; M.B.A., U. Calif., Berkeley, 1961. With IBM Corp., San Jose, Calif., 1965-72; founder, chief exec. officer Electronics Internat. Co., Santa Clara, Calif., 1968-72, owner, gen. mgr., 1972-81, reorganized as EIC Group, 1982, now chmn. bd., chief exec. officer; dir. Systek Electronics Corp., Santa Clara, 1970-73; founder, sr. ptnr. Wang Enterprises (name changed to Chen Kim Entrprises 1982), Santa Clara, 1974—; founder, sr. ptnr. Hanson & Wang Devel. Co., Woodside, Calif., 1977-85; chmn. bd. Golden Alpha Enterprises, San Mateo, Calif., 1979—; mng. ptnr. Woodside Acres-Las Pulgas Estate, Woodside, 1980-85; founder, sr. ptnr. DeVine & Wang, Oakland, Calif., 1977-83; Van Heal & Wang, West Village, Calif., 1981-82; founder, chmn. bd. EIC Fin. Corp., Redwood City, Calif., 1985—; chmn. bd. Maritek Corp., Corpus Christi, Tex., 1988-89; chmn. EIC Internat. Trade Corp., Lancaster, Calif., 1989—, EIC Capital Corp., Redwood City, 1990—. Served to 2d lt., Nationalist Chinese Army, 1955-56. Mem. Internat. Platform Assn., Tau Beta Pi. Mem. Christian Ch. Author: Monetary and Banking System of Taiwan, 1955, The Small Car Market in the U.S., 1961. Home: 195 Brookwood Rd Woodside CA 94062-2302 Office: EIC Group Head Office Bldg 2055-2075 Woodside Rd Redwood City CA 94061-2095

WANG, CHIA PING, physicist, educator; came to U.S., 1963, naturalized; (parents Chinese citizens).; s. Guan Can and Tah (Lin) W. BS, U. London, 1950; MS, U. Malaya (now U. Singapore), 1951; PhD in Physics, U. Malaya (now U. Singapore) and U. Cambridge, 1953; DSc in Physics, U. Singapore, 1972. Asst. lectr. U. Malaya, 1951-53; mem. faculty Nankai U., Tientsin, 1954-58, prof. physics, 1956-58, head electron physics div., 1955-58, mem. steering com. nuc. physics divsn., 1956-58; head electron physics Lanchow Atomic Project, 1958; mem. faculty Hong Kong U.; mem. faculty Chinese U., Hong Kong, 1958-63, prof. physics, 1959-63, acting head physics, math. depts., 1959; rsch. assoc. lab. nuclear studies Cornell U., Ithaca, N.Y., 1963-64; assoc. prof. space sci. and applied physics Cath. U. Am., Washington, 1964-68; assoc. prof. physics Case Inst. Tech. Case Western Res. U., Cleve., 1966-70; vis. scientist, vis. prof. U. Cambridge (Eng.), U. Leuven (Belgium), U.S. Naval Rsch. Labs., U. Md., MIT, 1970-75; rsch. physicist radiation lab. U.S. Army Natick (Mass.) R & D Command, 1975—, mem. steering com. sci. and tech. directorate, 1993—; pioneer in fields of nuclear sub-structure (now often referred to as parton), nucleon sub-unit structure, multiparticle prodn., cosmic radiation, picosecond time to pulse-height conversion, thermal physics, lasers, microwaves. Contbg. author: Atomic Structure and Interactions of Ionizing Radiations with Matter in Preservation of Food by Ionizing Radiation, 1982; contbr. numerous articles to profl. jours. Recipient Outstanding Performance award Dept. Army, 1980, Quality Increase award, 1980. Mem. Am. Phys. Soc., Inst. Physics London, N.Y. Acad. Scis., AAAS, Sigma Xi. Home: 28 Hallett Hill Rd Weston MA 02193-1753 Office: US Army Natick Rsch And Devel Ctr Natick MA 01760

WANG, DANIEL I-CHYAU, biochemical engineering educator; b. Nanking, China, Mar. 12, 1936; s. Shou Chin and Ling Nyi (Vee) W.; m. Victoria Dawn, Aug. 27, 1966; 1 child, Keith Fredric. B.S., MIT, 1959, M.S., 1961; Ph.D., U. Pa., 1963. Process engr. Esso. Research and Devel. Co., Linden, N.Y., 1963; asst. prof. MIT, Cambridge, 1965-70; asso. prof. MIT, 1970-74, prof. biochem. engring., 1974—, Chevron prof. chem. engring., 1985—, dir. Biotech. Process Engring. Ctr., 1985—. Co-author 3 books; contbr. articles to profl. jours. Served with U.S. Army, 1963-65. Recipient Outstanding Tchr. award MIT, 1972, 78, 89, Sci. Appreciation award Republic of China, 1978; AMF fellow, 1962-63. Mem. NAE, Am. Inst. Chem. Engrs. (food, pharm. and bioengring. award 1981, Inst. lectr. 1986), Am. Chem. Soc. (M.J. Johnson award 1983, David Perlman Meml. lectr. 1991), Am. Soc. Microbiology, Inst. Food Technologists (sci. lectr. 1984-87), Am. Acad. Arts and Scis., Sigma Xi, Tau Beta Pi. Patentee in field. Office: MIT 77 Massachusetts Ave Cambridge MA 02139-4301

WANG, FEI JUN, microbiologist, researcher; b. Zheng Zhou, Henan, China, May 7, 1964; arrived in U.S., 1991; s. You Min Zhao and Yuling Wang; m. Chao Wu, May 15, 1986. B, So. China Inst. Tech., Guang Zhou, 1985; M, Nat. Inst. Applied Scis., Toulouse, France, 1987; PhD, U. Paris-VI, 1991. Registered profl. engr., N.J. Postdoctoral rschr. U. Medicine and Dentistry N.J., Newark, 1991-92, rsch. assoc., 1993—; postdoctoral rschr. Jacques Monod Inst., Paris, 1992-93. Contbr. articles to profl. jours. Mem. Am. Assn. Cancer Rsch. (assoc.). Avocations: workout, cooking, movies.

WANG, FRANNY, electronics executive; b. 1946. Grad., Nat. Taiwan U., 1969; MBA, Temple U., 1970. Acct. PMI, Santa Clara, Calif., 1970-73; sec.-treas. Pantronix Corp., San Jose, Calif., 1974—. Office: Pantronix Corp 145 Rio Robles San Jose CA 95134-1807*

WANG, GUNG H., management consultant; b. Ningpo, Zhejiang, China, Feb. 3, 1909; s. Cheng V. and Zhao S. (Zhu) W.; m. Gladys Chen Wang, Sept. 10, 1938; children: Edward, Jo-Ann, Nancy, James. BA, U. Shanghai, China, 1928; MA, Tulane U., New Orleans, 1952; LLD (hon.), Loyola U., Chgo., 1989. Staff officer Mil. Fgn. Affairs, Nanking, China, 1928-30; vice cons. Consulate Gen. China, Chgo., 1930-38; cons. Consulate of China, New Orleans, 1938-50; exec. dir. Chinese Am. Civic Council, Chgo.; mng. dir. Chinatown Devel. Inc., Chgo., 1960-64; asst. dir. Chgo. Dwellings Assn., 1964-69; housing specialist Model Cities Program, Chgo., 1969-73; dir. Neighborhood Housing Services, Dept. Human Services, 1973-76; owner G.H. Wang Assocs., Chgo., 1976--; sec. Chinese Del. UN Gen. Assembly, Lake Success, N.Y., 1946-47; alt. del. UN Temporary Commn. on Korea, Seoul and Paris, 1948; pres. Neighborhood Redevel. Assn. Inc., Chgo., 1972—; exec. dir. South Side Planning Bd., 1977; adminstr. fund for intercultural edn. NRAI, 1989—. Author: The Chinese Mind 1946, Kinsiskt Tankande, 1948; contbr. articles to profl. jours. 1948-51. Mem. Nat. Assn. Housing and Redevel. Ofcls., Am. Planning Assn., Rotary Club Chgo., Phi Sigma Alpha. Presbyterian. Avocation: writing. Home: 8200 S Indiana Ave Chicago IL 60619-4725

WANG, GWO JAW, university educator. Recipient U. Va. Pres.'s Report award, 1992. Office: U Va Sch Medicine Charlottesville VA 22906

WANG, I-TUNG, atmospheric scientist; b. Peking, People's Republic of China, Feb. 16, 1933; came to U.S., 1958; s. Shen and Wei-Yun (Wen) W.; m. Amy Hung Kong; children: Cynthia P., Clifford T. BS in Physics, Nat. Taiwan U., 1955; MA in Physics, U. Toronto, 1957; PhD in Physics, Columbia U., 1965. Rsch. physicist Carnegie-Mellon U., Pitts., 1965-67, asst. prof., 1967-70; environ. systems engr. Argonne (Ill.) Nat. Lab., 1970-76; mem. tech. staff Environ. Monitoring and Svcs. Ctr. Rockwell Internat., Creve Coeur, Mo., 1976-80, Newbury Park, Calif., 1980-84; sr. scientist, combustion engr. Environ. Monitoring and Svcs. Inc., Newbury Park, Camarillo, 1984-88; sr. scientist ENSR Corp (formerly ERT), 1988; pres. EMA Co., Thosand Oaks, Calif., 1989—; tech. advisor Bur. of Environ. Protection, Republic of China, 1985; environ. cons. ABB Environ, 1989-92, ARCO, 1990-91, Du Pont (SAFER Sys. Divsn.), 1992-93, So. Calif. Edison, 1993-95, So. Coast Air Quality Mgmt. Dist., 1995—. Contbr. papers to profl jours. Grantee Bureau of Environ. Protection, Taiwan, 1985. Mem. N.Y. Acad. of Scis., Air and Waste Mgmt. Assn., Sigma Xi. Avocations: violin and chamber music. Office: EMA Co Ste 435 2219 E Thousand Oaks Blvd Thousand Oaks CA 91362-2905 *Personal philosophy: The pursuit of science is much like the pursuit of art. It requires one's complete involvement and devotion.*

WANG, JAMES CHIA-FANG, political science educator; b. Nanling, China, Apr. 4, 1926; came to U.S., 1946, naturalized, 1962; s. Chien-Yu and Lilian W.; m. Sarah Cutter, May 7, 1960; children—Sarah, Eric. BA in Polit. Sci., Oberlin Coll., 1950; postgrad., N.Y. U., 1951; PhD in Polit. Sci, U. Hawaii, 1971. Rsch. asst., internat. study group Brookings Instn., 1951-53; adminstrv. and tng. officer UN Secretariat, N.Y.C., 1953-57; editor-in-charge UN Documents Edit., Readex Corp., N.Y.C., 1957-60; lectr. far eastern politics NYU, N.Y.C., 1957-60; instr. Asian history and econs. Punahou Sch., Honolulu, 1960-64; program officer Inst. Student Interchange, East-West Ctr., Honolulu, 1964-69, acting dir. participant svcs., 1970, adminstrv. officer admissions, 1969-71; dir. freshmen integrated program Hilo (Hawaii) Coll., 1971-72; asst. prof. polit. sci. and internat. studies U. Hawaii, Hilo, 1971-72, assoc. prof., 1973-76, prof., 1976—; mem. U. Hawaii Contemporary China Study Group), Hilo, 1971—; chmn. dept. polit. sci. U. Hawaii, Hilo, 1973-75, 84—; profl. assoc. East-West Communications Inst., Honolulu, 1978, East-West Communications Inst. (Resource System Inst.), 1980-81; adviser to AAUW, Hawaii, 1978-79; cons. World Polit. Risk Forecast, Frost & Sullivan, Inc., N.Y.C., 1980-81. Author: The Cultural Revolution in China: An Annotated Bibliography, 1976, Contemporary Chinese Politics: An Introduction, 1980, rev. edit., 1985, 89, 92, 95, Hawaii State and Local Politics, 1982, Study Guide for Power in Hawaii, 1982, Ocean Law and Politics, 1992 (selected One of 1993 Outstanding Acad. Books ALA), Comparative Asian Politics, 1994; contbr. articles to profl. jours. Mem. Hawaii County Bicentennial Com., 1988-89; vice chmn. Dem. Party, County of Hawaii, 1972-76, chmn., 1982-84; mem. Dem. State Ctrl. Com., 1982-84; chmn. univ. adv. com. to Hawaii County Coun.; mem. coordinating com. Hawaii Polit. Studies Assn., 1986—; mem. Hawaii State Campaign Spending Commn., 1990-94, chmn., 1994—. U. Hawaii Rsch. Found. grantee, 1972-78. Mem. Assn. Asian Studies, Internat. Studies Assn., Coun. Ocean Law and the Law of the Sea Inst., Big Island Press Club. Home: PO Box 13 Hilo HI 96721-0013 Office: U Hawaii Dept Polit Sci Hilo HI 96720

WANG, JAW-KAI, agricultural engineering educator; b. Nanjing, Jiangsu, People's Republic of China, Mar. 4, 1932; came to U.S., 1955; s. Shuling and Hsi-Ying (Lo) W.; m. Kwang Mei Chow, Sept. 7, 1957 (div. Oct. 1989); children: Angela C.C., Dora C.C., Lawrence C.Y. BS, Nat. Taiwan U., 1953; MS in Agrl. Engring., Mich. State U., 1956, PhD, 1958. Registered profl. engr., Hawaii. Faculty agrl. engring. dept. U. Hawaii, Honolulu, 1959-93; assoc. prof., chmn. dept. U. Hawaii, 1964-68, prof., 1968—, chmn. dept. agrl. engring., 1968-75, dir. Aquaculture Program, 1990—; prof. biosystems engring. dept. U. Hawaii-Manoa, Honolulu, 1994—; spl. asst., Internat. Rsch. Dept., Office of Internat. Cooperation and Devel. U.S. Dept. Agr., 1988; pres. Aquaculture Tech., Inc., 1990—; co-dir. internat. sci. and ednl. coun. USDA; vis. assoc. dir. internat. programs and studies office Nat. Assn. State Univs. and Land-Grant Colls., 1979; vis. prof. Nat. Taiwan U., 1965, U. Calif., Davis, 1980; cons. U.S. Army Civilian Adminstrn., Ryukus, Okinawa, 1966, Internat. Rice Rsch. Inst., The Philippines, 1971, Pacific Concrete and Rock Co. Ltd., 1974, AID, 1974, Universe Tankships, Del., 1980-81, World Bank, 1981, ABA Internat., 1981-85, Internat. Found. for Agrl. Devel./World Bank, 1981, Rockefeller Found., 1980, Orizaba, Inc., 1983, Agrisys./FAO, 1983, Info. Processing Assocs., 1984, County of Maui, 1984, 85, Dept. of State, 1985, Alexander and Baldwin, 1986; mem. expert panel on agrl. mechanization FAO/UN, 1984-90; sr. fellow East-West Ctr. Food Inst., 1973-74; dir. Info. Sys. and Svcs. Internat., Inc., 1986-90; mem. Am. Soc. Agrl. Author: Irrigated Rice Production Systems, 1980; editor: Taro-A Review of Colocasia Esculenta and its Potentials, 1983; mem. editl. bd. Aquacultural Engring., 1982—. Recipient Exemplary State Employee award State of Hawaii, 1986, State of Hawaii Employee of Yr. award Office of Gov., 1990. Fellow Am. Soc. Agrl. Engrs. (chmn. Hawaii sect. 1962-63, chmn. grad. instrn. com. 1962-63, various coms., Engr. of Yr. 1976, Tech. Paper award 1978, Kishida Internat. award 1991), Am. Inst. Med. and Biol. Engring.; mem. Nat. Acad. Engring., Aquaculture Engring. Soc. (pres. 1993-95), Sigma Xi, Gamma Sigma Delta (pres. Hawaii chpt. 1974-75), Pi Mu Epsilon. Office: U Hawaii Biosystems Engring Dept 3050 Maile Way Honolulu HI 96822-2231 *To be allowed a continuing search for truth even when you are doubting its existence, is to be blessed.*

WANG, JOHN CHENG HWAI, communications engineer; b. Beijing, Feb. 12, 1934; s. Hwa Lung and Shu Shiang (Shia) W.; m. Rosa Jenny Chu, Sept. 9, 1967; children: Sophia, Maria, Nina, Amy. BS, U. Md., 1959; MS, U. Pitts., 1968. Engr. Chesapeake Instrument Corp., Shadyside, Md., 1959-64; rsch. scientist Rsch. Ctr. U.S. Steel Corp., Monroeville, Pa., 1964-67; asst. prof. Pa. State U., New Kensington, 1967-69; rsch. engr. FCC, Washington, 1969—; chmn. working party medium wave propagation Internat. Radio Consultative Com., Geneva, 1983—. Contbr. articles to profl. jours. Fellow IEEE. Avocations: astronomy, bridge, Chinese history. Office: FCC 1919 M St NW Washington DC 20036-3505

WANG, JOSEPHINE L. FEN, physician; b. Taiwan, China, Jan 2, 1948; came to U.S., 1974; d. Pao-San and Ann-Nam (Chen) Chao; m. Chang-Yang Wang, Dec. 20, 1973; children: Edward, Eileen. MD, Nat. Taiwan U., Taipei, 1974. Diplomate Am. Bd. Pediatrics, Am. Bd. Allergy and Immunology. Intern Nat. Taiwan U. Hosp., 1973-74; resident U. Ill. Hosp., Chgo., 1974-76; fellow Northwestern U. Med. Ctr., Chgo., 1976-78, instr. pediatrics, 1978—; cons. Holy Cross Hosp., Chgo., 1978—, Meth. Hosp. Ind., 1979—, St. Anthony Hosp., 1985—, Christ Hosp., 1995—. Fellow Am. Coll. Allergy; mem. AMA, Am. Acad. Allergy. Office: 9012 Connecticut Dr Merrillville IN 46410-7170 also: 4901 W 79th St Burbank IL 60459-1501

WANG, JUI HSIN, biochemistry educator; b. Peking, Republic of China, Mar. 16, 1921; s. Lieh and Sun Li (Sun) W.; m. Yen Chan Yang, Apr. 2, 1949; children: Jane, Nancy. BS, Nat. SW Assoc. U., Kunming, Republic of China, 1945; PhD, Washington U., St. Louis, 1949; MA (hon.), Yale U., 1960. Postdoctoral fellow radiochemistry Washington U., 1949-51; mem. faculty Yale U., New Haven, Conn., 1951—, prof. chemistry, 1960-62, Eugene Higgins prof. chemistry, 1962-65, Eugene Higgins prof. chemistry and molecular biophysics, 1965-72; Einstein prof. sci. SUNY, Buffalo, 1972—; rschr. molecular structure and biochem. activity, superconductivity. Contbr. articles to profl. jours., chapters in books. Guggenheim fellow Cambridge U., 1960-61. Fellow AAAS, Am. Acad. Arts and Scis.; mem. Am. Chem. Soc., Chem. Soc. London, Yale Chemists Assn., Am. Soc. for Biochemistry and Molecular Biology, Am. Phys. Soc., Biophys. Soc., Academia Sinica, Am. Soc. Photobiology, Electrochem. Soc., Materials Rsch. Soc., Sigma Xi. Home: 477 Lebrun Rd Buffalo NY 14226-4218 Office: SUNY Dept Chemistry Buffalo NY 14260-3000

WANG, JULIE CAROLINE, public relations executive; b. Petersfield, Hampshire, Eng., June 17, 1947; came to U.S., 1972; d. Raymond Garnier and Molly Eileen (Travers-Drapes) Dreyer; m. Paul Wang, Jan. 6, 1969 (div. Apr. 1981); children: Timothy, Katharine; m. Bronson Binger, June 26, 1982; 1 child, Walter. BA, McGill U., Montreal, Can., 1967; postgrad., Harvard Bus. Sch., 1994. Journalist Montreal Gazette, 1968-72; asst. dir. Univ. Hosp. Pa., Phila., 1972-74; editor Sci. and Medicine, N.Y.C., 1974-79; v.p. Manning Selvage and Lee, N.Y.C., 1979-82, Burson-Marsteller, N.Y.C., 1982-83; chmn., CEO Wang Assocs., N.Y.C., 1983—; adj. prof. NYU, 1989—. Author: Phobia Free and Flying High, 1979, Everything You Wanted to Know About Phobias but Were Afraid to Ask, 1981. Mem. Nat. Assn. Sci. Writers, Am. Soc. Journalists and Authors, N.Y. Acad. Scis., Heights Casino club. Episcopalian. Avocations: gardening, sailing, tennis, skiing. Home: 142 Dean St Brooklyn NY 11217-2212 Office: Wang Assoc Health Comm 373 Park Ave S New York NY 10016-8805

WANG, KUO-KING, manufacturing engineer, educator. BSME, Nat. Ctrl. U., China, 1947; MSME, U. Wis., 1962, PhD in Mech. Engring., 1968. Sibley prof. mech. engring. Cornell U., Ithaca, N.Y.; founder, dir. Cornell Injection Molding Program, 1974—; cofounder Cornell Mfg. Engring. and Productivity Program, Advanced CAE Tech., Inc. Recipient Disting. Svc. citation U. Wis., 1990. Fellow ASME (Blackall Machine Tool and Gage award 1968, William T. Ennor Mfg. Tech. award 1991), Soc. Mfg. Engrs. (Frederick W. Taylor Rsch. medal 1987); mem. CIRP, ASM Internat., Nat. Acad. Engring., Am. Welding Soc. (Adams Meml. Membership award 1976), Soc. Plastic Engrs., Polymer Processing Soc. Achievements include pioneering research in injection molding, friction welding and applications of solid modeling to CAD/CAM. Office: Cornell Univ Dept Mech/Aero Engring Upson Hall Ithaca NY 14853

WANG, L. EDWIN, church official; b. Medford, Oreg., Nov. 2, 1919; s. Lorang Edwin and Laura (Thomas) W.; m. Astrid H. Wikander, Sept. 4, 1942; children: David M., Linnea M., Judith L. Extension student, U. Calif., 1947-48, U. Minn., 1956-65; LHD, Midland Luth. Coll., 1970. CLU. Field underwriter, then asst. mgr. Mut. of N.Y., 1943-51; mgr. Standard Ins. Co., Oakland, Calif., 1951-56; exec. sec. Augustana Pension & Aid Fund, Mpls., 1956-62; pres. bd. pensions Luth Ch. Am., 1962-87; acting ins. commr., Minn., 1967; part-time ins. instr. Oakland Jr. Coll., Contra Costa Jr. Coll., 1954-56; pres. Oakland-East Bay Life Underwriters Assn., 1951, Oakland Mgrs. and Gen. Agts. Assn., 1955; pres. Ch. Pensions Conf., 1967; mem. pension research council U. Pa. Wharton Sch. Fin., 1971-92. Bd. dirs. Nat. Found. for Philanthropy, 1981—; pres. Lewis and Clark Trail Heritage Found. Inc., 1985-86; pres. Luth. Ch. Libr. Assn. 1988-90, bd. dirs., 1988—. Recipient Outstanding Service award Gov. Minn. Mem. Am. Risk and Ins. Assn., Am. Soc. CLU's (bd. dirs. 1980-84), Mpls. Chpt. CLU's (pres. 1973-74). Home: 6013 St Johns Ave Minneapolis MN 55424-1834

WANG, PAUL WEILY, materials science and physics educator; b. Kao-Hsiung, Taiwan, Republic of China, Nov. 4, 1951; came to U.S., 1979; s. Yao Wen Wang and Yue Hua Lo; m. Diana Chung-Chung Chow, June 9, 1979; children: Agnes J., Carol H., Alfred Z. PhD, SUNY, Albany, 1986. Rsch. asst. prof. Vanderbilt U., Nashville, 1986-90; asst. prof. U. Tex., El Paso, 1990-96, assoc. prof., 1996—; hon. prof. Dalian Inst. Light Industry, 1995—; cons. EOTec Inc., 1987-88, Midtex Comm. Instruments Inc., 1996—. Contbr. articles to Jour. Applied Physics, Nuclear Instru. and Math., Springer Series in Surface Scis., Applied Surface Sci., Applied Optics, Jour. of Am. Ceramic Soc., Jour. Materials Sci., Jour. Luminescence, Jour. Non-cyrs. Solids, Lasers. Fellow Inst. for Study of Defects in Solids; mem. Am. Ceramic Soc., Am. Phys. Soc., Materials Rsch. Soc., Am. Vacuum Soc. Achievements include iron in silicon gettered by thermally grown silicon dioxide thin film, dopants effects on the structure of fluoride glasses, surface modification of heavy metal doped glasses under x-ray and electron irradiations, luminescence centers in silica stimulated by particle bombardments, defects introducted by gamma-ray radiation enhance the luminescence in silica, development of defects creation mechanism in silica by 5 and 50 eV photons, investigation of silver diffuses and precipitates thermally on the surface in ion exchange sodium calcium silicate glass, investigate the radiation effects on lead silicate glasses, electron beam processing on trimethylsilane covered Si(100) surface, aluminum nitride/aluminum oxide composite films grown by plasma, conduct and manage numerous research projects in materials research. Home: 6890 Orizaba Ave El Paso TX 79912-2324 Office: U Tex Dept Physics/Materials Rsch El Paso TX 79968

WANG, SHIH-HO, electrical engineer, educator; b. Kiangsu, China, June 29, 1944; came to U.S., 1968; s. C.C. Wang and Man Shih. BEE, Nat. Taiwan U., Taipei, 1967; MEE, U. Calif., Berkeley, 1970, PhD in Elec. Engring., 1971. Asst. prof. elec. engring. U. Colo., Colo. Springs, 1973-76, Boulder, 1976-77; asst. prof. electrical engring. U. Md., College Park, 1977-78, assoc. prof., 1978-84; prof. U. Calif., Davis, 1984—; cons. Lawrence Livermore (Calif.) Nat. Lab., 1986—; scientific officer Office Naval Research, Arlington, Va., 1983-84. Assoc. editor Internat. Jour. Robotics and Automation, 1986—. Served to 2d lt. China Air Force, Taiwan, 1967-68. Mem. IEEE (hon. mention award control systems soc. 1975). Office: Univ Calif Dept Elec/Computer Engring Davis CA 95616

WANG, STANLEY, electronics executive; b. 1943. MBA, Temple U. Mgr. Philco-Ford, Sunnyvale, Calif., 1964-71; materials mgr., mktg. rep. Intersil Corp., Cupertino, Calif., 1971-73; with Pantronix Corp., San Jose, Calif., 1974—, pres. Office: Pantronix Corp 145 Rio Robles San Jose CA 95134-1807*

WANG, SU SUN, chemical company executive, chemist; b. Taipei, Taiwan, China, Jan. 11, 1934; s. Tuan King and Shane (Lai) W.; m. Beth Song-hwa, Aug. 6, 1964; children: Albert W., Fritz W. BS, Nat. Taiwan U., 1957, MS, 1959; PhD, U. Calif., Berkeley, 1966. Sr. chemist Hoffmann-La Roche Inc., Nutley, N.J., 1970-79; ptnr. Peninsula Labs. Inc., Belmont, Calif., 1979-81; founder, pres. Am. Biochems., San Carlos, Calif., 1981-82; v.p. Alpha 1 Biomeds. Inc., Bethesda, 1982—. invited vis. scholar Ministry Edn., Academia Sinica, Taipei Inst. Biochemistry, 1986. Patentee in field. U.S. Dept. Health and Edn. fellow Rockefeller U., 1968-70. Mem. AAAS, Am. Chem. Soc., Fedn. Am. Socs. for Exptl. Biology, Chinese Biochem. Soc. Republican. Home: 1512 Chula Vista Dr Belmont CA 94002-3614

WANG, TAYLOR GUNJIN, science administrator, astronaut, educator; b. Shanghai, China, June 16, 1940; came to U.S., 1963; m. Beverly Fung, 1966; children: Kenneth, Eric. BS, UCLA, 1967, MS, 1968, PhD, 1971. Mgr. microgravity sci. and applications program Jet Propulsion Lab., Pasadena, Calif., 1972-88, cons., 1987-89; Space Shuttle astronaut-scientist NASA, 1983-85; Centennial prof., dir. Ctr. for Microgravity Rsch. and Applications Vanderbilt U., Nashville, 1988—. Contbr. over 170 articles to profl. jours.; inventor living cellls encapsulation tech. as cure of hormone deficiency states in humans; over 20 patents in field. Bd. dirs. Com. of 100. Fellow Acoustical Soc. Am.; mem. AIAA, Am. Phys. Soc., Assn. Space Explorers-USA (pres. 1988), Sigma Xi. Office: Vanderbilt U Sta B Box 6079 Nashville TN 37235

WANG, VERA, fashion designer; b. 1950; d. Cheng Ching Wang; m. Arthur Becker; children: Cecilia, Josephine. Grad., Sarah Lawrence Coll., New York. Sr. fashion editor Vogue, N.Y.C.; design dir. Ralph Lauren Women's Wear, N.Y.C., 1987-89; prin. Vera Wang Bridal House Ltd., N.Y.C., 1990—. Office: Vera Wang Bridal House 225 W 39th St 10th Fl New York NY 10018*

WANG, WALTER, chemicals executive; b. 1947. Sec. asst. to pres. Formosa Plaztic Group, 1985-90; pres. J M Mfg Co, Livingston, N.J., 1990—. Office: J M Mfg Co 9 Peach Tree Hill Rd Livingston NJ 07039-5702*

WANG, WILLIAM KAI-SHENG, law educator; b. N.Y.C., Feb. 28, 1946; s. Yuan-Chao and Julia Ying-Ru (Li) W.; m. Kwan Kwan Tan, July 29, 1972; 1 child, Karen You-Chuan. B.A., Amherst Coll., 1967; J.D., Yale U., 1971. Bar: Calif. 1972. Asst. to mng. partner Gruss & Co., N.Y.C., 1971-72; asst. prof. law U. San Diego, 1972-74, asso. prof., 1974-77, prof., 1977-81; prof. Hastings Coll. Law, U. Calif., San Francisco, 1981—; vis. prof. law U. Calif., Davis, 1975-76, U. Calif., L.A., 1990; cons. to White House Domestic Policy Staff, Washington, 1979; vis. prof. Hastings Coll. Law, U. Calif., 1980; chair investment policy oversight group Law Sch. Admissions Coun.; mem. com. on audit and assn. investment policy Assn. of Am. Law Schs. Co-author: Inside Trading, 1996; contbr. articles to newspapers, mags., scholarly jours. Mem. State Bar Calif., Am. Law Inst. Home: 455 39th Ave San Francisco CA 94121-1507 Office: U Calif Hastings Coll Law 200 Mcallister St San Francisco CA 94102-4978

WANG, WILLIAM SHI-YUAN, linguistics educator; b. Shanghai, China, Aug. 14, 1933; came to U.S., 1948, naturalized, 1960; s. Harper and Lily W.; children: Eugene, Yulun, Yumei, Yusi. A.B., Columbia U., 1955; M.A., U. Mich., 1956, Ph.D., 1960. Assoc. prof., chmn. dept. linguistics Ohio State U., Columbus, 1963-65; prof. linguistics U. Calif., Berkeley, 1966—, dir. Project on Linguistic Analysis, 1966—; prof. grad. sch., 1994—; fellow Center Advanced Studies in Behavioral Scis., 1969-70, 83-84; sr. Fulbright lectr. in, Sweden, 1972, India, 1979. Author: Explorations in Language, 1991; editor: The Lexicon in Phonological Change, 1977, Human Communication, 1982, Language Writing and the Computer, 1986; co-editor: Individual Differences in Language Ability and Language Behavior, 1979; assoc. editor Language, 1967-73; founding editor Jour. Chinese Linguistics, 1973—; contbr. numerous articles to profl. jours. Guggenheim Found. fellow, 1978-79. Mem. Linguistic Soc. Am., Acoustical Soc. Am., Academia

Sinica, Internat. Assn. Chinese Linguistics (pres. 1992-93). Office: U Calif 2222 Piedmont Ave Berkeley CA 94720 *Because language penetrates so many aspects of life, my attempt to understand its nature has frequently led me into anthropology, biology, etc. These forays into neighboring fields have enhanced my awareness of the unity of knowledge, and of the importance of a broad perspective in any serious intellectual venture.*

WANG, XIN-MIN, molecular biologist; b. Shanghai, China, Oct. 30, 1949; came to U.S., 1986; s. Zheng-An and Wan-Zhu (Sun) W.; m. Su Wang, Feb. 14, 1980; children: Cheng-Xi, Cheng-Hua. BA in Biochemistry, Zhoung Shan U., Guangzhou, 1976; MS in Biochemistry, Beijing Med. U., 1983; MA in Molecular Biology, SUNY, Stony Brook, 1993. Rsch. asst. Beijing Med. U., 1977-79, rsch. assoc., lectr., 1983-86; vis. rsch. assoc. SUNY, Stony Brook, 1986-90; sr. rsch. scientist Sterling Winthrop Inc., Collegeville, Pa., 1991-93; prin. rsch. scientist Sterling Winthrop Inc., Collegevill, Pa., 1993-94; sr. scientist SmithKline Beecham Pharm., King of Prussia, Pa., 1994—. Author: (with others) Experimental Methods in Biochemistry, 1984; contbr. articles to profl. jours. Mem. AAAS. Office: SmithKline Beecham 709 Swedeland Rd King Of Prussia PA 19406

WANG, XINWEI, aeronautics educator; b. Wu County, Jiangsu, China, Feb. 25, 1948; s. Shiheng and Meizhen (Jiang) W.; m. Guoying Zhang, Dec. 2, 1975; children: Xia Ping, Xiongfei. BS, Nanjing Aero. Inst., China, 1975, MS, 1981; PhD, U. Okla., 1989. Farmer Constrn. People's Commune, Jiangsu, 1968-72; asst. prof. Nanjing Aero. Inst., 1976-78, lectr., 1981-84; vis. scholar UCLA, 1984-85; vis. rsch. prof. U. Okla., 1985-86, vis. asst. prof., 1989-92; prof. Nanjing U. Aeronautics and Astronautics, 1992—, dir. structural mechanics and strenght divsn., 1994—; vis. prof. UMBC, 1995-96. Mem. ASME (assoc.), Am. Acad. Mechanics, Chinese Soc. Theoretical and Applied Mechanics (Jiangsu br. dir.), Chinese Soc. Aeronautics, Chinese Soc. Vibration Engring. Avocations: traveling, American football, basketball, football, reading. Office: NUAA Dept Aircraft Engring, Dept Mech Engring Indsl Section, Nanjing 210016, China

WANG, ZENG-YU, neurologist, immunologist; b. Dongan Hunan, China, July 27, 1962; came to U.S., 1993; s. Xian-Zhun and Yue (Lu) W.; m. Jianhua, Oct. 1, 1989; 1 child, Rachel. MB, Hunan (China) Med. U., 1984, M of Medicine in Neurology, 1987; PhD, Karolinska Inst., Stockholm, Sweden, 1993. Resident Hunan Med. U., 1987-90; rsch. asst. Karolinski Inst., Stockholm, 1990-93; postdoctoral assoc. U. Minn., St. Paul, 1993-96; rsch. assoc. U Minn., 1996—. Contbr. articles to profl. jours. Recipient Rsch. fellowship Karolinska Inst., 1991, Rsch. fellowship Swedish NHR-fonden, 1992, Rsch. fellowship Muscular Dystrophy Assn., 1994. Mem. AAAS, N.Y. Acad Scis. Avocations: fishing, badminton, classical music. Achievements include induction of oral tolerance to experimental myaschenia gravis. Home: 1619 Carl St # 15 Saint Paul MN 55108 Office: Univ Minn Dept Biochemistry 1479 Gortner Ave Saint Paul MN 55108

WANGER, OLIVER WINSTON, federal judge; b. L.A., Nov. 27, 1940; m. Lorrie A. Reinhart; children: Guy A., Christopher L., Andrew G., W. Derek, Oliver Winston II. Student, Colo. Sch. Mines, 1958-60; BS, U. So. Calif., 1963; LLB, U. Calif., Berkeley, 1966. Bar: Calif. 1967, U.S. Dist. Ct. (ea. dist.) Calif. 1969, U.S. Tax Ct. 1969, U.S. Dist. Ct. (cen. dist.) Calif. 1975, U.S. Dist. Ct. (so. dist.) Calif. 1977, U.S. Dist. Ct. (no. dist.) Calif. 1989, U.S. Ct. Appeals (9th cir.) 1989. Dep. dist. atty. Fresno (Calif.) County Dist. Atty., 1967-69; ptnr. Gallagher, Baker & Manock, Fresno, 1969-74; sr. ptnr. McCormick, Barstow, Sheppard, Wayte & Carruth, Fresno, 1974-91; judge U.S. Dist. Ct. (ea. dist.) Calif., Fresno, 1991—; adj. prof. law Humphreys Coll. Law, Fresno, 1968-70. Fellow Am. Coll. Trial Lawyers, Internat. Acad. Trial Lawyers; mem. Am. Bd. Trial Advs. (pres. San Joaquin Valley chpt. 1987-89, nat. bd. dirs. 1989-91), Am. Bd. Profl. Liability Attys. (founder, diplomate), Calif. State Bar (mem. exec. com. litigation sect. 1989-92, mem. com. on fed. cts. 1989-90), San Joaquin Valley Am. Inn of Ct. (pres. 1992-93), Beta Gamma Sigma. Office: US Dist Ct 5104 US Courthouse 1130 O St Fresno CA 93721-2201

WANGLER, WILLIAM CLARENCE, retired insurance company executive; b. Buffalo, Dec. 7, 1929; s. Emil A. and Viola M. (Roesser) W.; m. Carol B. Sullivan, Aug. 17, 1957; children: Jeffrey W., Eric J. BS, SUNY, Cortland, 1951. Claims adjuster Liberty Mut. Ins. Co., Buffalo, 1954-60; claims supr. Liberty Mut. Ins. Co., Miami, Fla., 1960-65; home office examiner Liberty Mut. Ins. Co., Boston, 1965-68; asst. claims mgr. Liberty Mut. Ins. Co., Cleve., 1968-69; claims mgr. Liberty Mut. Ins. Co., Cleve, 1969-73; div. claims service mgr. Liberty Mut. Ins. Co., Pitts., 1973-79, div. claims mgr., 1979-86; v.p. asst. gen. claims mgr. adminstrn. Liberty Mut. Ins. Co., Boston, 1986-94; ret., 1994; pres. Claims Mgrs. Counsel, Cleve., 1970; chmn. Nationwide Intercompany Arbitration, Cleve., 1969-70. Loaned exec. Mass. Bay United Way, Boston, 1964; account exec. Pitts. United Way, 1985-86. Served to capt. USMC, 1951-54. Republican. Roman Catholic. Home: 64 Trout Farm Ln Duxbury MA 02332-4609

WANK, GERALD SIDNEY, periodontist; b. Bklyn., Jan. 20, 1925; s. Joseph and Sadie (Ikowitz) W.; m. Gloria Baum, June 4, 1949; children: David, Stephen, Daniel. B.A., NYU, 1945, D.D.S., 1949; cert. in orthodontia, Columbia U., 1951, cert. in periodontia, 1956. Intern in oral surgery Bellevue Hosp., 1949-50; practice dentistry specializing in oral rehab. and periodontal prosthetics N.Y.C., Great Neck, N.Y., 1949—; instr. dept. periodontia, oral medicine NYU Dental Sch., 1956-63, asst. clin. prof. dept. periodontia, 1963-67, asst. prof. periodontia, oral medicine, former postgrad. dir. periodontal-prosthesis dept. fixed partial prosthesis, 1970—, clin. assoc. prof. periodontia and oral medicine, 1970-77, clin. prof., 1977—, postgrad. dir. periodontia, 1968-71; staff lectr. periodontology Harvard U. Sch. Dental Medicine, 1973-74; vis. lectr. Albert Einstein Coll. Medicine, N.Y.C. Community Coll. Sch. Dental Hygiene; sr. asst. attending staff North Shore Univ. Hosp., 1974-77, sr. asst. attending div. surgery, 1977—; cons. orthodontic panel N.Y. State, N.Y.C. depts. health; cons. periodontal prosthesis, Goldwater Meml. Hosp., N.Y.C.; former postgrad. instr. 1st Dist. Dental Soc. Postgrad. Sch.; lectr. various socs. N.Y. U.; mem. com. admissions N.Y. U. Coll. Dentistry, 1975—, chmn. fund raising, 1976—. Contbr. to: Practice of Periodontia, 1960, Dental Clinics of North America, 1972, 81, Manual of Clinical Periodontics, 1973; contbr. articles to profl. jours. Served to capt. USAF, 1953-55. Recipient Alumni Meritorious Service award N.Y. U., 1981, Coll. Dentistry Alumni Achievement award N.Y. U., 1983. Fellow Acad. Gen. Dentistry, N.Y. Acad. Dentistry, Internat. Coll. Dentists, Am. Coll. Dentists, Am. Acad. Oral Medicine (pres. N.Y. sect. 1971-72), Am. Pub. Health Assn.; mem. N.Y. Coll. Dentists (dir.), ADA, Dental Soc. N.Y.C. (dir. 1st dist., chmn. ethics com. 1985-86), Fedn. Dentaire Internat., Am. Assn. Dental Schs., N.Y. State Pub. Health Assn., AAUP, Pan Am. Med. Assn. (life), AAAS, ADA, Am. Acad. Periodontology, Sci. Rsch. Soc. Am., Northeastern Soc. Periodontia, Am. Acad. Dental Medicine, Acad. Gen. Dentistry, Internat. Acad. Orthodontia, Am. Acad. Endodontia (life), Am. Acad. Periodontia (life), Am. Acad. Oral Medicine (life), NYU Coll. Dentistry Alumni Assn. (dir., sec. 1973-74, v.p. 1974-75, pres. 1976-77), Am. Soc. Anesthesiology, Am. Assn. Endodontists, NYU Coll. Dentistry Dental Assocs. (charter), Acad. Oral Rehab. (hon.), First Dist. Dental Soc. (program chmn. 1984, chmn. continuing edn. 1983, sec., 1985, v.p. Eastern Dental Soc. br. 1986, pres.-elect 1987, pres. br. 1988, bd. dirs.), First Dist. Dental Soc. (bd. dirs. 1989—), Am. Acad. Osseointegration, NYU Gallatin Assos., Alumni Fedn. N.Y. U. (dir. 1976-81), Omicron Kappa Upsilon, Alpha Omega. Jewish. Clubs: Fresh Meadow Country (Great Neck, N.Y.); N.Y. U. (charter N.Y. U. Coll. Dentistry), Century (charter N.Y. U. Coll. Dentistry); Masons. Home and Office: 40 Bayview Ave Great Neck NY 11021-2819 Office: 310 Madison Ave New York NY 10017-6009

WANKAT, PHILLIP CHARLES, chemical engineering educator; b. Oak Park, Ill., July 11, 1944; s. Charles and Grace Leona (Pryor) W.; m. Dorothy Nel Richardson, Dec. 13, 1980; children: Charles, Jennifer. BS in Chem. Engring., Purdue U., 1966, MS in Edn., 1982; PhD, Princeton U., 1970. From asst. prof. to prof. chem. engring. Purdue U., West Lafayette, Ind., 1970—, head freshman engring., 1987-95, interim dir. continuing engring. edn., 1996—; cons. pharm. firm, 1985-94. Author: Large Scale Ads and Chromatog, 1986, Equil Staged Separations, 1988, Rate Controlled Separations, 1990, Teaching Engineering, 1993; patentee in field. With AUS, 1962-64. Recipient award in Separations Sci. and Tech., Am. Chem. Soc., 1994. Mem. AIChE, Am. Soc. Engring. Edn., Am. Chem. Soc. Avocations: fishing, canoeing, camping. Office: Purdue U Dept Chemical Engring West Lafayette IN 47907-1283

WANKE, RONALD LEE, lawyer; b. Chgo., June 22, 1941; s. William F. and Lucille (Kleinwachter) W.; m. Rose Klonowski, Oct. 23, 1987. BSEE, Northwestern U., 1964; JD, DePaul U., 1968. Bar: Ill. 1968. Assoc. Wood, Dalton, Phillips, Mason & Rowe, Chgo., 1968-71, ptnr., 1971-84; ptnr. Jenner & Block, Chgo., 1984—; lectr. John Marshall Law Sch., Chgo., 1985-94. Contbr. articles to Software Law Jour., 1987, Internat. Legal Strategy, 1995. Mem. ABA, Chgo. Bar Assn. (lectr. 1985-87, chmn. computer law com. 1987-88), Computer Law Assn., Intellectual Property Law Assn. Chgo. (chmn. inventor svcs. com. 1976, chmn. fed. rules com. 1981). Home: 1806 N Sedgwick St Chicago IL 60614-5306 Office: Jenner & Block 1 E IBM Plz Chicago IL 60611-3608

WANKEL, ROBERT EDMOND, financial executive; b. Bklyn., Dec. 5, 1946; s. Ellery E. and Rose J. (Falco) W.; m. Helen Pfeiffer, Aug. 2, 1969; 1 child, Virginia. BBA, St. John's U., Jamaica, N.Y., 1968. CPA, N.Y. Acct. Laventhol & Horwath, N.Y.C., 1968-75; contr., v.p. fin. The Shubert Orgn., Inc., N.Y.C., 1975—, sr. v.p., CFO. Office: The Shubert Orgn Inc 234 W 44th St New York NY 10036-3909

WANN, LAYMOND DOYLE, petroleum research scientist; b. Magazine, Ark., Apr. 25, 1924; s. Vernon Cecil and Emma (McCrary) W.; B.S. in Physics (Phi Eta Sigma scholar), Okla. State U., 1949, M.S., 1950; m. Betty Lou Brown, Nov. 6, 1948; children: Jacqueline, Lyndall Doyle. With Conoco Inc., Ponca City, Okla., 1951—, sr. research scientist, 1957-60, research group leader, 1960-81, assoc. research dir., 1981-84, staff scientist, 1984-85, ret., 1985; cons. in disciplines of phys. . Mem. Mcpl. Airport Bd., Ponca City. Served with AUS, 1942-46; ETO. Decorated Bronze Star. Mem. Am. Petroleum Inst. chmn. well logging subcom.), IEEE, Aircraft Owners and Pilots Assn., Seaplane Pilots Assn., VFW, Am. Legion, Phi Kappa Phi, Pi Mu Epsilon, Sigma Pi Sigma. Republican. Episcopalian (vestryman). Contbr. articles on elec. and radioactive well-logging, elec. design to profl. jours. Patentee in field. Home: 1501 Monument Rd Ponca City OK 74604-3522 Office: 1000 S Pine St Ponca City OK 74601-7509

WANNER, ERIC, foundation executive, researcher, writer, editor; b. Wilmington, Del., Mar. 14, 1942; s. Edwin and Isabel Smith (Speakman) W.; m. Patricia Attix, June 13, 1964 (div. 1976); children: Noel Edwin, Erin Cole; m. Carla Francesca Seal, June 18, 1983; children: Lindzay Elizabeth. BA, Amherst Coll., 1963; PhD, Harvard U., 1969. Asst. to assoc. prof. Harvard U., Cambridge, Mass., 1968-76; behavioral sci. editor Harvard U. Press, Cambridge, Mass., 1976-82; program officer Alfred P. Sloan Found., N.Y.C., 1982-84, v.p., 1984-86; pres. Russell Sage Found., N.Y.C., 1986—; mem. adv. bd. Malcolm Weiner Ctr. for Social Policy, Harvard U., 1988—; trustee Ctr. for Advanced Study in Behavioral Scis., 1993—; bd. dirs. Life Trends Inc. Author: Remembering, Forgetting and Understanding Sentences, 1974; editor: Language Acquisition: the State of the Art, 1982; contbr. articles to profl. jours. Fulbright fellow Sussex U., Brighton, Eng., 1979, fellow N.Y. Inst. for Humanities, NYU, 1985-93, Am. Acad. Arts and Scis., 1994—. Mem. APA, Cognitive Sci. Soc., N.Y. Acad. Scis., Century Club, Sigma Xi. Office: Russell Sage Found 112 E 64th St New York NY 10021-7307

WANNSTEDT, DAVID RAYMOND, professional football team coach; b. Pitts., May 21, 1952; m. Jan Wannstedt; children: Keri, Jami. Student, U. Pitts. Player Green Bay Packers, 1974; asst. coach U. Pitts., 1975-79, Okla. State U., 1979-82, U. So. Calif., 1983-85; def. coord. U. Miami, 1986-89, Dallas Cowboys, 1989-93; head coach Chgo. Bears, 1993—. Named to NCAA 2nd team All-East; inducted into Western Pa. Hall of Fame, 1990. Office: Chgo Bears Halas Hall 250 N Washington Rd Lake Forest IL 60045-2471*

WAN-TATAH, VICTOR FON, theology educator; b. Kumbo, Bui, Cameroon, Nov. 28, 1949; came to U.S., 1977; s. Samuel and Miriam (Ngaibe) Tatah; m. Margaret Kernyui Wirsiy, Sept. 15, 1973; children: Nathan, Wuyuni, Simuben. MTS, Harvard U., 1979, ThD, 1984. Assoc. prof. Youngstown (Ohio) State U., 1987-92, 1992—. founder, coord. Concerned Citizens for Safer Youngstown, 1991. Mem. Phi Kappa Phi. Presbyterian. Avocations: jogging, table tennis, gardening. Office: Youngstown State U Dept Philosophy 410 Wick Ave Youngstown OH 44555-0001

WANTLAND, WILLIAM CHARLES, bishop, lawyer; b. Edmond, Okla., Apr. 14, 1934; s. William Lindsay and Edna Louise (Yost) W. BA, U. Hawaii, 1957; JD, Okla. City U., 1967; D in Religion, Geneva Theol. Coll., Knoxville, Tenn., 1976; DD (hon.), Nashotah House, Wis., 1983, Seabury-Western Sem., Evanston, Ill., 1983. With FBI, various locations, 1954-59, Ins. Co. of N.Am., Oklahoma City, 1960-62; law clk.-atty. Bishop & Wantland, Seminole, Okla., 1962-77; vicar St. Mark's Ch., Seminole, 1963-77, St. Paul's Ch., Holdenville, Okla., 1974-77; presiding judge Seminole Mcpl. Ct., 1970-77; atty. gen. Seminole Nation of Okla., 1969-72, 75-77; exec. dir. Okla. Indian Rights Assn., Norman, 1972-73; rector St. John's Ch., Oklahoma City, 1977-80; bishop Episcopal Diocese of Eau Claire, Wis., 1980—; interim bishop of Navajoland, 1993-94; adj. prof. Law Sch. U. Okla., Norman, 1970-78; instr. canon law Nashotah House, 1983—; mem. nat. coun. Evang. & Cath. Mission, Chgo., 1977-90; co-chmn. Luth.-Anglican Roman Cath. Commn. of Wis., 1987-95; mem. Episcopal Commn. on Racism, 1990-92, Episcopal Coun. Indian Ministries, 1990-95, Standing Commn. on Constitution and Canons, 1992-95. Author: Foundations of the Faith, 1982, Canon Law of the Episcopal Church, 1984, The Prayer Book and the Catholic Faith, 1994; co-author: Oklahoma Probate Forms, 1971; contbr. articles to profl. jours. Pres. Okla. Conf. Mcpl. Judges, 1973; v.p. South African Ch. Union, 1985-95; trustee Nashotah House, Wis., 1981—, chmn., 1992—; bd. dirs. SPEAK, Eureka Springs, Ark., 1983-89; mem. Wis. adv. com. U.S. Civil Rights Commn., 1990-91; mem. support com. Native Am. Rights Fund, 1990—; co-chmn. Luth.-Anglican-Roman Cath. Commn. of Wis., 1989-95; pres. Wis. Episc. Conf., 1995—. Recipient Most Outstanding Contbn. to Law and Order award Okla. Supreme Ct., 1975, Outstanding Alumnus award Okla. City U., 1980, Wis. Equal Rights Coun. award, 1986, Manitou Ikwe award Indian Alcoholism Coun., 1988, Episcopal Synod Pres.'s award, 1995. Mem. Okla. Bar Assn., Okla. Indian Bar Assn., Living Ch. Found., Oklahoma City Law Sch. Alumni Assn. (pres. 1968), Wis. Conf. Chs. (pres. 1985-86), Wis. Episcopal Conf. (pres. 1995—). Democrat. Avocations: canoeing, skin-diving, cross-country skiing. Home: 145 Marston Ave Eau Claire WI 54701-3911 Office: Diocese of Eau Claire 510 S Farwell St Eau Claire WI 54701-3723 *If we truly believe that God reigns, we will so order our lives that such a belief is clearly reflected in all that we do and say; further, such a belief will shape our relations, not only with all other people, but all of God's created order.*

WAPIENNIK, CARL FRANCIS, manufacturing firm executive, planetarium and science institute executive; b. Donora, Pa., Oct. 10, 1926; s. Karl and Rose (Kidzinski) W.; m. Elva Louise Bartron, Nov. 27, 1953; children: Carl Eric, Ellen Louise. B.S., U. Pitts., 1953. Prodn. supr. RCA, Canonsburg, Pa., 1953-54; staff physicist Buhl Planetarium and Inst. Popular Sci., Pitts., 1954-64; exec. dir. Buhl Planetarium and Inst. Popular Sci., 1964-82; owner, operator Work-o-Art Miniatures (small mfg. firm), 1983—. Mem. Rostraver Twp. Planning Commn., 1965-67; mem. adv. bd. Allegheny C. of C. (formerly North Side Pitts. C. of C.), 1966-67, dir., 1968-73, pres., 1970; mem. adv. coun. Salvation Army, 1978-82; bd. dirs. Bapt. Homes, Pitts., 1982-94; chmn. Rostraver Twp. Mcpl. Water Authority, 1990-94. With USNR, 1945-46. Recipient Man of Yr. award in sci. Pitts. Jaycees, 1969. Mem. Service Core Ret. Execs., Pitts. Bapt. Assn. (bd. dirs. 1976-82), Phi Beta Kappa, Sigma Pi Sigma. Patentee means for controlling liquid flow. Home: Salem Church Rd RR 4 Box 227 Belle Vernon PA 15012-9457 Office: Work-o-Art Miniatures RR 4 Box 227 Belle Vernon PA 15012-9457

WAPNER, SEYMOUR, psychologist, educator, administrator; b. Bklyn., Nov. 20, 1917; s. Hyman and Rose S. (Liese) W.; m. Lorraine E. Gallant, June 4, 1946; children: Jeffrey Gallant, Amy Beth. A.B., NYU, 1939; A.M., U. Mich., 1940, Ph.D., 1943. Instr., dir. U. Rochester Office Com. Selection and Tng. Aircraft Pilots, NRC, N.Y., 1943-46, 45-46; asst. prof. Bklyn. Coll., 1946-48, acting chmn. psychology dept., 1947-48; assoc. prof. dept. psychology Clark U., Worcester, Mass., 1948-56, prof., 1956-63, chmn. dept., 1960-86, G. Stanley Hall prof. genetic psychology, 1963-88; prof. emeritus Clark U., 1988—; chmn. exec. com. H. Werner Inst. Devel. Analysis, 1957—; mem. exec. bd. Council Grad. Depts. of Psychology, 1981-84; mem. U.S. Nat. Com. for Man and the Biosphere Directorate, 1975-86. Author: (with H.A. Watkin, et al), Personality Throuth Perception, 1954, (with H. Werner) Perceptual Development, 1957; editor: The Body Percept, 1965, (with W.A. Koelsch) Freud In Our Time, 1988, (with S.B. Cohen, B. Kaplan) Experiencing the Environment, 1976, (with B. Kaplan) Toward a Holistic Developmental Psychology, 1983, Perspectives in Psychological Theory, 1960, (with M. Bertini and L. Pizzamiglio) Field Dependence in Psychological Theory, Research and Application, 1986, (with L. Cirillo) Value Presuppositions in Theories of Human Development, 1986, (with L. Cirillo and B. Kaplan) Emotions in Ideal Human Development, 1989, (with J. Demick) Field Dependence-Independence, 1991, (with T. Yamamoto) Developmental Psychology of Life Transitions, 1992, Relations Between Psychology and Allied Fields, 1995. Fellow APA, AAAS; mem. AAUP, Soc. Rsch. in Child Devel., Eastern Psychol. Assn. (dir. 1968-70, 71-74, 85-88, 93—, pres. 1979-80), New Eng. Psychol. Assn. (pres. 1979-80), Mass. Psychol. Assn., Phi Beta Kappa, Sigma Xi. Office: Clark U Werner Inst for Devel Analysis 950 Main St Worcester MA 01610-1400

WAPPNER, REBECCA SUE, pediatrics educator; b. Mansfield, Ohio, Feb. 25, 1944; d. William Henry and Helen Elizabeth (Gilmore) W. BS in Zoology, Ohio U., 1966; MD, Ohio State U., 1970. Cert. Am. Bd. Pediatrics, clin. and clin. biochem. Am. Bd. Med. Genetics. Intern in pediatrics The Children's Hosp., Ohio State U., Columbus, 1970-71, resident in pediatrics, 1971-72, asst. chief resident, 1972-73; fellow in pediatric metabolism and genetics Ind. U. Sch. Medicine, Indpls., 1973-75, asst. prof. dept. pediatrics, 1975-78, assoc. prof. dept. pediatrics, 1978-92, prof. dept. med. & molecular genetics, 1993—, prof. med. and molecular genetics, 1993—. Mem. Am. Acad. Pediatrics, Am. Soc. for Human Genetics, Soc. for Inherited Metabolic Disease, Soc. for the Study of Inborn Errors of Metabolism, Soroptimist Internat., Mortar Bd., Iota Sigma Pi, Sigma Xi, Phi Beta Kappa. Office: Riley Hosp 702 Barnhill Dr Rm 0907 Indianapolis IN 46202-5225

WARAN, DAVID ANTHONY, naval officer; b. Chgo., July 18, 1957; s. Adam Joseph and Lorraine Marie (Chess) W. BS, U. So. Calif., 1979; MS, Salve Regina Coll., Newport, R.I., 1991; MA, U.S. Naval War Coll., Newport, 1991. Commd. ensign USN, 1979, advanced through grades to cmdr., 1994; officer aviation arm div. VS33, San Diego, 1982-86; asst. ops. officer VS35, San Diego, 1986-87; model mgr. USN and Lockheed Corp., San Diego, 1987-89; instr. pilot VS41, San Diego, 1987-89; safety and adminstrv. ops. officer VS37, San Diego, 1990-92; dir. Auto Submarine Warfare Ops. Center, San Diego, 1993—. Mem. Inst. Indsl. Engrs., Tailhook Assn., U. So. Calif. Alumni Assn., U.S. Naval Inst., Classic TBird Club Internat., Inland Empire Classic TBird Club. Republican. Roman Catholic. Avocations: stained glass, woodworking, collecting coins, German steins and Royal Doulton. Home: 4171 Mars Way La Mesa CA 91941-7249

WARBURTON, RALPH JOSEPH, architect, engineer, planner, educator; b. Kansas City, Mo., Sept. 5, 1935; s. Ralph Gray and Emma Frieda (Niemann) W.; m. Carol Ruth Hychka, June 14, 1958; children: John Geoffrey, Joy Frances, W. Tracey. B.Arch., MIT, 1958; M.Arch., Yale U., 1959, M.C.P., 1960. registered architect, Colo., Conn., Fla., Ill., La., N.J., Md., N.Y., Va., D.C.; registered profl. engr., Fla., N.J., N.Y.; registered cmty. planner, Mich., N.J. With various archtl. planning and engring. firms Kansas City, Mo., 1952-55, Boston, 1956-58, N.Y.C., 1959-62, Chgo., 1962-64; chief planning Skidmore, Owings & Merrill, Chgo., 1964-66; spl. asst. for urban design HUD, Washington, 1966-72, cons., 1972-77; prof. architecture, archtl. engring. and planning U. Miami, Coral Gables, Fla., 1972—, chmn. dept. architecture, archtl. engring. and planning, 1972-75, assoc. dean engring. and environ. design, 1973-74; dir. grad. urban and regional planning program, 1973-75, 81,, 87-93; advisor govt. Iran, 1970; advisor govt. France, 1973, govt. Ecuador, 1974, govt. Saudi Arabia, 1985; cons. in field, 1972—, lectr., critic design juror in field, 1965—; mem./chmn. Coral Gables Bd. Archs., 1980-82. Assoc. author: Man-Made America: Chaos or Control, 1963; editor: New Concepts in Urban Transportation, 1968, Housing Systems Proposals for Operation Breakthrough, 1970, Focus on Furniture, 1971, National Community Art Competition, 1971, Defining Critical Environmental Areas, 1974; contbg. editor: Progressive Architecture, 1974-84; editl. adv. bd.: Jour. Am. Planning Assn., 1983-88, Planning for Higher Edn., 1986-94, Urban Design and Preservation Quar., 1987—; contbr. numerous articles to profl. jours.; mem. adv. panel Industrialization Forum Quar., 1969-79, archtl. portfolio jury Am. Sch. and Univ., 1993. Mem. Met. Housing and Planning Coun., Chgo., 1965-67; mem. exec. com. Yale U. Arts Assn., 1965-70; pres. Yale U. Planning Alumni Assn., 1983—; mem. ednl. adv. com. Fla. Bd. Architecture, 1975; mem. frievance com. The Fla. Bar., 1996—. Recipient W.E. Parsons medal Yale U., 1960; recipient Spl. Achievement award HUD, 1972, commendation Fla. Bd. Architecture, 1974, Fla. Trust Historic Preservation award, 1983, Group Achievement award NASA, 1976; Skidmore, Owings & Merrill traveling fellow MIT, 1958; vis. fellow Inst. Architecture and Urban Studies, N.Y.C., 1972-74; NSF grantee, 1980-82. Fellow AIA (nat. housing com. 1968-72, nat. regional devel. and natural resources com. 1974-75, nat. systems devel. com. 1972-73, nat. urban design com. 1968-73, bd. dirs. Fla. S. chpt. 1974-75), ASCE, Nat. Acad. Forensic Engrs., Fla. Engring. Soc.; mem. Am. Inst. Cert. Planners (exec. com. dept. environ. planning 1973-74), Am. Soc. Engring. Edn. (chmn. archtl. engring. divsn. 1975-76), Nat. Soc. Archtl. Engrs. (founding profl.), Nat. Soc. Profl. Engrs., NAt. Sculpture Soc. (allied profl. mem.), Nat. Trust Hist. Preservation (principles and guidelines com. 1967), Am. Soc. Landscape Architects (hon., chmn. design awards jury 1971, 72), Am. Planning Assn. (Fla. chpt. award excellence 1983), Am. Soc. Interior Designers (hon.), Urban Land Inst., Omicron Delta Kappa, Sigma Xi, Tau Beta Pi. Home: 6910 Veronese St Coral Gables FL 33146-3846 Office: 420 S Dixie Hwy Coral Gables FL 33146-2222 also: U Miami Sch Architecture Coral Gables FL 33124-5010 *My contribution to society is made through comprehensive determination, design and development activity leading to habitats most suited to the optimum continuing progress of mankind.*

WARCH, RICHARD, academic administrator; b. Hackensack, N.J., Aug. 4, 1939; s. George William and Helen Anna (Hansen) W.; m. Margot Lynn Moses, Sept. 8, 1962; children: Stephen Knud, David Preston, Karin Joy. B.A., Williams Coll., 1961; B.D., Yale Div. Sch., 1964; Ph.D., Yale U., 1969; postgrad., U. Edinburgh, 1962-63; H.H.D., Ripon Coll., 1980. Asst. prof. history and Am. studies Yale U., 1968-73, asso. prof., 1973-77; assoc. dean Yale Coll.; dir. summer plans Yale U., 1976-77; asso. dir. Nat. Humanities Inst., New Haven, 1975-76; v.p. acad. affairs Lawrence U., Appleton, Wis., 1977-79; pres. Lawrence U., 1979—; cons. Nat. Humanities Faculty; ordained to ministry United Presbyn. Ch. in U.S.A., 1968; dir. Bank One of Appleton. Author: School of the Prophets, Yale College, 1701-1740, 1973; editor: John Brown, 1973. Rockefeller Bros. Theol. fellow, 1961-62. Mem. Am. Studies Assn., Soc. for Values in Higher Edn., Winnebago Presbytery. Club: Rotary. Home: 229 N Park Ave Appleton WI 54911-5414 Office: Lawrence U PO Box 599 Appleton WI 54912-0599

WARD, ALAN S., lawyer; b. Wilmington, Del., Jan. 1, 1931; s. Gilbert Hughes and Sarah Anna (Sparks) W.; m. Mariette S. Schneider, Apr. 4, 1959; children: Kathryn Ann Ward Koch, Guy Gilbert, Carolyn Alice. AB, Wesleyan U., 1952; JD, U. Chgo., 1955. Bar: Del. 1955, U.S. Supreme Ct. 1959, N.Y. 1962, D.C. 1964. Law clk. to judge U.S. Dist. Ct., Wilmington, 1955-56; trial atty. Antitrust div. Dept. Justice, Washington, 1956-61, asst. chief spl. litigation sect., 1960-61; assoc. Breed, Abbott & Morgan, N.Y.C., 1961-63; ptnr. Hollabaugh & Jacobs, Washington, 1963-70; dir. Bur. Competition, FTC, Washington, 1970-73; ptnr. Baker & Hostetler, Washington, 1973—, mem. mng. com., 1977-87; lectr. law George Washington U., 1967-70; lectr. profl. assns. Mem. bd. trustees Wesleyan U., 1986-89. Mem. ABA (chmn. antitrust com. litigation sect. 1986-87), Assn. of Bar of City of N.Y., Bar Assn. D.C., Del. Bar Assn., Wesleyan U. Alumni Assn. (chmn. 1983-86), U. Washington Club, Union Club (N.Y.C.), Union Club (Cleve.), Columbia County Club (Chevy Chase, Md.), Farmington Country Club (Charlottesville, Va.). Republican. Methodist. Avocations: squash, golf, tennis, sailing. Home: 5804 Cedar Pky Chevy Chase MD 20815-4252 Office: Baker & Hostetler 1050 Connecticut Ave NW Washington DC 20036-5303

WARD, ALICE FAYE, elementary education educator; b. Swartz, La.. BS, Grambling (La.) U., 1973; postgrad., N.E. U., 1976-79. Tchr. Robinson Elem. Sch., Monroe, 1971-73, Poinciana Elem. Sch., Boynton Beach, Fla., 1973-76, Melaleuca Elem. Sch., West Palm Beach, Fla.; tchr., dir. after sch.

program Melaleuca Elem. Sch., West Palm Beach. Dir. Just Say No Club, 1994-95, K-Kid Club, 1994-95, After Sch. Program, 1994. Named Tchr. of Week Palm Beach Post Newspaper, 1994. Mem. NEA, CTA. Democrat. Baptist. Avocations: reading, bowling, traveling, dancing, helping under privileged children. Office: Melaleuca Elem Sch 5759 W Gun Club Rd West Palm Beach FL 33415-2505

WARD, ANTHONY JOHN, lawyer; b. L.A., Sept. 25, 1931; s. John P. and Helen C. (Harris) W.; A.B., U. So. Calif., 1953; LL.B., U. Calif. at Berkeley, 1956; m. Marianne Edle von Graeve, Feb. 20, 1960 (div. 1977); 1 son, Mark Joachim; m. 2d, Julia Norby Credell, Nov. 4, 1978. Admitted to Calif. bar, 1957; asso. firm Ives, Kirwan & Dibble, Los Angeles, 1958-61; partner firm Marapese and Ward, Hawthorne, Calif., 1961-69; individual practice law, Torrance, Calif., 1969-76; partner firm Ward, Gaunt & Raskin, 1976—. Served to 1st lt. USAF, 1956-58. Mem. ABA, Blue Key, Calif. Trial Lawyers Assn., Lambda Chi Alpha. Democrat. Home: 4477 Wilshire Blvd Apt 209 Los Angeles CA 90010-3727 Office: Pavilion A 21525 Hawthorne Blvd Torrance CA 90503-6605

WARD, BETHEA, artist, small business owner; b. Montgomery, Ala., July 6, 1924; d. Charles E. and Lucy (Walter) W. BFA, Syracuse U., 1946; postgrad., Trinity U., San Antonio, 1965, 66, 68, San Antonio Art Inst., 1967, Houston Mus. Fine Arts Sch., 1973-75. Interior designer Davison-Paxon, Atlanta, 1946-47; assoc. prof. interior design U. Tex., Austin, 1947-51; interior designer Heminways-Bundrick, Shreveport, La., 1951-55; draftsman, supr. Ark. Fuel subs. Cities Service Co., Shreveport, 1955-60, Cities Svc. Co. Midland, San Antonio, 1961-82; visual artist, owner Tex. Notables Studio-Gallerie, Houston, 1983—. Juried shows include (watercolor paintings) Midland (Tex.) Art Fest. (2d place award, 1962), 35th Ann. Local Artist Exhbn., San Antonio (Wofford award 1965), Wichita, Kas. Centennial Nat. Exhbn. (inclusion award 1970), Cen. Tex. Hist. on Canvas Exhbn. (1st place award TFAA 1972), Laguna Gloria, Austin; group exhibits include U. Houston, 1986; contbr. ink drawing to Southwestern Hist. Quarterly, 1977; commns. include drawing for Moody Found. of Galveston; one person shows include Star of the Republic Mus., Houston Pub. Libr., Harris County Heritage Soc., San Antonio Pub. Libr. Recipient Award of Distinction Juried Art Fair, Houston Internat. Festival, 1987, numerous awards for watercolor paintings. Mem. Hoover Watercolor Soc. (founding mem. 1952), Watercolor Art Soc. Houston (chmn bd. social chmn., sec., co-founder), Art League Houston, Cultural Arts Council Houston, Coppini Acad. Fine Arts (life), Tex. Arts Alliance, Tex. Commn. on the Arts, Southwestern Watercolor Soc. (founding mem., pub. chmn.), Tex. State Hist. Assn., Tex. Hist. Found., Cultural Arts Council of Houston. Presbyterian. Avocations: classical music, ballet, Tex. history, exploring unknown streets and roads. Home and Studio: Tex Notables Studio-Gallerie 9614 Val Verde St Houston TX 77063-3702

WARD, C. BRUCE, entrepreneur; b. 1953. Graduate, U. Calif.; MBA, Stanford U., 1969. From sales mgr. to divsn. pres. Gunderson Bros. Engrng. divsn. of FMC Corp., Portland, 1985-89, chmn., 1989—; regional v.p. Midwest ops. FMC Corp., Chgo., 1974-78; v.p. American Steel, Portland, 1978-80; pres. Western Acquisitions Group, Portland, 1980-84, American Guaranty Fin. Corp., Portland, 1984-85; bd. dirs. Stimson Lumber Co., Portland, Greenbrier Cos., Inc., Oswego, Or. Office: Gunderson Inc 4350 NW Front Ave Portland OR 97210-1422*

WARD, CARL EDWARD, research chemist; b. Albuquerque, Oct. 16, 1948; s. Joe E. and Loris E. (Wenk) W.; m. Bertha R. Schloer, June 9, 1970. BS in Chemistry, N.Mex. Inst. Mining and Tech., 1970; MS in Chemistry, Oreg. Grad. Ctr., 1972; PhD in Chemistry, Stanford U., 1977. Research chemist Union Carbide Corp., Charleston, W.Va., 1977-79, Dynapol Corp., Palo Alto, Calif., 1979-80; research chemist Chevron Chem. Co., Richmond, Calif., 1980-85, sr. research chemist, 1986-88; apptd. supr. chemical synthesis Chevron Chem. Co., Richmond, 1988-90; sr. rsch. assoc. Chevron Rsch. & Tech. Co., Richmond, 1990-91, staff scientist, 1991—. Referee Jour. Organic Chemistry, 1983—; patentee in field; contbr. articles to profl. jours. Recipient NSF traineeship, Stanford U., 1972-73; Upjohn fellow, Stanford U., 1976-77; recipient Clarence E. Earle Meml. award, 1995. Mem. Soc. Tribologists and Lubrication Engrs., Nat. Lubricating Grease Inst. (Clarence E. Earle Meml. award 1995), Am. Chem. Soc., Calif. Acad. Sci., N.Mex. Inst. Mining and Tech. Pres. Club, Stanford U. Alumni Assn. Democrat. Avocations: gardening, camping, fishing. Home: 1355 Nisich Dr San Jose CA 95122-3061 Office: Chevron Rsch & Tech Co PO Box 1627 Richmond CA 94802-1796

WARD, CHARLES RICHARD, extension and research entomologist, educator; b. Tahoka, Tex., Mar. 25, 1940; s. James Henry and Bertrice Opha (Moore) W.; m. Norma Faye Martin, Aug. 25, 1960; children: Beverly Jan, Charles Edward. AA, South Plains Coll., 1960; BS, Tex. Tech U., 1962, MS, 1964; PhD, Cornell U., 1968. Entomology specialist N.Mex. State U., Santa Cruz, Bolivia, 1976-78; rsch. assoc., assoc. prof. entomology N.Mex. State U., Las Cruces, 1978-80; pest mgmt. specialist N.Mex. State U., Artesia, 1980-82, 1984-85; chief party, entomologist N.Mex. State U., San Pedro Sula, Honduras, 1983-84; supt. agrl. sci. ctr., prof. entomology N.Mex. State U., Alcalde, N.Mex., 1985-86; extension and rsch. entomologist, prof. N.Mex. State U., Albuquerque, 1986—; cons. entomologist Internat. Irrigation Ctr., Logan, Utah, 1985-86, Consortium for Internat. Crop Protection, College Park, Md., 1986-93, Cornell U., Ithaca, N.Y., 1993—, Tropical Rsch. and Devel., Gainesville, Fla., 1989—. Contbr. numerous articles to profl. jours. Mem. Bd. Cert. Entomologists (Outstanding Contbrn. award 1981), Entomol. Soc. Am. (sec. subsect. ea. 1992-93), Southwestern Entomol. Soc. (pres. 1993-94), Extension Specialists Assn., N.Mex. Acad. Sci. Avocations: insect collecting, hunting, fishing. Home: 12105 El Dorado Pl NE Albuquerque NM 87111-4059 Office: NMex State U Ste B495 9301 Indian School Rd NE Albuquerque NM 87112-2884

WARD, CHESTER LAWRENCE, physician, retired county health official, retired military officer; b. Woodland, Yolo, Calif., June 8, 1932; s. Benjamin Briggs and Nora Elizabeth (Cash) W.; m. Sally Diane McCloud, Dec. 10, 1960; children: Katharine, Lynda. BA, U. Calif., Santa Barbara, 1955; MD, U. So. Calif., 1962; MPH, U. Calif., Berkeley, 1966; grad., Indsl. Coll. Armed Forces, 1978. Commd. 2d lt., inf. U.S. Army, 1954; advanced through grades to brig. gen., 1980; chief aviation medicine, preventive medicine and aeromed. consultation service Ft. Rucker, Ala., 1967-68; surgeon Aviation Brigade and USA Vietnam Aviation Medicine Cons., 1968-69; flight surgeon Office of U.S. Army Surgeon Gen., 1970-71; physician The White House, Washington, 1971-75, 76; dir. environ. quality research U.S. Army Med. Research and Devel. Commd., 1975-76; comdr. Womack Community Hosp.; surgeon XVIII Airborne Corps, Ft. Bragg, N.C., 1978-80; comdr. William Beaumont Army Med. Center, El Paso, Tex., 1980-82; med. dir. Union Oil Co., Schaumburg, Ill., 1982-83; dir. domestic medicine Union Oil Co., Los Angeles, 1983-84; exec. dir. continuing med. edn. and clin. prof. emergency medicine U. So. Calif. Sch. Medicine, Los Angeles, 1984-85; dir., health officer Dept. Health, Butte County, Calif., 1985-95; cons., contractor, pvt. med. practice, 1996—. Apptd. by Gov. Wilson Calif. Commn. Emergency Med. Svcs. Decorated D.S.M., Legion of Merit (2), Bronze Star, Air medal (5). Fellow Am. Coll. Preventive Medicine, Aerospace Med. Assn., Health Officers Assn. Calif., Butte-Glenn County Med. Soc. (past pres.), Calif. Med. Assn. (del.), Calif. Commn. Emergency Med. Svcs., No. Calif. Emergency Med. Svcs. (dir.). Home: 4 Lemon Hill Ct Oroville CA 95966-3708 Office: Butte County 33 County Center Dr Oroville CA 95965-3335 also: Enloe Outpatient Ctr 888 Lakeside Village Common Chico CA 95928

WARD, DANIEL THOMAS, bishop; b. Umri, Yavatmal, India, Apr. 8, 1942; s. Thomas Tuckker and Sudina Thomas (Suhasini) W.; m. Suhasini Daniel, Nov. 27, 1968; children: Vandan, Prerana. BA, Amolakchand Coll., Yavatmal, 1964; BD, Union Bibl. Sem., Yavatmal, 1967; ThM, Fuller Sem., Pasadena, Calif., 1982. Bishop Free Meth. Ch. of N.Am., Indpls.; deacon, minister Free Meth. Ch., Yavatmal, 1969-71, elder, 1971-91, dist. supt., 1986-87, bishop, 1989—; mem. hosp. bd. Free Meth. Ch., Yavatmal, 1989, mem. sem. faculty, 1983, registrar, 1984, bishop on U.S. bd., 1989—. Editor, author (newsletter) Christ-Jyot, 1974, (monthly publ.) Ankur, 1985, (quar. publ.) The New Day, 1989. Speaker All Religions Platform Meeting Lions Club, Yavatmal, 1986, Nat. Integrity, 1987. Avocations: soccer, badminton, cricket, basketball, volleyball. Home: Bishop House Maharashtra, PO Box 27 Vanjari Fail Rd, 445001 Yavatmal India Office: Free Meth Ch N Am, PO Box 27, Bishop House, 445001 Yavatmal Maharashtra, India Office: PO Box 535002 Indianapolis IN 46253-5002

WARD, DAVID, academic administrator, educator; b. Manchester, Eng., July 8, 1938; came to U.S., 1960; s. Horace and Alice (Harwood) W.; m. Judith B. Freifeld, June 11, 1964; children: Michael J.H., Peter F.B. BA, U. Leeds, Eng., 1959; MA, U. Leeds, 1961; MS, U. Wis., 1961, PhD, 1963; LittD, U. Leeds, 1992. Lectr. Carleton U., Ottawa, Ont., Can., 1963-64; asst. prof. Univ. B.C., Vancouver, Can., 1964-66; asst. prof. U. Wis., Madison, 1966-67, assoc. prof., 1967-70, prof., 1970—, chmn. geography dept., 1974-77, assoc. dean Grad. Sch., 1980-88, provost and vice chancellor acad. affairs, Andrew Clark prof. geography, 1989—; now chancellor U. Wis. Madison; mem. exec. com. Argonne (Ill.) Nat. Lab., 1990-93; dir.-at-large Social Sci. Rsch. Coun., 1991-93. Author: Cities and Immigrants, 1970, Geographic Perspectives on Americas Past, 1978, Poverty Ethnicity and the American City, 1989, Landscape of Modernity, 1992; contbr. articles to profl. jours. Guggenheim fellow, 1970, Einstein fellow Hebrew U., 1980, Fulbright fellow, Australian Nat. U., 1979. Mem. Assn. Am. Geographers (pres. 1989). Office: U Wis-Madison 161 Bascom Hall 500 Lincoln Dr Madison WI 53706-1380

WARD, DAVID ALLEN, sociology educator; b. Dedham, Mass., June 21, 1933; s. Theodore Allen and Jessie Miller (Ketchum) W.; m. Carol Jane Barton, June 10, 1957 (div. 1964); children: Douglas Allen, Andrew Barton; m. Reneé Ellen Light, Mar. 10, 1967. BA, Colby Coll., 1955; PhD, U. Ill., 1960. Asst. prof. Wash. State U., Pullman, 1960-61; asst. research sociologist UCLA, 1961-64; assoc. prof. U. Minn., Mpls., 1965-68, prof., 1968—, chmn. dept. sociology, 1984-88, 92-95; chmn. Salzburg (Austria) Seminar in Am. Studies, 1977; mem. research adv. com. Fed. Bur. Prisons, Washington, 1983—; cons. jud. com. U.S. Ho. Reps., Washington, 1984. Co-author: Women's Prison, 1965, Prison Treatment, 1971; co-editor: Delinquency, Crime and Social Process, 1969, Confinement in Maximum Custody, 1981; editorial cons. Jour. Criminal Law and Criminology, 1968—. Liberal Arts fellow Harvard U. Law Sch., 1968-69; Fulbright research fellow, 1971-72; research fellow Norwegian Fgn. Office, Oslo, 1976. Mem. Am. Sociol. Assn. (chmn. sect. criminology 1976-77), Law and Soc. Assn., Am. Soc. Criminology. Office: Univ of Minn Dept of Sociology 909 Social Sci Bldg Minneapolis MN 55455

WARD, DAVID HENRY (DAVE WARD), television news reporter, anchorman; b. Dallas, May 6, 1939; s. H. M. and Mary W.; m. Glenda Lois Odom, Nov. 10, 1959 (div.); children—Linda Ann, David H.; m. 2d, Debra Rene Holland, Apr. 25, 1976 (div.); children: Jonathan H., Christopher H. Student Tyler Jr. Coll., Tex., 1957-59. Announcer Sta. KGKB, Tyler, 1958-60; program director Sta. WACO (Tex.), 1960-62; news dir. Sta. KNUZ, Houston, 1962-66; news reporter, photographer, writer, producer Sta. KTRK-TV, 1966—; freelance writer, producer, cons.; chmn. pub. affairs adv. bd. Houston Bus. Council; pub. info. com. Am. Cancer Soc.; pres. bd. dirs. Easter Seal Soc., Harris, Fort Bend counties. Recipient Best TV Newscast award Tex. UPI, 1968, 72, 73-80; TV Service award Houston Jaycees, 1982; named Man of Yr., Houston Sertoma Club, 1973; TV Personality of Yr. Am. Women in Radio and TV, 1983, Best TV Anchor, Houston Press, 1995. Mem. Sigma Delta Chi. Baptist. Club: Press (Houston). Office: 3310 Bissonnet Houston TX 77005

WARD, DAVID SCHAD, screenwriter, film director; b. Providence, Oct. 24, 1947; s. Robert McCollum and Miriam (Schad) W.; children: Joaquin Atwood, Sylvana Soto. B.A., Pomona Coll., 1967; M.F.A., UCLA, 1970. Scriptwriter: films include Steelyard Blues, 1971, The Sting, 1973 (Acad. award best original screenplay 1973), The Milagro Beanfield War, 1988, (with Nora Ephron and Jeff Arch) Sleepless in Seattle, 1993 (Academy award nominee Best Original Screenplay 1993); writer, dir. films include Cannery Row, 1981, Major League, 1989, King Ralph, 1991, The Program, 1993. Mem. Dirs. Guild Am., Acad. Motion Picture Arts and Scis. Office: care CAA/Ken Stovitz 9830 Wilshire Blvd Beverly Hills CA 90212-1804

WARD, DUANE, professional baseball player; b. Parkview, N.M., May 28, 1964. With Atlanta Braves, 1982-86, Toronto Blue Jays, 1986—; player Am. League All-Star Team, 1993.

WARD, EDWARD WELLS, telecommunications executive; b. Jacksonville, Fla., Nov. 17, 1947; s. Joe Terrell and Dorothy Robyn (Wells) W. AA, Fla. Jr. Coll., 1976; MBA, Jacksonville U., 1986; MA, George Washington U., 1991. Cert. data processor, systems profl. Tech. dir. Trader Glick's Dinner Theatre, Jacksonville, 1969-70; prodn. asst. William Cook Advt., Jacksonville, 1970-74; various positions Computer Power, Inc., Jacksonville, 1974-84; communications svcs. mgr. PractiComm, Jacksonville, 1984-87, CEO, founder, 1984-87; network svcs. mgr. Am. Mgmt. Systems, Inc., Arlington, Va., 1987-93; dir. data and voice communications Am. Mgmt. Systems, Inc., Fairfax, Va., 1993—; instr. Jones Coll., Jacksonville, 1985; dir. credit union Am. Mgmt. Systems, 1988-89. Contbr. articles to profl. jours. With U.S. Army, 1968. Mem. North Am. ISDN User's Forum (svc. ind. chmn. 1990-91), Met. Washington Area Mensa (testing coord. 1994), No. Va. Royal Scottish Country Dance Soc. (chmn. 1994). Avocations: skiing, Scottish country dancing, tennis. Office: Am Mgmt Systems Inc 4050 Legato Rd Fairfax VA 22033-4003

WARD, ELAINE, artist; b. Boston, June 4, 1927; d. Robert and Gertrude (Toibb) Winston; m. William Ward (dec.); 1 child, Heather; m. Arthur Lee Dann. BA, Ecole des Beaux Arts, Paris, 1958; student, Art Students League, N.Y.C.; hon. degree, Ecole des Beaux Arts, Cannes, France. Mem. Phoenix Gallery, N.Y.C., 8 yrs. Solo show at Phoenix Gallery, 1989; group shows include Lever House, N.Y.C., 1987-89, 93, 95, Guild Hall, Easthampton, N.Y., 1988, 95, Phoenix Gallery, N.Y.C., 1992-94, Elaine Benson Gallery, Bridgehampton, N.Y., 1992, Palmas Del Mar, P.R., 1993, C.W. Post Coll., 1993, Agora Gallery, N.Y.C., 1994, Meadowlands Ctr. for Arts, N.J., 1995, Marcella Geltman Gallery, N.J., 1995; East End Art Coun., N.Y.C., 1995 (winner), Focus on Art, Livingston, N.J., 1995 (prize); represented in collections at Coastal Steel Co., Carteret, N.H., Pandora and Co., Conway, N.H., Ardan Assocs., Ltd., N.Y.C.; subject of articles. Winner Juried Show, East End Arts Coun., 1995. Mem. Nat. Arts Club, Nat. Assn. Women Artists, Guild Hall Mus., Parrish Mus.

WARD, ERICA ANNE, lawyer, educator; b. Okiyama, Japan, Oct. 20, 1950; d. Robert Edward and Constance Regina (Barnett) W.; m. Ralph Joseph Gerson, May 20, 1979; children: Stephanie Claire, Madeleine Ward Gerson. B.A., Stanford U., 1972; J.D., U. Mich., 1975. Bar: Calif. 1975, D.C. 1976, U.S. Ct. Appeals (5th and D.C. cirs.) 1977, Temporary Emergency Ct. Appeals 1983, Mich. 1989. Assoc. Wilmer, Cutler & Pickering, Washington, 1975-77; staff counsel U.S. Senate Ethics Com., Washington, 1977-78; exec. asst. gen. counsel Dept. Energy, Washington, 1978-79, counsellor to dep. sec., 1980; assoc. dir. energy and natural resources, domestic policy staff White House, Washington, 1980-81; of counsel Skadden, Arps, Slate, Meagher & Flom, Washington, 1981-87, ptnr., 1987—; adj. prof. law U. Mich., Ann Arbor, 1984-85. Editor Mich. Law Rev., 1975. Commr. Mackinac Island (Mich.) State Park Commn., 1989-95; mem. adv. bd. Ctr. Edn. of Women U. Mich., Ann Arbor, 1989—; bd. trustees Cranbrook Ednl. Cmty., 1993—; mem. visitors com. U. Mich. Law Sch. Recipient Outstanding Svc. medal Dept. Energy, 1981. Mem. ABA, Women's Bar Assn. D.C. Democrat. Jewish. Office: Skadden Arps Slate Meagher Flom 1440 New York Ave NW Washington DC 20005-2111

WARD, FRED, actor; b. 1943. Film appearances include Escape From Alcatraz, 1979, Tilt, 1979, Carny, 1980, Southern Comfort, 1981, Timerider: The Adventures of Lyle Swann, 1982, Silkwood, 1983, Uncommon Valor, 1983, The Right Stuff, 1984, Swing Shift, 1984, Secret Admirer, 1985, UFOria, 1985, Remo Willaims: The Adventure Begins..., 1985, Train of Dreams, 1987, The Prince of Pennsylvania, 1988, Big Business, 1988, Off Limits, 1988, Tremors, 1990, Henry and June, 1990, Backtrack, 1990, Miami Blues, 1990 (also co-exec. prodr.), Thunderheart, 1992, The Player, 1992, Bob Roberts, 1992, Equinox, 1993, Short Cuts, 1993, The Naked Gun 33 1/3: The Final Insult, 1994; TV appearances (movies) Belle Star, 1980, Florida Straights, 1986, Cast A Deadly Spell, 1991, Four Eyes and Six Guns, 1992, (spls.) Noon Wine, 1985. Office: Paradigm Talent Agy 10100 Santa Monica Blvd Fl 25 Los Angeles CA 90067-4003

WARD, GEOFFREY CHAMPION, author, editor; b. Newark, Ohio, Nov. 30, 1940; s. Frederick Champion and Duira Rachel (Baldinger) W.; m. Diane Raines; children—Nathan, Kelly; 1 stepchild, Garrett Keim. BA, Oberlin Coll., 1962; DHL (hon.), Wilkes U., 1995. Sr. picture editor Ency. Britannica, Chgo., 1964-68; co-founder, editor Audience mag., Boston, 1969-73; mng. editor Am. Heritage Mag., N.Y.C., 1976-78; editor Am. Heritage Mag., 1978-82; Author: Lincoln's Thought and the Present, 1978, Treasures of the Maharajas, 1983, Before th Trumpet: Young Franklin Roosevelt, 1892-1905, 1985, A First Class Temperament: The Emergence of Franklin Roosevelt, 1989 (Nat. Book Critics Cir. award, Francis Parkman prize Soc. Am. Historians, L.A. Times biography prize, Ohioana award), The Civil War: An Illustrated History, 1990, American Originals: The Private Worlds of Some Singular Men and Women, 1991; (with Diane Raines Ward) Tiger Wallahs, Encounters with the Men Who Tried to Save the Greatest of the Great Cats, 1993, Baseball: An Illustrated History, 1994, Closest Companion: The Unknown Story of the Intimate Friendship between Franklin Roosevelt and Mrgaret Suckley, 1995, The West: An Illustrated History, 1996; (TV documentary) Huey Long, 1985, Thomas Hart Benton 1989, Lind.
Author: Lincoln's Thought and the Present, 1978, Treasures of the Maharajas, 1983, Before the Trumpet: Young Franklin Roosevelt, 1882-1905, 1985, A First-Class Temperament: The Emergence of Franklin Roosevelt, 1989 (Nat. Book Critics Cir. award, Francis Parkman prize Soc. Am. Historians, L.A. Times biography prize, Ohioana award), The Civil War: An Illustrated History, 1990, American Originals: The Private Worlds of Some Singular Men and Women, 1991; (with Diane Raines Ward) Tiger Wallahs, Encounters with the Men Who Tried to Save the Greatest of the Great Cats, 1993, Baseball: An Illustrated History, 1994, Closest Companion: The Unknown Story of the Intimate Friendship between Franklin Roosevelt and Margaret Suckley, 1995, The West: An Illustrated History, 1996; (TV documentaries) Huey Long, 1985, Thomas Hart Benton, 1989, Lindbergh, 1990, Nixon, 1990 (Writer's Guild Am. award), The Civil War, 1990 (Emmy award), Reminiscing in Tempo, 1991, Empire of the Air, 1992, The Kennedys, 1992 (Emmy award), George Marshall and the American Century, 1993, Baseball, 1994 (Emmy award), Daley: The Last Boss, 1995, The West, 1996, Theodore Roosevelt, 1996; columnist: The Life and Times for Am. Heritage; contbr. articles to mags., jours. Recipient Christopher awards for The Statue of Liberty, The Christophers, The Civil War, New Eng. Booksellers Assn. award, Am. Booksellers award, Lila Scheson Wallace Readers Digest writers award. Mem. Soc. Am. Historians, Writers Guild Am., East Inc., Century Assn. Home: 17 C 290 W End Ave New York NY 10023-8106 Office: Brandt & Brandt care Carl Brandt 1501 Broadway New York NY 10036

WARD, GEORGE FRANK, JR., foreign service officer; b. Jamaica, N.Y., Apr. 9, 1945; s. George Frank and Hildegard Louisa (Evans) W.; m. Peggy Elizabeth Coote, June 12, 1965; 1 child, Pamela Ward Priester. BA, U. Rochester, 1965; MPA, Harvard U., 1980. U.S. vice consul Am. Consulate, Hamburg, Germany, 1970-72; ops. officer Office Sec. State, Washington, 1972-74; U.S. consul Am. Consulate Gen., Genoa, Italy, 1974-76; polit. officer Am. Embassy, Rome, 1976-77, exec. asst., 1977-79; polit. officer Am. Embassy, Bonn, Germany, 1984-85, dep. chief mission, 1989-92; polit.-military officer U.S. Dept. State, Washington, 1980-84, deputy dir. European Security and Polit. Affairs, 1985-88, prin. dep. asst. sec. Bur. Internat. Orgns., 1992—. Capt. USMC, 1965-69. Decorated Vietnamese Cross Gallantry (Vietnam); Naval Commendaton medal; recipient Presdl. Meritorious Svc. awards, 1992, 94. Mem. Am. Fgn. Svc. Assn., Phi Beta Kappa. Episcopalian. Avocations: classical music, running, skiing, tennis. Home: 6407 Recreation Ln Falls Church VA 22041-1216 Office: Dept of State 2201 C St NW Washington DC 20520-0001

WARD, GEORGE TRUMAN, architect; b. Washington, July 24, 1927; s. Truman and Gladys Anna (Nutt) W.; m. Margaret Ann Hall, Sept. 10, 1949; children: Carol Ann Ward Dickson, Donna Lynne Ward Solomon, George Truman, Robert Stephen. BS, Va. Poly. Inst., 1951, MS, 1952; postgrad., George Washington U., 1966. Registered profl. architect, Va., Md., D.C., W.Va., Ohio, N.J., Del., N.C. Archtl. draftsman Charles A. Pearson, Radford, Va., 1950; head archtl. sect. Hayes, Seay, Mattern & Mattern, Radford and Roanoke, 1951-52; with Joseph Saunders & Assos., Alexandria, Va., 1952-57, asso. architect, 1955-57; ptnr. Vosbeck-Ward & Assos., Alexandria, 1957-64, Ward/Hall Assocs., Fairfax, Va., 1964—; dir. Crestar Bank/Greater Washington Region. Pres. PTA Burke (Va.) Sch., 1970-71; mem. bd. mgrs. Fairfax (Va.) County YMCA, 1964-76; chmn. adv. com. Coll. Architecture, Va. Poly. Inst., 1984-90; bd. dirs., mem. investment com. Va. Tech. Found., Inc., 1986-91, 93—; pres. Springfield Rotary Found., 1978-79; chmn. county adv. bd. Salvation Army, 1978-79, 86-95, co-chmn. Fairfax County Salvation Army Capital Campaign, 1991-95; mem. Gen. Bd. Va. Bapts., deacon, moderator; mem. bd. visitors Va. Poly. Inst. & State U., 1984-87; trustee Fairfax County Pub. Schs. Edn. Found., Inc. With AUS, 1946-47. Paul Harris fellow; recipient Disting. Svc. award Va. Tech. Alumni Assn., 1988, William H. Ruffner medal Va. Tech., 1996. Fellow Coll. AIA, mem. AIA (corp., charter Octagon Soc.), Va. Soc. AIA (chmn. polit. action com. 1991—. Disting. Svc. award 1990, treas. Va. soc. 1994—), Rowe Fellowship (charter mem. 1988), Alumni Assn. Va. Poly. Inst. & State U. (bd. dirs., v.p. 1992, pres. 1994), Interfaith Forum on Religion, Art and Architecture, Va. Found. for Architecture (trustee), Va. Assn. Professions, Va. C. of C., No. Va. Angus Assn. (pres. 1987-88), Masons, Shriners, KT, Rotary (charter mem., pres. Springfield 1973-74), Tau Sigma Delta, Omicron Delta Kappa, Phi Kappa Phi, Pi Delta Epsilon, Ut Prosim. Baptist. Home: Glenara Farm 10239 Glenara Ln Marshall VA 22115-2728 Office: Ward Hall Assoc AIA 12011 Lee Jackson Memorial Hwy Fairfax VA 22033-3310

WARD, HAROLD WILLIAM COWPER, oncologist, educator; b. Southend-On-Sea, Essex, Eng., Nov. 24, 1925; came to U.S., 1976; s. William Samuel and Winifred (Marjorie) W.; m. Barbara Mary Sanderson, Oct. 6, 1982; children: Belinda Mary Jane Morris, Rosemary Sylvia, Timothy Harold. MB BS, U. London, 1953; diploma in med. radiation therapy, Royal Coll. Physicians London, 1957. Cert. therapeutic radiology Am. Bd. Radiology, cert. basic cardiopulmonary resuscitation Am. Heart Assn. Intern Charing Cross Hosp., London, 1953, Royal Postgrad. Med. Sch., London, 1954-55; intern in surgery The Bolinbroke Hosp., London, 1954; sr. resident in radiotherapy Edinburgh Royal Infirmary, London, 1958-59; rsch. fellow in radiotherapy St. Bartholomew's Hosp., London, 1959-65; cons. radiotherapist Queen Elizabeth Hosp., Birmingham, Eng., 1965-75; clin. lectr. U. Birmingham, 1965-75; dir. radiation oncology Parkland Meml. Hosp., Dallas, 1976-78; prof. radiology U. Tex. Southwestern Med. Sch., Dallas, 1976-78; clin. prof. radiology divsn. radiation oncology U. Cin., 1978-82, assoc. prof. medicine divsn. hematology, 1980-82; dir. radiation oncology Meml. Med. Ctr., Corpus Christie, Tex., 1982—; clin. assoc. prof. radiation oncology U. Tex. Med. Br., Galveston, 1984—; mem. Oncology Assocs., Inc., Cin., 1978-92; travelling fellow in radiotherapy, 1965; staff Meml. Hosp. for Cancer and Allied Diseases, N.Y.C., M.D. Anderson Hosp., Houston, U. Calif. Med. Sch., San Francisco; mem. U.K. Med. Rsch. Coun. Working Party for study of embryonal tumors of childhood, 1967-75; mem. steering com. U.K. Nat. Ovarian Cancer Clin. Survey, 1967-75; site vis. team NCI, 1984-87; physician advisor Tex. Med. Found. Peer Rev. Orgn., 1985—; mem. regional quality rev. com., 1989—. Mem. exec. com. Symphony Orch., Corpus Christi, 1992—. Fellow Royal Coll. Radiology; mem. AMA, Internat. Soc. for Pediatric Oncology, Royal Coll. Surgeons Eng., Royal Coll. Physicians, Soc. Apothecaries, Am. Soc. Therapeutic Radiologists, Am. Coll. Radiology, Am. Cancer Soc. (Nueces County br. 1984-88), Brit. Inst. Radiology, Brit. Med. Assn., Brit. Assn. for Cancer Rsch., Ohio Med. Assn., Tex. Med. Assn., Southeastern Oncology Group, Southwestern Oncology Group, Acad. Medicine of Cin., Nueces County Med. Soc. (pub. rels., environ. pollution control, Cancer adv. com. 1984—, consultative fee review com. 1988—). Episcopalian. Avocations: music, gardening. Home: 131 Naples St Corpus Christi TX 78404-1828 Office: 1201 S 19th St Corpus Christi TX 78405-1527

WARD, HARRY PFEFFER, physician, university chancellor; b. Pueblo, Colo., June 6, 1933; s. Lester L. and Alysmai (Pfeffer) W.; m. Betty Jo Stewart, Aug. 20, 1955; children—Stewart, Leslie, Elizabeth, Mary Alice, Amy. A.B., Princeton U., 1955; M.D., U. Colo., 1959; M.S., U. Minn., 1963. Intern Bellevue Hosp., N.Y.C., 1959; resident Mayo Clinic, Rochester, Minn., 1960-63; practice medicine specializing in hematology; chief medicine Denver VA hosp., 1968-72; dean, asso. v.p. U. Colo. Sch. Medicine, 1972-78, prof. medicine, 1972; chancellor U. Ark. Med. Sci., Little Rock, 1979—; clin. investigator VA, 1964-67. Chmn. Assn. Acad. Health Ctr., 1993-94. Mem.

ACP, AMA, Am. Fedn. Clin. Research, Central Soc. Clin. Investigation, Am. Soc. Hematology, Internat. Soc. Hematology, Western Soc. Clin. Research. Home: 369 Valley Club Cir Little Rock AR 72212-2900 Office: U Ark Med Scis 4301 W Markham St Little Rock AR 72205-7101

WARD, HILEY HENRY, journalist, educator; b. Lafayette, Ind., July 30, 1929; s. Hiley Lemen and Agnes (Fuller) W.; m. Charlotte Burns, May 28, 1951 (div. 1971); children: Dianne, Carolee, Marceline, Laurel; m. Joan Bastel, Aug. 20, 1977. BA, William Jewell Coll., 1951; MA, Berkeley (Calif.) Bapt. Div. Sch., 1953; MDiv, McCormick Theol. Sem., Chgo., 1955; summer, evening student, Northwestern U., 1948, 54, 56-57; PhD, U. Minn., 1977. News asst. Christian Advocate, 1953-55; editor jr. publs. David C. Cook Pub. Co., 1956-59; editor Record, Buchanan, Mich., 1960; religion editor Detroit Free Press, 1960-73; asst. prof. journalism Mankato (Minn.) State U., 1974-76; assoc. prof. journalism Wichita (Kans.) State U., 1976; prof. journalism Temple U., Phila., 1977—, dir. news-editorial sequence, journalism dept., 1977-80, chmn. dept., 1978-80; instr. journalism Oakland U., Rochester, Mich., evenings 1963-66. Author: Creative Giving, 1958, Space-age Sunday, 1960, Documents of Dialogue, 1966, God and Marx Today, 1968, Ecumania, 1968, Rock 2000, 1969, Prophet of the Black Nation, 1969, The Far-out Saints of the Jesus Communes, 1972, Religion 2101 A.D., 1975, Feeling Good About Myself, 1983, Professional Newswriting, 1985, My Friend's Beliefs: A Young Reader's Guide to World Religions, 1988, Reporting in Depth, 1991, Magazine and Feature Writing, 1993; editor: Media History Digest, 1979-94; exec. editor: Kidbits, 1981-82; book editor: Editor and Publisher, 1989—; contbr. articles to profl. jours., feature articles to newspapers and mags.; also short stories and poems. Religious Pub. Rels. Coun. fellow, 1970; recipient citation Religious Heritage Am., 1962, Leidt award Epsic. Ch., 1969, citation U.S. Am. Revolution Bicentennial Adminstrn., 1976. Mem. Religion Newswriters Assn. (pres. 1970-72), Am. Soc. Journalists and Authors, Am. Journalism Historians Assn. (bd. dirs.), Overseas Press Club. Home: PO Box 399 1263 Folly Rd Warrington PA 18976-1422 Office: Temple U Dept Journalism Philadelphia PA 19122

WARD, HIRAM HAMILTON, federal judge; b. Thomasville, N.C., Apr. 29, 1923; s. O.L. and Margaret A. W.; m. Evelyn M. McDaniel, June 1, 1947; children: William McDaniel, James Randolph. Student, Wake Forest Coll., 1945-47; J.D., Wake Forest U., 1950. Bar: N.C. bar 1950. Practiced law Denton, N.C., 1950-51; staff atty. Nat. Prodn. Authority, Washington, 1951-52; partner firm DeLapp, Ward & Hedrick, Lexington, N.C., 1952-72; U.S. dist. judge Mid. Dist. N.C., 1972—, chief judge, 1982-88, sr. judge, 1988—; mem. com. on Codes of Conduct of Jud. Conf., U.S., 1990-95; mem. Fourth Cir. Jud. Coun., 1984-87. Contbr. legal opinions to Fed. Supplement, 1972—. Bd. visitors Wake Forest U. Sch. Law, 1973—; Mem. N.C. Bd. Elections, 1964-72; trustee Wingate Coll., 1969-72. Served with USAAF, 1940-45. Decorated Air medal, Purple Heart; recipient Liberty Bell award N.C. Bar Assn., 1994. Mem. ABA, N.C. Bar Assn., Am. Judicature Soc., N.C. State Bar, Masons, Lions, Phi Alpha Delta (hon. life). Republican. Baptist. Home: 188 Forest Park Dr Denton NC 27239 Office: US Courthouse 246 Fed Bldg 251 N Main St Winston Salem NC 27101-3914

WARD, HORACE TALIAFERRO, federal judge; b. LaGrange, Ga., July 29, 1927; m. Ruth LeFlore (dec.); 1 son (dec.). AB, Morehouse Coll., 1949; MA, Atlanta U., 1950; JD, Northwestern U., 1959. Bar: Ga. 1960. Instr. polit. sci. Ark. A.M. and N. Coll., 1950-51, Ala. State Coll., 1951-53, 55-56; claims authorizer U.S. Social Security Adminstrn., 1959-60; assoc. firm Hollowell Ward Moore & Alexander (and successors), Atlanta, 1960-69; individual practice law Atlanta, 1971-74; judge Civil Ct. of Fulton County, 1974-77, Fulton Superior Ct., 1977-79; U.S. Dist. Ct. judge No. Dist. Ga., Atlanta, 1979—; lectr. bus. and sch. law Atlanta U., 1965-70; dep. city atty., Atlanta, 1969-70, asst. county atty., Fulton County, 1971-74. Former Trustee Friendship Baptist Ch., Atlanta; mem. Ga. adv. com. U.S. Civil Rights Commn., 1963-65; assisting lawyer NAACP Legal Def. and Edn. Fund, Inc., 1960-70; mem. Jud. Selection Commn., Atlanta, 1972-74, Charter Commn., 1971-72; mem. Ga. Senate, 1964-74, jud. com., rules com., county and urban affairs com.; mem. State Democratic Exec. com., 1966-74; former bd. dirs. Atlanta Legal Aid Soc.; bd. dirs. Atlanta Urban League, Fed. Defender Program, No. Dist. Ga.; trustee Met. Atlanta Commn. on Crime and Delinquency, Atlanta U., Fledgling Found. Mem. Am. Bar Assn., Nat. Bar Assn. (chmn. jud. council 1978-79), State Bar Ga., Atlanta Bar Assn., Gate City Bar Assn. (pres. 1972-74), Atlanta Lawyers Club, Phi Beta Kappa, Alpha Phi Alpha, Phi Alpha Delta, Sigma Pi Phi. Office: US Dist Court 2388 US Courthouse 75 Spring St SW Atlanta GA 30303-3309

WARD, IVA NELL BELL, special education educator; b. Grapeland, Tex., Aug. 29, 1949; d. Frenchie and Eunice (Smith) Bell; m. Edward K. Ward Jr., Sept. 1969 (div. 1972); children: Eric Kendrick, Edward Kelly III. BS, Tex. So. U., 1978. Cert. tchr., Tex. Tchr. spl. edn. Houston Ind. Sch. Dist., 1978-85, reading specialist, program coord., 1990—; mem. steering com. Mayor's Hearing on Children and Youth, 1990, steering com. for restructuring Houston Ind. Sch. Dist., 1991, shared decision making com. for Sch. Campus. Active City of Houston Task Force for Infant Mortality Rate, 1993. Mem. NAACP, Nat. Women of Achievement (youth advisor, spelling bee coord., VI coord., Golden Apple award 1992), Assn. Tex. Profl. Tchrs., Houston Fedn. Tchrs. (svc. and recruitment com. 1985-86), Internat. Platform Assn., Houston Area Alliance of Black Sch. Educators, Africa Am. Reclaiming Our Cmty., Iota Phi Lambda (S.E. area coord., VIP). Home: 1660 W T C Jester Blvd Apt 511 Houston TX 77008-3265 Office: Houston Ind Sch Dist 3830 Richmond Ave Houston TX 77027-5864

WARD, JACQUELINE ANN BEAS, nurse, healthcare administrator; b. Somerset, Pa., Oct. 23, 1945; d. Donald C. and Thelma R. (Wable) Beas; divorced; children: Charles L. Jr., Shawn M. BS in Nursing, U. Pitts., 1966; MA in Counseling and Guidance, W.Va. Coll. Grad. Studies, 1976; MBA, Columbus Coll., 1983. Cert. in advanced nursing adminstrn. Staff nurse W.Va. U. Hosp., Morgantown, 1966-67; staff nurse, head nurse Meml. Hosp. Charleston, W.Va., 1967-69; staff nurse Santa Rosa Hosp., San Antonio, 1969; staff nurse, supr. Bexar County Hosp., San Antonio, 1970; charge, staff nurse Rocky Mountain Osteo. Hosp., Denver, 1971; staff nurse Charleston Area Med. Ctr., 1971-74, asst. dir. nursing, 1974-82; dir. nursing H.D. Cobb Meml. Hosp., Phenix City, Ala.; clin. instr. Chattahoochie Valley C.C., Phenix City, 1982-84; v.p. nursing Venice (Fla.) Hosp., 1984-90, v.p. ops., 1990-94, exec. dir., v.p. Life Counseling Ctr., Osprey, Fla., 1994-95, dir. skilled unit and spl. projects Bon Secours/Venice Hosp., 1995—. Mem. Am. Coll. Healthcare Exec., Fla. Hosp. Assn., Nat. League Nursing, Articulation Coun. Sarasota and Manatee Counties, Am. Orgn. of Nurse Execs. (pres. region II south Fla. 1985-86, 90-94), Fla. Orgn. Nurse Execs., Fla. Commn. on Nursing. Office: Bon Secours-Venice Hosp 540 The Rialto Venice FL 34285

WARD, JAMES FRANK, pension fund administrator; b. Chgo., May 29, 1938; s. Frank William and Josephine (Calderone) W.; m. Judith Evelyn Drake, Nov. 22, 1957 (dec. Sept. 1981); children: Jeffrey Thomas, Jason Banning. BEd in Acctg., Ill. State U.; MBA, DePaul U., 1967. Chartered fin. analyst. Asst. traffic mgr. Witco Chem. Co., Stickney, Ill., 1958-59; office mgr. R.E. Chatterton Indsl. Diamonds, Chgo., 1960-62; acctg. tchr. Chgo. Bd. Edn., 1963-66; asst. exec. dir. Chgo. Tchrs. Pension Fund, 1967-76, exec. dir., 1977—. Author, editor numerous newsletters, bulletins. Speaker on pension topics various civic & tchr. orgns. Mem. Nat. Coun. on Tchr. Retirement, Nat. Conf. Pub. Employee Retirement Systems, Govt. Fin. Officers Assn. U.S. & Canada (cert. of excellence in achievement for fin. acctg. & disclosures 1989, 90), Investment Analysts Soc. Chgo., Assn. for Investment Mgmt. & Rsch. Avocations: instrumental music, tennis, skiing. Home: 300 N State St Apt 5233 Chicago IL 60610-4808 Office: Chgo Tchrs Pension Fund 55 W Wacker Dr Chicago IL 60601

WARD, JAMES HUBERT, dean, social work educator, researcher, consultant; b. Lawndale, N.C., Apr. 8, 1937; s. Frank A. and Helen (Wray) W.; m. Jacqueline Ferman Ward, Dec. 29, 1966; children: Dawn Alese, Audran Maria, James H., Christopher F. BS, N.C. A&T State U., 1960; MSW, U. Md., 1968; PhD, Ohio State U., 1974. Tchr., counselor Ohio Youth Commn., Columbus, 1962-66, dep. dir., 1971-73; adj. instr. social work dept. sociology and anthropology, U. Dayton (Ohio), 1968-69; exec. dir. Montgomery County Cmty. Action Agy., Dayton, 1969-71; asst. prof. sociology and anthropology, Central State U., Wilberforce, Ohio, 1973; asst. prof., sr. research assoc. Sch. Applied Social Scis., Case Western Res. U., Cleve., 1975-76, asst. prof., assoc. dean, 1976-79, assoc. prof., assoc. dean, 1979-81; dean, prof. Sch. Social Work, U. Ala., Tuscaloosa, 1981-88; prof., dean, Grad. Sch. Social Work, Portland State U., Portland, Oreg., 1988—; cons. in field; mem. Ala. Juvenile Justice Adv. Com., 1983—; mem. adv. coun. on social work edn. Ala. Commn. on Higher Edn., 1982—; mem. ho. of dels. Coun. on Social Work Edn., 1981-87, bd. dirs., 1995—; mem. Coun. Social Work Edn. Accreditation Commn., 1987-93; mem. annual program planning com. Council on Social Work Edn., 1984-85; chmn. bd. dirs. United Way of Columbia-Willamette, 1988—, mem. exec. com., mem. community orgn. and planning com., chair agency rels. com., mem. strategic planning com.; bd. dirs. Urban League, Portland, 1988-89; bd. dirs. Mt. Hood Community Mental Health Ctr., 1988-91; mem. govs. panel on ecclesia, 1988-89; mem adv. coun. mental health edn. planning Dept. Human Resources, Mental Health Divsn., Salem, Oreg., 1988-91; mem. Portland City Club, 1988—; mem. task force on licensing for social work practice, Ala. State Bd. Social Work Examiners, 1985; mem.local human resources bd. Tuscaloosa County Dept. Pensions and Security, 1982-87, mem. external central adminstrv. rev. panel, 1985. Bd. dirs. Greater Tuscaloosa chpt. ARC, 1982-87; pres. Eastwood Middle Sch. PTA, Tuscaloosa Bd. Edn., 1983-84; hon. mem. bd. Parents Anonymous of Ala. State Bd., 1982; mem. W. Ala. Nat. Issues Forum, 1984-86; bd. dirs., chmn. fin. com. Tuscaloosa County Mental Health Assn., 1984-87. Served to capt. U.S. Army, 1960-68. Recipient Pace Setters award for disting. achievement Coll. Adminstrv. Sci., Ohio State U., 1974; named Outstanding Profl. in Human Services, Acad. Human Services, 1974. Mem. Acad. Cert. Social Workers (cert), Council on Social Work Edn., Internat. Assn. Schs. Social Work, Internat. Council on Social Welfare, Nat. Assn. Social Workers (mem.-at-large, bd. dirs. Ala. Chpt. 1985, nat. com. nom. and leadership indentification, 1986-88, v.p. Oreg. chpt. 1991—, edit. bd. jour. Social Work 1990-93), Am. Assn. Deans and Dirs. of Grad. Schs. of Social Work (chair deans group S.E. region 1985-87, v.p. 1987-89), Ala. Conf. of Social Work (chmn. program com.), Greater Tuscaloosa C. of C. Contbr. numerous articles to various profl. jours., also chpts. to books. Office: Portland State Univ Grad Sch Social Work PO Box 751 Portland OR 97207-0751

WARD, JANET LYNN, magazine editor, sports wire reporter; b. Albany, Ga., Feb. 20, 1955; d. Andrew Johnson and Dorothy Iris (Pepera) W.; m. William Thomas Hankins III, Apr. 25, 1981 (div. Feb. 1990); m. Jack Wilkinson, May 22, 1993. AB in Journalism, U. Ga., 1977; JD, Woodrow Wilson Coll. Law, 1984. Sports editor Marietta (Ga.) Daily Jour., 1977-79, North Fulton extra-Atlanta Jour. Constitution, 1979-80; asst. editor In town extra-Atlanta Jour. Constitution, 1980-84; lawyer Atlanta, 1984-89; editor Am. City & County Mag., Atlanta, 1989—. Democrat. Roman Catholic. Avocations: sports, reading. Home: 372 Oakdale Rd NE Atlanta GA 30307-2070 Office: Am City & County Ste 1200 6151 Powers Ferry Rd NW Atlanta GA 30339-2943

WARD, JASPER DUDLEY, III, architect; b. Flemington, N.J., Oct. 8, 1921; s. Jasper Dudley and Constance Fargis (Allen) W.; m. Lucretia Baldwin; children: Lucretia B., James R., Michael D., Alexander A., Abigail B. B.Arch., M.I.T., 1948. Designer Skidmore, Owings & Merrill, N.Y.C., 1948-50; partner Ward-Knight, N.Y.C., 1950; architect Kelly & Gruzen, N.Y.C., Knappen, Tippetts, Abbott & McCarthy, N.Y.C., Gen. Electric Co., Reynolds Metals Co., Louisville, 1951-58; pvt. practice architecture Louisville, 1958-93; chief architect Hazelet * Erdal Consulting Engrs. & Architects, various, 1993-95, The Stone Group, 1995—; Vis. critic archtl. design Pratt Inst., 1954-56, Columbia U., 1955, U. Ky., 1960-71; lectr. U. Louisville, 1983-86. Prin. works include: Neighborhood House, 1964 (award), Portland Sch., 1968 (award), Ky. Sch. for Blind, Recital Hall and Music Bldg., 1977 (award), Alice Lloyd Coll. Sci. Bldg., 1977 (award), St. Francis Sch, Goshen, Ky., 1000 Car Fed. Parking Garage, Louisville, Alice Lloyd Coll. Boy's and Girl's dormitory, Pippa Passes, Ky., John F. Kennedy Library, West Liberty, Ky., U. Louisville Radiation Center, Jefferson County Elementary Sch, Okolona, Ky., Ballard Mills Silo Apts. and Redevel. of Big 4 Bridge, U. Louisville Student Activities Ctr., 6th and Main Sts. Parking Garage, 1988 (award), Louisville Gardens Parking Garage, 1990 (award). Served to 1st lt. C.E. AUS, M41943-46. Recipient AIA award of merit for Swain House, Watching, N.Y. 1956, 1st Honor awards Ky. Soc. Architects for CIT Bldg., 1961; White Cement award of excellence for Drs. Office Bldg., Louisville, Portland Cement Assn. 1971; City Blue Print Co. Louisville in Archtl. Collection, Mus. of Modern Art. Home: 6601 Mayfair Ave Prospect KY 40059-9155 Office: 626 E Gray St Louisville KY 40202

WARD, JO ALICE, computer consultant, educator; b. Ft. Worth, Aug. 14, 1939; d. Boyd Wheeler and Frances Elizabeth (Wheeler) Patton; m. John Oliver Ward, Mar. 19, 1960 (div. Feb. 1976); children: Russell Scott, Pamela Joan Ward Watson. BA in Math., North Tex. State U., 1961, MA in Math., 1965, postgrad., 1969-72. Instr. math. North Tex. State U., Denton, 1965-67, grad. asst., 1968-72; instr. math. Tarrant County Jr. Coll., Ft. Worth, 1967-68; math. tchr. Aldine Ind. Schs., Houston, 1973-76; math. instr. U. Houston Downtown, 1974-80; sys. analyst Conoco Inc, Houston, 1981-93; computer cons. Quality First Computer Svcs., Houston, 1994—. Vol facilitator for family violence program Houston Area Women's Ctr., 1993-94; adminstrv. vol. Citizens for Animal Protection, 1993—; vol. Bering Cmty. Svc. Found., 1995—. Recipient Outstanding Adminstrv. Vol. award Citizens for Animal Protection, 1995. Home: 11943 Briar Forest Dr Houston TX 77077-4132

WARD, JOHN MILTON, music educator; b. Oakland, Calif., July 6, 1917; s. John Milton and Maud (Van Alstyne) W.; m. Ruth Marie Neils, Jan. 9, 1945. B.A., San Francisco State Coll., 1941; M.Mus., U. Wash., 1942; Ph.D., NYU, 1953; A.M. (hon.), Harvard U., 1955. Instr. lit. and fine arts Mich. State U., 1947-53; asst., later assoc. prof. music U. Ill., 1953-55; assoc. prof. music Harvard U., 1955-58, prof., chmn. dept., 1958-62, William Powell Mason prof., 1961-85, William Powell Mason prof. emeritus, 1985—. Author: The Dublin Virginal Manuscript, 1954, 3d edit., 1983, A Dowland Miscellany, 1977, Sprightly and Cheerful Musick, 1981, Music for Elizabethan Lutes, 1992, The Lute Music of John Johnson, 1994; editor series Pantomime, Dance, and Ballet; contbr. articles to profl. jours. Chmn. bd. dirs. Laura Boulton Found.; mem. adv. bd. London Entertainment, 1660-1800; hon. curator music and dance Harvard Theatre Collection. Mem. Am. Acad. Arts and Scis., Am. Musicol. Soc. (hon.), Internat. Musicological Soc., Internat. Coun. for Traditional Music, Soc. Ethnomusicology, Royal Mus. Assn. (hon. fgn. mem.), Lute Soc. (hon.). Home: 20 Follen St Cambridge MA 02138-3503

WARD, JOHN ORSON, economics educator, consultant; b. Toledo, Ohio, Jan. 10, 1942; m. Pamela S. Strada, Sept 21, 1985; children: Howard, Rachel, Blaine. BA, U. Toledo, 1965, MA, 1967; PhD, U. Okla., 1970; postgrad., Havard U., 1979. Systems analyst Nat. Lead, Toledo, 1965-67; teaching asst., lectr. U. Okla., Norman, 1967-69; chair econs. U. Mo., Kansas City, 1976-79, prof. econs., 1969—, assoc. dean arts and scis., 1978-85, chair comm., 1985-86, chair econs., 1992—; vis. prof. Fed. U. Ceara, Fortaleza, Brazil, 1975-76; Latin Am. teaching fellow Tufts U., Brazil, 1976. Mng. editor Jour. Forensic Econs., 1985—; author: over 40 articles, books and books chpts. Mem. Mo. Task Force on Tax Reform, 1986-87, Mo. Commn. on Global Warming, 1989. Weldon Spring grantee U. Mo., 1978. Fellow Acad. Econ. Arbitrators (bd. dirs. 1989-90); mem. Am. Econ. Assn., Nat. Assn. Forensic Economists (pres. 1985-87). Avocations: astronomy, tennis. Home: 11821 Washington St Kansas City MO 64114-5549 Office: U Mo Kans City Natl Assn Forensic Econs PO Box 30067 Kansas City MO 64112-0667

WARD, JOHN ROBERT, physician, educator; b. Salt Lake City, Nov. 23, 1923; s. John I. and Clara (Elzi) W.; m. Norma Harris, Nov. 5, 1948; children: John Harris, Pamela Lyn, Robert Scott, James Alan. BS, U. Utah, 1944, MD, 1946; MPH, U. Calif., Berkeley, 1967; Masters, Am. Coll. of Rheumatology, 1990. Diplomate Am. Bd. Internal Medicine. Intern Salt Lake County Gen. Hosp., 1947-48, asst. resident, 1949-50, resident physician internal medicine, 1950-51, asst. physician, 1957-58, assoc. physician, 1958-69; clin. fellow medicine Harvard U., Boston, 1955-57; instr. medicine U. Utah Med. Sch., Salt Lake City, 1954-58, asst. prof., 1958-63, assoc. prof., 1963, prof., 1966-93, chmn. dept. preventive medicine, 1966-70, emeritus prof. internal medicine, 1993—, chief div. rheumatology, 1957-88; prof. internal medicine emeritus U. Utah. Med. Sch., Salt Lake City, 1994—; attending physician internal medicine Salt Lake City VA Hosp., 1957-70; Nora Eccles Harrison prof. medicine, Am. Coll. Rheumatology. Served as capt. M.C. AUS, 1951-53. Master Am. Coll. Rheumatology; fellow ACP; mem. Am. Coll. Rheumatology (Disting. rheumatologist award 1994), Utah State Med. Assn. (hon. pres. 1994-95). Home: 1249 E 3770 S Salt Lake City UT 84106-2446 Office: U Utah Health Scis Ctr 50 N Medical Dr Salt Lake City UT 84132

WARD, JOHN WESLEY, retired pharmacologist; b. Martin, Tenn., Apr. 8, 1925; s. Charles Wesley and Sara Elizabeth (Little) W.; m. Martha Isabelle Hendley, Dec. 7, 1947; children: Judith Carol, Charles Wesley, Richard Little. A.A., George Washington U., 1948, B.S., 1950, M.S., 1955; Ph.D., Georgetown U., 1959. Research assoc. in pharmacology Hazleton Labs., Falls Church, Va., 1950-55; head dept. pharmacology Hazleton Labs., 1955-58, chief depts. biochemistry and pharmacology, 1958-59; with A. H. Robins Co., Richmond, Va., 1959-90, dir. biol. research, 1978-80, dir. research, 1980-82, v.p. research, 1982-89, v.p., gen. mgr. R & D div., 1989-90; ret., 1990; lectr. in pharmacology Med. Coll. Va., 1960-64, adj. assoc. prof. pharmacology, 1982-90; guest lectr. Seminar on Good Lab. Practices, FDA, Washington, 1979, Chgo., 1979, San Francisco, 1979; apptd. expert pharmacologue toxicologue, France, 1986. Contbr. articles on pharmacology, toxicology and medicinal chemistry to profl. publs. Served with USMC, 1943; Served with USN, 1944-46; Served with U.S. Army, 1944. Mem. AAAS, N.Y. Acad. Sci., Va. Acad. Sci., Am. Chem. Soc., Soc. Toxicology (charter), Am. Soc. Pharmacology and Exptl. Therapeutics, Internat. Soc. Regulatory Toxicology and Pharmacology (charter), Pharm. Mfrs. Assn. (chmn. animal care and use com. 1971-88), Am. Assn. for Accreditation Lab. Animal Care (chmn. bd. trustees 1976-80), Sigma Xi. Clubs: Willow Oaks (Richmond); Cosmos (Washington), Masons (Washington). Achievements include patents in field. Home: 10275 Cherokee Rd Richmond VA 23235-1107 *An appreciation of the responsibility we have to society has set the standards by which I live. These responsibilities are as important as the rights to be gained from society. Those who are unwilling to assume responsibility should have no rights.*

WARD, JULIE MCDUFF, real estate marketing specialist; b. Birmingham, Ala., Mar. 26, 1946; d. Oliver Tabor and Julia Frances (Cooper) McDuff; m. David William Ward, Jan. 19, 1968; 1 child, Brian William. BS in Edn., U. Ala., 1968. Mgmt. trainee Bell Telephone Co., Birmingham, 1964-68; tchr. elem. edn. Huntsville (Ala.) City Schs., 1969-73; real estate agt. Frontier Better Homes and Gardens, Littleton, Colo., 1988—. Mem. pers. com. Ken Caryl Bapt. Ch., Littleton, 1992-95. Mem. Colo. Assn. Realtors (grad. realtor inst. designation), Jefferson County Assn. Realtors. Avocations: reading, physical fitness, cross-country skiing. Office: Frontier Better Homes 5944 S Kipling St Ste 100 Littleton CO 80127-2590

WARD, KATHERINE MARIE, school system administrator; b. Raton, N.Mex., Oct. 31, 1936; d. Robert Lee and Lucille (Gasperetti) Davis; m. Leonard Carlin Ward, Aug. 30, 1953; children: Kathy Ann, Ronnie, Tonia, Jess. BS, Ea. N.Mex. U., 1972, MEd, 1977; edn. specialist, U. N.Mex., 1981. Data reduction tech. phys. sci. lab. N.Mex. State U., Las Cruces, 1955-61; 3d and 4th grade tchr. Clayton Pub. Schs., Amistad, N.Mex., 1972-74; 4th grade tchr. Grants/Cibola County (N.Mex.) Schs., 1974-76, Title I reading tchr., 1976-77, Title I coord., 1977-82, Chpt. I coord., 1982-89, coord. Chpt. I and drug free schs. and cmtys., 1989-90, coord. Chpt. I, drug free, DARE and Title II, 1990-92, coord. Chpt. I, Title I, drug free and Title II, 1992-96, fed. program coord., 1996—. Leader Girl Scouts U.S., Las Cruces, 1966-67, 4-H, Grants, 1977-80; mem., sec. Fighting Back Robert Wood Johnson Found. Prevent Drug and Alcohol Use Grants, 1991-96. Recipient Adminstrn. award N.Mex. Study and Rsch. Coun., 1986, Chpt. I Exemplary award U.S. Dept. Edn., 1988, Merit award DARE program Grants Police Dept., 1991. Mem. N.Mex. Sch. Adminstrs., Internat. Reading Assn., Malpais Internat. Reading Assn. (pres. 1977-79, Literacy award 1979), N.Mex. Internat. Reading Assn. (Land of Enchantment Book award com. 1983-86). Avocations: grandchildren, travel, writing children's literature, recreational reading. Home: PO Box 188 2100 Ann St Grants NM 87020 Office: Grants/Cibola County Schs Grants NM 87020

WARD, LARRY THOMAS, social program administrator; b. Abingdon, Va., Sept. 10, 1951; s. Manuel Thomas and Virginia June (Meade) W.; m. Jacqueline June Moore, Aug. 7, 1982 (div. June 1995); 1 child, Nicholas Lawrence. BSW cum laude in Clin. Social Work, Philosophy, U. Md., 1983, MSW in Social Program Adminstrn. and Community Orgn., 1984. Lic. social worker. Legis. lobbyist Citizen Action Coalition, Balt., 1982-83; mgmt. cons. United Way of Md., Balt., 1983-84; program adminstr. Adams County Office for Aging, Gettysburg, Pa., 1985-86; dir. social work Margaret E. Moul Home, York, Pa., 1986-87, Employee Assistance Program coordinator, family service supr., Family and Children's Service, Harrisburg, Pa., 1987-92; cons. Drug and Alcohol, Gettysburg, 1984-86; pres., CEO Impact Seminars, Guffey, Colo., 1988—; pub. Guffey, Co., 1992—. Author: Meditations on Descartes, 1979, A Philosophical Perspective, 1979, Heracles Reborn, 1983, Protective Services for the Elderly, 1984, Why A Psychiatrist, 1985, The Blue Ridge Summit Project, 1986, The Effects of Office Design on the Delivery of Therapeutic Social Work Services, 1987, Emotional Disorders of the Chronically Disabled Adolescent, 1987, Resistance to School-based EAPs, 1989, 2nd edit., 1993, What Healthy Couples Seem to Know, 1990, Good Relationships Have Certain Traits, 1991; exec. prodr. film on courtroom survival techniques, 1996. Ex-officio bd. dirs. Grass Roots, Inc., Columbia, Md., 1984; del. Gov.'s Youth Adv. Council, Annapolis, Md., 1970-72; mem. consumer adv. council Met. Edison Co., Harrisburg, 1986-87. Recipient Original Art award Md. Pub. Broadcasting, 1969. Democrat. Avocations: tennis; baseball. Home: 365 Eagles Nest Trl Guffey CO 80820-9624 Office: PO Box 324 Guffey CO 80820-0324

WARD, LESLIE ALLYSON, journalist, editor; b. L.A., June 3, 1946; d. Harold Gordon and Marilyn Lucille (Dahlstead) W.; m. Robert L. Biggs, 1971 (div. 1977); m. Colman Robert Andrews, May 26, 1979 (div. 1988). AA, Coll. San Mateo, 1966; BA, UCLA, 1968, MJ, 1971. Reporter, researcher L.A. Bur. Life mag., 1971-72; reporter, news asst. L.A. bur. N.Y. Times, 1973-76; sr. editor New West mag., L.A., 1976-78, 79-80; L.A. bur. chief US mag., 1978-79; Sunday style editor L.A. Herald Examiner, 1981-82, editor-in-chief Sunday mags., 1982-83, Olympics editor, 1984, sports editor, 1985-86, sr. writer, 1986; sr. editor L.A. Times Mag., 1988-90; travel editor L.A. Times, 1990—. Democrat. Office: LA Times Times Mirror Sq Los Angeles CA 90053

WARD, LESTER LOWE, JR., arts executive, lawyer; b. Pueblo, Colo., Dec. 21, 1930; s. Lester Lowe and Alysmai (Pfeffer) W.; m. Rosalind H. Felps, Apr. 18, 1964; children: Ann Marie, Alison, Lester Lowe. AB cum laude, Harvard U., 1952, LLB, 1955. Bar: Colo. 1955. Pvt. practice Pueblo, 1957-89; ptnr. Predovich, Ward & Banner, Pueblo, 1974-89; pres., COO Denver Ctr. for Performing Arts, 1989—. Trustee, Thatcher Found., Frank I. Lamb Found., Helen G. Bonfils Found.; pres. bd. trustees Pueblo Pub. Library, 1960-66; trustee St. Mary-Corwin Hosp., 1972-80, pres., 1979-80. With U.S. Army, 1955-57. Named Outstanding Young Man of Yr., Pueblo Jaycees, 1964. Fellow Am. Coll. Trust and Estate Counsel; mem. ABA (ho. of dels. 1986-88), Colo. Bar Assn. (bd. govs. 1977-79, 82-88, pres. 1983-84), Pueblo County Bar Assn. (Outstanding Young Lawyer award 1965, 67, pres. 1976-77), Denver Metro C. of C. (bd. dirs.), Denver Civic Ventures, Harvard Law Sch. Assn. Colo. (pres. 1972), Kiwanis (pres. 1969). Democrat. Roman Catholic. Home: 1551 Larimer St Apt 2601 Denver CO 80202-1638 Office: Denver Ctr Performing Arts 1050 13th St Denver CO 80204-2157

WARD, LLEWELLYN O(RCUTT), III, oil company executive; b. Oklahoma City, July 24, 1930; s. Llewellyn Orcutt II and Addie (Reisdorph) W.; m. Myra Beth Gungoll, Oct. 29, 1955: children: Casidy Ann, William Carlton. Student, Okla. Mil. Acad. Jr. Coll., 1948-50; BS, Okla. U., 1953; postgrad. Harvard U., 1986. Registered profl. engr., Okla. Dist. engr. Delhi-Taylor Oil Corp., Tulsa, 1955-56; ptnr. Ward-Gungoll Oil Investments, Enid, Okla., 1956—; owner L.O. Ward Oil Ops., Enid, 1963—; mem. Okla. Gov.'s Adv. Coun. on Energy; rep. to Interstate Oil Compact Commn.; bd. dirs. Community Bank and Trust Co. Enid. Chmn. Indsl. Devel. Commn., Enid, 1968—; active YMCA; mem. bd. visitors Coll. Engring., U. Okla.; mem. adv. coun. Sch. Bus., trustee Phillips U., Enid, Univ. Bd., Pepperdine, Calif.; Okla. chmn. U.S. Olympic Com., 1986—; chmn. bd. Okla. Polit. Action Com., 1974—, Bass Hosp.; Rep. chmn. Garfield County, 1967-69; Rep. nat. committeeman from Okla.; bd. dirs. Enid Indsl. Devel.

Found. Served with C.E., U.S. Army, 1953-55. Mem. Ind. Petroleum Assn. Am. (chmn. 1996—), Okla. Ind. Petroleum Assn. (pres., bd. dirs.), Nat. Petroleum Council, Enid C. of C. (v.p., then pres.), Alpha Tau Omega. Methodist. Clubs: Toastmasters (pres. Enid chpt. 1966), Am. Bus. (pres. 1964). Lodges: Masons, Shriners, Rotary (pres. Enid 1990-91). Home: 900 Brookside Dr Enid OK 73703-6941 Office: 502 S Fillmore St Enid OK 73703-5703

WARD, LOUIS EMMERSON, retired physician; b. Mt. Vernon, Ill., Jan. 19, 1918; s. Henry Ben Pope and Aline (Emmerson) W.; m. Nan Talbot, June 5, 1942; children—Nancy, Louis, Robert, Mark; m. Marian Mansfield, Jan. 27, 1979. A.B., U. Ill., 1939; M.D., Harvard, 1943; M.S. in Medicine, U. Minn., 1949. Intern Ill. Research and Ednl. Hosp., Chgo., 1943; fellow medicine Mayo Found., 1946-49; cons. medicine, rheumatology Mayo Clinic, 1950-83, chmn. bd. govs., 1964-75. Contbr. articles to profl. jours. Vice chmn. bd. trustees Mayo Found., 1964-76; past bd. dirs. Fund for Republic, Ctr. for Study Democratic Instns., Arthritis Found.; mem. Nat. Council Health Planning and Devel., 1976-83. Recipient U. Ill. Alumni Achievement award, 1968; recipient disting. alumnus award Mayo Found., 1983. Master Am. Coll. Rheumatology (pres. 1969-70); mem. AMA, Nat. Soc. Clin. Rheumatologists (pres. 1967-69), Ctrl. Soc. Clin. Rsch., Minn. Med. Soc., Zumbro Valley Med. Soc., So. Minn. Med. Assn., Phi Beta Kappa, Sigma Xi, Alpha Omega Alpha, Phi Delta Theta. Home: 30 Raeburn Ct Port Ludlow WA 98365-9796

WARD, LYNDA SUE SCOVILLE, special education educator, writer; b. Pampa, Tex., Jan. 5, 1945; d. Kenneth E. and Opal Myrle (Turner) Scoville; m. Bruce C. Ward, Oct. 1, 1976; children: J. Wade Bainum, Jennifer L. Bainum. BS in Edn., Emporia (Kans.) State U., 1967; MS in Edn., U. Kans., 1973; postgrad., Wichita (Kans.) State U. Cert. learning disabled, educable mentally handicapped, psychology, composition and lit., Kans., Tex. Tchr. educable mentally handicapped and learning disabled Shawnee Mission (Kans.) Pub. Schs., 1967-69; tchr. headstart program Hutchinson Pub. Schs., 1968; tchr. educable mentally handicapped Chanute High Sch., Iola, Kans., 1974-76; tchr. learning and behavior disabled Sedgwick County Area Spl. Edn. Svcs. Coop., Goddard, Kans., 1979-80; tchr. learning disabled coun. spl. edn. program Butler County Sch. Bd., El Dorado, Kans., 1986-87; tchr. learning disabled Wichita Pub. Schs., 1987-89; writer and researcher, Andover, Kans., 1989-91; legal adminstrv. asst., 1992-94; tchr. learning and behavior disabled So. Tex. Ind. Sch. Dist., Mercedes, 1995—. Author: A Scoville Branch in America: A Genealogy and Story (1660-1990). Grantee U. Kans. Mem. AAUW, ASCD, DAR (Eunice Sterling chpt. registrar), Coun. for Exceptional Children, Psi Chi.

WARD, MARTHA GAIL JOINER, adult education educator; d. Woffard Johnston and Tommie Lee Joiner; m. James Edward Ward; 1 child, Jonathan Calder. Student, Brunswick (Ga.) Jr. Coll., 1971; BFA in Art Edn., Valdosta State Coll., 1974; MEd in Early Childhood Edn., Ga. So. Coll., 1985, postgrad., 1987. Reading instr. Madison County (Fla.) Sch. Bd., 1974-76; tchr. David Emanuel Acad., Stillmore, Ga., 1976-78, Candler County Bd. Edn., Metter, Ga., 1979-87; learning svcs. coord. The Job Network Ctr., Ga. So. U., Statesboro, 1987-90; adult edn. instr. Swainsboro Tech. Inst., 1990—. Reviewer series of math books: Math Matters for Adults, 1992. Recipient Most Innovative Program of the Yr. award State of Ga.'s Job Tng. Partnership Act 8% Grant, 1989. Mem. Ga. Adult Literacy Assn., Profl. Assn. Ga. Educators (state student group liaison, Candler County chpt. pres. 1986), Ga. Adult Edn. Assn., Inc., Kappa Delta Pi (chpt. pres. 1989-90), Delta Kappa Gamma Soc. Internat. (Beta Beta chpt.). Avocations: pottery, painting, camping, fishing, scuba diving. Home: RR 2 Box 110 Metter GA 30439-9548 Office: Swainsboro Tech Inst 201 Kite Rd Swainsboro GA 30401-1852

WARD, MARVIN MARTIN, retired state senator; b. Newport News, Va., Feb. 10, 1914; s. Charles Tilden and Nora Belle (Martin) W.; m. Mary June Darden, Aug. 23, 1941; children: Elizabeth Darden Ward Cone, Marvin Thomas. BS, Appalachian U., 1934; MA, U. N.C., 1940. Tchr. Bethel Sch., Midland, N.C., 1934-37, Reynolds High Sch., Winston-Salem, N.C., 1937-46; prin. Granville Elem. Sch., Winston-Salem, N.C., 1946-49; asst. supt. Winston-Salem City Schs., 1949-62, supt., 1962-63; supt. Winston-Salem/Forsyth County Schs., 1963-76; mem. N.C. State Senate, Raleigh, 1979-94; ret., 1994; mem. exec. com. N.C. Pub. Sch. Forum, Raleigh, 1986—; mem. edn. com. Nat. Cong. State Legis., Denver, 1985—. Sunday sch. tchr. Centenary Meth. Ch., Winston-Salem, 1941—; mem. Forsyth County Emergency Planning Com., Winston-Salem, 1987—. Recipient Valand award Mental Health Assocs. Inc., Raleigh, 1982, Leadership award N.C. Assn. Educators, 1985; named Disting. Alumni Appalachian State U., 1986, The Educator A. Phillip Randolph Inst., 1989, Legis. of Yr. N.C. Nurses Assn., 1989. Mem. Winston-Salem C. of C., Lions, Ardmore Community Club (pres. 1950). Democrat. Avocations: golf, fishing, travel, photography, wood carving. Home: 641 Yorkshire Rd Winston Salem NC 27106-5541

WARD, MICHAEL DELAVAN, congressman, former state legislator; b. Jan. 7, 1951; s. Jasper Dudley III and Lucretia (Baldwin) W.; m. Christina Heavrin, July 18, 1975; children: Jasper Dudley IV, Kevin Michael. BS, U. Louisville, 1975. Salesperson Matthew Bender & Co., Louisville, 1979-83; owner Campaign Svcs., Polit. Cons., Louisville, 1983—; campaign mgr. Ron Mazzoli for Congress, Louisville, 1984; salesman Sta. WAVG, Louisville, 1984-85; spl. asst. Jefferson County, Louisville, 1985-88; state rep. Ky. Gen. Assembly, Frankfort, 1988-93; mem. 3rd congl. dist. U.S. Ho Reps., 1994—. State chair Common Cause/Ky. Louisville, 1975-77, 79-80; treas. Jefferson County Dem. Com., Louisville, 1984-91; bd. dirs. Ohio Valley March of Dimes, 1987-88. Mem. Kentuckiana Hemophilia Soc. (bd. dirs. 1987—), Action League for Physically Handicapped Adults (bd. dirs. 1987—). Home: 1905 Deer Park Ave Louisville KY 40205-1201 Office: 1032 Longworth Washington DC 20015*

WARD, MILTON HAWKINS, mining company executive; b. Bessemer, Ala., Aug. 1, 1932; s. William Howard and Mae Ivy (Smith) W.; m. Sylvia Adele Randle, June 30, 1951; children: Jeffrey Randle, Lisa Adele. BS in Mining Engring., U. Ala., 1955, MS in Engring., 1981; MBA, U. N.Mex., 1974; DEng (hon.), Colo. Sch. of Mines, 1994. Registered profl. engr., Tex., Ala. Supr., engr. San Manuel (Ariz.) Copper Corp., 1955-60; mine supt., divsn. supt., gen. supt. of mines, divsn. engr. Kerr-McGee Corp., Oklahoma City and Grants, N.Mex., 1960-66; gen. mgr. Homestake Mining Co., Grants, 1966-70; v.p. ops. Ranchers Exploration & Devel. Corp., Albuquerque, 1970-74; pres., bd. dirs. Freeport Minerals Co., N.Y.C., 1974-85; pres., COO Freeport-McMoRan, Inc., New Orleans, 1985-92, also bd. dirs.; chmn., pres. CEO Cyprus Amax Minerals Co., Englewood, Colo., 1992—; chmn., CEO Amax Gold Inc., 1993—; bd. dirs. Mineral Info. Inst., Inc., Internat. Copper Assn. Contbr. articles to profl. jours. Bd. trustees Western Regional Coun.; bd. dirs. Smithsonian Nat. Mus. Natural History, Nat. Mining Hall of Fame and Mus.; mem. adv. bd. bus. coun. Tulane U. Sch. Bus.; disting. engring. fellow U. Ala., also mem. minin engring. adv. coun., mem. Pres.'s cabinet. Recipient Daniel C. Jackling award and Saunders gold medal Soc. Mining, Metallurgy and Exploration, 1992; inductee Am. Mining Hall of Fame. Fellow Inst. Mining and Metallurgy (London); mem. NAE, AIME (former sect. chmn., Disting. Mem. award), Am. Mining Congress, Nat. Mining Assn. (dir.), Am. Australian Assn., Mining and Metall. Soc. Am. (pres. 1981-83, exec. com.), Can. Inst. Mining and Metall., NAM (natural resources com.), Internat. Copper Assn. (bd. dirs.), Copper Club, Cherry Hills Country Club (Englewood), Met. Club (Washington), Met. Club (Englewood). Republican. Presbyterian. Office: Cyprus Amax Minerals Co 9100 E Mineral Circle Englewood CO 80112

WARD, NEIL O., otolaryngologist; b. Chippewa Falls, Wis., 1934. MD, George Washington U., 1963. Rotating intern LDS Hosp., Salt Lake City, 1963-64; resident in gen. surgery Wadsworth/VA Hosp., L.A., 1964-65, resident in otolaryngoloty, 1965-68; mem. staff Good Samaritan Hosp., Phoenix; pvt. practice. Mem. AMA, ACS, AAO-HNS, ASHNS. Office: Ariz Phys Ctr 1331 N 7th St # 375 Phoenix AZ 85006-2772*

WARD, NICHOLAS DONNELL, lawyer; b. N.Y.C., July 30, 1941; s. Francis Xavier and Sarah Delamater (Donnell) W.; m. Elizabeth Reed Lowman, Sept. 6, 1968 (dec.); m. Virginia Ann McArthur, June 7, 1985 (div. 1993). BA, Columbia Coll., 1963; LLB, Georgetown U., 1966. Bar: D.C. 1967, U.S. Supreme Ct. 1977. Assoc. Hamilton & Hamilton, Washington, 1967-72, ptnr., 1973-85; ptnr. Muir & Ward, Chartered, 1986-87, Noterman and Ward, Washington, 1987-90; pvt. practice Washington, 1990—; instr. paralegal progams U. Md., College Park, 1975-77, Georgetown U., Washington, 1977, 89; mem. adv. com. on Superior Ct. rules of probate and fiduciary procedure, Superior Ct. of D.C., 1975—, cons. Register of Wills, 1987-88, rules cons., 1988-89; mem. Jud. Conf., D.C., 1981—, D.C. Cir., 1981, 84, 85; mem. faculty Mus. Mgmt. Inst., Berkeley, Calif., 1979-86; adj. prof. Sch. Law Cath. U., 1986-88. Editor legal form book: Will and Testamentary Trust Forms, 1974, 2d edit. 1982, 3d edit. 1993 (ABA Spl. Recognition award 1982); state editor Wilkins' Drafting Wills and Trust Agreements, D.C. Supplement; author-reviser Digest of D.C. Probate Law for The Probate Counsel, 1990—; contbr. articles to profl. jours.; performer and author phonograph record: The Roast Beef of Old England, Come Dance With Me In Ireland. Trustee Benjamin Franklin U., Washington, 1976-79; ann. corp. mem. Children's Hosp. of D.C., Washington, 1971-81; trustee Conf. Meml. Assn., Inc., Washington, 1975-77; knight Mil. and Hospitaller Order of Saint Lazarus of Jerusalem, 1977—; Receiver Commandery of the Atlantic, 1987—; officer The Am. Soc. Most Venerable Order of Hosp. of St. John of Jerusalem, 1992—; pres. gen. Gen. Soc. of War of 1812, 1984-87; gen. sec. Gen. Soc. SR, 1976-85; gov. gen. Hereditary Order of Descendants of Col. Govs., 1983-85; gov. Soc. of Col. Wars in D.C., 1982-84; mem. steering com. Friends of Music at Smithsonian, 1986—. Staff sgt. USAR, 1966-72. Recipient Samuel Green award N.H. Soc. of Cin., 1991. Fellow Am. Coll. Trust and Estate Counsel (state chmn. 1987-92), Nat. Assn. Coll. and Univ. Attys. (sec.-treas. 1979-86, chmn. sect. on univ. mus. and collections 1981-86); mem. Bar Assn. of D.C. (bd. dirs. 1979-81, treas. 1982-85, trustee rsch. found. 1986-88, 1990—, pres. 1992-93, Marvin E. Preis award 1980), D.C. Estate Planning Coun. (bd. dir. 1985-87, membership com. 1983-86), ABA (real property, probate and trust law sect., chmn. com. on charitable instns. 1985-89, chair com. on estate planning and drafting: charitable giving 1990-92, state reporter on current probate and trust law decisions 1983-92, mem. com. on exempt orgns. sect. taxation 1991—, mem. at large com. on nonprofit corps. sect. bus. 1989—), Am. Law Inst. (planning com. and faculty continuing legal edn. program, legal problems of mus. adminstn. 1975—), Selden Soc., Am. Soc. for Legal History, Associated Musicians of Greater N.Y., Am. Fedn. Musicians, D.C. Jaycees (bd. dir. Downtown chpt. 1971-72, legal counsel, 1972-74), D.C. Bar (trustee client's security fund 1981-1990, chmn. 1983-90, chmn. sect. 8, estates, trust and probate sect. 1984-86, cert. appreciation for contbns. to continuing legal edn. 1989), Am. Counsel Assn. (sec.-treas. 1987-89), Am. Arbitration Assn. (panel of arbitrators), Cosmos Club (bd. mgmt. 1984-86, 87-90, sec. 1986-87), Met. Club, City Tavern Club (reciprocity com. 1989—, bd. govs. 1992—), Union Club, St. Nicholas Soc. of City N.Y. (bd. mgrs. 1985-89), The Barristers (v.p. 1989-90), The Counsellors, Soc. Cin., N.H. Soc., Alpha Delta Phi, Phi Delta Phi (pres. Barrister Inn 1977-78, Samuel Green award 1991). Episcopalian. Avocation: golf, flutist. Home: 1690 32nd St NW Washington DC 20007-2969 Office: 1000 Potomac St NW Ste 300 Washington DC 20007-3501

WARD, PATRICIA SCOTT, secondary special education educator; b. Atlanta, Feb. 2, 1937; d. Daniel M. and Susie (Ramsey) Scott; m. Albert Ray Ward, Jan. 6, 1956; children: Albert Ray Jr., Felicia Gail. BA, Spelman Coll., Atlanta, 1963; MA, Atlanta U., 1974, EdS, 1979; cert. in computer literacy, Dartmouth Coll., 1986. Cert. learning disabilities, computer literacy, info. processing, ga. Tchr. handicapped Atlanta Pub. Schs.; adj. prof. Atlanta U. Computer literacy fellow, 1986; computer grantee, 1988. Mem. ASCD, Nat. Coun. Tchrs. Math., ASPEW.

WARD, PETER ALLAN, pathologist, educator; b. Winsted, Conn., Nov. 1, 1934; s. Parker J. and Mary Alice (McEvoy) W. B.S., U. Mich., Ann Arbor, 1958, M.D., 1960. Diplomate: Am. Bd. Anat. Pathology, Am. Bd. Immunopathology. Intern Bellevue Hosp., 1960-61; resident U. Mich. Hosp., Ann Arbor, 1961-63; postdoctoral fellow Scripps Clinic, La Jolla, Calif., 1963-65; chief immunobiology br. Armed Forces Inst. Pathology, Washington, 1967-71; prof. dept. pathology, chmn. dept. U. Conn. Health Center, Farmington, 1971-80; prof., chmn. dept. pathology U. Mich., Ann Arbor, 1980—; interim dean U. Mich. Med. Sch., 1982-85, 1st Godfrey D. Stobbe prof. pathology, 1987; Disting. faculty lectr. U. Mich. Biomed. Rsch. Coun., 1989; cons. VA Hosp., 1980—; mem. rsch. rev. com. NHLBI, NIH, Bethesda, Md., 1978-82, Inst. Medicine/NAS, 1990—; trustee Am. Bd. Pathology, 1988—, pres., 1996; bd. dirs. Univs. Assoc. for Rsch. and Edn. in Pathology, Inc., 1978—, pres. bd. dirs., 1988-90; chmn., mem. sch. adv. bd. Armed Forces Inst. Pathology, Washington, 1981-83; mem. pathology A study sect. NIH, 1972-76, chmn., 1976-768; pres.-elect U.S./Can. Acad. Pathology, 1991-92, pres., 1992-93. Capt., M.C. U.S. Army, 1965-67. Recipient Borden Research award U. Mich. Med. Sch., Ann Arbor, 1960; recipient Research and Devel. award U.S. Army, 1969, Meritorious Civilian Service award Dept. Army, 1970, Parke-Davis award Am. Soc. Exptl. Pathology, 1971. Mem. Am. Assn. Pathologists (pres. 1978-79), Am. Soc. Clin. Investigation, Am. Assn. Immunologists, U.S./Can. Acad. Pathologists (past pres. 1993-94), Assn. Pathology Chmn., Mich. Soc. Pathologists. Office: U Mich Med Sci I PO Box 0602 1301 Catherine Rd #M5240 Ann Arbor MI 48109-0602

WARD, R. J., bishop. Bishop of Ea. Md. Ch. of God in Christ, St. Louis. Office: Ch of God in Christ 4724 Palm St Saint Louis MO 63115-2017

WARD, RICHARD C., advertising executive; b. 1933. With Kenyon & Eckhardt, Detroit, Mich., 1962-73; dir. mktg. Monroe (Mich.) Auto Equipment, 1973-78; with Ross Roy, Inc., Bloomfield Hills, Mich., 1978-94, former pres.; vice chmn. Ross Roy Comm., Inc., 1994—. Office: Ross Roy Comm Inc 100 Bloomfield Hills Pky Bloomfield Hills MI 48304-2949

WARD, RICHARD JOSEPH, university official, educator, author; b. Beverly, Mass., Nov. 7, 1921; s. Ralph Woodbury and Margaret (Lyons) W.; m. Cecilia Butler, Sept. 1, 1951; children: Timothy, Mary, Richard, Christopher. BS, Harvard U., 1946; MA, U. Mich., 1948, PhD, 1958. Dir. planning U.S. Aid Mission to Jordan, 1961-63; chmn. econ. dept. C.W. Post Coll., L.I. U., 1960-61, 63-65; chief planning Bur. for Near East, S. Asia, U.S. Agy. for Internat. Devel., 1965-69; mgr. internat. cons. Peat, Marwick, Mitchell & Co., Washington, 1969-75; dean U. Mass. Coll. Bus., Dartmouth, 1975-87, dean, dir. rsch., prof., 1990—, Chancellor prof., 1996; dir. U.S. Internat. U. Sch. Bus., London, 1988-89; cons. in field. Author: Principles of Economics, 1967, Development Problems, 1973, The Palestine State, 1978, Development Horizon '80, 1980; editor: The Challenge of Development, 1967; editor Third Wave, 1995-96; contbr. articles to profl. jours. Bd. dirs. Indsl. Found., 1976-82, New Bedford Symphony, 1982-85; bd. dirs. Jr. Achievement, 1977—, also past pres.; mem. exec. com. World Congress on Violence and Human Co-existence. Lt. USN, 1943-46, PTO. Recipient Disting. Svc. award AID, Jordan Mission, 1963, Univ. Svc. award U. Mass. Alumni Assn., 1983; fellow Ford Found., 1957. Mem. Assn. Social Econs. (pres. 1970-71), Ea. Econ. Assn. (exec. com.), Am. Econ. Assn., Harvard Club (pres. 1984-87, regional bd. dirs. Mass. and R.I. 1989-92), U.S. Signatory/Found. for Human Co-Existence. Home: 20 Pleasant St South Dartmouth MA 02748-3813

WARD, RICHARD VANCE, JR., management executive; b. Montreal, Que., Can., Jan. 19, 1929; s. Richard Vance Ward and Isobel Eugene Moseley; m. Elizabeth Anne Gareau, Aug. 15, 1953; children: Carolyn, Jennifer, Philip, Karen, Katherine. BSc, McGill U., Montreal, 1951; diploma in bus. adminstrn., U. Western Ont., London, Can., 1952. Indsl. engr. CIL Inc., Montreal, 1952-63, prodn. mgr., 1963-65; prodn. dir. ICI Am. Inc., Stamford, 1965-73; prodn. dir. CIL Inc., Montreal, 1973-76, v.p., 1976-84; pres. CIL Corp. of Am., Stamford, Conn., 1984-89, Ward Assocs. Mgmt. Cons., 1989—; bd. dirs. Cornwall Chems. Inc., CIL Corp. Am., Cansco Chems. Inc., Can.; bd. dirs. Chlorine Inst., Washington, exec. com., 1984-86, Friends of McGill, Inc., N.Y.C. Mem. Chem. Mfrs. Assn., Sr. Men's Club (dir., pres.). Avocations: sailing, hiking, curling, skiing. Home: 45 Brushy Ridge Rd New Canaan CT 06840-4207

WARD, ROBERT, composer, conductor, educator; b. Cleve., Sept. 13, 1917; s. Albert E. and Carrie (Mollenkopf) W.; m. Mary Raymond Benedict, June 19, 1944; children: Melinda, Johanna, Jonathon, Mark, Timothy. B.Mus., Eastman Sch. Music, 1939; cert., Juilliard Grad. Sch. Music, 1946; student composition with, Bernard Rogers, Howard Hanson, Frederick Jacobi, Aaron Copland; conducting with, Albert Stoessel, Edgar Schenkman; D.F.A., Duke, 1972; Mus.D., Peabody Inst., 1975; D.F.A., U. N.C., Greensboro, 1992. Tchr. Juillard Sch. Music, 1946-56; mng. editor, mem. bd. Galaxy Music Corp., until 1967, dir., 1967—; exec. v.p. Highgate Press, 1967; pres. N.C. Sch. Arts, Winston-Salem, 1967-74; tchr. composition N.C. Sch. Arts, 1974-79; prof. composition Duke U., Durham, N.C., 1978-87, Mary Duke Biddle prof. music, 1978-87; chmn. bd. Triangle Music Theater Assocs. Composer: 1st Symphony, 1942, Hush'd Be the Camps Today, 1943, Second Symphony, 1947, Third Symphony, 1951, Fourth Symphony, 1958, Divertimento for Orchestra, 1961, Earth Shall Be Fair, 1960, He Who Gets Slapped (Pantaloon) (opera in 3 acts); opera in 4 acts The Crucible, 1962 (Pulitzer Prize in music); Hymn and Celebration (for orch.), 1962; for orch. Invocation and Toccata, 1963; opera in 2 acts The Lady From Colorado, 1964; Let the Word Go Forth, 1965; cantata Sweet Freedom's Song, 1965, Hymn To The Night, 1966; First String Quartet, 1966, Concerto for Piano and Orchestra, 1968; opera Claudia Legare, 1974; Fifth Symphony-Canticles for America, 1976, Sonic Structure (for orch.), 1980; opera Abelard and Heloise, 1981, Minutes Till Midnight, 1982, Dialogues for Violin, Cello and Orchestra, 1983, Concerto for Saxophone and Orchestra, 1984, Raleigh Divertimento for Wind Quintet, 1986, Festival Triptych, 1987, Sixth Symphony, 1988, First Symphonic Set for the New South, 1988, Fanfare, 1988, Second Symphonic Set, 1988, Appalachian Ditties and Dances, 1988, 5x5, 1989, Images of God, 1989, Ballet Music on The Scarlet Letter, 1990, Second Sonata for Violin and Piano, 1990, Bath County Rhapsody, 1991, Serenade for Mallarmé, 1991, one act opera Roman Fever, 1993, Love's Seasons, 1994, song cycle Sacred Canticles, 1994. Bd. dirs. Martha Baird Rockefeller Fund for Music, 1971-82, Am. Symphony Orch. League, 1977-89, Nat. Inst. Music Theatre, 1977-85; mem. music com. Henry St. Settlement; bd. dirs. Durham Arts Coun. Served with AUS, 1942-46. Decorated Bronze Star; MacDowell Colony fellow, 1938; recipient Juilliard Pub. award, 1942, Fine Arts award State of N.C., 1975, Gold Baton award Am. Symphony Orch. League, 1991, Disting. Faculty Alumnus award U. N.C., 1992, A.I. DuPont award of Del. Symphony, 1995; Alice M. Ditson fellow Columbia U., 1944, Guggenheim fellow, 1950, 52, 66-67; Am. Acad. Arts and Letters grantee, 1946. Mem. Nat. Acad. Arts and Letters. Home: The Forest at Duke # 4029 2701 Pickett Rd Durham NC 27705-5654

WARD, ROBERT ALLEN, textile company executive; b. Greensboro, N.C., Aug. 2, 1940; m. Margaret Cude; children: David, Robert Jr. BSBA, East Carolina U., 1962; cert. for postgrad. exec. program, U. N.C., 1976. CPA, N.C. Staff acct. A.M. Pullen & Co., Raleigh, N.C., 1962-65; acctg. mgr. Stedman Mfg. Co., Asheboro, N.C., 1965-67; v.p., treas. Universal Textured Yarns, Mebane, N.C., 1967-71; exec. v.p. fin. and adminstrn. Unifi Inc., Greensboro, 1971—, also bd. dirs. Mem. bd. visitors Elon (N.C.) Coll., 1987—; fellow bus. adv. coun. sch. bus. East Carolina U., Greenville, N.C., mem. ecec. com. Pirate Club, bd. dirs. Named Disting. Alumni East Carolina U., 1988. Mem. AICPA, Fin. Execs. Inst. (pres. 1987-88), N.C. Assn. CPAs, Rotary (fellow). Office: Unifi Spun Yarns Inc PO Box 19109 Greensboro NC 27419-9109*

WARD, ROBERT ALLEN, JR., advertising executive; b. Summit, N.J., Sept. 25, 1937; s. Robert Allen and Edith Allen (Edith) Seiberling; m. Nancy Prescott, Oct. 3, 1964; children: Victoria, Jennifer, Robert. BA, Yale U., 1959. Account exec. U.S. Trust Co., N.Y.C., 1959-62; v.p., dir. Progressive Mktg. Svcs., N.Y.C., 1962-63, Coin Depot Corp., Elizabeth, N.J., 1963-68; pres. J.S. Riley Co., Wayne, N.J., 1964-70; pres., dir., C.G.W. Enterprises, Butler, N.J., Carelli, Glynn & Ward Advt. Co., 1969-95, All Hours Answering Svc., Pompton Lakes, N.J., 1969-93; v.p., dir. N.J. Exchange, 1969-93, v.p. direct Anserve Inc., 1993—; pres., dir. B.E.K., Inc., real estate mgmt. co., Wayne, N.J., Litho Four Printers, 1970-88, Healthserve, 1996—; dir. Devon Pubs., Butler, N.J., 1977-78. Pres., Kinnelon PTA, N.J., 1972-73; councilman Kinnelon Borough Coun., 1978-83; police commr., Kinnelon, 1978-83; mem. Kinnelon Drug Adv. Coun., 1978-83; vestry St. David Episc. Ch., Kinnelon, 1969-72, 78-87, 90-93, sr. warden, 1978-87; bd. dirs. Morris Area Coun. Girl Scouts U.S.A., 1977-80; dir. Inner City Ensemble, 1983-90, Willing Hands, 1989—; mem. sports awards dinner com. North Jersey March of Dimes, 1986-90; chmn. Yale Alumni Schs. commn., 1984—. Served with USMC, 1959-60; served to capt. USAR, 1960-72. Mem. No. N.J. Advt. Club (bd. dirs. 1970-72), Commerce and Industry Assn. of N.J. (Penpac bd. dirs. 1982-90), N.J. Home Builder Assoc. (bd. dirs. 1967-70), Bank Mktg. Assn., Inner City Ensemble/N.J. Dance Troupe (bd. dirs. 1983-89). Republican. Clubs: Yale (trustee, v.p. 1981—, pres. 1993—, Montclair); Nippon (N.Y.C.); Smoke Rise (Kinnelon), Smoke Rise Paddle Tennis (pres. 1988—). Home: 393 Ski Trl Kinnelon NJ 07405-2247 Office: CGW Enterprises 1250 State Route 23 Butler NJ 07405-2026

WARD, ROBERT EDWARD, retired political science educator and university administrator; b. San Francisco, Jan. 29, 1916; s. Edward Butler and Claire Catherine (Unger) W.; m. Constance Regina Barnett, Oct. 31, 1942; children: Erica Anne, Katherine Elizabeth. B.A., Stanford U., 1936; M.A., U. Calif.-Berkeley, 1938, Ph.D., 1948. Instr. in polit. sci. U. Mich., 1948-50, asst. prof. polit. sci., 1950-54, assoc. prof., 1954-58, prof., 1958-73; prof. Stanford U., 1973-87, dir. Center for Research in Internat. Studies, 1973-87; cons. in field; advisor Center for Strategic and Internat. Studies, Washington, 1968-87. Author: Modern Political Systems: Asia, 1963, Political Modernization in Japan and Turkey, 1964. Mem. nat. council Nat. Endowment for Humanities, Washington, 1968-73; mem. Pres.'s Commn. on Fgn. Lang.-Internat. Studies, 1978-79; chmn. Japan-U.S. Friendship Commn., 1980-83; mem. Dept. Def. Univ. Forum, 1982-87. Served to lt. (j.g.) USN, 1942-45. Recipient Japan Found. award Tokyo, 1976; recipient Order of Sacred Treasure 2d class (Japan), 1983. Fellow Am. Acad. Arts and Scis.; mem. Am. Polit. Sci. Assn. (pres. 1972-73), Assn. Asian Studies (pres. 1972-73), Social Sci. Research Council (chmn. 1969-71), Am. Philos. Soc. Home: Box 8129 501 Portola Rd Portola Valley CA 94028

WARD, ROBERT JOSEPH, federal judge; b. N.Y.C., Jan. 31, 1926; s. Joseph G. and Honor V. (Hess) W.; m. Florence C. Maisel, Apr. 15, 1951 (dec. Mar. 1994); children: Laura Alice, Carolyn; m. Renée J. Sokolow, May 28, 1995. SB, Harvard Coll., 1945, LLB, 1949. Bar: N.Y. 1949. Practiced in N.Y.C., 1949-51, 61-72; asst. dist. atty. N.Y. County, 1951-55; asst. U.S. atty. So. Dist. N.Y., 1956-61; judge U.S. Dist. Ct. (so. dist.) N.Y., 1972—. With USNR, 1944-46. Mem. ABA, N.Y. State Bar Assn., Assn. of Bar of City of N.Y., Fed. Bar Coun. Office: US Dist Ct US Courthouse Foley Sq New York NY 10007-1501

WARD, ROBERTSON, JR., architect; b. Boston, Sept. 7, 1922; s. Robertson and Sylvia (Whiting) W.; m. Sara Weeks, June 2, 1948 (div. 1953); 1 child, Robin Regina. A.B. cum laude, Harvard Coll., 1944, M.Arch., 1951. Mem. faculty dept. advanced bldg. research Ill. Inst. Tech., Chgo., 1951-52; research designer Arnold Rosner, Chgo., 1952; architect Skidmore, Owings & Merrill, Tokyo, 1953, Breuer, Nervi and Zehrfuss, UNESCO, Paris, 1953-54; head dept. design research Skidmore, Owings & Merrill, Chgo., 1954-60; pvt. practice architecture, bldg. systems, research Chgo., from 1960; rep., cons. UNESCO archtl. environ. info. system, 1976-79, U.S. Nat. Com./Coun. Internat. Bldg. Rsch., 1973-78; rep. from U.S. Econ. Commn. for Europe, 1972; mem. Chgo. Urban Renewal Rev. Commn., 1965; mem. tech. adv. bd. U.S. Dept. Commerce, 1967; dir. ARCC/NSF Office Environ. Rsch., 1984—, AIA/R.W. Johnson Found./Health Facilities Rsch. Program on Oper. Costs., 1992—, others. Archtl. works include Sci., Visual and Performing Arts Centers, Bennington Coll., Exptl. Theater, Vassar Coll., Sci. Center, Deerfield Acad. Served with USNR, 1944-46. Recipient Gov. of Calif.'s Design award, 1966; Graham Found. fellow, 1963, 75; NSF grantee 1984, 89. Fellow AIA, 1970; mem. Illuminating Engring. Soc., U.S. Inst. Theater Tech., Environ. Design Research Assn. Clubs: Harvard (N.Y.C.), Tavern. Home: 17 Brimmer St Boston MA 02108-1041 Office: MIT Rm 5-41B Architecture/Bldg Tech Grp Cambridge MA 02139

WARD, RODMAN, JR., lawyer; b. Wilmington, Del., Apr. 8, 1934; s. Rodman and Dorcas (Andrews) W.; m. Susan Speakman Hill, Oct. 10, 1959; children: Margery Ward Garnett, Emily Ward Neilson, Rodman III, Jennifer Ward Oppenheimer. BA, Williams Coll., 1956; LLB, Harvard U., 1959. Bar: Del. 1959, D.C. 1959. Partner Prickett, Ward, Burt & Sanders, Wilmington, 1967-79, Skadden, Arps, Slate, Meagher & Flom, Wilmington, 1979—; bd. dirs. WMB Holdings, Inc. Author: (with Folk and Welch) Folk on the Delaware General Corporation Law, 1987; contbr. articles to profl. jours. Trustee, mem. fin. com. Med. Ctr. of Del. Served to capt. USAF, 1960-63. Fellow Am. Coll. Trial Lawyers, Am. Bar Found.; mem. ABA, Am. Law Inst., Del. State Bar Assn. (pres. 1989-90), D.C. Bar Assn., Assn.

of Bar of City of N.Y., Am. Judicature Soc., Wilmington Club, Wilmington Country Club, Vicmead Hunt Club. Home: 52 Selborne Dr Wilmington DE 19807-1216 Office: PO Box 636 Wilmington DE 19899-0636

WARD, ROGER COURSEN, lawyer; b. Newark, June 19, 1922; s. Waldron Merry and Aline Toppin (Coursen) W.; m. Katharine More Stevens, Oct. 22, 1949; children: James Olney, Alexander More. Grad., Phillips Exeter Acad., 1940; A.B., Princeton U., 1943; LL.B., Columbia U., 1949. Bar: N.J. 1949. Law clk. to justice N.J. Supreme Ct., 1951; since practiced in Newark, Morristown, Montclair, N.J.; ptnr. Pitney, Hardin, Kipp & Szuch, 1959-91, counsel, 1991-92; counsel Schwartz, Tobia & Stanziale, 1993—; bd. advisors Am. Inst. Law Tng. Within Office, Phila. 1986-88, Law Hiring and Tng. Report, Chgo., 1983-88. Bd. dirs. United Hosps. Newark, 1965-78, pres., 1973; trustee, v.p. Newark Mus. Assn., 1969-92; bd. dirs. Better Bus. Bur. Greater Newark, 1970-84; mem. Summit Zoning Bd. Adjustment, 1966-70; trustee Eye Inst. N.J., 1973, Pingry Sch., 1966-68, Summit YMCA, 1960-62, Newark Council Social Agys., 1956-60; vice chmn. Newark Mayor's Commn. on Youth, 1958-60. Served to lt. (j.g.) USNR, 1943-46, PTO, ETO. Harlan Fiske Stone scholar Columbia U., 1949. Mem. N.J. State Bar Assn., Essex County Bar Assn., Princeton Club N.Y., Short Hills (N.J.) Club, Phi Beta Kappa. Office: Schwartz Tobia Stanziale Becker Rosensweig & Sedita 22 Crestmont Rd Montclair NJ 07044-2902

WARD, ROSCOE FREDRICK, engineering educator; b. Boise, Idaho, Dec. 5, 1930; s. Roscoe C. W. and Alice E. (Ward); m. Julia Duffy, June 8, 1963; children: Eric R., David C. Student, U. Oreg., 1949-50; B.A., Coll. of Idaho, 1953; postgrad., U. Wash., 1955-57; B.S., Oreg. State U., 1959; M.S., Wash. State U., 1961; Sc.D., Washington U., St. Louis, 1964. Registered profl. engr., Ohio. Asst. prof. civil engring. U. Mo., Columbia, 1963-65, Robert Coll., Istanbul, Turkey, 1965-67; assoc. prof. civil engring. Asian Inst. Tech., Bangkok, Thailand, 1967-68; assoc. prof. civil engring., assoc. dean Sch. Engring. U. Mass., Amherst, 1968-75; prof. Bogazici U., Istanbul, 1974-75; br. chief biomass energy Dept. Energy, Washington, 1975-79; interregional advisor UN/World Bank, N.Y.C., 1979-83; dean Sch. Applied Scis. Miami U., Oxford, Ohio, 1983-88; prof. paper sci. and engring. Sch. Applied Scis. Miami U., Oxford, 1983—; vis. scientist Csir, Republic of South Africa, 1990-91. Contbr. chpts. to books, articles to profl. jours. Fellow ASCE. Home: 4818 Bonham Rd Oxford OH 45056-1423

WARD, SELA, actress; b. Meridian, Miss.; d. Granberry Holland and Annie Kate Ward. BA, U. Ala. Appearances include: (TV series) Emerald Point, N.A.S., 1983-84, Sisters, 1991— (Emmy award for Lead Actress in Drama Series 1994), (TV movies) Rainbow Drive, 1990, Double Jeopardy, 1993, Almost Golden: The Jessica Savitch Story, 1995, (films) Rustler's Rhapsody, 1985, Nothing in Common, 1986, Hello Again, 1987, The Fugitive, 1993. Office: Ste 469 289 S Robertson Blvd Beverly Hills CA 90211

WARD, SUSAN MARIE, cultural organization administrator; b. Detroit, Jan. 29, 1954; d. Richard Guerin and Helen Marie (Stone) W. BA in Art History, Wayne State U., 1983; MA in Decorative Arts, Parsons Sch. Design/Cooper-Hewitt Mus., 1985. Intern Met. Mus. Art, N.Y.C., 1985; asst. curator Biltmore Estate, Asheville, N.C., 1985-86, curator, 1987-92; exec. dir. Travellers Rest, Nashville, 1992-94; founder, dir. Heritage Comm., Brentwood, Tenn., 1994—; sec. Biltmore Village Hist. Mus., Asheville, 1989-91; adj. prof. O'More Coll. Design, Franklin, Tenn., 1995—. Author: The Gilded Age at Biltmore Estate, 1990. Vol. Big Bros. and Sisters, Asheville, 1988-92; com. mem. Bele Cher, Asheville, 1989; vol. cons. Jr. Achievement, 1994. Mem. Am. Assn. State and Local History (state membership chmn. 1989), N.C. Mus. Coun. (chmn. computers and museums com.), Southeast Museums Conf. (chmn. intern staff devel. com.), Asheville Mus. of Art (bd. dirs. 1991-92).

WARD, THOMAS JEROME, lawyer; b. New Kensington, Pa., May 6, 1936; s. Richard Thomas and Renatha Ann (Hruscienski) W.; m. Lindley Ann Bennett, Aug. 20, 1960; children: Christine Lester, Janice Nolte, Thomas, James, Jeffrey, Matthew. BS, Duquesne U., 1958; JD, Villanova U., 1961. Tax atty. Westinghouse Electric Corp., Pitts., 1961-65; successively atty., sr. atty., asst. gen. atty. Rockwell Mfg. Co., Pitts., 1965-71, mgr. corp. devel., 1971-73; v.p., gen. counsel, sec. Disston Inc., Pitts., 1973-78; ptnr. Meyer, Darragh, Buckler, Bebenek & Eck, Pitts., 1978-84; v.p. fin. and law, gen. counsel, sec. Dravo Corp., Pitts., 1984-87, sr. v.p. fin. and adminstrn., 1987-88, exec. v.p., 1988-90; sr. atty. Buchanan Ingersoll. PC, Pitts.; dir. Buchanan Ingersoll (Europa), Frankfurt, Fed. Republic Germany, 1990-91; sr. v.p., gen. counsel Federated Svcs. Co., Pitts., 1991—. Editor Villanova Law Rev., 1960-61. Bd. dirs., past pres. Cath. Charities of Pitts.; past bd. advisors Duquesne U. Sch. Bus. and Adminstrn., Pitts.; mem. bd. dirs., pres. Bethel Park Cmty. Found. Mem. ABA, Pa. Bar Assn., Allegheny County Bar Assn., Am. Soc. Corp. Secs., Century Club Disting. Alumni, Duquesne U. Democrat. Roman Catholic. Club: Duquesne. Office: Federated Investors Tower Pittsburgh PA 15222

WARD, THOMAS LEON, engineering educator; b. Norfolk, Va., May 12, 1930; s. Thomas Leon and Emma Anna (Meyer) W. B.S. in Physics, U. Tex., 1953; M.S. in Systems Engring., West Coast U., 1969; M.S. in Indsl. and Systems Engring., U. So. Calif., 1972, Ph.D. in Engring., 1975. Registered profl. engr., Ky., Calif. Engr. Glenn L. Martin Co., Balt., 1953-55, Convair, Edwards AFB, Calif., 1955-58; prin. engr. Rep. Aviation Corp., Edwards AFB, 1958-59; group engr. Giannini Controls Corp., Passadena, Calif., 1959-62; chief engr. Parsons Electronics, Pasadena, 1962-63; engr. Delta Semicondrs., Inc., Newport Beach, Calif., 1963-64; sr. engr. Electro-Optical Systems, Pasadena, 1964-65, 67-68; group engr. Hycon Mfg. Co., Morovia, Calif., 1965-66; mem. engring. staff Truesdail Labs., Los Angeles, 1966-67, 70-76; engring. specialist Aerojet-Gen. Corp., Azusa, Calif., 1968-69; chief engr. Giannini-Voltex, Whittier, Calif., 1969-70; lectr. indsl. and systems engring. U. So. Calif., 1972-75, asst. prof., 1975-78; prof., chmn. indsl. and mfg. engring. Calif. State Poly. U., Pomona, 1978-80; mem. tech. staff Jet Propulsion Lab., Calif. Inst. Tech., 1980-81; prof., chmn. dept. indsl. engring. Speed Sci. Sch., U. Louisville, 1981-86, prof., 1986—; dir. Instn. for Fuzzy Systems and Intelligent Control. Sr. mem. Am. Inst. Indsl. Engrs., IEEE, Soc. Mfg. Engrs.; mem. AAAS, ASME, Sigma Xi, Alpha Pi Mu, Omega Rho., Tau Beta Pi. Democrat. Office: Speed Sci Sch Louisville KY 40292

WARD, THOMAS MONROE, lawyer, law educator; b. Raleigh, N.C., Mar. 6, 1952; s. Melvin Francis and Margaret Alice (Fulcher) W.; m. Ann Frances Sharky, July 28, 1980. B.S.B.A., U. N.C., 1974, J.D., 1978. Bar: N.C. 1978, U.S. Dist. Ct. (ea. dist.) N.C. 1978. Ptnr. Ward, Ward, Willey & Ward, New Bern, N.C., 1978—; instr. bus. law Craven Community Coll., New Bern, 1982-85. Bd. dirs. Footlight Theatre/Lollipop Playhouse Inc., New Bern, 1980-89, Craven Chpt. N.C. Cmty. Found., 1994—; vol. Craven County Recreation Dept., New Bern, 1982-86; chmn. Richard Dobbs Spaight Constl. Commemorative Com., 1985-89; dir. Craven county affiliate N.C. Commns. Found. Mem. Craven County Bar Assn., N.D. Bar Assn., N.C. Acad. Trial Lawyers, Assn. Trial Lawyers Am., Phi Beta Kappa, Beta Gamma Sigma. Democrat. Methodist. Lodge: Rotary. Office: Ward Ward Willey & Ward 409 Pollock St New Bern NC 28560-4946

WARD, WALLACE DIXON, medical educator; b. Pierre, S.D., June 30, 1924; s. Edmund Dixon and Thelma Marie (Hill) W.; m. Edith Marion Bystrom, Dec. 27,1949; children: Edith Marion IV, Laurie Elizabeth, Kathryn Christine, Holly Lydene. BS in Physics, S.D. Sch. Mines and Tech., 1944, DSc, 1971; PhD in Exptl. Psychology, Harvard U., 1953. Research engr. Baldwin Piano Co., Cin., 1953-54; research assoc. Cen. Inst. for Deaf, St. Louis, 1954-57; assoc. dir. research Noise Research Ctr., Am. Acad. Ophthalmology and Otolaryngology, Los Angeles, 1957-62; prof., depts. communication disorders, otolaryngology, pub. health and psychology U. Minn., Mpls., 1962—; mem. com. on hearing, bioacoustics and biomechanics NRC, 1960-92, mem. exec. coun., 1970-75, chmn., 1971-73; mem. communicative scis. study sect. div. rsch. grants NIH, 1969-73; sci. adviser Callier Hearing and Speech Ctr., Dallas, 1968-86; cons. U.S. Army, 1972-88, EPA Office Noise Abatement and Control, 1973; mem., co-chmn. Internat. Sci. Noise Teams, 1973—. Editor: Noise as a Public Health Hazard, 1969, Noise as a Public Health Problem, 1974, Noise and Hearing Conservation Manual, 1986; contbr. articles to tech. jours. Served with USNR, 1944-46. Recipient Research Career Devel. award NIH, 1962. Fellow Acoustical Soc. Am. (mem. exec. coun. 1978-81, pres. 1988), Am. Speech and Hearing Assn.; mem. AAAS, Am. Audiology Soc. (v.p, 1973-75, pres. 1976), Internat. Soc. Audiology (governing bd., pres. 1978-80), Am. Otol. Soc., Am. Indsl. Hygiene Assn., Mensa, Triangle, Soc. for Music Perception and Cognition (v.p. 1992), Sigma Xi, Sigma Tau. Libertarian. Home: 1666 Coffman St #315 Falcon Heights MN 55108-1340 Office: U Minn Med Sch Dept Otolaryngology 2001 6th St SE Minneapolis MN 55455-3007

WARD, WILLIAM BINNINGTON, agricultural communicator; b. Idaho Falls, Ida., July 16, 1917; s. William A. and Daisy (Binnington) W.; m. Thora Bracken, Sept. 12, 1939; children—Ann Lyn, William Bracken, Cristen Lee, Alan Miller. B.S., Utah State Agrl. Coll., 1940; M.S., U. Wis., 1941. With editorial dept. Post Register (daily newspaper), Idaho Falls, 1935-36; asst. to extension editor Utah State Agrl. Coll., Logan, 1937-40; corr. A.P. and Rocky Mountain newspapers, 1938-40; asst. to extension editor, grad. instr. agrl. journalism U. Wis., 1940-41; information specialist dairy marketing, handling pub. relations on milk marketing agreements and orders U.S. Dept. Agr., 1941-42; chief information sect. Agrl. Marketing Adminstrn., then Food Distbn. Adminstrn., 1943-44; prof., head dept. communication arts, editor, chief of publs. N.Y. State Coll. Agr. Life Scis. and Human Ecology, Cornell U., Ithaca, N.Y., 1945-72; prof. N.Y. State Coll. Agr. Life Scis., Cornell U., 1973-88, prof. emeritus, 1988—; chmn. nat. adv. com. on information U.S. Dept. Agr., 1953-55; agr. com. adviser U. Philippines, 1956-57, 65; communcations adviser Argentine Govt., 1961-62; agr. communications cons. Ford Found., India, 1968-69, 70; communication adviser, chief of party U. Tenn./U.S. AID India Agrl. Programs, 1972; cons. ICRISAT, India, 1973, World Bank, Bangladesh, 1974—; vis. scientist Internat. Inst. Tropical Agr., Africa, 1976-77, cons., 1978-89, 92—; cons. Boyce Thompson Inst. Plant Research, 1981-82; communications cons., Indonesia, 1978-81, 87, Internat. Center Argrl. Rsch. in Dry Areas, 1981-86; cons., mem. adv. bd. Acad. Ednl. Devel., 1985-88. Author: Agricultural News in the Daily Press, 1941, Reporting Agriculture, 2d edit, 1959, Science and Rice in Indonesia, 1985; contbr. articles to internat., nat., regional agrl. publs. Mem. Am. Assn. Agrl. Coll. Editors (pres.), Agrl. Communicators in Edn., Rotarian Club, Blue Key, Sigma Delta Chi. Home: 402 Savage Farm Dr Ithaca NY 14850

WARD, WILLIAM FRANCIS, JR., real estate investment banker; b. Everett, Mass., Aug. 23, 1928; s. William Francis and Helen (Schriber) W.; m. Elaine L. Wilson, June 11, 1950 (dec. Oct. 1993); children: Jeffrey W., Gary T., Michelle A., Gregory W., Suzanne M.; m. Marie-Louise Buchheit, Nov. 5, 1994. B.S., U.S. Mil. Acad., 1950; M.B.A., Harvard U., 1956; LLB, La Salle U., 1966. Econ. analyst E.I. duPont de Nemours & Co., Inc., Wilmington, Del., 1956-58; sec. N.Y. State Bridge Authority, Poughkeepsie, 1958-60; div. controller, dir. marketing services GAF Corp., N.Y.C., 1960-63; asst. to pres. Grosset & Dunlap, Inc., 1963-65, v.p., 1965-67; controller Dun & Bradstreet, 1967-71, v.p., 1968-71; chmn. bd., pres. Dun-Donnelley Pub. Corp., 1971-77; v.p., treas. Gestam, Inc., 1981-83, pres., 1983-86; chief Army Res., 1986-91; chmn., pres. Realicam, 1985—; bd. dirs. Quotron Electronics, Inc., Empire Nat. Bank, Eastern Savs. Bank, Apple Bank for Savs., Greater N.Y. Bank for Savs.; trustee All-City Funds; faculty N.Y. U. Sch. Commerce, 1960-64. Pres. Ramapo Central Sch. Dist., 1966-72, 1982-87; mem. facilities and planning bd. Good Samaritan Hosp., 1980-85; County chmn. Citizen for Kennedy and Johnson, 1960; Dem. candidate for Ho. of Reps., 1962; chmn. Young Citizens for Johnson and Humphrey, 55 counties N.Y., 1964; exec. v.p. Am. Cancer Soc., 1976-81; bd. dirs. N.Y.C. div. Aerospace Edn. Found., U.S. Army War Coll. Found., West Point Fund, 1979, Franciscan Sisters of the Poor Found., 1980-92; trustee N.Y. Mil. Acad., 1982-86, 91—, Assn. Grads. U.S. Military Acad., 1993—, Hist. Soc. Rockland County, 1993—. Served to capt. AUS, 1950-54; maj. gen. U.S. Army Res. Decorated D.S.M. with 1 oak leaf cluster, Legion of Merit, Meritorious Service medal with oak leaf cluster, Air medal with 3 oak leaf clusters, Army Commendation medal with oak leaf cluster, Purple Heart. Mem. West Point Soc. (Washington chpt., Space Coast chpt., N.Y. chpt., pres. 1974-76), Antrim Players, Soc. Harvard Engrs. and Scientists, Fin. Execs. Inst., Newcomen Soc., Res. Officers Assn., Am. Friends of Viet Nam (nat. chmn.), VFW, Am. Legion, Disabled Am. Vets., Pilgrim Soc., Army and Navy Club, Squadron "A" Club, Univ. Club (N.Y.), Harvard Club (Washington), Nat. Press Club, KC. Roman Catholic. Home: Summit View Farm RJ17A PO Box 150 Goshen NY 10924 also: 1271 Continental Ave Melbourne FL 32970

WARD, WILLIAM REED, composer, educator; b. Norton, Kans., May 20, 1918; s. Joseph Aloysius and Maude (Jones) W.; m. Elizabeth Jane Adam, Aug. 8, 1943; children—Claudia Christine, Joseph Andrew, John David. Mus.B., Mus.Edn.B., U. Kans., 1941; Mus.M., Eastman Sch. Music, 1942, Ph.D., 1954; student, Charles S. Skilton, L.E. Anderson, Robert Palmer, Bernard Rogers, Howard Hanson. Instr. music Colo. State U., 1942-44; asst. prof. music, head composition and theory curriculum Lawrence U., 1944-47; faculty San Francisco State U., 1947—, head music dept., 1954-69, prof. music, 1959—; asso. dean San Francisco State U. (Sch. Creative Arts), 1977-80; Lectr. panelist music Idyllwild Inst. Arts; Lectr. panelist music Cal. Music Tchrs. Assn., Choral Condrs. Guild Calif., Am. Guild Organists, Music Educators Nat. Conf., Music Tchrs. Nat. Assn. Choir dir., First Christian Ch., Ft. Collins, Colo., 1942-44, Meml. Presbyn. Ch., Appleton, Wis., 1944-47, First Bapt. Ch., Burlingame, Calif., 1949-63, United Meth. Ch., 1967—; dir., Asian Arts Acad. and Music of Whole Earth Festival, San Francisco, 1978, World Arts Acad., San Francisco, 1979; compositions performed by Eastman-Rochester, Indpls., Oklahoma City, San Francisco symphony orchs., numerous others; composer: Lullaby for a Pinto Colt, 1941, A Vision of the World, 1955, Psalm 136, 1959, Fray Junipero Serra, The Great Walker; dramatic oratorio, 1960, Symphony 1, 1938, 2, 1947, 3, 1954, Variations on a Western Tune, 1948, Suite for Woodwind Quintet, 1954, A Psalm of Praise, 1964, The Crucufixion, 1971, Fun, Love, Joy, Trains, 1971, In Town Again, 1973, Arcs, 1973, O For A Thousand Tongues, 1973, They Shall Mount Up With Wings, 1980, Four Old American Songs of Merriment, 1994, Fantasia on St. Dunstan's Tune, 1996, others.; Author: Examples for the Study of Musical Style, rev. edit. 1970, American Bicentennial Song Book, 2 vols, 1975. Mem. City of Burlingame Beautification Commn., 1988—; mem. artistic adv. com. Music at Kohl Mansion, 1987—. Recipient Nat. Arrangers contest award, 1947. Mem. Assn. Univ. Composers, ASCAP, Music Tchrs. Nat. Assn., Music Educators Nat. Conf., Choral Condrs. Guild, AAUP. Home: 120 Occidental Ave Burlingame CA 94010-5268

WARD, WILLIAM T., insurance company executive; b. 1939. BS, Drexel U., 1961. Mgr. Smith, Kline & French, Phila., 1963-67; v.p. Cambridge Computer Corp., Saddlebrook, N.J., 1968-71; sr. v.p. Health Application Systems, Inc., Burlingame, Calif., 1972-76; pres. Deltanet, Inc., San Francisco, Calif., 1977-80, Delta Dental Plan of Calif., San Francisco, 1980—. Office: Delta Dental Plan of Calif 100 1st St San Francisco CA 94105-2634*

WARD, WILLIAM WEAVER, electrical engineer; b. Dallas, Feb. 19, 1924; s. Carroll Ross Ward and Dorothy Jane (Weaver) O'Rourke; m. Lydia Maeve McPeek, June 4, 1955; children: Geoffrey William, Christopher Andrew. BSEE, Tex. A & M Coll., 1948; MSEE, Calif. Inst. Tech., 1949, PhD in Elec. Engring., 1952. Registered profl. elec. engr., Mass. Engr. Texaco Geophys. Lab., Bellaire, Tex., summer 1948, Hughes Aircraft Co., Culver City, Calif., summer 1949, 50; teaching asst. Calif. Inst. Tech., Pasadena, 1949-52; staff mem. to group leader to mgr. satellite ops. Lincoln Lab., MIT, Lexington, 1952-94; cons. on various tech. matters U.S., Can., British, and Australian govts.; presenter, lectr. in field. Vestryman, treas. local ch., Newton Highlands, Mass. With U.S. Army, 1943-46, PTO. Mem. IEEE (reviewer, named regional outstanding lectr. 1974, disting. lectr. 1995—), AIAA (disting. lectr. 1986-87), Nat. Soc. Profl. Engrs., Mass. Soc. Profl. Engrs., Dalhousie Lodge, Masons, Sigma Xi, Tau Beta Pi. Democrat. Episcopalian. Achievements include research and development on UHF airborne-early-warning radar; development of worldwide tracking range for Project Mercury, ballistic-missile testing, UHF and EHF satellites for military communication. Home: 22 Carver Rd Newton MA 02161-1008 Office: Lincoln Lab MIT 244 Wood St Lexington MA 02173-9108

WARD, YVETTE HENNIG, advertising executive; b. St. Paul, June 15, 1910; d. Leo J. and Adele (Hennig) Borer; m. Charles Saunders, Nov. 30, 1931 (div.); 1 child, Charlene; m. Charles Allen Ward, Feb. 29, 1940 (dec. May 1959); children—Allen, Vida, Herbert. Publisher Hudson (Wis.) Star-Observer, 1952-58; with Brown & Bigelow, 1942—, pres., 1959—. Profl. dancer, 1918-28, free-lance interior decorator, 25 yrs; Author: Russia Through Women's Eyes, 1956, Around the World in 32 Days, 1958. Chmn. fine arts and jewelry funding Compas 11, Phoenix.; Chmn. bd. Hudson Meml. Hosp.; bd. dirs. Heard Mus., Phoenix, Barrows Neurol. Inst., trustee; trustee Harrington Arthritis Research Ctr., St. Luke's Hosp., Phoenix Art Mus.; bd. dirs. Florence Crittenton Home.; bd. dirs. Western Arts. The Nat. Livestock show honors Yvette Ward as a Pioneer Stockman and mem. of the Ariz. Living-Stockman Hall of Fame, 1991. Mem. Phoenix Zoo Aux., Phoenix Symphony Aux., Costume Design Inst. Club: Phoenix Country. Office: Brown & Bigelow 106 E San Miguel Ave Phoenix AZ 85012-1339

WARD DIDIO, PATTY, special education educator, educational diagnostician; b. McCamey, Tex., Dec. 10, 1934; d. Frank and Bertha Ellen (Hancock) McIlhaney; m. Arthur Ward Sr., Oct. 31, 1958 (div. May 1985); children: Candice Kama, Arthur Jr., Karen Guile; m. Ugo J. DiDio, June 26, 1989. BS, U. Tex., El Paso, 1974, MEd, 1979; PhD, U. So. Miss., 1988. Cert. supt., elem. adminstr., elem. supr., spl. subject supr., psychometrist, Miss.; cert. mid mgmt. adminstr., profl. supr., profl. ednl. diagnostician, profl. counselor, profl. spl. edn. counselor, tchr., Tex. Tchr. El Paso (Tex.) Ind. Sch. Dist., 1974-79, ednl. diagnostician, 1979-86, asst. prin., 1990-91; coord. assessment Ysleta Ind. Sch. Dist., El Paso, 1991-94; ednl. diagnostician Clint (Tex.) Ind. Sch. Dist., 1991—; part time instr. U. Tex., El Paso, 1990-93. Contbr. chpts. to book. Mem. Tex. Ednl. Diagnosticians Assn. Republican. Baptist. Avocations: reading, music, writing poetry, traveling. Home: 2205 Sea Palm Dr El Paso TX 79936-3032

WARDELL, DAVID JOSEPH, travel industry specialist; b. Portland, Oreg., Feb. 4, 1956; s. Joseph Lindsay and Alice Freda (Salvisburg) W.; m. Lydia Wilhelm. Computer software developer, svc. bur. operator PDQ Data Systems, Portland, 1973-76; owner The Book House, Portland, 1974-76; agt., account exec. Gateway Travel, Portland, 1976-83; v.p. tech. services Sontag, Annis & Assocs., Inc., Rockville, Md., 1984-87; various positions including v.p. mgr. product devel., dir. bus. devel., mng. dir. vendor rels. Citicorp Info Mgmt. Services, Rockville, 1987-90; aviation, hospitality and travel industry cons., 1990-91; chief info. officer, v.p. info. svcs. US Travel, Rockville, Md., 1991-94; v.p. bus. devel. Global Travel Computer Svcs., Toronto and Vienna, Va., Ont., Can., 1994-95; sr. v.p. info. systems OAG Travel Svcs. (Reed Elsevier), Secaucus, N.J., 1995-96; exec. v.p., COO Travelogue, Inc., Washington, 1996—; cons. software and travel, sys. design, planning and integration; featured speaker and seminar dir. Travel Weekly, Am. So. Travel Agts., Assn. Retail Travel Agts., other groups; program dir. Travel Weekly Conf., 1996. Pub., editor: (newsletter) Automation Guidelines, 1982-84, Tech. Reality, 1993—; columnist: (trade jour.) Travel Weekly, 1985—; author of textbooks; contbr. over 300 articles to profl. jours. and gen. interest publs. Mem. IEEE, Am. Soc. Artificial Intelligence, Soc. Bibl. Lit. Republican. Mem. LDS Ch. Avocations: computer science, machine intelligence, patristics, writing, history. Home: PO Box 1746 Vienna VA 22183-1746 Office: Travelogue Inc 1201 New York Ave Ste 280 Washington DC 20005-3917

WARDELL, JOE RUSSELL, JR., pharmacologist; b. Omaha, Nov. 11, 1929; s. Joe Russell and Marie Hamilton (Waugh) W.; m. Leta Harris, July 14, 1952 (div. Oct. 1981); children: Michael R., Susan E., John D.; m. Doris Erway, Aug. 27, 1983. BS in Pharmacy, Creighton U., 1951; MS in Pharmacology, U. Nebr., Omaha, 1959, PhD in Pharmacology, 1962. Lic. pharmacist Nebr. Pharmacist Osco Drug, Waterloo, Iowa, 1953-56; grad. asst. Coll. of Medicine U. Nebr., Omaha, 1956-62; sr. pharmacologist Smith Kline & French Labs., Phila., 1962-64, advanced to assoc. dir. biol. rsch., 1974-78; dir. R & D compound acquistions R&D, 1978-86; pres. Wardell Assocs., Park City, Utah, 1986—. Author: more than 40 articles in profl. pubs.; inventor/co-inventor 4 patents respiratory and cardiovascular drugs. Asst. scoutmaster, Boy Scouts of Am., N.J., 1969-75. Recipient Merck Award Creighton U., 1951. Mem. Soc. of Parmacology & Experimental Therapeutics, Am. Acad. of Pharmaceutical Scis., Am. Chem. Soc., Licensing Exec. Soc., Am. Arbitration Assn. Panel Neutrals. Avocations: recreational flying, skiing, fly fishing. Home and Office: Wardell Assocs 55 Thaynes Canyon Dr Park City UT 84060-6713

WARDELL, KEVIN STUART, hospital administrator; b. L.A., May 19, 1951; married. Bachelors degree, U. Calif., 1972, masters degree, 1975; masters degree, Duke U., 1976. Adminstrv. asst. Hoag Meml. Hosp. Presbyn., Newport Beach, Calif., 1974-75; asst. adminstr. Utah Valley Regional Med. Ctr., Provo, 1976-79; dir. shared svcs. Associated Hosp. System, Salt Lake City, 1979-80; asst. adminstr. McKay-Dee Hosp. Ctr., Ogden, Utah, 1980-82; sr. v.p., COO Miami Valley Hosp., Dayton, Ohio, 1983-88; exec. v.p., COO Luth. Gen. Hosp.-Lincoln Park, Park Ridge, Ill., 1988-89; pres. Luth. Gen. Hosp., Park Ridge, 1991-93; exec. v.p., COO Luth. Gen. Health System, Park Ridge, 1991-94; exec. v.p. regional ops. south Advocate Health Care, Oak Brook, Ill., 1995—. Contbr. articles to profl. jours. Home: 965 North Ave Deerfield IL 60015-2203 Office: Advocate Health Care 2025 Windsor Dr Oak Brook IL 60521-1586*

WARDELL, WILLIAM MICHAEL, drug development executive; b. New Zealand, Nov. 15, 1938; came to U.S., 1971; m. Dorothy Rile; children: Michael, Steven. MA in Physiology, U. Oxford, Eng., 1961, DPhil in Pharmacology, 1964, MD, 1967. Diplomate Am. Bd. Clin. Pharmacology. Faculty U. Otago (New Zealand) Med. Sch., 1967-71; also rsch. officer New Zealand Med. Rsch. Coun.; assoc. prof. pharmacology and medicine Med. Ctr., U. Rochester, N.Y., 1971-83; v.p., med. dir. Boehringer Ingelheim Pharms., Inc., Ridgefield, Conn., 1983-91; sr. v.p. drug devel., pharm. rsch. div. Parke-Davis Pharm., Ann Arbor, Mich., 1991-92; pres. Protein Engring. Corp., Cambridge, Mass., 1993—, Wardell Assocs Internat, Belmont, Mass. Author: Regulation and Drug Development, 1975, Systems for Controlling Drug Utilization: An International Comparison, 1978. Mem. AMA (coun. sect. on clin. pharmacology and therapeutics), Pharm. Mfrs. Assn. (steering com. med. sect.), Am. Soc. for Clin. Pharmacology and Therapeutics (former chmn. govt. affairs com.), Conn. Acad. Scis. and Engring. Home: 1225 Fair Oaks Pky Ann Arbor MI 48104-3628 also: Wardell Assocs Internat 49 Hill Rd # 21 Belmont MA 02178 Office: Protein Engring Corp 765 Concord Ave Cambridge MA 02138-1044

WARDEN, GAIL LEE, health care executive; b. Clarinda, Iowa, May 11, 1938; s. Lee Roy and Juanita (Haley) W.; m. Lois Jean Johnson, Oct. 9, 1965; children: Jay Christopher, Janna Lynn, Jena Marie. BA, Dartmouth Coll., 1960; MHA, U. Mich., 1962. Adminstrv. asst. Blodgett Meml. Hosp., Grand Rapids, Mich., 1962; adj. Dewitt Hosp., Ft. Belvoir, Va., 1963-65; adminstrv. asst. Presbyn.-St. Luke's Hosp., Chgo., 1965-68, asst. to pres., 1968, v.p. adminstrn., 1968-69; exec. v.p. Rush-Presbyn.-St. Luke's Med. Center, Chgo., 1970-76, Am. Hosp. Assn., Chgo., 1976-81; pres., CEO Group Health Coop. Puget Sound, Seattle, 1981-88, Henry Ford Health System, Detroit, 1988—; past chmn. Am. Hosp. Assn.; bd. dirs. Medicus Systems Corp., Evanston, Ill., Comerica Bank, Dartmouth-Hitchcock Med. Ctr.; mem. governing coun. Inst. Medicine of NAS; mem. Pew Health Professions Commn. Contbr. articles to profl. jours. Served to capt. AUS, 1965. Named one of Ten Outstanding Young Men in Chgo., Jr. Assn. Commerce and Industry, 1968, Nat. Health Care award B'nai B'rith Internat., 1992, CEO award Am. Hosp. Assn.'s Soc. for Healthcare Planning and Mktg., 1993. Mem. NAS, Am. Coll. Hosp. Adminstrs. (named Young Adminstr. of Yr. 1972), Am. Pub. Health Assn., Am. Healthcare Systems, Alpha Chi Rho. Office: Henry Ford Health System 1 Ford Pl Detroit MI 48202-3450

WARDEN, GLENN DONALD, burn surgeon; b. Palo Alto, Calif., Jan. 25, 1943; s. John and Thelma Warden; m. Nori Katherine Bartschi, Mar. 30, 1971; children: Glenn David, Nori Lei, Emilie Nicole, Lianna Katherine. Student, U. Ariz., 1961-64; MD, U. Utah, 1968. Diplomate Am. Bd. Surgery; qualifications in surg. critical care; lic., Utah, Tex., Ohio. Intern in surgery dept. surgery U. Utah Med. Ctr., Salt Lake City, 1968-69, resident in gen. surgery dept. surgery, 1969-71, 74-76; fellow in renal transplantation - nephrology dept. medicine divsn. nephrology VA Hosp., Salt Lake City, 1970-71; dir. Intermountain Burn Ctr. U. Utah Sch. Medicine, Salt Lake City, 1977-85, dir. trauma divsn. dept. surgery, 1978-85, co-dir. surg. ICU, 1983-84, from instr. to asst. prof. to assoc. prof. dept. surgery, 1976-85, prof. dept. surgery, 1985; prof. dept. surgery, dir. divsn. burn surgery U. Cin. Med. Ctr., 1985—; chief of staff Shriners Burn Inst., Cin., 1985—; mem.

exec. com. dept. surgery U. Cin. Med. Ctr., 1985, com. on reappointment, promotion and tenure, 1985—, chmn., 1991, dir. search com. oral surgery, 1991, adv. com. dept. phys. medicine & rehab., 1985-87, dir. search com., 1985-87, med. scis. scholars com., 1985-87, faculty forum exec. com., 1987-89, operating rm. subcom., 1985—, equipment control com., 1986—, trauma com., 1985—, spl. care units com., 1988—; critical care unit cons. emergency med. svcs. Salt Lake City Dept. Health, 1977-85, bd. dirs. emergency trng. coun., 1982-85, curricumum com., 1984-85; burn cons. Handicapped Children's Svcs., Utah State Dept. Health, 1981-85; mem. univ. senate U. Utah, 1984-85; chmn. I.V. subcom. U. Utah Med. Ctr., 1976-80, 82-85, oper. rm. exec. com., 1979-85, pharmacy and therapeutics com., 1979-85, infection ctrl. com., 1979-85, med. dir. disaster com., 1981-85, ambulatory svcs. com., 1982-85, emergency med. svcs. com., 1983-85, critical care com., 1984-85; contbr. (with others) various exhibits and posters ACS, U.S. Army Inst. Surg. Rsch., Brooke Army Med. Ctr., Am. Burn Assn.; lectures, presentations, symposiums ACS, Internat. Transplantation Soc., Am. Assn. Surgery of Trauma, Western Surg. Assn., Brooke Army Med. Ctr., Am. Burn Assn., Internat. Soc. for Burn Injuries, Assn. Acad. Surgery, Inst. Surg. Rsch., Intermountain Pediatric Soc., Nat. Inst. Gen. Med. Sci., Soc. Univ. Surgeons, Marion Labs., U. Cal., U. Texas S.W. Med. Ctr., Ky. Surg. Soc., Ohio Respiratory Care Soc., Ohio Burn Team Soc., Am. Soc. Parenteral and Enteral Nutrition, Grady Meml. Hosp., Atlanta, U. Iowa Hosps., Miami Valley Hosp., Christ Hosp., Cin., Internat. Soc. Surgery, Ohio State U., Fedn. Am. Socs. for Exptl. Biology, Am. Assn. Tissue Banks, U.S. Army Inst. Surg. Rsch., Am. Soc. Plastic & Reconstructive Surg. Nurses, others. Mem. editorial bd. Jour. Burn Care and Rehab., 1982—; contbr. numerous chpts. to books including Burns of the Upper Extremities, 1976, Surgery of the Ambulatory Patient, 1980, Management of the Burned Patient, 1987, Manual of Excision, 1988, Immune Consequences of Trauma, Shock and Sepsis, 1989, Total Parenteral Nutrition, 1991, The Critical Care of the Burned Patient, 1992, Host Defense Dysfunction in Trauma, Shock and Sepsis, 1993; contbr. numerous articles to profl. jours. Maj. U.S. Army, 1971-74. Named Internat. Hon. prof. surgery Third Mil. Med. Coll., People's Republic of China; Mel Ott scholar U. Ariz., 1962, Paul Spaulding scholar U. Ariz., 1963, Gen. Resident scholar U. Ariz., 1963, Martha Bamburger scholar U. Utah Sch. Medicine, 1965. Fellow ACS (Utah chpt. 1980, sec.-treas. 1984); mem. Internat. Soc. for Burn Injuries, Internat. Soc. of Surgery, Internat. Burn Found. of U.S. (bd. dirs. 1992), Pan-Pacific Surg. Assn., Pan-Am. Med. Assn., Am. Burn Assn (com. on orgn. and delivery of burn care 1976-80, com. edn. 1986, chmn. 1986-87, sec. 1987-90, 1st v.p. 1990-91, pres.-elect 1991-92, pres. 1992-93, bd. trustees 1993), Transplantation Soc., Soc. for Leukocyte Biology (formerly Reticuloendothelial ssn. for Acad. Surgery, Utah Med. Assn. (del. 1979-81), Am. Assn. Tissue Banks (inter-regional exch. com. 1977-79, skin coun. 1989-91), Western Transplant Assn., Am. Soc. Transplant Surgeons, Am. Soc. Parenteral and Enteral Nutrition (edn. com. 1981—), Southwestern Surg. Congress, Salt Lake Surg. Soc., Utah Soc. Certified Surgeons (treas. 1981, pres. 1982), Am. Assn. Surgery of Trauma, Univ. Surg. Soc., Surg. Infection Soc. (chmn. fellowship com. 1986-88), Soc. Univ. Surgeons, Western Surg. Assn., Soc. Critical Care Medicine, Acad. Medicine Cin., Ohio State Med. Assn., Cin. Surg. Soc., Surg. Biology Club III, Ohio Burn Team Soc., U. Cin. Grad. Surg. Soc., Eastern Great Lakes Burn Study Group, Am. Surg. Assn., Ctrl. Surg. Assn., Wound Healing Soc., Am. Trauma Soc. (liaison bd. 1990). Office: Shriners Burn Inst 3229 Burnet Ave Cincinnati OH 45229-3018*

WARDEN, HERBERT EDGAR, surgeon, educator; b. Cleve., Aug. 30, 1920; s. Fred Edgar and Eva Alethea (Powers) W.; m. Audrey Eleanor Flaten, June 14, 1958; children: Karen Eleanor, Bradford Edgar, Douglas Edward, Suzanne Elise. BS, Washington and Jefferson Coll., 1942, DSc (hon.), 1996, ScD, 1996; MD, U. Chgo., 1946. Diplomate Am. Bd. Surgery, Am. Bd. Thoracic Surgery. Intern U. Chgo. Clinics, 1946-47; med. officer U.S. Naval Hosp., Mare Island, Calif., 1947-49; surgeon USAF Hosp., Travis AFB, Calif., 1949-50; asst. resident in surgery U. Minn., Mpls., 1951-56, rsch. asst. cardio vascular surgery, 1953-56, chief resident, 1956-57, instr., 1957-60; assoc. prof. surgery W.Va. U., Morgantown, 1960-62, head cardiovascular surgery, 1960-82, prof., 1962—, vice chmn. dept. surgery, 1968-76; cons. Louis A. Johnson VA Hosp., Clarksburg, W.Va., 1962—; bd. dirs. W.Va. U. Med. Corp., Morgantown, 1987—; physician football team W.Va. U.; bd. dirs. First Nat. Bank, Morgantown. Contbr. articles to profl. jours. Trustee Drummond Chapel, Morgantown, 1974-78, Washington and Jefferson Coll., Washington, Pa., 1974—; bd. dirs. Am. Heart Assn., 1968-73. Lt. M.C., USNR, 1947-49. Recipient Albert Lasker award APHA, 1955, Disting. Svc. awards W. Va. Heart Assn., 1973, W. Va. U., 1976; named to the Order of Vandalia, W.Va. U., 1995; named Disting. Alumnus Washington and Jefferson Coll., 1968. Fellow ACS (gov. 1988—), Am. Coll. Cardiology (gov. 1982-85), Southeastern Surg. Congress; mem. AMA (Hektoen Gold medal 1957), Am. Surg. Assn., Am. Assn. Thoracic Surgery, Soc. Univ. Surgeons, Soc. Thoracic Sugeons (founder, chair program com. 1983-84, Chamberlin award 1985), So. Thoracic Surg. Assn., Halsted Soc., Lillehei Surg. Soc. (pres. 1988), Alpha Kappa Alpha, Alpha Omega Alpha, Sigma Xi. Republican. Methodist. Avocations: golfing, fishing, gardening, reading. Home: 616 Schubert Pl Morgantown WV 26505-2330 Office: Health Scis Ctr N W Va U Morgantown WV 26505

WARDEN, JACK, actor; b. Newark, Sept. 18, 1920; s. Jack Warden and Laura M. (Costello) Lebzelter; m. W. Dupree, 1958; 1 son, Christopher. Student, pub. schs., Newark; acting classes, N.Y.C. Appeared in repertory Margo Jones Theatre, Dallas, 1947-51; appeared in numerous dramatic TV shows including Playhouse 90, Kraft Television Theater, Goodyear Television Playhouse; Broadway play The Man in The Glass Booth, 1969; motion pictures include From Here to Eternity, 1953, Donovan's Reef, 1962, Shampoo, 1975, Heaven Can Wait, 1978, The Great Muppet Caper, 1981, Carbon Copy, So Fine, 1981, The Verdict, 1982, September, 1987, The Presidio, 1988, Everybody Wins, 1990, Problem Child, 1990, Problem Child 2, 1991, Passed Away, 1992, Night and the City, 1992, Toys, 1992, Guilty as Sin, 1993, Beyond Innocence, 1993, Bullets Over Broadway, 1994, While You Were Sleeping, 1995; appeared in TV series Mr. Peepers, 1952-55, Norby, 1955, The Asphalt Jungle, 1961, The Wackiest Ship in the Army, 1965-66, N.Y.P.D., 1967-69, Jigsaw John, 1976, The Bad News Bears, 1979-80, Crazy Like a Fox, 1984-86, TV motion picture A Memory of Two Mondays, Nat. Ednl. TV, Topper, 1979, Bad News Bears; (recipient Obie award 1963, Emmy award 1972). Served with USN, 1938-41, U.S. Maritime Service, 1941-42, U.S. Army, 1942-46, ETO. Mem. Screen Actors Guild, AFTRA, Actors Equity. Democrat. Office: care Agy for Performing Arts 888 7th Ave New York NY 10106*

WARDEN, JOHN L., lawyer; b. Evansville, Ind., Sept. 22, 1941; s. Walter Wilson and Juanita (Veatch) W.; m. Phillis Ann Rodgers, Oct. 27, 1960; children: Anne W. Clark, John L., W. Carson. AB, Harvard U., 1962; LLB, U. Va., 1965. Bar: N.Y. 1966, U.S. Ct. Appeals (2d cir.) 1966, U.S. Dist. Ct. (so. and ea. dists.) N.Y. 1967, U.S. Ct. Appeals (10th cir.) 1971, U.S. Supreme Ct. 1972, U.S. Ct. Appeals (D.C. cir.) 1980. Assoc. Sullivan & Cromwell, N.Y.C., 1965-73, ptnr., 1973—. Trustee U. Va. Law Sch. Found., Am. Ballet Theatre. Fellow Am. Coll. Trial Lawyers; mem. ABA, Am. Law Inst., N.Y. State Bar Assn., Assn. of Bar of City of N.Y., N.Y. County Lawyers Assn., Knickerbocker Club, Down Town Assn. Club, Bedford Golf and Tennis Club, Lyford Cay Club. Republican. Episcopalian. Editor-in-chief Va. Law Review, 1964-65. Office: Sullivan & Cromwell 125 Broad St New York NY 10004-2400

WARDEN, KAREN BARBARA, special education educator; b. Camden, N.J., Jan. 19, 1949; d. Russell James Jr. and Harriet May (Tupper) W. BS, Vanderbilt U., 1971; student, N.J. Tchr.-Artist Inst., 1990-91, 93-94, Peters Valley, 1994. Cert. elem. edn., spl. edn., and art edn. tchr., N.J. Tchr. of handicapped Camden County Tng. Ctr., Cherry Hill, N.J., 1979, sch. art coord., 1992; tchr., facilitator cmty. awareness program, vol. cmty. tng. program Camden County Libr., Voorhees, N.J., 1987—, Cherry Hill, N.J., 1991—; tchr., facilitator integration of spl. students Magnolia (N.J.) Pub. Schs., 1990-92. Mem. Coun. Exceptional Children, N.J. Art Educators Assn., Ctr. Arts Co. N.J., Love Apple Quilters, South Jersey Spinners and Weavers (asst. pres. 1995—), Third Star Fiber Arts Build, Garden Patch Quilters. Avocations: weaving, spinning, quilting, painting, gardening. Home: 216 Atlantic Ave SW Magnolia NJ 08049-1716

WARDEN, RICHARD DANA, government labor union official; b. Great Falls, Mont., Dec. 10, 1931; s. Robert Dickinson and Helen (Leach) W.; m. Barbara Freeman; children: Denise, Michael, Joseph, Jerome. B.A., Mont. State U., 1957, M.A., 1958. Reporter, then state editor Gt. Falls (Mont.) Tribune, 1959-61; legis. asst. to U.S. Senator Lee Metcalf of Mont., 1962-63; adminstrv. asst. to U.S. Congressman James G. O'Hara of Mich., 1963-67; dep. dir. Office Civil Rights, HEW, 1967-68; legis. rep. AFL-CIO, 1969-70; dir. Washington Research Project Action Council, 1970-72; legis. rep. UAW, 1972-75, legis. dir., 1975-77, 79-91, ret., 1991; asst. sec. legis. HEW, 1977-79. Served with USN, 1951-54. Congressional fellow, 1961-62; recipient Pub. Affairs Reporting award Am. Polit. Sci. Assn., 1960. Home: Apt 502 4700 Connecticut Ave NW Washington DC 20008-5629

WARDER, RICHARD CURREY, JR., dean, mechanical aerospace engineering educator; b. Nitro, W.Va., Sept. 30, 1936; s. Richard Currey and Edith Irene (Moser) W.; m. Carolyn Strickler, Mar. 7, 1964 (div. Dec. 1978); children: Jennifer, Jeffrey W.; m. Marjorie Dianne Forney, Jan. 10, 1981. B.S., S.D. Sch. Mines, 1958; M.S., Northwestern U., 1959, Ph.D., 1963. Registered profl. engr., Mo., Tenn. Asst. prof. Northwestern U., Evanston, Ill., 1963-65; mgr. energy processes research Litton Industries, Beverly Hills, Calif., 1965-68; assoc. prof. mech. and aerospace engring. U. Mo., Columbia, 1968-72, prof., 1972-94, James C. Dowell prof., 1989-94, chmn. mech. aerospace engring., 1988-94; dean Herff Coll. of Engring. U. Memphis, Tenn., 1994—; program mgr., head resources sect. NSF, Washington, 1974-76; cons. to industry U.S. govt. Bd. dirs. Columbia Montessori Soc., 1971-73; bd. dirs. Columbia Soccer Club, 1976-80, pres., 1978-80; referee Maj. Indoor Soccer League, 1979-83. Fellow AIAA (assoc.); mem. AAAS, Am. Phys. Soc., ASME, Am. Soc. Engring. Edn., Am. Assn. for Aerosol Research, Am. Soc. Heating, Refrigerating and Air Conditioning Engrs. Methodist.

WARD-MANSON, YVONNE ELAINE, television station official; b. Bklyn., Sept. 19, 1955; d. Benjamin Owen Woolsley and Elaine Vera (Taitt) Ward; m. Chauncey D. Manson III, Nov. 19, 1988; children: Chauncey D. IV, Owyn Simone. BA in Broadcast Comm., CUNY, 1978, MS in Broadcast Comm., 1982. Prodn. and program asst. Sta. WJLA-TV, Washington, 1982-87; account exec. for TV syndication Johnson Pub. Co., Chgo., 1987-88; unit prodn. mgr. Cape Cities/ABC News, Washington, 1988-93; ind. TV cons. Vision One Comm., Washington, 1993-94; mgr. program svcs. Sta. WHMM-TV, Washington, 1994—; cons. Comm. 2000, Landover, Md., 1994. Democrat. Episcopalian. Avocations: tennis, travel. Home: 20308 Cabana Dr Germantown MD 20876 Office: Sta WHMM-TV 2222 4th St NW Washington DC 20001-2312

WARDROPPER, BRUCE WEAR, language educator; b. Edinburgh, Scotland, Feb. 2, 1919; came to U.S., 1945; s. Joseph Blair and Edna (Bruce) W.; m. Joyce Vaz, Dec. 15, 1942 (dec. Mar. 1959); 1 son, Ian Bruce; m. Nancy Hélène Palmer, July 19, 1960. Student, King Edward's Sch., Birmingham, Eng., 1932-36; B.A., U. Cambridge, 1939, M.A., 1942; Ph.D., U. Pa., 1949. Head modern lang. dept. Wolmer's Sch., Kingston, Jamaica, 1940-45; instr. U. Pa., 1945-49; asst. prof. Johns Hopkins U., 1949-53, asso. prof., 1953-55, chmn. dept. Romance langs., 1954-55, prof. Spanish, 1959-62; William H. Wannamaker prof. Romance langs. Duke U., 1962-89, William H. Wannamaker prof. Romance studies emeritus, 1989—; prof. Spanish, Ohio State U., 1955-59; vis. Andrew Mellon prof. Romance langs. U. Pitts., 1965; vis. prof. U. N.C., 1967-68; cons. bd. overseers U. Louisville, 1976-78; NEH Fellowships in Residence Program, 1977-78; seminar dir. NEHSummer Seminars for Coll. Tchrs., 1975, 76, 81; mem. ednl. adv. bd. John Simon Guggenheim Meml. Found., 1978-82. Author: Introducción al teatro religioso, 1953, Historia de la poesía lírica a lo divino, 1958, Critical Essays on the Theatre of Calderón, 1965, Poesía elegiaca española, 1967, Teatro español del Siglo de Oro, 1970, Spanish Poetry of the Golden Age, 1971; co-author: Teoría de la comedia: La comedia española del Siglo de Oro, 1978; mem. editorial bd., PMLA (MLA), 1962-69, 73-75; assoc. editor: Purdue U. Monographs in Romance Langs., 1978-90; editor, translator: (Calderon) El Magico Prodigioso, 1982; editor Historia y Critica de la Literatura Española, vol. 3: Barroco, 1983. Guggenheim fellow, 1952, 59; Recipient award Am. Philos. Soc., 1957, award Am. Council Learned Socs., 1959, fellow, 1969. Mem. MLA (editorial bd. PMLA 1973-75), Internat. Assn. Hispanists (exec. com. 1971-77), Renaissance Soc. Am., South Atlantic MLA, Acad. Lit. Studies (membership com. 1973-78), Assn. Hispanists Gt. Britain and Ireland, Modern Humanities Research Assn. (Am. com. 1976-80), Cervantes Soc. Am. (v.p. 1980-83, pres. 1983-85, Am. com. 1976-90). Home: 3443 Rugby Rd Hope Valley Durham NC 27707

WARDROPPER, IAN BRUCE, museum curator, educator; b. Balt., May 11, 1951; s. Bruce Wear and Joyce (Vaz) W.; stepmother: Nancy Hélène (Palmer) W.; m. Laurel Ellen Bradley, May 22, 1982; 1 child, Chloe Bradley. BA, Brown U., 1973; MA, NYU, 1976, PhD, 1985. Asst. curator European sculpture Art Inst. Chgo., 1982-85, assoc. curator European decorative arts and sculpture, 1985-89, Eloise W. Martin curator European decorative arts and sculpture, and classical art, 1989—; adj. instr. Drew U., N.J., 1982; vis. asst. prof. Northwestern U., Evanston, Ill., 1986, Sch. of Art Inst. Chgo., 1988; guest scholar J. Paul Getty Mus., Malibu, Calif., 1995. Co-author: European Decorative Arts in the Art Institute of Chicago, 1991, Austrian Architecture and Design beyond Tradition in the 1990s, 1991, News from a Radiant Future: Soviet Porcelain from the Collection of Craig H. and Kay A. Tuber, 1992, Chiseled with a Brush: Italian Sculpture, 1860-1925, from the Gilgore Collections, 1994; contbr. articles to profl. jours. Mem. sculpture and garden ornament com. Chgo. Bot. Garden, Glencoe, Ill., 1988—. NEA fellow, 1976-77, Chester Dale fellow Met. Mus. Art, 1978-79; Kress Found. rsch. grantee, Paris, 1979-81, Am. Philos. Soc. grantee, 1991; named Chicagoan of the Yr. in Arts Chicago Tribune, 1994. Mem. Phi Beta Kappa. Office: The Art Inst Chgo 111 S Michigan Ave Chicago IL 60603-6110

WARDRUP, LEO C., JR., state legislator; married; 3 children. AB in English, U. N.C., 1958; MBA in Fin., George Wash. U., 1972; disting. grad., U.S. Naval War Coll., 1976. Capt. USN, ret., 1986, mil. asst. to sec. defense, 1968-70, comptroller Air Sta. Oceana, 1972-74, comptroller air forces Atlantic Fleet, 1976-78, comptroller Norfolk Naval Shipyard, 1979-83, commdg. officer Atlantic Fleet acctg. and disbursing ctr., 1983-86; dir. fin. and devel. Tidewater Consultants, Inc., 1986-90; cost and fin. analyst Virginia Beach, 1990—; rep. Commonwealth of Va. Ho. of Dels., Virginia Beach, 1991—; asst. prof. English and Lit., U.S. Naval Acad., 1960-63; sr. adj. prof. in econs. and fin. Golden Gate U., 1973-90; mem. econs. faculty Tidewater C.C. and St. Leo's, 1975-86; adj. prof. econs. Old Dominion U., 1992. Bd. dirs. Samaritan House; Heart Found., Prevention of Child Abuse; commr. econ. devel., Va. Beach, 1990-91; vice-chmn. Econ. Devel. Authority, Va. Beach, 1991. Mem. Disabled Am. Vets., Am. Legion, Fleet Res. Assn., Ret. Officers Assn., Phi Beta Kappa. Home: 2208 Sunvista Dr Virginia Beach VA 23455 Office: PO Box 5266 Virginia Beach VA 23455-0266

WARD-STEINMAN, DAVID, composer, music educator; b. Alexandria, La., Nov. 6, 1936; s. Irving Steinman and Daisy Leila (Ward) W.-S.; m. Susan Diana Lucas, Dec. 28, 1956; children: Jenna, Matthew. MusB cum laude, Fla. State U., 1957; MusM, U. Ill., 1958, DMA, 1961; studies with Nadia Boulanger, Paris, 1958-59; postdoctoral vis. fellow, Princeton U., 1970. Grad. instr. U. Ill., 1957-58; mem. faculty San Diego State U., 1961—, prof. music, 1968—, dir. comprehensive musicianship program, 1972—, composer in residence, 1961—, univ. research lectr., 1986-87; mem. summer faculty Eastman Sch. Music Workshop, 1969; Ford Found. composer in residence Tampa Bay (Fla.) Area, 1970-72, Brevard Music Ctr., N.C., summer 1986; acad. cons. U. North Sumatra (Indonesia), 1982; concert and lecture tour U.S. Info. Agy., Indonesia, 1982; mem. faculty Coll. Music Soc. Nat. Inst. for Music in Gen. Studies, U. Colo., 1983, 84, Calif. State Summer Sch. for the Arts, Loyola Marymount U., 1988; master tchr. in residence Atlantic Ctr. for the Arts, New Smyrna Beach, Fla., summer 1996. Composer: Symphony, 1959, Prelude & Toccata for orch., 1962, Concerto No. 2 for chamber orch., 1962, ballet Western Orpheus, 1964, Cello Concerto, 1966, These Three ballet, 1966, The Tale of Issoumbochi chamber opera, 1968, Rituals for Dancers and Musicians, 1971, Antares, 1971, Arcturus, 1972, The Tracker, 1976, Brancusi's Brass Beds, 1977; oratorio Song of Moses, 1964; Jazz Tangents, 1967, Childs Play, 1968; 3-act opera Tamar, 1977; Golden Apples, 1981; choral suite Of Wind and Water, 1982; Christmas cantata And In These Times, 1982; Moiré for piano and chamber ensemble, 1983, And Waken Green, song cycle on poems by Douglas Worth, 1983, Olympics Overture for orchestra, 1984, Children's Corner Revisited, song cycle, 1984, Summer Suite for oboe and piano, 1984, Quintessence for double quintet and percussion, 1985, Chroma concerto for multiple keyboards, percussion and chamber orch., 1985, Winging It for chamber orchestra, 1986, Elegy for Astronauts, for orchestra, 1986, What's Left for piano, 1987, Gemini for 2 guitars, 1988, Intersections II: Borobudur, Under Capricorn, 1989, 1989 Voices from the Gallery, 1990, Cinnabar for viola and piano, 1991, Seasons Fantastic for chorus and harp, 1992, Cinnabar Concerto for Viola and Chamber Orchestra, 1993, Night Winds Quintet # 2 for woodwinds, 1993, Double Concerto for Two Violins and Orchestra, 1995, Prisms and Reflections (3rd Piano Sonata), 1996; recs. include Fragments from Sappho, 1969; Duo for cello and piano, 1974, Childs Play for bassoon and piano, 1974, The Tracker, 1989, Brancusi's Brass Beds, 1984, concert suite from Western Orpheus, 1987, Sonata for Piano Fortified, 1987, Moiré, 1987, 3 Songs for Clarinet and Piano, 1987, Concerto #2 for Chamber Orchestra, 1990; commd. by Chgo. Symphony, Joffrey Ballet, numerous others; author: (with Susan L. Ward-Steinman) Comparative Anthology of Musical Forms, 2 vols, 1976, Toward a Comparative Structural Theory of the Arts, 1989. Recipient Joseph H. Bearns prize in Music Columbia U., 1961, SAI Am. Music award, 1962, Dohnanyi award Fla. State U., 1965, ann. BMI awards, 1970—, Broadcast Music prize, 1954, 55, 60, 61; named Outstanding Prof., Calif. State Univs. and Colls., 1968, Outstanding Alumnus of Yr., Fla. State U., 1976; Fulbright sr. scholar La Trobe U. and Victorian Coll. Arts, Victorian Arts Ctr., Melbourne, Australia, 1989-90. Mem. Coll. Music Soc. (nat. bd. for composition 1991-93), Broadcast Music, Inc., Soc. of Composers, inc., Nat. Assn. of Composers U.S.A., Golden State Flying Club. Presbyterian. Office: San Diego State U Dept Music San Diego CA 92182

WARDWELL, ALLEN, art historian; b. N.Y.C., Jan. 18, 1935; s. Edward Rogers and Lelia (Morgan) W.; m. Sarah Williams Tilghman, June 29, 1957; children: William Thomas, Lelia Morgan, Alexander Tilghman. Grad., Groton Sch., 1953; BA, Yale, 1957; MA, NYU, 1960. Asst. curator primitive art dept. Art Inst. Chgo., 1960-62, curator, 1962-73, acting curator decorative arts dept., 1963-70, asst. dir. mus. svcs., 1969-72; dir. Gallery Asia Soc., N.Y.C., 1974-84, Isamu Noguchi Garden Mus., 1985-90; sr. cons. on tribal art Christie's, N.Y.C., 1992—; vis. prof. art history Princeton (N.J.) U., 1994-95. Trustee Yale Art Gallery; adv. coun. U. Notre Dame Art Gallery, 1970-84; mem. mus. panel Indo-U.S. Subcomm. Edn. and Culture, 1975-84; mem. vis. com. Asian Art Met. Mus. Art, 1977—. Mem. Coll. Art Assn., Am. Mus. Assn. Office: 88 Central Park W New York NY 10023-5209

WARE, BRENDAN JOHN, electrical engineer, electric utility company executive; b. Dublin, Ireland, Aug. 27, 1932; came to U.S., 1959, naturalized, 1967; s. Michael and Rose Anna (Ryan) W.; m. Jane Mills Orth, Oct. 7, 1961; children—Michael, Henry, Frieda. B.E. with honors, Nat. U. Ireland, Dublin, 1954; M.S.E.E., Newark Coll. Engring., 1967. Various engring. positions Am. Elec. Power Service Corp., N.Y.C., 1960-76; mgr. elec. research and tech. svcs. Am. Elec. Power Service Corp., Columbus, Ohio, 1976—. Contbr. articles to profl. jours. Fellow IEEE; mem. Conf. Internat. de Grand Reseau. Roman Catholic. Home: 2478 Bryden Rd Columbus OH 43209-2132 Office: Am Elec Power Service Corp 1 Riverside Plz Columbus OH 43215-2355

WARE, CARL, bottling company executive; b. Newnan, Ga., Sept. 30, 1943; s. U.B. and Lois (Wimberly) W.; m. Mary Clark, Jan. 1 1966; 1 son, Timothy Alexander. B.A., Clark Coll., 1965; M.P.A., U. Pitts., 1968; post-grad., Carnegie Mellon U., 1965-66. Dir. Atlanta Housing Authority, 1970-73; pres. city council City of Atlanta, 1974-79; v.p. The Coca-Cola Co., Atlanta, 1974-86, sr. v.p., 1986—; dir. Ga. Power Co. Mem. adv. council U.S. Civil Rights Commn., 1983; bd. dirs. Nat. Council Black Agencies, 1983—, United Way of Met. Atlanta, 1983—; trustee Clark Coll. Mem. Gammon Theol. Sem. (trustee), Ga. State U. Found. (trustee), Sigma Pi Phi. Democrat. Methodist. Office: The Coca-Cola Co PO Drawer 1734 Atlanta GA 30301-1734*

WARE, D. CLIFTON, singer, educator; b. Newton, Miss., Mar. 15, 1937; s. Durward Clifton and Emma Edna (Blount) W.; m. Elizabeth Jean Oldham, June 20, 1958; children: Jon Clifton, David Michael, Stephen Alan. B.A., Millsaps Coll., 1959; MusM, U. So. Miss., 1962; MusD, Northwestern U., 1970. Voice instr. U. So. Miss., Hattiesburg, Miss., 1964-69; coord. voice instrn., chmn. Roy A. Schuessler Vocal Arts Ctr. U. Minn., Mpls., 1970—; clinician, cons., adjudicator. Author: (book, song collection and video) Voice Adventures, 1988, (text, song collection, audio cassette) Adventures in Singing, 1995; made recs. St. Nicolas, 1977, Paul Bunyan, 1988; tenor soloist opera, oratorio, recitals. Mem. Nat. Assn. Tchrs. Singing (pres. Minn. chpt. 1972-73, 81-82, bd. dirs. 1995—), Nat. Opera Assn. (pres. 1978-79), Pi Kappa Lambda, Phi Kappa Delta, Phi Mu Alpha Sinfonia, Pi Kappa Alpha. Avocations: travel, hiking, reading. Home: 1923 3rd St NW New Brighton MN 55112-7254 Office: U Minn Sch Music 100 Ferguson Minneapolis MN 55455

WARE, JAMES EDWIN, retired international company executive; b. Athens, Ga., Jan. 27, 1925; s. James Edwin and Marguerite (McCue) W.; m. Petronella J. Knoors, Dec. 13, 1952; children: Marguerite Linda, Jennifer Ellen. Student, St. Petersburg Jr. Coll., Fla., 1942-43, Rutgers U., 1943-44; M.E., Stevens Inst. Tech., 1948. Salesman Chgo. Pneumatic Tool Co., N.Y.C., N.Y., 1948-61; gen. sales mgr. Hoke, Inc., Cresskill, N.J., 1961-63; mgr. instrument systems sales McKiernan Terry div. Litton Industries, Clifton, N.J., 1963-66; dir. marketing, mining and constrn. div. Joy Mfg. Co., Claremont, N.H., 1966-67; v.p., gen. mgr. Picker X-Ray Co., White Plains, N.Y., 1967-70; pres., gen. mgr. Northrop Archtl. Systems, City of Industry, Calif., 1971-82; v.p. Northrop Corp., 1971-82, dir. comml. internat. offset trade program, 1982-84; dir. Shinko-Northrop, Japan, dir. Société d'Etudes et de Prefabrication, France., dir. Industry Mfrs. Council, City of Industry, Calif., 1971-74. Served with inf. AUS, World War II, ETO. Decorated Bronze Star. Home: 10952 Cherry Hill Dr Santa Ana CA 92705-2442

WARE, JAMES W., federal judge; b. 1946. BA, Calif. Luth. U., 1969; JD, Stanford U., 1972. Assoc. Blase, Valentine & Klein, Palo Alto, Calif., 1972-77, ptnr., 1977; judge Santa Clara County Superior Ct., U.S. Dist. Ct. (no. dist.) Calif., 1990—; pro bono East Palo Alto Law Project. Active Am. Leadership Forum; mem. bd. visitors Stanford Law Sch.; active Martin Luther King Papers Project. 2nd lt. USAR, 1969-86. Office: US Dist Cts US Courthouse Rm 4150 280 S 1st St San Jose CA 95113-3002*

WARE, LUCILE MAHIEU, child psychiatrist, educator, researcher; b. Kansas City, Mo., Feb. 23, 1929; d. Robert Georges and Lucile (Bailey) Mahieu; m. Jean Andre Demonchaux, Sept. 4, 1958; children: Elisabeth (dec.), Catherine, Theodore. AB cum laude, Bryn Mawr Coll., 1949; MD, Columbia U., 1953. Diplomate Am. Bd. Psychiatry and Neurology, Am. Bd. Child Psychiatry. Staff psychiatrist, Children's Div. Menninger Clinic, Topeka, 1968-93, dir. Presch. Day Treatment Ctr., 1972-93; dir. admissions and diagnosis Children's Div. Menninger Clinic, 1974-75,77,78; cons. No. Topeka Head Start, 1976-93, co-principle investigator, DHHS-NIMH (CPR) MH#39895, 1982-87; mem. faculty Karl Menninger Sch. of Psychiatry, Topeka, 1969-93, Topeka Inst. for Psychoanalysis, 1974; cons. C.F. Menninger Hosp. and Children's Hosp., Topeka, 1975-93, rschr. The Menninger Clinic, 1982—. Contbr. articles to profl. jours. Assoc. leader Campfire Girls, Topeka, 1968-72; bd. dirs. Dance Arts of Topeka, 1974-77; bd. dirs., founder Ballet Midwest, 1977-88; bd. dirs. Shawnee County Med. Soc., 1992-94. Fellow Albert Einstein Coll. Med. N.Y.C., 1957-58, Seeley Fellow Menninger Found. Children's Div.; named Kenworthy Prof., Menninger Found., 1983-84. Fellow Am. Assn. Child and Adolescent Psychiatry, Am. Psychiatric Assn. (life); mem. Kans. Assn. for Infant Mental Health (founder, pres., bd. dirs.). Club: Alliance Francaise (Topeka). Home: 1925 SW Wayne Ave Topeka KS 66604-3138 Office: Menninger Clinic Rsch Dept Children's Div PO Box 829 Topeka KS 66601-0829

WARE, MARCUS JOHN, lawyer; b. Yakima, Wash., Mar. 17, 1904; s. Marcus Clark and Ruby Marie (Cross) W.; m. Helen Gorton, June 6, 1933; children: Robert Gorton, Donald Frank (dec.), Barbara Jean (Mrs. Wray W. Featherstone, Jr.), Mary Elizabeth (Mrs. James H. Rathlesberger). LL.B., U. Idaho, 1927. Bar: Idaho 1927. Since practiced in Lewiston; with firm Ware, O'Connell & Creason, and predecessors, 1927-87, sr. ptnr., 1955-87; ret., 1987; pros. atty. Nez Perce County, Idaho, 1943, 44. Chmn. Lewis-Clark Sesquicentennial Celebration, Lewiston, also Clarkston, Wash., 1955-

56; chmn. Lewiston Centennial Celebration, 1961; former vice chmn. Lewis and Clark Trail Commn.; mem. Idaho Hist. Sites Rev. Bd., 1969-91, Idaho Bicentennial Commn., 1972-76, Lewiston Bicentennial Commn., 1973-76, Idaho TV History series adv. bd., 1988-91; mem. nat. adv. coun. on ethnic heritage studies Office Edn., HEW, 1975-76; bd. dirs. Pacific N.W. Nat. Parks Assn., 1976-82, Pacific N.W. Nat. Parks and Forests Assn., 1985-91; past dir. Lewis and Clark Trail Heritage Found. Recipient award of merit Am. Assn. State and Local History, 1961, citation Idaho Recreation and Park Soc., 1973, Disting. Service award Lewis and Clark Trail Heritage Found., 1983. Mem. ABA, Idaho State Bar Assn. (commr. 1959-62, pres. 1961-62, Outstanding Svc. award 1988, Idaho Disting. Lawyer award Idaho State Bar 1991), Clearwater Bar Assn., Am. Coll. Trial Lawyers, SAR (past state pres.), Soc. Mayflower Descendants (past gov. Idaho soc., past dep. gov. gen.), Nez Perce County Hist. Soc. (past pres.), James Willard Schultz Soc., Scottish Gaelic Texts Soc., Gaelic Soc. Inverness, An Comunn Gaidhealach, Mont. Hist. Soc., Nev. HIst. Soc., Idaho State Hist. Soc. (trustee 1971-91), The Nature Conservancy, Outlook Club (Lewiston), Ind. Order Odd Fellows, Masons (33 deg., Blue Lodge, Nez Perce #10 , grand master Idaho 1945-46), Scottish Rite, 33d Degree, York Rite, Red Cross Constantine, Shrine, Elks, Kiwanis (past pres.). Home: 308 Prospect Blvd Lewiston ID 83501-2153 Office: 1219 Idaho St Lewiston ID 83501-1940

WARE, PEGGY JENKINS, photographer, writer, artist, dancer; b. Santa Monica, Calif., Sept. 6, 1947; d. Stanley Lauder Mahony and Patricia Lou Chapman Covo; m. James Michael Jenkins, Feb. 5, 1966 (div. May 1982) 1 child, Cheryl Denise Jenkins; m. Wiley Neal Ware, Jan. 1, 1988. Dance student of Eugene Loring, U. Calif., Irvine, 1979; dance student Valentina Oumansky, Dramatic Dance Ensemble, North Hollywood, Calif., 1969-72; dance student, Jerry Bywaters Cochran, Dallas, 1972-75; photography student of James Baker, U. Tex., Dallas, Richardson, 1984-86; BA in English, U. Tex. at Dallas, Richardson, 1986, postgrad., 1987. Propr. Mahony/Jenkins & Assocs., Richardson, 1980-82; mng. editor, writer Happenings Mag., Dallas, 1983; prodn. supr. Publishing Concepts, Dallas, 1983-85; mem. book prodn. team David Marquis/Robin Sachs-Corp. for Edn., Dallas, 1990; freelance photographer and artist Dallas, 1984-95, Sedona, Ariz., 1995—; rsch. editor Prin. Fin. Securities, Dallas, 1994; dance rsch. interviewer Simon Semenoff, Ballet Russe, Sol Hurok, Impressario. Exhbns. include Allen St. Gallery, Dallas, 1985, Oak Cliff Art Festival, Dallas, 1991, 500 Inc. Artfest, Dallas, 1992, Sedona Art and Wine Festival, 1993, Good Dog/Bad Dog, Dallas, 1994, Internat. FotoFest, 1994, Lakewood Svc. League, Dallas, 1995, Bath House Cultural Ctr., 1995, Irvine (Calif.) Fine Arts Ctr., 1995-96, Select Art Gallery, Sedona, 1996; transcribing editor: I Am a Teacher, A Tribute to America's Teachers, 1990; photographer: Photo Essay of the Berlin Wall, 1988; contbr. articles and photos to mags. Exec. bd. Friends of Photography, Dallas Mus. Art, 1993-94; bd. dirs., trustee Dancers Unltd. Repertory Co., Dallas, 1990-91; contbr. photographer Lakewood Svc. League, Dallas, 1992; writer, video producer Women's Conf., Women's Caucus for Art, Dallas, 1986. Home: 62 Morning Sun Dr Sedona AZ 86336 Office: PO Box 1891 Sedona AZ 86339

WARE, RICHARD ANDERSON, foundation executive; b. N.Y.C., Nov. 7, 1919; s. John Sayers and Mabelle (Anderson) W.; m. Lucille Henney, Mar. 20, 1942 (div. 1972); children: Alexander W., Janet M., Bradley J., Patricia E.; m. Beverly G. Mytinger, Dec. 22, 1972. BA, Lehigh U., 1941; M in Pub. Adminstrn., Wayne State U., 1943; D in Social Sci. (honoris causa), Francisco Marroquin U., Guatemala, 1988. Research asst. Detroit Bur. Govt. Research, 1941-42; personnel technician Lend-Lease Adminstrn., Washington, 1942-43; research asso. to asst. dir. Citizens Research Council, Detroit, 1946-56; sec. Earhart and Relm Founds., Ann Arbor, Mich., 1956-70; trustee, pres. Earhart and Relm Founds., 1970-84, trustee, pres. emeritus, 1985—; prin. dep. asst. sec. Def. for internat. security affairs, Washington, 1969-70; cons. Office Asst. Sec. Def., 1970-73; dir. Citizens Trust Co., 1970-87. Vice pres. Ann Arbor United Fund and Community Svcs., 1968, pres., 1969; asst. dir. Mich. Joint Legis. Com. on State Reorgn., 1950-52; sec. Gov.'s Com. to Study Prisons, 1952-53; com. to chmn. Ann Arbor City Planning Commn., 1958-67; mem. Detroit Com. on Fgn. Rels., 1971-87; mem. coun. Woodrow Wilson Internat. Center for Scholars, 1977-85; vis. com. div. social scis. U. Chgo., 1977-85; mem. adv. com. The Citadel, 1977-85; mem. adv. coun. internat. studies program Fletcher Sch., Tufts U., 1979-85; trustee Greenhills Sch., 1973-80, Ann Arbor Area Found., 1977-83, Inst. Fgn. Policy Analysis, 1985—, Inst. Polit. Economy, 1985—, Ctr. for Study Social and Polit. Change Smith Coll., 1988—, Pequawket Found., 1989—; polit. analyst Republican Nat. Com., Washington, 1964; bd. dirs. The Liberty Fund, Inc., Indpls., 1980—, Bd. Fgn. Scholarships, 1984-90, chmn., 1987-89. With USAAF, 1943-46. Recipient Civilian Meritorious Service medal Dept. Def., 1970. Mem. Govtl. Research Assoc. (trustee, v.p. 1955-56), Am. Polit. Sci. Assn., Mont Pelerin Soc., Phi Beta Kappa, Phi Alpha Theta. Congregationalist. Clubs: Ann Arbor; North Conway Country, Cosmos (Washington). Home: PO Box 310 Intervale NH 03845-0310 Office: 2200 Green Rd Ste H Ann Arbor MI 48105-2948

WARE, THADDEUS VAN, government official; b. High Point, N.C., Mar. 31, 1935; s. Elsec and Irene (Myers) W.; m. Doretha Ardella Lee, June 18, 1960; children—Kimberly Melissa, Chrystal Lynn. B.A. cum laude, Va. Union U., 1957; J.D., Howard U., 1960. Bar: Va. bar 1961, D.C. bar 1970, U.S. Supreme Ct. bar 1970. Gen. atty. Office of Solicitor, Dept. Labor, 1961-66; trial counsel Chief Counsel's Office, Fed. Hwy. Adminstrn., 1966-69; staff asst. to Pres. Richard M. Nixon, 1969-70; chief adminstrv. judge, chmn. Bd. Contract Appeals, Dept. Transp., 1987—. Served with AUS, 1960-61. Mem. Va., D.C., U.S. Supreme Ct., Fed. Bar Assns., Urban League, NAACP, Bd. Contract Appeals Judges Assn. (pres. 1988-89), Alpha Phi Alpha, Sigma Delta Tau, Alpha Kappa Mu. Home: 2213 Parallel Ln Silver Spring MD 20904-5446 Office: 400 7th St SW Washington DC 20590-0001

WARE, WILLIAM BRETTEL, education educator; b. Glen Ridge, N.J., June 17, 1942; s. Howard Brettel and Helen Burd (Dickson) W.; m. Andrea Lou Gartley, June 24, 1967 (div. May 1989); children: Emily Dickson, Matthew Brettel, Erin Johanna Ware; m. Barbara Ann McClave Reynolds, Dec. 26, 1991; stepchildren: Dianne Catherine, Kristin Elise. AB, Dartmouth Coll., 1964; MA in Tchg., Northwestern U., 1965, PhD, 1968. Classroom tchr. Chgo. Pub. Schs., 1964-65; asst. prof. U. Fla., Gainesville, 1968-73, assoc. prof., 1973-76, prof., 1976-78; prof. U. N.C., Chapel Hill, 1978—. Contbr. chpts. to books and articles to profl. jours. Mgr. youth soccer team Ctrl. Carolina Youth Soccer Assn., Chapel Hill, 1980-86. Recipient J. Minor Gwynn professorship Sch. Edn., U. N.C., 1994-95. Mem. Am. Evaluation Assn., Am. Ednl. Rsch. Assn., Nat. Coun. on Measurement in Edn., The Psychometric Soc., N.C. Assn. for Rsch. in Edn. (bd. dirs. 1991—). Home: 110 Princeton Rd Chapel Hill NC 27516-3222 Office: Sch Edn U N C CB #3500 Chapel Hill NC 27599-3500

WARE, WILLIS HOWARD, computer scientist; b. Atlantic City, Aug. 31, 1920; s. Willis and Ethel (Rosswork) W.; m. Floy Hoffer, Oct. 10, 1943; children—Deborah Susanne Ware Pinson, David Willis, Alison Floy Ware Manoli. B.S.E.E., U. Pa., 1941; M.S.E.E., MIT, 1942; Ph.D. in Elec. Engring, Princeton U., 1951. Research engr. Hazeltine Electronics Corp., Little Neck, N.Y., 1942-46; mem. research staff Inst. Advanced Study, Princeton, N.J., 1946-51, North Am. Aviation, Downey, Calif., 1951-52; mem. corp. research staff Rand Corp., Santa Monica, Calif., 1952—; adj. prof. UCLA Extension Service, 1955-68; first chmn. Am. Fedn. Info. Processing Socs., 1961, 62; chmn. HEW sec.'s Adv. Com. on Automated Personal Data Systems, 1971-73; mem. Privacy Protection Study Commn., 1975-77, vice chmn., 1975-77; mem. numerous other adv. groups, spl. coms. for fed. govt., 1959—. Author: Digital Computer Technology and Design, vols. I and II, 1963. Recipient Computers Scis. Man of Yr. award Data Processing Mgmt. Assn., 1975, Exceptional Civilian Svc. medal USAF, 1979, Disting. Svc. award Am. Fedn. Info. Processing Socs., 1986, Nat. Computer Sys. Security award Nat. Computer Sys. Lab./Nat. Computer Security Ctr., 1989, Computer Pioneer award IEEE Computer Soc., 1993, Pioneer award Electronic Frontier Found., 1995; named one of Fed. 100 of 1994, Fed. Computer Week. Fellow IEEE (Centennial medal 1984), AAAS, Assn. for Computing Machinery; mem. NAE, AIAA, Sigma Xi, Eta Kappa Nu, Pi Mu Epsilon, Tau Beta Pi. Office: The Rand Corp 1700 Main St Santa Monica CA 90401-3208

WAREHAM, JAMES LYMAN, steel company executive; b. Clinton, Iowa, Oct. 8, 1939; s. Lyman Hugh and Ulainee Maria (Pitts) W.; m. Patricia Josephine Wrubel, June 18, 1966; children: Lisa Jo, Tara Lynn. BSEE, U. Notre Dame, 1961. Various mgmt. positions U.S. Steel-Gary Works, Ind., 1961-69, div. mgr., 1976-79; various mgmt. positions U.S. Steel-Tex. Works, Baytown, 1969-72; various mgmt. positions U.S. Steel-South Works, Chgo., 1972-76, gen. plant mgr., 1979-84; v.p. engring. U.S. Steel, Pitts., 1984-86; pres., CEO Bliss Salem, Inc., Ohio, 1986-89; pres., COO Wheeling-Pitts. Steel Corp., W.Va., 1989-92, chmn., pres., CEO, 1992—; pres., bd. dirs. Wheeling-Pitts. Corp.; bd. dirs. Bliss-Salem Inc., Wesbanco, Am. Iron and Steel Inst. Area coord. Thompson for Gov., Homewood, Ill., 1978; div. chmn. United Way, Gary, Ind., 1976; gen. chmn., United Way Wheeling, W.Va., 1990; bd. dirs. United Way of Upper Ohio Valley, Wheeling Jesuit Coll., 1989—, Wheeling Hosp., 1990—. Named Small Businessman of Yr. Salem C. of C., 1988, Entrepreneur of Yr. Ernst & Young, Pitts., 1989. Mem. Assn. Iron & Steel Engrs., Inst. Mining & Metall. Engrs., Ohio Steel Industry Adv. Commn., W.Va. Mfg. Assn., Wheeling C. of C. Home: 234 Greenwood Dr Canonsburg PA 15317-5211 Office: 1134 Market St Wheeling WV 26003-2906*

WAREHAM, RAYMOND NOBLE, investment banker; b. Rochester, N.Y., Nov. 20, 1948; s. Simon Harold and Barbara (Snell) W.; m. Cornelia Lee Clifford, June 28, 1975; children: Ellinor Park, Laura Stewart, Cornelia Ashley. BS in Indsl. Engring., Northwestern U., 1970; MBA, Harvard U., 1975. With J.P. Morgan & Co., N.Y., 1975-80; head-corp. fin. J.P. Morgan & Co., Tokyo, 1980-85; exec. dir. J.P. Morgan Securities Ltd., London, 1986-87; mngr. dir., head banking industry group J.P. Morgan & Co., N.Y., 1988-92; mng. dir. corp. fin. dept. J.P. Morgan Securities, N.Y.C., 1992—. Pres. bd. trustees Spence Sch., N.Y.C.; trustee Am. Sch., Tokyo, 1982-85; elder Brick Presbyn. Ch., N.Y.C., 1989-92; bd. dirs. Brick Ch. Day Sch., 1989-92. Lt. Supply Corps, USN, 1970-73. Mem. DERU (Northwestern hon.), Union Club (N.Y.), Duxbury Yacht Club, Century Club (Harvard Bus. hon.). Republican. Avocations: athletics, Japanese antique furniture, secondary school education. Home: 1148 Fifth Ave New York NY 10128-0807 Office: JP Morgan Securities Inc 60 Wall St New York NY 10005-2807

WAREN, STANLEY A., university administrator, theatre and arts center administrator, director; b. N.Y.C., Mar. 22, 1919; s. Maurice and Minnie (Rosen) W.; m. Florence Rigal, Nov. 21, 1949; 1 child, Mark. B.S.S., CCNY, 1938; M.A., Columbia U., 1939, Ph.D., 1953. Exec. producer, dir. theatre U.S. and abroad, 1953-70; prof., chmn. dept. speech and theatre CCNY, 1967-72; prof., exec. officer Ph.D. program theatre CUNY, 1972-81, v.p., provost, dep. pres. Grad. Sch., 1981-84; dir. Ctr. for Advanced Study in Theatre Arts, N.Y.C., 1979-82, 84-86; reviewer NEH, 1978-91; advisor humanities com. Bklyn. Acad. Music, N.Y.C., 1980-81; spl. edn. cons. Double Image Theatre, N.Y.C., 1982-90; mem. adv. council Roundabout Theatre, N.Y.C., 1985—; Fulbright-Hayes vis. prof. Nat. Taiwan U., 1986-87; vis. prof. Shanghai Drama Inst., 1988. Dir. musical The Chess King (Taiwan) 1987, Old B Hanging on the Wall (Shanghai), 1988, Judas, Mexico (N.Y.), 1989. Bd. dirs. Women's Inter. Art Ctr., N.Y.C., 1978-82; mem. grants panel N.Y.C. Dept. Cultural Affairs, 1979; bd. dirs. Frank Silvera Workshops for Writers, N.Y.C., 1979-81. Served to capt. USAF, 1942-46. Grantee Herman Goldman Found., 1980-82, NEH, 1980-81, N.Y. Coun. Humanities, USIA/Arts Am., Singapore, 1990. Mem. AAUP, Soc. Stage Dirs. and Choreographers, Profl. Staff Congress CUNY. Democrat. Club: The Century Assn. (resident 1984—). Avocations: arts; tennis; swimming. Home: 465 W End Ave New York NY 10024-4926 Office: CUNY Grad Sch 33 W 42nd St New York NY 10036-8003

WARFIELD, GERALD ALEXANDER, composer, writer; b. Ft. Worth, Feb. 23, 1940; s. George Alexander and Geraldine (Spencer) W. Student, Tex. Christian U., 1958-61; B.A., North Tex. State U., 1963, M.Mus., 1965; M.F.A., Princeton U., 1967; postgrad., Tanglewood, summers 1963-64. Instr. Princeton, 1968-71; asso. dir. Index of New Mus. Notation, N.Y.C., 1971-75; lectr. contemporary music notation. Mem. conf. com. Internat. Conf. on New Mus. Notation, Belgium, 1974; chmn. program com. 2d Nat. Conf. Music Theory, 1977. Author: A Beginner's Manual of Music 4B, 1967, Layer Analysis: a Primer of Elementary Tonal Structures, 1976, Writings on Contemporary Music Notations, 1977, How to Write Music Manuscript, 1977, (with others) Layer Dictation, 1978, The Investor's Guide to Stock Quotations, 1982, How To Buy Foreign Stocks and Bonds, 1984, How to Read the Financial News, 1986; (with others) Export-Import Financing, 1986; No Nonesence Guides to the Stock Market, Mutual Funds, Tax-Free Bonds, 1991, Managing Your Stock Portfolio, Money Market Funds, 1993; composer: Variations and Metamorphoses, 1973 (1st prize Ariz. Cello Soc.); filmstrip Introduction to Musical Notation, 1976; Fantasy Quintet, 1978 (2d prize New Music for Young Ensembles); contbr.: Grove's Dictionary of Music and Musicians, 1976; editor: Longman Music Series, 1976-85; contbr. articles to profl. jours. Mem. Soc. Composers, Inc. (chmn. exec. com. 1972-74, conf. chmn. 9th Ann. Conf., 1974, founding editor Jour. of Music Scores, gen. mgr. 1977—), Am. Composers Alliance (treas. 1979—), Coll. Music Soc. (coun., conf. chmn. 1981), Broadcast Music Inc. Home: 205 W 22nd St New York NY 10011-2702

WARFIELD, JOHN NELSON, engineering educator, consultant; b. Sullivan, Mo., Nov. 21, 1925; s. John Daniel and Flora Alice (Land) W.; m. Rosamond Arline Howe, Feb. 2, 1948; children: Daniel, Nancy, Thomas. BA, U. Mo., 1948, BSEE, 1948, MSEE, 1949; PhD, Purdue U., 1952. Assoc. prof. Pa. State U., University Park, 1949-55, U. Ill.-Urbana, 1955-57, Purdue U., West Lafayette, Ind., 1957-58; prof. elec. engring U. Kans., Lawrence, 1958-66; sr. research leader Battelle Meml. Inst., Columbus, Ohio, 1966-74; prof. elec. engring U. Va., Charlottesville, 1974-83; sr. mgr. Burroughs Corp., 1983-84; dir. Inst. for Info. Tech. George Mason U., Fairfax, Va., 1984-87, dir. Inst. for Advanced Study in Integrative Scis., 1987—; cons. IBM, Armonk, N.Y., 1979-82, Saudi Arabian Nat. Ctr. Sci. and Tech., Riyadh, 1978-82, Ghana Tech. Transfer Ctr., Accra, 1989—, Niagara-Mohawk Power Co., 1989, Ford Motor Co., 1990—, Defense Systems Mgmt. Coll., 1990—. Author: Societal Systems, 1976, A Science of Generic Design, 1990, A Handbook of Interactive Management, 1994; inventor interpretive structural modeling, 1973; editor: IEEE Transactions on Systems, Man, and Cybernetics, 1968-73, Systems Research, 1981-90. Recipient Excellence in Instrn. award Western Electric Co., 1966, Peace Pipe award Ams. for Indian Opportunity, 1987, Best Paper award European Conf. Cyberneti s and Systems, 1988, Mayour's cert. City of Austin, 1993, Plaque of Recognition, Mex. Ministry of Social Devel., 1994, Spl. Recognition award Internat. Soc. Design and Process Sci., 1995. Fellow IEEE (life, outstanding contbn. award 1977, Centennial medal 1984); mem. Systems, Man and Cybernetics Soc. (pres. 1972), Soc. Gen. Systems Research (pres. 1982-83), Assn. for Integrative Studies, Internat. Soc. Panetics. Home: 4308 Wakefield Dr Annandale VA 22003-3611 Office: George Mason U Inst. Advanced Study in Integrative Sci Fairfax VA 22030

WARFIELD, WILLIAM CAESAR, singer, actor, educator; b. West Helena, Ark., Jan. 22, 1920; s. Robert Elza and Bertha (McCamery) W.; m. Leontyne Price, Aug. 31, 1952 (div. Dec. 1972). MusB, Eastman Sch. Music, 1942; LLD (hon.), U. Ark., 1972; MusD (hon.), Lafayette Coll., 1978. Prof. music dept. U. Ill., Champaign, 1974—; Bd. dirs. N.Y. Coll. Music; also trustee; trustee Berkshire Boys Choir, 1966-70, Nat. Assn. Negro Musicians. Actor nat. co. Call Me Mister, 1946-47; Broadway plays include Regina, 1948-49; Town Hall debut, 1950, tour of, Australia, 1950; motion picture Showboat, 1951; toured with: govt. sponsored European prodn. Porgy and Bess; singing role of Porgy govt. sponsored European prodn., 1952, concerts, radio and TV appearances; Symphony soloist recitals, 1950—, concert tour for, Dept. State; as soloist with Phila. Orch. for its continental debut, 1955, tour, Africa, Nr. East, Europe, 1956, Asia, Australia, 1958, Cuba, 1959, Europe, 1966, recital, Brussels Fair, 1958; starred as De Lawd in: Green Pastures, NBC-TV, 1957, 59; star: N.Y.C. Opera revival Porgy and Bess, 1961, 64; also Vienna prodn., 1965-72; featured soloist, Casals Festival, P.R. and N.Y.C., 1962-63, Athens Festival, Greece, 1966; starred in: Richard Rodgers' prodn. Show Boat for, Music Theater of Lincoln Center, 1966; German lang. Show Boat for Vienna Volksoper, 1971-72; soloist (with Pablo Casals) German lang., Geneva, Switzerland, Pacem in Terris II Convocation, 1967; title role in: German lang. Mendelssohn's Elijah, 1969; presented by Central City Opera (Colo.) as: star prodn. Puccini opera Gianni Schicchi, 1972; performed concert, Carnegie Hall, 1975. Recipient hon. citation Eastman Sch. Music, 1954, Grammy award Nat. Acad. Rec. Arts and Scis., 1984. Mem. Actors Equity, Am. Guild Mus. Artists, Screen Actors Guild, AFTRA, NAACP (life), Phi Mu Alpha Sinfonia (life). Home: 247 E Chestnut St Apt 701 Chicago IL 60611

WARGA, JACK, mathematician, educator; b. Warsaw, Poland, Dec. 5, 1922; came to U.S., 1943, naturalized, 1944; s. Herman and Czarna (Lichtenstein) W.; m. Faye Kleinman, Feb. 27, 1949; children—Charna Ruth, Arthur David. Student, Brussels (Belgium) U., 1939-40; BA, Carleton Coll., 1944; PhD, NYU, 1950. Assoc. mathematician Reeves Instrument Corp., N.Y.C., 1951-52; Chief engring. computing sect. Republic Aviation Corp., Farmingdale, N.Y., 1952-53; head math dept. Burroughs Corp., Pasadena, Cal., 1954-56; mgr., math dept. Avco Research and Devel., Wilmington, Mass., 1957-66; prof. math. Northeastern U., Boston, 1966-93, prof. emeritus, 1993—. Author: Optimal Control of Differential and Functional Equations, 1972, expanded Russian transl., 1977; contbr. articles to profl. jours. Served with AUS, 1944-46. Weizmann Meml. fellow, 1956-57. Fellow AAAS; mem. Am. Math. Soc., Soc. Indsl. and Applied Math. (editor Jour. on Control and Optimization 1963-89). Home: 233 Clark Rd Brookline MA 02146-5847 Office: Northeastern U Dept Math Boston MA 02115

WARGA, JOHN, construction company executive; b. 1942. BS in Acctg., LaSalle U., 1969. CPA. With Dynalectric Co., McLean, Va., 1973—, treas., sr. v.p., 1988—. Office: Dynalectric Co 1420 Spring Hill Rd Ste 500 Mc Lean VA 22102-3006*

WARHAFTIG, SOLOMON L., lawyer; b. N.Y.C., Apr. 11, 1938; s. Paul and Sara (Raskin) W.; m. Toby Bremen, Dec. 25, 1965 (div. 1977); children: Jeremy Paul, Daniel Ethan; m. Susan Klein, July 4, 1984. BS, Columbia U., 1959; JD, Harvard U., 1964. Atty. U.S. Dept. Justice, Washington, 1964-67; ptnr. Kaye, Scholer, Fierman, Hays & Handler, N.Y.C., 1967-79, Gelbert & Abrams, N.Y.C., 1979-87, Proskauer, Rose, Goetz & Mendelsohn, N.Y.C., 1987—. Lt. USNR, 1959-61. Office: Proskauer Rose 1585 Broadway New York NY 10036-8200*

WARICK, LAWRENCE HERBERT, psychiatrist; b. Warsaw, Poland, May 2, 1936; came to U.S., 1949, naturalized, 1954; s. Joseph and Marsha (Beck) W.; m. Elaine Ruth Christensen, Feb. 24, 1963; children: Catherine Ann, David Mark. BS, CCNY, 1956; MD, Albert Einstein Coll. Medicine, 1960; PhD, So. Calif. Psychoanalytic Inst, 1980. Diplomate Am. Bd. Psychiatry and Neurology. Rotating intern L.A. County Gen. Hosp., 1960-61; resident neurology U. So. Calif. Sch. Medicine, L.A. County Gen. Hosp., 1961-62, resident psychiatry, 1962-65; clin. assoc. So. Calif. Psychoanalytic Inst., L.A., 1973-80, instr., 1981—; pvt. practice L.A., 1980—; asst. clin. prof. psychiatry UCLA Sch. Medicine, 1967—; instr. faculty Psychoanalytic Inst. So. Calif., L.A., 1980—. Contbr. articles to profl. jours., chpt. to book. Capt. USAF, 1962-68. Mem. Am. Psychiat. Assn., Am. Acad. Psychiatry and Law, So. Calif. Psychiatry Soc., So. Calif. Psychoanalytic Soc., Phi Beta Kappa. Avocations: swimming, music, hiking, tennis, racketball, reading. Office: 2444 Wilshire Blvd Ste 418 Santa Monica CA 90403-5808

WARING, MARY LOUISE, social work administrator; b. Pitts., Feb. 15, 1928; d. Harold R. and Edith (McCallum) W. AB, Duke U., 1949; MSS, Smith Coll., 1951; PhD, Brandeis U., 1974. Lic. clin. social worker, Tenn. Sr. supervising social worker Judge Baker Guidance Ctr., Boston, 1955-65; dir. social svc. Cambridge (Mass.) Mental Health Ctr., 1965-70; assoc. prof. Sch. Social Work Fla. State U., Tallahassee, 1974-77; prof. Fordham U., N.Y.C., 1977-82; cons. Dept. Human Svc., N.J., 1983-84; cons., sr. staff mem. Family Counseling Svc. Bergen County, Hackensack, N.J., 1984-86; dir. Step One Employee Assistance Program Fortwood Ctr., Inc., Chattanooga, 1986—; mem. ethics com. Chattanooga Rehab. Hosp., 1995. Contbr. articles to profl. jours. Mem. Citizen Amb. Program Human Resource Mgmt. Delegation to Russia, 1993; active Nat. Trust for Hist. Preservation, Nature Conservancy, Hunter Mus. Am. Art, Chattanooga Symphony and Opera Assn., Friends of Hamilton County Bicentennial Libr. Recipient Career Tchr. award Nat. Inst. Alchohol and Alchohol Abuse, 1972-74; traineeship NIMH, 1949-51. Mem. NASW (charter), Acad. Cert. Social Workers, Nat. Mus. Women in Arts (charter), Smithsonian Assocs., Cmty. Svcs. Club Greater Chattanooga (pres. 1995, 96, v.p. 1994, 97). Office: Fortwood Ctr Inc 1028 E 3rd St Chattanooga TN 37403-2107

WARING, WALTER WEYLER, English language educator; b. Sterling, Kans., May 13, 1917; s. Walter Wray and Bonnie Laura (Weyler) W.; m. Mary Esther Griffith, Feb. 8, 1946; children: Mary Laura, Helen Ruth, Elizabeth Anne, Claire Joyce. B.A., Kans. Wesleyan U., 1939; M.A., U. Colo., 1946; Ph.D., Cornell U., 1949. Tchr., English and chemistry Belleville (Kan.) High Sch., 1939-41; instr. U. Colo., Boulder, 1941-42, 46-47; mem. faculty Kalamazoo Coll., 1949—, prof. English, 1955-85, prof. emeritus, 1985—, chmn. dept., 1953-78, dir. humanities, 1978-83; Ednl. TV lectr.; vis. prof. Kenyon Coll., 1984-86, 90-91. Painter watercolors.; author: Thomas Carlyle, 1978, also articles. Served to 1st lt. AUS, World War II, PTO. Decorated Legion of Merit. Mem. Phi Beta Kappa. Home: 156 Monroe St Kalamazoo MI 49006-4475

WARING, WILLIAM WINBURN, pediatric pulmonologist, educator; b. Savannah, Ga., July 20, 1923; s. Antonio Johnston and Sue Cole (Winburn) W.; m. Nell Pape Williams, July 19, 1952; children—William Winburn, Benjamin Joseph, Antonio Johnston, Peter Ayraud, Patrick Houstoun. G-rad., Hotchkiss Sch., Lakeville, Conn., 1942; student, Yale U., 1942-43; M.D., Harvard U., 1947. Diplomate Am. Bd. Pediatrics (subbd. of pediatric pulmonology 1985-89). Intern Children's Hosp., Boston, 1947-48; intern, then resident Johns Hopkins Hosp., Balt., 1948-52; practice medicine specializing in pediatrics Jacksonville, Fla., 1955-57; instr. dept. pediatrics Sch. Medicine, Tulane U., New Orleans, 1957-58, asst. prof., 1958-61, assoc. prof., 1961-66, prof., 1966—, Jane B. Aron Prof. Pediatrics, 1987—; dir. Pediat. Pulmonary Ctr., New Orleans, 1969-88, Cystic Fibrosis Ctr., Tulane U., New Orleans, 1963-88; chmn. profl. tng. com. Cystic Fibrosis Found., 1978-86; cons. La. State Handicapped Children's Assn., 1963-88; mem. pulmonary diseases adv. com. NIH, 1978-80. Co-author, editor: Practical Manual of Pediatrics, 1975, 2d edit., 1982; editor: Harriet Lane Handbook: A Manual for Pediatric House Officers, 1952, Hospital Pediatric Manual, 1958; contbg. author books on pediatric pulmonary disease, also articles in field; assoc. editor Am. Jour. Diseases of Children, 1989-91; mem. editl. bd. Pediatric Pulmonology, 1985-94. Served to capt. M.C., U.S. Army, 1952-54. Recipient Research Career Devel. award NIH, 1970-72. Fellow Am. Acad. Pediatrics (exec. com. 1966-71), Am. Coll. Chest Physicians; mem. Am. Pediatric Soc., Am. Thoracic Soc. (v.p. 1977). Republican. Roman Catholic. Clubs: Boston, So. Yacht, Wyvern (New Orleans). Avocations: fly fishing; running; computing. Home: 123 Walnut St 123 Walnut St Ste 905 New Orleans LA 70118 Office: Tulane U Sch of Medicine Dept of Pediatrics 1430 Tulane Ave New Orleans LA 70112-2699

WARIS, MICHAEL, JR., lawyer; b. Phila., July 3, 1921; s. Michael and Esther (March) W.; m. Mary Luschyk, June 2, 1956. B.S. in Econs., U. Pa., 1942, J.D. cum laude, 1944. Bar: Pa., D.C. Law clk. to judge U.S. Tax Ct., Washington, 1946-48; trial counsel IRS, Washington, 1948-52; legis. atty. Legislation and Regulations div. IRS Washington, 1952-55; assoc. tax legis. counsel U.S. Treasury Dept., Washington, 1955-62; ptnr. Baker & McKenzie, Washington, 1962-88, of counsel, 1988—; adj. prof. Georgetown U. Law Sch., Washington, 1963-73. Bd. dirs. United Service Orgn. Nat. Capital Area, 1978-79; mem. adv. group to U.S. Commr. of IRS, Washington, 1979-80. Named Master of the Bench, J. Edgar Murdock Am. Inn of Ct., 1988. Fellow ABA; mem. Fed. Bar Assn., Bar Assn. D.C., Ukrainian-Am. Bar Assn. (past chmn. bd. govs.), Cosmos Club, Met. Club, Beta Gamma Sigma. Ukrainian Catholic. Home: 6707 Tusculum Rd Bethesda MD 20817-1521 Office: Baker & McKenzie 815 Connecticut Ave NW Washington DC 20006-4004

WARK, ROBERT RODGER, art curator; b. Edmonton, Can., Oct. 7, 1924; came to U.S., 1948, naturalized, 1970; s. Joseph Henry and Louise (Rodger) W. B.A., U. Alta., 1944, M.A., 1946, LLD (hon.), 1986; A.M., Harvard, 1949, Ph.D., 1952. Instr. art Harvard U., 1952-54; instr. history art Yale U., 1954-56; curator art Henry E. Huntington Library and Art Gallery, San Marino, Calif., 1956-90; lectr. art Calif. Inst. Tech., 1960-91, UCLA, 1966-80. Author: Sculpture in the Huntington Collection, 1959, French Decorative Art in the Huntington Collection, 1961, Rowlandson's Drawings for a Tour in a Post Chaise, 1963, Rowlandson's Drawings for the English Dance of Death, 1966, Isaac Cruikshank's Drawings for Drolls, 1968, Early British Drawings in the Huntington Collection 1600-1750, 1969, Drawings by John Flaxman, 1970, Ten British Pictures 1740-1840, 1971, Meet the Ladies: Personalities in Huntington Portraits, 1972, Drawings from the Turner Shakespeare, 1973, Drawings by Thomas Rowlandson in the Huntington Collection, 1975, British Silver in the Huntington Collection, 1978; editor: Sir Joshua Reynolds: Discourses on Art, 1959. Served with RCAF, 1944-45; Served with RCNVR, 1945. Mem. Coll. Art Assn. Home: 1330 Lombardy Rd Pasadena CA 91106-4120 Office: Huntington Library San Marino CA 91108

WARLICK, CHARLES HENRY, mathematician/computer science educator; b. Hickory, N.C., May 8, 1930; married; 1 child. BS, Duke U., 1952; MA, U. Md., 1955; PhD, U. Cin., 1964. Mathematician U.S. Dept. Army, 1952-53; programmer IBM Corp., 1954; from applied mathematician to supervisor applied math. GE Co., 1955-65; from lectr. to sr. lectr., dir. computer ctr. U. Tex., Austin, 1965—; v.p. VIM Users Orgn. Control Data Corp., 1968-70, pres., 1970-71. Mem. Assn. Computing Machinery. Office: U Tex Austin Computation Ctr Austin TX 78712*

WARLICK, KARLA JAN, school counselor; b. Levelland, Tex., Aug. 6, 1949; d. Milton Jr. and Mary Tom (Bradford) Tankersley; m. Philip Owen Warlick, Aug. 24, 1968 (div. Oct. 1994); children: Allyson Wynn, Philip Owen II. BS, Tex. Women's U., 1970; MA, U. Tex., Odessa, 1991. Tchr. Richardson (Tex.) Ind. Sch. Dist., 1970-72; agt. Irene Smith Realtors, Austin, 1977-79; broker Bohannan Realtors, Midland, Tex., 1979-80; broker in pvt. practice Midland, 1980-92; tchr. Hillander Sch., Midland, 1980-81; assessment coord. Midland Coll., Midland, 1988-90; therapist, substance abuse supr. Dept. Family Svcs., Midland, 1990-91; counselor Midland Ind. Sch. Dist., Midland, 1991—; counselor in pvt. practice Midland, 1992—; counselor Grapevine-Colleyville (Tex.) Ind. Sch. Dist., 1995—; mem. gifted and talented com. Midland Ind. Sch. Dist., 1992—. Active Midland Symphony Guild; bd. dirs. Am. Heart Assn., Midland, 1982-85. Mem. Am. Counseling Assn., Tex. Counseling Assn., Permian Basin Counseling Assn. (mem. legis. com. 1992—), Zeta Tau Alpha. Methodist. Avocations: snow skiing, travel, reading. Home: 365 Parkway Blvd Coppell TX 75019

WARLICK, ROGER KINNEY, history educator, assistant dean; b. San Diego, Oct. 1, 1930; s. John Portland and Bernice Catherine (Johnson) W.; m. Claudette Evans, Aug. 22, 1953 (div. 1972); m. Lorraine Vanden Bout, Dec. 13, 1973; children: David, Andrea, Kathryn, Dawn, Elizabeth, Sarah, Amy. BA, Ariz. State U., 1957; PhD, Boston U., 1965. Asst. to assoc. prof. history Bentley Coll., Boston and Waltham, Mass., 1963-70; prof., head history dept. Armstrong State Coll., Savannah, Ga., 1970-93, asst. dean Arts and Scis., 1993-94, prof. emeritus, 1994—; asst. program dir. Brit. studies U. Ga. system, London, 1982, 83, program dir., 1988, 89, 90, 92, 93, 94. Author: As Grain Once Scattered, 1988; contbr. articles to profl. jours. Bd. dirs. Hist. Savannah Found., 1980-86, Savannah Park and Tree Commn., 1976-87, vice chmn., 1983-87; gov. appointed mem. Ga. Hist. Records Adv. Bd., 1993—. Staff sgt. USAF, 1951-55. Cokesbury, resident fellow Boston U., 1961-63. Mem. Ga. Hist. Soc. (pres. 1990-94), Ga. Trust for Hist. Preservation, Nat. Trust for Hist. Preservation, Ga. Assn. Historians (various coms. 1978—), Savannah Symphony Soc. (bd. dirs. 1983-86).

WARM, JOEL SEYMOUR, psychology educator; b. Bklyn., Sept. 28, 1933; s. Abraham and Stella (Kaplan) W.; m. Frances Goldberg, July 31, 1966; children: Eric Jay, Ellen Sue. BS, CCNY, 1956, MS, 1958; PhD, U. Ala., 1966. Rsch. assoc. U.S. Army Med. Rsch. Lab., Ft. Knox, Ky., 1958-60; rsch. intern VA, Tuscaloosa, Ala., 1960-63; instr. U. Bridgeport (Conn.), 1963-64; adj. asst. prof. U. Louisville, 1964-67; asst. prof. U. Cin., 1967-72, assoc. prof., 1972-75, prof. psychology, 1975—. Co-author: Psychology of Perception, 1979, Ergonomics and Human Factors, 1987; editor: Sustained Attention in Human Performance, 1984; editorial bd. Human Factors, 1989—, Jour. Gen. Psychology, 1992—, Internat. Rev. Rsch. in Mental Retardation, 1992—. Knothole mgr. Finneytown (Ohio) Athletic Assn., 1980. Lt. (j.g.) USNR, 1963-70. Fellow Grad. Sch., U. Cin., 1984—, sr. postdoctoral fellow NRC, Cin., 1986, Disting. Summer Faculty fellow Naval Air Warfare Ctr., Warminster, Pa., 1992; grantee Fragrance Rsch. Fund, N.Y.C., 1987-89, NASA, 1992, Naval Air Warfare Ctr., 1995, Procter and Gamble Corp., 1995. Fellow AAAS, APA, Am. Psychol. Soc.; mem. Psychonomic Soc., Human Factors Soc. (pres. Tri-State chpt. 1988), So. Soc. Philosophy and Psychology (pres. 1991-92), Sigma Xi (treas. U. Cin. chpt. 1988-91, pres.-elect 1991, pres. U. Cin. chpt. 1992). Jewish. Office: Dept Psychology U Cin ML #376 Cincinnati OH 45221

WARMBROD, JAMES ROBERT, agriculture educator, university administrator; b. Belvidere, Tenn., Dec. 13, 1929; s. George Victor and Anna Sophia (Zimmerman) W.; m. Catharine P. Phelps, Jan. 30, 1965. B.S., U. Tenn., 1952, M.S., 1954; Ed.D. (Univ. fellow), U. Ill., 1962. Instr. edn. U. Tenn., Knoxville, 1956-57; tchr. high sch. Winchester, Tenn., 1957-59; asst. prof. U. Ill., Urbana, 1961-66; assoc. prof. U. Ill., 1966-67; prof. agrl. edn. Ohio State U., Columbus, 1968-95; ret., Presdl. prof., 1989, Presdl. prof. emeritus, 1995, Disting. univ. prof. emeritus, 1995—, chmn. dept., 1978-86, acting assoc. dean Coll. Agr., 1989, acting v.p. agrl. adminstrn., dean Coll. Agr., 1989-91; vis. prof. Pa. State U., 1970, U. Minn., 1971, Iowa State U., 1974, La. State U., 1986; vis. scholar Va. Poly. Inst. and State U., 1976, Univ. Coun. Vocat. Edn., 1988-89; mem. com. on agr. in secondary schs. Nat. Acad. Scis., 1985-87. Author: Review and Synthesis of Research on the Economics of Vocational Education, 1968, The Liberalization of Vocat. Education, 1974, (with others) Methods of Teaching Agriculture, 1986, 2d edit. 1993; editor: Agrl. Edn. mag., 1968-71. Served with USAF, 1954-56. Recipient Disting. Teaching award Ohio State U., 1972, 95, Teaching award Ohio State U. Chpt. Gamma Sigma Delta, 1977. Fellow Am. Assn. Agrl. Edn.; mem. Am. Vocat. Assn. (v.p. 1976-79, Outstanding Svc. award 1987), Am. Ednl. Rsch. Assn., Am. Vocat. Edn. Rsch. Assn. (pres. 1976), Am. Assn. Tchr. Educators in Agr. (Disting. Svc. award 1974, Disting. lectr. 1974). Home: 3853 Surrey Hill Pl Columbus OH 43220-4778 Office: 2120 Fyffe Rd Columbus OH 43210-1010

WARMENHOVEN, DANIEL JOHN, communications equipment executive; b. Jersey City, Nov. 27, 1950; s. Peter F. and Roseann E. (Fedkenheuer) W.; m. Charmaine C. Andre, June 16, 1973; children: Eric A., Laura A. BS in Elec. Engring., Princeton U., 1972. Program mgr. communication products div. IBM Corp., Research Triangle Park, N.C., 1972-85; gen. mgr. Info. Networks Group Hewlett-Packard Co., Cupertino, Calif., 1985-89; chmn., pres., chief exec. officer Network Equipment Techs., Redwood City, Calif., 1989—; pres., chief exec. officer Network Appliance, Mountain View, Calif. Avocations: golf, amatuer photography. Office: Network Appliance 319 Bernardo Ave Mountain View CA 94043*

WARMER, RICHARD CRAIG, lawyer; b. Los Angeles, Aug. 12, 1936; s. George A. and Marian L. (Paine) W.; children: Craig McEchron, Alexander Richard. AB, Occidental Coll., 1958; MA, Tufts U., 1959; LLB, NYU, 1962. Bar: Calif. 1963, D.C. 1976. Assoc. O'Melveny & Myers, Los Angeles, 1962-69, ptnr., 1970-75; mng. ptnr. O'Melveny & Myers, Washington, 1976-92, mem. mgmt. com., 1986-92; with O'Melveny & Myers, San Francisco, 1994—; speaker in field. Contbr. articles to profl. jours. Trustee Law Ctr. Found. NYU, 1981—. Mem. ABA, D.C. Bar, State Bar Calif., Order of Coif, Phi Beta Kappa, Cosmos Club. Home: 550 Davis St Apt 26 San Francisco CA 94111-1953 Office: O'Melveny & Myers Embarcadero Ctr W 275 Battery St San Francisco CA 94111-3305

WARNATH, MAXINE AMMER, organizational psychologist, mediator; b. N.Y.C., Dec. 3, 1928; d. Philip and Jeanette Ammer; m. Charles Frederick Warnath, Aug. 20, 1952; children: Stephen Charles, Cindy Ruth. BA, Bklyn. Coll., 1949; MA, Columbia U., 1951, EdD, 1982. Lic. psychologist, Oreg. Various profl. positions Hunter Coll., U. Minn., U. Nebr., U. Oreg., 1951-62; asst. prof. psychology Oreg. Coll. Edn., Monmouth, 1962-77; assoc. prof. psychology, chmn. dept. psychology and spl. edn. Western Oreg. St. Coll., Monmouth, 1978-83, prof. 1986—, dir. organizational psychology program 1983—; pres. Profl. Perspectives Internat., Salem, Oreg., 1987—; cons., dir. Orgn. R & D, Salem, Oreg., 1983-87, seminar leader Endeavors for Excellence program. Author: Power Dynamism, 1987. Mem. APA (com. pre-coll. psychology 1970-74), ASTD, N.Y. Acad. Sci., Oreg. Acad. Sci., Oreg. Psychol. Assn. (pres. 1980-81, pres.-elect 1979-80, legis. liaison 1977-78), Western Psychol. Assn. Office: Profl Perspectives Internat PO Box 2265 Salem OR 97308-2265

WARNE, ANDREW GEORGE, geologist, researcher; b. Marion, Ind., Nov. 18, 1954; s. Thomas Parkison Jr. and Ruth (Lang) W. BS in Geology, U. N.C., 1983, PhD in Geology, 1990; MS in Geology, Rutgers U., 1986. Cons. oil and gas Stonewall Gas Co., Jane Lew, W.Va., 1985-89; postdoctoral fellow Smithsonian Instn., Washington, 1991-93, rsch. assoc., 1994-95; contractor wetland rsch. program Waterways Expt. Sta., U.S. Army C.E., Vicksburg, Miss., 1993-94, rsch. geologist, 1994—. Contbr. articles to sci. jours. Mem. Geol. Soc. Am., Soc. Wetland Scientists, Sigma Xi. Avocations: running, bicycling, backpacking. Home: 1210 Mulvihill St Vicksburg MS 39180 Office: US Army CE Waterways Expt Sta CEWES-GG-YH Vicksburg MS 39180

WARNE, RONSON JOSEPH, mathematics educator; b. East Orange, N.J., June 14, 1930; s. Ronson Joseph and Mildred (Morton) W.; m. Gloria Jane La France, Oct. 24, 1950. BA, Columbia U., 1953; MS, NYU, 1955; PhD, U. Tenn., 1959. Teaching asst., instr. U. Tenn., Knoxville, 1955-59; asst. prof. Math. La. State U., New Orleans, 1959-63; assoc. prof. Math. Va. Polytech. Inst., Blacksburg, 1963-64; prof. Math. W.Va. U., Morgantown, 1964-70, U. Ala., Birmingham, 1970-89, King Fahd U. of Petroleum and Minerals, Dhahran, Saudi Arabia, 1989—. Contbr. articles to profl. jours. Oak Ridge Nat. Lab. fellow, 1960, Dryser fellow, U. Tenn., 1957; vis. rsch. scholar U. Calif., Berkeley, 1982. Mem. Am. Math. Soc. Avocations: body building, weightlifting, running. Office: KFUPM # 1564, Dhahran 31261, Saudi Arabia

WARNE, WILLIAM ROBERT, economist; b. Washington, Nov. 30, 1937. BA, Princeton U., 1960; MA, Johns Hopkins U., 1974. Provincial advisor U.S. Mission, Vinh Binh, Vinh Long, Vietnam, 1962-64; officer in charge trade, devel. and fin. policy U.S. Mission to European Communities, Brussels, 1974-77; dep. dir. East Asian Econ. Policy, 1977-79; dir. Caribbean affairs U.S. Dept. State, Kingston, Jamaica, 1979-81, charge d'affaires, dep. chief mission, 1981-84; dir. Latin Am. Econ. Policy U.S. Dept. State, Washington, 1984-86; counselor for trade, energy, social affairs and agr. U.S. Delegation OECD, Paris, 1986-88; v.p. Midwest Ctr. Exec. Coun. on Fgn. Diplomats, Indpls., 1988-89; pres. Korea Econ. Inst. Am., Washington, 1990—. With U.S. Army, 1960-62. Office: Korea Econ Inst Am 1101 Vermont Ave NW Ste 401 Washington DC 20005-3521

WARNECKE, MICHAEL O., lawyer; b. Chgo., June 28, 1941. BS, ME, Purdue U., 1963; JD, George Washington U., 1967. Bar: Ill. 1967. Ptnr. Keck, Mahin & Cate, Chgo.; lectr. in field. Mem. ABA, Am. Arbitration Assn. (mem. panel arbitrators), Am. Intellectual Property Law Assn., Chgo. Bar Assn., Bar Assn. 7th Cir., Intellectual Property Law Assn. Chgo., Internat. Patent and Trademark Assn. Office: Keck Mahin & Cate 77 W Wacker Dr Ste 4900 Chicago IL 60601-1629 Office: Mayer Brown Platt 190 S LaSalle St Chicago IL 60603*

WARNEMUNDE, BRADLEY LEE, insurance company executive; b. Norfolk, Nebr., Mar. 21, 1933; s. Erwin Theodore and Frances Irene (Render) W.; m. Mary Fauneil Carhart, Aug. 3, 1952 (div. Nov. 1981); children—Jon B., Ralph E., Brian C., Clay S. Student, Kans. State Coll., 1950-51, U. Nebr., 1952-53. With Ohio Nat. Life Ins. Co., 1954—; from agt. to exec. v.p. mktg. Ohio Nat. Life Ins. Co., Cin., 1969-84, pres., 1984-93, chmn., CEO, 1985-94, chmn. emeritus, 1994—, also bd. dirs.; mem. bd. advisers U. Cin. Coll. Bus. Adminstrn., 1978-79. Grad. Leadership Cin. Program, 1985, chmn. Leadership Cin. steering com., 1989-90; chmn. corp. div. Cin. Fine Arts Fund, 1990; bd. dirs. LOMA/Life Mgmt. Inst., Atlanta, 1988-92. Mem. Life Ins. Mktg. and Rsch. Assn. Hartford (past mem. bd. dirs.), Am. Coun. Life Ins. (bd. dirs. 1993-94), Assn. Ohio Life Cos. (pres. 1990), Cin. C. of C., Eastern Hills Tennis Club, Queen City Club, Comml. Club, Masons, Shriners. Republican. Lutheran. Avocations: tennis, golf, fishing, gardening. Home: 7081 Salem Rd Cincinnati OH 45230-2946 Office: Ohio Nat Life Ins Co Ste 205 250 William Howard Taft Rd Cincinnati OH 45219

WARNER, ALVINA (VINNIE WARNER), principal; b. Des Moines, Nov. 3, 1936; d. Harry and Pearl Walker; m. Robert M. Warner, June 8, 1958. BS, U. Mo., 1958; MEd, Saint Louis U., 1969. Adv. cert. specialist-prin. S.E. Mo., 1972. Tchr. Centralia (Mo.) Pub. Schs., 1958-59; tchr., curriculum coord., asst. prin. Webster Groves Sch. Dist., 1959-74; prin. Barretts Sch. Parkway Sch. Dist., Saint Louis County, 1974-96; ret., 1996; organizer Barretts Sch. Centennial Celebration, 1994-95. Recipient Elem. Sch. Recognition, Blue Ribbon Sch. of Excellence award, U.S. Dept. Edn., 1989-90. Home: 169 Horseshoe Dr Kirkwood MO 63122

WARNER, BARRY GREGORY, geographer, educator; b. Cambridge, Ont., Can., July 20, 1955; s. Gregory O. and Alma (Jansen) W. B in Environ. Studies, U. Waterloo, 1978, MS, 1980; PhD, Simon Fraser U., Burnaby, Can., 1984. Rsch. asst. prof. U. Waterloo, Ont., Ont., 1985-89; rsch. assoc. prof. U. Waterloo, Ont., 1989-91; assoc. prof. geography U. Waterloo, Ont., Ont., 1991-96; prof. geography U. Waterloo, Ont., 1996—; interim dir. Wetlands Rsch. Inst., 1991—; U. Neuchatel; vis. prof. U. Neuchatel, 1993; chair Can. Nat. Wetlands Working Group, 1993—. Editor: Methods in Quaternary Ecology, 1990; co-editor: Wetlands: Envigradients, Boundaries and Buffers, 1996; contbr. articles to profl. jours. Postdoctoral fellow Natural Scis. and Engring. Rsch. Coun. of Can., 1984-85, rsch. fellow, 1985-90; fellow Suisse Nat. Res. Fond, 1993. Fellow Geol. Assn. Can. Office: Univ of Waterloo, Dept Geography, Waterloo, ON Canada N2L 3G1

WARNER, BART C., retail executive; b. 1953. Grad., U. Utah. Pres. BCW Enterprises, Inc., Salt Lake City, 1975—. Office: BCW Enterprises Inc 310 W 1370 S Salt Lake City UT 84115*

WARNER, CECIL RANDOLPH, JR., lawyer; b. Ft. Smith, Ark., Jan. 13, 1929; s. Cecil Randolph and Reba (Cheeves) W.; m. Susan Curry, Dec. 10, 1955 (div. 1982); children: Susan Rutledge, Rebecca Jane, Cecil Randolph III, Matthew Holmes Preston, Katherine Mary; m. Barbara Ragsdale, May 26, 1983. B.A. magna cum laude, U. Ark., 1950; LL.B. magna cum laude, Harvard U., 1953, Sheldon fellow, 1953-54. Bar: Ark. 1953. Ptnr. Warner & Smith and predecessor firm, 1954-89; pres., CEO, Fairfield Communities Inc., Little Rock, 1973-81; chmn., CEO Fairfield Communities Inc., 1981-85, chmn., pres., CEO, 1985-91; chmn., pres., CEO Environ. Systems Co., Little Rock, 1991-93; cons., 1993-95; chmn. bd. Wortz Co., Poteau, Okla., 1993—; instr. U. Ark. Sch. Law, 1954, 56; vice chmn. Ark. Constl. Revision Study Commn., 1967; v.p. 7th Ark. Constl. Conv., 1969-70. Scoutmaster troop 23 Boy Scouts Am., Fort Smith, 1955-58; commr. Ark. State Police Commn., 1970; bd. dirs. St. Vincent Infirmary Found., Ctrs. for Youth and Family. Fellow Am. Bar Found., Ark. Bar Found.; mem. ABA, Ark. Bar Assn. (past chmn. exec. com., past chmn. young lawyers sect.), Pulaski County Bar Assn., Am. Law Inst., Fifty for the Future, Phi Beta Kappa, Phi Eta Sigma, Omicron Delta Kappa, Sigma Alpha Epsilon. Methodist. Office: PO Box 7462 Little Rock AR 72217-7462 also: 12332 Harbour Ridge Blvd Palm City FL 34990

WARNER, CHARLES COLLINS, lawyer; b. Cambridge, Mass., June 19, 1942; s. Hoyt Landon and Charlotte (Collins) W.; m. Elizabeth Denny, Aug. 24, 1964; children: Peter, Andrew, Elizabeth. BA, Yale U., 1964; JD cum laude, Ohio State U., 1970. Bar: Ohio 1970. Assoc. Porter, Wright, Morris & Arthur and predecessor, Columbus, 1970-76, ptnr., 1976—, also mgr. labor and employment law dept., 1988-92. Pres. Peace Corps Svc. Coun., Columbus, 1974-76, Old Worthington (Ohio) Assn., 1976-78, Alliance for Quality Edn., Worthington, 1987-89, Worthington Ednl. Found., 1994-96; chmn. lawyers sect. United Way, Columbus, 1983-84. Mem. ABA (subcom. chmn. EEO com. 1986-89, exec. com. Met. Bar Caucus 1992-94, chmn. state & local bar ADR com.), Ohio State Bar Assn. (coun. of dels. 1993—, chmn. fed. cts. com. 1992-94), Ohio Met. Bar Assn. (pres. 1991-92), Columbus Bar Assn. (pres. 1991-92, bd. govs. 1982-87, 88-93), FBA, Ohio Assn. Civil Trial Attys. (exec. bd. 1988—), Nat. Coun. Ohio State U. Law Alumni Assn., Capital Club, Univ. Club, Yale Club (pres. 1979-81). Avocations: clarinet, singing, tennis. Home: 145 E South St Worthington OH 43085-4129 Office: Porter Wright Morris & Arthur 41 S High St Columbus OH 43215-6101

WARNER, DARRELL DWAYNE, financial planner; b. Pratt, Kans., July 4, 1952; s. Leslie O. and Lona Marie (Craven) W.; m. Belinda K. Bales, Mar. 4, 1972; children: Lorinda K., Michael D. BBA in Fin., Ft. Hays State U., Hays, Kans., 1992. Sales cons. Coast to Coast, Osborne, Kans., 1972-73; materials coord. Gilmore & Tatge Mfg. Co., Osborne, 1973-80; mng. ptnr. Warner Farm Supply, Alton, Kans., 1980-82; asst. materials mgr. Schult Homes Corp., Plainville, Kans., 1982-90; night mgr. Holiday Inn, Hays, 1990-92; personal fin. planner Am. Express Fin. Advisors, Inc., Hays, 1992—; mem. Western Kans. Coun. on Estate Planning and Giving, Hays, 1993—. Leader Sumner 4-H Club, Alton, 1980-86; chmn. Osborne County Extension Coun., Osborne, 1981-86. Named to Outstanding Young Men of Am., 1977. Mem. Hays Area Wide C. of C., Alpha Kappa Psi. Republican. Avocations: hunting, fishing, golf. Home: 107 W 3d St PO Box 146 Liebenthal KS 67553 Office: Am Express Fin Advisors Inc PO Box 703 1200 Main Ste 407 Hays KS 67601

WARNER, DENNIS ALLAN, psychology educator; b. Idaho Falls, Idaho, Apr. 27, 1940; s. Perry and Marcia E. (Finlayson) W.; m. Charyl Ann DeHart, Dec. 12, 1962; children: Lisa Rae, Sara Michelle, David Perry, Matthew Aric. BS, Brigham Young U., 1964; MS with honors, U. Oreg., 1966, PhD, 1968. Asst. prof. edn. Wash. State U., Pullman, 1968-72, assoc. prof. edn., 1972-78, prof. edn., 1978-85, dir. tchr. edn., 1983-85, prof., chmn. ednl. counseling psychology, 1985-93, interim dir. Partnership Ctr., 1993-94; prof. edn. leadership and counseling psychology Wash. State U., Pulman, 1994—; vis. asst. prof. psychology U. Idaho, Moscow, 1971. Author: Interpreting and Improving Student Test Performance, 1982; contbr. articles to profl. jours. Postdoctoral research assoc. U. Kans., 1976-77. Mem. Am. Psychol. Assn., Council for Exceptional Children, Phi Delta Kappa. Mem. LDS Ch. Home: 645 SW Mies St Pullman WA 99163-2057 Office: Wash State Univ Dept Ednl and Counsel Psych Rm 371 Cleveland Hall Pullman WA 99164-2131

WARNER, DON LEE, dean emeritus; b. Norfolk, N.B., Jan. 4, 1934; s. Donald A. and Cleo V. (Slagel) W.; m. Patricia Ann Walker, Feb. 24, 1957; children: Mark J., Scott Lee. BS in Geol. Engring., Colo. Sch. Mines, 1956, MSc in Geol. Engring., 1961; PhD in Engring. Sci., U. Calif., Berkeley, 1964. Registered profl. engr., Mo., geologist, Mo. Geol. engr. Gulf Oil Corp., Casper, Wyo., 1956, Calif. Exploration Co., Guatemala, 1957-58; civil engr. U.S. Forest Svc., Gunnison, Colo., 1958-59; teaching asst. Colo. Sch. Mines, Golden, 1959-61; rsch. asst. U. Calif., Berkeley, 1962-64; rsch. geologist and engr. U.S. Pub. Health Svc., Cin., 1964-67; chief, earth scis. Ohio Basin Region Fed. Water Pollution Control Adminstrn., 1967-69; prof. geol. engring. U. Mo., Rolla, 1969-92, prof. emeritus geol. engring., 1992—, dean emeritus Sch. Mines and Metallurgy, 1992—, chmn., geol. engring., 1980-81, dean Sch. Mines and Metallurgy, 1981-93; bd. dirs. Underground Injection Practices Coun., 1985-89; mem. adv. com. to Sec. of Interior for Mineral Resources Rsch., 1985-92. Author: Subsurface Wastewater Injection, 1977. Special award scholarship Colo. Sch. Mines, 1951-56, grad. fellowship Colo. Sch. Mines, 1959-61, rsch. fellowship U. Calif., 1962-64; recipient Best Paper award Am. Water Works Assn., 1971. Mem. Am. Assn. Petroleum Geologists (cert.), ASTM, Geol. Soc. Am. (ground water protection coun.), Nat. Ground Water Assn. (sci. award 1984, disting. lectr. 1986), Blue Key, Soc. Petroleum Engrs., Scabbard and Blade, Theta Tau, Tau Beta Pi. Avocations: fishing, boating, tennis, golf. Office: U Mo-Rolla Sch Mines and Metallurgy 1870 Miner Circle Rolla MO 65409-0230

WARNER, DOUGLAS ALEXANDER, III, banker; b. Cin., June 9, 1946; s. Douglas Alexander Jr. and Eleanor (Wright) W.; m. Patricia Grant, May 13, 1977; children: Alexander, Katherine, Michael. BA, Yale U., 1968. Officer's asst. J.P. Morgan & Co. Inc., N.Y.C., 1968-70; asst. treas. Morgan Guaranty Trust Co., N.Y.C., 1970-72, asst. v.p., 1972-75, v.p., 1975-85; sr. v.p. J.P. Morgan & Co. Inc., N.Y.C., 1983-87, exec. v.p., 1987-89; mng. dir. Morgan Guaranty Trust Co., N.Y.C., 1989-90, pres., 1990-95, chmn., pres., CEO, 1995—, also bd. dirs.; bd. counselors Bechtel Group, Inc.; bd. dirs. GE Co., Anheuser-Busch Cos., Inc.; vice chmn. bd. mgrs., bd. overseers Meml. Sloan-Kettering Cancer Ctr.; active The Bus. Coun. Trustee Pierpont Morgan Libr., Cold Spring Harbor Lab. Mem. Bankers Roundtable, Links Club, River Club, Meadowbrook Club (L.I.). Avocations: golf, skiing, shooting. Home: PO Box 914 New York NY 10268-0914 Office: J P Morgan & Co Inc 60 Wall St New York NY 10005-2807

WARNER, E. JOHN, manufacturing financial executive; b. Chgo., Sept. 28, 1942; s. Eugene John and Kathryn (Jones) W.; m. Nan Shipley, Aug. 21, 1965; children: John Warner, Thomas Shipley. BSBA, Ohio State U., 1965; MCS, Harvard U., 1978; PEE, Carnegie Mellon U., 1981. Mgmt. trainee GM, Flint, Mich., 1965-68; asst. prodn. mgr. Diebold Inc., Canton, Ohio, 1968-70, prodn. mgr., 1970-77, gen. mgr. Wooster (Ohio) divsn., 1977-85, dir. strategic planning, 1985-88; pres. W.L. Jenkins Co., Canton, 1988—; guest lectr. Harvard U. Bus. Sch., Boston, 1979. Bd. dirs. United Way, Canton, 1987—, gen. campaign chmn., 1987; bd. dirs. Jr. Achievement, Wooster, 1980-85, YMCA, Wooster, 1980-85. Mem. Canton City Club, Glemoor Country Club. Episcopalian. Avocations: tennis, swimming, sailing, fishing, golf. Home: 3304 Croydon Dr NW Canton OH 44718-3220 Office: WL Jenkins Co 1445 Whipple Ave SW Canton OH 44710-1321

WARNER, EDWARD L., III, federal agency administrator; b. Detroit, 1940; m. Pam Melton; children: Kelly, Erika. BS, U.S. Naval Acad., 1962; MS in Politics, Princeton U., 1967, PhD in Politics, 1975; grad., Armed Forces Staff Coll., 1975; grad. in Russian, Def. Lang. Inst., 1976. Commd. 2d lt. USAF, 1962; analyst Office Strategic Rsch., CIA; asst. prof. polit. sci. USAF Acad., Colorado Springs, Colo.; asst. air attache Am. Embassy, Moscow; dep. chief strategy div. Hdqs. USAF, Washington, head staff group Office Chief of Staff; ret., 1982; sr. def. analyst RAND Corp., Washington, 1982-93; asst. sec. def. for strategy and requirements Dept. Def., Washington, 1993—; condr. grad. seminars on Soviet def. and arms control policy George Washington U., Johns Hopkins U. Sch. Advanced Internat. Studies, Princeton U., Columbia U.; former mem. mil. adv. panel to Nat. Intelligence Coun.; former mem. polit. consultative group Office Slavic and Eurasian Analysis, CIA. Mem. Coun. Fgn. Rels. Office: Dept Def Pentagon Washington DC 20000

WARNER, EDWARD WAIDE, JR., lawyer; b. St. Louis, Oct. 17, 1951; s. Edward Waide Sr. and Barbara (Hardy) W.; m. Cecilia Tso, Oct. 1, 1983; children: Edward Waide Tso, Sarah Liang, Rebecca Li, Genevieve An Hardy. AB magna cum laude, Boston Coll., 1973; JD, Rutgers U., 1977; postgrad., U. Chgo., 1974. Bar: Mo. 1978, N.Y. 1980. Law clk. to sr. cir. judge U.S. Ct. Appeals (8th cir.), St. Louis, 1977-78; assoc. Davis, Polk & Wardwell, N.Y.C., 1978-85, ptnr., 1986—; bd. advisors Morin Ctr. Banking Law Studies, Boston U. Sch. Law. Trustee Episcopal Sch., N.Y.C., 1994. Mem. ABA, Internat. Bar Assn., Assn. of Bar of City of N.Y., Mo. Bar Assn., Phi Beta Kappa. Home: 151 E 74th St New York NY 10021-3226 Office: Davis Polk & Wardwell 450 Lexington Ave New York NY 10017-3911

WARNER, ELIZABETH ROSE, librarian, educator; b. Phila., Pa., Dec. 10, 1952; d. Charles Hoffman and Elizabeth Mathilda Warner; m. Michael Joseph Dunn, Oct. 12, 1979; children: Brian Joseph Charles Warner Dunn, Colin Joseph Patrick Warner Dunn. BA, Holy Family Coll., 1974; MLS, Villanova U., 1977. Med. librarian JFK Meml. Hosp., Stratford, N.J., 1975-77; lib. coord. N.J. Sch. Osteopathic Medicine, Stratford, 1976-77; extension librarian Coll. Physicians Phila., 1977-79, reader's svcs. asst., 1975-77; med. librarian Crozer-Chester (Pa.) Med. Ctr., 1979-86; reference librarian Scott Meml. Lib. Thomas Jefferson U., Phila., 1986-90, edn. svcs. librarian, instr. info. skills workshops Scott Meml. Lib., 1991—; vol. librarian Mummers Mus., Phila., 1976; cons., presenter in field. Contbr. numerous articles to profl. jours. Mem. Am. Lib. Assn., Med. Lib. Assn. (chair legis. com. Phila. Regional chpt. 1980-81, pres. elect, program chair, 1981-82, pres. 1982-83, mem. com. 1981-83, rep. chpt. coun. 1985-87, nominating com. 1987-88, 94-95, Achievement award 1994, edn. com. nursing and allied health resources sect. 1988-89, sec., treas. 1991-93, nominating com. 1988-89, 93-94, editor newsletter, 1992—, course designer 1993—, instr. 1993—, com. chair pub. svcs. sect., 1985-87, jury chair Ida and George prize 1992-94, Disting. mem. Acad. Health Info. Profls. 1990—), Grtr. Phila. Health Care Congress, Phila. Area Reference Librarians Info. Exchange (Bibliotecaire Sans Sobriete cert. 1993), Kappa Gamma Pi, Phi Kappa Phi. Democrat. Roman Catholic. Home: 421 E Melrose Ave Westmont NJ 08108-2510 Office: Thomas Jefferson U Scott Meml Lib 1020 Walnut St Philadelphia PA 19107-5587

WARNER, FRANK SHRAKE, lawyer; b. Ogden, Utah, Dec. 14, 1940; s. Frank D. and Emma (Sorensen) W.; m. Sherry Lynn Clary; 1 child, Sheri. JD U. Utah 1964. Bar: Utah 1964. Assoc. Young, Thatcher, Glasmann &

Warner, and predecessor, Ogden, 1964-67, ptnr., 1967-72; chmn. Pub. Svc. Commn. Utah, Salt Lake City, 1972-76; ptnr. Warner & Wikstrom, Ogden, 1976-79, Warner, Marquardt & Hasenyager, Ogden, 1979-82; pvt. practice, Ogden, 1982—. Mem. Utah Gov.'s Com. on Exec. Reorgn., 1978-80. Mem. Utah Bar Assn. (ethics and discipline com. 1981-90), Ogden Gun Club (past pres.). Office: 505 27th St Ogden UT 84403-0101

WARNER, FRANK WILSON, III, mathematics educator; b. Pittsfield, Mass., Mar. 2, 1938; s. Frank Wilson Jr. and Charlotte (Walton) W.; m. Ada Woodward, June 6, 1958; children: Bruce Woodward, Clifford Powell. BS, Pa. State U., 1959; PhD, MIT, 1963. Instr. MIT, Cambridge, 1963-64; acting asst. prof. U. Calif., Berkeley, 1964-65, asst. prof., 1965-68; assoc. prof. U. Pa., Phila., 1968-73, prof. math., 1973—, assoc. dean Sch. Arts and Scis., 1992-95, dep. dean Sch. Arts and Scis., 1995—. Author: Foundations of Differentiable Manifolds and Lie Groups, 1971; contbr. articles to scholarly jours. Fellow Guggenheim Found., 1976. Fellow AAAS; mem. Am. Math. Soc., Math. Assn. Am., Sigma Xi. Achievements include research on the conjugate locus of a Riemannian manifold, on existence and conformal deformation of metrics with prescribed gaussian and scalar curvatures, on great circle fibrations of spheres. Office: U Pa 116 College Hall Philadelphia PA 19104-6377

WARNER, HAROLD CLAY, JR., banker, investment management executive; b. Knoxville, Tenn., Feb. 24, 1939; s. Harold Clay and Mary Frances (Waters) W.; m. Patricia Alice Rethorst, Sept. 1, 1961; children—Martha Lee, Carol Frances. B.S. in Econs, U. Tenn., 1961, Ph.D., 1965. Asst. to pres. First Fed. Savs., Savannah, Ga., 1965-67; v.p. and economist No. Trust Co., Chgo., 1967-73; sr. v.p. and chief economist Crocker Nat. Bank, San Francisco, 1974-79; sr. v.p. liability mgmt. Crocker Nat. Bank, 1979-82; exec. v.p., dir. fixed income mgmt. BA Investment Mgmt. Corp., 1982-84, dir., pres., chief operating officer, 1984-86; dir., pres. Montgomery St. Income Securities, Inc., 1984-86; sr. v.p. Bank of Am., San Francisco, 1982-86; chmn. BA Investment Mgmt. Internat., Ltd., 1985-86; pres. Arthur D. Gimbel, Inc., San Mateo, Calif., 1986-87; exec. v.p., chief investment officer Riggs Nat. Bank Washington, 1987-88; chmn. Riggs Investment Mgmt. Corp., 1988-89; sr. v.p., chief economist Bank of Calif., San Francisco, 1989-93; pres., chief investment officer MERUS Capital Mgmt., San Francisco, 1989-93; pres. Govett Asset Mgmt. Co., 1993-95, Govett Fin. Svcs. Ltd., 1993-95; pres., COO Fisher Investments, Inc., Woodside, Calif., 1996—; lectr. dept. econs. U. Tenn., 1962-63, Grad. Sch. Bus., Loyola U., Chgo., 1969-73; lectr. Pacific Coast Banking Sch., U. Wash., 1978-79. NDEA fellow, 1961-64. Mem. Burlingame Country Club, Phi Gamma Delta, Phi Eta Sigma, Beta Gamma Sigma, Omicron Delta Kappa, Phi Kappa Phi. Home: 1960 Broadway # 6 San Francisco CA 94109 Office: 13100 Skyline Blvd Woodside CA 94062-4547

WARNER, HARRY BACKER, JR., retired journalist, freelance writer; b. Chambersburg, Pa., Dec. 19, 1922; s. Harry Backer, Sr. and Margaret Caroline (Klipp) W. Student pub. schs., Hagerstown, Md. Reporter, editor, columnist Herald-Mail Co., Hagerstown, 1942-82. Author: All Our Yesterdays, 1969, A Wealth of Fable, 1976; editor, author (amateur jour.) Horizons, 1939—. Com. mem. Community Action Coun., Hagerstown, Civic Music Assn., Hagerstown, Washington County Adult Edn., Hagerstown; mem. publicity com. Washington County United Fund, Hagerstown. Recipient Hugo award World Sci. Fiction Convs., 1968, 72, 93, Hist. Preservation award Washington County Commrs., 1980, First Fandom Hall of Fame award, 1995. Mem. Spectator Amateur Press Soc. (v.p. 1982-95), So. Fandom Pubs. Alliance. Republican. Lutheran. Avocations: science fiction fandom, classical music. Home: 423 Summit Ave Hagerstown MD 21740-6229

WARNER, HARRY HATHAWAY, financial consultant; b. Staunton, Va., Nov. 30, 1935; s. Morris Thompson and Virginia Drury (Worthington) W.; m. Mary Elizabeth Patrick, Sept. 24, 1960; children—Harry Hathaway, Cabell Worthington, Ann Morris, Morris Patrick. B.A., Va. Mil. Inst., 1957; grad., U. Va. Sch. Bank Mgmt., 1963, Stonier Grad. Sch. Banking, 1969. With Met. Nat. Bank, Richmond, Va., 1965-71; exec. v.p. Met. Nat. Bank, 1969-71; pres., dir. Transohio Fin. Corp., Cleve., 1971-78; exec. v.p. VMI Found., Lexington, Va., 1978-90; cons. in field; bd. dirs. Chesapeake Corp., Pulaski Furniture Corp. Va., Am. Filtrona Corp., Allied Rsch. Corp. Served as 2d lt. AUS, 1957. Recipient Distinguished Service award Richmond Jaycees, 1969. Mem. Commonwealth Club, Lexington Country Club. Episcopalian. Address: PO Box 1577 Lexington VA 24450-1577

WARNER, HEIDI C., clinical research nurse; b. Thomasville, N.C., Nov. 7, 1962; d. Walter Vance and Virginia Ruth (Beck) Warner. BSN, N.C. U., Charlotte, 1985. RN, N.C.; cert. in audiometry. Clin. rsch. assoc. tng. The Blethen Group, Research Triangle Park, N.C.; clin. rsch. nurse Olsten-Kimberly Quality Care, Raleigh, N.C. Walter C. Teagle Found. nursing scholar, Exxon Co. USA. Mem. Phi Eta Sigma. Republican. Methodist.

WARNER, HOMER R., physiologist, educator; b. Salt Lake City, Apr. 18, 1922; married, 1946; 6 children. BA, U. Utah, 1946, MD, 1949; PhD in Physiology, U. Minn., 1953; Doctorate (hon.), Brigham Young U., 1971, U. Linkoping, Sweden, 1990. Intern Parkland Hosp., Dallas, 1949-50; resident in medicine U. Minn. Hosp., 1950-51; fellow Mayo Clinic, 1951-52, U. Minn., 1952-53; rsch. instr. dept. internal medicine U. Utah, Salt Lake City, 1953-54, asst. rsch. prof. dept. physiology, 1957-64, prof., chmn. dept. biophysiology and bioengring., 1964-73, rsch. prof. dept. surgery, 1966-83, spl. asst. info. mgmt. to v.p. health sci., 1983-93, prof., chmn. dept. medicine informatics, 1973—, dir., chmn. computer health sci., 1993—; dir. cardiovasc. lab. Latter-Day Sts. Hosp., 1954-70; mem. adv. com. computers NIH, 1961-63, chmn. computer rsch. study sect., 1963-66; vis. prof. U. Hawaii, 1968, U. So. Calif., 1972; mem. Biomed. Libr. Rev. Com., Nat. Libr. Medicine, 1982-86, chmn. grant rev. study sect., 1985-86. Recipient James E. Talmage Sci. Achievement award, 1968. Mem. Inst. Medicine-NAS (sr.), Am. Physiol. Soc., Am. Coll. Med. Informatics (pres. 1989). Office: U Utah Sch Medicine Dept Med Informatics AB193 Med Ctr Salt Lake City UT 84132*

WARNER, JACK, JR., motion picture and television producer, writer; b. San Francisco, Mar. 27, 1916; s. Jack Leonard and Irma Warner Rogell; m. Barbara Ann Richman, May 30, 1948; children—Elizabeth Susan, Sally Jo (dec.), Deborah. A.B. cum laude, U. So. Calif., 1938. Formerly with home office Warner Bros. Pictures, Inc. (distbn. and exhbn. of films), U.S., Can.; former exec. television div. Warner Bros. Pictures, Inc., past v.p. charge TV commls. and indsl. films div.; prodr. short subject films Warner Bros. Studios, Burbank, Calif., in theatre dept. and distbn., 1946-49; prodr. Warner Bros. Studios, London, 1948-49; other exec. positions, until 1959; organizer own co. Jack M. Warner Prodns., Inc., 1949. Author: (novels) Bijou Dream, 1983, The Dream Factory, 1986; co-author: (nonfiction) Hollywood Be Thy Name, 1994. Past pres. Los Angeles County Assn. Mental Health; v.p. Mental Health Found. Served as 2d lt. Signal Corps Photog. Co.; advanced through grades to col. photo officer ETO, World War II; col. Res. ret. Mem. Acad. Motion Picture Arts and Scis. (asso.), Assn. U.S. Army, 12th Army Group Assn., Zeta Beta Tau, Pi Sigma Alpha. Democrat. Jewish.

WARNER, JAMES JOHN, small business owner; b. Paw Paw, Mich., Feb. 22, 1942; s. James Kelley and Arleta Alice (Turner) W.; m. Lynne Ann McGuire, June 19, 1965 (div. Apr. 4, 1994); children: Todd M., Kirk T., Beth K. BA, Mich. State U., 1965; postgrad., Western Mich. U., 1968-72. Sales rep. Warner Vineyards, Paw Paw, 1965-70, gen. mgr., 1970-73, v.p., 1973-75, pres., 1976—, also bd. dirs.; bd. dirs. Peninsular Products Co., Lansing, Mich., 1975—. Chmn. Lakeview Found., Paw Paw, Mich., 1978, Van Buren County Econ. Devel. Corp., Paw Paw, 1977; dir. Van Buren Emergency Med. Svcs., Paw Paw, 1982, Hospice of Van Buren and Kalamazoo, 1988. With U.S. Army, 1966-68, Vietnam. Decorated Bronze Star. Mem. Am. Mktg. Assn. (Man of Yr. 1978), Am. Assn. Vintners (dir. 1981—), Young Pres.' Orgn. (chmn. 1982-83), Mich. Grape and Wine Industry Coun. Episcopalian. Avocations: reading, walking, sailing, gardening, swimming. Home: 304 S Kalamazoo St Paw Paw MI 49079-1528 Office: Warner Vineyards 706 S Kalamazoo St Paw Paw MI 49079-1558

WARNER, JOHN ANDREW, foundry executive; b. Kansas City, Mo., Jan. 1, 1924; s. Richard G. and Margaret (Falconer) W.; m. Patricia Pooley, Feb. 25, 1950; children: Katherine, Amanda. Sec. Warner Oil Co., Oklahoma City, 1948-50; pres., chief exec. officer Tyler Pipe Industries, Tex., 1950-89; ret., 1989; bd. dirs. Tex. Power & Light Co., Dallas. Past chmn. East Tex. Hosp. Found.; trustee Tex. Chest Found.; former mem. Tex. Gov.'s Commn. on Phys. Fitness. Served with USCGR, 1942-46. Named Tyler's Most Outstanding Citizen, 1973. Mem. Tyler C. of C. (dir., past pres.), Cast Iron Soil Pipe Inst. (dir., past pres.), Am. Foundrymen's Soc., Tex. Assn. Bus. (dir., past state chmn.), Country Club of the Rockies, Willow Brook Country Club (dir., past pres. Tyler), Masons, Shriners, Sigma Alpha Epsilon. Presbyterian. Home: 608 Rosemont Pl Tyler TX 75701-8643

WARNER, JOHN EDWARD, advertising executive; b. Troy, N.Y., Mar. 26, 1936; s. George Edward and Ann Frances (Teson) W.; m. Anne Elizabeth Hibbard, Sept. 19, 1959; children—Matthew J., Barbara A., Peter J., Christopher J. B.S. in Chemistry and Philosophy, Coll. Holy Cross, 1957. Promotion mgr. Union Carbide Corp., N.Y.C., 1957-62; account exec. McCann-Erickson, Inc., N.Y.C., 1962-64; pres. Warner, Bicking & Fenwick, Inc., N.Y.C., 1964-84; chmn. Warner, Bicking, Morris & Ptnrs. Inc., 1984—; Pres. Transworld Advt. Agy. Network, 1987—; speaker confs. advt. mktg. assns. Columnist advt. and mktg. publs. Home: 706 Hillcrest Rd Ridgewood NJ 07450-1110 Office: 866 UN Pla New York NY 10017

WARNER, JOHN HILLIARD, JR., technical services, military and commercial systems and software company executive; b. Santa Monica, Calif., Mar. 2, 1941; s. John Hilliard and Irene Anne (Oliva) W.; m. Helga Magdalena Farrington, Sept. 4, 1961; children: Tania Renee, James Michael. BS in Engring. with honors, UCLA, 1963, MS in Engring., 1965, PhD in Engring., 1967. Mem. staff Marquardt Corp., Van Nuys, Calif., 1963; mem. faculty West Coast U., Los Angeles, 1969-72; mem. staff TRW Systems Group, Redondo Beach, Calif., 1967-70, sect. mgr., 1970-73; mem. staff Sci. Applications Internat. Corp., San Diego, 1973-75, asst. v.p., 1975-77, v.p., 1977-80, corp. v.p., 1980-81, sr. v.p., 1981-87, sector v.p., 1987-89; exec. v.p. Sci. Applications Internat Corp., San Diego, 1989-96, bd. dirs., 1988—; corp. exec. v.p. Sci. Applications Internat. Corp., San Diego, 1996—; cons. Rand Corp., Santa Monica, 1964-66. Contbr. articles to profl. jours. AEC fellow, 1963, 66, NSF fellow, 1964, 65. Mem. AIAA, Assn. U.S. Army, Air Force Assn. Am. Def. Preparedness Assn., Am. Security Coun., Armed Forces Communications and Electronics Assn., Navy League U.S., La Jolla Chamber Music Soc. (bd. dirs. 1990—), Sigma Nu, Tau Beta Pi. Methodist. Avocations: bicycling, fishing, water skiing, music. Office: SAIC 10260 Campus Point Dr San Diego CA 92121-1522

WARNER, JOHN WILLIAM, senator; b. Washington, DC, Feb. 18, 1927; s. John William and Martha Stuart (Budd) W.; children: Mary Conover, Virginia Stuart, John William IV. BS Engring., Washington and Lee U., 1949; LL.B., U. Va., 1953. Law clk. to U.S. judge, 1953-54, spl. asst. to U.S. atty., 1956-57; asst. U.S. atty. Dept. Justice, 1957-60; ptnr. Hogan & Hartson, 1960-68; owner, operator Cattle Farm, 1961—; undersec. of navy, 1969-72, sec. of navy, 1972-74; adminstr. Am. Revolution Bicentennial Adminstrn., 1974-76; U.S. senator from Va., 1979—. Served with USNR, 1944-46; to capt. USMCR, 1949-52. Mem. Bar Assn. D.C. Republican. Episcopalian. Club: Metropolitan. Office: Office of Senate 225 Russell Senate Bldg Washington DC 20510-4601*

WARNER, JOHN WILLIAM, lawyer; b. Amarillo, Tex., June 4, 1936; s. Arthur Greeley and Janet Karen (Miller) W.; m. Judith Diane Mumma, Dec. 30, 1961; children: Michael Allan, Sandra Kay, Melanie Diane, Patricia Karen. B.A., Tex. A. and M. U., 1958; LL.B., U. Tex., 1962. Bar: Tex. 1962. Practice law Pampa, Tex., 1962—; judge Municipal Ct., 1963-68; county atty. Gray County, Tex., 1969-76; discovery task force Tex. Supreme Ct., 1991-94. Dist. commr. Boy Scouts Am., 1968-70; incorporator Pampa Youth Coun., Inc., S.W. Indian Orgn., Inc., Master's Home for Children, Inc.; dir., sec.-treas. PHS Scholarship Found., 1988—; trustee Happy Haven Children's Home, 1970-71; coach Little League, 1974—; chmn. Gray County Dem. Party, 1987—; pres. Gray County chpt. Am. Cancer Soc., 1976-77; Sunday sch. tchr. 1st United Meth. Ch., 1962—, chmn. adminstrv. bd., 1984, chmn. coun. ministries, 1986, lay leader, 1990-92; adv. bd. Samaritan Pastoral Counseling Ctr., 1996—. Recipient Adult Leader of Yr. award Pampa Jr. C. of C., 1969, Tru-Teens Leader of Yr. award, 1972, Pampa High Sch. Key Club Disting. Svc. award, 1966, 83, Spl. Achievement award Panhandle Sports Hall of Fame, 1994. Mem. ABA, Tex. Bar Assn., Coll. State Bar Tex., Gray County Bar Assn., Assn. Trial Lawyers Am. (sustaining) Tex. Trial Lawyers Assn. (bd. dirs. 1988-92), Tex. Criminal Def. Lawyers Assn., Pampa C. of C., Pampa Jaycees (pres. 1968-69), Tex. Jaycees (legal counsel 1970-71), Kiwanis (pres. 1985-86), Optimists (pres. 1983-84, Optimist of Yr. award 1987). Home: 2111 Dogwood Ln Pampa TX 79065-3825 Office: Warner Finney & Warner Box 645 Pampa TX 79066-0645 *The epitaph on my grandfather's grave reads: "He lived to serve." I have tried to live my life according to that philosophy.*

WARNER, JUDITH (ANNE) HUSS, educator; b. Plainfield, N.J., June 15, 1936; d. Charles and Martha McMullen (Miller) Huss; m. Howard R. Warner, June 14, 1958; children: Barbara, Robert. BS in Elem. Edn., Russell Sage Coll., 1959. Elem. tchr. Pitts. Bd. Edn., 1959-60; home tchr. Napa (Calif.) Sch. Bd., 1974-77; substitute tchr. Allegheny Intermediate Unit, Pitts., 1977—. Leader Girl Scouts U.S.A., Pitts., 1966-70; vol. Children's Hosp., PItts., 1967-74, Jefferson Hosp., Pitts., 1977-88; pres., trustee Whitehall Libr., Pitts., 1984-92; pres., bd. dirs. Friends of Whitehall Libr., Pitts., 1969-94. Mem. AAUW, DAR. Republican. Methodist. Avocations: sailing, skiing, swimming, hiking, travel. Home: 4985 Wheaton Dr Pittsburgh PA 15236-2064

WARNER, KENNETH E., public health educator, consultant; b. Washington, Jan. 25, 1947; s. Edgar W. Jr. and Betty (Strasburger) W.; m. Patricia A. Hilty, Oct. 1, 1977; children—Peter, Andrew. A.B., Dartmouth Coll., 1968; M.Phil., Yale U., 1970, Ph.D., 1974. Lectr. dept. health planning and adminstrn. Sch. Pub. Health, U. Mich., Ann Arbor, 1972-74; asst. prof. Sch. Pub. Health, U. Mich., 1974-77, assoc. prof., 1977-83, prof., 1983—, chmn., 1982-88, 92-95; Richard D. Remington Collegiate prof. pub. health, 1995—; cons. Office of Tech. Assessment, U.S. Congress, Washington, 1976-95, Office on Smoking and Health, USPHS, Rockville, Md., 1978—, Inst. Medicine, Nat. Acad. Scis., Washington, 1984—, numerous additional pub. and pvt. orgns.; mem. bd. sci. counselors divsn. cancer prevention and control Nat. Cancer Inst., Bethesda, Md., 1985-89. Author: (with Bryan Luce) Cost-Benefit & Cost Effectiveness Analysis in Health Care, 1982; contbr. articles to profl. jours. Trustee Am. Lung Assn., Mich., Lansing, 1982; mem. subcom. on smoking Am. Heart Assn., Dallas, 1983-87; mem. com. on tobacco and cancer Am. Cancer Soc., N.Y.C., 1984-92. Hon. Woodrow Wilson fellow, 1968; W.K. Kellog Found. fellow, 1980-83; vis. scholar Nat. Bur. Econ. Research, Stanford, Calif., 1975-76; recipient Surgeon Gen.'s medallion Dr. C. Everett Koop, 1989. Mem. Am. Pub. Health Assn., Am. Econ. Assn., Nat. Assn. Pub. Health Policy (sec. council on smoking prevention 1983-84), Phi Beta Kappa. Office: U Michigan Sch Pub Health Mgmt Policy 109 Observatory St Ann Arbor MI 48109-2029

WARNER, KENNETH WILSON, JR., editor, association publications executive; b. Chgo., Dec. 22, 1928; s. Kenneth Wilson and Ann S. (Knapp) W.; m. Deborah Ann Bollo, Dec. 28, 1982 (div. Apr. 1995); 1 child, Joseph; children by previous marriages: Sara, Seth, Katharin. B.S. Ed., No. Ill. U., 1950. Staff editor Bldg. Supply News, Chgo., 1953-56; staff editor Elec. Merchandising, 1956-60; free-lance writer Sarasota, Fla., 1960-66; editor Gunsport Mag., Alexandria and Falls Church, Va., 1966-67; editor Gunfacts Mag., Arlington, Va., 1968-70, pub., 1968-70; exec. editor Am. Rifleman, Nat. Rifle Assn., Washington, 1971-78, asst. dir. publs. div., 1972-78; editor Am. Hunter, 1973-78, Am. Rifleman, 1976-78; dir. publs. NRA, Washington, 1977-78; editor in chief Gun Digest, Knives Annual-DBI Books Inc., Greenville, W.Va., 1979—; design cons. Blackjack Knives, Effingham, Ill. Author: The Practical Book of Knives. 1976; The Practical Book of Guns, 1978. Editor: The Bolt Action, 1976. Contbr. articles to profl. jours. Cpl. U.S. Army. 1951-53. Recipient Cutlery Hall of Fame. Mem. NRA (life), Knifemaker's Guild. Am. (assoc.). Office: Gun Digest Editorial Office PO Box 52 Greenville WV 24945-0052

WARNER, MARK ROY, film editor. Editor: (films) (with Freeman Davies and Billy Weber) 48 Hours, 1982, (with Don Zimmerman) Rocky III, 1982, (with Zimmerman) Staying Alive, 1983, (with Caroline Biggerstaff) A Soldier's Story, 1984, (with Christopher Lebenzon and Scott Wallace) Weird Science, 1985, (with Steve Mirkovich and Edward A. Warschilka) Big Trouble in Little China, 1986, (with Warschilka and John Wright) The Running Man, 1987, Cocoon: The Return, 1988, Driving Miss Daisy, 1989 (Academy award nomination best film editing 1989), Pacific Heights, 1990, Rush, 1992, (with John F. Burnett and Zimmerman) Leap of Faith, 1992, Rich in Love, 1992, Intersection, 1994, Dolores Claiborne, 1995. Address: 20567 Paradise Lane Topanga CA 90290

WARNER, PATRICIA JOAN, psychotherapist; b. Greenville, N.C., Mar. 5, 1947; d. Joseph Ophir and Florence Genevieve (Jenkins) Teel; m. Richard Barr Cayton, May 21, 1971 (div. 1978); 1 child, Heather Jeanine; m. Michael Roy Warner, Jan. 9, 1987. BS in Elem. Edn., East Carolina U., 1968, MA in Guidance an Counseling, 1969. Lic. profl. counselor, Ga., Tenn.; nat. cert. counselor. Mental retardation counselor Pineland Mental Health, Jesup, Ga., 1983-85; mental health counselor Jesup, 1985-89; therapist, adolescence substance abuse Sci. Applications Internat., Nuernberg, Germany, 1989-92; adolescent therapist Harriett Cohn Ctr., Clarksville, Tenn., 1992—; chairperson Troubled Childrens Com., Baxley, Ga., 1988; presenter Am. Women's Activities in Germany, 1989. Recipient Letter of Commendation Comdr. U.S. Army Europe, 1991. Mem. Am. Counseling Assn., Erlangen Amateur Radio Soc. (sec. 1990-92), Clarksville Amateur Transmitting Soc., Assn. of Specialists in Group Work. Democrat. Avocation: amateur radio. Home: 447 Winding Way Rd Clarksville TN 37043-5191 Office: Harriett Cohn Mental Health Ctr 511 8th St Clarksville TN 37040-3093

WARNER, PETER DAVID, publishing executive; b. Phila., Aug. 15, 1942; s. Robert and Myra (Spector) W.; m. Ruth Bluestein (div. 1982); m. Jill Sansone, 1983; children: Emily, Cynthia, Nicholas. BA, NYU, 1964. Asst. dir. membership and devel. Mus. Modern Art, N.Y.C., 1973-76; editor, promotion dir. Book-of-the-Month Club, N.Y.C., 1976-79; pres. Thames and Hudson, N.Y.C., 1979—. Author: Loose Ends, 1972, Lifestyle, 1986. Mem. The Writers Room (bd. dirs.). Office: Thames & Hudson Inc 500 Fifth Ave New York NY 10110-0001

WARNER, RAWLEIGH, JR., oil company executive; b. Chgo., Feb. 13, 1921; s. Rawleigh and Dorothy (Haskins) W.; m. Mary Ann deClairmont, Nov. 2, 1946; children: Alison W. Pyne, Suzanne W. Parsons. Grad., Lawrenceville (N.J.) Sch., 1940; A.B. cum laude, Princeton U., 1943. Sec., treas. Warner Bard Co., Chgo., 1946-48; with Continental Oil Co., 1948-53; asst. treas. Continental Oil Co., Houston, 1952-53; treas. Socony-Vacuum Overseas Supply Co., 1953-55; asst. treas. Mobil Overseas Oil Co., 1955-56; mgr. econs. dept., then mgr. Middle East dept. Socony Mobil Oil Co. Inc., 1956-59; regional v.p. Mobil Internat. Oil Co., 1959-60, exec. v.p., 1960-63, pres., 1963-64; exec. v.p., dir. Mobil Oil Corp. (formerly Socony Mobil Oil Co., Inc.), 1964, pres., 1965-69, chmn. bd., chief exec. officer, 1969-86; chmn. Mobil Corp., 1976-86. Served to capt. F.A., AUS, 1943-45. Decorated Purple Heart, Bronze Star, Silver Star. Mem. Am. Petroleum Inst. Republican. Presbyn. Clubs: Augusta (Ga.) Nat. Golf; Links (N.Y.C.) ; New Canaan Country; Blind Brook (Rye Brook, N.Y.); Jupiter Island (Hobe Sound, Fla.); Chicago; Seminole (North Palm Beach, Fla.). Office: Mobil Corp PO Box 2072 New York NY 10163-2072

WARNER, ROBERT MARK, university dean, archivist, historian,; b. Montrose, Colo., June 28, 1927; s. Mark Thomas and Bertha Margaret (Rich) W.; m. Eleanor Jane Bullock, Aug. 21, 1954; children: Mark Steven, Jennifer Jane. Student, U. Denver, 1945; B.A., Muskingum Coll., 1949, LL.D. (hon.), 1981; M.A., U. Mich., 1953, Ph.D., 1958; H.H.D. (hon.), Westminster (Pa.) Coll., 1981; L.H.D. (hon.), DePaul U., 1983. Tchr. high sch. Montrose, Colo., 1949-50; lectr. dept. history U. Mich., 1958-66, asso. prof., 1966-71, prof., 1971—, prof. Sch. Info. and Library Studies, 1974—, dean Sch. Info. and Library Studies, 1985-92, univ. historian, 1992—, interim dir. Univ. Libraries, 1988-90; asst. in rsch. Bentley Hist. Libr., 1953-57, asst. curator, 1957-61, asst. dir., 1961-66, dir., 1966-80; archivist of U.S., 1980-85; mem. exec. com. Bentley Hist. Libr., 1988—; bd. visitors Sch. Libr. Sci., Case Western Res. U., 1976-80, chmn., 1980-84, Maxwell Sch. Govt., Syracuse U., 1982-87; chmn. Gerald R. Ford Presdl. Libr. Bldg. Com., 1977-79; bd. dirs., sec. Gerald R. Ford Found., 1987—; trustee Woodrow Wilson Internat. Ctr. for Scholars, 1980-85, chmn. fellowship com., 1983-85; chmn. Nat. Hist. Publs. and Records Commn., 1980-85; mem. exec. com. Internat. Coun. on Archives, 1984-88; pres. 2d European Conf. on Archives, 1989; comptroller gen. U.S. Rsch. and Edn. Adv. Com., 1988—; rsch. adv. com. Online Computer Libr. Ctr., 1990-93; bd. govs. Clements Libr., 1988-90, 93—, Clark Hist. Libr. Ctrl. Mich. U., 1987—; vis. prof. UCLA, 1993. Author: Chase S. Osborn, 1860-1949, 1960, Profile of a Profession, 1964, (with R. Bordin) The Modern Manuscript Library, 1966, (with C.W. Vanderhill) A Michigan Reader: 1865 to the Present, 1974, (with F. Blouin) Sources for the Study of Migration and Ethnicity, 1979, Diary of a Dream: A History of the National Archives Independence Movement, 1980-1985, 1995. Served with U.S. Army, 1950-52. Recipient Disting. Svc. award Muskingum Coll., 1990, Disting. Svc. award Nat. Hist. Pub. and Records Commn., 1992. Fellow Soc. Am. Archivists; mem. Am. Hist. Assn. (council 1981-85), Orgn. Am. Historians, ALA (council 1986-91), Assn. for Library and Info. Sci. Edn., Presbyn. Hist. Soc. (bd. dirs. 1987-91), Am. Assn. State and Local History, Hist. Soc. Mich. (trustee 1960-66, v.p. 1972-73, pres. 1973-74), Soc. Am. Archivists (mem. council 1967-71, sec., exec. dir. 1971-73, v.p. 1974-75, pres. 1976-77), Am. Antiquarian Soc., Phi Alpha Theta, Beta Phi Mu. Presbyterian. Club: U. Mich. Research. Lodge: Rotary. Home: 1821 Coronada Dr Ann Arbor MI 48103-5066 Office: U Mich Sch Info & Libr Studies 550 E University Ave Ann Arbor MI 48109-1092

WARNER, ROBERT S., company director, former accountant; b. Erie, Pa., Apr. 9, 1907; s. Spencer Roycraft and Anna Edith (MacDonald) W.; m. Doris Jean Squarey, June 29, 1931 (dec. Sept. 1987); children: Elizabeth S. (Mrs. Richard W. Bakenhus), Robert S. (dec.); m. Mary Catherine Moore, Oct. 13, 1990. Litt.B., Rutgers U., 1928. With Lybrand, Ross Bros. & Montgomery, C.P.A.s, N.Y.C., 1928-72; charge St. Louis office Lybrand, Ross Bros. & Montgomery, C.P.A.s, 1936-49; charge Los Angeles office Lybrand, Ross Bros. & Montgomery, C.P.A.s, Los Angeles, 1949-72; mem. firm Lybrand, Ross Bros. & Montgomery, C.P.A.s, 1944-72; mem. exec. com.; exec. com. Coopers & Lybrand; dir. Bixby Ranch Co. Trustee J.B. and Emily Van Nuys Charities, L.A., South Coast Med. Ctr. Found., South Laguna. Mem. Calif., N.Y. socs. C.P.A.s, Am. Inst. C.P.A.s. Clubs: Bohemian (San Francisco); Big Canyon Country (Newport Beach, Calif.). Home: 32 N La Senda Dr Laguna Beach CA 92677-3365

WARNER, SCOTT DENNIS, investment banker; b. York, Pa., July 13, 1963; s. Earl Dennis and Sandra Glee (Barnhart) W. SB in Elec. Engring., MIT, 1986, SB in Computer Sci. and Engring., 1986, SM in Elec. Engring. and Computer Sci., 1986; MBA in Fin., U. Chgo., 1990. Rschr., teaching asst. MIT Lab. for Computer Sci., Cambridge, Mass., 1982-86; intern IBM Corp., Yorktown Heights, N.Y., 1983-86; fin. analyst Merrill Lynch & Co., N.Y.C., 1986-88, assoc., 1990-94, v.p., 1994-95; summer assoc. Goldman, Sachs & Co., N.Y.C., 1989; v.p. Lipper & Co., N.Y.C., 1995—. Nat. Merit scholar, 1981, ROTC scholar, 1981, teaching asst. scholar MIT, 1985, 86; Leon C. Marshall scholar U. Chgo., 1988. Mem. Nat. Eagle Scout Assn., Delta Upsilon Frat. Republican. Presbyterian. Home: 235 E 95th St Apt 23E New York NY 10128 Office: Lipper & Co 101 Park Ave New York NY 10178

WARNER, SETH L., mathematician, educator; b. Muskegon, Mich., July 11, 1927; s. Seth LeMoyne and Agnes (Brustad) W.; m. Susan Emily Rose, June 16, 1962; children: Susan Emily, Sarah Southall, Seth Lawrence. B.S., Yale U., 1950; M.A., Harvard U., 1951, Ph.D., 1955. Rsch. instr. Duke U., 1955-57, asst. prof., 1957-61, asso. prof., 1961-65, prof. math., 1965-95, dir. grad. studies math., 1960-68; prof. emeritus math., 1995—; chmn. Duke U., 1968-70, 73-82; mem. Inst. Advanced Studies, 1959-60; vis. disting. prof. math. Reed Coll., 1970-71; visitor U. Paris, 1964-65, U. Oslo, 1982-83. Author: Modern Algebra, vols. I and II, 1965, re-issued, 1990, Classical Modern Algebra, 1971, Topological Fields, 1989, Topological Rings, 1993. Served with Med. Service Corps AUS, 1946-48. Mem. Phi Beta Kappa, Sigma Xi. Episcopalian. Home: 2433 Wrightwood Ave Durham NC 27705-5823 Office: Duke U Math Dept Box 90320 Durham NC 27708-0320

WARNER, THEODORE KUGLER, JR., lawyer; b. Phila., Sept. 13, 1909; s. Theodore Kugler and Anna (Allen) W.; m. Dorothy Wark Hoehler, Nov.

23, 1935 (dec. 1985); children: Betsy Ann, Peter Joyce; m. Lynn Howell, May 20, 1995. A.B., U. Pa., 1931, LL.B. cum laude, 1934. Bar: Pa. 1934. With Pa. R.R., Phila., 1934-70; chief tax counsel Pa. R.R., 1952-58, dir. taxation, 1958-68, v.p. taxes, 1968, v.p. accounting and taxes, 1968-69, v.p. corp. adminstrn., 1969-70; pres. Can. So. Ry., 1968-70; v.p. Pitts. & Lake Eric R.R., 1968-70; officer, dir. other Penn Central cos., 1968-70; counsel Duane, Morris & Heckscher, Phila., 1970-71, Harper & Driver, 1975—; lectr. on consol. returns various tax forums. Bd. suprs. Easttown Twp., Pa., 1962-70, chmn., 1966-70; bd. dirs. Independence Found., 1991—, sec. 1993, pres., 1993-95, sec.-treas., 1996—. Mem. Nat. Tax Assn. (pres. 1965-66), Am. Law Inst. (life mem.), ABA, Pa. Bar Assn., Order of Coif, Aronimink Golf Club, Union League, Masons (33 deg., mem. com. on masonic homes 1970-84, chmn. 1975-77, 81-83, Franklin medal 1983, bd. dirs., treas. Masonic libr. and mus. 1991—), Tau Kappa Epsilon. Republican. Lutheran. Home: 39 Old Covered Bridge Rd Newtown Square PA 19073-1211 Office: 1000 N American Bldg Philadelphia PA 19107

WARNER, VINCENT W., bishop. Bishop Diocese of Olympia, Seattle, 1990—. Office: Diocese of Olympia PO Box 12126 1551 10th Ave E Seattle WA 98102-4298*

WARNER, WALTER DUKE, corporate executive; b. Davenport, Iowa, Feb. 26, 1952; s. Robert Martin and Opal Louise (Gibbons) W.; m. Susan Dee Hafferkamp, Nov. 15, 1975 (div. 1982); 1 child, Natalie. BS, Drake U., 1975. Ops. officer Iowa-Des Moines Nat. Bank, 1975-78; from v.p. ops. to v.p. mktg. and pub. rels. Cen. Savs. and Loan Assn., San Diego, Calif., 1978-84; pres. The Lomas Santa Fe Cos., Solana Beach, Calif., 1985-91; pres., co-founder Ebert Composites Corp., San Diego, 1991—, also bd. dirs.; bd. dirs. Torrey Pines Bank, Solana Beach, Lomas Group Inc., Del Mar, Calif., Madison Valley Properties, Inc., La Jolla, Calif., Nature Preserved of Am. Inc., San Clemente, Calif.; pres., bd. dirs. Regents Pk. Comml. Asns., La Jolla. Bd. dirs. Inst. of the Ams., La Jolla, 1986—, mem. internat. council, 1986—; chmn. bd. dirs., pres. San Diego chpt. Arthritis Found., 1985-87; dir., pres. Gildred Found., Solana Beach, 1986—; founding dir., treas. Golden Triangle Arts Found. Mem. The Exec. Com., Calif. League of Savs. and Loans (mem. mktg. and ops. com. 1982-84), Internat. Forum for Corp. Dirs., Iowa Club of San Diego (founding dir. 1984-85). Republican. Protestant. Avocations: tennis, piano.

WARNER, WILLIAM HAMER, applied mathematician; b. Pitts., Oct. 6, 1929; s. John Christian and Louise (Hamer) W.; m. Janet Louise West, June 29, 1957; 1 dau., Katherine Patricia. Student, Haverford Coll., 1946-48; B.S., Carnegie Inst. Tech., 1950, M.S., 1951, Ph.D., 1953. Research asso. grad. div. applied math. Brown U., Providence, 1953-55; asst. prof. dept. aerospace engring. and mechanics U. Minn., Mpls., 1955-58; asso. prof. U. Minn., 1958-68, prof., 1968-95, prof. emeritus, 1995—. Author: (with L.E. Goodman) Statics, 1963, Dynamics, 1964; contbr. articles to profl. jours. Mem. Am. Math. Soc., Soc. Indsl. and Applied Math., Math. Assn. Am., Soc. Natural Philosophy. Office: U Minn 107 Akerman Hall Minneapolis MN 55455

WARNICK, WALTER LEE, mechanical engineer; b. Balt., May 31, 1947; s. Marvin Paul and Freda (Wilt) W.; m. Metta Ann Nichter, May 2, 1970; children: Ashlie Colleen, Leah Brooke. BS in Engring., Johns Hopkins U., 1969; PhD, U. Md., 1977. Registered profl. engr., Md. Engr. Westinghouse Electric Co., Linthicum, Md., 1969-71, U.S. Naval Rsch. Lab., Washington, 1971-77; engr. U.S. Dept. Energy, Washington, 1977-85, sr. exec., 1985—; Dept. Energy rep. Nat. Acid Precipitation Assessment Program, Washington, 1981—. Author: Warnick Families of Western Maryland, 1988, 95, Wilt Families of Western Maryland, 1991. Pres. citizen's adv. com. to Howard County Bd. of Edn., Ellicott City, Md., 1980-82. Mem. ASME, Sigma Xi. Office: US Dept Energy Washington DC 20585

WARNKE, DETLEF ANDREAS, geologist, educator; b. Berlin, Fed. Republic of Germany, Jan. 29, 1928; came to U.S., 1955; s. Aloys and Martha (Konetzky) W.; m. Holly M. Menkel, Nov. 14, 1964 (div. 1993); children: Erik, D. Christian. Diploma in Geology, U. Freiburg, Fed. Republic of Germany, 1953; PhD in Geology, U. So. Calif., 1965. Jr. exploitation engr. Shell Oil, Houston and Los Angeles, 1956-58; research asst. U. So. Calif., Los Angeles, 1959-61; instr. various colls., Los Angeles and Long Beach, Calif., 1959-63; research assoc., asst. prof. Fla. State U., Tallahassee, 1963-71; from asst. prof. to prof. geology Calif. State U., Hayward, 1971—, chair dept. geology, 1994—; exchange prof. Free U. Berlin, 1980-81. Contbr. articles to profl. jours. Fulbright scholar, 1987-88; NSF grantee. Mem. Geol. Soc. Am., Soc. Sedimentary Geology, Am. Geophys. Union, Am. Quaternary Assn., Geologische Vereinigung, Sigma Xi. Avocations: skiing, hiking. Office: Calif State U Dept Geol Scis Hayward CA 94542

WARNKE, PAUL CULLITON, lawyer; b. Webster, Mass., Jan. 31, 1920; s. Paul Martin and Lillian (Culliton) W.; m. Jean Farjeon Rowe, Sept. 9, 1948; children: Margaret Farjeon, Georgia Culliton, Thomas Martin, Stephen August, Benjamin Hyatt. A.B., Yale U., 1941; LL.B., Columbia U., 1948; LL.D. (hon.), Northland Coll., 1979, Franklin and Marshall Coll., 1983, George Washington U., 1984, Grinnell Coll., 1985, Amherst Coll., 1985, Haverford Coll., 1989. Bar: D.C. 1948. Assoc. Covington & Burling, Washington, 1948-57; ptnr. Covington & Burling, 1957-66; gen. counsel Dept. Def., 1966-67, asst. sec. def. for internat. security affairs, 1967-69; ptnr. Clifford, Warnke, Glass, McIlwain & Finney, 1969-77; dir. U.S. Arms Control and Disarmament Agy., Washington, 1977-78; chief U.S. arms control negotiator, 1977-78; ptnr. Clifford & Warnke, Washington, 1978-91, Howrey & & Simon, Washington, 1991—; adj. prof. Georgetown U. Sch. Fgn. Svc., 1996; spl. cons. to sec. state, 1978-81; mem. Md. and D.C. adv. coms. to U.S. Commn. Civil Rights, 1962-66; trustee Lawyers Com. for Civil Rights Under Law; dir. Internat. Vol. Svcs., 1973-76; exec. com. Trilateral Commn., 1973-77; mem. China coun. Asia Soc., 1976-77; mem. Presdl. Adv. Bd. on Arms Proliferation Policy, 1995—; mem. sci. and policy adv. commn. ACDA, 1995—; mem. disciplinary bd. D.C. Bar, 1973-75, bd. govs., 1976-77. Trustee Potomac Sch., 1958-66, chmn. bd., 1965-66; bd. dirs. Health and Welfare Coun. Nat. Capital Area, 1966-67, Franklin and Eleanor Roosevelt Inst., 1991—, Georgetown U., 1979-92, Wolftrap Found., 1978-83; trustee Northland Coll., 1970-76, Columbia U., 1984-90; mem. bd. visitors Columbia U. Sch. Law; chmn. selection com. Albert Einstein Peace Prize Found., 1991-93; mem. governing bd. Common Cause, 1983-86. Lt. USCGR, 1942-46. Fellow Am. Bar Found.; mem. ABA, Fed. Bar Assn., D.C. Bar Assn., Coun. Am. Ambs., Am. Soc. Internat. Law, Coun. Fgn. Rels., Atlantic Coun. of the U.S. (sr. councillor). Democrat. Clubs: Met. (Washington); Yale (N.Y.C.). Home: 5037 Garfield St NW Washington DC 20016-3465 Office: Howrey & Simon 3rd Fl 1299 Pennsylvania Ave NW Washington DC 20004-2402

WARNKE, ROGER ALLEN, pathology educator; b. Peoria, Ill., Feb. 22, 1945; s. Delmar Carl and Ruth Armanelle (Peard) W.; m. Joan Marie Gebhart, Nov. 18, 1972; children: Kirsten Marie, Lisa Marie. BS, U. Ill., 1967; MD, Washington U., St. Louis, 1971. Diplomate Am. Bd. Pathology. Intern in pathology Stanford (Calif.) U. Med. Sch., 1971-72, resident in pathology, 1972-73, postdoctoral fellow in pathology, 1973-75, postdoctoral fellow in immunology, 1975-76, asst. prof. pathology, 1976-82, assoc. prof., 1983-90; prof., 1991—; cons. Becton Dickinson Monoclonal Ctr., Mountain View, Calif., 1982-88, IDEC, Mountain View, 1985-90; sci. advisor Ventana Med. Systems, Inc., Tucson, 1986—. Contbr. over 200 articles to med. jours., chpts. to books. Recipient Benjamin Castleman award Mass. Gen. Hosp., 1981; Agnes Axtel Moule faculty scholar Stanford U., 1979-82; Nat. Cancer Inst. and NIH rsch. grantee, 1978-95. Mem. So. Bay Pathology Soc., Calif. Soc. Pathologists, U.S. Can. Acad. Path., Am. Assn. Pathologists, Soc. for Hematopathology, European Assn. for Haematopathology. Home: 845 Tolman Dr Stanford CA 94305 Office: Stanford U Dept Pathology Stanford CA 94305

WARNKEN, DOUGLAS RICHARD, publishing consultant; b. N.Y.C., Apr. 17, 1930; s. Richard William and Juliette (Lindsay) W.; m. Virginia M. Thompson, Sept. 16, 1957; 1 child, William Monroe. A.B., Norwich U., 1952. Sales rep. Prentice-Hall, Inc., Nashville, 1954-56; regional sales mgr. Wadsworth Pub. Co., Inc., Chgo., 1957-59; nat. sales mgr. Wadsworth Pub. Co., Inc., Belmont, Calif., 1960-64; v.p., marketing mgr. Wadsworth Pub. Co., Inc., Belmont, 1964-68; exec. v.p. Wadsworth Pub. Co., Inc., 1968-77, pres., 1977-78, dir., 1971-78; pres., dir. Wadsworth, Inc., 1978-85, chief exec. officer, 1980-84, vice chmn., 1985-86; chmn. bd. Wadsworth Pubs. of Can., Ltd., 1975-80; chmn. bd. Van Nostrand Reinhold Co. Inc., 1981-83, dir., 1983-85; chmn. bd. Anaheim Pub. Co., Inc., 1982-85; dir. Van Nostrand Reinhold Co., Inc., Lange Med. Pubs., Inc., Internat. Thomson Orgn., Inc., 1982-85; chmn. HDL Communications, Inc., 1988—. Active Boy Scouts Am. Served to 1st lt. AUS, 1952-54. Named hon. Ky. col., 1978. Mem. Vols. for Internat. Tech. Assistance, Belmont C. of C. (dir. 1970-80, pres. 1972-73), Western Book Pubs. Assn. (dir. 1971-78), Press Club of San Francisco. Republican. Presbyterian. Clubs: Carmel Valley Golf and Country, Monterey Country, Peninsula Golf and Country. Lodge: Knights of the Vine.

WARNOCK, DAVID GENE, nephrologist; b. Parker, Ariz., Mar. 5, 1945. MD, U. Calif., San Francisco, 1970. Diplomate Am. Bd. Internal Medicine, Am. Bd. Nephrology. Intern U. Calif., San Francisco, 1970-71, resident, 1971-73; fellow nephrology NIH, Bethesda, Md., 1973-75; prof. medicine and pharmacology U. Calif., San Francisco, 1983; prof. U. Ala., Birmingham, 1988—; chief nephrology sect. VA Med. Ctr., Birmingham, 1983-88; prof., dir. divsn. nephrology U. Ala., Birmingham, 1988—, prof. medicine & physiology, 1988—. Mem. AAAS, Am. Physiol. Soc., Am. Soc. Clin. Investigation, Am. Soc. Nephrology. Office: U Ala Nephrology Rsch & Tng Ctr UAB Sta Birmingham AL 35294

WARR, ROBERT, producer. Recipient Best Music Video-Long Form Grammy award, 1996. *

WARREN, ALBERT, publishing executive; b. Warren, Ohio, May 18, 1920; s. David and Clara W.; m. Margaret Virginia Yeomans, Jan. 9, 1947; children: Ellen, Paul, Claire, Daniel, Thomas, Joan. BA in Journalism, Ohio State U., 1942. Assoc. editor TV Digest, Washington, 1945-50, sr. editor, 1950-58, chief Washington Bur., 1958-61; pres., editor, pub. Warren Pub., Inc., Washington, 1961—; lectr. Columbia Grad. Sch. Journalism, N.Y.C., 1962-75; mem. alumni adv. coun. Ohio State U., Columbus, 1982-88. Contbr. articles to profl. jours. Mem. adv. coun. sch. of journalism Ohio State U., 1982—. With USNR, 1942-45, PTO. Recipient Disting. Alumnus award Ohio State U. Sch. Journalism, 1995. Mem. Ind. Newsletter Assn. (co-founder 1963, pres. 1965-66), Newsletter Pubs. Assn. (Pub. of Yr. 1985), Broadcast Pioneers (Annual Recognition award 1982), Cable TV Pioneers, Internat. Radio and TV Soc. Pubs., Mus. of Broadcasting, White House Corr. Assn., U.S. Congress Periodical Gallery, Soc. Profl. Journalists (Hall of Fame 1991). Home: 26 W Kirke St Chevy Chase MD 20815-4261 Office: Warren Pub Inc 2115 Ward Pl NW Washington DC 20037-1213

WARREN, ALEX MCLEAN, JR., automotive executive; b. Augusta, Ga., Aug. 4, 1940; s. Alex McLean and Bessie Clay (Farris) W.; m. Barbara Howell, Feb. 16, 1963 (div.); children: Elizabeth Clay, Brian Lee; m. Virginia A. Fitzgerald, Jan. 3, 1980. BA, U. Ky., 1962, LLB, 1965; MBA, U. Chgo., 1979. Bar: Ky. 1965, Pa. 1969. Labor atty. U.S. Steel Corp., Pitts., 1968-72; dir. indsl. rels. Rockwell Internat. Graphics Group, Chgo., 1972-75, dir. pers., 1975-77; corp. dir. human resources Allegheyn Internat. Chemetron Group, Chgo., 1977-80; v.p. human resources Leaseway Transp. Corp., Cleve., 1980-83, sr. v.p., 1983-86; sr. v.p. Toyota Motor Mfg. USA, Lexington, Ky., 1986—. Mem. task force Greater Cleve. Growth Assn., 1983-86, Ky. Econ. Devel. Corp., 1987—; bd. dirs. United Way Bluegrass, 1987—, Cleve. 500 Found., Fund for the Arts, 1988-90, Opera House Fund, 1988—, Ky. Ctr. for the Arts, 1993—; founder, co-chmn., bd. dirs. Bluegrass Tomorrow, 1988—. Capt. USAF, 1965-68. Mem. Georgetown C. of C., Champions of Golf Club. Republican. Presbyterian. Home: 927 Edgewater Dr Lexington KY 40502-2788 Office: Toyota Mfg USA Inc 1001 Cherry Blossom Way Georgetown KY 40324-9564

WARREN, ALVIN CLIFFORD, JR., lawyer, educator; b. Daytona Beach, Fla., May 14, 1944; s. Alvin Clifford and Barbara (Barnes) W.; m. Judith Blatt, Aug. 20, 1966; children—Allison, Matthew. B.A., Yale U., 1966; J.D., U. Chgo., 1969. Bar: Conn. 1970, Pa. 1975. Prof. law U. Conn.-West Hartford, 1969-73, Duke U., Durham, N.C., 1973-74, U. Pa., Phila., 1974-79, Harvard U. Law Sch., Cambridge, Mass., 1979—. Mem. ABA (tax sect.). Contbr. articles to law jours. Office: Law Sch Harvard U Cambridge MA 02138

WARREN, CHARLES DAVID, library administrator; b. Martin, Tenn., June 12, 1944; s. Charles Alton and Evelyn (Bell) W.; m. Linda Ann Hild, July 10, 1971; children: Aaron David, Meredith Hild, Julia Myers. BS, U. Tenn., 1967; MS, U. Ill., Urbana, 1969. cert. pub. library adminstr. Dir. Shiloh Regional Library, Jackson, Tenn., 1969-72, Cumberland County Pub. Library, Fayetteville, N.C., 1973-79; exec. dir. Richland County Pub. Library, Columbia, S.C., 1979—; v.p. LHW Creations, Inc., 1979—. Bd. dirs. Civic Music Assn., Fayetteville, N.C., 1973-79, Fayetteville Symphony, 1973-78, Fayetteville Arts Commn., 1975, Friends of Librs. U.S.A., 1994—; mem. Columbia Coord. Coun., 1987-88; chmn. Richland County History Commn., 1987-93; mem. John Cotton Dana Awards Commn., 1994—. Recipient Lucy Hampton Bostick award, 1993, S.C. Pub. Adminstr. Yr. award, 1993; named Young Man of Yr., Fayetteville Jaycees, 1977, S.C. Libr. of Yr., 1991. Mem. ALA (pres. Jr. Member Roundtable 1977, chmn. awards com. 1984), Southeastern Libr. Assn. (pres. pub. libr. sect. 1978), S.C. Libr. Assn. (bd. dirs. 1980), Caprician Club, Spring Valley Country Club, Rotary, Kiwanis. Democrat. Episcopalian. Home: 217 Cricket Hill Rd Columbia SC 29223-3003 Office: Richland County Pub Libr 1431 Assembly St Columbia SC 29201-3101

WARREN, CHRISTOPHER COLLINS, professional football player; b. Silver Spring, Md., Jan. 24, 1967. Degree in psychology, Ferrum Coll. Running back Seattle Seahawks, 1990—. Selected to Pro Bowl, 1993-94. Office: c/o Seattle Seahawks 11220 N E 53d St Kirkland WA 98033*

WARREN, CRAIG BISHOP, flavor and fragrance company executive, researcher; b. Phila., Oct. 21, 1939. AB, Franklin and Marshall Coll., 1961; MS, Villanova U., 1963; PhD, Cornell U., 1968. Rsch. chemist Monsanto Co., St. Louis, 1968-70, sr. rsch. chemist, 1970-72, rsch. specialist, 1973-75; group leader Internat. Flavors & Fragrances, Union Beach, N.J., 1975-77, sr. group leader, 1977-79, rsch. dir., 1979-83, v.p., 1983—. Editor: Odor Quality and Chemical Structure, 1981, Use of Computers in Flavor and Fragrance Research, 1983; contbr. 40 articles to profl. jours.; patentee in field. Mem. exec. coun. Boy Scouts Am., Monmouth County, N.J., 1981-85. Rsch. fellow NIH, 1964-68. Mem. Assn. Rsch. Dirs. (pres. 1989-90), Am. Chem. Soc. (chmn. Monmouth Country chpt. 1980-81), N.Y. Acad. Sci., Indsl. Rsch. Inst., ASTM. Avocations: bicycling, sailing, skiing, tropical fish, personal computers. Office: Internat Flavors & Frangrance 1515 State Route 36 Keyport NJ 07735-3542

WARREN, DAVID GRANT, lawyer, educator; b. Chgo.; m. Marsha White, 1959. A.B., Miami U., Oxford, Ohio, 1958; J.D., Duke U., 1964. Bar: N.C. 1964. Prof. Med. Ctr., Duke U., Durham, N.C., 1975—; exec. dir. N.C. Med. Malpractice Study Commn., 1986, Gov.'s Inst. on Alcohol and Substance Abuse, 1991—; faculty mem. U.N.C., U. London, Georgetown U., McGill U. News editor Jour. Health Politics, Policy and Law, 1977—. Office: Duke U Med Ctr PO Box 2914 Durham NC 27710-2914

WARREN, DAVID HARDY, psychology educator; b. Chelsea, Mass., July 28, 1943; s. Roland Leslie and Margaret (Hodges) W.; m. Katherine V. Warren; children: Michael Jonathan Warren, Gabriel Kristopher Coy. A.B. in Psychology, Yale U., 1965; Ph.D. in Child Devel, U. Minn., 1969. Prof. psychology U. Calif., Riverside, 1969—, dean Coll. Humanities and Social Scis., 1977-85, dir. Univ. honors program, 1989-92, chair dept. psychology, 1992-94, exec. vice chancellor, 1994—. Author: Blindness and Early Childhood Development, 1977, 84, Blindness and Children: An Individual Differences Approach, 1994; contbr. articles to profl. jours. Mem. Psychonomic Soc., AAAS. Office: U Calif Office of Exec Vice Chancellor Riverside CA 92521

WARREN, DAVID LILES, educational association executive; b. Goldsboro, N.C., Sept. 15, 1943; s. James Hubert and Katherine (Liles) W.; m. Ellen Elizabeth LeGendre, Mar. 1, 1969; children—Jamison, Mackenzie, Katrin. B.A. in English, Wash. State U., 1965; M. Urban Studies, Yale U., 1970, M.Div., 1970; Ph.D., U. Mich., 1976; LittD, Elmhurst Coll., 1994, Moravian Coll., 1994; LLD, Rider U., 1996. Gen. sec. Dwight Hall, Yale U., New Haven, 1969-76, bd. dirs., 1976—; assoc. dir. community relations Yale U., New Haven, 1976-78; sr. v.p., provost Antioch U., N.Y.C. and Yellow Springs, Ohio, 1978-82; chief adminstrv. officer City of New Haven, 1982-84; pres. Ohio Wesleyan U., Delaware, 1984-93, Nat. Assn. Indep. Colls. and Univs., Washington, 1993—; cons. to hosps., sch. systems, colls., univs.; bd. dirs. Delaware County Bank; chmn. NCAA Pres. Commn., Div. III, 1990-92. Contbr. chpts. to books, articles to Yale Alumni Mag. Mem. NEw Haven Bd. Alderman, 1973-75; vice chmn. New Haven Commn. on Poverty, 1981-82; pres. North Coast Athletic Conf., 1988-90; justice of peace New Haven Dem. Party, 1974-76; state chmn. People to People, 1987; chmn. Gov.'s Task Force on Dep. Registrar, 1987; chmn. Ohio Five Coll. Commn., 1985-95, Campus Compact Nat. Exec. Com., 1987-88; bd. dirs. U.S. Health Corp., Coun. Ethics and Econs.; exec. com. Great Lakes Colls. Assn., Ctrl. Ohio Symphony Orch.; chmn. Ohio Ethics commn. Fulbright scholar Wash. State U., 1965-66; Rockefeller fellow Yale U., 1966; disting. Centennial Alumnus Wash. State U. Mem. Am. Assn. Higher Edn., Assn. Ind. Colls. Univs. (sec. 1987-88), Phi Beta Kappa. Democrat. Methodist. Clubs: University (Columbus, Ohio); Graduate (New Haven). Avocations: jogging; writing; tennis. Office: Nat Assn Ind Colls & Univs Ste 700 1025 Connecticut Ave NW Washington DC 20036

WARREN, DEAN STUART, artist; b. Mpls., June 30, 1949; s. Jefferson Trowbridge and Dorothy Ann (Edin) W.; m. Betty Sharon Poe, Aug. 14, 1971; children: Jeremy, Adam. BFA, Fla. Atlantic U., 1973; MA, Northwestern State U., 1975; MFA, Stephen F. Austin State U., 1980. Instr. art Cisco (Tex.) Jr. Coll., 1976-78; staff craftsworker Walt E. Disney Show Prodn. Walt Disney World, Lake Buena Vista, Fla., 1981-83, staff craftsworker staff shop, 1983, property craftsworker, 1983-87, artist preparator animation dept., 1987—; lead prodn. artist Marvac, Inc., Seminole County, Fla., 1983; founder Dean S. Warren Studio, 1991—; cons. Mt. Dora (Fla.) Ctr. for Arts Children's Edn. Ctr. Author: Runemaster, 1991; project artist Youth Art Symposium, U. Ctrl. Fla., 1993, Children's Art program, Atlantic Ctr. for arts, 1993, 95; one-man shows include Ormond Beach (Fla.) Meml. Art Gallery and Gardens, 1987, U. Ctrl. Fla. Art Gallery, Orlando, 1991, Harris House Atlantic Ctr. for Arts, New Smyrna Beach, Fla., 1993; exhibited in group shows at U. Miami (Fla.) Sculpture Invitational, 1982, Valencia C.C. Fine Arts Gallery, Orlando, 1989, Polk C.C. Fine Arts Gallery, Winter Haven, Fla., 1990, U. Ga., Athens, 1990, U. Tampa (Fla.) Scarfone Gallery, 1991, World Cup Soccer, Valencia C.C., 1994, Mt. Dora Ctr. of Arts, 1996, others. Recipient Artist in the Schs. grant Tex. Commn. on the Arts, 1980, awards U. Ga. Bot. Gardens, Athens, 1980, Valencia C.C., East Campus, Orlando, 1983, Arts on The Park, Lakeland, Fla., 1995. Home: 8069 Wellsmere Cir Orlando FL 32835-5361

WARREN, DONALD WILLIAM, physiology educator, dentistry educator; b. Bklyn., Mar. 22, 1935; s. Sol B. and Frances (Plotkin) W.; m. Priscilla Girardi, June 10, 1956; children: Donald W. Jr., Michael C. BS, U. N.C., 1956, DDS, 1959; MS, U. Pa., 1961, PhD, 1963; d Odontology honoris causa, U. Kuopio, Finland, 1991. Asst. prof. dentistry U. N.C., Chapel Hill, 1963-65, dir. Craniofacial Ctr., 1963—, assoc. prof., 1965-69, prof., 1969-80, chmn. dept. dental ecology, 1970-85, Kenan prof., 1980—, rsch. prof. otolaryngology, 1985—; cons. NIH, Bethesda, Md., 1967—, R. J. Reynolds-Nabisco, Winston-Salem, N.C., 1986—. Contbr. articles to profl. jours. Recipient Honor award Am. Cleft Palate Assn./Craniofacial Assn., 1992, O. Max Garner award U. N.C. Bd. Govs., 1993. Fellow AAAS, Internat. Coll. Dentists, Am. Speech and Hearing Lang. Assn., Internat. Assn. Dental Rsch., Acoustical Soc. Am., Am. Cleft Palate Assn. (pres. 1981-82, Disting. Svc. award 1984), Am. Cleft Palate Edn. Found. (pres. 1976-77). Avocations: horse related activities, running, farming. Home: PO Box 1356 Southern Pines NC 28388-1356 Office: U NC Sch Dentistry CB # 7450 Chapel Hill NC 27599

WARREN, EDUS HOUSTON, JR., investment management executive; b. Danville, Va., Dec. 9, 1923; s. Edus Houston and Edith (Farley) W.; children: Ann Warren Ketchledge, Ralph Lounsbury, Sarah Randolph, Edus Houston III; m. Harriet C. Higgins, May 5, 1990. A.B., Harvard U., 1946. With Spencer Trask & Co., Inc., N.Y.C., 1951-77; gen. partner Spencer Trask & Co., Inc., 1959-68, pres., chief exec. officer, dir., 1974-77; vice chmn. Hornblower, Weeks, Noyes & Trask, Inc., (merger Spencer Trask & Co., Inc./Hornblower, Weeks, Hemphill, Noyes), 1977-78; exec. v.p., mem. fin. com., mem. exec. com. Loeb Rhoades, Hornblower & Co.; vice chmn. Capital Guardian Research Co., N.Y.C., from 1978; sr. v.p. Capital Internat. Ltd., London, 1989—; sr. v.p., dir. Capital Guardian Trust Co.; sr. ptnr. Capital Group Cos.; treas., trustee Fin. Acctg. Found. Served to 1st lt. USAAF, 1943-45. Decorated D.F.C., Air medal. Mem. N.Y. Soc. Security Analysts, Fin. Analysts Fedn. (chmn.), Securities Industry Assn., Inst. Chartered Financial Analysts. Republican. Episcopalian. Home: Lynch Mountain Rd Sautee Nacoochee GA 30571

WARREN, EDWARD W., lawyer; b. Louisville, Ky., Apr. 2, 1944. BA, Yale U., 1966; JD, U. Chgo., 1969. Bar: Ill. 1969, D.C. 1970. Law clk. to Hon. Luther M. Swygert U.S. Ct. Appeals (7th cir.), 1969-70; ptnr. Kirkland & Ellis, Washington. Mem. ABA, D.C. Bar. Office: Kirkland & Ellis 655 15th St NW Ste 1200 Washington DC 20005-5701

WARREN, FRANK M., JR., construction company executive; b. 1932. Grad., Ga. Inst. Tech., 1958. With Raymond Internat. Builders, Charlotte, N.C., 1958-61, 64-83, Nat. Bulk Carriers, Inc., Charlotte, 1961-64; pres., dir. Jones Group, Inc., Charlotte, 1983-86; pvt. cons. Charlotte, 1986-88; pres., CEO Rogers Group, Inc., Nashville, 1988—. Office: Rogers Group Inc 421 Great Circle Rd Nashville TN 37228-1407*

WARREN, GERALD LEE, newspaper editor; b. Hastings, Nebr., Aug. 17, 1930; s. Hie Elias and Linnie (Williamson) W.; m. Euphemia Florence Brownell, Nov. 20, 1965 (div.); children: Gerald Benjamin, Euphemia Brownell; m. Viviane M. Pratt, Apr. 27, 1986. A.B., U. Nebr., 1952. Reporter Lincoln Star, Nebr., 1951-52; reporter, asst. city editor San Diego Union, 1956-61; bus. rep. Copley News Service, 1961-63; city editor San Diego Union, 1963-68, asst. mng. editor, 1968-69, editor, 1975-92; editor San Diego Union-Tribune, 1992-95; ret., editor at large, 1995—; dep. press sec. to Pres. Gerald Ford, 1974-75. Mem. bd. Pacific coun. internat. policy Eureka Found., Freedoms Found. Lt. (j.g.) USNR, 1952-56. Mem. Am. Soc. Newspaper Editors, Coun. Fgn. Rels., Sigma Delta Chi, Sigma Nu. Republican. Episcopalian. Office: Copley Press Inc 350 Camino De La Reina San Diego CA 92108-3003

WARREN, HARRY VERNEY, geological sciences educator, consulting geological engineer; b. Anacortes, Wash., Aug. 27, 1904; s. Victor Mackenzie and Rosamond Ellice Burrell (Campion) W.; m. Margaret Bessie Tisdall, July 14, 1934; children: Charlotte Louisa Verney, Victor Henry Verney. BA, U. B.C., Vancouver, Can., 1926, BASc, 1927, DSc (hon.), 1978; postgrad., Rhodes Sch. for B.C., 1926-29; MSc, Oxford U., Eng., 1928, DPhil, 1929; DSc (hon.), Waterloo U., Ont., Can., 1975. Registered profl. engr., B.C. Lectr. U. B.C., 1932-35, asst. prof. geol. scis., 1935-39, assoc. prof., 1939-45, prof., 1945-73, hon. prof., 1973—; Commonwealth Fund fellow Calif. Inst. Tech., 1929-32. Contbr. articles to profl. jours. Mem. coun. Vancouver Bd. Trade, 1939-81 (life); pres. B.C. and Yukon Chamber of Mines, Vancouver, 1952-54, UN Assn. Can. (Vancouver br.), 1956-58. Decorated officer Order of Can., 1971, Order of B.C., 1991; named Disting. lectr. Can. Inst. Mining and Metallurgy, 1971; Hon. fellow Royal Coll. Gen. Practitioners, Eng., 1973; recipient "Spud" Huestis disting. prospectors award B.C./Yukon Chamber of Mines, 1986, Disting. Citizen award City of Vancouver Centennial, 1986, Disting. Svc. award Prospector and Developer's Assn. Can., 1990, Can. 125th Commemorative medal, 1992; inductee B.C. Sports Hall of Fame, 1990, U. B.C. Sports Hall of Fame, 1993. Fellow Inst. Mining and Metallurgy (life), Royal Soc. Can. (life), Geol. Soc. Am. (life); mem. Can. Coun. (Killam award), Assn. Profl. Engrs. B.C. (life), Sigma Xi. Mem. Ch. of England. Avocations: field hockey, rugby, cricket. Home: 1816 Western Pkwy, Vancouver, BC Canada V6T 1V4

WARREN, IRWIN HOWARD, lawyer; b. N.Y.C., May 16, 1950; s. Milton and Shirley (Glatman) W.; m. Elizabeth Vogel, Aug. 11, 1974. BA, Columbia U., 1971, JD, 1974. Bar: N.Y., U.S. Ct. Appeals (1st, 2d, 3d, 4th, 6th, 8th cirs.), U.S. Dist. Ct. (so. and ea. dists.). Assoc. Weil, Gotshal &

Manges, N.Y.C., 1974-82, ptnr., 1982—. Contbr. articles to profl. jours. Mem. ABA (litigation sect., co-chair task force on ind. lawyer). Office: Weil Gotshal & Manges 767 5th Ave New York NY 10153

WARREN, J. BENEDICT, retired history educator; b. Waterflow, N.Mex., June 30, 1930; s. Benedict Alfred and Mary Ursula (Clark) W.; m. Patricia Susan Hyde, June 15, 1968. BA, Duns Scotus Coll., 1953; postgrad., Holy Family Sch. Theology, 1953-57, Cath. U. of Am., 1957-58; MA, U. N.Mex., 1960, PhD, 1963. Franciscan priest various chs., 1957-67; asst. prof. history U. Md., Coll. Park, 1968-70, assoc. prof. hist., 1970-77, prof. history, 1977-93; ret., 1993; cons. Library of Congress, Washington, 1967-77. Author: Vasco de Quiroga and His Pueblo-Hospitals of Santa Fe, 1963 (rev. Spanish edits. 1977, 90), Hans P. Kraus Collection of Hispanic American Manuscripts, a Guide, 1974, La conquista de Michoacán, 1521-1530, 1977 (rev. edit., 1989,rev. English version, 1985); editor: books including Diego Basalenque, Arte, 1994, Gonzalo Gómez primer poblador espanol de Guayangareo (Morelia), 1991, Diccionario grande de la lengua de Michoacan, 1991 (2 vol.), Maturino Gilberti, Arte, 1987, Vocabulario, 1989, Juan Baptista de Lagunas, 1983, Latin America: a Guide to the Historical Literature, 1971; editor: The Americas: A Quarterly Rev. of Inter-Am. Cultural History, 1963-66. John Carter Brown Library fellow, 1965, Fulbright fellow 1981-82. Mem. Conf. on Latin Am. History, Academia Mexicana de la Historia (corr.). Democrat. Avocation: gardening. Office: Lic J Ma Mendoza Pardo 99, Col Nueva Chapultepec, 58280 Morelia Michoacan, Mexico

WARREN, JACK HAMILTON, former diplomat and trade policy advisor; b. Apr. 10, 1921; m. Hilary J. Titterington; children: Hilary Warren Nicolson, Martin, Jennifer Warren Part, Ian. Student, Queens U., Kingston, Ont., Can., 1938-41. Joined Dept. External Affairs, 1945; assigned London, 1948-51; fin. counsellor Washington, 1954-57; asst. dep. minister trade and commerce, 1958-64, dep. minister industry, trade and commerce, 1964-71, high commr. to U.K., 1971-75, ambassador to U.S., 1975-77, Can. coordinator for multilateral trade negotiations, 1977-79; vice chmn. Bank of Montreal, Que., Can., 1979-86; prin. trade policy advisor Govt. Que., 1986-94. Served with Royal Canadian Navy, 1941-45; officer Order of Can., 1982. Home: PO Box 282 RR 1, Chelsea, PQ Canada J0X 1N0

WARREN, JAMES RONALD, retired museum director, author, columnist; b. Goldendale, Wash., May 25, 1925; stepson H.S. W.; m. Gwen Davis, June 25, 1949; children: Gail, Jeffrey. B.A., Wash. State U., 1949; M.A., U. Wash., 1953, Ph.D., 1963. Adminstrv. v.p. Seattle Community Coll., 1965-69; pres. Edmonds Community Coll., Lynnwood, Wash., 1969-79; dir. Mus. of History and Industry, Seattle, 1979-89; lectr. in field. Author history books; columnist Seattle Post Intelligencer, 1979-92, Seattle Times, 1992—. Served with U.S. Army, 1943-45, ETO, prisoner-of-war, Germany. Mem. VFW, Am. Ex-POW Assn., 42d (Rainbow) Div. Vets., others. Lodge: Rotary (Seattle). Home and Office: 3235 99th Ave NE Bellevue WA 98004-1803

WARREN, JERRY ALLEN, lawyer; b. Bartlesville, Okla., Jan. 9, 1943; s. Alvin Harold and Cora Christena (Campbell) W.; m. Jolinda Joy Caldwell, Jan. 3, 1947; children: Bradley Wayne, Megan Reneé. BA, U. Okla., 1965, JD, 1968. Bar: Okla. 1968. Atty., shareholder McAfee & Taft, A Profl. Corp., Okla. City, 1968—. Mem. ABA, Okla. Bar Assn., Okla. Ct. Bar Assn. Home: 6000 Kingsbridge Dr Oklahoma City OK 73162-3208 Office: McAfee & Taft 2 Leadership Sq 10th flr Oklahoma City OK 73102

WARREN, JOHN HERTZ, III, lawyer; b. Charleston, S.C., June 6, 1946; s. John Hertz Jr. and Louise (Hammett) W.; m. Helen Smith, Oct. 7, 1968; children: Louise Capers, Caroline Gregorie, John Alexander. BS in English, Coll. Charleston, 1967; JD, U. S.C., 1972. Bar: S.C. 1972, U.S. Dist. Ct. S.C. 1973, U.S. Ct. Appeals (4th cir.) 1973. Assoc. Brockinton & Brockinton, Charleston, 1972-73; assoc., then ptnr. Sinkler, Gibbs & Simons, Charleston, 1973-85; ptnr. Hutcheson & Warren, Charleston, 1986-92, Warren & Sinkler, Charleston, 1993—. Pres. Charleston Symphony Orch., 1984-85; trustee Hist. Charleston Found., 1987—, pres., 1994—; trustee Coll. of Charleston Found., 1987—, pres., 1995—; bd. dirs. Med. Soc. Health Sys., Inc., 1993—. Mem. ABA, S.C. Bar Assn., Charleston County Bar Assn., Ocean Cruising Club (London), Carolina Yacht Club. Episcopalian. Home: 6350 Oak Grove Plantation Rd Wadmalaw Island SC 29487 Office: 171 Church St Ste 340 Charleston SC 29401-3140

WARREN, JOHN WILLIAM, professional society administrator; b. Clarksville, Ark., June 27, 1927; s. Frederick H. and Fannie Emily (Casey) W.; m. Marguerette Christine Cohoon, Oct. 9, 1948 (dec. Dec. 1987); children: Catherine Gail, Carolyn Anne, Eve Colette; m. Anna Jane Taylor, Feb. 10, 1990. BA, Abilene Christian U., 1949; MA, U. Ark., 1951; PhD, U. Tenn., 1961. Instr. U. Tenn., Knoxville, 1954-61; assoc. prof. David Lipscomb Coll., Nashville, 1961-62; prof., chmn. English Tenn. Tech. U., Cookeville, 1962-88; assoc. exec. dir. Phi Kappa Phi, Baton Rouge, 1988-92, exec. dir., 1992—. Author Ofcl. Lit. Map of Tenn., 1976; author: Tennessee Belles-Lettres-Guide to Tennessee Literature, 1976. Mem. Rotary (Cookeville pres. 1972-73), Phi Kappa Phi (Tenn. Tech. U. chpt. pres. 1980, SE region v.p. 1982-88, nat. bd. dirs. 1982-88). Republican. Mem. Ch. of Christ. Avocations: gardening, travel. Office: Honor Soc Phi Kappa Phi PO Box 16000 LSU Baton Rouge LA 70893

WARREN, KEITH ASHLEY, lawyer; b. Cambridge, Md., Dec. 26, 1943; s. William Lester and Exa Martha (Ashley) W.; m. Ingrid T. Peterson, July 20, 1968; children: Lisa, Mark, Blake. BA, U. Ky., 1965, JD, 1968. Bar: Ky. 1968, U.S. Ct. Mil. Appeals 1969, U.S. Supreme Ct. 1972, Tenn. 1977. Trial atty. Nat. Labor Rels. Bd., Memphis, 1973-76; assoc. McKnight, Hudson, Lewis, Memphis, 1976-80, ptnr., 1980—; spl. labor rels. coun. Govt. of Shelby County, Memphis, 1979-81; bd. advisors Hospitality Human Resources, Lincoln, Nebr., 1992—. Pres. Fisherville (Tenn.) Civic Club, 1992—. Capt. USAF, 1968-73. Mem. Ky. Bar Assn. (labor law sect. 1968—), Tenn. Bar Assn. (labor law sect. 1977—), Memphis Bar Assn. (employment law sect. 1977—), Nat. Law Network (labor litigation sect. 1994—). Republican. Methodist. Avocation: snow skiing. Home: 11590 Macon Rd Eads TN 38028 Office: McKnight Hudson Lewis 6750 Poplar Ave Ste 301 Memphis TN 38138

WARREN, KENNETH S., medical educator, physician; b. N.Y.C., June 11, 1929; m. Sylvia Marjorie Rothwell, Feb. 14, 1959; children: Christopher Harwood, Erica Marjorie. AB, Harvard U., 1951, MD, 1955; DSc (hon.), Mahidol U., Thailand, 1990. Intern, Harvard service Boston City Hosp., 1955-56; research assoc. Lab. Tropical Diseases, NIH, Bethesda, Md., 1956-62; asst. prof. medicine Case Western Res. U., 1963-68, assoc. prof., 1968-75, prof., 1975-77, prof. library sci., 1974-77; dir. health scis. Rockefeller Found., N.Y.C., 1977-87, assoc. v.p., 1988-89; adj. prof. Rockefeller U., 1977-89; prof. medicine NYU, 1977—; dir. sci. Maxwell Communication Corp., Maxwell Found., N.Y.C., 1989-92; Heath Clark lectr. London Sch. Hygiene and Tropical Medicine, 1988; adj. prof. medicine Tufts U., 1990—; cons. ed. Charles Scribner's Sons, 1992-93; CEO Comprehensive Med. Sys., Inc., 1992-94; v.p. acad. affairs Picower Inst. Med. Rsch., 1993—; chmn. Harvard Internat. Med. Libr., Inc. 1994—; mem. Inst. Medicine, Nat. Acad. Scis.; bd. dirs. Immunotherapy, Inc.; cons. WHO. Author: Schistosomiasis: The Evolution of a Medical Literature, Selected Abstracts and Citations, 1852-1972, 1973, Geographic Medicine for the Practitioner, 2d edit., 1985, Scientific Information Systems and the Principle of Selectivity, 1980, Coping with the Biomedical Literature, 1981, Tropical and Geographical Medicine, 2d edit., 1990, Immunology and Molecular Biology of Parasitic Infections, 1993, Doing More Good Than Harm, 1993; founding editor: Jour. Molecular Medicine; contbr. numerous articles to profl. jours. Recipient Career Devel. award NIH, 1966-71, Mary Kingsley medal Liverpool Sch. Tropical Med., 1987, Frohlich award N.Y. Acad. Sci., 1988, Van Thiel medal Dutch Soc. Parasitology, 1989. Fellow ACP, Royal Coll. Physicians, N.Y. Acad. Scis. (bd. govs. 1991-93); mem. Am. Soc. Clin. Investigation, Assn. Am. Physicians, Am. Assn. Immunologists, Am. Assn. Study Liver Diseases, Am. Soc. Tropical Medicine and Hygiene (Bailey K. Ashford award 1974), Infectious Diseases Soc. Am. (Squibb award 1975), Royal Soc. Tropical Medicine and Hygiene, Internat. Fedn. Sci. Editors (exec. bd.), N.Y. Acad. Scis. (bd. govs. 1991-93), Royal Soc. Medicine Found. (bd. dirs. 1992—, treas. 1994—), Internat. Molecular Medicine Soc. (founding sec., treas.). Patentee diagnostic methods, drugs. Office: Picower Inst Med Rsch 350 Community Dr Manhasset NY 11030-3849 *During my career in tropical medicine I have been fortunate to fulfill my three goals: to travel, to revel in the challenge of medical research and to contribute to the health of our fellows in the developing world.*

WARREN, LESLEY ANN, actress; b. N.Y.C., Aug. 16, 1948. Studied ballet, N.Y.C.; studied acting, The Actors Studio, N.Y.C. TV appearances include Rodgers and Hammerstein's Cinderella, 1964, Fight for Jenny, 1986, 27 Wagons Full of Cotton, 1990, A Seduction in Travis County, 1991, In Sickness and in Health, 1991; Broadway debut in 110 in the Shade, 1963, Drat the Cat, 1964, Metamorphosis, Three Penny Opera; films include The Happiest Millionaire, 1967, Harry and Walter Go to New York, 1976, Victor/Victoria, 1982, Songwriter, Choose Me, Clue, Apology, 1986, Burglar, 1987, Cop, 1988, Baja Oklahoma, 1988, Worth Winning, 1989, Life Stinks, 1991, Pure Country, 1992, The Color of Night, 1994; TV mini-series include 79 Park Ave., 1977, Beulah Land, 1980, Pearl, Evergreen, 1985, Family of Spies, 1990; TV films include Seven in Darkness, 1969, Love Hate Love, 1971, Assignment Munich, 1972, The Daughters of Joshua Cabe, 1972, The Letters, 1973, The Legend of Valentino, 1975, Betrayal, 1978, Portrait of a Stripper, 1979, Beulah Land, 1980, Portrait of a Showgirl, 1982, A Flight for Jenny, 1986, Baja Oklahoma, 1988, Family of Spies, 1990, A Seduction in Travis County, 1991, In Sickness and Health, 1992, Willing to Kill: The Texas Cheerleader Story, 1992, Joseph, 1995, Murderous Intent, 1995; films include Bird of Prey, 1995. Office: care ICM 8942 Wilshire Blvd Beverly Hills CA 90211

WARREN, MARK EDWARD, shipping company executive, lawyer; b. Rochester, Minn., Nov. 26, 1951; s. Edward Joseph and Eunice (Golberg) W.; m. Jasmine Margaret Syracuse, Feb. 18, 1984; children: Natalie, Stephanie. Cert., Instituto de Estudios Europeos, Madrid, 1972; BA, Gustavus Adolphus Coll., St. Peter, Minn., 1974; JD, U. Minn., 1977. Bar: Calif. 1977, U.S. Dist. Ct. (no. and cen. dists.) Calif. 1978, U.S. Ct. Appeals (9th cir.) 1985, U.S. Dist. Ct. (ea. dist.) Calif. 1986, U.S. Dist. Ct. (so. dist.) Calif. 1987, D.C. 1989, U.S. Supreme Ct. 1989, U.S. Ct. Appeals (D.C. cir.) 1989, U.S. Dist. Ct. (D.C. dist.) 1989, U.S. Dist. Ct. Md. 1991, Va. 1992. Assoc. Gibson, Dunn & Crutcher, L.A., 1977-78; spl. asst. to V.P. Walter Mondale Washington, 1979-80; assoc. Gibson, Dunn & Crutcher, L.A., 1980-84; ptnr. Gibson, Dunn & Crutcher, L.A. and Washington, 1985-93; sr. v.p., gen. counsel Princess Cruises, L.A., 1993-96. Mem. U. Minn. Law Alumni Assn. (bd. dirs.). Home: 11802 Carson Rd Mason Neck VA 22079

WARREN, PATRICIA J., arts association executive; b. Seattle, Dec. 12, 1950; d. Vernon Sidney and Ernestine Abernathy (Bilan) W. BA, U. Wash., 1972, BS, 1975, JD, 1978, MA, 1990. Atty. City Kirkland, Wash., 1978-80, City Bellevue, Wash., 1980-86; mus. dir. Jefferson County Hist. Soc., Port Townsend, Wash., 1990-94. Precinct chair 46th Dist., Seattle, 1985-88; mem. Jefferson County AIDS Task Force, Port Townsend, 1991-94; mem. Greater Seattle Bus. Assn., 1994—. U. Wash. fellow, 1988-89. Mem. Wash. State Bar Assn., Wash. Mus. Assn. (trustee 1991-93, v.p. 1993-95, pres. 1995—). Democrat. Office: Pratt Fine Arts Ctr 1902 S Main Seattle WA 98144

WARREN, RICHARD JORDAN, newspaper publisher; b. Bangor, Maine, May 28, 1945; s. Richard Kearney Warren and Joanne (Jordan) Van Namee; m. Barbara Burrowes Hall, Mar. 9, 1968 (div.); m. Elizabeth Carter, June 21, 1978; children: Courtney, George, Anne. BA, Trinity Coll., Hartford, Conn., 1968; postgrad. smaller cos. mgmt. program Harvard Bus. Sch., 1977-80. Reporter, The Courant, Hartford, Conn., 1968-71; asst. pub. The Bangor Daily News 1971-84, v.p., 1974—, editor, 1980—, pub., 1984—; pres. Northeast Pub. Co., Presque Isle, Maine; dir. Bangor Pub. Co., Northeast Pub. Co., Rockland Courier-Gazette, Inc., Alta Group Newspapers, Inc., Eastern Maine Med. Ctr., Affiliated Health Care, New Eng. Newspaper Assn., Action Com. Fifty, Quebec-Labrador Found., Maine Coast Heritage Trust, Nature Conservancy Maine chpt., Am. Mus. Fly Fishing, Atlantic Salmon Found., Bangor Symphony Orch.; mem. Am. Soc. Newspaper Editors, Maine Daily Newspaper Assn., Bangor Mechanic Assn., Land for Maine's Future Bd., Kent Moot Ct., Columbia U. Law Sch., N.Y.C.; adv. bd., past trustee Unity Coll. Served to 1st lt., Air N.G.. Mem. Alexander Graham Bell Assn. Deaf Centennial Bd. (steering com.), Nat. Press Club, Univ. Club, Anglers Club, Penobscot Salmon Club. Office: Bangor Daily News 491 Main St Bangor ME 04401-6296

WARREN, RICHARD KEARNEY, newspaper publisher; b. N.Y.C., Apr. 13, 1920; s. George Earle and Anna (Kearney) W.; m. Joanne Jordan, Sept. 18, 1943 (div. Oct. 1969); children: Richard J., Carolyn; m. Susan Atwood Thibodeau, Oct. 1, 1970. B.S., Yale U., 1942; Litt.D., Ricker Coll., 1971. Shift supt. W.Va ordnance works Gen. Chem. Co., Point Pleasant, 1942-43; dir. Bangor Pub. Co., Maine, chmn. exec. com.; pres. Rockland Courier-Gazette, Inc., also dir.; bd. dirs. N.E. Pub. Co. Bd. dirs. William A. Farnsworth Libr. and Art Mus.; past trustee Ricker Coll.; past bd. dirs. Bangor YMCA. Lt. (j.g.) USNR, 1943-46. Mem. Maine Daily Newspaper Assn. (pres. 1953-54, 73-74), N.E. Daily Newspaper Assn. (pres. 1959-60), Am. Newspaper Pubs. Assn., New Eng. Soc. N.Y., N.E. Harbor Fleet Club (Maine), Penobscot Valley Country Club, Yale Club (N.Y.C.), N.E. Harbor Tennis Club, Rotary. Home: 28 W Broadway Bangor ME 04401-4541 Office: 96 Harlow St Ste F Bangor ME 04401-4920 also: 3 Huntington Pl Northeast Harbor ME 04662-0663

WARREN, RICHARD M., experimental psychologist, educator; b. N.Y.C., Apr. 8, 1925; s. Morris and Rae (Greenberg) W.; m. Roslyn Pauker, Mar. 31, 1950. BS in Chemistry, CCNY, 1946; PhD in Organic Chemistry, N.Y. U., 1951. Flavor chemist Gen. Foods Co., Hoboken, N.J., 1951-53; rsch. assoc. psychology Brown U., Providence, 1954-56; Carnegie sr. rsch. fellow Coll. Medicine NYU, 1956-57; Carnegie sr. rsch. fellow Cambridge (Eng.) U., 1957-58, rsch. psychologist applied psychology Rsch. Unit, 1958-59; rsch. psychologist NIMH, Bethesda, Md., 1959-61; chmn. psychology Shimer Coll., Mt. Carroll, Ill., 1961-64; assoc. prof. psychology U. Wis., Milw., 1964-66, prof., 1966-73, rsch. prof., 1973-75, disting. prof., 1975-95, adj. disting. prof., 1995—; vis. scientist Inst. Exptl. Psychology, Oxford (Eng.) U., 1969-70, 77-78. Author: (with Roslyn Warren) Helmholtz on Perception: Its Physiology and Development, 1968, Auditory Perception: A New Synthesis, 1982; contbr. articles on sensation and perception to profl. jours. Fellow APA, Am. Psychol. Soc.; mem. AAAS, Acoustical Soc. Am., Am. Chem. Soc., Am. Speech and Hearing Assn., Sigma Xi. Office: U Wis Dept Psychology Milwaukee WI 53201

WARREN, ROBERT WILLIS, federal judge; b. Raton, N.M., Aug. 30, 1925; s. George R. and Clara (Jolliffe) W.; m. Laverne D. Voagen, Aug. 23, 1947; children: Cheryl Lynn, Iver Eric, Gregg Alan, Treiva Mae, Lyle David, Tara Rae. BA magna cum laude, Macalester Coll., 1950; MA, U. Minn., 1951; JD, U. Wis., 1956; postgrad., Fgn. Service Inst., 1951-52. Bar: Wis. 1956. Fgn. affairs officer U.S. Dept. State, 1951-53; mem. firm Godfrey, Godfrey & Warren, Elkhorn, 1956-57; ptnr. firm Warren & Boltz, Attys., Green Bay, 1957-59, Smith, Will & Warren, 1965-69; asst. dist. atty. Brown County, Wis., 1959-61; dist. atty., 1961-65; mem. Wis. Senate, 1965-69; atty. gen. Wis., 1969-74; U.S. dist. judge Milw., 1974—; Mem. Gt. Lakes Commn., Wis. Council on Criminal Justice, Wis. Bd. Commrs. Pub. Lands, Four Lakes council Boy Scouts Am., Wis. Controlled Substances Bd., Wis. Council on Drug Abuse, Wis. State Urban Affairs. Served with AUS, 1943-46, ETO. Decorated Purple Heart. Mem. ABA, Wis. Bar Assn., Nat. Assn. Attys. Gen. (pres. 1973-74), Midwestern Conf. Attys. Gen., Wis. Dist. Attys. Assn., VFW, DAV. Republican. Methodist. Club: Optimist. Office: US Dist Ct 364 US Courthouse 517 E Wisconsin Ave Milwaukee WI 53202*

WARREN, ROSANNA, poet; b. Fairfield, Conn., July 27, 1953; d. Robert Penn Warren and Eleanor Clark; m. Stephen Scully, 1981; children: Katherine, Chiara; stepson, Benjamin. BA summa cum laude, Yale U., 1976; MA, Johns Hopkins U., 1980. Private art tchr., 1977-78; clerical worker St. Martin's Pr., N.Y.C., 1977-78; asst. prof. English Vanderbilt U., Nashville, 1981-82; vis. asst. prof. Boston U., 1982-88, asst. prof. English and modern fgn. langs., 1989-95, assoc. prof. English, 1995—; poetry cons., contbg. editor Partisan Rev., 1985—; poet-in-residence Robert Frost Farm, 1990. Author: The Joey Story, 1963, Snow Day, 1981, Each Leaf Shines Separate, 1984, Stained Glass, 1993; editor, contbr.: The Art of Translation: Voices from the Field, 1989; editor: Eugenio Montale's Cuttlefish Bones, 1993; translator (with Stephen Scully) Euripides' Suppliant Women, 1995; contbr. to periodicals including Agni Rev., Am. Poetry Rev., Antioch Rev., Atlantic Monthly, Chelsea, Chgo. Rev., Georgia Rev., Nation, New Yorker, N.Y. Times, Partisan Rev., Ploughshares, Southern Rev., Washington Post. Recipient McLaughlin English prize Yale U., 1973, Charles E. Clark award Yale U., 1976, Nat. Discovery award in poetry 92nd St. YMHA-YWCA, 1980, Newton Arts Coun. award, 1983, Lavan Younger Poets prize Acad. Am. Poets, 1992, Lamont Poetry prize Acad. Am. Poets, 1993, Lila Wallace Writers' Fund award, 1994, Witter Bynner prize in poetry Acad. Arts and Letters, 1994, May Sarton award New End and Poetry Club, 1995; named Scholar of House Yale U., 1975-76; Yaddo fellow, 1980; Ingram Merrill grantee, 1983, 93; Guggenheim fellow, 1985-86; Am. Coun. Learned Societies grantee, 1989-90. Mem. MLA. Home: 11 Robinwood Ave Needham MA 02192 Office: Univ Professors Program Boston Univ 745 Commonwealth Ave Boston MA 02215

WARREN, RUSSELL GLEN, academic administrator; b. Balt., Apr. 29, 1942; s. Clarence N. and Kathryn (Butler) W. BBA, U. Richmond, 1964; PhD, Tulane U., 1968. Asst. prof., then assoc. prof. U. Richmond (Va.), 1971-74, dean of Richmond Coll., 1974-76, asst. to univ. v.p., then. asst. to univ. pres., 1976-78; v.p. for acad. affairs U. Montevallo, Ala., Ala., 1978-84; v.p. for acad. affairs James Madison U., Harrisonburg, Va., 1984-90, acting pres., 1986-87; pres. N.E. Mo. State U., Kirksville, 1990-95; Disting. prof. econs. and mgmt. Hardin-Simmons U., Abilene, Tex., 1995—, dir. Ctr. for Rsch. on Teaching and Learning, 1995—. Author: Antitrust in Theory and Practice, 1976, Carpe Diem, 1995. Bd. Dirs. Va. Rural Devel. Corp., Richmond, 1988-90. Capt. U.S. Army, 1969-71. Named One of Outstanding Young Men of Va., Va. Jaycees, 1976. Mem. Am. Assn. Colls. and Univs. (bd. dirs. 1994-95). Methodist. Avocations: golf, collecting cars. Home: 71 Tamarisk Cir Abilene TX 79606 Office: Hardin-Simmons U Sch Bus Box 16220 Abilene TX 79698

WARREN, RUSSELL JAMES, investment banking executive, consultant; b. Cleve., July 28, 1938; s. Harold Fulton and Agnes Elmina (Hawkswell) W.; BS, Case Western Res. U., 1960; MBA, Harvard U., 1962. CPA, Ohio; m. Doris Helen Kenyeres, June 6, 1964. With Ernst & Whinney, Cleve., 1962-87, ptnr. in charge merger and acquisition svcs., 1976-87; pres. The TransAction Group, 1987—. Co-author: Implementing Mergers and Acquisitions in the Fin. Svcs. Industry, 1985; assoc. editor Jour. Corp. Growth, 1986-87, mem. editorial bd., 1988; contbg. editor Jour. Buyouts and Acquisitions, 1984-86; contbg. author venture capital financing study conducted in five selected countries for Asian Devel. Bank, Malaysia, Indonesia, Pakistan, Sri Lanka, Thailand, 1986. Trustee Case Western Res. U., 1980—, chmn. audit com., 1991—, Cleve. Bot. Garden, 1995—, Fairmount Presbyn. Ch., 1987-93, elder, 1991-93, Cmty. Improvement Corp. Summit, Medina and Portage Counties, 1992—, Cascade CDC, 1992—; dir. Univ. Tech., Inc., 1986-88; adv. bd. Shaker Investments, 1992—; v.p. M & A Internat., Inc., 1990-91, pres., 1992; bd. zoning appeals City of Lyndhurst, 1978—, chmn., 1980-82, 91-93; mem. vis. com. Weatherhead Sch. Mgmt. Mem. AICPA, Brit.-Am. C. of C., Ohio Soc. CPAs, Assn. for Corp. Growth (bd. dirs internat. orgn. 1988, 91—, pres. 1994), Cleve. Com. on Fgn. Rels., Cleve. World Trade Assn. Clubs: Union, Mayfield Country, Catawba Island (Port Clinton, Ohio), Put-in-Bay (Ohio) Yacht. Lodge: Jesters. Office: The TransAction Group 1666 Hanna Bldg Cleveland OH 44115

WARREN, WILLIAM BRADFORD, lawyer; b. Boston, July 25, 1934; s. Minton Machado and Sarah Ripley (Robbins) W.; children: John Coolidge, Sarah Robbins; m. Arete B. Swartz, Sept. 20, 1985. AB magna cum laude, Harvard U., 1956, LLB cum laude, 1959. Bar: N.Y. 1960. Assoc. Dewey Ballantine, N.Y.C., 1959-68; ptnr. Dewey Ballantine, 1968—; lectr. Inst. Fed. Taxation, N.Y. U., So. Fed. Tax Inst., Practicing Law Inst. Pres. Cintas Found., N.Y.C.; bd. dirs. John Carter Brown Libr., Providence, R.I. Mem. Am. Law Inst., Am. Coll. Trust and Estate Counsel (former regent), Acad. Am. Poets (bd. dirs.), Internat. Acad. Estate and Trust Law (former exec. coun.), N.Y. State Bar Assn. (chmn. com. taxation of trust and estates sect. 1980-83), Assn. Bar City N.Y., Soc. Mayflower Descs., Harvard Club, Knickerbocker Club, Century Club, Grolier Club (pres.). Home: 520 E 86th St New York NY 10028-7534 Office: Dewey Ballantine 1301 Avenue Of The Americas New York NY 10019-6022

WARREN, WILLIAM CLEMENTS, law educator; b. Paris, Tex., Feb. 3, 1909; s. Archibald Levy and Elma (Clements) W.; m. Diana June Peel Willock, Jan. 13, 1945; children: Robert Peel, Larissa Eve, William Liversidge. AB, U. Tex., 1930, AM, 1931; LLB, Harvard U., 1935; LLD (hon.), L.I. U., 1955, Columbia U., 1981; D in Polit. Sci., U. Basle, 1965. Bar: Ohio 1937, N.Y. 1952, D.C. 1959. Assoc. Davis, Polk & Wardwell, N.Y.C., 1935-37, Holiday, Grossman & McAfee, Cleve., 1937-42, Milbank, Tweed, Hadley & McCloy, N.Y.C., 1942-47; prof. law Western Res. U., Cleve., 1937-42; mem. faculty Columbia Law Sch., N.Y.C., 1946-82, Kent prof. law, 1959-77, Kent prof. emeritus, 1977—, dean, 1952-70, dean emeritus, 1970—; ptnr., of counsel Roberts & Holland, N.Y.C., 1952; bd. dirs. Guardian Life Ins. Co. Am., Sterling Nat. Bank & Trust Co. N.Y.C., Barnwell Industries, Inc., Sterling Bancorp, CSS Industries, Aston-Martin LaGonda Group, Aladan Corp.; hon. chmn. bd. dirs. Sandoz U.S.; mem. N.Am. adv. bd. Swissair. Served as lt. col. U.S. Army, 1943-46. Decorated Bronze Star (2), Legion of Merit; comdr. Order of the Crown (Italy); recipient Medal for excellence Columbia Law Sch. Alumni Assn., 1969. Mem. ABA, Am. Judicature Soc., Am. Law Inst., Assn. of Bar of City of N.Y., N.Y. County Lawyers Assn., N.Y. State Bar Assn., Inst. Internat. Edn. (trustee), Order Moral Scis. (fgn. corr.), Accademia delle Scienze dell' Instituto di Bologna (fgn. corr. mem.; Order Moral Scis. 1971). Presbyterian. Clubs: Broad Street, Century Assn., Cosmos, Links, Metropolitan, Univ. Co-author: U.S. Income Taxation of Foreign Corporations and Nonresident Aliens, 1966; Cases and Materials on Accounting and the Law, 1978; Cases and Materials on Federal Wealth Transfer Taxation, 1982; Cases and Materials on Federal Income Taxation, Vol. I, 1972, supplement, 1983, Vol. II, 1980; pres., dir. Columbia Law Rev. Office: Roberts & Holland 825 8th Ave New York NY 10019-7416

WARREN, WILLIAM GERALD, lawyer; b. Detroit, Apr. 22, 1930; s. William Grant and Margaret Kathryn (Matthews) W.; m. Martha Elsie Artz, Apr. 20, 1974; children: Mary Katharine, Elizabeth Bogo. A.B. with honors, U. Mich., 1952, LL.B. (Frederick L. Leckie scholar), 1955. Bar: Mich. 1956. Assoc. firm Dickinson, Wright, Moon, Van Dusen & Freeman, Detroit, 1955-63, ptnr., 1964—; bd. dirs. Mackinac Fin. Corp., Mackinac Corp., V.G. Nahrgang Co.; gen. counsel, sec. bd. Detroit Savs. Bank. Contbr. articles to profl. jours. Mem., chmn. Wayne County (Mich.) Grievance Com., 1966—; spl. counsel 4-H Found. Mich., 1966-68. Recipient Henry M. Campbell award, 1954, Roberts P. Hudson award State Bar Mich., 1978. Fellow Am. Coll. Trial Lawyers, Internat. Soc. Barristers, Am. Bar Found., Mich Bar Found.; mem. Phi Beta Kappa, Phi Kappa Phi, Pi Sigma Alpha, Phi Alpha Delta. Republican. Roman Catholic. Clubs: Detroit, University, Otsego Ski, Grosse Pointe, Witenagemote. Office: Dickinson Wright Moon Van Dusen & Freeman One Detroit Ctr Ste 4000 Detroit MI 48226

WARREN, WILLIAM HERBERT, business administration educator; b. Newport News, Va., July 21, 1924; s. William Herbert and Helen Virginia (Cofer) W.; m. Mary Virginia Shaw, Sept. 11, 1948; children: Katherine Warren Butt, Constance Warren Desaulniers, Suzanne Warren Huhn, David, John. BSBA, U. Richmond, 1948; MS, Purdue U., 1950, PhD, 1969. Dir. indsl. rels., plant mgr. Albemarle Paper Co. div. Ethyl Corp., 1954-66; dir. labor relations, cons. Newport News Shipbldg. div. Tenneco, 1970-73; asst. prof. U. Richmond, Va., 1950-53; assoc. prof. Purdue U., 1966-70; mem. faculty Coll. William and Mary, Williamsburg, Va., 1972—, D. Hillsdon Ryan prof. bus. adminstrn., 1979-92; prof. emeritus Williamsburg, Va., 1992—; cons. to industry and govt.; labor arbitrator. Served with USN, 1943-46. Mem. APA, Acad. Mgmt., Kiwanis, Omicron Delta Kappa. Republican. Baptist. Home: 110 Bowstring Dr Williamsburg VA 23185-4952 Office: Sch Business Coll William and Mary Williamsburg VA 23185

WARREN, WILLIAM KERMIT, newspaper managing editor; b. Harlem, Ga., May 27, 1941; s. William Kermit and Willie Garnell (Thaxton) W.; m. Nancy Carolyn Andrews, Sept. 5, 1964; children—Wendy Karen, William Kermit. B.A. in Journalism, U. Ga., 1964. Reporter Augusta Ga. Chronicle, Ga., 1964-65; reporter Chattanooga Times, Tenn., 1965-66, reporter, city editor, 1971-80; mng. editor Roanoke (Va.) Times & World News, 1980—. Served to capt. USAF, 1966-70. Recipient Best Feature Story award Ga, AP, 1964. Mem. AP Mng. Editors Assn., Sigma Delta Chi.

Episcopalian. Avocation: reading. Home: 3355 Dawn Cir Roanoke VA 24018-3837 Office: Times World Corp PO Box 2491 201-209 W Campbell Ave Roanoke VA 24010

WARREN, WILLIAM ROBINSON, real estate broker; b. St. Louis, Nov. 14, 1931; s. Edgar Lovett and Katharine (Cope) W.; m. Margaret Dorothea Ogilvy, June 13, 1953; children: Anne W. Bretting, Christina Margaret, Erica W. Long. B.S. in Math. and Physics, Bethany Coll., 1953; M.B.A., U. So. Calif., 1963; student, UCLA, 1951-56, Am. U., summer 1952. Vice pres. System Devel. Corp., Santa Monica, Calif., 1958-69; v.p. King Resources Co., Los Angeles, 1969-71; pres. Consol. Mgmt. Systems, Los Angeles, 1971-72; sr. v.p. and region dir. Western Bancrop. and United Calif. Bank, Los Angeles, 1972-75; v.p. Fluor Corp., Irvine, Calif., 1975-84; pres. Consol. Realty, Newport Beach, Calif., 1984-93, Bishop Hawk, Newport Beach, 1993-95, Consol. Realty, Newport Beach, Calif., 1995—; instr. U. Calif. Irvine Grad. Sch. Mgmt., 1985-87. Mem. Orange County Blue Ribbon Com., Santa Ana, 1980-81; trustee, exec. com. South Coast Repertory, Costa Mesa, Calif. Mem. Soc. Info. Mgmt., Am. Mgmt. Assn., Mgmt. Info. Continuing Seminar (chmn. 1980-81, exec. com. 1978-82), Realty Investment Assn. Calif. (dir. 1994—), Beta Theta Pi. Republican. Presbyterian. Clubs: Big Canyon Country (Newport Beach). Home: 26 Pinehurst Ln Newport Beach CA 92660-5229 Office: 26 Pinehurst Ln Newport Beach CA 92660

WARRICK, JAMES CRAIG, banker; b. Bangor, Pa., Oct. 9, 1938; s. Walter John and Florence Elizabeth (Lentz) W.; m. Diane Marie Higham, May 29, 1965; children—Scott, John. BS, Rider U., 1961; MBA, Seton Hall U., 1968. CPA, N.J. With KPMG Peat Marwick, N.J., 1965-71; audit mgr. KPMG Peat Marwick, 1971-74; v.p., regional controller Crestar Fin. Corp., Richmond, 1974-77; sr. v.p., corp. controller Crestar Fin. Corp., 1977-85, group exec. v.p., 1985—. Mem. long range planning com. United Way Svcs., Richmond, Va., 1984-85, fin. com., 1984—, allocations com., 1975-84; councilman East Windsor Twp., N.J., 1969; bd. dirs. One Ocean Place Homeowners, Fin. Inst. Res. Risk Retention Group; fund raising chmn., class agt. Rider U. Lt. (j.g.) USN, 1961-64, capt. USNR. Fellow AICPA, Va. Soc. CPAs; mem. Fin. Execs. Inst. (pres. Va. chpt. 1985-86), Bryce Resort (dir. 1981-82, planning, fin. com. 1989—). Republican. Episcopalian. Avocations: skiing; swimming; golf; tennis. Home: 2120 Castlebridge Rd Midlothian VA 23113 Office: Crestar Fin Corp PO Box 26665 919 E Main St Richmond VA 23261-6665

WARRINGTON, CLAYTON LINWOOD, JR., advertising agency executive; b. Balt., Sept. 12, 1936; s. Clayton Linwood and Alice Theresa (Piccini) W.; m. Jacqueline Hoke Kiefer, Mar. 28, 1960 (div. 1974); children—Clayton Linwood, John Niles; m. Elizabeth Barbara Waizenegger, Sept. 28, 1974. B.S., U. Md., 1958; Postgrad. Am. U., 1962-63. Registered pharmacist. Mgr. market data systems Pfizer Labs., N.Y.C., 1966-68; v.p., account group supr. Dean L. Burdick Assocs. Inc., N.Y.C., 1968-72; sr. v.p., mgmt. supr. Sudler & Hennessey Inc., N.Y.C., 1972-74; pres., CEO Dugan/Farley Comm. (a divsn. Bozell, Jacobs, Kenyon & Eckhardt Inc.), Upper Saddle River, N.J., 1974—. Served to lt. USN, 1959-64. Mem. U. Md. Alumni Internat. Republican. Methodist. Club: Ridgewood Country. Home: 16 Highwood Ter Glen Rock NJ 07452-1512 Office: Dugan/Farley Comm 600 E Crescent Ave Saddle River NJ 07458-1846

WARRINGTON, JOHN WESLEY, lawyer; b. Cin., June 6, 1914; s. George Howard and Eliza (Holmes) W.; m. Suzanne Mooney, May 5, 1951; children: Anne McGrath Warrington Wilson, George Howard, John Wesley, Mary Warrington Cassidy, Elizabeth Warrington Ott, Sarah Warrington Selnick, Rachel Warrington Moss. A.B., Yale U., 1936; postgrad., Cambridge (Eng.) U., 1937; LL.B., Harvard U., 1940; D.F.A. (hon.), U. Cin., 1980. Bar: Ohio 1940. Since practiced in Cin.; sr. ptnr. Graydon, Head & Ritchey, 1951-89; dir. emeritus Fifth Third Bank. Chmn. emeritus planning commn., Indian Hill, Ohio, 1959-86; pres. emeritus Cin. Music Hall; chmn. Cin. Mus. Assn.; trustee emeritus Cin. Union Bethel, Am. Schs. Oriental Research, Seven Hills Schs., Cin. Natural History Mus., Cin. Inst. Fine Arts; sec. bd. trustees Episc. Diocese So. Ohio. Served to capt. Am. Field Service, 1942-45. Mentioned in dispatches Brit.). Mem. Am., Ohio, Cin. Bar Assns., Phi Beta Kappa. Republican. Episcopalian. Home: 8625 Camargo Club Dr Cincinnati OH 45243-3340 Office: PO Box 6464 Cincinnati OH 45201-6464

WARRINGTON, WILLARD GLADE, former university official; b. Macomb, Ill., Oct. 24, 1920; s. Henry K. and Farie V. (Prather) W.; m. A. Irene Windser, Aug. 9, 1945 (dec. 1969); m. Janette Moffatt Cooper, Apr. 26, 1972; children: David, Steven, Douglas, Jane Ann, Stephen Cooper. B.Ed., Western Ill. State Tchrs. Coll., 1941; M.S., U. Ill., 1949, U. Ill., 1950; Ed.D., U. Ill., 1952. Tchr. public high schs. Ill., 1941-42, 45-48; mem. faculty Mich. State U., 1952-58, dir. office evaluation services, 1958-74, asso. dean Univ. Coll., 1974-78, acting dean Univ. Coll., 1978-80, dir. undergrad. univ. div., 1980-85, dir., prof. emeritus, 1986—; cons. edn.; Ford Found. cons. U. Philippines. Contbr. articles on ednl. measurement to profl. publs.; editorial bd.: Ednl. and Psychol. Measurement, 1968-85. Active Boy Scouts Am., 1957-68. Served to lt. col. USAAF, 1942-45. Mem. Nat. Council on Measurement in Edn. (pres. 1973-74), Am. Ednl. Research Assn., Assn. for Gen. and Liberal Studies (sec.-treas. 1973-79). Methodist. Home: 9 Ashleigh Ct Lansing MI 48906

WARRIS, ANNA CUMMINGS, religious organization executive; b. Phila., Aug. 8, 1912; d. James Emlen and Anna May (Mock) Cummings; widow; 1 child, Joseph Emlen. Student, Wheaton Coll., 1931-32, Albany Bible Inst., 1933-34, Pa. State U., 1934-35, U. Ariz., 1955-56, Temple U., 1958-59. Cert. SEC, Nat. Assn. Security Dealers. Soil conservationist USDA, 1941-42; acctg. clk. Lansdale (Pa.) Tube Co., 1943-48; office mgr. Clark and Co., Tucson, 1952-54; head acctg. dept. Philco (formerly Lansdale Tube Co.), Spring City, Pa., 1956-61; comptr., then exec. asst. to pres. De Moss Assocs., King of Prussia, Pa., 1961-66; field underwriter, pension trust work and estate planning N.Y. Life Ins. Co., Phila., 1966-91; pres. Bible Women Internat., 1974—; spkr. in field. Author: Foretaste of Glory, 1979, 2nd edit., 1982, Braille edit., 1994, Come Travel with Me, 1984, Seed of David...Son of God, 1985, Navajo transl., 1986, Portugese transl., 1992, Nest in a Rock, 1991, 2nd edit., 1993. Mem. ad hoc fin. com. Ariz. State Opera, 1975-76; active Montgomery County War Bd., 1941-42, So. Ariz. Estate Planning Com., 1975, 76. Recipient Kemper Merriam award U. Ariz., 1972; named Hon. Citizen of South Korea. Mem. Nat. Assn. Accts. (emeritus, bd. dirs. Tuscon chpt.), Nat. Women's Leaders Round Table (nat. pension leader). Republican. Mem. Brethren Ch. Avocations: reading, writing books. Home: 3941 E Desmond Ln Tucson AZ 85712-3304 Office: Bible Women Internat 3941 E Desmond Ln Tucson AZ 85712-3304

WARSAWER, HAROLD NEWTON, real estate appraiser and consultant; b. N.Y.C.; s. Sidney L. and Alice (Frachtman) W.; m. Sally Kingsbury; children: Alice Cooper, Nancy Arkuss, Carole Greenblatt. BA, U. Mo.; MBA, Harvard U. Property mgr. and real estate broker Sidney L. Warsawer & Son, N.Y.C.; pres., dir. Consol. Capital, N.Y.C., 1962-68; pres. Atlantic Appraisal Co., Inc., N.Y.C., 1960—; pres., dir. Contemporary Enterprises, N.Y.C., 1974-76; pres. Mem. editorial bd. The Appraisal Jour., 1970-85. Candidate Teaneck (N.J.) Sch. Bd.; chmn. bldg. com. Temple Emeth, Teaneck, 1954-64. Mem. Appraisal Inst. (pres. N.Y. chpt. 1977, bd. dirs. 1970-80, 90-92, gov. counselor 1978), Nat. Assn. Rev. Appraisers, Real Estate Bd. N.Y., Nat. Realty Conf. (pres. 1992, bd. dirs.), Am. Arbitration Assn., Haworth Golf Club. Avocations: golf, clocks. Home: 430 Rutland Ave Teaneck NJ 07666-2823 Office: Ste 1446 60 E 42nd St New York NY 10165

WARSHAUER, IRENE CONRAD, lawyer; b. N.Y.C., May 4, 1942; d. A. Alfred and Sylvia (Bober) Conrad; m. Alan M. Warshauer, Nov. 27, 1966; 1 dau., Susan L. B.A. with distinction, U. Mich., 1963; LL.B. cum laude, Columbia U., 1966. Bar: N.Y. 1966, U.S. Dist. Ct. (so. and ea. dists.) N.Y. 1969, U.S. Ct. Appeals (2d cir.) 1969, U.S. Supreme Ct. 1972, U.S. Dist. Ct. (no. dist.) N.Y. 1980. With First Jud. Dept., N.Y. State Mental Health Info. Service, 1966-68; assoc. Chadbourne Parke Whiteside & Wolff, 1968-75; mem. Anderson Kill & Olick & Oshinsky, P.C., N.Y.C., 1975—; lectr. Def. Research Inst., Aspen Inst. Humanistic Studies, ABA, Rocky Mountain Mineral Law Found., CPR Inst. Dispute Resolution, panelist Am. Arbitration Assn., 1973—; mediator U.S. Dist. Ct. So. Dist., N.Y. Contbr. articles, chpts. to profl. lit. Mem. Democratic County Com., 1968—. Named to Hon. Order Ky. Cols. Mem. Assn. of Bar of City of N.Y. (judiciary com. 1982-84), N.Y. State Bar Assn. (chairperson subcom. mentally disabled and community 1978-82), ABA. Avocations: gardening, cooking, birding. Office: Anderson Kill Olick & Oshinsky 1251 Avenue Of The Americas New York NY 10020-1104

WARSHAUER, MYRON C., parking facility manager; b. 1939. BS in Fin., U. Ill., 1962; MBA, Northwestern U., 1963. With affiliate Standard Parking Corp., 1962—; now pres., CEO Standard Parking Corp., Chgo. Office: Standard Parking Corp Ste 4800 200 E Randolph Dr Chicago IL 60601

WARSHAVSKY, ELI SAMUEL, media company chief executive; b. Tel Aviv, July 2, 1930; s. Yechiel and Zipora Warshavsky; m. Carmela Warshavsky; children: Ofer Bernard, Sharon-Rina. Student, Tel Aviv U., 1952. Foodstuff wholesaler Tel Aviv, 1952; v.p. Imex Ltd., Ghana, 1952-58; dir. operations Super-Sol Ltd. Supermarkets, Israel, 1958-64; gen. mgr. Chen-Paldag Ltd., Israel, 1958-64, Jantzen (Israel) Bathing Suits Mfg., 1964-69; pres. Maximedia Group Outdoor Advt., Media, Ramat-Gan, Israel, 1969—, Golden-Wheels Ltd., Telruf Ltd., Terminal (Airports & Railways Advt.), Barak Silk Screen Printing Ltd., 1969—; acad. lectr. Author: Outdoor Advertising - the Powerful Medium; contbr. articles to profl. jours. Recipient Quality Mgmt. award Israel, CBI Yakir award Jerusalem. Mem. Internat. Advt. Assn. (world bd. dirs. 1986—, internat. adv. assn. N.Y., Internat. Medal for Merit 1992 Barcelona, pres. Israel chpt.), Forum Israeli Outdoor Advt. Assn. (chmn.), Coun. Beautiful Israel (hon. world treas. 1980—), Fe-Pe European Outdoor Advt. Fedn. Paris (bd. dirs.). Mem. D'Honneur FEPE (Rome) World Outdoor Advt. Assn. Home: 42 King David St, 46661 Herzliya Pituach Israel

WARSHAW, ALLEN CHARLES, lawyer; b. Harrisburg, Pa., Aug. 27, 1948; s. Julius and Miriam (Nepove) W.; m. Shirley Anne Nes, Aug. 23, 1970; children: Christopher James, Andrew Charles, William Robert. BA, U. Pa., 1970; JD, Villanova U., 1973. Bar: Pa. 1973, U.S. Dist. Ct. (ea. and mid. dists.) Pa. 1974, U.S. Ct. Appeals (3d cir.) 1975, U.S. Supreme Ct. 1977, Calif. 1978. Staff atty. Office Atty. Gen., State of Pa., Harrisburg, 1973-79, chief civil litigation, 1979-85, dir. civil law, 1985-86; ptnr. Duane, Morris & Heckscher, Harrisburg, 1986—. Coach, pres. Mechanicsburg Soccer Assn.; coach Upper Allen Baseball Assn. Fellow Am. Bar Found.; mem. ABA, Am. Bankruptcy Inst., Pa. Bar Assn., Pa. Def. Inst. Home: 1035 Mccormick Rd Mechanicsburg PA 17055-5970 Office: Duane Morris & Heckscher 305 N Front St Harrisburg PA 17101-1236

WARSHAW, ANDREW LOUIS, surgeon, researcher; b. N.Y.C., Feb. 18, 1939; s. David and Florence (Rand) W.; m. Brenda Rose Flavin, Jan. 4, 1986; children: Jordan, Abigail, Daniel; stepchildren: Heather, Gretchen, Brenda. AB, Harvard U., 1959, MD, 1963. Diplomate Am. Bd. Surgery. Intern in surgery Mass. Gen. Hosp., Boston, 1963-64, resident in surgery, 1964-65, 67-70, rsch. fellow in medicine, 1970, chief resident in surgery, 1971; clin. assoc. in gastroenterology NIH, Bethesda, Md., 1965-67; from instr. surgery to prof. surgery Harvard Med. Sch., Boston, 1972-90, Harold & Ellen Danser prof. surgery, 1990—; assoc. chief surg. svcs. Mass. Gen. Hosp., Boston, 1990—, chief gen. surgery, 1992—. Editor: Pancreatitis, 1989, Current Practice of Surgery, 1993; contbr. over 220 articles to med. jours., revs., 8 med. ednl. films, videos. Lt. comdr. USPHS, 1965-67. Mem. Am. Bd. Surgery (chmn. 1992-93, dir. 1985-93), New Eng. Surgical Soc. (pres. 1993-94), Am. Coll. Surgeons (pres. Mass. chpt. 1991-92). Avocations: photography, fly fishing. Office: Mass Gen Hosp WACC-336 Boston MA 02114

WARSHAW, JOSEPH BENNETT, pediatrician, educator; b. Miami Beach, Fla., July 17, 1936; s. Phillip Robert and Mona (Monashefsky) W.; m. Cynthia Ann Stober, June 6, 1961; children: Deborah, Kathryn, Lawrence. B.S., U. Fla., 1957; M.D., Duke U., 1961; M.S. (hon.), Yale U., 1976; M.D. (hon.), Catholic U.; Josiah Macy Jr. faculty scholar, U. Oxford, 1979-80. Diplomate Am. Bd. Pediatrics., subsplty bd. in neonatal-perinatal medicine. Intern, resident in pediatrics Strong Meml. Hosp., Rochester, N.Y., 1961-63; resident in pediatrics Duke Hosp., Durham, N.C., 1963-64; research assoc. NIH, 1964-66, Retina Found., Boston, 1966-68; assoc. in pediatrics Harvard U., 1968-71, asst. prof. pediatrics, 1971-72, assoc. prof., 1972-73; assoc. prof. pediatrics and ob-gyn Yale U., 1973-76, prof. pediatrics and ob-gyn, 1976-82; prof., chmn. dept. pediatrics U. Tex. Health Sci. Ctr., Dallas, 1982-87; chief staff Children's Med. Ctr., Dallas, 1982-87; chief pediatrics Parkland Meml. Hosp., Dallas, 1982-87; prof., chmn. dept. pediatrics Yale U. Sch. Medicine, New Haven, 1987—; physician-in-chief Children's Hosp. at Yale New Haven Hosp., 1987—, dep. dean for clin. affairs, 1995—; mem. human embryology and devel. study sect. NIH, 1974-78, nat. adv. council nat. inst. child health and human devel., 1987-91. Editor: Seminars in Perinatology, Principles and Practice of Pediatrics; contbr. articles on pediatrics, perinatology, devel. biology and biochemistry to profl. jours. Clin. research adv. com. Nat. Found. March of Dimes, 1978-92; mem. rsch. com. United Cerebral Palsy, 1987—. Served with USPHS, 1964-66. Fellow Am. Acad. Pediatrics; mem. Inst. Medicine of NAS, Am. Pediatric Soc. (coun. mem. 1988-94), Am. Soc. Clin. Investigation, Am. Soc. Biol. Chemistry, Am. Soc. Cell Biology, Soc. Devel. Biology, Soc. Pediatric Rsch. (pres. 1981-82), Assn. Am. Physicians, Internat. Pediatric Rsch. Found. (chmn. bd. 1989-93), Conn. Acad. Arts and Scis., Conn. Acad. Sci. & Engring. Home: 350 Vineyard Point Rd Guilford CT 06437-3255

WARSHAW, LEON J(OSEPH), physician; b. N.Y.C., July 20, 1917; s. Samuel and Bessie (Olken) W.; m. Mona Glassman, Aug. 31, 1941; children: Peter M., David C. A.B., Columbia U., 1938, M.D., 1942. Diplomate Am. Bd. Internal Medicine, Am. Bd. Preventive Medicine (occupational medicine). Intern, house physician 1st med. div. Bellevue Hosp., N.Y.C., 1942-44; from clin. asst. vis. physician to asso. vis. physician Bellevue Hosp., 1942-59; clin. asst., then adj. Beth Israel Hosp., N.Y.C., 1944-49; asso. attending physician Beth Israel Hosp., 1949-87, chief adult cardiac clinic, 1950-62; practice internal medicine N.Y.C., 1944-55, med. dir. and/or med. cons. various corps., 1944-69; with Equitable Life Assurance Soc., N.Y.C., 1970-80; v.p., chief med. dir. Equitable Life Assurance Soc., 1970-75, v.p., corp. med. dir., 1975-80; on leave as dep. dir. N.Y.C. Mayor's Office of Ops., 1978-80; clin. prof. environ. medicine NYU, 1980—; cons. health care delivery, 1980—; exec. dir. N.Y. Bus. Group on Health, 1980-94; mem. N.Y. Gov.'s Health Adv. Coun., 1978-84, N.Y. State Adv. Coun. on Alcoholism Svcs., 1988—, chmn., 1990—; mem. faculty Columbia U. Coll. Physicians and Surgeons, 1944-60, NYU Med. Sch., 1945-47; chmn. bd. Equitable Environ. Health, Inc., Woodbury, N.Y., 1973-75, dir., 1975-78; trustee Ins. Med. Scientist Scholarship Fund, 1975-78; mem. adv. bd. Ctr. Productive Aging, N.Y. Ctr. for Policy on Aging; bd. dirs. Med. & Health Rsch. Assn.; mem. nat. adv. com. Pres.'s Com. Employment Handicapped, 1965-89; mem. Pres.'s Coun. Phys. Fitness and Sports, 1970-85; bd. sponsors Twin Cities Health Care Devel. Project, 1972-75; chmn. med. adv. com. Washington Bus. Group Health, 1977-79; mental health adv. bd. Cornell U., 1970-80; Sappington Meml. lectr. Indsl. Med. Assn.; dir. Health Sys. Agy. N.Y.C., 1987-93; Thackrah lect. Soc. Occupl. Medicine/Leeds U., 1988. Author: Malaria: Biography of a Killer, 1949, Managing Stress, 1979, The Heart in Industry, 1969; contbr. articles to profl. jours.; mem. editorial bd. jours. Fellow Am. Coll. Occupational & Environ. Medicine, Am. Coll. Cardiology, ACP, Am. Coll. Preventive Medicine, Am. Occupational Medicine Assn. (past dir.), N.Y. Acad. Scis.; mem. AMA, N.Y. State, N.Y. County med. socs., Am. Arbitration Assn. (adv. health council 1972-80), Am. Heart Assn. (chmn. heart industry com. 1966-68, dir. 1969-73), Conf. Board, Nat. Safety Council (dir. 1972-74, v.p. research 1972-74), Greater N.Y. Safety Council (1970), N.Y. C. of C., N.Y. Heart Assn. (dir. 1968-70, 76-82), Occupational Health Inst. (dir. 1970-87), N.Y. Acad. Medicine (chmn. sec. occupational medicine 1964-66), N.Y. State Soc. Occupational Medicine (pres. 1965-67, exec. com. 1967-77), Occupational Psychiatry Group, Soc. Occupational Medicine, Med. and Health Rsch. Assn. N.Y.C. (bd. dirs.), Alpha Omega Alpha, Beta Sigma Rho, Phi Delta Epsilon. Office: 180 W End Ave Apt 6C New York NY 10023-4926

WARSHAW, MARTIN RICHARD, marketing educator; b. N.Y.C., Sept. 17, 1924; s. Irving Gregg and Adelaide (Klein) W.; m. Alice M. Present, Mar. 28, 1948; children: Gregg, Mark, Lynn, Laurie. A.B., Columbia U., 1947; M.B.A., U. Mich., 1957, Ph.D., 1960. Salesman Daniels Jewelry Co., Battle Creek, Mich., 1947-50; store mgr. Daniels Jewelry Co., 1950-55; v.p., dir. Daniels Jewelry Co., Lansing, Mich., 1955-64; instr. mktg. U. Mich., 1957-60, asst. prof., 1960-64, assoc. prof., 1964-67, prof., 1967-89, prof. emeritus, 1989—, chmn. mktg. faculty, 1973-79, 81-84. Author: (with Taylor and Scott) Introduction To Marketing Management, 5th edit, 1985, (with Engel and Kinnear) Promotional Strategy, 8th edit., 1994. Served with C.E. U.S. Army, 1943-46. Mem. Am. Mktg. Assn. (past pres. Detroit chpt.). Home: 5424 Parkgrove Rd Ann Arbor MI 48103-9202 Office: U Mich Sch Bus Adminstrn Ann Arbor MI 48109

WARSHAW, ROBERTA SUE, lawyer, financial specialist; b. Chgo., July 10, 1934; d. Charles and Frieda (Feldman) Weiner; m. Lawrence Warshaw, July 5, 1959 (div. June 1978); children: Nan R., Adam; m. Paul A. Heise, Apr. 2, 1994. Student, U. Ill., 1952-55; BFA, U. So. Calif., 1956; JD, Northwestern U., 1980. Bar: Ill. 1980. Atty., fin. specialist Housing Svcs. Ctr., Chgo., 1980-84, Chgo. Rehab. Network, 1985-91, 92-95; dir. housing State Treas., State of Ill., Chgo., 1991; sole practitioner, 1995—; legal worker Sch. of Law, Northwestern U. Legal Clinic, Chgo., 1977-80; real estate developer, mgr., marketer, Chgo., 1961-77; bd. dirs. Single Room Housing Assistance Corp. Co-author: (manual) The Cook County Scavenger Sale Program and The City of Chicago Reactivation Program, 1991, (booklet) Fix the Worst First, 1989; co-editor: The Caring Contract, Voices of American Leaders, 1996. Alderman 9th ward City of Evanston, Ill., 1985-93, mem. planning and devel., rules com., unified budget com., chair flood and pollution control com.; pres. Sister Cities Found.; mem. cmty. and econ. devel. policy Nat. League Cities, 1990-93; mem. Dem. Nat. Com.; bd. dirs. Dem. Ctrl. Com. Evanston, 1973—; elected committeeman Evanston Twp. Dem. Com., 1994—; del. Dem. Nat. Conv., 1996. Mem. ABA (affordable housing com.), Ill. State Bar Assn., Chgo. Bar Assn. (real estate coms.), Decalogue Soc. Lawyers, Chgo. Coun. Lawyers (housing com.). Avocations: politics, travel, hiking, camping, athletic activities. Home: 550 Sheridan Sq # 5G Evanston IL 60202-3169

WARSHAW, STANLEY IRVING, government official; b. Boston, Nov. 5, 1931; s. Alec and Sarah (Laserson) W.; m. Wanda Faye Capino, Feb., 12, 1992; 1 child from previous marriage, Karen Beth. B.S. in Ceramic Engring, Ga. Tech. Inst., 1957; Sc.D. in Ceramics, M.I.T., 1961; grad., Advanced Mgmt. Program, Harvard Bus. Sch., 1978. Sr. scientist research div. Raytheon Co., Waltham, Mass., 1961-64; with Am. Standard, Inc., New Brunswick, N.J., 1964-75, gen. mgr. engring. and devel., 1972-75; dir. Ctr. for Consumer Product Tech., Nat. Inst. Stds. and Tech. (formerly Nat. Bur. Stds.), Washington, 1975-80, dir. Office Product Standards Policy, 1981-86, assoc. dir., 1987-89; dir. Office Standards Svcs. Nat. Inst. Stds. and Tech. (formerly Nat. Bur. Stds.), Gaithersburg, Md., 1989-93; sr. policy advisor Internat. Trade Adminstrn., U.S. Dept. Commerce, Washington, 1994—. Served to capt. U.S. Army, 1951-53. Fellow N.Y. Acad. Scis., Washington Acad. Scis. Home: 8051 Rising Ridge Rd Bethesda MD 20817-6951 Office: US Dept Commerce Rm 3527 Internat Trade Adminstrn Washington DC 20230

WARSHAWSKY, ISIDORE, physicist, consultant; b. N.Y.C., May 27, 1911; s. Morris and Esther (Sherman) W. BS, CCNY, 1930. Physicist Nat. Adv. Com. Aeronautics, Langley Field, Va., 1930-42; chief instrumentation sect. Nat. Adv. Com. Aeronautics, Cleve., 1942-50; chief instrument rsch. br. Nat. Adv. Com. Aeronautics/ NASA, Cleve., 1950-72; instrumentation cons. NASA, Cleve., 1972-90, ret., 1990, disting. rsch. cons. (unsalaried), 1990-95. Author: (textbook) Foundations of Measurement and Instrumentation, 1990, 10 NACA/NASA tech. reports; contbr. 20 articles to sci. jours. and books. Fellow Instrument Soc. Am., Am. Phys. Soc., Combustion Inst., Am. Vacuum Soc.

WARTELL, ROGER MARTIN, biophysics educator; b. N.Y.C., Feb. 24, 1945; s. Hugh H. and Jennie (Silbermann) W.; m. Aila Irmeli Salo, Sept. 18, 1945; children: Zachary, Arlena. BSc, Stevens Inst. Tech., Hoboken, N.J., 1966; PhD, U. Rochester, N.Y., 1971. Postdoctoral fellow U. Wis., Madison, 1971-73; prof. physics and biology Ga. Inst. Tech., Atlanta, 1974—, dir. Sch. Biology, 1991—, dir. Bioscis. Ctr., 1991-95; vis. fellow U. Wis., Madison, 1978-79; vis. scientist NIH, Bethesda, Md., 1986-87; cons. SCI-EXPO Inc., Tucson, 1984-86. Contbr. articles to profl. jours. Mem. Biophys. Soc., ACS. Office: Ga Inst Tech Sch of Biology Atlanta GA 30332

WARTELLA, ELLEN ANN, communications educator, consultant; b. Kingston, Pa., Oct. 16, 1949; d. Nicholas and Margaret (Lipko) W.; m. D. Charles Whitney, Aug. 1, 1976; children: David Charles, Stephen Wright. BA, U. Pitts., 1971; MA, U. Minn., 1974, PhD, 1977. Asst. prof. Ohio State U., Columbus, 1976-79; rsch. asst. prof. communications U. Ill., Champaign, 1979-83, rsch. assoc. prof., 1983-89, rsch. prof., 1989-93; dean Coll. Comm., Walter Cronkite Regents Chair in Comm. U. Tex., Austin, 1993—; vis. prof. U. Calif., Santa Barbara, 1992-93; cons. Children's TV Workshop, N.Y.C., 1988-89, FTC, Washington, 1978, 1991-92, FCC, Washington, 1979. Co-author: How Children Learn to Buy, 1977; editor: Mass Communications Review Yearbook, 1982-83, Rethinking Communication, vols. I and II, 1989. Mem. bd. advisors Am. Children's TV Festival, Chgo., 1988—, The Learning Place, Champaign, 1992; bd. dirs. Headliners Found, Austin, 1993—, Sta. KLRU-TV (ex officio), Austin, 1993—. Recipient Krieghbaum award Assn. for Edn. in Journalism and Mass Communication, 1984; Univ. scholar U. Ill., 1989-93; Gannett Ctr. for Media Studies fellow, 1985-86. Fellow Internat. Comm. Assn. (pres. 1992-93), Broadcast Edn. Assn. (bd. dirs. 1990-94), Speech Comm. Assn., Soc. for Rsch. in Child Devel.

WARTH, ROBERT DOUGLAS, history educator; b. Houston, Dec. 16, 1921; s. Robert Douglas and Virginia (Adams) W.; m. Lillian Eleanor Terry, Sept. 18, 1945. B.S., U. Ky., 1943; M.A., U. Chgo., 1945, Ph.D., 1949. Instr. history U. Tenn., Knoxville, 1950-51; instr. Rutgers U., Newark, 1951-54; asst. prof. Rutgers U., 1954-58; vis. prof. Paine Coll., Augusta, Ga., 1960; asso. editor Grolier, Inc., N.Y.C., 1960-62, 63-64; lectr. Hunter Coll., N.Y.C., part time, 1962-63; asso. prof. S.I. Community Coll., 1964-68; prof. history U. Ky., Lexington, 1968-92; prof. emeritus history U. Ky., 1992—; Pres. So. Conf. Slavic Studies, 1982-83. Author: The Allies and the Russian Revolution, 1954, Soviet Russia in World Politics, 1963, Joseph Stalin, 1969, Lenin, 1973, Leon Trotsky, 1977. Served with AUS, 1943-44. Sr. scholar award So. Conf. Slavic Studies, 1992. Mem. Am. Hist. Assn., Am. Assn. Advancement Slavic Studies, AAUP. Home: 640 W Cooper Dr Lexington KY 40502-2277 Office: U Ky Dept History Lexington KY 40506

WARTHEN, HARRY JUSTICE, III, lawyer; b. Richmond, Va., July 8, 1939; s. Harry Justice Jr. and Martha Winston (Alsop) W.; m. Sally Berkeley Trapnell, Sept. 7, 1968; children: Martha Alsop, William Trapnell. BA, U. Va., 1961, LLB, 1967. Bar: Va. 1967, U.S. Ct. Appeals (4th cir.) 1967, U.S. Dist. Ct. (ea. dist.) Va. 1969. Law clk. to judge U.S. Ct. Appeals (4th cir.), Richmond, Va., 1967-68; assoc. Hunton & Williams, Richmond, 1968—; lectr. U. Va. Law Sch., Charlottesville, 1975-77, in field. Trustee exec. com. Hist. Richmond Found., 1986-95; dir. exec. com. Preservation Alliance of Va., 1991—, pres., 1994-96; elder, trustee endowment fund Grace Covenant Presbyn. Ch.; moderator Hanover Presbytery, Presbyn. Ch. (USA), 1988. Lt. U.S. Army, 1962-64. Fellow Am. Coll. Trust and Estate Counsel, Va. Law Found.; mem. ABA, Richmond Bar Assn., Va. Bar Assn. (chmn. sect. on wills, trusts and estates 1981-89), Antiquarian Soc. Richmond (pres. 1977-78), Country Club Va., Deep Run Hunt Club. Republican. Home: 1319 Shallow Well Rd Manakin-Sabot VA 23103-2305 Office: Hunton & Williams Riverfront Plaza East Tower 951 E Byrd St Richmond VA 23219-4040

WARTHEN, JOHN EDWARD, construction, leasing and finance executive; b. Cedar City, Utah, May 8, 1922; s. Mark Tew and Emma (Simkins) W.; student Branch Agrl. Coll. So. Utah, Cedar City, 1940-41; m. Norma Jane Hansen, June 22, 1943; children—Russel Edward, John Merrill, Judith Lally, Linda Fahringer, Carla Jean Thompson, Lauri Janette Sherratt. Pres., mgr. St. George Service, Inc. (Utah), 1945-61, Warthen Constrn. Co., Las Vegas, 1961—, Warthen Buick, 1961—; pres., gen. mgr. Diversified Investment & Leasing Corp., Las Vegas. Councilman, City of St. George, 1950-54. Past trustee, treas. Latter Day Saint Br. Geneal. Library, Las Vegas, 1964-76 ; co-founder Ctr. for Internat. Security Studies; past dist. dir. Freeman Inst.; past nat. dir. Liberty Amendment Com.; past chmn. Citizens for Pvt. Enterprise, Las Vegas; mem. Coun. Inter-Am. Security, Americanism Ednl. League; past fin. chmn. Boy Scouts Am.; past state chmn. Nev. Dealer Election Action Com.; mem. Nev. Devel. Authority. Mem. Ludwig Von Misses Inst. Econs. (charter), SAR (Good Citizenship award nat. soc.). Mormon (bishop 1957-

61). Clubs: Rotary, Kiwanis. Home: 2475 E Viking Rd Las Vegas NV 89121-4109 Office: 3025 E Sahara Ave Las Vegas NV 89104-4315

WARTHIN, THOMAS ANGELL, physician, educator; b. Ann Arbor, Mich., Aug. 11, 1909; s. Aldred Scott and Katharine Louise (Angell) W.; m. Virginia Carver Whittier, Oct. 15, 1938 (dec. Nov. 1995); children: Jonathan Carver, Richard Scott, Thomas Whittier. AB, U. Mich., 1930; MD cum laude, Harvard U., 1934. Diplomate Am. Bd. Internal Medicine. Intern medicine Boston City Hosp., 1934-36; resident intern medicine New Haven Hosp., Conn., 1936-37; fellow intern medicine Johns Hopkins Med. Sch., Balt., 1937-39; practice medicine Mass. Gen. Hosp., Boston, 1939-42; chief med. svc. VA Hosp., W. Roxbury, Mass., 1946-75; prof. of medicine Harvard Med. Sch., Boston, 1955-76, prof. of medicine emeritus, 1976—; cons. Surgeon Gen. U.S. Army, Washington, 1960-69, Internal Medicine VA Hosp., W. Roxbury, Mass., 1976-84. Contbr. articles to profl. jours. Brigadier Gen. U.S. Army, 1942-69. Recipient Legion of Merit, U.S. Army, 1969. Mem. ACP (master), Soc. Med. Cons. Armed Forces (pres. 1964), Internat. Soc. Internal Medicine (hon.), Mass. Med. Soc., Am. Clin. and Climatol. Assn. (coun., v.p. 1982), Aesculapian Club (pres. 1962), Alpha Omega Alpha. Avocation: gardening. Home: 180 Main St Apt 120 Walpole MA 02081-4033

WARWICK, DIONNE, singer; b. East Orange, N.J., Dec. 12, 1940; m. Bill Elliott (div. 1975); children: David, Damon. Ed., Hartt Coll. Music, Hartford, Conn. As teen-ager formed Gospelaires and Drinkard Singers, then sang background for rec. studio, 1966; debut, Philharmonic Hall, N.Y. Lincoln Center, 1966; appearances include London Palladium, Olympia, Paris, Lincoln Ctr. Performing Arts, N.Y.C.; records include Don't Make Me Over, 1962, Walk On By, Do You Know The Way to San José, What The World Needs Now, Message To Michael, I'll Never Fall In Love Again, I'll Never Love This Way Again, Deja Vu, Heartbreaker, That's What Friends are For; albums include Valley of the Dolls and Others, 1968, Promises, Promises, 1975, Dionne, 1979, Then Came You, Friends, 1986, Reservations for Two, 1987, Greatest Hits, 1990, Dionne Warwick Sings Cole Porter, 1990, Hidden Gems; The Best of Dionne Warwick, Vol. 2, 1992, (with Whitney Houston) Friends Can Be Lovers, 1993; TV appearance in Sisters in the Name of Love, HBO, 1986; screen debut Slaves, 1969, No Night, So Long, also, Hot! Live and Otherwise; co-host: TV show Solid Gold; host: TV show A Gift of Music, 1981; star: TV show Dionne Warwick Spl. Founder Dionne Warwick Scholarship Fund, 1968, charity group BRAVO (Blood Revolves Around Victorious Optimism), Warwick Found. to Help Fight AIDS; spokeswoman Am. Sudden Infant Death Syndrome; participant U.S.A for Africa; Am. Amb. of Health, 1987. Recipient Grammy awards, 1969, 70, 80; NAACP Key of Life award, 1990. Address: Arista Records Inc 6 W 57th St New York NY 10019-3913

WASAN, DARSH TILAKCHAND, university official, chemical engineer educator; b. Sarai, Salah, West Pakistan, July 15, 1938; came to U.S., 1957, naturalized, 1974; s. Tilakchand Gokalchand and Ishari Devi (Obhan) W.; m. Usha Kapur, Aug. 21, 1966; children: Ajay, Kern. BSChemE, U. Ill., 1960; PhD, U. Calif., Berkeley, 1965. Asst. prof. chem. engring. Ill. Inst. Tech., Chgo., 1964-67, assoc. prof., 1967-70, prof., 1970—, chmn. dept., 1971-77, 78-87, acting dean, 1977-78, 87-88, v.p. rsch. and tech., 1988-91, provost, 1991—, provost and sr. v.p., 1995—; cons. Inst. Gas Tech., 1965-70, Chgo. Bridge & Iron Co., 1967-71, Ill. EPA, 1971-72, NSF, 1971, 78-79, 87-89, Nelson Industries, 1976—, B.F. Goodrich Chem. Co., 1976-78, Exxon Rsch. & Engring. Co., 1977-89, Stauffer Chem. Co., 1980-88, ICI Ams., 1988-92. Editor-in0chief Jour. colloid and Interface sci.; mem. publs. bd. Chem. Engring. Edn. Jour.; mem. adv. bd. Interant. Jour. Powder Tech., Jour. Separations Tech., Surfaces and Colloids Jour., Current Opinion in Colloid and Interface Sci., Jour. of Dispersion Sci. and Tech.; contbr. articles to profl. jours. Recipient Donald Gage Stevens Disting. Lectureship award Syracuse U., 1991, Jakob J. Bikerman Lectureship award Case Western U., 1994, Robert Gilpin Lectr. award Clarkson U., 1995, MacMoran Disting. Lectrureship award Tulane U., 1996. Fellow Am. Inst. Chem. Engrs. (Ernest Thiele award 1989); mem. AAAS, Am. Chem. Soc., Soc. Rheology, Am. Soc. Engring. Edn. (Western Electric award 1972, 3M Lectureship award chem. engring. divsn. 1991), Am. Physics Inst., Fine Particles Soc. (pres. 1976-77, Hausner award 1982), Sigma Xi. Home: 8705 Royal Swan Ln Darien IL 60561-8433 Office: Ill Inst Tech 3300 S Federal St Chicago IL 60616-3732

WASELL, GÖSTA, auditor; b. Hudiksvall, Sweden, Mar. 14, 1930; s. Per-Alef and Henny (Bengtsson) W.; m. Siv Ingegerd Berggård, Aug. 13, 1955; children: Åsa-Helen, Per-Anders. Student, Stockholm U., 1952-55. Cert. internal auditor. Part-time railway and bldg. worker Swedish State Railways, 1946-51; officer, internal auditor, office mgr. Folksam Ins. Group, Stockholm, 1954-76; internal auditor, v.p. Swedish Trade Coun., Stockholm, 1976-81; mgr. audit dept. Swedish Trade Union Confederation, Stockholm, 1981-92; elected external auditor Stockholm, 1981-95. Fellow Nils Ferlin Soc.; mem. Inst. Internal Auditors. Social Democrat. Lutheran. Avocations: playing organ, reading biographies and memoirs, travel abroad. Home: Sparrisbacken 35, 16561 Hässelby Sweden

WASHBURN, BRADFORD (H.B. JR.), JR., museum administrator, cartographer, photographer; b. Cambridge, Mass., June 7, 1910; s. Henry Bradford and Edith (Hall) W.; m. Barbara Teel Polk, Apr. 27, 1940; children: Dorothy Polk, Edward Hall, Elizabeth Bradford. Grad., Groton Sch., 1929; A.B., Harvard U., 1933, A.M., 1960, D.H.L. (hon.), 1975; postgrad., Inst. Geog. Exploration, 1934-35; postgrad. hon. degrees; Ph.D., U. Alaska, 1951; D.Sc., Tufts U., 1957, Colby Coll., 1957, Northeastern U., 1958, U. Mass., 1972, Curry Coll., 1982; D.F.A., Suffolk U., 1965; D.H.L., Boston Coll., 1974; LL.D., Babson Coll., 1980. Instr. Inst. Geog. Exploration, Harvard U., 1935-42; dir. Mus. Sci., Boston, 1939-80, chmn. of the corp., 1980-85, hon. dir., 1985—; dir. Mountaineer in Alps, 1926-31; explorer Alaska Coast Range, 1930-40; served as leader numerous mountain, subarctic area explorations; cons. various govtl. agys. on Alaska and cold climate equipment; leader in spl. expdns. investigating high altitude cosmic rays, Alaska, 1947; rep. Nat. Geog. Soc., 17th Internat. Geog. Congress, 1952; leader Nat. Geog. mapping expdns. to, Grand Canyon, 1971-75; chmn. Mass. Com. Rhodes Scholars, 1959-64; chmn. arts and scis. com. UNESCO conf., Boston, 1961; mem. adv. com. John F. Kennedy Library, 1977; mem. vis. com. Internat. Mus. Photography, 1978; mem. U.S. Nat. Commn. for UNESCO, 1978; lectr. work of Yukon Expdn., Royal Geog. Soc., London, 1936-37, on mapping Grand Canyon, 1976; lectr. Mus. Imaging Tech., Bangkok, 1989, Royal Geog. Soc., London, on mapping Mt. Everest, 1990; lectr. Antarctica, 1994. Contbr. articles, photographs on Alaska, Alps, glaciers, and mountains to mags., books.; editor, pub. 1st large-scale map Mt. McKinley, Am. Acad. Arts and Scis.-Swiss Found. Alpine Rsch., Bern, 1960; mapped Mt. Kennedy for Nat. Geog. Soc., 1965, Grand Canyon, 1971-74, Muldrow Glacier (Mt. McKinley), 1977; editor new chart, Squam Lake, N.H., 1968, new Grand Canyon map for Nat. Geog. Soc., 1978, Bright Angel Trail map, 1981; photo-mapped Mt. Everest for Nat. Geog. Soc., 1984; dir., pub. large-scale map of Mt. Everest for Nat. Geog. Soc., 1984-88; project chief new 1:50,000 map of Mt. Everest for Nat. Geog. Soc. and Boston Sci. Mus., 1988; pub. Tourist Guide to Mt. McKinley, 1971, new map of Presdl. Range, N.H, 1989; completed new large-scale relief model Mt. Everest, 1990; one-man photographic shows Whyte Art Mus., Banff, Can., Internat. Mus. Photography, N.Y.C., Rochester, N.Y. Bd. overseers Harvard, 1955-61; trustee Smith Coll., 1962-68, Richard E. Byrd Found., 1979-84, Mt. Washington Obs., 1979—; mem. Task Force on Future Financing of Arts in Mass., 1978; hon. bd. dirs. Swiss Found. Alpine Research, 1984—. Recipient Royal Geog. Soc. Cuthbert Peek award for Alaska Exploration and Glacier Studies, 1938, Burr prize Nat. Geog. Soc., 1940, 65, Stratton prize Friends of Switzerland, 1970, Lantern award Rotary Club, Boston, 1978, New Englander of Yr. award New Eng. Coun., 1974, Gold Research medal Royal Scottish Geog. Soc. (with wife), 1979, Alexander Graham Bell award Nat. Geog. Soc., 1980, Disting. Grotonian award Groton Sch., 1979, Explorers medal Explorers Club, 1984, award for lifelong contbns. to cartography and surveying Engring. Socs. New Eng., 1985, King Albert medal of merit, 1994; named Bus. Statesman of Yr. Harvard Bus. Sch. Assn., Boston, 1970; named to Acad. Disting. Bostonians Boston C. of C., 1983; one of nine Photographic Masters, Boston U. Fellow Royal Geog. Soc. London, Harvard Travelers Club (Gold medal 1959), Nat. Geog. Soc. (with wife, Centennial award 1988), AAAS, Am. Acad. Arts and Scis., Am. Geog. Soc. (hon., major photographic exhibit for ann. conv. 1993—). Clubs: Commercial, Harvard Varsity, St. Botolph (hon. life), Aero Club of New Eng. (hon.), Harvard Mountaineering (Boston) (hon., past pres.); American Alpine (N.Y.C.) (hon.); Alpine (London) (hon.); Sierra of San Francisco (hon.); Mountaineers (Seattle) (hon.); Mountaineering of Alaska (hon.); hon. mem. several clu. Leader 1st ascent Mt. Crillon, Alaska, 1934, Nat. Geog. Soc. Yukon Expdn., 1935; leader 1st aerial photog. exploration Mt. McKinley, 1936, ascended its summit, 1942, 47, 51; leader 1st aerial exploration St. Elias range, 1938; 1st ascents Mount Sanford and Mount Marcus Baker in Alaska, 1938, Mt. Lucania, Yukon, 1937, Mt. Bertha, Alaska, 1940, Mt. Hayes, Alaska, 1941; 1st ascent West side Mt. McKinley 1951; leader Nat. Geog. Soc. Mt. Everest mapping project, 1981-88; expdn. to S.E. Asia, guest Chinese Acad. Scis., met with King of Nepal, 1988; leader expdn. to Nepal, 1992; 1st laser-distance observation to summit of Mt. Everest, 1992; 50th trip to Alaska to open exhibit of own photos Anchorage Art Mus., 1993. Home: 220 Somerset St Belmont MA 02178-2011 Office: Science Park Boston MA 02114

WASHBURN, DAVID THACHER, lawyer; b. Claremont, N.H., May 2, 1930; s. Walter Henry and Josephine Emmeline (Dana) W.; m. Joycemarie Springer, June 10, 1957 (div. Dec. 1975); children: Margaret Dana, David Thacher Jr., Robert Springer, John Putnam. BA, U. Vt., 1952; JD, NYU, 1955. Bar: N.Y. 1956, D.C. 1970, U.S. Supreme Ct 1970. Assoc. Paul, Weiss, Rifkind, Wharton & Garrison, N.Y.C., 1955-65, ptnr., 1965-95, counsel, 1996—. Trustee Rye Neck Bd. Edn., Mamaroneck, N.Y., 1971-73, Cambridge (Mass.) Coll., 1980-88, The Yard, N.Y.C., 1986-95, ARIA Found., Inc., Williston, Vt., 1991—; trustee, mem. exec. com. Rare Ctr. for Tropical Bird Conservation, Phila., 1979-80; dir. Sanctuary for Families, Inc., N.Y.C., 1994—, treas. 1995—. Mem. ABA, N.Y. State Bar Assn., Assn. of Bar of City of N.Y., The Coffee House (N.Y.C.), Doubles (N.Y.C.), Coveleigh Club (Rye, N.Y.), Westchester Country Club (Harrison, N.Y.). Home: 10 W 66th St New York NY 10023-6206 Office: Paul Weiss Rifkind Wharton & Garrison 1285 Avenue Of The Americas New York NY 10019-6064

WASHBURN, DOROTHY A., entrepreneur; b. Detroit, Oct. 28, 1934; d. Dajad and Mary (Pevrenkjian) Katchadoorian; m. Floyd Donald Washburn, June 23, 1956; children: Mary Susan, Dorothy Ann, Sherry Lynn, Tina Marie. Addressograph and graphotype instr. Burrough's Corp., Detroit, 1952-54; sec. to wire divsn. mgr. Mich. Oven Co., Detroit, 1954-58; exec. sec. to pres. Walch Metal Products, Detroit, 1961-62; sec. and treas. Record Distbrs. Corp., Detroit, 1963-65; fundraiser and trip coord. Edison High Sch., Huntington Beach, Calif., 1972-90; pres. Sunset Sales, Huntington Beach, 1977—. Editor: Annual Assembly Booklet of Ladies Society of the Armenian Church of North America Western Diocese, 1993-96. Campaign com. Gov. George Deukmejian, Doris Allen Campaign com.; chair band boosters Edison High Sch., 1975-77, chair choir boosters, 1988-90; vice chair parish coun. St. Mary Armenian Apostolic Ch., 1994, treas., social and entertainment com., 1993, advisor Ladies Soc., 1994—, advisor cultural com., 1993—, tchr. Sunday sch., 1992-96; corr. sec. Armenian ch. N.Am., Western Diocese, Ladies Ctrl. Coun., 1985—. Recipient Hon. Svc. award Calif. Congress of Parents, Tchrs. and Students, 1990. Armenian Orthodox. Avocations: creative cooking, music, folk dancing, swimming, travel.

WASHBURN, JOHN JAMES, lawyer, financial services company executive; b. Chelsea, Mass., Sept. 15, 1956; s. Frank Eugene and Kathryn Lorraine (Webster) W. BSBA cum laude, Suffolk U., Boston, 1978; MBA, Suffolk U., 1983; JD, New Eng. Sch. Law, 1987; LLM in Taxation, Boston U., 1989. Bar: Mass. 1987, Ill. 1996, U.S. Dist. Ct. Mass. 1988, U.S. Ct. Appeals (1st, 3d and 4th cirs.) 1988, U.S. Tax Ct. 1989, U.S. Ct. Claims 1991, U.S. Ct. Appeals (D.C. cir.) 1992, U.S. Ct. Appeals (7th cir.) 1996, U.S. Supreme Ct. 1996, U.S. Dist. Ct. (no. and ctrl. dists.) Ill. 1996. Assoc. Boxer & Assocs., Boston, 1987-88; pvt. practice North Reading, Mass., 1988-95, Westchester, Ill., 1996—; v.p. legal Nat. Translink Corp., Westchester, Ill., 1995—; cons. FGL Commodity Svcs. New England, 1988-92. Editor Confinement jour., 1986-87, B.U. Taxation jour., 1988-89; contbr. articles to profl. jours. Mem. North Reading Rep. Town Com., 1989-95, vice chmn., 1992-95; del. Mass. Rep. State Conv., 1990, 94; selectman North Reading, 1991-94, chmn., 1993-94, fin. com., 1994-95, clk., 1995; bd. dirs. Essex-Middlesex Sanitary Dist., 1991-95; Mass. Justice of Peace. Mem. ATLA, Ill. State Bar Assn., DuPage County Bar Assn., Chgo. Bar Assn., Am. Soc. Notaries, Phi Alpha Delta, Delta Sigma Pi. Republican. Avocations: golf, numismatics. Office: Nat Translink Corp 1127 S Mannheim Rd Ste 103 Westchester IL 60154 also: PO Box 264 4 Dodge Rd North Reading MA 01864

WASHBURN, ROBERT BROOKS, university dean, composer; b. Bouckville, N.Y., July 11, 1928; s. Robert Phelps and Florence (Brooks) W.; m. Beverly Jean Darnell, July 10, 1952; children: Brooks, Roberta. BS, SUNY, Potsdam, 1949, MS, 1956; PhD, Eastman Sch. Music, 1960. Dean, prof. music SUNY, Potsdam, 1954-95, dean emritus, sr. fellow music, 1995—; cons. NEH, Ogdensburg, N.Y., 1984-87, N.Y. State Sch. Music Assn., 1976-80, U.S. Office Edn., Washington, 1978-80; del. Music Educators Nat. Conf. Composer over 150 mus. works, 1955—. Served as sgt. USAF, 1950-54. Nat. Endowment for the Arts grantee, 1979; fellow Danforth Found., 1958-59, Ford Found. grantee, 1959-60, Fulbright fellow, 1986. Mem. ASCAP, Soc. for Ethnomusicology. Avocation: traveling. Home: 87 State Hwy 72 Potsdam NY 13676-3478 Office: SUNY Crane Sch Music Potsdam NY 13676

WASHBURN, STAN, artist; b. N.Y.C., Jan. 2, 1943; s. Sherwood Larned and Henrietta (Pease) W.; m. Andrea Aall Stub, Mar. 5, 1966; children: Anne Elizabeth, John Larned. MFA, Calif. Coll. Arts and Crafts, 1968. Founding ptnr. The Griffin Co., Oakland, Calif., 1968-70. Author: George's Dragon, 1974, A Moral Alphabet of Vice and Folly, 1986, Intent to Harm, 1994; one-man shows include Achenbach Found., San Francisco, 1977, St. Botolph Club, Boston, 1977, Pucker/Safrai, Boston, 1975, 77, 80, 85, Ames, Berkeley, Calif., 1974, 78, 81, 84, Thackrey & Robertson, San Francisco, 1981, 86, Charles Campbell, San Francisco, 1983, 86, 88, 90, 91, Bannatyne, Santa Monica, 1990, North Point, San Francisco, 1993, 96; represented in permanent collections at Bklyn. Mus., Achenbach Found., Chgo. Art Inst., Libr. of Congress, Houghton Libr., Phila. Mus. Art, Boston Mus. Fine Arts. Mem. Berkeley Police Res., 1973-78; mem. Berkeley Police Rev. Commn., 1979-83; trustee The Coll. Prep. Sch., Oakland, 1986—. Address: 2010 Virginia St Berkeley CA 94709-2138

WASHBURN, WILCOMB EDWARD, historian, educator; b. Ottawa, Kans., Jan. 13, 1925; s. Harold Edward and Sidsell Marie (Nelson) W.; m. Lelia Elizabeth Kanavarioti, July 14, 1951 (div. June 1981); children—Harold Kitsos, Edward Alexandros; m. Kathryn Laffler Cousins, Jan 2, 1985. Grad., Phillips Exeter Acad., 1943; AB summa cum laude, Dartmouth Coll., 1948; MA, Harvard U., 1951, PhD, 1955; HHD (hon.), St. Mary's Coll. Md., 1970, Assumption Coll., 1983, St. Lawrence U., 1991. Teaching fellow history and lit. Harvard, 1954-55; fellow Inst. Early Am. History and Culture, Williamsburg, Va., 1955-58; instr. Coll. William and Mary, 1955-58; curator div. polit. history Smithsonian Instn., U.S. Nat. Mus., Washington, 1958-65; dir. Am. studies program Smithsonian Instn., 1965—; Professorial lectr. Am. U., 1961-63, adj. prof., 1963-69; cons. in research Grad. Sch. Arts and Scis., professorial lectr. in Am. civilization George Washington U., 1966—; adj. prof. U. Md., 1975—; Civil info. and edn. officer Toyama Mil. Govt. Team, Toyama Prefecture, Japan, 1946-47. Author: The Governor and the Rebel: A History of Bacon's Rebellion in Virginia, 1957, Red Man's Land/White Man's Law: A Study of the Past and Present Status of the American Indian, 1971, revised edit., 1995, The Assault on Indian Tribalism: General Allotment Law (Dawes Act) of 1887, 1975, The Indian in America, 1975, (with others) The Federal City: Plans and Realities, The Exhibition, 1976; editor: (with others) The Indian and the White Man, 1964, Proc. of the Vinland Map Conf., 1971, The American Heritage History of the Indian Wars, 1977; contbr. articles to profl. jours. Past pres. Hist. Soc. of Washington; active Am. Hist Assn., Va. Hist. Assn., Md. Hist. Assn., Mass. Hist. Soc. With USMCR, 1943-45, 51-52. Fellow Am. Anthropol. Assn.; mem. AAAS, Am. Soc. Ethnohistory (past pres.), Am. Studies Assn. (past pres.), Colonial Soc. Mass., Am. Antiquarian Soc., Orgn. Am. Historians, Japan-Am. Soc. Washington (past trustee), Instituto Histórico e Geográfico Brasileiro, Anthropol. Soc. Washington, Phi Beta Kappa, Cosmos Club. Club: Cosmos (Washington). Office: Smithsonian Instn Am Studies Program Nat Postal Museum Washington DC 20560

WASHINGTON, DENNIS, production designer. Prodn. designer: (films) Crossing the Line, 1992, (with Robert Fortune) White Men Can't Jump, 1992, Nowhere to Run, 1993, The Fugitive, 1993, Angels in the Outfield, 1994. Office: Smith/Gosnell/Nicholson & Assocs PO Box 1166 1515 Palisades Dr Pacific Palisades CA 90272

WASHINGTON, DENNIS, construction executive. CEO Washington Cos., Missoula, Mont. Office: Washington Cos PO Box 8182 Missoula MT 59807

WASHINGTON, DENZEL, actor; b. Mt. Vernon, N.Y., Dec. 28, 1954; m. Paulette Pearson; children: John David, Katia, Malcolm and Olivia (twins). BA in Journalism, Fordham U.; student, Am. Conservatory Theatre, San Francisco. With N.Y. Shakespeare Festival, Manhattan Theatre Club, New Fed. Theatre. Actor: (stage prodns.) Coriolanus, 1979, Spell No. 7, The Mighty Gents, Richard III, One Tiger to a Hill, Ceremonies in Old Dark Men, When the Chicken Comes Home to Roost (Audelco award), A Soldier's Play (Obie award 1981), Checkmates, 1988, Split Second, (feature films) Carbon Copy, 1981, A Soldier's Story, 1981, Power, 1986, Cry Freedom, 1987, For Queen and Country, 1988, The Mighty Quinn, 1989, Glory, 1989 (Golden Globe award 1989, Acad. award 1990, NAACP Image award 1990), Heart Condition, 1990, Mo' Better Blues, 1990, Ricochet, 1991, Mississippi Masala, 1992, Malcolm X, 1992, Much Ado About Nothing, 1993, Philadelphia, 1993, The Pelican Brief, 1993, Crimson Tide, 1995, Virtuosity, 1995, Devel in a Blue Dress, 1995, Courage Under Fire, 1996, The Preacher's Wife, 1996; (TV movies) Wilma, 1977, License to Kill, 1984, The George McKenna Story, 1986, (TV miniseries) Flesh and Blood, 1979; regular (TV series) St. Elsewhere, 1982-88. Recipient Harvard Found. award, 1996; Am. Conservatory Theater scholar. Avocations: basketball, reading, cooking. Office: care ICM 8942 Wilshire Blvd Beverly Hills CA 90211*

WASHINGTON, GERALD, manufacturing executive; b. 1939. With Futorian Mfg. Co., New Albany, Miss., 1960-69, De Ville Furniture Co., Pontotoc, Miss., 1969-74, Astro Lounger Co., Okolona, Miss., 1974-76; with Washington Furniture Mfg. Co., Houlka, Miss., 1977—, now chmn. bd. Office: Washington Furniture Mfg Co 6496 Redlane Rd Houlka MS 38850*

WASHINGTON, GROVER, JR., musician, producer, composer, arranger; b. Buffalo, Dec. 12, 1943; m. Christine; children: Grover III, Shana. Student, Wurlitzer Sch. Music, Temple U.; also pvt. instrn. Worked for record distbr., 1969-70; pres. pub. co. G.W. Jr. Music, Inc.; pres. prodn. co. G-Man Prodns., Inc. Played with musical group Four Clefs, to 1963, with Keith McAllister, 1963-65, 19th Army Band, 1965-67; played with various groups in Phila. and N.Y., with Billy Cobham, with Don Gardner's Sonotones, 1967-68, Charles Earland, 1971; rec. for Kudu Records, Elektra Records, now under contract with Columbia Records; plays soprano, tenor, alto, baritone saxophones; over 24 solo albums including Come Morning, Mr. Magic, Winelight, The Best Is Yet to Come, Then and Now, Time Out of Mind, Next Exit, All My Tomorrows; numerous recs. as sideman or featured artist with Randy Weston, Bob James, Ralph MacDonald, Kathleen Battle, Don Sebesky, others; numerous TV and personal appearances throughout U.S., Can., Europe, Japan; performs Nat. Anthem regularly for Phila. Eagles and Phila. 76ers; prodr. 3 albums for group Pieces of a Dream, Jean Carne; first album of music from the Cosby Show. Performed at Inaugural events for Pres. Bill Clinton, 1993. Recipient numerous record industry awards including Grammy awards, 6 gold albums, platinum albums, also many prestigious industry, charitable and cmty. awards.

WASHINGTON, JAMES WINSTON, JR., artist, sculptor; b. Gloster, Miss., Nov. 10, 1909; s. James and Lizie (Howard) W.; m. Janie R. Miller, Mar. 29, 1943. Student, Nat. Landscape Inst., 1944-47; D.F.A., Center Urban-Black Studies, 1975. tchr. summer class N.W. Theol. Union Seattle U., 1988. One man shows U.S.O. Gallery, Little Rock, 1943, Foster-White Gallery, Seattle, 1974, 78, 80, 83, 89 (also at Bellevue Art Mus., 89), Charles and Emma Frye Art Mus., Seattle, 1980, 95, Mus. History and Industry, Seattle, 1981; exhibited in group shows Willard Gallery, N.Y.C., 1960-64, Feingarten Galleries, San Francisco, 1958-59, Grosvenor Gallery, London, Eng., 1964, Lee Nordness Gallery, N.Y.C, 1962 Woodside Gallery, Seattle, 1962-65, Foster-White Gallery, Seattle, 1974, 76, 89, 92, Smithsonian Instn., 1974, San Diego, 1977, others; retrospective exhbn. Bellevue Art Mus., Washington, 1989; represented in permanent collections Seattle, San Francisco, Oakland art museums, Seattle First Nat. Bank, Seattle Pub. Libr. YWCA, Seattle, Meany Jr. H.S., Seattle World's Fair, Expo 70 Osaka, Japan, Whitney Mus. Am. Art, N.Y.C.; commd. sculpture: Bird With Covey, Wash. State Capitol Mus., Olympia, 1983, Obelisk with Phoenix and Esoteric Symbols of Nature in granite, Sheraton Hotel Seattle, 1982, Life Surrounding the Astral Alter, In Matrix, owner T.M. Rosenblume, Charles Z. Smith & Assocs., Seattle, 1986, The Oracle of Truth (6 1/2 ton sculpture) Mt. Zion Bapt. Ch., Seattle, 1987, commd. sculptures King County Arts Commn., 1989, Bailey Gatzent Elem. Sch., Seattle, 1991, Twin Eaglets of the Cosmic Cycle (Quincy Jones), 1993, Fountain of Triumph (Bangasser Assocs. Inc.), 1992-93, Seattle, 1993-94, 94-95. Passover leader Mt. Zion Baptist Ch., Seattle, 1974-87. Recipient Spl. Commendation award for many contbns. to artistic heritage of state Gov., 1973, plaque City of Seattle, 1973, plaque Benefit Guild, Inc., 1973, arts service award King County Arts Commn., 1984, cert. of recognition Gov. of Wash., 1984, Editor's Choice award Outstanding Achievement in Poetry Nat. Libr. Poetry, 1993; named to Wash. State Centennial Hall of Honor, Wash. State Hist. Soc., 1984; home and studio designated historic landmark (city and state), 1991. Mem. Internat. Platform Assn., Internat. Soc. Poets (life, awards 1993), Profl. Artists Phila., Masons (33d degree). Home: 1816 26th Ave Seattle WA 98122-3110

WASHINGTON, MALIVAI, professional tennis player; b. Swartz Creek, MI, June 20, 1969. Student, U. Mich. Ranked 6th in U.S. Tennis Assn., 1993. Named All-American NCAA, 1988-89; mem. U.S. Davis Cup Team, 1993; winner of Australian Open, 1994, U.S. Clay Courts Championship, 1992.

WASHINGTON, PATRICIA LANE, retired school counselor; b. Junction City, Kans., June 23, 1943; d. LeRoy and Rose Mary (Strong) Lane; children: Janet Rosemarie, Kelly Edward. BS in Elem. Edn., Lincoln U., 1965; postgrad., U. Kans., 1968, 69, 70; specialist in counseling, U. Mo., Kansas City, 1972, postgrad., 1990-93; MS in Learning Disabilities, Ctrl. Mo. State U., 1975; postgrad., Met. C.C., Kansas City, Mo., 1979, Nat. Coll., Kansas City, 1983, Ottawa U., 1984, Avilla Coll., 1993. Cert. elem. and secondary tchr., tchr. of bevavioral disordered, learning disabled, psychol. examiner, counselor, Mo. 1st grade tchr. Kansas City Sch. Dist., 1965-68, head start instr., 1966-69, sr. instr., 1968-75, K-6 grade resource tchr., 1975-77, edni. resource tchr. with gifted and talented students, 1979, ednl. resource tchr. early identification screening program, 1980, mem. screening team, 1980-81; sr. H.S. learning disabilities instr. Kansas City Bd. Edn., 1981, mem. spl. edn. placement team., 1981-84, sch. psychol. examiner, 1984-88, placement advisor, psychol. examiner, 1988-89, learning disabilities high sch. instr., 1989-90, elem. guidance counselor, 1990-91, mid. sch. guidance counselor, 1991-92, high sch. guidance counselor, 1992-93, chpt. I counselor grades K-5, 1993-94, mid. sch. counselor, 1994-95; ret., 1995; exec. dir., owner Upper Pathways - The Wave of the Future, Kansas City, 1996—; dir., counselor Jackson County Ct., summer 1971; instr. Pioneer C.C., 1970-80, 80-81, 82; coord., instr. Second Bapt. Ch. Adminstr., 1983; spkr. in field. Pres. Host-Hostess ministry 2d Missionary Bapt. Ch. Mem. Am. Legion, Optimist Club. Democrat. Baptist. Avocations: reading, speaking, bowling, dance, travel. Home and Office: 9716 Elm Ave Kansas City MO 64134-2221

WASHINGTON, REGINALD LOUIS, pediatric cardiologist; b. Colorado Springs, Colo., Dec. 31, 1949; s. Lucius Louis and Brenette Y. (Wheeler) W.; m. Billye Faye Ned, Aug. 18, 1973; children: Danielle Larae, Reginald Quinn. BS in Zoology, Colo. State U., 1971; MD, U. Colo., 1975. Diplomate Nat. Bd. Med. Examiners, Am. Bd. Pediatrics, Pediatric Cardiology. Intern in pediatrics U. Colo. Med. Ctr., Denver, 1975-76, resident in pediatrics, 1976-78, chief resident, instr., 1978-79, fellow in pediatric cardiology, 1979-81, asst. prof. pediatrics, 1982-1988, assoc. prof. pediatrics, 1988-90, assoc. clin. prof. pediatrics, 1990—; staff cardiologist Children's Hosp., Denver, 1981-90; v.p. Rocky Mountain Pediatric Cardiology, Denver, 1990—; mem. admissions com. U. Colo. Sch. Medicine, Denver, 1985-89; chmn., bd. dirs. Coop. Health Care Agreements, 1994—. Cons. editor Your Patient and Fitness, 1989-92. Chmn. Coop. Health Care Agreements Bd.,

State of Colo., 1994—; adv. bd. dirs. Equitable Bank of Littleton, Colo., 1984-86; bd. dirs. Ctrl. City Opera, 1989-95, Cleo Parker Robinson Dance Co., 1992-94, Rocky Mountain Heart Fund for Children, 1984-89, Raindo Ironkids, 1989—; nat. bd. dirs. Am. Heart Assn., 1992-96; bd. dirs. Nat. Coun. Patient Info. and Edn., 1992—, Children's Heart Alliance, 1993-94, Regis U., Denver, 1994—, Colo. State U. Devel. Coun., 1994—; trustee Denver Ctr. Performing Arts, 1994—; mem. Gov.'s Coun. Phys. Fitness, 1990-91; bd. trustees Regis U.; mem. Colo. State Bd. Agr. Named Salute Vol. of Yr. Big Sisters of Colo., 1990; honoree NCCJ, 1994, Physician of Yr., Nat. Am. Heart Assn., 1995. Fellow Am. Acad. Pediatrics (cardiology subsect.), Am. Coll. Cardiology, Am. Heart Assn. (coun. on cardiovascular disease in the young, exec. com. 1988-91, nat. devel. program com. 1990-94, vol. of yr. 1989, pres. Colo. chpt. 1989-90, Torch of Hope 1987, Gold Heart award Colo. chpt. 1990, bd. dirs. Colo. chpt., exec. com. Colo. chpt. 1987—, grantee Colo. chpt. 1983-84, mem. editorial bd. Pediatric Exercise Scis. 1988—, Nat. Physician of the Yr., 1995), Soc. Critical Care Medicine; mem. Am. Acad. Pediatrics/Perinatology, N.Am. Soc. Pediatric Exercise Medicine (pres. 1986-87), Colo. Med. Soc. (chmn. sports medicine coun. 1993-94), Leadership Denver 1990, Denver Athletic Club, Met. Club, Glenmoor Golf Club. Democrat. Roman Catholic. Avocations: skiing, golf, fishing. Home: 7423 Berkeley Cir Castle Rock CO 80104-9278 Office: Rocky Mountain Pediatric Cardiology 1601 E 19th Ave Ste 5600 Denver CO 80218-1216

WASHINGTON, ROBERT ORLANDA, educator, former university administrator; b. Newport News, Va., Feb. 8, 1935; s. Robert Lee and Fannie (Bates) W.; m. Mary Louise Lewis, Apr. 7, 1955; children: Robert, Glynis, Cheryl, Nathan, Allyson, Terrence, Candace. B.S., Hampton Inst., 1956; M.S., Marquette U., 1966; M.A., U. Mo., 1968; Ph.D., Brandeis U., 1973. Pub. Milw. Post, weekly newspaper, 1960-64; research assoc. Greenleigh Assocs., N.Y.C., 1968-72; instr. social work Simmons Coll., Boston, 1970-72; prof. Case Western Res. U., Cleve., 1972-74; dean Sch. Social Work, Ohio State U., Columbus, 1976-82, U. Ill., Champaign, 1982-86; cons. U.S. AID, Nigeria, 1970, 72, Cairo, 1975, 77; commr. accreditation Coun. on Social Work Edn., N.Y.C., 1978-81; cons. U.S. HHS, Washington, 1981; pres., CEO Social Policy Rsch. Group, Inc., Boston, 1986-88; vice-chancellor for rsch. and grad. studies U. New Orleans, 1988-93. Author: Programm Evaluation in the Human Services, 1980, (with others) Social Policy and Social Welfare, 1980, Marco Practice in Social Work, 1982, Social Work in the 1980's, 1982, Children in Need of Roots, 1985, Social Work in Schools, 1985, Toward a Theory of Social Planning, 1994. NDEA fellow, 1967. Mem. Council on Social Work Edn., Nat. Assn. Social Workers, Champaign Urban League, Ill. Guardianship and Advocacy Commn. Democrat. Home: 7135 Benson Ct New Orleans LA 70127-2001 Office: U New Orleans Dept Social Work Lakefront New Orleans LA 70148

WASHINGTON, SHELLEY LYNNE, dancer; b. Washington, Nov. 3, 1954; d. Edward Freeman and Geraldine (Butler) W. Student, Interlochen Arts Acad., 1969-72, Juilliard Acad., N.Y.C., 1972-74. Dancer Martha Graham, N.Y.C., 1974-75, Twyla Tharp Dance Found., N.Y.C., 1975—, Am. Ballet Theatre, N.Y.C., 1988-91; ballet mistress and artistic assoc. dir. for Twyla Tharp, including repertory for Boston Ballet, Hubbard St. Dance Co., Martha Graham Dance Co., Am. Ballet Theatre, The Royal Ballet, London. Dancer in film Hair, 1978; in Broadway show Singin in the Rain, 1985-86. Recipient Bessie Schonberg award for Outstanding Performing, 1987. Office: Twyla Tharp Dance Found Tharp Prodns 336 Central Park W New York NY 10025-7111

WASHINGTON, VALORA, foundation administrator; b. Columbus, Ohio, Dec. 16, 1953; d. Timothy Washington and Elizabeth (Jackson) Barbour; children: Omari, Kamilah. BA in Social Sci. with honors, Mich. State U., 1974; PhD, Ind. U., 1978; PhD (hon.), Bennett Coll., 1992. Assoc. instr. sch. edn. Ind. U., Bloomington, 1975-77; dir., cons. Urban League Ind., Indpls., 1977-78; substitute tchr. Indpl. Pub. Schs., 1978; dir. U. N.C., Chapel Hill, 1980-82; congrl. sci. fellow Soc. for Rsch. in Child Devel., Washington, 1981-82; prof. edn. U. N.C., Chapel Hill, 1978-83; asst. dean, assoc. prof. Howard U., Washington, 1983-86, Am. U., Washington, 1986-87; prof., v.p. Antioch Coll., Yellow Springs, Ohio, 1987-90; v.p. Kellogg Found., Battle Creek, Mich., 1990—; cons. Ford Found., N.Y.C., 1990; project evaluator Carnegie Corp., N.Y.C., 1989-90, Ohio Bd. Regents, Columbus, 1990—. Author: (with others) Creating New Linkages for the Adoption of Black Children, 1984, Project Head Start: Past, Present and Future Trends in the Context of Family Needs, 1987, Black Children and American Institutions: An Ecological Review and Resource Guide, 1988, Affirmative Rhetoric, Negative Action: The Status of Black and Hispanic Faculty in Higher Education, 1989; contbr. articles to profl. jours; contbr. chapters to numerous books. Recipient Capital U. award, 1990, award Springfield Alliance Black Educators, 1989; named one of Ten Outstanding Young Women Am., 1980, Outstanding Young Woman N.C., 1980, one of 100 Young Women of Promise Good Housekeeping Mag., 1985. Mem. Nat. Coun. Negro Women (chmn. 1982-83), Am. Assn. for Higher Edn. (sec. black caucus 1989), Soc. for Rsch. in Child Devel. (pres. black caucus 1987-89), Nat. Assn. for the Edn. of Young Children (sec. of bd. dir. 1990—), Phi Delta Kappa, Delta Kappa Gamma.

WASHINGTON, VIVIAN EDWARDS, social worker, former government official; b. Claremont, N.H., Oct. 26, 1914; d. Valdemar and Irene (Quashie) Edwards; m. George Luther Washington, Dec. 22, 1950; 1 child, Valdemar Luther. AB, Howard U., 1938, MA, 1946, MSW, 1956; LHD (hon.), U. Balt., 1993. Tchr., guidance counselor, sch. social worker, asst. prin., prin. Edgar Allan Poe Sch. Program for Pregnant Girls, Balt., 1966-73; cons. Office Adolescent Pregnancy Programs, HEW, Washington, 1978-80, program devel. specialist, 1980-81; exec. dir. Balt. Coun. on Adolescent Pregnancy, Parenting and Pregnancy Prevention Inc., 1982-86, cons., 1986—; cons. to adolescent parents. Author: I Am Somebody, I Am Me, 1986; contbr. articles to profl. jours. Bd. dirs. Nat. Alliance Concerned with Sch.-Age Parents, 1970-76, pres., 1970-72; YWCA, Balt., 1966-69, United Way Central Md., 1971-80; mem. bd. visitors U. Balt., 1978-80, U. Balt. Ednl. Found., 1980, 92-94, chair, 1992-94; adv. commn. on social services City of Balt., 1978-85, Govs. Coun. on Adolescent Pregnancy, 1986; chmn. Md. Gov.'s Commn. on Children and Youth, 1972-77, active 1987. Recipient Alumni award Howard U. Sch. Social Work, 1966, Clementine Peters award United Way, 1980, Sojourner Truth award Nat. Bus. and Profl. Women, 1979, Vashti Turley Murphy award Balt. chpt. Delta Sigma Theta, 1981, Balt.'s Best Blue and Silver award, 1983, Pvt. Sector Vol. Svc. award Pres. Reagan, 1984, United Way Community Svc. award, 1985, H. Mebane Turner Svc. award U. Balt. Alumni Assn., 1991, 94, Disting. Black Marylander award Towson State U., 1992, Cmty. Svc. award For Sisters Only, 1994, Learn and Earn Program Pioneer award Balt. City 4-H, 1993; named to Balt. Women's Hall of Fame, 1989, Md.'s Outstanding Ch. Woman Nat. Episc. Triennial, 1991; Paul Harris fellow Balt. Rotary, 1985. Mem. Am. Heritage Soc., Great Cir. Md. Living Legend, Nat. Assn. Social Work, LWV, Nat. Coun. Negro Women (life), Balt. Urban League (Equal Opportunity award 1987), Balt. Mus. Art, Delta Sigma Theta (nat. treas. 1958-63, Las Amigas Svc. award Balt. chpt. 1973), Pierians Club. Democrat. Episcopalian. Home: 3507 Ellamont Rd Baltimore MD 21215-7422

WASHINGTON, WALTER, retired academic administrator; b. Hazlehurst, Miss., July 13, 1923; s. Kemp and Mable (Comous) W.; m. Carolyn Carter, July 31, 1949. BA, Tougaloo Coll., 1948, LLD (hon.), 1972; MS, Ind. U., 1952, LLD (hon.), 1983; Edn. Specialist, Peabody Coll., 1958; postgrad., Yale, 1953; EdD, U. So. Miss., 1969; postgrad., Harvard U., 1989; DSc (hon.), Purdue U., 1993. Tchr. Holtzclaw High Sch., Crystal Springs, Miss., 1948-49; asst. prin., tchr. Parrish High Sch., Hazlehurst, 1949-52; prin. Utica Jr. Coll. High Sch., Miss., 1951-54; dean Utica Jr. Coll., 1954-55, pres., 1957-69; prin. Sumner Hill High Sch., Clinton, Miss., 1955-57; pres. Alcorn (Miss.) State U., 1969-94, pres. emeritus, 1994—; past ptnr. Klinger Industries, Ltd.; bd. dirs. Blue Cross and Blue Shield Miss. Pres. Nat. Pan-Hellenic Council, 1964-67, Nat. Alumni Council of United Negro Coll. Fund, 1959-60; past. mem. adv. council Miss. Vocational Edn. Program, Miss. Regional Med. Programs; mem. Miss. Econ. Council; mem. S.E. regional exec. com. Boy Scouts Am.; mem. exec. com. Andrew Jackson council; past mem. adv. council Miss. 4-H Clubs; bd. dirs. Miss. Mental Health Assn., Miss. Easter Seal Soc.; past bd. dirs. Miss. Heart Assn. Recipient Presdl. citation for outstanding leadership to Univ./Industry Cluster, 1980-81, Disting. Alumni award Vanderbilt-Peabody, 1991, George Washington Carver Lifetime Achievement award Tuskegee Inst., 1993; named to U. So. Miss. Alumni Hall of Fame, 1987; Walter Washington Bldgs. named in his honor U. So. Miss., 1993, Alcorn State U., 1994. Mem. NEA, ASCD, Am. Assn. Sch. Adminstrs. (So. Regional Edn. bd.), Nat. Assn. State Univs. and Land Grant Colls., So. Assn. Colls. Secondary Schs. (past bd. dirs., past chmn. secondary commn., past chmn. commn. on colls., past trustee), Miss. Educators Assn. (pres. 1964-65), Miss. Tchrs. Assn., Nat. Soc. for Study of Higher Edn., Tougaloo Nat. Alumni Assn. (pres. 1960), George Peabody Coll. Alumni Assn. (past v.p. exec. com., Disting. Alumni of Yr. 1991), John Dewey Soc., Delta Kappa Pi, Phi Delta Kappa, Alpha Kappa Mu, Alpha Phi Alpha (gen. pres. 1974-76).

WASHINGTON, WARREN MORTON, meteorologist; b. Portland, Oreg., Aug. 28, 1936; s. Edwin and Dorothy Grace (Morton) W.; m. LaRae Herring, July 30, 1959 (div. Aug. 1975); children: Teri, Kim, Marc (dec.), Tracy; m. Jona Ann, July 3, 1978 (dec. Jan. 1987); m. Mary Elizabeth Washington, Apr., 1995. B.S. in Physics, Ore. State U., 1958, M.S. in Meteorology, 1960; Ph.D. in Meteorology, Pa. State U., 1964. Dir. of climate and global dynamics div. Nat. Center Atmospheric Research, Boulder, Colo., 1978-95; affiliate prof. meteorology oceanography U. Mich. at Ann Arbor, 1968-71; mem. Nat. Adv. Com. for Oceans and Atmospheres, 1978-84; mem. sec. of energy adv. bd. U.S. Dept. Energy, 1990-93. Contbr. articles to meteorol. jours. Mem. Boulder Human Relations Commn., 1969-71; mem. Gov.'s Sci. Adv. Com., 1975-78. Recipient Disting. Alumni award Pa. State U., 1994, E.B. Lemon Disting. Alumni award Pa. State U., 1996. Fellow AAAS (bd. dirs.), Am. Meteorol. Soc. (pres. 1994); mem. Am. Geog. Union, Nat. Sci. Bd. Home: 725 Pinehurst Ct Louisville CO 80027-3285 Office: PO Box 3000 Boulder CO 80307-3000

WASIELE, HARRY W., JR., diversified electrical manufacturing company executive; b. Chgo., June 29, 1926; s. Harry W. and Antoinette (Tuleja) W.; m. Loretta K. Anderson, Jan. 3, 1948; children: Kathleen Ann Wasiele Bach, Brian David, Larry Scott, Mark Thomas. Grad. high sch. Asst. sales mgr. Drake Mfg. Co., Chgo., 1950-55; sales engr. AMP, Inc., Chgo., 1955, Detroit, 1956-57; product mgr. AMP, Inc., Harrisburg, Pa., 1958-61; industry mgr. AMP, Inc., 1961-67, dir. marketing, 1967-68; div. gen. mgr. Brand-Rex div. Am. Enka Corp., Willimantic, Conn., 1968-70; pres. Brand-Rex Co., subs. Akzona Inc., 1970-83; chmn. Brand-Rex Ltd., Glenrothes, Scotland, 1974-83; v.p. sales and corp. devel. Cablec Corp., New City, N.Y., 1985—; dir. Berkel Inc.; chmn., pres. Tarpon Springs (Fla.) Internat. Tannery, Inc., 1990—. Bd. dirs. Eastern Conn. State Coll. Found., 1972-83; trustee Windham Community Hosp., Willimantic, 1969-83, trustee emeritus, 1983—, pres. bd. trustees, 1981-83. With USNR, 1944-46. Mem. Nat. Elec. Mfrs. Assn. (chmn. wire and cable div., bd. govs. 1982-84), Conn. Bus. and Industry Assn. (emeritus dir.), New Seabury Country Club, Mariner Sands Country Club. Republican. Roman Catholic. Home (summer): 53 Shore Dr W PO Box 826 New Seabury MA 02649 Home (winter): Mariner Sands 6755 SE Barrington Dr Stuart FL 34997-8639

WASIK, JOHN FRANCIS, editor, writer, publisher; b. Chgo., July 2, 1957; s. Arthur Stanley and Virginia Frances (Gray) W.; m. Kathleen Rose. BA in Psychology, U. Ill., Chgo., 1978, MA in Communication, 1988. Sr. editor Consumers Digest Inc., Chgo., 1986—; editor, pub. Conscious Consumer and Co. Newsletters. Author: Electronic Business Information Sourcebook, 1987, Green Company Resource Guide, 1992, The Green Supermarket Shopping Guide, 1993, The Investment Club Book, 1995. Mem. Soc. Profl. Journalists, Soc. Environ. Journalists. Office: Consumers Digest Inc 5705 N Lincoln Ave Chicago IL 60659-4707

WASILEWSKI, VINCENT THOMAS, retired lawyer; b. Athens, Ill., Dec. 17, 1922; s. Alex and Anna (Gillespie) W.; m. Patricia Callery, June 17, 1950 (dec. 1989); children: Jan, Susan, Catherine, Terese, Thomas, James; m. Marjorie Nohowel, June 19, 1992. A.B. in Polit. Sci, U. Ill., 1948, J.D., 1949. Bar: Ill. 1950, D.C. 1980. Mem. staff Nat. Assn. Broadcasters, Washington, 1949-82; v.p. govt. affairs Nat. Assn. Broadcasters, 1960-61, exec. v.p., 1961-65, pres., 1965-82; trustee Mus. Broadcasting. Served with USAAF, 1942-45. Decorated D.F.C. with oak leaf cluster; Air medal with oak leaf cluster.; Recipient David Sarnoff award, Am. Women in Radio and TV Silver Satellite award, Commonwealth award. Mem. ABA, Nat. Assn. Broadcasters (Disting. Svc. award 1982), Fed. Comms. Bar Assn., Internat. Radio and TV Soc., Internat. Club (Washington), Burning Tree Club (Washington), George Town Club (Washington), Congl. Club (Potomac, Md.), John's Island Club (Vero Beach, Fla.), Knights of Malta, Order of Coif, Sigma Phi Epsilon, Phi Kappa Phi, Phi Alpha Delta. Home: 6111 Davenport Ter Bethesda MD 20817-5827 Office: Dow Lohnes & Albertson 1255 23rd St NW Washington DC 20037-1125

WASIOLEK, EDWARD, literary critic, language and literature educator; b. Camden, N.J., Apr. 27, 1924; s. Ignac and Mary (Szczesniewska) W.; m. Emma Jones Thomson, 1948; children: Mark Allan, Karen Lee, Eric Wade. B.A., Rutgers U., 1949; M.A., Harvard, 1950, Ph.D., 1955; postgrad., U. Bordeaux, France, 1950-51. Teaching fellow Harvard U., Cambridge, Mass., 1953-54, research fellow Russian Research Ctr., 1952-54; instr. English Ohio Wesleyan U., 1954-55; asst. prof. U. Chgo., 1955-60, assoc. prof. English and Russian, 1960-64, prof. Russian and comparative lit., 1964-69, Avalon prof. comparative lit. and Russian, 1969-76, Disting. Services prof. of English, comparative lit., and Slavic studies, 1976—, chmn. comparative lit. program, 1965-83, chmn. dept. Slavic langs. and lit., 1971-77; vis. prof. Slavic and comparative lit. Harvard, 1966-67. Author: (with R. Bauer) Nine Soviet Portraits, 1955, Crime and Punishment and the Critics, 1961, Dostoevsky: The Major Fiction, 1964, The Notebooks for Crime and Punishment, 1967, The Brothers Karamazov and the Critics, 1967, The Notebooks for the Idiot, 1968, The Notebooks for the Possessed, 1968, The Notebooks for A Raw Youth, 1969, The Notebooks for the Brothers Karamazov, 1970, The Gambler, with Paulina Suslova's Diary, 1972, Tolstoy's Major Fiction, 1978, Critical Essays on Tolstoy, 1986, Fathers and Sons: Russia at the Crossroads, 1993. Addressed UN on Tolstoy, 1988. With USNR, 1943-46. Recipient Quantrell teaching prize U. Chgo., 1961; Laing Press prize, 1972; Research fellow USSR, 1963; Guggenheim fellow, 1983-84. Mem. Modern Lang. Assn., Phi Beta Kappa, Lambda Chi Alpha. Home: 1832 Butterfield Ln Flossmoor IL 60422-2107 Office: Univ Chicago Dept English Chicago IL 60637 *I believe in the life of the mind and I believe with Albert Camus that man's dignity lies in his lucidity: in seeing his fate clearly and in having the courage to accept it. Man is capable of sensitivity, courage, love, and compassion, and all of these are more human because he can think. He is also capable of cruelty, hatred, and destruction, and these are more tolerable because he can reason. Man is not man without reason.*

WASKOW, ARTHUR OCEAN, theologian, educator; b. Balt., Oct. 12, 1933; s. Henry B. and Hannah (Osnowitz) W.; m. Irene Elkin, 1956 (div. 1978); children: David, Shoshana; m. Phyllis Ocean Berman, 1986. B.A., Johns Hopkins, 1954; M.A., U. Wis., 1956, Ph.D., 1963. Legis. asst. Ho. of Reps., Washington, 1959-61; sr. staff mem. Peace Rsch. Inst., Washington, 1961-63; fellow Inst. Policy Studies, Washington, 1963-77; colleague Pub. Resource Ctr., Washington, 1977-82; faculty Reconstructionist Rabbinical Coll., Phila., 1982-89; dir. Shalom Ctr., 1983—; fellow ALEPH Alliance for Jewish Renewal, 1990—: mem. adv. bd. Temple of Understanding; vis. prof. religion Swarthmore Coll., 1982-83, Temple U., 1976-77, 87-88; sec.-treas. Conf. On Peace Rsch. in History, 1969-74. Author: The Limits of Defense, 1962, (with Stanley L. Newman) America in Hiding, 1962, Worried Man's Guide to World Peace, 1963, From Race Riot to Sit-In, 1966, The Freedom Seder, 1969, Running Riot, 1970, The Bush Is Burning, 1971, Godwrestling, 1978, Seasons of Our Joy, 1982, These Holy Sparks, 1983, (with David and Shoshana Waskow) Before There Was a Before, 1984, (with Howard Waskow) Becoming Brothers, 1993, Down-to-Earth Judaism: Food, Money, Sex, and the Rest of Life, 1995, Godwrestling—Round 2: Ancient Wisdom, Future Paths, 1996, (with Phyllis O. Berman) Tales of Tikkun: New Jewish Stories to Heal the Wounded World, 1996; editor: Debate Over Thermonuclear Strategy, 1965, Menorah Jour., 1979—; screenwriter: In Every Generation, 1988; editl. bd. Tikkun, Reconstructionist. Alt. del. Dem. Nat. Conv., 1968; fellow Chs. Ctr. for Theology and Pub. Policy, 1977-82; Gamaliel chair Luth. Student Ctr., Milw., 1996. Coolidge fellow Assn. Religion and Intellectual Life, 1983. Fellow Am. Acad. Arts and Scis. (colloquium on disarmament 1962); mem. Nat. Writers Union, Fabrangen, Nat. Havurah Com. (bd. dirs. 1979-80, 83-87), P'nai Or (bd. dirs. 1984-93, Aleph bd. dirs. 1993-95), Internat. Coord. Com. on Religion and Earth (steering com. 1990-93), Phi Beta Kappa. Address: 6711 Lincoln Dr Philadelphia PA 19119-3119 *For about 500 years the human race has made no "Sabbath" from ceaseless working, making, producing, doing and it therefore has raced to the brink of destroying itself and much of life on the planet. Just as individuals need rhythmic rest, so do societies—a spiritual truth that we should again learn from Torah. Time to be!.*

WASKOW, JOYCE ANN, school administrator; b. Meriden, Iowa, Aug. 15, 1941; d. Clarence Emory and Lucille Dorothy (Horstman) Smith; m. James R. Waskow, July 6, 1963; children: Susan, Brent. BS, Iowa State U., 1963; MA, U. Mo., St. Louis, 1992. Cert. edn. specialist, Mo. Home econs./sci. tchr. Collins (Iowa) H.S., 1963-64; home economist Met. Sewer Dist., Omaha, Nebr., 1964-65; home econs. tchr. Westbrook Jr. H.S., Omaha, 1965-67; home economist The Merchandising Group, N.Y.C., 1970-76; home econs. tchr. Pattonville H.S., St. Louis, 1976-79, Maplewood-Richmond Hts. H.S., St. Louis, 1979-80, Webster Groves H.S., St. Louis, 1980-93; dir. Tchr.'s Acad. Network for Ednl. Devel., St. Louis, 1989-92; asst. prin. Lafayette H.S., St. Louis, 1993—; spkr./workshop leader Network for Edn. Devel., 1987—. Mem. ASCD, Nat. Assn. Secondary Sch. Prins., Am. Home Econs. Assn. (nominating com.), Suburban Home Econs. Assn. (pres. 1986-87), Nat. Assn. Vocat. Home Econs. Tchrs. (Disting. Svc. award 1989), Mo. Home Econs. Tchrs. Assn. (Tchr. of the Yr. 1987, nominating com. 1987-88). Avocations: reading, whitewater rafting, hiking, antiquing, orienteering. Office: Lafayette High School 17050 Clayton Rd Ballwin MO 63011-1792

WASMUTH, CARL ERWIN, physician, lawyer; b. Pitts., Feb. 16, 1916; s. Edwin Hugo and Mary Blanche (Love) W.; m. Martha Conn., Aug. 25, 1939; children: Carl Erwin; m. Gertrude White Ruth, June 19, 1984; m. Wilhelmina Waterman Devine, May 12, 1990. BS, U. Pitts., 1935, MD, 1939; LLB, Cleve.- Marshall Law Sch., 1959. Bar: Ohio bar 1959; diplomate: Am. Bd. Anesthesiology. Intern Western Pa. Hosp., Pitts., 1939-40; fellow anesthesiology Cleve. Clinic Found., 1949-51, mem. emeritus staff, 1976—; pvt. practice medicine Dry Run, Pa., 1942-45, Scottdale, Pa., 1945-49; mem. dep. anesthesia Cleve. Clinic, 1951—, head dept., 1967-69; asso. prof. law Cleve.-Marshall Law Sch., 1959-66; adj. prof. Cleve. Marshall Law Sch., 1966-73. Author: Anesthesia and the Law, 1961, Law for the Physician, 1966, Law and the Surgical Team, 1968; Editor: Legal Problems in the Practice of Anesthesiology, 1973; contbg. editor: Hale's Anesthesiology; editorial bd.: Med. World News; Contbr. articles to profl. jours. Trustee Cleve.- Marshall Law Sch., chmn., 1969-71; bd. dirs. Scottdale Hosp. Found; chmn. bd. govs. Cleve. Clinic, 1969-77; trustee Cleve. Clinic Found., 1969-76, v.p., 1973-76; trustee Cleve. Clinic Ednl. Found., 1969-76, v.p., 1973-76; chmn. bd. trustees, pres. Cleve. Marshall Ednl. Found., 1972-81; bd. overseers Coll. Law, Cleve. State U., 1972-76; vis. com. Coll. Law, Case-Western Res. U., 1973-76; trustee United Torch Svcs., Tucson Symphony Soc., 1983-84, 88; trustee Santa Cruz Med. Found., 1977, pres., 1978; bd. govs. Ohio World Trade Center; trustee Cancer Center Cleve., Ohio Coll. Podiatric Medicine, 1976, Am. Coll. Legal Medicine Research Found., 1984—; mem. U. Ariz. Found., 1978, World Congress Med. Law, 1967—, Keynoter 3d World Congress, 1971; sec. Commn. Med. Malpractice, HEW, 1972-73; vestryman St. Francis-in-the-Valley Episcopal Ch., Green Valley. Named Distinguished Eagle Scout Nat. Council Boy Scouts Am., 1977; named Outstanding Citizen Eagle Cuyahoga council, 1976; Citizen of Year Cleve. Area Bd. Realtors, 1976. Fellow Am. Coll. Anesthesiologists, Am. Coll. Legal Medicine (pres. bd. govs. 1966-69), A.C.P., Am. Coll. Chest Physicians, Law Sci. Acad.; mem. Am. Soc. Anesthesiologists (dir., pres. 1968, speaker ho. of dels.), Ohio Soc. Anesthesiologists (dir. 1960-69), Cleve. Soc. Anesthesiologists (pres. 1963), Internat. Anesthesia Research Soc., World Fedn. Soc. Anesthesiologists (vice chmn. Am. delegation 1967), Acad. Anesthesiology (chmn. program com. 1967), Am., Ohio med. assns., N.Y. Acad. Scis., Nat. Acad. Sci., NRC, Com. Cadaver Utilization, Cleve. Acad. Medicine, AAAS, Transplantation Soc. (charter), Am., Ohio, Cuyahoga County, Cleve. bar assns., Phi Rho Sigma, Delta Theta Phi, Masons, Lions (past pres. local clubs), Old Pueblo Club, Tucson Club, Country of Green Valley Club, Pleasant Valley Country Club, Mt. Kenya Safari Club, Nanyuki, Kenya. Home: 727 W Quail Dr Green Valley AZ 85614-1740

WASS, HANNELORE LINA, educational psychology educator; b. Heidelberg, Germany, Sept. 12, 1926; came to U.S., 1957, naturalized, 1963; d. Hermann and Mina (Lasch) Kraft; m. Irvin R. Wass, Nov. 24, 1959 (dec.); 1 child, Brian C.; m. Harry H. Sisler, Apr. 13, 1978. B.A., Tchrs. Coll., Heidelberg, 1951; M.A., U. Mich., 1960, Ph.D., 1968. Tchr. W. Ger. Univ. Lab. Schs., 1958-60; mem. faculty U. Mich., Ann Arbor, 1958-60, U. Chgo. Lab. Sch., 1960-61, U. Mich., 1963-64, Eastern Mich. U., 1965-69; prof. ednl. psychology U. Fla., Gainesville, 1969-92; prof. emeritus, 1992—; faculty assoc. Ctr. for Gerontol. Studies U. Fla., Gainesville; cons., lectr. in thanatology. Author: The Professional Education of Teachers, 1974, Dying-Facing the Facts, 1979, 2d edit., 1988, 3d edit., 1995, Death Education: An Annotated Resource Guide, 1980, vol. 2, 1985, Helping Children Cope With Death, 1982, 2d edit., 1984, Childhood and Death, 1984; founding editor (jour.) Death Studies, 1977—; cons. editor: Ednl. Gerontology, 1977-92, (book series) Death Education, Aging and Health Care; contbr. approximately 200 articles to profl. jours. and chpts. in books. Mem. Am. Psychol. Assn., Gerontol. Soc., Internat. Work Group Dying, Death and Bereavement (bd. dirs.), Assn. Death Edn. and Counseling. Home: 6014 NW 54th Way Gainesville FL 32653-3265 Office: U Fla 346 Norman Hall Gainesville FL 32611-2053

WASS, WALLACE MILTON, veterinarian, clinical science educator; b. Lake Park, Iowa, Nov. 19, 1929; s. Authur Carl and Esther (Moberg) W.; m. Doreen McCollum, May 31, 1953; children: Karen, Kimberly, Christopher, Kirby. Student, Minn. Jr. Coll., 1947-48; B.S., U. Minn., 1951, D.V.M., 1953, Ph.D., 1961. Diplomate: Am. Coll. Vet. Internal Medicine. Veterinarian Medford Vet. Clinic, Wis., 1953-58; instr. U. Minn. Coll. Vet. Medicine, St. Paul, 1958-63; prof. vet. medicine Iowa State U., Ames, 1964—, head dept. vet. clin. scis., 1964-83, prof., 1983—; cons. U.S. AID, Bogota, Columbia, 1963, U. Yola, Nigeria, 1983; staff veterinarian for med. rsch. sect. Brookhaven Nat. Lab., Upton, N.Y., 1963-64; cons. investigator fur seal harvest U.S. Dept. Commerce, Pribilof Islands, 1971, South Africa, 1974; use of antibiotics in animal feed U.S. FDA, 1972; cons. Farmland Ins. Co., 1971—; spl. cons. Kasetsart U., Bangkok, Thailand, 1974, Min. of Edn., Thailand, 1994. Contbr. articles, papers in field to profl. lit. Chmn. collegiate-ch. paster parish rels. com. United Methodist Ch., 1979, chmn. stewardship and fin. com., 1982. Served to 1st lt. USAF, 1953-55. Mem. AVMA (del. 1973-88), Iowa Vet. Med. Assn., Central Iowa Vet. Med. Assn. (pres. 1977), Am. Assn. Vet. Clinicians (pres. 1971-73), Phi Kappa Phi (sec. 1984-88, Iowa State U. chpt. pres. 1989-90), Phi Zeta, Alpha Zeta, Gamma Sigma Delta. Club: Wiltco Flying (sec. 1966-74). Home: 2166 Ashmore Dr Ames IA 50014-7840 Office: Iowa State U Dept Vet Clin Scis Ames IA 50011

WASSELL, IRENE MARTIN, food editor; b. Siloam Springs, Ark., Sept. 19, 1931; d. Leslie and Cora Etna (Jones) Martin; m. Bill J. Wassell, Mar. 29, 1953; children: Lisa Annette, Cynthia Lenore, Eric Lyndon. BA, U. Ark., 1978; MA, U. Ark., Little Rock, 1983. Woman's editor The Times of North Little Rock, 1978-80; staff features writer Ark. Gazette, Little Rock, 1980-90, food editor, 1990-91; food editor Ark. Dem.-Gazette, Little Rock, 1992—. Office: Ark Dem Gazette 121 E Capitol Ave Little Rock AR 72201-3819

WASSENICH, LINDA PILCHER, health policy analyst, fund raiser; b. Washington, Aug. 27, 1943; d. Mason Johnson and Vera Bell (Stephenson) Pilcher; m. Mark Wassenich, May 14, 1965; children: Paul Mason, David Mark. BA magna cum laude, Tex. Christian U., 1965; MSW, U. N.C., 1970. Licensed advanced practitioner, cert. social worker, Tex. Counselor family ct. Dallas County Juvenile Dept., Dallas, 1970-73, 75-76; dir. govt. rels. Vis. Nurse Assn., Dallas, 1980-84, exec. officer of hospice, 1984-85; exec. dir. Incest Recovery Assn., Dallas, 1985-86; assoc. exec. dir. Lone Star Coun. Camp Fire, Dallas, 1986-89; exec. v.p. Vis. Nurse Assn. Found., Dallas, 1989-91; dir. policy & resource devel. Vis. Nurse Assn. Tex., Dallas, 1992—. Contbr. articles to profl. publs. Bd. dirs. Women's Coun. Dallas County, 1986-95, pres., 1992-93; chmn. Dallas County Welfare Adv. Bd., 1991-95; bd. dirs. United Way of Met. Dallas, 1992-94, Youth Impact Ctrs., Dallas, 1993-94; mem. adv. bd. Maternal Health and Family Planning Dallas, 1990-94; mem. Leadership Dallas, 1988-89. Recipient AAUW, Dallas, Laurel award, 1995. Mem. NASW (Tex. bd. dirs., nominating chmn. 1990-92, co-chmn. Dallas unit 1981-82, Social Worker of Yr. award 1988), LWV (bd. dirs. Dallas 1974-80, pres. 1995—), Acad. Cert. Social Workers, Nat. Soc.

Fundraising Execs. (cert.; bd. dirs. Dallas chpt. 1994—, v.p. governance 1995-96). Home: 6948 Kenwhite Dr Dallas TX 75231-5640 Office: 1440 W Mockingbird Ln Dallas TX 75247-4929

WASSER, HENRY, retired English educator; b. Pitts., Apr. 13, 1919; s. Nathan and Mollie (Mendelson) W.; m. Solidelle Felicité Fortier, Aug. 20, 1942; children: Michael Frederick (dec.), Eric Anthony (dec.), Frederick Anthony, Felicity Louise. B.A., M.A., Ohio State U., 1940; Ph.D., Columbia U., 1951. Teaching fellow George Washington U., 1940-42; analyst USAAF intelligence, 1941-43; chemist Goodyear Synthetic Rubber Co., 1943-45; from tutor to assoc. prof. City Coll., CUNY, 1946-66; prof. English, dean faculties Richmond Coll., CUNY, 1966-73; v.p. for acad. affairs Calif. State U., Sacramento, 1973-74; prof. English Coll. S.I., CUNY, 1974-89; dir. Center for European Studies, Grad. Sch. CUNY, 1979-93, prof. emeritus of sociology and English, 1989—; Fulbright prof. U. Salonika, Greece, 1955-56; seminar assoc. Columbia U., 1961—, co-=chair, 1982-87, chair, 1987-89; mem. Colloquium on Higher Edn., Yale U., 1974-75; Fulbright prof. Am. Lit. U. Oslo, 1962-64, dir., prof. Am. Inst., 1963-64; vis. prof. U. Sussex, Eng., 1972; lectr. in field, Sweden, Norway, Eng., Germany, Poland, Yugoslavia, Italy, Turkey; Fulbright prof. Am. Lit. and Civilization U. Bergen, Norway, 1989-90, U. Aveiro, Portugal, 1993; rsch. scholar comparative higher edn. CUNY, 1989—. Author: The Scientific Thought of Henry Adams, 1956, (with others) Higher Education in Western Europe and North America: A Selected and Annotated Bibliography, 1979, American Literature and Language: A Selected and Annotated Bibliography, 1980; editor: (with Sigmund Skard) Americana Norvegica; Norwegian Contributions to American Studies, 1968, (with others) The Compleat University, 1983, Problems of the Urban University: A Comparative Perspective, 1984, Impact of Changing Labor Force on Higher Education, 1987; editor (with Ulrich Teichler) German and American Universities: Mutual Influences, 1992; mem. bd. editors History of European Ideas, 1986—, guest editor, summer, 1987; guest editor Higher Edn. Policy, spring, 1994, contbr. articles to newspapers and profl. jours. Faculty trustee CUNY, 1981-86, trustee emeritus, 1986—; bd. dirs. Scandinavian Seminar, 1978-86, sec., 1980-83, vice chmn., 1983-86. Recipient Am. Scandinavian Found. award, 1969, 71, German Acad. Exchange Service award, 1973, 80, Swedish Info. Service award, 1979, Norwegian Ministry of Culture award, 1983, NEH award, 1984, Foscolo medal U. Pavia, Italy, 1986, German Marshall Fund award, 1985, 87, Atheneum medal U. Pavia, Italy, 1988; Finnish Ministry Culture grantee, 1989. Mem. Am. Studies Assn. (pres. Met. N.Y. chpt. 1961-62, mem. nat. exec. council 1968-74), Melville Soc. Am. (historian 1969-74), MLA, Am. Scandinavian Found. (fellow 1971), Internat. Assn. Univ. Profs. English, Assn. Upper Level Colls. and Univs. (2d v.p. 1971-72), Assn. for World Edn. (internat. council), Phi Beta Kappa (sec. City Coll. chpt. 1957-62, 64-67, pres. CUNY Acad. for Humanities and Scis. 1991—), Internat. Conf. Higher Edn. (steering com. 1989—), Henry Adams Soc. (exec. coun. 1994—). Home: 333 E 34th St Apt 16C New York NY 10016-4927 also: 5517 Fieldstone Rd Bronx NY 10471 Office: CUNY Academy Grad Sch 33 W 42d St New York NY 10036

WASSERBURG, GERALD JOSEPH, geology and geophysics educator; b. New Brunswick, N.J., Mar. 25, 1927; s. Charles and Sarah (Levine) W.; m. Naomi Z. Orlick, Dec. 21, 1951; children: Charles David, Daniel Morris. Student, Rutgers U.; BS in Physics, U. Chgo., 1951, MSc in Geology, 1952, PhD, 1954, DSc (hon.), 1992; Dr. Hon. Causa, Brussels U., 1985, U. Paris, 1986; DSc (hon.), Ariz. State U., 1987. Research assoc. Inst. Nuclear Studies, U. Chgo., 1954-55; asst. prof. Calif. Inst. Tech., Pasadena, 1955-59, assoc. prof., 1959-62, prof. geology and geophysics, 1962-82, John D. MacArthur prof. geology and geophysics, 1982—; served on Juneau Ice Field Rsch. Project, 1950; cons. Argonne Nat. Lab., Lamont, Ill., 1952-55; former mem. U.S. Nat. Com. for Geochem., com. for Planetary Exploration Study, NRC, adv. coun. Petroleum Rsch. Fund, Am. Chem. Soc.; me. lunar sample analysis planning team (LSAPT) manned Spacecraft Ctr., NASA, Houston, 1968-71, chmn., 1970; lunar sample rev. bd., 1970-72; mem. Facilities Working Group LSAPT, Johnson Space Ctr., 1972-82; mem. sci. working panel for Apollo missions, Johnson Space Ctr., 1971-73; advisor NASA, 1968-88, phys. scis. com., 1971-75, mem. lunar base steering com., 1984; chmn. com. for planetary and lunar exploration, mem. space sci. bd. NAS, 1975-78; chmn. divsn. Geol. and Planetary Scis., Calif. Inst. Tech., 1987-89; vis. prof. U. Kiel, Fed. Republic of Germany, 1960, Harvard U., 1962, U. Bern, Switzerland, 1966, Swiss Fed. Tech. Inst., 1967, Max Planck Inst., Mainz and Heidelberg, Fed. Republic of Germany, 1985; invited lectr., Vinton Hayes Sr. fellow Harvard U., 1980, Jaeger-Hales lectr. Australian Nat. U., 1980, Harold Jeffreys lectr. Royal Astron. Soc., 1981, Ernst Cloos lectr. Johns Hopkins U., 1984, H.L. Welsh Disting. lectr. U. Toronto, Can., 1986, Danz lectr. U. Washington, 1989, Goldschmidt Centennial lectr. Norwegian Acad. Sci. and Letters, 1989, Lindsay lectr. Goddard Space Flight Ctr., 1996; plenary spkr. 125th Anniversary Geol. Soc. Sweden, 1996; 60th Anniversary Symposium spkr. Hebrew U., Jerusalem, 1985. Served with U.S. Army, 1944-46. Decorated Combat Inf. badge. Recipient Group Achievement award NASA, 1969, Exceptional Sci. Achievement award NASA, 1970, Disting. Pub. Svc. medal NASA, 1973, J.F. Kemp medal Columbia U., 1973, Profl. Achievement award U. Chgo. Alumni Assn., 1978, Goldschmidt medal Geochem. Soc., 1978, Disting. Pub. Svc. medal with cluster NASA, 1978, Wollaston medal Geol. Soc. London, 1985, Sr. Scientist award Alexander von Humboldt-Stiftung, 1985, Crafoord prize Royal Swedish Acad. Scis., 1986, Holmes medal, 1987, Regents fellow Smithsonian Inst., Gold medal Royal Astron. Soc., 1991; named Hon. Fgn. fellow European Union Geoscis., 1983. Fellow Am. Acad. Arts and Scis., Geol. Soc. London (hon.), Am. Geophys. Union (planetology sect., Harry H. Hess medal 1985), Geol. Soc. Am. (life, Arthur L. Day medal 1970), Meteoritical Soc. (pres. 1987-88, Leonard medal 1975); mem. Nat. Acad. Scis. (Arthur L. Day prize and lectureship 1981, J. Lawrence Smith medal 1985), Norwegian Acad. Sci. and Letters, Am. Phil. Soc. Research interests include geochemistry and geophysics and the application of the methods of chemical physics to problems in the earth scis. Major researches have been the determination of the time scales of nucleosynthesis, connections between the interstellar medium and solar material, the time of the formation of the solar system, the chronology and evolution of the earth, moon and meteorites, the establishment of dating methods using long-lived natural radio-activities, the study of geologic and cosmic processes using nuclear and isotopic effects as a tracer in nature, the origin of natural gases, and the application of thermodynamic methods to geologic systems. Office: Calif Inst of Tech Divsn Geol & Planetary Scis Pasadena CA 91125

WASSERMAN, ALBERT, writer, director; b. N.Y.C., Feb. 9, 1921; s. Martin S. and Beatrice (Schaffer) W.; m. Della Newmark, Aug. 5, 1943 (div. Mar. 1965); children—Paul, Vicki; m. Barbara Alson, June 19, 1968. B.S., Coll. City N.Y., 1941. Pres. Wasserman Prodns., Inc., N.Y.C., 1968-75. Writer documentary, ednl. and indsl. films, 1946-53; free lance writer, dir. TV documentary films, 1953-55; staff writer, dir., producer, CBS-TV, 1955-60; producer, dir., writer: NBC News, 1960-67; producer: 60 Minutes, 1976-86; writer, prod., dir.: Out of Darkness; writer film: First Steps; writer, dir. films for: CBS Pub. Affairs Series The Search; prod., writer dir.: NBC White Paper programs; prod., dir.: TV Spl. The Making of the President, 1972; (Sylvania TV award, Robert Flaherty film award, Acad. award 1947, Peabody award CBS Pub. Affairs series.). Recipient Lasker Med. Journalism awards (2); Edinburgh Film Festival silver medal, 1948, George Polk award, 1960, Journalism award Ohio State U., 1961. Mem. Writers Guild Am. East (treas. 1965-66), Dirs. Guild Am. (eastern regional council 1965-66, 69-70). Home: 259 W 11th St New York NY 10014-2414

WASSERMAN, ARNOLD SAUL, academic dean, industrial design executive; b. Washington, June 15, 1934; s. Joseph and Mildred (Jacobs) W. BA in Indsl. Design, Carnegie Mellon U., Pitts., 1956; MA in Design History, U. Chgo., 1965. Project dir. Peter Muller-Munk Assocs., Pitts., 1956-59; asst. dir. Compagnie de l'Esthetique Industrielle, Paris, 1961-63; project dir. Latham, Tyler, Jensen, Inc., Chgo., 1963-68; exec. dir. Product Planning Assocs., Santa Barbara, Calif., 1968-72; pres. Arnold Saul Wasserman Design, Santa Barbara, 1972-79; chmn. bd.., dir. design TAG, Inc., Santa Barbara, 1976-79; dir. corp. indsl. design NCR Corp., Dayton, Ohio, 1979-80; mgr. indsl. design Xerox Corp., various locations, 1980-86; v.p. strategic planning RichardsonSmith, Inc., Columbus, Ohio, 1986-87; v.p. corp. indsl. design and human factors Unisys Corp., Blue Bell, Pa., 1987-91; dean Sch. Art & Design Pratt Inst., Bklyn., 1991—; mem. profl. adv. bd. Carnegie Mellon U., Pitts., 1987-89, Calif. State U., Long Beach, 1987-89, Stanford Design Forum, Palo Alto, 1988-89; design juror NEA, Washington, 1987-91. Author: Ergonomics, 1989. With U.S. Army, 1959-61. Carnegie Mellon U. fellow, 1952-55, U. Chgo. fellow, 1964-65, Ford Found. grantee, 1966, Nat. Endowment for Arts grantee, 1989. Mem. Indsl. Designers Soc. Am. (dir. 1979-80). Avocations: backpacking, art, music, sports. Home: 174 Emerson Pl Brooklyn NY 11205-3803 Office: Pratt Inst # Main-4 Brooklyn NY 11205

WASSERMAN, BARRY L(EE), architect; b. Cambridge, Mass., May 25, 1935; s. Theodore and Adelaide (Levin) W.; m. Wilma Louise Greenfield, June 21, 1957 (div. 1971); children: Tim Andrew, Andrew Glenn; m. Judith Ella Michaelowski, Apr. 22, 1979. B.A., Harvard U., 1957, M. Arch., 1960. Registered architect, Calif. Assoc. John S. Bolles Assocs., San Francisco, 1960-69; prin. Wasserman-Herman Assocs., San Francisco, 1969-72; prin., dir. Office Lawrence Halprin U Assocs., San Francisco, 1972-76; dep. state architect State of Calif., Sacramento, 1976-78, state architect, 1978-83; prof. dept. architecture, dir. Inst. Environ. Design, Sch. Environ. Design Calif. State Poly. U., Pomona, 1983-87, chair dept. architecture, Coll. Environ. Design, 1988—; cons. architecture, Sacramento, 1983—; program advisor Fla. A&M U., Tallahassee, 1981-83. Architect Wasserman House, San Rafael, Calif., 1963 ((AIA-Sunset Mag. award of Merit) 1965-66), Anna Waden Library, San Francisco, 1969 ((AIA award of Merit 1970)), Capitol Area Plan, Sacramento, 1977 (Central Valley chpt. AIA Honor award 1979). Recipient Awards citation Progressive Architecture 26th awards Program, 1979. Fellow AIA chmn. architecture in govt. com. (1979). Democrat. Jewish. Home: 6456 Fordham Way Sacramento CA 95831-2218

WASSERMAN, CHARLES, banker; b. Guayaquil, Ecuador, Aug. 31, 1929; came to U.S., 1948, naturalized, 1960; s. Mendel and Mary Wasserman; m. Jacqueline Royer, Oct. 4, 1960; children: Roger, Mark. BA, Farleigh Dickinson U., 1949; MBA, U. Havana, 1956. Trainee internat. dept. Chase Manhattan Bank, N.Y., 1958-60, Swiss Bank Corp., N.Y., 1960-64; area sr. credit analyst Am. Express Bank, N.Y., 1965-66; exec. v.p. Republic Nat. Bank, N.Y., 1967—, cons. to World Bank, 1989; chmn., pres. Republic Internat. Bank N.Y., L.A., 1988-89; hon. chmn. Meridian Capital Corp. Named Hon. Chmn., Meridian Capital Corp., 1994. Mem. Internat. Exec. Svc. Corps, Internat. Platform Assn. Home: 224 Nassau Ave Manhasset NY 11030-2440 Office: 127 E 59th St Rm 222 New York NY 10022-1225

WASSERMAN, DALE, playwright; b. Rhinelander, Wis., Nov. 2, 1917; s. Samuel and Hilda (Paykel) W. founder, artistic dir. Midwest Profl. Playwrights Lab.; Trustee, founding mem. Eugene O'Neill Theatre Center. Writer, producer, dir. for TV, motion pictures, theatre; author: (with Bruce Geller) musical Livin' the Life, 1957; stage plays The Pencil of God, 1961, 998, 1962, One Flew Over the Cuckoo's Nest, 1963, Man of La Mancha, 1965 (Tony award for best musical 1966, N.Y. Drama Critics' Circle award for best musical 1966, Outer Circle award 1966, Variety award 1966, Spanish Pavilion award 1966, others), Play with Fire, 1978, Great Big River, 1981, Shakespeare and The Indians, 1983; screenplays World of Strangers, 1955, The Vikings, 1958, Two Faces to Go, 1959, Aboard the Flying Swan, 1962, Jangadeiro, 1962, Cleopatra, 1963, Quick, Before It Melts, 1964; writer, co-prodr.: motion pictures Mister Buddwing, 1965, A Walk With Love and Death, 1969, Man of LaMancha, 1972; also numerous TV plays including Elisha and the Long Knives, 1954 (Publishers Guild award 1954), The Fog, 1957 (Writers Guild of Am. award 1957), Eichmann, 1958, Engineer of Death, 1959, The Citadel, 1959 (Writers Guild of Am. award 1959), I, Don Quixote, 1959, (Writers Guild of Am. award 1960), The Power and the Glory, 1960, The Lincoln Murder Case, 1961 (Writers Guild of Am. award 1961), Stranger, 1962, Burden of Proof, 1976, Scheherazade, 1977, The Seventh Dimension, 1984, My Name Is Esther, 1985, The Whole Truth, 1987, Green, 1987, A Fine American Family, 1988, Players in a Game, 1989, Murder Among the Saints, 1989, The Girl From Botany Bay, 1990, (mus.) Western Star, 1992, Beggar's Holiday, 1994; contbr. short stories, articles to Variety and other pubs. Recipient hon. degree U. Wis., 1980. Mem. ALA, Writers Guild Am. East (nat. coun. 1960-64), Writers Guild Am. West, Dramatists Guild, Am. Acad. Motion Picture Arts and Scis., French Soc. Authors and Composers, The Jaques Brel Found. (gov.), Players Club, Monte Cristo Soc. Office: c/o Harold Orenstein Atty 157 W 57th St New York NY 10019-2210

WASSERMAN, EDWARD ARNOLD, psychology educator; b. L.A., Apr. 2, 1946; s. Albert Leonard and May (Sabin) W. BA, UCLA, 1968; PhD, Ind. U., 1972. Postdoctoral fellow U. Sussex, Brighton, Eng., 1972; from asst. prof. to prof. psychology U. Iowa, Iowa City, 1972-83, prof., 1983—. Contbr. articles to profl. jours., chpts. to books; assoc. editor several jours. Bd. dirs. Big Bros., Big Sisters, Johnson County, Iowa, 1982-85. Ind. U. fellow, 1968, U. Iowa fellow, 1975, 82, NAS fellow, former USSR, 1976, James Van Allen Natural Scis. fellow, 1994-95. Fellow APA, Am. Psychol. Soc.; mem. Psychonomic Soc., Midwestern Psychol. Assn., Phi Beta Kappa. Office: U Iowa Dept Psychology Iowa City IA 52242

WASSERMAN, FRED, III, internist; b. Phila., May 17, 1955; m. Susan Valesky; 1 child, Sara Elisabeth. MBA, U. South Fla., 1990; MD, U. Miami, 1981. Diplomate Am. Bd. Internal Medicine. Resident in gen. surgery U. Miami (Fla.) Affiliated Hosps., 1981-82; resident in internal medicine Baylor Coll. Medicine Affiliated Hosps., Houston, 1982-85; chief med. officer, clin. of jurisdiction Dept. Vets. Affairs Bay Pines (Fla.) VA Med. Ctr., 1991—. Mem. ACP, Am. Coll. Physician Execs. Office: Dept Vets Affairs Bay Pines VAMC Bay Pines FL 33504

WASSERMAN, HARRY HERSHAL, chemistry educator; b. Boston, Mass., Dec. 1, 1920; s. Maurice Leonard and Rebecca (Franks) W.; m. Elga Ruth Steinherz, June 1, 1947; children: Daniel M., Diana R., Steven A. BS, MIT, 1941; MA, Harvard U., 1942, PhD, 1949; MA (hon.), Yale U., 1962. Rsch. asst. O.S.R.D. Penicillin Project, 1945; instr., asst. prof. dept. chemistry Yale U., New Haven, Conn., 1948-57, assoc. prof. dept. chemistry, 1957-62, prof. dept. chemistry, 1962-82, Eugene Higgins prof. chemistry, 1982-91; Eugene Higgins prof. chemistry emeritus, 1991—; cons. Union Carbide Corp., 1956-66, Sandoz Corp., 1966-=74, SmithKline Beckman Corp., 1974-80, Ortho Pharms., 1980-94; bd. dirs. Camille and Henry Dreyfus Found. Author numerous articles on organic chemistry in sci. jours. Capt. USAF, 1942-45. Recipient William Devane Tchr.-Scholar award Phi Beta Kappa, 1977, Catalyst Teaching award Chem. Mfrs. Assn., 1985, Oustanding Tchr. award Yale U., 1985, Aldrich Synthetic Chemistry award, Am. Chem. Soc., 1987, Arthur Cope scholar award, 1990. Mem. NAS, Am. Acad. Scis., Conn. Acad. Scis. Avocation: watercolor painting. Home: 192 Bishop St New Haven CT 06511-3718 Office: Yale U Dept Chemistry 225 Prospect St New Haven CT 06512-1958

WASSERMAN, HELENE WALTMAN, art dealer, artist; b. Phila., Jan. 29, 1929; d. William T. and Bertha (Brener) Waltman; m. Richard M. Wasserman, June 23, 1950 (div. 1972); children: Ann Zelver, Ellen Rubinfield, Stephen; m. Mark C. Cooper, Jan. 22, 1988. BFA, U. Pa., 1951. Pvt. practice art dealer, 1972—; apptd. appraiser Supreme Ct., State of N.Y., 1978. One-woman shows at Philmont Gallery, Phila., 1964, Roko Gallery, N.Y., 1965; exhibited in group shows at Phila. Mus. Art, Pa. Acad. Fine Arts, Philbrook Mus., Tulsa, Woodmere Gallery, Roko Gallery, 1953-68. Active Nassau County Art Commn., 1968-72; trustee, Sculpture Ctr., N.Y.C., bd. dirs., 1991. Mem. Pvt. Art Dealers Assn., Cosmopolitan Club, Nature Conservancy. Avocations: painting, sculpting, garden design.

WASSERMAN, LAWRENCE HARVEY, research astronomer; b. Bronx, N.Y., Oct. 19, 1945; married, 1970; 3 children. BS, Rensselaer Poly. Inst., 1967; MS, Cornell U., 1971, PhD in Astronomy, 1973. Rsch. assoc. in astronomy Lab. Planetary Studies Cornell U., 1973-74; fellow Lowell Observatory, Flagstaff, Ariz., 1974-77, astronomer, 1977—. Mem. Am. Astron. Soc., Sigma Xi. Office: 1400 W Mars Hill Rd Flagstaff AZ 86001*

WASSERMAN, LEW R., film, recording and publishing company executive; b. Cleve., Mar. 15, 1913; m. Edith T. Beckerman, July 5, 1936; 1 dau., Lynne Kay. D (hon.), Brandeis U., NYU. Nat. dir. advt. and publicity Music Corp. Am., 1936-38, v.p., 1938-39, became v.p. charge motion picture div., 1940; now chmn., chief exec. officer, dir., mem. exec. com. MCA, Inc., also chmn. bd., chief exec. officer, dir. subsidiary corps.; now chmn. emeritus; chmn. emeritus Assn. Motion Picture and TV Producers. Trustee John F. Kennedy Libr., John F. Kennedy Ctr. Performing Arts, Jules Stein Eye Inst., Carter Presdl. Ctr., Lyndon Baines Johnson Found.; pres. Hollywood Canteen Found.; chmn. Rsch. to Prevent Blindness Found.; hon. chmn. bd. Ctr. Theatre Group L.A. Music Ctr.; bd. dirs. Amateur Athletic Found. of L.A. (chmn. fin. com.), L.A. Music Ctr. Found.; bd. gov.'s Ronald Reagan Presdl. Found. Recipient Jean Hersholt Humanitarian award Acad. Motion Picture Arts and Scis., 1973. Democrat. Office: Universal City Studios Inc 100 Universal City Plz Universal City CA 91608*

WASSERMAN, LOUIS ROBERT, physician, educator; b. N.Y.C., July 11, 1910; s. Jacob and Ethel (Ballin) W.; m. Julia B. Wheeler, Feb. 20, 1957. A.B., Harvard U., 1931; M.D., U. Chgo., 1935. Diplomate: Am. Bd. Internal Medicine. Intern Michael Reese Hosp., Chgo., 1935-37; research fellow hematology Mt. Sinai Hosp., N.Y.C., 1937-39; research asst. Mt. Sinai Hosp., 1940-42, dir. dept. hematology, 1953-72, hematologist to hosp., 1950-72; research fellow med. physics U. Cal. at Berkeley, 1946-48, cons. radiation labs., 1948-51; asst. prof. Columbia Coll. Phys. and Surg., 1950-60, asso. clin. prof., 1960-66; prof. medicine Mt. Sinai Sch. Medicine, 1966-72, chmn. dept. clin. sci., 1967-72, Distinguished Service prof., 1972-79, emeritus, 1979—, Albert A. and Vera G. List prof. medicine (hematology), 1977-79, emeritus, 1979—; Research collaborator Brookhaven Nat. Labs., 1960-71; cons. practice specializing in hematology, N.Y.C., 1950—; Mem. nat. cancer planning com., chmn. polycythemia vera study group Nat. Cancer Inst., NIH, 1967—, mem. diagnostic research adv. com., 1972-75, co-chmn., 1975-77, chmn. bd. sci. counselors div. cancer treatment, 1974-76. Served to maj. AUS, 1942-46. Fellow ACP, AMA, N.Y. Acad. Medicine, N.Y. Acad. Sci., Internat. Soc. Hematology (v.p. 1972, counselor at-large 1973—); mem. Assn. Am. Physicians, Am. Soc. Hematology (exec. com. 1964-66, pres. 1968-69, adv. council 1969-74), Soc. Nuclear Medicine, Societe de Hopitaux de Paris, Soc. Exptl. Biology and Medicine, Harvey Soc., Soc. Study Blood, Am. Fedn. Clin. Research, Am. Soc. Clin. Nutrition, Am. Assn. Cancer Research, Am. Soc. Clin. Oncology, Reticulo-Endothelial Soc., Alpha Omega Alpha. Office: Mt Sinai Hosp 19 E 98th St New York NY 10029-6501

WASSERMAN, PAUL, library and information science educator; b. Newark, Jan. 8, 1924; s. Joseph and Sadie (Ringelescu) W.; m. Krystyna Ostrowska, 1973; children: Jacqueline R., Steven R. BBA, Coll. City N.Y., 1948; MS in L.S., Columbia, 1949, MS, 1950; PhD, U. Mich., 1960; postgrad., Western Res. U., 1963-64. Advt. mgr. Zuckerberg Co., N.Y.C., 1946-48; asst. to bus. libr. Bklyn. Pub. Library, 1949-51, chief sci. and industry div., 1951-53; librarian, asst. prof. Grad. Sch. Bus. and Pub. Adminstrn., Cornell U., 1953-56, libr., assoc. prof., 1956-62, librarian, prof., 1962-65; dean U. Md. Coll. Library and Info. Scis., 1965-70, prof., 1970—; vis. prof. U. Mich., summers 1960, 63, 64, Asian Inst. Tech., U. Hawaii, U. Hong Kong, summer 1988, Chulalongkorn U., Bangkok, 1990, U. Wash., summer 1991, U. Wis., summer 1991, U. Wis., summer 1992, C.W. Post Coll., L.I. U., 1993, Inst. Sci. and Tech. China, Beijing, 1996; Isabel Nichol lectr. Denver U. Libr. Sch., 1968; market rsch. cons. Laux Advt., Inc., 1955-59, Gale Rsch. Co., Detroit, 1959-60, 63-64; rsch. planning cons. Ind. U. Sch. Bus., 1961-62; cons. to USPHS as mem. manpower tng. rev. com. Nat. Libr. Medicine, 1966-69, Ohio Bd. Regents, 1969, Omngraphics Inc., 1988-91, VITA, summer 1987; dir. Documentation Abstracts, Inc., 1970-73, v.p., 1971-73; Fulbright prof. Warsaw U., 1993-94. Author: Information for Adminstrators, 1956, (with Fred Silander) Decision Making, 1958, Measurement and Evaluation of Organization Performance, 1959, Sources of Commodity Prices, 1960, 2d edit., 1974, Sources for Hospital Administrators, 1961, Decision Making: An Annotated Bibliography, supplement, 1958-63, 1964, Librarian and the Machine, 1965; Book rev. editor: Adminstrv. Sci. Quar, 1956-61; editor: Service to Business, 1952-53, Directory of University Research Bureaus and Institutes, 1960, Health Organizations of the U.S. and Canada, 1961, and 2d to 4th edit., 1977, Statistics Sources, 1962 and 4th to 8th edits., 1984, (with Bundy) Reader in Library Adminstration, 1968, Reader in Research Methods in Librarianship, 1969; mng. editor: Mgmt. Information Guide Series, 1963-83, Consultants and Consulting Organizations, 1966, 4th edit., 1979, 5th edit., 1982, Who's Who in Consulting, 1968, 2d edit., 1974, Awards, Honors and Prizes: A Sourcebook and Directory, 1969, 2d edit., 1972, 4th edit. Vol. 1, 1978, International and Foreign Awards, 1975, New Consultants, 1973-74, 76-77, 78-79, Readers in Librarianship and Information Science, 1968-78, Ency. Bus. Information Sources, 1971, 3d edit., 1976, 4th edit., 1980, 5th edit., 1983, Library and Information Services Today, 1971-75, Consumer Sourcebook, 1974, 2d edit., 1978, 3d edit., 1980, 4th edit., 1983; series editor: Contributions in Librarianship and Information Science, 1969—; coordinating mgmt. editor: Information Guide Library, 1971-83, The New Librarianship-A Challenge for Change, 1972; mng. editor: Museum Media, 1973, Library Bibliographies and Indexes, 1975, Ethnic Groups in the United States, 1976, 2d edit., 1982, Training and Development Organizations, 1978, 2d edit., 1983, Speakers and Lecturers: How to Find Them, 1979, 2d edit., 1982, Learning Independently, 1979, 2d edit., 1983, Recreation and Outdoor Life Directory, 1979, Law and Legal Information Directory, 1980, 2d edit., 1982, Ency. Health Info. Sources, 1986, Ency. Sr. Citizen Info. Sources, 1987, Ency. Pub. Affairs Info. Sources, 1987, Ency. Legal Info. Sources, 1987; mem. editorial bd. Social Scis. Citation Index, Inst. Scientific Info., 1972—, Jour. Library Adminstrn., 1979-89, Social Sci. Info. Studies, 1979—, 1991 Education for Info.: The Internat. Rev. of Education and Tng. in Library and Info. Sci., 1983-88. Active U.S. Com. on Edn. and Tng. for Internat. Fedn. for Info. and Documentation, 1993-94. Served with U.S. Army, 1943-46. Decorated Purple Heart, Bronze Star; Fulbright scholar, Sri Lanka, 1986-87. Mem. AAUP, ALA, Am. Soc. Info. Sci., Spl. Librs. Assn. (editor, chmn. publ. project.). Home: 4940 Sentinel Dr Apt 203 Bethesda MD 20816-3552 Office: U Md Coll Libr and Info Svcs College Park MD 20742

WASSERMAN, RICHARD LEO, lawyer; b. Balt., Aug. 6, 1948; s. Jack B. and Claire (Gutman) W.; m. Manuele Delbourgo, May 13, 1973; children: Alexander E., Lauren E. AB, Princeton U., 1970; JD, Columbia U., 1973. Bar: N.Y. 1975, Md. 1978, U.S. Dist. Ct. (so. and ea. dists.) N.Y. 1975, U.S. Dist. Ct. Md. 1978, U.S. Ct. Appeals (2d cir.) 1975, U.S. Ct. Appeals (4th cir.) 1979, U.S. Supreme Ct. 1982. Law clk. to hon. Roszel C. Thomsen U.S. Dist. Ct. Md., Balt., 1973-74; assoc. Proskauer Rose Goetz & Mendelsohn, N.Y.C., 1974-78; assoc. Venable, Baetjer & Howard, Balt., 1978-81, ptnr., 1982—. Mem. ABA (bus. bankruptcy com.), Md. Bar Assn. (sec. coun. bus. law sect. 1989-92), Bar Assn. Balt. City (chmn. banking, bankruptcy and bus. law com. 1987-88), Bankruptcy Bar Assn. Dist. Md. (bd. dirs. 1988—, pres. 1990-91), Assn. Bar City N.Y., Am. Bankruptcy Inst., Princeton U. Alumni Assn. Md. (bd. dirs. 1980—, pres. 1985-87), Suburban Club Baltimore County (bd. govs. 1982-89, 94—, 2d v.p. 1986-87, sec. 1987-88, pres.-elect 1994-95, pres. 1995—). Democrat. Jewish. Avocations: tennis, bridge. Office: Venable Baetjer & Howard 1800 Mercantile Bank Bldg Baltimore MD 21201

WASSERMAN, ROBERT HAROLD, biology educator; b. Schenectady, Feb. 11, 1926; s. Joseph and Sylvia (Rosenberg) W.; m. Marilyn Mintz, June 11, 1950; children: Diane Jean, Arlene Lee, Judith Rose. B.S., Cornell U., 1949, Ph.D., 1953; M.S., Mich. State U., 1951. Research assoc. AEC project U. Tenn., Oak Ridge, 1953-55; sr. scientist med. div. Oak Ridge Inst. Nuclear Studies, 1955-57; asso. prof. dept. phys. biology N.Y. State Vet. Coll., Cornell U., 1957-63, prof., 1963—, James Law prof. physiology, 1989—, acting head phys. biology dept., 1963-64, 71, 75-76, chmn. dept. / sect. physiology, 1983-87, mem. exec. com. div. biol. sci., 1983-87; vis. fellow Inst. Biol. Chemistry, Copenhagen, 1964-65; chmn. Conf. on Calcium Transport, 1962; co-chmn. Conf. on Cell Mechanisms for Calcium Transfer and Homeostasis, 1970; mem. adv. bd. Vitamin D Symposia, 1976—; mem. adv. bd. Symposia Calcium-Binding Proteins, 1977-88, chmn., 1977; mem. food and nutrition bd. NRC; cons. NIH, Oak Ridge Inst. Nuclear Studies; mem. pub. affairs com. Fedn. Am. Socs. Exptl. Biology, 1974-77 ; chmn. com. MPI, NRC. Bd. editors: Calcified Tissue Research, 1977-80, Procs. Soc. Exptl. Biol. Medicine, 1970-76, Cornell Veterinarian, Jour. Nutrition; contbr.: articles to profl. jours. Served with U.S. Army, 1944-45. Recipient Mead Johnson award, 1969, Andre Lichtwitz prize INSERM, 1982, W.F. Neuman award Am. Soc. Bone and Mineral Rsch., 1990, merit award NIH, 1993-96; Guggenheim fellow, 1964-65, 72, fellow NSF-OECD, 1964-65. Fellow Am. Inst. Nutrition, mem. Am. Physiol. Soc., Soc. Exptl. Biology and Medicine, AAAS, Nat. Acad. Scis., Sigma Xi, Phi Kappa Phi, Phi Zeta. Home: 207 Texas Ln Ithaca NY 14850-1758

WASSERMAN, STEPHEN IRA, physician, educator; b. Los Angeles, Dec. 17, 1942; m. Linda Morgan; children: Matthew, Zachary. BA, Stanford U., 1964; MD, UCLA, 1968. Diplomate Am. Bd. Internal Medicine, Am. Bd.

Allergy and Immunology. Intern, resident Peter B. Brigham Hosp., Boston, 1968-70; fellow in allergy, immunology Robert B. Brigham Hosp., Boston, 1972-75; asst. prof. medicine Harvard U., Boston, 1975-79, assoc. prof., 1979; assoc. prof. U. Calif.-San Diego, La Jolla, 1979-85, prof., 1985—, chief allergy tng. program Sch. Medicine, 1979-85, chief allergy div. Sch. Medicine, 1985-93, acting chmn. dept. medicine, 1986-88, chmn. dept. medicine, 1988—, Helen M. Ranney prof., 1992—; co-dir. allergy sect. Robert B. and Peter B. Brigham Hosps., 1977-79; dir. Am. Bd. Allergy and Immunology, Am. Bd. Internal Medicine. Contbr. articles to profl. jours. Served to lt. comdr. USPHS, 1970-72, San Francisco. Fellow Am. Acad. Allergy and Immunology; mem. Am. Soc. Clin. Investigation, Assn. Am. Physicians, Am. Assn. Immunologists, Collegium INternationale Allergologicum, Phi Beta Kappa, Alpha Omega Alpha. Office: U Calif Med Ctr 402 Dickinson St Ste 380 San Diego CA 92103-6902

WASSERMAN, STEPHEN M., communications manager; b. Chgo., Apr. 26, 1945; s. Samuel Isreal and Rayna (Krassner) W.; m. Faye Rita Samuelson, Oct. 17, 1971; children: Rayna, Alyssa. BA in Journalism, Bradley U., 1967. Mgr. corp. comms. Underwriter Labs., Inc., Northbrook, Ill., 1991—; mem. pub. rels. and fundraising com. Ill. Math. & Sci. Acad., Aurora, 1992—; comms. chair Nat. Electric Safety Found., Washington, 1994—. campaign chmn. United Way, Buffalo Grove, Ill., 1991-93, pres., 1994-95. Mem. Nat. Press Club. Office: Underwriter Labs Inc 333 Pfingsten Rd Northbrook IL 60062-2002

WASSERMAN, STEVE, publisher; b. Vancouver, Wash., Aug. 3, 1952; s. Abraham and Ann (Dragoon) W.; m. Michelle Krisel, Mar. 7, 1982; children: Claire, Paul, Isaac. AB in Criminology, U. Calif., Berkeley, 1974. Asst. editor City Mag. of San Francisco, 1975-76; dep. editor opinion sect. Los Angeles Times, 1977-83; editor in chief New Republic Books The New Republic, N.Y.C., 1984-87; pub. Hill and Wang div. Farrar, Straus and Giroux Inc., N.Y.C., 1987-90, The Noonday Press div. Farrar, Straus and Giroux Inc., N.Y.C., 1987-90; editorial dir. Times Books divsn. Random House, N.Y.C., 1990—; cons. editor The Threepenny Rev., Berkeley, Calif., 1980-86, Tikkun, Oakland, Calif., 1986-90. Contbr. articles and revs. to mags. and newspapers. Mem. PEN. Office: Times Books/Random House 201 E 50th St New York NY 10022-7703

WASSERMAN, SUSAN VALESKY, accountant; b. St. Petersburg, Fla., June 5, 1956; d. Charles B. Valesky and Jeanne I. (Schulz) Morgan; m. Fred Wasserman III, May 19, 1990; 1 child, Sara Elisabeth. BS in Merchandising, Fla. State U., 1978; BA in Acctg., U. South Fla., 1983; ChFC, Am. Coll., 1991. CPA, Fla.; ChFC, Fla. Mgmt. trainee Burdines Dept. Stores, Miami, Fla., 1978-79; store mgr. Levi Straus Inc., San Francisco, 1979; pvt. practice St. Petersburg, Fla., 1980—; internet practice, 1996—. Paintings shown at Longboat Key (Fla.) Art Ctr. Watercolor 10 Art Show, 1993, Fla. Suncoast Watercolor Soc. Aqueous Show, Sarasota, 1994. Mem. AICPA (personal fin. specialist), Am. Soc. CLUs and ChFCs (bd. dirs.), Fla. Inst. CPAs. Avocation: watercolor painting. Office: PO Box 406 Terra Ceia FL 34250

WASSERSPRING, FREDRIC ROY, securities trader; b. Bklyn., Jan. 12, 1947; s. Harold and Pearl W.; m. Barbara Grossman, Dec. 21, 1969; children: Karen, Amy. BS, U. R.I., 1969; MBA, NYU, 1970. CPA, N.Y. Acct. Peat Marwick Mitchell, N.Y.C., 1970-74; v.p. Prudential-Bache Securities, N.Y.C., 1974-81; exec. v.p. Prudential-Bache Metal Co., Inc., N.Y.C., 1981-93, pres. and COO, 1993—; securities advisor Michael Anthony Jewelers Inc. Trustee Village of Saddle Rock (N.Y.), 1986—. Office: Michael Anthony Jewelers Inc 115 S Macquesten Pky Mount Vernon NY 10550

WASSERSTEIN, BERNARD MANO JULIUS, historian; b. London, Jan. 22, 1948; came to U.S., 1980; s. Abraham and Margaret (Ecker) W.; m. Janet Barbara Sherrard, Nov. 29, 1981; 1 child, Charlotte Sophia. BA, Oxford U., 1969, MA, 1972, D.Phil., 1974. Rsch. fellow in politics Nuffield Coll. Oxford (Eng.) U., 1973-75, jr. lectr. politics Magdalen Coll., 1973, lectr. politics and internat. rels. Corpus Christi Coll., 1974-76; lectr. modern history U. Sheffield, Eng., 1976-80; assoc. prof. history Brandeis U., Waltham, Mass., 1980-82, prof. history, 1982-96; pres. Oxford Centre for Hebrew and Jewish Studies, Waltham, Mass., 1996—; chmn. dept. Brandeis U., Waltham, Mass., 1986-90, dean grad. sch., 1990-92; vis. lectr. Hebrew U. of Jerusalem, 1979-80. Author: The British in Palestine, 1978, Britain and the Jews of Europe, 1939-45, 1979, The Secret Lives of Trebitsch Lincoln, 1988 (Golden Dagger award 1988), Herbert Samuel: A Political Life, 1992, Vanishing Diaspora, 1996. Inst. for Advanced Studies fellow Hebrew U. of Jerusalem, 1984-85. Fellow Royal Hist. Soc., Royal Asiatic Soc.; mem. United Oxford Club, Cambridge Univs. Club, Athanaeum (London).

WASSERSTEIN, WENDY, playwright; b. Bklyn., Oct. 18, 1950; d. Morris and Lola W. BA, Mt. Holyoke Coll., 1971; MA, CCNY, 1973; MFA, Yale Drama Sch., 1976. Author: (plays) Any Woman Can't, 1973, Happy Birthday, Montpelier Pizz-zazz, 1974, (with Christopher Durang) When Dinah Shore Ruled the Earth, 1975, Uncommon Women and Others, 1975, Isn't It Romantic, 1981, Tender Offer, 1983, The Man in a Case, 1986, Miami, 1986, The Heidi Chronicles, 1988 (Pulitzer prize for drama 1989, Outer Critics Cir. award for best play 1989, N.Y. Drama Critics Cir. award 1989, Susan Smith Blackburn prize 1989), The Sisters Rosenzweig, 1991 (Outer Critics Cir. award 1993); (essays) Bachelor Girls, 1990; (screenplays) Uncommon Women and Others, 1978, The Sorrows of Gin, 1979, (with Durang) House of Husbands, Isn't It Romantic, The Heidi Chronicles; (children's book) Pamela's First Musical. Bd. dirs. Channel Thirteen MacDowell Colony, British Am. Arts. Assn. Am. Playwrights Project grantee, 1988, Brit.-Am. Arts Assn. grantee, Hale Matthews Found. award, Commissioning Program Phoenix Theater grantee, Guggenheim fellow, 1983. Mem. Coun. Dramatists Guild.

WASSHAUSEN, DIETER CARL, systematic botanist; b. Jena, Germany, Apr. 15, 1938; came to U.S., 1950, naturalized, 1957; s. Heinz P. and Elizabeth A. (Mueller) W.; m. Merrilee M. Locklin, Dec. 23, 1961; children—Lisa A., David B. B.S., George Washington U., 1962, M.S., 1965, Ph.D., 1972. Assoc. curator dept. botany Smithsonian Instn., Washington, 1969-76; chmn., curator dept. botany Nat. Mus. Natural History, Washington, 1976—. Recipient Smithsonian Research Found. awards, 1974, 75, Willdenow medal, 1979. Mem. Am. Soc. Plant Taxonomists, Internat. Assn. Plant Taxonomy, Neotropical Field Botanists Assn., Am. Inst. Biol. Scis., AAAS, Assn. Tropical Biology, Sigma Xi. Presbyterian. Research on systematics of neotropical Acanthaceae, floristic studies in Graminea of Brazil, floristic studies in Begoniaceae, revision of Nat. List Sci. Plant Names. Home: 9406 Chatteroy Pl Gaithersburg MD 20879-1424 Office: Nat Mus Natural History 10th St and Constitution Ave NW Washington DC 20560

WASSNER, STEVEN JOEL, pediatric nephrologist, educator; b. N.Y.C., Dec. 16, 1946; s. Abraham and Clara (Weitzner) W.; m. Enid K. Kling, June 11, 1972; children: Adam Jacob, Nancy Shane. B.S., CCNY, 1968; M.D., NYU, 1972. Diplomate Am. Bd. Pediatrics , Am. Bd. Pediatrics Nephrology. Intern, resident Children's Hosp. Los Angeles, 1972-74, fellow in pediatric nephrology, 1974-75; research fellow in pediatric nephrology U. Calif.-San Francisco, 1975-77; asst. prof. pediatrics Pa. State U. M.S. Hershey Med. Ctr., Hershey, 1978-83, assoc. prof. pediatrics, 1983-91, prof. pediatrics, 1991—, vice chmn. dept. pediatrics, 1990—, chief div. pediatrics nephrology, 1978—, chief div. pediatric diabetes, 1991—; vis. prof. human biochemistry Hebrew U., Hadassah Hosp., 1985-86; dir. Pediatric Diabetes Svc., 1988-91; bd. dirs. dialysis program for Pa. State U. students. Contbr. articles to med. jours. Mem. adv. bd. Kidney Found. South Ctrl. Pa., Harrisburg, 1980-90, sci. adv. coun. for pediatric nephrology/urology Nat. Kidney Found., 1986-92, Harrisburg com. for Hebrew U.; bd. dirs. Jewish Family Svc., Harrisburg, 1979-85, United Jewish Fedn., 1983-85, 94—, Yeshiva Acad., 1987-90. Recipient Rsch. Career Devel. award NIH, 1983; Musclar Dystrophy Assn. grantee, 1979-81; Sr. Internat. fellow Fogarty Internat. Ctr. NIH, 1985. Fellow Am. Acad. Pediatrics, Am. Bd. Pediatrics; mem. Am. Pediatrics Soc., Soc. Pediatric Rsch., Am. Soc. Nephrology, Internat. Soc. Nephrology, Am. Soc. Pediatr, Nephrology, Am. Physiol. Soc., Am. Diabetes Assn., Internat. Soc. Pediatric Nephrology, Internat. Pediatric Nephrology Assn. (counsellor 1989-95). Office: MS Hershey Med Ctr PO Box 850 Hershey PA 17033-0850

WASSON, RICHARD HOWARD, English language educator; b. Chgo., Oct. 7, 1930; s. Robert Rock W. and Anna Hilbert Witt; m. Audrey Dohmeyer, 1956 (div. 1971); 1 child, Kristen Anna Wasson-Mirskin. BA, Cornell Coll., 1952; MA, U. Iowa, 1956; PhD, U. Wisc., 1962. Profl. Cert. English. Instr. U. W.Va., Morgantown, 1956-57; teaching asst. U. Wis., Madison, 1956-62; asst. prof. U. Ill., Champaign, Urbana, 1962-70; prof. Rutgers U., New Brunswick, N.J., 1970—, now prof. emeritus; freshman com. dir. Rutgers U., 1977-81. Recipient Georgina Smith award for Creative and Disting. Leadership, 1992. Mem. AAUP (grievance chair 1987, 89, 92-95, pres. New Brunswick chpt. 1990-93), MLA. Home: 12 Talbot Somerset NJ 08873 Office: Rutgers U English Dept New Brunswick NJ 08903

WATABE, NORIMITSU, biology and marine science educator; b. Kure, Hiroshima, Japan, Nov. 29, 1922; came to U.S., 1957; s. Isamu and Matsuko (Takamatsu) W.; m. Sakuko Kobayashi, Dec. 12, 1952; children: Shoichi, Sachiko. BS, 1st Nat. High Sch., Tokyo, 1945; MS, Tohoku U., Sendai, Japan, 1948, DSc, 1960. Rsch. investigator Fuji Pearl Co., Mie-ken, Japan, 1948-52; instr. Prefect U. Mie, Tsu, Mie-ken, Japan, 1952-55, asst. prof., 1955-59; rsch. assoc. Duke U., Durham, N.C., 1957-70; assoc. prof. U. S.C., Columbia, 1970-72, prof. biology, marine sci., 1972-93, disting. prof., 1993-94; disting. prof. emeritus, 1994—. dir. Electron Microscopy Ctr., 1970-95; cons. in field. Author: Studies on Pearls, 1959. Editor: Mechanisms of Mineralization, 1976; Mechanisms of Biomineralization, 1980, Hard Tissue Mineralization and Demineralization, 1991. Contbr. numerous sci. articles to profl. jours. Recipient Pearl Research award Elmer W. Ellsworth, 1952, Alexander Von Humboldt award Govt. of Germany, 1976, Russel award U. S.C., 1981; grantee NIH, 1971-76, NSF, 1973-95. Fellow AAAS, Royal Micros. Soc. Gt. Britain; mem. Am. Micros. Soc. (rev. bd.), Am. Malacological Union (rev. bd.), Am. Soc. Zoologists, Micros. Soc. Am. Avocations: music; piano playing. Home: 3510 Greenway Dr Columbia SC 29206-3416 Office: Dept Biol Sci Univ S Carolina Columbia SC 29208

WATANABE, AUGUST MASARU, physician, scientist, medical educator, corporate executive; b. Portland, Oreg., Aug. 17, 1941; s. Frank H. and Mary Y. W.; m. Margaret Whildin Reese, Mar. 14, 1964; children: Nan Reiko, Todd Franklin, Scott Masaru. B.S., Wheaton (Ill.) Coll., 1963; M.D., Ind. U., 1967. Diplomate: Am. Bd. Internal Medicine. Intern Ind. U. Med. Center, Indpls., 1967-68; resident Ind. U. Med. Center, 1968-69, 71-72, fellow in cardiology, 1972-74; clin. asso. NIH, 1969-71; clin. instr. medicine Georgetown U. Med. Sch., Washington, 1970-71; mem. faculty Ind. U. Sch. Medicine, Indpls., 1972—, prof. medicine and pharmacology, 1978—, chmn. dept. medicine, 1983-90; dir. Regenstrief Inst. for Health Care Ind. U. Sch. of Medicine, Indpls., 1984-90; v.p. Lilly Rsch. Labs. Eli Lilly & Co., Indpls., 1990-92, group v.p. Lilly Rsch. Labs., 1992-94, pres. labs, 1994—; v.p. Eli Lilly and Co., Indpls., 1994—, also bd. dirs., 1994—; mem. pharmacology study sect. NIH, 1979-81, chmn., 1981-83; mem. cardiovasc.-renal adv. com. FDA, 1982-85; mem. com. A, Nat. Heart, Lung and Blood Inst., 1984-88, chmn., 1986-88; cons. to fed. govt. and industry. Contbr. articles to profl. jours.; editorial bds. sci. jours. Served with USPHS, 1969-71. NIH grantee, 1972-92. Fellow ACP, Am. Coll. Cardiology, Am. Heart Assn. (councils on clin. cardiology and circulation, research rev. com. Ind. affiliate 1978-82, research and adv. com. North Central region 1978-82, adv. com. cardiovascular drugs 1976-79, chmn. com. 1979-81, chmn. program com. council on basic sci. 1982-84, chmn. com. on sci. sessions programs 1985-88, bd. dirs. 1985-88), Am. Coll. Cardiology (govt. relations com. 1979-81, trustee 1982-87); mem. Am. Fedn. Clin. Research (councilor Midwest sect. 1976-77, chmn.-elect Midwest sect. 1977-78, chmn. sect. 1978-79, chmn. sect. nominating com. 1979-80), Am. Soc. Clin. Investigation, Am. Soc. Clin. Pharmacology and Therapeutics, Am. Soc. Pharmacology and Exptl. Therapeutics (exec. com. div. clin. pharmacology 1978-81), Cardiac Muscle Soc., Central Soc. Clin. Research (councillor 1983-86, pres.-elect 1989, pres. 1990), Internat. Soc. Heart Research, Assn. Am. Physicians, Assn. Profs. of Medicine, Sigma Xi. Office: Eli Lilly & Co Drop Code 1209 Lilly Corp Ctr Indianapolis IN 46285

WATANABE, KYOICHI A(LOYSIUS), chemist, researcher, pharmacology educator; b. Amagasaki, Hyogo, Japan, Feb. 28, 1935; s. Yujiro Paul and Yoshiko Francisca (Hashimoto) W.; m. Kikyoko Agatha Suzuki, Nov. 22, 1962; children: Kanna, Kay, Kenneth, Kim, Kelly, Katherine. BA, Hokkaido U., 1958, PhD, 1963. Lectr. Sophia U., Tokyo, 1963; rsch. assoc. Sloan-Kettering Inst., N.Y.C., 1963-66, assoc., 1968-72, assoc. mem., 1972-81, mem., prof., 1981-95; rsch. fellow U. Alta., Edmonton, Can., 1966-68; assoc. prof. Cornell U. Med. Coll., N.Y.C., 1972-81; prof. pharmacology Sloan-Kettering Inst., N.Y.C., 1981—; dir. organic chemistry OncorPharm, Inc., Gaithersburg, Md., 1996—; mem. study sect. NIH, Washington, 1981-84. Mem. Polish Chem. Soc. (hon.), Russian Acad. Sci. (bd. sci. cons. Engelhardt Inst. Molecular Biology 1994—). Achievements include total synthesis of nucleoside antibiotics, novel heterocycle ring transformation, C-nucleose chemistry; antiviral and anticancer nucleosides; intercalating agents; modified oligonucleotides. Office: OncoPharmInc 200 Perry Pkwy Gaithersburg MD 20877

WATANABE, MAMORU, former university dean, physician, researcher; b. Vancouver, B.C., Can., Mar. 15, 1933; s. Takazo and Nao (Suginobu) W.; m. Marie Katie Bryndzak, June 1, 1974; 1 child, David. M.D., McGill U., 1957, Ph.D., 1963. Intern Royal Victoria Hosp., Montreal, 1957-58, resident in medicine, 1958-63; prof. medicine U. Alta., Edmonton, 1967-74; head internal medicine U. Calgary, Alta., 1974-76, assoc. dean edn., 1976-80, assoc. dean research, 1980-81, acting dean medicine, 1981-82, dean faculty medicine, 1982-92; med. staff Foothills Hosp., Calgary, 1974—. Fellow Royal Coll. Physicians and Surgeons (Can.); mem. Endocrine Soc., Can. soc. Clin. Investigation, Can. Soc. Endocrinology and Metabolism, Can. Hypertension Soc. Home: 162 Pumpridge Place SW, Calgary, AB Canada T2V 5E6 Office: U Calgary, 3330 Hospital Dr NW, Calgary, AB Canada T2N 1N4

WATANABE, RUTH TAIKO, music historian, library science educator; b. Los Angeles, May 12, 1916; d. Kohei and Iwa (Watanabe) W. B.Mus., U. So. Calif., 1937, A.B., 1939, A.M., 1941, M.Mus., 1942; postgrad., Eastman Sch. Music, Rochester, N.Y., 1942-46, Columbia U., 1947; Ph.D., U. Rochester, 1952. Dir. Sibley Music Library Eastman Sch. of Music, Rochester, N.Y., 1947-84; prof. music bibliography Eastman Sch. of Music, 1978-85, historian, archivist, 1984—; adj. prof. Sch. Library Sci. State U. Coll. at Geneseo, 1975-83; coordinator adult edn. program Rochester Civic Music Assn., 1963-75; mem. adv. com. Hochstein Music Sch.; lectr. on music, book reviewer, 1966—; program annotater Rochester Philharmonic Orch., 1959—. Author: Introduction to Music Research, 1967, Madrigali-II Verso, 1978; editor: Scribners New Music Library, Vols. 2, 5, 8, 1973, Treasury of Four Hand Piano Music, 1979; contbr. articles to profl. jours., contbr. symphony orchs. of U.S., 1986, internat. music jours.; modern music librarianship, 1989; contbr. to Festschrift for Carleton Sprague Smith, 1989, De Mósica Hispana et aliis, 1990. Mem. overseers vis. com. Baxter Sch. Library Sci., Case Western Res. U., 1979-85, Alderman Book Com., 1986-89. Mem. ALA, AAUW (Pa.-Del. fellowship. 1949-50, 1st v.p. Rochester 1964-65, mem. N.Y. state bd. 1965-66, mem. nat. com. on soc.'s reflection on arts 1967-69, nat. com. Am. fellowships awards 1969-74, br. pres. 1969-71, hon. co-chair Capital Fund Drive, 1986-88, Woman of Yr. award 1990), Internat. Assn. Music Librs. (2d v.p. commn. on conservatory libraries, commn. research librs.), Am. Musicol. Soc., Music Libr. Assn. (v.p. 1968-70, citation 1986, mem. editl. bd. 1967-95, pres. 1979-81), Music Libr. Assn./Internat. Assn. Music Librs. (joint com., 1986-87), Civic Music Assn. Rochester, Riemenscheider Bach Inst. (hon.), Hanson Inst. Am. Music (bd. mem. 1981—), Univ. Club, Century Club, Phi Beta Kappa (pres. Iota chpt. of N.Y. 1969-71), Phi Kappa Phi, Mu Phi Epsilon (gen. chmn. nat. conv. 1956, nat. librarian 1958-60, recipient citation 1977, Ora Ashley Lambke award 1989), Pi Kappa Lambda (sec. 1978—, treas. 1980—), Delta Phi Alpha, Epsilon Phi, Delta Kappa Gamma (parliamentarian 1986-88). Home: 111 East Ave Apt 610 Rochester NY 14604-2539 Office: Eastman Sch Music Rochester NY 14604

WATANABE, TOSHIHARU, ecologist, educator; b. Kyoto, Japan, June 6, 1924; s. Seizo and Fusa Watanabe; m. Sumiko Isebo, Nov. 3, 1952; children: Ikuko, Naoki. DSc, Kyoto U., 1961. Prof. Nat. Kanazawa (Japan) U., 1972-75, Nat. Nara (Japan) Women's U., 1975-88; prof. fgn. studies Kansai U., Hirakata/Osaka, Japan, 1988—; owner Diamond Resort Hawaii Owner's Club, 1989—; pres. Inst. Sci. Rsch. to Hydrospherical Ecology, 1990-95, adviser, 1995—. Author: Encyclopedia of Environmental Control Technology, 1990; editor: Japanese Jour. Diatomology, 1985—, Japanese Jour. Water Treatment Biology, 1971—. Profl. mem. Ministry of Constrn., Kinki dist., 1980—; vice-chmn. Com. on environ. pollution, Nara Prefecture and City, 1982—, com. mem. Wakayama, 1980—. Recipient Blue Ribbon Order of the Navy, 1961. Avocations: Indian ink drawing, music. Home: Higashigawa-cho 518, Shinkyogoku St Nakagyo-ku, Kyoto 604, Japan Office: Kansai U Fgn Studies, Kitakatahoko-cho 16-1, Hirakata Osaka 573, Japan

WATARU, WESTON YASUO, civil engineer; b. Honolulu, Mar. 30, 1957; s. Ralph Mitsuo and Anna Setsuko (Ogami) W.; m. Celine Jacqueline Teasdale, Nov. 1, 1986; children: Maile, Hope, Amber, Adam. BS, U. Hawaii, 1980. Registered profl. engr., Hawaii. Asst. engr. Dames and Moore, Honolulu, 1980-82; civil engr. I City and County of Honolulu Dept. Pub. Works, 1982-84, civil engr. IV, 1985-87, civil engr. V, 1987-89, svc. engr., civil engr. VI, 1989—; mem. utilities coord. com. City and County of Honolulu, 1989—, mem. permit streamlining task force, 1995—. Mem. ASCE, NSPE, Am. Pub. Works Assn., Hawaii Govt. Employees Assn. Avocations: family, sporting events, basketball, reading. Office: City and County of Honolulu Dept Pub Works 650 S King St Honolulu HI 96813-3017

WATCHORN, WILLIAM ERNEST, diversified manufacturing executive; b. Toronto, Ont., Can., Aug. 8, 1943; s. Roy Elgin and Josephine (Swyrida) W.; m. Maureen Emmett, Dec. 28, 1967; 1 child, Meghan. Chartered Acct., Toronto, 1967. Mgr. fin. planning Found. Group of Cos., Toronto, 1968-70; cons. Pahang Tengarra Regional Master Planning Study, Malaysia, 1970-72; controller Selkirk Holdings, Ltd., Toronto, 1972-75; corp. contr. Torstar Corp., Toronto, 1975-78; v.p. fin. Canwest Capital Corp., Winnipeg, Man., 1978-82; exec. v.p. Kaiser Resources Ltd., Vancouver, B.C., 1982; sr. v.p., chief fin. officer Fed. Industries Ltd., Winnipeg, 1982-88; pres., chief exec. officer Fed. Industries Indsl. Group, Winnipeg, 1989-91, Ensis Corp., Inc., Winnipeg, 1991—; bd. dirs. Carte Internat. Inc., Ensis Corp., Inc., Heron Cable Industries Ltd., Infocorp Computer Solutions Ltd., Milltronics Ltds., Neo Industries Inc., Neo Europe, S.A. Chmn. Balmoral Hall Sch. Found., Winnipeg; bd. dirs., vice-chmn. western region com. C.D. Howe Inst., Toronto; dir. Can. Stds. Assn. Mem. Can. Inst. Chartered Accts., Fellowship Inst. of Chartered Accts., Man. Inst., Chartered Accts., Ont. Inst. Chartered Accts., Winter Club. Avocations: squash, golf, tennis. Home: 6453 Southboine Dr, Winnipeg, MB Canada R3R 0B7 Office: Ensis Corp Inc, Ste 1120/200 Graham Ave, Winnipeg, MB Canada R3C 4L5

WATERHOUSE, BLAKE E., health facility administrator; b. 1936. Physician Jackson Clinic, Madison, Wis., 1965-87, Physicians Plus Med. Group, Madison, 1987-90; with Straub Clinic Hosp. Inc., Honolulu, 1990—, pres., CEO. Office: Straub Clinic Hosp Inc 888 S King St Honolulu HI 96813-3009

WATERMAN, MICHAEL SPENCER, mathematics educator, biology educator; b. Coquille, Oreg., June 28, 1942; s. Ray S. and Bessie E. (Payne) W.; m. Vicki Lynn Buss, Aug. 14, 1962 (div. Mar. 1977); 1 child, Tracey Lynn. B.S., Oreg. State U., 1964, M.S., 1966; M.A., Mich. State U., 1968, Ph.D., 1969. Assoc. prof. Idaho State U., Pocatello, 1969-75; mem. staff Los Alamos Nat. Lab., 1975-82, cons., 1982—; USC Assocs. Endowed Chair U. So. Calif., L.A., prof. math. and biology, 1982—, U. So. Calif. Assocs. Endowed Chair, 1991—; vis. prof. math. U. Hawaii, Honolulu, 1979-80; vis. prof. structural biology U. Calif.-San Francisco, 1982; vis. prof. Mt. Sinai Med. Sch., N.Y.C., 1988. author: Introduction to Computational Biology, 1995; editor: Mathematical Methods for DNA Sequences; assoc. editor Bull. Math. Biology; mem. editl. bd. Jour. Advances in Applied math. jour., Molecular Phylongenetics and Evolution, Genomics, Soc. for Indsl. and Applied Math. Jour. Applied Math.; sr. editor: Jour. Computational Biology; contbr. numerous articles on math. stats., biology to profl. jours. Grantee NSF, 1971, 72, 75, Los Alamos Nat. Lab, 1976, 81, 88—, Sys. Devel. Found., 1982-87, NIH, 1986—, Sloan Found., 1990-91; Guggenheim Found. fellow, 1995. Fellow AAAS, Am. Acad. Arts and Scis., Inst. Math. Stats.; mem. Am. Stats. Assn., Soc. Math. Biology, Soc. Indsl. and Applied Math. Office: U So Calif Dept Math Los Angeles CA 90007

WATERMAN, ROBERT DAVID, academic administrator, mental health counselor; b. Columbia, Mo., May 18, 1941; s. Earl Lewis and Sarah Lee (Long) W.; m. Shereen Hume, Sept. 28, 1975 (div. Jan. 15, 1985); children: Craig Spencer, David Hamilton; m. Karey Colleen Thorne, Sept. 4, 1986; 1 stepchild, Joshua Byran Thorne. AA, Santa Barbara City Coll., 1965; BA, U. Calif., Santa Barbara, 1968; MA, N.Mex. State U., 1973, EdD, 1978. Lic. profl. clin. mental health counselor; cert. sec. sch. tchr., N.Mex.; ordained to ministry Ch. Movement Spiritual Awareness, 1978. Substitute tchr. Alamogordo Pub. Schs., N.Mex., 1969-71; therapist Quimby Ctr., Alamogordo, 1970-78; dir. and therapist Quimby Ctr., 1978-79; mem. faculty N.Mex. State U., Alamogordo, 1970; founder, pres., mem. core faculty Southwestern Coll., Santa Fe, 1978—; mem. adj. faculty Parsons Coll., Alamogordo, 1974-78, John F. Kennedy U., Orinda, Calif., 1978. Author: Curriculum of the Soul: An Introduction to Transformational Learning, 1992; contbr. monographs to profl. jours.; presenter numerous papers at profl. confs.; developer Mandal Process art therapy. Lobbied state legislature in N. Mex. and developed legis. to license counselors and art therapists. With U.S. Army, 1969-71. Recipient awards ednl. innovation and legis. leadership. Mem. Am. Assn. Art Therapists, Assn. Transpersonal Psychology, Global Assn. Tranforming Edn. (mem. steering comm.), Rotary. Avocations: construction remodeling, gardening, traveling, spiritual studies. Office: Southwestern Coll PO Box 4788 Santa Fe NM 87502

WATERS, BETTY LOU, newspaper reporter, writer; b. Texarkana, Tex., June 13, 1943; d. Chester Hinton and Una Erby (Walls) W. AA, Texarkana Jr. Coll., 1963; BA, East Tex. State U., 1965. Gen. assignment reporter Galveston County Pub. Co., Galveston and Texas City, 1965-68; news and feature writer Ind. and Daily Mail, Anderson, S.C., 1968-69; reporter Citizen-Times newspaper, Asheville, N.C., 1969-74; edn. and med. reporter News Star World Pub. Co., Monroe, La., 1974-79; reporter, writer Delta Democrat Times, Greenville, Miss., 1980-89; staff writer Tyler (Tex.) Morning Telegraph, 1990—. Recipient 1st place award for articles La. Press Women's Contest, 1978, 1st place for interview, 1979; news media award N.C. Easter Seal Soc., 1973; 3d place award for feature writing Miss. Press Assn., 1984, for gen. news, 1983, for investigative reporting, 1988, 1st place for best series of articles, 1990; hon. mentions Tex. AP, 1966. Mem. Sigma Delta Chi.

WATERS, CURTIS JEFFERSON, minister, retired; b. Spartanburg, S.C., Apr. 8, 1929; s. Leroy Belton and Lillian Isola (Tucker) W.; m. Nancy Carol Taylor, Oct. 25, 1947; children: Curtis Michael, Ronald Stephen, Gloria Lynn. BA, North Greenville Coll., Tigerville, S.C., 1953; BD, Luther Rice Sem., Jacksonville, Fla., 1973; DD (hon.), North Fla. Bapt. Theol. Sem., 1988, ThD, 1991. Ordained to ministry So. Bapt. Conv., 1950; lic. real estate broker, N.C. Pastor Gap Creek Bapt. Ch., Marietta, S.C., 1950-51, Fairmont (S.C.) Bapt. Ch., 1951-55, Francis Bapt. Ch., Palatka, Fla., 1955-60, Double Springs Bapt. Ch., Greer, S.C., 1960-63, Churchwell Avenue Bapt. Ch., Knoxville, Tenn., 1963-71, Tuxedo (N.C.) 1st Bapt. Ch., 1971-75, City View 1st Bapt. Ch., Greenville, S.C., 1975-93; retired, 1993; chmn. bd. dirs. Champions for Christ Found. City View 1st Bapt. Ch., Greenville, S.C., 1987-93; ret., 1993, evangelist, 1993—; dir. E.J. Daniels Crusade, Palatka, Fla.; evangelist 9 states and Jamaica; sem. commencement speaker North Fla. Bapt. Theol. Sem., 1989-90, 90-91; speaker Bible confs. Bd. dirs. Jacksonville (Fla.) Bapt. Theol. Sem. Republican. Home: 148 Pilot Rd Greenville SC 29609-6348 *The rewards of life are incredible when one gives himself completely to the will of God. Sharing life with others and ministering to their needs brings invaluable satisfaction.*

WATERS, CYNTHIA WINFREY, television show host, public service director; b. Atlanta, Feb. 25, 1951; d. Tommie Lee (Winfrey) W.; m. Leroy Hollaway Jr., June 7, 1970 (div. 1981); children: Marechalnelle, Geoffrey; m. Leamond Howard Waters, Sept. 1, 1985. Cert. in acctg., Atlanta Area Tech. Inst., 1982; cert. in human relations, Chattahoochee Tech. Inst., 1988. Customer svc. rep. Atlanta Gaslight Co., 1975-83; asst. mktg. mgr. Vorwerk, U.S.A., Atlanta, 1983-86; fg. sec. coordinator Focal Point Inc., Atlanta, 1986-91, safety facilitator, 1988-91; pub. svc. dir. Sta. WYZE Radio, Atlanta,

1991—; TV host A New Look in Gospel, Atlanta, 1991—; sec. Emory U., Atlanta, 1993-94; owner operator Water Print Media Creations, 1995—. Mem. Atlanta Prevention Connection, Edwin Hawkins Arts & Music Seminar Choir Metro Atlanta chpt.,Gateway Baptist Church youth job training pgm., cons. Avocations: reading, activities with youths, writing, comm. Home: 2968 Chipmunk Trl Marietta GA 30067 Office: PO Box 813056 Smyrna GA 30081-8056

WATERS, DANIEL W., electrical power industry executive. Exec. dir. So. Calif. Pub. Power Auth., Pasadena, Calif. Office: Southern Cal Pub Power Auth 225 S Lake Ave Ste 1410 Pasadena CA 91101*

WATERS, DAVID ROGERS, retail executive; b. Akron, Ohio, Apr. 27, 1932; s. Herbert H. and Winifred Elsie (Kearns) W.; children: Ann S. Rohrbaugh, David Rogers, Thomas J., Peter M., Christopher C., Elizabeth E. Brewer, Jeffrey P. BS in Econs., U. Pa., 1954. Trainee, asst. to controller W.R. Grace & Co., N.Y.C., 1954-55; buyer M. O'Neil Co., Akron, 1957-62; div. mdse. mgr. May-Cohens, Jacksonville, Fla., 1962-66, Rich's, Atlanta, 1967; pres., gen. mdse. mgr. DePinna, N.Y.C., 1967-69; gen. mdse. mgr., then pres. Garfinckel's, Washington, 1969-73; pres., dir. Garfinckel, Brooks Bros., Miller & Rhoads, Inc., Washington, 1972-76, chmn., pres., CEO, 1976-81; chmn., dir. Frederick Atkins, Inc., 1980-81; pvt. practice cons., 1982-85, 90-92, 94—; exec. v.p., mem. mgmt. policy com., pres. Splty Retailing Group Gen Mills., Inc., 1985-88; chmn., dir., chief exec. officer Joseph A. Bank Clothiers, Inc., 1988-90; founder, pres., dir. Douglass & Waters, Inc., 1992-94; v.p., gen. mgr. Waverly Home divsn. F. Schumacher & Co., 1995—; cons. DLJ Capital Corp., 1984-85; 1st vice-chmn. Nat. Retail Mchts. Assn., 1980-81; bd. dirs. Findings, Inc. Served with U.S. Army, 1955-57.

WATERS, DONALD JOSEPH, information services administrator; b. Balt., Sept. 16, 1952; s. Richard Hunter and Annette Catharine (Hannan) W.; m. Beverly Ann Brent, Apr. 5, 1974; children: Laura Elizabeth, Sarah Elizabeth. BA, U. Md., 1973; M Phil, Yale U., 1976, PhD, 1982. Resource specialist Yale Computer Ctr., New Haven, 1982-84; dir. computer services Yale Sch. Mgmt., New Haven, 1984-87; head, systems office Yale U. Library, New Haven, 1987-92, dir., libr. and adminstrv. systems, 1992-93, assoc. univ. librarian, 1993—. Author: Strange Ways and Sweet Dreams: Afro-American Folklore From the Hampton Institute, 1983. Mem. AAAS, ALA, Am. Soc. Info. Sci. Roman Catholic. Avocations: jazz, rowing, cabinet making. Home: 40 Overbrook Rd Madison CT 06443-1834 Office: Yale U Libr 120 High St New Haven CT 06511-6644

WATERS, GEORGE BAUSCH, newspaper publisher; b. Syracuse, N.Y., July 4, 1920; s. Louis Addison and Mildred Elaine (Bausch) W.; m. Shirley Kessinger Barnard, Sept. 23, 1943; children: Peter, Stephen, Nancy, Kristin, Dean. BA, Syracuse U., 1943. With Rome (N.Y.) Sentinel Co. Pub., 1947—, asst. gen. mgr., 1954-60, gen. mgr., 1960-66, pub., 1966-93, pres., 1993—; bd. dirs. N.Y. State Photonics Devel. Corp. Chmn. Rome Art and Community Ctr., 1967-85; trustee Stevens Kingsley Found., N.Y.C., 1966—, Kirkland Coll., Clinton, N.Y., 1973-79, Utica Coll. Syracuse U., Utica, 1963-78; past mem. Rome Bd. Edn., Rome Hosp.; bd. dirs. Cen. Assn. Blind. Capt. inf. U.S. Army, 1943-47, ETO. Mem. Am. Newspaper Pubs. Assn., N.Y. State Newspaper Pubs. Assn., N.Y. State Associated Dailies (pres. 1974), Am. Soc. Newspaper Editors, Jervis Libr. Assn. (pres. 1959-65), Soc. Profl. Journalists, Ft. Schuyler Club, Yale Club, Washington Press Club, Delta Kappa Epsilon. Republican. Presbyterian. Office: Rome Sentinel Co 333 W Dominick St Rome NY 13440-5701

WATERS, GEORGE GARY, financial service executive; b. Garyville, La., June 3, 1928; s. Elisha McCLendon and Lena Mae (Anderson) W.; m. Genevieve Corley, Aug. 15, 1952; children: Gary, George D., Gina, Glenda, Genevieve J., Grant. BA, U. Nebr., 1963; MBA, Nat. U., San Diego, 1979. Lic. ins. agt., securities aft., tax advisor, enrolled agent lic. to practice before IRS. Enlisted USAF, 1951, advanced through grades to lt. col.; stationed at Keesler AFB Biloxi, Miss., 1958-59; detachment comdr. Encampment, Wyo, 1959-61, AFTAC 415, Chiengmai, Thailand, 1962-65, AFTAC Det 333, Teheran, Iran, 1970-72; plans officer HQ USAF, Washington, 1966-69; sr. air force advisor 162 Mobile Command, Sacramento, Calif., 1976-78; systems analyst Planning Rsch. Corp., Camp Pendleton, Calif., 1979-80; tax practitioner, pres. Palomar Tax Svc. Inc., San Marcos, Calif., 1979—; speaker in field. Pub. Palomar Tax Svc. newsletter. Alt. del. Calif. Reps., 1992. Fellow Nat. Tax Practice Inst.; mem. Inland Soc. Tax Cons. (founding pres. No. San Diego 1985-86, past pres. 1987), Calif. Assn. Independent Accts. (pres.-elect, pres. 1993-94), Nat. Soc. Pub. Accts. (del. to conv. 1990-93), Nat. Soc. Enrolled Agts., Calif. Soc. Enrolled Agts., San Marcos C. of C. Republican. Roman Catholic. Avocations: golf, tennis, reading. Home: 326 Sunrise Cir Vista CA 92084-5834 Office: Palomar Tax Svc Inc 470 S Rancho Santa Fe Rd San Marcos CA 92069-3621

WATERS, H. FRANKLIN, federal judge; b. Hackett, Ark., July 20, 1932; s. William A. and Wilma W.; m. Janie C. Waters, May 31, 1958; children—Carolyn Denise, Melanie Jane, Melissa Ann. B.S., U. Ark., 1955; LL.B., St. Louis U., 1964. Engr., atty. Ralston-Purina Co., St. Louis, 1958-66; ptnr. Crouch, Blair, Cypert & Waters, 1967-81; judge U.S. Dist. Ct. (we. dist.) Ark., from 1981, now chief judge. Former bd. dirs. Springdale Schs.; former bd. govs. Washington Regional Med. Ctr. Mem. ABA, Ark. Bar Assn., Springdale C. of C. (past bd. dirs.). Office: US Dist Ct PO Box 1908 Fayetteville AR 72702-1908*

WATERS, JAMES LOGAN, analytical instrument manufacturing executive; b. Lincoln, Nebr., Oct. 7, 1925; s. Leland L. and Marian L. (Yungblut) W.; m. Faith Cabot Pigors, Sept. 11, 1948; children: Richard Cabot, Barbara Faith. B.S., Columbia U., 1946; DSc (hon.), Northeastern U., 1993. Project mgr. Baird Assocs., Inc., Cambridge, Mass., 1947; founder, pres. James L. Waters, Inc., Framingham, Mass., 1947-58, Waters Assocs., Inc., Milford, Mass., 1958-72; chmn. bd. Waters Assocs., Inc., 1972-80; founder, pres. Waters Bus. Systems, Inc., Framingham, 1978—; bd. dirs. Markem Corp., Keene, N.H., Transtek Corp., Ellington, Conn. Mem. Framingham Town Meeting, 1952-61; mem. Framingham Sch. Com., 1961-70, chmn., 1962, 64; trustee Babson Coll., Wellesley, Mass., 1979-85; founder, trustee Waters Found., 1955—; trustee Northeastern U., 1984—. Served as ensign USNR, 1943-46. Mem. Tau Beta Pi. Patentee in field. Home: 1153 Grove St Framingham MA 01701-3779 Office: New York Ave Framingham MA 01701

WATERS, JENNIFER NASH, lawyer; b. Bridgeport, Conn., Dec. 21, 1951; d. Lewis William and Patricia (Cousins) W.; m. Todd David Peterson, Sept. 19, 1981; children: Elizabeth, Andrew. BA, Radcliffe, 1972; JD, Harvard, 1976. Bar: D.C. 1977, U.S. Supreme Ct. 1980. Clk. U.S. Ct. Appeals (D.C. cir.), Washington, 1976-77; assoc. Jones, Day, Reavis & Poque, Washington, 1977-79; assoc. Crowell & Moring, Washington, 1979-83, ptnr., 1983—. Mem. Fed. Energy Bar Assn. (bd. dirs. 1988-94, v.p. 1994-95, pres. 1996—). Office: Crowell & Moring 1001 Pennsylvania Ave NW Washington DC 20004-2505

WATERS, JOHN, film director, writer, actor; b. Balt., Apr. 22, 1946; s. John Samuel and Patricia Ann (Whitaker) W. Student, NYU, 1966. Speaker various colls., comedy clubs, U.S., Europe, Australia, 1968—. Writer, dir. films Roman Candles, 1966, Eat Your Makeup, 1968, Mondo Trasho, 1969, Multiple Maniacs, 1970, Pink Flamingos, 1972, Female Trouble, 1974, Desperate Living, 1977, Polyester, 1981, Cry-Baby, 1990, Serial Mom, 1994; writer, dir., actor film Hairspray, 1987; actor Something Wild, 1988, Homer and Eddie, 1990, (TV show) 21 Jump Street, 1990; author: Shock Value, 1981, Crackpot, 1986, Trash Trio, 1988; contbr. articles to N.Y. Times, Am. Film, other mags. Fund raiser AIDS Action Balt.; spokesperson Anti-Violence Campaign, N.Y.C., 1991. John Waters Day named in his honor State of Md., 1985; John Waters Week named in his honor City of Balt., 1988. Mem. AFTRA, SAG, Dirs. Guild Am., Writers Guild Am., Acad. Motion Picture Arts and Scis. Avocation: study of extreme Catholic behavior before the Reformation.

WATERS, JOHN B., lawyer; b. Sevierville, Tenn., July 15, 1929; s. J. B. and Myrtle (Paine) W.; m. Patsy Temple, Apr. 8, 1953; children: John B., Cynthia Beth. BS, U. Tenn., 1952, JD, 1961, D in Environ. Sci. (hon.), Milligan Coll., 1993. Bar: Tenn. 1961, U.S. Dist. Ct. (ea. dist.) Tenn. 1961, U.S. Dist. Ct. D.C. 1970, U.S. Supreme Ct. 1969. Mem. hearing com. Bd. Profl. Responsibility, Supreme Ct., 1974-80 Fed. co-chmn. Appalachian Regional Commn., 1969-71; chmn. Sevier County Indsl. Bd., Sevierville Library Found.; mem. Gov.'s Com. Econ. Devel.; Tenn. rep. to So. Growth Policies Bd., 1970-74; appointed dir. by Pres. Reagan Tenn. Valley Authority, Knoxville, 1984, appointed chmn. bd. dirs. by Pres. Bush 1992; trustee East Tenn. Baptist Hosp., Knoxville; mem. Tenn.-Tombigbee Waterway Authority, 1978-84; bd. dirs. Inst. of Nuclear Power Ops., 1985. Lt. USN, 1952-55. Fellow Am. Bar Found., Am. Coll. Probate Counsel; mem. Tenn. Bar Assn. (pres. 1983-84), Sevier County Bar Assn. (past pres.); mem. bd. Met. Knoxville Airport Authority. Republican. Baptist. Home: 405 Burridge Waters Edge Sevierville TN 37862 Office: Long Ragsdale & Waters PC PO Box 90384 Knoxville TN 37990-0384 also: 119 Commerce St Sevierville TN 37862*

WATERS, LAUGHLIN EDWARD, federal judge; b. L.A., Aug. 16, 1914; s. Frank J. and Ida (Bauman) W.; m. Voula Davanis, Aug. 22, 1953; children: Laughlin Edward, Maura Kathleen, Deirdre Mary, Megan Ann, Eileen Brigid. A.B., UCLA, 1939; J.D., U. So. Calif., 1946. Bar: Calif. 1946. Dep. atty. gen. Calif., Los Angeles, 1946-47; individual practice law Los Angeles, 1947-53; sr. ptnr. Nossaman, Waters, Krueger & Marsh, 1961-76; U.S. atty. So. Dist. Calif., 1953-61; judge U.S. Dist. Ct. (cen. dist.) Calif., 1976—; cons. U.S. Dept. State in London, 1970; mem. U.S. Del. to Conf. Environ. Problems in Prague, 1971, White House Conf. on Aging, 1970-71; sr. dist. judge rep. Jud. Coun.; judge Atty Gen.'s Adv. Inst. Mem. Calif. Legislature, 1946-53; vice chmn. Rep. State Ctrl. Com., 1950-51, chmn., 1952-53; bd. dirs. Legal Aid Found., 1954-60; past pres. Cath. Big Brothers. Served as capt. U.S. Army, 1942-46. Decorated Bronze Star with oak leaf cluster, Purple Heart with oak leaf cluster, Combat Inf. badge. Fellow Am. Bar Found., Am. Coll. Trial Lawyers; mem. ABA (chmn. com. on housing and urban devel. 1977-79), Fed. Bar Assn. (founder, past pres.), L.A. County Bar Assn., Am. Judicature Soc., Assn. Bus. Trial Lawyers, U. So. Calif., UCLA Law Assn., Am. Legion, U. So. Calif. Legion Lex, Order Blue Shield, Town Hall, Polish Order Merit Cross with Swords, Hon. Citizen of Chambois, Trun, France, 10th Polish Dragoons (hon.), Soc. Friendly Sons St. Patrick (past pres., Medallion of Merit award), Knights of Malta, Anchor Club, Calif. Club, L.A. Club (past pres.). Roman Catholic. Office: US Dist Ct 255 E Temple St Los Angeles CA 90012-3334

WATERS, LOU, anchorman, correspondent; b. Mpls., July 7, 1938; s. Louis Joseph and Anne Marie Riegert; m. Marth Lee Morin Waters, Feb. 15, 1975; children: Scott, Christopher, Alexander. Student, U. Minn. Reporter Sta. KDWB, Mpls., 1959, Sta. WWTC, Mpls., Sta. KFWB, L.A., Sta. WLBS-FM, N.Y.C., Sta. KNEW, San Francisco; reporter, anchor Sta. KVOA-TV, Tucson, news dir.; news dir. Sta. KCST-TV, San Diego; asst. sta. mgr., evening anchor Sta. KOLD-TV, CBS, Tucson; co-anchor CNN Today CNN, Atlanta, 1980—, co-anchor Earlyprime, 1991—. Avocations: golf, photography, music. Office: CNN One CNN Ctr Atlanta GA 30348

WATERS, M. BRUCE, engineering technician; b. Houston, Apr. 17, 1950; s. Wayland O. and Snellah G. (Holt) W.; m. Jean H. Sudduth, June 26, 1971; 1 child, Tegan Joy. Student, La. State U., 1968-69, '70-74, U. Houston, 1969, San Jacinto Jr. Coll., Deer Park, Tex., 1969. Engring. aide I La. Dept. Highways, Baton Rouge, 1971-73, engring. aide II, 1973-74; sta. mgr. Cliff Brice Gas Stas., Boulder, Colo., 1975; mill worker Red Dale Coach, Longmont, Colo., 1975; engring. aide B Colo. Dept. Highways, Boulder, 1975-76, engring. aide C, 1976-91, engring tech. I, 1991—. Blood donor Belle Bonfils, Boulder, Colo., 1975—; mem. Vols. for Outdoor Colo.; sec. Libertarian Party of Boulder County, 1991-93, 95-96. Mem. Nat. Inst. Cert. Engring. Techs., Chpt. C Freewheelers (sec. 1993-95), Am. Motorcyclist Assn., Soc. for Preservation and Encouragement of Barbershop Quartet Singing in Am. Avocations: collecting antique motorcycles, skiing, reading, music. Office: Colo Dept Transp 1050 Lee Hill Dr Boulder CO 80302-9404

WATERS, M. JEAN, mortgage company executive; b. 1945. With Waters Mortgage Co., Ft. Lauderdale, Fla., 1976—, pres., COO. Office: Waters Mortgage corp Ste 500 8751 W Broward Blvd Plantation FL 33324

WATERS, MARY BASKIN, state government official; b. Sumter, S.C., Aug. 31, 1945; d. Norwood Fleming and Nan Richardson (Rickenbaker) Baskin; m. Samuel C. Waters, Sept. 14, 1968. Cert. d'Etude, Sorbonne U., Vichy, France, 1966; BA, U. S.C., 1985, MA in Tchg., 1987; grad. cert. in Women's Studies, S.C. Exec. Inst., 1993. Instr. art Newberry (S.C.) Coll., 1987-92; instr. women's studies U. S.C., Columbia, 1988—; instr. art U. S.C., Lancaster, 1990-92; dir. S.C. Commn. on Women, A Divsn. of Gov.'s Office, Columbia, 1992—; vis. lectr. U. S.C., Columbia, 1988; art cons., broker Carolina Editions Gallery, Columbia, 1990; instr. art Midlands Tech. Coll., Columbia, 1991; exec. bd. Advs. for Women on Bds. and Commns., Columbia; adv. bd. Pathways for Women at Richland Meml. Hosp., Columbia; mem. Leadership Inst., Columbia (S.C.) Coll.; lectr. in field. Contbr. articles to profl. jours. Mem. S.C. Dept. Edn. Visual and Performing Arts Transition Com., Columbia, 1991; adv. com. Women in State Work Force Symposium, 1993; adv. com. Women in State Work Force Symposium, 1993; adv. bd. S.C. Women in Higher Edn. Adminstrn., 1994; S.C Del. leader U.S. Southeastern Regional Conf. Beijing World Conf., 1995, commn. USIA Grant Commn. Exchange Program Women and Civic Participation, 1996—; adv. bd. The Leadership Inst. Columbia Coll. Mem. Nat. Art Edn. Assn., Nat. Coun. for Rsch. on Women, Southea. Women's Studies Assn., Nat. Assn. Commns. on Women (S.C. delegation leader U.S. southea. regl. conf. on women - UN prepatory meeting for Beijing World Conf., 1995, commr. USIA grant comm. exchange program, 1996, adv. bd. The Leadership Inst. Columbia Coll., 1996), Richland County Legal Aux. (pres. 1982-83), Brennen Elem. Sch. PTO (pres. 1980-81), Golden Key Honor Soc., Gamma Beta Phi, Kappa Phi Kappa. Office: Office of Gov SC Commn on Women 2221 Devine St Ste 408 Columbia SC 29205-2418

WATERS, MAXINE, congresswoman; b. St. Louis, Aug. 15, 1938; d. Remus and Velma (Moore) Carr; m. Sidney Williams, July 23, 1977; children: Edward, Karen. Grad. in sociology Calif. State U., L.A.; hon. doctorates, Spelman Coll., N.C. Agrl. & Tech. State U., Morgan State U. Former tchr. Head Start; mem. Calif. Assembly from dist. 48, 1976-91, Dem. caucus chair, 1984; mem. 102nd-104th Congresses from Dist. 35, Calif., 1991—; mem. Banking, Fin., Urban Affairs com., Ho. subcom. on banking, capitol subcom. on banking, employment and tng. subcom. on vets., veterans affairs com. Mem. Dem. Nat. Com., Dem. Congrl. Campaign com.; del. Dem. Nat. Conv., 1972, 76, 80, 84, 88, 92, mem. rules com. 1984; mem. Nat. Adv. Com. for Women, 1978—; bd. dirs. TransAfrica Found., Nat. Women's Polit. Caucus, Ctr. Nat. Policy, Clara Elizabeth Jackson Carter Found. Spellman Coll., Nat. Minority AIDS Project, Women for a Meaningful Summit, Nat. Coun. Negro Women, Black Women's Agenda; founder Black Women's Forum. Office: US Ho of Reps 330 Cannon HOB Washington DC 20515*

WATERS, RICHARD, retired publishing company executive; b. Sterling, Mass., May 13, 1926; s. Sherman Hoar and Viola (Arnold) W.; m. June Hollweg Dorer, Aug. 27, 1949; children: Karl (dec.), Kurt, Kris. B.A., Hobart Coll., 1950, LL.D. hon., 1970; M.B.A., Harvard U., 1951. Assoc. acct. Hunter & Weldon, N.Y.C., 1953-55; exec. v.p., chief fin. officer Reader's Digest Assn., Pleasantville, N.Y., 1955-77; assoc. dean Harvard U. Bus. Sch., Boston, 1977-81; pres., chief exec. officer Sporting News, St. Louis, 1981-90, ret., 1990; bd. dirs. Republic Bank for Savs. (formerly Manhattan Savs. Bank), N.Y.C., Republic Nat. Bank, N.Y.C. Trustee Hobart Coll., 1971-91, William Smith Coll., 1971-91; regional v.p. Associated Industries N.Y. State, Albany, 1965-79; chmn. bd. Westchester Heart Assn., Port Chester, N.Y., 1975-76; bd. dirs., vice-chmn. Gateway chpt. Nat. Multiple Sclerosis Soc., 1991—. With USN, 1944-46, PTO; 1st lt. USAF, 1951-53. Mem. Nat. Assn. Pub. Accts.; mem Baseball Writers Assn. Am. Republican. Clubs: Old Warson Country; University (St. Louis); Sky (N.Y.C.). Home: 20 Somerset Downs Saint Louis MO 63124-1007

WATERS, RICHARD W., SR., mortgage company executive; b. 1943. With Dade County Sch. Bd., Miami, Fla., 1964-71, Waters Mortgage Investment Co., Ft. Lauderdale, Fla., 1971-76, Cmty. Mortgage Corp., Ft. Lauderdale, 1977-78; with Waters Mortgage Corp., Ft. Lauderdale, 1976—, chmn. bd. dirs. Office: Waters Mortgage Corp 8751 W Broward Blvd Ste 500 Fort Lauderdale FL 33324*

WATERS, ROGER, rock musician; b. Cambridge, England, Sept. 6, 1947. Bassist Sigma-6, T-Set, Megga Death, Screaming Abdabs, Pink FLoyd Sound, Pink Floyd, 1964-86; solo musician, 1987—. Albums include Music from the Body, 1970, The Pros & Cons of Hitchhiking, 1986, Radio KAOS, 1987, The Wall: Berlin 1990, 1990, Amused to Death, 1992; (with Pink Floyd) Piper at the Gates of Dawn, 1967, More, 1969, Atom Heart Mother, 1970, Relics, 1971, Darkside of the Moon, 1973, Wish You Were Here, 1976, The FInal Cut, 1983, A Collection of Great Dance Songs, 1994, The Division Bell, 1994.;.

WATERS, RONALD W., educator, church executive, pastor; b. Kokomo, Ind., July 23, 1951; s. Ronald Lee and Carolyn Elizabeth (Myers) W.; m. Norma Lee Grumbling Waters, June 16, 1973; 1 child, Melinda Ronee Waters. BA magna cum laude, Ashland (Ohio) Coll., 1973; MA in Comms. with high honors, Wheaton (Ill.) Coll., 1975; MDiv with high honors, Ashland (Ohio) Theol. Seminary, 1985; postgrad., Asbury Theol. Seminary, Wilmore, Ky., 1993—. Ordained elder Brethren Ch., 1986; lic. minister, 1985-86. Asst. to dir. Bd. of Christian Edn. The Brethren Ch., Ashland, Ohio, 1971-74; mng. editor of publs. Brethren Pub. Co., Ashland, Ohio, 1975-78, asst. to dir. and gen. mgr., 1978-80, exec. dir., 1980-82; dir. of Denom. Bus. The Brethren Ch. Nat. Office, Ashland, Ohio, 1982-84; cons. in mgmt. and computer applications, 1984-85; pastor Mt. Olive Brethren Ch., McGaheyville, Va., 1985-89; dir. Brethren Ch. Ministries The Brethren Ch. Nat. Office, Ashland, Ohio, 1989-95; asst. prof. evangelism Ashland (Ohio) Theol. Sem., 1996—; cons. for evangelism and ch. growth The Brethren Ch. Nat. Office, Ashland, 1996—; bd. dirs. corp. sec. Brethren Printing Co., Ashland, 1989-96; mission bd. Brethern Ch. Southeastern Dist., 1987-89; mem. statement of faith task force Gen. Conf. Brethern Ch., 1981-84, policy com. 1986-91, bd. ref. congl. adv. The Andrew Ctr., Elgin, Ill., 1994—; founder, tchr. Young Adult Sunday Sch. class Park St Brethern Ch., Ashland, 1990-93; adv. com. Ashland Theol. Sem., 1990-95; mem. Evangelism Mgmt. Team, Elgin, 1992—; spkr. in field. Author: Promise for the Future, 1993, Leader's Manual for Inviting and Welcoming New People, 1995; editor: The Brethren Evangelist mag., 1975-78; editl. asst.: New Beginnings mag., 1995—; contbr. numerous articles to religious jours. Adv. coun. World Relief Corp., Wheaton, Ill., 1990-92. Mem. Am. Soc. Ch. Growth, Nat. Assn. Brethern Ch. Elders, Nat. Assn. Evangelicals, Denom. Prayer Leaders Network. Avocation: gardening. Office: Ashland Theological Sem 910 Center St Ashland OH 44805

WATERS, SYLVIA, dance company artistic director. Prin. dance Alvin Ailey Am. Dance Theater, N.Y.C.; artistic dir. Alvin Ailey Repertory Ensemble, N.Y.C., 1974—.

WATERS, TIMOTHY J., lawyer; b. Santa Rosa, Calif., Apr. 18, 1943. BS, U. San Francisco, 1965; JD with honors, George Washington U., 1968. Bar: Va. 1968, D.C. 1973. Atty. FTC, Washington, 1968-73, asst. to dir. Bur. Competition, 1971, asst. to Chmn., 1972; ptnr. McDermott, Will & Emory, Washington. Mem. D.C. Bar, Va. State Bar. Office: McDermott Will & Emery 1850 K St NW Ste 500 Washington DC 20006-2213*

WATERS, WILLIE ANTHONY, opera and orchestra conductor; b. Goulds, Fla., Oct. 11, 1951. BMus, U. Miami, 1973; postgrad., Memphis State U. Music dir. Greater Miami (Fla.) Opera, 1983-84, artistic dir., 1984-92, prin. condr., 1992-95; music dir. San Antonio Festival, 1983-85; guest condr. Detroit Symphony, Indpls. Orch., Norwegian Radio Orch., Philharm. Orch. Fla., Essen Philharm., Bavarian Radio Orch., Baden-Baden Radio Orch., Cologne Opera. Condr. San Diego Opera, Mich. Opera Theatre, Conn. Opera, San Francisco Opera, Australian Opera, Sydney, Opera De Montréal; conducted Otello, Salome, Die Walkure, Bianca e Falliero (U.S. premiere), other operas; appeared in concert with Detroit Symphony, Norwegian Radio Orch., Fla. Philharm., Dayton Philharm., Brucknerhaus Orch., Linz, Austria; rec. Philips Co. Recipient Prix de Martell, 1991.

WATERSTON, SAMUEL ATKINSON, actor; b. Cambridge, Mass., Nov. 15, 1940; s. George Chychele and Alice Tucker (Atkinson) W.; m. Lynn Louisa Woodruff, Jan. 26, 1976; children: Graham C., Elisabeth P., Katherine B.; child by previous marriage: James S. B.A., Yale U., 1962; student, Sorbonne, Paris, 1960-61. Theatrical appearances include: Indians, Oh Dad Poor Dad, Halfway Up the Tree, Lunch Hour, Hamlet, The Tempest, Measure for Measure, Much Ado About Nothing (recipient Obie, Drama Desk awards), Benefactors, 1986, A Walk in the Woods, 1988, Abe Lincoln in Illinois, 1993, Shakespeare & Szekspir, 1994, Abe Lincoln in Illinois, N.Y.C., 1993-95; film appearances include: The Great Gatsby, 1975, Rancho Deluxe, 1976, Capricorn One, 1978, Interiors, 1978, Sweet William, 1978, Heaven's Gate, 1979, Eagle's Wing, 1983, The Killing Fields, 1984, Warning Sign, 1985, Savages, Hopscotch, 1980, Hannah and Her Sisters, 1986, Just Between Friends, 1986, The Devil's Paradise, September, 1987, Welcome Home, 1989, The Man in the Moon, 1991, Mindwalk, 1991, Serial Mom, 1994, Nixon, 1995, Proprietor, 1995, Shadow Conspiracy, 1995; TV films include: Much Ado About Nothing, 1974, The Glass Menagerie, 1975, Diabolique, 1975, Friendly Fire, 1978, Oppenheimer, 1982, Q.E.D., 1982, Terrorist on Trial: The United States vs. Salim Ajami; TV miniseries appearance: Gore Vidal's Lincoln, 1988, Lost Civilizations, 1995; regular TV series I'll Fly Away, NBC-TV, 1991-93 (Emmy award nomination, Lead actor, Drama, 1993), I'll Fly Away: Then and Now, PBS, 1993 (Emmy nomination, Lead Actor - Special, 1994), Law and Order, 1994—. Mem. Actors Equity Assn., Screen Actors Guild, AFTRA. Office: care Addis/Wechsler & Assocs 955 Carrillo Dr Fl 3 Los Angeles CA 90048-5400

WATERSTON, WILLIAM KING, minister, educator, academic administrator; b. Elizabeth, N.J., Feb. 12, 1937; s. John Robert and Sylvia (Eadie) W.; m. Judith Jane Schramm, Aug. 29, 1959; children: John Scott, Gregory Glenn, Robert Ormsby; m. Kathryn Larsen, Dec. 17, 1983; 1 child, Chad. AB, Bates Coll., 1959; BD, Eastern Bapt. Sem., 1962, M.Div., 1973. Ordained to ministry Am. Bapt. Chs. USA, 1962. Bus. mgr., editorial asst. Missions Mag., 1962-66, Crusader Mag., 1964-66; assoc. dir. radio and TV Am. Bapt. Chs. USA, 1966-69, dir. electronic media, 1969-72; host Dialogue TV Show, Phila., 1969-85; assoc. dir. communications div. Am. Bapt. Chs. USA, 1972-73; Parker Ford Bapt. Ch., 1973-81; dir. group homes ch. rels. devel. Bapt. Children's Svcs., Phila., 1981-92; sr. minister First Bapt. Warren, Warren, Pa., 1992-95; pres. Warren County Ministerium, 1971-85; instr. Eastern Bapt. Coll., 1973-85, Eastern Bapt. Sem., 1970-85. Editor Medi-athink, 1973. Lodge: Rotary (pres. Cen. Perkiomen 1968). Home: 747 Ball Ave Watertown NY 13601 Office: First Baptist Watertown 207 State St Watertown NY 13601

WATFORD, MICHAEL D., marketing professional; b. Dec. 10, 1954; m. Joanne Watford; children: Amanda, Jason. BSBA, U. Fla., 1975; MBA, U. New Orleans, 1978. Supr. material control Norco Mfg. Complex, Houston, 1979; purschasing rep. Shell Oil Co., Houston, 1975-81; supr. sr. purchasing svcs. Superior Oil Co., Houston, 1981-85; mgr. materials Meridian Oil Inc., Houston, 1985, mgr. direct natural gas sales, 1986, dir. natural gas mktg., 1985-90; pres. Torch Energy Mktg. Inc., Houston, 1990—; pres., CEO Nuevo Energy Co., Houston. Mem. Natural Gas Men's Soc. (pres. N.W. mcpl. utility dist. 6). Office: Nuevo Energy Co 1221 Lamar St Ste 1600 Houston TX 77010-3039

WATHEN, DANIEL EVERETT, state supreme court chief justice; b. Easton, Maine, Nov. 4, 1939; s. Joseph Jackson and Wilda Persis (Dow) W.; m. Judith Carol Foren, July 14, 1960; children: Julanne Carol, Daniel Arthur. AB, Ricker Coll., 1962; JD, U. Maine, 1965; LLM (hon.), U. Va. Law Sch., 1988. Bar: Maine 1965. Atty. Wathen & Wathen, Augusta, Maine, 1965-77; trial judge Superior Ct. Maine, Augusta, 1977-81; appellate judge Supreme Jud. Ct. Maine, Augusta, 1981-92; state chief justice Supreme Jud. Ct. Maine, 1992—. Office: ME Supreme Jud Ct 142 Federal St Portland ME 04101-4151*

WATHNE, CARL NORMAN, hospital administrator; b. Johnstown, Pa., Oct. 16, 1930; s. Odd and Alice (Anderson) W.; m. Alice Adele Tucker, Jan. 25, 1958; children: John M., Carl K. BS, U. Pitts., 1952; MS, Columbia U., 1958. Asst. adminstr. Bayonne (N.J.) Hosp., 1958-60; assoc. adminstr.

Binghamton (N.Y.) Gen. Hosp., 1960-63; chief exec. officer Putnam Community Hosp., Carmel, N.Y., 1963-65; v.p. A.J.J. Rourke, Inc., New Rochelle, N.Y., 1965-72; exec. dir. Lahey Clinic, Boston, 1972-79; pres., chief exec. officer Leonard Morse Health System, Natick, Mass., 1980-85, Leominster (Mass.) Health System, 1985-92; pres. Wathne Health Strategists, 1992—; adj. asst. prof. Boston U., 1981—; pres. Cen. New Eng. PHO, Leominster, 1991-92; hosp. cons. Contbr. articles to profl. jours. Mem. Mass. Hosp. Assn. (pres. 1987-88, chmn. 1987), New Eng. Hosp. Supts. Club (pres. 1986-88), North Cen. Mass. C. of C. (dir. 1988-91). Avocations: painting, sailing, photography. Home: 6 Colony Rd Lexington MA 02173-2004 Office: Wathne Health Strategists 6 Colony Rd Lexington MA 02173-2004

WATKIN, DAVID, film director, cinematographer; b. Margate, Eng., Mar. 23, 1925. Filmmaker, 1948—; asst. cameraman Brit. Transport Films, 1950-55, cameraman, 1955-61; ind. filmmaker, 1961—. Motion pictures include The Knack, 1964, Help!, 1965, Marat/Sade, 1966, How I Won the War, 1967, Charge of the Light Brigade, 1968, Catch 22, 1970, The Devils, 1971, The Boyfriend, 1971, The Homecoming, A Delicate Balance, 1973, The Three Musketeers, 1974, The Four Musketeers, 1976, Jesus of Nazareth, Mahogany, 1975, To The Devil a Daughter, 1976, Robin and Marian, 1976, Joseph Andrews, 1977, Cuba, 1979 Endless Love, 1981, Chariots of Fire, 1981, Yentil, 1983, The Hotel New Hampshire, 1984, White Nights, 1985, Out of Africa (Acad. award 1985), Return of Oz, 1985, Sky Bandits, 1986, Moonstruck, 1987, The Good Mother, 1988, Masquerade, 1988, Memphis Belle, 1990, Hamlet, 1990, An Object of Beauty, 1991, The Cabinet of Dr. Ramirez, 1991, Used People, 1992, The Boy's Life, 1993, Bopha, 1993, Milk Money, 1993, Jane Eyre, 1994, Bogus, 1995, Night Falls on Manhatten, 1995, Through Roses, 1996. Home: 6 Sussex Mews, Brighton BN2 1GZ, England

WATKINS, BIRGE SWIFT, real estate investment executive; b. Grand Rapids, Mich., May 2, 1949; s. Robert Goodell and Betty Jane (Swift) W.; m. Elizabeth Beverly Price, Nov. 28, 1985; children: Elizabeth Porter, Benjamin Thorne Swift, Robert William MacIntosh. BA, Alma Coll., 1971; MBA, London Bus. Sch., 1981; MPA, Harvard U., 1989. Staff asst. to Pres. of U.S. Washington, 1974-77; congl. press sec. U.S. Ho. of Reps., Washington, 1977; v.p. Arbor Internat. Inc., McLean, Va., 1980-81; asst. office dir. AID, Washington, 1982-88; asst. dir. Pres.'s Task Force on Internal Pvt. Enterprise, Washington, 1983-85; dep. asst. sec. USDA, Washington, 1989-90; dir. investor outreach Resolution Trust Corp., Washington, 1991-94; ptnr. Benton Resources, Washington, 1994-95; cons. Com Mac, Washington, 1995; mng. dir. Thornfalcon Internat., 1996—; bd. dirs. Corp. Healthcare Svcs. Inc., Springfield, Va.; cons. Washington Campus Inc., 1977, Va. Med. Assocs. Inc., Springfield, 1988. Mem. campaign staff Reagan-Bush campaign, Washington, 1980, Bush for President, 1988; mem. transition team office of Pres.-elect Bush, 1988. Mem. Urban Land Inst., Harvard Club (Washington). Avocations: skiing, running, contemporary art. Home: 832 Blackwell Rd Warrenton VA 22186-2216 Office: 832 Blackwell Rd Warrenton VA 22186-2216

WATKINS, CARLTON GUNTER, retired pediatrician; b. Wilmington, N.C., Aug. 25, 1919; s. Edison Lee and Maysie (Gunter) W.; m. Charlotte Jean Metcalf, Mar. 21, 1943; children—Lloyd Dixon Hollingsworth, Carlton Gunter, Mary Melissa, Charlotte Lou. A.B., U. N.C., 1939; M.D., Washington U., St. Louis, 1943. Rotating intern, asst. resident, resident pediatrics St. Louis City Hosp., 1943-45; resident pediatrics Duke Hosp., 1945-46; pvt. practice Charlotte, N.C., 1946-51, 53-73; chmn. dept. pediatrics Charlotte Meml. Hosp., 1958-61, 63-67; founder, sr. mem. Charlotte Pediatric Clinic, 1963-73; med. dir. Mecklenburg Center for Human Devel., Charlotte, 1973-89. Contbr. articles to med. jours. Pres. Charlotte-Mecklenburg Assn. for Children with Learning Disabilities, 1971-73, Mecklenburg Sr. Dems., 1993-94; mem. profl. adv. bd. Epilepsy Assn. N.C., 1976-86, v.p., 1986-88; mem. cons. bd. CPC Cedar Spring Hosp., 1992-96; mem. Charlotte-Mecklenburg Bd. Edn., 1966-74, Mecklenburg Human Svcs. Coun., 1994—. Capt. M.C., U.S. Army, 1951-53. Fellow Am. Acad. Pediatrics (life); mem. AMA (life), N.C. Med. Soc., Mecklenburg County Med. Soc., N.C. Pediatric Soc., Charlotte Pediatric Soc. (founder, 1st sec. 1950, pres. 1962), N.C. PTA (life), N.C. Zool. Soc. (life), Friends of U. N.C. Charlotte (life), Alpha Kappa Kappa, Old Catawba (Charlotte) Club. Home: 8713 Gainsford Ct Charlotte NC 28210-5850

WATKINS, CHARLES BOOKER, JR., mechanical engineering educator; b. Petersburg, Va., Nov. 20, 1942; s. Charles Booker and Haseltine Lucy (Thurston) W.; m. Judith Griffin; children: Michael, Steven. B.S. in Mech. Engring. cum laude, Howard U., 1964; M.S., U. N.Mex., 1966, Ph.D., 1970. Registered profl. engr., D.C. Mem. tech. staff Sandia Nat. Labs., Albuquerque, 1964-71; asst. prof. dept. mech. engring. Howard U., Washington, 1971-73; prof., chmn. dept. mech. engring. Howard U., 1973-86; Herbert G. Keyser prof. mech. engring. dean Sch. Engring. CCNY, 1986—; cons. U.S. Army, U.S. Navy, NSF, pvt. industries, 1984-85; bd. dirs. Parsons Brinkerhoff, Inc., 1994—. Research grantee NSF, U.S. Navy, Nuclear Regulatory Commn.; research grantee Dept. Energy, NASA; recipient Ralph R. Teetor award Soc. Automotive Engrs., 1980; Sandia Labs. doctoral fellow; NDEA fellow. Fellow ASME, AIAA (assoc.); mem. AAAS, Soc. Automotive Engrs., Am. Soc. Engring. Edn., Sigma Xi, Omega Psi Phi, Tau Beta Pi. Home: 171 Sherman Ave Teaneck NJ 07666-4121 Office: CCNY Sch Engring Convent Ave New York NY 10031

WATKINS, CHERYL DENISE, special education educator; b. Chgo., Dec. 15, 1963; d. Henry Eugene and Jean (Ingram) W. BS Edn. in Spl. Edn., Chgo. State U., 1987; MEd, U. Ill., 1992. Tchr. children with spl. needs Chgo. Bd. Edn., 1987—; cons. in field; adj. faculty Columbia Coll., Chgo., 1993, Nat. Louis U., Chgo. State U.; spkr. ednl. topics Chgo., St. Louis, Ill., Iowa, Fla., Md., Ala., Tex. Author: You Can Do Anything: A Story for Ryan, 1993, Living with Autism, 1995. Scout master Scouting for People with Disabilities, 1989—; vol. workshops Cabrini Green Tutoring Program, Chgo. Recipient Golden Apple award Golden Apple Found., 1991, Disting. Alumni award Nat. Assn. for Equal Opportunity in Higher Edn./Chgo. State U., 1992, Kizzy award, 1992, Tchr. Achiever award Michael Jordan Found. Edn. Club, 1993; named Outstanding Young Woman in Am., 1986. Mem. Nat. Bd. Profl. Teaching Standards (spl. needs com.), Kappa Delta Pi, Phi Delta Kappa, Delta Sigma Theta. Avocations: roller skating, reading, cake decorating, writing, traveling.

WATKINS, DAYTON J., federal agency administrator. BA in Econs., Howard U.; BS in Acctg., U. Md.; MA in Mgmt. and Adminstrn., Ctrl. Mich. U.; postgrad., Mount Vernon Coll. Economist U.S. Dept. of Transp., 1972-74; various fin. positions, 1974-76; acad. advisor U. Md., 1976-78; prin. acctg. firm, 1987; asst. treas./cash mgr. D.C. Dept. of Fin. and Revenue, 1978-80, dept. comptr., 1980-82, chief real estate taxation divsn., 1982-84; exec. asst. to the dir. D.C. Dept. of Housing and Community Devel., 1984-86, gen. mgr. bur. of real estate, 1986-90, acting dep. dir. of program ops., 1990-92; acting SBA adminstr. U.S. SBA, 1993, coun. to the adminstr., 1993—. Office: Dept of Agrl Rural Bus & Coop Svc 14th & Independence Ave SW Washington DC 20250

WATKINS, DEAN ALLEN, electronics executive, educator; b. Omaha, Oct. 23, 1922; s. Ernest E. and Pauline (Simpson) W.; m. Bessie Ena Hansen, June 28, 1944; children—Clark Lynn, Alan Scott, Eric Ross. B.S., Iowa State Coll., 1944; M.S., Calif. Inst. Tech., 1947; Ph.D., Stanford, 1951. Engr. Collins Radio Co., 1947-48; mem. staff Los Alamos Lab., 1948-49; tech. staff Hughes Research Labs., 1951-53; asso. prof. elec. engring. Stanford, 1953-56; prof., dir. Electron Devices Lab., 1956-64, lectr. elec. engring., 1964-70; co-founder, pres., chief exec. officer, dir. Watkins Johnson Co., Palo Alto, Calif., 1957-67; chmn., chief exec. officer, dir. Watkins Johnson Co., 1967-80, chmn., dir., 1980—; cons. Dept. Def., 1956-66; mem. White House Sci. Coun., 1988-89. Patentee in field; contbr. articles to profl. jours. Legis. chmn., dir. San Meteo County Sch. Bds. Assn., 1959-69; gov. San Francisco Bay Area Coun., 1966-75; Rep. precinct capt. Portola Valley, 1964; vice chmn. San Mateo County Fin. Com., 1967-69; mem. Calif. Rep. Ctrl. Com., 1964-68; trustee Stanford, 1966-69; regent U. Calif., 1969-96, chmn., 1972-74; mem. governing bd. Sequoia Union H.S. Dist., 1964-68, chmn., 1967-68; mem. governing bd. Portola Valley Sch. Dist., 1958-66; mem. bd. overseers Hoover Instn. on War, Revolution and Peace, Stanford, 1969—, chmn., 1971-73, 85-86; adv. policy commn. Santa Clara County Jr. Achievement; trustee Nat. Security Indsl. Assn., 1965-78. Served from pvt. to 1st lt. C.E., O.R.C. AUS, 1943-46. Fellow IEEE (7th region Achievement award 1957, Frederik Philips award 1981), AAAS; mem. Am. Phys. Soc., Am. Mgmt. Assn., Western Electronic Mfrs. Assn. (chmn. San Francisco coun. 1967, v.p., dir.), Calif. C. of C. (dir. 1965-92, treas. 1978, pres. 1981), Nat. Acad. Engring., Mounted Patrol San Mateo County (spl. dep. sheriff 1960-70), San Mateo County Horseman's Assn., San Benito County Farm Bur., Calif. Cattlemen's Assn., Delta Upsilon. Clubs: Palo Alto (Palo Alto), University (Palo Alto); Shack Riders (San Mateo County); Commonwealth (San Francisco); Rancheros Visitadores. Office: Watkins-Johnson Co 3333 Hillview Ave Palo Alto CA 94304-1223

WATKINS, GEORGE DANIELS, physics educator; b. Evanston, Ill., Apr. 28, 1924; s. Paul F. and Lois V. (Daniels) W.; m. Carolyn Lenore Nevin, June 19, 1949; children: Lois Roberta, Paul Brent, Ann Romaine. B.S., Randolph-Macon Coll., 1943; D.Sc. (hon.), 1976; M.A., Harvard U., 1947, Ph.D., 1952. Research physicist Gen. Electric Research Lab., Schenectady, 1952-75; adj. prof. Rensselaer Poly. Inst., 1962-65, SUNY-Albany, 1969-72; Sherman Fairchild prof. physics Lehigh U., Bethlehem, Pa., 1975-95, prof. emeritus, 1995—; chmn. Gordon Research Conf. on Defects in Semiconductors, 1981; mem. solid state adv. com. Oak Ridge Nat. Lab., 1980-85. Mem. editorial bd. Phys. Rev. B, 1978-82; contbr. articles to profl. jours. Served to lt. (j.g.) USNR, 1943-46. NSF fellow, 1966-67; named Virginian of Yr. Va. Press Assn., 1980; recipient Alexander von Humboldt sr. U.S. Scientist award, 1983, 91. Fellow Am. Phys. Soc. (Oliver E. Buckley award 1978), AAAS, Nat. Acad. Scis. Democrat. Unitarian. Office: Lehigh U Dept Physics Bethlehem PA 18015

WATKINS, HAROLD D., SR., protective services official; b. Feb. 19, 1933; m. Jean Watkins; 3 children. AD, Macomb Coll.; grad., Nat. Fire Acad. Md. From trial fire fighter to chief fire ops. City of Detroit Fire Dept., 1955-93, exec. fire commr., 1994—. With USAF. Mem. NAACP (life), Internat. Bd. Fire Chiefs, Internat. Assn. Black Firefighters, Phoenix Black Profl. Fire Fighters Assn. (charter). Home: 571 New Town Detroit MI 48215 Office: Detroit Fire Dept 250 W Larned Detroit MI 48226

WATKINS, HAROLD ROBERT, minister; b. Wauseon, Ohio, July 30, 1928; s. Orra Lynn and Florence Margaret (Bruner) W.; m. Evelyn Norma Earlywine, June 18, 1950; children: Mark Edwin, Nancy Jo Watkins Boyd. AB, Bethany Coll., 1950; BD, Lexington Theol. Sem., 1953; DD, Phillips U., 1985, Christian Theol. Sem., Indpls., 1995. Ordained minister Disciples of Christ, 1950. Min. Park Ave. Christian Ch., Tucson, 1953-56, First Christian Ch., Tuscaloosa, Ala., 1956-57; gen. ch. adminstr. Bd. Ch. Extension of Disciples of Christ, Indpls., 1958-95, pres., 1980-95; chmn. bd. dirs. Discipledata, Inc., Indpls. Trustee Bethany (W.Va.) Coll., 1976—, Nat. City Christian Ch. Corp., Washington, 1981—; bd. dirs. Ecumenical Ch. Loan Fund, Geneva; pres. World Conv. Chs. of Christ, Nashville, 1988-92. Recipient Outstanding Alumnus award Bethany Coll., 1975. Mem. Interfaith Forum on Religion, Art and Arch. (dir. officer 1979-95, pres. 1981-82, Elbert M. Conover award 1989), Indpls. Athletic Club. Home: 7402 Somerset Bay # 118 Indianapolis IN 46240-3400

WATKINS, HAYS THOMAS, retired railroad executive; b. Fern Creek, Ky., Jan. 26, 1926; s. Hays Thomas Sr. and Minnie Catherine (Whiteley) W.; m. Betty Jean Wright, Apr. 15, 1950; 1 son, Hays Thomas III. BS in Acctg., Western Ky. U., 1947; MBA, Northwestern U., 1948; LLD (hon.), Baldwin Wallace Coll., 1975, Alderson Broaddus Coll., 1980, Coll. of William and Mary, 1982, Va. Union U., 1987. CPA, Ill., Ohio. With C. & O. Ry. Cleve., 1949-80, v.p. fin., 1964-67, v.p. adminstrv. group, 1967-71, pres., chief exec. officer, 1971-73, chmn. bd., chief exec. officer, 1973-80; with B. & O. R.R., 1964-80, v.p. finance, 1964-71, pres., chief exec. officer, 1971-73, vice chmn. bd., chief exec. officer, 1973-80; chmn., chief exec. officer Chessie System, Inc., 1973-80; pres. and co-chief exec. officer CSX Corp. (merger of Chessie System, Inc. and Seaboard Coast Line Industries, Inc.), Richmond, Va., 1980-82, chmn. bd., chief exec. officer, 1982-89, chmn. bd., 1989-91; chmn. emeritus, 1991—. Vice rector bd. visitors Coll. William and mary, 1984-87, rector, 1987-93. With AUS, 1945-47. Named Man of Yr., Modern R.R. mag., 1984; recipient Excellence in Mgmt. award Industry Week mag., 1982. Mem. Nat. Assn. Accts., Am. Inst. C.P.A.'s. Clubs: Commonwealth (Richmond, Va.); Country of Va. (Richmond). Home: 22 Lower Tuckahoe Rd W Richmond VA 23233-6108 Office: CSX Corp PO Box 85629 Richmond VA 23285-5629

WATKINS, JAMES DAVID, food products executive; b. Rochester, Minn., Sept. 17, 1947; s. John Frederick and Lillian Kay (Johnson) W.; m. Elizabeth Smith Cieslowski; children: James David Jr., Joseph John. BA, U. Minn., 1969. Venture mgr. Pillsbury, Mpls., 1971-78; chief exec. officer Golden Valley Microwave Foods, Mpls., 1978—; bd. dirs. Country Lake Foods, Mpls. Bd. dirs. Big Brothers/Big Sisters, 1987. Home: 10011 NW Highway 225A Ocala FL 34482-1268 Office: Golden Valley Microwave Foods 7450 Metro Blvd Minneapolis MN 55439-3037*

WATKINS, JERRY WEST, retired oil company executive, lawyer; b. Vernon, Tex., Dec. 10, 1931; s. Terrell Clark and Daisy (West) W.; m. Elizabeth Jill Cole, Sept. 3, 1955. Student, Hendrix Coll., 1949-50, La. Poly. Inst., 1950-51; JD, U. Ark., 1954. Bar: Ark. 1954. Law clk. Supreme Ct. Ark., Little Rock, 1954-55; with Murphy Oil Corp., El Dorado, Ark., 1955-89, sec., gen. atty., 1966-71, sec., gen. counsel, 1971-88, v.p., dir., 1975-88, exec. v.p., 1991-92, also dir., 1975-89; chief exec. officer, bd. dirs. Ocean Drilling and Exploration Co., New Orleans, 1989-91; mem. Ark. Bd. Law Examiners, 1969-74. Trustee Ark. State U., 1982-87; mem. Barton Libr. Bd., El Dorado, 1966-89; bd. dirs. South Ark. Arts Ctr., El Dorado, 1979-82, 85-88, Warner Brown Hosp., El Dorado, 1984-87, South Ark. Med. Systems, 1987-89. Mem. ABA, Ark. Bar Assn., Union County Bar Assn. Home: 111 Watkins Dr El Dorado AR 71730-2752

WATKINS, JOAN MARIE, osteopath, occupational medicine physician; b. Anderson, Ind., Mar. 9, 1943; d. Curtis David and Dorothy Ruth (Beckett) W.; m. Stanley G. Nodvik, Dec. 25, 1969 (div. Apr. 1974). BS, West Liberty State Coll., 1965; Cert. of Grad. Phy. Therapy, Ohio State U., 1966; DO, Phila. Coll. Osteo., 1972; M of Health Professions Edn., U. Ill., Chgo., 1986; MPH, U. Ill., 1989. Diplomate Osteo. Nat. Bds., Am. Bd. Preventive Medicine. Emergency osteo. physician Cooper Med. Ctr., Camden, N.J., 1974-79, Shore Meml. Hosp., Somers Point, N.J., 1979-81, St. Francis Hosp., Blue Island, Ill., 1981-82; emergency osteo. physician Mercy Hosp. and Med. Ctr., Chgo., 1982-90, dir. emergency ctr., 1984-88; resident in occupational and preventive medicine U. Ill., 1988-90; corp. med. dir. occupl. health svc. Univ. Cmty. Hosp., Tampa, 1992—. Fellow Am. Coll. Occupl. and Environ. Medicine, Am. Co.. Preventive Medicine. Avocations: sailing, needlework, swimming. Home: 4306 Harbor House Dr Tampa FL 33615-5408 Office: U Community Hosp Occupational Health Svcs 3100 E Fletcher Ave Tampa FL 33613-4613

WATKINS, JOHN CHESTER ANDERSON, newspaper publisher; b. Corpus Christi, Tex., Oct. 2, 1912; s. Dudley Warren and Ruth (Woodruff) W.; m. Helen Danforth, Nov. 20, 1943 (div. 1959); children: Fanchon Metcalf Burnham, Robert Danforth, Stephen Danforth, Jane Pierce; m. Izetta Jewel Smith, Feb. 1960 (dec. 1989). Litt.D., Bryant Coll.; D.J., Roger Williams Coll., 1983. Reporter, makeup editor, aviation editor Dayton (Ohio) Jour. and Herald, 1934-35; reporter, aviation editor, mil. corr. Balt. Sun, 1935-41; asst. to pub., assoc. pub. Providence Jour.-Bull., 1945-54, pub., 1954-79; chmn. Providence Jour. Co., 1961-85, chmn. emeritus, 1985—; pres. Interam. Press Assn., 1971-72; also mem. adv. council. Served as fighter pilot USAAF, 1941-45; ops. officer 325th Fighter Group MTO. Decorated D.F.C., Air medal with 9 oak leaf clusters; knight comdr. Order of Merit Italy), R.I. Heritage Hall of Fame. Fellow New Eng. Acad. Journalists (Yankee Quill award); mem. Air Force Assn., Am. Soc. Newspaper Editors, New Eng. Daily Newspaper Assn. (pres. 1966-68), Hope Club, Agawam Hunt Club, Cruising Am. Club, N.Y. Yacht Club, Spouting Rock Beach Assn. Home: PO Box 1085 Providence RI 02901-1085 Office: Providence Jour Co 75 Fountain St Providence RI 02902-0050

WATKINS, JOHN FRANCIS, management consultant; b. Alhambra, Calif., May 21, 1925; s. Edward F. and Louise (Ward) W.; divorced; children—Stephen, Katherine, John Francis, William. BSCE, U. Tex., Austin, 1947. With Earle M. Jorgensen Co., Lynwood, Calif., 1947-90, sr. v.p. adminstrn., 1978-90, ret.; owner John F. Watkins Assocs., Pasadena, Calif., 1990—. Bd. dirs. Boys Republic, Chino Hills, Calif., 1970—, pres., 1977-80; bd. dirs. St. Luke Hosp., Pasadena, 1979-86, chmn. bd., 1982-86; pres. bd. Poly. Sch., Pasadena, 1978-80, Holy Family Sch., 1994—; bd. dirs. Econ. Literacy Coun. Calif., 1980-87, Pasadena Hist. Mus., 1990—, Greater Pasadena Bus. Ptnrs., 1995—; tri-sch. consortium mem., commn. on cath. schs. mem. Archdiocese L.A., 1995—; pres. coun. Coll. Sci. and Engring./Loyola Marymount U.; posse sheriff Huntington Westerners; adv. bd. Bishop Mora Salesian H.S., 1994—; active Edn. Found. Archdiocese L.A., 1995—; St. Gabriel pastoral region bd. dirs. Cath. Charities, 1994—. Mem. U.S. Navy League (nat. bd. dirs. 1989—, pres. Pasadena coun. 1992-93), Calif. Club, Annandale Golf Club, Serra Club (pres. 1995—), Valley Club (San Marino, Calif.). Republican. Roman Catholic. Home & Office: 410 California Ter Pasadena CA 91105-2419

WATKINS, JOHN GOODRICH, psychologist, educator; b. Salmon, Idaho, Mar. 17, 1913; s. John Thomas and Ethel (Goodrich) W.; m. Evelyn Elizabeth Browne, Aug. 21, 1932; m. Doris Wade Tomlinson, June 8, 1946; m. Helen Verner Huth, Dec. 28, 1971; children: John Dean, Jonette Alison, Richard Douglas, Gregory Keith, Rodney Philip, Karen Stroobants, Marvin R. Huth. Student, Coll. Idaho, 1929-30, 31-32; BS, U. Idaho, 1933, MS, 1936; PhD, Columbia U., 1941. Instr. high sch. Idaho, 1933-39; faculty Ithaca Coll., 1940-41, Auburn U., 1941-43; assoc. prof. Wash. State Coll., 1946-49; chief clin. psychologist U.S. Army Welch Hosp., 1945-46; clin. psychologist VA Hosp., American Lake, Wash., 1949-50; chief clin. psychologist VA Mental Hygiene Clinic, Chgo., 1950-53, VA Hosp., Portland, Oreg., 1953-64; prof. psychology U. Mont., Missoula, 1964-84; prof. emeritus U. Mont., 1984—, dir. clin. tng., 1964-80; lectr. numerous univs.; clin. asso. U. Oreg. Med. Sch., 1957; pres. Am. Bd. Examiners in Psychol. Hypnosis, 1960-62. Author: Objective Measurement of Instrumental Performance, 1942, Hypnotherapy of War Neuroses, 1949, General Psychotherapy, 1960, The Therapeutic Self, 1978, (with others) We, The Divided Self, 1982, Hypnotherapeutic Techniques, 1987, Hypnoanalytic Techniques, 1992; contbr. articles to profl. jours. Mem. Internat. Soc. Clin. and Exptl. Hypnosis (co-founder, pres. 1965-67, recipient awards 1960-65), Soc. Clin. and Exptl. Hypnosis (pres. 1969-71, Morton Prince award), Am. Psychol. Assn. (pres. divsn. 30 1975-76, recipient award 1993), Sigma Xi, Phi Delta Kappa. Home and Office: 413 Evans Ave Missoula MT 59801-5827
For a complete life one needs a job, a home, a love, a friend, and an enemy. My "enemies" are injustice, war, poverty, illness, and suffering, not people. Make your existence as meaningful as possible. Enjoy life fully, and when it comes time to leave, have no fear or regrets. Seek to leave this world a little better off because you lived. These are my values. Would that I were mature enough always to live up to them.

WATKINS, LLOYD IRION, university president; b. Cape Girardeau, Mo., Aug. 29, 1928; s. Herman Lloyd and Lydia Mina (Irion) W.; m. Mary Ellen Caudle, Aug. 14, 1949; children: John Lloyd, Joseph William, Robert Lawrence. BEd, Southeast Mo. State U., 1949; MS, U. Wis., 1951, PhD, 1954; DH (hon.), U. Dubuque, 1974; EdD (hon.), Srinakharinwirot U., Thailand, 1986. Tchr. Jackson (Mo.) High Sch., 1948-50; asst. prof. Moorhead State Coll., 1954-56; asst., assoc. prof. Ohio U., 1956-64, asst. to acad. v.p., assoc. prof., 1964-66; exec. v.p. Ida. State U., 1966-69; pres. Iowa Assn. Pvt. Colls. and Univs. Des Moines, 1969-73, West Tex. State U., 1973-77; pres. Ill. State U., Normal, 1977-88, prof., pres. emeritus, 1988-91, pres. emeritus, 1991—. Contbr. articles to profl. jours. Recipient Baker grant for Research Ohio U., 1963, Alumni Merit award S.E. Mo. State U., 1978. Mem. McLean County Humane Soc., McLean County Hist. Soc., Citizens' Com., The Alumni Club, Crestwick Country Club, Kappa Delta Pi, Phi Alpha Theta, Rotary. Home: RR 13 Box 111 Bloomington IL 61704-8917

WATKINS, MICHAEL DEAN, town planner; b. Chillicothe, Ohio, June 14, 1961; s. James A. and Delores G. (Gloff) W. BArch, U. Cin., 1985. Registered architect, Md. Project architect Cho, Wilks & Benn, Balt., 1985-88; town architect Andres Duany & Elizabeth Plater-Zyberk, Architects, Washington, 1988—; speaker, panelist in field. Jr. high youth sponsor, mem. bldg. com., deacon Mountain Christian Ch., Joppa, Md. Recipient Young Arch.'s award Progressive Architecture mag., 1993. Office: DPZ Architects 320 Firehouse Ln Gaithersburg MD 20878-5643

WATKINS, MICHAEL JAMES, real estate broker; b. Crawfordsville, Ind., Dec. 18, 1945; s. James H. Gordon and Mary Jane Harlson; m. Jeanne Watkins, Apr. 3, 1971; children: Patrick, christopher. BS, U. Indpls., 1968; MS, Butler U., 1972. Tchr., coach New Palestine (Ind.) High Sch., 1968-69, Franklin (Ind.) High Sch., 1969-72; admissions counselor U. Indpls., 1972-73, dir. fin. aid, 1973-76, dean of students, 1975-78; owner Michael J. Realty, Indpls., 1978-80; sales mgr. Credence Contractors, Greenwood, Ind., 1980-83; broker, assoc. Tomlin Realtors, Greenwood, 1983-95; pres. Mike Watkins Real Estate Group, Greenwood, 1995—. Mem. Pres.'s Club, U. Indpls., 1984—; trustee Marian Coll., Indpls., 1989-92, U. Indpls., 1992—. Named to Outstanding Young Men of Am., 1974, 76. Mem. Met. Bd. Realtors (named Southside Realtor of Yr. 1984), Nat. Assn. Realtors, U. Indpls. Alumni Varsity Club (Alumnus of Yr. 1986). Republican. Roman Catholic. Avocations: golf, boating, family activities. Home: 3696 Saddle Club Rd Greenwood IN 46143-9230 Office: Mike Watkins Real Estate 633 Library Park Ste J Greenwood IN 46142

WATKINS, NANCY HOBGOOD, sales executive; b. Oxford, N.C., Mar. 7, 1949; d. Ruben Northington and Julia Clyde (Hobgood) W. AA, Vardell Hall Jr. Coll., Red Springs, N.C., 1967-68; BS in Edn., Atlantic Christian Coll., 1971. Tchr. Granville County Schs., 1972-74; with Combined Ins. Co., 1974-76; dist. mgr. Investors Heritage Life Ins. Co., 1976-80; mfrs. rep. Jerry Elsher Co., N.Y.C., 1982-85, Down South, Atlanta, 1985-90; nat. sales mgr. Chang Seng, Inc., Charlotte, N.C., 1990-93; mfrs. rep. Good Ship, Atlanta, 1993—. Mem. Young Reps., Charlotte, 1985-91. Episcopalian. Avocations: reading, walking, tennis.

WATKINS, PAUL B., academic research center administrator, medical educator; b. Schenectady, N.Y., Feb. 17, 1953; s. George Daniels and Carolyn Lenore (Nevin) W.; m. Joanne Carol Spalty, July 4, 1981; children: Andrew James, Melanie Ann. BA, Cornell U., 1975, MD, 1979. Intern N.Y. Hosp., 1979-80, resident, 1980-82; fellow Medical Coll. Va., 1982-84; physician admission ward Khao-I-Dang Cambodian Refuge Camp, Thailand, 1982; from instr. to asst. prof. Med. Coll. Va., 1984-86; asst. prof. U. Mich., Ann Arbor, 1986-91, assoc. prof. medicine, 1991—, assoc. dir. clin. rsch. ctr., 1991, dir. clin. rsch. ctr., 1991—; advisor toxic waste orgn. Inst. Medicine, Washington, 1993—; mem. toxicology study sect. NIH, Bethesda, Md., 1992—; sci. cons. Parke-Davis Pharm., Organon Internat., Wyeth-Ayerst, Proctor and Gamble, Abbott Labs., Bristol-Meyers Squibb. Contbr. articles to profl. jours. Asst. coach Burns Park Elem. Soccer Team, Ann Arbor, 1991—, softball team, 1993; mem. St. Andrews Ch., Ann Arbor, 1990—. Recipient VA Career Devel. Associate Investigator award, 1984-86, Rsch. Assoc. award, 1987-91. Fellow ACP; mem. AAAS, Am. Soc. Clin. Investigation (elected), Am. Assn. Study Liver Disease, Am. Gastroent. Assn., Am. Fedn. Clin. Rsch., Midwest Gut Club, Ctrl. Soc. Clin. Rsch., Internat. Assn. Study Liver, Internat. Soc. Study Xenobiotics. Avocations: jogging, skiing, wind surfing, tennis, scuba diving. Home: 2112 Wallingford Rd Ann Arbor MI 48104-4563 Office: U Mich Hosp Gen Clin Rsch Ctr 1500 E Med Ctr Dr A7119 Ann Arbor MI 48109-0108

WATKINS, STANLEY, academic director; b. Bklyn., Feb. 23, 1929; s. Harry and Rose (Smith) W.; m. Dorothy Yaffe, Aug. 3, 1953; children: Leonard, Ellen. BSME, Cooper Union, 1962; MBA, St. Johns U., 1972. Adminstr. Loral Corp., N.Y.C., 1958-70; rsch. adminstr. City Coll. of CUNY, N.Y.C., 1970—. Served with U.S. Army, 1951-53, Korea. Mem. Soc. Rsch. Adminstrs., Nat. Coun. Univ. Rsch. Adminstrs. Avocations: skiing, biking. Home: 60 W 13th St New York NY 10011-7959 Office: City Coll CUNY Convent Ave at 138th St New York NY 10031

WATKINS, STEPHEN EDWARD, accountant; b. Oklahoma City, Sept. 1, 1922; s. Ralph Bushnell and Jane (Howell) W.; m. Suzanne Fowler, Aug. 16, 1976; children—Elizabeth Ann Watkins Racicot, Stephen Edward. B.B.A., U. N.Mex., 1944. C.P.A., N.Mex. With Peat, Marwick, Mitchell & Co., 1944-67; pres. The New Mexican, Santa Fe, 1967-78, 90—; pvt. practice pub. acctg. Santa Fe, 1978—. Vestryman Ch. of Holy Faith; trustee St. Vincent Hosp., 1979-85, Orchestra Santa Fe, 1976-82, Hist. Santa Fe Found. (pres.

1990). Mem. AICPA, Sons of Am. Revolution, Rotary. Home: 1325 Don Gaspar Ave Santa Fe NM 87505-4627 Office: 223 E Palace Ave Santa Fe NM 87501-2044

WATKINS, SYDNEY LYNN, sports administrator; b. Hartford, Conn., Sept. 12, 1964; s. Robert Lee and Joan (Hardy) W. BS, Howard U., 1986, MS, 1989. Cert. U.S. Olympic Acad., Sport Adminstrn. Facility Mgmt. Inst. Water safety instr. Howard U. Satellite Youth Program, Washington, 1986; water safety instr. D.C. Dept. Recreation, Washington, 1986-87, phys. therapeutic recreation specialist, 1987-88; account rep. AT&T, Silver Spring, Md., 1988-90; program assoc. Amateur Athletic Found., L.A., 1991-95; program mgr. L.A. Team Mentoring, 1995—; spl. asst. to pres. Dr. LeRoy T. Walker Found., Durham, N.C., 1993. African Am. Summit fellow NAACP, L.A., 1994; Patricia Harris grantee Howard U., 1989. Mem. AAHPERD, Alpha Kappa Alpha. Home: 1233 1/2 S Citrus Ave Los Angeles CA 90019-1603

WATKINS, TED ROSS, social work educator; b. Terrell, Tex., Dec. 2, 1938; s. Daniel Webster and Iva Lucy (Lowrie) W.; m. Betty Diane Dobbs, May 30, 1959; children: Evan Scott, Brett Dobbs, James David. BA in Psychology, U. North Tex., 1961; MSW, La. State U., 1963; D of Social Work, U. Pa., 1976. Staff social worker Mercer County Mental Health Ctr., Sharon, Pa., 1963-65; chief social worker, assoc. exec. Talbot Hall Treatment Ctr., Jonestown, Pa., 1965-70; chief social worker Harrisburg (Pa.) Mental Health Ctr., 1970-71; asst. prof. social work U. Tex., Arlington, 1971-76; dir. counseling svcs. Family Svcs., Inc., Ft. Worth, 1976-79; assoc. prof. social work U. Tex., 1979-85, dir. criminal justice, 1985-87, chair dept. sociology, 1987-91, assoc. prof., grad. advisor social work, 1991—; cons. in field. Contbr. articles to profl. jours. Tex. del. to Pres.'s Commn. in Mental Health, Austin, 1978. Recipient Golladay Teaching award Coll. Liberal Arts, Arlington, 1990; named Outstanding Profl. Human Svcs., 1972. Mem. NASW (state bd. dirs. 1976-78, 80-82, unit chair, vol. lobbyist 1982), Acad. Cert. Social Workers (lic. master social worker, advanced clin. practitioner). Democrat. Methodist. Avocations: music, painting, camping. Office: U Tex Box 19129 UTA Arlington TX 76019

WATKINS, WILLIAM, JR., electric power industry executive; b. Jersey City, N.J., Aug. 12, 1932; s. William James and Willie Ree (Blount) W.; m. Sylvia I. Mulzac, Oct. 16, 1955; children: Cheryl, Rene, Linda. BBA, Pace U., 1954; MBA, N.Y.U., 1962; postgrad. advanced mgmt. program, U. Mich., 1979; postgrad. exec. program, Edison Electric Inst., 1988. Staff asst. Consol. Edison Co. N.Y., N.Y.C., 1957-64; sys. mgr. Volkswagen Am., Englewood Cliffs, N.J., 1964-71; v.p., dir. adminstrn. New Eng. Power Svc. Co., Westboro, Mass., 1972-82, v.p., dir. human resources, 1986-92; v.p., dist. mgr. Narragansett Electric Co., Providence, 1982-86, exec. v.p., 1992—; bd. dirs. Peerless Precision Corp., Lincoln, R.I., 1982-91. Chmn. R.I. Urban Project, Providence, 1984, R.I. Coun. for Econ. Edn., Providence, 1984; mem. Gov.'s Commn. on Health Care Reform, 1993-94; trustee R.I. Hosp., 1995—, Roger Williams U., Bristol, R.I., 1991-94; bd. dirs. R.I. Hosp. Trust Nat. Bank, Providence, 1987—, R.I. Hosp. Fin. Corp., Providence, 1987-91, Inroads, 1993—, Leadership R.I., 1993-95, NCCJ, 1993—; mem. resource and devel. commn. Episcopal Diocese Mass., 1988-92; vice chmn. bd. trustees RISD, 1995—. Recipient Cmty. Svc. award Urban League R.I., 1986, Paris V. Sterett award John Hope Settlement House, 1987, Small Bus. Adminstrn. Adv. of the Yr. award, 1994. Mem. N.E. Indsl. Developers Assn. (bd. dirs. 1993—), R.I. Urban Bankers Assn., Kappa Alpha Psi. Avocations: swimming, biking, hiking, traveling. Home: 61 Stone Ridge Rd Franklin MA 02038-3121 Office: Narragansett Electric Co 280 Melrose St Providence RI 02907-2152

WATKINS, WILLIAM LAW, retired lawyer; b. Anderson, S.C., Dec. 26, 1910; s. Thomas Franklin and Agnes (Law) W.; m. Frances Sitton, Oct. 23, 1937; children: Sarah Watkins Marshall, Anna Watkins Hattaway, Elizabeth Watkins Kinghorn, Jane Watkins Mudd. A.B., Wofford Coll., 1932; LL.B., U. Va., 1933; LLD, Anderson (S.C.) Coll., 1996. Bar: S.C. 1933. Practice law Anderson, S.C., 1933; mem. Watkins & Prince, 1934-46, Watkins & Watkins, 1946-54, Watkins, Vandiver & Freeman, 1954-64, Watkins, Vandiver, Kriven & Long, 1964-67, Watkins, Vandiver, Kirven, Long & Gable, 1968-77; ptnr. Watkins, Vandiver, Kirven, Gable & Gray, 1977-85, of counsel, 1985-92; bd. dirs. Duke Power Co., 1975-84, Perpetual Bank, F.S.B., 1953-92. Mem. S.C. Ho. of Reps., 1935-36; mem. S.C. Probation, Parole and Pardon Bd., 1954-69; trustee Presbyterian Coll., Clinton, S.C., 1966-75, Anderson County Hosp. Assn., S.C., 1964-74. Served with AUS, 1942-46. Decorated Bronze Star with oak leaf cluster. Fellow Am. Coll. Trial Lawyers, Am. Bar Found.; mem. ABA, S.C. Bar, Anderson Bar Assn., Phi Beta Kappa, Sigma Alpha Epsilon. Presbyterian. Lodge: Rotary. Home: 317 North St Anderson SC 29621-5814

WATKINSON, PATRICIA GRIEVE, museum director; b. Merton, Surrey, Eng., Mar. 28, 1946; came to U.S., 1972; d. Thomas Wardle and Kathleen (Bredl) Grieve. BA in Art History and Langs. with honors, Bristol U., Eng., 1968. Sec. Mayfair Fine Arts and The Mayfair Gallery, London, 1969-71; adminstr. Bernard Jacobson, Print Pub., London, 1971-73; freelance exhbn. work, writer Kilkenny Design Ctr., Davis Gallery, Irish Arts Council in Dublin, Ireland, 1975-76; curator of art Mus. Art, Wash. State U., Pullman, 1978-83, dir., 1984—; asst. prof. art history Wash. State U., Pullman, 1978. Co-author, co-editor: Gaylen Hansen: The Paintings of a Decade, 1985. Mem. Assn. Am. Colls. and Univ. Mus. and Galleries (western regional rep. 1987-89), Art Mus. Assn. Am. (Wash. state rep. 1986-87), Internat. Coun. Mus. (modern art com. 1986-89), Wash. Mus. Assn. (bd. dirs. 1984-87), Am. Fedn. Arts (western region rep. 1987-89), Wash. Art Consortium (pres. 1993-95), Western Mus. Assn. (bd. dirs. 1996—). Office: Wash State U Mus Art Pullman WA 99164-7460

WATKISS, ERIC JOHN, naval flight officer; b. East Point, Ga., May 17, 1964; s. George Philip Watkiss and Barbara Anne Seaman; m. Lynne Lee Novak, Nov. 25, 1989. B of Aerospace Engring., Ga. Inst. Tech., 1986; MS in Aero. Engring., Naval Postgrad. Sch., 1994; grad., U.S. Naval Test Pilot Sch., 1995. Airport mgr. Aerocountry Airport, McKinney, Tex., 1981-86; advanced through grades to lt. comdr. USN, 1996, naval flight officer, 1986—, naval flight test officer, 1995-96, naval test pilot sch. instr., 1996—. Mem. AIAA, MENSA. Republican. Episcopalian. Avocations: flying, mountain biking, skiing. Home: 20705 Hermanville Rd Lexington Park MD 20653 Office: US Naval Test Pilot Sch Aircraft Divsn Naval Air Warfare Ctr Patuxent River MD 20670-5304

WATLINGTON, JOHN FRANCIS, JR., banker; b. Reidsville, N.C., Mar. 23, 1911; s. John Francis and Frances (Byers) W.; m. Margaret Jones, Feb. 22, 1947; children: John Francis III, Anne Wilson Watlington Curtis. A.B., Washington and Lee U., 1933. With Wachovia Bank & Trust Co., Winston-Salem, N.C., 1933-82; transit clk., asst. cashier, asst. v.p., v.p., sr. v.p. Wachovia Bank & Trust Co., 1933-56, pres., 1956-74, chmn., 1974-76, chmn. exec. com., 1977-82, also chmn. Charlotte office, 1946-56; chmn. Wachovia Corp., 1968-76; chmn. exec. com., 1977-82; ret. dir. Piedmont Natural Gas Co., Inc.; dir. emeritus USAir Group Inc. Trustee Union Theol. Sem.; chmn. Union Theol-Sem., 1980-82; hon. life trustee Va. Found. for Ind. Colls.; hon. chmn. bd. visitors Bowman Gray Sch. Medicine; dir., past pres. Presbyn. Ch. U.S.A. Found. Mem. Winston-Salem C. of C. (pres. 1958-59), N.C. Citizens Assn. Presbyterian. Home: 17 Graylyn Place Ln Winston Salem NC 27106-5816 Office: 100 N Main St Winston Salem NC 27101

WATRING, WATSON GLENN, gynecologic oncologist, educator; b. St. Albans, W.Va., June 2, 1936; m. Roberta Tawell. BS, Washington & Lee U., 1958; MD, W.Va. U., 1962. Diplomate Am. Bd. Ob-Gyn, Am. Bd. Gynecol. Oncology. Intern The Toledo Hosp., 1963; resident in ob-gyn Ind. U., Indpls., 1964-66, Tripler Gen. Hosp., Honolulu, 1968-70; resident in gen. and oncologic surgery City of Hope Nat. Med. Ctr., Duarte, Calif., 1970-71, assoc. dir. gynecol. oncology, sr. surgeon, 1973-77; fellow in gynecol. oncology City of Hope Nat. Med. Ctr. and UCLA Med. Ctr., 1972-74; asst. prof. ob-gyn UCLA Med. Ctr., 1972-77; assoc. prof., sr. gynecologist, sr. surgeon Tufts New Eng. Med. Ctr. Hosp., Boston, 1977-80, asst. prof. radiation therapy, 1978-80; practice medicine specializing in ob-gyn Boston, 1980-82; assoc. prof. ob-gyn U. Mass., Worcester, 1982; regional dir. gynecol. oncology So. Calif. Permanente Med. Group, Los Angeles, 1982—, asst. dir. residency tng., 1985—; dir. gynecol. oncology St. Margarets Hosp. for Women, Dorchester, Mass., 1977-80; clin. prof. ob-gyn U. Calif., Irvine, 1982—. Contbr. articles to profl. jours. Mem. ch. council Luth. Ch. of the Foothills, 1973-75. Served to lt. col. M.C., U.S. Army, 1965-71. Fellow Am. Coll. Ob-Gyn, Los Angeles Obstet. and Gynecol. Soc.; mem. AAAS, ACS (Calif. and Mass. chpts.), Boston Surg. Soc., AMA, Mass. Med. Soc., Mass. Suffolk Dist. Med. Soc., Internat. Soc. Gynecol. Pathologists, Western Soc. Gynecologists and Obstetricians, Am. Soc. Clin. Oncology, Soc. Gynecol. Oncologists, Western Assn. Gynecol. Oncologists (sec.-treas. 1976-81, program chmn. 1984, pres. 1985—), New Eng. Assn. Gynecol. Oncologists (chmn. charter com.), New Eng. Obstet. and Gynecol. Soc., Obstet. Soc. Boston, Am. Radium Soc., Soc. Study Breast Disease, New Eng. Cancer Soc., Internat. Gynecol. Cancer Soc., Daniel Morton Soc., Sigma Xi. Republican. Avocations: golf, skiing, horticulture. Office: So Calif Permanente Med Group 4950 W Sunset Blvd Los Angeles CA 90027-5822

WATROUS, ROBERT THOMAS, academic director; b. Cleve., Apr. 20, 1952; s. Frank Thomas and Marie Anne (Kmeicik) W.; m. Robin Joyce Braun, Mar. 14, 1981 (div. 1993); 1 child, Michael Francis. BS, U. Dayton, 1974, MS, 1977. Dir. student ctr. for off campus community rels. Univ. Dayton, Ohio, 1974-76; resident dir. Univ. Dayton, 1976-78; dir. of housing St. Bonaventure Univ., Olean, N.Y., 1978-81; asst. dean of student life/housing Kutztown (Pa.) Univ. of Pa., 1981-86, dir. commuter and jud. affairs, 1986-89, 92-95; faculty senate Kutztown (Pa.) U., 1986-89, 92-95; mem. Pa. Task Force on Intergroup Behavior in Higher Edn., 1991-94; trainer Pa. Interagy. Task Force on Civil Tension, Harrisburg, Pa., 1989—; exec. coun. Adult Learners Consortium, Bloomsburg, Pa., 1990-91; mem. Lehigh Valley Svc. Learning Consortium, 1994—. Bd. mgr. Tri Valley YMCA, Fleetwood, Pa., 1983-94; adv. bd. Crossroads, Kutztown, 1989-94; bd. dirs. Jr. Achievement of Berks County, Reading, Pa., 1990, Reading, Pa., 1990, Reading and Berks Coun. YMCA, 1992-96; mem. Leadership Berks, Reading, 1990; bd. dirs. Leadership Berks, 1995—; co-founder Leading Sch. Bds., 1994—; mem. YMCA cultural diversity and internat. awareness com., 1994—. Mem. Nat. Assn. Student Pers. Adminstrs. (profl. affiliate), Hawk Mt. Coun. Boy Scouts Am. (sustaining mem.), Berks County C. of C. (sch. bd. governance com. 1993—), Fleetwood Youth Soccer Club treas., Fleetwood Youth Basketball Assn. coach. Avocations: golf, sports, gardening. Office: Kutztown Univ PO Box 37 Kutztown PA 19530-0037

WATROUS, WILLIAM RUSSELL, trombonist, composer, conductor; b. Middletown, Conn., June 8, 1939; s. Ralph Jarvas and Edna (Little) W.; m. Mary Ann Ackerman, Oct. 1978; children: Melody, Cheryl, Jason. Student pub. schs., New London, Conn. lectr. jazz edn., participant music seminars, brass confs.; bd. dirs. Internat. Trombone Workshop. Trombonist with bands of Woody Herman, Quincy Jones, Count Basie, leader own band, Manhattan Wildlife Refuge (now Calif. Wildlife Refuge), from 1970, composer: Dirty Dan and others (Voted Number One Trombonist, Downbeat Reader's Poll, 1975, 76, 77, 78, 79, 80, Internat. Critics Poll 1976, 77). Albums include The Tiger of San Pedro, Bone Straight Ahead, Watrous in Hollywood, I'll Play For You, Coronary Trombossa, La Zorra, Roarin' Back Into New York, New York, Someplace Else, 1986, Reflections, 1987, Bone-Ified, 1992, A Time for Love, 1993. Served with USNR, 1956-60. Mem. ASCAP, Am. Fedn. Musicians. Address: care Welk Records 1299 Ocean Ave Ste 800 Santa Monica CA 90401-1040

WATSON, ADA, secondary education educator; b. Memphis, Oct. 21, 1951; d. Leroy and Helen Marie (Sparks) Preyer; m. William Elton Watson, June 2, 1973; children: William Elton Jr., Moneka Nésha. BS in Edn., Memphis State U., 1974, care-guidance of children endorsement, 1976; MS in Human Resource Devel., U. Tenn., 1995. Parenting educator Sea Isle Adult Vocat.-Tech. Ctr., Memphis, 1975-76; tchr. child care Sheffield Vocat.-Tech. Ctr., Memphis, 1976-88; tchr. home econs. and teen parenting edn. Booker T. Washington H.S., Memphis, 1989—. Author teen parenting videos; co-author child care curriculum. Mem. adv. bd. Golden Leaf Day Care Ctr., Memphis, 1979-81; chmn. March of Dimes, Sheffield Vocat.-Tech. Ctr., 1985-86; craft coord. Vacation Bible Sch., Greater Imani Bapt. Ch., Memphis, 1991; Sunday sch. tchr. St. Matthew Bapt. Ch., Millington, Tenn., 1992—, dir. Vacation Bible Sch., 1992-95. Recipient svc. award Future Homemakers Am., 1986-89. Mem. NEA, Am. Vocat. Assn., Tenn. Edn. Assn., Memphis Edn. Assn. (faculty rep. 1978-86, bargaining com. 1981, ins. chmn. 1983, svc. awards 1981, 83), Nat. Assn. Home Econs. Tchrs. (local arrangements com., membership com., svc. award 1993), Tenn. Vocat. Assn. (v.p. home econs., svc. award 1994), Tenn. Assn. Vocat. Home Econs. Tchrs. (bd. dirs., v.p., pres.-elect, pres. 1995, svc. award 1985, 90, 91, 92-94), Assn. Supvsn. and Curriculum Devel. Democrat. Avocations: sewing and crafts, singing, working with youth groups. Home: 2614 Monette Ave Memphis TN 38127-6835 Office: Booker T Washington HS 715 S Lauderdale St Memphis TN 38126-3910

WATSON, ALEXANDER FLETCHER, organization executive, former ambassador; b. Boston, Aug. 8, 1939; s. Fletcher G. and Alice Victoria (Hodson) W.; m. Judith Dawson Tuttle, June 23, 1962; children: David F., Caitlin H. BA, Harvard U., 1961; MA, U. Wis., 1969. Consular officer Am. embassy, Santo Domingo, Dominican Republic, 1962-64, Madrid, 1964-66; internat. relations officer Dept. State, Washington, 1966-68, 73-75, spl. asst., 1975-77, dir. Office of Devel. Fin., 1978-79; polit. officer Am. embassy, Brasilia, Brazil, 1969-70; prin. officer Am. Consulate, Salvador, Brazil, 1970-73; dep. chief of mission Am. Embassy, La Paz, Bolivia, 1979-81; dep. chief of mission Bogota, Colombia, 1981-84, Brasilia, Brazil, 1984-86; U.S. ambassador to Lima, Peru, 1986-89; dep. U.S. permanent rep. to UN, 1989-93; asst. sec. of state for inter-Am. affairs Dept. of State, Washington, 1993-96; v.p., exec. dir. L.Am. and Caribbean program The Nature Conservancy, Arlington, Va., 1996—. Bd. dirs. Inter-Am. Found. Decorated Order of San Carlos, Govt. of Colombia, 1984; Order of the Condor, Govt. of Bolivia, 1985; Labor Justice Order of Merit, Govt. of Brazil, 1987; Order of the Sun, Govt. of Peru, 1989. Mem. Am. Soc., Am. Fgn. Svc. Assn., Coun. on Fgn. Rels. Office: The Nature Conservancy Internat Hdqs 1815 N Lynn St Arlington VA 22209

WATSON, ANDREW SAMUEL, psychiatry and law educator; b. Highland Park, Mich., May 2, 1920; s. Andrew Nicol and Eva Arvel (Barnes) W.; m. Catherine Mary Osborne, Sept. 1942; children: Andrew Nicol, John Lewis, David Winfield, Steven; m. Joyce Lynn Goldstein, July 21, 1967. BS in Zoology, U. Mich., 1942; MD, Temple U., 1950, M in Med. Sci., 1954. Intern, U. Pa. Grad. Hosp., 1950-51; resident in psychiatry Temple U., Phila., 1951-54; spl. lectr. Sch. Social Work, Bryn Mawr Coll., 1955-59; mem. med. faculty U. Pa., 1954-59, law faculty, 1955-59; prof. psychiatry U. Mich., Ann Arbor, 1959-80, mem. law faculty, 1959-90, prof. emeritus psychiatry and of law, 1990; pvt. practice medicine, specializing in psychiatry, Ann Arbor, 1959—. Mem. Mich. Law Enforcement and Criminal Justice Commn., 1968-72. Served to capt. Med. Service Corps, AUS, 1942-46. Recipient Issac Ray award Am. Psychiat. Assn., 1978. Mem. Am. Psychiat. Assn., Am. Coll. Psychiatry, ABA (assoc.). Democrat. Unitarian. Author: Psychiatry for Lawyers, rev. edit., 1978; The Lawyer in the Interviewing and Counseling Process, 1976; others. Home: 21 Ridgeway St Ann Arbor MI 48104-1739 Office: 555 E William St Apt 21D Ann Arbor MI 48104-2427

WATSON, ANTHONY L., health facility executive; b. 1942. Supervising pub. health advisor dept.health edn. and welfare Ctr. for Disease Control, Pub. Health Svc., 1966-70; dep. dir. Comprehensive Health Planning Agy., N.Y.C., 1970-76; exec. v.p. Health Systems Agency of N.Y.C., 1976-85; pres. Health Ins. Plan Greater N.Y., N.Y.C. Mem. Community Council of Greater N.Y.; pres, CEO The N.Y. Urban Coalition. Mem. Am. Health Planning Assn., Am. Hosp. Assn. Office: Health Ins Plan Greater NY 7 W 34th St New York NY 10001-8100*

WATSON, ARTHUR DENNIS, government official; b. Brownsville, Pa., May 11, 1950; s. Arthur Francis Puglia and Margaret Teresa Mastile; stepson of John Leslie Watson; m. Kathleen Frances Zaccardo, July 16, 1983; 1 child, Fiona Kathleen. BSBA, U. Richmond, 1972; MS in Bus.-Govt. Rels. Am. U., 1977, MA in Lit., 1979; PhD in English Lang. and Lit. Cath. U., 1987. Statisical asst. U.S. Postal Svc. Hdqrs., Washington, 1972-73, economist assoc., 1973-74, staff economist, 1974-77, mktg. analyst, 1977; rate analyst U.S. Postal Rate Commn., Washington, 1977-79, dir. pub. affairs, 1979-82; spokesman, pub. affairs officer ICC, Washington, 1982-89, dep. dir. pub. affairs, 1989-93, assoc. dir. congl. and pub. affairs, 1993-95, assoc. dir. congressional and pub. affairs surface transp. bd., U.S. DOT, 1995—; pres. Arthur D. Watson and Co., Clifton, Va., 1983—. Washington corr. Linn's Stamp News, Sidney, Ohio, 1983-84; pub. rels. columnist Arundel Communications, Reston, Va., 1991-92; contbr. articles to profl. jours.; reader Washington Ear, WETA-FM radio side channel, 1977. With USCG, 1972-78. Recipient Meritorious Svc. medal, Pub. Svc. award ICC, 1989. Mem. Nat. Assn. Govt. Communicators, E. Claiborne Robins Sch. Bus. Alumni Assn., Assn. Transp. Law, Logistics and Policy, USS Natoma Bay Assn., Pub. Rels. Soc. Am. Roman Catholic. Avocations: classical music, reading, writing, model building, travel. Home: 6521 Rockland Dr Clifton VA 22024-2415 Office: ICC 1201 Constitution Ave NW Washington DC 20423-0001

WATSON, BILLY, publishing executive, newspaper; b. Pitts, Ga., Sept. 7, 1938; m. Helen Turk; children: Kevin, Kim Holland. Degree in Journalism, U. Ga., 1960; postgrad., Ga. State U. With Cordele Dispatch, Wilcox County Chronicle, 1960-61; with Macon Telegraph, 1963, 67-78, bur. chief Atlanta, 1963-67; exec. editor Telegraph and News, 1978-83, gen. mgr., 1983-87; pres., pub. Columbus Ledger-Enquirer, 1987—; vis. instr. journalism Mercer U.; mem. journalism bd. U. Ga.; pres. Ga. AP, chmn. News Coun. AP. Founding chmn. Columbus Literate Community Program, Inc.; past chmn. Ga. Coun. Adult Literacy; bd. dirs. UPtown Columbus, Columbus Tech. Inst., Creek Indian Meml. Assn. With US Army. Mem. Ga. Press Assn. (former pres.), U. Ga. Journalism Alumni Assn. (former pres.), Columbus Rotary Club, Columbus Country Club, Chattahoochee River Club, Columbus C. of C. (bd. dirs.). Avocations: swimming, running, fishing, bluegrass music. Office: R W Page Corp 17 W 12th St Columbus GA 31901-2413

WATSON, C. L. (CHUCK WATSON), gas industry executive; b. 1950. Grad., Okla. State U., 1972. With Conoco, Inc., Houston, 1972-85; pres, CEO Natural Gas Clearinghouse, Houston, 1985—. Office: Natural Gas Clearinghouse 13430 Northwest Fwy Houston TX 77040-6000*

WATSON, CATHERINE ELAINE, journalist; b. Mpls., Feb. 9, 1944; d. Richard Edward and LaVonne (Slater) W.; m. Al Sicherman (div.); children: Joseph Sicherman, David Sicherman. B.A. in Journalism, U. Minn., 1967; M.A. in Teaching, Coll. of St. Thomas, 1971. Reporter Mpls. Star Tribune, 1966-72; editor Picture mag., 1972-78, Travel sect., 1978—; editor in chief Galena (Ill.) Gazette, 1990-91. Author: Travel Basics, 1984. Contbr. articles to newspapers and travel mags. Recipient Newspaper Mag. Picture Editor's award Pictures of Yr. Competition, 1974, 75, awards for writing and photography Soc. Am. Travel Writers, 1983-95, Photographer of Yr. award, 1990, Alumna of Notable Achievement award U. Minn. Coll. Liberal ARts, 1994; named Lowell Thomas Travel Journalists of Yr., 1990. Mem. Am. Newspaper Guild, Soc. Am. Travel Writers, Phi Beta Kappa, Kappa Tau Alpha, Alpha Omicron Pi. Office: 425 Portland Ave Minneapolis MN 55488-0001

WATSON, DEAN, agricultural products. Pres. Koch Nitrogen Co., Inc. (changed to Koch Agriculture Co.), Wichita, Kas. Office: Koch Agriculture Co 4111 E 37th St N Wichita KS 67220-3203*

WATSON, DENNIS WALLACE, microbiology educator, scientist; b. Morpeth, Ont., Can., Apr. 29, 1914; came to U.S., 1938, naturalized, 1946; s. William and Sarah (Verity) W.; m. Alicemay Whittier, June 15, 1941; children: Catherine W., William V. BSA, U. Toronto, 1934; MS, Dalhousie U., 1937; PhD, U. Wis., 1941, DSc (hon.), 1981. Rsch. assoc. U. Wis., 1942, asst. prof., 1946-49; vis. investigator Rockefeller Inst., 1942; investigator Connaught Lab. Med. Rsch. U. Toronto, 1942-44; assoc. prof. U. Minn., Mpls., 1949-52; prof. U. Minn., 1953-63, head dept. microbiology, 1964-84, Regents prof. microbiology, 1980-84, Regents prof. emeritus, 1984—; vis. prof. Med. Sch. U. Wash., 1950; mem. Commn. Immunization Armed Forces Epidemiology Bd., 1946-59; mem. bd. sci. counselors, div. biol. standards NIH, 1957-59, mem. allergy and immunology study sect., 1954-58; chmn. tgn. grant com. Inst. Allergy and Infectious Diseases, 1964, mem. adv. coun., 1967-71; mem. microbiology panel Office Naval Rsch., 1963-66; vice chmn. Am. Soc. Microbiology Found., 1973; bd. dirs. Nat. Found. Infectious Diseases, 1976-81. Editorial bd. Infection and Immunity, 1971-72; editorial cons. Medcom Faculty Medicine, 1973—. With AUS, 1944-46. Recipient USPHS Research Career award, 1962-64; Spl. research fellow USPHS, 1960-61. Mem. AAAS, Am. Assn. Immunologists, Am. Chem. Soc., Am. Acad. Microbiology (vice chmn. bd. govs. 1967), Am. Soc. Microbiology (pres. 1969, v.p. Found. 1972-73), Soc. Exptl. Biology and Medicine (coun. 1977-79, pres. 1977-78), Lancefield Soc., Sigma Xi, Phi Zeta. Home: 2106 Hendon Ave Saint Paul MN 55108-1419 Office: U Minn Med Sch Dept Microbiology PO Box 196 Minneapolis MN 55455

WATSON, DOC (ARTHEL LANE WATSON), vocalist, guitarist, banjoist, recording artist; b. Deep Gap, N.C., Mar. 2, 1923; s. General Dixon and Annie (Greer) W.; m. Rosa Lee Carlton; children—Eddy Merle (dec.), Nancy Ellen. Ind. rec. artist, touring performer. Made first appearance at Boone (N.C.) Fiddler's Conf., rec. artist for Folkways in 1960's, signed with Vanguard Records, 1964, also recorded for United Artists, Columbia, Poppy, Sugar Hill, Verve and Flying Fish labels; performed at Newport Folk Festival, 1963, Smithsonian Inst., White House, 1980, Carnegie Hall, 1985; toured in Africa for Dept. State, 1970, also toured in Europe and Japan; albums include (many with Merle Watson) Southbound, Red Rocking Chair, The Guitar Album, Riding the Midnight Train (Grammy award for Best Traditional Folk album, 1986), Portrait, Songs for Little Pickers, On Praying Ground (Grammay award for best traditional folk album 1990); performed music for film Places in the Heart. Recipient Grammy award Nat. Acad. Rec. Arts and Scis., 1973, 74, 79, 86, 90, N.C. award State of N.C., 1985, Carolina prize N.Y. Times Corp., 1985, Grammy award for Best Traditional Folk Rec., 1990. Office: care Folklore Inc 1671 Appian Way Santa Monica CA 90401-3258

WATSON, DONALD RALPH, architect, educator, author; b. Providence, Sept. 27, 1937; s. Ralph Giles W. and Ethel (Fletcher) Pastene; m. Marja Palmqvist, Sept. 8, 1966 (div. Jan. 1984); children: Petrik, Elise; m. Judith Criste, Jan. 3, 1986. A.B., Yale U., 1959, B.Arch., 1962, M.Ed., 1969. Lic. architect Nat. Council Archtl. Registration Bds. Architect Peace Corps, Tunisia, 1962-64; archtl. cons. Govt. of Tunisia, 1964-65; pvt. practice, Trumbull, Conn., 1969-90; dean Sch. Architecture, Rensselaer Poly. Inst., Troy, N.Y., 1990-95, prof., 1990—; Frederick C. Baker vis. prof. U. Oreg., 1995; chmn. environ. design program, Yale U., 1979-90; cons. UN, Bhutan, 1976, World Bank, North Yemen, 1979, Dept. of Energy, 1979, NAS, 1982, U.S. Advanced Bldg. Tech. Coun., 1991. Author: Designing and Building a Solar House, 1977, Energy Conservation Through Building Design, 1979, Climatic Design, 1983, Energy Design Handbook, 1993. Bd. dirs. Save the Children Fedn., 1979-82. Recipient Honor Design award Conn. Soc. Architects, 1974, Honor Design award region AIA, 1978, 84, 1st award Owens Corning Energy Conservation Bldg. Design Program, 1983, Excellence in housing award Energy Efficient Bldg. Assn., 1988, Lifetime Achievement award Passive and Low Energy Architecture, 1990; Assn. of Collegiate Schs. of Archtecture/Am. Metals Climax rsch. fellow, 1967-69; rsch. fellow Rockefeller Found., 1978. Fellow AIA; mem. Am. Solar Energy Soc. (editor). Home and Office: 54 Larkspur Dr Trumbull CT 06611-4652

WATSON, DOROTHY COLETTE, real estate broker; b. Boston, Oct. 26, 1938; d. Edward Vincent and Ethel May (Sanford) Walsh. Student, Regis Coll., 1957-59; BS, Harvard U., 1960; m. Gerald C. McDonald, May 23, 1959 (dec.); children: Gerald C., Deborah L. McDonald, Hermanson, Gregory Christopher (dec.); m. William G. Watson, May 29, 1993. Various secretarial positions, 1958-59. model, 1958-75; guidance counselor Newton High Sch., 1959-60; model, personal shopper Filene's, Chestnut Hill, Mass., 1974-78; designer program covers Boston Red Sox, 1974-76; TV facts girl for TV comml. T.V. Facts mag., 1974-75; real estate broker Channing Assocs., Inc., Wellesley, Mass., 1976-81, Boca Blossom Realty Co., Boca Raton, Fla., 1979-81, N.B. Taylor & Co., Inc., Sudbury, Mass., 1986—; fashion coord. Ava Botélle Fashions, Natick, Mass., 1988-90, mgr. Newton store, 1990-93. Roman Catholic. Home: 11 Saunders Rd Sudbury MA 01776-1282 Office: NB Taylor & Co Inc 356 Boston Post Rd Sudbury MA 01776-3007

WATSON, ELIZABETH MARION, protective services official; b. Phila., Aug. 25, 1949; d John Julian and Elizabeth Gertrude (Judge) Herrmann; m. Robert LLoyd Watson, June 18, 1976; children: Susan, Mark, David. BA in Psychology with honors, Tex. Tech. U., 1971. With Houston Police Dept.,

1972-92, detective homicide, burglary and theft, 1976-81, lt. records div. northeast patrol div., 1981-84, capt. inspections div., auto theft div., 1984-87, dep. chief west patrol bur., 1987-90, police chief, 1990-92; with Austin, Tex. Police Dept., 1992—, police chief, 1992—; mem. editorial bd. S.W. Law Enforcement Inst., Richardson,Tex., 1990—. Mem. editorial bd. Am. Jour. Police, 1991—. mem. Internat. Assn. Chiefs of Police (mem. exec. com., mem. civil rights com.), Police Exec. Rsch. Form, Tex. Police Chiefs Assn. Roman Catholic. Office: Police Department PO Box 1088 Austin TX 78767-8865

WATSON, ELLEN I., academic administrator; b. Sioux City, Iowa, Jan. 14, 1948; d. Homer V. and Elsie (Bertelsen) W. AB, Wellesley Coll., 1970; MLS, U. Md., 1973. Cataloger Eisenhower Libr. Johns Hopkins U., Balt., 1970-74; appointments sec. to mayor City of Balt., 1974-75; libr. C.C. Balt., 1975-82, acting dir. librs., 1982-83; dir. learning resources ctr. Ark. Coll., Batesville, 1983-88; dir. Cullom-Davis Libr. Bradley U., Peoria, Ill., 1988-95, assoc. provost info. resources and tech., 1995—; adv. bd. Ill. Valley Libr. System, Pekin, 1989-95. Contbr. articles to profl. jours. and chpts. to books. Mem. ALA, Assn. Coll. and Rsch. Librs., Libr. Adminstrn. and Mgmt. Assn., Libr. and Info. Tech. Assn., Ill. Libr. Assn., Ill. Assn. Coll. and Rsch. Librs., Phi Kappa Phi. Avocations: morgan horses, reading. Office: Bradley Univ 106 Bradley Hall 1501 W Bradley Ave Peoria IL 61625

WATSON, GEORGE HENRY, JR., broadcast executive, journalist; b. Birmingham, Ala., July 27, 1936; s. George Henry and Grace Elizabeth (Carr) W.; m. Ellen Havican Bradley, July 13, 1979; children—George H., III, Ellen Havican. B.A., Harvard U., 1959; M.S., Columbia U., 1960. Reporter Washington Post, 1960-61; corr. ABC News, 1962-75, Moscow bur. chief, 1966-69, London bur. chief, 1969-75, v.p., Washington bur. chief, 1976-80; v.p., mng. editor Cable News Network, 1980; v.p. news ABC News, N.Y.C., 1981-85; exec. in charge ABC News Viewpoint ABC News, 1981-85, v.p., Washington bur. chief, 1985-93, sr. contbg. editor, 1993—. Bd. advisors Grad. Sch. Journalism, Berkeley.Served with U.S. Army, 1958. Recipient Peabody award, 1982, DuPont Columbia award, 1983, nat. news Emmy award, 1984. Mem. Radio Television News Dirs. Assn., Soc. Profl. Journalists, Nat. Press Club, Overseas Press Club (award for best television documentary 1971, citation for excellence 1974), Washington Press Club, Com. to Protect Journalists. Club: Fed. City. Office: ABC News 1717 Desales St NW Washington DC 20036-4401

WATSON, GEORGE WILLIAM, lawyer, legal consultant; b. Eaton Rapids, Mich., Mar. 1, 1926; s. George W. and Agnes R. (Nissen) W.; m. Ruth Carpenter Murphy, Oct. 1, 1949; children: G. William, Linda, Daniel, Thomas, Rose Mary. AB, U. Mich., 1947, JD, 1950. Bar: Mich. 1951, U.S. Dist. Ct. (ea. and we. dists.) Mich. 1951, U.S. Ct. Military Appeals, 1991. Pvt. practice law Charlotte, Mich., 1951-53; dir. Kalamazoo Legal Aid Bur., 1953-54; asst. pros. atty. Kalamazoo County, 1955-56; gen. atty. Office Civil and Def. Mobilization, Battle Creek, Mich., 1956-62, Def. Civil Preparedness Agy., Washington, 1962-80; assoc. gen. counsel Fed. Emergency Mgmt. Agy., Washington, 1980=88, gen. counsel, 1988-91; cons. on adminstrn. law and govtl. affairs pvt. practice, Alexandria, Va., 1991—. Pres. Mt. Vernon/Lee Enterprises, Alexandria, Va., 1988-94; commordor Nat. Yacht Club, Washington, 1981. With USN, 1944-46, PTO. Mem. State Bar of Mich. Episcopalian. Avocations: community svc., sailboat racing. Home and Office: 2108 Huntington Ave Alexandria VA 22303-1534

WATSON, GEORGIANNA, librarian; b. Lock Haven, Pa., Feb. 18, 1949; d. George and Anna (Eisenhower) Rhine; children: Sharga Nicolle, George Winfield-Martin. BS in Edn., Lock Haven State U., 1971; MLS, Brigham Young U., 1978; M in Pub. Adminstrn., John Jay Coll. Criminal Justice, N.Y.C., 1986. Tchr. Mifflin County Sch. Dist., Lewistown, Pa., 1971-72; librarian Shiprock Boarding Sch. Bur. Indian Affairs, Shiprock, N.Mex., 1972-79, Ft. Sill Indian Sch. Bur. Indian Affairs, Lawton, Okla., 1979-80; librarian U.S. Mil. Acad., West Point, N.Y., 1980-83, head pub. services, library, 1983—. Mem. Southeastern N.Y. Library Resource Council (mem. continuing edn. com., chairperson govt. documents interest group), Southeastern N.Y. Reference Library Interest Group, Am. Quarter Horse Assn., Internat. Arabian Horse Assn., Pi Alpha Alpha. Republican. Home: 176 Plains Rd Walden NY 12586-2443 Office: US Mil Acad Dept Army West Point NY 10996-1799

WATSON, GLENN ROBERT, lawyer; b. Okla., May 2, 1917; s. Albert Thomas and Ethel (Riddle) W.; m. Dorothy Ann Mosiman, Feb. 25, 1945; 1 dau., Carol Ann. Student, East Cen. State U., Okla., 1933-36; LL.B., Okla. U., 1939. Bar: Okla. 1939, Calif. 1946. Pvt. practice law Okla., 1939-41; ptnr. Richards, Watson & Gershon, Los Angeles, 1946—; city atty. Industry, Calif., 1958-65, 78-83, Commerce, Calif., 1960-61, Cerritos, Calif., 1956-64, Victorville, Calif., 1962-63, Carson, Calif., 1968—, Rosemead, Calif., 1960-76, Seal Beach, Calif., 1972-78, South El Monte, Calif., 1976-78, Avalon, Calif., 1976-80, Artesia, Calif., 1976—. Served with USNR, 1942-46. Mem. ABA, Los Angeles County Bar Assn., Am. Judicature Soc., Lawyers Club of Los Angeles (past pres.), Los Angeles World Affairs Council, La Canada C. of C. (past pres.), Order of Coif, Phi Delta Phi, Delta Chi. Home: 800 W 1st St Los Angeles CA 90012-2412 Office: Richards Watson & Gershon 333 S Hope St Los Angeles CA 90071-1406

WATSON, HARLAN L(EROY), federal official, physicist, economist; b. Macomb, Ill., Dec. 17, 1944; s. Joseph Carroll and Helen Louise (Sanders) W.; m. Sharon Ann Rinkus Diguette, Apr. 22, 1977. BA in Physics, Western Ill. U., 1967; PhD in Physics, Iowa State U., 1973; MA in Econs., Georgetown U., 1981. Postdoctoral fellow Argonne (Ill.) Nat. Lab., 1973-75; project scientist, then sr. scientist B-K Dynamics, Inc., Rockville, Md., 1975-78; tech. staff TRW Energy Systems Planning Group, Mc Lean, Va., 1978-80; profl. staff mem. subcom. on energy nuclear proliferation and govt. processes Com. on Govtl. Affairs, U.S. Senate, Washington, 1980-81; tech. and sci. cons. Com. on Sci. and Tech., U.S. Ho. of Reps., 1981-86; rep. energy and environ., coord. Com. on Sci., Space and Tech., U.S. Ho. of Reps., 1986-89; sci. adviser to sec. Dept. Interior, Washington, 1989-93, dep. asst. sec. for sci.-water and sci., 1989-90, prin. dep. asst. to sec. for water and sci., 1990-93; rep. spl. asst. subcom. energy, com. sci., space, tech. U.S. Ho. of Reps., Washington, 1993-95, staff dir. subcom. energy and environment, com. sci., 1995—. Contbr. articles to profl. jours. Home: 6719 Tomlinson Ter Cabin John MD 20818-1328 Office: B 374 Rayburn House Office Bldg Washington DC 20515

WATSON, HAROLD GEORGE, ordnance company executive, mechanical engineer; b. Phoenix, Oct. 19, 1931; s. Clarence Elmer and Eunice A. (Record) W.; m. Ruth May Thomas, Aug. 30, 1951 (dec.); children: Patricia Ruth, Linda Darlene, Harold George; m. Katherina Anna Kish, Sept. 22, 1990. B.S., U. Ariz., 1954. Engr. Shell Oil Co., L.A., 1954; project engr. Talco Engring. Co., Hamden Conn., 1956, area mgr., Mesa, Ariz., 1956-57, chief engr. Rocket Power, 1958-61, dir. engring., 1961-64; dir. engring. Space Ordnance Systems, El Segundo, Calif., 1964-68; dir. engring. Universal Propulsion Co., Riverside, Calif., 1968-70, gen. mgr., v.p. engring., Tempe, Ariz., 1970-76, v.p., mgr., 1976-77, pres., gen. mgr., Phoenix, 1977—. Patentee in field. 1st lt. USAR, 1954-56. Mem. Am. Mgmt. Assn., SAFE Assn. (past pres.), AIAA, Air Force Assn., Internat. Pyronetics Soc., Am. Def. Preparedness Assn. Office: Universal Propulsion Co Inc 25401 N Central Ave Phoenix AZ 85027-7899

WATSON, HELEN RICHTER, educator, ceramic artist; b. Laredo, Tex., May 10, 1926; d. Horace Edward and Helen Mary (Richter) Watson. B.A., Scripps Coll., 1947; M.F.A., Claremont Grad. Sch. and U. Ctr., 1949; postgrad. Alfred U., 1966; Swedish Govt. fellow Konstfackskolan, Stockholm, 1952-53. Mem. faculty Chaffey Coll., Ontario, Calif., 1950-52; chmn. ceramics Mt. San Antonio Coll., Walnut, Calif., 1955-57; prof., chmn. ceramics dept. Otis Art Inst., Los Angeles, 1958-81; mem. faculty Otis-Parsons Sch. Design, 1983-88, ret. 1988; studio ceramic artist, Claremont, Calif. and Laredo, Tex., 1949—; design cons. Interpace, Glendale, Calif., 1963-64; artist-in-residence Clarement Men's Coll., 1977. Claremont Grad. Sch. fellow, 1948-49; Swedish Govt. grantee, 1952-53; recipient First Ann. Scripps Coll. Disting. Alumna award, Claremont, 1978. Mem. Artists Equity, Nat. Ceramic Soc., Am. Craftsmen's Council, Los Angeles County Mus. Art, Mus. Contemporary Art Los Angeles. Republican. Episcopalian. Address: 220 Brooks Ave Claremont CA 91711-4026 also: 1906 Houston St Laredo TX 78040-7709

WATSON, JACK CROZIER, state supreme court justice; b. Jonesville, La., Sept. 17, 1928; s. Jesse Crozier and Gladys Lucille (Talbot) W.; m. Henrietta Sue Carter, Dec. 26, 1958; children: Carter Crozier (dec.), Wells Talbot. BA, U. Southwestern La., 1949; JD, La. State U., 1956; completed with honor, Appellate Judges Seminar, N.Y. U., 1974, Sr. Appellate Judges Seminar, 1980. Bar: La. 1956. Atty. King, Anderson & Swift, Lake Charles, La., 1956-58; prosecutor City of Lake Charles, 1960; asst. dist. atty. Calcasieu Parish, La., 1961-64; ptnr. Watson & Watson, Lake Charles, 1961-64; judge 14th Jud. Dist., La., 1964-72; judge ad hoc Ct. Appeals, 1st Circuit, Baton Rouge, 1972-73; judge Ct. Appeals, 3rd Circuit, Lake Charles, 1973-79; asso. justice La. Supreme Ct., New Orleans, 1979—; faculty advisor Nat. Coll. State Judiciary, Reno, 1970, 73; adj. prof. law summer sch. program in Greece, Tulane U., 1988-95; del. NEH Seminar, 1976; La. del to Internat. Conf. Appellate Magistrates, The Philippines, 1977; mem. La. Jud. Coun., 1986-92. 1st lt. USAF, 1950-54. Mem. ABA, La. Bar Assn., S.W. La. Bar Assn. (pres. 1973), Law Inst. State of La., La. Coun. Juvenile Ct. Judges (pres. 1969-70), Am. Judicature Soc., S.W. La. Camellia Soc. (pres. 1973-74), Am. Legion (post comdr. 1963), Lake Charles Yacht Club (commodore 1974), Blue Key, Sigma Alpha Epsilon, Phi Delta Phi, Pi Kappa Delta. Democrat. Baptist. Office: La Supreme Ct 301 Loyola Ave New Orleans LA 70112-1800

WATSON, JACK H., JR., lawyer; b. El Paso, Tex., Oct. 24, 1938; children: Melissa Woodward, Lincoln Hearn. BA, Vanderbilt U., 1960; LLB, Harvard U., 1966. Bar: Ga. 1965, D.C. 1978. Assoc. King & Spalding, Atlanta, 1966-71; partner King & Spalding, 1972-77; asst. to Pres. for intergovtl. affairs and sec. to cabinet Washington, 1977-80; chief of staff White House, 1980-81; ptnr. Long, Aldridge & Norman, Atlanta, 1981—; mem. vis. com. Harvard Law Sch., 1987-93; permanent chmn. Ga. Joint Commn. on Alt. Dispute Resolution, 1990-93, chmn. Ga. Commn. on Dispute Resolution, 1993—. Counsel Met. Atlanta Commn. Crime and Juvenile Delinquency, 1966-67; trustee Milton S. Eisenhower Found., 1994—; pres. Met. Atlanta Mental Health Assn., 1971-72; chmn. Gov.'s Study Commn. Alcohol, 1971-72, Ga. Alcoholism Adv. Council, 1972; chmn. bd. Ga. Dept. Human Resources, 1972-77; candidate gov. of Ga., 1982; mem. nat. adv. com. Ctr. for Study of Presidency, 1983; mem. Franklin D. Roosevelt Library Bd., 1986—; chmn. 20th Century Fund Task Force on the U.S. Vice Presidency, 1987-88; active Franklin and Eleanor Roosevelt Instnl. Bd., 1990—. Served as officer USMC. Named One of Atlanta's Five Outstanding Young Men Jaycees, 1970. Mem. ABA (standing com. on dispute resolution 1991-93, coun. mem. sect. dispute resolution 1993—, chmn. ABA task force on N.Am. Free Trade Agreement 1993), State Bar Ga., Atlanta Bar Assn., Atlanta Lawyers Club, Phi Beta Kappa, Phi Eta Sigma, Omicron Delta Kappa. Office: Long Aldridge & Norman 701 Pennsylvania Ave NW Ste 600 Washington DC 20004-2608

WATSON, JAMES D., JR., principal; b. Phila., Apr. 8, 1943; s. James D. and Alice Geneva W.; m. Linda Watson, Aug. 1, 1987; children: D'Ana, Asher, Janine, Antonio. BS, Cheyney State Coll., 1966, MS; postgrad., Temple U.; student, Pa. State U. Cert. reading, elem. and secondary principalship, supt. Tchr., grade 6 Abington (Pa.) Sch. Dist.; tchr., grades 7-8 Chester (Pa.) Twp. Sch. Dist.; tchr., grades 5-8 Phila. (Pa.) Sch. Dist.; prin. Bensalem (Pa.) Sch. Dist.; developer High Expectations Program. Recipient commendations from Phila. City Coun., Mayor, Gov. and Bensalem Sch. Bd. Mem. Nat. Assn. for Elem. (Sch.) Prins., Pa. Assn. for Elem. Sch. Prins., Nat. Assn. Black Sch. Educators.

WATSON, JAMES DEWEY, molecular biologist, educator; b. Chicago, Ill., Apr. 6, 1928; s. James Dewey and Jean (Mitchell) W.; m. Elizabeth Lewis, 1968; children: Rufus Robert, Duncan James. BS, U. Chgo., 1947, DSc (hon.), 1961; PhD in Zoology, Ind. U., 1950, DSc (hon.), 1963; LLD (hon.), U. Notre Dame, 1965; DSc (hon.), L.I. U., 1970, Adelphi U., 1972, Brandeis U., 1973, Albert Einstein Coll. Medicine, 1974, Hofstra U., 1976, Harvard U., 1978, Rockefeller U., 1980, Clarkson Coll., 1981, SUNY, 1983; MD (hon.), U. Buenos Aires, Argentina, 1986; DSc (hon.), Rutgers U., 1988, Bard Coll., 1991, U. Cambridge, 1993, Fairfield U., 1993, U. Stellenbosch, 1993, U. Oxford. Rsch. fellow NRC, U. Copenhagen, 1950-51; Nat. Found. Infantile Paralysis fellow Cavendish Lab., Cambridge U., 1951-52, 55-56; sr. rsch. fellow biology Calif. Inst. Tech., 1953-55; asst. prof. biology Harvard U., 1955-58, assoc. prof., 1958-61, prof., 1961-76; dir. Cold Spring Harbor Lab., N.Y., 1968—, pres., 1994—; assoc. dir. Nat. Ctr. for Human Genome Rsch. NIH, 1988-89, dir. Nat. Ctr. for Human Genome Rsch., 1989-92; Newton-Abraham vis. prof. Oxford U., 1994. Author: Molceular Biology of the Gene, 1965, 4th edit., 1986, The Double Helix, 1968, (with John Tooze) The DNA Story, 1981, (with others) The Molecular Biology of the Cell, 1983, 2d edit., 1989, (with John Tooze and David Kurtz) Recombinant DNA, A Short Course, 1983, 2d edit., 1992. Named Hopn. fellow Clare Coll., Cambridge U.; recipient (with F.H.C. Crick) John Collins Warren prize Mass. Gen. Hosp., 1959, Eli Lilly award in biochemistry Am. Chem. Soc., 1959, Albert Lasker prize Am. Pub. Health Assn., 1960, (with F.H.C. Crick) Rsch. Corp. prize, 1962, (with F.H.C. Crick and M.H.F. Wilkins) Nobel prize in medicine, 1962, Presdl. Medal of Freedom, 1977, Kaul Found. award for excellence, 1993, Nat. Biotech. Venture award, 1993, Copley Medal, 1993, Royal Society. Mem. NAS (Carty medal 1971), Am. Philos. Soc., Am. Assn. Cancer Rsch., Am. Acad. Arts and Scis., Am. Soc. Biol. Chemistry, Royal Soc. (London) (Copley medal 1993), Acad. Scis. Russia, Danish Acad. Arts and Scis. Home: Bungtown Rd Cold Spring Harbor NY 11724 Office: Cold Spring Harbor Lab PO Box 100 Cold Spring Harbor NY 11724-0100

WATSON, JAMES LOPEZ, federal judge; b. N.Y.C., May 21, 1922; s. James S. and Violet (Lopez) W.; m. D'Jaris Hinton Watson, July 14, 1956 (dec. Nov. 1989); children: Norman, Karen, Kris. B.A. in Govt, N.Y. U., 1947; LL.B., Bklyn. Law Sch., 1951. Bar: N.Y. bar 1951. Mem. N.Y. Senate from 21st Senatorial Dist., 1954-63; judge Civil Ct. N.Y., 1964-66; acting judge N.Y. State Supreme Ct., 1965; judge U.S. Customs Ct., 1966-80, U.S. Ct. Internat. Trade, 1980—. Bd. dirs. N.Y.C. Police Athletic League. Served with inf. AUS, World War II, ETO. Decorated Purple Heeart, Combat Inf. badge. Mem. ABA, N.Y. State Bar Assn., Fed. Bar Council, World Peace Through Law. Home: 676 Riverside Dr New York NY 10031-5529 Office: US Ct Internat Trade 1 Federal Plz New York NY 10278-0001

WATSON, JERRY CARROLL, advertising executive; b. Greenville, Ala., Aug. 22, 1943; s. William J. and Georgia Katherine (Mixon) W.; m. Judith Zeigler Brooks, Sept. 16, 1988; 1 child, Theodore William. BS, U. Ala., Tuscaloosa, 1967. Staff writer Phillips, Eindhoven, The Netherlands, 1967-68; mgr. mktg. Fuller & Dees Mktg., Montgomery, Ala., 1968-70; v.p. Univ. Programs, Washington, 1970-73; pres. Coll. & Univ. Press, Washington, 1973-80; ptnr. Direct Response Consulting Svcs., McLean, Va., 1981—; bd. dirs. Foxhall Corp., The Art Co. Founding mem. Am. Inst. Cancer Rsch. Mem. Direct Mktg. Assn., Non-Profit Mailer Fedn., Promotional Mktg. Assn., Assn. Direct Response Fund Raising Coun., Am. Forestry Assn., Nature Conservancy, Sierra Club, Falls Church (Va.) C. of C. (bd. dirs.), Phi Kappa Psi. Avocation: gardening, astronomy. Home: 850 Dolley Madison Blvd Mc Lean VA 22101-1821 Office: Direct Response Cons Svcs 6849 Old Dominion Dr Ste 300 Mc Lean VA 22101-3705

WATSON, JOHN ALLEN, lawyer; b. Ft. Worth, Sept. 18, 1946; s. John and Mary (Barlow) W.; m. Patricia L. Clardy, Oct. 24, 1946; 1 child, Virginia E. B.A., Rice U., 1968; J.D., U. Tex., Austin, 1971. Bar: Tex. 1971. Assoc. Fulbright & Jaworski, Houston, 1971-78, ptnr., 1978—. Mem. ABA. Office: Fulbright & Jaworski LLP 1301 Mckinney St Ste 5100 Houston TX 77010

WATSON, JOYCE LESLIE, elementary educator; b. Riverside, N.J., May 31, 1950; d. Robert Eugene and Doris Virginia (Robinson) Stockton; m. Edward Donald Watson, Oct. 4, 1980; 1 child, Michelle Leslie. BS, Trenton State Coll., 1972, MEd, 1978. Cert. elem. tchr., N.J., Pa. Tchr. elem. Willingboro (N.J.) Sch. Dist., 1972-81, Pennsbury Sch. Dist., Fallsington, Pa., 1987—; tchr. gifted/talented Pennsbury Sch. Dist., Fallsington, 1987-88, 92—; elem. demonstration tchr. Pennsbury Sch. Dist., 1995—; coach Odyssey of Mind, Pennwood Mid Sch., Yardley, Pa., 1993-94; participant 8th Ann. Capital Area Space Orientation Program, Washington, 1996. Mem. NEA, ASCD, Coun. Exceptional Children, Talented and Gifted, Pa. Assn. for Gifted Edn., Pa. State Edn. Assn., Airplane Owners and Pilots Assn., Phi Delta Kappa. Home: 10 Shelley Ln Yardley PA 19067-7320 Office: Makefield Elem Sch Makefield Rd Yardley PA 19067

WATSON, JULIAN See BLAKE, BUD

WATSON, KATHARINE JOHNSON, art museum director, art historian; b. Providence, Nov. 11, 1942; d. William Randolph and Katharine Johnson (Badger) W.; m. Paul Luther Nyhus, Dec. 17, 1983; stepchildren: Kristina Victoria, Karen Ida, Katharine Ellen. BA, Duke U., 1964; MA, U. Pa., 1967, PhD, 1973. Teaching asst. U. Pa., 1966-67; instr., curator exhbns. U. Pitts., 1969-70; curator of art before 1800 Allen Meml. Art Mus., Oberlin, Ohio, 1973-77; lectr. Oberlin Coll., 1973-77; dir. Peary-MacMillan Artic Mus. Bowdoin Coll., Brunswick, Maine, 1977-83, dir. Mus. of Art, 1977—; trustee Mus. Art of Ogunquit, 1977-89, Regional Art Conservation Lab., Williamstown, 1977-90, Surf Point Found., York, Maine; mem. Smithsonian Coun. Author: Pietro Tacca, 1983; author text for exhbn. catalogues; co-editor: Allen Meml. Art Mus. Bull, 1974-77; contbr. articles to profl. jours. Mem. profl. adv. com. Victoria Soc. Maine, 1988-93; mem. adv. coun. Archives of Am. Art, 1982-90. Kress Found. fellow, 1967-68, Chester Dale Fellow, 1970-71, Am. Coun. Learned Socs. fellow, 1977-78, Villa I Tatti fellow, 1977-78. Mem. Am. Assn. Art Mus. Dirs., Am. Assn. Museums, Coll. Art Assn. Office: Bowdoin Coll Mus Art Walker Art Bldg Brunswick ME 04011

WATSON, KAY, school system administrator; b. Rotan, Tex., Feb. 5, 1942; d. C.M. and Marie (Reeder) W. BA, Baylor U., 1964; MA, Colo. State Coll., 1968; MEd, Sul Ross State U., Alpine, Tex., 1982; EdD, Tex. Tech. U., 1988. Tchr. grade 6 Dallas Ind. Sch. Dist., Dallas, 1964-67, counselor J.L. Long Jr. H.S., 1968-70, tchr. grade 7, 1970-72; tchr. grade 5 Weatherford (Tex.) Ind. Sch. Dist., 1972-73; spl. edn. counselor Parker County Coop., Weatherford, 1973-74; spl. edn. counselor Monahans (Tex.)-Wickett-Pyote Ind. Sch. Dist., 1974-78, dir. spl. edn., 1978-85; supr. pre-sch. ctr. Ector County Ind. Sch. Dist., Odessa, Tex., 1985-86, prin. elem. Magnet Sch. at Travis, 1986-89, prin. LBJ Elem. Sch., 1989-90, assoc. dir. elem. edn., 1990-92, assoc. exec. dir., clusters I and II, 1992; asst. supt. Calhoun County Ind. Sch. Dist., Port Lavaca, Tex., 1992—. Bd. dirs. Am. Cancer Soc., Odessa, 1991-92; mem. Odessa Symphony Guild, 1990-92, Port Lavaca Crisis Hotline Vol.; bd. dirs. United Way of Calhoun County, 1996—. Mem. ASCD, Tex. Elem. Prins. and Suprs. Assn., Tex. Assn. Secondary Sch. Adminstrs., Tex. Assn. Sch. Adminstrs., Tex. Assn. Profl. Educators, Pilot Club Internat. (dir. 1991-92, 93—), Rotary Club Internat. (dir. 1995—), Delta Kappa Gamma Soc. Internat. Baptist. Home: 1204 S Eric Monahans TX 79756 Office: Calhoun County Ind Sch Dist 525 N Commerce St Port Lavaca TX 77979-3034

WATSON, KENNETH MARSHALL, physics educator; b. Des Moines, Sept. 7, 1921; s. Louis Erwin and Irene Nellie (Marshall) W.; m. Elaine Carol Miller, Mar. 30, 1946; children: Ronald M., Mark Louis. B.S., Iowa State U., 1943; Ph.D., U. Iowa, 1948; Sc.D. (hon.), U. Ind., 1976. Rsch. engr. Naval Rsch. Lab., Washington, 1943-46; mem. staff Inst. Advanced Study Princeton (N.J.) U., 1948-49; rsch. fellow Lawrence Berkeley (Calif.) Lab., 1949-52, mem. staff, 1957-81; asst. prof. physics U. Ind., Bloomington, 1952-54; asso. prof. physics U. Wis., Madison, 1954-57; prof. physics U. Calif., Berkeley, 1957-81; prof. oceanography, dir. marine physics lab. U. Calif., San Diego, 1981-93; cons. Mitre Corp., Sci. Application Corp.; mem. U.S. Pres.'s Sci. Adv. Com. Panels, 1962-71; adviser Nat. Security Coun., 1972-75; bd. dirs. Ctr. for Studies of Dynamics, 1979-88; mem. JASON Adv. Panel; mem. sci. adv. bd. George C. Marshall Inst., 1989—. Author: (with M.L. Goldberger) Collision Theory, 1964, (with J. Welch and J. Bond) Atomic Theory of Gas Dynamics, 1966, (with J. Nutall) Topics in Several Particle Dynamics, 1970, (with Flatté, Munk, Dashen) Sound Transmission Through a Fluctuating Ocean, 1979. Mem. Nat. Acad. Scis. Home: PO Box 9726 Rancho Santa Fe CA 92067-4726 Office: U Calif Marine Physics Lab La Jolla CA 92093

WATSON, LEE ANN, lawyer; b. Huntington, Ind., Oct. 28, 1952. BS, Ind. U., 1973; JD, Washington U., 1976. Bar: Ill. 1976. Ptnr. Katten Muchin & Zavis, Chgo. Mem. ABA, Ill. State Bar Assn., Chgo. Bar Assn. Office: Katten Muchin & Zavis 525 W Monroe St Ste 1600 Chicago IL 60661-3629*

WATSON, LINDA ANNE, library director; b. New Milford, Conn., Nov. 26, 1951. Student, Georgetown U., 1969-71; BA summa cum laude, U. Conn., 1972; MLS, Simmmons Coll., 1973. Libr., project mgr. Tracor-Jitco, Inc., Rockville, Md., 1974-75, libr. assoc., then AVLINE coord., 1975-79; asst. head selection and acquisitions sect. Nat. Libr. Medicine, NIH, Bethesda, Md., 1979-80, chief materials utilization br., 1980-82, head audiovisual resources sect., 1982-85; dir. info. svcs. Houston Acad. Medicine-Tex. Med. Ctr. Libr., 1985-86, assoc. dir. for pub. svcs., 1986-89, assoc. exec. dir. for libr. ops., 1989-90; dir. Claude Moore Health Scis. Libr., U. Va. Health Scis. Ctr., Charlottesville, 1990—, mem. gen. med. faculty, 1990—; sr. assoc. Cooper and Assocs., Charlottesville, 1985—; mem. adv. com. arthritis info. clearinghouse NIH, 1980-82, diabetes info. clearinghouse, 1984-85; mem. adv. com. combined health info. database HHS, 1983-85; adj. asst. prof. Baylor Coll. Medicine, Houston, 1986-90; adj. asst. prof. U. Tex. Med. Sch., Houston, 1986-90; mem. pub. rels. adv. coun. Tex. Med. Ctr., 1987-89; mem. planning panel on edn. and tng. health sci. librs. Nat. Libr. Medicine, 1993-94; presenter in field. Contbr. articles to profl. jours. Mem. Leadership Charlottesville, 1990—. Grantee Nat. Libr. Medicine, 1990-93, 94-95, Va. State Libr. and Archives, 1993-94, NSF, 1993-94. Mem. ALA, Assn. Coll. and Rsch. Librs., Libr. Adminstrn. and Mgmt. Assn., Am. Med. Informatics Assn., Va. Libr. Assn., Med. Libr. Assn. (chmn. ann. meeting nat. program com. 1992-95, bd. dirs. 1996—), Acad. Health Info. Profls. (disting.), Assn. Acad. Health Scis. Libr. Dirs. (vice chmn. joint legis. task force with Med. Libr. Assn. 1990-94), Va. Coun. Health Scis. Librs. (chmn. 1991-94). Avocations: horses, sports. Home: 200 George Rogers Rd Charlottesville VA 22911-8402 Office: U Va Health Scis Ctr Claude Moore Health Scis Libr HSC Box 234 Charlottesville VA 22908

WATSON, MARY ELLEN, ophthalmic technologist; b. San Jose, Calif., Oct. 29, 1931; d. Fred Sidney and Emma Grace (Capps) Doney; m. Joseph Garrett Watson, May 11, 1950; children: Ted Joseph, Tom Fred, Pamela Kay Watson. Cert. ophthalmic med. technologist and surg. asst. Ophthalmic technician Kent W. Christoferson, M.D., Eugene, 1965-80; ophthalmic technologist, surg. asst., adminstr. I. Howard Fine, M.D., Eugene, 1980—; course dir. Joint Commn. Allied Health Pers. in Ophthalmolgy, 1976—, lectr., mem. faculty, 1983—, skill evaluator and site coord., Eugene, 1988—; internat. instr. advanced surgical techniques. Contbr. articles to profl. jours. Recipient 5-Yr. Faculty award Joint Commn. for Allied Health Pers. in Ophthalmology, 1989. Mem. Allied Tech. Pers. in Ophthalmology, Internat. Women's Pilots Assn. Avocation: flying. Home: 2560 Chaucer Ct Eugene OR 97405-1217 Office: I Howard Fine MD 1550 Oak St Eugene OR 97401-7701

WATSON, MARY JO, special education educator; b. Candandaigua, N.Y., May 7, 1947; d. Joseph William and Mary (Treble) W. BS, Pembroke State U., 1970; postgrad., U. N.C., 1970, East Carolina U., 1977; MS, SUNY, Geneseo, 1983. Cert. tchr. phys. edn., N.C., tchr. phys. edn. and spl. edn., N.Y. Tchr. 3rd grade Scurlock Elem. Sch., Raeford, N.C., 1970-71; tchr. phys. edn., tennis coach, creative dance instr. E.E. Smith Sr. High Sch., Fayetteville, N.C., 1971-73; tchr. social studies and art for gifted students Reilly Rd. Elem. Sch., Fayetteville, 1973-74, specialist elem. phys. edn. resource, 1974-78; devel. specialist Craig Devel. Ctr., Sonyea, N.Y., summer 1981; tchr. spl. edn. Naples (N.Y.) Ctrl. Sch., 1984—; mem. com. special edn. membership, Naples (N.Y.) Ctrl. Sch., special olympic com.- Cumberland County, Reilly Rd. Elem. Sch., Fayetteville, Curriculum Com. E.E. Smith Sr. High Sch., Fayetteville. Author, publisher (jour.) Teaching Exceptional Children, 1982, Learning Disabilities Advocacy Newsletter, The Advocator, 1993. Fellow ASCD, Coun. for Exceptional Children (presenter nat. conf. 1980, 81, Conn. and N.Y. state conf. 1981), N.Y. State United Tchrs., Naples Tchrs. Assn. Home: PO Box 277 Honeoye NY 14471-0277 Office: Naples Ctrl Sch 136 N Main St Naples NY 14512-9201

WATSON, MATHEW D., optical scientist; b. L.A., Feb. 9, 1958. BS in Physics, San Jose State U., 1984; MS in Optical Scis., U. Ariz., 1989, PhD in Optical Scis., 1991. Mem. tech. staff Uniphase, Inc., San Jose, Calif., 1984-86; rsch. assoc. Optical Scis. Ctr., Tucson, Ariz., 1986-91; electro optical engr. ILX Lightwave, Inc., Bozeman, Mont., 1991-93; sr. optical engr. Quest Integrated, Inc., Kent, Wash., 1994—. Contbr. articles to profl. jours.; patentee in field. Grad. rsch. scholar Optical Scis. Ctr., 1989; recipient ARCS scholarship ARCS Found., 1983. Mem. Optical Soc. Am., IEEE/ Laser and Electro-optic Soc., Soc. Photometric and Instrumentation Engrs. Home: 10439 NE 28th Pl Bellevue WA 98004 Office: Quest Integrated Inc 21414 68th Ave South Kent WA 98032

WATSON, MAX P., JR., computer software company executive; b. 1946. Graduate, La. U. With IBM Corp., Houston, 1967-83, Wang Labs., Houston, 1985-90; with BMC Software, Inc., Houston, 1990—, now pres., ceo, chmn. Office: BMC Software Inc 2101 Citywest Blvd Houston TX 77042-2827*

WATSON, PATRICIA L., library director; b. Jan. 15, 1939; m. Jack Samuel Watson, 1960; children: Bradley, Amanda. BA, Univ. Tenn., 1961, MS in Libr. and Info. Sci., 1975. Cataloging asst. tech. svcs. dept. Knoxville Pub. Libr., 1961-65; adminstrv. asst. Knoxville-Knox County Pub. Libr., 1975-78, head West Knoxville br. libr., 1978-85; dir. Knox County Pub. Libr. System, 1985—. Bd. dirs. Tanasi Girl Scout Coun., 1981-86; treas. Univ. Tenn. Grad. Sch. Libr. and Info. Sci. Alumni Orgn., 1983-84; elder Farragut Presbyn. Ch. Mem. ALA, Tenn. Libr. Assn. (pres. 1992-93), East Tenn. Libr. Assn. (pres. 1988-89), Rotary Internat. Office: Knox County Pub Libr System 500 W Church Ave Knoxville TN 37902-2505

WATSON, PAUL, photojournalist, correspondent. Photographer The Toronto Star, 1986—, Africa bur. chief, 1992-94, Asian bur. chief, 1994—. Recipient Robert Capa gold medal for photography, 1993, Nat. Newspaper award for spot news photography, 1994, Pulitzer Prize for spot news photography, 1994, Nat. Newspaper award for internat. reporting, 1994. Office: The Toronto Star, One Yonge St, Toronto, ON Canada M5E 1E6

WATSON, PAULA D., library administrator; b. N.Y.C., Mar. 6, 1945; d. Joseph Francis and Anna Julia (Miksza) De Simone; m. William Douglas Watson, Aug. 23, 1969; children—Lucia, Elizabeth. A.B., Barnard Coll., 1965; M.A., Columbia U., 1966; M.S.L.S., Syracuse U., 1972. Reference librarian U. Ill., Urbana, 1972-77, city planning and landscape architecture librarian, 1977-79, head documents library, 1979-81; asst. dir. gen. services U. Ill. Library, Urbana, 1981—, acting dir. gen. svcs., 1988-93, dir. ctrl. pub. svcs., 1989-93, asst. univ. libr., 1993-95, dir. electronic info. svcs., 1995—. Contbr. articles to profl. jours. N.Y. State Regents fellow Columbia U., N.Y.C., 1965-66; Council on Library Resources profl. edn. and tng. for librarianship grantee, 1983. Mem. ALA (sec. univ. librs. sect. ALA-Assn. Coll. and Rsch. Librs. 1989-91, mem. libr. adminstrn. mgmt. sect. com. on comparative libr. orgn. 1988-89, mem. conf. planning com. optical disk interest group 1988), Ill. Library Assn. Avocation: gardening. Home: 715 W Delaware Ave Urbana IL 61801-4806 Office: U Ill 246 A Library 1408 W Gregory Dr Urbana IL 61801-3607

WATSON, PETER S., federal agency administrator; married. LLB, Auckland U.; LLM, McGill U.; MIBA, West Coast U. Pvt. practice internat. and bus. law L.A., Washington, 1976, 78-88; spl. advisor to Pres. Overseas Pvt. Investment Corp.; dir. Asian affairs Nat. Security Coun., 1989-91; commr. U.S. Internat. Trade Commn., 1991—, vice chmn., 1992-94, chmn., 1994—; adj. prof. internat. trade and investment law and internat. bus. law. Contbr. articles to profl. jours. Republican. Office: International Trade Commission Office of the Chairman 500 E St SW Washington DC 20436-0003*

WATSON, RANDY JOHN, hospital administrator; b. Shreveport, La., July 2, 1954; s. Clifford and Sadie (Rebouche) Watson; m. Bonita Ann Behan, Feb. 10, 1977; children: Sean, John Thomas. Diploma in Med. Tech., La. State U., 1977; MBA, Centenery Coll. of La., 1992. Med. technologist Shumpert Med. Ctr., Shreveport, 1977-80, lab. supr., 1980-84; physicians asst. Pathologist Lab., Shreveport, 1984-86; adminstr. Diagnostic Pathology, Shreveport, 1986-89; asst. adminstr. Westbrook Hosp., Richmond, Va., 1989; adminstr. Glenwood Hosp., Midland, Tex., 1989—; ceo Charter Forest Hosp., Shreveport, La., 1989—. Capt. United Way, Shreveport, 1991. Mem. La. Hosp. Assn. (pres.-elect N.W. chpt. 1991-92, sec., treas. 1990-91), Rotary. Avocations: golf, hiking, writing, reading, volleyball. Office: Charter Forest Hosp 9320 Linwood Ave Shreveport LA 71106-7003

WATSON, RICHARD ALLAN, philosophy educator, writer; b. New Market, Iowa, Feb. 23, 1931; s. Roscoe Richard and Daisy Belle (Penwell) W.; m. Patty Jo Andersen, July 30, 1955; 1 child, Anna Melissa. B.A., U. Iowa, 1953, M.A., 1957, Ph.D. in Philosophy,, 1961; M.S. in Geology, U. Minn., 1959. Instr. philosophy U. Mich., Ann Arbor, 1961-64; asst. prof. Washington U., St. Louis, 1964-67; assoc. prof. Washington U., 1967-74, prof., 1974—; pres. Cave Research Found., Mammoth Cave, Ky., 1965-67; trustee Nat. Parks and Conservation Assn., Washington, 1969-81. Author: The Downfall of Cartesianism, 1966, Under Plowman's Floor, 1978, The Runner, 1981, The Philosopher's Diet, 1985, The Breakdown of Cartesian Metaphysics, 1987, The Philosopher's Joke, 1990, Writing Philosophy, 1992, Niagara, 1993, The Philosopher's Demise, 1995, Representational Ideas, 1995; (with others) Man and Nature, 1969, The Longest Cave, 1976; editor: Classics in Speleology, 1968-73, Speleologia, 1974-79, Cave Books, 1980—, Jour. History of Philosophy, 1983, Jour. History of Philosophy Monograph Series, 1985-95. Served to 1st lt. USAF, 1953-55. NEH grantee, 1975; fellow Ctr. Advanced Study in Behavioral Scis., Stanford, Calif., 1967-68, 81-82, 91-92, Am. Coun. Learned Socs., 1967-68, Princeton Ctr. Internat. Studies, 1975-76, Camargo Found., 1995. Mem. Nat. Speleological Soc. (hon. life), AAAS, Am. Philos. Assn., Cave Research Found. Office: Washington U Dept Philosophy Saint Louis MO 63130-4899

WATSON, ROBERT JAMES, lawyer; b. Oceanside, N.Y., Mar. 30, 1955; s. Ralph Joseph and Mildred Adeline (Knapp) W.; m. Ann M. Goade, May 27, 1988; children: Emily Allyn, Caroline Elisabeth. BA, Biscayne Coll., 1976; JD, U. Fla., 1979. Bar: Fla. 1979, U.S. Dist. Ct. (so. dist.) Fla. 1980, U.S. Dist. Ct. (no. dist.) Fla. 1981, U.S. Dist. Ct. (mid. dist.) Fla. 1982, U.S. Ct. Appeals (11th cir.) 1982. Asst. pub. defender Law Offices of Elton Schwarz, Ft. Pierce, Fla., 1979-81; ptnr. Wilkinson & Watson P.A., Stuart, Fla., 1981-86; pvt. practice Stuart, 1986-90; ptnr. Frierson & Watson, Stuart, 1990—. Mem. Fla. Bar Assn., Nat. Assn. Criminal Def. Lawyers, Acad. Fla. Trial Lawyers, Martin Assn. Criminal Def. Lawyers, Fla. Assn. Criminal Def. Lawyers. Democrat. Roman Catholic. Avocation: golf, marathon running, skiing. Home: 9 Emerita Way Stuart FL 34996-6704 Office: Frierson & Watson 3601 SE Ocean Blvd Ste 004 Stuart FL 34996-6737

WATSON, ROBERT JOE, hospital administrator, retired career officer; b. Wellington, Kans., Nov. 12, 1934; s. Charles Bruce and Marguerite B. (Scholes) W.; m. Ursula Eschenroeder, Dec. 26, 1983; children: Stephanie, Stacy Watson Bruce, Susannah Watson Gold; stepchildren: Jurgen Wanke, Claudia Wanke. MS in Edn., Kans. State Tchrs. Coll., 1963; MBA, U. Hawaii, 1969; MHA, George Washington U., 1973, EdD, 1976; student, Command-Gen. Staff Coll., 1973, U.S. Army War Coll., 1986. Commd. 2nd lt. U.S. Army, 1963, advanced through grades to col., 1989; stationed at Tripler Army Med. Ctr., Honolulu, 1967-69, USARV Surgeons Office, Long Binh, Vietnam, 1969-70, Surgeon Gen.'s Office, Washington, 1970-74, Walter Reed Med. Ctr., Washington, 1974-76, Acad. Health Svcs., Ft. Sam Houston, Tex., 1976-80, 87-89, 68th Med. Group, Ziegenberg, Germany, 1980-82, U.S. Army Hosp., Ft. Riley, Kans., 1982-84, 34th Gen. Hosp., Augsburg, Germany, 1984-87; ret., 1989; assoc. dir. Student Health Ctr. U. Fla., Gainesville, 1989—. Fellow Am. Coll. Healthcare Execs. (adv., regent 1982-84). Episcopalian. Avocations: tennis, golf, gardening. Office: U Fla Student Health Ctr Gainesville FL 32611

WATSON, ROBERT R., lawyer; b. Buffalo, N.Y., Mar. 10, 1944. BA, Wheaton Coll., 1967; JD, U. Chgo., 1972. Bar: Ill. 1972. Law clerk to Hon. Richard W. McLaren U.S. Dist. Ct. (no. dist.), Ill., 1972-74; ptnr. Sidley & Austin, Chgo. Office: Sidley & Austin 1 First Nat Plz Chicago IL 60603

WATSON, ROBERT TANNER, physical scientist; b. Columbus, Ohio, Sept. 25, 1922; s. Rolla Don and Gladys Margaret (Tanner) W.; m. Jean Mehlig, Oct. 7, 1944; children—Melinda Jean, Parke Tanner, John Mehlig, Todd Pennell, Kate Ann. B.A., DePauw U., 1943; Ph.D., MIT, 1951. With photo products dept. E. I. duPont de Nemours & Co., Inc., Parlin, N.J., 1951-55; with electron tube div. RCA, Marion, Ind., 1955-59; with Internat. Tel. & Tel. Corp., 1959-71, v.p., gen. mgr. indsl. labs. div., 1962-63, pres., 1963-68; dept. tech. dir., other positions Aerospace and Def. Group, 1968-71; gen. phys. scientist OT and NTIA U.S. Dept. Commerce, 1971-90. Mem. Gov.'s Air Pollution Control Bd., 1966-70; Allen County chmn. Ind. Sesquicentennial, 1965; trustee Ind. Ednl. Services Found., 1968-71; bd. dirs. YMCA of Greater Ft. Wayne and Allen County, 1966-69. Served to lt. (j.g.) USNR 1943-46, combat, PTO; USNR, 1946-55. Mem. Am. Inst. Mgmt. (fellow pres.'s council 1970), Ft. Wayne C. of C. (dir. 1966-68), Allen County-Ft. Wayne Hist. Soc. (Old Fort com.), Optical Soc. Am., IEEE, Sigma Xi, Phi Eta Sigma, Beta Theta Pi. Research and engring. in x-ray diffraction, radioactive scattering, solid state energy levels, electron emission, magnetic and photog. media, electro-optical, Laser and telecommunication systems. Mgr. several engring. firsts. Patentee in field. Home: 1770 Lang Dr Crofton MD 21114-9999

WATSON, ROBERT WINTHROP, poet, English language educator; b. Passaic, N.J., Dec. 26, 1925; s. Winthrop and Laura Berdan (Trimble) W.; m. Elizabeth Ann Rean, Jan. 12, 1952; children: Winthrop, Caroline. BA, Williams Coll., 1946; postgrad., U. Zurich, 1947; MA, Johns Hopkins, 1950, PhD in English, 1955. Instr. English Williams Coll., 1946, 47-48, 52-53, Johns Hopkins, 1950-52; mem. faculty U. N.C., Greensboro, 1953—; prof. English U. N.C., 1963-90; vis. poet, prof. English Calif. State U., Northridge, 1968-69. Author: (poetry) A Paper Horse, 1962, Advantages of Dark, 1966, Christmas in Las Vegas, 1971, Selected Poems, 1974, Island of Bones, 1977, Night Blooming Cactus, 1980, The Pendulum: New and Selected Poems, 1995; (novels) Three Sides of the Mirror, 1966, Lily Lang, 1977. Swiss-Am. exch. fellow, 1947; grantee Nat. Endowment for Arts, 1973; recipient Am. Scholar Poetry prize, 1959, Lit. award Am. Acad. Inst. Arts Letters, 1977. Home: 9D Fountain Manor Dr Greensboro NC 27405-8001

WATSON, SHARON GITIN, psychologist, executive; b. N.Y.C., Oct. 21, 1943; d. Louis Leonard and Miriam (Myers) Gitin; m. Eric Watson, Oct. 31, 1969; 1 child, Carrie Dunbar. B.A. cum laude, Cornell U., 1965; M.A., U. Ill., 1968, Ph.D., 1971. Psychologist City N.Y. Prison Mental Health, Riker's Island, 1973-74; psychologist Youth Services Ctr., Los Angeles County Dept. Pub. Social Services, Los Angeles, 1975-77, dir. clin. services, 1978, dir. Youth Services Ctr., 1978-80; exec. dir. Crittenton Ctr. for Young Women and Infants, Los Angeles, 1980-89, Assn. Children's Svcs. Agys. of So. Calif., L.A., 1989-92, L.A. County Children's Planning Coun., 1992—. Contbr. articles to profl. jours. Mem. Commn. for Children's Svcs. Family Preservation Policy Com., Mayor's Com. on Children, Youth and Families, L.A. Learning Ctrs. Design Team, Interagy. Coun. Child Abuse and Neglect Policy Com.; mem. commn. on student health and human svcs. L.A. City Bd. Edn.; bd. dirs. L.A. Roundtable for Children, 1988-94, Adolescent Pregnancy Childwatch, 1985-89; trustee L.A. Ednl. Alliance for Restructuring Now; co-chmn. L.A. County Drug and Alcohol Abuse Task Force, 1990; mem. cmty. adv. coun. Dept. Children's Svcs., 1991; mem. steering com. western region Child Welfare League Am., 1985-87; governing coun. sel. U.S. Olympic Festival Local Organizing Com., 1991, nat. judge. Mem. APA, Calif. Assn. Svcs. for Children (sec.-treas. 1983-84, pres. 1986-87), Assn. Children's Svcs. Agys. So. Calif. (sec. 1981-83, pres. 1984-85), Town Call Calif., U.S. Figure Skating Assn. (chair, membership com., sanctions and eligibility com. 1993-96), Inter-Club Assn. Figure Sakting Clubs (vice chair 1989-91, chair 1991-93), Pasadena Figure Skating Club (bd. dirs., pres. 1985-87, 89-90). Home: 4056 Camino Real Los Angeles CA 90065-3928 Office: LA County Children's Planning Coun 500 W Temple St Rm B-26 Los Angeles CA 90012-2713

WATSON, SOLOMON BROWN, IV, lawyer, business executive; b. Salem, N.J., Apr. 14, 1944; s. Solomon Brown and Denise Amelia W.; m. Bernadette Aldrich, Mar. 18, 1967 (div.); children: Katitti Madrid, Kira Pallis (twins); m. Brenda J. Wilson, Apr. 28, 1984. B.A. in English, Howard U., 1966; J.D., Harvard U., 1971. Bar: Mass. 1972, N.Y. 1977. Assoc. Bingham, Dana & Gould, Boston, 1971-74; corp. sec., asst. gen. counsel N.Y. Times Co., N.Y.C., 1979-89, gen. counsel, 1989-90, v.p., gen. counsel, 1990—. Active Vols. Legal Svc., Jobs for Youth Inc., until 1989; v.p. N.Y. Vietnam Vets. Leadership Program, Inc., until 1992, Agent Orange Assistance Fund, Vets. Adv. Bd. Lt. U.S. Army, 1966-68. Decorated Bronze Star with oak leaf cluster, Army Commendation medal with oak leaf cluster and V. Mem. ABA (com. on corp. law depts.), Am. Arbitration Assn. (bd. dirs.), Am. Corp. Counsel Assn. (dir.), Assn. Bar City N.Y., Mass. Bar Assn., Newspaper Assn. Am. (mem. legal affairs com.), Legal Aid Soc. (bd. dirs.). Home: 341 W 87th St New York NY 10024-2635 Office: NY Times Co 229 W 43rd St New York NY 10036-3913

WATSON, STEPHEN ALLISON, III, lawyer; b. Spokane, Wash., Aug. 17, 1957; s. Stephen Allison Jr. and Joan (Sauter) W. BA in Polit. Sci., Northwestern U., 1979; JD, Case We. U., 1982. Bar: Ohio 1983, U.S. Dist. (no. dist.) Ohio 1983. Counsel, environ. claims mgr. Argonaut Ins. Co., Cleve., 1982-86; mgr. hazardous waste unit Zurich Ins. Co., Schaumburg, Ill., 1989-91; mgr. environ. line bus. Zurich Ins. Co., Schaumburg, 1991-94; dir. regulatory svcs. Foster Wheeler Environ. Corp., Lyndhurst, N.J., 1995—; cons. Office Spl. Dep., Chgo., 1995—; lectr. in field. Contbr. articles to profl. jours. Mem. ABA (natural resource, energy and environ. law sect.), Def. Rsch. Inst. (environ. law com.). Republican. Avocations: golf, photography, sailing. Office: Foster Wheeler Environ Corp 1290 Wall St W Lyndhurst NJ 07071

WATSON, STEWART CHARLES, construction company executive; b. Brock, Sask., Can., Sept. 17, 1922; s. Samuel Henry and Elva Jane (St. John) W.; student U. Buffalo; m. Irene Lillian Ahrens, Aug. 4, 1943; children: Judith Gail (Mrs. David Stafford), Wendy Carolyn (Mrs. Rocco Amuso), Ronald James, Candyce Louise. With Acme Steel & Malleable Iron Works, Buffalo, 1940-42; with Acme Hwy. Products, Buffalo, 1946-69, internat. mktg. mgr., 1955-69; pres. Watson-Bowman Assocs., Inc., Buffalo, 1970—, pres., Kinematics, 1984—. chmn. bd. Air Stewart Inc.; internat. lectr. on kinetics of civil engring. structures; mem. U.S. Transp. Rsch. Bd.; bd. dirs. Internat. Bridge of Peace for Bering Strait Crossing. Served with AUS, 1943-45; ETO. Fellow Am. Concrete Inst. (dir. 1984—, Delmar Bloehm award 1984, Charles S. Whitney Medal 1987, hon. mem.); mem. Internat. Joints & Bearings Rsch. Coun. (chmn. 1988—), Internat. Activities Commn., ASTM, NAS, Masons (32 degree), Shriners. Home: 272 Lake Shore Rd, Fort Erie, ON Canada L2A 1B3

WATSON, SUSAN, newspaper columnist. Columnist Detroit Free Press. Office: Detroit Free Press 312 W Lafayette Blvd Detroit MI 48226-2701

WATSON, THOMAS C., lawyer; b. Poplar Bluff, Mo., Feb. 26, 1945; s. William C. and Dorothy E. (Whitson) W.; children: Thomas II, Nathan, Edward, Clay, Luke; m. Sharlene Wonders, Mar. 19, 1994. BS, U. Memphis, 1967, MEd, 1968; JD, Washington U., St. Louis, 1972. Bar: Mo. 1972, D.C. 1973. Assoc. Morgan, Lewis & Bockius, Washington, 1973-78, ptnr., 1978-79; ptnr. Crowell & Moring, Washington, 1979-95, Watson & Renner, 1996—. Avocations: hiking, biking, computers, hunting wild fowl. Home: Apt 87 2101 Connecticut Ave NW Washington DC 20008 Office: Watson & Renner 1001 Pennsylvania Ave NW Washington DC 20004

WATSON, THOMAS CAMPBELL, economic development consulting company executive; b. Pensacola, Fla., Feb. 19, 1931; s. Thomas Campbell and Lucie Davis (Yonge) W.; m. Norma Lynn Lofberg, June 20, 1959; children: Thomas C., Valerie Lynn, Pamela Lucie. Student, The Citadel, 1949-50; B.S., U.S. Naval Acad., 1954; B.S.E.E., U.S. Naval Postgrad. Sch., 1962; postgrad., Armed Forces Staff Coll., 1978. Commd. ensign U.S. Navy, 1954, advanced through grades to rear adm., 1980; comdg. officer Attack Squadron 81, 1970-72, comdr. Carrier Air Wing 9, 1972-73, comdr. Light Attack Wing 1, 1973-75; exec. asst. DCNO Air Warfare, The Pentagon Washington, 1975-76; comdg. officer USS Truckee, 1976-78, comdg. officer USS Independence, 1978-80; dep. dir. for current ops. Joint Chiefs of Staff, The Pentagon Washington, 1980-82; ret. U.S. Navy, 1982; pres. Mars Electronics, U.S.A., West Chester, Pa., 1982-88, ret., Omega Ventures, 1988—; exec. dir. Mus. Sci. and History, Jacksonville, Fla., 1989; pres. CAVUAssoc., 1990—. Decorated Legion of Merit, D.F.C., Bronze Star, Air medal. Mem. Assn. Naval Aviation, Naval Acad. Alumni Assn. Roman Catholic. Club: Rotary. Home: 2371 Bridgette Way Green Cove Springs FL 32043-8763

WATSON, THOMAS STURGES, professional golfer; b. Kansas City, Mo., Sept. 4, 1949; s. Raymond Etheridge and Sarah Elizabeth (Ridge) W.; m. Linda Tova Rubin, July 8, 1973; children: Margaret Elizabeth, Michael Barrett. BS, Stanford U., 1971. Profl. golfer, 1971—. Winner Western Open, 1974, 1977, 1984; winner Byron Nelson Tournament, 1975, 78, 79, 80; winner Brit. Open, 1975, 77, 80, 82, 83; winner, U.S. Open, 1982; winner World Series, 1975, 80; winner Andy Williams San Diego Open, 1977, 80; winner El Prat, 1977; winner Masters, 1977, 81; winner Bing Crosby Nat. Pro-Am Golf Tournament, 1977, 78; winner Tucson Open, 1978, 84; winner Colgate Hall of Fame Classic, 1978, 79; winner Anheuser Busch Golf Classic, 1978; winner Meml. Tournament, 1979; winner Heritage Classic, 1979, 83; winner Tournament of Champions, 1979, 80, 84; Los Angeles Open, 1980, 82; Greater New Orleans Open, 1980, 81; Dunlop Phoenix, 1980, Atlantic Classic, 1981; Nabisco Championship, 1987, Hong Kong Open, 1992; Recipient Vardon Trophy, 1977, 78, 79, Byron Nelson award, 1977-78, 79-80; named to Ryder Cup Team, 1977, 81, 83, 89 (elected capt. 1992—); named Player of Year Profl. Golf Assn., 1977, 78, 79, 80, 82, 84; elected to PGA World Golf Hall of Fame, 1988, Kans. Golf Hall of Fame, 1991, William H. Richardson award 1990. Mem. U.S. Golf Assn., Profl. Golfers Assn., Golf Course Supts. Assn. of Am. (Old Tom Morris award 1992), Butler Nat. Golf Club, Shadow Glen Club, Preston Trails Golf Club, Oakwood Country Club, Par Club, Blue Hills Country Club, Kansas City Country Club. Leading money winner PGA, 1977-80, 84. Office: 1901 W 47th Pl Ste 200 Shawnee Mission KS 66205-1834

WATSON, W. H., bishop. Bishop of N.W. Tex. Ch. of God in Christ, Lubbock.

WATSON, W. ROBERT, president, chief executive officer; b. Corvallis, Oreg., Sept. 3, 1943; s. John Ernest and Sara (Rice) W.; m. Janice Gayle Blair, Mar. 18, 1978; children: Shelly, Rhonda, Melody, Brian. BS in Fin., Fla. State U., 1965, MBA, 1968. Mktg. mgr. Coca-Cola U.S.A., Atlanta, 1969-79, mgr. strategic planning, 1979-82, dir. fin. svcs., 1982-88; sr. v.p. Tex. Commerce Bank, Houston, 1988-89; pres. Watson & Assocs., Inc., Marietta, Ga., 1989-94; pres., CEO Harrison Direct, Inc., Atlanta, 1995—. Elder Presbyn. Ch., Marietta, 1985-86; deacon Johnson Ferry Bapt. Ch.; mem. Fla. State U. Boosters Club, President's Club. Capt. U.S. Army, 1965-67.

WATSON, WARREN EDWARD, retired library administrator; b. Quincy, Mass., Apr. 5, 1925; s. Eimer Loring and Alice Loretta (Campbell) Watson; m. Elizabeth Mary Paul. AB, Boston Coll., 1948, MA, 1950; MLS, Simmons Coll., 1962. Broadcast news editor various radio stas., Mass., R.I., 1950-53; news editor Sta. WJAR-TV, Providence, 1953-55, spl. news assignments, 1958-59; spl. fgn. corr. on Operation Deepfreeze I CBS, Internat. News Svc., 1955-56; tech. writer Lincoln Lab., Lexington, Mass., 1956-58; libr. asst. Boston Pub. Libr., 1959-60, Boston Coll. Lib., 1960-61; asst. dir. Framingham (Mass.) Pub. Libr., 1961-64, dir., 1964-68; dir. librs. Thomas Crane Pub. Libr., Quincy, 1968-93; pres. Old Colony Libr. Network, Canton, Mass., 1984-86, Simmons Coll. Grad. Sch. of Libr. and Info. Sci. Alumni Bd., Boston, 1988-89. Mem. U.S. Power Squadrons, Raleigh, N.C., 1964—, Quincy (Mass.) Hist. Soc. Aviation Cadet US Army Air Corps, 1943-44. Mem. Mass. Libr. Assn. (pres. 1971), ALA, New England Libr. Assn. Democrat. Avocation: reading. Home: 7 Dorchester St # 3 Quincy MA 02171-1152

WATSON, WELLS, lawyer; b. Lake Charles, La., Apr. 11, 1963; s. Jack Crozier and Sue (Carter) W. BA, U. Miss., 1987; JD cum laude, Tulane U., 1990. Bar: La. 1990. Law clk. for Chief Judge Fred Heebe U.S. Dist. Ct., New Orleans, 1990-91; lawyer Baggett, McCall & Burgess, New Orleans, 1991—. Mem. La. Trial Lawyers Assn. (chmn. new lawyers, bd. govs. 1994), Am. Trial Lawyers (La. gov. of new lawyers). Home: 6916 Shadow Ln Lake Charles LA 70605 Office: Baggett McCall & Burgess 3006 Country Club Rd Lake Charles LA 70605

WATSON, WILLIAM A. J., law educator; b. 1933; MA, U. Glasgow, 1954, LLB, 1957; BA, Oxford U., 1957, MA, 1958, PhD, 1960. Lectr. Wadham Coll., Oxford U., 1957-59; fellow in jurisprudence Oriel Coll., Oxford U., 1959-65; pro-proctor Oxford U., 1962-63; Douglas prof. civil law U. Glasgow, 1965-68; prof. civil law U. Edinburgh, 1968-79; prof. law U. Pa., Phila., 1979-84, Gallichio prof., 1984-86, Univ. prof. law, 1986-89; Ernest P. Rodger prof., U. Ga., 1989—; vis. prof. Tulane U., 1967, U. Va., 1970, Cape Town (South Africa) U., 1974-75, U. Mich., 1977. Mem. Soc. Jean Bodin, Soc. Internationale des Droits de l'Antiquité, Soc. de l'Histoire du Droit, Am. Law Inst. Office: U Ga Law Sch Athens GA 30602

WATSON, WILLIAM D., lawyer; b. Buffalo, Sept. 1, 1943; s. William E. and Dorothy J. (Bowman) W.; m. Andrea L. Ehudin, Dec. 18, 1971; children: William A., Graham H. BA, Princeton U., 1965; LLB, Harvard U., 1968. Atty. Holme Roberts & Owen, LLC, Denver, 1970—; dir. Colo. Oil & Gas Assn. Author: The Gas Sellers Companion, 1992; editor Public Land and Resource Law Digest, 1990—. Capt. U.S. Army, 1968-70, Vietnam. Decorated 8 Bronze stars. Mem. Colo. Bar Assn., Fed. Energy Bar Assn., Rocky Mountain Princeton Club (pres. 1991-94). Office: Holme Roberts & Owen LLC 1700 Lincoln St Ste 4100 Denver CO 80203-4541

WATSON-BOONE, REBECCA A., associate dean; b. Springfield, Ohio, Mar. 7, 1946; d. Roger S. and Elizabeth Lupton (Walker) Boone; m. Dennis David Ash, 1967 (div. 1975); m. Frederick Kellogg, 1979 (div. 1988); m. Peter G. Watson-Boone, May 26, 1989. Student, Earlham Coll., 1964-67; BA, Case Western Res. U., 1968; MLS, U. N.C., 1971; PhD, U. Wis., 1995. Asst. reference libr. Princeton (N.J) U., 1970-76; head cen. reference dept. U. Ariz., Tucson, 1976-83, assoc. dean Coll. Arts and Scis., 1984-89; loaned exec. Ariz. Bd. Regents, 1988-89; pres. Ctr. for Study of Info. Profls., 1995—. Contbr. articles to profl. jours. Mem. ALA (div. pres. 1985-86, councilor 1988-92), Assn. for Libr. and Info. Sci. Edn., NAFE. Mem. Soc. of Friends. Office: 4333 W Grace Ave Mequon WI 53092-2136

WATT, DEAN DAY, retired biochemistry educator; b. McCammon, Idaho, Sept. 21, 1917; s. George William and Mary Amelia (Day) W.; m. Frances Elaine Murdock, Aug. 23, 1945; children: Sharon (Mrs. William E. Shull, Jr.), Nola Jean (Mrs. Thomas E. Barzee, Jr.), Barbara (Mrs. Robert Lauritzen), David, Stuart. Student, Idaho State U., 1936-37, 38-40; BS, U. Idaho, 1942; PhD, Iowa State U., 1949; postgrad., Case-Western Res. U., 1946-47. Research chemist Westvaco Chlorine Products, Newark, Calif., 1942-44; instr. Iowa State U., 1947-49; asst. prof. Purdue U., 1949-53; head dept. physiol. scis. Southeast La. Hosp., Mandeville, 1953-60; asso. prof. Tulane U., 1955-60, Ariz. State U., 1960-63; prin. biochemist Midwest Research Inst., Kansas City, Mo., 1963-69; prof. biochemistry Creighton U., 1969-88, prof. emeritus, 1988—. Fellow AAAS; mem. Internat. Soc. Toxinology (founding mem.), Sigma Xi. Mem. Ch. of Jesus Christ of Latter-day Saints. Research on animal venoms, biochemistry mental diseases. Home: 618 S 130th St Omaha NE 68154-2910

WATT, DOUGLAS (BENJAMIN WATT), writer, critic; b. N.Y.C., Jan. 20, 1914; s. Benjamin Douglas and Agnes Rita (Neimann) W.; m. Ray Mantel, Nov. 5, 1937 (div.); children—Richard David, James Douglas; m. Ethel Madsen, Aug. 13, 1951; children—Patricia, Katherine. A.B., Cornell U., 1934. Copy boy N.Y. News, 1936-37, radio columnist, 1937-40, drama reporter, 1940-71, sr. drama critic, 1971-87, critic-at-large, 1987-93; staff writer New Yorker mag., 1946-95; profl. song writer; columnist Small World, 1955-70. Pres. Hampton Animal Shelter, 1965-79. Served with USAAF, World War II. Mem. ASCAP, N.Y. Drama Critics Circle (pres. 1975-77). Club: Dutch Treat (N.Y.C.) (bd. govs.). Home: 27 W 86th St New York NY 10024-3615 *To say one has achieved success, except perhaps in isolated instances, is an exercise in vanity and contrary to man's experience. At best, some satisfaction can be gained in one's career, and then almost always because of intense effort.*

WATT, (ARTHUR) DWIGHT, JR., computer programming and microcomputer specialist; b. Washington, Jan. 25, 1955; s. Arthur Dwight and Myrtle Lorraine (Putnam) W.; m. Shari Elizabeth Gambrell, July 30, 1988. BA, Winthrop U., 1977, MBA, 1979; EdD, U. Ga., 1989. Cert. computer profl. Inst. Cert. Computer Profls.; cert. instr. cmty. first aid and safety, ARC. Data processing instr. York Tech. Coll., Rock Hill, S.C., 1977-

78; computer ctr. asst. Winthrop U., Rock Hill, 1976-79; data processing instr. Brunswick (Ga.) Coll., 1979-80; system operator, asst. programmer Sea Island (Ga.) Co., The Cloister, 1981; pvt. practice data processing cons. Swainsboro, Ga., 1981—; computer programming/microcomputer specialist instr. Swainsboro Tech. Inst., 1981—; cons., speaker in field; chmn. exec. bd. computer curricula Ga. Dept. Tech. and Adult Edn., 1990-92, mem. exec. bd. computer curricula, 1994—; chmn. East Ctrl. Ga. Consortium for Computer Occupations, 1990-93, 94—. Author: District Revenue Potential and Teachers Salaries in Georgia, 1989; co-author: District Property Wealth and Teachers Salaries in Georgia, 1990, Factors Influencing Teachers Salaries: An Examination of Alternative Models, 1991, Local Wealth and Teachers Salaries in Pennsylvania, 1992, School District Wealth and Teachers' Salaries in South Carolina, 1993. Chmn. Emanuel County chpt. ARC, Swainsboro, 1989-90, 92-93, bd. dirs., 1989—; pres. United Meth. Men. Swainsboro, 1984-86; trustee Greater Swainsboro Tech. Inst. Found., Inc., 1995—. Recipient Nat. Tech. Tchr. of Yr. finalist award Am. Tech. Edn. Assn., 1994; named Olpympic Cmty. Hero Torchbearer, 1996. Mem. Ga. Bus. Edn. Assn. (dir. dist. 1 1986, 96—, dist. sec.-treas. 1993-95, dist. 1 dir.-elect 1995-96, Dist. 1 Postsecondary Tchr. of Yr. 1985, state postsecondary tchr. of yr. 1995), Ga. Vocat. Assn., Data Processing Mgmt. Assn., Swainsboro Jaycees (Outstanding Young Citizen 1985, treas. 1984-89, pres. 1987-88, pres. S.E. Ga. Jaycee Fair 1995, treas. S.E. Ga. Jaycee Fair 1995), Ga. Jaycees (v.p. area C. mem. 1988-89, chaplain 1989-90, dir. region 6 1990-91, chmn. state shooting edn. 1991-92), U.S. Jr. C. of C. (nat. rep. shooting edn. program 1992-95, Shooting Edn. State Program Mgr. of Yr. 1992). Methodist. Home: PO Box 1637 Swainsboro GA 30401-4637 Office: Swainsboro Tech Inst 346 Kite Rd Swainsboro GA 30401-1822

WATT, JAMES GAIUS, lawyer, former government official, legal consultant; b. Lusk, Wyo., Jan. 31, 1938; s. William G. and Lois M. (Williams) W.; m. Leilani Bomgardner, Nov. 2, 1957; children: Erin Gaia, Eric Gaius. B.S., U. Wyo., 1960, J.D., 1962. Bar: Wyo. 1962, U.S. Supreme Ct. 1966. Legis. asst., counsel to Senator Simpson of Wyo., 1962-66; sec. to natural resources com. and environ. pollution adv. panel C. of C. of U.S., 1966-69; dep. asst. sec. water and power devel. Interior Dept., 1969-72; dir. Bur. Outdoor Recreation, Washington, 1972-75; mem., vice chmn. Fed. Power Commn., 1975-77; pres., chief legal officer Mountain States Legal Found., Denver, 1977-80; sec. Dept. Interior, Washington, 1981-83; bus. cons. Washington, 1983-86, Jackson Hole, Wyo., 1986—; chmn. bd. Environ. Diagnostics, 1984-87, Disease Detection Internat., 1986-90; instr. Coll. Commerce and Industry, U. Wyo. Author: (with Doug Wead) The Courage of a Conservative, 1985. Mem. Phi Kappa Phi, Delta Theta Phi. Office: PO Box 3705 755 E Paintbrush Dr Jackson WY 83001-3705

WATT, JOHN H., financial executive; b. Jersey City, Aug. 31, 1927; s. John and Mary (Tollan) W.; m. Margaret Johnstone, Feb. 15, 1958; children: John, Jennifer, Andrew, R. Cameron. BS, Rutgers U., 1953; MBA cum laude, Fairleigh Dickinson U., 1965. Mgr. bus. planning NL Industries, Inc., N.Y.C., 1960-65, fin. mgr., 1965-69, asst. treas., 1969-82, treas., 1982-87; treas. Omnicom Group Inc., N.Y.C., 1988-92; prin. John H. Watt Assocs., Weston, Conn., 1993—. Served with USN, 1945-46, U.S. Army, 1953-55. Mem. Nat. Assn. Corp. Treas., Soc. Internat. Treas., University Club (N.Y.C.).

WATT, KENNETH EDMUND FERGUSON, zoology educator; b. Toronto, July 13, 1929; s. William Black Ferguson Watt and Irene Eleanor (Hubbard) Dodd; m. Genevieve Bernice Bendig, Oct. 28, 1955; children: Tanis Jocelyn, Tara Alexis. BA with honor, U. Toronto, 1951; PhD in Zoology, U. Chgo., 1954; LLD, Simon Fraser U., 1970. Biometrician Rsch. div. Dept. Lands and Forests, Ont., Canada, 1954-57; sr. biometrician Can. Dept. Agr., Ottawa, Ont., 1957-60; head, statis. rsch. and svcs. Canadian Dept. Forestry, Ottawa, 1960-63; from assoc. prof. to prof. dept. zoology Dept. Zoology, U. Calif., Davis, 1963—. Author: Ecology and Resource Management, 1968, Principles of Environmental Sciences, 1973, Understanding the Environment, 1982, Taming the Future, 1991; editor-in-chief The Macloscope. Recipient Gold medal Entomol. Soc., 1969. Achievements include development of new approach to forecasting future based on exhaustive statistics testing of nonlinear math. equations to long runs of historical data; discovery that change through time in real world systems violates Markov principles. Home: 1116 Dartmouth Pl Davis CA 95616-2312 Office: U Calif Dept of Zoology Davis CA 95616 *The actual causes of present events are much further back in time than most people suspect. Failure to understand this is why forecasting is such a disaster area.*

WATT, MELVIN L., congressman, lawyer; b. Mecklenburg County, N.C., Oct. 26, 1945; m. Eulada Paysour; children: Brian, Jason. BS in Bus. Adminstrn., U. N.C., 1967; JD, Yale U., 1970. Atty. Ferguson, Stein, Watt, Wallis, Adkins, & Grensham, 1971—; U.S. senator from N.C. 95th Congress, 1985-86; co-owner East Towne Manor, 1989—; mem. 103rd-104th Congress from 12th N.C. dist., Washington, D.C., 1993—; pres. Mecklenburg County Bar. Active Ctrl. Piedmont C.C. Found., Legal Aid of Southern Piedmont, N.C. NB Community Devel. Corp., Auditorium-Coliseum-Civic Ctr. Authority, United Way, Mint Mus., Family Housing Svcs., Pub. Edn. Forum, Dilworth Community Devel. Assn., Cities in Schs., Housing Authority Scholarship Bd., Morehead Scholarship Selection Com.; bd. visitors Johnson C. Smith Univ. Mem. N.C. Assn. Black Lawyers, N.C. Acad. Trial Lawyers, Charlotte C. of C. (sports action coun.), West Charlotte Bus. Incubator, Inroads Inc., Phi Beta Kappa. Democrat. Presbyterian. Office: US Ho of Reps 1230 Longworth Ho Office Bldg Washington DC 20515-3312*

WATT, RONALD WILLIAM, public relations executive; b. Cleve., Oct. 10, 1943; s. Archie Gordon and Molly (Champa) W.; m. Elizabeth K. Strasshofer, May 15, 1965 (div. Dec. 1973); children: Cheryl Marie, Laurie Michelle; m. Simona Catherine Yesbak, Dec. 21, 1973; children: Ronald William Jr., Amanda Catherine. BJ, Bowling Green State U., 1965. Reporter Sta. WSPD-TV and Radio, Toledo, 1965-66; mgr. pub. relations Toledo-Lucas County Port Authority, Toledo, 1966-68; account exec. Flournoy & Gibbs, Toledo, 1968-73; v.p. Edward Howard and Co., Cleve., 1973-79; pres. Watt-Jayme Pub. Relations, Cleve., 1979-81; pres., chief operating officer Watt, Roop & Co., Cleve., 1981-86, chmn., chief exec. officer, 1987—. Grad. Leadership Cleve., 1988, alumni steering com., 1991—; chmn. Centennial ARC, Cleve., 1981; mem. vis. com. Coll. Urban Affairs Cleve. State U., chmn. In Tribute to Pub. Svc. program; co-founder Browns Buddies Program, Rainbow Babies, Childrens Hosp., Cleve., 1981; bd. dirs. Youth Opportunities, Inc., 1984-89, Downtown Cleve. Bus. Coun., 1987—, Cleve. chpt. NCCJ, 1988—, Citizens League of Cleve., 1988—, Marymount Hosp., 1988—, Cleve. chpt. Am. Cancer Soc., 1988—, N.E. Ohio Jazz Soc., Singing Angels, 1990—, Hiram House, 1991—, Clean-Land, Ohio, 1991—; co-chmn. Tri-C Jazzfest, 1990—, Tri-C Found., 1993—; leadership giving adv. com., image and presence Task Force Greater Cleve., United Way; voluntary communications dir., cabinet mem. 1990 campaign; steering com. Walter Hagen Invitational Golf Tournament; dir. Brian Brennan Boys Hope Golf Tournament, 1989—. Named one of Outstanding Young Men Am., 1971. Fellow Pub. Relations Soc. Am. (nat. chmn. profl. standards and bus. practices, bd. dirs. Counselors Acad. 1989—, chmn. 1993—, pres. Greater Cleve. chpt. 1981-82, 6 Silver Anvil awards 1969, 73, 87, 88, accredited); mem. Nat. Media Conf. (bd. dirs. 1985—), Cleve. Advt. Club (bd. dirs. 1985—, pres. 1991-92), Cleve. Press Club (bd. dirs. 1986-90), Greater Cleve. Press Club (co-chmn. centennial 1987), ARC Cleve. chpt. (vice chmn 1991-93, mktg. chair, 1989-92)Canterbury Golf Club (Shaker Heights, Ohio), Firestone Country Club (Akron, Ohio), Lakewood Country Club (Westlake, Ohio), Hermit Club (Cleve.), Clifton Club (Lakewood, Ohio), Union Club (Cleve.). Republican. Roman Catholic. Avocations: jazz music, piano, writing comedy. Office: Watt Roop & Co 1100 Superior Ave E Ste 1350 Cleveland OH 44114-2518*

WATT, STUART GEORGE, engineering contracting company executive; b. Warsaw, N.Y., Apr. 26, 1934; s. George James and Elizabeth Fern (Fullington) W.; m. Dorothy Elayne McLeod, Aug. 13, 1957; children: Stuart George II, Eric Duncan. BS in Mineral Engring., Pa. State U., 1956, MS in Mineral Engring. (NSF fellow), 1958. Ops. research cons. Lukens Steel Co., Coatesville, Pa., 1959; sr. research engr. Internat. Minerals & Chems. Co., Mulberry, Fla., 1959-62; project mgr. Internat. Minerals & Chems. Co., Skokie, Ill., 1962-64; prodn. mgr. Internat. Minerals & Chems. Co., Carlsbad, N.Mex., 1964-66; exec. engr. Davy Powergas, Inc., Lakeland, Fla., 1966-69, v.p. bus. devel., 1970-71, sr. v.p., 1972-74; exec. v.p., chief exec. ops. Davy Powergas, Inc., Houston, 1974-78; exec. v.p. Davy Internat. Inc., 1978—, also dir.; exec. v.p. Davy McKee, 1979—; pres. Stuart G. Watt & Co., Pensacola, Fla.; bd. dirs. McKee-Kearney, Bricmont Enterprises, Aker Oil and Gas Tech., Inc., Aker Omega Inc. Mem. Am. Inst. Mining and Metal. Engrs., Pa. State Alumni Assn., Toastmasters Club, Jr. Achievement, Sigma Gamma Epsilon. Republican. Lutheran. Clubs: Houston University, Lone Palm Golf; Lakeside Country (Houston); University (Salt Lake City); Walden Golf. Home and Office: 14456 River Rd Pensacola FL 32507-9684

WATT, WILLIAM JOSEPH, academic administrator, chemistry educator; b. Carbondale, Ill., Dec. 15, 1925; s. Phillip Clinton and Ella (Dickey) W.; m. Helen Stevens Gravatt, Sept. 1, 1956; children: John Gravatt, Phyllis Cary, William Joseph. Student, U. Mich., 1943; B.S. in Chemistry, U. Ill., 1949; M.S., Cornell U., 1951, Ph.D., 1956. Asst. prof. chemistry Davidson (N.C.) Coll., 1951-53; asst. prof. to assoc. prof. Washington and Lee U., Lexington, Va., 1955-65, prof. chemistry, 1965-94; prof. and dean emeritus, 1994—; assoc. dean of coll. Washington and Lee U., Lexington, Va., 1968-71, dean, 1971-84, head dept. chemistry, 1986-91; vis. prof. NSF Inst. High Sch. Tchrs., Ala. Coll., summers 1959-61, U. Va., summers 1964-66; Summer research participant Cornell U., 1956; Oak Ridge Nat. Lab., 1957, 58, U. Va., 1962. Contbr. articles to profl. jours. Pres. Rockbridge chpt. Va. Mus. Fine Arts, 1963-65; bd. dirs. Rockbridge Concert Theater Series, 1960—, pres., 1971-77; trustee Episcopal High Sch., 1974-80; vestryman, sr. warden Episcopal Ch.; bd. dirs. Botetourt-Rockbridge Regional Library, 1971-80, chmn., 1975-77; sec.-treas. Conf. Acad. Deans of So. States, 1978-79, v.p., 1979-80, pres., 1980-81; chmn. Nat. Deans Conf., 1983, Commn. Ministry Higher Edn. Diocese of Southwestern Va., 1989—. Served with AUS, 1944-46. Mem. AAAS, Am. Chem. Soc., English-Speaking Union (nat. bd. dirs. 1993—), Soc. Chimique de France, Va. Acad. Sci., N.Y. Acad. Sci., Phi Eta Sigma, Alpha Chi Sigma, Omicron Delta Kappa (hon.). Democrat. Home: 7 Providence Pl # 753 Lexington VA 24450-1833 Office: Washington and Lee U Dept Chemistry Lexington VA 24450

WATT, WILLIAM VANCE, surgeon; b. Thomasville, Ga., Apr. 10, 1924; s. Charles Hansell and Elizabeth Gilkeson (Pancake) W.; m. Mary Mercer Pendleton, Apr. 7, 1951; children: Mercer Pendleton Watt Pember, Elizabeth Vance Watt Finch, Philip Cargill. Student, Davidson Coll., 1942-43, Duke U., 1943-44; MD, Johns Hopkins U., 1948. Diplomate Am. Bd. Surgery. Intern Union Meml. Hosp., Balt., 1948-49; resident surgery Jefferson Hosp., Roanoke, Va., 1949-51, 53-54; fellow surgery Lahey Clinic, Boston, 1954-55; mem. surg. staff Archbold Meml. Hosp., Thomasville, Ga., 1955-94. Founder Brookwood Sch., Thomasville, 1970, All Saints Episcopal Ch., Thomasville, 1980. Recipient Silver Beaver award Boy Scouts Am., 1974, Golden Eagle award, 1995. Mem. ACS, AMA, Am. Soc. Gastrointestinal Endoscopy, Southeastern Surg. Soc., Rotary. Republican. Episcopalian. Avocations: hunting, golfing, fishing. Home: 1104 Old Monticello Rd Thomasville GA 31792

WATT, WILLIS "BILL" MARTIN, communications educator; b. Ottawa, Kans., Dec. 20, 1950; s. Gerald Omry and Shirley Arlene (Tush) W.; m. Katherine Ann Young, Feb. 14, 1970; 1 child, Derek Lee. BS in Christian Edn., Manhattan Christian Coll., 1976; BS in Secondary Edn.-Speech/Drama, Kans. State U., 1976, MA in Speech/Drama, 1978, PhD in Curriculum/Instrn./Speech, 1980. Ordained to ministry Christian Ch., 1976. Grad. tchg. asst. dept. speech, theatre and dance Kans. State U., Manhattan, 1976-78, instr., 1978-80; teaching intern speech/drama Manhattan (Kans.) Christian Coll., 1979; asst. prof. dept. speech comm. Iowa State U., Ames, 1980-84; dir. forensics dept. comm. Ft. Hays (Kans.) State U., 1984-91, chair, 1991—; dir. Talking Tiger Rsch. Inst., Hays, 1985-91, Comm. Tng. Svcs., Hays, 1986—; exec. dir. Chi Rho Players Religious Drama Troupe, Ames, Iowa, 1981-84; adjudicator Am. Coll. Theatre Festival, Region V, 1982—. Author: Fundamentals of Speech, 1988, Theory and Application for Effective Bus. and Profl. Presentations, 1994, Fundamentals of Oral Communication: Theory and Practice, 1995; editor Kans. Speech Jour., 1994—; assoc. editor Nat. Forensic Jour., 1987—. Edn. divsn. leader United Way of Ellis County, Hays, 1989, Ft. Hays State U. chmn. leader, 1992; baseball coach Little League, Ames, Iowa and Hays, 1982-86. With U.S. Army, 1971-74. Mem. World Comm. Assn., Speech Comm. Assn., Speech Comm. Assn. P.R., Ctrl. State Comm. Assn., Kans. Speech Comm. Assn. (mem. exec. bd., dist. rep., Outstanding Coll. Tchr. award 1996), Theta Alpha Phi, Pi Kappa Delta (gov. plains province 1986-88, 90-91, Exemplary Svc. award 1987, 91, Svc. award 1993, Order of Highest Distinction 1995), Pi Delta Kappa, Alpha Psi Omega. Avocations: racketball, chess, reading, writing, travel. Home: 1309 Holmes Rd Hays KS 67601-2515 Office: Ft Hays State U Dept Comm 600 Park St Hays KS 67601-4099

WATTEL, HAROLD LOUIS, economics educator; b. Bklyn., Sept. 30, 1921; s. David Max and Carolyn (Abrams) W.; m. Sara Gordon, Sept. 1, 1946; children: Karen, Jill. B.A., Queens Coll., 1942; M.A., Columbia U., 1947; Ph.D. magna cum laude, New Sch. Social Research, 1954. Jr. economist WPB, 1942; economist Dept. Agr., 1946; econ. cons. Boni, Watkins & Mounteer, 1952; economist Bur. Bus. and Community Research, Hofstra U., 1954, 57, dir., 1957-58; prof. econs. Bur. Bus. and Community Rsch., Hofstra U., 1957-86, prof. emeritus, 1986—, chmn. dept. econs., 1957-61, chmn. div. bus., 1961—, dean Sch. Bus., 1965-73; econ. cons. to consumer counsel, staff Gov. N.Y., 1956-58; cons. N.Y. State Moreland Commn. on Alcoholic Beverage Control Law, 1963-64, Legislative Reference Bur., U. Hawaii, 1966, Schenley Industries, 1967—, Ralston Purina Co., 1967—, Am. Can Co., 1965—; econ. cons. Nat. Millinery Planning Bd., 1959-70; edn. cons. U.S. Mcht. Marine Acad., Kings Point, 1972, Bulova Watch Co., 1975-82. Author ann. publ.: The Millinery Industry; Editor: Planning in Higher Education, 1975, Chief Executive Officer Compensation, 1978, The Gross Personal Income Tax, 1981; Contbr. chpts. to books, encys., dictionaries, also reports.; Editor, contbr.: L.I. Bus, 1954-59. Mem. Comprehensive Health Planning Coun., 1970-75; bd. dirs., v. p., N.Y. State unit Am. Lung Assn.; pres. Nassau-Suffolk unit; bd. dirs. Comprehensive Health Planning Coun., Nassau-Suffolk, N.Y., N.Y. State Citizen Coun., Consumer Farmer Found., Regional Med. Program Nassau-Suffolk, consumer rep., bd. dirs. Island Peer Rev. Orgn. , 1990. Lt. USNR, 1942-46. Edn. fellow, 1949; Hazen Found. fellow, 1952; Ford Found. regional fellow, 1960. Mem. AAUP (chpt. pres. 1953), Middle Atlantic Assn. Colls. Bus. Adminstrn. (pres. 1970-71), Am., Met. econs. assns., N.Y. State Environ. Health Assn. (v.p.), Island Peer Rev. Orgn. (consumer/AARP rep. 1990—), Pi Gamma Mu, Omicron Chi Epsilon, Beta Gamma Sigma (hon. assoc.). Home: 181 Shepherd Ln Roslyn Heights NY 11577-2525 Office: Hofstra U Dept Econ Hempstead NY 11550

WATTENBERG, ALBERT, physicist, educator; b. N.Y.C., Apr. 13, 1917; s. Louis and Bella (Wolff) W.; m. Alice von Neumann, May 23, 1992; children from a previous marriage: Beth, Jill, Nina Diane. B.S., Coll. City N.Y., 1938; M.A., Columbia, 1939; Ph.D., U. Chgo., 1947. Spectroscopist Schenley Distilleries, N.Y.C., 1939-42; physicist Manhattan Project, Metall. Lab., Chgo., 1942-46; group leader Argonne Nat. Lab., Chgo., 1946-50; asst. prof. U. Ill., Urbana, 1950-51; prof. physics U. Ill., 1958—; research physicist Mass. Inst. Tech., 1951-58. Recipient award for 1st nuclear reactor Am. Nuclear Soc., 1962; Nuclear Pioneer award Soc. Nuclear Medicine, 1977; NSF fellow U. Rome, 1962-63. Pioneered controlled nuclear reactor.

WATTENMAKER, RICHARD JOEL, archive director, art scholar; b. Phila., Feb. 22, 1941; s. Nathan H. and Frances (Rynes) W.; m. Eva Augusta Oscarsson, June 25, 1968; children: Adrian Ezra, Barnaby Leo. B.A., U. Pa., 1963; M.A., NYU Inst Fine Arts, 1965; Ph.D., NYU Inst Arts, 1972. With The Barnes Found., 1959-66, Rutgers U. Art Gallery, New Brunswick, N.J., 1966-69; chief curator Art Gallery Ont., Toronto, Can., 1972-78; dir. Chrysler Mus., Norfolk, Va., 1979-80, Flint (Mich.) Inst. Arts, 1980-88, Archives of Am. Art, Smithsonian Instn., Washington, 1990—; lectr. Barnes Found., 1991-92. Author: The Art of Charles Prendergast, 1968, The Art of Jean Hugo, 1973, Puvis de Chavannes and the Modern Tradition, 1975, Maurice Prendergast, 1994. Trustee Intermus. Conservation Lab., Oberlin, Ohio, 1982-88. Recipient Founders Day award NYU, 1972. Office: Smithsonian Instn Archives of Am Art 8th and G Sts NW Washington DC 20560

WATTERS, EDWARD MCLAIN, III, lawyer; s. Edward McL. and Lucy F. (Disston) W.; m. Susan Secor, May 12, 1979; children—Jennifer Susan, Ann Elizabeth. B.A. cum laude, Yale U., 1965; J.D. cum laude, U. Pa., 1970. Bar: Pa. 1970. Ptnr., Pepper, Hamilton & Scheetz, Phila., 1977—; lectr. programs on estate planning and will drafting Pa. Bar Inst. Bd. dirs. Children's Cruise and Playground Soc. Pa., Sanitarium Playgrounds of N.J., others. Served to lt. USNR, 1965-75. Fellow Am. Coll. Trust and Estate Counsel (mem. com. state laws); mem. Phila. Bar Assn. , Pa. Bar Assn. (past chmn. legis. com. probate sect.), ABA (mem. com. on significant legislation probate sect.), Phila. Estate Planning Council (past pres.), Yale Club of Phila., Penn Club, Merion Golf Club. Office: Pepper Hamilton & Scheetz 1235 Westlakes Dr Ste 400 Berwyn PA 19312-2416

WATTERS, RICHARD JAMES, professional football player; b. Harrisburg, Pa., Apr. 7, 1969. Degree in design, U. Notre Dame. With San Francisco 49'ers, 1991-94; running back Phila. Eagles, 1995—. Selected to Pro Bowl, 1992-94. Achievements include member San Francisco 49'ers Super Bowl XXIX Champions, 1994, holds NFL postseason single game for most points (30), most touchdowns (5), Jan. 15, 1994 vs N.Y. Giants. Office: Philadelphia Eagles 3501 S Broad St Philadelphia PA 19148-5298

WATTERS, TERESA MARIE, health care administrator; b. Columbus, Ohio, Dec. 11, 1961; d. James Lilburn Banner and Eleanor Jane (Lewis) Smith; m. Jerome Wendell Watters, Sept. 9, 1989; 1 child, Ashley Lauren. BS, Howard U., 1984; M in Health Svc. Adminstrn., George Washington U., 1991. From adminstrv. asst. to exec. asst. for clin. ops. George Washington U. Med. Ctr., Washington, 1987-91; from exec. assoc. to dir. bus. ops. VITAS Healthcare Corp., Miami, Fla. and Ft. Worth, 1991-93; regional dir. bus. ops. VITAS Healthcare Corp., Dallas, Ft. Worth, 1993-95; branch dir. Olsten Kimberly Quality Care, Dallas, 1995—. Coord. D.C. CARE Health Directory, 1989. Adminstrv. vol. Dept. Health and Human Svcs., Washington, 1987. Mem. Am. Coll. Healthcare Execs. (assoc. 1991—), Nat. Assn. Healthcare Exec., Nat. Hospice Assn., Tex. Hospice Assn. Avocations: skiing, horseback riding. Home: 717 Bear Run Dr Grapevine TX 76051

WATTERS, THOMAS ROBERT, geologist, museum administrator; b. West Chester, Pa., Feb. 1, 1955; s. Frank Edward Sr. and Beatrice Josephine (Speirs) W.; m. Nancy Rae Tracey, June 18, 1983; children: James T. Samantha E., Adam T. BS in Earth Scis., West Chester U., 1977; MA in Geology, Bryn Mawr Coll., 1979; PhD in Geology, George Washington U., 1985. Rsch. fellow Am. Mus. Natural History, 1978-80; rsch. asst. dept. terrestrial magnetism Carnegie Instn. Washington, 1980-81; rsch. geologist Ctr. for Earth and Planetary Studies Smithsonian Instn., Washington, 1981-89, supervisory geologist Ctr. for Earth and Planetary Studies, Nat. Air and Space Mus., 1989—, acting. chmn. Ctr. for Earth and Planetary Studies, 1989-92, chmn. Ctr. for Earth and Planetary Studies, 1992—; lectr. in field. Author: Plants: A Smithsonian Guide; contbr. over 100 abstracts and papers. Active Plum Point Elem. PTA, 1991—, mem. exec. bd. 1991-92; coach Calvert T-Ball, 1992-93; coach Babe Ruth, 1994—. William P. Phillips Meml. scholar; grantee NASA, 85-89, 86-88, 87-88, 87-90, 89-94, 89-95, 91-95, 95—; recipient cert. award Nat. Air Space Mus., 1983, 86, 89-94. Mem. AAAS, Geol. Soc. Am. (mem. editl. bd. GEOLOGY 1993—), Am. Geophys. Union (Editor's citation 1992), Nat. Youth Sports Coaches Assn., Kappa Delta Phi. Achievements include research in terrestrial and planetary tectonics and tectonophysics; morphological and structural comparisons of tectonic features on the terrestrial planets and analogous features on Earth; geologic mapping of Mars. Office: Smithsonian Instn Nat Air & Space Museum Rm 3789 Ctr Earth & Planetary Studies Washington DC 20560

WATTERSON, BILL, cartoonist; b. Washington, 1958; s. James and Kathryn W.; m. Melissa Watterson. Grad. polit. sci., Kenyon Coll., 1980. Editorial cartoonist Cincinnati Post, Cincinnati, OH, 1980; syndicated cartoon strip, Calvin and Hobbes Universal Press Syndicate, 1985—. Author, illustrator: Calvin and Hobbes, 1987, The Essential Calvin and Hobbes: A Calvin and Hobbes Treasury, 1988, Something Under the Bed is Drooling: A Calvin and Hobbes Collection, 1988, Yukon Ho!, 1989, The Calvin & Hobbes Lazy Sunday Book, 1989, The Authoritative Calvin and Hobbes, 1990, Weirdos from Another Planet!, 1990, The Revenge of the Baby-Sitter, 1991, Scientific Progress Goes "Boink", 1991, Attack of the Deranged Mutant Killer Monster Snow Goons, 1992, Indispensible Calvin and Hobbes: A Calvin and Hobbes Treasury, 1992, The Days are Just Packed, 1993, Homicidal Psycho Jungle Cat: A Calvin & Hobbes Collection, 1994; illustrator The Komplete Kolor Krazy Kat, vol. I, 1990; wrote forward Fox Trot, 1989. Office: Universal Press Syndicate 4900 Main St Fl 9 Kansas City MO 64112-2630

WATTERSON, JOYCE GRANDE, editor, publisher; b. Cleve., May 15, 1937; d. Anthony John Sr. and Helen Bernice (Kramer) Grande; m. Thomas Batchelor, Sept. 27, 1968; children: Sean Anthony, William Grande. BA, Notre Dame Ohio, 1960; Cert. Pratique, U. Paris, 1964; MA, Case Western Res., 1967. Cert. sales profl.; cert. tchr., Ohio. Tchr. Cleve. Bd. Edn., 1960-63, 64-65; asst. pers. dir. Cleve., Ohio Retail, 1965-66; tchr. Shaker Heights (Ohio) Bd. Edn., 1966-69, 71-72, 1983-85; lectr. Cleve. State U., 1987-88, Notre Dame Coll. Ohio, Cleve., 1990-91; adminstrv. dir. No. Ohio Acad. Pharmacy, Cleve., 1991-94; editor, pub. Concord Gazette GrandeLine Custom Comms., 1994—. Author, editor, pub.: Cascade Valley Soups, 1989, Cascade Valley Beans, 1992; editor/pub. Concord Gazette, 1994—. Advisor Alateens, Cleve., 1970-73; pres. Parents of U. Sch., Hunting Valley, Ohio, 1986-87; mem. adv. com. Painesville Adult Basic and Literacy Edn. Project, 1995—; mem. 50th anniversary com. Lake County Soil and Water Conservation Dist. Mem. Lake County Soil and Water Conservation Dist. (50th Ann. Com.), Le Cercle des Conferences Francaises of Cleve. (pres. 1986-88, life). Republican. Roman Catholic. Avocations: swimming, embroidery, crafts, book clubs. Home: 7067 Cascade Rd Concord OH 44077-9509 Office: GrandeLine Custom Comm 7067 Cascade Rd Concord OH 44077-9509

WATTERSON, SCOTT, home fitness equipment manufacturer. Chmn., CEO ICON Health & Fitness, Inc., Logan, Utah. Office: ICON Hlth & Fitness Inc 1500 S 1000 W Logan UT 84321

WATTLES, JOSHUA, motion picture studio executive. Sr., v.p. dep. gen. counsel Paramount Pictures Corp., subs. Gulf & Western Inc., N.Y.C. Office: Paramount Pictures Corp 1 Gulf Western Plz New York NY 10023

WATTLETON, (ALYCE) FAYE, educational association administrator; b. St. Louis, July 8, 1943; d. George and Ozie (Garret) Wattleton; m. Franklin Gordon (div.); 1 child, Felicia. BS in Nursing, Ohio State U., 1964; MS in Maternal and Infant Health Care, Columbia U., 1967; LLD (hon.), Northeastern Univ. Law Sch., 1990; LHD (hon.), Long Island Univ., 1990, Univ. of Pa., 1990, Bard Coll., 1991; HHD (hon.), Oberlin Coll., 1991; LLD (hon.), Wesleyan Univ., 1991. Tchr. Miami Valley Hosp. Sch. Nursing, Dayton, Ohio, 1964-66; asst. dir. Montgomery County Combined Pub. Health Dist., Dayton, 1967-70; exec. dir. Planned Parenthood, Dayton, 1970-78; pres. Planned Parenthood Fedn. Am., Inc., N.Y.C., 1978-92; host syndicated TV show Tribune Entertainment, Chgo., 1992—. Author: How to Talk to Your Child About Sexuality, 1986. Bd. dirs. Kaiser Family Found., Calif. Wellness Found., WNET, Inst. for Internat. Edn., Quidel, Empire Blue Cross Blue Shield, Leslie Fay Cos. Recipient Claude Pepper Humanitarian award Internat. Platform Assn., 1990, Pioneer of Civil Rights and Human Rights award Nat. Conf. of Black Lawyers, 1990, Florina Lasker award N.Y. Civil Liberties Union Found., 1990, Whitney M. Young Jr. Service award Boy Scouts of Am., 1990, Ministry of Women award Unitarian Universalist Women's Fed., 1990, Spirit of Achievement award Albert Einstein Coll. of Med. Yeshiva Univ., 1991, 20th Anniversary Advocacy award Nat. Family Planning and Reproductive Health Assn., 1991, Women of Achievement award Women's Projects and Production, 1991, Margaret Sanger award, 1992, Jefferson Public Service award, 1992, Dean's Distinguished Service award Columbia Sch. of Public Health, 1992. Office: care Fischer-Ross Agy 211 E 49th St New York NY 10017*

WATTMAN, MALCOLM PETER, lawyer; b. N.Y.C., June 27, 1941; s. William and Irma (Turtletaub) W.; m. Donna Weber, Sept. 1, 1963. BS in Indsl. Engring., U. Buffalo, 1963; postgrad., Syracuse U., 1963-64; JD, Fordham U., 1968. Bar: N.Y. 1969. Engr. US Air Material Command, Rome, N.Y., 1963-64, Uniroyal, Passaic, N.J., 1964-66, M&M Candies, Hackettown, N.J., 1966-68; cons. Touche Ross Co., N.Y.C., 1968-69; assoc. Cadwalader Wickersham & Taft, N.Y.C., 1969-78, ptnr., 1978—. Mem.

ABA, N.Y. State Bar Assn., Assn. of Bar of City of N.Y. Home: 1185 Park Ave Apt 8K New York NY 10128-1130 Office: Cadwalader Wickersham & Taft 100 Maiden Ln New York NY 10038-4818

WATTO, DENNIS PAUL, school system administrator, researcher, writer; b. Upland, Pa., Oct. 31, 1945; s. Paul and Helen (Kashlak) W.; m. Andrea Franzosa; children: Julie, Joseph. BS, Millersville U., 1971; MEd, East Stroudsburg U, 1977, Pa. State U., 1981; DEd, Pa. State U., 1987. Tchr. North Schuylkill (Pa.) Sch. Dist., 1971-77; adminstr. Tamaqua (Pa.) Area Sch. Dist., 1978-88, Downingtown (Pa.) Area Sch. Dist., 1988—; v.p. Schuylkill County Inter-Scholastic Athletic Assn., Pottsville, Pa., 1978-79, 85-87, pres., 1979-85; instr. Pa. State U., 1988. Active mem. Downingtown-Uwchlan Recreation Bd.; coach Valley West Baseball Assn.; active Am. Heart Assn., Jr. Miss Pageant. With Pa. N.G., 1966-72. Mem. ASCD, Am. Ednl. Rsch. Assn., Nat. Assn. Secondary Sch. Prins., Pa. Assn. Secondary Sch. Prins., Phi Delta Kappa. Avocations: reading, music, golf, fishing, tennis. Home: 48 Carlson Way Downingtown PA 19335-2262 Office: Downingtown Area Sch Dist Wallace Ave Downingtown PA 19335

WATTS, ANDRÉ, concert pianist; b. Nüremberg, Germany, June 20, 1946; s. Herman and Maria Alexandra (Gusmits) W. Student, Phila. Mus. Acad.; grad., Peabody Conservatory, Balt.; hon. doctorate, Yale U., 1973; HHD, Albright Coll., 1975; MusD (hon.), U. Pa., 1984. First pub. appearance at age 10, Phila. Orch. Children's Concerts, 1955, performed with Phila. Orch., 1956, with Leonard Bernstein and the N.Y. Philharm., 1963, European debut, London Symphony Orch., 1966, made world concert tour to 16 Asian and Western European cities for U.S. State Dept., 1967, including an appearance at the Berlin Festival, Soviet Union tour with San Francisco Symphony, 1972, appearances as soloist with all major U.S. and European orchs., solo tours, Europe, U.S., Japan, Israel; TV appearances include Live from Lincoln Ctr., Great Performers series Lincoln Ctr., NET TV Spl. with Zubin Mehta and L.A. Philharm., Eugene Ormandy and the Phila. Orch., Casals Festival in P.R. on Arts and Entertainment Network (emmy award nomination for Outstanding Individual Achievement in Cultural Programming); rec. artist with Angel/EMI label. Decorated Order of Zaire Congo; recipient Grammy award Nat. Acad. Rec. Arts and Scis., 1963; Lincoln Center medallion, 1974, Avery Fisher prize, 1988. Address: care IMG 22 E 71st St New York NY 10021-4911

WATTS, BARBARA GAYLE, law academic administrator; b. Covington, Ky., Oct. 18, 1946; d. William Samuel and LaVerne Barbara (Ziegler) W. BA, Purdue U., 1968; MEd, U. Cin., 1969, JD, 1978. Bar: Ohio 1978, U.S. Dist. Ct. (so. dist.) Ohio 1978. Residence dir. Ohio State U., Columbus, 1969-71, asst. dean students, 1971-75; assoc. Frost & Jacobs, Cin., 1978-81; asst. dean U. Cin. Coll. Law, 1981-84, assoc. dean, 1984—. Trustee Summerfair Inc., Cin., 1982-85; bd. dirs. Pro-Srs., 1995—; mem. Summerfair Cmty. Adv. Com. Schleman fellow Purdue U., 1968, Castleberry fellow AAUW, 1977. Mem. ABA, Ohio State Bar Assn., Cin. Bar Assn. (trustee 1992—, sec.1993-94), Nat. Assn. Women in Edn., Order of Coif, Chi Omega. Democrat. Office: U Cin Coll Law Clifton & Calhoun Sts Cincinnati OH 45221-0040

WATTS, CHARLES DEWITT, surgeon, corporate medical director; b. Atlanta, Sept. 21, 1917; s. Lewis G. and Ida H. (Hawes) W.; m. Constance Merrick, Jan. 5, 1945; children: Eileen Constance Watts Welch, Deborah Hill (dec.), Charles D., Winifred Anita Watts Hemphill. B.S., Morehouse Coll., 1938; M.D., Howard U., 1943; LHD (hon.), St. Pauls Coll., 1984; DSc (hon.), Duke U., 1991. Diplomate: Am. Bd. Surgery. Practice medicine specializing in surgery Durham, N.C., 1950—; med. dir. N.C. Mut. Life Ins. Co., Durham, 1960—; mem. faculty dept. surgery Howard U. Coll. Medicine, 1947-50; instr. surgery Howard U., Washington; asst. clin. prof. surgery Duke Med. Center; attending surgeon Durham County Gen. Hosp.; chmn. bd. Capital Health Systems Regional Agy., 1976; founder, dir. Lincoln Community Health Center, Durham, 1970. Trustee Howard U., Washington. Fellow Am. Coll. Surgery; mem. Inst. of Medicine of NSF. Home: 829 E Lawson St Durham NC 27701-4534 *As one looks back, he is impressed with the fact that whatever one accomplished was done with the help of others. It is an humbling experience to realize how interdependent we are as we go through life.*

WATTS, CHARLES HENRY, II, university administrator; b. N.Y.C., Oct. 17, 1926; s. Charles Henry and Mabel (Lamborn) W.; m. Patricia Dorothy McQuillen, June 9, 1951; children: Katharine L., Caroline W. Collins, Charles Henry III. AB, Brown U., 1947, PhD, 1953, LLD, 1975; MA, Columbia, 1948; LittD, Franklin Coll., 1965; LLD, Dickinson Sch. Law, 1968; HHD, Alderson-Broaddus Coll., 1969; LHD, Bucknell U., 1979. Mem. English dept. faculty Brown U., 1948-62, dean coll., 1958-62; exec. assoc. Am. Council on Edn., 1962-64; pres. Bucknell U., 1964-76; pres., chief exec. officer Wolf Trap Found. Performing Arts, 1976-77; cons., 1977-78; dir. campaign Brown U., 1978-80; dir. Beneficial Corp., Wilmington, Del., 1953—, gen. dir., 1980-87. Trustee emeritus Bucknell U., Lewisburg, Pa.; trustee St. John's Coll. Ensign USNR, WWII. Mem. Century Assn. (N.Y.C.), Knickerbocker Club (N.Y.C.), St. Botolph Club. Home: 191 Commonwealth Ave Apt 41 Boston MA 02116-2211

WATTS, CLAUDIUS ELMER, III, retired air force officer; b. Bennettsville, S.C., Sept. 22, 1936; s. Claudius Elmer and Blanche Robey (Wannamaker) W.; m. Patricia Jane Sims, July 23, 1960; children: Claudius Elmer IV, Patricia Watts Heck. A.B. in Polit. Sci., The Citadel, 1958; postgrad. (Fulbright scholar), London Sch. Econs. and Polit. Sci., 1958-59; M.B.A., Stanford U., 1967. Commd. officer USAF, 1958, advanced through grades to lt. gen., 1986; comdr. 438th Mil. Airlift Group USAF, McGuire AFB, N.J., 1978-80; comdr. 63d Mil. Airlift Wing USAF, Norton AFB, Calif., 1980-82; asst. dep. chief staff plans Mil. Airlift Command USAF, Scott AFB, Ill., 1982-83, dep. chief staff plans Mil. Airlift Command, 1982-84; dir. budget Hdqrs. U.S. Air Force, Washington, 1984-85; sr. mil. asst. to dep. sec. def. U.S. Dept. Def., Washington, 1985-86; compt. USAF, Washington, 1986-89; pres. The Citadel, Charleston, S.C., 1989-96; ret.; former mem. adv. coun. grad. sch. bus. Stanford U.; former mem. bd. visitors Air U.; mem. NCAA Coun., rep. on acad. requirements, chmn. peer rev. teams for cert. Bd. trustees Palmetto Partnership; chmn. Marion Sq. Commn.; bd. dirs., mem. fin. com. Air Force Aid Soc. Decorated Def. Disting. Svc. medal, USAF Disting. Svc. medal, Legion of Merit with oak leaf cluster, DFC with two oak leaf clusters, Air Medal with 10 oak leaf clusters, Gallantry Cross with Palm (Vietnam), Vietnamese Svc. Cross with 2 svc. stars. Mem. Air Force Assn. (audit com. nat. hdqrs.), Am. Soc. Mil. Comptrollers, Mil. Order World Wars, Air Force Sgts. Assn., Airlift Assn., VFW, Royal Order of St. Stanislas, Order of Daedalians, Soc. of the Cincinnati (hon.), Assn. Mil. Colls. and Schs. of U.S. (exec. com.), Rotary. Methodist. Avocations: golf; reading. Office: Mil Coll of SC Pres Office The Citadel Charleston SC 29409

WATTS, DAVE HENRY, corporate executive; b. Montgomery, Ala., Jan. 18, 1932; s. Lawson Tate and Annie (Sherman) W.; m. Eleanor Lewis, Nov. 5, 1950; children—Anne Watts Durham, Martha Watts Keens, Susan Watts Balla. Student, U. Ala., 1950, U. Va., 1962; B.B.A., George Washington U., 1968, M.B.A., 1970, D.B.A., 1974. Constrn. clk. So. Ry., Birmingham, Ala., 1950-51, safety supr., various other positions, 1951-77; v.p. personnel So. Ry., Washington, 1977-82; v.p. personnel and corp. devel. Norfolk So. Corp., Va., 1982-85, exec. v.p. planning and devel., 1985-86, exec. v.p. mktg., 1986-95, vice-chmn., 1995—; lectr. George Washington U., 1974—. Contbr. articles to pubIs. in field. Mem. Va. Opera Bd.; bd. trustees Va. Wesleyan Coll. Mem. Nat. Freight Transp. Assn. (exec. com.), Am. Soc. Transp. and Logistics, Nat. Indsl. Transp. League, Washington Golf and Country Club (Arlington, Va.), Princess Anne Country Club (Virginia Beach, Va.), Town Pt. Club (Norfolk, Va., bd. dirs.). Methodist. Avocations: tennis; golf. Office: Norfolk So Corp 3 Commercial Pl Norfolk VA 23510-2191

WATTS, DAVID EIDE, lawyer; b. Fairfield, Iowa, June 13, 1921. B.A., U. Iowa, 1941, J.D., 1942; postgrad., Columbia Law Sch., 1946-47. Bar: Iowa 1942, Mass. 1950, N.Y. 1954. Instr. U. Iowa, Iowa City, 1947-48; asst. prof. U. Pa., 1948-49, Harvard Law Sch., 1949-52; ptnr. Dewey Ballantine, N.Y.C., 1958-90; of counsel Dewey Ballantine, N.Y.C., 1990—; adj. assoc. prof. NYU, 1952-55; vis. lectr. Columbia U., 1954. Contbr. articles to legal jours. Mem. ABA, N.Y. State Bar Assn., Assn. Bar City N.Y., Am. Law Inst., Am. Coll. Tax Counsel, Am. Inst. Tax Policy. Home: 33 W 74th St New York NY 10023-2402 Office: Dewey Ballantine 1301 Avenue Of The Americas New York NY 10019-6022

WATTS, EMILY STIPES, English language educator; b. Urbana, Ill., Mar. 16, 1936; d. Royal Arthur and Virginia Louise (Schenck) Stipes; m. Robert Allan Watts, Aug. 30, 1958; children: Benjamin, Edward, Thomas. Student, Smith Coll., 1954-56; A.B., U. Ill., 1958, M.A. (Woodrow Wilson Nat. fellow), 1959, Ph.D., 1963. Instr. English U. Ill., Urbana, 1963-67, asst. prof., 1967-73, assoc. prof., 1973-77, prof., dir. grad. studies dept. English, 1977—; bd. dirs. U. Ill. Athletic Assn., chmn., 1981-83; mem. faculty adv. com. Ill. Bd. Higher Edn., 1984—, vice chmn., 1986-87, chmn., 1987-88. Author: Ernest Hemingway and The Arts, 1971, The Poetry of American Women from 1632 to 1945, 1977, The Businessman in American Literature, 1982; contbg. editor: English Women Writers from the Middle Ages to the Present, 1990; contbr. articles on Jonathan Edwards, Anne Bradstreet to lit. jours. John Simon Guggenheim Meml. Found. fellow, 1973-74. Mem. MLA, AAUP, Midwest MLA, Am. Inst. Archaeology, Authors Build, Ill. Hist. Soc., Phi Beta Kappa, Phi Kappa Phi. Presbyterian. Home: 1009 W University Ave Champaign IL 61821-3317 Office: U Ill 208 English Urbana IL 61801

WATTS, ERNEST FRANCIS, manufacturing company executive; b. Chgo., Mar. 23, 1937; s. Ernest Francis and Frances A. (Roche) W.; student Spring Hill Coll., 1955-57; student No. Ill. U., 1958-59; m. Sept. 10, 1960; children: Ernest Francis, Peggy, Colin. Sales rep. Binks Mfg. Co., Dallas, 1960-62, Memphis, 1962-65, asst. regional mgr., Dallas, 1971, v.p., gen. mgr., Mexico City, 1971-75, v.p. gen. mgr., Toronto, 1975-81, v.p. mktg., Franklin Park, Ill., 1981—; dir. Binks Can., Japan, Australia, Mex. Trustee, mem. exec. bd. Fenwick High Sch., 1983-89, lifetime trustee, 1989; trustee Rosary Coll., 1990. Served with USAR, 1960. Republican. Roman Catholic. Club: K.C. Office: Binks Mfg Co 9201 Belmont Ave Franklin Park IL 60131-2807

WATTS, GERALD DALE, software engineer, researcher; b. Norman, Okla., July 7, 1959; s. Gerald Dale Sr. and Berle Janet (Orr) W.; m. Loretta Olline Meurer, July 2, 1988 (div.); 1 child, Michael A. Grad., Moore Norman Vocat. Tech., 1978, postgrad., 1978—. System operator Cablistic Rsch., Norman, 1987—. Author: (software) Cipher version 1.0, 1992, version 2.0, 1993, version 3.0, 4.0, 1994, Generator version 1.0, 1992, version 2.0, 1993, version 3.0, 4.0, 1994. Home: 110 W Haddock St Norman OK 73069-8720

WATTS, GLENN ELLIS, union official; b. Stony Point, N.C., June 4, 1920; s. George Dewey and Nellie Viola (Ellis) W.; m. Bernice Elizabeth Willett, Nov. 8, 1941; children: Glenn Ellis II, Sharon Elizabeth Ann, Marianne Elizabeth Watts Erickson. With Chesapeake & Potomac Telephone Co., Washington, 1941-48; with Communications Workers Am., Washington, 1942-85, pres. div. 36, 1948-51, dir. dist. 2, 1951-56, asst. to pres., 1956-65, v.p., 1965-69, sec.-treas. union, 1969-74, pres., 1974-85, pres. emeritus, 1985—; v.p. exec. council AFL-CIO, 1974-85, v.p. emeritus, 1985—; v.p. indsl. union dept., 1968-85, mem. exec. bd. maritime trades dept., 1974-85; mem. Nat. Labor Com. for U.S. Savs. Bonds, 1975; nat. adv. bd. Labor Council for Latin Am. Advancement, 1975-85; mem. labor policy adv. com. for trade negotiations Dept. Labor, 1975-79; mem. industry-labor council White House Conf. on Handicapped Individuals, 1976; chmn. labor subcom. Pres.'s Com. on Employment of Handicapped, 1977; mem. sec.'s adv. council Dept. Commerce, 1976-77; mem. Pres.'s Commn. on Mental Health, 1977-78. Mem. Pres.'s Commn. on the Holocaust, 1978-79; mem. U.S. Holocaust Meml. Coun., 1979-93; past mem. D.C. Appeals and Rev. Bd., D.C. Wage and Hour Rev. Panel, Home Rule for D.C. Com.; mem. nat. advisory com. Nat. Congress Community Econ. Devel., 1974; past chmn. community chest relations com. Nat. Capital Area council Boy Scouts Am., past chmn. James E. West Dist., 1969-71; pres. Health and Welfare Council of Nat. Capital Area, 1967-69; mem. Inter-Am. adv. com. Postal Tel. and Tel. Internat., 1968-74, mem. exec. com., 1977-85, v.p., 1978-81, pres., 1981-85; gen. chmn. United Giver's Fund, 1968, pres., 1971-75; sec. United Way of Am., 1971-76; bd. dirs., treas. United Way Internat., 1974-78; mem.-at-large Dem. Nat. Com., 1974-85, mem. incomes policy study group of domestic affairs task group, 1974-76; trustee, sec.-treas. Am. Inst. Free Labor Devel., 1974-85; mem. U.S. Assn. for Club of Rome, 1978-80; trustee AFL-CIO Human Resources Devel. Inst., 1974-85, George Meany Ctr. for Labor Studies, 1976-85; trustee Ford Found., 1976-88; trustee Aspen Inst. for Humanistic Studies, 1974-89, trustee emeritus, 1989—; trustee Nat. Planning Assn., 1974-80; governing bd. Common Cause, 1974-77; sec.-treas. Ctr. for Mgmt. Services, 1974; hon. vice chmn. Am. Trade Union Council for Histadrut, 1974; mem. nat. adv. council Ariz. Heart Inst., 1974-80; bd. dirs. Am. Arbitration Assn., 1975-79, Am. Productivity Ctr., 1978-82, New Directions, 1977-80, Alliance to Save Energy, 1977-80; mem. nat. com. on coping with interdependence Aspen Program of Humanistic Studies, 1975-77; bd. dirs. Council on Fgn. Rels., 1987-90, Initiative Com. for Nat. Econ. Planning, 1975-76, Overseas Devel. Council, 1987-91; trustee, mem. exec. com. Joint Council Econ. Edn., 1976-79, Collective Bargaining Forum, 1983—, co-chmn. 1983-87, adv. bd. Collective Bargaining Inst. George Washington U., 1987-92; mem. Commn. on a Nat. Inst. Justice, 1976-79, Trilateral Commn., 1977—, Helsinki Watch, 1978-90, commn. Future U.S.-Mex. Relations, 1987-89, exec. com. Am. Agenda, 1988. Recipient Urban Trade Unionist award Nat. Urban Coalition, 1978, Silver Beaver award, 1965. Unitarian.

WATTS, HAROLD ROSS, hospital administrator; b. Tillsonburg, Ont., Can., June 7, 1944; s. Leo Kirkland and Beatrice Josephine (Williams) W. MD, U. Western Ont., 1968. Licentiate Med. Coun. Can. Dist. med. officer Dept. of Health, Catalina, Nfld., Can., 1972-74; sr. med. officer Dept. of Health, Bell Island, Nfld., 1975-78; med. dir. Western Meml. Regional Hosp., Corner Brook, Nfld., 1978-79, chief exec. officer, med. dir., 1979-95; CEO Western Health Care Corp., Stephenville, Nfld., 1995—; exec. mem. N.E. Can.-Am. Health Coun., Boston, 1988—; co-chmn. Royal Commn. Implementation Com., St. John's, Nfld., 1986-91. Pres. Soc. Prevention Cruelty to Animals, Corner Brook, 1983-86, 87-89, mem. exec. com.; mem. adv. com. on sci. and tech. Nfld., 1990-92; bd. dirs. Stephenville Festival of the Arts, 1986-91. Med. officer Royal Can. Navy, 1965-72. Mem. Nfld. Med. Assn. (bd. dirs. 1988-89, chmn. polit. action com. 1988—, pres. 1992-93, co-chmn. joint mgmt. com.), Can. Med. Assn. (gen. coun. 1991—, bd. dirs. 1994—), Corner Brook C. of C. (pres. 1990-91), Humber-St. Barbe-Baie Verte Progresive Conservative Assn. (past pres.), Alpha Omega Alpha. Anglican. Home: 64 Ohio Dr, Stephenville, NF Canada A2N 2V2 Office: Sir Thomas Roddick Hosp, 89 Ohio Dr, Stephenville, NF Canada A2N 2V6

WATTS, HAROLD WESLEY, economist, educator; b. Salem, Oreg., Sept. 30, 1932; s. Elton and Claire W.; m. Doris A. Roth, Sept. 28, 1951 (div. 1973); children—Michael Lee, Suzanne, Jane Marie, Kristin. B.A., U. Oreg., 1954; M.A., Yale U., 1956, Ph.D., 1957. From instr. to assoc. prof. Yale U., New Haven, 1957-63; from assoc. prof. to prof. econs. U. Wis., Madison, 1963-76, dir. Inst. Research on Poverty, 1966-71; prof. econs. and pub. policy Columbia U., N.Y.C., 1976—, dir. Pub. Policy Rsch. Ctr., 1988—; sr. fellow Mathematica Policy Research Princeton, N.J., 1979-92; sr. rsch. assoc. Urban Inst., 1994-95. Recipient Paul Lazarsfeld award, 1980; Guggenheim fellow, 1975. Fellow Assn. Pub. Policy Analysis and Mgmt., Econometric Soc.; mem. Am. Econ. Assn., Am. Statis. Assn. Democrat. Home: 448 Riverside Dr # 82 New York NY 10027-6818 Office: Columbia U Dept Economics New York NY 10027

WATTS, HEATHER, ballerina; b. Long Beach, Calif., Sept. 27, 1953; d. Keith Nevin and Sheelagh Maud (Woodhead) W. Student, Sch. Am. Ballet, N.Y.C. Mem. corps de ballet N.Y.C. Ballet Co., 1970-78, soloist, 1978-79, prin., 1979-95, retired, 1995; dir. N.Y. State Summer Sch. of Arts Sch. of Dance, Saratoga Springs, from 1982; organized dance troupe, Dancers, 1986. Created roles in George Balanchine's Robert Schumann's Davidsbündlertänze, Peter Martin's Rossini Pas de Deux, Lille Suite, Suite from Histoire du Soldat, Calcium Light Night, Sonate di Scarlatti, Concerto for Two Solo Pianos, Tango, A Schubertiad, Song of the Aurenge, Ecstatic Orange, Jerome Robbins' Piano Pieces, Chamber Works, I'm Old Fashioned, & The Four Seasons; performed in N.Y.C. Ballet's Balanchine Celebration, 1993; PBS-TV appearances include Bournonville Dances, The Magic Flute, A Choreographer's Notebook (all Dance in America series), and Lincoln Center Special: Balanchine Celebrates Stravinsky. Recipient Dance Mag. award, 1985; L'Oreal Shining Star award, 1985, Lions of the Performing Arts award N.Y. Pub. Library, 1986.

WATTS, HELENA ROSELLE, military analyst; b. East Lynne, Mo., May 29, 1921; d. Elmer Wayne and Nellie Irene (Barrington) Long; m. Henry Millard Watts, June 14, 1940; children: Helena Roselle Watts Scott, Patricia Marie Watts Foble. B.A., Johns Hopkins U., 1952, postgrad., 1952-53. Assoc. engr., Westinghouse Corp., Balt., 1965-67; sr. analyst Merck, Sharp & Dohme, Westpoint, Pa., 1967-69; sr. engr. Bendix Radio div. Bendix Corp., Balt., 1970-72; sr. scientist Sci. Applications Internat. Corp., McLean, Va., 1975-84; mem. tech. staff The MITRE Corp., McLean, 1985-94, ret., 1994; adj. prof. Def. Intelligence Coll., Washington, 1984-85. Contbr. articles to tech. jours. Mem. IEEE, AAAS, AIAA, Nat. Mil. Intelligence Assn., U.S. Naval Inst., Navy League of U.S., Air Force Assn., Assn. Former Intelligence Officers, Assn. Old Crows, Mensa, N.Y. Acad. Sci. Republican. Roman Catholic. Avocations: photography, gardening, reading. Home: 4302 Roberts Ave Annandale VA 22003-3508

WATTS, J. C., JR., congressman; b. Eufaula, Okla., Nov. 8, 1957; m. Frankie Watts; 5 children. BA in Journalism, U. Okla., 1981. Profl. football player Ottawa and Toronto Teams Can. Football League, 1981-86; youth min. Sunnyland So. Bapt. Ch., Del City, 1987-94; mem. Okla. Corp. Commn., 1990-94, chmn., 1993-94; mem. 104th Congress from 4th Okla. dist., 1995—; mem. Nat. Drinking Water Adv. Coun.; mem. electricity com. Nat. Assn. Regulatory Utility Commrs. Republican. Office: US House Reps 1713 Longworth Washington DC 20515-3604

WATTS, JOHN MCCLEAVE, financial services executive; b. Salt Lake City, July 20, 1933; s. Newell Edward and Mildred (McCleave) W.; m. Sharon Lee Sewell, Apr. 4, ž954 (div. Nov. 1969); children: John McCleave Jr., Christopher A., Kelly Lee Watts Cramer; m. Janis Marie Duncan, July 4, 1971; 1 stepson, Kenneth D. McCoy; BS, Mass. Inst. Tech., 1956; CLU; registered prin. Nat. Assn. Securities Dealers. In sales mgmt., Gen. Am. Life, Corpus Christi, Tex., 1957-65 ; mktg. dir., Am. Gen. Life, Houston, 1965-71; exec. v.p., Rsch. Mgmt. Assocs., Kansas City, Mo., 1971-79; pres., E.F. Hutton Agys., La Jolla, Calif., 1979-83; pres., Hartford (Conn.) Equity Corp., 1983-85; sr. v.p., Washington Nat. Corp., Evanston, Ill, 1985-90; chmn bd. Washington Equity Corp., 1985-90, Washington Nat. Fin. Services, Evanston, 1985-90; pres., CEO Xelan Inc., San Diego, 1991-93, bd. dirs., 1991-93; exec. v.p. Lamar Life Ins. Co., Jackson, Miss., 1993—; speaker mgmt., sales and data processing confs. Author: The Financial Services Shockwave, 1987; contbr. numerous articles to trade and profl. jours. City councilman, Leawood, Kans., 1973-78; chmn. Nueces County (Tex.) Republican Party, 1962-65; chmn. bd. dirs. Nat. Ctr. Fin. Edn., San Francisco, 1984—; bd. regents Coll. for Fin. Planning, Denver, 1986-91. Capt. AUS, 1956-57. Recipient Life Ins. Mktg. Inst. Achievement award Purdue U., 1960. Mem. Internat. Assn. Fin. Planners, Am. Soc. CLU's. Republican. Introduced nation's first universal life ins. product. Avocation: piloting. Home: 1537 Brobridge Dr Jackson MS 39211-2114 Office: Lamar Life Ins Co PO Box 880 Jackson MS 39205-0880

WATTS, JOHN RANSFORD, university administrator; b. Boston, Feb. 9, 1930; s. Henry Fowler Ransford and Mary Marion (Macdonald) W.; m. Joyce Lannon, Dec. 20, 1975; 1 child, David Allister. AB, Boston Coll., 1950, MEd, 1965; MFA, Yale U., 1953; PhD, Union Grad. Sch., 1978.Prof., asst. dean Boston U., 1958-74; prof., dean of fine arts Calif. State U., Long Beach, 1974-79; dean and artistic dir. The Theatre Sch. (Goodman Sch. of Drama), DePaul U., Chgo., 1979—; mng. dir. DePaul U. Blackstone Theatre, 1988—; gen. mgr. Boston Arts Festivals, 1955-64; adminstr. Arts Programs at Tanglewood, 1966-69; producing dir. Theatre Co. of Boston, 1973-75. Chmn., Mass. Council on Arts and Humanities, 1968-72; dir., v.p. Long Beach (Calif.) Pub. Corp. for the Arts, 1975-79; mem. theatre panel, Ill. Arts Council, 1981-90. Served with U.S. Army, 1953-55. Mem. Mass. Ednl. Communications Commn., Am. Theatre Assn., Nat. Council on Arts in Edn., Met. Cultural Alliance, U.S. Inst. Theatre Tech., League Chgo. Theatres, Chgo. Internat. Theatre Festival, Phi Beta Kappa, Phi Kappa Phi. Clubs: St. Botolph (Boston); University (Chgo.). Office: De Paul U The Theatre Sch 2135 N Kenmore Ave Chicago IL 60614-4111

WATTS, MALCOLM S(TUART) M(CNEAL), physician, medical educator; b. N.Y.C., Apr. 30, 1915; s. Malcolm S.M. and Elizabeth (Forbes) W.; m. Genevieve Moffitt, July 12, 1947; children: Pauline, Elizabeth, Malcolm, James. A.B., Harvard U., 1937; M.D., 1941. Diplomate: Pan Am. Med. Assn. Group practice internal medicine San Francisco, 1948-76; clin. prof. medicine U. Calif. Sch. Medicine, 1972-89, assoc. dean, 1966-89, clin. prof. medicine emeritus, 1989—, dir. Extended Programs in Med. Edn., 1973-82; dir. Calif. Statewide Area Health Edn. System, 1979-89; chmn. bd. trustees San Francisco Consortium, 1968-74, trustee, 1974-80, exec. dir., 1981-94; dir. Soc. Med. Coll. Dirs. Continuing Med. Edn., 1975-82, pres., 1980-81; trustee Hospice of San Francisco, v.p., 1979-85; pres. Alliance Continuing Med. Edn., 1979-81. Editor Western Jour. Medicine, 1968-90, Jour. Continuing Edn. in the Health Professions, 1988-91. Served to capt. M.C. AUS, 1942-46. Recipient Outstanding Community Funds and Councils Am., 1964, U. Calif. San Francisco medal, 1983, Disting. Svc. award Alliance for Continuing Med. Edn., 1990, Disting. Svc. award soc. Med. Coll. Dirs. of Continuing Med. Edn., 1991. Master ACP; fellow Am. Coll. Hosp. Adminstrs. (hon.); mem. AMA, AAAS, Calif. Acad. Scis., Calif. Acad. Medicine, Am. Med. Writers Assn. (John T. McGovern award 1986), San Francisco Med. Soc. (pres. 1961), Am. Soc. Internal Medicine (pres. 1964-65), Calif. Med. Assn. (bd. dirs. 1962-90), Nat. Inst. Medicine, Soc. Med. Friends Wine, Acad. Mexicana Ciencias Mexicano de Cultura (corr.). Home: 270 Sea Cliff Ave San Francisco CA 94121-1028

WATTS, MARVIN LEE, minerals company executive, chemist, educator; b. Portales, N.Mex., Apr. 6, 1932; s. William Ellis and Jewel Reata (Holder) W.; m. Mary Myrtle Kiker, July 25, 1952; children: Marvin Lee, Mark Dwight, Wesley Lyle. BS in Chemistry and Math., Ea. N.Mex. U., 1959, MS in Chemistry, 1960; postgrad. U. Okla., 1966, U. Kans., 1967. Analytical chemist Dow Chem. Co., Midland, Mich., 1960-62; instr. chemistry N.Mex. Mil. Inst., Roswell, 1962-65, asst. prof., 1965-67; chief chemist AMAX Chem. Corp., Carlsbad, N.Mex., 1967-78, gen. surface supt., 1978-84; pres. N.Mex. Salt and Minerals Corp., 1984—; chem. cons. Western Soils Lab., Roswell, 1962-67; instr. chemistry N.Mex. State U., Carlsbad, 1967—; owner, operator cattle ranch, Carlsbad and Loving, N.Mex., 1969—; bd. dirs. Mountain States Mutual Casualty Co., 1991; gen. mgr. Eddy Potash, Inc., 1987—; dir. Soil Conservation Svc.; mem. Roswell dist. adv. bd. Bur. Land Mgmt. Bd. dirs. Southeastern N.Mex. Regional Sci. Fair, 1966; mem. adv. bd. Roswell dist. Bur. Land Mgmt.; mem. Eddy County Fair Bd., 1976—, chmn., 1978, 82; mem. pub. sch. reform com.; chmn. higher edn. reform com.; mem. sponsor of N.Mex. Pub. Sch. Reform Act; bd. dirs. Carlsbad Regional Med. Ctr., 1976-78; pres. bd. Carlsbad Found., 1979-82; adv. bd. N.Mex. State U. at Carlsbad, 1976-80; vice chmn. bd. Guadalupe Med. Ctr.; bd. dirs. N.Mex. State U. Found.; state senator N.Mex. Legis., 1984-89. Mem. Rep. State Exec. com., 1972—; Rep. chmn. Eddy County (N.Mex.), 1970-74, 78-82. dirs. Conquistador coun. Boy Scouts Am., Regional Environ. Ednl. Rsch. and Improvement Orgn. Served with Mil. Police Corps, AUS, 1953-55; Germany. Recipient Albert K. Mitchell award as outstanding Rep. in N.Mex., 1976; hon. state farmer N.Mex. Future Farmers Am.; hon. mem. 4-H. Fellow N.Mex. Acad. Sci.; mem. Am. Chem. Soc. (chmn. subsect.), Western States Pub. Lands Coalition, Carlsbad C. of C. (dir. 1979-83), N.Mex. Mining Assn. (dir.), AIME (chmn. Carlsbad potash sect. 1975), Carlsbad Mental Health Assn., N.Mex. Inst. Mining and Tech. (adv. bd. mining dept.), Am. Angus Assn., Am. Quarter Horse Assn., N.Mex. Cattle Growers Assn. (bd. dirs. 1989—), Carlsbad Farm and Ranch Assn., Nat. Cattleman's Assn. Baptist. Kiwanis (Disting. lt. gov.), Elks. Home: PO Box 56 Carlsbad NM 88221-0056 Office: PO Box 31 Carlsbad NM 88221-5601

WATTS, OLIVER EDWARD, engineering consultancy company executive; b. Hayden, Colo., Sept. 22, 1939; s. Oliver Easton and Vera Irene (Hockett) W.; m. Charla Ann French, Aug. 12, 1962; children—Erik Sean, Oliver Eron, Sherilyn. BS, Colo. State U., 1962. Registered profl. engr., Colo., Calif.; profl. hand surveyor, Colo. Crew chief Colo. State U. Rsch. Found., Ft. Collins, 1962; with Calif. Dept. Water Resources, Gustine and Castaic, 1964-70; land and water engr. CF&I Steel Corp., Pueblo, Colo., 1970-71; engring. dir. United Western Engrs., Colorado Springs, Colo., 1971-76; ptnr. United Planning and Engring Co., Colorado Springs, 1976-79; owner Oliver E. Watts, Cons. Engr., Colorado Springs, 1979—. Dir. edn. local Ch. of Christ, 1969-71, deacon, 1977-87, elder, 1987-96. 1st lt. C.E., AUS, 1962-64.

Recipient Individual Achievement award Colo. State U. Coll. Engring., 1981. Fellow ASCE (v.p. Colorado Springs br. 1975, pres. 1978); mem. NSPE (pres. Pike's Peak chpt. 1975, sec. Colo. sect. 1976, v.p. 1977, pres. 1978-79, Young Engr. award 1976, Pres.'s award 1979), Cons. Engrs. Coun. Colo. (bd. dirs. 1981-83), Am. Cons. Engrs. Coun., Profl. Land Surveyors Colo., Colo. Engrs. Coun. (del. 1980—), Colo. State U. Alumni Assn. (v.p., dir. Pike's Peak chpt. 1972-76), Lancers, Lambda Chi Alpha. Home: 7195 Dark Horse Pl Colorado Springs CO 80919-1442 Office: 614 Elkton Dr Colorado Springs CO 80907-3514

WATTS, QUINCY, track and field athlete. Olympic track and field participant Barcelona, Spain, 1992; Gold medalist and world record holder (with Valmon, Reynolds, Johnson) 4 x400 relay World Track and Field Championships, Stuttgart, Germany, 1993. Recipient 400m Track and Field, 4x4 Relay Gold medals Olympics, Barcelona, 1992. Office: c/o First Team Mktg 10100 Santa Monica Blvd Ste 46 Los Angeles CA 90067-4003*

WATTS, ROBERT, wholesale distribution executive; b. 1948. Prin. Robert Watts, CPA, Atlanta, 1969-85; with EIS Mgmt. Corp., Atlanta, 1985—, sec.-treas., 1990—, v.p., sec.- treas. Office: EIS Mgmt Corp 1255 Collier Rd NW Atlanta GA 30318*

WATTS, ROBERT GLENN, retired pharmaceutical company executive; b. Norton, Va., Apr. 28, 1933; s. Clifford Amburgey and Stella Lee (Cornette) W.; m. Doris Juanita Slaughter, Aug. 29, 1953 (dec. 1980); children: Cynthia L. Watts Waller, Robert Glenn, Kelly L.; m. Sara Lowry Childrey, Aug. 20, 1982; stepchildren: J. Eric Alexander, Matthew R. Alexander. B.A., U. Richmond, 1959. Dir. ops. A.H. Robins Co., Inc., Richmond, Va., 1967-71, asst. v.p., 1971-73, v.p., 1973-75, sr. v.p., 1975-79, exec. v.p., 1979-92; ret., 1992; bd. dirs. Little Oil Co., Richmond, Fidelity Fed. Savs. Bank, Richmond. Bd. dirs. United Way, Richmond, 1982—; Pvt. Industry Council, Richmond, 1983—; sec. YMCA, Richmond, 1984—. Served with USN, 1952-56. Mem. Met. Richmond C. of C. (chmn. 1985-86), Bull and Bear Club, Hermitage Country. Episcopalian. Home: 2409 Islandview Dr Richmond VA 23233-2525

WATTS, RONALD LESTER, retired military officer; b. Seneca, Mo., June 27, 1934; s. Lester N. and Naomi (Montgomery) W.; m. Anita Abelquist, Sept. 26, 1981; 1 child, Christina; children by previous marriage—Elizabeth Ann, Ronald Allen. B.S. in Edn., Pitts. State U., 1956; M.S. in Polit. Sci., Auburn U., 1976. Commd. officer U.S. Army, 1956, advanced through grades to lt. gen., 1987; asst. div. comdr. 1st Inf. Div., Ft. Riley, Kans., 1981-83; comdg. gen. U.S. Army Readiness, Fort Meade, Md., 1983; dep. comdg. gen. 1st U.S. Army, Fort Meade, Md., 1983-84; comdg. gen. 1st Inf. Div., Ft. Riley, Kans., 1984-86; chief staff Hdqrs. Forces Command, Ft. McPherson, Ga., 1986-87; commdg. gen. VII Corps, 1987-89, ret., 1989; pres. Watts Leadership Devel. Svcs., Greensboro, Ga., 1990—. Decorated D.S.M. with oak leaf cluster, Legion of Merit with 2 oak leaf clusters, Bronze Star, Air medal with 10 oak leaf clusters, Combat Inf. badge, Def. Superior Svc. medal with cluster.

WATTS, STEPHEN HURT, II, lawyer; b. Lynchburg, Va., Feb. 21, 1947; s. James Owen Jr. and Sarah Webb (Key) W.; m. Beverley Allan Brockenbrough, July 16, 1969 (div. 1986); children: Day Lowry, Stephen Hurt Jr.; m. Sally Yates Wood, May 24, 1986 (div. 1995). BA, Washington & Lee U., 1968; JD, U. Va., 1972. Bar: Va. 1972, W.Va. 1973. Law clk. Taylor, Michie & Callahan, Charlottesville, Va., 1970-72; assoc. Spilman, Thomas, Battle & Klostermeyer, Charleston, W.Va., 1972-75; ptnr. Watts & Watts, Lynchburg, Va., 1975-77; v.p., counsel Commonwealth Gas Pipeline Corp., Richmond, 1977-81; gen. counsel Commonwealth Natural Resources, Inc., Richmond, 1980-81; assoc. McGuire, Woods & Battle, Richmond, 1981-83; ptnr. McGuire, Woods, Battle & Boothe, L.L.P., Richmond, 1983—. Bd. dirs. Lower Fan Civic Assn., Richmond, 1987-91, TheatreVirginia, Richmond, 1992-93, Va. Oil and Gas Assn., 1993; pres., bd. dirs. Studio Theatre Richmond, 1991-93; chmn. outreach com. Grace and Holy Trinity Episcopal Ch., Richmond, 1993. Mem. ABA, Va. State Bar (dir. adminstrv. law sect., chmn. 1995-96), Fed. Energy Bar Assn. Home: 3420 Grove Ave Richmond VA 23221-2734 Office: McGuire Woods Battle et al One James Center 901 E Cary St Richmond VA 23219-4057

WATZ, MARTIN CHARLES, brewery executive; b. St. Louis, Oct. 31, 1938; s. George Michael and Caroline Theresa (Doggendorf) W.; m. Deborah Perkowski; children: Pamela, Kathlene, Karen. BS in Chemistry and Microbiology, SE Mo. State U., 1961; MBA, Washington U., 1966-67. Safety engr. McDonnell-Douglas, 1962-64; sr. brewing chemist Anheuser-Busch, Inc., St. Louis, 1965-68, asst. brewmaster, Columbus, Ohio, 1968-79, sr. asst. brewmaster, St. Louis, 1979-82, resident brewmaster, Baldwinsville, N.Y., 1982-84, Williamsburg, Va., 1984-87; v.p. bakers yeast divsn. Anheuser-Busch Indsl. Products Corp., St. Louis, 1987-88, dir. brewing ops., 1988-89; sr. resident brewmaster Anheuser-Busch, Ft. Collins, Colo., 1989—. Patentee in field. With USAF, 1962-65. Mem. Master Brewers Assn. Am. (pres., nat. bd. govs.), Am. Soc. Brewing Chemists, Internat. Food Tech. Assocs., Aircraft Owners and Pilots Assn., U.S. Pilots Assn. Avocation: flying. Home: 1417 North County Rd #3 Fort Collins CO 80524-9312 Office: Anheuser-Busch Ft Collins Brewery 2351 Busch Dr Fort Collins CO 80524-9400

WAUD, ROGER NEIL, economics educator; b. Detroit, Mar. 26, 1938; s. Othneil Stockwell and Mary Josephine (Gough) W.; children: Heather, Neil. B.A., Harvard U., 1960; M.A., U. Calif., Berkeley, 1962; Ph.D. (Ford Found. fellow), U. Calif., Berekley, 1965. Asst. prof. bus. econs. Grad. Sch. Bus. U. Chgo., 1964-69; assoc. prof. econs. U. N.C., Chapel Hill, 1969-72; prof. U. N.C., 1972—; sr. economist, bd. govs. Fed. Res. System, Washington, 1973-75; cons. Dept. Labor; mem. adv. bd. Taxpayers Ednl. Coalition, 1981; research assoc. Nat. Bur. Econ. Research, 1982-92; mem. N.C. Energy Policy Council, 1986-92. Author: Macroeconomics, 5th edit., 1992, Microeconomics, 5th edit., 1992; contbr. articles to profl. jours.; mem. editorial bd.: So. Econ. Jour, 1970-73. Mem. Am. Econ. Assn., Econometric Soc., So. Econ. Assn. (exec. com. 1977-79). Office: Univ NC Dept Econs Chapel Hill NC 27599-3305

WAUGAMAN, RICHARD MERLE, psychiatrist, psychoanalyst, educator; b. Easton, Pa., Apr. 27, 1949; s. Charles Hoffmeier and Ruth Alviene (Melee) W.; m. Elisabeth Leone Pearson, June 20, 1970; children: Adele Marie, Garrett Dennis. AB, Princeton U., 1970; MD, Duke U., 1973. Cert. psychiatry, 1978, psychoanalysis, 1984. Resident in psychiatry Sheppard-Pratt Hosp., Towson, Md., 1973-76; mem. faculty Washington Sch. Psychiatry, 1983—; grad. Washington Psychoanalytic Inst., 1984, tng. and supervising analyst, 1989—; from clin. instr. to clin. assoc. prof. Georgetown U. Sch. Medicine, Washington, 1978-92, clin. prof. psychiatry, 1992—; staff psychiatrist Chestnut Lodge, Rockville, Md., 1986—; cons. psychiat. residency program Nat. Naval Med. Ctr., Bethesda, Md., 1994—. Contbr. articles to profl. jours. Mem. Washington Psychoanalytic Soc., Am. Psychoanalytic Assn. (exec. coun. 1995—), Internat. Psychoanalytic Assn., Am. Psychiat. Assn. Methodist. Home: 8109 Horseshoe Ln Potomac MD 20854-3834 Office: Chestnut Lodge 500 W Montgomery Ave Rockville MD 20850-3892

WAUGH, DOUGLAS OLIVER WILLIAM, pathology educator; b. Hove, Sussex, Eng., Mar. 21, 1918; emigrated to Can., 1918; s. Oliver Sayles and Helen (Champion) W.; m. Sheila Louise Duff, Jan. 16, 1971. Student, U. Man., 1935-38; M.D.C.M., McGill U., 1942, M.S., 1948, Ph.D., 1950; LL.D. (hon.), Dalhousie U., 1992. Assoc. prof. pathology U. Alta., Edmonton, Can., 1950-51, McGill U., Montreal, Que., Can., 1951-57; assoc. prof. Queens U., Kingston, Ont., Can., 1958-60, prof., 1960-64, dean medicine, 1970-75, vice prin. health sci., 1971-72; prof., head pathology Dalhousie U., Halifax, N.S., Can., 1964-70; exec. dir. Assn. Can. Med. Colls., Ottawa, Ont., 1975-83; free-lance writer, essayist, biographer, 1983—; columnist Can. Med. Assn. Jour., 1983—; adj. prof. pathology U. Ottawa, 1978-83; chmn. adv. com. Can. Tumour Reference Ctr., NCI, Toronto, Ont., 1958-70; chmn. med. rsch. coun. Survey Path. Rsch., Ottawa, 1967; cons. Lab. Tech. Govt., B.C., 1977; sec. com. on accreditation Can. Med. Schs., 1978-83; mem. bd. accreditation Can. Assn. Univ. Schs. Nursing, 1984-93, cons. Ont. region, 1983. Editor: ACMC Forum, 1975-83; contbr. articles to profl. jours. Served to capt. M.C., RCA, 1942-46. Named Prof. of Yr. Med. Undergrads., Dalhousie U., 1967; recipient Jubilee medal Queen Elizabeth II, 1977. Mem. Can. Med. Assn. (sr.), Can. Cytology Coun., Nat. Cancer Inst. Can. (pres. 1974-76), Social and Behavior Coun., Alcoholic Beverages Med. Rsch. Found., Royal Coll. Physicians and Surgeons Can. (coun. 1969-70), Can Authors Assn. (nat. v.p. 1991-94, Alan Sangster award 1995). Home: 183 Marlborough Ave, Ottawa, ON Canada K1N 8G3

WAUGH, JOHN STEWART, chemist, educator; b. Willimantic, Conn., Apr. 25, 1929; s. Albert E. and Edith (Stewart) W.; married 1983; children: Alice Collier, Frederick Pierce. AB, Dartmouth Coll., 1949; PhD, Calif. Inst. Tech., 1953; ScD (hon.), Dartmouth Coll., 1989. Rsch. fellow in physics Calif. Inst. Tech., 1952-53; mem. faculty MIT, Cambridge, 1953—, prof. chemistry, 1962—, Albert Amos Noyes prof. chemistry, 1973-88, inst. prof., 1989—; vis. prof. U. Calif.-Berkeley, 1963-64; lectr. Robert Welch Found., 1968; Falk-Plaut lectr. Columbia U., 1973; DuPont lectr. U. S.C., 1974; Lucy Pickett lectr. Mt. Holyoke Coll., 1978; Reilly lectr. U. Notre Dame, 1978; Spedding lectr. Iowa State U., 1979; McElvain lectr. U. Wis., 1981; Vaughan lectr. Rocky Mountain Conf., 1981; G.N. Lewis meml. lectr. U. Calif., 1982; Dreyfus lectr. Dartmouth Coll., 1984; G.B. Kistiakowsky lectr. Harvard U., 1984; O.K. Rice lectr. U. N.C., Chapel Hill, 1986, Baker lectr. Cornell U., 1990; Smith lectr. Duke U., 1992; sr. fellow Alexander von Humboldt-Stiftung; also vis. prof. Max Planck Inst., Heidelberg, 1972; vis. scientist Harvard U., 1976; mem. chemistry adv. panel NSF, 1966-69, vice chmn., 1968-69; mem. rev. com. Argonne Nat. Lab., 1970-74; mem. sci. and edn. adv. com. Lawrence Berkeley Lab., 1980-86; exchange visitor USSR Acad. Scis., 1962, 75; mem. vis. com. Tufts U., 1966-69, Princeton, 1973-78; mem. fellowship com. Alfred P. Sloan Found., 1977-82; Joliot-Curie prof. École Supérieure de Physique et Chemie, Paris, 1985. Author: New NMR Methods in Solid State Physics, 1978; editor: Advances in Magnetic Resonance, 1965-87; assoc. editor: Jour. Chem. Physics, 1965-67, Spectrochimica Acta, 1964-78; mem. editorial bd. Chem. Revs., 1978-82, Jour. Magnetic Resonance, 1989—, Applied Magnetic Resonance, 1989—. Recipient Irving Langmuir award, 1976, Gold Pick Axe award, 1976, Pitts. award Spectroscopic Soc. Pitts., 1979, Wolf prize, 1984, Pauling medal, 1985, Calif. Inst. Tech. disting. alumnus award, 1987, Killian award, 1988, ISMAR prize, 1989, Richards medal, 1992, Evans award, 1994; Sloan fellow, 1958-62, Guggenheim fellow, 1963-64, 72; Sherman Fairchild scholar Calif. Inst. Tech., 1989. Fellow AAAS, Am. Acad. Arts and Scis., Am. Phys. Soc. (chmn. divsn. chemistry and physics 1983-84); mem. NAS, Internat. Soc. Magnetic Resonance (mem. coun. 1989-95, mem. exec. com. 1996—), Slovenian Acad. Sci. and Arts (fgn. corr.), Phi Beta Kappa, Sigma Xi. Office: MIT 77 Massachusetts Ave Cambridge MA 02139-4301

WAUGH, THEODORE ROGERS, orthopedic surgeon; b. Montreal, Sept. 21, 1926; s. Theodore Rogers and Anne Maude (Lawlor) W.; children: Susanne Rogers, Margaret Stewart, Theodore Rogers. BA, Yale U., 1949; MD, CM, McGill U., 1953; D Med.Sci., U. Goteborg, Sweden, 1968. Diplomate Am. Bd. Orthopaedic Surgery. Intern Royal Victoria Hosp., Montreal, 1953-54; asst. resident in pathology McGill U., 1954-55; asst. resident in surgery N.Y. U. Bellevue Med. Center, 1955-56; asst. resident, resident, fellow N.Y. Orthopedic Hosp., Columbia U., 1958-62, instr., clin. asst. prof. orthopedic surgery, 1962-68; asst. attending Presbyn. Hosp., N.Y.C., 1962-68; prof., chief div. orthopedic surgery U. Calif., Irvine, 1968-78; prof., chmn. dept. orthopedic surgery N.Y. U. Med. Center, 1978—. Contbr. numerous articles to profl. jours. Capt., M.C. USAF, 1956-58. Fellow ACS, Royal Coll. Surgeons (Can.), Am. Acad. Orthopaedic Surgeons, Scoliosis Research Soc., Assn. Bone and Joint Surgeons, Am. Orthopaedic Assn., Am. Orthopaedic Soc. for Sports Medicine.; mem. Soc. Colonial Wars, Alpha Omega Alpha. Presbyterian. Club: 20th Century Orthopedic. Designer surg. devices used in orthopaedic surgery. Office: NYU Med Ctr 550 1st Ave New York NY 10016-6481

WAUGH, WILLIAM HOWARD, biomedical educator; b. N.Y.C., May 13, 1925; s. Richey Laughlin and Lyda Pearl (Leamer) W.; m. Eileen Loretta Garrigan, Oct. 4, 1952; children: Mark Howard, Kathleen Cary, William Peter. Student, Boston U., 1943, W.Va. U., 1944; MD, Tufts U., 1948, postgrad., 1949-50. Cardiovascular rsch. trainee Med. Coll. Ga., Augusta, 1954-55, asst. rsch. prof. physiology, 1955-60, assoc. medicine, 1957-60; assoc. prof. medicine U. Ky., Lexington, 1960-69; Ky. Heart Assn. Chair in cardiovascular rsch. Ky. Heart Assn., Lexington, 1963-71; prof. medicine U. Ky., Lexington, 1969-71; prof. medicine and physiology East Carolina U., Greenville, N.C., 1971—; head renal sect. U. Ky. Coll., Lexington, 1960-68; chmn. dept. clin. scis. E.Carolina U., Greenville, 1971-75; chmn. E. Carolina U. Policy and Rev. Com. on Human Rsch., Greenville, N.C., 1971-90. Contbr. articles to profl. jours. With AUS, 1943-46; capt. USAF, 1952-54. Fellow ACP; mem. AAAS, Am. Physiology Soc., Am. Heart Assn., Am. Soc. Nephrology, Microcirculatory Soc. Republican. Achievements include basic advances in excitation contraction coupling in vasc. smooth muscle; basic advances in autoregulation of renal blood flow and urine flow; adj. therapy in acute lung edema; noncovalent antisickling agents in sickle cell hemoglobinopathy. Home: 119 Oxford Rd Greenville NC 27858-4954 Office: E Carolina U Sch Medicine Dept Physiology Greenville NC 27858

WAVLE, ELIZABETH MARGARET, music educator, college official; b. Homer, N.Y., Jan. 18, 1957; d. John Andrew Jr. and Louise Hayford (Estey) W. BMus, SUNY, Potsdam, 1979; AM in Libr. Sci., U. Mich., 1980; MS in Edn., Elmira Coll., 1990. Sr. libr. asst. U. Mich., Ann Arbor, 1979-80; pub. svcs. libr. Elmira (N.Y.) Coll., 1980-84, instr. music, 1981—, head tech. svcs., 1984—, coord. women's studies, 1992, 96-97; mem. South Ctrl. Rsch. Libr. Coun. Interlibr. Loan Adv. Com., Ithaca, N.Y., 1991-93; mem. South Ctrl. Rsch. Libr. Coun. Regional Automation Com., Ithaca, 1994-95, resource sharing com., 1996—. Contbr. revs., essays to profl. publs. Mem. Ithaca Concert Band, 1st Unitarian Ch. of Ithaca. Mem. ALA. Democrat. Avocations: music, reading, antiques. Home: 700 Comfort Rd Spencer NY 14883-9622 Office: Elmira Coll PO Box 7023 Elmira NY 14901

WAWRZYN, RONALD M., lawyer; b. Milw., July 25, 1945; s. Edmund T. and Virginia Marie (Mandt) W.; m. Mary Anne Koenig, June 20, 1970; children: Robert, Matthew, James. BS, U. Wis., 1968, JD, 1972. Bar: Wis. 1972, U.S. Dist. Ct. (ea. dist.) Wis. 1974, U.S. Dist. Ct. (we. dist.) Wis. 1978, U.S. Dist. Ct. (no. dist.) Ill. 1975, U.S. Ct. Appeals (7th and 10th cirs.). Trial atty. U.S. Dept. Justice, Washington, 1972-74; ptnr. Foley & Lardner, Milw., 1974—. Contbr. articles to law jours. Mem. ABA, Milw. Bar Assn. Clubs: Milw. Athletic, Ozaukee Country (Mequon, Wis.). Office: Foley & Lardner Firstar Ctr 777 E Wisc Ave Milwaukee WI 53202

WAX, BERNARD, research and development consultant, lecturer; b. Phila., Apr. 4, 1930; s. Samuel and Anna (Kaminker) W.; m. Dolores Helen Nemchek, Mar. 21, 1953; children—Ann Susan Wax Loeb, Steven Albert, Stuart Michael, Rebecca Mara. B.A., U. Chgo., 1950, M.A., 1955; postgrad., U. Wis., 1955-59. Field rep., field services supr. Ill. State Hist. Library, 1959-66; dir. Am. Jewish Hist. Soc., Waltham, Mass., 1966-91, dir. spl. projects, 1991-93, dir. emeritus, 1993—; mem. Ill. State Records Commn., 1961-66, Cook County State Records Commn., 1961-66. Editor: Assn. Jewish Libraries Bull, 1970-72, Bay State Hist. League Bull, 1971-73. Co-founder Joint Cultural Appeal, 1972; pres. Coun. on Archives and Rsch. Librs. in Jewish Studies, 1983-85. With Signal Corps, U.S. Army, 1953-55. Mem. Bay State Hist. League (editor, bd. dirs. 1971-76, pres. 1976-78). Home: 21 Blake Rd Brookline MA 02146-5803

WAX, EDWARD L., advertising executive; b. 1937; 2 children: Elizabeth, Alex. BS, Northeastern U., 1959; MBA, U. Pa., 1961. Chmn., CEO Saatchi & Saatchi Advt. Worldwide, 1963-68; account exec. Compton Advt., N.Y.C., 1963-68; gen. mgr. Ace Compton Manila, Manila, Philippines, 1968-72; sr. v.p. Compton Advt., N.Y.C., 1972-77; pres. Saatchi & Saatchi Compton, Inc. (now Saatchi/Saatchi Advt.), N.Y.C., 1983-87; chief exec. officer Saatchi & Saatchi Compton Inc. (now Saatchi & Saatchi Advt.), N.Y.C., 1983-87, 1988-89; CEO Saatchi & Saatchi Compton, Inc. (now Saatchi/Saatchi Advt.), N.Y.C., 1987-89; chmn. Saatchi & Saatchi Compton Inc. (now Saatchi & Saatchi Advt.), N.Y.C., 1988-89; pres., chief exec. officer Saatchi & Saatchi Advt. Inc., N.Y.C., 1989—, also bd. dirs.; chmn., CEO Saatchi & Saatchi Compton, Inc. (now Saatchi/Saatchi Advt.), N.Y.C., 1989-92; past pres., CEO Saatchi & Saatchi N. Am., now chmn., CEO, dir.; pres., chief ops. officer Richard K. Manoff, Inc. (later Geers Gross Advt.), 1977-81. Capt. signal corps U.S. Army, 1965-67. Office: Saatchi & Saatchi Advt Worldwide 375 Hudson St Fl 12 New York NY 10014-3658*

WAX, GEORGE LOUIS, lawyer; b. New Orleans, Dec. 6, 1928; s. John Edward and Theresa (Schaff) W.; LL.B., Loyola U. of South, 1952, B.C.S., 1960; m. Patricia Ann Delaney, Feb. 20, 1965; children: Louis Jude, Joann Olga, Therese Marie. Admitted to La. bar, 1952, practiced in New Orleans, 1954—. Served with USNR, 1952-54. Mem. La., New Orleans bar assns., Am. Legion. Roman Catholic. Kiwanian. Clubs: New Orleans Athletic, Suburban Gun and Rod, Southern Yacht. Home: 6001 Charlotte Dr New Orleans LA 70122-2731 Office: Nat Bank Commerce New Orleans LA 70112

WAX, NADINE VIRGINIA, retired banker; b. Van Horne, Iowa, Dec. 7, 1927; d. Laurel Lloyd and Viola Henrietta (Schrader) Bobzien; divorced; 1 child, Sharlyn K. Wax Munns. Student, U. Iowa, 1970-71; grad. Nat. Sch. Real Estate and Fin., Ohio State U., 1980-81. Jr. acct. McGladrey, Hansen, Dunn (now McGladrey-Pullen Co., CPAs), Cedar Rapids, Iowa, 1944-47; office mgr. Iowa Securities Co. (now Norwest Mortgage Co.), Cedar Rapids, 1954-55; asst. cashier Mchts. Nat. Bank, Cedar Rapids, 1956-75, asst. v.p., 1976-78, v.p., 1979-91; ret., 1991. Bd. dirs., v.p. Kirkwood C.C. Facilities Found., Cedar Rapids, 1970-96; bd. dirs., treas. Kirkwood C.C., 1984-91; trustee Indian Creek Nature Ctr., Cedar Rapids, 1974—, pres., 1980-81; vol. St. Luke's Hosp. Aux., Cedar Rapids, 1981-85; mem. Linn County Regional Planning Commn., 1982-92, Cedar Rapids-Marion Fine Arts Coun., 1994—; bd. suprs. Compensation Commn. for Condemnation, 1987-92; bd. dirs. Am. Heart Assn., Cedar Rapids, 1983-94; mem. Iowa Employment and Tng. Coun., Des Moines, 1982-83. Recipient Outstanding Woman award Cedar Rapids Tribute to Women and Industry, 1984. Mem. Fin. Women Internat. (state edn. chmn. 1982-83), Am. Inst. Banking (bd. dirs. 1968-70), Soc. Real Estate Appraisers (treas. 1978-80), Linn. County Bankers Assn. (pres. 1979-80), Cedar Rapids Bd. Realtors, Cedar Rapids C. of C. (bus.-edn. com. 1986-91), Cedar Rapids Country Club. Republican. Lutheran. Avocations: travel, reading, walking. Home: 147 Ashcombe SE Cedar Rapids IA 52403-1700

WAX, WILLIAM EDWARD, photojournalist; b. Miami, Fla., Dec. 7, 1956; s. Ira and Rita (Gunshor) W. A.S., Berry Coll., Rome, Ga., 1976; B.S. in Engring., U. Fla., 1983. With Ind. Fla. Alligator, Gainesville, Fla., 1977-79; staff photographer Gainesville (Fla.) Sun, 1979-87; photo cons. N.Y. Times regional newspapers, 1984—; freelance photographer Miami, 1987—; pres. Wax Photographics, Inc., Miami Beach, Fla., 1989—; owner Studio SoBe, Miami Beach, 1992—; guest lectr. various univs.; faculty So. Short Course in News Photography, 1985—. named So. Photographer of Yr., 1980, Regional Photographer of Yr., 1979, 82, 85; recipient Mark of Excellence, Sigma Delta Chi, 1978, Best of Show award Atlanta Seminar on Photojournalism, 1982, Best of Show and Silver medal Hearst awards, 1978, Design Gold award Fla. Tech. Writers Assn., 1992, Design award, Gold award, Excellence award Soc. Tech. Comm. Internat. Tech. Art Competition, 1993, 94, Best of Show, 1994, Disting. Design award, 1993, Excellence Design award, 1993, 2 Design Excellence awards and award of merit, 1995, Best of Show award Ann. Report Fla. Pub. Rels., 1995, Silver and Bronze awards Fla. Mag. Assn., 1994, Gold, Silver and Bronze awards Fla. Mag. Assn., 1995, Merit award STC, 1995; nominated for Pulitzer prize, 1979, 89. Mem. Nat. Press Photographers Assn., Fla. Mag. Assn., Profl. Photographers Am., Nikon Profl. Svcs., Fla. Press Photographers Assn. Democrat. Jewish. Office: 350 Lincoln Rd Ste 516 Miami FL 33139

WAXENBERG, ALAN M., publisher; b. Davenport, Iowa, Mar. 1, 1935; s. George and Rose Waxenberg; m. Suzanne C. Ecker, Oct. 26, 1958; children: Robin Lynn, Scott Stephen. BA, U. Iowa, 1956. Cen. advt. dir. Look mag., Detroit, 1958-71; mgr. Petersen Pub. Co., Detroit, 1971-72; v.p. nat. advt. dir. Petersen Pub. Co., N.Y.C., 1972-76; pub. Motor, N.Y.C., 1976-79; v.p., pub. Redbook, N.Y.C., 1982-88; sr. v.p., pub. Good Housekeeping, Hearst Pub. Co., N.Y.C. Active United Jewish Appeal Fedn., Anti-Defamation League, Jr. Achievement, United /fund; bd. dirs. adv. coun. Am. Health Found. Served with U.S. Army, 1956-58. Mem. Am. Advt. Fedn. (bd. dirs.), Mag. Pubs. Assn., Adcraft Club Detroit, U. Iowa Alumni Assn. Clubs: Metropolis Country (White Plains, N.Y.); University (N.Y.). Office: Good Housekeeping Mag Hearst Mags 959 8th Ave New York NY 10019-3767

WAXLER, BEVERLY JEAN, anesthesiologist, physician; b. Chgo., Apr. 11, 1949; d. Isadore and Ada Belle (Gross) Marcus; m. Richard Norman Waxler, Dec. 24, 1972; 1 child, Adam R. BS in Biology, No. Ill. U., 1971; MD, U. Ill., Chgo., 1975. Diplomate Am. Bd. Anesthesiology, Am. Bd. Pathology. Intern dept. pathology Northwestern U., Chgo., 1975-76, resident, 1976-79; instr. Rush Presbyn. St. Luke's Med. Ctr., Chgo., 1979-81; asst. prof. pathology Loyola U., Maywood, Ill., 1981-84; resident dept. anesthesiology Cook County Hosp., Chgo., 1984-87, attending anesthesiologist, 1987—; clin. asst. prof. U. Ill., Chgo., 1988—. Contbr. papers to Tissue and Cell, British Jour. Exptl. Pathology, Biochem. Medicine, Calcified Tissue Internat., Jour. Lab. Clin. Med. Recipient B.B. Sankey Anesthesia Advancement award Internat. Anesthesia Rsch. Soc., 1989; Nat. Rsch. Svc. award fellow Nat. Cancer Inst., 1980; grantee Varlen Corp., 1982. Mem. AAAS, Internat. Anesthesia Rsch. Soc., Am. Soc. Anesthesiologists, Sigma Xi. Achievements include research with future implications for the delivery of anesthesia for cancer patients and the effects of anesthetics on proteinase inhibitors and tumor behavior. Home: 7615 Church St Morton Grove IL 60053-1618 Office: Cook County Hosp Chicago IL 60612

WAXLER, ROBERT PHILLIP, university educator, consultant; b. Cambridge, Mass., Dec. 16, 1944; s. Felix Benjamin and Helen Ruth (Fonfara) W.; m. Linda Davida Lassoff, June 25, 1967; children: Jonathan Blake, Jeremy Regan. BA, Brown U., 1967; MA, Boston Coll., 1969; PhD, SUNY, Stony Brook, 1976. Instr. Whitman Coll., Walla Walla, Wash., 1974-75, asst. prof., 1975-80, assoc. prof., 1980-86, prof. lit., 1986—, asst. dean, 1987-88; assoc. dean Whitman Coll., Walla Walla, Wsh., 1988-89; dean continuing edn. and summer programs U. Mass., Dartmouth, 1994—, co-dir. Ctr. for Jewish Culture, 1981—, chmn. Judaic studies, 1984—, chmn. English dept., 1993-94; ptnr. Comm. Mgmt. co., Inc., South Dartmouth, 1981-85; comm. cons. Tricom, Inc., South Dartmouth, 1981-90; NEH vis. fellow Princeton U., summer 1983; participant 12th ann. seminar Am. Jewish Com., Israel, 1981. Contbg. editor Compass Mag., 1981-85; contbr. lit. and communcation articles to profl. jours. and anthologies. Founding mem. Jewish Student Svc. Ctr., North Dartmouth, 1978-85; co-founder Changing Lives Through Lit. program, 1991—; mem. steering com. Labor Edn. Ctr., North Dartmouth, 1981—; mem. bd. of regents Mass. Task Force on Undergrad. Experience, Boston, 1988; bd. dirs. Tifereth Israel Synagogue, New Bedford, Mass., 1976-80, Jewish Fedn., New Bedford, 1980-81; chmn. Azorean Synagogue Restoration Com., 1989—. NEH summer grantee UCLA, 1978; grantee So. Mass. U. Found. 1984; recipient Eisner Citizenship award Boy Scouts Am., 1987, Richard M. Fontera award Labor Edn. Ctr., 1988, Hon. medal U. of the Azores, 1989. Mem. Mass. Speech Communication Assn. (exec. com. 1984-85). Avocation: tennis. Home: 25 Strathmore Rd North Dartmouth MA 02747-3113 Office: U Mass-Dartmouth Dept Lit Old Westport Rd North Dartmouth MA 02747

WAXMAN, DAVID, physician, university consultant; b. Albany, N.Y., Feb. 7, 1918; s. Meyer and Fannie (Strosberg) W.; m. Jane Zabel; children: Gail, Michael, Dan, Ann, Steve, Abby. B.S., Syracuse U., 1942, M.D., 1950. Intern Grace Hosp., Detroit, 1950-51; resident in medicine, fellow in cardiology Kans. U. Med. Ctr., Kansas City, 1958-61; instr. internal medicine Kans. U. Med. Ctr., 1961-64; asst. prof. internal medicine Kans. City Med. Ctr., 1964-69, assoc. prof., 1969-77, prof., 1977—, dir. dept. medicine outpatient service, 1970-74, asst. dean, 1970-71, assoc. dean for student affairs, 1971-72, dean of students, 1972-74, vice chancellor for students, 1974-76, vice chancellor, 1976-77, exec. vice chancellor, 1977-83, spl. cons. to chancellor for health affairs, 1983-94; ret.; nat. cons. to surgeon gen. USAF. Contbr. articles to med. jours. Mem. Kans. State Bd. Healing Arts, 1984-88. Maj. gen. USAFR ret. Decorated D.S.M., Legion of Merit with one oak leaf cluster. Fellow ACP, Alpha Omega Alpha; mem. Kans. Med. Soc., Soc. Med. Cons. to the Armed Forces. Office: Kans U Med Ctr 39th and Rainbow Blvd Kansas City KS 66103

WAXMAN, HENRY ARNOLD, congressman; b. Los Angeles, Sept. 12, 1939; s. Louis and Esther (Silverman) W.; m. Janet Kessler, Oct. 17, 1971; children: Carol Lynn, Michael David. B.A. in Polit. Sci, UCLA, 1961, J.D., 1964. Bar: Calif. 1965. Mem. Calif. State Assembly, 1969-74, chmn. com. on health, until 1974; mem. 94th-104th Congresses from 24th (now 29th)

Calif. dist., 1975—, ranking minority mem. house subcom. on health and environment, 1979—; mem. govt. reform & oversight com. Pres. Calif. Fedn. Young Democrats, 1965-67. Mem. Calif. Bar Assn., Guardians Jewish Home for Aged, Am. Jewish Congress, Sierra Club, B'nai B'rith, Phi Sigma Alpha. Office: US Ho of Reps 2408 Rayburn HOB Washington DC 20515

WAXMAN, MARGERY HOPE, lawyer; b. N.Y.C., Oct. 21, 1942; d. Lee and Florence Waxman; m. Willard H. Mitchell, Apr. 4, 1982. A.B., Smith Coll., 1964; J.D. with honors, George Washington U., 1967. Bar: D.C. 1968, U.S. Supreme Ct. 1971. Law clk. Honorable Spottswood W. Robinson III, U.S. Ct. Apls. for D.C. Cir., 1967-68; assoc. Covington & Burling, 1968-72; asst. gen. counsel Office Consumer Affairs, 1972-73; dep. gen. counsel Cost of Living Council, 1973-74; exec. asst. to chmn. FTC, 1975, asst. dir., dep. dir., acting dir. Bur. Consumer Protection, 1976-77, exec. dir., 1977-79; gen. counsel Office Personnel Mgmt., Washington, 1979-81; dep. gen. counsel Dept. Treasury, Washington, 1981-86; ptnr. Sidley & Austin, Washington, 1986-94, Mediation Coun., Washington, 1995—. Recipient Meritorious Rank award, 1980, Presdl. Disting. Rank award, 1985. Mem. ABA, Am. Law Inst., Fed. Bar Assn., D.C. Bar Assn., Womens Bar Assn. Office: Mediation Coun 3921 Idaho Ave NW Washington DC 20008

WAXMAN, RONALD, computer engineer; b. Newark, Nov. 28, 1933; s. Benjamin and Rose (Lifson) W.; m. Pearl Latterman, June 19, 1955; children: David, Roberta, Benjamin. BSEE, N.J. Inst. Tech., 1955; MEE, Syracuse U., 1963. Engr. IBM, Poughkeepsie, N.Y., 1955-56, 58-64, East Fishkill, N.Y., 1964-70, Poughkeepsie and Kingston, N.Y., 1970-80; sr. engr. IBM, Manassas, Va., 1980-87; prin. scientist U. Va., Charlottesville, 1987—; IEEE rep. and tech. advisor to Internat. Elec. Commn. U.S. tech. activities group for internat. design automation stds.; mem. steering com. very high speed integrated circuits hardware description lang. VHDL Users Group, 1987-91. Contbr. numerous articles to profl. jours. and tech. presentations. 1st lt. USAF, 1956-58. Fellow IEEE, IEEE Computer Soc. (bd. govs. 1989-94, 86—, chmn. fellows evaluation com. 1995-96, founder, chmn. design automation stds. subcom. 1983-88, steering com. 1989—, chmn. design automation tech. com. 1988-90, steering com. 1991—, vice-chmn. tech. activities bd. 1991-92, chmn. awards com. 1993, disting. visitor 1986-88, v.p. mem. activities bd. 1994, Meritorious Svc. cert. 1988, Disting. Svc. cert. 1994, TAB Pioneer award 1989), Internat. Fedn. Info. Processing Orgns. (working group hardware description langs. rep. to tech. com.), Assn. for Computing Machinery (spl. interest group DA). Achievements include patents in field. Office: U Va Ctr for Semicustom Integrated Systems Dept EE Thornton Hall Charlottesville VA 22903

WAXMAN, SETH PAUL, lawyer; b. Hartford, Conn., Nov. 28, 1951; s. Felix H. and Frieda (Goodman) W.; m. Debra F. Goldberg, Mar. 20, 1977; children: Noah, Sarah, Ethan. AB summa cum laude, Harvard U., 1973; JD, Yale U., 1977. Bar: D.C. 1978, U.S. Dist. Ct. D.C., U.S. Ct. Appeals (D.C., 3d, 4th, 5th, 9th and 11th cirs.) 1979, U.S. Supreme Ct. 1981. Law clk to Judge Gerhard A. Gesell Washington, 1977-78; mng. ptnr. Miller Cassidy Larroca & Lewin, Washington, 1978-94; assoc. dep. atty. gen. U.S. Dept. Justice, Washington, 1994—; instr. Nat. Inst. for Trial Advocacy. Contbr. numerous articles on litigation to legal jours. Michael C. Rockefeller fellow Harvard U., 1973-74; recipient Cardozo award for civil rights Anti-Defamation League, 1987. Mem. ABA (steering com. postconviction death penalty representation project, com. chmn. litigation sect., Pro Bono Publico award 1988), Jud. Conf. U.S. Office: US Dept Justice Rm 4208 Washington DC 20530

WAXMAN, SHELDON ROBERT, lawyer; b. Chgo., Apr. 22, 1941; s. Henri and Ann (Sokolsky) W.; m. Katherine Slamski, Aug. 23, 1979; children: Josiah, Zoe. BA, U. Ill., 1963; JD, DePaul U., 1965. Bar: Ill. 1965, U.S. Supreme Ct. 1976, Mich. 1985. Staff atty. Argonne (Ill.) Nat. Lab., 1968-71; asst. U.S. Atty., Chgo., 1971-74; owner firm Shelly Waxman & Assocs., Chgo. and South Haven, Mich., 1976—. Author: In the Teeth of the Wind--Memoirs of a Libertarian Lawyer, 1995; editor-in-chief New Z Letter; contbr. articles to profl. jours. Founder Freedom Lawyers of Am., People for Simplified Tax Law, Nukes to the Sun. Office: PO Box 309 South Haven MI 49090-0309

WAXMAN, STEPHEN GEORGE, neurologist, neuroscientist; b. Newark, Aug. 17, 1945; s. Morris and Beatrice (Levitch) W.; m. Merle Applebaum, June 25, 1968; children: Matthew, David. AB, Harvard U., 1967; PhD, Albert Einstein Coll. Med., Yeshiva U., 1970, MD, 1972; MA (hon.), Yale U., 1986. Rsch. fellow in neurosci. Albert Einstein Coll. Medicine, Bronx, N.Y., 1970-72; clin. fellow Boston City Hosp., 1972-75; asst. prof. neurology Med. Sch. Harvard U., Boston, 1975-77, assoc. prof., 1977-78; prof. Stanford (Calif.) U., 1978-86; chief neurology unit Palo Alto (Calif.) VA Hosp., 1978-86; prof., chmn. dept. neurology Yale U., New Haven, 1986—; chief neurology Yale-New Haven Hosp., 1986—; vis. asst. prof. biology MIT, Cambridge, 1975-77, vis. assoc. prof., 1977-78; vice chmn. dept.neurology Stanford, 1981-86, chmn. neuroscis. program, 1982-86; mem. adv. bd. Regeneration Programs VA, Washington, 1982-86; mem. sci. adv. com. Nat. Spinal Cord Injury Assn., 1982—, Paralized Vets Am., 1981-81; dir. Ctr. Rsch. Neurol. Disease, VA Med. Ctr., West Haven, Conn., 1986—; mem. corp. Marine Biol. Labs., Woods Hole, Mass., 1988; mem. sci. adv. coun. Am. Paralysis Assn., 1990, mem. bd. sci. counselors NINDB, 1990—; mem. bd. biobehavioral scis. Inst. Medicine, 1990; Geschwind vis. prof. Harvard U., 1996. Author: Spinal Cord Compression, 1990, Correlative Neuroanatomy, 1993, The Axon, 1995; editor: Physiology and Pathbiology of Axons, 1978; editor-in-chief The Neuroscientist; assoc. editor Jour. Neurol. Scis.; mem. editl. bd. Brain Rsch., Muscle and Nerve, Internat. Rev. Neurobiology, Annals of Neurology, Jour. Neurol. Rehab., Glia, Devel. Neurosci., Jour. Neurotrauma, Neurobiology of Disease, Cerebrovascular Disease, Synapse. Recipient Trygve Tuve Meml. award NIH, 1973, Rsch. Career Devel. award NIH, 1975, Disting. Alumnus award Albert Einstein Coll. Medicine, 1990; rsch. fellow Univ. Coll., London, 1969; Nat. Multiple Sclerosis Soc. established investigator, 1987; numerous vis. lectureships. Fellow Royal Soc. Medicine (Gr. Britain), Am. Heart Assn. (stroke coun.); mem. Am. Soc. Cell Biology, Am. Acad. Neurology, Internat. Brain Rsch. Orgn. (U.S. nat. com.), Soc. Neurosci., Am. Neurol. Assn. (counsillor 1980), World Fedn. Neurology, Assn. Rsch. in Nervous and Mental Diseases (trustee, pres. 1992), Assn. Univ. Profs. Neurology. Office: Yale U Sch Medicine 33 Cedar St New Haven CT 06519-2314

WAXSE, DAVID JOHN, lawyer; b. Oswego, Kans., June 29, 1945; s. I. Joseph and Mary (Poole) W.; m. Linda Schilling (div.); children: Rachel, Ryan, Rebecca; m. Judy Pfannenstiel, May 29, 1982; 1 child, Elayna. BA, U. Kans., 1967; teaching cert., Columbia U., 1968, JD, 1971. Bar: Kans. 1971, U.S. Ct. Appeals (10th cir.) 1971, U.S. Supreme Ct. 1975. Dean of students Intermediate Sch. 88, N.Y.C., 1968-70; spl. edn. tchr. Peter Cooper Sch., N.Y.C., 1970-71; assoc. Payne & Jones, Olathe, Kans., 1971-74, ptnr., 1974-84; of counsel Shook, Hardy & Bacon, Overland Park, Kans., 1984-86, ptnr., 1986-95; ptnr. Shook, Hardy & Bacon L.L.P., Overland Park, Kans., 1995—; shareholder Shook, Hardy & Bacon P.C., Overland Park, 1993-95, v.p., asst. gen. counsel, 1995—; mcpl. judge City of Shawnee, Kans., 1974-80; atty. City of DeSoto, Kans., 1972-79; adj. prof. U. Kans. Sch. Law, Lawrence, 1981-82; mem. juv. code adv. com. Kans. Jud. Coun., 1979-83, guardianship adv. com., 1982-83, atty. fees adv. com., 1986-87; mem. Civil Justice Reform Act Adv. Com., U.S. Dist. Ct. for Dist. Kans., 1991—; mem. Kans. Commn. on Jud. Qualifications, 1992-94, vice-chmn. 1994—; v.p. Kans. Legal Svcs., Inc., 1980-82, pres., 1985-87; bd. advisors Kans. Coll. Advocacy, 1979-80. Author: (with others) Kansas Employment Law, 1985, Litigating Employment Law Cases, 1987, Kansas Employment Law Handbook, 1991, supplements, 1992, 95, Kansas Annual Survey, 1990—. Mem. Kan. Gov.'s Adv. Com. on Criminal Justice, 1974-77; gen. counsel Western Mo. Dist. ACLU, 1976-78, 86—, v.p., 1983-86, nat. bd. dirs., 1979-86, 91—, chmn. children's rights com., 1980-86; mem. AIDS Pol. Network, 1987—, med. treatment issues com., 1991—, constn. com., 1991—; mem. med./tech. com. AIDS Coun. Greater Kans. City, 1986—, ethics com. consortium Midwest Bioethics Ctr., 1990—; bd. dirs. Parents Anonymous Kans., 1978-83, pres., 1979; bd. dirs., mem. fin. com. Kans. Com. for Prevention Child Abuse, 1980-83. Mem. ABA (chmn. children's rights com. and family law sects. 1985-86), Am. Employment Law Coun., Kans. Bar Assn. (chmn. legal aid com. 1978-83, bd. govs. 1988—, v.p. 1996—, Pres.' Outstanding Svc. award 1982), Johnson County Bar Assn. (chmn. legal aid com. 1975-82, 92—), Amnesty Internat. (legal com. Kansas City chpt.), Common Cause, Sierra Club. Home: 9976 Hemlock Dr Shawnee Mission KS 66212-3447 Office: Shook Hardy and Bacon LLP 40 Corporate Woods 6th flr 9401 Indian Creek Pky Overland Park KS 66210-2005

WAY, BARBARA HAIGHT, dermatologist; b. Franklin, N.J., Dec. 27, 1941; d. Charles Padley and Alice Barbara (Haight) Shoemaker; m. Anthony Biden Way; children: Matthew Shoemaker Way, Sarah Shoemaker Way. AB in Music cum laude, Bryn Mawr Coll., 1962, postgrad., 1963-64; MD, U. Pa., 1968. Diplomate Am. Bd. Dermatology. Systems engr. IBM, Balt., 1962-63; mem. dean's staff Bryn Mawr (Pa.) Coll., 1963-64; med. intern U. Wis. Hosps., Madison, 1968-69, resident in dermatology, 1969-72; physician emergency rm. St. Francis Hosp., La Crosse, Wis., 1969-72, founder dept. of dermatology, 1972; asst. prof. dept. dermatology Tex. Tech U. Sch. Medicine, Lubbock, 1972-73, from asst. clin. to assoc. clin. prof., 1973-74, asst. prof., assoc. chair, 1974-76, assoc. prof., chair, 1976-81; assoc. clin. prof. Tex. Tech U. Health Scis. Ctr. (formerly Tex. Tech U. Sch. Medicine), Lubbock, 1981-92; clin. prof. Tex. Tech. U. Health Scis. Ctr., Lubbock, 1995—; founder, dir. dermatology residency tng. program Tex. Tech U. Health Scis. Ctr. (formerly Tex. Tech U. Sch. Medicine), Lubbock, 1978-81; pvt. practice Lubbock, 1973-74, 81—; acting dir. Lubbock City Health Dept., 1982-83; active staff Meth. Hosp., Lubbock, subsection chief, 1992, 94; active staff St. Mary of Plains Hosp., Lubbock, mem. credentials com., 1990, 92, 94, 95, founding dir. phototherapy unit, 1990-91, 93, mem. exec. com., 1991, 93, chief dermatology sect., 1991, 93. Alumna admissions rep. Bryn Mawr Coll., 1972-75, 87-95; mem. selection com. outstanding physician Lubbock chpt. Am. Cancer Soc., 1991-94, chmn., 1991; bd. dirs. Tex. Tech. U. Med. Found., 1987-89, Double T. Connection, 1988-90. Fellow Am. Acad. Dermatology (reviewer jour.); mem. AMA, Am. Soc. Dermatologic Surgery, Tex. Dermatol. Soc. (chmn. roster com. 1980), Tex. Med. Assn. (mem. sexually transmitted diseases com. 1986-90, mem. coun. pub. health 1990-92, vice councillor dist. III 1992—, chmn. reference com. fin. and orgnl. affairs ann. session 1992), Lubbock County-Garza County Med. Soc. (mem. various coms. 1980—, chmn. sch. and pub. health com. 1983, mem. bd. censors 1983-85, chair 1985, sec. 1986, v.p. 1987, liaison with Tex. Tech. U. Health Scis. Ctr. com. 1988-91, co-chmn. pub. rels. com. 1988-89, alt. Tex. Med. Assn. del. 1988-89, del. 1990-95, pres.-elect 1989, pres. 1990, chmn. ad hoc bylaws com. 1991-94, chmn. Hippocratic award 1991), Soc. Pediatric Dermatology, Women's Dermatologic Soc. (founding mem.). Office: 4102 24th St Ste 201 Lubbock TX 79410-1801

WAY, E(DWARD) LEONG, pharmacologist, toxicologist, educator; b. Watsonville, Calif., July 10, 1916; s. Leong Man and Lai Har (Shew) W.; m. Madeline Li, Aug. 11, 1944; children: Eric, Linette. BS, U. Calif., Berkeley, 1938, MS, 1940; PhD, U. Calif., San Francisco, 1942. Pharm. chemist Merck & Co., Rahway, N.J., 1942; instr. pharmacology George Washington U., 1943-46, asst. prof., 1946-48; asst. prof. pharmacology U. Calif., San Francisco, 1949-52; assoc. prof. U. Calif., 1952-57, prof., 1957-87, prof. emeritus, 1987—, chmn. dept. pharmacology, 1973-78; USPHS spl. rsch. fellow U. Berne, Switzerland, 1955-56, China Med. Bd.; rsch. fellow, vis. prof. U. Hong Kong, 1962-63; Sterling Sullivan disting. vis. prof. martin Luther King U., 1982; hon. prof. pharmacology and neurosci. Guangzhou Med. Coll., 1987; mem. adv. com. Pharm. Rsch. Mfrs. Assn. Found., 1968—; mem. coun. Am. Bur. for Med. Advancement in China, 1982; bd. dirs. Li Found., 1970—, pres., 1985—, bd. dirs. Haight Ashbury Free Clinics, 1986-93; Tsumura prof. neuropsychopharmacology med. sch. Gunma U., Maebashi, Japan, 1989-90; sr. staff fellow Nat. Inst. on Drug Abuse, 1990-91; researcher on drug metabolism, analgetics, devel. pharmacology, drug tolerance, drug dependence and Chinese materia medica. Editor: New Concepts in Pain, 1967, (with others) Fundamentals of Drug Metabolism and Drug Disposition, 1971, Endogenous and Exogenous Opiate Agonists and Antagonists, 1979; mem. editl. bd. Clin. Pharmacology, Therapeutics, 1975-87, Drug, Alcohol Dependence, 1976-87, Progress in Neuro-Psychopharmacology, 1977-91, Research Communications in Chem. Pathology and Pharmacology, 1978-91, Alcohol and Drug Dependence, 1986-91, Asian Pacific Jour. Pharm., 1985—, Jour. Chinese Medicine, 1993; contbr. numerous articles and revs. to profl. publs. Recipient Faculty Rsch. Lectr. award U. Calif., San Francisco, 1974, San Francisco Chinese Hosp. award, 1976, Cultural citation and Gold medal Ministry of Edn., Republic of China, 1978, Nathan B. Eddy award Coll. on Problems in Drug Dependence, 1979, Chancellor's award for pub. svc. U. Calif., 1986, Disting. Alumnus award U. Calif., San Francisco, 1990, Asian Pacific Am. Systemwide Alliance award, 1993. Fellow AAAS, Am. Coll. Neuropsychopharmacology, Am. Coll. Clin. Pharmacology (hon.), Coll. on Problems of Drug Dependence (exec. com. 1978-92, chmn. bd. dirs. 1978-82); mem. Am. Soc. Pharmacology, Exptl. Therapeutics (bd. editors 1957-65, pres. 1976-77, Torald Sollman award 1992), Fedn. Am. Socs. Exptl. Biology (exec. bd. 1975-79, pres. 1977-78), Am. Pharm. Assn. (life, Rsch. Achievement award 1962), AMA (affiliate), Soc. Aid and Rehab. Drug Addicts (Hong Kong, life), Western Pharmacology Soc. (pres. 1963-64), Japanese Pharm. Soc. (hon.), Coun. Sci. Soc. Pres.' (exec. com. 1979-84, treas. 1980-84), Chinese Pharmacology Soc. (hon.), Academia Sinica. Office: U Calif Dept of Pharmacology San Francisco CA 94143-0450

WAY, JACOB EDSON, III, museum director; b. Chgo., May 18, 1947; s. Jacob Edson Jr. and Amelia (Evans) W.; m. Jean Ellwood Chappell, Sept. 6, 1969; children: Sarah Chappell, Rebecca Stoddard, Jacob Edson IV. BA, Beloit Coll., 1968; MA, U. Toronto, 1971, PhD, 1978. Instr. Beloit (Wis.) Coll., 1972-73, asst. prof., 1973-80, assoc. prof., 1980-85; dir. Logan Mus. Anthropology, Beloit, 1980-85, Wheelwright Mus. Am. Indian, Santa Fe, 1985-89; interim dir. N.Mex. Mus. Natural History, Albuquerque, 1990-91; exec. dir. Space Ctr. Internat. Space Hall of Fame, Alamogorgo, N.Mex., 1991-94; dir. N.Mex. Farm and Ranch Heritage Mus., 1994—; evaluator Nat. Park Service, Denver, 1986. Contbr. articles to profl. jours. Mem. Nuke Watch, Beloit, 1983-84. Research grants Wis. Humanities Com., 1984, NSF, 1981; grantee Cullister Found., 1978-84; fellow U. Toronto, 1971. Mem. Am. Assn. Mus., Am. Assn. Phys. Anthropology, Can. Assn. for Phys. Anthropology, N.Mex. Assn. Mus. (pres. 1994-96), Soc. Am. Archaeology, Wis. Fedn. Mus. (adv. bd. 1982-85). Mem. Soc. Friends. Avocations: camping, skiing, fishing, reading, horseback riding. Office: N Mex Farm & Ranch Heritage Mus PO Drawer 1898 Las Cruces NM 88004

WAY, JAMES LEONG, pharmacology and toxicology educator; b. Watsonville, Calif., Mar. 21, 1926; s. Wong Bung Wee and Wow Wee (Wong) W.; m. Diana; children: Lani, Jon, Lori. BA, U. Calif., Berkeley, 1951; PhD, George Washington U., 1955. Asst. prof. U. Wis., Madison, 1959-62; assoc. prof. Marquette Med. Sch., Milw., 1962-67; prof. Washington State U., Pullman, 1967-82; endowed Shelton prof. pharmacology Tex. A&M U., College Station, 1982—; mem. toxicology study sect. NIH, Bethesda, Md., 1974-78; mem. toxicology data bank peer rev. com., NIH-NLM, 1978-85; mem. environ. health sci. study sect. NIEHS, 1985-90; vis. prof. pharmacology Nat. Def. Med. Ctr., Taipei, Taiwan, 1981-82; mem. toxicology data bank NLM, 1976-85; vis. scientist Med. Rsch. Coun./Nat. Inst. Med. Rsch., London, 1973-75. Contbr. over 200 articles to profl. jours. Recipient rsch. career devel. award NIH, 1959-72; Greenwald scholar U. Calif., Berkeley, 1960, Disting. scholar of U.S. NAS, 1986-88; N.Am. Baxter fellow, 1954-55, fellow NIH, 1979-80, Nat. Cancer Inst., 1955-58, also others. Mem. Am. Soc. Pharmacology and Exptl. Therapeutics (treas. 1989-90), Soc. Toxicology, Western Pharmacology Soc. (pres. 1978-79, mem. editorial bd. Toxicology and Applied Pharmacology 1978-90, Ann. Rev. Pharmacology and Toxicology 1986-91, assoc. editor 1991—), Internat. Soc. Resealed Erthrocyte (pres. 1994-96). Avocations: skiing, sky diving, windsurfing, scuba, handball. Office: Tex A&M U Health Sci Ctr Dept Med Pharmacology Med Sci Bldg College Station TX 77843-1114

WAY, KENNETH L., seat company executive; b. 1939. BS, Mich. State U., 1961, MBA, 1971. V.p. Lear Siegler, Inc., Southfield, Mich., 1966-88; chmn., chief exec. officer Lear Seating Co., Southfield, Mich., 1988—. With USAF, 1962-66. Office: Lear Seating 21557 Telegraph Rd Southfield MI 48034*

WAYANS, DAMON, actor; b. N.Y.C., 1961. TV appearances include Saturday Night Live, 1985-86, Take No Prisoners: Robert Townsend and His Partners in Crime, 1988, The Mutiny Has Just Begun: Robert Townsend and His Partners in Crime, III, 1989, In Living Color, 1990-92 (Emmy Outstanding writing in variety program 1990, 91, Outstanding individual in variety program 1991); exec prodr., actor: Damon Wayans: The Last Stand?, 1991 (film appearances) Beverly Hills Cop, 1984, Hollywood Shuffle, 1987, Roxanne, 1987, Colors, 1988, I'm Gonna Git You Sucka, 1988, Punchline, 1988, Earth Girls Are Easy, 1989, Look Who's Talking Too (voice), 1990, The Last Boy Scout, 1991; co-exec. prodr., screenwriter, actor Mo' Money, 1992, Blankman, 1994, Major Payne, 1995. Office: care CAA 9832 Wilshire Blvd Beverly Hills CA 90212*

WAYANS, KEENEN IVORY, actor, producer; b. N.Y.C., June 8, 1958; s. Howell and Elvira W. Film appearances include Star 80, 1983, Hollywood Shuffle (also co-screenwriter), 1987, Raw (also co-prodr., co-screenwriter), 1987, I'm Gonna Git You Sucka (also dir., screenwriter), 1988, Low Down Dirty Shame (also dir., screenwriter), 1994; co-screenwriter The Five Heartbeats; TV series For Love and Honor, 1983-84, (also exec. prodr., creator) In Living Color (Emmy award outstanding variety, music or comedy program 1990), 1990-93; TV specials Robert Townsend and His Partners in Crime, HBO (also co-prodr., writer), 1987. Office: CAA 9832 Wilshire Blvd Beverly Hills CA 90212*

WAYCASTER, BILL, chemicals executive; b. 1942. With Tex. Olefins Co., Houston, 1969—, CEO; with Tex. Petrochems., Houston, 1969—, CEO. Office: Tex Olefins Co 8707 Katy Fwy Ste 300 Houston TX 77024-1706 also: Tex Petrochems 8600 Park Place Blvd Houston TX 77017*

WAYGOOD, ERNEST ROY, plant physiology educator; b. Bramhall, Cheshire, Eng., Oct. 26, 1918; s. Edward Samuel and Alice (Harrison) W.; m. Adoree Magdalyn Woolf-LeBrooy, Dec. 30, 1950; 1 child, Pamela Mimi. B.S. in Agr., Ont. Agrl. Coll., 1941; M.S. in Agr., U. Toronto, 1947, Ph.D., 1949. Asst. prof. botany McGill U., Montreal, Que., Can., 1949-52, assoc. prof, 1952-54; prof., head dept. botany U. Man., Winnipeg, Can., 1954-74, prof. emeritus, 1979—. Flight lt. RCAF, 1941-45. Recipient Research award Lalor Found., 1956. Fellow Royal Soc. Can., Chem. Inst. Can.; mem. Can. Bot. Assn., Can. Soc. Plant Physiologists (pres. 1960), Am. Soc. Plant Physiologists, Am. Inst. Biol. Sci., Sigma Xi. Anglican. Home: 802-1245 Quayside Dr, New Westminster, BC Canada V3M 6J6

WAYLAND, J(AMES) HAROLD, biomedical scientist, educator; b. Boise, Idaho, July 2, 1909; s. Charles William and Daisy (McConnell) W.; m. Virginia Jane Kartzke, June 24, 1933; children—Ann Marie Peters, Elizabeth Jane (Mrs. Paul T. Barber). B.S., U. Idaho, 1931, D.Sc. (hon.), 1977; M.S., Calif. Inst. Tech., 1935, Ph.D., 1937. Am. Scandinavian Found. fellow U. Copenhagen, 1937; asst. prof. physics U. Redlands, 1938-41; mil. research in mine warfare and torpedo devel., 1941-48; assoc. prof. applied mechanics Calif. Inst. Tech., Pasadena, 1949-57; prof. Calif. Inst. Tech., 1957-63, prof. engring. sci., 1963-79, prof. emeritus, 1979—; U.S. coordinator U.S.-Japan Coop. Seminars on Peripheral Circulation, 1967, 70; mem. cardiovascular and renal study sect. NIH, 1973-77; vis. prof. Shinshu U., Matsumoto, Japan, 1973, U. Limburg, Maastricht, The Netherlands, 1979, U. New South Wales, Australia, 1980, U. Heidelberg, 1982, U. of Tsukuba, Japan, 1987; Disting. vis. prof. U. Del., 1985. Contbr. articles to profl. publs., also books and articles on history of playing cards. Recipient Ordnance Devel. award U.S. Navy, 1945, Cert. of Recognition, NASA, 1975, Humboldt Sr. Scientist Rsch. award U. Heidelberg, 1982, 91, Malpighi prize, 1988; named to Alumni Hall of Fame, U. Idaho, 1990; Guggenheim fellow, 1953-54; rsch. grantee NIH, NSF, John A. Hartford Found., Kroc Found. Fellow AAAS (chmn. med. scis. sect. 1976); founding fellow Am. Inst. Med. and Biol. Engring.; mem. AAUP, Microcirculatory Soc. (pres. 1971-72, Landis award 1981), Am. Phys. Soc., Am. Physiol. Soc., European Microcirculatory Soc. (hon.), German Microcirculatory Soc. (hon.), Internat. Soc. Biorheology, Am. Heart Assn., Am. Inst. Archeology, Am. Soc. Enologists, Playing Card Soc., Sigma Xi, Phi Beta Kappa, Sigma Tau. Democrat. Unitarian. Club: Athenaeum. Achievements include patents for scanning confocal microscopy; development of quantitative methods for measuring blood flow in microvessels and macromolecular diffusion in living tissues, of servo-microscope for maintaining focus on moving tissue. Home: 900 E Harrison Ave Apt B-21 Pomona CA 91767 Office: Calif Inst Tech Mail Code 104 # 44 Pasadena CA 91125

WAYLAND, NEWTON HART, conductor; b. Santa Barbara, Calif., Nov. 5, 1940; s. L.C. Newton and Helen Bertha (Hart) W.; m. Judith Anne Curtis, July 3, 1969 (div. 1986). MusB, New Eng. Conservatory Music, 1964, MusM, 1966. Host, composer, performer Sta. WGBH-TV, Boston, 1963-82; pianist, harpsichordist Boston Symphony Orch., 1964-71; music dir. Charles Playhouse, 1965-67; pianist, guest condr., arranger Boston Pops Orch., 1971-74; resident Pops condr. Midwest Pops Orch., South Bend, Ind., 1979-91, Oakland Symphony Orch., Calif., 1980-85, Houston Symphony Orch., 1986-93; prin. Pops condr. Denver Symphony Orch., 1987-89, Vancouver (B.C.) Symphony Orch., 1993—; guest condr. numerous orchs. U.S. and Canada, 1977—. Recs. include: Music for Zoom (PBS Emmy-winning TV show), 1971-78, Music for Nova (award-winning PBS-TV show), 1972-78, America Swings, 1987, Gershwin Plays Gershwin, 1987, Pop Go the Beatles, 1987, Classical Jukebox, 1988, Stompin' at the Savoy, 1988, Sophisticated Ladies, 1988, A Touch of Fiedler, 1989, Prime Time, 1989; arranger, performer: Jazz Loves Bach, 1968, Fiedler in Rags, 1974; arranger, condr.: Berlin to Broadway with Kurt Weill, 1972; condr. Oedipus Tex (Grammy award 1991); arranger, composer, performer (songs A&M Records) Come On and Zoom, Zoom Tunes. Recipient highest honors New Eng. Conservatory Music, 1974, Chadwick Disting. Achievement medal New Eng. Conservatory Music, 1966. Avocations: hiking, history, theatre. Home and Office: 2970 Hidden Valley Ln Santa Barbara CA 93108-1619

WAYLAND, RUSSELL GIBSON, JR., retired geology consultant, government official; b. Treadwell, Alaska, Jan. 23, 1913; s. Russell Gibson and Fanchon (Borie) W.; m. Mary Mildred Brown, 1943 (div. 1964); children: Nancy, Paul R.; m. Virginia Bradford Phillis, Dec. 24, 1965. B.S., U. Wash., 1934; A.M., Harvard, 1937; M.S., U. Minn., 1935, Ph.D., 1939. Engr., geologist Homestake Mining Co., Lead, S.D., summers 1930-39; with U.S. Geol. Survey, 1939-42, 1952-80, chief conservation div., 1966-78; research phys. scientist Office of Dir., 1978-80; energy minerals cons., 1980—; Washington rep. Am. Inst. Profl. Geologists, 1982-88; commr. VA Oil and Gas Conservation Bd., 1982-90; with Army-Navy Munitions Bd., 1942-45, Office Mil. Govt. and Allied High Commn., Germany, 1945-52; instr. geology U. Minn., 1937-39. Author sci. bulls. in field. Served to lt. col. AUS, 1942-46. Decorated Army Commendation medal; recipient Distinguished Service award Dept. Interior. Mem. AIME, Mineral Soc. Am., Geol. Soc. Am., Am. Inst. Profl. Geologists, Soc. Econ. Geologists, Assn. Engring. Geologists, Cosmos Club, Sigma Xi, Tau Beta Pi, Phi Gamma Delta, Sigma Gamma Epsilon, Gamma Alpha, Phi Mu Alpha Sinfonia. Episcopalian. Home and Office: 4660 35th St N Arlington VA 22207-4462

WAYLAND, SHARON MORRIS, law librarian; b. Ft. Worth, July 5, 1951; d. Wesley B. Morris and Lelia L. Curl; children: Brian, Curtis. BA magna cum laude, U. Tex., Arlington, 1973; MLS summa cum laude, U. North Tex., 1982. Asst. dir. Tarrant County Law Libr., Ft. Worth, 1982-89, dir., 1990—; law book reviewer Legal Info. Alert, Chgo., 1989—. Mem. Am. Assn. Law Librs., Southwestern Assn. Law Librs., Tarrant County Assn. Law Librs. (past pres.), Dallas Assn. Law Librs. Avocations: gardening, oil painting, sewing. Office: Tarrant County Law Libr 100 W Weatherford St Rm 420 Fort Worth TX 76102-2115

WAYLAND-SMITH, ROBERT DEAN, banker; b. Oneida, N.Y., July 2, 1943; s. Robert and Prudence Cragin (Skinner) W.-S.; m. Kathleen Anne Schultz, Aug. 24, 1968; children: Kristin, Debra. BA in Econs., U. Rochester, 1965. Mgr. equipment svc. Strong Meml. Hosp., Rochester, N.Y., 1965-67; mgmt. trainee Chase Lincoln First Bank, N.A., Rochester, 1967-68, mgr. mcpl. securities, 1968-81, mgr. portfolio mgmt. depart., 1981-84, mgr. fin. and investment svc. dept., 1984-87, mgr. trust and fin. svc. dept., 1987-88; pres. and CEO Rochester region Chase Manhattan Bank, N.A., 1988-93, upstate wealth segment exec., 1993—; mem. adv. bd. Roberts Wesleyan Coll., Rochester, 1989—; mem. adv. coun. J.W. Jones Sch. Bus. SUNY, Geneseo, 1990—. Trustee Ctr. for Govtl. Rsch., 1985—, Rochester Visitors Assn., 1990-93, Rochester Downtown Devel. Corp., 1991-93; dir. United Neighborhood Ctrs., Greater Rochester Found., 1992—; mem. fin. execs. adv. bd. Coll. Bus. Rochester Inst. Tech., 1994—; mem. adv. bd. Help Our World Found., 1990—. Fellow Assn. for Investment Mgmt. and Rsch.; mem. Internat. Assn. Fin. Planners, Rochester Soc. Security Analysts, Greater Rochester Met. C. of C. (dir. 1992-95), Genesee Valley Club, Oak

Hill Country Club. Avocations: golf, gardening, reading. Office: Chase Manhattan Bank NA One Chase Sq Rochester NY 14643

WAYLETT, THOMAS ROBERT, management consultant executive; b. Toronto, Ont., Can., Apr. 27, 1941; s. Robert George and Frances Jean (Thomson) W.; m. Nancy Jean Parkinson, May 12, 1961 (div.); children: Cherie Lynne, Matthew; m. Karen P. Pritchard, Jan. 23, 1989. With Nat. Life, Imperial Life, Indsl. Life, Toronto; v.p. William M. Mercer Ltd., Toronto, 1966-75; dir. William M. Mercer, Inc., N.Y.C., 1975-82; mng. dir. Marsh & McLennan Cos., N.Y.C., 1982-91; exec. v.p. William M. Mercer Cos., N.Y.C., 1991—; chmn. Mercer Mgmt. Consulting, Inc., N.Y.C., 1992—; bd. dirs. Nat. Econ. Rsch. Assocs., White Plains, N.Y., William M. Mercer Cos., Inc., N.Y.C. Office: Mercer Mgmt Consulting 1166 Avenue Of The Americas New York NY 10036-2708

WAYMAN, COOPER HARRY, environmental legal counsel; b. Trenton, N.J., Jan. 29, 1927; s. Cooper Ott and Helen Viola (Unverzagt) W.; m. Ruth Treier, June 16, 1951; children: Carol Beth Withers, Andrea Lee Daschbach. BS, Rutgers U., 1951; MS, U. Pitts., 1954; PhD, Mich. State U., 1959; JD, U. Denver, 1967. Bar: Colo. 1969, Tex. 1972; registered profl. engr., Colo.; cert. real estate broker, Colo. Rsch. chemist U.S. Geol. Survey, Lakewood, Colo., 1960-65; assoc. prof. chemistry Colo. Sch. Mines, Golden, 1965-70; regional counsel EPA, Dallas, 1971-74; asst. to regional adminstr. EPA, Denver, 1974-83; exec. asst. to mayor City of Denver, 1981-85; dir. environment compliance Cord Labs., Inc., Broomfield, Colo., 1986-88; environ. and permits mgr. Chem. Waste Mgmt. Inc., Port Arthur, Tex., 1988-92; regional regulatory mgr. Chem. Waste Mgmt., Inc., Houston, 1992-94; compliance branch mgr. Adv. Scis., Inc., Carlsbad, N.Mex., 1994-95; area office legal counsel Waste Isolation Project, Dept. Energy, Carlsbad, N.Mex., 1995—; dir. energy office EPA, Denver, 1974-78; adj. prof. law U. Denver, 1981-84; mem. State of Colo. Air Pollution Commn., Denver, 1969-70. Author: Detergents and Environment, 1965, Permits Handbook, 1981; contbr. articles to profl. jours. V.p. WE Lockwood Civic Assn., Lakewood, 1985-86. With USNR, 1945-46. Grantee U.S. Fish and Wildlife Svc., 1967; fellow, rsch. assoc. MIT, 1956-58. Fellow Am. Inst. Chemists, 1993. Avocations: skiing, golf, photography, art. Home: 1408-A W Church St Carlsbad NM 88220 Office: US Dept Energy Carlsbad Area Office PO Box 3090 Carlsbad NM 88221

WAYMIRE, BONNIE GLADINE, nursing administrator; b. Williamsport, Ind., Dec. 16, 1954; d. Jackie Lee and Mary Lou (Jennings) W. LPN diploma, Danville Jr. Coll., 1978; diploma, Lakeview Sch. Nursing, 1986; BS in Bus. Mgmt., Ind. Inst. of Tech., 1996. RN, Ind., Ill., Tenn. Supr. evening shift Vermillion Manor, Danville, Ill., 1986; staff nurse, rsch. coord. VA Med. Ctr., Indpls., 1986-92; vis. nurse Vis. Nurse Svc., Indpls., 1992; charge nurse Eagle Valley Health Care, Indpls., 1992; DON Vinewood Health Care, Plainfield, Ind., 1992-93, Records Autumn Care, Franklin, Ind., 1993, Bloomfield (Ind.) Health Care, 1993-94, Shakamak Good Samaritan, Jasonville, Ind., 1994—, 1996—. Co-author: Am. Jour. Vascular Surgery, 1992. Mem. Soc. Vascular Nursing (nursing standard and practice Acte com. 1988-92), Nat. Assn. Dirs. Nursing Adminstrn. in Long Term Care, VFW Aux., Women of the Moose (Acad. Friendship award 1992, Am. Legion Aux., Shakamak Women's Civic Club, Wednesday Rsch. Club. Roman Catholic. Avocations: collecting stamps, coins and Star Trek memorabilia. Home: 387 E Main St Bloomfield IN 47424-1458

WAYMOUTH, JOHN FRANCIS, physicist, consultant; b. Barahona, Dominican Republic, May 24, 1926; came to U.S., 1936; s. John Francis and Margaret Logan (Postell) W.; m. Frances O'Bannon Pope, Sept. 3, 1949; children: John F., George L., Anne K., Mark D. BS, U. of South, 1947; PhD in Physics, MIT, 1950. From sr. engr. to sect. head Sylvania Electric Products Co., Salem and Danvers, Mass., 1950-69; lab. dir. GTE Products Corp., Danvers, 1969-88; cons. physicist Marblehead, Mass., 1988—; chmn. exec. com. Phys. Electronic Conf., 1969-72; mem. evaluation panel heat div. Nat. Bur. Standards, Gaithersburg, Md., 1972-74; mem. tech. elec. products radiol. saftey standards com. Bur. of Radiol. Health, Rockville, Md., 1977-79; mem. adv. com. for physics NSF, Washington, 1981-83. Author: Electric Discharge Lamps; contbr. articles to profl. jours.; patentee in field. With U.S. Army, 1944-46, PTO. Recipient Elenbaas prize Dutch Phys. Soc., 1973. Fellow Am. Phys. Soc., Illuminating Engring. Soc. N.Am. (medal 1991).

WAYNE, LOWELL GRANT, air pollution scientist, consultant; b. Washington, Nov. 27, 1918; s. Glenn Lytten and Bonnie Jean (Leming) W.; m. Martha Lee Dolson, June 21, 1942; children: Garth Lee, Randall Rush. BS, U. Calif., Berkeley, 1937; student, U. Calif., Davis, 1939-41, Harvard U., 1942; PhD, Calif. Inst. Technology, 1948. Diplomate Am. Bd. Indsl. Hygiene. Fellow Mellon Inst. for Indsl. Rsch., Pitts., 1949-52; phys. chemist Stanford Rsch. Inst., Menlo Park, Calif., 1953-54; occupational health engr. U. Calif., L.A., 1954-56; rsch. photochemist Air Pollution Control Dist., L.A., 1956-62; rsch. analyst Hancock Found. U. So. Calif., L.A., 1962-72, section head Air Pollution Control Inst., 1966-72; v.p., sr. scientist Pacific Environ. Svcs., Inc., Santa Monica, Calif., 1972-85; cons. L.A., 1985—; sr. scientist Valley Rsch. Corp., Van Nuys, Calif., 1987—. Lt. comdr. USNR, 1942-46. Fellow AAAS; mem. So. Calif. Fedn. Scientists, Air and Waste Mgmt. Assn., Am. Chem. Soc., Sigma Xi (chmn. Humboldt State U. chpt., 1995—). Unitarian. Avocation: chamber music. Home: 285 Bayside Rd Arcata CA 95521-6463

WAYNE, ROBERT ANDREW, lawyer; b. Newark, Oct. 4, 1938; s. David Michael and Charlotte (Chesler) W.; m. Charlotte Fainblatt, Aug. 14, 1969; children—Andrew Mark, Gary Howard, Deborah Jill. B.A., Princeton U., 1960; J.D., Columbia U. 1963. Bar: N.J. 1964, U.S. Dist. Ct. N.J. 1964, U.S. Dist. Ct. (ea. and so. dists.) N.Y. 1966, U.S. Ct. Apls. (3d cir.) 1967, N.Y. 1981, U.S. Ct. Apls. (2d cir.) 1984, U.S. Supreme Ct. 1984, U.S. Claims Ct., 1984, U.S. Tax Ct. 1984. Assoc., Shanley & Fisher, Newark, 1964-69, ptnr., 1969-71; ptnr. Robinson, St. John & Wayne, Newark, 1971—. Mem. Democratic County Com., Livingston, N.J., 1971-74. Served with AUS, 1963-69. Mem. ABA, N.J. Bar Assn., Essex County Bar Assn., Monmouth County Bar Assn., Fed. Bar Assn., Am. Coll. Real Estate Lawyers. Jewish. Office: Robinson St John & Wayne 2 Penn Plz E Newark NJ 07105-2246

WAYNE, STEPHEN J., government educator, academic director, writer; b. N.Y.C., Mar. 22, 1939; s. Arthur G. and Muriel (Marks) W.; m. Cheryl Beil, May 22, 1982; children: Jared B., Jeremy B. BA with honors, U. Rochester, 1961; MA, Columbia U., 1963, PhD, 1968. Instr. polit. sci. U.S. Naval Postgrad. Sch., 1963-65; instr. politics and govt. Ohio Wesleyan U., 1966-68; asst. prof. polit. sci. and pub. affairs The George Washington U., 1968-73, assoc. prof., 1973-79, prof., 1979-89; prof. govt. Georgetown U., Washington, 1989—; adviser Pres.-Elect Portillo and staff, Mexico City, 1976; dir. U.S. Studies program Ctr. Advanced Study of Am., 1985-87; presenter and lectr. in field. Author: The Legislative Presidency, 1978, The Road to the White House, 1980, post election edit., 1981, 2d edit., 1984, 3d edit., 1988, 4th edit., 1992, (with George C. Edwards) Presidential Leadership: Politics and Policy Making, 1985, 2d edit., 1990, 3d edit., 1994; editor: Investigating the American Political System: Problems, Methods, and Projects, 1974, (with George C. Edwards) Studying the Presidency, 1983, (with Clyde Wilcox) The Quest for National Office, 1992; appeared on 3 one-hour programs on presidency Every Four Years, sta. WHYY-TV, PBS, 1980; election night analyst ARD-German TV, 1992; adv. editor Polit. Sci. McGraw Hill Coll. Divsn., 1982—; series editor Am. Political Institutions and Pub. Policy, M. E. Sharpe, Inc., 1990—; contbr. numerous articles, chpts. and book revs. to books and profl. jours. Office: Georgetown U Dept Govt 37th and O NW Washington DC 20057

WAYTE, (PAUL) ALAN, lawyer; b. Huntington Park, Calif., Dec. 30, 1936; s. Paul Henry and Helen Lucille (McCarthy) W.; m. Beverly A. Bruen, Feb. 19, 1959 (div. 1972); children: David Alan, Lawrence Andrew, Marcia Louise; m. Nancy Kelly Wayte, July 5, 1975. AB, Stanford U., 1958, JD, 1960. Bar: Calif. 1961, U.S. Dist. Ct. (so. dist.) Calif. 1961, U.S. Supreme Ct. 1984. Ptnr. Adams, Duque & Hazeltine, Los Angeles, 1966-85, Dewey Ballantine, Los Angeles, 1985—. Mem. L.A. County Bar Assn. (chmn. real property sect. 1981-82), Am. Coll. Real Estate Lawyers (bd. govs. 1989—, pres. 1994), Am. Coll. Mortgage Attys., Anglo-Am. Real Property Inst. (bd. govs. 1989-91), L.A. Philharm. Assn. (exec. com. bd. dirs. 1973—), Chancery Club, Calif. Club (L.A.), Valley Hunt Club (Pasadena). Home: 1745 Orlando Rd Pasadena CA 91106-4131 Office: Dewey Ballantine 333 S Hope St Los Angeles CA 90071-1406

WAZZAN, AHMED R(ASSEM) FRANK, engineering educator, dean; b. Lattakia, Syrian Arab Republic, Oct. 17, 1935; married, 1959; 3 children. BS, U. Calif., Berkeley, 1959, MS, 1961, PhD in Engring. Sci., 1963. From asst. prof. to assoc. prof. engring. UCLA, 1962-69, prof. engring. and applied sci., 1974—, assoc. dean Sch. Engring. and Applied Sci., 1981-86, dean Sch. Engring. and Applied Sci., 1986—; cons. McDonnell Douglas Corp., 1962-71, Lawrence Radiation Lab., 1965-67, Westinghouse Electric Corp., 1974-76, N.Am. Aviation, 1975-78, Rand Corp., 1975—; Honeywell Corp., 1976-78; vis. scholar Electricité de France, Paris, Office of Commr. Atomic Energy, Saclay, France, 1973-79. Reviewer Applied Mech. Rev., 1971-87. Guggenheim fellow, 1966. Fellow Am. Nuclear Soc. Research in modeling of fuel elements for fast breeder reactor, stability and transition of laminar flows, thermodynamics of solids and of dense gases, and thermal hydraulics of pressurized water reactors. Office: UCLA Sch of Engring Dean Box 951600 Los Angeles CA 90095-1600

WEADOCK, DANIEL PETER, corporate executive; b. N.Y.C., June 21, 1939; m. Florence Towey, Oct. 5, 1961; children: Daniel, Bryan, Kevin, Ann, Kathleen. B.S. in Fin, Fordham U., 1967; PhD (hon.), Georgian Ct. Coll., Lakewood, N.J., 1991. With central bookkeeping Chase Manhattan Bank, 1957-61; with ITT Corp., 1961—; spl. asst. to office of pres. ITT, 1969-75; dir. ops. ITT Africa and Middle East, Brussels, 1975-79; pres. ITT Africa and Middle East, 1979; v.p. ITT, 1979-83; pres. ITT Europe Inc., Brussels, 1983—; exec. v.p. ITT, 1983—, group exec.-Europe; pres. ITT-Europe, Inc.; chmn., pres., CEO ITT Comms. and Info. Svcs., Seacucus, N.J., 1988-93; pres., CEO ITT Sheraton Corp., Boston, 1993—. Named Knight of the Order of the Crown by the King of Belgium, 1988. Office: ITT Sheraton Corp 60 State St Boston MA 02109-1803

WEAKLAND, ANNA WU, artist, art educator; b. Shanghai, China, May 1, 1924; came to the U.S., 1947; d. Tse-Chien and Kwei-Ying (Sze) Wu; m. John H. Weakland, Feb. 11, 1950; children: Alan Wade, Lewis Francis, Joan. BA, U. Shanghai, China, 1943; MA, Columbia U., 1948; postgrad., Stanford U., 1953-55. art instr. U. Calif., 1968, 72, 78, 82, 84, Stanford (Calif.) U., 1990; vis. art prof. Zhejiang Acad. Arts, Hangzhou, China, 1991. One-woman shows include De Young Mus., San Francisco, 1959, San Francisco Mus. Modern Art, 1961, Chathan Gallery, Hong Kong, 1963, Seattle Art Mus., 1964, Ashmolian Mus., Oxford, Eng., 1964, Sale Internat./ Palacio De Bellas, Mexico City, 1966, Downtown Gallery, N.Y., 1967, Victoria (Can.) Art Mus., 1967, Heritage Gallery, L.A., 1971, Wells Fargo Bank Hdqs., San Francisco, 1973, Macy's, Palo Alto, 1976, I. Magnin, Palo Alto, 1981, Tresidor Union Gallery, Stanfor U., 1982, Palo Alto (Calif.) Med. Found., 1984, Stanford (Calif.) Mus. Art, 1988, Hewlett-Packard Co. Art Gallery, Palo Alto, 1989, Gump's Art Gallery, San Francisco, 1990, Marin County Civic Ctr., San Rafael, Calif., 1994; represented in permanent collections including Ashmolean Mus., Oxford, Eng., U. B.C., Vancouver, Fukuoka (Japan) U., Stanford U., Seattle (Wash.) Art Mus., IBM Corp., others. Named Artist of the Yr., Friends of The Libr. award, Palo Alto, Calif., 1979, Artist of the Month, No. Calif. Home and Garden Mag., Redwood City, Calif., 1992. Mem. Am. Women Caucus for Art, Asian Am. Women Artists Assn. Avocations: music, tennis, aerobic dancing, cooking, photography. Home: 4245 Manuela Ct Palo Alto CA 94306-3731

WEAKLAND, REMBERT G., archbishop; b. Patton, Pa., Apr. 2, 1927; s. Basil and Mary (Kane) W. AB, St. Vincent Coll., Latrobe, Pa., 1948, DD (hon.), 1963, LHD (hon.), 1987; MS in Piano, Juilliard Sch. Music, 1954; grad. studies sch. music, Columbia U., 1954-56; LHD (hon.), Duquesne U., 1964, Belmont Coll., 1964, Cath. U. Am., 1975, Loyola U., Chgo., 1986, Xavier U., Cin., 1988, DePaul U., 1989, Loyola U., New orleans, 1992, Dayton U., 1993, Villanova U., Fond du Lac, 1992, Marian Coll., Fond du Lac, Wis., 1995; HHD (hon.), St. Ambrose U., Davenport, 1990, Aquinas Inst. Theology, St. Louis, 1991, St Mary's Coll., Notre Dame, Ind., 1994; LLD (hon.), Cardinal Stritch Coll., Milw., 1978, Marquette U., 1981, U. Notre Dame, 1987, Mt. Mary Coll., Milw., 1989, John Carroll U., Cleve., 1992, Fairfield U., 1994; D of Sacred Music (hon.), St. Joseph's Coll., Rensselaer, Ind., 1979; DST (hon.), Jesuit Sch. Theology, Berkeley, Calif., 1989, St. John's U., Collegeville, Minn., 1991, Santa Clara U., 1991, Yale U., 1993; DD (hon.), Lakeland Coll., Sheboygan, 1991, Ill. Benedictine Coll., Lisle, Ill., 1992, Regis Coll., Toronto, 1993. Joined Benedictines, Roman Cath. Ch., 1945, ordained priest, 1951. Mem. faculty music dept. St. Vincent Coll., 1957-63, chmn., 1961-63, chancellor chmn. of bd. of Coll., 1963-67; elected co-adjutor archabbot, 1963; abbot primate Benedictine Confederation, 1967-77; archbishop of Milw., 1977—. Mem. Ch. Music Assn. Am. (pres. 1964-66), Am. Guild Organists. Office: PO Box 07912 Milwaukee WI 53207-0912

WEARLY, WILLIAM LEVI, business executive; b. Warren, Ind., Dec. 5, 1915; s. Purvis Gardner and Ethel Ada (Jones) W.; m. Mary Jane Riddle, Mar. 8, 1941; children: Patricia Ann, Susan, William Levi, Elizabeth. B.S., Purdue U., 1937, Dr. Engring. (hon.), 1959. Student career engr. C.A. Dunham Co., Michigan City, Ind., 1936; mem. elec. design staff Joy Mfg. Co., Franklin, Pa., 1937-39; v.p., gen. sales mgr. Joy Mfg. Co., 1952-56, exec. v.p., 1956-57, pres., dir., 1957-62; v.p., dir. Ingersoll-Rand Co., 1964-66, exec. v.p., 1966-67, chmn., chief exec. officer, 1967-80, chmn. exec. com., 1981-85; dir. ASA Ltd., Med. Care Am.; trustee LMI; speaker engring. groups. Author tech. publs. relating to mining. Bd. dirs. Boys Clubs Am. Mem. NAE, IEEE, AIME, Nat. Acad. of Engring., C. of C., Sky Club N.Y.C., Blind Brook Golf Club, Desert Forest Golf Club, Ariz. Club, Masons, Shriners, Eta Kappa Nu, Tau Beta Pi, Beta Theta Pi. Republican. Methodist. Patentee in field. Home: One Milbank IIF Greenwich CT 06830 also: PO Box 1072 Carefree AZ 85377-1072

WEARN, WILSON CANNON, retired media executive; b. Newberry, S.C., Oct. 7, 1919; s. George F. and Mary (Cannon) W.; m. Mildred Colson, Feb. 21, 1948; children: Jean Wearn Held, Joan Wearn Gilbert, Wilson Cannon Jr. B.E.E., Clemson U., 1941. Engr. Westinghouse Electric Corp., Pitts., 1941, FCC, Washington, 1946-48; assoc. cons. electronic engr. firm Weldon & Carr, Washington, 1948-50; ptnr. Vandivere, Cohen & Wearn (cons. engrs.), Washington, 1950-53; with Multimedia Broadcasting Co., Greenville, S.C., 1953-68; organizer of corp. Multimedia Broadcasting Co., 1953, became corp. officer, 1960, pres., 1966-77; pres. Multimedia, Inc., Greenville, 1977-81; chief exec. officer Multimedia, Inc., 1978-84, chmn. bd., 1981-89; chmn. emeritus Multimedia, Inc., Greenville, 1989-95; instr. electronic engring. Clemson U., 1946. Mem. S.C. Hosp. Adv. Council, 1969-71; bd. dirs. Family and Children Service of Greenville County, 1967-69, pres., 1969; bd. dirs. Newspaper Advt. Bur., 1981-85; trustee Greenville Symphony Assn., 1960-62, 71-77, pres., 1977; trustee Greenville Hosp. System, 1964-70, chmn., 1968-70; trustee Broadcast Rating Council, 1969-73, chmn., 1971-73; trustee Clemson U. Found., 1973-79, pres., 1979; trustee Presbyn. Coll., F.W. Symmes Found. Served to capt. Signal Corps, AUS, 1941-45, PTO. Decorated Bronze Star; recipient Outstanding Alumni award Clemson U., 1972. Mem. Nat. Assn. Broadcasters (chmn. bd. 1975-77), S.C. Broadcasters Assn. (pres. 1967), Greater Greenville C. of C. (pres. 1972), Nat. Assn. Securities Dealers (bd. govs. 1985-88), Kiwanis (Greenville), Poinsett Club (Greenville), Green Valley Country Club (Greenville), Augusta (Ga.) Nat. Golf Club. Presbyterian (elder).

WEART, SPENCER RICHARD, historian; b. Detroit, Mar. 8, 1942; s. Spencer Augustus and Janet (Streng) W.; m. Carole Ege, June 30, 1971; children: Lara Kimi, Spencer Gen. BA, Cornell U., 1963; PhD, U. Colo., 1968. Postdoctoral fellow Calif. Inst. Tech., 1968-71, U. Calif., Berkeley, 1971-74; dir. Ctr. for History Physics, Am. Inst. Physics, College Park, Md., 1974—. Author: Scientists in Power, 1979, Nuclear Fear, 1988; contbr. articles to profl. jours. Recipient Andrew Gemant award Am. Inst. of Physics, 1994. Fellow AAAS. Home: 12 Buena Vista Dr Hastings Hdsn NY 10706-1104 Office: Am Inst Physics One Physics Ellipse College Park MD 20740-3843

WEARY, PEYTON EDWIN, medical educator; b. Evanston, Ill., Jan. 10, 1930; s. Leslie Albert and Conway Christian (Fleming) W.; m. Janet Edsall Gregory, Aug. 23, 1952; children—Terry, Conway Christian, Carolyn Fielder. B.A., Princeton U., 1970; M.D., U. Va., 1955. Diplomate: Am. Bd. Dermatology (dir. 1978-88, pres. 1987-88). Intern, case Western Res. U. Hosps., Cleve., 1955-56; rotating intern Univ. Hosp. Cleve., 1955-56; asst. resident dermatology U. Va., Charlottesville, 1958-60; resident dermatology U. Va., 1960-61, instr. dept. dermatology, 1961-62, asst. prof., 1962-65, asso. prof., 1965-70, prof., chmn. dept. dermatology, 1970-93; mem. staff Univ. Hosp., mem. cancer com., 1979—, sec.-treas.; Univ. Hosp. house staff, 1960-61, clin. staff, 1965-66, pres. clin. staff, 1966-67. Mem. editorial bd. Jour. Am. Acad. Dermatology, 1978-87; editorial adv. bd. Skin and Allergy News, 1978—; contbr. articles to profl. jours. Bd. dirs. Lupus Found. Am., 1980-84; trustee, mem. exec. com. Dermatology Found., 1975-79; pres. Albermarle County unit Am. Cancer Soc., 1967-69. Served from 1st lt. to capt., M.C. U.S. Army, 1956-58. Mem. Nat. Assn. Physicians Environ. (pres. 1995—), Va. Dermatol. Soc. (sec.-treas. 1965-71), Am. Acad. Dermatology (hon. bd. dirs. 1973-76, Gold medal 1990, pres. 1993-95), Soc. Investigative Dermatology (bd. dirs. 1976-81, v.p.1985, hon. mem. 1996), Assn. Profs. Dermatology (sec.-treas. 1976-79), Am. Dermatol. Assn. (bd. dirs. 1987-93, pres. 1992-93), Dermatology Found., Albermarle County Med. Soc., Med. Soc. Va., So. Med. Assn., Reven Soc., Am. Bd. Med. Specialties (v.p. 1988, pres-elect 1989, pres. 1990-92), Coun. Med. Specialty Socs. (bd. dirs. 1989-92, sec. 1992-95), Alpha Omega Alpha, Sigma Xi. Republican. Presbyn. Club: Boar's Head Sports. Home: 110 Magnolia Dr Charlottesville VA 22901-2015 Office: Dept Dermatology Univ Va Hosp Charlottesville VA 22908

WEATHERBEE, DONALD EMERY, political scientist, educator; b. Portland, Maine, June 21, 1932; s. Perley Emery and Ruby Francis (Smith) W.; m. Mary Ellen Bailey, Sept. 4, 1954; children: Mercy Meria, Donald Bailey, Thais Elizabeth, Amy Francesca, Oliver Parks Emery. A.B. magna cum laude, Bates Coll., 1954; M.A., Johns Hopkins U. Sch. Advanced Internat. Studies, 1956, Ph.D. (Earhart dissertation fellow), 1968. Spl. lectr. Gajah Mada State U., Jogjakarta, Indonesia, 1957-61; Ford Found. fellow The Hague, Netherlands, 1962-64; asst. prof. to prof. U. S.C., 1964-74; Donald S. Russell prof. contemporary fgn. policy, 1981—; sr. Fulbright fellow Inst. Southeast Asian Studies, Singapore, 1981-82; asst. dean Coll. Social Scis., 1972; Henry L. Stimson prof. polit. sci. U.S. Army War Coll., 1974-77; vis. asst. prof. U. R.I., 1965; exchange prof. Free U. Berlin, 1969; vis. fellow Inst. Security and Internat. Studies, Chulalongkorn U., Bangkok, Thailand, 1988-89; panelist reviewer Nat. Endowment for Humanities; cons., lectr. for U.S. govt. agys. Author: Ideology in Indonesia, 1965, The United Front in Thailand, 1970, Ancient Indonesia, 1974, Indonesian Security Policy and Perceptions, 1978, Southeast Asia Divided: The Asean-Indochina Crisis, 1985; editorial bd.: Asian Survey; exec. editor: Asian Affairs; contbr. numerous articles, revs. to publs. on S.E. Asian politics and internat. relations. Recipient Disting. Civilian Service decoration Dept. of the Army, 1977. Fellow Inter-Univ. Seminar on Armed Forces and Soc.; mem. Assn. Asian Studies, Internat. Studies Assn., Koninklijke Instituut voor Taal, Land- en Volkenkunde (Leiden, Netherlands). Office: Dept Govt and Internat Studies U SC Columbia SC 29208

WEATHERFORD, GEORGE EDWARD, civil engineer; b. Oakdale, Tenn., Jan. 8, 1932; s. Walter Clyde and Kathleen (Hinds) W.; m. Martha Jeannette Beck, July 9, 1960; children: Kathleen Jeannette Weatherford-Hommeltoft, Elizabeth Lynn. BSCE, Ind. Inst. Tech., Fort Wayne, 1957; BS Engr. in Constrn., U. Mich., 1959; MSBA, St. Francis Coll., 1975. Registered profl. engr., Ind., Ga., Ohio, Minn., Iowa, S.C., Pa., Ky., Ill., Md., La., Tenn., Mich. Plant engr. Cen. Soya Co., Inc., Decatur, Ind., 1959; civil engr. Cen. Soya Co., Inc., Decatur, 1959-64; county hwy. engr. Allen County Ind. Govt., Ft. Wayne, 1964-66; sr. civil engr. Cen. Soya Co., Inc., Fort Wayne, 1966-69, engring. mgr., 1969-77, prin. engr., 1977—; ind. cons. 1964—. Author book chpts.; contbr. articles to profl. jours. Trustee Ft. Wayne YWCA, 1973-76, North Christian Ch. and Endowment Trust. Sgt. USMC, 1950-54. Mem. ASCE (state treas. 1957), NSPE, Am. Concrete Inst., Am. Inst. Steel Constrn., Nat. Grain and Feed Assn. (fire and explosion rsch. and edn. com.), Ill. Assn. Structural Engrs., Grain Elevator and Processing Soc. (edn. programming com.). Republican. Home: 3617 Delray Dr Fort Wayne IN 46815-6012

WEATHERFORD, WILLIS DUKE, JR., college president emeritus; b. Biltmore, N.C., June 24, 1916; m. Anne Smith, 1954; children: Edith, Julia, Willis III, Susan, Alice. B.A., Vanderbilt U., 1937; B.D., Yale U., 1940; postgrad., U. N.C., 1940-41; M.A., Harvard U., 1943, Ph.D. in Econs., 1952; LL.D., Carleton Coll., 1969, Swarthmore Coll., 1981; L.H.D., Blackburn U., 1983, Transylvania U., 1983, Berea Coll., 1984; L.L.D., Tusculum Coll., 1987. Dir. youth work Methodist Commn. World Peace, 1943-44; relief worker Am. Friends Service Com., Europe, 1944-47; asst. prof. econs. Swarthmore Coll., 1948-54, asso. prof., 1954-64; acad. dean Carleton Coll., 1965-67; pres. Berea Coll., Ky., 1967-84; pres. emeritus, asst. to pres. Berea Coll., 1984-91. Author: Geographic Differentials in Agricultural Wages, 1957; co-author: Economies of the World Today, 1962, 65, 76; contbg. author: Labor in Developing Countries, 1962; Editor: The Goals of Higher Education, 1960. Rural devel. specialist Am. Friends Svc. Com., India, 1950-51, UN, Malaya, 1959-60, Rotary Club, India, 1993; bd. chmn. Pine Mountain Settlement Sch., 1967-84; pres. Black Mountain Pairing Project, 1988-89, 92-93; bd. dirs. Frontier Nursing Svc., Warren Wilson Coll., Blue Ridge YMCA Assembly N.C., The Morgan Sch., Black Mountain Rotary Club. Recepient Chevalier de la Santé Publique award by French government, 1946; Ford Found. fellow India, 1954-55. Mem. Am. Econ. Assn., Assn. Asian Studies, AAUP (pres. chpt. 1965), Grace Episcopal Ch., Phi Beta Kappa, Omicron Delta Kappa, Phi Kappa Phi. Address: 1 Briar Branch Rd Black Mountain NC 28711

WEATHERFORD-BATMAN, MARY VIRGINIA, rehabilitation counselor, educator; b. St. Louis, Mar. 28; d. John Ely and Virginia Louise (Cox) Weatherford; m. Aug. 28, 1965 (div. Jan. 1976); 1 child, Christopher James Batman. Cert. med. technologist, Jackson Meml. Hosp., Miami, Fla., 1966; BS, Barry U., 1984, MBA, 1986, EdS, 1992; postgrad., Union Inst. Cert. rehab. counselor, case mgr., hypnotherapist. Crossmatch technologist John Elliott Blood Bank, Miami, 1966-68; nurse D. E. Fortner MD, P.A. Gutlohn MD, Miami, 1969-75; allergy technologist Dadeland Allergy, Ear, Nose and Throat Assocs., Miami, 1975-78; tech. mgr. Morris Beck MD, Miami, 1978-86; sales rep. Glaxo, Inc., Research Triangle Park, N.C., 1987-88; med. ctr. specialist Wyeth Ayerst, Phila., 1988-90; hosp. rep. Allen & Hanburys, Div. Glaxo, Inc., Research Triangle Park, 1990; sales cons. Profl. Detailing Network, Princeton, N.J., 1991—; adj. prof. Union Inst., Miami, 1993—; chief psychology intern Miami Heart Inst., 1994-95; adj. prof. Union Inst., 1993—; rehab. counselor Nat. Health & Rehab. Cons., Inc., Miami, 1991-94; therapist Ctrs. for Psychol. Growth, 1994; chief psychology intern Miami Heart Inst., 1994-95. Vocat. devel. vol. Jackson Meml. Hosp., U. Miami, 1991—; vol. Crippled Children's Soc., Miami, 1968-69, South Miami Hosp., 1959-63. Recipient award DAR, 1962; Training scholar NIH, 1962, Lucille Funk Keely Trust scholar, 1991. Mem. ACA, APA, Assn. for Adult Devel. and Aging, Am. Rehab. Counseling Assn., Fla. Counseling Assn., Fla. Assn. for Adult Devel. and Aging (pres.), Fla. Soc. Med. Technologists, Barry U. Counseling Assn., Miami Parrot Club, Country Club of Coral Gables, Delta Epsilon Sigma. Methodist. Avocations: aviculture, scuba diving, orchid growing, flying. Office: PO Box 141217 Coral Gables FL 33114-1196 Office: PO Box 141217 Coral Gables FL 33114-1196

WEATHERHOLTZ, DONNA BAKER, education educator; b. Savannah, Ga., Dec. 6, 1950; m. Ruben Earnest Weatherholtz III, Dec. 19, 1970; children: Kathern Kinnett, James Earnest. BS in Elem. Edn., Coll. Charleston, S.C., 1980; MEd in Adminstrn. and Supervision, U. Va., 1988; postgrad., Ohio State U., 1993—. Cert. elem. tchr. and prin., Va. Tchr. Charleston County Pub. Schs., 1980-83; adminstr. law libr. U.S. Senate Jud. Com., Washington, 1983-84; spl. asst. Office Intergovtl. & Interagy. Affairs U.S. Dept. of Edn., Washington, 1984-86; asst. prin. Shenandoah County Pub. Schs., Woodstock, Va., 1986-89; grad. teaching asst. Ohio State U., Columbus, 1993-96; bd. govs. S.C. Med. Malpractice Patient Compensation Fund, Columbia, S.C., 1976-83; edn. adv. bd. Shenandoah County Sch. Bd, 1990-92. Mem. nat. exec. com. S.C. Young Reps., Columbia, 1976. Named Outstanding Young Women of Am., 1976, Earl W. Anderson Leadership award, 1994, Campbell Meml. Scholarship Fund in Edn. Adminstrn., 1995, John A. Ramseyer Meml. fellowship, 1995. Mem. Am. Assn. Sch. Adminstrs., Nat. Assn. Elem. Sch. Prins., Nat. Assn. Gifted Children, Am. Ednl. Rsch. Assn., Assn. Faculty and Profl. Women, Univ. Coun. for Ednl. Adminstrn., Phi Detla Kappa. Home: 5815 Woodlawn Gable Dr Alexandria VA 22309 Office: Ohio State U Dept Ednl Theory & Practice 1945 N High St Columbus OH 43210-1120

WEATHERILL, JOHN FREDERICK WILLIAM, arbitrator; b. Oakville, Ont., Can., Aug. 3, 1932; s. John Francis and Elda Evelyn (Stinson) W.; m. Stephanie Goodman, 1957 (div. 1985); children: Timothy, Andrew, Katherine. B.A., U. Toronto, 1954, LLB, 1957; LLM, Harvard U., 1958. Bar: Ont. 1960. Asst. prof. Osgoode Hall Law Sch., 1960-63, U. Western Ont., 1963-64; part-time prof. U. Ottawa, 1975-78; vice chmn. Ont. Labour Rels. Bd., 1964-67; labour-mngt. arbitrator, 1968-89; arbitrator Can. Ry. Office Arbitration and Grievance Commr. , Inco Metals Ltd., United Steelworkers Am., 1968-83; chmn. Crown employees Grievance Settlement Bd., Ont., 1980-84; bd. dirs., adjudicator PSSRB, 1970-86; v.p. Nat. Acad. Arbitrators, 1971-76, bd. govs., 1974-77, chmn., 1971-76, co-chmn., 1986-89, pres., 1995-96, dir. rsch. and edn. found., 1985-89; chmn. Can. Labour Rels. Bd. Author: A Practical Guide to Labour Arbitration Procedure, 1987; contbr. articles to profl. jours. Fellow Chartered Inst. Arbitrators (U.K.), Ont. Labour Mngt. Arbitrators Assn. (past pres.), Internat., Can. Bar Assns., Cercle univ. d'Ottawa. Avocations: reading, music, tennis. Home: 24 Belvedere Cres, Ottawa, ON Canada K1M 2G4 Office: Can Labour Rels Bd, CD Howe Bldg 4th Fl W, 240 Sparks St, Ottawa, ON Canada K1A 0X8

WEATHERLEY-WHITE, ROY CHRISTOPHER ANTHONY, surgeon, consultant; b. Peshawar, India, Dec. 1, 1931; S. Roy and Elfreda (Milward) Boehm, m. Dorian Jeanne Freeman Weatherley-White, Dec. 27, 1961; children: Carl Christopher, Matthew Richard, Larissa Chantal. MA, Cambridge U., 1953; MD, Harvard U., 1958. Surgeon Biomedical Cons., Denver, 1970—; pres., 1992—; chmn. Plastic Surgery Rsch. Coun., 1975-76; pres. Rocky Mountain Assn. Plastic Surgeons, 1973-74; v.p. Am. Cleft Palate Assn. Author: Plastic Surgeru of the Female Breast, 1982; contbr. over 45 articles to profl. jours. Cons. Colo. Biomedical Venture Ctr., Denver, 1993—. Recipient Rsch. award Am. Soc. Plastic Surgery, 1962, 64. Mem. Harvard Club of N.Y., Oxford-Cambridge Club, Denver Country Club, Denver Athletic Club. Episcopalian. Avocations: flying, skiing, scuba diving, archaeology. Home: 100 S Humboldt Denver CO Office: 4500 E 9th Ave Ste 470 Denver CO 80220-3923

WEATHERLY, ROBERT STONE, JR., banker; b. Birmingham, Ala., May 12, 1929; s. Robert Stone and Gladys (Manning) W.; m. Mary Anne Burr, May 1, 1955; children: Robert Stone, III, Henry, William. A.B., Princeton U., 1950; LL.B., Harvard U., 1953, grad. advanced mgmt. program, 1972. Bar: Ala. 1953. Assoc. firm Burr, McKamy Moore & Thomas, Birmingham, 1955-62; asst. gen. atty. Vulcan Materials Co., Birmingham, 1962-69; v.p. chems. div. Vulcan Materials Co., Wichita, Kans., 1969-71; treas. Vulcan Materials Co., 1971-74, v.p. and controller, 1974-77; pres. metals div. Vulcan Materials Co., Birmingham, Ala., 1977-87, pres. Middle East div., 1982-87; chmn., chief exec. officer Jefferson Fed. Savings, Birmingham, 1987-91; dir. All Seasons Travel, Birmingham, 1991—; disting. lectr.-practitioner U. Ga. Served with U.S. Army, 1953-55. Mem. Nat. Assn. Accts. (cert. mgmt. acct.). Presbyterian. Club: Country of Birmingham, Chattooga (Cashiers, N.C.). Home: 4608 Old Leeds Rd Birmingham AL 35213-1802 Office: All Seasons Travel 120 Office Park Dr Birmingham AL 35223-2422

WEATHERMON, SIDNEY EARL, elementary school educator; b. Abilene, Tex., Jan. 20, 1937; s. Sidney Elliot Weathermon and Evelyn Marie (Landreth) Parker. BA, U. Colo., 1962, MA, 1968, EdD, 1976. Cert. K-12 reading tchr., elem. edn. tchr., K-12 reading specialist. Tchr. Jefferson County (Colo.) Pub. Schs., 1963-66; grades 5-6 tchr. Boulder (Colo.) Valley Pub. Schs., 1962-63, reading tchr., 1968-71, consortium dir. right-to-read project Louisville Mid. Sch., 1974-75, comm. skills program coord. Vocat.-Tech. H.S., 1976, K-12 dist. reading specialist, 1971-85, chpt. 1 tchr. grades 1-6, 1985-89, chpt. 1 kindergarten project coord., 1985-89, grade 1 tchr., 1989—; instr. U. Colo., Boulder, 1971-72, U. No. Colo., Greeley, 1977; adj. faculty Regis U., Denver, 1972—, dept. edn. instr., 1982. Contbr. articles to profl. jours. Recipient Celebrate Literacy award, Boulder Coun. Internat. Reading Assn., 1986, IBM Corp. Tchr. of Yr. award, 1989, Colo./Nat. Educator, Milkin Family Found., 1990; NDEA fellow, 1966-68. Mem. NEA, Internat. Reading Assn., Colo. Edn. Assn., Boulder Valley Edn. Assn. (chair tchr. adv coun., assoc. rep., tchrs. rights and activities commn., negotiations team, profl. leave com.), Phi Delta Kappa (certs. of recognition 1987, 90), Kappa Delta Pi. Democrat. Avocation: Southwest Indian art. Home: 449 S Shore Dr Osprey FL 34229-9657 Office: Martin Park Elem Sch 3740 Martin Dr Boulder CO 80303-5448

WEATHERS, MELBA ROSE, hospital administrator; b. Ladonia, Tex., Mar. 31, 1940; d. E. Carl and Rosa Lee (Evans) W. BSN, Holy Family Coll., 1974; BS, Tex. Woman's U., 1989. Staff/charge nurse maternal and child health St. Paul Med. Ctr., Dallas, 1974-87; rev. coord. Tex. Med. Found., Austin, 1989-95; utilization review mgmt. coord. Marshall (Tex.) Meml. Hosp., 1995—. Mem. Am. Health Info. Mgmt. Assn., VFW Ladies Aux. Roman Catholic. Avocation: collecting nursing memorabilia. Home: 100 Stonecreek Dr #210 Marshall TX 75670-4580

WEATHERS, MILLEDGE WRIGHT, retired economics educator; b. Augusta, Ga., May 11, 1926; s. Robert Edward Lee and Margaret Elizabeth (Johnson) W.; m. Anna-Maria Helene von Bertrab; children: Helene Boehnlein, Martin, Margarete, Banjamin. BA, George Washington U., 1949, MA, 1957; Dr. oec. publ., U. Munich, 1961. Rsch. analyst U.S. Dept. Air Force, Washington, 1951-57, Gen. Electric Co., Santa Barbara, Calif., 1959-62; pvt. practice cons. Munich, 1962-64; cons. Gesellschaft fuer Anlagewerte, Munich, 1964-66; sr. staff analyst Lockheed-Ga. Co., Marietta, 1966-68; prof. econs. Adrian (Mich.) Coll., 1968-91. Contbr. articles to profl. jours. With U.S. Army, 1944-46. Mem. Am. Econs. Assn., Assn. for Evolutionary Econs., Nat. Tax Assn., Economists Allied for Arms Reduction, Kappa Sigma. Avocations: music, walking. Home: 930 Lincoln Ave Adrian MI 49221-3230

WEATHERSBY, GEORGE BYRON, investment management executive; b. Albany, Calif., Dec. 9, 1944; s. Byron and Fannie A. W.; m. Linda Rose Scheirer, June 29, 1979; children: Deborah Jane, Geoffrey Byron. BS, U. Calif., Berkeley, 1965, MS, 1966, MBA, 1967; MS, Harvard U., 1968, PhD, 1970; DHL (hon.), U. San Francisco, 1987; LLD (hon.), U. So. Ind., 1992. Mem. faculty, assoc. dir. analytical studies, dir. Ford Found. rsch. program U. Calif., Berkeley, 1969-72; spl. asst. to U.S. Sec. of State Washington, 1972-73; dir. rsch. Nat. Commn. on Financing Higher Edn., Washington, 1973-74; assoc. prof. mgmt. Harvard U., Cambridge, Mass., 1974-78; commr. higher edn. State of Ind., 1977-83; pres. Curtis Pub. Co., 1983-86, New UPI Inc., Washington, 1985-86; corp. v.p. fin. Ontario Corp., Muncie, Ind., 1986-88, pres., 1988-91, also bd. dirs.; ptnr. Founders Court Inc., Princeton, N.J., 1991-93; independant cons., 1975—; pres. Oxford Mgmt. Corp., 1994—; chmn. bd. dirs. Otis Conner Cos., 1984-86, Curtis Media Corp., 1984-86, Curtis Internat. Ltd., 1985-86, Prince Gardner, Inc., 1991-93, Alma Industries, 1992-93, Hanes Holding Co., 1992-93; bd. dirs. Holnam Inc., Farm Fans Inc., Delta Consol. Industries, Cambridge Parallel Processing, Advanced Retail Mktg. Author: (books) Financing Postsecondary Education in the U.S, 1974, Colleges and Money, 1976; contbr. numerous articles to profl. jours., 1967—; cons. editor: Jour. Higher Edn., 1974—; exec. editor: Change mag., 1980-84. Bd. dirs. Nat. Ctr. for Higher Edn Mgmt. Sys., 1980-83, U.S.A. Group, 1989—; mem. steering com. Edn. Commn. of States, 1978-82; mem. Ind. Com. Humanities, 1981-87; trustee U. So. Ind., 1985-91, Park Tudor Sch. Indpls., 1986-91, Butler U., 1987-93. Calif. Regents scholar, 1963-65; NSF fellow, 1966-67; AEC fellow, 1966-67; Kent fellow, 1967-70; White House fellow, 1972-73; named 1 of 100 Outstanding Young Leaders in Higher Edn. Change Mag., 1978. Mem. Am. Coun. Edn., Ops. Rsch. Soc. Am., Inst. Mgmt. Scis., Econometrica, Young Pres. Orgn. Republican. Office: 660 Madison Ave Fl 18 New York NY 10021

WEATHERSBY, JAMES ROY, lawyer; b. Pine Bluff, Ark., Aug. 28, 1935; s. Willard Alton and Francis (McCormick) W.; children: Jim, Brad; m. Lydia Huber, Jan. 20, 1990. BScE, U. Tenn., 1958; JD, Vanderbilt U., 1964. Bar: Ala. 1965, Tenn. 1965, Ga. 1971, U.S. Dist. Ct. (no. dist.) Ala. 1966, U.S. Dist. Ct. (no. dist.) Ga. 1971, U.S. Dist. Ct. (middle dist.) Ga. 1985, U.S. Dist. Ct. (so. dist.) Ga. 1990. Labor counsel Rust Engring. Co., Pitts., Birmingham, Ala., 1964-70; ptnr. Wilson & Wilson, Atlanta, 1971-76; ptnr., head labor sect. Powell Goldstein Fraser & Murphy, Atlanta, 1976-90; mng. ptnr. Ogletree Deakins Nash Smoak & Stewart, Atlanta, 1991-95; ptnr. Littler, Mendelson, Fastiff, Tichy & Mathiason, Atlanta, 1996—; dep. atty. gen. State of Ga., Atlanta, 1974—; gen. counsel Gen. Assocs. Ga. Associated Builders & Contractors, Atlanta, 1976—; bd. dirs. Kamtech Inc., Glen Falls, N.Y. Mem. ABA, Lawyers Club Atlanta, Ga. Bar Assn., Atlanta Bar Assn. Home: 510 Valley Rd Atlanta GA 30305 Office: Littler Mendelson Fastiff Tichy & Mathiason 1100 Peachtree St Ste 2000 Atlanta GA 30309

WEATHERSTONE, DENNIS, trust company executive; b. London, Nov. 29, 1930; s. Henry Philip and Gladys (Hart) W.; m. Marion Blunsum, Apr. 4, 1959; children—Hazel, Cheryl, Gretel, Richard Paul. Student, Northwestern Poly., London, 1946-49. Sr. v.p. Morgan Guaranty Trust Co. N.Y., N.Y.C., 1972-77, exec. v.p., 1977-79, treas., 1977-79, vice chmn., 1979-80, chmn. exec. com., 1980-86; pres. J.P. Morgan & Co., Inc. (formerly Morgan Guaranty Trust Co. N.Y.), N.Y.C., 1987-90, chmn., chief exec. officer, 1990-95; bd. dirs. GM Corp., Merck & Co., Inc.; mem. internat. adv. council Inst. Internat. Studies. Mem. Assn. Res. City Bankers (bd. dirs.). Office: Morgan Guaranty Trust Co of NY 60 Wall St New York NY 10005-2807*

WEATHERUP, ROY GARFIELD, lawyer; b. Annapolis, Md., Apr. 20, 1947; s. Robert Alexander and Kathryn Crites (Hesser) W.; m. Wendy Gaines, Sept. 10, 1977; children: Jennifer, Christine. AB in Polit. Sci., Stanford U., 1968, JD, 1972. Bar: Calif. 1972, U.S. Dist. Ct. 1973, U.S. Ct. Appeals (9th cir.) 1975, U.S. Supreme Ct. 1980. Assoc. Haight, Brown & Bonesteel, L.A., Santa Monica and Santa Ana, Calif., 1972-78, ptnr., 1979—; judge Moot Ct. UCLA, Loyola U., Pepperdine U.; arbitrator Am. Arbitration Assn.; mem. com. Book Approved Jury Instructions L.A. Superior Ct. Mem. ABA, Calif. Acad. Appellate Lawyers, Town Hall Calif., L.A. County Bar Assn. Republican. Methodist. Home: 17260 Rayen St Northridge CA 91325-2919 Office: Haight Brown & Bonesteel 1620 26th St Santa Monica CA 90404

WEATHERUP, WENDY GAINES, graphic designer, writer; b. Glendale, Calif., Oct. 20, 1952; d. William Hughes and Janet Ruth (Neptune) Gaines; m. Roy Garfield Weatherup, Sept. 10, 1977; children—Jennifer, Christine. B.A., U. So. Calif., 1974; Lic. ins. agt. Freelance graphic designer, desktop pub., Northridge, Calif. Mem. Nat. Assn. Female Execs., U. So. Calif. Alumni Assn., Alpha Gamma Delta. Republican. Methodist. Avocations: photography; travel; writing novels; computers. Home: 17260 Rayen St Northridge CA 91325-2919

WEAVER, ALBERT BRUCE, university administrator; b. Mont., May 27, 1917; s. John B. and Myrtle (Dragstedt) W.; m. Adeline Okerberg, Sept. 1945; children: Janet, Gail, John. Student, Mont. Sch. Mines, 1935-37; AB, U. Mont., 1940; MS, U. Ida., 1941; postgrad., U. Minn., 1941-42; PhD, U. Chgo., 1951. Physicist Naval Ordnance Lab., 1942-45; research asso. U. Chgo., 1952, U. Wash., 1952-54; mem. faculty U. Colo., 1954-58, asso. prof., 1957-58, chmn. dept. physics, 1956-58; prof., head dept. physics U. Ariz., 1958-70, asso. dean, 1961-70, provost acad. affairs, 1970-72, exec. v.p., 1972-83, exec. v.p. emeritus, 1983—. Fellow Am. Phys. Soc., AAAS; mem. Am. Assn. Physics Tchrs., Ariz. Acad. Sci., Sigma Xi. Home: 5726 E Holmes St Tucson AZ 85711-2426

WEAVER, BARBARA FRANCES, librarian; b. Boston, Aug. 29, 1927; d. Leo Francis and Nina Margaret (Durham) Weisse; m. George B. Weaver, June 6, 1951; 1 dau., Valerie S. Clark. B.A., Radcliffe Coll., 1949; M.L.S., U. R.I., 1968; Ed.M., Boston U., 1978. Head libr. Thompson (Conn.) Pub. Libr., 1961-69; dir. Conn. State Libr. Svc. Ctr., Willimantic, 1969-72; regional adminstr. Cen. Mass. Regional Libr. System, Worcester, 1972-78; asst. commr. of edn., state libr. State of N.J., Trenton, 1978-91; dir. R.I. Dept. State Libr. Svcs., Providence, 1991—; lectr. Simmons Coll., Boston, 1976-78. Mem. ALA, R.I. Libr. Assn., Chief Officers State Libr. Agys. Office: State Libr Svcs Dept 300 Richmond St Providence RI 02903-4222

WEAVER, CARLTON DAVIS, retired oil company executive; b. Grantsville, W.Va., May 27, 1921; s. Arley Ezra and Grace (Davis) W.; m. Nancy Mason McIntosh, Mar. 21, 1951; 1 child, Nancy Mason. B.S. Engr. Mines, W.Va. U., 1948. Office engr. E.I. du Pont de Nemours & Co., 1941-42, tech. service rep., 1948-51; with Ashland (Ky.) Oil, Inc., 1951-81, exec. asst., 1960-67, v.p., 1967-72, sr. v.p., 1972-81, group operating officer, 1976-81, pres. Ashland Resources Co. div., 1970-74; chmn. bd. Ashland Coal, Inc., 1981-84, Ven-Black, Inc., 1983-86; chmn. vis. com. Coll. Mineral and Energy Resources, W.Va. U., 1967-80. Served to maj. USMCR, 1942-46, 52-53. Mem. Nat. Coal Assn. (dir.). Home: PO Box 2036 White Sulphur Springs WV 24986-6036 Office: 1409 Winchester Ave Ashland KY 41101-7555

WEAVER, CARRIE ETTA, sales executive; b. Brenham, Tex., Oct. 5, 1935; d. Arthur and Matilda Marietha (Atkinson) Correthers; m. Frank Jay Weaver, July 13, 1956; children: Deborah Lene Weaver Nash, Dianna Lynn Weaver Baronville. AS, Seminole Community Coll., 1978. With Emerson Electric Co., Sanford, Fla., 1976-88; buyer Emerson Electric Co., 1978-86, sr. buyer, 1986-88; beauty cons. Mary Kay Cosmetics, Inc., Winter Springs, Fla., 1982-89, sales dir., 1989—. Chmn. Winter Springs Bd. Adjustment, 1975-80; chmn. adminstrv. com. St. Augustine Cath. Ch., Casselberry, Fla., 1987-89; chmn. pers. policy, bd. dirs. Seminole Cmty. Vol. Program, Sanford, 1988-93, Seminole County Ret. Srs. Vol. Program. Democrat. Avocations: Star Trek memorabilia, reading science fiction, travel, attending Mary Kay seminars.

WEAVER, CHARLES HENRY, business consulting executive; b. Phila., Aug. 10, 1914; s. Charles Henry and Isabel (Walker) W.; m. Louise Schildecker, Sept. 7, 1940 (dec. Nov. 1977); children—Patricia Ann Weaver Tekins, William Schildecker, Peter Charles; m. Lois S. Amper, May 20, 1979. B.S., U. Pa., 1936. With Westinghouse Electric Corp., 1936-79; beginning as trainee, successively sales dept. transp. and generator div., sales engr. marine sect., mgr. marine sect., mgr. marine dept. Westinghouse Electric Corp., Pitts., 1953-55, mgr. marine and aviation sales dept., mgr. ctrl. dist. sales office; mgr. atomic power div. Westinghouse Electric Corp., 1948-55, v.p. charge atomic power activities, 1955-62, group v.p. atomic, def. and space group, 1962-67, v.p. govt. affairs, 1967-71, pres. world regions, 1971-75, exec. v.p. corp. world relations, 1975-79; pres. Pitts. Cons. Group, Inc., 1979—; dir., vice chmn. IEM (S.A.), Mexico, 1973-78. Trustee Moore Sch. Elec. Engring. of U. Pa., also bd. overseers Sch. Engring. and Applied Sci.; chmn. Allegheny County Air Pollution Adv. Com., 1959-67; mem. Coun. on Fgn. Rels., Nat. Fgn. Trade Coun. (past dir.), World Affairs Coun. Pitts. (past pres.), trustee Pitts. Coun. Internat. Visitors; past trustee Bus. Coun. Internat. Understanding; adv. coun. Japan-U.S. Econ. Rels.; past vice chmn. U.S.-Korea; past chmn. U.S.-Yugoslav Econ. Coun., Polish-U.S. Econ. Coun. Recipient order of merit Westinghouse Elec. Corp., 1948; ann. Nat. Transp. award for outstanding contbns. transp. industry, 1955. Mem. IEEE, ASME, Atomic Indsl. Forum (past pres.), Soc. Naval Archs. and Marine Engrs., Am. Nuclear Soc., Nat. Security Indsl. Assn. (past chmn.), Coun. Def. and Space Industry Assn. (past chmn.), Internat. C. of C. (past dir. U.S. coun.), Duquesne Club, Concordia Club, River Forest Country Club. Home: 540 N Neville St Pittsburgh PA 15213

WEAVER, CHARLES HORACE, architect; b. Statesville, N.C., Nov. 11, 1927; s. Lucius Stacy and Elizabeth Roderick (Hallyburton) W.; m. Nancy Jane Veale, June 24, 1955; 1 child, Charles Horace. BA, Wofford Coll., Spartanburg, S.C., 1951; MA, Columbia U., 1956; PhD, U. N.C., 1961. Tchr. English Oak Ridge Mil. Inst., N.C., 1951-54, High Point (N.C.) Cen. High Sch., 1954-56; asst. prin. Ferndale Jr. High Sch., High Point, 1956-58; prin. N.E. Jr. High Sch., High Point, 1959-60, Ferndale Jr. High Sch., High Point, 1960-62; asst. supt. Asheboro (N.C.) City Schs., 1962-65; supt. Elizabeth City (N.C.) pub. schs., 1965-69, Burke County Pub. Schs., Morganton, N.C., 1969-79; with State Dept. Pub. Instrn., Raleigh, N.C., 1979—; asst. state supt. aux. svcs. State Dept. Pub. Instrn., 1989-96; architect Shook Design, Charlotte, N.C., 1996—; bd. dirs. We. Carolina Bank & Trust Co., Wilmington Food Sys., Inc., Greenville Food Sys., Inc. Contbr. articles to profl. ours. Bd. dirs. Burke County United Fund, Burke County Council on Alcoholism, We. Piedmont Mental Health Assn., We Piedmont Symphony. Mem. Am. Assn. Sch. Adminstrs., N.C. Assn. Sch. Adminstrs., Horace Mann League (pres. 1975-76), High Point Jr. C. of C. (bd. dirs.), Burke Country C. of C., Rotary, Asheboro Country Club, Raleigh Capital City Club. Democrat. Methodist. Avocations: reading, golf, antiques.

WEAVER, CHARLES LYNDELL, JR., educational administrator; b. Canonsburg, Pa., July 5, 1945; s. Charles Lyndell and Georgia Lavelle (Gardner) W.; m. Ruth Marguerite Uxa, Feb. 27, 1982; children: Charles Lyndell III, John Francis. BArch, Pa. State U., 1969; cert. in assoc. studies U. Florence (Italy), 1968. Registered architect, Pa., Md., Mo., Va., Mass., Ky. With Celento & Edson, Canonsburg, Pa., part-time 1966-71; project architect Meyers & D'Aleo, Balt., 1971-76, corp. dir., v.p., 1974-76; ptnr. Borrow Assocs.-Developers, Balt., 1976-79, Crowley/Weaver Constrn. Mgmt., Balt., 1976-79; pvt. practice architecture, Balt., 1976-79; cons., project mgr. U. Md., College Park, 1979-80; corp. cons. architect Bank Bldg. & Equipment Corp., Am., St. Louis, 1980-83; dir. archtl. and engring. svcs. Ladue Bldg. & Engring. Inc., St. Louis, 1983-84; v.p., sec. Graphic Products Corp.; pres. CWCM Inc. Internat., 1987—; dir. K-12 Edn. Market Ctr. and sr. program mgr., Sverdrup Corp., 1989-95; prin. Benham Internat. Eurasia, 1995; v.p., dir. mktg. and bus. devel. The Benham Group, St. Louis, 1995—; vis. Alpha Rho Chi lectr. Pa. State U., 1983; vis. lectr. Washington U. Lindenwood Coll., 1987, Wentworth Inst., Boston, Am. Assn. Cost Engrs., So. Fla., 1994; panel mem. Assn. Univ. Architects Conv., 1983. Project bus. cons. Jr. Achievement, 1982-85; mem. cluster com., advisor Explorer Program, 1982-85. Recipient 5 brochure and graphic awards Nat. Assn. Indsl. Artists, 1973; 1st award Profl. Builder/Am. Plywood Assn., 1974; Honor award, 2 articles Balt. chpt. AIA, 1974; Better Homes and Gardens award Sensible Growth, Nat. Assn. Home Builders, 1975; winner Ridgely's Delight Competition, Balt., 1976. Mem. ASCD, BBC Credit Union (bd. dirs. 1983-85), AACE (conv. speaker So. Fla. sect. 1994), Vitruvius Alumni Assn., Penn State Alumni Assn., BOCA, NFPA, Am. Assn. Sch. Adminstrs. (nat. coun., panel moderator 1994), Coun. Ednl. Facilities Planners, Assn. Sch. Bus. Officials (Mehlville Mo. schs. program mgmt. 1992-94, Chelsea, Mass., 1993-95. Orange County, Fla., 1994-95), Alpha Rho Chi (nat. treas. 1980-82, dir. nat. found. treas. 1989—). Office: 1318 Shenandoah Saint Louis MO 63104

WEAVER, CONNIE MARIE, foods and nutrition educator; b. LaGrande, Oreg., Oct. 29, 1950; d. Robert Chesley and Averil Jean (Harris) Shelton; m. Lloyd Rollin Weaver, Dec. 22, 1971; children: Douglas, Mark, Richard. BS, Oreg. State U., 1972, MS, 1974; PhD, Fla. State U., 1978. Teaching asst. Oreg. State U., Corvallis, 1973-74; instr. Grossmont Coll., El Cajon, Calif., 1974-75; rsch. assoc. U. R.I., Kingston, 1975; teaching asst. Fla. State U., Tallahassee, 1975-78, mem. adj. faculty, 1977-78; asst. prof. foods and nutrition Purdue U., West Lafayette, Ind., 1978-84, assoc. prof., 1984-88, prof., 1988—, head, 1991—; rsch. fellow Kraft, Inc., Glenview, Ill., 1988—. Contbr. articles to profl. jours. Mem. Inst. Food Technologists (exec. com. 1991—, Outstanding Svc. and Recognition award Ind. sect. 1984), Am. Chem. Soc., Am. Inst. Nutrition (treas. 1992—), Soc. for Exptl. Biology and Medicine, Sigma Xi, Gamma Sigma Delta. Office: Purdue U Foods-Nutrition Stone Hall West Lafayette IN 47907

WEAVER, DAVID HUGH, journalism educator, communications researcher; b. Hammond, Ind., Dec. 23, 1946; s. David W. and Josephine L. Weaver; m. Gail Shriver, June 28, 1969; children: Quinn David, Lesley Jo. BA, Ind. U., Bloomington, 1968, MA, 1969; PhD, U. N.C., 1974. Copy editor The Post-Tribune, Gary, Ind., 1968; wire editor, reporter The Courier-Tribune, Bloomington, Ind., 1968; wire editor The Chapel Hill Newspaper, N.C., 1973; asst. prof. journalism Ind. U., Bloomington, 1974-78, assoc. prof., 1978-83, prof., 1983-88; Roy W. Howard prof. Ind. U., Bloomington, Ind., 1988—. Author: Videotex Journalism, 1983; co-author: Newsroom Guide to Polls and Surveys, 1980, 90, Media Agenda-Setting, 1981, The American Journalist, 1986 (award Soc. Profl. Journalists 1987), 2d edit., 1991, The Formation of Campaign Agendas, 1991, Contemporary Public Opinion, 1991, The American Journalist in the 1990's, 1996. Lt. U.S. Army, 1969-71. Fellow Midwest Assn. Pub. Opinion Rsch. (pres. 1986-87); mem. Assn. for Edn. in Journalism and Mass Comm. (pres. 1987-88, Krieghbaum award 1983), Soc. Profl. Journalists, Internat. Comm. Assn. Avocations: guitar, music. Office: Ind U Sch of Journalism Ernie Pyle Hall Bloomington IN 47405-6201

WEAVER, DELBERT ALLEN, lawyer; b. Shoshone, Idaho, May 28, 1931; s. Arlo Irving and Kate Rosamond (McCarter) W.; m. Jeanne Carol Alford, June 1959; children: Tobin Elizabeth, Michael Andrew, Matthew Stewart, Edward Malcolm. BA, U. Oreg., 1953, LLB, 1956. Bar: Oreg. 1956, U.S. Dist. Ct. Oreg. 1956, U.S. Ct. Appeals (9th cir.) 1968. Ptnr. Weaver & Oram, Eugene, Oreg., 1956-59; dep. atty. City of Portland, Oreg., 1959-68; assoc. Winfree, Latourette, Murphy, et al., Portland, 1968-71; stockbroker Dupont Glore Forgan, Portland, 1971-73; securities examiner corp. div. State of Oreg., Salem, 1973-75, dep. commr. corp. div., 1975-80; pvt. practice Portland, 1980-87; counsel Schwabe, Williamson & Wyatt, Portland, 1987-90, sr. ptnr., 1991-96; pvt. practice Portland, 1996—. Office: 1207 SW 6th Ave Portland OR 97204

WEAVER, DENNIS, actor; b. Joplin, Mo., June 4, 1924; s. Walter and Lenna Weaver; m. Gerry Stowell, Oct. 20, 1945; children: Rick, Robby, Rusty. BFA, U. Okla., 1948. Appeared on N.Y. stage, 1948-52; appeared in Streetcar Named Desire, Hollywood, Calif., 1953; under contract to Universal Internat., Hollywood, 1952-53, freelance actor, Hollywood, 1953-55; appeared on: TV series Gunsmoke, 1955-64, Kentucky Jones, 1964-65, Gentle Ben, 1967-69, McCloud, 1970-77, Stone, 1980, Buck James, 1985-87, Lonesome Dove, 1994; also Movies of the Week: Duel, 1971, Forgotten Man, 1971, Rolling Man, 1973, Terror on the Beach, 1973, Female Artillery, 1973, Patty Hearst, 1979; spls. Intimate Strangers, 1977, Police Story-A Cry for Justice, 1977, Pearl, 1978, Ishi, 1978, Islander, 1978, Centennial-The Longhorns, 1978, Amber Waves, 1979, The Ordeal of Dr. Mud, 1979, The Day the Loving Stopped, 1981, Don't Go to Sleep, 1982, Cocaine: One Man's Seduction, 1983, Winners Never Quit, 1986, Bluffing It, 1987, Disaster at Silo 7, 1988, The Return of Sam McCloud, 1989, Mastergate, 1991, (pilot) Greyhounds, 1993, "Buffalo Bill" in Lonesome Dovs, the series, 1994-95, (pilot) called "The Wolfe Pack" for CBS, 1996—. Mem. SAG (pres. 1973-75), AFTRA, Dirs. Guild. Office: care Alice Billings PO Box 257 Ridgway CO 81432

WEAVER, DON L., lawyer; b. Inglewood, Calif., Dec. 1, 1951. BA with highest honors, U. Calif., Santa Barbara, 1973; JD, U. So. Calif., 1977. Bar: Calif. 1977. Ptnr. Mayer, Brown & Platt, L.A. Mem. ABA (mem. sect. corp., banking and bus. law, mem. sect. antitrust law), Beverley Hills Bar Assn. (mem. exec. com., chmn. corps. and comml. law sect. 1982), State Bar Calif. (mem. exec. com. bus. law sect. 1987-91, chmn. franchise legislation com. 1986-87), Am. Law Inst. Office: Mayer Brown & Platt 350 S Grand Ave Los Angeles CA 90071-3406*

WEAVER, EDWARD T., foundation executive, educator; b. Beggs, Okla., Dec. 13, 1931; s. Thurmon Wesley and Thelma Cleo (Wright) W.; m. Judith A. DeVliegher; children: Mark E., Kirk B. Student, S.W. Mo. State U., 1958-59; BA, Cen. Bible Coll., Springfield, Mo., 1959; M Social Work, Washington U., 1961; MPA, U. So. Calif., 1981, D Pub. Adminstrn., 1985. Adminstr. Lake Bluff (Ill.) Children's Home, 1961-64; regional dir. Ill. Dept. Children and Family Services, Champaign, 1964-66, Chgo., 1966-68; dir. Ill. Dept. Children and Family Services, Springfield, 1968-72, Ill Dept. Pub. Aid, Springfield, 1971-73; sr. assoc. Booz, Allen & Hamilton, Washington, 1973-74; exec. dir. Am. Pub. Welfare Assn., Washington, 1974-85; v.p. Paramount Communications, Inc. (formerly Gulf & Western Inc.), N.Y.C., 1985-89; pres. Paramount Communications Found., N.Y.C., 1985-91; prof. Henry W. Bloch Sch. Bus. and Pub. Adminstrn. U. Mo.-Kansas City, 1989—; v.p., chief adminstrv. officer Ewing Marion Kauffman Found., 1992—; lectr. U. Ill., Champaign, 1966; vis. prof. Washington U., St. Louis, 1978-85, 90-92; bd. dirs. Independent Sector, Washington, 1987-92; trustee Lois and SamuelSilberman Fund, N.Y.C., 1988-91, Am. Humane Assn., 1990-94, Camp Fire Inc., 1992—, Mid-Am. Care Found., 1991—, Midwest Care Ctrs., Inc., 1995—. Mem. Internat. Council on Social Welfare (asst. treas. gen., treas. gen., v.p.). Presbyterian.

WEAVER, FRANK CORNELL, government agency administrator; b. Tarboro, N.C., Nov. 15, 1951; s. Frank Byrd and Esther (Lewis) W.; m. Kathryn Weaver, Nov. 11, 1980; 1 child, Christina. BSEE, Howard U., 1972; MBA in Mktg., U. N.C., 1976; DSc (hon.), Saint Augustine's Coll., 1995; LHD (hon.), Shaw Divinity Sch., 1995. Asst. sales engr. Westinghouse, Phila., 1972-73; asst. prof. N.C. Ctrl. Univ., Durham, 1975; credit analyst Mellon Bank, Pitts., 1976-77; mktg. mgr., comm. RCA ASTRO-

Electronics, Princeton, N.J., 1977-88; dir. Gen. Dynamics Com. Launch, Washington, 1988-90; pres. UNET Comm., Inc., Ft. Washington, Md., 1990-93; assoc. adminstr. fed. aviation adminstrn. office of comml. space transp. Dept. of Transp., Washington, 1993—; lectr. comm. sattellite sems.; tech. coord. RCA Minorities in Engring. Program, 1977-83; mem. brain trust Congrl. Black Caucas. Contbr. articles to profl. jours. Mem. Dem. Nat. com., Washington, Suburban Md. High Technology Coun. Mem. Wash. Space Bus. Roundtable Space Club (sec., bd. dirs.), Tau Beta Pi. Baptist. Avocation: tennis. Home: 602 Luxor Ct Fort Washington MD 20744

WEAVER, FRANKLIN THOMAS, newspaper executive; b. Johnstown, N.Y., Oct. 11, 1932; s. Edwin K. and Bertha J. (Wendt) W.; children: Thomas, James, Michael, David, Tammy, Kelly, Anna; m. Joyce W. Phelps, Oct. 23, 1991. B.A. with high honors in Journalism, Mich. State U., 1954. Advt. sales rep. Grand Rapids Press, Mich., 1955-64; controller Muskegon (Mich.) Chronicle, 1964-66; mgr. Bay City (Mich.) Times, 1966-73; mgr. Jackson (Mich.) Citizen Patriot, 1973-84, pub., 1984—. Trustee, pres. Ella Sharp Mus. Mem. Newspapers Assn. Am., Mich. Press Assn. (pres. 1991), Greater Jackson C. of C., Jackson Country Club. Office: Jackson Citizen Patriot 214 S Jackson St Jackson MI 49201-2213

WEAVER, FRITZ WILLIAM, actor; b. Pitts., Jan. 19, 1926; s. John Carson and Elsa (Stringaro) W.; m. Sylvia Short, Feb. 7, 1953; children: Lydia Charlotte, Anthony Ballou. Mem. Barter Theatre Va., 1951, 52, Group 20 Players, Wellesley, Mass., 1953, 54, Stratford Shakespeare Festival, 1956, 58, Vancouver Festival, 1961, Phoenix Theatre, N.Y.C., 1959-60, Ednl. TV Channel 13, N.Y.C., 1960, 65; Off-Broadway appearances include Doctor's Dilemma, 1953, The Way of the World, 1954, L'Histoire du Soldat, 1954, Family Reunion, 1958, Power and Glory, 1958, Peer Gynt, 1959, Henry IV, parts I and II; Broadway appearances include White Devil, 1955 (Carence Derwent award), Chalk Garden, 1956, Miss Lonelyhearts, 1957, A Shot in the Dark, 1962, Protective Custody, 1958, All American, 1962, Lorenzo, 1962-63, The White House, 1964, Baker Street, 1965, Child's Play, 1969-70, The Price, 1979, The Crucible; appearances with Am. Shakespeare Festival, 1955, 56, 57, 58, 73, Cambridge Drama Festival, 1960, N.Y. Philharm., 1962; starred in world premiere Sorrows of Frederick, Los Angeles, 1967, Absurd Person Singular, 1975, Lincoln, 1976, Cocktail Hour, 1990, Love Letters, 1989, 90, King Lear, 1991, The Professional, 1995; motion pictures include The Crimson Curtain, 1955, Fail-Safe, 1963, The Guns of August, 1965, The Maltese Bippy, 1969, A Walk in the Spring Rain, 1969, Company of Killers, 1970, The Day of the Dolphin, 1973, Marathon Man, 1976, Demon Seed, 1976, Black Sunday, 1976-77, The Big Fix, 1979, Creepshow, 1983, Power, 1986; numerous TV appearances, including The Borgia Stick, 1967, Berlin Affairs, 1970, Heat of Anger, 1972, The Snoop Sisters, 1972, Hunter, 1973, The Legend of Lizzy Borden, 1975, Captains Corageous, 1977, The Hearst and Davies Affair, 1985, A Death in California, 1985, My Name is Bill W, 1989, Ironclads, 1991, Citizen Cohn, 1992, Blind Spot, 1993. Recipient Antoinette Perry award; Drama Desk award Outer Critics Circle, also Variety. Office: The Gersh Agy 130 w 42nd St Ste 1804 New York NY 10036*

WEAVER, HOWARD C., newspaper executive; b. Anchorage, Oct. 15, 1950; s. Howard Gilbert and Lurlene Eloise (Gamble) W.; m. Alice Laprele Gauchay, July 16, 1970 (div. 1974); m. Barbara Lynn Hodgin, Sept. 16, 1978. BA, Johns Hopkins U., 1972; MPhil, Cambridge U., 1993. Reporter, staff writer Anchorage Daily News, 1972-76, columnist, 1979-80, mng. editor, 1980-83, editor, 1983-95; editor, owner Alaska Advocate, Anchorage, 1976-79; asst. to pres., McClatchy Newspapers, 1995—; internat. co-chair Northern News Svc., 1989-94; disting. lectr. journalism U. Alaska, Fairbanks, 1991. Pulitzer Prize juror, 1988, 89, 94, 95. Recipient Pulitzer prize, 1976, 89, Pub. Svc. award AP Mng. Editor's Assn., 1976, 89, Headliner award Press Club of Atlantic City, 1976, 89, Gold medal Investigative Reporters and Editors, 1989. Mem. Am. Soc. Newspaper Editors, Investigative Reporters and Editors, Sigma Delta Chi (Nat. award 1989), Alaska Press Club (bd. dirs. 1972-84), Upper Yukon River Press Club (pres. 1972). Avocations: ice hockey, foreign travel, opera.

WEAVER, JERRY, entrepreneur, holding company executive; b. 1931. Chmn. bd. Mid South Industries, Inc., Gadsden, Ala., 1964—. Office: Mid South Industries Inc 418 Stone St Gadsden AL 35906*

WEAVER, JO NELL, elementary school educator; b. Dallas, Apr. 22, 1941; d. Robert Glen and Lottie (Harris) Bryant; m. L. Ben Weaver, Sr., June 20, 1963 (div. Mar. 1968); children: Carolyn Cantrell, L. Ben Weaver, Jr. BA, So. Meth. U., Dallas, 1968; MEd, U. North Tex., 1974. Cert. elem. tchr., elem. supr. Tchr. Richardson (Tex.) Ind. Sch. Dist., 1968—. Curriculum writer Delta Edn., Inc., 1984-85; critic reader Silver Burdett & Ginn, 1989. Mem. Sch. Dist. edn. coun., Richardson, Ind., 1994-95; area communication coun. R.I.S.D., 1995-96. Recipient Tex. Congress of Parents and Tchrs. scholarship/grant Tex. PTA, 1974, Ross Perot award for Excellence in Tchg., 1978; named one of Outstanding Elem. Tchrs. of Am., 1975. Mem. Richardson Edn. Assn., North Tex. Reading Assn., Assn. Tex. Profl. Educators, ASCD, TEx. State Tchrs.' Assn., Alpha Delta Kappa. Republican. Baptist. Avocations: travel, photography, reading. Home: 4505 Hanover Dr Garland TX 75042-5131 Office: Richardson Ind Sch Dist 2100 Copper Ridge Dr Richardson TX 75080-2312

WEAVER, LINDA, textiles executive. Chmn. bd. dirs., sec., treas. Diamond Rug & Carpet Mills, Eton, Ga., 1969—. Office: Diamond Rug & Carpet Mills Hwy 411 Eton GA 30724*

WEAVER, LYNN EDWARD, academic administrator, consultant, editor; b. St. Louis, Jan. 12, 1930; s. Lienous E. and Estelle F. (Laspe) W.; m. JoAnn D., 1951 (div. 1981); children: Terry Sollenberger, Gwen, Bart, Stephen, Wes; m. Anita G. Gomez, Oct. 27, 1983. BSEE, U. Mo., 1951; MSEE, So. Meth. U., 1955; PhD, Purdue U., 1958. Devel. engr. McDonnell Aircraft, St. Louis, 1952-53; aerophysics engr. Convair Corp., Ft. Worth, 1953-55; instr. elec. engring. Purdue U., Lafayette, Ind., 1955-58; assoc. prof., then prof., dept. head U. Ariz., Tucson, 1959-69; assoc. dean coll. engring. U. Okla., Norman, 1969-70; exec. asst. to pres. Argonne Univs., Chgo., 1970-72; dir. sch. nuclear engring. and health physics Ga. Inst. Tech., 1972-82; dean engring., disting. prof. Auburn (Ala.) U., 1982-87; pres. Fla. Inst. Tech., Melbourne, 1987—; cons. Ga. Power; bd. dirs. Oak Ridge Associated Univs., 1984-87, DBA Systems, Inc., Melbourne, Fla.; chmn. pub. affairs coun. Am. Assn. Engring. Socs., Washington, 1984-87; bd. advisors Ctr. for Sci., Tech. & Media, Washington. Author: (textbook) Reactor Dynamics & Control, State Space Techniques, 1968; exec. editor Annals of Nuclear Energy; contbr. numerous articles to tech. jours. U.S. rep. World Fedn., Engring. Orgn. Energy Com., 1981-86. Served to lt. USAF, 1951-53. Recipient Mo. Honors award for disting. svc. in engring., 1995. Fellow Am. Nuclear Soc.; mem. IEEE (sr.), Am. Soc. Engring. Edn., Sigma Xi. Republican. Roman Catholic. Club: Eau Gallie Yacht. Avocations: tennis, jogging. Office: Fla Inst Tech 150 W University Blvd Melbourne FL 32901-6988

WEAVER, MARGUERITE MCKINNIE (PEGGY WEAVER), plantation owner; b. Jackson, Tenn., June 7, 1925; d. Franklin Allen and Mary Alice (Caradine) McKinnie; children: Elizabeth Lynn, Thomas Jackson III, Franklin A. McKinnie. Student, U. Colo., 1943-45, Am. Acad. Dramatic Arts, 1945-46, S. Meisner's Profl. Classes, 1949, Oxford U., 1990, 91. Actress, 1946-52; mem. staff Mus. Modern Art, N.Y.C., 1949-50; journalist radio sta. WTJS-AM-FM, Jackson, Tenn., 1952-55; editor, radio/TV Jackson Sun Newspaper, 1952-55; columnist Bolivar (Tenn.) Bulletin-Times, 1986—; chmn. Ho. of Reps. of Old Line Dist., Hardeman County, Tenn., 1985-91, 94—. Founder Paris-Henry County (Tenn.) Arts Coun., 1965; pres. Assn. Preservation of Tenn. Antiquities, Hardeman County chpt., 1991-95; charter mem. adv. bd. Tenn. Arts Commn., Nashville, 1967-74, Tenn. Performing Arts Ctr., Nashville, 1972—; chmn. Tenn. Libr. Assn., Nashville, 1973-74; regional chmn. Opera Memphis, 1979-91; mem. nat. coun. Met. Opera, N.Y.C., 1980-92, Tenn. Bicentennial Com., Hardeman County, 1993—. Mem. DAR, Nat. Soc. Colonial Dames Am. (treas. Memphis chpt. 1996—), Am. Women i Radio and TV, Jackson Golf and Country, English Speaking Union (London chpt.), Summit (Memphis), Dilettantes (Memphis). Methodist. Avocations: horseback riding, travel, theatre.

WEAVER, MICHAEL JAMES, lawyer; b. Bakersfield, Calif., Feb. 11, 1946; s. Kenneth James and Elsa Hope (Rogers) W.; m. Valerie Scott, Sept. 2, 1966; children: Christopher James, Brett Michael, Karen Ashley. AB, Calif. State U., Long Beach, 1968; JD magna cum laude, U. San Diego, 1973. Bar: Calif., 1973, U.S. Dist. Ct. (so. dist.) Calif. 1973, U.S. Ct. Appeals (9th cir.) 1975, U.S. Supreme Ct. 1977. Law clk. to chief judge U.S. Dist. Ct. (so. dist.) Calif., San Diego, 1973-75; assoc. Luce, Forward, Hamilton & Scripps, San Diego, 1975-80, ptnr., 1980-86; ptnr. Sheppard, Mullin, Richter & Hampton, San Diego, 1986—; judge pro tem San Diego Superior Ct.; master of the Bench of the Inn, Am. Inns of Ct., Louis M. Welch chpt.; lectr. Inn of Ct., San Diego, 1981—, Continuing Edn. of Bar, Calif., 1983—, Workshop for Judges U.S. Ct. Appeals (9th cir.) 1990. Editor-in-chief: San Diego Law Rev., 1973; contbr. articles to profl. jours. Bd. dirs., pres. San Diego Kidney Found., 1985-90; bd. dirs. San Diego Aerospace Mus., 1985—; trustee La Jolla (Calif.) Playhouse, 1990-91. Served to lt. USNR, 1968-74. Fellow Am. Coll. Trial Lawyers; mem. San Diego Assn. Bus. Trial Lawyers (founding mem., bd. govs.), San Diego Def. Lawyers Assn. (dir.), Am. Arbitration Assn., 9th Cir. Jud. Conf. (del. 1987-90), Safari Club Internat. (San Diego chpt.), San Diego Sportsmen's Club. Republican. Presbyterian. Avocations: reading, family activities, flying, skiing. Office: Sheppard Mullin Richter & Hampton 501 W Broadway Fl 19 San Diego CA 92101-3536

WEAVER, MOLLIE LITTLE, lawyer; b. Alma, Ga., Mar. 11; d. Alfred Ross and Annis Mae (Bowles) Little; m. Jack Delano Nelson, Sept. 12, 1953 (div. May 1970); 1 dau., Cynthia Ann; m. 2d, Hobart Ayres Weaver, June 10, 1970; stepchildren: Hobart Jr., Mary Essa, Robert. BA in History, U. Richmond, 1978; JD, Wake Forest U., 1981. Bar; N.C. 1982, Fla. 1983; Cert. profl. sec.; cert. adminstrv. mgr. Supr., Western Electric Co., Richmond, Va., 1952-75; cons., owner Cert. Mgmt. Assocs., Richmond, 1975-76; sole practice, Ft. Lauderdale, Fla., 1982-86, Emerald Isle, N.C., 1986-89, Richmond, 1989—. Author: Secretary's Reference Manual, 1973. Mem. adv. coun. to Bus. and Office Edn., Greensboro, N.C., 1970-73, adv. com. to bus. edn. Va. Commonwealth U., Richmond, 1977. Recipient Key to City of Winston-Salem, N.C., 1963; Epps award for scholarship, 1978. Mem. ABA, N.C. Bar Assn., Fla. Bar Assn., Word Processing Assn. (v.p., founder Richmond 1973-75), Adminstrv. Mgmt. Soc. (com. chmn. Richmond, 1973-75), Phi Beta Kappa, Eta Sigma Phi, Phi Alpha Theta. Republican. Home: 12301 Renwick Pl Glen Allen VA 23060-6959

WEAVER, PAMELA ANN, hospitality research professional; b. Little Falls, N.Y., July 7, 1947; d. Floyd Aron Weaver and Norma May (Putnam) Hoyer; m. Ken Ward McCleary, Mar. 2, 1947; children: Brian Wilson, Blake McCleary, Ryan McCleary. AA, Fulton Montgomery Community Co, Amsterdam, NY, 1968; BA, SUNY, 1970; MA, U. S. Fla., 1973; PhD, Mich. State U., East Lansing, 1978. Mem. Mathematics Dept., Riviera Jr. High Sch., Miami, Fla., 1970-72; grad. asst. Office of Med., Edn. Research and Devel., Mich. State U., East Lansing, 1973-74, Dept. of Mktg., Mich. State U., East Lansing, 1974-75; instr. mktg. Mich. State U., East Lansing; asst. prof. mktg., hospitality svcs. adminstrn. Cen. Mich. State U., Mt. Pleasant, 1978-79, Cen. Mich. U., 1982-86; chair acad. senate Cen. Mich. U., Mt. Pleasant, 1985-86, prof. mktg., hospitality svcs. adminstrn., 1986-89; prof. Dept. Hospitality and Tourism Mgmt. Va. Poly. Inst. and State U., Blacksburg, 1989—. Contbr. articles to profl. jours. Recipient John Wiley and Sons award for Lifetime Achievent to Hospitality Industry, 1994. Mem. Coun. on Hotel, Restaurant and Instln. Edn., Acad. Mktg. Sci., So. Mktg. Assn. Office: Va Poly Inst and State U Wallace Hall Blacksburg VA 24061-0429

WEAVER, RICHARD L., II, writer, educator; b. Hanover, N.H., Dec. 5, 1941; s. Richard L. and Florence B. (Grow) W.; m. Andrea A. Willis; children: R. Scott, Jacquelynn Michelle, Anthony Keith, Joanna Corinne. AB, U. Mich., 1964, MA, 1965; PhD, Ind. U., 1969. Asst. prof. U. Mass., 1968-74; assoc. prof. speech communication Bowling Green State U., 1974-79, prof., 1979-96, dir., basic speech communication course, 1974-96; vis. prof. U. Hawaii-Manoa, 1981-82, Bond U., Queensland, Australia, 1990, St. Albans, Melbourne, Australia, 1990, Western Inst., Perth, Australia, 1990. Author: (with Saundra Hybels) Speech/Communication, 1974, 2d edit., 1979, Speech/Communication: A Reader, 1975, 2d edit., 1979, Speech/Communication: A Student Manual, 1976, 2d edit., 1979, Understanding Interpersonal Communication, 1978, 2d edit., 1981, 3d edit., 1984, 4th edit., 1987, 5th edit., 1990, 6th edit., 1993, 7th edit., 1996, (with Raymond K. Tucker, Cynthia Berryman-Fink) Research in Speech Communication, 1981, Foundations of Speech Communication: Perspectives of a Discipline, 1982, Speech Communication Skills, 1982, Understanding Public Communication, 1983, Understanding Business Communication, 1985, Understanding Speech Communication Skills, 1985, Readings in Speech Communication, 1985, (with Saundra Hybels) Communicating Effectively, 1986, 2d edit., 1989, 3d edit., 1992, 4th edit., 1995, Skills for Communicating Effectively, 1985, 2d edit., 1988, 3d edit., 1991, 4th edit., 1993, rev. edit., 1995, (with Howard W. Cotrell) Innovative Instructional Strategies, 1987, 2d edit., 1988, 3d edit., 1989, 4th edit., 1990, 5th edit., 1992, 6th edit., 1993, (with Curt Bechler) Listen to Win: A Guide to Effective Listening, 1994, Study Guide to Accompany Communicating Effectively, 1995, Essentials of Public Speaking, 1996. Mem. Internat. Comm. Assn., Internat. Soc. Gen. Semantics, Speech Comm. Assn., World Comm. Assn., Ctrl. States Speech Assn., Ohio Speech Assn., Internat. Listening Assn., Midwest Basic Course Dirs. Conf., Golden Key, Phi Kappa Phi (Bowling Green Faculty Excellence award 1989). Home and Office: 9583 Woodleigh Ct Perrysburg OH 43551-2669

WEAVER, ROBIN GEOFFREY, lawyer, educator; b. Columbus, Ohio, Aug. 19, 1948; s. Eugene Rudolph and Lois Ann (Banks) W.; m. Valerie Cheryl Waller, June 28, 1980; children: Allyson, Lauren, Meridith. BA, Ohio State U., 1970; JD, U. Mich., 1973. Bar: Ohio 1974, U.S. Dist. Ct. (no. dist.) Ohio 1974, U. S. Ct. Appeals (6th cir.) 1980. Assoc. Squire, Sanders & Dempsey, Cleve., 1973-83, ptnr., 1983—; mem. faculty Nat. Inst. for Trial Adv. Northwestern U., Chgo., 1983—; mem. Ohio Supreme Ct. Bd. of Commrs. on Grievances and Discipline, chair, 1996. With U.S. Army, 1974. Fellow Am. Coll. Trial Lawyers, Internat. Soc. Barristers; mem. ABA, Ohio Bar Assn., Cleve. Assn. Trial Attys. (life), 8th Appellate Jud. Conf., Am. Inns of Ct. (master bencher Cleve. chpt.). Episcopalian. Office: Squire Sanders & Dempsey 4900 Society Ct Cleveland OH 44114

WEAVER, SIGOURNEY (SUSAN ALEXANDRA WEAVER), actress; b. N.Y.C., Oct. 8, 1949; d. Sylvester (Pat) Weaver and Elizabeth Inglish; m. James Simpson, 1984; 1 child, Charlotte. BA in English, Stanford U., 1971; MA in Drama, Yale U., 1974. First profl. theater appearance in The Constant Wife, 1974; other roles in Beyond Therapy, Hurlyburly, 1984, The Merchant of Venice, 1987; films include: Annie Hall, 1977, Alien, 1979, Eyewitness, 1981, The Year of Living Dangerously, 1982, Deal of the Century, 1983, Ghostbusters, 1984, Aliens, 1986 (Acad. award nomination for best actress), Half Moon Street, 1986, One Woman or Two, 1987, Working Girl, 1988, Gorillas in the Mist, 1988 (Golden Globe award 1989), Ghostbusters II, 1989, Alien 3, 1992, 1492: Conquest of Paradise, 1992, Dave, 1993, Death and the Maiden, 1994, Jeffrey, 1995. Office: ICM 8942 Wilshire Blvd Beverly Hills CA 90211*

WEAVER, THOMAS HAROLD, health facility administrator; b. Asheville, N.C., July 21, 1943; s. Thomas Harold and Evelyn (Morris) W.; m. Marsha Va Fossen, Dec. 17, 1982; 1 child, Sallie Jayne. BA, Va. Mil. Inst., 1964; MEd, U. Ga., 1970; MAHA, George Washington U., 1973. Vol. EMS, various locations, 1965-94; mgmt. analyst VA Med. Ctr., Martinez, Calif., 1972-74; health planner VA Ctrl. Hdqs., Washington, 1974-76, sr. health sys. specialist, 1976-79; asst. dir. VA Med. Ctr., Lexington, Ky., 1979; COO, assoc. dir. VA Med. Ctr., Ft. Howard, Md., 1980-82; sr. exec. sys. specialist VA Med. Ctr., Durham, N.C., 1982-85; COO, assoc. med. dir. VA Med. Ctr., Pitts., 1985-89; CEO, med. ctr. dir. VA Med. Ctr., Martinsburg, W.Va., 1989-94; CEO, dir. VA Med. Ctr., Bay Pines, Fla., 1994—; v.p., bd. dirs. Berkeley County Emergency Ambulance Authority, Martinsburg, 1989-94; pres., chmn. bd. Bedington Vol. Fire and Rescue Dept., 1989-93; disting. vis. lectr. W.Va. U., 1992-94; lectr., cons. in field. Contbr. articles to profl. jours. Emergency med. svcs. instr. various locations, 1967-94, W.Va., 1990-94; bd. dirs. Pinellas County EMS Med. Control Bd., 1995-96, Hurricanes and Health Care Consortium, 1994-96. Recipient Nat. Cmty. Svc. award Sec. Vets. Affairs, Washington, 1975, Cert. of Merit, Geico Pub. Svc., Washington, 1985, Spl. Act Commendation award DVA and County Commn. for outstanding actions during cmty. disaster, 1993. Fellow Am. Coll. Healthcare Execs. (Fed. Exec. of Yr. W.Va. chpt. 1994); mem. Nat. Registry EMTs, Rotary. Office: Dept VA Affairs Med Ctr 10000 Bay Pines Bay Pines FL 33504

WEAVER, VELATHER EDWARDS (VAL WEAVER), small business owner; d. Willie and Ethel Edwards; m. Ellerson Weaver; children: Frank Mattox Jr., Terence Mattox, Christopher Williams, Sharon, Shelley, Stephanie. Student, Sonoma State Coll., 1972, U. Calif., Berkeley, 1972; BA, Calif. State U., Hayward, 1973; MBA, St. Mary's Coll., Moraga, Calif., 1989. Coach, counselor Opportunities Industrialization Ctr., Oakland, Calif., 1967-69; tchr. Berkeley Headstart, 1969-70; instr., cons. external degree program Antioch Coll.-West, San Francisco, 1971-74; market analyst World Airways, Inc., Oakland, 1972-75, affirmative action adminstr., 1975-78; cons. A.C. Transit, Oakland, 1982; owner, mgr. Val's Designs and Profl. Svcs., Lafayette, Calif., 1980—; mgr. adminstrn., tng. supr. North Oakland Pharmacy, Inc., 1970—, also bd. dirs.; adv. bd. The Tribune, Oakland, 1982-88. Author RAPRO Self Mgmt. Program, 1985. Program coord., mem. publicity com. Lafayette Arts and Sci. Found., 1982-83; mem. admission bd. St. Mary's Coll. Grad. Sch. Bus., 1990; bd. dirs. Acalanes H.S., Lafayette, 1980-82, Lafayette Elem. Sch., 1975-80; mem. Lafayette Econ. Devel. Task Force, 1994-95; vice chmn. Lafayette Econ. Devel. Commn., 1995—. Mem. Calif. State Pharmacists Assn. Aux. (pres. Contra Costa Aux. 1980, pres. state aux. 1986-88, recognition award 1987), Calif. Pharmacists Polit. Action Com. (appreciation award 1988), Diablo Valley Bus. and Profl. Women (pub. rels. com. 1986-87, best local orgn. award 1987, author yearbook 1987), No. Calif. Med., Dental and Pharm. Assn. Aux. (bd. dirs., com. chair 1975—, pres. elect 1991, pres. 1991-93), Internat. Platform Assn., Links, Inc. Avocations: reading, researching family businesses, travel, attending auctions. Office: North Oakland Pharmacy Inc 5705 Market St Emeryville CA 94608-2811

WEAVER, WILLIAM BRUCE, astronomer, research administrator; b. Catskill, N.Y., Sept. 1, 1946; s. William Ray and Bette (Martino) W.; m. Sandra Dale Wilford; children: Cristina Dawn, Robert Bruce Glen. BS, U. Ariz., 1968; MS, Case Western Res. U., 1971, PhD, 1972. Sr. prin. staff mem. BDM, Monterey, Calif., 1973—; astronomer Monterey Inst. for Rsch. in Astronomy, 1972—, pres., 1985-92, 94—, dir. rsch., 1992—, also bd. dirs., 1972-92, 94—. Contbr. articles to profl. jours. Recipient NSF traineeship, 1968-72. Fellow Royal Astron. Soc., Am. Astron. Soc.; mem. Calif. Acad. Sci., Astron. Soc. Pacific, Internat. Astron. Union. Office: Monterey Inst Rsch Astronomy 900 Major Sherman Ln Monterey CA 93940-4633

WEAVER, WILLIAM CHARLES, retired industrial executive; b. Pitts., Nov. 10, 1941; s. Curtis D. and Mary (Yahres) W.; BS in Edn., Indiana U. of Pa., 1963; postgrad. in acctg. Tex. Christian U., 1964-65; m. Karla Lee Kottas, June 13, 1964; children: Michael, Kelli. With Price Waterhouse & Co., Pitts., 1965-73, audit mgr., 1970-73; corp. contr. Kennametal Inc., Latrobe, Pa., 1973-78, v.p., contr., 1978-83, v.p., treas., 1983-86, v.p., CFO, 1987-89; sr. v.p., CFO Oak Industries, Inc., Waltham, Mass., 1990-95; ret., 1995. Trustee, Hampton United Presbyn. Ch., 1972-73; pres. Mountain View Parent Tchrs. Orgn., 1976-77; bd. dirs. East High Acres Civic Assn., 1976-77; treas. Greater Latrobe Hockey Club, 1982-87; chmn. bd. dirs., mem. adv. coun. Jr. Achievement, Latrobe, 1982-85; chmn. bd. trustees Latrob United Way, 1988-89. 1st lt. U.S. Army, 1963-65. CPA, Pa. Mem. AICPA, Pa. Inst. CPAs, Nat. Investors Rels. Inst., Fin. Execs. Inst., MAPI Fin. Coun.

WEAVER, WILLIAM CLAIR, JR. (MIKE WEAVER), human resources development executive; b. Indiana, Pa., Apr. 11, 1936; s. William Clair and Zaida (Bley) W.; m. Janet Marcelle Boyd, Sept. 18, 1963 (div. 1978); 1 child, William Michael; m. Donna June Hubbuch, Feb. 10, 1984. B Aero Engring., Rensselaer Poly. Inst., 1958; MBA, Washington U., St. Louis, 1971; postgrad., Rutgers U.; grad., Armed Forces Indsl. Coll. Registered profl. engr. Engr. aerodynamics N.Am. Aviation, Los Angeles, 1959-60; engr. flight test ops. Boeing/Vertol, Phila., 1963-66; engr. flight test project Lockhead Electronics, Plainfield, N.J., 1966-69; project engr. advanced systems, sr. staff engr. Emerson Electric Co., St. Louis, 1969-72; pres. Achievement Assocs., Inc., St. Louis, 1972—; founder, charter mem. Catalyst, 1978—; speaker in field. Contbr. articles to profl. jours.; author: Winning Selling, 1983, Winning Manager, 1990. Mem. adv. com. Boy Scouts Am., Bridgeton, Mo., 1974. Served to capt. USAF, 1960-63, USAFR. Mem. Nat. Soc. Profl. Engrs.,Am. Soc. Bus. and Mgmt. Cons., Am. Ordnance Soc., Am. Inst. Aeronautics and Astronautics, Assn. MBA Execs., Air Force Assn., Am. Helicopter Soc., Acacia Frat., St. Louis C. of C., Mensa, Beta Gamma Sigma. Republican. Lutheran. Avocations: photography, music, sports. Home and Office: 13018 Ray Trog Ct Saint Louis MO 63146-1802

WEAVER, WILLIAM H., newspaper editor; b. Burlington, Iowa, Oct. 10, 1950; s. William Otis and Margaret (Hall) W.; m. Erin Therese Malloy, June 29, 1974; children: Molly, Michael, Daniel. BA, U. Iowa, 1972. Editor, mgr. Des Moines County News, West Burlington, Iowa, 1972-73; mng. editor Nevada (Iowa) Evening Jour., 1973-75, Centerville (Iowa) Iowegian, 1975-81; editor The Union-Recorder, Milledgeville, Ga., 1981-86; metro editor The Macon (Ga.) Telegraph, 1986-93, asst. mng. editor, 1993—; mem. news coun. Ga. AP, Atlanta, 1987-88. Sec., coach Vine-Ingle Little League, Macon, 1993—; bd. dirs. Miller Mid. Sch., Macon, 1993-94; den leader Cub Scouts, Macon, 1990-91, cubmaster, 1991-93. Mem. Ga. Press Assn. (mem. contest com. 1990, mem. edn. com. 1993-94, chmn. edn. com. 1994-95). Avocations: golf, desktop publishing, woodworking, fishing, camping. Home: 811 Winchester Cir Macon GA 31210-3429 Office: Macon Telegraph Pub Co 120 Broadway PO Box 4167 Macon GA 31201-3444

WEAVER, WILLIAM MERRITT, JR., investment banker; b. Phila., Jan. 7, 1912; s. William Merritt and Frances (Jones) W.; m. Rosemary R. Fine, May 9, 1972; children by previous marriage: Judith (Mrs. Ross Campbell), Patricia (Mrs. Clarence Wurts), Wendy, Alison M. Grad., Phillips Exeter Acad., 1930; BA, Princeton, 1934. Ptnr. Nathan Trotter & Co., Phila., 1934-40; pres., dir. Frank Samuel & Co., Inc., Phila., 1945- 59, Haile Mines, N.Y.C., 1957-58; pres. Howmet Corp., N.Y.C., 1958-65; chmn. bd. dirs. Howmet Corp., 1965-66; ptnr. Alexander Brown & Sons, Balt., 1966-86, ltd. ptnr. emeritus, 1986—; dir. Allen Group, Inc. Served to col. AUS, 1941-45. Decorated Legion of Merit, Bronze Star, Croix de Guerre (France and Belgium).. Mem. Knickerbacker Club, River (N.Y.C.) Club, Lyford Cay (Nassau) Club, Country Club of Fairfield (Southport, Conn.), Phi Beta Kappa. Home: Lazy W Ranch Smith NV 89430

WEAVER, WILLIAM SCHILDECKER, electric power industry executive; b. Pitts., Jan. 15, 1944; s. Charles Henry and Louise (Schildecker) W.; m. Janet Kae Jones, Mar. 7, 1981. BA, Hamilton Coll., 1965; JD, U. Mich., 1968. Bar: Wash. 1968. Assoc. Perkins Coie, Seattle, 1968-74; ptnr. Perkins COIE, Seattle, 1975-91; exec. v.p., CFO Puget Sound Power & Light Co., Bellevue, Wash., 1991—; bd. dirs. Puget Sound Power & Light Co., Hydro Electric Devel. Co., Bellevue. Bd. dirs. Wash. Rsch. Coun., Seattle, 1991—, chmn., 1995—; trustee Seattle Repertory Theatre, 1992-95. Mem. ABA, Wash. State Bar Assn., Seattle Yacht Club, Rainier Club. Office: Puget Sound Power & Light Co PO Box 97034-obc- Bellevue WA 98009

WEAVER, WILLIAM TOWNSEND, laywer; b. Chgo., Sept. 10, 1943; s. William H. and Lorraine (Matthews) W.; m. Nancy Fleming (div.); children: Kristin, Karin; m. Amy L. Sherrard, July 10, 1982; children: Kelsey, Matthew. AB, Stanford U., 1965; JD, U. Calif., San Francisco, 1968. Bar: Ill. 1968, U.S. Dist. Ct. (no. dist.) Ill. 1970. Ptnr. Lord, Bissell & Brook, Chgo., 1970—. With U.S. Army, 1968-70, Vietnam. Mem. ABA, Ill. Bar Assn., Chgo. Bar Assn., Order of Coif., Union League Club (Chgo.). Avocations: skiing, tennis, squash. Office: Lord Bissell & Brook Harris Bank Bldg 115 S La Salle St Ste 3200 Chicago IL 60603-3801*

WEAVER, WILL(IAM WELLER), English educator, writer; b. 1950. Farmer Park Rapids, Minn., 1977-81; with Bemidji (Minn.) State U., part-time writing instr., 1979-81, assoc. prof., 1981-90, prof. English, 1990—. Author: Red Earth, White Earth, 1986, A Gravestone Made of Wheat, 1989, Striking Out, 1993; contbr. articles to profl. publs. Office: Bemidji State U. Dept English Bemidji MN 56601*

WEAVIL, DAVID CARLTON, clinical laboratory services executive; b. Winston-Salem, N.C., Feb. 13, 1951; s. Kenneth George and Dorothy Elvira (Kiser) W.; m. Teresa Ann Houser (div. 1988); children: Heather Leigh, Chelsea Anne, Lucas Alexander, Kendall McKenzie; m. Mila Dicecco, Mar. 2, 1991. BBA, U. N.C., 1974. CPA, N.C. Auditor Peat Marwick Main Co., Greensboro, N.C., 1974-77; treas. Biomed. Reference Labs., Inc., Burlington, N.C., 1977-79, v.p. fin., 1979-82; sr. v.p. fin. Roche Biomed. Labs., Inc. (acquired by Hoffmann-LaRoche Inc.), Burlington, 1982-87; sr. v.p. ops. Roche Biomed Labs., Inc., Burlington, 1988-89; chief oper. officer, sr. v.p. Roche Biomed. Labs., Inc. (acquired by Hoffman-LaRoche), Burlington, 1989-95; COO, exec. v.p. Lab. Corp. Am., Inc., Burlington, 1995—. Bd. dirs. YMCA, Burlington, 1984—; treas./sec. T.E. Powell Jr. Biology Found. Elon Coll., N.C., 1978-88; bd. dirs. First United Meth. Ch., Graham, N.C., 1983, 84. Fellow N.C. Assn. CPAs; mem. AICPA, U. N.C. Alumni Assn. (life), Rams Club U. N.C., Beta Gamma Sigma.. Office: Lab Corp Am Inc 430 S Spring St Burlington NC 27215-5865

WEBB, ALEXANDER, III, investment company executive; b. Raleigh, N.C., Aug. 19, 1945; s. Alexander Jr. and Mary (Hall) W.; m. Laura Lee Robinson; children: Alexander IV, William Robinson. BA, U. N.C., 1968; MBA, Columbia U., 1972. Investment analyst First Union Nat. Bank, Charlotte, N.C., 1968-69; investment officer New Eng. Life Ins. Co., Boston, 1972-73; exec. v.p., dir., chief investment officer State Street Research & Mgmt. Co., Boston, 1973-89; pres. Fidelity Mgmt. Trust Co. (Fidelity Investments), Boston, 1990-95, also bd. dirs.; vice chmn., chief investment officer The Boston Co. Asset Mgmt. Inc., 1995—; adv. com. Investment Counseling, Inc., 1995—. Investment com. Soc. Preservation New England Antiquities. Mem. Boston Security Analysts Soc., Fin. Anaylsts Fedn. Episcopalian. Avocations: running, hiking. Office: Fidelity Mgmt Trust Co 82 Devonshire St Boston MA 02109-3605

WEBB, ALI, federal agency administrator; b. South Pasadena, Calif.. BJ, Stanford U., 1979; MPA, Harvard U., 1989. Reporter The Eagle, Bryan-College-Station, Tex., 1979; Calif. press sec. Walter Mondale for Pres., L.A., 1984; state press sec. Bradley for Gov., L.A., 1986; press sec. to L.A. mayor Tom Bradley, 1980-87; nat. press sec. Dick Gephardt for Pres., 1987-88; teaching asst., rsch. fellow Barone Ctr. Press, Politics and Pub. Policy Kennedy Sch. of Govt., Harvard U., Cambridge, Mass., 1988-89; instr. polit. comm. Emerson Coll., Boston, 1989; assoc. dir. League of Conservation Voters, Washington, 1989-93; dir. pub. affairs USDA, Washington, 1993—. Home: 9006 Eton Rd Silver Spring MD 20902 Office: USDA Dept Comm 14th & Independence Ave SW Washington DC 20250

WEBB, ANTHONY ALLAN, banker; b. Lincoln, Nebr., May 24, 1943; s. Robert McGraw and Ruth Irene (Good) W.; m. Micheline Touchette, July 10, 1971; children—Annie, Christian. B.A., U. Colo., 1965; B.Internat. Mgmt., Am. Grad. Sch. Internat. Mgmt., 1970. Various positions Royal Bank Can., Montreal and London, 1970-77; assoc. mgr. Royal Bank Can., Toronto, Ont., Can., 1977-80; v.p. Royal Bank Can., Toronto, 1980-83, sr. v.p. merchant banking, 1983-84; dir. gen. Royal Bank Can., Geneva, 1984-88; sr. v.p. personal fin. svcs. Royal Bank Can., Montreal, 1988-93; chmn. Royal Bank Can. Suisse, Royal Bank Can., Channel Islands; pres., CEO Royal Trust, Toronto, 1993—. Served to lt. comdr. USNR, 1965-69. Home: 48 Suncrest Dr, Don Mills, ON Canada M3C 2L3 Office: PO Box 7500 Sta A, Toronto, ON Canada M5W 1P9

WEBB, BRAINARD TROUTMAN, JR., lawyer, distribution company executive; b. Brooklyn, Conn., Feb. 13, 1943; s. Brainard Troutman and Loretta (Dwyer) W.; m. Leigh Wickersham, Apr. 6, 1968; children: Patrick Brewster, Elizabeth Ryan. B.S., Spring Hill Coll., 1965; J.D., Emory U., 1968. Bar: Ga. 1968. Assoc. Tarleton & Zion, Decatur, Ga., 1970-73; corp. counsel Barwick Industries, Inc., Chamblee, Ga., 1973-75; corp. counsel Genuine Parts Co., Atlanta, 1975—, sec. 1984-95, v.p. 1988—. Served to capt. AUS, 1968-70; Vietnam. Decorated Bronze Star, Air medal. Mem. Ga. Bar Assn., Greater Atlanta Corp. Counsels Assn., Lawyers Club Atlanta, Am. Soc. Corp. Secs. Roman Catholic. Home: 7990 Innsbruck Dr Dunwoody GA 30350-4308 Office: Genuine Parts Co 2999 Circle 75 Pky NW Atlanta GA 30339-3050

WEBB, CHARLES HAIZLIP, JR., university dean; b. Dallas, Feb. 14, 1933; s. Charles Haizlip and Marion (Gilker) W.; m. Kenda McGibbon, June 21, 1958; children: Mark, Kent, Malcolm, Charles Haizlip III. AB, So. Meth. U., 1955, MMus, 1955; DMus, Ind. U., 1964; DMus (hon.), Anderson. Coll., 1979. Asst. to dean Sch. Music, So. Meth. U., 1957-58; mem. faculty Sch. Music, Ind. U., 1960—, dean, 1973—. dir. Indpls. Symphony Choir, 1967-81; guest condr. chorus and orch. festivals throughout U.S.; duo-pianist with Wallace Hornibrook in U.S. and Australian tour, 1973; organist First Meth. Ch., Bloomington, 1961—, mem. hymnal revision com. Meth. Ch.; mem. jury Chopin competition; mem. jury internat. piano competitions in Munich, Budapest, South Africa, Paris, Chile, Warsaw, Bolzano, London, Cologne, Japan. Chmn. adv. bd. Internat. Music Festivals, Inc.; mem. Ind. Arts Commn., 1975-83, U.S.-USSR Commn. on Music Performance Edn., Am. Coun. Learned Socs./USSR Ministry of Culture; mem. adv. panel The Music Found.; mem. recommendation bd. Avery Fisher Prize Program; bd. dirs. Busoni Found.; mem. bd. advisors Van Cliburn Internat. Piano Competition; mem. nat. adv. bd. Am. Guild Organists; trustee Indpls. Symphony Orch. With U.S. Army, 1955-57. Decorated D.S.M.; recipient Disting. Alumni award So. Meth. U., 1980, Sagamore of Wabash Gov. award, 1987, 89, Thomas Hart Benton medal Ind. U., 1987, Disting. Alumni award Highland Park High Sch., Dallas, 1989, Ind. Gov. award for arts, 1989. Mem. Ind. Acad., Century Assn. of N.Y., Pi Kappa Lambda, Phi Mu Alpha, Phi Delta Theta. Home: 648 S Woodcrest Dr Bloomington IN 47401-5417 Office: Ind U Sch Music Bloomington IN 47405

WEBB, CHARLES RICHARD, retired university president; b. Berkeley, Calif., Oct. 4, 1919; s. Charles Richard and Adele (McDaniel) W.; m. Andrée Bonno; 1 child, Charles Richard III. AB, U. Calif., Berkeley, 1942, MA, 1944; MA, Harvard U., 1947, PhD, 1949. Faculty San Diego State Coll., 1949-64, prof., 1958-64, chmn. dept. history, 1956-58; dean acad. affairs Stanislaus State Coll., Turlock, Calif., 1964-66; prof. history San Diego State Coll., 1966-70; pres. Eastern Conn. State U., Willimantic, 1970-88; ret., 1988; former assoc. dean acad. planning Calif. State Colls., 1966-69, former dep. state coll. dean acad. planning. Author: Workbook in Western Civilization, 2 vols, 1959, Western Civilization vol. 1 (with Schaefer), vol. 2 (with Palm), 1958, (with Crosby) The Past as Prologue, 2 vols, 1973; contbr. articles to profl. jours. Bd. dirs. Santa Rosa Symphony Assn., New Eng. Program, Windham Meml. Cmty. Hosp., Sea Rsch. Found.; mem. Commn. on Conn.'s Future. With USNR, 1941-45. Mem. AAUP, Am. Hist. Assn., Am. Fedn. Musicians, Nat. Pks. and Conservation, Sonoma Land Trust, Sierra Club, Nature Conservancy, New Eng. Hist. Assn., Assn. Calif. State Coll. Profls. (v.p. 1958-60), Save the Redwoods League, Conn. Employees Assn., Am. Assn. State Colls. and Univs., Phi Alpha Theta, Kappa Delta Pi, Omicron Delta Pi. Clubs: University (San Diego), Commonwealth of Calif., Willimantic Country, Saddle Club, Santa Rosa, Montecito Heights Health & Raquet Club, Santa Rosa. Home: 6495 Timber Springs Dr Santa Rosa CA 95409-5900

WEBB, CLIFTON ALAN, anchorman, writer; b. New London, Conn., Nov. 3, 1950; s. Robert Lee Sr. and June Mildred (Hargrove) W.; m. Jacqueline Diana gales, Oct. 14, 1988; children: Diana Rose, Joanna Joy. BA, So. Conn. State, 1972; postgrad., U. Conn., 1972-73. Lic. radiotelephoner. Announcer Sta. WSUB-AM/FM, Groton, Conn., 1974-78; program dir. Sta. WYBC-FM, New Haven, Conn., 1978-81; prodr. Conn. Radio Network, Hamden, 1981-82; news anchor Nat. Black Network, N.Y.C., 1982-83; editor UPI Radio Network, N.Y.C., 1983-85; correspondent NBC News, Washington, 1985-87; news anchor Media Gen. Cable, Fairfax, Va., 1987-91, News Channel 8, Springfield, Va., 1991—; dir. Wolf Trap Asscs., Vienna, Va., 1990-96. TV reporter Blacks & Koreans, 1992, Teen Moms, 1992, Election Diary, 1994. Spokesman No. Va. Mental health, Fair Oaks, 1994—, Alexandria (Va.) Valor Awards, 1994—, Urban League Ann. Dinner, Alexandria, 1994—. Baptist. Avocations: diving, swimming. Home: 805 W Tantallon Dr Fort Washington MD 20744 Office: Newschannel 8 7600 D Boston Blvd Springfield VA 22153

WEBB, DAN K., lawyer; b. Macomb, Ill., Sept. 5, 1945; s. Keith L. and Phyllis I. (Clow) W.; student Western Ill. U., 1963-66; J.D., Loyola U., 1970; m. Laura A. Buscemi, Mar. 15, 1973; children—Jeffrey, Maggie, Michael, Melanie. Bar: Ill. 1970. Chief spl. prosecutions div. U.S. Atty.'s Office, Chgo., 1970-76; ptnr. firm Cummins, Decker & Webb, Chgo., 1976-79; dir. Ill. Dept. Law Enforcement, Chgo., 1979-80; ptnr. Pierce, Webb, Lydon & Griffin, Chgo., 1980-81; U.S. atty., Chgo., 1981-84; ptnr. Winston & Strawn, Chgo., 1984—; instr. John Marshall Law Sch., 1975—, Loyola U. Sch. Law, 1980—. Vice chmn. Met. Fair and Expn. Authority, 1978—; bd. advisers Mercy Hosp. and Med. Ctr.; mem. Chgo. Council on Arson. Recipient spl. commendation award U.S. Justice Dept., 1975; named 1 of 10 Outstanding Young Chicagoans, Chgo. Jaycees, 1979. Mem. ABA, Ill. Bar Assn., Chgo. Bar Assn., Fed. Bar Assn., Legal Club Chgo., Execs. Club Chgo. Republican. Home: 10020 S Damen Ave Chicago IL 60643-2004 Office: Winston & Strawn 35 W Wacker Dr Chicago IL 60601-1614

WEBB, DONALD ARTHUR, minister; b. Wales, May 4, 1926; came to U.S., 1958; s. Arthur and Emily W.; m. Renee Mowbray, May 18, 1946; children—Cheryl, Marian, Christopher, Alison, Ian. Student, Queen's Coll., Cambridge (Eng.) U., 1944-45; BA, Ohio Wesleyan U., 1960; MDiv, Methodist Theol. Sch. in Ohio, 1963; PhD, Drew U., 1966; postdoctoral, Lincoln Coll., Oxford (Eng.) U., 1969, 72; LLD, Centenary Coll. La., 1991. Ordained to ministry Methodist Ch., 1960. Insp. Brit. Social Services, 1953-58; pastor various chs. Ohio and N.J., 1958-68; dean admissions, asst. prof. theology and lit. Meth. Theol. Sch. in Ohio, 1968-75, v.p. adminstrn., 1975-77; pres. Centenary Coll. La., Shreveport, 1977-91; sr. pastor First United Meth. Ch., Shreveport, 1991—. Author: The Flame and Dusty Miller, 1970, We Hold These Truths, 1960; author: Dostoevsky and Christian Agnosticism, 1971; contbr. articles, revs. to profl. jours. With Brit. Royal Navy, 1945-53. Mem. Shreveport C. of C. (bd. dirs. 1978-80). Home: 5709 Lakefront Dr Shreveport LA 71119-3913 Office: Centenary Coll La 2911 Centenary Blvd Shreveport LA 71104-3335

WEBB, E. PHILIP, retired textile engineer; b. Birmingham, Ala., May 18, 1928; s. Evan Hall and Mary Lee (Hough) W.; m. Mary Ann Pritchett, 1954; children: Phyllis Ann, Rebecca Hough Webb Campbell, Jeffery, Richard. BS in Textiles, Ga. Inst. Tech., 1954, MS in Indsl. Mgmt., 1955. Textile mfr. Callaway Mills, Manchester and LaGrange, Ga., 1954-59; devel. engr. Firestone Tire and Rubber Co., Akron, Ohio, 1959-62, tire and process engr. radial tires, 1962-65, mgr. internat. radial tire engring., 1965-68; sales engr., mgr. water mgmt. Firestone Coated Fabrics Co., Magnolia, Ark., 1968-70, product sales mgr. fuel cells and allied products worldwide, 1970-75, developer of rubber-coated fuel tank for GM Corvette, 1973-75, sales mgr. coated fabrics northern divsn. and internat., 1975-79, sales mgr. Ea. U.S., Can. and all exports, 1979-80, staff prodn., processing, testing and R & D engr., 1980-83; staff prodn., processing, testing and R & D engr. Am. Fuel Cell and Coated Fabric Co., Magnolia, 1983-92, ret., 1992; exec. v.p. TFR Financial Svcs., Magnolia, 1990-93; participant Internat. Conf. London, Rome, Spain and Germany for Radial Tire Devel. and Engring. Program, 1965; served on team NATO, 1974. Asst. scoutmaster Troop 54 Boy Scouts Am., Anchorage, 1947-50; asst. scoutmaster and scoutmaster Troop and Post 24, Manchester, Ga., 1955-56, explorer advisor, 1956-58, explorer, scout commr., 1957-59, instl. rep., 1957-58; asst. scoutmaster, mem. troop com. Troop 50, Akron, Ohio, 1960-70; asst. scoutmaster Troop 49, Magnolia, Ark., 1971-73, scoutmaster, 1973-76, dist. chmn., dist. vice chmn., 1973-76, mem. coun. exec. bd., 1974—, dist. commr., 1976-79, 90-92, fin. chmn., 1977-78; numerous other positions Boy Scouts Am.; chmn. mfg. com. Am.'s Pub. Works Assn. 85th Congress FWPA, 1968-69; deacon Presbyn. Ch., Ohio and Ga., supt. Sunday Sch., Ohio and Ga., asst. supt. Sunday Sch., Ark.; pres. Men of Ch., Ohio, Ark. and Ga.; pres. Couples Club, Ohio; elder, trustee 1st Presbyn. Ch., Magnolia; tchr. Sunday Sch.; Stephen's min. Peachtree Presbyn. Ch., Atlanta, 1995—; mem. various chs. orgnl. coms.; mem. Vols. in Probation, Vols.-in-Drug-Abuse Edn. Program, Ohio and Ark.; mem. adv. bd. Magnolia Adult Drug Edn. Program; mem. DeSoto Area Coun. Exec. Bd., 1971-93; exec. bd. Atlanta Area coun., 1993-94, v.p. camping com., 1993-94; asst. leader Boy Scouts Am. Atlanta group to 1st Russian Boy Scouts Am. Jamboree, Russia, 1994. Staff sgt. USAF, 1946-49, USAFR, 1949-52. Recipient Wood Badge award Boy Scouts Am., 1972, Scouter Trainer award and cert. Boy Scouts Am., 1977, Scouter Key Tng. Recognition award Boy Scouts Am., 1978, Silver Beaver award, 1978, cub scout cub master and dist. cub commr., 1978-90, Man of Achievement award, 1979, Vigil Honor Order of Arrow award, 1980, Dist. Merit award, 1991; recognized for 50 years in scouting as a vol., 1996—, Com. Nat. Jamboree Boy Scouts Am.; recipient Good Neighbor award City of Magnolia, 1993. Mem. Am. Assn. Textile Chemists and Colorists, Nat. Fire Protection Assn., So. Overseers Assn., Soc. Automotive Engrs. (mem. and cons. G9 and AE5 com.), Kiwanis, Jaycees, Rotary, Masons, Toastmasters Internat. (pres. club 151, dist. commr.), Scottish Rite, Akron Rubber Group, Sigma Nu, Alpha Phi Omega (pres., commr. of scouting). Avocations: camping, hiking, tennis, golf, photography. Home: 1631 Willow Way Woodstock GA 30188-4649

WEBB, EMILY, retired plant morphologist; b. Charleston, S.C., Apr. 10, 1924; d. Malcolm Syfan and Emily Kirk (Moore) W.; m. John James Rosemond, Apr. 23, 1942 (div. 1953); 1 child, John Kirk; m. Julius Goldberg, Sept. 9, 1954; children: Michael, Judith. AB in Liberal Arts and Sci. with honors, U. Ill., Chgo., 1968, MS in Biol. Scis., 1972, PhD in Biol. Scis., 1985. Undergrad. fellow in bacteriology Med. Coll. S.C., Charleston, 1952-54; teaching asst. U. Ill., Chgo., 1969-72, 77-84, rsch. asst., 1977; teaching fellow W.Va. U., Morgantown, 1974, instr., 1974-75; rsch. in N.Am. bot. needlework art, 1986—. Author: Studies in Several North American Species of Ophioglossum, 1986; translator Nat. Transl. Ctr., Chgo., 1976; contbr. articles to profl. jours. James scholar U. Ill., 1968-69. Mem. DAR. Democrat. Episcopalian. Avocations: garden design, writing, money management. Home and Office: 1356 Mandel Ave Westchester IL 60154-3433

WEBB, ERMA LEE, nurse educator; b. Hitchcock, Okla., Mar. 16, 1933; d. Edward B. and Annabelle G. (Schnell) Haffner; m. James M. Webb, Apr. 4, 1959; children: Scott, Sandee, Steve. BSN, Union Coll., 1957; MSN, Loma Linda (Calif.) U., 1976. Charge and staff nurse pediatrics and surg. units Porter Meml. Hosp., Denver; dir. LPN program Hialeah (Fla.) Hosp.; asst. prof. Loma Linda U.; assoc. prof. So. Coll. 7th Day Adventists, Orlando, Fla., coord. BS program Fla. campuses. Mem. Fla. Nurse's Assn., Fla. League Nursing, So. Regional Edn. Bd., Sigma Theta Tau. Home: 3233 Holiday Ave Apopka FL 32703-6635

WEBB, EUGENE, English language educator; b. Santa Monica, Calif., Nov. 10, 1938; m. Marilyn Teruko Domoto, June 4, 1964. B.A., U. Calif., Los Angeles, 1960; M.A., Columbia U., 1962, Ph.D., 1965. Asst. prof. Simon Fraser U., 1965-66; asst. prof. U. Wash., Seattle, 1966-70, assoc. prof., 1970-75, prof. comparative lit. and comparative religion, 1975—. Author: Samuel Beckett: A Study of His Novels, 1970, The Plays of Samuel Beckett, 1972, The Dark Dove: The Sacred and Secular in Modern Literature, 1975, Eric Voegelin: Philosopher of History, 1981, Philosophers of Consciousness: Polanyi, Lonergan, Voegelin, Ricoeur, Girard, Kierkegaard, 1988, The Self Between: From Freud to the New Social Psychology of France, 1993. Active Colloquium on Violence and Religion. Mem. Am. Acad. Religion, Phi Beta Kappa. Episcopalian. Home: 6911 57th Ave NE Seattle WA 98115-7834 Office: U Wash Thomson Hall Jackson Sch Intrnat Studies Box 353650 Seattle WA 98195-3650

WEBB, HOWARD WILLIAM, JR., humanities educator, university official; b. Dayton, Ohio, June 23, 1925; s. Howard William and Martha (Brown) W.; m. Joyce Moore Cooper, Nov. 20, 1947; children: Howard William (dec.), Amy Forrest, Sarah Winship. BA, Denison U., 1947; MA, State U. Iowa, 1950, PhD, 1953. Asst. prof. English Central Mo. State Coll., 1953-56, So. Ill. U., Carbondale, 1956-62; assoc. prof. So. Ill. U., 1962-67, prof., 1967-90, dir. grad. studies in English, 1961-67, acting chmn., 1968, chmn., 1968-72, acad. affairs officer on bd. trustees staff, 1974-79, system acad. officer on chancellor's staff, 1979-85, vice chancellor for acad. affairs, 1985-90; interim dir. SIU Press, 1993. Editor: Illinois Prose Writers: An Anthology, 1968; contbr. articles to profl. jours. With USNR, 1943-46. Mem. MLA, Melville Soc. Home: 904 S Oakland St Carbondale IL 62901-2557

WEBB, IGOR MICHAEL, academic administrator; b. Malacky, Czechoslovakia, Nov. 8, 1941; came to U.S., 1952; s. Michael and Josephine (Nash) W.; m. Catherine Lamb (div. 1989); 1 child, Kelly Webb-Lamb; m. Marianne F. Walters, 1990; children: Rebecca Alice, Sarah Elizabeth, Benjamin Oliver. BA, Tufts U., 1963; MA, Stanford U., 1966, PhD, 1971. Asst. prof. English Loyola U. Montreal, Can., 1968-70; asst. prof. English U. Mass., Boston, 1971-77, assoc. prof., 1977-78; chair div. humanities Richmond Coll., London, 1979-86; spl. asst. to pres. Adelphi U., Garden City, N.Y., 1986-87, acting provost, 1987-89, provost, 1989—, sr. v.p., 1992—. Author: From Custom to Capital, 1981, Against Capitulation, 1984. Creative Writing fellow Nat. Endowment for Arts, 1978. Mem. Phi Beta Kappa. Office: Adelphi U Office of Provost Garden City NY 11530

WEBB, JACK M., lawyer; b. Monroe, La., Feb. 23, 1936; s. Sam L. and Lillian Etta (McCowen) W.; m. Diane Adele Waterman, Aug. 22, 1964; children: Julia Lillian Pogue, Kathryn Joy, Samuel Logan. BS in Geology, Centenary Coll. La., 1957; JD, Tulane U., 1960. Bar: La. 1960, Tex. 1962. Atty. Standard Oil Co. Tex., Houston, 1961-66; staff atty. Trunkline Gas. Co., Houston, 1966-71; sr. atty. M.W. Kellogg Co., Houston, 1971-73; sec., asst. gen. counsel Gulf Resources & Chem. Corp., Houston, 1973-78, v.p. govt. rels., adminstrv. asst. to chmn. bd., 1978-82; pres. Jack M. Webb & Assocs., 1983—; U.S. spl. amb. Bolivia, 1985; spl. amb. Finland, 1986, Haiti, 1991, Angola, 1992, Ghana, 1993; hon. consul gen. of Ghana, 1996; bd. dirs. Houston Nat. Bank, Scotia Pacific Holding Co., Employers Indemnity Co. Bd. dirs. U.S. Peace Corps, 1985-86, Nat. Park Found., 1986-92. Capt. U.S. Army, 1960-61. Mem. Tex. Bar Assn., La. Bar Assn., Houston Bar Assn. Methodist. Home: 3434 Locke Ln Houston TX 77027-4139 Office: 2028 Buffalo Ter Houston TX 77019-2408

WEBB, JAMES OKRUM, JR., insurance company executive; b. Cleve., Nov. 25, 1931; s. James Okrum and Bessie Ruth (Eubanks) W.; m. Frankie L. Lowe, Feb. 19, 1954; children: Pamela Ruth, Lisa Suzanne. B.A., Morehouse Coll., Atlanta, 1953; M.B.A. in Actuarial Sci, U. Mich., 1955-57. Actuarial asst. Mut. of N.Y., N.Y.C., 1957-62; asst. to pres., actuary Supreme Life Ins. Co. Am., Chgo., 1962-64; v.p., actuary Supreme Life Ins. Co. Am., 1964-66; asst. actuary Health Care Service Corp. (Blue Cross and Blue Shield), Chgo., 1966-68; asst. v.p. product devel. Health Care Service Corp. (Blue Cross and Blue Shield), 1968-69, v.p. product and project mgmt., 1969-73, v.p. finance, asst. treas., 1973-74, v.p. finance, treas., 1974-75, v.p. corp. planning and devel., 1975-79, sr. v.p. planning and devel., 1979-85; pres., chief exec. officer Effective Data Processing, Inc., Oakbrook Terrace, Ill., 1985-94; pres. Managed Dental Care of Can., Toronto, 1987-94; chmn., pres., CEO Dental Network Am., 1985-94; pres. Village of Glencoe, Ill., 1993—; dir. South Shore Nat. Bank Chgo., 1975-87, Harris Bank Glencoe/Northbrook, 1994—, Harris Bankcorp, 1995—, Harris Bankmont, 1995—, Harris Trust and Savings Bank, 1995—; Mem. Ill. Ins. Adv. Com., 1965-67; mem. Ill. Commn. Urban Area Govt., 1970-72. Mem. Glencoe (Ill.) Sch. Bd., 1970-77, pres., 1976-77; pres. Glencoe Human Relations Com., 1970-71; Bd. dirs., mem. budget and finance com. Mid-Am. chpt. ARC, 1974-75; v.p., mem. exec. com., chmn. devel. com. Chgo. Black United Fund, 1974-76; pres., bd. dirs. Chgo. Caucus; founder, past pres. bd. dirs. Home Investments Fund, 1968—; mem. Gov.'s Commn. on Health Assistance Programs; bd. dirs., v.p. Leadership Coun. for Met. Open Cmtys. Served with C.E. AUS, 1953-55. Mem. Am. Acad. Actuaries (dir., treas. 1975-78), Conf. Actuaries in Pub. Practice (assoc.), Alpha Phi Alpha. Clubs: Economics, Executives (Chgo.). Home: 260 Wentworth Ave Glencoe IL 60022-1932

WEBB, JAMES WILLIAM, food products executive; b. Dayton, Ohio, Apr. 16, 1938; s. Jesse Allen Lucille (Bevan) W.; m. Susan Bay Hayes, Aug. 12, 1961; children: Scott Charles, Julie Elizabeth. BBA, U. Cin., 1960. Mgr. sales Procter & Gamble, Cin., 1961-69, Clorox Co., Oakland, Calif., 1969-80; mgr., v.p. sales, now pres. Challenge Dairy Products, Dublin, Calif., 1980—. Served with U.S. Army, 1961-62. Mem. U. Cin. Alumni Assn. (pres. Bay Area chpt. 1975). Republican. Lutheran. Avocations: tennis, running, bonsai gardening. Home: 204 Via Mantilla Walnut Creek CA 94598-3526 Office: Challenge Dairy Products PO Box 2369 11875 Dublin Blvd B200 Dublin CA 94568-0706*

WEBB, JANE MARIE, lawyer; b. Wellington, Shropshire, Eng., Jan. 14, 1945; came to the U.S., 1969; BA, U. London, Eng., 1966; BA in English summa cum laude, Waynesburg Coll., 1981; JD, U. Pitts., 1984. Bar: Pa. 1984. Law clk. presiding judge Glenn R. Toothman Jr. Greene County, Waynesburg, Pa., 1982-84; assoc. McCall, Stets & Hardisty, Waynesburg, 1984-86; asst. dist. atty. Greene County Dist. Atty.'s Office, Waynesburg, 1986-87; assoc. Nernberg & Laffey, Pitts., 1988-89, Toothman & Toothman, Waynesburg, 1989-91; ptnr., founding mem., shareholder, dir., officer Chambers Webb, P.C., Waynesburg, 1991-96; pvt. practice Waynesburg, 1996—; instr. Waynesburg (Pa.) Coll., 1986—. Editor (legal jour.) The Greene Reports, 1992—; editor, author (newsletter) The Greene Sheet, 1992—. Lt., treas., mem. Morris Twp. Vol. Fire Co., Nineveh, Pa., 1972-81; asst. dir. Greene County Emergency Mgmt. Agy., 1977-79; bd. dirs. Nat. Football League Players Assn.-Greene County Celebrity Golf Classic, Waynesburg, 1995. Mem. NAFE, Pa. Bar Assn. (del. ho. of dels. 1994, exec. com. conf. of county bar leaders 1994—, gov.-at-large bd. govs. 1995—), Greene County Bar Assn., Allegheny County Bar Assn., Xi Psi Epsilon. Avocations: skiing, long distance running. Home: RD 1 Box 192A Graysville PA 15337 Office: 32 Church St Ste 208 Waynesburg PA 15370

WEBB, JERE MICHAEL, lawyer; b. Portland, Oreg., July 28, 1944; s. Jesse F. Webb and Olive Rea (Coble) Chin; m. Judith A. Hartmann, Sept. 11, 1966. AB with distinction, Stanford U., 1966; JD, U. Chgo., 1969. bd. dirs. Oreg. Law Inst., Pacific Rim Computer Law Inst. Law clk. to justice Oreg. Supreme Ct., Salem, 1969-70; with Stoel, Rives, Boley, Portland, 1970—; bd. dirs. Oreg. Law Inst., Pacific Computer Law Inst. Editor Advising Oreg. Businesses, 1994, Marketing and Trade Regulation Law News; contbr. articles to numerous profl. jours. Mem. Oreg. State Bar (bd. govs. 1986-89, chmn. continuing legal edn. com. 1984-85). Home: 5433 SW Vacuna St Portland OR 97219-7260 Office: Stoel Rives & Boley 900 SW 5th Ave Ste 2300 Portland OR 97204-1232

WEBB, JOHN, state supreme court justice; b. Rocky Mount, N.C., Sept. 18, 1926; s. William Devin and Ella (Johnson) W.; m. Martha Carolyn Harris, Sept. 13, 1958; children: Caroline Webb Smart, William Devin. Student, U. N.C., 1946-49; LLB, Columbia U., 1952. Judge Superior Ct., Wilson, N.C., 1971-77, N.C. Ct. Appeals, Raleigh, 1977-86; justice Supreme Ct. N.C., Raleigh, 1986—. Served with USN, 1944-46. Mem. N.C. Bar Assn. Democrat. Baptist. Home: 808 Trinity Dr W Wilson NC 27893-2131 Office: NC Supreme Ct PO Box 1841 Raleigh NC 27602-1841

WEBB, JOHN GIBBON, III, lawyer; b. Flint, Mich., June 1, 1944; s. John Gibbon Jr. and Martha Elizabeth (Sweet) W.; m. Fain Murphey, July 6, 1968; children: Jennifer, Philip, Andrew, Matthew. AB, Davidson Coll., 1966; JD, Vanderbilt U., 1970. Bar: N.Y. 1971, N.J. 1981. Assoc. Curtis, Mallet, Prevost, Colt & Mosle, N.Y.C., 1970-80; gen. counsel, sec. J.M. Huber Corp., Edison, N.J., 1980-95; v.p. J.M. Huber Corp., Rumson, N.J., 1991-95. Lay eucharistic min. Episcopal chs., S.I., N.Y., Milburn, N.J., Rumaon, 1972-80, 89-90; trustee Lunch Break, Red Bank, N.J., 1986-89, pres., 1988-89; chair standing com. on constn. and census Diocese of N.J., 1996—. Named Vol. of Yr., Jr. League of Monmouth County, Red Bank, 1990. Avocations: jogging, tennis.

WEBB, LEWIS M., retail executive; b. 1934. Owner Webb's Texaco Svc., Los Alamitos, Calif., 1960-72; pres. Bargain Rent-A-Car Inc., Cerritos, Calif., 1960—, L.M. Webb & Sons, Inc., Mission Viejo, Calif., 1988—; pres., CFO Webb Automotive Group, Inc., Cerritos, Calif., 1989—; pres. Buick Mart Inc., Cerritos, Cerritos Body Works, Inc., Irvine, Calif., Kit Fit Inc., Buena Park, Calif., Lew Webb's Irvine Toyota, Mr. Wheels Inc., Cerritos. Office: Webb Automotive Group Inc 18700 Studebaker Rd Cerritos CA 90703-5335*

WEBB, LOUIS, automotive company executive. CEO Webb Automotive Group, Irvine, CA. Office: Webb Automotive Group 44 Auto Center Dr Irvine CA 92718

WEBB, MARTY FOX, principal; b. Des Moines, July 15, 1942; d. Joseph John and Jean (Way) Fox; m. Andrew H. Rudolph, Aug. 17, 1963 (div. Jan. 1988); children: Kristen Ann, Kevin Andrew; m. Eugene J. Webb, Nov. 23, 1991. BS, U. Mich., 1964; MEd, Houston Bapt. U., 1982; EdD, U. San Francisco, 1993. Cert. adminstr., Tex., elem. and spl. edn. educator, Mich., Tex. Tchr. spl. edn. Hawthorn Ctr., Northville, Mich., 1964-70; tchr. Bellaire (Tex.) Sch. for Children, 1977-80; dir., owner Ednl. Consulting, Houston, 1979-80; prin. Corpus Christi Sch., Houston, 1980—; cons. Hawthorn Ctr., Northville, 1970-72, Bellaire Sch. for Young Children, 1974-78; instr. Excellence in Edn. Seminars, Galveston, Houston, 1985—; speaker in field. Recipient Elem. Sch. Recognition award U.S. Dept. Edn., 1989-90, Blue Ribbon Sch. award, 1990, Outstanding Doctoral Student award, 1994. Mem. ASCD, Nat. Cath. Edn. Assn., Child Abuse Prevention Network, U. Mich. Alumni. Avocations: reading, flyfishing, camping, exercise, hiking. Home: 3531 Sun Valley Dr Houston TX 77025-4148 Office: Corpus Christi Sch 4005 Cheena Dr Houston TX 77025-4701

WEBB, MICHAEL A., food products executive; b. 1957; s. Erman A. W. With father's grocery store; supr. Tropicana Foods, San Jose, Calif., 1981-83; with Sav Max Foods, Inc., Modesto, Calif., 1983—; pres. Sav Max Foods, Inc., Calif. Office: Sav Max Foods Inc 1101 Sylvan Ave Ste A25 Modesto CA 95350*

WEBB, MYRTLE BAILEY, elementary school reading teacher; b. Balt., Jan. 3, 1943; d. Henry Sailie and Myrtle (Dalton) Bailey; m. Harold Webb, Oct. 6, 1990; 1 child, Michele Elaine Cockrell Rochon. BS with honors, Morgan State U., 1965; MEd, Johns Hopkins U., 1970, cert. advanced studies, 1976; EdD, Temple U., 1982. Elem. sch. tchr. Balt. City Pub. Schs., 1965-67; day care tchr. Balt. Dept. Social Svcs., 1967-69; elem. sch. tchr. Balt. City Pub. Schs., 1969-77, reading specialist, 1977-95; title I facilitator/parent educator, 1995—. Mem. NAACP, Women Power, Nat. Assn. Black Sch. Educators, State of Md. Internat. Reading Assn. (bd. dirs.), Balt. City Coun. Internat. Reading Assn. (pres. elect 1992). Democrat. Roman Catholic. Avocations: reading, writing, walking. Office: Balt City Pub Schs 101 S Ellwood Ave Baltimore MD 21224-2244

WEBB, O. GLENN, farm supplies company executive; b. 1936; married. B.S., U. Ill., 1957; Ph.D., So. Ill. U., 1973. With Growmark, Inc., Bloomington, Ill., 1965—, sec., 1968-72, v.p., 1972-80, pres., from 1980, chmn., 1980—, also dir.; trustee, chmn. Am. Inst. Coop.; dir. St. Louis Farm Credit Banks, Farmers Export Co., Nat. Coop. Refinery Assn., Ill. Agr. Leadership Found.; trustee Grad. Inst. Coop. Leadership. Office: Growmark Inc Box 2500 1701 N Towanda Ave Bloomington IL 61701-2040*

WEBB, O(RVILLE) LYNN, physician, pharmacologist, educator; b. Tulsa, Aug. 29, 1931; s. Rufus Aclen and Berla Ophelia (Caudle) W.; m. Joan Liebenheim, June 1, 1954 (div. Jan. 1980); children—Kathryn, Gilbert, Benjamin; m. Jeanne P. Heath, Aug. 24, 1991. B.S., Okla. State U., 1953; M.S., U. Okla., 1961; Ph.D. in Pharmacology, U. Mo., 1966, M.D., 1968. Diplomate Nat. Bd. Med. Examiners, Am. Bd. Family Practice. Research assoc. in pharmacology U. Okla., 1959-61; research fellow NIH, 1962-66; instr. pharmacology U. Mo., Columbia, 1966-68, asst. prof., 1968-69; intern, U. Mo. Med. Center, 1968-69; family practice, New Castle, Ind., 1969-89, med. dir. VA Clinic, Lawton, Okla., 1989-94, Comanche County Hosp., 1994—; clin. assoc. prof. family medicine U. Okla. Coll. Medicine, 1989—; adj. assoc. prof. pharmacology U. Okla. Coll. Medicine, 1989—; mem. U. Okla. Coll. Medicine Admissions Bd., 1995—; mem. staff Henry County Meml. Hosp., New Castle, 1969-89; guest prof. pharmacy and pharmacology Butler U. Coll. Pharmacy, Indpls., 1970-75; owner, dir. Carthage Clinic, 1975-89; clin. assoc. prof. family medicine Ind. U. Coll. Medicine, 1986-89; county physician, jail med. dir. Henry County, Ind., 1976-89. Bd. dirs. Lawton Philharmonic, 1990-95. Recipient Cert. of merit in Pharmacol. and Clin. Med. Research, 1970; Med. Student Research Essay award Am. Acad. Neurology, 1968. Fellow Am. Acad. Family Physicians, Am. Coll. Physician Execs.; mem. AMA (ann. award recognition 1975—), Ind. State Med. Assn., Am. Coll. Sports Medicine, AAAS, N.Y. Acad. Sci., Am. Soc. Contemporary Medicine and Surgery, Festival Chamber Music Soc. (bd. dirs. Indpls. 1981-87), Mensa, Phi Sigma, Sigma Xi. Clubs: Columbia, Skyline (Indpls.), Country, Kiwanis. Lodge: Elks. Author: (with Blissitt and Stanaszek, Lea and Febiger) Clinical Pharmacy Practice, 1972; contbr. 30 articles to profl. jours. Home: 30 Quail Creek Dr NW Lawton OK 73501-9026

WEBB, PATRICK MCIVOR, artist, educator; b. N.Y.C., July 20, 1955; s. Dwight Willson and Nancy Webb. BFA, Md. Inst., 1976; postgrad., Skowhegan Sch., 1977; MFA, Yale U., 1979. lectr. U. Wis. Oshkosh, 1979-81; asst. prof. Cornell U., Ithaca, N.Y., 1981-83; vis. artist Yale U., New Haven, 1985, Brandeis U., Waltham, Mass., 1988, Mpls. Coll. Art and Design, 1989, St. Mary's Coll., 1990, Truro Ctr. for the Arts at Castle Hill, Princetown Art Assn., 1992, R.I. Sch. Design, 1993, Fla. Internat. U., Miami, Cranbrook, Detroit, 1992, 94; instr. N.Y. Acad. Art, Grad. Sch. in Figurative Art, N.Y.C., 1992-94, Swarthmore Coll., 1996, Pratt Inst., 1995-96. One man show includes Ripon (Wis.) Coll., 1980, Allen Priebe Gallery, 1981, Kendall Gallery, 1985-89, Alpha Gallery, Boston, 1987-95, Capricorn Galleries, Bethesda, 1988, Forum Gallery, Mpls., 1990, Amos Eno Gallery, N.Y.C., 1993, Mercer Gallery, N.Y.C., 1995; two person shows include East End Galleries, 1987-88, Provincetown Group Gallery, 1992, 93, 450 Broadway Gallery, 1994, Tatistcheff-Rogers Gallery, 1995; exhibited in group shows at Forum Gallery, Mpls., 1989, Robert I. Kahn Gallery, 1989-90, Minn. Mus. of Art, 1989-90, AMMO Exhbn. Space, 1989, Provincetown Art Assn. and Mus., 1990, 91, 92, Clocktowner Gallery, Longwood Gallery, 37 Gallery, 1990, 55 Mercer St., 1990, Claude Gallery, 1991, Daniel Quinn Gallery, 1991, Contemporary Realist Gallery, 1993, Marymount Coll., 1993, Open Space Gallery, 1993, Multi Media Gallery, N.Y.C., 1994, Lowe Art Gallery at the Hudson Guild, N.Y.C., 1994, Leslie-Lohman Gay Art Found., N.Y.C., 1995, Warren Street Gallery, Hudson, 1995, Peter Madero Gallery, 1995, Atrium at Park Avenue, N.Y.C., 1995; work represented in permanent collections, Fred Alger & Co., Boston Pub. Libr., Chem. Bank, Horton & Calamifde, N.Y., Houstatonic Mus., Interneuron, Inc., Boston, Glickenhause & Co., Otis Elevator, Pier-Fine Assocs., Queensboro Coll. Mus., CUNY, Michelle Rosenfeld, Inc., Fine Arts, Sharf Mktg. Group, Shearson Lehman, U. Wis.-Oshkosh. Fellowship Art Matters Inc., 1992, Nat. Endowment for the Arts, 1984, 86, 88, Ford Matching grant, 1978, Skowhegan scholarship, 1977; recipient Ingram Merrill award, 1989, 95. Mem. Provincetown Art Assn., Art Group, Artists Equity, Coll. Art Assn. Avocation: running. Office: PO Box 903 New York NY 10011

WEBB, RALPH LEE, mechanical engineering educator; b. Parker, Kans., 1934; m. Sylvia Apple; children: Janet, Laura. BSME (with honors), Kans. State U., 1957; MME, Rensselaer Poly. Inst., 1962; PhD, U. Minn., 1969. Registered profl. engr., Wis. Instr. mech. engring. Kans. State U., 1957; engring. maintenance officer USAF, Nellis AFB, Nev., 1957-59; engr. Knolls Atomic Power Lab., Schenectady, N.Y., 1960-62; mgr. heat transfer rsch. Trane Co., La Crosse, Wis., 1963-77; assoc. prof. mech. engring. Pa. State U., University Park, 1977-81, prof., 1981—; lectr., cons. in field; condr. various workshops. Author: Principles of Enhanced Heat Transfer, 1994; contbr. articles to profl. jours. Recipient Hall-Thermotank gold medal Inst. Refrigeration, 1989; rsch. grantee NSF, 1978-80, 83-86, Dept. Energy, 1979-82, 90-92, Internat. Copper Assn., 1984—, EPRI, 1988-92, Improved Radiators Studies Assn., 1988—, Wolverine, 1988-89, York Internat., 1988-89, 94—, Olin Brass Corp., 1992—, Marlow Industries, 1994—, Showa Aluminum Corp., 1992—, Thermo King Corp., 1994—, LG Electronics, Inc., 1995—. Fellow ASME (chmn. heat transfer divsn., honors and awards com. 1987-90, nat. nominating com. 1983-86, heat transfer divsn. rep. to basic engring. group 1980-86, exec. com. heat transfer divsn. 1976-81, tech. editor Jour. Heat Transfer 1972-76, nat. heat transfer conf. coordinating com. 1972-77, Outstanding Svc. award 1973-76, 82, Heat Transfer Meml. award 1987); mem. AIChE, ASHRAE (tech. editor Heat Transfer Engring. 1978—, Jour. Heat Recovery 1981—, editor-in-chief Jour. Enhanced Heat Transfer 1992—, Jour. Paper award 1985). Office: Pa State Univ Dept Mech Engring University Park PA 16802

WEBB, RICHARD ALAN, physicist; b. L.A., Sept. 10, 1946; married; 2 children. BA, U. Calif., Berkeley, 1968; MS, U. Calif., San Diego, 1970, PhD, 1973. Rsch. assoc. U. Calif., San Diego, 1973-75; from asst. to assoc. rsch. physicist Argonne Nat. Lab., 1975-78; mem., mgr. rsch. staff T.J. Watson Ctr. IBM, Yorktown Heights, 1978-93; Alford Ward chaired prof. semicondr. physics, dept. physics Ctr. Superconductivity Rsch., Univ. Md., College Park, 1993—. Recipient Simon Mem prize, 1989. Fellow Am. Physics Soc. (Oliver E. Buckley condensed Malter Physics prize 1992). Achievements include research in macroscopic quantum tunneling in Josephson junctions at low temperatures, investigations of the Aharonov-Bohm effect and universal conductance fluctuations in very small semiconducting and normal metal rings, measurement of temperature, magnetic field and Fermi Engery dependencies of the conduction process of very small Si MOSFET devices in both insulating and metallic regimes. Office: U Md Dept Physics College Park MD 20742

WEBB, RICHARD C., engineering company executive; b. Omaha, Sept. 2, 1915; m. Virginia; 1 son. B.S.E.E., U. Denver, 1937; M.S.E.E., Purdue U., 1944, Ph.D., 1951. Registered profl. engr., Colo. Traffic engr. Mountain States Telephone and Telegraph Co., Denver, 1937-39; research engr. RCA Labs. Div., Princeton, N.J., 1945-53; pres., founder, tech. dir. Colo. Research Corp. (subs. Carrier Corp.), Syracuse, N.Y., 1956-61; pres., founder. tech. dir. Colo. Instruments, Inc., Broomfield, Colo., 1961-71; pres., gen. mgr. Colo. Instruments div. Mohawk Data Scis. Corp., Utica, N.Y.C., 1971-73; pres. Webb Engring. Co. (name changed to Data Ray Corp.), Boulder, Colo., 1973-85; vis. lectr. U. Colo., 1962-82; prof. elec. engring. U. Denver, 1953-56, Iowa State Coll., 1950. Contbr. articles to profl. jours. Recipient Disting. Engring. Alumnus award Purdue U., 1970, Profl. Achievement award U. Denver Alumni Assn., 1983, Outstanding Elec. Engr. award Purdue U., 1992. Fellow IEEE; mem. Soc. Motion Picture and TV Engrs., Acoustical Soc. Am., Inst. Aerospace Scis., Am. Ordnance Assn., Western Electronics Mfrs. Assn. (past v.p., dir.), Sigma Xi, Tau Beta Pi, Eta Kappa Nu. Patentee in field. Home: PO Box 3078 Estes Park CO 80517-3078

WEBB, RICHARD GILBERT, financial executive; b. Tulsa, May 11, 1932; s. William Leslie and Cora (Kroshus) W.; m. Patricia S. Wagdin, Apr. 13, 1957 (dic. Sept. 1974); children: Catherine, Andrea, Nicholas; m. Judith A. Burke, Jan. 12, 1980; stepchildren: Mara, Karen, Jennifer, Christopher. Student, U. Okla., 1950-52; BBA, So. Meth. U., 1954; MBA, Harvard U., 1956. CPA, Okla. Mgmt. cons. McKinsey & Co., N.Y.C., 1959-61; planning analyst Mobil Oil Co., N.Y.C., 1961-64; sub controller, treas. ITT, N.Y.C., 1964-66; v.p., mgr. corp. devel. Ill. Tool Works, Chgo., 1966-70; v.p. planning, treas., chief fin. officer Interstate Bakers, Kansas City, Mo., 1970-78; v.p., treas., chief fin. officer Gen. Host Corp., Stamford, Conn., 1979-81; v.p., treas., chief fin. officer Grolier, Inc., Danbury, Conn., 1981-89, fin. cons., 1989—; cons. to State Ill., Springfield, 1969; adj. prof. fin. dept. We. Conn. State U., 1984; adv. bd. Conn. Bank and Trust Co., Danbury, 1986-88. Fundraiser, bd. dirs. United Way, Danbury, Conn., 1982-86; bd. dirs. Danbury YMCA, 1983-89, treas., 1985-87, chmn. bd. dirs., 1987-89, chmn. bd. trustees, 1981-91, trustee, 1991—; mem. bd. advisors dept. fin. U. Conn., 1984-88; trustee Conn. Pub. Expenditure Coun., 1986-88. 1st lt. U.S. Army, 1956-59. Mem. AICPA, Okla. Soc. CPAs, Greater Danbury C. of C. (bd. dirs. 1985-89, treas. 1986-88, chmn. bd.dirs. 1988-89), Harvard Club (N.Y.C.). Republican. Avocations: swimming, reading, antiques, golf. Home and Office: 37 Saddle Ridge Rd Pound Ridge NY 10576-1111

WEBB, RICHARD STEPHEN, manufacturing executive; b. Nottingham, Eng., Aug. 3, 1944; came to U.S., 1988; s. Sydney and Kathleen Florence (Day) W.; m. Pamela Anne Fowlds, Sept. 3, 1966 (dec. July 1976); children: Jane, Simon, Elizabeth; m. Anne Hessel, Aug. 19, 1978; children: Clare, Penelope. BSc, U. Sheffield, Eng., 1966, PhD, 1970. Rsch. scientist U. Sheffield, 1966-69; tech. asst. C.E. Ramsden & Co. Ltd., Stoke-on-Trent, Eng., 1969-74; mktg. exec. Magnesium Elektron Ltd., Manchester, Eng., 1974-80, mktg. mgr., 1980-84; bus. devel. mgr. Alcan Aluminium, Mont., Can., 1984-88; bus. mgr. Alanx Products Inc., Newark, Del., 1988-91; pres. Alanx Products Inc., Newark, 1992-95, Lanxide Coated Products (Div. Lanxide Corp.), Newark, Del., 1995—; chmn. Del. Mfg. Alliance, 1993-95, bd. dirs., 1995—. Contbr. articles to profl. jours. Fellow Inst. Materials U.K.; mem. Am. Ceramic Soc., Can. Ceramic Soc., Am. Chem. Soc. Avocations: marathon and road running. Office: Lanxide Coated Products PO Box 6077 1300 Marrows Rd Newark DE 19714-6077

WEBB, RICHMOND JEWEL, professional football player; b. Dallas, Jan. 11, 1967. BA in Indsl. Distbn., Texas A&M. Offensive tackle Miami Dolphins, 1990—. Named NFL Rookie of Yr., Sporting News, 1990, Sporting News All-Pro Team, 1992. Played in Pro Bowl, 1990-93. Office: Miami Dolphins 2269 NE 199th St Miami FL 33180

WEBB, ROBERT KIEFER, history educator; b. Toledo, Nov. 23, 1922; s. Charles Ellis and Melva Marie (Kiefer) W.; m. Patty Bradburn Shull, Dec. 28, 1957; children: Emily, Margaret. A.B., Oberlin Coll., 1947; A.M., Columbia U., 1948, Ph.D., 1951; postgrad., London Sch. Econs., 1949-51. Instr. history Wesleyan U., 1951-53; from asst. prof. to prof. history Columbia U., 1953-70; editor Am. Hist. Rev., Washington, 1968-75; prof. history U. Md. Baltimore County, 1975-89, Presdl. Rsch. prof., 1989-93, acting vice-chancellor for acad. affairs, 1978-79, prof. emeritus, 1993—; vis. professorial fellow Victorian Studies Ctr. U. Leicester, Eng., 1967; mem. Inst. Advanced Study, Princeton, 1982-83; vis. fellow Australian Nat. U., 1986, Humanities Rsch. Ctr. Australian Nat. U., 1996; fellow Ctr. for History of Freedom, Washington U., 1988; assoc. fellow Manchester Coll. Oxford, Eng., 1988—; Sorenson rsch. fellow St. Catherine's Coll. Oxford, 1992; hon. fellow Australian Acad. Humanities, 1995—. Author: The British Working-Class Reader, 1790-1848: Literacy and Social Tension, 1955, Harriet Martineau, a Radical Victorian, 1960, Modern England, from the Eighteenth Century to the Present, 2d edit., 1980, (with Peter Gay) Modern Europe, 1973; editor: bull. AAUP, 1975-78, Academe, 1979-81. Served with AUS, 1943-46. Fulbright scholar, 1950-51; Guggenheim fellow, 1959-60, 73-74, Am. Coun. Learned Socs. fellow, 1966-67; NEH rsch. grantee, 1978-80, 85-88. Democrat. Club: Cosmos (Washington). Home: 3309 Highland Pl NW Washington DC 20008-3234

WEBB, RODNEY SCOTT, judge; b. Cavalier, N.D., June 21, 1935; s. Chester and Aylza (Martin) W.; m. Betty M. Lykken, Aug. 31, 1957; children: Sharon, Crystal, Todd, Wade, Susan. BS, U. N.D., 1957, JD, 1959. Bar: N.D. 1959, U.S. Dist. Ct. N.D. 1965, U.S. Ct. Appeals (8th cir.) 1981. Assoc. Ringsak, Webb, Rice & Metelman, Grafton, N.D., 1959-81; state's atty. Walsh County, Grafton, 1966-74; mcpl. judge City of Grafton, 1975-81; spl. asst. atty. gen. State of N.D., 1970-81; U.S. atty. Dist. of N.D., Fargo, 1981-87, judge U.S. Dist. Ct. N.D., 1987—. Col. JAG, N.D. Army N.G., ret. Mem. N.D. State Attys. Assn. (past pres.). Lutheran. Office: US Dist Ct PO Box 3164 Fargo ND 58108-3164*

WEBB, RONALD WAYNE, hospital administrator; b. Tunica, Miss., Oct. 8, 1953; s. Norris Nall and Ruby Jean (Frazier) W.; m. Annette d'Allemand, Oct. 17, 1981. AS, Phillips County Community Coll., 1973; BS, Ark. State U., Jonesboro, 1975; MBA, MS, U. Mo., 1977. Adminstrv. asst. St. Elizabeth Community Health Ctr., Lincoln, Nebr., 1977-79, v.p., 1979-81; adminstr. Holdenville (Okla.) Gen. Hosp., 1981-85; v.p. St. Anthony Hosp., Oklahoma City, 1985-91; adminstr. Pike County Meml. Hosp., Louisiana, Mo., 1991-94; pres. St. Eugene Cmty. Hosp., Dillon, S.C., 1994—; treas. Task Force on Emergency Med. Svcs., Lincoln, 1979-81; chmn. exhibits com. Midwest Health Congress, 1987-88. Pres. bd. dirs. Lancaster County March of Dimes, Lincoln, 1980-81; bd. dirs. Holy Apostles Episc. Ch., Oklahoma City, 1987-91. Recipient Outstanding Com. Mem. award Boy Scouts Am., Shawnee, Okla., 1985. Fellow Am. Coll. Healthcare Execs.; mem. Ctrl. Okla. Young Adminstrs. Group, Retail Mchts. Assn. (pres. 1983-84), Holdenville C. of C. (pres. 1984-85), Kiwanis (bd. dirs. Holdenville chpt. 1983-85), Rotary. Avocations: camping, running, music. Home: 804 Edgewood Blvd Dillon SC 29536-2616 Office: St Eugene Cmty Hosp 301 Jackson St Dillon SC 29536

WEBB, THEODORE STRATTON, JR., aerospace scientist, consultant; b. Oklahoma City, Mar. 4, 1930; s. Theodore S. and Helen (Klabzuba) W.; m. Cuba Evans, Sept. 2, 1952; children: Theodore S. III, Kelly Elizabeth. BS in Physics, Okla. U., 1951; PhD in Physics and Math., Calif. Inst. Tech., 1955. Engr. Ft. Worth div. Gen. Dynamics, 1955-62, program mgr., 1962-69, dir. aero. tech., 1969-75, v.p. rsch. and engring., 1975-80, v.p. F-16 programs, 1980-89; pvt. practice cons. Ft. Worth, 1989—; engring. adv. bd. U. Okla., Norman, 1983—; mem. aerospace coun. Soc. Automotive Engrs., 1975-81; bd. dirs. Lear Astronics Inc. Bd. mem. Engring. Found. U. Tex., Austin, 1975-81, Found. for Sci. and Engring. So. Meth. U., Dallas, 1974-81, Tarrant County Day Care Assn., Ft. Worth, 1975-80, 89—; All Saints Episcopal Hosp., 1989—, Goodwill Industries of Tarrant Country, 1989—. Mem. AAAS, Am. Phys. Soc., Rivercrest Country Club. Home: 4901 Westridge Ave Fort Worth TX 76116-8222 Office: 6100 Western Pl Ste 901 Fort Worth TX 76107-4679

WEBB, THOMAS EVAN, biochemistry educator; b. Edmonton, Alta., Can., Mar. 4, 1932; came to U.S., 1970, naturalized, 1978; s. Donald John and Sarah Jane (McMinis) W.; m. Ellen Adair Armstrong, Sept. 4, 1961; children: Linda Carol, Sharon Laura. B.S., U. Alta., 1955, M.S., 1957; Ph.D., U. Toronto, 1961. Rsch. assoc. Nat. Rsch. Coun., Ottawa, Can., W. Wis., Madison, 1963-65; 1961-63; asst. prof. biochemistry U. Man. (Can.), Winnipeg, 1965-66; asst. prof. McGill U., Montreal, Que., Can., 1966-70, acting dir. cancer unit., 1969-70; assoc. prof. med. biochemistry Ohio State U., Columbus, 1970-74, prof., 1974—. Contbr. numerous articles on biochemistry of cancer to profl. jours. Grantee NIH/Nat. Cancer Inst., 1970—; fellow Air Force Office Sci. Rsch., 1982. Mem. Am. Soc. Biol. Scientists, Am. Assn. Cancer Research, AAAS, Sigma Xi. Home: 1772 Colhasset Ln Columbus OH 43220-4412 Office: Ohio State U 1645 Neil Ave Columbus OH 43210-1218

WEBB, THOMAS IRWIN, JR., lawyer; b. Toledo, Sept. 16, 1948; s. Thomas Irwin and Marcia Davis (Winters) W.; m. Polly S. DeWitt, Oct. 11, 1986; 1 child, Elisabeth Hurst. BA, Williams Coll., 1970; postgrad., Boston U., 1970-71; JD, Case Western Res. U., 1973. Bar: Ohio. Assoc. Shumaker, Loop & Kendrick, Toledo, 1973-79, ptnr., 1979—, chmn. corp. law dept., 1992-94, mgmt. com., 1994—; dir. Comml. Aluminum Cookware Co., York Oldsmobile, Inc. Coun. mem. Village of Ottawa Hills, Ohio, Divsn. Securities, 1979—, adv. com.; trustee Kiwanis Youth Found. of Toledo, 1982—; dir. Toledo Area Regional Transit Authority, 1989-91; trustee Arts Commn. Greater Toledo, 1993—, exec. com., 1994—, v.p., 1994-96, pres., 1996—; trustee Jr. Achievement of Northwestern Ohio, Inc., 1992—, Lourdes Coll. Found., 1995—. Mem. ABA, Ohio Bar Assn. (corp. law com. 1989—), Toledo Bar Assn., Northwestern Ohio Alumni Assn. of Williams Coll. (pres. 1974-83), Toledo-Rowing Found. (trustee 1985—), Toledo Area C. of C. (trustee 1991—, exec. com. 1993—), Order of Coif, Crystal Downs Country Club, Toledo Country Club, The Toledo Club (trustee 1984-90, pres. 1987-90), Williams Club N.Y. Republican. Episcopalian. Office: Shumaker Loop & Kendrick 1000 Jackson St Toledo OH 43624-1515

WEBB, THOMPSON, geological sciences educator, researcher; b. L.A., Jan. 13, 1944; s. Thompson and Diana (Stimson) W.; m. Joan Moscovitch Webb, Aug. 10, 1969; children: Rosanna, Sarah. BS with honors, Swarthmore Coll., 1966; PhD, U. Wis., 1971. Rsch. assoc. U. Mich., Ann Arbor, 1970-72; asst. prof. geol. sci. Brown U., Providence, 1972-75, assoc. prof., 1975-84, prof., 1984—; vis. prof. U. Wis., Madison, summer 1976; chmn. paleoclimate adv. panel NOAA, 1994; chmn. terrestrial earth sys. history com. NSF, 1996. Author: (book chpt.) Late Quat. Environments of the US, vol. 2, 1983; editor: (book) Vegetation History, 1988 (publ.) Geographie Physique et Quat. v. 39, no. 2, 1985, Global Climates Since the Last Glacial Maximum, 1993. Interviewer Swarthmore Coll., Providence, 1972—, pres. 30th ReunionClass of 1966; sec. Seekonk Land Trust, 1995—. NSF postdoctoral fellow, 1970; vis. fellow Clare Hall, U. Cambridge, Eng., 1977; CIRES fellow U. Colo., Boulder, 1988; Bullard fellow Harvard U., 1995. Fellow AAAS; mem. Am. Meteorol. Soc. Office: Brown U Dept Geol Sci 324 Brook St Providence RI 02912-9019

WEBB, TODD (CHARLES CLAYTON WEBB), photographer, writer; b. Detroit, Sept. 15, 1905; s. Joseph Franklin and Bertha (Hollingshead) W.; m. Lucille Minqueau, Sept. 10, 1949. Student, U. Toronto, Ont., Can., 1924-25. Free-lance photographer Standard Oil, N.Y.C., 1947-48, Marshall Plan, Paris, 1948-52, UN, N.Y.C., Togoland, Ghana, Sudan, Italian Somaliland, Tanganyika, Kenya,, Rhodesia, Zanzibar, 1956-60, Santa Fe, N.Mex., 1961-71, St. Restitut, Provence, France, 1971-74; free-lance photographer Avon, Eng., 1974-75, Bath, Maine, 1975—. Photographer Tex. Homes of 19th Century, 1968, Pub. Tex. Bldgs., 1974, Georgia O'Keeffe: The Artist and Her Landscape, 1986, photos of N.Y.C., 1986, Paris, 1987; author: (Western U.S. history) Gold Strikes and Ghost Towns, 1961, The Gold Rush Trail and the Road to Oregon, 1963; (memoirs) Looking Back, 1991. With USN, 1942-45, PTO. Guggenheim fellow, 1955, 56; NEA grantee for Photography, 1979. Democrat. Mem. Soc. of Friends. Avocation: traveling. Home and Studio: 120 North St Bath ME 04530-2224 also: Betsy Evans Sea View Cape Elizabeth ME 04107

WEBB, VERONICA, fashion model, journalist; b. Detroit, Feb. 25, 1965; d. Leonard Douglas and Marion (Stewart) W. Student, New Sch. Social Rsch., 1983; signed with, Ford Models, Inc., N.Y.C., 1992—. Contbg. editor, columnist Paper Mag., 1989—; contbg. editor features column Interview Mag., 1990—; spokesmodel Revlon, 1992—. First featured on cover of Vogue, 1988. First African-Am. to receive exclusive cosmetics contract. Mem. Lifebeat (bd. dirs. 1994—). Office: NS Bienstalk 1740 Broadway 24th flr New York NY 10019

WEBB, WATT WETMORE, physicist, educator; b. Kansas City, Mo., Aug. 27, 1927; s. Watt Jr. and Anna (Wetmore) W.; m. Page Chapman, Nov., 1950; children: Watt III, Spahr C., Bucknell C. BS, MIT, 1947, ScD, 1955. Rsch. engr., asst. dir. rsch. Union Carbide Metals Co., Niagara Falls, N.Y., 1947-52, 55-61; prof. applied physics Cornell U., Ithaca, N.Y., 1961—, dir. Sch. Applied and Engring. Physics, 1983-88; dir. NIH-NSF Resource Biophysical Imaging and Opto-electronics, 1988—, dir. Biophysics Program, 1991—; NIH scholar-in-residence Fogarty Internat. Ctr. for Advanced Study, 1988-92; mem. adv. panels Materials Adv. Bd., 1958-59, 63-64, NSF, 1974—; co-chair NAS panel on sci. interfaces and tech. applications, Physics Through the 90s, 1983-86. Mem. adv. com. Physics Today, 1991—; assoc. editor Phys. Rev. Letters, 1975-91; mem. editorial bd. Biophysics Jour., 1975-78, mem. publ. com., 1976-83; contbr. 200 articles to profl. jours. Guggenheim fellow, 1974-75. Fellow AAAS, Am. Phys. Soc. (chmn. 1988-89, exec. com. divsn. biol. physics 1975-77, Biol. Physics prize 1991), Am. Inst. Med. and Biol. Engrs. (founding 1992); mem. Nat. Acad. Engring., Biophys. Soc. (mem. coun. 1972-75, 82-85), Nat. Acad. Scis., Am. Soc. Cell Biology, Am. Soc. Gen. Physiology, Optical Soc. Am., Cornell Rsch. Found. (bd. dirs., exec. com. 1983—), Ithaca Yacht Club, Rochester Yacht Club, N.Y. Yacht Club. Achievements include patents in optical instruments, two photon laser microscopy, fluorescent probes, microcrystals, welding technology. Office: Cornell U Clark Hall Ithaca NY 14853

WEBB, WATTS RANKIN, surgeon; b. Columbia, Ky., Sept. 8, 1922; s. Frank Elbert and Susie Josephine (Rankin) W.; m. Frances Luella Cooke, Aug. 19, 1944; children: Andrew Michael, Paul Alan, Harvey Elbert, Gordon Lewis. BA, U. Miss., 1942; MD, Johns Hopkins U., 1945. Diplomate Am. Bd. Surgery, Am. Bd. Thoracic Surgery, Am. Bd. Surg. Critical Care. Intern Barnes Hosp., St. Louis, 1945-48; resident in surgery VA Hosp., Biloxi, Miss., 1946-48; resident in gen. and thoracic surgery Barnes Hosp., 1948-52; chief surgeon Miss. State Sanatorium, 1952-63; instr. surgery U. Miss., 1955-56, asst. prof. surgery, 1956-58, prof., 1958-63; prof., chmn. div. thoracic and cardiovascular surgery U. Tex. Southwestern Med. Sch., Dallas, 1964-70; prof., chmn. dept. surgery SUNY Upstate Med. Center, Syracuse, 1970-77; prof. surgery Tulane U., New Orleans, 1977-93, La. State U., New Orleans, 1993—; chmn. dept. Tulane U., New Orleans, 1977-89. Author: Pulmonary Problems in Surgery, 1974, Surgery in Acute Coronary Problems, 1974, Aneurysms, 1983, Cardiovascular Emergencies, 1986, Atlas of Pulmonary Resections, 1988, (with others) Surgical Management for Chest Injuries, Vol. VII, 1990; editorial bd.: Annals of Thoracic Surgery, 1968-79, Surg. Rounds, 1978-82, Surgery Clinics, 1980-82, Microcirculation, 1983-84, Brit. Jour. Surgery, 1981-89; contbr. over 450 articles to profl. jours. Recipient award Hadassah, 1965, Knockers Soc. Outstanding Tchr. award SUNY Upstate Med. Ctr., 1972, Owl Club Clin. Tchr. of Yr. award Tulane U. Med. Sch., 1978, 86, 88-93, Gloria P. Walsh award for best tchr. in Med. Sch., 1992, Aesculapian Tchr. of Yr. award La. State U., 1995. Fellow ACS, Am. Coll. Chest Physicians; mem. AMA, Am. Assn. Thoracic Surgery, Am. Coll. Cardiology, Am. Fedn. Clin. Research, Am. Heart Assn. (Silver medal 1963), Am. Physiol. Soc., Am. Surg. Assn., Am. Thoracic Soc., Halsted Soc., La. Med. Soc., Orleans Parish Med. Soc., New Orleans Surg. Soc., Societe International de Chirurgie, Soc. Cryobiology, Soc. Thoracic Surgeons, Soc. Univ. Surgeons, Southeastern Surg. Congress, So. Med. Assn., So. Soc. Clin.

Research, So. Surg. Assn. (Shipley medal 1961), So. Thoracic Soc., So. Thoracic Surg. Assn., Surg. Assn. La., Surg. Biology Club II, Internat. Soc. Heart Transplantation, Gulf Coast Vascular Soc., Sigma Xi, Alpha Omega Alpha, Pi Kappa Pi, Beta Beta Beta, Alpha Epsilon Delta. Methodist. Home: 21 Park Island Dr New Orleans LA 70122-1228 Office: La State U Dept Surgery 1542 Tulane Ave New Orleans LA 70112-2825

WEBB, WAYNE EARL, JR., lawyer, engineer; b. East St. Louis, Ill., Apr. 3, 1951; s. Wayne E. and Esther T. (Koesterer) W.; m. Carla J. Lemons, June 24, 1975; children: Jennifer, Casey. BEE, Rice U., 1973; JD, U. Tex., 1976. Bar: Tex. 1976, U.S. Dist. Ct. (so. dist.) Tex. 1980, U.S. Ct. Appeals (Fed cir.) 1982, U.S. Ct. Appeals (5th cir.) 1983, U.S. Ct. Appeals (7th cir.) 1985, U.S. Dist. Ct. (no. and we. dists.) Tex. 1990. Assoc. Pravel, Gambrell, et al, Houston, 1980-84, ptnr., 1984-89; ptnr. Fulbright & Jaworski, Austin, Tex., 1989—. Contbr. articles to profl. jours. Lt. USN JAGC, 1976-80. Mem. Tex. Bar Assn. (intellectual property law sect. 1980-90, sec. 1984), Am. Intellectual Property Law Assn. (chmn. membership com. 1987-89), Houston Intellectual Property Law Assn. (chmn. trademark law com. 1985), Austin Intellectual Property Law Assn. Republican. Avocations: golf, guitar. Home: 603 Las Lomas Dr Austin TX 78746-5493 Office: Fulbright & Jaworski 600 Congress Ave Ste 2400 Austin TX 78701-3248*

WEBB, WELLINGTON E., mayor; BA in Edn. Colo. State Coll., 1964, MA in Edn. Univ. No. Colo., 1970; teacher, 1964-76; elected Colo. House of Reps., 1972, 74, 76; regional dir. HEW, 1977-81, governor's cabinet, 1981-87; elected auditor City of Denver, 1987-91, mayor, 1991—. Chmn. U.S. Conf. of Mayor's Task Forces on Violence, 1993—. Office: Office of Mayor City & County Bldg Rm 350 1437 Bannock St Denver CO 80202-5308*

WEBB, WILLIAM DUNCAN, lawyer, investment executive; b. Dayton, Ohio, Feb. 14, 1930; s. Herbert Henry and Dorothy (Chamberlain) W.; m. Nancy Helen Regester, June 12, 1953; children: Joseph Chamberlain (dec.), Mary Helen, Nancy Katherine, Sarah Elizabeth, Lucy Ellen. AB, U. Mich., 1952, JD, 1956. Bar: Mo. 1956, Kans. 1958, U.S. Supreme Ct. 1969. Assoc. Stinson, Mag, Thomson, McEvers & Fizzell, Kansas City, Mo., 1956-58; sec. Kansas City (Mo.) Power & Light Co., 1960-78, asst. treas., 1969-78, asst. v.p. communications, 1978-79, asst. v.p. fed. affairs, 1979-84; legal counsel Fellowship of Christian Athletes. Mem. city coun. Roeland Park, Kans., 1960-62; chmn. Kansas City Myasthenia Gravis Found., 1965-67; bd. dirs. Boys Club of Kansas City, Mo., 1969-74, Greater Kansas City YMCA, Greater Kansas City chpt. ARC; chmn. bd. councilors Avila Coll., 1969-70; trustee, asst. sec., 1970-89; bd. dirs. Rural Water Dist. # 7, Johnson County, Kans., 1992-94. Mem. Internat. Maine-Anjou Assn. (dir., sec.-treas. 1969-76), Theta Delta Chi, Phi Alpha Delta. Presbyterian. Home: 37000 W 155th St Gardner KS 66030-9617 Office: 7500 College Blvd Ste 225 Overland Park KS 66210-4035

WEBB, WILLIAM HESS, lawyer; b. Scottdale, Pa., Sept. 10, 1905; s. Austin Allison and Gertrude (Hess) W.; m. Marian Elizabeth Wellings, Nov. 26, 1931; children: John M., Patricia Ann (Mrs. Terence S. Small). BS, U. Pitts, 1926, LLB, 1929. Bar: Pa. 1929. Practiced in Pitts., 1929—; sr. ptnr. Webb, Ziesenheim, Bruening, Logsdon, Orkin & Hanson, Pitts., 1948—. Bd. dirs., v.p., treas. Pitts. Opera, Inc.; mem. Pitts. Symphony Soc. Served to lst lt. U.S. Army Res., 1926-34. Mem. ABA (ho. of dels. 1961-65), Am. Intellectual Property Law Assn. (bd. mgrs. 1953-62, pres. 1959-60), Pa. Bar Assn., Allegheny County Bar Assn., Am. Law Inst., Duquesne Club, Univ. Club (Pitts.), Edgeworth Club (Sewickley, Pa.), Allegheny Country Club, Delta Theta Phi, Theta Chi. Home: 201 Grant St Apt 305 Sewickley PA 15143-1337 Office: Webb Ziesenheim Bruening Logsdon Orkin & Hanson 436 7th Ave Pittsburgh PA 15219-1818

WEBB, WILLIAM JOHN, public relations counsel; b. Chgo., Jan. 9, 1922; s. Archibald Roy and Nina Spencer (Brown) W.; m. Madeline Betty Calkins, Oct. 24, 1989. BA, U. Calif., L.A., 1947; MA in Polit. Sci. and Pub. Adminstrn., Am. U., 1976. Spl. projects, plans and policy staff officer CIA, Washington, 1951-58; press sec., spl. asst. Senator William Knowland of Calif., Washington, 1958-59; spl. asst. pub. info. Army Chief R & D, 1959-63; spl. asst. Senator John Tower of Tex., Washington, 1963-64; spl. asst. to asst. dir. inspections and spl. projects OEO, 1965, spl. asst. regional rels., sr. pub. affairs officer, 1973-74; spl. asst. pub. affairs, chief public info. Navy Seabees Naval Facilities Engring. Command, Washington, 1966-69; dir. spl. projects Maritime Adminstrn., 1969-70; spl. asst. regional liaison-coordination Office of Sec. Dept. Transp., 1970-71; dir. congl. and pub. affairs Nat. Reading Ctr., 1972-73; spl. asst. communication liaison-coordination White House, Washington, 1974; regional and intergovtl. liaison officer Office of Adminstr. EPA, 1975; staff specialist in indsl. rels. communication Fed. Energy Adminstrn., Washington, 1976; sr. public affairs officer, dir. Pubs. Health Care Financing Adminstrn. HHS, 1976-79; sr. staff officer intergovt. and regional affairs Office of Sec. Dept. Energy, 1980-81; dep. spl. asst. public affairs to Sec. of Labor, 1981. Mem. Pub. Rels. Soc. Am. (Nat. Capital chpt. bd. dirs. 1963, 65-67, 69-70, 72, 74, 76-77, 79, Silver Anvil award 1968), Nat. Assn. Govt. Communicators (bd. dirs. 1977-78, pres. Nat. Capital chpt. 1977-78, Blue Pencil awards), Mensa, Nat. Press Club, Am. Legion, Kappa Sigma. Home: 2124 Powhatan St Falls Church VA 22043-1910

WEBB, WILLIAM LOYD, JR., army officer; b. Mineral Wells, Tex., Sept. 30, 1925; s. William Loyd and Francis (Mayer) W.; m. Muriel Emma Hinson, Dec. 27, 1947; children: George Sidney, William Loyd III, Lucinda Adrienne, Alicia Muriel. Student, Tex. A & M Coll., 1942-44; B.S., U.S. Mil. Acad., 1947; M.A., U. Pa., 1958. Commd. 2d lt. U.S. Army, 1947, advanced through grades to maj. gen., 1974; co. comdr. Korea, 1950, Ft. Riley, Kans., 1951-52, Germany, 1953-54; assoc. prof. English U.S. Mil. Acad. West Point, N.Y., 1958-61; regimental comdr., dep. comdt. of cadets U.S. Mil. Acad., 1969-71; squadron comdr. 14th Armored Cavalry Germany, 1963-64; mem. faculty U.S Army War Coll., 1965-68; comdr. support command 1st Inf. Div. Vietnam, 1969; dep. comdg. gen. Ft. Ord, Calif., 1971-73; ops. officer 8th Army, U.S. Forces Korea, UN Command Korea, 1973-75, sr. mem. UN Command Mil. Armistice Commn., 1975; comdr. 1st Armored Div., U.S. Army Europe W.Ger., 1975-78; dep. comdg. gen. V Corps, U.S. Army Europe W. Ger., 1978; asst. dep. chief of staff for personnel Dept. Army Washington, 1978-82. Decorated D.S.M., Legion of Merit with oak leaf cluster, D.F.C., Bronze Star medal with oak leaf cluster, Air medal with 5 oak leaf clusters, Army Commendation medal with 2 oak leaf clusters, Purple Heart. Mem. Assn. U.S. Army, Armor Assn. Episcopalian. Office: 10148 Hillington Ct Vienna VA 22182-2908

WEBBER, CHRIS, III (MAYCE EDWARD CHRISTOPHER WEBBER), professional basketball player; b. Detroit, Mar. 1, 1973; s. Mayce and Doris Webber. Student, U. Mich., 1991-93. Drafted Orlando (Fla.) Magic, 1993; forward Golden State Warriors, San Francisco, 1993-94, Washington Bullets, 1994—. Founder Timeout Found. Drafted 1st round Orlando Magic, 1993; named Nat. H.S. Player of Yr., 1990-91, Mr. Basketball State of Mich., 1991, Coca-Cola Classic NBA Player of Yr., 1994, Brut Bullets Player of Yr., 1994-95, NBA All-Rookie 1st Team, 1994. Avocations: collecting signed historical documents of prominent African-Americans. Office: Washington Bullets US Air Arena Landover MD 20785

WEBBER, HOWARD RODNEY, computer company executive; b. Berlin, N.H., Oct. 20, 1933; s. Robert Alfred and Amelia (Rousseau) W.; m. Helen Margaret McCubbin, May 6, 1959; children: Benjamin James, Adam Brooks, Holly Isabella. A.B., Dartmouth Coll., 1956; postgrad., Lehigh U., 1956-57. Editor in chief U. N.C. Press, Chapel Hill, 1960-63, Johns Hopkins Press, Balt., 1963-65; dir. Case Western Res. U. Press Cleve., 1965-70, MIT Press, Cambridge, 1970-74; v.p., gen. mgr., pub. Open Court Pub. Co., LaSalle, Ill., 1974-83; v.p., pub. Reference div. Houghton Mifflin Co., Boston, 1983-87; mgr. advanced devel. Groupware Systems Digital Equipment Corp., Nashua, N.H., 1987-95; chmn. FutureTense, Inc., Acton, Mass., 1995—. Served with AUS, 1957-59. Mem. Phi Beta Kappa. Democrat. Episcopalian. Home: 49 Wilson Rd Bedford MA 01730-1340 Office: FutureTense Inc 33 Nagog park Acton MA 01720

WEBBER, JOHN BENTLEY, orthopedic surgeon; b. Morritown, N.J., Jan. 27, 1941; s. George Bentley and Gladys (Moody) W.; m. Mary Christina Thometz, Feb. 25, 1978; children: John Bentley, Edward Alan. B.A., Lehigh U., 1962; M.D., Temple U., 1966. Intern Rochester Gen. Hosp., N.Y., 1966-67; resident Temple U. Med. Ctr., Phila., 1967-70; Stelrling Bunnell fellow in hand surgery Pacific Med. Ctr., San Francisco, 1971; practice medicine specializing in orthopedic surgery and surgery of hand Phila., 1973—; assoc. prof. orthopedic surgery and rehab. Hahnemann Med. Coll. and Hosp., Phila., 1973—, chief sect. on hand surgery, 1973—; cons. in hand surgery Mcpl. Med. Svcs., Phila., 1973-87, USPHS, Phila., 1973-76, burn ctr. St. Agnes Med. Ctr., Phila., 1973—, Phila. unit Shriners' Hosp. for Crippled Children, 1979-95. Served to maj. USAF, 1971-73. Fellow ACS (Pa. com. on trauma), Am. Acad. Orthopedic Surgeons; mem. AMA, Am. Soc. for Surgery of Hand, Bunnell Hand Club (pres. 1978-80), Assn. for Acad. Surgery, Eastern Orthopedic Soc., Pa. Med. Soc., Phila. Orthopedic Soc., Phila. Hand Soc. (pres. 1987-89), Phila. County Med. Soc., Phila. Coll. Physicians, Meigs Med. Assn., Rotary, Union Leauge, Riverside Yacht Club (fleet surgeon), Phila. Country Club, Delaware Valley Ducks Unltd. (chmn. 1983-88). Republican. Congregationalist. Home: 1139 Rock Creek Rd Gladwyne PA 19035-1439 Office: 221 N Broad St Philadelphia PA 19107-1511

WEBBER, RICHARD JOHN, lawyer; b. Mpls., July 27, 1948; s. Richard John and Mary Lee (Moore) W.; m. Susan Barbara Listerman, Jan. 8, 1972; children: Hillary, Joanna. BA, Princeton U., 1970; JD, U. Mich., 1973. Bar: D.C. Ct. Appeals 1974, U.S. Ct. Appeals (9th and D.C. cirs.) 1980, U.S. Dist. Ct. D.C. 1980, U.S. Claims Ct. 1974, U.S. Supreme Ct. 1980. Law clk. U.S. Ct. Claims, Washington, 1973-75; trial atty. U.S. Dept. Justice, Washington, 1975-80; assoc. Arent, Fox et al, Washington, 1980-85, ptnr., 1985—. Mem. ABA (chmn. fed. contract claims and remedies com. sect. pub. contract law 1986-91), Fed. Bar Assn. (chmn. ADP procurement com. govt. contracts sect. 1992-94, chmn. govt. contracts sect. 1994—). Office: Arent Fox Washington Sq 1050 Connecticut Ave NW Washington DC 20036-5303

WEBBER, ROSS ARKELL, management educator; b. New Rochelle, N.Y., July 18, 1934; s. Richard and Muriel (Arkels) W.; m. Mary Louise Foradora, Sept. 29, 1956; children: Sarah Ruth, Judith Mary, Gregory Ross, Jennifer Louise, Stephen Andrew. BSE, Princeton U., 1956; PhD, Columbia U., 1966; MS (hon.), U. Pa., 1972. Indsl. engr. Eastman Kodak Co., Rochester, N.Y., 1959-61; instr. Columbia U., New York, N.Y., 1961-64; lectr. Wharton Sch. U. Pa., Phila., 1964-65, asst. prof., 1965-70, assoc. prof., 1970-76, prof., 1976—; v.p. U. Pa., Phila., 1981-86; chmn. dept. mgmt. Wharton Sch. U. Pa., Phila., 1992-95; dir. Wharton-Industry Exec. Program, U. Pa., 1966-68, chmn. Wharton Internat. Bus. com., 1968-69, coord. Orgn. Behavior and Mgmt. Group, 1968-75, asst. dept. chmn., PhD com., 1972-75, coord. Orgnl. and Mgmt. Component, Advanced Mgmt. Program in Health Care Adminstrn., 1973-74, mem. Univ. Coun., 1975-77, adv. com. Pub. Mgmt. Unit, The Wharton Sch., 1977-81, chmn. Grad. Admissions com.; mem. editl. bd. The Wharton Mag.; bd. dirs. Heidemij N.V., Am. Water Works Co., N.J.-Am. Water Co.; owner, prin. Ross A. Webber Assocs., 1970—. Author: Organizational Behavior and the Practice of Management, 1968, 5th rev. eit., 1987; Spanish lang. edit., 1982, Culture and Management: Text and Reading in Comparative Management, 1969, Management: Basic Elements of Managing Organizations, 1979, 3rd rev. edit., 1984, Polish lang. edit., 1984, Management Pragmatics: Readings and Cases on Managing Organizations, 1979, Time is Money!: The Key to Managerial Success, 1980, Japanese lang. edit. 1983, Swedish edit. 1983, Spanish lang. edit., 1985, Portugese lang. edit., 1989, To Be a Manager, 1981, A Guide to Getting Things Done, 1984, Becoming a Courageous Manager: Overcoming Career Problems of New Managers, 1991, Breaking Your Time Barriers: Becoming a More Effective Strategic Time Manager, 1992; also over 55 articles to profl. jours. Past mem. bd. dirs. United Way Southeastern Pa.; coach youth athletics, fund raiser for church and religious educator. Lt. (jg) USN, 1956-59. Avocations: painting, tennis, skiing. Office: Univ Pa The Wharton Sch 2000 Steinberg Hall Philadelphia PA 19104

WEBBER, WILLIAM ALEXANDER, university administrator, physician; b. Nfld., Can., Apr. 8, 1934; s. William Grant and Hester Mary (Constable) W.; m. Marilyn Joan Robson, May 17, 1958; children—Susan Joyce, Eric Michael, George David. M.D., U. B.C., Can., Vancouver, 1958. Intern Vancouver Gen. Hosp., 1958-59; postdoctoral fellow Cornell U. Med. Coll., N.Y.C., 1959-61; asst. prof. medicine U. B.C., 1961-66, assoc. prof., 1966-69, prof., 1969—, dean faculty medicine, 1977-90, assoc. v.p. acad., 1990—. Mem. B.C. Med. Assn., Can. Assn. Anatomists, Am. Assn. Anatomists, Can. Nephrological Soc. Research on renal structure and function. Home: 2478 Crown St, Vancouver, BC Canada V6R 3V8 Office: U BC Old Adminstrn Bldg, 6328 Memorial Rd Rm 132, Vancouver, BC Canada V6T 1Z2

WEBEL, RICHARD KARL, landscape architect; m. Janet Darling, July 25, 1947 (dec.); 1 son, Richard Crawford; m. Pauline Dodge Pratt, Sept. 27, 1969. BA, Harvard U., 1923, M.Landscape Architecture, 1926; hon. degrees, Wofford Coll., 1979, Furman U., 1983. Fellow Am. Acad. in Rome, 1926-29; asst. prof. Harvard U. Sch. Design, Cambridge, Mass., 1929-39; pvt. practice landscape architecture, 1931—; mem. N.Y.C. Fine Arts Commn.; mem. vis. com. Grad. Sch. Design, Harvard U., 1962-68. Prin. works include, colls., univs., racetracks, clubs and redesign of Washington Mall and Lincoln Meml. areas, Washington. Recipient numerous awards Am. Assn. Nurserymen, 1955-81, Nat. Landscape award Am. Assn. Nurserymen, 1991, Mrs. Oakleigh Thorne medal Garden Club Am., 1970. Fellow Am. Soc. Landscape Architects (pres. N.Y. chpt. 1954); mem. NAD, Archtl. League N.Y. Clubs: Harvard; Century Assn. (N.Y.C.); Jupiter Island (Hobe Sound, Fla.); Piping Rock (Locust Valley, N.Y.). Home: Cedar Swamp Rd Glen Head NY 11545 Office: Innocenti & Webel 85 Forest Ave Box 506 Locust Valley NY 11560

WEBER, ALFONS, physicist; b. Dortmund, Germany, Oct. 8, 1927; s. Alexander and Ilona (Banda) W.; m. Jeannine K. Weber, Oct. 8, 1955; children: Karl, Louise, Paul. PhD, Ill. Inst. Tech., 1956. Instr. physics Ill. Inst. Tech., Chgo., 1953-56; from asst. prof. physics to prof. Fordham U., Bronx, N.Y., 1957-81, prof. physics and chemistry, 1976-81, chmn. dept. physics, 1964-70; rsch. physicist Nat. Inst. Stds. and Tech., Gaithersburg, Md., 1977—, acting chief molecular spectroscopy divsn., 1980-81, chief molecular physics divsn., 1982-96, sr. scientist physics lab., 1996—; with chem scis. divsn. U.S. Dept. Energy, 1991-92, chem. divsn. NSF, 1992-95. Editor: Raman Spectroscopy of Gases and Liquids, 1979; Structure and Dynamics of Weakly Bound Molecular Complexes, 1987, Spectroscopy of the Earth's Atmosphere and Interstellar Medium, 1992; mem. editorial bd. Jour. of Raman Spectroscopy, Jour. Chem. and Phys. Reference Data. V.p. Union Free Dist. # 1 Sch. Bd., Eastchester, N.Y., 1970-73. Postdoctoral fellow NRC Can., U. Toronto, 1956-57. Fellow Am. Phys. Soc. (councillor 1987-91); mem. AAAS, Optical Soc. Am., Coblentz Soc. Office: Nat Inst Stds and Tech Optical Tech Divsn Rm B208 Bldg 221 Gaithersburg MD 20899

WEBER, ARNOLD R., academic administrator; b. N.Y.C., Sept. 20, 1929; s. Jack and Lena (Smith) W.; m. Edna M. Files, Feb. 7, 1954; children: David, Paul, Robert. B.A., U. Ill., 1951; M.A., MIT, 1958, Ph.D. in Econs., 1958. Instr., then asst. prof. econs. MIT, 1955-58; faculty U. Chgo. Grad. Sch. Bus., 1958-69, prof. indsl. relations, 1963-69; asst. sec. for manpower Dept. Labor, 1969-70; exec. dir. Cost of Living Council; also spl. asst. to Pres. Nixon, 1971; Gladys C. and Isidore Brown prof. urban and labor econs. U. Chgo., 1971-73; former provost Carnegie-Mellon U.; dean Carnegie-Mellon U. (Grad. Sch. Indsl. Adminstrn.), prof. labor econs. and pub. policy, 1973-80; pres. U. Colo., Boulder, 1980-85; pres. Northwestern U., Evanston, Ill., 1985-95, chancellor, 1995—; vis. prof. Stanford U., 1966; cons. union, mgmt. and govt. agys., 1960—, Dept. Labor, 1965; mem. Pres.'s Adv. Com. Labor Mgmt. Policy, 1964, Orgn. Econ. Coop. and Devel., 1987; vice chmn. Sec. Labor Task Force Improving Employment Svcs., 1965; chmn. rsch. adv. com. U.S. Employment Svc., 1966; assoc. dir. OMB, Exec. Office of Pres., 1970-71; chmn. Presdl. R.R. Emergency Bd., 1982; trustee Com. for Econ. Devel.; bd. dirs. Aon Corp., Burlington No., Inc., Inland Steel Co., Pepsico Inc., Tribune Corp., Deere & Co. Author: Strategies for the Displaced Worker, 1966; Contbr. articles to profl. jours. Trustee com. econ. devel., U. Notre Dame; bd. dirs. Chgo. Coun. Fgn. Rels., Eurasia Found. Lt. (j.g.) USCGR, 1952-54. Laureate, Lincoln Acad. Ill.; Ford Found. Faculty Rsch. fellow, 1964-65. Mem. Am. Acad. Arts and Scis., Indsl. Rels. Rsch. Assn. (bus.-higher edn. forum), Nat. Acad. Pub. Adminstrn., Comml. Club Chgo. (pres., civic com.), Econ. Club Chgo. (pres.), Phi Beta Kappa. Jewish. Office: Northwestern U Office of Chancellor 555 Clark St Evanston IL 60208-0805

WEBER, ARTHUR, magazine executive; b. Chgo., Feb. 1, 1926; s. Philip and Mary (Arlinsky) W.; m. Sylvia Zollinger, Aug. 19, 1950; children—Randy, Lori. Student, Ill. Inst. Tech., 1943-44; BSEE, Northwestern U., 1946. Elec. design engr. Corn Products Refining Co., 1946-48, Naess & Murphy (architects & engrs.), Chgo., 1949-51, Ford Motor Co., 1952-53, Skidmore, Owings & Merill, Chgo., 1954-57, Shaw, Metz & Dolio, Chgo., 1958-59; pres. Consumers Digest mag., Chgo., 1959—; pub. Money Maker mag. (name changed to Your Money mag., 1991), 1979-91, U. Chgo. Better Health Letter, 1995—. Served with USNR, 1944-46. Office: Consumers Digest Inc 5705 N Lincoln Ave Chicago IL 60659-4707

WEBER, BARBARA M., sales executive, consultant; b. Oneonta, N.Y., Apr. 27, 1945; d. Peter J. and Helen (Bettiol) Macaluso; m. Peter Biddle Weber, July 29, 1972 (div. July 1988). Student, SUNY, Cortland, 1963-67; AAS in Merchandising and Retail Mgmt., SUNY, Mohawk Valley. Service cons. N.Y. Telephone, Albany, N.Y., 1966-68; sr. service advisor N.Y. Telephone, Albany, 1970-73; data communications instr. AT & T, nationwide, 1968-70; equipment mgr. Rushmore & Weber, Albany, 1978-82; v.p. ops. Rushmore & Weber, 1983-92, gen. mgr., v.p., 1987-88, pres., chief exec. officer, 1988-92, also bd. dirs.; ind. cons. Orange Handling, Inc., Latham, N.Y., 1992-93; owner The Weber Group, Newtonville, N.Y., 1993—. Republican. Roman Catholic. Club: Schuyler Meadows Country. Avocations: skiing, tennis, golf, sailing, knitting. Home: PO Box 236 Newtonville NY 12128-0236

WEBER, CHARLES L., electrical engineering educator; b. Dayton, Ohio, Dec. 2, 1937. BSEE, U. Dayton, 1958; MSEE, U. So. Calif., 1960; PhD, UCLA, 1964. Tech. staff Hughes Aircraft Co., Calif., 1958-62; from asst. prof. to prof. elec. engring. U. So. Calif., 1964—. Mem. IEEE. Office: U So Calif Comm Scis Inst Dept Elec Engring-Systems Los Angeles CA 90089-0272*

WEBER, DAVID C(ARTER), librarian; b. Waterville, Maine, July 25, 1924; s. Carl J. and Clara (Carter) W.; m. Natalie McLeod, Dec. 26, 1952; children: L. Jefferson, Christopher Q., Douglas McLeod, Sarah N. A.B., Colby Coll., 1947; student, Bowdoin Coll., 1946; B.S., Columbia U., 1948; A.M., Harvard U., 1953; postgrad., Rutgers U., 1956. Cataloger, asst. to dir., asst. dir. libraries Harvard U., 1948-61; asst. dir., assoc. dir. Stanford (Calif.) U., 1961-69, dir. libraries, 1969-91, Ida M. Green chair, 1987-91, dir. librs. emeritus, 1991; cons. to acad. libraries, pub. and pvt. instns. and orgns., U.S. and Can. Author: (with others) College and University Accreditation Standards, 1958, (with R.D. Rogers) University Library Administration, 1971; (with P.D. Leighton) Planning Academic and Research Library Buildings, 1986; editor: Studies in Library Administrative Problems, 1960; contbr. articles to profl. jours. Served with AUS, 1943-46. Council on Library Resources fellow, 1970. Mem. ALA, Assn. Coll. and Rsch. Libraries (pres. 1981-82), Assn. Libr. Collections and Tech. Svcs. (pres. 1967-68). Clubs: Roxburghe (San Francisco); Book of Calif. Office: 863 Lathrop Dr Stanford CA 94305-1054

WEBER, DELBERT DEAN, academic administrator; b. Columbus, Nebr., July 23, 1932; s. Charles and Ella M. (Hueschen) W.; m. Lou Ann Ross, Dec. 29, 1954; children: William, Bethany, Kelly. BA, Midland Coll., Fremont, Nebr., 1954; MEd, U. Nebr., 1958, EdD, 1962; LittD (hon.), Shizuoka (Japan) U., 1982; LLD (hon.), U. City of Manila, 1984. Tchr. social studies and English, prin. Creston (Nebr.) High Sch., 1956-58; instr. ednl. founds. U. Nebr., Lincoln, 1958-60, instr. and coord. jr. high lab. sch., 1960-62; chancellor U. Nebr., Omaha, 1977—; from asst. to assoc. prof. edn. Ariz. State U., Tempe, 1962-65, dean and prof. edn., 1969-77; asst. to pres. and sec. to trustees Cleve. State U., 1965-69; chmn. commn. on culture and edn. to Pakistan, U.S. Dept. of State, 1984; bd. dirs. Norwest Bank, Omaha. Author: (with N.L. Haggerson, L.H. Griffith) Secondary Education Today, 1968; contbr. articles to profl. jours. trustee Nebr. Meth. Hosp., Omaha Home for Boys, Nebr. Meth. Hosp., 1980—; bd. dirs. Midlands region NCCJ, Omaha Community Playhouse, numerous others; gen. campaign chmn. United Way of Midlands, 1983; chmn. midlands region Nat. Conf. Christians and Jews, 1989-92; mem. consultation com. Strategic Command, 1988—, adv. bd. Salvation Army, 1991—, Nebr. state exec. bd. U.S. West Comm., Inc., 1992—, merit selection panel for Magistrate Judge, 1992. With U.S. Army, 1954-56. Named Citizen of Yr., United Way of Midlands, 1984, Disting. Educator N. Cen. Region Bosy Scouts Am., 1989, Outstanding Citizen, Woodmen of the World, 1990, King of Ak-Sar-Ben, 1990, Man of Yr. Omaha Club 1992, Merry Makers 1992; recipient Vision award Soc. Prevention of Blindness, 1991, Svc. to Mankind award Sertoma Club, 1994. Mem. Am. Assn. Colls. for Tchr. Edn. (bd. dirs. 1976-79, chmn. ann. conv. 1975, appeals bd. 1984-85, task force 1984-85), Am. Assn. State Colls. and Univs. (task force on excellence in edn. 1982-84, bd. dirs., exec. com. 1983-86, com. communications tech. 1984-86, resource ctr. bd. liaison 1985, com. acad. affairs, com. on internat. programs 1987, com. on urban affairs 1987), Assn. Urban Univs. (bd. dirs. 1980-85), Nat. Assn. State Univs. and Land Grant Colls. (mem. exec. com. 1982-83, chmn. urban affairs div. 1982-83), Nat. Assn. Colls. and Schs. of Edn. in State Univs. and Land Grant Colls. (bd. dirs. 1974-77, pres. 1977-78), Nat. Collegiate Athletic Assn. (pres. commn. 1984-89), Nat. Coun. for Accreditation of Tchr. Edn. (appeals bd. 1983), Omaha C. of C., Strategic Air Command (bd. dir. consultation com.). Lutheran. Avocation: golf. Home: 1816 N 132nd Avenue Cir Omaha NE 68154-3898 Office: U Nebr Eppley 201 Omaha NE 68182

WEBER, DON, finance company executive. Pres. Norwest Funding, Inc., Mpls., Norwest Direct, Colorado Springs, CO, 1995—. Office: Norwest Direct 4455 Arrow West Colorado Springs CO 80907*

WEBER, DONALD B., advertising and marketing executive; b. Jersey City, Nov. 6, 1932; s. John William and Rose Ann (Saroshi) W.; m. Ann McDermaid, 1955 (div. 1975); children: Martha Elizabeth, Margaret Ann; m. Jean Host, 1980. BA, Rollins Coll., 1954; MBA, Northwestern U., 1959. Account exec. Leo Burnett Co., Inc., Chgo., 1958-63; sr. v.p., mgmt. supr. Foote, Cone & Belding, Chgo., 1963-76; pres. Blau Bishop Assocs., 1976-79; v.p. Russell Reynolds Assocs., Chgo., 1979-82; sr. v.p., regional mgr. MSL Internat., Chgo., 1982-85; exec. v.p. Rumrill-Hoyt, Inc., Rochester, N.Y., 1985-88; sr. v.p. D'Arcy Masius Benton & Bowles, Chgo., 1988-95; sr. v.p. mgmt. dir. Cramer-Krasselt, Chgo., 1996—; lectr. Northwestern U. Mem. Am. Cancer Soc., chmn. Chgo. Area Crusade, 1994—; bd. dirs. Am. Inst. of Wine and Food, 1995—. Lt. commdr. USNR, 1955-58. Mem. Chgo. Advtg. Fedn. (bd. dirs. 1988-93), Oak Hill Country Club, Exmoor Country Club, Tavern Club. Republican. Episcopalian. Office: Cramer-Krasselt 225 North Michigan Av Chicago IL 60601

WEBER, ERNESTO JUAN, educator, counselor, industrialist; b. Mexico City, Aug. 20, 1930; m. Vera Elisa Engels, Oct. 25, 1958; children: Frank, Ernesto Jr., Monica. BS in Mech. Engring., Calif. Inst. Tech., 1952; PhD in counseling, U. Iberoamericana, Mexico City, 1980. Gen. mgr. Schultz y Cia, S.A., Mexico City, 1961-68, owner, pres., 1968-76; prof. U. Iberoamericana, Mexico City, 1976-85, dean dept. human devel. and edn., 1982-84; gen. corp. dir. Grupo Indsl., Aloymex, Mex., 1987-84; dir. dept. psychology Centro Medico la Pascua, Mexico City, 1980-81; profl. counselor, Mexico City, 1976—; dir. Metron S.A., 1966-70, Sycmatica, S.A. de C.V., 1967-76, Ascomatica, S.A. de C.V., 1967-76 (all Mexico City); pres. Weber y Asociados, S.C. Author: Der Integrierte Mensch, 1988; patentee in automatic controls; contbr. articles to profl. jours. Recipient Achievement award United Inventors and Scientists, 1974; award Automatic Switch Co., 1976. Mem. Assn. de Profs. e Inv. de La U.I.A., Assn. Mex. de Terapia Familiar, Assn. Suiza de Mex., A.C. (pres.). Club: Assoc. Empresarial Mexicano-Suiza, A.C. Home and Office: Alabama 196-502, Mexico City 03810, Mexico

WEBER, EUGEN, historian, educator, author; b. Bucharest, Romania, Apr. 24, 1925; came to U.S., 1955; s. Emanuel and Sonia (Garrett) W.; m. Jacqueline Brument-Roth, June 12, 1950. Student, Inst. d'études politiques, Paris, 1948-49, 51-52; M.A., Emmanuel Coll., Cambridge U., 1954, M.Litt., 1956. History supr. Emmanuel Coll., 1953-54; lectr. U. Alta., 1954-55; asst. prof. U. Iowa, 1955-56; asst. prof. history UCLA, 1956, assoc. prof., 1959-63, prof., 1963—, Joan Palevsky prof. modern European history, 1984—, chmn. dept., 1965-68; dir. study center U. Calif., France, 1968-70; dean social scis. UCLA, 1976-77, dean Coll. Letters and Scis., 1977-82; Ford faculty lectr. Stanford U., 1965; Patten lectr. Ind. U., 1981; vis. prof. Collège de France, Paris, 1983; dir. d'ètudes Ecole des hautes ètudes, Paris, 1984-85;

Christian Gauss lectr., Princeton U., 1990. Author: Nationalist Revival in France, 1959, The Western Tradition, 1995, Paths to the Present, 1960, Action Française, 1962, Satan Franc-Maçon, 1964, Varieties of Fascism, 1964; (with H. Rogger) The European Right, 1965, A Modern History of Europe, 1970, Europe Since 1715, 1972, Peasants into Frenchmen, 1976 (Commonwealth prize Calif. 1977), La Fin des Terroirs, 1983 (Prix de la Sociéè des gens de lettres 1984), France Fin-de-siècle, 1986 (Commonwealth prize Calif. 1987), The Western Tradition (WGBH/PBS TV series), 1989, My France, 1990, Movements, Currents, Trends, 1991, The Hollow Years, 1994, La France des annèes trente (Prix littèraire Etats-Unis/France, 1995, Prix Maurice Baumont 1995), 1995; adv. editor Jour. Contemporary History, 1966—, French History, 1985—, French Cultural Studies, 1990—, Am. Scholar, 1992—. Served as capt. inf. Brit. Army, 1943-47. Recipient Luckman Disting. Teaching award UCLA Alumnae Assn., 1992; decorated Ordre Nat. des Palmes Academiques, France; Fulbright fellow, 1952, 82-83; research fellow Am. Philos. Soc., 1959, Social Sci. Research Council, 1959-61, Am. Council Learned Socs., 1962; Guggenheim fellow, 1963-64; NEH sr. fellow, 1973-74, 82-83. Fellow Netherlands Inst. Advanced Studies, Assn. française de science politique, Am. Acad. Arts and Scis.; mem. Am. Hist. Assn., Soc. d'histoire moderne, Soc. French Hist. Studies, Phi Beta Kappa (hon., Ralph Waldo Emerson prize 1977, senator 1988—).

WEBER, FREDERICK EDWIN, management recruiter; b. Quincy, Ill., Aug. 9, 1924; s. Edwin Frederick and Minnie Catherine (Boschulte) W.; m. Wanda Lou Woody, Aug. 10, 1946; children: Barbara L., Marcia A. (dec. 1990), William F. BS in Indsl. Mgmt., U. Ill., 1948. Cert. personnel cons. Foreman US Rubber Co., Mishawaka, Ind., 1948-56, supt., 1956-59; plant mgr. US Rubber Co., Stoughton, Wis., 1959-65, Uniroyal Inc., Port Clinton, Ohio, 1965-67; mng. dir. Uniroyal Inc., Edinburgh, Scotland, 1968-70; factory mgr. Masland Duraleather, Phila., 1971-74; indsl. cons. J.L. Tunnel Co., Blue Bell, Pa., 1974-76; pres. Mgmt. Recruiters, Cedar Rapids, Iowa, 1976—; farm mgr., 1993—; regional rep. Midwest Region Mgmt. Recruiters, 1994—. Mem. Iowa Job Svc. Adv. Coun., Des Moines, 1982-95, chmn., 1984, 87, 93; mem. Bd. Edn., Stoughton, Wis., 1962-65; pres. Iowa Assn. Pers. Cons., 1982-83. With USN, 1943-46, PTO. Mem. Am. Legion, Rotary (bd. dirs. 1980-83). Republican. Lutheran. Avocations: travel, golf, photography, poetry. Home: 360 Red Fox Rd SE Cedar Rapids IA 52403-2056 Office: Mgmt Recruiters 150 1st Ave NE Ste 400 Cedar Rapids IA 52401-1110

WEBER, FREDRIC ALAN, lawyer; b. Paterson, N.J., July 31, 1948; s. Frederick Edward and Alida (Hessels) W.; m. Mary Elizabeth Cook, June 18, 1983. BA in History, Rice U., 1970; JD, Yale U., 1976. Bar: Tex. 1976, U.S. Dist. Ct. (so. dist.) Tex. Assoc. Fulbright & Jaworski, Houston, 1976-80, participating assoc., 1980-83, ptnr., 1983—. Dir. Houston Symphony Soc., 1993—. Recipient Benjamin Scharps prize Yale Law Sch., 1976, Ambrose Gherini prize Yale Law Sch., 1976. Mem. ABA, Am. Coll. Bond Counsel, Nat. Assn. Bond Lawyers (bd. dirs. 1988-89, treas. 1989-90, pres.-elect 1991, pres. 1991-92), Houston Bar Assn. Office: Fulbright & Jaworski LLP 1301 Mckinney St Ste 5100 Houston TX 77010

WEBER, FREDRICK LOUIS, JR., hematologist, medical researcher; b. Syracuse, N.Y., June 8, 1944; s. Fredrick L. and Jean (Caldwell) W.; m. Gayle Christine Weber; children: Luke, Laura, Nell, Charles, Andrew. BA, Wesleyan U., 1966; MD, Cornell U., 1970. Resident in internal medicine Bellevue Hosp./NYU Med. Ctr., N.Y.C., 1970-73; fellow in gastroenterology Johns Hopkins Hosp., Balt., 1973-75; asst. prof. medicine U. Ky. Med. Ctr., Lexington, 1975-81; assoc. prof. medicine Case Western Res. U., Cleve., 1981-93; dir. liver unit U. Cin. Med. Ctr., 1993—. Achievements include research in hepatic encephalopathy and intestinal nitrogen metabolism. Office: U Cin Med Ctr Liver Unit ML 595 Cincinnati OH 45267

WEBER, GEORGE, oncology and pharmacology researcher, educator; b. Budapest, Hungary, Mar. 29, 1922; came to U.S., 1959; s. Salamon and Hajnalka (Arvai) W.; m. Catherine Elizabeth Forrest, June 30, 1958; children: Elizabeth Dolly Arvai, Julie Vibert Wallace, Jefferson James. BA, Queen's U., 1950, MD, 1952; MD (hon.), U. Chieti, Italy, 1979, Med. Faculty, Budapest, 1982, U. Leipzig, Fed. Republic of Germany, 1987, Tokushima (Japan) U., 1988; Kagawa (Japan) U., 1992. Rsch. assoc. Montreal Cancer Inst., 1953-59; prof. pharmacology Ind. U. Sch. Medicine, Indpls., 1959—; dir. Lab for Exptl. Oncology Sch. Medicine, Ind. U., Indpls., 1974—; Milan Panič prof. oncology Ind. U., Indpls., 1994—, Wellcome prof., 1995—; prof. Lab. for Exptl. Oncology Sch. Medicine, Ind. U., Indpls., 1974-90, disting. prof. Lab. for Exptl. Oncology, 1990—; chmn. study sect. USPHS, Washington, 1976-78; sci. adv. com. Am. Cancer Soc., N.Y.C., 1972-76, 94—, Damon Runyon Fund, N.Y.C., 1971-76; mem. U.S. Nat. Com., Internat. Union Against Cancer, Washington, 1974-80, 90-94, NAS, Washington, 1974-80, 90-94. Editor: Advances in Enzyme Regulation, Vols. 1-36, 1962—; assoc. editor Jour. Cancer Rsch., 1969-80, 82-89. Recipient Alecce Prize for cancer rsch. Tiberine Acad., Rome, 1971, Best Prof. award Student AMA, Indpls., 1966, 68, G.F. Gallanti prize for enzymology Internat. Soc. Clin. Chemists, 1984, Outstanding Investigator award Nat. Cancer Inst., NIH, 1986-94. Mem. Am. Soc. for Pharmacology and Exptl. Therapeutics, Am. Assn. Cancer Rsch. (G.H.A. Clowes award 1982), Am. Physiol. Soc., Biochem. Soc., Russian Acad. Sci. (hon.), Hungarian Cancer Soc. (hon.), Hungarian Acad. Scis. (hon.), Acad. Scis. Bologna (Italy) (hon.). Home: 7307 Lakeside Dr Indianapolis IN 46278-1618 Office: Ind U Sch Medicine Lab Exptl Oncology 702 Barnhill Dr Indianapolis IN 46202-5200

WEBER, GEORGE RICHARD, financial consultant, writer; b. The Dalles, Oreg., Feb. 7, 1929; s. Richard Merle and Maud (Winchell) W.; m. Nadine Hanson, Oct. 12, 1957; children: Elizabeth Ann Weber Katooli, Karen Louise Weber Zaro, Linda Marie. BS, Oreg. State U., 1950; MBA, U. Oreg., 1962. CPA, Oreg. Sr. trainee U.S. Nat. Bank of Portland (Oreg.), 1950-51; jr. acct. Ben Musa, CPA, The Dalles, 1954; tax and audit asst. Price Waterhouse, Portland, 1955-59; sr. acct. Burton M. Smith, CPA, Portland, 1959-62; pvt. practice, Portland, 1962—; lectr. acctg. Portland State Coll.; expert witness fin. and tax matters. Sec.-treas. Mt. Hood Kiwanis Camp, Inc., 1965. Exec. counselor SBA; mem. fin. com., powerlifting team U.S. Powerlifting Fedn., 1984, amb. People to People, China, 1987. With AUS, 1951-53. Decorated Bronze Star. Mem. AICPA, Internat. Platform Assn., Oreg. Hist. Soc.,Oreg. City Traditional Jazz Soc., Order of the Holy Cross Jerusalem, Order St. Stephen the Martyr, Order St. Gregory the Illuminator, Knightly Assn. St. George the Martyr., World Literary Acad., Portland C.S. Lewis Soc., Beta Alpha Psi, Pi Kappa Alpha. Republican. Lutheran. Clubs: Kiwanis, Portland Track, City (Portland); Multnomah Athletic; Sunrise Toastmasters. Author: Small Business Long-term Finance, 1962, A History of the Coroner and Medical Examiner Offices, 1963, CPA Litigation Service References, 1991, Letters to a Friend, 1995; contbr. to profl. publs. and poetry jours. Home: 2603 NE 32nd Ave Portland OR 97212-3611 Office: 4380 SW Macadam Ave Ste 210 Portland OR 97201-6404 *My basic beliefs are in faith, family and freedom through limited government and personal responsibility, with personl responsibility including development and use of capabilities.*

WEBER, GLORIA RICHIE, minister, retired state representative; married; 4 children. BA, Washington U., St. Louis; MA, MDiv, Eden Theol. Sem., Webster Groves, Mo. Ordained to ministry Evang. Luth. Ch. Am., St. Louis, 1974;. Min. Am. Luth. Ch., St. Louis, 1974; family life educator Luth. Family & Children's Svcs. Mo.; state representative State of Mo., 1993-94; Mo. state organizer, dir. comm. Mainstream Voters C.A.R.E., 1995. Exec. dir. Older Women's League, 1990-95; Dem. candidate for Mo. State Senate, 1996. Recipient Woman of Achievement award St. Louis Globe-Dem., 1977, Unselfish Cmty. Svc. award St. Louis Sentinel Newspaper, 1985, Faith in Action award Luth. Svcs. St. Louis, 1994, Outstanding Woman award Coalition of St. Louis Labor Women, 1994; named Woman of Yr., Variety Club, 1978, Woman of Worth, Older Women's League, 1993. Democrat. Home and Office: 4910 Valley Crest Dr Saint Louis MO 63128-1829

WEBER, HANNO, architect; b. Barranquilla, Colombia, Sept. 24, 1937; came to U.S., 1952; s. Hans and Ester (Oks) W. BA magna cum laude, Princeton U., 1959, MArch, 1961. Registered architect, Ill., Fla., Mo., Pa., N.J., Va. Urban designer, research assoc. Guayana project MIT and Harvard U., Caracas, Venezuela, 1961-63; project architect Paul Schweikher Assocs., Pitts., 1963-67; asst. prof. architecture Princeton U., 1967-73; assoc. prof. architecture Washington U., St. Louis, 1973-80; sr. design architect, studio head, assoc. Skidmore, Owings & Merrill, Chgo., 1980-83; prin. Hanno Weber & Assocs., Chgo., 1984—; vis. lectr. Escuela Nacional de Arquitectura Universidad Nacional de Mex., 1975; research assoc. Research Ctr. Urban and Environ. Planning, Princeton, N.J., 1967-70; project dir. The Community Design Workshop, Washington U. Sch. Architecture, St. Louis, 1973-78; assoc. prof. architecture U. Wis., Milw., 1983—. Contbr. articles to profl. jours. Mem. Pres.'s Commn. on Education of Women Princeton U., 1968-69. Fellow NEH, 1970, Graham Found., 1973; 1st prize winner Flagler Dr. Waterfront Master Plan design competition, West Palm Beach, Fla., 1984, 1st prize winner Mcpl. Ctr. design competition, Leesburg, Va., 1987, Chgo. AIA Disting. Bldg. award Citation of Merit, Altamira, Terrace, Highland Park, Fla., 1987. Mem. AIA (Urban Design award Mcpl. Govt. Ctr., Leesburg, Va., 1992, Chgo. AIA Interior Architecture award citation of merit, Mcpl. Govt. Ctr., Leesburg, 1992), The Arch. Assn., Phi Beta Kappa. Office: Hanno Weber & Assocs 417 S Dearborn St Chicago IL 60605-1120

WEBER, HARM ALLEN, college chancellor, former college president; b. Pekin, Ill., Sept. 28, 1926; s. Harm Allen and Hilda (Meyer) W.; m. Arlene Olson, Dec. 18, 1948; children: Jan Christine, Harm Allen III, Matthew Karl. B.A., Bethel Coll., St. Paul, 1950; B.D., Bethel Sem., 1954; M.R.E., Christian Theol. Sem., Indpls., 1959; postgrad., Ball State U., Muncie, Ind., 1961-62; D.D., Judson Coll., Elgin, Ill., 1964. Ordained to ministry Baptist Ch., 1953; pastorates at Isle (Minn.) Bapt. Ch., 1950-53, Central Bapt. Ch., Indpls., 1954-60, First Bapt. Ch., Muncie, 1960-64, Covenant Bapt. Ch., Detroit, 1964-69; pres. Judson Coll., Elgin, 1969-91; vice chmn. bd. trustees Judson Coll., chancellor, 1992—; chmn. Indpls. Fedn. Chs., 1955-59; pres. Delaware County (Ind.) Coun. Chs., 1963-64; chmn. evangelism Detroit Coun. Chs., 1967-69; v.p. Am. Bapt. Home Mission Soc., 1969—; mem. exec. com. Gt. Lakes Coun. on Ministry, 1969—; mem. Ministers and Missionaries Benefit Bd., 1974-75; mem. gen. bd. Am. Bapt. Chs./USA; mem. nat. adv. com. Ednl. Assistance Ltd., 1987—. Mem. Ind. Gov.'s Multiple Sclerosis Bd., 1957-60; bd. dirs. Camp Isongal, Delaware County Crippled Children's Assn.; chmn. bd. dirs. Galloway Meml. Youth Camp, Wahkon, Minn.; mem. state exec. bd. Vols. of Am.-Minn., 1976—; trustee Am. Bapt. Sem. of the West, 1984-86. Mem. Am. Assn. Pres. Ind. Colls. and Univs., Elgin Area C. of C. (dir. 1975-78), Am. Bapt. Assn. Colls. and Univs. (pres. 1986-89). Club: Rotary. Office: Judson Coll 1151 N State St Elgin IL 60123-1404

WEBER, HERMAN JACOB, federal judge; b. Lima, Ohio, May 20, 1927; s. Herman Jacob and Ada Minola (Esterly) W.; m. Barbara L. Rice, May 22, 1948; children: Clayton, Deborah. BA, Otterbein Coll., 1949; JD summa cum laude, Ohio State U., 1951. Bar: Ohio 1952, U.S. Dist. Ct. (so. dist.) Ohio 1954. Ptnr. Weber & Hogue, Fairborn, Ohio, 1952-61; judge Fairborn Mayor's Ct., 1956-58; acting judge Fairborn Mcpl. Ct., 1958-60; judge Greene County Common Pleas Ct., Xenia, Ohio, 1961-82, Ohio Ct. Appeals (2d dist.), Dayton, 1982-85, U.S. Dist. Ct. (so. dist.) Ohio, Cin., 1985—; chmn. Ohio Jud. Conf., Columbus, 1980-82; pres. Ohio Common Pleas Judges Assn., Columbus, 1975. Vice mayor City of Fairborn, 1955-57, council mem., 1955-59. Served with USNR, 1945-46. Office: US Dist Ct 801 Potter Stewart US Courthse 5th & Walnut Sts Cincinnati OH 45202

WEBER, JANET M., nurse; b. Lansdale, Pa., Mar. 12, 1936; d. Russell H. and Naomi (dec.) Moyer W. Diploma in nursing, Washington County Hosp. Sch. Nursing, 1959; B.S. in Nursing, Grace Coll., 1960; M.Ed., Duquesne U., 1969. Staff nurse, supr. Murphy Med. Ctr., Warsaw, Ind., 1959-60; coll. nurse Grace Coll., Winona Lake, Ind., 1959-60; med. surg. nursing instr. Washington County Hosp. Sch. Nursing, Hagerstown, Md., 1961-64; pvt. duty nurse Washington County Hosp., Hagerstown, 1964; chmn. found. of nursing Presbyn. Univ. Hosp. Sch. Nursing, Pitts., 1964-72; curriculum coordinator Albert Einstein Med. Ctr. Sch. Nursing, Phila., 1972-73; assoc. dir. Albert Einstein Med. Ctr. Sch. Nursing, 1973-74, acting dir., 1974, dir., 1974-87; staff nurse ARC Penn-Jersey Blood Drive Donor Services, Phila., 1988-92, asst. nurse mgr., 1992—; nurse mgr. ARC Penn-Jersey Blood Drivce Donor Svcs., Phila., 1992—; cons. Md. Bd. Higher Edn., 1981-82. Author: The Faculty's Role in Policy Development, 1981, Assisting Students with Educational Deficiencies, 1975. Mem. Washington County Hosp. Nurses Alumni Assn. (pres. 1962-64), Grace Coll. Alumni Assn., Duquesne U. Alumni Assn. Republican. Home: 5640 Arbor St Philadelphia PA 19120-2502 Office: ARC Blood Donor Svcs 700 Spring Garden St Philadelphia PA 19123-3508

WEBER, JEROME CHARLES, education and human relations educator, former academic dean and provost; b. Bklyn., Sept. 1, 1938; s. Meyer and Ethel (Shier) W.; m. Elizabeth Lynn Wiley, July 18, 1975; children: Amy Elizabeth, Jeffrey Glenn. B.S., Bklyn. Coll., 1960; M.A., Mich. State U., 1961, Ph.D., 1966. Mem. faculty U. Okla., Norman, 1964—, prof. edn., phys. edn., human rels. and social work, 1973—, Regents' prof. edn. and human rels., 1991—, asst. and acting dean, 1969-72, dean Univ. Coll., 1973-91, vice provost instructional svcs., 1979-91; chmn. ednl. leadership and policy studies, 1993. Author: (with D.R. Lamb) Statistics and Research in Physical Education, 1970, (with G. Henderson) College Survival for Student-Athletes, 1985; contbr. articles to profl. jours. Bd. dirs. Univ. div. United Way, 1970; pres. Norman Kindergarten Assn., 1968; commr. Norman Bd. Parks, 1971-79. Fellow Am. Coun. Sports Medicine; mem. Am. Assn. Higher Edn., Coun. Sports Psychology, Am. Coun. on Edn. Democrat. Jewish. Home: 5 Pebble Creek Rd Norman OK 73072-2822 Office: 630 Parrington Oval Norman OK 73069-8813

WEBER, JOHN BERTRAM, architect; b. Evanston, Ill., Oct. 15, 1930; s. Bertram Anton and Dorothea Hennecke (Brammer) W.; m. Sally Ann French; children: Suzanne French Weber Roulston, Jane Marie Weber McCarthy, Patricia Ann Weber Blodgett, Nancy Brammer. AB in Architecture, Princeton U., 1953; postgrad., Ill. Inst. Tech., 1959. Lic. architect. Field engr. United Constrn. Co., Riverdale, N.D., 1952; draftsman Bertram A. Weber Architect, Chgo., 1947- 53, architect, 1958-1973; field engr. Atkinson United Constrn. Co., Greenup and Ashland, Ky., 1956-58; ptnr., proprietor Weber & Weber Architects, Chgo., Northbrook and Winnetka, Ill., 1973—; Mem. Ill. Architecture Act Revision task force, 1982-89. Prin. works include Prestwick Country Club, the 3175 Commercial Ave. Bldg., Northbrook, med. office bldg. and additions to Bi-county hospital, Warren, Mich., additions and alterations to Detroit Osteopathic Hosp., addition to Duraclean Internat. Bldg., Deerfield, additions to The Admiral (a retirement home in Chgo.), and numerous pvt. residences, churches, comml., ednl., and recreational bldgs. Active Winnetka (Ill.) Cmty. Caucus, 1965, 74; mem. Mayor's adv. com. on bldg. codes, Chgo., 1975-80; chmn. bldg. com. Winnetka Cmty. House, 1977-81; mem. Winnetka Zoning Bd. Appeals, 1983-88, chmn., 1987-88; mem. Winnetka Ad Hoc Zoning Com., 1995-96; deacon, elder Winnetka Presbyn. Ch. With USN, 1953-56. Fellow Ill. Soc. Architects (bd. dirs. 1969-84, 91—, pres. 1976-78); mem. AIA (health com. 1969-76), Ill. Architect-Engr. Coun. (chmn. 1981-82, del. 1976-87, 92—), Northbrook C. of C., Architects Club Chgo. (pres. 1981, bd. dirs. 1976-86, 94), Builders Club Chgo. (bd. dirs. 1986—, pres. 1973-74), Am. Legion, Old Willow Club, Mchts. and Mfrs. Club, Dairymen's Country Club. Home: 415 Berkeley Ave Winnetka IL 60093-2109 Office: Weber & Weber Architects 415 Berkeley Ave Winnetka IL 60093-2109 also: 464 Central Ave Northfield IL 60093-3040 *Do what you should do, not what you have to do. In the end, it is only the things that we do that impact on other people's and other living being's lives that have real meaning.*

WEBER, JOSEPH H., communications company executive; b. N.Y.C., Dec. 10, 1930; s. Sol and Minna (Hoffman) W.; m. Sophie Ruderman, Apr. 10, 1954 (div. 1973); m. J. V. Hammar, Jan. 10, 1976; children—Leslie, Jonathan, David. B.E.E., Rensselaer Poly. Inst., 1952; M.S.E., George Washington U., 1956. Engr. Hazeltine Electronics Co., Little Neck, N.Y., 1952-53; mem. tech. staff Bell Telephone Labs., N.Y.C., 1956-61; head network analysis dept. Bell Telephone Labs., Holmdel, N.J., 1961-72; dir. data services AT&T Long Lines, N.Y.C., 1972-75; dir. network services planning Bell Telephone Labs., Holmdel, 1975-80; dir. tech. standards and regulatory planning AT&T, Basking Ridge, N.J., 1980-84; dir. strategic planning AT&T, N.Y.C., 1984-85; dir. venture tech. AT&T, Berkeley Heights, N.J., 1985-87; v.p. tech. Global Transactions Services Co., Parsippany, N.J., 1987-88; ptnr. T.E.L.A. Group, 1989-94, Weber Temin & Co., 1995—. Vice-pres. Holmdel Twp. Bd. Edn., 1970-72; mem. Morris Twp. Planning Bd., 1988—. Served with U.S. Navy, 1953-56. Mem. IEEE (sr.), IEEE Communications Soc. (chmn. switching com. 1972-73). Patentee in field. Home: Box 224 16 Canfield Rd Convent Station NJ 07961

WEBER, JULIAN L., lawyer, former publishing and entertainment company executive; b. Des Moines, July 19, 1929; s. Milton and Zelda (Robinson) W.; m. Idelle Feinberg, Apr. 17, 1957; children—Jonathan Todd, Suzanne. B.A., UCLA, 1951; J.D., Harvard U., 1955. Bar: N.Y. 1956. Partner Botein Hays & Sklar, 1964-79; pres. Nat. Lampoon, Inc., N.Y.C., 1979-84; pvt. practice law N.Y.C., 1984—. Mem. ABA, Assn. of Bar of City of N.Y.

WEBER, KATIE, special education educator; b. Delhi, La., Dec. 6, 1933; d. Sullivan and Teresa McClain Aytch; m. Hilliard Weber Jr., June 16, 1956; children: Barrett Renwick, Sandra Anita, Dawna Lynn, Thaddeus Marc. BA, So. U., 1957; MEd, Tex. So. U., 1982. Cert. elem. and spl. edn. tchr., La., Tex. Elem. tchr. Port Arthur (Tex.) Ind. Sch. Dist., 1957-73, elem. spl. edn. tchr., 1974-85, secondary spl. edn. tchr., 1985—; part-time prin. Port Arthur Ind. Sch. Dist., 1976-83, interim prin., 1983-85; mem. Tex. assessment acad. skills test Tex. Edn. Agy., Austin, 1988-90, scorer master tchr. test, 1990; also curriculum writer. Candidate for city coun. City of Port Arthur, Tex., 1974; active Rock Island Bapt. Ch., Port Arthur, 1975—, Buchanan Cir., 1980—, Port Child Svc. League, Port Arthur, 1989—, Life PTA-Tex. PTA, 1985, Clean Cmty. Commn., Port Arthur, 1990—. Named One of Top 20 Tchrs. in Tex., Leadership Edn., 1984-85, Bus. Assoc. of Yr. plaque Energy City chpt. Am. Women Bus. Assn., 1984. Mem. Assn. Tex. Profl. Educators (Leadership cert. 1989), Zeta Phi Beta. Democrat. Avocations: walking, gardening, cooking, reading, classical music. Home: 741 E 10th St Port Arthur TX 77640

WEBER, LAVERN JOHN, marine science administrator, educator; b. Isabel, S.D., June 7, 1933; s. Jacob and Irene Rose (Bock) W.; m. Shirley Jean Carlson, June 19, 1959 (div. 1992); children: Timothy L., Peter J., Pamela C., Elizabeth T.; m. Patricia Rae Lewis, Oct. 17, 1992. AAS, Everett Jr. Coll., 1956; BA, Pacific Luth. U., 1958; MS, U. Wash., 1962, PhD, 1964. Instr. U. Wash., Seattle, 1964-67, asst. prof., 1967-69, acting state toxicologist, 1968-69; assoc. prof. Oreg. State U., Corvallis, 1969-75, prof., 1976—, asst. dean grad. sch., 1974-77; dir. Hatfield Marine Sci. Ctr. Oregon State U., Newport, 1977—, supt. Coastal Oreg. Marine Exptl. Sta., 1989—. Pres., trustee Newport Pub. Libr., 1991-92, Yaquina Bay Econ. Found., Newport, 1991-92; chmn. Oreg. Coast Aquarium, 1983-95. Recipient Pres. award Newport Rotary, 1984-85. Mem. South Slough Mgmt. Commn., Am. Soc. Pharm. and Exptl. Therapy, West Pharm. Soc., Soc. Toxicology, Soc. Exptl. Biol. Med. (n.w. divsn., pres. 1978, 82, 87), Pacific N.W. Assn. Toxicologists (chair 1985-86, coun. 1991-93), Western Assn. Marine Lab. (pres. 1993). Avocations: woodworking, reading, walking, scuba, gardening. Office: Oregon State Univ Hatfield Marine Sci Ctr Aquarium 2030 SE Marine Science Dr Newport OR 97365-5229

WEBER, MARY E., lawyer; b. June 21, 1948; d. George H. and Arlis A. (Holleman) Weber; m. Robert Duggan, May, 1977; children: Sarah Duggan, Anne Duggan, Laurence Duggan. BA, Northwestern U., 1970; JD, U. Pa., 1973. Bar: Mass. 1973, Pa. 1973. Ptnr. Ropes & Gray, Boston, 1973—. Trustee Greater Boston Legal Svcs., 1985—, Mass. Continuing Legal Edn., Inc., Boston, 1987—, pres., 1989-92. Office: Ropes & Gray 1 Internat Plz Boston MA 02110

WEBER, MARY ELLEN HEALY, economist; b. San Francisco, May 28, 1943; d. Ignatius Bernard and Grace Marie (Hogan) Healy; B.A., Dominican Coll., 1965; postgrad. Nat. U. Mex., 1967, (vis. scholar) Stanford U., 1969-70, Cath. U. Chile, 1970-71, U. Chile, 1971-72; Ph.D., U. Utah, 1974; m. Stephen Francis Weber, Dec. 21, 1971. U. Utah teaching fellow, 1965-68; asst. prof. Smith Coll., 1972-75; country economist World Bank, IBRD, 1975-76; sr. economist Internat. Research & Tech. Corp., McLean, Va., 1976-78; dir. regulatory analysis, chief economist OSHA, U.S. Dept. Labor, Washington, 1979-84; pres. Weber Software Enterprises, 1984-86, Web-Wolf Data Systems, Inc., 1986-90; dir. econs., exposure and tech divsn. Office of Pollution Prevention & Toxics US EPA, Washington, 1990—. Social Sci. Research Council fgn. area fellow 1969-71. Mem. Sr. Execs. Assn., Exec. Women in Govt. Roman Catholic.

WEBER, MARY LINDA, preschool educator; b. Hermon, N.Y., May 21, 1947; d. Stanley Albert and Shirley Lucille (Holland) Morrill; m. John Weber, July 23, 1966 (div. Nov. 1980); children: James, Mark. AAS, Agrl. and Tech. Coll., Canton, N.Y., 1971; BA, SUNY, Potsdam, 1973; MA, U. South Fla., 1981. Cert. pre-sch., elem. and reading K-12 tchr., N.Y., Fla.;. Tchr. elem. Hermon-DeKalb Ctrl. Sch., DeKalb Junction, N.Y., 1974-76, Westside Elem. Sch., Spring Hill, Fla., 1976-77; tchr. kindergarten Spring Hill Elem. Sch., 1977-89; tchr. pre-kindergarten Deltona Elem. Sch., Spring Hill, 1989—. Author mini-grant Home-Sch. Partnerships, 1990, Multi-Cultural Ctr., 1992, Family Info. Ctr., 1993. Mem. NEA (Young Children sect.), Assn. Childhood Edn. Internat., Internat. Reading Assn., So. Early Childhood Assn., Fla. Reading Assn., Hernando County Reading Coun. Avocations: reading, cross-stitch, bicycling. Home: 4132 Redwing Dr Spring Hill FL 34606-2425 Office: Deltona Elem Sch 2055 Deltona Blvd Spring Hill FL 34606-3216

WEBER, MERRILL EVAN, lawyer, business executive; b. Chgo., Sept. 1, 1956; s. Robert and Mildred (Kurchitzer) W.; m. Mindy Kallus, Mar. 29, 1987; children: Stephanie Margalit, Sarah Abigail. BA, Columbia Coll., 1978, MS in Journalism, 1978, JD, 1984. Bar: N.Y. 1985, U.S. Dist. Ct. (so. and ea. dists.) N.Y. 1985. Assoc. Fried, Frank, Harris, Shriver & Jacobson, N.Y.C., 1984-85, Mayer, Brown & Platt, N.Y.C., 1985-87, Paul, Weiss, Rifkind, Wharton & Garrison, N.Y.C., 1987-91, D'Ancona & Pflaum, Chgo., 1991-92; CEO, gen. counsel Merrill Weber & Co., Inc. (formerly Weber, Halpert & Co., Inc.), Chgo., 1992—. Harlan Fiske Stone scholar, Columbia Law Sch., 1982-83, 1983-84. Mem. ABA, N.Y. State Bar Assn., Assn. of Bar of City of N.Y. Jewish. Office: Merrill Weber & Co Inc Ste A 95 Revere Dr Northbrook IL 60062

WEBER, MICHAEL, editor; b. N.Y.C., Sept. 25, 1945; s. David and Dorothy (Silverberg) W. BA in History magna cum laude, CUNY, 1966; postgrad., U. Wis., 1966-67; MA in Am. Civilization, NYU, 1968. Asst. editor in regional studies gen. ency. dept. Macmillan Pub. Co., N.Y.C., 1970-71; assoc. editor in regional studies New Columbia Ency. project Columbia U. Press, N.Y.C., 1971-74; editing supr. coll. divsn. McGraw-Hill Book Co., N.Y.C., 1974-76; assoc. editor in social studies sch. dept. Harcourt Brace Jovanovich, N.Y.C., 1976-79; project editor coll. divsn. St. Martin's Press, N.Y.C., 1979-81, acquisitions editor and devel. editor coll. divsn., 1981-89; exec. editor history and polit. sci. M. E. Sharpe, Inc., Armonk, N.Y., 1989-95; copyeditor, proofreader, fact-checker for several pubs. house and Met. Mus. of Art. Author: Our National Parks, 1994, Our Congress, 1994, three books on U.S. Presidents; contbr. articles to the New Columbia Ency., 1975, also to other books in field. Mem. Phi Beta Kappa, Phi Alpha Theta. Democrat. Avocations: classical music, wines, hiking, photography. Home: 6 Peter Cooper Rd # 2D New York NY 10010 Office: ME Sharpe 80 Business Park Dr Armonk NY 10504

WEBER, MORTON M., microbial biochemist, educator; b. N.Y.C., May 26, 1922; s. Morris and Mollie (Scherer) W.; m. Phyllis Stern Levy, July 31, 1955; children—Stephen Abbott, Ethan Lenard. B.S., Coll. City N.Y., 1949; Sc.D., Johns Hopkins, 1953. Instr. microbiology Sch. Medicine, Johns Hopkins, 1951-55; Am. Cancer Soc. fellow in biochemistry McCollum-Pratt Inst., 1953-56; instr. bacteriology and immunology Med. Sch., Harvard, 1956-59; asst. prof. Sch. Medicine, St. Louis U., 1959-61, assoc. prof., 1961-63, prof., 1963—, chmn. dept. microbiology, 1964-87, chmn. emeritus, 1987—, prof. emeritus, 1992—; vis. scientist microbiology unit U. Oxford (Eng.) Dept. Biochemistry, 1970—; sr. mem. Linacre Coll. Oxford U., 1970—; mem. microbial chemistry study sect. NIH, USPHS, 1969-73. Served with USAAF, 1942-46. Fellow AAAS, Am. Acad. Microbiology, Infectious Disease Soc. Am., Johns Hopkins Soc. Scholars; mem. Am. Soc. Biol. Chemists, Am. Soc. Microbiology (sec. physiology div. 1964-65, vice chmn. 1965-66, chmn. 1966-67), Soc. Gen. Microbiology, N.Y. Acad. Scis., St. Louis Biochemistry Group (pres. 1968-69), Phi Beta Kappa (hon.), Sigma Xi. Research in biochemistry of microorganisms, with emphasis on pathways and mechanisms of electron transport, enzymatic regulatory mechanisms, and mode of action of antimicrobial drugs and antibiotics.

Home: 7068 Waterman Ave Saint Louis MO 63130-4323 Office: St Louis U Sch Medicine Dept Microbiology Saint Louis MO 63104

WEBER, NANCY WALKER, charitable trust administrator; b. Adrian, W.Va., Aug. 26, 1936; d. James Everett and Wanna Virginia (Alderman) Walker; m. J. Raymond Jacob, Jr., June 12, 1955 (div. 1967); children: Paul M., Sharon L.; m. George Harry Weber, Apr. 27, 1983 (dec. Mar. 1995). Student, Peabody Prep. Mus., 1946-53, Peabody Conservatory Mus., 1954-56. Asst. buyer cosmetics Hutzler's Dept. Store, Balt., 1967-69; exec. sec. to exec. v.p. Martin Marietta Corp., Bethesda, Md., 1969-75; asst. exec. to exec. dir. hosp. U. Utah, Salt Lake City, 1976-80; dir. program adminstrn. Lucille P. Markey Charitable Trust, Miami, Fla., 1983—. Pianist, organist Middle River Bapt. Ch., Balt., 1953-61. Named Mrs. Del. in Mrs. Del./Am. Pagent, 1966. Avocations: piano, organ. Office: Lucille P Markey Charitable Trust 3250 Mary St Ste 405 Miami FL 33133-5232

WEBER, OWEN, broadcast executive; b. N.Y.C., Apr. 29, 1946; s. Francis and Margaret (Korn) W.; m. Barbara Burke, Oct. 28, 1978. BS in Broadcasting, U. Fla., 1968. Program dir. Sta. WLYH-TV, Lancaster, Pa., 1970-72; dir. affiliate rels. Mut. Radio Networks, Washington, 1972-77; account exec. Sta. WCBM, Balt., 1977-78; local sales mgr. Sta. WTOP, Washington, 1979-80; gen. sales mgr. Sta. WTOP-Radio Outlet Co., Washington, 1980-81; gen. sales mgr. Sta. WCBM-Radio Metromedia, Balt., 1981-83; gen. sales mgr. Sta. WPGC-AM-FM First Media Corp., Washington, 1983-85; v.p., gen. mgr. Stas. WCAO-Radio and WXYV-Radio Summit Broadcasting Corp., Balt., 1985-88; exec. v.p. Summit Broadcasting Corp., Atlanta, 1988-93; pres., CEO HMW Comm., Inc., Atlanta, 1993-95; v.p., gen. mgr. Sta. KIKK-AM-FM and Sta. KILT-AM-FM CBS-Radio, Houston, 1995—. Office: CBS Radio Houston Ste 1900 24 E Greenway Plz Houston TX 77046

WEBER, PHILIP JOSEPH, retired manufacturing company executive; b. Chgo., Mar. 15, 1909; s. Joseph and Theresa (Zollner); m. Esther P. White, Aug. 29, 1941; 1 child, Patricia G. B.B.A., Northwestern U., 1938. With Ernst & Ernst, Chgo., 1938-41; with Doall Co., Des Plaines, Ill., 1941—88; exec. v.p. Doall Co., 1960-69, pres., 1969-74, chmn. bd., 1974-88, ret. Clubs: Mason (Shriner), Elk, Park Ridge Country. Home: 709 N Merrill St Park Ridge IL 60068-2701 also: 4545 N Ocean Blvd Apt 9-d Boca Raton FL 33431-5344

WEBER, ROBERT CARL, lawyer; b. Chester, Pa., Dec. 18, 1950; s. Robert Francis and Lucille (Nobili) W.; m. Linda Brediger, June 30, 1972; children: Robert F., Mary Therese, David P., Joseph T. BA cum laude, Yale U., 1972; JD, Duke U., 1976. Bar: Ohio 1976, U.S. Dist. ct. (no. dist.) Ohio 1976, U.S. Ct. Claims 1980, U.S. Ct. Appeals (6th cir.) 1981, U.S. Ct. Appeals (5th cir.) 1995. Assoc. Jones, Day, Reavis & Pogue, Cleve., 1976-83, ptnr., 1983—. Bd. dirs. United Way Svcs. of Cleve., 1992—. Fellow Am. Coll. Trial Lawyers; mem. Ohio Bar Assn., Am. Law Inst., Product Liability Adv. Coun., Cleve. Bar Assn. (chmn. jud. selection com. 1985-86, trustee 1990-93, pres.-elect 1994-95, pres. 1995-96), Jud. Conf. for 8th Jud. Dist. Ohio (life), Order of Coif. Roman Catholic. Office: Jones Day Reavis & Pogue 901 Lakeside Ave E Cleveland OH 44114-1116

WEBER, ROBERT MAXWELL, cartoonist; b. L.A., Apr. 22, 1924; p. Milton and Edith (Huston) W.; m. Marilyn Baum, Oct. 11, 1953 (div.); children—Peter, Lee; m. Debora Graves, Dec. 24, 1988. Student, Pratt Inst., 1945-48, Art Students League, 1948-50. Fashion illustrator, 1949-54; artist New Yorker mag., 1962—; work commd. by IBM, N.Y. Telephone, Am. Airlines, Mobil, Blue Cross/Blue Shield, U.S. Healthcare, Goodyear Co., J.C. Penney Co., Air Canada, Swissair, others; contbr. cartoons to nat. mags. Served with USCGR, 1942-45. Office: New Yorker 20 W 43rd St New York NY 10036-7400

WEBER, ROBYN VICTORIA, environmental engineer; b. Landover, Md., June 7, 1965. BS in Petroleum Engring., U. Mo., Rolla, 1987; postgrad., U. Okla., 1995—. Ops. engr. Mobil Oil Corp., Ada, Countyline, Okla., 1988-92; project mgr., environ. engr. StanTech Environ. Svcs., Oklahoma City, Okla., 1992-94, Gulf-Pacific Environ. Engring., Oklahoma City, Okla., 1994-95; pres. Advantage Environ. Svcs., Oklahoma City, Okla., 1995—; reservoir mgmt. team leader Mobil Oil Corp., Countyline, 1990-92; presenter at confs. Vol. Second Chance Animal Sanctuary, 1991-92. Mem. ASTM, DAR, Soc. Petroleum Engrs., Okla. Soc. Environ. Profls., Nat. Groundwater Assn., Air and Waste Mgmt. Assn., Okla. Hazardous Materials Assn. Avocations: travelling, music, hiking. Home: 11637 SW 4th Terr Yukon OK 73099 Office: Advantage Environ Svcs P O Box 890566 Oklahoma City OK 73189

WEBER, RONALD GILBERT, retired college president; b. Bergholz, Ohio, Feb. 18, 1916; s. George John and Elizabeth (Davis) W.; m. Mary Evelyn Cook, May 25, 1940 (dec. Dec. 1979); children: Constance (Mrs. Norman G. Coates), Judith L. (Mrs. Charles C. Watts). A.B., Mt. Union Coll., 1938; D.B.A. (hon.), Ohio No. U., 1963; LL.D. (hon.), Baldwin-Wallace Coll., 1976; L.H.D. (hon.), Mt. Union Coll., 1980. Loan rep., comml. rep., mgr. Household Finance Corp. & Beneficial Mgmt. Corp., Canton, O., Pitts., and McKeesport, Pa., 1938-43; alumni sec., dir. admissions and publicity Mt. Union Coll., Alliance, O., 1943-44; bus. mgr., sec. trustees Mt. Union Coll., 1945-50, v.p., sec., 1950-67, acting pres., 1967-68, pres., 1968-80, pres. emeritus, 1980—; comml. rep. First Nat. Bank McKeesport, 1944-45; cons. Ohio No. U., 1984—. Past bd. dirs. United Fund Alliance; past treas. Alliance Citizens Hosp. Assn.; past chmn. Ohio Meth. Commn. High Edn., life trustee Ohio Found. Ind. Colls.; past trustee, past vice chmn., mem. exec. com. Assn. Ind. Colls. and Univs. Ohio; hon. trustee Mt. Union Coll.; past pres. East Central Coll. Consortium. Recipient Alumni award Mt. Union Coll., 1943, Ohio No. U., 1991. Mem. Alliance Country Club, Blue Key, Psi Kappa Omega, Pi Gamma Mu, Alpha Tau Omega. Methodist. Home: 440 Vincent St Alliance OH 44601-3952

WEBER, SAMUEL, editor; b. N.Y.C., July 31, 1926; s. Bernard and Gertrude (Ellenberg) W.; m. Eileen Gloria Hornstein, Mar. 5, 1950; children—Bruce Jay, Robert Matthew. B.S. in Elec. Engring, Va. Poly. Inst., 1947. Engr. N.Y. Bd. Transp., 1948-50, U.S. Naval Shipyard, Bklyn., 1950-52, Barlow Engring. Co., N.Y.C., 1952-54; engring. supr. Curtiss Wright Corp., Woodridge, N.J., 1954-56; electronics engr. Loral Electronics Corp., N.Y.C., 1957-58; with Electronics mag., N.Y.C., 1958-67, assoc. mng. editor, 1968-70, exec. editor, 1970-79, editor in chief, 1979-84, exec. tech. editor, 1984-88, editor-at-large, 1988-92; editor in chief Electrotechnology mag., N.Y.C., 1968—; pres. Samuel Weber & Assocs., 1988-91, Samuel Weber & Assocs., Inc., 1991—; contbg. editor Asic & Eda Magazine, 1991—; spl. projects editor Electronic Engring. Times, 1992—. Author: Modern Digital Circuits, 1964, Optoelectronic Devices and Circuits, 1968, Large and Medium Scale Integration, 1974, Circuits for Electronics Engineers, 1977, Electronic Circuits Notebook, 1981. Served with AUS, 1944-46. Mem. IEEE (life). Home and Office: 4242 E Allison Rd Tucson AZ 85712-1039

WEBER, SAMUEL LLOYD, tap dancer, choreographer; b. Washington, Oct. 16, 1950; s. Abe Charles and Mary Louise (Walker) W.; m. Rosine Anne Bena, July 28, 1973 (div. May 1986); 1 child, Ananda Bena. Grad., Calif. State U., L.A. Prin. dancer Peninsula Ballet Theatre, San Mateo, Calif., 1972-86; ballet master, prin. dancer Sacramento Ballet, 1986; prin. dancer Jazz Tap Ensemble, L.A., 1986—; instr. dance artist-in-residence L.A. County H.S. for Arts, 1989-91, Calif. State U., Fullerton, 1990, 94. Tap dancer Joyce Theatre season, 1992 (Bessie award 1993), soloist with Lyon Symphony Biennial, 1991. Home: 1163 Guerrero St San Francisco CA 94110-2934 Office: 1433 Yale St # B1 Santa Monica CA 90404-3133

WEBER, SHIRLEY BOWERS, retired management analyst, networking communicator; b. Columbus, Miss., Nov. 9, 1942; d. Durant Jr. and Myra Waldene (Davis) Bowers; m. Frank Thomas Weber, Sept. 28, 1963 (div. May 26, 1966). Student, Ga. State Coll. Bus. Adminstrn., 1960-61, Montgomery Coll., 1977-79. Budget & mgmt. analyst U.S. Dept. Commerce/NOAA, Rockville, Md., 1977-81; sr. budget & mgmt. analyst Nat. Weather Svc., Silver Spring, Md., 1981-88; chief, prodn. mgmt. branch U.S. Dept. Commerce/NEXRAD, Silver Spring, Md., 1988-92; sr. mgmt. analyst U.S. Dept. Commerce/NOAA, Silver Spring, Md., 1992-94. Author, editor: Animal Organizations-VA & DC, 1985, Directory of Animal Org's-MD & DC, 1986, Project BREED Directory Vol. 1, 1989, Project BREED Directory-Red Book, 1993. Named humanitarian of yr. Montgomery County (Md.) Humane Soc., 1990, Pres.'s award SPCA of Anne Arundel County (Md.), 1992, top dog award Washington Animal Rescue League, 1994. Mem. Project BREED (v.p., co-founder). Democrat. Established a nationwide vol. coalition currently comprising approximately 10,000 vols. who specialize in rescue of specific breeds or species of animals. Avocations: gardening, reading. Office: Project BREED, Inc. PO Box 15888 Chevy Chase MD 20825-5888

WEBER, STEPHEN LEWIS, university president; b. Boston, Mar. 17, 1942; s. Lewis F. and Catherine (Warns) W.; m. Susan M. Keim, June 27, 1965; children: Richard, Matthew. BA, Bowling Green State U., 1964; postgrad., U. Colo., 1964-66; PhD, U. Notre Dame, 1969; EdD (hon.), Capital Normal U., China, 1993. Asst. prof. philosophy U. Maine, Orono, 1969-75, assoc. prof., 1975-79, asst. to pres., 1976-79; dean arts and scis. Fairfield (Conn.) U., 1979-84; v.p. acad. affairs St. Cloud (Minn.) State U., 1984-88; pres. SUNY Oswego, 1988—; interim provost SUNY, Oswego, 1995-96; pres. San Diego State U., 1996—; participant Harvard Inst. Ednl. Mgmt., Cambridge, Mass., 1985; cons. Sloan Found., 1981. Contbr. numerous articles on philosophy and acad. adminstrn. to profl. jours. Mentor Am. Coun. Edn. Fellowship Program; co-chair Minn. State Bd. Edn. Curriculum Task Force on Educating the Black Learner, 1988; mem. Minn. Tech. Alliance, 1987; mem. program adv. com. Minn. Higher Edn. Coordinating Bd., 1986-88; mem. Gov.'s Commn. on Internat. Edn., 1988. Named Outstanding Humanities Tchr., U. Maine, 1975; Rsch. fellow U. Notre Dame, 1968-69. Mem. Am. Philos. Assn., Am. Assn. Higher Edn. Democrat. Avocations: art, woodworking, swimming, boating. Office: Office of President San Diego State Univ La Jolla CA

WEBER, THOMAS WILLIAM, chemical engineering educator; b. Orange, N.J., July 15, 1930; s. William A. and Dorothy (Negus) W.; m. Marianne S. Hartmann, June 4, 1966; children—Anne Louise, William Alois. B.Chem. Engring., Cornell U., 1953, Ph.D., 1963; M.S. in Chem. Engring., Newark Coll. Engring., 1958. Registered profl. engr., N.Y. Chem. engr. econs. and planning Esso Research & Engring., Linden, N.J., 1955-58; instr. Cornell U., 1961-62; asst. prof. SUNY-Buffalo, 1963-66, assoc. prof. chem. engring., 1966-82, prof., 1982—, assoc. chmn. dept., 1980-82, chmn. dept., 1982-89. Author: An Introduction to Process Dynamics and Control, 1973. Named Prof. of Yr., Tau Kappa Chi, 1965; recipient Chancellor's award for excellence in teaching, 1981, Tchr. of Yr. award Tau Beta Pi, 1982. Fellow Am. Inst. Chem. Engrs. (chmn. we. N.Y. sect. 1969-70, Profl. Achievement award we. N.Y. sect. 1978), Am. Soc. Engring. Edn. (chmn. instrumentation divsn. 1975-77, chmn. St. Lawrence sect. 1979-80, 92-94, chmn. divsn. experimentation and lab.-oriented studies 1985-86, Outstanding Zone Campus Rep. award 1988, AT&T Found. award 1987-88), Tech. Socs. Coun. Niagara Frontier (sec. 1973-75, pres. 1975-76, treas. 1978—), Sigma Xi, Phi Kappa Phi, Tau Beta Pi, Theta Xi. Presbyterian. Club: Swedish of Buffalo (pres. 1974-76). Home: 52 Autumnview Rd Buffalo NY 14221-1602

WEBER, WALTER JACOB, JR., engineering educator; b. Pitts., June 16, 1934. Sc.B., Brown U., 1956; M.S.E., Rutgers U., 1959; A.M., Harvard, 1961, Ph.D., 1962. Registered profl. engr. Diplomate Am. Acad. Environ. Engrs. Engr. Caterpillar Tractor Co., Peoria, Ill., 1956-57; instr. Rutgers U., 1957-59; engr. Soil Conservation Service, New Brunswick, N.J., 1957-59; research, teaching asso. Harvard, 1959-63; faculty U. Mich., Ann Arbor, 1963—; prof., chmn. water resources program U. Mich., 1968-91, The Earnest Boyce Disting. Prof. of Engring., 1987-94; The Gordon Maskew Fair and Earnest Boyce Disting. U. Prof. U. Mich., Ann Arbor, 1994—; dir. Great Lakes & Mid-Atlantic Hazardous Substance Rsch. Ctr., Nat. Ctr. for Integrated Bioremediation R & D; Internat. cons. to industry, govt. Author: (with K.H. Mancy) Analysis of Industrial Wastewaters, 1971, Physicochemical Processes for Water Quality Control, 1972, (with F.A. DiGiano) Process Dynamics in Environmental Systems, 1996; editor, author: (with E. Matijevic) Adsorption for Aqueous Solution, 1968; contbr. numerous articles and chpts. to tech. and profl. jours. and books. Recipient Disting. Faculty awards U. Mich., 1967, 78, Rsch. Excellence award, 1980, Stephen S. Attwood award, 1977; Disting. Faculty award Mich. chpt. Assn. Gov. Bds. of State Univs., 1989; Disting. Scientist award U.S. EPA, 1991; Athalie Richardson Irvine Clarke prize Nat. Water Rsch. Inst., 1996. Mem. NAE, Am. Acad. Environ. Engrs. (Diplomate 1975, Gordon Maskew Fair award, 1995), Am. Chem. Soc. (cert. of merit 1962, F.J. Zimmerman award 1982), Am. Inst. Chem. Engrs., ASCE (Rudolph Hering medal 1980, Thomas R. Camp award 1982, Simon W. Freese award 1984, G. Brooks Earnest award 1985), Am. Water Works Assn. (life, Acad. Achievement awards 1981, 89, A.P. Black Rsch. award 1991), Assn. Environ. Engring. Profs. (Disting. Faculty award 1968, NALCO rsch. award 1979, Engring. Sci. rsch. award 1984, Outstanding Publ. award 1989, Disting. Lectr. award 1990), Internat. Assn. for Water Pollution Rsch. and COntrol (Founders Outstanding Publ. award 1987, 92), Water Pollution Control Fedn. (John R. Rumsey Meml. award 1975, Willard F. Shepard award 1980, Thomas R. Camp medal 1988, Gordon Maskew Fair medal 1990), Tau Beta Pi, Sigma Xi, Chi Epsilon, Delta Omega. Home: PO Box 7775 Ann Arbor MI 48107-7775 Office: U Mich Coll Engring Environ Engring Program Ste 181 EWRE Bldg Ann Arbor MI 48109-2125

WEBER, WENDELL WILLIAM, pharmacologist; b. Maplewood, Mo., Sept. 2, 1925; s. Theodore William and Flora Ann (Holt) W.; m. La Donna Tavis, Sept. 29, 1952; children—Jane Holt, Theodore Wendell. A.B., Central Coll., 1945; Ph.D. in Phys. Chemistry, Northwestern U., 1950; M.D., U. Chgo., 1959. Diplomate Am. Bd. Pediatrics; lic. Mich., N.Y., Calif. Asst. prof. chemistry U. Tenn., Knoxville, 1949-51; mem. ops. research staff U.S. Army Chem. Center, Edgewood, Md., 1951-55; successively instr., asst. prof., asso. prof., prof. pharmacology N.Y. U. Sch. Medicine, N.Y.C., 1963-74; prof. U. Mich., Ann Arbor, 1974—; Disting. Lectureship in Biomedical Rsch. U. Mich., 1993; mem. pharmacology-toxicology com. NIH, 1969-73, rev. coms., 1968—. Editorial bd. Bioessays, 1984-91, Pharmacogenetics, 1990—. NIH spl. fellow, 1962-65; research grantee, 1967—; recipient Career Scientist awards N.Y.C. Health Research Council, 1965-70, 70-74. Fellow N.Y. Acad. Scis.; mem. Am. Soc. Pharmacology and Therapeutics, Am. Chem. Soc., Am. Soc. Human Genetics, Soc. Toxicology (hon.), AAAS, Sigma Xi, Phi Lambda Upsilon. Research specialty in pharmacogenetics. Home: 14 Geddes Hts Ann Arbor MI 48104-1724 Office: Dept Pharmacology U Mich Ann Arbor MI 48109-0632

WEBER, WILFORD ALEXANDER, education educator; b. Allentown, Pa., Apr. 29, 1939; s. Alexander F. and Kathryn A. (Campbell) W.; children from previous marriage: Kendra L., Brad A.; m. Cheryl Angelo. BA, Muhlenberg Coll., 1963; EdD, Temple U., 1967. Tchr., counselor New Life Boys Ranch, Harleysville, Pa., 1963-65; rsch. asst. Temple U., Phila., 1965-67; asst. prof. Syracuse (N.Y.) U., 1967-71; prof. U. Houston, 1971—, chair dept. curriculum & instrn. Author approximately 165 books, monographs, papers and articles. Grantee, Syracuse U., U. Houston. Mem. Am. Ednl. Rsch. Assn., Assn. Tchr. Educators. Avocation: sports. Home: 2015 Swift Blvd Houston TX 77030-1213

WEBER, WILLIAM P., electronics company executive; b. 1940; married. BS, Lamar U., 1962; MS, So. Meth. U., 1966. With Tex. Instruments, Inc., Dallas, 1962—, mgr. assembly and test equipment group, 1965-70, mfr. mgr. electro-optics div. equipment group, 1970-71, mgr. ops. digital systems, 1971-75, asst. v.p., mgr. missile div. equipment group, 1975-79, 1979-80, mgr. Lewisville site, 1979-80, v.p., mgr. electro optics div., 1980-81, mgr. Forest Ln. site, 1980-81, v.p., mgr. equipment group, 1981-82, v.p. and pres. defense systems and electronics group, 1982-84, exec. v.p., mgr. corp. devel., 1984-87, exec. v.p., pres. semiconductor group, 1987—, also bd. dirs. Office: Tex Instruments Inc PO Box 655474 13500 N Central Expy Dallas TX 75265*

WEBER-ROOCHVARG, LYNN, English second language adult educator, consultant; b. Long Beach, Calif., Jan. 5, 1945; d. Bernard R. and Ruth M. (Oehler) Weber; m. Edward A. Birge (div.); 1 child, Colin E.; m. Alan C. Roochvarg. BA, U. Wis., 1966, MA in Libr. Sci., 1967; PhD, Ariz. State U., 1980. Teaching asst. U. Wis., Madison, 1966-67; libr. Madison Pub. Libr., 1967-70, New Haven Free Pub. Libr., 1970-72; ESL instr. Tempe (Ariz.) Adult Basic Education Program, 1972-77, supr., 1977-80; pvt. practice Phoenix, 1980-82; libr. Phoenix Coll., 1982-84, Lansdale (Pa.) Sch. Bus., 1985-92; pres. LWR Assocs., Colmar, Pa., 1991—. Author: Serving Adult Learners, 1981; contbr. articles to profl. jours. Ford Found fellow, 1966; Ariz. Dept. Edn. grantee, 1978-80. Mem. ALA, Pa. TESOL, Phi Beta Kappa. Office: LWR Assocs PO Box 501 Colmar PA 18915-0501

WEBRE, SEPTIME, ballet company artistic director, choreographer; b. New Orleans, Dec. 7, 1961; s. Alfred L. and Juanita (Chisholm) W. BA, U. Tex., 1984. Dancer Merce Cunningham Dance Co., N.Y.C., 1991; dancer Am. Repertory Ballet/Princeton (N.J.) Ballet, 1987—, choreographer, 1988—, artistic dir., 1993—; freelance choreographer various ballet cos., 1988—; guest master tchr. various ballet cos., 1990—. Former mem. exec. bd. Young Dems. Am., Austin. Choreographic fellow N.J. Coun. on Arts, 1992. Roman Catholic. Office: Am Repertory Ballet 80 Albany St New Brunswick NJ 08901

WEBSTER, ALBERT KNICKERBOCKER, consultant in performing arts; b. Bklyn., Oct. 14, 1937; s. Albert Noyes and Janet (Knickerbocker) W.; m. Sara Beyer, Feb. 19, 1961; children: Albert Van Berghen, Katherine Lee. BA, Harvard Coll., 1959; student, L'Ecole de Musique de Fontainebleau, summers 1958-59. Asst. to mgr., asst. mgr. N.Y. Philharm., 1962-71, mng. dir., 1975-90, exec. v.p., 1978-90; gen. mgr. Cin. Symphony Orch., 1971-75; mem., co-chmn. planning sect., orch. sect., music panel Nat. Endowment for Arts, 1974-80, mem. inter-arts panel, 1981-82. Bd. dirs., treas. Am. Music Ctr.; bd. dirs. Harvard Pieriou Found. Mem. Am. Symphony Orch. League (exec. com., bd. dirs.), Am. Arts Alliance (founding dir., bd. dirs., exec. com., sec.). Office: 5316 S Dorchester Ave Apt 408 Chicago IL 60615-5365

WEBSTER, DANIEL ROBERT, lawyer; b. Wayne, Mich., June 23, 1945. B.A. with high distinction, Ind. U., 1967; J.D., Harvard U., 1970. Bar: Ind. 1971, U.S. Dist. Ct. (so. dist.) Ind. 1971, U.S. Ct. Appeals (7th cir.) 1972, U.S. Supreme Ct. 1982; assoc. Hogan and Hartson, Washington, 1970-1; assoc. Ice, Miller, Donadio & Ryan, Indpls., 1971-77, 84—; dir. research Ind. Lawyers Commn., Indpls., 1977-81; sr. atty. Cummins Engine Co., Columbus, Ind., 1981-83; of counsel Ice Miller Donadio & Ryan, Indpls., 1983-85, ptnr., 1986-92; mng. ptnr. Bamberger & Feibleman, Indpls., 1994—; chmn. corrections com. Indpls. Lawyers Commn., 1979-80, chmn. pub. defender com., 1977-80, mem. community services com., 1973-74, bd. dirs., 1974-80; mem. Greater Indpls. Progress Com. Task Force on Criminal Justice; mem. Legal Def. Panel; adv. com. The Carl Duisberg Soc., Ind. U. East Asian Studies Ctr.; mem. speakers bur. Indpls. Co-editor: An Anatomy of Criminal Justice, 1980, Juvenile Intervention, 1982; contbr. articles to profl. jours.; producer TV Spl. Violence and the Public Response, 1978. Dem. nominee for Ind. Atty. Gen., 1980; Indpls., 1976-80; Am. del. Internat. YMCA Conf. on Disarmament and Detente, 1981; counsel Ind. Dem. Policy Com., 1980-81; mem. culture com. Ind. Ptnrs. for the Americas, 1983—; bd. dirs. Am. Ctr. for Internat. Leadership, Indpls. Pan Am. Games Planning Com.; bd. dirs. Indpls. Internat. Ctr., CEO Indpls. World Trade Ctr., chmn. Ind. Asean Coun. Served with U.S. Army, 1971. Ind. U. merit scholar, 1966-67; Wheeler scholar, 1966-67; Ford P. Hall scholar, 1967. Mem. Ind. Assn. (internat. law sect.), Indpls. Bar Assn. NAACP, Ind. Hist. Soc., Ind. Lawyers Commn. (bd. dirs. 1982—), Ind. Council Fgn. Relations, Indpls. Lit. Club. Indpls. Econ. Club (bd. dirs.), Forum for Internat. Profl. Services, Inc. (bd. dirs., pres.), Internat. Sch. of Indpls. (bd. dirs.), Blue Key, Phi Beta Kappa, Phi Eta Sigma. Club: Phoenix. Office: Bamberger & Feibleman 54 Monument Cir Ste 600 Indianapolis IN 46204-2942

WEBSTER, DAVID A., lawyer; b. Jacksonville, Fla., Aug. 25, 1948. BBA summa cum laude, U. Ga., 1975, JD cum laude, 1977; LLM Taxation, NYU, 1979. Bar: Ga. 1977, U.S. Tax Ct. 1978, Fla. 1980. Ptnr. Baker & Hostetler, Orlando, Fla., 1980-94, Mahoney Adams & Criser PA, Jacksonville, 1994-96; v.p., sec. general counsel St Anthony Publishing Inc., Reston, VA, 1996—; mem. Fla. Coun. Internat. Devel. 1981—, World Trade Coun. Ctrl. Fla. 1979—; chmn. Internat. Tax Discussion Group, 1989-90. Contbr. articles to profl. jours. Capt. U.S. Army, 1967-73. Mem. ABA (con. sect. taxation 1981-85), Internat. Bar Assn., Fla. Bar. Assn. (exec. com. internat. law, co-chmn. internat. tax com. 1986-87), State Bar Ga., Am. Assn. Atty. Cert. Pub. Accts., Orange County Bar Assn. (chmn. tax sect. 1986-87), adjunct prof. Unity of North Fla. Grad. Acctg. Program, Phi Kappa Phi. Office: St Anthony Publishing Inc Issac Newton Sq Reston VA 22090*

WEBSTER, DAVID ARTHUR, life insurance company executive; b. Downs, Ill., July 20, 1937; s. Harold Sanford and Carmen Mildred (Moore) W.; m. Anna Elizabeth Prosch, June 10, 1956; children: Theodore David, Elizabeth Anna, Arthur Lee, William Harold. B.S., U. Ill., 1960. Actuarial asst. Mass. Mut. Life Ins. Co., Springfield, 1960-64; cons. actuary George Stennes & Assocs., Mpls., 1964-68; v.p., actuary Piedmont Life Ins. Co., Atlanta, 1968-72, Pacific Fidelity Life Ins. Co., Los Angeles, 1972-74; v.p., chief actuary U.S. Life Corp., N.Y.C., 1974-76; exec. v.p. U.S. Life Corp., 1976-78, dir., 1976-78; pres., dir. Beneficial Pension Svcs, BPS Agy., Inc.; v.p., treas., dir. Beneficial Assurance Co., 1978-82; asst. sec., dir. Beneficial Computer Svcs., Inc.; treas. Tel-Assurance Corp.; exec. v.p., dir. Beneficial Standard Life, 1978-82; pres., dir. U.S. Life Ins. Co. of Calif., 1982-84, Western World Fin. Group Inc., 1984-86; exec. v.p., COO R.W. Durham and Co., 1987—. Fellow Soc. Actuaries; mem. Am. Acad. Actuaries. Clubs: Actuaries of Pacific States, Woodland Hills Country. Home: 5131 Encino Ave Encino CA 91316-2523

WEBSTER, EDWARD GLEN, principal, school system administrator; b. Chester, Pa., Sept. 13, 1946; s. Joseph Armiger and Lois Dean (Wise) W.; m. Janice Kay Bigelow, Apr. 10, 1982; 1 child, Caitlin Bigelow. AB in English Lit., Niagara U., 1972; MA in English Lit., Gannon U., 1977; MAEd in Elem. and Secondary Adminstrn., George Wash. U., 1986; EdD in Curriculum and Instrn., W.Va. U., 1989. Cert. adminstrn., Md., Maine, Va., S.C., N.C., W.Va. English tchr. Lake Forest H.S., Felton, Del., 1972-75; grad. asst. in English Gannon U., Erie, Pa., 1975-77; English tchr. Ryken H.S., Leonardtown, Md., 1979-81; grad. asst. in secondary edn. W.Va. U., Morgantown, 1981-83; chmn. English Dept. Cumberland (Va.) County H.S., 1983-84; English tchr. Leonardtown (Md.) H.S., 1984-86; prin. Forest Hills Mid. Sch., Jackman, Maine, 1986-87; asst. prin., athletic dir. Livermore Falls (Maine) H.S., 1987-88, prin., 1988-93; prin. Easton (Md.) H.S., 1993-95, Tucker County H.S. & Career Ctr., Hambleton, W.Va., 1995—. Contbr. articles to profl. jours. Mem. fin. com. Eaton United Meth. Ch., Livermore Falls, 1991-93. Sgt. U.S. Army, 1965-68. Recipient honorarium Allyn & Bacon, Inc., 1992, Cert. of Appreciation New Eng. Assn. Schs. and Colls., 1991. Mem. ASCD, Am. Assn. Sch. Adminstrs., Am. Ednl. Rsch. Assn., Md. Secondary Sch. Prins. Assn., Nat. Assn. Secondary Sch. Prins., W.Va. Assn. Secondary Sch. Prins., Kappa Delta Pi, Phi Delta Kappa (Cert. of Recognition 1983, 10-Yr. Membership award 1991), Rotary. Republican. Avocations: computers, jogging, reading. Home: 6 Apple Creek Estates Elkins WV 26241

WEBSTER, EDWARD WILLIAM, medical physicist; b. London, Apr. 12, 1922; came to U.S., 1949, naturalized, 1957; s. Edward and Bertha Louisa (Cornish) W.; m. Dorothea Anne Wood, June 24, 1961; children: John Stein, Peter Wood, D. Anne, Edward Russell, Mark Vincent, Susan Victoria. BSc in Elec. Engring., U. London, 1943, PhD, 1946; postgrad., MIT, 1949-51, 65-66, Columbia U., 1966; AM (hon.), Harvard U., 1989. Diplomate: Am. Bd. Radiology in radiol. physics (examiner 1958-84, chmn. physics com. 1966-76), Am. Bd. Health Physics. Research engr. English Electric Co., Stafford, Eng., 1945-49; travelling fellow lab. for nuclear sci. MIT, 1949-50, staff scientist, 1950-51; lectr. U. London, 1952-53; physicist Mass. Gen. Hosp., Boston, 1953—, chief radiol. scis. div., 1970—; prof. radiology Harvard U. Med. Sch., Boston, 1975—; prof. radiology div. health scis. and tech. Harvard-MIT, 1978-86; Langham lectr. U. Ky. Coll. Medicine, 1989; mem. biol. effects of ionizing radiation com. NAS, 1977-80; adv. com. on environ. hazards VA, 1985—, Med. Use of Isotopes, U.S. Nuclear Regulatory Commn., 1971-93; U.S. del. UN Sci. Com. on Effects of Atomic Radiation, 1987—; lectr. Harvard Sch. Pub. Health, 1971-86; cons. Radiation Effects Rsch. Found., Hiroshima, Japan, 1988; Taylor lectr. Nat. Coun. on Radiation Protection, 1992, mem., 1965-89, hon. mem., 1989—, cons. Presdl. Adv. Com. on Human Radiation Experiments, 1994-95. Author: A Basic Radioisotopes Course, 1959, Atlas of Radiation Dose Distributions, 1965, Radiation Safety Manual of MGH, 1965, Physics in Diagnostic Radiology, 1970; co-author: Instrumentation and Monitoring Methods for Radiation Protection, 1978, Low-level Radiation Effects, 1982; co-editor: Advances in Medical Physics, 1971, Biological Risks of Medical Irradiations, 1980; inventor composite shields against low energy X-rays, 1970. Robert

Blair travelling fellow London County Council, 1949; USPHS fellow, 1965; NIH grantee, 1958-80. Fellow Health Physics Soc. (Landauer award 1985, Failla award 1989), Am. Coll. Radiology (commn. mem. 1963—, Gold medal 1991), Am. Assn. Physicists in Medicine (dir. 1958-65, pres. 1963-64, Coolidge medal 1983); mem. Soc. Nuclear Medicine (trustee 1973-77), Radiol. Soc. N.Am. (v.p. 1977-78), New Eng. Roentgen Ray Soc. (hon., exec. com. 1976-77), Radiation Rsch. Soc., Sigma Xi (nat. lectr. 1988-89). Office: Mass Gen Hosp Fruit St Boston MA 02114-2620 *My efforts have focused on increasing and spreading knowledge which will improve man's control over his environment, including his health. Important principles include freedom to discuss and publish, respect for the rights of others and the acceptance of calls for difficult service.*

WEBSTER, ELROY, diversified supplies and machinery executive. Former 2d v.p., now chmn. Farmers Union Cen. Exch., Inc. Office: Farmers Union Cen Exch Inc 5500 Cenex Dr Inver Grove MN 55077-1733 also: Cenex PO Box 64089 Saint Paul MN 55164-0089*

WEBSTER, FREDERICK ELMER, JR., marketing educator, consultant; b. Auburn, N.Y., Oct. 22, 1937; s. Frederick Elmer and Evelyn May (Dudden) W.; m. Mary Alice Powers, Dec. 27, 1957; children: Lynn Marie, Mark Andrew (dec.), Lisa Ann. AB, Dartmouth Coll., 1959, MBA, 1960; PhD, Stanford U., 1964; Artium Magistrum (hon.), Dartmouth Coll., 1974. Asst. prof. mktg. Columbia U., N.Y.C., 1964-65; from asst. prof. to prof. bus. adminstrn. Dartmouth Coll., Hanover, N.H., 1965-79; assoc. dean Amos Tuck Sch. Dartmouth Coll., Hanover, 1976-83, E.B. Osborn prof. mktg., 1979-93, Charles Henry Jones Third Century prof. mgmt., 1993—; vis. prof. Internat. Mgmt. Inst., Geneva, 1970-88; vis. prof. bus. sch. Harvard U., Boston, 1987-89; exec. dir. Mktg. Sci. Inst., Cambridge, Mass., 1987-89; bd. dirs. Samuel Cabot, Inc., Mascoma Savs. Bank, Lebanon, N.H. Author: Marketing Communications, 1968, Social Aspects of Marketing, 1974, Marketing for Managers, 1974, Industrial Marketing Strategy, 1979, 3d edit., 1991, Marketing Management Casebook, 1980, 4th edit., 1984, Field Sales Management, 1983, Market-Driven Management, 1994; editor: Ronald Series on Marketing Management, 1975-91; mem. editorial bd., sect. editor Jour. Mktg., 1968—, Mktg. Letters, 1989—, Mktg. Mgmt., 1991—, Jours. Market-Focused Mgmt., 1995—; contbr. articles to profl. jours. Trustee Alice Peck Day Meml. Hosp., Lebanon, N.H., 1970-87, Mktg. Sci. Inst., 1989-94, exec. dir. coun. 1994—; bd. overseers Hanover Inn, N.H., 1985-92; firefighter Town of Hanover, 1970—, lt. Etna Divsn., 1991; bd. dirs., v.p. Vt. Pub. Radio, 1978-91, 92—; mem. fin. com. Dresden Sch. Dist., Hanover, 1973-76, chmn. 1976-77; vestryman, treas. St. Thomas Episc. Ch., Hanover, 1967-70, 76-78, 91-92; mem. missions com. Episc. Diocese N.H., Concord, 1988—. Gulf Oil fellow, 1959-60, U.S. Steel Found. fellow, 1961-63, Nat. Assn. Purchasing Agts. Doctoral fellow, 1963-64. Mem. Am. Mktg. Assn. (dir. 1972-74), Norford Lake Club. Republican. Episcopalian. Home: Deer Run Farm 80 Stevens Rd Hanover NH 03755-3114 Office: Dartmouth Coll Amos Tuck Sch Bus Adminstrn Hanover NH 03755

WEBSTER, GEORGE DRURY, lawyer; b. Jacksonville, Fla., Feb. 8, 1921; s. George D. and Mary Gaines (Walker) W.; m. Ann Kilpatrick; children: Aen Walker, George Drury, Hugh Kilpatrick. BA, Maryville Coll., 1941, LLD (hon.), 1984; LLB, Harvard U., 1948. Bar: Tenn. 1948, D.C. 1952, Md. 1976. Atty. tax div. Dept Justice, 1949-51; sr. partner Webster, Chamberlain & Bean, Washington; lectr. numerous tax. insts. Author: Business and Professional Political Action Committees, 1979, The Law of Associations, 1995. Trustee U.S. Naval Acad. Found., Annapolis, Md.; spl. U.S. ambassador, 1972. Served to lt. USNR, 1942-46. Mem. Am. Law Inst., Am. Bar Assn. Presbyn. Clubs: Chevy Chase (Md.); Metropolitan (Washington); Racquet and Tennis (N.Y.C.). Home: 5305 Cardinal Ct Bethesda MD 20816-2908 also: Webster Angus Farm Rogersville TN 37857 Office: Webster Chamberlain & Bean 1747 Pennsylvania Ave NW Washington DC 20006-4604

WEBSTER, HENRY DEFOREST, neuroscientist; b. N.Y.C., Apr. 22, 1927; s. Leslie Tillotson and Emily (deForest) W.; m. Marion Havas, June 12, 1951; children: Christopher, Henry, Sally, David, Steven. AB cum laude, Amherst Coll., 1948; MD, Harvard U., 1952. Intern Boston City Hosp., 1952-53, resident, 1953-54; resident in neurology Mass. Gen. Hosp., 1954-56, research fellow in neuropathology, 1956-59; prin. investigator NIH research grants for electron microscopic studies of peripheral neuropathy, 1959-69; mem. staffs Mass. Gen., Newton-Wellesley hosps.; instr. neurology Harvard Med. Sch., 1959-63, assoc. in neurology, 1963-66, asst. prof. neuropathology, 1966; assoc. prof. neurology U. Miami Sch. Medicine, 1966-69, prof., 1969; head sect. cellular neuropathology Nat. Inst. Neurol. Diseases and Stroke, Bethesda, Md., 1969—; assoc. chief Lab. of Neuropathology and Neuroanat. Scis., 1975-84; chief Lab. Exptl. Neuropathology, 1984—; disting. scientist, lectr. dept. anatomy Tulane U. Sch. Medicine, 1973; Royal Coll. lectr. Can. Assn. Neuropathologists, 1982; Saul Korey lectr. Am. Assn. Neuropathologists, 1992; chmn. Winter Conf. on Brain Rsch., 1985, 86; head neuropathology delegation to visit China in 1990, Citizen Amb. Program, People to People Internat.; mem. exec. com. rsch. group on neuromuscular disease World Fedn. Neurology, 1986-93. Author: (with A. Peters and S.L. Palay) The Fine Structure of the Nervous System, 1970, 76, 91; contbr. articles to sci. jours. Recipient Superior Svc. award USPHS, 1977, A. von Humboldt award Fed. Republic Germany, 1985, Sci. award Peripheral Neuropathy Assn., 1994; named hon. prof. Norman Bethune U. of Med. Scis., Chanchun, China, 1991. Mem. Am. Assn. Neuropathologists (v.p. 1976-77, pres. 1978-79, Weil award 1960), Internat. Soc. Neuropathology (councillor 1976-80, v.p. 1980-84, exec. com. 1980-84, 86-94, pres. 1986-90), Internat. Congress Neuropathology (sec. gen. VIII 1978), Peripheral Nerve Study Group (exec. com. 1975-93, chmn. 1977 meeting), Japanese Soc. Neuropathology (hon.), Am. Neurol. Assn., Am. Acad. Neurology, Am. Soc. Cell Biologists, Am. Assn. Anatomists, Soc. Neurosci., Rotary Internat., Washington Ctr. Photography, Ausable Club. Office: NIH Bldg 36 Rm 4A 29 Bethesda MD 20892

WEBSTER, JAMES RANDOLPH, JR., physician; b. Chgo., Aug. 25, 1931; s. James Randolph and Ruth Marian (Burtis) W.; m. Joan Burchfield, Dec. 28, 1954; children: Susan, Donovan, John. B.S., U. Chgo.-Northwestern U., 1953; M.D., M.S., Northwestern U., 1956. Diplomate: Am. Bd. Internal Medicine (sub bd. pulmonary disease and geriatrics). Resident in medicine, NIH fellow in pulmonary disease Phila. Gen. Hosp., 1956-57; resident in medicine and fellow in pulmonary disease Northwestern U., 1957-60, 62-64; asst. chief medicine Northwestern Meml. Hosp., Chgo., 1968-73; chief medicine Northwestern Meml. Hosp., 1973-88; prof. medicine Northwestern U. Med. Sch., 1977—, chief gen. med. sect. Dept. Medicine, 1987-88; chief exec. officer Northwestern Med. Group Practice, 1978-88; dir. ctr. on aging/geriatrics Northwestern U. Med. Ctr., 1988—; chief staff Northwestern Meml. Hosp., 1988-90. Contbr. chpts. to books, articles to med. jours. Served with U.S. Army, 1960-62. Recipient Outstanding Clin. tchr. award Northwestern U. Med. Sch., 1974, 77, 84, 86, Alumni Merit award Northwestern U., 1979. Mem. Am. Fedn. Clin. ACP (gov. for Ill. 1988-92, chair sub-com. on aging 1993—, Claypoole award 1994), Am. Thoracic Soc., Am. Geriatrics Soc., Ill. Geriatrics Soc. (pres. 1992-94), Soc. Rsch. and Edn. in Geriatrics. Home: 227 E Delaware Pl Chicago IL 60611-1713 Office: 750 N Lake Shore Dr Rm 601 Chicago IL 60611-4403 *Life should best be measured not by how long you live, but how.*

WEBSTER, JILL ROSEMARY, historian, educator; b. London, Sept. 29, 1931; arrived in Can., 1965; d. Harold James and Dora Elena (Andreini) W. BA in Hispanic Studies with honors, U. Liverpool, Eng., 1962, postgrad. cert. in edn., 1965; PhD in Spanish, U. Toronto, Can., 1969; MA in Spanish, U. Nottingham, Eng., 1964; BA in History with honors, U. London, Eng., 1978. Prof. U. Toronto, 1968-94, assoc. dean, 1978-81, dir. Ctr. for Medieval Studies, 1979-94, grad. chair dept. Spanish and Portuguese, 1993-94; prof. emeritus, 1995—. Author: Els Menorets: The Franciscans in the Realms of Aragon from St. Francis to the Black Death (1348), 1993. Fellow Royal Soc. Can.; mem. Am. Hist. Assn., Am. Cath. Hist. Assn., Medieval Acad. Am., Am. Acad. Rsch. Historians of Medieval Spain (pres. 1990-95). Office: U Toronto St Michaels Coll, 81 St Mary St, Toronto, ON Canada M5S 1J4

WEBSTER, JOHN CHAS, human resources management consultant; b. L.A., May 5, 1944; s. Leo Paul and Agnes (Melavic) W.; m. Dawn Thompson, Nov. 13, 1993; children from a previous marriage: Miriam, Mark. BA in Sociology, German, Benedictine Coll., 1973; cert., Johns Hopkins U., 1974; MA in Social Psychology, U. No. Colo., 1975; PhD, U. L.C., Modesto, 1982. Cert. alcohol, drug therapist. Staff psychologist, alcohol and drug programs U.S. Army, Ft. Carson, Colo., 1965-76; dir. alcohol and drug program Coconino County, Flagstaff, Ariz., 1976-78; dir. univ. rels. Intel Corp., Phoenix, Ariz., 1978-80; dir. employment G.T.E. Microcircuits, Phoenix, 1980-81; v.p. Monarch Computer Corp., Phoenix, 1981-83; dir. Found. for Human Resources, Santa Cruz, Calif., 1982—, v.p., 1983—; lectr. No. Ariz. U., Flagstaff, 1977-78, Regis Coll., Colorado Springs, Colo., 1985-88, U. Colo., Colorado Springs, 1985-88, Calif. State Employment Com., Sunnyvale, 1991-92; cons. Seagate Tech., Scotts Valley, Calif., Oracle Corp., Adaptec, Inc., Radius, Inc., Starlight Networks, Inc, NASA, Ames, Inc., 1991-96. Contbr. numerous articles to profl. jours. Designed Navajo Tribal Mental Health Program, Window Rock, Ariz., 1978. With U.S. Army, 1965-75. Recipient Outstanding Contbn. award Mental Health Dept., Colo., 1974, Ariz. Hwy. Patrol, 1978, Ariz. Adult Probation, 1978, Navajo tribe, Window Rock, Ariz., 1978. Mem. U. No. Colo. Alumni Assn. (Recognition award 1978), Benedictine Coll. Alumni Assn. (Svc. award 1991). Republican. Avocations: pilot, parachuting, Alpinist. Home: 14035 Saratoga Ave Saratoga CA 95070-5437 Office: Found for Human Resources 14035 Saratoga Ave Saratoga CA 95070-5437

WEBSTER, JOHN GOODWIN, biomedical engineering educator, researcher; b. Plainfield, N.J., May 27, 1932; s. Franklin Folger and Emily Sykes (Boody) W.; m. Nancy Egan, Dec. 27, 1954; children: Paul, Robin, Mark, Lark. BEE, Cornell U., 1953; MSEE, U. Rochester, 1965, PhD, 1967. Registered profl. engr., Wis. Engr. North American Aviation, Downey, Calif., 1954-55; engr. Boeing Airplane Co., Seattle, 1955-59, Radiation Inc., Melbourne, Fla., 1959-61; staff engr. Mitre Corp., Bedford, Mass., 1961-62, IBM Corp., Kingston, N.Y., 1962-63; asst. prof. elec. engring. U. Wis.-Madison, 1967-70, assoc. prof. elec. engring., 1970-73, prof. elec. and computer engring., 1973—. Author: (with others) Medicine and Clinical Engineering, 1977, Sensors and Signal Conditioning, 1991; editor: Medical Instrumentation: Application and Design, 1978, 2d. edit., 1992, Clinical Engineering: Principles and Practices, 1979, Design of Microcomputer-Based Medical Instrumentation, 1981, Therapeutic Medical Devices: Application and Design, 1982; Electronic Devices for Rehabilitation, 1985; Interfacing Sensors to the IBM-PC, 1988, Encyclopedia of Medical Devices and Instrumentation, 1988, Tactile Sensors for Robotics and Medicine, 1988, Electrical Impedance Tomography, 1990, Teaching Design in Electrical Engineering, 1990, Prevention of Pressure Sores, 1991, Design of Cardiac Pacemakers, 1995. Recipient Rsch. Career Devel. award NIH, 1971-76; NIH fellow, 1963-67. Fellow IEEE, Am. Inst. Med. and Biol. Engring., Instrument Soc. Am. (Donald P. Eckman Edn. award 1974), Am. Soc. Engring. Edn. (Western Electric Fund award 1978, Theo C. Pilkington Outstanding Educator award 1994). Office: Univ Wis Dept Elec Computer Engring 1415 Engineering Dr Madison WI 53706-1691

WEBSTER, JOHN KIMBALL, investment executive; b. N.Y.C., June 7, 1934; s. Reginald Nathaniel and Lillian (McDonald) W.; m. Katherine Taylor Mulligan; children: John McDonald, Katherine Kimball. B.A., Yale U., 1956; postgrad., Wharton Sch., U. Pa., 1957-58. With Dominick & Dominick, N.Y.C., 1961-73; v.p. Dominick & Dominick, 1968-73; v.p., sec. Dominick Fund, Inc., also Barclay Growth Fund, N.Y.C., 1971-73; v.p. Dominick Mgmt. Corp., N.Y.C., 1971-73, Monumental Capital Mgmt., Inc., Balt., 1974-75, Bernstein-Macaulay, Inc., N.Y.C., 1975-78; v.p., dir. Penmark Investments, Inc., Chgo., 1978-79; sr. v.p. Penmark Investments, Inc., 1979-80, exec. v.p., 1980-84; exec. v.p. Trust Banking Group, Sun Banks, Inc., 1984-85; v.p. MPT Assocs., 1986-90, Value Line Asset Mgmt., N.Y.C., 1990-96, M&T Capital Advisors Group, 1996—; mem. no-load com. Investment Co. Inst., Washington, 1971-73; exec. com. No Load Mut. Fund Assn., N.Y.C., 1971-73; treas. No Load Mut. Fund Assn., 1972-73. Chmn. Nat. Telethon Com., Lawrenceville, Sch., 1986-88, chmn. Ann. Giving, 1988-89; vice chmn. Parents Fund Trinity Coll., Conn., 1987-90. Capt. USAF, 1958-61. Mem. Church Club (N.Y.C.), Yale Club (N.Y.C.), Rumson (N.J.) Country Club, Seabright (N.J.) Lawn Tennis Club, Baltusrol Golf Club, Summit Paddle Tennis Club. Episcopalian. Home: 46 Meadowview Ln Berkeley Heights NJ 07922-1308 Office: M&T Capital Adv Group 350 Park Ave 6th Flr New York NY 10022

WEBSTER, LARRY RUSSELL, artist; b. Arlington, Mass., Mar. 18, 1930; s. James Burpee and Ethel (Hughes) W.; m. Rosemary Siekman, June 13, 1953; children: Wendy Lyn, Ricky Stewart, Holly Jean. B.F.A., Mass. Coll. Art, 1952; M.S., Boston U., 1953. Package designer Union Bag & Paper Co., N.Y.C., 1953-54; art dir., graphic designer, v.p., dir. Thomas Todd Co., Boston, 1956-78; asst. prof. design Mass. Coll. Art, 1964-66. Paintings in permanent collections including, DeCordova Mus., Lincoln, Mass., Grand Rapids (Mich.) Art Mus., Springfield (Mo.) Art Mus., Davenport (Iowa) Municipal Gallery, Colby Coll. Art Mus., Waterville, Maine, Peabody Mus. Salem, Mass. Served with U.S. Army, 1954-56. Recipient Silver medal Am. Watercolor Soc., 1968, 72; recipient C.F.S. award, 1963, Ed Whitney award, 1973, High winds medal, 1983, Rhinehold award, 1967, Ranger Fund Purchase prize, 1965, Adolph and Clara Obrig prize in watercolor NAD, 1970, gold medal Allied Artists Am., 1971, Washington Sch. Art award, 1977, Lena Newcastle award, 1978, Colo. Watermedia award, 1978, Golden award Rocky Mountain Nat. Watermedia Exhbn., 1979, Lorraine Fetzer Meml. award, 2d prize N.Am. Open Competition, 1990. Mem. NAD, Soc. Printers Boston (past mem. council), Am. Watercolor Soc. (Dolphin fellow 1981), Boston Watercolor Soc. (pres. 1974-75), Guild of Boston Artists. Home: 116 Perkins Row Topsfield MA 01983-1923

WEBSTER, LESLIE TILLOTSON, JR., pharmacologist, educator; b. N.Y.C., Mar. 31, 1926; s. Leslie Tillotson and Emily (de Forest) W.; m. Alice Katharine Holland, June 24, 1955; children—Katharine White, Susan Holland, Leslie Tillotson III, Romi Anne. B.A., Amherst Coll., 1947, Sc.D. (hon.), 1982; student, Union Coll., 1944; M.D., Harvard U., 1948. Diplomate: Am. Bd. Internal Medicine. Rotating intern Cleve. City Hosp., 1948-49, jr. asst. resident in medicine, 1949-50; asst. resident medicine Bellevue Hosp., N.Y.C., 1952-53; research fellow medicine Harvard and Boston City Hosp. Thorndike Meml. Lab., 1953-55; from demonstrator to instr. Sch. of Medicine Western Res. U., 1955-60; research assoc. to sr. instr. biochemistry Case Western Res. U. Sch. Medicine, 1959-60, asst. prof. medicine, 1960-70, asst. prof. biochemistry, 1960-65, asst. prof. pharmacology, 1965-67, asso. prof., 1967-70, prof. pharmacology, 1976-92, chmn. pharmacology dept., 1976-91, prof. pharmacology dept. emeritus, 1992, prof. medicine, 1980-86; prof., chmn. pharmacology dept. Northwestern U. Med. and Dental Sch., 1970-76. Served to lt. USNR, 1950-52. Russell M. Wilder fellow Nat. Vitamin Found., 1956-59; Sr. USPHS Research fellow, 1959-61; Research Career Devel. awardee, 1961-69; Macy faculty scholar, 1980-81. Mem. ACP (life), Central Soc. Clin. Rsch. (emeritus), Am. Soc. Clin. Investigation (emeritus), Am. Soc. Biochemistry and Molecular Biology (emeritus), Assn. Med. Sch. Pharmacology (emeritus), Am. Soc. Pharmacology and Exptl. Therapeutics (emeritus). Home: 2728 Leighton Rd Cleveland OH 44120-1325 Office: Univ Hosps of Cleve Rainbow Babies and Childrens Hosp 2074 Abington Rd Cleveland OH 44106-2602

WEBSTER, MELVILLE JAY, III, bank executive; b. South Bend, Ind., Feb. 21, 1944; s. Melville Jay Jr. and Mildred Grace (Spear) W. AB, Ind. U., 1966, MS, 1968. Cert. data processor, quality analyst. Scientific programmer Uniroyal, Inc., Mishawaka, Ind., 1968-71; sr. systems analyst G.D. Searle & Co., Skokie, Ill., 1971-74; systems mgr. Baxter Labs., Deerfield, Ill., 1974-77; data base adminstr. Union Spl. Machine Corp., Chgo., 1977-79; data base analyst Blue Cross of Calif., Oakland, 1979-81; sr. tech. specialist McKesson Corp., San Francisco, 1981-83; consulting systems engr. Bank of Am., San Francisco, 1983-89; cons. Computer Power Group, Oak Brook, Ill., 1989-91; systems mgr., v.p. First Bank Sys., Mpls., 1991—. Tchr. Jane Addams Resource Ctr., Chgo., 1990-91; mem. adv. coun. Mpls. Pub. Schs./Adult Basic Edn. Program, 1992-93. Mem. Twin Cities Quality Assurance Assn., Am. MENSA, Lions. Republican. Avocations: reading, gardening, contract bridge, urban renewal. Home: 4929 3rd Ave S Minneapolis MN 55409-2629 Office: First Bank System MPFP1901 601 2nd Ave S Minneapolis MN 55402-4303

WEBSTER, MURRAY ALEXANDER, JR., sociologist, educator; b. Manila, Philippines, Dec. 10, 1941; s. M.A. and Patricia (Morse) W.; A.B., Stanford U., 1963, M.A., 1966, Ph.D., 1968. Asst. prof. social relations Johns Hopkins U., Balt., 1968-74, assoc. prof., 1974-76; prof. sociology, adj. prof. psychology U. S.C., Columbia, 1976-86; vis. prof. sociology Stanford U., 1981-82, 85, 88-89; sr. lectr. San Jose State U., 1987-89; sociology program dir. NSF, 1989-91; prof. sociology U. N.C., Charlotte, 1993—; NIH fellow, 1966-68; grantee NSF, Nat. Inst. Edn. Mem. AAAS, Am. Sociol. Assn., So. Sociol. Soc., Am. Psychol. Assn., Am. Psychol. Soc., N.Y. Acad. Scis. Presbyterian. Author: (with Barbara Sobieszek) Sources of Self-Evaluation, 1974; Actions and Actors, 1975, (with Martha Foschi) Status Generalization: New Theory and Research, 1988; mem. editorial bd. Am. Jour. Sociology, 1976-79, Social Psychology Quar., 1977-80, 84-87, 93—, Social Sci. Research, 1975—. Office: Univ NC Dept Sociology Charlotte NC 28223

WEBSTER, NORMAN ERIC, journalist, charitable foundation administrator; b. Summerside, P.E.I., Can., June 4, 1941; s. Eric and Elizabeth (Paterson) W.; m. Pat Roop, 1966; children: David, Andrew, Derek, Gillian, Hilary. BA, Bishop's U., Que., Can.; MA, St. John's Coll., Oxford, Eng. Corr. Globe and Mail, Que. and Ottawa, Ont., Can.; editor Globe Mag., Toronto, Ont.; corr. Globe and Mail, Peking, China, 1969-71; columnist Ont. affairs Globe and Mail, Toronto; European corr. Globe and Mail, London; editor-in-chief Globe and Mail, Toronto, 1983-89, Montreal (Que.) Gazette, 1989-93; pres. R. Howard Webster Found., Montreal, 1993—. Recipient Nat. Newspaper award for Peking corr., 1971, for editl. writing, 1988; Rhodes scholar; mem. Order of Can. Office: R Howard Webster Found Ste 2912, 1155 Rene Levesque Blvd W, Montreal, PQ Canada H3B 2L5

WEBSTER, ROBERT KENLY, lawyer; b. N.Y.C., May 16, 1933; s. Francis Kenly and Mary Louise (Rathbone) W.; m. Sally Irene Stratton, Apr. 16, 1960; children: Timothy Kenly, Kimberly Anne. AB, Princeton U., 1955; LLB, U. Va., 1960. Assoc. Cadwalader, Wickersham & Taft, N.Y.C., 1960-65; asst. U.S. atty. Dept. of Justice, Washington, 1965-68; prin. dep. gen. counsel Dept. of Army, Washington, 1968-73; ptnr. Kennedy & Webster, Washington, 1973-81, Shaw, Pittman, Potts & Trowbridge, Washington, 1981—; spl. investigator Iran FMS program Sec. of Def., Washington, 1977; advisor conflict of interest issues Watergate defendants Dept. Justice, Washington, 1977. Sec., gen. counsel, bd. dirs. Princeton (N.J.) Project 55, Inc., 1989—. Lt. (j.g.) USN, 1955-57. Mem. ABA, Fed. Bar Assn., Met. Club. Avocations: pottery, reading, traveling, squash, tennis. Office: Shaw Pittman Potts 2300 N St NW Washington DC 20037-1122

WEBSTER, ROBERT LEE, accounting educator, researcher; b. Little Rock, Oct. 4, 1946; s. Daniel and Mildred LaNette (Patishall) W.; m. Mary Katherine Fiske, Aug. 26, 1967; children: Elizabeth Ashley, Jessica Lee. BA, Ouachita Bapt. U., 1968; MBA, Syracuse U., 1975; MS, L.I. U., 1986; DBA, La. Tech. U., 1993. Cert. govt. fin. mgr. Commd. 2d lt. U.S. Army, 1968, advanced through grades to lt. col., 1985; dep. contr. U.S. Army Electronics R&D Command, Adelphi, Md., 1975-80; chief of ops., comms. security NATO, Mons, Belgium, 1980-83; asst. prof. acctg. and fin. U.S. Mil. Acad., West Point, N.Y., 1983-86; prof. mil. sci. Henderson State U., Arkadelphia, Ark., 1986-88; ret. U.S. Army, 1988; asst. prof. acctg. Henderson State U., 1988-91, chair dept. acctg., econs. and bus. edn., 1991-93; chair dept. acctg. Ouachita Bapt. U., Arkadelphia, 1993—; George Young chair bus. Ouachita Bapt. U., 1995—; bd. dirs. Hospitality Care Ctr., Arkadelphia, 1992-93; speaker in field. Editor Jour. Bus. & Behavioral Scis., 1995; author articles. Army scholar Syracuse U., 1974-75; Exch. Educator to Republic of Kazakhstan, 1994-95; recipient Dean's award for acad. achievement L.I. U., 1986. Mem. Nat. Social Sci. Assn. (bd. govs. 1992—, Outstanding Conf. Paper award 1992), Am. Acctg. Assn., MidSouth Acad. Econs. and Fin., Beta Gamma Sigma. Avocations: coin collecting, exercising. Home: 205 Forrest Park Dr Arkadelphia AR 71923-2811 Office: Ouachita Bapt U PO Box 3689 Arkadelphia AR 71998-3689

WEBSTER, RONALD B., lawyer; b. Cle Elum, Wash., June 11, 1942; s. Burnette O. and Lucille (Beck) W.; m. M. Gail Skinner, June 26, 1971; children: Noel, Michelle. BA, U. Wash., 1964; JD, Gonzaga U., 1969. Bar: Wash., U.S. Dist. Ct. (ea. and we. dists.) Wash., U.S. Ct. Appeals (9th cir.). Dep. pros. atty. Cowlitz County, Kelso, Wash., 1970-73; ptnr. Hickman, Webster, Ensley & Carpenter, Colfax, Wash., 1973-90, Hickman, Webster & Moulton, 1973-92, Hickman & Webster, P.S., 1992-95. Mem. Whitman County Bd. Mental Health, Pullman, Wash., 1973-83; chmn. civil svc. commn. Whitman County Sheriffs Office, Colfax, 1973—; pres. Colfax and Cmty. Fund, 1973-74; pres. Whitman Cmty. Concerts, 1990-93. Mem. Whitman County Bar Assn. (pres. 1981-82), Wash. State Bar Assn. (inter profl. com. 1986-89—, disciplinary com. 1986—). Club: Colfax Golf and Country. Lodge: Rotary (pres. Colfax club 1983-84). Home: 1801 N Oak St Colfax WA 99111-9705 Office: Hickman Webster & Moulton 302 N Mill St Colfax WA 99111-1826

WEBSTER, STEPHEN BURTIS, physician, educator; b. Chgo., Dec. 3, 1935; s. James Randolph Webster and Ruth Marion (Burtis) Holmes; m. Katherine Griffith Webster, Apr. 4, 1959; children: David Randolph, Margaret Elizabeth, James Lucian. BS, Northwestern U., 1957, MD, 1960. Diplomate Am. Bd. Dermatology. Intern Colo. Gen. Hosp., Denver, 1960-61; resident Walter Reed Gen. Hosp., Washington, 1962-65; staff physician Henry Ford Hosp., Detroit, 1969-71, Gundersen Clinic, La Crosse, 1971—; assoc. clin. prof. U. Wis., Madison, 1976—, U. Minn., Mpls., 1978—. Lt. col. U.S. Army, 1962-69. Fellow Am. Acad. Dermatology (sec.-treas. 1985-88, pres. 1991), Am. Bd. Dermatology (dir. 1992—); mem. AMA, Am. Dermatol. Assn., Wis. State Med. Soc., La Crosse County Med. Soc., Soc. Investigative Dermatology, Alpha Omega Alpha. Republican. Congregationalist. Avocations: bagpipes, model R.R. Home: 2062N Wedgewood Dr E La Crosse WI 54601 Office: Gundersen Clinic Ltd 1836 South Ave La Crosse WI 54601-5429

WEBSTER, THOMAS GLENN, psychiatrist; b. Topeka, Jan. 23, 1924; s. Guy Welland and Iva Amanda (Keefover) W.; m. Mary Tupper Dooly, June 27, 1948; children—Warnie Louise, Guy Weyman, David Michael. AB, Ft. Hays State Coll., 1946; MD, Wayne State U., 1949. Intern Los Angeles County Gen. Hosp., Calif., 1949-50; resident in psychiatry Mass. Mental Health Ctr., Boston, 1953-55, resident in child psychiatry, 1955-56; resident in child psychiatry James Jackson Putnam Children's Ctr., Boston, 1956-58; dir. presch. program for retarded children Greater Boston, 1958-62; coordinator 3d yr. med. student psychiatry clerkship Harvard U. Med. Sch.-Mass. Mental Health Ctr., Boston, 1960-63; practice medicine specializing in psychiatry Boston, 1953-62, Bethesda, Md., 1963-72, Washington, 1972—; tng. specialist psychiatry, then chief continuing edn. br. NIMH, Bethesda, Md., 1963-72; prof. psychiatry George Washington U., Washington, 1972-86, chmn. dept. psychiatry and behavioral scis., 1972-75, prof. emeritus, 1986—; vis. prof. Harvard U. Med. Sch., 1980-83, McLean Hosp., 1980-86; U.S.-Poland exchange health scientist, 1981. Pres. Woodhaven Citizens Assn., 1971-72. Served with AUS, 1943-46; as sr. asst. surgeon USPHS, 1951-53. Fellow Am. Psychiat. Assn., Am. Coll. Psychiatrists, Am. Coll. Psychoanalysts; mem. Assn. Acad. Psychiatry (pres. 1976-78), Group Advancement Psychiatry. Home: 8506 Woodhaven Blvd Bethesda MD 20817-3117 Office: 2112 F St NW Washington DC 20037-2715

WEBSTER, WILLIAM HEDGCOCK, lawyer; b. St. Louis, Mar. 6, 1924; s. Thomas M. and Katherine (Hedgcock) W.; m. Drusilla Lane, May 5, 1950 (dec. 1984); children: Drusilla Lane Busch, William Hedgcock, Katherine Hagee Roessle; m. Lynda Clugston, Oct. 20, 1990. AB, Amherst Coll., 1947, LLD, 1975; JD, Washington U., 1949, LLD, 1978; LLD (hon.), William Wood Coll., 1978, DePauw U., 1978, Drury Coll., Columbia Coll., U. Dayton, U. Notre Dame, Center Coll., Dickinson Coll., U. Miami, DePaul U., Am. U., John Jay Coll., Westminster Coll., Georgetown U., Rockhurst Coll., Pepperdine U. Bar: Mo. 1949, D.C. 1981. With Armstrong, Teasdale, Kramer and Vaughan (and predecessors), St. Louis, 1949-50, 52-59, 61-70; U.S. atty. U.S. Dist. Ct. (ea. dist.) Mo., 1960-61, judge, 1971-73; judge U.S. Ct. Appeals (8th cir.), 1973-78; dir. FBI, 1978-87, CIA, 1987-91; sr. ptnr. Milbank, Tweed, Hadley & McCloy, Washington, 1991—; mem. Mo. Bd. Law Examiners, 1964-69, mem. adv. com. on criminal rules, 1971-78, mem. ct. adminstrs. com., 1975-78; bd. dirs. Anhauser-Busch Cos., Maritz Inc., Pinkertons Inc. Trustee Washington U., 1974—; bd. dirs. Atlantic Coun., Nat. Legal Ctr. for Pub. Interest, Police Found; hon. life pres. Big Bros. Orgn. St. Louis; bd. dirs. Big Bros. Am., 1966, hon. bd. dirs., 1978—. Lt. USN, 1943-46, 50-52. Recipient Disting. Alumnus award Washington U., 1977, Stein award Fordham U., Law award U. Va., Nat. Svc. medal Freedoms Found., Theodore Roosevelt award, Presdl. medal of Freedom,

Nat. Security medal; named Father of Yr., 1986, Man of Yr., St. Louis Globe Dem., 1980. Fellow Am. Bar Found.; mem. ABA (chmn. sect. on corp. banking and bus. law 1977-78), FBA, Mo. Bar Assn., St. Louis Bar Assn., Am. Law Inst. (mem. coun. 1978—), Wash. U. Alumni Fedn. (pres. 1956-57), Wash. U. Law Alumni (pres. 1961), Mo. Assn. Reps. (pres. 1958), Rotary, St. Louis Country Club, Noonday Club (St. Louis), Met. Club, Alfalfa Club, St. Alban's Tennis Club, Order of Coif, Psi Upsilon, Delta Sigma Rho, Phi Delta Phi. Office: 1825 I St NW Ste 1100 Washington DC 20006-5403

WECHSLER, ALFRED ELLIOT, engineering executive, consultant, chemical engineer; b. Suffern, N.Y., Sept. 12, 1934; m. Nancy L. Lyons, Apr. 22, 1961; children: Charles, Elizabeth, Abigail. BS in Chem.Engring., MIT, 1955, MS, 1958; ScD. in Chem. Engring, M.I.T., 1961; ScD in Ghem. Engring., MIT. Registered profl. engr., Mass. Staff engr. Chevron Research Corp., 1957; asst dir. field sta. MIT Sch. Chem. Engring. Practice, Bangor, Maine, 1958; rsch. asst. chem. engring. MIT, Cambridge, 1959-61; sr. research engr. engring. div. Arthur D. Little, Inc., Cambridge, 1961-66, leader research and experiments group, 1966-73, mgr. bio/enviro systems sect., v.p., 1973-80, corp. staff v.p., 1980—, sr. v.p., mgr. profl. ops. bus. unit, 1980-83, sr. v.p., gen. mgr. profl. ops., 1983-85, sr. v.p., chief profl. officer, 1985—. Contbr. articles to profl. jours. Trustee Environ. Careers Orgn. With U.S. Army, 1956-57. Fellow AAAS; mem. NSPE, Am. Chem. Soc., Am. Inst. Chem. Engrs. (bd. dirs. 1991-93). Office: Arthur D Little Inc 25 Acorn Park Cambridge MA 02140-2301

WECHSLER, ARNOLD, osteopathic obstetrician and gynecologist; b. N.Y.C., June 10, 1923; s. David and Eva (Kirsch) W.; m. Marlene Esta Jurnovoy, Sept. 11, 1955 (div. Sept. 1986); children: Diane, Paul, Stewart. Grad., Rutgers U.; DO, Phila. Coll. Osteo. Medicine, 1952. Diplomate Am. Bd. Osteo. Obstetricians and Gynecologists; lic. physician, Pa., N.Y., Fla. Intern Hosps. of Phila. Coll. Osteo. Medicine, 1952-53, resident in obstetrics/gynecology and gen. surgery, 1953-56; lectr. in obstetrics and gynecology Nursing Sch. Phila. Coll. Osteo. Medicine; founder, mem. staff Tri County Hosp., Delaware County, Pa., from 1960, chief staff, 1960-62, chief dept. obstetrics and gynecology surgery, 1960-77, dir. med. edn., 1968-71; attending and cons. in obstetrics and gynecol. surgery Met. Hosp., Phila., 1956-60, 71-75; chief dept. obstetrics and gynecology Humana Hosp.-South Broward, Hollywood, Fla., 1980-84; cons. and attending in gynecol. surgery Drs. Hosp. of Hollywood, 1982-86; insp. for intern and resident tng. programs Bur. Hosps. of Am. Osteo. Assn., 1965-66; founder, med. dir. Women's Med. Svcs., 1973-77, Nutrients Inc., Phila., 1977-79, Supplements Inc., Phila., 1979-80, Alternative Lifestyle Ctr., Fla., 1983-86; founder, dir. A.W. Profl. Consultants, Inc.; cons. Practice Mgmt. Group, Med Temps Plus, Plantation, Fla.; provider ambulatory gyn. surgery for multiple gyn ctrs. in Dade, Broward and Palm Beach Counties, Fla. Author: Dr. Wechsler's New You Diet, 1978. Staff Sgt. Signal Corps, USAF, 1942-46, PTO, Japan. Fellow Am. Coll. Osteo. Obstetricians and Gynecologists, Internat. Coll. Applied Nutrition; mem. Am. Osteo. Assn., Pa. Osteo. Med. Assn., Philadelphia County Osteo. Soc., Fla. Osteo. Med. Assn., Broward County Osteo. Med. Assn., Am. Soc. Bariatric Physicians, Assn. Maternal and Child Welfare, Internat. Acad. Preventive Medicine, Inst. Food Technologists, Coun. for Responsible Nutrition, Internat. Coll. Gynecologic Laparoscopists, Assn. Reproductive Health Profls. Avocations: photography, sculpture, woodworking.

WECHSLER, GIL, lighting designer; b. N.Y.C., Feb. 5, 1942; s. Arnold J. and Miriam (Steinberg) W. Student Rensselaer Poly. Inst., 1958-61; BS, NYU, 1964; MFA, Yale U., 1967. Lighting designer Harkness Ballet, N.Y.C., 1967-69, Pa. Ballet, Phila., 1969-70, Stratford Shakespeare Festival, Ont., Can., 1969-78, Guthrie Theatre, Mpls., 1971, Lyric Opera Chgo., 1972-76, Met. Opera, N.Y.C., 1976-96; guest lectr. Teatro Colon, Buenos Aires, Argentina, 1985, Yale U., New Haven, 1980, Rensselaer Polytech. Inst., 1994-96; guest lighting designer Am. Ballet Theatre, N.Y.C., 1980, Paris Opera, 1983, Chatelet Theatre, Paris, 1991. Cons. editor Opera Quar., 1983-90. Recipient Emmy award nominations. Mem. U.S. Inst. for Theatre Tech., Illuminating Engring. Soc., United Scenic Artists. Avocations: collecting ocean liner memorabilia, gardening, kayaking. Home: 1 Lincoln Plz New York NY 10023-7129

WECHSLER, HENRY, research psychologist; b. Warsaw, Poland, Aug. 16, 1932; came to U.S., 1941, naturalized, 1953; s. William and Lucy (Fryd) W.; m. Joan Goldstein, Oct. 16, 1955; children: Stephen Bruce, Pamela Jane, Peter Thomas. A.B. summa cum laude, Washington and Jefferson Coll., 1953; M.A. (Harvard Found. Advanced Study fellow, resident fellow), Harvard U., 1955, Ph.D. in Social Psychology, 1957. USPHS postdoctoral rsch. fellow, 1957; rsch. assoc. Joint Commn. Mental Illness and Health, 1957-58; rsch. assoc., asst. prof. Clark U., 1958-59; rsch. social psychologist Mass. Mental Health Ctr., 1959-65; rsch. assoc. in psychology Med. Sch., Harvard U., 1960-66; rsch. assoc. in psychology Harvard Sch. Pub. Health, 1963-66, lectr. social psychology, 1966—, dir. Youth Alcohol-Drug Program, dept. health & social behavior, 1988—; dir. rsch. and community health programs Med. Found., Inc., Boston, 1965-88; vis. lectr. Boston U., 1967-68; pres. SocioTech. Systems, 1969-74; lectr. in rsch. Simmons Coll. Sch. Social Work, 1969-80, adj. prof., 1981-84. Author, editor: The Threat of Impending Disaster; contbr. to books Psychology of Stress, 1964, Social Psychology and Mental Health, 1970, Emergency Medical Services: Behavioral and Planning Perspectives, 1973, Social Work Research in the Human Services, 1976, Handbook of Medical Specialties, 1976, The Horizons of Health, 1977, Explorations in Nursing Research, 1978, Handbook of Dental Specialties, 1979, Minimum Drinking Age Laws, 1980, The Social Context of Medical Research, 1981, Medical School Admissions, 1982; contbr. numerous articles to profl. jours. Fellow Am. Psychol. Assn., Mass. Psychol. Assn. (treas. 1967-68), Am. Sociol. Assn., Am. Pub. Health Assn.; mem. Mass. Pub. Health Assn., Phi Beta Kappa. Club: Harvard (Boston). Home: 148 Puritan Dr Quincy MA 02169-1739 Office: Harvard Sch Pub Health Dept Health & Social Behavior 677 Huntington Ave Boston MA 02115-6028

WECHSLER, HERBERT, retired legal educator; b. N.Y.C., Dec. 4, 1909; s. Samuel and Anna (Weisberger) W.; m. Elzie S. Stix, May 29, 1933 (div. 1957); m. Doris L. Klauber, Apr. 13, 1957. AB, CCNY, 1928; LLB, Columbia U., 1931, LLD (hon.), 1978; LLD (hon.), U. Chgo., 1962, Harvard U., 1967, Georgetown U., 1984, CUNY, 1988, Yale U., 1991. Bar: N.Y. 1933. Editor Columbia U. Law Rev., 1929-31; instr. law Columbia U., 1931-32, asst. prof., 1933-38, assoc. prof., 1938-45, prof., 1945—, Harlan Fiske Stone prof. constl. law, 1957-78, emeritus, 1978—; law sec. to Mr. Justice Harlan F. Stone, 1932-33; counsel to minority leader N.Y. State Constl. Conv., 1938; asst. atty. gen. of N.Y. (assigned Bklyn. investigation), 1938-40; exec. sec. U.S. Bd. Legal Examiners, 1941-42; mem. adv. com. on rules criminal procedure U.S. Supreme Ct., 1941-45; spl. asst. to atty. gen. of U.S., 1940-44; asst. atty. gen. of U.S., in charge war div. U.S. Dept. Justice, 1944-46; tech. adviser to U.S. mems. Internat. Mil. Tribunal, 1945-46; vis. prof. Harvard Law Sch., 1956-57, Oliver Wendell Holmes lectr., 1958-59; Am. Law Inst. reporter Model Penal Code, 1952-62; exec. dir. Am. Law Inst., 1963-84, mem. council, 1984—; dir. Social Sci. Research Council, 1953. Author: (with J. Michael) Criminal Law and Its Administration, 1940, The Federal Courts and the Federal System, (with H. Hart Jr.), 1953, 3d edit. (with others), 1988, Principles, Politics and Fundamental Law, 1961, The Nationalization of Civil Liberties and Civil Rights, 1969. Mem. Pres.'s Commn. on Law Enforcement and Adminstrn. of Justice, 1965-67, N.Y. Temporary Commn. Rev. Penal Law and Criminal Code, 1961-70; mem. permanent com. for Oliver Wendell Holmes Devise, 1966-74; mem. com. on rev. fed. ct. appellate system, 1973-75; chmn. N.Y. Jud. Nomination Commn., 1978-82. Recipient Henry J. Friendly medal Am. Law Inst., 1993. Fellow Am. Acad. Arts and Scis., Brit. Acad. (corr.); mem. ABA, Assn. of Bar of City of N.Y. (past v.p., medal), Am. Philos. Soc. (Townsend Harris medal, Learned Hand award), Order of Coif (hon.). Democrat. Club: Century Assn. Home: 179 E 70th St New York NY 10021-5154 Office: 435 W 116th St New York NY 10027-7201

WECHSLER, RAYMOND HENRY, management company executive; b. Taunton, Mass., Apr. 2, 1945; s. Kurt and Ann (Schlessinger) W.; BA, Queens Coll., 1966; MBA, Columbia U., 1968; m. Louise Austin, July 29, 1979. CPA, N.Y. Mgmt. cons. Touche Ross & Co., N.Y.C., 1968-72; with RCA, N.Y.C., 1972-80, dir. internat. financing, 1976-77, dir. internat. treasury ops., 1977-80; CFO AT&T Internat., Basking Ridge, N.J., 1980-81, v.p., treas., CFO, 1981-83; pres. United Press Internat., Inc., 1985, Wechsler Mgmt. Corp. Inc., N.Y.C., 1983—; vice chmn. Protect Svcs. Industries, Inc., 1987—; chmn. bd., CEO ERC Industries, Inc., 1989-91, Mueller Industries, 1990-91, Accessory Place, Inc., 1993—; chmn., pres. Am. Equity Ptnrs., Inc., 1992—; bd. dirs. Crystal Oil Co., Jos. A. Bank Clothiers Inc.

WECHSLER, SUSAN LINDA, software design engineer; b. Burbank, Calif., Oct. 7, 1956; d. Robert Edward and Sharron Ilene Wechsler; m. Gary Daniel Grove, Aug. 24, 1975 (dec. Dec. 1980); m. Dane Bruce Rogers, Feb. 28, 1987; children: Shayna Marneen Rogers, Ayla Corinne Rogers. BA in Math., Calif. State U., Long Beach, 1979. R&D software engr. Hewlett-Packard Co., Corvallis, Oreg., 1980—; Presenter N.W. Software Quality Conf., 1984. Contbr. articles to profl. publs.; co-developer nine calculators and handheld computers; patentee in field; co-designer HP 200LX Palmtop PC/Organizer, 1994; writer software for laptop computers. Pres. Gifts for a Better World, Corvallis, Oreg., 1994, bd. dirs. 1990-1995. Democrat. Avocations: gardening, sewing, hiking, running, reading. Office: Hewlett-Packard 1000 NE Circle Blvd Corvallis OR 97330-4239

WECHTER, CLARI ANN, paint manufacturing company executive; b. Chgo., June 1, 1953; d. Norman Robert and Harriet Beverly (Golub) W.; m. Gordon Jay Siegel, Feb. 10, 1980; 1 child, Alix Jessica. BA, U. Ariz., 1975; BE, Loyola U., Chgo., 1977. Cert. tchr., Ill. Saleswoman, v.p. sales Federated Paint Mfg. Co., Chgo., 1979—. Republican. Jewish. Avocation: travel. Home: 25 E Cedar St Chicago IL 60611-1151 Office: Federated Paint Mfg Co 1882 S Normal Ave Chicago IL 60616-1013

WECHTER, IRA MARTIN, tax specialist, financial planner; b. Bkyn., June 26, 1947; s. Nathan Harris and Mollie (Bauer) W.; m. Myrna Ellen Rosenbaum, Dec. 22, 1968; 1 child, Megan Jill. BA, CCNY, 1969; MPA, Bernard Baruch Coll., 1973. CFP; cert. practitioner of taxation; registered investment advisor; enrolled to practice before IRS; lic. in gen. securities, life, health and disability ins., N.J., N.Y.; accredited tax advisor. Dir. adminstrv. svcs. N.Y.C. Dept. City Planning, 1971-77; dep. asst. budget dir. N.Y., N.Y.C. Office Mgmt. and Budget, 1977-81; dep. commr. N.Y.C. Dept. Environ. Protection, 1981-84; pres. Wechter Fin. Svcs., Inc., Parsippany, N.J., 1984—. Mem. Community Bd. No. 1 S.I., 1973-76, 1st v.p., 1976-77; treas. S.I. Coun. on Arts, 1974-75. Recipient Outstanding Citizenship award Borough Pres. of S.I., 1977. Mem. Nat. Assn. Enrolled Agts., Inst. Cert. Fin. Planners, Nat. Assn. Tax Practitioners, Nat. Soc. Tax Preparers, Nat. Soc. Pub. Accts. Republican. Jewish. Avocations: U.S. mint stamp collecting, organist. Office: Wechter Fin Svcs Inc 1719 Rte 10 Ste 310 Parsippany NJ 07054

WECHTER, VIVIENNE THAUL, artist, poet, educator; b. N.Y.C.; d. Samuel Joshua and Hilda (Thaul) Rosenthal; m. Nathan Wechter; 1 dau., Robyrta Joan Wechter Rapoport. B. Pedagogy, Jamaica Tchrs. Coll.; post-grad., Columbia U., N.Y. U., New Sch. for Social Research, Art Students League, Sculpture Center, Pratt Inst. Graphic Center; Ph.D. in Interarts and Psychology of Creativity, Union Inst. Artist in residence Fordham U., 1964—, asst. prof. art and esthetics, 1964, now prof. interdisciplinary creative arts, chmn. acquisitions and exhbns.; vis. poet-artist Kansas City Art Inst., 1975, Md. Inst. Coll. Art, 1975, New Sch., N.Y.C., 1976, Marist Coll., Poughkeepsie, N.Y., 1977; vis. prof. New Sch. for Social Rsch., spring 1986; past chmn. coll. liaison divsn. Bronx Coun. on Arts; vis. prof. creative devel. Miami (Fla.) Jewish Home and Hosp. for Aged, 1993; lect. Sch. Internat. Affairs U. Malta; sole U.S. rep. Internat. Brennale, Malta, 1995. Moderator: weekly radio broadcast Today's World, WFUV, 1951—, created 6 programs in South Pacific, 1986-87; illustrator: (Alfeo Marzi) book cover Park of Jonas, 1965; author: A View from the Ark, 1973; contbr. articles to profl. jours.; one-woman shows Castellane Gallery, East Hampton Gallery, N.Y.C., Cornell U., Ithaca, N.Y., Neville Pub. Mus., Green Bay, Wis., Nashville Fine Arts Ctr., Fairleigh Dickinson U., Rutgers U., Waterloo (Iowa) Mcpl. Galleries, Bodley Gallery, Gloria Cortella Gallery, N.Y.C., Manhattan Coll., N.Y.C., Kouros Gallery, N.Y.C., Everson Mus. Art, Syracuse, N.Y., CCNY, B.R. Kornblatt Gallery, Balt., New Sch. Social Research, N.Y.C., Arts Interaction, N.Y.C., 1993, Douglass Gardens, Miami, also Paris, Rejik, Yugoslavia, multimedia show, Everson Mus. Fine Art, Syracuse, 1979, Dyansen Gallery, N.Y.C., 1981, L.I. U., 1986, Schiller-Wapner, N.Y.C., Shapolsky Gallery, N.Y.C., 1989, New England Mus. Contemporary Arts, 1991, 92, Douglas Gardens, Miami, 1992, Nassau County Mus. Art, 1994; solo shows and poetry readings New Sch., N.Y.C., Arts Interaction, N.Y.C., L.I. U., 1988, Arts Interaction Gallery 12, N.Y.C., 1988, 93, Fordham U., N.Y.C., 1994; represented in permanent collections Corcoran Gallery, Washington, Houston Mus. Fine Arts, Jewish Mus. N.Y.C., Fordham U., N.Y.C., Univ. Art Museum Berkeley, Calif., Museum Art and Sci., Norfolk, Va., NYU, Mus. of Fine Arts, Moscow, Russia, Mus. of Fine Art, Newark, Ohio State U., Phoenix Mus. Fine Arts, Fairleigh Dickinson U., Madison, N.J., UN, Internat. Culture Ctr., Jerusalem, Mus. Modern Art Warsaw, Poland, Mus. Fine Arts Moscow, N.J. State Mus., Trenton, others; monumental outdoor sculpture The Emerging Sun commd. for Manhattan Psychiat. Ctr., Ward's Island, N.Y.C.; permanent sculpture installed George Meany Internat. Ctr. Labor Studies, Washington, 1981, Simple Justice on Columbus Ave. nr. Lincoln Ctr., N.Y.C., 1989; logo sculpture Miami Jewish Home & Hosp. for Aged; developer, curator, 1st Biennial of Outdoor Sculpture, Fordham U. Rose Hill Campus, 1983. Author: Art, Where We Today and Why?, 1985; solo exbn. and video presentation New Sch. for Social Research, Mar. and Apr., 1986, Wagner-Schiller Galleries, Sept., 1986; solo painting, sculpture, video presentation and poetry reading, Nov. Dec., 1986; sole exhbn. and poetry reading, The Silver Dream, Provincetown Art Assn. and Mus., July, 1987; chair, moderator Influences in Art (Italian Am. Roundtable Art & Lit., 1988, video on RAI TV, Rome, 1989; panelist St. Bartholomew's, N.Y.C., 1987; rep., exhbns. Leister Fine Arts, Ltd., London; prin. speaker annual cong. Arts Interaction, N.Y.C., 1993. Bd. dirs. Urban Arts Corps; founder, trustee, past pres. Bronx Mus. Art; v.p. U.S. Com. IAA-UNESCO; trustee Bronx Soc. Arts and Letters, 1988—, New England Ctr. Contemporary Arts, 1992—. Recipient awards Am. Acad. Arts and Letters, awards Am. Soc. Contemporary Art. Mem. Am. Abstract Artists, Univ. Council of Art Educators, Urban League Center Greater N.Y. (dir., mem. advisory bd. 1952—), United World Fedelists (1st chmn.), Fedn. Modern Painters and Sculptors (v.p.), Alpha Mu Gamma, Kappa Pi. *To be an artist-poet who requires solitude in order to create yet has the urgent need to be actively involved in the human community is a frightening challenge. Yet I know that to live one without the other will be for me, neither.*

WECK, THOMAS LINCOLN, consulting company executive; b. Norwalk, Conn., June 3, 1942; s. Frank A. and Wilnor Weck; m. Sandra L. Larson, Aug. 19, 1967; children: David Scot, Peter Michael, Kathryn Ann, Andrew Alan. AB, Stanford (Calif.) U., 1964; MBA, Harvard U., 1969. Assoc. Louis Berger & Assocs., Inc., East Orange, N.J., 1969-74; asst. v.p. Louis Berger Internat., Inc., East Orange, N.J., 1974-75, v.p., 1975-81, group v.p., 1981-93; pres. East Orange, N.J., 1993—; mem. transp. rsch. bd. Nat. Acad. Sci., 1981—; chmn. Com. on Environ. Analysis in Transp., 1992—. Author: Moving Up Quickly, 1979, Back-Back and The Lima Bear, 1985; contbr. articles to profl. jours. Mem. Environ. Commn., Madison, N.J., 1979-82, Rep. Nat. Com., Washington, 1986—. Hon. fellow Harvard U., 1967. Mem. Am. Econs. Assn., ASCE (affiliate). Office: Louis Berger Internat Inc 100 Halsted St East Orange NJ 07018-2612*

WECKER, WILLIAM A., preventive medicine physician, neuropsychiatrist; b. N.Y.C., Mar. 14, 1923; s. Philip and Ruth (Frumkin) W.; m. Norma Cairney (dec. 1993); 1 child, Lyle Jeffery. BA, NYU, 1943, MD, 1946; MPH in Adminstrn., Harvard U., 1950; diploma Sch. Aviation Medicine, USAF, 1953. Lic. physician, surgeon, psychiatrist, N.Y.; cert. treating physician N.Y. State Workmen's Compensation Bd.; qualified psychiatrist N.Y. State Dept. Mental Health. Intern Bellevue Hosp., N.Y.C., 1946, Bayonne Gen. Hosp., 1946-47; health officer N.Y.C. Health Dept., 1948-50; dist. health officer N.Y. State Health Dept., Albany, 1950-52; pvt. practice medicine N.Y.C., 1954-59; grad. Sch. Aviation Medicine USAF, 1953; resident in psychiatry U.S. VA Hosp., N.Y.C., 1959-62, psychiatrist, 1962-64; psychiatrist Riverside Hosp., N.Y.C. Hosp. Dept., 1964-65, Postgrad. Ctr. for Mental Health, N.Y.C., 1964-65; pvt. practice preventive medicine, neuropsychiatry N.Y.C., 1948—; advisor Pan Am. Med. Assn., N.Y.C., 1952-55; cons. World Med. Assn., N.Y.C., 1954-61; staff physician Meml. Hosp., Queens, N.Y., 1955-64, Springfield (Mass.) Hosp., 1970-71; civil def. lectr. N.Y.C. Dept. of Health, 1955-58; advisor, charter mem. Acad. Religion and Mental Health, N.Y.C., 1959-62; psychiatrist, mgmt. cons., advisor in staff devel. program Youth House, N.Y.C., 1963-71; psychiatrist, cons. Mahoney Health Ctr., N.Y.C. Dept. Health, Bklyn., 1964-71; psychiatrist N.Y. State Narcotic Addiction Control Commn., 1970-71; med. examining physician N.Y.C. Workers Compensation Bd., 1971-76. Author: 3rd World Economics, 1981, Psychecology for Everybody, 1983, Comprehensive Psychenomics, 1983, American Confetti, 1990, Anatomy of an Asylum, 1968, The Story of "H", 1971, The Honduran Syndrome, 1973, Devil's Den, 1978, Growing Up in Honduras, 1980. Cons. Allen Haus, Zurich, 1990-91; advisor English Gentlemen's Club, Zurich, 1982-87, Centro Cultural, Honduras, 1978-82; corr. Harry Schulz Internat. Newsletter, Switzerland and monaco, 1983-91. 2d lt. U.S. Army, 1943-45, ATO, capt. MC-USAF, 1952-54, ETO. Fellow Nat. Poliomyelitis Found., 1949-50, U.S. VA, 1960-61, NIMH fellow Postgrad. Ctr. for Mental Health, N.Y.C., 1964-65; recipient 50th Anniversary cert. NYU, 1996. Mem. Acad. Medicine Bklyn. (life), Nat. Inst. Mental Health, N.Y. State Med. Soc. (life, citation for 50 yrs. of svc. 1996), N.Y. Coun. Child Psychiatry, Kings County Med. Soc. (life), Royal Soc. Health (London). Avocations: medical astrology and medical psychecology, writing science books, esperanto and languages. Home and Office: 52 Macdougal St # 1-a New York NY 10012-2937

WECKESSER, ERNEST PROSPER, JR., publisher, educator; b. Akron, Ohio, Mar. 23, 1933; s. Ernest Prosper and Sadie (Liken) W.; m. Mary B. Hunter, Jan. 12, 1959; children—Jeffrey, Franz, Kathleen, Lynne. B.A., Bowling Green State U., 1955, M.A., 1960; Ph.D., Mich. State U., 1963. Asst. prof. speech SUNY-Oneonta, 1962-63, Kent State U., 1963-64; mem. faculty Purdue U., 1964-70, assoc. prof., 1968-70; prof. speech Montclair (N.J.) Coll., 1970-71; assoc. prof. speech Pa. State U., 1971-72; dir. Ernest Weckesser Assos.; chmn. bd. dirs. Green Tree Press, Inc., Dunkirk, N.Y.; pres. Bierhaus Internat., Inc., Erie, Pa. Author: The Radio Rhetoric of John L. Lewis, 1963, How To Succeed in College, 1971, The 12,000 Housewife, 1975, Dollars in Your Mailbox, 1975, Alternatives: A Network of Small Business Opportunities, 1992; co-author: The Bradley-Cooper Smoke Cessation Program, 1995. Bd. dirs. Florerence Crittenden Home, Erie.; Mem. Pres.'s Council Gannon U.; Mem. adv. bd. Villa Maria Coll. Served to capt. USAF, 1955-59. Named Disting. Pennsylvanian William Penn Soc., 1983.

WECKSTEIN, RICHARD SELIG, economics consultant; b. N.Y.C., Feb. 11, 1924; s. Isidore and Flo (Litwin) W.; m. Muriel Watenmaker, June 11, 1947; children: Beth Alison Harris, Leslie Ellen Hyman. Ph.B., U. Wis.-Madison, 1947; M.A., Yale U., 1948, Ph.D., 1953. Asst. prof. NYU, N.Y.C., 1951-53; asst. prof. U. Buffalo, 1953-57; vis. faculty Gadjah Mada U., Jogjakarta, Indonesia, 1957-58; vis. assoc. prof. U. Rochester, N.Y., 1958-59; asst. prof. Williams Coll., Williamstown, Mass., 1959-62; assoc. prof. Brandeis U., Waltham, Mass., 1962-66, prof., 1967-73, Carl Marks prof. econs., 1973-93, prof. emeritus, forensic economist, 1971—; mem. Consumers Council, Mass., 1964-72; cons. mission to Liberia Harvard Devel. Adv. Service, Cambridge, Mass., 1964, 66; cons. to Internal Bank of Reconstrn. Devel., Washington, 1971-72; vis. scholar Nuffield Coll., Oxford, 1972; lectr. Flaschner Jud. Inst. of Mass. Bar Found., 1981-83; lectr. Mass. Council Trial Attys., 1986-87. Editor: Expansion of World Trade and the Growth of National Economies, 1968; contbr. articles to profl. jours., ency. Bd. dirs. Beacon Hill Civic Assn., Boston, 1980-83; trustee Longy Sch. Music, Inc., Cambridge, Mass., 1990. Served to 1st lt. USAF, 1942-46. Social Sci. Research Council grantee, 1963-66; vis. fellow Harvard Law Sch., 1978. Mem. Am. Econ. Assn., Atlantic Econ. Soc., Nat. Assn. Forensic Econs., North Haven Yacht Club (Maine) (bd. dirs. 1983—, pres. 1988-92). Avocations: sailing, tennis, flying. Home: 22 Gray Gdns E Cambridge MA 02138-1402 Office: Brandeis U Dept Econs Waltham MA 02254

WECLEW, ROBERT GEORGE, lawyer, educator; b. Chgo., Oct. 30, 1911; s. Victor T. and Mary (Tadrowski) W.; m. Jean Helen Vinson, Jan. 5, 1942; children: Harlene Villio, Robert Vinson Weclew. B.S. in Law, Northwestern U., 1932, J.D., 1935. Bar: Ill. 1934, U.S. Dist. Ct. (no. dist.) Ill. 1937, U.S. Supreme Ct. 1966. Assoc. Case and Lynn, Chgo., 1935-40; atty. Employers of Wausau, Chgo., 1940-42, VA, Chgo., 1945-57; prof. Law Sch., DePaul U., Chgo., 1957-78; acting dean Law Sch., DePaul U., 1968-71, prof. emeritus, 1978—; sole practice Chgo., 1978—; Mem. Am. Law Inst., 1968-71; counsel, co-founder Acad. of Gen. Dentistry, 1952-70. Contbr. articles on constl. law to profl. jours. Mem. Ill. Constl. Study Commn., Chgo., 1968-69. Fellow Acad. Continuing Edn. (counsel, co-founder 1974—); mem. Ill. Bar Assn. (council legal edn. 1969-71), Advocates Soc., Phi Kappa Theta, Delta Theta Phi. Home and Office: 5766 N Kercheval Ave Chicago IL 60646

WECLEW, VICTOR T., dentist; b. Chgo., Mar. 18, 1916; m. Gertrude David, 1945; 1 child, Victor T. III. B.S., U. Ill., 1939, D.D.S., 1943. Gen. practice dentistry Chgo., 1946—. Contbr. articles to profl. jours. Active Boy Scouts Am. Served to maj. AC, U.S. Army, 1943-46. Fellow Acad. Gen. Dentistry (co-founder 1952, bd. dirs., asst. editor jour. 21 yrs.), Acad. Continuing Edn. (co-founder 1974), Am. Coll. Dentists, Acad. of Dentistry Internat. (trustee); mem. ADA, Ill. State Dental Soc., Chgo. Dental Soc. (various coms., past. dir., pres. N.W. br. 1969-70), U. Ill. Dental Alumni Assn. (bd. dirs. 10 yrs., Disting. Alumnus award 1991), Omicron Kappa Upsilon, Psi Omega. Roman Catholic. Home: 5781 N Forest Glen Ave Chicago IL 60646-6610

WEDDIG, LEE J(OHN), trade association executive; b. Fon du Lac, Wis., Sept. 22, 1935; s. Edward K. and Rose M. (Weddig); m. June M. Hennig, Jan. 28, 1956; children: Andrew J., Lisa M. B.S. in Journalism, Marquette U., 1956. Reporter UP, Milw., 1956, Fairchild Publs., Chgo., 1957; nat. merchandising mgr. Motorola, Inc., Chgo., 1957-67; exec. dir. Nat. Fisheries Inst., Washington, 1967-73, exec. v.p., 1975—; pres. C.L. Watt, Inc., and Fin. Mgmt. Svcs., Inc., Dayton, Ohio, 1973-74. Mem. Lakewood Club. Republican. Roman Catholic. Club: Lakewood.

WEDDING, CHARLES RANDOLPH, architect; b. St. Petersburg, Fla., Nov. 16, 1934; s. Charles Reid and L. Marion (Whitaker) W.; m. Audrey Whitsel, Aug. 18, 1956 (div. Apr. 1979); children: Daryl L., Douglas R., Dorian B.; m. Vonnie Sue Hayes, June 22, 1984 (div. Dec. 1991); stepchildren: Stephanie M., Brian E.; m. June A. Free, Mar. 31, 1993; stepchildren: Gregory, Kristine. BArch, U. Fla., 1957. Registered architect, Fla., Ga., N.C., S.C., Del., Va., Tex., Ill., Ind., Kans., La., Mo., Okla., Tenn. Architect in tng. Harvard & Jolly AIA, St. Petersburg, 1957-60; architect, prin., pres. Wedding & Assocs., St. Petersburg, 1960—. Mayor City of St. Petersburg, 1973-75; past chmn. Pinellas County Com. of 100, Bldg. Dept. Survey Team, City of St. Petersburg; trustee All Children's Hosp., 1968-70; sect. leader St. Petersburg United Fund, 1965-70; mem. city council Action Team for Pier Redevel., 1967-68; mem. exec. com. Goals for City of St. Petersburg, 1970-72; den. leader Weblos, Boy Scouts Am., 1971-72; chmn., trustee Canterbury Sch. YMCA, 1968-72; mem. adv. com. Tomlinson Vocat. Sch., 1969-79; past trustee Mus. Fine Arts; past bd. dirs. Neighborly Ctr., Jr. Achievement Pinellas County. Served to 1st lt. U.S. Army, 1958-60. Fellow AIA (5 Silver Spike awards, Merit of Honor, Medal of Honor); mem. Am. Soc. Landscape Architects, St. Petersburg Assn. Architects (past. pres.), Fla. Assn. Architects (8 Merit Design awards). Republican. Episcopalian. Clubs: Suncoasters; St. Petersburg Yacht. Avocations: sailing, hunting, golfing, tennis. Home: 6900 10th Ave N Saint Petersburg FL 33710-6152 Office: Wedding & Assocs Inc 300 1st Ave S Saint Petersburg FL 33701-4236

WEDDINGTON, SARAH RAGLE, lawyer, educator; b. Abilene, Tex., Feb. 5, 1945; d. Herbert Doyle and Lena Catherine (Morrison) Ragle. BS magna cum laude, McMurry Coll., 1965, hon. doctorate, 1979; JD, U. Tex., 1967; hon. doctorate, Hamilton Coll., 1979, Southwestern U., 1989, Austin Coll., 1993. Bar: Tex. 1967, D.C. 1980, U.S. Dist. Ct. (we., no. and ea. dists.) Tex., U.S. Ct. Appeals (5th cir.), U.S. Supreme Ct. Pvt. practice law Austin, 1967-77; gen. counsel Dept. Agr., Washington, 1977-78; spl. asst. to Pres., Washington, 1978-79, asst. to Pres., 1979-81; chmn. Interdepartmental Task Force on Women, 1978-81; mem. Pres.'s Commn. on Exec. Exchange, 1981; Carl Hatch prof. law and pub. adminstrn. U. N.Mex., Albuquerque, 1982-83; pvt. practice law Austin, Tex., 1985—; dir. Tex. Office State-Fed. Relations, Austin, 1983-85; vis. prof. govt. Wheaton Coll., Norton, Mass., 1980-81; sr. lectr. Tex. Woman's U., Denton, 1981-93, U. Tex., Austin, 1986—. Author: A Question of Choice, 1992; contbg. editor Glamour mag., 1981-83. Mem. Tex. Ho. of Reps., 1973-77. Recipient Woman of Yr. award Tex. Women's

Polit. Caucus, 1973, Elizabeth Boyer award Equity Action League, 1978, Outstanding Woman award, 1979, Leadership awards Ladies Home Jour., 1979, spl. recognition Esquire mag., 1984, Woman Who Dares award Nat. Coun. Jewish Women, 1993, Woman of Distinction award Nat. Conf. for Coll. Women Student Leaders, 1993; named Lectr. of Yr. Nat. Assn. for Coll. Activities, 1990, 91. Mem. Tex. Bar Assn., Bus. and Profl. Women's Club, AAUW. Office: S Weddington Law Offices 709 W 14th St Austin TX 78701-1707

WEDDLE, STEPHEN SHIELDS, manufacturing company executive; b. Boston, Nov. 9, 1938; s. Harold Mansfield and Esther Letha (Bales) W.; m. Meredith Baldwin, June 10, 1961; children: Christopher, Timothy, Justin, Jamien. A.B., Harvard, 1960; LL.B., Columbia, 1963. Bar: N.Y. 1966, Conn. 1989. Lectr. in law (supported by Ford Found. Project for Staffing African Instns. for Legal Edn. and Research) Ahmadu Bello U., Zaria, Nigeria, 1963-65; assoc. firm Debevoise & Plimpton, N.Y.C., 1965-71; corporate counsel Technicon Corp., Tarrytown, N.Y., 1971-74; sec. Technicon Corp., 1972-78, sr. v.p., gen. counsel, 1974-78; v.p., gen. counsel, sec. Stanley Works, New Britain, Conn., 1978—. Mem. Assn. Bar City N.Y. (sec. com. on fgn. and comparative law 1968-70), Am., Conn., N.Y. bar assns., Am. Soc. Corp. Secs., Am. Corp. Counsel Assn. Office: Stanley Works 1000 Stanley Dr New Britain CT 06053-1675

WEDEEN, MARVIN MEYER, hospital executive; b. Perth Amboy, N.J., Jan. 3, 1926; s. Nathan and Gertrude (Rappaport) W.; m. Hannah Haas; children: Rachel, Miriam. BS, Cornell U., 1949; MSc in Hosp. Adminstrn., Columbia U., 1971. Rsch. asst. Sealtest div. Kraft Foods, Schenectady, N.Y., 1949-55, dir. work simplification, 1955-59; pers. mgr. Dellwood Foods, Yonkers, N.Y., 1959-63; asst. v.p. Dellwood Foods, Yonkers, 1964-69; cons. pers. N.Y. Infirmary, N.Y.C., 1971; asst. adminstr. Sewickley Valley Hosp., Sewickley, Pa., 1971-80; v.p. Sewickley Valley Hosp., Sewickley, 1980-90; spl. advisor to pres. Sewickley (Pa.) Valley Hosp., 1991; ret., 1992; cons. Exec. Svc. Corp., 1992—; bd. dirs. Valley Care Assn., Sewickley, pres., 1993; mem. Human Resources com., Hosp. Coun. Western Pa., 1987-89; cons. Sr. Med. Cons., N.Y.C., 1971. Chmn. oper. com. Health Sys. Agy., Pitts.; class fund rep. Cornell U. Alumni Fund, 1967-72; bd. dirs. United Jewish Fedn. Bd., 1991-94. Named Man of the Yr., Sewickley Hist. Soc. and Gateway Press, 1980. Fellow, Am. Coll. Health Care Execs.; mem. Am. Pub. Health Assn., Am. Hosp. Assn., Hosp. Assn. (planning and mktg. section, 1984—), Edgeworth Club. Avocations: racket sports, music, theater art. Home: RR 4 Sewickley PA 15143-9804

WEDEL, MILLIE REDMOND, secondary school educator; b. Harrisburg, Pa., Aug. 18, 1939; d. Clair L. and Florence (Heiges) Aungst; BA, Alaska Meth. U., 1966; MEd, U. Alaska, Anchorage, 1972; postgrad. in comm. Stanford U., 1975-76; m. T.S. Redmond, 1956 (div. 1967); 1 child, T.S. Redmond II; m. Frederick L. Wedel, Jr., 1974 (div. 1986). Lic. third class broadcasting, FCC. Profl. model Charming Models & Models Guild of Phila., 1954-61; public rels. staff Haverford (Pa.) Sch., 1959-61; asst. dir. devel. in charge public rels. Alaska Meth. U., Anchorage, 1966, part-time lectr., 1966, 73; comm. tchr. Anchorage Sch. Dist., 1967—; owner Wedel Prodns., Anchorage, 1976-86; pub. rels. staff Alaska Purchase Centennial Exhibit, U.S. Dept. Commerce, 1967; writer gubernatorial campaign, 1971; part-time instr. Chapman Coll., 1990-93; adj. instr. U. Alaska, Anchorage, 1972, 77-79, 89—; cons. Cook Inlet Native Assn., 1978, No. Inst., 1979; judge Ark. Press Women's Writing Contest, 1990-91; sec. exec. bd. Alaska Dept. Edn. Profl. Tchg. Practices Commn., 1993—. Bd. dirs. Sta. KAKM, Alaska Pub. TV, membership chmn., 1978-80, nat. lay rep. to Pub. Broadcasting Svc. and Nat. Assn. Pub. TV Stas., 1979; bd. dirs. Ednl. Telecom. Consortium for Alaska, 1979, Mid-Hillside Community Coun., Municipality of Anchorage, 1979-80, 83-88, Hillside East Cmty. Coun., 1984-88, pres. 1984-85; rsch. writer, legal asst. Vinson & Elkins, Houston, 1981; v.p., bd. dirs. inlet view ASD Cmty. Sch., 1994-95, pres. 1995—; mem. Valley Forge Freedoms Found., Murdoch Scholarships, Valley Forge; bd. dirs. Rev. Richard Gay Trust, Alaska and Pa., 1992—, Inlet View ASD Cmty. Sch., 1995—; commn. dept. edn. profl. teaching practices commn. State Alaska, 1993-95, sec. exec. bd. 1993—; active Anchorage Opera Guild, Anchorage Concert Assn. Recipient awards for newspapers, lit. mags.; award Nat. Scholastic Press Assn., 1968, 74, 77, Am. Scholastic Press Assn., 1981, 82, 83, 84; Alaska Coun. Econs., 1982, Merits award Alaska Dept. Edn., 1982, 93, Legis. commendation State of Alaska, Blue Ribbon award State Alaska, 1982, 93. Mem. NEA (AEA bldg. rep., state del. 70s, 80s, 94-95), Nat. Assn. Secondary Sch. Prins., Nat. Fedn. Interscholastic Speech and Debate Assn., Assn. Pub. Broadcasting (charter mem., nat. lay del. 1980), Indsl. TV Assn. (San Francisco and Houston 1975-81), Alaska Press Club (chmn. high sch. journalism workshops, 1968, 69, 73, awards for sch. newspapers, 1972, 74, 77), Alaska Fedn. Press Women (dir. 1978-86, 94-95, pres. 1995—, h.s. journalism competition youth projects dir., award for brochures, 1978, chair youth writing contest, 1994-95, pres. 1995—), Internat. Platform Assn., World Affairs Coun., Alaska Coun. Tchrs. of English, Chugach Electric (chair 1990, nomination com. for bd. dirs. 1988-90) Stanford Alumni Club (pres. 1982-84, 90-92), Capt. Cook Athletic Club, Alaska (Anchorage), Edgewater Beach Club, Glades Country Club (Naples, Fla.), Delta Kappa Gamma. Presbyterian. Office: PO Box 730 Girdwood AK 99587-0730

WEDEL, PAUL GEORGE, retired hospital administrator; b. Elizabeth, N.J., Jan. 1, 1927; s. Paul John and Helen (Cleary) W.; m. Jean Marie Martin, June 18, 1949; children: Dana Lyn Wedel, Laurie Ann Wedel Musser, Paul John II, Kurt Frederick. Grad., Peddie Sch., Hightstown, N.J., 1944; B.S. in Bus. Adminstrn., Am. U., 1952; M.S. in Hosp. Adminstrn., Northwestern U., 1955. Adminstrv. resident Harrisburg (Pa.) Polyclinic Hosp., 1953-54; asst. adminstr. Williamsport (Pa.) Hosp., 1954-59, adminstr., 1959-64; pres. Lancaster (Pa.) Gen. Hosp., 1964-89; pres. Lancaster Gen. Hosp. Found., 1989-92, pres. emeritus, 1992-94; ret., 1994. Bd. dirs. Inter-County Hospitalization Plan, Inc., 1966-84, James Buchanan Found., Preservation Wheatland, 1968-80, Linden Hall Sch., 1984-91; sr. warden St. Thomas Episcopal Ch., 1979-81; trustee Millersville U., 1991—. Served with USNR, 1944-46, 50-51. Named Outstanding Young Man, Williamsport Jr. C. of C., 1957. Fellow Am. Coll. Health Care Execs. (regent Pa. 1984-89); mem. Am. Hosp. Assn., Hosp. Assn. Pa. (bd. dirs. 1970-73, 84-89), Lancaster Assn. Commerce and Industry (bd. dirs.), Hamilton Club, Pirates Club, Rotary (pres. 1978-79), Masons. Home: Rock Rimmon Ridges 203 Riveredge Dr Leola PA 17540-9745

WEDEMEYER, SALLY EILEEN, special education educator; b. Arverne, N.Y., Mar. 10, 1960; d. Albert J. and Ethel I. (Graf) W. BS in Edn., Keene (N.H.) State Coll., 1982, MEd, 1988. Cert. experienced tchr., N.H. Remedial tchr. Tobey Sch., Concord, N.H., 1982-87; resource tchr. Belmont (N.H.) Elem. Sch., 1988—. Head coach Belmont Spl. Olympics Team, 1991—; participant Project Star Tree, Belmont, 1992—. Named Tchr. of Yr., Belmont Elem. Sch., 1993. Mem. NEA, Coun. for Exceptional Children (emotionally handicapped com. Shaker Regional sch. dist., workshop copresenter Internat. Conf. Learning Disabilites, Austin, Tex. 1990). Avocations: reading, travel. Home: 897 Farrington Corner Rd Hopkinton NH 03229-2022 Office: Belmont Elem Sch 89 Gilmanton Rd E Belmont NH 03220-4813

WEDEPOHL, LEONHARD M., electrical engineering educator; b. Pretoria, Republic of South Africa, Jan. 26, 1933; s. Martin Willie and Liselotte B.M. (Franz) W.; m. Sylvia A.L. St. Jean; children: Martin, Graham. B.Sc. (Eng.), Rand U., 1953; Ph.D., U. Manchester, Eng., 1957. Registered profl. engr., B.C. Planning engr. Escom, Johannesburg, Republic of South Africa, 1957-61; mgr. L.M. Ericsson, Pretoria, Republic of South Africa, 1961-62; sect. leader Reyrolle, Newcastle, Eng., 1962-64; prof., head dept. Manchester U., 1964-74; dean engring. U. Man., Winnipeg, Can., 1974-79; dean applied sci. U. B.C., Vancouver, Can., 1979-85, prof. elec. engring., 1985—; mem. Sci. Rsch. Coun., London, 1968-74; dir. Man. Hydro, Winnipeg, 1965-69, B.C. Hydro, Vancouver, 1980-84, B.C. Sci. Coun., 1981-84; cons. Horizon Robotics, Saskatoon, 1986; chmn. implementation team Sci. Place Can., 1985; cons. CEPEL, Rio de Janeiro; adv. Man. High Voltage D.C. Rsch. Ctr.; tech. advisor RTDS Techs., Inc., Winnipeg, 1994—. Contbr. articles to sci. jours.; patentee in field. Named Hon. Citizen City of Winnipeg, 1979. Fellow Instn. Elec. Engrs. (premium 1967); mem. Assn. Profl. Engrs. B.C. Avocations: music; cross-country skiing; hiking. Office: U BC Dept Elec Engring, 2356 Main Mall, Vancouver, BC Canada V6T 1Z4

WEDGEWORTH, ANN, actress; b. Abilene, Tex., Jan. 21, 1935; m. Rip Torn (div.); 1 child, Danae; m. Ernest Martin; 1 child, Dianna. Attended, U. Tex.; B.A. in Drama, So. Methodist U. Broadway debut in Make A Million, 1958; other Broadway appearances Chapter Two (Tony award), Thieves, Blues for Mr. Charlie, The Last Analysis; off-Broadway appearances Line, Chapparal, The Crucible, Days and Nights of Beebee Fenstermaker, Ludlow Fair, The Honest to God Shnozzola, A Lie of the Mind; toured with nat. cos. of The Sign in Sidney Brustein's Window and Kennedy's Children; appeared: in TV series Three's Company, The Edge of Night, Another World, Somerset, Filthy Rich, Evening Shade; other TV appearances All That Glitters, The Defenders, Bronk, Evening Shade, Twilight Zone, Trapper John, M.D.; TV film The War Between the Tates, Bogey, Right to Kill, A Stranger Waits; movies Handle With Care (Nat. Soc. Film Critics award), Thieves, Bang the Drum Slowly, Scarecrow, Catamount Killing, Law and Disorder, One Summer Love, Dragon-Fly, Birch Intervals, Soggy Bottom, USA, No Small Affair, Sweet Dreams, Mens Club, A Tiger's Tale, Made in Heaven, Far North, Miss Firecracker, Green Card. Office: care Paradigm Talent Agy 10100 Santa Monica Blvd 25th Fl Los Angeles CA 90067

WEDGEWORTH, ROBERT, university librarian, dean, former association executive; b. Ennis, Tex., July 31, 1937; s. Robert and Jimmie (Johnson) W.; m. Chung Kyun, July 28, 1972; 1 child, Cicely Veronica. AB, Wabash Coll., 1959, DHL (hon.), 1980; MS, U. Ill., 1961; LittD, Park Coll., 1973; LLD, Atlanta U., 1982; DHL, Western Ill. U., 1983, Coll. William & Mary, 1988. Cataloguer Kansas City Pub. Library, 1961-62; asst. librarian, then acting librarian Park Coll., Parkville, Mo., 1962-64; librarian Meramec Community Coll., Kirkwood, Mo., 1964-66; acquisitions librarian Brown U. Library, Providence, 1966-69; asst. prof. Rutgers U., New Brunswick, N.J., 1971-72; exec. dir. ALA, Chgo., 1972-85; dean Sch. Library Service Columbia U., N.Y.C., 1985-92; univ. libr., prof. libr. adminstrn. U. Ill., Urbana, 1992—; mem. Nat. Commn. on New Technol. Uses of Copyrighted Works, 1975-78, biomed. library rev. com. Nat. Library Medicine, 1975-78, chmn., 1978-79; mem. network adv. com. Library of Congress, 1977-78; nat. adv. bd., exec. com., council Ctr. for the Book, Library of Congress, 1978-82; bd. dirs. Newberry Library, Chgo., 1979—, Pub. Service Satellite Consortium, 1975-85; bd. visitors U. Miami Libraries, Air U.; mem. exec. bd. Internat. Fedn. Library Assns. and Instns., The Hague, 1985-91, pres. 1991—; trustee Am. Library in Paris, 1986-92; trustee Wabash Coll., 1988—; alumni bd. Wabash Coll., pres. 1987-89; vis. prof. Sch. Library Sci. U. N.C., Chapel Hill, 1985; mem. adv. coun. Princeton U. Libraries, 1977-78, Stanford U. Librs., 1989—; mem. nat. adv. com. Gannett Ctr. for Media Services; mem. Accrediting Council on Edn. in Journalism and Mass Communication. Editor: Library Resources and Tech. Services, 1971-73; editor-in-chief: ALA Yearbook, 1976-85, World Encyclopedia of Library and Information Services, 3d edit., 1994. Chmn. U.S. Nat. Com. for UNESCO/PGI, 1976-81. Council on Library Resources fellow, 1969. Mem. ALA (life), NAACP (life), Am. Soc. Info. Sci., Grolier Club, Am. Antiquarian Soc. Home: 2008 Bentbrook Dr Champaign IL 61821-9204 Office: Univ of Illinois 1408 W Gregory Dr Rm 230 Urbana IL 61801-3607

WEDZICHA, WALTER, foreign language educator; b. Jezor, Poland, June 5, 1920; came to U.S., 1946; s. Wladyslaw and Maria (Kruczek) W.; m. Sabina Purzynska, Nov. 28, 1945; children: John M., Christine S. AB, U. Miami, 1965; MA, U. Pitts., 1966. Attaché Consulate Gen. of Poland, N.Y.C., 1946-49; acct. Miami, 1950-65; asst. prof. German and Russian Clarkson U., Potsdam, N.Y., 1967-86, prof. emeritus, 1986—. Author: Song of the City, 1957, From Love of God and All Creation, 1992. Fellow NDEA, U. Pitts., 1965-66; grantee NEH, Ohio State U., 1977, NEH, U. Ill., 1978. Mem. MLA. Democrat. Avocations: photography, music, gardening. Home: 2311 SE Bowie St Port Saint Lucie FL 34952-7317

WEED, EDWARD REILLY, marketing executive; b. Chgo., Jan. 25, 1940; s. Cornelius Cahill and Adelaide E. (Reilly) W.; student Fordham U., 1959-61, Loyola U., 1961-62; m. Lawrie Irving Bowes, Feb. 2, 1969. Account exec. Leo Burnett Co., Chgo., 1961-71; pres. GDC Ad Inc., corporate officer, Miami, Fla., 1971-74; v.p., account supr. D'Arcy Mac Manus & Masius, Chgo., 1975; group v.p. mktg. Hart Schaffner & Marx (Hartmarx), Chgo.; pres. Hart Services, Inc., 1975-82; v.p. mktg. Tishman, 1983-86; exec. v.p. Hannah Marine, 1986-87; exec. v.p., dir. U.S. Auction, 1988-92; v.p. mktg. Telemedia, 1992—; mng. dir. Southward, 1996—; dir. First Nat. Bank So. Miami; seminar instr. Grad. Sch. Notre Dame U., South Bend, Ill.; guest faculty Loyola U., Chgo. Contbr. articles to profl. jours. Trustee, Latin Sch. Found., 1976—; bd. dirs. North Ave. Day Nursery, 1969-73, Santa for Poor, 1975-87, Off-the-Street, 1982-87, Chgo. Boys' and Girls' Clubs, 1983-87, Map Inc., 1988—, Geneva Lake Conservancy, 1994—. Recipient Chi Ad Club award. Served with Ill. N.G. Republican. Roman Catholic. Clubs: Tavern, Cliff Dwellers, Saddle and Cycle. Office: Southward 120 S Riverside Plz S 422 Chicago IL 60606

WEED, ITHAMAR DRYDEN, life insurance company executive; b. Pomeroy, Ohio, Sept. 3, 1914; s. Ithamar B. and Besse (Smith) W.; m. Sally Lemert, July 5, 1941; children—Judith Lynne (Mrs. Lloyd Lindner), Charles Boyd, Donald Lemert. A.B., Ohio U., 1938; J.D. summa cum laude, Ohio State U., 1939. Bar: Ohio 1939. Clk. U.S. Dist. Ct. So. Dist. Ohio, Columbus, 1939-41; assoc. firm Vorys, Sater, Seymour and Pease, Columbus, 1946-54; assoc. counsel Western and So. Life Ins. Co., Cin., 1954-63; v.p., chief counsel Western and So. Life Ins. Co., 1963-73, sr. v.p., chief counsel, 1973-81; sec., dir Eagle Savs. Assn., Cin., 1970-81, West Ad, Inc., Cin., 1970-81; lectr. Coll. Law, Ohio State U., 1949-53. Served to lt. col. AUS, 1941-46. Mem. Order of Coif, Beta Theta Pi, Phi Delta Pi. Home: 5538 E Galbraith Rd Apt 34 Cincinnati OH 45236-2849

WEED, MAURICE JAMES, composer, retired music educator; b. Kalamazoo, Oct. 16, 1912; s. Frank Eugene and Ella May (Britton) W.; m. Berneice Laverne Pope, Aug. 23, 1937; children: Allison Gilbert (Mrs. Walter D. Herrick), Laurice Ellen (Mrs. Samuel L. Rich). BA, Western Mich. U., 1934; MusB, Eastman Sch. Music, 1940, MusM, 1952, PhD, 1954. Supr. instrumental music pub. schs. Ionia, Mich., 1934-36, Three Rivers, Mich., 1937-43; asst. prof. music, dir. instrumental music, tchr. music theory Ripon Coll., 1946-51; tchr. Eastman Sch. Music, summer 1954; prof., head dept. music No. Ill. U., 1954-61, prof. music, 1961-74; adj. prof. music Western Carolina U., 1974-75; ret., 1975. Composer in residence, MacDowell Colony, 1961; performances include: Serenity for chamber orch. Eastman-Rochester Symphony, 1953, Symphony Number 1, Nat. Symphony Orch., Washington, 1956, Symphony of the Air, Carnegie Hall, 1957, Wonder of the Starry Night, 1st ann. symposium Contemporary Am. Music, U. Kans., 1959, Serenity and Fanfare for Two Trumpets and Organ, 8th ann. symposium Univ. Composers Exchange, Valparaiso, Ind., 1959; Sept Cinquains for Soprano Voice and chamber instrumental group, No. Ill. U., 1964, 67, Symphonie Breve, 6th ann. symposium Contemporary Am. Music U. Kans., 1967, Symphonie Breve, Oklahoma City Symphony Orch.; MBS broadcast, 1965, U. Redlands, 1964, Asheville (N.C.) Symphony Orch., 1979; condr. symposium of 8 sacred choral and 2 organ works by 6 coll., univ., high sch. and ch. choirs, Atlanta, 1975; Serenity, Asheville Symphony Orch., 1977; composer: over 65 works including Ships, Witchery (songs for soprano and piano), 1937, Rain, for contralto and piano, 1940, Three Preludes for Organ, 1945, Introduction and Scherzo, symphonic band, 1948, Gratitude, for contralto with organ, 1950, An After Easter Prayer, 1950, Serenity, for chamber orch., 1953, Wonder of the Starry Night, a capella choir, 1958, Symphonie Breve, 1959, Trio for violin, cello and piano, 1961, Concertino for cello and orch, 1962, Psalm XIII (mixed choir and organ), 1964, Hopkins Park, concert march, 1966, Triptych for Voices, a cappella choir, 1966, Vestigia Nulla Retrorsum, processional march, 1968, Praise Ye the Lord (mixed choir), 1968, A Wedding Song (soprano and organ), 1969, In the Midnight Hour (soprano and organ), 1970, In Te, Domini, Speravi (mixed choir), 1970, 4 Anthems for Mixed Choir, 1973, Postlude for Organ, 1974, The Catamounts, concert march for band, 1974, Duo for Viola and C Trumpet, 1977, Choral Fanfare No. 2, 1977, An Appalachian Celebration for Choir and Band, 1978; Celebration (hymn-anthem), 1981; 3 anthems for mixed voices Let All the People Praise Thee, 1980, Sing Praises to God, 1981, Praise Ye the Lord, 1982, The 3Bs-Brass Sextet, 1982, Voices of Appalachia, 1986; numerous others. Recipient 25th Anniversary award Nat. Symphony Orch., 1956, Ostwald award, 1959, J. Fisher & Bro. Centennial award, 1964, Pedro Paz award, 1966; Eastman Sch. Music teaching fellow, 1951-54. Mem. Nat. Assn. Composers U.S.A., Am. Music Ctr., Music Edn. Nat. Conf., N.C. Music Educators, Am. Soc. Univ. Composers, ASCAP, Phi Mu Alpha. Methodist. Home: Givens Estates Sweeten Creek Rd Wesley Dr N Villa 21-F Asheville NC 28803

WEED, RAY ARNOLD, lawyer; b. Lubbock, Tex., May 30, 1934; s. Thomas Arnold and Rosalie (Syfrett) W.; m. Barbara Ware, Dec. 22, 1955 (div. 1961); children: Stanley Arnold, Stephen Kelsey; m. Kathleen Burks, Dec. 19, 1987. BBA, Tex. Tech. U., 1957; JD, U. Tex., 1964. Bar: Tex. 1964, U.S. Dist. Ct. (we. and so. dists.) Tex., U.S. Ct. Appeals (5th cir.), U.S. Supreme Ct. Assoc. Groce, Hebdon, Fahey and Smith, San Antonio, 1964-69; ptnr., shareholder Groce, Locke & Hebdon, San Antonio, 1969-91; shareholder, pres. Ball & Weed, PC, San Antonio, 1991. Capt. U.S. Army, 1957-64. Fellow Am. Coll. Trial Lawyers, Tex. Bar Found., San Antonio Bar Found.; mem. Tex. Assn. Def. Counsel, Fed. Inst. and Corp. Counsel, Am. Bd. Trial Advs. (pres. San Antonio chpt. 1990), Def. Counsel San Antonio (founder 1992, pres. 1993). Republican. Avocation: ranching. Office: Ball & Weed 745 E Mulberry Ave San Antonio TX 78212-3137

WEED, ROGER OREN, rehabilitation educator and counselor; b. Bend, Oreg., Feb. 2, 1944; s. Chester Elbert and Ruth Marie (Urie) W.; m. Paula J. Keller; children: Nicholette, Andrew. BS in Sociology, U. Oreg., 1967, MS in Rehab. Counseling, 1969; PhD in Rehab. Counseling, U. Ga., 1986. Cert. rehab. counselor; cert. disability mgmt. specialist; lic. profl. counselor. Vocat. rehab. counselor State of Alaska, Anchorage, 1969-71; instr. U. Alaska, Anchorage, 1970-76; counselor Langdon Psychiat. Clinic, Anchorage, 1971-74; from asst. dir. to exec. dir. Hope Cottages, Anchorage, 1974-79; owner Profl. Resources Group, Anchorage, 1978-80; mng. ptnr. Collins, Weed & Assocs., 1980-84; assoc. dir. Ctr. for Rehab. Tech. Ga. Tech. U., Atlanta, 1986-87; catastrophic injury rehab. Weed & Assocs., Atlanta, 1984—; assoc. prof. Ga. State U., Atlanta, 1987—; adj. faculty Ga. Inst. Tech. Co-author: Vocational Expert Handbook, 1986, Transferable Work Skills, 1988, Life Care Planning: Spinal Cord Injured, 1989, 94, Life Care Planning: Head Injured, 1994, Life Care Planning for the Amputee, 1992, Rehab Consultant Handbook, 1994; mem. editl. bd. Jour. of Pvt. Sector Rehab., Athens, Ga., 1986—; mem. Disting. Editl. Bd. Vanguard Series in Rehab., Athens, 1988—; contbr. articles to profl. publs. Recipient Gov.'s award Gov.'s Com. on Employment, Alaska, 1982, Goldpan Svc. award Gov.'s Com. on Employment, Alaska, 1978, Profl. Svcs. award Am. Rehab. Counselors Assn., 1993. Fellow Nat. Rehab. Assn. (chair legis. com., bd. dirs. met. Atlanta chpt. 1988—, pres. Pacific region 1983-85, pres.'s award Pacific region 1986), Nat. Assn. Rehab. Profls. in Pvt. Sector (chair resh. and tng. com. 1988-93, pres. 1994-95, Educator of the Yr. award 1991), Nat. Brain Injury Assn., Pvt. Rehab. Suppliers Ga., Rehab. Engring. Soc. N.Am., Anchorage Amateur Radio Club. Republican. Methodist. Avocations: sailing, skiing, bicycling, flying, computers. Office: 9th Fl College of Education Ga State U Dept Counseling Atlanta GA 30303

WEEDEN, DEBBIE SUE, early childhood education educator; b. Tenn., Nov. 7, 1952; d. Edward Jr. and Ann Arrants; m. Gordon H. Weeden, May 5, 1979; children: Lance Edward, Lindsey Brooke. BS in Early Child Edn. magna cum laude, Va. Intermont U., 1975; MA in Reading Rsch., East Tenn. State U., 1979. Cert. K-8 reading tchr., Tenn. Kindergarten tchr. Weaver Sch., Bristol, Tenn., 1975—. V.p. Weaver Sch. PTA; tchr. rep. Weaver Sch. Mem. Career Ladder Tchrs., Alpha Delta Kappa (historian). Methodist. Avocations: crafts, volleyball. Home: 328 Orchard Ln Bluff City TN 37618-1160 Office: Weaver Sch Rte 1 Bristol TN 37620

WEEDER, DANA NIXON, surgeon; b. Phila., July 30, 1934; s. Stephan Dean and Caroline Denny (Nixon) W.; m. Astrid Sundt, May 19, 1962; children: Dana Sundt, Kristian Nixon, Kari Sundt. AB, Princeton U., 1955; MD, U. Pa., 1959. Diplomate Am. Bd. Surgery. Staff surgeon Doylestown (Pa.) Hosp., 1965-66, 68-70, Exeter (N.H.) Hosp., 1970—. Lt. cmdr. USN, 1966-68. Fellow Am. Coll. Surgeons; mem. N.E. Surgical Soc. Avocations: boat building, tennis, golf. Office: Saltonstall Med Bldg Buzell Ave Exeter NH 03833

WEEDON, ALAN CHARLES, chemist, educator, university dean; b. Oxford, Eng., Mar. 29, 1951; arrived in Can., 1976; s. Charles Arthur Reginald and Marjorie Elsie (Cook) W. BSc, London U., 1973, PhD, 1976. Rsch. assoc. U. Western Ont., London, Can., 1976-80, asst. prof., 1980-86, assoc. prof., 1986-91, prof., 1991—, dean Faculty Grad. Studies, 1996—. Contbr. articles to sci. jours. Recipient Merck-Frosst award Can. Soc. Chemistry, 1991. Fellow Chem. Inst. Can.; mem. Am. Chem. Soc. Office: U Western Ont, Dept of Chemistry, London, ON Canada N6A 5B7

WEEKES, TREVOR C., astrophysicist; b. Dublin, Ireland, May 21, 1940; came to U.S. 1966; s. Gerard and Florence (Murtagh) W.; m. Ann Katherine Owens, Sept. 30, 1964; children: Karina, Fiona, Lara. BSc, U. Coll. Dublin, 1962, PhD, 1966; DSc, Nat. U. Ireland, 1978. Lectr. Univ. Coll. Dublin, 1964-66; postdoctoral fellow NRC, Cambridge, Mass., 1966-67; astrophysicist Smithsonian Astrophys. Obs., 1967-92, sr. astrophysicist, 1992—; resident dir. Whipple Obs., Amado, Ariz., 1969-76; vis.prof. Royal Greenwich Obs., U.K., 1980-81; adj. prof. physics U. Ariz., 1995—. Assoc. editor astrophysics Phys. Rev. Letters, 1994—. Mem. Am. Astron. Soc., Am. Phys. Soc., Royal Astron. Soc. Democrat. Roman Catholic. Office: Whipple Obs PO Box 97 Amado AZ 85640-0097

WEEKLEY, DAVID, real estate developer; b. 1954. Student, Trinity Univ., 1975. General Homes, Inc., Houston, 1975-76; CEO David Weekley Homes, Houston, 1976—. Office: 1300 Post Oak Blvd Houston TX 77056

WEEKLEY, FREDERICK CLAY, JR., lawyer; b. San Antonio, Aug. 29, 1939; s. F. Clay and Topsy (Stevens) W.; m. Lynda Freeman; children: Amber Lee, Caroline Lee. BBA, Baylor U., 1962, JD, 1963; LLM, NYU, 1969. Bar: Tex. 1963. Ptnr. Bracewell & Patterson, Houston, 1974-90; trust counsel Bank One, Tex., N.A., 1990—; mem. coun. real property, probate and trust law sect., State Bar of Tex., 1987-90; mem. trust divsn. Tex. Bankers Assn., 1992—, chmn. legis. com., 1992-95. Editor: Texas Wills System, 1984. Mem. Commn. Probate Law Examiners, Tex. Bd. Legal Specialization, 1978-82. Fellow Am. Coll. Trust and Estate Counsel. Home: 1821 Mossy Oak St Arlington TX 76012-5619 Office: Bank One Texas NA Legal Dept 1717 Main St Fl 9 Dallas TX 75201-4605

WEEKLY, JOHN WILLIAM, insurance company executive; b. Sioux City, Iowa, June 21, 1931; s. John E. Weekly and Alyce Beatrice (Preble) Nichols; m. Bette Lou Thomas, Dec. 31, 1949; children: John William Jr., Thomas Patrick, Michael Craig, James Mathew, Daniel Kevin. Grad. high sch., Omaha. V.p. First Data Resources, Inc., Omaha, 1969-74; v.p. Mut. of Omaha/United of Omaha Ins. Co., Omaha, 1974-81, sr. exec. v.p., 1981-87, pres., COO, 1987-95, vice chmn., pres., COO, 1995—, vice chmn., pres., CEO, 1996—; CEO Mutual of Omaha Ins. Co., 1996—; also bd. dirs. Mut. of Omaha/United of Omaha Ins. Co., Omaha, 1996—; bd. dirs. KPM Investment Mgmt., Midwest Express Airlines, Inc., Harbor Holdings, Inc., Companion Life Ins. Co., Kirkpatrick, Pettis, Smith, Polian, Inc., Tele-Trip Co., Inc., Omaha Property and Casualty Co., United World Life Ins., Mut. Asset Mgmt. Co., Norwest Bank Nebr., N.A., Omaha Airport Authority, Mut. of Omaha Investor Svcs., Preferred HealthAlliance, Inc. Bd. dirs. Bellevue (Nebr.) U., 1986—. Mem. Health Ins. Assn. Am. (chmn. of bd. 1996), Am. Coun. Life Ins. (bd. dirs. 1995—), Greater Omaha C. of C. (bd. dirs. 1991—). Avocations: hunting, fishing, golf. Office: Mut Omaha Ins Co Mutual Omaha Plz Omaha NE 68175

WEEKS, ALBERT LOREN, author, educator, journalist; b. Highland Park, Mich., Mar. 28, 1923; s. Albert Loren and Vera Grace (Jarvis) W. Student, U. Mich., 1942-43; MA, U. Chgo., 1949; PhD, Columbia U., 1965; cert., Russian Inst., 1960. Reporter Chgo. City News Bur., 1946; polit. analyst U.S. Dept. State, 1950-53, Free Europe Com., Inc., 1953-56; editorial asst. Newsweek mag., 1957-58; Russian tech. glossary compiler McGraw-Hill Book Co., 1960-61; prof. continuing edn. NYU, 1959-89; lectr. U.S. diplomatic history and soviet govt. Columbia U., 1951-52; mem. adv. coun. Nat. Strategy Info. Ctr., 1979-89; instr. Ringling Sch. Art and Design, 1991—. Host: A Week's View of Red Press, Sta. WNBC, 1965-68; series Myths That Rule America, NBC-TV, 1979-82; author: Reading American History, 1963, The First Bolshevik: A Political Biography of Peter Tkachev, 1968, The Other Side of Coexistence: An Analysis of Russian Foreign Policy, 1970, Richard Hofstadter's The American Political Tradition and the Age of

Reform, 1973, Andrei Sakharov and the Soviet Dissidents, 1975, The Troubled Detente, 1976, Solzhenitsyn's One Day in the Life of Ivan Denisovich, 1976, Myths That Rule America, 1980, War and Peace: Soviet Russia Speaks, 1983; editor/compiler Brassey's Soviet and Communist Quotations, 1987, The Soviet Nomenklatura, 1987-1991; internat. affairs editor Def. Sci. mag., 1982-85; columnist Def. Report, 1982-90; nat. sec., editor N.Y.C. Tribune, 1982-90; contbr. articles N.Y. Times, New Republic, New Leader, Annals, Russian, Slavic revs., Christian Sci. Monitor, Problems of Communism, Survey, Mil. Intelligence, Strategic Rev., World War II mag., Air Univ. Rev., L.A. Times, Washington Times, Orbis, Global Affairs, Panorama, Sarasota Herald-Tribune, Bradenton Herald, Defense and Diplomacy, Am. Intelligence Jour., USA Today, Rossiiskiye Vesti. Home: 4884 Kestral Park Cir Sarasota FL 34231-3369

WEEKS, ARTHUR ANDREW, lawyer, law educator; b. Hanceville, Ala., Dec. 2, 1914; s. A.A. and Anna S. (Seibert) W.; m. Carol P. Weeks; children: John David, Carol Christine, Nancy Anna. A.B., Samford U., 1936; LL.B., U. Ala., 1939, J.D., 1939; LL.M., Duke U., 1950; LL.D. (hon.), Widener U., 1980. Bar: Ala. 1939, Tenn. 1948. Sole practice Birmingham, Ala., 1939-41, 1946-47, 1954-61; dean, prof. law Cumberland U. Sch. Law, 1947-54; dean, prof. Samford U., 1961-72, prof. law, 1972-74; prof. law Cumberland Sch. Law, Samford U., 1984—; prof. law Del. Sch. Law of Widener U., Wilmington, 1974-82, dean, 1974-80, interim dean, 1982-83, dean emeritus, prof., 1983—. Served to capt. AUS, 1941-46. Mem. ABA, Tenn. Bar Assn., Ala. Bar Assn., Birmingham Bar Assn., Del. Bar Assn. (assoc.), Phi Alpha Delta, Phi Kappa Phi, Delta Theta Phi. Home: 1105 Water Edge Ct Birmingham AL 35244-1437

WEEKS, BRIGITTE, publishing executive; b. Whitchurch, Hants, Eng., Aug. 28, 1943; came to U.S., 1965; d. Jack and Margery May (Millett) W.; m. Edward A. Herscher, Sept. 6, 1969; children—Hilary, Charlotte, Daniel. Student, Univ. Coll. of North Wales, Bangor, 1962-65. Asst. editor Boston Mag., 1966-70; editor Kodansha Internat., Tokyo, 1969-72, Resources for the Future, 1973-74; asst. editor The Washington Post Book World, 1974-78, editor, 1978-88; sr. v.p., editor-in-chief Book-of-the-Month Club, N.Y.C., 1988-94; editor-in-chief Guideposts Books, N.Y.C., 1994—; pres. Nat. Book Critics Circle, 1984-86; bd. dirs. Nat. Book Found. Office: Guideposts Books 16 E 34th St New York NY 10016-4328

WEEKS, DAVID FRANK, foundation administrator; b. Salt Lake City, Sept. 9, 1926; s. Frank Harold and Myrtle June (Larsen) W.; m. Betty Alice Tellin, Aug. 14, 1949; children: David Rice, Clayton Frank. Student, So. Meth. U., 1945, U. Tex., 1946; B.S. (Union Pacific Carl Raymond Gray scholar), U. Idaho, 1949; HHD (hon.), U. Louisville, 1993. Pres. Assoc. Students U. Idaho, 1948-49; announcer Sta. KBIO, Burley, Idaho, 1949; Idaho rep. Nat. Found. for Infantile Paralysis, Boise, 1949-53; asst. to nat. dir. fund raising Nat. Found. for Infantile Paralysis, N.Y.C., 1953-57; asst. nat. dir. March of Dimes, N.Y.C., 1957-59; account exec. Kersting, Brown & Co., N.Y.C., 1959-61; exec. dir. Rsch. to Prevent Blindness, Inc., N.Y.C., 1961-70, exec. v.p., 1970-83, pres., 1983—; pres., trustee RPB Endowment Fund Inc., N.Y.C., 1988—; mem. borough coun. Borough of Ho-Ho-Kus, N.J., 1966-68; mayor Borough of Ho-Ho-Kus, 1968-75; consumer rep. sub-com. ophthalmic prostheses HEW, 1976-79; cons. Bur. Med. Devices, FDA, 1977-80; mem. nat. adv. eye coun. NIH, HHS, 1985-90; trustee Okla. Eye Found., 1988-92. Mem. Ho-Ho-Kus Planning Bd., 1962-65, chmn., 1965; mem. Zoning Bd., 1975-85, Bergen County (N.J.) Ethics Bd., 1977-82; founder, pres. Ho-Ho-Kus Republican Club, 1983-86. Served with USN, 1944-46. Recipient Bronze Palm Eagle Scout award Boy Scouts Am., 1941, Disting. Pub. Svc. award Am. Acad. Ophthalmology and Otolaryngology, 1976, cert. of recognition Johns Hopkins U. Schs. Medicine, Hygiene and Pub. Health, 1984, Nat. Vision Rsch. Leadership award Assn. U. Profs. Ophthalmology, 1989, Disting. Svc. award Johns Hopkins Med. Instns.-Wilmer Ophthal. Inst., 1989; named Ky. col., 1969, U. of Idaho Alumni Hall of Fame award, 1992. Mem. Assn. Rsch. in Vision and Ophthalmology (hon.), Pan Am. Ophthalmol. Assn. (assoc.), Am. Soc. Assn. Execs., Internat. Assn. Eye Rsch., Bergen County Mayors Assn. (pres. 1975-77), Am. Tentative Soc. (treas. and trustee 1974-94, v.p. 1982-94), Assn. U. Profs. Ophthalmology (hon.), Met. Club. Home: 4058 NW Northcliff Bend OR 97701 Office: Rsch Prevent Blindness 645 Madison Ave New York NY 10022

WEEKS, DEBORAH CAROL, special education educator; b. Wilmington, Del., Sept. 24, 1963; d. James Irivin Jr. and Carol Evelyn (Mumford) W. AAS, Del. Tech., 1983; BS cum laude, Del. State U., 1988. Cert. elem. tchr., elem. spl. edn. tchr. Tchr. Greensboro (Md.) Elem. Sch., 1988-89; resource tchr. Lake Forest South Elem. Sch., Harrington, Del., 1989-90; tchr. presch. Children 1st Inc., Hockessin, Del., 1991; tchr. Seaford (Del.) Elem. Sch., 1991—; spl. edn. tchr. Polytech H.S., 1993—. Mem. CEC, Make A Wish Found., Spl. Olympics, Del. Blue/Gold Com. Mem. NEA, Kappa Delta Pi, Alpha Chi. Republican. Episcopalian. Home: RR 1 Box 812 Dover DE 19904-6027

WEEKS, GERALD, psychology educator; b. Morehead City, N.C., Nov. 20, 1948; s. Marion G. and Ada (Willis) W.; m. Kathleen Glass, Sept. 2, 1972. BA in Philosophy and Psychology, East Carolina U., 1971, MA in Gen. Psychology, 1973; PhD in Clin. Psychology, Ga. State U., 1979. Diplomate Am. Bd. Profl. Psychology (pres. 1987-88, bd. dirs. 1982-87), Am. Bd. Family Psychology, Am. Bd. Sexology; cert. marital and family therapist; lic. practicing psychologist, N.C., Pa.; registered Health Care Providers in Psychology. Intern in family therapy Harlem Valley Psychiatric Ctr., Wingdale, N.Y., 1978-79; assoc. prof. psychology U. N.C., Wilmington, 1979-85; dir. tng. Penn Coun. for Relationships, 1985—; clin. asst. prof. psychology Sch. Medicine U. Pa., Phila., 1985-87, clin. assoc. prof., 1988—; pvt. practice Carolina Ob-gyn Ctr., Wilmington, 1980-85. Author: Promoting Change Through Paradoxical Therapy, 1985, Treating Couples: The Intersystem Model of the Marriage Council of Philadelphia, 1989, Promoting Change through Paradoxical Therapy, 1991, (with L. L'Abate) Paradoxical Psychotherapy: Theory and Practice with Individuals, Couples, and Families, 1982, (with R. Sauber, L. L'Abate) Family Therapy: Basic Concepts and Terms, 1985, (with L. Hof) Integrating Sex and Marital Therapy: A Clinicians Guide, 1987, (with S. Treat) Couples in Treatment, 1992, Integrative Solutions: Treating Common Problems in Coupld Therapy, 1995; mem. editl. bd. Am. Jour. Family Therapy, Am. Jour. Family Psychology; contbr. articles to profl. jours. Fellow Am. Assn. Marital and Family Therapy (clin. mem., nat. adv. bd., approved supr.); mem. APA, Acad. Family Psychology, Interpersonal and Social Skills Assn. (founding mem.), Acad. Psychologists in Marital, Sex, and Family Therapy. Home: 210 Church St # D Philadelphia PA 19106-4519 Office: Penn Coun for Relationships 4025 Chestnut St Fl 2 Philadelphia PA 19104-3054

WEEKS, JEROME C., writer, drama critic; b. Detroit, Dec. 10, 1953; s. William Lawrence and Frances (Podgurski) W.; m. Sara Rankin; 1 child, Suzanna Beckett. Bachelor, U. Detroit, 1975; Master, U. Conn., 1977; postgrad., U. Tex., 1977-80. Rsch. asst. Detroit Free Press, 1973-75; columnist, editor Third Coast Mag., Austin, Tex., 1982-84; entertainment writer Houston Post, 1984-86; drama critic Dallas Morning News, 1986—. Recipient Katy award Dallas Press Club, 1993. Mem. Am. Theatre Critics Assn. Office: Dallas Morning News 508 Young St Dallas TX 75202-4808*

WEEKS, JOHN DAVID, chemistry and physical science educator; b. Birmingham, Ala., Oct. 11, 1943; s. Arthur Andrew Weeks and Grace Hicks (Ezell) Marquez; m. Kaja Parming, May 27, 1987; 1 child, Aili. AB, Harvard U., 1965; PhD, U. Chgo., 1969. Postdoctoral fellow U. Calif., San Diego, 1969-71, U. Cambridge, Eng., 1971-72; mem. tech. staff AT&T Bell Labs., Murray Hill, N.J., 1972-90; prof. Inst. Phys. Sci. and Tech., dept. chemistry U. Md., College Park, 1990-95, disting. univ. prof., 1995—. Contbr. articles to profl. jours. Fellow Am. Phys. Soc.; mem. AAAS, Am. Chem Soc. (chair, theoretical chem. subdiv. 1992-93, Hildebrand award 1990). Home: 15301 Watergate Rd Silver Spring MD 20905-5779 Office: U Md Inst Phys Sci and Tech College Park MD 20742

WEEKS, JOHN ROBERT, geographer, sociology educator; b. Sacramento, June 1, 1944; s. Robert Louis and Thelma Hope (Evans) W.; m. Deanna Jean Hosea, May 16, 1965; children: John Robert, Gregory, Jennifer. AB, U. Calif., Berkeley, 1966, MA, 1969, PhD, 1972. Asst. prof. sociology Mich. State U., East Lansing, 1971-74; asst. prof. sociology San Diego State U., 1974-78, assoc. prof., 1978-81, prof., 1981-92; prof. geography, 1992—; chmn. dept. San Diego State U., 1978-85; adminstrv. dir. Internat. Population Ctr., 1985—; vis. research demographer U. Calif.-Berkeley, 1972; cons. Allied Home Health Assn., 1978-80, Area Agy. on Aging, San Diego, 1979-81, Los Angeles Regional Family Planning Council, 1986—, East County Econ. Devel. Coun., 1986—. Author: Teenage Marriages, 1976, Population, 6th edit., 1996, Aging, 1984, Demography of Islamic Nations, 1988, High Fertility Among Indochinese Refuges, 1989, Demographic Dynamics of the U.S.-Mexico Border, 1992. Grantee USPHS, 1983-84, 87-88, 88-89, 90—, U.S. Administrn. on Aging, 1979-80, U.S. Bur. of Census, 1988-89; trainee USPHS, 1967-71. Mem. Population Assn. Am., Am. Sociol. Assn., Internat. Union for Sci. Study Population, Am. Assn. Geographers. Democrat. Office: San Diego State U Dept Geography San Diego CA 92182

WEEKS, MARIE COOK, health and physical education educator; b. High Point, N.C., Jan. 21, 1949; d. Paul Hue Cook and Beulah Edna (Smith) Townsend; m. Lewis Tirey Weeks, June 5, 1970; children: Gina, Corby. BS in Edn., Western Carolina U., 1971. Tchr. grades 6,7,8, math. science, health, physical edn. Ramseur (N.C.) Elem. Sch., 1971-91; tchr. grades 6,7,8, health and physical edn. Archdale-Trinity Middle Sch., Trinity, N.C., 1991—; coach girls softball and volleyball Randolph County Schs., Asheboro, N.C., 1971—; mentor tchr. Randolph County Schs., Asheboro, 1989—; student tchr. supr. Archdale Trinity Middle Sch. 1993—, head of health and phys. edn. dept., 1993—. Coach girls' softball Hillsville (N.C.) Civitan's Youth Softball League, 1984—. Named Ramseur Sch. Tchr. of Yr., Ramseur Faculty, 1983, 89, Outstanding Young Educatior Asheboro/Randolph County, Asheboro Jaycees, 1989. Mem. NEA, N.C. AAHPERD, Nat. Fedn. Coaches, N.C. Assn. Educators. Baptist. Avocations: arts and crafts, softball, family. Home: 3725 Lynn Oaks Dr Trinity NC 27370-9445 Office: Archdale-Trinity Mid Sch 5105 Archdale Rd Trinity NC 27370

WEEKS, MARTA JOAN, priest; b. Buenos Aires, May 24, 1930; came to U.S., 1932; d. Frederick Albert and Anne (Newman) Sutton; m. Lewis Austin Weeks, Aug. 17, 1951; children: Kermit Austin, Leslie Anne. BA in Polit. Sci., Stanford U., 1951; MDiv, Episcopal Theol. Sem. S.W., 1991. Ordained priest Episcopal Ch., 1992. Legal libr., sec. Mene Grande Oil Co., Caracas, Venezuela, 1948; English tchr. Centro-Venezolano Americano, Caracas, 1948; sec. Household Fin. Corp., Salt Lake City, 1951; legal sec. McKelvey & McKelvey Attys., Durango, Colo., 1952; sec., dir. Weeks Air Mus., Miami, Fla., 1985—; chaplain Jackson Meml. Hosp., 1992-93; priest-at-large Episcopal Diocese of S.E. Fla., until 1996; interim asst. St. James Episcopal Ch., Salt Lake City, 1994-95. Trustee Beloit (Wis.) Coll., 1980-82, U. Miami, 1983-88, 95—, Bishop Gray Inns, Lake Worth and Davenport, Fla., 1992—. Mem. Am. Soc. Order St. John of Jerusalem. Address: 7350 SW 162nd St Miami FL 33157-3820

WEEKS, PAUL MARTIN, plastic surgeon, educator; b. Clinton, N.C., June 11, 1932; m. Doris Hill, Apr. 28, 1956; children: Christopher, Heather, Paul, Thomas, Susan, Phillip. AB, Duke U., 1954; MD, U. N.C., 1958. Diplomate Am. Bd. Surgery, Am. Bd. Plastic Surgery. Intern N.C. Meml. Hosp., Chapel Hill, 1959-62, asst. resident in surgery, 1962-63, chief resident in gen. surgery, 1962-63, chief resident in plastic surgery, 1963-64; from instr. to asst. prof. surgery U. Ky., Louisville, 1964-68, assoc. prof. surgery, 1968-70; prof. surgery, plastic and reconstructive surgery, head of div. Washington U. Sch. Medicine, St. Louis, 1971—; plastic surgeon-in-chief Barnes Hosp., St. Louis, 1971—, St. Louis Children's Hosp., 1971—. Assoc. editor Jour. Hand Surgery, 1976—, Plastic and Reconstructive Surgery, 1978-84; contbr. articles to profl. jours. Mem. AMA, ACS (gov. 1991—), Soc. Univ. Surgeons, So. Med. Assn., Am. Surg. Assn., So. Surg. Assn., Assn. Academic Surgeons, Am. Cleft Palate Assn., Am. Soc. Plastic and Reconstructive Surgeons, Am. Soc. Surgery of the Hand, Plastic Surgery Research Council, Am. Burn Assn., Am. Assn. Plastic Surgeons (pres. elect 1990-91, pres. 1991-92), Am. Assn. Plastic and Reconstructive Surgeons, Mo. State Med. Assn., St. Louis Med. Soc., Canadian Soc. Plastic and Reconstructive Surgeons, Nathan Womack Soc. Republican. Avocations: golf, sailing, skiing. Home: 6470 Ellenwood Ave Saint Louis MO 63105-2229 Office: Barnes Hosp Barnes Hospital Plz Saint Louis MO 63110

WEEKS, RICHARD RALPH, marketing educator; b. Champaign, Ill., Sept. 18, 1932; s. Frank Cook and B. Caroline (Pool) W.; m. Sue Ann Grunwald, Aug. 29, 1953; children: Kimberly Sue, Bret William. B.S., U. Ill., 1955; M.B.A., Washington U., St. Louis, 1960, D.B.A., 1966. Exec. sec., editor bull. Am. Assembly Collegiate Schs. Bus., St. Louis, 1960-64; exec. sec. Beta Gamma Sigma; also editor Beta Gamma Sigma Exchange, 1961-64; 1st ann. A.A.C.B.S. doctoral fellow in bus. adminstrn., 1964-65; dir. MBA program, asst. prof. mktg. Coll. Bus., Okla. State U., 1965-66, asst. dean, dir. MBA program, asso. prof. mktg., 1966-67; dean, prof. mktg. Walter E. Heller Coll. Bus. Adminstrn., Roosevelt U., 1967-70; dean Coll. Bus. Adminstrn. U. R.I., 1970-85, acting v.p. bus. and fin., 1976-77, provost for pub. policy, pub. service and mgmt., 1979-85, prof. mktg., 1970-92, prof. emeritus, dean emeritus, 1992—; dir. Potter Hazlehurst Inc., Providence Gas. Co., Providence Energy Co., Newport Am. Corp., Daly & Walcott, Inc. Editor: Faculty Personnel, 9th edit, 1965; contbg. editor Ency. Bus. Information Sources, 1964; editorial adv. bd. Bus. and Soc, 1968-70. Bd. dirs. Chgo. Econ. Devel. Corp., 1968-70, v.p., 1969-70; bd. dirs. Chgo. Fin. Devel. Corp., 1970, Progress Assn. for Econ. Devel., 1972-73; bd. dirs. Coun. on Postsecondary Accreditation, 1974-83, mem. exec. com., 1977-82, chmn., 1979-81; bd. dirs. Friends of Jamestown Philomenian Library, 1972-77, pres., 1974-76; mem. adv. bd. Intercollegiate Case Clearinghouse, 1976-79; pres. Friends of URI Library, 1986-88. Served to capt. USAF, 1955-63. Fulbright grantee, 1986. Mem. Am. Mktg. Assn. (dir. acad. placement 1966, 68), Ea. Fin. Assn. (dir. 1974-77), Council Profl. Edn. Bus. (sec.-treas. 1960-64, exec. com. 1961-64), Nat. Assn. State Univs. and Land-grant Colls., Commn. on Edn. for Bus. Professions (sec. 1973-76, chmn. 1976-78), New Eng. Assn. Schs. and Colls. (sec.-treas. 1983-85), Am. Assn. Collegiate Schs. Bus. (various com., bd. dirs. 1976-85, pres. 1983-84), Greater Providence C. of C. (dir. 1979-82), Delta Sigma Pi, Alpha Kappa Lambda, Beta Gamma Sigma (various comms., pres. 1978-80), Mu Kappa Tau, Pi Sigma Epsilon, Phi Kappa Phi. Home: 2048 Imperial Cir Naples FL 33942-1089

WEEKS, ROBBIE C., elementary education educator, administrator; b. Mulga, Ala., Oct. 13, 1936; d. Jesse Lewis and Ruby Pearl (Miles) Jackson; m. Cleophus James Weeks, June 10, 1956; children: Cleophus, Reginald Darnell. BS, Daniel Payne Coll., Ala., 1966; MEd, Ala. State U., 1976; postgrad. in edn., U. Ala.-Birmingham, 1977. Cert. educator, administr., Ala.; cert instrn. supervision K-12, 1988. Instr. J.A. Davis Elem. Sch., Bessemer, Ala., 1968—, coord. programs Bessemer City Sch. System, 1971—, supr. comm., 1979-83, coord. workshops, 1984-85, coord. in-svc. tng. tchrs., 1990—, resource curriculum specialist; coord. creative writing, oratorical contests, sponsor Red Cross Club, 1985—. Contbr. articles to profl. jours., scripts for video presentations in edn.. Coord. programs Allen Temple AME Ch., Bessemer, 1970-95, pro tem steward, 1985—; mem. Unserv Coun., Birmingham, Ala., 1984— (past pres.); coun. pres. U.S. Postal, Bessemer; block capt. March of Dimes Mothers, Bessemer, 1986; pres. Bessemer Edn. Assn., 1985—, U.S. Postal Coun., 1993-94. Mem. NEA (mem. supervision/curriculum 1993-94), NAFE, Ala. Edn. Assn. (mem. supervision, curriculum 1993-94), Nat. Reading Assn., Edn. Assn. Bessemer. Democrat. Methodist. Club: Auxiliary (Bessemer), Gamma Phi Delta. Avocations: writing; singing; speaking; sports; traveling. Home: 1314 21st Ave N Bessemer AL 35020-3943

WEEKS, ROBET ANDREW, materials science researcher, educator; b. Birmingham, Ala., Aug. 23, 1924; s. William Andrew and Annie Bell (Hammond) W.; m. Jane Sutherland, Mar. 20, 1948; children—Kevin Dale, Robin Dee, Loren Hammond, Kerry Andrew. B.S., Birmingham-So. Coll., 1947; M.S., U. Tenn., 1951; Ph.D., Brown U., 1966. Sr. physicist Union Carbide Corp., Oak Ridge, Tenn., 1951-84; research prof. material sci. Vanderbilt U., 1984—; disting. vis. prof. Am. U. in Cairo, 1970-71; invited prof. Ecole Poly. Federale de Lausanne, Switzerland, 1981; vis. prof. Cath. U., Leuven, Belgium, 1983; cons. numerous pvt. corps. and fed. agys. Coeditor: Effects of Modes of Formation on Structure of Glass, 1985, 88, Editing the Refereed Scientific Journal, 1994; assoc. editor Jour. Geophys. Rsch., 1968-74; editor Jour. Noncrystalline Solids, 1988—; contbr. numerous articles to profl. jours. Served with U.S. Army, 1943-46. Union Carbide fellow, 1964; Fulbright lectr., 1980; research fellow Reading U., 1971. Fellow Am. Ceramic Soc. (R. A. Weeks Symposium on Sci. and Tech. Si02 and Related Materials named in his honor, Honolulu 1993); mem. AAAS, Am. Phys. Soc., Materials Rsch. Soc. Avocation: photography. Home: 331 Southshore Dr Greenback TN 37742-2301 Office: Vanderbilt U PO Box 1678 Nashville TN 37240

WEEKS, ROLAND, JR., newspaper publisher; b. Knoxville, Tenn., July 8, 1936. B.S., Clemson (S.C.) U., 1958. Sales engr. Metal Products, Inc., Greenville, S.C., 1961-63; mgmt. trainee, then bus. mgr. Columbia Newspapers, Inc.; pubs. The State and Columbia (S.C.) Record newspapers, 1963-68; pres., pub. Gulf Pub. Co., Inc.; pubs. Biloxi-Gulfport (Miss.) Sun Herald, 1968—; dir. Hancock Bank, Gulfport. Pres. Pine Burr area council Boy Scouts Am., 1980; chmn. Miss. Bd. Corrections, 1982-88. Served to 1st lt. USAF, 1958-61. Mem. Am. Newspaper Assn., So. Newspaper Pubs. Assn. (pres. 1981), Young Pres. Orgn., Gulf Coast C. of C. (pres. 1989). Presbyterian. Office: Gulf Pub Co Inc 205 DeBuys Rd PO Box 4567 Biloxi MS 39535-4567

WEEKS, ROSS LEONARD, JR., museum executive; b. Jamestown, N.Y., Sept. 11, 1936; s. Ross Leonard and Cecile Forbes (Carrie) W.; AB, Colgate U., 1958; MS, George Washington U., 1971, cert. Fed. Exec. Inst., 1988; m. Patricia Ann Earley, June 10, 1951; children: Susan Woodall, Ross Leonard, III, William Andrew, David James. Reporter, Jamestown Post-Jour., 1958-60, Richmond (Va.) News Leader, 1960-65; dir. public info. Coll. William and Mary, Williamsburg, Va., 1965-71, asst. to exec. v.p. 1971-74, asst. to pres., dir. univ. communications, 1974-81; exec. dir. Jamestown (Va.)-Yorktown Found., 1981-91; exec. dir. Historic Crab Orchard Mus., Inc., Tazewell, Va., 1992—; grant reviewer U.S. Inst. Mus. Svcs., Va. Arts Commn. Editor William & Mary Alumni Gazette, 1966-81. Chmn. Williamsburg-James City Bicentennial, 1975-77; bd. dirs. Coalfield Regional Tourism Devel. Authority S.W. Va., 1993—; Va. Southwest Blue Ridge Highlands, Inc., 1993-95, v.p., 1996—; sec., treas. Frontier Culture Found., 1982-86; exec. dir. Va. Independence Bicentennial Commn., 1981-83; trustee council, Thirteen Original States, 1982-87; chair Tazewell County Tourism Devel. Commn., 1993—; mem. exhibition mine com. Town of Pocahontas, Gov.'s Va. History Initiative, 1995—; lay reader Stras Meml. Episc. Ch., Tazewell. Mem. Am. Assn. Mus. (mus. assessment cons. 1988—), Am. Assn. State and Local History, St. Andrews Soc., Masons, Rotary (Paul Harris fellow 1987), Clan Ross Assn. U.S. Sigma Delta Chi, Kappa Delta Rho (Ordo Honora 1986). Avocations: travel, landscaping, antiquities, historical research. Home: Hemlock Ridge PO Box 82 Tazewell VA 24651-0082 Office: Hist Crab Orchard Mus Rt 1 Box 194 Tazewell VA 24651

WEEKS, SANDRA KENNEY, healthcare administrator; b. Akron, Ohio. BSN, Stockton State Coll.; MSN, Trenton State Coll., 1995. RN, N.J., cert. rehab. registered nurse Assn. Rehab. Nurses. Staff nurse Akron (Ohio) Childrens Hosp., William Beaumont Hosp., Royal Oak, Mich.; elected pub. official Twp. of Cranford (N.J.); rehab. nurse Kessler Inst. Rehab., West Orange, N.J.; supr. HIP/HMO Ambulatory Care Ctr., Medford, N.J.; rehab. nurse mgr. Lourdes Rehab. Ctr., Camden, N.J.; rschr. in nursing. Contbr. articles to profl. jours. Bd. dirs. United Way; trustee pub. libr.; mem. Twp. Com. Bd. Health. Mem. Am. Nurses Assn., N.J. Nurses Assn., Assn. Rehab. Nurses, Sigma Theta Tau. Avocations: golf, bicycling. Home: 3 Dewberry Ct Medford NJ 08055-9159 Office: Lourdes Regional Rehab Ctr 1600 Haddon Ave Camden NJ 08103-3101

WEEKS, STEVEN WILEY, lawyer; b. Topeka, Mar. 7, 1950; s. Glen Wiley and Grace Aileen (West) W.; m. Lee Nordgren, Aug. 1, 1974 (div. 1985); 1 child, Kirstin Nordgren. BS summa cum laude, Washburn U., 1972; JD cum laude, Harvard U., 1977. Bar: Ohio. Project leader Nat. Sanitation Found., Ann Arbor, Mich., 1972; engr. Kans. Dept. Health and Environ., Topeka, 1972-74; ptnr. Taft, Stettinius & Hollister, Cin., 1977—; dir. The Myers Y. Cooper Co., Cin.; adj. faculty Chase Coll. Law, 1987-88. Mem. adv. com. prosecuting atty., Hamilton County, Cin., 1992; mem. Hamilton County Rep. Ctrl. Com., 1994—. Mem. Ohio State Bar Assn., Cin. Bar Assn. Republican. Methodist. Avocations: computers, golf. Home: 3641 Michigan Ave Cincinnati OH 45208-1411 Office: 425 Walnut St Cincinnati OH 45202-3957

WEEKS, THOMAS WESLEY, bishop; b. Boston, July 14, 1945; s. Thomas J. and Susan Weeks; m. Leona Brown, Sept. 3, 1966; children: Thomas Wesley Jr., Abdullah Azeez. B in Applied Sci., Boston U., 1969, M in Urban Affairs, 1974; MDiv, Luther Rice Sem., Jacksonville, Fla., 1990; DD (hon.), Aenon Bible Coll., 1984. Ordained to ministry Pentecostal Assemblies of the World, Inc. Asst. site mgr. rsch. ops. Rand Corp., South Bend, Ind., 1974-76, site mgr., 1974-80; pastor Greater Bethel Apostolic Temple, Wilmington, Del., 1980—; pastor, bishop Pentecostal Assemblies of the World, Inc., 1987—; pres. Aenon Bible Coll., Indpls., 1984—; pres. Mass. State Young People, 1960-67, Internat. Pentecostal Young People's Union, 1976-82, Interdenominational Mins. Coun. Del., 1986—; mem. com. Planning for Internat. Ministerial Conf., 1990—. Author: Pagan Holidays, 1983; editor Reachout jour. and newsletter. With USAR, 1963-71. Recipient Outstanding award Internat. Pentecostal Young People's Union, 1982, Betterment of Community award City of Indpls., 1982, commendations U.S. Senate, State of Del., Wilmington City Coun., 1984-87. Mem. NAACP (Disting. Svc. award Del. chpt. 1989). Home: PO Box 527 Wilmington DE 19899-0527 Office: Greater Bethel Apostolic Temple 2900 N Van Buren St Wilmington DE 19802-2956

WEEKS, WALTER LEROY, electrical engineering educator; b. Utica, N.Y., Mar. 30, 1923; s. Walter William and Emma (Conley) W.; children: Patricia, Walter William, Daniel, Sheryl, Joseph, Kathryn. BS, U. Mich., 1947; MS, Mich. State U., 1949; PhD, U. Ill., 1958. Instr. Mich. State Coll., 1947-51; asst. prof. N.Mex. State Coll., 1951-54, prof., 1959-60; asso. prof. U. Ill., 1954-59; asst. dir. research and devel. Collins Radio Co., Cedar Rapids, Iowa, Dallas, 1960-63; prof. elec. engring. Purdue U., 1963-89, prof. emeritus, 1989—; chmn. Purdue Electric Power Ctr., 1985-88; cons. Terronics Devel. Corp., Elwood, Ind., 1985—. Author: Electromagnetic Theory for Engineering Applications, 1964, Antenna Engineering, 1968, Transmission and Distribution of Electrical Energy, 1981. With USAAF, 1942-46. Inventor radiation leak detector, 1975, partial discharge locator, 1982, power cable fault locator, 1989. Home: 5517 Inverness Dr Sarasota FL 34243-4734 also: PO Box 2162 West Lafayette IN 47906-0162

WEEKS, WILFORD FRANK, geophysics educator, glaciologist; b. Champaign, Ill., Jan. 8, 1929; married; 2 children. BS, U. Ill., 1951, MS, 1953; PhD in Geology, U. Chgo., 1956. Geologist mineral deposits br. U.S. Geol. Survey, 1952-55; glaciologist USAF Cambridge Research Ctr., 1955-57; asst. prof. Washington U., St. Louis, 1957-62; adj. prof. earth scis. Dartmouth Coll., Hanover, N.H., 1962-85; glaciologist Cold Regions Rsch. and Engring. Lab., Hanover, 1962-89; chief scientist Alaska Synthetic Aperture Radar Facility, Fairbanks, 1986-93; prof. geophysics Geophys. Inst. U. Alaska, Fairbanks, 1986—; vis. prof. Inst. Low Temperature Sci. Hokkaido U., Sapporo, Japan, 1973; chair Arctic marine sci. USN Postgrad. Sch., Monterey, Calif., 1978-79; mem. earth sys. sci. com. NASA, Washington, 1984-87; advisor U.S. Arctic Rsch. Commn., divsn. polar programs NSF, Washington, 1987-88; chmn. NAS Com. on Cooperation with Russia in Ice Mechanics, 1991-92; mem. environ. task force MEDEA Cons. Group, 1992—. Capt. USAF, 1955-57. Recipient Emil Usibelli Prize for Rsch., 1996. Fellow Arctic Inst. N.Am., Am. Geophys. Union; mem. NAE, Internat. Glaciological Soc. (v.p. 1969-72, pres. 1973-75, Seligman Crystal award 1989). Avocations: skiing, diving, contrabassist. Office: U Alaska Fairbanks Geophys Inst PO Box 757320 Fairbanks AK 99775-7320

WEEMS, CARRIE MAE, photographer. BA, Calif. Inst. Arts, Valencia, 1981; MFA, U. Calif., San Diego, 1984; postgrad., U. Calif., Berkeley, 1984-87. Asst. prof. Hampshire Coll., Amherst, Mass., 1987-91, Calif. Coll. Arts and Crafts, Oakland, 1991; vis. prof. Hunter Coll., N.Y., 1988-89. One-person shows include Inst. Contemporary Art, 1991, Trustman Gallery, Simmons Coll., Boston, 1991, The New Mus. Contemporary Art, N.Y., 1991, Matrix Gallery, Wadsworth Atheneum, Hartford, Conn., 1991, Albright Coll., Reading, Pa., 1991, Greenville County Mus. Art, S.C., 1992, San Francisco Art Inst., 1992, Linda Carthcart Gallery, Santa Monica, Calif., 1993, Rhonda Hoffman Gallery, Chgo., 1993, New Langton Arts, San Francisco, 1993, Hood Mus. Art, Dartmouth Coll., N.H., 1994, Mus. Modern Art, N.Y., 1995, Reframing the Family Artists Space, 1991, Whitney Mus. Am. Art, 1991, Mus. Modern Art, 1992, Randy Alexander,

1992, Artists of Conscience: 16 Years of Social and Polit. Commentary, Alt. Mus. N.Y., 1991-92, Through the Kitchen Door, NAME, 1991-92, Disclosing the Myth of Family, Art Inst. Chgo., The Betty Rymer Gallery, Chgo., 1992, The Theater of Refusal: Black Art and the Mainstream Criticism (traveling), 1993-94, States of Loss: Migration, Displacement, Colonialism and Power, Jersey City Mus., N.J., 1993-94, Gesture and Pose, Mus. Modern Art, N.Y., 1994, Bad Girls, Part 1, New Mus. Contemporary Art, N.Y., 1994, Who's Looking at the Family? Barbican Art Gallery, London, 1994, Equal Rights and Justice, High Mus. Art and Nat. Black Arts Fest, Atlanta, 1994, Imaging Families: Images and Voices, Smithsonian Instn., 1994-95, Black Male, Representations of Masculinity in Contemporary Am. Art, Whitney Mus. Am. Art, N.Y., 1994-95. Office: c/o PPOW 532 Broadway 3d Fl New York NY 10012

WEEMS, JOHN EDWARD, writer; b. Grand Prairie, Tex., Nov. 2, 1924; s. J. Eddie and Anna Lee (Scott) W.; m. Jane Ellen Homeyer, Sept. 11, 1946; children: Donald (dec.), Carol, Mary, Barbara, Janet. BJ, U. Tex., 1948, M.Journalism, 1949; MA in Libr. Sci., Fla. State U., 1954. Tel. editor Temple (Tex.) Daily Telegram, 1950; instr. Calif. State Poly. Coll., San Dimas, 1950-51; night news editor San Angelo (Tex.) Standard-Times, 1951; copy editor Dallas Morning News, 1952-53; asst. prof., head cataloger main library Baylor U., 1954-57; asst. prof. U. Ala., also asst. mgr. Ala. Press Assn., 1957-58; asst. to dir. U. Tex. Press, 1958-68; prof. English, Baylor U., 1968-71, lectr. creative writing, fall 1979; reference librarian McLennan Community Coll., Waco, Tex., 1969-70; freelance writer, 1971—. With USNR, 1943-46, 51-52; lt. Res. (ret.). Am. Philos. Soc. grantee, 1964. Fellow Tex. State Hist. Assn., Tex. Inst. Letters; mem. PEN, Nat. Book Critics Circle, Authors Guild, Western Writers Am., Sigma Delta Chi, Beta Phi Mu. Author: A Weekend in September, 1957; The Fate of the Maine, 1958; Race for the Pole, 1960; Peary: The Explorer and the Man, 1967; Men Without Countries, 1969; Dream of Empire (Amon G. Carter award), 1971; To Conquer a Peace: The War Between the United States and Mexico (Richard Fleming award), 1974; Death Song, 1976; The Tornado, 1977; (with John Biggers and Carroll Simms) Black Art in Houston, 1978; "If You Don't Like the Weather," 1986; editor: A Texas Christmas: A Miscellany of Art, Poetry, Fiction, Vol. I, 1983, Vol. II, 1986; (San Antonio Conservation Soc. Spl. award), The Story of Texas, 1986, Austin (Texas): 1839-1989, 1989 (Tex. Inst. Letters Barbara McCombs Lon Tinkle award lifetime Writing achievement 1989). Address: 2012 Collins St Waco TX 76710-2626

WEEMS, ROBERT CICERO, economist, educator; b. Meridian, Miss., July 22, 1910; s. Robert Cicero and Susie (Vaughan) W.; m. Frances Dodds, Aug. 13, 1941; 1 dau., Susan. B.S. with honors, Miss. State U., 1931; M.B.A., Northwestern U., 1934; Ph.D. in Econs., Columbia U., 1951. Part-time staff Bank of Shubuta, Miss., 1924-33; teaching fellow econs. La. State U., 1933-34; instr. bus. adminstrn. Miss. State Coll., 1934-35, asst. prof. banking and finance, 1935-38, asso. prof., 1938-40, acting dean Sch. Bus. and Industry, 1940-42; dean Miss. State Coll. Sch. Bus. and Industry, 1942-56; dir. Bus. Research Sta. of Coll. Miss. State Coll., 1940-56, asst. dir. engring. sci. and mgmt. War Tng. Program, 1941-43; dean Coll. Bus. Adminstrn., dir. Bur. Research U. Nev., 1956-77; adviser-cons. U. Nev. Endowment Fund, 1975—; chmn. Regional (Nev.) Export Expansion Council, 1960-74; mem. Nat. Export Expansion Council, U.S. Dept. Commerce, 1960-74; chmn. adv. council Miss. Employment Security Commn., 1952-56; mem. Western Indsl. Nev., Nev. Public Employees Retirement Bd., 1963-78, vice chmn., 1975-78; mem. employment security council Nev. Employment Security Dept.; mem. nat. adv. council SBA, 1975-77. Trustee U.S. Travel Data Center, 1973-76, Calif.-Nev. Meth. Found., 1980—; trustee Am. Inst. Econ. Research, 1964—, chmn. bd., 1972-76. Served to lt. comdr. USN, 1943-46. Recipient cert. of appreciation U.S. Dept. Commerce, 1968, 1973. Mem. Am. Hotel and Motel Assn. (trustee ednl. inst.), Travel Research Assn. (treas.), Western Econ. Assn., Nev. World Trade and Internat. Tourism Assn. (trustee 1974—, pres. 1976-77), Blue Key, Omicron Delta Kappa (hon.), Chi Lambda Rho, Delta Sigma Pi, Beta Gamma Sigma (nat. exec. com. 1970-74), Phi Kappa Phi, Pi Kappa Alpha, Kappa Kappa Psi. Methodist. Club: Rotary (Reno). Home: 1135 Williams Ave Reno NV 89503-2648

WEERTMAN, JOHANNES, materials science educator; b. Fairfield, Ala., May 11, 1925; s. Roelof and Christina (van Vlaardingen) W.; m. Julia Ann Randall, Feb. 10, 1950; children: Julia Ann, Bruce Randall. Student, Pa. State Coll., 1943-44; BS, Carnegie Inst. Tech. (now Carnegie Mellon U.), 1948, DSc, 1951; postgrad., Ecole Normale Superieure, Paris, 1951-52. Solid State physicist U.S. Naval Rsch. Lab., Washington, 1952-58, cons., 1960-67; sci. liaison officer U.S. Office Naval Rsch., Am. Embassy, London, 1958-59; faculty Northwestern U., Evanston, Ill., 1959—, prof. materials sci. dept., 1961-68, chmn. dept., 1964-68, prof. geol. scis. dept., 1963—, Walter P. Murphy prof. materials sci., 1968—; vis. prof. geophysics Calif. Inst. Tech., 1964, Scott Polar Rsch. Inst., Cambridge (Eng.) U., 1970-71, Swiss Fed. Inst. Reactor Rsch., 1986; cons. Cold Regions Rsch. and Engring. Lab., U.S. Army, 1960-75, Oak Ridge (Tenn.) Nat. Lab., 1963-67, Los Alamos (N.Mex.) Sci. Lab., 1967—; co-editor materials sci. books MacMillan Co., 1962-76. Author: Dislocated Based Fracture Mechanics, 1996, (with Julia Weertman) Elementary Dislocation Theory, 1964, 2d edit., 1992; mem. editorial bd. Metal. Trans., 1967-75, Jour. Glaciology, 1972—; assoc. editor Jour. Geophys. Rsch., 1973-75; contbr. articles to profl. jours. With USMC, 1943-46. Honored with naming of Weertman Island in Antarctica.; Fulbright fellow, 1951-52; recipient Acta Metallurgica gold medal, 1980; Guggenheim fellow, 1970-71. Fellow Am. Soc. Metals, Am. Phys. Soc., Geol. Soc. Am., Am. Geophys. Union (Horton award 1972, AIME Mathewson Gold medal 1977); mem. AAAS, Nat.. Acad. Engring., Am. Inst. Physics, Internat. Glaciol. Soc. (Seligman Crystal award 1983), Arctic Inst., Am. Quaternary Assn., Explorers Club, Fulbright Assn., Sigma Xi, Tau Beta Pi, Phi Kappa Phi, Alpha Sigma Mu, Pi Mu Epsilon. Home: 834 Lincoln St Evanston IL 60201-2405 Office: Northwestern U Materials Sci Dept Evanston IL 60208

WEERTMAN, JULIA RANDALL, materials science and engineering educator; b. Muskegon, Mich., Feb. 10, 1926. BS in Physics, Carnegie-Mellon U., 1946, MS in Physics, 1947, DSc in Physics, 1951. Physicist U.S. Naval Rsch. Lab., Washington, 1952-58; vis. asst. prof. dept. materials sci. and engring. Northwestern U., Evanston, Ill., 1972-73, assoc. prof., 1978-82, prof., 1982—, Walter P. Murphy prof., 1989, chmn. dept., 1987-92, asst. to dean grad. studies and rsch. Tech. Inst., 1973-76; mem. various NRC coms. and panels. Co-author: Elementary Dislocation Theory, 1964, 1992, also pub. in French, Japanese and Polish; contbr. numerous articles to profl. jours. Mem. Evanston Environ. Control Bd., 1972-79. Recipient Creativity award NSF, 1981, 86; Guggenheim Found. fellow, 1986-87. Fellow Am. Soc. Metals Internat., Minerals, Metals and Materials Soc.; mem. ASTM, NAE, Am. Phys. Soc., Materials Rsch. Soc., Soc. Women Engrs. (disting. engring. educator award 1989, achievement award 1991). Home: 834 Lincoln St Evanston IL 60201-2405 Office: Northwestern U Dept Material Sci & Engring 2225 N Campus Dr Evanston IL 60208-3108

WEESE, BENJAMIN HORACE, architect; b. Evanston, Ill., June 4, 1929; s. Harry Ernest and Marjorie (Mohr) W.; m. Cynthia Rogers, July 5, 1963; children: Daniel Peter, Catharine Mohr. B.Arch., Harvard U., 1951, M.Arch., 1957; cert., Ecole des Beaux Arts, Fontainebleau, France, 1956. Assoc., Harry Weese & Assocs., Architects, Chgo., 1957-77; prin. Weese Langley Weese, Chgo., 1977—; co-founder, pres. Chgo. Arch. Found., Glessner House, Chgo., 1966—. Trustee Graham Found. for Advanced Studies in Fine Arts, 1988—, pres. 1995—. Fellow AIA; mem. Nat. Council Archtl. Registration Bds. Home: 2133 N Hudson Chicago IL 60614 Office: Weese Langley Weese Ltd 9 W Hubbard St Chicago IL 60610-4605

WEESE, BRUCE ERIC, pharmaceutical industry lobbyist; b. Chewelah, Wash., Mar. 22, 1942; s. Harry M. and Roberta B. (Carman) W.; m. Elaine M. Smith, June 18, 1962 (div. July 1972); children: Sandra G., Michael D.; m. Vera B. Reed, Mar. 22, 1975; stepchildren: Kevin E. Bayron, Kelly M. Bayron. BA in Edn., Ea. Wash. State U., Cheney, 1964; MBA, Pepperdine U., 1981. Tchr. Grant Joint Union High Sch. Dist., Sacramento, 1964-70; pharm. sales McNeil Labs., San Jose, Calif., 1970-77, Adria Labs., San Francisco, 1977-83, Serono Labs., San Francisco, 1983-84, Boehringer Ingelheim, Santa Rosa, Calif., 1984-91; mgr. govt. affairs (lobbyist) Boehringer Ingelheim, 9 western states, 1991—. Bd. dirs. Russian River Health Ctr., Guerneville, Calif., 1994-95. Mem. United Anglers, Sequoia Paddlers, Santa Rosa Sailing Club. Democrat. Avocations: kayaking, sailing, fishing. Home: 20303 NE 226th Circle Battle Ground WA 98604-4943 Office: Boehringer Ingelheim PO Box 368 Ridgefield CT 06877-0368

WEESE, CYNTHIA ROGERS, architect, educator; b. Des Moines, June 23, 1940; d. Gilbert Taylor and Catharine (Wingard) Rogers; m. Benjamin H. Weese, July 5, 1963; children: Daniel Peter, Catharine Mohr. B.S.A.S., Washington U., St. Louis, 1962; B.Arch., Washington U., 1965. Registered architect, Ill. Pvt. practice architecture Chgo., 1965-72, 74-77; draftsperson, designer Harry Weese & Assocs., Chgo., 1972-74; prin. Weese Langley Weese Ltd., Chgo., 1977—; design critic Ball State U., Muncie, Ind., Miami U., Oxford, Ohio, 1979, U. Wis.-Milw., 1980, U. Ill.-Chgo., 1981, 85, Iowa State U., Ames, 1982, Washington U., St. Louis, 1984, U. Ill., Champaign, 1987-92, Kans. State U., 1992; dean sch. architecture Washington U., St. Louis, 1993—. Bd. regents Am. Architecture Found., 1990-93. Recipient Alpha Rho Chi award Washington U., 1965, Met. Chgo. YWCA Outstanding Achievement award, 1990. Mem. AIA (bd. dirs. Chgo. chpt. 1980-83, v.p. 1983-85, 1st v.p. 1986-87, pres. 1987-88, regional dir. 1990-92, Disting. Bldg. awards 1977, 81-83, 86, 91, 95, Interior Architecture award 1981, 90, 92, nat. v.p. 1993), AIA/ACSA Coun. on Archtl. Rsch. (chair 1991-92), AIA Found. (pres. Chgo. chpt. 1988-89), Soc. Archtl. Historians (bd. dirs. 1992—), Chgo. Women Architecture, Chgo. Network, Nat. Inst. Archtl. Edn. (bd. dirs. 1988-90), Chgo. Archtl. Club (pres. 1988-89), Washington U. Sch. Architecture Alumni (nat. coun. 1988-93), Lambda Alpha. Democrat. Clubs: Arts, Chgo. Archtl. Office: Washington University Architecture DEpt. 1 Brookings Drive Saint Louis MO 63130

WEESE, SAMUEL H., academic administrator; b. Morgantown, W.Va., Mar. 28, 1935; m. Ellen C. Carros, Feb. 14, 1981; children: Marguerite, James. BS, W.Va. U., 1957, MBA, 1962; MA, U. Pa., 1967, PhD, 1969. Ins. commr. State of W.Va., Charleston, 1969-75; gen. mgr. Nat. Flood Insurers Assn., Arlington, Va., 1975-78; prof. ins. U. Hartford, Conn., 1978-81; prof., chair ins. Ea. Ky. U., Richmond, 1981-85; v.p., exec. asst. to pres., sec. bd. trustees Am. Coll., Bryn Mawr, Pa., 1985-86, v.p. acad. affairs, sec. bd. trustees, 1986-87, acting pres., v.p. acad. affairs, sec. bd. trustees, 1988, pres., CEO, 1988—; bd. dirs. Am. Soc., 1988—, Ins. Soc. Phila., 1989—; instr. dept. bus. and econs. Davis and Elkins (W.Va.) Coll., 1962-67; asst. prof. dept. fin. and ins. Coll. Bus. Adminstrn., U. Fla., Gainesville, 1967-69; adj. lectr. Coll. Bus. Adminstrn., George Washington U., Washington, 1977-78. Author: Non-Admitted Insurance in the United States, 1971; contbr. articles, studies to profl. publs. 1st lt. USAF, 1958-60. Mem. Am. Risk and Ins. Assn., Am. Soc. CLU, Risk and Ins. Mgmt. Soc., Soc. Ins. Rsch. Office: Am Coll 270 S Bryn Mawr Ave Bryn Mawr PA 19010-2105

WEG, JOHN GERARD, physician; b. N.Y.C., Feb. 16, 1934; s. Leonard and Pauline M. (Kanzleiter) W.; m. Mary Loretta Flynn, June 2, 1956; children: Diane Marie, Kathryn Mary, Carol Ann, Loretta Louise, Veronica Susanne, Michelle Celeste. BA cum laude, Coll. Holy Cross, Worcester, Mass., 1955; MD, N.Y. Med. Coll., 1959. Diplomate: Am. Bd. Internal Medicine. Commd. 2nd lt. USAF, 1958, advanced through grades to capt., 1967; intern Walter Reed Gen. Hosp., Washington, 1959-60; resident, then chief resident in internal medicine Wilford Hall USAF Hosp., Lackland AFB, Tex., 1960-64; chief pulmonary sect. Wilford Hall USAF Hosp., 1964-66, chief inhalation sect., 1964-66, chief pulmonary and infectious disease service, 1966-67; resigned, 1967; clin. dir. pulmonary disease div. Jefferson Davis Hosp., Houston, 1967-71; from asst. prof. to assoc. prof. medicine Baylor U. Coll. Medicine, Houston, 1967-71; assoc. prof. medicine U. Mich. Med. Sch. Univ. Hosp., Ann Arbor, 1971-74; prof. U. Mich. Med. Sch. Univ. Hosp., 1974—; physician-in-charge pulmonary div., 1971-81, physician-in-charge pulmonary and critical care med. div., 1981-85; cons. Ann Arbor VA, 1971—, Wayne County Gen. hosps., 1971-84; mem. adv. bd. Washtenaw County Health Dept., 1973—; mem. respiratory and nervous system panel, anesthesiology Sect. Nat. Ctr. Devices and Radiol. Health, FDA, 1983—, chmn., 1985-88. Contbr. med. jours., reviewer, mem. editorial bds. Decorated Air Force Commendation medal; travelling fellow Nat. Tb and Respiratory Disease Assn., 1971; recipient Aesculpaius award Tex. Med. Assn., 1971. Fellow Am. Coll. Chest Physicians (chmn. bd. govs. 1976-79, gov. Mich. 1975-79, chmn. membership com. 1976-79, prof.-in-residence 1972—, chmn. critical care coun. 1982-85), Am. Coll. Chest Physicians and Internat. Acad. Chest Physicians (exec. council 1976-82, pres. 1980-81), ACP (chmn. Mich. program com. 1974); mem. AAAS, Am. Fedn. Clin. Rsch., AMA, Am. Thoracic Soc. (sec.-treas. 1974-76), Am. Assn. Inhalation Therapy, Air Force Soc. Internists and Allied Specialists, Soc. Med. Consultants to Armed Forces, Internat. Union Against Tb, Mich. Thoracic Soc. (pres. 1976-78), Mich. Lung Assn. (dir., Bruce Douglas award 1981), Am. Lung Assn., Rsch. Club U. Mich., Assn. Advancement Med. Instrumentation, Central Soc. Clin. Rsch., Am. Bd. Internal Medicine (subsplty. com. on pulmonary disease 1980-86, critical care medicine test com. 1985-87, critical care medicine policy com. 1986-87), N.Y. Med. Coll. Alumni Assn. (medal of honor 1990), Alpha Omega Alpha. Home: 3060 Exmoor Rd Ann Arbor MI 48104-4132 Office: B I H 245 Box 0026 1500 E Medical Center Dr Ann Arbor MI 48109-0026

WEGENER, MARK DOUGLAS, lawyer; b. Cedar Rapids, Iowa, Nov. 1, 1948; s. Virgil Albert and Jean Frances (Wilke) W.; m. Donna Chait, May 28, 1972; children: Tara, David, Marisa. BA cum laude, Cen. Coll., Pella, Iowa, 1970; JD, Rutgers U., 1973. Bar: D.C. 1974, U.S. Dist. Ct. D.C. 1974, U.S. Ct. Appeals (D.C. cir.) 1974. Assoc. Howrey & Simon, Washington, 1973-79, ptnr., 1979—. Mem. ABA (anti-trust sect., litigation sect.), D.C. Bar Assn., The Metropolitan Club, Stage Harbor Yacht Club. Home: 7523 Old Dominion Dr Mc Lean VA 22102-2500 Office: Howrey & Simon 1299 Pennsylvania Ave NW Washington DC 20004-2400

WEGENER, PETER PAUL, engineering educator, author; b. Berlin, Aug. 29, 1917; came to U.S., 1946; naturalized, 1953.; m. Annette Schleiermacher, Aug. 14, 1961; children: Paul, Christopher, Philip. Dr rer. nat., U. Berlin, 1943; MA (priv.), Yale U., 1960; Dr. Ing. (E.h.) (hon.), U. Karlsruhe, Germany, 1979. Researcher supersonic wind tunnels Kochel, Germany, 1943-45; researcher gasdynamics, hypersonic wind tunnels U.S. Naval Ordnance Lab., 1946-53, Jet Propulsion Lab. Calif. Inst. Tech., 1953-60; prof. applied sci. Yale U., New Haven, 1960-72, Harold Hodgkinson prof. engring. and applied sci., 1972—, chmn. dept. engring. applied sci., 1966-71, prof. emeritus, 1987—; sr. Am. scientist Humboldt Found., 1979;. Researcher and contbr. articles on hypersonics, condensation metastable state, chem. kinetics, flow systems real gases, bubbles to profl. jours. Inst. Advanced Study Berlin fellow, 1986. Fellow Am. Phys. Soc., Conn. Acad. Sci. & Engring. (charter). Home: 29 Montgomery Pky Branford CT 06405-5128 Office: Yale U PO Box 208286 New Haven CT 06520-8286

WEGENKE, GARY L., school systems administrator; b. South Bend, Ind., Feb. 28, 1938; s. Edward and Blanche Wegenke; m. Sandra S. Gard, Aug. 17, 1963; children: Bart and Bret (twins), Blake. BA, DePauw U., 1961; MS, Ind. U., 1964; PhD, Ohio State U., 1971. Secondary tchr. South Bend (Ind.) Cmty. Sch. Corp., 1961-69; grad. rsch. assoc. Coll. Edn. Ohio State U., Columbus, 1969-71; prin. Hill H.S., Lansing, Mich., 1972-76; dir. adminstrv. svcs. Lansing Sch. Dist., 1976-78, asst. supt. Fiscal and Adminstrv. Svcs., 1979-81, dep. supt., 1981-83; supt. schs. Waterloo (Iowa) Cmty. Sch. Dist., 1983-88, Des Moines Ind. Cmty. Sch. Dist., 1988—; adj. asst. prof. Ohio State U., Columbus, 1971-72; adj. prof. Mich. State U., East Lansing, 1980-84, U. Northern Iowa, Cedar Falls, 1984—, Drake U., 1991; nat. adv. panel chairperson Ctr. for Rsch. on Ednl. Accountability and Tchr. Evaluation, Western Mich. U., Kalamazoo, 1990—, Danforth Found. Leadership Initiative, 1994—; chairperson state outcomes and assessment Iowa State Dept. Edn., 1992-93; project dir. Statewide Libr. Planning and Evaluation, Ohio State U., 1971-72; lectr. various symposia. Contbr. articles to profl. jours. Bd. dirs. Cedar Valley United Way, 1985-88, Leadership Investment for Tomorrow, Waterloo/Cedar Falls, 1986-88, HMO Iowa, 1990-92, Boy Scouts Am., 1991—, Jr. Achievement, Des Moines, 1988—, Polk County United Way, 1989—, Community Focus, 1992—; chairperson Urban Edn. Network, 1987. Named Exec. Educator 100 Best Sch. Execs., 1993, Iowa Supt. of Yr., 1993-94; recipient Lansing Concerned Citizen award Jr. C. of C., 1972. Mem. Am. Assn. Sch. Adminstrs. (finalist Supt. of Yr. 1994), Sch. Adminstrs. Iowa, Des Moines Sch. Adminstrs. Assn., Des Moines C. of C. (bd. dirs. 1990), Waterloo C. of C. (bd. dirs. 1985-87, Pub. Servant of Yr. award 1985), Phi Delta Kappa (v.p. U. No. Iowa chpt., Des Moines area Outstanding Educator of Yr. award 1992). Office: Des Moines Pub School 1800 Grand Ave Des Moines IA 50309-3310

WEGGE, LEON LOUIS FRANÇOIS, economics educator; b. Breendonk, Antwerp, Belgium, June 9, 1933; came to U.S., 1959; s. Petrus Maria and Alberta (De Maeyer) W.; m. Beate Maria Teipel, Nov. 22, 1962; children: Simone, Robert, Elizabeth. B in Thomistical Philosophy, Cath. U. Louvain, Belgium, 1957, Licentiate in Econ. Sci., 1958; PhD in Indsl. Econs., MIT, 1963. Assoc. lectr. U. New S. Wales, Kensington, Australia, 1963-66; prof. econs. U. Calif., Davis, 1966—; vis. prof. U. Bonn, Fed. Republic Germany, 1980-81. Assoc. editor Jour. Internat. Econs., 1971-84; contbr. articles to profl. jours. Rsch. fellow Ctr. for Ops. Rsch. and Econometrics, 1972-73, fellow The Netherlands Inst. for Advanced Study, 1987-88. Mem. Econometric Soc., Am. Statistical Assn. Roman Catholic. Home: 26320 County Rd # 98 Davis CA 95616 Office: U Calif Davis Dept Econs Davis CA 95616

WEGMAN, HAROLD HUGH, management consultant; b. Cin., June 29, 1916; s. Clarence H. and Lillian (de Tellem) W.; m. Ruth Ellen Volk, May 1, 1937; children—Susan Ruth (Mrs. Michael Manning), Sally Ann (Mrs. Jerry Fine). B.B.A., U. Cin., 1941; M.B.A., Xavier U., 1954. Band leader, studio mgr. Rudolph Wurlitzer Co., 1946-50; Tng. supr., then asst. to v.p. Gruen Watch Co., 1950-55; personnel dir., asst. to pres. Bavarian Brewing Co., Covington, Ky., 1955-59; dir. indsl. relations, asst. to pres. Howard Paper Co., Dayton, Ohio, 1959-62; v.p., gen. mgr. Elano Corp., Xenia, Ohio, 1962-64; v.p., dir. indsl. relations Champion Papers Inc., Hamilton, Ohio, 1964-67; v.p. U.S. Plywood Champion Papers, Inc., 1967-71, Champion Internat., 1971-72; pres. PEP Group, 1972—; dir. Mgmt. Center, Sacred Heart U., 1974—. Contbr. articles to profl. publs. Trustee Foreman Found., 1965-71. Served to lt. (j.g.) USNR, 1944-46. Mem. Am. Soc. Personnel Adminstrs. (bd. dirs. 1969—, treas. 1970), Am. Soc. for Tng. and Devel., NAM, Am. Paper Inst., Am. Mgmt. Assn., Conn. songwriters assn., Lambda Chi Alpha. Home: 3400 S Ocean Blvd Ste 7-d Highland Beach FL 33487

WEGMAN, MYRON EZRA, physician, educator; b. Bklyn., July 23, 1908; s. Max and Nettie (Finkelstein) W.; m. Isabel Howe, July 4, 1936; children: Judith (Mrs. John A. Hirst), David Howe, Jane (Mrs. David D. Dunatchik), Elizabeth Gooding (Mrs. Ralph A. Petersen). A.B., CCNY, 1928; M.D. cum laude, Yale U., 1932; M.P.H., Johns Hopkins U., 1938. Diplomate Am. Bd. Preventive Medicine, Am. Bd. Pediatrics (ofcl. examiner). Intern, asst. resident, resident in pediatrics New Haven Hosp., 1932-36; instr. pediatrics Yale U., 1933-36; cons. pediatrics Md. State Health Dept., 1936-41; asst. prof. child hygiene sch. Tropical Medicine, San Juan, P.R., 1941-42; dir. research and tng. in child health, dir. sch. health N.Y.C. Health Dept., 1942-46; instr. pediatrics and lectr. public health adminstrn. Johns Hopkins U., 1939-46; asst. prof. pediatrics and pub. health Cornell U., 1942-46; asst. prof. pub. health Columbia U., 1940-46; prof. pediatrics, head dept. La. State U., 1946-52; pediatrician-in-chief Charity Hosp., New Orleans, 1946-52; prof. public health Sch. Public Health, U. Mich., Ann Arbor, 1960-74; dean Sch. Public Health, U. Mich., 1960-74, dean emeritus, 1974—; prof. pediatrics U. Mich. Med. Sch., 1961-78, prof. emeritus, 1978—, chmn. div. health sci., 1970-74; John G. Searle prof. public health, 1974-78, emeritus, 1978—; vis. prof. U. Malaya, 1974, Centro Universitario de Salud Publica, U. Autónoma Madrid, 1990—, U Cin., 1993; external examiner Nat. U. Singapore, 1983; cons. Internat. Sci. and Tech. Inst., 1986—, Sch. Pub. Health U. Kinshasa, Zaire, 1987, Schs. Pub. Health Jakarta, Surabaya, Ujung Pandang, Medan, Semarang, Indonesia, 1988; coord. Mich.-Madrid Sch. Pub. Health collaboration, 1990—. Editor: Public Health in the People's Republic of China, 1973; author: also pediatrics and public health textbooks, articles in med. jours. Status of Pan American Centers; mem. editorial bd. Revista Mexicana de Salud Publica, 1990—. Chief div. edn. and tng. Pan-Am. San. Bur., Regional Office for Ams., WHO, 1952-56; sec. gen Pan Am. San. Bur., WHO Regional Office, 1957-60; pres. Assn. Schs. Public Health, 1963-66; pres. Comprehensive Health Planning Council, SE Mich., 1970-74; trustee Pan Am. Health and Edn. Found., 1970-85, 86-92, 94—, pres. 1984-85, chmn. Devel. com., 1991-96, v.p. 1996—; trustee Nat. San. Found., 1969-84, emeritus trustee, 1984—; pres. Physicians for Social Responsibility, Ann Arbor, 1987-92; mem. com. on carcinogenesis of pesticides Nat. Acad. Sci., 1977-79, com. on advanced study in China, 1978-82; chmn. Task Force on Nat. Immunization Policy, HEW, 1975-76; adv. com. Kellogg Nat. Fellowship Program, 1982—; rsch. adv. com. Resources for Future, 1978-84; spl. cons. State U. System Fla., 1982-87; mem. com. on prevention ctrs. CDC, 1986-94. Recipient Man of Yr. award CCNY, 1955; Clifford G. Grulee award Am. Acad. Pediatrics, 1958; Townsend Harris medal CCNY, 1961; Bronfman prize Am. Public Health Assn., 1967; Disting. Service award Mich. Public Health Assn., 1974; Walter P. Reuther award for disting. service United Auto Workers, 1974; Sedgwick medal Am. Pub. Health Assn., 1974; Outstanding Alumnus award Johns Hopkins Sch. Hygiene, 1982; Disting. Service award Delta Omega Soc., 1982; Spes Hominum award Nat. Sanitation Found., 1986, Disting. Alumnus award Yale U. Med. Sch., 1987; Spl. award Korean Soc. Preventive Medicine, 1989. Fellow Royal Soc. Health (hon.), AAAS; mem. Johns Hopkins U. Soc. Scholars, Am. Pediatric Soc., Soc. Pediatric Research, Am. Acad. Pediatrics, Am. Assn. World Health (v.p. 1979-82, 85-88, pres. 1982-84), Am. Public Health Assn. (chmn. exec. bd. 1965-70, pres. 1971-72), Fedn. Assn. Schs. Health Professions (1st pres. 1968-70), Soc. Exptl. Biol. and Medicine, Peruvian, Ecuadorian, Argentinian pediatric socs. (hon.), P.R. Pub. Health Assn. (hon.), Sigma Xi, Alpha Omega Alpha, Delta Omega, Phi Kappa Phi, Phi Beta Kappa (hon.). Club: Cosmos (Washington). Home: 2760 Overridge Dr Ann Arbor MI 48104-4049 Office: Sch Public Health U Mich Ann Arbor MI 48109-2029

WEGMAN, ROBERT B., food service executive; b. 1918; married. BBA, Niagara Univ. With Wegman's Food Markets, Inc., Rochester, pres., 1950—, chmn., 1969—. With USMC, ret. Office: Wegmans Food Markets Inc 1500 Brooks Ave Rochester NY 14624-3512*

WEGMAN, WILLIAM GEORGE, artist; b. Holyoke, Mass., Dec. 2, 1943; s. George W. and Eleanor (Vezina) W. BFA in Painting, Mass. Coll. Art, 1965; MFA, U. Ill., 1967. One-man shows include Gallerie Sonnabend, Paris, 1971, Pomona Coll. Art Gallery, 1971, Sonnabend Gallery, N.Y.C., 1972, 77, Gallerie Ernst, Hanover, Ger., 1972, Situation, London, 1972, Konrad Fischer Gallery, 1972, 75, 79, Courtney Sale Gallery, 1972, Tex. Gallery, Houston, 1973, 75, 79, L.A. County Mus. of Art, Calif., 1973, 112 Greene St., N.Y.C., 1974, Mayor Gallery, London, 1975, Galleria Alessandra Castelli, Milan, 1975, The Kitchen, N.Y., 1976, Bruna Soletti Gallery, Milan, 1977, 82, Rosamund Felsen Gallery, 1978, Holly Solomon Gallery, N.Y.C., 1979, 80, 82, 84, 86, 88, 90, 92, Arnolfini Gallery, Eng., 1979, U. Wis., Milw., 1979, U. Colo. Art Galleries, Boulder, 1980, Marianne Deson Gallery, Chgo., 1980, Vivianne Esders Gallery, Paris, 1981, Magnuson Lee Gallery, Boston, 1981, Robert Hull Fleming Mus., Burlington, Vt., 1981, Locus Solus, Genoa, Italy, 1982, Dart Gallery, Chgo., 1982, Fraenkel Gallery, San Francisco, 1982, 88, 90, 92, 93, James Corcoran Gallery, Los Angeles, 1982, 90, Nancy Drysdale Gallery, Washington, 1982, 87, 94, Walker Art Ctr, Mpls., 1982, Ft. Worth Art Mus., Tex., 1982, De Cordova & Dana Mus. & Park, Mass., 1982, Southeastern Ctr. for Contemporary Art, Winston-Salem, N.C., 1982, The Contemporary Arts Ctr., Ohio, 1982, Newport Harbor Mus., Calif., 1982, Inst. Contemporary Arts at Va. Mus., Richmond, 1983, Fine Arts Gallery, U. Mass., Amherst, 1983, Tex. Gallery, Houston, 1983, 86, Greenville County Mus. Art, 1984, Lowe Mus. Art, Miami, Fla, 1985, Cleve. Mus. Art, 1986, Honolulu Acad. Arts, 1987, Mass. Coll. Art, Boston, 1987, U San Diego, La Jolla, Calif., 1988, Pace MacGill Gallery, N.Y., 1988, 90, 92, 93, San Francisco Mus. Modern Art, Calif., 1988, Galerie Durand-Dessert, Paris, 1989, Budoin Lebon, Paris, 1989, Maison de la Culture et de la Communication de Saint Etienne, France, 1989, Linda Cathcart Gallery, L.A., 1990, 92, 94, The Taft Mus. Cin., 1990, The Butler Inst., Ohio, 1990, Sperone Westwater Gallery, N.Y., 1992, Kunstmuseum, Lucerne, Switzerland, 1990, ICA, London, 1990, Stedelijk Mus., The Netherlands, 1990, Frankfurt Kunstverein, Germany, 1990, Pompidou Ctr., Paris, 1990, ICA, Boston, 1990, Ringling Mus., Fla., 1990, Whitney Mus., N.Y., Contemporary Arts Mus., Tex., 1990, Neuberger Mus., SUNY, 1991, Galerie Andreas Binder, Germany, 1992, Athenaeum Music & Arts Library, Calif., 1992, Lisa Sette Gallery, Phoenix, 1994, Greg Kucera Gallery, Seattle, 1994, George Eastman House: Internat. Mus. Photography and Film, 1995, Aspen Art Mus., ACC Galerie, Weimar, Germany, 1995, Pace Wildenstein, L.A., 1995, others; exhibited in group shows at Walker Art Ctr., Mpls., 1968, N.J. State Mus., Trenton, 1968, Detroit Inst. Art, 1969, Mus. Contemporary Art, Chgo., 1969, 77, Allen Meml. Mus., 1970, L.A. County Mus., Calif., 1971, Pasadena Art Mus., 1972, Contemporary Arts Mus., Houston, 1972, Whitney Mus. Am. Art, N.Y.C., 1973, 81, 89,

Sonnabend Gallery, N.Y.C., 1974, Milw. Art Ctr., 1975, Sarah Lawrence Coll. Gallery, 1975, Phila. Mus. Art, 1976, San Francisco Mus. Modern Art, 1976, U. Calif.-Berkeley Art Mus., 1976, U. Chgo., 1976, Ringling Mus. Art, Sarasota, Fla., 1977, Walker Art Gallery, Eng., 1978, Holly Solomon Gallery, N.Y.C., 1978, 82, 87, Mus. Fine Arts, Houston, 1978, Aspen Ctr. Visual Arts, 1979, Santa Barbara Mus. Art, 1979, Mus. Modern Art, N.Y.C., 1980, 82, 83, Sidney Janis Gallery, 1981, Art Inst. Chgo., 1981, 82, Young Hoffman Gallery, Chgo., 1983, Inst. Contemporary Art, Boston, 1983, Castelli Graphics, N.Y.C., 1983, Queens Mus., N.Y., 1986, James Madison U., Harrison, Va, 1987, Fay Gold Gallery, Atlanta, 1988, Hudson River Mus., 1989, Volcano Arts Ctr., 1989, Pace/MacGill, N.Y.C., 1990, The History of Travel, The Taft Museum, Cin., The Butler Inst. Youngstown, Ohio, 1990, William Wegman: Paintings, Drawings, Photographs, Videotapes, Kunstmuseum, Luzern, Stedelijk Museum, Amsterdam, Frankfurt Kunstverein Frankfurt, Centre Nat. d'Art et cle Culture Georges Pompidou, Paris, Inst. of Contemporary Art, London, Inst. of Contemporary Arts, Boston, Contemporary Arts Mus., Houston, J.M. Ringling Mus., Sarasota, Whitney Mus., of American Art, N.Y., 1990-92, Outdoor Photographs, Neuberger Mus., State U. of N.Y. at Purchase, 1991, William Wegman: L'oeuvre photographique, 1969-76, Fonds Regional d'Art Contemporary, Limousin, France, 1991, New Polaroids, Holly Solomon Gallery, N.Y.C., Early Black and White Photographs, Pace/MacGill Gallery, N.Y.C., New Paintings, Sperone Westwater Gallery, N.Y.C., 1992, many others; contbr. articles to profl. jours.; videography: Reel 1, 1970-72, Reel 2, 1972, Reel 3, 1972-73, Reel 4, 1973-74, Reel 5, 1975, Reel 6, 1975-76, Reel 7, 1976-77, Spit Sandwich, 1970, Gray Hairs, 1974-75, Man Ray, Man Ray, 1978, The World of Photography, 1985, Sesame Street Videos, 1989, 92, 93; film: Dog Baseball, 1986; filmography; The Hardy Boys in Hardly Gold; publications: Man's Best Friend, 1982, Everyday Problems, 1984, William Wegman: Paintings, Drawings, Photographs, Videotapes, 1990, Cinderella, 1993, Little Red Riding Hood, 1993, ABC, 1994. Recipient Creative Artists Pub. Svc. award, 1979; Guggenheim Found. fellow, 1975, 86, Nat. Endowment for the Arts grantee, 1976, 82. Office: 431 E 6th St New York NY 10009-6305

WEGNER, GARY ALAN, astronomer; b. Seattle, Dec. 26, 1944; s. Herbert Edward and Melba Jean (Gardner) W.; m. Cynthia Kay Goodfellow, June 25, 1966; children: Josef, Kurt, Christian, Peter-Jürgen, Emma. Student, Wash. State U., Pullman, 1963-65; BS, U. Ariz., 1967; PhD, U. Wash., Seattle, 1971. Fulbright fellow Mount Stromlo Obs., Camberra, A.C.T., 1971-72; departmental demonstrator in astrophysics Oxford U., Eng., 1972-75; sr. sci. rsch. officer South African Astron. Obs., Capetown, Republic of South Africa, 1975-78; Annie J. Cannon fellow U. Del., Newark, 1978-79; asst. prof. Pa. State U., State College, 1979-82; asst. prof. to assoc. prof. physics and astronomy Dartmouth Coll., Hanover, N.H., 1982-88, Margaret Anne and Edward Leede Disting. prof. physics and astronomy, 1988—; dir. Mich.-Dartmouth-MIT Obs., 1991—; vis. astronomer Cornell U., 1992. Editor: White Dwarfs, 1989; contbr. articles to jours. in field. Keeley fellow Wadham Coll., Oxford, 1992-93, vis. fellow in astrophysics Oxford U., 1992-93; vis. prof. Astron. Inst. Ruhr U. Bochum, Germany, 1993-94; recipient rsch. prize The Alexander von Humboldt Found., Germany, 1993-94, numerous grants NSF, NASA. Mem. Am. Astron. Soc., Internat. Astron. Union. Lutheran. Office: Dartmouth Coll Dept Physics & Astronomy Wilder Lab Hanover NH 03755

WEGNER, JUDITH WELCH, lawyer, educator, university dean; b. Hartford, Conn., Feb. 14, 1950; d. John Raymond and Ruth (Thulen) Welch; m. Warren W. Wegner, Oct. 13, 1972. BA with honors, U. Wis., 1972; JD, UCLA, 1976. Bar: Calif. 1976, D.C. 1977, N.C. 1988, U.S. Supreme Ct. 1980, U.S. Ct. Appeals. Law clk. to Judge Warren Ferguson, U.S. Dist. Ct. for So. Dist. Calif., L.A., 1976-77; atty. Office Legal Counsel and Land & Natural Resources Divsn. U.S. Dept. Justice, Washington, 1977-79; spl. asst. to sec. U.S. Dept. Edn., Washington, 1979-80; vis. assoc. prof. U. Iowa Coll. Law, Iowa City, 1981; asst. prof. U. N.C. Sch. Law, Chapel Hill, 1981-84, assoc. prof., 1984-88, prof., 1988—, assoc. dean, 1986-88, dean, 1989—; spkr. in field. Chief comment editor UCLA Law Rev., 1975-76; contbr. articles to legal publs. Mem. ABA (chmn. planning com. African Law Sch. Initiative 1994, co-chmn. planning com. 1994 mid-yr. deans meeting sect. on legal edn. and admission to bar), AAUP, N.C. Assn. Women Attys. (Gweneth Davis award 1989), N.C. State Bar Assn., Assn. Am. Law Schs. (mem. exec. com. sect. on law & edn. 1985-88, mem. exec. com. sect. on local govt. law 1989-92, mem. accreditation com. 1986-88, chmn. 1989-91, program chmn. 1992 ann. meeting, program chmn. 1994 ann. meeting, mem. exec. com. 1992-94, pres. 1995), Soc. Am. Law Tchrs., Nat. League Cities (coun.-mentor program 1989-91), Women's Internat. Forum, Order of Coif (nat. exec. com. 1989-91), Phi Beta Kappa. Democrat. Office: U NC Sch Law Van Hecke-Wettach Hall Campus Box 3380 Chapel Hill NC 27599-3380

WEGNER, KARL HEINRICH, physician, educator; b. Pierre, S.D., Jan. 5, 1930; s. Lester Fred and Nellie (Norbeck) W.; m. Mary Josephine Waddell, June 15, 1957; children: Madeleine Jean, Peter Norbeck, Mary Nell. B.A., Yale U., 1952; M.D., Harvard U., 1959. Intern, resident Mass. Gen. Hosp./Harvard U., 1959-62; pathologist Sioux Valley Hosp., Sioux Falls, S.D., 1962-90; pathologist, dir. Lab. Clin. Medicine, Sioux Falls, 1962-90; prof., chmn. dept. pathology U. S.D., 1968-73, v.p. health affairs, dean Sch. Medicine, 1973-79, Regents Disting. prof. emeritus, 1992—; owner, operator Meadowlark Farms, Montrose, S.D.; mem. Bd. of Regents for Higher Edn., State of S.D. Bd. dirs. U. S.D. Found., Sioux Valley Hosp. Found., Sioux Falls Area Found. With USMC. Karl H. Wegner Endowed Professorship, Bd. of Regents for Higher Edn., 1979; recipient Disting. Svc. award S.D. State Med. Assn., 1984, Community Svc. award, 1975; inducted to S.D. Hall of Fame, 1987. Fellow Coll. Am. Pathologists, Internat. Acad. Pathologists, Am. Soc. Pathologists; mem. Am. Pathology Found. (pres. 1984-85, Am. pathologist of Yr award, 1989), Alpha Omega Alpha. Home: Sunnymede S Minn Rd Sioux Falls SD 57106 Office: 1212 S Euclid Ave Sioux Falls SD 57105-0413

WEGNER, LAURA SHOWN, social services director; b. Ft. Lee, Va., Sept. 26, 1955; d. Edward R. and Laura Louise (Jones) Shown; m. Robert Carl Wegner, Aug. 29, 1975; children: Eamon Colin-Shown, Cyrus Sharpe. BA in Sociology, Mary Baldwin Coll., 1990. Social work aid/eligibility worker Nottoway (Va.) Social Svcs., 1979-84; fraud investigator Lunenburg (Va.) Social Svcs., 1984-85; benefit programs specialist Va. Dept. Social Svcs., Lynchburg, 1985-89; benefit programs supr. Va. Dept. Social Svcs., Richmond, 1989-91; dir. social svcs. Charlotte County (Va.) Social Svcs., 1991—; cons. Piedmont Humanities Coun., Farmville, Va., 1992—; bd. dirs. Va. League Social Svcs. Execs. Vol. Nottoway County Emergency Squad, Crewe, Va., 1987—; bd. dirs. Nottoway Regional Arts Coun., Crewe, 1991—, Southside Va. Food Distbn. Ctr., Dolphin, Va., 1991—. Named Squadman of Yr., Nottoway County Emergency Squad, 1992. Democrat. Episcopalian. Avocations: painting, calligraphy. Home: RR 1 Box 143 Blackstone VA 23824-9763 Office: Charlotte County Dept Social Svcs PO Box 440 Charlotte Court House VA 23923-0440

WEGNER, SAMUEL JOSEPH, historical society executive; b. Twin Falls, Idaho, Aug. 27, 1952; s. Albert Henry and Eleanor Esther (Wright) W.; m. Linda Louise Talley, May 27, 1972; children: Ethan, Elena. BA, U. Ariz., 1973; MA, U. Idaho, 1975. Curator Mansion Mus.-Oglebay Inst., Wheeling, W.Va., 1975-76; curator of edn. State Hist. Soc. Wis., Madison, 1976-78; asst. supt. Region I Mo. Dept. Nat. Resources, Brookfield, 1978-85; dir. ops. So. Oregon Hist. Soc., Jacksonville, Oreg., 1985-87; exec. dir. So. Oregon Hist. Soc., Medford, Oreg., 1987-96; dep. exec. dir. Jamestown-Yorktown Found., Williamsburg, Va., 1996—; mem. Nat. Adv. Com. Common Agenda for History Mus., 1990-92, Nat. Adv. Com. Phila. Documentation Project for Common Agenda, 1989-91; chmn. Region 11 Am. Assn. State and Local History Awards Program, 1989-90, chmn. Oregon State chpt., 1987-88; chmn. Western Region Assn. Living History Farms and Agrl. Mus., 1986-87; mem. Am. Assn. Mus. Ad Hoc Com. for Hist. Sites and Mus. in Pks., 1984-85. Mem. adv. com. Medford (Oreg.) Vis. and Conv. Bur., 1988-96; bd. dirs. Oreg. Trail Coordinating Coun., 1994-96, So. Oreg. Visitors Assn., 1995-96; bd. dirs., coord. Applegate Trail Coalition, 1993-96; mem. Jacksonville Transp. Com., 1993-95. Mem. Am. Assn. Mus., Nat. Trust for Hist. Preservation, Oreg. Mus. Assn., Medford Rouge Rotary Club. Office: Jamestown-Yorktown Found PO Drawer JF Williamsburg VA 23187-3630

WEGNER, SANDRA SUE, library director; b. Hutchinson, Kans., July 30, 1938; d. John Wilbur and Evelyn Lucille (White) DeFore; m. Leroy Gene Wegner, Oct. 7, 1960; children: Ross Eugene, Barry John. BS in Journalism, Tex. Woman's U., 1960; MS in LS, North Tex. State U., 1985. Cert. county libr., Tex. Reporter oil sect. Midland (Tex.) Reporter-Telegram, 1960; libr. clk. Midland County Pub. Libr., Midland, 1974-82, spl. collections libr., 1982-85, asst. dir., 1985-90, dir., 1990—. Literacy tutor Midland Need To Read, 1987-90, bd. dirs., 1988—. Mem. ALA, Tex. Libr. Assn., Midland Geneal. Soc. (bd. dirs.), DAR (registrar Col. Theunis Dey chpt. 1993-95), Beta Phi Mu. Republican. Methodist. Avocation: genealogy. Home: 1502 Seaboard Midland TX 79705 Office: Midland County Pub Libr 301 W Missouri Ave Midland TX 79701

WEHMEIER, HELGE H., chemical, health care and imaging technologies company executive; b. Goettingen, Germany, 1943; married; 2 children. Attended, Internat. Mgmt. Devel. Inst., Switzerland, Inst. Europeen d'Adminstrn. des Affaires, France. With Bayer AG, 1965; mktg. synthetic fibers U.S. and Can. Mobay, N.Y.C., 1969; mktg. mgr. Leverkusen, Ger., 1974-78; gen. mgr. U.K., 1978-80; mgr. organic chem. divsn., 1981-84; head indsl. photographic divsn. Agfa-Gevaert AG subs. Leverkusen, 1984-89; pres., CEO Agfa Corp., Ridgefield Park, N.J., 1989-91; also bd. dirs., exec. com. Agfa Corp., Ridgefield Park, N.J.; pres., CEO Bayer Corp. (formerly Miles Inc.), 1991—; bd. dirs. PNC Bank Corp. Bd. dirs. Pitts. Symphony Soc.; mem. exec. com., officer Allegheny Conf. Cmty. Devel., Pitts.; mem. Conf. Bd., Trilateral Commn. Mem. Chem. Mfrs. Assn. (exec. com., internat. com.). Office: Bayer Corp One Mellon Bank Ctr 500 Grant St Pittsburgh PA 15219-2502

WEHNER, ALFRED PETER, inhalation toxicologist, biomedical scientist; b. Wiesbaden, Germany, Oct. 23, 1926; came to U.S., 1953, naturalized, 1958; s. Paul Heinrich and Irma (Schulze) Wl; m. Ingeborg Hella Miller, Aug. 30, 1955; children: Patricia Ingeborg, Alfred Peter, Jr., Jackie Diane, Peter Hermann. Cand. med., Johannes Gutenberg U., 1949, Zahnarzt DDS, 1951, D.M.D. cum laude, 1953. Diplomate Acad. Toxicol. Scis., 1988. Individual practice dentistry Wiesbaden, 1951-53; fellow clin. pedodontia Guggenheim Dental Clinic, N.Y.C., 1953-54; dentist 7100th Hosp., USAF, 1954-56; rsch. asst. Mobil Oil Co., Dallas, 1957-62; sr. rsch. scientist Biometrics Instrument Corp., Plano, Tex., 1962-64; pres. Electro-Aerosol Inst., Plano, Tex.; dir. Electro-Aerosol Therapy Centers, 1964-67; prof., chmn. dept. sci. U. Plano, 1966-67; sr. rsch. scientist biology dept. Battelle Pacific Northwest Labs., Richland, Wash., 1967-78; mgr. environ. and indsl. toxicology Battelle Pacific Northwest Labs., 1978-80, project dir., task leader indsl. toxicology, 1980-89; founder, pres. Biomed. & Environ. Cons., Inc., 1989—; cons. VA Hosp., McKinney, Tex., 1963-65; chmn., guest speaker 16 internat. sci. congresses and symposia. Author: From Hitler Youth to U.S. Citizenship, 1972; more than 120 sci. publs., including chpts. to books.; editor-in-chief: Am. Inst. Biomed. Climatology Bull.; editor: MEDICEF Direct Information (Federal Republic of Germany); reviewer various sci. jours.; patentee in field. Chmn. citizen adv. bd. Richland Police Dept. Fellow Internat. Soc. Med. Hydrology, Tex. Acad. Sci.; mem. Am. Inst. Biomed. Climatology (bd. dirs. 1972-90, sec. 1972-83, pres. 1984-90), Accademia degli Abruzzi per le Scienze e le Arti, Italy (hon. academician, v.p.), Pacific N.W. Assn. Toxicologists, Internat. Soc. of Biometeorology (USA rep. 1972-79), Internat. Soc. Aerosols in Medicine (exec. bd. 1970-80, diploma for highest merits in med. sci. 1980), Dallas County Dental Soc. (hon.), Internat. Assn. Aerobiology, Sigma Xi.

WEHNER, HENRY OTTO, III, pharmacist, consultant; b. Birmingham, Ala., Mar. 3, 1942; s. Henry O. Jr. and Carolyn (Kirkland) W.; m. Sammye Ruth Murphy, June 8, 1974 (div. July 1989). AA, Daytona Beach Community Coll., 1967; BS in Biology, North Ga. Coll., Dahlonega, 1971; BS in Pharmacy, U. Ga., 1978. Registered pharmacist, Fla., Ga.; cert. sci. tchr. grades 7-12, Ga. Tchr. biology Irwin County High Sch., Ocilla, Ga., 1971-75; extern Eckerd Drugs, Athens, Ga., 1977; intern/extern St. Mary's Hosp., Athens, 1977; pharmacy intern Button Gwinnett Hosp., Lawrenceville, Ga., 1978; co-owner, mgr. Hiawassee (Ga.) Pharmacy, 1978-79; staff pharmacist Dyal's Pharmacy, Daytona Beach, Fla., 1979, Little Drug Co., New Smyrna Beach, Fla., 1979-80; staff pharmacist, mgr. Super X Drugs, New Smyrna Beach, 1980-81; staff pharmacist Fish Meml. Hosp., New Smyrna Beach, 1981-92, Halifax Med. Ctr., Daytona Beach, Fla., 1992—. With USAF, 1961-65. Mem. Am. Pharm. Assn., Fla. Soc. Hosp. Pharmacists, Volusia County Pharm. Assn., Ea. Shores Soc. Hosp. Pharmacists (charter, pres. 1995-96), Phi Lambda Sigma, Phi Theta Kappa. Methodist. Avocations: painting, cycling, tennis. Office: Halifax Med Ctr PO Box 1350 303 N Clyde Morris Blvd Daytona Beach FL 32114-2709

WEHR, LYNN, food products executive. V.p. T. Marzetti Co., Columbus, Ohio. Office: T Marzetti Co 1105 Schrock Rd Ste 600 Columbus OH 43229-1174*

WEHR, THOMAS A., psychiatrist, researcher; b. Louisville, Ky., Oct. 15, 1941; s. Elmer A. and Lillian (Ashby) W.; m. Elizabeth Barker Jones, Mar. 30, 1963; 1 child, David Rowan. BA in English Lit., Yale U., 1965; MD, U. Louisville, 1969. Diplomate Am. Bd. Psychiatry. Intern Michael Reese Hosp. and Med. Ctr., Chgo., 1969-70; resident in psychiatry Yale U. Sch. Medicine, New Haven, 1970-73; clin. assoc. sect. psychiatry NIMH, Bethesda, Md., 1973-75, med. rsch. officer, 1975-76, staff psychiatrist, 1976, chief clin. rsch. unit, clin. psychobiology br., 1977-84, chief clin. psychobiology br., 1982—; pvt. practice psychiatry Bethesda, Md., 1977—; instr. Washington Sch. Psychiatry, 1976-78; vis. prof. U. Naples Med. Sch., Italy, 1984; adj. prof. dept. biol. scis. U. Md., 1986—; internat. adv. bd. Ctr. Design Industrial Schedules; adv. bd. Soc. Rsch. Biol. Rhythms. Author: (with D. Oren, N.E. Rosenthal and W. Reich) How To Beat Jet Lag: The Travelers' Guide, 1993; co-editor: Circadian Rhythms in Psychiatry, 1983; mem. editorial bd. Experimental and Clinical Psychiatry, 1987-93, Lithium, 1989-95, Jour. Biol. Rhythms, 1985-94; patentee portable light delivery system; contbr. articles to profl. jours. Med. dir. USPHS, 1973-75, 76—. Recipient Nat. Rsch. Svc. award, 1975-76, award for Rsch. in Depression Anna-Monika Found., 1981, 91; grantee NIMH 1966-68, 69. Mem. Am. Psychiat. Assn., Am. Coll. Neuropsychopharmacology, Soc. Biol. Psychiatry, Soc. Light Treatment and Biol. Rhytms (v.p. 1992-93, chmn. ann. meeting sci. program com. 1992-93), Internat. Soc. Psychoneuroendocrinology, Internat. Soc. Chronobiology, Soc. Rsch. Biol. Rhythms, Sleep Rsch. Soc. Office: Nat Inst of Mental Health Rm 4S-239 Bldg 10 10 Center Dr MSC 1390 Bethesda MD 20892-1390

WEHRER, CHARLES SIECKE, business and education educator; b. Norfolk, Nebr., July 13, 1914; s. Charles C. and Ella (Augusta) W.; m. May Winther Hansen, Aug. 21, 1982 (dec. Oct. 27, 1991). BA, Nebr. State Tchrs. Coll., 1940; MA in Sch. Adminstrn., U. Nebr., 1950, postgrad., 1950; postgrad., Columbia U., 1950, U. So. Calif., 1954-55; PhD without dissertation, Ohio State U., 1961; LHD (hon.), Sioux Empire Coll., 1967. Asst. commandant, basketball coach Black-Foxe Mil. Inst., Hollywood, Calif., 1945-46; coach, supt. local schs. Wood Lake, Nebr., 1947-49; prin. Scottsbluff (Nebr.) Jr. High Sch., 1950-51; grad. asst. in edn. U. Nebr., 1949-50, U. So. Calif., 1954-55; grad. asst. prof. elem. edn. Ohio State U., 1960; tchr. pub. schs. Paramount, Calif., 1953-54; tchr. Excelsior Adult Sch., Norwalk, Calif., 1953-57; supt. local schs. Shandon, Calif., 1956-57; assoc. prof. edn., supr. student teaching Ohio No. U., Ada, 1958-60; assoc. prof., supr. elem. student teaching Capital U., Columbus, Ohio, 1961-62; prin. Norwalk Iowa Elem. Jr. High Sch., 1962-63; prof. edn., dir. student affairs, asst. to pres. Grand View Coll., Des Moines, 1962-64; with depts. youth, TV, ednl. programming City of Des Moines, 1965; cons. program Iowa Civil Def./Health Dept., 1966; prof. edn. and psychology S.W. Community Coll., Creston, Iowa, 1967; acad. dean Sioux Empire Coll., Hawarden, Iowa, 1967-68; chmn. depts. edn., psychology, dir. tchr. edn. J.F. Kennedy Coll., Wahoo, Nebr., 1970-71; prodr., emcee youth radio/TV program Let's Listen to Youth, Lincoln, Nebr., 1971, Des Moines, Sioux City, Iowa, 1952-74, L.A., Columbus, Ohio, 1952-74; prof. edn. Concordia Coll., Seward, Nebr., 1973; tng. coord., dir. spl. tng. programs for mgmt. State of Nebr., 1974-75; prof. bus. Metro Tech., Omaha, 1976-82; prof. mgmt. tng. Bus. Devel. Ctr. U. Nebr., Omaha, 1976-82; prof. bus. Nebr. State Coll., Wayne, 1982-88, ret.; pres. Bus. Mgmt. Cons. Co., Wisner, Nebr., 1982-90; lectr. in field. Author: Keep in Touch, My Students, 1966; contbr. articles to profl. jours. Phys. dir. YMCA, Norfolk, 1934-36, McCook, Nebr., 1937-38, L.A. Downtown Y, 1940-41; counselor, adv. Nebr. Boys' State, 1949-50; Nebr. del. White House Conf. on Children and Youth, 1950; chmn. Nebr. Com. on Juvenile Delinquency; mem. Gov.'s Com. on Youth, Calif., Nebr.; spl. youth cons. radio program Art Linkletter House Party, Calif., 1952; dir. dept. guest rels. NBC, Hollywood, Calif., 1952; dir. spl. project Iowa Dept. Health, 1965-66; contbr. to sub-com. on poverty-youth programs U.S. Congress, 1964-65; chmn. youth sect. Iowa Congress Parents & Tchrs., 1966-67; lay min. Protestant Chs., 1967—, past ch. official First Cong. United Ch. of Christ, Norfolk, Elkhorn Valley Hist. Soc. Capt. USAAF, 1941-45. Decorated Bronze Star, Soldiers medal, 3 Battle Stars, 15th AF Unit citation, Pres. Unit citation, others; recipient spl. awards/commendations for radio/TV programs State PTA and other civic and youth groups, 1960-75, numerous awards for tchg. and youth work; named Outstanding Sch. Adminstr. in Nebr. dept. sch. adminstrn. U. Nebr., 1994, Nebr. Dept. Edn., 1948-50; named to Hall of Honor, Nebr. Softball Assn., 1993, Norfolk H.S. Students honor as Sr. Citizens of Yr., 1995, Spl. Proclamation for Edn. and Youth Svcs. State of Nebr., 1994. Mem. NEA (Spl. Commendation for tchr. edn. programs), AAUP, Am. Assn. Ret. Persons (Nebr. Sr. Citizen Spl. Commendation 1980-810, Assn. for Higher Edn., Nat. Assn. Sch. Adminstrs., Nat. Soc. for Study of Edn., Internat. Platform Assn. (spl. spkr. conv. 1970), Am. Legion, VFW (post 1684), SCORE, Lions (bd. dirs., past pres.), Kiwanis (past pres.), Rotary, Delta Sigma, Phi Delta Kappa (Spl. Recognition award 1992), Sigma Tau Delta (past pres.). Address: 1000 Village Green Dr Apt 1 Norfolk NE 68701-2279 *We are living in a dangerous world of unrest, a difficult time for all of us to adjust to the emotional and mental problems of this changing environmental world. If we can be of help to those who are in need of a friendly act then let us do our best to be of help and service to young and old alike as we may not pass this way again.*

WEHRING, BERNARD WILLIAM, nuclear engineering educator; b. Monroe, Mich., Aug. 3, 1937; s. Bernard Albert and Alma Christina (Graf) W.; m. Margaret Mary Robinson, Sept. 5, 1959; children: Mary Ann, James, Susan, Barbara. B.S.E. in Physics, U. Mich., 1959, B.S.E. in Math, 1959; M.S. in Physics, U. Ill., 1961, Ph.D. in Nuclear Engring, 1966. Asst. prof. nuclear engring. U. Ill., Urbana, 1966-70, assoc. prof., 1970-77, prof., 1977-84, asst. dean engring., 1981-82; prof. nuclear engring. N.C. State U., Raleigh, 1984-89, dir. nuclear reactor program, 1984-89; prof. mech. engring. U. Tex., Austin, 1989—, dir. Nuclear Engring. Teaching Lab., 1989—; cons. Argonne and Los Alamos nat. labs.; mem. crosssect. evaluation working group Brookhaven Nat. Lab. Contbr. sects. to books, articles to profl. publs. AEC fellow, 1963-65; NSF grantee, 1968—. Fellow Am. Nuclear Soc.; mem. Am. Soc. Engring. Edn., Am. Nuclear Soc. (standards com.), Am. Phys. Soc., IEEE. Achievements include contributing in the generation of basic nuclear data and development of new instruments and experimental techniques. Home: 8907 Spring Lake Dr Austin TX 78750-2932 Office: U Tex Nuclear Engring Teaching Lab J J Pickle Rsch Campus Austin TX 78712

WEHRLE, HENRY BERNARD, JR., diversified manufacturing company executive; b. Charleston, W.Va., 1922. Grad., Princeton U., 1943. Chmn. McJunkin Corp., Charleston, also bd. dirs.; bd. dirs. Bank One W. Va., Petroleum Equipment Supplies Assn. Office: McJunkin Corp 835 Hillcrest Dr E Charleston WV 25311-1627*

WEHRLE, LEROY SNYDER, economist, educator; b. St. Louis, Feb. 5, 1932; s. Fred Joseph and Eleanor (Snyder) W.; m. JoAnn Griffith, Aug. 29, 1959; children—Chandra Lee, Lon Joseph. B.S., Washington U., St. Louis, 1953; M.A. in Econs, Yale, 1956, Ph.D. with honors, 1959. Asst. instr. Yale, 1958-59; with econ. sect. AID mission to Laos, 1960-61; sr. staff economist President's Council Econ. Advisers, 1961-62; spl. econ. adviser to U.S. Ambassador Unger, Vientiane, 1962; dep. dir. AID mission to Laos, 1963-64; asst. dir. AID mission, also econ. counsellor to U.S. ambassador, Saigon, 1964-67; asso. dir. AID Mission, Saigon, 1964-67; dept. asst. adminstr. Vietnam, AID, Dept. State, 1967-68; univ. fellow Harvard, 1968-69; sr. fellow Brookings Instn., 1969-70; dir. Ill. Inst. for Social Policy, Springfield, 1970-72; aide to Lt. Gov. Paul Simon, 1972; prof. economics Sangamon State U., 1972-88; founding ptnr., chief exec. officer Health Econs. and Mkt. Analysis Inc., Springfield, 1987-94; pres. Healthcare Cost Analysis, Inc., 1994—; chmn. bd. Tie Collar, Ltd. Mem. spl. study group Alliance Progress, 1962; mem. Rockefeller Latin Am. Mission, 1969; chmn. study team world food and nutrition study Nat. Acad. Sci., 1976-77. Served with AUS, 1953-55. Recipient William A. Jump meml. award, 1966. Home and Office: 2001 S Bates Ave Springfield IL 62704-3304

WEHRLI, JOHN ERICH, biotechnology executive; b. Bogota, Colombia, Dec. 1, 1963; came to U.S., 1969; s. Werner Friederich and Graciela Wehrli; m. Vicki Lee Burnett, Aug. 18, 1991; children: Sophia Cristina, Sarina Darlene. BS summa cum laude in Mgmt. and Econs., Golden Gate U., 1993; Tax cert., Foothill Coll., 1994; postgrad., U. Calif., San Francisco, 1994—, U. Calif., Berkeley, 1995—. Analytical chemist dept. Chem. Analysis Syva Diagnostics Co., 1985-87; part-time fin. cons. assoc. Shearson Lehman Bros., San Francisco, 1989; robotics specialist dept. Automation Tech. Syntex Rsch. Inc., 1987-89; v.p. Precision Instrument Design Inc., Tahoe City, Calif., 1989—; rsch. chemist Inst. Pharm. Scis., dept. Pharm. Chemistry Syntex Rsch. Inc., 1987-91, sr. sci. analyst programmer, sys. mgr. Rsch. Info. Sys., 1991-93, sys. analyst, sr. sys. mgr., 1993-94; legal intern patent and tech. licensing Lawrence Berkeley Nat. Lab., 1995—; pres. Wehrli Tech. Cons., Mountain View, Calif., 1995—. Contbr. articles to profl. jours. Enterprise scholar Golden Gate U., 1992, Kanze scholar, 1993, Univ. Honors scholar, 1993, Pres.'s scholar Foothill Coll., 1993. Mem. AAAS, ABA (sci. and tech. sect.), Am. Chem. Soc. (chem. info. and computer scis. sect.), Assn. Univ. Tech. Mgrs., Licensing Execs. Soc., Am. Intellectual Property Law Assn., Phi Alpha Delta. Avocations: wildlife preservation, animal cruelty prevention, fractal mathematics, non-linear systems, Graeco Roman history. Home: 1879 Springer Rd Apt B Mountain View CA 94040-4052 Office: Precision Instrument Design Tahoe City CA 96145

WEHRLY, JOSEPH MALACHI, industrial relations executive b. County Armagh, Ireland, Oct. 2, 1915; s. Albert and Mary Josephine (Gribbon) W.; came to U.S., 1931, naturalized, 1938; student L.A. City Coll., evenings 1947-49; certificate indsl. relations U. Calif. at Berkeley Extension, 1957; m. Margaret Elizabeth Banks, July 3, 1946; children: Joseph Michael, Kathleen Margaret, Stephen Patrick. Mgr. interplant relations Goodyear Tire & Rubber Co., L.A., 1935-42; dir. indsl. rels. Whittaker Corp., L.A., 1946-60, Meletron Corp., L.A., 1960-61; asst. indsl. rels. mgr. Pacific Airmotive Corp., Burbank, Calif., 1961-63; pers. mgr. Menasco Mfg. Co., Burbank, 1963-66; indsl. rels. adminstr. Internat. Electronic Rsch., Burbank, 1966; dir. indsl. rels. Adams Rite Industries, Inc., Glendale, Calif., 1966-75, cons., 1975-76; pers. mgr. TOTCO div. Baker Hughes Corp., Glendale, 1975-80; instr. indsl. rels. and supervision L.A. Pierce Coll., 1949-76. Served with U.S. Army, 1942-46. Mem. Pers. and Indsl. Rels. Assn., Mchts. and Mfrs. Assn. Republican. Roman Catholic. Home: 90 Shorebreaker Dr Laguna Niguel CA 92677-9304

WEI, JAMES, chemical engineering educator, academic dean; b. Macao, China, Aug. 14, 1930; came to U.S., 1949, naturalized, 1960; s. Hsiang-chen and Nuen (Kwok) W.; m. Virginia Hong, Nov. 4, 1956; children: Alexander, Christina, Natasha, Randolph (dec.). B.S. in Chem. Engring, Ga. Inst. Tech., 1952; M.S., Mass. Inst. Tech., 1954, Sc.D., 1955; grad., Advanced Mgmt. Program Harvard, 1969. Research engr. to research assoc. Mobil Oil, Paulsboro, N.J., 1956-62; sr. scientist Princeton, N.J., 1963-68; mgr. corp. planning N.Y.C., 1969-70; Allan P. Colburn prof. U. Del., Newark, 1971-77; Sherman Fairchild distinguished scholar Calif. Inst. Tech., 1977; Warren K. Lewis prof. MIT, Cambridge, 1977-91, head dept. chem. engring., 1977-88; Pomeroy and Betty Smith prof. chem. engring., dean Sch. Engring. and Applied Sci. Princeton (N.J.) U., 1991—; vis. prof. Princeton, 1962-63, Calif. Inst. Tech., 1965; cons. Mobil Oil Corp.; cons. com. on motor vehicle emissions Nat. Acad. Sci., 1972-74, 79-80; mem. sci. adv. bd. EPA, 1976-79; mem. Presdl. Pvt. Sector Survey Task Force on Dept. Energy, 1982-83. Bd. editors Chem. Tech, 1971-80, Chem. Engring. Communications, 1972—; cons. editor chem. engring. series, McGraw-Hill, 1964—; editor-in-chief: Advances in Chemical Engineering, 1980; Contbr. papers, monographs to profl. lit., The Structure of Chemical Processing Industries, 1979. Recipient Am. Acad. Achievement Golden Plate award, 1966. Mem. AIChE (dir. 1970-72, Inst. lectr. 1968, Profl. Progress award 1970, Walker award 1980,

Lewis award 1985, v.p. 1987, pres. 1988, Founders award 1990), Am. Chem. Soc. (award in petroleum chemistry 1966), Nat. Acad. Engring. (nominating com. 1981, peer com. 1980-82, membership com. 1983-85, Draper award com. 1995), AAAS, Am. Acad. Arts and Scis., Academica Sinica of Taiwan, Sigma Xi. Home: 571 Lake Dr Princeton NJ 08540-5632 Office: Princeton U Engring Quadrangle Princeton NJ 08544-5263

WEI, TAM DANG, mental health specialist, educator; b. Nghe An, Vietnam, Jan. 2, 1926; came to U.S., 1955; d. Huong Dang Van and Hien Hoang Thi; m. Lun Shin Wei, Aug. 18, 1955; children: Michael, Max, Manuel, Aline. BA in Philosophy, U. Hanoi, Vietnam, 1949; licentiate in edn. and psychology, U. Geneva, 1955; MEd in Ednl. Psychology, U. Ill., 1958, PhD in Ednl. Psychology, 1966. Cert. sch. psychologist, administrator, bilingual tchr. French and Vietnamese, Ill. Tche. elem. and h.s. Thanh Quan and Dong Khanh Schs., Vietnam, 1948-52; instr. ednl. psychology U. Ill., Urbana, 1962-67, asst. prof., 1967-69; sch. psychologist Ford-Iroquois Counties Spl. Edn. Coop., Ford County, Ill., 1970-81; dir. bilingual edn. program Champaign (Ill.) Sch. Dist. 4, 1982-85; mental health specialist East Ctrl. Ill. Refugee Mut. Assistance Ctr., Urbana, 1986—; cons. psychology and mental health various schs., 1975—; mem. adv. bd. Ill. Coun. Multi-Cultural Edn., Springfield, 1977-79, Ill. Adv. Home Econ. Extension, Urbana, 1978-79, Opportunity Industrialization Ctr., Champaign, 1979-81, East Ctrl. Ill. Refugee Assistance Ctr., 1981-86. Author: Piaget's Concept of Classification, 1971, Handbook for Teachers of Refugee Students, 1977, Bilingual Exceptional Child, 1984, Vietnamese Refugee Students, 1980-84. Mem. Internat. Coun. Psychologists, Ill. Sch. Psychologists, Ill. Registry Psychologists with Spl. Skills, Nat. Assn. Vietnamese, Laotian and Cambodian Educators, Bilingual Educators. Avocations: reading, walking, bicycling, music, family activities. Office: East Ctrl Ill Ref Asst Ctr 302 S Birch St Urbana IL 61801-3201

WEIANT, WILLIAM MORROW, investment banking executive; b. Perth Amboy, N.J., Nov. 30, 1938; s. Monroe Alden and Lois May (Dayer) W.; m. Joan Claire Eberstadt, June 10, 1967; children: Clarissa Leigh, Pamela Anne. BA, Amherst Coll., 1960; MBA, NYU, 1964. Chartered fin. analyst. Ptnr. Blyth Eastman Dillon, N.Y.C., 1963-75; mng. dir. CS 1st Boston, N.Y.C., 1976-91, Dillon, Read & Co. Inc., N.Y.C., 1991-94, Morgan Stanley & Co., N.Y.C., 1994—. With USAF, 1960-61. Mem. Bank and Fin. Analysts (pres. 1976, 87). Avocations: tennis, golf, skiing, piano. Home: 46 Northover Pl Red Bank NJ 07701-6311

WEIBLE, ROBERT A., lawyer; b. Dover, Ohio, June 25, 1953. BA summa cum laude, Wittenberg U., 1975; JD summa cum laude, Ohio State U., 1978. Ptnr. Baker & Hostetler, Cleve. Editor Ohio State Law Jour., 1977-78. Mem. Order of Coif. Office: Baker & Hostetler 3200 Nat City Ctr 1900 E 9th St Cleveland OH 44114-3401*

WEICH, RONALD H., lawyer; b. N.Y.C., Nov. 19, 1959. Student, London Sch. Econs., 1979; BA, Columbia U., 1980; JD, Yale U., 1983. Bar: N.Y. 1984, U.S. Ct. Appeals (D.C. cir.) 1988. Asst. dist. atty. N.Y. Dist. Atty's Office, N.Y.C., 1983-87; spl. counsel U.S. Sentencing Commn., Washington, 1987-89; minority counsel Senate Constitution Subcom., Washington, 1989; chief counsel drug policy Senate Labor & Human Resources Com., Washington, 1990-95, gen. counsel, 1992-95; chief counsel to Senator Kennedy Senate Judiciary Com., Washington, 1995—. Guest editor Federal Sentencing Reporter, 1991; contbr. articles to profl. jours. Mem. ABA (criminal justice sect., sentencing/prison coms.), Bar Assn. State N.Y. Office: The Judiciary 520 Dirksen Office Bldg Washington DC 20510

WEICHENTHAL, BURTON A., educational administrator, beef specialist; b. Stanton, Nebr., Nov. 7, 1937; s. Arthur W. and Bertha M. (Topp) W.; m. Phyllis A. Bonner, June 12, 1960; 1 child, Susan. BS, U. Nebr., 1959; MS, S.D. State U., 1962; PhD, Colo. State U., 1967. Beef specialist U. Ill., Urbana, 1967-81; assoc. dir. U. Nebr. Panhandle Ctr., Scottsbluff, 1982—, beef specialist, 1987—. Mem. Sugar Valley Singers (past pres., treas.), Lions (past pres.), Elks. Avocations: barbershop chorus singing. Office: U Nebr Panhandle Ctr 4502 Avenue I Scottsbluff NE 69361-4939

WEICHERT, DIETER HORST, seismologist, researcher; b. Breslau, Silesia, Germany, May 2, 1932; came to Can., 1954; s. Kurt Herman and Margarete Adelheid (Buresch) W.; m. Edith Struning (div. 1983), children: Thomas, Andreas. BASc, U. B.C., Vancouver, Can., 1961, PhD, 1965; MS, McMaster U., Hamilton, Ont., Can., 1963. Rsch. scientist earth physics br. Dominion Obs., Ottawa, Ont., 1965-78; rsch. scientist Pacific Geosci. Ctr., Sidney, B.C., 1978-81, head earthquake studies, 1981-88, assoc. dir., acting dir., 1988-90; rsch. scientist Geol. Survey Can., Sidney, B.C., 1990-96, emeritus, 1996—; cons. U.K. Atomic Energy Authority, Blacknest, Eng., 1970; guest lectr. Fredericiana U., Karlsruhe, Germany, 1971; mem. Can. Earthquake Engring. Com., Ottawa, 1982—; supt. constrn. industry, Germany, 1951-57. Contbr. over 80 articles to profl. jours. Woodrow Wilson fellow, 1961; Inco fellow, 1962-64. Mem. Seismol. Soc. Am. Achievements include research on underground nuclear explosion detection and identification; seismic hazard and strong seismic ground motion. Office: Geol Survey Can, 9860 W Saanich Box 6000, North Saanich, BC Canada V8L 4B2

WEICKSEL, CHARLENE MARIE, principal; b. York, Pa., June 16, 1945; d. Edward A. and Mary Elizabeth (Hoffman) Debes; m. Stephen A. Weicksel, Aug. 27, 1967; children: Ann, Andrew. B Music Edn., Westminster Choir Coll., 1967; MEd, Trenton State Coll., 1986. Cert. tchr., prin., supr., N.J. Tchr. Hillsborough Twp. Bd. Edn., Neshanic, N.J., 1967-87, curriculum supr. fine and performing arts, 1987-93; prin. Triangle Rd. Elem. Sch., Hillsborough, N.J., 1993—. Bd. dirs. Lenape Swim Club, Skillman, N.J., 1990-93, Raritan Valley Chorus, Belle Mead, N.J., 1991-92. Mem. NEA, Nat. Art Educators Assn., Nat. Assn. Elem. Sch. Prins., Art Educators N.J., N.J. Edn. Assn., Jazz Educators, N.J. Prins. and Suprs. Assn. Democrat. Presbyterian. Avocations: cross-stitch, crochet, knitting, writing, travel. Home: 302 Sunset Rd Skillman NJ 08558-1628 Office: Hillsborough Twp Bd Edn 555 Amwell Rd Neshanic Station NJ 08853-3409

WEIDA, LEWIS DIXON, marketing analyst, consultant; b. Moran, Ind., Apr. 23, 1924; s. Charles Ray and Luella Mildred (Dixon) W.; student Kenyon Coll., 1943, Purdue U., 1946; B.S., Ind. U., 1948; M.S., Columbia U., 1950. Mgr. statis. analysis unit Gen. Motors Acceptance Corp., N.Y.C., 1949-55; asst. to exec. v.p. Am. Express Co., 1955-82. Served with USAAF, 1943-46; PTO. Mem. Internat. Platform Assn. Democrat. Club: Masons. Home: 25 Tudor City Pl New York NY 10017-6819

WEIDE, WILLIAM WOLFE, housing and recreational vehicles manufacturer; b. Toledo, Aug. 19, 1923; s. Samuel and Pearl Celia (Weide) W.; m. Beatrice Lieberman, June 4, 1950; children: Brian Samuel, Bruce Michael, Robert Benjamin. Student, U. Toledo, 1942, Marquette U., 1943-44; B.S., U. So. Calif., 1949. Asst. controller Eldon Mfg., 1950; mem. Calif. Franchise Tax Bd., 1951; controller Sutone Corp., 1951-53; contr., treas. Pacific Concessions Corp., 1953; treas. Descoware Corp., 1953-58; sr. v.p., dir. Fleetwood Enterprises, Inc., Riverside, Calif., 1958-73, pres., chief oper. officer, 1973-82, vice chmn., 1982—, dir.; treas. So. Eastern Manufactured Housing Inst., Atlanta., 1972-74; vice chmn. bd. dirs. Fleetwood Enterprises, Inc.. Mem. City of Riverside Housing Com.; mem. exec. com. of policy adv. bd. Joint Ctr. for Urban Studies, Harvard-MIT, Cambridge; trustee City of Hope Hosp., Duarte, Calif.; Orange County chmn. United Jewish Welfare Fund, 1982-83; mem. Pres.'s Circle of U. So. Calif.; pres. Orange County Jewish Community Found., 1986-88; chmn. Calif. Mfrs. Housing Inst. Polit Action Com., 1986-92; vice chmn., chmn. devel. Wellness Community of Orange County. With USNR, 1942-46. Recipient Jack E. Wells Meml. award for service to manufactured housing industry, 1976; named to Recreational Vehicle/Manufactured Housing Industry Hall of Fame Elkhart, Ind., 1981; named Man of Yr., City of Hope, 1986. Mem. Nat. Assn. Accts. (past v.p., dir. Los Angeles and Orange County chpt.), Manufactured Housing Inst. (chmn., founding com. Calif. chpt. 1986), Western Manufactured Housing Inst. (vice-chmn.), Trailer Coach Assn., NAM (public affairs com.), Riverside C. of C. Office: Fleetwood Enterprises Inc PO Box 7638 Riverside CA 92513-7638 *Love your family. Love your job. Give all you can for what you wish to achieve. Be a Jonathan Livingston Seagull.*

WEIDEMANN, CELIA JEAN, social scientist, international business and financial development consultant; b. Denver, Dec. 6, 1942; d. John Clement and Hazel (Van Tuyl) Kirlin; m. Wesley Clark Weidemann, July 1, 1972; 1 child, Stephanie Jean. BS, Iowa State U., 1964; MS, U. Wis.-Madison, 1970, PhD, 1973; postgrad. U. So. Calif., 1983. Advisor, UN Food & Agr. Orgn., Ibadan, Nigeria, 1973-77; ind. researcher, Asia and Near East, 1977-78; program coord., asst. prof., rsch. assoc. U. Wis., Madison, 1979-81; chief institutional and human resources U.S. Agy. for Internat. Devel., Washington, 1982-85, team leader, cons., Sumatra, Indonesia, 1984; dir. fed. econs. program Midwest Rsch. Inst., Washington, 1985-86; pres., CEO Weidemann Assocs., Arlington, Va., 1986—; cons. U.S. Congress, Aspen Inst., Ford Found., World Bank, Egypt, Nigeria, Gambia, Pakistan, Indonesia, AID, Thailand, Jamaica, Panama, Philippines, Sierra Leone, Kenya, Jordan, Poland, India, Egypt, Russia, Finnish Internat. Devel. Agy., Namibia, pvt. client, Estonia, Lativa, Russia, Japan, Internat. Ctr. Rsch. on Women, Zaire, UN Food and Agriculture Orgn., Ghana, Internat. Statis. Inst., The Netherlands, Global Exchange, 1986-87, Asian Devel. Bank, Mongolia, Nepal, Vietnam, Bangladesh, Indonesia, Philippines. Author: Planning Home Economics Curriculum for Social and Economic Development, Agricultural Extension for Women Farmers in Africa, 1990, Financial Services for Women, 1992, Egyptian Women and Microenterprise: The Invisible Entrepreneurs, 1992, Small Enterprise Development in Poland: Does Gender Matter?, 1994; contbr. chpts. to books and articles to profl. jours. Am. Home Econs. Assn. fellow, 1969-73 (recipient research grant Ford Found. 1987-89). Mem. Soc. Internat. Devel., Am. Sociol. Assn., U.S. Dirs. of Internat. Agrl. Programs, Assn. for Women in Devel. (pres. 1989, founder, bd. dirs.), Internat. Devel. Conf. (bd. dirs., exec. com.), Am. Home Econs. Assn. (Wis. internat. chmn. 1980-81), Internat. Fedn. Home Econs., Internat. Platform Assn., Pi Lambda Theta, Omicron Nu. Roman Catholic. Avocations: mountain trekking, piano/pipe organ, canoeing, photography, poetry. Home and Office: 2607 24th St N Arlington VA 22207-4908

WEIDEMANN, JULIA CLARK, principal, educator; b. Batavia, N.Y., May 21, 1937; d. Edward Thomas and Grace Eloise (Kenna) Clark; m. Rudolph John Weidemann, July 9, 1960; 1 child, Michael John. BA in English, Daemen Coll., 1958; MS in Edn., SUNY, Buffalo, 1961, MEd in Reading Edn., 1973, postgrad, 1985-86. Cert. sch. adminstr., supr. Tchr Buffalo Pub. Schs., 1958-61, 66-67; remedial reading tchr. West Seneca (N.Y.) Cen. Sch. Dist., 1972-79, coord. chpt. I reading program, 1974-79, reading coord., 1980-87; prin. Parkdale Elem. Sch. East Aurora (N.Y.) Union Free Sch., 1987—; adj. prof. edn. Canisius Coll., Medaille Coll.; tchr. cons. Scott Foresman Lang. Arts Textbooks; chmn. elem. com. staff devel. West Seneca Ctrl. Sch., 1985-87; mem. adv. coun. Medaille Coll.; chmn. various confs.; lectr. in field. Author numerous poems. Mem. West Seneca Dist. Computer Adv. Com., 1980-87, East Aurora Hist. Soc., 1990—; mem. cmty. adv. coun. SUNY, Buffalo, 1994—, Women's Health Initiative, 1994—; Women's Action Coalition of Buffalo, 1994; pres. Roycroft Wordsmiths. Scholar Rosary Hill Coll., 1954, N.Y. State Regents, 1954; recipient Reading award Niagara Frontier Reading Coun., 1986. Mem. AAUW (life, pres. Buffalo br. 1994-95, exec. bd. dirs., named gift ednl. found., state bd. dirs. equity in edn. com. 1995—), Assn. Compensatory Edn. (pres. 1984-85, exec. bd. Region VI 1983-87, conf. chmn. Region VI 1985-87), Internat. Reading Assn. (acting chmn. 3d ea. regional reading conf. 1980), Niagara Frontier Reading Assn. (pres. 1979-80, fin. com. chmn., bd. dirs. 1973—), Daemen Coll. Alumni Assn. (bd. govs. 1987, chmn. alumni reunion weekend, chmn. sr. reception, Disting. Alumna 1989), Assn. Supervision and Devel., Assn. Tchr. Educators, Delta Kappa Gamma (pres., Ruth Fraser scholar 1986), Beta Zeta (pres.), Phi Delta Kappa (Buffalo-South chpt. 1989). Democrat. Roman Catholic. Home: 50 Boxwood Cir Hamburg NY 14075-4212 Office: Parkdale Elem Sch 80 Parkdale Ave East Aurora NY 14052-1615

WEIDEMEYER, CARLETON LLOYD, lawyer; b. Hebbville, Md., June 12, 1933. BA in Polit. Sci., U. Md., 1958; JD, Stetson U., 1961. Bar: Fla. 1961, D.C. 1971, U.S. Dist. Ct. (mid. dist.) Fla. 1963, U.S. Ct. Appeals (5th cir.) 1967, U.S. Ct. Appeals (D.C. cir.) 1976, U.S. Supreme Ct. 1966, U.S. Ct. Appeals (11th cir.) 1982. Research asst. Fla. 2d Dist Ct. Appeals, 1961-65; ptnr. Kalle and Weidemeyer, St. Petersburg, Fla., 1965-68; asst. pub. defender 6th Jud. Cir., Fla., 1966-69, 81-83; ptnr. Wightman, Weidemeyer, Jones, Turnbull and Cobb, Clearwater, Fla., 1968-82; pres. Carleton L. Weidemeyer, P.A. Law Office, 1982—; guest lectr., Stetson U., 1978-80; lectr. estate planning seminars; bd. dirs. 1st Nat. Bank and Trust Co., 1974-78, Fla. Bank of Commerce, 1973-77. Author: (handbook) Arbitration of Entertainment Claims, Baltimore County's Second District, The Emerging Thirties, 1990, Area History, Baltimore County, 1990; editor: Ad Lib mag., 1978-81; contbr. numerous articles to profl. jours. & geneal. pubs.; performer This Is Your Navy Radio Show, Memphis, 1951-52; leader Polka Dots, The Jazz Notes, 1976—; mem. St. Paul Ch. Orch., Fla. Hist. Soc., 1973—, Md. Hist. Soc., 1990—; performer Clearwater Jazz Holiday, 1980, 81, co-chmn., 1981. Bd. advisors Musicians Ins. Trust; trustee Francis G. Prasse Meml. Scholarship Trust, 1984—. Served with USN, 1951-54. Mem. SAR, Musicians Assn. Clearwater (pres. 1976-81), Fla.-Ga. Conf. Musicians (sec., treas. 1974-76), NRA, ABA (sr. bar sect.), Fed. Bar Assn., Fla. State Hist. Soc., Greater St. Petersburg Musicians Assn., Clearwater Fla. Bar Assn. (probate divsn.), Am. Fedn. Musicians (internat. law com.; pres. so. conf. musicians 1979-80), Clearwater Genealogy Soc., Md. Geneal. Soc., Pa. Geneal. Soc., Pinellas (Fla.) Geneal. Soc., Balt. County Geneal. Soc., Lancaster (Pa.) Mennonite Hist. Soc., Navy Hurricane Hunters, Sons Union Vets. Civil War, Md. Hist. Soc., Catonsville (Md.) Hist. Soc., Am. Legion, German Am. Geneal. Assn. D.A.V. Fleet Res., Masons, Egypt Temple Shrine, Scottish Rite, Moose, Sertoma (bd. dirs. Clearwater chpt. 1984-86, v.p. 1989—), Phi Delta Phi, Sigma Pi, Kappa Kappa Psi. Home: 2261 Belleair Rd Clearwater FL 34624-2761 Office: 501 S Fort Harrison Ave Clearwater FL 34616

WEIDENAAR, DENNIS JAY, college dean; b. Grand Rapids, Mich., Oct. 4, 1936; s. John and Jennie (Beukema) W.; m. Kristin Andrews, July 14, 1963; children: Kaarin Jaye, John Andrews. AB, Calvin Coll., Grand Rapids, 1958; MA, U. Chgo., 1961; PhD, Purdue U., W. Lafayette, 1969. Asst. prof. of econs.. Purdue U., West Lafayette, 1966-72, assoc. prof. of econ., 1972-77, prof. of econ., 1977—; interim dean Krannert Sch. of Mgmt., West Lafayette, 1983-84, assoc. dean, 1984—; dean Krannert Grad. Sch. Mgmt., West Lafayette, Ind., 1990—; cons. TRW, B.F. Goodrich, Ea. Panhandle. Author: Economics. Contbr. articles to profl. jours. Bd. dirs. Ind. Coun. on Econ. Edn., Lafayette, 1974-83, St. Elizabeth Hosp., Lafayette, Greater Lafayette Comty. Found., Lafayette Ins. Co. Recipient The Leavey Awd for Excellence in Pvt. Enterprise Edn., Freedom's Found., Valley Forge, 1983, Distinguished Service Awd., Joint Council on Econ. Edn., N.Y., 1986, Golden Key Nat. Honor Soc., 1985. Mem. Rotary, Delta Sigma Pi, Beta Gamma Sigma (bd. dirs. 1996—), Phi Delta Kappa. Presbyterian. Home: 3703 Moss Hill Dr West Lafayette IN 47906-8885 Office: Purdue U Krannert Sch Mgmt West Lafayette IN 47907

WEIDENBAUM, MURRAY LEW, economics educator; b. Bronx, N.Y., Feb. 10, 1927; s. David and Rose (Warshaw) W.; m. Phyllis Green, June 13, 1954; children: Susan, James, Laurie. BBA, CCNY, 1948; MA, Columbia U., 1949; MPA, Princeton U., 1954, PhD, 1958; LLD, Baruch Coll., 1981, U. Evansville, 1983, McKendree Coll., 1993. chmn. rsch. adv. com. St. Louis Regional Indsl. Devel. Corp., 1965-69; exec. sec. Pres.'s Com. on Econ. Impact of Def. and Disarmament, 1964; mem. U.S. Fin. Investment Adv. Panel, 1970-72; cons. various firms and instns. Fiscal economist Bur. Budget, Washington, 1949-57; corp. economist Boeing Co., Seattle, 1958-62; sr. economist Stanford Rsch. Inst., Palo Alto, Calif., 1962-63; mem. faculty Washington U., St. Louis, 1964—, prof., chmn. dept. econs., 1966-69, Mallinckrodt prof., 1971—; dir. Ctr. for Study Am. Bus. Ctr. for Study Am. Bus., St. Louis, 1974-81, 82-95; chmn. Ctr. for Study Am. Bus. Washgnton U., St. Louis, 1995—; asst. sec. econ. policy Treasury Dept., 1969-71; chmn. Coun. of Econ. Advs., 1981-82. Author: Federal Budgeting, 1964, Modern Public Sector, 1969, Economics of Peacetime Defense, 1974, Economic Impact of the Vietnam War, 1967, Government-Mandated Price Increases, 1975, Business, Government, and the Public, 1990, The Future of Business Regulation, 1980, Rendezvous With Reality: The American Economy After Reagan, 1988, paperback edit., 1990, Small Wars, Big Defense, 1992, Business and Government in the Global Marketplace, 1995, The Bamboo Network, 1996; mem. editl. bd. Publius, 1971—, Jour. Econ. Issues, 1972-75, Challenge, 1974-81, 83—. With AUS, 1945. Recipient Alexander Hamilton medal U.S. Dept. Treasury, 1971, Disting. Writer award Georgetown U., award for disting. teaching Freedoms Found., 1980, award for best book in econs. Assn. Am. Pubs., 1992; named to Free Market Hall of Fame, 1983; Banbury fellow Princeton U., 1954. Fellow AIAA, Nat. Assn. Bus. Economists, City Coll. Alumni Assn. (Townsend Harris medal 1969), Assn. for Pvt. Enterprise Edn. (Adam Smith award 1986), Cosmos Club. Office: Washington Univ Ctr for Study Am Bus 1 Brookings Dr Saint Louis MO 63130-4899

WEIDENFELD, EDWARD LEE, lawyer; b. Akron, Ohio, July 15, 1943; s. Sam and Beatrice (Cooper) W.; m. Sheila Rabb, Aug. 11, 1968; children: Nicholas, Daniel. BS, U. Wis., 1965; JD, Columbia U., 1968. Bar: N.Y. 1968, U.S. Supreme Ct. 1972, D.C. 1973. Pvt. practice N.Y.C., 1969-71, 73-82, Washington, 1982—; counsel, dir. energy staff Com. on Interior and Insular Affairs, U.S. Ho. of Reps., 1971-73; mem. faculty Am. Law Inst.-Am. Bar Assn. Continuing Legal Edn. Programs; mem. Internat. del. to observe Philippine Election, 1986, internat. del. to observe Republic Korea Election, 1987, Pakistan Election, 1988, Chilean Election, 1989; lectr. to profl. groups; spl. cons. N.Y.C. Dept. Bldgs., 1967. Editor in chief Atomic Energy Law Jour., 1975-76. Mem. Pres.'s Commn. on White House Fellowships, 1977; nat. chmn. Lawyers for Reagan/Bush, 1980; chief dep. counsel Reagan/Bush Campaign, 1980; chmn. Reagan/Bush '84 Legal Adv. Bd., 1984; mem. D.C. Rep. Com., 1984-92, vice chmn., 1984-88; mem. Coun. Adminstrv. Conf. of U.S., 1981-92, sr. fellow, 1992-95; trustee Danny Kaye and Sylvia Fine Kaye Found. Mem. ABA, D.C. Bar Assn., Fed. Communications Bar Assn., Internat. Bar Assn., Am. Law Inst., Assn. Bar City N.Y., Internat. Human Rights Law Group (vice chmn. bd. dirs.). Club: Met. (Washington). Home: 3059 Q St NW Washington DC 20007-3081

WEIDENFELD, SHEILA RABB, television producer, author; b. Cambridge, Mass., Sept. 7, 1943; d. Maxwell M. and Ruth (Cryden) Rabb; BA, Brandeis U., 1965; m. Edward L. Weidenfeld, Aug. 11, 1968; children: Nicholas Rabb, Daniel Rabb. Assoc. producer Metromedia, Inc., WNEW-TV, N.Y.C., 1965-68; talent coord. That Show with Joan Rivers, NBC, N.Y.C., 1968-71; coord. NBC network game programs, N.Y.C., 1968-71; producer Metromedia, Inc., WTTG-TV, Washington, 1971-73; creator/producer Take It From Here, NBC (WRC-TV), Washington, 1973-74; press sec. to first lady Betty Ford and spl. asst. to Pres. Gerald R. Ford 1974-77; mem. Pres.'s Adv. Commn. on Historic Preservation, 1977-81; TV producer, moderator On the Record, NBC-TV, WRC-TV, Washington, 1978-79; pres. D.C. Prodns., Ltd., 1978; producer, host Your Personal Decorator, 1987; mem. Sec. State's Adv. Commn. on Fgn. Service Inst., 1972-74; founding mem. Project Censured Panel of Judges, 1976—. Author: First Lady's Lady, 1979. Mem. U.S. Holocaust Meml. Council, 1987—; corporator, Dana Hall Sch., Wellesley, Mass; bd. dirs. Wolf Trap Found., Women's Campaign Fund, 1978-79; bd. dirs. D.C. Contemporary Dance Theatre, 1986-88, D.C. Rep. Cen. Com., 1984—, D.C. Preservation League, 1987-90; chmn. C&O Canal Nat. Hist. Park Commn, 1988—; bd. dirs. Am. Univ. Rome, 1988—. Recipient awards for outstanding achievement in the media AAUW, 1973, 74, Silver Screen award A Campaign to Remember for the U.S. Holocaust Meml. Coun., 1989, Bronze medal Internat. Film and Video Festival N.Y., 1990; named hon. consul gen. of Republic of San Marino to Washington; knighted by Order of St. Agatha, Republic of San Marino, 1986. Mem. NATAS (Emmy award 1972), Washington Press Club, Am. Newspaper Women's Club, Am. Women in Radio and TV, Cosmos Club, Consular Corps, Sigma Delta Chi. Home and Office: 3059 Q St NW Washington DC 20007-3081

WEIDENFELLER, GERALDINE CARNEY, speech and language pathologist; b. Kearny, N.J., Oct. 12, 1933; d. Joseph Gerald and Catherine Grace (Doyle) Carney; BS, Newark State U., 1954; postgrad. Northwestern U., summer 1956, U. Wis., summer 1960; MA, NYU, 1962; m. James Weidenfeller, Apr. 4, 1964; children: Anne, David. Lic speech/language pathologist, N.J. Speech pathologist Kearny (N.J.) Public Schs., 1954-61, North Brunswick (N.J.) Public Schs., 1961-65, Bridgewater (N.J.) Public Schs., 1969-72; speech therapist Somerset County Ednl. Commn., 1983-88; real estate agt., N.J., 1982-89; pvt. practice speech therapy, Somerville, N.J., 1980-92; speech therapist no. br. Midland Sch., 1989, No. Plainfield, N.J., 1989-90. V.p. Rosary Soc., Hillsborough, N.J., 1986—; Rep. county com. woman, 1989-90, 91—; chmn. fedn. of Rep. women program com., Somerset, program chmn., scholarship chmn. 1991—; dancer Hillsborough Rockettes, 1994—; tudor Literacy Vol. of Am., 1993-96; storyteller Cath. Charities, 1992-93. Mem. Am. Speech and Hearing Assn., N.J. Speech and Hearing Assn. Roman Catholic. Club: Toastmasters (winner dist. humorous speech contest 1984, sec. 1985, advanced Toastmaster 1986). Home: 3 Banor Dr Somerville NJ 08876-4501

WEIDENSAUL, THOMAS CRAIG, university administrator, researcher; b. Reedsville, Pa., Apr. 4, 1939; s. Thomson Becker and Grace Elizabeth (Kendig) W.; married, June 12, 1965; children: T. Luke, Susan E., Daniel J. BA in Biology, Gettysburg Coll., 1962; MF in Forest Mgmt. and Forest Pathology, Duke U., 1963; PhD in Plant Pathology, Pa. State U., 1969. Plant pathologist forests and forest products USDA U.S. Forest Svc., Harrisonburg, Va., 1963-66; grad. asst. dept. plant pathology Pa. State U., University Park, 1966-69; head lab. for environ. studies, asst. prof. plant pathology and forestry Ohio Agrl. Rsch. and Devel. Ctr., Lab. For Environ. Studies, Wooster, 1970; assoc. prof. Ohio State U., Ohio Agrl. Rsch. and Devel. Ctr., Lab. For Environ. Studies, 1973-79, prof., 1979-95, asst. dir. experiment sta., 1986-87, asst. dir. sch. natural resources, 1990-95; ret., 1995, Christmas tree grower, forestry cons., 1995—; mem. NAS panel on sulfur oxides. Contbr. articles to profl. publs. Chmn. environ. quality task force Ohio Agrl. Rsch. and Devel. Ctr., mem. exec., 1973—, mem. stats. adv. com., 1976-87, mem. adminstrv. and program rev. panel for rsch. and extension analytical lab., 1988, mem. adminstrv. cabinet, 1986—, mem. steering com. centennial open house, 1982, chmn. task force on global change rsch., 1990; mem. steering com. Nat. Air Pollution Workshop, 1974-76. With USAR, 1963-69. Recipient Ohio League Sportsmen and Nat. Wildlife Fedn. Gov's. award, 1980; Pa. State Senatorial scholar, 1957-58, Duke U. scholar, 1962-63, Pa. State U. post doctoral, 1969-70. Fellow NASA; mem. Am. Phytopathological Soc. (air pollution damage to crops com. 1973-75, 77-81, 83-86, vice chmn. environ. quality com. 1974, environ. quality and plant health com. 1989-90, 91—), Am. Soc. Agronomy, Pa. Christmas Tree Growers Assn., Am. Phytopath. Soc., Soc. Am. Foresters, Soil Sci. Soc. Am., Ohio Acad. Sci., Phi Kappa Phi, Sigma Xi, Phi Sigma, Phi Epsilon Phi. Achievements include research in effects of gaseous and metallic pollutants on microorganisms and higher plants, sources and effects of atmospheric deposition, predisposing and/or protecting capabilities of gaseous, acidic and metallic materials re infectious plant diseases, epidemiology and etiology of forest and shade tree diseases, uses and effects of municipal sewage sludge on soils, plant growth and nutrient availability, control of plant diseases: silvicultural and/or horticultural, chemical and resistance, sustaining and enhancing income to sugar maple sap producers through identifying, modeling, and managing risks associated with maple stresses and subsequent tree decline, idenfitication and assessment of air pollution injury and damage to plants, chirstmas tree production and forest pathology extension, determination of presence of stable pollutants in soils, water and plant and animal tissues. Home: RR # 1 Box 521-B Centre Hall PA 16828

WEIDENTHAL, MAURICE DAVID (BUD WEIDENTHAL), educational administrator, journalist; b. Cleve., Nov. 26, 1925; s. William and Evelyn (Kolinsky) W.; m. Grace Schwartz, Apr. 14, 1957; 1 child, Susan Elizabeth Weidenthal Saltzman. B.A., U. Mich., 1950. Mem. staff Cleve. Press, 1950-81, editorial writer, 1950-51, asst. city editor, 1956-58, edn. editor, 1958-81; v.p. public affairs Cuyahoga Community Coll. Dist., Cleve., 1981-88; dir. Urban Colls. Project RC 2000, Tempe, Ariz., 1989—. Editor The Urban Report. Mem. pub. affairs com. Greater Cleve. Growth Assn., 1981-88; mem. bd. advisors Coun. for Advancement and Support of Edn., 1981-88, Nat. Coun. Mktg. and Pub. Rels., 1981—; alt. bd. dirs. St. Vincent Quadrangle, 1983-88; trustee Hebrew Free Loan Assn., 1975-86; mem. philanthropic adv. com. Jewish Community Fedn. Served with AUS, 1944-45. Decorated Air medal. Mem. Edn. Writers Assn., Soc. Profl. Journalists, Edn. Press Assn., Cleve. City Club (bd. dirs. 1969-76), Cleve. Press Club. Home: 25858 Fairmount Blvd Cleveland OH 44122-2214 Office: 4250 Richmond Rd Cleveland OH 44122-6104

WEIDER, JOSEPH, wholesale distribution executive. Chmn. bd., treas. Weider Health and Fitness, Woodland Hills, Calif.; Mem. chmn. bd. Weider

Health and Fitness, Great Am. Foods. Office: Men's Fitness 21100 Erwin St Woodland Hills CA 91367-3712*

WEIDERHOLZ, CONRAD, magazine publisher. Pub. First for Women mag., Englewood Cliffs, N.J. Office: First for Women Bauer Pub Co 270 Sylvan Ave Englewood Cliffs NJ 07632*

WEIDLINGER, PAUL, civil engineer; b. Budapest, Hungary, Dec. 22, 1914; came to U.S., 1944; s. Andrew and Juliete W.; m. Solveig Hojberg, Dec. 24, 1964; children—Thomas, Pauline, Jonathan. B.S., Tech. Inst., Brno, Czechoslovakia, 1934; M.S., Swiss Poly. Inst., Zurich, 1937. Registered profl. engr. 17 states. Chief engr. Atlas Aircraft Products, N.Y.C., 1944-46; chief tech. cons., dir. Nat. Housing Agy., Industrialization Program Div., Washington, 1946-47; dir. engring. div. United Indsl. Assocs., Washington, 1947-48; sr. ptnr. Weidlinger Assocs., cons. engrs., N.Y.C., 1948—; mem. seismic loads com. Am. Nat. Standards Inst., 1978-80; chmn. Nat. Acad. Scis. Evaluation Panel, Nat. Bur. Standards, 1978-80; mem. sci. adv. bd. to chief staff USAF, 1957-58; vis. lectr. Harvard U., 1955-64, MIT, 1952-64. Author: Aluminum in Modern Architecture, Vol. II, 1956; contbr. papers to profl. jours. Recipient award Engring. News-Record, 1966. Fellow ASCE (Ernest E. Howard award, Moisseiff award 1975, J. James R. Cross medal 1963), Franklin Inst. (Frank P. Brown medal 1987); mem. AIAA, Am. Concrete Inst., Nat. Acad. Engring., Earthquake Engring. Rsch. Inst., Internat. Assn. Bridge and Structural Engrs., N.Y. Acad. Scis., Nat. Bldg. Mus. (bd. dirs. 1982-88). Office: Weidlinger Assocs 333 7th Ave New York NY 10001-5004

WEIDMAN, ANNA KATHRYN, publishing company financial executive; b. Redwood City, Calif., July 6, 1962; d. Ronald Frank and Jane (Cotton) W.; m. Charles Shaw Robinson, Nov. 1, 1993. BA, U. Calif., Berkeley, 1984, MBA, 1992. Asst. to dir. U. Calif. Press, Berkeley, 1985-91, exhibits/sales mgr., 1991-93, CFO, 1993—; bd. dirs. Mercury House Pubs.; ind. cons., Berkeley, 1991-93; treas., bd. dirs. Assocs. of U. Calif. Press, Berkeley, 1992—. Mem. vestry, bd. dirs. St. Mark's Episcopal Ch., Berkeley, 1993-95. Democrat. Avocations: theatre, reading, cross-country skiing. Office: U Calif Press 2120 Berkeley Way Berkeley CA 94720

WEIDMAN, HAZEL HITSON, anthropologist, educator; b. Taft, Calif., Aug. 3, 1923; d. Frederick Dhu and Estell M. (Griesemer) Hitson; m. William H. Weidman, Sept. 9, 1960; children: William, Charles. B.S. in Social Anthropology, Northwestern U., 1951; A.M. (Thomas Dana Scholar in Social Anthropology), Radcliffe Coll., 1957; USPHS fellow, Burma, 1957-59; PhD, Radcliffe Coll., 1959. Staff anthropologist Mass. Dept. of Pub. Health, Boston, 1959-60; cons. social sci. USPHS, Washington, 1960, Calif. Dept. Pub. Health, 1964; asst. prof. sociology and anthropology Coll. of William and Mary, Williamsburg, Va., 1964-65; asst. prof. social anthropology dept. psychiatry U. Ala. Med. Center, Birmingham, 1965-67; asso. research fellow Social Sci. Research Inst., U. Hawaii, Honolulu, 1967-68; assoc. prof. social anthropology dept. psychiatry U. Miami Sch. Medicine, Miami, 1968-72; prof. U. Miami Sch. Medicine, 1972-89, prof. emerita, 1989—, staff anthropologist and sr. social scientist, 1979-81, dir. Office Transcultural Edn. and Research, 1981-89, ret., 1990; assoc. prof. dept. anthropology U. Miami, Coral Gables, 1968-72, prof., 1972-77; Cons. social sci. U. Ala. Hosps. and Clinics, Birmingham, 1965-67; cons. social anthropology Nat. Center for Health Services Research and Devel., 1970-71; social sci. cons. Am. Found. Blind, 1973-76; cons. to Miccosukee Indian tribe and sec. higher edn. exec. com. Miccosukee Corp., 1978-82; mental health research edn. rev. com. NIMH, 1980-84; mem. vis. com. So. Assn. Colls. and Schs., 1980; mem. med. adv. bd. Ednl. Film Prodn., Riverside, Calif., 1969-72; dir. programs in cross-cultural tng. health profls., 1981-89. Founding editor: Med. Anthropology Newsletter, 1968-71; Contbr. articles and book revs. on social anthropology to profl. jours.; contbr. book chpts. on social anthropology. Mem. nat. adv. com. for cross-cultural demonstration project, Epilepsy Found. Am., 1985-89; mem. nat. adv. council Transcultural Nursing Rsch. Inst. U. Miami, 1986-89. Am. Philos. Soc. research grantee, 1965; Commonwealth Fund research grantee, 1971-73; Continuation grantee, 1973-75; State of Fla. Community Hosp. Edn. Council research and tng. grantee, 1979-81. Fellow Soc. Applied Anthropology, Am. Anthrop. Assn. (chmn. steering com. group for med. anthropology 1967-69, mem. com. on membership 1968-70, chmn. organizing com. group for med. anthropology 1969-70); mem. So. Anthrop. Soc., Assn. for Behavioral Scis. and Med. Edn., Soc. for Med. Anthropology, Council on Anthropology and Edn., Soc. Anthropology of Visual Communication, Soc. Psychol. Anthropology (mem. bd. dirs. 1979-81), Assn. Anthropology and Gerontology, World Fedn. Mental Health, World Future Soc., Phi Beta Kappa. Home: 58 Park St Camden ME 04843-2012

WEIDMAN, JEROME, author; b. N.Y.C., Apr. 4, 1913; s. Joseph and Annie (Falkovitz) W.; m. Peggy Wright, 1943; children: Jeffrey, John Whitney. Ed., CCNY, 1930-33, Washington Sq. Coll., N.Y.C., 1933-34, N.Y.U. Law Sch., 1934-37. Author: (novel) I Can Get It for You Wholesale, 1937, (novel) What's in It for Me?, 1938; (short stories) The Horse that Could Whistle Dixie, 1939; (travel) Letter of Credit, 1940; (novel) I'll Never Go There Any More, 1941, (novel) The Lights Around the Shore, 1943, (novel) Too Early To Tell, 1946; (short stories) The Captain's Tiger, 1947; (novel) The Price is Right, 1949, (novel) The Hand of the Hunter, 1951, (novel) The Third Angel, 1953; (essays) Traveler's Cheque, 1954; (novel) Give Me Your Love, 1954, (novel) Your Daughter, Iris, 1955; (short stories) A Dime A Throw, 1957; (novel) The Enemy Camp, 1958; (play) Fiorello!, 1959; (novel) Before You Go, 1960; (play) Tenderloin, 1961; (short stories) My Father Sits In The Dark, 1961; (novel) The Sound of Bow Bells, 1962; (play) I Can Get It For You Wholesale, 1962; (essays) Back Talk, 1963; (short stories) Nine Stories, 1964; (novel) Word Of Mouth, 1964; (short stories) The Death of Dickie Draper, 1965; (novel) Other People's Money, 1968; (novel) The Center of The Action, 1969; (play) Ivory Tower, 1969, (play) Asterisk, 1969; (novel) Fourth Street East, 1971, (novel) Last Respects, 1972, (novel) Tiffany Street, 1974, (novel) The Temple, 1976, (novel) A Family Fortune, 1978; (novel) Counsellors-at-Law, 1980, (autobiography) Praying For Rain, 1986. Co-recipient Pulitizer prize in drama for play Fiorello!, 1960; recipient Antoinette Perry award, N.Y. Drama Critics Circle award. Mem. Authors League Am. (pres. 1969-74). Home: 1230 Park Ave New York NY 10128-1724

WEIDMAN, JOHN CARL, II, education educator, consultant; b. Ephrata, Pa., Oct. 3, 1945; s. John Carl and Mary Elizabeth (Grube) W.; m. Carla Sue Fassnacht, Aug. 20, 1967; children: Jonathan Scott, Rebecca Mary. AB in Sociology cum laude, Princeton U., 1967; AM, U. Chgo., 1968, PhD, 1974. Acting asst. prof. edn. U. Minn., Mpls., 1970-74, asst. prof. edn., sociology and Am. studies, 1974-77; sr. rsch. assoc. Bur. Social Sci. Rsch., Inc., Washington, 1977-78; assoc. prof. edn. and sociology U. Pitts., 1979-86, prof. edn. and sociology, 1986—, chmn. dept. adminstrv. and policy studies, 1986-93; cons. Nat. Ctr. Adminstrv. Justice, Youthwork, Inc., Upper Midwest Tri-Racial Gen. Assistance Ctr., Acad. for Ednl. Devel., Asian Devel. Bank; UNESCO chair higher edn. rsch. Maseno U. Coll., Kenya, 1993. Mem. editl. bd. Rev. of Higher Edn., 1984-88, Am. Ednl. Rsch. Jour., 1991-92; cons. editor Jour. Higher Edn., 1989—; contbr. chpts. to books, articles to profl. jours. Bd. dirs. Sch. Vol. Assn. Pitts., 1982-90, pres., 1984-87. Grantee, U.S. Office Edn., 1971-73, Spencer Found., 1973-76, Nat. Inst. Edn., 1976-79, NEH, 1985-86; Fulbright scholar U. Augsburg, Germany, 1986-87. Mem. Am. Ednl. Rsch. Assn. (sec. postsecondary divsn. 1987-89), Am. Sociol. Assn., Assn. Study of Higher Edn., Comparative and Internat. Edn. Soc. Office: U Pitts 5S01 Forbes Quadrangle 230 S Bouquet St Pittsburgh PA 15260

WEIDNER, DONALD J., geophysicist educator; b. Dayton, Ohio, Apr. 26, 1945; s. Virgil Raymond and Aletha Winifred Weidner; m. Deborah Mary Ray, April 13, 1968; children: Raymond V., Jennifer L. AB in Physics cum laude, Harvard, 1967; PhD in Geophysics, Mass. Inst. Tech., 1972. Asst prof. SUNY, Stony Brook, N.Y., 1972-77, assoc. prof., 1977-82, prof. geophysics, 1982—; dir. Mineral Physics Inst., SUNY, 1988—, Ctr. for High Pressure Rsch, SUNY, 1991—. Am. Geophysical Union fellow, 1981; recipient James B. Macelwane award Am. Geophysical Union, 1981. Achievements include building (with others) the high pressure facility at Stony Brook SUNY; large volume high pressure studies with synchrotron radiation; determining the equation of state of earth materials; phase stability fields of minerals and has pioneered the use of this system to determine the yield strength of these materials; design team leader for the large volume experiments that the GeoCars program is preparing for the Advanced Photon Source. Office: SUNY Sci & Tech Ctr High Pressure Rsch Dept Earth & Space Scis Stony Brook NY 11794

WEIDNER, EDWARD WILLIAM, university chancellor, political scientist; b. Mpls., July 7, 1921; s. Peter Clifford and Lillian (Halbe) W.; m. Jean Elizabeth Blomquist, Mar. 23, 1944; children: Nancy Louise, Gary Richard, Karen, William. BA magna cum laude, U. Minn., 1942, MA, 1943, PhD, 1946; postgrad., U. Wis., 1943-45; LHD (hon.), No. Mich. U., 1969; PhD (hon.), Linköping U., Sweden, 1975. Staff mem. Nat. Mcpl. League, 1944, research assoc., 1944-45; cons. govts. div. U.S. Bur. Census, 1945; statistician U.S. Bur. Census, Washington, 1946; lectr. U. Wis., Madison, 1945; instr. U. Minn., Mpls., 1945-47, asst. prof., 1947-49, asst. dir. research in inter-govtl. relations, 1946-53; asst. prof. UCLA, 1949-50; faculty Mich. State U., East Lansing, 1950-62, from assoc. prof., dir. govtl. research bur., to prof. polit. sci., 1952-62, chmn. polit. sci. dept., 1952-57; coordinator, chief adviser Vietnam Project, 1955-57; dir. Inst. Research on Overseas Programs, 1957-61; vice chancellor E.W. Ctr., 1962-65; prof. polit. sci., dir. ctr. for devel. change U. Ky., Lexington, 1965-67; chancellor U. Wis., Green Bay, 1966-86, prof. polit. sci., 1966-89, chancellor emeritus, prof. emeritus, 1989—, dir. Cofrin Arboretum, 1986-89; project dir. Edward W. Weidner Ctr. for Performing Arts, U. Wis., Green Gay, 1987-92; bd. dirs. Univ. Bank, Green Bay; cons. Fgn. Ops. Adminstrn., Vietnam, 1954-55, Baltimore County (Md.) Reorgn. Commn., 1953-54, Ford Found., Pakistan, 1956, Nat. Assn. Fgn. Student Advisers, 1959-60, Pres.'s Task Force Fgn. Econ. Assistance, 1961, Dept. State, 1962-63, AID, 1964-65, Lees Coll., 1971-72, Mcpl. Clks. Edn. Found., 1992—; mem. Gov. Mich. Commn. Inter-Govtl. Rels., 1954-55, UN Univ. Coun., 1974-80. Author: (with William Anderson) American Government, 1951, State and Local Government, 1951, (with others) The International Programs of American Universities, 1958, Intergovernmental Relations as Seen by Public Officials, 1960, (with William Anderson, Clara Penniman) Government for the Fifty States, 1960, The World Role of Universities, 1962, Technical Assistance in Public Administration Overseas, 1964; editor: Development Administration in Asia, 1970. Mem. Wis. Gov.'s Commn. on UN, 1975-81; trustee Prairie Sch., 1969-91, mem. adv. bd., 1991—; bd. dirs. Inst. for Shipboard Edn., 1976-89, Lab. Ornithology, Cornell U.; chmn. adv. bd. Lakeland chpt. ARC, 1981-84; mem. N.Am. adv. group UN Environ. Programme, 1983-90; bd. advisers Nature Conservancy Wis., 1984-91; bd. dirs. Heritage Hill Found., 1987-92, 95—, pres. 1991-92; bd. dirs. Family Svc. Assn., 1988-93; chmn. Brown County Cultural Coun., 1991-94; mem. nat. coun. ASPA, 1947-50; mem. internat. coun. UN U., 1974-80; bd. dirs. Am. Coun. on Edn., 1971-74, sec. bd., 1971-72; mem. nat. coun. Am. Polit. Assn., 1950-52. Recipient Outstanding Achievement award U. Minn., 1975. Mem. Assn. Am. Colls. (bd. dirs. 1978-80), Internat. Assn. Mcpl. Clks. Found., Nature Conservancy, Audubon Soc., Am. Birding Assn., Phi Beta Kappa, Pi Sigma Alpha. Home: 5953 N Shore Acres New Franken WI 54229-9443

WEIDNER, RICHARD TILGHMAN, physicist, educator; b. Allentown, Pa., Mar. 31, 1921; s. Miles Percival and Mabel (Aichroth) W.; m. Jean Elizabeth Fritsch, June 28, 1947 (dec. 1995); children: Christopher, Allegra, Timothy. B.S. summa cum laude, Muhlenberg Coll., 1943; M.S., Yale U., 1943, Ph.D., 1948. Instr. physics Yale U., 1943-44; instr. Rutgers U., 1947-48, asst. prof., 1948-53, assoc. prof., 1953-63, prof. physics, 1963-88, prof. emeritus, 1988—; asst. dean Rutgers Coll., 1966-69, assoc. dean, 1969-77, acting dean, 1977-78; physicist U.S. Naval Research Lab., Washington, 1944-46. Author: (with R.L. Sells) Elementary Modern Physics, 3rd edit., 1980, Elementary Classical Physics, 2d edit., 1973, Elementary Physics, Classical and Modern, 1975, (with H.Y. Carr) Physics from the Ground Up, 1971, Physics, 1985, rev. edit., 1988 (transls. in German, Spanish, Vietnamese); also articles in field; contbr. Physics sect. Ency. Britannica, 15th edit., 1974; assoc. editor Jour. Internat. Trumpet Guild, 1984-96. Mem. Bd. Edn. Bridgewater Twp., N.J., 1957-63. Lt. (j.g.) USNR, 1944-45. Recipient Alumni Achievement award Muhlenberg Coll., 1994; Lindback award Rutgers U., 1984. Fellow Am. Phys. Soc.; mem. Internat. Trumpet Guild, Sigma Xi. Lutheran. Home: 1426 Calypso Ave Bethlehem PA 18018-4740 Office: 56 W Market St Bethlehem PA 18018-5734

WEIDNER, ROSWELL THEODORE, artist; b. Reading, Pa., Sept. 18, 1911; s. Harry and Amelia (Hughes) W.; m. Marilyn Kemp, Dec. 1, 1957; children: Roslyn, Janice. Student, Pa. Acad. Fine Arts, 1930-35, Barnes Found., 1933-35. sr. instr. Pa. Acad. Fine Arts, 1938-96, Dawson Metal, 1965, 72. One-man shows include Pa. Acad. Fine Arts, 1940, 60, 65, Reading Mus., 1961, William Penn Meml. Mus., Harrisburg, Pa., 1966, McCleaf Gallery, Phila., 1970, Newman Galleries, Phila., 1978, 87, Marion Locks Gallery, 1981, So. Alleghenies Mus. Art, Loretto, Pa., 1991, F.A.N. Gallery, Phila., 1995; represented in permanent collections Pa. Acad. Fine Arts, Phila. Mus. Art, Met. Mus. Art, Libr. Congress, U. Pa., Conn. State Libr., Hahnemann Hosp., Phila., Temple U., Phila. Maritime Mus., Free Libr. Phila., Smith Kline, Berwin Corp., Price Waterhouse, Nat. Assn. Broadcasters, Washington, Bell Atlantic Corp., Phila., Dauphin Deposit Bank and Trust Co., Harrisburg, Phila. Conv. Ctr.; work represented by Art Communication Internat., Phila.; contbr. articles to profl. jours. Cresson Fgn. Travelling scholar, 1935-36; recipient Percy Owens award, 1975. Fellow Pa. Acad. Fine Arts (pres. 1955-70).

WEIERSTALL, RICHARD PAUL, pharmaceutical chemist; b. Jersey City, N.J., Nov. 5, 1942; s. William August and Emily Lois (Haughey) W.; m. Gail Janet Thomsen, Aug. 17, 1968; children: Eric, Kurt, Karen. BS, Rutgers U., 1966, MS, 1969; PhD, U. Calif., San Francisco, 1973. Unit head drug metabolism Sandoz Pharm., East Hanover, N.J., 1973-74; dir. tech. svc. Banner Gelatin Products, Chatsworth, Calif., 1974-76; v.p. tech. svc. Banner Gelatin Prod., Chatsworth, Calif., 1976-81; dir. pharm. sci. Ayerst Labs Inc., Rouses Point, N.Y., 1981-87; asst. v.p. Wyeth Ayerst Rsch., Rouses Point, 1987—. Mem. Am. Assn. Pharm. Sci., Am. Pharm. Assn. Home: 7 Stewart St Rouses Point NY 12979-1511

WEIGAND, JAMES GARY, utility company executive, former military officer; b. Sheridan, Wyo., Aug. 11, 1935; s. Harold Frederick and Maribel (Ragan) W.; m. Mary Alice Moosey, Apr. 21, 1962; children: Janet, Gretchen, Caroline. BS, U.S. Naval Acad., 1958; MS, U. Wash., Seattle, 1962, PhD, 1964. Commd. ensign USN, 1958, advanced through grades to comdr., 1973, nuclear submarine officer, served in Vietnam; ret., 1978; asst. to chmn. Gulf States Utitlites Co., Beaumont, Tex., 1978-79, v.p., 1979-86; pres., chief exec. officer Vt. Yankee Nuclear Power Co., Brattleboro, 1986—, also bd. dirs.; bd. dirs. Seyton Inc., Tacoma. Trustee BMH Inc. Mem. Assoc. Industries Vt. (bd. dirs. 1987—), Am. Nuclear Soc. (regional v.p. 1982-83). Episcopalian. Avocation: tennis. Office: Vt Yankee Nuclear Power Corp Ferry Rd Brattleboro VT 05301

WEIGAND, WILLIAM KEITH, bishop; b. Bend, Oreg., May 23, 1937. Ed., Mt. Angel Sem., St. Benedict, Oreg., St. Edward's Sem. and St. Thomas Sem., Kenmore, Wash. Bishop Diocese Salt Lake City, 1980—; Ordained priest Roman Cath. Ch., 1963. Office: See of Sacramento 2110 Broadway Sacramento CA 95851-2541*

WEIGEL, GEORGE S., JR., think tank executive; m. Joan Weigel; 3 children. Student, St. Mary's Seminary, Balt., U. St. Michael's Coll., Toronto, Can. Asst. prof. theology, from asst. to dean of studies St. Thomas Sem. Sch. of Theology, Kenmore, 1975-77; scholar-in-residence World Without War Coun. Greater Seattle, 1977-84; founding pres. James Madison Found., 1986-89; pres. Ethics and Pub. Policy Ctr., Washington, 1989—; bd. dirs. numerous orgns. Author: Tranquillitas Ordinis: The Present Failure and Future Promise of American Catholic Thought on War and Peace, 1987; author, editor 14 books including Catholicism and the Renewal of American Democracy, 1989, The Final Revolution: The Resistance Church and the Collapse of Communism, 1992, Idealism Without Illusions: U.S. Foreign Policy in the Nineties, 1994; columnist Cath. Northwest Progress, 1977-84, 93—, Seattle Weekly, 1977-84; mem. editl. bd. First Things, The Washington Quar., Orbis. Fellow Woodrow Wilson Internat. Ctr. for Scholars, 1984-85. Office: Ethics and Pub Policy Ctr 1015 15th St NW Washington DC 20005

WEIGEL, JOHN J., lawyer; b. New Orleans, Feb. 4, 1932; s. George Edward and Marian Rose (Martin) W.; m. Barbara Ann Laporte, July 9, 1955; children: Leslie Ann, John J. Jr., Lynn Ann, Guy Edward. LLB, Tulane U., 1956. Bar: La. 1956, U.S. Dist. Ct. (ea., mid., we. dists.) La. 1959, U.S. Ct. Appeals (5th cir.) 1959, U.S. Supreme Ct. Law clk. La. Supreme Ct., New Orleans, 1958-59; from assoc. to sr. ptnr. Jones, Walker, Waechter, Poitevent, Carrere & Denegre, New Orleans, 1959—. Pers. bd. Jefferson Parish, La., 1974-83; bd. dirs. La. Civl Svc. League, New Orleans, 1975—. Fellow Am. Coll. Trial Lawyers; mem. ABA, Am. Bd. Trial Advocates, La. Bar Assn., New Orleans Bar Assn. Office: Jones Walker Waechter Poitevent Carrere & Denegre 201 Saint Charles Ave New Orleans LA 70170-1000

WEIGEL, PAUL HENRY, biochemistry educator, researcher, consultant; b. N.Y.C., Aug. 11, 1946; s. Helmut and Jeanne (Wakeman) W.; m. Nancy Shulman, June 15, 1968 (div. Dec. 1987); 1 child, Dana J.; m. Janet Oka, May 17, 1992. BA in Chemistry, Cornell U., 1968; MS in Biochemistry, Johns Hopkins U., Balt., 1969, PhD in Biochemistry, 1975. NIH postdoctoral fellow Johns Hopkins U., Balt., 1975-78; asst. prof. U. Tex. Med. Br., Galveston, Tex., 1978-82, assoc. prof., 1982-87; prof. biochemistry and cell biology U. Tex. Med. Br., Galveston, 1987-94, vice chmn. dept. human biol. chemistry and genetics, 1990-93, acting chmn. dept. human biology, chemistry and genetics, 1992-93; prof., chmn. dept. biochemistry and molecular biology U. Okla. Health Scis. Ctr., Okalahoma City, 1994—; mem. NIH Pathobiochemistry Study Sect., Washington, 1985-87; cons. Teltech, Mpls., 1985—. Contbr. articles to profl. jours.; patentee in field. Treas. Bayou Chateau Neighborhood Assn., Dickinson, Tex., 1981-83, v.p., 1983-84, pres., 1984-86. With U.S. Army, 1969-71. Grantee NIH, 1979—, Office Naval Rsch., 1983-87, Tex. Biotech., 1989-94; recipient Disting. Tchr. award U. Tex. Med. Br., 1989, Disting. Rsch. award, 1989. Mem. Am. Chem. Soc., Am. Soc. Cell Biology, Am. Soc. Biochemistry and Molecular Biology. Democrat. Lutheran. Avocations: raquetball, basketball card collecting, poetry, camping. Home: 817 Hollowdale Edmond OK 73003-3022 Office: U Okla Health Scis Ctr Dept Biochem & Mol Biology BMSB Rm 860 Oklahoma City OK 73190

WEIGEL, RAINER R., lawyer; b. Thalheim, Germany, Nov. 22, 1933. BA, Lake Forest Coll., 1955; JD, U. Mich., 1958. Bar: Ill. 1958, Fla. 1977, D.C. 1989. Ptnr. McDermott Will & Emory, Miami, Fla., now off-counsel. Contbr. articles. to profl. jours. Mem. ABA, Ill. State Bar, Chgo. Bar Assn., Fla. Bar Assn., D.C. Bar Assn., Am. Coll. Trust and Estate Counsel. Office: McDermott Will & Emery 700 Brickell Ave Miami FL 33131-2804 also: McDermott Will & Emery 227 W Monroe St Chicago IL 60606-5016*

WEIGEL, STANLEY ALEXANDER, judge; b. Helena, Mont., Dec. 9, 1905; s. Louis and Jennie (Hepner) W.; m. Anne Kauffman, Apr. 21, 1940; children: Jane Anne, Susan Mary. AB, Stanford U., 1926, JD, 1928. Bar: Calif. 1928. Pvt. practice law San Francisco, 1928-62; judge U.S. Dist. Ct. (no. dist.) Calif., from 1962, now sr. judge; non-resident lectr. Stanford Law Sch., 1952—; mem. Jud. Panel on Multidist. Litigation, 1968-79; mem. temporary emergency Ct. Appeals of U.S., 1980—; pres. Internat. Hospitality Ctr. Bay Area, 1959-68, Nat. Council for Community Services to Internat. Visitors, 1972-73; adv. gov. Calif. on Automobile Accident Commn., 1959; chmn. bd. visitors Stanford Law Sch., 1958-63; trustee World Affairs Council No. Calif., 1960—, pres., 1973-74; chmn. Ford Found. vis. com. to study behavioral sci. depts. Stanford U., 1956-57; mem. jud. conf. com. on jud. ethics, 1982-87. Served to lt. USNR, 1943-45. Decorated chevalier Order Leopold II (Belgium). Mem. Delta Sigma Rho, Phi Alpha Delta, Sigma Delta Chi. Office: US Ct Appeals PO Box 36060 450 Golden Gate Ave San Francisco CA 94102-3400*

WEIGEND, GUIDO GUSTAV, geographer, educator; b. Zeltweg, Austria, Jan. 2, 1920; came to U.S., 1939, naturalized, 1943; s. Gustav F. and Paula (Sorgo) W.; m. Areta Kelble, June 26, 1947 (dec. 1993); children: Nina, Cynthia, Kenneth. B.S., U. Chgo., 1942, M.S., 1946, Ph.D., 1949. With OSS, 1943-45; with mil. intelligence U.S. War Dept., 1946; instr. geography U. Ill., Chgo., 1946-47; instr. then asst. prof. geography Beloit Coll., 1947-49; asst. prof. geography Rutgers U., 1949-51, assoc. prof., 1951-57, prof., 1957-76, acting dept. chmn., 1951-52, chmn. dept., 1953-67, assoc. dean, 1972-76; dean Coll. Liberal Arts, Prof. geography Ariz. State U., Tempe, 1976-84, prof. geography, 1976-89; ret., 1989; Fulbright lectr. U. Barcelona, 1960-61; vis. prof. geography Columbia U., 1963-67, NYU, 1967, U. Colo., summer 1968, U. Hawaii, summer 1969; liaison rep. Rutgers U. to UN, 1950-52; invited by Chinese Acad. Scis. to visit minority areas in Chinese Cent. Asia, 1988; mem. U.S. nat. com. Internat. Geog. Union, 1951-58, 61-65; chmn. Conf. on Polit. and Social Geography, 1968-69. Author articles, monographs, bulls. for profl. jours.; contbr.: (4th edit.) A Geography of Europe, 1977; geog. editor-in-chief: Odyssey World Atlas, 1966. Bd. adjustment Franklin Twp., N.J., 1959; mem. Highland Park (N.J.) Bd. Edn., 1973-75, v.p., 1975; mem. Ariz. Coun. on Humanities and Pub. Policy, 1976-80; vice chmn. Phoenix Com. on Fgn. Rels., 1976-79, chmn., 1979-81; mem. exec. com. Fedn. Pub. Programs in Humanities, 1977-82; bd. dirs. Coun. Colls. Arts and Scis., 1980-83, Phoenix Chamber Music Soc., 1995—; commr. N. Cen. Assn. Colls. and Schs., 1976-80, bd. dirs. commn. on instns. of higher edn., 1980-83. Research fellow Office Naval Research, 1952-55, Rutgers Research Council, 1970-71; grantee Social Sci. Research Council, 1956, Ford Found., 1966, Am. Philos. Soc., 1970-71, German Acad. Exchange Service, 1984; Fulbright travel grantee Netherlands, 1970-71. Mem. Assn. Am. Geographers (chmn. N.Y. Met. divsn. 1955-56, editl. bd. 1955-59, mem. coun. 1965-66, chmn. N.Y.-N.J. divsn. 1965-66), Am. Geog. Soc., Phoenix Chamber Mus. Soc. (bd. dirs. 1995—), Sigma Xi (pres. Ariz. State U. chpt. 1989-91). Home: 2094 E Golf Ave Tempe AZ 85282-4046 Office: Ariz State U Dept Geography Tempe AZ 85287

WEIGER, JOHN GEORGE, foreign language educator; b. Dresden, Germany, Feb. 6, 1933; came to U.S., 1938, naturalized, 1945; s. Willy and Elisabeth (Prinz) W.; m. Leslie Lawrence Carpenter, Dec. 28, 1955; children: Robert Boyden, Mark Owen, Heidi Elaine. B.A., Middlebury Coll., 1955; M.A., U. Colo., 1957; Ph.D. (NDEA fellow), Ind. U., 1966. Instr. U. Colo., Boulder, 1955-57, Lawrence Coll., Appleton, Wis., 1957-58; instr. Romance langs. U. Vt., Burlington, 1958-62, asst. prof., 1964-67, assoc. prof., 1967-73, prof., 1973—, vice chmn. Romance lang. dept., 1964-68; chmn., 1994-96; asst. dean U. Vt. (Coll. Arts and Scis.), Burlington, 1968-69, assoc. dean, 1969-71, dean, 1971-76; instnl. rep. for Rhodes scholarships, Danforth fellowships, Turrell Fund scholarships, 1971-76; program chmn. George Aiken lecture series, 1975; vis. lectr. U. Bologna, 1978, 87, U. Venice, Italy, 1987, U. Valencia, Spain, 1987; Cervantes lectr. Fordham U., 1990; cons. Eirik Borve, Inc., 1979—. Author: Introduction to the Youthful Deeds of the Cid, 1969, The Valencian Dramatists of Spain's Golden Age, 1976, Cristobal de Virues, 1978, Hacia la Comedia, 1978, The Individuated Self: Cervantes and the Emergence of the Individual, 1979, The Substance of Cervantes, 1985, In the Margins of Cervantes, 1988; editor: Las Hazañas del Cid, 1981, La Infelice Marcela, 1985; mem. editorial bd.: Bull. of Comediantes, 1978—; editorial bd.: Hispania, 1993—; contbr. articles to profl. jours., also chpts. to books. U. Vt. Faculty Research fellow, 1967, 83, 86; Am. Council Learned Socs. grantee, 1978; U. Vt. Univ. scholar for the humanities, 1985-86. Mem. MLA (chmn. comedia sect. 1970-71), Renaissance Soc. Am., Am. Assn. Tchrs. Spanish and Portuguese (chmn. com. hon. mems. and fellows 1984), The Comediantes, Internat. Assn. Hispanists, Cervantes Soc. Am., Phi Beta Kappa, Phi Sigma Iota, Phi Eta Sigma (hon.). Home: 8 Woodbine Rd Shelburne VT 05482-7268 Office: U Vermont 506A Waterman Bldg Burlington VT 05405

WEIGERT, ANDREW JOSEPH, sociology educator; b. N.Y.C., Apr. 8, 1934; s. Andrew Joseph and Marie Teresa (Kollmer) W.; m. Kathleen Rose Maas, Aug. 31, 1967; children: Karen Rose, Sheila Marie. BA, St. Louis U., 1958, PhL, 1959, MA, 1960; BTh, Woodstock (Md.) Coll., 1964; PhD, U. Minn., 1968. NIMH trainee U. Minn., Mpls., 1965-67; asst. prof. sociology U. Notre Dame, Ind., 1968-72, assoc. prof., 1972-76, prof., 1976—, chmn. dept., 1980-84, 88-89; vis. assoc. prof. Yale U., New Haven, 1973-74; participant nat. and regional profl. meetings. Co-author: Family Socialization, 1974, Interpretive Sociology, 1978, Society and Identity, 1986; author: Everyday Life, 1981, Social Psychology, 1983, Life and Society, 1983, Mixed Emotions, 1991; adv. editor various sociology jours.; contbr. over 50 articles to profl. jours., chpts. to books. Grantee NSF, 1969. Mem. Soc. for Study Symbolic Interaction, Soc. for Sci. Study Religion, Assn. for Sociology Religion. Avocation: woodlot management. Office: U Notre Dame Dept Sociology Notre Dame IN 46556

WEIGHT, GEORGE DALE, banker, educator; b. Salt Lake City, Mar. 25, 1934; s. Sheldon J. and Florence (Noe) W.; m. Carilee Kesler, June 16, 1959; children: Camille, Kristene, Denise, Marcie, Nancy. BS, U. Utah, 1961; MS, U. Oreg., 1965, PhD, 1968. Instr. U. Oreg., Eugene, 1963-68; economist Fed. Res. Bank, Cleve., 1968-69; asst. v.p. fiscal ops. Fed. Res. Bank, Pitts., 1969-71; v.p. bank ops. Fed. Home Loan Bank Bd., Pitts., 1971-73; exec. v.p. Syracuse Savs. Bank, N.Y., 1972-73, pres., chief exec. officer, 1973-83; chmn., chief exec. officer Ben Franklin Fed. Savs. and Loan Assn., Portland, Oreg., 1983-90; dean Atkinson Grad. Sch. Mgmt. Willamette U., Salem, Oreg., 1990—; adj. prof. Oreg. Grad. Inst. Sci. & Tech., 1994—, Syracuse U., 1974; chmn. bd. Savs. Banks Life Ins. Fund, N.Y.C., bd. dirs. Onondaga County Indsl. Devel. Agy., Fed. Res. Bank San Francisco, Portland Br., State Accident Ins. Fund, Fed. Home Loan Bank Seattle; chmn. Oreg. State Bd. Edn., 1991. Pres. Hiawatha coun. Boy Scouts Am., Syracuse, 1974-77; chmn. bd. Crouse-Irving Meml. Hosp., 1978-83; mem. Gov.'s Commn. Edn. Reforms, 1988, Oreg. State Bd. Edn., 1989-95, chmn., 1991-92; chmn. Associated Oreg. Industries Found., 1993-95; pres. Canal Mus.; bd. dirs. Oreg. Bus. Coun. Recipient Silver Beaver award Boy Scouts Am., 1978; recipient Vol. of Yr. award Am. Heart Assn., 1980, Community Service award Rotary, Syracuse, 1982. Mem. Am. Fin. Assn., Arlington Club, Beta Gamma Sigma. Republican. Home: 16057 NW Claremont Dr Portland OR 97229-7841 Office: Willamette U Atkinson Grad Sch Mgmt 900 State St Salem OR 97301-3930

WEIGHTMAN, JUDY MAE, lawyer; b. New Eagle, Pa., May 22, 1941; d. Morris and Ruth (Gutstadt) Epstein; children: Wayne, Randall, Darrell. BS in English, California U. of Pa., 1970; MA in Am. Studies, U. Hawaii, 1975; JD, U. Hawaii, 1981. Bar: Hawaii 1981. Tchr. Fairfax County Sch. (Va.), 1968-72, Hawaii Pub. Schs., Honolulu, 1973-75; lectr. Kapiolani Community Coll., Honolulu, 1975-76; instr. Olympic Community Coll., Pearl Harbor, Hawaii, 1975-77; lectr. Hawaii Pacific Coll., Honolulu, 1977-78; law clk. to atty. gen. Hawaii & Case, Kay & Lynch, Davis & Levin, 1979-81, to chief judge Intermediate Ct. Appeals State of Hawaii, 1981-82; dep. pub. defender Office of Pub. Defender, 1982-84; staff atty. Dept. Commerce & Consumer Affairs, State of Hawaii 1984-86; pres., bd. dirs. Am. Beltwrap Corp., 1986—; asst. prof. law, dir. pre-admission program, asst. prof. Richardson Sch. Law, U. Hawaii, 1987—, faculty senator; faculty senate exec. com. U. Hawaii Manoa. Author: Days of Remembrance: Hawaii Witnesses to the Holocaust; producer (documentary) The Panel: The First Exchange, Profile of An Aja Soldier, Profile of a Holocaust Survivor; prodr., dir. From Hawaii to The Holocaust: A Shared Moment in History; patentee in field; mem. Richardson Law Rev., 1979-81. Mem. neighborhood bd. No. 25 City and County Honolulu, 1976-77; vol. Legal Aid Soc., Honolulu, 1977-78; bd. dirs. Jewish Fedn., Protection and Advocacy Agy.; parent rep. Wheeler Intermediate Adv. Coun., Honolulu, 1975-77; trustee Carl K. Mirikitani Meml. Scholarship Fund, Arts Coun. Hawaii; membership dir. ACLU, 1977-78, bd. dirs., Hawaii, 1988—, treas. Amicus; founder Hawaii Holocaust Project; trustee Jewish Fedn. Hawaii. Community scholar, Honolulu, 1980; Internat. Rels. grant Chaminade U., 1976; recipient Hawaii Filmmakers award Hawaii Internat. Film Festival, 1993, Golden Eagle award CINE, 1995, Silver Apple Nat. Edn. Film & Video Festival, 1995, Bronze World medal N.Y. Festivals, 1996, CINDY Bronze medal, 1996. Mem. ABA, Afro-Am. Lawyers Assn. (bd. trustee), Hawaii Women Lawyers, Assn. Trial Lawyers Am., Hawaii State Bar Assn., Am. Judicature Soc., Richardson Sch. Law Alumni Assn. (alumni rep. 1981-82), Advocates for Pub. Interest Law, U. Hawaii Senate Faculty (senator), Phi Delta Phi (v.p. 1980-81), Hadassah Club, Women's Guild Club. Democrat. Jewish. Office: U Hawaii William S Richardson Sch Law 2515 Dole St Honolulu HI 96822-2328

WEIGLE, ROBERT EDWARD, civil engineer, research director; b. Shiloh, Pa., Apr. 27, 1927; s. William Edgar and Hilda Geraldine (Fans) W.; m. Mona Jean Long, Aug. 13, 1949; 1 child, Geoffrey Robert. BCE in Structures, Rensselear Poly. Inst., 1951, MS in Mechanics, 1957, PhD in Mechanics, 1959. Registered profl. engr., N.Y., Pa. Assoc. rsch. scientist Rensselear Poly. Inst., Troy, N.Y., 1955-59; chief scientist Watervliet Arsenal, 1959-77; technical dir. U.S. Army and Armament R & D Command, 1977-82; dir. U.S. Army Rsch. Office, 1982-88; dir. phys. sci. lab. N.Mex. State U., Las Cruces, 1988-96; dir. emeritus phys. sci. lab. N. Mex. State U., Las Cruces, 1996—; tech. dir., then dir. Benet Weapons Lab., 1959-77; chmn. numerous DoD and Army coms. Contbr. articles to profl. jours. Recipient Meritorious Civilian Service award for cannon breech design U.S. Army, 1964, U.S. Army Materiel Command citation for engineering achievement in Vietnam, 1966, Presidential citation for development of cannon firing simulator, 1965, Exceptional Civilian Svc. medal U.S. Army; elected to Am. Acad. of Mechanics, 1972. Mem. NSPE, ASME, AAAS, ASTM, Soc. Exptl. Mechanics, Am. Def. Preparedness Assn. (Corzier prize 1985), Nat. Conf. Advancement Rsch. (program com. 1987, exec. conf. com., host rep. NCAR-46 ann. conf. 1992), Army Sci. Bd. (chmn. rsch. and new initiatives group 1982), Tau Beta Pi, Chi Epsilon, Sigma Xi. Office: N Mex State U Physical Sci Lab 607 Upper Sondley Dr Asheville NC 28805

WEIGLE, WILLIAM OLIVER, immunologist, educator; b. Monaca, Pa., Apr. 28, 1927; s. Oliver James and Caroline Ellen (Alsing) W.; m. Kathryn May Lotz, Sept. 4, 1948 (div. 1980); children—William James, Cynthia Kay; m. Carole G. Romball, Sept. 24, 1983. B.S., U. Pitts., 1950, M.S., 1951, Ph.D., 1956. Research assoc. pathology U. Pitts., 1955-58, asst. prof. immunochemistry, 1959-61; assoc. div. exptl. pathology Scripps Rsch. Inst., La Jolla, Calif., 1961-62, assoc. mem. div., 1962-63; mem. dept. exptl. pathology Scripps Rsch. Inst., La Jolla, 1963-74, mem. dept. immunopathology, 1974-82, chmn. dept. immunopathology, 1980-82, mem., vice chmn. dept. immunology, 1982-85, mem. dept. immunology, 1982—, chmn. dept. immunology, 1985-87; adj. prof. biology U. Calif., San Diego; McLaughlin vis. prof. U. Tex., 1977; mem. adv. bd. Immunetech Pharms., San Diego, 1988—; cons. in field. Author: Natural and Acquired Immunologic Unresponsiveness, 1967; assoc. editor: Clin. and Exptl. Immunology, 1972-79; Jour. Exptl. Medicine, 1974-84; Immunochemistry 1964-71; Procs. Soc. Exptl. Biology and Medicine, 1967-72; Jour. Immunology, 1967-71; Infection and Immunity, 1969-86, Aging: Immunology and Infectious Disease, 1987—; sect. editor: Jour. Immunology, 1971-75; editorial bd.: Contemporary Topics in Immunobiology, 1971-93; Cellular Immunology, 1984—; contbr. articles to profl. jours. Trustee Lovelace Med. Found., Albuquerque. With USNR, 1945-46. Pub. Health Research fellow, Nat. Inst. Neurol. Diseases and Blindness, 1956-59; NIH sr. research fellow, 1959-61, Research Career award, 1962. Mem. Am. Assn. Immunologists, Am. Soc. Exptl. Pathology (Parke Davis award 1967), Am. Soc. Microbiology, N.Y. Acad. Scis., Am. Assn. Pathologists, Soc. Exptl. Biology and Medicine. Home: 688 Via De La Valle Solana Beach CA 92075-2461 Office: Scripps Rsch Inst Dept Immunology IMM9 10666 N Torrey Pines Rd La Jolla CA 92037-1027

WEIGLEY, RUSSELL FRANK, history educator; b. Reading, Pa., July 2, 1930; s. Frank Francis and Meta Beulah (Rohrbach) W.; m. Emma Eleanor Seifrit, July 27, 1963; children: Jared Francis Guldin, Catherine Emma Rohrbach. BA, Albright Coll., 1952; MA, U. Pa., 1953, PhD, 1956; HLD (hon.), Albright Coll., 1978. Instr. history U. Pa., Phila., 1956-58; asst. prof. Drexel Inst. Tech., Phila., 1958-60, assoc. prof., 1960-62; assoc. prof. Temple U., Phila., 1962-64, prof. history, 1964-85, Disting. Univ. prof., 1985—; vis. prof. Dartmouth Coll., Hanover, N.H., 1967-68; U.S. Army vis. prof. mil. history rsch. U.S. Army War Coll., U.S. Army Mil. History Rsch. Collection, Carlisle Barrakcs, Pa., 1973-74; pres. Am. Mil. Inst., Washington, 1975-76. Author: Quartermaster General of the Union Army: A Biography of M.C. Meigs, 1959, Towards an American Army: Military Thought from Washington to Marshall, 1962, History of the United States Army, 1967, 84, The Partisan War: The South Carolina Campaign of 1780-82, 1970, The American Way of War, 1973, Eisenhower's Lieutenants, 1981 (Athenaem of Phila. Spl. award for Nonfiction by a Phila. Author, 1983), The Age of Battles: The Quest for Decisive Warfare from Breitenfeld to Waterloo, 1991; editor: The American Military: Readings in the History of the Military in American Society, 1969, New Dimensions in Military History, 1976, Philadelphia: A 300-Year History, 1982. Mem. hist. adv. commn. Dept. of Army, Washington, 1976-79, 88—, Pa. Hist. Records Adv. Com., Harrisburg, 1977-79; bd. dirs. Masonic Libr., Mus. of Pa., The Grand Lodge of Masons of Pa., Phila., 1990-95. Penrose Fund grantee Am. Philos. Soc., 1958; fellow John Simon Guggenheim Meml. Found., 1969-70; recipient Samuel Eliot Morison prize Am. Mil. Inst., 1989. Mem. Hist. Soc. Pa. (vice chmn. 1989-93, councilor 1983-89, 92—), Pa. Hist. Assn. (pres. 1975-78, v.p. 1967-75, coun. 1967—, editor jour. 1962-67), Am. Hist. Assn., Orgn. Am. Historians, Soc. Mil. Hist. (Disting. Book award 1992), So. Hist. Assn., Soc. Am. Historians Inc., Interuniv. Seminar on Armed Forces and Soc., Am. Philos. Soc. Democrat. Unitarian. Home: 327 S Smedley St Philadelphia PA 19103-6717 Office: Temple U Dept History Philadelphia PA 19122

WEIGMANN, HANS-DIETRICH H., chemist; b. Rostock, Germany, Jan. 12, 1930; m. Christa Weigmann; 2 children, Stefanie, Jessica. Vordiplom. in Chemistry, U. Hamburg, Germany, 1954, Diplom. in Organic Chemistry, 1958; Dr. rer. nat. in Organic Chemistry, Technische Hochschule, Aachen, Germany, 1960. Scientist German Wool Rsch. Inst., 1960-61; postdoctoral fellow Textile Rsch. Inst., Princeton, N.J., 1961-63, sr. scientist, 1963-67, assoc. dir. chem. rsch., 1967-70, assoc. dir. rsch., 1970-93, v.p. rsch., 1993-95, rsch. assoc., 1995—; cons. to cosmetic industry; com. tech. programs 4th Internat. Wool Textile Rsch. Conf., 1969-70; chmn. Gordon Rsch. Conf. Fiber Sci., 1975. Co-recipient Best Paper award Textile Chemist and Colorist, 1982, Lit. award Soc. Cosmetic Chemists, 1986. Mem. Am. Chem. Soc. (chmn. sumposium 1970, Inst. Textile Sci. Can. 1982), Soc. Cosmetic Chemists, Am. Assn. Textile Chemists and Colorists (chmn. internat. dyeing symposium 1983, Olney medal for achievement in textile chemistry 1990), Fiber Soc. (hon.). Office: Textile Research Institute PO Box 625 Princeton NJ 08542-0625

WEIHAUPT, JOHN GEORGE, geosciences educator, scientist, university administrator; b. La Crosse, Wis., Mar. 5, 1930; s. John George and Gladys Mae (Ash) W.; m. Audrey Mae Reis, Jan. 28, 1961. Student, St. Norbert Coll., De Pere, Wis., 1948-49; B.S., U. Wis., 1952, M.S., 1953; M.S., U. Wis.-Milw., 1971; Ph.D., U. Wis., 1973. Exploration geologist Am. Smelting & Refining Co., Nfld., 1953, Anaconda Co., Chile, S.Am., 1956-57; seismologist United Geophys. Corp., 1958; geophysicist Arctic Inst. N.Am., Antarctica, 1958-60, Geophys. and Polar Research Center, U. Wis., Antarctica, 1960-63; dir. participating Coll. and Univ. program, chmn. dept. phys. and biol. sci. U.S. Armed Forces Inst., Dept. Def., 1963-73; assoc. dean for acad. affairs Sch. Sci., Ind. U.-Purdue U., Indpls., 1973-78; prof. geology Sch. Sci., Ind. U.-Purdue U., 1973-78; asst. dean (Grad. Sch., prof. geoscis. Purdue U.), 1975-78; prof. geology, assoc. acad. v.p., dean grad. studies and research, v.p. Univ. Research Found., San Jose (Calif.) State U., 1978-82; vice chancellor for acad. affairs U. Colo., Denver, 1982-86, prof. geoscis., 1987—; Sci. cons., mem. sci. adv. bd. Holt Reinhart and Winston, Inc., 1967—; sci. editor, cons. McGraw-Hill Co., 1966—; hon. lectr. U. Wis., 1963-73; geol. cons., 1968—; editorial cons. John Wiley & Sons, 1968; editorial adv. bd. Dushkin Pub. Group, 1971—. Author: Exploration of the Oceans: An Introduction to Oceanography; mem. editorial bd. Internat. Jour. Interdisciplinary Cycle Research, Leiden; co-discoverer USARP Mountain Range (Arctic Inst. Mountain Range), in Victoria Land, Antarctica, 1960; discoverer Wilkes Land Meteorite Crater, Antarctic. Mem. Capital Community Citizens Assn.; mem. Madison Transp. Study Com., Found. for Internat. Energy Research and Tng.; U.S. com. for UN Univ.; mem. sci. council Internat. Center for Interdisciplinary Cycle Research; mem. Internat. Awareness and Leadership Council; mem. governing bd. Moss Landing Marine Labs.; bd. dirs. San Jose State U. Found. Served as 1st lt. AUS, 1953-55, Korea. Mt. Weihaupt in Antarctica named for him, 1966; recipient Madisonian medal for outstanding community service, 1973; Outstanding Cote Meml. award, 1974; Antarctic medal, 1968. Fellow Geol. Soc. Am., Explorers Club; mem. Antarctican Soc., Nat. Sci. Tchrs. Assn., Am. Geophys. Union, Internat. Council Corr. Edu., Soc. Am. Mil. Engrs., Wis. Alumni Assn., Soc. Study Biol. Rhythms, Internat. Soc. for Chronobiology, Marine Tech. Soc., AAAS, Univ. Indsl. Adv. Council, Am. Council on Edn., Expdn. Polaire France (hon.), Found. for Study Cycles, Assn. Am. Geographers, Nat. Council Univ. Research Adminstrs., Soc. Research Adminstrs., Man-Environ. Communication Center, Internat. Union Geol. Scis., Internat. Geog. Union, Internat. Soc. Study Time, Community Council Pub. TV, Internat. Platform Assn., Ind., Midwest assns. grad. schs., Western Assn. Grad. Schs., Council Grad. Schs. in U.S., Wis. Alumni Assn. of San Francisco, Kiwanis, Carmel Racquet Club (Rinconada), The Ridge at Hiwan (Evergreen, Colo., pres. 1991-93). Achievements include discoveryof the Wilkes Land Anomaly in Antarctica; also credited with revision of the discovery date of Antarctic continent by 3 centuries. Home: 23906 Currant Dr Golden CO 80401-9243 Office: U Colo Campus Box 172 PO Box 173364 Denver CO 80204-5310

WEIHE, STARR CULVER, biology educator; b. Salisbury, Md.; d. Frederick A. and Violet (Timmons) Culver; m. Rudolph George Weihe, Oct. 20, 1967. BA, Hood Coll., 1959; MA, Duke U., 1961; EdD, Nova U., 1978. Biology asst. Fla. Presbyn. Coll., 1961-62; prof. biology St. Petersburg Jr. Coll., Fla., 1963—, chair natural scis. dept., 1989-93. Contbr. articles profl. jours. Active St. Petersburg Symphony Guild, St. Petersburg Mus. Fine Arts. Hood Coll. scholar, 1958; recipient Nat. Tchg. Excellence award U. Tex., 1989. Mem. AAAS, AAUW, Am. Inst. Biol. Scis., Fla. Acad. Scis., Beta Beta Beta. Democrat. Methodist. Clubs: St. Petersburg Yacht, Lakewood Country. Avocation: piano. Home: 5108 Brittany Dr S Apt 901 Saint Petersburg FL 33715-1540 Office: St Petersburg Jr Coll Saint Petersburg FL 33710

WEIHING, JOHN LAWSON, plant pathologist, state senator; b. Rocky Ford, Colo., Feb. 26, 1921; s. Henry John and Clara Adele (Krull) W.; m. Shirley Ruth Wilkerson, Aug. 18, 1948; children: Lawson James, Martin Roy, Adell Ann, Warren John. BS in Agronomy, Colo. State U., 1942; MSc in Agronomy, U. Nebr., 1949, PhD in Botany and Plant Pathology, 1954. Instr. plant pathology U. Nebr., Lincoln, 1950-54, asst. prof., 1954-56, assoc. prof., 1956-60, prof., 1960-61, 62-64, 66-71, prof., interim chmn. plant pathology dept., 1961-62; prof., dir. Panhandle Rsch. and Extension Ctr. U. Nebr., Scottsbluff, 1971-84; with Alumni Office, Panhandle Found. U. Nebr., Scottsbluf, 1984-86; prof., chmn. plant sci. dept. Ataturk U., Erzurum, Turkey, 1964-66; mem. dist. 48 Nebr. Legislature, Lincoln, 1987-91; cons. Am. Hydrponics Systems, Inc., Grapevine, Tex., 1969-72. Creator U. Nebr. TV series Backyard Farmer, The Equation of Nature, 1959-60. Campaign chmn. United Way, Scottsbluff and Gering, Nebr., 1978. Lt. U.S. Army, 1942-46. Recipient Honor award Soil Conservation Soc. Am., 1982, Merit award Gamma Sigma Delta, 1977, Disting. Svc. award Nebr. Turfgrass Found., 1982, Nebr. Coop. Extension, 1970; named to Nebr. Hall Agrl. Achievement, 1987. Mem. Am. Phytopathol. Soc. (chmn. nat. extension com. 1963, pres. north cen. dir. 1971-72), AAAS, Am. Inst. Biol. Scis., Scottsbluff/Gering United C. of C. (pres. 1980-81), Rotary (bd. dirs. 1977-80), Elks. Republican. Presbyterian. Avocation: archeology. Home: 1605 Holly Dr Gering NE 69341-1954

WEIHRICH, HEINZ, management educator; came to U.S., 1959; s. Paul and Anna Weihrich; m. Ursula Weihrich, Aug. 3, 1963. BS, UCLA, 1966, MBA, 1967, PhD, 1973. Assoc. Grad. Sch. Mgmt. UCLA, 1968-73; from asst. to assoc. prof. Ariz. State U., Tempe, 1973-80; prof. global mgmt. and behavioral sci. U. San Francisco, 1980—; internat. mgmt. cons. in field. Author: (with Harold Koontz and Cyril O'Donnell) Management, 7th edit., 1980, Japanese, Chinese and Indonesian edits., 8th edit., 1984, Singapore edit., 1985, Indonesian edit., 1986, Philippines edit., Bengali edit., 1989, Taiwan edit., 1985 (with Harold Koontz) 9th edit., 1988, Singapore edit., 1988, Chinese edit., 1989, Spanish edit., 1990, best-seller Spanish speaking world, Korean edit., 1988, 90, Pengurusan (Malaysian) edit., 1991, Management: A Global Perspective, 10th edit. (with Harold Koontz), 1993, Administracão Fundamentos da Teoriae da Cienca, Primeiro Volume 1986, Administracão Organizacão Planejamento e Controle, Segundo Volume, 1987, Administracão Recursos Humanos: Desenvolvimento de Administradores, Terceiro Volume, 1987, (with Harold Koontz and Cyril O'Donnell) Management: A Book of Readings, 5th edit., 1980, (with George Odiorne and Jack Mendleson) Executive Skills: A Management by Objectives Approach, 1980, (with Harold Koontz) Measuring Managers--A Double-Barreled Approach, 1981, (with Harold Koontz and Cyril O'Donnell) Essentials of Management, 3d edit. 1982, Taiwan, Philippines, Chinese and India edits., 4th edit., 1986, Singapore edit., 1986, 5th edit., 1990, (with Harold Koontz) Manajamen, Jilid 1, Indonesian edit., 1987, Manajamen, Jilid 2, 1986, Elementos de Administracion, 3d edit., 1983, 4th edit. 1988, Management Excellence--Productivity through MBO, 1985, Singapore edit. 1986, Japanese edit., 1990, Greek edit., Produttivita con L' Italian edit. 1987, Administracion, 1985, Management Basiswissen, 1986, Excelencia Administrativa (Mex.), 1987, (with Harold Koontz and Cyril O'Donnell) Adminstracion Moderna, Tomo 1, 1986, (with Harold Koontz) Management: A Global Perspective, internat. edit., 1993, Administración: Una Perspectiva Global, 1994; editor: (with Jack Mendleson) Management: An MBO Approach, 1978; contbr. numerous articles and papers to profl. jours. Grantee Am. Mgmt. Assn., 1970. Fellow Internat. Acad. Mgmt., mem. Acad. Mgmt., Assn. Mgmt. Excellence (trustee 1985-87), Assn. Bus. Simulation Exptl. Learning, Acad. Internat. Bus., Beta Gamma Sigma, Sigma Iota Epsilon. Roman Catholic. Office: U San Francisco 2130 Fulton St San Francisco CA 94117-1080

WEIKART, DAVID POWELL, educational research foundation administrator; b. Youngstown, Ohio, Aug. 26, 1931; s. Hubert James and Catherine (Powell) W.; m. Phyllis Saxton, Aug. 24, 1957; children: Cynthia, Catherine, Jennifer, Gretchen. AB, Oberlin Coll., 1953, DSc (hon.), 1992; PhD, U. Mich., 1966. Cert. sch. psychologist, Mich. Dir. spl. svcs. Ypsilanti (Mich.) Pub. Schs., 1957-70; pres. High Scope Ednl. Rsch. Found., Ypsilanti, 1970—; dir. High Scope Inst., London, 1991—. Author: Young Children in Action, 1979, Changed Lives, 1984, Challenging the Potential, 1992, Significant Benefits, 1993, Educating Young Children, 1995; editor: How Nations Serve Young Children, 1991, Families Speak, 1994. Mem., Nat. Commn. on Children, 1990-93. 1st lt. USMC, 1953-55. Recipient Lela Rowland award Nat. Mental Health Assn., Washington, 1987. Mem. Nat. Assn. for Edn. of Young Children. Avocation: camping.

WEIKERT, JERARD LEE, real estate broker; b. Zanesfield, Ohio, Dec. 25, 1929; s. Paul Hoover and Thelma May (McKeever) W.; m. Beth Ann Houston, Aug. 24, 1983. Grad., Officer Candidate Sch., 1952; BA, Wittenberg U., 1961; MS, George Washington U., 1966. Enlisted U.S. Army, 1951, advanced through grades to col., 1967, ret., 1972; self-employed profl. horse trainer and judge Fairfax County, Va., 1972—; v.p. sales and plans Keyes Gateway, Inc., Dayton, Ohio, 1983—; pres. Darrowby Inc. Real Estate Brokerage Consultancy, 1994—; judge Am. Horse Show Assn., 1972—. Contbr. articles to U.S. Army and horse jours. Chmn. Human Rels. Bd., Springfield, Ohio, 1991-92; mem. Planning Commn., Clark County, Ohio, 1991-93; v.p., exec. bd. Community Leadership Acad., Springfield, 1991-93; fin. dir. Tackett for State Senate, Ohio, 1992. Decorated Legion of Merit (2), Combat Infantry Badge. Mem. U.S. Dressage Fedn. (exec. bd.), Dayton Dressage Assn. (chmn. bd. dirs. 1995—), Dayton Area Bd. Realtors (chmn. equal opportunity com. 1988-90, profl. stds. com. 1991-93, grievance com. 1993-94, chmn. grievance com. 1995—), Dayton Racquet Club, Troy Country Club. Democrat. Avocations: antique bronzes and icons, geneaology.

WEIL, DAVID S., plastics manufacturing executive; b. Germany, Apr. 6, 1925; came to U.S., 1943; s. William and Martha Weil; m. Grace K. Pollack, Mar. 20, 1949; children: Aryeh L., Esther R. Weil Sturm. BA, CCNY, 1949. Pres., chief exec. officer Ampacet Corp., Tarrytown, N.Y., 1958—. Sgt. U.S. Army, 1943-46, CBI. Decorated Bronze Star. Mem. Soc. Plastics Engrs. (Internat. Excellence award 1986), Soc. Plastics Industry (bd. dirs. 1983-86). Avocations: tennis, swimming. Office: Ampacet Corp 660 White Plains Rd Tarrytown NY 10591*

WEIL, D(ONALD) WALLACE, business administration educator; b. Cleve., July 20, 1923; s. Laurence J. and Carol S. (Wallace) W.; m. Jane A. Bittel, Dec. 29, 1947; children—John Wallace, Charles Andrew, Margaret Jane, Carol Wyn. B.A., Oberlin Coll., 1947; J.D., Willamette U., 1950. Pres. James Foundry Corp., Fort Atkinson, Wis., 1960-70; faculty bus. adminstrn. U. Wis., Eau Claire, 1971-74; chmn. dept. bus. adminstrn. U. Wis., 1974-77, prof., 1985—; pres. Diversified Industries, Inc., St. Louis, 1977-81, UHI Corp., Los Angeles, 1981-85; dir. U.H.I. Corp. Diversified Industries, Inc., St. Louis, Sales Investments, Mgmt. Inc., Elmwood, Wis., Jane B. Inc., Eau Claire. Served with AUS, 1942-45. Mem. Am. Security Council, Nat. Council Small Bus. Mgmt. Devel., Phi Kappa Phi, Beta Gamma Sigma. Republican. Congregationalist. Home: 1530 Canfield St Eau Claire WI 54701-4018 Office: U Wis-Eau Claire Dept Bus Adminstrn Eau Claire WI 54701

WEIL, EDWARD DAVID, chemistry researcher, consultant, educator; b. Phila., June 13, 1928; s. Irving E. and Minna M. (Stainbrook) W.; m. Barbara Joy Hummel, Sept. 11, 1952; children: David L., Claudia E. BS in Chemistry, U. Pa., 1950; PhD in Organic Chemistry, U. Ill., 1953; MBA, Pace U., 1982. Chemist, supr. Hooker Chem. Co., Niagara Falls, N.Y., 1950-65; supr., sr. scientist Stauffer Chem. Co., Dobbs Ferry, N.Y., 1965-86; ind. cons., patent agt., propr. Intertech. Svcs., 1986—; dir. exploratory rsch. Adelphi Rsch. Ctr., Garden City, 1986-87; rsch. prof., Poly. U., Bklyn., 1987—; . Contbr. articles to Kirk-Othmer Ency., Ency. Polymer Sci., Rsch. Mgmt. Jour., others. Recipient IR-100 award Indsl. Rsch. Mag. Achievements include over 220 patents for commercial pesticides, flame retardants, processes, agricultural chemicals, others. Mem. Am. Chem. Soc. (chmn. profl. rels. com. N.Y. sect. 1980-95), Assn. Cons. Chemists and Chem. Engrs., Sigma Xi. Home: 6 Amherst Dr Hastings On Hudson NY 10706 Office: Polytechnic U 6 Metrotech Ctr Brooklyn NY 11201

WEIL, FRANK A., investment banker, lawyer; b. Bedford, N.Y., Feb. 14, 1931; s. Sylvan and Ruth Alice (Norman) W.; m. Denie Sandison, Feb. 10, 1951; children: Deborah Weil Harrington, Amanda, Sandison, William. A.B. cum laude, Harvard U., 1953, LL.B., 1956. Bar: N.Y. 1956. Practiced in N.Y.C., 1957-60; gen. partner Loeb, Rhoades & Co., N.Y.C., 1960-71; pres. Abacus Fund, Inc., 1968-72; chief fin. officer, dir. Paine, Webber, Jackson & Curtis, N.Y.C., 1972-77; asst. sec. industry and trade Dept. Commerce, Washington, 1977-79; partner firm Ginsburg, Feldman, Weil & Bress, Washington, 1979-83, Wald, Harkrader & Ross, Washington, 1983-85; chmn., chief exec. officer Abacus and Assocs., Inc., 1985—; dir. Dorr-Oliver, Inc., Stamford, Conn., 1968-77, Hamburg Savs. Bank, N.Y.C., 1975-77, J.B. Lippincott Co., Phila., 1975-77, Govt. Research Corp., 1975-77, 79-85; dir., pres. Norman Found., 1953-77, 79—. Trustee Tchrs. Coll., Columbia U., 1976-79, Montefiore Hosp., 1960-77; trustee, vice chmn. No. Westchester Hosp., 1971-77; past vice chmn. bd. govs. Atlantic Inst. Internat. Affairs; past pres. Ednl. Alliance, trustee, 1957-77; trustee, sec. Fedn. Jewish Philanthropies, N.Y.C., 1965-77; trustee, chmn. Harvey Sch., 1969-76; trustee Hurricane Island Outward Bound Sch., 1974—, Washington Opera, 1984-85, Asia Soc., 1993—; bd. dirs., pres. Hickrill Found., Inc., 1953-77, 79—; bd. dirs. Coun. Excellence in Govt., 1984—, chmn., 1988-93, Am. Assembly, 1992—, Smithsonian Inst., 1994—; mem. vis. com. Kennedy Sch. Govt., Harvard U.; chmn. tax com., mem. N.Y. State Econ. Devel. Bd., 1975-77; chmn., mem. N.Y. State Bd. Equalization and Assessment, 1976-77; adv. bd. Sch. Advanced Internat. Studies, Johns Hopkins U., 1979-88; mem. N.Y. State Council on Fiscal and Econ. Priorities, 1985-89, N.Y. Coun. Fgn. Rels.; mem. N.Y. State Adv. Commn. on Liability Ins., 1986. Mem. Century Assn., Harvard Club, The Links, River Club, Met. Club. Home: 1516 28th St NW Washington DC 20007-3058 Office: Abacus & Assocs Inc 147 E 48th St # 3fl New York NY 10017-1223

WEIL, GILBERT HARRY, lawyer; b. N.Y.C., Aug. 31, 1912; s. Alexis and Esther (Marks) W.; m. Louise Rhoda Cohen, Mar. 14, 1936; children: Allen Charles, Jeffrey Lee. B.S., NYU, 1933, J.D., 1937. Bar: N.Y. 1937, U.S. Dist. Ct. (so. dist.) N.Y. 1941, U.S. Ct. Appeals (2d cir.) 1949, U.S. Ct. Appeals (4th cir.) 1950, U.S. Dist. Ct. (ea. dist.) N.Y. 1952, U.S. Ct. Appeals (3d cir.) 1956, U.S. Dist. Ct. D.C. 1961, U.S. Supreme Ct. 1964, U.S. Ct. Appeals (9th cir.) 1968, U.S. Ct. Appeals (5th cir.) 1969, U.S. Ct. Appeals (7th cir.) 1976, U.S. Ct. Appeals (fed. cir.) 1982. Law clk. and assoc. to Isaac W. Digges, 1935-53; pvt. practice, 1953-65; partner Weil and Lee, N.Y.C., 1966-69, Weil, Lee & Bergin, N.Y.C., 1969-76, Weil, Guttman & Davis, N.Y.C., 1976-82, Weil, Guttman, Davis & Malkin, N.Y.C., 1982-86, Weil, Guttman & Malkin, N.Y.C., 1986—; lectr. in field, 1952—. Contbr. articles to profl. jours. Served to lt (j.g.) USNR, 1943-45. Office: Weil Guttman & Malkin 60 E 42nd St New York NY 10165

WEIL, IRWIN, Slavic languages and literature educator; b. Cin., Apr. 16, 1928; s. Sidney and Florence (Levy) W.; m. Vivian Weil, Dec. 27, 1950; children: Martin, Alice, Daniel. A.B., U. Chgo., 1948, M.A., 1951; Ph.D., Harvard U., 1960. Sr. social sci. research analyst Library of Congress, 1951-54; teaching fellow Harvard U., 1956-58; mem. faculty Brandeis U., 1958-65; mem. faculty dept. Slavic langs. and lit. Northwestern U., Evanston, Ill., 1966—; chmn. dept. Northwestern U., 1976-82; vis. prof. U. Moscow, Soviet Acad. Scis.; set up series of internat. symposia between Am. scholars and USSR Acad. Scis.; founder 1st Soviet-Am. TV Student Competition in Lit., 1988-89. Author books and articles pub. in field, pub. in U.S.A. and Russia. Recipient Pushkin Internat. gold medal for outstanding teaching and research, 1984, Outstanding Teaching award Northwestern U. Alumni Assn.,

1987, Tempo All-Professor Team, Humanities, Chicago Tribune, 1993; Ford Found. fellow, 1954-55. Mem. Am. Assn. Tchrs. Slavic and East European Langs. (exec. sec. 1962-68, Excellence in Teaching award 1993), Am. Coun. Tchrs. Russian (v.p. 1975-79, pres. 1980-84), Internat. Assn. Profs. Russian (founding U.S. mem.). Jewish. Established TV competition on American and Russian literature between American and Russian high schoolers. Office: Northwestern U Slavic Dept Evanston IL 60208 *As a scholar and teacher trying hard to develop mutual understanding and cultural exchange with the USSR, I have discovered how important and fruitful it is to apply the normal standards of friendly discourse with people from an entirely different country and historical background.*

WEIL, JEFFREY GEORGE, lawyer; b. Allentown, Pa., Apr. 28, 1951; s. Russel G.E. and Irene Marie (Kozlowski) W.; divorced; children: Michael, Stephen, Brooke; m. Rachel Eisner, 1994. AB, Princeton U., 1973; JD, Harvard U., 1976. Bar: Pa. 1976, U.S. Dist. Ct. (ea. dist.) Pa. 1976, U.S. Ct. Appeals (3d cir.) 1976, U.S. Supreme Ct., 1988. Assoc. Dechert, Price & Rhoads, Phila., 1976-84, ptnr., 1984—, chmn. firm hiring com., 1987-89, mem. firm exec. com., 1990-94. Chmn. com. United Way Southeastern Pa., Phila., 1982-85, trustee, 1983-89, mem. funding policy com., 1987-90; participant Community Leadership Seminar Program, Phila., 1986; bd. dirs. Hawk Mountain Sanctuary, 1993—. Mem. ABA (vice chmn. admsntrn. law com. on pub. advs. and pub. representation 1985-88, mem. antitrust sect. pvt. litigation subcom. 1991—), Pa. Bar Assn., Phila. Bar Assn. (fed. cts. com. 1985—), Princeton U. Alumni Schs. Com., Princeton Club Phila. Avocations: fly-fishing, reading, sports. Home: 2 Esprit Ter Wayne PA 19087-5713 Office: Dechert Price & Rhoads 1717 Arch St Philadelphia PA 19103-2713

WEIL, JERRY, animator. MS, Brown U. Sr. animator MetroLight Studios, L.A. Creator fringe animation opening sequence (TV program) ABC World of Discovery; producer several films. Office: MetroLight Studios 5724 W 3rd St Ste 400 Los Angeles CA 90036-3078*

WEIL, JOHN DAVID, envelope company executive; b. Chgo., Sept. 28, 1947; s. Leslie Joseph and Carlyne (Strauss) W.; m. Marcie Bornfriend, July 4, 1981; children: Jessica Lauren, Michael Brandon, Samantha Leigh. BS in Econs., U. Ill., 1969; MBA in Fin., Northwestern U., 1971. Asst. to chmn. bd. Stanwood Industries, Lake Forest, Ill., 1971-74; pres. Kent Paper Co., Ridgewood, N.Y., 1974-81; pres., CEO Am. Envelope Co., Chgo., 1982-94; dir. Sage Enterprises, Inc., 1995—; operating affiliate McCown De Leeuw & Co., 1995—; bd. dirs., chmn. bd., 1995—; dir. Specialty Paperboard Inc., 1996—, Tiara Motorcoach Corp., 1996—. Mem. Envelope Mfrs. Am. (bd. dirs. 1986-94), Northmoor Country Club, Stonebridge Country Club. Office: McCown DeLeeuw & Co 5 Revere Dr Ste 200 Northbrook IL 60062

WEIL, JOHN WILLIAM, technology management consultant; b. N.Y.C., Feb. 3, 1928; s. Frank Leopold and Henrietta Amelia (Simons) W.; m. Joan Leatrice Landis, June 15, 1950; children—Nancy Ellen, Linda Jill. B.S., MIT, 1948; Ph.D., Cornell U., 1953. Various positions in nuclear reactors and computers Gen. Electric Co. (various locations), 1953-70; v.p. advanced systems and tech. Honeywell Info. Systems, Inc., Waltham, Mass., 1970-74; v.p., chief tech. officer Bendix Corp., Southfield, Mich., 1974-77; sr. v.p., chief tech. officer Bendix Corp., Southfield, 1977-83; v.p. advanced tech. and engrng. Allied Corp., Southfield, 1983; pres. Modular Bio Systems, Inc., 1983-85, Weil Assocs., Inc., Bloomfield Hills, Mich., 1985—; bd. dirs. Access Corp., Maxwell Labs.; founder Met. Detroit Sci. and Engrng. Coalition, 1977, sec., 1977-80, pres., 1980-82; chmn. Mich. Biotech. Inst., 1981-85, trustee, 1985-92; mem. Army Sci. Bd., 1982-84. Contbr. articles to prof. jours. AEC fellow, 1950-51. Home and Office: 218 Guilford Rd Bloomfield Hills MI 48304-2737

WEIL, LEON JEROME, diplomat; b. N.Y.C., June 15, 1927; m. Mabel Selig, Apr. 8, 1952; children: Leon Jerome Jr., Katherine A., Caroline E. A.B. cum laude, Princeton U. Ptnr. Herzfeld & Stern, N.Y.C., 1974-84, Steiner Rouse & Co., 1950-74; now with Gruntal & Co., N.Y.C.; U.S. ambassador to Nepal, 1984-87; cons. UN Devel. Programme, Financial Svcs. Vol. Corps., Internat. Found. for Electoral Systems; exch. ofcl. Am. Stock Exchange. Trustee Berkshire Sch., Sheffield, Mass., Outward Bound Inc., Greenwich, Conn., Robert Taft Inst. Govt., N.Y.C.; mem. Pres.'s Council on Phys. Fitness and Sports; bd. dirs. Media Rsch. Center of Alexandria, Va. Served with USN, 1945-46. Republican. Club: City Athletic (N.Y.C.). Home: 213 E 48th St New York NY 10017-1538

WEIL, LEONARD, banker; b. 1922; married. With U.S. Dept. State, Vienna, Austria, 1946; with Union Bank, Los Angeles, 1946-62; pres., CEO Mfrs. Bank, Los Angeles, 1962-86; pres. emeritus Mfrs. Bank, 1986—; bd. dirs. Bond Fund of Am., Inc., Capital World Bond Fund, Inc., Tax-Exempt Bond Fund of Am., Inc.; adj. asst. prof. fin. Anderson Grad. Sch. Mgmt., UCLA. Trustee UCLA Found.; bd. visitors UCLA Grad. Sch. Mgmt.; past pres. Town Hall; bd. dirs. Braille Inst. Served with U.S. Army, 1943-45. Mem. Calif. Bankers Assn. (bd. dirs., past pres.), Am. Mgmt. Assn., Am. Econs. Assn., Am. Bankers Assn. Office: 233 Wilshire Blvd Fl 6 Santa Monica CA 90401-1205

WEIL, LOUIS ARTHUR, III, newspaper publishing executive; b. Grand Rapids, Mich., Mar. 14, 1941; s. Louis Arthur, Jr. and Kathryn (Halligan) W.; m. Mary Elizabeth Buckingham, Sept. 7, 1963 (div. June 1977); children: Scott Arthur, Christopher Davison, Timothy Buckingham; m. Daryl Hopkins Goss, Jan. 26, 1980. B.A. in English, Ind. U., 1963; DHL (hon.), Mercy Coll., Grand Valley State U. Various positions Times Herald, Port Huron, Mich., 1966-68; personnel dir., pub. Journal and Courier, Lafayette, Ind., 1968-73; gen. mgr., pub. Gannett Westchester Rockland Newspapers, White Plains, N.Y., 1973-74, pres., gen. mgr., 1974-77, pres., pub., 1977-79; v.p. devel. Gannett Co., Inc., N.Y.C., 1979-83, sr. v.p. planning and devel., 1982-86; chmn., pub. Gannett Westchester Rockland Newspapers, White Plains, 1984-86; pres. The Detroit News, 1986-89, pub., 1987-89; U.S. pub. Time Mag., 1989-91; pub., chief exec. officer, exec. v.p. Ariz. Republic, Phoenix Gazette, Ariz. Bus. Gazette, 1991-96; pres., CEO Central Newspapers, Inc., Phoenix, 1996—; bd. dirs. Ctrl. Newspapers, Inc., Prudential. Chmn. membership Trustee Found. for Am. Comm.; bd. trustees, adv. bd. Ariz. Cancer Ctr. at U. Ariz.; chmn. adv. bd. Kids Voting USA; bd. dirs. Ariz. Cmty. Found., Ariz. Cities in Schs., Ind. U. Found.; campaign chmn. Valley of the Sun United Way, 1992; past chmn. Greater Phoenix Leadership; past pres. bd. trustees Phoenix Art Mus. With USN. Office: Phoenix Newspapers Inc 120 E Van Buren St Phoenix AZ 85004-2227

WEIL, MAX HARRY, physician, medical educator, medical scientist; b. Baden, Switzerland, Feb. 9, 1927; came to U.S., 1937, naturalized, 1944; s. Marcel and Gretl (Winter) W.; m. Marianne Judith Posner, Apr. 1955; children: Susan Margot, Carol Juliet. AB, U. Mich., 1948; MD, SUNY, N.Y.C., 1952; PhD, U. Minn., 1957. Diplomate Am. Bd. Internal Medicine and Critical Care Medicine, Nat. Bd. Med. Examiners. Intern in internal medicine U. Cin. Med. Ctr., 1952-53; resident U. Minn. Hosps., Heart Hosp., VA Hosp., Mpls., 1953-55; rsch. fellow U. Minn., Mpls., 1955-56; sr. fellow Nat. Heart Inst., Mayo Clinic, Rochester, Minn., 1956-57; chief cardiology City of Hope Med. Ctr., Duarte, Calif., 1957-59; asst. clin. prof. U. So. Calif. Sch. Medicine, L.A., 1957-59, asst. prof., 1959-63, assoc. prof., 1963-71, prof., 1971-81; chmn. L.A. Com. on Emergency Med. Svcs., 1968-73; prof., chmn. dept. medicine, chief divsn. cargiology Chgo. Med. Sch., Finch U. Health Scis., North Chicago, Ill., 1981-91, disting. univ. prof., 1992-94, disting. univ. prof. emeritus, 1994—; prof. clin. med. bioengring. U. So. Calif., 1972-91, adj. prof. medicine, 1981—, dir. Shock Rsch. Unit, 1961-81, Inst. Critical Care Medicine Ann. Symposium, 1963—, Ctr. Critically Ill., 1968-80; pres. Inst. Critical Care Medicine, Palm Springs, Calif. and Northbrook, Ill., 1974—; attending cardiologist children's divsn. L.A. County/U. So. Calif. Med. Ctr., 1958-65, attending physician, 1958-71, sr. attending cardiologist, 1968-73, sr. attending physician, 1971-81; vis. prof. anesthesiology/critical care medicine U. Pitts., 1972—; clin. prof. anesthesiology UCLA, 1981-95; adj. prof. Northwestern U. Med. Sch., Chgo., 1992—; clin. prof. anesthesiology U. So. Calif. Sch. Medicine, L.A., 1995—, Weil Internat. lectr. in critical care medicine, 1987; numerous vis. professorships and lectureships; cons. in field; prin. rschr. numerous grants and rsch. projects. Sect. editor Archives Internal Medicine, 1983-86, JAMA, 1969-72; guest editor Am. Jour. Cardiology, 1982, Critical Care Medicine, 1985; mem. editl. bd. Am. Jour. Medicine, 1971-79, Chest, 1980-95, Jour. Circulatory Shock, 1979-92, Clin. Engring. Newsletter, 1980—, Methods of Info. in Medicine, 1977-91, Jour. Clin. Illness, 1986—, Clin. Intensive Care, 1989—; mem. editl. adv. bd. Emergency Medicine, 1978—, Issues in Health Care Tech., 1983-86; assoc. editor Critical Care Medicine, 1973-74, mem. editl. bd., 1973-91, 94—; editor-in-chief Acute Care, 1983-90; contbr. articles to profl. jours.; patentee in field. Pres. Temple Brotherhood, Wilshire Blvd. Temple, L.A., 1967-68; bd. dirs. Hollywood Presbyn. Med. Ctr., 1976-81, L.A. chpt. Met. Am. Heart Assn., 1962-67, Chgo. chpt. Met. Am. Heart Assn., 1982—. Served with U.S. Army, 1946-47. Recipient prize in internal medicine SUNY, 1952, Alumni medallion SUNY, 1970; Disting. Svc. award Soc. Critical Care Medicine, 1984; numerous rsch. grants, 1959—; named Disting. Alumni Lectr., 1967, Oscar Schwindetzky Meml. Lectr. Internat. Anesthesia Rsch. Soc., 1978; recipient Lawrence R. Medoff award Chgo. Med. Sch., 1987, Morris L. Parker Rsch. award, 1989; Lilly scholar, 1988-89. Master ACP; fellow Am. Coll. Cardiology (chmn. emergency cardiac care com. 1974-81), Am. Coll. Chest Physicians (coun. clin. cardiology, coun. critical care medicine), Am. Coll. Clin. Pharmacology, Am. Coll. Critical Care Medicine (Disting. Investigator award 1990, 96), Am. Heart Assn. (coun. circulation, coun. basic sci., coun. cardiopulmonary and critical care, coun. clin. cardiology), N.Y. Acad. Sci., Chgo. Soc. Internal Medicine; mem. AMA (sect. editor jour. 1969-72), IEEE, Ill. Med. Assn., Lake County Med. Assn., L.A. County Med. Assn., Am. Physiol. Soc. Am. Soc. Pharmacology and Exptl. Therapeutics, Am. Soc. Echocardiography, Am. Soc. Nephrology, Am. Trauma Soc. (founding mem.), Assn. Computing Machinery, Assn. Am. Med. Colls., Ctrl. Soc. Clin. Rsch., Chgo. Cardiol. Group (sec.-treas. 1986-88, chmn. 1988-90), Chgo. Medicine, Lake County Heart Assn. (bd. govs. 1983-86), Intensive Care Soc. U.K., L.A. Soc. Internal Medicine, Soc. Exptl. Biology and Medicine, Western Soc. Clin. Rsch., Fedn. Am. Socs. Exptl. Biology, Am. Soc. Parenteral and Enteral Nutrition, Nat. Acad. Practice (disting. practitioner), Skull and Dagger, Sigma Xi, Alpha Omega Alpha. Jewish. Avocations: swimming, tennis, photography, philosophy-economics. Office: Inst Critical Care Medicine Bldg 1695 N Sunrise Way #3 Palm Springs CA 92262-5309

WEIL, MYRON, retired banker; b. Lincoln, Nebr., Apr. 17, 1918; s. Julius and Fannie (Livingston) W.; m. Pauline Clayton, Sept. 26, 1945; children—Michele Susan, Judy Lynn, Layla. B.S., Yale, 1939. Exec. v.p., dir. Nat. Bank Commerce, Lincoln, 1939-67; bd. dir. First Nat. Bank, Clinton, Iowa, 1967-91, chmn. bd. dirs., 1984-91; exec. v.p. Hawkeye Bancorp., Des Moines, 1967-83, bd. dirs., 1967-91; vice chmn. bd Hawkeye Bancorp., 1983-86. Served to maj., Q.M.C. AUS, 1939-45. Decorated Bronze Star. Home: 1025 Crescent Dr Clinton IA 52732-4739

WEIL, NANCY HECHT, psychologist, educator; b. Chgo., Apr. 15, 1936; d. Theodore R. and Jenice (Abrams) Hecht; children: Lynda Jo, Edward S. Student Cornell U., 1954-57; MEd, Nat. Coll. Edn., Ill., 1974; PhD, Northwestern U., 1976; postgrad. Chgo. Inst. Psychoanalysis, 1972-74; attending staff Michael Reese Hosp., 1978—; clin. asst. prof. U. Chgo. Pritzker Sch. of Medicine, 1985-90; asst. prof. psychiatry Coll. Medicine, U. Ill. at Chgo., 1990; med. staff, clin. asst. prof. psychiatry U. Ill. Abraham Sch. Medicine, Chgo., 1990—; mental health cons., State of Ill., writer mental health prevention plan; vice-chair Ill. Mental Health Planning Bd., 1973-75; cons. Ill. Comprehensive Health/Planning Agency, 1974; bd. trustees Chgo Inst. for Psychoanalysis, 1973—, faculty continuing edn., 1976, 87; asst. prof. Northwestern U. Med. Sch., 1976-77, assoc. prof., 1977-79; lectr. U. Chgo. Pritzker Sch. Medicine, 1978-85; chmn. adv. council Ill. Dept. Mental Health 5-Yr. Plan, 1975-80. Bd. dirs. Chgo. Focus. Fellow Am. Orthospsychiat. Assn.; mem. Am. Psychol. Assn., Ill. Psychol. Assn., Nat. Health Register Assn., Chgo. Assn. Psychoanalytic Psychology, AAUP. Contbr. articles to profl. jours.; lectr. applied psychoanalysis. Home: 200 E Delaware Pl Apt 24 C Chicago IL 60611-1736 Office: 180 N Michigan Ave Chicago IL 60601-7401

WEIL, PAUL PERES, lawyer; b. Evansville, Ind., Jan. 30, 1936; s. Henry A. and Clarice Emy (Peres) W.; m. Barbara Ann Podell; children: Cynthia Marie Weil Connolly, Leslie Renee Weil Masaki. Student, U. Pa., 1953-55; BSBA, Washington U., 1959, JD, 1959. Bar: Mo. 1960. Assoc. Thomas, Busse, Cullen & Godfrey, St. Louis, 1959-68, ptnr., 1968-73; ptnr. Bryan Cave (formerly Bryan, Cave, McPheeters & McRoberts), St. Louis, 1973—. Mem. handicapped budget panel United Way, 1976-77; bd. dirs. Kammergild Chamber Orch. St. Louis, 1986-88; trustee Rosalie Tilles Non-Sectarian Charity Fund, 1987—; pres. Congregation Temple Israel, St. Louis, 1980-83. Mem. ABA (IRS regional liaison), Mo. Bar Assn. (vice chmn. tax sect. 1970), St. Louis Bar Assn. (v.p. 1969-72, treas. 1972-73), Noonday Club, Mo. Athletic Club (chmn. art com. 1978-80, mem. bd. govs. 1988-91). Republican. Jewish. Office: Bryan Cave 1 Metropolitan Sq 211 N Broadway Saint Louis MO 63102-2733

WEIL, PETER HENRY, lawyer; b. N.Y.C., Nov. 20, 1933; s. Frank L. and Henrietta Amelia (Simons) W.; m. Helen Fay Kolodkin, Dec. 18, 1960; children: Karen W. Markus, Frank L. BA cum laude, Princeton U., 1954; LLB cum laude, Harvard U., 1957. Bar: N.Y. 1957, U.S. Dist. Cts. (so. and ea. dists.) N.Y. 1972. Assoc. Weil, Gotshal & Manges, N.Y.C., 1958-62; from assoc. to ptnr. Kaye Scholer, N.Y.C., 1962-95, ret., 1995; lectr. SMU Inst. on Comml. Financing, 1985-94, Banking Law Inst., 1987-89. Author: Asset Based Lending: An Introductory Guide to Secured Financing, PLI, 1989, 3d edit., 1996. Fellow Am. Coll. of Commercial Fin. Lawyers; former chmn. N.Y. bd. overseers, former bd. govs. Hebrew Union Coll., Jewish Inst. Religion, Cin., N.Y.C., Los Angeles, Jerusalem. With U.S. Army 1957-58. Mem. Ringwood Golden Master Volleyball Team, U.S. Nat. Champions, 1983. Mem. ABA, Assn. of Bar of City of N.Y. (banking law com. 1975-78).

WEIL, RAYMOND RICHARD, soil scientist; b. Detroit, May 27, 1948; s. Ulrich L. and Hilde C. (Levy) W.; m. Susan R. Boscov, Feb. 22, 1968 (div. Feb. 1982); children: Benjamin S., Joshua J.; m. Patricia Lynn Driggers, Feb. 5, 1983. BS, Mich. State U., 1970; MS, Purdue U., 1972; PhD, Va. Poly. Inst. and State U., 1977. Cert. profl. soil scientist. Vol Peace Corps, Ethiopia, 1970; Farm mgr. Nat. Sharecropper's Fund, Wadesboro, N.C., 1972-73; instr. Va. Poly. Inst. and State U., Blacksburg, 1975-77; lectr. U. Malawi, Lilongwe, 1977-79; asst. prof. U. Md., College Park, 1979-84, assoc. prof., 1984-91, prof., 1991—; cosn. Forest Dept., Sri Lanka Govt., 1981; adv. bd. Com. on Agr. Sustainability for Developing Countries, Washington, 1988—; mem. task force Ecosystem Farm, Accokeek (Med.) Found., 1990—, chair medium size farm bd. Future Harvest Project, 1995—. Author: Lab Manual for Soil Science, 1993; co-author: Nature and Properties of Soil: A Study Guide, 1984; co-author: Nature and Properties of Soils, 11th edit., 1996; contbr. articles to profl. jours. Named Fulbright-Hayes Scholarship Exch. fellow, Zimbabwe, 1985, Fulbright-Hayes Africa Regional Rsch. scholar, Tanzania, 1994, Nat. Def. Edn. Act fellow, Ind., Md., 1991, Md. Agr. Exptl. Sta., 1991, 92, 93, 94, U.S. AID, Malawi, 1988-92, USDA Agrl. Rsch. Edn., 1996—. Mem. Am. Soc. Agronomy (internat. div. chair 1993-94), Soil Sci. Soc. Am., Internat. Soil Sci. Soc. Achievements include development of new methods of matching fertilizer use to soil requirements in peasant farming sectors by mapping soil and plant nutrient status, of improved cropping system for sustainable production of cereals and legumes; development of new soil management system to reduce groundwater contamination by nitrates; contributions to understanding how best to manage organic wastes such as animal manure and sewage sludge in farming systems; development of new method for indigenous nutrient sources to enhance soil fertility, practical measures of soil quality. Office: U Md Agronomy Dept College Park MD 20742

WEIL, ROLF ALFRED, economist, university president emeritus; b. Pforzheim, Germany, Oct. 29, 1921; came to U.S., 1936, naturalized, 1944; s. Henry and Lina (Landauer) W.; m. Leni Metzger, Nov. 3, 1945; children: Susan Linda, Ronald Alan. B.A., U. Chgo., 1942, Ph.D., 1950; D. Hebrew Letters, Coll. Jewish Studies, 1967; L.H.D., Loyola U., 1970; D.H.L., Bowling Green State U., Ohio, 1986; LHD, Roosevelt U., 1988. Rsch. asst. Cowles Commn. for Rsch. in Econs., 1942-44; rsch. analyst Ill. Dept. Revenue, 1944-46; mem. faculty Roosevelt U., Chgo., 1946—, prof. fin. and econs., also chmn. dept. fin., 1954-65, dean Coll. Bus. Adminstrn., 1957-64, acting pres., 1965-66, pres., 1966-88, pres. emeritus, 1988—; past pres. Selfhelp Home for the Aged, Chgo.; cons. to non-profit orgns., 1988—. Author: Through these Portals-from Immigrant to College President, 1991; contbr. articles on fin. Bd. dirs. trustees Roosevelt U., Selfhelp of Chgo., Inc. Mem. Am. Econ. Assn., Cliff Dwellers Club.

WEIL, ROMAN LEE, accounting educator; b. Montgomery, Ala., May 22, 1940; s. Roman L. and Charlotte (Alexander) W.; children: Alexis Cherie, Charles Alexander Roman, Lacey Lorraine. B.A., Yale U., 1962; M.S. in Indsl. Adminstrn, Carnegie-Mellon U., 1965, Ph.D. in Econs., 1966. C.P.A.; Cert. Mgmt. Acct. From instr. to prof. U. Chgo., 1965-93, Sigmund E. Edelstone prof. acctg., 1993—; Mills B. Lane prof. indsl. mgmt. Ga. Inst. Tech., 1974-76; adv. com. replacement cost implementation SEC, 1976-77; prof. acctg. Stanford U., 1984, prof. econs., 1985, prof. law, 1990-96; prof. acctg. and law NYU Sch. Law, 1985; mem. adv. coun. Fin. Acctg. Stds., 1989-94; mem. task force on consolidations Fin. Acctg. Stds. Bd., 1984-89, mem. task force on discounting, 1989—, mem. task force on fin. instruments, 1994—, mem. adv. coun., 1989-94. Author: Fundamentals of Accounting, 1975, Financial Accounting, 7th edit., 1994, Accounting: The Language of Business, 9th edit., 1994, Inflation Accounting, 1976, Replacement Cost Accounting, 1976, Managerial Accounting, 1979, 5th edit., 1994, Litigation Services Handbook, 1990-96, editor: Handbook of Modern Accounting, 1977, 3d edit., 1983, Handbook of Cost Accounting, 1980, 4th edit., 1985, Acctg. Rev., 1974-79, Fin. Analysts Jour., 1980-88. NSF grantee, 1967-81. Mem. AICPA, Ill. Soc. CPAs, Am. Econ. Assn., Inst. Mgmt. Scis., Nat. Assn. Accts. (cert. mgmt. acct.), Am. Acctg. Assn., Inst. Managerial Acctg., Assembly Am. Collegiate Schs. Bus. (acctg. accreditation com. 1987-88), Oenonomy Soc. (co-chmn.). Home: 175 E Delaware Pl Apt 8302 Chicago IL 60611-1732 Office: U Chgo Grad Sch Bus 1101 E 58th St Chicago IL 60637-1511

WEIL, STEPHEN EDWARD, museum official; b. N.Y.C., June 24, 1928; s. Sidney and Beatrice (Sachs) W.; m. Rose Reicherson, Oct. 15, 1950 (div.); children: Rachel J., David N., Michael D.; m. Elizabeth Carbone, Sept. 7, 1974 (div.); m. Wendy Luke, Apr. 8, 1990. A.B., Brown U., 1949; LL.B., Columbia U., 1956. Bar: N.Y. 1956. Assoc. firm Rosenman, Colin, Kaye, Petschek & Freund, N.Y.C., 1956-63; v.p., gen. mgr. Marlborough-Gerson Gallery, N.Y.C., 1963-67; adminstr., sec., trustee Whitney Mus. Am. Art, N.Y.C., 1967-74; dep. dir., sec. Hirshhorn Mus. and Sculpture Garden, Smithsonian Instn., Washington, 1974-95; emeritus sr. scholar, 1995—; mem. cultural property adv. com. USIA, 1995—; chair adv. com. Museum Loan Network, 1995—. Co-author: Art Works - Law, Policy, Practice, 1974, Art Law - Rights and Liabilities of Creators and Collectors, 1986; author: Beauty and the Beast, 1983, Rethinking the Museum, 1990, A Cabinet of Curiosities, 1995; co-editor: Art Galleries and Museums, 1973. Mem. mus. adv. panel N.Y. State Coun. on Arts, 1974-78; mem. adv. panel Inst. for Mus. Scis.; trustee Brown U., 1989-95. Mem. Am. Assn. Mus. (treas., v.p., councilor), Am. Fedn. Arts (trustee 1988-95). Jewish. Home: 2936 28th St NW Washington DC 20008-3413 Office: Ctr for Museum Studies Smithsonian Instn Washington DC 20560

WEIL, THOMAS ALEXANDER, electronics engineer; b. N.Y.C., Jan. 22, 1930; s. Frank Leopold and Henrietta Amelia (Simons) W.; m. Dianne Isaacs; children: Deborah, Elizabeth, Alexander. BSEE, MIT, 1951. Engr. modulator sect. Raytheon Co., Watertown, Mass., 1951-55, sect. mgr. transmitters, 1955-69, dept. mgr. transmitters, 1969-77, staff scientist equipment devel. labs., 1972-95; ret., lab. mgr. radar systems, 1977-79, lab. mgr. advanced devel., 1979-80, program mgr. oil shale program, 1980-84; cons. in field, 1995—. Contbr. 33 articles to profl. jours., 3 chpts. to books; patentee (10) in field. Recipient Excellence in Tech. award Raytheon co., 1990; Raytheon Co. fellow, 1989. Fellow IEEE (tech. papers com. Modulator Symposia Microwave Tube Symposia, Germeshausen award 1994). Republican. Mem. Universalist-Unitarian Ch. Avocations: classical music, photography, mountain climbing. Home: 14 Lanark Rd Wellesley MA 02181-3029 *Evolution and survival of the fittest have left mankind aggressive and prone to make war. Peace depends on finding how to overcome this heritage. Shouldn't we be working on how to resteer mankind's instincts?.*

WEIL, THOMAS P., health services consultant; b. Mount Vernon, N.Y., Oct. 2, 1932; s. H.M. and Alice (Franc) W.; m. Janet Whalen, Feb. 13, 1965. BA, Union Coll., 1954; MPH, Yale U., 1958; PhD, U. Mich., 1964. S.S. Goldwater fellow Mount Sinai Med. Ctr., N.Y.C., 1957-58; assoc. cons. J.G. Steinle Assocs., Garden City, N.Y., 1958-61; asst. prof. UCLA, 1962-65; assoc. dir. Touro Infirmary, New Orleans, 1964-66; prof., dir. U. Mo., 1966-71; v.p. E.D. Rosenfeld Assocs., N.Y.C., 1971-75; pres. Bedford Health Assocs. Inc., N.Y., N.C., 1975—; chmn. Health Edn. & Applied Rsch. Found., Washington, 1981-83; bd. dirs. Albany (N.Y.) Med. Ctr., Inc., 1974-77; cons. to numerous hosps., med. schs., health related orgs., 1958—. Contbr. articles profl. jours. Named vis. prof. W.K. Kellogg Found., Sydney, Australia, 1969; recipient svc. award Am. Assn. Healthcare Cons., 1982; Weil Disting. Profl. in Health Svcs. Mgmt., U. Mo. established in 1991. Fellow APHA, Am. Assn. Healthcare Cons. (emeritus), Am. Coll. Healthcare Execs. (emeritus). Jewish. Avocations: mantrailing bloodhounds, quarter horses. Home: 1400 Town Mountain Rd Asheville NC 28804-2936 Office: Bedford Health Assocs Inc Flat Iron Bldg Ste 900A Asheville NC 28801

WEILAND, CHARLES HANKES, lawyer; b. Billings, Mont., Feb. 19, 1921; s. George Michael and Elizabeth (Hankes) W. A.B. cum laude, Johns Hopkins U., 1942; J.D., Harvard U., 1948. Bar: Ill. 1949, U.S. Dist. Ct. (no. dist.) Ill. 1949, U.S. Ct. Appeals (7th cir.) 1949, U.S. Supreme Ct. 1968. Assoc. Lord, Bissell & Brook, Chgo., 1948-55, ptnr., 1956-83; chmn. Cook County Inquiry Bd., Supreme Ct. Ill. Atty. Regis. and Disciplinary Commn., 1974-75. Served with AUS, 1942-46. Mem. Ill. Bar Assn., Chgo. Bar Assn. Republican. Clubs: Law; Legal (Chgo.).

WEILBACHER, WILLIAM MANNING, advertising and marketing consultant; b. Albany, N.Y., June 23, 1928; s. William Carl and Gladys (Manning) W.; m. Martha Ethel Meyer, May 19, 1962; children: Barbara Taylor, Elizabeth Manning. BS, Yale U., 1949; MS, Columbia, 1951. Supr. product analysis Nat. Biscuit Co., 1951-53; v.p., dir. rsch. Dancer-Fitzgerald-Sample, Inc., 1953-62, sr. v.p., 1971-73, exec. v.p., 1973-74, vice chmn., 1974-79; bd. dir., sr. v.p. McCaffrey & McCall, 1962-66; exec. dir. Ctr. for Advanced Practice, 1966; ptnr. Jack Tinker and Ptnrs., Interpub. Inc., 1966-69; v.p., dir. rsch. J. Walter Thompson Co., 1969-70; pres. Master Jazz Recs., Inc., 1967—, D-F-S Realty Inc., 1975-79, D-F-S Holdings Inc., 1974-79, Bismark Corp., 1979—, Second Mktg. Opinion, Inc., 1981—; lectr. advt. Grad. Sch. Bus., Columbia U., 1956-64, adj. prof. mktg., 1976-77, 81-82, 83; lectr. mktg. CCNY, 1955-57; adj. prof. mktg. Grad. Sch. Bus., NYU, 1965-70, 80-81, 88; Spencer vis. prof. S.I. Newhouse Sch. Pub. Comms., Syracuse U., 1982-86; mem. Radio-TV Ratings Rev. Com., 1958-65; bd. dirs. Audit Bur. Circulation, 1964-71, Broacast Rating Coun., 1963-67; mem. tech. adv. com. Robert Wood Johnson Found., 1994—. Author: (with L.O. Brown, R. S. Lessler) Advertising Media, 1957, (with H.C. Barksdale) Marketing Research; Selected Readings and Analytic Commentaries, 1966, (with R.A. Bauer, S.A. Greyser) Advertising in America: The Consumer View, 1968, Marketing Management Cases, 1970, 4th edit. 1986, Advertising, 1979, 2d edit. 1984, Cases in Advertising, 1981, Auditing Productivity, 1981, Choosing an Advertising Agency, 1983, Current Advertiser Practices in Compensating Their Advertising Agencies, 1983, 86, 89, 92, 95, Choosing and Working with Your Advertising Agency, 1991, Managing Agency Relations, 1991, Brand Marketing, 1993, contbg. editor: Marketing Handbook, 1965. Vice chmn. tech. com. Advt. Rsch. Found., 1960-63, chmn., 1963-65, bd. dirs., 1965-67. Mem. Am. Assn. Advt. Agys. (past vice chmn. rsch. com.), Market Rsch. Coun. (pres. 1970-71), Yale Club of N.Y.C., Eastward Ho Country Club, Alpha Kappa Psi, Beta Gamma Sigma. Home: Box 2002 30 Bismark Way Dennis MA 02638-2207

WEILER, JEFFRY LOUIS, lawyer; b. N.Y.C., Dec. 31, 1942; s. Kurt and Elaine (Kabb) W.; m. Susan Karen Goodman, June 8, 1964; children: Philip K., June M. BS, Miami U., Oxford, Ohio, 1964; JD, Cleve. State U., 1970. Bar: Ohio 1970, Fla. 1981; CPA, Ohio 1968. Acct. Meaden & Moore, CPAs, Cleve., 1964-65; IRS agt. U.S. Dept. Treasury, Cleve., 1965-70; assoc. Ulmer & Berne, Cleve., 1970-71; ptnr. Benesch, Friedlander, Coplan & Aronoff, Cleve., 1971—; adj. assoc. prof. Cleve.-Marshall Coll. Law, Cleve. State U., 1980-87. Contbr. to profl. pubs. Former trustee, Jewish Community Fedn., Cleve., 1978-83. Fellow Am. Coll. Trust and Estate Counsel; mem. ABA (sect. taxation, estate and gift tax subcom.), Cleve. Estate Planning Inst. (chmn. 1980), Cleve. Tax Inst. (chmn. 1983), Cleve. Bar Assn. (treas. 1993-96, trustee 1988-91). Avocations: photography, sailboat racing, ice skating. Home: 24714 Maidstone Ln Cleveland OH 44122-1614 Office:

Benesch Friedlander 2300 BP America Bldg 200 Public Sq Cleveland OH 44114-2378

WEILER, KURT WALTER, radio astronomer; b. Phoenix, Mar. 16, 1943; s. Henry Carl and Dorothy (Esser) w.; m. Geertje Stoelwinder, June 8, 1979; children: Corinn Nynke Yoon, Anil Erick Jivan, Sanna Femke Lee. BS, U. Ariz., 1964; PhD, Calif. Inst. Tech., 1970. Guest investigator Netherlands Found. for Radioastronomy, Groningen, 1970-74; sci. collaborator Inst. for Radioastronomy, Bologna, Italy, 1975-76; sr. scientist Max Planck Inst. for Radioastronomy, Bonn, W.Ger., 1976-79; program dir. NSF, Washington, 1979-85; radio astronomer Naval Rsch. Lab, Washington, 1985—; Halley steering com. NASA, Washington, 1981-85. Author: WSRT Users Guide, 1973, 75; editor Radio Astronomy from Space, 1987; editor: Low Frequency Astrophysics from Space, 1990; contbr. over 150 articles to profl. jours. and mags. Mem. Am. Astron. Soc., Royal Astron. Soc., Internat. Astron. Union, Internat. Sci. Radio Union, Nederlandse Astronomen Club, Jaguar Club, Nat. Capital Club. Home: 6232 Cockspur Dr Alexandria VA 22310-1504 Office: Naval Rsch Lab Code 7214 4555 Overlook Ave SW Washington DC 20375-5351

WEILER, PAUL CRONIN, law educator; b. Port Arthur, Ont., Can., Jan. 28, 1939; s. G. Bernard and Marcella (Cronin) W.; m. Florrie Darwin, 1988; children: Virginia, John, Kathryn, Charles. B.A. with honors, U. Toronto, 1960, M.A. with honors, 1961; LL.B., Osgoode Hall Law Sch., 1964; LLM, Harvard Law Sch., 1965; LL.D., U. Victoria, 1981. Bar: Ont. Prof. law Osgoode Hall Law Sch., 1965-72; chmn. Labour Relations Bd. B.C., 1973-78; Mackenzie King prof. Can. studies Harvard Law Sch., 1978-80, prof. law, 1980—, Henry J. Friendly prof. law, 1993—; prof. law, 1993—; chief counsel U.S. Commn. Future of Worker-Mgmt. Rels.; prin. legal investigator Harvard U. Med. Practice Study Group; impartial umpire AFL-CIO; chief reporter Am. Law Inst. Tort Reform Project; cons. to U.S. Commn. on Comprehensive Health Care (Pepper Commn.); spl. counsel Govt. of Ont. Rev. of Workers' Compensation, 1980-88; mem. pub. rev. bd. United Auto Workers, chief counsel Pres.' commn. Future Worker-Mgmt. Rels., 1993—; panelist, US/Canada Free Trade Agreement Softwood Lumber Arbitration, 1992-93. Author: Labor Arbitration and Industrial Change, 1970; In the Last Resort: A Critical Study of the Supreme Court of Canada, 1974; (with others) Labor Relations Law in Canada, rev. edit. 1974; (with others) Studies in Sentencing in Canada, 1974; Reconcilable Differences: New Directions in Canadian Labour Law, 1980; Reforming Workers Compensation, 1980; MEGA Projects: The Collective Bargaining Dimensions, 1981; Protecting the Worker From Disability, 1983; Governing the Workplace: The Future of Labor and Employment Law, 1990; (with others) Patients, Doctors, and Lawyers: Medical Injury, Malpractice Litigation and Patient Compensation, 1990; Medical Malpractice on Trial, 1991; (with others) A Measure of Malpractice, 1992; Cases, Materials and Problems on Sports & the Law, 1993; contbr. articles to profl. jours. Mem. Nat. Acad. Arbitrators, Nat. Acad. Social Ins., Nat. Acad. Sci., Inst. Medicine. Roman Catholic. Club: Cambridge Tennis (Cambridge, Mass.). Office: Harvard U Law Sch 1525 Massachusetts Ave Cambridge MA 02138-2903

WEILER, TODD ALAN, army official; b. Texarkana, Tex., Oct. 7, 1964; s. Gerald and Mamie Ruth (Clements) Penny. BA, Tex. Christian U., 1987. Cert. comml. rated rotorcraft aviator. Mem. campaign staff Clinton for Pres., 1992; White House liaison Dept. Def., Washington, 1993; dep. asst. sec. U.S. Army, Washington, 1993—; Dept. of Army rep. Civil-Tiltrotor Commn., Washington, 1993—. With U.S. Army, 1987-91, Desert Storm. Decorated 2 Air medals. Mem. VFW, Am. Legion, Ind. Charities Am., 101st Airborne Assn., Clinton-Gore Adminstrn. Assn. Democrat. Avocations: boating, flying, skiing. Home: 326 Cloudes Mill Dr Alexandria VA 22304-3077 Office: OASA M&RA The Pentagon Rm 2E 580 Washington DC 20310

WEIL-GARRIS BRANDT, KATHLEEN (KATHLEEN BRANT), art historian; d. Kurt Hermann and Charlotte (Garris) Weil; m. Werner Brandt (dec. 1983). BA with honors, Vassar Coll., 1956; postgrad., U. Bonn, Germany, 1956-57; MA, Radcliffe U., 1958; PhD, Harvard, 1966. Asst. prof. NYU, N.Y.C., 1963-67, assoc. prof., 1967-72, prof., 1973—; asst. prof. NYU Inst. Fine Arts, N.Y.C., 1966-67, assoc. prof., 1967-72, prof., 1973—; vis. prof. Harvard U., Cambridge, Mass., 1980; editor in chief The Art Bulletin, N.Y.C., 1977-81; cons. on Renaissance art Vatican Mus., 1987—; vis. fellow Bibliotheca Hartziana (Max-Planck Inst.) Rome. Author: Leonardo and Central Italian Art, 1974, Problems In Cinquecento Sculpture, 1977; author: (with J. d'Amico) The Renaissance Cardinal's Ideal Palace, 1981; contbr. numerous articles to profl. jours. Decorated officer Order of Merit (Italy); recipient rsch. award Humboldt Found., 1985, Disting. Tchg. award Lindback Found., 1967, Golden Dozen Tchr. award NYU, 1993; Guggenheim fellow, 1976; grantee Henkel Found., 1987. Mem. Coll. Art Assn. (bd. dirs. 1973-74, 77-81), Renaissance Soc. Am. (editl. bd. 1992—), Soc. Archtl. Historians, N.Y. Acad. Scis., Phi Beta Kappa (v.p. NYU chpt. 1979-81). Avocations: art films, conservation, music, dance. Office: NYU Inst Fine Arts 1 E 78th St New York NY 10021-0102

WEILL, GEORGES GUSTAVE, mathematics educator; b. Strasbourg, France, Apr. 9, 1926; came to U.S., 1956; s. Edmond and Germaine (Falck) W. Ed., Ecole Polytechnique, Paris, 1950; E.N.S., Telecom., Paris, 1952; Licence de Mathematiques, U. Paris, France, 1954, D.Sc. in Physics, 1955; Ph.D. in Math, U. Calif. at Los Angeles, 1960. Research scientist Compagnie Generale de Telegraphie Sans Fil, France, 1952-56; research fellow dept. elec. engring. Calif. Inst. Tech., Pasadena, 1956-59; teaching asso. math. U. Calif. at Los Angeles, 1959-60; research fellow math. Harvard, 1960-62; lectr., research asso. Yale, 1962-64; vis. asst. prof. Belfer Grad. Sch. Sci., Yeshiva U., 1964-65; assoc. prof. math. Poly. U., Bklyn., 1964-65, prof., 1966—. Mem. Am. Math. Soc., Societe Mathematique de France, IEEE (sr. mem.), Sigma Xi, Pi Mu Epsilon. Office: Polytechnic Univ 333 Jay St Brooklyn NY 11201-2907

WEILL, HANS, physician, educator; b. Berlin, Aug. 31, 1933; came to U.S., 1939; s. Kurt and Gerda (Philipp) W.; m. Kathleen Burton, Apr. 3, 1958; children: Judith, Leslie, David. B.S., Tulane U., 1955, M.D., 1958. Diplomate: Am. Bd. Internal Medicine. Intern Mt. Sinai Hosp., N.Y.C., 1958-59; resident Tulane Med. Unit, Charity Hosp. La., New Orleans, 1959-60; chief resident Tulane Med. Unit, Charity Hosp. La., 1961-62, sr. vis. physician, 1972—; NIH research fellow dept. medicine and pulmonary lab. Sch. Medicine Tulane U., New Orleans, 1960-61; instr. medicine Sch. Medicine Tulane U., 1962-64, asst. prof. medicine, 1964-67, assoc. prof., 1967-71, prof. medicine, 1971—, Schlieder Found. prof. pulmonary medicine, 1985—; chief Environ. Medicine sect. Tulane Med. Center, 1980—; dir. univ. Ctr. for Bioenviron. Rsch., 1989-93; dir. interdisciplinary research group in occupational lung diseases Nat. Heart, Lung and Blood Inst., 1972-92, mem. nat. adv. council, 1986-90, chmn. pulmonary disease adv. com., 1982-84; active staff Tulane Med. Center Hosp., 1976—; program dir. Nat. Inst. for Environ. Health Sci., 1992—; cons. pulmonary diseases Touro Infirmary, New Orleans, 1962—; cons. NIH, Nat. Inst. Occupational Safety and Health, Occupational Safety and Health Adminstrn., USN, NAS, EPA; lectr., participant workshops and confs. profl. groups in U.S., France, Can., U.K.; dir. Nat. Inst. Environ. Health Scis Superfund. Basic Rsch. Program, 1992—. Mem. editorial bd. Am. Rev. of Respiratory Disease, 1980-85, CHEST, 1987-91; editor Respiratory Diseases Digest, 1981; guest editor Byssinosis conf. supplement, CHEST, 1981. Fellow Am. Acad. Allergy, Royal Soc. Medicine, ACP; mem. Am. Thoracic Soc. (pres. 1976), Am. Lung Assn. (bd. dirs. 1975-78), New Orleans Acad. Internal Medicine (sec., treas. 1973-75), Am. Coll. Chest Physicians (gov. for La. 1970-75), Am. Fedn. Clin. Research, So. Soc. Clin. Investigation, N.Y. Acad. Scis., Brit. Thoracic Assn., Internat. Epidemiol. Assn., Am. Heart Assn. (task force on environment and cardiovascular system 1978), Brit. Thoracic Soc., Phi Beta Kappa, Alpha Omega Alpha. Home: 755 Hearthstone Dr Basalt CO 81621 Office: Tulane U Sch Medicine Sect Environ Medicine 1430 Tulane Ave New Orleans LA 70112-2699

WEILL, (LIGE) HARRY, SR., lawyer; b. Chattanooga, Sept. 12, 1916; s. David Robert Weill Sr. and Elsie Rose (Wertheimer) W.; m. Marcelle Baum, Dec. 10, 1947; children: Lige Harry Jr., Elsie Florence, Marcelle Audrey. BA, U. Va., 1936; JD, Harvard U., Cambridge, Mass., 1940; LLD, Harvard U., New Haven, Conn., 1940. Bar: Tenn. 1948, U.S. Ct. Appeals (6th cir.) 1954, U.S. Tax Ct. 1976, U.S. Supreme Ct. 1983. Assoc. Frazier & Roberts, 1940, 1944-59; ptnr. Roberts & Weill, 1959-62; sr. ptnr. Weill & Weill, Chattanooga; instr. contract law, McKenzie Coll.; founder Rossville (Ga.) Bank, 1963. Past pres. Mizpah congregation Julius and Bertha Ochs Meml. Temple; bd. dirs. Girls Club Chattanooga; mem. Estate Planning Coun. Chattanooga; past pres. Jaycees Jr. C of C Chattanooga; mem. bd. dirs. Kiwanis Club; Lt. U.S. Army, 1941-44, PTO. Named mem. of Thomas Jefferson Soc. of Alumni Univ. Va., 1986; scholar Univ. Va., 1932. Mem. ABA, Assn. Trial Lawyers Am., Am. Judicature Soc., Tenn. Bar Assn. (bd. dirs.), Tenn. Trial Lawyers Assn., Chattanooga Bar Assn., Chattanooga Trial Lawyers Assn., B'Nai Brith Internat. Assn., Walden Club, Am. Legion, Zeta Beta Tau. Avocations: gardening, skiing, walking.

WEILL, RICHARD L., lawyer; b. Lincoln, Nebr., Jan. 28, 1943; s. Walter and Irma (Heineman) W.; m. Judy A. Brumm, July 11, 1965; children: David, John. BS, U. Nebr., 1964; LLB, NYU, 1967. Bar: N.Y. 1967, Nebr. 1969. Assoc. Proskauer Rose Goetz & Mendelsohn, N.Y.C., 1967-69; ptnr. Kutak Rock, Omaha, 1969-89; pres. MBIA Inc., Armonk, N.Y., 1989-91, exec. v.p., 1994, pres., 1994—. Office: MBIA Inc 113 King St Armonk NY 10504-1611

WEILL, SAMUEL, JR., automobile company executive; b. Rochester, N.Y., Dec. 22, 1916; s. Samuel and Bertha (Stein) W.; student U. Buffalo, 1934-35; m. Mercedes Weil, May 20, 1939 (div. Aug. 1943); children: Rita and Eric (twins); m. Cléanthe Kimball Carr, Aug. 12, 1960 (div. 1982); m. Jacqueline Natalie Bateman, Jan. 5, 1983. Co-owner, Brayton Air Coll., St. Louis, 1937-42; assoc. editor, advt. mgr., bus. mgr. Road and Track Mag., Los Angeles, 1951-53; pres. Volkswagen Pacific, Inc., Culver City, Calif., 1953-73, Porsche Audi Pacific, Culver City, 1953-73; chmn. bd. Minto Internat., Inc., London; v.p. fin. Chieftain Oil Co., Ojai, Calif. Recipient Tom May award Jewish Hosp. and Research Center, 1971. Served with USAAF, 1943-45. Home: 305 Palomar Rd Ojai CA 93023-2432 Office: Chieftain Oil Co 214 W Aliso St Ojai CA 93023-2502 *Try to find a position that can utilitze whatever knowledge and abilities you have. Learn all you can about that company and its workings and then work as hard as you can, giving more than is expected of you, much more, but not more than you can capably handle.*

WEILL, SANFORD I., banking executive; b. N.Y.C., Mar. 16, 1933; s. Max and Etta (Kalika) W.; m. Joan Mosher, June 20, 1955; children: Marc P., Jessica M. B.A., Cornell U., 1955, student Grad. Sch. Bus. and Pub. Adminstrn., 1954-55. Chmn. bd., chief exec. officer Carter, Berlind & Weill (name changed to CBWL-Hayden, Stone, Inc. 1970, to Hayden Stone, Inc. 1972, to Shearson Hayden Stone 1974, to Shearson Loeb Rh, N.Y.C., 1960-84; dir., chmn. exec. com. Carter, Berlind & Weill (name changed to CBWL-Hayden, Stone, Inc. 1970, to Hayden Stone, Inc. 1972, to Shearson Hayden Stone 1974, to Shearson Loeb Rh, 1981-83, pres., 1983-85; chmn. Fireman's Fund, 1984-85; past pres., chmn. exec. com., mem. fin. com. Am. Express Co., until 1989; chmn., chief exec. officer Primerica Corp., N.Y.C., 1989—, pres., until 1992; chmn. Primerica Holdings Inc., N.Y.C.; chmn., pres., chief exec. officer Comml. Credit Co., Balt., 1986—; dir. IDS Mutual Funds Group; vice chmn. adv. council The Johnson Grad. Sch. of Mgmt.; founder Acad. of Fin. Mem. bd. overseers Cornell Med. Coll.; chmn. Carnegie Hall, N.Y.C.; mem. bus. com. Mus. of Modern Art, N.Y.C. Mem. N.Y. Soc. Security Analysts. Clubs: Cornell (N.Y.C.), Century Country (Purchase, N.Y.), Harmonie (N.Y.C.). Office: Travelers Inc 388 Greenwich St New York NY 10013*

WEIMAN, ENRIQUE WATSON, lawyer; b. Rio de Janeiro, Jan. 1, 1946; came to U.S., 1947; BA, U. Tampa, 1968; LLM, Atlanta U., 1977, JD, 1976. Bar: Ga.1984. Staff atty. Easton Kennedy, Atlanta, 1984-85; mng. ptnr. Hyatt Legal Svcs., Sandy Springs, Ga., 1985-90; ptnr. Weiman & Perry, Stone Mountain, Ga., 1990—. Contbr. to local newspaper. Capt. USMC, 1969-71, Res., 1972-80. Avocations: tennis, swimming, sailing. Home: 5575 S Pines Ct Stone Mountain GA 30087 Office: Weiman & Perry 739 Main St Ste 9 Stone Mountain GA 30083

WEIMER, GREGORY ALOYISUS, lawyer; b. Ridgewood, N.J., June 15, 1961; m. Allison Ruth Hastings, Sept. 12, 1992. BA, U. Vt., 1984; JD cum laude, Vt. Law Sch., South Royalton, 1988. Bar: Vt. 1989, Maine 1990, N.H. 1993. Law clk. Vt. Trial Cts., Bennington, 1988-89; assoc. Wilson Powell Lang & Faris, Burlington, Vt., 1989-90, Friedman & Babcock, Portland, Maine, 1990-92; ptnr. Hastings Law Office, Fryeburg, Maine, 1992—; rsch. editor Vermont Law Review, 1987-88. Mem. Fryeburg Planning Bd., 1994—; soccer coach Fryeburg Acad., 1992—. Avocations: bird hunting, soccer. Office: Hastings Law Office 71 Main St Fryeburg ME 04037-1105

WEIMER, JEAN ELAINE, nursing educator; b. Denver, June 8, 1932; d. John and Marquerite Christina (Friehauf) Jacoby; m. James David Weimer, Aug. 5, 1956; 1 dau., Lisa Marie. Diploma in nursing Children's Hosp. Sch. Nursing, Denver, 1953; BS in Nursing, U. Denver, 1954; MA, NYU, 1962. RN, Colo., S.D., N.Y., Ill. Staff nurse Children's Hosp., Denver, 1953-54, head nurse, 1954-56; dir. nursing edn. Yankton (S.D.) State Hosp., 1956-60; instr. Mt. Sinai Hosp. Sch. Nursing, N.Y.C., 1962-63, curriculum coord., 1964-67; asst. prof. nursing City Colls. Chgo., 1968-78, assoc. prof., 1978-85, prof., 1985—, Disting. prof., 1995-96, co-chmn. nursing dept. Truman Coll., 1984-93, chmn. 1993—; chmn. program com. RN Tutoring project, 1988-92. Deacon United Ch. of Christ, 1988-90. NIMH grantee, 1960-62. Mem. Am. Nurses Assn., Coun. Advanced Practioners Psychiat. Coun. of Dirs. of Assoc. Degree Nursing Programs, Nursing Truman Coll. Faculty Coun., City Coll. Faculty Coun., Kappa Delta Pi, Pi Lambda Theta. Home: 50 E Bellevue Pl Apt 904 Chicago IL 60611-1167 Office: Truman Coll 1145 W Wilson Ave # 184 Chicago IL 60640-5616

WEIMER, PAUL K(ESSLER), electrical engineer, consultant; b. Wabash, Ind., Nov. 5, 1914; s. Claude W. and Eva V. (Kessler) W.; m. Katherine E. Mounce, July 18, 1942; children: Katherine Weimer Lasslob, Barbara Weimer Blackwell, Patricia Weimer Hess. A.B., Manchester Coll., 1936, D.Sc. (hon.), 1968; M.A. in Physics, U. Kans., 1938; Ph.D. in Physics, Ohio State U., 1942. Prof. phys. sci. Tabor Coll., 1937-39; rsch. engr. David Sarnoff Research Center, RCA Labs., Princeton, N.J., 1942-65; fellow tech. staff David Sarnoff Research Center, RCA Labs., 1965-81, cons., 1981—. Recipient TV Broadcasters award, 1946, Zworykin TV prize Inst. Radio Engrs., 1959, Sarnoff award in sci. RCA, 1963, Kulturpreis award German Photographic Soc., 1986, Albert Rose Electronic Imager of Yr. award, 1987, Pioneer award N.J. Inventors Hall of Fame, 1991. Fellow IEEE (Outstanding Paper award Solid State Cirs. Conf. 1963, 65, Morris Liebmann prize 1966); mem. NAE. Holder 90 patents in field; active in initial devel. of TV camera tubes, solid state sensors and thin-film transistors. Home and Office: 112 Random Rd Princeton NJ 08540-4146

WEIMER, ROBERT JAY, geology educator, energy consultant, civic leader; b. Glendo, Wyo., Sept. 4, 1926; s. John L. and Helen (Mowrey) W.; m. Ruth Carol Adams, Sept. 12, 1948; children: Robert Thomas, Loren Edward (dec.), Paul Christner, Carl Scott. BA, U Wyo., 1948, MA, 1949; PhD, Stanford U., 1953. Registered profl. engr., Colo. Geologist Union Oil Co. Calif., 1949-54; cons. geologist U.S. and fgn. petroleum exploration, 1954—; prof. geology Colo. Sch. Mines, 1957-83, prof. emeritus, 1983—, Getty prof. geology, 1978-83; vis. prof. U. Colo., 1961, U. Calgary, Can., 1970, Inst. Tech., Bandung, Indonesia, 1975; Fulbright lectr. U. Adelaide, South Australia, 1967; disting. lectr. and continuing edn. lectr. Am. Assn. Petroleum Geologists, Soc. Expl. Geophysicists; ednl. cons. to petroleum cos., 1964—; mem. energy rsch. adv. bd. Dept. Energy, 1985-90, Bd. on Mineral and Energy Resources, NAS, 1988. Editor: Guide to Geology of Colorado, 1960, Symposium on Cretaceous Rocks of Colorado and Adjacent Area, 1959, Denver Earthquakes, 1968, Fossil Fuel Exploration, 1974, Studies in Colorado Field Geology, 1976. Trustee Colo. Sch. Mines Research Found., 1967-70; pres. Rockland Found., 1982-83. With USNR, 1944-46. Recipient Disting. Alumnus award U. Wyo., 1982, Mines medal Colo. Sch. Mines, 1984, Brown medal, 1990, Parker medal Am. Inst. Profl. Geologists. Fellow Geol. Soc. Am. (chmn. Rocky Mountain sect. 1966-67), AAAS; mem. Am. Assn. Petroleum Geologists (pres. 1992, Sidney Powers medal, Dist. Educator award 1996), Soc. Econ. Paleontologists and Mineralogists (hon., sec.-treas. 1966-67, v.p. 1971, pres. 1977, Twenhofel medal 1995), Colo. Sci. Soc. (hon., pres. 1981), Rocky Mountain Assn. Geologists (pres. 1969, hon. mem., Scientist of Yr. 1982), Wyo. Geol. Assn. (hon.), Colo. Sch. Mines Alumni Assn. (hon., Coolbaugh award), Am. Geol. Inst. Found. (sec., treas. 1984-88), Nat. Acad. Engring., Mt. Vernon Country Club (Golden, bd. dirs. 1956-59, 81-84, pres. 1983-84). Home: RR 3 25853 Mt Vernon Rd Golden CO 80401-9699

WEIN, ALAN JEROME, urologist, educator, researcher; b. Newark, Dec. 15, 1941; s. Isadore R. and Jeanette Frances (Abrams) W. A.B. cum laude, Princeton U., 1962; M.D., U. Pa., 1966. Diplomate Am. Bd. Urology. Intern mixed surgery Hosp. U. Pa., Phila., 1966-67, resident surgery, 1967-68; resident urology U. Pa., Phila., 1969-72, fellow Harrison Dept. Surg. Rsch. Urology Sch. Medicine, 1968-69, asst. instr. surgery Sch. Medicine, 1967-68, asst. instr. urology, 1969-71, instr., 1971-72, asst. prof., 1974-76, assoc. prof., 1976-83, prof., 1983—, asst. chief urology, 1974-79, dir. Urodynamic Evaluation Ctr., 1974—, chmn. div. urology, 1981—, chief urology, 1981—; dir. resident edn. com. div. urology Sch. Medicine U. Pa., 1976—, coord. program urologics oncology, 1976—; chief urology VA Hosp., Phila., 1974-82, attending urologist, 1982—; asst. surgeon Children's Hosp. Phila., 1974—; cons. CDC Coun. Incontinence, 1990—; assoc. surgeon Pa. Hosp., Phila., 1977—; attending urologist Grad. Hosp., Phila., 1980—. Author: (with D.M. Barrett) Controversies in Neuro-Urology, 1984, Voiding Function and Dysfunction: A Logical and Practical Approach, 1988, 2d edit., 1995, (with A.R. Mundy and T.P. Stephenson) Urodynamics: Principles, Practice and Application, 1984, 2d edit., 1994, (with P.M. Hanno) A Clinical Manual of Urology, 1987, 2d edit., 1994, (with Hanno, Staskin and Krane) Interstitial Cystitis, 1990; editl. bd. asst. editor Urol. Survey, 1978-81; editl. bd. cons. Investigative Urology, 1978-81; mem. editl. bd. World Jour. Urology, 1982—, Am. Urol. Assn. Update series, 1983—, Urol. Survey, 1987—, Internat. Jour. Impotence Rsch.: Basic and Clin. Studies, 1989—, Urology, 1991—; ad hoc reviewer Cancer, 1985—; cons. editor Sexuality and Disability, 1985—; asst. editor Jour. Urology, 1980-89, ad hoc reviewer clin. sect., 1989—, editl. bd. investigative sect., 1989—; assoc. editor Neurology and Urodynamics, 1982—; contbr. over 560 articles and abstracts to profl. jours. Mem. coun. urology Nat. Kidney Found., Inc.; mem lectrs. bur. Am. Cancer Soc., 1984—; mem. adv. panel Help for Incontinent People, 1987—; mem. adv. bd. Simon Found., 1987—; mem. med. adv. bd. Institial Cystitis Assn., 1987—; chmn. bladder health coun. Am. Found. Urologic Disease, 1990—; trustee Am. Bd. Urology, 1990-96. Maj. MC, U.S. Army, 1972-74. Grantee VA, 1974-79, 79, 81, 81-84, 82-85, 85-88, 88-92, Eaton Labs., 1975-76, 78-80, McCabe Rsch. Fund, 1975-82, 87-88, Merrell Nat. Labs., 1979-82, 1980-82, Nat. Kidney Found., 1980-81, NIH, 1980-83, 83-88, 84-87, 87—, Roche Labs., 1981, Smith Kline and French Labs., 1982, 86-88, Eli Lilly Labs., 1986-88, 91, Found. Interstitial Cystitis, 1986-87, 87-88, Sterling Drug Co., 1991. Fellow ACS; mem. AAAS, AMA (cons. com. drug evaluation 1977—), Am. Acad. Clin. Neurophysiology, Am. Assn. Surgery of Trauma, Am. Assn. Clin. Urologists, Am. Assn. Genito-Urinary Surgeons, Am. Fertility Soc., Am. Inst. Ultrasound in Medicine, Am. Soc. Pharmacology and Exptl. Therapeutics, Am. Soc. Andrology, Am. Soc. Clin. Oncology, Am. Urol. Assn. (chmn. practical cases urology 1982—, rsch. com. 1985—, editl. com. mid-Atlantic sect. 1988—), Assn. Acad. Surgery, Can. Urol. Assn., Clin. Soc. Genito-Urinary Surgeons, Ea. Coop. Oncologic Group, Endourol. Soc., Internat. Continence Soc., Nat. Assn. VA Physicians, N.Y. Acad. Scis., Coll. Physicians Phila., John Morgan Soc., Pa. Med. Assn., Pa. Oncologic Soc., Phila. Acad. Surgery, Phila. County Med. Soc., Phila. Profl. Standards Rev. Orgn., Phila. Urologic Soc. (pres. 1990-91), Ravdin-Rhoads Surg. Soc., Urol. Assn. Pa., Radiation Therapy Oncology Group (genitourinary working com. 1980—), Royal Soc. Medicine, Soc. Internat. d'Urologie, Soc. Basic Urologic Rsch., Soc. Sex Therapy and Rsch., Soc. Govt. Svc. Urologists, Soc. Pelvic Surgeons, Soc. Univ. Surgeons, Soc. Univ. Urologists, Soc. Urologic Oncology, Univ. Urologic Forum, Urodynamics Soc. (exec. com. 1980—), Urologic Rsch. Soc., Urologist's Corrnson Ln Haverford PA 19041-1921 Office: Hosp U Pa 1 Rhoads Pavilion 3400 Spruce St Philadelphia PA 19104

WEINACHT, JOHN WILLIAM, lawyer; b. Orange, Tex., Nov. 13, 1963; s. Charles and Mary Ann W.; m. Luz Marina Lara, Aug. 21, 1985; children: Lara, Jake, Claire. BA, U. Tex., 1987; JD, Baylor U., 1989. Bar: Tex. 1989, N. Mex. 1994, U.S. Dist. Ct. (all dists.) Tex. 1993, U.S. Dist. Ct. N. Mex. 1994, U.S. Ct. Appeals (5th cir.) 1993, U.S. Ct. Appeals (10th cir.) 1995, U.S. Ct. Internat. Trade 1995; U.S. Supreme Ct. 1995. Atty. pvt. practice, Pecos, Tex., 1989—; county atty. Reeves County, Pecos, Tex., 1993—. Mem. ABA, Tex. Trial Lawyers Assn., Reeves County Bar Assn., Trans-Pecos Bar Assn. Democrat. Office: 420 S Cypress Pecos TX 79772

WEINBACH, ARTHUR FREDERIC, computing services company executive; b. Waterbury, Conn., May 3, 1943; s. Max and Winifred (Eckstein) W.; m. Joanne Kaplan, Nov. 20, 1970; children: Michael Scott, Jonathan David. BS in Econs., U. Pa., 1965, MS in Acctg., 1966. CPA. Various positions with Touche Ross & Co., N.Y.C., 1966-75; ptnr. Touche Ross & Co., Stamford, Conn., 1976-79; v.p. Automatic Data Processing, Inc., Roseland, N.J., 1980-81; v.p. fin. Automatic Data Processing, Inc., Clifton, N.J., 1981-82, sr. v.p. adminstrn. and fin., 1982-91, exec. v.p., 1992-94, pres., 1994—; also bd. dirs. Automatic Data Processing, Inc., Roseland, 1989—. Editor mag. sect. Conn. CPA Mag., 1978-79. Chmn. task force Stamford Area Commerce and Industry Assn., 1979; bd. dirs. Boys Hope, 1991—, Overlook Hosp. Found., 1991—, Metro N.J. U. Pa. Club, 1993—. Mem. Fin. Execs. Inst. Jewish. Home: One Twin Oak Rd Short Hills NJ 07078-1208 Office: ADP Inc 1 A D P Blvd Roseland NJ 07068-1728

WEINBACH, LAWRENCE ALLEN, financial executive; b. N.Y.C., Jan. 8, 1940; s. Max N. and Winifred E. Weinbach; m. Patricia Leiter, Dec. 1961; children: Wendy, Peter, Daniel. BS in Econs., U. Pa., 1961. CPA, Conn., N.Y., other states. With Arthur Andersen & Co. (CPA's), N.Y.C., 1961—; mng. ptnr. Arthur Andersen & Co. (CPA's), Stamford, Conn., 1974-80; ptnr.-in-charge N.Y. acctg. and audit practice Arthur Andersen & Co., N.Y.C., 1980-83, mng. ptnr. N.Y. and N.Y. Met. area, 1983-87, mem. bd. ptnrs., 1984-87, chmn. bd. ptnrs., 1986-87, mng. ptnr., COO, 1987-89, mng. ptnr., chief exec., 1989—; bd. dirs. Asia Soc., 1995—, U.S.-Japan Bus. Coun., 1989-94. With Hartman Regional Theatre, Stamford, 1978-80, chmn. bd. dirs., 1977-78; mem. bd. incorporators Stamford Hosp., 1976-84; bd. dirs. United Way, Stamford, 1976-78, Phoenix House Inc., 1984-92, Coun. on Fgn. Rels., 1986—, catalyst, 1991—; trustee Carnegie Hall, 1985—, Northwestern U., 1990—; mem. bd. overseers Wharton Sch., U. Pa., 1988—; mem. bd. Stern Sch., 1989—, Pub. Policy Inst., 1990—, Am. Bus. Conf., 1994—, YMCA-Greater N.Y., 1995—. Mem. AICPA, N.Y. Soc. CPAs, Conn. Soc. CPAs, Econs. Club N.Y., Asia Soc. (bd. dirs. 1995—), Chgo. Club, Harmonie Club, Univ. Club, Beta Gamma Sigma, Beta Alpha Psi. Office: Andersen Worldwide 1345 Avenue Of The Americas New York NY 10105

WEINBAUM, SHELDON, biomedical engineer; b. Bklyn., July 26, 1937; s. Alexander Weinbaum and Frances Clare (Stark) Colby; m. Alexandra Tamara, June 10, 1962; children: Alys Eve, Daniel Eden. BAE, Rensselaer Polytech. Inst., Troy, 1959; MS, Harvard U., 1960, PhD, 1963. Mem. rsch. staff Sperry Rand Rsch. Lab., Sudbury, Mass., 1963-64; prin. rsch. scientist Avco Everett Rsch. Lab., Everett, Mass., 1964, G.E. Space Sci. Lab., Valley Forge, Pa., 1964-67; assoc. prof. CUNY, N.Y.C., 1967-72, H. Kayser Prof., 1980-85, CUNY Disting. Prof., 1986—, dir. Ctr. Biomed. Engring., 1994—; vis. prof. Imperial Coll. Sci. and Tech., London, 1973-74, MIT, 1980-81; Russell S. Springer vis. prof. U. Calif., Berkeley, 1979-80; sr. fellow scientific rsch. coun. of Gt. Britain, 1973-74. Chair legal action com. CUNY, 1992. Recipient rsch. award European Soc. Biomechanics, 1994; Gordon McKay prize fellow Harvard U., 1959-60, NSF fellow Harvard U., 1961-63; spl. creativity grantee NSF, 1985-87, H.R. Lissner award Am. Soc. of Mechanical Engineers, 1994. Fellow ASME, Am. Phys. Soc., Am. Inst. Med. Bio. Engring.; mem. NAE (Melville medal 1996), Biomed. Engring. Soc. (bd. dirs. 1989-92). Achievements include contributions in the broad application of engineering principles to the understanding of biological and medical processes including water and solute transport in capillary interendothelial clefts, bioheat transfer, plasma skimmings and red cell screening in blood flow, leaky junction-cell turnover mechanism for LDL transport, intraocular fluid mechanics, convective transport in the arterial intima and atherogenesis and the mechano-sensory mechanism for bone growth. Office: City Coll City of New York Convent Ave & 138th St New York NY 10031

WEINBERG, ALVIN MARTIN, physicist; b. Chgo., Apr. 20, 1915; s. J.L. and Emma (Levinson) W.; m. Margaret Despres, June 14, 1940 (dec. 1969); children: David, Richard; m. Gene K. DePersio, Sept. 20, 1974. A.B., U.

Chgo., 1935, A.M., 1936, Ph.D., 1939; LL.D., U. Chattanooga, Alfred U.; D.Sc., U. Pacific, Denison U., Wake Forest U., Kenyon Coll., Worcester Poly. Inst., U. Rochester, Stevens Inst. Tech., Butler U., U. Louisville, U. Bridgeport. Research assoc. math. biophysics U. Chgo., 1939-41, Metall. Lab., 1941-45; joined Oak Ridge Nat. Lab., 1945, dir. physics div., 1947-48, research dir. lab., 1948-55, dir. lab., 1955-74; dir. Office Energy R&D, Fed. Energy Adminstrn., 1974, Inst. Energy Analysis, Oak Ridge, 1975-85; disting. fellow Oak Ridge Associated Univs., 1985—; mem. Pres.'s Sci. Adv. Com., 1960-62, Pres.'s Medal of Sci. Com. Author: Reflections on Big Science, (with E.P. Wigner) Physical Theory of Neutron Chain Reactors, 1958, Continuing the Nuclear Dialogue, 1985, Nuclear Reactions: Science and Trans-Science, 1992, The First Nuclear Era: The Life and Times of a Technological Fixer, 1994; co-author: The Second Nuclear Era, 1985; co-editor: The Nuclear Connection, 1985, Strategic Defenses and Arms Control, 1987; editor: Eugene Wigner's Collected Works on Nuclear Energy. Recipient Atoms for Peace award, 1960, E.O. Lawrence award, 1960, U. Chgo. Alumni medal, 1966, Heinrich Hertz award, 1975, N.Y. Acad. Scis. award, 1976, Enrico Fermi award, 1980, Harvey prize, 1982, Eugene Wigner award in reactor physics, 1992. Mem. Nat. Acad. Scis. (applied sci. sect.), Am. Nuclear Soc. (pres. 1959-60), Nat. Acad. Engring., Am. Acad. Arts and Scis., Am. Philos. Soc., Royal Netherlands Acad. Sci. (fgn. asso.). Home: 111 Moylan Ln Oak Ridge TN 37830-5351 Office: Oak Ridge Associated Univs PO Box 117 Oak Ridge TN 37831-0117

WEINBERG, DAVID, chemicals executive. Co-chmn. bd., CEO Fel-Pro Inc., Skokie, Ill., 1965—. Office: Fel-Pro Inc 7450 Mccormick Blvd Skokie IL 60076-4046

WEINBERG, DAVID B., lawyer; b. Chgo., Feb. 19, 1952; s. Judd A. and Marjorie (Gottlieb) W.; m. Lynne Ellen Mesirow, July 6, 1980; children: Julie, Jane, Jonathan. AB cum laude, Harvard U., 1974; JD, Georgetown U., 1977. Bar: Ill. 1977, U.S. Dist. Ct. (no. dist.) Ill. 1977, U.S. Ct. Appeals (7th cir.) 1978. Law clerk to Hon. William G. Clark Supreme Ct. Ill., 1977-79; assoc. Lord, Bissell & Brook, Chgo., 1979-84, ptnr., 1985-89; ptnr. Mayer, Brown & Platt, Chgo., 1989—; Ill. Supreme Ct. com. Profl. Responsibility, Chgo., 1984-94, chmn. subcom. lawyers certification. Founding mem. Friends of Prentice, Chgo., 1986-87; assocs. bd. Rush-Presbyn. St. Luke's Med. Ctr., 1989—; founder, 1st pres., sec., trustee Ravinia Festival Assn., Highland Park, Ill., 1989—; jr. gov. bd. Chgo. Symphony Orchestra, 1979-86, chmn. fundraising com. 1981-82, chmn. nominating com. 1984-85; trustee Northwestern U., 1994—. Mem. ABA (sect. bus. law, com. fed. regulation securities), Harvard Club Chgo. (v.p. 1985-89), Chgo. Club, Standard Club Chgo. (dir. 1988-90), Econ. Club Chgo., Lake Shore Country Club, Arts Club Chgo. Office: Mayer Brown & Platt 190 S La Salle St Chicago IL 60603-3410*

WEINBERG, EUGENE DAVID, microbiologist, educator; b. Chgo., Mar. 4, 1922; s. Philip and Lenore (Bergman) W.; m. Frances Murl Izen, Sept. 5, 1949; children—Barbara Ann, Marjorie Jean, Geoffrey Alan, Michael Benjamin. B.S., U. Chgo., 1942, M.A., 1948, Ph.D., 1950. Instr. dept. microbiology Ind. U., Bloomington, 1950-53; asst. prof. Ind. U., 1953-57, asso. prof., 1957-61, prof., 1961—, head microbiology sect., med. sci. program, 1978—. Served with AUS, 1942-45. Mem. AAAS, Am. Soc. Microbiology. Office: Ind U Biology Dept Jordan Hall Bloomington IN 47405

WEINBERG, GERHARD LUDWIG, history educator; b. Hannover, Germany, Jan. 1, 1928; came to U.S., 1940, naturalized, 1949; s. Max Bendix and Kate Sarah (Gruenebaum) W.; m. Janet Kabler White, Apr. 29, 1989. BA, N.Y. State Coll. Tchrs., Albany, 1948; MA, U. Chgo., 1949, PhD, 1951; LHD honoris causa, SUNY, Albany, 1989. Research analyst War Documentation project Columbia U., 1951-54; vis. lectr. history U. Chgo., 1954-55, U. Ky., Lexington, 1955-56; dir. project microfilming captured German documents Am. Hist. Assn., 1956-57; asst. prof. U. Ky., 1957-59; mem. faculty U. Mich., Ann Arbor, 1959-74; prof. history U. Mich., 1963-74, chmn. dept., 1972-73; William Rand Kenan, Jr. prof. history U. N.C., Chapel Hill, 1974—; acting chmn. dept., 1989-90; vis. prof. Bonn U., 1983, USAF Acad., 1990-91; bd. dirs. World War II Studies Assn., 1968—; cons. in field. Author: Guide to Captured German Documents, 1952, Germany and the Soviet Union, 1939-41, 1954, The Foreign Policy of Hitler's Germany, 1933-36, 1970, The Foreign Policy of Hitler's Germany, 1937-39, 1980, World in the Balance: Behind the Scenes of World II, 1981, A World at Arms: A Global History of World War II, 1994, Germany, Hitler and World War II, 1995; co-author: Soviet Partisans in World War II, 1964; editor: Hitlers zweites Buch, 1961, 95, Transformation of a Continent, 1975; bd. editors Jour. Modern History, 1970-72, Central European History, 1970-72, Kansas Humanities Series, 1987—, Internat. History Rev., 1990—. Chmn. Ann Arbor Democratic Com., 1961-63; mem. Mich. Dem. Central Com., 1963-67; mem. adv. com. on the air force history program Sec. of Air Force, 1987-90. Wwith AUS, 1946-47. Fellow Social Sci. Research Council, 1962-63; fellow Am. Council Learned Socs., 1965-66; fellow Guggenheim Found., 1971-72; fellow Nat. Endowment Humanities, 1978-79. Mem. Am. Hist. Assn. (George Louis Beer prize 1971, 95, v.p. rsch. 1982-84), So. Hist. Assn. (chmn. European sect. 1989), Conf. Group for Ctrl. European History (chmn. 1982), Coordinating Com. Women in Hist. Profession, German Studies Assn. (exec. com. 1989-92, Halverson prize 1981, v.p. 1994—), World War II Studies Assn., Phi Beta Kappa. Jewish. Home: 1416 Mount Willing Rd Efland NC 27243-9646 Office: Dept History Univ NC Chapel Hill NC 27599-3195

WEINBERG, H. BARBARA, art historian, educator, curator paintings and sculpture; b. N.Y.C., Jan. 23, 1942; d. Max and Evelyn Kallman; m. Michael B. Weinberg, Aug. 30, 1964. AB, Barnard Coll., 1962; MA, Columbia U., N.Y.C., 1964, PhD, 1972. From asst. prof. to prof. art history Queens Coll. and Grad. Sch., CUNY, 1972-94; curator dept. Am. paintings and sculpture Met. Mus. Art., 1990—. Author: The Decorative World of John La Farge, 1977, The American Pupils of Jean-Léon Gérome, 1984, The Lure of Paris: Nineteenth-Century American Painters and Their French Teachers, 1991, Thomas Eakins and the Metropolitan Museum of Art, 1994; co-author: American Impressionism and Realism: The Painting of Modern Life, 1885-1915, 1994; mem. editorial bd. Am. Art Jour., 1984—. Mem. Coll. Arts Assn., Gallery Assn. N.Y. State (bd. trustees), Phi Beta Kappa. Office: Met Mus Art 1000 5th Ave New York NY 10028-0113

WEINBERG, HARRY BERNARD, cardiologist; b. Fremont, Nebr., Apr. 29, 1913; s. Ephraim and Goldie (Levynsky) W.; m. Evelyn Waxenberg, Mar. 26, 1939; 1 son, Steven M. B.S. in Medicine, U. Nebr., 1935, M.D., 1936. Intern, Univ. Hosp., Omaha, 1936-37; resident cardiovascular disease Michael Reese Hosp., Chgo., 1938-40; pvt. practice internal medicine and cardiology Davenport, Iowa, 1940-69; coordinator Iowa Regional Med. Program, clin. prof. internal medicine U. Iowa Coll. Medicine, 1969-72; dir. med. edn. Meml. Hosp., Hollywood, Fla., 1972-74; pvt. practice medicine specializing in cardiology Hollywood, 1974-82; hon. med. staff Meml. Hosp., Hollywood, Fla., 1982—; physician utilization rev. cons., 1982-91; Bd. dirs. Iowa Heart Assn., 1953-64, pres., 1955-56. Bd. dirs. Davenport C. of C., 1958-61, v.p., 1961. Served to lt. col. AUS, 1940-46. Fellow ACP, Am. Coll. Cardiology; mem. AMA, Am. Heart Assn. (bd. dirs. 1956-69, fellow council clin. cardiology 1965—), Alpha Omega Alpha. Home: 4040 N Hills Dr Apt 37 Hollywood FL 33021-2453

WEINBERG, HELEN ARNSTEIN, American art and literature educator; b. Orange, N.J., June 17, 1927; d. Morris Jerome and Jeannette (Tepperman) Arnstein; m. Kenneth Gene Weinberg, Sept. 12, 1949; children: Janet Sue Weinberg Strassner, Hugh Benjamin, John Arnstein. BA in English Lit., Wellesley Coll., 1949; MA in English Lit., Western Res. U., 1953, PhD in English Lit., 1966. Teaching fellow Ohio State U., Columbus, 1949-51, Western Res. U., Cleve., 1953-57; instr. to prof. Cleve. (Ohio) Inst. Art, 1958—; standing officer Coll. English Assn. Ohio, 1987-90; vis. tchr. NYU, 1985, Sch. Visual Art's, 1981; lecture tours Israel, 1968, 70, 71. Author: The New Novel in America: The Kafkan Mode in Contemporary Fiction, 1970. Recipient fellowship in art history NEH, Columbia U., N.Y.C., 1977-78; Recipient Am. Culture grantee NEH/Vassar Coll., 1993. Mem. AAUP, Modern Lang. Assn., Coll. Art Assn. Democrat. Jewish. Home: 3015 Huntington Rd Shaker Hts OH 44120-2407 Office: Cleve Inst Art 11141 East Blvd Cleveland OH 44106-1710

WEINBERG, HENRY, mathematician, researcher; b. Bronx, N.Y., Feb. 27, 1940; s. Albert and Freda (Nathanson) W.; m. Jane Sharon Rifkin, June 6, 1964; children: Michele Robin, Scott Adam. BS, CCNY, 1960, MS, 1961; PhD, NYU Courant Inst., 1974. Mathematician Naval Undersea Warfare Ctr., New London, Conn., 1964-85, Syntek, North Stonington, Conn., 1985-88; comdr. Naval Undersea Warfare Ctr., New London, 1988—; instr. U. Conn., Groton, 1980-90. Contbr. articles to profl. jours. Recipient Founders Day award NYU, 1974. Mem. Acoustical Soc. Am. Republican. Jewish. Achievements include devel. of computer models of sonar systems; rsch. in ocean acoustic propagation. Home: 23 Colonial Dr Waterford CT 06385-3307

WEINBERG, HERSCHEL MAYER, lawyer; b. Bklyn., Oct. 13, 1927; s. Jacob and Gertrude (Wernick) W. B.A., Bklyn. Coll., 1948; LL.B., Harvard U., 1952. Bar: N.Y. 1952. Atty. firm Payne & Steingarten, N.Y.C., 1952-57, Jacobs, Persinger & Parker, N.Y.C., 1957-61; partner firm Rubin, Rubin, Weinberg, & Di Paola, N.Y.C., 1961-78, Weinberg Tauber & Pressman, 1979-90; pvt. practice N.Y.C., 1990—; dir. Milgray Electronics, Inc. Served with AUS, 1946-47. Mem. Assn. of Bar of City of N.Y., N.Y. State Bar Assn. Club: Harvard (N.Y.C.). Home: 50 Sutton Pl S New York NY 10022-4167 Office: 110 E 59th St New York NY 10022-1306

WEINBERG, JEFFREY J., lawyer; b. N.Y.C., Aug. 27, 1948; s. Arnold Mitchell and Lucile (Barton) W.; m. Bonnie J. Sandhaus, Aug. 23, 1970; children: Seth, Andrew. BA, SUNY, Stony Brook, 1969; JD, Georgetown U., 1973. Bar: N.Y., U.S. Dist. Ct. (so. and ea. dists.). Assoc. Weil, Gotshal & Manges, N.Y.C., 1973-81, ptnr., 1981—; acting judge Village of Roslyn Estates. Author: Sales of Troubled Business, 1991, 92, 93, 94. Former trustee Village of Roslyn Estate. Mem. Knickerbocker Y.C. (gov. 1990-91). Avocation: sailing. Office: Weil Gotshal & Manges 767 5th Ave New York NY 10153*

WEINBERG, JOHN LEE, federal judge; b. Chgo., Apr. 24, 1941; s. Louis Jr. and Jane Kitz (Goldstein) W.; m. Sarah Kibbee, July 6, 1963; children: Ruth, Leo. BA, Swarthmore Coll., 1962; JD, U. Chgo., 1965. Bar: Ill. 1966, Wash. 1967, U.S. Dist. Ct. (we. dist.) Wash. 1967, U.S. Ct. Appeals (9th cir.) 1967. Law clk. to Hon. Henry L. Burman Ill. Appellate Ct., Chgo., 1965-66; law clk. to Hon. Walter V. Schaefer Ill. Supreme Ct., Chgo., 1966; law clk. to Hon. William T. Beeks U.S. Dist. Ct. Wash., Seattle, 1967-68; atty. Perkins Coie Law Firm, Seattle, 1968-73; magistrate judge U.S. Dist. Ct.; U.S. Magistrate judge Seattle, 1973—. Author: Federal Bail and Detention Handbook, 1988. Mem. ABA, Am. Judicature Soc., Wash. State Bar Assn., Seattle-King County Bar Assn., Fed. Magistrate Judges Assn. (nat. pres. 1982-83). Avocations: sports and physical fitness activities, bridge. Office: US Magistrate Judge 304 US Courthouse 1010 5th Ave Seattle WA 98104-1130

WEINBERG, JOHN LIVINGSTON, investment banker; b. N.Y.C., Jan. 5, 1925; s. Sidney James and Helen (Livingston) W.; m. Sue Ann Gotshal, Dec. 6, 1952; children: Ann K. (dec.), John, Jean. A.B. cum laude, Princeton U., 1948; M.B.A., Harvard U., 1950. With Goldman, Sachs & Co., N.Y.C., 1950—, ptnr., 1956-76, sr. ptnr., 1976-90, co-chmn. mgmt. com., 1976-84, chmn. mgmt. com., 1984-90; sr. chmn. Goldman, Sachs & Co., 1990—; bd. dirs. Knight-Rider, Inc., Seagram Co. Ltd., Champion Internat. Corp.; mem. Conf. Bd. Bd. govs. N.Y. Hosp.-Cornell Med. Ctr.; mem. DeWitt Wallace fund for meml. Sloan-Kettering Cancer Ctr. Capt. USMCR, 1942-46, 51-52. Fellow AAAS; mem. Va. Neurol. Inst., Coun. on Fgn. Rels., Bus. Coun., DeWitt Wallace Fund for Meml. Sloan Kettering Cancer Ctr. Office: Goldman Sachs & Co 85 Broad St Fl 22 New York NY 10004-2434

WEINBERG, LEONARD BURTON, political scientist; b. N.Y.C., Nov. 10, 1939; s. Max R. and Rose (Levin) W.; m. Ellen Bach, Aug. 23, 1966 (div.); 1 son, David; m. Sinikka Palomaki, June 4, 1986. B.A., Syracuse U., 1961, Ph.D., 1967; M.A., U. Chgo., 1963. Instr. polit. sci. U. Wis., Milw., 1966-67; asst. prof. polit. sci. U. Nev., Reno, 1967-71; assoc. prof. U. Nev., 1971-78, prof., 1978—, chmn. dept., 1979-82; vis. prof. U. Florence, Italy, 1992. Author: Comparing Public Policies, 1977, After Mussolini, 1979, The Rise and Fall of Italian Terrorism, 1987, Introduction to Political Terrorism, 1989; editor: Political Parties and Terrorist Groups, 1992, Revival of Right-Wing Extremism in the 1990s, 1996; co-editor: Encounters with the Radical Right, 1992, The Transformation of Italian Communism, 1994. Recipient Fulbright Rsch. award, 1984; Italian Govt. Borsa di Studio, 1965-66; Fulbright grantee, 1965-66, Harrs F. Guggenheim grantee, 1995-96. Mem. Am. Polit. Sci. Assn., Internat. Polit. Sci. Assn. (political sociology com.), Conf. Group on Italian Politics of Am. Polit. Sci. Assn., Phi Kappa Phi. Jewish. Office: Dept Political Science U Nevada Reno NV 89557

WEINBERG, LILA SHAFFER, writer, editor; d. Sam and Blanche (Hyman) Shaffer; m. Arthur Weinberg, Jan. 25, 1953; children: Hedy Merrill Cornfield, Anita Michelle Miller, Wendy Clare Rothman. Editor Ziff-Davis Pub. Co., 1944-53; assoc. chief manuscript editor jours. U. Chgo. Press, 1966-80, sr. manuscript editor books, 1980—; mem. faculty Sch. for New Learning DePaul U., Chgo., 1976—; vis. faculty continuing edn. programs U. Chgo., 1984—. Author: (with A. Weinberg) The Muckrakers, 1961 (selected for White House Library 1963), Verdicts Out of Court, 1963, Instead of Violence, 1963, Passport to Utopia, 1968, Some Dissenting Voices, 1970, Clarence Darrow: A Sentimental Rebel, 1980; contbr. articles and revs. to various publs. Bd. dirs. Hillel Found. U. Chgo. Recipient Friends of Lit. award Chgo. Found. Lit., 1980, Social Justice award Darrow Community Ctr., 1980, Disting. Body of Work award Friends of Midwest Authors, 1987. Mem. Soc. Midland Authors (dir. 1977-83, pres. 1983-85, Best Biography award 1980), ACLU, Clarence Darrow Commemorative Com., YIVO, Authors' League. Home: 5421 S Cornell Ave Chicago IL 60615-5608

WEINBERG, LOUISE, lawyer, educator, author; b. N.Y.C.; m. Steven Weinberg; 1 child, Elizabeth. AB summa cum laude, Cornell U.; LLM, Harvard U., 1974, JD, 1969. Bar: Mass. Sr. law clk. Hon. Chas. E. Wyzanski, Jr., Boston, 1971-72; assoc. in law Bingham, Dana & Gould, Boston, 1969-72; teaching fellow Harvard Law Sch., Boston, 1972-74; lectr. law Brandeis U., Waltham, Mass., 1974; assoc. prof. law Suffolk U., Boston, 1974-76, prof., 1977-80; vis. assoc. prof. law Stanford U., Palo Alto, Calif., 1976-77; vis. prof. law U. Tex., Austin, 1979; prof. law Sch. Law, U. Tex., Austin, 1980-84, Thompson prof., 1984-90, Andrews and Kurth prof. law, 1990-92; Fulbright and Jaworski regents rsch. prof. U. Tex., Austin, 1991-92, Angus G. Wynne, Sr. prof. civil jurisprudence, 1992—, Fondren chair faculty excellence, 1995-96, Eugene R. Smith Centennial rsch. prof. law, 1993; vis. scholar Hebrew U., Jerusalem, 1989; Forum fellow World Econ. Forum, Davos, Switzerland, 1995—; lectr. in field. Author: Federal Courts: Judicial Federalism and Judicial Power, 1994, and ann. supplements; co-author: Conflict of Laws, 1990; contbr. chpts. to books, articles to profl. jours. Bd. dirs. Ballet Austin, 1986-88, Austin Coun. on Fgn. Affairs, 1985—. Recipient Disting. Educator award Tex. Exes Assn., 1996. Mem. Am. Law Inst. (consultative com. complex litigation 1989-93, consultative com. enterprise liability 1990—), The Philos. Soc. Tex., Assn. Am. Law Schs. (chmn. com. on conflict laws 1991-93, exec. coun. 1989-90), Maritime Law Assn., Scribes, Phi Beta Kappa, Phi Kappa Phi. Office: U Tex Sch Law 727 E 26th St Austin TX 78705-3224 *The right thing is usually also the humane and liberal thing.*

WEINBERG, MARTIN HERBERT, psychiatrist; b. Bklyn., Sept. 3, 1923; s. Abe and Ida (Levine) W.; m. Elizabeth Carwardine, Sept. 20, 1951; children: Mark David, Sheila Ann, Keith Warren. B.S., CCNY, 1947; licentiate, Royal Coll. Surgeons, Edinburgh, Royal Coll. Physicians, Edinburgh, Royal Faculty Physicians and Surgeons, Glasgow. Diplomate: Am. Bd. Psychiatry and Neurology, certified mental hosp. adminstr. Intern Kings County Med. Center, Bklyn., 1952; resident psychiatry Essex County Overbrook Hosp., Cedar Grove, N.J., 1954-56; staff psychiatrist Ancora State Hosp., Hammonton, N.J., 1956; chief service Ancora State Hosp., 1957, clin. dir., 1958-60, asst. med. dir., 1960-62, dep. med. dir., 1962-67; med. dir. Trenton Psychiat. Hosp., 1967-73; dir. div. mental health and hosps. N.J. Dept. Instns. and Agys., 1973-74; med. dir. Trenton Psychiat. Hosp., 1974-79; surveyor psychiat. programs Joint Commn. Accreditation of Hosps., 1979-80; asst. supt. clin. services Phila. State Hosp., 1980-81; individual practice medicine specializing in psychiatry, 1981-86; staff psychiatrist Woods Sch., Langhorne, Pa., to 1986; cons. N.J. Neuropsychiat. Inst., 1981-83, New Lisbon State Sch., to 1985. Fellow Am. Psychiat. Assn., AAAS; mem. N.J. Psychiat. Assn. (past pres.). Home: 26 Diane Dr Trenton NJ 08628-2621

WEINBERG, MARYLIN LYNN, foreign language educator; b. Kansas City, Mo., June 26, 1940; d. Mildred Marie Goetsch; m. Richard Lee Weinberg, Dec. 26, 1962 (div. Oct. 1988); children: Eric H., Kerstin I. BA, Cornell Coll., 1962; MA, Marycrest Coll., 1982. English tchr. Galesburg (Ill.) Community Schs., 1962-63, Grant Community Schs., Fox Lake, Ill., 1963-64, Saydel Community Schs., Des Moines, 1965-66; English instr. Grandview Coll., Des Moines, 1966-70; behavior disorders cons. Western Ill. Assn., Galesburg, Ill., 1976-77; prevocational coord. Knox-Warren Spl. Edn. Dist., Galesburg, 1977-78; Spanish tchr. Winola Community Schs., Viola, Ill., 1979-80; spl. edn. tchr. Pleasant Valley (Iowa) Community Schs., 1980-86; English instr. Ea. Iowa Community Coll. Dist., Davenport, 1983-86; spl. edn. tchr. Davenport Community Schs., 1986-94, fgn. lang. tchr., 1994—. Author: (with others) Parent Prerogatives, 1979. Recipient Tchr. Incentive award State of Iowa Dept. Edn., 1982; chpt. II grant U.S. Office of Edn., Williams Jr. High, 1988. Mem. NEA, Iowa State Edn. Assn., Am. Coun. Tchg. Fgn. Langs., Davenport Edn. Assn., Coun. for Exceptional Children (divsn. learning disabled). Republican. Lutheran. Avocations: home decorating, bird watching, selling securities. Home: 4614 Hamilton Dr Davenport IA 52807-3427

WEINBERG, MEYER, humanities educator; b. N.Y.C., Dec. 16, 1920; s. Charles and Anna (Palatnik) W.; m. Erica C. Mueller, Sept. 5, 1943; children: Rachel (dec.), David, Daniel, Carl, Benjamin. B.A., U. Chgo., 1942, M.A., 1945; A.A., Herzl Jr. Coll., 1940. Faculty history Wright br. City Coll. Chgo., 1945-67, coordinator master planning, 1968-69, coordinator innovations center, 1970-71; prof. history City Coll. Chgo. (Loop br.), 1971-78; dir. Ctr. for Equal Edn. Northwestern U., Evanston, Ill., 1972-78, prof. Sch. Edn., 1978-88; prof. Afro-Am. studies, dir. Horace Mann Bond Center for Equal Edn., U. Mass., Amherst, 1978-90, prof. emeritus, 1990-92, 94—; inaugural holder Veffie Milstead Jones chair in multicultural edn. Calif. State U., Long Beach, 1992-94; chmn. edn. com. Coordinating Council Community Orgns., 1963-67; cons. Howard U., 1964-65, Am. Inst. for Research, 1972, bds. of edn. various cities, univs., 1964-79; bds. of edn. various cities, univs. Fla. Desegregation Center, U. Miami, 1973, NAACP Legal Def. Fund, 1972, Ford Found., 1978, System Devel. Corp., 1975, Nat. Cath. Conf. on Interracial Justice, 1977-78, Stanford Research Inst., 1976, WTTW-TV, Chgo., 1975-78, Edn. Commn. of States, 1978, Cemrel, Inc., 1977, System Devel. Corp., 1979, ESAA Human Relations Study, 1977; mem. tech. adv. com. Ill. Bd. Edn., 1971-72. Author: (with O.E. Shabat) Society and Man, 1956, 65, TV in America-The Morality of Hard Cash, 1962, Race and Place-A Legal History of the Neighborhood School, 1968, Desegregation Research-An Appraisal, 1968, 70, Minority Students-A Research Appraisal, 1977, A Chance to Learn (A History of the Education of Black, Mexican American, American Indian and Puerto Rican Children), 1977, 95, In Search of Quality Integrated Education, 1983, Because They Were Jews: A History of Antisemitism, 1986; editor: Issues in Social Science, 1959, Learning Together, 1964, Integrated Education-A Reader, 1968, Education of the Minority Child-A Comprehensive Bibliography of 10,000 Selected Entries, 1970, W.E.B. DuBois-A Reader, 1970, The Education of Poor and Minority Children: A World Bibliography Supplement, 1986, America's Economic Heritage: A Documentary History, 2 vols., 1983, Racism in the United States, 1990, World Racism and Related Inhumanities: A Country-by-Country Bibliography, 1992, The World of W.E.B. DuBois, 1992, Racism in Contemporary America, 1996; editor Rsch. Rev. of Equal Edn., 1977-79, Integrateducation mag., 1963-86; contbr. chpts. to books, articles to profl. jours. Recipient Center for Human Relations award for creative leadership in edn. NEA, 1971, Human Relations award Mass. Tchrs. Assn., 1988. Mem. Am. Hist. Assn., Soc. for History of Tech., Am. Soc. for Legal History. Home: Apt 7-D 5140 S Hyde Park Blvd Chicago IL 60615-4261

WEINBERG, MICHAEL, JR., commodities broker; b. Chgo., Mar. 19, 1925; s. Michael H. and Leila (Eichberg) W.; m. Joan F. Rusnak, Feb. 25, 1951; children: Michael Alan, Wendy Lee, Jill Diane (Mrs. Avrum Miller). B.A., U. Chgo., 1943; student, Grad. Sch. Bus., 1946-49. Chmn. Assn. of Coll. Unions, 1948; Pres. Great Lakes Pub. Co., Chgo., 1950-53; editor Hyde Park Herald, also Oakland-Kenwood Outlook, Chgo., 1950-53; dir., sec. U. Chgo. Settlement, 1954-58; commodity broker, v.p. Weinberg Bros. & Co. (commodity brokers and wholesalers), Chgo., 1953-83; mem. Chgo. Mercantile Exch., 1954—; pres. Am. Futures Corp., 1983-88; exec. dir. Lincoln Park Zool. Soc., 1963-65; Chmn. bd. govs., chmn. exec. com. Chgo. Merc. Exchange, 1972-73; dir. Internat. Monetary Market; mem. adv. com. Commodity Futures Trading Commn., Washington, 1975-76. Monitor Cook County (Ill.) Ct. Watchers, 1994—. Served with AUS, World War II. Mem. U. Chgo. Alumni Assn., Zeta Beta Tau. Home and Office: 800 Deerfield Rd Highland Park IL 60035-3531

WEINBERG, MILTON, JR., cardiovascular-thoracic surgeon; b. Sumter, S.C., Aug. 8, 1824; s. Milton and Ethel (Harper) W.; m. Joan Ehrenstrom, Nov. 24, 1956; children: Caryl, Susan, Amy. Student, Duke U., 1941-43, MD, 1947. Diplomate Am. Bd. Surgery, Am. Bd. Thoracic Surgery. Attending surgeon Rush Presbyn.-St. Luke's Med. Ctr., Chgo., 1957-90, emeritus attending, 1990—; attending surgeon Cook County Hosp., Chgo., 1956—, Luth. Gen. Hosp., Park Ridge, Ill., 1986—; assoc. prof. Rush Med. Coll., Chgo., 1969-78, prof. surgery, 1978-90, emeritus prof., 1990—; clin. prof. U. Chgo., 1990—; chmn. dept. surgery Luth. Gen. Hosp., Park Ridge, 1988-94, vice-chmn. dept. surgery, 1994—; pres. med. staff Rush Med. Ctr., Chgo., 1977-79; presenter movies at mtgs. ACS. Mem. editorial bd. Annals of Thoracic Surgery, 1968-79; contbr. articles to profl. jours., chpts. to surg. textbooks. Trustee The Presbyn. Home, Evanston, Ill., 1984-94; bd. dirs. Chgo. Symphony Orch., 1985-95, Advocate Charitable Found., 1996—; chmn. Luth. Gen. Hosp. Devel. Coun., 1996—; mem. Luth. Gen. Hosp. Governing Coun., 1996—. Decorated Bronze Star. Fellow ACS, Am. Coll. Chest Physicians, Am. Coll. Cardiology; mem. Am. Assn. Thoracic Surgery, Soc. Thoracic Surgeons, Soc. Vascular Surgery, Internat. Cardiovascular Soc., Ctrl. Surg. Soc. Avocations: fly fishing, fly rod building. Home: 2550 Princeton Ave Evanston IL 60201-4941 Office: Luth Gen Hosp 1775 Dempster St Park Ridge IL 60068-1143

WEINBERG, NORMAN LOUIS, electrochemist; b. Toronto, Ont., Can., May 6, 1936; s. Samuel and Helen (Wise) W.; m. Hannah Rita Cohen, Aug. 30, 1959; children: Eric, Laurie. BSc, U. Toronto, 1959, MSc, 1960; PhD, U. Ottowa, Can., 1963; postdoctoral studies, Technion, Israel, 1963-64. Sr. rsch. chemist Bristol Labs. Can., Candiac, Que., 1964-66, Am. Cyanamid Co., Stamford, Conn., 1966-70; group leader Hooker Chems. & Plastics Corp., Grand Island, N.Y., 1970-74, supr./program leader, 1974-77; pres. Berg Color-Tone, Inc., Lancaster, N.Y., 1977—, The Electrosynthesis Co., inc., Lancaster, 1977—, Benham Electrosynthesis Co., Inc., Lancaster, 1995—; lectr. electrochem. courses Buffalo, 1986, 87, 89; lectr. in-house course DuPont, 1987, 88; lectr./editor Internat. Forum on Electrolysis in the Chem. Industry, 1987-96. Editor: Technique of Electroorganic Synthesis, vol. 1, 1974, vol. 2, 1975, (with Tilak) Technique of Electroorganic Synthesis: Scale-Up, vol. 3, 1982, (with Little) Electroorganic Synthesis: Festschrift in Honor of Manuel Baizer, 1991; contbr. numerous articles to profl. jours. including Jour. Am. Chem. Soc., Can. Jour. Chemistry, Jour. Organic Chemistry, Jour. Applied Electrochemistry. Recipient Inventor of Yr. award Niagara Frontier Patent Law Assn., 1990. Mem. ECS, ISE, Am. Chem. Soc. (lectr. 1972-78). Achievements include 27 patents including for Radiographic Image Enhancement, Methods for the Electrosynthesis of Polyols, Fluorinated Carbons and Method of Manufacture, (with others) Modified Carbons and Electrochemical Cells Containing Same, (with others) Reactions in an Electrochemical Cell Including an Electrode Comprising Magneli Phase Titanium Oxide, (with others) Methods for Paired Electrosynthesis with Simultaneous Ethylene Glycol Formation, (with other) Membrane Divided Aqueous-Nonaqueous System for Electrochemical Cells, others; 9 patent applications for fluorinated carbons and uses thereof, (with others) porous electrodes for use in electrochemical gas sensors, (with others) methods for purification of air, (with others) manufacture of flourinated carbons, (with others) high surface area electrodes. Office: Electrosynthesis Co Inc 72 Ward Rd Lancaster NY 14086-9779

WEINBERG, RICHARD ALAN, psychologist, educator; b. Chgo., Jan. 28, 1943; s. Meyer and Mollie I. (Soell) W.; m. Gail E. Blumberg Aug. 25, 1964; children: Eric, Brett. BS, U. Wis., 1964; MAT, Northwestern U., 1965; PhD,

U. Minn., 1968. Lic. psychologist, Minn. Asst. prof. Tchrs. Coll., Columbia U., N.Y.C., 1968-70; prof. ednl. psychology, psychology and child psychology U. Minn., Mpls., 1970—, Birkmaier professorship, 1994—; dir. Inst. Child Devel., former dir. Ctr. for Early Edn. and Devel., former chair adv. coun. Children, Youth & Family Consortium; cons. EPA; reviewer Office of Edn., NSF, NRC; guest speaker TV and radio shows. Former mem. adv. com. Children's Mus. Minn.; past pres. Am. Assn. State Psychol. Bds.; liaison Nat. Register for Health Care Providers in Psychology. Grantee Bush Found.; NSF; NIH. Fellow APA, Am. Psychol. Soc.; mem., Soc. Rsch. in Child Devel. (former chair pub. policy coun.), Behavior Genetics Assn., Am. Psychol. Soc. (bd. dirs.), Phi Beta Kappa, Phi Kappa Phi. Author: (with A. Boehm) The Classroom Observer: Developing Observation Skills in Early Childhood Settings, 1996; (with Scarr and Levine) Understanding Development, 1986; former assoc. editor Contemporary Psychology; editor: Applied Developmental Science. Office: U Minn 180 Child Devel 51 E River Rd Minneapolis MN 55455-0365

WEINBERG, ROBERT ALLAN, biochemist, educator; b. Pitts., Nov. 11, 1942; s. Fritz E. and Lore (Reichhardt) W.; m. Amy Shulman, Nov. 19, 1976; children—Aron, Leah Rosa. S.B., MIT, 1964, Ph.D, 1969; Ph.D. (hon.), Northwestern U., 1984. Instr. Stillman Coll., Tuscaloosa, Ala., 1965-66; research fellow Weizmann Inst., Rehovoth, Israel, 1969-70, Salk Inst., LaJolla, Calif., 1970-72; from asst. prof. to assoc. prof. dept. biology & ctr. cancer rsch. MIT, Cambridge, 1973-82, prof. biology, 1982—; mem. Whitehead Inst., Cambridge, 1984—. Contbr. articles to profl. jours. Recipient Bristol Myers award, 1984, Armand Hammer award, 1984, Brown-Hazen award N.Y. State Dept. Health, 1984, Sloan prize Gen. Motors Cancer Rsch. Found., 1987, Rsch. Recognition award Samuel Roberts Noble Found., 1990, Gairdner Found. Internat. award, 1992, Harvey Prize, Technion, 1994. Mem. Nat. Acad. Sci. (sci. award 1984). Avocations: genealogy, house building. Office: Whitehead Inst 9 Cambridge Ctr Cambridge MA 02142-1401

WEINBERG, STEVEN, physics educator; b. N.Y.C., NY, May 3, 1933; s. Fred and Eva (Israel) W.; m. Louise Goldwasser, July 6, 1954; 1 child, Elizabeth. BA, Cornell U., 1954; postgrad., Copenhagen Inst. Theoretical Physics, 1954-55; PhD, Princeton U., 1957; AM (hon.), Harvard U., 1973; ScD (hon.), Knox Coll., 1978, U. Chgo., 1978, U. Rochester, 1979, Yale U., 1979, CUNY, 1980, Clark U., 1982, Dartmouth Coll., 1984, Columbia U., 1990, U. Salamanca, 1992, U. Padua, 1992; U. Barcelona, 1996, U. Barcelona, 1996; PhD (hon.), Weizmann Inst., 1985; DLitt (hon.), Washington Coll., 1985. Rsch. assoc., instr. Columbia U., 1957-59; rsch. physicist Lawrence Radiation Lab., Berkeley, Calif., 1959-60; mem. faculty U. Calif., Berkeley, 1960-69, prof. physics, 1964-69; vis. prof. MIT, 1967-69, prof. physics, 1969-73; Higgins prof. physics Harvard U., 1973-83; sr. scientist Smithsonian Astrophys. Lab., 1973-83; Josey prof. sci. U. Tex., Austin, 1982—; sr. cons. Smithsonian Astrophys. Obs., 1983—; cons. Inst. Def. Analyses, Washington, 1960-73, ACDA, 1973; Sloan fellow, 1961-65; chair in physics Coll. de France, 1971; mem. Pres.'s Com. on Nat. Medal of Sci., 1979-82, Coun. of Scholars, Libr. of Congress, 1983-85; sr. adv. La Jolla Inst.; mem. Com. on Internat. Security and Arms Control, NRC, 1981, Bd. on Physics & Astronomy, 1989-90; dir. Jerusalem Winter Sch. Theoretical Physics, 1983-94; mem. adv. coun. Tex. Superconducting Supercollider High Energy Rsch. Facility, 1987; Loeb lectr. in physics Harvard U., 1966-67, Morris Loeb vis. prof. physics, 1983—; Richtmeyer lectr., 1974; Scott lectr. Cavendish Lab., 1975; Silliman lectr. Yale U., 1977; Lauritsen Meml. lectr. Calif. Inst. Tech., 1979; Bethe lectr. Cornell U., 1979; de Shalit lectr. Weizman Inst., 1979; Cherwell-Simon lectr. Oxford U., 1983; Bampton lectr. Columbia U., 1983; Einstein lectr. Israel Acad. Arts and Scis., 1984; Hilldale lectr. U. Wis., 1985; Clark lectr. U. Tex., Dallas, 1986; Dirac lectr. U. Cambridge, 1986; Klein lectr. U. Stockholm, 1989; Brittin lectr. U. Colo., 1994; Sackler lectr. U. Copenhagen, 1994; Gibbs lectr. Am. Math. Soc., 1996; Sloan fellow, 1961-65; mem. Supercollider Sci. Policy Com., 1989-93. Author: Gravitation and Cosmology: Principles and Application of the General Theory of Relativity, 1972, The First Three Minutes: A Modern View of the Origin of the Universe, 1977, The Discovery of Subatomic Particles, 1982; co-author (with R. Feynman) Elementary Particles and the Laws of Physics, 1987, Dreams of a Final Theory, 1992, The Quantum Theory of Fields - Vol. I: Foundations, 1995, Modern Applications, Vol. II, 1996; rsch. and publs. on elementary particles, quantum field theory, cosmology; co-editor Cambridge U. Press, monographs on math. physics; mem. adv. bd. Issues in Sci. and Tech., 1984-87; mem. sci. book com. Sloan Found., 1985-91; mem. editl. bd. Jour. Math. Physics, 1986-88; mem. bd. editors Daedalus, 1990—; mem. bd. assoc. editors Nuclear Physics B. Bd. advisors Santa Barbara Inst. Theoretical Physics, 1983-86; bd. overseers SSC Accelerator, 1984-86; bd. dirs. Headliners Found., 1993—. Recipient J. Robert Oppenheimer meml. prize, 1973, Dannie Heineman prize in math. physics, 1977, Am. Inst. Physics-U.S. Steel Found. sci. writing award, 1977, Nobel prize in physics, 1979, Elliott Cresson medal Franklin Inst., 1979, Madison medal Princeton U., 1991, Nat. Medal of Sci. NSF, 1991. Mem. Am. Acad. Arts and Scis. (past councilor), Am. Phys. Soc. (past councilor at large, panel on faculty positions com. on status of women in physics), NAS (supercollider site evaluation com. 1987-88), Einstein Archivess (adv. bd. 1988—), Internat. Astron. Union, Coun. Fgn. Rels., Am. Philos. Soc., Royal Soc. London (fgn. mem.), Am. Mediaeval Acad., History of Sci. Soc., Philos. Soc. Tex. (pres. 1994), Tex. Inst. of Letters, Phi Beta Kappa. Clubs: Saturday (Boston); Headliners, Tuesday (Austin); Cambridge Sci. Soc.

WEINBERG, SYDNEY STAHL, historian; b. N.Y.C., Oct. 2, 1938; d. David Leslie and Berenice (Jarvis) Stahl; B.A., Barnard Coll., 1960; M.A., Columbia U., 1964; Ph.D., 1969; divorced; children: Deborah Sara, Elisa Rachel; m. Gerald Tenenbaum, Mar. 23, 1996. Instr. history N.J. Inst. Tech., 1967-69, asst. prof., 1969-72; asso. prof. history Ramapo Coll. N.J., Mahwah, 1972-74, prof., 1974—; dir. Master of Arts Program in Liberal Studies, 1994—; dir. Garden State Immigration History Consortium, 1987-89. Nat. Endowment for Humanities fellow, 1977-78; sec./treas. Berkshire Conf. Women Historians, 1994—. Mem. Inst. for Rsch. in History, Am. Hist. Assn., Orgn. Am. Historians, Am. Studies Assn., Jewish Studies Assn., Assn. of Graduate Liberal Studies Programs. Author: The World of Our Mothers: The Lives of Jewish Immigrant Women, 1988; contbr. articles to profl. jours. Home: 80 La Salle St Apt 19F New York NY 10027-4760 Office: Ramapo Coll MA Liberal Studies Program Office Mahwah NJ 07430

WEINBERG, SYLVAN LEE, cardiologist, educator, author, editor; b. Nashville, June 14, 1923; s. Abraham J. and Beatrice (Kottler) W.; m. Joan Hutzler, Jan. 29, 1956; children: Andrew Lee, Leslie. BS, Northwestern U., 1945, BM, 1946, MD, 1947. From intern to resident, fellow Michael Reese Hosp., Chgo., 1947-51; attending physician Good Samaritan Hosp., Dayton, Ohio, 1953—, chief of cardiology, 1966—, founding dir. coronary care unit, 1967—; clin. prof. medicine Wright State U., Dayton, 1975—; panelist Med. Affairs, nat. TV; pres. Weinberg Marcus Cardiomed. Group, Inc. Author: An Epitaph for Merlin and Perhaps for Medicine, 1983; founding editor Dayton Medicine, 1980—, Heart & Lung, 1972-87; contbr. articles to profl jours. Capt. U.S. Army, 1951-53, Korea. Recipient Army Commendation medal; Outstanding Pub. Svc. award Ohio State Senate, 1980. Fellow Am. Coll. Cardiology (editor in chief jour. ACCEL 1985—, pres. 1993-94, chmn. bd. Inst. for Study of Cardiovascular Medicine 1993—), Am. Coll. Chest Physicians (pres. 1984); mem. Montgomery County Med. Soc. (pres. 1980). Avocations: writing, travel, golf. Home: 4555 Southern Blvd Dayton OH 45429-1118 Office: Weinberg Marcus Cardiomed Group 9000 N Main St Ste 402 Dayton OH 45415-1165

WEINBERG, WILLIAM HENRY, chemical engineer, chemical physicist, educator; b. Columbia, S.C., Dec. 5, 1944; s. Ulrich Vivian and Ruth Ann (Duncan) W. BS, U. S.C., 1966; PhD in Chem. Engring, U. Calif., Berkeley, 1970; NATO postdoctoral fellow in phys. chemistry, Cambridge U., Eng., 1971. Asst. prof. chem. engring. Calif. Inst. Tech., 1972-74, asso. prof., 1974-77, prof. chem. engring. and chem. physics, 1977-89, Chevron disting. prof. chem. engring. and chem. physics, 1981-86; prof. chem. engring. and chemistry U. Calif., Santa Barbara, 1989—, assoc. dean Coll. Engring., 1992—; CTO Symyx Technologies, Sunnyvale, Calif., 1996—; vis. prof. chemistry Harvard U., 1980, U. Pitts., 1987-88, Oxford U., 1991; Alexander von Humboldt Found. fellow U. Munich, 1982; cons. E.I. DuPont Co. Author: (with Van Hove and Chan) Low-Energy Electron Diffraction, 1986; editor 4 books in field; mem. editorial bd. Jour. Applications Surface Sci., 1977-85, Handbook Surfaces and Interfaces, 1978-80, Surface Sci. Reports, 1980—, gen. editor, 1992—, Applied Surface Sci., 1985—, Langmuir, 1990—, Surface Sci., 1992—; contbr. articles to profl. jours., chpts. to books. Recipient Giuseppe Parravano award Mich. Catalysis Soc., 1989, Disting. Teaching award Coll. of Engring., U. Calif. Santa Barbara, 1995, Arthur W. Adamson awardAm. Chem. Soc., 1995; fellow NSF, 1966-69, Alfred P. Sloan Found., 1976-78, Camille and Henry Dreyfus Found. fellow, 1976-81. Fellow AAAS, Am. Phys. Soc. (Nottingham prize 1972), Am. Vacuum Soc.; mem. AIChE (Colburn award 1981), Am. Chem. Soc. (LaMer award 1973, Kendall award 1991, Arthur W. Adamson award 1995), N.Am. Catalysis Soc., Nat. Acad. Engring., Phi Beta Kappa. Home: 25 Hidden Valley Ln Woodside CA 94062 Office: U Calif Dept Chem Nuclear Engr Santa Barbara CA 93106 Office: Symyx technologies 420 Oakmead Pkwy Sunnyvale CA 94086

WEINBERGER, ALAN DAVID, corporate executive; b. Washington, July 31, 1945; s. Theodore George and Shirley Sunshine (Gross) W.; m. Lauren Myra Kaminski, Dec. 2, 1979; children: Mark Henry, Benjamin Charles. BA, NYU, 1967, JD, 1970; LLM, Harvard U., 1973. Bar: N.Y. 1971, D.C. 1978, U.S. Supreme Ct. 1980. Assoc. White & Case, N.Y.C., 1970-72; founding law prof. Vt. Law Sch., South Royalton, 1973-75; atty. SEC and Fed. Home Loan Bank Bd., Washington, 1977-81; founder, chmn. bd., CEO The ASCII Group Inc., Washington, 1984—; mem. adv. bd. Ashton Tate Inc., Torrance, Calif., 1986-87; sponsor, agt. All Union Fgn. Trade Acad., Acad. Nat. Economy of USSR in U.S.A., 1988-90; chmn. U.S. adv. bd. Moscow State U. of Commerce, 1992—; chmn. govt. affairs com. Computer Tech. Industry Assn., 1993-95. Author: White Paper to Reform Business Education in Russia, 1996; law rev. editor NYU Sch. Law, 1970. Named one of Top 25 Most Influential Execs. in Computer Industry, Computer Reseller News, 1988. Mem. Nat. Orgn. on Disability (CEO coun.), D.C. Bar Assn., Order of Coif, Kenwood Country Club. Avocation: tennis. Office: ASCII Group Inc 7475 Wisconsin Ave Bethesda MD 20814-3412

WEINBERGER, ARNOLD, retired electrical engineer; b. Bardejov, Czechoslovakia, Oct. 23, 1924; came to U.S., 1939; s. Henry C. and Bina (Shapira) W.; widowed; children: Paul I., Ronda B., Keith A. BSEE, CCNY, 1950. Engr. Nat. Bur. Standards, Washington, 1950-60; rsch. staff mem. IBM, Yorktown Heights, N.Y., 1960-66; engr., Poughkeepsie, N.Y. IBM, 1966-91, ret., 1991. Contbr. articles on computer arithmetic, logic, large-scale integration, system organization, memories, design automation. Patentee in field. With U.S. Army, 1944-46, ETO. Fellow IEEE (Outstanding sect. award 1981). Avocation: table tennis.

WEINBERGER, CASPAR WILLARD, publishing executive, former secretary of defense; b. San Francisco, Aug. 18, 1917; s. Herman and Cerise Carpenter (Hampson) W.; m. Jane Dalton, Aug. 16, 1942; children: Arlin Cerise, Caspar Willard. AB magna cum laude, Harvard U., 1938, LLB, 1941; LLD (hon.), U. Leeds, Eng., 1989; LittD (hon.), U. Buckingham, 1995. Bar: Calif., U.S. Ct. Appeals (D.C. cir.) 1990. Law clk. U.S. Judge William E. Orr, 1945-47; with firm Heller, Ehrman, White & McAuliffe, 1947-69, ptnr., 1959-69; mem. Calif. Legislature from 21st Dist., 1952-58; vice chmn. Calif. Rep. Cen. Com., 1960-62, chmn., 1962-64; chmn. Com. Calif. Govt. Orgn. and Econs., 1967-68; dir. fin. Calif., 1968-69; chmn. FTC, 1970; dep. dir. Office Mgmt. and Budget, 1970-72, dir., 1972-73; counsellor to the Pres., 1973; sec. HEW, 1973-75; gen. counsel, v.p., dir. Bechtel Power Corp., San Francisco, 1975-80, Bechtel, Inc., 1975-80, Bechtel Corp., 1975-80; sec. Dept. Def., Washington, 1981-87; counsel Law Firm of Rogers & Wells, Washington and N.Y.C., 1988-94; chmn. Forbes Magazine, New York, 1989—; formerly staff book reviewer San Francisco Chronicle; moderator weekly TV program Profile, Bay Area, sta. KQED, San Francisco, 1959-68; Frank Nelson Doubleday lectr., 1974. Writer column on Calif. govt., 1959-68; author: Fighting for Peace: Seven Critical Years in the Pentagon, 1990. Chmn. Pres.'s Com. on Mental Retardation, 1973-75; former mem. Trilaterial Commn.; former mem. adv. coun. Am. Ditchley Found.; former bd. dirs. Yosemite Inst.; former trustee St. Luke's Hosp., san Francisco, Mechanics Inst.; former chmn. nat. bd. trustees Nat. Symphony, Washington; former bd. govs. San Francisco Symphony; chmn. bd. USA-ROC Econ. Coun., 1991-94; co-chmn. Winston Churchill Travelling Fellowships Found., 1989—. Served to capt., inf. AUS, 1941-45; PTO. Decorated Bronze Star, Grand Cordon of Order of the Rising Sun (Japan), Hon. Knight Grand Cross Civil Div. Order of Brit. Empire; recipient Presdl. medal Freedom with distinction, 1987, George Catlet Marshall medal, 1988, Civil award Hilal-i-Pakistan, 1989. Mem. ABA, State Bar Calif., D.C. Ct. Appeals, Century Club (N.Y.), Bohemian Club (San Francisco), Pacific Union Club (San Francisco), Harvard Club (Washington). Episcopalian (former treas. Diocese of Calif.). Office: Forbes Mag 60 5th Ave New York NY 10011-8802 also: Forbes Inc 1901 L St NW Washington DC 20036-3506

WEINBERGER, DANIEL R., psychiatrist, neurologist; b. N.Y.C., May 24, 1947; married; 1 child. BA, Johns Hopkins U., 1969; MD, U. Pa., 1973. Diplomate Am. Bd. Psychiatry and Neurology. Intern L.A. County-Harbor Gen. Hosp., Torrance, Calif., 1973-74; grad. fellow in medicine UCLA Sch. Medicine, 1973-74; clin. fellow in psychiatry Harvard U., 1974-77; resident in psychiatry Mass. Mental Health Ctr., Boston, 1974-76, chief resident, 1976-77; assoc. in medicine, divsn. psychiatry Peter Bent Brigham Hosp., Boston, 1974-76; asst. clin. prof. psychiatry George Washington U., Washington, 1978-81, assoc. clin. prof., 1982, assoc. clin. prof. neurology and psychiatry, 1984; resident in neurology George Washington U. Med. Ctr., Washington, 1980-83; dir. rsch. ward adult psychiatry br., intermural rsch. program NIHM, Washington, 1977-78, staff psychiatrist, 1977-81; head clin. neuropsychiatry and neurobehavior unit NIMH/St. Elizabeth's Hosp., Washington, 1981-82, chief sect., 1983-86, chief clin. brain disorders br., 1986—; dir. movement disorder, dementia clinic, experimental therapeutics br. Nat. Inst. Neurol. Diseases and Stroke, Washington, 1983-86; dir. behavioral neurology svc. St. Elizabeth's Hosp., Washington, 1983-88; part-time gen. practice Bridgewater Med. Ctr., East Bridgewater, Mass., 1974-76; emergency rm. physician Cardinal Cushing Gen. Hosp., Brockton, Mass., 1974-77; examiner Am. Bd. Psychiatry and Neurology; part-time gen. practice psychiatry and neurology, Washington, 1978—; scientists promotion review com. NIMH, 1984-87; elected to coun. Assembly of Scientists NIMH/Nat. Inst. Neurological Diseases and Stroke, 1985-88; Roerig vis. prof. U. N.Mex., 1990, U. Mich., 1992; adv. bd. Alzheimer Disease Found., 1990—, Adams Super Ctr. Brain Studies, Tel Aviv, 1993—; Neal Mysell lectr. Harvard Med. Sch., 1993; steering com. in vivo NMR Ctr., NIH, 1993—. Mem. editorial bd. Biol. Psychiatry, 1986—, Internat. Jour. Schizophrenia Rsch., 1987—, Jour. Neuropsychiatry and Clin. Neurosci., 1987—, Psychiatry, 1987—, Progress in Neuropsychiatry and Psychopharmacology, 1989—, Jour. Clin. Brain Imaging, 1989—, Psychiatry Research: Neuroimaging, 1990—, Jour. Psychiatry and Neurosci., 1990—, Neuropsychopharmacology, 1991—, Development and Psychopathology, 1991—, Harvard Review of Psychiatry, 1992—; contbr. articles to profl. jours.; patentee in field. Capt. USPHS, 1977-86. Recipient Morton Prince award Am. Psychopathol. Assn., 1984, Judith B. Silver award Nat. Alliance for Mentally Ill, 1985, Arthur S. Flemming award Washington Jaycees, 1986, Established Investigator award NARSAD, 1990, Lieber award, 1993, Dean award Am. Coll. Psychiatrists, 1994. Fellow Am. Coll. Neuropsychopharmacology (Joel Elkes internat. award 1989); mem. AMA, AAAS, Am. Psychiat. Assn. (Found. Fund prize for rsch. 1991), Am. Acad. Neurology (sci. program com. 1993—), Am. Neuropsychiatric Assn., Soc. Biol. Psychiatry (A.E. Benett Found. award clin. science 1981), Behavioral Neurology Soc., Soc. Neurosci. (pub. lectr. 20th ann. meeting 1990), Washington Neurology Soc., Washington Psychiat. Soc., Phi Beta Kappa, Alpha Omega Alpha. Office: St Elizabeth's Hosp Chief Clin Brain Disor Br Washington DC 20032

WEINBERGER, FRANK, information systems advisor; b. Chgo., Sept. 18, 1926; s. Rudolph and Elaine (Kellner) W.; m. Beatrice Natalie Fixler, June 27, 1953; children: Alan J., Bruce I. BSEE, Ill. Inst. of Tech., 1951; MBA, Northwestern U., Evanston, 1959; DBA, U.S. Internat. U., 1996. Registered profl. engr., Ill, Calif. Engr. Admiral Corp., Chgo., 1951-53; sr. engr. Cook Rsch., Chgo., 1953-59; mem. tech. staff Rockwell Internat., Downey, Calif., 1959-80, info. systems advisor, 1980-95; info. mgmt. cons., 1995—. Pres. Temple Israel, Long Beach, Calif., 1985-87, bd. dirs. 1973-85. With USN, 1944-46. Mem. Assn. for Computer Machinery. Democrat. Jewish. Avocation: microcomputers. Home and Office: 3231 Yellowtail Dr Los Alamitos CA 90720-5253 *Don't ask "what can I do?" Instead, survey the needs, prepare the information, and give your best recommendation.*

WEINBERGER, HAROLD PAUL, lawyer; b. N.Y.C., Mar. 12, 1947; s. Fred and Elaine (Schonfeld) W.; m. Toby Ann Strassman, Dec. 15, 1968; children—James David, Karen Ellen. B.A., CCNY, 1967; J.D., Columbia U., 1970. Bar: N.Y. 1971, U.S. Dist. Cts. (so., ea. and no. dists.) N.Y. 1972, U.S. Ct. Appeals (2d cir.) 1972. Law clk. to presiding justice U.S. Ct. Appeals (2d cir.) N.Y.C., 1970-71; assoc. Kramer, Levin, Naftalis, Nessen, Kamin & Frankel, N.Y.C., 1971-77, ptnr., 1978—. Recipient John Ordronaux prize Columbia U. Law Sch., 1970. Mem. Assn. Bar City N.Y. (com. fed. legislation 1975-78, com. on products liability 1983-86, mem. com. on trademarks and unfair competition 1995—). Democrat. Jewish. Home: 336 Central Park W New York NY 10025-7111 Office: Kramer Levin Naftalis Nessen Kamin & Frankel 919 3rd Ave New York NY 10022

WEINBERGER, LEON WALTER, sanitary engineer; b. N.Y.C., Aug. 28, 1923; s. Nathan and Margaret (Feldman) W.; m. Greta Stovsky, Dec. 16, 1950; children: Jeffrey Howard, Paula Lynn, Gayle Ellen. BS in Civil Engring., Cooper Union Coll., 1943; MS, MIT, 1947, ScD, 1949. Diplomate, Am. Assn. Environ. Engrs. Rsch. assoc. MIT, Cambridge, Mass., 1947-49; assoc. prof. Case Inst. Tech., Cleve., 1949-63; asst. com. R&D water pollution Depts. Interior & HEW, Washington, 1963-68; group v.p. Zurn Industries, Erie, Pa., 1968-70; v.p. EnviroControl, Washington, 1970; prin. Leon W. Weinberger & Assocs., Rockville, Md., 1970-76; chief engr. Peer Cons., Rockville, Md., 1978-96. Contbr. articles to profl. jours., presentations to sci. meetings. Lt. US Navy 1943-46, PTO. Fellow ASCE; mem. Water Pollution Control Fed., Am. Water Works Assn., Sigma Xi. Jewish. Home: 7400 Masters Dr Potomac MD 20854-3852

WEINBERGER, MILES M., physician, pediatric educator; b. McKeesport, Pa., June 28, 1938; divorced; 4 children; m. Leslie Kramer, Aug. 22, 1992. A.B., U. Pitts., 1960, M.D., 1965. Diplomate Am. Bd. Pediatrics, Am. Bd. Allergy and Immunology, Am. Bd. Pediatric Pulmonology. Intern U. Calif. Med. Ctr., San Francisco, 1965-66, pediatric resident, 1965-67; research assoc NIH, Bethesda, Md., 1967-69; allergy and pulmonary fellow U. Colo., Denver, 1969-71; staff Ross Valley Med. Clinic, Greenbrae, Calif., 1971-73; clin. pharmacology fellow U. Colo., Denver, 1973-75; div. chmn. U. Iowa, Iowa City, 1975—; cons. D.C.Hosp. for Sick Children, 1967-69, allergy and immunology Family Practice Program, Sonoma County Community Hosp., U. Calif. Sch. Medicine, 1972-73; clin. instr. pediatrics Georgetown U. Sch. Medicine, Washington, 1967-69; staff pediatrician part-time West Side Neighborhood Health Ctr., Denver, 1970-71; pediatric sr. staff mem. Nat.Jewish Hosp. and Research Ctr., 1973-75; clin. asst. U. Colo. Med.Ctr., 1974-75; assoc. prof. pediatrics, chmn. pediatric allergy and pulmonary div. U. Iowa Coll. Medicine, 1975-80, assoc. prof. pharmacology, 1975-79, dir. Cystic Fibrosis Ctr., 1977—, prof. pediatrics, 1980—, dir. pediatric allergy and pulmonary div., 1975—. Author: Managing Asthma, 1990; contbr. numerous articles to profl. jours., chpts. to books, also audio-visual materials, commentaries, pub. letters and presentations in field. Recipient Clemens von Pirquet award Am. Coll. Allergy, 1974; grantee NIH, 1980-85, Cystic Fibrosis Ctr., Pharm. Mfrs. Assn. Fellow Am. Acad. Pediatrics (allergy sect. 1972, sect. on clin. pharmacology and therapeutics 1978, diseases of chest 1978); mem. Am. Acad. Allergy, Am. Soc. Clin. Pharmacology and Therapeutics, Soc. for Pediatric Rsch., Am. Thoracic Soc. (pres. Iowa Thoracic Soc. 1992-93), Camp Superkids of Iowa (adv. bd. 1981—), Am. Lung Assn. (pediatric pulmonbary ctr. task force com. 1984-86). Home: 7 Cottage Grove Dr NE Iowa City IA 52240-9171 Office: U Iowa Dept Pediatrics Iowa City IA 52242

WEINBERGER, MYRON HILMAR, medical educator; b. Cin., Sept. 21, 1937; s. Samuel and Helen Eleanor (Price) W.; m. Myrna M. Rosenberg, June 12, 1960; children: Howard David, Steven Neal, Debra Ellen. BS, Ind. U., Bloomington, 1959, MD, 1963. Intern Ind. U. Med. Ctr., Indpls., 1963-64, resident in internal medicine, 1964-66, asst. prof. medicine, 1969-73, assoc. prof., 1973-76, prof., 1976—, dir. Hypertension Research Ctr., 1981—; USPHS trainee in endocrinology and metabolism Stanford U. Med. Ctr., Calif., 1966-68, USPHS spl. fellow in hypertension, 1968-69. Contbr. articles to profl. jours. Recipient Tigerstedt award Am. Soc. Hypertension, 1996. Fellow ACP, Am. Coll. Cardiology, Am. Coll. Nutrition, Am. Soc. for Clin. Pharmacology and Therapeutics; mem. AAAS, Am. Fedn. Clin. Research, AMA, Am. Heart Assn., Am. Soc. Nephrology, Internat. Soc. Nephrology, Central Soc. Clin. Research, Endocrine Soc., Internat. Soc. Hypertension, Soc. for Exptl. Biology and Medicine. Home: 135 Bow Ln Indianapolis IN 46220-1023 Office: Ind U Hypertension Research Ctr 541 Clinical Dr Indianapolis IN 46202-5111

WEINBRENNER, GEORGE RYAN, aeronautical engineer; b. Detroit, June 10, 1917; s. George Penbrook and Helen Mercedes (Ryan) W.; BS, M.I.T., 1940, MS, 1941; AMP, Harvard U., 1966; ScD (hon.), Mapua Inst. Tech., Manila, 1994; m. Billie Marjorie Elwood, May 2, 1955. Commd. 2d lt. USAAF, 1939, advanced through grades to col., 1949; def. attaché Am. embassy, Prague, Czechoslavakia, 1958-61; dep. chief staff intelligence Air Force Systems Command, Washington, 1962-68; comdr. fgn. tech. div. U.S. Air Force, Wright-Patterson AFB, Ohio, 1968-74; comdr. Brooks AFB, Tex., 1974-75; ret., 1975; exec. v.p. B.C. Wills & Co., Inc., Reno, Nev., 1975-84; lectr. Sch. Aerospace Medicine Brooks AFB, Tex., 1975-84; chmn. bd. Hispaño-Technica S.A. Inc., San Antonio, 1977—; adv. dir. Plaza Nat. Bank, San Antonio; cons. Def. Dept., 1981, Dept. Air Force, 1975-84. Decorated D.S.M., Legion of Merit, Bronze Star, Air medal, Purple Heart; Ordre National du Merite, Medaille de la Resistance, Croix de Guerre (France). Fellow AIAA (asso.); mem. World Affairs Council, Air Force Assn. (exec. sec. Tex. 1976-94), Assn. Former Intelligence Officers (nat. dir.), Air Force Hist. Found. (dir.), U.S. Strategic Inst., Nat. Mil. Intelligence Assn., Tex. Aerospace & Nat. Def. Tech. Devel. Coun., Am. Astronautical Soc., Aerospace Ednl. Found. (trustee), Disabled Am. Vets. (life), Mil. Order World Wars, Am. Legion, Assn. Old Crows, Kappa Sigma. Roman Catholic. Clubs: Army-Navy (Washington). Home: 7400 Crestway Dr Apt 903 San Antonio TX 78239-3094 Office: PO Box 8121 San Antonio TX 78208-0121

WEINBROT, HOWARD DAVID, English educator; b. Bklyn., May 14, 1936; s. William and Rose (Shapiro) W. BA, Antioch Coll., Yellow Springs, Ohio, 1958; MA with honors (Woodrow Wilson fellow 1959, grad. fellow 1959-63), U. Chgo., 1959, PhD, 1963. Teaching fellow U. Chgo., 1962-63; instr. English Yale U., 1963-66; asst. prof., then assoc. prof. U. Calif., Riverside, 1966-69; mem. faculty U. Wis., Madison, 1969—, prof. English, 1972-84, Ricardo Quintana prof., 1984-87, Vilas prof., 1987—; Andrew Mellon vis. prof. Inst. Advanced Studies, Princeton, N.J., 1993-94. Author: The Formal Strain, 1969, Augustus Caesar in Augustan England, 1978, Alexander Pope and the Traditions of Formal Verse Satire, 1982, Essays on 18th-Century Satire, 1988, Britannia's Issue, 1993; also numerous articles, revs.; editor: New Aspects of Lexicography, 1972, Northrop Frye and 18th Century Studies; co-editor: The 18th Century: A Current Bibliography for 1973, 1975, Poetry in English, An Anthology, 1987. Fellow Inst. for Advanced Studies, Princeton, N.J, 1993-94; Guggenheim fellow, 1988-89. Mem. Am. Soc. 18th Century Studies (mem. editl. bd. 1977-80, 96—), Johnson Soc. (sec.-treas. ctrl. region 1970-95), Johnsonians, Midwest Soc. 18th Century Studies (pres. 1980). Home: 1505 Wood Ln Madison WI 53705-1456 Office: U Wis Dept English 600 N Park St Madison WI 53706-1403

WEINER, ANDREW JAY, lawyer; b. Hartford, Conn., Dec. 19, 1950; m. Debra Lewin, May 29, 1977; children: Joshua Isaac, Hannah Leah. BA, Yale Coll., 1972; JD, Harvard U., 1976. Bar: N.Y. 1977. Planner N.Y.C. Dept. City Planning, 1972-73; assoc. Shearman & Sterling, N.Y.C., 1976-84; ptnr. Gordon Hurwitz Butowsky Weitzen Shalov & Wein, N.Y.C., 1984-89, Morrison & Foerster, N.Y.C., 1990—. Office: Morrison & Foerster 1290 Avenue Of The Americas New York NY 10104

WEINER, ANNETTE BARBARA, university dean, anthropology educator; b. Philadelphia, Pa., Feb. 14, 1933; d. Archibald W. and Phyllis M. (Stein-Goldman) Cohen; m. Martin Weiner, 1953 (div. 1973); children: Linda Matisse, Jonathan Weiner; m. Robert Palter, 1979 (div. 1982); m. William E. Mitchell, 1987. B.A., U. Pa., 1968; Ph.D., Bryn Mawr Coll., 1974. Vis. asst. prof. Franklin and Marshall Coll., Lancaster, Pa., 1973-74; assoc. prof. Clare Hall, Cambridge, Eng., 1976; asst. prof. anthropology U. Tex., Austin, 1974-80, assoc. prof., 1980-81; prof., chmn. dept. anthropology NYU, N.Y.C., 1981-91; David B. Kriser prof. NYU, 1985—; dean Grad. Sch. Arts and Scis. NYU, N.Y.C., 1991—, dean Social Scis., 1993—; mem. adv. com. NRC, 1993—; bd. dirs. Social Sci. Rsch. Coun. Author: Women of Value:

Men of Renown: New Perspectives in Trobriand Exchange, 1976, The Trobrianders of Papua New Guinea, 1989; editor (with J. Schneider) Cloth and Human Experience, 1989, (film, with D. Wason) The Trobriand Islanders of Papua New Guinea, Bilan du Film Ethnographique, Paris, 1991 (Grand Prix award), Inalienable Possessions: The Paradox of Keeping-While-Giving, 1992. Guggenheim fellow, 1980; grantee Wenner-Gren Found. Anthrop. Rsch., 1982, 85, 86, NEH, 1976, 85, Am. Council Learned Socs., 1976, NIMH, 1972-73. Fellow Am. Anthrop. Assn. (pres. 1991-93), Royal Anthrop. Inst. Gt. Britain and Ireland, Assn. Social Anthropology in Oceania, Soc. Cultural Anthropology (bd. dirs. 1985-87, pres. 1988-89), N.Y. Inst. of the Humanities; mem. Cibola Anthrop. Assn. (pres. 1977-79), Commn. Visual Anthropology, Nat. Rsch. Coun. (adv. com. 1993—), Social Sci. Rsch. Coun. (bd. dirs. 1993-95). Office: NYU Dean Grad Sch 6 Washington Sq N New York NY 10003-6635

WEINER, CARL DORIAN, historian; b. N.Y.C., Mar. 26, 1934; s. Alexander and Ann (Goodson) W.; m. Ruth Ann Feinglass, Sept. 6, 1959; children—Nicholas, Kevin, Daniel. B.A., Queens Coll., 1955; postgrad., U. Wis., 1958-61; M.A., Columbia U., 1959. Instr. U. Pitts., 1961-62; mem. faculty Carleton Coll., Northfield, Minn., 1964—, chmn. dept. history, 1974-77, 95—; prof. Carleton Coll., 1982—. Served with U.S. Army, 1957. Recipient 2d Century award Carleton Coll., 1968; Bush grantee, 1983-84. Jewish. Home: 403 Laurel Ave Saint Paul MN 55102-2015

WEINER, CHARLES R., federal judge; b. Phila., June 27, 1922; s. Max and Bessie (Chairney) W.; m. Edna Gerber, Aug. 24, 1947; children: William, Carole, Harvey. Grad., U. Pa., 1947, M.A., 1967, Ph.D., 1972; LL.B., Temple U., 1950. Bar: Pa. bar 1951. Asst. dist. atty. Philadelphia County, 1952-53; mem. Pa. Senate from Phila. County, 1952-67, minority floor leader, 1959-60, 63-64, majority floor leader, 1961-62; U.S. dist. judge Eastern Dist. Pa., 1967—; Mem. Phila. County Bd. Law Examiners, 1959—. Mem. Pres.'s Adv. Commn. Inter-Govtl. Rels., Phila., Pub. Policy Com., Phila. Crime Prevention Assn., Big Bros. Assn.; mem. Pa. Bd. Arts and Scis.; trustee, exec. com. Fedn. Jewish Philanthropies of Phila., Allied Jewish Appeal of Phila.; bd. dirs. Mental Health Assn. of Pa., Phila. Psychiat. Ctr., Phila. Tribune Charities, Phila. Wharton Ctr. Parkside YMCA, Jewish Publ. Soc. Am., The Athenaeum, and others. Recipient Phila. Fellowship award; Founder's Day award Temple U.; Alumni award U. Pa.; Founder's award Berean Inst.; others. Mem. ABA, Pa. Bar Assn., Phila. Bar Assn., Am. Law Inst. Office: US District Ct 6613 US Courthouse Ind Mall W 601 Market St Philadelphia PA 19106-1510

WEINER, EARL DAVID, lawyer; b. Balt., Aug. 21, 1939; s. Jacob Joseph and Sophia Gertrude (Rachanow) W.; m. Gina Helen Priestley Ingoglia, Mar. 30, 1962; children: Melissa Danis Balmain, John Barlow. A.B., Dickinson Coll., 1960; LL.B., Yale U., 1968. Bar: N.Y. 1969. Assoc. Sullivan & Cromwell, N.Y.C., 1968-76, ptnr., 1976—; adj. prof. Rutgers U. Sch. Law, 1987-88; bd. dirs. Solvay Techs. Inc., Hedwin Corp., The Acting Co., vice chair, 1992—, v.p., 1991-92. Gov. Bklyn. Heights Assn., 1980-87, pres., 1985-87, adv. com., 1987—; gov. The Heights Casino, 1979-84, pres., 1981-84; trustee Bklyn. Bot. Garden, 1985—, vice chmn., 1989—; trustee Green-Wood Cemetery, 1986—, vice chmn., 1991—; bd. advisors Dickinson Coll., Carlisle, Pa., 1986-90, chmn., 1988-90, trustee, 1988—; mem. adv. com. East Rock Inst., 1988—. Lt. USN, 1961-65. Mem. ABA, N.Y. State Bar Assn., Assn. of Bar of City of N.Y. Office: Sullivan & Cromwell 125 Broad St New York NY 10004-2400

WEINER, IRVING BERNARD, university administrator, psychologist, educator; b. Grand Rapids, Mich., Aug. 16, 1933; s. Jacob H. and Mollie Jean (Laevin) W.; m. Frances Shair, June 9, 1963; children: Jeremy Harris, Seth Howard. B.A., U. Mich., Ann Arbor, 1955, M.A., 1957, Ph.D., 1959. Diplomate: Am. Bd. Profl. Psychology. From instr. to prof. psychiatry and pediatrics U. Rochester, N.Y., 1959-72; head div. psychology U. Rochester Med. Center, 1968-72; prof. psychology, chmn. dept. Case Western Res. U., 1972-77, dean grad. studies, 1976-79; vice chancellor for acad. affairs U. Denver, 1979-83, prof. psychology, 1979-85; v.p. for acad. affairs Fairleigh Dickinson U., Teaneck, N.J., 1985-89; prof. psychology Fairleigh Dickinson U., 1985-89; prof. psychiatry U. South Fla., Tampa, 1989—; adv. editor John Wiley & Sons, 1967-93, Lawrence Erlbaum Assocs., 1993—; psychology edn. rev. com. NIMH, 1977-81. Author: Psychodiagnosis in Schizophrenia, 1966, Psychological Disturbance in Adolescence, 1970, rev. edit., 1992, Rorschach Handbook, 1971, Child Development, 1972, Principles of Psychotherapy, 1975, Development of the Child, 1978, Child and Adolescent Psychopathology, 1982, Rorschach Assessment of Children and Adolescents, 1982, rev. edit., 1995, Adolescence, 1985, rev. edit., 1995, Handbook of Forensic Psychology, 1987; editor: Readings in Child Development, 1972, Clinical Methods in Psychology, 1976, 83, Jour. Personality Assessment, 1985-93, Rorschachiana, 1989—; mem. editl. bd. Profl. Psychology, 1971-76, Jour. Adolescent Health Care, 1979-87, Children and Youth Svcs. Rev., 1979-91, Jour. Pediatric Psychology, 1981-87, Devel. and Behavioral Pediatrics, 1985—, Studi Rorschachiani, 1985—, European Jour. Psychol. Assessment, 1985—, Jour. Adolescent Rsch., 1986-91, Jour. Personality Disorders, 1986-92, Psychol. Assessment, 1994—. Recipient Disting. Profl. Achievement award Genesee Psychol. Assn., 1974. Fellow APA, Am. Psychol. Soc., Acad. Clin. Psychology, Acad. Forensic Psychology; mem. Assn. Advancement Psychology, Soc. Personality Assessment (pres. 1976-78, Disting. Contbn. award 1983), Assn. Internship Ctrs. (exec. com. 1971-76), Soc. Rsch. in Adolescence, Soc. for Rsch. in Child and Adolescent Psychopathology, Soc. for Exploration Psychotherapy Integration, Soc. Pediat. Psychology, Am. Psychol. Law Soc., Phi Beta Kappa, Sigma Xi, Phi Kappa Phi. Home: 13716 Halliford Dr Tampa FL 33624-6903 Office: U South Florida Psychiatry Ctr 3515 E Fletcher Ave Tampa FL 33613-4706

WEINER, IRWIN M., medical educator, college dean, researcher; b. N.Y.C., Nov. 5, 1930; s. Samuel and Pearl (Levine) W.; m. Lois M. Fuxman, Apr. 18, 1961 (div. 1980); children: Stefanie F., Jeffrey N.; m. Lieselotte Roth, June 20, 1981. AB, Syracuse U., 1952; MD, SUNY-Syracuse, 1956. Postdoctoral fellow Johns Hopkins Sch. Medicine, Balt., 1956-58, instr., 1958-60, asst. prof., 1960-66; assoc. prof. SUNY, Upstate Med. Ctr., Syracuse, 1966-68, prof., chmn. dept., 1968-87, v.p. rsch., 1982-88, dean Coll. Medicine, 1987-91, v.p. for med. and biomed. edn., 1988-91; dean Coll. Medicine Health Sci. Ctr., SUNY, Bklyn., 1991-96; vis. asst. prof. Albert Einstein Coll Medicine, Bronx, N.Y., 1964-65; cons. Sterling-Winthrop Rsch. Inst., N.Y., 1968-82, mem. rsch. bd., 1973-76; mem. study sect. Pharmacology and Exptl. Therapeutics "A", NIH, 1965-72, ad hoc com. on comparative pharmacology, Nat. Inst. Gen. Med. Scis., 1966-68, ad hoc com. rsch. career devel. awards and fellowships pharmacology, 1975-76; mem. consensus devel. panel analgesic associated kidney disease NIH, 1984; mem. pharmacology com. Nat. Bd. Med. Examiners, 1977-82; mem. rsch. com. Am. Heart Assn., 1969-74, chmn., 1969-74; mem. pharmacology adv. com. Pharm. Mfrs. Assn. Found., 1981—, chmn. basic pharmacology adv. com., 1987—; mem. N.Y. State Health Rsch. Coun., 1987—, chmn., 1991—. Field editor for renal pharmacology Jour. Pharmacology & Exptl. Theapeutics, 1965-72, editorial adv. bd., 1981-86; editorial bd. Life Scis. jour., 1973-79, renal, fluid and electrolyte physiology Am. Jour. Physiology, 1982-86; editorial com Ann. Rev. Pharmacology and Toxicology, 1982-86; contbr. over 90 articles to profl. jours., chpts. to books. Trustee Loretto Geriatric Ctr., 1989-91; bd. regents L.I. Coll. Hosp., 1993—; bd. dirs. Rsch. Found. SUNY, 1994—. Predoctoral fellow in physiology SUNY Upstate Med. Ctr., 1953-54; recipient numerous fed. fellowships, grants, 1956—, Rsch. Career Devel. award NIH, 1964-65. Mem. AAAS, Am. Soc. Pharmacology and Exptl. Therapeutics (bd. publs. trustees 1973-79), N.Y. Acad. Scis., Am. Soc. Nephrology, Internat. Soc. Biochem. Pharmacology, Internat. Soc. Nephrology, Assn. Med. Sch. Pharmacologists, N.Y. Acad. Medicine. Democrat. Jewish. Home: 39 Plaza St W Apt 10A Brooklyn NY 11217-3932

WEINER, JEROME HARRIS, mechanical engineering educator; b. N.Y.C., Apr. 5, 1923; s. Barnet and Dora (Muchar) W.; m. Florence Mensch, June 24, 1950; children: Jonathan David, Eric Daniel. B. Mech. Engring., Cooper Union U., 1943; A.M., Columbia U., 1946, Ph.D., 1952. Mem. faculty Columbia U., N.Y.C., 1952-68; prof. mech. engring. Columbia U., 1960-68, acting chmn. dept., 1961-62; L. Herbert Ballou Univ. prof. Brown U., Providence, 1968-93; L. Herbert Ballou Univ. prof. emeritus, 1993—. Author: (with B.A. Boley) Theory of Thermal Stresses, 1960, Statistical Mechanics of Elasticity, 1983. Fulbright research scholar Rome, Italy, 1958-59, Haifa, Israel, 1965- 66; Guggenheim fellow, 1965-66. Mem. Am. Phys. Soc., Am. Math. Soc., ASME. Home: 24 Taber Ave Providence RI 02906-4113 Office: Brown U 79 Waterman St Providence RI 02912-9079

WEINER, JOEL DAVID, retired consumer packaged goods products executive; b. Chgo., Aug. 27, 1936; m. Judith L. Metzger; children: Beth, David. BBA, Northwestern U. Dir. new products and household div. Alberto-Culver Co., Melrose Park, Ill., 1963-66; group mktg. mgr. Bristol Myers Co., N.Y.C., 1966-74; v.p. new products Carter Wallace Co., N.Y.C., 1974-78; exec. v.p. Joseph E. Seagram Corp., N.Y.C., 1979-84; exec. v.p. corp. mktg. Kraft, Inc., Glenview, Ill., 1984-89. Home: 550 Park Dr Kenilworth IL 60043-1005

WEINER, JONATHAN DAVID, writer; b. N.Y.C., Nov. 26, 1953; s. Jerome Harris and Ponnie (Mensch) W.; m. Deborah Heiligman, May 29, 1982; children: Aaron, Benjamin. BA cum laude, Harvard U., 1977. Asst. editor Moment, Boston, 1978; sr. editor The Sciences N.Y. Acad. of Scis., N.Y.C., 1978-84, contbg. editor, 1984—, columnist "Field Notes", 1984—; columnist "Quanta", The Sciences, "Tech Photo", Close-Up. Author: Planet Earth, 1986 (award Am. Geol. Inst. 1986), The Next One Hundred Years: Shaping the Fate of Our Living Earth, 1991, The Beak of the Finch: A Story of Evolution in Our Time, 1994 (L.A. Sci. Book prize 1994, Pulitzer prize for nonfiction 1995). Mem. Nat. Assn Sci. Writers. Office: care Victoria Pryor Arcadia 20A Old Neversink Danbury CT 06811-3337

WEINER, LAWRENCE, lawyer; b. Phila., Aug. 20, 1942; s. Robert A. and Goldie (Miller) W.; m. Jane M. Coulthard, Feb. 28, 1976; 1 child, Kimberly. BS in Econs., U. Pa., 1964, JD, 1967. Bar: Pa. 1967, U.S. Dist. Ct. (ea. dist.) Pa. 1967, Fla. 1970, U.S. Dist. Ct. (so. dist.) Fla. 1976, U.S. Ct. Appeals (5th cir.) 1976, U.S. Tax Ct. 1984. Assoc., ptnr. Blank, Rome, Klaus & Comisky, Phila., 1967-71, 1975-77; ptnr. Weiner & Weisenfeld, P.A., Miami Beach, Fla., 1971-73, Pettigrew & Bailey, Miami, Fla., 1973-75; pres. Lawrence Weiner, P.A., Miami, 1977-83; ptnr. Spieler, Weiner & Spieler, P.A., Miami, 1983-89, Weiner & Cummings, P.A., Miami, 1989-94, Weiner, Cummings & Vittoria, Miami, 1994—; lectr. Wharton Sch. U. Pa., Phila., 1968-70; instr. bus. law and acctg. Community Coll. Phila., 1967-70; lectr. estate planning various non-lawyer groups, Miami, 1972—. Mem. ABA (pension, profit sharing trust coms. 1976-77), Fla. Bar (liaison non-lawyers groups 1980-87), Pa. Bar Assn., Phila. Bar Assn., Dade County Bar Assn. (chmn. ins. com. 1977-78, probate law com. 1992—). Democrat. Jewish. Office: Weiner Cummings & Vittoria 1428 Brickell Ave Ste 400 Miami FL 33131-3436

WEINER, LAWRENCE CHARLES, sculptor; b. Bronx, N.Y., Feb. 10, 1942. One-man shows include Hirshhorn Mus. and Sculpture Garden, Washington, 1990, San Francisco Mus. Modern Art, 1992, Walter Art Ctr., Mpls., 1994, Städtische Galerie Chemnitz, Germany, 1994, Phila. Mus. Art, 1994, Radio Düsseldorf, Germany, 1994, Leo Castelli Gallery, N.Y., 1994; exhibited in group shows Mus. Modern Art, N.Y., 1970, Art Inst. Chgo., 1974, Tate Gallery, London, 1982, Mus. Contemporary Art, L.A., 1983; represented in permanent collections Mus. Modern Art, N.Y., Guggenheim Mus., N.Y., Vanabbe Mus., Eindhoven, The Netherlands, Staatiches Mus. Monchengladbach, Germany, Ctr. Georges Pompidou, Paris, Nat. Gallery Australia, Canberra, others. Recipient Arthur Kopcke prize, Copenhagen, 1991; fellow Nat. Endowment Arts, 1976, 83; John Simon Guggenheim fellow, 1994. Home: 297 W Fourth New York NY 10014

WEINER, LESLIE PHILIP, neurology educator, researcher; b. Bklyn., Mar. 17, 1936; s. Paul Larry and Sarah (Paris) W.; m. Judith Marilyn Hoffman, Dec. 26, 1959; children: Patrice Weiner Miller, Allison Hope, Matthew, Jonathan. BA, Wilkes Coll., 1957; MD, U. Cin., 1961. Diplomate Am. Bd. Psychiatry and Neurology. Intern in medicine SUNY, Syracuse, 1961-62; resident in neurology Johns Hopkins Hosp., Balt., 1962-65, fellow, 1967-69; resident Balt. City Hosp., 1962-63; fellow in virology Slow Virus Lab., Nat. Inst. Neurol and Communicative Disorders-Stroke, NIH, Balt., 1969; asst. prof. neurology Johns Hopkins U., 1969-72, assoc. prof., 1972-75; prof. neurology and microbiology U. So. Calif. Sch. Medicine, L.A., 1975—, chmn. dept. neurology, 1979—, Richard Angus Grant Sr. chair in neurology, 1987—; chief neurologist U. So. Calif. Univ. Hosp., 1979—, mem. bd. govs.; chief neurologist L.A. county-U. So. Calif. Med. Ctr., 1979—; bd. dirs. John Douglas French Found., L.A., 1987—; mem. neurosci. tng. study sect. NIH, 1990-93, chmn., mem. sci. adv. bd. Hereditary Disease Found., 1992—. Contbr. over 120 articles on neurology, immunology and virology to med. jours., chpts. to books. Bd. dirs. Starbright Found., L.A., 1991. Capt. M.C., U.S. Army, 1965-67. Grantee NIH, 1995-99, Kenneth Norris Found., 1995-97, Conrad Hilton Found., 1995-97. Fellow Am. Acad. Neurology; mem. AAAS, Am. Health Assistance Found., Am. Neurology Assn., Soc. Neurosci., Johns Hopkins U. Soc. Scholars, L.A. Acad. of Medicine, Assn. of Univ. Profs. of Neurology, Alpha Omega Alpha. Democrat. Jewish. Avocations: collecting books, concerts, plays. Home: 625 S Rimpau Blvd Los Angeles CA 90005-3842 Office: U So Calif Sch Medicine 1510 San Pablo St Ste 646 Los Angeles CA 90033-4606

WEINER, LOUIS MAX, retired mathematics educator; b. Chgo., Nov. 11, 1926; s. Samuel and Lena (Adelman) W.; m. June Belmont, Aug. 18, 1957; children: Howard, Joel, Todd. BS, U. Chgo., 1947, MS, 1948, PhD, 1951. Examiner Civil Svc. Commn., Chgo., 1951-52; asst. prof. DePaul U., Chgo., 1952-58; rsch. engr. Gen. Am. Rsch. Divsn., Niles, Ill., 1958-64; prof. math. Northeastern Ill. U., Chgo., 1964-93, chmn. dept., 1968-74; ret., 1993; instr. Oakton C.C., Des Plaines, Ill., 1974-92. Assoc. editor Math. mag., 1968-72; author: Introduction to Modern Algebra, 1970, Basic Mathematical Concepts, 1972. Mem. Am. Math. Soc., Math. Assn. Am., Sigma Xi, Phi Beta Kappa. Avocation: photography.

WEINER, MAX, educational psychology educator; b. Hartford, Conn., May 7, 1926; s. Harry Sam and Gertrude (Cohen) W.; m. Gloria Sall, Feb. 24, 1960; children: William Ronald, Jennifer Sharon. BA, U. Conn., 1950; MA, Trinity Coll., 1953; PhD, Yale U., 1957. Sci. tchr. Meriden (Conn.) Pub. Schs., 1952-55; guidance dir. White Plains (N.Y.) Pub. Schs., 1956-59; assoc. prof. Bklyn. Coll., CUNY, 1959-68; prof. Grad. Sch. CUNY, 1968-81, acting univ. dean, tchr. edn., 1973-74, exec. officer PhD program edn. psychology, 1970-76, dir. Ctr. for Advanced Study Edn., 1970-78, acting dean rsch. Grad. Sch., 1978-79; dean edn. Fordham U., N.Y.C., 1981-93, prof. ednl. psychology, 1981—; cons. psychologist SUNY Health Sci. Ctr., Bklyn., 1967-89; mem. nat. commn. on excellence in edn. adminstrn. Univ. Coun. for Edn. Adminstrn., 1985-87; mem. nat. adv. commn. Coll. Bd. Equity 2000, 1993—. Contbr. articles to profl. jours. Treas. N.Y. Alliance for Pub. Schs., N.Y.C., 1987-93; mem. Mayor's Commn. on Spl. Edn., N.Y.C., 1984-85; bd. dirs. Arthritis Found., Atlanta, 1974-76; trustee Beth El Synagogue, New Rochelle, N.Y., 1985—, La Scuola, N.Y., 1986—; mem. bd. visitors Sch. Edn., Scranton U., 1992—. Fellow Japan Soc. Promotion Scis., 1978. Fellow APA, Am. Psychol. Soc., N.Y. Acad. Scis.; mem. ACA (life), AAAS, Arthritis Health Professions Assn. (pres. 1974-75), Am. Ednl. Rsch. Assn., Assn. Colls. and Schs. Edn. in State Univs. and Land Grant Colls. and Affiliated Pvt. Univs. (mem. exec. com. 1986-89, 92-93), Assn. for Measurement and Evaluation in Guidance (senator 1966-72, sec. 1973-75), Nat. Coun. Measurement in Edn., Westchester Assn. Hebrew Schs. (pres. 1982-84), Sigma Xi, Phi Delta Kappa, Kappa Delta Pi. Office: Fordham U Grad Sch Edn 113 W 60th St New York NY 10023-7471

WEINER, MORTON DAVID, banker, insurance agent; b. Balt., Aug. 19, 1922; s. Max and Rose (Wolfe) W.; m. Joan M. Maggin; children: Bruce, Lori, Julie, Jeff. B.S., Towson State Coll., 1942; grad. exec. program, UCLA, 1959. Pres., dir. AVNET, Inc., N.Y.C., 1963-69; pres., owner Morton D. Weiner & Co., Inc., N.Y.C., 1969-70; dir. USLIFE Corp., 1970-77; chmn. bd. Nat. Investors Life Ins. Cos., 1970-78; exec. v.p. Norris Grain Co., 1971-78; pres., chief exec. officer Norin Corp., 1971-78; chmn. bd. Maple Leaf Mills, Ltd., Toronto, Ont., Can., 1974-78; chmn., dir. South Atlantic Fin. Corp., 1978-80, Atico Fin. Corp., 1980-81; chmn. Morton D. Weiner & Co., 1981—; bd. dirs. City Nat. Bank Fla. Served to capt. Signal Corps, U.S. Army, 1942-46, CBI. Office: 200 SE 1st St Miami FL 33131

WEINER, MYRON, political science educator; b. N.Y.C., Mar. 11, 1931; s. Hyman and Anna (Peretz) W.; m. Sheila Leiman, June 29, 1952; children: Beth, Saul Jeremy. B in Social Scis., CCNY, 1951; MA in Politics, Princeton U., 1953, PhD, 1955. Instr. Princeton (N.J.) U., 1951-52; asst. prof. U. Chgo., 1956-61; mem. faculty MIT, 1961—, prof. polit. sci., 1965—, Ford prof. polit. sci., 1977—, chmn. dept., 1974-77; sr. staff mem. Under Ctr. Internat. Studies, MIT, 1965—, dir., 1967-92, 95—; mem. com. on comparative politics Social Sci. Rsch. Coun., 1961-71; NAS chmn. project population policy in less-developed countries, 1972-75; mem. Ctr. for Population Studies, Sch. Pub. Health, Harvard U., 1973—; co-chmn. joint Harvard-MIT faculty seminar on polit. devel.; vis. prof. Inst. Econ. Growth, Delhi (India) U., 1970; vis. scholar U. Paris, 1966-67, Harry S Truman Inst., Hebrew U., 1979; chmn. joint com. on South Asia, Am. Coun. Learned Socs./Social Sci. Rsch. Coun., 1980-84; vis. prof. Harvard U., 1984; vis. scholar Balliol Coll., Oxford, 1992; cons. to govt. and founds. Author: Party Politics in India, 1957, The Politics of Scarcity, 1962, Political Change in South Asia, 1963, Party Building in a New Nation: The Indian National Congress, 1967, Sons of the Soil, 1978, India at the Polls: The Parliamentary Elections of 1977, 1978, India at the Polls-1980, 1983, The Indian Paradox: Essays in Indian Politics, 1989, The Child and the State in India, 1993, The GLobal Migration Crisis: Challenge to States and to Human Rights, 1995; co-author: Politics of the Developing Areas, 1960, Rapid Population Growth: Consequences and Policy Implication, 1972, Crises and Sequences in Political Development, 1972, Policy Sciences and Population, 1975, India's Preferential Policies: Migrants, the Middle Classes and Ethnic Equality, 1981; editor: Modernization: The Dynamics of Growth, 1966, Political Parties and Political Development, 1966, State Politics in India, 1968, International Migration and Security, 1993; co-editor: Indian Voting Behavior, 1963, Electoral Politics in Indian States, 4 vols., 1974-77,The State, Religion and Ethnic Politics: Afghanistan, Iran and Pakistan, 1986, Understanding Political Development, 1987, Competitive Elections in Developing Countries, 1987, The Political Culture of Foreign Area and International Studies, 1991, The New Politics of Central Asia and Its Borderlands, 1995, Threatened Peoples, Threatened Borders: World Migration and U.S. Policy, 1995; editorial bd.: Global Political Assessment, Asian Survey, Jour. Commonwealth and Comparative Studies, Jour. Interdisciplinary History, Third World Quarterly. Mem. adv. com. UN High Commr. for Refugees. Named Fulbright 40th Anniversary Disting. fellow, 1986-87; fellow Fulbright Found., 1953, Ford Found., 1953, 87, Soc. Sci. Rsch. Coun., 1957, 79, Rockefeller Found., 1961, Guggenheim Found., 1961, Carnegie Found., 1966, NSF, 1969, Rockefeller-Ford Found. program population policy, 1975, Nat. Inst. Child Health and Human Devel. NIH, 1976, Smithsonian Instn., 1985, MacArthur Found., 1992, Japan Found., 1994. Mem. Assn. Asian Studies (dir. 1961-69, chmn. adv. com. rsch. and devel. 1966-69, chmn. Indian state politics com. 1960-70), New Eng. Assn. Asian Studies (pres. 1980), Am. Polit. Sci. Assn. (sec. 1986, chmn. nominating com. 1987, editl. bd. rev. 1966-70), Am. Acad. Arts and Scis. (dir. joint German-Am. project on migration and refugee policies 1993—), Internat. Union for Sci. Study of Population, Coun. Fgn. Rels. Home: 1258 Beacon St Brookline MA 02146-3715 Office: MIT Dept Polit Sci E53-369 Cambridge MA 02142-1320

WEINER, RICHARD, public relations executive; b. Bklyn., May 10, 1927; s. George M. and Sally (Kosover) W.; m. Florence Chaiken, Dec. 9, 1956; children: Jessica Weiner Lampert, Stephanie Weiner Iosbaker. B.S., U. Wis., 1949, M.S., 1950. Pres. Creative Radio Assocs., Madison, Wis., 1951-52, Weiner-Morton Assocs., Madison, 1952-53; sr. v.p. Ruder & Finn, Inc., N.Y.C., 1953-68; pres. Richard Weiner, Inc., N.Y.C., 1968-86; pres. N.Y. div. Porter/Novelli, N.Y.C., 1987-88, sr. counselor, 1988—. Author: Professional's Guide to Public Relations Services, 1968, New Bureaus in the U.S., 1970, Syndicated Columnists, 1972, Professional's Guide to Publicity, 1979, Military Publications, 1979, College Alumni Publications, 1980, Investment Newsletters, 1981, Webster's New World Dictionary of Media and Communications, 1996. Fellow Pub. Rels. Soc. Am. (accredited counselor, Silver Anvil award 1965, 84, 86, 87, John Hill award 1984, Gold Anvil award 1990), Am. Acad. Physician and Patient (bd. dirs.), Am. Arbitration Assn. Jewish. Office: Porter/Novelli 437 Madison Ave New York NY 10022-7001 *The essence of life is growth, adaptation, change. I hope to continue to succeed in living vigorously.*

WEINER, ROBERT MICHAEL, engineering design company executive, consulting engineer; b. N.Y.C., Jan. 20, 1936; s. Dudley John and Ruth Alice (McCormick) W.; m. Mary Carole Soetje, June 8, 1957; children: Michael, David, Therese, Paul, Kathryn, John, Thomas, James. BS in Chem. Engring. maxima cum laude, U. Notre Dame, 1957; grad., Bettis Reactor Engring. Sch., 1958; MS in Nuclear Engring., U. Md., 1965. Power systems engr. br. naval reactors AEC, Washington, 1957-62, sect. leader br. naval reactors, 1962-65; systems engr. MPR Assocs. Inc., Washington, 1965-68, sect. supr., 1968-87, prin. officer, 1987—. Contbr. articles to profl. jours. Parish rep., charter mem. Annandale (Va.) Christian Community for Action, 1967—; active Christian Family Movement, No. Va.); coach, leader youth activities Boys Sports Clubs, Boy Scouts Am., 1967-82. Served to lt. USN, 1957-61. Mem. K.C. Avocations: photography, camping, ch. related edn. and social action work. Home: 4820 Randolph Dr Annandale VA 22003-6222 Office: MPR Assocs Inc 320 King St Alexandria VA 22314

WEINER, ROBERT STEPHEN, federal agency administrator; b. Paterson, N.J., Apr. 3, 1947; s. Jess Joseph Weiner and Dorothea Violet (Slavin) Tabor. BA, Oberlin Coll., 1969; MA, U. Mass., 1974. Student coord. Hampshire County, dir. telephone bank Kennedy for U.S. Senate, Amherst, Mass., 1970; dir. nat. voter registration Young Dems. Am., Washington, 1971-72; dir. voter registration, media dir. get out the vote Dem. Nat. Com., Washington, 1972; legis. asst. Congressman Edward Koch, Washington, 1974-75; staff dir. subcom. health and long-term care U.S. Ho. of Reps., Washington, 1975-76, staff dir. com. aging, 1976-80, media dir., press sec. com. narcotics, 1987-90, press sec./comms. dir. com. on govt. ops., 1990-95; nat. campaign aide Kennedy for Pres., Washington, 1980; sr. assoc. Mgmt. Recruiters Internat., Springfield, Mass., 1981-83; dir. Robert Weiner Assocs., Amherst, 1983-86; dir. comm. Ho. Judiciary com. Minority and Cong. John Conyers Jr., 1995; dir. pub. affairs White House Drug Policy Office, Washington, 1995—; dir. gen. press room Dem. Nat. Convention, Atlanta, 1988, N.Y.C, 1992; cons. Carter-Mondale Transition, Washington, 1976-77, Congressman Claude Pepper, Washington, 1975-89. Represented in permanent exhbns. Nat. Mus. Am. History, Smithsonian Instn., Washington; contbr. numerous articles to profl. jours. Dem. nominee for U.S. Congress, Mass., 1986; chmn. Road Runners Am. Nat. 10 Mile Championship, Amherst, 1984; vice chmn. Dem. Town Com., Amherst, 1984-87; legis. chmn. Pioneer Valley Gray Panthers, Amherst, 1981-87. Named Communicator of Yr., Washington Crime News Svcs., 1988, 89, 90; 2d place U.S. Nat. 1500 Meter Age 45+ Indoor Track Championship, 1994. Mem. Assn. House Dem. Press Assts., Congl. Staff Club, Nat. Dem. Club, Sugarloaf Mountain Athletic Club (pres. 1984-86), Potomac Valley Track Club, Capitol Hill Runners (pres. 1991—). Avocations: running, attending performing arts. Home: 1104 Sanford Ln Accokeek MD 20607-2324 Office: Exec Office of Pres Office Nat Drug Control Pol Washington DC 20500

WEINER, RONALD GARY, accounting firm executive; b. Newark, N.J., Nov. 24, 1945; s. Seymour and Beatrice (Goldberg) W.; m. Vicki Miles, Sept. 8, 1973; children: Jennie, Maureen. BSBA, Babson Coll. (Mass.), 1966; postgrad. NYU, 1968-69; Harvard U., 1982. CPA, N.Y., N.J., Pa. Mgmt. cons., acct., pres. Perelson Weiner, N.Y.C., 1971—. Bd. dirs. Jewish Cmty. Rels. Coun. N.Y.; officer; trustee Babson Coll., Citizens Budget Com., N.Y.C.; dir., v.p. Jewish Guild for the Blind, N.Y.C.; treas., dir. Roundtable Polit. Action Com., N.Y.C.; officer, bd. govs. Am. Jewish Com.; dir. Irvington Inst.; mem. adv. com. Muehlenberg Coll., Nat. Polish Am. Jewish Am. Coun.; dir. Irvington House. Fellow Wexner Heritage Found, Adenauer Exch. Program; mem. AICPA, Accts. Club Am., Pa. State Soc. CPAs, N.J. State Soc. CPAs (dir.), N.Y. State Soc. CPAs., Chief Execs. Orgn., Young Pres.'s Orgn., Econ. Club, Harmonie Club, Harvard Club, Mt. Ridge Country Club, Pottsville Club. Office: Perelson Weiner One Dag Hammarskjold Plz New York NY 10017-2286

WEINER, SANDRA SAMUEL, critical care nurse, nursing consultant; b. N.Y.C., Jan. 12, 1947; d. Herbert A. and Ruth (Wallerstein) Samuel; m. Neil D. Weiner, June 15, 1969 (div. June 1980); 1 child, Jaime Michelle. BS in Nursing, SUNY, Buffalo, 1968; cert. in critical care, Golden West Coll., 1982; postgrad. UCLA, U. West L.A. Sch. of Law, 1992. RN, Pa., Calif. Staff nurse N.Y. Hosp.-Cornell Med. Ctr., 1968-69; head nurse med.-surg. nursing Abington (Pa.) Hosp., 1969; assoc. prof. Sch. Nursing, U. Pa., Phila., 1970; instr. nursing Coll. of Med. Assts., Long Beach, Calif., 1971-72; surg. staff nurse Med. Ctr. of Tarzana, Calif., 1978-79, Cedar-Sinai Med. Ctr., L.A., 1979-81; supr. recovery room Beverly Hills Med. Ctr., L.A., 1981-92;

Post Anesthesia Care Unit nurse Westside Hosp., 1992—; med. cons. RJA & Assocs., Beverly Hills, Calif., 1984-92; instr. CPR, L.A., 1986-95. Mem. women's aux. Ctr. Theater Group Vols., L.A., 1986—, Maple Ctr., Beverly Hills, 1987—. Mem. Am. Nursing Assn., Am. Soc. Post-Anesthesia Nursing, Am. Assn. Critical Care Nurses, Heart and Lung Assn., Post Anesthesia Nurses Assn., U.S. Ski Assn. Democrat. Jewish. Avocations: skiing, running, travel, theater, ballet. Home: 12633 Moorpark St Studio City CA 91604-4537

WEINER, STEPHEN ARTHUR, lawyer; b. Bklyn., Nov. 20, 1933; s. Joseph Lee W. and Ruth Lessall (Weiner); m. Mina Rieur, Sept. 1, 1958; children: Karen, James. B.A. summa cum laude, Harvard U., 1954; J.D. cum laude, Yale U., 1957. Bar: N.Y. 1958, U.S. Supreme Ct. 1963. Assoc. Winthrop, Stimson, Putnam & Roberts, N.Y.C., 1958-65, ptnr., 1968—; vice chmn. mgmt. com., 1984—; acting prof. law U. Calif., Berkeley, 1965-68; lectr. Practising Law Inst., 1971—. Contbr. articles to legal publs. Comment editor Yale Law Jour., 1956-57. Fellow Am. Coll. Trial Lawyers, Am. Bar Found.; mem. Assn. Bar City N.Y. (chmn. recruitment of lawyers com., chmn. com. on Stimson medal), Fed. Bar Coun. (chmn. com. on 2d cir. cts., trustee), Order of Coif, Phi Beta Kappa. Home: 190 Harbor Rd Port Washington NY 11050-2636 Office: Winthrop Stimson One Battery Park Pla New York NY 10004-1490

WEINER, STEPHEN L., lawyer; b. N.Y.C., Sept. 9, 1946; m. Nan E. Weiner. AB, Columbia Coll., 1967, JD cum laude, 1970. Bar: N.Y. 1971, U.S. Dist. Ct. (so. and ea. dists.) N.Y. 1971, U.S. Ct. Appeals (2d cir.) 1971. Assoc. Hughes Hubbard & Reed, N.Y.C., 1970-72; asst. dist. atty. N.Y. County Dist. Atty., N.Y.C., 1972-75; law sec. to Hon. Leon B. Polsky N.Y. Supreme Ct., N.Y.C., 1975-78; spl. counsel N.Y. State Commn. Investigation, N.Y.C., 1978-79; ptnr. Hoffinger Friedland, N.Y.C., 1979-96; pvt. practice N.Y.C., 1996—; chmn. and commr. N.Y. State Commn. Investigation, 1996—; mem. nat. evaluation team, assigned counsel plan, 1st jud. dept., sch. pub. affairs, Am. U., Washington, 1991. Mem. ind. jud. screening panel Supreme Ct. Dem. County Com., 1986, ind. jud. screening panel surrogates ct. and civil ct., 1990; mem. N.Y. Gov. George E. Pataki's transition team, 1994-95; bd. dirs. Legal Aid Soc., 1995—, Ctr. Cmty. Alternatives, 1995—; mem. N.Y. Unified Ct. Sys. Office Ct. Adminstrn. Adv. Com. Criminal Law and Procedure, 1994—; mem. appellate divsn. N.Y. Supreme Ct. First Jud. Dept. Disciplinary com., policy com., 1989-92, hearings panel, 1986—. Mem. ABA (criminal justice, family law, litigation sects.), Nat. Assn. Criminal Def. Lawyers (mem. ethics adv. com. 1989—), Fed. Bar Coun., N.Y. State Bar Assn. (del. ho. of dels. 1991—, mem. second century com., 1993—, mem. various coms. and sects.), N.Y. Criminal Bar Assn. (co-chair com. legislation 1981-84), N.Y. State Assn. Criminal Def. Lawyers (charter), Assn. Bar City of N.Y. (chair com. criminal justice ops. and budget 1987-90, coun. criminal justice 1990—, mem. delegation to N.Y. State Bar Assn. ho. of dels. 1991—, mem. various coms. and couns.), Phi Delta Phi. Avocations: fishing, sailing, boating, photography. Office: care White & Case 1155 Ave of the Americas New York NY 10036

WEINER, STEPHEN MARK, lawyer; b. Boston, Mar. 20, 1943; s. Meyer and Esther (Lowenstein) W.; m. Roslyn G. Weiner, Dec. 19, 1967 (div. 1992); children: Jeremiah, Ben, Miriam, Isaac. AB magna cum laude, Harvard U., 1964; LLB, Yale U., 1968. Bar: Mass. 1968. Teaching fellow Boston Coll. Law Sch., Chestnut Hill, Mass., 1968-69; assoc. Goodwin, Proctor & Hoar, Boston, 1969-71; spl. asst. to Gov. Francis W. Sargent Commonwealth of Mass., Boston, 1971-74; chmn. Mass. Rate Setting Commn., Boston, 1972-78; assoc. prof. Boston U. Sch. Law, 1978-81, dir. Ctr. for Law and Health Scis.; mem. Goulston & Storrs, Boston, 1981-90, Mintz, Levin, Cohn, Ferris, Glovsky and Popeo, P.C., Boston, 1990—; co-chair and sect. coord. health law sect. Mintz, Levin, Cohn, Ferris, Glovsky and Popeo, P.C.; adj. prof. law Boston U. Sch. Law, 1993-94; vis. lectr. Yale Law Sch., 1994-95. Mem. editorial bd. New Eng. Jour. Human Svcs., 1979-81; mem. adv. bd. Hosp. Risk Mgmt., 1979-83; contbr. articles to profl. jours. Mem. gov. task to evaluate Mass. Determination of Need Program, 1979-80; profl. adv. coun. Mass. Dept. Elder Affairs,1979-81; dir., treas. AIDS Action Com. Mass.; bd. dirs. Boston Film/Video Found.; del. Mass. Easter Seal Soc.; trustee Beth Israel Hosp., Boston, 1979-95, Spaulding Rehab. Hosp., Boston, 1979-95; corp. Ptnrs. HealthCare Sys., Inc., Boston. Mem. ABA, Nat. Health Lawyers Assn., Mass. Bar Assn., Boston Bar Assn. Home: 65 Heron St West Roxbury MA 02132 Office: Mintz Levin Cohn Ferris Glovsky and Popeo PC 1 Financial Ctr Boston MA 02111-2621

WEINER, TIMOTHY EMLYN, newspaper journalist; b. June 20, 1956; s. Herbert and Dora B. Weiner. BA, Columbia U., 1978, MS in Journalism, 1979. Reporter, freelance writer N.Y.C., 1979-81; reporter Kansas City (Mo.) Times, 1981-82, Phila. Inquirer, 1982-93, N.Y. Times, Washington, 1993—. Author: Blank Check: The Pentagon's Black Budget, 1990. Recipient Pulitzer prize (with others) Kansas City Times, 1982, for nat. reporting, 1988. Office: NY Times 1627 I St NW Washington DC 20006-4007

WEINER, WALTER HERMAN, banker, lawyer; b. Bklyn., Aug. 29, 1930; s. Harry and Sylvia (Freifeld) W.; m. Nina Ester Avidar, Oct. 11, 1966; children: Thomas Field, Jon Michael. BA, U. Mich., 1952, JD, 1953. Bar: N.Y. 1953. Sr. ptnr. Kronish, Lieb, Weiner & Hellman, N.Y.C., 1965-79; chmn. exec. com., chief exec. officer Republic N.Y. Corp., 1980-81, pres., chief exec. officer, 1981-83, chmn. bd., chief exec. officer, 1983—; chmn. exec. com., chief exec. officer Republic Nat. Bank of N.Y., 1980-82, pres., chief exec. officer, 1981-86, chmn. bd., chief exec. officer, 1986—, also bd. dirs.; bd. dirs. Republic N.Y. Corp., Republic Nat. Bank of N.Y. Assoc. editor U. Mich. Law Rev. Bd. dirs., treas. Bryant Park Restoration Corp., Internat. Sephardic Edn. Found.; trustee Guild Hall, East Hampton, N.Y.; mem. N.Y. Holocaust Meml. Commn.; bd. visitors U. Mich. Law Sch. Recipient Humanitarian award NAACP, 1987, Human Rels. award Accts., Bankers, Factors and Fin. divsn. Am. Jewish Com., 1988, Man of Yr. award Bklyn. Sch. for Spl. Children, 1988, Good Scout award Greater N.Y. Couns./Boy Scouts Am., 1994, Jewish Theol. Sem.'s Louis Marshall award, 1994, numerous others. Mem. ABA, N.Y. State Bar Assn., Assn. of Bar of City of N.Y., Am. Bankers Assn., N.Y. Clearing House Assn., Bankers Roundtable. Home: 876 Park Ave New York NY 10021-1832 Office: Republic Nat Bank of NY 452 5th Ave New York NY 10018-2706

WEINER-HEUSCHKEL, SYDELL, theater educator; b. N.Y.C., Feb. 18, 1947; d. Milton A. and Janet (Kay) Horowitz; children: Jason, Emily; m. Rex Heuschkel, Sept. 3, 1992. BA, SUNY, Binghamton, 1968; MA, Calif. State U., L.A., 1974; PhD, NYU, 1986; postgrad. in acting, Yale U., 1968-70. Prof. theater arts, chmn. dept., dir. honors program Calif. State U. Dominguez Hills, Carson, 1984—; guest lectr. Calif. Inst. Arts, 1988. Appeared in play Vikings, Grove Shakespeare Festival, 1988; dir. Plaza Suite, Brea (Calif.) Civic Theatre, 1982, Gypsy, Carson Civic Light Opera, 1990, Same Time Next Year, Muckehthaler, 1987, Slow Dance on the Killing Ground, Alternative Repertory Theatre, 1989; co-author: School and Community Theatre Problems: A Handbook for Survival, 1978, (software) Public Speaking, 1991. Yale U. fellow, 1969; recipient Lyle Gibson Disting. Tchr. award, 1989. Mem. Screen Actors Guild, Am. Fedn. TV and Radio Artists, Calif. State U. Women's Coun. (treas. 1989-91), Phi Kappa Phi.

WEINERT, DONALD G(REGORY), association executive, engineer; b. Aberdeen, S.D., Sept. 16, 1930; s. McDonald Donnegan and Susan Mae (Mathis) W. B.S., U.S. Mil. Acad., 1952; M.S.E., Purdue U., 1958; grad., Northwestern U. Inst. for Mgmt., 1974, Command Staff Gen. Coll., 1965, Armed Forces Staff Coll., 1967, Army War Coll., 1969. Registered profl. engr., Tex. Commd. 2d lt. U.S. Army C.E., 1952, advanced through grades to brig. gen., 1977; troop comdr. Korea, 1953-54, Ger., 1958-60, 67-68; dist. engr. Little Rock, Ark., 1972-75; staff officer Hdqrs. Dept. Army, Washington, 1970-72; dir. Engr. Studies Group, Washington, 1975-77; spl. asst. to Chief Engrs., C.E., Washington, 1978, ret., 1978; exec. dir., sec. NSPE, 1978-95; bd. dirs. Jr. Engring. Tech. Soc., Nat. Mathcounts. Decorated Legion of Merit (3), Bronze Star medal (2), Army Commendation medal (4). Mem. NSPE (exec. dir. emeritus), Soc. Am. Mil. Engrs., Assn. U.S. Army. Republican. Home: 8121 Dunsinane Ct Mc Lean VA 22102-2719

WEINERT, HENRY M., biomedical company executive; b. Nordhausen, Kassel, Fed. Republic Germany, May 31, 1940; s. Heinrich V. Nennenstiehl and Martha H. Weinert; m. Helen Koopmans, Feb. 14, 1966 (div. June 1982); children: Jason C., Brian T.; m. Kerri V. Keaton, Sept. 25, 1989. BA in Sci., Columbia Coll., 1962; MBA, Harvard Grad. Sch. Bus., 1970. Med. rsch. assoc. Columbia Univ., N.Y.C., 1964-65; exec. v.p., founder Clin. Diagnostic Lab., New Haven, Conn., 1966-68; dir. planning, bus. devel. Lederle Labs./Am. Cyan., Pearl River, N.Y., 1970-73, mktg. dir., 1973-74; bus. devel. mgr. Corning (N.Y.) Glass Works, 1974-77; pres., founder Boston Biomed. Cons., Waltham, Mass., 1977—; spl. ltd. ptnr. MedVenture Assocs., San Francisco, 1965—, Interwest Ptnrs., San Francisco, 1989; presenter, lectr. in field. Patentee laser fabrication of microsuture needles; contbr. articles to profl. jours. Pres. Svc. Soc., Columbia Coll., 1959; chmn. Student Union Com., Columbia Coll., 1961; treas. Class 1962, Columbia Coll., 1962-64; others. Recipient Alumni Achievement award Columbia Coll., 1962; grantee NIH, 1964-66. Mem. Biomed. Mktg. Assn. (bd. dirs. 1978-86, Recognition award 1986), Am. Assn. Clin. Chemistry, Van Slyke Soc. (bd. mem. 1991—). Lutheran. Avocations: reading sci. fiction and mystery novels, sailing, cars, landscaping. Home: 86 Myles Standish Rd Weston MA 02193-2124 Office: Boston Biomed Cons 100 5th Ave Waltham MA 02154-8703

WEINGAND, DARLENE ERNA, librarian educator, consultant; b. Oak Park, Ill., Aug. 13, 1937; d. Edward Emil and Erna (Heidenway) W.,; m. Wayne Anthony Weston, Sept. 7, 1957 (div. June 1976); children: Kathleen Mary, Lynda Anne, Judith Diane, Barbara Jeanne; m. James Elberling, May 1977 (div. 1980); m. Robert Paul Couture, Apr. 7, 1984. BA in History and English, Elmhurst Coll., 1972; MALS, Rosary Coll., 1973; PhD in Adult Edn./Libr. Sci., U. Minn., 1980. Asst. prof. U. Wis., Madison, 1981-86, assoc. prof., 1986-92, prof., 1992—, SLIS acting dir., 1991, summer 86, SLIS asst. dir., 1990-94, adminstr. SLIS Continuing Edn. Svcs., 1981—; cons. in mktg., continuing edn., libr. futures, info. issues, and mgmt., 1980—; invited mentor Snowbird Leadership Inst., 1990, 92; vis. fellow Curtin U. Tech. Perth, Australia, 1990; Fulbright lectr. U. Iceland, 1988; lectr. 2d World Conf. on Continuing Edn. for Libr. and Info. Sci., Barcelona, 1993, Internat. Fedn. Libr. Assn. Author: Marketing/Planning Library and Information Services, 1987, Administration of the Small Public Library, 3d edit., 1992, Budgeting and the Political Process in Libraries: Simulation Games, 1992 (with others), Connections: Literacy and Cultural Heritage: Lessons from Iceland, 1992, Managing Today's Public Library: Blueprint for Change, 1994, author (with others) Continuing Professional Education and Internat. Fed. of Libr. Assoc.: Past, Present, and a Vision for the Future, 1993, Keeping the Book$: Public Library Financial Management, 1992; contbr. articles to profl. jours. Recipient excellence award Nat. Univ. Continuing Edn. Assn., 1989, Econ. and Cmty. Devel. award, 1989, outanding achievement in audio applications award Internat. Teleconferencing Assn., 1991, LITA/Libr. Hi-Tech award, 1996. Mem. ALA, Internat. Fedn. Libr. Assns. (ALA rep.), Assn. for Libr. and Info. Sci. Edn. (bd. dirs. 1990-93, rsch. grantee 1992, Russia project fellow 1994), Wis. Libr. Assn., Wis. Assn. for Adult and Continuing Edn., Phi Delta Kappa, Beta Phi Mu. Office: U Wis-Madison Helen White Hall 600 N Park St Madison WI 53706-1403

WEINGART, JEANNE, public relations executive. Ptnr., adminstv. dir. Fin. Rels. Bd., Chgo. Office: Fin Rels Bd John Hancock Ctr 875 N Michigan Ave Chicago IL 60611-1801*

WEINGARTEN, JOSEPH LEONARD, aerospace engineer; b. N.Y.C., June 5, 1944; s. Herman H. and Irene Jane (Binzer) W.; 1 child, Toby. B of Mech. Engring., NYU, 1966; postgrad., Air War Coll., 1976. Chief engr. Air Transportability Test Loading Agy. Wright-Patterson AFB, Wright-Patterson AFB, Ohio, 1972-74; project engr. dept. engring. USAF, Wright-Patterson AFB, 1966-72, sr. project engr. dept. engring., 1974-76, planning and project engr. dept. engring., 1976-81, chief mgmt. ops. dept. engring., 1981-83, sr. tech. planner dept. engring., 1983-92; tech. asst. DCS Engring. and Tech. Mgmt. Air Force Material Command, Wright-Patterson AFB, 1992-93; founder, CEO Huffman Wright Inst., 1993—; CEO Weingarten Gallery, Dayton, Ohio, 1967—; v.p., sec., treas., bd. dirs. Ohio Designer Craftsmen, Columbus; sec. Ohio Designer Craftsmen Enterprise, Columbus, 1982—; chmn. continuing edn. design dept. Affiliate Socs. Coun., Dayton, 1971-74, chmn. edn. coord. com. Kettering Inst., Wright State U., 1974-76, chmn. scientist and engr. awards panel, 1990-91, mem., 1992-94. Contbr. articles on systems engring. to Aeronautical Sys. divsn. Mech. Engring. Jour. (1st place award nat. contest 1970), Procs. 4th Intersoc. Conf. on Transp., Air Force Sys. Command, USAF Spl. Purpose Report, Gems and Minerals, Friends Jour. USAF Mus., Ceramics Monthly, The Crafts Report, Macintosh Software. Scoutmaster Troop 81 Boy Scouts Am., Kettering, Ohio, 1985-91, com. mem., 1991-93, dist. chmn. Sequoia Dist. Miami Valley Coun., 1991-93, asst. coun. commr., 1993—; pres. Friends of Montessori Sch. South Dayton, 1978-94. Capt. USAF, 1967-71. Named Eagle Scout Boy Scouts Am., 1962; recipient Disting. Eagle award Boy Scouts Am., 1992, Silver Beaver award Boy Scouts Am., 1995. Mem. AIAA (sr. mem., air transport systems tech. com. 1976-78, 80-82, Lawrence Sperry award 1977), ASME (sr. mem.), Am. Nat. Standards Inst. (materials handling 5 com. 1968-70), Soc. Automotive Engrs. (aircraft ground support equiment com. 1969-75). Achievements include 11 patents for expendable air cargo pallet, mail container, collapsible air cargo container, process for reinforcing extruded articles, process for large scale extrusions, air flotation cargo handling system, integral aircraft barrier net, load distributive cargo platform, laminated plastic packaging material, computer printer paper support, and investment casting mold base; developments include 3g cargo restraint criteria used worldwide on aircraft/spacecraft/shuttles, rope extraction system for C-5A, system for large scale structural plastics extrusions, advanced planning documents for Air Force, report in new type of DOD procurement system; other achievements include the design and creation of jewelry sold in museums and retail stores.

WEINGARTEN, MURRAY, manufacturing executive; b. N.Y.C., Feb. 8, 1925; s. Ellis and Ethel (Gaies) B.; m. Shirley L. Bowersox, Apr. 30, 1955; children—Steven Ellis, Betsy Lori. E.E., Rensselaer Poly. Inst., 1947. With J.R. Rider, N.Y.C., 1947-48; engr. Bendix Radio, Towson, Md., 1948-50; with Bendix Field Engring. Corp., Columbia, Md.; became v.p. Bendix Field Engring. Corp., 1963; chmn. bd., pres., dir.; chmn. bd., pres., dir. Bendix Comml. Services Corp., Columbia, 1974; ret. Bendix Comml. Services Corp., 1989; chmn. bd., pres. Morrison & Knudsen Svcs. Inc., ret., 1992—; pres. United Geophys. Corp. (subs. Bendix Corp.); also dir.; pres. Skagit Corp. (subs. Bendix Corp.), Sedro-Woolley, Wash. Served with USNR, 1943-45. Mem. IEEE (sr.), Armed Forces Communication and Electronics Assn., Soc. Exploration Geophysicists (asso.), Engring. Soc. Balt. Home: 9442 Dunloggin Rd Ellicott City MD 21042-5148

WEINGARTEN, SAUL MYER, lawyer; b. Los Angeles, Dec. 19, 1921; s. Louis and Lillian Dorothy (Alter) W.; m. Miriam Ellen Moore, Jan. 21, 1949; children: David, Steven, Lawrence, Bruce. AA, Antelope Valley Coll., 1940; AB, UCLA, 1942; cert., Cornell U., 1943; JD, U. Southern Calif., 1949. Prin. Saul M. Weingarten, Inc., Seaside, Calif., 1954—; pres, CEO Quaestor Inc., Seaside, Calif., 1995—, also bd. dirs.; atty. City of Gonzales, Calif., 1968-74, City of Seaside, 1955-70; gen. counsel Redevel. Agy., Seaside, 1955-76, Security Nat. Bank, Monterey, Calif., 1968-74; bd. dirs., exec. com. Frontier Bank, Cheyenne, Wyo., 1984—, Mariposa Hall Inc., 1989—. Author: Practice Compendium, 1950; contbr. articles to profl. jours. Del. Internat. Union of Local Authorities, Brussels, Belgium, 1963, 73; candidate state legislature Dem. Com., Monterey County, 1958; counsel Monterey Peninsula Mus. of Art, Inc., 1972-80; gen. counsel Monterey County Symphony Assn., Carmel, Calif., 1974—, Mountain Plains Edn. Project, Glasgow, Mont., 1975-81; chmn. fund raising ARC, Monterey, 1964; chmn., bd. dirs. fund raising United Way, Monterey, 1962-63; pres., bd. dirs. Alliance on Aging, Monterey, 1968-82; bd. dirs. Family Svc. Agy., Monterey, 1958-66, Monterey County Cultural Coun., 1986—; dir., mem. exec. com. Monterey Bay Performing Arts Ctr., 1990. Served to commdr. USN, 1942-46, 50-54, Korea. Grad. fellow Coro Found., 1949-50. Mem. Calif. Bar Assn., Monterey County Bar Assn., Monterey County Trial Lawyers Assn., Rotary (pres. 1970-71, 82-83), Commonwealth Club, Meadowbrook Club. Jewish. Avocations: tennis, travel. Home: 4135 Crest Rd Pebble Beach CA 93953-3008 Office: 1123 Fremont Blvd Seaside CA 93955-5759

WEINGARTEN, VICTOR I., engineering educator; b. N.Y.C., Jan. 18, 1931; s. Arnold and Sophia (Dickerman) W.; m. Myrna Marcia Rosenthal, July 31, 1954; children: Scott, Barbara. BME, CCNY, 1952; MSME, NYU, 1954; PhD in Engring., UCLA, 1964. Prof. computer structural mechanics U. So. Calif., Los Angeles, 1964—; br. head, cons. Northrop Aircraft, Hawthorne, Calif., 1964-66; cons. Hughes Aircraft, Canoga Park, Calif., 1964-86, Rockwell Internat., El Segundo, Calif., 1983-85; pres. Structural Rsch. and Analysis Corp., L.A., 1983—. Contbr. articles to profl. jours. Mem. ASME, ASCE. Office: Structural Rsch & Analysis 7th Fl 12121 Wilshire Blvd Los Angeles CA 90025-1170

WEINGARTNER, H(ANS) MARTIN, finance educator; b. Heidelberg, Germany, Apr. 4, 1929; came to U.S., 1939, naturalized, 1944; s. Jacob and Grete (Kahn) W.; m. Joyce Trellis, June 12, 1955; children—Steven M., Susan C., Eric H., Kenneth L. A.B., S.B., U. Chgo., 1950, A.M., 1951; M.S., Carnegie Mellon U., 1956, Ph.D., 1962. Economist Dept. Commerce, 1951-53; instr. Grad. Sch. Indsl. Adminstrn., Carnegie Mellon U., 1956-57; instr., then asst. prof. Grad. Sch. Bus., U. Chgo., 1957-63; assoc. prof. fin. Alfred P. Sloan Sch. Mgmt., Mass. Inst. Tech., 1963-66; prof. Grad. Sch. Mgmt., U. Rochester, N.Y., 1966-77; Brownlee O. Currey prof. fin. Owen Grad. Sch. Mgmt., Vanderbilt U., Nashville, 1977—; dir. Computer Consoles, Inc., 1974-89; cons. to industry. Author: Mathematical Programming and the Analysis of Capital Budgeting Problems, 3d edit, 1974, (with George Benston and Dan Horsky) An Empirical Study of Mortgage Redlining, 1978; also articles.; Deptl. editor: Mgmt. Sci, 1967-73. Served with AUS, 1951-53. Mellon fellow, 1954-55; Ford Found. fellow, 1955-56, recipient first prize Dissertation Competition, 1963. Mem. Inst. Mgmt. Scis. (v.p. fin. 1978-84, pres. 1985-86), Coun.Sci. Soc. Pres.s, Am. Econ. Assn., Am. Fin. Assn., Beta Gamma Sigma. Home: 1616 Ash Valley Dr Nashville TN 37215-4202 Office: Vanderbilt U Owen Grad Sch Mgmt 401 21st Ave S Nashville TN 37203

WEINGARTNER, RUDOLPH HERBERT, philosophy educator; b. Heidelberg, Germany, Feb. 12, 1927; came to U.S., 1939, naturalized, 1944; s. Jacob and Grete (Kahn) W.; m. Fannia Goldberg-Rudkowski, Dec. 28, 1952 (dec. Nov. 1994); children: Mark H., Eleanor C. A.B., Columbia U., 1950, M.A., 1953, Ph.D., 1959. Fellow Inst. Philos. Research, San Francisco, 1953-55; instr. philosophy Columbia, 1955-59; from asst. prof. to prof., chmn. dept. philosophy San Francisco State Coll., 1959-68; prof. philosophy Vassar Coll., Poughkeepsie, 1968-74, chmn. dept., 1969-74, Taylor prof. philosophy, 1973-74, dean Coll. Arts and Scis.; prof. philosophy Northwestern U., Evanston, Ill., 1974-87; provost U. Pitts., 1987-89, prof. philosophy, 1987-94, fellow Ctr. for the Philosophy of Sci., 1990-94, chmn. dept. philosophy, 1991-93. Author: Experience and Culture: The Philosophy of Georg Simmel, 1962, The Unity of the Platonic Dialogue: The Cratylus, The Protagoras, The Parmenides, 1973, Undergraduate Education, Goals and Means, 1992 (Frederick W. Ness book award 1993), Fitting Form to Function: A Primer on the Organization of Academic Institutions, 1996; editor: (with Joseph Katz) Philosophy in the West, 1965; exhibited sculptures in Mendelson Gallery, 1992, 94, UP Gallery, 1992; contbr. articles to profl. jours. Bd. dirs. Chamber Music Chgo., 1982-87, pres., 1986-87; mem. bd. advisors Pitts. Symphony, 1991—; mem. adv. bd. dept. music Carnegie Mellon U., Pitts., 1992—. Social Sci. Rsch. Coun. fellow, 1958-59; Guggenheim fellow, 1965-66; Am. Coun. Learned Socs. fellow, 1971-72; residency Rockefeller Found. Study and Conf. Ctr. in Bellagio, 1994. Mem. Am. Philos. Assn., Assn. Am. Colls. (bd. dirs. 1985-89, task force on gen. edn. 1985-88, editorial bd. liberal edn. jours. 1986-94), Assoc. Artists Pitts. (artist mem.), Phi Beta Kappa. Home: 5448 Northumberland St Pittsburgh PA 15217-1129

WEINGAST, MARVIN, laboratory executive; b. Bklyn., Jan. 1, 1943; s. Abe and Rose (Altein) W. BS, L.I. U., 1967, MS, 1971; postgrad., Poly. Inst., 1967-68. Analytic and pollution chemist Amerada Hess Corp., Pt. Reading, N.J., 1969-73; asst. lab. dir. Chem. Constrn., North Brunswick, N.J., 1973-74; dir. Indsl. Hygiene Lab. Nat. Starch and Chemical, Bridgewater, N.J., 1974—; grant com. mem. Ctr. for Hazardous and Toxic Substance Mgmt., Newark, 1988—; mem. Sourland Regional Citizens Planning Coun., Neshanic, N.J., 1989—. Contbr. to book: Small Business Programs, 1980; contbr. articles to profl. jours. Recipient Chemistry Dept. award L.I. U., 1967, Teaching fellowship Poly. Inst., 1967, L.I. U., 1968. Mem. MENSA, Am. Chem. Soc., Am. Conf. Chem. Labeling, Soc. Toxicology. Achievements include development of improved system for identification of hazardous chemicals; organization of first global monitoring of indsl. workers to hazardous workplace chemicals. Office: Nat Starch & Chem Co 10 Finderne Ave Bridgewater NJ 08807-3355

WEINGEIST, THOMAS ALAN, ophthalmology educator; b. N.Y.C., Jan. 28, 1940; s. Samson and Fausta (Haim) W.; m. Carol Perera, Mar. 19, 1963 (div. Aug. 1977); children: Aaron P., Rachel; m. Catherine McGregor, Aug. 18, 1977; children: Robert M., David M. BA, Earlham Coll., 1963; PhD, Columbia U., 1969; MD, U. Iowa, 1972. Resident in ophthalmology U. Iowa, 1972-75, fellow in retina, 1976; asst. prof. ophthalmology U. Iowa, Iowa City, 1976-80, assoc. prof., 1980-83, prof., 1983—, prof., head dept. ophthalmology, 1986—. Mem. editl. bd. Documenta Ophthalmologica, The Netherlands, 1989-94, Ophthalmology World News, vice chair, 1994. Fellow Am. Acad. Ophthalmology (editorial bd. jour. 1982—, Honor award 1979, Sr. Honor award 1989, assoc. sec. for self-assessment 1988-93, sec. continuing edn. 1993—, trustee 1993—, sr. sec. clin. edn. 1994—); mem. Macula Soc., Retina Soc., Vitreous Soc., Am. Medico-Legal Found., Assn. Univ. Profs. Ophthalmology (bd. dirs., pres.-elect. 1994, pres. 1995). Avocations: photography, tennis. Home: 3 Heather Ct Iowa City IA 52245-3226 Office: U Iowa Dept Ophthalmology Iowa City IA 52242

WEINGOLD, ALLAN B., obstetrician, gynecologist, educator; b. N.Y.C., Sept. 2, 1930; s. Irving and Evelyne (Gold) W.; m. Marjorie Nassau, Dec. 21, 1952; children: Beth, Roberta, Matthew, Daniel. B.A., Oberlin Coll., 1951; M.D., N.Y. Med. Coll., 1955. Diplomate Am. Bd. Ob-Gyn. Instr. N.Y. Med.Coll., N.Y.C., 1960-63, asst. prof., 1963-67, assoc. prof., 1967-70, prof., 1970-73; prof., chmn. dept. ob-gyn George Washington U., Washington, 1973-92, v.p. med. affairs and exec. dean, 1992—; cons. NIH, Bethesda, Md., 1974—, Walter Reed Army Med. Ctr., Washington, 1974—. Author: Principles and Practices of Clinical Gynecology, 1988; editor: Monitoring the Fetal Environment, 1969, Surgical Complications of Pregnancy, 1984. Bd. dirs. Mayor's Adv. Bd. Maternal Health, Washington, 1981-87; mem. host com. John Glenn Campaign Com., Washington, 1983-85. Maj. U.S. Army, 1957-66. Recipient Alumni award N.Y. Med. Coll., 1974. Fellow Am. Coll. Obstetricians and Gynecologists (program chmn. 1975-77), Am. Gyn.-Ob. Soc. (coun. 1988-90); mem. Assn. Profs. Ob-Gyn. (sec. 1981-84, pres. 1985-86), Soc. Perinatal Rsch. Republican. Office: George Washington U Dept Ob-Gyn 2150 Pennsylvania Ave NW Washington DC 20037-2396

WEINGROW, HOWARD L., financial executive, investor; b. N.Y.C., Dec. 6, 1922; s. Nathan and Anna (Mintzes) W.; m. Muriel Corrine Franzblau, Nov. 24, 1946; children: Terry Vaccaro, Caron Abby Haim. Owner Legion Fluorescent Corp., N.Y.C., 1946-56; ptnr. Hechler & Weingrow, Inc., N.Y.C., 1956-58, Hechler, Lifton & Weingrow, Inc., N.Y.C., 1958-78; exec. v.p. Tanscontinental Investing Corp., N.Y.C., 1960-67; pres. Tanscontinental Investing Corp., 1967-70; prin. Lifton & Weingrow, N.Y.C., 1970—; co-chmn. Marcade Group, Inc., N.Y.C., 1986-91, bd. dirs., 1986-93; pres. Cell Diagnostics, Inc. and Medis Ltd., 1992—, Stanoff Corp., 1980—, Wesak Internat., chmn. Wesak Chrysler, 1992-94; bd. dirs. Preferred Health Care, N.Y.C., Four Winds Inc., N.Y.C.; founder Weingrow Family Pediatric Urology Lab., L.I.J. Hosp., 1990. Treas. Dem. Nat. Com., Washington, 1970-72; mem. bd. govs. Hofstra U. Law Sch., 1977-79; dep. fin. chmn. Pres. Carter, Washington, 1980; trustee Hofstra U., Hempstead, N.Y., 1973-76, James S. Brady Presdl. Found., 1982, Children's Med. Fund, L.A. Jewish Children's Hosp., Lake Success, N.Y., 1986—, Am. Jewish Congress, 1988—; treas. Nassau County Mus. Fine Arts, 1988—; advisor to Pres. Lyndon Johnson, OEO, Washington; fin. advisor to the Govt. of Grenada and Office of Prime Minister Garry, 1977-79; founder Howard and Muriel Weingrow Collection of Avant Garde Arts and Lit., Hofstra U. Libr., 1972; founder Weingrow Family Pediatric Urology Lab., L.I.J. Hosp., 1990. Decorated Air medal, Disting. Flying Cross, Presdl. Citation; recipient of Hofstra U. Presdl. medal. Office: Stanoff Corp 805 3rd Ave Fl 15 New York NY 10022-7513

WEINHAUER, WILLIAM GILLETTE, retired bishop; b. N.Y.C., Dec. 3, 1924; s. Nicholas Alfred and Florence Anastacia (Davis) W.; m. Jean Roberta Shanks, Mar. 20, 1948; children: Roberta Lynn, Cynthia Anne, Doris Jean. BS, Trinity Coll., Hartford, Conn., 1948; MDiv, Gen. Theol.

Sem., 1951, STM, 1956, ThD, 1970. Ordained to ministry Episcopal Ch., 1951. Pastor Episcopal parishes Diocese N.Y., 1951-56; prof. N.T. St. Andrews Theol. Sem., Manila, Philippines, 1956-60; asst. prof. N.T. Gen. Theol. Sem., 1961-71; rector Christ Ch., Poughkeepsie, N.Y., 1971-73; bishop Episcopal Diocese of Western N.C., Black Mountain, 1973-90, ret., 1990; vis. prof. religion Western Carolina U., Cullowhee, N.C., 1991-96; adj. faculty Seabury-Western Theol. Sem., Evanston, Ill., 19991-94. Served with USN, 1943-46. Mem. Soc. Bibl. Lit.

WEINHOLD, VIRGINIA BEAMER, interior designer; b. Elizabeth, N.J., June 21, 1932; d. Clayton Mitchell and Rosemary (Behrend) Beamer; divorced; children: Thomas Craig, Robert Scott, Amy Linette. BA, Cornell U., 1955; BFA summa cum laude, Ohio State U., 1969; MA in Design Mgmt., Ohio State U., 1982. Freelance interior designer, 1969-72; interior designer, dir. interior design Karlsberger and Assocs. Inc., Columbus, Ohio, 1972-82; assoc. prof. dept. indsl. design Ohio State U., 1982—, grad. studies chairperson, 1995-96; lectr. indsl. design Ohio State U., 1972, 79-80. Trustee Found. for Interior Design Edn. and Research. Mem. Inst. Bus. Designers (chpt. treas. 1977-79, nat. trustee 1979-81, nat. chmn. contract documents com. 1979-84, chpt. pres. 1981-83), Constrn. Specifications Inst., Interior Design Educator's Coun. (nat. treas. 1989-93), Interior Design Educator's Coun. Found. (nat. treas. 1992-94), Illuminating Engring. Soc., AIA (assoc.), Internat. Interior Design Assn. (nat. dir. 1994—). Prin. works include Grands Rapids (Mich.) Osteo. Hosp., Melrose (Mass.) Wakefield Hosp., Christopher Inn, Columbus, John W. Galbreath Hdqrs., Columbus, Guernsey Meml. Hosp., Cambridge, Ohio, Trinity Epis. Ch. and Parish House, Columbus, Hale Hosp., Haverhill, Mass., Ohio State U. Dept. Indsl. Design Lighting Lab., others. Author: IBO Forms and Documents Manual, Interior Finish Materials for Health Care Facilities, Subjective Impressions: Lighting Hotels and Resturants, 1989, Effects of Lighting on The Perception of Interior Spaces, 1993. Home: 112 Glen Dr Columbus OH 43085-4010 Office: Ohio State U/Grad Studies 128 N Oval Mall Columbus OH 43210-1318

WEINHOUSE, SIDNEY, biochemist, educator; b. Chgo., May 21, 1909; s. Harry and Dora (Cutler) W.; m. Sylvia Krawitz, Sept. 15, 1935 (dec. Aug. 1957); children: Doris Joan, James Lester, Barbara May; m. Adele Klein, Dec. 27, 1969. B.S., U. Chgo., 1933, Ph.D., 1936; D.M.S. (hon.), Med. Coll. Pa., 1973; D.Sc. (hon.), Temple U., 1976, U. Chieti, Italy, 1979, Jefferson Med. Coll., 1983. Eli Lilly fellow U. Chgo., 1936-38, Coman fellow, 1939-41; staff OSRD, 1941-44; with Houdry Process Corp., 1944-47; biochem. research dir. Temple U. Research Inst., 1947-50, prof. chemistry, 1952-77; emeritus prof. biochemistry Temple U. Med. Sch., 1977—; emeritus prof. Jefferson Med. Coll., 1991; sr. scientist Lankenau Med. Research Ctr., 1987—; head dept. metabolic chemistry Lankenau Hosp. Research Inst. and Inst. Cancer Research, 1950-57; chmn. div. biochemistry Inst. Cancer Research, 1957-61; assoc. dir. Fels Research Inst., Temple U. Med. Sch., Phila., 1961-64, dir., 1964-74; mem. bd. sci. advisers Inst. Environ. Health, NIH. Contbr. articles on original research to sci. jours.; editor: Jour. Cancer Research, 1969-79. Bd. dirs. Am. Cancer Soc. Mem. Am. Chem. Soc., Am. Soc. Biol. Chemists, Am. Assn. Cancer Research, Nat. Acad. Sci. Home: 1919 Chestnut St Phildelphia PA 19103-3401 Office: Lankenau Med Rsch Ctr 100 E Lancaster Ave Wynnewood PA 19096-3411 also: Jefferson Cancer Inst Rm 1034 273 S 10th St Philadelphia PA 19107

WEINKAUF, MARY LOUISE STANLEY, clergywoman; b. Eau Claire, Wis., Sept. 22, 1938; d. Joseph Michael and Marie Barbara (Holzinger) Stanley; m. Alan D. Weinkauf, Oct. 12, 1962; children: Stephen, Xanti. BA, Wis. State U., 1961; MA, U. Tenn., 1962, PhD, 1966; MDiv Luth. Sch. Theology, Chgo., 1993. Grad. asst., instr. U. Tenn., 1961-66; asst. prof. English, Adrian Coll., 1966-69; prof., head dept. English, Dakota Wesleyan U., Mitchell, S.D., 1969-89; instr. Columbia Coll., 1989-91; pastor Siloa Lutheran Ch., Ontonagon Faith, White Pine, Mich., Gowrie, Iowa. Mem. Mitchell Arts Council; bd. trustees, The Ednl. Found., 1986—; bd. dirs. Ontonagon County Habitat for Humanity, 1995—. Author: Hard-Boiled Heretic, 1994, Sermons in Science Fiction, 1994, Murder Most Poetic, 1996. Mem. Nat. Council Tchrs. English, S.D. Council Tchrs. English, Sci. Fiction Research Assn., Popular Culture Assn., Milton Soc., AAUW (div. pres. 1978-80), S.D. State Poetry Soc. (pres. 1982-83), Delta Kappa Gamma (pres. local chpt., mem. state bd. 1972-89 , state v.p. 1979-83, state pres. 1983-85), Sigma Tau Delta, Pi Kappa Delta, Phi Kappa Phi. Republican. Lutheran.

WEINKAUF, WILLIAM CARL, instructional media company executive; b. Fond du Lac, Wis., Apr. 7, 1934; s. Carl Alfred and Erma Gertrude (Lueck) W.; m. Carole Jean Hill, May 3, 1958 (div.); children: Carl William, Mary Gretchen, Donald Hill; m. Jean Boyne Hawks, Sept. 10, 1988. BA, Ripon (Wis.) Coll., 1955; postgrad. U. Wis., 1954, 57-58. Dir. Wis. Cen. Lumber Co., 1959-63; with Carlton Films, Beloit, Wis., 1965-68; founder, pres. IMCO Inc., Green Lake, Wis., 1968—; founder, pres. initiator of distribution of ednl. instructional materials catalogs, IMCO Pub. Co., 1978—; bd. dirs. The Peterson System, Inc.; co-founder, chmn. Affluence Unltd., Inc., Dallas, 1986; Chmn. council Cub Scouts Am., 1968-69; mem. exec. com. county Reps., 1970-71. Served to maj. AUS, 1955-57. Mem. Nat. Audio Visual Assn. (chmn. legis. com. Wis. 1975—), Nat. Sch. Supply and Equipment Assn. (bd. dirs. 1986-87), U.S. Res. Officers Assn. (chpt. pres. 1966-70), Green Lake C. of C., Sigma Nu. Mem. United Ch. Christ (bd. trustees Green Lake, Wis. 1965-66, mem. bd. deacons Dallas 1989-93, chmn. 1992-93). Lodges: Mason (32 degree), KT. Office: 2215 Commerce St Dallas TX 75201-4345

WEINKOPF, FRIEDRICH J., lawyer; b. Bautsch, Germany, Feb. 17, 1930. Referendar, U. Marburg, Germany, 1954; LLM, U. Pa., 1958; JD, Chgo.-Kent Coll. Law, 1967. Bar: Ill. 1967. Ptnr. Baker & McKenzie, Chgo. Office: Baker & McKenzie 1 Prudential Plz 130 E Randolph Dr Chicago IL 60601

WEINLANDER, MAX MARTIN, retired psychologist; b. Ann Arbor, Mich., Sept. 9, 1917; s. Paul and Emma Carol (Lindemann) W.; BA, Ea. Mich. Coll., 1940; MA, U. Mich., 1942, PhD, 1955; M.A., Wayne U., 1951; m. Albertina Adelheit Abrams, June 4, 1946; children: Bruce, Annette. Psychometrist, VA Hosp., Dearborn, Mich., 1947-51; sr. staff psychologist Ohio Div. Corrections, London, 1954-55; lectr. Dayton and Piqua Centers, Miami U., Oxford, Ohio, 1955-62; chief clin. psychologist Child Guidance Clinic, Springfield, Ohio, 1956-61, acting dir., 1961-65; clin. psychologist VA Center, Dayton, Ohio, 1964-79; cons. Ohio Divsn. Mental Hygiene; summer guest prof. Miami U., 1957, 58, Wittenberg U., 1958; adj. prof. Wright State U., Dayton, 1975-76; cons. State Ohio Bur. Vocat. Rehab., Oesterlen Home Emotionally Disturbed Children. Pres. Clark County Mental Health Assn., 1960, Clark County Health and Welfare Club, 1961; mem. Community Welfare Coun. Clark County, 1964; chmn. Comprehensive Mental Health Planning Com. Clark County, 1964; trustee United Appeals Fund, 1960. Mem. citizens adv. coun. Columbus Psychiat. Inst., Ohio State U. Served as sgt. AUS, 1942-46. Fellow Ohio Psychol. Assn. (chmn. com. on utilization of psychologists; treas., exec. bd. 1968-71); mem. Am. Psychol. Assn., Ohio Psychol Assn., Mich. Psychol. Assn., DAV, U. Mich. Pres. Club, Pi Kappa Delta, Pi Gamma Mu, Phi Delta Kappa. Republican. Lutheran. Lodge: Kiwanis. Contbr. 18 articles to psychology jours. Home: 17185 Valley Dr Big Rapids MI 49307-9523

WEINMAN, DAVID PETER, elementary education educator; b. Allentown, Pa., May 25, 1957; s. Leonard Edward and Esther (German) W.; m. Teresa Modafferi, Aug. 7, 1982; children: Christopher, Joseph. AA, Lehigh County C.C., Schnecksville, Pa., 1977; BS in Elem. Edn., Kutztown State Coll., 1979; MEd, reading specialist, East Stroudsburg U., 1983; prin. cert., Pa. State U., 1986. Fourth grade tchr. Pleasant Valley Sch. Dist., Brodheadsville, Pa., 1979-82; reading specialist grades K-4 Chestnuthill Elem.-Pleasant Valley Sch. Dist., Brodheadsville, 1982-89; reading specialist grades 3-5 J.C. Mills Elem.-Pleasant Valley Sch. Dist., Brodheadsville, 1989-93, instrnl. support tchr., 1993—. Scoutmaster Troop 98 Boy Scouts Am., Brodheadsville, 1983—. Mem. Internat. Reading Assn., Keystone State Reading Assn., Colonial Assn. Reading Educators (v.p. 1984-86, 92-94, pres., 1986-87, 94-95), Phi Delta Kappa. Democrat. Roman Catholic. Avocations: photography, camping, traveling. Office: Pleasant Valley Sch Dist Pleasant Valley Elem Sch Brodheadsville PA 18322

WEINMAN, GLENN ALAN, lawyer; b. N.Y.C., Dec. 9, 1955; s. Seymour and Iris Rhoda (Bergman) W. BA in Polit. Sci., UCLA, 1978; JD, U. So. Calif., 1981. Bar: Calif. 1981. Assoc. counsel Mitsui Mfrs. Bank, Los Angeles, 1981-83; assoc. McKenna, Conner & Cuneo, Los Angeles, 1983-85, Stroock, Stroock & Lavan, Los Angeles, 1985-87; sr. counsel Buchalter, Nemer, Fields & Younger, Los Angeles, 1987-91; ptnr. Keck, Mahin & Cate, 1991-93; sr. v.p., gen. counsel Western Internat. Media Corp., L.A., 1993-96; gen. counsel Guess?, Inc., L.A., 1996—. Mem. ABA (corp. banking and bus. law sect., com. on savs. instns., com. on banking law), Calif. Bar Assn. (bus. law sect., com. fin. instns. 1989-91, com. consumer svcs. 1991-94), L.A. County Bar Assn. (corp. legal depts. sect., bus. and corps. law sect., subcom. on fin. instns.), Legion Lex., U. So. Calif. Law Alumni Assn., Phi Alpha Delta. Avocation: tennis. Office: Guess? Inc 1444 S Alameda St Los Angeles CA 90021

WEINMAN, HOWARD MARK, lawyer; b. N.Y.C., May 6, 1947; s. Joseph and Kate (Dorn) W.; m. Pamela Eve Brodie, Jan. 6, 1980; children: David Lewis, Nathaniel Saul. B.A. magna cum laude, Columbia U., 1969; M.P.P., Harvard U, 1973, J.D. cum laude, 1973; LL.M. with highest honors in Taxation, George Washington U., 1981. Assoc., Fried, Frank, Harris, Shriver & Kampelman, Washington and N.Y.C., 1973-78; legis. atty. Joint Com. on Taxation, U.S. Congress, Washington, 1978-80; assoc. Sachs, Greenebaum, & Tayler, Washington, 1980-82; assoc. Crowell & Moring, Washington, 1982-84, ptnr., 1984—; adj. prof. internat. tax Georgetown U. Law Ctr., 1988-89. Contbr. articles to profl. jours. Mem. ABA (sect. on taxation), Kenwood Club, Phi Beta Kappa. Jewish. Home: 5404 Center St Bethesda MD 20815-7101 Office: Crowell & Moring 1001 Pennsylvania Ave NW Washington DC 20004-2505

WEINMAN, ROBERT ALEXANDER, sculptor; b. N.Y.C., Mar. 19, 1915; s. Adolph Alexander and Margaret Lucille (Landman) W.; m. Jane Morrison, July 14, 1945; children: Paul Alexander, Christopher Robert. Student, NAD, 1931-39, Art Students League, N.Y.C., 1939-40. Exhbns. include, NAD, 1937, 38, 49, 53, 71, 83, Pa. Acad. Fine Arts, 1939, N.Y. State Nature Assn., 1939, Nat. Arts Club, 1941, Georg Jensen, Inc., 1941, Allied Artists Am., 1946, 3d Sculpture Internat., Phila., 1949, Nat. Sculpture Soc., 1952, 64, 68, 69, 71, 79, 81, Soc. Animal Artists, 1970, 72; works include bronze doors, Baylor U., Tex.; bronze overdoor motif, U. Tenn. Ctr.; bronze dolphin fountain group, S.I. Community Coll.; small bronze, Bessie the Belligerent; study of an Indian rhinoceros, and a watercolor, Great Blue Heron, Brookgreen Gardens, Georgetown, S.C.; Stations of the Cross, chapel Manhattanville Coll. Sacred Heart, Purchase, N.Y., bronze airman, Tulsa Mcpl. Airport, granite eagle, Fed. Res. Bank, Buffalo, rood group and twelve apostles, Our Lady of Perpetual Help, Queens, N.Y., others; creator numerous medals for athletic, ednl., bus., mil., religious and cultural orgns. Served to sgt. U.S. Army 1942-45. Recipient Sanford Saltus medal award Am. Numis. Soc., 1964, Sculptor of Year award Am. Numis. Assn., 1975. Fellow Nat. Sculpture Soc. (pres. 1973-76, Bennett Prize 1952, Henry Hering medal 1985); mem. Nat. Acad. Design (academician). Address: 941 Old Post Rd Bedford NY 10506-1223

WEINMANN, JOHN GIFFEN, lawyer, diplomat; b. New Orleans, Aug. 29, 1928; s. Rudolph John and Mary Victoria (Mills) W.; m. Virginia Lee Eason, June 11, 1955; children: Winston Eason, Robert St. George Tucker, John Giffen Jr., Mary Virginia Lewis; m. Peter Daniel Coffman; 1 child, George Gustaf. BA, Tulane U., 1950, JD, 1952. Bar: La. 1952. Pvt. practice law Phelps Dunbar and predecessor firm, New Orleans; ptnr. Phelps Dunbar and predecessor firm, 1955-80, of counsel, 1981-83, 85-89; of counsel, 1993—; gen. counsel Times-Picayune Pub. Corp., 1968-80; pres., dir. Waverly Oil Corp., 1981-89; amb. to Finland Am. Embassy, Helsinki, 1989-91; amb., chief of protocol of White House Dept. of State, Washington, 1991-93; lectr. bills and notes New Orleans chpt. Am. Inst. Banking, 1958-59; bd. dir. Eason Oil Co., 1961-81, chmn., 1977; bd. dir. 1st Nat. Bank of Oklahoma City, 1978-84, Am. Life Ins. Co. of N.Y., 1981-88, Allied Investment Corp., 1985-88; asst. sec. Am. Bar Endowment, 1971-74, bd. dirs., sec., 1975-80. Mem. adv. bd. Tulane Law Rev., 1965-92. Bd. govs. Tulane Med. Ctr., 1968-81; bd. adminstrs. Tulane Ednl. Fund, 1981—, chmn. devel. com., 1985-89, co-chmn. Tulane Parents Fund, 1980-81, bd. chmn., 1993—; nat. chmn. ann. giving Campaign for Tulane, 1983-85; bd. dirs. Coun. for Better La., 1987-89, Tulane Children's Ctr., 1981-84, WYES Ednl. TV Sta., 1981-82; trustee S.W. Legal Found., 1978-80, Metairie Park Country Day Sch., v.p., 1976-77, pres., 1978-80, U.S. commr. gen. for 1984 La. Workd Expn., 1983-85; U.S. del. Bur. Internat. Expositions, Paris, 1984-85, chmn. del., 1985; state fin. chmn. George Bush for Pres., and Victory La. '88, 1987-89. Named Outstanding Law Alumnus Tulane U., 1985; selected Rex, King of Carnival, New Orleans, 1996. Mem. ABA (chmn. jr. bar conf. 1963-64, mem. ho. dels. 1964-66, 70, 72-76, sec. com. ethics evaluation 1965, rep. to conv. Union des Jeunes Avocats de France, 1964, chmn. sect. bar activities 1969-70), La. Bar Assn. (sec. treas. 1965-67, Outstanding Young Lawyer award), La. Soc. Colonial Wars (gov. 1976), Swiss-Am. Cultural Exch. Found. (hon. com. 1994—), Phi Beta Kappa, Order of Coif, Delta Kappa Epsilon, Omicron Delta Kappa. Episcopalian. Home: 611 Hector Ave Metairie LA 70005-4415 Office: Waverly Enterprises 601 Poydras St Ste 2690 New Orleans LA 70130

WEINMANN, ROBERT LEWIS, neurologist; b. Newark, Aug. 21, 1935; s. Isadore and Etta (Silverman) W.; m. Diana Weinmann, Dec. 13, 1980 (dec. Dec. 1989); children: Paul, Chris, Dana, Paige. BA, Yale U., 1957; MD, Stanford U., 1962. Diplomate Am. Bd. of EEG and Neurophysiology, v.p.; diplomate Am. Acad. Pain Mgmt. Intern Pacific Presbyn. Med. Ctr., San Francisco, 1962-63; resident in neurology Stanford U. Hosp., 1963-66, chief resident, 1965-66; pvt. practice San Jose, Calif., 1969—. Chmn. editorial bd. Clin. EEG Jour.; mem. editorial bd. Jour. Am. Acad. Pain Mgmt.; formerly mem. editorial bd. Clin. Evoked Potentials Jour.; contbr. articles to various publs. Capt. M.C., U.S. Army, 1966-68, Japan. Award recipient State of R.I., Santa Clara County Med. Soc., Epilepsy Soc., other orgns.; fellow Univ. Paris, 1957-58. Union of Am. Physicians and Dentists (pres. 1990—, bd. dirs. 1972—, pres. Calif. fedn. 1990—). Avocations: softball, tennis, music, theater, martial arts. Office: Union Am Physicians & Dentists 1330 Broadway Ste 730 Oakland CA 94612-2506

WEINREB, LLOYD LOBELL, law educator; b. N.Y.C., Oct. 9, 1936; s. Victor and Ernestine (Lobell) W.; m. Ruth Plaut, May 5, 1963; children—Jennifer, Elizabeth, Nicholas. B.A., Dartmouth, 1957; B.A., U. Oxford, 1959, M.A., 1963; LL.B., Harvard, 1962. Bar: N.Y. 1963, Mass. 1969. Faculty Harvard Law Sch., Cambridge, Mass., 1965—; prof. law Harvard Law Sch., 1968—. Home: 119 Russell Ave Watertown MA 02172-3453 Office: Law Sch Harvard U Cambridge MA 02138

WEINREICH, GABRIEL, physicist, minister, educator; b. Vilnius, Lithuania, Feb. 12, 1928; came to U.S., 1941, naturalized, 1949; s. Max and Regina (Szabad) W.; m. Alisa Lourié, Apr. 19, 1951 (dec. 1970); m. Gerane Siemering Benamou, Oct. 23, 1971; children: Catherine, Marc, Daniel, Rebecca, Natalie. A.B., Columbia U., 1948, M.A., 1949, Ph.D., 1954. Ordained priest Episcopal Ch., 1986. Mem. staff Bell Telephone Labs., Murray Hill, N.J., 1953-60; mem. faculty U. Mich., Ann Arbor, 1960—; prof. physics U. Mich., 1964-95; prof. emeritus, 1995—; Collegiate prof. U. Mich., 1974-76; adj. min. St. Clare's Episcopal ch., Ann Arbor, 1986-90; rector St. Stephen's Episcopal Ch., Hamburg, Mich., 1993-96. Author: Solids: Elementary Theory for Advanced Students, 1965, Fundamental Thermodynamics, 1968, Notes for General Physics, 1972. Recipient Disting. Teaching award U. Mich., 1968, Klopsteg award Am. Assn. Physics Tchrs., 1992, Internat. medal French Acoustical Soc., 1992. Fellow Acoustical Soc. Am. (assoc. editor Jour. 1987-89). Home: 754 Greenhills Dr Ann Arbor MI 48105-2718 Office: Randall Lab U Mich Ann Arbor MI 48109-1120

WEINRIB, SIDNEY, retired optometric and optical products and services executive; b. N.Y.C., Sept. 29, 1919; s. David and Rose (Lichtig) W.; m. Ruth Lois Simon, Aug. 25, 1946 (dec. 1988); children: Irene Henry, Donna Acker, Jeri Taylor. BS in Optometry, Columbia U., 1941. Practice optometry Sterling Optical, N.Y.C., 1947-66, from sec. treas. to chmn. bd., 1966-87; v.p. Ipco Corp., White Plains, N.Y., 1971-87; tchr. Bernard Baruch Sch. Bus., N.Y.C., 1953-54. Served with U.S. Army Signal Corps, 1942-46. Recipient commendation U.S. War Dept., 1946. Mem. Nat. Assn. Optometrists and Opticians (pres. 1978-87), Am. Nat. Standards Inst. Pioneer in modern optical chain retailing. Home: 270 Grand Central Pky # 32D Floral Park NY 11005

WEINS, LEO MATTHEW, retired publishing executive; b. Racine, Wis., Sept. 2, 1912; s. Leo Matthew and Lula (Vollman) W.; m. Margaret Killion, Oct. 19, 1955. Student, Loyola U., Chgo., 1935-36, Northwestern U., 1946-47, U. Chgo., 1937-38. Comptroller ALA, 1952-57; with H. W. Wilson Co., N.Y.C., 1957-95; pres., treas. H. W. Wilson Co., 1967-95; retired, 1995; chmn. bd. Mansell Pub., Ltd., London, 1981-87; mem. editorial bd. Choice, 1963-70, 77-81; mem. govt. adv. com. book and library programs Dept. State, 1973-76; mem. Bronx adv. com. Chase Manhattan Bank, 1968-78; trustee Dollar Dry Dock Savs. Bank N.Y., 1969-87; trustee, treas. N.Y. Met. Reference and Research Library Agency, 1979-83. Mem. sci. info. coun. NSF, 1968-72; bd. dirs. Highbridge Conservation Program, Bronx, 1966-69; pres. H.W. Wilson Found., 1967-95; trustee Maritime Coll. at Ft. Schuyler Found., Bronx, 1978-90. Served with AUS, 1943-46. Mem. ALA, Am. Anitquarian Soc., Fgn. Policy Assn. (gov. 1981-94). Home: 20 Beekman Pl New York NY 10022-8032

WEINSCHEL, ALAN JAY, lawyer; b. Bklyn., Feb. 9, 1946; m. Barbara Ellen Schure, Aug. 20, 1967; children: Lawrence, Adam, Naomi. BA, Bklyn. Coll., 1967; JD, NYU, 1969. Bar: N.Y. 1970, U.S. Dist. Ct. (so. and ea. dists.) N.Y. 1973, U.S. Ct. Appeals (2d cir.) 1979, U.S. Ct. Appeals (9th cir.) 1986, U.S. Ct. Appeals (3d cir.) 1993. Assoc. Breed, Abbott & Morgan, N.Y.C., 1969-74; assoc. Weil, Gotshal & Manges, N.Y.C., 1974-78, ptnr., 1978—; lectr. Practising Law Inst., Ohio Legal Ctr., Am. Mgmt. Assn., Law Jour. Seminars, Law and Bus. Seminars. Trustee N.Y. Inst. Tech., Old Westbury, N.Y., 1969-76, Temple Sinai, Roslyn, N.Y., 1981-87, 89-95. Capt. U.S. Army res., 1969-74. Mem. ABA (editl. bd. dirs. Antitrust Devels. 1981-87), N.Y. State Bar Assn. (chmn. antitrust sect. 1993-95), Assn. Bar of City of N.Y. Office: Weil Gotshal & Manges 767 5th Ave New York NY 10153

WEINSCHEL, BRUNO OSCAR, engineering executive, physicist; b. Stuttgart, Germany, May 26, 1919; came to U.S., 1939; m. Shirley Kittredge; 6 children. BA in Physics, Technische Hochschule, Stuttgart, 1938; Dr. Engring., Technische Hochschule, Munich, Fed. Republic of Germany, 1966; DSc (hon.), Capitol Inst. Tech., 1984. Registered profl. engr., Md., D.C. Sr. engr. Western Electric, 1943-44; chief engr. Indsl. Instruments Co., Jersey City, 1944-48; group leader, rsch. scientist Nat. Bur. of Standards, 1949-52; chief engr., pres. Weinschel Engring. Co., Inc., Gaithersburg, Md., 1952-86, cons., 1987-88; pres., chief engr. Weinschel Rsch. Found., Gaithersburg, Md., 1987—; chief engr. Weinschel Assocs., Gaithersburg, 1988—. Contbr. over 50 articles to profl. jours.; inventor and co-inventor with 20 patents. Mem. Pres. Reagan's Com. Medal of Sci., 1986-87. Recipient William A. Wildhack award Nat. Conf. of Standards Labs., 1985. Fellow IEEE (pres. 1986, Richard M. Emberson award 1992), Instn. Elec. Engrs.-U.K.; mem. Annapolis Yacht Club, Cosmos Club, Univ. Club. Republican. Avocations: sailing, snow and water skiing.

WEINSHEIMER, WILLIAM CYRUS, lawyer; b. Chgo., Jan. 12, 1941; s. Alfred John and Coress (Searing) W.; m. Roberta Limarzi, June 5, 1965; children: William C. Jr., Kurt R., Robert L. BBA in Mktg., U. Notre Dame, 1962; JD, Northwestern U., 1965. Bar: Ill. 1965, U.S. Dist. Ct. (no. dist.) Ill. 1967, U.S. Tax Ct. 1968. Assoc. Hopkins & Sutter, Chgo., 1967-73, ptnr., chmn. trust and estates sect., 1973—; lectr. continuing legal edn. programs; mem. estate planning adv. coun. Northwestern U. Author: (with others) The New Generation Skipping Tax; Analysis, Planning & Drafting, 1987; Drafting Wills and Trust Agreements, 1990; contbr. articles to profl. jours. Bd. dirs. The Ragdale Found., Lake Forest, Ill., 1987—, Lawyers for Creative Arts, 1973-90, Winnetka United Way, 1989-92; pres. Family Svc. Winnetka-Northfield, Inc., 1978-79. Capt. U.S. Army, 1965-67. Fellow Am. Coll. Trust and Estate Coun. (bus. planning com. 1993—, chair Ill. chpt. 1989-92, editor Actec Notes 1991-92, bd. regents 1992—, chair edit. bd. 1993—); mem. ABA (vice chmn. con. on generation-skipping tax 1988-92), Ill. Bar Assn., Chgo. Bar Assn. (chmn. probate practice com. 1989), Chgo. Bar Found. (bd. dirs. 1992—), Ill. Bar Found. (bd. dirs. 1985-91), Law Club, Econ. Club, Mid-Day Club, Skokie Country Club, Notre Dame Club Chgo. (bd. govs. 1984-90). Roman Catholic. Avocations: golf, visual arts, performing. Office: Hopkins & Sutter 3 First National Plz Chicago IL 60602

WEINSHIENK, ZITA LEESON, federal judge; b. St. Paul, Apr. 3, 1933; d. Louis and Ada (Dubov) Leeson; m. Hubert Troy Weinshienk, July 8, 1956 (dec. 1983); children: Edith Blair, Kay Anne, Darcy Jill; m. James N. Schaffner, Nov. 15, 1986. Student, U. Colo., 1952-53; BA magna cum laude, U. Ariz., 1955; JD cum laude, Harvard U., 1958; Fulbright grantee, U. Copenhagen, Denmark, 1959; LHD (hon.), Loretto Heights Coll., 1985; LLD (hon.), U. Denver, 1990. Bar: Colo. 1959. Probation counselor, legal adviser, referee Denver Juvenile Ct., 1959-64; judge Denver Mcpl. Ct., 1964-65, Denver County Ct., 1965-71, Denver Dist. Ct., 1972-79, U.S. Dist. Ct. Colo., Denver, 1979—. Precinct committeewoman Denver Democratic Com., 1963-64; bd. dirs. Crime Stoppers. Named one of 100 Women in Touch with Our Time Harper's Bazaar Mag., 1971, Woman of Yr., Denver Bus. and Profl. Women, 1969; recipient Women Helping Women award Soroptimist Internat. of Denver, 1983, Hanna G. Solomon award Nat. Coun. Jewish Women, Denver, 1986. Fellow Colo. Bar Found., Am. Bar Found.; mem. ABA, Denver Bar Assn., Colo. Bar Assn., Nat. Conf. Fed. Trial Judges (exec. com.), Dist. Judges' Assn. of 10th Cir. (past pres.), Colo. Women's Bar Assn., Fed. Judges Assn., Denver Crime Stoppers Inc. (bd.dirs.), Devner LWV, Women's Forum Colo., Harvard Law Sch. Assn., Phi Beta Kappa, Phi Kappa Phi, Order of Coif (hon. Colo. chpt.). Office: US Dist Ct US Courthouse Rm C-550 1929 Stout St Denver CO 80294-2900*

WEINSIER, ROLAND LOUIS, nutrition educator and director. MD, D in Nutrition, Harvard U., 1973. Prof. nutrition U. Ala., Birmingham, 1975—. Office: U Ala at Birmingham Med Ctr Dept Nutrition Scis U Sta PO Box 188 Birmingham AL 35294-0001

WEINSTEIN, ALAN, health care management executive; b. Orange, N.J., Oct. 31, 1942; s. Herbert Milton and Evelyn (Schneider) W.; m. Ronni Jane Klorman, July 1, 1967 (div.); children: Renée S., Kevin M.; m. Harriet Rose Grumet, May 2, 1987. BS, Allegheny Coll., 1994; postgrad., Cornell U., 1994—. Sr. asst. Colorado-Wyoming Regional Med. Program, Denver, 1968-69; exec. dir. Midtown Hosp. Assn., Denver, 1969-73, North Suburban Assn. for Health Resources, Glenview, Ill., 1973-78; sr. v.p. Ill. Hosp. Assn., Naperville, Ill., 1978-83; pres. Premier Health Alliance, Westchester, Ill., 1983—; bd. dirs. Am. Internat. Health Alliance, Washington. With USPHS, 1966-68. Avocations: tennis, fishing, gardening. Office: Premier Health Alliance 3 Westbrook Corp Ctr Fl 9 Westchester IL 60154*

WEINSTEIN, ALAN EDWARD, lawyer; b. Bklyn., Apr. 20, 1945; s. John and Matilda W.; m. Patti Kantor, Dec. 18, 1965; children: Steven R., David A. AA, U. Fla., 1964; BBA, U. Miami (Fla.), 1965, JD cum laude, 1968. Bar: Fla. 1968, U.S. Dist. Ct. (so. dist.) Fla. 1968, U.S. Ct. Appeals (5th cir.) 1969, U.S. Supreme Ct. 1973, U.S. Ct. Appeals (4th & 11th cirs.) 1981. Assoc. Cohen & Hogan, Miami Beach, Fla., 1968-71; pvt. practice Miami Beach, 1972-81; sr. ptnr. Weinstein & Preira, Miami Beach, 1981-92; prin. Law Offices of Alan E. Weinstein, Miami, 1992—; lectr. continuing legal edn. programs. Mem. ABA (criminal and family law sect. 1968—), Nat. Assn. Criminal Def. Lawyers, Fla. Bar Assn. (criminal and family law sect. 1968—, ethics com. 1987-88, bench/bar com. 1988-89), Fla. Criminal Def. Attys. Assn. (pres. 1978-79), Fla. Assn. Criminal Def. Lawyers (treas. 1989-90), Miami Beach Bar Assn., Soc. Wig and Robe, Phi Kappa Phi. Avocations: marlin fishing, reading, travel. Office: 1801 West Ave Miami FL 33139-1431

WEINSTEIN, ALLAN M., medical device company executive; b. Bklyn., June 25, 1945; s. Henry I. Weinstein and Hannah L. (Broidy) Glasser; m. Phyllis Fishman, Aug. 28, 1965; children: Craig, Brett, Danielle. BS, Poly. Inst., Bklyn., 1965, MS, 1966, PhD, 1972. Registered profl. engr. Postdoctoral fellow U. Pa., Phila., 1971-72; asst. prof. Clemson U., 1972-75; prof., dir. biomaterials Tulane U., New Orleans, 1975-81; v.p. tech. affairs Intermedics Orthopaedics, Dublin, Calif., 1981-83, also bd. dirs.; pres., chief exec. officer Harrington Arthritis Rsch. Ctr., Phoenix, 1983-87; co-founder, chmn., pres., chief exec. officer OrthoLogic Corp., Phoenix, 1987—. Editor:

spl. publs. 472, 601, Nat. Bur. Stds., 1977, 81; contbr. numerous articles to profl. jours.; patentee (3) in field. Rsch. grantee NIH, 1973-91. Mem. Soc. for Biomaterials (charter mem., pres. 1985-86, Clemson Award for contbns. to biomaterials lit. 1995), Orthopaedic Rsch. Soc., Am. Soc. Metals, N.Y. Acad. Scis., Sigma Xi. Republican. Jewish. Avocations: tennis, skiing, golf. Home: 11629 E del Timbre Scottsdale AZ 85259-5908 Office: OrthoLogic Corp 2850 S 36th St Phoenix AZ 85034-7239

WEINSTEIN, ALLEN, educator, historian, non-profit administrator; b. N.Y.C., Sept. 1, 1937; s. Samuel and Sarah (Popkoff) W.; m. Adrienne Dominguez, June 14, 1995; children: Andrew Samuel, David Meier. BA, CCNY; MA, Yale U., PhD, 1967. Prof. Smith Coll., Northampton, Mass., 1966-81, Georgetown U., Washington, 1981-83; pres. R.M. Hutchins CSDI, Santa Barbara, Calif., 1984; prof. Boston U., 1985-89; founder, pres. The Ctr. for Democracy, Washington, 1985—. Author: Prelude to Populism, 1970, Freedom and Crisis, 1974, 3d edit., 1981, Perjury, 1978 (NISC award 1978), new edit., 1996, Between the Wars, 1978; editor: Am. Negro Slavery, 1968, 3d edit., 1981, HST and Israel, 1981; mem. editorial bd. The Washington Post, 1981; exec. editor The Washington Quar., 1982-83. Exec. dir. The Democracy Program, Washington, 1982-83; acting pres. Nat. Endowment for Democracy, Washington, 1983-84; chmn. edn. com. U.S. Inst. Peace, Washington, 1986—; mem. U.S. Observer del., Feb., 1986 Philippines election, co-author report; vice chmn. U.S. del. UNESCO World Conf. on Culture, 1982, UNESCO/IPDC meeting, 1983. Recipient Meade prize in history CCNY, 1960, Egleston prize Yale U., 1967, Binkley-Stephenson prize Orgn. Am. Historians, 1968, UN Peace medal, 1986, Coun. of Europe silver medal, 1990, 96; Fulbright lectr., Australia, 1968, 71; Commonwealth Fund lectr. U.S. History, U. London, 1981; Fourth of July Orator Faneuil Hall, Boston, 1987. Fellow Woodrow Wilson Ctr., NEH; mem. Soc. Am. Historians. Democrat. Jewish. Office: The Ctr for Democracy 1101 15th St NW Ste 505 Washington DC 20005-5002

WEINSTEIN, DAVID CARL, investment compaany executive, lawyer; b. Flushing, N.Y., Nov. 21, 1951; s. Philip and Molly (Rencoff) W.; m. Clare Villari, Aug. 14, 1988; 1 child, Matthew Charles. BA, Boston U., 1972; JD, Boston Coll., 1975. Bar: Mass. 1975. Assoc. gen. counsel Prucapital, Inc., Cambridge, Mass., 1976-84; v.p., corp. counsel Fidelity Investments, Boston, 1984-95, sr. v.p. adminstrn., 1995—; bd. dirs. Empire Fidelity Investments Life Ins. Co., N.Y.C. Trustee Hebrew Coll., Brookline, Mass., 1993—; bd. dirs. Goodwill Industries, Boston, 1990—. Mem. Am. Corp. Counsel Assn., Mass. Bar Assn. Office: Fidelity Investments 82 Devonshire St Boston MA 02109-3605

WEINSTEIN, DIANE GILBERT, federal judge, lawyer; b. Rochester, N.Y., June 14, 1947; d. Myron Birne and Doris Isabelle (Robie) Gilbert; m. Dwight Douglas Sypolt; children: Andrew, David. BA, Smith Coll., Northampton, Mass., 1969; postgrad., Stanford U., 1977-78, Georgetown U., 1978; JD, Boston U., 1979. Bar: D.C. 1979, Mass. 1979. Law clk. to judge D.C. Ct. Appeals, Washington, 1979-80; assoc. Peabody, Lambert & Meyers, Washington, 1980-83; asst. gen. counsel Office of Mgmt. and Budget, Washington, 1983-86; dep. gen. counsel U.S. Dept. Edn., Washington, 1986-88, acting gen. counsel, 1988-89; legal counselor to V.P. of U.S., White House; counsel Pres.'s Competitiveness Coun., Washington, 1989-90; judge U.S. Ct. Fed. Claims, Washington, 1990—. Recipient Young Lawyer's award Boston U. Law Sch., 1989. Mem. Fed. Am. Inn of Ct., Federalist Soc., Univ. Club. Republican. Home: 3927 Massachusetts Ave NW Washington DC 20016-5104

WEINSTEIN, EDWARD MICHAEL, architect, consultant; b. Bklyn., May 5, 1947; s. Hyman and Freda (Rochkes) W.; m. Melanie Jane Ross, June 22, 1969; children: Valerie, David. BS, CCNY, 1969. Registered architect; lic. N.Y., N.J. Jr. architect N.Y.C. Dept. Ports and Terminals, 1970-72, architect, 1972-75, sr. urban designer, 1975-80, dir. waterfront devel., 1980-84, asst. commr., 1984-87; pres. EMW Assocs., Hastings-On-Hudson, N.Y., 1984—; ptnr. The Hastings Design Group, Hastings-On-Hudson, 1987—; adv. bd. Metro Marine Express Ltd., N.Y.C., 1989-91. Active Planning Bd., Hastings-on-Hudson, 1990—, Waterfront Ctr.; trustee Greenburgh Hebrew Ctr., Dobbs Ferry, N.Y., 1986-89, 92—; v.p. N.Y. Port Promotion Assn., N.Y.C., 1984-87; adv. com. on waterfront devel. N.Y. State Assembly. Recipient Gold Key award House Plan Assn., 1969. Mem. AIA, Am. Assn. Port Authority, N.Y. Soc. Architects, The Waterfront Ctr., CCNY Alumni Assn. Democrat. Jewish. Avocations: tennis, art. Office: The Hastings Design Group 14 Spring St Hastings On Hudson NY 10706

WEINSTEIN, EILEEN ANN, elementary education educator; b. Phila., Sept. 11, 1947; d. Bernard and Eleanor (Cohen) Cobert; m. Philip Weinstein, Aug. 16, 1970; children: Lawrence, Steven. BS in Edn. with honors, Temple U., 1969, MEd with honors, 1972. Cert. elem. tchr., psychology of reading, Pa. 1st grade tchr. Phila. Sch. Dist., 1969-70; 1st grade tchr. Neshaminy Sch. Dist., Langhorne, Pa., 1970-74, tchr. reading and 3d grade, 1985—; kindergarten tchr. Jewish Cmty. Ctr., Phila., 1981-85; mem. instrnl. support team Neshaminy Sch. Dist., 1987—, mem. student assistance team, 1992—. Active Dem. Nat. Com., 1992—. Recipient Teaching award Children with ADD, 1994-95. Mem. Internat. Reading Assn., Neshaminy Fedn. Tchrs. (union rep. 1986—), Women's Am. ORT (officer, bd. mem. 1973—), Hadassah (officer and bd. mem. 1969—). Jewish. Avocations: reading, travel, music, impressionist art. Home: 83 Cypress Cir Richboro PA 18954-1653 Office: Neshaminy Sch Dist Oliver Heckman Sch Cherry St Langhorne PA 19047

WEINSTEIN, GEORGE WILLIAM, ophthalmology educator; b. East Orange, N.J., Jan. 26, 1935; s. Henry J. and Irma C. (Klein) W.; m. Sheila Valerie Wohlreich, June 20, 1957; children: Bruce David, Elizabeth Joyce, Rachel Andrea. AB, U. Pa., 1955; MD, SUNY, Bklyn., 1959. Diplomate Am. Bd. Ophthalmology (bd. dirs. 1981-89). Intern then resident in ophthalmology Kings County Hosp., Bklyn., 1959-63; asst. prof. ophthalmology Johns Hopkins U., Balt., 1967-70; head ophthalmology dept. U. Tex., San Antonio, 1970-80; prof., Jane McDermott Shott chmn. W.Va. U., Morgantown, 1980-95. Author: Key Facts in Ophthalmology, 1984; editor: Open Angle Glaucoma, 1986; editor Ophthalmic Surgery jour., 1971-81, Current Opinion in Ophthalmology jour., 1988—; contbr. articles to profl. jours. Served to lt. comdr. USPHS, 1963-65. Sr. Internat. fellow Fogarty Internat. Ctr. NIH, 1987. Mem. ACS (bd. govs. 1983-85, bd. regents 1987-92), Assn. Univ. Profs. Ophthalmology (pres. 1986-87, exec. v.p. 1994), Am. Acad. Ophthalmology (bd. dirs. 1980-92, chmn. long range planning com. 1986-89, pub. and profl. sec. 1983-89, pres.-elect 1990, pres. 1991, Honor award, Sr. Honor award), Alpha Omega Alpha (faculty 1987), Am. Ophthalmology Soc. (coun. 1992—). Jewish. Avocations: jazz, banjo, photography, tennis, basketball. Home: 100 Ironwood Dr Apt 124 Ponte Vedra Beach FL 32082

WEINSTEIN, GERALD D., dermatology educator; b. N.Y.C., Oct. 13, 1936; m. Marcia Z. Weinstein; children: Jeff, Jon, Debbie. BA, U. Pa., 1957, MD, 1961. Diplomate Am. Bd. Dermatology. Intern Los Angeles County Gen. Hosp., 1961-62; clin. assoc. dermatology br. Nat. Cancer Instn. NIH, Bethesda, Md., 1962-64; resident dept. dermatology U. Miami, Fla., 1964-65; asst. prof. Dept. Dermatology U. Miami, Fla., 1966-71, assoc. prof., 1971-74, prof., 1975-79; prof., chmn. dept. dermatology U. Calif., Irvine, 1979—, acting dean Coll. Medicine, 1985-87; attending staff VA Med. Ctr., Long Beach, Calif., 1979—, UCI Med. Ctr., Orange, Calif., 1979—, St. Joseph Hosp., Orange, 1980—. Contbr. articles to profl. jours., chpts. to books. Recipient Lifetime Achievement award Nat. Psoriasis Found., 1994; co-recipient award for psoriasis rsch. Taub Internat. Meml., 1971; NIH spl. postdoctoral fellow, 1965-67. Mem. Am. Acad. Dermatology (chmn. task force on psoriasis 1986—, bd. dirs. 1984-88). Office: U Calif Irvine Coll Medicine Dept Dermatology Irvine CA 92697-2400

WEINSTEIN, HARRIS, lawyer; b. Providence, May 10, 1935; s. Joseph and Gertrude (Rusitzky) W.; m. Rosa Grunberg, June 3, 1956; children: Teme Feldman, Joshua, Jacob. BS in Math., MIT, 1956, MS in Math., 1958; LLB, Columbia U., 1961. Bar: D.C. 1962. Law clk. to judge U.S. Ct. Appeals (3d cir.), Phila., 1961-62; with Covington & Burling, Washington, 1962-67, 69-90, 1993—; chief counsel Office of Thrift Supervision U.S. Dept. of Treasury, Washington, 1990-92; asst. to solicitor gen. U.S. Dept. Justice, 1967-69; pub. mem. Adminstrv. Conf. of U.S., 1982-90; lectr. U. Va. Law Sch., 1996. V.p. Jewish Social Svc. Agy.; mem. MIT Corp., 1989-95. Mem. Nat. Press Club. Home: 7717 Georgetown Pike Mc Lean VA 22102-1411 Office: Covington & Burling PO Box 7566 1201 Pennsylvania Ave NW Washington DC 20004-2401

WEINSTEIN, HARVEY, film company executive. Co-chmn. Miramax Films Corp., L.A. Office: Miramax Films Corp 375 Greenwich St New York NY 10013-2338*

WEINSTEIN, HERBERT, chemical engineer, educator; b. Bklyn., Mar. 10, 1933; s. Abraham and Pauline (Feldman) W.; m. Judith Cooper, Apr. 6, 1957; children: Michael Howard, Edward Marc, Ellen Rachel. B.Engring. in Chem. Engring. Coll. City N.Y., 1955; M.S. in Chem. Engring, Purdue U., 1957; Ph.D., Case Inst. Tech., 1963. Staff mem. Los Alamos Sci. Lab., 1956-58; research engr. NASA Lewis Research Center, Cleve., 1959-63; asst. prof. chem. engring. Ill. Inst. Tech., 1963-66, assoc. prof., 1966-72, prof., 1972-77; dir. Center for Biomed. Engring., 1973-77; prof. CUNY, 1977—; Herbert G. Kayser prof. of chem. engring., 1987—; vis. rsch. assoc., mem. Med. Rsch. Inst. Michael Reese Hosp. and Med. Ctr., Chgo., 1965-77; vis. prof. mech. engring. Technion-Israel Inst. Tech., 1972-73; vis. prof. biomed. engring. Rush Med. Coll., Chgo., 1973-76; summer prof. Exxon Rsch. and Engring. Co., annually, 1981-92; Lady Davis vis. prof. Technion-Israel Inst. Tech., 1985; cons. to industry, rsch. labs. Mem. Am. Inst. Chem. Engrs., Sigma Xi. Jewish. Research and publs. on fluidization, chem. reactor engring., fluid mechanics, biomed. engring. Office: CUNY Dept Chem Engring New York NY 10031

WEINSTEIN, I. BERNARD, oncologist, geneticist, research administrator; b. Madison, Wis., Sept. 9, 1930; married, 1952; 3 children. BS, U. Wis., 1952, MD, 1955. Nat. Cancer Inst. spl. rsch. fellow bacteriology/immunology Harvard Med. Sch./MIT, Boston, 1959-61; career scientist Health Rsch. Coun., City of N.Y., 1961-72; assoc. vis. physician Francis Delafield Hosp., 1961-66; from asst. attending physician to assoc. attending physician Presbyn. Hosp., 1967-81, attending physician, 1981—; from asst. to assoc. prof. medicine Coll. Physicians & Surgeons, divsn. Environ. Sci., N.Y.C., 1978-90; prof. medicine Columbia U., N.Y.C., 1973—, prof. pub. health, 1978—, dir. divsn. oncology, prof. genetics and devel., 1990—, Frode Jensen prof. medicine, dir. comprehensive cancer ctr., 1985—; advisor Lung Cancer Segment, Carcinogenesis Program, Nat. Cancer Inst., 1971-74, Chem. and Molecular Biol. Segment, 1973-76; mem. interdisciplinary comm. program Smithsonian Inst., 1971-74, Pharmacology B Study ect., NIH, 1971-75, numerous sci. and adv. coms. Nat. Cancer Inst., Am. Cancer Soc., 1976-88; advisor Roswell Park Meml. Inst., Buffalo, Brookhaven Nat. Lab., Divsn. Cancer Cause and Prevention, Nat. Cancer Inst., Coun. on Analysis and Projects, Am. Cancer Soc., Internat. Agy. for Rsch. on Cancer, WHO, Lyon, France; Nakasone vis. prof., Tokyo, 1987; GM Cancer Rsch. Found. vis. prof. Internat. Agy. Rsch. Cancer, Lyon, 1988. Assoc. editor Cancer Rsch., 1973-76, 86—, Jour. Environ. Pathology and Toxicology, 1977-84, Jour. Cellular Physiology, 1982-89. Recipient Meltzer medal, 1964, Dlowes award Am. Assn. Cancer Rsch., 1987, Silvio O. Conte award Environ. Health Inst., 1990; Louise Weissberger lectr. U. Rochester, 1981, Mary Ann Swetland lectr. Case Western Res. U., 1983, Daniel Laszlo Meml. lectr. Montefiore Med. Ctr., 1983, Samuel Kuna Disting. lectr. Rutgers U., 1985, Ester Langer lectr. U. Chgo., 1989, Harris Meml. lectr. MIT, 1989; European Molecular Biology Orgn. travel fellow, 1970-71. Mem. AAAS (coun. del. 1985-88, pres. 1990-91), Inst. Medicine/Nat. Acad. Sci., Am. Soc. Microbiology, Internat. Soc. Quantum Biology, Am. Assn. Cancer Rsch., Am. Soc. Clin. Investigation, N.Y. Acad. Sci. Achievements include research in oncology, cellular and molecular aspects of carcinogenesis, environmental carcinogenesis, control of gene expression. Office: Inst Cancer Rsch Columbia Univ 701 W 168th St New York NY 10032

WEINSTEIN, IRA PHILLIP, advertising executive; b. Chgo., June 10, 1919; s. Phillip Marshall and Lillian (Greenblatt) W.; m. Norma Randall; children: Terri, Laura Temkin. Student, Crane Tech. Inst., 1937, Northwestern U., 1945-46. Chmn. bd. Schram Advt. Co., Chgo., 1945—. 1st lt. USAAF, 1942-45, ETO. Decorated D.F.C., Air medal, Purple Heart, Ex-Prisoner of War medal; recipient Presdl. citation, 1988. Mem. Chgo. Direct Mail Assn., Air Force Assn., Ex-POW Assn., Bombardiers Assn., Caterpillar Assn., Air Force Heritage League, 2d Air Divsn. Assn., Mil. Order of Purple HEart, 8th Air Force Hist. Soc. Office: The Schram Advt Co 450 Skokie Blvd Ste 800 Northbrook IL 60062-7916

WEINSTEIN, IRWIN MARSHALL, internist, hematologist; b. Denver, Mar. 5, 1926; m. Judith Braun, 1951. Student, Dartmouth Coll., 1943-44, Williams Coll., 1944-45; MD, U. Colo., Denver, 1949. Diplomate Am. Bd. Internal Medicine (assoc. bd. govs. hematology subcom.). Intern Montefiore Hosp., N.Y.C., 1949-50; jr. asst. resident in medicine Montefiore Hosp., 1950-51; sr. asst. resident in medicine U. Chgo., 1951-52, resident in medicine, 1952-53, instr. in medicine, 1953-54, asst. prof. medicine, 1954-55; vis. assoc. prof. medicine U. Calif. Center for Health Scis., L.A., 1955-56, assoc. clin. prof., 1957-60, clin. prof., 1970—; sect. chief in medicine, hematology sect. Wadsworth Gen. Hosp., VA Center, L.A., 1956-59; pvt. practice medicine specializing in hematology and internal medicine Los Angeles, 1959—; mem. staff Cedars-Sinai Med. Center, L.A., 1959—; chief of med. staff Cedars-Sinai Med. Ctr., 1972-74, bd. govs., 1974—; mem. staff U. Calif. Ctr. Health Scis., Wadsworth Gen. Hosp., VA Ctr.; vis. prof. Hadassah Med. Ctr., Jerusalem, 1967; adv. for health affairs to Hon. Alan Cranston, 1971-92; mem. com. on space biology and medicine Space Sci. Bd.; active UCLA Comprehensive Cancer Ctr. Contbr. articles to profl. pubs.; editor: (with Ernest Beutler) Mechanisms of Anemia, 1962. Master ACP (gov. So. Calif. Region I 1989-93); fellow Israel Med. Assn. (hon.); mem. AAAS, Am. Fedn. Clin. Rsch., Am. Soc. Hematology (exec. com. 1974-78, chmn. com. on practice 1978-87, mem. council 1974-78), Am. Soc. Internal Medicine, Assn. Am. Med. Colls., Internat. Soc. Hematology, Internat. Soc. Internal Medicine, L.A. Acad. Medicine, L.A. Soc. Nuclear Medicine, Inst. of Medicine NAS, N.Y. Acad. Sci., Reticulo-Endothelial Soc., Royal Soc. Medicine, Western Soc. Clin. Rsch., Alpha Omega Alpha. Office: 8635 W 3rd St Ste 665 Los Angeles CA 90048-6101

WEINSTEIN, JACK BERTRAND, federal judge; b. Wichita, Kans., Aug. 10, 1921; s. Harry Louis and Bessie Helen (Brodach) W.; m. Evelyn Horowitz, Oct. 10, 1946; children: Seth George, Michael David, Howard Lewis. BA, Bklyn. Coll., 1943; LLB, Columbia, 1948; LLD (hon.), Bklyn. Law Sch., Yeshiva U., Albany Law Sch., Hofstra Law Sch., L.I. U.; Yale U. Bar: N.Y. 1949. Assoc. Columbia Law Sch., 1948-49; law clk. N.Y. Ct. Appeals Judge Stanly H. Fuld, 1949-50; ptnr. William Rosenfeld, N.Y.C., 1950-52; mem. faculty Columbia Law Sch., 1952-67, prof. law, 1956-67, adj. prof., 1967—; U.S. judge (Eastern Dist. N.Y.), 1967-93, chief judge, 1980-88; sr. judge Ea. Dist. N.Y., 1993—; vis. prof. U. Tex., 1957, U. Colo., 1961, Harvard U., 1982, Georgetown U., 1991, Bklyn. Law Sch., 1988—, others; counsel N.Y. Joint Legis. Com. Motor Vehicle Problems, 1952-54, State Sen. Seymour Halpern, 1952-54; reporter adv. com. practice and procedure N.Y. State Temp. Commn. Cts., 1955-58; adv. com. practice N.Y. Judicial Conf., 1963-66; adv. com. rules of evidence U.S. Jud. Conf., 1965-75, mem. com. jurisdiction, 1969-75, mem., 1983-86; mem. 2d Cir. Jud. Coun., 1982-88, U.S. Jud. Conf., 1983-86, others in past. Author: (with Morgan and Maquire) Cases and Materials on Evidence, 4th edit., 1965, (with Maguire, Chadbourne and Mansfield, 5th edit.), 1971, 6th edit., 1975, (with Mansfield, Abrams and Bergen), 8th edit., 1988, (with Rosenberg) Cases and Materials on Civil Procedure, 1961, rev. edit, (with Smit), 1971, (with Smit, Rosenberg and Korn), 1976, (with Korn and Miller) New York Civil Procedure, 9 vols., rev. edit, 1966, Manual of New York Civil Procedure, 1967, Basic Problems of State and Federal Evidence, 1976, (with Berger) Weinstein's Evidence, 7 vols., 1967, rev. edit., 1993, Revising Rule Making Procedures, 1977, A New York Constitution Meeting Today's Needs and Tomorrow's Challenges, 1967, Disaster, A Legal Allegory, 1988, (with Greenawalt) Readings for Seminar on Equality and Law, 1979, (with Murphy) Readings for Seminar in Individual Rights in a Mass Society, 1990-91, (with Berger) Readings for Seminar in Science and Law, (with Feinberg) Mass Torts, 1992, 94, Individual Justice in Mass Litigation, 1995. Chmn. N.Y. Dem. adv. com. on Constl. Conv., 1955; bd. dirs. N.Y. Civil Liberties Union, 1956-62, Cardozo Sch. Law, Conf. on Jewish Social Studies, 1980-88; nat. adv. bd. Am. Jewish Congress, 1960-67, CARE, 1985-90, Fedn. Jewish Philanthropies, 1985-94; chmn. lay bd. Riverside Hosp. Adolescent Drug Users, 1954-55. Lt. USNR, 1943-46. Mem. ABA, N.Y. State Bar Assn., Assn. of Bar of City of N.Y., Nassau County Bar Assn., Am. Law Inst., Soc. Pub. Tchrs. Law (Eng.), Am. Acad. Arts and Scis. Jewish. Office: US Dist Ct US Courthouse 225 Cadman Plz E Brooklyn NY 11201-1818

WEINSTEIN, JAY A., social science educator, researcher; b. Chgo., Feb. 23, 1942; s. Lawrence E. and Jacqueline L. (Caplan) W.; m. Diana S. Staffin, Sept. 16, 1961; m. Marilyn L. Schwartz, Nov. 25, 1972; children—Liza, Bennett. A.B., U. Ill., 1963, Ph.D., 1973; M.A., Washington U., St. Louis, 1965. Teaching fellow U. Ill., Urbana, 1963-64; teaching asst. McGill U., Montreal, Que., Can., 1966-68; instr. Sir George Williams U., Montreal, Que., Can., 1967-68; lectr. Simon Fraser U., Vancouver, B.C., Can., 1968; asst. prof. North Central Coll., Naperville, Ill., 1970-71, U. Iowa, 1973-77; prof. social sci. Ga. Inst. Tech., Atlanta, 1977-86; head dept. sociology Eastern Mich U., 1986-90, faculty rsch. fellow, 1990-91; U.S. Info. Agy. and Soros Found. grantee ednl. devel. project, Bulgaria and Albania,, 1992—; researcher; cons. pub. and pvt. agys. Author: Madras: An Analysis of Urban Ecological Structure in India, 1974, Demographic Transition and Social Change, 1976, Sociology-Technology: Foundations of Postacademic Social Science, 1982, The Grammar of Social Relations: The Major Essays of Louis Schneider, 1984; editor: Paradox and Society, 1986; (with Vinod Tewari and V.L.S. Prakash Rao) Indian Cities: Ecological Perspectives, 1987; Studies in Comparative International Development, 1978-88; mem. editorial bd. Social Development Issues, 1977-85; specialized contbr. Calcutta Mcpl. Gazette, 1979—; editor: Social and Cultural Change, 1974-75; editorial reviewer Jour. Asian Studies, Social Devel. Issues, Tech. and Culture, Am. Sociologist, Technol. Forecasting and Social Change; contbr. chpts. to books, articles to profl. jours. Fulbright prof. Ahmedabad, India, 1975-76, Hyderabad, India, 1981-82; grantee Ga. Tech. Found., 1981-82, World Order Studies Course, 1974-75, State of Mich. Rsch. Excellence Fund; Steinberg fellow, 1967. Mem. Am. Sociol. Assn., Soc. for Applied Sociology, Soc. South Indian Studies, Mich. Sociol. Assn. (pres. 1988-89, v.p. 1994-95), Sigma Xi. Jewish. Office: Eastern Mich U Sociology Dept Ypsilanti MI 48197

WEINSTEIN, JEFFREY ALLEN, consumer products company executive, lawyer; b. N.Y.C., Jan. 20, 1951; s. Herbert and Pearl (Linksman) W.; m. Kyle D. Jacobson, Mar. 30, 1996; children: Jamie Kate, Jonathan Alexander. BA, Pa. State U., 1972; JD, Villanova U., 1975. Bar: Pa. 1975, N.H. 1983, U.S. Dist. Ct. (ea. dist.) Pa. 1975, U.S. Dist. Ct. N.H. 1983. Litigator Arthur Alan Wolk Assocs., Phila., 1975-78; v.p. adminstrn., sec., gen. counsel Centronics Data Computer Corp., Hudson, N.H., 1978—; exec. v.p., sec., gen. counsel Ekco Group, Inc., also bd. dirs.; sec., bd. dirs. Ekco Housewares, Inc., Woodstream Corp.; sec. Ekco Can. Inc., Wright-Bennet, Inc.; asst. clk. Kellogg Brush Mfg. Co., B.VIA Internat. Housewares, Inc., Ekco Consumer Products Ltd.; asst. clk., bd. dirs. Frem Corp. Bd. dirs. Boys Club, Nashua, N.H., 1982-83; mem. N.H. Library Adv. Bd., Concord. Mem. Pa. Bar Assn., N.H. Bar Assn. Office: Ekco Group Inc 98 Spit Brook Rd Nashua NH 03062-5737

WEINSTEIN, JOSH, television producer; m. Lisa Weinstein. Student Stanford U. Co-writer Lampoon parodies USA Today, Time, also others; writer Spy, Nat. Lampoon America's Most Waanted. Writer The Simpsons, from 1992, also story editor, supervising prodr., now exec. prodr. (Emmy award 1995). Office: care Fox Publicity PO Box 900 Beverly Hills CA 90213

WEINSTEIN, MARK MICHAEL, lawyer; b. N.Y.C., Apr. 20, 1942; s. Nathan and Caroline (Levine) W.; m. Adrienne Peni Kuba, Aug. 15, 1965; children: Samantha Beth, Caleb Jonathan. AB, Columbia Coll., 1964; LLB, U. Pa., 1968. Assoc. Paul Weiss, Rifkind, Wharton and Garrison, N.Y.C., 1968-76; asst. v.p., dep. gen. counsel Warner Communications Inc., N.Y.C., 1976-78, v.p., 1978-85; v.p., gen. counsel Viacom Internat. Inc., N.Y.C., 1985-87, sr. v.p., gen. counsel and sec., 1987-93, sr. v.p. govt. affairs, 1993—. Office: Viacom Inc 1515 Broadway New York NY 10036 also: Viacom/DC 1501 M St NW Washington DC 20005-1700

WEINSTEIN, MARTIN, aerospace manufacturing executive, materials scientist; b. Bklyn., Mar. 3, 1936; s. Benjamin and Dora (Lemo) W.; m. Sandra Rebecca Yaffie, June 5, 1961; children: Hilary Ann, Sarah Elizabeth, Joshua Aaron. BS in Metals Engring., Rensselaer Poly. Inst., 1957; MS, MIT, 1960, PhD, 1961. Mgr. materials sci. Tycolabs, Waltham, Mass., 1961-68; tech. dir. turbine support div. Chromalloy Am. Corp., San Antonio, 1968-71, v.p., asst. gen. mgr., 1971-74, pres. 1975-79; pres. Chromalloy Compressor Techs., San Antonio, 1979-82; group pres. Chromalloy Gas Turbine, San Antonio, 1982-86, chmn., chief exec. officer, N.Y.C., 1986—; supervisory mng. dir. Turbine Support Europe, Tilburg, Netherlands, 1975—; bd. dirs. Turbine Support Thailand, Bankok, Chromalloy U.K., Nottingham, Eng., Internat. Coating Co., Tokyo, Japan, Heurchrome, Paris, Malichaud Orleans, France. Bd. dirs. Jewish Fedn., 1981-85, Chamber Players of San Antonio, 1979-83, NCCJ, 1982-85; mem. vis. com. dept. metallurgy and materials sci. MIT, 1992—. Recipient Turner Meml. award Electrochem. Soc., 1963; Achievement award NASA, 1965; Am. Iron and Steel Inst. fellow, 1960. Mem. Am. Soc. Metals, Am. Inst. Metall. Engrs., N.Y. Acad. Sci., Sigma Xi. Patentee diffusion coating of jet engine materials. Contbr. articles to profl. jours. Home: 111 Sheffield San Antonio TX 78213-2626 Office: Chromalloy Gas Turbine Corp 200 Park Ave New York NY 10166-0005

WEINSTEIN, MICHAEL ALAN, political science educator; b. Bklyn., Aug. 24, 1942; s. Aaron and Grace (Sosin) W.; m. Deena Schneiweiss, May 31, 1964. B.A. summa cum laude, NYU, 1964; M.A. in Polit. Sci., Case Western Res. U., 1965, Ph.D., 1967. Asst. prof. polit. sci. Case Western Res. U., summer 1967, Va. Poly. Inst., 1967-68; asst. prof. Purdue U., 1968-70, assoc. prof., 1970-72, prof., 1972—; Milward Simpson disting. prof. polit. sci. U. Wyo., 1979. Author: (with Deena Weinstein) Living Sociology, 1974, The Polarity of Mexican Thought, 1976, The Tragic Sense of Political Life, 1977, Meaning and Appreciation, 1978, The Structure of Human Life, 1979, The Wilderness and the City, 1982, Unity and Variety in the Philosophy of Samuel Alexander, 1984, Finite Perfection, 1985, Culture Critique: Fernand Dumont and New Quebec Sociology, 1985, (with Helmut Loiskandl and Deena Weinstein) Georg Simmel's Scopenhauer and Nietzsche, 1986; (with Deena Weinstein) Deconstruction as Cultural History/The Cultural History of Deconstruction, 1990, La Déconstruction un Jeu Symbolique, 1990, (with Deena Weinstein) Georg Simmel: Sociological Flâmeur/Bricoleur, 1991, Photographic Realism as a Moral Practice, 1992, (with Deena Weinstein) Postmodern(ized) Simmel, 1993, (with Arthur Kroker) Data Trash: The Theory of the Virtual Class, 1994, Culture/Flesh: Explorations of Postcivilized Modernity, 1995; mem. editorial bd. Humanitas, Social Philosophy Rsch. Book Series. Recipient Best Paper prize Midwest Polit. Sci. Assn., 1969; Guggenheim fellow, 1974-75; Rockefeller Found. humanities fellow, 1976; fellow Center Humanistic Studies, Purdue U., 1981. Mem. Phi Beta Kappa. Home: 800 Princess Dr West Lafayette IN 47906-2038 Office: Dept Polit Sci Purdue U West Lafayette IN 47907 *And which is worse, to be arbitrary or to be contradictory? I have attempted to be the most consistent rationalist of all by refusing to harmonize what is irreconcilable in the name of reason.*

WEINSTEIN, MILTON CHARLES, health policy educator; b. Brookline, Mass., July 14, 1949; s. William and Ethel (Rosenbloom) W.; m. Rhonda Kruger, June 14, 1970; children: Jeffrey William, Daniel Jay. AB, AM, Harvard U., 1970, MPP, 1972, PhD, 1973. Asst. prof. John F. Kennedy Sch. Govt., Harvard U., Cambridge, Mass., 1973-76, assoc. prof., 1976-80; prof. policy and decision scis. Harvard Sch. Pub. Health, Boston, 1980-86, Henry J. Kaiser prof. health policy and mgmt., 1986—; adj. prof. community and family medicine Dartmouth Med. Sch., Hanover, N.H., 1981-87; cons. U.S. office Tech. Assessment, 1979-87, HHS, 1979—, VA, 1984-86, EPA, 1983—, Smith Kline and French, 1984-87, Ciba-Geigy, 1987—, New Eng. Med. Ctr., 1986-87, Intermountain Health Care, 1987—, Bristol Myers-Squibb, 1989-92, E.I. DuPont de Nemours Co., 1989-91, Schering-Plough Corp., 1991—, Marion Merrell Dow, Inc., 1992—, Upjohn Corp., 1993—; mem. adult treatment panel Nat. Cholesterol Edn. Program, NIH; co-chair Cost-Effectiveness Panel on Clin. Prevention Svcs, USPHS, 1993—. Author: Clinical Decision Analysis, 1980, Hypertension: A Policy Perspective, 1976; mem. editl. bd. Med. Decision Making, 1981—, Jour. Environ. Econs. and Mgmt., 1986-88; assoc. editor Med. Decision Making, 1994—. NSF fellow, 1972. Mem. Inst. Ops. Rsch. Mgmt. Scis., Inst. Medicine of NAS (com. on priorities for new vaccine devel., com. to evaluate the NIH artificial heart program), Soc. Med. Decision Making (trustee 1980-82, pres. 1984-85), Internat. Health Econs. Assn., Soc. Risk Analysis, Internat. Soc. Tech. Assessment in Health Care,

Am. Med. Joggers Assn., Phi Beta Kappa. Office: Harvard U Sch Pub Health Dept Health Policy & Mgmt Boston MA 02115

WEINSTEIN, NORMAN JACOB, chemical engineer, consultant; b. Rochester, N.Y., Dec. 31, 1929; s. Sol. and Anne (Trapunsky) W.; m. Ann Francine Keiles, June 30, 1957; children: Maury S., Aaron S., Kenneth B. BChemE, Syracuse U., 1951, MChemE, 1953; PhD, Oreg. State Coll., 1956. Registered profl. engr.; diplomate Am. Acad. Environ. Engrs. Chem. engr. ESSO Rsch. Engring. Co., Linden, N.J., 1956-60; sr. engr. ESSO Rsch. Engring. Co., Baton Rouge, 1960-65; engring. assoc. ESSO Rsch. Engring. Co., Florham Park, N.J., 1965-66; asst. dir. engring. and devel. Princeton Chem. Rsch. Inc., 1966-67, dir. engring. and devel., 1967-69; pres. Recon Environ. Corp., Raritan, N.J., 1969—. Author: Thermal Processing of Municipal Solid Waste for Resource and Energy Recovery, 1976; contbr. numerous articles to profl. jours. Fellow AIChE (chmn. air sect., environ. divsn.); mem. ASTM, Am. Chem. Soc., Assn. Cons. Chemists and Chem. Engrs., N.Y. Acad. Scis. Democrat. Achievements include 8 patents in chemical processing; expert in waste oil technology. Home: 1005 Canal Rd Princeton NJ 08540-8629 Office: Recon Environ Corp 5 Johnson Dr Raritan NJ 08869-0130

WEINSTEIN, PETER M., lawyer, state senator; b. N.Y.C., Feb. 3, 1947; s. Moses and Muriel W.; m. Barbara Ann Forman; children: Andrew, Michael. BS, NYU; JD, Bklyn. Law Sch. Bar: N.Y., Fla. Asst. dist. atty. Queens County, N.Y.; asst. state's atty., Broward County, Fla.; pvt. practice, Ft. Lauderdale, Fla.; mem. Fla. State Senate, Tallahassee, 1982—, chmn. Broward County legis. del., 1985-86. Mem. Broward County Charter Rev. Commn.; mem. Coral Springs Planning and Zoning Bd. Capt. U.S. Army. Recipient Allen Morris award Fla. Senate; named Most Effective Freshman, Fla. Senate. Mem. Jewish War Vets., Coral Springs Dem. (pres. 1980-82). Avocation: photography. Office: 7880 N University Dr Ste 301 Fort Lauderdale FL 33321-2124

WEINSTEIN, RHONDA KRUGER, elementary mathematics educator, administrator; b. Boston, May 18, 1948; d. David Solomon and Henrietta Reina (Slocum) Kruger; m. Milton Charles Weinstein, June 14, 1970; children: Jeffrey William, Daniel Jay. AB, Mt. Holyoke Coll., 1970; MA, Suffolk U., 1973. Cert. supr./dir.; math. 7-12; elem. K-8; elem. prin.; supt., Mass. Tchr. grade 3 Brookline (Mass.) Pub. Schs., 1974-78, math. resource tchr. K-6, 1980-81, math. resource tchr. K-8, 1981-82, elem. curriculum coord. for math., 1982—; program evaluator Newton (Mass.) Pub. Schs., 1992-93; part-time instr. Suffolk U., Boston, 1976, 79; mem. math. adv. bd. Ency. Britannica, Chgo., 1993-95; cons. Mass. sch. sys. including Northborough/Southborough, 1978-88, Sudbury, 1987, North Andover, 1993; speaker profl. meetings Assn. Tchrs. Math. in New Eng., 1990, 94, 95, ASCD, Boston, 1988. Co-author: Calculator Activities, 1987; reviewer 2 books Arithmetic Teacher, 1991. Alumnae fund vol. Mt. Holyoke Coll., South Hadley, Mass., 1985-90; vol. Am. Heart Assn., Brookline, 1982-93; mem. PTO, Baker Sch., Brookline, 1983-95. Sarah Williston scholar Mt. Holyoke Coll., 1967; grantee Brookline Found., 1994, Tchrs. and Adminstrs. Tng. Fund, 1992, 96. Mem. Nat. Coun. Tchrs. Math. (nat. conv. com. chair 1995, speaker profl. meeting 1993), Nat. Coun. Suprs. of Math., Assn. Tchrs. of Math. in Mass., Boston Area Math. Specialists, Phi Beta Kappa. Avocations: cross-country skiing, gourmet cooking, walking, swimming, playing piano. Home: 50 Princeton Rd Chestnut Hill MA 02167-3061 Office: Brookline Pub Schs 88 Harvard St Brookline MA 02146-6899

WEINSTEIN, ROBERT, film company executive. Co-chmn. Miramax Films Corp., L.A. Office: Miramax Films Corp 375 Greenwich St New York NY 10013-2338*

WEINSTEIN, ROY, physics educator, researcher; b. N.Y.C., Apr. 21, 1927; s. Harry and Lillian (Ehrenberg) W.; m. Janet E. Spiller, Mar. 26, 1954; children: Lee Davis, Sara Lynn. B.S., MIT, 1951, Ph.D., 1954; Sc.D. (hon.), Lycoming Coll., 1981. Research asst. Mass. Inst. Tech., 1951-54, asst. prof., 1956-59; asst. prof. Brandeis U., Waltham, Mass., 1954-56; assoc. prof. Northeastern U., Boston, 1960-63, prof. physics, 1963-82, exec. officer, chmn. grad. div. of physics dept., 1967-69, chmn. physics dept., 1974-81; spokesman MAC Detector Stanford U., 1981-82; dean Coll. Natural Scis. and Math. U. Houston, 1982-88; prof. physics, 1982—; dir. Inst. Beam Particle Dynamics U. Houston, 1985—; assoc. dir., spokesman Tex. Ctr. for Superconductivity, 1987-89; vis. scholar and physicist Stanford (Calif.) U., 1966-67, 81-82; bd. dirs. Perception Tech., Inc., Winchester, Mass., Omniwave Inc., Gloucester, Mass., Wincom Inc., Woburn, Mass.; cons. Visidyne Inc., Burlington, Mass., Houston Area Rsch. Ctr., Stanford U., Hodotector Inc., Houston Park Square Engring., Marietta, Ga., Harvard U., Cambridge, Mass., Cambridge Electron Accelerator, mem. adv. com., 1967-69; mem. adv. com. and portfolio evaluation com. Houston Venture Ptnrs., 1990—; chmn. bd. dirs. Xytron Corp., 1986-91; dir., mem. exec. com. Houston Area Rsch. Ctr., 1984-87; 3d ann. faculty lectr. Northeastern U., 1966; chmn. organizing com. 4th ann. Internat. Conf. on Meson Spectroscopy, 1974, chmn. program com. 5th ann., 1977, mem. organizing com. 6th ann.,, 1980, 83; chmn. mgmt. group Tex. Accelerator Ctr., Woodlands, 1985-90; chmn. Tex. High Energy Physicists, 1989-91; keynote spkr. MIT Alumni series, 1988; permanent mem. exec. com. Large Vol. Detector (Underground Neutrino Telescope, Italy); organizer session High Temperature Superconducting Magnets 3d and 4th World Congress on Superconductivity, Munich, 1993, Orlando, 1994. Author: Atomic Physics, 1964, Nuclear Physics, 1964, Interactions of Radiation and Matter, 1964; editor: Nuclear Reactor Theory, 1964, Nuclear Materials, 1964; editor procs.: 5th Internat. Conf. on Mesons, 1977; contbr. numerous articles to profl. jours. Mem. Lexington (Mass.) Town Meeting, 1973-76, 77-84; vice chmn. Lexington Coun. on Aging, 1977-83. With USNR, 1945-46. Recipient Founders award World Congress Superconductivity, 1988, Materials/Devices award Internat. Superconductivity Technology Ctr. and Materials Rsch. Soc., 1995, Tex. Rsch. awards, 1986-87, 90—, U.S. Dept. Energy award 1974, 77, 87—, NASA award, 1990—, ARO award, 1994—, Elec. Power Rsch. Inst. award, 1990-95, Founders award World Congress on Superconductivity, 1988; NSF fellow Bohr Inst., Copenhagen, 1959-60, Stanford U. 1969-70, Guggenheim fellow Harvard U., 1970-71; NSF grantee, 1961—. Fellow Am. Phys. Soc. (organizer session SSC and High Energy Physics 1984); mem. Am. Assn. Physics Tchrs., Masons, Sigma Xi, Phi Kappa Phi (chpt. pres. 1977-79, Nat. Triennial Disting. Scholar prize 1980-83, keynote spkr. MIT Alumni series 1988), Pi Lambda Phi. Unitarian. Achievements include measurement of fine structure of positronium; first measurement of rho meson coupling to gamma rays, of phi meson decay to two muons; early observation of break down in SU3 symmetry; demonstration of electron-muon universality, discovery of non-applicability of Lorentz contraction to length measured by a single observer; disproof of splitting of A2 meson; independent discovery of upsilon meson (bottom quark); achievement of highest magnetic field for any permanent magnet, in $YBa_2Cu_3O_7$, 10.1 Tesla. Home: 4368 Fiesta Ln Houston TX 77004-6603 Office: U Houston IBPD Rm 632 SR1 Houston TX 77204

WEINSTEIN, RUTH JOSEPH, lawyer; b. N.Y.C., Mar. 26, 1933; d. David Arthur and Toby (Landau) Joseph; m. Marvin Walter Weinstein, June 3, 1962; children: Rosalyn S., Steven M., Barbara E. AB magna cum laude, Radcliffe Coll., 1954; LLB, Harvard U., 1957. Bar: N.Y. 1957, D.C. 1966. Assoc. Hale Russell & Gray and predecessor firms, N.Y.C., 1957-66, ptnr., 1966-85; ptnr. Winthrop Stimson Putnam & Roberts, N.Y.C., 1985—; chairperson Practising Law Inst. Forum, N.Y.C., 1978. Mem. sch. bd. Union Free Sch. Dist. 5, Rye Town, N.Y., 1976-79, pres., 1978-79. Mem. ABA, Assn. of Bar of City of N.Y. (com. on Aeronautics Assn. 1987-90), Harvard-Radcliffe Club of Westchester, The Wings Club Inc. Avocations: boating, skiing. Home: 21 Meadowlark Rd Rye Brook NY 10573-1209 Office: Winthrop Stimson 1 Battery Park Plz New York NY 10004-1403

WEINSTEIN, SIDNEY, university program director; b. N.Y.C., July 1, 1920; s. Jacob and Yetta W.; m. Celia Kahn, Mar. 6, 1943 (dec.); children: Risa, Jeri; m. Florence Landau, June 21, 1988. B.A., Bklyn. Coll., 1951; M.A., Columbia U., 1955; DPA, Indsl. Coll. Armed Forces, 1964. Contract adminstr. U.S. Corps Engrs., 1941-43; mgmt. analyst Dept. Army, N.Y.C., 1946-55; dir. data processing procurement GSA, 1956-68; dep. asst. commr. automated data mgmt. services GSA, Washington, 1968-72; asst. commr. automated data and telecommunications GSA, 1972-75; exec. dir. Assn. Computing Machinery, N.Y.C., 1975-85; assoc. prof., dir. affiliates program Ctr. Research Info. Systems, Leonard N. Stern. Sch. Bus. NYU, 1985—; cons. to chmn. U.S. CSC. Served with USAF, 1943-46. Recipient Exceptional service award U.S. Govt., 1975. Mem. ABA (arbitrator 1989—), Coun. Engring. and Sci. Soc. Execs. (dir.), N.Y. Soc. Assn. Execs., Assn. Indsl. Coll. Armed Forces, Assn. Fed. Execs. Inst., Assn. Computing Machinery, Soc. Info. Mgmt. Home: 360 E 72nd St New York NY 10021-4753 Office: 44 W 4th St New York NY 10012-1126

WEINSTEIN, STANLEY, Buddhist studies educator; b. Bklyn., Nov. 13, 1929; s. Louis Arthur and Ruth (Appleson) W.; m. Lucie Ruth Krebs, Sept. 23, 1951; 1 son, David Eli. BA, Komazawa U., Tokyo, 1954-58; MA, U. Tokyo, 1960; PhD, Harvard U., 1966; MAH (hon.), Yale U., 1974. Lectr. Sch. Oriental and African Studies, London, 1962-68; assoc. prof. Buddhist studies Yale U., New Haven, 1968-74, prof., 1974—, chmn. council East Asian studies, 1982-85. Author: Buddhism under T'ang, 1987. Served with U.S. Army, 1952-54. Ford Found. fgn. area fellow, 1958-62; NEH sr. fellow, 1974-75. Mem. Am. Oriental Soc., Assn. Asian Studies. Home: 270 Ridgewood Ave Hamden CT 06517-1426 Office: Yale U Hall Grad Studies New Haven CT 06520

WEINSTEIN, STEPHEN BRANT, communications executive, researcher, writer; b. N.Y.C., Nov. 25, 1938; s. Max S. and Evelyn A. (Brandt) W.; m. Judith Louise Benham, June 10, 1961; children: Brant M., Anna M. SB, MIT, 1960; MS, U. Mich., 1962; PhD, U. Calif. at Berkeley, 1966. Mem. tech. staff Philips Rsch. Labs., Eindhoven, The Netherlands, 1967-68, Bell Labs., Holmdel, N.J., 1968-79; v.p. tech. strategy Am. Express Co., N.Y.C., 1979-84; exec. dir. subscriber systems rsch. Bellcore (formerly, Bell Communications Rsch.), Morristown, N.J., 1984-93; fellow C&C Rsch. Lab. NEC USA, Inc., 1994—. Author: Getting the Picture: A Guide to CATV and the New Electronic Media, 1986; co-author: Data Communication Principles, 1992; contbr. articles to profl. jours.; patentee in field. Fellow IEEE (editor-in-chief Comms. mag. 1984-89, chmn. press 1979-82, Centennial medal 1984), IEEE Comms. Soc. (pres. 1996-97, v.p. tech. affairs 1994-95, dir. publs. 1990-93). Avocations: skiing, woodworking, video editing. Home: 150 Woodland Ave Summit NJ 07901-2029 Office: NEC USA Inc C & C Res Lab 4 Independence Way Princeton NJ 08540-6634

WEINSTEIN, STEVEN DAVID, lawyer; b. Phila., May 3, 1946; s. Leon and Elizabeth (Evantash) W.; m. Karin Elkis, Feb. 16, 1986. BA, Rutgers U., 1968, JD, 1975. Bar: N.J. 1975, Pa. 1975, U.S. Dist. Ct. N.J. 1975, U.S. Dist. Ct. (ea. dist.) Pa. 1975, U.S. Supreme Ct. 1979, U.S. Ct. Appeals (3d cir.) 1981, U.S. Ct. Claims 1986. Assoc. Lewis Katz P.C., Cherry Hill, N.J., 1975-78; pvt. practice law Collingswood, N.J., 1978-84; ptnr. Blank, Rome, Comisky & McCauley, Cherry Hill, 1984—; atty. Camden (N.J.) County Counsel, 1982-84; v.p. N.J. County Counsels Assn. 1983. Trustee Camden County Coll., Blackwood, N.J., 1983, West Jersey Hosps. Found., Camden, 1984-96, chmn. 1989-91; trustee Rowan Coll., N.J., 1990—, chmn. 1992-94, trustee devel. fund. bd., 1989-90; mem. N.J. Bus.-Higher Edn. Forum. Mem. ABA, N.J. Bar Assn., Camden County Bar Assn. Democrat. Jewish. Office: Blank Rome Comisky & McCauley Woodland Falls Corporate Park 210 Lake Dr E Ste 200 Cherry Hill NJ 08002-1163

WEINSTEIN, WILLIAM JOSEPH, lawyer; b. Detroit, Dec. 9, 1917; s. Joseph and Bessie (Abromovitch) W.; m. Evelyn Ross, Apr. 5, 1942 (dec.); children: Patricia, Michael; m. 2d, Rose Sokolsky, Oct. 25, 1972. LL.B., Wayne State U., 1940. Bar: Mich. 1940, U.S. Dist. Ct. (ea. and so. dists.) Mich. 1940, U.S. Ct. Appeals (6th cir.) 1951, U.S. Ct. Appeals (9th cir.) 1972. Ptnr. Charfoos, Gussin & Weinstein, Southfield, Mich., 1951-54, Charfoos, Gussin, Weinstein & Kroll, Detroit, 1955-59, Gussin, Weinstein & Kroll, Detroit, 1959-65, Weinstein & Kroll, P.C., Detroit, 1965-73, Weinstein, Kroll & Gordon, P.C., Detroit, 1973-85; pvt. practice, Southfield, 1985—; apptd. to standard jury instrn. com. Mich. Supreme Ct. 1965-72. Maj. gen. USMCR, 1941-75. Decorated Bronze Star with Combat V, Legion of Merit (2), Purple Heart (2). Recipient Disting. Alumnus award Wayne State U., 1973. Mem. Mich. Bar Assn. (chmn. negligence sect. 1962-63), Am. Coll. Trial Lawyers, Internat. Acad. Trial Lawyers, USN League (nat. v.p. 1971-72), Tam-o-Shanter Club (Orchard Lake, Mich.), St. Andrews Country Club (Boca Raton, Fla.). Contbr. articles to legal jours. Home and Office: 3922 Wabeek Lake Dr E Bloomfield Hills MI 48302-1261

WEINSTEIN-BACAL, STUART ALLEN, lawyer, educator; b. Stuttgart, Germany, May 23, 1948; s. Marvin Stuart and Mae (Beal) W.; m. Holly Laurette Thompson, Aug. 7, 1982; children: Rachel Lee, Maximillian II, Sarah Nicole. BA, U. Va., 1970, MEd, 1973; JD cum laude, U. Miami, 1979. Bar: D.C. 1979, Va. 1981, V.I. 1985, P.R. 1988. Tchr., pvt. tutor various schs., Conn., Fla., Costa Rica, 1973-76; mem. prof. staff Merchant Marine and Fisheries Com. U.S. Ho. of Reps., Washington, 1977; assoc. Cameron, Hornbostel & Adelman, Washington, 1979-80, Burch, Kerns & Klimek, P.C., Washington, 1980, 81; staff atty. C.A.C.I., Washington, 1982, 83; sr. assoc. Dudley, Dudley & Topper, St. Thomas, U.S. Virgin Islands, 1984, 85; v.p. , gen. counsel Redondo Construction Corp., San Juan, P.R., 1985-89; pvt. practice law San Juan, 1989—; sr. ptnr. Indiano, Williams & Weinstein-Bacal; early neutral evaluator U.S. Dist. Ct. P.R.; dir. Caribbean Medi Bank. Contbr. articles to profl. jours. Mem. Commn. Pro Sede Olimpiades 2004, San Juan, 1988—; bd. dirs. Bucaplaa Libr. Capt. USAR, 1970-85. Mem. ABA, Am. Arbitration Assn. (pres., adv. coun. 1988—, arbitrator 1989—), Res. Officers Assn., Colegio de Abogados de P.R., U. Va. Alumni Assn., Nature Conservancy, Sovereign Order of the Oak (knight comdr.), Rotary, Club of San Juan (bd. dirs. 1991—), Phi Alpha Delta. Avocations: scuba diving, golf, tennis, gourmet cooking, traveling. Home: 11 Vanda St Los Filtros Guaynabo PR 00969 also: 2810 Farm Rd Alexandria VA 22302-2404 Office: Hato Rey Tower 21st Fl 268 Muñoz Rivera Ave San Juan PR 00918

WEINSTOCK, HAROLD, lawyer; b. Stamford, Conn., Nov. 30, 1925; s. Elias and Sarah (Singer) W.; m. Barbara Lans, Aug. 27, 1950; children—Nathaniel, Michael, Philip. B.S. magna cum laude, N.Y. U., 1947; J.D., Harvard, 1950. Bar: Conn. bar 1950, Ill. bar 1950, Calif. bar 1958. Atty. SEC, Washington, 1950-52, IRS, 1952-56; tax atty. Hunt Foods & Industries, Inc., Los Angeles, 1956-58; pvt. practice Beverly Hills, Calif., 1958-71, Los Angeles, 1971—; mem. Weinstock, Manion, Reisman, Shore & Neumann (and predecessor firms), 1958—; Lectr. extension div., estate planning courses U. Calif. at Los Angeles, 1959—; estate planning and taxation courses Calif. Continuing Edn. of the Bar, 1960—. Author: Planning An Estate, 4th edit., 1995; contbr. articles to profl. publs. Nat. trustee Union Am. Hebrew Congregations, 1976-79; bd. trustees Jewish Cmty. Found., L.A.; adv. bd. Estate Planning Inst. UCLE Law Sch., 1979-92, NYU Inst. on Fed. Taxation, 1986-95. Mem. ABA, Calif. Bar Assn., Beverly Hills Bar Assn. (chmn. probate and trusts com. 1967-68), Los Angeles Bar Assn., Beverly Hills Estate Planning Council (pres. 1968-69), Estate Counselors Forum of Los Angeles (pres. 1963-64). Jewish (pres. temple 1974-76). Office: Weinstock Manion 1888 Century Park E Los Angeles CA 90067-1702

WEINSTOCK, HERBERT FRANK, public relations executive; b. Los Angeles, July 26, 1913; s. Frank and Sarah (Mantel) W.; m. Evelyn June Hanson, July 27, 1940; children—Allan Herbert, William Jay, Joan Louise. A.A., Los Angeles City Coll., 1933. Financial editor Los Angeles Daily News, 1939-54; pub. relations assoc. H. F. Weinstock & Assocs., 1955-61, 80-91; public relations dir. Burton, Booth & Weinstock, Inc., 1961-63; with Eisamen, Johns & Laws (advt.), Los Angeles, 1964; v.p. charge corporate and financial pub. relations Kennett Pub. Relations Assos., 1966-71; pres. Conway/Weinstock/ Assos., Inc., 1971-80. Pres. Intercommunity Care Centers, Inc., Long Beach, Calif. Served with AUS, 1943-45; with 3d Army 1944-45. Home: 533 21st St Manhattan Beach CA 90266-2201

WEINSTOCK, JOEL VINCENT, immunologist; b. Detroit, Mar. 21, 1948; s. Herman and Esther B. (Frazein) W.; m. Allison Lee Rose, July 15, 1979; children: Lisa, Jeffrey, Andrew. BS, U. Mich., 1969; MD, Wayne State U., 1973. Diplomate Am. Bd. Internal Medicine, subspeciality gastroenterology; lic. physician, Mich., Iowa. Straight med. intern Univ. Hosp., Ann Arbor, Mich., 1973-74, resident internal medicine, 1974-76, fellow gastroenterology dept. internal medicine, 1976-78; asst. prof. internal medicine Wayne State U. Sch. Medicine, Detroit, 1978-83, assoc. prof., 1983-86, adj. assoc. prof. dept. immunology and microbiology, 1983-86, vice chief divsn. gastroenterology, 1984-86; assoc. prof., dir. gastroenterology divsn. U. Iowa, Iowa City, 1986-91, prof., dir., 1991—, dir. Ctr. Digestive Diseases, 1990—, dir. divsn. gastroenterology-hepatology, 1986—, dir. Ctr. Digestive Diseases, 1990—; mem. exec. bd. Crohn's and Colitis Found. Am., N.Y.C., 1993—, mem. tng. awards rev. com., 1991-93, chmn., 1993—; chief sect. gastroenterology Hutzel Hosp., Detroit, 1978-84, dir. endoscopy unit, 1978-84, dir. nutritional support svc., 1980-84; vice chief gastroenterology dept. medicine Wayne State U. Sch. Medicine, 1984-86; dir. gastroenterology subspecialty unit Harper Hosp., Detroit, 1984-86, vice-chief gastroenterology, 1984-86; mem. sci. adv. ang grant rev. com. Crohn's and Colitis Found. Am., 1987—; mem. NIH Task force for developing nat. agenda for IBD rsch., 1989; mem. Lederle award selection com., 1989; mem. study sect. NIH Core Ctr. Rev. Com., 1990, 92; mem. abstract rev. com. ASCI, 1990; vis. prof. Washington U., St. Louis, 1990, U. Tex., Houston, 1991, Cleve. Clinic, 1992, U. Md., Balt., 1993; participant various conferences and meetings; mem. Digestive Diseases Ctr. Planning Com., 19886—; mem. Adult TPN Subcom., 1986—; chmn. coord. com. Ctr. Digestive Diseases, 1986—; mem. grant rev. coms. NIH, 1980—; mem. gastroenterology subspecialty coun. CSCR, 1993—. Mem. editl. bd. Autoimmunity Forum: Gastroenterology Edit., 1989-92; mem. internat. adv. bd. Alimentary Pharmacology and Therapeutics, 1990—; sect. editor Jour. Inflammatory Bowel Disease, 1994; reviewer Am. Jour Gastroenterology, Jour. Clin. Investigation, Jour. Immunology, Jour. Clin. Immunology, Gastroenterology, Digestive Diseases and Scis.; contbr. articles to profl. jours., chpts. to books. Rsch. grantee NIH, 1982—, Sandoz Pharm., 1993, Marion Merrell Dow, 1994, Centocor, 1995. Mem. AAAS, Am. Inst. Nutrition, Am. Soc. Clin. Nutrition, Ctrl. Soc. Clin. Rsch., Am. Soc. Gastrointestinal Endoscopy, Am. Assn. Study Liver Disease, Am. Fedn. Clin. Rsch., Am. Assn. Immunologists, Ileitis and Colitis Found. Am., Am. Soc. Clin. Investigation, Clin. Immunology Soc., Am. Gastroenterological Assn. (rsch. com. 1987-90, chmn. task force rsch. fellowship awards 1989-90, program evaluation com. 1990—), Midwest Gut Club (councillor 1990—), Alpha Omega Alpha. Achievements include research in elucidaiton of immunoregulatory circuits that control granulomatous inflammation; characterization of how neurokines help control inflammatory responses; avocations: stamp collecting, reading, gardening, exercising, child rearing. Office: U Iowa Internal Medicine 4607JCP UIHC Iowa City IA 52242

WEINSTOCK, LEONARD, lawyer; b. Bklyn., Aug. 18, 1935; s. Samuel Morris and Evelyn (Reiser) W.; m. Rita Lee Itkowitz, May 25, 1963; children—Gregg Douglas, Valerie Lisa, Tara Diane. B.S., Bklyn. Coll., 1956; J.D., St. John's U., Bklyn., 1959. Bar: N.Y. 1961, U.S. Supreme Ct. 1964, U.S. Ct. Appeals (2d cir.) 1963, U.S. Dist. Ct. (ea. and so. dists.) N.Y. 1963, U.S. Tax Ct. 1963. Assoc. Bernard Helfenstein law practice, Bklyn., 1962-63; supr. All State Ins. Co., Bklyn., 1963-64; atty. Hertz Corp., N.Y.C., 1964-65; ptnr. Nicholas & Weinstock, Flushing, N.Y., 1965-68; v.p., ptnr. Garbarini & Scher, P.C., N.Y.C., 1968—; lectr. Practicing Law Inst., N.Y.C., 1975—; arbitrator Nassau County Dist. Ct., Mineola, N.Y., 1979—, U.S. Dist. Ct. (ea. dist.) N.Y. 1986—; mem. Med. Malpractice Mediation Panel, Mineola, 1978—. Legal counsel Massapequa Soccer Club (N.Y.), 1981—; county committeeman Democratic Party, Massapequa Park, N.Y., 1979—. Served with U.S. Army, 1959-62. Mem. ABA, N.Y. State Bar Assn., Nassau County Bar Assn. (mem. med. jurisprudence ins. com. 1978), N.Y. Trial Lawyers Assn., Queens County Bar Assn. (mem. legal referral com. 1969). Avocations: stamp collecting, softball, racquetball. Home: 38 Barstow Rd Great Neck NY 11021-2218 Office: Garbarini and Scher PC Ste 1111 1114 Avenue Of The Americas Fl 35 New York NY 10036-7703

WEINSTOCK, WALTER WOLFE, systems engineer; b. Phila., Aug. 18, 1925; s. Abraham and Jeanne (Feldman) W.; m. Doris Alpert, Sept. 21, 1946; children—Steven Eric, Bruce Alan. B.S.E.E., U.Pa., 1946, M.S.E.E., 1954, Ph.D., 1964. Design engr. Philco, 1946-49; with RCA Corp., 1949-87; prin. scientist RCA Corp. (Missile and Surface Radar div.), Moorestown, N.J., 1979-87; cons., 1987—; mem. planning and steering adv. group Surface Ship Security Panel, Dept. Navy, 1979-82. Contbg. author: Modern Radar, 1965, Practical Phased Array Antenna Systems, 1991; contbr. articles to profl. jours. Recipient David Sarnoff award for Outstanding Achievement in Engring. RCA, 1972. Fellow IEEE; mem. Tau Beta Pi, Eta Kappa Nu, Sigma Tau, Pi Mu Epsilon. Patentee in field. Home: 6 Beryl Rd Cheltenham PA 19012-1206

WEINTRAUB, ALLEN, diversified financial services executive. With Putnam, Coftin & Burr, Hartford, Conn., 1955-77; chmn. bd., CEO. pres. Advest Group Inc., Hartford, Conn., 1977—. Office: Advest Inc 90 State House Hartford CT 06103*

WEINTRAUB, DANIEL RALPH, social welfare administrator; b. N.Y.C., Apr. 23, 1939; s. Benjamin Zion and Ida (Barman) W.; BA in Biology, NYU, 1959; DDS, Columbia U., 1963; certificate pub. health U. Wash., 1963; m. Sally Ann Franco, Mar. 16, 1968; children—David Arlo, Jeremy Michael. Rural community devel. adviser AID, Dominican Republic, 1966-68, population and pub. health adviser, 1968-69; asso. planning dir. Alan Guttmacher Inst. (formerly Center for Family Planning Program Devel.), N.Y.C., 1969-74; dep. dir. Family Planning Internat. Assistance, N.Y.C., 1974-76, COO, 1977—; v.p. internat. programs Planned Parenthood Fedn. Am., N.Y.C., 1978—, mem. speaker's bur., 1982—; vol. leader, coordinator U.S. Peace Corps, Bolivia, 1964-65; cons. HEW, 1971-74, Nat. Center Health Statistics, 1974. Recipient Certificate of Honor, Dominican Republic, 1969; commendation Dept. Interior, Cochabamba, Bolivia, 1965. Mem. ACLU, Nat. Geog. Soc., Nature Conservancy, Choice in Dying. Author books and manuals on community devel. theory and practice, plans for area-wide family planning programs in met. areas, family planning tech. assistance in developing nations, nat. studies including Need for Subsidized Family Planning Services: United States, Each State and County, 1971. Home: 8 Dock Ln Port Washington NY 11050-1732 Office: FPIA 810 7th Ave New York NY 10019-5818

WEINTRAUB, JERRY, motion picture producer, executive; b. Sept. 26, 1937; m. Jane Morgan. Prodr.: (films) including Nashville, 1975, Oh God!, 1977, Cruising, 1980, All Night Long, 1981, Diner, 1982, The Karate Kid, 1984, The Karate Kid, Part II, The Karate Kid, Part III, 1989, Pure Country, 1992, The Next Karate Kid, 1994, The Specialist, 1994; appeared in (film) The Firm, 1993. Office: Weintraub Prodns 4000 Warner Blvd # 1 Burbank CA 91522-0001

WEINTRAUB, JOSEPH BARTON, publishing executive; b. Phila., Dec. 2, 1945; s. George and Edith (Lubner) W.; m. Denise Waters, June 14, 1974. BA, U. Pitts., 1966; MA, U. Chgo., 1967, PhD, 1973. Assoc. faculty U. Ind., Gary, Ind., 1970-74; mktg. specialist journalism div. U. Chgo. Press, 1974-75, sr. copywriter journalism div., 1975-78; periodical specialist ABA Press, Chgo., 1978-80, mktg. mgr., 1980-92, dir. publ. planning, 1992—; mktg. cons. Teachers Coll. Record, N.Y.C., 1977-79, Repertoire Internat. de la Litterature de l'Art, N.Y.C., 1977-79, Am. Lung Assn., 1980-82. Contbr. essays, translations, plays, poems, short fiction to lit. revs. and small press anthologies. Recipient award Ill. Art Coun., Barrington Art Coun. Mem. Phi Beta Kappa. Avocations: writing, language study. Office: Am Bar Assn 750 N Lake Shore Dr Chicago IL 60611-4403

WEINTRAUB, MICHAEL IRA, neurologist; b. N.Y.C., Aug. 14, 1940; s. Abraham and Mildred Weintraub (Kuttner) W.; m. Anita Bellin, Aug. 2, 1964; children: Jeffrey Brian, Lisa Ellen. B.A., N.Y. U., 1962; M.D., State U. N.Y., Buffalo, 1966. Diplomate: Am. Bd. Psychiatry and Neurology, Am. Bd. EEG., Am. Acad. Pain Mgmt., Am. Bd. Prof. Disability Cons., Am. Soc. of Neurorehabilitation. Intern E. J. Meyer Hosp., Buffalo, 1966-67; fellow neurology State U. N.Y., Buffalo, 1967-68; fellow neurology Yale U.-New Haven Med. Center, 1968-70, chief resident, 1969-70; instr. neurology Boston U. Sch. Medicine, 1970-72; instr. Albert Einstein Sch. Medicine, Bronx, N.Y., 1972-73; asst. prof. neurology N.Y. Med. Coll., 1974-77, assoc. clin. prof., 1977-83, clin. prof. neurology, 1983—; chief pediatric neurology Westchester County Med. Center, Valhalla, N.Y., 1974-77; practice medicine specializing in neurology/pain mgmt. Briarcliff, N.Y., 1972—; attending neurologist Phelps Meml. Hosp., 1972—, chief of neurology, 1981—; sr. neurologist Putnam Community Hosp., 1981—. Contbr. articles to med. jours. Recipient Outstanding Young Men of Am. award U.S. Jr. C. of C., 1971. Fellow ACP, Am. Coll. Angiology, Am. Acad. Neurology, Am. Bd. Electroencephalography; mem. AMA, Westchester County Med. Soc. Home: Quaker Bridge Rd E Croton On Hudson NY 10520 Office: 325 S Highland Ave Briarcliff Manor NY 10510-2031

WEINTRAUB, RUSSELL JAY, lawyer, educator; b. N.Y.C., Dec. 20, 1929; s. Harry and Alice (Lieberman) W.; m. Zelda Kresshover, Sept. 6, 1953; children—Sharon Hope, Harry David, Steven Ross. BA, NYU, 1950; JD, Harvard U., 1953. Bar: N.Y. 1955, Iowa 1961, Tex. 1980. Teaching fellow Harvard U. Law Sch., 1955-57; asst. prof. law U. Iowa, 1957-61, prof., 1961-65; prof. U. Tex., 1965—, Marrs McLean prof. law, 1970-80, Bryant Smith chair, 1980-82, John B. Connally chair, 1982—; vis. prof. law U. Mich., 1965, UCLA, 1967, U. Calif., Berkeley, 1973-74, Bklyn. Law Sch., 1990, 95, Inst. Internat. Comparative Law, Paris, 1975, U. Houston, 1979-80, Inst. Internat. and Comparative Law, Oxford, Eng., 1982, 83, 86, 87, 92, Dublin, Ireland, 1991, La. State U., Aix-en-Provence, France, 1993; lectr. Hague Acad. Internat. Law, 1984; cons. in field. Author: International Litigation and Arbitration, 1994, (with Eugene Scoles) Cases and Materials on the Conflict of Laws, 1967, 2d rev. edit., 1972, supplement, 1978, Commentary on the Conflict of Laws, 1971, 3d rev. edit., 1986, supplement, 1991, (with Hamilton and Rau) Cases and Materials on Contracts, 1984, 2d rev. edit., 1992, (with Rosenberg and Hay) Cases and Materials on the Conflict of Laws, 10th rev. edit., 1996; contbr. articles to profl. jours. Trustee U. Iowa Sch. Religion, 1960-65. Served with U.S. Army, 1953-55. Recipient Disting. Prof. award U. Tex. Sch. Law, 1977, Teaching Excellence award, 1979, cert. of meritorious service Am. Bar Assn., 1977, cert. of meritorious service Tex. Bar Assn., 1978, Best Tchr. award U. Houston, 1980, Carl Fulda award scholarship in internat. law, 1993. Mem. Am. Law Inst., Am. Bar Found., Tex. Bar Found., Scribes. Jewish. Home: 7204 Sungate Dr Austin TX 78731-2141 Office: U Tex Sch Law 727 E 26th St Austin TX 78705-3224 *The only true happiness lies in useful work done to the best of your ability.*

WEINTRAUB, SIDNEY, economist, educator; b. N.Y.C., May 18, 1922; s. Reuben and Anna Weintraub; m. Gladys Katz, Aug. 11, 1946; children: Jeffrey, Marcia Weintraub Plunkett, Deborah Weintraub Chilewich. B.B.A., CCNY, 1943; B.J., M.A. in Journalism, U. Mo., 1948; M.A. in Econs., Yale U., 1958; Ph.D. in Econs, Am. U., 1966. Commd. fgn. service officer Dept. State, 1949; dep. asst. sec. of state for internat. fin. and devel. Dept. State, Washington, 1969-74; asst. adminstr. for interagy. devel. coordination AID, 1974-75, exec. dir. interagy devel. coordination com., 1974-75; ret., 1975; sr. fellow Brookings Instn., Washington, 1978-79; Dean Rusk prof. Lyndon B. Johnson Sch. Public Affairs, U. Tex., Austin, 1976—; also dir. Program for U.S.-Mex. Policy Studies Lyndon B. Johnson Sch. Public Affairs, U. Tex.; William E. Simon chair in polit. economy Ctr. Strategic and Internat. Studies, 1993—; Disting. vis. scholar Ctr. for Strategic and Internat. Studies, Washington, 1990. Author: Free Trade with Mexico, 1984, A Marriage of Convenience: Relations Between Mexico and The United States, 1990, NAFTA: What Comes Next, 1994; contbr. articles to profl. jours. Served with U.S. Army, 1943-46. Recipient Disting. Career Service award AID, 1975. Mem. Coun. on Fgn. Rels., Am. Econ. Assn., Am. Fgn. Service Assn. Club: Cosmos (Washington). Office: Lyndon B Johnson Sch Pub Affairs Drawer Y University Sta Austin TX 78712 *Once having been thrust into the Second World War, my main intellectual interest has been in foreign affairs. I had concluded, as President Kennedy did later, that domestic issues can hurt but misplaced foreign policy can kill. My drive has been to understand what motivates nations, what stimulates people within different nations, what is the U.S. national interest, and to become as expert as my talents would allow about such crucial issues as domestic security, international economic interaction, social mobility, and human development generally. This remains my ambition.*

WEINTRAUB, STANLEY, arts and humanities educator, author; b. Phila., Apr. 17, 1929; s. Ben and Ray (Segal) W.; m. Rodelle Horwitz, June 6, 1954; children: Mark, David, Erica. BS, West Chester (Pa.) State Coll., 1949; MA, Temple U., 1951; PhD, Pa. State U., 1956. Instr. Pa. State U., University Park, 1953-59; asst. prof. Pa. State U., 1959-62, asso. prof., 1962-65, prof. English, 1965-70, research prof., 1970-86, Evan Pugh prof. Arts and Humanities, 1986—; dir. Inst. for Arts and Humanistic Studies, 1970-90; Vis. prof. U. Calif. at Los Angeles, 1963, U. Hawaii, 1973, U. Malaya, 1977, Nat. U. Singapore, 1982. Author: Private Shaw and Public Shaw, 1963, The War in the Wards, 1964, Reggie, 1965, The Art of William Golding, 1965, Beardlsey, 1967, The Last Great Cause, The Intellectuals and the Spanish Civil War, 1968, Evolution of a Revolt: Early Postwar Writings of T.E. Lawrence, 1968, The Literary Criticism of Oscar Wilde, 1968, Journey to Heartbreak, 1971, Whistler: A Biography, 1974, Lawrence of Arabia: the Literary Impulse, 1975, Four Rossettis, A Victorian Biography, 1977, Aubrey Beardsley: Imp of the Perverse, 1976, The London Yankees: Portraits of American Writers and Artists in England, 1894-1914, 1979, The Unexpected Shaw. Biographical Approaches to G.B. Shaw and His Work, 1982, A Stillness Heard Round the World: The End of the Great War, 1985, Victoria. An Intimate Biography, 1987, Long Day's Journey into War: December 7, 1941, 1991, Bernard Shaw: A Guide to Research, 1992, Disraeli: A Biography, 1993, The Last Great Victory-The End of World War II, July/August 1945, 1995, Shaw's People, 1996, Victoria to Churchill, 1996; editor: An Unfinished Novel by Bernard Shaw, 1958, C.P. Snow: A Spectrum, 1963, The Yellow Book: Quintessence of the Nineties, 1964, The Savoy: Nineties Experiment, 1966, The Court Theatre, 1966, Biography and Truth, 1967, Evolution of a Revolt: Early Postwar Writings of T.E. Lawrence, 1968, The Literary Criticism of Oscar Wilde, 1968, Shaw: An Autobiography 1856-1898, 1969, Shaw: An Autobiography, The Playwright Years, 1898-1950, 1970, Bernard Shaw's Nondramatic Literary Criticism, 1972, Directions in Literary Criticism, 1973, Saint Joan Fifty Years After: 1923/24-1973/74, 1973, The Portable Bernard Shaw, 1977, (with Anne Wright) Heartbreak House. A Facsimile of the Revised Typescript, 1979, (with Richard Aldington) The Portable Oscar Wilde, 1981, Modern British Dramatists, 1900-1945, 1982, The Playwright and the Pirate. Bernard Shaw and Frank Harris: A Correspondence, 1982, British Dramatists Since World War II, 1983, Bernard Shaw, the Diaries, 1885-1897, 1986, Bernard Shaw on the London Art Scene, 1885-1950, 1989, also editor Comparative Literature Studies, 1987-92, Shaw, The Ann. of Bernard Shaw Studies, 1956-89. Pres. Jewish Community Council of Bellefonte (Pa.) State Coll., 1966-67. Served to 1st lt. AUS, 1951-53, Korea. Decorated Bronze Star medal.; Guggenheim fellow, 1968-69; recipient Disting. Humanist award Pa. Humanities Council, 1985. Mem. The Authors' Guild, PEN. Home: 840 Outer Dr State College PA 16801-8233 Office: Pa State U 202 Ihlseng Bldg University Park PA 16802-1705 *I subscribe to Bernard Shaw's declaration in the Preface to Man and Superman that "This is the true joy in life, the being used for a purpose recognized by yourself as mighty one; the being thoroughly worn out before you are thrown on the scrap heap; the being a force of Nature instead of a feverish selfish little clod of ailments and grievances complaining that the world will not devote itself to making you happy.".*

WEINTZ, CAROLINE GILES, non-profit association consultant, travel writer; b. Columbia, Tenn., Dec. 8, 1952; d. Raymond Clark Jr. and Caroline Higdon (Wagstaff) Giles; m. Walter Louis Weintz; children: Alexander Harwood, Elizabeth Pettus. AB, Princeton U., 1974; postgrad. diploma, U. London, 1976. Dir. advt. and promotion E.P. Dutton Pubs., N.Y.C., 1977-86; advt. cons. Assn. Jr. Leagues Internat., N.Y.C., 1986-91, advt. mgr., 1992-94, dir. of systems, 1994—. Author: The Discount Guide for Travelers over 55, 4th edit., 1988. Vol. researcher St. Paul's Nat. Hist. Site and Bill of Rights Mus., Westchester, N.Y., 1986—; treas. Soc. Nat. Shrine of The Bill of Rights; mem. Jr. League, Pelham, N.Y. Mem. Authors Guild, Nat. Soc. Colonial Dames, Huguenot Soc. Am., Daus. Cin., Mensa. Episcopalian. Home: 444 Wolfs Ln Pelham NY 10803-2127

WEIR, ALEXANDER, JR., utility consultant, inventor; b. Crossett, Ark., Dec. 19, 1922; s. Alexander and Mary Eloise (Field) W.; m. Florence Forschner, Dec. 28, 1946; children: Alexander III, Carol Jean, Bruce Richard. BSChemE, U. Ark., 1943; MChemE, Poly Inst. Bklyn., 1946; PhD, U. Mich., 1954; cert., U. So. Calif. Grad. Sch. Bus. Adminstrn., 1968. Chem. engr. Am. Cyanamid Co., Stamford Rsch. Labs., 1943-47; with U. Mich., 1948-58; rsch. assoc., project supr. Engring. Research Inst., U. Mich., 1948-57; lectr. chem. and metall. enging. dept. U. Mich., 1954-56, asst. prof., 1956-58; cons. Ramo-Wooldridge Corp., L.A., 1956-57; mem. tech. staff, sect. head, asst. mgr. Ramo-Wooldridge Corp., Los Angeles, 1957-60, incharge Atlas Missile Captive test program, 1956-60; tech. adv. to pres. Northrop Corp., Beverly Hills, Calif., 1960-70; prin. scientist for air quality So. Calif. Edison Co., Los Angeles, 1970-76, mgr. chem. systems research and devel., 1976-86, chief research scientist, 1986-88; utility cons. Playa Del Rey, Calif., 1988—; rep. Am. Rocket Soc. to Detroit Nuclear Council, 1954-57; chmn. session on chem. reactions Nuclear Sci. and Engring. Congress, Cleve., 1955; U.S. del. AGARD (NATO) Combustion Colloquium, Liege, Belgium, 1955; Western U.S. rep. task force on environ. research and devel. goals Electric Research Council, 1971; electric utility advisor Electric Power Research Inst., 1974-78, 84-87; industry advisor Dept. Chemistry and Biochemistry Calif. State U., Los Angeles, 1981-88. Author: Two and Three Dimensional Flow of Air through Square-Edged Sonic Orifices, 1954; (with R.B. Morrison and T.C. Anderson) Notes on Combustion, 1955, also tech. papers; inventor acid rain prevention device used in 5 states. Sea scout leader, Greenwich, Conn., 1944-48, Marina del Rey, Calif., 1965-70; bd. govs., past pres. Civic Union Playa del Rey, chmn. sch., police and fire, nominating, civil def., army liaison coms.; mem. Senate, Westchester YMCA, chmn. Dads sponsoring com., active fundraising; chmn. nominating com. Paseo del Rey Sch. PTA, 1961; mem. L.A. Mayors Cmty. Adv. Com.; asst. chmn. advancement com., merit badge dean Cantinella dist. L.A. Area coun. Boy Scouts Am. Recipient Nat. Rsch. Coun. Flue Gas Desulfurization Industrials Scale Reliability award NAS, 1975, Power Environ. Achievement award EPA, 1980, Excellence in Sulfur Dioxide Control award EPA, 1985. Mem. AICE, Am. Geophys. Union, Navy League U.S. (v.p. Palos Verdes Peninsula coun. 1961-62), N.Y. Acad. Scis., Sci. Rsch. Soc. Am., Am. Chem. Soc., U.S. Power Squadron, St. Andrew Soc. So. Calif., Clan Macnachtan Assn., Clan Buchanan Soc. Am., Betty Washington Lewis Soc. of Children of Am. Revolution (past pres.), Ark. Soc. of Children of Am. Revolution (past pres.), Santa Monica Yacht Club, Sigma Xi, Phi Kappa Phi, Phi Lambda Upsilon, Alpha Chi Sigma, Lambda Chi Alpha. Office: 8229 Billowvista Dr Playa Del Rey CA 90293-7807

WEIR, BRYCE KEITH ALEXANDER, neurosurgeon, neurology educator; b. Edinburgh, Scotland, Apr. 29, 1936; came to U.S., 1992; s. Ernest John and Marion (Stewart) W.; m. Mary Lou Lauber, Feb. 25, 1976; children: Leanora, Glyncora, Brocke. BSc, McGill U., Montreal, Que., Can., 1958, MD, CM, 1960, MSc, 1963. Diplomate Am. Bd. Neurol. Surgery, Nat. Bd. Med. Examiners. Intern Montreal Gen. Hosp., 1960-61; resident in neurosurgery Neurological Inst., Montreal, 1962-64, 65-66, N.Y. Neurol. Inst., N.Y.C., 1964-65; neurosurgeon U. Alta., Edmonton, Can., 1967-92, dir. div. neurosurgery, 1982-86, Walter Anderson prof., chmn. dept. surgery, 1986-92; surgeon-in-chief U. Alta. Hosps., 1986-92; Maurice Goldblatt prof. surgery and neurology U. Chgo., 1992—, dir. Brain Rsch. Inst., 1993—; past pres. V Internat. Symposium on Cerebral Vasospasm; mem. neurology A study sect. NIH, 1991-93; invited speaker at over 100 profl. meetings; vis. prof. over 50 univs., including Yale U., Cornell U., Columbia U., Duke U., U. Toronto, U. Calif., San Francisco; over 10 named lectureships, including White lectr. Harvard U., Gainey lectr., Mayo Clinic. Author: Aneurysms Affecting the Nervous System, 1987; mem. editl. bd. Jour. Neurosurgery, chmn. bd., 1993-94; mem. editl. bd. Neurosurgery Quar., Jour. Cereborvascular Disease; contbr. over 250 articles to med. jours. Named Officer of the Order of Can., 1995. Fellow ACS, Royal Coll. Surgeons Can., Royal Coll. Surgeons Edinburgh (hon.); mem. Am. Surg. Assn., James IV Assn. Surgeons, Am. Acad. Neurol. Surgeons, Soc. Neurol. Surgeons (Grass gold medal 1992). Achievements include contributions to the understanding of cerebral vasospasm and the surgical management of intracranial aneurysms. Office: U of Chgo Pritzker Sch of Medicine 5841 S Maryland Ave Chicago IL 60637-1463

WEIR, EDWARD KENNETH, cardiologist; b. Belfast, No. Ireland, Jan. 7, 1943; came to U.S. 1973; s. Thomas Kenneth and Violet Hilda (ffrench) W.; m. Elizabeth Vincent Pearman, May 29, 1971; children: Fergus G., Conor K. BA, U. Oxford, U.K., 1964; MA, BM, BCh, U. Oxford, 1967, DM, 1976. Diplomate Am. Bd. Internal Medicine. Sr. house physician Nuffield Dept. Medicine, Radcliffe Infirmary, Oxford, 1970-71; registrar in cardiology Groote Schuur Hosp., Cape Town, South Africa, 1971-73; postdoctoral rsch. fellow U. Colo., Denver, 1973-75; cons. pediatric cardiologist U. Cape Town Med. Sch., 1975-76; cons. cardiologist U. Natal Med. Sch., Durban, South Africa, 1976-77; assoc. prof. medicine U. Minn., Mpls., 1978-85, prof. medicine, 1985—; staff physician Va. Med. Ctr., Mpls., 1978—; dir. Grover Confs. on Pulmonary Circulation, 1984—. Co-editor: Pulmonary Hypertension, 1984, The Pulmonary Circulation in Health and Disease, 1987, Pulmonary Vascular Physiology and Pathophysiology, 1989, The Diagnosis and Treatment of Pulmonary Hypertension, 1992, Ion Flux in Pulmonary Vascular Control, 1993, The Pulmonary Circulation and Gas Exchange, 1994, Nitric Oxide and Radicals in the Pulmonary Vasculature, 1996. Fulbright scholar, 1973-75; Sr. Internat. Fogarty fellow, 1993. Fellow Am. Coll. Cardiology, Royal Coll. Physicians London; mem. Am. Heart Assn. (Minn. affiliate bd. dirs. 1989-93, Nat. Cardiopulmonary Coun. (exec. com. 1992—), Pulmonary Circulation Found. (treas. 1985—). Office: VA Med Ctr 1 Veterans Dr # 111C Minneapolis MN 55417-2300 *What you "achieve" in life is much less important than what you do for those around you. One hundred years after their death, very few people are remembered for what they achieved.*

WEIR, KENNETH WYNN, marine corps officer, experimental test pilot; b. Sherman, Tex., Oct. 20, 1930; s. Kenneth Herbert and Berye Lee (Wynn) W.; m. Nancy Corr Mosher, Oct. 10, 1953; children—Kenneth Mosher, David Wynn, William Scott. B.S., U.S. Naval Acad., 1952; M.S., U. So. Calif., 1968. Commd. 2d lt. USMC, 1952, advanced through grades to maj. gen., 1977, comdg. gen. 65th Marine Amphibian Brigade, 1978, dep. comdg. gen. Fleet Marine Force Pacific, 1981, comdg. gen. 4th Marine Air Wing, 1985; chief U-2/TR 1 Test Pilot Lockheed Skunk Works, Burbank, Calif., 1966-93; ret., 1993. Fellow Soc. Exptl. Test Pilots (pres. 1980-81). Achievements include more flight test experience above 60,000 feet altitude in high performance airplanes than anyone else in the world.

WEIR, MORTON WEBSTER, retired academic administrator, educator; b. Canton, Ill., July 18, 1934; s. James and Frances Mary (Johnson) W.; m. Cecelia Ann Rumler, June 23, 1956; children: Deborah, Kevin, Mark. AB, Knox Coll., 1955; MA, U. Tex., 1958, PhD, 1959. Rsch. assoc., asst. prof. child devel. U. Minn., Mpls., 1959; asst. prof. child devel. U. Ill., Urbana, 1960-64, assoc. prof., 1964-68, prof., 1968-93, prof. emeritus, 1993—, head dept. psychology, 1969-71, vice chancellor acad. affairs, 1971-79, v.p. acad. affairs, 1982-88, chancellor, 1988-93, chancellor emeritus, 1993—, sr. found. rep., 1993—; dir. Boys Town Center Study Youth Development, 1979-80. Contbr. numerous articles to profl. jours. Chmn. bd. trustees Knox Coll., 1995—. With AUS, 1960. NSF Predoctoral fellow, 1957-59. Fellow AAAS; mem. Soc. Rsch. in Child Devel. (chmn. bd. publs. 1971, chmn. fin. com. 1993-95), Sigma Xi, Phi Beta Kappa, Phi Kappa Phi. Office: U Ill Found Harker Hall 1305 W Green St Urbana IL 61801-2919

WEIR, PETER FRANK, lawyer; b. Stuttgart, Germany, Mar. 26, 1933; s. Robert Henry and Ruth Sophie W.; m. Jean M., Sept. 27, 1958; children: Bradford F., Elizabeth A. BA, Williams Coll., 1955; LLB, Harvard U., 1958; MBA, N.Y.U., 1967. Bar: N.Y. 1959, Ga. 1957. Assoc. Winston & Strawn (formerly Cole & Deitz), N.Y.C., 1959-66, ptnr., 1966-92, ret. ptnr., 1992; pvt. practice, 1993—. Bd. dirs. Episc. Ch. Found., 1981-93, sec., 1989-93, also treas., chmn. fin. com., 1982-89, chmn. audit com., 1982-88; mem. exec. com. N.Y. Regional Coun., 1975-81, chmn. 1979-81, mem. steering com., 1981-93; mem. adv. bd. First Am. Title Ins. Co. of N.Y., Inc., 1984-95. Bd. dirs., counsel Point O'Woods Assn., N.Y., 1976-91, v.p., 1982-91; alt. bd. dirs. Fire Island Assn., 1976-86, 92—; sec. and dir. Elderworks Found., 1982-92; dir. Episc. Evangelism Found., 1995—. Served with Air N.G., 1958-63. Mem. ABA, Internat. Bar Assn., N.Y. State Bar Assn., Assn. of Bar of City of N.Y., Church Club (trustee 1988-91), Down Town Assn. Club, Williams Club, Club at Point O'Woods (v.p., gov. 1970-79), Hillsboro Club. Republican. Home: 530 E 86th St Apt 11C New York NY 10028-7535 Office: c/o Winston & Strawn 200 Park Ave New York NY 10166-4193

WEIR, PETER LINDSAY, film director; b. June 21, 1944, Sydney; s. Lindsay Weir and Peggy Barnsley; m. Wendy Stites, 1966; 2 children. Ed. Scots Coll., Sydney, Vaucluse Boys High Sch., Sydney U. Worked in real estate until 1965; worked as stagehand in TV, Sydney, 1967; dir. film sequences in variety show, 1968; dir. amateur univ. revs., 1967-69; dir. for Film Australia, 1969-73; made own short films, 1969-73, ind. feature film producer, dir. and writer, 1973—. Films include: Cars that Ate Paris, 1973, Picnic at Hanging Rock, 1975, The Last Wave, 1977, The Plumber (TV), 1978, Gallipoli, 1980, The Year of Living Dangerously, 1982, Witness, 1985, The Mosquito Coast, 1986, Dead Poets Society, 1989, Green Card, 1990, Fearless, 1993. Mem. Australia A.M. Recipient various film awards. Office: CAA care John Ptak 9830 Wilshire Blvd Beverly Hills CA 90212-1804

WEIR, RICHARD DALE, elementary education educator; b. Diamond Springs, Calif., Oct. 2, 1940; s. Martin Gaines and Phyllis Lorene (Sargent) W.; m. Carol Jean Baker, Dec. 25, 1976; children:; David Richard, Barbara Anne, Susan Michelle, Roger Allen. BS in Elem. Edn., Oklahoma City U., 1976, MEd, 1988; BS in Mgmt. Info. Sys., Coleman Coll., LaMesa, Calif., 1987. Cert. tchr. K-8, Okla. Joined USCG, 1976, advanced through grades to chief warrant officer, 1982; adminstrv. officer USCG, Washington, 1976-82; platform instr. IBM Corp., Oklahoma City, 1985-86; mid. sch. tchr. Archdiocese Oklahoma City, 1987-88; adj. prof. Oklahoma City U., 1988-91; elem. tchr. Oklahoma City Pub. Schs., 1988—; cons. in tng. math.-sci. tchrs.; trainer for Activities Integrating Math./Scis. Nat. Leadership Network. Recipient Presdl. award for excellence in sci. and math. teaching NSF, Washington, 1993. Mem. ASCD, Nat. Sci. Tchrs. Assn., Nat. Coun. Tchrs. Math., Coun. Presdl. Awardees Math., Okla. Coun. Tchrs. Math. (advisor Metro Oklahoma City), Soc. Elem. Presdl. Awardees. Republican. Methodist. Avocation: golf. Home: 9109 NW 99th Pl Yukon OK 73099-8313 Office: Quail Creek Elem Sch 11700 Thorn Ridge Rd Oklahoma City OK 73120-5920

WEIR, ROBERT H., lawyer; b. Boston, Dec. 7, 1922; s. Abraham and Beatrice (Stern) W.; A.B., Harvard U., 1944, LL.B., 1948; m. Ruth Hirsch, July 2, 1954 (dec. Nov. 1965); children—Anthony, David, Michael H.; m. 2d, Sylvia T. Frias; children—Nicole F., Daniella F. Admitted to Mass. bar, 1948, Wash. bar, 1952, Calif. bar, 1957; spl. asst. to atty. gen. U.S. Dept. Justice, Seattle, 1948-53, Washington, 1953-56; practiced in San Jose, also Palo Alto, Calif., 1957—. Instr. taxation of real estate U. Calif. at San Jose and San Francisco, 1957—; lectr. U. So. Calif. Tax Inst. Mem. prison com. Am. Friends Service Com. Bd. dirs. San Jose Light Opera Assn., Inc. Served with U.S. Army, 1942-45. Mem. Am., Santa Clara County bar assns., State Bar Calif., Am. Judicature Soc. Author: Advantages in Taxes, 1960. Tax columnist Rural Realtor, Chgo., 1959—. Speaker taxation annual meetings Nat. Assn. Real Estate Bds., 1958-60. Author: Taxes Working for You, 1966; How to Make the Most of Depreciation Write Off. Contbr. articles to profl. jours. Address: 27743 Via Ventana Los Altos CA 94022-3224

WEIR, STEPHEN JAMES, financial executive; b. Calgary, Alta., Can., Mar. 22, 1940; s. Jack W. and Elizabeth T. (Speirs) W.; m. Janet R Suggitt, July 1961; children: James, Jennifer. C.A., U. Man., 1962; M.B.A., U. Western Ont., Can., 1967. Accountant Winnipeg, Man., 1957-63; mgr. credit and control 3M Co. of Can., London, Ont., 1963-65; asst. credit mgr. corporate credit Bank of Montreal, 1967-72; treas. Dominion Textile Inc., Montreal, 1972-77; compt., 1977-81; v.p. internat. divsn. Dominion Textile Inc., 1981-83, v.p. consumer div., 1983-84, v.p. ops. service, 1984-85, v.p. APP/IND div., 1985-87, v.p. fin. ops., 1987-88; v.p. fin. Telemedia Inc., Montreal, 1988-90, exec. v.p., chief fin. officer, 1990—. Mem. Can. Inst. Chartered Accountants, Financial Execs. Inst.. Office: Telemedia Inc, 1411 Peel St, Montreal, PQ Canada H3A 1S5

WEIR, THOMAS CHARLES, banker; b. Sandwich, Ill., Oct. 18, 1933; s. Glendon V. and Eleanor (Hoge) W.; m. Angela Di Giovanni. Grad., Pacific Coast Banking Sch., U. Wash., 1966. Mgr. consumer loans Barnett Nat. Bank, Cocoa, Fla., 1955-58; with 1st Interstate Bank Ariz., 1958-79; head retail banking div. 1st Nat. Bank Ariz., various locations, 1974-79, exec. v.p., 1975-79; chmn., chief exec. officer Home Fed. Savs., Tucson, 1979-87; chmn. Ariz. Commerce Bank, 1987-88; pres. Tucson Resources, Inc., 1988-89; pres., chief exec. officer Tucson Electric Power Co., 1989-90; fin. cons. Tucson, 1990—; pres. WD Enterprises, Inc., 1994—, Dependable Personnel, Inc., 1994—; bd. dirs. Apollo Group, Inc.; pres. Dependable Nurses, Inc., 1994—. With AUS, 1953-55. Republican. Episcopalian. Clubs: Tucson Country, White Mountain Country.

WEIR, WILLIAM C., III, lighting manufacturing company executive; b. Orlando, Fla., Oct. 17, 1937. Grad. high sch., Orlando. Mail clk. Hughes Supply, Inc., Orlando, 1955-56; warehouse mgr., 1957-59, gen. oper. mgr., 1959-64, gen. mgr., 1964-72, v.p., gen. mgr., 1972-83, exec. v.p., 1983-90; ptnr. Accord Industries, Winter Park, Fla., 1990—; mem. nat. adv. coun. U.S. Small Bus. Adminstrn., 1986—; dir. Associated Gen. Contractors, 1970-72, Cen. Fla. Builders & Exchange, 1972-76, Associated Builders & Contractors, 1988—. Bd. dirs. Tri County Transp. Authority, 1985-90, Better Bus. Bur. Cen. Fla., 1985-90; chmn. Cen. Fla. Crime Line Program, 1986-89. Mem. Illuminating Engring. Soc. Republican. Methodist. Avocations: playing golf, fishing, photography. Office: Accord Industries 4001 Forsyth Rd Winter Park FL 32792-6814*

WEIRICH, RICHARD DENIS, government official; b. Aurora, Ill.. BS, U. Notre Dame, 1966; MBA, U. Chgo., 1968. Computer programmer/analyst Armour & Co., Chgo., 1966-68; software specialist NIMH, Washington, 1968-70; mgr. software support State of Ill., Springfield, 1970-73; dir. info. requirements U.S. Postal Svc., Washington, 1973-75, mgr. tech. support, 1975-80; dir. postal data ctr. U.S. Postal Svc., San Bruno, Calif., 1980-84; dir. comms. and tech. U.S. Postal Svc., Washington, 1984-88, asst. postmaster gen. tech. resources, 1988-89, asst. postmaster gen., v.p. info. systems, 1989—. Office: US Postal Svc Information Systems 475 Lenfant Plz SW Washington DC 20260-1500

WEIS, JOSEPH FRANCIS, JR., federal judge; b. Pitts., Mar. 12, 1923; s. Joseph Francis and Mary (Flaherty) W.; m. Margaret Horne, Dec. 27, 1958; children: Maureen, Joseph Francis, Christine. BA, Duquesne U., 1941-47; J.D., U. Pitts., 1950; LLD (hon.), Dickinson Coll., 1989. Bar: Pa. 1950. Individual practice law Pitts., 1950-68; judge Ct. Common Pleas, Allegheny County, Pa., 1968-70, U.S. Dist. Ct. (we. dist.) Pa., 1970-73, U.S. Ct. Appeals (3d cir.), Pitts., 1973—; lectr. trial procedures, 1965—; adj. prof. law U. Pitts., 1986—; chmn. Fed. Cts. Study Com., Jud. Conf. Com. on Experiment to Videotape Trial Proceedings within the 3rd Cir., Internat. Jud. Conf. the Joint Am.-Can. Appellate Judges Conf., Toronto, 1986, London, 1985, futurist subcom. bicentennial com. Ct. Common Pleas, Allegheny County, Pa., 1988; participant programs legal medicine, Rome, London; mem. Am.-Can. Legal Exchange, 1987. Contbr. articles to legal jours. Mem. Mental Health and Mental Retardation Bd., Allegheny County, 1970-73; mem. Leukemia Soc., 1970-73, Knights of Malta, Knights of Equity, Am. Legion, 4th Armored Div. Assn., Disabled Am. Vets., Cath. War Vets., Mil. Order of the World Wars; mem. bd. adminstrn. Cath. Diocese Pitts., 1971-83; trustee Forbes Hosp. System, Pitts., 1969-74. Capt. AUS, 1943-48. Decorated Bronze Star, Purple Heart with oak leaf cluster; recipient St. Thomas More award, 1971, Phillip Amram award, 1991, Edward J. Devitt Disting. Svc. to Justice award, 1993. Fellow Internat. Acad. Trial Lawyers (hon.), Am. Bar Found.; mem. ABA (chmn. appellate judges' conf. 1981-83), Pa. Bar Assn., Allegheny Bar Assn. (past v.p.), Acad. Trial Lawyers Allegheny County (past pres), Am. Judicature Soc., Jud. Conf. U.S. (chmn. civil rules com. 1986-87, com. on adminstrn. bankruptcy system 1983-87, subcom. on jud. improvements 1983-87, chmn. standing com. rules of practice and procedure 1988), Inst. Jud. Adminstrn., KC. Home: 225 Hillcrest Rd Pittsburgh PA 15238-2307 Office: US Ct Appeals 513 US PO & Courthouse 7th Grant St Pittsburgh PA 15219*

WEIS, JUDITH SHULMAN, biology educator; b. N.Y.C., May 29, 1941; d. Saul B. and Pearl (Cooper) Shulman; m. Peddrick Weis; children: Jennifer, Eric. BA, Cornell U., 1962; MS, NYU, 1964, PhD, 1967. Lectr. CUNY, 1964-67; asst. prof. Rutgers U., Newark, 1967-71, assoc. prof., 1971-76, prof., 1976—; Congl. sci. fellow U.S. Senate, Washington, 1983-84; mem. grant rev. panel NSF, Washington, 1976-82, program dir., 1988-90; mem. rev. panel EPA, 1984-92; vis. scientist EPA Lab., Gulf Breeze, Fla., 1992. Mem. marine bd. NAS, 1991—. Grantee NOAA, 1977—, N.J. EPA Rsch., 1978-79, 81-83, N.J. Marine Scis. Consortium Rsch., 1987—; NSF fellow, 1962-64. Mem. Am. Inst. for Biol. Scis. (bd. dirs. 1986-88, 89-91), Soc. Environ. Toxicology and Chemistry (bd. dirs. 1990-93), Estuarine Rsch. Fedn., Ecol. Soc. Am., NOW (pres. Essex County 1972), Sierra Club (bd. dirs. N.J. chpt. 1986-88). Avocations: choral singing, swimming, jogging. Office: Rutgers U Dept Biol Scis Newark NJ 07102

WEISBERG, ADAM JON, lawyer; b. Cocoa Beach, Fla., June 5, 1963; s. Melvin H. Weisberg and Joan Julie (Carney) Vargo; m. Cheryl Lynn Scupp, June 25, 1994. BS in Bus. Econs., Rider Coll., 1985; JD, N.Y. Law Sch.,

1988. Bar: N.Y. 1989, N.J. 1989, U.S. Dist. Ct. 1989, Fla. 1991. Law clk., asst. prosecutor Middlesex County Prosecutors Office, New Brunswick, N.J., 1988-90; workers' compensation atty. Levinson Axelrod Wheaton, Edison, N.J., 1990-91; trial atty. workers compensation Richard J. Simon, Esq., New Brunswick, 1991-92; pvt. practice lawyer New Brunswick, 1992—. Mem. ABA, N.J. Bar Assn., Middlesex County Bar Assn., Monmouth County Bar Assn., Assn. Criminal Def. Lawyers. Avocations: fishing, surfing. Office: Monmouth Exec Plz II 1300 Hwy 35 Ste 201 Ocean NJ 07712 Office: 9 Spring St New Brunswick NJ 08901

WEISBERG, HERBERT FRANK, political science educator; b. Mpls., Dec. 8, 1941; s. Nathan R. and Jean (Schlessinger) W.; m. Judith Ann Robinson, Dec. 16, 1979; 1 child, Bryan Bowen. BA, U. Minn., 1963; PhD, U. Mich., 1968. Asst. prof. polit. sci. U. Mich., Ann Arbor, 1967-73, assoc. prof. polit. sci., 1973-74; assoc. prof. polit. sci. Ohio State U., Columbus, 1974-77, prof. polit. sci., 1977—. Author: Central Tendency and Variation, 1992; co-author: Theory Building and Data Analysis, 1984, Controversies in Voting Behavior, 1992, Survey Research and Data Analysis, 1996; editor: Political Science: Science of Politics, 1985, Democracy's Feast: Elections in America, 1995; co-editor Am. Jour. Polit. Sci., 1979-82. Mem. Midwest Polit. Sci. Assn. (v.p. 1983-85), Am. Polit. Sci. Assn. (program chmn. 1983), Phi Beta Kappa, Pi Sigma Alpha, Phi Kappa Phi. Home: 742 Gatehouse Ln Columbus OH 43235-1732 Office: Ohio State U Dept Polit Sci Columbus OH 43210-1330

WEISBERG, JONATHAN MARK, public relations executive; b. Troy, N.Y., Dec. 5, 1943; s. David G. and Elizabeth (Cohn) W.; m. Pamela Crowe, Apr. 30, 1972; children: Zoe, Amanda. BA, Syracuse U., 1965; MA, Newhouse Communications Ctr., Syracuse U., 1968. V.p. Harshe, Rotman & Druck, N.Y.C., 1972-74, Rowland Co., N.Y.C., 1974-76; exec. v.p. Richard Weiner Inc., N.Y.C., 1976-84; dir. consumer, med. device and nutritional communications Bristol-Myers Squibb Co., N.Y.C., dir. corp. comms., 1984—; dir. internat. pub. affairs Bristol-Myers Squibb Co., 1994—; cons. Interbank Card Assn., N.Y.C., 1972-74, Ky. Fried Chicken, Louisville, 1974-76, Cigar Assn. Am., Washington, 1984, Am. Soc. Journalists and Authors, N.Y.C., 1980-84, Belgian Endive Mktg. Bd., Brussels, 1982-84. Office: Bristol Myers Squibb Co 345 Park Ave New York NY 10154-0004

WEISBERG, LEONARD R., retired research and engineering executive; b. N.Y.C., Oct. 17, 1929; s. Emanuel E. and Esther (Raynes) W.; m. Frances Simon, Mar. 23, 1980; children: Glenna Weisberg Andersen, Orren Weisberg Falk, Frances Weisberg Brookner. BA magna cum laude, Clark U., 1950; MA, Columbia U., 1952. Rsch. asst. Watson Labs. IBM, N.Y.C., 1953-55; with RCA Labs., Princeton, N.J., 1955-71; mem. tech. staff RCA Labs., 1955-66, head rsch. group, 1966-69, dir. semicondr. device rsch. lab., 1969-71; dir. materials rsch. lab. Itek Corp., Lexington, Mass., 1972-74; v.p., dir. ctrl. rsch. lab. Itek Corp., 1974-75; dir. electronics tech U.S. Dept. Def., Washington, 1975-79; v.p. rsch. and engring. Honeywell Inc., Mpls., 1980-94, ret., 1994; mem. adv. group on electron devices U.S. Dept. Def.; bd. dirs. SubMicron Sys. Corp., XLI Corp. Contbr. articles to profl. jours. Recipient award for initiating VHSIC program U.S. Dept. Def., 1979. Fellow IEEE; mem. Am. Phys. Soc., Sigma Xi. Home: 1225 Lasalle Ave Apt 1407 Minneapolis MN 55403-2331

WEISBERG, LOIS, museum administrator. Commr. Chgo. Cultural Ctr. Office: Chicago Cultural Center 78 E Washington St Chicago IL 60602-4801*

WEISBERG, MORRIS L., retired lawyer; b. Phila., June 7, 1921; s. Alexander and Hilda (Lichtenstein) W.; m. Mildred Norma Lubich, July 7, 1948; children—Richard, James, John. B.A., U. Pa., 1943, LL.B., 1947; M.A., Yale U., 1944. Bar: Pa. 1950, U.S. Dist. Ct. (ea. dist.) Pa. 1950, U.S. Supreme Ct. 1962. Bigelow teaching fellow U. Chgo. Law Sch., 1947-48, Raymond grad. fellow, 1948-49; Gowen fellow U. Pa. Law Sch., Phila., 1948-49; ptnr. Harry Norman Ball, Phila., 1950-56; assoc. Blank, Rome, Comisky & McCauley, and predecessor, Phila., 1956-60, ptnr., 1960-93; permanent mem. Jud. Conf. 3d Cir. Fellow Am. Bar Found.; mem. Order of Coif, Phi Beta Kappa Assocs. Office: Blank Rome Comisky & McCauley 4 Penn Center Plz Philadelphia PA 19103-2521

WEISBERG, STUART ELLIOT, federal official, lawyer; b. Bklyn., Feb. 2, 1949; s. Julius and Esther Weisberg; m. Elizabeth Jane Krucoff, June 24, 1979; children: Andrew Jonathan, Eric Nathaniel. BA, Brandeis U., 1971; JD, U. Pa., 1974. Bar: N.Y. 1976, D.C. 1976, U.S. Ct. Appeals (9th cir.) 1976, U.S. Supreme Ct. 1979. Assoc. NLRB, Washington, 1975-84; staff dir., counsel employment and housing subcom. U.S. Ho. of Reps., Washington, 1984-93; now chmn. Occupational Safety and Health Review Commission, Washington. Democrat. Jewish. Avocations: basketball, tennis. Office: Occupational Safety and Health Review Commission 1120 20th St NW Washington DC 20036-3419

WEISBERGER, BARBARA, choreographer, artistic director, educator; b. Bklyn., Feb. 28, 1926; d. Herman and Sally (Goldstein) Linshes; m. Sol Spiller, Sept. 3, 1945 (div. 1948); m. Ernest Weisberger, Nov. 15, 1949; children: Wendy, Steven. B.S. in Edn., Psychology, Pa. State U., 1945; L.H.D. (hon.), Swarthmore Coll., 1970; D.F.A. (hon.), Temple U., 1973, Kings Coll., 1978, Villanova U., 1978. Founder, dir., tchr. Wilkes-Barre (Pa.) Ballet Theater, 1953-63; founder, dir. Pa. Ballet, Phila., 1962-82, Carlisle (Pa.) Project, 1984—; vice chmn. dance panel Nat. Endowment for the Arts, Washington, 1975-79. Performed with Met. Opera Ballet, N.Y.C., 1937, 38, Mary Binney Montgomery Co., Phila., 1940-42, ballet mistress, choreographer, Ballet Co. of Phila. Lyric Opera, 1961-62, ; choreographic works include Italian Concerto, Bach, Symphonic Variations, Franck; also operas for, Phila. Lyric Opera Co. Named Disting. Dau. of Pa., 1972, Disting. Alumna, Pa. State U., 1972; recipient 46th ann. Gimbel Phila. award, 1978. Mem. Psi Chi. Office: 571 Charles Ave Kingston PA 18704-4711

WEISBERGER, JOSEPH ROBERT, state supreme court chief justice; b. Providence, Aug. 3, 1920; s. Samuel Joseph and Ann Elizabeth (Meighan) W.; m. Sylvia Blanche Pigeon, June 9, 1951; children: Joseph Robert, Paula Ann, Judith Marie. AB, Brown U., 1942; JD, Harvard U., 1949; LLD, R.I. Coll., Suffolk U., Mt. St. Joseph Coll.; DCL, Providence Coll.; DHL, Bryant Coll.; LLD, Roger Williams Coll., 1992, Brown U., 1992. Bar: Mass. 1949, R.I. 1950. With Quinn & Quinn, Providence, 1951-56; solicitor Glocester, R.I., 1953-56; judge Superior Ct. R.I., Providence, 1956-72; presiding justice R.I. Supreme Ct., Providence, 1972-78, chief justice, 1993—; adj. prof. U. Nev., 1986—; mem. faculty Nat. Jud. Coll.; vis. lectr. Providence Coll., Suffolk Law Sch., Roger Williams Coll.; Chmn. New Eng. Regional Conf. Trial Judges, 1962, 63, 65; chmn. New Eng. Regional Commn. Disordered Offender, 1968-71, R.I. Com. Adoption on Rules Criminal Procedure, 1968-72, chmn. of R.I. Adv. Com. Corrections, 1973, Nat. Conf. State Trial Judges ABA, 1977-78; exec. com. Appelate Judges Conf. ABA, 1979—, vice chmn., 1983-85, chmn., 1985-86; bd. dirs. Nat. Ctr. for State Cts., 1975-81. Chmn. editorial bd. Judges Jour., 1973-75. Pres. R.I. Health Facilities Planning Coun., 1967-70; chmn. Gov. R.I. Coun. Mental Health, 1968-73; moderator Town of East Providence, 1954-56; mem. R.I. Senate, 1953-56, minority leader, 1955-56; vice chmn. bd. trustee R.I. Hosp., 1968-92, St. Joseph's Hosp., trustee, 1962—. Lt. comdr. USNR, 1941-46. Recipient Erwin Griswold award Nat. Jud. Coll., 1989; named to R.I. Hall of Fame; Paul Harris fellow Rotary Internat. Fellow Am. Bar Found.; mem. ABA (ho. of dels., task force on criminal justice stds. 1977-79, exec. com. appellate judges' conf. 1979-95), R.I. Bar Assn., Am. Judges Assn. (gov.), Inst. Jud. Adminstrn., Am. Judicature Soc. (Herbert Harley award 1990), Am. Law Inst., KC, Order of St. Gregory (knight comdr. with star 1989, Goodrich award for Svc. 1995), Phi Beta Kappa (past pres. Alpha chpt. Brown U.). Home: 60 Winthrop St Riverside RI 02915-2624 Office: RI Supreme Ct 250 Benefit St Providence RI 02903-2719 *My professional life for the last 40 years has been occupied with judicial duties. I have been blessed with the opportunity to meet ever changing challenges and to attempt to solve a myriad of problems. These opportunities have been rewarding and absorbing. I consider judicial work to be a great privilege.*

WEISBROD, CARL BARRY, lawyer, public official; b. N.Y.C., Oct. 5, 1944; s. Walter and Hilda (Pelzer) W.; m. Jody Adams, Jan. 21, 1979; 1 child, William. BS, Cornell U., 1965; JD, NYU, 1968. Bar: N.Y., 1968; U.S. Dist. Ct. (so. dist.) N.Y., 1969. Asst. commr. N.Y.C. Housing Dept., 1970-72; counsel, chief exec. officer Wildcat Svc. Corp., N.Y.C., 1972-77; gen. counsel Manpower Demonstration Rsch. Corp., N.Y.C., 1977-78; dir. Mayor's Office of Midtown Enforcement, N.Y.C., 1978-84; exec. dir. City Vol. Corps, N.Y.C., 1984-86, N.Y.C. Planning Commn., 1986-87; pres. 42d St. Devel. Project, N.Y.C., 1987-90; pres., chief exec. officer N.Y.C. Econ. Devel. Corp., 1990-94; pres. Alliance for Downtown N.Y., 1995—; chmn. N.Y.C. Loft Bd., 1982-84. Contbr. articles to profl. jours. Office: Alliance for Downtown NY 120 Broadway New York NY 10271

WEISBUCH, ROBERT ALAN, English educator; b. Rochester, N.Y., Nov. 22, 1946; s. Irving Arthur and Ferne (Paull) W.; m. Susan Ann Remington, July 23, 1972 (div. 1979); 1 child, Max; m. Louise Wicks Freymann, Aug. 6, 1983 (div. 1994); children: Sarah, Michael; m. Candy Jaye Cooper, Aug. 27, 1994. BA magna cum laude, Wesleyan U., Middletown, Conn., 1968; MPhil in English, Yale U., 1970, PhD in English, 1972. Asst. prof. English U. Mich., Ann Arbor, 1972-76, assoc. prof., 1976-85, prof., 1985—, assoc. chmn. dept. English, 1981-84, chmn., 1987-94, assoc. prof. rsch., assoc. dean faculty programs Rackham Sch. Grad. Studies, 1994-95, assoc. v.p. rsch., 1994-95, interim dean Grad. Sch., 1995-96. Author: Emily Dickinson's Poetry, 1975, Atlantic Double-Cross, 1986; co-editor Dickinson and Audience, 1995; radio columnist Ann Arbor News, 1984-87. Am. Coun. Learned Socs. fellow, 1976-77, Rackham fellow, U. Mich., 1983; recipient Amoco teaching award U. Mich., 1986. Mem. MLA, Emily Dickinson Soc. (bd. dirs. 1987—), Phi Beta Kappa. Democrat. Avocations: radio, baseball, automobiles. Office: U Mich Dept English 7601 Haven Hall Ann Arbor MI 48109

WEISBURGER, ELIZABETH KREISER, retired chemist, editor; b. Greenlane, Pa., Apr. 9, 1924; d. Raymond Samuel and Amy Elizabeth (Snavely) Kreiser; m. John H. Weisburger, Apr. 7, 1947 (div. May 1974); children: William Raymond, Diane Susan, Andrew John. BS, Lebanon Valley Coll., Annville, Pa., 1944, DSc (hon.), 1989; PhD, U. Cin., 1947, DSc (hon.), 1981. Rsch. assoc. U. Cin., 1947-49; col. USPHS, 1951-89; postdoctoral fellow Nat. Cancer Inst., Bethesda, Md., 1949-51, chemist, 1951-73, chief carcinogen metabolism and toxicology br., 1972-75, chief Lab. Carcinogen Metabolism, 1975-81, asst. dir. chem. carcinogenesis, 1981-89, ret.; cons. in field; lectr. Found. for Advanced Edn. in Scis., Bethesda, 1980-95; adj. prof. Am. U., Washington, 1982—. Asst. editor-in-chief Jour. Nat. Cancer Inst., 1971-87; mem. editl. adv. bd. Environ. Health Perspectives, 1993—; mem. editl. bd. Chem. Health and Safety, 1994—; contbr. articles to profl. jours. Trustee Lebanon Valley Coll., 1970—, pres. bd. trustees, 1985-89. Recipient Meritorious Svc. medal USPHS, 1973, Disting. Svc. medal, 1985; Hillebrand prize Chem. Soc. Washington, 1981. Fellow AAAS (nominating com. 1978-81); mem. Am. Chem. Soc. (Garvan medal 1981), Am. Assn. Cancer Research, Soc. Toxicology, Am. Soc. Biochem. and Molecular Biology, Royal Soc. Chemistry, Am. Conf. Govtl. Indsl. Hygienists (Herbert Stokinger award 1996), Grad. Women in Sci. (hon.), Iota Sigma Pi (hon.). Lutheran.

WEISBURGER, JOHN HANS, medical researcher; b. Stuttgart, Germany, Sept. 15, 1921; came to U.S., 1943, naturalized, 1944; s. William and Selma (Barth) W.; children: William, Diane, Andrew. AB, U. Cin., 1947, MS, 1948, PhD, 1949; MD (hon.), U. Umeå, Sweden, 1980. Mem. staff Nat. Cancer Inst., NIH, Bethesda, Md., 1950-61, head carcinogen screening sect., 1961-72; dir. bioassay segment, Carcinogenesis Programs Nat. Cancer Inst., Bethesda, Md., 1971-72; v.p. rsch. Am. Health Found., Valhalla, N.Y., 1972-87; dir. Naylor Dana Inst. for Disease Prevention, Valhalla, 1972-87, dir. emeritus, sr. mem., 1987—; rsch. prof. pathology N.Y. Med. Coll., Valhalla, 1974—; pres. Weisburger Assocs., North White Plains, N.Y., 1987—; mem. biochemistry and nutrition study sect. NIH, 1957-58; mem. interdepartmental panel on carcinogens FDA, USDA, USPHS, 1962-71; chmn. subcom. Nat. Cancer Program Strategic Plan, 1971-74; chmn. carcinogenesis subcom. Nat. Large Bowel Cancer Project, 1972-75; chmn. subcom. positive controls NAS-NRC Conf. on Carcinogen Testing of New Drugs, 1973; mem. expert panel on nitrites and nitrosamines USDA, 1973-77; chmn. Workshop Colorectal Cancer, Unio Internat. Contra Cancrum, Geneva, 1975; mem. Nat. Cancer Inst. Clearinghouse on Environ. Carcinogens, 1976-78; program chmn. Toxicology Forum, 1977; co-chmn. organizing com. U.S.-Japan Coop. Workshop on GI Tract Cancer, 1979, Internat. Workshop on Nutrition and Cancer, 1982, Workshop on Dietary Fats and Fiber in Human Cancer, 1986; chmn. symposium on large bowel cancer 7th congress OMGE, 1982; chmn. symposium on natural carcinogens in human cancer devel. Unio Internat. Contra Cancrum, 1982; mem. program com. Internat. Congress of Toxicology III, 1982-83; mem. panel on irritants and vesicants Commn. on Life Scis., NRC, NAS, 1983; mem. cancer edn. com. N.Y. Med. Coll., 1983-88; bd. dirs., co-chmn. profl. edn. com. Westchester div. Am. Cancer Soc., 1983-89; mem. pancreas cancer working group, organ systems program Nat. Cancer Inst., 1985-86; mem. sci. adv. bd. Am. Water Works Assn., 1988; chmn. sci. rev. panel N.J. State Commn. Cancer Rsch., 1988-90; chmn. nutrition and cancer sect. 15th meeting Unio Internt. Contra Cancrum, Hamburg, Fed. Republic Germany, 1990; chmn. internat. discussion group Belgian Soc. Psychosocial Aspects of Cancer, Brussels, 1990; internat. lectr. on nutrition and cancer prevention, S.E. Asia, 1991; co-chmn. internat. symposium on health effects of tea, N.Y., 1991; chmn. nutrition and cancer sect. 3d anticarcinogenesis and antimutagenesis conf., Italy, 1991; chmn. study sect. NIH-Nat. Cancer Inst., Bethesda, Md., 1991; co-chmn. mechanisms nutrition cancer European Sch. Oncology, Venice, Italy, 1992; rsch. fellow Japanese Found. for Promotion of Cancer Rsch. Nat. Cancer Ctr. Rsch. Inst, Tokyo, 1992; advisor com. rev. RDA Food and Nutrition Bd. NAS, 1993; lectr. German Acad. Nutritional Medicine, Freiburg, 1994, 2d conf. Internat. Fedn. Socs. Toxicologic Pathol., Tours, France, 4th Internat. Congress Amino Acids, Vienna, Austria, 3d Internat. Symposium Green Tea, Seoul, Korea, 6th Internat. Conf. Carcinogenic Mutagenic N-Aryl Compounds, Forum Alcohol-Cancer, Frankfurt, Germany, Internat. Conf. Food Factors, Hamamatsu, Japan, 4th Internat. Yakult Intestinal Flora Symposium, Tokyo, 1995. Assoc. editor Jour. Nat. Cancer Inst., 1960-62, Xenobiotica, 1971—, Archives of Toxicology, 1977-87, Jour. Am. Coll. Toxicology, 1982—, Preventive Medicine, 1988—; mem. internat. editl. adv. bd. Food and Chem. Toxicology, 1967—; assoc. editor Cancer Rsch., 1969-80, mem. cover editl. bd., 1987—; mem. editl. bd. Chemico-Biol. Interactions, 1969-88, Carcinogenesis, 1979-87, Inst. Sci. Info. Atlas of Sci., 1987-89, Cancer Epidemioloyg Biomarkers Prevention, 1991—, Cnacer Detection Prevention, 1994—; mem. guest editl. bd. Japanese Jour. Cancer Rsch., 1987—. With AUS, 1944-46; col. USPHS, 1950-72. Decorated D.S.M., 1964; recipient Meritorious Svc. medal USPHS HEW, 1970, Outstanding Service awstchester div. Am. Cancer Soc., 1984, Meyer and Anna Prentis award Mich. Cancer Ctr., 1987; named one of 1000 most cited scientists, ISI List, 1981. Leadership plaque N.J. State Commn. Cancer Rsch., 1990. Fellow N.Y. Acad. Scis., Am. Coll. Nutrition; mem. Am. Assn. Cancer Rsch. (rep. to European Assn. Cancer Rsch. 1985-89), Am. Chem. Soc. (com. environ. improvement 1992-94), Am. Gastroent. Assn., Am. Conf. Govt. Indsl. Hygienists, Am. Soc. Biochem. Molecular Biologists, Am. Soc. Pharmacology and Exptl. Therapeutics, Am. Soc. Preventive Oncology (founding mem., bd. dirs. 1983-90, Disting. Svc. award 1990), Biochem. Soc. (London, emeritus), Environ. Mutagen Soc., European Assn. Cancer Rsch. (coun. 1985-90), Japan Cancer Assn. (hon. life), Soc. Exptl. Biol. Medicine, Soc. Toxicology (chmn. bd. publs. 1968-71, councilor 1972-74, amb. toxicology Mid-Atlantic divsn. 1990, hon. mem. 1995, Award of Merit 1981), Westchester Chem. Soc. (Disting. Scientist 1996), Sigma Xi, Alpha Chi Sigma (pres. Washington profl. chpt. 1967-68), Phi Lambda Upsilon. Achievements include research on lifestyle and chronic disease prevention, relevant mechanisms, and medical care cost reduction. Home: 4 Whitewood Rd White Plains NY 10603-1137 Office: Am Health Found Naylor Dana Inst Valhalla NY 10595-1599 *In my lifetime a revolutionary change occurred in our knowledge of the causes and the mechanisms involved in the major premature killing diseases—heart disease, hypertension, stroke, many forms of cancer. These key advances stemmed from the partnership between the federal government, public-supported societies and academic institutions that encourage health research. The impact of these diseases can be reduced in virtually all countries of the world provided their political bodies can agree that peaceful endeavors and cooperation in fostering better health for their people can be made a high priority goal. Medical science now can implement successful prevention efforts. I am glad I have lived through this period and have played a role in this development.*

WEISE, CHARLES MARTIN, zoology educator; b. Bridgeville, Pa., July 8, 1926; s. Louis August and Alice (Martin) W.; m. Joan C. Spencer, July 18, 1951; children—Patricia, Carla, Christopher, Charles, Robert. B.S., Ohio U., 1950; M.S., U. Ill., 1951; Ph.D., 1956. Asst. prof. biology Fisk U., Nashville, 1953-56; asst. prof. zoology U. Wis., Milw., 1956-60, assoc. prof., 1960-66, prof., 1966—, 1966-95, prof emeritus, 1995. Served with USMCR, 1945-46. Mem. Am., Brit. ornithologists unions, Wis. Soc. Ornithology, Am. Soc. Zoologists, Phi Beta Kappa. Research physiology of bird migration, population ecology of vertebrates. Home: 2314 E Stratford Ct Milwaukee WI 53211-2630 Office: U Wis Dept Biol Sci Milwaukee WI 53201

WEISE, FRANK EARL, III, food products company executive; b. Williamsport, Pa., July 30, 1944; s. Frank E. and Marian (Hagerman) W.; m. Deborah Dunstan; children: Frank E. IV, Alison S. BA in Econs., Lehigh U., 1966, MS in Bus. Econs., 1967. Various fin. mgmt. Procter & Gamble Co., Cin., 1967-79, comptr., CFO health and personal care div., 1983-86, dir. pers. and fin., 1986-88, comptr., CFO food and beverages div., 1988-91; fin. dir., CFO Procter & Gamble Benelux, Brussels, 1979-83; sr. v.p. fin., CFO Campbell Soup Co., Camden, N.J., 1992-95, sr. v.p., pres. confectionary divsn., 1995—. Mem. Fin. Execs. Inst., Cin. Country Club, Merion Golf Club (Ardmore, Pa.). Presbyterian. Avocations: golf, tennis. Office: Campbell Soup Co Campbell Pl Camden NJ 08101*

WEISE, GEORGE JAMES, commissioner; b. Scranton, Pa., Mar. 3, 1949; s. George Franklin and Rita Marie W.; m. Therese Lee Palmer, Oct. 20, 1984; children: Michelle Lyddane, Melissa Anne. BS, U. Md., 1971, JD with honors, 1975; MBA with honors, George Washington U., 1983. Bar: Md. 1975, Ct. Internat. Trade 1984. Import specialist U.S. Customs Svc., Dept. Treasury, Washington, 1972-75, commr., 1993—; atty. U.S. Internat. Trade Commn., Washington, 1975-83, IBM Corp., Armonk, N.Y., 1983-84; profl. staff mem. Subcom. on Trade, Ho. of Reps. Ways and Means Com., Washington, 1984-89, staff dir., 1989-93. Office: US Customs Svc Dept Treasury 1301 Constitution Ave NW Washington DC 20229-0001

WEISE, RICHARD HENRY, lawyer, corporate executive; b. Davenport, Iowa, Apr. 5, 1935; s. F. Roe and Jane (Neiger) W.; m. Virginia Armstrong, Aug. 25, 1956; children: Kimberley, Steven, Richard. B.A., DePauw U., 1956; J.D., Northwestern and DePaul U., 1961. Bar: Ill. 1961. Cons. Standard Oil, 1958-61; atty. E.J. Brach & Sons, Chgo., 1961-65; div. counsel Kraft Co., Chgo., 1965-68; various positions law dept. Motorola, Schaumburg, Ill., 1968-77, v.p., gen. counsel, sec., 1977-85; sr. v.p., gen. counsel, sec. Motorola Inc., Schaumburg, Ill., 1985—; lectr. ITT Kent Coll., Chgo., 1982-83; adj. lectr. Loyola U. Law Sch., Chgo., Fla. Bar Edn.; sr. v.p. & sec. Motorola, Schaumburg, 1996—; pres. 1550 Corp. Mem. ABA, Ill. Bar Assn., Chgo Bar Assn. Republican. Episcopalian. Club: Meadow (Roselle, Ill.). Office: Motorola Inc 1303 E Algonquin Rd Schaumburg IL 60196-4041

WEISENBURGER, RANDALL, company executive; b. 1958. With Coopers & Lybrand, 1980-85, First Boston Corp., 1987-88; mng. dir. Wasserstein Perella & Co., 1988—; CEO Wickes Mfg. Co., Inc., Southfield, Mich., 1990-93; co-chmn. Collins & Aikman; vice-chmn. Maybelline, Inc.; chmn. Yardley of London. Office: Wasserstein Perella & Co 31 W 52nd St New York NY 10019-6118

WEISER, MARK DAVID, computer scientist, researcher; b. Chgo., July 23, 1952; s. David Warren and Audra Laverne (Hunsaker) W.; m. Victoria Ann Reich, Dec. 16, 1976; children: Nicole Reich-Weiser, Corinne Reich-Weiser. Student, New Coll., Sarasota, Fla., 1969-71; MS, U. Mich., 1976, PhD, 1979. V.p. Cerberus Video, Ann Arbor, Mich., 1972-75; programmer Omnitext, Ann Arbor, Mich., 1971-76; project leader MIS, Internat., Romulus, Mich., 1975-76; from asst. to assoc. prof. computer sci. U. Md., College Park, 1979-87; prin. scientist Xerox Palo Alto (Calif.) Rsch. Ctr., 1987—, lab. mgr., 1988—; founder Cerberus Video, Ann Arbor, 1972-75. Contbr. over 70 articles to profl. jours. Mem. IEEE, AAAS, Assn. for Computing Machinery. Avocations: existential philosophy, Go, drummer for rock band Severe Tire Damage. Office: Xerox PARC Computer Sci Lab 3333 Coyote Hill Rd Palo Alto CA 94304-1314

WEISER, PAUL DAVID, manufacturing company executive; b. N.Y.C., May 30, 1936; s. Irving Julius and Rose (Peckerman) W.; m. Paula Lee Block, June 19, 1960; children: Amy Helen, Deborah Susan. B.S. in Metallurgy, M.I.T., 1959; LL.B. (editor law rev.), U. Calif., Berkeley, 1963. Bar: Calif. 1963. Assoc. firm Mitchell, Silberberg & Knupp, Los Angeles, 1963-68; with Dataproducts Corp., Woodland Hills, Calif., 1968—; sec., gen. counsel Dataproducts Corp., 1968—, sr. v.p., 1980—; chmn. adv. com. shareholder communications SEC, 1981. Contbr. articles legal publns. Served with USAR, 1959-60. Mem. Am. Bar Assn., Am. Soc. Corp. Secs. Jewish. Office: 6219 De Soto Ave Woodland Hills CA 91367-2602

WEISER, RALPH RAPHAEL, business executive; b. N.Y.C., May 25, 1925; children: Jane, Jeffrey. BA, NYU, 1947; JSD, Harvard U., 1950. Bar: N.Y. 1950. Ptnr. Lotterman & Weiser, Esq., N.Y.C., 1955-64; pres. Dragor Shipping Inc., N.Y.C., 1964-65; chmn. Nat. Equipment Rental, N.Y.C., 1965-67; exec. v.p. Am. Export Industries, N.Y.C., 1967-69; pvt. practice investment, 1970-84; chmn. World Fuel Svcs. Corp., Miami, Fla., 1984—. Sgt. USAAF, 1943-45, PTO. Office: World Fuel Svcs Corp 700 S Royal Poinciana Blvd Miami FL 33166-6600

WEISER, SHERWOOD MANUEL, hotel and corporation executive, lawyer; b. Cleve., Mar. 9, 1931; s. Aaron A. and Helen (Scheiner) W.; m. Judith A. Zirkin, July 31, 1955; children: Douglas J., Warren P., Bradley A. BS, Ohio State U., 1952; LLB, Case Western Res. U., 1955. Bar: Ohio 1955. Ptnr. Weiser & Weiser, Attys., Cleve., 1955-65, Weiser & Lefton, Attys., Cleve., 1965-69; chmn., chief exec. officer TCC, Miami, Fla., 1970—; bd. dirs. United Nat. Bank, Miami, Carnival Cruise Lines, Miami. Trustee Fla. Internat. U. Found., Miami, 1984-94, U. Miami, 1988—, New World Symphony, Miami, 1987—; trustee, chmn. bd. Ransom-Everglades Sch., Miami, 1974-84; co-chmn. bd. advisors Coconut Grove Playhouse, 1986—. Mem. Am. Hotel and Motel Assn., Cleve. Bar Assn., Soc. of Benchers, Order of Coif. Jewish. Avocations: tennis, sailing, art. Office: CHC Internat Inc 3250 Mary St Miami FL 33133-5232

WEISFELDT, MYRON LEE, physician, educator; b. Milw., Apr. 25, 1940; s. Simon Charles and Sophia (Price) W.; m. Linda Nan Zaremski, Dec. 29, 1963; children—Ellyn Joy, Lisa Janel, Sara Michelle. Student, Northwestern U., 1958-60; BA, Johns Hopkins U., 1962, MD, 1965. Intern and resident Columbia-Presbyn. Med. Ctr., N.Y.C., 1965-67; fellow in cardiology Mass. Gen. Hosp., Boston, 1970-72; asst. prof. medicine Johns Hopkins U., Balt., 1972-78, prof. medicine, 1978-91, Robert L. Levy prof. cardiology, 1979-91; Samuel Bard prof. medicine, chair dept. Columbia-Presbyn. Med. Ctr., N.Y.C., 1991—; dir. cardiology Johns Hopkins Med. Inst., Balt., 1975-91, Peter Belfer Lab. for Johns Hopkins, Ischemic Heart Disease Spl. Ctr. Rsch., 1977-91; nat. pres. Am. Heart Assn., 1989-90; cardiology adv. com. Nat. Heart, Lung and Blood Inst., 1986-90, chmn., 1988-90. Editor: The Aging Heart, 1980; editorial bd. Jour. Clin. Investigation, 1984-88, Circulation, 1980-86, 88—, Jour. Am. Coll. Cardiology, 1987-93, Jour. Molecular and Cellular Cardiology, 1975-80, 86-89, Circulation Rsch., 1988-94. Served with USPHS, 1967-69. NIH grantee, 1977-91. Fellow AAAS, ACP, Am. Coll. Cardiology; mem. Assn. Univ. Cardiologists, Am. Soc. Clin. Investigation, Assn. Am. Physicians, Assn. Prof. Medicine, Phi Beta Kappa, Alpha Omega Alpha, Interurban Clin. Club. Jewish. Home: 47 Havermeyer Rd Irvington NY 10533-2642 Office: Columbia Presbyn Med Ctr 630 W 168th St New York NY 10032-3702

WEISGALL, HUGO DAVID, composer, conductor; b. Ivancice, Czechoslovakia, Oct. 13, 1912; came to U.S., 1920, naturalized, 1926; s. Adolph Joseph and Aranka (Stricker) W.; m. Nathalie Shulman, Dec. 28, 1942; children: Deborah, Jonathan. Student, Johns Hopkins, 1929-31, Ph.D., 1940; musical edn., Peabody Conservatory, Baltimore, 1927-30, Curtis Inst., Phila., 1936-39; studied composition with, Roger Sessions. Instr. composition Cummington Sch. Arts, 1948-51; instr. Julliard Sch. Music Arts, 1957-69; Disting. prof. composition Queens Coll., 1960-83; disting. vis. prof. Penn State U., 1959-60; disting. prof. Peabody Inst., Balt., 1974-75; chmn. faculty Sem. Coll. of Jewish Music, Jewish Theol. Sem. of Am.; pres. Am. Music

Ctr., 1964-73; assoc. Lincoln Ctr. Fund, 1965-68; dir. Hilltop Mus. Co., Balt., 1951-54. Condr. Har Sinai Temple Choir, 1931-42, Y-Alliance Orch., 1935-42, Balt. String Symphony, 1936-38, Md. N.Y.A. Orch., 1940-41; guest condr. London Symphony, London Philharmonic, BBC Symphony orchs., Orchestre de la Chapelle Musicale de la Reine Elizabeth, Belgium, Radio National Belge, dir. Balt. Inst. Mus. Arts, 1949, composer in residence Am. Acad. in Rome, 1966-67, 84; composer Songs, 1929, Quest; ballet, 1937, One Thing Is Certain, ballet, 1939, Hymn for chorus and orch, 1941; Overture in F, 1942, Soldier Songs, 1944-45, Outpost, 1947; opera The Tenor, 1949-50, The Stronger, 1952, Three Symphonic Songs for high voice and orch, 1952, Six Characters in Search of an Author, 1956, Purgatory, 1958, Athaliah, 1963, Nine Rivers from Jordan, 1968; song cycle Fancies and Inventions, 1970, Translations, 1971, End of Summer, 1974; cantata for soprano, tenor, chorus and orch. Song of Celebration, 1976; (opera) Jenny or the Hundred Nights, 1976, The Golden Peacock, 1976; song cycle Liebeslieder, 1979; opera The Gardens of Adonis, 1981, Piano Sonata, 1982, Prospect, 1983, 4 Birthday Cards, 1983, Lyrical Interval, song cycle for low voice and piano, 1984, Tekiatot: Rituals for Rosh Hashannah for orch., 1985, Tangents, 4 episodes for flute and marimba, 1985, Arioso and Burlesca for cello and piano, 1983, Loves Wounded 2 songs for baritone and orch., 1986, opera Will You Marry Me?, 1987, opera Esther, 1992; Ditson Opera commn., Columbia, 1952, Koussevitzky commn., 1961, Psalm of the Distant Dove canticle for mezzo soprano and piano, 1992. Enlisted as pvt. AUS, 1942; asst. mil. attache to govts. in exile, London, later to Czechoslovakia cultural attache Am. embassy 1946-47, Prague. Awarded Bearns prize Columbia, 1931; traveling fellow Curtis Inst., 1938; Ditson fellow Columbia, 1944; grantee Nat. Inst. Arts and Letters, 1952; Guggenheim fellow, 1955-56, 61-62, 66-67. Mem. Nat. Inst. Arts and Letters, Am. Acad.-Inst. Arts and Letters (pres. 1990—), Phi Beta Kappa. Home: 81 Maple Dr Great Neck NY 11021-1909 Office: Jewish Theol Sem Broadway & 122d St New York NY 10027

WEISGERBER, DAVID WENDELIN, editor, chemist; b. Delphos, Ohio, May 20, 1938; s. Hubert Louis and Catherine Margaret (Laudick) W.; m. Carole Ann Friemoth, Oct. 23, 1965; children: Jason, Erik. B.S., Bowling Green State U., 1960; Ph.D., U. Ill., 1965. Research chemist E.I. duPont de Nemours & Co., Inc., Deepwater, N.J., 1964-69; indexer Chem. Abstracts Service, Columbus, Ohio, 1969-73, asst. to editor, 1973-77, mgr. chem. substance handling, 1977-79, dir. editorial ops., 1979-82, editor, 1982—. Mem. Am. Chem. Soc., N.Y. Acad. Sci., Am. Soc. Info. Sci. Roman Catholic. Home: 6178 Middlebury Dr E Worthington OH 43085-3375 Office: PO Box 3012 Columbus OH 43210-0012

WEISGERBER, JOHN SYLVESTER, provincial legislator; b. Barrhead, Alta., Can., June 12, 1940; s. Sylvester and Eva (Kilshaw) Harrison; m. Judith Muriel Janke, June 30, 1961; children: Joanne, Pamela. BBA, N. Alta. Inst. Tech., 1962. Owner Carland Ltd., 1975-81; econ. devel. commr. Peace River-Liard Regional Dist., Dawson Creek, 1982-84; sales mgr. Timberline Pontiac Buick GMC Ltd., Dawson Creek, 1984-86; mem. legis. assembly Govt. of B.C. (Can.), Victoria, 1986—, parliamentary sec. to min. of state, 1987-88, min. of state for Nechako and N.E., 1988-89, min. native affairs, 1989—; chmn. Cabinet Com. on Native Affairs, Victoria, 1988-90; mem. Cabinet Com. on Sustainable Devel., Victoria, 1988-90; mem. Select Standing Com. of Forests and Lands, Victoria, 1988-90; mem. Select Standing Com. on Agr. and Fisheries, Victoria, 1988-90; interim leader B.C. Social Credit Party, 1992-93; leader Reform Party of B.C., 1995. Bd. dirs., pres. Dawson Creek and Dist. Fall Fair, 1980-86. Mem. Rotary (past pres.), Mile O Riding Club (bd. dirs., pres. 1976-81). Avocations: hunting, fishing, downhill skiing. Office: Parliament Bldgs, Rm 101, Victoria, BC Canada V8V 1X4

WEISHEIT, JON CARLETON, physicist, educator; b. Mt. Vernon, Wash., Oct. 10, 1944; s. O. George and Shirley Ann (Spickerman) W.; m. Janet Carolyn Lucas, Nov. 24, 1965; children: Krista Marie, Lara Elizabeth. BS, U. Tex., 1966; MS, Rice U., 1969, PhD, 1970. Rsch. fellow astronomy Harvard U., Cambridge, Mass., 1970-72; rsch. physicist Lawrence Livermore Nat. Lab., Livermore, Calif., 1972-79, assoc. div. leader physics, 1981-88; rsch. physicist, lectr. Princeton (N.J.) U., 1979-81; prof. space physics and astronomy Rice U., Houston, 1988—, dept. chmn. space physics and astronomy, 1992—; cons. Los Alamos (N.Mex.) Nat. Lab., 1988—, Lawrence Livermore Nat. Lab., 1988—; mem. adv. com. NRC, Washington, 1984-87. Author: (with others) Applied Atomic Collision Physics Vol. 2, 1984, Advances Atomic: Molecular Physics, 1989; contbr. approx 60 articles to profl. jours. Dir. swim meets AAU, Calif., 1975-79; mem. fellowship com. Hertz Found., Livermore, 1977-92. Recipient fellowship Dept. Defense, 1966-69, post-doctoral fellowship NSF, 1970. Fellow Am. Phys. Soc.; mem. Am. Assn. Physics Tchrs., Am. Astron. Soc., Internat. Astron. Union. Achievements include patent related to tokamak plasma heating; comprehensive research on atomic processes in dense plasmas; role of Auger transitions in astrophysics; interpretation of quasar spectra; intense magnetic field phenomena. Office: Rice U PO Box 1892 Houston TX 77251-1892

WEISKITTEL, RALPH JOSEPH, real estate executive; b. Covington, Ky., Jan. 1, 1924; s. Nelson I. and Hilda (Nieman) W.; m. Audrey Bushelman, June 19, 1948; children—Thomas, Carol Anne, Barbara Jane. Eve. student, Xavier U., Cin., 1946-47. Mem. staff Cin. Enquirer, 1942-43, 45—, home sect. editor, 1958-63, bus. editor, 1963-77; v.p. corp. markets Koetzle Corp. (Realtors), 1977-79; v.p. Devitt and Assocs. (Realtors), 1979-90; v.p. sales and mktg. Toebben Cos., 1990-91; sr. v.p. The Chelsea-Moore Co., 1991-94; v.p. sales Cline Realtors, 1994—; dir. New Comty. Developers, Inc. Mem. city council, Ft. Wright, Ky., 1960-68; mem. St. Agnes Parish Council, 1974-77; mem. bishop's adv. council Diocese of Covington. Served with AUS, 1943-46. Mem. Nat. Assn. Real Estate Editors, Soc. Am. Bus. Writers. Club: Cin. Athletic. Home: 1571 St Anthony Dr Covington KY 41011-3752 Office: The Federated Bldg 7 W 7th St Ste 1900 Cincinnati OH 45202

WEISL, EDWIN LOUIS, JR., foundation executive, lawyer; b. N.Y.C., Oct. 17, 1929; s. Edwin L. and Alice (Todriff) W.; m. Barbara Butler, June 12, 1974; 1 child, by previous marriage, Angela Jane. A.B., Yale, 1951; LL.B., Columbia, 1956. Bar: N.Y. 1956, D.C. 1968. Assoc. Simpson Thacher & Bartlett, N.Y.C., 1956-64; mem. firm Simpson Thacher & Bartlett, 1964-65, 69-73; adminstr. parks, recreation and cultural affairs, commr. parks City of N.Y., 1973-75; asst. atty. gen. of U.S. in charge of land and natural resources division, 1965-67, asst. atty. gen. in charge civil div., 1967-69; asst. spl. counsel, preparedness investigating com. U.S. Senate, 1957-58; former pres. Internat. Found. for Art Research. Dir. N.Y. State Dem. campaign, 1964; mem. The 1001, World Wildlife Fund; mem. vis. com. dept. European paintings Met. Mus. Art; bd. dirs. Robert Lehman Found.; mem. corp. Presbyn. Hosp., N.Y.C.; bd. dirs. Old Master Exhbn. Soc. N.Y.; mem. Villa I Tatti Coun, Harvard Ctr. for Renaissance Studies. Lt. U.S. Navy, 1951-53. Mem. Explorers Club, Warrenton Hunt Club, Century Assn. Office: 50 E 77th St New York NY 10021-1836

WEISMAN, IRVING, social worker, educator; b. N.Y.C., May 6, 1918; s. Max and Sadie (Berkowitz) W.; m. Cyrille Gold, May 1, 1941; children: Seth, Adam. B.S., CCNY, 1939; M.S., U. Buffalo, 1942; Ed.D., Columbia U., 1962. Cert. social worker N.Y. State. Caseworker Nat. Refugee Service, N.Y.C., 1941; warden's asst. Fed. Detention Hdqrs., Bur. Prisons, Dept. Justice, N.Y.C., 1942-43; mil. svc. psychiat. social worker to chief social worker VA, Camden and Union City, N.J., 1946-49; case supr. Altro Health and Rehab. Service, N.Y., 1949-50; field instr., lectr. Columbia U. Sch. Social Work, 1950-57, assoc. prof., 1957-62, prof., 1962-84, prof. emeritus, 1984, adj. prof., 1984, acting dean, 1964-65; assoc. dean Hunter Coll. Sch. Social Work, 1967-69; exec. officer doctoral program social work Grad. Ctr. CUNY, 1975-78; clin. practice William Alanson White Inst., 1976-79; vis. prof. Sch. Social Work, Barry U., 1984-85; adj. prof. Sch. Social Work, San Diego State U., 1988—; UN adv. on social welfare to Ceylon Sri Lanka, 1963-64; sr. Simon research fellow U. Manchester (Eng.), 1970-71; cons. U.S. Office Juvenile Delinquency and Youth Devel., U.S. Children's Bur., NIMH, NIDA, HEW, N.Y.C. Dept. Personnel, Westchester County (N.Y.) Dept. Mental Health, Community Service Soc., Council Social Work Edn., Moblzn. for Youth, N.Y.C., Universidad Católica Madre y Maestra, Santo Domingo, Dominican Republic, 1983-84, United Jewish Appeal-Fedn. Jewish Philanthropies of N.Y.C., 1986-87, U. Puertorriqueña de los Antillas Aguadilla, P.R., 1993; condr. continuing edn. workshops, various univs. Contbr. articles to profl. jours., also monographs. Served with USAAF, 1943-46. HEW and HHS grantee, 1961-62, 64-76, 77-81. Home: 4612 Monongahela St San Diego CA 92117-2415

WEISMAN, JOEL, nuclear engineering educator, engineering consultant; b. N.Y.C., July 15, 1928; s. Abraham and Ethel (Marcus) W.; m. Bernice Newman, Feb. 6, 1955; 1 child, Jay (dec.). B.Ch.E., CCNY, 1948; M.S., Columbia U., 1949; Ph.D., U. Pitts, 1968. Registered profl. engr., N.Y., Ohio. Plant engr. Etched Products, N.Y.C., 1950-51; from jr. engr. to assoc. engr. Brookhaven Nat. Lab., Upton, N.Y., 1951-54; from engr. to fellow engr. Westinghouse Nuclear Energy Systems, Pitts., 1954-59, from fellow engr. to mgr. thermal and hydraulic analysis, 1960-68; sr. engr. Nuclear Devel. Assocs., White Plains, N.Y., 1959-60; assoc. prof. nuclear engrng. U. Cin., 1968-72, prof. nuclear engrng., 1972—, dir. nuclear engrng. program, 1977-86, dir. lab. basic and applied nuclear research, 1984-94. Co-author: Thermal Analysis of Pressurized Water Reactors, 1970, 2d edit., 1979, 3rd edit., 1996, Introduction to Optimization Theory, 1973, Modern Power Plant Engineering, 1985; editor: Elements of Nuclear Reactor Design, 1977, 2d edit., 1983; contbr. tech. articles to profl. jours.; patentee in field. Mem. Cin. Environ. Adv. Council, 1976-78; mem. Cin. Asian Art Soc., 1977—, v.p., 1980-82, pres., 1982-84; mem. exec. bd. Air Pollution League Greater Cin., 1980-90. Sr. NATO fellow, Winfrith Lab., U.K. Atomic Energy Authority, 1972; sr. fellow Argonne Nat. Lab., Ill., 1982; NSF research grantee, 1974-78, 82-85, 86-89; recipient Dean's award U. Cin. Coll. Engrng., 1987. Fellow Am. Nuclear Soc. (v.p. Pitts. sect. 1957-58, mem. exec. com. thermal-hydraulics div. 1989-92); mem. Am. Inst. Chem. Engrs., Sigma Xi. Democrat. Jewish. Avocation: Japanese art. Home: 3419 Manor Hill Dr Cincinnati OH 45220-1562 Office: U Cin Dept Mech Ind & Nuclear Engrng Cincinnati OH 45221

WEISMAN, JOHN, author; b. N.Y.C., Aug. 1, 1942; s. Abner I. Weisman and Syde (Lubowe) Kremer; m. Susan Lee Povenmire, Feb. 12, 1983. AB, Bard Coll., 1964. Mng. editor Coast mag., Los Angeles, 1969-70; staff writer Rolling Stone, San Francisco, 1971, Detroit Free Press, 1971-73; assoc. editor TV Guide, Radnor, Pa., 1973-77; bur. chief TV Guide, Washington, 1977-89; sr. fellow Annenberg Washington program Northwestern U., Washington, 1989-91; bd. dirs. Va. Writing mag. Author: (nonfiction) Guerrilla Theatre, 1973, Shadow Warrior, 1989, Rogue Warrior, 1992 (#1 bestseller N.Y. Times Book Rev.), (novels) Evidence, 1980, Watchdogs, 1983, Blood Cries, 1987, Rogue Warrior II, Red Cell, 1994 (bestseller N.Y. Times), Green Team, 1995 (bestseller N.Y. Times), Task Force Blue, 1996 (bestseller N.Y. Times). Mem. Bard Coll. Alumni Assn. (bd. govs. 1975-81, pres. 1981-83). Club: Army and Navy (Washington). Home: 5522 Trent St Chevy Chase MD 20815-5512 also: Ground Zero Lodge PO Box 170 Bluemont VA 20135

WEISMAN, LORENZO DAVID, investment banker; b. Guatemala, Apr. 22, 1945; came to U.S., 1957; s. Eduardo Tobias and Suzanne (Loeb) W.; m. Danielle Maysonnave, June 22, 1971; children—Melissa Anne, Alexia Maria, Thomas Alexander. B.A. in History and Lit. cum laude, Harvard U., 1966; postgrad., Conservatoire Nat. D'Art Dramatique, Paris, 1966-71; M.B.A. in Fin., Columbia U., 1973. V.p. Dillon, Read & Co., Inc., N.Y.C., 1977-80, sr. v.p., 1980-82; mng. dir. Dillon, Read & Co., Inc., London, 1982-84; pres., chief exec. officer Dillon Read Ltd., London, 1984-93; head Internat. Dillon Read & Co., N.Y.C., 1993—; bd. dirs. Sudimer Buy-Out Fund, Spain, Corporacion Borealis, Spain, France Capital Devel., France, Dillon, Read & Co., Inc., N.Y.C., Dillon, Read, Ltd., London; com. univ. resources Harvard U., 1991, mem. adv. com. David Rockefeller Ctr. for L.Am. Studies, 1995—; mem. internat. bd. overseers Columbia Bus. Sch., 1992; mem. bd. overseers Institut Français/Alliance Française, N.Y., 1995—. Trustee Institut Français/Alliance Française, N.Y.C., 1995. Mem. Harvard Club (N.Y.C.), Travelers Club (Paris), RAC Club (London).

WEISMANN, DONALD LEROY, art educator, artist, filmmaker, writer; b. Milw., Oct. 12, 1914; s. Friedrich Othello and Stela Priscilla (Custer) W.; m. M. Virginia Stant; children: Anne Wilder, Christopher Thomas. B.S., U. Wis., Milw., 1935; Ph.M., U. Wis., Madison, 1940; Ph.D., Ohio State U., 1950. Asst. prof. art Ill. State U., Normal, 1940-42, 47-48, Wayne U., Detroit, 1949-51; prof., head dept. art U. Ky., Lexington, 1951-54; prof., chmn. dept. art U. Tex., Austin, 1954-58, Univ. prof. arts, 1959-81, prof. emeritus, 1981—; cons. Ford Found., N.Y.C., 1958, 66, U.S. Nat. Com. UNESCO, 1953, Rockefeller Found., 1956, Nat. Council Arts., 1966-72; spl. cons. USIS, Forence, Italy, 1961-62. Author: Language and Visual Form, 1968, Visual Arts as Human Experience, 1970, Duncan Phyfe & Drum, 1984, Follow the Bus with the Greek License Plates, 1981, Frank Reaugh, Painter to the Longhorns, 1985; contbr. articles, poems, stories and revs. to profl. jours.; painter, collagist one-man shows, Cushman Gallery, Houston, Nye Gallery, Dallas, Petite Gallery, N.Y.C., Art Mus. U. N. Mex., group shows, Bocur Gallery, N.Y.C., Chgo. Art Inst., Dallas Mus. Fine Arts, Rockefeller Ctr., N.Y.C., Vanucci Gallery, Pistoia, Italy, Villa Monte Carlo Chapala, Jalisco, Mexico; film-maker numerous productions. Served to lt. (j.g.) USN, 1942-45, PTO. Recipient Letter of Commendation Pres. U.S., 1972; recipient Teaching awards U. Tex., 1963, 65, 70, 77, honor for book Some Folks Went West 12th Annual Writers Conf., Austin, 1960; grantee U. Tex. Research Inst., Italy, Eng., 1961-62, 71, Pub. Broadcast Corp., 1970, 72; named fine arts scholar Harvard U., 1941. Mem. Nat. Humanities Faculty. Home: 1108 Yaupon Valley Rd Austin TX 78746-4329 Office: Am Studies U Tex Austin TX 78712

WEISMANTEL, GREGORY NELSON, management consultant and software executive; b. Houston, Sept. 8, 1940; s. Leo Joseph and Ellen Elizabeth (Zudis) W.; m. Marilyn Ann Fanger, June 18, 1966; children: Guy Gregory, Christopher Gregory, Andrea Rose. BA in English, U. Notre Dame, 1962; MBA in Internat. Bus., Loyola U., Chgo., 1979. With mgmt. staff Gen. Foods Corp., White Plains, N.Y., 1966-80; pres., chief exec. officer Manor House Foods, Inc., Addison, Ill., 1980-82, Weismantel & Assocs., Downers Grove, Ill., 1982-84; v.p. perishable div. Profl. Marketers, Inc., Lombard, Ill., 1984-86; group v.p. sales and mktg. services, dir. corp. strategy Profl. Marketers, Inc., Lombard, 1986-87; v.p. mng. prin. CPG Industry, Louis A. Allen Assoc. Inc., Palo Alto, Calif., 1987-88; pres., chief exec. officer The Vista Group, St. Charles, Ill., 1989—; bd. dirs. Epicurean Foods, Ltd., Chgo.; pres., CEO The Vista Tech. Group, Ltd., The Vista Mgmt. Group. Chmn. fin. St. Edward's High Sch. Jubilee, Elgin, Ill., 1982-85; bd. dirs. Dist. 301 Sch. Bd., Burlington, Ill., 1980-84, St. Edward's Found., Elgin, 1982—. Capt. U.S. Army, 1962-66. Recipient ICP/Chgo. Software Assoc. Re-Engrng. award, 1994; State of Ill. grantee, 1989, Build Ill. Investment Fund. Mem. Grocery Mfg. Sales Execs., Chgo. Software Assn., Chg. C. of C. (small bus. com.). Roman Catholic. Clubs: Merchandising Execs., Food Products, Am. Mktg. (Chgo.). *Success can only occur when a person realizes that life is not a rehearsal.*

WEISMILLER, DAVID R., library administrator; b. Victoria, B.C., Can., Feb. 12, 1943. BA, U. B.C., 1967; B Library Sci., U. Toronto, 1968, MLS, 1972; MPA, Queen's U., Kingtson, Ont., Can., 1986. Cataloguer, MAP libr., acquisitions libr. Trent U., Peterborough, Ont., 1968-74; asst. dist. libr. Scarborough (Ont.) Pub. Libr., 1974-77; cons. Waterloo-Brazil-CIDA Programme in Engrng., Brazil, 1977-79; chief libr. Belleville (Ont.) Pub. Libr., 1979-85, Nepean (Ont.) Pub. Libr., 1985-88; dir. librs. Winnipeg (Man., Can.) Pub. Libr., 1988—. Mem. ALA, Inst. Pub. Adminstrn. Can., Can. Library Assn. Office: Winnipeg Pub Libr, 251 Donald St, Winnipeg, MB Canada R3C 3P5

WEISNER, MAURICE FRANKLIN, former naval officer; b. Knoxville, Tenn., Nov. 20, 1917; s. Clinton Hall and Adra Inez (Ogg) W.; m. Norma Holland Smith, May 30, 1942; children: Maurice Hall, Franklin Lee, Stewart Holland. B.S., U.S. Naval Acad., 1941; aviation tng., 1943; grad., Nat. War Coll., 1959. Commd. ensign U.S. Navy, 1941, advanced through grades to adm., 1972; assigned U.S.S. Wasp, 1941-42; various aircraft squadrons in PTO, 1942-46, (U.S.S. Badoeng Strait), 1947-48; comdr. Patrol Squadron 46, 1949-51; assigned Office Chief Naval Operations, 1951-53; comdr. Fighter Squadron 193, 1954-55; assigned air striking forces study sect. Office Chief Naval Operations, 1955-58; comdr. Fighter Squadron 101, 1959-60, U.S.S. Guadalupe, 1960-61, U.S.S. Coral Sea, 1961-62; assigned Bur. Naval Personnel, 1962-64; dir. air weapons systems analysis staff Office Chief Naval Operations, 1964-65; comdr. Carrier Div. 1, 1965-67; dep. chief naval personnel, 1967-69; comdr. Attack Carrier Striking Force 7th Fleet, 1969-70, 7th Fleet, 1970-71; dep. chief naval operations (air warfare), 1971-72, vice chief of naval operations, 1972-73; comdr. in chief U.S. Pacific Fleet, 1973-76, Unified Pacific, 1976-79. Decorated Def. D.S.M., Navy D.S.M. with 4 gold stars, Army D.S.M., Air Force D.S.M.; Legion of Merit with gold star; D.F.C. with gold star; Air medal with 5 gold stars; Navy Commendation medal. Home: 351 Woodbine Dr Pensacola FL 32503-3202

WEISS, ALLAN JOSEPH, transport company executive, lawyer; b. Boston, Nov. 1, 1932; s. Mark and Eve S. (Kane) W.; m. Sherrill Roecker, Feb. 18, 1973; children: Stephanie Eve, Mark Allan. B.S., U.S. Mcht. Marine Acad., 1955; J.D., Cornell U., 1961. Bar: N.Y. 1961, D.C. 1962, Calif. 1965, U.S. Supreme Ct. 1965. Trial atty. admiralty and shipping U.S. Dept. Justice, 1961-67; chief trial atty. admiralty office U.S. Dept. Justice, San Francisco, 1967-74; Pacific counsel Sea-Land Service, Inc., Oakland, Calif., 1974-76; dep. gen. counsel Sea-Land Service, Inc., 1977-78, gen. counsel, 1978-82, sec., 1979-82; assoc. gen. counsel Sea-Land Industries, 1979-82; pres. Freights Unltd., Inc., 1982—; gen. counsel Toledo, Peoria & Western Rwy., 1991-96; adj. prof. law McGeorge Sch. Law, 1974-76. Served with U.S. Navy, 1956-57. Mem. Fed. Bar Assn., Calif. Bar Assn., D.C. Bar Assn., San Francisco Bar Assn., Maritime Law Assn. U.S., Cornell U. Law Assn., Kings Point Alumni Assn. Home: 126 Seney Dr Bernardsville NJ 07924-1818 Office: Freights Unlimited Inc PO Box 428 Peapack NJ 07977-0428

WEISS, ALVIN HARVEY, chemical engineering educator, catalysis researcher and consultant; b. Phila., Apr. 28, 1928; s. Louis and Helen F. (Wilinsky) W.; children: Linda S., Louis B.; m. Devorah Schwartz, June 10, 1979. BSChemE, U. Pa., 1949, PhD in Phys. Chemistry, 1965; MSChemE, Newark Coll. Engring., 1955. Registered profl. engr., Mass., Del. Chem. engr. Fiber Chem. Corp., Cliffwood, N.J., 1949-51, Colgate-Palmolive Co., Jersey City, 1953-55, Houdry Process and Chems. Co., Linwood, Pa., 1956-63; research assoc., lectr. U. Pa., Phila., 1963-66; prof. chem. engring. Worcester Poly. Inst., Mass., 1966-94, prof. emeritus, 1994—; NASA-ASEE summer faculty fellow Stanford U., Ames Research Ctr., 1967, 68; affiliate scientist Worcester Found. Exptl. Biology, 1972-74; Fulbright-Hays sr. faculty fellow to dept. chem. engring. Ben-Gurion U. of Negev, Beersheva, Israel, 1973-74, vis. prof. chem. engring., 1974; U.S. coord. U.S.-USSR Coop. Sci. Program in Chem. Catalysis, Topic IV, 1973-76, prin. investigator (with M.M. Sakharov), 1976-78; prin. investigator (with K.I. Ione) U.S.-USSR Coop. Sci. Program in Chem. Catalysis, Topic III, 1978-80; Fulbright-Hays vis. lectr. dept. chem. engring. Middle East Tech. U., Ankara, Turkey, 1974, vis. prof., 1991; vis. research scientist dept. organic chemistry Weizmann Inst., Rehovoth, Israel, 1974; vis. lectr. Inst. Isotopes and Central Inst. Chemistry, Hungarian Acad. Scis., Budapest, 1976; vis. prof. Inst. Cultural Relations and Inst. Isotopes, Hungarian Acad. Scis., 1978, 80; UNIDO chief tech. advisor to Petrochem. Complex of Bahia Blanca, Argentina, 1980; sr. research fellow chem. systems lab. Army Chem. Ctr., Md., 1981; UNIDO expert in chem. process devel. Rsch. Inst. for Chem. Industry, Beijing, Peoples Republic of China, 1982; UNIDO expert in catalysis to YARPET Petrochemical Complex, Yarimca, Turkey, 1986-87; bd. dirs. U.S. com. for sci. coop. with Vietnam; vis. lectr. Nat. Ctr. for Sci. Rsch., Hanoi, Inst. of Indsl. Chemistry, Ho Chi Minh City, 1986. translator: (with M. Delleo, G. Dembinski and J. Happel) Catalysis by Non-Metals (O.V. Krylov), 1970; contbr. articles to profl. jours.; patentee in field. With U.S. Army, 1951-53. Named Outstanding Researcher and Creative Scholar, Worcester Poly. Inst., 1984; recipient Sci. Achievement award Worcester Engring. Soc., 1984; research grantee NSF, PRF, NASA, DOD, DOE. Fellow Am. Inst. Chem. Engrs. (rsch. com. 1968-80, symposia chmn. 1973-84); mem.AAUP, ACS, Am. Inst. Chem. Engrs., Catalysis Soc. (bd. dirs., sec. 1968-88), Catalysis Soc. New England (founding pres. 1967-68, bd. dirs. 1968—), Am. Chem. Soc. (New England petroleum div. rep. 1970-88, session chmn. 1973—), Deutsche Gesellschaft für Chemische Apparatwesen. Office: Worcester Poly Inst 100 Institute Rd Worcester MA 01609-2247

WEISS, ANDREW RICHARD, lawyer; b. Hartford, Conn., Jan. 11, 1945; s. Irving and Clara E. (Miller) W.; m. Sara N. Brookwood, Apr. 3, 1981 (dec. June 1982); m. Avril M. Bell, Oct. 14, 1989. BA, Dartmouth Coll., 1967; MA, U. Wis., 1968; postgrad., Boston U., 1970, JD, 1977. Bar: Mass. 1977, U.S. Dist. Ct. Mass. 1978, U.S. Supreme Ct. 1992. Tchr. English Saddle River (N.J.) County Day Sch., 1968-69; rsch. & writing asst. Soun-View Throg's NEck Cmty. Mental Health Ctr., Bronx, 1969-70; legal advocate Mass. Advocacy Ctr., Boston, 1975-77; atty. pvt. practice, Boston, 1978-89, RESOLUTION, Wellesley, Mass., 1989—. Trustee Thacher Montessori Sch., Milton, Mass., 1981—, Newbury Insight Meditation Ctr., 1995—; pres. Zaltho Found., Inc., Concord, Mass., 1994—. Mem. Mass. Bar Assn., Soc. Profls. Dispute Resolution, Internat. Alliance Holistic Lawyers. Avocations: hiking, music, pets. Home: 64 Winslow Rd Belmont MA 02178-2263 Office: RESOLUTION 40 Grove St Wellesley MA 02181-6326

WEISS, ANN, filmmaker, editor, writer, photographer, information specialist, educational association administrator, consultant, researcher; b. Modena, Italy, July 17, 1949; came to U.S., 1951, naturalized, 1959; d. Leo and Athalie Weiss; children: Julia Emily, Rebecca Lauren. BA magna cum laude in English Lit. and Edn., U. Rochester, 1971; MA in Info. Sci. summa cum laude, Drexel U., 1973; MA in Comm., U. Pa., 1994, postgrad. in Edn., Folklife and Ethnography, 1993—. Editor, chief cons. monographs, articles, freelance photographer, 1974—; cataloguer Drexel U., Phila., 1971-73; libr. Akiba Lower Sch., Merion, Pa., 1973; head children's dept. Tredyffrin Pub. Libr., Strafford, Pa., 1973-79, co-head reference dept., 1979-87; cons. in edn. and librs. Gulf Arab States Edn. and Rsch. Ctr. UNESCO, 1977—, cons. Rabbi Zalman Schachter-Shalomi, P'nai or Fellowship, 1987-88; photojournalist in Ea. Europe, mainly Poland, Ukraine and Czechoslovakia, 1987—; mem. editl. bd. Studies of Shoah, 1991—; primary investigator Holocaust rsch. team U. Pa., Transcending Trauma: Psychological Mechanism of Survival, 1989—; exec. dir. Eyes From the Ashes, 1988—, curator, 1995—. Dir., exec. producer (video documentary and archive creation) oral history project Inst. Pa. Hosp. U. Pa., (video documentary) The Institute: An Intimate History, 1992; dir., producer, writer, narrator, photographer (video documentary) Eyes From The Ashes, Archival Photographs from Auschwitz, 1989-90; dir., producer, writer, narrator, photographer; author, lyricist (with Thaddeus Lorentz/musical), Zosia: An Immigrant's Story; chief editorial cons. Puppetry and the Art of Story Creation, 1981, Puppetry in Early Childhood Education, 1982, Puppetry, Language and the Special Child: Discovering Alternative Language, 1984, Humanizing the Enemy...and Ourselves, 1986, Imagination, 1987; one-person photographic shows in U.S., Europe, Israel; represented in permanent collections including Martyr's Meml. Mus./Yad Vashem, Simon Wiesenthal Ctr./Mus. Tolerance. Active So. Poverty Law Ctr., Common Cause, promoting dialogue and understanding between Jews and Arabs, Jews and Poles; active Coun. for Soviet Jews, Internat. Network Children Holocaust Survivors; photographer Bob Edgar's Campaign U.S. Senate, 1985-86, David Landau's Congl. Campaign, 1986; mem. adv. coun. U.S. Holocaust Meml. Mus., 1995—. Mem. ACLU, NOW, SANE, Free Wallenberg Alliance, Physicians for Social Responsibility, Amnesty Internat., New Israel Fund, Sierra Club, Shefa Fund. Office: PO Box 1133 Bryn Mawr PA 19010-7133

WEISS, ARMAND BERL, economist, association management executive; b. Richmond, Va., Apr. 2, 1931; s. Maurice Herbert and Henrietta (Shapiro) W.; BS in Econs., Wharton Sch. Fin., U. Pa., 1953, MBA, 1954; D.B.A., George Washington U., 1971; m. Judith Bernstein, May 18, 1957; children: Jo Ann Michele, Rhett Louis. Cert. assn. exec. Officer, U.S. Navy, 1954-65; spl. asst. to auditor gen. Dept. Navy, 1964-65; sr. economist Center for Naval Analyses, Arlington, Va., 1965-68; project dir. Logistics Mgmt. Inst., Washington, 1968-74; dir. systems integration Fed. Energy Adminstrn., Washington, 1974-76; sr. economist Nat. Commn. Supplies and Shortages, 1976-77; tech. asst. to v.p. System Planning Corp., 1977-78; chmn. bd., pres., chief exec. officer Assns. Internat., Inc., 1978—; chmn. bd. dirs., chief fin. officer RAIL Digital Corp., 1988-91; v.p., treas. Tech. Frontiers, Inc., 1978-80; sr. v.p. Weiss Pub. Co., Inc., Richmond, Va., 1960—; v.p. Condo News Internat., Inc., 1981; v.p., bd. dirs. Leaders Digest Inc., 1987-88; sec., bd. dirs. Mgmt. Svcs. Internat. Inc., 1987-88; adj. prof. Am. U., 1979-80, 89-90; vis. lectr. George Washington U., 1971; assoc. prof. George Mason U., 1984; treas. Fairfax County (Va.) Dem. Com. 1992-94, assisted Pres. Clinton, v.p. Gore transition at White House, 1993, pres. Washington Mgnt. and Business Assn., 1993—; chmn. U.S. del., session chmn. NATO Symposium on Cost-Benefit Analysis, The Hague, Netherlands, 1969, NATO Conf. on Operational Rsch. in Indsl. Systems, St. Louis, France, 1970; pres. Nat. Council Assns. Policy Scis., 1971-77; chmn. adv. group Def. Econ. Adv. Council

Dept. Def., 1970-74; resident asso. Smithsonian Instn., 1973—; expert cons. Dept. State, GAO; undercover agt. FBI, 3 yrs. Del. Pres.'s Mid-Century White House Conf. on Children and Youth, 1950; scoutmaster Japan, U.S., leader World Jamborees, France, Can., U.S., 1945-61; Eagle scout, 1947; U.S. del. Internat. Conf. on Ops. Rsch., Dublin, Ireland, 1972; organizing com. Internat. Cost-Effectiveness Symposium, Washington, 1970; speaker Internat. Conf. Inst. Mgmt. Scis., Tel Aviv, 1973, del., Mexico City, 1967. Mem. bus. com. Nat. Symphony Orch., 1968-70, Washington Performing Arts Soc., 1974-88; bus. mgr. Nat. Lyric Opera Co., 1983—; mem. mktg. com. Fairfax Symphony Orch., 1984-91; bd. dirs. Mc Lean (Va.) Orch., 1992-94; exec. com. Mid Atlantic council Union Am. Hebrew Congregations, 1970-79, treas., 1974-79, mem. nat. MUM com., 1974-79; mem. dist. com. Boy Scouts Am., 1972-75; bd. dirs. Nat. Council Career Women, 1975-79; Va. Acad. Scis., 1991—. Recipient Silver medal 50-yard free style and half mile swimming meet No. Va. Sr. Olympics, 1990. Fellow AAAS, Washington Acad. Scis. (gov. 1981-92, v.p. 1987-88, pres.-elect 1989-90, pres. 1990-91, past pres. 1991-92); mem. Ops. Research Soc. Am. (chmn. meetings com. 1969-71; chmn. cost-effectiveness sect. 1969-70, Moving Spirit award 1994), Washington Ops. Research/Mgmt. Sci. Council (editor newsletter 1969-93, sec. 1971-72, pres. 1973-74, trustee 1975-77, bus. mgr. 1976-93), Internat. Inst. Strategic Studies (London), Am. Soc. Assn. Execs. (membership com. 1981-82, assn. mgmt. co. com. 1995—, cert.), Inst. for Mgmt. Sci., Inst. for Ops. Rsch. and the Mgmt. Scis., Am. Econ. Assn., Wharton Grad. Sch. Alumni Assn. (exec. com. 1970-73), Am. Acad. Polit. and Social Sci., Nat. Eagle Scout Assn., Am. Legion, Navy League of the U.S., Greater Wash. Soc. Assn. Execs. (new ventures com. 1995—), Fairfax County C. of C., Vienna, Va. C. of C., Alumni Assn. George Washington U. (governing bd. 1974-82, chmn. univ. publs. com. 1976-78, Alumni Service award 1980), Alumni Assn. George Washington U. Sch. Govt. and Bus. Adminstrn. (exec. v.p. 1977-78, pres. 1978-79), George Washington U. Doctoral Assn. (sr. v.p. 1968-69), Nat. Assn. Acad. Sci. (del. 1991-93). Jewish. (pres. temple 1970-72). Club: Wharton Sch. Washington (sec. 1967-69, pres. 1969-70, exec. dir. 1987—, Joseph Wharton award 1991). Co-editor: Systems Analysisal Problems, 1970, The Relevance of Economic Analysis to Decision Making in the Department of Defense, 1972, Toward More Effective Public Programs: The Role of Analysis and Evaluation, 1975. Editor: Cost-Effectiveness Newsletter, 1966-70, Operations Research/Systems Analysis Today, 1971-73, Operation Research/Mgmt. Sci. Today, 1974-87; Feedback, 1969-93, Condo World, 1981; assoc. editor Ops. Research, 1971-75; publisher: IEEE Scanner, 1983-89, Spl. and Individual Needs Tech. (SAINT) Newsletter, 1987-88, Jour. Parametrics, 1984-88. Home: 6516 Truman Ln Falls Church VA 22043-1821

WEISS, BRUCE JORDAN, academic administrator; b. N.Y.C., Mar. 17, 1945; s. Robert and Margolith (Goldsmith) W.; m. Dianne Mary McConville, Sept. 1, 1968; children: Jenna Lynn, Evan Michael. BA in Psychology, CUNY, 1965; MA in Psychology, U. Toledo, 1967; PhD in Psychology, U. Md., 1971. Lic. psychologist, Mass. Counseling psychologist Am. U., Washington, 1970-71, U. Calif., Berkeley, 1971-72; clin. dir. Pedregal House, San Mateo, Calif., 1973-74; dir. Berkeley Day Treatment Ctr., 1974-77; program dir. Mass. Sch. Profl. Psychology, Newton, 1977-79; dean Dedham, 1979-86; pres., 1986—. Contbr. chpt. to book. Fellow Mass. Psychol. Assn.; mem. Am. Psychol. Assn. Jewish.

WEISS, CARL, aerospace company executive; b. Bklyn., Dec. 6, 1938; s. Morris Harold and Sonia B. (Botwinick) W.; m. Judith Fellner, Jan. 27, 1963; children: Daniel Oren, Jonathan Michael. BBA, CUNY, 1961, MBA, 1968; postgrad., Harvard U., Boston, 1971. CPA, N.Y. Acct. Joseph Warren & Co., N.Y.C., 1965-68; asst. contr. Fisher Radio Corp., L.I., N.Y., 1968-69; sr. v.p. Deutsch Relays, Inc., East Northport, N.Y., 1969-83; owner, exec. v.p. Logical Solutions, Inc., Melville, N.Y., 1983-92; owner, pres., COO G&H Tech., Inc., Camarillo, Calif., 1992—. Bd. dirs. Deutsch Dagan, Inc. With U.S. Army, 1961-67. Mem. AICPA (future issues com. 1985-88); N.Y. Soc. CPA. Office: G & H Tech Inc 750 W Ventura Blvd Camarillo CA 93010-5804

WEISS, CHARLES ANDREW, lawyer; b. Perryville, Mo., Jan. 24, 1942; s. Wallace Francis and Iola Frances Weiss; m. Marie Suzanne Desloge, June 10, 1972; children—Christopher, Robert, Julie, Anne. B.J. with highest honors, U. Mo., 1964, A.B. in History, 1965; J.D. cum laude, Notre Dame U., 1968. Bar: Mo. 1968, U.S. Dist. Ct. (ea. dist.) Mo. 1968, U.S. Ct. Appeals (8th cir.) 1968, U.S. Ct. Appeals (9th cir.) 1974. Law clk. to chief judge U.S. Ct. Appeals (8th cir.), 1968-69, U.S. Ct. Appeals (5th cir.) 1992; ptnr. Bryan Cave, St. Louis, 1969—; lectr., researcher St. Louis U. Law Sch., 1970-73. Supr., Red Cross Water Safety Program, Perry County, Mo., 1962-64; dir. Neighborhood Youth Corps., Perry County, 1965-66; pres. Perry County Young Democrats Club, 1965-67; committeeman Boy Scouts Am., 1982-86. Fellow Am. Coll. Trial Lawyers; mem. ABA (ho. of dels. 1986—), Met. Bar Assn. St. Louis (pres. 1984-85), Mo. Bar Assn. (bd. govs. 1985, v.p. 1994-95, pres-elect 1995—). Roman Catholic. Clubs: Mo. Athletic (St. Louis), The Riverlands Assn., Inc. (pres. 1991-93), Jefferson Nat. Expansion Hist. Assn. (chmn. 1993—), Notre Dame of St. Louis (dir. 1983—). Office: Bryan Cave 211 N Broadway Saint Louis MO 63102-2733

WEISS, CHARLES MANUEL, environmental biologist; b. Scranton, Pa., Dec. 7, 1918; s. Morris and Fannie (Levy) W.; m. Shirley Friedlander, June 7, 1942. BS, Rutgers U., 1939, postgrad., 1939-40; postgrad., Harvard U., 1940; PhD, Johns Hopkins U., 1950. Fellow in marine microbiology, research assoc. in marine biology Woods Hole Oceanographic Instn., Mass., 1939-47; chemist, biologist Balt. Harbor Project, Johns Hopkins U. Dept. San Engring., 1947-50; basin biologist div. water pollution control USPHS, N.Y.C., 1950-52; biologist med. labs. Army Chem. Ctr., Edgewood, Md., 1952-56; prof. environ. biology U. N.C., Chapel Hill, 1956-89, prof. emeritus, 1989—, creator/sponsor C. & S. Weiss Urban Livability program, 1992—; cons. limnology Duke Power Co.; mem. ad hoc panel waste treatment Space Sci. Bd., Nat. Acad. Sci., 1966-68, chmn. panel mgmt. of spacecraft solid and liquid wastes, 1968-69, subcom. atmosphere and water contaminants of manned spacecraft, 1971; mem. triennial water quality standards rev. com. N.C. Dept. Natural Resources and Community Devel., 1982-83; cons. Nat. Health Service, Santiago, Chile, 1971. Author: Water Quality Investigations, Guatemala: Lake Atitlan 1968-70, 1971, Water Quality Investigations, Guatemala: Lake Amatitlan 1969-70, 1971, The Trophic State of North Carolina Lakes, 1976, The Water Quality of the Upper Yadkin Drainage Basin, 1981, Water Quality Study, B. Everett Jordan Lake, N.C., 1981-85, 87; editor N.C. Conf. AAUP Newsletter, 1985-91. Mem. Chapel Hill Planning Bd., 1969-76, chmn., 1970-72, 75-76; trustee Chapel Hill Preservation Soc., 1972; bd. dirs. Triangle Theatre Opera, 1986, 89, 91—; mem. adv. coun. Santa Fe Chamber Music Festival, 1990-91, trustee, 1991—. Bigelow fellow Woods Hole Oceanographic Instn., 1970—. Fellow AAAS, APHA, N.Y. Acad. Scis.; mem. AAUP (chpt. pres. 1980-81, pres. N.C. conf. 1982-83, William S. Tacey award Assembly of State Confs. 1992), Am. Chem. Soc., Am. Geophys. Union, Am. Fisheries Soc., Am. Soc. Limnology and Oceanography, Ecol. Soc. Am., Soc. Internat. Limnologie, Water Pollution Control Fedn. (chmn. rsch. com. 1966-71), Am. Water Works Assn. (chmn. subcom. water quality sampling for quality control in reservoirs 1978-80), Am. Soc. Microbiology, Sigma Xi, Delta Omega. Home: 155 N Hamilton Rd Chapel Hill NC 27514-5628 Office: U NC Sch Pub Health CB7400 Rosenau Chapel Hill NC 27599-7400

WEISS, DANIEL EDWIN, clergyman, educator; b. Kenosha, Wis., June 9, 1937; s. Edwin and Ruth J. (Stromquist) W.; m. Rachel A. Johnson, Aug. 9, 1958; children: Daniel E., Kristen R. BA, Wheaton Coll., 1959, MA, 1962; MDiv, Gordon Conwell Theol. Sem., South Hamilton, Mass., 1962; PhD, Mich. State U., 1964; DD (hon.), Judson Coll., 1976, Franklin Coll., 1990. Ordained to ministry Am. Bapt. Chs., 1962. Prof. ministry Gordon Div. Sch., Wenham, Mass., 1964-69; v.p. Gordon Coll., Wenham, 1969-73; pres. Eastern Coll., St. Davids, Pa., 1973-81, Eastern Bapt. Theol. Sem., Phila., 1973-81; exec. v.p. Pace U., N.Y.C., 1981-83; exec. dir. Am. Bapt. Bd. Edn. and Publ., Valley Forge, Pa., 1983-88; gen. sec. Am. Bapt. Chs. U.S.A., Valley Forge, 1988—; mem. ctrl. com. World Coun. Chs., Geneva, 1989—; mem. gen. bd. Nat. Coun. Chs., N.Y.C., 1989—; mem. gen. coun. Bapt. World Alliance, Washington, 1985—. Office: Am Bapt Chs USA PO Box 851 Valley Forge PA 19482-0851

WEISS, DAVID, construction executive. CFO Beazer Homes USA, Inc., Atlanta. *

WEISS, DAVID, religion educator; b. Sighet, Rumania, Dec. 21, 1928; came to U.S., 1947, naturalized, 1953; s. Callel and Fanny (Weiss) Wiederman; m. Tzipora Hager, Dec. 9, 1953; children—Baruch, Ephraim, Isaiah. B.A., Bklyn. Coll., 1953; M.A., N.Y.U., 1956; M.H.L., Jewish Theol. Sem., 1957, D.H.L., 1958; PhD (hon.), Haifa U., Israel, 1993; DHL (hon.), Gratz Coll., 1994; DTh (hon.), U. Lund, Sweden, 1995. Instr. religion and Talmud Jewish Theol. Sem., 1957-62, asst. prof. Talmud, 1962-68, assoc. prof., 1968-86, prof. Rabbinics, 1970-86; lectr. religion Columbia U., N.Y.C., 1961-63, adj. asst. prof., 1963-65, adj. assoc. prof., 1965-68, adj. prof., 1968-86, prof., 1986—, Lucius N. Littauer prof. classical Jewish civilization, 1995—; vis. prof. Talmud Bar-Ilan U., Israel, 1974; Lady Davis vis. prof. Talmud Hebrew U., Israel, 1984; vis. prof. Harvard U. Law Sch., 1996. Author: (under name Halivni): Sources and Traditions: A Source Critical Commentary on the Talmud, Vol. 1. on Seder Nashim, 1968; author: Vol. II on Seder Nashim, 1975, Vol. III on Tractate Shabbath, 1983, Vol. IV on Tracrate Erubin and Pesahim, 1983, Vol. V on Tractate Baba Qama, 1993, Midrash, Mishnah and Gemara, 1986, Peshat and Derash, 1991, The Book and the Sword: A Life of Learning in the Throes of Holocaust, A Memoir, 1996. Recipient Blalik prize City of Tel-Aviv, Israel, 1984; grantee Council Research Humanities Columbia, 1964; Guggenheim fellow, 1970-71; recipient L. Ginzberg award Jewish Theol. Sem., 1971-72; Nat. Endowment for Humanities fellow, 1980; fellow Inst. for Advanced Studies Hebrew U., Jerusalem, Israel, 1981. Mem. Am. Acad. Jewish Rsch. (past pres.), Am. Acad. Arts and Scis. Home: 435 Riverside Dr New York NY 10025-7743 Office: Columbia U 626 Kent Hall New York NY 10027

WEISS, DENIS ANTHONY, manufacturing executive, mechanical engineer; b. Cleve., July 25, 1942; s. William Richard and Mary Margaret (Ragazinskas) W.; m. Joan Hilda Hammink, Sept. 1, 1962; children: Eric, Mark, Alan, Lori. BMSE, Gen. Motors Inst. Engring., 1968; MS in Engring., U. Mich., 1967; MBA, Bowling Green (Ohio) State U., 1987. Plant engr. McLouth Steel, Detroit, 1973-74, supt. maintenance, 1974-75; with Rockwell Internat., 1975-87; plant mgr. Rockwell Internat., Kenton, Ohio, 1983-87; v.p. mfg. div. Huffy Bicycle Co., Celina, Ohio, 1987-89; v.p. mfg. Kirby Co., div. Scottfetzer Corp., Cleve., 1989-92; v.p. ops. Crown Leisure Products, Inc., Owosso, Mich., 1992-94, Taylor Bldg. Products, West Branch, Mich., 1994—; asst. prof. part-time Oakland Community Coll., Pontiac, Mich., 1971-72. Mem. Charter Study Commn., Pontiac, 1974, Pontiac Zoning Bd. of Appeals, 1974-75; mem. engring. adv. bd. Wright State U. Lake Campus, Celina, Ohio, 1988; co-founder Bay St. Block Club, Pontiac, 1971, Pontiac Citizens Watch, 1973. Recipient Resolution of Appreciation, Pontiac City Commn., 1975; named Boss of the Yr., Am. Bus. Women's Assn., 1981. Mem. Assn. Mfg. Excellence, Soc. Mfg. Engrs., Am. Mgmt. Assn., Home Owners Assn. (trustee Lima, Ohio chpt. 1988-89). Roman Catholic. Avocations: gunsmiths, stained glass, golf. Home: 2980 Arrowhead Tr West Branch MI 48661 Office: Taylor Bldg Products PO Box 280 631 N 1st St PO Box 457 West Branch MI 48861

WEISS, DONALD L(OGAN), retired sports association executive; b. Aurora, Ill., Aug. 22, 1926; s. Harry H. and Esther (Cook) W.; m. Charlene Thomas, Aug. 23, 1947; children: Deborah Lynn Weiss Geline, Barbara Jane Weiss Juckett, Pamela Sue Weiss Van der Lee. Student, Cornell Coll., Mt. Vernon, Iowa, 1943, 46; B.J., U. Mo., 1949. Newsman AP, Huntington, W.Va., 1949-51; sports writer-editor AP, N.Y.C., 1951-63; publs. editor, info. dir. U.S. Golf Assn., N.Y.C., 1963-65; dir. info. Nat. Football League, N.Y.C., 1965-68; dir. public relations Nat. Football League, 1968-77; exec. dir. Nat. Football League, N.Y.C., 1977-94. Contbr. articles on golf and football to profl. publs., 1963—. With submarine svc., USN, 1944-46. Recipient Journalistic Achievement awards Sigma Delta Chi, Kappa Tau Alpha, 1948-49, Trustees' award Ohio U., 1978, Nat. citation Nat. H.S. Athletic Coaches Assn., 1990. Methodist. Office: 410 Park Ave New York NY 10022-4407

WEISS, EARLE BURTON, physician; b. Waltham, Mass., Nov. 23, 1932; s. Murray E. and Ruth R. (Pill) W.; m. Ruth Lithwick, Dec. 1, 1963; children—Ilana, Joshua. BS with honors, Northeastern U., 1955; MS, M.I.T., 1957; MD, Albert Einstein Coll. Medicine, 1961. Intern King's County Hosp., Bklyn., 1961-62; resident Boston City Hosp., 1962-64, Nat. Heart Inst. fellow, 1964-66; assoc. dir. Tufts Med. Svc., 1969-71; dir. respiratory ICU, physician pulmonary svc. Boston City Hosp., 1964-71; dir. div. respiratory diseases St. Vincent Hosp., Worcester, Mass., 1971-89; also acting med. dir. St. Vincent Hosp., 1985-87; prof. medicine U. Mass. Med. Sch., 1977—; sr. pulmonary rsch. scientist, dept. anesthesia Rsch. Labs. Brigham and Womens Hosp., Boston, 1989—; lectr. Tufts Med. Sch.; assoc. affiliated prof. life scis. Worcester (Mass.) Poly. Inst.; vis. prof. Faculty of Medicine, dept. of anesthesia Harvard Med. Sch., 1990—; med. dir. Found. Rsch. in Bronchial Asthma and Related Diseases; Tb cons. Commonwealth of Mass., 1964-71. Author: Bronchial Asthma, 2d edit., 1976, 3d edit., 1993, Status Asthmaticus, 1978; contbr. (with artist Frank H. Netter) Ciba Collection: The Respiratory System and Clinical Symposia, An Anthology of Medical Classics, 1995—. Served to capt. USAF, 1965-70. Recipient Dr. J. McKeever award for outstanding educator St. Vincent Hosp., 1970, Chadwick medal for meritorious contbn. thoracic diseases Mass. Thoracic Soc., 1990. Fellow ACP, Am. Coll. Chest Physicians, Royal Coll. Physicians (assoc.); mem. AAAS, AMA, Mass. Thoracic Soc. (pres. 1976-78, Chadwick medal for meritorious contbn. 1990), Mass. Med. Soc., Am. Thoracic Soc. (co-founder clin. assembly), Am. Assn. Clin. Scientists, Am. Soc. Internal Medicine, Soc. Free Radical Rsch., N.Y. Acad. Scis., Interasthma. Avocation: research in the role of calcium and oxygen toxic products in asthma and airways reactivit. Home: 57 South St Natick MA 01760-5526 Office: Brigham and Womens Hosp Dept Anesthesia Rsch L Boston MA 02115

WEISS, EDITH BROWN, law educator; b. Salem, Oreg., Feb. 19, 1942; d. Leon Michael and Edith E. Brown; A.B., Stanford U., 1963; J.D., Harvard U., 1966; Ph.D., U. Calif.-Berkeley, 1973; DDL (hon.) Chgo.-Kent Coll. Law, 1993; m. Charles Weiss, Jr., July 24, 1969; children—Jed, Tamara. Bar: D.C., 1967, U.S. Ct. Claims, 1967, U.S. Ct. Customs and Patent Appeals, 1967, U.S. Ct. Mil. Appeals, 1967; atty. adv. ACDA, Washington, 1966-68; rsch. assoc. Columbia U., N.Y.C., 1970-72, Brookings Instn., Washington, 1972-74; asst. prof. civil engring. and politics Princeton (N.J.) U., 1974-78; prof. law Georgetown U., Washington, 1978—, Francis Cabell Brown prof. internat. law, 1996—; cons. UN Environ. Program, 1974-78, 94—, UN U., 1983—; assoc. gen. coun. internatl law, EPA, 1990-92; chmn. Social Sci. Rsch. Coun. Com. on Rsch. on Global Environ. Change, 1989-94. Bd. editors Am. Jour. Internat. Law, Internat. Legal Materials, Global Governance. Recipient Dinkelspiel award Stanford U., 1963, Leland T. Chapin award, 1962, Mellinkoff award, 1963; Harold and Margaret Sprout award, 1979, Elizabeth Haub prize, 1994; Woodrow Wilson fellow, 1968. Mem. ABA (standing com. world order), Am. Soc. Internat. Law (chmn. ann. meeting 1979, nominating com. 1979-80, exec. coun. 1981-85, v.p. 1983-85, pres. 1994-96, Cert. Merit 1990), Nat. Acad. Scis. (environ. studies bd. 1981-84, vice chmn. U.S. nat. com. for SCOPE 1984-85, water sci. and tech. bd. 1985-88, commn. on geoscis., environment and resources 1992-95, U.S. Dept. State adv. com. pub. internat. law 1994—), Coun. Fgn. Relations, Am. Law Inst., Internat. Coun. Environ Law, Cousteau Soc. (coun. advs.), Phi Beta Kappa, Sigma Xi. Club: Bannockburn Civic Assn. Author: (with Brown, Fabian, Cornell) Regimes for the Oceans, Outer Space and Weather, 1977, In Fairness to Future Generations: International Law, Common Patrimony and Intergenerational Equity, 1989, Environmental Change and International Law, 1992; contbr. articles to profl. jours. Office: Georgetown U Law Ctr 600 New Jersey Ave NW Washington DC 20001

WEISS, EGON ARTHUR, retired library administrator; b. Vienna, Austria, June 7, 1919; Came to U.S., 1938; s. Arthur and Martha (Schrecker) W.; m. Renee Hansi Weiss, July 11, 1942; children—Helen Louise, Steven Arthur. Student, Berea Coll., Ky., 1938-40; A.B., Harvard U., 1947; M.A., Boston U., 1949; M.S.L.S., Simmons Coll., Boston, 1951. Prof. asst. Brookline (Mass.) Pub. Library, 1949-51, br. dir., 1951-58; asst. dir. library U.S. Mil. Acad., West Point, N.Y., 1958-62, libr., dir. libr., 1962-87, libr. emeritus, 1987—; libr. cons., 1987—; trustee Southeast N.Y. Libr. Rsch. Coun., Poughkeepsie, 1966—; mem. John Cotton Dana Com., N.Y.C., 1975-79; cons. Pergamon Press, McLean, Va., 1983—. Co-author: Catalog Military Science Coll., 4 vols., 1969; contbr. to Funk & Wagnalls Ency., 1965—; appraiser rare books and spl. collections. Chmn. Black Rock Forest Preservation Council, Cornwall, N.Y., 1981—; trustee Mus. Hudson Highlands, Cornwall-on-Hudson, N.Y., 1968; vice chmn. Citizens Adv. Com., Cornwall, 1963-64; pres. Friends of Cornwall (N.Y.) Pub. Libr., 1989—, chmn. gifts and bequests, 1984—; counsellor Friends of West Point Libr., 1987—; trustee David Libr. of Am. Revolution, Pa., 1986—; alt. del. The White House Conf. on Libr. and Info. Svcs., 1991. Served to lt. col. U.S. Army, 1942-46, ETO. Mem. ALA (pres. armed forces sect. 1966), Spl. Libraries Assn. (chmn. mil. library div. 1970), Archons of Colophon, Res. Officers Assn. (pres. Orange County 1965—), Assn. U.S. Army (bd. govs. 1984—). Club: Harvard (v.p. schs. and scholarship) (Poughkeepsie, N.Y.) Lodges: Toastmasters (edn. v.p. Newburgh, N.Y. 1968), Masons. Avocations: reading; swimming; tennis; playing violin. Home: 33 Spruce St Cornwall On Hudson NY 12520-1124

WEISS, ELLYN RENEE, lawyer; b. Phila., Aug. 11, 1947; d. Samuel J. and Ruth G. (Miller) Paul; m. Robert Lowell Weiss Jr., June 26, 1969; 1 child, Nora Caroline. BA cum laude, Smith Coll., Northampton, Mass., 1969; JD cum laude, Boston U., 1972. Bar: Mass. 1972, D.C. 1978, U.S. Dist. Ct., Mass., U.S. Dist. Ct., D.C., U.S. Ct. Appeals (D.C., 1st and 3d cirs.), U.S. Supreme Ct. Lectr. environ. law Boston U., 1976-77; asst. atty. gen. Mass. Atty. Gen., Boston, 1973-77; ptnr. Harmon & Weiss, Washington, 1977-88, Foley, Hoag & Eliot, Washington, 1988—; mem. Clinton/Gore Presdl. Transition Team, 1992; spl. counsel, dir. human radiation experiments investigation U.S. Dept. Energy, dep. asst. sec. Office of Environment, Safety and Health, 1994-95. Recipient Disting. Svc. Citation Mass. Atty. Gen., Boston, 1975. Mem. Union Concerned Scientists (dir. 1988—). Avocation: painting. Office: Foley Hoag & Eliot 1615 L St NW Washington DC 20036-5610

WEISS, GAIL ELLEN, legislative staff director; b. N.Y.C., Apr. 11, 1946; d. Joseph and Elaine (Klein) W.; m. John A. Kelly. BA, U. Md., 1967. Staff asst. U.S. Office Econ. Opportunity/Job Corps, Washington, 1967-69; legis. asst. Hon. William L. Clay, Mem. Congress, Washington, 1969-72; rsch. asst. Rt. Hon. Roy Hattersley, Mem. Parliament, London, 1972-73; legis. asst. various coms. U.S. Ho. of Reps., Washington, 1973-90, staff dir. Com. on P.O. and Civil Svc., 1991-94, Dem. staff dir. Com. on Econ. and Ednl. Opportunities, 1995&; mem. working group Pres.'s Task Force on Nat. Health Reform, 1993. Democrat. Jewish. Office: Com on Econ and Ednl Opp 2100 Rayburn Ho Office Bldg Washington DC 20515

WEISS, GEORGE C., lawyer; b. Cornwall, N.Y., Dec. 18, 1946; s. George Joseph and Ella (Vacca) W.; m. Donna Irene Rysinger, June 17, 1967; children: Matthew, Christopher, Nora, Claire, Delia. BA, St. John's U., 1968, JD, 1971. Bar: N.Y. 1972, U.S. Dist. Ct. (so. dist.) N.Y. 1975, U.S. Ct. Appeals (2d cir.) 1975, Ct. Appeals (D.C. cir.) 1988. Ptnr. Dewey, Ballantine, Bushy, Palmer & Wood, N.Y.C., 1971—. Pres. parish coun. St. John the Evangelist Roman Cath. Ch., Goshen, N.Y., 1977-81, trustee, 1981-83. Mem. N.Y. State Bar Assn. (real property and banking law sects.). Republican. Office: Dewey Ballantine 1301 Avenue Of The Americas New York NY 10019-6022*

WEISS, GEORGE HERBERT, mathematician, consultant; b. N.Y.C., Feb. 19, 1930; s. Morris and Violet (Mayer) W.; m. Delia Esther Orgel, Dec. 20, 1961; children: Miriam Judith, Alan Keith, Daniel Mordechai. BA, Columbia U., 1951; MA, U. Md., 1953, PhD, 1958. Physicist USN, White Oak, Md., 1951-61; asst. prof. U. Md., College Park, 1959-63; fellow Rockefeller U., N.Y.C., 1963-64, Weizmann Inst., Rehovot, Israel, 1958-59; mathematician NIH, Bethesda, Md., 1964—; cons. GM, IBM, GE. Author: Lattice Dynamics in the Harmonic Approximation, 1963, 2d edit., 1971, The Master Equation in Chemical Physics, 1977, Contemporary Problems in Statistical Physics, 1994, Aspects and Applications of the Random Walk, 1994, Introduction to Crystallographic Statistics, 1995. With U.S. Army, 1954-56. Recipient Disting. Svc. in Math. award Washington Acad. Sci., 1967, Disting. Svc. award NIH, 1970. Avocations: photography, music. Office: NIH Bethesda MD 20816

WEISS, GERALD FRANCIS, JR., secondary education educator, coach; b. Pottsville, Pa., Nov. 22, 1961; s. Gerald Francis Sr. and Joan (Marx) W.; m. Patricia Ann Lengel, Nov. 22, 1985; children: Matthew, Nicole, Caitlin. BS in Edn./Physics, Kutztown (Pa.) U., 1985; MS in Edn., Wilkes U., Wilkes-Barre, Pa., 1991. Cert. tchr., Pa. Tchr. sci. Tri-Valley Sch. Dist., Higgins, Pa., 1985-86; tchr. physics and chemistry St. Clair (Pa.) Sch. Dist., 1986-87; tchr. physics Hamburg (Pa.) Area Sch. Dist., 1987—. Program dir. Camp Duportail, Hawk Mountain coun. Boy Scouts Am., 1995—, Indian Run Dist. membership chair, 1995—. Named Disting. Tchr. of Honor Students Pa. State U., 1994; recipient Outstanding Educator award Phila. Coll. Textiles and Sci., 1994. Mem. ASCD. Avocations: fishing, boating. Home: 439 Mohave Dr Auburn PA 17922-9512 Office: Hamburg Area Sch Dist Windsor St Hamburg PA 19526

WEISS, GERHARD HANS, German language educator; b. Berlin, Aug. 6, 1926; came to U.S., 1946; s. Curt Erich and Gertrud (Grothus) W.; m. Janet Marilyn Smith, Dec. 27, 1953; children: John Martin, Susan Elizabeth Weiss Spencer, James David. BA, Washington U., St. Louis, 1950, MA, 1952; PhD, U. Wis., 1956. Prof. German U. Minn., Mpls., 1956—, assoc. dean, 1967-71, 79, chmn. dept. German, 1987-95; mem. German-Am. Textbook Commn., Braunschweig, Fed. Republic Germany, 1985-88. Author: Begegnung mit Deutschland, 1970; editor: Unterrichtspraxis, 1975-80, Minn. Monographs in the Humanities, 1964-70; contbr. articles to profl. jours. Served to lt. col. USAR, 1946-75. Recipient Cross Merit, Fed. Republic Germany, 1982. Mem. MLA, Am. Assn. Tchrs. German (pres. 1982-83, cert. of merit 1981, Disting. German Educator award 1991, elected hon. mem. 1995), German Studies Assn., Am. Coun. Tchg. Fgn. Langs. (Nelson Brooks award 1987). Methodist. Home: 4101 Abbott Ave S Minneapolis MN 55410-1004

WEISS, GERSON, physician, educator; b. N.Y.C., Aug. 1, 1939; s. Samuel and Lillian (Wolpe) W.; m. Linda Gordon, Dec. 24, 1959; children: Jonathan, David, Michele, Andrew. B.A., NYU, 1960, M.D., 1964. Diplomate Am. Bd. Ob-Gyn. (mem. div. reproductive endocrinology 1985-90). Intern, fellow dept. medicine Johns Hopkins Sch. Medicine, 1964-65; resident ob-gyn NYU Med. Center, 1964-69; research fellow physiology U. Pitts. Sch. Medicine, 1971-73; asst. prof. ob-gyn NYU Med. Center, 1971-76, asso. prof., 1976-80, prof., 1980-85, dir. div. reproductive endocrinology, 1975-85; prof. ob-gyn U. Med. and Dentistry N.J.-N.J. Med. Sch., 1986—, chmn. dept., 1986—. Mem. editorial bd. Fertility and Sterility Jour., Gyn.-Ob. Investigation; contbr. rsch. articles reproductive endocrinology and gynecology to med. jours. Served to maj. MC U.S. Army, 1969-71. Rsch. grantee NIH, 1975—, United Cerebral Palsy Found., 1977-83, Mellon Found., 1982-85; John Polachek Found. Med. Rsch. fellow. Mem. Am. Coll. Ob-Gyn., Am. Ob-Gyn. Soc., Am. Bd. Ob-Gyn. (bd. dirs. 1993—, ob-gyn. residency rev. com. 1995—), Endocrine Soc. Gynecol. Investigation, N.Y. Obstet. Soc. (pres. 1990-91), N.Y. Gynecol. Soc. (pres. 1989-90), Soc. Study of Reprodn., Phi Beta Kappa, Sigma Xi, Alpha Omega Alpha. Home: 390 1st Ave Apt 11D New York NY 10010-4935 Office: UMDNJ NJ Med Sch Dept Ob-Gyn 185 S Orange Ave Newark NJ 07103-2714

WEISS, HEDY, theater critic. Theater critic Chgo Sun-Times. Office: Chgo Sun-Times Inc 401 N Wabash Ave Chicago IL 60611-3532

WEISS, HERBERT KLEMM, retired aeronautical engineer; b. Lawrence, Mass., June 22, 1917; s. Herbert Julius and Louise (Klemm) W.; m. Ethel Celesta Giltner, May 14, 1945 (dec.); children: Janet Elaine, Jack Klemm (dec.). B.S., MIT, 1937, M.S., 1938. Engr. U.S. Army Arty. Bds., Ft. Monroe, Va, 1938-42, Camp Davis, N.C., 1942-44, Ft. Bliss, Tex., 1944-46; chief WPN Systems Lab., Ballistic Research Labs., Aberdeen Proving Grounds, Md, 1946-53; chief WPN systems analysis dept. Northrop Aircraft Corp., 1953-58; mgr. advanced systems devel. mil. systems planning aeronutronic div. Ford Motor Co., Newport Beach, Calif., 1958-61; group dir., plans devel. and analysis Aerospace Corp., El Segundo, Calif., 1961-65; sr. scientist Litton Industries, Van Nuys, Calif., 1965-82; cons. mil. systems analysis, 1982-90; Mem. Sci. Adv. Bd. USAF, 1959-63, sci. adv. panel U.S. Army, 1965-74, sci. adv. commn. Army Ball Research Labs., 1973-77; advisor Pres.'s Commn. Law Enforcement and Adminstrn. Justice, 1966; cons. Office Dir. Def., Research and Engring., 1954-64. Contbr. articles to profl. jours. Patentee in field. Recipient Commendation for meritorious civilian service USAF, 1964, cert. appreciation U.S. Army, 1976. Fellow AAAS, AIAA (assoc.); mem. IEEE, Ops. Research Soc. Am. Republican. Presbyterian. Club: Cosmos. Home: PO Box 2668 Palos Verdes Peninsula CA 90274-8668 *The difference between having something to do and having* *to do something is a pain in the neck. Anything worth doing takes more doing than it is worth except for the fun of it.*

WEISS, HOWARD A., violinist, concertmaster, conductor, music educator; b. Chgo.; s. Morris X. and Rose (Weiner) W. B.Music, Chgo. Musical Coll. of Roosevelt U., 1960; M.Music with honors, Roosevelt U., 1966. Founder, music dir., condr. Rochester Philharm. Youth Orch., N.Y., 1970-89; prof. violin Eastman Sch. Music, Rochester, 1981—, Nazareth Coll., Rochester, 1983-85; mem. adv. bd. Young Audiences of Rochester, 1975—, Rochester Chamber Orch., 1981—. Concertmaster Rochester Philharm. Orch., 1967-87, concertmaster emeritus, 1987— , concertmaster Rochester Oratorio Soc., 1987—, Chgo. Chamber Orch., 1962-70, Va. Symphony, 1964, San Francisco Ballet Orch., 1962, Eastern Music Festival, Greensboro, N.C., 1976-80, Grand Teton Music Festival Seminar, Jackson Hole, Wyo., 1983-86, Bear Lake Mus. Festival, Utah, 1992-93; 1st violinist Cleve. Orch., 1965-67; violin soloist more than 40 concertos with Cleve. Orch., Rochester Philharm., New Orleans Philharm., Chgo. Grant Park Symphony, Cin. Chamber Orch., Chgo. Chamber Orch., Rochester Chamber Orch.; soloist in complete concerti, (5) of J.S. Bach for Violin and Orch. with Rochester Bach Festival; soloist in complete concerti, (3) of Haydn for Violin and orch. with Rochester Chamber Orch.; soloist rec. Amram Elegy for Violin and Orchestra, David Zinman, Rochester Philharm. Orch., on RCA Red Seal; performed chamber music with: Misha Dichter, Leonard Rose, Lynn Harrell, Yo-Yo Ma, Elly Ameling, Jaime Laredo, Walter Trampler, Lillian Fuchs, James Buswell, Gary Karr, Alan Civil, Lukas Foss; leader of Hartwell String Quartet, 1975-78; participant Casals Festival, Puerto Rico, 1975-80. As music dir. and condr. Rochester Philharm. Youth Orch. recorded 21 LPs including symphonies by Franck, Sibelius, Shostakovich, Dvorak, Borodin and Rachmaninoff, made 12 tours, including 4 abroad, Eng. and Scotland, 1984, Germany, Austria and Switzerland, 1986, Dominican Republic, 1987, Jamaica, 1989, and appears on Voice of Am. Named Outstanding Grad. of 1966, Roosevelt U., 1973; recipient Monroe County (N.Y.) Medallion, 1986. Home: 228 Castlebar Rd Rochester NY 14610-2914

WEISS, IRA FRANCIS, retired banker; b. Providence, R.I., Oct. 19, 1909; s. Abraham and Minnie (Chernoff) W.; m. Gladys Abbott (div. 1966); children: Abbott, Michael, John. Student, CCNY, 1926-28; LL.B., St. Lawrence U., 1931; postgrad., Columbia U., 1931-33, St. John's Coll., Annapolis, 1975-78; B.A., Seminar Coll., New Sch., 1980, M.A., 1982; postgrad., CUNY Grad. Ctr. Bar: N.Y. 1934. Pvt. practice N.Y.C., 1934-37; asst. sec. Credit Utility Co., Inc., N.Y.C., 1937-42; successively asst. sec., asst. v.p., v.p., adminstrv. v.p., sr. v.p. Trade Bank & Trust Co., 1926-33, 45-70; sr. v.p. Nat. Bank N. Am., N.Y.C., 1970-74; sr. cons. Nat. Bank N.Am. (now NatWest Bank), 1975. Mem. Jewish Com. on Scouting, N.Y.C., 1950-53; asst. mgr. United Fund, Glen Ridge, N.J., 1959; mem. Civic Conf. Com., 1961-64, Mayor's Transp. Com., 1962-65, Speakers Bur. of United Cerebral Palsy Soc., N.Y.C., 1946-50; treas., exec. bd. N.Y. chpt., mem. nat. exec. council Am. Jewish Com., 1962-75; mem. Nat. Com. on Am. Fgn. Policy. Sgt. U.S. Army, 1942-45. Mem. AIM, N.Y. Credit and Financial Mgmt. Assn., Am. Arbitration Assn. (nat. panel), Robert Morris Assocs., Fgn. Policy Assn., Carnegie Council on Ethics and Internat. Affairs, Ctr. for Study Presidency, Acad. Polit. Sci. Home: 8 Reservoir Rd Apt 101 Hanover NH 03755-1315

WEISS, JAMES LLOYD, cardiology educator; b. Chgo., Jan. 15, 1941; s. Edward Huhner and Ruth (Wingerhoff) W.; m. Susan Forscher Weiss, July 23, 1967; children: Ethan James, Lisa Fleur. BA, Harvard Coll., 1963; MD, Yale U., 1968. Intern, resident U. Mich. Hosp., Ann Arbor, 1968-70; staff fellow NIH, Bethesda, Md., 1970-72; resident medicine Johns Hopkins Hosp., Balt., 1972-73; fellow cardiology, 1973-75, dir. Heart Station, 1976—, asst. prof. Medicine, 1975-81, assoc. prof. Medicine, 1981-90, prof. Medicine, Cariology, 1990—; Michael J. Cudahy prof. of cardiology Johns Hopkins Hosp., 1992—; editorial bd. Johns Hopkins Med. Ctr., 1991—. Contbr. 100 articles to profl. jours. Recipient Harvard Book prize, 1959. Fellow Am. Coll. Cardiology, AHA Coun. on Circulation; mem. Harvard Club N.Y.C., Ctr. Club. Office: Cariology Div. Johns Hopkins Hosp. 600 N Wolfe St Baltimore MD 21287

WEISS, JAMES MICHAEL, financial analyst, portfolio manager; b. Chgo., July 20, 1946; s. Harold Cornelius and Elizabeth Josephine (Jesse) W.; m. Kathleen Jane Postorino, July 18, 1970; children: Elizabeth, Ann, Jane, William. BA, Marquette U., 1968; MBA, U. Pa., 1972. CFA; chartered investment counselor. Credit analyst Provident Nat. Bank, Phila., 1972; ptnr., sr. portfolio mgr. Stein Roe & Farnham Investment Counselors, Chgo., 1972-87, 1st v.p., sr. portfolio mgr., 1987-90, sr. v.p., prin., sr. portfolio mgr., 1991-92; exec. v.p., sr. portfolio mgr. IDS Adv. Group, Inc., Mpls., 1993-95; pres., chief investment officer IDS Equity Advisors, 1995; sr. v.p., dep. chief investment officer Equities, State St. Rsch. & Mgmt. Co., Boston, 1995—; bd. dirs. Colie & Harris, Inc., Tropp & Co., Chgo.; v.p. Stein Roe Cash Reserves Fund, Chgo., 1982-87. Author: (with others) Handbook of Cash Flow and Treasury Management, 1987; contbr. articles to profl. jours. Commr. Glenview (Ill.) Zoning Bd., 1978-80; trustee Glenview Village Bd. Trustees, 1980-86; chmn. Marquette U. Exec. Senate, Chgo., 1984-87; mem. Glenview Bus. Area Redevel. Com., 1990-93; mem. bus. adv. coun. Elmhurst (Ill.) Coll., 1986-93; founding bd. dirs. Glenview Edn. Found., 1990-93. With U.S. Army, 1968-70. Recipient Cert. Merit Village of Glenview, 1987. Mem. Investment Analysts Soc., Fin. Analysts Fedn., Investment Counsel Assn., Marquette U. Alumni Assn. (nat. bd. dirs. 1989-91, Nat. Svc. award 1995), North Shore Country Club (Glenview). Avocations: golf, travel, writing. Home: 251 Caterina Heights Concord MA 01742-4774 Office: 1 Financial Ctr Boston MA 02111-2690

WEISS, JAMES MOSES AARON, psychiatrist, educator; b. St. Paul, Oct. 22, 1921; s. Louis Robert and Gertrude (Simon) W.; m. Bette Shapera, Apr. 7, 1946; children: Jenny Anne Weiss Ford, Jonathan James. AB summa cum laude, U. Minn., 1941, ScB, 1947, MB, 1949, MD, 1950; MPH with high honors, Yale U., 1951. Diplomate: Am. Bd. Psychiatry and Neurology (examiner 1963-83). Teaching asst. psychology St. Thomas Coll., St. Paul, 1941-42; intern USPHS Hosp., Seattle, 1949-50; resident, fellow psychiatry Yale Med. Sch., 1950-53; from instr. to asst. prof. psychiatry Washington U., St. Louis, 1954-60; mem. faculty U. Mo., 1959—, First Prof. psychiatry, 1961—, founding chmn. dept., 1960-91, prof. community medicine, 1971—, univ. prof. emeritus, 1991—; vis. prof. Inst. Criminology, Cambridge (Eng.) U., 1968-69, All-India Inst. Med. Scis. and U. Malaya, 1984; internat. cons., 1958—; founding co-chmn. Asian-Am. Consortium on Psychiat. Disorders, 1986—; Kohler disting. lectr. St. Louis U., 1988. Author numerous articles in field; editor, co-author: Nurses, Patients, and Social Systems, 1968; corr. editor: Jour. Geriatric Psychiatry, 1967—; founding editor, chmn. bd. Jour. Operational Psychiatry, 1970-90; editorial advisor Community Mental Health Jour., 1979-87; trustee Mo. Rev., 1982-83. Served with M.C., AUS, 1942-46, PTO; to capt. M.C., AUS, 1953-54. Decorated Philippine Liberation medal, 1945; recipient Sir Henry Wellcome award, 1955, Israeli bronze medal, 1963, Basic Books award, 1974, Disting. Service commendation Nat. Council Community Mental Health Ctrs., 1982, 83, 86, Guhleman award for Clin. Excellence U. Mo., 1987, Hon. Achievement award U.Mo., 1991, Disting. Svc. award VA, 1991; named Chancellor's Emissary U. Mo., 1979; faculty fellow Inter-Univ. Council, 1958, sr. research fellow Am. Council Edn. and NSF, 1984. Found. fellow Royal Coll. Psychiatrists; fellow Royal Soc. Medicine, Am. Psychiat. Assn. (life), Am. Pub. Health Assn. (life), Am. Coll. Preventive Medicine (emeritus), Royal Soc. Health, AAAS, Am. Coll. Psychiatrists (life), Am. Assn. Psychoanalytic Physicians (hon.); mem. Assn. Mil. Surgeons U.S. (hon. life), Assn. Western Profs. Psychiatry (chmn. 1970-71), Mo. Acad. Psychiatry (1st pres. 1966-67), Mo. Psychiat. Assn. (life, pres. 1987-88), Assn. de Methodologie et Documentation en Psychiatrie, Mil. Order World Wars, Phi Beta Kappa, Sigma Xi, Psi Chi, Alpha Omega Alpha, Alpha Epsilon Sigma, Gamma Alpha. Clubs: Scholars (Cantab.); Wine Label (London); Yale (St. Louis); Univ. (Columbia). Research on suicide, homicide, antisocial behavior, aging, social psychiatry. Home: Crow Wing Farm RR 2 Box 2 Columbia MO 65201-9802 Office: U Mo Dept Psychiatry Columbia MO 65212 *Only this endures: creativity, the pursuit of excellence, and continuing concern for human civilization.*

WEISS, JAMES ROBERT, lawyer; b. Munich, Oct. 27, 1949; s. Norman Emanuel and Zelda Jane (Klein) W.; m. Lynn Marcia Levey, June 25, 1972; children: Allana, Tessa. BA, Northwestern U., 1971; JD, Cath. U. Am., 1974. Bar: Pa. 1974, D.C. 1985, Md. 1985. Trial atty. anti-trust div. U.S. Dept. Justice, Washington, 1974-80, asst. chief transp. sect. anti-trust div., 1980-86, chief transp., energy and agr. sect. anti-trust div., 1986-88; ptnr. Preston Gates Ellis & Rouvelas Meeds, Washington, 1988—. Contbr. articles to profl. jours. Mem. ABA (anti-trust sect. rep. to coordinating group on energy law 1988-91), D.C. Bar Assn., Fed. Energy Bar Assn., Md. Bar Assn. Jewish. Avocations: tennis, bicycling, hiking. Office: Preston Gates Ellis & Rouvelas Meeds 1735 New York Ave NW Washington DC 20006-5209

WEISS, JAY M(ICHAEL), psychologist, educator; b. Passaic, N.J., Mar. 20, 1941; s. Benjamin and Anne (Pearl) W.; m. Meryl Etta Levenson, June 9, 1963; children: Jennifer, Jason. BA, Lafayette Coll., 1962; PhD, Yale U., 1967. Asst. prof. Rockefeller U., N.Y.C., 1969-73, assoc. prof., 1973-84; prof. dept. psychiatry Med. Ctr., Duke U., Durham, N.C., 1984-92; prof. dept psychiatry behavioral scis. Emory U. Sch. Medicine, Atlanta, Ga., 1992-95, Jenny Culbreth Adams prof. psychiatry and behavioral scis., 1995—; adj. assoc. prof. NYU, 1973-84, CCNY, 1979-84. MacArthur Found. fellow, 1984-89. Fellow AAAS, Soc. for Behavioral Medicine. Office: Emory Univ Sch Medicine Ga Mental Health Inst 1256 Briarcliff Rd NE Atlanta GA 30306-2636

WEISS, JEFFREY L., federal agency director; b. New Haven, July 13, 1945; s. Robert Weiss and Elsie (Altschuler) Janis; m. Hemlata Nazli Pisharody, June 1, 1969; children: Vasanta, Jack. BA, Yale U., 1968; MPA, So. Meth. U., 1977. Vol. Peace Corps, India, 1968-72; country dir. Peace Corps, Seychelle Islands, 1977-80; agy. exec. ACTION, Tex., 1972-76, Small Bus. Agy., Washington, 1981-88; with Cmty. Rels. Svc., Dept. Justice, Washington, 1989-92, acting dir., 1993—. Vol. Orr Sch., Washington, 1991—, DuPont Cir. Citizens Assn., Washington, 1991—; active YMCA, 1988—. Mem. Am. Soc. Stoopers, Yale Club. Office: Dept Justice 10th and Constitution NW Washington DC 20530

WEISS, JEROME PAUL, lawyer; b. Binghamton, N.Y., May 16, 1934; s. Milton I. and Irene (Freeman) W.; m. Marion Levitt, June 30, 1963; children: Jonathan Peter, Andrew Stephen. AB magna cum laude, Princeton U., 1956; JD, Harvard U., 1961. Bar: N.Y. 1962, D.C. 1975. Assoc., Hiscock, Cowie, Bruce, Lee & Mawhinney, Syracuse, N.Y., 1961-64; asst. gen. counsel Agway, Inc., Syracuse, 1964-72; dep. gov. and gen. counsel Farm Credit Adminstrn., Washington, 1972-73; assoc. Hamel, Park, McCabe & Saunders, Washington, 1974-76, ptnr., 1976-78, sr. ptnr., 1978-83, mng. ptnr., 1983-86; mng. ptnr. Sonnenschein, Nath & Rosenthal, Washington, 1986—; adj. prof. Syracue U. Sch. Law, 1970-74, Antioch Sch. Law, 1974-76. Trustee Landon Sch., Bethesda, Md., 1982-88. Lt. USNR, 1956-58. Mem. ABA, N.Y. State Bar Assn., D.C. Bar Assn. Clubs: Riverbend Country (Great Falls, Va.); Naples (Fla.) Bath and Tennis. Contbr. articles to legal jours. Home: 488 River Rd Great Falls VA 22066 Office: Sonnenschein Nath & Rosenthal 1301 K St NW Washington DC 20005-3317

WEISS, JOANNE MARION, writer; b. Wayne, N.J., Mar. 16, 1960; d. Henry Daniel and Florence Frances (Zaratkiewicz) W. BA, Bennington Coll., 1982; MA, U. Cambridge, Eng., 1988. Prodn. mgr. The Suburban News, N.J., 1982-83; gardener Artistic Landscaping, N.J., 1983; case mgr. Mid-Bergan Mental Health Ctr., N.J., 1985-86; founder Isis Farm Writers, 1995—. Author, dir.; (play) The Gift, 1987, 88. Translator Solidarity, Poland, 1983; co-leader Vols. for Peace, 1986; mem., worker Pregnancy Adv. Svc., Cambridge, 1991-92. Recipient scholarship Inst. for Brit. and Irish Studies, Trinity Coll., Dublin, 1985, Chancellor's medal for poetry U. Cambridge, Eng., 1988, grants for Edinburgh, Sir John Gielgud, 1988, grant Judith Wilson Fund, U. Cambridge, Eng., 1988. Mem. People for Ethical Treatment of Animals. Avocations: dog and horse training, animal welfare, singing, classical Greek, organic farming. Home: Isis Farm 265 River Rd Suncook NH 03275

WEISS, JOSEPH JOEL, consulting company executive; b. Newark, July 27, 1931; s. Harry H. and Belle (Sass) W.; m. Leah Kneller, Apr. 10, 1954 (div. 1961); children: Sara, Daniel; m. Carol Lynn Seegott, Sept. 29, 1967; children: Laura, John. BSBA, Rutgers U., 1953, MBA, 1958. Dist. mgr. N.J. Bell Telephone Co., 1955-61; asst. comptroller ITT P.R. Telephone Co., San Juan, 1964-68; sr. cons. N.Y.C., 1968-71; v.p. data services Rio De Janeiro, 1971-74; dir. ops. N.Y.C., 1975-80; v.p. Control Data Corp., Rio De Janeiro, 1974-75; exec. v.p., chief adminstrv. officer Burger King Corp., Miami, 1980-89; chief oper. officer Goode, Olcott, Knight & Assocs., Coral Gables, Fla., 1989-90; pres. Contraband Detection Internat., Miami, Fla., 1990-92, Cons. Group Internat., Solon, Ohio, 1992—, Seegot Environ., Solon, 1992—; bd. dirs. WPB TV. Pres. Civic Betterment Assn., Franklin Twp., N.J., 1961; trustee U. Miami Citizens Bd., 1987—; bd. dirs. Boy Scouts Am., 1982—. Maj. USAF, 1954-63. Recipient Strategic Planning Achievement award Boy Scouts Am., 1985. Mem. Hist. Soc. Fla. (bd. dirs. 1986—). Republican. Presbyterian. Club: Fisher Island. Avocations: oil painting, tennis. Home: 8216 Chagrin Rd Chagrin Falls OH 44023-4746 Office: Seegot Environ 10040 Aurora-Hudson Rd Streetsboro OH 44241

WEISS, JUDITH MIRIAM, psychologist; b. Chgo., June 29, 1939; d. Louis and Annette (Frazin) Schmerling; m. Jon Howard Kaas, May 19, 1963 (div. Dec. 1984); children: Lisa Karen, Jon Michael; m. Stephen Fred Weiss, Dec. 22, 1988. AB in Liberal Arts, Northwestern U., 1961; PhD, Duke U., 1969. Lic. clin. psychologist, Tenn. Postdoctoral fellow U. Wis. Hosp., Madison, 1969-71; neuropsychologist Mental Health Assocs., Madison, 1971-72; asst. prof. George Peabody Coll., Nashville, 1972-77, Vanderbilt U., Nashville, 1972-77; neuropsychologist Comprehensive Clin. Svcs., Nashville, 1977—; advocate, cons. Tenn. Protection and Advocacy, Inc., Nashville, 1976—. Mem. CABLE, Nashville. Mem. APA, Tenn. Psychol. Assn., Internat. Neuropsychol. Assn., Nat. Acad. Neuropsychology, U.s.-China Peoples Friendship Assn., Tenn. Head Injury Assn., B.R.A.I.N., Tenn. Assn. for the Talented and Gifted, Tenn. Assn. Audiologists and Speech-Lang. Pathologists, Nashville Area Psychol. Assn., Coun. for Learning Disabilities, Assn. for Children with Learning Disabilities. Jewish. Home: 893 Stirrup Dr Nashville TN 37221-1918 Office: Comprehensive Clin Svcs 102 Woodmont Blvd Ste 215 Nashville TN 37205-2287

WEISS, JULIE, costume designer. Costume designer: (stage) The Elephant Man, 1979 (Tony award nomination best costume design 1979); (films) I'm Dancing as Fast as I Can, 1982, Independence Day, 1983, Second Thoughts, 1983, Spacehunter: Adventures in the Forbidden Zone, 1983, Testament, 1983, The Mean Season, 1985, Creator, 1985, F/X, 1986, Masters of the Universe, 1987, The Whales of August, 1987, 1969, 1988, Tequila Sunrise, 1988, Steel Magnolias, 1989, Wicked Stepmother, 1989, The Freshman, 1990, Married to It, 1991, Honeymoon in Vegas, 1992, House of Cards, 1993, Searching for Bobby Fischer, 1993, Naked in New York, 1993, It Could Happen to You, 1994, 12 Monkeys, 1995 (Acad. award nominee for best costume design 1996); (TV movies) The Gangster Chronicles, 1981, The Elephant Man, 1982 (Emmy award nominee for best costume design 1982), Little Gloria...Happy at Last, 1982 (Emmy award nominee for best costume design 1983), The Dollmaker, 1984 (Emmy award for best costume design 1984), Do You Remember Love?, 1985, Evergreen, 1985 (Emmy award nominee for best costume design 1985), Conspiracy of Love, 1987, A Woman of Independant Means, 1994 (Emmy award for best costume design), Love She Sought, 1990, The Portrait, 1993; costume cons.: (films) Cherry 2000, 1988. Office: care Costume Designer's Guild 13949 Ventura Blvd Ste 309 Sherman Oaks CA 91423-3570*

WEISS, KENNETH ANDREW, lawyer, law educator; b. New Orleans, Jan. 16, 1951; s. Irving and Julia (Mayer) W.; m. Barbara Hollingsworth, June 30, 1979. BA, Tulane U., 1972, JD with honors, 1975; LLM in Taxation with highest honors, George Washington U., 1981. Bar: La. 1975, D.C. 1976. Edit. writer, Washington corr. The Times-Picayune, New Orleans and Washington, 1973-79; news editor Congl. Quarterly, Washington, 1979-81; mng. editor Reporters Com. for Freedom of the Press, Washington, 1981-82; assoc. atty. McGlinchey Stafford Lang, New Orleans, 1982-84, dir., 1984—; prof. Tulane U. Law Sch., New Orleans, 1987—; mem. trust code com. La. Law Inst., Baton Rouge, 1993—; mem. planning com. Tulane Tax Inst., 1996—. Co-author: Bankers' Guide to Establishing, Managing and Operating Common Trust Funds, 1986, Business Uses of Life Insurance, 1986, Executive Compensation, 1990; assoc. editor Tulane Law Rev., 1974-75, mem. bd. adv. editors, 1992—; contbr. articles to profl. jours. Bd. dirs. Longue Vue House and Gardens Adv. Corp., 1993-95, bd. dirs. Longue Vue Found., 1995—; trustee Greater New Orleans Ednl. TV Found., Sta. WYES-TV, 1994—; mem. profl. adv. com., Jewish Endowment Found., 1982—; mem. planned gifts adv. com. Tulane U., 1989—; active Met. Area Com. Leadership Forum, New Orleans, 1983; fellow Inst. Politics Loyola U., New Orleans, 1989-90; mem. devel. com. Greater New Orleans Found., 1995—. Recipient Addy award for polit. advt., 1989, awards for investigative reporting; Phi Delta Phi scholar, 1972-73. Fellow Am. Coll. Trust and Estate Counsel; mem. La. State Bar Assn. (taxation sect., bd. cert. tax atty.), New Orleans Bar Assn., New Orleans Estate Planning Coun., Order of the Coif. Republican. Jewish. Office: McGlinchey Stafford Lang 643 Magazine St New Orleans LA 70130-3405

WEISS, KENNETH JAY, education educator, reading specialist, administrator; b. N.Y.C., Mar. 26, 1950; s. Daniel and Ida (Berson) W.; m. Roberta Carol Ungar, June 10, 1973; children: Seth, Marc, Richard. BA, C.W. Post Coll., 1972; MBA, Long Island U., 1982; EdM, Rutgers U., 1989, EdD, 1993. Cert. tchr. reading specialist, adminstr., N.J. Tchr. Rabbi Pesach Raymon Yeshiva, Edison, N.J., 1988-92; ednl. cons. New Brunswick (N.J.) Tomorrow, 1992-93; teaching rsch. asst. Rutgers U. Grad. Sch. of Edn., New Brunswick, 1991-93; asst. prof. edn., dir. grad. reading program Nazareth Coll., Rochester, N.Y., 1993—; spkr., facilitator, Rutgers Annual Summer Inst. on Literature and Literacy, New Brunswick, N.J., 1991, 92, 93, IRA Confs. Editl. rev. bd. Reading Teacher, 1995—, NYS Lang. and Literacy Spectrum. Bd. dirs. IRA SIG Children's Reading and Lit. Named Holmes Group Scholar, 1992-93. Mem. NCTE, Internat. Reading Assn., N.Y. State Reading Assn., Nat. Reading Conf., Nat. Rsch. Fon. Lit. & Lang. Arts, Kappa Kelta Pi (counselor Rho Psi chpt. 1996—).

WEISS, LAWRENCE N., lawyer; b. N.Y.C., Aug. 9, 1942; s. Joseph and Martha (Guggenheimer) W.; m. Osnat Gad. BA, CCNY, 1963; LLB summa cum laude, Columbia U., 1966. Bar: N.Y. 1966, U.S. Ct. Appeals (2d cir.) 1967, U.S. Dist. Ct. (so. and ea. dists) N.Y. 1968, U.S. Supreme Ct. 1971, U.S. Tax Ct. 1977, U.S. Ct. Appeals (3d cir.) 1968, U.S. Ct. Appeals (6th cir.) 1980, U.S. Tax Ct. 1977. Assoc. Kaye, Scholer, Fierman, Hays & Handler, N.Y.C., 1966-67, 67-73; law clk. to judge N.Y. Ct. Appeals, Albany and N.Y.C., 1967; assoc. Botein, Hays, Sklar & Herzberg, N.Y.C., 1973-76; assoc. Weisman, Celler, Spett, Modlin & Wertheimer, N.Y.C., 1976, ptnr., 1977-79, counsel, 1979-81; prin. Lawrence N. Weiss, P.C., N.Y.C., 1981—; Pantaleoni Govens & Weiss, N.Y.C., 1993—; arbitrator Am. Arbitration Assn., 1968—, Civil Ct., N.Y.C., 1985—, Better Bus. Bur., N.Y.C., 1987—; mediator U.S. Dist. Ct. (ea. dist.) N.Y. and N.Y. Supreme Ct. Mem. Assn. Bar of City of N.Y. (com. on legal edn. and admission to bar), N.Y. State Bar Assn. (chair com. on fed. judiciary, spl. com. on copyright, vice chair com. on UN, subcom. internat. cts., com. continuing legal edn. litig. sect., judiciary com.). Avocations: Shakespearean studies, equestrian, scuba. Home: 230 Central Park W New York NY 10024-6029

WEISS, LEONARD, mathematician, engineer, senate staff director; b. N.Y.C., Mar. 14, 1934; s. Max and Sadie (Albert) W.; m. Sandra Joyce Raynes, June 15, 1958; children: Madelyn, Eugene. B.E.E., CCNY, 1956; M.S., Columbia U., 1959; Ph.D., Johns Hopkins U., 1962. Lectr. CCNY, 1956-59; staff scientist Research Inst. for Advanced Studies, Balt., 1962-64; asst. prof. Brown U., Providence, 1964-66; assoc. prof. Brown U., 1966-68; prof. U. Md., College Park, 1968-78; legis. asst. to Senator John Glenn of Ohio, 1976-77; cons. Naval Research Lab., Washington, 1970-77; staff dir. Senate Subcom. on Energy, Nuclear Proliferation and Govt. Processes, 1977-86, Senate Com. Govtl. Affairs., 1987—. Editor: Ordinary Differential Equations, 1972; contbr. articles to profl. jours.; author legislation on nuclear proliferation, energy, govt. orgn., and govt. mgmt. Alfred P. Sloan research fellow, 1966-68; IEEE Congl. fellow, 1976. Mem. AAAS, IEEE, Sigma Xi. Home: 11701 Auth Ln Silver Spring MD 20902-1644 Office: 326 Dirksen Bldg Washington DC 20510-0010

WEISS, LINDA WOLFF, health systems administrator; b. Albany, N.Y., Apr. 12, 1953; d. Charles Vincent and Hilda Bertha (Kitzman) Wolff; divorced; 1 child, Russell. AAS, Hudson Valley C.C., Troy, N.Y., 1973; BS, Empire State Coll., 1983; MS in Health Sys. Mgmt., Union Coll., 1987. Staff nuc. medicine technologist VA Med. Ctr., Albany, 1973-83, chief technologist nuc. medicine, 1983-84, asst. chief radiology/nuc. medicine svc., 1984-87, area mgr. emergency medicine preparedness office, 1987-94; area mgr. emergency medicine preparedness office U.S. Dept VA, Albany and Syracuse, N.Y., 1994-96; dir. managed care and planning Upstate N.Y. VA Healthcare Network, Albany, 1996—; mem. N.Y. State Disaster Preparedness Commn., Albany; charter mem. human needs in disaster standing com., 1989-96, Albany County Local Emergency Preparedness Commn., 1987-96, N.Y. State Vol. Orgns. Active in Disaster, 1989; mem. adj. faculty, tutor Empire State Coll., Albany; investigator Northridge Earthquake Epidemiology Study, 1995—. Contbg. editor Jour. Clin. Ultrasound, 1981-85, Med. Ultrasound, 1981-83; mem. editl. bd. EMPO News, 1992-96. W.K. Kellogg Found. Ptnrs. fellow, 1990-93; Leadership VA class, 1996; recipient Dir.'s cert. Hurricane Andrews Response, 1992. Mem. Ptnrs. of the Am. (W.K. Kellogg Found. fellow 1990-93, chair emergency preparedness com. 1991—), Proctor's Theater, Barn Raisers. Lutheran. Avocations: travel, project devel., swimming, bungee jumping. Office: Upstate NY VA Healthcare PO Box 8980 Albany NY 12208-0980

WEISS, LIONEL EDWARD, geology educator; b. London, Eng., Dec. 11, 1927; came to U.S., 1956, naturalized, 1972; s. S. and E. (Carney) W.; m. Liv Mariane Nissen-Sollie, Dec. 27, 1964; children: Nicholas Erling, Elin Katrina. B.Sc. with 1st class honours, U. Birmingham, Eng., 1949, Ph.D., 1953; Sc.D., U. Edinburgh, Scotland, 1956. Commonwealth Fund fellow U. Calif. at Berkeley, 1951-53; sr. research fellow U. Edinburgh, 1953-56; mem. faculty U. Calif. at Berkeley, 1956—, prof. geology, 1964-89, emeritus prof. geology, 1989—, Miller research prof., 1965, 66; cons. in field. Author: (with F.J. Turner) Structural Analysis of Metamorphic Tectonites, 1963, (with others) The Earth, 1970, The Minor Structures of Deformed Rocks, 1972; also articles. Guggenheim fellow, 1962, 69; Fulbright scholar Norway, 1975. Home: 1954 Patricia Dr Pleasant Hill CA 94523-2930

WEISS, MAREDA RUTH, dean; b. Chgo., Sept. 23, 1941; d. William Arthur and Ruth Emily (Schauble) W. BBA, U. Wis., 1963. Acct., then supr. rsch. adminstrn./fin. U. Wis. System, Madison, 1964-69; specialist, asst. dean, now assoc. dean, dir. rsch. svcs. U. Wis., Madison, 1969—; univ. chair State Employees Combined Campaign, Madison, 1986. Treas. Wis. Cen. Ctr. Aux., Madison, 1971-73, 75-77, 79-81, Frineds of WHA-TV pub. tv, Madison, 1989-91; chair nominating com. U. Wis. Credit Union, 1982-88. Mem. Nat. Coun. Univ. Rsch. Adminstrs. (presenter workshops, sec.-treas. 1980-83, chair, vice-chair mid-Am. region 1989-91, Disting. Svc. award 1989), Univ. Ins. Assn. (bd. dirs. 1982—). Avocations: skiing, golf, photography, travel. Office: U Wis Grad Sch 500 Lincoln Dr Madison WI 53706-1314

WEISS, MARK, public relations executive; b. N.Y.C., Mar. 5, 1950. BA in Psychology, Queens Coll., 1972; MA om Social Psychology, New Sch. for Social Rsch., 1975. With Multimedia Advt./Pub. Rels., 1970-74; account rep. Edward Baker, Inc., 1974-78; account exec. Rowland Co., 1978-81, v.p., 1980-84, sr. v.p., 1984-86, exec. v.p., 1986-90, sr. exec. v.p., COO, 1991-92, pres., CEO, 1992—. Office: Rowland Worldwide Inc 1675 Broadway New York NY 10019-5820*

WEISS, MARK ANSCHEL, lawyer; b. N.Y.C., June 20, 1937; s. George and Ida (Galin) W.; m. Joan Roth, June 8, 1958; children—Rebecca, Sarabeth, Jonathan, Deborah. A.B., Columbia U., 1958; LL.B. magna cum laude, Harvard U., 1961; Bar: N.Y. 1961, D.C. 1962, U.S. Supreme Ct. 1965. Assoc. Covington & Burling, Washington, 1961-66, 69-70, ptnr., 1970—; spl. asst. to Under Sec. Treasury Dept., Washington, 1966-68, spl. asst. to sec., 1968-69. Mem. D.C. Bar, ABA, Fed. Bar Assn., City Club (Washington). Office: Covington & Burling PO Box 7566 1201 Pennsylvania Ave NW Washington DC 20044

WEISS, MARK LAWRENCE, anthropology educator; b. Bklyn., Nov. 1, 1945; s. Arthur A. and Ruth E. Heilbrunn W.; m. Linda K. Spangler, July 31, 1993; children: Evan M., Emily C. BA, SUNY, Binghamton, 1966; MA, U. Calif., Berkeley, 1968, PhD, 1969. Asst. prof. anthropology Wayne State U., Detroit, 1969-73, assoc. prof., 1973-87, prof., 1987—; program dir. phys. anthropology NSF, Washington, 1990-92, 95—. Co-author: Human Biology and Behavior, 1975; contbr. articles to Nature, Am. Jour. Primatology, Yearbook, Phys. Anthropology, Jour. Molecular Biology; mem. editorial bd. Human Biology, 1988—, Yearbook of Phys. Anthropology, 1992—, Jour. Human Evolution, 1994—. Recipient award in excellence in teaching and rsch. Probus Club, 1973. Fellow Am. Anthrop. Assn., Am. Assn. Phys. Anthropologists (exec. com. 1993-96). Jewish. Office: Dept Anthropology Wayne State Univ. Detroit MI 48202

WEISS, MARTIN HARVEY, neurosurgeon, educator; b. Newark, Feb. 2, 1939; s. Max and Rae W.; m. R. Debora Rosenthal, Aug. 20, 1961; children: Brad, Jessica, Elisabeth. AB magna cum laude, Dartmouth Coll., 1960, BMS, 1961; MD, Cornell U., 1963. Diplomate Am. Bd. Neurol. Surgery (bd. dirs. 1983-89, vice chmn. 1987-88, chmn. 1988-89). Intern Univ. Hosps., Cleve., 1963-64; resident in neurosurgery Univ. Hosps., 1966-70; sr. instr. to asst. prof. neurosurgery Case Western Res. U., 1970-73; asso. prof. neurosurgery U. So. Calif., 1973-76, prof., 1976-78, prof., chmn. dept., 1978—; chmn. neurology B study sect. NIH; mem. residency rev. com. for neurosurgery Accreditation Commn. for Grad. Med. Edn., 1989—, vice chmn., 1991-93, chmn., 1993-95, mem. appeals coun. in neurosurgery, 1995—; Courville lectr. Loma Linda U. Sch. Medicine, 1989; Edgar Kahn vis. prof. U. Mich., 1987; W. James Gardner lectr. Cleve. Clinic, 1993; Edwin Boldrey vis. prof. U. Calif., San Francisco, 1994; hon. guest San Francisco Neurol. Soc., 1994, Australian Neurosurg. Soc., 1996; Arthur Ward vis. prof. U. Wash., 1988; John Raff vis. prof. U. Oreg., 1995; Afrox traveling prof. South African Congress Neurol. Surgeons, 1989; Loyal Davis lectr. Northwestern U., 1990. Author: Pituitary Diseases, 1980; editor-in-chief Clin. Neurosurgery, 1980-83; assoc. editor Bull. L.A. Neurol. Socs., 1976-81, Jour. Clin. Neurosci., 1981—; mem. editl. bd. Neurosurgery, 1979-84, Neurol. Rsch., 1980—, Jour. Neurosurgery, 1987—, chmn., 1995—, assoc. editor, 1996. Served to capt. USAR, 1964-66. Spl. fellow in neurosurgery NIH, 1969-70; recipient Jamieson medal Australian Neurosurg. Soc., 1996. Mem. ACS (adv. coun. neurosurgery 1985-88), Soc. Neurol. Surgeons, Neurosurg. Soc. Am., Am. Acad. Neurol. Surgery (exec. com. 1988-89, v.p. 1992-93), Rsch. Soc. Neurol. Surgeons, Am. Assn. Neurol. Surgeons (bd. dirs. 1988-91, sec. 1994-97), Congress Neurol. Surgeons (v.p. 1982-83), Western Neurosurg. Soc., Neurosurg. Forum, So. Calif. Neurosurg. Soc. (pres. 1983-84), Phi Beta Kappa, Alpha Omega Alpha. Home: 357 Georgian Rd La Canada-Flintridge CA 91011-3520 Office: 1200 N State St Los Angeles CA 90033-4525

WEISS, MAX TIBOR, aerospace company executive; b. Hajduananas, Hungary, Dec. 29, 1922; came to U.S., 1929, naturalized, 1936; s. Samuel and Anna (Hornstein) W.; m. Melitta Newman, June 28, 1953; children: Samuel Harvey, Herschel William, David Nathaniel, Deborah Beth. BEE, CCNY, 1943; MS, MIT, 1947, PhD, 1950. Rsch. assoc. MIT, 1946-50; mem. tech. staff Bell Tel. Labs., Holmdel, N.J., 1950-59; assoc. head applied physics lab. Hughes Aircraft Co., Culver City, Calif., 1959-60; dir. electronics rsch. lab. The Aerospace Corp., L.A., 1961-63, gen. mgr. labs. div., 1963-67, gen. mgr. electronics and optics div., 1968-78, v.p., gen. mgr. lab. ops., 1978-81, v.p. engring. group, 1981-86; v.p. tech. and electronics system group Northrop Corp., L.A., 1986-91; v.p., gen. mgr. electronics systems div. Northrop Corp., Hawthorne, Calif., 1991-94; corp. v.p., dep. gen. mgr. electronics/systems integration Northrop Grumman Corp., Bethpage, N.Y., 1994-96, corp. v.p., 1996—; asst. mgr. engring. ops. TRW Systems, Redondo Beach, Calif., 1967-68; mem. sci. adv. bd. USAF. Contbr. articles to physics and electronics jours.; patentee in electronics and communications. With USNR, 1944-45. Fellow Am. Phys. Soc., IEEE (Centennial medal, 1983, Fredrik Philips award, 1993), AIAA, AAAS; mem. NAE, Sigma Xi. Office: 1840 Century Park E Los Angeles CA 90067

WEISS, MORDECHAI, principal. Prin. Hebrew Acad. Atlantic County, Margate City, N.J. Recipient Elem. Sch. Recognition award U.S. Dept. Edn., 1989-90. Office: Hebrew Acad Atlantic County 6814 Black Horse Pike Pleasantville NJ 08232-4132

WEISS, MORRY, greeting card company executive; b. Czechoslovakia, 1940; m. Judith Stone. Grad., Wayne State U. Salesman, field mgr. Am. Greetings Corp., Cleve., 1961-66, advt. mgr., 1966-68, v.p., 1969-73, group v.p. mktg. and sales, 1973-78, formerly chief operating officer, from 1978, pres., 1978-92, also bd. dirs., chief exec. officer, 1987—, chmn., 1992—. Office: Am Greetings Corp 10500 American Rd Cleveland OH 44144-2301*

WEISS, MYRNA GRACE, business consultant; b. N.Y.C., June 22, 1939; d. Herman and Blanche (Stiftel) Ziegler; m. Arthur H. Weiss; children: Debra Anne Huddleston, Louise Esther. BA, Barnard Coll., 1958; MA, Hunter Coll., 1968; MPA, NYU, 1978; cert. in Mktg., U. Pa. Tchr. N.Y.C. and Vallejo, Calif., 1959-68; dir. admissions Columbia Prep. Sch., N.Y.C., 1969-72; dir. PREP counselling NYU, N.Y.C., 1973-74; dept. head Hewitt Sch., N.Y.C., 1974-79; mgr. Met. Ins. Co., N.Y.C., 1979-84; mktg. exec. Rothschild, Inc., N.Y.C., 1984-85; pres. First Mktg. Capital Group Ltd., N.Y.C., 1985—; mng. dir. Wrap Co. Internat. N.V., 1992—; advisor Lared Group, N.Y.C., 1987—; advisor Gov.'s Hwy. Safety Com., N.Y.C., 1985-88; pres. Fin. Women's Assn. N.Y., 1984-85. Bd. dirs. 92nd Y, N.Y.C., 1972-90, ARC, N.Y.C., 1989—, asst. treas., 1993—. Mem. Internat. Women's Forum (bd. dirs. 1990-92), Econ. Club N.Y., Women's Econ. Roundtable (bd. dirs. 1988-90). Office: 1st Mktg Capital Group Ltd 1056 Fifth Ave New York NY 10028-0112

WEISS, PAUL, philosopher, educator; b. N.Y.C., May 19, 1901; s. Samuel and Emma (Rothschild) W.; m. Victoria Brodkin, Oct. 27, 1928 (dec. Dec. 31, 1953); children: Judith, Jonathan. BSS, CCNY, 1927; MA, Harvard U., 1928, PhD (Sears Travelling fellow), 1929; hon. degrees, Grinnell Coll., 1960, Pace Coll., 1969, Bellarmine Coll., 1973, Haverford Coll., 1974, Boston U., 1989. Instr., tutor philosophy Harvard U., also instr. Radcliffe Coll., 1930-31; assoc. in philosophy Bryn Mawr (Pa.) Coll., 1931-33, assoc. prof., 1933-40, prof., 1940-46, chmn. dept., 1944-46; Guggenheim fellow, 1938; vis. prof. Yale U., 1945-46, prof. philosophy, 1946-62, Sterling prof. philosophy, 1962-69, Sterling prof. emeritus, 1969—; fellow Ezra Stiles Coll.; vis. prof. philosophy Hebrew U., Jerusalem, 1951; Luce-Rabinowitz grantee for study, Israel and India, 1954; lectr. Aspen Inst., 1952, Chancellor's Forum, U. Denver, 1952; Orde Wingate lectr., 1954; Powell lectr. U. Ind., 1958; Gates lectr. Grinnell Coll., 1960; Matchette lectr. Purdue U., 1961, Wesleyan Coll., 1963; Aquinas lectr. Marquette U., 1963; Townsend Harris medalist, 1963; Rhoades lectr. Haverford Coll., 1964; Phi Beta Kappa lectr., 1968-69; resident scholar State U. N.Y., 1969, 70; vis. prof. U. Denver, spring 1969; Eliot lectr. Marquette U., 1970; William De Vane medalist Yale, 1971; Aquinas lectr. St. Mary's, 1971; medalist City Coll., 1973, Hofstra U., 1973; B. Means lectr. Trinity Coll.; lectr., Japan, 1981; Ann. McDermott Lectr. U. Dallas, 1983; vis. Heffer prof. Philosophy Cath. U. Am., 1969-91, 93-94. Author: Reality, 1938, Nature and Man, 1947, Man's Freedom, 1950 (Portugese transl., 1960), Modes of Being, 1958, Our Public Life, 1959, World of Art, 1961 (Hebrew transl., 1970), Nine Basic Arts, 1961, History: Written and Lived, 1962, Religion and Art, 1963, The God We Seek, 1964, Philosophy in Process, 12 vols., 1955-88, The Making of Men, 1967, Sport: A Philosophic Inquiry, 1969 (Japanese transl., 1985, Korean transl., 1993), Beyond All Appearances, 1974, Cinematics, 1975, First Considerations, 1977, You, I and The Others, 1980, Privacy, 1983, Toward a Perfected State, 1986, Creative Ventures, 1991, Being and Other Realities, 1995; co-author: Right and Wrong: A Philosophical Dialogue Between Father and Son, 1967, 71 (Hebrew transl., 1971), Approaches to World Peace, 1944, Perspectives on a Troubled Decade, 1950, Moral Principles of Action, 1952, Personal Moments of Discovery, 1953, Perspectives on Peirce, 1965, Dimensions of Job, 1969, Mid-Century American Philosophy, 1974, Philosophy of Baruch Spinoza, 1980, Existence and Actuality, 1984, When the Worst That Can Happen Already Has, 1992, The Philosophy of Paul Weiss: Autobiography, Replies to Critics, Drawings, and Bibliography, 1995; co-editor: Collected Papers of Charles S. Peirce, 6 vols.; founder, editor Rev. Metaphysics, 1947-63; mem. editl. bd. Judaism, Jour. Speculative Philosophy; contbr. articles to profl. jours. Mem. Assn. for Symbolic Logic (councillor 1936), Am. Philos. Assn. (co-pres. 1966), Conf. on Sci., Philosophy and Religion (founding), C.S. Peirce Soc. (founding, pres.), Metaphys. Soc. Am. (founder, pres. 1951-52, councillor 1953-58), Philos. Soc. for Study of Sport (co-founder, pres. 1973), Am. Friends Hebrew U., Philos. Edn. Soc. (founder), Washington Philosophic Club (C.S. Peirce award), European Soc. Culture, Internat. Acad. Philosophy of Art, Am. Assn. Mid. East Studies, Aurelian Club, Elizabethan Club, Phi Beta Kappa. Address: 2000 N St NW Washington DC 20036-2336

WEISS, PAUL THOMAS, management consultant; b. Bismarck, N.D., Nov. 18, 1944; s. Earl Paul and Hazel Lucretia (Baker) W.; children: Mark David, Clare Elizabeth. BS, U. N.D., 1967. Pers. mgmt. specialist Dept. Justice, Washington, 1970-72; labor employee relations specialist Dept. Treasury, Washington, 1972-77; assoc. dir. human resources Comptr. of Currency, Washington, 1977-80; dep. dir. pers. Dept. Treasury, Washington, 1980-83, dir. pers., 1984-85; assoc. adminstr. for adminstrn. GSA, Washington, 1985-89; assoc. dir. mgmt. and budget U.S. Action Agy., Washington, 1989-90; dep. asst. sec. for adminstrn. Dept. Transp., Washington, 1990-95; pvt. practice mgmt. cons., 1995—; mem. Pres. Coun. Mgmt. Improvement, 1985-89; mem. panel on pub. svc. Nat. Acad. Pub. Adminstrn., 1986—; v.p., mem. exec. com. Am. Consortium for Internat. Pub. Adminstrn., 1986—; bd. dirs. Worldwide Assurance for Employees of Pub. Agys., Inc., 1986—. Author (booklet) You and Your Employees, 1974; author, reviewer numerous reports and govt. manuals. With Med. Svc. Corps, U.S. Army, 1969-70, Vietnam. Decorated Bronze Star medal with 3 oak leaf clusters; recipient Pres. Rank Meritorious Svc. award Pres. U.S., 1987, awards U.S. Treas., 1979, 85, Govt. Exec. Mag. Leadership award, 1992. Mem. Sr. Execs. Assn., Am. Soc. Pub. Adminstrs. (bd. dirs. Nat. Capital area chpt.). Roman Catholic. Avocations: bridge, jogging, reading. Office: US Dept Transp 400 7th St NW Washington DC 20590-0001

WEISS, RANDALL A., television producer, supermarket executive; b. Gary, Ind., Sept. 3, 1952; s. Arthur and Sylvia (Mednick) W.; m. Adrienne J. Weiss, Feb. 5, 1973; children: Benjamin, Caleb, Joshua, James, Abigail, Emma. AA, Coll. DuPage, 1977; BA, Dallas Bapt. U., 1993; MA in Religious Studies, Greenwich U., 1994; diploma of practical theology, Christ for the Nations Inst., 1993; PhD, Greenwich U., 1995; MS in Jewish Studies, Spertus Inst. Jewish Studies, 1996; DMin, Faraston Theol. Sem., 1996. Gen. mgr. We Care Food Stores, Inc., Knox, Ind., 1975-84; pres., CEO We Care Food Stores, Inc. subs. Five Star Foods, Knox, Ind., 1984—; asst. prof. on adj. faculty ICI U.; dean Jewish studies dept. Faraston Theol. Sem. Author: Jewish Sects of the New Testament Era, Does Jacob's Trouble Wear a Cross?: Christianity: A Jewish Religion; pub. Lordship Music, Excellence inChristian Books; writer, artist: (TV show) Crosstalk, 1994, 95, 96. Internat. dir. Lesea Global Feed the Hungry, South Bend, Ind., 1988—. Recipient Excellence in Christian Broadcasting award. Mem. Full Gospel Bus. Men's Fellowship Internat. (life, banquet spkr.), Soc. for Pentecostal Studies, Evang. Theol. Soc. Avocations: fishing, travel, reading, music. Office: Five Star Foods 1209 S Heaton St Knox IN 46534-2311

WEISS, RENÉE KAROL, editor, writer, musician; b. Allentown, Pa., Sept. 11, 1923; d. Abraham S. and Elizabeth (Levitt) Karol; m. Theodore Weiss. BA, Bard Coll., 1951; student, Conn. Sch. Dance; studied violin with Sascha Jacobinoff, Boris Koutzen, Emile Hauser, Ivan Galamian. Mem. Miami U. Symphony Orch., 1941, N.C. State Sympnony, 1942-45, Oxford U. Symphony, Opera Orchs., Eng., 1953-54, Woodstock String Quartet, 1956-60, Bard Coll. Chamber Ensemble, 1950-66, Hudson Valley Philharmonic, 1960-66, Hudson Valley String Quartet, 1965, Princeton Chamber Orch., 1980-93; orchestral, chamber, solo work, 1966—; mem. Theodore Weiss poetry writing workshops Princeton U., 1985, Hofstra Coll., 1985, modern poetry workshop Cooper Union, 1988; tchr. modern dance to children Bard Coll., Kindergarten Tivoli, N.Y. Pub. Sch., 1955-58. Author: (children's books) To Win A Race, 1966, A Paper Zoo, 1968 (best books for children N.Y. Times, Book World 1968, N.J. Author's award 1968, 70, 88), The Bird From the Sea, 1970, David Schubert: Works and Days, 1984; co-editor, mgr. Quar. Rev. Lit., 1945—; contbr. poems to various jours.; poetry readings (with Theodore Weiss) at various colls. in U.S. and abroad, including China. Office: Q R L Poetry Series 26 Haslet Ave Princeton NJ 08540-4914

WEISS, RICHARD RONALD, rocket propulsion technology executive; b. Detroit, Nov. 4, 1934; s. Charles Max and Edna May (Guard) W.; m. Sally Anita Sparkman, Aug. 10, 1957; children: Mark, Kevin, Todd, Scott. BS in Aero. Engring., U. Mich., 1957; MSME, U. So. Calif., 1964; PhD in Mech. Engring., Purdue U., 1970. Devel. engr. Jupiter Missile rocket engine Rocketdyne, 1957-58; unit chief, test condr. THOR Missile test program Air Force Rocket Prop. Lab., 1958-61, various tech. positions, 1961-65, various engring. mgmt. positions, 1965-74, chief scientist, 1974-89, 1st dir. Strategic Def. Initiative Tech. Office, 1985-87; chief scientist Air Force Rocket Prop. Lab. (renamed Astronautics Lab.), 1987-89; dir. Astronautics Lab., 1989-90; chief scientist, dir. Astronautics Lab. (merger Phillips Lab.), 1990-91; dir. Propulsion Directorate Phillips Lab. Operating Location, Edwards AFB, Calif., 1991-93; dep. dir. space launch systems and tech. Office of Under Sec. of Def., Strategic and Space Systems, Missiles and Space Systems, 1993-94; ret., 1994; past tech. panel chmn. Space Launch Modernization Plan, 1994; mem. Nat. Rsch. Coun. Aeronautics & Space Engring. Bd., Advanced Space Tech. Panel, Washington, 1992-94; U.S. rep. Agard Propulsion & Energetics Panel, Paris, 1987—; mem. ad hoc panel on space launch USAF Sci., 1993—; chmn. Joint Army, Navy, AF (JANNAF) Interagy. Chem. Propulsion Exec. Com.; contbr. to rocket propulsion devels. for most of the nation's space and missile sys. including Apollo, Space Shuttle, Titan, Atlas, Peacekeeper, Minuteman, Strategic Def. Initiative;. 1st lt. USAF, 1958-61. Co-recipient Air Force Sys. Command Aerospace Primus award, 1986. Fellow AIAA (assoc., AIAA Wyld Propulsion award 1994). Home: 5912 Walnut Way Palmdale CA 93551-2812

WEISS, ROBERT BENJAMIN, lawyer; b. Perth Amboy, N.J., Aug. 27, 1948; s. Denes and Patricia (Chazin) W.; m. Susan Stern, June 11, 1972; children: Elana, Shira, Danielle. BA, Yeshiva U., 1971; JD, Case Western U., 1975. Bar: Mich. 1977, U.S. Dist. Ct. (ea. dist.) Mich. 1978. Assoc. Ulmer, Berne, Laronge, Glickman & Curtis, Cleve., 1975-76; staff atty. Gen. Motors Corp., Detroit, 1976-82; ptnr. Honigman Miller Schwartz & Cohn, Detroit, 1982—. Office: Honigman Miller Schwartz & Cohn 2290 1st National Bldg Detroit MI 48226

WEISS, ROBERT FRANCIS, former academic administrator, religious organization administrator, consultant; b. St. Louis, Aug. 27, 1924; s. Frank L. G. and Helen M. (Beck) W. B.A., St. Louis U., 1951, Ph.L., 1953, M.A., 1953, S.T.L., 1961; Ph.D., U. Minn., 1964. Joined Soc. of Jesus, 1946; ordained priest Roman Catholic Ch., 1959; tchr. Rockhurst High Sch., Kansas City, Mo., 1953-56; adminstrv. asst. to pres. St. Louis U., 1961-62; asst. dean Rockhurst Coll., Kansas City, Mo., 1964-66, dean, v.p., asst. prof. edn., 1966-72, pres., 1977-88; pres. St. Louis U. High Sch., 1973-77, interim pres., 1992; asst. for higher edn. and continuing formation Mo. Province S.J., St. Louis, 1989-92, treas., 1992—; mem. Commn. on Govtl. Rels., Am. Coun. Edn., 1985-87; bd. dirs. Kansas City Regional Coun. for Higher Edn., 1978-88, Boys Hope/Girls Hope, 1977—. Contbr. chpts. to books, articles to profl. jours. Trustee St. Louis U., 1973-87, 91—, Loyola U., New Orleans, 1973-82, 85-88, United Student Aid Funds, Inc., 1977-94, U. San Francisco, 1987—, Marymount Coll., Salina, Kans., 1986-88, St. Louis U. H.S., 1989—, Fontbonne Coll., St. Louis, 1973-77, Sacred Heart Program, Radio and TV Apostolate, St. Louis, 1990-96, pres., 1992-96; bd. dirs. Creighton U., Omaha, Our Little Haven. With U.S. Army, 1943-46. Decorated Bronze Star. Mem. Am. Assn. for Higher Edn., Rainbow Divsn. Vets. Assn. (nat. chaplain 1976-84, 88-90, pres.-elect 1990-91, pres. 1991-92, assoc. nat. chaplain 1992—), Alpha Sigma Nu, Alpha Phi Omega. Home and Office: 4511 W Pine Blvd Saint Louis MO 63108-2109 *The only way for me to look at life is in the light of faith, which I consider one of God's greatest gifts. Life for me is an opportunity to serve God and as many of my neighbors as I can. I am basically an optimist. There is so much beauty around us, so many good people, so many marvels to behold—that I thank the Lord for giving me the ability to know and experience this life and to look forward to eternal life with God, the Source of all life. Any success I have had I attribute to taking advantage of the opportunities that God has put in my path.*

WEISS, ROBERT JEROME, psychiatrist, educator; b. West New York, N.J., Dec. 9, 1917; s. Harry and Dora (Samuels) W.; m. Minnie Thompson Moore, Apr. 21, 1945; children—Scott Tillman, James Woodrow, Elizabeth Thompson. Student, Johns Hopkins, 1937; A.B., George Washington U., 1947; M.D., Columbia, 1951; M.A. (hon.), Dartmouth, 1964. Intern Columbia div. Bellevue Hosp., 1951, asst. resident medicine, 1953; resident psychiatry N.Y. Psychiat. Inst., 1954-56; asst. attending Vanderbilt Clinic, 1957-58, Presbyn. Hosp., N.Y.C., 1958-59; chief psychiatry Mary Hitchcock Meml. Hosp., 1959-70; career tchr. trainee Nat. Inst. Mental Health, 1956-58; tchr., research Columbia Coll. Phys. and Surg., 1956-59; prof. psychiatry, chmn. dept. Dartmouth Med. Sch., 1959-70; psychiatrist Beth Israel Hosp., 1988-90; attending physician Presbyn. Hosp., 1975-85, cons., 1985—; vis. prof. comty. medicine Harvard Med. Sch., 1970-75, assoc. dir. comty. health, 1970-95, assoc. dean health care planning; prof. psychiatry and social medicine Columbia Coll. Physicians and Surgeons, 1975-86, also dir. Ctrs. for Comty. Health, 1975-86; De Lamar prof. pub. health practice, dean Columbia U. Sch. Pub. Health, 1980-86, dean and De Lamar prof. of pub. health practice, prof. psychiatry, prof. social medicine, prof. emeritus, 1986—; vis. prof. comty. medicine U. N.Mex. Med. Sch., 1986-89; cons. Nat. Ctr. for Health Svcs. Rsch., 1975-86, NIMH, 1977-86; chmn. psychiatry tng. com. NIMH, 1967-68, mem. coord. panel, 1965-67, ad hoc com. interdisciplinary tng. program, 1966, mem. agenda com., 1966; cons. AT&T, 1990-92; chmn. bd. Academica, 1992, Employee Managed Care Corp., 1994—. Co-editor: Columbia U. Coll. Physicians and Surgeons Complete Home Medical Guide, 1986, editor emeritus 2d and 3d edits., 1989; contbr. articles to profl. jours., chpts. to books. Served to maj. AUS, 1941-46. Recipient Bi-Centennial medal Columbia Coll. Phys. and Surg., 1967. Fellow Am. Psychiat. Assn. (life); mem. Am. Assn. Chmn. Depts. Psychiatry (pres. 1979-80). Achievements include demonstrated social supports reduce disability due to mental illness; research in special health care delivery, health care preventive psychiatry. Home: 92 Falmouth Ct Bedford MA 01730

WEISS, ROBERT M., urologist, educator; b. N.Y.C., Jan. 13, 1936; s. David and Laura W.; m. Ilana Shemer, May 20, 1973; children—Erik Daniel, Dana Alexandra. B.S. magna cum laude, Franklin and Marshall Coll., Lancaster, Pa., 1957; M.D., SUNY, Bklyn., 1960; M.A. (hon.), Yale U., 1976. Diplomate: Am. Bd. Urology, Nat. Bd. Med. Examiners. Intern Cornell Med. Div., Bellevue Hosp., N.Y.C., 1960-61; resident in gen. surgery Beth Israel Hosp., N.Y.C., 1961-62; resident in urology Squier Urol. Clinic, Presbyn. Hosp., N.Y.C., 1963-64, 65-67; vs. fellow Columbia U. Coll. Physicians and Surgeons, N.Y.C., 1964-65, adj. assoc. prof. pharmacology, 1975-77, adj. prof. pharmacology, 1977—; mem. faculty Yale U. M.ed. Sch., New Haven, 1967—, prof. urology, 1976-88, prof., chief sect. of urology, 1988—; attending urology Yale-New Haven Hosp., New Haven, 1967-88, head sect. of urology, 1988—; cons. West Haven VA Hosp., Waterbury (Conn.) Hosp. Contbr. articles to med. publs. Served with USAR, 1962-63. Fellow ACS, Am. Acad. Pediatrics; mem. Am. Assn. Genito-Urinary Surgeons, Am. Physiol. Soc., Soc. Gen. Physiologists, Assn. Univ. Urologists, Soc. Pediatric Urology, Am. Urol. Assn., Am. Soc. Clin. Pharmacology and Therapeutics, Internat. Urodynamics Soc., AAAS, Internat. Soc. Dynamics of Upper Urinary Tract, Clin. Soc. Genito-Urinary Surgeons, Phi Beta Kappa, Sigma Xi. Office: Yale U Sch of Medicine 333 Cedar St New Haven CT 06510-3206

WEISS, ROBERT ORR, speech educator; b. Kalamazoo, Apr. 8, 1926; s. Nicholas John and Ruth (Orr) W.; m. Ann Lenore Lawson, Sept. 16, 1951; children: Elizabeth Ann, John Lawson, James Robert, Virginia Lenore. BA, Albion Coll., 1948; MA, Northwestern U., 1949, PhD, 1954. Instr. speech Wayne State U., Detroit, 1949-51; instr. pub. speaking Northwestern U., Evanston, Ill., 1954-55; mem. faculty DePauw U., Greencastle, Ind., 1955—, H.B. Gough prof. speech, 1965—, dir. forensics, head communication arts and scis., 1963-78, 85-86, 93. Author: Public Argument, 1995; editor: Speaker and Gavel, 1968-75; co-editor: Current Criticism, 1971; contbr. articles to profl. jours. Served with AUS, 1945-46. Recipient Fred C. Tucker Disting. Career award, 1995. Mem. AAUP (pres. DePauw U. chpt. 1961-62), Speech Communication Assn. (legis. assembly 1966-68), Am. Forensic Assn. (sec.-treas. 1958-59), Cen. States Communication Assn., Internat. Communication Assn., Phi Beta Kappa, Delta Sigma Rho-Tau Kappa Alpha (nat. v.p. 1981-83, pres. 1983-85), Theta Alpha Phi, Omicron Delta Kappa, Sigma Nu. Home: 722 Highridge Ave Greencastle IN 46135-1402

WEISS, ROBERT STEPHEN, medical manufacturing and services company financial executive; b. Honesdale, Pa., Oct. 25, 1946; s. Stephen John and Anna Blanche (Lescinski) W.; BS in Acctg. cum laude, U. Scranton, 1968; m. Marilyn Annette Chesick, Oct. 29, 1970; children: Christopher Robert, Kim Marie, Douglas Paul. CPA, N.Y. Supr., Peat, Marwick, Mitchell & Co., N.Y.C., 1971-76; asst. corp. contr. Cooper Labs., Inc., Parsippany, N.J., 1977-78, v.p., corp. contr. Palo Alto, Calif., 1981-83; v.p., corp. contr. The Cooper Cos., Inc. (formerly CooperVision, Inc.), Palo Alto, Calif., 1984-89; v.p., treas., CFO The Cooper Cos., Inc., Pleasanton, Calif., 1989—, sr. v.p., 1992-95, exec. v.p., 1995—; v.p. fin., contr. CooperVision Pharms., Mountain View, Calif., 1979, v.p. fin., group contr., 1980; bd. dirs. The Cooper Cos., Inc., Ft. Lee, N.J., 1992-94. With U.S. Army, 1969-70. Decorated Bronze Star with oak leaf cluster, Army Commendation medal. Mem. AICPA, N.Y. State Soc. CPAs. Home: 446 Arlington Ct Pleasanton CA 94566-7708 Office: The Cooper Cos Inc 6140 Stoneridge Mall Rd Pleasanton CA 94588-3232

WEISS, RONALD WHITMAN, real estate executive, lawyer; b. N.Y.C., Aug. 13, 1939; s. Rudolph and Sandra (Walters) W.; m. Ellen Klein, Oct. 25, 1980; children: Hilary, Carolyn, Christopher. B.S. in Econs., U. Pa., 1961; J.D., L.L.B., Columbia U., 1964. Bar: N.Y. 1964; cert. prin. N.Y. Stock Exchange. Pvt. practice N.Y.C., 1964—; pres. Shearson Hamill Real Estate Corp., N.Y.C., 1971-73; pres., chmn. Shearson Hayden Stone Real Estate Corp., N.Y.C., 1973-75, Shearson Loeb Rhodes Real Estate Corp., N.Y.C., 1975-78, Shearson Am. Express Real Estate Corp., N.Y.C., 1979-84, Shearson Lehman Bros. Real Estate Corp., N.Y.C.; exec. v.p. Shearson Lehman Bros., Inc., N.Y.C., 1984-89; chmn., pres. CWS Fin. Group, N.Y.C., 1989—; exec.v.p., dir. Balcor/Am. Express, Inc.; pres., chmn. CWS Fin. Groupo, 1989—; mng. dir., asst. gen. counsel Primerica Corp., 1991—; sr. real estate analyst, v.p. First Albany Corp., N.Y.C., 1994-96; sr. v.p. Gilford Securities, Inc., N.Y.C., 1996—. Mem. ABA, New York County Lawyers Assn., Real Estate Bd. N.Y., Security Industry Assn. Clubs: Quaker Ridge (Scarsdale, N.Y.); Harmonie (N.Y.C.). Home: 737 Park Ave New York NY 10021-4256 Office: Gilford Securities Inc 850 3rd Ave New York NY 10022

WEISS, SHIRLEY F., urban and regional planner, economist, educator; b. N.Y.C., Feb. 26, 1921; d. Max and Vera (Hendel) Friedlander; m. Charles M. Weiss, June 7, 1942. BA, Rutgers U., 1942; postgrad., Johns Hopkins U., 1949-50; M in Regional Planning, U. N.C., 1958; PhD, Duke U., 1973. Assoc. research dir. Ctr. for Urban and Regional Studies U. N.C., Chapel Hill, 1957-91, lectr. in planning, 1958-62, assoc. prof., 1962-73, prof., 1973-91, prof. emeritus, 1991—; joint creator-sponsor Charles and Shirley Weiss Urban Livability Program, U. N.C., Chapel Hill, 1992—; research assoc. Inst. for Research in Social Sci., U. N.C., 1957-73; research prof. U. N.C., Chapel Hill, 1973-91, acting dir. women's studies program Coll. Arts and Scis., 1985, faculty marshal, 1988-91; mem. tech. com. Water Resources Rsch. Inst., 1976-79; mem. adv. com. on housing for 1980 census Dept. Commerce, 1976-81; cons. Urban Inst., Washington, 1977-80; mem. rev. panel Exptl. Housing Allowance Program, HUD, 1977-80; mem. adv. bd. on built environ. Nat. Acad. Scis.-NRC, 1981-83, mem. program coordinating com. fed. constrn. coun. of adv. bd. on built environ., 1982-83; mem. Planning Accreditation Bd., Site Visitation Pool, Am. Inst. Cert. Planners and Assn. Collegiate Schs. Planning, 1985—; mem. discipline screening com. Fulbright Scholar awards in Architecture and City Planning, Coun. for Internat. Exchange of Scholars, 1985-88. Author: The Central Business District in Transition: Methodological Approaches to CBD Analysis and Forecasting Future Space Requirements, 1957, New Town Development in the United States: Experiment in Private Enterpreneurship, 1973; co-author: A Probabilistic Model for Residential Growth, 1964, Residential Developer Decisions: A Focused View of the Urban Growth Process, 1966, New Communities U.S.A, 1976; co-author, co-editor: Urban Growth Dynamics in a Regional Cluster of Cities, 1962; co-editor: New Community Development: Planning Process, Implementation and Emerging Social Concerns, vols. 1, 2, 1971, City Centers in Transition, 1976, New Communities Research Series, 1976-77; mem. editorial bd.: Jour. Am. Inst. Planners, 1963-68, Rev. of Regional Studies, 1969-74, 82—, Internat. Regional Sci. Rev, 1975-81. Trustee Friends of Libr., U. N.C., Chapel Hill, 1988-94, Santa Fe Chamber Music Festival, adv. coun., 1990-91, trustee, 1991—; bd. dirs. Triangle Opera Theatre, 1986-89, 91—. Recipient Disting. Alumni award in recognition of outstanding contributions in the field of city and regional planning Alumni Assn. Dept. City and Regional Plannning, U. N.C. at Chapel Hill, 1996,

Mary Turner Lane award Assn. Women Faculty, 1994; Adelaide M. Zagoren fellow Douglass Coll., Rutgers U., 1994. Fellow Urban Land Inst. (sr., exec. group, community devel. coun. 1978—); mem. Am. Inst. Planners (sec., treas. southeast chpt. 1957-59, v.p. 1960-61), Am. Inst. Cert. Planners, Am. Planning Assn., Am. Econ. Assn., So. Regional Sci. Assn. (pres. 1977-78), Regional Sci. Assn. (councillor 1971-74, v.p. 1976-77), Nat. Assn. Housing and Redevelopment Ofcls., Interamerican Planning Soc., Internat. Fedn. Housing and Planning, Town and Country Planning Assn., Internat. Urban Devel. Assn., Econ. History Assn., Am. Real Estate and Urban Econs. Assn. (regional membership chmn. 1976-82, 84-85, dir. 1977-80), AAUP (chpt. pres. 1976-77, pres. N.C. Conf. 1978-79, mem. nat. council 1983-86, William S. Tacey award Assembly of State Confs.), Douglass Soc., Order of Valkyries, Phi Beta Kappa. Recipient Disting. Alumni award in Recognition of Outstanding Contbns. in the field of city and regional planning, The Alumni Assn. of Dept. of City and Regional Planning, U. N.C. at Chapel Hill, 1996, Mary Turner Lane award Assn. Women Faculty, 1994; Adelaide M. Zagoren fellow Douglass Coll., Rutgers U., 1994. Home: 155 N Hamilton Rd Chapel Hill NC 27514-5628

WEISS, STANLEY ALAN, mining, chemicals and refractory company executive; b. Phila., Dec. 21, 1926; s. Walter Joseph and Anne Betty (Lubin) W.; m. Lisa Popper, May 23, 1958; children: Lori Christina Lurie, Anthony Walter. Student, Pa. Mil. Coll., 1947-48, Georgetown U., 1950-51; fellow Ctr. for Internat. Affairs, Harvard U., Cambridge, Mass., 1977-78; LHD (hon.), Point Park Coll., Pitts., 1994. Founder Minera La Mundial, SA, San Luis Potosi, Mexico, 1954-56, Manganeso Mexicano SA, Mexico City, 1957-61, Mercurio Internacional SA, Mexico City, 1957-61; founder Flux, SA, Mexico City, 1960-82, Sao Paulo, Brazil, 1964-74; founder, chmn. bd., chief exec. officer Am. Minerals, Inc., El Paso, Tex., 1960-91; co-founder, exec. v.p. Ralstan Trading & Devel. Corp., 1968-91, chmn. bd. dirs., 1991; chmn. bd. dirs. Am. Premier, Inc., King of Prussia, Pa., 1991—. Author: Manganese: The Other Uses, 1976; contbr. articles on nat. security and internat. trade issues. Founder, chmn. Bus. Exec. for Nat. Security, Washington, 1982—; bd. dirs. New Am. Schs. Devel. Corp., Washington; mem. Coun. on Fgn. Rels., Am. Friends of Bilderberg, The Coun. for Excellence in Govt. With U.S. Army, 1944-46, ATO. Mem. Am. Bus. Conf., Am. Ditchley Found., Internat. Inst. Strategic Studies (Eng.), World Econ. Forum (Switzerland), Royal Inst. Gt. Britain (London), Garrick Club (London). Jewish. Avocations: tennis, skiing. Office: Am Premier Inc 1615 L St NW Ste 330 Washington DC 20036-5610

WEISS, STANLEY C., electrical and electronics products wholesale distribution executive; b. Chgo., Apr. 20, 1929; s. Edward and Belle Rose (Heifler) W.; m. Fern Adrienne Dellheim, Feb. 26, 1956;children: Sharon Anne Weiss Maluth, Lisa Karen. BBA, So. Meth. U., 1951; postgrad., Northwestern U., Chgo., 1953. Asst. mgr. men's furnishings Gassman's, Chgo., 1951-53; restaurant and hotel supplies salesman Edward Don & Co., Chgo., 1953; sales trainee, mgr. EDP, Kuppenheimer Clothing, Chgo., 1954-56; with EESCO, Inc. (Englewood Electric), Chgo., 1956—; bd. dirs. Cameron Ashley Bldg. Material Supply; speaker at profl. meetings; adv. cons. various elec. mfrs., 1980-92. Contbr. articles to profl. mags. Banquet co-chmn. Better Boys Found., Chgo., 1984-93; bd. dirs. Jewish Cmty. Ctrs. of Chgo., 1994—. Recipient Banquet Co-chmn.'s award Better Boys Found., 1984-92. Mem. Nat. Assn. Elec. Distbrs. (bd. dirs., chmn. 1991-92), Nat. Assn. Wholesalers (product liability com. Chgo. 1984, bd. dirs. 1991-92), Nat. Assn. Credit Mgmt. (chmn. WES group Chgo. 1970-74), Lake Michigan Club (chmn., bd. dirs. 1975-85), Twin Orchard Country Club (Longwood, Ill., bd. dirs. 1988-92), DuPage Club (Oak Brook Terrace, Ill.), B'nai Brith (officer Chgo. 1954-64, bd. dirs. 1962-64). Avocations: reading, travel, golf. Office: EESCO Inc 3939 S Karlov Ave Chicago IL 60632-3813*

WEISS, STEPHEN JOEL, lawyer; b. N.Y.C., Sept. 12, 1938; s. Morris and Frances (Dinkin) W.; m. Madeline Adler, Aug. 12, 1962; children: Lowell Andrew, Valerie Elizabeth, Bradley Lawrence. B.S., Queens Coll., 1959; LL.B., Cornell U., 1962; LL.M., Georgetown U., 1966. Bar: N.Y. 1963, D.C. 1966, U.S. Supreme Ct. 1975. Atty. SEC, Washington, 1962-65; assoc. firm Arent Fox Kintner Plotkin & Kahn, Washington, 1965-70, ptnr., 1971-94; ptnr. Holland & Knight, Washington, 1994—; lectr. securities and corp. law Am. Law Inst., ABA, Fed. Bar Assn., Practicing Law Inst., Bur. Nat. Affairs, Exec. Enterprises, Aspen Law & Bus. Orgn. Mgmt., Inc. Mem. adv. bd.; Securities Regulation and Law Report, Bus. Nat. Affairs, 1980—; contbr. articles on securities, corp. dirs. and officers liability and ins. law to legal and bus. jours.; author: Regulation D-A Practical Guide, 1994. Mem. nat. com. Cornell Law Sch. Fund, 1987-88. Mem. ABA (fed. regulation securities com. 1970—, chmn. Rule 10b-5 subcom. 1976-78, chmn. civil liabilities subcom. 1978-81, chmn. ad hoc com. fgn. corrupt practices legislation 1976-77, Guiding Principles Task Force bus. ins. com. 1994—, devels. in bus. financing com. 1982—), Fed. Bar Assn. (chmn. securities law comm. 1968-70, mem. exec. com. of securities law com. 1971—, chmn. coun. on financing and taxation 1971-72, chmn. publs. bd. 1977-78, nat. coun. 1972-80, Leadership commednation 1973). Club: Cornell Law (Washington) (pres. 1971-79). Office: Holland & Knight 2100 Pennsylvania Ave NW Washington DC 20037-3202

WEISS, STUART LLOYD, lawyer; b. N.Y.C.. JD, Bklyn. U., 1985. Bar: N.Y. 1986. Assoc. Malen & Assocs., P.C., Hicksville, N.Y., 1985-86; supervising atty. Malen & Assocs., P.C., 1986-87; pvt. practice N.Y.C., 1987—. Mem. ABA, Counsel N.Y. Coop. Community Assn. Inst., Rho Epsilon. Office: 2 Park Ave New York NY 10016-5603

WEISS, SUSAN, newspaper editor. Managing editor Life Section, USA Today, Arlington, Va. Office: USA Today 1000 Wilson Blvd Arlington VA 22209-3901

WEISS, THEODORE RUSSELL, poet, editor; b. Reading, Pa., Dec. 16, 1916; s. Nathan and Mollie T. (Weinberg) W.; m. Renée Karol, July 6, 1941. B.A., Muhlenberg Coll., 1938, Litt.D. (hon.), 1968; M.A., Columbia U., 1940, postgrad., 1940-41; Litt.D. (hon.), Bard Coll., 1973. Instr. English U. Md., 1941, U. N.C., 1942-44, Yale U., 1944-46; prof. English, Bard Coll., 1946-68; vis. prof. poetry MIT, 1961-62; resident fellow creative writing Princeton U., 1966-67, prof. English and creative writing, 1968-87, emeritus, William and Annie S. Paton prof. ancient and modern lit., 1977-87, emeritus; Fannie Hurst prof. lit. Washington U., St. Louis, 1978; prof. English poetry Cooper Union, 1988; poet-in-residence Monash U., Melbourne, Australia, 1982; lectr. New Sch. Social Research, 1955-56, N.Y.C. YMHA, 1965-67; lectr. for USIS in various countries; guest Inst. for Advanced Study, Princeton, N.J., 1986-87, 87-88, Villa Serbelloni, Bellagio, Italy, 1989; guest lectr. Peking U., Shanghai U., People's Republic China, 1991. Editor, pub. Quar. Rev. Lit., 1943—; editor poetry series Princeton U. Press, 1974-78; mem. poetry bd. poetry series Wesleyan U. Press, 1964-70; juror in poetry for poetry series, Bollingen Com., 1965, Nat. Book Awards, 1967, 77; author: Selections from the Note-Books of G.M. Hopkins, 1945; author: The Breath of Clowns and Kings: Shakespeare's Early Comedies and Histories, 1971, The Man from Porlock, Selected Essays, 1982; (poems) The Catch, 1951; Outlanders, 1960, Gunsight, 1962, The Medium, 1965, The Last Day and the First, 1968, The World Before Us: Poems, 1950-70, 1970, Fireweeds, 1976, Views and Spectacles, Selected Poems, 1978, Views and Spectacles, New and Selected Shorter Poems, 1979, Recoveries, 1982, A Slow Fuse, 1984, Collected Poems, 1987, paper back edit., 1988, A Sum of Destructions, 1994, Selected Poems, 1995; also articles and recs. Recipient Wallace Stevens award, 1956, Creative Arts award Brandeis U., 1977, Shelley Meml. award Poetry Soc. Am., 1989; fellow Ford Found., 1953-54, Ingram Merrill Found., 1974-75, Guggenheim Found., 1986-87 hon. fellow Ezra Stiles Coll., Yale U.; grantee Nat. Found. Arts and Humanities, 1967-68; subject of films Living Poetry, 1988, Yes, With Lemon, 1996. Home: 26 Haslet Ave Princeton NJ 08540-4914

WEISS, THOMAS EDWARD, physician; b. New Orleans, June 15, 1916; s. Carl Adam and Viola Maine W.; m. Catherine Torres Edwards, June 29, 1950; children: Thomas Edward, Hampton Carl. Student, La. State U., 1933-34; M.D., Tulane U., 1940. Diplomate: Am. Bd. Internal Medicine. Intern Touro Infirmary, New Orleans, 1940-41; resident in pathology Touro Infirmary, 1940; fellow in internal medicine Alton Ochsner Med. Found., New Orleans, 1946-47; staff physician specializing in internal medicine Ochsner Clinic, New Orleans, 1947-50; head rheumatology sect. Ochsner Clinic, 1960-77, now mem. staff emeritus rheumatology sect., bd. mgrs. clinic, 1966-74; mem. staff Ochsner Found. Hosp.; sr. vis. physician Charity Hosp. La., New Orleans; mem. faculty Tulane U. Med. Sch., 1960-84, emeritus prof. clin. medicine, 1989—; chmn. vol. support com. Alton Ochsner Med. Found., 1984—, dir. alumni affairs, 1984-95. Contbr. articles to profl. jours. Bd. dirs. Vis. Nurses Assn., Alton Ochsner Med. Found., also trustee; founder, bd. govs. La. Arthritis Found.; nat. bd. govs. Arthritis Found., 1968-74. Maj. AUS, 1941-45, ETO and PTO. Fellow ACP (Laureate award 1991); mem. AMA, Orleans Parish Med. Soc. (dir.), La. Med. Soc., Soc. Med. Assn., Nat. Soc. Rheumatologists, Am. Coll. Rheumatology (master, pres. 1973-74, exec. com.), Vis. Nurses Assn., New Orleans Country Club, Sigma Chi, Alpha Kappa Kappa. Democrat. Roman Catholic. Home: 401 Metairie Rd Apt 625 Metairie LA 70005-4305 Office: 1514 Jefferson Hwy New Orleans LA 70121-2429

WEISS, WALTER STANLEY, lawyer; b. Newark, Mar. 12, 1929; s. Jack and Mollie (Orkin) W.; m. Misty M. Moore; children from previous marriage: Jack Stephen, Andrew Scott. A.B., Rutgers U., 1949, J.D., 1952. Bar: D.C. 1952, N.J. 1956, Calif. 1961. Trial atty. IRS, Phila., Los Angeles, 1957-62; asst. U.S. atty., chief tax div. Los Angeles, 1962-63; ptnr. firm Goodson & Hannam, Los Angeles, 1963-67; mng. ptnr. firm Long & Levit, Los Angeles, 1967-79; ptnr. firm Greenberg & Glusker, Los Angeles, 1979-81, Rosenfeld, Meyer and Susman, Beverly Hills, Calif., 1981-93; prin. Law Office of Walter S. Weiss, L.A., 1993—. Contbr. articles to legal jours. Served to capt. JAGC USAF, 1953-56. Named Arbitrator Nat. Assn. Securities Dealers, 1974. Fellow Am. Coll. Trial Lawyers; mem. Am., Los Angeles County, Beverly Hills, Century City bar assns. Home: 1805 Westridge Rd Los Angeles CA 90049-2215 Office: Law Office Walter S Weiss 9th Flr 12424 Wilshire Blvd Los Angeles CA 90025-1052

WEISSBACH, HERBERT, biochemist; b. N.Y.C., Mar. 16, 1932; s. Louis and Vivian (Ruhalter) W.; m. Renee Kohl, Dec. 27, 1953; children—Lawrence, Nancy, Marjorie, Robert. B.S., CUNY, 1953; M.S., George Washington U., 1955, Ph.D., 1957. Chemist Nat. Heart Inst., Bethesda, Md., 1953-68; acting chief NIH, Bethesda, Md., 1968-69; assoc. dir. Roche Inst. Molecular Biology, Nutley, N.J., 1969-83, dir., 1983—; v.p. Hoffmann-La Roche, Nutley, N.J., 1983—; adj. prof. George Washington U., 1964-69, Columbia U., 1969-85, U. Medicine and Dentistry N.J., Newark, 1981-93, Princeton U., 1984-85. Editor: Molecular Mechanisms of Protein Biosynthesis, 1977, Archives of Biochemistry and Biophysics; contbr. articles to profl. jours. Recipient Superior Svc. award NEW, 1968, Enzyme award Am. Chem. Soc., 1970, Disting. Alumni award George Washington U., 1994. Mem. Am. Soc. Biol. Chemists, Am. Soc. Pharmacology and Exptl. Therapeutics, Nat. Acad. Scis., AAAS. Home: 5 Blackfoot Cir Wayne NJ 07470-4942 Office: Roche Inst Molecular Biology 340 Kingsland St Nutley NJ 07110-1150

WEISSBARD, DAVID RAYMOND, minister; b. Albany, N.Y., July 10, 1940; s. Alfred Henry and E. Ramona (Van Wie) W.; m. Mary Linda Roberts, Mar. 31, 1963 (dec. May 1987); children: Melissa Anne, Michele Lee Weissbard Burns, Andrew Van Wie (dec.), Meredith Lynn Weissbard Andrews; m. Karen Wells, Sept. 1, 1990; 1 child, Hilary Rebecca. BA, St. Lawrence U., 1962, MDiv., 1965; diploma in applied social studies, U. Southampton, Eng., 1973. Ordained to ministry Unitarian Universalist Assn., 1965; cert. social worker, Eng. Student min. 1st Universalist Ch., Dexter, N.Y., 1963-65, Henderson, N.Y., 1963-65; min. 1st Parish in Bedford (Mass.) Unitarian Universalist Ch., 1965-74; sr. min. Fairfax Unitarian Ch., Oakton, Va., 1974-79, The Unitarian Universalist Ch., Rockford, Ill., 1979—; v.p. Cen. Midwest Dist. Unitarian Universalist Assn., 1989-92. Producer, host weekly TV program Fusion, WIFR-TV, 1980—. Mem. religious policy com. Rockford Sch. Dist., 1991. Recipient Skinner award Unitarian Universalist Assn., 1979; named One of Rockford's 15 Most Interesting People, 1990. Mem. ACLU (co-pres. No. Ill. chpt.), Greater Rockford Clergy Assn., Unitarian Universalist Mins. Assn. (treas. 1976-78). Democrat. Home: 1805 Clinton St Rockford IL 61103-4805 Office: The Unitarian Ch 4848 Turner St Rockford IL 61107-5029

WEISSBARD, SAMUEL HELD, lawyer; b. N.Y.C., Mar. 3, 1947; children: Andrew Joshua, David S. BA, Case Western Res. U., 1967; JD with highest honors, George Washington U., 1970. Bar: D.C. 1970, U.S. Supreme Ct. 1974. Assoc. Fried, Frank, Harris, Shriver & Kampelman, 1970-73, Arent, Fox, Kintner, Plotkin & Kahn, 1973-78; prin. Weissbard & Fields, P.C., 1978-83; shareholder, v.p. Wilkes, Artis, Hedrick & Lane, Washington, 1983-86; ptnr. Foley & Lardner, Washington, 1986—; co-chair Creditors' Rights Workout and Bankruptcy Group, 1992-95. Editor in chief George Washington U. Law Rev., 1969-70. Bd. dirs. Luther Rice Soc., George Washington U., 1985-87, Atlanta Coll. Art, 1993, Nat. Learning Ctr. Capital Children's Mus., 1993—; bd. dirs., gen. counsel Georgetown Arts Commn., 1995—; chmn. steering com. Lawyers Alliance for Nat. Learning Ctr. and Capital Children's Mus., 1989-90; mem. steering com. D.C./NLC Don't Drop Out Campaign, 1992, 93. Recipient John Bell Larner medal, 1970. Mem. ABA, D.C. Bar, Georgetown Bus. and Profl. Assn. (bd. dirs. 1993—, sec., gen. counsel 1994—), Order of Coif. Office: Foley & Lardner 3000 K St NW Ste 500 Washington DC 20007-5109

WEISSENBUEHLER, WAYNE, bishop. Bishop of Rocky Mountain Evang. Luth. Ch. in Am., Denver. Office: Rocky Mountain Synod ABS Bldg #101 7000 Broadway Denver CO 80221-2907

WEISSKOPF, BERNARD, pediatrician, child behavior, development and genetics specialist, educator; b. Berlin, Dec. 11, 1929; came to U.S., 1939, naturalized, 1944; s. Benjamin and Bertha (Loew) W.; m. Penelope Allderdice, Dec. 26, 1965; children: Matthew David, Stephen Daniel. BA, Syracuse U., 1951; MD, U. Leiden, Netherlands, 1958. Diplomate Am. Bd. Med. Mgmt. Intern Meadowbrook Hosp., East Meadow, N.Y., 1958-59; resident Meadowbrook Hosp., 1959-60, Johns Hopkins Hosp., Balt., 1962-64; fellow child psychiatry Johns Hopkins U. Sch. Medicine, Balt., 1962-64; asst. prof. pediatrics U. Ill. Coll. Medicine, Chgo., 1964-66; faculty U. Louisville, 1966—, prof. pediatrics, 1970—; also assoc. in psychiatry, pathology and Ob-gyn, dir. Child Evaluation Ctr., Louisville, 1966—; chmn. Gov.'s Adv. Com. Early Childhood, Gov.'s Council on Early Childhood, Ky., 1986-88. Contbr. articles to profl. jours. Trustee Jewish Hosp., Louisville, 1974-77. Served to capt. USAF, 1960-62. Fellow Am. Acad. Pediatrics, Am. Assn. Mental Deficiency; mem. Am. Soc. Human Genetics, So. Soc. Pediatric Rsch., Am. Soc. Law and Medicine, Am. Coll. Physician Execs. Home: 6409 Deep Creek Dr Prospect KY 40059-9422 Office: Child Evaluation Ctr 571 S Floyd St Louisville KY 40202

WEISSMAN, DANIEL, journalist; b. N.Y.C., Nov. 19, 1938; s. Herman Reuben and Fanny (Goldstein) W.; m. Marcia Deborah Kaufman, June 2, 1962; children: Neil Edward, Charles Todd, Glen Scott. BS, NYU, 1962. Special asst. N.J. Dept. Commerce and Economic Devel., Trenton, N.J., 1965-67; newspaper reporter columnist Herald News, Passaic, N.J., 1967-71; newspaper columnist, political reporter The Star Ledger, Newark, N.J., 1971—. Bd. dirs. Easter Seal Soc., 1967—. With USAR, 1960-67. Recipient Opinion Writing award Sigma Delta Chi, 1993, Investigative Writing award Headline Club, 1993, Bus. Writing award C.I.T. Club, 1993. Home: 915 Pickering Dr Yardley PA 19067-4309 Office: The Star Ledger The State House Cn # 021 Trenton NJ 08625

WEISSMAN, EUGENE YEHUDA, chemical engineer; b. Bucharest, Romania, Sept. 23, 1931; came to U.S., 1958; s. Alfred A. and Paula D. (Braunstein) W.; children: Ian A., Michael L. BS, Israel Inst. Tech., 1953; MS, U. Mich., 1959; PhD in chem. engr., Case Western Reserve U., 1963; MBA, U. Chgo., 1972. Registered profl. engr. Mgr. Israel Atomic Energy Comm., 1953-58; process engr. Hercules Powder Co., 1960-61; sr. engr. Gen. Electric Co., 1963-65, mgr. R&D, 1965-68; head rsch. dept. Johnson Controls, 1968-73; dir. rsch. B.A.S.F. Corp., 1973-91; dir. technology transfer Nat. Ctr. for Mfg. Scis., 1991-92; exec. dir. Ctr. for Process Analytical Chemistry U. Wash., 1992-94; pres. Weissman Assocs., Seattle, 1994—; adv. coun. Coll. Engring. U. Akron; mem. editorial and tech. adv. bd. PI Quality. Contbr. articles to profl. jours.; patentee in field. Fellow USPHS, 1959, 62. Mem. AAAS, AIChE (dir. heat transfer and energy conversion divsn.), NRC (co. rep.), Catalysis Soc. New Eng. (dir.), Electrochem. Soc., Nat. Membership Com., Am. Soc. for Quality Control, Indsl. Rsch. Inst. (bd. dirs., chmn. bd. editors, chmn. nominating com., univ. rels. com., advanced study groups com., fin. com.), Am. Chem Soc. (corp. assocs. com.), Nat. Coun. Advancement Rsch. (conf. com.), Coun. Chem. Rsch. (Univ. Ind. interaction com.), Tech. Transfer Soc., Inst. Mgmt. Cons., Product Devel. and Mgmt. Assn., Am. Translators Assn. N.W. Translators and Interpreters Soc., Mich. Materials Processing Inst. (bd. dirs.), Internat. Forum Process Analytical Chemistry (sci. bd.). Home and Office: 4119 NE 142nd St Seattle WA 98125-3841

WEISSMAN, IRVING L., medical educator; b. Great Falls, Mont., Oct. 21, 1939; married, 1961; 4 children. BS, Mont. State Coll., 1960; MD, Stanford U., 1965. NIH fellow dept. radiology Stanford U., 1965-67, rsch. assoc., 1967-68, from asst. prof. to assoc. prof. dept. pathology, 1969-81, prof. pathology Sch. Medicine, 1981—, prof. devel. biology, 1989—; James McGinnis Meml. lectr. Duke U., 1982; George Feigen Meml. lectr. Stanford U., 1987; Albert Coons Meml. lectr. Harvard U., 1987; Jame Stahlman lectr. Vanderbilt U., 1987; R. E. Smith lectr. U. Tex. Sys. Cancer Ctr., 1988; Chauncey D. Leake lectr. U. Calif., 1989; Harvey lectr. Rockefeller U., 1989; Rose Litman lectr., 1990; sr. Dernham fellow, Calif. divsn. Am. Cancer Soc., 1969-73; mem. immunobiology study sect. NIH, 1976-80; mem. sci. rev. bd. Howard Hughes Med. Inst., 1986—; mem. sci. adv. com. Irvington House Inst., 1987—; co-founder Systemik, Inc., 1988; Karel & Avice Beekhuis prof. cancer biology, 1987; 5th Ann. vis. prof. cancer biology U. Tex. Health Sci. Ctr., 1987; disting. lectr. Western Soc. Clin. Investment, 1990. Recipient Pasarow award, 1989, Faculty Rsch. award Nat. Am. Cancer Soc., 1974-78; Josiah Macy Found. scholar, 1974-75. Fellow AAAS; mem. NAS, Am. Acad. Arts and Scis., Am. Assn. Immunologists (pres. 1994-95), Am. Assn. Univ. Pathologists, Am. Assn. Pathologists, Am. Soc. Microbiology, Am. Assn. Cancer Rsch., Inst. Immunology. Office: Stanford U Dept Pathology B257 Beckman Ctr Sch Medicine Stanford CA 94305

WEISSMAN, JACK (GEORGE ANDERSON), editor; b. Chgo., June 6, 1921; s. Ben and Ida (Meyerson) W.; m. Bernice Platt, Nov. 13, 1949; children: Bruce, David, Ellen Montgomery. B.A. in Edn., Northwestern U., 1943, M.S. in Journalism, 1944. Asst. editor Bankers Monthly, Chgo., 1944-45; mng. editor Practical Knowledge, Chgo., 1945-50; with pub. relations dept. Roosevelt U., Chgo., 1947-50; editor Opportunity Mag., Chgo., 1950-89, ret. Author: Make Money at Home, 1963, How to Make Correct Decisions, 1964, Money Making Businesses You Can Start for $500 Or Less, 1965, Making It Big in Selling, 1987. Served to cpl. USAAF, 1945-46. Mem. Sigma Delta Chi, Phi Delta Kappa. Jewish.

WEISSMAN, MICHAEL LEWIS, lawyer; b. Chgo., Sept. 11, 1934; s. Maurice and Sue (Goldberg) W.; m. Joanne Sherwin, Dec. 19, 1961; children: Mark Douglas, Greg Steven, Scott Adam, Brett Anthony. Student (White scholar), U. Chgo., 1951-52; BS in Econs, Northwestern U., 1954; MBA in Accounting, U. Pa., 1956; JD, Harvard U., 1958; postgrad. (Fulbright scholar), U. Sydney, Australia, 1958-59; postgrad., Hague Acad. Internat. Law, 1959. Bar: D.C. 1958, Ill. 1959. Asst. prof. bus. law Roosevelt U., Chgo., 1959-61; practice in Chgo., 1959—; mem. firm Aaron, Aaron, Schimberg & Hess, 1969-78; sr. ptnr. Boorstein & Weissman, 1978-82, Weissman, Smolev & Solow, 1982-88, Foley & Lardner, 1988-92, McBride Baker & Coles, 1992—; asst. prof. Roosevelt U., 1960-62; lectr. Lake Forest (Ill.) Coll., 1979-80; chmn. Banking Group, Union League Club Chgo.; mem. Com. on Bank Counsel Ill. Bankers Assn., 1987-88, vice chmn., 1988-89; panelist Robert Morris Assocs., Banking Law Inst., Midwest Fin. Conf., Greater O'Hare Assn., Miss. Law Inst., Bank Lending Inst., Chgo. Assn. Commerce and Industry, State of Art Seminars, Infocast Inc., SBA, Fed. Res. Bank Chgo., Lenders Ednl. Inst., Bank Adminstrn. Inst. Found., Lender's Forum. Author: Lender Liability, 1988, Commercial Loan Documentation and Secured Lending, 1990; mem. bd. editors Commercial Damages, 1985—; contr. articles to profl. jours. and bus. orgns. Mem. adv. bd. Affective Disorders Clinic, U. Ill. Med. Sch., 1979-81. Mem. ABA, Ill. Bar Assn., Chgo. Bar Assn., Ill. Bankers Assn., Ill. Inst. Continuing Legal Edn. (bd. dirs. 1989-96), Assn. Comml. Fin. Attys. (bd. dirs.), HArvard Law Soc. Ill., Turnaround Mgmt. Assn. (steering com. Chgo. chpt.), Comml. Fin. Assn. Ednl. Found. (adv. bd.), Robert Morris Assn., Beta Alpha Psi. Home: 2067 Old Briar Rd Highland Park IL 60035-4245 Office: McBride Baker & Coles 500 W Madison St Ste 4000 Chicago IL 60661-2511

WEISSMAN, MORRIS, printing compnany company; b. 1942. Grad., NYU, 1962. Assoc. Demou Morris Levin & Shein, 1965-70; mng. dir. Gen. Mortgage Investments, 1971; pres. Midwest, 1973-86; vice chmn. U.S. Banknote; chmn., chief exec. Am. Banknote Co. and Am. Banknote Holographics; trustee UN Bus. Coun. Office: Am Banknote Corp 51 W 52nd St New York NY 10019-6119

WEISSMAN, NORMAN, public relations executive; b. Newark, Apr. 12, 1925; s. Julius and Lenora (Schimmel) W.; m. Sheila Holtz, Dec. 12, 1950 (div. Dec. 1973); 1 son, Lee; m. Natalie Ruvell, Aug. 31, 1984. BA in English, Rutgers U., 1949; MA in Journalism, U. Wis., 1951. Asst. editor McGraw Hill Pub. Co., Inc., 1951-54; sec. to Dept. Air Pollution Control, N.Y.C., 1954-56; account exec. Ruder & Finn, N.Y.C., 1956-59, v.p., 1959-62, sr. v.p., 1962-68, pres., 1968-85, vice-chmn., 1983-85; vice-chmn. G.C.I. Group, Inc., N.Y.C., 1986-90; chmn. Edward Aycoth Worldwide, 1991-93, Citigate, Inc., N.Y.C., 1993—. Served with USN, 1943-46. Mem. Advt. Women N.Y. (hon.), Internat. Pub. Rels. Assn., Phi Beta Kappa, Sigma Delta Chi. Lodge: Rotary. Home: 162 E 93rd St New York NY 10128-3711 Office: Citigate Inc 850 Third Ave New York NY 10022

WEISSMAN, PAUL MARSHALL, investment company executive; b. New Haven, Apr. 3, 1931; s. Abraham S. and Regina (Sanditz) W.; m. Harriet Levine, Sept. 30, 1961; children: Michael A., Peter A., Stephanie T. BA, Harvard U., 1952; MBA, U. Pa., 1954. Mng. dir. emeritus Bear, Stearns & Co., N.Y.C., 1958—. Bd. dirs., v.p. Grand Street Settlement, N.Y.C.; bd. dirs. N.Y. Svc. for Handicapped, 1963-75, treas., 1969-71; mem. exec. com., chmn. Harvard Coll. Fund; mem. nominating com. bd. overseers Harvard U., 1983-86; trustee Conn. Coll., New London, Rye Country Day Sch., N.Y., 1982-91, Hopkins Grammar Sch., New Haven, 981-86. 1st lt. U.S. Army, 1955-58. Recipient Richard T. Flood award Harvard U., 1977. Mem. Harvard Club of N.Y., Harvard Alumni Assn. (dir. 1978-81, sr. v.p. 1986-87, pres. 1987-88). Jewish. Home: 2 Oxford Rd White Plains NY 10605-3603 Office: 245 Park Ave New York NY 10167-0002

WEISSMAN, ROBERT EVAN, information services company executive; b. New Haven, May 22, 1940; s. Samuel and Lillian (Warren) W.; m. Janet Johl, Aug. 27, 1960; children: Gregory, Christopher, Michael. BSBA, Babson Coll., Wellesley, Mass., 1964. Exec. v.p. Rediffusion Inc., Saugus, Mass, 1972-73; dir. corp. devel. Nat. CSS, Wilton, Conn., 1973-74, chmn., 1975-81; exec. v.p. Dun & Bradstreet Corp., N.Y.C., 1981-84, pres., 1985-93, CEO, 1995—, chmn., CEO, 1995—; bd. dirs. State St. Boston Corp.; mem. bus. roundtable com. econ. devel. U.S.-Japan Bus. Coun. Vice chmn. Babson Coll. Mem. IEEE, Info. Tech. Assn. Am., Inst. Mgmt. Accts., Soc. Mfg. Engrs. (sr.). Office: Dun & Bradstreet Corp 187 Danbury Rd Wilton CT 06897-4003

WEISSMAN, WILLIAM R., lawyer; b. N.Y.C., Aug. 16, 1940; s. Emanuel and Gertrude (Halpern) W.; m. Barbra Phylis Gershman; 1 child, Adam; stepchildren: Eric, Jace, Julie Greenman. BA, Columbia U., 1962, JD cum laude, 1965. Bar: N.Y. 1965, D.C. 1969, U.S. Dist. Ct. (no. dist.) Tex. 1965, U.S. Dist. Ct. (so. and ea. dists.) N.Y. 1977, U.S. Ct. Appeals (5th cir.) 1966, U.S. Ct. Appeals (D.C. cir.) 1969, U.S. Ct. Appeals (9th cir.) 1973, U.S. Ct. Appeals (2d and 3d cirs.) 1974, U.S. Ct. Appeals (10th cir.) 1979, U.S. Ct. Appeals (11th cir.) 1981, U.S. Supreme Ct. 1968. News dir., program dir. WKCR-FM, N.Y.C., 1960-62; law clk. U.S. dist. judge, Dallas, 1965-66; trial atty. antitrust div. Dept. Justice, Washington, 1966-69; spl. asst. U.S. atty., Washington, 1967; assoc. Wald, Harkrader & Ross, Washington, 1969-72, ptnr., 1973-85; ptnr. Piper & Marbury, Washington, 1986—; instr. Georgetown U. Law Sch.-D.C. Bar Continuing Legal Edn. Program, 1980-89, environ. regulation course Exec. Enterprises, Inc., 1985-95. Mem. Arlington (Va.) County Tenant-Landlord Commn., 1973-77, chmn., 1975-77; parliamentarian Arlington County Dem. Com., 1971-75; sec. Columbia Law Sch. Alumni Assn. of Washington, 1982-84, pres., 1984-86, bd. dirs. 1984-88. Mem. editorial adv. bd. Jour. Environ. Regulation, 1991-95, Environ. Regulation & Permitting, 1995—. Recipient James Gordon Bennett prize Columbia U., 1962, E.B. Convers prize Columbia U., 1965. Mem. ABA, Fed. Bar Assn., D.C. Bar Assn. Jewish. Club: Columbia U. of Washington (bd. dirs. 1987-93). Home: 3802 Lakeview Ter Falls Church VA 22041-1313 Office: Piper & Marbury LLP 1200 19th St NW Washington DC 20036

WEISSMANN, GERALD, medical educator, researcher, writer, editor; b. Vienna, Austria, Aug. 7, 1930; came to U.S., 1938; s. Adolf and Greta (Lustbader) W.; m. Ann Raphael, Apr. 1, 1953; children: Lisa, Andrew. BA with honors, Columbia U., N.Y.C., 1950; MD, NYU, 1954. Diplomate Am. Bd. Internal Medicine. Intern Mt. Sinai Hosp., N.Y.C., 1954-55, asst. resident medicine, 1957-58; chief resident medicine Bellevue Hosp., N.Y.C., 1959-60; fellow depts. biochemistry and medicine Arthritis and Rheumatism Fedn., NYU, 1958-59; rsch. asst. dept. medicine NYU Sch. Medicine, 1959-60, instr. medicine, 1959-62, asst. prof., 1962-65, assoc. prof., 1966-70, prof., 1970—, dir. div. cell biology, 1969-73, dir. div. rheumatology of dept. medicine, 1973—; USPHS spl. rsch. fellow dept. biophysics Strangeways Lab., Cambridge, Eng., 1960-61; sr. investigator Arthritis and Rheumatism Found., N.Y.C., 1961-65; career rsch. scientist Health Rsch. Coun. N.Y.C., 1966-71; instr. physiology Marine Biol. Lab., Woods Hole, Mass., 1973-77, investigator, 1970—, trustee, 1993—; vis. investigator ARC Inst. Animal Physiology, Babraham, Eng., 1964-69, Centre de Physiologie et d'Immunologie Cellulaires, Hosp. St. Antoine, Paris, 1973-74, William Harvey Rsch. Inst., London, 1987; mem. postdoctoral fellowships rev. com. Pfizer Internat., N.Y.C., 1983—; mem. scholarship selection com. Pew Scholars in Biomed. Scis., New Haven, 1984—; lectr. Johns Hopkins U., 1976, 89, Med. Coll. Ga., Augusta, 1980, Med. Coll. Pa., 1988, William Harvey Rsch. Inst., London, 1987, others; nat. adv. bd. Pew Scholars Biomed. Sci., 1984-95. Author: The Woods Hole Cantata, 1995, They All Laughed at Christopher Columbus, 1987, The Doctor With Two Heads, 1990, The Doctor Dilemma, 1992, Democracy and DNA, 1996; editor-in-chief Inflammation, 1975—, Advances in Inflammation Rsch., 1979—, MD Mag., 1989-94; mem. editl. bd. Clin. Immunology and Immunopathology, 1972-88, Advances in Prostaglandin, Thromboxane and Leukotriene Rsch., 1975—, Am. Jour. Medicine, 1976-88, Tissue Reactions, 1979, Immunopharmacology, 1982; contbr. over 300 articles to profl. jours. Capt. M.C., U.S. Army, 1955-57. Recipient Allessandro Robecchi prize Internat. League Against Rheumatism, 1972, Marine Biol. Lab. award, 1974, 1979, U. Bologna medal, Italy, 1978, Lila Gruber Cancer Rsch. award Am. Acad. Dermatology, 1979, Solomon A. Berson Med. Alumni Achievement award NYU, 1980, Merit award NIH, 1987, Centennial award Marine Biol. Lab., 1988, C.M. Plotz award N.Y. Arthritis Found., 1993, others; Guggenheim Found. fellow, N.Y.C., 1973-74. Fellow AAAS; mem. Am. Coll. Rheumatology (pres. 1982-83, Disting. Investigator award 1992), Am. Fedn. Clin. Rsch., Soc. Exptl. Biology and Medicine, Am. Soc. Pharmacology and Exptl. Therapeutics, Am. Soc. Exptl. Pathology, Assn. Am. Immunologists, Am. Soc. Cell Biology, Am. Soc. Clin. Investigation, Am. Soc. Biol. Chemistry and Molecular Biology, Assn. Am. Physicians, Harvey Soc. of N.Y. (pres. 1981-82), Interurban Clin. Club, PEN Am. Ctr., Phi Beta Kappa, Alpha Omega Alpha. Avocation: tennis. Office: NYU Med Ctr Dept Medicine 550 1st Ave New York NY 10016-6481

WEISS-SWEDE, FRANCES ROBERTA See **ZAMIR, FRANCES ROBERTA**

WEISSTEIN, ULRICH WERNER, English literature educator; b. Breslau, Germany, Nov. 14, 1925; came to U.S., 1950, naturalized, 1959; s. Rudolf and Berta (Wende) W.; m. Elisabeth Rieckh; children: Cristina, Cecily, Eric Wolfgang, Anton Edward. Student, Goethe-Universität, Frankfurt, 1947-50, 51-52, U. Iowa, 1950-51; MA, Ind. U., 1953, PhD, 1954; Doctorate (hon.), U. Lund, Sweden, 1993. Instr. Lehigh U., Bethlehem, Pa., 1954-58; asst. prof. Lehigh U., 1958; asst. prof. English and comparative lit. Ind. U., Bloomington, 1959-62; assoc. prof. Ind. U., 1962-66, prof. German and comparative lit., 1966-90, chmn. comparative lit. program, 1985-89; dir. Ind. U.-Purdue U. Studienprogramm U. Hamburg, 1981-82; vis. prof. U. Wis., summer 1966, Middlebury Sch. German, summer 1970, U. Hamburg (Germany), spring 1971, U. Vienna, 1976, Stanford U., 1979, U. Hamburg, spring 1982, Grax U., Austria, 1985, U. Bologna, Italy, 1991, U. Antwerp, Belgium, 1992, U. Graz, Austria, 1995, 96; external examiner comparative lit. U. Hong Kong, 1974-76. Author: Heinrich Mann, 1962, The Essence of Opera, 1964, Max Frisch, 1967, Einführung in die Vergleichende Literaturwissenschaft, 1968, English version: Comparative Literature and Literary Theory, 1973; Spanish version: Introducción a la Literatura Comparada, 1975, Chinese version, 1987, Japanese version, 1976, Korean version, 1979; Forschungsbericht zur Vergleichenden Literaturwissenschaft, 1968-1977, 1981, Links und links gesellt sich nicht: Gesammelte Aufsätze zum Werk Heinrich Manns und Bertolt Brechts, 1985; editor: Literatur und Bildende Kunst: Ein Handbuch zur Theorie und Praxis eines komparatistischen Grenzgebiets, 1992; editor German sect. Twayne World Authors series, 1964-86, Yearbook of Comparative and General Literature, 1960-90, Expressionism as an International Literary Phenomenon, 1973; co-editor: Literature and the Other Arts, 1981, Texte und Kontexte: Festschrift für Norbert Fuerst, 1973, Intertextuality: German Literature and Visual Art from the Renaissance to the Twentieth Century, 1993; translator: The Grotesque in Art and Literature (W. Kayser), 1963. Recipient Grosses goldenes Ehrenzeichen des Landes Steiermark, 1996; Guggenheim fellow, 1974-75; MLA grantee, 1958-59. Mem. MLA (exec. coun. 1983-86), Internat. Comparative Lit. Assn. (exec. coun. 1979-85, sec. 1985-89), Am. Comparative Lit. Assn., Coun. Internat. Exchange Scholars (area com. for W. Ger. and Austria 1983-85). Home: Baiernstrasse 54/IV, 8020 Graz Austria

WEISWASSER, STEPHEN ANTHONY, lawyer, broadcast executive; b. Detroit, Nov. 21, 1940; s. Avery and Eleanor (Sherman) W.; m. July 3, 1962 (div. 1985); children: Jonathan, Gayle; m. Andrea Timko, Apr. 19, 1986; children: Anne, Emily. BA, Wayne State U., 1962; student, Johns Hopkins U., 1962-63; JD, Harvard U., 1966. Bar: D.C. 1967, U.S. Supreme Ct. 1970. Law clk. to chief judge U.S. Ct. Appeals, Washington, 1966-67; assoc. Wilmer, Cutler and Pickering, Washington, 1967-74, ptnr., 1974-86; sr. v.p., gen. counsel Capital Cities/ABC, Inc., N.Y.C., 1986-91, sr. v.p., exec. v.p. ABC-TV network group, 1991, sr. v.p., exec. v.p. ABC News, 1991-93, sr. v.p., 1993; sr. v.p., pres. Multimedia Group, N.Y.C., 1993-95; pres., CEO Americast, L.A., 1995—; bd. dirs. Ctr. Comm.; pres. Internat. Radio and TV Soc. Found., Inc., 1995—. Trustee Woodrow Wilson Found., 1994—. Mem. ABA, Fed. Comm. Bar Assn. Jewish. Home: 2718 32nd St NW Washington DC 20008 Office: Americast 1800 Wilshire Blvd Ste 1750 Burbank CA 90024

WEISZ, PAUL B(URG), physicist, chemical engineer; b. Pilsen, Czechoslovakia, July 2, 1919; naturalized, 1946; s. Alexander and Amalia (Sulc) W.; m. Rhoda A.M. Burg, Sept. 4, 1943; children: Ingrid B., P. Randall. Student, Tech. U. Berlin, 1938-39; BS, Auburn U., 1940; ScD, Swiss Fed. Inst. Tech., Zurich, 1965, ScD (hon.), 1980. Research physicist Bartol Research Found., Swarthmore, Pa., 1940-46; Research physicist Mobil Oil Corp. (formerly Socony Mobil Oil Corp.), 1958-61, sr. scientist, 1961-69, mgr. process research sect., 1967-69; mgr. Central Research Lab. Mobil Research & Devel. Corp., Princeton, N.J., 1969-82, sr. scientist and sci. adv., 1982-84; Disting. prof. chem. and bio-engring. sci. U. Pa., 1984-90, prof. emeritus, 1990—; adj. prof. Pa. State U., 1992—; cons. rsch. and tech. strategy, 1984—; vis. prof. Princeton U., 1974-76, mem. adv. council dept. chem. engring., 1973-78; mem. adv. and resource council Princeton U. Sch. Engring., 1974-78; chmn. center policy bd. Center for Catalytic Sci. and Tech., U. Del., 1977-81; mem. energy research adv. bd. U.S. Dept. Energy, 1985-90. Editor: Advances in Catalysis, 1956-93; editl. bd. Jour. Catalysis, 1962-83, Chem. Engring. Comms., 1972-78, Heterogenous Chem. Reviews, 1993—; monthly columnist Sci. of the Possible, Chemtech, 1980-83; contbr. numerous articles to sci. jours.; holder 80 patents. Recipient ann. award Catalysis Club Phila., 1973, Lavoisier medal, Société Chimique de France, 1983, Perkin medal Soc. Chem. Industries, 1985, Nat. Medal of Tech., 1992. Fellow Am. Phys. Soc., Am. Inst. Chemists (Chem. Pioneer award 1974); mem. AIChE (R.H. Wilhelm award 1978), Am. Chem. Soc. (sci. award South Jersey sect. 1963, E.V. Murphree award 1972, Leo Friend award 1977, Chemistry of Contemporary Tech. Problems award 1986, Carothers award 1987), N.Y. Acad. Sci., Nat. Acad. Engring., Nassau Club (Princeton). Quaker. Office: Univ of Pa Dept Bio-Engring Philadelphia PA 19104

WEISZ, WILLIAM JULIUS, electronics company executive; b. Chgo., Jan. 8, 1927; m. Barbara Becker, Dec. 25, 1947; children: George, Terri, David. B.S. in Elec. Engring, MIT, 1948; D.B.A. (hon.), St. Ambrose Coll., 1976. With Motorola, Inc., Chgo., 1948-90, exec. v.p., 1969-70, pres., 1970-80, chief oper. officer, 1972-86, vice chmn., 1980-93, chief exec. officer, 1986-87, officer of bd., 1988-89, ret., 1990, chmn. bd. dirs., 1993—; Pres. Motorola Communications Internat., 1966-69; Motorola Communications and Electronics, Inc., 1966-69; dir. (Motorola Israel.), Harris Bankcorp Harris Trust and Savs. Bank; mem. exec. com. land mobile adv. com. to FCC. Com. chmn. Cub Scout Pack Evanston coun. Boy Scouts Am., 1960-62; trustee MIT, 1975-85, 91—; mem. Def. Policy Adv. Com. on Trade, 1988-92. Recipient award of merit Nat. Electronics Conf., 1970; Freedom Found. of Valley Forge award, 1974; MIT Corp. Leadership award, 1976. Fellow IEEE (past nat. chmn. vehicular communications group); mem. Electronic Industries Assn. (past chmn., bd. govs., past chmn. indsl. elec. div., medal of honor 1981), Bus. Roundtable, MIT Club (bd. dirs. Chgo.), Sigma Xi, Tau Beta Pi, Eta Kappa Nu. Office: Motorola Inc 1303 E Algonquin Rd Schaumburg IL 60196-4041

WEITKAMP, WILLIAM GEORGE, retired nuclear physicist; b. Fremont, Nebr., June 22, 1934; s. Alvin Herman and Georgia Ann (Fuhrmeister) W.; m. Audrey Ann Jensen, June 2, 1956; children—Erick, Jay, Gretchen, Laurie. B.A., St. Olaf Coll., 1956; M.S., U. Wis., 1961, Ph.D., 1965. Research asst. prof. U. Wash., Seattle, 1965-67; asst. prof. U. Pitts., 1967-68; tech. dir., research prof. Nuclear Physics Lab., U. Wash., Seattle, 1968-95; retired, 1995, rsch. prof. emeritus, 1995—. Served with USAF, 1956-59. Acad. guest Eidgenossische Technische Hochschule Zurich, Switzerland, 1974-75. Mem. Am. Phys. Soc. Home: 2019 E Louisa St Seattle WA 98112-2207 Office: Univ Wash Nuclear Physics Lab GL-10 Seattle WA 98195

WEITZ, JOHN, fashion designer, writer; b. Berlin, May 25, 1923; came to U.S., 1940, naturalized, 1943; s. Robert and Hedy (Jacob) W.; m. Susan Kohner, Aug. 30, 1964; children: Paul John, Christopher John; children by previous marriage: Karen Weitz Curtis, Robert. Student, Hall Sch., London, 1936, St. Paul's Sch., London, 1936-39; certificate, Oxford-Cambridge Sch., 1938. Founder John Weitz Designs, Inc., N.Y.C., 1954—. Designer various cos., until 1954; author: Value of Nothing, Man in Charge (Best Seller list 1974), Friends in High Places, 1982, Hitler's Diplomat, 1992. Bd. dirs. emeritus The Allen-Stevenson Sch., N.Y.C.; bd. dirs. Phoenix House, William J. Donovan Found., Vets. of OSS; mem. pres.'s coun. Mus. City of N.Y. Capt. M.I. AUS, 1942-46, ETO. Decorated First Class Cross Order of Merit (Fed. Republic Germany), 1988, Comdr.'s Cross (Fed. Republic Germany), 1995; recipient Sports Illustrated award, 1959, NBC Today award, 1960, Phila. Mus. award, 1960, Caswell Massey awards 1963-66, Harpers Bazaar medallion, 1966, Moscow diploma, 1967, Coty award, 1974, Cartier Design award, 1981, Mayor's Liberty medal, N.Y.C., 1986, Cutty Sark Career Achievement award, 1986, Dallas Menswear Mart award, 1990, Pres.'s award of Fashion Inst. of Tech., 1990, Ellis Island medal of Honor, 1992; named to Internat. Best Dressed List Hall of Fame, 1971. Mem. The Pilgrims, Union Club, Century Assn., Spl. Forces Club, Old Pauline Club (v.p., London), Confrerie des Chevaliers du Tastevin, Beach Club (Palm Beach), Vintage Sports Car Club Am., Sports Car Club Am., Road Racing Drivers Club, USN Acad. Sailing Squadron, Sag Harbor Yacht Club. Office: 600 Madison Ave New York NY 10022-1615

WEITZEL, JOHN PATTERSON, lawyer; b. Pitts., Aug. 24, 1923; s. Albert Philip and Elizabeth (Patterson) W.; m. Elisabeth Swan, Mar. 20, 1965; children: Mary Middleton, Paul Patterson. Student, Deerfield (Mass.) Acad., 1937-40; A.B., Yale U., 1946; LL.B., Harvard U., 1949. Bar: Mass. 1949, U.S. Supreme Ct. 1960. Asso. Herrick, Smith, Donald, Farley & Ketchum (now Herrick & Smith), Boston, 1949-53, ptnr., 1961-86; ptnr. Palmer & Dodge, Boston, 1986-93; of counsel, 1993—, spl. asst. to asst. sec. treasury, 1953-55, asst. to under sec. treas, 1955-56; asst. gen. counsel Treasury Dept., 1956-59, dep. to sec. treasury, 1959-60, asst. sec. treasury, 1960-61; U.S. exec. dir. IBRD, 1960-61; mem. planning bd. NSC, 1959-61; cons. to sec. def., 1973. Mem. Mass. Council Arts and Humanities, 1966-71; overseer, dir. sec. Boys and Girls Clubs, Boston; mem. corp. Mass. Gen. Hosp., Boston Mus. Sci.; trustee Roxbury Latin Sch. Served with USAAF, 1943-45. Mem. Am., Boston bar assns., Am. Law Inst. Clubs: Harvard (Boston), Union Boat (Boston). Home: 45 Devon Rd Chestnut Hill MA 02167-1851 Office: Palmer & Dodge 1 Beacon St Boston MA 02108-3190

WEITZEL, JOHN QUINN, bishop; b. Chgo., May 10, 1928; s. Carl Joseph and Patricia (Quinn) W. BA, Maryknoll (N.Y.) Sem., 1951, M of Religious Edn., 1953; PMD, Harvard U. Ordained priest Roman Cath. Ch., 1955. With ednl. devel. Cath. Fgn. Mission Soc. of Am., Maryknoll, 1955-63, nat. dir. vocations for Maryknoll, dir. devel. dept. and info. services, 1963-72, mem. gen. council, 1972-78; asst. parish priest Cath. Ch., Western Samoa, 1979-81, pastor, vicar gen., 1981-86; consecrated bishop, 1986; bishop Cath. Ch., Am. Samoa, 1986—. Office: Diocese Samoa-Pago Pago Fatuoaiga PO Box 596 Pago Pago AS 96799-0596

WEITZEL, PETER ANDRE, editor, newspaper; b. Akron, Ohio, July 5, 1936; s. Anthony Edmund Weitzel and Dorothy (Leininger) Simons; m. Sara Mitchell, June 28, 1958 (div. 1978); m. Linda Goodridge Steckley, Jan. 10, 1981; children: Tony, Philip, Mark, Matthew, Adam. AB Polit. Sci., U. Ill., 1958. Reporter Miami Herald, 1958-65, asst. city editor, 1965-69, govt. editor, 1969-71, state editor, 1971-78, asst. mng. editor, 1978-83, mng. editor, 1983-93, sr. mng. editor, 1993-95; ret., 1995; Pres. Fla. Soc. Newspaper Editors, 1979-80. Pres. Fla. First Amendment Found., Tallahassee, 1985—; chmn. Nat. Freedom Info. Coalition, Dallas, 1993—. Mem. Am. Soc. Newspaper Editors, Fla. Soc. Newspaper Editors (Freedom info. com. 1981—), Fla. First Amendment Found., Nat. Freedom Info. Coalition. Avocations: softball, swimming. Home: 721 Biltmore Way Apt 702 Coral Gables FL 33134-7524 Office: The Miami Herald 1 Herald Plz Miami FL 33132-1609

WEITZEL, WILLIAM CONRAD, JR., lawyer; b. Washington, Feb. 6, 1935; s. William Conrad and Pauline Lillian (Keeton) W.; m. Loretta LeVeck, Mar. 10, 1978; children: William Conrad III, Richard S., Sarah L., Andrew K. AB, Harvard U., 1956, LLB, 1959; postgrad., MIT, 1974. Bar: D.C. 1961. Law clk., chief judge U.S. Cts. Md., Balt., 1959-60; asst. U.S. atty., Washington, 1961-66; atty. Texaco, Inc., White Plains, N.Y., 1966-73; assoc. gen. counsel Texaco, Inc., 1973-76, gen. counsel, 1977-82, v.p., gen. counsel, 1982-84, sr. v.p., gen. counsel, 1984-90; Pres. Texaco Philanthropic Found., Inc., 1980-90; ptnr., chmn. bus. clients dept. Cummings & Lockwood, Stamford, Conn., 1991—. Trustee, chmn. adv. bd. Southwestern Legal Found.; bd. dirs. Forum for World Affairs, 1995—. With USN, 1960-61. Fellow Ctr. for Pub. Resources; mem. ABA, Am. Law Inst., Conn. Bar Assn., D.C. Bar Assn., Assn. Gen. Counsel (v.p., bd. dirs. 1988-90), Westchester-Fairfield Corp. Counsel Assn. (pres. 1981, chmn., chief legal officers com. 1982-90), Am. Petroleum Inst. (gen. com. on law, chmn. 1983-84), Darien (Conn.) Country Club, Harvard Club (dir. Harvard Alumni Assn. for Conn. 1990-93, pres. Fairfield County club 1987—). Republican. Episcopalian. Office: Cummings & Lockwood 4 Stamford Plz PO Box 120 Stamford CT 06904

WEITZER, BERNARD, telecommunications executive; b. Bronx, N.Y., Sept. 22, 1929; s. Morris R. and Eva (Kurtz) W.; m. Anne DeHaven Jones, Nov. 5, 1982. BS, CCNY, 1950; MS, NYU, 1951, postgrad., 1951-54. Mgr., asst. v.p. systems engring and analysis Western Union Telegraph Co., Upper Saddle River, N.J., 1966-71, v.p. engring. and computer systems, 1976-85, sr. v.p. ops., 1985-90; cons. pvt. practice, Fort Lee, N.J., 1990—; exec. v.p., gen. mgr. Western Union Teleprocessing Industries, Inc., Mahwah, N.J., 1971-76; dir. U.S. Telecomm. Tng. Inst.; mem. adv. com. TV comm. U.S. Info. Agy. Pres. Ft. Lee Bd. Edn.; pres., bd. trustees Ft. Lee Pub. Libr. Served to lt. U.S. Army, 1954-57. Mem. Chaines des Rotisseurs, Internat. Wine Food Soc. Home: 6 Horizon Rd Apt 2509 Fort Lee NJ 07024-6622

WEITZMAN, ARTHUR JOSHUA, English educator; b. Newark, Sept. 13, 1933; s. Louis I. and Cecele W.; m. Catherine Ezell, Aug. 8, 1982; children: Peter A., Anne E. B.A., U. Chgo., 1956, M.A., 1957; Ph.D., NYU, 1964. Instr. English, Bklyn. Coll., 1960-63; asst. prof. Temple U., Phila., 1963-69; assoc. prof. Northeastern U., Boston, 1969-72; prof. Northeastern U., 1972—; field editor G.K. Hall (Macmillan Pub.). Editor: Letters Writ by a Turkish Spy (G.P. Marana), 1970; founder, co-editor: The Scriblerian, 1968—; co-editor: Milton and the Romantics, 1980-81; contbr.: revs. and articles to profl. jours. and newspapers including Los Angeles Times, Boston Globe, Miami Herald. NEH fellow, 1972-73; Mellon fellow, 1976; research grantee Temple U.; research grantee Northeastern U. Mem. MLA, Am. Soc. 18th Century Studies, Conf. Editors Learned Jours. Jewish. Home: 4 Bellis Ct Cambridge MA 02140-3240 Office: Northeastern U Dept English 406 Holmes Boston MA 02115

WEITZMAN, HOWARD L., lawyer; b. L.A., Sept. 21, 1939. BS, U. So. Calif., 1962, JD, 1965. Bar: Calif. 1966, U.S. Dist. Ct. (ctrl., ea. and so. dists.) Calif., U.S. Ct. Appeals (9th cir.), U.S. Supreme Ct. 1976, U.S. Ct. Appeals (6th cir.) 1983. Ptnr., now exec. v.p. of corp. oper. Katten Muchin Zavis & Weitzman, L.A.; lectr. U. So. Calif., 1973-83. Mem. ABA, L.A. County Bar Assn., Beverly Hill Bar Assn. Office: Katten Muchin Zavis & Weitzman 100 Universal City Plaza Universal City CA 91608*

WEITZMAN, ROBERT HAROLD, investment company executive; b. Chgo., July 15, 1937; s. Nathan and Selma Weitzman; m. Marilynn Beth Felzer, Sept. 5, 1965; children—Joshua C., Eliza S. B.A. in Bus., Econs., Grinnell Coll., 1959; J.D., DePaul U., 1963. Bar: Ill 1963. Vice pres. Weitzman Enterprises, Chgo., 1955-63; assoc. Lissner, Rothenberg, Reif & Barth, Chgo., 1963-68; real estate counsel Continental Ill. Nat. Bank and Trust Co., Chgo., 1968-74; v.p., group head Continental Ill. Investment Trust, Chgo., 1974-76; founding ptnr. Group One Investments, Chgo., 1977—; lectr. in field. Editor: Real Estate Finance Handbook, 1979. Contbr. articles to profl. jours. Trustee, advisor Weitzman Found., 1963-77, mng. trustee, 1978—; cons., advisor Ill. chpt. Big Bros. Am. Orgn., 1969-72; trustee The Wis. Real Estate Investment Trust, 1980, 81. Recipient Outstanding Young Man Am. award U.S. Jaycees, 1973. Mem. Ill. Bar Assn., Chgo. Bar Assn., Nat. Assn. Rev. Appraisers and Mortgage Underwriters (charter mem. cert. rev. appraiser designation), Real Estate Securities and Syndication Inst. (bd. dirs. Ill. chpt. 1982-90, pres. 1984, regional v. p. 1988, specialist in real estate securities designation 1988, chmn. nat. com. on continuing edn. 1989, 90). Real Estate Investment Assn. (founding mem., Nat. bd. dirs. 1990—, exec. com. nat assn. and Ill. chpt. 1990—, chmn. nat. com. for advanced edn., 1990—, specialist in real estate investment designation 1990), Am. Inst. Banking, Internat. Coll. Real Estate Cons. Profls., Internat. Real Estate Bd. Home: 535 Carriage Way Deerfield IL 60015-4534 Office: Group One Investments Suite 1005 77 W Washington St Chicago IL 60602-2805

WEITZNER, HAROLD, mathematics educator; b. Boston, May 19, 1933; s. Morris and Alice Savitz W.; m. Lois S. Friedlander, June 12, 1962; children: Daniel J., Henry D. AB, U. Calif., Berkeley, 1954; AM, Harvard U., 1955, PhD, 1958. Assoc. rsch. scientist Courant Inst. NYU, N.Y.C., 1959-60, rsch. scientist, 1960-62, asst. prof., 1962-65, assoc. prof., 1965-69, prof., 1969—; assoc. dir. Magneto-Fluids div. Courant Inst. NYU, N.Y.C., 1988—, dir., 1973-79, 84-88; chmn. Math. Dept. Courant Inst. NYU, N.Y.C., 1989-91; cons. Oak Ridge Nat. Labs., Oak Ridge, Tenn., 1980—; mem. magnetic fusion adv. com. U.S. Dept. Energy, 1986-89, fusion energy adv. com., 1991-93; mem. adv. com. Gen. Atomics Corp., 1994—. Contbr. articles to sci. jours. Fellow Am. Phys. Soc.; mem. Soc. for Indsl. and Applied Math., Univ. Fusion Assn. (exec. com. 1993—). Home: 10 Cedar Ave Larchmont NY 10538-4121 Office: NYU Courant Inst 251 Mercer St New York NY 10012-1110

WEKSEL, WILLIAM, electronics executive. Chmn. bd. dirs., CEO E. F. Johnson Co., Burnsville, Minn. Office: E F Johnson Co 438 Gateway Blvd Burnsville MN 55337-2564*

WEKSLER, MARC EDWARD, physician, educator; b. N.Y.C., Apr. 16, 1937; s. Jacob J. and Lillian W.; m. Babette Barbash; children: David J., Jennifer Lee. B.A., Swarthmore Coll., 1958; M.D., Columbia U., 1962. Intern Bronx (N.Y.) Mcpl. Hosp., 1962-63, resident in medicine, 1963-64; asst. prof. medicine Cornell U. Med. Coll., N.Y.C., 1970-75; asso. prof. Cornell U. Med. Coll., 1975-78, Wright prof. medicine, 1978—, dir. div. geriatrics and gerontology, 1978—; attending physician N.Y. Hosp., Meml. Hosp., N.Y.C.; vis. prof. Pasteur Inst., Paris; cons. NIH, VA, N.Y.C., WHO, Pontifical Acad. Scis., Nat. Acad. Scis.; James Day lectr. Cornell U., 1980; pres. bd. trustees Am. Fedn. Aging Rsch., 1992-94. Editorial bd.: Jour. Clin. Immunology, Annals of Internal Medicine, Proc. Soc. Exptl. Biology and Medicine; asso. editor: Exptl. Aging Research. Founder, pres. Graphic Arts Coun. N.Y.; pres. Am. Fedn. Aging Rsch. Fellow Morgan Libr., Frick Collection. Fellow ACP; mem. Am. Soc. Clin. Investigation, N.Y. Acad. Medicine (chmn. geriatric sect.), Gerontol. Soc. (humanities and arts com.), Assn. Am. Physicians, Interurban Clin. Club, Alpha Omega Alpha. Office: Cornell U Med Coll 1300 York Ave New York NY 10021-4805

WELANDER, BO, chemicals executive; b. 1942. Degree, U. Tech., Stockholm, 1966. With Nobel Industries Sweden, 1966-87; pres., sec., treas. Eka Nobel, Inc., Marietta, Ga., 1987—. Office: Eka Nobel Inc 1519 Johnson Ferry Rd Marietta GA 30062-6494*

WELBER, DAVID ALAN, accountant; b. York, Pa., Oct. 14, 1949; s. Harry and Julia Welber. BS in Acctg., York Coll., 1975. CPA, Pa.; cert. fin. planner, Coll. for Fin. Planners. Acct. Einhorn, Butler, Gingerich & Co., York, 1974-82; ptnr. Bergdoll & Martin, York, 1984-86; prin. David A. Welber, CPA, York, 1982-84, 86—; v.p. Bell Socialization Svcs., 1994-96. Bd. dirs. Jewish Family Svcs.,Exch. Club Ctr. for Prevention of Child Abuse, Harrisburg, Pa.,1979—, Rehab. and Indsl. Tng. Ctr., York, 1987-90, Bell Socialization Svcs., 1991—, pres.1996—; mem. coun. Colony Park Homeowners Assn., York, 1982-84; co-chmn. Ohev Sholom Bd. Edn., York, 1987-90. Mem. Pa. Inst. CPAs (mem. personal fin. planning com. 1987—, Edn. award 1973), Exch. Club York (treas. 1984-90, pres. 1991-92), Greater York Rep. Club (treas. 1995—). Republican. Jewish. Avocations: reading, dancing, history, tropical birds, Compuserve network. Office: 212 E Market St York PA 17403-2013

WELBORN, CARYL BARTELMAN, lawyer; b. Phila., Jan. 29, 1951; d. Raymond C. and Helen Ann (Roach) Bartelman; m. Lucien Ruby, Apr. 11, 1987. AB, Stanford U., 1972; JD, UCLA, 1976. Bar: Ill. 1976, Calif. 1978. Assoc. Isham Lincoln & Beale, Chgo., 1976-78; from assoc. to ptnr. Morrison & Foerster, San Francisco and L.A., 1978—; now prin. Law Office of Caryl Welborn; lectr. real property law. Mem. ABA (chmn. com. on partnerships, real property sect. 1989-93), Am. Coll. Real Estate Lawyers (bd. govs. 1994). Office: Law Office of Caryl Welborn 126 S Park Sta St San Francisco CA 94107-2635*

WELBORN, JOHN ALVA, former state senator, small business owner; b. Kalamazoo, Mich., Dec. 20, 1932; s. H. Sterling and Elizabeth Catherine (Dougherty) W.; m. Dorothy Yeomans, Aug. 15, 1952; children: Kayla, John, Kami. Grad. high sch., Richland, Mich. Previously supr. Cooper Twp., Mich.; Mich. state rep. Lansing, 1972-74, Mich. sen., 1974-82, 85-94; dairy farmer Kalamazoo area, 1985-94; agt. Welborn Ins. Agy., Kalamazoo area; owner Welborn's Yesteryear Antiques. Candidate for gov. Mich., 1982; past chmn. Kalamazoo Rep. Exec. Com.; past mem. Gull Lake (Mich.) Sch. Bd.; past bd. suprs. Kalamazoo County, dir. Kalamazoo Soil Conservation Dist.; vol. fireman Cooper Twp. Fire Dept. Named Legislator of Yr. Police Officers Assn. Mich., 1988; recipient Golden Eagle Nat. Fedn. Police. Home: 6304 N Riverview Dr Kalamazoo MI 49004-9649

WELBORN, REICH LEE, lawyer; b. Winston-Salem, N.C., Nov. 1, 1945; s. Bishop M. and Hazel (Weatherman) W.; m. Martha Huffstetler, Aug. 27, 1966; children: Judson Allen, Spencer Brooks. AB, U. N.C., 1968, JD with honors, 1971. Bar: N.C. 1971. Assoc. Moore & Van Allen, PLLC and predecessor Powe Porter & Alphin, P.A., Durham, N.C., 1971-76; ptnr. Moore & Van Allen and predecessor Powe Porter & Alphin, P.A., Durham, N.C., 1976—; v.p. Family Counseling Svc., Durham, 1978-79. Recipient Order of Long Leaf Pine award Gov. of N.C., 1981, Spl. Citation, 1983. Mem. ABA, N.C. Bar Assn., Durham County Bar Assn. (v.p. 1987-89, pres. 1989-90), N.C. State Bar, Croasdaile Club (pres. 1989-90), Sertoma (pres. Durham chpt. 1987-88), N.C. Jaycees (pres. 1981-82), Durham C. of C. (bd. dirs. 1992-93). Home: 7 Lanecrest Pl Durham NC 27705-1854 Office: Moore & Van Allen PLLC 2200 W Main St Ste 800 Durham NC 27005

WELCH, ARNOLD DEMERRITT, pharmacologist, biochemist; b. Nottingham, N.H., Nov. 7, 1908; s. Lewis H. and Stella M. (Batchelder) W.; m. Mary Grace Scott, June 15, 1933 (dec.); children: Michael Scott, Stephen Anthony, Gwyneth Jeanne Sinizer; m. Erika Petrová, Mar. 15, 1966. B.S.,

U. Fla., 1930, M.S., 1931, D.Sc. (hon.), 1973; Ph.D., U. Toronto, 1934; M.D., Washington U., 1939. Research asst. U. Fla., 1929-31; fellow pharmacology U. Toronto, 1931-35; asst. pharmacology Washington U., 1935-36, instr., 1936-40; dir. pharmacol. research Sharp and Dohme, Inc., Phila., 1940-44, dir. research, 1943-44; prof. pharmacology, dir. dept. Sch. Medicine, Western Res. U., 1944-53; Fulbright sr. research scholar Oxford U., 1952; prof. pharmacology, chmn. dept. Sch. Medicine, Yale U., 1953-67, Eugene Higgins prof. pharmacology, 1957-67; dir. Squibb Inst. Med. Research, 1967-72; pres. Squibb Inst. Med. Research, Princeton, N.J., 1972-74; chmn. dept. biochem. and clin. pharmacology St. Jude Children's Research Hosp., Memphis, 1974-81, rschr., mem. emeritus, 1981-83; cancer expert Nat. Cancer Inst., 1983-86, acting dep. dir. divsn. of cancer treatment, 1984; scientist emeritus NIH, 1988—; mem. com. on growth NRC, chmn. panel mech. action, 1946-48, chmn. sect. chemotherapy, 1948-52, chmn. com. on growth, 1952-54; mem. sci. adv. bds. Leonard Wood Meml., 1947-53, Nat. Vitamin Found., 1953-56, St. Jude Children's Rsch. Hosp., Memphis, 1968-71; mem. divsn. biology and medicine NSF, 1953-55; mem. study sect. pharmacology and exptl. therapeutics USPHS, 1952-56, 1959-63, chmn., 1960-63, chmn. study sect. chemotherapy, 1963-65; mem. coordinating com. cancer chemotherapy Nat. Cancer Svc. Ctr., USPHS, 1955-57; mem. rsch. adv. coun. Am. Cancer Soc., 1956-59; mem. adv. coun. biol. sci. Princeton U., 1969-75; mem. working cadre Nat. Large Bowel Cancer program Nat. Cancer Inst., 1975-80; sci. adv. bd. La Jolla Cancer Rsch. Found., 1978-81; mem. Memphis Med. Seminar, 1977-83, pres., 1981-82. Assoc. editor: Cancer Research, 1950-58, Pharmacological Revs., 1962-66, Ann. Rev. Pharmacol., 1965-69; editor: Biochem. Pharmacology, 1958-62, vice chmn. internat. bd. editors, 1962-83, chmn., 1983-93; mem. adv. bd. Advances in Pharmacology and Chemotherapy, 1962-85; mem. bd. editors Handbuch der experimentellen Pharmakologie, 1966-85; contbr. articles to profl. jours., chpts. to books. Recipient alumni award U. Fla., 1953, Washington U., 1957, Torald Sollmann award Am. Soc. Pharmacology and Exptl. Therapeutics, 1966, Chester Stock award Meml. Sloan-Kettering Cancer Ctr., 1987, J. Heyrovsky gold medal Czechoslovak Acad. Scis., 1989; Commonwealth fellow Inst. für Therapeutische Biochemie, U. Frankfurt, Germany and Acad. Scis., Prague, Czechoslovakia, 1964-65. Fellow AAAS; mem. Am. Soc. Pharmacol. and Exptl. Therapeutics, Assn. Am. Physicians, Am. Assn. Cancer Rsch., Am. Soc. Biol. Chemistry and Molecular Biology, Am. Soc. Clin. Pharmacology and Therapeutics, Am. Soc. Hematology, Am. Chem. Soc., Soc. Exptl. Biology and Medicine, Biochem. Soc. Gt. Britain, Cosmos Club (Washington), Phi Beta Kappa, Phi Kappa Phi, Sigma Xi, Alpha Omega Alpha, Delta Tau Delta. Home: 5333 Renaissance Ave San Diego CA 92122

WELCH, ASHLEY JAMES, engineering educator; b. Ft. Worth, May 3, 1933; married, 1952; 3 children. BS, Tex. Tech U., 1955; MS, So. Meth. U., 1959; PhD in Elec. Engring., Rice U., 1964. Aerophys. engr. Gen. Dynamics, Ft. Worth, 1957-60; instr. elec. engring. Rice U., 1960-64, from asst. to assoc. prof., 1964-74, dir. engring. computing facility, 1970-71, dir. biomed. engring. program, 1971-75, 96—; prof. elec. and biomed. engring. U. Tex., Austin, 1975—, Marion E. Forsman Centennial prof. engring., 1985—; dir. biomed. engring., 1996—. Fellow IEEE, Am. Soc. Lasers Surg. Medicine (bd. dirs. 1989-92). Research in laser-tissue interaction, application of lasers in medicine. Office: U Tex at Austin Dept Elec & Computer Engring Austin TX 78712

WELCH, BO (ROBERT W. WELCH, III), production designer; m. Catherine O'Hara. BArch., Univ. of Ariz., 1975. Works include: (prodn. designer films) Lost Boys, 1987, Beetle Juice, 1988, Accidental Tourist, 1988, Ghostbusters II, 1989, Joe Versus the Volcano, 1990, Edward Scissor Hands, 1990 (Brit. Acad. Award 1992), Grand Canyon, 1991, Batman Returns, 1992, Wolf; (TV films) Heart of Steel, Stark II; (art dir. films) Mommy Dearest, 1981, Star Chamber, 1983, Deal of the Century, 1983, Best Defense, 1984, Swing Shift, 1984, The Color Purple, 1985 (Acad. award nominee for best art direction1986), Violets Are Blue, 1986, A Little Princess, 1995 (Acad. award nominee for best art direction 1995), Men in Black. Mem. Acad. of Motion Pictures Arts & Scis., Soc. of Motion Picture and TV Art Dirs. Office: The Mirisch Agency Ste 700 10100 Santa Monica Blvd Los Angeles CA 90067

WELCH, BYRON EUGENE, communications educator; b. Kansas City, Mo., Mar. 3, 1928; s. Paul C. and Lucile Irene (Sherman) W.; m. Mabel Holmberg, May 18, 1947; 1 son, Byron Eugene, II. Ed., Swarthmore Coll., Tex. Christian U., U. Tex., Austin. Dir. devel. and planning Atlantic Christian Coll., Wilson, N.C., 1956-58; dir. devel. Chapman Coll., Orange, Calif., 1958-59; asst. to pres. Calif. Western U., San Diego, 1959-60, William Woods Coll., Fulton, Mo., 1960-62; pres. Welch Assocs., Inc.; fund raising and devel. cons. Welch Assocs., Inc., Houston, 1962-94; adj. prof. communication U. Tex., Austin, 1968—. Mem. exec. bd. Sam Houston Area coun. Boy Scouts Am., 1974-91; bd. dirs. population program Baylor U. Coll. Medicine, 1975—; sec., mem. exec. com. U. Amas., Pueblo, Mex., 1978—; chmn. bd. elders, chmn. ch. bd. Bethany Christian Ch., Houston, 1972-79, mem. pension fund bd., 1979-86; pers. Houston Community Found., 1980-91; chmn. bd. Excape Ctr., 1989-91. With USNR, 1945-46. Recipient Silver Beaver award Boy Scouts Am., 1981. Mem. Nat. Soc. Fund Raisers (pres. 1975-77, chmn. bd. 1977-78, mem. cert. bd. 1981-86), Southwest Soc. Fund Raisers (pres. 1968-70), U. Tex. Southwest Inst. Fund Raising (dean 1974-85, dean Rice U. fund raising 1986-91), Nat. Soc. Fund Raising Execs. Found. (pres. 1980-83). Home: 4515 W Alabama St Houston TX 77027-4803 *The supreme satisfaction is to give without counting the cost. I have tried to make it a rule of my life never to remember what I do for others, but never to forget what others do for me.*

WELCH, CAROL MAE, lawyer; b. Rockford, Ill., Oct. 23, 1947; d. Leonard John and LaVerna Helen (Ang) Nyberg; m. Donald Peter Welch, Nov. 23, 1968 (dec. Sept. 1976). BA in Spanish, Wheaton Coll., 1968; JD, U. Denver, 1976. Bar: Colo. 1977, U.S. Dist. Ct. Colo. 1977, U.S. Ct. Appeals (10th cir.) 1977, U.S. Supreme Ct. 1981. Tchr. State Hosp., Dixon, Ill., 1969, Polo Cmty. Schs., Ill., 1969-70; registrar Sch. Nursing Hosp. of U. Pa., Phila., 1970; assoc. Hall & Evans, Denver, 1977-81, ptnr., 1981-92, spec. counsel, 1993-94; mem. Miller & Welch, L.L.C., Denver, 1995—. mem. Colo. Supreme Ct. Jury Inst., Denver, 1982—; vice chmn. com. on conduct U.S. Dist. Ct., Denver, 1982-83, chmn., 1983-84; lectr. in field. Pres. Family Tree, Inc. Named to Order St. Ives, U. Denver Coll. Law, 1977. Mem. ABA, Am. Coll. Trial Lawyers (state com.), Internat. Soc. Barristers, Internat. Assn. Def. Counsel, Am. Bd. Trial Advs. (treas. Colo. chpt. 1991-92, pres. 1992-93), Colo. Def. Lawyers Assn. (treas. 1982-83, v.p. 1983-84, pres. 1984-85), Denver Bar Assn., Colo. Bar Assn. (mem. litigation sect. coun. 1987-90), Colo. Bar Found. (trustee 1992—, pres. 1995), Def. Rsch. Inst. (chmn. Colo. chpt. 1987-90, regional v.p. 1990-93, bd. dirs. 1993—), William E. Doyle Inn. Office: Miller & Welch LLC 730 17th St # 370 Denver CO 80202-3503

WELCH, CHARLES DAVID, diplomat; b. Munich, Germany, Dec. 25, 1953; s. Donald Mansel and Jackie (Brown) W.; m. Gretchen Anne Gerwe, May 14, 1983; children: Emma Frances, Margaret Elizabeth, Hannah Alice. Student, London Sch. Econs., 1973-74; BS in Fgn. Svc., Georgetown U., 1975; MA in Law and Diplomacy, MA, Tufts U., 1977. Staff asst. office of undersecretary U.S. State Dept. Security Assistance, Washington, 1977-79; polit. officer U.S. Embassy, Islamabad, Pakistan, 1979-81; country officer Syria desk U.S. State Dept. Bur. of Near Ea. and South Asian Affairs, Washington, 1981-82, country officer Lebanon desk, 1982-83; polit. sect. chief U.S. Embassy, Damascus, Syria, 1984-86; polit. counselor U.S. Embassy, Amman, Jordan, 1986-88; mem. sr. seminar fgn. policy U.S. State Dept. Fgn. Svc. Inst., Washington, 1988-89; dir. near Ea. and South Asian affairs Nat. Security Coun., White House, Washington, 1989-91; exec. asst. to undersec. for polit. affairs Dept. of State, Washington, 1991-92; dep. chief mission U.S. Embassy, Riyadh, Saudi Arabia, 1992-95; prin. dep. asst. sec. for near ea. affairs Dept. of State, Washington, 1995—. Mem. Coun. Fgn. Rels., Am. Fgn. Svc. Assn., Phi Beta Kappa, Phi Alpha Phi. Presbyterian. Avocations: sports, books, music, history. Home and Office: Rm 6242 Dept State Washington DC 20520

WELCH, CLAUDE (RAYMOND), theology educator; b. Genoa City, Wis., Mar. 10, 1922; s. Virgil Cleon and Deone West (Grenelle) W.; m. Eloise Janette Turner, May 31, 1942 (div. 1970); children—Eric, Thomas, Claudia; m. Theodosia Montigel Blewett, Oct. 5, 1970 (dec. 1978); m. Joy Neuman, Oct. 30, 1982. BA summa cum laude, Upper Iowa U., 1942; postgrad., Garrett Theol. Sem., 1942-43; BD cum laude, Yale U., 1945, PhD, 1950; DD (hon.), Ch. Div. Sch. of Pacific, 1972, Jesuit Sch. Theology, 1982; LHD (hon.), U. Judaism, 1976. Ordained to ministry Meth. Ch., 1947. Instr. religion Princeton (N.J.) U., 1947-50, asst. prof., 1950-51, vis. prof., 1962; asst. prof. theology Yale U. Div. Sch., New Haven, 1951-54, assoc. prof., 1954-60; Berg prof. religious thought, chmn. dept. U. Pa., Phila., 1960-71, assoc. dean Coll. Arts and Scis., 1964-68, acting chmn. dept. philosophy, 1965-66; prof. hist. theology Grad. Theol. Union, Berkeley, Calif., 1971—, dean, 1971-87, pres., 1972-82; vis. prof. Garrett Theol. Sem., 1951, Pacific Sch. Religion, 1958, Hartford Sem. Found., 1958-59, Princeton Theol. Sem., 1962-63, U. Va., 1987; Fulbright sr. lectr. U. Mainz, Germany, 1968; Sprunt lectr. Union Theol. Sem., Richmond, Va., 1958; Willson lectr. Southwestern U., Georgetown, Tex., 1994; dir. study of grad. edn. in religion Am. Coun. Learned Socs., 1969-71; del. World Conf. on Faith and Order, 1963. Author: In This Name: the Doctrine of the Trinity in Contemporary Theology, 1952, (with John Dillenberger) Protestant Christianity, interpreted through its Development, 1954, 2d rev. edit., 1988, The Reality of the Church, 1958, Graduate Education in Religion: A Critical Appraisal, 1971, Religion in the Undergraduate Curriculum, 1972, Protestant Thought in the 19th Century, vol. 1, 1799-1870, 1972, vol. 2, 1870-1914, 1985; Editor, translator: God and Incarnation in Mid-19th Century German Theology (Thomasius, Dorner and Biedermann), 1965; Contbr. to publs. in field. Recipient decennial prize Bross Found., 1970; Guggenheim fellow, 1976; NEH research fellow, 1984, Fulbright research fellow, 1956-57. Mem. Am. Acad. Religion (pres. 1969-70), Coun. of Socs. for Study of Religion (chmn. 1969-74, 85-90), Soc. for Values in Higher Edn. (pres. 1967-71), Am. Soc. Ch. History, Am. Theol. Soc., Phi Beta Kappa. Home: 123 Fairlawn Dr Berkeley CA 94708-2107

WELCH, DAVID WILLIAM, lawyer; b. St. Louis, Feb. 26, 1941; s. Claude LeRoy Welch and Mary Eleanor (Peggs) Penney; m. Candace Lee Capages, June 5, 1971; children: Joseph Peggs, Heather Elizabeth, Katherine Laura. BSBA, Washington U., St. Louis, 1963; JD, U. Tulsa, 1971. Bar: Okla. 1972, Mo. 1973, U.S. Dist. Ct. (we. dist.) Mo. 1973, U.S. Dist. Ct. (ea. dist.) Mo. 1974, U.S. Ct. Appeals (8th cir.) 1977, U.S. Ct. Appeals (7th cir.) 1991. Contract adminstr. McDonnell Aircraft Corp., St. Louis, 1965-66; bus. analyst Dun & Bradstreet Inc., Los Angeles, 1967-68; atty. U.S. Dept. Labor, Washington, 1972-73; ptnr. Moller Talent, Kuelthau & Welch, St. Louis, 1973-88, Lashly & Baer, St. Louis, 1988-96, Armstrong, Teasdale, Schlafly & Davis, St. Louis, 1996—. Author: (handbook) Missouri Employment Law, 1988; contbr. book chpts. Missouri Bar Employer-Employee Law, 1985, 87, 89, 92, 94; co-editor: Occupational Safety and Health Law, 1996. Mem. City of Creve Coeur Ethics Commn., 1987-88, Planning and Zoning Commn., 1988—; bd. dirs. Camp Wyman, Eureka, Mo., 1982—, sec., 1987-88, 2nd v.p. 1988-89, 1st v.p. 1990-92, pres., 1992-94. Mem. ABA, Fed. Bar Assn., Mo. Bar Assn., Okla. Bar Assn., St. Louis Bar Assn., Tulsa County Bar Assn., Kiwanis (bd. dirs. St. Louis 1979—, sec. 1982-83, 93-94, v.p. 1983-84, 88-90, 92-93, Man of Yr. award 1985). Democrat. Mem. Christian Ch. (Disciples of Christ). Avocations: travel, landscaping, music. Home: 536 N Mosley Rd Saint Louis MO 63141-7633 Office: Armstrong Teasdale Schlafly & Davis 1 Metropolitan Sq 2600 Saint Louis MO 63102

WELCH, DOUGLAS LINDSAY, physics educator; b. Karamursel, Turkey, Oct. 8, 1958; s. Gene Armour and Katharin (Lindsay) W.; m. Carol Marie Gibbons, Aug. 28, 1982. BSc, U. Toronto, Ont., Can., 1981, MSc, 1983, PhD, 1985. Rsch. assoc. Nat. Rsch. Coun. Dom Astrophys. Obs., Victoria, B.C., Can., 1986-88; from asst. prof. to assoc. prof., univ. rsch. fellow McMaster U., Hamilton, Ont., 1988—. Office: McMaster U Dept Physics & Astron, 1280 Main St W, Hamilton, ON Canada L8S 4M1

WELCH, EDWARD P., lawyer; b. Columbus, Ohio, Mar. 12, 1950; s. Charles E. and Charma L. (Overbeck) W.; m. Noreen R. Welch, Sept. 8, 1973. BS in Bus. Administrn., Georgetown U., 1972; JD, Villanova U., 1976. Bar: Del. 1976, U.S. Dist. Ct. Del. 1977, U.S. Ct. Appeals (3d cir.) 1981, U.S. Supreme Ct. 1981, N.Y. 1982, U.S. Ct. Appeals (fed. cir.) 1985, (5th cir.) 1992. Law clk. Del Ct. Chancery, Wilmington, 1976-77; assoc. Prickett, Ward, Burt & Sanders, Wilmington, 1977-79; assoc. Skadden, Arps, Slate, Meagher & Flom, Wilmington, 1979-84, ptnr., 1984—; mem. com. charged with drafting evidence code Del., com. charged with drafting dir. liability legis., Wilmington 1977-78, Ct. Chancery Rules Com., Wilmington, 1990—. Author: Folk, Ward & Welch: Folk on the Delaware General Corporation Law, 1988, 2d edit., 1992; bimonthly Nat. Law Jour.; co-editor: Folk On The Delaware General Corporation Law Fundamentals, 1993. Bd. dirs. United Cerebral Palsy of Del., Wilmington, 1977-87, The Mary Campbell Ctr., 1987—; co-chmn. United Cerebral Palsy's Camp Manito, Wilmington, 1982-83; trustee The Tatnall Sch., Wilmington, 1992-95. Recipient Community Svc. award United Cerebral Palsy of Del., Wilmington, 1981. Mem. Del. Bar Assn. (mem. coun. corp. law, Young Lawyers award 1986), The Rodney Square Club, Corp. Law Coun. Office: Skadden Arps Slate Meagher & Flom PO Box 636 One Rodney Sq Wilmington DE 19801

WELCH, EDWIN HUGH, academic administrator; b. Balt., Apr. 11, 1944; s. Lester Kenneth and Catherine (Dodrer); m. Janet Gail Boggess, Nov. 22, 1977. BA, Western Md. Coll., 1965; STB, Boston U. Sch. Theology, 1968; postgrad., London Sch. Econs. and Polit. Sci., 1968-69; PhD, Boston U., 1971. Assoc. prof., chmn. W.Va. Wesleyan Coll., Buckhannon, 1971-75; assoc. prof., chmn. Lebanon Valley Coll., Annville, Pa., 1975-79, dir. weekend coll., 1979-80; dean Lakeland Coll., Sheboygan, Wis., 1980-81; provost Wartburg Coll., Waverly, Iowa, 1981-89; pres. U. Charleston, W.Va., 1989—; chmn. Iowa Deans Confs., Des Moines, 1984-89; title III evaluator Iowa Wesleyan Coll., Mt. Pleasant, 1983-85. Contbr. articles to edn. jours. Bd. dirs. Bus. and Indsl. Devel. Corp., One Valley Bank, Charleston Area Med. Ctr.; v.p. Nat. Inst. Chem. Studies; creator, dir. Community Leadership Devel. Program, Waverly, 1986-88; bd. dirs., pres. Lebanon (Pa.) Family Planning Assn., 1976-81. Named Tchr. of Yr., W.Va. Wesleyan Coll., 1974. Mem. Nat. Assn. Ind. Colls. and Univs., Balt. Conf. United Meth. Ch. (ordained), Appalachian Coll. Assn., Coun. Ind. Colls., Rotary Internat. (bd. dirs. Charleston). Democrat. Methodist. Office: U Charleston Office of Pres Charleston WV 25304-1099

WELCH, GARTH LARRY, chemistry educator; b. Brigham City, Utah, Feb. 14, 1937; s. Samuel and Minnie Jane (Hughes) W.; m. Melba Lael Coombs, Sept. 9, 1960; children: Larry Kent, Kathryn Louise, Richard Samuel, Garth Edward, Robert Irvine, David Jonathan. B.S., U. Utah, 1959, Ph.D., 1963. Teaching asst. U. Utah, 1959-62; postdoctoral research fellow UCLA, 1962-64; asst. prof. Weber State U., Ogden, Utah, 1964-68; assoc. prof. Weber State U., 1968-72; prof. Weber State U., Ogden, 1972—, dean Sch. Natural Sci., 1974-83, exec. dir. bus. affairs, 1983-89, assoc. v.p. phys. facilities, 1990-91; mem. Utah State Council on Sci. and Tech., 1980-84. Mem. Mormon Tabernacle Choir, Salt Lake City, 1958-62, Jay Welch Chorale, 1983—, Pleasant View Planning Commn., 1988-91, chmn., 1990-91, sci. adv. com. Salt Lake C.C., 1994—. Mem. Am. Chem. Soc., Sigma Xi, Phi Kappa Phi. Mem. LDS Ch. (bishop 1966-74). Home: 3910 N 800 W Ogden UT 84414

WELCH, HARRY SCOVILLE, lawyer, retired gas pipeline company executive; b. Hugo, Okla., Nov. 14, 1923; s. John Calvin and Gaynell (Potts) W.; m. Peggy Joyce Weis, Dec. 18, 1954; children—Marshall Porter, Gay, Harry Scoville, Mary Margaret, Anne. B.B.A., U. Tex. at Austin, 1947, LL.B., 1949. Bar: Tex. 1948. Atty. Am. Republics Corp., Houston, 1949-51; ptnr. Turner, White, Atwood, McLane & Francis, Dallas, 1951-59; exec. asst., then v.p. Tenneco Inc., Houston, 1959-73; v.p., gen. counsel Panhandle Ea. Corp., Houston, 1973-74, sr. v.p., gen. counsel, 1975-85; v.p., gen. counsel Tex. Ea. Corp., Houston, 1987-89; mem. bd. adjustment Hunter's Creek Village, Tex., 1970-77, chmn., 1973-77; mem. adv. bd. Internat. Oil and Gas Ednl. Ctr., Southwestern Legal Found., Dallas, 1975-85; bd. dirs. Barrett Resources Corp. Served with USNR, 1943-46. Fellow Tex. Bar Found.; mem. Am., Houston Bar Assns., State Bar Tex., Phi Kappa Sigma, Phi Alpha Delta. Presbyterian. Club: Ramada (Houston). Home: 10611 Twelve Oaks Dr Houston TX 77024-3135

WELCH, JERRY, oil company executive; b. Marion, Ohio, Mar. 13, 1963; s. Arthur Leroy and Donna R. (Ellwood) W. BA, U. Colo., 1984. Exec. Amoco Oil, Houston, 1984—. Mem. Internat. Platform Assn. Republican. Avocations: auto racing, sailing, swimming. Home: 31650 E State Road 44 Eustis FL 32726-8920

WELCH, JOHN DANA, urologist, performing arts association executive; b. Canton, Ill., Mar. 14, 1938; m. Myrna Lee Loring, Dec. 23, 1962; children: Timothy Lance, Christina Dawn. BS, U. Ill., 1960, MD, 1963. Diplomate Am. Bd. Urology, Nat. Bd. Med. Examiners, Fla. Bd. Med. Examiners. Rotating intern Tampa (Fla.) Gen. Hosp., 1963-64, resident in urology, 1964-68; pvt. practice, Sarasota, Fla., 1970—; bd. dirs. Bay Area Renal Stone Ctr.; chief surgery HCA Doctors Hosp., 1981, chief of staff, 1983, trustee, 1988-91. Bd. dirs. Asolo Ctr. for Performing Arts, 1982-95, sec., 1989-90, v.p., 1990-93, pres., 1993-94. Maj. USAF, 1968-70. Mem. Fla. Med. Assn., Sarasota County Med. Soc., Am. Urological Assn. (SE sect.), Fla. Urological Soc. (pres. 1986), Am. Lithotripsy Soc. Home: 650 Mourning Dove Dr Sarasota FL 34236 Office: 1921 Waldemere St Sarasota FL 34239

WELCH, JOHN FRANCIS, JR. (JACK WELCH), electrical manufacturing company executive; b. Peabody, Mass., Nov. 19, 1935; s. John Francis and Grace (Andrews) W.; m. Carolyn B. Osburn, Nov. 1959 (div. 1987); children: Katherine, John, Anne, Mark; m. Jane Beasley, Apr. 1989. B.S. in Chem. Engring, U. Mass., 1957; M.S., U. Ill., 1958, Ph.D., 1960. With Gen. Electric Co., Fairfield, Conn., 1960—, v.p., 1972, v.p., group exec. components and materials group, 1973-77, sr. v.p., sector exec., consumer products and services sector, 1977-79, vice chmn., exec. officer, 1979-81, chmn., chief exec. officer, 1981—; also dir. Gen. Electric Capital Services. Patentee in field. Mem. NAE, The Bus. Coun. (former chmn.), Bus. Roundtable. Office: Gen Electric Co 3135 Easton Tpke Fairfield CT 06431-0002

WELCH, JOSEPH F., investment company executive; b. Binghamton, N.Y., Aug. 3, 1934; s. James Joseph and Winifred Frances (Doyle) W.; m. Marcia Pyle, Oct. 6, 1962; children: Winifred, Lorraine, Suzanne, Lucinda, Elizabeth. BS, Lehigh U., 1956; MBA, Cornell U., 1961. Mgmt. positions with Gen. Electric Co., Benton & Bowles, Internat. Salt, 1963-70; pres. Penske Corp., Reading, Pa., 1974-76; pres., owner J.F. Welch Interests, Inc., 1970—, The Bachman Co., Reading, 1980—; bd. dirs. Detroit Diesel Corp., Snack Food Assn., chmn.; mem. adv. bd. Meridian Bank, Del. to White House Conf. on Small Bus. Bd. dirs. YMCA, Phila. Zoo; mem. Pa. Ethics Commn., 1980-82; bd. dirs., treas. Pa. Energy Devel. Authority; mem. pres.'s council U. Vt. Bus. Sch.; trustee Miss Hall's Sch., St. Joseph Hosp., Lehigh U.; chmn. Bus. Adv. Coun., Coll. Bus. & Econs., Lehigh Univ. Mem. adv. coun. Johnson Grad. Sch. Mgmt. Served to maj. U.S. Army, 1956-58. Mem. Am. Mgmt. Assn. (pres. sect.), Berks County C. of C. (bd. dirs., v.p.), Lehigh U. Alumni Assn. (bd. dirs., pres.), Saucon Valley Country Club, Berkshire Country Club, Ocean Reef Club, Sankaty Head Club, Nantucket Yacht Club. Office: 1 Washington Tower Plz Reading PA 19601

WELCH, LLOYD RICHARD, electrical engineering educator, communications consultant; b. Detroit, Sept. 28, 1927; s. Richard C. and Helen (Felt) W.; m. Irene Althea Main, Sept. 12, 1953; children: Pamela Irene Welch Towery, Melinda Ann Bryant. BS in Math., U. Ill., 1951; PhD in Math., Calif. Inst. Tech., 1958. Mathematician NASA-Jet Propulsion Lab., Pasadena, Calif., 1956-59; staff mathematician Inst. Def. Analyses, Princeton, N.J., 1959-65; prof. elec. engring. U. So. Calif., L.A., 1965—; cons. in field of elec. comms. Contbr. articles to profl. jours. Served with USN, 1945-49, 51-52. Fellow IEEE; mem. Nat. Acad. Engring., Am. Math. Soc., Math. Assn. Am., Soc. for Indsl. and Applied Math., Phi Beta Kappa, Sigma Xi, Phi Kappa Phi, Pi Mu Epsilon, Eta Kappa Nu. Office: U So Calif Elec Engring Bldg 500A Los Angeles CA 90089

WELCH, MICHAEL JOHN, chemistry educator, researcher; b. Stoke-on-Trent, Staffordshire, Eng., June 28, 1939; came to U.S., 1965; s. Arthur John W. and Mary (Welch); m. Teresa Jean Conocchiolli, Apr. 22, 1967 (div. 1979); children: Colin, Lesley. B.A., Cambridge U., Eng., 1961; M.A., Cambridge U., 1964; Ph.D., London U., 1965. Asst. prof. radiation chemistry in radiology Washington U. Sch. Medicine, St. Louis, 1967-70, assoc. prof., 1970-74; assoc. prof. dept. chemistry Washington U. Sch., St. Louis, 1971-75, prof. dept. chemistry, 1978—; prof. radiology Washington U. Sch. Medicine, St. Louis, 1991—, prof. molecular biology and pharmacology, 1993—; dir. radiol. scis. dept. Washignton U., 1990—; mem. diagnostic radiology study sect. NIH, 1986-89, chmn., 1989-91; mem. sci. adv. com. Whitaker Found., 1995—. Author: Introduction to the Tracer Methods, 1972; editor: Radiopharmaceuticals and Other Compoounds Labeled with Shortlived Radionuclides, 1977; assoc. editor Jour. Nuclear Medicine, 1989—; contbr. chpts. to books, more than 400 articles to profl. jours. Recipient Georg Charles de Hevesy Nuclear Medicine Pioneer award, 1992; scholar St. Catharine Coll. Cambridge U., 1958-61. Mem. Soc. Nuclear Medicine (trustee, pres. 1984, Paul C. Aebersold award 1980), Radiopharm. Sci. Coun. (pres. 1980-81), Am. Chem. Soc. (St. Louis award 1988, award for nuclear chemistry 1990, Mid-West award 1991), Chem. Soc. London, Radiation Rsch. Soc., Sigma Xi. Home: 1 Spoede Ln Saint Louis MO 63141-7708 Office: Washington U Sch Medicine Edward Mallinckrodt Inst Radiology 510 S Kingshighway Blvd Saint Louis MO 63110-1016

WELCH, NEAL WILLIAM, retired electric company executive; b. North Adams, Mass., Sept. 16, 1908; s. Owen William and Mary Gertrude (McGovern) W.; m. Harriet Flood, June 27, 1935; children—Marian, Mary. Grad., Bently Coll., 1930. With Sprague Electric Co., North Adams, 1932-82; v.p. sales Sprague Electric Co., 1953-60, sr. v.p. mktg. and sales, 1960-67, exec. v.p., 1967-71, chmn. exec. com., 1968-71, chmn., chief exec. officer, 1971-81, chmn. bd., chmn. exec. com., 1981-82; dir. GK Techs.; chmn., cons., mem. exec. com. Spelco; ret., 1984. Home: Laurie Dr Williamstown MA 01267

WELCH, OLIVER WENDELL, retired pharmaceutical executive; b. Jacksonville, Tex., Jan. 9, 1930; s. Jackson Andrew and Annie Laura (Trapp) W.; m. Wanda Virginia Urrey, Nov. 14, 1948. BA, Tex. Tech U., 1952; MA, Columbia U., 1958. Pharm. rep., supr. mktg. rsch., manpower devel. Warner Lambert Co., Morris Plains, N.J., 1962-72; mgr. corp. devel. Boehringer Mannheim Corp., N.Y.C., 1972-75; v.p. Biomed. Data Co., N.Y.C., 1975-77; assoc. dir., dep. dir. regulatory affairs Sterling Winthrop Inc., N.Y.C., 1977-94; ret., 1994; cons. Sanofi Winthrop, Inc., N.Y.C., 1995. Mem. Regulatory Affairs Profls. Soc., Drug Info. Assn., Order St. John of Jerusalem. Republican. Episcopalian. Avocations: music, travel, theatre. *Pursue excellence. Pay attention to detail. Expect a positive result.*

WELCH, PATRICK DANIEL, state senator; b. Chgo., Dec. 12, 1948; s. William C. and Alice W. Student, So. Ill. U., 1970; JD, Chgo. Kent Coll. Law, 1974. Bar: Ill. 1974. Pvt. practice, Peru, Ill., 1974—; mem. Ill. Senate, 1983—; asst. minority leader, 1993—; former chmn. energy and environ. comm.; nat. Del., mem. credentials com. Dem. Nat. Conv., 1976, del., 1980, 84, 88, 92; precinct committeeman Peru Dem. Party, 1976-86; del. Dem. Nat. Mid-Term Conf., 1978, 82; committeeman Ill. Dem. Cen. Com., 1978—, mem. exec. com., 1983—; mem. Peru Citizens' Svc. Orgn.; vice-chmn. Ill. Dem. Party, 1990-94, chmn. party platform com., 1994. Recipient Disting. Svc. award Ill. Bicentennial Commn., 1976. Mem. Ill. Bar Assn., La Salle County Bar Assn. Office: State Senate State Capitol Springfield IL 62706

WELCH, PATRICK E., diversified financial services company executive; b. 1947. Student, Seattle U.; MS in Physics, U. Wash., 1970, MBA, 1973. Fin. analyst Ford Motor Com, Seattle, 1973-74; mgr. investment evaln. dept. Weyerhaeuser Co., Inc., Federal Way, Wash., 1974-81; with Great Northern Insured Annuities, Seattle, 1981—, GNA Securities, Inc., Federal Way, Seattle; pres., CEO Gen. ELC Capital Assurance Co., Seattle, 1993—; now pres., CEO GNA Corp., Seattle. Office: First GNA Life Insur Co of NY Two Union Sq 601 Union St Ste 5600 Seattle WA 98101-2336*

WELCH, PHILIP BURLAND, electronics and office products company executive; b. Portland, Maine, Nov. 15, 1931; s. Philip Gerald Welch and Clara Jenny (Berry) Hawxwell; m. Sheila May Preston, May 19, 1960; children: Jahna Holly Welch Roth, Victoria Preston Welch Johnsen. Student, Berklee Coll., 1955-58. Nat. sales mgr. Akai Am. Ltd., Anaheim, Calif., 1970-73, BSR, USA, Blaupunkt, N.Y., 1973-76; nat. sales and mktg. mgr. Philips High Fidelity Labs, Ft. Wayne, Ind., 1976-79; dir. mktg. Pioneer

Electronics, Moonachie, N.J., 1979-82; pres. Schneider N.Am. Ltd., Dayton, N.J., 1982-83; v.p. Lyons Assn., Indpls., 1986-88; pres. Nat. Electric Mktg. Co., Jacksonville, Fla., 1975—, Hemisphere Enterprises Corp., Jacksonville, 1988-91; v.p., gen. mgr. Atlantic office Sources, Inc., Jacksonville, Fla., 1996—; pres. Phil Welch Enterprises, Jacksonville, 1989—; cons. ContraTech Corp., Portland, Oreg., 1986-87, Kukje Internat., N.Y.C., 1986, FCI Inc., N.J., 1985, others; cons. Multiform Products, Inc., Jacksonville, 1989-90, gen. mgr., v.p., 1990-96. Contbr. articles to profl. jours. With USAF, 1950-54. Named Man of Decade Audio/Video Cons. USA, 1982, Man of Yr. Soc. of Audio Cons., 1974. Republican. Avocations: flying, golf. Office: Ste 141 10991-55 San Jose Blvd Jacksonville FL 32223

WELCH, RAQUEL, actress; b. Chgo., Sept. 5, 1940; d. Arm and Josepha (Hall) Tejada; m. James Westley Welch, May 8, 1959 (div.); children: Damon, Tahnee; m. Patrick Curtis (div.); m. Andre Weinfeld, July 1980 (div.). Actress: (films) including Fantastic Voyage, 1966, One Million B.C, 1967, The Biggest Bundle of Them All, 1968, Fathom, 1967, The Queens, 1967, 100 Rifles, 1969, Magic Christian, 1970, Bedazzled, 1971, Fuzz, 1972, Bluebeard, 1972, Hannie Caulder, 1972, Kansas City Bomber, 1972, Myra Breckinridge, 1970, The Last of Sheila, 1973, The Three Musketeers, 1974 (Golden Globe award for best actress), The Wild Party, 1975, The Four Musketeers, 1975, Mother, Jugs and Speed, 1976, Crossed Swords, 1978, L'Animal, 1979, (TV movies) The Legend of Walks Far Woman, 1982, Right to Die, 1987, Scandal in a Small Town, 1988, Trouble in Paradise, 1989, Torch Song, 1993, Naked Gun 33 1/3, 1993, (Broadway debut) Woman of the Year, 1982; author: The Raquel Welch Total Beauty and Fitness Program, 1984. Address: Innovative Artists 1999 Ave of the Stars Ste 2850 Los Angeles CA 90067*

WELCH, ROBERT BOND, ophthalmologist, educator; b. Balt., May 24, 1927; s. Robert S.G. and Sally (Bond) W.; m. Elizabeth Truslow, May 30, 1953. A.B., Princeton U., 1949; M.D., Johns Hopkins U., 1953. Diplomate: Am. Bd. Ophthalmology. Intern in internal medicine Duke U. Hosp., 1953-54; resident in ophthalmology Wilmer Inst., Johns Hopkins U., 1954-57, chief resident in ophthalmology, 1959, co-dir. retina service, 1959-84, dir. retina service, 1984-85; retinal cons. in ophthalmology Walter Reed Army Hosp., 1961—, Bethesda Naval Hosp, 1976—; assoc. prof. ophthalmology Johns Hopkins U.; chmn. dept. ophthalmology Greater Balt. Med. Ctr., 1985-91. Author: (with others) The Wilmer Institute 1925-1975, 1976; editor Transactions Am. Ophthal. Soc., 1984-91; mem. editorial staff Retina mag., 1980-86. Served with USNR, 1945-47. Mem. Am. Ophthal. Soc. (v.p. 1992-93, pres. 1993-94, editor 1984-90), Retina Soc. (pres. 1981-83), Pan. Pacific Surg. Assn. (v.p. 1972-80), Md. Soc. Eye Physicians and Surgeons (pres. 1963-64), Md. Club., Elkridge Club, South River Club. Democrat. Episcopalian. Home: 4409 Atwick Rd Baltimore MD 21210-2811 Office: 6565 N Charles St Baltimore MD 21204-6800 also: 86 State Cir Annapolis MD 21401-1906

WELCH, ROBERT MORROW, JR., lawyer; b. Wichita Falls, Tex., Dec. 17, 1927; s. Robert Morrow and Sue (Hays) W.; children: Catherine C., Robert Morrow III, Candice C.; m. Annette Y. Apodaca, Dec. 17, 1985. LLB, Baylor U., 1951. Bar: Tex. 1951, Colo. 1989. Briefing clk. Supreme Ct. Tex., Austin, 1951-52; assoc., then ptnr. Fulbright & Jaworski, Houston, 1952-92, ret. sr. ptnr., 1992—. Sgt. USMC, 1946-48. Fellow Tex. Bar Found.; mem. ABA, Am. Acad. Matrimonial Lawyers (cert. matrimonial arbitrator), Internat. Acad. Matrimonial Lawyers, Houston Bar Assn. Home: 1436 W Gray Ste 189 Houston TX 77019 also: PO Box 10000 Ste 127 Silverthorne CO 80498 Office: Fulbright & Jaworski 1301 Mckinney St Houston TX 77010

WELCH, ROBERT W., production designer, art director. Prodn. designer: (TV movies) Heart of Steel, 1983, Slow Burn, 1986, Stark: Mirror Image, 1986, (films) The Lost Boys, 1987, The Accidental Tourist, 1988, Beetlejuice, 1988, Ghostbusters II, 1989, Joe Versus the Volcano, 1990, Edward Scissorhands, 1990, Grand Canyon, 1991, Batman Returns, 1992, Wolf, 1994; art dir.: (films) The Star Chamber, 1983, Deal of the Century, 1983, Swing Shift, 1984, Best Defense, 1984, The Color Purple, 1985 (Academy award nomination best art direction 1985). Office: care Lawrence Mirisch The Mirisch Agency 10100 Santa Monica Blvd Ste 700 Los Angeles CA 90067-4011

WELCH, (WILLIAM) ROGER, artist; b. Westfield, N.J., Feb. 10, 1946; s. Herbert Russell and Yvonne (Miller) W.; m. Carla M. Stellweg. BFA, Miami U., Oxford, Ohio, 1969; MFA, Chgo. Art Inst., 1971. visiting artist Univ. of Tex., Austin, 1988, 90, Univ. Tenn., Knoxville, 1989. One-man shows include Miami U., Oxford, Ohio, 1984, Whitney Mus. of Am. Art, N.Y.C., 1982, Museo Nacional, Havana, Cuba, 1981, Museo De Arte Moderno, Mex. City, 1980, Albright Knox Art Gallery, Buffalo, 1977, Milw. Art Ctr., 1974, Sonnabend Gallery, Paris and N.Y.C., 1972, Ewing Gallery, U. Tenn., Knoxville, 1990, Liverpool Gallery, Brussels, 1991. Grantee Nat. Endowment for the Arts, 1980, 74, N.Y. State Coun. on the Arts, 1976, 73. Democrat. Methodist. Home: 87 E Houston St New York NY 10012-2805

WELCH, RONALD J., actuary; b. Luling, Tex., June 26, 1945; s. Billie C. and Irene (Anton) W.; m. Leslie Ann Herman, Oct. 9, 1971; children: Kelley, Stephen. BBA, U. Tex., 1966; MS, Northeastern U., 1968. V.p., actuary Am. Nat. Ins. Co., Galveston, Tex., 1975-80, sr. v.p., actuary, 1980-86, sr. v.p., chief actuary, 1986—; bd. dirs. Standard Life & Accident Ins. Co., Oklahoma City, Am. Nat. Property & Casualty Ins., Springfield, Mo., Am. Nat. Life Ins. Co. of Tex., Galveston; chmn. bd. Garden State Life Ins. Co., Newark. Fellow Soc. of Actuaries; mem. Am. Acad. Actuaries. Office: Am Nat Ins Co 1 Moody Plz Galveston TX 77550-7948

WELCH, ROSS MAYNARD, plant physiologist, researcher, educator; b. Lancaster, Calif., May 8, 1943; s. Lloyd C. and Theda W. (Slane) W.; m. Jill Susanne Varley, Aug. 22, 1965; children: Renell Cherie, Brent Ross. BS, Calif. Poly. U., 1966; MS, U. Calif., Davis, 1969, PhD, 1971. Plant physiologist USDA Agrl. Rsch. Svc., Ithaca, N.Y., 1971—; rsch. assoc. Cornell U., Ithaca, 1971-75, asst. prof. plant physiology, 1975-81, assoc. prof., 1981-87, prof., 1987-94; co-organizer food sys. for improved health program Coll. Agr. and Life Scis., Cornell U., Ithaca, 1994—; disting. vis. scientist Murdoch U., Perth, Australia, 1980-81; vis. disting. scholar and lectr. U. Adelaide, Australia, 1991—; coord. food systems for health program coll. agriculture and life sci. Cornell U., 1994—. Editor: Crops as Sources of Nutrients for Humans, 1984; co-editor: Micronutrients in Agriculture, 2d edit., 1989; contbr. over 100 rsch. articles and 20 rev. articles to profl. jours. Fellow Am. Soc. Agronomy (Rsch. award N.E. br. 1992), Soil Sci. Soc. Am.; mem. Am. Soc. Plant Physiologists, AAAS, N.Y. Acad. Scis., Masons (master 1984-85), Sigma Xi. Republican. Mem. United Ch. of Christ. Achievements include discovery that nickel is an essential element for all higher plants; discovery that zinc plays a role in maintaining the integrity of root-cell plasma membranes. Home: 24 Hickory Cir Ithaca NY 14850-9673 Office: US Plant Soil & Nutrition Lab Tower Rd Ithaca NY 14853

WELCH, S(TEPHEN) ANTHONY, university dean, Islamic studies and arts educator; b. Phila., Apr. 29, 1942; s. Arnold DeMerritt and Mary Scott Welch; m. Hyesoon Kim; children: Nicholas, Bronwen, Emily. Student, U. Munich, Free U. of Berlin; BA in German Lit. with honors, Swarthmore Coll., 1965; MA, Harvard U., 1967, PhD (Fine Arts) History of Islamic Art and Architecture, 1972. Lectr. dept. history in art U. Victoria, B.C., 1971-72, asst. prof., 1972-75, assoc. prof., 1975-80, prof., 1980—, assoc. dean, 1982-85, Dean of Faculty of Fine Arts, 1985—; vis. prof. U. Minn., U. Wash., U. Chgo.; specialist in Iranian painting, Mughal painting in India, Islamic calligraphy and Sultanate architecture in medieval India. Author: Shah 'Abbas and the Arts of Isfahan, 1973, Artists for the Shah, 1976, Collection of Islamic Art, Prince Sadruddin Aga Khan, 4 Vols., 1972-78, Calligraphy in the Arts of the Muslim World, 1979, Arts of the Islamic Book, 1982, Treasures of Islam, 1985; contbr. articles to scholarly and profl. jours. Office: Dean Faculty Fine Arts, Univ Victoria, Victoria, BC Canada V8W 2Y2

WELCH, SUSAN, political science educator, dean; b. Galesburg, Ill.; d. Delbert Franklin and Marie S. Welch; m. Alan Booth, Feb. 16, 1974; 1 child, Andrew Welch Booth. AB in History, U. Ill., 1965, MA in Polit. Sci., 1966, PhD in Polit. Sci., 1970. From asst. prof. to prof. U. Nebr., 1970-80, Happold prof., 1980-91; prof. dept. polit. sci., dean Coll. Liberal Arts Pa. State U., University Park, 1991—; bd. examiners Ednl. Testing Svc., Grad. Record Exam., Advances Polit. Sci. Exam., 1978-88; mem. polit. sci. rev. panel NSF, 1978-80, com. of visitors, 1990; presenter papers to profl. assns.; prin. investigator rsch. grants nat. funding agys. Author: (with others) Black Representation and Urban Policy, 1981, Quantitative Methods for Public Administration, 1982, 2d edit., 1988, The Political Life of American Jewish Women, 1984, 85, Understanding American Government, 1991, 3d edit., 1995, American Government, 1986, 6th edit., 1996, Women: Elections and Representation, 1987, 2d edit., 1994, Urban Reform and Its Consequences: A Study in Representation, 1988, Black Americans' Views of Racial Inequality: The Dream Deferred, 1991, rev. edit., 1993; editor: Am. Politics Quar., 1987-92; mem. editl. bd. several profl. jours.; contbr. articles to profl. jours. Mem. AAUP, Am. Polit. Sci. Assn. (exec. coun. 1982-85, mem. com. on status of women, treas. 1983-85, chair trust and devel. fund 1983-85, sec. 1995-96), Midwest Polit. Sci. Assn. (exec. coun. 1978-81, pres. 1992-93), Women's Caucus for Polit. Sci., Phi Beta Kappa, Pi Sigma Alpha (coun. mem. 1990-94). Office: Pa State U Coll of the Liberal Arts 110 Sparks University Park PA 16802

WELCH, THOMAS ANDREW, lawyer; b. Lincoln, Nebr., Dec. 22, 1936; s. Lawrence William and Edna Alberta (Tangeman) W.; m. Ann Reinecke, Sept. 12, 1959; children: Jonathan Thomas, Michael Andrew, Susan Jennifer. Student, Stanford U., 1955-56; BA, UCLA, 1959; JD, Harvard U., 1965. Bar: Calif. 1966, U.S. Dist. Ct. (no. dist.) 1966, U.S. Ct. Appeals (9th cir.) 1966, U.S. Supreme Ct. 1976. Assoc. Brobeck, Phleger & Harrison, San Francisco, 1965-71, ptnr., 1972—; exec. com. Asia/Pacific Ctr. Resolution Internat. Disputes, San Francisco; bd. dirs. Ctr. Internat. Dispute Resolutions, Honolulu. Chmn. bd. dirs. Youth Law Ctr., San Francisco, 1990—. Lt. USNR, 1959-66. Mem. ABA, Calif. Bar Assn., Am. Law Inst., Am. Arbitration Assn. (large complex case panel of neutrals). Republican. Presbyterian. Club: World Trade (San Francisco). Home: 38 Irving Ln Orinda CA 94563-1108 Office: Brobeck Phleger & Harrison 1 Market Pla 2800 Spear Tower San Francisco CA 94105

WELCH, WILLIAM HENRY, oil service company executive, consultant; b. Pharr, Tex., Nov. 24, 1929; married. AA, Edinburg (Tex.) Jr. Coll., 1949; BS, Trinity U., 1951. Sales engr. NL Baroid div. NL Industries, Inc., Liberty, Tex., 1955-58; dist. mgr. NL Industries, Inc., Liberty, Alvin (Tex.), New Orleans, Ardmore (Okla.), 1958-65; gen. mgr. Baroid de Venezuela NL Industries, Inc., Marcaibo, 1965-69; mgr. Latin Am. ops. Baroid Internat. NL Industries, Inc., Houston, 1969-71; mgr. Latin Am. ops. NL Industries, Inc., 1971-74, dir. internat. drilling svcs. NL Baroid div., 1974-77, pres. NL Atlas Bradford, 1977-81; sr. v.p. NL Ind., 1981; pres. NL Oilfield Svcs. NL Industries, Inc., 1981-83, pres. NL Baroid, 1983-86, pres., chief operating officer NL Petroeum Svcs., 1986-87, cons., 1987; retired, 1987—; chmn. Valley Shamrock Inc., 1987—; chmn. bd. dirs. Cottonwood Ctrs., 1993. Bd. dirs. Jr. Achievement Southeast Tex., Houston, 1985-86; fund raiser United Way, Houston, 1985-86. 1st lt. U.S. Army, 1952-55. Mem. Petroleum Equipment Supplies Assn. (1st v.p. 1988-89), Nat. Oilfield Material and Del. Soc. (pres. 1984-85), Am. Petroleum Inst., Soc. Petroleum Engrs., Nat. Oil-Equipment Mfrs. and Dels. Soc., Petroleum Club, Sugar Creek Country Club. Avocations: golf, fishing, travel. Home: 26 Bendwood Dr Sugar Land TX 77478-3701

WELCH-HILL, CONSTANCE MARCELLA, speech and language therapist, consultant; b. Wichita, Kans., Nov. 28, 1958; d. Winfred Du Bois and Graydie Marie (Bennett) Welch; m. Steven Joseph Hill, Aug. 11, 1984; 1 child, Matthew Christopher; stepson from previous marriage: Steven Marcus Hill. BS, Fontbonne Coll., 1981. Cert. speech correction K-12, Mo. Speech and lang. therapist Ware County Bd. Edn., Waycross, Ga., 1981; speech and lang. asst. Chgo. Bd. Edn., 1981-83; speech therapist in behavior mgmt. Judevine Ctr. for Autism, St. Louis, 1985—; speech and lang. therapist Franklin County Coop., St. Clair, Mo., 1989—, cons., 1992—; speech and lang. therapist R-II Sch., New Haven, Mo., 1989—; cons. New Haven Sch. Dist., 1994—. Campaign worker Horace White for Alderman, Chgo., summer 1982. Mem. Mo. Tchrs. Accreditation Orgn. Democrat. Roman Catholic. Avocations: reading, crafts. Home: 704 Brownbert Ct Saint Louis MO 63119-1302

WELCH-MCKAY, DAWN RENEE, legal assistant; b. Lincoln, Nebr., Jan. 21, 1965; d. David Eugene and Helen Bessie (Hypes) W. BA in Pre-Law, Hawaii Pacific U., 1988; postgrad., U. Alaska, Anchorage, 1995—. Cert. Emergency Med. Tech., Alaska, 1994. Supr. Sizzler Family Steakhouse, Anchorage, 1981; dept. mgr. sales Jay Jacobs, Anchorage, 1982-83; resident asst. Hawaii Pacific U., Kaneohe, 1987-88; legal asst., intern Atkinson, Conway & Gagnon, Anchorage, 1988; contract paralegal Anchorage, 1989—; legal asst. Bogle & Gates, Anchorage, 1989, Bradbury, Bliss & Riordan, Anchorage, 1990-91; owner Welch's Ind. Paralegal Svc., Anchorage, 1991—; ind. contractor, Anchorage, 1991—. Vol. Rep. Party of Alaska, 1987, State of Alaska Cmty. Clean-Up, 1981-82, Concerned Citizens of Anchorage, 1981-82. Hawaii Pacific U. grantee, 1987-88; named to Outstanding Young Women Am., 1987. Mem. NAFE, Nat. Fedn. Paralegal Assns., Alaska Assn. Legal Assts., Nat. Assn. Legal Assts. Avocations: hiking, body surfing, biking, softball. Home and Office: Box 110230 Anchorage AK 99511

WELD, JONATHAN MINOT, lawyer; b. Greenwich, Conn., Feb. 25, 1941; s. Alfred White and Sally (Duggan) W.; m. Jane Paige, June 19, 1965; children: Elizabeth, Eric. A.B. in History cum laude, Harvard U., 1963; J.D., Cornell U., 1967. Bar: N.Y. 1967, U.S. Ct. Appeals (2d cir.) 1969, U.S. Dist. Ct. (ea. and so. dist.) N.Y. 1970. Assoc. Shearman & Sterling, N.Y.C., 1967-75, ptnr., 1976—; ptnr. Shearman & Sterling, London, 1982-85; bd. dirs. Bank of N.S. Internat. Bd. dirs. Bklyn. Hosp., St. Ann's Sch.; former bd. dirs. Bklyn. Home for Children, Harvard Coll. Fund, Winant and Clayton Vols. Mem. ABA, N.Y. State Bar Assn. Office: Shearman & Sterling 599 Lexington Ave New York NY 10022-6030

WELD, ROGER BOWEN, clergyman; b. Greenfield, Mass., Dec. 1, 1953; s. Wayland Mauney and Luvycie (Bowen) W.; m. Patricia Ann Kaminski, June 7, 1978 (div. 1979); m. Cynthia Lou Lang, Apr. 15, 1995. Grad., Sacred Acad. Jamilian U. of the Ordained, Reno, 1976-77, Seminary, 1978-82; student, U. Nev., 1983-85; postgrad., Sacred Coll. Jamilian Theology, 1988-90. Ordained to ministry, Internat. Comty. of Christ Ch. of Second Advent, 1977; appointed Rabban priest Internat. Comty. of Christ, 1993. Adminstrv. staff Internat. Community of Christ Ch. of Second Advent, Reno, 1977—, exec. officer dept. canon law, 1985—, exec. officer advocates for religious rights and freedoms, 1985—, exec. officer speakers bur., 1985—, exec. officer office pub. info., 1986—, mgr. Jamilian Univ. Press, 1987—, dir. advt. prodns., 1988—; founder, pres. Crown Rsch. Found., 1992—. Author: Twelve Generations of the Family of Weld: Edmund to Wayland Mauney, 1986; dir. photography, supervising editor: (video documentary) Gene Savoy's Royal Roads to Discovery. Staff sgt. USAF, 1971-75. Named Life Mem., Sacred Oversee, 1991. Mem. Nev. Clergyman's Assn., Andean Explorers Found. (Explorer's medal 1990), Ocean Sailing Club (exec. sec. 1988—, v.p. 1994—, Participant's Silver Medallion 1989). Avocations: photography, cinematography, videography, print media. Office: Internat Cmty Christ Ch Second Advent 643 Ralston St Reno NV 89503-4436 *In the volatile arena of international politics, mankind's hope rests upon the acceptance of its spiritual destiny, not dwelling on its material past.*

WELD, TUESDAY KER (SUSAN KER WELD), actress; b. N.Y.C., Aug. 27, 1943; d. Lathrop Motley and Aileen (Ker) W.; m. Claude Harz, Oct., 1965 (div. 1971); 1 dau., Natasha; m. Dudley Moore, Sept. 20, 1975 (div.); 1 son, Patrick; m. Pinchas Zukerman, Oct. 18, 1985. Attended Hollywood (Calif.) Profl. Sch. Actress: (TV programs) including Cimarron Strip, Playhouse 90, Kraft Theatre, Alcoa Theatre, Climax, Ozzie and Harriet, The Many Loves of Dobie Gillis, 77 Sunset Strip, The Millionaire, Tab Hunter Show, Zane Grey Theatre, Follow the Sun, Bus Stop, Dick Powell Theatre, Adventures in Paradise, Naked City, Eleventh Hour, DuPont Show of the Month, The Greatest Show on Earth, Mr. Broadway, Fugitive, The Crucible, (films) including debut in Rock, Rock, Rock, 1956, Rally Round the Flag Boys, The Five Pennies, 1959, The Private Lives of Adam and Eve, 1960, Return to Peyton Place, Wild in the Country, Bachelor Flat, 1961, Lord Love A Duck, 1966, Pretty Poison, 1968, I Walk the Line, 1970, A Safe Place, 1971, Play It As It Lays, 1972, Because They're Young, 1960, High Time, Sex Kittens Go to College, 1960, The Cincinnati Kid, 1965, Soldier in the Rain, I'll Take Sweden, 1965, Who'll Stop the Rain, 1978, Looking for Mr. Goodbar, 1977, Serial, 1980, Thief, 1981, Author! Author!, 1982, Once Upon a Time in America, 1984, Heartbreak Hotel, 1988, Falling Down, 1993 (TV movies) including Reflections of Murder, 1974, F. Scott Fitzgerald in Hollywood, 1976, A Question of Guilt, 1978, Mother and Daughter: The Loving War, 1980, Madame X, 1981, The Rainmaker, 1982, The Winter of Discontent, 1983, Scorned and Swindled, 1984, Circle of Violence, 1986. Began childhood career as fashion and catalogue model at age of three; by age of twelve appeared regularly on covers of mags. and performed child roles on TV programs, including Playhouse 90, Kraft Theatre, Alcoa Theatre, Climax. *

WELD, WILLIAM FLOYD, governor, lawyer; b. Smithtown, N.Y., July 31, 1945; s. David and Mary Blake (Nichols) W.; m. Susan Roosevelt, June 7, 1975; children: David Minot, Ethel Derby, Mary Blake, Quentin Roosevelt, Frances Wylie. A.B. summa cum laude, Harvard U., 1966, J.D. cum laude, 1970; diploma with distinction, Oxford (Eng.) U., 1967. Bar: Mass. 1970. Law clk. to Hon. R.A. Cutter, Supreme Jud. Ct. Mass., 1970-71; ptnr. firm Hill & Barlow, Boston, 1971-81; assoc. minority counsel U.S. Ho. of Reps. Judiciary Com. Impeachment Inquiry, 1973-74; U.S. atty. for the Dist. of Mass., 1981-86; asst. atty. gen., criminal div. U.S. Justice Dept., Washington, 1986-88; sr. ptnr. Hale & Dorr, Boston, Washington, 1988-90; gov. Commonwealth of Mass., 1990—. Republican nominee for atty. gen., Mass., 1978. Republican. Office: Office of Gov Executive Office State House Boston MA 02133

WELDEN, ARTHUR LUNA, biology educator; b. Birmingham, Ala., Jan. 27, 1927; s. Arthur Luna and Mary Woodson (Smith) W.; m. Frances Merkl Colvin, Aug. 19, 1950; children: Charles Woodson, Arthur Frederick. AB, Birmingham-So. Coll., 1950; MS, U. Tenn., 1951; PhD, U. Iowa, 1954. Asst. prof. Millikin U., Decatur, Ill., 1954-55; instr. in botany Tulane U., New Orleans, 1955-59, asst. prof., 1959-63, assoc. prof., 1963-68, prof. biology, 1968-79, Ida Richardson prof. botany, 1979—, chmn. dept. biology, 1979-93, prof. emeritus, 1994—; panel chmn. So. Assembly, Biloxi, Miss., 1970-71; program dir. Mesoam. Ecology Inst., New Orleans, 1982-87. Assoc. editor Tulane Studies in Zoology and Botany, 1966-78; contbr. articles to profl. jours. Served with U.S. Army, 1945-47. Grantee Am. Philos. Soc., 1957, NSF, 1960-75, NSF and Consejo Nacional de Mex., 1976-79, fellow AAAS, 1992; named to Socio Honorario, Sociedad Mexicana de Mex., 1982. Mem. Mycol. Soc. Am. (councilor 1967-69), Assn. for Tropical Biology, Swiss Mycol. Soc., Orgn. for Tropical Studies (life), Sigma Xi. Democrat. Home: 7826 Willow St New Orleans LA 70118-4056 Office: Tulane U Dept Biology 6823 Saint Charles Ave New Orleans LA 70118-5665

WELDON, DAVID BLACK, financial executive; b. London, Ont., Can., June 27, 1925; s. Douglas Black and Margaret (Black) W.; m. Ina G. Perry, July 7, 1951; children: Susan, Douglas, Anthony, Mardie, Kate. BA with honors, U. Western Ont., London, 1947, LLD (hon.). With Midland Doherty Fin. Corp. and predecessor cos., Toronto, Ont., 1950—, ret., 1989; chancellor U. Western Ont., 1984-88, chancellor emeritus, 1994—; dir. Dover Industries Ltd., Toronto, Emco Ltd., London, Goderich Elevators Ltd., Ont. Trustee Ont. Jockey Club; bd. dirs. Royal Agrl. Winter Fair, Toronto, 1970—, pres., 1980-82. Served with inf. Can. Army, 1944-45. Progressive Conservative. Anglican. Clubs: Toronto (bd. mgrs. 1983-85), York, Toronto Golf; London Hunt, London; Ristigouche Salmon (Quebec, Que., Can.); Griffith Island. Avocations: breeding and racing standardbred horses; fishing; hunting. Home: Prospect Farms, Arva, ON Canada N0M 1C0 also: 18A Hazelton Ave Apt 408, Toronto, ON Canada M5R 2E2 Office: Denison Mines Ltd, 40 Dundas St W Ste 320, Toronto, ON Canada M5G 2C2

WELDON, DAVID JOSEPH, JR., congressman, physician; b. Amityville, N.Y., Aug. 31, 1953; s. David Joseph and Anna (Mallardi) W.; m. Nancy Sourbeck, Nov. 26, 1956; 1 child, Kathryn. BS, SUNY, Stony Brook, 1978; MD, SUNY, Buffalo, 1981. Elder Zion Christian Fellowship, Palm Bay, Fla., 1991—; mem. 104th Congress from 15th Fla. dist., Washington, DC, 1995—; pvt. practice, Melbourne, Fla., 1987—; pres. Space Coast Family Forum, Melbourne, 1988-91. Maj. USAR, 1981—. Mem. AMA, Am. Coll. Physicians, Fla. Med. Assn. Home: 1602 Willard Rd NW Melbourne FL 32907-6320 Office: US House of Reps 216 Cannon Bldg Washington DC 20515-1015

WELDON, DEBORAH A., historical site director. Dir. Hearst Castle Hearst San Simeon State Hist. Monument, Calif. Office: Hearst San Simeon State Hist Monument 750 Hearst Castle Rd San Simeon CA 93452-9740

WELDON, JEFFREY ALAN, state senator, lawyer; b. Billings, Mont., May 6, 1963; s. Richard Allen and Monica (Michaud) W.; m. Leslie Helen Boileau, July 7, 1990. BA, U. Mont., 1986, MPA, 1994, postgrad., 1994-96. Rsch. analyst Heritage Rsch. Ctr., Missoula, Mont., 1989-91, v.p., 1991—; state senator Mont., 1993—. Democrat.

WELDON, NORMAN ROSS, manufacturing company executive; b. Greencastle, Ind., July 21, 1934; s. David M. and Lenora F. (Evens) W.; m. Carol J. Warne, Oct. 2, 1954; children: Thomas D., Cynthia M. B.S., Purdue U., 1956, M.S. in Indsl. Mgmt, 1962, Ph.D., 1964. With CTS Corp., Elkhart, Ind., 1964-79; exec. v.p. CTS Corp., 1970-76, pres., 1976-79, chief exec. officer, 1977-79, also dir.; pres. Cordis Corp., Miami, Fla., 1979-87; also chief exec. officer Cordis Corp.; pres., dir. Corvita Corp., Miami, 1987-96; mem. adv. bd. Investment Co. Am., Inc.; trustee New Economy Fund; bd. dirs. SMALLCAP World Fund, Inc., Novoste Corp., Enable Med. Corp. Trustee Fla. Internat. U. Served to capt. USAF, 1956-60. Recipient Disting. Alumnus award Krannert Grad. Sch. Mgmt., Purdue U., 1979; NSF fellow, 1962-63; Ford Found. fellow, 1963-64. Mem. Tau Kappa Epsilon, Phi Eta Sigma, Alpha Zeta. Presbyterian. Club: Royal Palm Tennis, Weston Hills Country Club. Office: Corvita Corp 8210 NW 27th St Miami FL 33122-1900

WELDON, THEODORE TEFFT, JR., retail company executive; b. Evanston, Ill., July 19, 1932; s. Theodore Tefft and Dorothe Galbraith (Stover) W.; m. Barbara Ann Eskilson, Aug. 17, 1957; children: Lisa Courtney Weldon LeFevre, Theodore Tefft III, Margaret Helen. BA, Dartmouth Coll., 1954. Retail store salesman Sears Roebuck & Co., Gary, Ind., 1954-58; retail store mgr. Sears Roebuck & Co., Kankakee, Ill., 1958-62; sales mgr. Craftsman Sears Roebuck & Co., Chgo., 1962-69, advt. mgr. Craftsman, 1969-70, mktg. mgr. tires, 1970-81, sr. buyer sporting goods, 1981-82, nat. gen. catalog mgr., 1982-86; dir. home TV shopping Sears/QVC, Chgo., 1986-92; cons. Drake, Beam, Morin, Inc., Chgo., 1992-94, Focus Media, Inc., L.A., 1993—, Std. Mktg. Corp., Naperville, Ill., 1993—, King World Direct, L.A., 1993—. Mem. Jr. Achievemnt, Chgo., 1966-68; rep. Winnetka (Ill.) Village Caucus, 1972-74; advisor Children's Theatre of Winnetka, 1972—; pres. Sunset Improvement Assn., Winnetka, 1975—. Avocations: internat. travel, theatre, swimming, biking, golf. Home: 426 Sunset Rd Winnetka IL 60093-4232

WELDON, VIRGINIA V., corporate executive, physician; b. Toronto, Sept. 8, 1935; came to U.S., 1937; d. John Edward and Carolyn Edith (Swift) Verral; children: Ann Stuart, Susan Shaeffer. A.B. cum laude, Smith Coll., 1957; M.D., SUNY-Buffalo, 1962; L.H.D. (hon.), Rush U., 1985. Diplomate Am. Bd. Pediatrics in pediatric endocrinology and metabolism. Intern Johns Hopkins Hosp., Balt., 1962-63, resident in pediatrics, 1963-64; fellow pediatric endocrinology Johns Hopkins U., Balt., 1964-67, instr. pediatrics, 1967-68; instr. pediatrics Washington U., St. Louis, 1968-69, asst. prof., 1969-73, assoc. prof. pediatrics, 1973-79, prof. pediatrics, 1979-89, v.p. Med. Ctr., 1980-89, dep. vice chancellor med. affairs, 1983-89; v.p. sci. affairs Monsanto Co., St. Louis, 1989, v.p. pub. policy, 1989-93, sr. v.p. pub. policy, 1993—; mem. gen. clin. rsch. ctrs. adv. com. NIH, Bethesda, Md., 1976-80, mem. rsch. resources adv. coun., 1980-84; bd. dirs. Gen. Am. Life Ins. Co., Security Equity Life Ins. Co., G.D. Searle & Co.; bd. dirs., advisor Monsanto Co., 1989—. Contbr. articles to sci. jours. Commr. St. Louis Zool. Park, 1983-92; bd. dirs., vice chmn. St. Louis Symphony Orch.; bd. dirs. United Way Greater St. Louis, 1978-90, St. Louis Regional Health Care Corp., 1985-91; mem. risk assessment mgmt. commn. EPA, 1992—; mem. Pres.'s Com. of Advisors on Sci. and Tech., 1994—. Fellow AAAS, Am. Acad. Pediatrics; mem. Inst. Medicine, Assn. Am. Med. Colls. (del., chmn. coun. acad. socs. 1984-85, chmn. assembly 1985-86), Am. Pediatric Soc., Nat. Bd. Med. Examiners (bd. dirs. 1987-89), Endocrine Soc., Soc. Pediatric Rsch., St.

Louis Med. Soc., Sigma Xi, Alpha Omega Alpha. Roman Catholic. Home: 242 Carlyle Lake Dr Saint Louis MO 63141-7544 Office: Monsanto Co DIA 800 N Lindbergh Blvd Saint Louis MO 63141-7843

WELDON, W(AYNE) CURTIS, congressman; b. Marcus Hook, Pa., July 22, 1947; m. Mary Gallagher; children: Karen, Kristin, Kimberly, Curt, Andrew. BA in Humanities, West Chester State Coll., 1969; AAS in Fire Sci., Del. County Community Coll., Media, Pa., 1972; state instrn. cert., Cheyney State Coll.; postgrad., Cabrini Coll., Temple U., St. Joseph's U. Lic. tchr. Pa. From tchr. to head tchr. Walnut St. Sch., Darby-Colwyn-William Penn Sch. Dist., Pa., 1972-76; dir. tng. and manpower CIGNA (INA Corp.), Del. County, 1976-87; mayor City of Marcus Hook, 1977-81; councilman Del. County Council, 1981-87, vice chmn. then chmn., 1984-87; mem. 100th-103rd Congresses from 7th Pa. dist., Washington, D.C., 1987—; former chmn. Del. Valley Regional Planning Commn.; asst. dir. Elem. Secondary Edn. Act Title I Program, 1972-76; environ. specialist Project KARE, 1972-76; chmn. readiness Com. on Nat. Security R & D; mem. Com. on Sci. Energy and Environ. Basic Rsch.; co-chmn. Congl. Fire Svcs. Caucus, The Empowerment Caucus, Globe Ocean Protection Task Force, Congl. Missil Def. Caucus, US-FSU Energy Caucus. Named Man of Yr. Chester Bus. and Profl. Assn., Most Effective Freshman Legislator Am. Security Coun., Citizen of the Yr. Del. County C. of C., Clean Air Champion Sierra Club, Man of Yr. Internat. Soc. Fire Protection Engrs., 1988, taxpayers hero Citizen's Against Government Waste; recipient Outstanding Govt. Leadership award Nat. Recycling Coalition, Fed. Legis. award Pa. Dirs. Assn. Community Action Agys., Spirit of Enterprise award U.S. C. of C., Golden Bulldog Watchdogs of Treasury award. Office: US Ho of Reps Office Ho Mems 2452 Rayburn Bldg Washington DC 20515-0005

WELDON, WILLIAM FORREST, electrical and mechanical engineer, educator; b. San Marcos, Tex., Jan. 12, 1945; s. Forrest Jackson and Rubie Mae (Wilson) W.; m. Morey Sheppard McGonigle, July 28, 1968; children: William, Embree, Seth Forrest. BS in Engring. Sci., Trinity U., San Antonio, 1967; MSME, U. Tex., 1970. Registered profl. engr., Tex. Engr. Cameron Iron Works, Houston, 1967-68; project engr. Glastron Boat Co., Austin, Tex., 1970-72; chief engr. Nalle Plastics Co., Austin, 1972-73; rsch. engr. U. Tex., Austin, 1973-77, tech. dir. Ctr. Electromechanics, 1977-85, dir. Ctr. Electromechanics, 1985-93, prof., 1985—; mem. permanent com. Symposium on Electromagnetic Launch Tech., 1978—, naval rsch. adv. com., 1992-96; cons. numerous cos. and govts., 1973—. Contbr. over 285 articles to profl. publs. Bd. dirs. Water Control & Improvement Dist. No. 10, Travis County, Tex., 1984—. Recipient Peter Mark medal Electromagnetic Launch Symposium, 1986, IR 100 award Indsl. Rsch. mag., 1983. Fellow ASME; mem. IEEE (sr.), NSPE. Achievements include 31 patents for rotating electrical machines, pulsed power, and electromagnetic propulsion.

WELDON-PETERSON, KAREN JEAN, school counselor; b. Jamestown, N.Y., Jan. 30, 1945; d. Donald Clair and Betty Ruth (Murbach) Schmonsky; divorced; children: Shellee L. Gard Weldon, Sherrie L. Gard Weldon; m. David R. Peterson, Dec. 23, 1994. AA in Liberal Arts, Jamestown Community Coll., 1964; BA in English, SUNY, Fredonia, 1966, MS in Edn., 1986; MS in Counseling, St. Bonaventure U., 1993. Cert. tchr., English tchr., N.Y., provisional sch. counselor. Kindergarten tchr. Dept. of Def. Schs., Clark AFB, The Philippines, 1967-68; English tchr. Burkburnett (Tex.) Schs., 1968-69; English tchr. Jamestown Pub. Schs., 1970-92, counselor, 1992—; tchr. adult edn. GED program, Jamestown, 1978-79; facilitator E.P.I.C. Parenting Skills Workshops, Jamestown, 1993—. Author poems, articles Tier Drops, 1990, 91. program dir. Agnes Home for Battered Women, Jamestown, 1987-88; cand. Town Justice, town of Kiantone, N.Y., 1993. Recipient scholarship AAUW, 1962-66. Mem. AAUW, NEA, Am. Counseling Assn., Chautauque County Counselors Assn., Delta Kappa Gamma, Delta Epsilon Sigma. Democrat. Lutheran. Avocations: reading, hiking, nature, sewing, real estate. Home: 2487 Donelson Rd Jamestown NY 14701-9349

WELFELD, JOSEPH ALAN, healthcare consultant; b. Bklyn., May 8, 1948; s. Morris Welfeld and Shirley Schachner; m. Blossom Yablon, June 15, 1969; children: Robyn Elise, Michael Evan. BE, The Cooper Union, 1970; MBA, Baruch Coll., 1975. Asst. dir. Kings County Hosp., Bklyn., 1972-75; exec. dir. L.I. Cancer Coun., Inc., Melville, N.Y., 1975-78, Nassau Physicians Rev. Orgn., Inc., Westbury, N.Y., 1978-82; CEO Ocean State Physicans Health Plan, Providence, 1982-86; regional v.p. United Healthcare Corp., Providence, 1986-87; pres. Managed Care Resources, Inc., Miami, Fla., 1987-93; regional dir. healthcare cons. The Hay Group, N.Y.C., 1993-96; prin. assoc. McManis Assocs., Ft. Lee, N.J., 1996—. Author: Contracting with Managed Care Organizations: A Guide for the Health Provider, 1996. Fellow Am. Coll. Healthcare Execs. (chmn. managed care execs. com. 1994-95), Metro N.Y. Healthcare Fin. Mgmt. Assn. (chmn. managed care com. 1992-96). Office: McManis Assocs Inc Parker Plz Ste 1500 400 Kelby St Fort Lee NJ 07024

WELFER, THOMAS, JR., utility company executive; b. Pitts., Sept. 21, 1936; s. Thomas and Gertrude (Myers) W.; m. Kathleen Ward, Aug. 25, 1962; children: Karen A. Welfer Rapp, Sharon A., Thomas III, Gary, Jeff, Kathy. BSBA cum laude, Duquesne U., 1961; postgrad., U. Pitts., 1962, C.C. Allegheny County, 1977. Lic. real estate salesman, Pa. Union relations statistician Duquesne Light Co., Pitts., 1965-68, union relations analyst, 1968-70, mgr. office of pres., 1970-80, corp. sec., 1980-84, coordinator human resources, 1984-85, benefits compliance coordinator, 1985—. Com. chmn. troop 670 Boy Scouts Am., 1975-87, mem.-at-large Seneca dist. Allegheny Trails coun., 1983-92; coach Westview-Ross Athletic Assn., Pitts., 1985-86; chmn. adminstrv. bd. McKnight United Meth. Ch., Pitts., 1976-77, mem. fin. com., 1978—, chmn., 1986—, mem. bldg. com. and bldg. fund steering com., 1995—. Mem. Pa. Electric Assn. (mem. econ. survey com. 1972-80, supr. ann. conv. registration 1975, 77, 79), Beta Alpha Phi. Republican. Avocations: travel; camping; fishing; photography; bowling. Office: Duquesne Light Co PO Box 1930 411 Seventh Ave Pittsburgh PA 15230-1930

WELGE, DONALD EDWARD, food manufacturing executive; b. St. Louis, July 11, 1935; s. William H. and Rudelle (Fritze) W.; m. Mary Alice Childers, Aug. 4, 1962; children: Robert, Tom. B.S., La. State U., 1957. With Gilster-Mary Lee Corp., Chester, Ill., 1957—, pres., gen. mgr., 1965—; dir. Buena Vista Bank of Chester; pres. Buena Vista Bankcorp. Former chmn. St. John's Luth. Bd. Edn. 1st lt. Transp. Corp, U.S. Army, 1958-63. Named So. Ill. Bus. Leader of Yr. So. Ill. U., 1988. Mem. Perryville C. of C. (pres. 1989), Chester, Ill. C. of C. (past pres.), Alpha Zeta, Phi Kappa Phi. Republican. Lutheran. Home: 5 Knollwood Dr Chester IL 62233-1416 Office: Gilster Mary Lee Co 1037 State St Chester IL 62233-1657

WELGE, JACK HERMAN, JR., lawyer; b. Austin, Tex., Sept. 12, 1951; s. Jack Herman and Regina Victoria (Hunger) W.; m. Frances Ava Roddy Avent, Dec. 23, 1977; children: Kirsten Frances Page Welge, Kathleen Ava Regina Welge. BA, U. Tex., 1974; JD, St. Mary's U., 1977. Bar: Tex. 1977, U.S. Dist. Ct. (ea. dist.) Tex. 1979, U.S. Dist. Ct. (no. dist.) Tex. 1982, U.S. Ct. Appeals (5th cir.) 1983, U.S. Supreme Ct., 1984; cert. family law Tex. Bd. Legal Specialization. Asst. dist. atty. Gregg County Criminal Dist. Atty., Longview, Tex., 1978-79; assoc. Law Office of G. Brockett Irwin, Longview, 1979-81; judge Mcpl. Ct. of Record, Longview, 1979-81; ptnr. Adams & Sheppard, Longview, 1981-83; pvt. practice, 1983—; of counsel East Tex. Assn. for Abused Families, Longview, 1985-90. Bd. dirs. Longview Mus. and Arts Ctr., 1991-94, East Tex. Coun. on Alcoholism and Drug Abuse, Longview, 1981-83, Longview Comty. Theater, 1979-82, East Tex. Assn. for Abused Families, Longview, Salvation Army, 1994—; vestry Trinity Episcopal Ch., Longview, 1993-96. Mem. State Bar of Tex. (pro bono coll., contested custody case panel, protective case panel, Gregg County lawyers pro bono project, Outstanding Contbn. award 1990, Disting. Svc. award 1993), Rotary (pres. Longview club 1987-88, Paul Harris fellow 1982), Gregg County Bar Assn. (pres. 1983), Gregg County Family Law Coun., Tex. Acad. Family Law Specialists, East Tex. Knife and Fork Club (pres. 1983-84), Mason, Delta Theta Phi (dean 1977). Office: 211 E Tyler St Longview TX 75601-7209

WELHAN, BEVERLY JEAN LUTZ, nursing educator, administrator; b. Phila., Dec. 7, 1950; d. Winfield E. and Mary Helen (James) Lutz; m. Robert John LeBar, Aug. 28, 1971 (div. July 1978); m. Joseph Welhan, Jan. 7, 1984; children: James Benjamin, Jillian Grace. Diploma, Montgomery Hosp. Sch. Nursing, 1971; B.S.N., Gwynedd Mercy Coll., 1974; M.Ed., Lehigh U., 1977; M.S.N., Villanova U., 1983; postgrad., Widener U. Staff nurse recovery room Montgomery Hosp., Norristown, Pa., 1971-72; charge nurse North Penn Convalescent Residence, Lansdale, Pa., 1972-74; instr. med./surg. nursing Episcopal Hosp., Phila., 1974-78; staff nurse Montgomery Hosp., Norristown, Pa., 1978-79; asst. dir. nursing edn. Episcopal Hosp., Phila., 1979-85, assoc. dir. nursing edn., 1985-89, dir. nursing edn., 1989—; adj. instr. Pa State U., 1983-84. Author: Testing Program for Scherer's Introductory Medical/Surgical Nursing, 1986. Mem. Nat. League Nursing (program evaluator 1990—, bd. rev. 1993-96), Southeastern Pa. League for Nursing (mem. nominating com. 1982-83, bd. dirs. 1983-85), Northeast Coalition of Hosp. & Diploma Schs. of Nursing (bd. dirs., 1993-94, chair nominating com., 1993-94, nominating com. 1991-92), Montgomery Hosp. Alumni Assn., Nurses' Alumni Assn. of Episcopal Hosp. (hon.), Sigma Theta Tau, Phi Kappa Phi. Republican. Home: 607 Overbrook Ln Oreland PA 19075-2403 Office: Episc Hosp Sch Nursing Front St and Lehigh Ave Philadelphia PA 19125

WELIKSON, JEFFREY ALAN, lawyer; b. Bklyn., Jan. 8, 1957; s. Bennet Joseph and Cynthia Ann Welikson; m. Laura Sanders, Aug. 19, 1979; children: Gregory Andrew, Joshua Stuart. BS, U. Pa., 1976, MBA, 1977; JD, Harvard U., 1980. CPA, N.Y.; bar: N.Y. 1981. Assoc. Shearman & Sterling, N.Y.C., 1980-83; staff counsel Reliance Group Holdings Inc., N.Y.C., 1983-84, dir. legal dept., 1984-85, asst. v.p., corp. counsel, 1985-88, v.p., asst. gen. counsel, asst. sec., 1988-94; exec. v.p., gen. counsel, sec. Reliance Nat. Ins. Co., N.Y.C., 1994—. Contbg. editor Harvard U. Internat. Law Jour., 1979-80. Mem. ABA, N.Y. State Bar Assn., Am. Inst. CPAs. Office: Reliance Nat Ins Co 77 Water St New York NY 10005-4401

WELIN, WALTER, financial advisor; b. Lund, Sweden, Sept. 20, 1908; s. Lars and Adele (Hellegren) W.; m. Ulla Olsson, Nov. 25, 1950; 1 child, Lars. Grad. Econs. and Fin., U. Lund, MA in Polit. Sci. 1943, grad. law sch. 1945. Dir. dept. The Royal Swedish Patent Office, Stockholm, 1948-74; fin. advisor/cons. in pvt. practice, Lund. Club: St. Knut Guild. Mem. AAAS, N.Y. Acad. Scis., Nat. Geographic Soc., Planetary Soc. Address: Siriusgatan 25 S-224, 57 Lund Sweden

WELKE, ELTON GRINNELL, JR., publisher, writer; b. Berkeley, Calif., June 15, 1941; s. Elton Grinnell Sr. and Elsie Maud (Shattuck) W.; m. Anna Lange, July 28, 1963 (div. 1980); children: Allison Espy, Erik Grinnell; m. Bonnie Jean Lum, Jan. 24, 1981; 1 child, Erin Irene. BA in Zoology, U. Calif., Berkeley, 1962. Staff writer Sunset mag., Menlo Pk., Calif., 1962-65, assoc. editor, 1965-69, sr. editor, 1978-80; travel editor Better Homes & Gardens, Des Moines, 1969-71; mng. editor Apt. Life mag., Des Moines, 1971-72; exec. editor Sunset Spl. Interest mags., Menlo Pk., 1972-78; free-lance editorial cons. San Francisco and Seattle, 1981-84; v.p., dir. Livingston & Co., Seattle, 1984-89; publisher Microsoft Press, 1989—; cons. Holland Am. Line, Seattle, 1983-84, Livingston & Co. Advt., Seattle, 1983-84. Author: How to Survive Being Alive, 1977, Place's to go With Children Around Puget Sound, 1987. Bd. dirs. Olympic Nat. Pk. Assocs., Washington, 1965-69, March of Dimes, Western Washington, 1987-92, chmn. campaign com., 1989-92. Recipient 1st Pl. award Washington Press Assn., 1985, 86, 88, WPA award, 1987. Mem. Soc. A. Travel Writers, PRSA, Internat. Assn. Bus. Communicators (Golden Quill award 1985), Washington Athletic Club, Safari Club, Sierra Club. Avocations: gardening, plant collecting, fly fishing, cattle ranching, Asian art. Home: 11329 NE 103rd St Kirkland WA 98033-5178 Office: Microsoft Corp 1 Microsoft Way Redmond WA 98052

WELKER, WALLACE IRVING, neurophysiologist, educator; b. Batavia, N.Y., Dec. 17, 1926. Ph.D. in Psychology, U. Chgo., 1954. Mem. faculty U. Wis. Med. Sch., 1957—, prof. neurophysiology, 1965-90, emeritus prof., 1990—. Served with AUS, 1945-47. Sister Kenny Found. scholar, 1957-62; recipient NIH Career Devel. award, 1962-67. Mem. Am. Anat. Soc., Neurosci. Soc. Office: U Wis 275 Med Sci Bldg Madison WI 53706

WELKER, WILLIAM ANDREW, reading specialist; b. Shamokin, Pa., Apr. 26, 1947; s. William Howard and Dorothy Irene (Bertolette) W.; m. Margaret Jean Bainbridge, Mar. 1, 1969; children: William, Richard, Tiffany, Daniel. BS, U. Pitts., 1969, MEd, 1970; EdD, W.Va. U., 1989. Cert. tchr. health, phys. edn. K-12, Pa., W.Va., reading specialist K-12, Pa., W.Va., secondary prin. 5-12, W.Va., elem. prin. K-5, Pa., lang. arts 7-9, W.Va. Tchr. health phys. edn. Philip Murray Elem. Sch., Pitts., 1969-70, Swissvale (Pa.) Elem. Sch., 1970; tchr. 6th grade Edgington Lane Elem. Sch., Wheeling, W.Va., 1970-72; tchr. reading and English Ctrl. Cath. H.S., Wheeling, 1972-76; tchr. reading Warwood Mid. Sch., Wheeling, 1976—; adj. asst. prof. W.Va. U., Morgantown, 1991—; mem. steering com. Rschrs. In-Sch. Environ, Ohio County Schs., Wheeling, 1990-94. Contbr. articles to profl. jours. Commr. Wheeling Human Rights Commn., 1990-93. Minigrantee W.Va. Edn. Fund, Charleston, 1987, 89, 90. Mem. Internat. Reading Assn. (Columnist Svc. award 1991), Wheeling Island Lions Club. Avocations: writing, sports officiating, wrestling clinician, interpreter. Home: 110 N Huron St Wheeling WV 26003-2226 Office: Warwood Mid Sch 1 Viking Ln Wheeling WV 26003

WELKOWITZ, WALTER, biomedical engineer, educator; b. Bklyn., Aug. 3, 1926; s. Samuel and Shirley (Rosenblum) W.; m. Joan Horowitz, June 17, 1951; children: David, Lawrence, Julie. BS, The Cooper Union, N.Y.C., 1948; MS, U. Ill., 1949, PhD, 1954. Profl. engr., N.J. Rsch. assoc. U. Ill., Urbana, 1948-54, Columbia U., N.Y.C., 1954-55; asst. to pres., gen. mgr. Gulton Industries, Inc., Metuchen, N.J., 1955-64; prof., chmn. elec. engring. Rutgers U., Piscataway, N.J., 1964-86, prof. biomed. engring., 1986—, chmn. biomedical engring., 1986-90; cons. Gulton Industries, Metuchen, N.J., 1964-74. Author: Engineering Hemodynamics: Application to Cardiac Assist Devices, 1977, 2d edit., 1987; co-author: Biomedical Instruments: Theory and Design, 1976, 2d edit., 1992; author numerous chpts. in books; contbr. more than 100 articles to profl. jours. With U.S. Navy, 1944-46. Rutgers U. Rsch. Coun. fellow, 1974-75; recipient Centennial medal IEEE, 1984, Excellence in Rsch. award Rutgers Bd. Trustees, 1985, IEEE Career Achievement award Soc. Engring. Med. Biology, 1991; Llewellyn Thomas vis. prof. U. Toronto, Can., 1989. Fellow IEEE (engring. in medicine and biol. soc. career achievement award 1991), N.Y. Acad. Medicine, Am. Inst. of Medicine and Biol. Engring. Achievements include 26 patents for Electron Tube, Ultrasonic Flowmeter, Ultrasonic Transducer, Piezoelectric Heart Assist Apparatus, Method and Apparatus for Non-Invasive Monitoring Dynamic Cardiac Performance, and others. Home: 138 Highland Ave Metuchen NJ 08840-1942 Office: Rutgers U Biomed Engring PO Box 909 Piscataway NJ 08855-0909

WELL, IRWIN, language educator; b. Cin., Apr. 16, 1928; s. Sidney and Florence (Levy) W.; m. Vivian Max, Dec. 27, 1950; children: Martin, Alice, Daniel. BA, U. Chgo., 1948, MA, 1951; PhD, Harvard U., 1960. Teaching fellow Harvard U., Cambridge, Mass., 1955-58; asst. prof. Brandeis U., Waltham, Mass., 1958-65; assoc. prof. Northwestern U., Evanston, Ill., 1966-70, prof. Russian, Russian Lit., 1970—; pres., mem. bd. dirs. Am. Coun. Tchrs. of Russian., Washington, 1967—. Author numerous books in field; contbr. articles to scholarly jours. Recipient Pushkin medal Internat. Assn. of Russian Profs. Jewish. Avocations: music, singing. Office: Northwestern U Slavic Dept Evanston IL 60208

WELLBERG, EDWARD LOUIS, JR., insurance company executive; b. Eagle Pass, Tex., June 5, 1945; s. Edward L. Wellberg and Nell L. (Kownslar) Walker; children: Elizabeth, Ashley, Jennifer; m. Yvonne Hill, Feb. 4, 1989. Student, St. Mary's U., San Antonio, 1978. CLU, Life Underwriters Tng. Coun. Fellow. Sales agt. Washington Nat. Ins. Co., San Antonio, 1969-82; ptnr. Mazur Bennett Wellberg Assocs., San Antonio, 1982-91; mktg. exec. Wellberg Assocs., San Antonio, 1991—; bd. dirs. Tex. State Ins. Bd. Adv. Coun., Austin, 1988-94. Contbr. articles to trade publs. Mem. Am. Soc. CLU's, Tex. Assn. Life Underwriters (bd. dirs. 1983-86, 92-93, pres. 1995), Tex. Life Underwriters Polit. Action Com. (vice chmn. 1981-83, 88-90, chmn. 1990-92), San Antonio Assn. Life Underwriters (pres. 1982). Home: 1707 Ashley Cir San Antonio TX 78232-4710 Office: Wellberg Assocs 12500 San Pedro Ave Ste 650 San Antonio TX 78216-2858

WELLBORN, CHARLES IVEY, science and techology patenting company executive, lawyer; b. Houston, Dec. 9, 1941; s. Fred W. and Emily R. (Gladu) W.; m. JD McCausland, Aug. 14, 1965; children: Westly O., Kerry S. BA in Econs., U. N.Mex., 1963, JD, 1966; LLM, NYU, 1972. Bar: N.Mex. 1966, U.S. Dist. Ct. N.Mex. 1966. Assoc. Neal & Matkins, Carlsbad, N.Mex., 1966-68; Robinson & Stevens, Albuquerque, 1969-71; ptnr. Schlenker, Parker, Payne & Wellborn, Albuquerque, 1971-76, Parker & Wellborn, Albuquerque, 1976-82; ptnr. Modrall, Sperling, Roehl, Harris & Sisk, Albuquerque, 1982-95; pres., CEO Sci. and Tech. Corp. at U. N.Mex., Albuquerque, 1995—. Bd. dirs. N.Mex. Symphony Orch., 1988-91; bd. dirs. U. N.Mex. Anderson Schs. Mgmt. Found., 1989-94; vice chair U. N.Mex. Found., Inc., 1990-94; mem. Gov.'s Bus. Adv. Coun., 1989—; Small Bus. Adminstrn. Fin. Svcs. Adv., N.Mex., 1989; mem. venture capital mgmt. adv. com. N.Mex. State Investment Coun., 1991—; mem. Econ. Forum, vice-chair, 1993-94, chmn., 1995—; chmn. Roots & Wings Found., 1989—; v.p. N.Mex. Dem. Bus. Coun., 1992—; bd. dirs. Accion N.Mex., 1994—. Contbr. articles to law revs. Sgt. USAF, 1968-69, Korea. Fellow Am. Bar Found.; mem. ABA (ho. of dels. 1984-91), Albuquerque Bar Assn. (pres. 1977-78), N.Mex. Bar Found. (pres. 1980-82), State Bar N.Mex. (pres. 1982-83). Democrat. Roman Catholic. Office: Sci and Tech Corp at U NMex 851 University Blvd SE Ste 200 Albuquerque NM 87106

WELLBORN, OLIN GUY, III, law educator; b. Galveston, Tex., Oct. 21, 1947; s. Olin Guy Jr. and Betty Jean (Merriman) W.; m. Jodi Boston, July 1, 1983; children: Olivia Boston, Olin Guy IV. AB in English magna cum laude, Harvard U., 1970, JD magna cum laude, 1973. Law clk. U.S. Ct. Appeals, San Francisco, 1973-74; asst. prof. Sch. Law U. Tex., 1974-77, prof. Sch. Law, 1977—, William C. Liedtke sr. prof. Sch. Law, 1985—, assoc. dean acad. affairs Sch. Law, 1987-91; vis. prof. Harvard Law Sch., 1978, U. Mich. Law Sch., summer 1987; co-reporter liaison com. rules evidence State Bar Tex., 1981-83, adv. com. subcom. on criminal matters Tex. Senate-House Select Com. on Judiciary, 1984, standing com. adminstrn. rules of evidence State Bar Tex., 1983-88, 94—, faculty Criminal Justice Conf., Tex. Ctr. for Judiciary, 1985-86, Tex. Coll. Advanced Judicial Studies, 1992—. Author: (with John F. Sutton Jr.) Cases and Materials on Evidence, 6th edit., 1987, 7th edit., 1992, 8th edit., 1996, Teacher's Manual to Accompany Cases and Materials on Evidence, 1992, 96, (with Steven Goode and M. Michael Sharlot) Guide to the Texas Rules of Evidence: Civil and Criminal, 1988, 2d edit., 1993, Courtroom Handbook on Texas Evidence, 1994, 2d edit., 1995, 3d edit., 1996, (with Steven Goode) Courtroom Evidence Handbook, 1995, Courtroom Handbook on Federal Evidence, 1995, 2d edit., 1996; contbr. articles to profl. jours. Mem. Phi Beta Kappa. Office: U Tex Sch Law 727 E 26th St Austin TX 78705-3224

WELLBURN, TIMOTHY, film editor. Editor: (films) The Irishman, 1978, Cathy's Child, 1979, Chain Reaction, 1980, Caddie, 1981, (with Michael Balson and David Stiven) The Road Warrior, 1982, The Killing of Angel Street, 1983, The Coolangatta Gold, 1984, Burke and Wills, 1985, The Fringe Dwellers, 1987, Dangerous Game, 1989, Judgment Night, 1993, Blown Away, 1994. Office: The Lyons/Sheldon Agency 8344 Melrose Ave Ste 20 Los Angeles CA 90069-5496

WELLEK, RICHARD LEE, business executive; b. Chgo., Dec. 2, 1938; s. William I. and Mae (Silbert) W.; m. Susan Lee Pollack, Aug. 20, 1960; children: Jeffrey Alan, Marcia Rae, Deborah Lynn. BS, U. Ill., 1960. Material mgr. National Metalwares Inc., Aurora, Ill., 1963-65, sales mgr., 1968-73, exec. v.p. ops., 1977-80, pres., 1980-83; sales mgr. Decar Corp., Middleton, Wis., 1965-68; group exec. Varlen Corp., Naperville, Ill., 1983, pres., chief exec. officer, 1983—, also bd. dirs.; bd. dirs. AMCO Corp. Bd. dirs. Ill. Math. & Sci. Acad., Bus. Adv. Coun., Coll. Commerce & Bus. U. Ill., 1986—; bd. trustees Temple Bnai Israel, 1983—. Served to capt. USAF, 1960-63. Club: Economic (Chgo.). Avocations: motor sports, tennis. Office: Varlen Corp 55 Schuman Blvd PO Box 3089 Naperville IL 60566

WELLEN, ROBERT HOWARD, lawyer; b. Jersey City, Aug. 19, 1946; s. Abraham Louis and Helen Rose (Krieger) W.; m. Anita Fass, June 16, 1968; children: Elizabeth, Judith Maria. BA, Yale Coll., 1968; JD, Yale U., 1971; LLM in Taxation, Georgetown U., 1975. Bar: Conn. 1971, D.C. 1972, Colo. 1982. Assoc. Fulbright & Jaworski, Washington, 1975-76, participating assoc., 1976-79, ptnr., 1979-93; ptnr. Ivins, Phillips & Barker, Washington, 1993—; adj. prof. law Georgetown U. Law Ctr., 1982-85. Mem. lawyers com. Democratic Nat. Com., Washington, 1988. Served to lt. JAGC, USNR, 1971-75. Mem. ABA (past chmn. com. on corp. tax, sect. taxation, supr. editor sect. taxation newsletter), Fed. Bar Assn. (council taxation), Phi Beta Kappa. Jewish. Contbr. articles to legal publs. Office: Ivins Phillips & Barker 1700 Pennsylvania Ave NW Washington DC 20006-4704

WELLER, EDGAR O., transportation executive; b. 1915. LLB, 1938. Sole practice Dallas, 1938-69; with Frozen Food Express Industries, Inc., Dallas, 1947—, now vice chmn. bd. dirs. Office: Frozen Food Express Industries Inc 1145 Empire Central Pl Dallas TX 75247-4305

WELLER, ELIZABETH BOGHOSSIAN, child and adolescent psychiatrist; b. Aug. 7, 1949; m. Ronald A. Weller, Feb. 18, 1978; children: Andrew, Christine. BS, American U., Beirut, Lebanon, 1971, MD, 1975. Lic. psychiatrist, Lebanon, Mo., Kans., Ohio. Intern Am. U. of Beirut, 1974-75; resident Renard Hosp./Washington U., St. Louis, 1975-78; fellow U. Kans. Med. Ctr., Kansas City, 1978-79; asst. prof. psych. U. Kans. Med. Sch., Kansas City, Kans., 1979-84; chief child/adolescent psychiatry Ohio State U., Columbus, 1985-94, assoc. chair dept. psychiatry, 1994—; cons. Am. Psychiat. Assn. Task Force. Co-author: Psychiatric Disorders in Child/Adolescent, 1990, Current Perspectives on Major Depression Disorders in Children, 1984. Fellow APA, Am. Acad. Child/Adolescent Psychiatry; mem. Kans. Med. Soc., World Federation for Mental Health, Central Ohio Psychiat. Assn., Ohio Psychiat. Assn.,Soc. of Biological Psychiatry. Office: Ohio State U 273 W 12th Ave Columbus OH 43210-1303

WELLER, FRANK HARLOW, JR., lawyer, consultant; b. Washington, Nov. 11, 1938; s. Frank H. and Amelia Victoria (Alfaro) W.; m. Eleanor Jenkins Constable Keyser, Mar. 12, 1966; 1 dau., Eleanor Whedbee. BA, Yale U., 1960; LLB, U. Va., 1964. Bar: Va. 1964, Md. 1967, N.Y. 1982. Law clk. presiding justice U.S. Dist. Ct. Md., Balt., 1964-65; atty., adviser Robert Trent Jones, Inc., Montclair, N.J., 1965-67; assoc., then ptnr. Ober, Kaler, Grimes & Shriver and predecessors, Balt., 1967-88; assoc., atty. to Robert Trent Jones, 1988-90; pvt. practice Monkton, Md., 1990—. Bd. dirs. Balt. Ballet Co., 1973-85; pres., trustee Md. Hist. Soc., Balt., 80—, pres., 1980-83; cons. pvt. golf courses, 1990—; pres. Concert Artists Balt., 1994—; active Democratic Party nat. campaigns, 1960, 62, 68, 76. Mem. ABA (various coms.), Md. Bar Assn., Va. Bar Assn., Assn. of Bar of State of N.Y., Elkridge Harford Hunt (pres. 1975-82), Chevy Chase Club, Robert Trent Jones Golf Club, Nantucket Yacht Club. Roman Catholic. Office: 1901 Monkton Rd PO Box 363 Monkton MD 21111

WELLER, GERALD C., congressman; b. Streator, Ill., July 7, 1957. Degree in Agriculture, U. Ill., 1979. Aide to U.S. Congerssman Tom Corcoran, 1977-78, aide to U.S. Sec. of Agriculture John R. Block, 1981-85; active family farm, 1985-88; rep. State of Ill., 1988-94; mem. 104th Congress from 11th Ill. dist., 1994—; asst. majority whip; rep. House Republican steering com.; mem. Newt Gingrich's policy com.; exec. com. NRCC, House Banking Com., House Veterans Affairs Com., House Transp. and Infrastructure Com. Mem. 1st Christian Ch. of Morris, Ill. Mem. Nat. Republican Legis. Assn. (nominated Legislator of Yr.). Office: US House Reps 1710 Longworth House Office Bldg Washington DC 20515-1311

WELLER, GUNTER ERNST, geophysics educator; b. Haifa, June 14, 1934; came to U.S., 1968; s. Erich and Nella (Lange) W.; m. Sigrid Beilharz, Apr. 11, 1963; children: Yvette, Kara, Britta. BS, U. Melbourne, Australia, 1962, MS, 1964, PhD, 1968. Meteorologist Bur. Meteorology, Melbourne, 1959-61; glaciologist Australian Antarctic Exps., 1964-67; from asst. prof. to assoc. prof. geophysics Geophys. Inst., U. Alaska, Fairbanks, 1968-72, prof., 1973—, dep. dir., 1984-86, 90—; project dir. NASA-UAF Alaska SAR Facility, Fairbanks, 1983-93; program mgr. NSF, Washington, 1972-74; pres. Internat. Commn. Polar Meteorology, 1980-83; chmn. polar rsch. bd. NAS, 1985-90, Global Change Steering Com. Sci. com. on Antarctic Rsch., 1988-92; chmn. Global Change Working Group Internat. Arctic Sci. Com., 1990—; dir. Ctr. for Global Change and Arctic System Rsch., U. Alaska,

1990; dir. Coop. Inst. Arctic Rsch., 1994—. Contbr. numerous articles to profl. jours. Recipient Polar medal Govt. Australia, 1969; Mt. Weller named in his honor by Govt. Australia, Antarctica; Weller Bank named in his honor by U.S. Govt., Arctic. Fellow AAAS (exec. sec. arctic divsn. 1982—), Arctic Inst. N.Am.; mem. Internat. Glaciological Soc., Am. Meteorol. Soc. (chmn. polar meteorology com. 1980-83), Am. Geophys. Union. Home: PO Box 81024 Fairbanks AK 99708-1024 Office: U Alaska Geophys Institute Fairbanks AK 99775

WELLER, JANET LOUISE, lawyer; b. Boston, Sept. 17, 1953; d. Thomas Huckle and Kathleen (Fahey) W.; m. John Lee Holloway; children: Kelly Brianna, Janine Fahey. BA, Harvard U., 1975; JD, U. Mich., 1978. Bar: D.C. 1978, U.S. Dist. Ct. D.C. 1978, U.S. Ct. Appeals (D.C. cir.) 1979. Assoc. Cleary, Gottlieb, Steen & Hamilton, Washington, 1978-86, ptnr., 1986—. Office: Cleary Gottlieb Steen 1752 N St NW Washington DC 20036-2806

WELLER, JOSEPH C., brokerage house executive; b. 1939. BA, U. Miss., 1961. CPA. CPA Minor & Moore, Memphis, 1961-67; exec. v.p., sec., treas. Morgan, Keegan & Co. Inc., Memphis, 1969—. Office: Morgan Keegan & Co Inc Morgan Keegan Tower 50 Front St Memphis TN 38103*

WELLER, MICHAEL, playwright, screenwriter; b. Sept. 26, 1942; s. Paul and Rosa (Rush) W. BA, Brandeis U.; student, Manchester U. Author: plays Cello Days at Dixon's Place, 1965, How Ho-Ho Rose and Fell in Seven Short Scenes, 1966, Happy Valley, 1969, The Bodybuilders, 1969, Open Space, 1969, Poison Come Poison, 1970, Cancer, 1970, Moonchildren, 1972, Grant's Movie, 1971, Tira Tells Everything There is to Know About Herself, 1971, Twenty Three Years Later, 1973, Fishing, 1975, Alice, 1976, Split, 1978, Loose Ends, 1979, Dwarfman, 1980, The Ballad of Soapy Smith, 1983-84, Ghost On Fire, Broadway, 1985, Spoils of War, 1988, Lake No Bottom, 1990, Help!, 1995, Buying Time, 1996, The Heart of Art, 1994; lyricist (with Jim Steinman) More Than You Deserve, 1973; screenwriter Hair, 1979, Ragtime, 1980 (Academy award nomination for best adapted screenplay 1981), Lost Angels, 1989, Writing on the Wall, God Bless You Mr. Rosewater, 1991, Getting Rid of Alex, 1995, The Sixteen Pleasures, 1996 (TV) Spoils of War, 1994, Stranger at the Gate, 1996; adapter, composer: Fred, 1965, The Making of Theodore Thomas, Citizen, 1968. Recipient Drama Desk award for most promising playwright, 1971; Rockefeller fellowship, 1973; Creative Artists Pub. Svc. grantee, 1976. Office: CAA care David Styne care Rob Scheidlinger 9830 Wilshire Blvd Beverly Hills CA 90212-1804 also: McNaughton Lowe Representation, 200 Fulham Rd, London SW10 9PN, England

WELLER, PETER, actor; b. Stevens Point, Wis., June 24, 1947; s. Frederick and Dorothy Weller. BA, North Tex. State U., 1970; cert., Am. Acad. Dramatic Arts, N.Y.C., 1972; studies with Uta Hagen, H.B. Studios, N.Y.C., 1974-77. Appeared in various plays including Sticks and Bones, Streamers, The Woods, Daddy Wolf, Rebel Women, The Woolgatherer, Cat on a Hot Tin Roof; TV prodns. Kentucky Woman, 1983, Two Kinds of Love, 1983, Women and Men: Stories of Seduction, 1990, Rainbow Drive, 1990; films include Butch and Sundance: The Early Years, 1979, Just Tell Me What You Want, 1980, Shoot the Moon, 1982, Of Unknown Origin, 1983, Adventures of Buckaroo Bonzai, 1984, Firstborn, 1984, Robocop, 1987, Shakedown, 1988, A Killing Affair, 1988, Leviathan, 1989, Robocop II, 1990, Naked Lunch, 1992, Fifty-Fifty, 1993, The New Age, 1994; cable film My Sister's Keeper. Mem. Actor's Studio, 1979. Avocation: jazz. Office: care CAA 9830 Wilshire Blvd Beverly Hills CA 90212*

WELLER, ROBERT N(ORMAN), hotel executive; b. Harrisburg, Pa., Feb. 1, 1939; s. Charles Walter and Martha Ann (MacPherson) W.; m. Nancy M. Wood, June 21, 1975; children—Wendi Elizabeth, Terrie Lynn, Nikki Ann. B.S., Cornell U., 1969. Mgr. Hall's Motor Transit Co., Harrisburg, Pa., 1961-65; market research analyst Carrolls Devel. Corp., Syracuse, N.Y., 1970-72; asst. to pres. Econo-Travel Motor Hotel Corp., Norfolk, Va., 1972-74; dir. franchise sales Econo-Travel Motor Hotel Corp., 1975, pres., dir., 1976-84; pres., dir. Econo-Travel Devel. Corp., Norfolk, 1977-84; pres. Internat. Data Bank Ltd., 1985-86; pres., dir. Econo Lodges of Am., 1986-90; group pres., exec. v.p. Choice Hotels Internat., Silver Spring, Md., 1990-91; with Hospitality Ventures, Virginia Beach, 1991—; pres. Super 8 Motels, Inc. divsn. Hospitality Franchise Systems, Parsippany, N.J., 1993—. Served in USMC, 1957-60. Home: 3027 Lynndale Rd Virginia Beach VA 23452-6233 Office: 339 Jefferson Rd Parsippany NJ 07054

WELLER, SOL WILLIAM, chemical engineering educator; b. Detroit, July 27, 1918; s. Ira and Bessie (Wieselthier) W.; m. Miriam Damick, June 11, 1943; children—Judith, Susan, Robert, Ira. B.S., Wayne State U., 1938; Ph.D., U. Chgo., 1941. Asst. chief coal hydrogenation U.S. Bur. Mines, Pitts., 1945-50; head fundamental rsch. Houdry Process Corp., Linwood, Pa., 1950-58; mgr. propulsion rsch. Ford Aeronutronic Co., Newport Beach, Calif., 1958-61; dir. chem. lab. and materials rsch. lab. Philco-Ford Co., Newport Beach, 1961-65; prof. chem. engring. SUNY-Buffalo, 1965—; emeritus, 1989; C.C. Furnas prof. SUNY-Buffalo, 1983—; vis. fellow Oxford U., 1989. Author numerous sci. papers, book chpts., ency. entries. Fulbright lectr. Madrid, 1975, Istanbul, 1980. Mem. Am. Chem. Soc. (chmn. Orange County sect. 1964, H.H. Storch award 1981, E.V. Murphree award 1982, Schoellkopf medal 1984, Dean's award 1991), ASTM (founder com. D32 on catalysts). Achievements include patents in field. Office: SUNY Buffalo 305 Furnas Hall Buffalo NY 14260

WELLER, THOMAS HUCKLE, physician, emeritus educator; b. Ann Arbor, Mich., June 15, 1915; s. Carl V. and Elsie A. (Huckle) W.; m. Kathleen R. Fahey, Aug. 18, 1945; children: Peter Fahey, Nancy Kathleen, Robert Andrew, Janet Louise. A.B., U. Mich., 1936; M.S., 1937, LL.D. (hon.), 1956; M.D., Harvard, 1940; Sc.D., Gustavus Adolphus U., 1975, U. Mass., 1985; L.H.D., Lowell U., 1977. Diplomate Am. Bd. Pediatrics. Teaching fellow bacteriology Harvard Med. Sch., 1940-41, research fellow tropical medicine, pediatrics, 1947-48, instr. comparative pathology, tropical medicine, 1948-49, asst. prof. tropical pub. health Sch. Pub. Health, 1949-50, assoc. prof., 1950-54, Richard Pearson Strong prof. tropical pub. health, 1954-85, prof. emeritus, 1985—, head dept., 1954-81; intern bacteriology and pathology Children's Hosp., Boston, 1941; intern medicine Children's Hosp., 1942, asst. resident medicine, 1946, asst. dir. research div. infectious diseases, 1949-55; mem. commn. parasitic diseases Armed Forces Epidemiol. Bd., 1953-72, dir., 1953-59. Author sci. papers. Served to maj. M.C. AUS, 1942-46. Recipient E. Mead Johnson award for devel. tissue culture procedures in study virus diseases Am. Acad. Pediatrics, 1953, Kimble Methodology award, 1954, Nobel prize in physiology and medicine, 1954, George Ledlie prize, 1963, Weinstein Cerebral Palsy award, 1973, Stern Symposium honoree, 1972, Bristol award Infectious Diseases Soc. Am., 1980, Gold medal and diploma of honor U. Costa Rica, 1984, First Sci. Achievement award VZV Rsch. Found., 1993. Fellow Am. Acad. Arts and Scis.; mem. Harvey Soc., AMA, Am. Soc. Parasitologists, Am., Royal socs. tropical medicine and hygiene, Am. Pub. Health Assn., AAAS, Am. Epidemiological Soc., Nat. Acad. Scis., Am. Pediatric Soc., Assn. Am. Physicians, Soc. Exptl. Biology and Medicine, Am. Assn. Immunologists. Soc. Pediatric Research, Phi Beta Kappa., Sigma Xi, Alpha Omega Alpha. Home and Office: 56 Winding River Rd Needham MA 02192-1025

WELLES, JAMES BELL, JR., lawyer; b. Schenectady, N.Y., Aug. 27, 1918; s. James Bell and Grace E. (Frazer) W.; m. Ann Bouton Thom, Apr. 26, 1946; children—Ann, James Bell, III, William (dec.), Thomas, Amy. A.B., Columbia U., 1939, J.D., 1942. Bar: N.Y. 1943. Assoc. Mitchell, Capron, Marsh, Angulo & Cooney, N.Y.C., 1946-56; mem. firm. Angulo, Cooney, Marsh & Ouchterloney, N.Y.C., 1956-59, Debevoise & Plimpton, N.Y.C., 1960-93. Bd. visitors Columbia Law Sch., N.Y.C., 1974-94; bd. dirs. Burke Found., White Plains, N.Y., 1959—, pres.; trustee Emma Willard Sch., Troy, N.Y., 1974-82. Maj. USAAF, 1942-45. Fellow Am. Coll. Trust and Estate Counsel; mem. ABA, N.Y. State Bar Assn., Assn. of Bar of City of N.Y., Delta Phi, Phi Delta Phi. Republican. Episcopalian. Club: University (N.Y.C.). Home: 25 Ivy Hill Rd Chappaqua NY 10514-1805 Office: Debevoise & Plimpton 875 3rd Ave New York NY 10022-6225

WELLES, JOHN GALT, museum director; b. Orange, N.J., Aug. 24, 1925; s. Paul and Elizabeth Ash (Galt) W.; m. Barbara Lee Chrisman, Sept. 15, 1951; children: Virginia Chrisman, Deborah Galt, Barton Jeffery, Holly Page. BE, Yale U., 1946; MBA, U. Pa., 1949; LHD (hon.) U. Denver, 1994. Test engr. Gen. Electric Co., Lynn, Mass., 1947; labor relations staff New Departure div. Gen Motors Corp., Bristol, Conn., 1949-51; mem. staff Mountain States Employers Coun., Denver, 1952-55; head indsl. econs. div. U. Denver Research Inst., Denver, 1956-74; v.p. planning and devel. Colo. Sch. Mines, Golden, 1974-83; regional adminstr. EPA, Denver, 1983-87; exec. dir. Denver Mus. Natural History, 1987-94, exec. dir. emeritus, 1994—. Sr. cons. Secretariat, UN Conf. Human Environment, Geneva, 1971-72; cons. Bus. Internat., S.A., Geneva, 1972; trustee Tax Free Fund of Colo., N.Y., 1987—, Denver Pub. Libr. Friends Found., 1996—; exec. com. Denver Com. on Fgn. Rels., 1987—; bd. dirs Gulf of Maine Found., 1995—; chmn. Colo. Front Range Project, Denver, 1979-80. Contbr. articles to profl. jours., newspapers. Recipient Disting. Svc. award Denver Regional Coun. Govts., 1980, Barnes award EPA, 1987. Mem. AAAS, Am. Assn. Museums (ethics commn. 1991-94, v.p. 1992-95), Sustainable Futures Soc. (nat. adv. bd. 1994—), Met. Denver Exec. Club (pres. 1967-68), World Future Soc., Univ. Club (Denver) Denver Athletic Club, Tau Beta Pi, Blue Key. Republican. Episcopalian.

WELLES, MELINDA FASSETT, artist, educator; b. Palo Alto, Calif., Jan. 4, 1943; d. George Edward and Barbara Helena (Todd) W. Student, San Francisco Inst. Art, 1959-60, U. Oreg., 1960-62; BA in Fine Arts, UCLA, 1964, MA in Spl. Edn., 1971, PhD in Ednl. Psychology, 1976; student fine arts and illustration Art Ctr. Coll. Design, 1977-80. Cert. ednl. psychologist, Calif. Asst. prof. Calif. State U., Northridge, 1979-82, Pepperdine U., L.A., 1979-82; assoc. prof. curriculum, teaching and spl. edn. U. So. Calif., L.A., 1980-89; prof. liberal studies Art Ctr. Coll. Design, 1978—; mem. acad. faculty Pasadena City Coll., 1973-79, Otis Coll. Art and Design, L.A., 1986—, UCLA Extension, 1980-84, Coll. Devel. Studies, L.A., 1978-87, El Camino C.C., Redondo Beach, Calif., 1982-86; cons. spl. edn.; pub. adminstrn. analyst UCLA Spl. Edn. Rsch. Program, 1973-76; exec. dir. Atwater Park Ctr. Disabled Children, L.A., 1976-78; coord. Pacific Oaks Coll. in svc. programs for L.A. Unified Schs., Pasadena, 1978-81; mem. Southwest Blue Book, Freedom's Found. at Valley Forge, The Mannequins, bd. dirs. Costume Coun. L.A. County Mus. of Art., Assistance League of So. Calif. Author: Calif. Dept. Edn. Tech. Reports, 1972-76; editor: Teaching Special Students in the Mainstream, 1981, Educating Special Learners, 1986, 88, Teaching Students with Learning Problems, 1988, Exceptional Children and Youth, 1989; group shows include: San Francisco Inst. Art, 1960, U. Hawaii, 1978, Barnsdall Gallery, L.A., 1979, 80; represented in various pvt. collections. HEW fellow, 1971-72; grantee Calif. Dept. Edn., 1975-76, Calif. Dept. Health, 1978. Mem. Am. Psych. Assn., Calif. Learning Disabilities Assn., Am. Council Learning Disabilities, Calif. Scholarship Fedn. (life), Alpha Chi Omega. Office: 700 Levering Ave Apt 1 Los Angeles CA 90024-2795

WELLFORD, HARRY WALKER, federal judge; b. Memphis, Aug. 6, 1924; s. Harry Alexander and Roberta Thompson (Prothro) W.; m. Katherine E. Potts, Dec. 8, 1951; children: Harry Walker, James B. Buckner P., Katherine T., Allison R. Student, U. N.C., 1943-44; BA, Washington and Lee U., 1947; postgrad. in law, U. Mich., 1947-48; LLD, Vanderbilt U., 1950. Bar: Tenn. 1950. Atty. McCloy, Myar & Wellford, Memphis, 1950-60, McCloy, Wellford & Clark, Memphis, 1960-70; judge U.S. Dist. Ct., Memphis, 1970-82; judge U.S. Ct. Appeals (6th cir.), Cin. and Memphis, 1982-92, sr. judge, 1992—; mem. pres.' adv. coun. Rhodes Coll. Chair Senator Howard Baker campaigns, 1964-66; chair Tenn. Hist. Commn., Tenn. Constnl. Bicentennial Commn., 1987-88; mem. charter drafting com. City of Memphis, 1967, Tenn. Am. Revolution Bicentennial Commn., 1976, com. on Adminstrn. Fed. Magistrates Sys., Jud. Conf. Subcom. Adminstrn. of Criminal Law Probation; clk. session, commr. Gen. Assembly; elder Presbyn. Ch.; moderator Memphis Presbytery, 1994. Recipient Sam A. Myar award for svc. to profession and community Memphis State Law U., 1963. Mem. Phi Beta Kappa, Omega Delta Kappa. Home: 91 N Perkins Rd Memphis TN 38117-2425 Office: US Ct Appeals 1176 Federal Bldg 167 N Main St Memphis TN 38103-1816

WELLFORD, HILL B., JR., lawyer; b. Tulsa, Okla., Apr. 30, 1942. AB, Davidson Coll., 1964; JD, U. N.C., 1967. Bar: Va. 1968. Ptnr. Hunton & Williams, Richmond, Va.; lectr. in field. Mem. ABA, Va. Bar Assn. (chmn. com. labor rels. and employment law 1977-87), Assn. Trial Lawyers Am., Phi Delta Phi. Office: Hunton & Williams Riverfront Plaza East Tower 951 E Byrd St Richmond VA 23219-4040*

WELLIN, KEITH SEARS, investment banker; b. Grand Rapids, Mich., Aug. 13, 1926; s. Elmer G. and Ruth (Chamberlin) W.; m. Carol D. Woodhouse, Sept. 5, 1951 (dec. 1970); children: Cynthia Wellin Plum, Peter, Marjorie Wellin King; m. Nancy Brown Negley, Aug. 2, 1985. B.A., Hamilton Coll., 1950; M.B.A., Harvard U., 1952. With E.F. Hutton & Co., Inc., Chgo., 1952-71; regional v.p., dir. E.F. Hutton & Co., Inc., 1962-66; pres. E.F. Hutton & Co., Inc., N.Y.C., 1967-71; vice chmn. E.F. Hutton & Co., Inc., 1970-71; sr. v.p., treas., dir. Reynolds Securities Inc., 1971-74, pres., dir., 1974-78; exec. v.p., dir. Dean Witter Reynolds Orgn., from 1978; chmn. Dean Witter Reynolds Inter-Capital, from 1978; former vice chmn. Dean Witter Reynolds Inc.; chmn. bd. Moorco Internat., Houston; former gov., mem. exec. com. Assn. Stock Exchange Firms; mem. governing council Securities Industry Assn. Mem. investment com., trustee Hamilton Coll. Served to 2d lt., inf. AUS, 1945-47. Clubs: Knickerbocker (N.Y.C.); Clove Valley Rod and Gun (La Grangeville, N.Y.); Round Hill (Greenwich, Conn.); River Club. Home: El Tule Ranch Drawer C Falfurrias TX 78355 Office: c/o Dean Witter Reynolds 1345 Avenue of the Americas New York NY 10105

WELLINGTON, CAROL STRONG, law librarian; b. Altadena, Calif., Jan. 30, 1948; d. Edward Walters and Elizabeth (Leonards) Strong; m. David Heath Wellington, May 27, 1978; 1 child, Edward Heath. BA, Lake Forest (Ill.) Coll., 1969; MLS, Simmons Coll., 1973. Libr. Hill & Barlow, Boston, 1973-88, Peabody & Arnold, Boston, 1988—. Mem. Am. Assn. Law Librs., Assn. Boston Law Librs. (v.p. 1979-80, pres. 1980-81), Spl. Librs. Assn., Law Librs. New England. Office: Peabody & Arnold 50 Rowes Wharf Boston MA 02110-3342

WELLINGTON, HARRY HILLEL, lawyer, educator; b. New Haven, Aug. 13, 1926; s. Alex M. and Jean (Ripps) W.; m. Sheila Wacks, June 22, 1952; children: John, Thomas. AB, U. Pa., 1947; LLB, Harvard U., 1952; MA (hon.), Yale U., 1960. Bar: D.C. 1952. Law clk. to U.S. Judge Magruder, 1953-54, Supreme Ct. Justice Frankfurter, 1955-56; asst. prof. law Stanford U., 1954-56; mem. faculty Yale U., 1956—, prof. law, 1960—, Edward J. Phelps prof. law, 1967-83, dean Law Sch., 1975-85, Sterling prof. law, 1983-92, Sterling prof. emeritus law, 1992—, Harry H. Wellington prof. lectr., 1995—; pres., dean, prof. law N.Y. Law Sch., N.Y.C., 1992—; Ford fellow London Sch. Econs., 1965; Guggenheim fellow; sr. fellow Brookings Instn., 1968-71; Rockefeller Found. fellow Bellagio Study and Conf. Ctr., 1984; faculty mem. Salzburg Seminar in Am. Studies, 1985; John M. Harlan disting. vis. prof. N.Y. Law Sch., 1985-86; review person ITT-SEC; moderator Asbestos-Wellington Group; cons. domestic and fgn. govtl. agys.; trustee N.Y. Law Sch.; bd. govs. Yale U. Press; mem. jud. panel, exec. com. Ctr. Public Resources Legal Program; Harry H. Wellington lectr., 1995—. Author: with Harold Shepherd) Contracts and Contract Remedies, 1957, Labor and the Legal Process, 1968, (with Clyde Summers) Labor Law, 1968, 2d edit., 1983, (with Ralph Winter) The Unions and the Cities, 1971, Interpreting the Constitution, 1990; contbr. articles to profl. jours. Mem. ABA, Bar Assn. Conn., Am. Law Inst., Am. Arbitration Assn., Am. Acad. Arts and Scis., Common Cause (nat governing bd.). Office: NY Law Sch 57 Worth St New York NY 10013-2926 also: Yale U Sch Law New Haven CT 06520

WELLINGTON, JEAN SUSORNEY, librarian; b. East Chicago, Ind., Oct. 23, 1945; d. Carl Matthew and Theresa Ann Susorney; m. Donald Clifford Wellington, June 12, 1976; 1 child, Evelin Patricia. BA, Purdue U., 1967; MA in LS, Rosary Coll., River Forest, Ill., 1969; MA, U. Cin., 1976. Head Burnam Classical Libr. U. Cin., 1970—. Compiler: Dictionary of Bibliographic Abbreviations Found in the Scholarship of Classical Studies and Related Disciplines, 1983. Mem. Art. Librs. Soc. N.Am. (chair Ohio br. 1984-85). Office: U Cin Classics Libr Box 210191 Cincinnati OH 45221-0191

WELLINGTON, JUDITH LYNN, cultural organization administrator; b. Yonkers, N.Y., Feb. 4, 1947; d. James William Wellington and Ardath (Sweet) Longden; m. Charles L. Lerman (div.); 1 child, Michael J. BA, Wheaton Coll., Norton, Mass., 1969; MA, Harvard U., 1971, PhD, 1975. Asst. prof. Juniata Coll., Huntingdon, Pa., 1974-76; asst. dir., assoc. mem. Monell Chem. Senses Ctr., Phila., 1976-86; v.p. Zool. Soc. Phila., 1986-92; pres., CEO N.J. Acad. for Aquatic Scis., Camden, N.J., 1992-95; pres. N.J. Aquarium Found., Camden, 1995—. Bd. dirs. South Jersey Performing Arts Ctr., Camden, N.J., 1989—. Office: Thomas H Kean NJ State Aquarium 1 Riverside Dr Camden NJ 08103-1037 Home: 18 Allendale Rd Philadelphia PA 19151

WELLINGTON, ROBERT HALL, manufacturing company executive; b. Atlanta, July 4, 1922; s. Robert H. and Ernestine V. (Vossbrinck) W.; m. Marjorie Jarchow, Nov. 15, 1947; children: Charles R., Robert H., Christian J., Jeanne L. BS, McCormack Sch. of Engring. and Applied Scis. (formerly Northwestern Tech. Inst.), 1944; MSBA, MBA, U. Chgo., 1958. With Griffin Wheel Co., 1946-61; v.p. parent co. Amsted Industries, Inc., Chgo., 1961-74, exec. v.p., 1974-80, pres., chief exec. officer, 1981-88, chmn. bd., chief exec. officer, 1988-90; bd. dirs. Prudential Money Market Assets, Prudential Intermediate Income Fund, Inc. Served to lt. USN, 1943-46. Mem. Chgo. Athletic Club, Mid-Am. Club. Office: Amsted Industries Inc 205 N Michigan Ave Fl 44 Chicago IL 60601-5925

WELLINGTON, SHEILA WACKS, foundation administrator, psychiatry educator; b. N.Y.C., Feb. 24, 1932; d. Louis and Rose Feldman; m. Harry Hillel Wellington, June 22, 1952; children: John, Thomas. BA in Polit. Sci., Wellesley Coll., 1952; traineeship, USPHS, 1966-68; MUS, Yale U., 1968, MPH, 1968. Lectr. dept. psychiatry Sch. Medicine Yale U., New Haven, 1974-93; dir. Hill-West Haven div. Conn. Mental Health Ctr., 1977-80, Greater Bridgeport Community Mental Health Ctr., 1980-86; sec. Yale U., New Haven, Conn., 1987-93; pres. Catalyst, N.Y.C., 1993—; mem. plan and rev. pnel Pres.'s Com. Mental Health; mem. exec. com. Conn. conf. Ind. Colls., Am. Coll. Mental Health Adminstrn.; fellow Berkeley Coll.; trustee Nuveen Select Portfolios. Contbr. articles to profl. jours. Bd. dirs. N.Y. Women's Agenda, Bus. Coun. N.Y. State, Inst. for Women's Policy Rsch. Recipient New Haven Mayoral Citation for Cmty. svc., 1981, Conn. Gov.'s Com. to Employ Handicapped Outstanding Svc. award, 1984, Ofcl. Citation Gen. Assembly of Conn., 1985, Spl. Citation for Pub. Svc. Gov. William O'Neill, 1986, New Haven YWCA Women in Leadership award, 1990, Marrakech Founders award, 1990, Elm Ivy award, 1993. Mem. Phi Beta Kappa. Home: 55 Huntington St New Haven CT 06511-1332 Office: Pres Catalyst 250 Park Ave S New York NY 10003-1402

WELLINGTON, WILLIAM GEORGE, plant science and ecology educator; b. Vancouver, B.C., Can., Aug. 16, 1920; s. George and Lilly (Rae) W.; m. Margret Ellen Reiss, Sept. 22, 1959; children: Katherine Jean, Stephen Ross. B.A., U. B.C., 1941; M.A., U. Toronto, 1945, Ph.D., 1947. Meteorol. officer Can. Meteorol. Service, Toronto, 1942-45; research entomologist Can. Dept. Agr., Sault Ste. Marie, Ont., 1946-51; head bioclimatology sect. Can. Dept. Forestry, Sault Ste. Marie, Ont., Victoria, B.C., 1951-67; prin. scientist Can. Dept. Forestry, Victoria, 1964-68; prof. ecology U. Toronto, 1968-70; dir. Inst. Animal Resource Ecology, U. B.C., Vancouver, 1973-79; prof. plant sci. and resource ecology Inst. Animal Resource Ecology, U. B.C., 1970-86, hon. prof. dept. plant sci., 1986—, prof. emeritus, 1986—; Killam sr. research fellow U. B.C., 1980-81; inaugural lectr. C.E. Atwood Meml. Seminar Series, Dept. Zoology, U. Toronto, 1993. Contbr. articles to profl. jours. Named Prof. of Yr., Faculty Agrl. Sci., U. B.C., 1986. Fellow Entomol. Soc. Can. (Gold medal 1968), Royal Soc. Can., Explorers Club; mem. Am. Meteorol. Soc. (award 1969), Entomol. Soc. Am. (C. J. Woodworth award 1979), Japanese Soc. Population Ecology, Entomol. Soc. Ont. Anglican. Club: Am. Philatelic Soc. Home: 2350 130A St, Surrey, BC Canada V4A 8Y5 Office: U BC, ARE and Dept Plant Sci, Vancouver, BC Canada V6T 1W5

WELLIVER, CHARLES HAROLD, hospital administrator; b. Wichita, Kans., Feb. 14, 1945; married. BA, Wichita State U., 1972; MHA, U. Mo., 1974. Asst. dir. St. Luke's Hosp., Kansas City, 1974-79, assoc. dir., 1979-80; adminstr. Spelman Meml. Hosp., Smithville, Mo., 1980-82; sr. adminstr., COO Good Samaritan Med. Ctr., Phoenix, 1982-86, v.p., CEO, 1989—; v.p., CEO Thunderbird Samaritan Hosp., Glendale, Ariz., 1986-89. Office: Good Samaritan Regional Med Ctr 1441 N 12th St Phoenix AZ 85006-2837*

WELLIVER, WARREN DEE, lawyer, retired state supreme court justice; b. Butler, Mo., Feb. 24, 1920; s. Carl Winfield and Burdee Marie (Wolfe) W.; m. Ruth Rose Galey, Dec. 25, 1942; children: Gale Dee (Mrs. William B. Stone), Carla Camile (Mrs. Dayton Stone), Christy Marie. BA, U. Mo., 1945; JD, U. Mo., 1948. Bar: Mo. 1948. Asst. pros. atty. Boone County, Columbia, 1948-54; sr. ptnr. Welliver, Atkinson and Eng, Columbia, 1960-79; tchr. law Law Sch. U. Mo., 1948-49; mem. Mo. Senate, 1977-79; justice Supreme Ct. Mo., Jefferson City, 1979-89; mem. Gov. Mo. Adv. Coun. Alcoholism and Drug Abuse, chmn. drug coun., 1970-72; chmn. Task Force Revision Mo. Drug Laws, 1970-71; liaison mem. coun. Nat. Inst. Alcoholism and Alcohol Abuse, 1973-76; mem. Cen. Regional Adv. Coun. Comprehensive Psychiat. Svcs., 1990-92. Bd. dirs. Nat. Assn. Mental Health, 1970-76, regional v.p., 1973-76; pres. Mo. Assn. Mental Health, 1968-69, Stephens Coll. Assocs., 1965-79; pres. Friends of Libr., U. Mo., 1976, bd. dirs., 1979-92; chmn. Dem. Com., 1954-64; hon. fellow Harry S. Truman Libr. Inst., 1979—; bd. dirs. Supreme Ct. Hist. Soc., 1982—; vice chair adv. bd. U. Mo. Multiple Sclerosis Inst., 1992—; bd. curators Stephen's Coll., 1980-92. With USNR, 1941-45. Recipient Disting. Alumni medal and award U. Mo., 1994. Fellow Am. Coll. Trial Lawyers, Am. Bar Found.; mem. ABA, Mo. Bar Assn. (pres. 1967-68), Boone County Bar Assn. (pres. 1970), Am. Judicature Soc., Am. Legion (past post comdr.), Multiple Sclerosis Soc. (Gateway chpt. bd. dirs. 1986-92), Order of Coif, Country Club of Mo., Columbia Country Club (past pres.). Home: 3430 Woodrail Ter Columbia MO 65203-0926

WELLMAN, BARCLAY ORMES, furniture company executive; b. Jamestown, N.Y., May 13, 1936; s. Albert Austin and Leona (Greenlund) W.; m. Diane Taylor, July 2, 1960; children: Barclay Ormes Jr., Taylor A., Alexandra C. BA, Dartmouth Coll., 1959; grad., U.S. Army War Coll., 1982. Interior designer Wellman Bros., Inc., Jamestown, 1963-64, treas., 1964—, pres., 1978—. Trustee Lakeview Cemetery Assn., Jamestown, 1978—, Sheldon Found., Jamestown, 1981—, Emma Willard Sch. Maj. gen. USAR. Mem. Am. Soc. Interior Designers (v.p. 1972-74), Am. Appraisers Assn., Am. Legion, Res. Officers Assn., Sr. Army Res. Comdrs. Assn., Sportsmens Club, Moon Brook Country Club, Delta Kappa Epsilon. Republican. Presbyterian. Avocation: fishing. Home: 1235 Prendergast Ave Jamestown NY 14701-3146 Office: Wellman Bros Inc 130 S Main St Jamestown NY 14701-6623

WELLMAN, BONNIE WADDELL, school nurse, educator, substance abuse counselor; b. Phila., May 5, 1952; d. Russell and Arlene (Spencer) Waddell; m. Ned Allen Wellman, Sept. 14, 1974 (div. 1981); 1 child, Jeffrey Allen. BSN, Ohio State U., 1974; MA in Counseling, Trenton State Coll., 1991. RN, Pa. Sch. nurse Pennsbury Sch. Dist., Fallsington, Pa., 1985—. Bd. dirs. YWCA, Newtown, Pa., 1990; mem. Pennsbury Year Round Edn. Task Force. Mem. NEA, ACA, Pa. State Edn. Assn., Pennsbury Edn. Assn., Pa. Sch. Nurse Assn., Nat. Assn. Sch. Nurses, Bucks County Sch. Nurses Assn., Chi Sigma Iota. Republican. Presbyterian. Avocations: travel, reading. Home: 131 Windham Ct Newtown PA 18940-1750 Office: Pennsbury Sch Dist Yardley Ave Fallsington PA 19058

WELLMAN, CARL PIERCE, philosophy educator; b. Lynn, Mass., Sept. 3, 1926; s. Frank and Carolyn (Heath) W.; m. Farnell Parsons, June 20, 1953; children: Timothy, Philip, Lesley, Christopher. B.A., U. Ariz., 1949; M.A., Harvard U., 1951, Ph.D., 1954; postgrad., U. Cambridge, Eng., 1951-52. Instr. Lawrence U., Appleton, Wis., 1953-57; asst. prof. Lawrence U., 1957-62, assoc. prof., 1962-66, prof., chmn. dept. philosophy, 1966-68; prof. philosophy Washington U., St. Louis, 1968-88, Hortense and Tobias Lewin Disting. prof. humanities, 1988—; Mem. rev. panel research grants NEH, 1968-71. Author: The Language of Ethics, 1961, Challenge and Response: Justification in Ethics, 1971, Morals and Ethics, 1975, Welfare Rights, 1982, A Theory of Rights, 1985, Real Rights, 1995. Recipient Uhrig Distinguished Teaching award Lawrence U., 1968; Am. Council Learned Socs. fellow, 1965-66; NEH sr. fellow, 1972-73; Nat. Humanities Center fellow,

1982-83. Mem. Am. Philos. Assn., Internat. Assn. for Philosophy Law and Social Philosophy. Home: 625 S Skinker Blvd # 902 Saint Louis MO 63105-2301

WELLMAN, GERALD EDWIN, JR., safety and fire inspector; b. Steubenville, Ohio, Feb. 27, 1948; s. Gerald Edwin Sr. and Rose Marie (Bonacci) W.; 1 child, Jerad Anthony. AS Data Processing, West Liberty State Coll., 1974, BSBA, 1974; MS in Safety Mgmt., W.Va. U., 1991, cert. of advanced study, 1995. With production, mechanical Wheeling and Pitts. Steel Corp., Beech Bottom, W.Va., 1966-76; with production, mechanical, safety Wheeling and Pitts. Steel Corp., Steubenville, Ohio, 1976—, also safety and fire insp., safety coord.;, 1993, 95; mem. wellness com. Wheeling and Pitts. Steel Plant; safety coord. Wheeling and Pitts. Steel Corp. Hazardous Material Team; safety chmn., trustee local 1190 United Steel Workers Am.; mem. Am. Iron and Steel Inst. R.R. Com. Contbr. articles to profl. jours. With U.S. Army, 1967-69, Vietnam. Mem. Am. Iron and Steel Inst. (railroad com.), West Liberty State Coll. Alumni Club, West Liberty State Coll Hilltops Club, W.Va. U. Alumni Club, Mountaineer Athletic Club, Dapper Dan Club Upper Ohio Valley, Brooke High Sch. Boosters Club, W.Va. Sheriffs Assn., Follansbee Blue Waves Boosters Club, Nat. Fire Protection Assn., Nat. Safety Coun., W.Va. Safety Coun., Western Pa. Safety Coun., U.S. Steel Workers Am., Eagles Club, Am. Soc. Safety Engrs. (nominating com. 1989—), Alpha Kappa Psi. Avocations: golf, swimming, basketball, baseball, coaching youth football and baseball. Home: 311 Hillcrest Dr Wellsburg WV 26070-1943

WELLMAN, RICHARD VANCE, legal educator; b. Worthington, Ohio, Sept. 10, 1922; s. Burton Singley and Blanche (Gardner) W.; m. Louise Dewey Laylin, Oct. 18, 1944 (dec. Dec. 1982); children: Martha, Anne, Jane, Sarah, Peter Burton, Charles Dewey; m. Natalie Lancaster Robertson, Dec. 12, 1983. A.B., U. Mich., 1947; J.D., 1949. Bar: Ohio 1949, Mich. 1960. Practice in Cleve., 1949-51, Mt. Vernon, Ohio, 1951-54; mem. faculty U. Mich. Law Sch., 1954-74; Alston prof. law U. Ga. Sch. Law, 1974-90, prof. emeritus, 1990—. Engaged in nat. effort to encourage state probate code revisions, 1965—; commr. Mich. Uniform State Laws, 1970-73, Ga. Uniform State Laws, 1974—; exec. dir. Joint Editorial Bd. Uniform Probate Code, 1990—. Served to 1st lt. AUS, 1943-46. Mem. Am. Bar Assn., Mich. Bar Assn., Am. Law Inst., Am. Coll. Trust and Estate Counsel. Home: 190 Tipperary Rd Athens GA 30606-3833

WELLMAN, THOMAS PETER, lawyer; b. Farrell, Pa., Feb. 25, 1932; s. Peter Michael and Bessie Thomas (George) W.; m. Jeanne Ann Harding, July 9, 1971; children: Elizabeth Thomas, Katherine Thomas. BA, Miami U., Oxford, Ohio, 1956; JD, Ohio State U., 1959. Bar: Ohio 1959, U.S. Dist. Ct. (no. dist.) Ohio 1961. Asst. atty. gen. State of Ohio, Columbus, 1959-60; sr. atty. Wellman & Jeren Co., L.P.A., Youngstown, Ohio, 1960—; mng. ptnr. Tablack, Wellman, Jeren, Hackett & Skoufatos Co., L.P.A., Youngstown, 1973—. Mem. Canfield (Ohio) Income Tax Rev. Bd., 1981—. With U.S. Army, 1952-54. Mem. ABA, Ohio Bar Assn., Mahoning County Bar Assn. (chmn. unauthorized practice of law wcom. 1984-85, mem. inquiry com. 1990—). Presbyterian. Avocation: sailing. Office: 67 Westchester Dr Youngstown OH 44515-3902

WELLMAN, WILLIAM WALTER, printing executive; b. Lansing, Mich., Feb. 19, 1933; s. Lyle O. and Vera May (Barns) W.; m. Joelene Stella Richards, Apr. 24, 1954; children: Jeffrey William, Sherri Ann. B of Communications, Mich. State U., 1955. With pub. relations Farm Bur. Ins., Lansing, Mich., 1955-56; brand mgr. Kimberly-Clark Corp., Neenah, Wis., 1956-59; v.p. Wellman Press, Inc., Lansing, 1960-78, pres., 1978-86; sr. mgr. John Henry Co., Lansing, 1986—; ptnr. Wellman Enterprises, Lansing, 1986—; pres. Mich. Advt. Roundtable, Marshall, 1964. Mem. Nat. Assn. Photolithographers, Mich. Communicators Assn. (pres. 1963), Mid Mich. Alumni (pres. 1981), Lansing Regional C. of C. (bd. dirs. 1978-80). Clubs: Lansing Press (pres. 1969), Walnut Hills Country (East Lansing) (bd. dirs., v.p. 1972-86). Home: 1837 Foxcroft Rd East Lansing MI 48823-2123 Office: John Henry Co 5800 W Grand River Ave Lansing MI 48906-9111

WELLNER, MARCEL NAHUM, physics educator, researcher; b. Antwerp, Belgium, Feb. 8, 1930; came to U.S., 1949; s. Jules and Lucie (Rapoport) W.; m. Magdeleine Misselyn, Apr. 7, 1961; children: Pierre, Lucie. BS, MIT, 1952; PhD, Princeton U., 1958. Instr. Brandeis U., Waltham, Mass., 1957-59; mem. Inst. Advanced Study, Princeton, N.J., 1959-60; rsch. assoc. Ind. U., Bloomington, 1960-63; vis. scientist Atomic Energy Rsch. Establishment, Harwell, Eng., 1963-64; from asst. prof. to prof. Syracuse (N.Y.) U., 1964-95, prof. emeritus, 1995—; rsch. prof. Health Sci. Ctr. SUNY, Syracuse, 1995—. Author gen. physics textbook; contbr. numerous articles on quantum field theory to profl. jours. Mem. Am. Phys. Soc. Office: Syracuse U Dept Physics Syracuse NY 13244

WELLON, ROBERT G., lawyer; b. Port Jervis, N.Y., Apr. 18, 1948; s. Frank Lewis and Alice (Stephens) W.; m. Jan Montgomery, Aug. 12, 1972; children: Robert F., Alice Wynn. AB, Emory U., 1970; JD, Stetson Coll. Law, 1974. Assoc. Turner, Turner & Turner, Atlanta, 1974-78; ptnr. Ridley, Wellon, Schwieger & Brazier, Atlanta, 1978-86; of counsel Wilson, Strickland & Benson, Atlanta, 1987—; adj. prof. Atlanta Law Sch., 1981-94; adj. prof. law Emory U. Sch. of Law, 1995—. Gov.'s task force chmn. Atlanta 2000, 1978; exec. com., treas., 2d v.p. Atlanta Easter Seals Soc., 1983-88; rep. Neighborhood Planning Unit, 1981-83; adminstrv. bd. Northside United Meth. Ch.; bd. dirs. Atlanta Found. for Psychoanalysis, Inc. Served with USAR, 1970-76. Recipient Judge Joe Morris award Stetson Coll. Law, St. Petersburg, 1974, Charles E. Watkins svc. award 1995). Mem. Fla. Bar, State Bar. Ga. (professionalism com. 1994—), Atlanta Bar Assn. (bd. dirs. 1978-88, pres. 1986-87, bd. trustees CLE), Lawyers Club Atlanta, Old War Horse Lawyers Club. Methodist. Office: 1100 One Midtown Pla 1360 Peachtree St NE Atlanta GA 30309-3214

WELLS, ARTHUR STANTON, retired manufacturing company executive; b. Kingsport, Tenn., Jan. 8, 1931; s. Arthur Stanton and Blanche Welch (Duncan) W.; m. Ellen N. Blackburn, June 15, 1957; children: Arthur S., Thomas B., Emily B., Richard R. B.S., Yale U., 1953; M.B.A., Harvard U., 1957. Fin. analyst Eastman Kodak Co., Kingsport, Tenn., 1957-65; mgr. profit analysis Xerox Corp., Rochester, N.Y., 1966-68; asst. treas. Xerox Corp., Stamford, Conn., 1969-76, treas., 1976-79; v.p. fin. Barnes Group Inc., Bristol, Conn., 1979-86, exec. v.p. fin., 1987-93, pres., CEO, 1994-96, also dir., 1994—; bd. dirs. ValueCare Inc., Hartford. Trustee, treas. Wilton (Conn.) Libr. Assn., 1972-78; bd. dirs. New Eng. Opera Assn., 1972-78; assoc. bd. dirs. Conn. Bank and Trust Co., Hartford, 1984-90; chmn. bd. trustees, exec. com. Conn. Pub. Expenditure Coun., Inc., 1990-93. With AUS, 1953-55. Mem. Fin. Execs. Inst. Democrat. Home: 1 Wilton Crest Wilton CT 06897-4052 Office: Barnes Group Inc 123 Main St Bristol CT 06010-6307

WELLS, BENJAMIN GLADNEY, lawyer; b. St. Louis, Nov. 13, 1943; s. Benjamin Harris and Katherine Emma (Gladney) W.; m. Nancy Kathryn Harpster, June 7, 1967; children: Barbara Gladney, Benjamin Harpster. BA magna cum laude, Amherst (Mass.) Coll., 1965; JD cum laude, Harvard U., 1968. Bar: Ill. 1968, Tex. 1973, U.S. Tax Ct. 1973, U.S. Ct. Claims 1975, U.S. Ct. Appeals (5th cir.) 1981, U.S. Dist. Ct. (so. dist.) Tex. 1985, U.S. Dist. Ct. (we. dist.) Tex. 1993. Assoc. Kirkland & Ellis, Chgo., 1968-69; assoc. to ptnr. Baker & Botts, L.L.P., Houston, 1973—; mem. Harvard Legal Aid Bur., 1966-68. Contbr. articles to profl. jours. Mem. devel. com. St. John's Sch., Houston, 1987—, chmn. planned giving com., 1987—; active Harvard Legal Aid Bureau, 1966-68. Capt. U.S. Army, 1969-72. Mem. Houston Tax Roundtable (pres. 1994-95), The Forest Club, The Houston Club, Phi Beta Kappa. Presbyterian. Office: Baker & Botts LLP One Shell Plaza 910 Louisiana St Houston TX 77002-4995

WELLS, CAROLYN CRESSY, social work educator; b. Boston, July 26, 1943; d. Harris Shipman Wells and Marianne Elizabeth (Monroe) Glazier; m. Dale Reed Konle, Oct. 11, 1970 (div. Sept. 3, 1982); m. Dennis Alan Loefler, Sept. 29, 1990. BA, U. Calif., Berkeley, 1965; MSW, U. Wis., 1968, PhD, 1973. Cert. ind. clin. social worker, marriage and family therapist. Vol. VISTA, Espanola, N.Mex., 1965-66; social worker Project Six Cen. Wis. Colony, Madison, 1968, Milw. Dept. Pub. Welfare, 1969, Shorewood (Wis.) Manor Nursing Home, 1972; sch. social worker Jefferson (Wis.) County Spl. Edn., 1977-78; lectr. sociology and social work Marquette U., Milw., 1972-73, dir. social work program, 1973-90, 93—, assoc. prof. social work, 1981-94, prof. social work, 1994—; social work therapist Lighthouse Counseling Assocs., Racine, Wis., 1989-91, The Cambridge Group, 1991-92; Achievement Assocs., 1992-95; vis. lectr. social work U. Canterbury, Christchurch, N.Z., 1983. Author: Social Work Day to Day, 1982, rev. edit., 1988, Social Work Ethics Day to Day, 1986; co-author: The Social Work Experience, 1991, rev. edit., 1996. Mem. Wis. Coun. on Social Work Edn., pres., 1980-82, sec., 1985-87, mem. exec. com., 1993—. Mem. NASW, Am. Assn. Profl. Hypnotherapists, Coun. on Social Work Edn. (mem. publs. and media com. 1989-91, site visitor for accreditation 1987—), Acad. Cert. Social Workers, Assn. Baccalaureate Program Dirs. Democrat. Avocations: writing, silent sports. Home: 4173 Sleeping Dragon Rd West Bend WI 53095-9296 Office: Marquette U Social Work Program 526 N 14th St Milwaukee WI 53233-2211

WELLS, CHARLES ROBERT, secondary education educator; b. Chgo., Jan. 11, 1952; s. Samuel and Wanda Jean (Few) W. BA, Harris Tchrs. Coll., St. Louis, 1978; MS in Edn., Ind. U., 1992. Cert. tchr., Ind., Mo. Tchr. social studies Gary (Ind.) Cmty. Schs., 1984—; mem. adv. com. Ind. Dept. Edn., Indpls. Mem. Ind. Social Studies Coun., Gary Reading Coun. Lutheran. Home: PO Box 6563 Gary IN 46406-0563

WELLS, CHRISTINE, foundation executive; b. Grayling, Mich., Aug. 6, 1948; d. Chester John and Mary W. BA, Mich. State U., 1970, MLIR, 1982; MLS, U. Mich., 1976. Head libr. Lansing State Jour., E. Lansing, Mich., 1973-82; mng. editor libr. svcs. USA TODAY, Washington, 1982-87; libr. dir. Gannett Co., Inc., Washington, 1985-87, chief staff, chmn. and CEO office, 1988-89; v.p. adminstrn. Gannett Found., Washington, 1989-90; v.p. internat. The Freedom Forum, Washington, 1991—; exec. dir. The Newseum, 1993-94; sr. v.p. The Freedom Forum, 1994—. Mem. bd. overseers Internat. Press Ctr. and Club, Moscow; mem. bd. visitors Coll. Sci., Mich. State U. Recipient Dising. Alumni award U. Mich., 1991. Mem. ALA, Spl. Librs. Assn. (Profl. award 1994). Office: The Freedom Forum 1101 Wilson Blvd Arlington VA 22209-2248

WELLS, CHRISTOPHER BRIAN, lawyer; b. Belleville, Ill., Jan. 23, 1948; s. Frederick Meyers and Ethel Pauline (Morris) W.; m. Gaynelle Vansandt, June 6, 1970. BA in Econs., U. Kans., BS in Bus., 1970, JD, 1973. Enforcement atty. SEC, Seattle, 1977-82; ptnr. Lane, Powell, Moss & Miller, Seattle, 1982—. Served to capt. U.S. Army, 1973-77. Mem. ABA, Wash. State Bar Assn., King County Trial Lawyers Assn., Wash. Soc. CPA's., Kans. Bar Assn. Democrat. Office: Lane Powell Spears Lubersky 1420 5th Ave Ste 4100 Seattle WA 98101-2333

WELLS, DAMON, JR., investment company executive; b. Houston, May 20, 1937; s. Damon and Margaret Corinne (Howze) W.; BA magna cum laude, Yale U., 1958; BA, Oxford U., 1964, MA, 1968; PhD, Rice U., 1968. Owner, CEO Damon Wells Interests, Houston, 1958—, pres.,Damon Wells Found., 1993—. Bd. dirs. Child Guidance Ctr. of Houston, 1970-73; trustee Christ Ch. Cathedral Endowment Fund, 1970-73, 84-88, chmn., 1987-88, Kinkaid Sch., 1972-86, Kinkaid Sch. Endowment Fund, 1981-86; hon. friend of Somerville Coll., Oxford U., 1988—; mem. Sr. Common Room, Pembroke Coll., Oxford U., 1972—; trustee Camp Allen retreat of Episc. Diocese of Tex., 1976-78; founding bd. dirs. Brit. Inst. U.S., 1979-80; mem. pres.'s coun. Tex. A&M U., 1983-89. Named Hon. Comdr. Most Excellent Order of Brit. Empire by Her Majesty Queen Elizabeth II, 1991, Outstanding Alumnus Yr. by Kinkaid Sch., 1994. Fellow Jonathan Edwards Coll. (assoc.), Yale U., 1982—; hon. fellow Pembroke Coll., Oxford U., 1984—. Mem. English-Speaking Union (nat. dir. 1970-72, v.p. Houston br. 1966-73), Coun. Fgn. Rels., Phi Beta Kappa, Pi Sigma Alpha. Episcopalian. Clubs: Houston Country, Houston, Yale (N.Y.C.), United Oxford and Cambridge U. (London); Cosmos (Washington), Buck's (London), Coronado (Houston), Little Ship Club (London) . Author: Stephen Douglas: The Last Years, 1857-1861, 1971 (Tex. Writer's Roundup prize 1971), paperback edit., 1990. Home: 5555 Del Monte Dr Houston TX 77056-4116 Office: 2001 Kirby Dr Ste 806 Houston TX 77019-6033

WELLS, DAVID LEE, professional baseball player; b. Torrance, Calif., May 20, 1963. Grad. high sch., San Diego. With Toronto Blue Jays, 1987-92, Detroit Tigers, 1992-95; pitcher Cin. Reds, 1995—. Named Am. League All-Star Team, 1995. Achievements include mem. Am. League East Divsn. Champions, 1989, 91, 92, World Series Champions, 1992, Cin. Reds Nat. League Ctrl. Divsn. Champions. Office: Cin Reds 100 Riverfront Stadium Cincinnati OH 45202

WELLS, DEWEY WALLACE, lawyer; b. Raleigh, N.C., Oct. 14, 1929; s. B.C. and Alma (Blanchard) W.; m. Ann D. Wells, Aug 25, 1951; children: Robert, Betty W., Daniel, Brady, Jeff. AA, Mars Hill Coll., 1950; BS, Wake Forest U., 1952, JD, 1954. Bar: N.C. 1954, U.S. Dist. Ct. (ea. dist.) N.C. 1960, U.S. Ct. Appeals (4th cir.) 1961, U.S. Dist. Ct. (mid. dist.) N.C. 1985. Exec. sec. N.C. Jud. Council, Raleigh, 1954-55; trust officer Planter's Nat. Bank & Trust Co., Rocky Mt., N.C., 1955-57; ptnr. LeRoy, Wells, Shaw, Hornthal & Riley, Elizabeth City, N.C., 1958-85, Womble, Carlyle, Sandridge & Rice, Winston Salem, N.C., 1985-95; judge Superior Ct., 1st Jud. Dist. N.C., 1974. Trustee N.C. Natural Heritage Trust, 1990-95, chmn. 1995—. 1st lt. USAR, 1954-58. Fellow Am. Coll. Trial Lawyers, Am. Bar Found.; mem. ABA, N.C. Bar Assn. (pres. 1980-81), Rotary. Republican. Baptist. Home: 1890 Pilot Ridge Rd Collettsville NC 28611 Office: Womble Carlyle Sandridge & Rice PO Drawer 84 1600 Southern Nat Fin Ctr Winston Salem NC 27102-0084

WELLS, DONALD EUGENE, hospital administrator; b. Phoenix, May 10, 1940; married. BHA, Ga. State U., 1970, MHA, 1972. Adminstrv. resident Emory Univ. Hosp., Atlanta, 1971-72, asst. adminstr., 1972-77, assoc. adminstr., 1977-78, dep. exec. dir., 1978-81, adminstrv. dir., 1981-91, exec. dir., 1991—. Mem. Ga. Hosp. Assn. (del., mem. coms.). Office: Emory U Hosp 1364 Clifton Rd NE Atlanta GA 30322-1059*

WELLS, EVERETT CLAYTON, JR., economic development executive; b. Hopkinsville, Ky., May 11, 1954; s. Everett Clayton and Lois Gertrude (Aday) W.; m. Suzanne Walden. BS, Murray State U., 1977; postgrad., Memphis State U., 1978. Credit mgr. Dunlap Sales, Hopkinsville, 1979-85; asst. exec. dir. Hopkinsville C. of C., 1985-86; exec. dir. Hopkinsville Christian County C. of C., 1986-87; sr. econ. devel. coord. Mcpl. Electric Authority of Ga., Atlanta, 1987—; bd. dirs., vice-chmn. of promotions Ky. Western Waterways, Grand Rivers, 1986-87. Pres. Murray State U. Alumni Assn., 1985-86. Mem. Nat. Assn. Corp. Real Estate Execs., Am. Econ. Devel. Coun. (editorial rev. com. 1996), Ga. C. of C. Execs. Assn., Ga. Ind. Developers (chmn. Vol. of Yr. com. 1991), So. Econ. Devel. Coun. (alt. state bd. dirs. 1993, bd. dirs. 1992-95, exec. com. 1995, chair constn. and bylaws 1996), Rotary (chmn. pub. rels. 1981-82, chmn. youth com. 1986-87, chmn. free enterprise 1986-87), Little River Road Runners Club (co-founder, pres. 1981-83, state rep. 1983-88). Republican. Baptist. Avocations: running, basketball, reading, weight lifting. Home: 455 Amberidge Tr NW Atlanta GA 30328 Office: Mcpl Electric Authority Ga Ste 550 5660 New Northside Dr Atlanta GA 30328

WELLS, FAY GILLIS, writer, lecturer, broadcaster; b. Mpls., Oct. 15, 1908; d. Julius Howells and Minnie Irene (Shafer) Gillis; student Mich. State Coll., 1925-28; m. Linton Wells, Apr. 1, 1935 (dec. 1976); 1 son, Linton Wells, II. Free-lance corr. in USSR for N.Y. Herald Tribune and AP, 1930-34, aviation mags., 1930-36; fgn. corr. N.Y. Herald Tribune, 1935-36, spl. Hollywood corr., 1937-38; contbr. book revs. Saturday Review, 1939-42; dep. chief of mission for U.S. Comml. Co., Portuguese W. Africa, 1942-46, syndicated boating columnist, 1960-62; White House corr. Storer Broadcasting Co., 1964-77; aircraft pilot, 1929; designer yacht interiors Alta Grant Samuels, 1958-62; now co-chmn. Internat. Forest of Friendship; hon. co-chmn. Nat. Air Heritage Council; mem. com. to select 1st journalist in space, 1985—; judge of trophy winners Nat. Air Space Mus., 1988—. Recipient Sherman Fairchild Internat. Air Safety Writing award, 1965, Amelia Earhart medal, 1967, Golden Age of Flight award Nat. Air and Space Mus.-Dept. Transp., 1984, Elder Statesman of Aviation, 1984, award Internat. Conf. Women Engrs. and Scientists, 1984; named to Hall of Fame Women In Aviation Pioneers, 1992; Honors award Women in Aviation, 1990. Mem. Aviation/Space Writers Assn., Am. Women in Radio and TV (pres. Washington chpt. 1968-69, CBS Charlotte Friel award 1972), Radio-TV Corrs. Assn., White House Corrs. Assn. (hon. life), Aircraft Owners and Pilots Assn., The Ninety-Nines (charter mem.; Most Valuable Pilot, Washington chpt. 1975), OX5 Aviation Pioneers (Outstanding Woman of Year award 1972), Internat. Soc. Woman Geographers, Broadcast Pioneers, Zonta Internat. (life hon.), DAR, Nat. Aero. Assn. (named elder statesman 1984). Clubs: Georgetown, Overseas Press (founding mem. 1939), Nat. Assn. Female Execs., Nat. Press, Internat. Forest Friendship (co-gen. chmn. 1976—, Fay Gillis Wells Gazebo dedicated 1991). Home: 4211 Duvawn St Alexandria VA 22310-2024

WELLS, FAY R., food products executive; b. 1925. Attended, U. Iowa, 1946-50. With Wells Dairy, Inc., Le Mars, Iowa, 1951—, ptnr., 1954-77, pres., 1977-80, chmn. bd. dirs., 1980—. With U.S. Army, 1943-46. Office: Wells Dairy Inc 1 Blue Bunny Dr Le Mars IA 51031-2207*

WELLS, FRED D., food products executive; b. 1925. With Wells Dairy, Inc., Le Mars, Iowa, 1946—, ptnr., 1954-77, v.p., 1977-80, pres., 1980—. With U.S. Army, 1943-46. Office: Wells Dairy Inc 1 Blue Bunny Dr Le Mars IA 51031-2207*

WELLS, HERMAN B, university chancellor; b. Jamestown, Ind., June 7, 1902; s. Joseph Granville and Anna (Harting) W. Student, U. Ill., 1920-21; BS, Ind. U., 1924, AM, 1927, LLD, 1962; postgrad., U. Wis., 1927-28, LLD (hon.), 1946; LLD (hon.), Butler U., Rose Poly. Inst., DePauw U., 1939, Wabash Coll., 1942, Earlham, 1948, Valparaiso U., 1953, Miami U., Tri-State Coll., 1959, U. Louisville, 1961, Franklin Coll., Anderson Coll., 1962, Ball State Tchrs. Coll., Washington U., 1963, U. Notre Dame, St. Joseph's Coll., U. Calif., Ind. State Coll., 1964, Drury Coll., 1968, Columbia, 1969, Chgo. Circle Campus U. Ill., 1973, Howard U., 1976, U. S.C., 1980, L.H.D., 1963, Marian Coll., 1970; hon. doctorate in edn., Coll. Edn., Bangkok, 1968. Asst. cashier First Nat. Bank, Lebanon, Ind., 1924-26; asst. dept. econs. U. Wis., 1927-28; field sec. Ind. Bankers Assn., 1928-31; sec., research dir. Study Commn. for Ind. Fin. Instns., 1931-33; instr. econs. Ind. U., 1930-33, asst. prof., 1933-35, prof. acting dean sch. bus. adminstrn., 1935-72, dean sch. bus. adminstrn., 1935-37, acting pres. sch. bus. adminstrn., 1937-1938, pres. sch. bus. adminstrn., 1938-62, univ. chancellor, 1962—, interim pres., 1968; supr. div. of banks and trust cos., div. of research and statistics Ind. Dept. Fin. Instns., 1933-35; sec. Commn. for Ind. Fin. Instns., 1933-36; chmn. Ind. U. Found., 1937-62, 69-72, vice chmn., 1975—, pres., 1962-69, chmn. exec. com., 1969—; chmn. Fed. Home Loan Bank of Indpls., 1940-71; dir. Ind. Bell Telephone Co., 1951-72, Chemed Corp., 1970—, Lilly Endowment, Inc., 1973—; Spl. adviser on Liberated Areas, U.S. Dept. State, 1944; cons. U.S. delegation San Francisco Conf. for Am. Council on Edn., 1945; Mem. Allied Missions for Observation Greek elections, rank of Minister, 1946; adviser on cultural affairs to mil. gov. U.S. Zone, Germany, 1947-48; del. 12th Gen. Assembly of UN, 1957; adviser Ministry Edn., Pakistan, 1959; head U.S. delegation SEATO Prep. Commn. on Univ. Problems, Bangkok, 1960; mem. UN com. experts to rev. activities and orgn. UN Secretariat, 1960-61, Nat. Citizen's Commn. Internat. Cooperation, Com. Econ. Devel., 1958-61; chmn. legislature's cons. higher edn. State N.Y., 1963-64; mem. Pres.'s Com. U.S. Soviet Trade Relations, 1965; mem. rev. com. on Haile Sellassie I U., Addis Ababa, 1966-75; mem. pres.'s Spl. Com. on Overseas Vol. Activities, 1967; mem. Nat. Commn. on U.S.-China Relations, 1969; tech. adv. bd. Milbank Meml. Fund, 1973-78; Ex-pres. Nat. Assn. State Univs., State U. Assn.; exec. com. Am. Council on Edn. (chmn. council), 1944-45; mem. 1st bd. regents Am. Savs. & Loan Inst. Grad. Sch. Savs. and Loan.; Trustee Edn. and World Affairs, 1963-71, chmn., 1963-70; trustee Howard U., 1956-75, Am. U. at Cairo, 1957-75, Ind. Inst. Tech. (emeritus), Earlham Coll. (hon.), Carnegie Found. for Advancement Teaching, 1941-62; former mem. adv. council Am. Sch. of Madrid; mem. nat. com. on govt. fin. Brookings Instn.; bd. visitors Tulane U.; chmn. Aerospace Research Applications Center, Ind. U., 1962-72; nat. bd. dirs. Goodwill Industries Am., 1962-69; bd. dirs. James Whitcomb Riley Meml. Assn. (hon. chmn.), Sigma Nu Ednl. Found., 1946—, Arthur R. Metz Foundation (v.p.), Learning Resources Inst., 1959-65, Council on Library Resources, Historic Landmarks Found. Ind., 1974—; chmn. adv. com. Acad. in Pub. Service, 1976-83; founder, active mem. Ind. Acad., 1971—. Author: (with others) Report of Study Commission for Indiana Financial Institutions, 1932, Being Lucky: Reminiscences and Reflections, 1980, articles in mags. Recipient Distinguished Service award Ind. Jr. C. of C., 1938; 1st ann. award N.Y. Alumni chpt. Beta Gamma Sigma, 1939; Gold medal award Internat. Benjamin Franklin Soc., 1959; Comdrs. Cross of Order of Merit Germany, 1960; Radio Sta. WHAS Ind. Man of Year, 1960; Man of Year awards Indpls. Times, 1961; Man of Yr. awards Ind. Optometric Assn., 1961; comdr. Most Exalted Order White Elephant, Thailand, 1962; knight comdr. 2d class Most Noble Order Crown, 1968, Most Exalted Order of White Elephant, Thailand, 1986; Nat. Interfrat. Conf. award, 1962; Hoosier of Yr. award Sons of Ind. in N.Y., 1963; Interfrat. Service award Lambda Chi Alpha, 1964; Robins of Am. award, 1964; Distinguished Service Sch. Adminstrn. award Am. Assn. Sch. Adminstrs., 1965; Ind. Arts award, 1977; Liberty Bell award, 1978, Lifetime Achievement award Ind. Coun. Fund-Raising Execs., 1985; Disting. award for Lifetime Achievement Am. Coun. on Edn., 1985; Diamond Jubilee award Kappa Alpha Psi, 1986; Hon. mem. United Steelworkers Am., Dist. 30, Nat. Exchange Clubs, DeMolay Legion of Honor, 1975; hon. v.p. AM. Sunday Sch. Union; recipient Ind. U. medal, 1989; Great Am. Traditions award B'nai B'rith Internat., 1991, Lifetime Achievement award Entrepreneur of Yr., 1992, Maynard K. Hine medal Ind. U.-Purdue U. Indpls., 1993. Fellow Internat. Coll. Dentists (hon.), Am. Coll. Dentists (hon.), Am. Acad. Arts and Scis.; mem. NEA (ex. pres. div. higher edn.), AAUP, Am. Philos. Soc., Am. Assn. Sch. Adminstrs., Royal Soc. Art London (Benjamin Franklin fellow), Am. Econ. Assn., Internat. Assn. Univs. (v.p. 1955-60), Am. Research Inst. for Arts (chmn. bd. 1975-77), Nat. Commn. on Humanities (vice chmn. 1964-65), Ind. Acad. Social Scis. (past pres.), Ind. Soc. of Chgo., Ind. Soc. Pioneers, Ind. Hist. Soc. (dir. 1968—), Ind. Tchrs. Assn., Mortar Bd., Blue Key, Phi Beta Kappa, Phi Mu Alpha, Kappa Delta Pi, Beta Gamma Sigma, Alpha Kappa Psi, Kappa Kappa Psi, Sigma Nu (regent 1968-70). Methodist (trustee). Clubs: Mason (33 deg.), Kiwanian (hon.), Rotarian (hon.), Athenaeum; Columbia (Indpls.), Athletic (Indpls.); Century Assn. (N.Y.C.), University (N.Y.C.); University (Chgo.); Cosmos (Washington). Home: 1321 E 10th St Bloomington IN 47408-3964 Office: Ind U Owen Hall Office of Chancellor Bloomington IN 47405

WELLS, HERSCHEL JAMES, physician, former hospital administrator; b. Kirkland, Ark., Feb. 23, 1924; s. Alymer James and Martha Thelma (Cross) W.; m. Carmen Ruth Williams, Aug. 5, 1946; children: Judith Alliece Wells Jarecki, Pamela Elliece Wells McKinven, Joanne Olivia Wells Bennett. Student, Emory U., 1941-42, U. Ark., 1942-43; MD, U. Tenn., 1946. Rotating intern, then resident internal medicine Wayne County Gen. Hosp. (and Infirmary), Eloise, Mich., 1946-50; dir. infirmary div. Wayne County Gen. Hosp. (and Infirmary), 1955-65, gen. supt., 1965-74; dir. Wayne County Gen. Hosp. (Walter P. Reuther Meml. Long Term Care Facility), 1974-78; rev. physician DDS, SSA, Traverse City, Mich., 1978—. Served to maj. M.C. AUS, 1948-55. Mem. AMA, Mich. Med. Soc., Am. Fedn. Clin. Rsch., Masons (32 deg.), Alpha Kappa Kappa, Pi Kappa Alpha. Home and Office: 9651 N 3 Rd Copemish MI 49625-9608

WELLS, HOYT MELLOR, manufacturing executive; b. 1926; married. BME, U. Nebr., 1949, MME, 1951. V.p. Goodyear Can. Inc., 1972; with Goodyear Tire & Rubber Co., 1951—, from v.p. to exec. v.p., from 1980, pres., COO, vice-chmn. the bd., pres., COO, 1994-95; ret., 1995.

WELLS, J. LYLE, JR., bank executive. V. chmn. United Mo. Bank, Kansas City. Office: United Mo Bank 1010 Grand Blvd Kansas City MO 64106-2225*

WELLS, JAMES M., III, bank executive; b. 1946. Student, U. N.C., Rutgers U., U. Colo. Mgmt. trainee United Va. Bankshares, 1968-71, corporate adminstrv. officer, sec., 1971; br. officer, mgr. United Va. Bankshares/State-Planters, 1971-74; v.p. and treas. United Va. Mortgage Corp., 1974-79; pres., CEO United Va. Leasing Corp., 1974-79; exec. v.p. United Va. Bank, Norfolk, Va., 1979-83, pres. Ea. region, 1983-85, exec. v.p. corporate banking, 1985-86, exec. v.p. banking group, 1986-88; pres. Crestar Fin Corp, Richmond, Va., 1988—. Office: Crestar Fin Corp 919 E Main St PO Box 26665 Richmond VA 23261-6665*

WELLS, JOEL FREEMAN, editor, author; b. Evansville, Ind., Mar. 17, 1930; s. William Jackson and Edith (Strasell) W.; m. Elizabeth Louise Hein, June 5, 1952; children: William, Eugenia, Susan, Steven, Daniel. A.B. in Journalism, U. Notre Dame, 1952; Litt.D. (hon.), Rosary Coll., 1980. Advt. and promotion dir. Thomas More Assn., Chgo., 1955-64; v.p. Thomas More Assn., 1967—, dir., 1968—; editor The Critic, Chgo., 1964-80; editor-in-chief Thomas More Press, Chgo., 1975-94; lectr. grad. dept. library sci. Rosary Coll., River Forest, Ill., 1964-67; mem. assoc. grad. faculty Loyola U., Chgo., 1984—. Author: Grim Fairy Tales for Adults: Parodies of the Literary Lions, 1967, A Funny Thing Happened To The Church, 1969, Under the Spreading Heresy, 1971, The Bad Children's Book, 1972, Second Collection, 1973, Here's to the Family, 1977, How To Survive with Your Teenager, 1982, Coping in the 80s: Eliminating Needless Stress and Guilt, 1986, No Rolling in the Aisles, 1987, Who Do You Think You Are?, 1989, The Manger Mouse, 1990; also articles. revs.; editor: Pilgrim's Regress, 1979; co-editor: anthologies Bodies and Souls, 1961, (with Dan Herr) Blithe Spirits, 1962, Bodies and Spirits, 1964, Through Other Eyes, 1965, Moments of Truth, 1966, Contrasts, 1972; contbr. to: Ann Landers Ency., A to Z, 1978. Served to lt. (j.g.) USNR, 1952-55. Home: 1500 Oak Ave # 5D Evanston IL 60201-4217 Office: Thomas More Assn 205 W Monroe St Chicago IL 60606-5001

WELLS, JOHN CALHOUN, federal agency administrator. Dir. Fed. Mediation and Conciliation Svc., Washington, 1994—. Office: Fed Mediation Concilation Svc 2100 R St NW Washington DC 20427*

WELLS, KITTY (MURIEL DEASON WRIGHT), country western singer; b. Nashville, Aug. 30, 1919; d. Charles Carey and Murtle Bell (Street) Deason; m. Johnnie Robert Wright, Oct. 30, 1937; children: Ruby Jean Wright Taylor, Bobby, Carol Sue Wright-Sturdivant. Grad. high sch. Country music singer; sang gospel in chs. as a child; performed on radio, early 1930s; with John and Jack and the Tenn. Mountain Boys, late 1930's-early 1940's, regular on Grand Ole Opry, from 1952, now with Johnny Wright, Bobby Wright and the Tennessee Mountain Boys; songs include: Release Me, It Wasn't God Who Made Honky Tonk Angels, Making Believe; author: Kitty Wells Cookbook. Bd. dirs. Nashville Meml. Hosp. Recipient award as number 1 female singer Cashbox Mag., 1953-62, Billboard 1954-65, award of yr. for top female country vocalist Record World mag. 1965, award for highest artistic achievement in rec. arts 1964, various awards Downbeat mag., award as all-time queen of country music Music Bus. mag. 1964, Woman of Yr. award 1974, named Top Female Artist of Decade, Record World mag. 1974, named to Country Music Hall of Fame 1976. Mem. Country Music Assn., Nat. Assn. Rec. Arts and Scis. Mem. Ch. of Christ. First woman to hit No. 1 on the country charts with "It Wasn't God Who Made Honky Tonk Angels." Office: 240 Old Hickory Blvd Madison TN 37115

WELLS, LEONARD NATHANIEL DAVID, JR., lawyer; b. Akron, Ohio, Aug. 24, 1914; s. Leonard Nathaniel David and Lida Holmes (Carr) W.; m. Louise Cauker, July 31, 1937; children—Leonard Nathaniel David III, Sarah Ann (Bennett), Lida Louise (Angione), Joe Cauker. B.A., Tex. Christian U., 1934; LL.B., Columbia U., 1937. Bar: Tex. 1937. Regional atty. for NLRB Ft. Worth, 1937-39, NLRB, St. Louis, 1939-41; sr. atty. NLRB, Washington, 1941-44; assoc. dir. field div. NLRB, 1944-46; founding ptnr. Mullinax, Wells, Baab & Cloutman (and predecessors), Dallas, 1947-89; gen. counsel Tex. State Fedn. Labor, 1947-57; counsel So. Conf. Teamsters, 1956-92; monitor Internat. Brotherhood Teamsters, 1958-59; bd. dirs. lawyers coordinating com. AFL-CIO, 1984-93. Trustee Gulf Coast Trades Ctr., 1990—. Mem. Am. Bar Assn. (mem. Ho. of Dels. 1959-60, chmn. labor law sect. 1954-55), Tex. State Bar (chmn. labor law sect. 1951-52). Democrat. Home: 7525 Fisher Rd Dallas TX 75214-2908 Office: 3301 Elm St Dallas TX 75226

WELLS, LESLEY BROOKS, judge; b. Muskegon, Mich., Oct. 6, 1937; d. James Franklin and Inez Simpson W.; m. Arthur V.N. Brooks, June 20, 1959; (div.); children: Lauren Elizabeth, Caryn Alison, Anne Kristin, Thomas Eliot. BA, Chatham Coll., Pitts., 1959; JD cum laude, Cleve. State U., 1974; cert. Nat. Jud. Coll., Reno, 1983, 85, 87, 89. Bar: Ohio 1975, U.S. Dist. Ct. (no. dist.) Ohio 1975. Pvt. practice, Cleve., 1975; ptnr. Brooks & Moffet, Cleve., 1975-79; dir., atty. ABAR Litigation Ctr., Cleve., 1979-80; assoc. Schneider, Smeltz, Huston & Ranney, Cleve., 1980-83; judge Ct. of Common Pleas Cleve., 1983-94; judge, U.S. District Ct. (no. Ohio)6th Cir., Cleveland, 1994—; adj. prof. law and urban policy Cleve. State U., 1979-82. Editor, author: Litigation Manual, 1980. Past pres. Cleve. Legal Aid Soc.; legal chmn. Nat. Women's Polit. Caucus, 1981-82; chmn. Gov.'s Task Force on Family Violence, Ohio, 1983-87; mem. biomedical ethics com. Case Western Res. U. Med. Sch., 1985-94; master Inns of Ct., 1989—, Northwest Ordinance U.S. Constitution Commn., Ohio, 1986-88; trustee Miami U., 1988-92, Urban League of Clevel., 1989-90, Rosemary Ctr., 1986-92, Chatham Coll., 1989-94. Recipient Disting. Alumna award Chatham Coll., 1988, Superior Jud. award Supreme Ct. of Ohio, 1983; J. Irwin award Womenspace, Ohio, 1984, award Womens City Club, 1985, Alumni Civic Achievement award Cleve. State U., 1992, Golden Gavel award Ohio Judges Assn., 1994, Outstanding Alumi award Cleve. Marshall Law Alumni Assn., 1994, Greater Cleve. Achievement award YWCA, 1995. Mem. ABA, Ohio Bar Assn., Cleve. Bar Assn. (Merit Svc. award 1983), Cuyahoga County Bar Assn., Nat. Assn. Women Judges, Philosophy Club. Office: US Courthouse 201 Superior Ave E Ste 338 Cleveland OH 44114-1201

WELLS, LINDA ANN, editor-in-chief; b. N.Y.C., Aug. 9, 1958; d. H. Wayne and Jean (Burchell) W.; m. Charles King Thompson, Nov., 1993. BA in English, Trinity Coll., 1980. Edit. asst. Vogue Mag., N.Y.C., 1980-83, assoc. editor beauty, 1983-85; style reporter New York Times, N.Y.C., 1985, beauty editor, food editor, 1985-90; founding editor, editor-in-chief Allure Mag., N.Y.C., 1990—; speaker Am. Womens' Econ. Devel., N.Y., 1988-89. Contbr. numerous articles to N.Y. Times Mag., Allure Mag., 1985—. Chmn. N.Y. Shakespeare Festival, 1993, 94. Recipient Fragrance Found. award, 1991, Nat. Mag. Design award, 1994, Legal Def. and Edn. Fund Equal Opportunity award NOW, 1994. Mem. Am. Soc. Mag. Editors (bd. dirs. 1993—). Office: Allure Mag Condé Nast Publs 360 Madison Ave New York NY 10017-3136

WELLS, LINTON, II, federal official; b. Luanda, Angola, Apr. 7, 1946; s. Linton and Helen Fay (Gillis) W.; m. Linda Marie Motta; children: Linton III, Frank. BS in Physics and Oceanography, U.S. Naval Acad., 1967; MSE in Math. Scis., PhD in Internat. Rels., Johns Hopkins U., 1975; student, Boueikeushusho (Japanese Nat. Def. Coll.), Tokyo. Commd. ensign USN, 1967; commdr. USS Joseph Strauss, 1984-86, Destroyer Squadron 21, 1989-91; advanced through grades to capt. USN, 1994, ret., 1994; asst. to under sec. for policy Dept. Def., The Pentagon, Washington, 1991-93, dept. to under sec. for policy, 1993—. Decorated Def. Superior Svc. medal, Legion of Merit (2), others; recipient C.N.G. Hendrix award for excellence in oceanography, 1967, Arleigh Burke Leadership award, 1975, Silver medal Naval Inst. Prize Essay Contest, 1985. Mem. Nat. Space Soc., Army and Navy Club, U.S. Naval Inst., Soc. Physics Students, Tau Beta Pi (hon.). Avocations: flying, scuba diving, reading, travel. Office: Dep to Under Sec Def for Policy The Pentagon Rm 2E812 Washington DC 20301-2200

WELLS, MARTHA JOHANNA, elementary education educator; b. Rock Springs, Wyo., Feb. 25, 1941; d. Harold Richard and Mae Amber Rose (Langmack) Frey; divorced; children: Timothy, Duane, Amber Jo Wells Sutter. BA, Wayne State, 1964. Cert. tchr. grades K-9. Kindergarten tchr. Cherokee (Iowa) Cmty. Schs., 1960-63, Harris-Lake Park (Iowa) Cmty. Schs., 1964-66, Norfolk (Nebr.) Cmty. Schs., 1966-68; sr. primary tchr. Emmetsburg (Iowa) Cmty. Schs., 1969-75, first grade tchr., 1975-82, kindergarten tchr., 1982-92, second grade tchr., 1992—; critical reader adv. bd. Perfection Form Co., Des Moines, 1985-86; team mem. for evaluation on Paulina (Iowa) Schs.-Dept. Edn., 1985; presenter in field. Vol. helper Party for John Glenn, Marcie Frevert's Home, Emmetsburg, 1983. Mem. Internat. Reading Assn., Iowa Reading Assn. (zone coord. 1983-93, dir. membership 1993—, hospitality chairperson regional conf. 1995—, Appreciation cert. 1993), Iowa State Edn. Assn. (team interviewer 1994), Emmetsburg Edn. Assn. (profl. rights and responsibilities com. 1992—), Palo Alto Clay Kossuth Reading Coun. (newspaper in edn. com. 1990-92), Meth. Women. Democrat. Avocations: golf, bridge, dance, walking, reading. Home: 1603 8th St Emmetsburg IA 50536-1442

WELLS, MERLE WILLIAM, historian, state archivist; b. Lethbridge, Alta., Can., Dec. 1, 1918; s. Norman Danby and Minnie Muir (Huckett) W.; student Boise Jr. Coll., 1937-39; A.B., Coll. Idaho, 1941, L.H.D. (hon.), 1981; M.A., U. Calif., 1947, Ph.D., 1950; L.H.D., U. Idaho, 1990. Instr. history Coll. Idaho, Caldwell, 1942-46; assoc. prof. history Alliance Coll., Cambridge Springs, Pa., 1950-56, 58, dean students, 1955-56; cons. historian Idaho Hist. Soc., Boise, 1956-58, historian and archivist, 1959—; hist. preservation officer, archivist State of Idaho, Boise, 1968-86. Treas., So. Idaho Migrant Ministry, 1960-64, chmn., 1964-67; nat. migrant adv. com. Nat. Council Chs., 1964-67, gen. bd. Idaho council, 1967-75; bd. dirs. Idaho State Employees Credit Union, 1964-67, treas., 1966-67; mem. Idaho Commn. Arts and Humanities, 1966-67; mem. Idaho Lewis and Clark Trail Commn., 1968-70, 84-88; mem. Idaho Bicentennial Commn., 1971-76; bd. dirs. Sawtooth Interpretive Assn., 1972—, dept. history United Presbyn. Ch., 1978-84; v.p. Idaho Zool. Soc., 1982-84, bd. dirs., 1984-94, treas., 1988-90, historian, 1990—. State Hist. Preservation Officers (dir. 1976-81, chmn. Western states council on geog. names 1982-83), Am. Hist. Assn., Western History Assn. (council 1973-76), AAUP, Am. Assn. State and Local History (council 1973-77), Soc. Am. Archivists, Assn. Idaho Historians (pres., 1994), others. Author: Anti-Mormonism in Idaho, 1978, Boise: An Illustrated History, 1982, Gold Camps and Silver Cities, 1984, Idaho: Gem of the Mountains, 1985. Office: Idaho State Hist Soc 210 Main St Boise ID 83702-7264 *Those of us in government positions need to focus upon helping people: when reviewing projects that may be harmful, we should help make them acceptable, rather than simply express opposition or reject them.*

WELLS, NORMAN, JR., metal products executive. BS metallurgy, indsl. engrng., U. Wash., 1971; MBA, Gonzaga U., 1980. With Castech Aluminum Group Inc., Akron, Ohio, 1989—. Office: Castech Aluminum Group Inc. 753 W Waterloo Rd Akron OH 44314

WELLS, RAYMOND O., JR., mathematics educator, researcher; b. Dallas, June 12, 1940; s. Raymond O. and Hazel (Rand) W.; m. Rena Schwarze, Aug. 1, 1963; children: Richard Andrew, René Michael. BA, Rice U., 1962; MS, NYU, 1964, PhD, 1965. Asst. prof. math. Rice U., Houston, 1965-69, assoc. prof., 1969-74, prof. math., 1974—, prof. edn., 1993—, chmn. dept. edn., 1994—, dir. sch. math. project, 1987—, dir. computational math. lab., 1990—, prof. edn., 1993—, chmn. dept. edn., 1994—; vis. asst. prof. Brandeis U., Waltham, Mass., 1967-68, U. Göttingen, Germany, 1974-75, U. Colo., Boulder, 1983-84; adj. prof. cmty. medicine Baylor Coll. Medicine, 1994—; active Inst. for Advanced Study, Princeton, N.J., 1970-71, 79-80; exch. visitor NAS, Sofia, Bulgaria, 1984. Author: Differential Analysis on Complex Manifolds, 1973, Mathematics in Civilization, 1973, Twister Geometry and Field Theory, 1990; editor: Mathematical Heritage of Herman Weyl, 1989; contbr. numerous articles to sci. jours. Pres. Stages Repertory Theater, Houston, 1989-90. Recipient Alexander von Humboldt Sr. U.S. Scientist award U. Göttingen, 1974-75; Fulbright fellow, 1968, Guggenheim fellow, 1974. Fellow AAAS (coun. 1989—), Aware, Inc.; mem. Am. Math. Soc. (coun., editor 1978-88), Cosmos Club Washington. Home: 5000 Montrose Blvd Apt 21B Houston TX 77006-6564 Office: Rice U Dept Math PO Box 1892 Houston TX 77251-1892

WELLS, RICHARD LEWIS, insurance company executive. Pres. Farmers Ins. Columbus, Columbus, Ohio. Office: Farmers Ins Columbus 2400 Farmers Dr Columbus OH 43235-2762*

WELLS, ROBERT STEVEN, law association executive; b. Pitts., July 7, 1951; s. Richard H. and Mary J. (Kimball) W. BS, Purdue U., 1972; JD, Ohio State U., 1976. Bar: Ohio 1977, U.S. Dist. Ct. (so. dist.) Ohio 1977, Ill. 1980, U.S. Dist. Ct. (no. dist.) Ill. 1981, U.S. Supreme Ct. 1983. Pvt. practice, Columbus, Ohio, 1977-78; rsch. counsel ABA Ctr. for Profl. Responsibility, Chgo., 1979-84, ethics counsel, 1985; exec. dir. S.C. Bar, 1985—. Editor: ABA/BNA Lawyers' Manual on Profl. Conduct, 1984, ABA Disciplinary Law and Procedure Rsch. System, 1979. Mem. S.C. Bar, Am. Judicature Soc., Nat. Assn. Bar Execs. (past chmn. long-range planning com., past chmn. bylaws com.). Office: SC Bar 950 Taylor St Columbia SC 29201-2745

WELLS, ROGER STANLEY, software engineer; b. Seattle, Apr. 13, 1949; s. Stanley A. and Margaret W. BA, Whitman Coll., 1971; postgrad., U. Tex., Austin, 1973-74; BS, Oreg. State U., 1977. Software evaluation engr. Tektronix, Beaverton, Oreg., 1979-83; computer engr. Aramco, Dhahran, Saudi Arabia, 1983-84; software engr. Conrac Corp., Clackamas, Oreg., 1984-85, Duarte, Calif., 1985; software analyst Lundy Fin. Systems, San Dimas, Calif., 1986-89; contract software analyst for various orgns. Seattle, 1989-92; software engr. U.S. Intelco, Olympia, Wash., 1993—. Bd. dirs. The Sci. Fiction Mus., Salem, Oreg., 1993—; co-founder, bd. dirs., pres. Oreg. Sci. Fiction Conv., 1979-81. Mem. IEEE, Am. Philatelic Soc., Am. Inst. Parliamentarians (chpt. v.p. 1996-97), Portland Sci. Fiction Soc., N.W. Sci. Fiction Soc., Internat. Platform Assn., Mensa, Assn. Computing Machinery, L.A. Sci. Fantasy Soc. Avocations: travel, public speaking, science fiction, stamp collecting. Home: 4820 Yelm Hwy SE Apt B-102 Lacey WA 98503

WELLS, SAMUEL ALONZO, JR., surgeon, educator; b. Cuthbert, Ga., Mar. 16, 1936; s. Samuel Alonzo and Martha (Steele) W.; m. Barbara Anne Atwood, Feb. 13, 1964; children: Sarah, Susan. Student, Emory U., 1954-57, M.D., 1961. Diplomate: Am. Bd. Surgery (bd. dirs., exec. com. 1986-89, vice chmn. 1987-88, chmn. 1988-89). Intern Johns Hopkins Hosp., Balt., 1961-62, resident in internal medicine, 1962-63; asst. resident in surgery Barnes Hosp., St. Louis, 1963-64; resident in surgery Duke U., Durham, N.C., 1966-70; guest investigator dept. tumor biology Karolinska Inst., Stockholm, 1967-68; asst. prof. surgery Duke U., Durham, N.C., 1970-72, assoc. prof., 1972-76, prof., 1976-81; clin. assoc. surgery br. Nat. Cancer Inst., NIH, Bethesda, Md., 1964-66, sr. investigator surgery br., 1970-72, cons. surgery br., 1975—; prof., chmn. dept. surgery Washington U., St. Louis, 1981—; dir. Duke U. Clin. Rsch. Ctr., 1978-81. Mem. editl. bd. Annals of Surgery, 1975-93, Surgery, 1975-93, Jour. Surg. Rsch., 1981-93; editor in chief World Jour. Surgery, 1983-92, Current Problems in Surgery, 1989—. Served to lt. comdr. USPHS, 1964-66. Mem. ACS (bd. regents 1989—, residency rev. com. for surgery 1987-93, chmn. 1991-93, vice chmn. 1995—; mem. editl. bd. Current Problems in Surgery 1988—, editor-in-chief 1989—), Am. Surg. Assn. (recorder, mem. coun. 1986-91, pres. 1995-96), Soc. Univ. Surgeons (exec. coun. 1976-78), Soc. Clin. Surgery (treas. 1980-86, v.p. 1986-88, pres. 1988-90), Am. Soc. Clin. Investigation, Inst. of Medicine of NAS, Am. Bd. Surgery (vice chmn. 1987-88, chmn. 1988-89), Nat. Cancer Adv. Bd., Halsted Soc. (pres. 1987), Soc. Surg. Oncology (pres. 1993-94), Alpha Omega Alpha. Home: 46 Westmoreland Pl Saint Louis MO 63108-1244 Office: Washington U Sch Medicine 660 S Euclid Ave Saint Louis MO 63110-1010

WELLS, SAMUEL FOGLE, JR., research center administrator; b. Mullins, S.C., Sept. 13, 1935; s. Samuel Fogle and Mildred Inez (Meeks) W.; m. Novella R. Cloninger, June 15, 1957 (div. 1969); children: Lauren, Anthony (dec.), Jeffrey (dec.); m. Sherrill Perkins Brown, June 7, 1969; 1 child, Christopher Wentworth. AB, U. N.C., 1957; MA, Harvard U., 1961, PhD, 1967. Instr. Wellesley (Mass.) Coll., 1963-65; asst. prof. U. N.C., Chapel Hill, 1965-70, assoc. prof., 1970-78; dir. internat. security studies program Woodrow Wilson Ctr., Washington, 1977-87, assoc. dir., 1985-88, dep. dir., 1988—; cons. Office of Sec. of Def., Washington, 1974-77; trustee Z. Smith Reynolds Found., Winston-Salem, 1977-83. Author: The Challenges of Power: American Diplomacy, 1900-1921, 1990; editor and contbr. to books: Economics and World Power: An Assessment of American Diplomacy Since 1789, 1984, Limiting Nuclear Proliferation, 1985, Strategic Defenses and Soviet-American Relations, 1987, Security in the Middle East: Regional Change and Great Power Strategies, 1987, Superpower Competition and Security in the Third World, 1988, The Helsinki Process and the Future of Europe, 1990, New European Orders, 1919 and 1991, 1996; contbr. articles to profl. jours. Capt. USMC, 1957-60. Woodrow Wilson fellow, 1957, Danforth Found. fellow, 1957, Peace fellow Hoover Instn., 1972-73, Woodrow Wilson Internat. Ctr. for Scholars fellow, 1976-77. Mem. Am. Hist. Assn., Internat. Inst. for Strategic Studies, Orgn. Am. Historians, Soc. for Historians of Am. Fgn. Rels., Internat. Studies Assn., Coun. on Fgn. Rels. Avocations: hiking, soccer. Home: 1509 Woodacre Dr Mc Lean VA 22101-2538 Office: Woodrow Wilson Internat Ctr 1000 Jefferson Dr SW Washington DC 20560

WELLS, SAMUEL JOSEPH, insurance company executive; b. Cass City, Mich., Aug. 12, 1946; s. Harold J. and Evelyn E. (Schmidt) W.; m. Leslie Ann Buhs, Dec. 26, 1970; children: Samuel Joseph, Dace Elyse. BS in Mktg., Ferris State U., 1970; postgrad., Am. Coll., 1980, Am. Coll., 1983. CLU, chartered fin. cons. Agt. Farm Bur. Ins. Mich., Cass City, 1970-72; agy. mgr. Farm Bur. Ins. Mich., Kalamazoo, 1972-75; dir. sales Farm Bur. Mktg. Mich., Adrian, 1975-76, dir. agys.; regional dir. agys. Vol. State Life, Adrian, 1982-84; v.p., gen. mgr. Farm Progress Ins. Co., Ill., 1984-88; pres. Allied Life Ins. Co., Des Moines, 1988-93, Allied Life Fin. Corp., Des Moines, 1993—. Officer Adrian Maples Rd Runner, 1983. Mem. Town Life Underwriters, Iowa Soc. CLUs, Sigma Phi Epsilon. Republican. Methodist. Home: 105 S 32nd St West Des Moines IA 50265-6410 Office: Allied Life Ins Co 701 5th Ave Des Moines IA 50309-1304

WELLS, THEODORE V., JR., lawyer; b. 1950. BA, Holy Cross, 1972; MBA, Harvard U., 1976; JD, Harvard Law Sch., 1976. Bar: N.J. 1977. Law clerk to Hon. John J Gibbons U.S. Ct. Appeals (3rd cir.), 1976-77; ptnr. Lowenstein, Sandler, Kohl, Fisher & Boylan P.C., Roseland, N.J.; mem. adj. faculty trade regulation Sch. Law, Seton Hall U., 1980-81; mem. faculty trial advocacy Practicing Law Inst., 1982—; mem. lawyers adv. com. U.S. Ct. Appeals (3rd cir.), 1982-85, 88—. Bd. trustees Coll. Holy Cross, 1977—, Newark Mus., 1979-82; bd. dirs. Essex County Urban League, 1979-88. Mem. ABA (antitrust law sect., state antitrust law subcom. 1980—), Assn. Crimiunal Def. Lawyers (trustee 1984—), N.J. State Bar Assn. (antitrust law com. 1980—). Office: Lowenstein Sandler Kohl Fisher & Boylan 65 Livingston Ave Roseland NJ 07068-1725*

WELLS, THOMAS B., federal judge; b. 1945. BS, Miami U., 1967; JD, Emory U., 1973; LLM, NYU, 1978. Atty. Graham & Wells, Vidalia, Ga., Hurt, Richardson, Garner, Todd & Cadenhead, Vidalia, Ga., Shearer & Wells, Vidalia, Ga.; city atty. City of Vidalia; county atty. Toombs County, Ga.; judge U.S. Tax Ct., Washington, 1986—. With USNR, 1970. Mem. ABA. Office: US Tax Ct 400 2nd St NW Washington DC 20217-0001*

WELLS, VICTOR HUGH, JR., advertising agency executive; b. Bloomington, Ill., Apr. 19, 1924; s. Victor Hugh and Wilma Julia (Codlin) W.; m. Jacqueline L. Wade, Nov. 25, 1949; children—Victor Hugh, III, Polly Jo, Ken Douglas. B.S., Bradley U., 1948. Copywriter Chgo. Tribune, 1949-54; copywriter Earle Ludgin & Co., Chgo., 1954-58, creative dir., 1959-64; group creative dir. Tatham-Laird, Chgo., 1958-59; founder, creative dir., pres. Rink Wells & Assos. (advt. agy.), Chgo., 1964-72; exec. v.p., dir. creative services N.W. Ayer Inc., Chgo., 1972-84; exec. v.p., dir. creative services N.W. Ayer Inc., N.Y.C., 1984-86, also bd. dirs.; cons. N. W. Ayer Inc., N.Y.C., 1986—. Served to 2d lt. AC U.S. Army, 1943-45. Recipient various advt. creative awards, including Clio, Andy awards. Office: One Worldwide Plaza 825 8th Ave New York NY 10019-7416

WELLS, WALTER E., prefabricated housing manufacturing executive; b. 1936. Exec. v.p. Schult Homes Corp., Middlebury, Ind., 1970-72, pres., 1972-84, CEO,dir., 1984—. Office: Schult Homes Corp 221 Us Highway 20 Middlebury IN 46540-9713*

WELLS-CARR, ELIZABETH ANTOINETTE, educational leadership trainer; b. Taft, Okla., Aug. 23, 1930; d. Horace Charlie and Daisy Magnolia (Smith) Wells; m. Columbus Carr, Dec. 13, 1953; children: Lisa Michelle, Kimberly, Trudy Eleane. BA, Oklahoma U., 1951; specialist credential, Calif. State U., San Francisco, 1976, MS in Secondary Edn., Edn. Adminstrn., 1977, '78; grad. supt.'s acad., Trinity U., 1984; postgrad., U. San Francisco, 1978-83; PhD, Calif. Coast U., 1991. Tchr. Richmond (Calif.) Unified Sch. Dist., 1964-69, tchr., acting counselor, adminstrv. curriculum designer, dept. head, 1969-79; regional dir. for right-to-read program Calif. Dept. Edn., Sacramento, 1976-77; prin. and adminstrv. vice prin. Southwood Jr. High Sch., 1978-81; prin. Am. Inst. Foreign Study, 1981-85; acting prin. and admistrv. vice prin. Oroville (Calif.) High Sch.; prin. Biggs Jr., Sr. High Sch., 1985-89; programs cons. Calif. Dept. Edn., 1989-91; trainer Calif. Sch. Leadership Acad., Sacramento, 1989-91; dir. new products devel. Josten's Learning Corp., San Diego, 1991-93; cons. pvt. practice, San Diego; owner, trainer, cons. Visions of Success; mem. Ethnic Adv. Bd. U. Chico (Calif.), 1985-88, Tchr. Prep. Adv. Bd., U. Calif., Davis, 1988-91; assoc. prof. Butte (Calif.) C.C., 1989; liaison officer Calif. Dept. Edn., 1989—. Calif. del. Nat. Dem. Conv., 1992; chmn. Third Assembly Dist. Dem. Orgn., 1992;. Recipient Martin Luther King Jr. award Butte C.C. Black Student Union, 1985; named Outstanding Reading Specialist of Yr., Calif. Dept. Edn., 1957, Outstanding Adminstr. of Year, S. San Francisco, PTA Coun., 1979, Tchrs. Assn. S. San Francisco, 1980, Grand Nat. Speaker, Bus. and Profl. Women, 1983, Outstanding Speaker, 1985, Outstanding Prin., Lions Club Internat., 1986, Calif. Gold Star Adminstr., 1989; nominee for Reader's Digest Am. Heroes award, 1988, and others. Mem. Nat. Assn. Sch. Adminstrs., Nat. Assn. Black Sch. Educators, Bus. and Profl. Women, Calif. Women in Agrl., Concow Grange 735, Sacramento Alliance of Black Scholars, Host Internat., Nat. Coun. of Negro Women, Project Literacy, Pi Lambda Theta, Phi Delta Kappa, Delta Sigma Theta and others. Presbyterian. Avocations: research, story writing, reading, travel.

WELLSTONE, PAUL, senator; b. Washington, July 21, 1944; s. Leon and Minnie W.; m. Sheila Wellstone, 1963; children: David, Marcia, Mark. BA, U. N.C., 1965, PhD Polit. Sci., 1969. Tchr. Carleton Coll., Minn.; U.S. senator from Minn., 1991—, mem. coms. on small bus., energy and natural resources, Indian affairs, labor and human resources, sen. dem. policy com., chmn. subcom. rural economy and family farming. Author: How the Rural Poor Got Power, Powerline. Dir. Minn. Community Energy Program. Office: US Senate 717 Hart Senate Office Bldg Washington DC 20510*

WELNA, CECILIA, mathematics educator; b. New Britain, Conn., July 15; d. Joseph and Sophie (Roman) W. B.S., St. Joseph Coll., 1949; M.A., U. Conn., 1952, Ph.D., 1960. Instr. Mt. St. Joseph Acad., 1949-50; asst. instr. U. Conn., 1950-55; instr. U. Mass., Amherst, 1955-56; prof., chmn. dept. math. and physics U. Hartford, 1957-82, dean Coll. Edn., Nursing and Health Professions, 1982-91, prof. math., 1991—. Mem. Math. Assn. Am., Nat. Council Tchrs. Math., Assn. Tchrs. Math. Conn., Sigma Xi. Office: U Hartford Dana 295A Bloomfield Ave West Hartford CT 06117

WELNETZ, DAVID CHARLES, human resources executive; b. Antigo, Wis., Apr. 12, 1947; s. Francis P. and Marquette A. (Stengl) W.; m. Mary L. McCulley, Aug. 25, 1973; children: Andrew, Timothy. BS in Biology, U. Wis., Stevens Point, Wis., 1969; MS in Indsl. Rels., U. Wis. Madison, 1975. Mgr. coll. recruitment tng. Rexnord Inc., Milw., 1975-77; personnel mgr. Rexnord Inc., Sarasota, Fla., 1977-80; corp. dir. employee rels. Rexnord Inc., Milw., 1980-83; sr. cons. The Thompson Group, Brookfield, Wis., 1983-87; v.p. The Thompson Group, Brookfield, 1987-91; pres. Thompson Cons., Brookfield, 1991—; adv. bd. SUNY, Buffalo, 1982-88; bd. dirs. Matarah Industries. Mem. adv. bd. Am. Cancer Soc., 1994—; bd. dirs. Matarah Ind., 1994—, Lutheran Social Svcs., Milw. Ctr. for Independence. Recipient Bronze Star U.S. Army, 1972. Mem. Pers. Indsl. Rels. Assn. (program com. 1988-91, chmn. pers. rsch. 1980-82), Human Resources Planning Soc., Human Resources Mgmt. Assn. Roman Catholic. Home: 1918 Forest St Wauwatosa WI 53213-2153 Office: Thompson Cons Ltd 17700 W Capitol Dr Brookfield WI 53045-2006

WELPOTT, JACK WARREN, photographer, educator; b. Kansas City, Kans., Apr. 27, 1923; s. Ray Calvert and Dolores (Davenroy) W.; m. Doris Jean Franklin, June 12, 1949; children—Jan Marie, Matthew David; m. Judy Dater, May 22, 1969; m. Wendy Brooke Gray, May 11, 1986. B.S., Ind. U., 1949, M.S., 1954, M.F.A., 1959. Mem. acad. staff Ind. U., 1949-59; mem. faculty San Francisco State U., 1959-93, ret., 1993; artist in residence RISD, 1984; workshop leader Columbia Coll., 1985, Friends of Photo, 1985, Humboldt State U., 1985, Parsons Sch. Design, Paris, 1985, Volcano Hawaii, 1986, numerous others in France, England, Switzerland, Japan and Mexico. One man shows include, U. Calif., Davis, Art Inst. Chgo., 1972, Wall Street Gallery, Spokane, 1973, Gallery 113, Santa Cruz, Calif., 1974, San Francisco Mus. Art, 25 year retrospective, 1976, U. So. Calif., 25 year retrospective, 1977, Ind. U., 25 year retrospective, 1977, Silver Image Gallery, Seattle, 1977, Ohio State U., 1978, Center for Creative Photography, U. Ariz., 1979, Colo. Mountain Coll., 1980, Bard Coll., 1981, Jehu Gallery, San Francisco, 1981, Galerif Voor Fotografie, Antwerp, Belgium, 1983, R.I. Sch. Design, 1984, La Photographie Creative, Pavillon des Arts, Paris, 1984, New Sch.

Social Research, N.Y.C., 1984, Foto Biennale Enschede, Netherlands, 1984, Vision Gallery, San Francisco, 1984, Min Gallery, Tokyo, 1987, Osaka (Japan) Cultrual Ctr., 1989, Retrospective Vision Gallery, San Francisco, 1992; two man shows include Musee Reattu, Arles, France, 1976, Photographers Gallery, Palo Alto, Calif., 1986, group exhbns. include Santa Barbara Mus., Mus. Modern Art, Mexico City, Photography in Am, Whitney Mus., N.Y.C., Photography in the 20th Century, George Eastman House, California Photography, Oakland Mus., San Francisco Mus. Art, U. Oreg. Commitment to Vision, 1986, U. Colo. Photographics, 1986, numerous others, Met. Mus. Art, N.Y.C., De Cordova Mus., Lincoln, Mass.; represented in permanent collections Graham Nash Collection, Mus. Modern Art, N.Y.C., Whitney Mus. Art, N.Y.C., Art Inst. Chgo., Biblioteque Nat, Paris, Tokyo Coll. Photography, Open U., London, Internat. Mus. Photography, Rochester, N.Y., San Francisco Mus. Art, Musee Reattu, Arles, Frances, Oakland (Calif.) Mus., U. Colo., Center Creative Photography, Tucson, U. N.Mex., Pasadena Art Mus., Australian Nat. Gallery, Houston Mus. Fine Arts, Fogg Art Mus., Cambridge, Mass., Gallery Van Haarlem, Netherlands; author: The Halide Conversion, 1989; contbr. photos to books. Served with USAAF, 1943-46. NEA fellow, 1979; grantee Polaroid, 1983, Marin Arts Coun., 1991. Home: PO Box 496 Inverness CA 94937-0496

WELSCH, GLENN ALBERT, accounting educator; b. Woodward, Okla., Apr. 1, 1915; s. George Franklin and Minnie Melissa (Bowers) W.; m. Irma Richards, Apr. 5, 1942; children: Glenn Andrew, Linden Richards, Mary Ann Welsch Williamson. B.S., Northwestern State Coll., Alva, Okla., 1935; grad., Army Staff and Command Sch., 1943; M.S., Okla. State U., 1949; Ph.D., U. Tex., 1952. CPA, Okla., Tex. Comml. tchr. pub. high sch. Alva, Okla., 1937-40; mem. faculty Coll. Bus. Adminstrn., U. Tex., 1952-85, prof. acctg., 1956-85, chmn. dept., 1959-62, assoc. dean grad. studies, 1962-67, John Arch White prof. acctg., 1968-78, Peat, Marwick, Mitchell prof. acctg., 1978-83, Bayless chair in free enterprise, 1984-85, Bayless chair emeritus, 1985—; instr. Exec. Devel. Program, 1956-72; vis. prof. Carman G. Blough Disting. prof. U. Va., 1970-71; Prickett Disting. vis. prof. Ind. U., 1975; cons. various companies on fin. acctg. and profit planning and control; expert witness. Author: (with Ronald W. Hilton and Paul Gordon) Budgeting: Profit Planning and Control, 5th edit., 1988, (with B.H. Sord) Business Budgeting: A Survey of Management Planning and Control Practices, 1958, (with C.T. Zlatkovich) Intermediate Accounting, 8th edit., 1989, (with C.H. Griffin and T.H. Williams) Advanced Accounting, 1966, (with Daniel G. Short) Fundamentals of Financial Accounting, 6th edit., 1987, (with R.N. Anthony) Fundamentals of Management Accounting, 4th edit., 1984. Served to maj. AUS, 1940-46. Recipient numerous awards for teaching excellence and service to acctg. profession, including Outstanding Educators award Amn. Acctg. Assn., 1985; named to Hall of Fame, Coll. and Grad. Coll. of Bus. Adminstrn., U. Tex., 1988. Mem. Tex. Soc. CPA's (v.p. 1959-60), Am. Acctg. Assn. (pres. 1963), Am. Inst. CPA's (council 1968-73, acctg. prins. bd. 1970-73), Nat. Assn. Accts., Fin. Execs. Inst., Planning Execs. Inst., Beta Alpha Psi, Beta Gamma Sigma. Home: 3405 Taylors Dr Austin TX 78703-1047

WELSCH, JAMES LESTER, municipal judge; b. Catskill, N.Y., Oct. 2, 1917; s. Wolfgang Frederick and Hazel Juene (Lester) W.; m. Rosemary Hopkins, June 6, 1995. BS, Purdue U., 1942; MA, L.A. State Coll., 1954; PhD Golden State U., 1957; grad., Nat. Jud. Coll., 1985. Lic. ednl. adminstr., N. Mex., Ariz., Colo. real estate broker, N.Mex. Pers. mgr., safety dir. Nat. Cash Register Co. electronics div., Hawthorne, Calif., 1952-55; dir. indsl. rels., safety dir. Mercast Mfg. Corp., LaVerne, Calif., 1955-57; asst. prof. mgmt. Eastern N.Mex. U., Portales, 1957-58; asst. prof. indsl. mgmt. Calif. Western U., San Diego, 1958-63; dir. Montelores Multicultural Ctr., Cortez, Colo., 1967-68; chmn. Assn. Dirs. Colo. Bds. Cooperative Svcs., 1968; guidance counselor Dzilth-Na-o-dith-hle Sch., Bur. Indian Affairs, Bloomfield, N.Mex., 1974-76, supervisory guidance counselor, Huerfano, N.Mex., 1976-80, realty specialist, rights protection Bur. Indian. Affairs, Juneau, Alaska, 1980, supervisory realty specialist, safety mgr. Alaska Native Claims Settlement Act, Anchorage, 1981-83; ret., 1983; mcpl. judge, Bloomfield, N.Mex., 1983—. Chmn. San Juan County (N.Mex.) planning and zoning commn., 1973; bd. dirs. San Juan County Mus. Assn., 1978-79, San Juan County chpt. ARC, 1980, dir. of bd., 1987-88; bd. dirs. Salvation Army Bd., 1987-88, Anasazi Pageant Found., 1988—; chmn. Bloomfield Pride Commn., 1988—; mem. House Arrest and Intensive Supervision, 1987-88; del. N.Mex., State Republican Conv., 1974, 76; sustaining mem. Rep. Nat. Com.; bd. dirs. Farmington Conv. and Visitors Bur., 1988—, N.Mex. Supreme Ct. Jud. Edn. and Tng. Adv. Com., 1991—; mem. World Safety Orgn., 1990—; mem. San Juan County Juvenile Cmty. Corrections Local Selection Panel, 1994. Served to lt. USN, 1942-46, WWII; Korean War, 1951-52; ret. USNR, 1960. Recipient Cert. of Award, U.S. Coast Guard, 1971, Outstanding Achievement and Exceptional Accomplishment award N.Mex1 Legislature, 1990; named adm. Tex. Navy, Citizen of Yr., 1990, Man of the YearAm. Bio. Inst., 1992. Mem. Am. Judges Assn., Nat. Judges Assn. (chaplain 1987—, named Outstanding Non-Atty. Judge of the U.S., Kenneth L. MacEachern Meml. award, 1993), Am. Soc. Safety Engrs., N.Mex. Mcpl. Judges Assn. (pres. 1988-89),, Bloomfield C. of c. (pres. 1987-88), Phi Delta Kappa (pres. Mesa Verde, Colo. chpt., 1979), Am. Legion, VFW, Disabled Am. Vets., Elks (disting. Elk award, 1995), Masons, Red Cross Constantine, Nat. Sojourners, KYCH, Lambda Chi Alpha. Office: 915 N 1st St Bloomfield NM 87413-5221

WELSCH, ROY ELMER, statistician; b. Kansas City, Mo., July 31, 1943. AB, Princeton U., 1965; MS, Stanford U., 1966, PhD in math., 1969. Dir. Stats Ctr. MIT, Cambridge, Mass., asst. prof. ops. rsch. Sloan Sch. Mgmt., 1969-73, assoc. prof., 1973-79, prof. mgmt. sci. and stats., 1979—. Assoc. editor: Jour. Am. Statist. Assn. Fellow Am. Statis. Assn., Inst. Math. Stats. Office: MIT Stats Ctr E40-111 77 Massachusetts Ave Cambridge MA 02139-4301 Office: MIT Dept Mgmt & Stats 77 Massachusetts Ave Cambridge MA 02139*

WELSH, ALFRED JOHN, lawyer, consultant; b. Louisville, May 10, 1947; s. Elvin Alfred and Carol (Kleymeyer) W.; m. Lee Mitchell, Aug. 1, 1970; children: Charles Kleymeyer, Kathryn Thomas. BA, Centre Coll., 1969; JD, U. Ky., 1972; LLM in Internat. Law cum laude, U. Brussels, 1973. Bar: Ky. 1972, U.S. Dist. Ct. (we. and ea. dists.) Ky. 1972, U.S. Ct. Appeals (6th cir.) 1972. Atty. Ky. Atty. Gen. Office, Frankfort, 1973-74; legis. counsel to congressman Ho. of Reps., Washington, 1974-77; mng. ptnr. Nicolas Welsh Brooks & Hayward, Louisville, 1977—, Boone Welsh Brooks and Hayward Internat. Law; hon. counsel of Belgium, 1983—; econ. devel. advisor Kimgdom of Belgium; mem. Ky. Econ. Adv. Coun.; pres. Transcontinental Trading Cons., Ltd.; participant in North African Mideast Econ. Summit Conf., Morocco, 1994. Bd. dirs. Greater Louisville Swim Found., 1983—, Louisville com. Coun. Fgn. Rels., 1983—, Jefferson County Alcohol and Drug Abuse Found., Louisville, 1986—. Decorated knight Order of the Crown (Belgium). Mem. ABA (internat. law sect., commn. on impairment), Ky. Bar Assn. (bd. dirs. 1981-82, pres. young lawyers divsn. 1981-82), Am. Judicature Soc., Louisville C. of C. Democrat. Presbyterian. Avocations: swimming, water polo, soccer. Office: Barristers Hall 1009 S 4th St Louisville KY 40203-3207

WELSH, DENNIE M., business machines company executive. Gen. mgr. industry solutions IBM Corp., White Plains, N.Y. Office: IBM Corp 44 S Broadway White Plains NY 10601-4411*

WELSH, DONALD EMORY, publisher; b. Youngstown, Ohio, Oct. 6, 1943; s. Edward Francis and Clevelle Rose W.; m. Elizabeth Bourne Floyd, June 25, 1966; children: Leah Bourne, Emory Philip. A.B., Columbia U., 1965; J.D., Cleveland Marshall Sch. Law, 1969. Bar: Ohio 1969. Trust devel. officer Cleve. Trust Co., 1968-70; advt. sales rep. Fortune mag., Time, Inc., N.Y.C., 1970-75; advt. dir. Rolling Stone mag., N.Y.C., 1975-77; v.p., assoc. pub. Rolling Stone mag., 1977-78; pub. Outside mag., N.Y.C., 1978-82; pub. Muppet mag. and pres. Lorimar Pub. Group (formerly Telepictures Publs., Inc.), 1982-87; pres. Welsh Pub. Group, Inc., 1987-94; exec. v.p. Marvel Comics Group, N.Y.C., 1994—. Trustee Outward Bound, U.S.A.; bd. dirs. Big Apple Circus. Mem. ABA, Mag. Pubs. Assn. (past bd. dirs.), Ohio Bar Assn., Cleve. Bar Assn., Century Assn., Racquet and Tennis Club, Sharon Country Club (Conn.), Ocean Reef Club (Fla.). Home: 501 E 79th St New York NY 10021-0735 Office: Marvel Comics Group 387 Park Ave S New York NY 10016

WELSH, JOHN RICHARD, state official; b. Neillsville, Wis., May 27, 1938; s. Francis Richard and Bernice Margaret (Schneider) W.; m. Carol Kay Ableidinger, Sept. 30, 1961; children: Tony, Becky, Cathy, Michael, Chelley. BBA, Loyola U., Chgo., 1977; postgrad., No. Ariz. State U. Benefit mgr. George F. Brown & Sons, Chgo., 1968-69, Marsh & McLennon, Chgo., 1969-71; adminstrv. mgr. Kemper Ins. Group, Long Grove, Ill., 1971-73; benefits mgr. 1st Nat. Bank of Chgo., 1973-79, The Arizona Bank, Phoenix, 1979-81; cons. Phoenix, 1981-84; benefits mgr., arbitrator Frontier Airlines, Inc., Denver, 1984-85; benefits mgr. Dept. Adminstrn., State of Ariz., Phoenix, 1985-91; retirement officer, seminar facilitator Ariz. State Retirement Sys., Phoenix, 1991—; team leader, benefits adv. Total Quality Mgmt. Ariz. State Retirement System, Phoenix, 1995. High sch. football ofcl. Ariz. Interscholastic Assn., Phoenix, 1980-93; football coach Portage Park Sports, Chgo., 1969-79, baseball coach, 1969-79; basketball coach K.C., Durand, Wis., 1966-68. With USN, 1956-59. Mem. Nat. Assn. for Pre-Retirement Edn., Loyola U. Alumni Assn. (Phoenix chpt.). Roman Catholic. Avocations: golf, snow skiing, reading, walking, swimming. Home: 4141 W Hayward Ave Phoenix AZ 85051-5751 Office: Ariz State Retirement Sys 3300 N Central Ave Phoenix AZ 85012-2501

WELSH, JOHN ROBERT, musician; b. Seward, Nebr., Oct. 27, 1924; s. Frank Harrison and Ethel Mae (Steele) W.; children: Maxine, Fred, John, Richard. MMus, Cin. Conservatory of Music, 1946. Ptnr. Welsh, Hamilton & Ford, Deerfield, Ill., 1954-58; owner Hampshire House Gallery, Muskegon, Mich., 1976-89; ret., 1989; ednl. clinician Orff-Kodaly, 1975—. Author: Making Music at the Keyboard, 1979. Dir. Port City Playhouse, Muskegon, 1979-83. With U.S. Army, 1941-42. Democrat. Episcopalian. Avocations: music, antiques. Home: 487 W Webster Ave Muskegon MI 49440-1047

WELSH, KELLY RAYMOND, lawyer, telecommunications company executive; b. Chgo., July 6, 1952; s. Raymond J. and Mary Jane (Kelly) W.; m. Ellen S. Alberding, June 28, 1985; children: Katherine A., Julia S. AB cum laude, Harvard U., 1974, JD magna cum laude, 1978; MA, Sussex U., Eng., 1975. Assoc. Mayer, Brown & Platt, Chgo., 1979-85, ptnr., 1985-89; corp. counsel City of Chgo., 1989-93; v.p., assoc. gen. counsel Ameritech Corp., Chgo., 1993—. Chmn. Met. Pier and Exposition Authority, Chgo., 1994—. Mem. Chgo. Bar Assn., Chgo. Coun. Lawyers, Chgo. Coun. Fgn. Rels. (mem. Chgo. com.), Legal Club Chgo. Office: Ameritech Corp 30 S Wacker Dr 39th fl Chicago IL 60606

WELSH, MICHAEL L., business executive; b. Clayton, Ga., June 14, 1959; s. John F. and Mary Ann (Casimes) W.; m. Susie Googe, June 5, 1982; children: Sarah Alex, Daniel. BBA magna cum laude, U. Ga., 1981, MACC, 1986. Consolidation acct. Tex. Instruments, Dallas, 1981-82, fin. analyst, 1982-84; v.p. cons. MISA, Atlanta, 1986-87; consolidation analyst Coca-Cola Enterprise, Atlanta, 1987-88; mid-Atlantic supr., mgr. Coca-Cola Bottling Co., Columbia, Md., 1988-90; div. mgr. Coca-Cola Enterprises-North, Columbia, 1990-91; ops. contr. Cott Beverages USA, Columbus, Ga., 1993-95; v.p. adminstrn. Thompson Hardwoods, Inc., Hazlehurst, Ga., 1995—, v.p., adminstrn., 1995—; acctg. and system implementation cons., Dallas and Athens, Ga., 1982-86. Youth leader Ascension Ch., Dallas, 1982-83, St. Michael's Ch., Stone Mountain, Ga., 1986-88, St. John's Episc. Ch., Ellicott City, Md., 1988-91. Mem. Internat. Platform Assn., U. Ga. Alumni Soc. (pres. Dallas chpt. 1983-84), Blue Key, Golden Key, Phi Kappa Phi, Beta Gamma Sigma, Phi Eta Sigma, Beta Alpha Psi, Phi Kappa Psi. Baptist. Avocations: sports, reading, rapelling. Home: PO Box 1067 Hazlehurst GA 31539 Office: Thompson Hardwoods Inc PO Box 646 Hazlehurst GA 31539

WELSH, PETER CORBETT, museum consultant, historian; b. Washington, Aug. 28, 1926; s. Arthur Brinkley and Susan Jane (Putney) W.; m. Catherine Beatrice Allen, Nov. 27, 1951 (div. 1969); children—Susan Jane, Peter Corbett; m. Caroline Levert Mastin, Sept. 8, 1970; 1 child, James Munson Corbett. BA, Mt. Union Coll., Alliance, Ohio, 1950; postgrad., U. Va., 1950-51; M.A. (Hagley fellow), U. Del., 1956. Research asst., fellowship coordinator Eleutherian Mills-Hagley Found., Wilmington, Del., 1956-59; assoc. curator dept. civil history Mus. History and Tech., Smithsonian Instn., 1959-61; curator Growth U.S., 1962-64, curator dept. civil history, 1964-69, asst. dir. gen. mus. of instn., 1969-70, dir. Office Mus. Programs, 1970-71; dir. N.Y. State Hist. Assn., Cooperstown, 1971-74; vis. prof. Cooperstown Grad. Program, N.Y. State Hist. Assn.; dir. Cooperstown Grad. Programs, 1971-74; dir. spl. projects N.Y. State Mus., Albany, 1975-76; dir. Bur. Mus., Pa. Hist. and Mus. Commn., 1976-84; pres. The Welsh Group, 1984-86; curator The Adirondack Mus., Blue Mountain Lake, N.Y., 1986-88, sr. historian, 1988-89; mus. cons., lectr., 1989—; adj. prof. SUNY; cons. FDR Mus. and Little White House, Warm Springs, Ga., 1968-72; trustee Landon Sch., Bethesda, Md., 1964-70; bd. dirs., mem. exec. com. Ctr. for Conservation of Hist. Art and Artifacts, 1979-83; bd. dirs. Lake Placid Ctr. for the Arts, 1992-96. Author: Tanning in the United States: A Brief History, 1964, American Folk Art: The Art and Spirit of the People, 1967, Track and Road: The American Trotting Horse, 1820-1990, 1968, The Art of Enterprise: A Pennsylvania Tradition, 1983, Jacks, Jobbers and Kings: Logging the Adirondacks, 1850-1950, 1996; contbr. articles to profl. publs.; editor Smithsonian Jour. History, 1967-70. Served to 1st lt. AUS, 1951-54. Mem. Am. Hist. Assn., Am. Studies Assn., Am. Assn. Mus., N.Y. State Assn. Mus. (council 1971-75), Am. Assn. State and Local History (publ. com.), Soc. History of Tech., Sigma Nu. Democrat. Roman Catholic. Club: Country of Harrisburg. Office: 34 2nd St Tupper Lake NY 12986-2011

WELSH, ROBERT K., relgious organization executive. Pres. Ch. Fin. Coun. Office: Ch Fin Coun PO Box 1986 Indianapolis IN 46206

WELSH, RONALD ARTHUR, physician, educator; b. Houston, Oct. 13, 1926; s. Leo Arthur and Octavia Virginia (Franssen) W.; m. Mary Jeanne Duncan, June 24, 1950; children: Mary Jeanne, William, James. A.B., U. Tex., 1947, M.D., 1950. Intern USPHS, Hosp., New Orleans, 1950-51; resident in pathology USPHS, Balt., 1951-55; chief pathology USPHS Hosp., Galveston, Tex., 1955-57; asst. prof. pathology L. Tex. Med. Br., Galveston, 1955-57, La. State U., New Orleans, 1957-59; asso. prof. La. State U., 1959-61, prof., 1961—; chief surg. pathology Charity Hosp., New Orleans, 1975-93; cons. forensic pathology Orleans Parish Coroner, 1961-79; cons. path. Va. Hosp., New Orleans, 1971—; Mem. La. Commn. on Narcotics and Rehab., 1970-72; Bd. dirs. La. div. Am. Cancer Soc., 1960-89, La. div. Am. Cancer Soc. (nat. div.), 1966-68, nat. del. dir., 1980-86. Served with USNR, 1944-46; Served with USPHS, 1950-57. Recipient Distinguished Prof. award La. State U. Alumni Assn., 1973-74, Asclepian award Am. Cancer Soc., New Orleans unit, 1992. Mem. AMA, Internat. Acad. Pathology, Am. Soc. Clin. Pathologists, Coll. Am. Pathologists, Assn. Pathologists, La., Orleans Parish med. socs., Phi Beta Kappa, Alpha Omega Alpha, Nu Sigma Nu. Republican. Episcopalian. Home: 2429 Octavia St New Orleans LA 70115-6533 Office: 1901 Perdido St New Orleans LA 70112-1328

WELSH, STACEY LAU, investment banker; b. Honolulu, Nov. 30, 1960; d. Timothy Shao Yu and Violet Yuk Kung (Lee) Lau; m. John Anthony Welsh, May 15, 1993. BS, San Francisco State U., 1984; MBA, U. Chgo., 1989. CPA, Calif. Office mgr. Markle, Stuckey, Clark & Co., San Francisco, 1982-84, acct., 1984-87; v.p. Citicorp Securities, Inc., N.Y.C., 1989—; pres. Capajava, Stamford, Conn., 1992-94. Sponsor, Student/Sponsor Partnership, N.Y.C., 1990-94. Avocations: entrepreneurial ventures, golf, skiing. Home: 170 East 87th St New York NY 10128 Office: Citicorp Securities Inc 599 Lexington Ave Fl 26 New York NY 10022-4614

WELSH, THOMAS J., bishop; b. Weatherly, Pa., Dec. 20, 1921. Grad., St. Charles Borromeo Sem., Phila., Cath. U. Am. Ordained priest Roman Cath. Ch., 1946. Ordained titular bishop of Scattery Island and aux. bishop of Phila., 1970-74; 1st bishop of Arlington Va., 1974-83; bishop of Allentown Pa., 1983—. Office: Bishop of Allentown PO Box F 202 N 17th St Allentown PA 18105*

WELSHANS, MERLE TALMADGE, management consultant; b. Murphysboro, Ill., June 17, 1918; s. Arthur Isaac and Martha Ellen (Blair) W.; B.Ed., So. Ill. U., 1940; M.A., Washington U., St. Louis, 1947, Ph.D., 1951; m. Mary Katherine Whitenbaugh, June 2, 1942; children: Elizabeth Margaret Van Steenbergh, Arthur Edmund, Janice Ann. Asst. v.p. Merc. Mortgage Co., Olney, Ill., 1940; exec. officer, dept. bus. adminstrn. George Washington U., 1950-54; prof. fin. Grad. Sch. Bus. Adminstrn., Washington U., 1954-69; v.p. fin. Union Electric Co., St. Louis, 1969-83; mgmt. cons., 1983—; dir. Prudential Mutual Funds, Hotchkis & Wiley Funds. Trustee United Meth. Found. Served to capt. U.S. Army, 1942-45. Decorated Bronze Star medal. Mem. Fin. Mgmt. Assn. (dir.), Am. Econ. Assn., Am. Fin. Assn., Am. Soc. Fin. Analysis, Fin. Analysts Assn. St. Louis (trustee), Alpha Kappa Phi, Beta Gamma Sigma, Artus. Methodist. Author: (with R.W. Melicher) Finance, 8th edit., 1992; cons. economist, editor Fin. Newsletter, 1965-69. Address: 14360 Ladue Rd Chesterfield MO 63017-2524

WELSHIMER, GWEN R., state legislator, real estate broker, appraiser, tax consultant; b. Poughkeepsie, N.Y., Nov. 5, 1935; d. Freanor Ralph and Beulah M. (Reedy) Grant; m. Billy L. Blake (div. 1979); children: Donald E., Jerry A.; m. Robert E. Welshimer. Student, Kans. State U., 1953-54; cert., Jones Real Estate Coll., Colorado Springs, Colo., 1975. Cert. real estate appraiser, 1993. Exec. sec. Coll. Bd. Trustees, Bellevue, Wash., 1967-69; exec. sec. to chmn. bd. dirs. Garvey Industries, Wichita, Kans., 1969-73, adminstrv. asst. pers. and pub. affairs, 1969-73; copywriter Walter Drake & Sons, Colorado Springs, 1973-75; real estate agt. UTE Realty, Colorado Springs, 1975-76; newspaper pub., owner Black Forrest News, Colorado Springs, 1976-79; real estate broker, appraiser Gwen Welshimer Real Estate, Wichita, 1979—; coord. Epic Real Estate Sch., Wichita, 1988—; legislator Kans. Ho. of Reps., Topeka, 1990—; mem. taxation com., mem. banking and ins. com. Kans. Ho. or Reps., Topeka, 1991-96; minority leader local govt. and joint com. adminstrv. rules regulations Kans. Ho. of Reps., Topeka, 1994-96. Dem. precinct committeewomen, Wichita; bd. dirs. United Meth. Urban Ministries, Wichita, 1990—. Mem. NOW, Nat. Women's Polit. Caucus, Nat. Order Women Legislators (state dir. 1994-96), Nat. Conf. State Legislators (Kans. mem. Art and Tourism Ctr.). Democrat. Methodist. Home: 6103 Castle Dr Wichita KS 67218-3601 Office: Kans Ho of Reps State Capitol Topeka KS 66612

WELSOME, EILEEN, journalist; b. N.Y.C., Mar. 12, 1951; d. Richard H. and Jane M. (Garity) W.; m. James R. Martin, Aug. 3, 1983. BJ with honors, U. Tex., 1980. Reporter Beaumont (Tex.) Enterprise, 1980-82, San Antonio Light, 1982-83, San Antonio Express-News, 1983-86, Albuquerque Tribune, 1987-94. Recipient Clarion award, 1989, News Reporting award Nat. Headliners, 1989, John Hancock award, 1991, Mng. Editors Pub. Svc. award AP, 1991, 94, Roy Howard award 1994, James Aronson award, 1994, Gold Medal award Investigative Reporters and Editors, 1994, Sigma Delta Chi award, 1994, Investigative Reporting award Nat. Headliners, 1994, Selden Ring award, 1994, Heywood Broun award, 1994, George Polk award, 1994, Sidney Hillman Found. award, 1994, Pulitzer Prize for nat. reporting, 1994; John S. Knight fellow Stanford U., 1991-92.

WELT, PHILIP STANLEY, lawyer, consultant; b. Freeport, N.Y., July 5, 1959; s. Morris and Rose (Offenberg) W.; m. Karen Teresa Gault, May 22, 1994. BBA summa cum laude, Hofstra U., 1983; MBA, Columbia U., 1988; JD cum laude, NYU, 1995. Bar: N.J. 1995, N.Y. 1995; U.S. Dist. Ct. N.J. 1995. Sr. mgr. Deloitte & Touche, N.Y.C., 1983-92; assoc. Reboul MacMurray Hewitt Maynard & Kristol, N.Y.C., 1993, Davis Polk & Wardwell, N.Y.C., 1994, 96—; jud. clk. U.S. Dist. Ct. N.J., Newark, 1995-96; pres. Louis Michael Coins & Jewelry, Inc., Woonsocket, R.I., 1993-95, also bd. dirs.; bd. dirs., treas. Pub. Interest Law Found., N.Y.C., 1993-94; guest spkr. Boy Scouts Am., Nassau County, 1984-91, Nat. Assn. Accts., N.Y./N.J., 1988-92, others. Sr. editor Columbia Jour. World Bus., 1986-88; sr. exec. editor Ann. Survey Am. Law, 1993-95; contbr. articles to profl. jours. Vol. income tax asst. Dept. Treasury, IRS, N.Y.C., 1981-87; vol. Variety-The Children's Charity, N.Y.C., 1985-87; advisor Friends of Jon Kaiman, Nassau County, 1995. Provost's scholar Hofstra U., 1981-83, Deloitt & Touche fellow Columbia U., 1986-88; recipient Appreciation cert. Dept. Treasury, IRS, 1981-87, Variety, 1985-87, Bovenaan Outstanding Cmty. Svc. award Hofstra U., 1983; named Best Oralist, NYU Sch. Law, 1993. Mem. ABA, ATLA, AICPAs, N.Y. State Soc. CPAs, Beta Alpha Psi, Beta Gamma Sigma. Avocations: golf, rock climbing, photography, philately, amateur radio. Home: 157 Mountain Wood Rd Stamford CT 06903 Office: Davis Polk and Wardwell 450 Lexington Ave New York NY 10017

WELTER, WILLIAM MICHAEL, marketing and advertising executive; b. Evanston, Ill., Nov. 18, 1946; s. Roy Michael and Frances (DeShields) W.; m. Pamela Bassett, June 11, 1971; children: Barclay, Robert Michael. BS, Mo. Valley Coll., 1966. Account exec. Leo Burnett Co., Inc., Chgo., 1966-74; v.p., account supr. Needham Harper Worldwide, Chgo., 1974-80; v.p. mktg. Wendy's Internat., Inc., Dublin, Ohio, 1981, sr. v.p. mktg., 1981-84, exec. v.p., 1984-87; owner, chief exec. officer Haunty & Welter Advt. Agy., Worthington, Ohio, 1987-91; sr. exec. v.p. mktg. Rax Restaurants Inc., Dublin, 1992; exec. v.p. mktg. Metromedia Steakhouses, Inc., Dayton, 1992-93; sr. v.p. mktg. Metromedia Co., Dayton, 1993-95; exec. v.p., chief mktg. officer Heartland Foods Inc., Dublin, Ohio, 1995-96; exec. v.p. brand mgmt. Late Nite Magic, Inc., Columbus, Ohio, 1996—. Founder Santa's Silent Helpers, Columbus, Ohio, 1985. Mem. Advt. Fedn. Columbus, Scioto Country Club, Lakes Golf and Country Club. Avocations: golf, fishing. Home: 4311 Woodhall Rd Columbus OH 43220-4379 Office: Heartland Food Systems Inc 4150 Tuller Rd Dublin OH 43017-5014

WELTMAN, DAVID LEE, lawyer; b. Springfield, Mass., Jan. 12, 1933; s. Sol Walter and Esther (Ziskind) W.; m. Lois Handmaker, Sept. 2, 1956; children: John, Elizabeth, Herman, Sally. AB, Yale U., 1954; LLB, Harvard U., 1957. Bar: Mass. 1957. Assoc. Mintz, Levin & Cohn, Boston, 1957-60; v.p. Ansonia Mills, Inc., Taunton, Mass., 1960-63; assoc. Foley, Hoag & Eliot, Boston, 1963-67, ptnr., 1967—; sec., clk. Charles River Assocs., Boston, 1965—, Brigham Med. Group Found., 1972—, Siemens-Nixdorf Info. Systems, Burlington, Mass., 1979—, Am. Brush Co., Clairmont, N.H., 1982-92. Chmn. leadership devel. coun. Jewish Fedn. and Welfare Funds, 1966-68; trustee New Eng. Med. Ctr., Boston, 1970-82, Combined Jewish Philanthropies, Boston, 1970—, Hebrew Coll., Boston, 1995—; chmn. Newbury Coll., Boston, 1972—, Lown Cardiovascular Rsch. Found., 1993—; incorporator Mus. Sci., Boston, 1972—, Boston U. Med. Ctr., 1965—'; pres. Beaver Country Day Sch., Chestnut Hill, Mass., 1975-80, Jewish Cmty. Ctr., Brookline and Newton, 1968-71; bd. overseers South Shore Hosp. Found., Weymouth, Mass., 1990—; trustee, dir. Hebrew Coll., Brookline, 1995—. Recipient Young Leadership award Combined Jewish Philanthropies, 1968, Class of 1954 award Yale U., 1989, Founders Day award Beaver Country Day Sch., 1991. Mem. ABA, Boston Bar Assn., Nat. Health Lawyers Assn., Cohasset Yacht Club (Mass.), Downtown Club. Avocations: tennis, sailing. Home: 90 Gammons Rd Cohasset MA 02025-1406 Office: Foley Hoag & Eliot 1 Post Office Sq Boston MA 02109-2103

WELTS, RICK, sports association executive. V.p. comms. Nat. Basketball Assn., N.Y.C., 1984-88, dir. nat. promotions, then v.p. mktg., exec. v.p., 1988—; pres. Nat. Basketball Assn. Properties. Office: N B A Properties Inc 645 5th Ave New York NY 10022-5910 Office: Nat Basketball Assn 645 5th Ave New York NY 10022*

WELTY, EUDORA, author; b. Jackson, Miss.; d. Christian Webb and Chestina (Andrews) W. Student, Miss. State Coll. for Women; B.A., U. Wis., 1929; postgrad., Columbia Sch. Advt., 1930-31. Author: A Curtain of Green, 1941, The Robber Bridegroom, 1942, The Wide Net, 1943, Delta Wedding, 1946, Music From Spain, 1948, Short Stories, 1949, The Golden Apples, 1949, The Ponder Heart, 1954 (William Dean Howells medal Am. Acad. Arts and Letters 1955), The Bride of the Innisfallen, 1955, Place in Fiction, 1957, The Shoe Bird, 1964, Thirteen Stories, 1965, A Sweet Devouring, 1969, Losing Battles, 1970 (Nat. Book award nomination 1971), One Time, One Place, 1971 (Christopher Book award 1972), The Optimist's Daughter, 1972 (Pulitzer prize in fiction 1973), The Eye of the Story, 1978, The Collected Stories of Eudora Welty, 1980 (Notable Book award ALA 1980, Am. Book award 1981), One Writer's Beginnings, 1985 (Am. Book award 1984, Nat. Book Critics Circle award nomination 1984), Eudora Welty Photographs, 1989, A Writer's Eye: Collected Book Reviews, 1994, Monuments to Interruption: Collected Book Reviews, 1994; editor: (with Ronald A. Sharp) The Norton Book of Friendship, 1991; contbr.: New Yorker. Recipient O. Henry award, 1942, 43, 68, Creative Arts medal for fiction Brandeis U., 1966, Nat. Inst. Arts and Letters Gold Medal, 1972, Nat. Medal for Lit., 1980, Presdl. Medal of Freedom, 1980, Commonwealth medal MLA, 1984, Nat. Medal of Arts, 1987; Lit. grantee Nat. Inst. Arts and Letters, 1944; Guggenheim fellow, 1942; Chevalier de l'Ordre des Arts et

Lettres (France), 1987. Mem. Am. Acad. Arts and Letters. Home: 1119 Pinehurst Pl Jackson MS 39202-1812

WELTY, JOHN DONALD, academic administrator; b. Amboy, Ill., Aug. 24, 1944; s. John Donald and Doris (Donnelly) W.; children: Anne, Elisabeth. B.S., Western Ill. U., 1965; M.A., Mich. State U., 1967; Ed.D., Ind. U., 1974. Asst. v.p. for student affairs SW State U., Marshall, Minn., 1973-74; dir. residences SUNY-Albany, 1974-77, assoc. dean for student affairs, 1977-80; v.p. for student and univ. affairs Indiana U. of Pa., 1980-84, pres., 1984-91; pres. Calif. State U., Fresno, 1991—; lectr. in field. Contbr. articles to profl. jours. Chmn. Small Bus. Incubator of Indiana, 1985-91; bd. dirs. Open Door Crises and Counseling Ctr., Indiana, Big Bros./Big Sisters, Indiana, 1980-84. Recipient Chancellor's award SUNY, 1977. Mem. Pa. Assn. Student Personnel Adminstrs., Am. Coll. Personnel Assn., Am. Assn. State Colls. and Univs., Nat. Assn. Student Personnel Adminstrs., Indiana C. of C. (bd. dirs.), Assn. Gov. Bds. Roman Catholic. Lodge: Rotary. Office: Calif State U 5241 N Maple Ave Fresno CA 93740-8027

WELTZ, MARTIN DAVID, oncologist, hematologist; b. Phila., Jan. 18, 1948; m. Sharon Frankfort; children: Michael, Adam. BS in Biology, Bklyn. Coll., 1969; DO, U. for Health Scis., 1973. Diplomate Nat. Bd. Med. Examiners for Osteo. Physicians and Surgeons, Am. Bd. Internal Medicine, (subspecialty of med. oncology, subspecialty of hematology). Commd. 2d lt. USMC, 1973, advanced through grades to lt. col., 1981; intern Walter Reed Army Med. Ctr., Washington, 1973-74, resident, 1974-76, fellow hematology and med. oncology sect., 1976-79, attending physician dept. internal medicine, 1979-81, staff hematologist, med. oncologist, dir. med. edn., 1979-80, chief divsn. head Clin. Cancer Chemo-Pharmacology Rsch. Lab., 1979-80, asst. chief, dir. clin. pharmacy hematology-med. oncology, 1980-81; resigned USMC, 1981; pvt. practice Hematology-Oncology Cons., Greenbelt, Md., 1983—, v.p., sec., 1986—; v.p., sec., 1986—; attending med.staff AMI Drs. Hosp., Prince George's County, Lanham, Md., 1983, Washington Adventist Hosp., Takoma Park, Md., 1983—, sec.-treas. dept. internal medicine, 1991-94, asst. chmn., 1994; asst. chief hematology/med. oncology Prince Georges Hosp. Ctr., 1986—; staff Laurel Regional Hosp., 1983—, chmn. hematology-med. oncology, 1989—, med. dir. Hospice in Prince George's County, 1989—, chmn. dept. internal medicine, 1989-92, chmn. tumor bd., 1989—, chmn. employees ann. benefit med.-dental staff, 1990—, chmn. med. exec. com., 1993—, pres. med. and dental staff, 1993—, trustee, 1993—; bd. dirs. Dimensions Corp., Landover, Md., sec.-treas. bd. dirs., 1990—; pres. Med. Dental Staff laurel Regional Hosp., 1993—; vice chmn. Dept. Internal Medicine, Washington Adventist Hosp., 1994—; sec., treas. Dimensions Health Care Network PHO, 1994—; med. dir. Hospice in Prince Georges County, 1990—; bd. dirs. Universal Health Care Network, Medi-Cen of Md. Contbr. articles to profl. jours. Bd. dirs. Am. Cancer Soc., Prince George's County, 1981—; med. advisor cansurmount program Am. Cancer Soc., Montgomery County, Md., 1982-90; ring dir. Ea. Regional Karate Tournament, Montgomery Coll., Rockville, Md., 1987—; mem. advisor Md. Blood Ctr., 1987-88; mem. med. adv. bd. Hospice Prince George's County, Largo, Md., 1991—, active archtl. and design com., capital campaign com., bldg. com., 1992—; bd. dirs. Found. Laurel Regional Hosp., 1993—, others. Fellow ACP, Acad. Medicine N.J.; mem. AMA, Am. Soc. Internal Medicine, Am. Soc. Clin. Oncology, Am. Soc. Hematology, Acad. Hospice Physicians, Am. Coll. Clin. Pharmacology, Am. Coll. Osteo. Internists, Am. Soc. Clin. Oncologists, Am. Soc. Clin. Pharmacology and Therapeutics, Am. Soc. Contemporary Medicine and Surgery, Am. Fedn. for Clin. Rsch., Royal Soc. Medicine (London), Universal Health Care Network, Cancer Care, Inc., Med-Cen of Md., Md. Osteo. Assn., Oncology Soc. N.J., N.J. Soc. Internal Medicine, N.Y. Acad. Scis., N.Y. Oncology Soc., Md. Soc. Clin. Oncology. Office: Greenway Center Dr Greenbelt MD 20770

WELU, JAMES A., art museum director; b. Dubuque, Iowa, Dec. 15, 1943; s. Andrew L. and Anna E. (Riley) W. BA, Loras Coll., 1966; MA, U. Notre Dame, 1967, MFA, 1968; PhD, Boston U., 1977. Instr. St. Mary-of-the-Woods (Ind.) Coll., 1968-70; asst. curator Worcester (Mass.) Art Mus., 1974-76, assoc. curator, 1976-80, instr., 1977-78, 80-81, chief curator, 1980-86, dir., 1986—; instr. Clark U., Worcester, 1980. Panelist Mass. Coun. on Arts and Humanities, Boston, 1981-82, 90, Utilization of Mus. Resources Nat. Endowment for the Arts, 1988; trustee Williamstown Regional Art Conservation Lab., Inc., Mass., 1981-86; mem. panel Utilization Mus. Resources, NEA, 1988. Boston U. grantee, 1973, NEA Mus.' Profl. grantee, 1976-81; Samuel H. Kress Found. fellow, 1973; recipient Netherland-Am. Found. award Netherland Found., 1973, Disting. Alumni award Boston U. Grad. Sch., 1986. Mem. Assn. Art Mus. Dirs. (trustee), Am. Fedn. Arts (trustee), Coll. Art Assn. Am., Am. Assn. Mus., New Eng. Mus. Assn., Historians Netherlandish Art. Home: 16 Rutland Ter Worcester MA 01609-1664 Office: Worcester Art Mus 55 Salisbury St Worcester MA 01609-3123

WEMPLE, JAMES ROBERT, psychotherapist; b. Hardin, Mont., May 31, 1943; s. Charles Clifford and Lillian Louise (Smith) W.; m. Sarah Ann House, May 7, 1983; children: Brian Matthew, Laura Ashley. BA, U. Mont., 1966, MA, 1970, postgrad., 1970-71; PhD, Wash. State U., 1979. Diplomate Am. Acad. Pain Mgmt. Tchr., coach Custer County High Sch., Miles City, Mont., 1966-67; sch. psychologist Missoula, Mont., 1970-71; grad. asst. U. Mont., Missoula, 1970-71; dir. counseling Medicine Hat (Alberta) Coll., Canada, 1971-73; counselor Lethbridge (Alberta) C.C., 1973-76; head resident Wash. State U., Pullman, 1976-79; mental health specialist Missoula Rehab., 1979-82; clin. mental health counselor Missoula, 1982—. With U.S. Army, 1960-69, Korea. Fellow Am. Bd. Med. Psychotherapists; mem. Am. Psychol. Assn., Soc. for Clin. and Exptl. Hypnosis, Am. Soc. for Clin. Hypnosis, Internat. Soc. for Hypnosis, Nat. Acad. Cert. Clin. Mental Health Counselors, Soc. for Personality Assessment, AACD, Phi Kappa Phi. Avocations: fishing, hunting. Home: 2410 Clydesdale Ln Missoula MT 59801-9297 Office: 715 Kensington Ave Ste 9 Missoula MT 59801-5700

WEMPLE, WILLIAM, lawyer; b. N.Y.C., Nov. 3, 1912; s. William Lester and Dorothy (Gunnels) W.; m. Dorothea Dutcher, Nov. 1, 1941; children: Littlepaige, Katharine Holland, William Barent, Leslie, Wendy, Stephanie, Liana Ashley. AB, Harvard U., 1934; LLB, Columbia U., 1937. Bar: N.Y. 1938. Assoc. Cravath, deGersdorff, Swaine & Wood, N.Y.C., 1937-42; civilian with Office Gen. Counsel, Navy Dept., 1942-43, 45-46; assoc. Dewey, Ballantine, Bushby, Palmer & Wood, N.Y.C., 1946-52, ptnr., 1952—. Mem. planning commn. Village of Scarsdale, N.Y., 1957-64; bd. dirs. Scarsdale Community Fund and Council, 1955-60. Served to lt. comdr. USNR, 1943-45. Fellow Am. Bar Found.; mem. ABA (council corp., banking and bus. law sect. 1976-80), Am. Law Inst., N.Y. State Bar Assn. (chmn. banking, corp. and bus. law sect. 1969-70). Republican. Club: Town (Scarsdale) (gov. 1959-62, 75-76, chmn. edn. com. 1976-77). Home: 36 Old Farm Rd Charlottesville VA 22903-4723 Office: Dewey Ballantine 1301 Avenue Of The Americas New York NY 10019-6092

WEMPNER, GERALD ARTHUR, engineering educator; b. Waupun, Wis.; s. Paul Christian and Thekla Nelda (Jung) W.; m. Lorraine Bischel, Sept. 6, 1952 (div. Apr. 1983); children: Susan K., Paul J. BS, U. Wis., 1952, MS, 1953; PhD, U. Ill., 1957. Instr. U. Ill., Urbana, 1953-57, asst. prof., 1957-59; assoc. prof. U. Ariz., Tucson, 1959-62; prof. U. Ala., Huntsville, 1964-73; prof. Ga. Inst. Tech., Atlanta, 1973-91, prof. emeritus, 1991—; vis. prof. U. Calif., Berkeley, 1962-63. Author: Mechanics of Solids, 1973; co-author: Mechanics of Deformable Bodies, 1961, Mechanics of Solids, 1995; contbr. articles to profl. jours. With U.S. Army, 1946-48. NSF fellow, Stanford (Calif.) U., 1963-64, Sr. fellow Alexander von Humboldt Found., Germany, 1973, Killam fellow U. Calgary, Can., 1983. Fellow ASME (asssoc. editor 1976-83), Am. Acad. Mechanics. Avocations: art, sculpture, photography, woodwork. Home and Office: Ga Inst Tech Sch Engring 3397 Hidden Acres Dr Doraville GA 30340-4445

WEN, SHIH-LIANG, mathematics educator; came to U.S., 1959; s. S.W. and C.F. (Hsiao) W.; children: Dennis, Andy, Jue. BS, Nat. Taiwan U., Taipei, 1956; MS, U. Utah, 1961; PhD, Purdue U., 1968. Assoc. research engr. The Boeing Co., Seattle, 1961-63; with dept. math. Ohio U., Athens, 1968—, successively asst. prof., assoc. prof. and prof., chmn. dept. math., 1985-93; rsch. analyst Applied Math Rsch. Lab. USAF, Wright-Patterson AFB, Ohio, summer, 1972; vis. rsch. scientist Courant Inst. Math. Scis. NYU, 1978-79; hon. prof. Jiangxi U., People's Republic of China, 1985; disting. vis. prof. Lanzhou U., People's Republic of China, 1989. Mem. Am. Math. Soc., Soc. for Indsl. and Applied Math., Math. Assn. Am. Avocations: fishing, bridge, music. Office: Ohio Univ Dept Of Math Athens OH 45701

WENDEBORN, RICHARD DONALD, retired manufacturing company executive; b. Winnipeg, Man., Can.; came to U.S., 1976; naturalized, 1988; s. Curtis and Rose (Lysecki) W.; m. Dorothy Ann Munn, Aug. 24, 1957; children: Margaret Gayle, Beverley Jane, Stephen Richard, Peter Donald, Ann Elizabeth. Diploma, Colo. Sch. Mines, 1952; grad. advanced mgmt. program, Harvard U., 1974. With Can. Ingersoll-Rand Co., Montreal, 1952—, gen. mgr., v.p., dir., 1968, pres., 1969-74, chmn. bd., 1976—; exec. v.p. Ingersoll-Rand Co., Woodcliff Lake, N.J., 1976-89; ret., 1989; mem. Can Govt. Oil and Gas Tech. Exch. Program with former USSR, 1972—, Minerals and Metals Mission to China, 1972—. Mem. Resource Fund Colo. Sch. Mines; past pres., dir. Town and River Civic Assn. Mem. Machinery and Equipment Mfrs. Assn. Can. (bd. dirs. 1974—, past chmn.), Royal Palm Yacht Club (commodore 1994), Useppa Island Club, Tau Beta Pi. Home: 9990 Cypress Lake Dr Fort Myers FL 33919-6020

WENCK, WILLIAM ARISTÉ, marketing data and financial analyst; b. New Orleans, Apr. 20, 1947; s. William Aristé and Esther Hardy (Bragg) W.; m. Marian Gould Ruggles, May 28, 1983; 1 child, Alexander Ruggles. BS in Indsl. Engring., Cornell U., 1969; MEd, Columbia U., 1975, PhD in Social Psychology, 1981. Owner Wenck Capital Ventures, Essex, Conn., 1982-92, William A. Wenck and Assocs., Old Lyme, Conn., 1992-93, CIGNA Fin. Advisors Inc., New Haven, Conn., 1993-94, William A. Wenck & Assocs., Old Lyme, Conn., 1994—. Bd. dirs. Phoebe Griffen Noyes Libr.; chmn. Old Lyme Harbor Mgmt. Commn., 1989-94; mem. bd. edn. region dist. #18, 1995—. Mem. Am. Assn. for Pub. Opinion rsch., A.K. Rice Inst., N.Y. Yacht Club. Home: 110 Mile Creek Rd Old Lyme CT 06371-1716

WENDEL, RICHARD FREDERICK, economist, educator, consultant; b. Chgo., Apr. 29, 1930; s. Elmer Carl and Victoria Matilda (Jeffrey) W.; m. Leslie Jane Travis, June 15, 1957; children: John Travis, Andrew Stewart. A.B., Augustana Coll., 1951; M.B.A., U. Pa., 1957, Ph.D. (fellow 1962-64), 1966. Asst. to pres. Flexonics Corp., Maywood, Ill., 1957-59; sales rep., product mgr. Kordite div. Nat. Distillers Corp., Macedon, N.Y., 1959-62; instr. Wharton Sch., U. Pa., 1964-65; asst. prof. mktg. Grad. Sch. Bus. Adminstrn., Washington U., St. Louis, 1965-69; asso. prof. U. Conn., 1969-74, prof., 1974-90, prof. emeritus, 1990; mem. U.S. Census Field Adv. Commn., 1967-69; mem. acad. adv. commn. Bur. Labor Stats., U.S. Bur. Census Survey of Consumer Expenditures, 1971-76; mem. Conn. Export Devel. Council, Dept. Commerce, 1972-76; dir. Neon Software Inc. Author: (with M.L. Bell) Economic Importance of Highway Advertising, 1966; (with W. Gorman) Selling: Preparation. Persuasion. Strategy., 1983, 88; editor: Readings in Marketing, 1973-74, 75-76, 77-78, 78-79, 79-80, 80-81, (with C.L. Lapp) Add to Your Selling Know-How, 1968; editorial staff: jour. Mktg., 1965-74. Bd. dirs. Roper Center. Served with USAF, 1951-55. Center for Real Estate and Urban Econs. grantee, 1969-70. Mem. Am. Mktg. Assn., N.Y. Acad. Scis. Republican. Episcopalian. Home: 106 S Queen St Chestertown MO 21620

WENDELN, DARLENE DORIS, English language educator; b. Indpls., July 18, 1956; d. Robert Edward and Doris Mae (Brabender) W. BS, U. Indpls., 1978; MS, Ind. U., 1986. Lic. tchr., Ind. Secondary English tchr., coach Centerville (Ind.)-Abington Sch. Corp., 1978—; coach girls' tennis regional and sectional championships. Mem. NEA, Nat. Coun. Tchrs. English, Ind. H.S. Tennis Coaches Assn., U.S. Tennis Assn. Lutheran. Avocations: bicycling, tennis, golf, reading. Office: Centerville High Sch Willow Grove Rd Centerville IN 47330

WENDELSTEDT, HARRY HUNTER, JR., umpire; b. Balt., July 27, 1938; m. Cheryl Maher, Nov. 2, 1970; children: Harry III, Amy. Student, Essex Community Coll.; BS in Edn., U. Md. Profl. baseball umpire, 1962—; with minor leagues, Ga.-Fla., 1962, (Northwest), 1963, Tex., 1964, (Internat.), 1965; with maj. leagues (Nat.), 1966—; umpire All-Star Game, 1968, 76, 83, 92, Nat. League championship series, 1970, 72, 77, 80, 82, 84, 88, 90, World Series, 1973, 80, 86, 91, 95; owner, operator Harry Wendelstedt Umpire Sch. Named Top Umpire in Maj. League Baseball Md. Profl. Baseball Players Assn., 1975, Best Umpire in Nat. League Chgo. Tribune, 1982, Best Ball and Strike Umpire Sports Illustrated, 1982, Major League Umpire of Yr., 1992, Fla. Diamond Club, 1993. Mem. Major League Umpires Assn. (4 term past pres.). Office: Major League Umpires Assn 88 S St Andrews Dr Ormond Beach FL 32174-3857

WENDER, DEBORAH ELIZABETH, policy consultant, social worker; b. Sacramento, June 30, 1954; d. Joseph Andrew Sr. and Caroline Elizabeth (Wulff) Wender; adopted children: Alexander Darius Andrew, Zodie Miriam Caroline. AA, American River Coll., Sacramento, 1974; BA, Calif. State U., Sacramento, 1980, MSW, 1988. Counselor coord. Sacramento Women's Ctr., 1980-81, rape crisis project dir., 1981-84; program coord. Rape Prevention Edn. Program, U. Calif., Davis, 1984-87; criminal justice specialist Calif. Office Criminal Justice Planning, Sacramento, 1988-89; assoc. health program advisor Office of AIDS Calif. Dept. Health Svcs., Sacramento, 1989-91, pub. health social work cons. maternal and child health, 1991-93, assoc. govtl. program analyst Medi-Cal Eligibility, 1993-95; social svcs. consultant III Child Welfare Svcs. Bur. Calif. Dept. Social Svcs., 1995—; contract social worker Family Connections Adoptions, 1995—. Bd. dirs. Child Sexual Abuse Treatment Ctr., Yolo County, Woodland, Calif., 1984-86, WomanKind Health Clinic, Sacramento, 1984-86; bd. dirs. Sacramento Women's Ctr., 1987-91, bd. pres. 1989-91. Democrat. Avocations: camping, baking, holiday crafts, reading. Home: 8649 Glenroy Way Sacramento CA 95826-1743

WENDER, IRA TENSARD, lawyer; b. Pitts., Jan. 5, 1927; s. Louis and Luba (Kibrick) W.; m. Phyllis M. Bellows, June 24, 1966; children: Justin B., Sarah T.; children by previous marriage: Theodore M., Matthew G., Abigail A., John B. Student Swarthmore Coll., 1942-45; JD, U. Chgo., 1948; LLM, NYU, 1951. Atty. Lord, Day and Lord, N.Y.C., 1950-52, 54-59; asst. dir. internat. program in taxation Harvard U. Law Sch., 1952-54; lectr. N.Y. U. Sch. Law, N.Y.C., 1954-59; ptnr. Baker and McKenzie, Chgo., 1959-61, founding ptnr. N.Y.C. office, 1961-71; sr. ptnr. Wender, Murase & White, 1971-82, of counsel, 1982-86; chmn. C. Brewer and Co., Ltd., Honolulu, 1969-75; pres., chief exec. officer A.G. Becker Paribas Inc., 1978-82; chmn., chief exec. officer Sussex Securities Inc., 1983-85; of counsel Patterson, Belknap, Webb & Tyler, N.Y.C., 1986-87, ptnr., 1988-93, of counsel, 1994—; chmn. Perry Ellis Internat., Inc., N.Y.C., 1994; bd. dirs. REFAC Tech. Devel. Corp., N.Y.C., South West Property Trust, Inc., Dallas, Dime Bancorp, Inc. Bd. mgrs. Swarthmore Coll.. 1978-89; pres., bd. mgrs. PARC Vendome Condominium, 1990-94; trustee Brearley Sch., N.Y.C., 1980-85, Putney (Vt.) Sch., 1985—; active Council on Fgn. Relations. Mem. Am., N.Y. State bar assns., Assn. of Bar of City of N.Y. Author: (with E.R. Barlow) Foreign Investment and Taxation, 1955. Home: 340 W 57th St New York NY 10019-3706 Office: Patterson Belknap Webb & Tyler 1133 Avenue Of The Americas New York NY 10036-6710

WENDER, PAUL ANTHONY, chemistry educator. BS, Wilkes Coll., 1969; PhD, Yale U., 1973; PhD (hon.), Wilkes U., 1993. Asst. prof., assoc. prof. Harvard U., 1974-81; prof. chemistry Stanford U., 1981—; Bergstrom prof. chemistry, 1994—; cons. Eli Lilly & Co., 1980—, lectr. Am. Chem. Soc.. Recipient ICI Am. Chem. award Stuart Pharm., merit award NIH, Pfizer rsch. award, 1995, Pfizer Rsch. award, 1995. Mem. AAAS, Am. Chem. Soc. (Arthur C. Cope Sholan award 1990, Guenther award). Office: Stanford U Dept Chemistry Stanford CA 94305

WENDER, PHYLLIS BELLOWS, literary agent; b. N.Y.C., Jan. 6, 1934; d. Lee and Lillian (Frank) Bellows; m. Ira Tensard Wender, June 24, 1966; children: Justin Bellows, Sarah Tensard. B.A., Wells Coll., 1956. Asst. advt dir. Book Find Club, N.Y.C., 1957-58; publicity dir. Grove Press, N.Y.C., 1958-61, Dell Pub. Co., N.Y.C., 1961-63; theatrical agt. Artists Agy. Inc., N.Y.C., 1963-68; agt. Wender & Assocs., N.Y.C., 1968-81; writers' agt. Rosenstone/Wender, N.Y.C., 1981—. Bd. dirs. Just Women Inc., Bklyn., 1982, mem. adv. com., 1983-87; bd. dirs. Fortune Soc., N.Y.C., 1977-80; trustee Wells Coll., Aurora, N.Y., 1981-90. Mem. Women's Media Group (dir. 1988-90). Club: Cosmopolitan (N.Y.C.). Office: Rosenstone Wender 3 E 48th St New York NY 10017-1027

WENDEROTH, COLLIER, JR., food products executive; b. 1923. Chmn. bd. O. K. Instries Inc., Fort Smith, Ariz., 1985—. With U.S. Army, 1948-55. Office: O K Industries Inc PO Box 1119 Fort Smith AR 72902*

WENDERS, WIM, motion picture director; b. Dusseldorf, Germany, Aug. 14, 1945. Dir. films including Summer in the City, 1970, The Goalie's Anxiety at the Penalty Kick, 1972, The Scarlet Letter, 1974, Alice in the Cities, 1974, The Wrong Move, 1975, Kings of the Road, 1976, The American Friend, 1977, Lightning Over Water (Nick's Movie) (with Nicholas Ray), 1980, The State of Things, 1982, Hammett, 1982; Paris, Texas, 1984 (Palme d'Or, Cannes Internat. Film Festival), Tokyo-Ga, 1985, Wings of Desire, 1987 (Best Dir., Cannes Internat. Film Festival), Aufzeichnungen zu Kleiderund Stadten, 1989, Until the End of the World, 1991, Far Away, So Close, 1993 (Cannes Internat. Film Festival Grand Prize). Office: Gray City Inc 853 Broadway New York NY 10003-4703

WENDLER, WALTER V., dean. B in Environ. Design, Texas A&M U.; MArch, U. Calif., Berkeley; PhD, U. Tex. Cert. Nat. Coun. Archtl. Registration Bd. Lic. Tex., La. Pvt. practice, 1977-81; faculty Tex. A&M U. Coll. Architecture, College Sta., 1981—, assoc. dean acad. affairs, 1988-89, head dept. architecture, 1989-92, dean, 1992—. Contbr. articles to profl. jours. Office: Texas A&M U College of Architecture College Station TX 77843-3137

WENDORF, DENVER FRED, JR., anthropology educator; b. Terrell, Tex., July 31, 1924; s. Denver Fred and Margaret (Hall) W.; children: Frederick Carl, Michael Andrew, Gail Susan, Cynthia Ann, Kelly Peta, Scott Frederick. B.A., U. Ariz., 1948; M.A., Harvard U., 1950, Ph.D., 1953. Research assoc. Mus. N.Mex., Santa Fe, 1950-56; assoc. dir. Mus. N.Mex., 1958-64; assoc. prof. Tex. Tech U., Lubbock, 1956-58; prof. anthropology So. Meth. U., Dallas, 1964—; chmn. dept. anthropology So. Meth. U., 1968-74, Henderson-Morrison prof. prehistory, 1974—; dir. Ft. Burgwin Research Ctr., Taos, N.Mex., 1957-76. Author: numerous books including The Prehistory of Nubia, 1968, The Midland Discovery, 1955, Paleoecology of the Llano Estacado, 1961, A Guide to Salvage Archaeology, Prehistory of the Eastern Sahara, 1980; also articles. Chmn. Tex. State Antiquities Com., 1969-82; mem. Nat. Park System Adv. Bd., 1983-87, chmn., 1985-87; mem. Cultural Properties Adv. Bd., 1984-90. Served with AUS, 1943-47. Decorated Purple Heart; decorated Bronze Star. Mem. Soc. for Am. Archaeology (treas. 1974-77, pres. 1979-81), Nat. Acad. Scis. Home: 401 S Centre Ave Lancaster TX 75146-3830

WENDORF, HULEN DEE, law educator, author, lecturer; b. West, Tex., Oct. 29, 1916; s. Reinhardt and Laura (Blume) W.; m. Mary Jane Pfeffer, June 13, 1939; children: Robert Joseph, Donald Joseph, Florence Ann. BS, U.S. Mil. Acad., 1939; JD, Yale U., 1951. Bar: Conn. 1951, Tex. 1961, U.S. Ct. Mil. Appeals 1952, U.S. Supreme Ct. 1958, U.S. Dist. Ct. 1960. Commd. 2d lt. U.S. Army, 1939, advanced through grades to col., ret. as chief of adminstrv. law div. Office Judge Adv. Gen., 1959; practice El Paso, Tex., 1959-61; prof. law Baylor U. Law Sch., 1961-86, prof. emeritus, 1986—; former chmn. and long-time mem. Citizens Adv. Com. to Juvenile Judge; former dir. Heart of Tex. Legal Aid Assn. Author: Texas Law of Evidence Manual, 1983, 4th rev. edit., 1995, also 3 law sch. casebooks; columnist United Retirement Bull.; contbr. various articles to law revs. Rsch. dir. Texans War on Drugs, 1980-81; chmn. Food For People, 1981—. Decorated Legion of Merit, Bronze Star, Army Commendation medal. Mem. Waco-McLennan County Bar Assn. (former dir., former v.p.), Phi Delta Phi. Home: 2808 Cumberland Ave Waco TX 76707-1324 *Enjoying the work you do and a strong religious faith are the cornerstones of a good life. Do your best work when the boss is not looking.*

WENDORF, RICHARD HAROLD, library director, educator; b. Cedar Rapids, Iowa, Mar. 17, 1948; s. Harold Albert and Jeanne Ellen (Hamblin) W.; m. Barbara Hilderman, 1970 (div. 1983); m. Diana Thanet French, 1984 (div. 1995); children: Reed Thanet Wendorf-French, Carolyn Thanet Wendorf-French. BA, Williams Coll., 1970; PhB, U. Oxford, Eng., 1972; MA, Princeton U., 1974, PhD, 1976. From asst. prof. English to assoc. prof. English Northwestern U., Evanston, Ill., 1976-86, assoc. dean, 1984-88, prof. English and art history, 1986-89; libr. dir. Houghton Libr., Harvard U., Cambridge, Mass., 1989—; sr. lectr. fine arts Harvard U., 1990—, acting libr. Fine Arts Libr., 1991-92; lectr. Phi Beta Kappa Assocs., 1992—; dir. NEH summer seminars for coll. tchrs. Northwestern U., 1987, Harvard U., 1990, 92, 96; Robert Sterling Clark vis. prof. art history Williams Coll., 1993. Aauthor: William Collins and Eighteenth-Century English Poetry 1981, The Elements of Life: Biography and Portrait Painting in Stuart and Georgian England, 1990, paperback edit., 1991, Sir Joshua Reynolds: The Painter in Society, 1996—; editor: Articulate Images: The Sister Arts from Hogarth to Tennyson, 1983, Rare Book and Manuscript Libraries in the Twenty-First Century, 1993, (eith Charles Ryskamp) The Works of William Collins, 1979; contbr. essays in field; mem. editl. bd. Studies in 18th Century Culture, 1985-89, Word and Image, 1992-95, Yale edit. Writings of Samuel Johnson, Old-Time New Eng. Rsch. grantee Folger Shakespeare Libr., Washington, 1976, Am. Philos. Soc., Phila., 1977, 82, Henry E. Huntington Libr., 1979, Yale Ctr. for Brit. Art, 1983; jr. rsch. fellow Am. Coun. Learned Socs., 1978-79; summer stipend NEH, 1979; sr. rsch. fellow Am. Coun. Learned Socs., 1981-82; NEH rsch. fellow Newberry Libr., Chgo., 1988-89; fellow John Simon Guggenheim Meml. Found., 1989-90. Mem. Signet Soc. (assoc.), Keats-Shelley Assn. Am. (bd. dirs. 1993—), Am. Antiquarian Soc., Am. Soc. for 18th Century Studies (pres. Midwest regional soc. 1986), Coll. Art Assn., Soc. Brit. Art Historians, Colonial Soc. Mass., Nat. Com. on Stds. in Arts, The Johnsonians (chmn. 1994-95), Harvard Faculty Shop Club, Saturday Club, Cambridge Sci. Club, Club of Odd Volumes, Williams Club, Grolier Club, Phi Beta Kappa (exec. bd. Chgo. 1984-87). Office: The Houghton Library Harvard U Cambridge MA 02138

WENDT, ALLAN, ambassador. BA, Yale U., 1957; MPA, Harvard U., 1967. U.S. amb. to Slovenia U.S. Dept. State, Washington, 1993—. Office: Am Embassy Ljubljana Dept of State Washington DC 20521-7140*

WENDT, CHARLES WILLIAM, soil physicist, educator; b. Plainview, Tex., July 12, 1931; s. Charles Gottlieb and Winnie Mae (Bean) W.; m. Clara Anne Diller, Oct. 15, 1955; children: Charles Diller, John William, Elaine Anne, Cynthia Lynne. B.S. in Agronomy, Tex. A&M U., 1951, Ph.D. in Soil Physics, 1966; M.S. in Agronomy, Tex. Tech U., 1957. Research asst. Tex. Tech Coll., 1953-55, instr. agronomy, 1957-61, asst. prof., 1961-63; research asst. soil physics Tex. A&M U., 1963-65, research assoc., 1965-66; asst. prof. Tex. A&M U. (Agrl. Research and Extension Center), Lubbock, 1966-69; assoc. prof. Tex. A&M U. (Agrl. Research and Extension Center), 1969-74, prof., 1974-91, prof. emeritus, 1991—; cons. cotton prodn. Ministry of Agr. Sudan, summer 1960; cons. Irrigation Assn., 1977-81, Office of Tech. and Assessment, 1982, S.E. Consortium for Internat. Devel., 1989, Rhone Poulenc Agrl. Co., 1992-93; prin. backstop scientist U.S. AID West African Rsch. Program on Soil-Plant0Water Mgmt., 1982-91; chmn. agrl. sect. Southwestern and Rocky Mountain divsn. AAAS, 1982-83. Contbr. articles to profl. jours., chpt. to book. Del. Lubbock County Rep. Conv., 1978; elder Westminster Presbyn. Ch.; Tex. rep. to Great Plains Coun. 1 com. on evapotranspiration. 1st lt. U.S. Army, 1951-53. Named Outstanding Researcher High Plains Research Found., 1982; recipient Superior Achievement award for rsch., soil and crop scis. dept. Tex. A&M Univ., 1987; grantee industry and water dists. Dept. Interior, U.S. AID, EPA. Mem. Soil Sci. Soc. Am., Am. Soc. Agronomy, Brit. Plant Growth Regulator Soc., Optimist Club (1st v.p., bd. dirs.), Sigma Xi, Phi Kappa Phi. Home: 4518 22nd St Lubbock TX 79407-2515 Office: Texas Agrl Expt Station RR 3 Lubbock TX 79401-9803

WENDT, E. ALLAN, ambassador; b. Chgo., Nov. 8, 1935; s. John Arthur Frederick and Dorothy Hannah (Stephenson) W. BA magna cum laude, Yale U., 1957; Certificat d'Etudes Politques, Institut d'Etudes Politiques, Paris, 1959; MPA, Harvard U., 1967. Econ. comml. officer Am. Embassy, Saigon, Vietnam, 1967-71; fin. officer U.S. Mission to European Cmtys.,

Brussels, 1971-74; State Dept. fellow Coun. on Fgn. Rels., N.Y.C., 1974-75; dir. Office Internat. Commodities, Dept. State, Washington, 1975-79; counselor for econ. and comml. affairs Am. Embassy, Cairo, 1979-81; dep. asst. sec. of state for internat. energy and resources policy Dept. State, 1981-86, sr. rep. for strategic tech. policy, 1987-92, with rank of amb., 1988-92; amb. to Republic of Slovenia Ljubljana, 1993-95. Contbr. articles to profl. jours. Recipient award for heroism Dept. State, 1968, Presdl. Meritorious Svc. award, 1986, Superior Honor award Dept. State 1992. Mem. Coun. Fgn. Rels. Episcopalian. Avocation: tennis. Office: 3234 Volta Pl NW Washington DC 20007-2731

WENDT, GEORGE ROBERT, actor; b. Chgo., Oct. 17, 1948; m. Bernadette Birkette; children: Joshua, Andrew, Hilary. BA in Econs., Rockhurst Coll., 1971. Mem. Second City comedy troupe, Chgo., 1974-81. Actor: (feature films) My Bodyguard, 1980, Somewhere in Time, 1980, Airplane II: The Sequel, 1982, Jeckyl & Hyde: Together Again, 1982, The Women in Red, 1984, Thief of Hearts, 1984, No Small Affair, 1983, Fletch, 1985, House, 1986, Plain Clothes, 1988, Guilt by Suspicion, 1991, Forever Young, 1992, Man of the House, 1995; guest-star: (TV shows) Alice, Soap, Taxi, Hart to Hart, The American Dream; regular (TV show) Cheers, 1982-1993, The George Wendt Show, 1995; appeared in various comml.s.; appeared on stage with the Second City comedy troupe, also Wild Men, 1993. *

WENDT, HANS W(ERNER), life scientist, educator; b. Berlin, July 25, 1923; s. Hans O. and Alice (Creutzburg) W.; m. Martha A. Linger, Dec. 23, 1956 (div. 1979); children: Alexander, Christopher, Sandra; m. Judith A. Hammer, June 25, 1988. MSc, U. Hamburg, Germany, 1949; PhD in Psychopharmacology, U. Marburg, Germany, 1953. Diplomate in psychology. Rsch. asst. U. Marburg, 1949-53; rsch. assoc. Wesleyan U. and Office Naval Rsch., Middletown, Conn., 1952-53; asst. prof., field dir. internat. project U. Mainz, Germany, 1955-59; engring. psychologist to prin. human factors scientist Link Aviation, Apollo Simulator Systems, Binghamton, N.Y., 1959-61; assoc. to prof. psychology Valparaiso (Ind.) U., 1961-68; prof. psychology Macalester Coll., St. Paul, 1968-93; sr. rsch. fellow Chronobiology Labs. U. Minn., 1980—; prin. investigator Behavioral Geomedicine Collaboration Minn. Br., 1994—; cons. and reviewer, 1961—; hon. prof. sci. U. Marburg, Germany, 1971—; vis. prof. U. Victoria, B.C., Can., U. Marburg, U. Bochum, U. Bielefeld, U. Goettingen, all Germany, 1966-89. Contbr. articles to profl. jours., chpts. to books. Recipient Disting. Sr. Scientist award, Alexander von Humboldt Found., 1976. Mem. Internat. Soc. Biometeorology, Internat. Soc. Chronobiology, Bioelectromagnetics Soc., Soc. Sci. Exploration, Planetary Soc., others. Home: 2180 Lower Saint Dennis Rd Saint Paul MN 55116-2831

WENDT, LLOYD, writer; b. Spencer, S.D., May 16, 1908; s. Leo L. and Marie (Nylen) W.; m. Helen Sigler, June 16, 1932 (dec. Jan. 1980); 1 child, Bette Joan; m. Martha Toale, 1981. Student, Sioux Falls Coll., 1928-29; S.B., Northwestern U., 1931, MS, 1934. Reporter, later columnist, drama reviewer Sioux Falls (S.D.) Press, 1927-28; publicity dir. S.D. Democratic Central Com., 1928; reporter Daily Argus-Leader, 1929, telegraph editor, 1932-33; also tchr. journalism Sioux Falls Coll.; joined staff Chgo. Tribune, 1934; as reporter, becoming spl. feature writer mag. sect., later editor Grafic mag., Sunday editor, until 1961, asso. Sunday editor, asso. editor, 1975-77; editor Chgo.'s Am. newspaper, 1961-69; pub., editor Chgo. Today, 1969-74, also pres.; lectr. fiction writing Northwestern U., 1946; chmn. fiction div. Medill Sch. Journalism, 1950-53. Free lance writer, 1977—; author: (with Herman Kogan) Lords of the Levee, 1943, Gunners Get Glory, 1944, Bright Tomorrow, 1945, Bet a Million, 1948, Give the Lady What She Wants, 1952, Big Bill of Chicago, 1953, Chicago: A Pictorial History, 1958, Chicago Tribune, the Rise of a Great American Newspaper, 1979, The Wall Street Journal, the Story of Dow Jones and the Nation's Busniess NEwspaper, 1982, Swift Walker, Informal Biography of Gurdon Saltonstall Hubbard, 1986 (non-fiction award Chgo. Found. for Lit. 1986), Dogs: A Historic Journey, 1996. Pres. Soc. Midland Authors, 1947-50. Served to lt. comdr. USNR, 1942-46. Recipient Disting. Svc. award Nat. Soc. Journalists, 1980. Home: 2332 Harrier Way Nokomis FL 34275

WENDT, RICHARD L., manufacturing executive; b. 1931. From mgr. of frame factory to mgr. ops. Caradco; CEO Jeld-Wen Inc., Klamath Falls, Oreg. Office: Jeld-Wen Inc 3303 Lakeport Blvd Klamath Falls OR 97601-1017 Office: 3250 Lakeport Blvd Klamath Falls OR 97601*

WENDTLAND, MONA BOHLMANN, dietitian, consultant; b. Schulenburg, Tex., Mar. 30, 1930; d. Willy Frank and Leona A. (Bruns) Bohlmann; m. Charles William Ewing, Mar. 8, 1953 (div. Sept. 1975); children: Charles William Jr., Deborah Susan Ewing Richmond; m. William Wolters Wendtland, Jan. 12, 1991. BS in Home Econs., U. Tex., 1952, postgrad., 1952-57. Registered dietitian, Tex. Dietitian sch. lunch program Port Arthur (Tex.) Ind. Sch. Dist., 1952-53; elem. tchr. Portsmouth (Va.) Sch. Dist., 1953-54; dietitian, mgr. lunch room E.M. Scarbrough Dept. Store, Austin, Tex., 1955-57; asst. chief adminstrv. dietitian John Sealy HOsp., Galveston, Tex., 1957-59; chief therapeutic dietitian USPHS Hosp., Galveston, 1959-60, asst. chief dietitian, 1960-62; cons. dietitian Sinton (Tex.) Nursing Home, 1963-65; dietary cons. Deaton Hosp., Galena Park, Tex., 1966-68; dir. food svcs. Nat. Health Enterprises, Houston, 1975-76; dietary cons. to nursing homes, retirement & drug abuse ctr. Houston, 1976—. Del. Internat. Congress Arts & Comm., 1993. Mem. Am. Dietetic Assn. (registered), Tex. Dietetic Assn., South Tex. Dietetic Assn. (chmn. cons. interest group 1978-79), U. Tex. Home Econs. Assn., Dietitians in Bus. and Industry (nat. rep. to mgmt. practices group 1980-83, treas. Houston chpt. 1980-81, pres. 1981-82, advisor 1983-84), Tex. Gerontol Nutritionists (sec. 1994-95), Tex. Cons. Dietitians in Healthcare Facilities, Tex. Nutrition Coun., Dietary Mgrs. Assn. (advisor Houston dist. 1979-92). Republican. Methodist. Avocations: cooking, gardening, interior decorating, genealogy. Home and Office: 5463 Jason St Houston TX 77096-1238

WENDZEL, ROBERT LEROY, political science educator; b. May 28, 1938; married; 3 children. BA in Polit. Sci. magna cum laude, Kalamazoo Coll., 1960; PhD in Polit. Sci., U. Fla., 1965. Assoc. prof. polit. sci. U. Maine, Orono, 1977-81, 82-83; prof. internat. affairs U.S. Air War Coll., Maxwell AFB, Ala., 1981-82; asst. dean arts & scis., prof. polit. sci., coord. internat. affairs program U. Maine, 1984-86; prof. internat. politics U.S. Air War Coll., Maxwell AFB, 1986-87, ednl. advisor to the Commandant, 1987—; mem. internat. affairs com., U. Maine, 1970-86, budget adv. com., 1983-86, coord. internat. affairs program, 1984-86. Author: International Relations: A Policymaker Focus, Thai edit., 1989, Relacoes Internacionais, 1985, International Politics: Policymakers and Policymaking, 1981, International Relations: A Policymaker Focus, 1977, 2d edit., 1980; co-author: American's Foreign Policy in a Changing World, 1994, Defending America's Security, 1988, 2d edit., 1990, To Preserve the Republic: The Foreign Policy of the United States, 1985, Games Nations Play, 9th edit., 1996; contbr. articles to profl. jours. Mem. Phi Beta Kappa. Home: 160 Oldfield Dr Montgomery AL 36117-3938 Office: Air War Coll Maxwell AFB AL

WENG, CHUAN, mechanical engineer; b. Guang Zhou, China, July 13, 1963; came to U.S., 1986; B of Engring., Changsha (China) Ry. U., 1983; MSME, Ohio U., 1990. Registered profl. engr., N.C. Asst. engr. Guang Zhou Railway Adminstrn., Guang Zhou, 1983-86; rsch. asst. Ohio U./Forma Sci., Athens, Ohio, 1988-90; project engr. Revco/Lindberg, Asheville, N.C., 1990—. Patentee in field. Mem. NSPE, N.C. Soc. Profl. Engrs. Avocations: biking, hiking, tennis. Home: 43 Blue Ridge Ave Asheville NC 28806-3123

WENG, JOHN JUYANG, computer science educator, researcher; b. Shanghai, Apr. 15, 1957; came to U.S., 1983; m. Min Guo, 1985; children: Colin S., Rodney D. BS in Computer Sci., Fudan U., Shanghai, 1982; MS in Computer Sci., U. Ill., 1985, PhD in Computer Sci., 1989. Rsch. asst. U. Ill., Urbana, 1984-88; rschr. Computer Rsch. Inst. Montreal, Can., 1989-90; vis. asst. prof. U. Ill., 1990-92; asst. prof. Mich. State U., East Lansing, 1992—; mem. com. Internat. Symposium on Computer Vision, Coral Gables, Fla., 1995, 12th Internat. Conf. Pattern Recognition, Jerusalem, 1994. Author: (chpt.) Early Visual Learning, 1996; co-author: (chpt.) Handbook of Pattern Recognition and Computer Vision, 1993, Motion and Structures from Image Sequences, 1993. Recipient Rsch. Initiation award NSF, 1994. Mem. IEEE (Computer Soc., assoc. editor IEEE Transactions on Image Processing 1994—), Am. Soc. Engring. Edn., Sigma Xi, Phi Beta Delta. Achievements include contributions to understanding and computation of estimation of motion and structure from image sequences; co-inventor of Cresceptron, an experimental system for recognizing and segmenting objects from natural images; introducer of the concept of comprehensive visual learning for intelligent sensor-based machines; inventor of SHOSLIF, a general framework for visual learning by computers. Office: Mich State Univ A714 Wells Hall East Lansing MI 48824

WENGER, LARRY BRUCE, law librarian, law educator; b. Everett, Wash., Dec. 21, 1941; s. Lester Edwin Wenger and Selma Marie (Norberg) W. Saterstrom; m. Marilyn Diane Watt, June 26, 1965; children: Bruce Daniel, Kathleen Marie. BA, U. Wash., 1964, JD, 1967; MLS, Simmons Coll., 1969. Reference libr. Sch. Law Harvard U., Cambridge, Mass., 1967-69; asst. law libr. SUNY, Buffalo, 1969-71, law libr., assoc. prof. law, 1971-76; law libr., prof. law U. Va., Charlottesville, 1976—; cons. to law librs.; bd. dirs. Nat. Ctr. for Preservation Law. Mem. Am. Assn. Law Librs., Internat. Assn. Law Librs. (pres.), Bibliog. Soc., Bibliog. Soc. Am. Home: 2630 Meriwether Dr Charlottesville VA 22901-9513 Office: U Va Law Libr N Grounds Charlottesville VA 22901

WENGER, LUKE HUBER, educational association executive, editor; b. Ephrata, Pa., Oct. 23, 1939; s. Luke Martin and Elva B. (Huber) W. B.A., Eastern Mennonite Coll., Harrisonburg, Va., 1962; postgrad., U. Gottingen, W.Ger., 1962-63, U. Munich, W.Ger., 1967-78; Ph.D., Harvard U., 1973. Editor, asst. exec. dir. Medieval Acad. Am., Cambridge, Mass., 1973-81, exec. dir., 1981—. Editor: Speculum: A Jour. of Medieval Studies, 1981—. Fulbright fellow, 1962-63; Woodrow Wilson fellow, 1963-64; German Acad. Exchange fellow, 1967-68. Office: Speculum Jour Medieval Studies Medieval Acad of America 1430 Massachusetts Ave Cambridge MA 02138-3810

WENGER, VICKI, interior designer; b. Indpls., Aug. 30, 1928. Ed., U. Nebr., Internat. Inst. Interior Design, Parsons in Paris. Pres. Vicki Wenger Interiors, Bethesda, Md., 1963-71, Washington, 1982-95; pres. Beautiful Spaces Inc., Washington, 1982-95; chief designer Creative Design, Capitol Heights, Md., 1969-84; lectr. Nat. Assn. Home Builders, 1983-88; mem. programs com. D.C. Assn. Home Builders, 1983-88. Author-host: (patented TV interior design show) Beautiful Spaces 1984; producer, host (cable TV show) Design Edition, 1988—. Designer Gourmet Gala, March of Dimes, Washington, 1986-88; decorator showhouse Nat. Symphony Orch., Washington, 1983-94, chmn. women's com., 1991-92; decorator showhouse Am. Cancer Soc., Washington, 1983, Alexandria Comty. YWCA, 1990. Mem. Am. Soc. Interior Designers (profl., nat. bd. dirs. 1973-75, nat. examining com. 1977-78, pres. Md. chpt. 1976, bd. dirs. Washington Metro chpt. 1989-91, pres. 1995-96, mem. pres.'s barrier free com. 1980), Nat. Trust Hist. Preservation, Smithsonian Instn. (sponsor), Nat. Press Club. Democrat. Presbyterian.

WENGERT, NORMAN IRVING, political science educator; b. Milw., Nov. 7, 1916; s. Eugene F. and Lydia (Semmann) W.; m. Janet Mueller, Oct. 9, 1940; children: Eugene Mark, Christine Ann, Timothy John. B.A., U. Wis., 1938, J.D., 1942, Ph.D., 1947; M.A., Fletcher Sch., 1939. With TVA, 1941-48; faculty City Coll. N.Y., 1948-51; mem. program staff Office Sec. Dept. Interior, 1951-52; prof., chmn. social sci. dept. N.D. State U., Fargo, 1952-56; research asso. Resources for Future, Inc., 1956; prof. pub. adminstrn. U. Md., 1956-59; dep. dir. Nat. Outdoor Recreation Resources Rev. Com., 1959-60; prof., chmn. dept. polit. sci. Wayne State U., Detroit, 1960-68; vis. prof. pub. adminstrn. Pa. State U., 1968-69; prof. polit. sci. Colo. State U., Ft. Collins, 1969-87, prof. emeritus; mem. policy analysis staff Office of Chief, U.S. Forest Service, 1978-79; vis. rsch. prof. U.S. Army Engr. Inst. Water resources, 1969-70; Royer lectr. U. Calif., Berkeley, 1975; lectr. U. Sarajevo, Yugoslavia, summer 1978, NATO Adv. Study Inst., Sicily, summer 1981; lectr. U. Linkoping, Sweden, summer, 1984; spl. adviser Govt. of India on food, agr., 1959; cons. U.S. Army Corps Engrs., 1968, Thorne Ecol. Inst., 1972-75, FAA, 1963, Atlantic Richfield Oil Corp., 1973-74, Nat. Water Quality Commn., 1974—, Office Water Resources and Tech., USDI, 1973-75, and states Colo., Md., Ga., Mich., also Western Interstate Nuclear Bd.; summer fellow Fonds für Umweltstudien, Bonn, Germany, 1973; cons. No. Colo. Water Conservancy Dist., 1988—; mem. com. NAS/NRC. 1990. Author: Valley of Tomorrow: TVA and Agriculture, 1952, Natural Resources and the Political Struggle, 1955, Administration of Natural Resources, 1961, (with George M. Walker, Jr.) Urban Water Policies and Decision Making in Detroit Metro Region, 1970, Urban-Metropolitan Institutions for Water Planning, Development and Management, 1972, Impact on the Human Environment of Proposed Oil Shale Development in Garfield County, 1974, Property Rights in Land: A Comparative Exploration of German and American Concepts and Problems, 1974, Public Participation in Water Resources Development, 1974, The Political Allocation of Burdens and Benefits: Externalities and Due Process in Environmental Protection, 1976, Regional Factors in Siting and Planning Energy Facilities in the Eleven Western States, 1976, The Purposes of the National Forests, 1979; also chpts. in other books.; editor: (with others) Institutions for Urban-Metropolitan Water Management, 1972, Natural Resources Jour. issue, 1979; co-editor: (with others) The Energy Crisis: Reality or Myth, 1973; contbg. author: Planning the Use and Management of Land, 1979, Unified River Basin Management, 1981, Encyclopedia of Policy Studies, 1983, Operation of Complex Water Systems, 1983. Served as ensign USNR, 1944-45. Mem. Western Polit. Sci. Assn., Am. Soc. Pub. Adminstrn., State Bar Wis. (emeritus), Forest Hist. Soc. , Soil Conservation Soc. Am. (Nat. Honor award 1982), Order of Coif, Sigma Xi, Phi Kappa Phi. Home: 4914 Whitcomb Dr Apt 5 Madison WI 53711-2653

WENGLOWSKI, GARY MARTIN, economist; b. Rochester, N.Y., Sept. 2, 1942; s. Henry Bernard and Isabelle (Franc) W.; m. Joyce Richards, Oct. 3, 1964; children: Gary Martin, Catherine Jean. B.S. in Econs., U. Pa., 1964, M.A. (NDEA fellow), 1965, Ph.D. in Econs. (NDEA fellow), 1967. With Goldman Sachs & Co., N.Y.C., 1967—, v.p., economist, 1972-78, ptnr., dir. econ. research, 1978-86, ltd. ptnr., 1986—; adj. prof. NYU, Pace U.; tech. cons. The Bus. Coun., 1982-85; chmn. vis. com. econ. dept. U. Pa., 1985—. Author: Industry Profit Forecasting, 1972, Industry Profit Forecasting—Progress Report, 1975. Trustee CARE Found., 1991—, Haystack Mountain Sch., 1993—. Named Best Economist on Wall St., Ann. Instnl. Investor Mag. Polls, 1976-86. Fellow Nat. Assn. Bus. Economists; mem. Am. Econ. Assn., Deer Isle Yacht Club (vice commodore 1993-94, commodore 1994—). Office: Goldman Sachs & Co 85 Broad St Fl 2 New York NY 10004-2434

WENK, EDWARD, JR., civil engineer, policy analyst, educator, writer; b. Balt., Jan. 24, 1920; s. Edward and Lillie (Heller) W.; m. Carolyn Frances Lyford, Dec. 27, 1941; children: Lawrence Shelley, Robin Edward Alexander, Terry Allan. BE, Johns Hopkins U., 1940, DEng, 1950; MSc, Harvard U., 1947; DSc (hon.), U. R.I., 1968; LHD (hon.), Johns Hopkins U., 1989. Registered profl. engr. Head structures div. USN David Taylor Model Basin, Washington, 1942-56; chmn. dept. engring. mechanics S.W. Research Inst., San Antonio, 1956-59; sr. specialist sci. and tech. Legis. Reference Service, Library of Congress, Washington, 1959-61; chief sci. policy research div. Legis. Reference Service, Library of Congress, 1964-66; tech. asst. to U.S. President's sci. adviser and exec. sec. Fed. Council for Sci. and Tech., White House, Washington, 1961-64; exec. sec. Nat. Council on Marine Resources and Engring. Devel., Exec. Office of Pres., Washington, 1966-70; prof. engring. and pub. affairs U. Wash., Seattle, 1970-83, prof. emeritus, 1983—; dir. program in social mgmt. tech. U. Wash., 1973-79; tech. advisor to gov. State of Wash., 1993—; lectr. numerous univs.; cons. in pub. policy for environ. and tech. affairs, risk assessments, ocean engring., decision theory; Nat. Adv. Com. on Oceans and Atmosphere, 1972-73; vice chmn. U.S. Congress Tech. Assessment Adv. Coun., 1973-79; adviser Congress, GAO, NSF, EPA, NOAA, White House, UN Secretariat, Wash. State, Alaska, U.K., Australia, Sweden, The Philippines, Alaska Oil Spill Commn., 1989, Wash. State Marine Oversight Bd., 1992, pub. interest groups; vis. scholar Woodrow Wilson Internat. Ctr. for Scholars, 1970-72, Harvard U., 1976, Woods Hole Oceanographic Instn., 1976, U. Sussex, 1977. Author: The Politics of the Ocean, 1972, Margins for Survival, 1979, Tradeoffs-Imperatives of Choice in a High-Tech World, 1986, Making Waves--Engineering, Politics and the Social Management of Technology, 1995; editor: Engring. Mechs. Jour., 1958-60, Exptl. Mechs. Jour., 1954-56; mem. editl. bd. Tech. Forecasting, Tech. in Soc.; contbr. articles to profl. jours.; designer Aluminaut submarine, 1959; author of concept of tech. assessment, 1964. Bd. dirs. Human Interaction Rsch. Inst., 1980-90, Smithsonian Sci. Info. Exch., 1977-82, URS Corp., 1973-88; mem. Interfaith Alliance. Ensign USNR, 1944-45. Recipient Navy Meritorious Civilian Svc. award, 1946; named Disting. Alumnus Johns Hopkins U., 1979, Tchr. of Yr., Wash. State Engrs., 1980, Tchr. of Yr., Students in Pub. Adminstrn., 1986, Disting. Alumnus, Balt. Poly. Inst., 1991; Ford Found. grantee, 1970; Rockefeller Found. Belagio fellow, 1976, 90; 1st Stuckenburg lectr. Wash. U., 1988; Regents lectr. U. Calif., Berkeley, 1989. Fellow ASME (exec.), AAAS; mem. ASCE, NSPE, Soc. Exptl. Stress Analysis (past pres. and William M. Murray lectr.), Internat. Assn. Impact Assessment (pres. 1981-82), NAE (chmn. com. on pub. policy 1970-75), Nat. Acad. Pub. Adminstrn., Am. Soc. for Pub. Adminstrn. (chmn. com. on sci. and tech. in govt. 1974-78), Assembly Engring. and Marine Bd. NRC, Nat. Oceanography Assn. (v.p. pub. affairs 1979-72), Cousteau Soc. (chmn. adv. bd.), Explorers Club, Sigma Xi (nat. lectr.), Tau Beta Pi, Chi Epsilon. Club: Cosmos (Washington). Home: 111 Lake Ave W #302 Kirkland WA 98033-6155 *Each of us has the opportunity, indeed responsibility, to contribute to the human experience and to enrich the lives of future generations. In a world of change, cultural diversity and uncertainty, we must be ourselves and not merely slaves of conventional thought. We must act on the basis of what we believe to be right rather than only from the desire to be loved.*

WENNER, CHARLES RODERICK, lawyer; b. New Haven, Jan. 10, 1947; s. Charles Bellew and Joan Rhoda (Morrison) W. BS, Coll. Charleston, 1969; JD, U. Conn., 1973. Bar: Conn. 1974, D.C. 1977. Law clk. Conn. Superior Ct., Hartford, 1973-74; staff atty. SEC, Washington, 1974-76, spl. counsel to chmn., 1976-77; assoc. Fulbright & Jaworski, Washington, 1977-81, ptnr., 1981—; lectr. law Sch. Law U. Conn., 1973-74. Trustee Calvary United Meth. Ch., Arlington, Va., 1993-95; counselor Gospel Mission of Washington, 1991—; bd. dirs. Operation Friendship Internat., Inc., Washington, 1993—. Recipient Am. Hist. award DAR, Charleston, 1969. Mem. ABA, D.C. Bar Assn. Methodist. Avocations: running. Home: 1101 S Arlington Ridge Rd Arlington VA 22202-1951 Office: Fulbright & Jaworski 801 Pennsylvania Ave NW Washington DC 20004-2615

WENNER, GENE CHARLES, arts foundation executive; b. Catasauqua, Pa., Dec. 21, 1931; s. Clinton G. and Bertha (Taggert) W.; m. Carole Brunner, Aug. 15, 1953; children: Robert Larren, Laurel E. Wenner Carsell. B.S. in Music, West Chester (Pa.) State Coll., 1953; M.Ed. in Music, Pa. State U., 1954. Tchr. music Phila. pub. schs., 1945-55, 56-60; assoc. prof. Kutztown (Pa.) State Coll., 1960-66, dir. coll. choir, 1960-66; fine arts adv. Pa. Dept. Edn., 1966-69, U.S. Office Edn., 1969-71; asst. dir. arts in edn. program John D. Rockefeller 3d Fund, 1971-78; arts edn. coordinator Office Commr., U.S. Office Edn., 1978-79; pres. Am. Music Conf., Wilmette, Ill., 1979-81; v.p. for programs Nat. Found. Advancement in Arts, Miami, Fla., 1983-87; pres. Arts and Edn. Cons., Inc., Reston, Va., 1987-91; sr. cons. Bus. & Industry for Arts Edn., 1990-91; exec. dir. Charlotte (N.C.) Community Sch. for the Arts, 1991—; fund raising cons. Nat. Pub. Radio, Funding Ctr., S.C. Gov. Sch.; sr. cons. Spl. Kids in Pub., 1991; master tchr. Inst. Arts; guest lectr. U. N.C., U. Tex., Loyola U.; mus. dir. Allentown (Pa.) Mcpl. Opera, 1962-63, Allentown Civic Little Theatre, 1964, Little Theatre Alexandria, Va., 1971; dir. Hershey (Pa.) Little Theatre, 1967-68, Hershey Community Chorus, 1967-69. Composer: I'll Never Forget You, 1968, Chorale of Dedication, 1974, Turn Thou to Me, 1975, Are You Nobody, Too?, 1976, Great Things God Hath Done, 1986, In My Father's House, 1986; original music and script Adventures in the Arts, Hershey, 1968; also original TV music, I Am the Way, 1985, When You Remember, 1985; author papers, reports in field. Served with AUS, 1955-56. Named Best Mus. Dir. Little Theatre Alexandria. Mem. Music Educators Nat. Conf., Nat. Guild of Community Schs. of the Arts. Club: Masons. Home and Office: 4100 B Bannockburn Pl Charlotte NC 28211-4532

WENNER, HERBERT ALLAN, pediatrician; b. Drums, Pa., Nov. 14, 1912; s. Herbert C. and Verna (Walp) W.; m. Ruth I. Berger, June 27, 1942; children—Peter W., James M., Susan T., Thomas H. B.S., Bucknell U., 1933; M.D., U. Rochester, 1939. Diplomate: Am. Bd. Microbiology, Am. Bd. Pediatrics. Intern in pathology Sch. Medicine, U. Colo., Denver, 1939-40; intern in pediatrics Yale Sch. Medicine, 1940-41, asst. resident and fellow in pediatrics, 1941-43, instr. preventive medicine, 1944-46; NRC fellow Yale U.-Johns Hopkins U., 1943-44; asst. prof. pediatrics and bacteriology Sch. Medicine, U. Kans., Kansas City, 1946-49; asso. prof. Sch. Medicine, U. Kans., 1949-51, research prof. pediatrics, 1951-69, adj. prof., 1975—; Joyce C. Hall Disting. prof. pediatrics U. Mo. Sch. Med., Kansas City, 1969-83; emeritus adj. prof. U. Mo. Sch. Med. (Sch. Dentistry), 1970—; formerly cons. epidemiology Kans. Bd. Health, Mo. Bd. Health. Asso. editor: Am. Jour. Epidemiology, 1967-79; mem. editorial bd.: Intervirology, 1972-79; past mem. editorial adv. bd.: Archives of Virology, 1975-79; contbr. articles to med. books and jours. NIH Research Career awardee, 1962. Fellow AAAS, Am. Public Health Assn., Am. Coll. Epidemiology, Am. Acad. Pediatrics; mem. Soc. Pediatric Research, Am. Pediatric Soc., Soc. Exptl. Biology and Medicine, Biometrics Soc., Mo. Med. Assn., AMA, Royal Soc. Health, AAUP, N.Y. Acad. Scis., Am. Epidemiology Soc., Infectious Disease Soc. Am. Episcopalian. Home: 9711 Johnson Dr Shawnee Mission KS 66203-3147 *Good parents, a devoted family, superb teachers and hard work have contributed to my career, and the rewards therein.*

WENNER, JANN SIMON, editor, publisher; b. N.Y.C., Jan. 7, 1946; s. Edward and Ruth N. (Simmons) W.; m. Jane Ellen Schindelhiem, July 1, 1968; children: Alexander Jann, Theodore Simon, Edward Augustus. Student, U. Calif.-Berkeley, 1964-66. Editor, pub. Rolling Stone mag., N.Y.C., 1967—, Record, N.Y.C., 1981-86, Look mag., N.Y.C., 1979, Men's Jour., 1992—; editor in chief Outside Mag., San Francisco, 1977-78, US Mag., N.Y.C., 1985—, Men's Jour., 1992—; exec. v.p. Rock & Roll Hall of Fame. Author: Lennon Remembers, 1971, Garcia, 1972. Bd. dirs. Robinhood Found. Recipient Disting. Achievement award U. So. Calif. Sch. Journalism and Alumni Assn., 1976, Nat. Mag. award, 1970, 77, 86, 87, 88, 89. Mem. Am. Soc. Mag. Editors. Office: Rolling Stone Wenner Media Inc 1290 Avenue Of The Americas New York NY 10104*

WENNERSTROM, ARTHUR JOHN, aeronautical engineer; b. N.Y.C., Jan. 11, 1935; s. Albert Eugene and Adele (Trebus) W.; m. Bonita Gay Westenberg, Sept. 6, 1969 (div. Jan. 1989); children: Bjorn Erik, Erika Lindsay; m. Vicki Lynn Merrick, Feb. 17, 1990. BS in Mech. Engring., Duke U., 1956; MS in Aero. Engring., MIT, 1958; DSc of Tech., Swiss Fedn. Inst. Tech., Zurich, 1965. Sr. engr. Aircraft Armaments, Inc., Cockeysville, Md., 1958-59; rsch. engr. Sulzer Bros., Ltd., Winterthur, Switzerland, 1960-62; project engr. No. Rsch. and Engring. Corp., Cambridge, Mass., 1965-67; rsch. leader Air Force Aerospace Rsch. Lab., Dayton, Ohio, 1967-75, Air Force Aero Propulsion Lab., Dayton, 1975-91; dir. NATO Adv. Group for Aerospace R & D, Paris, 1991-94; engring. cons. Hillsborough, N.C., 1994—; mem. tech. adv. com., von Karman Inst. for Fluid Dynamics, Rhode-St-Genese, Belgium, 1988-94, bd. dirs.; lectr. in field. Contbr. articles to profl. jours. 1st lt., USAF, 1962-65. Recipient Cliff Garrett Turbo Machinery award Soc. Automotive Engrs., 1986; named Fed. Profl. Employee of Yr. Dayton C. of C., 1975; fellow Air Force Wright Aeronautical Labs., 1987. Fellow AIAA (assoc. editor 1980-82, Air Breathing Propulsion award 1979), ASME (chmn. turbomachinery com. gas turbine div. 1973-75, mem. exec. com. 1977-82, chmn. 1980-81, program chmn. internat. gas turbine conf. 1976, Beijing internat. gas turbine symposium 1985, mem. nat. nominating com. 1985-87, mem. TOPC bd. on rsch. 1985-88, mem.-at-large energy conversion group 1986-88, mem. bd. comm. 1989-91, editor Jour. Engring. for Gas Turbines and Power 1983-88, chmn. bd. editors 1989-91, founder, editor Jour. Turbomachinery 1986-88, R. Tom Sawyer award 1993). Achievements include introduction of wide-chord integrally-bladed fan, introduction of swept blading into mil. aircraft turbine engines; 5 patents in field. Home: 58 Blvd Emile Augier, 75016 Paris France Office: Adv Group for Aerospace, 7 Rue Ancelle, 92200 Neuilly sur Seine France

WENRICH, JOHN WILLIAM, college president; b. York, Pa., June 8, 1937; s. Ralph Chester and Helen Louise (McCollam) W.; m. Linda Larsen, June 23, 1961 (dec. Sept. 1966); 1 child, Thomas Allen; m. Martha Gail Lofberg, Sept. 1, 1967; 1 child, Margaret Ann. A.B., Princeton U., 1959; M.A., U. Mich., 1961, Ph.D., 1968. Fgn. service officer Dept. State, Washington, 1962-65; rep. Internat. Devel. Found., N.Y.C., 1965-66; project dir. U. Mich., Ann Arbor, 1966-69; asst. to pres. Coll. San Mateo, Calif., 1969-

71; v.p. Ferris State U., Big Rapids, Mich., 1971-75, pres., 1984-88; pres. Canada Coll., Redwood City, Calif., 1975-79, Santa Ana Coll., Calif., 1979-84; chancellor San Diego Community Coll. Dist., 1988-90, Dallas County Community Coll., 1990—. Co-author: Leadership in Administration of Technical and Vocational Education, 1974, Administration of Vocational Education. Recipient Meritorious Service medal Dept. State, 1966; Hinsdale scholar Sch. Edn. U. Mich., 1968. Avocations: bridge; tennis; travel. Home: 1520 Wyndmere Dr De Soto TX 75115-7808 Office: 701 Elm St Dallas TX 75202-3250

WENSINGER, ARTHUR STEVENS, language and literature educator, author; b. Grosse Pointe, Mich., Mar. 9, 1926; s. Carl Franklin and Suzanne (Stevens) W. Grad., Phillips Acad. Andover, 1944; BA, Dartmouth Coll., 1948; MA, U. Mich., 1951; postgrad., U. Munich, 1948, 50-51, U. Innsbruck, 1953-54; PhD, U. Mich., 1958. Instr., asst. prof., assoc. prof. Wesleyan U., Middletown, Conn., 1955-68, prof. German and humanities, 1968-93, Marcus Taft prof. German and humanities, 1977-93, prof. emeritus, 1994—, chmn. dept. German lang. and lit., 1971-93, also sr. tutor Coll. Letters; pres. Friends of Davison Art Ctr.; mem. selection com. German Acad. Exch. Svc., 1980-92. Author: Hogarth on High Life, 1970, Plays by Arthur Schnitzler, 1982-83, 95; translator, editor: The Theater of the Bauhaus, 1961, rev. edit., 1996, The Letters and Journals of Paula Modersohn-Becker, 1983, 2d edit., 1990; translator, editor: Querelle: The Film Book, 1983; translator: Franz Kafka: Pictures of a Life, 1984, The Sons, 1989, Marlene Dietrich: Portraits, 1984, Shabbat (Peter Stefan Jungk), 1985, (reprinted 1994), Hanna Shygulla and R.W. Fassbinder, 1986, Kaethe Kollwitz: The Work in Color, 1988, Niklas Frank, In the Shadow of the Reich, 1991; co-translator: Günter Grass, Two States-One Nation?, 1990; contbr. to R.W. Fassbinder, The Anarchy of the Imagination, 1992; editor: Stone Island (Peter S. Boynton), 1973; co-editor: Hesse's Siddhartha, 1962; continuing editor: Correspondence of Norman Douglas, 1868-1952; contbr. to Columbia U. Database CD-ROM for quotations, aphorisms, 1995—; contbr. articles to profl. jours.; translator in field. Wesleyan Ctr. for Humanities fellow, 1974, Reynolds fellow, 1950-51, Fulbright fellow, 1954-55, Danforth fellow, 1959, Ford Found. fellow, 1970-71; Inter Nations grantee, 1978, 82, NEH rsch. grantee, 1993. Mem. MLA, Am. Assn. Tchrs. German, Heinrich von Kleist Gesellschaft, Internat. Brecht Soc., Kafka Soc. Am., Auden Soc., Soc. Preservation New Eng. Antiquities, Conn. Acad. Arts and Scis., Yale Libr. Assocs., Haddam, Conn. Land Trust, Phi Beta Kappa, Phi Kappa Phi, Delta Tau Delta. Home: Candlewood Farm 95 Jacoby Rd Higganum CT 06441-4225 Office: Wesleyan U PO Box 6090 Middletown CT 06459-6082

WENSITS, JAMES EMRICH, newspaper editor; b. South Bend, Ind., Oct. 8, 1944; s. John Andrew and Melva Mae (Betz) W.; m. Wendy Anne Reygaert, June 12, 1965; children: Cheryl Wensits Lightfoot, John, Kristin Wensits Hough, Amy; m. Catherine Marie Palmer Pope, Nov. 27, 1987; stepdaughter, Christina Pope. BA in Journalism, Purdue U., 1966. Reporter South Bend Tribune, 1966-92, assoc. editor, 1992—. Office: South Bend Tribune 225 W Colfax Ave South Bend IN 46626-1000

WENSTROM, FRANK AUGUSTUS, state senator, city and county official; b. Dover, N.D., July 27, 1903; s. James August and Anna Petra (Kringstad) W.; student public schs., Carrington, N.D.; LLD (hon.), U. N.D., 1990. m. Mary Esther Pickett, June 10, 1938. In oil bus., Carrington, 1932-38, Williston, N.D., 1938-45; mgr. Williston C. of C., 1945-51; pub. rels. officer 1st Nat. Bank, Williston, 1951-53, mng. officer real estate mortgage dept., 1953-60; exec. officer Northwestern Fed. Savs. and Loan Assn. Williston, 1964-68; spl. cons. Am. State Bank Williston, 1968-73; mem. N.D. Senate, 1957-60, 67—, pres. pro tem, 1973-74; lt. gov. State of N.D., 1963-64; dir., sec. Williston Cmty. Hotel Co., 1950—; chmn. subscriber's com. N.W. dist. N.D. Blue Cross-Blue Shield, 1972—. Mem. Williston Public Housing Authority, 1951—, Williams County Park Bd., 1951—, N.D. Yellowstone-Ft. Union Commn., 1957-64, Legis. Rsch. Coun., 1957-60, Legis. Coun., 1969-70; del. N.D. 2d Constl. Conv., 1970, pres., 1971-72; Williams County chmn. U.S. Savs. Bonds Com., 1958-69; creator Frank A. Wenstrom Libr. for Student Rsch., Grank Forks, N.D., 1984; co-chair N.D. Constitution subcom. for developing and displaying hist. papers pertaining to U.S. constitution; mem. Constitutional Celebration com., 1985; pres. N.D. 2d Constitutional Conv., 1971-72; co-chair archives search com. N.D. Const. Conv., 1971-72; bd. dirs. N.D. Easter Seals Soc., 1960-75, state pres., 1970-71; bd. advisors Salvation Army, 1960-75; bd. dirs. Univ. Found., U. N.D., Williston Center, 1965—; mem. joint legis. com. Nat. Assn. Ret. Tchrs.-Am. Assn. Ret. Persons, 1975—, chmn., 1979-80. Recipient Liberty Bell award N.D. Bar Assn., 1977, Disting. Svc. award Bismarck Jr. Coll., 1981; award Nature Conservancy, 1982; Svc. award Greater N.D. Assn., 1983, C.P. Lura award Disting. Service to Edn. Minot State Coll., 1986, Award of Excellence Com. of Gov.'s Council on Human Resources, 1986. Mem. Upper Missouri Purebred Cattle Breeders Assn. (sec.-treas. 1947-62), N.D. Wildlife Fedn. (state pres. 1947-48), Greater N.D. Assn. (dir. 1955-56, mem. Roosevelt Nat. Meml. Park com. 1957-63), U.S. Savs. and Loan League (legis. com. 1965-67). Republican. Congregationalist. Clubs: Rotary, Elks, Masons (hon. grand master), Shriners, Order Eastern Star. Office: PO Box 187 Williston ND 58802-0187

WENSTRUP, H. DANIEL, chemical company executive; b. Cin., Sept. 27, 1934; s. Carl D. and Lucille (Cahill) W.; m. Eileen O'Brien, Nov. 24, 1956; children: Gary, Julie, Patrick, Kevin, Katy, Greg. BSBA, Xavier U., 1956. Sales rep. Chemcentral Corp., Cin., 1958-66; sales mgr. Chemcentral Corp., Detroit, 1966-72, gen. mgr., 1972-75, v.p. regional mgr., 1975-82; v.p. dir. mktg. Chemcentral Corp., Chgo., 1982-86, pres., 1986—, pres., chief exec. officer, 1988—, bd. dirs.; bd. dirs. Prove Quim S.A. de C.V. Mem., supporter Mus. Sci. Industry, Chgo., 1991—, Ravinia Chgo. Symphony, 1991—, adv. com. Gov. Edgar. 1st lt. U.S. Army, 1956-58. Mem. Chem. Mfrs. Assn. (dir. 1990-92), Chem. Industry Coun. Ill. (dir. 1989—, pres.), Nat. Paint & Coatings Assn., Nat. Petroleum Refiners Assn., Ill. Mfrs. Assn., Ill. C. of C., Medinah Country Club, Oak Brook Tennis Club, Am. Cancer Soc., NACD Edn. Found. (trustee). Republican. Roman Catholic. Avocations: golf, tennis, jogging, reading, theatre. Office: Chemcentral Corp 7050 W 71st St Bedford Park IL 60638-5902

WENTE, PATRICIA ANN, radio executive; 1 child, Jessica. BA in Communications, Sangamon State U., 1978, MA in Communications, 1981. Vol. coord. Sta. WSSR-FM, Springfield, Ill., 1977-79; sta. mgr. Stas. WRRS, KMUW, Wichita, Kans., 1979-85; gen. mgr. Sta. KGOU, Norman, Okla., 1985-87; mgr. sta. grant programs Corp. for Pub. Broadcasting, Washington, 1987-89; dir., gen. mgr. Sta. KWMU-FM, St. Louis, 1989—; participant NPR Pub. Radio Conf., 1979-90, Pub. Broadcasting Svc. Conf., 1987-89, Corp. for Pub. Broadcasting Conf., 1977-80, Rocky Mountain Pub. Radio Meetings, 1987-89, SECA Meetings, 1987-89; bd. dirs. Pub. Radio in Mid-Am. Conf., 1986-88; mem. gerontology faculty Wichita State u., 1983-84; promotion & pub. svc. announcer Sta. KPTS-TV, Wichita, 1979-80; judge coord. Ohio State Awards, 1986-87. Mem. adv. com. for handicapped svcs. Wichita State U., 1980-82. Mem. Pub. Telecommunication Fin. Mgmt. Assn. (bd. dirs. 1990—), Alpha Epsilon Rho (pres. 1979-84, advisor 1990). Office: Sta KWMU-FM Univ Mo-St Louis 8001 Natural Bridge Rd Saint Louis MO 63121-4401

WENTORF, ROBERT HENRY, physical chemist; b. West Bend, Wis., May 28, 1926; s. Robert H. and Sophia Wentorf; m. Vivian Marty, Aug. 20, 1949; children: Jill, Laine, Rolf; m. 2d Frances Cohen Gillepsie, 1993. B.S. in Chem. Engring, U. Wis., 1948, Ph.D. in Chemistry, 1952. Teaching and research asst. U. Wis., Madison, 1948-52; vis. prof. U. Wis., 1966-67; mem. R & D staff GE Co., Schenectady, 1952-88; disting. research prof. Rensselaer Poly. Inst., Troy, N.Y., 1988—. Editor: Modern Very High Pressure Techniques, 1962, Advances in High Pressure Research, vol. IV, 1974; contbr. articles to sci. jours. Served with USN, 1944-45. Recipient New Materials prize Am. Phys. Soc., 1977. Mem. Am. Chem. Soc. (Ipatieff prize 1965), Nat. Acad. Engring., Mohawk Soaring Club (dir., instr. gliding), Sigma Xi, Alpha Chi Sigma, Tau Beta Pi. Patentee in field. Home: RR 3 Box 154A Greenwich NY 12834-9111 Office: Rensselaer Poly Tech Inst Chem Engring Dept Troy NY 12180

WENTWORTH, DIANA VON WELANETZ, author; b. L.A., Mar. 4, 1941; d. Eugene and Marguerite (Rufi) Webb; m. Frederic Paul von Welanetz, Nov. 2, 1963 (dec. Mar. 19, 1989); 1 child, Lisa Frances von Welanetz; m. Theodore S. Wentworth, Dec. 9, 1989; stepchildren: Christina Linn, Kathryn Allison. Student, UCLA, 1958-60. Ptnr. von Welanetz Cooking Workshop, L.A., 1968-85; host New Way Gourmet, 1983-86; founder Inside Edge Found. Edn., Calif., 1985-93. Author: The Pleasure of Your Company, 1976 (Cookbook of Yr.), With Love from Your Kitchen, 1976, The Art of Buffet Entertaining, 1978, The Von Welanetz Guide to Ethnic Ingredients, 1983, L.A. Cuisine, 1985, Celebrations, 1985, Chicken Soup for the Soul Cookbook, 1995. Treas. Louise L. Hay Found., Carson, Calif., 1988—; advisor Women of Vision, Calif., 1995—. Mem. Internat. Food, Wine & Travel Writers Assn., Internat. Assn. Cooking Profls., Angels of Arts/Orange County Performing Arts Ctr., Ctr. Club. Avocations: painting, fine art, travel writing, design. Home: 3 Malibu Cir Corona Del Mar CA 92625 Office: 4631 Teller Ave Ste 100 Newport Beach CA 92660

WENTWORTH, JACK ROBERTS, business educator, consultant; b. Elgin, Ill., June 11, 1928; s. William Franklin and Elizabeth (Roberts) W.; m. Rosemary Ann Pawlak, May 30, 1956; children—William, Barbara. Student, Carleton Coll., 1946-48; BS, Ind. U., 1950, MBA, 1954, DBA, 1959. Coord. displays Cadillac divsn., Gen. Motors Corp., Detroit, 1954-56; asst. prof. bus., assoc. dir. research Sch. of Bus. Ind. U., Bloomington, 1957-60, assoc. prof., dir. rsch., 1960-70, prof., 1970-93, chmn. MBA program, 1970-76, chmn. dept., faculty rep. NCAA, 1978-85, dean Sch. of Bus., 1984-93, Arthur M. Weimer prof., 1993—; mktg. cons., Bloomington, 1960—; bd. dirs. Kimball Internat., Jasper, Ind., Bank One, Bloomington, Market Facts Inc., Chgo., KPT Corp., Bloomfield, Lone Star Industries, Stamford, Conn. Editor: (monograph) Marketing Horizons, 1965; exec. editor Bus. Horizons, 1960-70. Served to 1st lt. USAF, 1950-53. Recipient Teaching award MBA Assn., 1973, 78, 81, 84, 85, Svc. award Assn. for Bus. and Econ. Rsch., 1983. Mem. Am. Mktg. Assn. (v.p. 1971-73), Grad. Mgmt. Admissions Coun. (chmn. bd. trustees 1977-78), Univ. Club, Masons, Beta Gamma Sigma (pres. Alpha of Ind. chpt. 1971-72, bd. govs. 1986—, nat. pres. 1994—). Republican. Episcopalian. Avocations: athletic events; travel; bicycling; model railroading; magic. Office: Indiana Univ Sch Bus Bloomington IN 47405

WENTWORTH, MICHAEL JUSTIN, curator; b. Detroit, June 15, 1938; s. Harold Arnold and Marian (Jones) W. MFA, U. Mich., 1962; PHD, Harvard U., 1976. Curator, acting dir. Smith Coll. Mus. Art, Northhampton, Mass., 1968-69; dir. Rose Art Mus., Brandies U., Waltham, Mass., 1970-74; assoc. prof. Wellesley Coll., Mass., 1976; curator Boston Athenaeum, Mass., 1985—. Author: Tissot: Catalogue Raisonné of Prints, 1976, James Tissot, 1984, Tissot, 1988, 50 Books in the Collection of the Boston Athenaeum, 1994, The Boston Library Society, 1995. Office: Boston Athenaeum 10 1/2 Beacon St Boston MA 02108-3703

WENTWORTH, MURRAY JACKSON, artist, educator; b. Boston, Jan. 18, 1927; s. Harold Squires and Mary Louise (Murray) W.; m. Elaine Magnuson, June 16, 1953; 1 child, Janet Louise. Diploma, Art Inst. Boston, 1950. Advt. artist Agy. Art Svcs., Boston, 1950-58; instr. Art Inst. Boston, 1958-78; artist, instr. Norwell, Mass., 1968—. Group shows, Allied Artists Am., 1980, 82 (Silver medal 1980), Allied Art Am., 1982 (Obrig prize 1982), Am. Watercolor Soc., 1980 (Dolphin fellow 1980), Rocky Mount Nat. Exhibition, 1982 (Grumbacher award 1982). Cpl. U.S. Army, 1945-47. Recipient Hudson Valley Art Assn. award, 1991, Guild Boston Artists award, 1992. Mem. Allied Artists Am., Nat. Acad. Design (Pike Meml. award 1986), Am. Watercolor Soc., New England Watercolor Soc. (Grumbacher Gold medal award 1989). Home: 132 Central St Norwell MA 02061-1306

WENTWORTH, THEODORE SUMNER, lawyer; b. Bklyn., July 18, 1938; s. Theodore Sumner and Alice Ruth (Wortmann) W.; AA, Am. River Coll., 1958; JD, U. Calif., Hastings, 1962; m. Sharon Linelle Arkush, 1965 (dec. 1987); children: Christina Linn, Kathryn Allison; m. Diana Webb von Welanetz, 1989; 1 stepchild, Lexi von Welanetz. Bar: Calif. 1963, U.S. Dist. Ct. (no., ctrl. dists.) Calif., U.S. Ct. Appeals (9th cir.), U.S. Supreme Ct.; cert. civil trial specialist; diplomate Nat. Bd. Trial Advocacy; assoc. Am. Bd. Trial Advocates. Assoc. Adams, Hunt & Martin, Santa Ana, Calif., 1963-66; ptnr. Hunt, Liljestrom & Wentworth, Santa Ana, 1967-77; pres. Solabs Corp.; chmn. bd., exec. v.p. Plant Warehouse, Inc., Hawaii, 1974-82; prin. Law Offices of Theodore S. Wentworth, specializing in personal injury, product liability, profl. malpractice, bus. fraud, fire loss litigation, human rights issues, Newport Beach and Temecula, Calif.; judge pro tem Superior Ct. Attys. Panel, Harbor Mcpl. Ct.; owner Eagles Ridge Ranch, Temecula, 1977—. Pres., bd. dirs. Santa Ana-Tustin Community Chest, 1972; v.p., trustee South Orange County United Way, 1973-75; pres. Orange County Fedn. Funds, 1972-73; bd. dirs. Orange County Mental Health Assn. Mem. ABA, Am. Bd. Trial Advocates (assoc.), State Bar Calif., Orange County Bar Assn. (dir. 1972-76), Am. Trial Lawyers Assn., Calif. Trial Lawyers Assn. (bd. govs. 1968-70), Orange County Trial Lawyers Assn. (pres. 1967-68), Lawyer-Pilots Bar Assn., Aircraft Owners and Pilots Assn., Bahia Corinthian Yacht Club, Balboa Bay Club, Corsair Yacht Club, The Center Club, Pacific Club, Newport, Fourth of July Yacht Club (Catalina Island). Research in vedic prins., natural law, quantum physics and mechanics. Office: 4631 Teller Ave Ste 100 Newport Beach CA 92660-8105 also: Wells Fargo Bank Bldg 41530 Enterprise Cir S Temecula CA 92590-4816

WENTZ, BILLY MELVIN, JR., finance executive; b. Charlotte, N.C., Aug. 11, 1953; s. Billy M. Wentz and Betty Jane (Harper) Bass; m. Cynthia Gardner, Aug. 2, 1975; children: Jessica, Kyle. BSBA, U. of N.C., 1975; MBA, U. of Tampa, 1979. CPA, N.C. Contr. Kerley and Edwards, Charlotte, N.C., 1975-76; plant acct. Rexham Corp., Charlotte, 1976-77; acctg. mgr. Rexham Corp., Sarasota, Fla., 1977-79, div. controller, 1979-80, group controller, 1980-82; corp. cost mgr. Rexham Corp., Charlotte, 1982-86, corp. dir. acctg., 1986-87, corp. contr., 1987-89, fin. dir., 1989—. Bd. dirs. YMCA, Charlotte. Mem. AICPA, N.C. Assn. CPA's, Country Haven Swim and Racquet Club (treas.).. Office: 4201 Congress St Ste 340 Charlotte NC 28209-4621

WENTZ, CHARLES ALVIN, JR., environmentalist, chemical engineer; b. Edwardsville, Ill., Oct. 12, 1935; s. Charles Alvin and Frances Margaret (Bohm) W.; m. Sandra Niederecker, Dec. 11, 1961 (div. Jan. 1982); children: Sharon, Christopher, Suzanne, Sheila; m. Joan Domigan, Aug., 1983. BSChemE, U. Mo., 1957, MSChemE, 1959; PhDChemE, Northwestern U., 1961; MBA, So. Ill. U., 1985. Cert. safety profl.; registered profl. engr. Various exec. positions Phillips Petroleum Co., Bartlesville, Okla., 1961-82; pres. New Park Waste Treatment, Inc., New Orleans, 1982-83, ENSCO, Inc., El Dorado, Ark., 1983-84; pres., CEO Wentz Healthcare, Inc., Lebanon, Ill., 1984—; CEO Internat. Sci. Mgmt., Inc., Edwardsville, Ill., 1985—; mgr., waste and safety Argonne (Ill.) Nat. Lab., 1988-91; assoc. dean Chulalongkorn U., Bangkok, 1994; vis. prof. So. Ill. U., Edwardsville, 1984-86. Author: Hazardous Waste Management, 1989, 2d edit., 1995, (with others) Occupational and Environmental Safety, 1990, Encyclopedia of Environmental Control Technology, vol. 5, 1992; editor spl. issues Environ. Progress, 1988, 89; patentee in field; contbr. articles to profl. jours. Mem. adv. bd. Ill. Hazardous Waste Rsch. and Info. Ctr., 1989-91. Mem. Am. Soc. Safety Engrs. (instr. 1989—), Am. Chem. Soc. , Am. Inst. of Chem. Engrs. (instr. 1989—), Am. Inst. for Pollution Prevention, Nat. Safety Coun., Water Pollution Control Fedn., Air and Waste Mgmt. Assn., Sigma Xi. Avocations: hunting, fishing, gardening, cooking. Home and Office: Internat Sci Mgmt Inc 5953 Old Poag Rd Edwardsville IL 62025-7341

WENTZ, JANET, principal. Prin. Los Ranchos Elem. Sch. Recipient Doe Elem. Sch. Recognition award, 1989-90. Office: Los Ranchos Elem Sch 5785 Los Ranchos Rd San Luis Obispo CA 93401-8247

WENTZ, JEFFREY LEE, information systems consultant; b. Philippi, W.Va., Nov. 29, 1956; s. William Henry and Edith Marie (McBee) W. AS in Data Processing, BS in Acctg., Fairmont (W.Va.) State Coll., 1978. Programmer/analyst U.S. Dept. Energy, Morgantown, W.Va., 1978-79; analyst Middle South Svcs., New Orleans, 1979-81; sr. analyst Bank of Am., San Francisco, 1981-83; pres., cons. Wentz Cons. Inc., San Francisco, 1983—. Office: Wentz Consulting Inc 1378 34th Ave San Francisco CA 94122-1309

WENTZ, SIDNEY FREDERICK, insurance company executive, foundation executive; b. Dallas, Mar. 27, 1932; s. Howard Beck and Emmy Lou (Cawthon) W.; m. Barbara Strait, Sept. 9, 1961; children: Eric, Jennifer, Robin. AB, Princeton U., 1954; LLB, Harvard U. Bar: N.Y. 1961. Atty. White & Case, N.Y.C., 1960-65, Western Electric Co., 1965-66, AT&T Corp., 1966-67; with Crum & Forster Inc., Morristown, N.J., 1967—, v.p., gen. counsel, 1967-71, sr. v.p., gen. counsel, 1971-72, exec. v.p., 1972, pres., 1972-87, chmn. bd., 1987-88, chmn. exec. com., 1988-90, also bd. dirs.; chmn. bd. Robert Wood Johnson Found., Princeton, N.J., 1989—. Trustee Morristown Meml. Hosp., 1974—, Drew U., 1991—. Served to lt. (j.g.) USNR, 1954-57. Mem. Morris County Golf Club, Morristown Field Club, Sakonnet (R.I.) Golf Club, Baltusrol Golf Club, Jupiter Hills (Fla.) Golf Club, Loblolly Pines (Fla.) Golf Club. Office: Robert Wood Johnson Found PO Box 2316 College Rd E Princeton NJ 08540-6672

WENTZ, WALTER JOHN, health administration educator; b. Newburgh, Ohio, June 17, 1928; s. Walter John and Gladys Marjory W.; m. Lynne E. Putnam; children: Marcia, Sharon, Diane, Courtney, Richard, Jerry, Rick. B.A., U. Iowa, 1949, M.A., 1950, Ph.D., 1963. Pres. Meml. Hosp., Saulte Ste Marie, Mich., 1965-71; assoc. prof. Central Mich. U., Mt. Pleasant, 1977-78; prof. health adminstrn. Wichita State U., 1978-87, chmn. dept. health adminstrn. Coll. Health Professions., 1978-87; prof. div. health adminstrn. Gov's State U., Univ. Pk., Ill., 1987—. Contbr. articles to profl. jours., chpts. to books.; Mem. editorial bd.: Jour. Hosp. and Health Services Adminstrn. Fellow Am. Pub. Health Assn., AAAS, Royal Soc. Health, Am. Coll. Healthcare Execs.; mem. Phi Kappa Phi, Sigma Iota Epsilon, Omicron Delta Kappa, Beta Gamma Sigma, Alpha Eta. Republican. Methodist. Club: Rotary (dir.). Office: Governors State U Divsn Health Adminstrn University Park IL 60466

WENTZ, WILLIAM HENRY, JR., aerospace engineer, educator; b. Wichita, Kans., Dec. 18, 1933. BS in Mech. Engring. cum laude, Wichita State U., 1955, MS in Aeronautical Engring., 1961; PhD in Engring. Mechanics, U. Kans., 1969. Lic. profl. engr., Kans. Liaison engr. Beech Aircraft, 1952-53; propulsion engr. Boeing Co., Wichita, Kans., 1955; instr. mech. engring. Wichita State U., 1957-58; aerodynamicist Boeing Co., Wichita, 1958-63; from asst. prof. to assoc. prof. aeronautical engring. Wichita State U., 1963-75, prof. aeronautical engring., 1975-83, Gates-Learjet prof. aeronautical engring., 1983-86, disting. prof. aerospace engring., 1986—, dir. Ctr. Basic and Applied Rsch. Inst. Aviation Rsch., 1986-89, exec. dir. Nat. Inst. Aviation Rsch., 1988—; dir. rsch. projects Boeing Co., 1960, 61, NASA, 1964-66, 66-68, 70-71, 71-83, 86-87, 86-88, 82-87, Dept. of Def., 1986-88, Kans. Tech. Enterprise Corp., 1988—, FAA, 1986—. Contbr. articles to profl. jours. With USAF, 1955-57. Sci. Faculty fellow NSF, 1967-68. Fellow AIAA (assoc., past chmn. Wichita sect., Outstanding advisor student chpt. 1964, 65, 70, Gen. Aviation award 1981, Engr. of Yr. award Wichita sect. 1992, Engr. of Yr. award Region V 1991-92; mem. Soc. Automotive Engrs. (Ralph R. Teeter award 1973), Sigma Gamma Tau, Tau Beta Pi. Office: Wichita State U Nat Inst Aviation Rsch Campus Box 93 Wichita KS 67260-0093

WENZ, RICHARD L., school system and church administrator; b. Lincoln, Nebr., Sept. 24, 1934; s. Arthur Frederick and Mildred Iretha Wenz; m. Janet Helen, July 25, 1959; children: Jennifer, Jeffrey. BA, Concordia Tchrs. Coll., 1956; MA, Washington U., St. Louis, 1961. Tchr. Concordia Luth. Sch., Maplewood, Mo., 1956-61; prin. St. John's Luth. Sch., Hannibal, Mo., 1961-72, Ellisville, Mo., 1972-79; prin., ch. adminstr. Trinity Luth. Sch., Davenport, Iowa, 1979—; mem. Mo. Dist. Patterns Performance Com. 1960-71; pres. Mo. Dist. Tchrs. Conf., 1971, Mo. Dist. Prins. Conf., 1979, St. Louis Prins. Conf., 1979; chmn Mo. Dist. Sch. Com., 1974-76, Iowa Dist. East Sch. Com. 1981-84, evaluator, 1982-85; mem. evaluation team Concordia Tchrs. Coll., 1979; mem. Iowa Gov.'s Adv. Coun. for Non-Pub. Schs., 1984—; site visitor Blue Ribbon Sch. Award, 1986-88; mem. coors. coun. Iowa Dept. Edn., 1988-89; Iowa rep. to sch., Russia, 1989; evaluator Iowa Outcomes, 1992-93. Bd. dirs. Jr. C. of C., 1968-70; active doctinal review com. L.C.M.S., 1981-88, planning coun. for mission and ministry, 1990-92, reconciler, 1993—, tchr. rep. on 150th anniversary, 1993—. Named Alumnus of Yr., Concordia Tchrs. Coll., 1987, Iowa Exemplary Luth. Educator, 1988, Nat. Disting. Luth. Prin, 1993, Nat. Disting. Prin., U.S. Dept. Edn., 1993. Mem. Luth Edn. Assn. (treas. 1986-90), Dept. Luth. Elem. Sch. Prins. (conv. program com. 1986, conv. chmn. 1992), Iowa Assn. Non-Pub. Schs., Iowa Dist. East (bd. dirs. 1982—). Office: Trinity Luth Sch 1122 W Central Park Ave Davenport IA 52804-1805

WENZ, RODNEY E., public relations executive; b. North Platte, Nebr., Dec. 21, 1935. Student in Journalism, U. Nebr. Reporter, city editor Fremont Guide and Tribune, 1954-59; reporter, bur. chief Rockford Newspapers, 1959-66; coord. comm. Chrysler Corp., 1966-67; bus. editor Louisville Courier-Jour., 1967-70; pres. Wenz-Neely Co., Louisville, 1971-85, chmn.; consultant Wenz-Neely Co. (now Shadwick USA), Louisville. Recipient newswriting awards AP, UPI, Disting. Newswriting award Am. Polit. Sci. Assn., 1963; nominee Pulitzer prize, 1963. Mem. NIRI, Pub. Rels. Soc. Am. (counselors acad.). Office: Shadwick USA 950 Breckenridge Ln Louisville KY 40207*

WENZEL, FRED WILLIAM, apparel manufacturing executive; b. St. Louis, Jan. 14, 1916; s. Frederick H. and Ella M. (Heuerman) W.; m. Mary Edna Cruzen; 1 child, Robert F. Grad., U. Wis., 1937. Chmn. H. Wenzel Tent & Duck Co. St. Louis, 1937-52; pres. Hawthorn Co., New Haven, Mo., 1952-64; v.p. Kellwood Co., Chgo., 1961-64; chmn. bd. Kellwood Co., St. Louis, 1964, pres., chmn., 1965-76, chmn., chief exec. officer, 1976-84, chmn., from 1984, now chmn. emeritus. Home: 13315 Fairfield Square Dr Chesterfield MO 63017-5925 Office: Kellwood Co PO Box 14374 Saint Louis MO 63178-4374*

WENZEL, JAMES GOTTLIEB, ocean engineering executive, consultant; b. Springfield, Minn., Oct. 16, 1926; s. Gottlieb Henry and Elvira Wilhemina (Runck) W.; m. Elaine Joyce Abrahamson, June 17, 1950; children: Lori Lynn, Jodi Ann, Sheri Lee, James G. II. BA in Aero Engring. with high distinction, U. Minn., 1948, MS, 1950; DHL (hon.), Calif. Luth. U., Thousand Oaks, 1985. Mgr. aerodynamics Convair, San Diego, 1950-56, asst. to v.p engring., 1956-58; asst. to sr. v.p. engring. Gen. Dynamics Corp., N.Y.C., 1958-60, mgr., govt. planning, 1960-62; v.p. ocean systems Lockheed Missiles & Space Co., Sunnyvale, Calif., 1962-84; pres., chmn. Ocean Minerals Co., Sunnyvale, 1977-84, Marine Devel. Assocs. Inc, Saratoga, Calif., 1984—; chmn. Oreg. Resource Exploration Co., Portland, 1985—; pres. Centry Systems Inc., Saratoga, 1994—; bd. dirs. Yr. of the Ocean Found., Washington, 1984-8; pres., chmn. Sea/Space Symposium, Phila., 1971—. Author (with others) Ocean Engineering, 1968; author 58 published papers on ocean engring., 1966-88; patentee in field. Regent Calif. Luth. U., Thousand Oaks, 1975-78, 85-87; pres., chmn. Jr. Achievement, Santa Clara County, Calif., 1976-81; chmn. Luth. Lay Renewal, No. Calif., 1975-81, 88—; pres. Immanuel Luth. Trusts, Saratoga, Calif., 1989-94. With USN, 1944-46. Recipient Mayor's award for Oceanology City of L.A., 1967, Japan Govt. Contbns. award Marine Facilities Panel, 1992. Fellow Marine Tech. Soc. (ocean sci. and engring. award 1988); mem. NAE (life) , NRC Marine bd. 1978-84), Cosmos Club (Washington), Saratoga Mens Club, Tau Beta Pi, Tau Omega. Republican. Lutheran. Avocations: scuba diving, wood working, fishing. Office: Marine Devel Assocs Inc PO Box 3409 Saratoga CA 95070-1409

WENZEL, JOAN ELLEN, artist; b. N.Y.C., July 23, 1944; d. Irwin S. and Pearl (Silverman) Rever; m. Allen Jay Wenzel, June 12, 1966 (div. June 1987); 1 child, Kimberly Anne; m. Robert Harold Messing, July 23, 1987 (dec.). Student, Syracuse U., 1962-64; BS in Painting, NYU, 1966, MA in Painting, 1976; postgrad., Harvard U., 1967. One-woman shows include Helander Gallery, Palm Beach, Fla., 1985, 89, 95, Adamar Fine Art, Miami, 1993, Gallery Contemporena, Jacksonville, Fla., 1993, Alexander Brest Mus., Jacksonville, 1993, Albertson Peterson Gallery, Winter Park, Fla., 1992, Amerifest, Miami, 1991, Gallery Yves Arman, N.Y.C., 1982, Palm Beach County Court House, West Palm Beach, Fla., 1991, One Brickall Square, Miami, 1992, Lighthouse Gallery, Tequesta, Fla., 1995-96; exhbns. include Aldrich Mus., Ridgefield, Conn., 1977, Queens Mus., N.Y.C., 1981. Democrat. Jewish. Home: 2275 Ibis Isle Rd W Palm Beach FL 33480-5307

WENZEL, LEONARD ANDREW, engineering educator; b. Palo Alto, Calif., Jan. 21, 1923; s. Robert N. and Frances A. (Browne) W.; m. Mary E. Leathers, Oct. 21, 1944; children: Frances B., Alma L., Jesse R., Sara V. BSChemE, Pa. State U., 1943; MSChemE, U. Mich., 1948, PhD in

Chem. Engring., 1950. Registered profl. engr., Pa. Jr. rsch. engr. Phillips Petroleum Co., Bartlesville, Okla., 1943-44; jr. rsch. scientist Mellon Inst., Pitts., 1944; rsch. engr. Colgate-Palmolive, Jersey City, 1949-51; asst. prof. engring. Lehigh U., Bethlehem, Pa., 1951-56—, assoc. prof., 1956-60, prof., 1960-88, chmn. dep. chem. engring., 1962-83, prof. emeritus, 1988—; project dir. UNESCO, Bucaramanga, Colombia, 1969-70, cons. in chem. engring., Maracaibo, Venezuela,, 1970-73; cons. Air Products and Chems., Allentown, Pa., 1951-80, Exxon, Baytown, Tex., 1983-86; chief scientist Arencibia Techs., Inc., Allentown, 1987-93; pres. L.A. Wenzel, Inc., Bethlehem, 1988—; dir. of tech. Eco-Gen Techs., Inc., Bethlehem, 1993—. Co-author: Principles of Unit Operations, 1960, Introduction to Chemical Engineering, 1961, Chemical Process Analysis: Mass and Energy Balances, 1987. Bd. dirs. S.E. Neighborhood Assn., Bethlehem, 1986—, Bethlehem Housing Authority, 1988—. Lt. (j.g.) USN, 1944-46, PTO. Fellow Am. Inst. Chem. Engrs.; mem. Am. Chem. Soc., Am. Soc. for Engring. Edn. Avocations: stamps, gardening, travel. Home: 517 15th Ave Bethlehem PA 18018-6429 Office: Lehigh Univ Bldg #111 Bethlehem PA 18015

WENZEL, RICHARD PUTNAM, internist; b. Phila., Jan. 8, 1940; m. Jo Gail Wenzel; children: Amy, Richard. BS, Haverford (Pa.) Coll., 1961; MD, Jefferson Med. Coll., 1965; MSc, London U., 1986. Diplomate Am. Bd. Internal Medicine. Intern Phila. Gen. Hosp., 1965-66; resident in internal medicine U. Md. Hosp., Balt., 1966-68, fellowship infectious diseases, 1968-69, chief resident in internal medicine, 1969-70; asst. in medicine U. Md. Med. Sch., Balt., 1969-70; hosp. epidemiologist U. Va. Med. Ctr., Charlottesville, 1972-86; asst. prof. internal medicine U. Va. Sch. of Medicine, Charlottesville, 1972-76, assoc. prof., 1976-81, prof. internal medcine, 1981-86; dir. divsn. clin. epidemiology U. Iowa Coll. Medicine, Iowa City, 1986-89, prof. medicine, preventive medicine, 1986—, dir. hosp. epidemiology and statewide epidemiology svcs., 1986—, dir. divsn. gen. medicine, clin. epidemiology and health svcs. rsch., 1989—; founding chair dept. epidemiology MS degree granting program Grad. Sch. Arts and Scis., U. Va., Charlottesville, 1981-86; pres. ho. staff assn. of interns, residents and fellows U. Md. Hosp., 1968-69; cons. U.S. HO. Reps. Ethics Adv. Bd. Ethics Regarding Freedom of Info. and Infection Surveillance Data, Washington, 1979-80, NIH small bus. innovation rsch, 1988; infection control cons. U. Calif. Systemwide Task Force on AIDS, 1987; spl. cons. NIH Study Sect. Epidemiology and Disease Control (#2), 1987-92. Author: Assessing Quality Care: Perspective for Clinicians, 1992, Prevention and Control of Nosocomial Infections, 1987, Handbook on Hospital Acquired Infections, 1981; founding editor Infection Control and Hospital Epidemiology, 1979—, Clinical Performance and Quality Health Care, 1993—; editorial bd. Jour. of Hosp. Infection, London, 1984—, Enfermedades Infecciosas y Microbiologia Clinica, 1990—, New England Jour. of Medicine, 1992—, others; contbr. numerous articles to profl. jours. Recipient Sir Henry S. Wellcome medal prize, 1971, Major Louis Livingston Seaman prize, 1974, Burlington No. Found. Faculty Achievement award, 1990; Sr. Internat. fellowship, NIH, 1985-86. Fellow ACP, Infectious Diesease Soc. of Am. (coun. mem. 1988-91), Am. Coll. Epidemiology, Am. Acad. of Microbiology; sr. internat. fellow NIH, 1985-86; mem. Am. Assn. of Physicians, Am. Soc. for Clin. Investigation, Am. Clin. and Climatological Assn., Am. Epidemiological Soc., So. Soc. for Clin. Investigation, Cen. Soc. for Clin. Investigation, Am. Fedn. for Clin. Rsch., Am. Soc. for Microbiology, Assn. for Practitioners in Infection Control, Surg. Infection Soc., Soc. for Epidemiologic Rsch., Hosp. Infections Soc. (Europe). Office: U Iowa Coll Medicine Dept Internal Medicine 200 Hawkins Dr # C41 Gh Iowa City IA 52242-1009

WENZEL, SANDRA LEE ANN, pediatrics nurse; b. Peoria, Ill., July 4, 1940; d. Henry M. and Gertrude R. (Burchell) W. Diploma, St. Mary's Sch. Nursing, Kankakee, Ill., 1962; BSN, Bradley U., Peoria, 1966; cert. PNP, Wilford Hall Med. Ctr., San Antonio, 1972. RN, Ill., Tex.; cert. sch. health nurse. Asst. clin. instr. pediatrics St. Francis Sch. Nursing, Peoria, 1962-66; commd. 1st lt. USAF, 1966, advanced through grades to lt. col., 1981; staff nurse cardiology, ICU and pediatrics units, PNP, Wilford Hall Med. Ctr., 1966-68, 72-74; ret., 1986; charge nurse newborn nursery USAF Hosp., Lakenheath Air Base, Eng., 1968-72; PNP USAF Hosp., Goodfellow AFB, Tex., 1974-77; dir. nursing, part-time PNP USAF Clinic, Vance AFB, Okla., 1978-80; PNP USAF Hosp., Scott AFB, Ill., 1980-86; sch. health nurse Marissa, Ill., 1987-89; PNP Family Care Ctr. Corondolet, St. Louis, 1989—. Fellow Nat. Assn. Pediatric Nurse Assocs. and Practitioners (cert.); mem. Am. Diabetic Assn., Uniformed Mil. Practitioners Assn., Sigma Theta Tau.

WERBA, GABRIEL, public relations consultant; b. Paris, Feb. 28, 1930; came to U.S., 1941; s. Aron and Dina (Lewin) W.; m. Barrie Celia Sakolsky, June 1, 1952; children: Dean Steffen, Annmarie Alexandra. BA in Journalism, U. Tex., 1948; postgrad., NYU Grad. Sch. Bus., 1948-49, NYU Sch. Law, 1961-62. Account exec. Harold C. Meyers & Co., N.Y.C., 1959-61; dir. pub. rels. and advt. Yardney Electric Corp., N.Y.C., 1961-63; sr. assoc. Shiefman & Assocs., Detroit, 1963-66; account exec. Merrill Lynch, Detroit, 1966-70; exec. v.p. Shiefman Werba & Assocs., Detroit, 1970-73; sr. v.p., exec. v.p., pres., chief oper. officer Anthony M. Franco, Inc., Detroit, 1973-88; pres., chief exec. officer The Werba Group, Inc. and Gabriel Werba and Assocs., Inc., Detroit, 1988-94; prin. Durocher, Dixson, Werba, L.L.C., Detroit, 1994—; bd. dirs. Environ. Recovery Technologies, Inc., Troy, Mich., Intrepid World Comm., Inc., Birmingham, Mich. Contbr. articles to profl. jours. Bd. dirs. Oakland Citizens League, Detroit, Detroit Symphony Orch. Hall, Detroit Chamber Winds, 1985-91, Common Ground, Royal Oak, Mich., The Attic Theatre, Detroit, 1989-93, The Children's Ctr., Detroit, mem. strategic planning com., 1989-95, adv. bd., 1995-96; bd. dirs. NATAS, Detroit, The Jewish Cmty. Coun. Met. Detroit, 1989-95, Margaret W. Montgomery Hosp., 1993-95, adv. bd. 1988-93; mem. comm. com. Detroit Inst. Arts, 1986—, exhibits com., 1990—; chmn. comm. com. Mem. Nat. Investor Rels. Inst. (past dir., pres. Detroit chpt., spkr., panelist), Pub. Rels. Soc. Am. (bd. dirs. Detroit chpt. 1988-94, pres. 1992-93, past treas. Detroit Counselors' sect., nat. membership com., nat exec. com. fin. sect., spkr., panelist), Fin. Analysts Soc. Detroit (past chmn. pub. info. com.), Am. Mensa (bd. dirs. 1975-91, nat. chmn. 1979-83), Internat. Mensa (bd. dirs. 1979-83, 85-93). Avocations: art collecting, concerts, theater. Home: 20775 Indian Creek Dr Farmington Hills MI 48335-9999 Office: Durocher Dixson Werba LLC 400 Renaissance Ctr Ste 2250 Detroit MI 48243-1602

WERBER, STEPHEN JAY, lawyer, educator; b. N.Y.C., Apr. 20, 1940; s. Murray H. and Teddie Werber; m. Mary Jo Weinberg (dec. June 1965); m. Joan C. Kirsh, May 30, 1968; children: David S., Lauren F. BA, Adelphi U., 1961; JD, Cornell U., 1964; LLM, NYU, 1970. Bar: N.Y. 1965, U.S. Dist. Ct (no. dist.) Ohio 1970, U.S. Supreme Ct. 1970, U.S. Dist. Ct. (so. dist.) Ohio 1980, U.S. Ct. Appeals (6th cir.) 1982. Atty. FCC, Washington, 1964-65; assoc. Sidney G. Hollander, N.Y.C., 1965-67, Herzfeld & Rubin, N.Y.C., 1967-70; asst. prof. law Cleve. State U., 1970-73, assoc. prof.law, 1973-76, prof. law, 1976—; of counsel Guren, Merritt, Feibel, Sogg & Cohen, 1979-84; of counsel Weston, Hurd, Fallon, Paisley & Howley, 1984-89, cons. spl. litigation, 1989—; asst. dean Cleve. State U., 1973-74; sec., treas. Am. Inns of Ct. Harold H. Burton chpt., 1990-91, counsellor, 1991-92, pres., 1993-94. Contbr. numerous articles on product liability to profl jours. Former bd. dirs. NE Ohio Multiple Sclerosis Soc., Bur. Jewish Edn.; v.p. Temple Emanu-El, 1983-85; dir. continuing legal edn. programs Cleve.-Marshall Alumni Assn. Mem. ABA (litigation sect., com. on mfrs. liability), Fed. Bar Assn., Am. Arbitration Assn., Assn. Trial Lawyers Am., Am. Assn. Univ. Profs., N.Y. State Bar Assn., Ohio Bar Assn., Ohio Assn. Civil Trial Lawyers, Scribes. Democrat. Avocations: bridge, golf. Home: 2560 Lafayette Dr Cleveland OH 44118-4608

WERBOS, PAUL JOHN, neural research director; b. Darby, Pa., Sept. 4, 1947; s. Walter Joseph and Margaret Mary (Donohue) W.; m. Lily Fountain, July 13, 1979; children: Elizabeth, Alexander, Maia. BA magna cum laude, Harvard U., 1967; MSc, London Sch. Econs., 1968; MA, Harvard U., 1969, PhD, 1974. Rsch. assoc. MIT, Cambridge, Mass., 1973-75; asst. prof. U. Md., College Park, 1975-78; math. statistician U.S. Census Bur., Suitland, Md., 1978-79; energy analyst U.S. Dept. Energy, Washington, 1979-88, 89; program dir. NSF, Washington, 1988, 89—. Author: The Roots of Backpropagation: From Ordered Derivatives to Neural Network & Political Forecasting, 1993; contbr. chpt. to Handbook of Intelligent Control, 1992. Regional dir., Washington rep. L-5 Soc. (merged with Nat. Space Soc.), Washington, 1980s. Mem. Internat. Neural Network Soc. (pres. 1991-92, sec. 1990). Quaker-Universalist. Achievements include patent pending for elastic fuzzy logic and associated adaptation techniques; devised theory of intelligence; created alternative formulation of quantum theory. Home: 8411 48th Ave College Park MD 20740-2403 Office: NSF 4201 Wilson Blvd Rm 675 Arlington VA 22230

WERBOW, STANLEY NEWMAN, language educator; b. Phila., Apr. 19, 1922; s. Morris and Sadie (Newman) W.; m. Naomi Esther Ecker, June 1, 1952; children: Susan Linda, Emily Frances, Carol Martha. B.A., George Washington U., 1946; postgrad., Middlebury Coll., 1946, 47, U. Mich., 1948; Ph.D., Johns Hopkins, 1953. Tchr. Ea. High Sch., Washington, 1946-47; research analyst specialist U.S. Dept. Def., Washington, 1952-53; mem. faculty U. Tex., Austin, 1953—, prof., 1965-69, 78—, chmn. dept. Germanic langs., 1969-71, dean Coll. Humanities, 1971-78, acting dean Coll. Fine Arts, 1980-81; vis. prof. U. Marburg, 1963, U. N.Mex. German Summer Sch., 1984, 87, 89. Author: Martin von Amberg, 1957, (with Lehmann, Rehder, Shaw) Review and Progress in German, 1959; Editor: Formal Aspects of Medieval German Poetry, 1970. Served with Signal Corps AUS, 1943-45. Decorated Bronze Star medal; Bundesverdienstkreuz erster klasse W. Ger.; recipient Fulbright award to Netherlands, 1950-51; Guggenheim fellow, 1960; Fulbright research scholar Germany, 1960-61. Mem. Modern Lang. Assn. (pres. South Central assn. 1976—), Medieval Acad., Internat. Assn. Germanists, Phi Beta Kappa, Phi Kappa Phi, Delta Phi Alpha. Home: 4205 Prickly Pear Dr Austin TX 78731-2017 Office: Univ Texas Dept Germanic Langs Austin TX 78712

WERCKMEISTER, OTTO KARL, art historian and educator; b. Berlin, Apr. 26, 1934; came to U.S., 1965; s. Karl and Rose (Petzold) W.; m. Maria Eugenia Lacarra, July 3, 1965 (div. 1985); children: Christina, Robert, Veronica. PhD, Freie U., Berlin, 1958. Research assoc. German Archeol. Inst., Madrid, Spain, 1962-65; assoc. prof. to prof. UCLA, 1965-84; Mary Jane Crowe Disting. prof. Northwestern U., 1984—. Author: Ende der Ästhetik, 1971, 1972, Ideologie und Kunst bei Marx und andere Essays, 1974, Versuche über Paul Klee, 1981, Zitadellenkultur, 1989, Eng. edit., 1991, The Making of Paul Klee's Career, 1914-20, 1989. Guggenheim fellow, 1981, Wissenschaftskolleg (Berlin) fellow, 1986. Office: Northwestern U Dept Art Hist Evanston IL 60208

WERGER, PAUL MYRON, bishop; b. Greenville, Pa., June 13, 1931; s. Jacob Paul and Laura Annetta (Greenwalt) W.; m. Diane Mae Ellison, July 26, 1957; children: Paul Myron, Jonathan David, Matthew James, Mary Dianne. BA, Thiel Coll., 1954; MDiv, Northwestern Theol. Sem., Mpls., 1957, DD (hon.), 1976; LHD (hon.), Grand View Coll., 1985. Ordained to ministry, Luth. Ch. Am., 1957. Pastor Apostles Luth. Ch., St. Paul, 1957-61, St. Luke's Luth. Ch., Bloomington, Minn., 1961-78; bishop Iowa Synod Luth. Ch. Am., Des Moines, 1978-88, S.E. Iowa Synod, Iowa City, 1987—; chmn. Conf. Bishops Evang. Luth. Ch. Am. 1987-91, mem. ch. coun. 1988-91, bishop adv. mem., 1988, stewardship and evangelism com. NW Synod, 1959-62; mem. bd. social ministry Minn. Synod, 1963-70, mem. exec. bd., dean south suburban dist.; pres., bd. dirs. Luth. Social Services in Minn.; mem. mgmt. com. dir. mission N.Am. Luth. Ch. Am., 1983—; del. Luth. Ch. Am. convs.; pastor evangelist Evang. Outreach; corp. bd. dirs. Fairvi. Contbr. articles to profl. jours. Mem. Bloomington Human Rights Commn.; mem. citizens adv. com. Bloomington Sch. Dist. 271; bd. dirs. Luther Northwestern, 1976, Luth. Sch. Theology, Chgo., 1978-88, Luth. Ch. Am. Found., Grandview Coll., 1978, GrandView Coll., 1978-92, Iowa Luth. Hosp., 1978—, Luth. Soc. Svc. Iowa, 1978—, Fairview Corp., 1985— ; bd. fellows Sch. Religion, U. Iowa; Luth. Ch. in Am. observer Wartburg Theol. Sem., 1986-88. Recipient Thiel Coll. Alumni award for profl. achievement, 1979. Mem. Assn. Bloomington Clergy, Conf. of Luth./Roman Cath. Bishops. Avocations: travel, photography, golf, fishing, sports. Office: SE Iowa Synod Hdqrs PO Box 3167 2635 Northgate Dr Iowa City IA 52244-3167

WERKING, RICHARD HUME, librarian, historian, academic administrator; b. Charleston, S.C., Sept. 29, 1943; s. F. Woody and Mary S. (Prissinger) W. BA, U. Evansville, 1966; MA in Am. History, U. Wis., 1967, PhD in Am. History, 1973; MA in Librarianship, U. Chgo., 1975. Instr. history Northland Coll., Ashland, Wis., 1967-68; pers. staffing specialist U.S. Civil Svc. Commn., Indpls., 1968-69; reference libr. Lawrence U., Appleton, Wis., 1975-77; head reference dept., asst. prof. history U. Miss., Oxford, 1977-79, asst. libr. dir., asst. prof. history, 1979-80, acting libr. dir., asst. prof. history, 1980-81; assoc. libr. dir., asst. prof. history Trinity U., San Antonio, Tex., 1981-83, libr. dir., assoc. prof. history, 1983-91; libr. dir., assoc. dean, prof. history U.S. Naval Acad., Annapolis, Md., 1991—; With OCLC Adv. Com. on Coll. and Univ. Librs., Dublin, Ohio, 1986-92; sr. fellow Grad. Sch. Libr. & Info. Sci., UCLA, 1989. Author: The Master Architects: Building the U.S. Foreign Service, 1977; contbr. articles to profl. jours., chpts. to books, also papers, monographs and revs. With U.S. Army, 1962. Sparks fellow Phi Kappa Phi, 1966, postdoctoral fellow Coun. on Libr. Resources, 1974. Mem. ALA (chmn. coll. librs. sect. 1987-88), Orgn. Am. Historians. Office: US Naval Acad Nimitz Libr 589 Mcnair Rd Annapolis MD 21402-1317

WERKMAN, ROSEMARIE ANNE, past public relations professional, civic worker; b. Washingtonville, N.Y., Apr. 21, 1926; d. Alexander and Michelina (Russo) Di Benedetto; m. Henry J. Werkman, June 29, 1947; children: Elizabeth, Kristine, Hendrik. Student, U. Miami, Fla. Billing clk. Stern's Dept. Store, N.Y.C., 1945; clk., typist Doubleday-Doran Book Pub., N.Y.C., 1945-46; receptionist Moser & Cotins Advt. Agy., Utica, N.Y., 1947-48, Washingtonville Sch., N.Y., 1960-75. Author: (biography/autobiography) Love, War and Remembrance, 1992; author short stories; poetry pub. in several anthologies. Mem. Dem. Com., Blooming Grove; bd. dirs. Blooming Grove Hist. Assn.; mem. com. Update: Blooming Grove Master Plan; mem. Orange County Coun. Disabled; bd. dirs. Rehab. Support Svcs. Named Poet of Merit, Am. Poetry Assn., 1989; recipient Blooming Grove/Washingtonville C. of C. award, 1996. Mem. Blooming Grove C. of C. (v.p.), Orange County Classic Choral Soc., Clearwater (Fla.) Chorus. Democrat. Roman Catholic. Avocations: reading, gardening, furniture refinishing, singing.

WERKMAN, SIDNEY LEE, psychiatry educator; b. Washington, May 3, 1927. A.B., Williams Coll., 1948; M.D., Cornell U., 1952. Diplomate Am. Bd. Psychiatry and Neurology, Am. Bd. Child Psychiatry. Intern U. Va. Hosp., Charlottesville; resident in psychiatry Yale U., 1953-55, St. Elizabeth's Hosp., Washington, 1955-56; assoc. prof. psychiatry George Washington U., Washington, 1960-69; prof. U. Colo. Sch. Medicine, Denver, 1969-87; dir. div. adolescent psychiatry Children's Hosp. of Washington, 1965-69; clin. prof. Georgetown U. Sch. Medicine, Washington, 1989—; psychiatrist Capital Area Permanente Med. Group, Washington, 1990—; cons. grants NIMH, Washington, 1982—, guest researcher, 1984-85. Author: The Role of Psychiatry in Medical Education, 1966, Only a Little Time: A Chronicle of Dying, 1972, Bringing Up Children Overseas, 1977. Bd. dirs. Med. U. So. Africa, Performing Arts Soc., Washington Concert Operas. Master sgt. U.S. Army. Fellow Commonwealth Fund, Florence, Italy, 1963-64, NEH, 1979. Mem. Am. Psychiat. Assn., Am. Acad. Child Psychiatry, Group for Advancement Psychiatry, Am. Orthopsychiat. Assn. (bd. dirs. 1970-73), Colo. Psychiat. Soc. Office: Ste AG62 3636 16th St NW Washington DC 20010

WERLEIN, EWING, JR., federal judge, lawyer; b. Houston, Sept. 14, 1936; s. Ewing and Ruth (Storey) W.; m. Kay McGibbon Werlein, June 29, 1963; children: Ewing Kenneth, Emily Kay. BA, So. Meth. U., 1958; LLB, U. Tex., 1961. Bar: Tex. 1961, U.S. Dist. Ct. (so. dist.) Tex. 1965, U.S. Dist. Ct. (ea. dist.) Tex. 1990, U.S. Ct. Appeals (5th cir.) 1970, U.S. Ct. Appeals (10th cir.) 1980, U.S. Claims Ct. 1985, U.S. Tax Ct. 1985, U.S. Supreme Ct. 1983. Ptnr. Vinson & Elkins, Houston, 1964-92; dist. judge U.S. Dist. Ct. (so. dist.) Tex., 1992—. Trustee So. Meth. U., Dallas, 1976-92, Asbury Theol. Sem., Wilmore, Ky., 1989—; mem. gen. bd. pub. United Meth. Ch., Nashville, 1974-84, chmn., 1980-84, chancellor Tex. ann. conf., 1977—; mem. exec. com. World Meth. Counh., 1981—, treas., 1991-93. Capt. USAF, 1961-64. Fellow Am. Coll. Trial Lawyers, 1984, Internat. Soc. Barristers, 1987; recipient Disting. Alumni award SMU Alumni Assn., 1994. Fellow Am. Bar Found., Tex. Bar Found., Houston Bar Found.; mem. State Bar Tex. (dir. 1990-93), Nat. Conf. Bar Pres., Houston Bar Assn. (pres. 1988-89), Houston C. of C. (life), SAR, Order of Coif, Ramada Club (Houston), Houston Club, Phi Beta Kappa. Office: US Dist Ct Tex US Courthouse 515 Rusk St Ste 9136 Houston TX 77002-2605

WERLING, DONN PAUL, environmental educator; b. Ft. Wayne, Ind., Oct. 14, 1945; s. Paul Henry and Lydia Sophia (Rebber) W.; m. Diane Mueller, July 11, 1970; 1 child, Benjamin Paul. BS, Valparaiso U., 1967; MS, Mich. State U., 1968; MEd, Loyola U., 1970; Ph.D., U. Mich., 1979. Dir. nature project Raymond Sch., Chgo. Bd. Edn., 1969-72; dir. Evanston Environ. Assn., Ill., 1973-81; dir. Henry Ford Estate, U. Mich.-Dearborn, 1983—, adj. asst. prof. edn., 1984-95, adj. assoc. prof., 1996—; founder N.Am. Voyageur Conf., 1977. Author: Environmental Education and Your School Site, 1973; A School-Community Stewardship Model, 1979; Lake Michigan and Its Lighthouses, 1982, Lakes and Lighthouses, 1989, Lighthouse Library of the Great Lakes, 1993, Lore and Legacy, 1994. Mem. state master plan com. on environ. edn. State of Ill., Springfield, 1970; mem. adv. com. Ill. Coastal Zone, Chgo., 1978; bd. dirs. Ill. Shore council Girl Scouts U.S., 1978-82, Chgo. Maritime Soc., 1982. Recipient Mayor's award City of Evanston, 1976, Russell E. Wilson award U. Mich. Sch. Edn., 1979, Service award Ill. Shore council Girl Scouts U.S., 1978, J. Lee Barrett award Met. Detroit Tourist & Conv. Bur., 1986, award for interpretative excellence Nat. Assn. for Interpretation, 1989; named to Outstanding Young Men Am., Jaycees, 1975. Mem. Nat. Assn. Interpretation (founder), Am. Assn. Mus., Great Lakes Lighthouse Keepers Assn. (founder, pres. 1982-86), Tourist and Travel Assn. Southeast Mich. (chmn. 1984-86), Kiwanis. Avocations: historic restoration, gardening, writing, composing, singing Christian and bluewater music. Address: Henry Ford Estate-Fair Lane U of Michigan-Dearborn Evergreen Rd Dearborn MI 48128

WERMAN, DAVID SANFORD, psychiatrist, psychoanalyst, educator; b. N.Y.C., Jan. 1, 1922; s. Morris and Blanche (Heftel) W.; m. Marjolijn R. de Jager, Oct. 25, 1958 (div. 1975); children: Marco W., Claudia J. B.A., Queens Coll., 1942; postgrad., Columbia U., 1946-47; M.D., Cert. d'Etudes Medicales, U. Lausanne, Switzerland, 1952. Diplomate Am. Bd. Obstetrics and Gynecology, Am. Bd. Psychiatry and Neurology. Intern Beth Israel Hosp., N.Y.C., 1953-54, resident, 1954-57; resident Montefiore Hosp., Bronx, N.Y., 1964-67; pvt. practice specializing in ob-gyn. N.Y.C., 1957-64; faculty acad. psychiatry U. N.C., Chapel Hill, 1967-76, assoc. prof., instr. psychoanalytic tng. program, 1974—; prof. psychiatry Duke U. Med. Ctr., Durham, N.C., 1976—, supervising and tng. analyst psychoanalytic tng. program, 1981—, Honored prof. psychiatry, 1990—, prof. emeritus, 1992—; cons. Durham VA Hosp. Author: The Practice of Supportive Psychotherapy, 1984. Contbr. chpts. to books, articles to profl. jours. With AUS, 1943-45. Named Outstanding Tchr. psychiatry U. N.C., 1975, honored tchr. psychiatry Duke U., 1978, hon. prof., 1990. Fellow ACS, Am. Psychiat. Assn., Am. Coll. Psychoanalysts, others. Home: 1503 Michaux Rd Chapel Hill NC 27514-7637 Office: Duke Univ Med Ctr Dept Psychiatry PO Box 3812 Durham NC 27702-3812

WERMAN, THOMAS EHRLICH, record producer; b. Newton, Mass., Mar. 2, 1945; s. Lester and Ruth (Ehrlich) W.; m. Susan Lynne Gould, Aug. 25, 1968; children—Julia Gould, Nina Eve, Daniel Lester. B.A., Columbia U., 1967, M.B.A., 1969. Asst. account exec. Grey Advt., N.Y.C., 1969-70; asst. to dir. Epic Records Artistes and Repertoire, 1970-73; dir. talent acquisition Epic Records, 1973-76, staff producer, 1976-80; v.p., exec. producer CBS Records, Inc., L.A., 1980-81; sr. v.p. Elektra Records, 1981-82; pres. Julia's Music Inc., 1981—. Recipient N.Y.C. Civilian Commendation award for heroism, 1968, 14 platinum records awards Rec. Industry Assn. Am., 1977—, 8 Gold Record awards, 1977—. Mem. Nat. Assn. Recording Arts and Scis. Democrat. Jewish.

WERMUTH, PAUL CHARLES, retired English educator; b. Phila., Oct. 28, 1925; s. Paul C. and Susan (Manga) W.; m. Barbara Ethel Braun, Aug. 26, 1951; children—Geoffrey Paul, Paul Charles, Alan John, Stephen Mark. A.B., M.A., Boston U., 1951; Ph.D., Pa. State U., 1955. Instr. Clarkson Coll., Potsdam, N.Y., 1951-52; part-time instr., grad. asst. Pa. State U., 1952-55; asst. prof. Coll. William and Mary, 1955-57; mem. faculty Central Conn. State Coll., New Britain, 1957-68; assoc. prof. English Central Conn. State Coll., 1966-68; prof. English Northeastern U., 1968-90, prof. emeritus, 1990—, chmn. dept., 1968-75; vis. prof. Middlebury Coll., 1963-64. Author: Modern Essays on Writing and Style, 2d edit, 1969, Essays in English, 1967, Bayard Taylor, 1974, also articles. Served with USAAF, 1943-46. Danforth summer study grantee, 1961. Mem. Modern Lang. Assn., AAUP, Mensa. Home: 73 Mostyn St Swampscott MA 01907-1616 Office: English Dept Northeastern Univ Boston MA 02115

WERNER, CHARLES GEORGE, cartoonist; b. Marshfield, Wis., Mar. 23, 1909; s. George J. and Marie (Tippelt) W.; m. Eloise Robertson, Oct. 5, 1935 (dec. Jan. 1993); children: David, Jean, Stephen. Spl. courses at, Northwestern U.; student, Art Ins. Chgo., 1943. Artist, photographer Springfield Leader, 1930-35; mem. art dept. Daily Oklahoma, 1935-37, editorial cartoonist, 1937-41; chief polit. cartoonist Chgo. Sun, 1941-46; cartoonist Indpls. Star, 1947-95; instr. cartooning pub. schs., Oklahoma City, 1939-41, lectr. history polit. cartoons. Recipient Pulitzer prize for cartoon, 1938; honorable mention for cartoon in auto safety contest, 1939; hon. mention Nat. Safety Council cartoons, 1943; Sigma Delta Chi award best cartoon, 1943; Nat. Headliners Club 1st place award, 1951; Freedoms Found. awards, 1951, 52, 53, 55, 56, 58, 62, 63; 1st place award Nat. Found. Hwy. Safety, 1965; winner one of 6 best caricatures Internat. Salon of Cartoons, Montreal, 1969. Hon. lifetime mem. Oklahoma City Jr. C. of C.; mem. Am. Assn. Editl. Cartoonists (pres. 1959-60), Nat. Cartoonists Soc., Masons (33 deg.), Shriners, Jesters, Indpls. Athletic Club (Indpls.), Sigma Delta Chi (hon.). Episcopalian. Clubs: Masons (33 deg.), Shriners, Jesters, Indianapolis Athletic (Indpls.), Columbia (Indpls.). Address: 4445 Brown Rd Indianapolis IN 46226-3147

WERNER, CLARENCE L., transportation executive; b. 1937. Asst. mgr. Larson Grain Co., Omaha, 1958-61; with Bus. Motor Express, Inc., Omaha, 1961-62; with Werner Enterprises, Inc., Omaha, 1956-82, pres., 1982-84, chmn. bd., CEO, 1984—. Office: Werner Enterprises Inc I-80 Highway 50 Omaha NE 68138*

WERNER, ELIZABETH HELEN, librarian, Spanish language educator; b. Palo Alto, Calif., June 21, 1944; d. Fielding and Lucy Elizabeth (Hart) McDearmon; m. Michael Andrew Werner, Aug. 21, 1976. BA, Mills Coll., 1966; MA, Ind. U., 1968; MLS, U. Md., 1973. Instr. Spanish, Western Md. Coll., Westminster, 1968-72; libr., assoc. prof. Clearwater (Fla.) Christian Coll., 1975—; sec. Sunline Libr. users group Tampa Bay Libr. Consortium, Tampa, Fla., 1993-94. Contbr. book revs. to profl. jours. Com. mem. Upper Pinellas County Post Office Customers' Adv. Coun., Clearwater, 1992—. Mem. Fla. Libr. Assn., Assn. Christian Librs., Fla. Assn. Christian Librs. (pres. 1991-94), Friends of the Clearwater Libr., Am. Assn. Tchrs. Spanish and Portuguese. Avocations: reading, choir, travel, language study. Office: Clearwater Christian Coll 3400 Gulf To Bay Blvd Clearwater FL 34619-4514

WERNER, GERHARD, pharmacologist, psychoanalyst, educator; b. Vienna, Austria, Sept. 28, 1921; came to U.S., 1957, naturalized, 1965; s. Rudolf and Elizabeth (Lukas) W.; m. Marion E. Hollander, July 25, 1958; children—Philip Ralph, Karen Nicole. M.D., U. Vienna, 1945. With dept. pharmacology U. Vienna, 1945-50; prof. pharmacology, head dept. U. Calcutta (India) Sch. Tropical Medicine, 1952-54, U. Sao Paulo (Brazil) Med. Sch. of Ribeirao Preto, 1955-57; assoc. prof. Cornell U. Med. Sch., 1957-61; assoc. prof. pharmacology and physiology Johns Hopkins U. Med. Sch., 1963-65; v.p. prof. affairs Univ. Health Ctr., Pitts., 1975-78; prof. pharmacology, head dept. U. Pitts. Med. Sch., 1965-75, dean, 1975-78, prof. psychiatry, 1978-89, F.S. Cheever Disting. prof., emeritus prof., 1990; pres. Med. Comp, Inc., 1990—; assoc., chief of staff Dept. Vets. Affairs Med. Ctr. Highland Drive, Pitts., 1991; cons. Ctr. for Emergent Technology, Motorola, Inc., 1995—; cons. psychobiology program NSF, 1970-75, mem. adv. panel regulatory biology div. biology and med. sci., 1969-70, mem. primate ctr. rev. com., 1973-79; mem. chem. biol. info. panel NIH, 1967-70, mem. study sect. pharmacology and exptl. therapeutics, 1964-68; mem. study sect. Pitts. Psychoanalytic Inst., 1973-79; external examiner for Ph.D (med. scis.) U. Calcutta, 1953—; mem. adv. bd. Indian Coun. Med. Rsch., 1952-54. Mem. editorial bd. Jour. Neurophysiology, 1970-78, Internat. Jour. Neuropharmacology, Jour. Clin. Pharmacology; asso. editor Pharmacol. Revs, 1969-70; contbr. articles to profl. jours. Recipient Humboldt prize, 1984. Fellow N.Y. Acad. Sci.; mem. Soc. Neurosci., AAAS, Harvey Soc., Am. Soc. Pharmacology and Exptl. Therapeutics, Am. Physiol. Soc., Soc. Gen. Systems Research, Internat. Union for Psychobiology, Soc. for Artificial Intelligence, Assn. for Computing Machinery, Internat. Brain Research Orgn., Am. Psychoanalytic Assn., Indian Soc. Biochemistry and Physiology, German Pharmacol. Soc., Sigma Xi. Home: PO Box 161178 Austin TX 78716

WERNER, GLORIA S., librarian; b. Seattle, Dec. 12, 1940; d. Irving L. and Eva H. Stolzoff; m. Newton Davis Werner, June 30, 1963; 1 son, Adam Davis. BA, Oberlin Coll., 1961; ML, U. Wash., 1962; postgrad. UCLA, 1962-63. Reference librarian UCLA Biomed Library, 1963-64, asst. head pub. services dept., 1964-66, head pub. services dept., head reference div., 1966-72, asst. biomed. librarian public services, 1972-77, asso. biomed. librarian, 1977-78, biomed. librarian, assoc. univ. librarian, dir. Pacific S.W. regional Med. Library Service, 1979-83; asst. dean library services UCLA Sch. Medicine, 1980-83; assoc. univ. librarian for tech. services, 1983-89, dir. libraries, acting univ. librarian, 1989-90, univ. librarian, 1990—; adj. lectr. UCLA Grad. Sch. Library and Info. Sci., 1977-83. Editor, Bull. Med. Library Assn., 1979-82, asso. editor, 1974-79; mem. editorial bd. Ann. Stats. Med. Sch. Libraries U.S. and Can., 1980-83; mem. accrediting commn. Western Assn. Schs. and Colls., N.W. Assn. Schs. and Colls. Mem. ALA, Assn. Rsch. Librs. (bd. dirs. 1993—, v.p./pres.-elect 1995-96). Office: UCLA Rsch Libr Libr Adminstrv Office 405 Hilgard Ave Los Angeles CA 90024-1301

WERNER, MARLIN SPIKE, speech pathologist and audiologist; b. Portland, Maine, Aug. 15, 1927; s. Leonard Matthews and Margaret (Steele) W.; m. Caroline Emma Paul, Dec. 23, 1985; children: Leo Hart, Joseph Hart. BA in Sociology and Social Work, U. Mo., 1950; ScM in Audiology and Speech Pathology, Johns Hopkins U., 1957; PhD in Speech and Hearing Sci., Ohio State U., 1966. Lic. in audiology, hearing aid dispensing, speech pathology, Hawaii; lic. in audiology and speech pathology, Calif. Audiologist/speech pathologist, dir. Speech and Hearing Ctr. Asheville (N.C.) Orthopedic Hosp., 1960-64; assoc. prof. speech pathology and audiology We. Carolina U., Cullowhee, N.C., 1965-69; assoc. prof. speech pathology, audiology and speech sci. Fed. City Coll. (now U. D.C.), Washington, 1969-73; pres. Friends of Nepal's Hearing Handicapped, Oakland, Calif., 1979-84; audiologist, speech pathologist pvt. practice, Oakland and Lafayette, Calif., 1973-85; pvt. practice Lafayette, 1985-87; pvt. practice speech pathology and audiology Hilo, Hawaii, 1987—; speech and hearing cons. VA Hosp., Oteen, N.C., 1960-64; clin. cons. Speech and Hearing Clinic, Asheville Orthopedic Hosp., 1966-67; lectr., presenter in field. Contbr. articles to profl. jours.; contbr. to Ency. Brit., Am. Heritage Book of Natural Wonders, others. Mem. hearing impaired svcs. task force State of Hawaii Dept. Health, 1987-88; mem. Hawaii County Mayor's Com. for Persons with Disabilities, 1988-94; adv. bd. Salvation Army, 1992; bd. dirs. Hawaii chpt. Am. Arthritis Found.; past pres. Big Island Safety Assn.; mem. Hawaii Gov.'s Bd. Hearing Aid Dealers and Fitters; mem. adv. com., pres. Older Adult Resource Ctr., Laney Coll., Oakland, Calif.; v.p. Hawaii Speleol. Survey; chmn. Hawaii Grotto of Nat. Speleol. Soc., others. MCH fellow Johns Hopkins U., 1954, Pub. Health fellow Ohio State U., 1964. Fellow Nat. Speleological Soc.; mem. AAAS, Am. Speech and Hearing Assn., Acoustical Soc. Am., Calif. Speech and Hearing Assn., Calif. Writers Club (bd. dirs., past pres.), Hawaii Speech/Lang. Hearing Assn. Avocations: collecting and making musical instruments, graphic arts, photography, cave exploring, writing. Home: PO Box 11509 Hilo HI 96721-6509 Office: 400 Hualani St Ste 191-a Hilo HI 96720-4378

WERNER, R(ICHARD) BUDD, retired business executive; b. Lorain, Ohio, Aug. 27, 1931; s. Paul Henry and Bessie Marie (Budd) W.; m. Janet Sue Kelsey, Aug. 28, 1932; children: Richard Budd, David Kelsey, Mary Paula. BS in Commerce, Ohio U., 1953. CPA, Ohio. Sr. auditor Arthur Andersen & Co., Cleve., 1955-59; various fin. positions Glidden Co., Cleve., 1959-65; v.p., asst. treas. Harshaw divsn. Kewanee Oil Co., Cleve., 1965-72; v.p. fin., treas. Weatherhead Co., Cleve., 1973-77; v.p. finance, treas. Hauserman, Inc., Cleve., 1977-81; v.p. fin., CFO SPX Corp., Muskegon, Mich., 1981-94, sr. v.p. planning and devel., 1994-95; exec. in residence coll. of bus. Ohio U., Athens, 1995—. Mem. Lakewood (Ohio) City Coun., 1972-73; mem. North Muskegon (Mich.) Sch. Bd., 1981-85. Lt. Q.M.C., U.S. Army, 1953-55. Mem. Fin. Execs. Inst., Fin. Execs. Rsch. Found., Athletic Club Columbus, Ohio. Office: Ohio U Copeland Hall Athens OH 45701

WERNER, ROBERT JOSEPH, college dean, music educator; b. Lackawanna, N.Y., Feb. 13, 1932; s. Edward Joseph and Marian L. (Gerringer) W.; m. Sharon Lynne Mohrfeld, June 22, 1957; children: Mark J., Kurt M., Erik J. BME, Northwestern U., 1953, MusM, 1954, PhD, 1967. Dir. instrumental music Evanston (Ill.) Twp. High Sch., 1956-66; assoc. prof. mus. Harpur Coll. SUNY, Binghamton, 1966-68, dir. Contemporary Music Project, 1968-73; dir. Sch. Mus. U. Ariz., Tucson, 1973-85, deanfine arts, 1981-82; dean Coll.-Conservatory of Music U. Cin., 1985—. Editor: Comprehensive Musicianship: An Anthology of Evolving Thought, 1971; contbtr. articles to profl. jours. Mem. exec. bd. Tucson Symphony Orch., 1974-85; bd. dirs. Cultural Commn. Tucson, 1974-75, Cin. Symphony Orch., 1985—, Cin. Opera, 1985—, Cin. Ballet, 1985—. With U.S. Army, 1954-56. Mem. Nat. Assn. Schs. Music (pres. 1989-91), Coll. Music Soc. (pres. 1977-78), Internat. Soc. for Music Edn. (pres. 1984-86, treas. 1986—), Music Educators Nat.Conf., McDowell Soc., Coll. Music Soc., Psi Upsilon, Phi Mu Alpha Sinfonia. Office: U Cin Coll Conservatory of Music Cincinnati OH 45221-0003

WERNER, ROBERT L., lawyer; b. N.Y.C., Feb. 28, 1913; s. Abraham L. and Elsa (Ludwig) W.; m. Raye Davies, Oct. 13, 1945; children: William, John. A.B., Yale U., 1933; L.L.B., Harvard U., 1936. Bar: N.Y. 1936, U.S. Supreme Ct. 1936, also various fed. cts. and adminstrv. agys. 1936. Spl. asst. to U.S. atty. So. Dist. N.Y., 1936, asst. U.S. atty, 1937-40, confidential asst., 1940-42; 1st asst. civil div. U.S. Dept. Justice, Washington, 1946-47; spl. asst. to atty. gen. U.S., 1946-47; mem. law dept. RCA, N.Y.C., 1947; v.p., gen. atty. RCA, 1951-62, exec. v.p., gen. atty., 1962-66, exec. v.p., gen. counsel, 1966-78, dir., 1963-79, cons., 1978-83; mem. adv. bd. Internat. and Comparative Law Ctr. Southwestern Legal Found., Dallas, 1966—, treas., 1970-72, vice chmn., 1972-73, chmn. advisory bd., 1974-76, found. trustee 1976-88, hon. trustee 1988—; lectr. Conf. Bd., Practicing Law Inst., others; mem. nat. adv. council corp. law depts. Practising Law Inst., 1974-78; com. on restrictive bus. practices U.S. council Internat. C. of C., 1973-78; N.Y. Lawyers' Com. for Civil Rights under Law, 1972-78. Trustee Ithaca Coll., N.Y., 1968-88, hon. trustee, 1988—, chmn. bd., 1976-78; trustee Salisbury (Conn.) Sch., 1975-77, N.Y. Chiropractic Coll., 1986-89; bd. dirs. Midtown Arts Common at St. Peter's Ch., 1983-89. Capt. U.S. Army, 1942-44; to lt. col. USAAF, 1944-46, ETO. Recipient Disting. Service award Ithaca Coll., 1988. Fellow Am. Bar Found.; mem. Internat., Fed., Am., N.Y. State, City N.Y., FCC bar assns., IEEE (sr.), Am. Legion, Harvard Law Sch. Assn., Assn. Gen. Counsel (emeritus), U.S. Naval Inst., Internat. Law Assn. (Am. br.), Nat. Legal Aid and Defender Assn. (dir. 1974-79), Am. Judicature Soc., Newcomen Soc., N.Y. County Lawyers' Assn., Am. Soc. Internat. Law, Yale Club, Harvard Club N.Y., The Rockefeller Ctr. Club, Nat. Lawyers Club, Army and Navy Club (Washington), Coral Beach Club (Bermuda). Home: 116 E 68th St New York NY 10021-5956

WERNER, SETH MITCHELL, advertising executive; b. N.Y.C., Sept. 23, 1954; s. Michael M. and Helen (Barasch) W.; 1 child, Zachary Michael. BS in Pub. Rels., Boston U., 1976. Writer Monett Media, Atlanta, Ga., 1976-77; writer, copy chief Goldberg/Marchesano, Washington, 1977-79; writer The Marshalk Co., N.Y.C., 1979-86, Foote, Cone & Belding, San Francisco, 1986-87; then pres., exec. creative dir. Bloom FCA! (now Publicis/Bloom), Dallas, now vice chmn., exec. creative dir. Allstar Writer of Yr. Adweek mag., 1984, 87, Advt. Exec. of Yr., 1988. Office: Publicis Bloom Ste 450 3500 Maple Ave Dallas TX 75219-3901*

WERNER, STUART LLOYD, computer services company executive; b. N.Y.C., June 2, 1932; s. Leroy Louis and Frances Werner; m. Davideen Price, Jan. 6, 1990; children by previous marriage: Joan Leslie, Susan Lyn, Richard Wayne. BArch, Rensselaer Poly. Inst., 1954. Ptnr. in charge architecture Werner-Dyer & Assos., Washington, 1959-68; v.p. Rentex Corp., Phila., 1968-70; pres. Werner & Assos., Inc., Washington, 1970-81; v.p. spl. projects ARA Svcs., Inc.; v.p. ARA, 1981-83; chmn. STN Computer Svcs., Inc., Falls Church, Va., 1982-83; pres. Werner & Monk, Inc., 1983—; pres. STN Computer Svcs.; mem. indsl. engring. terminology U.S. Stds. Inst. Bd. dirs. Watergate South, Washington Opera Soc., Friends of the Corcoran Gallery, Washington. With AUS, 1955-57. Mem. AIA, Am. Inst. Indsl. Engrs., Marinette Yacht Club, Masons,Tau Beta Pi. Republican. Contbr. articles to tech. jours. Home: 700 New Hampshire Ave NW Washington DC 20037-2406 Office: STN Inc 5113 Leesburg Pike Falls Church VA 22041-3204

WERNER, THOMAS LEE, hospital administrator; b. Hazen, N.D., Dec. 8, 1945; married. BA, Union Coll., 1967; MA, U. Nebr., 1969. Asst. dir. pers. Portland (Oreg.) Adventist Med. Ctr., 1971-72; v.p. Verticare Ambulatory Care Program, Portland, 1972-73; adminstr. Tillamook (Oreg.) CountyGen. Hosp., 1973-77, Walla Walla (Wash.)Gen. Hosp., 1977-81; exec. v.p. Fla. Hosp. Med. Ctr., Orlando, 1981-85, pres., 1985—. Office: Fla Hosp Med Ctr 601 E Rollins St Orlando FL 32803-1248*

WERNER, TOM, television producer, professional baseball team executive; m. Jill Werner; 3 children, Teddy, Carolyn, Amanda. BA, Harvard Univ., 1971. With ABC Television, Inc., 1972-82; co-owner Carsey-Werner Co., Studio City, Calif., 1982—; chmn. San Diego Padres, 1991—; mem. bd. dirs.: Old Globe Theatre; Sharp Hospital. Co-exec. producer TV series: Oh, Madeline, 1983; exec. producer: The Cosby Show, (Emmy awd. Outstanding Comedy Series-1985), 1984-92, A Different World, 1987-93, Roseanne, 1988—, Chicken Soup, 1989-90, Grand, 1990, Davis Rules, 1991, You Bet Your Life, 1992-93, Frannie's Turn, 1992. also: San Diego Padres PO Box 2000 San Diego CA 92112-2000*

WERNER, UTAA, diversified financial services company executive. V.p. Marakon Assocs., Stamford, Conn. Office: Marakon Associates 300 Atlantic St Stamford CT 06901*

WERNER, WILLIAM ARNO, architect; b. San Francisco, Dec. 11, 1937; s. William Arno and Sophie (Menutis) W.; m. Wendy Rolston Wilson, Feb. 3, 1963 (div. Jan. 1983); 1 child, Christa Nichol. BA with honors, Yale U., 1959, BArch, 1962, MArch, 1963. Drafter Serge Chermayeff, Paul Rudolph and Charles Brewer, New Haven, 1961-63; project designer Johnson, Poole & Storm, San Francisco, 1963-64; project designer Leo S. Wou & Assocs., Honolulu, 1965-66, v.p. of design, 1971-72; project architect John Tatom Assocs., Honolulu, 1965-66; sr. designer Skidmore, Owings & Merrill, San Francisco, 1968-71, assoc./project architect, 1972-76; prin. W.A. Werner Assocs., San Francisco, 1976-80; ptnr. Werner & Sullivan, San Francisco, 1980—; mem. planning commn. City of Sausalito, Calif.; bd. govs. Yale U., New Haven; visitorship in architecture U. Auckland Found., New Zealand, 1994. Prin. works include Alameda Mcpl. Credit Union, Lane Pub. Co., Menlo Park, Calif., Pacific Data Images, Mountain View, Calif., Saga Corp., Menlo Park, Tiffany & Co., Union Square, San Francisco, Somerset Collection, Troy, Mich., Touche Ross & Co., Oakland, U.S. Post Office, San Francisco, (renovations) Fed. Express Co., San Francisco, KD's Grog N' Grocery, San Francisco, Jessie Street. Substation, San Francisco, Lakeside Tower Health Ctr./Mt. Zion Hosp., Qantas Bldg, San Francisco, Women's Care, San Francisco, Moon Residence, Dillon Beach, Calif., Shenkar Residence, San Francisco, Tacker Residence, Denver, Lasky Residence, San Francisco, Starring Residence, San Francisco, Whitehead Residence, Monte Rio, Calif., various laboratories, theatres and rsch. facilities, urban design. Recipient Progressive Architecture Design award Jessie St. Substation, 1980, DuPont Co. Design award Touche Ross & Co., 1983, award of Excellence Woodwork Inst. of Calif., 1989, USPS/NEA Nat. Honor award for Design Excellence, 1990, Tucker Design Excellence award Bldg. Stone Inst., Tiffany & Co., 1992. Mem. AIA (San Francisco chpt.), Found. for San Francisco's Architectural Heritage (hon.). Home: 213 Richardson St Sausalito CA 94965-2422

WERNER-JACOBSEN, EMMY ELISABETH, developmental psychologist; b. Eltville, Germany, May 26, 1929; came to U.S., 1952, naturalized, 1962; d. Peter Josef and Liesel (Kunz) W. B.S., Johannes Gutenberg U., Germany, 1950; M.A., U. Nebr., 1952, Ph.D., 1955; postgrad., U. Calif., Berkeley, 1953-54. Research asso. Inst. Child Welfare, U. Minn., 1956-59; vis. scientist NIH, 1959-62; asst. prof. to prof. human devel., rsch. child psychologist U. Calif., Davis, 1962-94, rsch. prof., 1995—. Sr. author: The Children of Kauai, 1971, Kauai's Children Come of Age, 1977, Cross-Cultural Child Development: A View from the Planet Earth, 1979, Vulnerable, but Invincible, 1982, 2d edit., 1989, Child Care: Kith, Kin and Hired Hands, 1984, Overcoming the Odds, 1992, Pioneer Children on the Journey West, 1995; contbr. articles to profl. jours. Mem. Internat. Assn. Cross-Cultural Psychologists, Am. Psychol. Soc., German Acad. Social Pediats. (hon.), Soc. for Rsch. in Child Devel.

WERNICK, EDWARD RAYMOND, company executive, computer consultant; b. Irvington, N.J., Mar. 11, 1955; s. Edward Joseph and Ann (Czech) W.; m. Ione Sharon Greenbaum, Nov. 2, 1984; 1 child, Elissa Ann. BS in Computer Sci., Kean Coll., 1977. Computer analyst N.Y. Life Ins., N.Y.C., 1978-81; computer cons. Horizons, N.Y.C., 1981-84; data base adminstr. oracle Standard & Poors, N.Y.C., 1984-88; tchr. sybase Sybase, N.Y.C., 1988-89; data base adminstr. sybase Merrill Lynch, N.Y.C., 1989-91, Paramount Comms., Old Tappan, N.J., 1991-95; v.p. Crossmar, Parsippany, N.J., 1995—; computer, fin. cons., pvt. practice, Oradell, N.J., 1981—. Designer stage lighting for more than 80 plays, 1978-84; writer relational scripts for Australian govt., 1994; exhibited sculpture in India, 1991, Brazil, 1992, Oslo, Norway, 1994. Mem. Rep. Nat. Com.; sec. Stockton (N.J.) Rifle Club, 1974; pres. Irvington (N.J.) Masquers, 1978. Named Outstanding Young Rep. Union, N.J., Rep. Com., 1976; Best of Show sculpture Art Assoc., Irvington, N.J., 1979; 100 yd. standing rifle champion Stockton (N.J.) Rifle Club, 1974. Mem. Assn. for Computing Machinery, Sybase Internat. Users Group, Relational Database Users Group, Oradell Arts Com., Internet Users Group. Roman Catholic. Avocations: lighting design, theater, logic. Home: 920 Oradell Ave Oradell NJ 07649-1925 Office: Crossman 4 Sylvan Way Parsippany NJ 07054

WERNICK, JACK HARRY, chemist; b. St. Paul, May 19, 1923; s. Joseph and Eva (Legan) W.; B.Met.E., U. Minn., 1947, M.S., 1948; Ph.D., Pa. State U., 1954; m. Sylvia Katz, Dec. 20, 1947 (dec.); children—Phyllis Roberta Wernick Lauer, Rosanne Pauline; m. 2d, Charlotte Adler, 1983. Staff, Manhattan Project, Los Alamos, 1944-46; mem. staff Bell Labs., Murray Hill, N.J., 1954-84, head solid state chemistry research dept., 1963-81, head device materials research dept., 1981-83; div. mgr. Bell Comm. Rsch., 1983-92; cons. U.S. Office Sci. and Tech., Nat. Bur. Standards, NSF; mem. steering com. div. nuclear fusion ERDA, 1977-79; mem. Gov.'s Roundtable on Superconductivity, N.J., 1989-90. Served in U.S. Army, 1944-46. Fellow N.Y. Acad. Scis., Am. Phys. Soc., AIME, Am. Soc. Metals (McFarland award 1969); mem. Nat. Acad. Engring., AAAS, IEEE, Electrochem. Soc., Sigma Xi, Phi Lambda Upsilon. Jewish. Author: (with E.A. Nesbitt) Rare Earth Permanent Magnets, 1973, (with J.L. Shay) Chalcopyrite Crystals, 1975; editor: Materials and Energy: Selected Topics, 1977; Materials Letters; contbr. articles to profl. jours. Home: 21 Haran Cir Millburn NJ 07041-1403 Office: AT&T Bell Labs New Providence NJ 07974

WERNICK, RICHARD FRANK, composer, conductor; b. Boston, Jan. 16, 1934; s. Louis and Irene (Prince) W.; m. Beatrice Messina, July 15, 1956; children: Lewis, Adam, Peter (dec.). BA, Brandeis U., 1955; MA, Mills Coll., 1957. Instr. music U. Buffalo, 1964-65; asst. prof. music, dir. univ. symphony U. Chgo., 1965-68; prof. emeritus Pa. Contemporary Players, U. Pa., 1968-96; co-founder Community Youth Orch. of Delaware County; cons. Contemporary Music, The Phil. Orch., 1983-89, spl. cons. to the music dir., 1989-93; bd. dirs. Theodore Presser Co. Music dir. Royal Winnipeg Ballet Can., 1957-58; composer: Haiku of Basho, 1967, A Prayer for Jerusalem, 1971 (Naumburg award 1975), Moonsongs from the Japanese, 1972, Kaddish Requiem, 1973, String Quartet 2, 1973, Songs of Remembrance, 1974, Visions of Terror and Wonder, 1976 (Pulitzer prize 1977), Contemplations of the Tenth Muse, Book I, 1976, Book II, 1978, Introits and Canons, 1977, A Poison Tree, 1979, Concerto for Cello and Ten Players, 1980, In Praise of Zephyrus, 1981, Piano Sonata: Reflections of a Dark Light, 1982, Sonata for cello and piano: Portraits of Antiquity, 1982, The Oracle of Shimon bar Yochai, 1983, Concerto for Violin and Orch., 1983-84 (Friedheim 1st prize 1986); Oracle II for soprano, oboe and piano, 1985, Concerto for Viola and Orch., 1985-86, Musica Ptolemeica brass quintet, 1987, Symphony #1, 1988, String Quartet #3, 1988, Concerto for Piano and Orch. (Friedheim award 1992), 1989-90, Fragments of Prophecy, 1990, String Quartet #4, 1991 (Friedheim 1st prize 1991), Concerto for Saxophone Quartet and Orch., 1991, Cello Concerto #2, 1992, Symphony #2, 1993, ...and a time for peace, 1994, String Quartet #5, 1995, Cassation music Tom Jefferson Knew, 1995, trio for violin, cello, piano, 1996. Recipient music award Nat. Inst. Arts and Letters, 1976, Nat. Endowment Arts grantee, 1975, 79, 82; Fellow Ford Found., 1962-64, Guggenheim Found., 1976. Mem. ASCAP. Democrat. Office: 201 S 34th St Philadelphia PA 19104-6313

WERNTZ, CARL WEBER, physics educator; b. Washington, Aug. 7, 1931; s. Walter Hartman and Elizabeth Katherine (Weber) W.; m. Margaret Anne Bjerke, Aug. 23, 1958; children: Heidi, Paul. BS, George Washington U., 1953; PhD, U. Minn., 1960. Postdoctoral fellow U. Wis., Madison, 1960-62; asst. prof. Cath. U. Am., Washington, 1962-65, assoc. prof., 1965-70, prof. physics, 1970—, chmn. physics dept., 1974-77, 92—; vis. prof. Calif. Inst. Tech., Pasadena, 1969-70. Nat. Rsch. Ctr. fellow, 1975-76. Office: Catholic U Physics Dept Cardinal Sta Washington DC 20064

WERRIES, E. DEAN, food distribution company executive; b. Tescott, Kans., May 8, 1929; s. John William and Sophie E. Werries; m. Marjean Sparling, May 18, 1962. B.S., U. Kans., 1952. With Fleming Foods Co., Topeka, 1955-89, exec. v.p., 1973-76; exec. v.p. Eastern ops. Fleming Foods Co., Phila., 1976-78; pres. Fleming Foods Co., Oklahoma City, 1978-81; pres., chief operating officer Fleming Cos., Inc., Oklahoma City, 1981-88, also dir.; pres., chief exec. officer Fleming Cos., Inc., 1988-89, chmn., CEO, 1989-93; chmn. bd. Sonic Corp., 1995—. Sec. of Commerce State of Okla., 1995. With U.S. Army, 1952-54, Korea. Mem. Nat. Am. Wholesale Grocers Assn. (bd. dirs. 1979-93), Food Mktg. Inst. (bd. dirs. 1984—, chmn. 1989-91), Ind. Grocers Alliance (bd. dirs. 1984-94). Republican. Presbyterian. Office: Fleming Cos Inc PO Box 26647 6301 Waterford Blvd Oklahoma City OK 73126-0647

WERT, BARBARA J. YINGLING, special education educator; b. Hanover, Pa., May 18, 1953; d. Richard Bruce and Jacqueline Louise (Myers) Yingling; m. Barry Thomas Wert, Aug. 23, 1975; children: Jennifer Allison, Jason Frederick. BS in Elem. Edn., Kutztown (Pa.) U., 1975; MS in Spl. Edn., Bloomsburg (Pa.) U., 1990. Cert. in elem. edn., spl. edn., Pa. Dir. children's program Coun. for United Ch. Ministries of Reading, Reading, Pa., 1975-76; instr. Berks County Vo-Tech., Oley Valley, Pa., 1976-77; asst. tchr. Ostrander Elem. Sch., Wallkill, N.Y., 1982-85; spl. needs surp., instrnl. support tchr., cons. Danville (Pa.) Child Devel. Ctr., 1986—; dir. Little Learners Pre-Sch., Northumberland, Pa., 1991-94, ednl. cons., 1991—; pvt. cons. Families with Spl. Needs, Northumberland, 1991—. Recipient Parent Profl. Partnership award 1993. Mem. ASCD, Coun. for Exceptional Children (exec. bd. dirs. divsn. early childhood 1991—, sec. 1991-93, newsletter editor, v.p. 1993-94, pres. 1995-96), Nat. Assn. for Edn. Young Children (v.p. Pa. divsn. for early childhood 1993—, tchr. edn. divsn., coun. for behavior disorders divsn., learning disabilities divsn.), Local Autism Support and Advocacy Group. Avocations: photography, needlework, hiking, reading. Home: RR 1 Box 372-n Northumberland PA 17857-9717 Office: Danville Child Devel Ctr PO Box 183 Danville PA 17821-0183

WERT, CHARLES ALLEN, metallurgical and mining engineering educator; b. Battle Creek, Iowa, Dec. 31, 1919; s. John Henry and Anna (Spotts) W.; m. Lucille Vivian Mathena, Sept. 5, 1943; children: John Arthur, Sara Ann. B.A., Morningside Coll., Sioux City, 1941; M.S., State U. Iowa, 1943, Ph.D., 1948. Mem. staff Radiation Lab., Mass. Inst. Tech., 1943-45; instr. physics U. Chgo., 1948-50; mem. faculty U. Ill. at Urbana, 1950—, prof., 1955, head dept. metall. and mining engring., 1967-86, prof. emeritus, 1989; cons. to industry. Author: Physics of Metals, 1970, Opportunities in Materials Science and Engineering, 1977; also articles.; Cons. editor, McGraw Hill Book Co. Recipient sr. scientist award von Humboldt-Stiftung. Fellow Am. Phys. Soc., Am. Soc. Metals, AAAS, AIME; mem. Sigma Xi. Home: 1708 W Green St Champaign IL 61821-3721 Office: U Ill Metallurgy & Mining Bldg Urbana IL 61801

WERT, JAMES JUNIOR, materials scientist, educator; b. Barron, Wis., Jan. 9, 1933; s. James Lewis and Bernice Janet (Walker) W.; m. Jane Alice Thornton, Aug. 16, 1958; children: Thaddeus Thornton, Melissa Jane. B.S., U. Wis., 1957, M.S., 1958, Ph.D., 1961; postgrad., Carnegie Tech. Inst., 1958-59. Assoc. engr. Westinghouse Electric Corp., Pitts., 1958-60; rsch. scientist A.O. Smith Corp., Milw., 1961-62; mem. faculty Vanderbilt U., Nashville, 1962—; prof. material sci. and engring. Vanderbilt U., 1967—, chmn. dept., 1969, chmn. materials, mechanics and structures div., 1969-72, chmn. materials sci. dept., 1975-82, chmn. dept. mech. and materials engring., 1976-82, George A. Sloan prof. metallurgy, 1976—; mayor City of Forest Hills, Tenn., 1990-95; dir. Ctr. for Coatings Sci. and Tech., Vanderbilt U., 1969-74; co.-dir. Ctr. for Materials Tribology, 1987—; vis. prof. Cambridge U., 1974; sr. Fulbright lectr. Mid. East; cons. Avco, 1964-71, Temco, 1964-71, Arnold Engring. Ctr., Tullahome, Tenn., 1966-71, Nat. Acad. Scis., 1969-70; pres. Technology Assocs., Inc., Nashville, 1975-85; pres. James Wert & Assocs., 1985—. Contbr. articles to profl. jours. Served with AUS, 1953-55. Ampco fellow, 1957-58; Westinghouse-Bettis fellow, 1958-59; Foundry Edn. fellow, 1952-57; recipient Adams award Am. Welding Soc., 1969, Teaching award Tau Beta Pi, 1970, 78. Fellow ASME, ASM Internat.; mem. ASTM, AIME, Am. Welding Soc., Am. Soc. Metals, Hillwood Country Club, Sigma Xi, Tau Beta Pi, Phi Eta Sigma, Alpha Sigma Mu, Pi Kappa Alpha, Pi Tau Sigma, Omicron Kappa Delta. Methodist. Patentee nuclear fuels and cladding materials. Home: 2510 Ridgewood Dr Nashville TN 37215-4518

WERT, JONATHAN MAXWELL, II, management consultant; b. Port Royal, Pa., Nov. 8, 1939; s. Jonathan Maxwell I and Helen Leona (Leonard) W.; m. Monica Kay Manbeck; children: Jonathan Maxwell III, Kimberly Dee, Jon Adam, Justin Tyler, Amanda Elizabeth. B.S. in Biology, Austin Peay State U., 1966, M.S. in Biology, 1968; Ph.D. in Adminstrn., U. Ala., 1974. Park supt., chief interpretive services Bur. State Parks Pa. Dept. Environ. Resources, Harrisburg, 1968-69; chief naturalist Bays Mountain Park Environ. Edn. Ctr., Kingsport, Tenn., 1969-71; environ. and energy edn. specialist TVA, Knoxville, 1971-75; cons. energy, environment, conservation U. Tenn., Knoxville, 1975; sr. assoc.-energy Energy Extension Svc., Coop. Extension Svc., Pa. State U., 1977-80; pres. Energy-Environ. Consultants, Port Royal, Pa., 1981-85, Mgmt. Diagnostics, Inc., Port Royal, 1985—. Author: Writing Environmental Education Grant Proposals, 1974, Environmental Education Study Projects for High School Students, 1974, Environmental Education Study Projects for College Students, 1974, Developing Environmental Study Areas, 1974, Developing Environmental Education Curriculum Material, 1974, Finding Solutions to Environmental Problems . . . A Process Guide, 1975, Assessing an Issue in Relation to Environmental, Economic, and Social Impact . . . A Process Guide, 1976, Energy Conservation Measures for Mobile Home Dwellers, 1978, Selected Energy Conservation Options for the Home, 1978, Selected Energy Management Options for Small Business and Local Government, 1978, Life Lines: A Book of Poetry, Prose, and Axioms, 1983, Survivorship and Growth in Employment: A Question and Answer Guide, 1983; mem. adv. bd.: Environ. Edn. Report, 1974—; cons. editor: Jour. Environ. Edn, 1975; contbr. articles to profl. jours. Counselor Boy Scouts Am., 1975. Served with USMC, 1958-61. Recipient Conservation award Am. Motors Co., 1976. Mem. U.S. Energy Assn., Inst. Mgmt. Cons., Orgn. Devel. Inst., Phi Delta Kappa. Lutheran. Office: Mgmt Diagnostics Inc PO Box 240 Port Royal PA 17082-0240

WERT, LAWRENCE JOSEPH, radio executive; b. Berwyn, Ill., May 27, 1956; s. Ronald J. and Joan (Damore) W.; m. Julia Anne Arneson, Aug. 25, 1984; children: Kathryn Ellis, Kristina Joanne, Sara Elizabeth, Charles Damore. BS in Journalism, U. Wis., 1978. Media buyer, planner Leo Burnett Advt., Chgo., 1978-79; account exec. Sta. KABC-TV, L.A., 1980-83, ABC-TV Nat. Sales, Chgo., 1983-84; sr. account exec. ABC-TV Nat. Sales, N.Y.C., 1984; local sales mgr. Sta. WLS-TV, Chgo., 1985-89; pres., gen. mgr. Sta. WLUP-AM-FM, Chgo., 1989—; officer Arbitron Adv. Coun. Bd. dirs. Children's Brittle Bone Found., Chgo., 1984—; gen. chmn. Little City Found. '90 Fundraiser, Chgo.; chmn. ann. Jim Shorts Charity Golf, 1989—. Mem. Broadcast Advt. Club, Radio Broadcast Com. (v.p.). Avocations: family, golf. Home: 226 Scottswood Rd Riverside IL 60546-2224 Office: WLUP Radio 875 N Michigan Ave Chicago IL 60611-1803

WERT, LINDA ARLENE, kindergarten educator; b. York, Pa., June 26, 1948; d. Daniel O. Sr. and Teresa M. (Phillips) Bumbaugh. BS,

Elizabethtown Coll., 1970. Cert. tchr., Pa. Tchr. kindergarten Red Lion (Pa.) Area Sch. Dist., 1969—, elem. computer coord., 1985-86; mem. tchr. adv. bd. York campus Pa. State U., 1991—. Mem. St. Paul's U.C.C. Ch., Dallastown, 1996—, Fools for Christ clown ministry, 1989—, York Symphony Chorus, 1995—. Recipient Presdl. award for Excellence in Sci. and Math. Teaching NSF, 1992, 93. Mem. ASCD, Pa. Coun. Tchrs. Math., Nat. Coun. Tchrs. Math., Red Lion Area Math. Com., York Quilters Guild, NEA, Pa. State Edn. Assn., Red Lion Area Edn. Assn. Avocations: quilting, making teddy bears, reading historical fiction, composing music, playing oboe. Home: 17 W Crestlyn Dr York PA 17402-4958 Office: North Hopewell Winterstown Elem Sch 12165 Winterstown Rd Red Lion PA 17356

WERTH, ANDREW M., telecommunications executive; b. Saarbruck, Germany, Mar. 2, 1934; came to U.S., 1944; s. Steven S. and Margot Werth; m. Eileen B. Pighini, Jan. 30, 1954; children: Gregory, Jeffrey, Karen. BS, Columbia U., 1955, MS, 1961. Project engr. ITT Labs., Nutley, N.J., 1959-64; mem. tech. staff Comsat Corp., Washington, 1964-68; br. mgr. Comsat Labs., Clarksburg, Md., 1968-72; pres. Hughes Network Systems Internat., Germantown, Md., 1972—. Patentee in field. Capt. USAF, 1955-57. Fellow IEEE; mem. AIAA, Cosmos Club. Roman Catholic.

WERTH, SUSAN, lawyer; b. N.Y.C., Nov. 29, 1948. BA, Barnard Coll., 1970; JD, Columbia U., 1973. Bar: Fla. 1973, U.S. Dist. Ct. (so. dist.) Fla. 1974, U.S. Dist. Ct. (mid. dist.) Fla. 1975, U.S. Dist. Ct. (no. dist.) Fla. 1976, U.S. Ct. Appeals (5th cir.) 1974, U.S. Ct. Appeals (11th cir.) 1978, U.S. Supreme Ct. 1978, U.S. Ct. Appeals (11th cir.) 1981. Ptnr. Weil, Gotshal & Manges, Miami, Fla., 1989-96; sr. v.p. of law Vistana Development, Miami, Fla.; adj. prof. law Sch. Law U. Miami, 1976-77. Mem. Fla. Bar Found. (bd. dirs. 1986-88, sec.-treas. 1988-90, pres.-elect 1991-92, pres. 1992-93), Fla. Bar. Office: Weil Gotshal & Manges 701 Brickell Ave Ste 2100 Miami FL 33131-2861*

WERTHAMER, N. RICHARD, physicist; b. Milw., Feb. 9, 1935. BS, Harvard Coll., 1956; PhD in physics, U. Calif., 1961. Rsch. assoc. U. Calif., San Diego, 1961-62; mem. tech. staff Bell Labs, 1962-75; chmn. N.Y. State Energy Rsch. and Devel. Authority, 1976-78; dir. Becton Dickinson Devel. Corp., 1983-89; exec. officer Am. Phys. Soc., 1990-93; mgmt. cons. Chelsea Technols, N.Y.C., 1993—. Fellow AAAS, Am. Phys. Soc., mem. Am. Assn, Clin. Chem. Office: Chelsea Technols 43 W 16th St Ste 7-D New York NY 10011

WERTHEIM, HARVEY J., human resource specialist. Grad., City Coll. N. Y., 1962. Acct. Price Waterhouse, N.Y., 1964-69, v.p., dir., 1969-81; v.p., dir. Rsch. and Sci. Dir., N.Y., 1969-81; pres. Harvest Ventures Inc., N.Y., 1981—; chmn. bd. Career Horizons, Inc., Woodbury, N.Y., 1990—. With U.S. Army, 1962-64. Office: Career Horizons Inc 177 Crossways Park Dr Woodbury NY 11797-2016*

WERTHEIM, MITZI MALLINA, technology company executive; b. N.Y.C.; d. Rudolf and Myrtle B. (McGraw) Mallina; m. Ronald P. Wertheim, Feb. 25, 1965 (div. July 1988); children: Carter, Christiana. B.A., U. Mich., 1960. Asst. dir. div. research Peace Corps, Washington, 1961-66; sr. program officer Cafritz Found., Washington, 1970-76; dep. undersec. navy, 1977-81; with Fed. Sector Div. IBM, 1981-94; v.p. enterprise solutions Systems Rsch. and Applications Corp., 1994—; Woodrow Wilson vis. fellow, 1979, 80. Bd. dirs. Nat. Coalition for Sci. and Tech., 1983—, Youth Policy Inst., 1986-91, VITA, 1990—; mem. vis. com. MIT, 1983-89. Recipient Federally Employed Women award Def. Dept., 1980; Disting. Pub. Svc. medal Navy Dept., 1981; fellow Maxwell Sch. Syracuse U., 1996—. Mem. Coun. on Fgn. Rels. Episcopalian. Home: 3113 38th St NW Washington DC 20016-3726

WERTHEIM, ROBERT HALLEY, air, aerospace transportation executive; b. Carlsbad, N.Mex., Nov. 9, 1922; s. Joseph and Emma (Vorenberg) W.; m. Barbara Louise Selig, Dec. 26, 1946; children: Joseph Howard, David Andrew. Student, N.Mex. Mil. Inst., 1940-42; B.S., U.S. Naval Acad., 1945; M.S. in Physics, M.I.T., 1954; postgrad., Harvard U., 1969. Commd. ensign U.S. Navy, 1945, advanced through grades to rear adm., 1972; assigned Spl. Projects Office, Washington, 1956-61, Naval Ordnance Test Sta., China Lake, 1961-62, Office Sec. Def., Washington, 1962-65; head Missile br. Strategic Systems Project Office, Washington, 1965-67; dep. tech. dir. Missile br. Strategic Systems Project Office, 1967-68, tech. dir., 1968-77, dir., 1977-80; sr. v.p. Lockheed Corp., 1981-88; cons. nat. def., 1988—; emeritus mem. Charles Stark Draper Lab., Inc.; mem. U. Calif. Pres. Adv. Coun.; mem. sci. adv. group Dept. Def., Dept. Energy, Inst. for Def. Analysis, Ctr. for Naval Analysis, U.S. Strategic Command; mem. nat. security adv. Los Alamos Nat. Lab., Lawrence Livermore Nat. Lab. Decorated D.S.M. with cluster, Legion of Merit, Navy Commendation medal, Joint Svc. Commendation medal; recipient Rear Adm. William S. Parsons award Navy League U.S., 1971. Fellow AIAA; mem. Am. Soc. Naval Engrs. (hon. mem., Gold medal 1972), Nat. Acad. Engring., U.S. Naval Inst., Nat. Acad. Scis. (com. on internat. security and arms control), Bernardo Heights Country Club, Masons, Sigma Xi, Tau Beta Pi. Home: 17705 Devereux Rd San Diego CA 92128-2084 Office: Sci Applications Internat Corp 1200 Prospect St La Jolla CA 92037

WERTHEIM, SALLY HARRIS, academic administrator, dean, education educator; b. Cleve., Nov. 1, 1931; d. Arthur I. and Anne (Manheim) Harris; m. Stanley E. Wertheim, Aug. 6, 1950; children: Kathryn, Susan B., Carole J. BS, Flora Stone Mather Coll., 1953; MA, Case Western Res. U., 1967, PhD, 1970. Cert. elem. and secondary edn. tchr., Ohio. Social worker U. Hosps., Cleve., 1953-54; tchr. Fairmount Temple Religious Sch., Cleve., 1957-72; mem. faculty John Carroll U., Cleve., 1969—, prof., 1980—, dean grad. sch., rsch. coord., 1986-93, acad. v.p., 1993-94, 95; dean Grad. Sch., coord. faculty rsch. John Carrol U., Cleve., 1994—; cons. in field; cons. Jennings Found., Cleve.; chmn. sch. com. Cleve. Commn. on Higher Edn., 1987—. Contbr. articles to profl. jours. Sec. Cuyahoga County Mental Health Bd., Cleve., 1978-82; pres. Jewish Family Svc. Assn., Cleve., 1974-77, Montefiore Home for Aged, Cleve., 1987-90; bd. dirs. Mt. Sinai Med. Ctr., Cleve., 1984-93, Cleve. Edn. Fund, 1992-94; v.p. Jewish Cmty. Fedn., 1988-91, pres., 1994—, bd. trustees, 1992—; chairperson edn. com. Cleve. Found. Commn. on Poverty, 1988-93, Cleve. Cmty. Bldg. Initiative, 1993—, United Way Svcs., 1994—. Named One of 100 Most Influential Women, Cleve. mag., 1983; recipient award Jewish Communty Fedn.; grantee Jennings Found., 1984-87, Cleve. and Gund Found., 1987-90, Lilly Found., 1988. Mem. Am. Assn. Colls. for Tchrs. Edn. (bd. dirs. 1982-85), Ohio Assn. Colls. for Tchrs. Edn. (pres. 1981-83), Coun. of Grad. Schs. Avocations: flower arranging, travel, antiques. Office: John Carroll U Grad Sch Cleveland OH 44118

WERTHEIM, STEVEN BLAKE, orthopedist; b. Apr. 1, 1956; m. Melinda Mitchell; children: Meredith, Julia, Eve. BA, Northwestern U., 1977; MD, Case Western Reserve U., 1981. Cert. Am. Bd. orthopaedic Surgery, Ga., 1989. Intern in Surgery Univ. Hosp. Cleve., 1981-82; resident in Orthipaedics, 1982-86; fellow in Sports Medicine U. Pa., 1986-87; asst. prof. Orthopaedic Surgery U. Pa. Sch. Medicine, 1987-88; faculty U.S. Sports Acad., 1995—; clin. asst. prof. Orthopaedics Emory U. Sch. Medicine, 1989—; bd. trustees Atlanta Jewish Fedn.,;; com. Am. Israeli Pub. Affairs; regional v.p. Macabah USA/Sports for Israel; team physician East Paulding H.S., 1993-94 Atlanta Fire Ants U.S. Profl. roller Hockey League, 1993-94; chmn. Promina Windy Hill Bd. Dirs. 1993, 94, Kennestone Hosp at Windy Hill, 1992, 93; chief of staff elect Kennestone Hosp. at Windy Hill, 1991, 92; chief of Orthopaedics Kennestone Hosp. at Windy Hill, 1989, 91; Ambulatory Care Com., Cobb Hosp. and Med. Ctr., 1989, 91; O.r. Com. Kennestone Hosp. at Windy Hill, 1989-92. Numerous lectures and exhibits in field; contbr. articles to profl. jours. Recipient Jesse T. Nicholson award, U. Pa. Dept. Orthopaedics, 1988, James Scholar award Psychology, 1977, Bus. Atlanta Forty Under Forty award, 1993. Mem. AMA, Am. Acad. Orthopaedic Surgeons, Arthroscopy Assn. N.Am., U.S. Olympic Com. Sports Medicine Soc., Nat. Athletic Trainers Assn., Southern Orthopaedic Assn., Southern Med. Assn. Office: C/O Resurgens Orthopaedics Ste 900 5671 Peachtree Dunwoody Rd Atlanta GA 30342*

WERTHEIMER, FRANC, retired corporate executive; b. Nuremberg, Germany, Sept. 26, 1927; came to U.S., 1938; s. Erich Z. and Sophie (Prager) W.; m. Sidelle Shaiken, Sept. 2, 1951; children: Laura S., David F. BA summa cum laude, Bklyn. Coll., 1950; MA, Columbia U., 1951. Head dept. systems analysis Vitro Labs., West Orange, N.J., 1952-68; pres., chief exec. officer ManTech Internat. Corp., Alexandria, Va., 1968-91; vice chmn. Forensic Techs. Internat. Corp., Annapolis, Md., 1968-92; adj. prof. math. Bklyn. Coll., CUNY, 1951-53, Fairleigh Dickinson U., Rutherford, N.J., 1954-58, Kean Coll., Union, N.J., 1968-72; instr. math. Emeritus Found., program dir. Emeritus Scientists, Mathematicians and Engrs. Program, 1991—; instr. math. Project Apply, AAAS, 1991—; mentor Dingman Ctr., U. Md. Sch. Bus. and Mgmt., 1991—, adj. prof. mgmt., 1995—. Contbr. over 500 reports, monographs, position papers, concept documents pub. and submitted to U.S. Govt. and pvt. sector clients, articles to profl. jours.; guest editor Technical Jour., 1969; session chmn. tech. seminar, 1980. Bd. dirs. Washington Urban League, 1979-84; bd. dirs., pres., v.p., sec. Sumner Village Condominium, Bethesda, Md., 1988-95; mem. Com. on Coms., Montgomery County, Md., 1991-93; docent Nat. Archives and Records Adminstrn., 1991-93; docent Phillips Collection, 1991—, mgrs. vols., 1994—; asst. to dir. men's group OASIS, 1993—. With U.S. Army. Grad. scholar Columbia U., 1950. Mem. Ops. Rsch. Soc. Am., Navy League U.S. (life), Bklyn. Coll. Alumni Assn. (pres. D.C. chpt. 1989), Cosmos Club, B'nai B'rith, Phi Beta Kappa, Pi Mu Epsilon. Home: 4956 Sentinel Dr Bethesda MD 20816-3594

WERTHEIMER, FREDRIC MICHAEL, professional society administrator; b. Bklyn., Jan. 9, 1939; s. Irving Wertheimer and Mildred (Klein) Van Brink; m. Linda Cozby, June 15, 1969. B.A., U. Mich., 1959; LL.B., Harvard U., 1962. Bar: N.Y. bar 1963. Atty. SEC, 1963-66; legis. counsel Congressman Silvio Conte, 1967-68; counsel House Small Bus. Com., 1969-70; lobbyist, legis. dir., v.p. Common Cause, Washington, 1971-81; pres. Common Cause, 1981-95. Author: Common Cause Manual on Money and Politics, 1972. Served with U.S. Army, 1962-63. Fellow Inst. Politics Harvard U., 1972. Jewish. Home: 3502 Macomb St NW Washington DC 20016

WERTHEIMER, ROBERT E., paper company executive; b. 1928; married. BSME, U. Wash., 1950; MBA, Harvard U., 1952. With Longview (Wash.) Fibre Co., 1952—, package engr., 1955-59, asst. mgr. container ops., 1959-60, asst. mgr. container sales, 1960-63, v.p. container sales West, 1963-75, v.p. prodn., 1975, group v.p. containers, now exec. v.p., dir. Office: Longview Fibre Co 120 Montgomery St Ste 2200 San Francisco CA 94104-4325 Office: Longview Fiber Co Longview WA 98632*

WERTKIN, GERARD CHARLES, museum director, lawyer; b. N.Y.C., Oct. 3, 1940; s. Murray and Cecelia (Bregman) W.; m. Barbara Susan Dansky, Sept. 18, 1965; children: Jennifer, Andrew Murray, Rebecca. AB, Syracuse U., 1962; LLB, NYU, 1965, LLM, 1970. Bar: N.Y. 1966. Assoc. Saxe, Bacon & O'Shea, N.Y.C., 1965-67; atty. Kayser-Roth Corp., N.Y.C., 1967-76; pvt. practice law N.Y.C., 1976-80; asst. dir. Mus. Am. Folk Art, N.Y.C., 1980-91, assoc. dir., then acting dir., 1991, dir., 1991—; instr. grad. program dept. folk art studies NYU, 1982-90, adj. assoc. prof., 1990—; cons. British Broadcasting Corp., 1990, 94. Author: The Four Seasons of Shaker Life, 1986; co-author: The Jewish Heritage in American Folk Art, 1984; author forewords and introductions to many books and exhbn. catalogs and essays in Folk Art and other jours. Bd. dirs. Friends of Shakers, Sabbathday Lake, Maine, 1975—, pres., 1979-82; trustee United Soc. of Shakers, Sabbathday Lake, 1979—; adv. com. grad. program mus. professions, Seton Hall U., South Orange, N.J., 1993—; bd. overseers Hancock Shaker Village, Pittsfield, Mass., 1993—; bd. adv. Hist. Soc. Early Am. Decoration, 1993—; nat. adv. com. Folk Art Soc. Am., 1992—; bd. dirs. Arts and Bus. Coun., Inc., N.Y.C., 1995—. Mem. Univ. Club N.Y.C. Office: Mus Am Folk Art 61 W 62nd St New York NY 10023-7015

WERTS, JOSEPHINE STARR, artist; b. Osage, Iowa, Aug. 5, 1903; d. William Jessie and Edna Lavinia (Wheeland) Starr; m. Leo Robert Werts, June 15, 1929 (div. 1947); 1 child, Barbara Werts Blatt. BA in Phys. Edn., Iowa State Tchrs. Coll., 1926; postgrad., Art Inst. Chgo., 1945, 46, U. Chgo., 1945, 46; MA in Fine Arts, U. So. Calif., 1961. One-woman shows include Cambria (Calif.) Coast Gallery, Ten Directions Gallery, Baywood Park, Calif., San Luis Obispo (Calif.) Art Ctr.; group shows include San Luis Obispo Art Ctr., U. So. Calif., Oakland (Calif.) Art Mus., Pasadena (Calif.) Art Mus., M.H. de Young Meml. Mus., San Francisco, Richmond (Calif.) Art Mus., Otis Art Inst., L.A., Long Beach (Calif.) Mus. Art, La Jolla (Calif.) Art Ctr., Ten Directions Gallery, Baywood Park, Calif., 1994, Kings County Art Ctr., Hanford, Calif., 1995, Paso Robles (Calif.) Art Ctr., 1996; represented in permanent collections Va. Mus. Fine Arts, Richmond, U. So. Calif. Fisher Gallery, also pvt. collections. Recipient award Palos Verdes Community Arts Assn., 1954, 57. Mem. Nat. Watercolor Soc. (bd. dirs. 1965, corr. sec. 1965, D'Arches award 1969), Watercolor U.S.A. Honor Soc. (Jurors award 1990), Ctrl. Coast Printmakers Soc., San Luis Art Assn. Democrat. Avocations: swimming, reading, stretching, music composition, dance. Home and Studio: 2050 Emmons Rd Cambria CA 93428-4510

WERTS, MERRILL HARMON, management consultant; b. Smith Center, Kans., Nov. 17, 1922; s. Mack Allen and Ruth Martha (Badger) W.; BS, Kans. State U., 1947; MS, Cornell U., 1948; m. Dorothy Wilson, Mar. 22, 1946; children: Stephen M., Riley J., Todd J., Kelly M. Beef sales mgr. John Morrell & Co., Topeka and Memphis, 1948-53; dir. mktg. Kans. Dept. Agr., Topeka, 1953-55; sec.-treas. Falley's Markets, Inc., Topeka, 1955-58; v.p. S.W. State Bank, Topeka, 1958-65; pres. First Nat. Bank, Junction City, Kans., 1965-78; pvt. practice mgmt. cons., Junction City, 1978—; mem. Kans. Senate, 1978-88; mem. Kans. Pub. Employee Rels. Bd., 1989-94, Kans. Comsn. on Future of Health Care, 1991-94; chmn. Kans. WWII Commemoration Com. 1995—, Kans. Commn. on Vets. Affairs, 1995—; chmn. Geary County Pub. Bldg. Commn., 1996—; dir. Stockgrowers State Bank, Maple Hill, Kans., J.C. Housing & Devel., Inc., Kans. State Hist. Soc., Transformer Disposal Specialists, Inc. Mem. Kans. Bank Mgmt. Commn., 1967-71; mem. adv. com. U.S. Comptroller of Currency, 1971-72. Mem. Topeka Bd. Edn., 1957-61; pres. Junction City-Geary County United Fund, 1967-68; pres. Junction City Indsl. Devel., Inc., 1966-72. Trustee Kans. State U. Endowment Assn., Kans. Synod Presbyn. Westminster Found., 1965-72. 1st lt., inf., AUS, 1943-46. Decorated Bronze Star medal, Purple Heart, Combat Inf. badge; named to Inf. Officer Candidate Hall Fame, 1981, Civilian Aide to Sec. of Army for Kans., 1991-95; named Outstanding State Legis. Am. Legis. Exchange Coun., 1988. Mem. Kans. State U. Alumni Assn. (pres. 1957), Am. Legion, VFW, Kans. Bankers Assn., Assn. U.S. Army, U.S., Kans. (bd. dirs., v.p. 1979-84), Junction City (pres. 1975-76) chambers commerce, Kans. Farm Bur., Kans. Livestock Assn., DAV, Junction City Country Club (past pres.), Masons, Shriners, Jesters, Rotary (dist. gov. 1973-74), Sigma Phi Epsilon. Republican. Presbyterian. Address: 1228 Miller Dr Junction City KS 66441-3312 *I believe that parents have no greater responsibility than that of being positive role models for their children, whether it be in their private, vocational or public pursuits.*

WERTSMAN, VLADIMIR FILIP, librarian, information specialist, author; b. Secureni, Romania, Apr. 6, 1929; came to U.S., 1967; s. Filip and Anna Wertsman. LLM summa cum laude, U. A.I. Cuza, Romania, 1953; MLS, Columbia U., 1969. Judge lower and appellate cts. Romania, 1953-67; examiner stock certs. 1st Nat. City Bank, N.Y.C., 1967-68; reference libr. sci. div. Bklyn. Pub. Libr., N.Y.C., 1969-74, sr. libr. Canarsie br., 1974-77, sr. libr. Greenpoint br., 1977-80, sr. libr. Leonard br., 1980-82; sr. libr., Slavic and Romanian specialist Donnell Libr. Ctr. N.Y. Pub. Libr., 1982-86; sr. libr. Learner's Adv. and Job Info. Ctr., 1987-93. Author, editor: The Romanians in America, 1748-1974, 1974, The Ukrainians in America, 1608-1975, 1976, The Russians in America, 1727-1970, 1977, The Armenians in America, 1618-1976, 1978, The Romanians in America and Canada, 1980, Librarian's Companion: A Handbook of Thousands of Facts and Figures on Libraries/Librarians, 1987, 2d edit., 1996, Career Opportunities for Bilinguals and Multilinguals: A Directory of Resources in Education, Employment and Business, 1991, 2d eidt., 1994, What's Cooking in Multicultural America, 1996, New York: The City in Over 500 Memorable Quotations From American & Foriegn Sources, 1996, Directory of Ethnic and Multicultural Publishers, Distributors and Resource Organizations, 3d edit., 1995; co-author: Ukrainains in Canada and United States, 1981, Free Voices in Russian Literature, 1950s-1980s, 1986; editl. cons. Harvard Ency. Am. Ethnic Groups, 1980; contbr. Books, Libraries and Information in Slavic and East European Studies, 1986, Immigrant Labor Press in North America, 1840s-1970s, 1987, Through American Eyes, 1989, Ency. of N.Y.C., 1995; mem. adv. bd., contbr.: Gale Ency. Multicultural Am., 1995; contbr. articles, book revs. to profl. jours. Recipient Disting. Lit. Achievement award Am. Soc. Writers, 1977. Mem. ALA, Am. Pub. Libr. Assn. (chair multilingual libr. materials and svcs. com. 1976-88, spl. merit award 1988, chair pub. & ethnic materials com. ethnic materials info. exch. roundtable 1989—), Am. Assn. Advancement of Slavic Studies, Am. Romanian Acad. Arts & Scis., Delta Tau Kappa. Avocations: chess playing, travel, stamp collecting, dancing. Home: 330 W 55th St New York NY 10019-5159 *America is by its very nature of historical formation and development a multiethnic, multicultural and multilingual society. And if variety is the spice of life then American ethno-linguistic and cultural mosaique is the spice of our society. America's pluralism is also a microcosm of the entire world its citizens representing virtually all continents.*

WERTZ, JOHN ALAN, secondary school educator; b. Mpls., May 28, 1945; s. John Edward and Florence (Carlson) W.; m. Margaret M. Schlangen, 1993. BS, Hamline U., 1967; MS, St. Cloud State Coll., 1973; postgrad., George Washington U., 1985. Tchr. social sci. St. Cloud (Minn.) Community Schs., 1967—; trainer and field rep. New Games Found., San Francisco, 1980-83; tchr.-coach Apollo H.S. Mock Trial team, 1987—, co-chair site coun., 1995-96. Mem. com. social action Minn. Synod, Luth. Ch. Am., 1971-74; chair social action com. Salem Luth. Ch. Coun., St. Cloud, 1974-76; mem. affirmative action com. St. Cloud Cmty. Schs., 1975-78, co-chair student assistance com., 1982-83, mem. site coun. Apollo H.S., 1994-96, co-chair site coun. Apollo H.S., 1995—; chair St. Cloud Human Rights Commn., 1979-86; adv. Ctrl. Minn. Sexual Assault Ctr., 1981-83; bd. dirs. St. Cloud Area Tenants' Assn., 1975-77, St. Cloud Area Spl. Olympics, 1982-83, United Way St. Cloud Area, 1996, Minn. Edn. Assn., 1996. Recipient Merit award St. Cloud Area Coun. for Handicapped, 1976; grad. St. Cloud Area Leadership Program, 1995. Mem. ASCD, NEA, Minn. Edn. Assn. (bd. dirs. 1996), St. Cloud Edn. Assn. (chair govtl. rels. coun. 1978-83, 88-96), Am. Hist. Soc. of Germans from Russia, St. Cloud Area C. of C. (edn. divsn. 1992—, vice-chmn. PreK-12 com. 1993-94, chair edn. recognition com. 1994-96). Avocations: theatre arts, camping, computing. Home: 816 Rilla Rd Saint Cloud MN 56303-1037 Office: Apollo High Sch 1000 44th Ave N Saint Cloud MN 56303

WERTZ, KENNETH DEAN, real estate executive; b. Oklahoma City, July 14, 1946; s. Walter K. and Kathryn L. (Moore) W.; children: Adam Troy, Kirsten Paige. B.S. in Acctg., Okla. State U., 1968, M.S. in Acctg. and Econs., 1969; JD, U. San Francisco, 1978. CPA, Okla., Calif; lic. real estate broker, Okla. Sr. acct. Deloitte, Haskins & Sells, San Francisco, 1969-70, 71-75; v.p. acquisitions, mng. dir. Landsing Corp., Menlo Park, Calif., 1975-86; pres. Detrick Salsberry Mgmt. Inc., Tulsa, 1987-88; v.p. asset mgmt. Corporex Co., Cin., 1989-90; exec. v.p. real estate Brunner Cos., Dayton, Ohio, 1990-92; pres. Pillar Real Estate Advisors, Dayton, Ohio, 1992—. Lt. col. Med. Svc. corps U.S. Army, 1968—. Decorated Army Commendation medal with three oak leaf clusters. Mem. Am. Inst. CPA's, Okla. Soc. CPA's, Calif. Soc. CPA's, Nat. Assn. Securities Dealers (fin. prin., registered sales rep.). Republican. Methodist. Avocations: running, snow and water skiing, racquetball, camping, fishing. Home: 835 Huntersknoll Ln Cincinnati OH 45230-4343 Office: Pillar Real Estate Advisors 5335 Far Hills Ave Ste 318 Dayton OH 45429-2317

WERTZ, SPENCER K., philosophy educator; b. Amarillo, Tex., Oct. 27, 1941; s. Ralph E. and Pauline (Tressler) W.; m. Linda Loflin, Aug. 12, 1967. BA, Tex. Christian U., 1965, MA, 1966; PhD, U. Okla., 1970. Instr. Austin Coll., Sherman, Tex., 1969; from instr. to full prof. philosophy Tex. Christian U., Ft. Worth, 1969—, chmn. dept. philosophy, 1983-92; instr. Tex. Christian U. Div. Extended Edn., Ft. Worth, 1975—. Author: Talking a Good Game, 1991; co-editor: Sport Inside Out, 1985; contbr. over 60 articles to profl. jours. and mags. Mem. N.Mex.-West Tex. Philos. Soc. (pres. 1980-81), Southwestern Philos. Soc. (pres. 1985-86), Philos. Soc. Study Sport (pres. 1985-86), North Tex. Philos. Assn. (pres. 1987-88), Phi Sigma Tau, Phi Beta Kappa. Avocations: tennis, gardening, wilderness travel. Home: 303 Mini Ranch Rd Weatherford TX 76088-8410 Office: Tex Christian Univ Dept Of Philosophy Fort Worth TX 76129

WERZBERGER, ALAN, pediatrician; b. Toronto, Dec. 4, 1954; came to U.S., 1985; s. Bernard and Clara (Hilman) W.; m. Sabina Fischman, June 18, 1978; children: Samuel, Moshe, Yehuda, Jacob Joseph, Mayer, Joel, Susan, Henry, Rochelle Werzberger. MD, U. Toronto, 1981. Intern, resident Hosp. for Sick Children, Toronto, 1981-85; pvt. practice Monroe, N.Y., 1985—; attending dept. pediatrics Good Samaritan Hosp., Suffern, N.Y., 1985—; assoc. attending dept. pediatrics St. Agnes Hosp., White Plains, N.Y., 1992—; clin. asst. prof. pediatrics N.Y. Med. Coll., Valhalla, 1991—; asst. prof. pediatrics NYU Med. Ctr., N.Y.C., 1994—, dir., 1994—; vlin. asst. Dept. Pediatrics Bellevue Hosp. Ctr., N.Y.C., 1995—; pres. Kiryas Joel Med. Rsch. Inst., Monroe, 1991—. Fellow Am. Acad. Pediatrics; mem. Med. Group Mgmt. Assn. Achievements include publication of the first demonstration of efficacy of a vaccine against Hepatitis A. Office: RR 5 Box 157 Monroe NY 10950-2633

WESBERRY, JAMES PICKETT, JR., financial management consultant, auditor, international organization executive; b. Columbia, S.C., Sept. 22, 1934; s. James P. and Ruby L. (Perry) W.; m. Lea Esdras Casteneda, June 13, 1975; children: Jonathan Jesse, Perry Latimer, Ruby Lee Nilda; children by previous marriage: James Pickett III, Elisa Marie, Lillian Sue, Paul Armand. BBA, Ga. State U., 1955; LLD (hon.), Atlanta Law Sch., 1967; MPA, Am. U., 1983. CPA, Ga.; cert. internal auditor; cert. fraud examiner; cert. govt. fin. mgr. Page, U.S. Ho. of Reps., 1949-51; acct., mgmt. cons., Atlanta, 1956-67; v.p. fin. and adminstrn. Computer Tech. South, Atlanta, 1969-70; sr. cons. Inst. Pub. Adminstrn., N.Y.C., 1967-69, 70-76; cons. to comptroller gen. of Peru, 1970-74, of Ecuador, 1974-78; adv., prof. Latin Am. Inst. Auditing Scis., Peruvian and Ecuadorean Sch. Govtl. Auditing, 1971-78; pres. Internat. Profl. Devel. Inst., 1976-78; condr. seminars; dir. systems, standards and procedures Days of Inns Am., Inc., 1979-80; chief auditor OAS, Washington, 1980-82; cons. World Bank, 1982-83, prin. advisor acctg. and auditing pub. sector modernization divsn. Latin Am. and Caribbean region, 1994—; sr. adv. to comptroller gen. U.S., 1983-85; dir. internat. ops. Price Waterhouse, 1985-88; sr. fin. adviser AID, 1988-93, pres., CEO, Inst. Pub. Adminstrn., 1993-94, trustee, 1993-94; dir. N.Y. Bur. Mcpl. Rsch., 1993-94; mem. panel of experts in acctg. and auditing UN, 1972—; adj. prof. Am. U., Washington, 1981-85; founding dir. Internat. Consortium Govtl. Fin. Mgmt., 1977-88, 94—, pres., 1984-87; cons./tchr., all Spanish-speaking Western Hemisphere nations, Brazil,, Haiti, Jamaica, The Netherlands Antilles, Peoples Republic of China, The Philippines, Can., U.S. Co-author: UN Handbook on Government Auditing for Developing Countries, editor: Latin American Manual of Professional Auditing in the Public Sector; editor Spanish lang. newsletter Pistas de Auditoria, 1985-92; mem. editorial bd. Pub. Budgeting and Fin. Mgmt.; mem. editorial bd., 1982-92. The Govt. Accts. Jour.; contbr. articles to profl. jours. Mem. Ga. Senate, 1962-67; mem. Fulton County Democratic Exec. Com. (Ga.), 1962-66. Decorated Order of Merit (Peru), 1972; recipient Outstanding Career Achievement award USAID, 1993. Mem. AICPA (chmn. interam. com. 1988-95), Interam. Acctg. Assn. (cert. assoc., bd. dirs. 1989-95, chmn. pub. sector com. 1989-91, mem. exec. com. 1994-95, Vet. Acct. Am. award 1987, lifetime acct. of Am. 1995), Am. Acctg. Assn., Assn. Govt. Accts. (Authors award 1981-82, 89-90); chmn. internat. affairs com. 1981-82, 89-91), Inst. Internal Auditors (v.p. Latin Am. 1978-79, internat. relations com. 1977-82, 84-88, regional dir. Latin Am. 1986-88, chpt. bd. govs. 1981-87, v.p. 1982-84, pres. 1984-85, vice chmn. internat. membership com. 1989-90, chpt. Disting. Svc. award 1987, Bradford Cadmus Meml. award internat. orgn. 1989, Outstanding Contbr. Author's award 1990), Honduras CPA Soc. (hon. award 1990), Jr. Chamber Internat. (life senator), Quito (Ecuador) Inst. Internal Auditors (life bd. dirs.), Lima (Peru) Coll. Pub. Accts. (hon.), Lima Jr. C. of C. (hon.), No. Va. Inst. Internal Auditors (hon.). Baptist. Home: 4004 Franconia Rd Alexandria VA 22310-2136 Office: World Bank Pub Sector Modernization Divsn Rm I-8383 Washington DC 20433 *Accountability to a higher authority is the cornerstone of human existence. Those who do not recognize this in their personal lives have great difficulty being accountable and responsible in their business and professional lives.*

WESBURY, STUART ARNOLD, JR., health administration and policy educator; b. Phila., Dec. 13, 1933; s. Stuart Arnold and Jennie (Glazewska)

W.; m. June Carol Davis, Feb. 23, 1957; children: Brian, Brent, Bruce, Bradford. BS, Temple U., 1955; MHA, U. Mich., 1960; PhD, U. Fla., 1972. Commd. pharmacist USPHS, 1955, served as adminstrv. officer, hosp. and clinic pharmacist, resigned, 1958; adminstrv. asst. Del. Hosp., 1960-61; asst. adminstr. Bronson Meth. Hosp., 1961-66; assoc. dir., asst. prof. U. Fla. Tchg. Hosp., 1966-67, dir., assoc. prof., 1967-69; v.p. Computer Mgmt. Corp., Gainesville, Fla., 1969-72; dir., prof. grad. studies in health svcs. mgmt. U. Mo., Columbia, 1972-78; pres. Am. Coll. Healthcare Execs., Chgo., 1979-91; sr. v.p. TriBrook Group, Inc., Westmont, Ill., 1992-94; prof. Sch. of Health Adminstrn. and Policy Ariz. State U., Tempe, 1994—. Co-author: Why We Spend Too Much on Health Care; contbr. articles to profl. jours. Bd. dirs. Health Task, Inc., Atlanta, Blood Sys., Inc., Scottsdale, Ariz., Boys Clubs, Gainesville, Heartland Inst.; chmn. bd. dirs. Mid-Am. chpt. ARC, 1988-91, DuPage County Dist., 1984-87; active Boy Scouts Am.; chmn. adminstrv. bd. Meth. Ch.; trustee Nat. Blood Found.; Rep. Congl. candidate Dist. 13, Ill. Fellow Am. Coll. Health Care Adminstrs. (hon.), Am. Coll. Healthcare Execs. (Silver Medal award 1991); mem. APHA, Am. Hosp. Assn., Hosp. Mgmt. Sys. Soc., Assn. Univ. Programs in Health Adminstrn. (chmn. 1977-78), Am. Assn. Healthcare Cons. (hon.), Rotary (past pres.). Home: 6711 E Camelback Rd Unit 25 Scottsdale AZ 85251-2064 Office: Ariz State Univ Sch Health Adminstrn Policy PO Box 874506 Tempe AZ 85287-4506

WESCHLER, ANITA, sculptor, painter; b. N.Y.C.; d. J. Charles and Hulda Eva (Mayer) W.; married. del. U.S. Com. Internat. Assn. Art, Fine Arts Fedn., N.Y. Exhibited in group shows at Met. Mus. Art, Mus. Modern Art, Art Inst. Chgo., Phila. Mus. Internat., Am. Acad., Inst. Arts and Letters, Bklyn. Mus., Newark Mus., Hofstra Mus., U. Conn., Carnegie Inst. Internat., Whitney Mus. Annuals, Storm King Art Ctr., mus. and galleries throughout U.S.; represented in permanent collections U. Pa., Michael Wolfson Found., Miami, Fla., Met. Mus. Art, Syracuse U., Butler Art Inst., Whitney Mus., Norfolk Mus., Brandeis U., Middlebury Coll., Amherst Coll., Yale U., Wichita State Mus., SUNY-Binghamton, U. Iowa, N.Y. Design Ctr., La Salle U., Pa. Acad. Fine Arts, Insts. for Achievement of Human Potential in Pa., Italy, and Brazil, Art Students League; one-man shows include Birmingham (Ala.) Mus. Art, Main Libr., Winston-Salem, N.C., U. Wis., Milw., Miami Beach Art Ctr., Tel Fair Acad., Savannah, Ga., Columbia (S.C.) Mus., U. N.C.-Chapel Hill, Stover Mill Gallery, Erwinna, Pa., Suffolk Art Mus., Stony Brook, N.Y., Cast Iron Gallery, N.Y., 1994, Kyoto Japan, also 50 traveling and stationary shows in N.Y.C. and nationwide, 1993; exhibited in over 500 shows; creator plastic resins and fiberglass as sculpture medium (bonded bronze), synthetic glazes as painting medium; author; (poetry) Nightshade, A Sculptor's Summary. Recipient prizes Corcoran Gallery, San Francisco Mus., Am. Fedn. Arts Traveling Show, Montclair Art Mus.; fellow MacDowell Colony, Yaddo. Mem. Archtl. League Sculptors Guild (past bd. dirs., treas.), Nat. Assn. Women Artists, Nat. Mus. Women in the Arts, Artist Craftsmen N.Y., Fedn. Modern Painters and Sculptors. Address: 136 Waverly Pl New York NY 10014-6821 *Imposed overall are multiple work hours. The deliberate shift is in periods, to another form—a contrasting medium. A life can be won or lost for work. The focus of attention remains entirely on the creative project. It is replenished by travel and forays into the outer world, a cultural and human renascence.*

WESCHLER, LAWRENCE MICHAEL, writer, journalist; b. Van Nuys, Calif., Feb. 13, 1952; s. Irving R. and Franzi (Toch) W.; m. Joanna S. Wegrzynowicz, Feb. 22, 1984; 1 child, Sara Alice. BA in Philosophy and Cultural History, U. Calif., Santa Cruz, 1974. Interviewer, editor Oral History Program UCLA, 1974-78; freelance writer L.A., 1978-80; staff writer The New Yorker mag., N.Y.C., 1981—. Author: Seeing is Forgetting the Name of the Thing One Sees: A Life of Contemporary Artist Robert Irwin, 1982, The Passion of Poland, 1984 , David Hockney's Cameraworks, 1986 (Kodakpreis 1986), Shapinsky's Karma, Boggs's Bills and Other True-Life Tales, 1988 (George Polk award 1988), A Miracle, A Universe: Settling Accounts with Torturers, 1990, Mr. Wilson's Cabinet of Wonder, 1995; contbr. to Village Voice, L.A. Times, Internat. Herald Tribune, L.A. Weekly, Rolling Stone, N.Y. Times, Artforum, ArtNews, The Nation, others. Co-dir. Ernst Toch Archive & Soc., L.A., 1972—. Recipient Hemingway prize Overseas Press Club, 1982, Sidney Hillman award, 1989, George Polk award for best mag. reporting, 1992; Pointer fellow Yale U., 1982, Guggenheim fellow, 1986-87, N.Y. Inst. for Humanities fellow, 1991—, Bard Ctr. fellow, 1992—. Mem. PEN, Nat. Writers Union. Jewish. Office: The New Yorker 20 W 43rd St New York NY 10036-7400*

WESCOE, W(ILLIAM) CLARKE, physician; b. Allentown, Pa., May 3, 1920; s. Charles H. and Hattie G. (Gilham) W.; m. Barbara Benton, Apr. 29, 1944; children: Barbara, William, David. BS, Muhlenberg Coll., 1941; ScD, 1957; MD, Cornell U., 1944. Intern N.Y. Hosp., 1944-45, resident, 1945-46; asst. prof. pharmacology Med. Coll., Cornell U., 1949-51; prof. pharmacology and exptl. medicine U. Kans. Med. Center, from 1951, dir., 1953-60; dean U. Kans. Med. Center (Sch. Medicine), 1952-60; chancellor U. Kan., 1960-69; v.p. med. affairs Sterling Drug Inc., N.Y.C., 1969-71; exec. v.p. Sterling Drug Inc., 1971-72, vice chmn., 1972-74, chmn., 1974-85; bd. dirs. N.Y. Stock Exch., 1986-92, Biofield Corp. Editor: Jour. Pharmacol. and Exptl. Therapeutics, 1953-57. Chmn. China Med. Bd. N.Y., N.Y.C., 1960-90; bd. dirs. Tinker Found., 1968-93, Minn. Opera; trustee emeritus Samuel Kress Found., Columbia U.; chmn. John Simon Guggenheim Meml. Found., 1983-91, Muhlenberg Coll. Markle scholar med. scis., 1949-54. Fellow ACP; mem. Am. Soc. Pharmacology and Exptl. Therapeutics, Phi Beta Kappa, Sigma Xi, Alpha omega Alpha, Alpha Tau Omega, Nu Sigma Nu. Home: 8935 N Shore Dr Spicer MN 56288

WESCOTT, ROGER WILLIAMS, anthropologist; b. Phila., Apr. 28, 1925; s. Ralph Wesley and Marion (Sturges-Jones) W.; m. Hilja J. Brigadier, Apr. 11, 1964; children: Walter, Wayne. Grad., Phillips Exeter Acad., 1942; B.A. summa cum laude, Princeton U., 1945, M.A., 1947, Ph.D., 1948; M.Litt., Oxford U., 1953. Asst. prof. history and human relations Boston U. and Mass. Inst. Tech., 1953-57; assoc. prof. English and social sci., also dir. African lang. program Mich. State U., 1957-62; prof. anthropology and history So. Conn. State Coll., 1962-66; prof., chmn. anthropology and linguistics Drew U., Madison, N.J., 1966—; Presdl. prof. Colo. Sch. Mines, 1980-81; first holder endowed Chair of Excellence in Humanities U. Tenn., 1988-89; shipboard lectr., 1980—; fgn. lang. cons. U.S. Office Edn., 1961; pres. Sch. Living, Brookville, Ohio, 1962-65; exec. dir. Inst. Exploratory Edn., N.Y.C., 1963-66; Korzybski lectr. Inst. Gen. Semantics, N.Y.C., 1976; forensic linguist N.J. State Cts., 1982-83; host Other Views, N.J. Cable TV, Trenton, 1985-87. Author: A Comparative Grammar of Albanian, 1955, Introductory Ibo, 1961, A Bini Grammar, 1963, An Outline of Anthropology, 1965, The Divine Animal, 1969, Language Origins, 1974, Visions, 1975, Sound and Sense, 1980, Language Families, 1986, Getting It Together, 1990; also poems and articles; host, program dir. Other Views, N.J. Cable TV, 1985-87. Rhodes scholar, 1948-50; Ford fellow, 1955-56; Am. Council Learned Socs. scholar, 1951-52. Fellow AAAS, Am. Anthrop. Assn., African Studies Assn.; mem. Acad. Ind. Scholars (life mem.), Assn. for Poetry Therapy, Internat. Soc. Comparative Study Civilizations (co-founder, pres. 1992—), Linguistic Assn. Can. and U.S. (pres. 1976-77), Internat. Linguistic Assn., Com. for Future, Soc. for Hist. Rsch. (v.p.), Internat. Orgn. for Unification Terminological Neologisms (1st .p.), World Hist. Assn., Assn. for Study of Lang. in Prehistory (bd. dirs.), Phi Beta Kappa. Home: 16A Heritage Crest Southbury CT 06488-1370 *Since our lives are short, it seems appropriate that our reflections on them should be comparably brief. Success is transient and high regard, relative. Though my occupational classification is that of a teacher and administrator, I have rarely been able seriously to picture myself as an educational careerist. I have thought of myself, rather, as an intellectual explorer, perennially fascinated by the inadequately explained aspects of man and his world and powerfully impelled to share that sense of fascination with fellow explorers.*

WESELY, DONALD RAYMOND, state senator; b. David City, Nebr., Mar. 30, 1954; s. Raymond Ely and Irene (Sabata) W.; m. Geri Williams, 1982; children: Sarah, Amanda, Andrew. BA, U. Nebr., 1977; LLD (hon.), Kirksville Coll. Osteopathic Medicine, 1989. Mem. Nebr. Legislature, Lincoln, 1978—; exec. assoc. Selection Rsch., Inc., Lincoln, 1984-86; sr. rsch. assoc. Lincoln Telephone Co., 1985—. Del., Dem. Nat. Conv., 1984, 88, 92; chair Assembly on Legislature, Nat. Conf. State Legislatures., 1992-93, exec. com., 1993-96; del. Am. Coun. Young Polit. Leaders, 1993. Recipient Friend of Edn. award Nebr. State Edn. Assn., 1982, Disting. Svc. award Nebr. Pub. Health Assn., 1984, Disting. Alumni award Lincoln Northeast High Sch., 1991, Disting. Health Care award Nebr. Nurse Anesthetists Assn., 1992, Leadership award for Quality in Health Care, Nebr. League Nursing, 1992, Pres.'s award Nebr. Acad. Physicians Assts., 1993, U. Nebr.- Lincoln Outstanding Young Alumni award, 1994; named Mental Health Citizen of Yr., Nebr. Mental Health Assn., 1984, Outstanding Young Man, Nebr. Jaycees, 1985, Pub. Official of Yr., Nebr. Assn. Retarded Citizens, 1992, Advocate of Yr, Nebr. Family Day Care Assn., 1993. Roman Catholic. Office: State Capitol Lincoln NE 68509

WESELY, EDWIN JOSEPH, lawyer; b. N.Y.C., May 16, 1929; s. Joseph and Elizabeth (Peles) W.; children: Marissa Celeste, Adrienne Lee; m. Marcy Brownson, Sept. 23, 1992. Ed., Deep Springs Coll., 1945-47; AB, Cornell U., 1949; JD, Columbia U., 1954. Bar: N.Y. 1954, D.C. 1985, U.S. Supreme Ct. 1960, others. Law clk. to judge U.S. Dist. Ct. (so. dist.) N.Y., 1954-55; asst. U.S. atty. So. Dist. N.Y., 1955-57; assoc. Winthrop, Stimson, Putnam & Roberts, N.Y.C., 1957-63, ptnr., 1964—; spl. master numerous cases; chmn. spl. com. on effective discovery in civil cases U.S. Dist. Ct. (ea. dist.) N.Y., 1982-84, com. on civil caseflow, 1985-88, com. on civil litigation, 1988—, civil justice reform adv. group, 1990-95; com. on pretrial phase civil cases Jud. Coun. 2d Cir., 1984-86, standing com. on improvement civil litigation, 1986-89; ex-officio Civil Justice Reform Act adv. group U.S. Dist. Ct. (so. dist.) N.Y.; pres. CARE, 1986-89, chmn., 1978-86, 89-90, internat. bd. dirs., 1981-90, pres., 1986-89; bd. dirs. Internat. Rescue Com.; bd. dirs., exec. com. Internat. Ctr. in N.Y., 1990—. Trustee Deep Springs Coll., 1991—. Decorated Order of Civil Merit (Republic of Korea); recipient World Humanitarian award Fgn. Press Assn., 1988, Commendation Bd. Judges U.S. Dist. Ct. (ea. dist.) N.Y., 1993. Fellow Am. Coll. Trial Lawyers (internat. com. 1990—); mem. ABA (spl. adv. com. on internat. activities 1990-93, litigation sect. chmn. com. on discovery 1977-78, spl. com. study discovery abuse 1977-82, chmn. task force on liaison with internat. profl. assns. on matters of mutual concern 1989-93, Civil Justice Reform Act task force 1991-93, task force on the state of the justice sys. 1993-95, fed. initiatives task force 1995—), UN Assn. U.S.A. (bd. govs. 1991—), Assn. of Bar of City of N.Y. (com. mem., organized demostration observation panel), Coun. on Fgn. Rels., India House. Office: Winthrop Stimson One Battery Park Pla New York NY 10004-1490

WESELY, MARISSA CELESTE, lawyer; b. N.Y.C., Apr. 25, 1955; d. Edwin Joseph and Yolanda Teresa (Pyles) W.; 1 child, Emma Elizabeth Wesely Allen. BA magna cum laude, Williams Coll., 1976; JD cum laude, Harvard U., 1980. Bar: N.Y. 1981. Assoc. Simpson Thacher & Bartlett, N.Y.C., 1980-82, 84-88, ptnr., 1989—; assoc. Simpson Thacher & Bartlett, London, 1982-84; lectr., cons. Harvard Inst. Internat. Devel., Beijing, 1981, Jakarta, Indonesia, 1982; guest lectr. Yale Law Sch., New Haven, 1991; spkr. ACI, PIL, BAFT confs., 1993—. Bd. dirs. City Lore, N.Y.C. Mem. N.Y.C. Bar Assn., N.Y. State Bar Assn. (mem. exec. com. sect. internat. law and practice), Internat. Bar Assn., Phi Beta Kappa.

WESENBERG, JOHN HERMAN, professional society administrator; b. Davenport, Iowa, Jan. 16, 1927; s. Herman B. and Nell (Watterson) W.; m. Alice Jane McMahill, Sept. 10, 1949; children: Anne, John, Sue, James. Student, Iowa State U., 1944-45, 47, Amherst Coll., 1946; B.A., U. Iowa, 1951, M.A., 1952; postgrad., Northwestern U., 1952-55, Mich. State U., 1956-67. Research asso. Bur. Bus. and Econ. Research, U. Iowa, 1949-52; asst. mgr. Danville (Ill.) C. of C., 1952-54; exec. v.p. Belleville (Ill.) C. of C., 1954-57; sec. Retail Mchts. and Central Dist. Bur., Des Moines, 1957-62; exec. v.p. Greater Des Moines C. of C., 1963-80; sec. Greater Des Moines Com., 1963-80; sr. exec. v.p. Greater Albuquerque C. of C., 1980-82, Met. Tulsa C. of C., 1982-91; dir. mgmt. adv. program Okla. State C. of C. and Industry, Tulsa, 1992—; sr. exec. counselor U.S. C. of C., 1993—; trustee Employee Stock Ownership Plan, Internat. Bank, Washington, 1977-80, 83-84; lectr. Inst. Orgn. Mgmt., Mich. State U., 1959-67, 69-70, U. Colo., 1970, 75, 78, 79, 81, 85, 87, 90, 91, Syracuse U., 1971, U. Santa Clara, Calif., 1972, 74-75; lectr. Tex. Christian U., 1971, 73, U. Del., 1973-76, 80, 82, U. Ga., 1973, 82, 86, U. Notre Dame, 1975, 81, So. Meth. U., 1975-76, 81, 84, 85, 87, 88, 89, 90, 91, Mills Coll., 1976, San Jose Coll., 1981, U. Okla., 1984, 86, 88, 90-91, Stanford U., 1990, Econ. Devel. Inst. U. Okla., 1994. Co-chmn. Des Moines Mail Users Council, 1963-68; sec.-treas. Des Moines Housing Corp., Baseball, Inc., 1963-80; sec. Des Moines Devel. Corp., Des Moines Industries, Inc., 1963-80, Community Improvement, Inc., 1968-80, Greater Des Moines Community Found., 1968-80; treas. Greater Des Moines Shippers Assn., 1971-80; trustee Fringe Benefits, Inc., Washington, 1969-82; mem. exec. com. Iowa Council on Econ. Edn., 1978-80; mem. planning com. Grand View Coll., 1976-80; mem. adv. council, region VIII SBA, 1973-80; Mem. bd. regents Inst. Orgn. Mgmt., Mich. State U., 1962-67, chmn., 1965-66; bd. regents U. Colo., 1977-80, So. Meth. U., 1980-81; vice chmn. nat. bd. regents Inst. for Orgn. Mgmt., 1978-79, chmn., 1979-80; trustee U. Albuquerque, 1980-82. Served with USAAF, 1944-46. Recipient Outstanding Community Leadership award Religious Heritage of Am., 1978. Mem. Am. Arbitration Assn., Am. Retail Execs. Assn. (dir. 1962-63), Am. C. of C. Execs. (dir. 1965-73, 84-91, hon. life dir./mem. 1992—, pres. 1971-72), U.S. C. of C. (dir. 1979-81, liaison officer 1989-91), Iowa C. of C. Execs. (dir. 1960-66, pres. 1964), Okla. C. of C. Execs. (dir. 1983-86, pres. 1986), Ill. Mfrs. Assn. (exec. com. So. div. 1955-57), St. Louis Indsl. Coun. (v.p. 1957), Okla. C. of C. and Industry (mem. exec. com. bd. dirs. 1986, fin. com. 1986-94), Industries for Tulsa (sec. 1986-91), Beta Theta Pi (gen. sec. 1974-81, adv. coun. former trustees 1981—), Mtn. States Assn. (v.p. 1980-81—), Des Moines Club, Petroleum Club. Home: 6718 E 65th Pl Tulsa OK 74133-4007 Office: Met Tulsa C of C 616 S Boston Ave Tulsa OK 74119

WESLER, KEN, theater company manager; b. Phila., Apr. 3, 1964; s. Irwin Harvey and Marcia Elaine (Trilling) W.; m. Deborah Lee Rader, Nov. 2, 1986; children: Alexander, Samantha. BA, Temple U., 1994. Prodn. mgr. The Wilma Theatre, Phila., 1983-89; gen. mgr. Gretna Prodns., Inc., Mt. Gretna, Pa., 1989, 90, Walnut St. Theatre, Phila., 1989-95; exec. dir. The Grand Opera House, Wilmington, 1995—; guest lectr. Cabrini Coll., Phila., 1988, Temple U., Phila., 1988—. Mem. Stage Mgr.'s Assn., Actor's Equity. Office: The Grand Opera House 818 N Market St Wilmington DE 19801

WESLER, OSCAR, mathematician, educator; b. Bklyn., July 12, 1921; s. Israel Edward and Sarah (Hartman) W. B.S., Coll. City N.Y., 1942; M.S., N.Y. U., 1943; postgrad., Princeton U., 1943-46; Ph.D., Stanford U., 1955. Mem. faculty Stanford U., 1952-56, vis. prof. stats., 1978; mem. faculty U. Mich., 1956-64; prof. stats. and math. N.C. State U., Raleigh, 1964—; cons. Inst. Sci. and Tech., U. Mich., 1957-64, IBM, 1966; vis. prof. statistics Stanford, 1962-63, 73, 74, 78, U. Calif., Berkeley, 1972-73; vis. lectr. NSF Program vis. lectrs. in statistics, 1963—. Author: Solutions to Problems in Theory of Games and Statistical Decisions, 1954; also articles in profl. jours. Recipient Outstanding Tchr. award N.C. State U., 1966. Mem. Inst. Math. Statistics, Am. Math. Soc., Sigma Xi, Phi Kappa Phi. Research in statis. decision theory, probability, stochastic processes. Home: 1926 Smallwood Dr Raleigh NC 27605-1302

WESLEY, JOHN MERCER, artist; b. Los Angeles, Nov. 25, 1928; s. Ner Wesley and Elsa Marie (Patzwaldt) W.; m. Hannah Allen Green, Dec. 18, 1971; children: Christine Alice, Ner. Student, Los Angeles City Coll., UCLA, 1947-50. One-man shows include, Robert Elkon Gallery, N.Y.C., 1963-80, 84, Premio Internat., Instituto Torcuato di Tella, Buenos Aires, 1967, Documenta 5, Kassel, 1972, Carl Solway Gallery, Cin., 1972, 85, 89, Galerie Rudolf Zwirner, Cologne, 1973, Rush Rhees Gallery, U. Rochester, 1974, PS 1, N.Y.C., 1978, Reinhard Onnasch Ausstellungen, Berlin, 1982-83, 101 Spring St. Gallery, N.Y.C., 1987, fiction/non fiction, N.Y.C., 1990, 91, Chinati Found., Marfa, Tex., 1990, Daniel Weinberg Gallery, Santa Monica, Calif., 1992, Portikus, Frankfurt, 1993, Stedelijk Mus., Amsterdam, 1993, Kunstverein, Ludwigsburg, Germany, 1993, daad-Galerie, Berlin, 1993, Galerie Rolf Ricke, Cologne, 1994, José Freire Gallery, N.Y.C., 1994, Jessica Fredericks Gallery, N.Y.C., 1996; group exhbns. include, Whitney Mus., 1968, 69, 76, Indpls. Mus., 1976, Royal Academy, London, 1991, Mus. Contemporary Art, L.A., 1992-93, Mus. Beaux Arts, Montreal, 1992-93; represented in permanent collections, Albright-Knox Mus., Buffalo, Mus. Modern Art, N.Y.C., U. Tex., Austin, Mpls. Soc. Fine Arts., Chinati Found., Marfa, Tex., Rose Art Gallery, Brandeis U., Waltham, Mass., U. Kentucky, Lexington, Kunstmuseum, Basel, Switzerland, Dayton (Ohio) Mus. Art, Portland (Oreg.) Art Mus., Whitney Mus., Stedelijk Mus., Speed Mus., Louisville, Ky. Guggenheim fellow, 1976; grantee Nat. Endowment Arts, 1989. Address: 52 Barrow St New York NY 10014-3723

WESLEY, NORMAN H., metal products executive; b. 1949. BA, MBA, U. Utah, 1973. With Crown Zellerbach Corp., San Francisco, 1973-83; pres., CEO ACCO World Corp., Wheeling, Ill., 1983—. Office: ACCO World Corp 500 Lake Cook Rd Ste 150 Deerfield IL 60015-5255*

WESLING, DONALD TRUMAN, English literature educator; b. Buffalo, May 6, 1939; s. Truman Albert and Helene Marie (Bullinger) W.; m. Judith Elaine Dulinawka, July 28, 1961; children: Benjamin, Molly, Natasha. BA, Harvard U., 1960, PhD, 1965; BA, Cambridge U., Eng., 1962. Asst. prof. U. Calif. at San Diego, La Jolla, 1965-67, assoc. prof., 1970-80, prof., 1981—; lectr. U. Essex, Colchester, Eng., 1967-70. Author: Wordsworth and Landscape, 1970, Chances of Rhyme, 1981, The New Poetries, 1985, The Scissors of Meter, 1996, (with T. Slawek) Literary Voice, 1995. Mem. Amnesty Internat. Home: 4968 Foothill Blvd San Diego CA 92109-2234 Office: U Calif Lit # 0410 La Jolla CA 92093

WESSE, DAVID JOSEPH, academic administrator; b. Chgo., May 5, 1951; s. Herman Theodore and Lorraine Joan (Holland) W.; m. Deborah Lynn Smith, Oct. 11, 1975; children: Jason David, Eric Joseph. AA, South Suburban Coll., 1971; postgrad., Purdue U., 1971-72; BEd, Ill. State U., 1973; MS, Loyola U., 1983. Adminstr. Don Tech, Inc., Chgo., 1974-76; adminstrv. mgr. Loyola U., Chgo., 1976-79, Joint Commn. on Accreditation of Healthcare Orgns., Oak Brook Terrace, Ill., 1979-81; adminstrv. dir., asst. sec. Northwestern U., Evanston, Ill., 1981—. Pres., bd. dirs. Riverdale (Ill.) Libr. Dist., 1975, Riverdale Youth Commn., 1975; bd. dirs. Better Bus. Bur. Chgo. and No. Ill., 1991—. Recipient Svc. Recognition award Riverdale Libr. Dist., 1975, Excellence in Journalism award Nat. Assn. Coll. Aux. Svcs., 1989. Mem. Adminstrv. Mgmt. Soc. (bd. dirs. Chgo. chpt. 1983-88, pres. 1986-87, bd. regents 1986-88), Acad. Adminstrv. Mgmt. (bd. regents 1992-94), Profl. Office Mgmt. Assn. Chgo. (bd. dirs. 1992-93, sec. 1993-95, pres. 1995), Nat. Mgmt. Assn. (chpt. pres. 1995), Nat. Assn. Coll. and Univ. Bus. Officers (com. mem. 1986-87, 89-90, cost reduction awards 1986-88, 90, 92), Midwest Higher Edn. Commn. (com. mem. 1996—), Assn. Coll. Adminstrn. Profls. (seminar leader 1995), Chgo. Area Bus. and Support Svc. Adminstrs. (founder), Big Ten Bus. and Support Svc. Adminstrs. (founder), Lambda Epsilon. Lutheran. Home: 207 S Washington St Wheaton IL 60187-5429 Office: Northwestern U 633 Clark St Evanston IL 60208-1121

WESSEL, HENRY, photographer; b. Teaneck, N.J., July 28, 1942; s. Henry and Jennie (Cincotta) W.; children by previous marriage: Nicholas, Rider. B.A., Pa. State U., 1966; M.F.A., SUNY, Buffalo, 1972. Propr., mgr. comml. photog. studio State Coll., Pa., 1966-68; cinematographer for documentary film Dept. HEW, 1967; instr. dept. art Pa. State U., Phila., 1967-69; prof. dept. photography San Francisco Art Inst., 1973-96, chmn. grad. program photography, 1977-78, chmn. dept. photography, 1987-93; asst. prof. San Francisco State U., 1974-75; vis. lectr. photography various colls. and art schs., 1967-81; propr., dir. Photographic Resources, Point Richmond, Calif., 1977—; vis. artist Mills Coll., 1987-88;. One-man show at Mus. Modern Art, N.Y.C., 1973; represented in permanent collections, Mus. Modern Art, N.Y.C., Phila. Mus. Art, Boston Mus. Fine Arts, Library of Congress, Am. Arts Documentation Center, Exeter, Eng., Nat. Gallery of Can., Ottawa; author: Henry Wessel, 1987, House Pictures, 1992. Guggenheim fellow, 1971, 78; Nat. Endowment Arts fellow, 1975, 77, 78. Home: PO Box 475 Richmond CA 94807-0475 Office: Photographic Resources PO Box 475 Richmond CA 94807-0475

WESSEL, MORRIS ARTHUR, pediatrics educator; b. Providence, Nov. 1, 1917; s. Morris Jacob and Bessie (Bloom) W.; m. Irmgard Rosenzweig, June 1, 1952; children: David, Bruce, Paul, Lois. BA, Johns Hopkins U., 1939; MD, Yale U., 1943. Diplomate Am. Bd. Pediatrics. Intern Babies Hosp., N.Y.C., 1943-44; asst. dir. pediatric outpatient clinic Yale New Haven (Conn.) Hosp., 1951-52, dir. pediatric outpatient clinic, 1952-57; staff pediatrician, collaboration project Yale U. Sch. Medicine, 1957-62, instr. in pediatrics, 1950-53, clin. asst. prof., 1963-61, clin. assoc. prof. of pediatrics, 1961-75, clin. prof. pediatrics, 1975—; cons. pediatrician Clifford Beers Child Guidance Clinic, 1967—; bd. dirs. Clifford Beers Guidance Clinic, New Haven, 1950-55, Women's Health Svc., New Haven, 1992—, Child Welfare League, N.Y.C., 1979-91. Author: Parents Book on Raising a Healthy Child, 1987. Maj. AUS, 1944-47, ETO. Mem. Am. Acad. Pediat. (Practitioner Rsch. award 1994), Soc. Adolescent Medicine, Conn. Med. Soc., New Haven County Med. Soc.

WESSEL, PETER, lawyer; b. N.Y.C., N.Y., Feb. 2, 1952; s. Harry Nathan Jr. and Charlene (Freimuth) W.; children: Daniel, Elizabeth. BS, Syracuse U., 1974, M in Pub. Adminstrn., JD, 1980. Bar: N.Y. 1981, U.S. Dist. Ct. (no., so., ea. and we. dists.) N.Y. 1981, Fla. 1984, U.S. Ct. Mil. Appeals, 1988, U.S. Ct. Appeals (2d cir.) 1988, U.S. Supreme Ct. 1988. Confidential law clk. to Hon. David F. Lee Jr. N.Y. Supreme Ct., 1980-82; sr. atty. criminal def. div. The Legal Aid Soc., N.Y.C., 1982-87; pvt. practice N.Y.C., 1987—. Notes and comments editor Syracuse Law Rev., 1979-80; contbr. articles to profl. jours. Robert M. Anderson award for Writing and Legal Scholarship, 1980, Neal Brewster scholar, 1977-78, Syracuse U. Coll. Law scholar 1978-79, Louis Waters Meml. scholar, 1979-80, Hiscock, Cowie, Bruce & Lee scholar, 1979-80. Mem. ABA, N.Y. State Bar Assn., Assn. of Bar of City of N.Y., Fla. Bar Assn., Nat. Assn. Criminal Def. Lawyers, N.Y. State Assn. Criminal Def. Lawyers, N.Y. State Defender Assn., N.Y. State Trial Lawyers Assn., N.Y. County Lawyers Assn., N.Y. Criminal Bar Assn.

WESSELINK, DAVID DUWAYNE, finance company executive; b. Webster City, Iowa, Sept. 5, 1942; s. William David and Lavina C. (Haahr) W.; m. Linda R. DeWitt, Dec. 27, 1971; children: Catherine, Bill. BA in Bus., Cen. Coll., 1964; MBA, Mich. State U., 1970. Tchr. Peace Corps, Turkey, 1964-66, Karabuk Koleji, Turkey, 1967-68, Robert Koleji, Turkey, 1969-70; research analyst Household Fin. Corp., Chgo., 1971-73, asst. dir. research, 1973-77; asst. treasurer Household Fin. Corp., Prospect Heights, Ill., 1977, v.p., dir. research, 1977-82, group v.p., chief fin. officer, 1982-86, sr. v.p., chief fin. officer, 1986—; v.p., treas. Household Internat., Prospect Heights, 1988-93; sr. v.p., CFO Advanta Corp., 1993—. Bd. dirs. Am. Cancer Soc., Northbrook, Ill., 1988—, Glenkirk Found., Northbrook, 1988—, Ctrl. Coll., Pella, Iowa, 1990—, CFC Internat., Chgo. Heights, Ill., 1992—. Mem. Fin. Execs. Inst., Chgo. Coun. on Fgn. Rels., Econ. Club Chgo. Office: Advanta Corp 300 Welsh Rd Horsham PA 19044-2209

WESSELMANN, GLENN ALLEN, hospital executive; b. Cleve., Mar. 21, 1932; s. Roy Arthur and Dorothy (Oakes) W.; m. Genevieve De Witt, Sept. 6, 1958; children: Debbie, Scott, Janet. A.B., Dartmouth, 1954; M.B.A. with distinction, Cornell U., 1959. Research aide Cornell U., Ithaca, N.Y., 1958-59; adminstrv. resident Meml. Hosp., N.Y.C., 1957-58; adminstrv. asst. Meml. Hosp., 1959-61, asst. adminstr., 1961-65, asst. v.p., 1965-68; v.p. for adminstrn. Meml. Hosp. for Cancer and Allied Diseases, N.Y.C., 1968-79; exec. v.p., chief operating officer St. John Hosp., Detroit, 1979-84; pres., CEO St. John Health System, 1984-95—, vice chmn., 1995—; chmn., pres., CEO St. John Hosp. & Med. Ctr., 1984-94; mem. bus. adv. bd. City of Detroit, 1991-95, chmn., 1993-94; mem. exec. com. Greater Detroit Area Health Coun.; bd. dirs. Caymich Ins. Co. Ltd., Mich. Health Care Alliance, SelectCare, Detroit Econ. Growth Corp. Trustee Sisters of St. Joseph Health System 1981-94, Sisters of St. Joseph Health Svc., 1983—, St. John Hosp. and Med. Ctr., 1979-95, St. John Health System, 1984—, The Oxford Inst., 1984-95, Eastwood Clinics, 1992-95; mem. bus. adv. bd., City of Detroit, 1991—, chmn. 1993-94. Served with MC AUS, 1955-57. Fellow ACHE; mem. Am. Hosp. Assn., Internat. Hosp. Fedn., Mich. Hosp. Assn. (trustee, chmn. 1994—, mem. exec. com.), Assn. Am. Med. Colls. (Coth rep.), Am. Cancer Soc. (regional adv. bd. 1994—), Med. Group Mgmt. Assn., Soc. Health Service Adminstrs., Sigma Phi Epsilon. Home: 63 Big Woods Dr Hilton Head Island SC 29926 Office: St John Health Sys Office of the Pres 22101 Moross Rd Detroit MI 48236-2148

WESSELS, BRUCE W., materials scientist, educator; b. N.Y.C., Oct. 18, 1946; m. Beverly T. Wessels; children: David, Kirsten. BS in Metallurgy and Materials Sci., U. Pa., 1968; PhD in Materials Sci., MIT, 1973. Mem. tech. staff GE R&D Ctr., 1972-77, acting branch mgr., 1976; from asst. prof. to assoc. prof. Northwestern U., Evanston, Ill., 1977-83, prof. materials sci. and engring., 1984—; vis. sci. Argonne Nat. Lab., 1978; mem. program com.

3d Internat. Conf. Superlattices, Microdevices and Microstructures, 1987; vice chair TMS electronic, magnetic and photonic materials divsn. exec. coun., 1991-92, chair, 1993—. Editor 4 books including (with G.Y. Chin) Advances in Electronic Materials, 1986; mem. editl. bd. Jour. Electronic Materials, 1982-88; contbr. numerous articles to profl. jours.; patentee in field. Fellow ASM; mem. The Minerals, Metals and Materials Soc.-AIME (chmn. electronic materials com. 1987-89, conf. program chmn. 1986-87, key reader Trans. of AIME 1985—, bd. dirs. 1993—, v.p. 1995, bd. trustees AIME), TMS (bd. trustees, pres. 1996), Electrochem. Soc. Materials Rsch. Soc. (symposium organizer 1993, 95), Sigma Xi, Tau Beta Pi. Office: Materials Science & Engring Northwestern U 2225 N Campus Dr Evanston IL 60208

WESSINGER, W. DAVID, management consultant; b. Leesville, S.C., Aug. 8, 1924; s. Noah F. and Willye W. (Quattlebaum) W.; m. Virginia Lou Hinsch, June 30, 1945; children: David, Clifford, Carol, Virginia Anne. BS in Bus., George Washington U., 1962; MS in Mgmt., U.S. Navy Postgrad. Sch., 1963. Cert. mgmt. cons. Ensign USN, 1943, advanced through grades to capt., 1964; cons. Orgn. Resources Counselors, Inc., N.Y.C., 1968-78, v.p., 1978-85, sr. v.p., 1985-93, sr. counselor, 1993—. Mem. Am. Arbitration Assn., Am. Compensation Assn., Inst. Mgmt. Cons. Presbyterian. Avocations: woodworking, fishing, tennis, golf. Office: Organization Resources Counselors Inc 1211 6th Ave New York NY 10036-8701

WESSLER, MELVIN DEAN, farmer, rancher; b. Dodge City, Kan., Feb. 11, 1932; s. Oscar Lewis and Clara (Reiss) W.; grad. high sch.; m. Laura Ethel Arbuthnot, Aug. 23, 1951; children: Monty Dean, Charla Cay, Virgil Lewis. Farmer-rancher, Springfield, Colo., 1950—; dir., sec. bd. Springfield Co-op. Sales Co., 1964-80, pres. bd., 1980—. Pres., Arkansas Valley Co-op. Council, SE Colo. Area, 1965-87, Colo. Co-op. Council, 1969-72, v.p. 1974, sec. 1980-86; community com. chmn. Baca County, Agr. Stablzn. and Conservation Svc., Springfield, 1961-73, 79—, vice chmn. Baca County Com., 1980-90; mem. spl. com. on grain mktg. Far-Mar-Co.; mem. adv. bd. Denver Bapt. Bible Coll., 1984-89; chmn., bd. dirs. Springfield Cemetery Bd., 1985—; apptd. spl. com. Farmland Industries spl. project Tomorrow, 1987—. Recipient The Colo. Cooperator award The Colo. Coop Coun., 1990. Mem. Colo. Cattlemen's Assn., Colo. Wheat Growers Assn., Southeast Farm Bus. Assn. (bd. dirs. 1991-95), Big Rock Grange (treas. 1964-76, master 1976-82), Southeast Kans. Farm Bus. Assn. (dir. 1996—). Address: 18363 County Road Pp Springfield CO 81073-9210

WESSLER, RICHARD LEE, psychology educator, psychotherapist; b. St. Louis, Sept. 11, 1936; s. Harry Edward and Lorraine Grace (Hoffman) W.; m. Sheenah Hankin, Mar. 28, 1984; 1 child, Lisa. Student, U. Mo., 1954-55; A.B., Washington U., 1958, Ph.D., 1966. Research assoc. St. Louis U., 1962-66, asst. prof. sociology, 1966-69; assoc. prof. psychology Parsons Coll., Farifield, Iowa, 1969-73; prof. psychology Pace U., Pleasantville, N.Y., 1974—; postdoctoral fellow, dir. tng. Inst. for Rational-Emotive Therapy, N.Y.C., 1973-75, 76-82; pvt. practice psychotherapy N.Y.C., 1976—; vis. prof. Rijksuniversiteit te Leiden, Netherlands, 1981-82, U. Aston, Eng., 1982; cons. govt. agys., hosps., bus. Author: (with R.A. Wessler) The Principles and Practice of Rational Emotive Therapy, 1980, (with S.R. Wolen and R.D. Giuseppe) A Practioner's Guide to Rational-Emotive Therapy, 1980; editor: Rational Living, 1974-83; assoc. editor: Brit.. Jour. Cognitive Psychotherapy. Mem. Am. Psychol. Assn., Assn. for Advancement Behavior Therapy.

WESSLER, SHEENAH HANKIN, psychotherapist, consultant; b. Tamworth, England, Nov. 4, 1939; came to U.S., 1982; d. Alexander Rolfe Mackenzie and Irene May Richards; m. Philip Raymond Hankin, Apr. 16, 1962 (div. Mar. 1984); children: Stuart, James, Robin, Nicholas; m. Richard L. Wessler, Mar. 28, 1984. BA with honors, Birmingham Univ., 1961, diploma in sr. edn., 1963; diploma in counseling psychology, Aston Univ., 1979; PhD, Internat. U., 1995. Dir. Irish Pregnangy Counseling Clinic, Dublin, Ireland, 1979-81; counselor trainer Well Woman Clinic, Dublin, Ireland, 1979-81; pvt. practice Dublin, Ireland, 1979-81; co-dir. Cognitive Psychotherapy Assocs., N.Y.C., 1983—; cons. Coolemine Therapeutic Cmty., Dublin, 1983—; expert presenter Breakfast Time, Fox Cable Network, 1994—. Contbr. articles to profl. jours. Mem. Am. Counseling Assn. Office: Cognitive Psychotherapy Svcs 18 E 93rd St New York NY 10128-0610

WESSLER, STANFORD, physician, educator; b. N.Y.C., Apr. 20, 1917; S. Hugo and Minerva (Miller) W.; m. Margaret Barnet Muhlfelder, Dec. 17, 1942; children—John Stanford, Stephen Lawrence, James Hugh. Grad., Fieldston Sch., N.Y.C., 1934; B.A., Harvard, 1938; M.D., N.Y.U., 1942. From fellow to asst. prof. medicine Harvard U. Med. Sch., 1946-64; from resident to assoc. chief med. svc. Beth Israel Hosp., Boston, 1946-64; prof. medicine Washington U. Sch. Medicine, St. Louis, 1964-74; John L. and Adalaine Simon prof. Washington U. Sch. Medicine, 1966-74; prof. medicine, assoc. dean postgrad. programs NYU Sch. Medicine, 1974-90; physician in chief Jewish Hosp., St. Louis, 1964-74; assoc. physician Barnes Hosp., St. Louis, 1964-74; attending physician NYU Med. Center, Univ. Hosp., N.Y.C., 1974-90, Bellevue Hosp. Center, N.Y.C., 1974-90, Manhattan VA Hosp. Med. Ctr., 1974-90; Mem. coms. NRC, Inst. of Medicine, Nat. Heart, Lung and Blood Inst.; bd. dirs. N.Y. Heart Assn., 1980-86; pres. Council Continuing Med. Edn., N.Y., 1979-85. Contbr. articles on vascular disease.; mem. editorial bds. jours. in field. Served with M.C. AUS, 1943-46. Recipient James A. Mitchell award, 1972. Mem. Am. Physiol. Soc., Am. Soc. Clin. Investigation, Assn. Am. Physicians, Am. Heart Assn. (investigator 1955-59, bd. dirs. 1971-76, chmn. publs. com. 1972-76, chmn. coun. on thrombosis 1974-76, v.p. 1974-76, mem. sci. adv. com. 1986-90, Merit award 1978, Disting. Achievement award 1989), Alpha Omega Alpha. Home: 60 Rye Rd Rye NY 10580-2228

WESSLING, ROBERT BRUCE, lawyer; b. Chgo., Oct. 8, 1937; s. Robert Euans and Marguerite (Rickert) W.; m. Judith Ann Hanson, Aug. 26, 1961; children: Katherine, Jennifer, Carolyn. BA, DePauw U., 1959; JD, U. Mich., 1962. Bar: Calif. 1963, U.S. Dist. Ct. (cen. dist.) Calif. 1963, U.S. Ct. Appeals (9th cir.) 1965. Assoc. Latham & Watkins, L.A., 1962-70, ptnr., 1970-94, of counsel, 1995—; bd. govs. Fin. Lawyers Conf., Los Angeles, 1974—. Mem. World Affairs Coun., L.A., Town Hall, L.A.; trustee DePauw U. Mem. ABA, Calif. Bar Assn., Los Angeles Bar Assn., Phi Beta Kappa, Phi Delta Phi, Phi Eta Sigma, Order of Coif. Democrat. Methodist. Avocations: tennis, travel. Office: Latham & Watkins 633 W 5th St Ste 4000 Los Angeles CA 90071-2005

WESSNER, DEBORAH MARIE, telecommunications executive, computer consultant; b. St. Louis, Aug. 15, 1950; d. John George and Mary Jane (Beetz) Eyerman; m. Brian Paul Wessner, Sept. 15, 1972; children: Krystin, David. BA in Math. and Chemistry, St. Louis U., 1972; M Computer Info. Sci., U. New Haven, 1980. Statistitian Armstrong Rubber Co., New Haven, 1972-74; programmer analyst Sikorsky div. United Techs., Stratford, Conn., 1974-77; project engr. GE, Bridgeport, Conn., 1977-79; software mgr. GE, Arlington, Va., 1979-81; mgr. software ops. Satellite Bus. Systems, McLean, Va., 1981-83; v.p. ops. DAMA Telecommunications, Rockville, Md., 1983-87; dir. network ops. and adminstrn. Data Gen. Network Svcs., Rockville, 1987-91; dir. bus. ops. Sprint Internat., Reston, Va., 1991-92; v.p. network adminstrn. Citicorp, Washington, 1992-93; v.p. telecomm. product mgmt. Citicorp, Reston, Va., 1994—; assoc., cons. KDB Assocs., Columbia, Md., 1986—. Mem. Am. Bus. Women's Assn., NAFE. Avocations: sailing, windsurfing, tennis. Office: Citicorp Reston VA 22091

WESSON, WILLIAM SIMPSON, retired paper company executive; b. Seattle, June 5, 1929; s. Edward Phineas and Margaret (Simpson) W.; m. Janet Hudson Knowles, Jan. 31, 1981; children by previous marriage: Edward, Anne, Lee. A.B., Cornell U., 1951, M.B.A., 1954. With Scott Paper Co., Phila., 1954-87; v.p. Edn. div. Scott Paper Co., Holyoke, Mass., 1969-74; pres. Scott Graphics, 1974-76; mng. dir. Bowater-Scott Corp. Ltd., U.K., 1976-81; pres. Scott Paper Internat., Phila., 1981-87; chmn. bd. Bowater-Scott Corp., Ltd., 1978-87, ret., 1987. Pres. Nat. Grocers Benevolent Fund, U.K., 1977-78; mem. Cornell U. Coun., N.Y., 1982-86; trustee Colby-Sawyer Coll., 1995—. 1st lt. U.S. Army, 1951-53. Republican.

WEST, ALFRED PAUL, JR., financial services executive; b. Brooksville, Fla., Dec. 7, 1942; s. Alfred Paul Sr. and Jane (Coogler) W.; m. Loralee Smith, June 16, 1964; children: Angela Paige, Alfred Paul III, Andrew Palmer. B in Aerospace Engring., Ga. Inst. Tech., 1964; MBA, U. Pa., 1967, postgrad., 1967-68. Chmn., chief exec. officer SEI Corp., Wayne, Pa., 1968—, pres., 1978—. Bd. dirs. All-Star Forum, Phila., 1983—, Paoli Meml. Hosp., 1990—, grad. exec. bd. Wharton Sch. of Bus., 1983—; chmn. bd. dirs. Wharton's SEI Ctr. for Advanced Studies in Mgmt., 1989—; bd. dirs. World Affairs Council, Phila., 1985-89, mem. exec. com., 1989, chmn. adv. com., 1989—. Republican. Presbyterian. Avocations: skiing, golf, photography. Office: SEI Corp 680 E Swedesford Rd Wayne PA 19087-1610*

WEST, ANN LEE, nursing educator, trauma nurse coordinator; b. Terre Haute, Ind., Aug. 11, 1943; d. Paul Everette and Margaret Alice (Roush) Corbin; m. Donald J. West, Aug. 29, 1964; children: Lee Ann, Kevin, Brian, Christopher. Diploma in nursing, St. Vincent's Hosp., 1964; BS, St. Joseph's Coll., 1983; MSN, Med. Coll. Ohio, 1992. RN, Ohio; ACLS, Advanced Cardiac Life Support provider instr.; cert. pediatric advanced life support, emergency nurse, trauma nurse core curriculum, basic life support; emergency nursing pediatric course provider, instr. Staff nurse St. Vincent Med. Ctr., Toledo, Ohio, 1964-67; office nurse Dr. Richard Leahy, Tiffin, Ohio, 1976-77; project nurse, relief nurse Clinicas Migrantes Reg., Fremont, Ohio, 1977-79; head nurse emergency dept. Bellevue Hosp., 1979-81; relief charge nurse Fireland's Cmty. Hosp., Sandusky, Ohio, 1981-95; staff devel. educator Med. Coll. Hosps., Toledo, 1993-96; trauma nurse coord. Med. Coll. Hosps., 1995—; med. and nursing educator Firelands Cmty. Hosp., Sandusky, 1987-95; trauma prevention/outreach, patient educator Med. Coll. Hosp., Toledo, 1994-96; disting. lectr. Am. Acad. Allergy and Immunology, 1993. Author booklet for Am. Lung Assn.; contbr. articles to profl. jours. Mem. Am. Acad. Poison Ctr., Am. Lung Assn. (bd. dirs., sec., sch. edn. chair 1984-96), Seagate Emergency Nurse Assn. (pres. 1996), Rolls Royce Owner's Club, Lion's Club Internat. (v.p.). Roman Catholic. Avocations: travel, camping, oil painting, Rockwell Foundation. Home: 320 Douglas Dr Bellevue OH 44811-1305 Office: Med Coll Ohio 3000 Arlington Ave Toledo OH 43699-0008

WEST, A(RNOLD) SUMNER, chemical engineer; b. Phila., Jan. 12, 1922; s. Arnold and Mary (Sumner) W.; m. Beverly Helen Lehman, Oct. 5, 1946; children: Barbara Ann, Richard Sumner. BSChemE, U. Pa., 1943; MS, Pa. State U., 1946. With Rohm and Haas Co., Phila., 1946-87, rsch. engr., 1946-62, rsch. supr., 1962-72, mgr. research dept., 1972-77, sr. tech. specialist govt. and regulatory affairs, 1978-87; owner, prin. A.S. West Assocs., Huntingdon Valley, Pa., 1987—; cons. dept. chem. engring. U. Pa., 1952-72; mem. indsl. and profl. adv. com. Coll. Engring., Pa. State U., 1978-84, chmn. chem. engring. div., 1980-81, chmn. com., 1982-83. Mem. Lower Moreland Twp. (Montgomery County) Authority, 1970, sec., 1971—; vice-chmn. bd. dirs. Chemical Heritage Found., 1984-92; pres. United Engring. Trustees, 1986-87. Fellow Am. Inst. Chem. Engrs. (dir. 1964-66, treas. 1973-75, v.p. 1976, pres. 1977); mem. Engrs. Joint Council (dir. 1976-79), Am. Assn. Engring. Socs. (vice chmn. public affairs council 1981, chmn. council 1982-83), Am. Chem. Soc., Nat. Soc. Profl. Engrs., Soc. Automotive Engrs., Water Environ. Fedn. Club: The Valley (Huntingdon Valley). Home and Office: 3896 Sidney Rd Huntingdon Valley PA 19006-2347

WEST, ARTHUR JAMES, II, biologist; b. Boston, Dec. 14, 1927; s. Arthur James and Lillian (Laming) W.; BS, Suffolk U., 1951, MA in Edn., 1956; MS, U. N.H., 1962, PhD in Zoology, 1964; m. Carolyn Barbara Ross, June 4, 1948 (div. May 1972); children: Arthur James, Gregory Thomas, Donald Robert; m. Linda Jean Cummings, July 21, 1985 (div. Sept. 1993); children: Melissa Ida, Benjamin Cummings. Faculty, Suffolk U., Boston, 1952-68, asso. prof. biology, 1964-65, prof., 1965-68, co-chmn. biology, 1964-68; dean, prof. div. natural sci. New Eng. Coll., Henniker, N.H., 1968-70; prof. chmn. dept. biology Suffolk U., 1970-72, 78-88; assoc. program dir. Pre-coll. Edn. in Scis., NSF, 1972-73; prof. dept. biology Suffolk U., 1973-89, prof. emeritus, 1989—; acad. v.p. for curriculum devel. U. San Juan Capistrano, 1992-93; owner, operator Subway of Farmington and Skowhegan, Maine, chmn.adv. coun. 1993-94; dir. R.S. Friedman Cobscook Bay Lab., 1975-88; exec. com. M.I.T./Sea Grant Consortium Program, 1979-85; asst. prof., chmn. biology Mass. Coll. Optometry, 1957-60; instr., chmn. sci. Emerson Coll., 1956-59; staff Norwich U., 1960; cons. Ginn & Co. Sci. Publs., 1967-70; hon. cons., parasitologist Akvapatologisk Lab., 1987; civil svc. examiner Mass. Dept. Natural Resources, 1965-72. Founding pres. Keltown Civic Assn., 1954; chmn. Woburn United Fund, 1958; mem. Woburn Sch. Com., 1955-60, chmn. 1957; chmn. Woburn YMCA, 1958, Woburn Rep. City Com., 1959, New Vineyard Town Com., 1990; vice chmn. Franklin County Rep. Com.; mem. commn. on ocean mgmt. Mass. Served with USN, 1946-47, with Res., 1947-52. NSF grantee, 1968-71, 70-71, 75-82. Mem. Mass. Bay Marine Studies Consortium (pres. 1982-85), Mass. Marine Educators, Inc. (com. 1978-86), AAAS, Am. Inst. Biol. Scis., Nat. Marine Edn. Assn. (dir. 1976-78, pres. 1985-86), Ea. Star, Rotary, Masons, Sigma Xi (Suffolk U. club pres. 1972), Sigma Zeta, Phi Beta Chi (pres. 1951), Beta Beta Beta, Phi Sigma. Research and publs. on Acanthocephala and undergrad. marine edn. Home: PO Box 104 New Vineyard ME 04956-0104 *To live with conscience is to live a life in grace. Helping others find and achieve their goals is the greatest reward a teacher may achieve.*

WEST, BOB, pharmaceutical company executive; b. Ellenville, N.Y., Mar. 7, 1931; s. Harry and Elsie May Wicentowsky; m. Betty Parker, May 9, 1957 (div.); children: Debra Ellen, Elizabeth Ann, Sharon Lynn; m. Jacqueline Cutler, Jan. 3, 1982. BS, Union U., 1952; MS, Purdue U., 1954, PhD, 1956; postgrad. mgmt. seminar, U. Chgo., 1972. Pres., dir. research Food, Drug, Chem. Svcs., Stamford, Conn., 1975—; pres., dir. research Bob West Assocs., Inc., Stamford, 1975—; pres. Drug Info. Assn., Phila., 1974-75; sci. adv. bd. Fountain Pharms., Inc., Largo, Fla., 1993—. Editorial bd. Drug Info. Assn. Jour., Phila., 1977-85; contbr. articles to profl. jours. Mem. ASPET, Am. Soc. Toxicology, Acad. Pharm. Scis., Assn. Rsch. Dirs., Drug Info. Assn., Assn. Univ. Tech. Mgrs. Home and office: Food Drug Chem Svcs 3771 Center Way Fairfax VA 22033-2602

WEST, BURTON CAREY, physician; b. Pitts., Feb. 21, 1941; s. Pemberton Burton and Maree (Van Scoyoc) W.; m. Katherine Ann Young, Dec. 27, 1963; children: Amy Fay Chandler, Holly Katherine Brewer, John Pemberton, Abigail Coleman, Emily Van Scoyoc. AB, AMherst Coll., 1963; MD, Cornell U., 1967. Diplomate Am. Bd. Internal Medicine and Infectious Diseases. Resident U. Hosps., Seattle, 1967-69; clin. assoc., sr. staff fellow NIAID, NIH, Bethesda, Md., 1969-72; resident, chief resident Vanderbilt Hosp., Nashville, 1972-74; from asst. prof. to prof. medicine La. State U. Sch. Medicine, Shreveport, 1974-89, chief sect. infectious diseases, 1974-89; chmn. dept. medicine Meridia Huron Hosp., Cleve., 1989—. Contbr. articles to profl. jours. Lt. comdr. USPHS, 1969-71. Fellow ACP (chmn. program dirs. Ohio chpt. 1995—), Infectious Diseases Soc. Am. (pres. Ohio chpt. 1996-97). Office: Meridia Huron Hosp 13951 Terrace Rd Cleveland OH 44112-4308

WEST, CHARLES CONVERSE, theologian, educator; b. Plainfield, N.J., Feb. 3, 1921; s. George Parsons and Florence (Farish) W.; m. Ruth Floy Carson, Sept. 6, 1944; children: Russell Arthur, Walter Lawrence, Glenn Andrew. B.A., Columbia U., 1942; B.D., Union Theol. Sem., N.Y.C., 1945; Ph.D., Yale U., 1955. Ordained to ministry Presbyterian Ch. U.S.A., 1946; missionary, fraternal worker Bd. Fgn. Missions Presbyn. Ch. U.S.A., 1946-56; instr., chaplain Cheeloo U., Hangchow, China, 1948-49; instr. Nanking Theol. Sem., 1949-50; indsl. mission work Gossner Mission, Mainz-Kastel, Germany, 1950-51; lectr. Kirchliche Hochschule, Berlin, 1951-53; Lectr. Hartford Sem. Found., 1955-56; asso. dir. Ecumenical Inst., Bossey, Switzerland under World Council Chs., 1956-61; chargé de cours U. Geneva, 1956-61; instr. Peking Nat. U., 1948; assoc. prof. Christian ethics Princeton Theol. Sem., 1961-63, Stephen Colwell prof. Christian ethics, 1963-91, prof. emeritus, 1991—, acad. dean, 1979-84; mem. Commn. to Form Statement Faith U.P. Ch. U.S.A., 1961-67, chmn. internat. affairs adv. com., 1963-66; Chmn. U.S. Com. for Christian Peace Conf., 1965-72; chmn. working com. Dept. Studies in Mission, Evangelism World Council Chs., 1967-68; member Commn. on Internat. Affairs, Nat. Council Chs., 1968-73. Author: Communism and the Theologians, 1958, Outside the Camp, 1959, Ethics, Biolence and Revolution, 1969, The Power to be Human, 1971, Perspective on South Africa, 1985; editor: The Sufficiency of God, Essays in Honor of Dr. W.A. Visser't Hooft, 1963; assoc. editor: Religion in Eastern Europe, 1985—; translator: J. Hamel-A Christian in East Germany, 1960. Mem. Am. Soc. Christian Ethics (v.p. 1972-73, pres. 1973-74), Am. Theol. Soc. (v.p. 1982-83, pres. 1983-84), Presbytery N.Y.C., Ams. for Dem. Action., Christians Associated for Rels. with Eastern Europe (pres. 1988-92). Home: 157 Mountain Rd Ringoes NJ 08551-1402 Office: Princeton Theological Seminary CN821 Princeton NJ 08542

WEST, CLARK DARWIN, pediatric nephrologist, educator; b. Jamestown, N.Y., July 4, 1918; s. Clark Darwin and Frances Isabel (Blanchard) W.; m. Ruthann Asbury, Apr. 12, 1944 (div.); children: Charles Michael, John Clark, Lucy Frances; m. Dolores Lachenman, Mar. 1, 1986. A.B., Coll. of Wooster, 1940; M.D., U. Mich., 1943. Intern Univ. Hosp., Ann Arbor, Mich., 1943-44; resident in pediatrics Univ. Hosp., 1944-46; fellow in pediatrics Children's Hosp. Research Found., Cin., 1948-49; research asso. Children's Hosp. Research Found., 1951—, asso. dir., 1963—, dir. div. immunology and nephrology, 1958—; with cardiopulmonary lab. chest service Bellevue Hosp., N.Y.C., 1949-51; attending pediatrician Children's Hosp., 1951—; asst. prof. pediatrics U. Cin., 1951-55, asso. prof., 1955-62, prof., 1962—; mem. coms. NIH, 1965-69, 1972-73. Mem. editorial bd.: Jour. Pediatrics, 1960-79, Kidney Internat., 1977-89, Clin. Nephrology, 1989—; contbr. articles to profl. jours. Served to capt. M.C., AUS, 1946-47. Decorated Army commendation medal; recipient recognition award Cin. Pediat. Soc., 1980, Mitchell Rubin award, 1986, Henry L. Barnett award, 1995, Daniel Drake medal, 1996. Mem. Soc. Pediatric Research (sec.-treas. 1958-62, pres. 1963-64), Am. Pediatric Soc., Am. Soc. Pediatric Nephrologists (pres. 1973-74), Am. Physiol. Soc., Am. Assn. Immunologists, Am. Soc. Nephrology, Internat. Pediatric Nephrology Assn., Sigma Xi, Alpha Omega Alpha. Research on immunopathogenesis and treatment of glomerulonephritides and in the complement system. Home: 11688 Aristocrat Dr Harrison OH 45030-9753 Office: Children's Hosp Med Ctr Cincinnati OH 45229

WEST, DANIEL JONES, JR., hospital administrator, rehabilitaton counselor, health care consultant, educator; b. Coaldale, Pa., Sept. 19, 1949; s. Daniel J. and Mildred Elizabeth (Kreiger) W.; m. Linda Jean Werdt, Sep. 18, 1971; children: Jeffrey Bryan, Christopher Jones, Danielle K. BS cum laude, Pa. State U., 1971, EdM summa cum laude, 1972, PhD in Counseling Psychology summa cum laude, 1982; postgrad., Montgomery County Community Coll., 1973, Rutgers U., 1974. Diplomate Am. Acad. Behavioral Medicine, Am. Acad. Med. Adminstrn. Adminstr. Good Samaritan Hosp., Pottsville, Pa., 1975-78, asst. v.p. ambulatory svcs., 1978-83; adminstr. MEDIQ, Inc., Scranton (Pa.) State Hosp., 1983-85; pres., CEO HTC Consulting Group, Inc., Gouldsboro, Pa., 1986—; dir., assoc. prof. U. Scranton, 1990—; adj. prof. Pa. State U., 1974-83, U. Scranton, 1983-90, Wilkes Coll., 1986; CEO Medi-Group, Inc., Penn Health Care, Inc., A.I.R., Inc., Med. Sci. Lab., Inc., Lackawanna Med. Group, P.C., Scranton, 1986-91; stockholder, ptnr. Penn Health Care, Inc., 1987—, Health Care Support Svcs., Scranton, 1993—; stockholder, bd. dirs. Northeast Women's Diagnostic Ctr., Scranton, 1989—; regional dir. ops. HCP Consulting Group, Inc., Willow Grove, Pa., 1990—; moderator First Ann. Conf. on Drug and Alcohol Abuse, Bedford, Pa., 1977; mem. adv. com. to rehab. counseling programs Pa. State U., 1983—; numerous positions Stte Bd. of Medicine, Commonwealth of Pa., 1991—; mem. departmental review bd. for rsch. U. Scranton, 1991—; mem. Scranton Temple residency program instnl. rev. bd. Mercy Hosp., 1991—; mem. Fedn. of State Med. Bd. of U.S., Inc., 1994—, mem. editl. adv. bd., 1984-85, voting del. from Pa. for osteopathic bd.; bd. dirs. comm. com. Midwest Regional Med. Bd., 1994—; mem. task force on health care Econ. Devel. Coun. Northeast Pa., 1994—; bd. dirs. Friendship House, 1995—; bd. dirs. Robert Charles Zaloga Found., 1994—; spkr. in field. Author manuals on mgmt. and healthcare; contbr. articles to profl. jours. Chmn. planning and implementation coun. Schuylkill County Gov.'s Coun. on Drug and Alcohol Abuse, State of Pa., 1973-74; mem. Drug Adv. Task Force, 1973-74, Task Force Child and Family Resource Devel. Program, Schuylkill County, 1973—, Criminal Justice Sys. Task Force, Schuylkill County, 1975—; mem. adv. bd. Holy Family Home Health Care Agy., Schuylkill County, 1977—, chmn. bd. edn. com., 1977—; bd. dirs. St. David's Soc. Schuylkill and Carbon Counties, 1976—, Health Sys. Agy., Northeast Pa., 1977—; mem. instnl. review bd. Cmty. Med. Ctr., 1986—; bd. dirs. Scranton Counseling Ctr., 1990—, mem. long range planning com. and personnel com.; bd. dirs. Telespond Sr. Svcs., Inc., 1991—; mem. Diocesan health care com. Diocese of Scranton, 1992—; mem. steering com. Citizen Advocacy Ctr., AARP Health Advocacy Svcs., 1992—; bd. dirs., v.p. Citizen Advocacy Ctr., Arlington, Va., 1994—; mem. ad hoc com. on children health United Way, 1995—. Recipient Rsch. award Am. Ednl. Rsch. Assn., 1983, Svc. and Leadership award Schuylkill County Drug and Alcohol Exec. Comm., 1982, Dedication and Leadership award Gov.'s Coun. Drug and Alcohol Abuse Drug Adv. Task Force, 1978; Fellow Accreditating Commn. Edn. for Health Svcs. Adminstrn., 1994-95. Fellow Am. Acad. Med. Adminstrs. (editl. com. 1993—), Internat. Acad. Behavioral Medicine, Counseling and Psychotherapy, Inc., Am. Coll. Healthcare Execs. (regents adv. bd. Pa. Area B 1995—), Fedn. State Med. Bds. US, Inc. (editl. com. 1994—), Coll. Osteo. Healthcare Execs. (editl. com. 1991—), Am. Coll. Med. Practice Execs., Am. Coll. Health Care Adminstr., Assn. Mental Health Adminstrs. (cert., editl. com. 1992—); mem. APHA, AAAS, Nat. Rehab. Assn., Nat. Rehab. Adminstrn. Assn., Am. Hosp. Assn., Med. Group Mgmt. Assn., Hosp. Assn. Pa., Pa. Rehab. Assn., Pa. Med. Group Mgmt. Assn., Phi Kappa Phi, Iota Alpha Delta. Address: RD # 1 Skyline Acres 101 Birch St Gouldsboro PA 18424

WEST, DOE, bioethicist, human rights activist; b. Tucson, July 14, 1951; d. George Oliver and Dorothy Marie (Watson) W.; m. Bruce Malcolm Gale, Feb. 1, 1980. AA, Dutchess C.C., 1975; BS, SUNY, New Paltz, 1977; BA, Logos Bible Coll., 1986, MDiv, 1993; MS, Boston U., 1980; PhD, Northeastern U., 1996. Dir. 504/compliance officer dept. health and hosps. City of Boston, 1979-81, commr. handicap affairs, 1981-84; pres. Myth Breakers, Inc., 1984—; writer, photographer; exec. dir. Social Action Ministries of Gtr. Boston, 1996—; lectr. Northeastern U., Mt. Ida Coll., 1982—; dir. chaplaincy svcs. Quincy (Mass.) Hosp., 1991-92; chief of staff State House Boston, 1992-94; project coord. task force on human subject rsch. Fernald State Sch., 1994. Home: PO Box 2006 Brookline MA 02146

WEST, DONALD VALENTINE, editor, journalist; b. Memphis, Tex., Jan. 5, 1930; s. Raynes V. and Kathleen Inez (Thornton) W.; m. Carroll Virginia Warren, July 24, 1951 (div.); children: Kathleen, Susan, James, Teresa, Michael, Mark, Thomas. BA, N.Mex. A&M U., 1950. Mng. editor Roswell (N.Mex.) Dispatch, 1947-48; desk editor El Paso (Tex.) Times, 1950-51; writer Broadcasting Mag., Washington and N.Y.C., 1953-60; mng. editor Television Mag., N.Y.C., 1961-66; asst. to pres. CBS Inc., N.Y.C., 1966-70; mng. editor, editor Broadcasting Mag., Broadcasting & Cable Mag., Washington, 1971—; TV prodr. SQN Prodns., 1970-71. Sgt. U.S. Army, 1951-53. Recipient Presdl. award Reed Pub. U.S.A., 1994. Office: Broadcasting & Cable Mag 1705 Desales St NW Washington DC 20036-4405

WEST, DORCAS JOY, women's health nurse; b. Friend, Nebr., Apr. 4, 1940; d. Ernest Emerson and Ruth Louise (Stuemky) Horner; m. Paul N. West, Nov. 8, 1969; children: Dale E., Charles B., Natalie Joy. RN, Bryan Meml. Sch. Nursing, Lincoln, Nebr., 1963; BS, Nebr. Wesleyan U., 1964; cert., Spanish Lang. Inst., San José, Costa Rica, 1964, Domestic Violence Coun., N.Mex., 1985. RN, N.Mex., Nebr.; cert. domestic violence counselor, N.Mex. RN obstetrics Bryan Meml. Hosp., Lincoln, 1963-64; missionary nurse Bd. Global Ministries, United Meth. Ch., Mex., 1964-66, Malaysia, 1970-75; office and surg. RN G. William LeWorthy MD, Reconstructive and Plastic Surgery, Lincoln, 1966-69; RN obstetrics Evanston (Ill.) Hosp., 1970; dir. Home for Women & Children, Shiprock, N.Mex., 1978-86; cons. RN quality assurance Shiprock (N.Mex.) Cmty. Health Ctr., 1988; RN obstetrics Navajo Area Indian Health Svc., Shiprock, 1989—; cons. Home for Women and Children, Shiprock, 1986—. Patricipant Internat. Christian Youth Exch., N.Y.C., 1958, Germany, 1958-59, host, 1985; pres. United Meth. Women, 1971-73, dist. pres., 1973-74, sec., 1988-91, mem., 1970—; mem. Four Corners Native Am. Ministry, 1977—; mem. Camp Farthest Out, 1984—, sec., 1990—; mem. social concerns com. United Meth. Ch., Shiprock, 1984-91, Sunday sch. tchr., 1966-69, 74-95; mem., asst. scoutmaster Anasazi dist. Boy Scouts Am., Shiprock, 1985—; mem. Concerned Women for Am., Washington, 1987—, Walk to Emmaus, 1991—. Recipient cert. of appreciation Home for Women and Children, Shiprock, 1984, appreciation award, 1994; named Nursing Employee of Month, Indian Health Svc., USPHS, 1991. Mem. Women's Soc. Christian Svc. (life). Avocations: quilting, sewing, reading, family camping, speaking. Home: PO Box 400 Shiprock NM 87420-0400

WEST, D(RUEY) TOM, JR., school administrator; b. Macon, Ga., Dec. 8, 1948; s. D.T. and Dovie Mae (Daniel) W.; m. Mary Nancy Swiney, Aug. 5, 1978; children: Dronda Sue, Leanna Marie, Ansley Hamlin, Jamie Hamlin. BA in Edn., Ga. Coll., 1971; MEd, U. Ga., 1976. Cert. sch. adminstr., Ga. Tchr. Boddie Jr. High Sch., Milledgeville, Ga., 1976-81, asst. prin., 1981-86; asst. prin. Baldwin High Sch., Milledgeville, 1983-91; elem. sch. prin. Southside Sch., Milledgeville, 1983-91; pers. dir. Baldwin County Schs., Milledgeville, 1991—; dist. legis. rep. Ga. Assn. Elem. Sch. Prins., Milledgeville, 1989-91; adv. bd. Ga. Coll. Career Ctr., Milledgeville, 1989-90; prin. Nat. Sch. Excellence, 1986. Mem. ASCD, Nat. Assn. Elem. Sch. Prins., Ga. Assn. Elem. Prins., Profl. Assn. Ga. Educators, Ga. Assn. Ednl. Leaders, Milledgeville Allied Arts Assn., Ga. Sch. Pers. Assn., Phi Delta Kappa. Avocation: restoring antique jukeboxes. Home: 129 Snyder Rd NE Milledgeville GA 31061-8015 Office: Baldwin County Bd Edn PO Box 1188 Milledgeville GA 31061-1188

WEST, E. JOSEPH, financial analyst, investment portfolio manager; b. Kingston, Pa., Nov. 24, 1940; s. David Dimon and Elizabeth Irene (Emery) W.; m. Darla Jean Payne, Oct. 13, 1962 (div. Aug. 1972); 1 child, Emery Joseph II; m. Karen Marie Rowlands, Jan. 1, 1981. Grad., Mercersburg Acad., 1959, U.S. Air Force Acad., 1962; cert., Northwestern U., Evanston, Ill., 1964, U. Windsor, Ont., 1972, 73, 79, Rockford Coll., Ill., 1982; cert. investment mgmt., Princeton U., 1984; MBA, Coll. William & Mary, 1990. Chartered fin. analyst. Jr. investment analyst Tech. Stock Rev., Inc., N.Y.C., 1962-63; analyst, broker Grant, Jones & Co., Inc., Washington, 1963-64; sr. account exec. W.E. Hutton & Co., Washington, 1964-74; investment exec. E.F. Hutton & Co., Inc., Washington, 1974-78; 1st v.p. investments and portfolio mgr. Drexel Burnham Lambert, Inc., Washington, 1978-89; 1st v.p., portfolio mgr. Smith Barney Inc., Washington, 1989—; bd. dirs. Fairfax Cable Channel 10, 1985-88; trustee and chmn. investment com. Fairfax County Retirement System, 1985-89. Active Fairfax County (Va.) Rep. Com., 1983—, Fairfax County Econ. Adv. Commn., 1992—, Fairfax County Com. 100, 1984—, No. Va. Tech. Coun. Recipient Award Appreciation County of Fairfax Retirement System, 1989. Fellow Fin. Analysts Fedn., Inst. Chartered Fin. Analysts, Internat. Soc. Fin. Analysts; mem. Assn. for Investment Mgmt. and Rsch., Washington Soc. Investment Analysts, Nat. Assn. Bus. Economists, Nat. Economists Club, Washington Assn. Money Mgrs., Mercersburg Acad. Alumni Coun., Fairfax County C. of C., Belle Haven Country Club, The Tower Club. Republican. Lutheran. Avocations: golf, crossword puzzles, backgammon, bridge. Office: Smith Barney Inc 1776 I St NW Washington DC 20006-3709

WEST, FELTON, retired newspaper writer; b. Houston, May 9, 1926; s. Felton Eber and Clara Viola (Ross) W.; m. Jean Frances Osborn, Oct. 27, 1945; children—Felton Dale, Bruce Eugene, Wade Osborn, Barbara Jean. Student, U. N.Mex., 1944-46; B.S., U. Houston, 1952, M.Litt., 1957. Mem. staff Houston Post, 1943-95, Washington corr., 1961-65, chief Austin (Tex.) capitol bur., 1966-85, columnist, 1985-93, editorial writer, 1993-95, ret., 1995. Served with USNR, World War II. Mem. Soc. Profl. Journalists, Phi Kappa Phi. Home and Office: 2251 CR 284 Liberty Hill TX 78642-9761

WEST, GAIL BERRY, lawyer; b. Cin.; d. Theodore Moody and Johnnie Mae (Newton) B.; m. Togo D. West, Jr., June 18, 1966; children: Tiffany Berry, Hilary Carter. B.A. magna cum laude, Fisk U., 1964; M.A., U. Cin., 1965; J.D., Howard U., 1968. Bar: D.C. 1969, U.S. Supreme Ct. 1978. Staff atty. IBM, 1969-76; spl. asst. to sec. HUD, 1977-78; staff asst. to spl. asst. to Pres., Washington, 1978-80; dep. asst. sec. for manpower res. affairs installations Dept. Air Force, 1980-81; atty. AT&T, Washington, 1983-84; exec. dir. govt. affairs Bell Comms. Rsch. Inc., Washington, 1984-95; dir. govt. rels. Armstrong World Industries, Inc., Washington, 1995—. Mem. exec. com. ARC, Washington, 1974-85; bd. dirs. Family and Child Svcs., Washington, 1974-87; trustee Corcoran Gallery Art, Arena Stage, Decatur House, WETA; bd. dirs. Meridian House. Ford Found. fellow, 1965-68. Mem. ABA, D.C. Bar Assn., Unified Bar D.C. Democrat. Episcopalian. Home: 4934 Rockwood Pky NW Washington DC 20016-3211 Office: 1025 Connecticut Ave NW Washington DC 20036-5405

WEST, GEORGE EDGAR (BUDDY WEST), congressman; b. Ballinger, Tex., Oct. 9, 1936; s. George Mitchell and Virginia Orr Lea (Carter) W.; m. Shirley Jean Porter, Mar. 22, 1956; children: Richie, Lori, Ami. BBA, U. Tex., Permian Basin. Various positions Amoco Prodn. Co.; rep. Tex. Ho. of Reps., 1992—; mem. pub. edn. com. Tex. Ho. of Reps., pub. edn. subcom. on mandates, energy resources com. Deacon Crescent Park Bapt. Ch.; active Protect Lakes Buchanan and Inks Assn.; trustee Presdl. Mus.; mem. ECISD Tech. High Sch. Task Force. Named Outstanding Freshman Legislator Ind. Brokers Assn., Most Outstanding Legislator Young Conservatives Tex. Mem. Nat. Conf. State Legislatures, Am. Legis. Exch. Coun., Tex. Legis. Sportsman's Caucus, Rural Legis. Coalition, Tex. Conservative Coalition Task Force on Property Rights, Tex. Conservative Coalition, Rep. Caucus, Am. Soc. Safety Engrs., Rotary, Odessa C. of C. Baptist. Home: 2408 Quail Park Pl Odessa TX 79761-2230 Office: Tex Ho of Reps PO Box 2910 Austin TX 78768-2910

WEST, GLENN EDWARD, business organization executive; b. Kansas City, Mo., Nov. 19, 1944; s. Ernest and Helen Cecil (Johnson) W.; m. Vicki Lynn Knox, May 22, 1970; children: Keele Kay, Kollen Chandler, Ashley Knox. BS in Acctg. and Mktg. cum laude, Northwest Mo. State U., 1966; student U. Colo. Inst. Orgn. Mgmt., 1974; student Notre Dame U. Acad. Orgn. Mgmt., 1977. Auditor Arthur Young & Co., Kansas City, Mo., 1966-68; sales mgr. Procter & Gamble, Kansas City, Mo., 1968-69; mgr. pub. relations St. Joseph Area C. of C., Mo., 1969-71, mgr. econ. devel., 1971-74; exec. v.p. Lawrence C. of C., Kans., 1974-81, Greater Macon C. of C., Ga., from 1981; now pres. Austin C. of C.; mem. bd. dirs. Tex. Assn. Bus. and C. of C., 1995, U.S. C. of C., 1995. Contbr. articles to profl. jours. Chmn. chpt. ARC, Macon, 1984; pres. Quality of Life Found. Austin, Greater Austin Sports Found.; cen. campaign chair Capital Area United Way, 1995. Recipient Leadership award Kiwanis Club, St. Joseph, Mo., 1974. Served with USNG, 1967-73. Mem. Kans Assn. Commerce and Industry (bd. dirs. 1977-79, leadership award 1981), Kans. C. of C. Execs. (bd. dirs. 1977-80, pres. 1979), Ga. C. of C. Execs. (bd. dirs. 1982—), Am. C. of C. Execs. (bd. dirs. 1979-81, 83-84, vice chmn. 1989—, chmn.-elect 1990, chmn. 1991, cert. chamber exec. 1980), C. of C. of U.S. (adv. com. 1981-89, bd. dir. 1995), Rotary, Barton Creek Country Club. Republican. Methodist. Office: Greater Austin C of C PO Box 1967 111 Congress Ave Plz Austin TX 78767-1967

WEST, HUGH STERLING, aircraft leasing company executive; b. Kansas City, Kans., Apr. 5, 1930; s. Gilbert Eugene and Dorothy (Johnson) W.; BS, U. Va., 1952; BS in Aero., U. Md., 1959; grad. U.S. Naval Test Pilot Sch., 1959; m. Willa Alden Reed, Jan. 16, 1954; children: Karen, Phillip, Susan. Commd. 2d lt. U.S. Marine Corps., 1948, advanced through grades to maj., 1961; exptl. flight test pilot, U.S. Naval Air Test Center, Patuxent River, Md.; resigned, 1961; program mgr. Boeing Aircraft Co., Seattle and Phila., 1961-66, dir. airworthiness, comml. airplane divsn., 1969-71; dir. aircraft sales Am. Airlines, Tulsa, 1971-76; v.p. equipment mgmt. GATX Leasing Corp., San Francisco, 1976-80; v.p. tech., partner Polaris Aircraft Leasing Corp., San Francisco, 1980-85; v.p., co-founder U.S. Airlease, Inc. divsn. Ford Motor Co., 1986-96, ret., 1996; aircraft cons. Mem. Soc. Exptl. Test Pilots, Army Navy Country Club. Republican. Episcopalian. Home: 387 Darrell Rd Hillsborough CA 94010-6763 Office: US Airlease Inc 733 Front St San Francisco CA 94111-1808

WEST, JAMES HAROLD, accounting company executive; b. San Diego, Oct. 11, 1926; s. Robert Reed and Clara Leona (Moses) W.; m. Norma Jean, 1953 (div.); 1 son, Timothy James; m., Jerel Lynn Smith, Nov. 16, 1976; 1 child, James Nelson. BS, U. So. Calif., Los Angeles, 1949. CPA, Calif. Ptnr., McCracken & Co., San Diego, 1950-61; mgr. Ernst & Ernst, San Diego, 1961-64; ptnr. West Turnquist & Schmitt, San Diego, 1964—. Bd. govs. ARC, Washington, 1981-87; pres., bd. dirs. Combined Arts and Edn. Coun., San Diego, 1980-83; pres. Francis Parker Sch., 1988-90; bd. dirs. San Diego Hosp. Assn., 1981—, San Diegans Inc., 1989-92, Mus. Photographic Arts, 1990-92; trustee Calif. Western Sch. Law, 1985—; mem. bd. advisors U. So. Calif. Sch. Acctg., 1985—; treas. San Diego Nat. Sports Tng. Found., 1988-92; mem. acctg. exec. bd. U. San Diego, 1992—. With AUS, 1945-46; PTO. Mem. AICPA, Calif. Soc. CPAs (bd. dirs. 1963-64), University Club (San Diego), Capital Hill Club (Washington), Masons. Republican. Home: 3311 Lucinda St San Diego CA 92106-2931 Office: West Turnquist & Schmitt 2550 5th Ave Fl 10 San Diego CA 92103-6612

WEST, JAMES JOSEPH, lawyer; b. Tarentum, Pa., Nov. 26, 1945; s. Samuel Elwood and Rose (McIntyre) W.; m. Kathleen Geslak, Aug. 19, 1967; children: Joseph Allen, Yvonne Michelle, KaiLynn Ann. BS in Econs., St. Vincent Coll., 1967; JD, Duquesne U., 1970. Bar: Pa. 1971, U.S. Dist. Ct. (we. dist.) Pa. 1971, U.S. Ct. Appeals (3d cir.) 1971, U.S. Dist. Ct. (mid. dist.) Pa., 1980. Law clk. to presiding justice U.S. Dist. Ct., Pa., 1970-74; asst. U.S. atty. chief appellate sect. U.S. Atty.'s Office, Pitts., 1974-79; dep. dir. criminal law Pa. Atty. Gen.'s Office, Harrisburg, 1979-82; 1st asst. U.S. atty. U.S. Dist. Ct. (mid. dist.) Pa., Harrisburg, 1982-84, U.S. atty., 1984-93; assoc. Sprague & Sprague, Phila., 1993-95; pvt. practice Harrisburg, Pa., 1995—. Mem. Nat. Environ. Enforcement Council. Recipient Outstanding Performance award U.S. Dept. Justice, 1974-78, Commendation Gov. of Pa., 1981. Mem. Pa. Bar Assn., Allegheny County Bar Assn., Dauphin County Bar Assn. Republican. Roman Catholic. Home: 129 Oxford Ln North Wales PA 19454-4402 Office: James West 105 N Front St Harrisburg PA 17011

WEST, JERRY ALAN, professional basketball team executive; b. Chelyan, W.Va., May 28, 1938; s. Howard Stewart and Cecil Sue (Creasey) W.; m. Martha Jane Kane, May, 1960 (div. 1977); children: David, Michael, Mark; m. Karen Christine Bua, May 28, 1978; 1 son, Ryan. BS, W.Va. Coll.; LHD (hon.), W.Va. Wesleyan Coll. Mem. Los Angeles Lakers, Nat. Basketball Assn., 1960-74, coach, 1976-79, spl. cons., 1979-82, gen. mgr., 1982-94; exec. v.p. basketball operations L. A. Lakers, 1994—; mem. first team Nat. Basketball Assn. All-Star Team, 1962-67, 70-73, mem. second team, 1968, 69; mem. NBA champion L.A. Lakers, 1972. Author: (with William Libby) Mr. Clutch: The Jerry West Story, 1969. Capt. U.S. Olympic Basketball Team, 1960; named Most Valuable Player NBA Playoff, 1969, All-Star Game Most Valuable Player, 1972; named to Naismith Meml. Basketball Hall of Fame, 1979, NBA Hall of Fame, 1980; mem. NBA 35th Anniversity All-Time Team, 1980; named NBA Exec. of Yr. Sporting News, 1994-95. Office: LA Lakers 3900 W Manchester Blvd PO Box 10 Inglewood CA 90306*

WEST, JOHN BURNARD, physiologist, educator; b. Adelaide, Australia, Dec. 27, 1928; came to U.S., 1969; s. Esmond Frank and Meta Pauline (Spehr) W.; m. Penelope Hall Banks, Oct. 28, 1967; children: Robert Burnard, Joanna Ruth. M.B.B.S., Adelaide U., 1951, M.D., 1958, D.Sc., 1980; Ph.D., London U., 1960; Dr. honoris causa, U. Barcelona, Spain, 1987. Resident Royal Adelaide Hosp., 1952, Hammersmith Hosp., London, 1953-55; physiologist Sir Edmund Hillary's Himalayan Expdn., 1960-61; dir. respiratory research group Postgrad. Med. Sch., London, 1962-67; reader medicine Postgrad. Med. Sch., 1968; prof. medicine and physiology U. Calif. at San Diego, 1969—; Wiltshire lectr., London, 1977, Schwidetzky lectr., 1975, Fleischner lectr., 1977, Robertson lectr. Adelaide U., 1978, McClement lectr. NYU, 1996; leader Am. Med. Rsch. Expdn. to Mt. Everest, 1981; U.S. organizer China-U.S. Conf. on respiratory failure, Nanjing, 1986; mem. life scis. adv. com. NASA, 1985-88, task force sci. uses of space sta., 1984-87, aerospace med. adv. com., 1988-89, chmn. sci. verification com. Spacelab SLS-1, 1983-92; prin. investigator Spacelabs SLS 1, 2, LMS, Neurolab, 1983—; co-investigator European Spacelabs, D2, Euromir, 1987—; mem. commn. on respiratory physiol., 1985—; mem. commn. on clin. physiol., 1991—, mem. commn. gravitation physiol., 1986—; mem. U.S. nat. com. Internat. Union Physiol. Scis., 1984-87; mem. study sect. NIH, chmn., 1973-75; external examiner Nat. U. Singapore, 1995. Author: Ventilation/Blood Flow and Gas Exchange, 1965, Respiratory Physiology-The Essentials, 1974, Translations in Respiratory Physiology, 1975, Pulmonary Pathophysiology-The Essentials, 1977, Translations in Respiratory Physiology, 1977, Bioengineering Aspects of the Lung, 1977, Regional Differences in the Lung, 1977, Pulmonary Gas Exchange (2 vols.), 1980, High Altitude Physiology, 1981, High Altitude and Man, 1984, Everest-The Testing Place, 1985, Best and Taylor's Physiological Basis of Medical Practice, 1985, 91, Study Guide for Best and Taylor, 1985, High Altitude Medicine and Physiology, 1989, The Lung: Scientific Foundations, 1991, Lung Injury, 1992. Recipient Ernest Jung prize for medicine, Hamburg, 1977, Presdl. citation Am. Coll. Chest Physicians, 1977, Reynolds Prize for history Am. Physiol. Soc., 1987; I.J. Flance lectr. Washington U., 1978; G.C. Griffith lectr. Am. Heart Assn., 1978; scholar Macy Found., 1974; Kaiser teaching award 1980; W.A. Smith lectr. Med. Coll. S.C., 1982; S.C., 1982; S. Kronheim lectr. Undersea Med. Soc., 1984; D.W. Richards lectr. Am. Heart Assn., 1980, E.M. Papper lectr. Columbia U., 1981, I.S. Ravdin lectr. ACS, 1982, Burns Amberson lectr. Am. Thoracic Soc., 1984, Harry G. Armstrong lectr. Aerospace Med. Assn., 1984, Annual Space Life Scis. lectr. Federation Associated Socs. of Exptl. Biology, 1991, Hermann Rahn lectr. SUNY Buffalo, 1992, Menkes lectr. Johns Hopkins, 1992, Jeffries Med. Rsch. award AIAA, 1992; Macallum lectr. U. Toronto, Can., 1989, Macleod lectr. Southampton U., U.K., 1990, Bulatto lectr. U. Philippines, Manila, 1990, Mohaideen lectr. L.I. Coll., Bklyn., 1992, Bullard lectr. Uniformed Svcs. U., Bethesda, Md., 1993, Raven lectr. Am. Coll. Sports Medicine, Dallas, 1995; external examiner Nat. U. Singapore, 1995. Fellow Royal Coll. Physicians (London), Royal Australasian Coll. Physicians, Royal Geog. Soc. (London), AAAS (med. sci. nominating com. 1987-93, coun. del. sect. med. scis.), Am. Inst. for Med. and Biol. Engring. (founder fellow 1992), Internat. Soc. for Mountain Medicine (pres. 1991-94); mem. NAS (com. space biology and medicine 1986-90, subcom. on space biology 1984-85, com. advanced space tech. 1992-94, panel on small spacecraft tech. 1994), Nat. Bd. Med. Examiners (physiology test com. 1973-76), Am. Physiol. Soc. (pres. 1984-85, coun. 1981-86, chmn. sct. on history of physiology 1984-92, hist. pubs. adv. com.), Am. Soc. Clin. Investigation, Physiol. Soc. Gt. Britain, Am. Thoracic Soc., Assn. Am. Physicians, Westessn. Physicians, Russian Acad. Sci. (elected fgn. mem.), Explorers Club, Fleischner Soc. (pres. 1985), Harveian Soc. (London), Royal Instn. Gt. Britain, Royal Soc. Medicine (London), Hurlingham Club (London), La Jolla Beach & Tennis Club. Home: 9626 Blackgold Rd La Jolla CA 92037-1110 Office: U Calif San Diego Sch Medicine 0623 Dept Medicine La Jolla CA 92093

WEST, JOHN CARL, lawyer, former ambassador, former governor; b. Camden, S.C., Aug. 27, 1922; s. Shelton J. and Mattie (Ratterree) W.; BA, The Citadel, 1942; LB magna cum laude, U. S.C., 1948; D. (hon.) The Citadel, U. S.C., Davidson Coll., Presbyn. Coll., Francis Marion Coll., Wofford Coll., Coll. Charleston; m. Lois Rhame, Aug. 29, 1948; children: John Carl Jr., Douglas Allen, Shelton West Bosley. Bar: S.C. 1947. Ptnr. West, Holland, Furman & Cooper, Camden, S.C., 1947-70; state senator Kershaw County State of S.C., 1954-66; lt. gov. State of S.C., 1966-70; gov. State of S.C., 1971-75; ptnr., West, Cooper, Bowen, Beard & Smoot, Camden, S.C., 1975-77; amb. to Saudi Arabia, 1977-81; sr. ptnr. West & West, P.A., Hilton Head Island and Camden, S.C., 1981-88; prin., pvt. practice John C. West, P.A., Hilton Head Island and Camden, 1981—; disting. prof. Middle East Studies U. S.C., 1981—; of counsel McNair Law Firm, Hilton Head Island, S.C., 1988-92, of counsel, Bethea, Jordan & Griffin, P.A., Hilton Head Island and Camden, S.C., 1993—; bd. dirs., chmn. Seibels Bruce Group, Inc., Donaldson, Lufkin & Senretta, Inc. Trustee So. Ctr. Internat. Studies. Maj. AUS, 1942-46. Decorated Army Commendation medal; comdr. Order of Merit (W. Ger.), Freedom award S.C. C. of C. Mem. Phi Beta Kappa. Democrat. Presbyterian. Address: PO Box 13 Hilton Head Island SC 29938-0013

WEST, JOHN MERLE, retired physicist, nuclear consultant; b. Stilwell, Okla., Jan. 18, 1920; s. James M. and Maude B. (Bacon) W.; m. Navlion F. Farmer, Oct. 5, 1945; children: J. Cornel, L. Clark. BS in Phys. Sci. and Math. with highest honors, Northeastern State U., 1939; MS in Physics, U. Iowa, 1941. Physicist, supr. Du Pont Co., Carney's Point, N.J., 1941-42, Pryor, Okla., 1942-43; physicist, supr. U. Chgo. Manhattan Project, 1943-44, Hanford Works Manhattan Project, 1944-46, GE, Hanford Works, Richland, Wash., 1946-49; asst. dir. reactor engring., project mgr. Argonne Nat. Lab., Lemont, Ill., 1949-57; exec. v.p. Gen. Nuclear Engring. Corp., Dunedin, Fla., 1957-65; v.p. nuclear activities Combustion Engring. Inc., Windsor, Conn., 1965-84; sr. v.p. Nuclear Combustion Engring. Inc., Windsor, Conn., 1984-85; nuclear cons., Cape Coral, Fla., 1985—. Contbr. numerous articles to profl. jours., papers at profl. meetings; holder numerous patents. Recipient Charles Coffin award GE, 1949. Fellow Am. Nuclear Soc. (charter mem., Walter Zinn award 1983); mem. NAE, Engrs. Club. Republican. Presbyterian. Home and Office: 1608 SE 40th Ter Cape Coral FL 33904-7467

WEST, KIM DENISE, university administrator; b. Mar. 19, 1957; d. Vaughn Edward and Maryln Margaret (Shults) W. B.A., Skidmore Coll., 1979; M.A., Columbia U., 1983. Residence hall dir. SUNY-Stony Brook, 1979-81, acting quad dir., 1981-82, complex dir., 1982-83; area coordinator Hofstra U., Hempstead, N.Y., 1983-85; asst. dir. residential life U. So. Calif., L.A., 1985-89, assoc. dir., 1989-90; dir. residence life Calif. Inst. Tech., Pasadena, 1990—; mem. residential life staff devel. com. SUNY-Stony Brook, 1981-83, instr. psychology, 1982-83; instr. ednl. counseling U. So. Calif., 1985-90, mem. student affairs divsn. staff devel. com., 1985-87, chair, 1989-90, mem. AIDS awareness task force, 1988-89, mem. gay and lesbian assembly for student svcs. adv. bd., 1989-90, mem. univ. peer rev. appeals panel, 1989-90; mem. AIDS awareness task force, Calif. Inst. Tech., 1990—, mem. student affairs divsn. staff devel. com., 1991-93; coord. various confs. in field. Sec. Skidmore Coll. Class of 1979, Saratoga Springs, N.Y., 1990—, co-chair reunion com., 1993-94; vol. Spl. Olympics, SUNY-Stony Brook, 1980; vol. All Saints AIDS Svc. Ctr., Pasadena, 1991—; mem. alumni awards com. Skidmore Coll., 1992—; mem. Pasadena Area Colls. Drug and Alcohol Consortium, Pasadena, 1992—; active Check-Out L.A., UCC Tng. Presdl. fellow Leadership Inst. U. So. Calif., 1994-95. Mem. Nat. Assn. Student Pers. Adminstrs. (acad. new profls. 1987), U. So. Calif. Assocs., Phi Delta Kappa. Office: Calif Inst Tech Winnett 115-51 Pasadena CA 91125

WEST, LEE ROY, federal judge; b. Clayton, Okla., Nov. 26, 1929; s. Calvin and Nicie (Hill) W.; m. MaryAnn Ellis, Aug. 29, 1952; children: Kimberly Ellis, Jennifer Lee. B.A., U. Okla., 1952, J.D., 1956; LL.M. (Ford Found. fellow), Harvard U., 1963. Bar: Okla. 1956. Individual practice law Ada, Okla., 1956-61, 63-65; faculty U. Okla. Coll. Law, 1961-62; Ford Found. fellow in law teaching Harvard U., Cambridge, Mass., 1962-63; judge 22d Jud. Dist. Okla., Ada, 1965-73; mem. CAB, Washington, 1973-78; acting chmn. CAB, 1977; practice law Tulsa, 1978-79; spl. justice Okla. Supreme Ct., 1965; judge U.S. Dist Ct. (we. dist.) Okla., 1979-94; sr. judge U.S. Dist. Ct. (we. dist.), Okla., 1994—. Editor: Okla. Law Rev. Served to capt. USMC, 1952-54. Mem. U. Okla. Alumni Assn. (dir.), Phi Delta Phi (pres. 1956), Phi Eta Sigma, Order of Coif. Home: 6500 E Danforth Rd Edmond OK 73034-7601 Office: US Dist Ct 3001 US Courthouse 200 NW 4th St Oklahoma City OK 73102-3003

WEST, LORETTA MARIE, underwriter; b. N.Y.C., Feb. 2, 1950; d. James L. and Alice (Richardson) W. AB, Washington Coll., Chestertown, Md., 1972. CPCU; cert. profl. ins. woman. Disbursements cashier Middlesex Ins. Co., Concord, Mass., 1972-76, tech. asst., 1976-78, comml. lines underwriter, 1978-83; sr. comml. lines underwriter Sentry Ins. Co., Concord, 1983-86, large acct. underwriter, 1986-88, sr. large account underwriter, 1988-92; with Hoffman Ins. Svcs., Inc., Wellesley, Mass., 1992—. Mem. Framingham (Mass.) Rep. Town Com., 1988-92; sec. Mass. Fedn. Rep. Women, 1992-94; trustee Prescott Gardens Condos, 1984-88; pres. Greater Precinct 12 Neighborhood Assn., 1990-92; pres. Framingham Rep. Women's Club, 1990-92; co-founder Framington Condominium Coalition, 1992—. Mem. Soc. CPCU, Nat. Assn. Ins. Women, Mass. Assn. Ins. Women (treas. 1990-92, various coms. Middlesex and South Middlesex chpts., co-dir. South Middlesex chpt. 1986-88, bd. dirs. South Middlesex chpt. 1988-90, Woman of Yr. award 1980), Women's Rep. Club Mass., Middlesex Club. Roman Catholic. Home: 6 Prescott St Framingham MA 01701-7511 Office: Hoffman Ins Svcs 200 Linden St Wellesley MA 02181-7914

WEST, MARJORIE EDITH, elementary education educator; b. Lawrence, Kans., Aug. 18, 1940; d. Merwin Hales and Helen Aletha (Fellows) Wilson Polzin; m. Hammond Dean Watkins, Feb. 17, 1968 (div. 1971); 1 child, Michele Dawn; m. Merlin Avery West, Apr. 2, 1975 (div. 1984). BA in Elem. Edn., U. No. Colo., 1962, MA in Reading, 1970; postgrad., La. State U., 1981-82, U. New Orleans, 1981-82. Cert. tchr., Colo. Tchr. Sch. Dist. 11, Colorado Springs, Colo., 1962-64, Nat. Def. Overseas Teaching Program, Wiesbaden, Fed. Republic Germany, 1964-65, Alaska On-Base Schs., Fairbanks, 1965-66, Great Bend (Kans.) Sch. Dist., 1966-67, Killeen (Tex.) Sch. Dist., 1967-68, Jefferson County Schs., Lakewood, Colo., 1969—. Recipient Alumni Trail Blazer award U. No. Colo., 1988; named Colo. Tchr. of Yr., 1994, finalist Nat. Tchr. of Yr., 1994; inductee into Nat. Tchrs.' Hall of Fame, 1995. Mem. NAFE, AAUW, NEA, PTA (by-laws com. 1989-90, hon. life mem.), Colo. Edn. Assn. (del. to assembly 1985-90), Jefferson County Edn. Assn. (spl. svcs. com. 1989-90), Internat. Reading Assn., Phi Delta Kappa, Pi Lambda Theta, Epsilon Sigma Alpha (edn. chair 1989-90, chair ways and means com. 1990-91, publicity chair 1991-93). Democrat. Avocations: football, travel, golf, reading. Home: 10810 W Exposition Ave Lakewood CO 80226-3818

WEST, MARSHA, elementary school educator; b. DeQueen, Ark., Sept. 1, 1950; d. Marshall T. and Mildred L. (Davis) Gore; m. Larry T. West, May 19, 1972; 1 child, Zachary. BS in Edn., So. State Coll., Magnolia, Ark., 1971; MEd, U. Ark., 1975; postgrad., Henderson State Coll., Arkadelphia, Ark., Purdue U.; specialist's degree, U. Ga., 1991. Cert. elem. and spl. edn. tchr., Tex., elem. tchr., early childhood, mid. sch. tchr., media specialist, Ga. Spl. edn. resource tchr. Gatesville (Tex.) Ind. Sch. Dist.; tchr. early childhood spl. edn. Bryan (Tex.) Ind. Sch. Dist.; elem. tchr. Tippecanoe Sch. Corp., Lafayette, Ind.; elem. tchr. Clarke County Sch. Dist., Athens, Ga., media specialist. Mem. ALA, NEA, Am. Assn. Sch. Librs., Internat. Reading Assn., Ga. Assn. Educators, Ga. Assn. Instrnl. Tech., Ga. Libr. Media Assn. (dist. V chair), N.E. Ga. Reading Coun., Clarke County Assn. Educators (faculty rep.), Kappa Delta Pi.

WEST, MARVIN LEON, managing editor; b. Knoxville, May 1, 1934; s. Alvin Leon and Alma Oneta (Bishop) W.; m. Sarah Jane Blackburn, July 24, 1954; children: Michael, Gary, Jayne, Donna. BA in Journalism, U. Tenn., 1955. Sports writer Knoxville News-Sentinel, Tenn., 1955-80, sports editor, 1980-83, mng. editor, 1983-85; nat. sports editor Scripps Howard News Svc., Washington, 1985-95, mng. editor, 1995—. Named Sportswriter of Yr., Tenn. Nat. Broadcasters and Sports Writers Assn., Salisbury, N.C., 1967, 1974. Mem. U.S. Basketball Writers Assn. (pres. 1983-84). Presbyterian. Avocation: fishing. Home: PO Box 327 Mount Vernon VA 22121-0327 Office: Scripps Howard News Svc 1090 Vermont Ave NW Washington DC 20005-4905

WEST, MARY ELIZABETH, psychiatric management professional; b. Spartanburg, S.C., Aug. 27, 1939; d. Thomas Benjamin and Virginia Milster (Smith) Anderson; m. William Duane West, Sept. 13, 1960; children: William Kevin, Walter Duane, Litia Allyn West Harrison, Thomas Anderson. Diploma in nursing, Ga. Bapt. Hosp., 1960; BS in Nursing Leadership, Tift Coll., 1966; MS in Counseling, U. Scranton, 1972; EdD, Nova U., 1979. RNC, Tenn.; cert. profl. counselor, Tenn., nurse adminstr. advanced. Staff nurse pub. health Fulton County Health Dept., Atlanta, 1960-61; instr. in nursing Macon (Ga.) Hosp. Sch. Nursing, 1965-66, Western Piedmont C.C., 1973-74; dir. nursing Tyler Meml. Hosp., Tunkhannock, Pa., 1967-70; assoc. dir. nursing Nesbitt Meml. Hosp., Kingston, Pa., 1971; assoc. adminstr. Home Health Svcs. Luzerne County, Wilkes-Barre, Pa., 1972; cons. nursing Hosp. Affiliates Internat., Nashville, 1974-76, v.p. nursing, 1976-78, v.p. quality assurance, 1978-80; v.p. nursing cons. svc. Advanced Mgmt. Sys., Nashville, 1981; sr. v.p. planning Hosp. Affiliates Devel. Corp., Nashville, 1982-83; v.p. ops. Winter Haven (Fla.) Hosp., 1986-90; pres. Hope Psychiat. Mgmt., Inc., Winter Haven, 1994—. Contbg. author: Political Action Handbook for Nurses, 1985 (Am. Jour. Nursing Book of Yr. 1986); co-author, editor manual Hosp. Affiliates International, 1978; contbr. articles to mags., chpt. to book. V.p. part time svcs. Winter Haven Hosp., 1987-90; insvc. tng. dir. Rotary Internat., Winter Haven, 1989-91; v.p. Winter Haven C. of C., 1988-90; pres. Polk County Nurse Exec. Orgn., Lakeland, Fla., 1989-90; bd. dirs. Women's Resource Ctr., Inc., Winter Haven, 1989-91; bd. dirs., founder Mothers Alone, Haines City, Fla., 1991—; nat. chair Sunhealth Nursing Coun., Charlotte, N.C., 1990; founder, bd. chmn. Hope Christian Counseling Inc., 1994; state bd. dirs., dir. profl. edn. Bapt. Nursing Fellowship, 1995—. Mem. ANA, Fla. Nursing Assn., Am. Orgn. Nurse Execs., Inner Wheel (v.p., treas., bd. dirs. 1992—), Theta Chi Omega. Republican. Baptist. Avocations: piano, reading, travel, walking, hiking. Home: 3208 Lake Breeze Dr Haines City FL 33844-9333 Office: HOPE Psychiat Mgmt Ste 5013 5665 Cypress Gardens Blvd Winter Haven FL 33884-2273

WEST, MICHAEL ALAN, hospital administrator; b. Waseca, Minn., Aug. 4, 1938; s. Ralph Lel and Elizabeth Mary (Brann) W.; m. Mary Thissen, Jan. 21, 1961; children—Anne, Nancy, Douglas. B.A., U. Minn., 1961, M.H.A.,

1963. Sales corr. Physicians and Hosps. Supply Co., Mpls., 1959-60; adminstrv. resident R.I. Hosp., Providence, 1962-63; adminstrv. asst. R.I. Hosp., 1963-65, asst. dir., 1965-68; exec. asst. dir. Med. Center U. Mo., Columbia, 1968-70; assoc. dir. Med. Center U. Mo., 1970-74, asst. prof. community health and med. practice, 1968-74; v.p. for adminstrn. Luth. Gen. Hosp., Park Ridge, Ill., 1974-80; exec. v.p. Luth. Gen. Hosp., 1980-84; pres., CEO Akron Gen. Med. Ctr., Ohio, 1984—; bd. dirs. Vol. Hosps. Am. Inc.; chair VHA-Ctrl., Inc. Mem. Am. Coll. Healthcare Execs., Akron Regional Hosp. Assn. (chmn.), Portage Country Club, Akron City Club, Rotary. Home: 495 Woodbury Dr Akron OH 44333-2780 Office: Akron Gen Med Ctr 400 Wabash Ave Akron OH 44307-2433

WEST, MORRIS LANGLO, novelist; b. Melbourne, Australia, Apr. 26, 1916; s. Charles Langlo and Florence Guilfoyle (Hanlon) W.; m. Joyce Lawford, Aug. 14, 1952. BA, U. Melbourne, Australia, 1937; DLitt. (hon.), Santa Clara U., 1968, Mercy Coll., Dobbs Ferry, N.Y., 1982, U. Western Sydney, 1993; DLitt (hon.), Australian Nat. U., Canberra, 1995. Tchr. modern langs. and math New South Wales, Australia and Tasmania, 1933-39; sec. to William Morris Hughes, Prime Minister Australia, 1943; mng. dir. Australian Radio Prodns., 1943-53; publicity mgr. Mudroch Newspaper Chain, Melbourne, Australia, 1945-46; film, drama writer Shell Co. and Australian Broadcasting Network, from 1954. Author: Moon in My Pocket, 1945, Gallows on the Sand, 1955, Kundu, 1956, Children of the Shadows (English title: Children of the Sun), 1957, The Crooked Road (English title: The Big Story), 1957, McCreary Moves In, 1958, Backlash (English title: The Second Victory), 1958, The Devil's Advocate, 1959 (Nat. Brotherhood award Nat. Coun. Christians and Jews, 1960, James Tait Black Meml. award 1960, William Heinemann award Royal Soc. 1959), The Naked Country, 1960, Daughter of Silence, 1961, The Shoes of the Fisherman, 1963 (Bestsellers Paperback of Yr. award 1965), The Ambassador, 1965, Tower of Babel, 1967, (with R. Francis) Scandal in the Assembly, 1970, The Heretic, A Play in Three Acts, 1970, Summer of the Red Wolf, 1971, The Salamander, 1973, Harlequin, 1974, the Navigator, 1976, Proteus, 1979, The Clowns of God, 1981 (Universe Lit. prize 1981), The World is Made of Glass, 1983, Cassidy, 1986, Masterclass, 1988, Lazarus, 1990, The Ringmaster, 1991, The Lovers, 1993, Vanishing Point, 1996, A View From the Ridge, 1996. Served to lt. Australian Imperial Forces, 1939-43, PTO. Recipient Internat. Dag Hammarskjold prize Diplomatic Acad. of Peace (grand collar of merit), 1978. Fellow Royal Soc. Lit., World Acad. Arts and Sci., Order of Australia. Clubs: Royal Prince Alfred Yacht (Sydney, Australia), Australian (Sydney). Office: PO Box 102, Avalon NSW 2107, Australia

WEST, PAUL NODEN, author; b. Eckington, Derbyshire, Eng., Feb. 23, 1930; came to U.S., 1961, naturalized, 1971; s. Alfred Massick and Mildred (Noden) W. Student, Oxford U., 1950-53; MA, Columbia U., 1953. Asst. prof. English Meml. U. Nfld., Can., 1957-58; assoc. prof. Meml. U. Nfld., 1958-60; faculty Pa. State U., 1962-95, prof. English and comparative lit., 1968-95; prof. emeritus, 1995—; Crawshaw prof. Colgate U., 1972; Melvin Hill disting. vis. prof. Hobart and William Smith Colls., 1973; vis. English prof. Cornell U., 1986; disting. writer in residence Wichita State U., 1982; vis. prof. English Brown U., 1992; fiction judge Creative Artists Pub. Svc. Program, N.Y.C., 1974, 81; writer-in-residence U. Ariz., 1984; judge Katherine Ann Porter Prize for Fiction, 1984, Artists Found. Author: Byron and the Spoiler's Art, 1960, rev. edit., 1990, I Said the Sparrow, 1963, The Snow Leopard, 1965, Tenement of Clay, 1965, The Wine of Absurdity, 1966, Alley Jaggers, 1967, I'm Expecting to Live Quite Soon, 1970, Words for a Deaf Daughter, 1970, Caliban's Filibuster, 1972, Colonel Mint, 1973, Gala, 1976, The Very Rich Hours of Count von Stauffenberg, 1980, Out of My Depths: A Swimmer in the Universe, 1983, Rat Man of Paris, 1986, Sheer Fiction, 1987, The Universe and Other Fiction, 1988, The Place in Flowers Where Pollen Rests, 1988, Lord Byron's Doctor, 1989, Portable People, The Women of Whitechapel and Jack the Ripper, 1991, Sheer Fiction: II, 1991, James Ensor, 1991, Love's Mansion, 1992, Tenement of Clay, 2d edit., 1993, Sheer Fiction, III, 1994, A Stroke of Genius, 1995, The Tent of Orange Mist, 1995 (memoir) My Mother's Music, 1996 (novel) Sporting with Amaryllis, 1996; contbr. Washington Post and N.Y. Times, 1962—, Harper's Mag., GQ Mag., Paris Rev., Yale Rev., Boston Phoenix, Bookpress; fiction judge N.Y. Found. for the Arts, Nat. Book award, 1990. Served with RAF, 1954-57. Recipient Aga Khan Fiction prize, 1973, Hazlett Meml. award for Excellence in Arts (lit.), 1981, Lit. award Am. Acad. and Inst. Arts and Letters, 1985, Pushcart prize 1987, 91, The Best Am. Essays award, 1990, Outstanding Achievement medal Pa. State U., 1991, Grand Prix Halpérine Kaminsky award 1992, Lannan Fiction award 1993, Tchg. award Northeastern Assn. Grad. Schs. 1994; named Lit. Lion N.Y. Pub. Libr. 1987; Guggenheim fellow, 1963; Nat. Endowment for Arts Creative Writing fellow, 1979, 84; nominated for Médicis, Femina and Meilleur Livre Etranger prizes, France, 1991, Lannan Lit. Videos # 35, Nat. Book Critics award for Fiction, 1996; named to Honor Roll The Yr. in Fiction, DLB Yearbook, 1996. Mem. Authors Guild. Office: Elaine Markson Agy 44 Greenwich Ave New York NY 10011-8347 *The unexamined life may not be worth having, but the examined life is endurable only to an open mind, through which life holistically flows, keeping that mind as incomplete as our knowledge of the universe itself.*

WEST, PHILIP WILLIAM, chemistry educator; b. Crookston, Minn., Apr. 12, 1913; s. William Leonard and Anne (Thompson) W.; m. Tenney Constance Johnson, July 5, 1935 (dec. Feb. 1964); children: Dorothy West/Farwell, Linda West Gueho (dec.), Patty West Elstrott; m. Foymae S. Kelso, July 1, 1964. B.S., U. N.D., 1935, M.S., 1936, D.Sc. (hon.), 1958; Ph.D., State U. Iowa, 1939; postgrad., Rio de Janeiro, 1946. Chemist N.D. Geol. Survey, 1935-36; research asst. san. chemistry U. Iowa, 1936-37; asst. chemist Iowa Dept. Health, 1937-40; research microchemist Econ. Lab., Inc., St. Paul, 1940; faculty La. State U., 1940-80, prof. chemistry, 1951-80, Boyd prof., 1953-80, emeritus, 1980—, chmn. ann. symposium modern methods of analytical chemistry, 1948-65, dir. Inst. for Environmental Scis., 1967-80; co-founder, chmn. bd. West-Paine Labs. Inc., Baton Rouge, 1980-93; O. M. Smith lectr. Okla. State U., 1955; vis. prof. U. Colo., 1963, Rand Afrikaans U., 1980; adj. prof. EPA, 1969-80; founder Kem-Tech. Labs., Inc., Baton Rouge, 1954, chmn. bd., 1965-74; co-founder West-Paine Labs., Inc., Baton Rouge, 1978, pres., 1978-93, chmn. bd., lab dir., 1990; mem. 1st working party sci. com. on problems of environment, 1971-74; pres. analytical sect. Internat. Union Pure and Applied Chemistry, 1965-69, mem. sect. indsl. hygiene and toxicology, 1971-73, mem. air quality sect., 1973-75; mem. tech. adv. com. La. Air Pollution Control Com., 1979—; mem. Gov.'s Task Force Environ. Health, 1983-85; mem. sci. adv. bd. EPA, 1983-84; cons. WHO; tech. expert Nat. Bur. Standards Nat. Vol. Lab. Accreditation Program, 1988—; chmn. bd., CEO West & Assoc., Inc., 1992—. Author: Chemical Calculations, 1948, (with Vick) Qualitative Analysis and Analytical Chemical Separations, 2d edit., 1959, (with Bustin) Experience Approach to Experimental Chemistry, 1975; editor: (with Hamilton) Science of the Total Environment, 1973-78, (with Macdonald) Analytica Chimica Acta, 1959-78, Reagents and Reaction for Qualitative Inorganic Analysis; co-editor: Analytical Chemistry, 1963; asst. editor: Mikrochemica Acta, 1952-78, Michrochem. Jour, 1957-75; adv. bd.: Analytical Chemistry, 1959-60; publ. bd.: Jour. Chem. Edn, 1954-57; contbr. articles to profl. jours. Recipient Honor Scroll award La. sect. Am. Inst. Chemistry, 1972. Fellow AAAS; mem. Am. Chem. Soc. (Southwest award 1954, Charles E. Coates award 1967, Analytical Chemistry award 1974, award for Creative Advances in Environ. Sci. and Tech.), La. Acad. Sci., Air Pollution Control Assn., Am. Indsl. Hygiene Assn., Austrian Microchem. Soc. (hon.), Soc. of Analysts Eng. (hon.), Internat. Union Pure and Applied Chemistry (pres. commn. I, pres. analytical div.), Japan Soc. for Analytical Chemistry (hon.), La. Cancer and Health Found., Sigma Xi, Phi Lambda Upsilon, Phi Kappa Phi, Alpha Epsilon Delta, Alpha Chi Sigma, Tau Kappa Epsilon. Office: West-Paine Labs Inc 7979 G S R I Rd Baton Rouge LA 70820-7402

WEST, RALPH LELAND, veterinarian; b. Grand Rapids, Minn., Apr. 23, 1915; s. Ralph Leland and Elsie (Wardall) W.; m. Mary Elizabeth Brann, June 14, 1937; children: Michael Alan, Janet Lee West Friedrich, Thomas James. DVM, Iowa State U., 1936; MS, Purdue U., 1972. Pvt. practice Waseca, Minn., 1936-42, 46-70; grad. asst. Sch. Vet. Medicine Purdue U., West Lafayette, Ind., 1970-72; asst. dir. sci. activities Am. Vet. Med. Assn., Schaumburg, Ill., 1972-77, dir. sci. activities, 1977-87. Contbr. articles to jours. in field. Mem. Pk. Bd., Waseca, 1948-50, Youth Commn., 1948-52; mem., chmn. Waseca Hosp. Bd., 1954-64; trustee Sunny Acres Village Inc., Denver, 1988-95. Maj. U.S. Army, 1942-46, ETO. Recipient Stange award Iowa State U., 1983. Mem. AMVA (award 1990), Am. Assn. Ret. Vets. (dir. 1987-90), Am. Vet. History Soc., Colo. Vet. Med. Assn., Minn. Vet. Med. Assn., Iowa State U. Vet. Alumni Assn., Phi Zeta. Republican. Avocations: reading, bridge, stock market. Home: 1719 E Bijou St Apt 611 Colorado Springs CO 80909-5732

WEST, REXFORD LEON, banker; b. Syracuse, N.Y., Feb. 18, 1938; s. Rexford A. and Nina (Crysler) W.; m. Pamela Hanlon, June 1, 1995; children from previous marriage: Lisa, Julie, Gregory, Kristen. A.A.S., Auburn Community Coll., N.Y., 1957; B.S. magna cum laude, Syracuse U., N.Y., 1972; Advanced Mgmt. Program, Harvard Bus. Sch., Boston, 1984. Accountant Marine Midland Bank, Syracuse, N.Y., 1959-67, v.p., asst. treas., 1967-72; v.p., controller Marine Midland Services Corp., Buffalo, N.Y., 1972-76; v.p. ops. div. Marine Midland Bank, N.A., Buffalo, N.Y., 1976-77, sr. v.p., sr. ops. officer, 1977-79, exec. v.p., sr. ops. officer, 1979-85, divsn. exec. ops., 1985-87, sector exec. ops. and fin. mgmt., 1987-90, sr. exec. v.p. corp. engring., 1990-92; exec. v.p. adminstrv. svc. Fleet Bank, Melville, N.Y., 1992-94; exec. v.p. loan servicing Fleet Mortgage Group, Columbia, S.C., 1994—. Served with U.S. Army, 1957-61. Office: Fleet Mortgage Group 1333 Main St Columbia SC 29201-3201

WEST, RICHARD LUTHER, military association executive, defense consultant, retired army officer; b. Ithaca, N.Y., Jan. 8, 1925; s. Luther W. and Beatrice E. (Ryan) W.; m. June D. Kirby, June 5, 1945; children—John R., Lesley A., Peter L. Student, No. Mich. Coll., 1941-42; B.S., U.S. Mil. Acad., 1945; M.S., Princeton U., 1954; M.S. in Bus. Adminstrn, George Washington U., 1965. Commd. 2d lt. U.S. Army, 1945, advanced through grades to lt. gen., 1977; comptr. of the Army Washington, 1977-81, ret., 1981, cons. def., 1982—; dir. Inst. Land Warfare Assn. U.S. Army, 1988—. Decorated D.S.M., Legion of Merit with 3 oak leaf clusters, Bronze Star, Air medal with 2 oak leaf clusters, Army Commendation medal with oak leaf cluster. Mem. Assn. U.S. Army (v.p. 1992—), Am. Mil. Engrs., Am. Soc. Mil. Comptrs., Am. Def. Preparedness Assn., Sigma Xi. Home: 1509 Laurel Hill Rd Vienna VA 22182-1713

WEST, RICHARD VINCENT, art museum official; b. Prague, Czechoslovakia, Nov. 26, 1934; came to U.S., 1938, naturalized, 1947; s. Jan Josef and Katherine Frieda (Mayer) Vysloužil; 1 child, Jessica Katherine. Student, UCLA, 1952-55, Music Acad. of the West, 1958-60; BA with highest honors, U. Calif., Santa Barbara, 1961; postgrad., Akademie der Bildenden Kuenste, Vienna, 1961-62, Hochschule fur Musik und darstellende Kuenste, Vienna, 1961-62; MA, U. Calif., Berkeley, 1965. Curatorial intern Cleve. Art Mus., 1965-66, Albright-Knox Art Gallery, Buffalo, 1966-67; curator Mus. Art Bowdoin Coll., Brunswick, Maine, 1967-69, dir., 1969-72; dir. Crocker Art Mus., Sacramento, Calif., 1973-82, Santa Barbara Mus. Art, Calif., 1983-91; pres. Artmuse Assocs., Benicia, Calif., 1991-92; dir. Newport (R.I.) Art Mus., 1992-94, Frye Art Mus., Seattle, 1995—; mem. Joint Yugoslav-Am. Excavations at Sirmium, 1971; bd. dirs. Sacramento Regional Art Coun., 1973-77; bd. overseers Strawbery Banke, 1993—. Author: Painters of the Section d'Or, 1967, Language of the Print, 1968; The Walker Art Building Murals, 1972, Munich and American Realism in the 19th Cen., 1978, An Enkindled Eye: The Paintings of Rockwell Kent, 1985, Standing in the Tempest: Painters of the Hungarian Avant-Garde, 1991, America in Art, 1991, A Significant Story: American Painting and Decorative Arts from the Karolik Collection, 1993; exhbn. catalogues, also various revs. and articles. Active Newport Reading Room; founding mem. New England Community Mus. Consortium. Served with USN, 1956-57. Ford Found. fellow, 1965-67; Smithsonian fellow, 1971. Mem. Am. Assn. Mus., Coll. Art Assn., Internat. Coun. Mus., Western Assn. Art Mus. (pres. 1975-78), Calif. Assn. Mus. (bd. dirs. 1980-82, v.p. 1986-91), Newport Reading Rm., Rotary. Office: Frye Art Mus PO Box 3005 Seattle WA 98114-3005

WEST, ROBERT COOPER, geography educator; b. Enid, Okla., June 30, 1913; s. George Washington and Elva A. (Cooper) W.; m. Phyllis Devereaux, May 11, 1968. A.B., U. Calif. at Los Angeles, 1935, M.A., 1938; Ph.D., U. Calif. at Berkeley, 1946. Cartographer OSS, Washington, 1941-45; geographer Smithsonian Instn. (Mexico City office), 1946-48; asst. prof. to prof. La. State U. at Baton Rouge, 1948—, Boyd prof., 1970-80, prof. emeritus, 1980—; vis. prof. U. Wis. at Madison, 1966, U. Calif. at Los Angeles, 1968, U. Ariz. at Tucson, 1972, 76. Co-author: Middle America: Its Lands and Peoples, 3d edit., 1989, others; co-editor: Handbook of Middle American Indians, vol. 1, Nat. Environment and Early Cultures, 1964, Sonora: It's Geographical Personality, 1993, In Quest of Mineral Wealth, 1994. Recipient Alumni Faculty award La. State U., 1965; Guggenheim fellow, 1955. Mem. A.A.A.S., Assn. Am. Geographers (citation for meritorious contbn. 1964, Outstanding Achievement award 1973), Latin Am. Studies Assn., Conf. Latin Amercanist Geographers, Sigma Xi. Home: 4815 Tulane Dr Baton Rouge LA 70808-4762 Office: Dept Geography and Anthropology La State U Baton Rouge LA 70803

WEST, ROBERT CULBERTSON, chemistry educator; b. Glen Ridge, N.J., Mar. 18, 1928; s. Robert C. and Constance (MacKinnon) W.; children: David Russell, Arthur Scott, Derek. B.A., Cornell U., 1950; A.M., Harvard U., 1952, Ph.D., 1954; ScD (hon.), G. Asachi Tech. U., Iasi, Romania, 1995. Asst. prof. Lehigh U., 1954-56; mem. faculty U. Wis.-Madison, 1956—, prof. chemistry, 1963—, Eugene G. Rochow prof., 1980; indsl. and govt. cons., 1961—; Fulbright lectr. Kyoto and Osaka U., 1964-65; vis. prof. U. Würzburg, 1968-69, Haile Selassie I U., 1972, U. Calif.-Santa Cruz, 1977, U. Utah, 1981, Inst. Chem. Physics Chinese Acad. Sci., 1984, Justus Liebigs U., Giessen, Fed. Republic Germany, U. Estadual de Campinas, Brazil, 1989; Abbott lectr. U. N.D., 1964, Seydel-Wooley lectr. Ga. Inst. Tech., 1970, Sun Oil lectr. Ohio U., 1971, Edgar C. Britton lectr. Dow, Midland, Mich., 1971, Jean Day Meml. lectr. Rutgers U., 1973; Japan Soc. for Promotion Sci. vis. prof. Tohoku U., 1976, Gunma U., 1987; Lady Davis vis. prof. Hebrew U., 1979; Cecil and Ida Green honors prof. Tex. Christian U., 1983; Karcher lectr. U. Okla., 1986; Broberg lectr. N.D. State U., 1986; Xerox lectr. U. B.C., 1986, McGregory lectr. Colgate U., 1988; Lady Davis vis. prof. Technion Israel Inst. Tech., 1990; Humboldt prof. Tech. U. Munich, Fed. Republic Germany, 1990; George W. Watt lectr. U. Tex., Austin, 1992; vis. prof. U. Estadual de Campinas, Brazil, 1993; Dozor vis. fellow Ben Gurion U. of the Negev, Israel, 1993. Co-editor: Advances in Organometallic Chemistry, Vols. I-XXXVI, 1964—, Organometallic Chemistry--A Monograph Series, 1968—; contbr. articles to profl. jours. Pres. Madison Community Sch., 1970-81; founder, bd. dirs. Women's Med. Fund, 1971—; nat. bd. dirs. Zero Population Growth, 1980-86; bd. dirs., v.p. Protect Abortion Rights Inc., 1980; lay minister Prairie Unitarian Universalist Soc., 1982. Recipient F.S. Kipling award, 1970, Outstanding Sci. Innovator award Sci. Digest, 1985, Chem. Pioneering award Am. Inst. Chemists, 1988, Wacker Silicon prize, 1989, Humboldt U.S. Scientist award, 1990. Mem. Am. Chem. Soc., Chem. Soc. (London), Japan Chem. Soc., AAAS, Wis. Acad. Sci. Home: 305 Nautilus Dr Madison WI 53705-4333

WEST, ROBERT MACLELLAN, science education consultant; b. Appleton, Wis., Sept. 1, 1942; s. Clarence John and Elizabeth Ophelia (Moore) W.; m. Jean Sydow, June 19, 1965; 1 child, Christopher. BA, Lawrence Coll., 1963; SM, U. Chgo., 1964, PhD, 1968. Rsch. assoc. Princeton (N.J.) U., 1968-69; asst. prof. Adelphi U., Garden City, N.Y., 1969-74; curator of geology Milw. Pub. Mus., 1974-83; dir. Carnegie Mus. Natural History, Pitts., 1983-87, Cranbrook Inst. Sci., Bloomfield Hills, Mich., 1987-91; prin. RMW Sci. Action, Washington, 1992-95; pres. Informal Sci., Inc., Washington, 1993—; adj. prof. U. Wis., Milw., 1974-83; com. mem. Indo-U.S. Subcom., 1990—. Contbr. articles to profl. jours. Bd. dirs. Friends of the New Zoo, Pitts., 1984-87; treas. East Mich. Environ. Action Coun., Birmingham, Mich., 1987-92. Recipient Arnold Guyot prize Nat. Geographic Soc., 1982; named Man of Yr. in Sci. by Vectors Pitts., 1988; NSF fellow, 1965-68, NSF rsch. grantee, 1970-82, Nat. Geographic Soc. rsch. grantee, 1973, 76, 77, 79, 80, 82. Mem. Nat. Ctr. Sci. Edn. (bd. dirs. 1984-88, 92—), Nepal Natural History Soc. (advisor 1992—), Soc. Vertebrate Paleontology, Geol. Soc. Am., Paleontology Soc., Am. Soc. Mammalogists, Am. Assn. Mus., Nepal Geol. Soc., Rotary. Avocations: nature, history, sports. Office: Informal Sci Inc PO Box 42328 Washington DC 20015-0928

WEST, ROBERT SUMNER, surgeon; b. Bowman, N.D., Nov. 20, 1935; s. Elmer and Minnie (DeBode) W.; m. Martha W. Hopkins, Mar. 23, 1957; children: Stephen, Christopher, Anna Marie, Catherine, Sarah. BA, U. N.D., 1957, BS in Medicine, 1959; MD, Harvard U., 1961. Diplomate Am. Bd. Surgery. Intern U.S. Naval Hosp., Chelsea, Mass., 1961-62; resident in surgery U. Vt. Med. Ctr. Hosp., 1965-69; pvt. practice Coeur d'Alene, Idaho, 1969—; coroner Kootenai County, Coeur d'Alene, 1984—. Trustee, pres. Coeur d'Alene Sch. Dist. 271 Bd. Edn., 1973-77. Lt. M.C., USN, 1960-65. Fellow ACS (pres. Idaho chpt. 1985, gov. at large); mem. Idaho Med. Assn. (pres. 1989-90, trustee), Kiwanis. Republican. Lutheran. Avocation: sailing. Office: 920 W Ironwood Dr Coeur D Alene ID 83814-2643

WEST, ROBERT VAN OSDELL, JR., retired petroleum executive; b. Kansas City, Mo., Apr. 29, 1921; s. Robert Van Osdell and Josephine (Quistgaard) W.; divorced; children: Robert Van Osdell III, Kathryn Anne, Suzanne Small, Patricia Lynn; m. Helen L. Boecking, 1978. BS, U. Tex., 1942, MS, 1943, PhD, 1949. Registered profl engr., Tex. Petroleum engr. Slick Urschel Oil Co., 1949-56; pres. Slick Secondary Recovery Corp., 1956-59; v.p. Texstar Corp., 1959; pres. Texstar Petroleum Co. subs. Texstar Corp., 1959-64; founder Tesoro Petroleum Corp., San Antonio, 1964, chmn. bd. dirs., chief exec. officer, 1971-88, chmn. bd., 1989-92; chief exec. officer Tesoro Petroleum Corp., 1964-92; bd. dirs. Frost Nat. Bank. Mem. engring. found. adv. coun. U. Tex., mem. at large and life Centennial Commn.; former bd. visitors McDonald Obs. and Astronomy; mem. devel. bd. U. Tex. San Antonio Health Sci. Ctr.; assoc. mem. bd. visitors U. Tex. M.D. Anderson Cancer Ctr., Houston; Trinity U. Assoc., San Antonio; mem. adv. coun., trustee St. Mary's U. Sch. Bus.; past trustee San Antonio City Public Service Bd.; trustee S.W. Research Inst.; past chmn. San Antonio Econ. Devel. Found.; bd. dirs. World Affairs Council, San Antonio; chmn. St. Luke's Luth. Hosp. Found., San Antonio; emeritus chmn. bd. trustees San Antonio Symphony; founder, former chmn. bd. dirs. Tiwanaku Archaeol. Found., Bolivia.; founder, former chmn. exec. com. Caribbean/L.Am. Action, Washington; trustee Ams. Soc. N.Y.; chmn. gen. campaign United Way of San Antonio and Bexar County, 1986, vice chmn. bd. trustees, 1988—; chmn. pub. sector campaign subcom. United Way of Am., 1988—. Named Disting. Grad., U. Tex. Coll. Engring., 1973; recipient People of Vision award Nat. Soc. Prevention of Blindness, 1982, Internat. Citizens award World Affairs Coun., 1986, Good Scout award Boy Scouts Am., 1987, Alexis de Tocqueville award United Way of San Antonio and Bexar County, 1990. Mem. Ind. Petroleum Assn. Am., Soc. Petroleum Engrs. (past chmn. San Antonio-Austin chpt.), 25 Yr. Club Petroleum Industry, Pvt. Enterprise Edn. (Herman W. Lay Meml. award 1986), Am.'s Soc., All-Am. Wildcatters Club, Sigma Chi (Significant Sig award 1979). Episcopalian. Office: 1250 NE Loop 410 Ste 805 San Antonio TX 78209-1533*

WEST, ROBERTA BERTHA, writer; b. Saline County, Mo., Sept. 7, 1904; d. Robert and Amanda Melvina (Driver) Baur; m. Harold Clinton West, Aug. 27, 1932; children: Arle Faith W. Lohof, Lydia Ann (Lyda) F H. Hyde, Danna Rose F H. Burns. AB, William Jewell Coll., 1928; AM, U. Mo., 1930. Cert. tchr., Mo., Mont. Elem. and secondary sch. tchr. Mo. and Mont. Schs., 1922-47; supt. schs. Hogeland (Mont.) Schs., 1947-48, 55; prof. fgn. langs. Will Mayfield Coll., Marble Hill, Mo., 1930; columnist Quad County Star, Viburnum, Mo., 1982—; writer and researcher ch. history, 1964-91; cons. hist. com. Yellowstone Conf. Meth. Ch., 1971-84; compiler Mont. list of Meth. Mins. 1784-1984. Author: Northern Montana Methodist History, 3 vols., 1974, Faith, Hope and Love in the West, 1971; editor: Brother Van by Those Who Knew Him, 1975, reprinted, 1989,; also contbr. articles. Recipient 1st John M. Templeton prize, 1959. Mem. Alpha Zeta Pi. Democrat. Avocation: crocheting. Home: PO Box 583 Viburnum MO 65566-0583 Office: Quad County Star Viburnum MO 65566

WEST, STEPHEN ALLAN, lawyer; b. Salt Lake City, Mar. 23, 1935; s. Allan Morrell and Ferne (Page) W.; m. Martha Sears, Mar. 21, 1960; children: Stephen Allan, Jr., Page, Adam. JD, U. Utah, 1961, BS in Philosophy, 1962. Law clk. to judge U.S. Dist. Ct., Utah, 1961-62; assoc. Marr, Wilkins & Cannon, Salt Lake City, 1962-65; ptnr. Marr, Wilkins & Cannon, 1965-67; atty. Jennings, Strouss, Salmon & Trask, Washington, 1967-68; atty. Marriott Corp., Washington, 1968-71, asst. gen. counsel, 1971-74, v.p. and assoc. gen. counsel, 1974-87, v.p. and dep. gen. counsel, 1987-93; sr. v.p., gen. counsel Marriott Internat., Inc., Washington, 1993-94; pres. Tex. San Antonio mission Ch. of Jesus Christ of Latter-Day Saints, 1995—. Bishop LDS Ch., 1977-81; mem. exec. bd. Interfaith Conf. Met. Washington, 1989-93, vice chmn., 1992-93; mem. exec. bd. Christa McAuliffe Inst. Task Force of Nat. Found. for Improvement Edn. Mem. ABA (exec. coun. young lawyers sect. 1964-65), Utah Bar Assn. (exec. com. young lawyers sect. 1962-67), D.C. Bar Assn., Utah Profl. Rels. Com., U. Utah Alumni Assn. (Disting. Alumni award 1971), Skull and Bones, Owl and Key, Phi Delta Phi, Sigma Chi. Office: Ch Jesus Christ Latter-Day Tex San Antonio Mission 404 E Ramsey Ste 105 San Antonio TX 78216 also: 15818 Mission Ridge San Antonio TX 78232

WEST, STEPHEN KINGSBURY, lawyer; b. Pittsfield, Mass., Sept. 28, 1928; s. William Bradford and Ruth (Osteyee) W.; m. Ann Wick, Apr. 30, 1955; children: Timothy Wick, Lucy West Engebretson, Todd Kingsbury, Daniel Wick. B.A., Yale U., 1950; LL.B., Harvard U., 1953. Assoc. Sullivan & Cromwell, N.Y.C., 1957-64, ptnr., 1964—; dir. ING Am. Life Ins. Co., Netherlands Ins. Co., Pioneer Mut. Fund, Boston, Aim, Inc., Houston, Winthrop Focus Funds, N.Y.C. Served to 1st lt. inf. U.S. Army, 1953-56. Mem. ABA, N.Y. State Bar Assn., Assn. Bar City N.Y. Office: Sullivan & Cromwell 125 Broad St New York NY 10004-2400

WEST, THOMAS LOWELL, JR., insurance company executive; b. Cedar Bluff, Va., June 7, 1937; s. Thomas Lowell and Kathleen (Bowling) W.; m. Katharine Thompson, Feb. 13, 1960; children: Thomas Lowell III, John Gardner, Katharine Covington. BS in Indsl. Engring., U. Tenn., 1959. CLU, 1967; chartered fin. cons., 1987. Asst. supr. Aetna Life Ins. Co., Memphis, 1960-62, supr., 1962-67, asst. gen. agt., 1967-69; gen. agt. Aetna Life Ins. Co., Jackson, Miss., 1969-80; regional v.p. Aetna Life & Casualty, Hartford, Conn., 1980-85; v.p. Aetna Life Ins. and Annuity Co., Hartford, 1985-88, sr. v.p. exec. com. and investment com., 1988-94, also bd. dirs.; v.p. Aetna Fin. Services, Hartford, 1986-87; pres., bd. dirs. Structured Benefits, Inc., Hartford, 1985-94, Systemized Benefits Adminstrn., Inc., SBFI, 1988; pres., dir. exec. com., mgmt. com., investment com. The Variable Annuity Life Ins. Co., 1994—; exec. v.p., dir. Am. Gen. Series Portfolio Co.; mem. bd. dirs. Houston Symphony. Named to Hall of Fame, Jackson Assn. Life Underwriters, 1977. Mem. Am. Soc. CLU's and CHFC, Am. Soc. Pension Actuaries (assoc.), Assn. for Advanced Life Underwriters (assoc.), Nat. Assn. Life Underwriters, Internat. Assn. Fin. Planners. Republican. Presbyterian. Avocations: tennis, running, E-type Jaguars, Mercedes Benz. Home: 2120 Brentwood Dr Houston TX 77019-3512 Office: The Variable Annuity Life Ins Co 2929 Allen Pky Houston TX 77019-2197

WEST, THOMAS MEADE, financial services strategic consultant; b. Owensboro, Ky., Aug. 15, 1940; s. Frank Thomas and Vivian (Brown) W.; children: Thomas Meade, Alexandra, Theodora. B.A. cum laude, Vanderbilt U., 1962; M.A. magna cum laude, U. Mich., 1964. Various mgmt. positions Lincoln Nat. Life Ins. Co., Fort Wayne, Ind., 1964-75, v.p., 1975-78, sr. v.p., 1978-81, exec. v.p., 1981-94; pres., CEO Lincoln Nat Reins. Cos.; prin. West Cons. Corp.; bd. dirs. Union Fed. Savs. Bank of Indpls., Union Acceptance Corp. Area pres. Boy Scouts Am., Ind.; dir. Jr. Achievement, Ft. Wayne. With U.S. Army, 1964-66. Fellow Soc. of Actuaries; mem. Am. Acad. Actuaries, Fort Wayne C. of C. (bd. dirs.). Presbyterian. Home: 2201 Turnberry Ln Fort Wayne IN 46804-2827

WEST, TOGO DENNIS, JR., secretary of Army, former aerospace executive; b. Winston-Salem, N.C., June 21, 1942; s. Togo Dennis and Evelyn (Carter) W.; m. Gail Estelle Berry, June 18, 1966; children: Tiffany Berry, Hilary Carter. BSEE, Howard U., 1965, JD cum laude, 1968. Bar: D.C. 1968, N.Y. 1969, U.S. Ct. Mil. Appeals 1969, U.S. Supreme Ct. 1978, U.S. Ct. Claims 1981. Elec. engr. Duquesne Light and Power Co., 1965; patent researcher Sughrue, Rothwell, Mion, Zinn and McPeak, 1966-67; legal intern U.S. EEOC, 1967; law clk. firm Covington & Burling, Washington, 1967-68; summer assoc. Covington & Burling, 1968, assoc., 1973-75, 76-77; law clk. to judge U.S. Dist. Ct. for So. Dist. N.Y., 1968-69; assoc. dep. atty. gen. U.S. Dept. Justice, Washington, 1975-76; gen. counsel Dept. Navy, Washington, 1977-79; spl. asst. to sec. and dep. sec. Dept. Def., Washington, 1979-80, gen. counsel, 1980-81; ptnr. Patterson, Belknap, Webb & Tyler, Washington, 1981-90; sr. v.p. govt. rels. Northrop Corp., Washington, 1990-93; sec. of Army, Washington, 1993—; adj. prof. Duke U. Sch. Law, 1980-81; bd. cons. Riggs Nat. Bank, Washington, 1990-93. Mng. editor: Howard Law Jour, 1968. Commr. D.C. Law Rev. Comm., 1982-89, chmn., 1985-89; mem. Nat.

Council of Friends of John F. Kennedy Ctr. for Performing Arts, 1984-91, treas., 1987-91; bd. govs. Antioch U. Sch. Law, 1983-87, vice chmn., 1986-87; chmn. Greater Washington Bd. Trade, legis. bur., 1987-89, bd. dirs., 1987-93, mem. exec. com. 1987-92; mem. fed. legis. com., 1990-93; chmn. Kennedy Ctr. Community and Friends Bd., 1991—; mem. Washington Lawyers' Com. Civil Rights Under Law, 1987-93, D.C. Com. on Pub. Edn., 1988-93, chmn., 1990-91; trustee The Aerospace Corp., 1983-90, Ctr. for Strategic and Internat. Studies, 1987-90, Nat. Lawyers Com. for Civil Rights Under Law, 1987-93, Inst. for Def. Analyses, 1989-91, Protestant Episcopal Cathedral Found., 1989—, Shakespeare Theatre at The Folger, 1990-93, N.C. Sch. Arts, 1990—, Aerospace Edn. Found. of Air Force Assn., 1991-93; bd. dirs. D.C. Law Students in Ct. Program, 1986-92, World Affairs Coun., 1991-93, Atlantic Coun., 1991-93; mem. fin. com. Episcopal Diocese of Washington, 1989—, mem. standing com., 1990-92; sr. warden St. John's Ch., Lafayette Sq.; chmn. trustee coun. YMCA Metro. Wash., 1990-92; mem. nat. adv. com. UN Assn. USA, 1991-93; D.C. Ct. Appeals Admissions Com., 1990-93.. Served to capt. Judge Adv. Gen. Corps U.S. Army, 1969-73. Decorated Legion of Merit; recipient Disting. Pub. Svc. medal Dept. Def., 1981, Eagle Scout award with Bronze Palm Boy Scouts Am., 1957, Disting. Eagle Scout award 1995, Svc. to Howard U. award, 1965. Mem. ABA, Nat. Bar Assn., Washington Coun. Lawyers (dir. 1973-75), Sigma Pi Phi, Phi Alpha Delta, Omega Psi Psi, Alpha Phi Omega, Met. Club, Univ. Club (Washington), F St. Club. Democrat. Episcopalian. Clubs: Metropolitan, University (Washington). Democrat. Episcopalian. Office: Office of Sec Army 101 Army Pentagon Washington DC 20310-0101

WEST, W. RICHARD, JR., museum director; b. San Bernardino, Calif., Jan. 6, 1943; s. W. Richard Sr. and Maribelle (McCrea) W.; m. Mary Beth Braden, June 29, 1968; children: Amy Elizabeth, Benjamin Braden. BA magna cum laude in Am. History, U. Redlands, 1965; AM in Am. History, Harvard U., 1968; JD, Stanford U., 1971; LHD (hon.), Bacone Coll., 1992, Ottawa U., 1994, U. Okla., 1995. Bar: Calif., D.C., U.S. Ct. Appeals (8th cir.), U.S. Supreme Ct. Clk. to Hon. Benjamin C. Duniway U.S. Ct. Appeals (9th cir.), 1971-72; assoc. Fried, Frank, Harris, Shriver & Jacobson, Washington, 1973-79, ptnr., 1979-88; dir. direct support component Am. Indian Lawyer Tng. Program, Inc., 1976-77; ptnr. Gover, Stetson Williams & West P.C., Albuquerque, 1988-90; founding dir. Smithsonian Instn's Nat. Mus. Am. Indian, Washington, 1990—; treas. Am. Indian Lawyer Tng. Program, Inc., 1973—; adj. prof. Indian law Stanford U., 1977. Mem. edit. bd. Am. Indian Historian, 1969-71; note editor Stanford Law Review, 1970-71; contbr. articles to profl. jours. Coord., treas. Native Am. Coun. Regents Inst. Am. Indian Arts, 1975-80; bd. visitors Stanford Law Sch., 1978-81; trustee Phelps Stokes Fund, 1981-87, Bush Found., 1991—, Bacone Coll., 1986-89, chmn., 1988-89, Morning Star Found., 1987-93, U. Redlands, 1991—, alumni bd., 1987-89, Ednl. Found. Am., 1993—; bd. dirs. Amerindian Circle, Inc., 1981-88, Nat. Indian Justice Ctr., 1982-89; cultural edn. com. Smithsonian Inst., 1987-90; nat. support com. Native Am. Rights Fund, 1990—; adv. com. Winslow Found., 1991—; hon. coun. Wings Am., 1993—; mem. Environ. Def. Fund, bd. trustees, 1986—. Recipient Career Achievement award U. Redlands, 1987, Disting. Svc. award, 1992, award Appreciation and Recognition, Cheyenne and Arapaho Tribes Okla., 1990, Spirit of the People award Okla. Inst. Indian Heritage, 1990; named (with another) Amb. of Yr. Red Earth Indian Ctr. Okla., 1993. Mem. Am. Indian Bar Assn. (charter pres. 1976-77). Mem. Cheyenne and Arapaho Tribes Okla. Home: 3311 Rowland Pl NW Washington DC 20008-3226 Office: Nat Mus of Am Indian 470 Lenfant Plz SW Ste 7102 Washington DC 20024-2124

WEST, WARREN HENRY, securities trader; b. Chgo., Sept. 18, 1956; s. Wiley and Naomi (Coleman) W.; m. Laraine Capobianco, Feb. 23, 1985; children: Jake, Lee. V.p. Drexel Burnham Lambert, N.Y.C., 1981-83; pres. Strategic Investors Inc., Phila., 1983-93, Comml. Credit Group, Voorhees, N.J., 1993—. Mem. Phila. Stock Exchange (mktg. com. 1982-84, options com. 1988-89).

WEST, WILLIAM BEVERLEY, III, lawyer; b. Ft. Worth, Feb. 5, 1922; s. William Beverley Jr. and Ella Louise (Moore) W. B.A., U. Tex., 1942, LL.B., 1948; Indsl. Adminstr., Harvard Grad. Sch. Bus. Adminstrn., 1943; LL.M., Columbia, 1949; grad., Command and Gen. Staff Sch. Bar: Tex. 1949. Practice in Ft. Worth; asst. U.S. atty. No. Dist. Tex., 1953, 1st asst. U.S. atty., 1957-58, U.S. atty., 1958-61; exec. asst. to asst. atty. gen., lands div. Dept. Justice, 1961-63; ptnr. Clark, West, Keller, Butler & Ellis, Dallas, 1963-89, of counsel, 1989—; mem. adv. bd. Southwestern Law Enforcement Inst., Dallas, 1959-82; mem. adv. com. on criminal rules U.S. Jud. Conf., 1973-77; mem. lawyers adv. com. U.S. Ct. Appeals, 5th Cir., 1985-87. Bd. dirs. prison ministry Kairos, Inc. of Tex., 1990-96, chmn., 1992; mem. nat. bd. Kairos Inc., 1991-96, sec., 1992-96; lay eucharistic min. Episc. Ch. Capt. AUS, 1942-46. Decorated Bronze Star. Fellow Tex. Bar Found., Southwestern Legal Found.; mem. ABA (chmn. sect. jud. adinstrn. 1970-71, ho. dels. 1971-74, sect. litigation, co-editor Antitrust Litigator 1988-92), Inst. Jud. Adminstrn. N.Y.C., Nat. Assn. Former U.S. Attys. (bd. dirs. 1990-93), Nat. Inst. for Trial Advocacy (dir. 1970-83), Fed. Bar Assn., Am. Judicature Soc., Ft. Worth Club, City Club (Dallas), Delta Tau Delta, Phi Alpha Delta, Pi Sigma Alpha. Home: 3701 Turtle Creek Blvd Apt 8H Dallas TX 75219-5530 Office: Clark West Keller Butler & Ellis 4800 Renaissance Tower Dallas TX 75270-2146

WESTBERG, JOHN AUGUSTIN, lawyer; b. Springfield, Mass., Oct. 12, 1931; s. Carl Joseph and Elizabeth Rebecca (Glassmire) W.; BA, Coll. William and Mary, 1955; JD, U. Va., 1959; m. Mina Lari, Aug. 21, 1976; children: Christine, Steven, Jennifer, Saman. Bar: N.Y. 1960, D.C. 1969, U.S. Supreme Ct. 1968. Assoc. Lord, Day and Lord, N.Y.C., 1959-64; legal adv. AID, Washington, 1964-65, regional legal adv. for Mid. East, Am. Embassy, Teheran, Iran, also AID affairs officer, 1965-68; founder John A. Westberg & Assocs., Inc., Teheran, 1968, pres., 1968-79; ptnr. Wald, Harkrader & Ross, London and Washington, 1981-87; pvt. practice, Washington, 1987-89; ptnr., Westberg & Johnson, Washington, 1989—; bd. dirs. Damavand Coll. Mem. N.Y. County Dem. com., 1963. Served as 1st lt. U.S. Army, 1955-57, Korea. Mem. ABA, Internat. Bar Assn., Am. Soc. Internat. Law, D.C. Bar, Fed. Bar Assn., Iran Am. C. of C. (bd. govs. 1973-77), Shaybani Soc. (v.p.), Cosmos Club. Author: International Transactions and Claims Involving Government Parties--Case Law of the Iran-United States Claims Tribunal, 1991; contbr. articles to bus. and law jours. Avocations: tennis, skiing, biking. Home: 4296 Massachusetts Ave NW Washington DC 20016-5548 Office: 1300 19th St NW Ste 700 Washington DC 20036-1609

WESTBERG, ROBERT MYERS, lawyer; b. Seattle, July 12, 1932; s. Alfred John and Jean Jackson (Myers) W.; m. Nancy Lyon, June 18, 1955; children: R. Britt, Jennifer J., Catherine C. Student, Princeton U., 1950-53; LL.B., U. Wash., 1956. Bar: Calif. 1957, Wash. 1957, D.C. 1981, N.Y. 1983. Ptnr. Pillsbury, Madison & Sutro, San Francisco, 1957—. Bd. dirs. Legal Aid Soc. San Francisco, 1972—. Mem. State Bar Calif., Wash. State Bar Assn., D.C. Bar Assn. Democrat. Episcopalian. Club: Princeton of N.Y. Office: Pillsbury Madison & Sutro 225 Bush St San Francisco CA 94104-4207*

WESTBERRY, BILLY MURRY, lawyer; b. Georgetown, La., Nov. 5, 1926; s. Iley Donley and Julia Frances (Thornton) W.; m. Nancy Elizabeth Kent, Aug. 7, 1953; children—Robert Kent, William Bishop. Student, Murray (Ky.) State U., 1946-48; LL.B., U. Louisville, 1950. Bar: Ky. 1950. Since practiced in Marion; county atty. Crittenden County, 1954-62, 1967-73; city atty. Marion, 1965-67; partner firm Westberry & Hibbs, 1968—; chmn. Jud. Ethics Com. Ky., 1979—; mem. Ky. Commn. Law Enforcement and Crime Prevention, 1968—. Served with USAAF, 1944-45; Served with USAF, 1951-53. Mem. Am. Bar Assn., Ky. Bar Assn. (pres. 1978-79), Crittenden County Bar Assn., Am. Legion. Republican. Episcopalian. Clubs: Rotary, Shriners. Home: 125 Brookfield Dr Paducah KY 42001-5380 Office: 113 S 4th St Paducah KY 42001-0794

WESTBERRY, DAVID M., executive search consultant; b. Savannah, Ga., Aug. 26, 1951; s. John R. and Marianne (Stopfer) W.; m. Carolyn Diane Manton, Apr. 27, 1987. AA, Pensacola Jr. Coll., 1976; BA in Acctg., U. West Fla., Pensacola, 1978. CPA, Fla. Sr. acct. KPMG Peat Marwick, Jacksonville, Fla., 1979-81; v.p. Robert Half Internat., Jacksonville, 1981-82, Pierce Catterton, Houston, 1983; sr. mgr. exec. search KPMG Peat Marwick, Dallas, 1983-89; mng. dir. Ward Howell Internat., Dallas, 1989—, exec. com., 1992—; bd. dirs. Global Am. Trade Corp., Dallas; mem. adv. coun. U. West Fla. Coll. Bus., Pensacola, 1992—. Trustee U. West Fla. Found., Pensacola, 1994—; mem. govt. rels. and met. devel. adv. coun. Greater Dallas Chamber, 1994—; bd. dirs. Girl Scouts of Met. Dallas, 1987-93, Girl Scouts Tejas Coun., 1995—. Sgt. USAF, 1971-74, South Korea. Office: Ward Howell Internat 1601 Elm St Ste 900 Dallas TX 75201-4733

WESTBO, LEONARD ARCHIBALD, JR., electronics engineer; b. Tacoma, Wash., Dec. 4, 1931; s. Leonard Archibald and Agnes (Martinson) W.; B.A. in Gen. Studies, U. Wash., 1958. Electronics engr. FAA, Seattle Air Route Traffic Control Center, Auburn, Wash., 1961-72; asst. br. chief electronics engring. br. 13th Coast Guard Dist., Seattle, 1972-87. Served with USCG, 1951-54, 1958-61. Registered profl. engr., Wash. Mem. Aircraft Owners and Pilots Assn., IEEE, Am. Radio Relay League. Home and Office: 10528 SE 323rd St Auburn WA 98092-4734

WESTBROOK, DON ARLEN, minister; b. Clinton, N.C., June 2, 1941; s. Ennis and Geneva (Gainey) W.; m. Carrol Ann Holder, Sept. 15, 1963; children: Felisha Ann, Neal Vance. Student, Logos Bible Coll./Grad. Sch., 1989, Duke Univ. Ordained to ministry Full Gospel Fellowship Chs. and Mins. Internat., 1965. Pastor Bethel Christian Ctr., Durham, N.C., 1969—; v.p. Full Gospel Fellowship Chs. and Mins. Internat., Dallas, 1982—; missionary to India, Nicaragua and Haiti, 1990. Chmn. Concerned Citizens for Moral Govt., Durham, 1989. Home: 5311 Emeraldwod Dr #B Durham NC 27705 Office: Bethel Christian Ctr 3518 Rose Of Sharon Rd Durham NC 27712-3306

WESTBROOK, JAMES EDWIN, lawyer, educator; b. Camden, Ark., Sept. 7, 1934; s. Loy Edwin and Helen Lucille (Bethea) W.; m. Elizabeth Kay Farris, Dec. 23, 1956; children: William Michael, Robert Bruce, Matthew David. BA with high honors, Hendrix Coll., 1956; JD with distinction, Duke U., 1959; LLM, Georgetown U., 1965. Bar: Ark. 1959, Okla. 1977, Mo. 1982. Assoc. Mehaffy, Smith & Williams, Little Rock, 1959-62; asst. counsel, subcom. of U.S. Senate Jud. Com., Washington, 1963; legis. asst. U.S. Senate, Washington, 1963-65; asst. prof. law U. Mo., Columbia, 1965-68, asst. dean, 1966-68, assoc. prof., 1968-70, prof., 1970-76, 80—, James S. Rollins prof. law, 1974-76, 80—, Earl F. Nelson prof. law, 1982—, interim dean, 1981-82; dean U. Okla. Coll. Law, Norman, 1976-80; George Allen vis. prof. law, U. Richmond, 1987; vis. prof. law Duke U., 1988; arbitrator on roster of Fed. Mediation and Conciliation Service, 1974—; reporter Mid-Am. Assembly on Role of State in Urban Crisis, 1970; dir. Summer Internship Program in Local Govt., 1968; cons. various Mo. cities on drafting home-rule charters; mem. Gov.'s Adv. Council on Local Govt. Law, 1967-68, Fed. Practice Com. U.S. Dist. Ct. (we. dist.) Mo., 1986-90; chmn. Columbia Charter Revision Commn., 1973-74; mem. spl. com. labor relations Mo. Dept. Labor and Indsl. Relations, 1975; mem. Task Force on Gender and Justice, Mo. Jud. Conf., 1990-93; mem. com. to rev. govtl. structure of Boone County, Mo., 1991. Author: (with L. Riskin) Dispute Resolution and Lawyers, 1987, supplement, 1993; contbr. articles to profl. jours. Chair search com. for chancellor U. Mo., Columbia, 1992. Mem. ABA, Nat. Acad. Arbitrators, Assn. Am. Law Schs. (chmn. local govt. law round table coun. 1972), Ctrl. States Law Sch. Assn. (pres. 1982-83), Mo. Bar Assn. (vice chmn. labor law com. 1986-87, chmn. 1987-88, Spurgeon Smithton award 1995), Order of Coif, Blue Key, Alpha Chi. Roman Catholic. Home: 3609 S Woods Edge Rd Columbia MO 65203-6606 Office: U Mo Sch Law Columbia MO 65211

WESTBROOK, JAY LAWRENCE, law educator; b. Morristown, N.J., Dec. 11, 1943; s. Joel W. and Elaine Frances (Summers) W.; m. Pauline June Travis, Feb. 15, 1969; 1 child, Joel Mastin. BA in Polit. Sci./Philosophy, U. Tex., 1965, JD, 1968. Bar: Tex. 1968, D.C. 1969, U.S. Ct. Appeals (D.C. cir.) 1969, U.S. Supreme Ct. 1976, U.S. Ct. Appeals (4th cir.) 1978, U.S. Ct. Appeals (2d cir.) 1979. Assoc. Surrey & Morse (name now Jones, Day, Reavis, Pogue), Washington, 1969-74; ptnr. Surrey & Morse (name now Jones, Day, Reavis, Pogue, Surrey & Morse), Washington, 1974-80; mem. law faculty U. Tex., Austin, 1980—, Benno C. Schmidt Chair Bus. Law, 1991—; vis. prof. U. London, 1990, Harvard Law Sch., 1991-92; advisor Tex. Internat. Law Jour., 1985-91; reporter Am. Law Inst. Transnat. Insolvency Project, 1994—; co-leader U.S. delegation to UN Commn. on Internat. Trade Law Working Group on Model Law Internation Insolvency, 1995—. Co-author: As We Forgive Our Debtors: Bankruptcy and Consumer Credit in America, 1989 (Silver Gavel award ABA 1989), The Law of Debtors and Creditors: Text, Cases and Problems, 3d edit., 1996, Teacher's Manual, The Law of Debtors and Creditors, 3d edit., 1996; contbr. articles to profl. jours. Grantee U. Tex. Law Sch. Found., 1982, U. Rsch. Inst., 1982-83, NSF, 1983-86, Policy Rsch. Inst., Lyndon Johnson Sch. Pub. Affairs, 1984, Tex. Bar Found., 1985, Nat. Inst. Child Health and Human Devel., 1986, Nat. Conf. Bankruptcy Judges, 1991, 93. Mem. ABA (bus. bankruptcy com., internat. bankruptcy subcom., internat. sect., Meyer rsch. grant 1986), Am. Law Inst., Am. Coll. Bankruptcy, Nat. Bankruptcy Conf., State Bar Tex. (governing coun. internat. sect. 1987-89), Internat. Bar Assn., Internat. Bankruptcy Com. (com. J), Internat. Acad. Comml. and Consumer Law, Order of Coif. Office: U Tex Sch Law 727 E 26th St Austin TX 78705-3224

WESTBROOK, JOEL WHITSITT, III, lawyer; b. San Angelo, Tex., June 19, 1916; s. Lawrence Whittington and Minnie Frances (Millspaugh) W.; m. Elaine Frances Summers, Feb. 13, 1943; 1 son, Jay Lawrence. Student, U. Va., 1934-35; B.A., U. Tex., 1937, J.D., 1940. Bar: Tex. 1940. 1st asst. U.S. Atty., San Antonio, 1946-51; 1st asst. dist. atty. Bexar County, San Antonio, 1951-52; dist. atty. pro tem, 1956; pvt.practice San Antonio, 1952-54; partner Trueheart, McMillan, Russell & Westbrook, San Antonio, 1954-61; ptnr. Jones, Boyd, Westbrook & Lovelace, Waco, Tex., 1962-68, Sheehy, Cureton, Westbrook, Lovelace & Nielsen, Waco, 1968-74, Trueheart, McMillan, Westbrook & Hoffman, San Antonio, 1974-80, Westbrook & Goldston, 1980-81, Westbrook Schroeder & Piker, San Antonio, 1981-84; pvt. practice San Antonio, 1984—; adj. prof. criminal law, legal ethics and evidence St. Mary's Sch. Law, San Antonio, 1957-61, 74-76; adj. prof. med. malpractice U. Tex. Law Sch., Austin, 1985, 86. Author: (with others) Texas Torts and Remedies, 1987; contbr. articles to legal and mil. jours. Chmn. San Antonio Crime Prevention Com., 1954-56; pres. Action Planning Coun., Waco, 1966-68; chmn. Waco-McLennan County Mental Health-Mental Retardation Bd. Trustees, 1967-70; pres. adv. bd. Providence Hosp., Waco, 1969-70, Model City com., Waco, 1969-72, chmn., 1971-72. Served to maj., inf. AUS, 1940-46, ETO, MTO. Decorated Combat Inf. badge, Silver Star, Bronze Star, Purple Heart. Fellow Tex. Bar Found. (life sustaining, charter); mem. Waco-McLennan County Bar Assn. (bd. dirs. 1963-66), San Antonio Bar Assn. (pres. 1957-58), State Bar of Tex. (bd. dirs. 1965-68, chmn. com. for local bar svcs. 1968-76, chmn. com. for legal svcs. to elderly 1976-79, mem. com. for ct. costs and delay 1980-81, mem. coll. bd. 1981-83, vice chmn. membership rels. 1981-83, mem. history and traditions of bar 1983—, chmn. spl. projects), Tex. Assn. Def. Counsel (v.p. 1970-71), U. Tex. Law Sch. Alumni Assn. (dir. 1969-72), Mil. Order World Wars (comdr. San Antonio chpt. 1952-53), Delta Theta Phi, Sigma Alpha Epsilon. Episcopalian. Clubs: Giraud (San Antonio); Army-Navy (Washington). Episcopalian. Home: 7709 Broadway St Apt 208 San Antonio TX 78209-3203 *I have expected responsibility in others, and I have wanted others to expect responsibility in me.*

WESTBROOK, JUANITA JANE, school administrator; b. Clarksville, Tex., July 15, 1947; d. James L. and S. Juanita (Dawson) Jamison; children: Jennifer L. Westbrook Cooper, Jayme Lee Westbrook. BS in Bus. Adminstrn./Edn., East Tex. State U., 1968; MS in Adult/Continuing Edn./Pers. Mgmt., U. North Tex., 1986. Cert. in mid-mgmt. adminstrn., supt. Tchr. Carroll Ind. Sch. Dist., Southlake, Tex., 1968-69; exec. sec. Tex. Instruments, Dallas, 1969-70; part-time instr. San Jacinto Coll., Pasadena, Tex., 1975-77, North Tex. State U., Denton, 1977-78; adminstrv. asst./sec. Halliburton Svcs., Duncan, Okla., 1978-80; part-time instr. Weatherford (Tex.) Coll., 1980-81; cmty. edn. coord., high sch. tchr. Weatherford Ind. Sch. Dist., 1981-82, cmty. svcs. dir., 1986—; cmty. edn. dir. Springtown (Tex.) Ind. Sch. Dist., 1982-86; cons. Tri-County Tech. Consortium, Hubbard, Tex., 1994—; cons./grant writer Parker County Counseling Coop, Poolville, Tex., 1992-93; presenter/lectr. in field. Editor: Texas Star newspaper, 1990-92, Texas Community Educator's Practitioners Manual, 1993. Bd. dirs. Palo Pinto Cmty. Svcs., Mineral Wells, Tex., 1994—, United Way, Springtown Friends of Libr., Tex. Bus. and Edn. Coalition; grant rev. com. North Ctrl. Tex. COG, Arlington, 1994—; bd. dirs. Parker County Com. on Aging, Weatherford, 1990-93; exec. dir. Parker County Adult Literacy Coun., Weatherford, 1987—; exec. bd. Practical Parent Edn., Parker County Parenting Coalition. Named First Lady of Springtown, City of Springtown, 1984. Mem. ASCD, Tex. Cmty. Edn. Assn. (sec., pres. 1988-93, Bright Idea award 1983), Tex. Sch. Pub. Rels. Assn. (Star awards 1989-94), Tex. Assn. Sch. Adminstrs., Tex. Assn. for Alternative Edn., Assn. Tex. Profl. Educators, Nat. Assn. Ptnrs. in Edn., Nat. Cmty. Edn. Assn. (Region IV conf. program chair 1991-92, nat. conf. program co-chair 1990), Nat. Com. State Cmty. Edn. Assns. (liaison 1991-92), Nat. Dropout Prevention Network, Nat. Sch. Pub. Rels. Assn., Tex. Assn. for Continuing Adult Edn., Tex. Assn. Supervision and Curriculum Devel., Tex. Coun. of Adult Edn. Coop Dirs., Tex. Assn. for Sch.-Age Childcare, Weatherford C. of C. Avocations: reading, crafts, sewing, gardening. Office: Weatherford Ind Sch Dist PO Box 439 Weatherford TX 76086-0439

WESTBROOK, NICHOLAS KILMER, museum administrator, historian; b. Boston, July 10, 1948; s. Jack Hall and Elizabeth (Kirkland) W.; m. Virginia Lee Macleod, June 12, 1971; children: Benjamin Macoun, Samuel Farley. AB cum laude, Amherst Coll., 1971; MA, U. Conn., 1973; post-grad., U. Pa., 1973-76. Seasonal ranger-historian Nat. Park Svc., Stillwater, N.Y., 1969-71; asst. to v.p. for interpretation Old Sturbridge Village, Sturbridge, Mass., 1972-75; ednl. materials developer Uni-Coll Corp., Phila., 1975-76; exhibits coord. Minn. Hist. Soc., St. Paul, 1976-78, curator of exhibits, 1978-88; exec. dir. Ft. Ticonderoga, Ticonderoga, N.Y., 1989—; panelist NEH, Washington, 1985—, Inst. Mus. Svcs., Washington, 1991—; bd. dirs. N.Y. State Mil. Heritage Mus. Editor: Industrial Archeology of the Twin Cities, 1983, Bull. Ft. Ticonderoga Mus., 1991—; book rev. editor Indsl. Archeology, 1983-89; curator several exhibits. Trustee Fedn. for Hist. Svcs., 1990-94, treas., 1992-94; bd. dirs. Mohican coun. Boy Scouts Am. Winston Churchill travelling fellow Gt. Britain, 1981, Andrew W. Mellon fellowship, 1995. Mem. Soc. for Indsl. Archaeology (bd. dirs. 1983-85, sec. 1986-91), Am. Assn. for State and Local History, Am. Assn. Mus., Soc. for History of Tech., Am. Printing History Assn., Mus. Assn. N.Y. (councillor 1995-98), Ticonderoga C. of C. (v.p. 1989-94, bd. dirs. 1995—), Antiquarian Soc., Kiwanis. Presbyterian. Avocation: letterpress printing. Home: Creek Rd Box 8 Crown Point NY 12928 Office: Ft Ticonderoga Fort Rd Ticonderoga NY 12883

WESTBROOK, SUSAN ELIZABETH, horticulturist; b. Canton, Ohio, Sept. 27, 1939; d. Walter Simon and Rosella Hunt Tolley; m. Edward D. Westbrook, July 2, 1966 (div. 1980); 1 child, Tyler Hunt. Student, Smithdeal-Massey, Richmond, Va., 1958-59; student in Spanish, U. Honduras, 1960; student biology/geology, Mary Washington Coll., 1960, 72, 73; student hort., Prince Georges Community Coll., 1987-88. Farm owner Spotsylvania, Va., 1972-83; office mgr. Tolley Investments, Inc., Fredericksburg, Va., 1980-83; real estate agt. Cooper Realty, Fredericksburg, Va., 1981-83; salesperson Meadows Farms Nursery, Chantilly, Va., 1986-93; student Geology Dept. Mary Washington Coll., Fredericksburg, Va., 1993—; master gardener Va. Poly. Inst., 1993. Author booklets: Japanese Maples, 1990, Fruit Trees, 1989; author radio format: Gardening in Virginia, 1960; co-author computer program: Plantscape, 1990. Sec. Rep. Party, Spotsylvania, 1972-83, Elko County, Nev., 1968; judge Bd. Elections, Spotsylvania, 1980-83, cand. bd. suprs., 1979. Named Master Gardener Va. Poly. Inst., Blacksburg, Va., 1993. Mem. Nat. Wildlife Fedn., Md. Nurserymen's Assn., Friends of the Nat. Arboretum. Avocations: travel, gardening, plant research and identification. Home: 6110 S Virginia Ln PO Box 8 Dahlgren VA 22448

WESTBROOK, T. L., bishop. Bishop of Wash. Ch. of God in Christ, Spanaway.

WESTER, KEITH ALBERT, film and television recording engineer, television executive; b. Seattle, Feb. 21, 1940; s. Albert John and Evelyn Grayce (Nettell) W.; m. Judith Elizabeth Jones, 1968 (div. Mar. 1974); 1 child, Wendy Elizabeth. AA, Am. River Coll., Sacramento, 1959; BA, Calif. State U., L.A., 1962; MA, UCLA, 1965. Lic. multi-engine rated pilot. Prodn. asst. Sta. KCRA-TV, Sacramento, 1956; announcer Sta. KSFM, Sacramento, 1960; film editor, sound rec. technician Urie & Assocs., Hollywood, Calif., 1963-66; co-owner Steckler-Wester Film Prodns., Hollywood, 1966-70; owner Profl. Sound Recorders, Studio City, Calif., 1970—, Aerocharter, Studio City, 1974—; owner Wester Devel., Sun Valley, Coeur d'Alene, Idaho, 1989—, also Studio City, 1989—; majority stockholder Sta. KDQ-TV, Coeur d'Alene/Spokane, Idaho, 1993—. Prodn. sound mixer for following films: Shadow Conspiracy, 1996, Navy Cross, 1996, The Rock, 1996, Waterworld, 1995 (Acad. award nominee with Steve Maslow and Gregg Landaker for best sound 1996), The Shadow, 1994, Wayne's World II, 1993, Coneheads, 1993, Body of Evidence, 1992, Indecent Proposal, 1992, School Ties, 1991, Frankie and Johnny, 1991, Thelma and Louise, 1990, Shattered, 1990, Desperate Hours, 1989, Joe vs the Volcano, 1989, Black Rain, 1989, Sea of Love, 1988, Real Men, 1985, Mask, 1984, Thief of Hearts, 1983, Young Doctors in Love, 1982, First Monday in October, 1981. Mem. NATAS (Emmy award An Early Frost 1986, Emmy nominations in 1982, 84, 85, 87), Acad. Motion Picture Arts and Scis. (Acad. award nomination for best sound Black Rain 1990), Cinema Audio Soc. (sec. 1985-91, Sound award 1987), Soc. Motion Picture and TV Engrs., Internat. Sound Technicians, Local 695, Assn. Film Craftsmen (sec. 1967-73, treas. 1973-76), Screen Actors Guild, Aircraft Owners and Pilots Assn. (Confederate Air Force col.), Am. Radio Relay League. Home: 4146 Bellingham Ave Studio City CA 91604-1601 Office: Profl Sound Recorders 22440 Clarendon St Woodland Hills CA 91367-4467

WESTERBECK, DANIEL J., lawyer; b. Cin., Mar. 21, 1944; s. Daniel John and Marie Therese (Flaherty) W.; m. Annabelle Parry, Oct. 19, 1968; 1 child, Scott. BSBA, Ohio State U., 1967; JD, U. Cin., 1972, MBA, 1973. Bar: Ohio 1972, Ind. 1972, U.S. Tax Ct. 1972, Mich. 1974, U.S. Supreme Ct. 1976, U.S. Ct. Appeals (10th cir.) 1983, U.S. Ct. Appeals (7th cir.) 1985. Salesman IBM Corp., Cin., 1967-69; trial atty. Office Regional Counsel, IRS, Detroit, 1972-77; asst. tax counsel Santa Fe Pacific Corp., Chgo., 1977-84, asst. v.p., gen. tax counsel, 1984-88; v.p., tax counsel Santa Fe So. Pacific Corp., Chgo., 1988—. Mem. ABA, Ohio Bar Assn., Ind. Bar Assn., Mich. Bar Assn., Chgo. Athletic Assn., Beta Theta Pi. Avocations: tennis, golf, sailing. Office: Burlington Northern Santa Fe 1700 E Golf Rd Schaumburg IL 60173

WESTERBECK, KENNETH EDWARD, retired insurance company executive; b. Des Moines, Sept. 5, 1919; s. Joseph David and Florence Alice (King) W.; m. Miriam M. Martens, Jan. 24, 1942; children: Kent E., Marcia M. Westerbeck Waltersheide. D.B.A., Upper Iowa U., 1979. With Equitable Life Ins. Co. of Iowa, 1938-84; v.p., chief fin. officer Equitable of Iowa Cos., 1977-84, v.p., treas., 1980-84; v.p., sec. Equitable Life Ins. Co. of Iowa, 1973-84; ret., 1984; pres. Equitable Investment Svcs. Inc., Des Moines, 1982-84. Bd. Trustees Upper Iowa U.; bd. dirs. A.R.C.; mem. West Des Moines City Council, 1976-93. Mem. Des Moines Soc. Fin. Analysts. Republican. Presbyterian. Home: 715 10th St West Des Moines IA 50265-3506

WESTERBERG, ARTHUR WILLIAM, chemical engineering educator; b. St. Paul, Oct. 9, 1938; s. Kenneth Waldorf and Marjorie Claire (Darling) W.; m. Barbara Ann Dyson, July 14, 1963; children: Kenneth, Karl. B.S., U. Minn., 1960; M.S., Princeton U., 1961; Ph.D., Imperial Coll., London, 1964. Pres. Farm Engring. Sales Inc., Savage, Minn., 1964-65; sr. analyst Control Data Corp., San Diego, Calif., 1965-67; asst. prof., assoc. prof., prof. U. Fla., Gainesville, 1967-76; prof. chem. engring. Carnegie-Mellon U., Pitts., 1976—, chmn. dept., 1980-83, Swearingen prof., 1982—, dir. Design Research Ctr., 1978-80, Univ. prof., 1992—; dir. Engring. Design Research Ctr., 1986-89. Co-author: Process Flowsheeting, 1979. Fellow AIChE (lectr. 1989, Computers and Systems Tech. divsn. award 1983, Walker award 1987, McAfee award 1990, Founders Outstanding Contbns. Chem. Engring. award 1995); mem. NAE, Am. Soc. Engring. Edn. (chem. engring. divsn. lectr. 1981). Home: 5564 Beacon St Pittsburgh PA 15217-1972 Office: Engring Dept Carnegie Mellon U Pittsburgh PA 15213

WESTERDAHL, JOHN BRIAN, nutritionist, health educator; b. Tucson, Dec. 3, 1954; s. Jay E. and Margaret (Meyer) W.; m. Doris Mui Lian Tan, Nov. 18, 1989. AA, Orange Coast Coll., 1977; BS, Pacific Union Coll., 1979; MPH, Loma Linda U., 1981. Registered dietitian; chartered herbalist;

cert. nutrition specialist. Nutritionist, health educator Castle Med. Ctr., Kailua, Hawaii, 1981-84, health promotion coord., 1984-87, asst. dir. health promotion, 1987-88, dir. health promotion, 1988-89; dir. nutrition and health rsch. Health Sci., Santa Barbara, Calif., 1989-90; sr. nutritionist, project mgr. Shaklee Corp., San Francisco, 1990-96; dir. nutrition Dr. McDougall's Right Foods, Inc., South San Francisco, 1996—; talk show host Nutrition and You, Sta. KGU Radio, Honolulu, 1983-89; nutrition com. mem. Hawaii div. Am. Heart Assn., Honolulu, 1984-87; mem. nutrition study group Govs. Conf. Health Promotion and Disease Prevention for Hawaii, 1985. Editor: Nourish Mag.; nutrition editor: Veggie Life Mag., 1995—. Mem. AAAS, Am. Coll. Sports Medicine, Am. Dietetic Assn., Am. Nutritionists Assn., Am. Coll. Nutrition, Soc. for Nutrition Edn., Nat. Wellness Assn., Nutrition Today Soc., Am. Soc. Pharmacognosy, Inst. Food Technologists, Hawaii Nutrition Coun. (v.p. 1983-86,m pres.-elect 1988-89, pres. 1989), Hawaii Dietetic Assn., Calif. Dietetic Assn., N.Y. Acad. Scis., Seventh-day Adventist Dietetic Assn., several other profl. assns. Republican. Seventh-Day Adventist. Avocations: swimming, scuba diving. Office: Dr McDougall's Right Foods 101 Utah Ave South San Francisco CA 94080 *Personal philosophy: "Beloved, I wish above all things that thou mayest prosper and be in health, even as thy soul prospereth." 3 John 2.*

WESTERFIELD, HOLT BRADFORD, political scientist, educator; b. Rome, Italy, Mar. 7, 1928; s. Ray Bert and Mary Beatrice (Putney) W.; m. Carolyn Elizabeth Hess, Dec. 17, 1960; children: Pamela Bradford, Leland Avery. Grad., Choate Sch., 1944; BA, Yale U., 1947; MA, Harvard U., 1951, PhD, 1952. Instr. govt. Harvard U., 1952-56; asst. prof. polit. sci. U. Chgo., 1956-57; mem. faculty Yale U., 1957—, prof. polit. sci., 1965—, chmn. dept., 1970-72, Damon Wells prof. internat. studies, 1985—; research asso. Washington Center Fgn. Policy Research, Johns Hopkins Sch. Advanced Internat. Studies, 1965-66; vis. prof. Wesleyan U., Middletown, Conn., 1967, 71. Author: Foreign Policy and Party Politics: Pearl Harbor to Korea, 1955, The Instruments of America's Foreign Policy, 1963; editor: Inside CIA's Private World: Declassified Articles from the Agency's Internal Journal, 1955-92, 1995. Sheldon traveling fellow Harvard, 1951-52; Henry L. Stimson fellow Yale, 1962, 73; sr. Fulbright-Hays scholar, 1973; hon. vis. fellow Australian Nat. U., 1973. Mem. Am. Polit. Sci. Assn. (Congl. fellow 1953-54), Internat. Polit. Sci. Assn., Internat. Studies Assn. Home: 115 Rogers Rd Hamden CT 06517-3533 Office: Yale Univ Dept Polit Sci PO Box 208301 New Haven CT 06520-8301

WESTERFIELD, PUTNEY, management consulting executive; b. New Haven, Feb. 9, 1930; s. Ray Bert and Mary Beatrice (Putney) W.; m. Anne Montgomery, Apr. 17, 1954; children: Bradford, Geoffrey, Clare. Grad., Choate Sch., 1942-47; B.A., Yale, 1951. Co-founder, v.p. Careers, Inc., N.Y.C., 1950-52; mgr. S.E. Asia Swen Publs., Inc., Manila, Philippines, 1952; mem. joint adv. commn. Korea, 1953-54; polit. officer Am. embassy, Saigon, Vietnam, 1955-57; asst. to pub. Time mag., N.Y.C., 1957-59, asst. circulation dir., 1959-61; circulation dir. Time mag., 1961-66, asst. pub., 1966-68; asst. pub. Life mag., N.Y.C., 1968; pub. Fortune mag., N.Y.C., 1969-73; pres. Chase World Info. Corp., N.Y.C., 1973-75; v.p. Boyden Assocs. Internat., San Francisco, 1976-80, sr. v.p., western mgr., 1980-84; pres., chief exec. officer Boyden Assocs. Internat., N.Y.C. and San Francisco, 1984-90, mng. dir., 1990—; bd. dirs. Upside Publ. Co. Bd. dirs. Urban League, N.Y.C., 1969-71, Children's Village, 1968-71, Mediterranean Sch. Found., 1969-71, Nat. Boys Club, 1970-73, U.S. -S. Africa Leaders Exch. Program, 1971—, Bus. Coun. for Internat. Understanding, 1974-76, Yale-China Assn., 1975-78, East Meets West Found., 1991—; trustee Choate Sch., Wallingford, Conn., 1967-76, Westover Sch., Middlebury, Conn., 1975-79, Watch Hill Chapel Soc., 1963-77, Assn. Yale Alumni, 1972-75, 80-83. Mem. Burlingame Country Club, Pacific Union Club, Bohemian Club. Home: 10 Greenview Ln Hillsborough CA 94010-6424 Office: Boyden Internat 275 Battery St Ste 420 San Francisco CA 94111-3331

WESTERGAARD, NEIL, editor; b. Chgo.; m. Cynthia; children: Ben, Rachel. Polit. reporter, asst. city editor Colorado Springs Sun; with The Denver Post, 1982—, exec. editor, 1991—. Office: Denver Post 1560 Broadway Denver CO 80202-5133

WESTERGAARD, PETER TALBOT, composer, music educator; b. Champaign, Ill., May 28, 1931; s. Harald Malcolm and Rachel (Talbot) W.; m. Barbara Jay, Sept. 11, 1955; children: Elizabeth, Margaret. BA, Harvard, 1953; MFA, Princeton, 1956. Fulbright guest lectr. Staatliche Hochschule, Freiburg, Germany, 1957-58; instr. Columbia, 1958-63, asst. prof., 1963-66; vis. lectr. Princeton U., 1966-67; assoc. prof. Amherst Coll., Mass., 1967-68; from assoc. prof. music to prof. Princeton U., 1968—, chmn. dept. music, 1974-78, 83-86, William Shubael Conant prof. music, 1995—, acting chair, Dept. Music, 1995—; vis. prof. U. B.C., 1987; lectr. internat. music seminar Univ. Bahia, Brazil, 1992; endowed prof. U. Ala., 1995. Condr. Princeton U. Orch., 1968-73; dir. Princeton U. Opera Theater, 1970—, June Opera Festival of N.J., 1983-86; composer: Cantata I (The Plot Against the Giant, 1956, Five Movements for Small Orchestra, 1958, Cantata II (A Refusal to Mourn the Death, by Fire, of a Child in London), 1985, Quartet for Violin, Vibraphone, Clarinet and Violoncello, 1960, Spring and Fall, To a Young Child, 1960, 64, Cantata III (Leda and the Swan), 1961, Trio for Flute, Violoncello and Piano, 1962, Variations for Six Players, 1963, Mr. and Mrs. Discobbolos, 1965, Divertimento on Discobbolic Fragments, 1967, Noises, Sounds and Sweet Airs, 1968, Tuckets and Sennets, 1969, Moto Perpetuo for Six Wind Industruments, 1976, Alonso's Grief, 1977, There Was a Little Man, 1979, Ariel Music, 1987, Two Fanfares, 1988, Ariel Songs, 1988, Ode, 1989,The Tempest, 1990, Ringing Changes (for orchestra), 1995; author: Introduction to Tonal Theory, 1975; translator operas: The Magic Flute, 1977, Don Giovanni, 1979, Der Freischutz, 1980, Fidelio (original version of 1805), 1982, Cosi fan tutte, 1983, The Marriage of Figaro, 1984, Cinderella, 1986. Guggenheim fellow, 1964-65, N.J. State Council on the Arts fellow, 1986-87, 89-90; grantee Nat. Endowment for Arts, 1990-91. Office: Princeton U Dept Music Princeton NJ 08544

WESTERHAUS, CATHERINE K., social worker; b. Corydon, Ind., Oct. 13, 1910; d. Anthony Joseph and Permelia Ann (Mathes) Kannapel; m. George Henry Westerhaus, Apr. 15, 1950. BEd in Music, Kans. U., 1934; MSW, Loyola U., Chgo., 1949. Cert. Acad. Cert. Social Workers. Clin. social worker Friendly Acres Home of Aged, Newton, Kans.; county welfare dir., state adult svcs. supr. Newton-Harvey County, State of Kans.; vol. cert. social worker Newton. Project dir.: Memories of War Years, 1995, The War Years Including Veterans of Harvey County, Kansas, 1995; contbr. articles to profl. jours. With USNR, 1945-46. Named Kans. Social Worker of Yr., 1975. Mem. NASW (cert.), Kans. Soc. Cert. Social Work, Am. Legion (comdr. Wayne G. Austin post 1981-82). Home: 313 W Broadway St Newton KS 67114-2631

WESTERHOFF, GARRET PETER, environmental engineer, executive; b. Fairlawn, N.J., Oct. 12, 1935; s. Garret Peter and Elizabeth (Ullmer) W.; m. Helga Ann Kasch, May 31, 1958; children: Garret Peter, Eric John, Paul Keith. BS in Civil Engring., N.J. Inst. Tech., 1957, MS in Sanitary Engring., 1967. Registered profl. engr., N.J., N.Y., Ohio, Va., Ariz., Calif., Md., Fla., Ala., La., Maine, Mass., Nebr., N.Mex., Nev., N.C., Pa., Wash.; cert. profl. planner; diplomate Am. Acad. Environ. Engrs. Loss prevention engr. Factory Mutual Engring. Co., 1960-64; project engr. Jersey Engring. Assocs., 1964-65; from v.p. to exec. v.p. Malcolm Pirnie, Inc., White Plains, N.Y., 1967—; mem. rsch. adv. coun. Nat. Water Rsch. Inst.; internat. rapporteur on water quality and treatment in U.S. Internat. Water Supply Assn., World Congress, Budapest, 1993, Durbon, S. Africa, 1995; tech. cons. Office Drinking Water U.S. EPA; presenter in field. Contbr. articles to profl. jours. 1st lt. USAF, 1957-60. Mem. Am. Water Works Assn. (former stds. coun., chmn. Internat. Water Supply Assn. N.Am. com., former chmn. water supply planning and coord. com., former trustee engring. and constrn. divsn., former chmn. water reuse com., former chmn. water treatment plant wastes disposal com., former chmn. alum recovery rsch. adv. com., rsch. adv. coun. Rsch. Found.), Am. Soc. Civil Engrs., NSPE, Water Environment Fedn. Avocations: fishing, photography, writing. Office: Malcolm Pirnie Inc 102 Corporate Park Dr White Plains NY 10604-3802

WESTERHOFF, JOHN HENRY, III, clergyman, theologian, educator; b. Paterson, N.J., June 28, 1933; s. John Henry and Nona Celia (Walsh) W.; m. Alberta Louise Barnhart, Dec. 27, 1955 (div. 1991); childen: Jill Louise, John Jeffrey, Beth Anne; m. Caroline Askew Hughes, Oct. 27, 1991. BS, Ursinus Coll., 1955; STB, Harvard U., 1958; EdD, Columbia U., 1974; DD, Ursinus Coll., 1990. Ordained to ministry United Ch. of Christ, 1958, Episcopal Ch., 1978; pastor Congl. Ch., Presque Isle, Maine, 1958-60; assoc. pastor Congl. Ch., Needham, Mass., 1960-64; pastor 1st Congl. Ch., Williamstown, Mass., 1964-66; edn. sec., editor Colloquy (United Ch. Bd. for Homeland Ministries), N.Y.C., 1966-73; Lentz lectr. Harvard U. Div. Sch., 1973-74; prof. Duke U. Div. Sch., Durham, N.C., 1974-94; dir. Inst. Pastoral Studies, Atlanta, 1992—; interim rector St. Bartholomew Episcopal Ch., Atlanta, 1993-94; assoc. rector St. Lukes Episcopal Ch., Atlanta, 1994—. Author: Values for Tomorrows Children, 1970, A Colloquy on Christian Education, 1972, Generation to Generation, 1974, Tomorrow's Church, 1976, Will Our Children Have Faith?, 1976, McGuffey and His Readers, 1978, Who Are We?, 1978, Learning Through Liturgy, 1978, Inner Growth-Outer Change, 1979, The Church's Ministry in Higher Education, 1979, Liturgy and Learning Through the Life Cycle, 1980, Christian Believing, 1980, Bringing Up Children in The Christian Church, 1980, A Faithful Church, 1981, The Spiritual Life: Learning East and West, 1981, Building God's People, 1983, A Pilgrim People, 1984, Living the Faith Community, 1985, On the Threshold of God's Future, 1986, Living Into Our Baptism, 1990, Schooling Christians, 1992, The Spiritual Life: Foundation for Preaching and Teaching, 1994; editor: Religious Edn, 1979-89. Mem. Assn. Profs. and Researchers in Religious Edn., Religious Edn. Assn. Democrat. Episcopalian. Office: Saint Luke's Episcopal Ch 435 Peachtree St NE Atlanta GA 30308-3219

WESTERHOUT, GART, retired astronomer; b. The Hague, The Netherlands, June 15, 1927; came to U.S., 1962, naturalized, 1969; s. Gerrit and Magdalena (Foppe) W.; m. Judith Mary Monaghan, Nov. 14, 1956; children: Magda C., Gart T., Brigit M., Julian C., Anthony K. Drs., Leiden U., Netherlands, 1954, Ph.D., 1958. Asst. Leiden U. Observatory, 1952-56, sci. officer, 1956-59, chief sci. officer, 1959-62; prof., dir. astronomy U. Md., 1962-73, chmn. div. math. and phys. scis. and engring., 1972-73, prof. astronomy, 1973-77; sci. dir. U.S. Naval Observatory, Washington, 1977-93; vis. astronomer Max Planck Inst. Radio Astronomy, Bonn, Germany, 1973-74, mem. adv. bd., 1976-79; vice chmn. divsn. phys. sci. NRC, 1969-73; mem. com. on radio frequencies, 1971-92; trustee Assoc. Univs. Inc., 1971-74; mem. Intern Union Commn. on Allocation of Frequencies, 1974-82; mem. sci. coun. Stellar Data Ctr., Strasbourg, France, 1978-84, chmn., 1981; chmn. working group on astrometry, astronomy survey com. NAS, 1979-81; mem. adv. bd. Haystac-N.E. Radio Obs. Consortium, 1974-77; mem. Arecibo adv. bd. Nat. Astronomy and Ionosphere Ctr., 1977-80, chmn., 1979-80. Contbr. on radio astronomy, spiral structure of our galaxy and astrometry to profl. jours. Recipient citation for teaching excellence Washington Acad. Scis., 1972; U.S. Sr. Scientist award Alexander von Humboldt Stiftung, Ger., 1973; NATO fellow, 1959. Mem. Internat. Astron. Union (chmn. working group on astron. data 1985-91), Internat. Sci. Radio Union (pres. commn. on radio astronomy 1975-78), Am. Astron. Soc. (councilor 1975-78, v.p. 1985-87), Royal Astron. Soc. Roman Catholic. Home: 811 W 38th St Baltimore MD 21211-2203

WESTERMAN, ROSEMARY MATZZIE, nurse, administrator; b. Sewickley, Pa., May 20, 1949; d. Joseph Edward and Martha (Aquino) Matzzie; m. Philip M. Westerman, Aug. 7, 1971. BSN, Duquesne U., 1971, MSEd, 1975. RN, Pa. Head nurse Dept. Vet. Affairs VA Med. Ctr., Pitts.; assoc. chief, nursing svc., edn. W. S Middleton Meml. VA Hosp., Madison, Wis.; assoc. chief, nursing svc., edn. Dept. VA Affairs VA Med. Ctr., Chilicothe, assoc. chief nursing svc., long term. care; assoc. chief nurse VA Med. Ctr., Augusta, Ga.; chief nurse VA Med. Ctr., Muskogee, Okla. Active Literacy Vol. of Am. Mem. ANA (cert. nursing adminstrn. advanced), Assoc. Am. Coll. Health Care Execs., Okla. Orgn. Nurse Execs., Okla. Nurses Found., Nursing Orgn. of VA, Okla. Nurses Assn., VA Nurse Execs., Sigma Theta Tau. Home: 1409 E Concord St Broken Arrow OK 74012-9259

WESTERMANN, HORACE CLIFFORD, sculptor; b. Los Angeles, Dec. 11, 1922; s. Horace Clifford and Florita Lynd (Bloom) W.; m. Joanna May Beall, Mar. 31, 1959. Student, Art Inst. Chgo., 1947-50, 52-54. Exhibited in one-man shows Frumkin Gallery, Chgo., 1958, 74, Corcoran Gallery, Los Angeles, 1974, Moore Coll., Phila., 1972, others; group shows Smithsonian Instn., 1974, Guggenheim Mus., N.Y.C., 1970, Carnegie Mus., 1971, Mus. Modern Art, N.Y.C., 1960, Whitney Mus. Am. Art, 1976, Venice Biennale, 1976, others; retrospective exhbns. Los Angeles County Mus., Calif., 1968, Mus. Contemporary Art, Chgo., 1968, Galerie Thomas Borgmann, Cologne, Fed. Republic Germany, 1970, Galerie Neuendorf, Hamburg, Fed. Republic Germany, 1973, Whitney Mus. Am. Art, New Orleans Mus. Art, Des Moines Mus. Art, Seattle Mus. Art, San Francisco Mus. Modern Art, 1978, Serpentine Gallery, London, 1980, Xavier Fourcade, N.Y.C., 1981, John Berggruen Gallery, San Francisco, 1985, Lennon, Weinberg Inc., N.Y.C., 1988, 90; author: Letters from H.C. Westermann, 1988; represented in pvt. collections. Served with USMC, 1942-46, 50-52. Recipient Nat. Arts Council award, 1967, Sao Paulo Biennial award, 1972. Studio: PO Box 5028 Brookfield CT 06804-5028

WESTERTERP, K. ROEL, chemistry educator; b. Beilen, Netherlands, Mar. 5, 1928; s. Murk and Albertine G. (Heijn) W.; m. Lucy G. Schwarz, June 12, 1979; 8 children. MS in Chem. Engring., Delft U., 1952, PhD in Tech. Scis., 1962. Plant supt. Shell, South America, 1952-58; mgr. pilot plants Delft (Netherlands) U., 1958-62; mng. dir. Petrochemie N.V., Delfzijl, 1962-70, Philips Duphar, Amsterdam, 1970-79; prof. chem. tech. Twente U., Enschede, Netherlands, 1979—; cons. in field. Author: Chemical Reactor Design and Operation, 1987; contbr. more than 300 articles to profl. jours. Pres. SCHC Hockey Club, Bilthoven, Netherlands, 1974-79. Mem. European Fedn. Chem. Engring. (pres. gen. assembly 1973, 78), Dechema (hon. mem.). Avocations: golf, electric model trains, history. Home: Mozartlaan 137, 7522 HM Enschede The Netherlands Office: Twente U, PO Box 217, 7500 AE Enschede The Netherlands

WESTERVELT, JAMES JOSEPH, insurance company executive; b. Bklyn., July 8, 1946; s. Cornealius V. and Regina Elizabeth (May) W.; m. Sue Jane Brubaker, Aug. 5, 1972; children: Kevin K., Natalie M. BBA, Manhattan Coll., 1967. Mgr. auditing Peat, Marwick & Mitchell, N.Y.C., 1967-78; dir. auditing City Investing, N.Y.C., 1978-81; asst. v.p., asst. contr. ITT Hartford, Conn., 1981-89, v.p., group contr., 1989-94; sr. v.p., group contr. ITT, Hartford, Conn., 1994—. With U.S. Army, 1968-69. Mem. AICPA, Hawaii Soc. CPAs, Conn. Soc. CPAs, Am. Ins. Assn. Roman Catholic. Avocations: skiing, wine tasting, tennis, chess, electronics. Office: Hartford Fire Insurance Co Hartford Plz Hartford CT 06115*

WESTFALL, BERNARD G., university hospital executive; b. Lockney, W.Va., July 12, 1941; s. Edward C. and Wilma (Dotson) W.; m. Marion Williams, July 26, 1969; 1 child, Gregory. BS, W. Va. U., 1963, MBA, 1972. Tchr. sci. Monongalia County Schs., Morgantown, W.Va., 1963-65; assoc. dir. purchasing W. Va. U., Morgantown, 1965-73; hosp. computer mgr. W. Va. U. Hosp., Morgantown, 1973-74, assoc. adminstr. fin. and systems, 1974-82; interim adminstr. W.Va. U. Hosp., Morgantown, 1982-83, sr. assoc. adminstr., 1983-84, exec. v.p., adminstr., 1984-87, pres., 1987—; bd. dirs. One Valley Bank; guest lectr. W. Va. U., 1984—. Author: Central Breakout at West Virginia University, 1970. Trustee W.Va. Hosp. Assn. Mem. Am. Coll. Hosp. Adminstrs., Hosp. Fin. Mgmt. Assn. Lodge: Rotary. Home: RR 9 Box 69A Morgantown WV 26505-9809*

WESTFALL, CARROLL WILLIAM, architectural historian; b. Fresno, Calif., Dec. 23, 1937; s. Carroll W. and Alice Margaret (DeVore) W.; m. Cheryl Ludwig, June 6, 1964 (div. 1971); m. Relling Rossi, June 26, 1982; children: Nicholas William, John Salvatore. BA, U. Calif., Berkeley, 1961; MArch, U. Manchester, Eng., 1963; PhD, Columbia U., 1967. Asst. prof. Amherst (Mass.) Coll., 1966-72; asst. prof. U. Ill., Chgo., 1972-75, assoc. prof., 1975-82; assoc. prof. U. Va., Charlottesville, 1982-88, prof. archtl. history, 1988—, chmn. dept., 1983-89; cons. in field. Author: In This Most Perfect Paradise, 1974, Italian edit., 1984, (with Robert Jan van Pelt) Architectural Principles in the Age of Historicism, 1991; contbr. articles to profl. jours. Bd. dirs. Landmarks Preservation Coun., Chgo., 1973-82, pres., 1974-76. Mem. Soc. Archtl. Historians, Coll. Art Assn., Nat. Trust Historic Preservation, Cliffdwellers (Chgo.). Republican. Avocation: travel. Home: 1 Cottage Ln Charlottesville VA 22903 Office: Univ Va Sch Architecture Charlottesville VA 22903

WESTFALL, DAVID, lawyer, educator; b. Columbia, Mo., Apr. 16, 1927; s. Wilhelmus David A. and Ruth (Rollins) W.; children: Elizabeth Stewart, William Beatty, Thomas Curwen, Katharine Putnam. AB, U. Mo., 1947; LLB magna cum laude, Harvard U., 1950. Bar: Ill. 1950, Mass. 1956. Assoc. Bell, Boyd, Marshall & Lloyd, Chgo., 1950-55; asst. prof. law Harvard Law Sch., 1955-58, prof., 1958—, John L. Gray prof., 1983—. Author: Estate Planning Cases and Text, 1985, Everly Woman's Guide to Financial Planning, 1984, Family Law, 1993; co-author: Estate Planning Law and Taxation, 3rd edit., 1994; co-editor: Readings in Federal Taxation, 1983. Served as 1st lt. JAGC, AUS, 1951-53. Fellow Am. Coll. Trust and Estate Counsel (acad.); mem. ABA, Mass. Bar Assn., Am. Law Inst., Phi Beta Kappa, Phi Delta Theta. Home: 106 Kendall Rd Lexington MA 02173 Office: Law Sch Harvard U Cambridge MA 02138

WESTFALL, GREGORY BURKE, lawyer; b. Stamford, Tex., June 30, 1963; s. William Jake Westfall and Martha Ann Burke; m. Mollee Elizabeth Bennett, Oct. 1, 1994. BBA with highest honors, U. Tex., Arlington, 1990; JD summa cum laude, Tex. Tech. U., 1993. Bar: Tex. 1993, U.S. Dist. Ct. Tex. (no. dist.) 1993. Assoc. Law Office of Tom Hall, Ft. Worth, 1990-94; assoc. Jeff Kearney & Assocs., Ft. Worth, 1994—. Contbr. articles to profl. jours. Sgt. U.S. Army, 1984-87. Recipient Order of the Coif Tex. Tech. U., 1993. Mem. ATLA, Nat. Assn. Criminal Def. Lawyers, Tex. Trial Lawyers Assn., Tex. Criminal Def. Lawyers Assn., Coll. of State Bar of Tex., Tarrant County Trial Lawyers Assn. (bd. dirs. 1995—), Tarrant County Criminal Def. Lawyers Assn. Office: Jeff Kearney & Assocs 120 W 3rd St Ste 300 Fort Worth TX 76102-7415

WESTFALL, RICHARD SAMUEL, historian; b. Fort Collins, Colo., Apr. 22, 1924; s. Alfred Rensselaer and Dorothy (Towne) W.; m. Gloria Marilyn Dunn, Aug. 23, 1952; children: Alfred, Jennifer, Kristin. B.A., Yale U., 1948; M.A., 1949, Ph.D., 1955; postgrad., London U., 1951-52. Instr. history Calif. Inst. Tech., Pasadena, 1952-53; instr., asst. prof. history State U. Iowa, Iowa City, 1953-57; asst. prof. history Grinnell Coll., 1957-60, assoc. prof., 1960-63; prof. history of sci. Ind. U., Bloomington, 1963-89; prof. history Ind. U., 1965-89, disting. prof. of history and philosophy of sci., 1976-89, chmn. dept., 1967-73; prof. emeritus Ind. U., Bloomington, 1989—. Author: Science and Religion in Seventennth Century England, 1958, Force in Newton's Physics, 1971, Construction of Modern Science, 1971, Never at Rest: A Biography of Isaac Newton, 1980, Essays on the Trial of Galileo, 1990, Life of Isaac Newton, 1993; editor: (with V. E. Thoren) Steps in the Scientific Tradition, 1969, (with I. B. Cohen) Newton, 1995. Mem. United Ministry Bd., Bloomington, 1964-73; elder First Presbyterian Ch., Bloomington. Served with USNR, 1944-46. Fellow Am. Acad. Arts and Scis., Royal Soc. Lit.; mem. AAUP, Am. Hist. Assn. (Leo Gershoy award 1981), History of Sci. Soc. (2d v.p. 1973-74, v.p. 1975-76, pres. 1977-78, Pfizer award 1972, 83, Sarton medal 1985), Societe internationale d'histoire des sciences. Home: 2222 N Browncliff Ln Bloomington IN 47408-1302 Office: Ind Univ Dept Hist & Phil Sci Bloomington IN 47405

WESTFALL, ROBERT VALLEN, religious organization executive; b. Akron, Ohio, July 21, 1961; s. Robert Austin Westfall and Dixie Lee (Engler) Wigbels; m. Sherri Wynn Knight, Aug. 6, 1988; children: Brittni Ann, Jessica Leigh, Austin James. Mgr. restaurant Taco Bell, Atlanta, 1979-81; sales cons. Olan Mills Studios, Atlanta, 1981-82, Photo Promotions Assocs., Atlanta, 1982-84; exec. v.p. Portrait One Studios, Atlanta, 1984-87; v.p. devel., pub. rels. Walk Thru the Bible Ministries, Charlotte, N.C., 1988—; cons. Coppinger & Affiliates, Cleve., Tenn., 1987, Joy Ranch Home for Children, Hixson, Va., 1992—. Republican. Avocations: sports, Bible reading, classical movies. Office: Walk Thru The Bible 1420 Convention Dr Fort Mill SC 29715

WESTFIELD, FRED M., economics educator; b. Essen, Germany, Nov. 7, 1926; came to U.S., 1940; s. Dietrich and Grete (Stern) W.; m. Joyce A. Horwitz Nochlin, Nov. 15, 1968; stepchildren: Steven Nochlin, Keith Nochlin. BA magna cum laude, Vanderbilt U., 1950; PhD in Indsl. Econs., MIT, 1957. Teaching asst., instr. MIT, Cambridge, 1952-53; lectr. Northwestern U., Evanston, Ill., 1953-57, asst. prof., 1957-60, assoc. prof., 1960-65; prof. econs. Vanderbilt U., Nashville, 1965—, mem. faculty coun. Coll. Arts and Sci., 1974-76, mem. faculty senate, 1979-82, 94-95, dir. undergrad. studies dept. econs. and bus. adminstrn., 1984-87, mem. grad. faculty coun., 1991; vis. prof. U. Colo., summers 1973-74; condr. seminars, lectr., participant univs. and rsch. orgns.; Fulbright sr. lectr. U. Nac. del Sur, Argentina, 1986; cons. Coun. Econ. Advisers, Exec. Office Pres., 1968, World Bank and Water and Power Devel. Authority, Pakistan, 1970-72, World Bank and East African Power and Light Co., Kenya, 1975, NSF, 1975, FTC, 1976-78, World Bank, UN Devel. Program and Econ. Planning Bd. South Korea, 1975-76; expert witness Tenn. Pub. Svc. Commn., 1980-89, Consumer Advocate Tenn. Atty. Gen., 1994; also others. Mem. editorial bd. Utilities Policy, 1990—; mem. bd. editors So. Econ. Jour., 1973-75; editorial referee Am. Econ. Rev., Jour. Polit. Economy, Econometrica, So. Econ. Jour., Econ. Inquiry; contbr. articles and book revs. to profl. jours. With U.S. Army, 1945-46. Fellow Gen. Edn. Bd., MIT, Ford Found., 1958-59. Mem. Am. Econ. Assn., Econometric Soc. (program com. 1967, chmn. conf. sessions), So. Econ. Assn. (v.p. 1976-77, chmn. conf. sessions), Phi Beta Kappa. Home: 1097 Lynnwood Blvd Nashville TN 37215-4540 Office: Vanderbilt U PO Box 1681 Sta B Nashville TN 37235

WESTHAVER, LAWRENCE ALBERT, electronics engineer, consultant; b. Washington, Oct. 24, 1936; s. James Waldo and Hattie Virginia (Bush) W.; m. Jo Ann Turner, Jan. 5, 1957; children: Lawrence Albert Jr., Wendy Jo Westhaver Burke, Bonnie Jo. Cert. engring., U. Va., 1966. Electronic design, cons. Westhaver Assocs., Inc., Laurel, Md., 1971—; engring. draftsman Office Rsch. and Devel. Nat. Security Agy., Arlington Hall, Va., 1955-57; engring. technician Office Rsch. and Engring. Nat. Security Agy., Ft. G.G. Meade, Md., 1958-66, electronic engr. Office Rsch. and Engring., 1967-82, sr. engr. Office of Rsch. and Engring., 1982-84; sr. engr. Communications Systems Support Group, Laurel, Md., 1984-93. Patentee method for photographic aperture control, photographic light integrator, switching current regulator, photographic test equipment, electronic tuner for stringed musical instruments, microcomputer-based Ni-Cd battery charger, and color-correcting filter for underwater photography. Avocations: scuba diving, snorkeling, biking, hiking, bird watching. Home: 8609 Portsmouth Dr Laurel MD 20708-1819

WESTHEIMER, DAVID KAPLAN, novelist; b. Houston, Apr. 11, 1917; s. Adolf and Esther (Kaplan) W.; m. Doris Gertrude Rothstein, Oct. 9, 1945; children: Fred, Eric. B.A., Rice Inst., Houston, 1937. Successively asst. amusement editor, radio editor, mag. editor, TV editor Houston Post, 1939-41, 45-46, 50, 53-60, columnist, 1984-88. Author: Summer on the Water, 1948, The Magic Fallacy, 1950, Watching Out for Dulie, 1960, Von Ryan's Express, 1964, My Sweet Charlie, 1965, Song of the Young Sentry, 1968, Lighter Than a Feather, 1971, Over the Edge, 1972, Going Public, 1973, Tha Avila Gold, 1974, The Olmec Head, 1974, Rider on the Wind, 1979, Von Ryan's Return, 1980, (with John Sherlock) The Amindra Gamble, 1982, Sitting It Out, 1992, Death Is Lighter Than a Feather, 1995, (with Karen Westheimer) LoneStar Zodiac, 1995, (play) My Sweet Charlie, 1966, (TV films) Trouble Comes to Town, 1972, A Killer Among Us, 1990. Served to capt. USAAF, 1941-45, ETO; served to capt. USAF, 1950-53; lt. col. USAF; ret. Decorated Air medal, D.F.C. Mem. ACLU, NAACP, PEN, Writer's Guild Am. West. Author's Guild, Ret. Officer Assn., Calif. Writers Club. Democrat. Avocations: travel, reading, walking. Home and Office: 11722 Darlington Ave Apt 2 Los Angeles CA 90049-5525

WESTHEIMER, FRANK HENRY, chemist, educator; b. Balt., Jan. 15, 1912; s. Henry Ferdinand and Carrie (Burgunder) W.; m. Jeanne Friedmann, Aug. 31, 1937; children: Ruth Susan, Ellen. AB, Dartmouth Coll., 1932, ScD (hon.), 1961; MA, Harvard U., 1933, PhD, 1935; ScD (hon.), U. Chgo., 1973, U. Cin., 1976, Tufts U., 1978, U. N.C., 1983, Bard Coll., 1983, Weizmann Inst., 1987, U. Ill. at Chgo., 1988. Rsch. assoc. U. Chgo., 1936-37, instr., 1937-41, asst. prof., 1941-44, assoc. prof., 1946-48, prof. chemistry, 1948-53; vis. prof. Harvard U., 1953-54, prof. chemistry, 1954-82, sr. prof., 1982-83, prof. emeritus, 1983—, chmn. dept., 1959-62; Overseas fellow Churchill Coll., U. Cambridge, Eng., 1962-63; mem. Pres.'s Sci. Adv. Com., 1967-70; research supr. Explosives Research Lab., Nat. Def. Research Com., 1944-45; chmn. com. survey chemistry Nat. Acad. Scis., 1964-65. Assoc. editor Jour. Chem. Physics, 1942-44, 52-54; editorial bd. Jour. Am. Chem.

Soc, 1960-69, Procs. Nat. Acad. Scis., 1983-89; contbr. articles to profl. jours. Recipient Naval Ordnance Development award, 1946, Army-Navy cert. of appreciation, 1946, James Flack Norris award in phys.-organic chemistry, 1970, Willard Gibbs medal, 1970, Theodore W. Richards medal, 1976; award in chem. scis. Nat. Acad. Sci., 1980, Richard Kokes award, 1980, Charles Frederick Chandler medal, 1980, Rosenstiel award, 1981, Nichols medal, 1982, Robert A. Welch award, 1982, Ingold medal, 1983, Cope award, 1982, Nat. Medal of Sci., 1986, Paracelsus medal, 1988, Priestley medal, 1988, Repligen award, 1992; fellow Columbia U. NRC, 1935-36, Guggenheim Found., 1962-63, Fulbright-Hays Found., 1974. Mem. Nat. Acad. Sci. (council 1971-75, 76-79), Am. Philos. Soc. (council 1981-84), Am. Acad. Arts and Scis. (sec. 1985-90), Royal Soc. (fgn. mem.). Home: 3 Berkeley St Cambridge MA 02138-3409

WESTHEIMER, GERALD, optometrist, educator; b. Berlin, Germany, May 13, 1924; naturalized, 1944, came to U.S., 1951; s. Isaak and Ilse (Cohn) W. Optometry diploma, Sydney (Australia) Tech. Coll., 1943, fellowship diploma, 1950; BSc, U. Sydney, 1947; PhD, Ohio State U., 1953; DSc (hon.), U. NSW, Australia, 1988; ScD (hon.), SUNY, 1990. Practice optometry Sydney, 1945-51; research fellow Ohio State U., 1951-53; prof. physiol. optics U. Houston, 1953-54; asst. prof., then assoc. prof. physiol. optics Ohio State U., 1954-60; postdoctoral fellow neurophysiology Marine Biol. Lab., Woods Hole, Mass., 1957; vis. researcher Physiol. Lab., U. Cambridge, Eng., 1958-59; mem. faculty U. Calif. at Berkeley, 1960—, prof. physiol. optics, 1963-68, chmn. group physiol. optics, 1964-67, prof. physiology, 1968-89, prof. neurobiology, 1989—, head div. neurobiology, 1987-92; adj. prof. Rockefeller U., N.Y., 1992—; Sackler lectr. Tel Aviv U. Med. Sch., 1988, D.O. Hebb lectr. McGill U., 1991, Grass Found. lectr. U. Ill., 1991; mem. com. vision NRC, 1957-72; mem. visual scis. study sect. NIH, 1966-70, chmn. visual scis. B study sect., 1977-79; mem. vision, research and tng. com. Nat. Eye Inst., NIH, 1970-74, chmn. bd. sci. counselors, 1981-83; mem. exec. council com. vision NAS-NRC, 1969-72; mem. communicative scis. cluster Pres.'s Biomed. Rsch. Panel, 1975. Author rsch. papers; editor: Vision Rsch., 1972-79; editl. bd. Investigative Ophthalmology, 1973-77, Exptl. Brain Rsch., 1973-89, Optics Letters, 1977-78, Spatial Vision, 1985—, Ophthalmic and Physiological Optics, 1985—, Vision Rsch., 1985-92, Jour. of Physiology, 1987-94; editor: procs. of Royal Soc. London, 1990—. Recipient Von Sallman prize Columbia U., 1986; Prentice medal Am. Acad. Optometry, 1986, Bicentennial medal Australian Optometric Assn., 1988. Fellow AAAS, Royal Soc. London (Ferrier lectr. 1992), Am. Acad. Arts and Scis., Optical Soc. Am. (Tillyer medal 1978, assoc. editor jour. 1980-83), Am. Acad. Optometry; mem. Royal Soc. New So. Wales, Soc. Neurosci., Assn. Rsch. in Vision and Ophthalmology (Proctor medal 1979), Internat. Brain Rsch. Orgn., Physiol. Soc. Gt. Britain, Sigma Xi. Home: 582 Santa Barbara Rd Berkeley CA 94707-1746

WESTIN, ALAN FURMAN, political science educator; b. N.Y.C, Nov. 11, 1929; s. Irving and Etta (Furman) W.; m. Beatrice Patricia Shapoff, June 20, 1954; children: David, Debra, Jeremy, Carla. B.A., U. Fla., 1948; LL.B., Harvard U., 1951; Ph.D. teaching fellow, 1965. Bar: D.C. 1951. Sr. fellow Yale U. Law Sch., New Haven, 1956-57, vis. prof. polit. sci., 1960-61; asst. prof. govt. Cornell U., Ithaca, N.Y., 1957-59; assoc. prof. pub. law and govt. Columbia U., N.Y.C., 1959-66; prof. Columbia U., 1966—; dir. Ctr. Research and Edn. in Am. Liberties, 1965-71; founder, pres. Ednl. Fund Individual Rights, N.Y.C., 1978-86; pres. Changing Workplaces, Englewood, N.J., 1982-87; program assoc. Harvard U., 1968-72; cons. IBM, 1973-75, U.S. Office Tech. Assessment, 1973—; pres. Ctr. Social and Legal Rsch., 1987—, Ref. Point Found., 1987—; ptnr. Privacy and Legis. Assocs., Washington, 1993—; chmn., CEO Toolkit Software, 1996—; cons. on privacy to Equifax, Citicorp, IBM, Am. Express, U.S. Social Security Adminstrn., Chrysler, Health Data Exch., N.Y. State Identification and Intelligence Sys., Bell Atlantic, Glaxo Wellcome, Eli Lilly; cons. on employee rights Fed. Express, Aetna Life and Casualty, Citicorp, IBM, 1980-86; acad. advisor nat. pub. surveys on privacy Louis Harris and Assocs., 1979, 90, 91, 92, 93, 94, 95, 96, nat. pub. surveys on cons. privacy, Can., 1992, 94; dir. privacy and human genome project U.S. Dept. Energy, 1992-95; chmn. emm. adv. panels U.S. Office Tech. Assessment, 1975-92; chmn. Res. Coun. Healthy Cos., 1991-95; spkr. nat. bus., profl., govt. confs., 1960—. Author: The Anatomy of a Constitutional Law Case, 1958, reprinted, 1990 (put in Notable Trials Libr. 1995), Privacy and Freedom, 1967 (George Polk award, Sidney Hillman award, Melcher award, Van Am. Soc. award 1967), (with Barry Mahoney) The Trial of Martin Luther King, 1975, (with Michael A. Baker) Databanks in a Free Society, 1972; editor: Whistle Blowing! Loyalty an Dissent in the Corporation, 1980, Information technology in a Democracy, 1971 (with Alfred Feliu) Resolving Employment Disputes Without Litigation, 1988, (with John D. Aram) Managerial Delemmas: Cases in Social, Legal, and Technological Change, 1988; editor-in-chief: The Civil Liberties Rev., 1973-79; polit. sci. editor: Casebook Series, 1960-66; contbr. numerous chpts. to books, articles to legal and popular publs.; mem. editl. bd. Employee Rights and Responsibilities Jour., Information Age, Jour. Computing and Society, Transnational Data Report: writer-narrator: CBS-TV Series, The Road to the White House, 1964; cons. spl. programs: ABC-TV; advisor Off Limits: Your Health, Your Job, Your Privacy, PBS Network, 1994; pub. editor-in-chief Privacy and American Business, 1993—. Mem. Nat. Wiretapping Commn., 1973-76; vice-chmn. N.J. Commn. Individual Liberty, 1977-81; sr. cons. U.S. Privacy Protection Study Commn., 1975-77. Recipient Mark Van Doren award Columbia U., 1972; recipient Disting. Alumnus award Delta Sigma Rho-Tau-Kappa Alpha, 1965; grantee Rockefeller Found., 1983, Russell Saga Found., 1969-71, 81-82. Mem. Nat. Acad. Scis. (computer sci. and engring. bd. 1969-72), Am. Polit. Sci. Assn., Assn. Computing Machinery (chmn. task force privacy 1972-73). Home: 1100 Trafalgar St Teaneck NJ 07666-1928 Office: Polit Sci Dept Coll U 118th St And Amsterdam Ave New York NY 10027 also: Ref Pt & Ctr Social Legal Rsch Ste 414 2 University Plz Hackensack NJ 07601-6202 *As fast as technological and social changes are in our age, the enduring matters are how we try to live our personal lives, how we relate to the people we work with, and how strongly we support civility and democratic values in our communities and nation.*

WESTIN, DAVID, broadcast executive. Pres. ABC TV Network Group, N.Y.C. Office: ABC TV Network Group 77 W 66th St New York NY 10023*

WESTIN, DAVID LAWRENCE, lawyer; b. Flint, Mich., July 29, 1952; s. Lawrence Rae and Mary Louise (Holman) W.; m. Victoria Peters; children: Victoria, Elizabeth, Matthew. BA, U. Mich., 1974, JD, 1977. Bar: D.C. 1979. Law clk. U.S. Ct. Appeals (2d cir.), N.Y.C., 1977-78, U.S. Supreme Ct., Washington, 1979; assoc. Wilmer, Cutler & Pickering, Washington, 1979-84, ptnr., 1985-91; sr. v.p., gen. counsel Capital Cities/ABC, Inc., N.Y.C., 1991-93; pres. of prodn. ABC TV Network, N.Y.C., 1993-94; lectr. Harvard U. Law Sch., Cambridge, Mass., 1986; adj. prof. Georgetown U. Law Ctr., Washington, 1989-91. Bd. dirs. Lincoln Ctr. Film. Soc., 1994—, Am. Arbitration Assn., 1991—. Democrat. Presbyterian. Club: Chevy Chase (Md.). Home: 1717 Desales St NW Washington DC 20036-4401 Office: Capital Cities/ABC Inc 77 W 66th St New York NY 10023-6201*

WESTLAKE, ROBERT ELMER, SR., physician; b. Jersey City, Oct. 2, 1918; s. Henry Ebenezer and Bertha (Fowle) W.; m. Agnes Vivian Kumpf, Oct. 1, 1944; children—Robert Elmer, Barbara Elizabeth, Richard Louis. Grad., Lawrenceville Sch., 1936; A.B., Princeton, 1940; M.D., Columbia, 1943. Diplomate: Am. Bd. Internal Medicine. Intern Englewood (N.J.) Hosp., 1944, 46-47; resident Univ. Hosp., Syracuse, N.Y., 1947-49; instr. medicine State U. N.Y. Med. Center, Syracuse, 1949-50; asst. prof. State U. N.Y. Med. Center, 1950-52, clin. asso. prof., 1956-67, clin. prof., 1967-81, clin. prof. emeritus, 1981—; pvt. practice internal medicine Syracuse, 1952-81; mem. staff State Univ., Crouse-Irving-Meml. VA hosps.; dir. profl. services Community Gen. Hosp., 1967-81; cons. USPHS, 1966-72, Social Security Adminstrn., 1968-71; mem. Com. Rev. Regional Med. Programs, NIH, 1966-67; med. adv. council Dept. Def., 1969-74; pres. Profl. Standards Rev. Orgn. Central N.Y., 1974-77. Contbr. articles to profl. jours. Pres. Onondaga Found. Med. Care, 1961-68; v.p. Blue Shield Central N.Y., 1965-73, chmn. bd., 1973-81. Served to lt. (j.g.) M.C. USNR, 1944-46. Fellow A.C.P.; mem. Am. Soc. Internal Medicine (pres. 1965-66), Onondaga County Heart Assn. (pres. 1963-64). Home: 5056 SE Bent Wood Dr Stuart FL 34997-1603

WESTLEY, JOHN RICHARD, foreign service officer; b. Fairmont, Minn., Feb. 25, 1939; s. Richard and Margaret (Kindschi) W.; m. Sidney Kathryn Bohanna, Mar. 26, 1966(div. Sept. 1977); children: Elizabeth Laura, Karen Margaret, Marian Bohanna; m. Joan Nancy Ehrlich, Apr. 12, 1980; 1 child, Katherine Matthea. BA in Philosophy, Yale U., 1961; MA in Econs., Columbia U., 1966; PhD in Econs., Am. Univ., 1983. Internat. economist U.S. Dept. Treasury, Washington, 1966-69; loan officer U.S. AID, Addis Ababa, Ethiopia, 1970-72; economist U.S. AID, Nairobi, Kenya, 1973-75, Washington, 1976-78; program officer U.S. AID, New Delhi, India, 1979-84; dir. mission to Bangladesh U.S. AID, Dhaka, 1985-87; assoc. asst. adminstr. bur. Africa U.S. AID, Washington, 1987-90; dir. mission to Kenya U.S. AID, Nairobi, 1990-94; dir. Mission to Egypt US AID, Cairo, 1994—. Author: Agriculture and Equitable Growth, 1986. With U.S. Army, 1961-64. Mem. Am. Econ. Assn., Soc. for Internat. Devel., Phi Beta Kappa. Presbyterian. Home and Office: USAID Unit 64902 APO AE 09839

WESTLING, JON, university administrator; b. Yakima, Wash., June 7, 1942; s. Norman L. and Jean R. (Bergamini) W.; m. Elizabeth A. Wüthrich, Oct. 14, 1977; children: Emma E., Matthew R., Andrew N. BA, Reed Coll., 1964; postgrad., St. John's Coll. Oxford (Eng.) U., 1964-67, UCLA, 1971-74. Instr. history Centre Coll., Danville, Ky., 1967-68; asst. prof. history and humanities Reed Coll., Portland, Oreg., 1968-71; assoc. dir. Boston Univ. Prodns., 1974-76; asst. to pres. Boston U., 1976-79, assoc. provost, 1979-83, provost ad interim, 1983-84, provost, 1984-88, exec. v.p., 1988-90, interim pres., 1990, exec. v.p., provost, 1991-95, provost, pres.-elect, 1995—; bd. dirs. Century Bank. Bd. dirs. Mass. Corp. for Ednl. Telecomms., 1990—; trustee Boston Mus. Sci., 1990—. Gen. Motors Nat. scholar, 1960-64, Rhodes scholar, 1964-67. Home: 7 Churchill Ln Lexington MA 02173-5801 Office: Boston U Office Provost 145 Bay State Rd Boston MA 02215-1708

WESTMAN, CARL EDWARD, lawyer; b. Youngstown, Ohio, Dec. 12, 1943; s. Carl H. and Mary Lillis (Powell) W.; m. Carolyn J., July 17, 1965; children: C. Forrest, Stephanie A. BBA, Sam Houston State U., 1966; JD, U. Miami, 1969, LLM in Taxation, 1972. Bar: Fla. 1969. Ptnr. Frost & Jacobs, 1983-93, Roetzel & Andress, Naples, Fla., 1993—. S.W. Fla. coun. Boy Scouts Am. Eagle Bd. of Review, 1987—; trustee David Lawrence Found. for Mental Health, Inc., 1976-86, chmn. 1985-86; trustee Pikeville Coll., 1993—, Naples Cmty. Hosp., 1992—; past pres. bd. trustees, elder Moorings Presbyn. Ch. Mem. ABA, Fla. Bar, Collier County Bar Assn., Estate Planning Coun, Coral Reef Yacht Club, Useppa Island Club. Home: 1952 Crayton Rd Naples FL 33940-5070 Office: Roetzel & Andress 850 Park Shore Dr Naples FL 33940

WESTMAN, JACK CONRAD, child psychiatrist, educator; b. Cadillac, Mich., Oct. 28, 1927; s. Conrad A. and Alice (Pedersen) W.; m. Nancy K. Baehre, July 17, 1953; children—Daniel P., John C., Eric C. M.D., U. Mich., 1952. Diplomate: Am. Bd. Psychiatry and Neurology. Intern Duke Hosp., Durham, N.C., 1952-53; resident U. Mich. Med. Center, 1955-59; dir. Outpatient Services, Children's Psychiatric Hosp., Ann Arbor, Mich., 1961-65; assoc. prof. U. Mich. Med. Sch., 1964-65; coordinator Diagnostic and Treatment Unit, Waisman Center, U. Wis., Madison, 1966-74; prof. psychiatry, 1965—; cons. Joint Commn. on Mental Health of Children, 1967-69, Madison (Wis.) Pub. Schs., 1965-74, Children's Treatment Center, Mendota Mental Health Inst., 1965-69. Author: Individual Differences in Children, 1973, Child Advocacy, 1979, Handbook of Learning Disabilities, 1990, Who Speaks for the Children?, 1991, Licensing Parents, 1994; editor: Child Psychiatry and Human Development; contbr. articles to profl. jours. Vice-pres. Big Bros. of Dane County, 1970-73; v.p. Wis. Assn. Mental Health, 1968-72; co-chmn. Project Understanding, 1968-75. Served with USNR, 1953-55. Fellow Am. Psychiat. Assn., Am. Coll. Psychiatrists, Am. Acad. Child and Adolescent Psychiatry, Am. Orthopsychiat. Assn. (bd. dirs. 1973-76); mem. Am. Assn. Psychiat. Svcs. for Children (pres. 1978-80), Multidisciplinary Acad. Clin. Edn. (pres. 1992—). Home: 1234 Dartmouth Rd Madison WI 53705-2214 Office: 600 Highland Ave Madison WI 53792-0001

WESTMORE, MICHAEL GEORGE, make-up artist; b. Hollywood, Calif., Mar. 22, 1938; s. Montague George and Edith Adeline W.; m. Marion Christine Bergeson, Dec. 4, 1966; children: Michael George, Michele, McKenzie. BA, U. Calif., Santa Barbara, 1961. Apprentice make-up artist Universal City Studios, Universal City, Calif., 1961-63, staff make-up artist, 1964, asst. head dept. make-up lab., 1965-71; freelance make-up artist various studios, Hollywood, Calif., 1971-87; make-up supr. and designer Paramount Studios, Hollywood, 1987—; instr. theatre arts dept. Los Angeles Valley Coll., 1966-71; pres. Cosmetic Control Ctrs., Inc., 1971-76; pres. Hollywood Magic Cosmetics, 1985-87; rsch. cons., lectr. therapeutic cosmetics for med. assns. Author: The Art of Theatrical Make-Up for Stage and Screen, 1971, also chpts. in books; co-author: Star Trek Makeup FX Journal; make-up artist for TV spls. Eleanor and Franklin (emmy award NATAS 1976), Why Me? (Emmy award 1984), Three Wishes of Billy Grier (Emmy award 1985), Star Trek (Emmy award 1988, 92, 93, 95), Amazing Stories (Emmy award 1987), (films) 2010 (Acad. award nomination Acad. Motion Picture Arts and Scis. 1985), Mask (Acad. award 1986), Clan of the Cave Bear (Acad. award nomination 1987). Served with AUS, 1956. Mem. Internat. Alliance Theatrical Stage Employees, Soc. Make-up Artists, Vikings of Scandia, Lambda Chi Alpha (life). Address: 3830 Sunswept Dr Studio City CA 91604-2328

WESTMORELAND, BARRY KEITH, state legislator; b. Kingsport, Tenn., Aug. 26, 1946; s. Horace Arnold and Ruth (Taylor) W.; m. Alice Charles, Feb. 1, 1977; children: Joel Keith, Stoney Lee. BS in Criminal Justice cum laude, East Tenn. State U., 1973; postgrad., U. Tenn., Walter State C.C. Policeman Kingsport Police Dept., 1968-69; dep. sheriff Sullivan County Sheriff's Dept., Blountville, Tenn., 1973-75, chief dep., adminstr., 1976-86; law enforcement planner 1st Tenn. Regional Law Enforcement Planning Agy., Johnson City, 1975-76; CEO Sullivan County, Blountville, 1986-90; mem. Tenn. Ho. of Reps., Nashville, 1992—; cons. Alternative Correction Systems, Johnson City, 1993—; mem. criminal justice adv. bd. Walters State C.C., East Tenn. State U. Former chmn. exec. com. Tri-Cities Airport Commn.; former chmn. Sullivan County Indsl. Commn.; former mem. bd. dirs. 1st Tenn. Devel. Dist., Upper East Tenn. Human Devel. Agy.; bd. dirs. Holston Valley Hosp. and Med. Ctr.., Upper East Tenn. Jevenile Detention Ctr., 1st Tenn. Human Resource Agy.; mem. adv. bd. Salvation Army; mem. adv. bd. N.E. Tenn. Community Coll.; mem. Kingsport Visitors Coun., Legis. Com. for Econ. Devel., East Tenn. Tourism Coun.; also others. Sgt. USAF, 1964-68; bd. dirs. Sullivan County Children's Advocacy Ctr.. Job Tng. Partnership Act. Recipient award of merit Tenn. Human Resources Agy., 1994; named Legislator of Yr., Tenn. Devel. Dists., 1994, 95, Human Resources Agy., 1996, Tenn. County Ofcls. Assn., 1995; named Outstanding Legislator, Tenn. Forestry Assn., 1994. Mem. NRA, Tenn. County Execs. Assn. (v.p.), Tenn. County Svcs. Assn., United Comml. Travelers, Outdoorsman, Kingsport Interfraternal Coun., Eagles, Moose. Republican. Methodist. Avocations: hunting, fishing, golf. Address: 3216 Kenridge St Kingsport TN 37664-4034 Office: Tenn Ho of Reps 214 War Memorial Bldg Nashville TN 37243

WESTMORELAND, KENT EWING, lawyer; b. Tulsa, May 17, 1949; s. Earl E. and Adeline (Burckhalter) W.; m. Mary Kathleen Price, June 14, 1981. B.B.A., So. Meth. U., 1971; J.D., U. Tex., 1975. Bar: Tex. 1975, U.S. Dist. Ct. (so. dist.) Tex. 1976, U.S. Dist. Ct. (ea. dist.) Tex. 1977, U.S. Ct. Appeals (5th cir.) 1977, U.S. Ct. Appeals (11th cir.) 1982, U.S. Dist. Ct. (no. dist.) Tex. 1984, U.S. Supreme Ct. 1985; cert. Tex. Bd. Legal Specialization, Civil Trial Law, Personal Injury Trial Law. Atty., Kronzer, Abraham & Watkins, Houston, 1975-76, Eastham, Watson, Dale & Forney, Houston, 1976-79, Ross, Griggs & Harrison, Houston, 1979-90, Phelps Dunbar, 1990—. Served with USNR, 1972-78. Mem. Maritime Law Assn. U.S. (proctor 1977), Tex. Assn. Def. Lawyers, Metro. Racquet Club, Sweetwater Country Club. Republican. Methodist. Home: 5303 Pine St Bellaire TX 77401-4810 Office: Phelps Dunbar 1331 Lamar St Ste 501 Houston TX 77010-3026

WESTMORELAND, THOMAS DELBERT, JR., chemist; b. near Vivian, La., June 2, 1940; s. Thomas Delbert and Marguerite Beatrice (Moore) W.; BS, N. Tex. State U., 1963, MS, 1965; PhD, La. State U., 1971, postdoctoral fellow, 1971-72; m. Martha Verne Beard, Jan. 1, 1966; children: Anne Laura, Kyle Thomas. Chemistry tchr., rsch. dir. Lewisville (Tex.) H.S., 1964; summer devel. program student Tex. Instruments, Inc., Dallas, 1966; sr. exptl./analytical engr. Power Systems div. United Technologies, South Windsor, Conn., 1972-76; sr. research chemist Pennzoil Co., Shreveport, La., 1976-82, rsch. assoc., 1983-93, sr. environ. engr. Pennzoil Products Co. Tech. Ctr., The Woodlands, Tex., 1993—; chem. cons. Recipient E.I. du Pont tchng. award La. State U., 1968-69. Mem. Am. Chem. Soc. (treas. 1978-79, chmn. 1979-80), Assn. Rsch. and Enlightenment, Soc. Automotive Engrs., Sigma Xi (sec.), Phi Eta Sigma (pres. 1959-60), Alpha Chi Sigma, Kappa Mu Epsilon. Clubs: Jaycees (state dir. Conn. 1976, gov.'s civic leadership award Conn. 1975-76, C. William Brownfield Meml. award 1976), Masons (Scottish Rite, 32d degree). Contbr. sci. articles to profl. jours; patentee in field. Home: 143 Melmont Ln Conroe TX 77302-1022 Office: PO Box 7569 The Woodlands TX 77387-7569

WESTOFF, CHARLES FRANCIS, demographer, educator; b. N.Y.C., July 23, 1927; s. Frank Barnett and Evelyn (Bales) W.; m. Joan P. Uszynski, Sept. 11, 1948 (div. Jan. 1969); children: David, Carol; m. Leslie Aldridge, Aug. 1969 (div. Feb. 1993). AB, Syracuse U., 1949, MA, 1950; PhD, U. Pa., 1953. Instr. sociology U. Pa., 1950-52; research assoc. Milbank Meml. Fund, N.Y.C., 1952-55; research assoc. Office Population Research Princeton U., 1955-62, prof. sociology, 1962—, Maurice P. During '22 prof. demographic studies and sociology, 1972—, chmn. dept. sociology, 1965-70, assoc. dir. Office Population Research, 1962-75, dir., 1975-92; assoc. prof. sociology N.Y.U., also chmn. dept. sociology Washington Sq. Coll., 1959-62; vis. sr. fellow East-West Population Inst., Honolulu, 1979, 81; Disting. vis. prof. Am. U., Cairo, 1979; mem. vis. com. Harvard-M.I.T. Joint Center for Urban Studies, 1980-83; exec. dir. Commn. Population growth and Am. Future, 1970-72; mem. adv. com. on population stats. U.S. Bur. Census, 1973-79; chmn. Nat. Com. for Rsch. on 1980 Census, 1981-88; bd. dirs. Alan Guttmacher Inst., 1977-88, 89—; sr. tech. advisor Demographic Health Surveys, 1984—; bd. dirs. Population Resource Ctr., 1985—, Population Ref. Bur., 1988-94, Population Comms. Internat., 1992—; com. on population NAS, 1983-88. Co-author: Family Growth in Metropolitan America, 1961, The Third Child, 1963, College Women and Fertility Values, 1967, The Later Years of Childbearing, 1970, From Now to Zero, 1971, Reproduction in the United States, 1965, 71, Toward the End of Growth: Population in America, 1973, The Contraceptive Revolution, 1976, Demographic Dynamics in America, 1977, Age at Marriage, Age at First Birth and Fertility in Africa, 1992, Unmet Need: 1990-1994, 1994; contbr. artiles on demography and sociology to profl. jours. Fellow Am. Sociol. Assn., Am. Acad. Arts and Scis.; mem. Inst. Medicine Nat. Acad. Sci., Planned Parenthood Fedn. Am. (dir. 1978-81), Population Assn. Am. (bd. dirs. 1960-62, 68-70, 1st v.p. 1972-73, pres. 1974-75), Internat. Union Sci. Study Population. Home: 537 Drakes Corner Rd Princeton NJ 08540-7515

WESTON, ARTHUR WALTER, chemist, scientific and business executive; b. Smith Falls, Ont. Can., Feb. 13, 1914; came to U.S., 1935, naturalized, 1952; s. Herbert W. and Alice M. (Houghton) W.; m. V. Dawn Thompson, Sept. 10, 1940; children: Roger L., Randall K., Cynthia B. BA, Queen's U., Kingston, Ont., 1934, MA, 1935; PhD, Northwestern U., 1938. Postdoctoral fellow Northwestern U., Evanston, Ill., 1938-40; with Abbott Labs., North Chgo., Ill., 1940-79, dir. rsch. and devel., 1959-61, v.p. rsch. and devel., 1961-68, dir. company, 1959-68, v.p. sci. affairs, 1968-77, v.p. corp. licensing, 1977-79; v.p., dir. San-Abbott, Japan, 1976-79; cons. Abbott Labs., North Chgo., Ill., 1979-85; pres. Arthur W. Weston & Assocs., Lake Forest, Ill., 1979—. Contbr. profl jours. and books. Patentee in field. Mem. Office Sci. Rsch. and Devel., War Manpower Commn., 1942-45; mem. exec. com. indsl. chemistry, div. chemistry and chem. tech. NRC, 1961-65; mem. indsl. panel on sci. and tech. NSF, 1974-80; mem. ad hoc com. chem. agts. Dept. Def., 1961-65. Mem. Rsch. Dirs. Assn. Chgo. (pres. 1965-66), Am. Chem. Soc. (trustee Chgo. 1965—, dir. Chgo. sect. 1952-59, nat. com. corp. assocs. 1967-72), Dirs. Indsl. Rsch., Indsl. Rsch. Inst. (bd. dirs. 1970-73), Phi Beta Kappa, Sigma Xi, Phi Lambda Upsilon. Home and Office: 349 Hilldale Pl Lake Forest IL 60045-3031

WESTON, BARBARA ELLEN, community health nurse; b. Boston, Dec. 29, 1939; d. Francis R. and Margaret E. Dalton; m. Marvin L. Weld, June 8, 1963 (div. May 29, 1971); children: Ann M., Susan L.; m. John C. Weston, June 14, 1974. Diploma in Nursing, St. Elizabeth's Hosp., Boston, 1962; BSN, Salem (Mass.) State Coll., 1984, MSN, 1988. RN, Mass. Staff nurse pediatrics Addison Gilbert Hosp., Gloucester, Mass., 1962-63, 67-69, Franklin County Hosp., Greenfield, Mass., 1963-64; office nurse pediatrics Dr. Tanner, Plattsburgh, N.Y., 1965-67; sch. nurse Hogan Regional Ctr., Hathorne, N.Y., 1969-73, nursing supr., 1973-77; health care coord. North Shore Spl. Edn. Consortium, Peabody, N.Y., 1977-88; clin. nurse specialist devel. disabilities The Shriver Ctr., Waltham, N.Y., 1988-90; clin. nurse specialist cmty. health Children's Hosp., Boston, 1990-92; nat. corp. dir. pediatrics Kimberly Quality Care, Boston, 1992-94; maternal child health program mgr. Vis. Nurse Assn., Cambridge, Mass., 1994-95; program devel. mgr. VNA Care Network, Inc., 1995—; mem. Pediatric Home Care Coalition, Boston, 1991—, chmn., 1994—; mem. Immunization Action Project, Cambridge, 1994—; mem. Early Childhood Adv. Project, Cambridge, 1994—. Mem. State Adv. Coun. for Children, Boston, 1988-93, Charter Preparation Team, Chelsea, Mass., 1994, Chelsea Bd. Health, 1991—. Mem. ANA, Mass. Nurse Assn., Mass. Pub. Health Assn., Assn. for Care of Children's Health, Am. Assn. Mental Retardation, Sigma Theta Tau. Democrat. Roman Catholic. Avocation: sailing. Home: 15 Boatswains Way Chelsea MA 02150-4017

WESTON, BURNS HUMPHREY, law educator; b. Cleve., Nov. 5, 1933; s. Stephen Burns and Simonne Humphrey Weston; m. Marta Cullberg; children: Timothy Bergmann, Rebecca Burns. Student, Oberlin Conservatory of Music, 1952-53, Western Res. U., 1954, U. Edinburgh, Scotland, 1954-55; BA, Oberlin Coll., 1956; LLB, Yale U., 1961, D of Jud. Sci., 1970. Bar: N.Y. 1963, Iowa 1968. Assoc. Paul, Weiss, Rifkind, Wharton & Garrison, N.Y.C., 1961-64; asst. prof. law U. Iowa, Iowa City, 1966-67, assoc. prof. law, 1967-69, prof. law, 1969-83, Bessie Dutton Murray disting. prof. law, 1983—, founding dir. ctr. for world order studies, 1972-76, chair internat. and comparative law program, 1990-92; assoc. dean for internat. and comparative legal studies, 1992—, chair grad. program in internat. and comparative law, 1992—; vis. prof. Grinnell Coll., 1974, UCLA, 1981; sr. fellow, dir. Transnational Acad. Program Inst. for World Order, 1976-78; vis. prof. summer program La. State U., Aix-en-Provence, 1991; cons. internat. law Naval War Coll., 1968-69, Club of Rome Project on Global Learning, 1977-79. Author: International Claims: Postwar French Practice, 1971, (with Richard B. Lillich) International Claims: Their Settlement by Lump Sum Agreements, 2 vols., 1975; editor, author: (with W. Michael Reisman) Toward World Order and Human Dignity: Essays in Honor of Myres S. McDougal, 1976, Peace and World Order Studies: A Curriculum Guide, 1978; (with Richard A. Falk and Anthony A. D'Amato) International Law and World Order, 1980, (with Lillich) International Claims: Contemporary European Practice, 1982, Toward Nuclear Disarmament and Global Security: A Search for Alternatives, 1984, (with Richard P. Claude) Human Rights in the World Community: Issues and Action, 1989, Alternative Security: Living Without Nuclear Deterrence, 1990, (with Richard A. Falk and Anthony D'Amato) International Law and World Order: A Problem-Oriented Coursebook, 2d ed., 1990, Basic Documents in International Law and World Order, 2d ed., 1990; (with Lakshman D. Guruswamy and Sir Geoffrey W.R. Palmer) International Environmental Law and World Order: A Problem-Oriented Coursebook, 1994, International Law and World Order: Basic Documents (vols. 1-5), 1994; contbr. numerous writings to many publs. in field; mem. bd. editors Am. Jour. Internat. Law; series editor Procedural Aspects of International Law; mem. editl. adv. bd. Innovation in Internat. Law Series, Transnational Pubs.; mem. editl. rev. bd. Human Rights Quarterly; mem. editl. bd. Jour. World Peace. Mem. Internat. Studies Assn. Consortium of Peace Rsch. Edn. and Devel., Coun. on Fgn. Rels., Global Edn. Assocs., Iowa City Fgn. Rels. Coun., World Future Studies Fedn., Lawyers Com. on Nuclear Policy, Internat. Assn. of Lawyers Against Nuclear Arms; mem. peace law and edn. project Meiklejohn Civil Liberties Inst.; bd. dirs. Iowa divsn. UN Assn.-USA. Rockefeller Found. and Sterling fellow Yale U. Law Sch., 1964-66, rsch. fellow Procedural Aspects Internat. Law Inst., 1967-74; sr. fellow World Policy Inst., 1974-91, World Order Teaching fellow, 1980-83, World Acad. Art and Sci. fellow, 1982—; recipient Scroll of Honor award UN Assn. Iowa div., 1991. Mem. ABA (past standing com. on World order under law, internat. law and practice sect., individual rights and responsibility sect.), Am. Assn. for Internat. Commn. on Jurists, Am. Soc. Internat. Law (spl. commendation 1978, award 1982), Internat. Human Rights Law Group, Lawyers Alliance for World Security, Internat. Peace Rsch. Assn., Procedural Aspects Internat. Law Inst., Am.

Soc. Internat. Law (v.p. 1992—), U.S. Assn. for Club of Rome. Avocations: music, mountain climbing, gardening. Office: Univ Iowa Coll Law Boyd Law Bldg Iowa City IA 52242

WESTON, FRANCINE EVANS, secondary education educator; b. Mt. Vernon, N.Y., Oct. 8, 1946; d. John Joseph and Frances (Fantino) Pisaniello. BA, Hunter Coll., 1968; MA, Lehman Coll., 1973; cert., Am. Acad. Dramatic Arts, N.Y.C., 1976; PhD, NYU, 1991. Cert. elem., secondary tchr., N.Y. Tchr. Yonkers (N.Y.) Bd. Edn., 1968—; aquatic dir. Woodlane Day Camp, Irvington-on-Hudson, N.Y., 1967-70, Yonkers Jewish Community Ctr., 1971-75; creative drama tchr. John Burroughs Jr. H.S., Yonkers, 1971-77; stage lighting designer Iona Summer Theatre Festival, New Rochelle, N.Y., 1980-81, Yonkers Male Glee Club, 1981-89, Roosevelt H.S., 1980—; rsch. specialist Scholarship Locating Svc., 1992-94, Yonkers Civil Def. Police Aux., 1994—; master electrician NYU Summer Mus. Theatre, 1979-80. Actress in numerous community theatre plays including A Touch of the Poet, 1979; dir. stage prodns. including I Remember Mama, 1973, The Man Who Came to Dinner, 1975; author: A Descriptive Comparison of Computerized Stage Lighting Memory Systems With Non-Computerized Systems, 1991, (short stories) A Hat for Louise, 1984, Old Memories: Beautiful and Otherwise, 1984; lit. editor: (story and poetry collection) Beautifully Old, 1984. Steering com. chairperson Roosevelt H.S.-Middle States Assn. of Schs. and Colls. Self-Evaluation, 1985-88; mem. Yonkers Civil Def. Police Aux., 1994—. Named Tchr. of Excellence, N.Y. State English Coun., 1990; recipient Monetary award for Teaching Excellence, Carter-Wallace Products, 1992, Educator of Excellence award N.Y. State English Coun., 1995; named to Arrid Tchrs. Honor Roll, 1992. Mem. U.S. Inst. for Theatre Tech., Nat. Coun. Tchrs. English, N.Y. State English Coun., N.Y. State United Tchrs. Assn., Yonkers Fedn. Tchrs., Port Chester Obedience Tng. Club, Inc., Kappa Delta Pi. Republican. Roman Catholic. Avocations: swimming, target shooting, animal related activities, anything theatrical. Office: Roosevelt High Sch Tuckahoe Rd Yonkers NY 10710

WESTON, I. DONALD, architect; b. Bklyn., Feb. 16, 1928; s. Martyn N. and Betty (Lash) W.; m. Sylvia Stone, Oct. 23, 1952; children: Suzanne, Pamela. BArch, MIT, 1950; MArch, Pratt Inst., 1959, M in City and Regional Planning, 1981. Cert. Nat. Coun. Archtl. Regis. Bd.; lic. architect N.Y., Mass. Ptnr., prin. Martyn & Don Weston Architects, Bklyn., 1956—. Co-authored 2 studies for determining methods of reducing the cost of pub. housing, 1960. Mem. Mayor's Blue Ribbon Panel to Investigate the Bldg. Process in N.Y.C., 1987-88; pro bono pub. mem., sec. Cadman Plz. Co-op., Bklyn., 1972-78. Fellow AIA (mem. Bklyn. chpt. 1954—, pres. 1964-65); mem. Architects Coun. of N.Y.C. (pres. 1970-72), N.Y.C. Art Commn.; mem. Nat. Sculpture Soc. (v.p. 1990—), Fine Arts Fedn. N.Y. (v.p. 1981—, pres. 1984-87, 90-91), Art Commn. Assocs. (pres. 1991-92). Avocations: tennis, golf, community activism. Office: Martyn & Don Weston Arch 100 Remsen St Brooklyn NY 11201-4256

WESTON, JOAN SPENCER, production director; b. Barton, Vt., Aug. 11, 1943; d. Rolfe Weston and Dorothy Lena (Spencer) Schoppe. BA magna cum laude, U. Mass., 1965. Tchr. high sch. Gorham (Maine) Schs., 1965-66; tchr. Sherwood Hall Sch., Mansfield, Eng., 1966-67; tchr. middle sch. Meden Sch., Warsop, Eng., 1967-68; dept. head high sch. Goffstown (N.H.) Schs., 1968-82; dir. circulation T.H.E. Jour., Acton, Mass., 1982-83; prodn. mgr. The Robb Report, Acton, 1983-87, prodn. dir., 1988; prodn. dir. New Age Pub. Inc., Watertown, Mass., 1993—. Mem. Boston Prodn. Mgrs. Group, Phi Beta Kappa. Avocations: travel, music, psychology, antiques. Office: New Age Jour 42 Pleasant St Watertown MA 02172-2316

WESTON, JOHN FREDERICK, business educator, consultant; b. Ft. Wayne, Ind., Feb. 6, 1916; s. David Thomas and Bertha (Schwartz) W.; children: Kenneth F., Byron L., Ellen J. B.A., U. Chgo., 1937, M.B.A., 1943, Ph.D., 1948. Instr. U. Chgo. Sch. Bus., 1940-42, asst. prof., 1947-48; prof. Anderson Grad. Sch. Mgmt. UCLA, 1949—, Cordner prof. Anderson Grad. Sch. Mgmt., 1981-94; prof. emeritus recalled Anderson Grad. Sch. Mgmt. UCLA, 1986—; econ. cons. to pres. Am. Bankers Assn., 1945-46; disting. lecture series U. Okla., 1967, U. Utah, 1972, Miss. State U., 1972, Miami State U., 1975; dir. UCLA Anderson Grad. Sch. Mgmt. Rsch. Program in Competition and Bus. Policy, 1969—, Ctr. for Managerial Econs. and Pub. Policy, 1983-86. Author: Scope and Methodology of Finance, 1966, International Managerial Finance, 1972, Impact of Large Firms on U.S. Economy, 1973, Financial Theory and Corporate Policy, 1979, 2d edit., 1983, 3d edit., 1988, Managerial Finance, 9th edit, 1992; assoc. editor: Jour. of Finance, 1948-55; mem. editorial bd., 1957-59; editorial bd. Bus. Econs., Jour. Fin. Rsch., Managerial and Decision Econs.; manuscript referee Am. Econ. Rev., Rev. of Econs. and Statistics, Engring. Economist. Bd. dirs. Bunker Hill Fund. Served with Ordnance Dept. AUS, 1943-45. Recipient Abramson Scroll award Bus. Econs., 1989-93; McKinsey Found. grantee, 1965-68; GE grantee, 1967; Ford Found. Faculty Rsch. fellow, 1961-62. Fellow Nat. Assn. Bus. Economists; mem. Am. Finance Assn. (pres. 1966, adv. bd. 1967-71), Am. Econ. Assn., Western Econ. Assn. (pres. 1962), Econometric Soc., Am. Statis. Assn., Royal Econ. Soc., Fin. Analysts Soc., Fin. Mgmt. Assn. (pres. 1979-80). Home: 258 Tavistock Ave Los Angeles CA 90049-3229 Office: UCLA Anderson Sch Los Angeles CA 90095-1481

WESTON, JOSH S., data processing company executive; b. Bklyn., Dec. 22, 1928; married. B.S., CCNY, 1950; M.A., U. New Zealand, 1951. Exec. v.p. Popular Services, Inc., 1955-70; v.p. planning adminstrn. Automatic Data Processing, Inc., Roseland, N.J., 1970-75, exec. v.p., 1975-77, pres., 1977—, CEO, 1982—, former COO, now also chmn.; bd. dirs. Shared Med. Sys., Pub. Svc. Electric and Gas Co., Olsten Corp., Vanstar Corp. Office: ADP Inc 1 A D P Blvd Roseland NJ 07068-1728

WESTON, M. MORAN, II, educator, real estate developer, banker, clergyman; b. Tarboro, N.C., Sept. 10, 1910; s. Milton Moran and Catharine C. (Perry) W.; m. June 27, 1946; children: Karann Christine, Gregory. BA, Columbia U., 1930, PhD, 1954, STD (hon.), 1968; DD (hon.), Va. Theol. Sch., 1964; DHL (hon.), Fordham U., 1988. Bus. mgr. St. Philips Episcopal Ch., N.Y.C., 1948-51; exec. sec. Christian Citizenship Nat. Council, Episcopal Ch., N.Y.C., 1951-57; rector, chief executive officer St. Philips Ch. and Community Svc. Council, N.Y.C., 1957-82; sr. prof. SUNY, Albany, 1959-77, prof. emeritus, 1977—; pvt. housing developer, 1982—; vis. prof. U. Ife, Ile-Ife, Nigeria, 1977; chmn. bd. Carver Fed. Savs. Bank, N.Y.C., 1980-95, vice chmn., 1995—; bd. dirs., founder Carver Fed. Bank, N.Y.C.; pres. 6 housing corps., providing over 1,200 rental apts.; co-developer 2 24-story, 600 apts. condominium bldgs. Towers-on-the-Park, 1986; founding developer, pres. Greater Harlem Nursing Home, 200 beds, nonprofit. Author: Social Policy, 1964. Founder, pres. Weston United for Cmty. Devel., N.Y.C., 1981—, Tri-Continental Assn.; trustee Columbia U., 1969-81, trustee emeritus, 1981—; trustee St. Augustine Coll., Raleigh, N.C., 1970—, Mt. Sinai Hosp. Med. Sch. and Ctr., N.Y.C., 1971—, NAACP Legal Def. Fund, N.Y.C., 1965—, Fgn. Policy Assn., N.Y.C., 1980-89, Phelps Stokes Fund, N.Y.C., 1970-80; cons. 3d Internat. UN Conf. Against Apartheid, 1977. Recipient St. Augustine's Cross, Archbishop of Canterbury, London, 1981, Excellence award Columbia Grad. Sch., N.Y.C., 1982, Humanitarian awards N.Y. Urban League, N.Y.C., 1982, N.Y. YMCA, 1982, Mickey Leland award Hope for the Homeless, 1989, Lifetime of Excellence in Pub. Svc. award Nat. Housing Assn., 1991, Phoenix award Abyssinian Devel. Corp. Mem. Housing for People (founder, pres. 1980—), Nat. Assn. for Affordable Housing (founder, pres. 1987—), Lotos Club (N.Y.C.), Sigma Pi Phi (pres. Zeta chpt. 1983-86). Club: Lotos (N.Y.C.). Lodge: Elks (Hon. Supreme Exalted Ruler 1946-50). Home: 228 Promenade Cir Heathrow FL 32746-4379 Office: Carver Fed Savs Bank 75 W 125th St New York NY 10027-4512

WESTON, MICHAEL C., lawyer; b. Asheville, N.C., Aug. 13, 1938; m. May Ann Damme; two children. AB in English, Brown U., 1960; JD, U. Mich., 1963. Bar: Mich. 1964, Ill. 1973. Assoc. Hill, Lewis, Adams, Goodrich & Tait, Detroit, 1963-68; from sec. to pres. corp. and indsl. consortium Econ. Devel. Corp. of Greater Detroit, 1969-73; chief staff atty. Northwestern U., Evanston, Ill., 1973-81, v.p. legal affairs, 1981-89; v.p. and gen. counsel, 1990—; lectr. minority bus. devel. Inst. Continuing Legal Edn., conflicts of interest Nat. Coun. Univ. Rsch. Adminstrs. Contbr. articles to profl. jours. Chmn. Univ. Gallery Com., 1982-85; bd. dirs. Northwestern U. Press. Mem. ABA (sec. taxation, com. on exempt orgns., lectr. Inst. on Minority Bus. Devel.), Chgo. Coun. Lawyers, Nat. Assn. Coll. and Univ. Attys. (lectr. fed. tax matters, outside activities faculty mems. univ.-cmty. rels., med. risk mgmt., bd. dirs. 1985-88, 92—, pres. 1995—). Office: Northwestern U 633 Clark St Evanston IL 60208-0001

WESTON, PAUL, composer, arranger, conductor; b. Springfield, Mass.; m. Jo Stafford, 1952; children: Tim, Amy. B in Econs. cum laude, Dartmouth U., 1933; postgrad., Columbia U. Currently pres. Hanover Music Corp., Corinthian Records. free lance arranger for Rudy Vallee, Phil Harris and his Orch., Joe Haymes, Fleischman Radio Hour, 1934-35; worked for Tommy and Jimmy Dorsey, 1935-40, arranged Song of India, Stardust, Night and Day, Who, other songs; 1st motion picture arranging with Bing Crosby Band for Holiday Inn, 1941; other work at Parmount Pictures for Crosby, Bob Hope, Bett Hutton, etc.; as musical dir. at Capitol Records made his own albums in style to be known as Mood Music and accompanied Johnny Mercer, Gordon MacRae, Jo Stafford, Betty Hutton, Dean Martin, others; 1st Capitol album Music for Dreaming; from 1943-50 on radio and making albums; in 1950 with Columbia Records, making instrumental albums, working as West Coast dir. of Artists and Repertoire, and with his own orch. accompanying singers Doris Day, Rosemary Clooney, Jo Stafford, Frankie Laine, others; CBS radio series The Paul Weston Show aired 1951-52; musical dir. NBC-TV, 1957-62; musical dir. Danny Kaye TV show, 1963-67, then with Jonathan Winters and Jim Nabors on CBS; after retiring from TV served as musical dir. for Disney on Parade for 3 yrs. Composer: (pop songs) Day By Day, I Should Care, Shrimp Boats, Autumn in Rome, When April Comes Again; (symphonic suites) Crescent City Suite, The Mercy Partridge Suite; (choral work) The Bells of Santa Ynez: also various religious works including two masses; 4 comedy albums with Jo Stafford including Grammy award winner Jonathan and Darlene in Paris. Former pres. Crippled Children's Soc. Los Angeles; bd. dirs. Westlake Sch.; active internat. hymnal project with Maryknoll Mission Soc. Mem. Phi Beta Kappa. Founder, 1st nat. pres. Nat. Acad. Recording Arts and Scis., awarded the Acad.'s Trustees award, 1971. Office: Corinthian Records PO Box 6296 Beverly Hills CA 90212-1296

WESTON, RANDY (RANDOLPH EDWARD WESTON), pianist, composer; b. Bklyn., Apr. 6, 1926; s. Frank Edward and Vivian (Moore) W.; children: Cherryl, Pamela, Niles, Kim. Student, Parkway Music Inst., Bklyn., 1950-52. lectr. on African music UN. Pianist Am. Soc. African Culture tour, Lagos, Nigeria, 1961, 63; toured with Randy Weston's sextet for State Dept., North and West Africa, 1967; appearances include Newport Festival, 1958, Monterey Festival, 1966, Carnegie Hall, 1973, Philharm. Hall, N.Y.C., 1973; appearances maj. jazz clubs in N.Y.C.; also numerous UN concerts, Billie Holiday Theatre, N.Y.U.; European tours include Kingsberg Jazz Festival, Oslo, 1974, Montreux (Switzerland) Jazz Festival, 1974, Festival de Costa del Sol, Marbella, Spain, 1974, Ahus Jazz Festival, Kristianstad, Sweden, 1974, Festival at Antibes, 1974; Tour of Brazil, 1981, Festival de Vienne, France, 1985, Pompeii Jazz Festival, Italy, 1985, Internat. Festival Marrahesh, Marocco, 1986, 1st Festival Gnaoua Culture, Marocco, 1987, Lygano Festival Jazz, Switzerland, 1988, Jazzaldia, San Sebastian, Spain, 1988; Caribbean Cultural Ctrs. Expressions Festival, N.Y.C., 1988, Roots Festival, Lagos, Nigeria, 1988; featured quest artist One Hundred Yrs. of Jazz, Amsterdam, The Netherlands, 1989; lecture-concerts in Europe including Bern, Basel, Zurich, Lyons, 1975; recs. include Blue Moses, 1972 (number 1 in Record World's jazz chart), Volcano Blues, 1993, Monterey '66, 1994; compositions include Pam's Waltz, 1950, Little Niles, 1950, Hi Fly, 1958, Portrait of Vivian, 1959, Berkshire Blues, 1960, Uhruru Africa suite, 4 movements, 1960, African Cook Book, 1965, The Last Day, 1966, The Ganawa, 1971, Portrait of F.E. Weston, 1974, Carnival, Blues to Africa, Nuits Americani, Blue, Trilogy: Portraits of Ellington; Portraits of Monk; Self-Portrait of Weston, Verve, The Spirits of Our Ancestors, 1992; concert artist for radio-TV and maj. U.S. museums including Smithsonian Instn.; performed benefit concerts for anti-apartheid com. at UN through African-Am. Musicians Soc., 1961; appeared in film Jamboree, 1966; commd. The Africans, Spoleto Festival, U.S.A., 1981, The African Queens, Boston Pops, 1981, Portrait of Billie Holiday, Orch. Symphonique de Lyons and Ensemble Instrumental et Big Band de Grenoble, France, 1985, African Sunrise, City of Chicago, 1985; Spanish TV films: Jazz Entre Amigos, 1987, Randy in Tangier; Randy Weston, African Rhythms, Boston TV, 1989. Recipient New Star Pianist award Down Beat Internat. Critics Poll 1955, Pianist Most Deserving of Wider Recognition award, 1972, Broadway award Hollywood Advt. Club 1965, Premier prix de l'Academie du Jazz, France 1975; named World's Best Jazz Pianist Internat. Roots Festival, Lagos, Nigeria, 1988; Randy Weston Week declared in his honor Bklyn. Borough Pres.'s Office/Bklyn. Acad. Music, 1986; French Office Nationale de Diffusion Artistique grantee, 1976; Nat. Endowment for Arts grantee, 1974. Mem. ASCAP (Composers awards), Am. Fedn. Musicians. Sufi. Address: PO Box 749 Maplewood NJ 07040-0749 also: care Louise Billotte 595 Connecticut St San Francisco CA 94107-2832

WESTON, ROGER LANCE, banker; b. Waukegan, Ill., Mar. 2, 1943; s. Arthur Walter and Vivian Dawn (Thompson) W.; m. Kathleen Plotzke, Sept. 15, 1979; children: Cynthia Page, Kent Andrew, Arthur Eladio, Rebecca Dawn, Alice Sinclair, Elliott Churchill, Evan Walter, Spencer Lance. BS, MacMurray Coll., 1965; MBA, Washington U., St. Louis, 1967. Investment adviser Harris Trust & Savs. Bank, Chgo., 1967-69; sr. investment counselor Security Suprs., Chgo., 1969-70; exec. v.p., treas., chief fin. officer Telemed Corp., Hoffman Estates, Ill., 1971-79; vice chmn. Bank Lincolnwood, Ill., 1979-85; pres., chief exec. officer GSC Enterprises, Lincolnwood, 1979-85, EVCO, Inc., Itasca, Ill., 1985-87; vice chmn., chief exec. officer Evanston (Ill.) Bank, 1985-88; chmn. bd. dirs., pres., chief exec. officer GreatBanc, Inc., Aurora, Ill., 1986—. Mem. Barrington Hills (Ill.) Zoning Bd. Appeals, 1987, com. Asian art Art Inst. Chgo., 1987. Mem. Washington U. Eliot Soc. (chmn. membership com. 1986-91), Univ. Club. Republican. Presbyterian. Office: Great Banc Inc 2300 Barrington Rd Hoffman Estates IL 60195

WESTON, ROY FRANCIS, environmental consultant; b. Reedsburg, Wis., June 25, 1911; s. Charles Frederick and Hattie (Jensen) W.; m. Madeleen Elizabeth Kellner, Dec. 31, 1934; children: Susan Weston Thompson, Katherine Weston Swoyer Fittipaldi. B.C.E., U. Wis., 1933; M.C.E., NYU, 1939; D.Engring. (hon.), Drexel U., 1981; DSc (hon.), U. Wis. Madison, 1995. Registered profl. engr., 18 states; diplomate Am. Acad. Environ. Engrs. (pres. 1973-74). Jr. hwy. engr. Wis. Hwy. Dept., 1934-36; dist. engr. Wis. Dept. Health, 1936-37; san. engring. research fellow NYU, N.Y.C., 1937-39; san. engr. Atlantic Refining Co., Phila., 1939-55; chmn. bd. Roy F. Weston, Inc., West Chester, Pa., 1955-91, chmn. emeritus, 1991-96; chmn. bd., 1996—, environ. cons. Contbr. numerous articles on environ. control and sustainable devel. to profl. publs. vis. com. dept. civil and urban engring. U. Pa., Phila., also Ctr. for Marine and Environ. Studies, Lehigh U.; bd. overseers Sch. Engring., Pa. State U., former mem. indsl. and profl. adv. com. Pa. State U.; past bd. overseers Duke U. Sch. Engring.; past trustee Phila. Coll. Pharmacy and Sci.; former mem. Pa. Gov.'s Energy Coun. Recipient Disting. Svc. citation U. Wis., 1975, George Washington medal Phila. Engrs., 1973, Samual S. Baxter Meml. award Water Resources Assn. of Delaware River Basin, 1994, Nat. Engring. award Am. Assn. Engring. Socs., 1994, Gordon Maskew Fair award Am. Acad. Environ. Engrs., 1977. National Engineering Award, 1994; American Assn of Engineering Societies. Mem. ASCE (Simon W. Freese Environ. Engring. award and lecture 1995, Hon. Mention award 1994), APHA, NSPE (Engr. of Yr. award 1973), NAE, AIChE (environ. divsn. Lawrence K. Cecil award 1993), Am. Assn. Engring. Socs. (nat. engring. award 1994), Am. Chem. Soc., Air Pollution Control Assn., Cons. Engrs. Coun., Water Resources Assn., Pa. Soc. Profl. Engrs. (Engr. of Yr. 1970, 73), Water Pollution Control Fedn. (Arthur Sidney Bedell award 1959, Indsl. Wastes medal 1950, hon.), Delaware River Assn. (pres. 1976-77), Overbrook Golf Club, Phila. Engrs. Club. Office: Roy F Weston Inc 1 Weston Way West Chester PA 19380-1469

WESTON, WILLARD GALEN, diversified holdings executive; b. Eng., Oct. 29, 1940; s. W. Garfield Weston and Reta L. Howard; m. Hilary Frayne, 1966; 2 children. BA, U. Western Ont., LLD (hon.). Chmn. bd. Wittington Investments, Ltd., George Weston Ltd., Toronto, Ont., Can., Holt, Renfrew & Co. Ltd., Loblaw Cos. Ltd., Weston Foods Ltd., Weston Resources Ltd.; vice chmn. bd. dirs. Fortnum and Mason PLC (U.K.); bd. dirs. Assoc. Brit. Foods PLC (U.K.), Can. Imperial Bank Commerce, Brown Thomas Group Ltd. (Ireland). Pres. The W. Garfield Weston Found.; bd. dirs. Lester B. Pearson Coll. Pacific; life mem. Royal Ont. Mus., Art Gallery Ont. Officer Order of Can. Mem. Badminton and Racquet Club, York Club, Toronto Club, Guards Polo Club, Lyford Cay Club, Windsor Club (Fla.). Avocations: polo, tennis. Office: George Weston Ltd. 22 St Clair Ave E Ste 1900, Toronto, ON Canada M4T 2S7

WESTON, WILLIAM LEE, dermatologist; b. Grand Rapids, Minn., Aug. 13, 1938; s. Eugene and Edith Kathryn (Lee) W.; m. Janet J. Atkinson, June 9, 1964; children: Elizabeth Carol, William Kemp. AB, Whitman Coll., 1960; B in Med. Sci., U. S.D., 1963; MD, U. Colo., 1965. Resident in pediatrics U. Calif., San Francisco, 1967-68; intern, then resident in pediatrics U. Colo., Denver, 1965-67, resident in dermatology, 1970-72, asst. prof. dermatology and pediatrics, 1972-76, prof., 1976—, chmn. dept. dermatology, 1976—. Author: Practical Pediatric Dermatology, 1979, rev. edit., 1985, Color Textbook of Pediatric Dermatology, 1991, rev. edit., 1996; editor-in-chief Current Problems in Dermatology, 1988-93. With AUS, 1968-70. Mem. Soc. Pediatric Dermatology (founder, sec.-treas. 1975-80, pres. 1984-85), Colo. Dermatol. Soc. (pres.), Soc. Investigative Dermatology (bd. dirs.), Am. Acad. Dermatology (bd. dirs.). Methodist. Home: 8550 E Ponderosa Dr Parker CO 80134-8233 Office: 4200 E 9th Ave Denver CO 80220-3706

WESTOVER, SAMUEL LEE, managed health care executive; b. Soap Lake, Wash., May 30, 1955; s. Gordon Kent Westover and Janice Lelia (Matlock) Jensen; m. Susan Kern, July 13, 1977; children: Michael, S. Fielding, Austin, Clinton, Cassandra. BS in Acctg., Brigham Young U., 1978. Acct. Price Waterhouse, L.A., 1978-80; chief fin. officer, sr. v.p. Maxicare Health Plans, Inc., L.A., 1981-88; chief exec. officer and chief operating officer Western Health Plans, Inc., San Diego, 1988-90; chief fin. officer, sr. v.p. Blue Cross of Calif., Woodland Hills, 1990-93; CFO, sr. v.p. WellPoint Health Networks, Inc., Woodland Hills, 1993; pres., CEO Systemed Inc., Torrance, Calif., 1993—. Office: Systemed Inc 970 W 190th St Ste 400 Torrance CA 90502-1000

WESTPHAL, KLAUS WILHELM, university museum administrator; b. Berlin, Mar. 20, 1939; came to U.S., 1969; s. Wilhelm Heinrich and Irmgard (Henze) W.; m. Margaret Elisabeth Dorothea Wagner, May 16, 1969; children: Barbara, Marianne, Christine. BS in Geology, Eberhard-Karls Universität, Tübingen, Germany, 1960, MS, 1964, PhD in Paleontology, 1969. Dir. geology mus. U. Wis. Madison, 1969—; bd. dirs. natural history coun. U. Wis. Madison, 1973—, Friends of Geology Mus., Inc., 1977—; nat. speaker on paleontology Outreach, 1977—; instr. paleontology U. Wis., 1977—; leader expeditions fossil vertebrates including dinosaurs, 1977—. Participant various tchr.-tng. projects Wis. Pub. Schs. Lutheran. Home: 3709 High Rd Middleton WI 53562-1003 Office: U Wis Geology Mus 1215 W Dayton St Madison WI 53706-1600

WESTPHAL, RAINER JOHN, software company executive; b. Huntington Station, N.Y., July 7, 1935; s. Frank and Gertrude M. (Zebedies) W.; m. Antoinette M. Passo, May 7, 1960; children: Jeffrey, Stefanie, Amanda. BS in Bus. Adminstrn., Drexel U., 1959. Programmer RCA, Camden, N.J., 1960-62; sys. analyst, mgr. Ednl. Testing Svc., Princeton, N.J., 1962-67; cons. Peat, Marwick, Mitchell, Phila., 1968-72; v.p. Sorbus, Inc., King of Prussia, Pa., 1973-78; pres. Vertex, Inc., Berwyn, Pa., 1978—; ptnr. Westford Devel., Berwyn, Pa., 1990—; mem. Drexel U. Adv. Bd., Phila., 1992—. Author: (directory) National Sales Tax Rate, 1973; contbr. articles to profl. jours. Mem. N.J. Jaycees, Somerville, 1965; vol. mem. Phila. (Pa.) City Task Force, 1992. Mem. Inst. Property Taxation, Union League Phila., Chester Valley Golf Club (treas. 1985-86), Bear's Paw Golf Club. Republican. Roman Catholic. Avocations: golf, travel, bridge, chess, hiking. Office: Vertex Inc 1041 Old Cassatt Rd Berwyn PA 19312

WESTPHAL, WILLIAM HENRY, staff nurse; b. Pt. Washington, Wis., Oct. 29, 1946; s. Henry Vernon and Milda Emma (Sudbrink) W.; m. R. Elaine Stumreiter, Dec. 14, 1974. Cert. oper. rm. technician, Brook Army Med. Ctr., 1967; LPN with honors, Lakeshore Tech. Coll., 1971, ADN with honors, 1979; BBA, Lakeland Coll., 1993. LPN, RN, Wis. Staff nurse, surg. nurse orthopedics, gen. surgery, urology St. Nicholas Hosp., Sheboygan, Wis., 1969-79; surg. asst. orthopedics Sheboygan Clinics, 1979-89; staff nurse Sheboygan County Instns., 1989-95, Flambeau Med. Ctr., Park Falls, 1996—; owner, operator Edge of Town Motel, Park Falls, Wis., 1995—; treas. LPN state chpt. Wis. Fedn. LPN, Sheboygan, 1971-79. Mem. Park Falls planning comm., 1995—. Sgt. 1st class U.S. Army, 1967-77, Vietnam, 1968-69. Mem. Am. Fedn. Nurses and Health Profls. (Wis. nurses union 1989-95), , Wis. Innkeepers Assn., Price County C. of C., KC (1st degree knight). Roman Catholic. Avocations: world travel, photography, woodcraft, golf. Home: North Hwy 13 900 4th Ave N Park Falls WI 54552

WESTWATER, JAMES WILLIAM, chemical engineering educator; b. Danville, Ill., Nov. 24, 1919; s. John and Lois (Maxwell) W.; m. Elizabeth Jean Keener, June 9, 1942; children: Barbara, Judith, David, Beverly. B.S., U. Ill., 1941; Ph.D., U. Del., 1948. Mem. faculty U. Ill., Urbana, 1948—; prof. chem. engring. U. Ill., 1962—, head dept., 1962-80; papers chmn. 5th Nat. Heat Transfer Conf., Buffalo, 1960; chmn. 3d Internat. Heat Transfer Conf., Chgo., 1966; Reilly lectr. Notre Dame U., 1958; Donald L. Katz lectr. U. Mich., 1978. Contbr. articles profl. jours. Recipient Conf. award 8th Nat. Heat Transfer Conf., 1965. Fellow AIChE (dir., past divsn. chmn., inst. lectr. 1964, named eminent chem. engr., William H. Walker award 1966, Max Jakob award with ASME 1972, Founders award 1984, heat transfer and energy conversion award 1989, Ernest Thiele award 1994); mem. ASME, NAE, Am. Chem. Soc., Am. Soc. Engring. Edn. (Vincent Bendix award 1974). Home: 116 W Iowa St Urbana IL 61801-5035

WESTWICK, CARMEN ROSE, nursing educator, consultant; b. Holstein, Iowa, Feb. 2, 1936; d. J. Alfred and Hazel C. (Lage) Armiger; m. Richard A. Westwick, Dec. 28, 1957; children: Timothy, Ann. BS in Nursing, U. Iowa, 1958; MS, U. Colo., 1960; PhD, Denver U., 1972. RN, Tenn. Instr. Sch. Nursing West Suburban Hosp., Oak Park, Ill., 1958-59, 60-62; nurse Navajo Presch., Carson's Trading Post, N.Mex., 1967; lectr. then prof. U. Colo., Denver, 1968-69, 72-77; program dir. Western Coun. on Higher Edn. in Nursing, Boulder, Colo., 1976-77; prof. nursing, dean U. N.Mex, Albuquerque, 1977-81, Boston U., 1982-85, S.D. State U., Brookings, 1988-91; NHC chair of excellence in nursing NHC, Murfreesboro, 1993—; exec. dir. N.H. Bd. Nursing, Concord, 1986-87; case reviewer Joint Underwriters Assn., Boston, 1983-92; mem. publs. and rsch. com. Aberdeen (S.D.) Area Indian Health Svc., 1989-91; manuscript reviewer Midwest Alliance in Nursing, Indpls., 1989-92, Holistic Nursing Jour.; mem. adv. coun. S.D. Office Rural Health, Pierre, 1989-91. Contbr. articles to profl. jours. Nurse trainee fellow Nursing div. Dept. Health and Human Svcs., 1959-60, Predoctoral fellow, 1969-72; Nat. Merit scholar, 1954-56. Fellow Am. Acad. Nursing; mem. Sigma Theta Tau (nat. 1st v.p. 1968, disting. lectr. 1996—), Phi Kappa Phi, Kappa Delta Pi. Lutheran. Avocations: antiques, quilting. Office: Mid Tenn State U Dept Nursing Box 81 Murfreesboro TN 37132

WESTWOOD, ALBERT RONALD CLIFTON, retired engineer; b. Birmingham, Eng., June 9, 1932; came to U.S., 1958, naturalized, 1974; s. Albert Sydney and Ena Emily (Clifton) W.; m. Jean Mavis Bullock, 1956; children: Abigail, Andrea. B.S. with honors, U. Birmingham, 1953, Ph.D. in Phys. Metallurgy, 1956, D.Sc. in Materials Sci., 1968. Chartered engr. and physicist, U.K. Tech. officer research dept., metals div. Imperial Chem. Industries, Birmingham, 1956-58, successively scientist, sr. scientist, assoc. dir., head materials sci. dept., dep. dir., 1958-74; dir. Martin Marietta Labs., Balt., 1974-84, corp. dir. R & D, 1984-87; v.p. R & D Martin Marietta Corp., Bethesda, Md., 1987-90, v.p. sci., 1990, v.p. rsch. and tech., 1990-93; v.p. rsch. and exploratory tech. Sandia Nat. Labs. divsn. Lockheed Martin Corp., Albuquerque, 1993-96; mem. various govt. and univ. adv. coms. including Office Sci. and Tech. Policy, NASA, NRC, NAE, NSF, Nat. Inst. Standards and Tech., U. Md., U. Fla., MIT, Ga. Inst. Tech., Coun. on Competitivemenss; dir. Martin Marietta Energy Systems. mem. various govt. and univ. adv. coms. including Office of Sci. and Tech. Policy, NASA, NRC, NAE, NSF, Nat. Inst. Standards and Tech., U. Md., U. Fla., MIT, Ga. Inst. Tech., Coun. of Competitiveness; dir. Martin Marietta Energy Sys.; bd. dirs. U.S. Civilian Rsch. and Devel. Found. for Former Soviet Union. Chmn. Md. Humanities Coun.; bd. dirs. N.Mex. Symphony Orch., Santa Fe Opera; mem. N.Mex. Endowment for Humanities. Recipient disting. young scientist award Md. Acad. Scis., 1966, centennial award U. Md., 1994, Beilby gold medal Royal Inst. Chemistry, 1970, Herbert J. Holloman award Acta Metallurgica, 1996, Tewksbury lectr. U. Melbourne, 1974. Fellow

AAAS (chmn. indsl. sci. sect.), Am. Soc. Metals Internat. (Burgess lectr. 1984, Campbell meml. lectr. 1987, disting. lectr. materials and soc. 1995), the Minerals, Metals and Materials Soc. (dir., fin. officer, pres. 1990, Krumb lectr. 1988, leadership award 1992); mem. NRC (chmn. com. engring. and tech. sys.), ASME (disting. lectr. 1989), NAE, Royal Swedish Acad. Engring. Scis., Russian Acad. Engring., Md. Acad. Scis. (mem. coun.), Md. Inst. Metals (pres.), Indsl. Rsch. Inst. (bd. dirs., pres. 1989-90). Home: 1413 Pinnacle View Dr NE Albuquerque NM 87112-6558

WESTWOOD, JAMES NICHOLSON, lawyer; b. Portland, Oreg., Dec. 3, 1944; s. Frederick Alton and Catherine (Nicholson) W.; m. Janet Sue Butler, Feb. 23, 1980; children: Laura, David. BA, Portland State U., 1967; JD, Columbia U., 1974. Bar: Oreg. 1974, U.S. Dist. Ct. Oreg. 1974, U.S. Ct. Appeals (9th cir.) 1978, U.S. Supreme Ct. 1981, U.S. Ct. Appeals (fed. cir.) 1984. Assoc. Miller, Anderson, Nash, Yerke & Wiener, Portland, 1974-76, 78-81; asst. to pres. Portland State U., 1976-78; ptnr. Miller, Nash, Wiener, Hager & Carlsen, Portland, 1981—. Recipient Disting. Svc. award Portland State U. Found., 1984, Outstanding Alumni award Portland State U., 1992. Mem. ABA (chmn. forest resources com. 1987-89), Oreg. Bar Assn. (chmn.-elect appellate practice sect. 1995-96), Am. Acad. Appellate Lawyers, Univ. Club (bd. govs. 1994), City Club (pres. 1991-92). Republican. Unitarian. Home: 3121 NE Thompson St Portland OR 97212-4908 Office: Miller Nash Wiener Hager & Carlsen 111 SW 5th Ave Portland OR 97204-3604

WESTWOOD, MELVIN NEIL, horticulturist, pomologist; b. Hiawatha, Utah, Mar. 25, 1923; s. Neil and Ida (Blake) W.; m. Wanda Mae Shields, Oct. 12, 1946; children: Rose Dawn, Nancy Gwen, Robert Melvin, Kathryn Mae. Student, U. Utah, 1948-50; BS in Pomology, Utah State U., 1952; PhD in Pomology, Wash. State U., 1956. Field botanist Utah State U., Logan, 1951-52, supt. Howell Field Sta., 1952-53; rsch. asst. State Coll. Wash., 1953-55; rsch. horticulturist Agrl. Rsch. Svc. USDA, Wenatchee, Wash., 1955-60; assoc. prof. Oreg. State U., Corvallis, 1960-67, prof., 1967-80, prof. emeritus, 1986—; rsch. dir. Nat. Clonal Germplasm Repository, Corvallis, 1980-82, nat. tech. advisor, 1984-86. Author: Deciduous Fruit and Nut Production, 1976, Temperate-Zone Pomology: Physiology and Culture, 1978, 3d edit., 1993, Contract Military Air Transport: From the Ground Up, 1995; co-author: Cherry Nutrition, 1966, Pear Rootstocks, 1987, Management and Utilization of Plant Germplasm, 1988, Maintenance and Storage: Clonal Germplasm, 1989, Genetic Resources of Malus, 1991; contbr. more than 200 articles to profl. jours. With USAAF, 1946-47. Grantee NSF, 1966; recipient Hartman Cup award Oreg. Hort. Soc., 1989. Fellow Am. Soc. Hort. Sci. (bd. dirs. 1974-75, chmn. com. environ. quality 1971, adv. coun. 1974-79, mem. pomology sect. 1967-74, publs. com. 1971-74, pres. western region 1974, Joseph Harvey Gourley award for Pomology 1958, 77, Stark award for Pomology 1969, 77, Outstanding Researcher award 1986); mem. AAAS, Am. Soc. Plant Physiologists, Am. Pomological Soc. (adv. bd. 1970-75, exec. bd. 1980-84, Paul Howe Shepard award 1968, 82, Wilder medal 1980), UN Assn. USA, Ams. United for Separation of Ch. and State, Amnesty Internat., Phi Kappa Phi, Gamma Sigma Delta. Baptist. Achievements include patent for Autumn Blaze ornamental pear; research on Pyrus (pear), Malus (apple) and Prunus (plum, cherry, peach) and on the physiology of rootstock genera. Office: Oreg State U Dept Horticulture Corvallis OR 97331

WESTWOOD, VIVIENNE, fashion designer; 2 children. Dr. h.c., Royal Coll. Art, 1992. Prof. Hochschule der Künste-Berlin, 1993—. Created Pirate Collection, 1980; launched Mini Crini, 1985; developed new glamourmovement; introduced corset as pret-a-porter garmet Harris Tweed Collection, 1987; introduced Anglomania collection, 1992, Café Society collection, 1993, On Liberty, 1994, Erotic Zones, 1994, Vive la Cocotte, 1985, Les Fremmes S/S, 1996, Stormin a Tea Cup Alm, 1996-97. Named Brit. Designer of Yr., 1990, 91.

WETHERALD, MICHELE WARHOLIC, lawyer; b. Lakewood, Ohio, June 17, 1954; d. Michael and Veronica (Walkuski) Warholic; m. Gary R. Wetherald, Nov. 26, 1987. AAB, Lorain County C.C., Elyria, Ohio, 1977; BA, Hiram Coll., 1980; JD, U. Akron, 1985. Bar: Ohio, 1986; U.S. Dist. Ct. (no. dist.) Ohio, 1987. Sec., dispatcher State Highway Patrol Ohio Turnpike Commn., Berea, Ohio, 1973-77; pers. and employee benefits rep. Terex Div. Gen. Motors Corp., Hudson, Ohio, 1978-83; labor relations rep. Lordstown Assembly Div. Gen. Motors Corp., Warren, Ohio, 1984-86; supr. labor relations and hourly employment Inland Div. Gen. Motors Corp., Livonia, Mich., 1986-87; staff atty. Hyatt Legal Svcs., Niles, Ohio, 1987-89; mng. atty. Hyatt Legal Svcs., Boardman, Ohio, 1990; assoc. Newman, Olson & Kerr, Youngstown, Ohio, 1990-95; human resources adminstr. W.Va. No. C.C., 1996—; instr. Hiram (Ohio) Coll. Mem. exec. bd. Hiram (Ohio) Coll. Alumni, 1990-93; mem. pub. affairs com., profl. connections, bd. trustees YMCA; mem. Cath. Svc. League; trustee, exec. com. Ursuline Ctr. Bd. Mem. ABA, AAUW (pres. Warren Ohio br., Ohio bd. and legal advocacy fund chair), Ohio State Bar Assn., Trumbull County Bar Assn., Mahoning County Bar Assn., The Pers. Assn. Roman Catholic. Avocations: skiing, running, reading. Home: 49376 S Park Cir Calcutta OH 43920-9530 Office: WVa No C C 1704 Market St Wheeling WV

WETHERILL, EIKINS, lawyer, stock exchange executive; b. Phila., Oct. 3, 1919; s. A. Hecksher and Edwina (Brunner) W. LL.B., U. Pa., 1948. Practiced in Phila., 1948-55, Norristown, 1955—; assoc. firm Evans, Bayard & Frick, 1948-50; ptnr. Reilly, Hepburn, Earle & Wetherill, 1950-55; firm Henderson, Wetherill, O'Hey & Horsey, 1955—; pres. Phila. Stock Exchange, Inc., 1965-81; bd. dirs. Germantown Savs. Bank; fin. commentator CBS-TV News, 1966-68; chmn. bd. Sta. WHYY-TV, 1970-76, dir., 1976-90; dir. 1st Pa. Corp., 1st Pa. Bank, solicitor to lt. gov. Pa., 1951-55, asst. U.S. atty. gen., 1953-55, treas., Montgomery County, 1956-59; pres. Montgomery County Bd. Commrs., 1960-63; chmn. Pa. Securities Commn., 1963-65; commr. Delaware Valley Regional Planning Commn., 1965—, chmn., 1968-69, 70-71, 78-79. Former bd. dirs. Greater Phila. Partnership; chmn. Phila. Drama Guild, 1975-80, dir., 1980-87; trustee Davis and Elkins Coll., 1973-91. Served to capt., cav. Signal Corps, OSS, AUS, 1941-45. Mem. Am., Phila. bar assns., Delta Psi. Episcopalian. Clubs: Phila. (Phila.), Racquet (Phila.). Office: 1 Montgomery Ave Ste 902 Norristown PA 19401-1948

WETHERILL, GEORGE WEST, geophysicist, planetary scientist; b. Phila., Aug. 12, 1925; s. George West and Leah Victoria (Hardwick) W.; m. Phyllis May Steiss, June 17, 1950 (wid. 1995); children: Rachel, George, Sarah. Ph.B., U. Chgo., 1948, S.B. in Physics, 1949, S.M., 1951, Ph.D. in Physics, 1953. Mem. staff dept. terrestrial magnetism Carnegie Inst., Washington, 1953-60; prof. geophysics and geology UCLA, 1960-75, chmn. dept. planetary and space sci., 1968-72; dir. dept. terrestrial magnetism Carnegie Inst., Washington, 1975-91, mem. sci. staff, 1991—; cons. NASA, NSF, Nat. Acad. Sci. Editor Ann. Rev. of Earth and Planetary Sci.; assoc. editor, Meteoritics, Icarus; contbr. articles to profl. jours. With USN, 1943-46. Recipient G.K. Gilbert award Geol. Soc. Am., 1984, Profl. Achievement Citation U. Chgo. Alumni Assn., 1985. Fellow Am. Acad. Arts and Scis., Am. Geophys. Union (pres. planetology sect. 1970-72, recipient H.H. Hess medal, 1991), Meteoritical Soc. (v.p. 1971-74, 81-83, pres. 1983-85, Leonard medal 1981); mem. NAS, Geochem. Soc. (v.p. 1973-74, pres. 1974-75), Internat. Assn. Geochem. and Cosmochemistry (pres. 1977-80), Internat. Astron. Union, Am. Astron. Soc. Div. Planetary Scis. and Div. Dynamic Astronomy (G.P. Kuiper prize 1986), Religious Soc. Free Quakers, Internat. Soc. for Study of Origin of Life. Episcopalian. Office: Carnegie Inst 5241 Broad Branch Rd NW Washington DC 20015-1305 *Seek him that maketh the Pleiades and Orion, and turneth the shadow of death into morning. Amos 5:8.*

WETHERINGTON, ROGER VINCENT, journalism educator, newspaper copy editor; b. Jacksonville, Fla., Mar. 12, 1942; s. Roger Vincent and Ruby Estelle (Jones) W.; m. Andra Marie Miller, Aug. 31, 1972; 1 child, Brady Miller. BA in English Lit., Columbia U., 1965; MA in Journalism (with hons.), U. So. Calif., 1979, PhD in Comm., 1986. Copyboy, reporter, asst. city editor Daily News, N.Y.C., 1963-76; lectr. journalism Calif. State U., Long Beach, 1976-78, 87-90; asst. prof. Calif. State U., Northridge, 1979-84; asst. prof. comm. St. John's U., Jamaica, N.Y., 1990-93, assoc. prof., 1993—; copy editor N.Y. Times, N.Y.C., 1992—. Recipient media award for incisive reporting Cancer Care, Inc., 1974, faculty devel. award Calif. State U.-Northridge, 1983; teaching fellow Gannett Found., 1977. Mem. AAUP, Assn. for Edn. in Journalism and Mass Comm., Soc. Profl. Journalists, Investigative Reporters and Editors, Newspaper Guild, Deadline Club. Avocation: opera. Office: St John's U 8000 Utopia Pky Jamaica NY 11439

WETHINGTON, CHARLES T., JR., academic administrator. AB, Ea. Ky. U., 1956; postgrad., Syracuse U., 1958-59; MA, U. Ky., 1962, PhD, 1965. Instr. ednl. psychology U. Ky., Lexington, 1965-66; dir. Maysville (Ky.) C.C., 1967-71; asst. v.p. c.c. system U. Ky., Lexington, 1971-81, v.p. c.c. system, 1981-82, chancellor c.c. system, 1982-88, chancellor c.c. system and univ. rels., 1988-89, interim pres., 1989-90, pres., 1990—; chmn. legis. com. State Dirs. Community and Jr. Colls., 1983-85, chmn. nat. coun., 1985-86; mem. commn. on colls. So. Assn. Schs. and Colls., 1978-84, vice chmn. exec. coun., 1984, trustee, 1986-89; mem. So. Regional Edn. Bd., 1988—, mem. exec. com., 1989-93, vice chmn., 1991-93. Bd. dirs. Bluegrass State Skills Corp., 1984-91, vice-chmn. bd. dirs., 1986-87; bd. visitors Community Coll. of Air Force, 1986-90; mem. Ky. Ednl. TV Adv. Com., 1984—; mem. jud. nominating commn. 22nd Jud. Dist., Fayette County, Ky., 1988-91; mem. Ky. Coal Authority, 1990—, So. Growth Policies Bd., 1990—; served with sec. svc. USAF, 1957-61. Home: Maxwell Pl 471 Rose St Lexington KY 40508 Office: U Ky 104 Administration Bldg Lexington KY 40506

WETHINGTON, JOHN ABNER, JR., retired nuclear engineering educator; b. Tallahassee, Apr. 18, 1921; s. John Abner and Mary McQueen (Hale) W.; m. Kathryn Kemp Greene, Aug. 19, 1943; 1 son, John Abner III. A.B., Emory U., 1942, M.A., 1943; Ph.D., Northwestern U., 1950. Vis. research asst. Princeton, 1943-44; chemist Fercleve Corp., Oak Ridge, 1944-46; chemist to sr. chemist Oak Ridge Nat. Lab., 1949-53; asst. prof. to prof. nuclear engring. U. Fla., 1953-85, prof. emeritus, 1985—; on leave as fellow Lawrence Livermore Lab., Calif., 1971-72; vis. scientist P.R. Nuclear Center, 1962-63, Oak Ridge Nat. Lab., 1979-80; U.S. del. to Radiation Congress, Haregate, Eng., 1963, 2d Internat. Conf. Peaceful Uses of Atomic Energy, Switzerland, 1958; faculty participant Oak Ridge Sch. Reactor Tech., 1957-58. Contbr. articles to profl. jours. Fellow AAAS; mem. Am. Chem. Soc., Am. Nuclear Soc., Phi Beta Kappa, Sigma Xi, Alpha Chi Sigma. Democrat. Methodist. Home: 109 NW 22nd Dr Gainesville FL 32603-1426

WETHINGTON, NORBERT ANTHONY, college administrator; b. Dayton, Ohio, Sept. 14, 1943; s. Norbert and Sophie Lillian W.; m. Martha M. Vannice, Aug. 13, 1966; children: Paula, Mark, Eric, Kristen, Rebecca, Lisa, Bethany. BA, U. Dayton, 1965; MA, John Carroll U., 1967; postgrad. Baldwin Wallace Coll., 1968-70, U. Toledo, 1990—. Grad. asst., teaching assoc. John Carroll U., Cleve., 1965-67; English tchr. Padua Franciscan High Sch., Parma, Ohio, 1967-70; instr., chmn. dept. tech. writing and speech N. Central Tech. Coll., Mansfield, Ohio, 1970-74; dir. evening div. Terra Tech. Coll., Fremont, Ohio, 1974-80, dir. public and cmty. svc. technologies, 1980-94; dir. humanities Terra State C.C., 1994—; cons. several profl. assns. and non-profit groups. Vice pres. Sandusky County Bd. Health, 1979-80. Mem. Am. Vocat. Assn., Ohio Vocat. Assn. (pres. tech. edn. div. 1985-86, Disting. Svc. award 1987), Nat. Council Tchrs. English. Democrat. Roman Catholic. Contbr. articles to profl. jours. Home: 1036 Hazel St Fremont OH 43420-2115 Office: Terra State Cmty Coll 2830 Napoleon Rd Fremont OH 43420-9670

WETLAUFER, DONALD BURTON, biochemist, educator; b. New Berlin, N.Y., Apr. 4, 1925; s George C. and Olga (Kirckhoff) W.; m. Lucille D. Croce, May 5, 1950; children—Lise, Eric. B.S. in Chemistry, U. Wis., Madison, 1946, M.S. in Biochemistry, 1952, Ph.D., 1954. Chemist Argonne (Ill.) Nat. Lab., 1944, 46-47, Bjorksten Lab., Madison, 1948-50; Carlsberg Lab., Copenhagen, 1955-56; research asso. Harvard U., 1956-61, tutor biochem. sci., 1958-61; asst. prof. biochemistry Ind. U. Med. Sch., 1961-62; asso. prof., then prof. biochemistry U. Minn. Med. Sch., 1962-75; DuPont prof. chemistry U. Del., Newark, 1975—, chmn. dept., 1975-85; vis. investigator Max Planck Inst. Ernahrungsphy., 1974-78; mem. fellowship rev. com. NATO, 1970; cons. Nat. Inst. Gen. Med. Sci., 1964—, NSF, 1980—. Author rsch. papers in field of protein biochemistry, protein folding and high performance protein purification; severl editl. positions; indsl. cons. NSF predoctoral fellow, 1952-54; Nat. Found. Infantile Paralysis postdoctoral fellow, 1955-56; Am. Heart Assn. postdoctoral fellow, 1956-58; grantee USPHS, 1961—; grantee NATO, 1974-77; grantee NSF, 1977—; grantee AEC, 1962; recipient Career Devel. award USPHS, 1961-62. Mem. AAAS, Am. Chem. Soc. (councilor, alt. councilor divsn. biol. chemistry 1975-87), Am. Soc. Biochemistry and Molecular Biology, The Protein Soc., Chromatography Forum, Phi Beta Kappa. Office: U Del Dept Chemistry & Biochemistry Newark DE 19716

WETMORE, BYRON F., construction company executive; b. 1932. Grad., Mansfield State Coll., 1954, Pa. State U., 1957. Joined Lane Constrn. Corp., Meriden, Conn., 1957, from various mgmt. positions to pres., 1957—. Office: Lane Constrn Corp 965 E Main St Meriden CT 06450-6006*

WETMORE, THOMAS TRASK, III, retired foundation administrator, retired coast guard officer; b. New London, Conn., Oct. 15, 1925; s. Thomas Trask and Vivian (Brown) W.; m. Joan M. Hancock, Feb. 5, 1949; children: Thomas Trask IV, James R., Jennifer Wetmore Sellers, Daniel H., Judith J. Wetmore Logan. Student, Yale U., 1943-44; B.S. in Marine Engring, U.S. Coast Guard Acad., 1948; postgrad., U.S. Naval Postgrad. Sch., 1951; M.A., N.Y. U., 1973. Commd. ensign U.S. Coast Guard, 1948, advanced through grades to rear adm., 1977; instr. profl. studies dept. C. G. Acad., New London, Conn., 1957-61; comdg. officer tender USCGC Papaw, Charleston, S.C., 1961-63; chief communications br. 5th C. G. Dist., Portsmouth, Va., 1963-67; comdg. officer USCGC Chincoteague, Norfolk, Va., 1967-69; communications officer C. G. Atlantic Area, Governors Island, N.Y., 1969-72; chief aids to nav. br. 3d C. G. Dist., Governors Island, 1972-74; chief ops. div. 3d C. G. Dist., 1974-75; dep. comdr. Atlantic Area, 1975-76; asst. supt. C. G. Acad., New London, 1976-77; chief Office of Reserve, U.S. C. G. Hdqrs., Washington, 1977-79; dist. comdr. 5th C. G. Dist., 1979-81; ret., 1981; exec. dir. Pequot Community Found., 1983-93; ret., 1993. Effective cycling instr. League Am. Bicyclists. Decorated Legion of Merit, Meritorious Service medal with gold star, C. G. Commendation medal with gold star, C. G. Achievement medal with ops. disting. device. Mem. U.S. C. G. Acad. Alumni Assn., Ret. Officers Assn., Pequot Cycling Club. Club: Rotary. Home: 62 Glenwood Pl New London CT 06320-2907

WETSCH, JOHN ROBERT, information systems specialist; b. Dickinson, N.D., Aug. 27, 1959; s. Joseph John and Florence Mae (Edwards) W.; m. Laura Jean Johnson, Aug. 29, 1981; children: Julie Elizabeth, Katherine Anne, John Michael. BS, U. State of N.Y.-Regents Coll., Albany, 1984; MA, Antioch U., 1989; PhD, Nova S.E. U., 1994. Radiation physics instr. Grand Forks (N.D.) Clinic, 1983-85; sr. programmer PRC, Inc., Cavalier Air Force Sta., N.D., 1987-91, PARCS project-SAFEGUARD sys.; pres. Dakota Sci. Inc., Langdon, N.D., 1988-95; instr. U. N.D.-Lake Region, Devils Lake, 1988-91; systems adminstr. U.S. Courts Nat. Fine Ctr., Raleigh, N.C., 1991-94; bus. sys. specialist Raleigh (N.C.) Info. Sys. Svc. Ctr., 1994—; cons. on Wave Obs./N.D. Proposal, Gov.'s Office, Bismarck, 1991; founder, developer Dakota Sci., Inc., Langdon, 1988-95; instr. divsn. continuing edn. Wake Tech. C.C., 1993—. Author: (with others) COMPUTE!'s 2nd Book of Amiga, 1988; contbr. articles to COMPUTE! Jour. of Progressive Computing, 1987, other profl. jours. Mem. coll. scholarship selection com. Cavalier Air Force Sta., N.D., 1990; program coord. Lake Region Outreach, U. N.D., Cavalier Air Force Sta., 1988-91; mem. Bd. Alumni Trustees, SUNY-Regents Coll., Albany, 1995—; pres. Zeta Rho chpt. Pi Kappa Alpha, Grand Forks, 1981. SMITS scholar N.D. Acad. Sci., 1990; Larimore-Mathews scholar U. N.D., Grand Forks, 1978, N.D. Acad. Sci. scholar, 1978; recipient Westinghouse Sci. Talent Search award, 1978. Mem. AAAS, IEEE, IEEE Computer Soc., N.Y. Acad. Scis., Assn. Computing Machinery, Regents Coll. Degrees (grad. resource network), Assn. for Computing Machinery, Dakota Astron. Soc. (co-founder, pres. 1987-91). Republican. Roman Catholic. Achievements include missile simulation; microcomputer short range weather forecasting algorithm, model of the motion of freely falling bodies in 3 dimensions as an elliptic paraboloid, study in astronomy and culture, and astronomy's impact on devel. on Western civilization, system administration assessment of U.S. Courts and establishment and assessment of information control systems for the U.S. Courts National Fine Center. Home: 5069 Tall Pines Ct Raleigh NC 27609-4662 Office: RAISSC 4200 Wake Forest Rd Raleigh NC 27668-9000

WETSCH, PEGGY A., nursing informaticist, educator; b. San Diego; d. Harvey William Henry and Helen Catherine (Thorpe) Brink; m. Gerald M. Wetsch, June 26, 1971; children: Brian Gearald, Lynette Kirstiann Nicole. Diploma, Calif. Hosp. Sch. Nursing, 1971; BSN cum laude, Pepperdine U., 1980; MS in Nursing, Calif. State U., L.A., 1985. Cert. in nursing adminstrn., human resource devel. Clin. nurse Orange County Med. Ctr./U. Calif. Irvine Med. Ctr., Orange, Calif., 1971-75; pediatric head nurse U. Calif. Irvine Med. Ctr., 1975-79; clin. nurse educator Palm Harbor Gen./Med. Ctr. Garden Grove, Calif., 1980-81; dir. ednl. svcs. Med. Ctr. of Garden Grove, 1981-85; dir. edn. Mission Hosp. Regional Med. Ctr., Mission Viejo, Calif., 1986-92; coord. computer and learning resources L.A. Med. Ctr. Sch. Nursing, 1992-95; assoc. part time faculty Saddleback Coll., 1990-94; cons. ptnr. nur.SYS-Edn. systems Cons., 1995—; lectr. statewide nursing program Calif. State U., Dominguez Hills, 1986-92; ednl. cons. Author: (with others) Nursing Diagnosis: Guidelines to Planning Care, 1993, 2d edit., 1994, 3d edit., 1996; contbr. articles to profl. jours. Treas. Orange County Nursing Edn. Coun., 1986-87, 88-90, pres., 1987-88. Mem. ANA, NLN, Am. Nursing Informatics Assn. (pres.-elect 1996—, elections com. So. Calif. chpt. 1994, coord. continuing edn., conf. planning com.), Am. Soc. Health Edn. and Tng., N.am. Nursing Diagnosis Assn. (secondary reviewer Diagnostic Rev. 1989-90, expert adv. panel 1990-92, mem. diagnosis rev. com. 1992-96), Soc. Calif. Nursing Diagnosis Assn. (membership chmn. 1984-92, pres. 1992-94), Nat. Am. Mgmt. Assn. (charter L.A. County, U. So. Calif. Med. Ctr. chpt.), Spina Bifida Assn. Am., Phi Kappa Phi, Sigma Theta Tau (pres. Iota Eta chpt. 1990-92). Home: 1520 San Clemente Ln Corona CA 91720-7949

WETSTEIN, GARY M., accountant, company executive. CPA, Mich., N.Y. BDO Seidman, LLP; Chmn., chief exec. officer BDO Seidman, Detroit, 1990—. Office: BDO Seidman LLP Ste 1900 755 W Big Beaver Rd Troy MI 48084-4903 also: BBO Seidman LLP 330 Madison Ave New York NY 10017-5001

WETTACK, F. SHELDON, academic administrator. AB, San Jose State U., 1960, MA, 1962; PhD, U. Tex., Austin, 1967. From asst. prof. to prof. Hope Coll., Holland, Mich., 1967-82, dean nat. and social scis., 1974-82; dean faculty arts and scis. U. Richmond, 1982-89; pres. Wabash Coll., Crawfordsville, Ind., 1989-93; v.p., dean of faculty Harvey Mudd Coll., Claremont, Calif., 1993—. Office: Harvey Mudd Coll 301 E 12th St Claremont CA 91711-5901

WETTELAND, JOHN KARL, professional baseball player; b. San Mateo, Calif., Aug. 21, 1966. Ed., Coll. of San Mateo. With L.A. Dodgers, 1989-91, Montreal Expos, 1992-94; pitcher N.Y. Yankees, 1995—. Office: Yankee Stadium E 161st St and River Ave Bronx NY 10451

WETTER, EDWARD, broadcasting executive; b. Hoboken, N.J., Feb. 2, 1919; s. Edward and Ottilie (Steup) W.; m. Alice Kornat, Nov. 6, 1940 (div. 1946); 1 son, Robert Edward; m. Ruth Lowenstein, Oct. 26, 1954 (div. 1971); 1 dau., Karen Deborah; m. Virginia F. Pate, Apr. 7, 1972. B.A., U. Mich., 1939, M.S., 1941. Dir. spl. ops. Office Sec. Def., 1946-57; bus. broker Allen Kander & Co., N.Y.C., 1957-59; pres. Edward Wetter & Co., Inc., Havre de Grace, Md., 1959—, Harford Enterprises, Havre de Grace, 1978—; v.p. Edwin Tornberg and Co., Inc., N.Y.C., 1959-73; sec-treas. Radio One Five Hundred, Inc., Indpls., 1964—, Radio 900, Inc., Louisville, 1966-90, Radio 780, Inc., Arlington, Va., 1977—. Contbr. to: Biol. Scis., Vol. 2, 1955. Chmn. Zoning Appeals Bd., Havre de Grace, 1982. Served to capt. AUS, 1941-46. Lodge: Rotary. Home and Office: 1000 Chesapeake Dr Havre De Grace MD 21078-3902

WETTERHAHN, KAREN ELIZABETH, chemistry educator; b. Plattsburgh, N.Y., Oct. 16, 1948; d. Gustave George and Mary Elizabeth (Thibault) W.; m. Leon H. Webb, June 19, 1982; children—Leon Ashley, Charlotte Elizabeth. B.S., St. Lawrence U., 1970; Ph.D., Columbia U., 1975. Chemist, Mearl Corp., Ossining, N.Y., 1970-71; research fellow Columbia U., N.Y.C., 1971-75, postdoctoral fellow, 1975-76; asst. prof. chemistry Dartmouth Coll., Hanover, N.H., 1976-82, assoc. prof., 1982-86, prof., 1986—, Albert Bradley 3rd Century prof. in the scis., 1996—; assoc. dean faculty scis., 1990-94, acting dean faculty, 1995. Contbr. articles to profl. jours. A.P. Sloan fellow, 1981. Mem. Am. Chem. Soc., Am. Assn. Cancer Research, AAAS, N.Y. Acad. Scis. Office: Dartmouth Coll Dept Chemistry 6128 Burke Lab Hanover NH 03755-3564

WETTIG, PATRICIA, actress; b. Cin., Dec. 4, 1951; m. Ken Olin, 1982; children: Clifford, Roxanne. Student, Ohio Wesleyan U., U. Aberdeen, Scotland; grad. in drama, Temple U.; studies with Bill Esper, Neighborhood Playhouse, N.Y.C. Personal dresser to Shirley MacLaine; mem. Circle Repertory Co. Appeared in theater prodns. including The Woolgatherer, 1980, The Diviners, 1981, Talking With, 1984, TV series St. Elsewhere, 1986-88, thirtysomething, 1987-91 (Emmy award for best supporting actress in drama 1988, for best lead actress in drama 1990, 1991), Courthouse, 1995—; guest appearances on L.A. Law, Hill Street Blues; appeared TV movies Silent Motive, 1992, Taking Back my Life: The Nancy Ziegenmeyer Story, 1992, Parallel Lives, 1994, The Langoliers, 1995; appeared in motion pictures, Guilty by Suspicion, 1991, City Slickers, 1991, City Slickers II: The Legend of Curley's Gold, 1994.

WETZEL, CARROLL ROBBINS, lawyer; b. Trenton, N.J., Apr. 5, 1906; s. William and V. Caroline (Wieand) W.; m. Phoebe Meade Francine, June 21, 1935; children: Anne F., Phoebe Wetzel Griswold, Carroll Robbins. A.B., Wesleyan U., Middletown, Conn., 1927; LL.B., U. Pa., 1930, Gowen fellow, 1931. Bar: Pa. 1931, N.J. 1931, U.S. Suprene Ct. 1962. Since practiced Phila.; partner firm Dechert, Price & Rhoads, 1934-73, of counsel, 1973—; mem. adv. com. to Comptroller of Currency, 1962. Bd. dirs. Libr. Co. Phila., 1952-83, pres., 1975-83; trustee Phila. Gen. Hosp., 1958-67; bd. dirs. Bok Tower Gardens, 1962-88, bd. dirs. emeritus, 1989—; bd. dirs. Phila. Maritime Mus., 1976-86, U. Pa. Law Sch., 1978-83. With USAAF, 1942-45, ETO. Mem. ABA (chmn. sect. bus. law 1966-67, editor Bus. Lawyer 1964-65), Pa. Hort. Soc. (bd. dirs. 1954-70, pres. 1967-70), Phila. Club. Democrat. Episcopalian. Home: 353 Lewis Ln Ambler PA 19002-5166 Office: Dechert Price & Rhoads 4000 Bell Atlantic Tower 1717 Arch St Philadelphia PA 19103-2713

WETZEL, EDWARD THOMAS, investment company executive; b. Indpls., Apr. 16, 1937; s. Edward George and Sarah Catherine Wetzel; children from previous marriage: Raymond, Cynthia; m. Christine E. Healy. BA, Bethany (W.Va.) Coll., 1959; MBA, U. Mass., Amherst, 1963. Market research analyst Gen. Electric Co., Pittsfield, Mass., 1960-63; editor, spl. projects dir., asst. v.p. DMS, Inc., Greenwich, Conn., 1964-70; pres. Industry News Service, Inc., Wilton, Conn., 1970-92; v.p. Wright Investor's Svc., Bridgeport, Conn., 1992—. Pres. Wilton Vol. Ambulance Corps, 1976-81, 83-87. Served to 2d lt. USAFR, 1959-65. Recipient Disting. Citizen award Town of Wilton, 1986. Mem. Strategic Leadership Forum, Info. Industry Assn., Kiwanis (pres. bd. dirs. Wilton chpt. 1991-92). Office: Wright Investor's Svc 1000 Lafayette Blvd Bridgeport CT 06604-4700

WETZEL, GRACE EMERY, occupational health nurse; b. N.Y.C., July 12, 1946; d. George W. and Alice (Cousins) Emery; m. Henry M. Wetzel III, Oct. 28, 1967; children: Sherry Ann, Charlea. Diploma, St. Peter's Gen. Hosp., New Brunswick, N.J., 1967. Cert. occupl. hearing conservationist, spirometry testing in workplace; cert. occupl. health nurse, Am. Bd. Occupl. Health Nurses. Occupl. health nurse Kimberly Clark Corp., Spotswood, N.J., 1976-90, Asbury Park Press, Neptune, N.J., 1990-93, N.Y. Times Co., Edison, N.J., 1993—. Trustee Jamesburg N.J. Pub. Libr., 1972-90. Mem. Cen. N.J. Assn. Occupational Health Nurses (pres. 1989-91, bd. dirs. 1992—), N.J. State Assn. Occupational Health Nurses (bd. dirs., nominee Schering award 1990).

WETZEL, HEINZ, foreign language educator; b. Ziesar, Germany, May 11, 1935; immigrated to Can., 1965; s. Ernst and Katharina (Jentzsch) W.; m. Marianne Dummin, Mar. 19, 1957; children: Andreas, Suzanne, Claudia. Staatsexamen, Free Univ., Berlin, 1960; Dr. phil., U. Göttingen, Fed. Republic Germany, 1967. Asst. prof. German dept. Queen's U., Kingston, Can., 1965-69; assoc. prof., grad. sec. German dept. U. Toronto, Can., 1969-72, prof. German dept., 1972—; chmn. German dept. U. Toronto, 1984-89;

vis. prof. U. Calif., San Diego, 1973, Technische U. Braunschweig, Germany, 1973, Humboldt U. Berlin, 1995. Author: (book) Konkordanz zu den Dichtungen Georg Trakis, 1971, Klang und Bild in den Dichtungen Georg Trakis, 2d edit., 1972, Banale Vitalitaet und laehmendes Erkennen, Drei vergleichende Studien zu T.S. Eliots, The Waste Land; editor: Seminar: A Journal of Germanic Studies, 1980-85; contbr. 50 articles to German and comparative lit. to profl. jours. Fellowships and grants from Social Scis. and Humanities Rsch. Coun. of Can. Mem. MLA of Am., Can. Assn. Univ. Tchrs. German. Office: U Toronto, Univ College, Toronto, ON Canada M5S 3H7

WETZEL, JODI (JOY LYNN WETZEL), history and women's studies educator; b. Salt Lake City, Apr. 5, 1943; d. Richard Coulam and Margaret Elaine (Openshaw) Wood; m. David Nevin Wetzel, June 12, 1967; children: Meredith (dec.), Richard Rawlins. BA in English, U. Utah, 1965, MA in English, 1967; PhD in Am. Studies, U. Minn., 1977. Instr. Am. studies and family social sci. U. Minn., 1973-77, asst. prof. Am. studies and women's studies, 1977-79, asst. to dir. Minn. Women's Ctr., 1973-75, asst. dir., 1975-79; dir. Women's Resource Ctrs. U. Denver, 1980-84, mem. adj. faculty history, 1981-84, dir. Am. studies program, dir. Women's Inst., 1983-84; dir. Women in Curriculum U. Maine, 1985-86, mem. coop. faculty sociology, social work and human devel., 1986—; dir. Inst. Women's Studies and Svcs. Met. State Coll. Denver, 1986—, assoc. prof. history, 1986-89, prof. history, 1990—; speaker, presenter, cons. in field; vis. prof. Am. studies U. Colo., 1985. Co-author: Women's Studies: Thinking Women, 1993; co-editor: Readings Toward Composition, 2d edit., 1969; contbr. articles to profl. publs. Del. at-large Nat. Women's Meeting, Houston, 1977; bd. dirs. Rocky Mountain Women's Inst., 1981-84; treas. Colo. Women's Agenda, 1987-91. U. Utah Dept. English fellow, 1967; U. Minn. fellow, 1978-79; grantee NEH, 1973, NSF, 1981-83, Carnegie Corp., 1988; named to Outstanding Young Women of Am., 1979. Mem. Am. Hist. Assn., Nat. Assn. Women in Edn. (Hilda A. Davis Ednl. Leadership award 1996), Am. Assn. for Higher Edn., Am. Studies Assn., Nat. Women's Studies Assn., Golden Key Nat. Honor Soc. (hon.), Alpha Lambda Delta, Phi Kappa Phi. Office: Met State Coll Denver Campus Box 36 PO Box 173362 Denver CO 80217-3362

WETZEL, JOE STEVEN, principal; b. Sherman, Tex., Aug. 7, 1948; s. Oscar Lee and Mary Elizabeth (Hash) W.; m. Patricia Fay Quattlebaum, Apr. 18, 1970; children: Jennifer Lea, Joseph Patrick. AS, Grayson County Jr. Coll., 1968; BS, East Tex. State U., 1970, MS, 1972. Tchr. Garland (Tex.) Ind. Sch. Dist., 1972-89, asst. prin., 1989—. Mem. Citizen Police Acad., membership com., 1994, v.p., 1993-94; mem. Southeastern Devel. Lab., Austin, Tex., 1993—. Mem. ASCD, Tex. Assn. Secondary Sch. Prins., Masons. Democrat. Presbyterian. Avocations: golf, reading, target shooting. Home: 514 Colonial Dr Garland TX 75043-2305 Office: South Garland High Sch 600 Colonel Dr Garland TX 75043-2302

WETZEL, ROBERT GEORGE, botany educator; b. Ann Arbor, Mich., Aug. 16, 1936; s. Wilhelm and Eugenia (Wagner) W.; m. Carol Ann Andree, Aug. 9, 1959; children: Paul Robert, Pamela Jeanette, Timothy Mark, Kristina Marie. BS, U. Mich., 1958, MS, 1959; PhD, U. Calif. at Davis, 1962; PhD (hon.), U. Uppsala, Sweden, 1984. Research assoc. Ind. U., Bloomington, 1962-65; asst. prof. botany Mich. State U., Hickory Corners, 1965-68; assoc. prof. Mich. State U., 1968-71, prof., 1971-86; prof. U. Mich., Ann Arbor, 1986-90; Bishop prof. biology U. Ala., Tuscaloosa, 1990—; cons. Internat. Biol. Program, London, 1967-75; chmn. Internat. Seagrass Commn., 1974-75; founding mem. Internat. Lake Environment Com., 1986—. Author: Limnology, 1975, 2d rev. edit., 1983, Limnological Analyses, 1979, 2d rev. edit., 1990, To Quench Our Thirst: Present and Future Freshwater Resources of the United States, 1983, Freshwater Ecosystems: Revitalizing Educational Programs in Limnology, 1996; editor: Periphyton of Freshwater Ecosystems, 1983, Wetlands and Ecotones, 1993, Recent Studies on Ecology and Management of Wetlands, 1994, Wetland Ecology, 1995, Lake Okeechobee: A Synthesis, 1995, Limnology of Developing Countries, vol. 1, 1995; mem. editl. bd. Aquatic Botany, 1975—, Jour. Tropical Freshwater Ecology, 1987—, Internat. Jour. Salt Lake Resources, 1991—, Biogeochemistry, 1993—, Lakes and Reservoirs, 1995—; N.Am. editor Archiv f. Hydrobiologie, 1989—; contbr. numerous articles on ecology and freshwater biology sys. to profl. jours. Served with USNR, 1954-62. Recipient First T. Erlander Nat. professorship Swedish Nat. Research Council and U. Uppsala, 1982-83, award of Distinction U. Calif. at Davis, 1989; AEC grantee, 1965-75; NSF grantee, 1962—; ERDA grantee, 1975-77; Dept. Energy grantee, 1978—. Home: 16 Dunbrook Tuscaloosa AL 35406-1962 Office: U Ala Dept Biol Scis Tuscaloosa AL 35487-0206

WETZLER, JAMES WARREN, economist; b. N.Y.C., Dec. 27, 1947; s. Benjamin and Deborah (Rabinowitz) W. B.S., U. Pa., 1969; Ph.D., Harvard U., 1973. Economist Joint Com. on Taxation, U.S. Congress, Washington, 1973-76; chief economist Joint Com. on Taxation, U.S. Congress, 1976-83, dep. chief staff, 1983-84; investment banker Bear Stearns and Co., Inc., N.Y.C., 1985-88; commr. N.Y. State Dept. Taxation and Finance, Albany, 1988-94; dir. Deloitte & Touche LLP, N.Y.C., 1995—. Office: Deloitte & Touche LLP 2 World Fin Ctr New York NY 10281

WETZLER, MONTE EDWIN, lawyer; b. N.Y.C., May 7, 1936; s. Alvin and Sally (Epstein) W.; m. Sally Jane Elsas, Dec. 19, 1963; 1 child, Andrew Elsas. AB, Brown U., 1957; LLB, U. Va., 1960; LLM in Taxation, NYU, 1966. Bar: N.Y. 1960, Calif. 1979. Assoc. Regan Goldfarb Heller Wetzler & Quinn, N.Y.C., 1960-66, ptnr., 1966-73, mng. ptnr., 1973-81; sr. v.p., gen. counsel Damson Oil Corp., N.Y.C., 1981-86, exec. v.p., CFO, 1986-88; pres. B&D Equities Inc., 1986-88; ptnr. Breed, Abbott & Morgan, N.Y.C., 1988-93, mng. ptnr., 1992-93; ptnr., exec. com. Whitman Breed Abbott & Morgan, N.Y.C., 1993—. Editor: Selected Problems in Securities Law, 1972, Joint Ventures and Privatization in Eastern Europe, 1991-92. Counsel, N.Y. State Senate Com. on Housing, N.Y.C. Recipient Svc. award Practicing Law Inst., N.Y.C., 1973. Mem. ABA, N.Y. State Bar Assn. (exec. com. bus. law sect. 1993-94, securities law com.), Bar Assn. City N.Y., Corp. Law com.; Harmonie Club (gov. 1983-84, 86-88), Cedar Point Yacht Club, Essex Yacht Club, Phi Delta Phi, Order of Coif. Republican. Jewish. Home: 8 River Road Dr Essex CT 06426-1377 Office: Whitman Breed Abbott & Morgan 200 Park Ave New York NY 10166-0005

WEVERS, JOHN WILLIAM, retired Semitic languages educator; b. Baldwin, Wis., June 4, 1919; emigrated to Can., 1951; s. Bernard and Wilemina (Te Grootenhuis) W.; m. Grace Della Brondsema, May 22, 1942; children: Robert Dick, John William, Harold George, James Merritt. A.B., Calvin Coll., Grand Rapids, Mich., 1940; Th.B., Calvin Sem., 1943; Th.D., Princeton Theol. Sem., 1945; D.D. (hon.), Knox Coll., Toronto, 1973; D.H.C. (hon.), Leiden U., 1985. Lectr., then asst. prof. O.T. and Semitic langs. Princeton Theol. Sem., 1946-51; mem. faculty U. Toronto, Ont., Can., 1951—, prof. Near Eastern studies, 1963—, prof. emeritus, 1984—, grad. chmn., 1972-75, chmn. dept., 1975-80; chmn. adminstrv. council Presbyn. Ch. Can., 1960-65. Author: Commentary on the Book of Ezekiel, 1969, Septuaginta Vetus Testamentum Graecum: Genesis, 1974, Deuteronomium, 1977, Numeri, 1981, Leviticus, 1986, Exodus, 1991; also text histories, 1974, 78, 83, 86, 92, Notes on the Greek Text of Exodus, 1990, Genesis, 1993, Deuteronomy, 1995. Bd. govs. Ctrl. Hosp., Toronto, 1963-96, chmn., 1967-80; chmn. Hosp. Coun. Met. Toronto, 1974-75; bd. govs. Ont. Hosp. Assn., 1974-84, pres., 1978-79. Recipient Queen's Jubilee medal, 1978. Fellow Royal Soc. Can.; mem. Oriental Club Toronto, Internat. Orgn. Septuagint and Cognate Studies (pres. 1972-80, hon. pres. 1989—), Can. Bibl. Studies (hon. life), Akademie Wissenschaften Goettingen (corr.), Arts and Letters Club (Toronto). Home: 116 Briar Hill Ave, Toronto, ON Canada M4R 1H9 Office: U Toronto, Dept Near Middle Eastern, Civilizations, Toronto, ON Canada M5S 1A1

WEXLER, ANNE, government relations and public affairs consultant; b. N.Y.C., Feb. 10, 1930; d. Leon R. and Edith R. (Rau) Levy; m. Joseph Duffey, Sept. 17, 1974; children by previous marriage: David Wexler, Daniel Wexler. B.A., Skidmore Coll., 1951, LL.D. (hon.), 1978; D.Sc. in Bus. (hon.), Bryant Coll., 1978. Assoc. pub. Rolling Stone mag., 1974-76; personnel adviser Carter-Mondale transition planning group, 1976-77; dep. undersec. regional affairs Dept. Commerce, 1977-78; asst. to Pres. of U.S., Washington, 1978-81; pres. Wexler and Assocs., Washington, 1981-82; govt. relations and pub. affairs cons., chmn. Wexler, Reynolds, Harrison & Schule, Inc., Washington, 1981-90; vice chmn. Hill and Knowlton PA Worldwide, Washington, 1990-92; chmn. The Wexler Group, div. Hill & Knowlton, Washington, 1992—; bd. dirs. Alumax, Inc., NOVA, Nat. Park Found., New Eng. Electric System, Comcast Corp., Dreyfus Index Funds; mem. vis. com. J.F. Kennedy Sch. Govt., Harvard U. Mem. bd. advisors Carter Ctr., Emory U.; mem. bd. visitors U. Md. Sch. Pub. Affairs. Named Outstanding Alumna Skidmore Coll., 1972, recipient most disting. alumni award, 1984, Bryce Harlow award, 1989. Mem. Coun. on Fgn. Rels., Nat. Women's Forum. Jewish. Office: Wexler Group 1317 F St NW Ste 600 Washington DC 20004-1105

WEXLER, GINIA DAVIS, singer, association executive; b. Phila., Mar. 10, 1923; d. Meyer and Hilda (Emery) D.; m. Morris M. Wexler, Oct. 1968. Student drama, Carnegie Inst. Tech., 1939-41; vocal pupil, Frances Lewando, Doris Monteux, 1939-50; coached with, Povla Frijsh, Pierre Monteux, Queena Mario, Pablo Casals, Madeleine Grey. Voice tchr. Mich. State U., East Lansing, 1962; dir. Hancock County Chamber Music Soc. (now Hancock County Friends of Arts), East Sullivan, Maine, 1962—; dir. free programs for children Farmstead Barn, Sullivan, Maine, 1970—. Performed as Polly Peachum in The Beggar's Opera, 1941, Bar Harbor (Maine) Stock Co., Chautauqua, N.Y. Bucks County Playhouse; leading roles New Moon, Toledo Light Opera Co., 1945; appeared on Broadway in Susan and God, 1942, Call Me Mister, 1946; made operatic debut as Gretel in Hansel and Gretel with Pitts. Opera Soc., 1943; ann. recital N.Y.C., 1948-65; toured U.S.A., 1947-67, Europe, 1949, 50; appeared at Holland Festival, 1950; in 1st U.S. performances of Flaminio of Pergolesi, 1953; performances at Royal Opera of Brussels, 1955, broadcasts, U.S., Europe; appeared with symphony orch., U.S., Europe, Middle-East, 1955-67; made six months world tour, Africa, Asia, 1966, guitar concerts, 1965; dir. performing arts for children series, Hancock Grand County Auditorium, 1976-89, high sch. touring program, 1980-89, recs. songs Music Library Records, Inc., folk music div., Library of Congress; mem. Surry, Maine Opera Co., 1984-90; dir. Sullivan Bicentennial Chorus, 1989; lead role in play All Thru the Night, 1989; appearances Am. Folksong Festival; adviser folk music, Nat Arts Found.; authority on folksongs; collecter, transcriber, interpreter: (with Jean Thomas) folklore Ky. mountains (the Traipsin' Woman), 1950-55, also other locations; entertainer Armed Forces, U.S., Europe. (Recipient grand prize Internat. contest interpretation French song 1958). Chmn. Sullivan (Me.) Conservation Commn., 1973-83. Developer unique recital program Portraits in Song, 1947. Home: 3850 Galt Ocean Dr Apt 1211 Fort Lauderdale FL 33308-7648 also: The Farmstead Box 8 Rte 1 Gouldsboro ME 04607-9703

WEXLER, HASKELL, film producer, cameraman; b. Chgo., 1922; s. Simon Wexler; m. Nancy Ashenhurst (div.); two children; m. Marian Witt (div.); 1 son, Mark; m. Rita Taggart. Grad., U. Chgo. Ednl. documentaries, Chgo., for eleven years; cinematographer films: The Hoodlum Priest, The Best Man, America America, The Loved One, In the Heat of the Night, Who's Afraid of Virginia Woolf? (Acad. award), The Thomas Crown Affair, American Graffiti, One Flew Over the Cuckoo's Nest, Introduction to the Enemy, Bound for Glory (Acad. award), Coming Home, Colors, Three Fugitives, 1988, Blaze, 1989, Lookin' to Get Out, Matewan, Other People's Money, The Babe, Mulholland Falls, 1995, Rich Man's Wife, 1995, (with others) Days of Heaven, (with others) Rolling Stones-IMAX, The Secret of Roan Inish, Canadian Bacon; producer, writer, dir., photographer: (with others) films Medium Cool, 1969; wrote and directed Latino, 1985. Received star on Hollywood's Walk of Fame, 1996. Mem. Acad. Motion Picture Arts and Scis. (bd. govs. cinematographers br.). Address: 626 Santa Monica Blvd #111 Santa Monica CA 90401-1066 Agent: Internat Creative Mgmt c/o Paul Hook 8942 Wilshire Blvd Beverly Hills CA 90211-1934

WEXLER, HERBERT IRA, retail company executive; b. Newark, Sept. 6, 1916; s. Irving and Jeanette (Lesser) W.; m. Elaine L. Ellis, Oct. 10, 1948; children: Susan, Peter, Toni. Student, Rutgers U., 1939-41; student advanced mgmt. program, Harvard U., 1956. Stock boy, salesman, asst. buyer L. Bamberger & Co., 1935-41, asst. buyer, 1946-47; buyer appliances R.H. Macy & Co., N.Y.C., 1947-48, TV radio buyer, 1949-54, mdse. adminstr., v.p., 1955-67, sr. v.p., mem. exec. com., dir., 1968-73; pres., chmn. bd., chief exec. officer Marcade Group Inc., N.Y.C., 1973-86, bd. dirs., cons., 1987—. Vice chmn. Greater N.Y. council Boy Scouts Am.; organizer, fundraiser Yale Grace New Haven Hosp.; mem. Gov. Harriman's Com. to Investigate Fraud and Misrepresentation in Consumer Products; mem. adv. council to bd. trustees Greens Farms Acad., Westport, Conn.; gen. chmn. State of Israel Bond Drive, 1980, testimonial, 1978; gen. chmn. N.Y. Community Service Soc.; chmn. N.Y. sect. for fundraising Denver Jewish Hosp; dir. Children's Blood Found. N.Y. Hosp. Served to capt. AUS, 1941-46. Named Key Man of Yr. Am. Jewish Com. and B'nai B'rith, 1957; named B'nai B'rith Man of Yr., 1976; recipient Disting. Service award Am. Jewish Com. and Anti-Defamation League, 1960, Award of Honor Fedn. Jewish Philanthropies of N.Y., 1961, Scroll of Honor United Jewish Appeal of Greater N.Y., 1964, Man of Yr. award Conn. Digestive Disease Soc., 1973. Clubs: Harvard, Harmonie, Birchwood Country. Home: 26 Burr Farms Rd Westport CT 06880-3817

WEXLER, JACQUELINE GRENNAN (MRS. PAUL J. WEXLER), former association executive and college president; b. Sterling, Ill., Aug. 2, 1926; d. Edward W. and Florence (Dawson) Grennan; m. Paul J. Wexler, June 1, 1969; stepchildren: Wendy, Wayne. A.B., Webster Coll., 1948; M.A., U. Notre Dame, 1957; LL.D., Franklin and Marshall Coll., 1968, Phila. Coll. Textiles and Sci., 1987; D.H.L., Brandeis U., 1968; LL.D., Skidmore Coll., 1967, Smith Coll., 1975; HHD, U. Mich., 1967, U. Ohio, 1976; D.H.L., Carnegie Inst., 1966, Colo. Coll., 1967, U. Pa., 1979, U. South Fla., 1991; HHD (hon.), U. Hartford, 1987; DH, St. Ambrose Coll., 1981; DD, Lafayette Coll., 1990. Tchr. English and math. Loretto Acad., El Paso, Tex., 1951-54; tchr. English and math. Nerinx Hall, St. Louis, 1954-59; tchr. English Webster Coll., 1959-60, asst. to pres., 1959, v.p. devel., 1960, exec. v.p., 1962-65, pres., 1965-69; v.p., dir. internat. univ. studies Acad. for Ednl. Devel., N.Y.C., 1969; pres. Hunter Coll., City U. N.Y., 1969-79, Acad. Cons. Assoc., N.Y.C., 1982-90; ret., 1990; pres. NCCJ, 1982-90; writer, commentator, cons.; mem. Am. Council on Edn., Commn. on Internat. Edn., 1967; mem. adv. com. to dir. NIH, 1978-80; mem. exec. panel chief naval ops. U.S. Navy, 1978-81; bd. examiners Fgn. Service, Dept. State, 1981-83; mem. Pres.'s Adv. Panel on Research and Devel. in Edn., 1961-65; mem. Pres.'s Task Force on Urban Ednl. Opportunities, 1967. Author: Where I Am Going, 1968; contbr. articles to profl. jours. Trustee U. Pa. Recipient NYU Sch. Edn. Ann. award for creative leadership in edn., 1968, Elizabeth Cutter Morrow award YWCA, 1978, Abraham L. Sachar Silver medallion Brandeis U.'s Nat. Women's Com., 1988, The Albert Einstein award Am. Soc. Technion, 1989; named One of Six Outstanding Women of St. Louis Area St. Louis chpt. Theta Sigma Phi, 1963, Woman of Achievement in Edn. St. Louis Globe-Democrat, 1964, Woman of Accomplishment Harpers Bazaar, 1967, one of Am.'s Most Important 100 Women Ladies Home Jour., 1988; Kenyon lectr. Vassar Coll., 1967. Mem. Mo. Acad. Squires, Kappa Gamma Pi.

WEXLER, JEFFREY F., education educator; b. Casper, Wyo., Apr. 3, 1941; s. Daniel Louis and Florence (Jamison) W.; m. Jennifer Forest, May 9, 1966; children: Paul, Jared, Denise, Flora. BEd, U. So. Calif., 1964, M in Early Childhood Edn., 1965. Cert. elem. sch. tchr. and early childhood edn. Teller Casper Fed. Savs., 1961-63, loan officer, 1963-65; teacher to asst. dir. Early Childhood Trng. Ctr., 1964-78; asst. dir. Montessori Trng. Inst., Syracuse, N.Y., 1978-89; dir., CEO Little Flower Montessori Sch., Syracuse, N.Y., 1989—; Vis. instr. Montessori Sch., Casper, Wyo., Summers 1990—, Montessori instr. Syracuse, 1992—; bd. dirs. Little Flower Montessori Sch. Elem. tchrs. assn., 1989—, Montessori tchrs. group, 1979—, (pres. Syracuse chpt. 1988-91, 95—), Edn. Found.

WEXLER, LEONARD D., federal judge; b. Bklyn., Nov. 11, 1924; s. Jacob and Bessie (Herman) W.; m. Barbara Blum, Mar. 1953; children: Allison Wexler Smeitanka, Robert, William. BS, Ind. U., 1947; JD, NYU, 1950. Bar: N.Y. 1983, U.S. Dist. Ct. (ea. dist.) N.Y. 1983. Assoc. Siben & Siben Esqs., Bay Shore, N.Y., 1950-56; ptnr. Meyer & Wexler Esqs., Smithtown, N.Y., 1956-83; judge U.S. Dist. Ct. (eastern dist.) N.Y., 1983—; atty. Suffolk County Police Conf., 1956-83; 1st atty. Suffolk County Patrolmen's Benevolent Assn., 1960-75; 1st atty. Suffolk County Detectives Assn., 1964-70; temporary state chmn., legal counsel Com. for Rev. Juvenile Justice System, N.Y. State Bar Assn.; speaker, lectr.; 1st adminstr. Assigned Counsel Plan N.Y. State, 1966-83. Served with U.S. Army, 1943-45. Mem. Suffolk County Criminal Bar Assn. (founder 1965, dir. 1956-60). Republican. Jewish. Avocations: travelling; sailing. Home: 94 W Bayberry Rd Islip NY 11751-4905 Office: US Dist Ct 300 Rabro Dr Hauppauge NY 11788-4256*

WEXLER, PETER JOHN, producer, director, set designer; b. N.Y.C., Oct. 31, 1936; s. S. David and Berda (Sarnoff) W.; m. Constance Ann Ross, Nov. 30, 1962. BS in Design, U. Mich., 1958; student, Yale Sch. Drama, 1958. cons. temp. quarters project San Francisco Ballet, 1994. Designs include White House stage, 1961, War and Peace, 1964, The White Devil, 1965, A Joyful Noise, 1966, The Happy Time, 1967, In the Matter of J. Robert Oppenheimer, 1968, Merv Griffin TV show, 1965, Terra Nova, 1979 (L.A. Dramalogue Critics award); prin. designer, Center Theatre Group, L.A., 1967-70, designer, N.Y. Philharmonic Promenades, 1965-78; play and film The Trial of the Catonsville 9, 1971-72; Leonard Bernstein's Mass, L.A., 1973, N.Y. Philharmonic Rug Concerts, 1973-77, Les Troyens, Met. Opera Co., 1973, Le Prophète, Met. Opera Co., 1977, Un Ballo in Maschera, Met. Opera Co., 1980, Theatre Space Prodns., Pitts. Pub. Theatre, 1975-77; mem. design team for Frank O. Gehry & Assocs., redesign Hollywood Bowl; designer: Albert Herring, Savonlinna Opera Festival, Finland, 1981; centennial prodn. Les Troyens, Met. Opera, 1983; directed: Cold Storage, Ariz. Theatre Co., 1978, Terra Nova, Pitts. Public Theatre, 1981; producer, Dallas Symphony Orch.'s Star Fest 80; producer Rocky Mountain Music Festival, Denver Symphony Orch., 1983-84, Star Spangled Banner, Permanent Exhibition U.S. Nat. Emblem, Smithsonian Instn., Washington, 1982; producer, design exhbn. Am. Anthem, LTV Ctr., Dallas/Smithsonian Instn., 1985; designer, broker exhbn. Liberties with Liberty, Trammell Crow Co./Mus. Am. Folk Art, 1985; designer Horizons '86, N.Y. Philharmonic, 1986; co-producer, designer video, exhbn. and space Albany Urban Cultural Park, Albany, N.Y., 1986; producer, dir. Pletka, multimedia theatre piece for orch., Dallas Symphony Orch., 1987; programmer, designer Trans-Hudson Ferry for the Port Authority of N.Y. and N.J., 1987-88; producer The Search for Life, Smithsonian Inst., 1987; producer Mstislav Rostropovich 60th Anniv. Gala Concert, Nat. Symphony Orch., Kennedy Ctr., Washington, 1987, Navy 87, Navy 89, USN multi-media orchestral prodn., Washington, 1987; producer, artistic dir. Spring Creek Music Festival, Garland, Tex. Dallas Ft. Worth Metroplex, 1992-94; dir. Lost in the Stars, A.C.O., Carnegie Hall, 1989; visual cons. Lifetime Med. (cable TV), 1989-90; design cons. Reebok River Stage - Radio City Music Hall Prodns, 1989; program designer Mega-Mall, Oxford Devel. Co., Pitts.; designer Infinished Stories, 1994, Boston Pops Orch., 1995; prodr. A Salute to Slava, Kennedy Ctr., Washington, 1994. Project leader Outdoor Performance Facility, Met. Opera Co., N.Y. Philharmonic Symphony, Dept. Cultural Affairs City of N.Y. Recipient Internat. Theatre Inst. competition award ANTA, 1965, most imaginative use of scene design award Saturday Rev., 1965, Drama Desk-Joseph Maharam award for The Happy Time as best designer of mus., 1968, L.A. Drama Critics Circle award, 1971. Address: 277 W End Ave New York NY 10023-2604

WEXLER, RICHARD LEWIS, lawyer; b. Chgo., June 19, 1941; s. Stanley and Lottie (Pinkert) W.; m. Roberta Seigel, June 13, 1962; children: Deborah (Mrs. Jonathan Sokobin), Joshua, Jonathan. Student, U. Mich., 1959-1962; JD cum laude, John Marshall Law Sch., 1965. Bar: Ill. 1965, US. Dist. Ct. (no. dist.) Ill. 1967. Gen. counsel Metro. Planning Council, Chgo., 1965-67; ptnr. Wexler, Kane, Rosenzweig & Shaw, Chgo., 1967-71, Taussig, Wexler & Shaw, Chgo., 1971-78, Wexler, Siegel & Shaw, Ltd., Chgo., 1978-83; ptnr. Sachnoff & Weaver, Ltd., Chgo., 1983-91, chair real estate dept., 1985-91, mng. ptnr., 1985-90; ptnr., co-chairperson real estate dept. Lord Bissell & Brook, Chgo., 1991—; legal cons. Zoning Laws Study Commn., Ill. Gen. Assembly, Springfield, 1969-71, Urban Counties Study Commn., Springfield, 1971-72; legal counsel Ill. Coastal Zone Mgmt. Program, Springfield, 1979-81, Northeastern Ill. Planning Commn., Chgo., 1969—. Contbr. numerous articles to profl. jours. Pres. Jewish Fedn. Met. Chgo., 1986-88, mem. numerous coms., also bd. dirs., 1978-90; pres. Jewish United Fund, 1986-88; bd. dirs. Coun. Jewish Fedns., 1980, mem. exec. com., 1985—, v.p., 1988—, chmn. planning steering com., 1990-95, chmn. fedn./agy. rels. com., 1988-90; co-chmn. Task Force on Poverty and Low Income, 1985-87; nat. vice-chmn. United Jewish Appeal, 1988—, nat. chmn., 1996—, regional allocations chmn., 1987-88, chmn. region II, 1988-90, budget com., 1989-92, allocations com., 1990-91, campaign exec., 1991—; chmn. Operation Exodus II, 1993-94, chmn. nat. mktg. com., 1994-95, chmn. 1997 campaign planning and budget com., 1995—; bd. dirs. Jewish Edn. Soc. N.Am., 1982-85, Hebrew Immigrant Aid Soc., 1988—, Nat. Conf. on Soviet Jewry, 1989—, vice chmn., 1989-92, nat. chmn., 1992—; bd. dirs. Nat. Jewish Cmty. Rels. Adv. Coun., 1988-90, vice chmn., 1988-92; chmn. Jewish Com. Rels. Coun. Chgo., 1988-89. Fellow Eta Lambda; mem. ABA, Ill. State Bar Assn. (Lincoln award, Legal Writing, 1966). Avocations: tennis, reading, travel. Office: Lord Bissell & Brook 115 S La Salle St Ste 3400 Chicago IL 60603-3801

WEXLER, ROBERT, university administrator. Pres. U. of Judaism, L.A. Office: U Judaism 15600 Mulholland Dr Los Angeles CA 90077-1519

WEXLER ROBOCK, STEPHANIE ELLEN, human services and career development specialist, researcher; b. Bronx, N.Y., July 28, 1952; d. Benjamin and Pauline (Zalewitz) Wexler; m. Jerry Robock, May 4, 1980; children: Zachary, Maxwell. BA in Cultural Anthropology cum laude with honors, Lehman Coll., CUNY, 1973; MA in Counselor Edn., NYU, 1979; postgrad., Columbia U., 1982, Mercy Coll., 1985, Fordham U., 1994. With social work, dir. recreational therapy area nursing homes and health-related facilities, Bronx, Mt. Vernon, N.Y., 1972-77; ind. rschr. Hellenic Gerontol. Inst., Athens, Greece, 1979; dir. R & D N.Y. State Divsn. Youth, 1980-83; sr. pers. cons., assessment, outplacement Pers. Systems, Inc., N.Y.C., Peekskill, Pomona, N.Y., 1986—; advisor, mem. grant com. Gerontol. Ctr., NYU, N.Y.C., 1980; career devel. specialist, trainer Fedn. Employment and Guidance Svc., 1982-86; cons., trainer, evaluator in field, Westchester, N.Y.C. and Conn., 1983—; coord./trainer Profl. Devel. Inst., N.Y.C., 1984-90; co-ordinator career devel. Croton Sch. Dist., 1984; dir. Career Devel., Transition and Assessment Svcs. JCC on the Hudson, Tarrytown, N,Y, 1995—; presenter in field. Designer Computer Based Career Devel. software, 1986. Mem. Environ. Def. Fund, N.Y.C., 1992—, Yorktown PTA, 1991—, Nat. PTA, 1991—. Rsch. grantee Hellenic Gerontol. Inst., 1980. Mem. ACA, AHEAD, NCDA, NECA, Nat. Career Devel. Assn., Nat. Cert. Career Counselors, Nat. Cert. Counselors. Avocations: ice skating, rock climbing, reading, computer programming. Office: Wexler-Robock PO Box 421 Baron de Hirsch Rd Crompond NY 10517

WEXNER, LESLIE HERBERT, retail executive; b. Dayton, Ohio, 1937. BSBA, Ohio State U., 1959, HHD (hon.), 1986; LLD (hon.), Hofstra U., 1987; LHD (hon.), Brandeis U., 1990; PhD (hon.), Jewish Theol. Sem. Founder, pres., chmn. bd. The Limited, Inc., fashion chain, Columbus, 1963—; dir., mem. exec. com. Banc One Corp., Sotheby's Holdings Inc., vis. com. Grad. Sch. Design Harvard U.; mem. bus. adminstrn. adv. coun. Ohio State U.; chmn. Retail Industry Trade Action Coalition. Bd. dirs. Columbus Urban League, 1982-84, Hebrew Immigrant Aid Soc., N.Y.C., 1982—; co-chmn. Internat. United Jewish Appeal Com.; nat. vice chmn., treas. United Jewish Appeal; bd. dirs., mem. exec. com. Am. Jewish Joint Distbn. Com., Inc.; trustee Columbus Jewish Fedn., 1972, Columbus Jewish Found., Aspen Inst., Ohio State U., Columbus Capital Corp. for Civic Improvement; former trustee Columbus Mus. Art, Columbus Symphony Orch., Whitney Mus. Am. Art, Capitol South Community Urban Redevel. Corp.; former mem. Governing Com. Columbus Found.; founding mem., first chair The Ohio State U. Found; exec. com. Am. Israel Pub. Affairs Com. Decorated cavaliere Republic of Italy. Named Man of Yr. Am. Mktg. Assn., 1974. Mem. Young Presidents Orgn., Sigma Alpha Mu. Club: B'nai B'rith. Office: Limited Inc PO Box 16000 3 Limited Pky Columbus OH 43216-6000*

WEYAND, FREDERICK CARLTON, retired military officer; b. Arbuckle, Calif., Sept. 15, 1916; s. Frederick C. W. and Velma Semans (Weyand); m. Lora Arline Langhart, Sept. 20, 1940; children: Carolyn Ann, Robert Carlton, Nancy Diane. A.B., U. Calif.-Berkeley, 1939; LL.D. (hon), U. Akron, 1975. Officer U.S. Army, advanced to gen. chief of staff, 1940-76; sr. v.p. First Hawaiian Bank, Honolulu, 1976-82; trustee Estate of S.M. Damon, Honolulu, 1982—; bd. dirs. First Hawaiian, Inc., Ltd., First Hawaiian Bank, First Hawaiian Credit Corp. Chmn. ARC, Honolulu, 1982, Hawaiian Open golf Tourney, 1981-82. Decorated D.S.C. U.S. Army, 1967, D.S.M. Army (3), Dept. Def. (1), 1966-76, other U.S. and fgn. mil. decorations. Mem. Am.

Def. Preparedness Assn., Assn. U.S. Army, U.S. Strategic Inst. (v.p. 1976—), USAF Assn. Lutheran. Clubs: Waialae Country. Lodge: Masons. Home: 2121 Ala Wai Blvd Ph 1 Honolulu HI 96815-2211 Office: SM Damon Estate 1132 Bishop St Ste 1520 Honolulu HI 96813-2830

WEYANDT, DANIEL SCOTT, technologist, naval officer; b. Altoona, Pa., Dec. 26, 1962; s. Blair Sherwood and Madolyn Rae (Dunmire) W. BS, Juniata Coll., Huntingdon, Pa., 1984; MS in Physics, Pa. State U., 1992; MBA, U. R.I., 1995. Commd. USN, 1984, advanced through grades to lt., 1988; divsn. officer USS John C. Calhoun, Charleston, S.C., 1987, USS Simon Bolivar, Charleston, 1986-89; rsch. officer Naval Undersea Warfare Ctr. Divsn., Newport, R.I., 1992-95; sr. engr. electronic sys. divsn. Westinghouse Elec. Corp., Sykesville, Md., 1995—. Decorated Navy achievement medal, Navy commendation medal. Mem. Altoona Horseshoe Chorus (assoc. dir. 1978—), Alexandria Harmonizers, Sigma Pi Sigma. Republican. Methodist. Avocations: music, water sports, fitness. Home: 1216 Country View Dr Duncansville PA 16635-7622 Office: Westinghouse Elec Corp 7301 Sykesville Rd Sykesville MD 21781-5101

WEYENBERG, DONALD RICHARD, chemist; b. Glenvil, Nebr., July 11, 1930; s. Clyde H. and Elva I. (Hlavaty) W.; m. Barbara Ann Oppenheim, Dec. 26, 1955; children: Ann Louise, Thomas Richard. B.S. in Chemistry, U. Nebr., 1951; Ph.D., Pa. State U., 1958; P.M.D. Program, Harvard U., 1968. Research chemist Dow Corning Corp., Midland, Mich., 1951-65, research mgr., 1965-68, dir. corp. devel., 1968-69, dir. silicone research, 1969-71, bus. mgr., 1971-76, dir. research, 1976-79, v.p. research and devel., 1979-86, chief sci. and sr. v.p. research and devel., 1987-93, sci. emeritus, 1993—; bd. dirs. Dow Corning, Dendritech; Hurd lectr. Northwestern U., 1992—. Bd. editors Organometallics Jour., 1980-86; contbr. articles to sci. jours., chpts. to books; patentee silicone materials. Bd. visitors Memphis State U., 1981-87; mem. indsl. bd. advisors U. Nebr., 1988. Named Alumni fellow Pa. State U., 1988. Mem. Am. Chem. Soc. (chmn. Midland sect. 1967, Outstanding Achievement in Promotion Chem. Scis. award Midland sect.), Indsl. Rsch. Inst., Sigma Xi. Lodge: Rotary. Home: 4601 Arbor Dr Midland MI 48640-2644 Office: Dow Corning Corp PO Box 994 2200 Salzburg St Midland MI 48640-8594

WEYERHAEUSER, GEORGE HUNT, forest products company executive; b. Seattle, July 8, 1926; s. John Philip and Helen (Walker) W.; m. Wendy Wagner, July 10, 1948; children: Virginia Lee, George Hunt, Susan W., Phyllis A., David M., Merrill W. BS with honors in Indsl. Engring., Yale U., 1949. With Weyerhaeuser Co., Tacoma, 1949—, successively mill foreman, br. mgr., 1949-56, v.p., 1957-66, exec. v.p., 1966-88, pres., chief exec. officer, 1988, chmn. bd., chief exec. officer, 1988-91, chmn. bd., past CEO, also bd. dirs.; bd. dirs. Boeing Co., SAFECO Corp., Chevron Corp.; mem. Bus. Coun., Bus. Roundtable, Wash. State Bus. Roundtable. Office: Weyerhaeuser Fin Svcs 33663 Weyerhaeuser Way S Federal Way WA 98003-9646*

WEYGAND, ROBERT A., lieutenant governor, landscape architect; b. Attleboro, Mass., May 10, 1948. BA in Fine Arts, U. R.I., 1971, BS in Civil and Environ. Engring., 1976. Project mgr. R.I. Dept. Nat. Resources, 1973-82; owner Weygand, Orciuch & Christie, Inc., 1982-92; mem. R.I. Ho. of Reps. from 84th dist., 1984-92; lt. gov. State of R.I., 1993—; chmn. house com. on corps., 1990; chmn. E. Providence Planning Bd., 1978-84, R.I. Small Bus. Advocacy Coun., 1992—, R.I. Long Term Care Coord. Coun., 1992—, R.I. Delegation/White House Conf. on Aging, 1995; bd. dirs. R.I. Scenic Hwy., 1988-92; presdl. appointee White House Conf. on Small Bus., 1995. Bd. dirs. Save the Bay, 1984-87, United Way, 1993—, Meeting St. Ctr., 1993—; pres., bd. dirs. R.I. Parks Assn., 1983-92; chmn. R.I. Land Use Commn., 1987-92. Recipient Legislator of Yr. award R.I. League Cities and Towns, 1988, Exceptional Pub. Svc. award FBI, 1992, Disting. Svc. Star State of R.I., 1992. Mem. Am. Soc. Landscape Architects; Am. Planning Assn. (Outstanding Pub. Svc. award New Eng. chpt. 1992).

WEYHER, HARRY FREDERICK, lawyer; b. Wilson, N.C., Aug. 19, 1921; s. Harry Frederick and Laura Gray (Carter) W.; m. Barbara Dore McCusker, Sept. 9, 1950 (div. May 1971); children: Barbara Brandon, Harry Frederick III, Laura Carter; m. Laura Hyman Harvey, Oct. 17, 1971 (div. Sept. 1986); m. Michelle Eimers, Dec. 29, 1989. B.S., U. N.C., 1946; student, U. Glasgow, Scotland, 1946; LL.B. magna cum laude, Harvard U., 1949. Bar: N.Y., 1950. Assoc. Cravath, Swaine & Moore, N.Y.C., 1949-54; sr. assoc. counsel N.Y. State Crime Commn., 1950-52; ptnr., counsel Olwine, Connelly, Chase, O'Donnell & Weyher, N.Y.C., 1954-91; adj. assoc. prof. N.Y.U. Sch. Law, 1952-62; bd. dirs. AFA Protective Systems, Inc., The Pioneer Fund, Inc. Author: (with Hiram Knott) ESOP--Employee Stock Ownership Plan, 2d ed., 1985, Hanging Out a Shingle, 1987; contbr. articles to profl. jours. Mem. ABA, N.Y. State Bar Assn., Assn. of Bar of City of N.Y., Phi Beta Kappa, Beta Gamma Sigma, Zeta Psi. Clubs: Harvard, Racquet and Tennis (N.Y.C.), Lyford Cay (Nassau), Boone & Crockett. Home: 211 E 70th St Apt 17B New York NY 10021-5207 Office: 551 Fifth Ave 27th FL New York NY 10176

WEYHER, HARRY FREDERICK, III, metals company executive; b. N.Y.C., Mar. 9, 1956; s. Harry F. and Barbara (McCusker) W.; m. Anda Gailitis, July 7, 1984; children: Harry F. IV, Jesse D. BA, Middlebury Coll., 1977. Treas. Bunge Corp., N.Y.C., 1977-90; v.p. fin. Gerald Metals Inc., Stamford, Conn., 1990—. Mem. Racquet & Tennis Club. Home: 215 Ridgefield Rd Wilton CT 06897-2432 Office: Gerald Metals Inc High Ridge Park Stamford CT 06904

WEYLAND, DEBORAH ANN, learning disabilities teacher consultant; b. Fayetteville, N.C., Aug. 19, 1959; d. William Frederick Louis and Carol Joyce (Varhall) W. BA, Fairleigh Dickinson U., 1981; MA, Montclair (N.J.) State U., 1994. Cert. tchr. nursery sch., K-8, tchr. of handicapped; cert. learning disabilities tchr. cons. Permanent substitute tchr. Franklin Jr. H.S., Nutley, N.J., 1981-82, asst. tchr. SCE program, 1982-83; tchr. grade 2 and kindergarten Saint Peter's Sch., Belleville, N.J., 1983-85; tchr. grade 5 and kindergarten Belleville Pub. Schs., 1985-91, tchr. pre-sch. handicapped program, 1991-95; learning cons. Belleville Pub. Schs., 1994—; adv. bd. Belleville Alliance for Substance Edn., 1993—, exec. bd. 1994—; cons. Assn. of Learning, State of N.J., 1994—; cons. in field. Mem. Spl. Edn. Parent and Profls. Orgn., Belleville Edn. Assn., Women's Club Belleville, Phi Zeta Kappa, Phi Omega Epsilon. Avocations: arts and crafts, reading, walking. Office: Belleville Pub Schs 100 Passaic Ave Belleville NJ 07109

WEYLER, WALTER EUGEN, manufacturing company executive; b. Berwyn, Ill., Sept. 21, 1939; s. Eugen J. and Else E. (Deeg) W.; m. Nancy Prudence Haines; children—Walter Eugen, Peter C., Amy H. B.E.E., Mich. State U., 1961; M.B.A., Harvard U., 1963. Mktg. mgr. integrated circuits Tex. Instruments Corp., Dallas, 1963-68; mfg. mgr. semicondr. div. ITT, West Palm Beach, Fla., 1968-74; various positions Gen. Electric Co., Waterford, N.Y., 1974-82; v.p., gen. mgr. mobile communications Gen. Electric Co., Lynchburg, Va., 1982-85; pres., chief operating officer Graco, Inc., Mpls., 1985-93; pres. Kinetics, Inc., 1995—. Trustee Minn. Orch., Mpls., 1985. Mem. Mpls. C. of C. (trustee 1987). Clubs: Interlachen (Mpls.), Minneapolis. Home: 2878 NW Cumberland Rd Portland OR 97210

WEYRAUCH, PAUL TURNEY, retired army officer; b. Alpine, Tex., July 22, 1941; s. Paul Russell and Margaret Fischer (Fletcher) W.; m. Nancy Virginia Haight, Dec. 18, 1965; children: Julie Lynn, Paul C. BS, U.S. Mil. Acad., West Point, N.Y., 1963; MBA, Tulane U., 1976; Tchg. Cert., S.W. Tex. State U., 1995. Commd. 2d lt. U.S. Army, 1963, advanced through grades to brig. gen.; bn. comdr. 1st Bn., 5th F.A., Ft. Riley, Kans., 1978-80; asst. chief of staff 1st Inf. Div., Ft. Riley, 1980-81; comdr. 1st Cav. Div. Arty., Ft. Hood, 1982-85; chief of staff U.S. Army F.A. Ctr., Ft. Sill, Okla., 1985-86; asst. chief of staff for plans and policy Allied Forces So. Europe, Naples, Italy, 1986-89; chief of staff III Corps and Ft. Hood, 1989-91; ret., 1991; tchr. math. Richarte H.S., Georgetown, Tex., 1995—; planning and zoning commr. City of Georgetown, 1994-96, chmn. planning and zoning commn., 1995-96. Tchr. Sunday sch. local Protestant chs., pres. chapel couns., leader, coord. Bible studies. Decorated D.S.M., Def. Superior Svc. Medal, Legion of Merit, Bronze Star medal with V. device, Bronze Star medal with 1 oak leaf cluster, Meritorious Svc. medal with 3 oak leaf clusters. Mem. 1st Cav. Div. Assn. Avocations: running, collecting military insignia. Home: 320 S Ridge Cir Georgetown TX 78628-8213

WEYRAUCH, WALTER OTTO, law educator; b. Lindau, Germany, Aug. 27, 1919; came to U.S., 1952; s. Hans Ernst Winand and Meta Margarete (Lönholdt) W.; m. Jill Carolyn White, Mar. 17, 1973; children from previous marriages—Kurt Roman, Corinne Harriet Irene, Bettina Elaine (dec.). Student, U. Freiburg, 1937, U. Frankfurt Main, Germany, 1940-43; Dr. iur, U. Frankfurt Main, Germany, 1951; LL.B., Georgetown U., 1955; LL.M., Harvard, 1956; J.S.D., Yale, 1962. Referendar Frankfurt, Germany, 1943-48; atty. German cts. U.S. Ct. Appeals, Allied High Commn., Frankfurt, 1949-52; expert on trade regulations, visit in U.S. under auspices Dept. State, 1950; Harvard U. Dumbarton Oaks Library and Collection, Washington, 1953-55; asst. in instrn. Law Sch., Yale, 1956-57; assoc. prof. law U. Fla., Gainesville, 1957-60, prof., 1960-89, Clarence J. TeSelle prof. law, 1989-94, Stephen C. O'Connell chair, 1994—; hon. prof. law Johann Wolfgang Goethe U., Frankfurt Main, 1980—; vis. cons. U. Calif. at Berkeley, Space Scis. Lab., 1965-66; vis. prof. law Rutgers U., 1968; vis. prof. polit. sci. U. Calif. at Berkeley, 1968-69; vis. prof. law U. Frankfurt, 1975; cons. Commn. of Experts on Problems of Succession of the Hague Conf. on Pvt. Internat. Law, U.S. Dept. State, 1968-71; Rockefeller Found. fellow, Europe, 1958-59. Author: The Personality of Lawyers, 1964, Zum Gesellschaftsbild des Juristen, 1970, Hierarchie der Ausbildungsstätten, Rechtsstudium und Recht in den Vereinigten Staaten, 1976, Gestapo V-Leute: Tatsachen und Theorie des Geheimdienstes, 1989, 2d edit., 1992; co-author: (with Sanford N. Katz) American Family Law in Transition, 1983, (with Katz and Frances E. Olsen) Cases and Materials on Family Law: Legal Concepts and Changing Human Relationships, 1994; contbr. to: Clinical Law Training-Interviewing and Counseling, 1972, Law, Justice, and the Individual in Society-Psychological and Legal Issues, 1977, Marriage and Cohabitation in Contemporary Societies: Areas of Legal, Social and Ethical Change-An International and Interdisciplinary Study, 1980, Dutch trans., 1981, Group Dynamic Law: Exposition and Practice, 1988. Mem. Am. Acad. Fgn. Law, Law and Soc. Assn., Internat. Soc. on Family Law, Assn. Am. Law Schs. (chmn. com. studies beyond 1st degree in law 1965-67), Order of Coif. Home: 2713 SW 5th Pl Gainesville FL 32607-3113 Office: U Fla Coll Law Gainesville FL 32611

WEYRICH, PAUL MICHAEL, political organizations executive; b. Racine, Wis., Oct. 7, 1942; s. Ignatius A. and Virginia M. (Wickstrom) W.; m. Joyce Anne Smigun, July 6, 1963; children: Dawn, Peter, Diana, Stephen, Andrew. AA, U. Wis., 1962. Ordained deacon Melkite Greek Eparchy, 1990. News dir. Service Broadcasting, Kenosha, Wis., 1962-63; reporter Milw. Sentinel, 1963-64; polit. reporter, newscaster CBS, Milw., 1964-65; news dir. Sta. KQXI, Denver, 1966; asst. U.S. Sen. Gordon Allott of Colo., 1966-73; asst. to Sen. Carl T. Curtis, Nebr., 1973-77; founder, pres. Heritage Found., 1973-74; nat. chmn. Free Congress PAC, Coalitions for Am., BOD, AMTRAK, 1987-93; pres. Free Congress Found., Krieble Inst. of Free Congress Found., NET-Polit. Newstalk Network; Washington editor The Wanderer, 1969-71; nat. editor Transport Central, 1968-73; treas. Coun. Nat. Policy, 1981-92; bd. dirs. All News Radio WEEI, Boston, 1984-90; vice chmn. Com. for Effective State Govt. Recipient Youth of Yr. award Racine Optimist Club, 1960, Excellence in Reporting citation Milw. Common Council, 1964, Documentary of Yr. award for Wis. TV, 1965. Mem. Central Electric Railroaders Assn., Internat. Policy Forum (chmn. 1983-94); former mem. HUD Adv. Commn. on Regulatory Barriers to Affordable Housing. Greek Catholic. Author: The Role of Rails series, 1964; pub. Polit. Report, 1975-89, The New Electric Rwy. Jour., 1988—, Spotlight on Congress, 1989-93; host (daily talk show) Direct Line, 1993—; co-host The New Electric Railway Jour., 1994—, Ways & Means, 1994—. Home: 12615 Lake Normandy Ln Fairfax VA 22030-7262 Office: Free Congress Found 717 2nd St NE Washington DC 20002-4368

WHALE, ARTHUR RICHARD, lawyer; b. Detroit, Oct. 28, 1923; s. Arthur B. and Orpha Louella (Doak) W.; m. Roberta Lou Donaldson, Oct. 29, 1949; children: Richard Donaldson, Linda Jean. BSChemE, Northwestern U., 1945; LLB, George Washington U., 1956. Bar: D.C. 1957, Mich. 1957, Ind. 1977, Office of U.S. Patent and Trademark 1957. Chem. engr. Ansul Chem. Co., Marinette, Wis., 1946-47, Parke, Davis & Co., Detroit, 1947-50; writer med. lit. Parke, Davis & Co., 1950-52; chem. engr. Bur. Ships, U.S. Dept. Navy, Washington, 1952-55; dep. sect. head, indsl. gas sect. Bur. Ships, U.S. Dept. Navy, 1954-55; patent engr. Swift & Co., Washington, 1955-56; patent atty. Upjohn Co., Kalamazoo, 1956-65; asst. mgr. organic chems. sect. patent dept. Dow Chem. Co., Midland, Mich., 1965-66; mgr. Dow Chem. Co., 1967-73, mng. counsel, 1973-75; asst. sec., gen. patent counsel Eli Lilly & Co., Indpls., 1975-86; of counsel Miller, Morriss, & Pappas, Lansing, Mich., 1986-89, Baker & Daniels, Indpls., 1987—; bd. dirs. Wyckoff Chem. Co., South Haven, Mich.; lectr. Practicing Law Inst., John Marshall Law Sch. Contbr. articles to profl. jours. Pres. Nat. Inventors Hall of Fame Found., 1978-79; bd. dirs. Holcomb Rsch. Inst., INdpls, 1982-86. Served to lt. (j.g.) USNR, 1943-46. Mem. State Bar Mich. (chmn. patent trademark copyright sect. 1967-69), D.C. Bar Assn. (mem. patent trademark copyright div.), Midland County Bar Assn. (pres. 1974-75), Am. Bar Assn. (mem. patent trademark copyright sect.), Assn. Corp. Patent Counsel, Nat. Coun. Patent Law Assns. (chmn. 1979-80), Am. Intellectual Property Law Assn. (pres. 1974-75), Ashlar Lodge, Masons, Shriners. Republican. Presbyterian. Avocation: golf. Home: 3513 Admiralty Ln Indianapolis IN 46240-3568 also: 2363 Gulf Shore Blvd N Naples FL 33940-4356 Office: Baker & Daniels 300 N Meridian St Ste 2700 Indianapolis IN 46204-1755

WHALEN, CHARLES WILLIAM, JR., author, business executive, educator; b. Dayton, Ohio, July 31, 1920; s. Charles William and Colette (Kelleher) W.; m. Mary Barbara Gleason, Dec. 27, 1958; children—Charles E., Daniel D., Edward J., Joseph M., Anne E., Mary B. B.S., U. Dayton, 1942, H.H.D. (hon.), 1980; M.B.A., Harvard U., 1946; postgrad., Ohio State U., 1959-60; LL.D., Central State U., Ohio, 1966. Vice pres. Dayton Dress Co., 1946-52; faculty U. Dayton, 1952-66; mem. 90th-95th Congresses 3d Dist. Ohio; pres. New Directions, Washington, 1978-79; fellow Woodrow Wilson Internat. Center for Scholars, 1980; adj. prof. Sch. Internat. Service, Am. U., 1981. Mem. Ohio Ho. of Reps., 1954-60, Ohio Senate, 1960-66; mem. Internat. Vol. Svcs., Inc.; v.p. Washington Inst. Fgn. Affairs; mem. U. Dayton adv. bd. Ctr. for Internat. Studies; bd. dirs. Harvard Bus. Sch., Washington. 1st lt. AUS, 1943-46. Recipient Disting. Alumnus award U. Dayton Alumni Assn., 1975;. Roman Catholic. Clubs: Capitol Hill, Kenwood Country, Dayton Bicycle.

WHALEN, JAMES JOSEPH, college president; b. Pottsville, Pa., Mar. 6, 1927; s. Frank Leo and Mary M. (McCusker) W.; m. Gillian Stuart Hamer, Sept. 29, 1956. AB, Franklin and Marshall Coll., 1950; MS (VA fellow), Pa. State U., 1952, PhD in Clin. Psychology (VA fellow), 1955; LLD (hon.), Newton (Mass.) Coll., 1975. Lic. psychologist, Mass. VA tng. intern clin. psychology Roanoke (Va.) VA Hosp., 1951-52, Wilkes-Barre (Pa.) VA Hosp., 1954-55; clin. psychologist VA Hosp., Pitts., 1955-58; asst. dean, psychologist European div. U. Md., Munich, Germany, 1958-60; prof. psychology, lectr. European div. U. Md., Heidelberg, Germany, 1960-63; asst. dir., asst. prof. psychology U. Md., European Div., 1963-64; assoc. prof., prof. psychology Ohio U., 1964-69, dir. ctr. for psychol. services, 1964-65, dean students, 1965-66, adminstrv. v.p., 1966-67, exec. v.p., 1967-69; pres., prof. Newton Coll., 1969-75; pres. Ithaca (N.Y.) Coll., 1975—, prof., 1975—; past chmn. Am. Coun. Edn., chmn. nominating com., 1994, Ad Hoc study com., Commn. on Ednl. Credit and Credentials, 1992—, chmn. membership com., 1988-90, bd. dirs., 1984-91, chmn. constn. and by-laws rev. com., 1991-92; past mem. pres.'s commn. NCAA, past chmn. div. III subcom., mem. com. on rev. and planning, 1990—; co-chair NCAA Gender Equity Task Force, 1992-93; mem. Edn. Commn. States Task Force on State Policy and Ind. Higher Edn.; past chmn. bd. visitors Air U. USAF; cons., chmn. Joint Chiefs of Staff Profl. Mil. Edn. Rev. Panel, mem. exec. com. Joint Chiefs of Staff Process for Accreditation of Joint Edn., 1991—; mem. Knight Found. Commn. on Intercoll. Athletics, 1989-93; mem. bd. visitors U. N.C., Asheville, 1986-89; past chmn. Nat. Assn. Ind. Colls. and Univs., bd. dirs., 1982-85, mem. pub. rels. adv. com., 1989-90, mem. govt. rels. com., 1985-89, chmn. govt. rels. com. on state rels., 1988-89; mem. Commn. on Ind. Colls. and Univs. in N.Y. State, past chmn. bd., past chmn. fed. rels. Com., trustee, 1978-84, 89-92, chmn. fin. com., 1990-92, treas. CICU/NYSCICU bd. 1991-92; mem. regents adv. coun. for Planning in Higher Edn., State of N.Y.; mem. nat. adv. com. Ctr. for Study of Sports in Soc.; mem. commr. edns. adv. coun. State N.Y., mem. commrs. edns. task force to reorganize state edn. dept.; chmn. adv. bd. Fleet Bank, Ithaca; bd. dirs. Fleet Investment Svcs., Rochester, N.Y. Contbr. articles on exec. leadership and ednl. adminstrn. to profl. jours. Served with USNR, 1945-46. Recipient Keiper award Franklin and Marshall Coll., 1948, medal USAF, 1990; Pa. State U. scholar, 1950-52. Mem. Am. Psychol. Assn., Mass. Psycho. Assn., Internat. Assn. Univ. Pres., N.Y. Acad. Scis., N.Y. State C. of C. (edn. com.), Ind. Coll. Fund N.Y. State (past mem. exec. com.), Assn. Colls. and Univs. N.Y. State (past mem. exec. com., bd. trustees), Oracle Soc., Univ. Club, Royal Auto Club, Ithaca Garden Club, Rotary, Phi Kappa Phi (editorial adv. bd. Nat. Forum 1989-94), Phi Delta Kappa, Psi Chi, Phi Kappa Tau, Phi Mu Alpha, Delta Phi Alpha. Home: 2 Fountain Pl Ithaca NY 14850-4428 Office: Ithaca Coll 953 Danby Rd Ithaca NY 14850-7000

WHALEN, JAMES LAWRENCE, protective services official, lawyer, educator; b. Cin., Jan. 8, 1962; s. Lawrence Edward and Donna Lee (Faulkner) W.; m. Mary Colleen Anneken, Apr. 28, 1984; children: Kelly, Amy, Nicholas, Julie. BS in Criminal Justice, U. Cin., 1988; JD, No. Ky. U., 1992. Bar: Ohio, D.C. Police officer Metro-Dade Police Dept., Miami, Fla., 1982-85; police officer Cin. (Ohio) Police Divsn., 1986-92, police sgt., 1992—; pvt. practice lawyer Cin., 1992—; cert. instr. Ohio Police Officers Tng. Assn., State of Ohio, 1990—; prof. No. Ky. U., Highland Heights, 1994—; instr. in field. Recipient Career Enhancement award Rotary Club, Cin., 1991. Mem. ABA, Ohio Bar Assn., Cin. Bar Assn., Fraternal Order of Police. Roman Catholic. Avocations: family activities, home remodeling, athletics. Office: Cin Police Divsn 310 Ezzard Charles Dr Cincinnati OH 45214

WHALEN, JEROME DEMARIS, lawyer; b. Portland, Oreg., Feb. 9, 1943; s. William F. and Rose (Demaris) W. BA, U. Wash., 1965; JD, Harvard U., 1969. Bar: Wash. 1969. Assoc. Foster Pepper & Shefelman, Seattle, 1969-74, ptnr., 1974-91, mng. ptnr., 1982-85; ptnr. Whalen & Firestone, Seattle, 1991—; adj. prof. corps. Law Sch., U. Puget Sound, Tacoma, 1976-77; instr. securities regulation Law Sch., U. Wash., Seattle, 1979; bd. dirs. Wright Runstad & Co., Seattle. Author: Commercial Ground Leases, 1988. Mem. Port of Seattle Ctrl. Waterfront Devel. Panel, 1988-90; trustee Corp. Coun. for Arts, Seattle, 1989—; trustee Pratt Fine Arts Ctr., Seattle, 1989-94, pres., 1991-93, Seattle Internat. Music Festival, 1992—. Mem. Wash. State Bar Assn. (chmn. corp. bus. and banking law sect. 1980-81), Phi Beta Kappa. Office: Whalen & Firestone 1221 2nd Ave Ste 410 Seattle WA 98101-2942

WHALEN, JOHN PHILIP, retired educational administrator, clergyman, lawyer; b. Troy, N.Y., Jan. 4, 1928; s. Philip Joseph and Mary Catherine (Doyle) W.; B.A. summa cum laude, St. Mary's Sem. and Univ., Balt., 1949; S.T.L., Cath. U., 1953, M.A., 1954, S.T.D. summa cum laude, 1965; J.D., George Washington U., 1976; postgrad. Johns Hopkins U., 1959-60, U. Md., College Park, 1958-59, Fordham U., 1953-54; LHD (hon.), Marymount U., 1987. Ordained priest Roman Cath. Ch., 1953. Instr. Mater Christi Sem., Albany, N.Y., 1953-58; asst. prof. Mt. St. Mary's Coll., Emmitsburg, Md., 1959-61; assoc. prof. Cath. U. Am., Washington, 1961-67, acting pres., 1968-69; pastor St. Mary's Ch., Oneonta, N.Y., 1970-72; pres. Consortium of Univs. of Washington area, 1972-88; mng. editor New Cath. Ency., 1963-67; pres., editor-in-chief Corpus Publs., 1967-94; ret. 1994. cons. 12 colls. and univs.; chmn. Univ. Support Services Inc., 1986-94, pres., chief exec. officer; cons. student loans, capital access trust, capital loans to colls.; bd. dirs. U.S. Fund for Improvement Postsecondary Edn., 1988-91. Bd. dirs. Sta. WETA-TV, 1968-69, Washington Ctr. for Met. Studies, 1968-69, Met. Bd. Trade, D.C., 1975-90, sec. bd. dirs., 1983-85; bd. dirs. Cath. U. Am., 1968-69, Nat. Shrine of Immaculate Conception, 1968-69, Dumbarton Coll., 1970-72, Trinity Coll., 1969-72, St. Mary's Coll. (South Bend, Ind.), 1970-74, St. Anselm's, 1979-85, Mt. Vernon Coll., 1982-84; pres. Univ. Extension Ednl. Corp., 1974-94; mem. Fed. City Council, 1982—; mem. Council for Ct. Excellence, 1984-90; chmn. Ctr. Advanced Studies of the Ams., 1984-90. Named Man of the Yr. 1984; recipient Disting. Alumnus award George Washington U., 1988. Mem. Nat. Cath. Edn. Assn., Cath. Theol. Soc. Am. (dir. 1966-68), Higher Edn. Group Washington (pres. 1974-75). Clubs: Tired Hands (pres. 1982-84), Cosmos (Washington), City Club; Rotary. Editorial bd. Law and Edn.; weekly columnist Evangelist, Albany; contbr. to Nat. Geog. mag.; contbr. articles to ednl. and theol. jours. Office: 1614 Parham Rd Silver Spring MD 20903-2256

WHALEN, JOHN SYDNEY, management consultant; b. Moncton, N.B., Can., Sept. 26, 1934; s. Harry Edward and Sarah Maude (Bourgeois) W.; m. Margaret Joan Carruthers, May 3, 1958; children: Bradley Graham, Elizabeth Ann. Grad., Can. Inst. Chartered Accts., 1959. Chartered acct. Coopers & Lybrand (formerly McDonald, Currie & Co.), St. John, N.B., 1954-63; with Kaiser Services, Oakland, Calif., 1963-75; telecommunications mgr. Kaiser Services, 1966-69, asst. controller, 1969-70, controller, 1970-74; mgr. corp. acctg. Kaiser Industries Corp., Oakland, 1975; controller Kaiser Engrs., Inc., Oakland, 1975-76; v.p. fin. and adminstrn. Kaiser Engrs., Inc., 1976-82; mgmt. cons., owner Whalen & Assocs., Inc., Alamo, Calif., 1983—; prin. Corp. Restructuring Group, Inc., Alamo, Calif., 1989—; pres. Round Hill Holdings, Inc., 1993—. Mem. Fin. Execs. Inst., Turnaround Mgmt. Assn. Club: Round Hill Golf and Country; Commonwealth. Home: 2216 Nelda Way Alamo CA 94507-2004 Office: 3191 Danville Blvd Alamo CA 94507-1540

WHALEN, LAURENCE J., federal judge; b. 1944. BA, Georgetown Coll., 1967; JD, Georgetown U., 1970, LLM in Taxation, 1971. Judge U.S. Tax Ct., Washington, 1987—; atty. Crowe & Dunlevy, Oklahoma City, Hamel & Park, Washington; spl. asst. to Asst. Atty. Gen.; trial atty., tax div. U.S. Dept. Justice. With USAR, 1971. Mem. ABA (taxation, litigation and bus. law sects.), Fed. Bar Assn. Office: US Tax Ct 400 2nd St NW Washington DC 20217-0001

WHALEN, LUCILLE, academic administrator; b. Los Angeles, July 26, 1925; d. Edward Cleveland and Mary Lucille (Perrault) W. B.A. in English, Immaculate Heart Coll., Los Angeles, 1949; M.S.L.S., Catholic U. Am., 1955; D.L.S., Columbia U., 1965. Tchr. elem. and secondary parochial schs. Los Angeles, Long Beach, Calif., 1945-52; high sch. librarian Conaty Meml. High Sch., Los Angeles, 1950-52; reference/serials librarian, instr. in library sci. Immaculate Heart Coll., 1955-58; dean Immaculate Heart Coll. (Sch. Library Sci.), 1958-60, 65-70; assoc. dean, prof. SUNY, Albany, 1971-78, 84-87; prof. Sch. Info. Sci. and Policy SUNY, 1979-83; dean grad. programs, libr. Immaculate Heart Coll. Ctr., Los Angeles, 1987-90; ref. libr. (part-time) Glendale Community Coll., 1990—; dir. U.S. Office Edn. Instn. Author, editor: (with others) Reference Services in Archives, 1986. author: Human Rights: A Reference Handbook, 1989. Mem. ACLU, Common Cause, Amnesty Internat. Democrat. Roman Catholic. Home: 320 S Gramercy Pl Apt 101 Los Angeles CA 90020-4542 Office: Glendale Community Coll 1500 N Verdugo Rd Glendale CA 91208-2809

WHALEN, PHILIP GLENN, poet, novelist; b. Portland, Oreg., Oct. 20, 1923; s. Glenn Henry and Phyllis Bush W. B.A., Reed Coll., 1951. Ordained Zen Buddhist priest, 1973. Head monk Dharma Sangha, Santa Fe, 1984-87; abbot Hartford St. Zen Ctr., San Francisco, 1991; lectr., tchr., 1955—. Author: poetry Three Satires, 1951, Self-Portrait, From Another Direction, 1959, Like I Say, 1960, Memoirs of an Inter-Glacial Age, 1960, Every Day, 1965, Highgrade, 1966, On Bear's Head, 1969, Severance Pay, 1971, Scenes of Life at the Capitol, 1971, The Kindness of Strangers, 1975, Enough Said, 1980, Heavy Breathing, 1983; novels You Didn't Even Try, 1967, Imaginary Speeches for a Brazen Head, 1972; interviews Off the Wall, 1978; prose text The Diamond Noodle, 1980; juvenile The Invention of the Letter, 1967; Recipient Poet's Found. award 1962, V.K. Ratcliff award 1964; By & Large, tape cassette reading his own poems, 1987. Served with USAAF, 1943-46. Am. Acad. Arts and Letters grantee-in-aid, 1965, 91, Morton Dauwen Zabel award for Poetry, 1986, Fund for Poetry award, 1987, 91; Com. on Poetry grantee, 1968, 70, 71. Office: 57 Hartford St San Francisco CA 94114-2013

WHALEN, STEPHANIE A., chemist,enviornmentalist and pharmacologist; b. Glendale, Calif., Apr. 7, 1944. BS in Chemistry magna cum laude, Holy Names Coll., 1966; MS in Pharmacology, U. Hawaii, 1973. Rsch. asst. forestry divsn. U. Calif., Berkeley, 1966; tchr. physical, biological scis. Sacred Hearts Acad., 1966-67; sr. chemist EPA, Honolulu, 1972-73; assoc. chemist crop scis. dept. Hawaiian Sugar Planters' Assn., 1973-79, assoc. chemist, supr. analytical labs. crop scis. dept., 1979-87, head environ. sci. dept., experiment sta., 1988—, pres., dir. experiment sta., 1994—; rsch. asst. U. Hawaii, 1967-69, rsch. assoc., 1969-73. Contbr. articles to profl. pubs. Mem. Am. Chem. Soc., Nat. Assn. Environ. Profls., Kappa Gamma Pi,

Sigma Xi. Office: Hawaiian Sugar Planters PO Box 1057 99-193 Aiea Heights Dr Aiea HI 96701*

WHALEN, THOMAS EARL, psychology educator; b. Toledo, June 26, 1938; s. T. Mylo and Alice E. (Tallman) W.; m. Carolyn Margaret Lapham, Dec. 24, 1960; children: Jennifer Susan, Holly Elizabeth. BA, UCLA, 1960; MA, San Diego State U., 1967; PhD, U. Conn., 1970. Cert. secondary tchr., Calif. Secondary tchr. San Diego City Schs., 1964-68; rsch. assoc. Southwest Regional Lab., Inglewood, Calif., 1969; prof. Calif. State U., Hayward, Calif., 1970—; chair ednl. psychology dept. Calif. State U., Hayward, 1987-89, 95-96; assoc. dean sch. edn. Calif. State U., 1987-89; ednl. psychology dept. chair Calif. State U., Hayward, 1977-79, assoc. dean. sch. edn., 1987-89, 95-96; rsch. con. Evaluation Assocs., San Sanfrancisco Bay Area Schs., 1971-88, Lawrence Livermore (Calif.) Nat. Lab., 1982-83. Author: (text book) Ten Steps to Behavioral Research, 1989; contbr. articles to profl. jours. Lt. USN, 1960-63. U.S. Office of Edn. fellow U. Conn., 1968-70, post doctoral scholar Am. Edn. Rsch. Assn., U. Iowa, 1972; recipient Loebner prize Cambridge Ctr. for Behavioral Studies, 1994. Mem. Am. Ednl. Rsch. Assn., APA, Calif. Ednl. Rsch. Assn. (bd. dirs. 1982-84), Bay Area Coun. on Measurement and Evaluation in Edn. (pres. 1976-77), United Profs. of Calif. (exec. bd. Calif. State U. Hayward 1975-76). Avocations: golf, travel, gardening. Home: 325 Conway Dr Danville CA 94526-5511 Office: Calif State U 25800 Carlos Bee Blvd Hayward CA 94542-3001

WHALEN, WAYNE W., lawyer; b. Savanna, Ill., Aug. 22, 1939; s. Leo R. and Esther M. (Yackley) W.; m. Paula Wolff, Apr. 22, 1970; children: Amanda, Clementine, Antonia, Nathaniel. BS, U.S. Air Force Acad., 1961; JD, Northwestern U., 1967. Bar: Ill. 1967, U.S. Ct. Appeals (7th cir.) 1968, U.S. Supreme Ct. 1972. Commd. 1st lt. USAF, 1961, ret., 1964; assoc. Mayer, Brown & Platt, Chgo., 1967-74, ptnr., 1974; ptnr. Skadden, Arps, Slate, Meagher & Flom, Chgo., 1984—; bd. dirs. Van Kampel Am. Capital Family Mut. Funds, Oak Brook, Ill. Author: Annotated Illinois Constitution, 1972. Del. 6th Ill. Constitutional Conv., 1969-70, chmn. style drafting and submission com. Named Outstanding Young Lawyer, Chgo. Bar Found., 1970. Mem. Chgo. Club. Home: 4920 S Greenwood Ave Chicago IL 60615-2816 Office: Skadden Arps Slate 333 W Wacker Dr Chicago IL 60606-1218

WHALEY, CAROLYN LOUISE, primary school educator; b. Jackson, Tenn., Apr. 4, 1952; d. James M. and Allie L. (Williams) Brown; m. Roy Lynn Whaley, Aug. 13, 1978. BA, Union U., 1974; M of Music, Southwestern Bapt. Sem., Ft. Worth, 1976, MA, 1979; postgrad., Tex. Woman's U., 1996. Cert. elem., early childhood, music tchr. $D, $D, $D; Preschool tchr. Naval Acad. Primary Sch., Annapolis, Md., 1983-87; kindergarten tchr. Bosqueville Ind. Sch. Dist., Waco, Tex., 1987-94, mulit-age primary tchr., 1994-95, music tchr., 1995—. Guest columnist Waco Tribune Herald, 1994. Vol. Prison Fellowship, Waco, 1988-94, Habitat for Humanity, Waco, 1990-94. Mem. Assn. for Childhood Edn. Internat., Nat. Assn. for Edn. of Young Children, Moo Duk Kwan Fedn. (Tae Kwon Do), Internat. Reading Assn. Home: 708 N 15th St Waco TX 76707-3513 Office: Bosqueville Ind Sch Dist 7636 Rock Creek Rd Waco TX 76708-7225

WHALEY, CHRISTOPHER D., manufacturing engineer; b. Fulton, N.Y., Feb. 21, 1965; s. Lawrence Arthor and Shirley May (Beebe) W.; m. Nina Terresa Barucco; children: Stefan, Aric. BS in Physics, SUNY, Oswego, 1986; BS in Polit. Sci., SUNY, Cortland, 1991; AAS in Mech. Engring. Tech., Ononadoga C.C., Syracuse, N.Y., 1988. Rsch. and devel. toolmaker The Eraser Co., Syracuse, 1983-85; design engr. Greno Industries, Scota, N.Y., 1985-87; mfg. and design engr. Majestic Mold, Phoenix, N.Y., 1987-89; mfg. engr. GE Co., Syracuse, 1989-92; v.p. mfg. engr. Display Prodrs., Bronx, N.Y., 1992-95; v.p. engring. and ops. Viz Mold & Die Ltd., Northvale, N.J., 1995—; cons. Viz Plastics & Mold, Northvale, N.J., 1992—, Shar-Jo Industries, Fulton, N.Y., 1989—; tooling designer GTS Industries, Clifton, N.J., 1992—. Author: U.S. Naval Repair Manual, 1986. Asst. wrestling coach Mexico (N.Y.) Acad. Schs., 1983-85. Mem. Soc. Plastic Engrs. Republican. Avocations: formula style road racing, motorcross racing, remote control gas car racing. Home: 8 Walnut Ln Harrison NY 10528 Office: Viz Mold & Die Ltd 210 Industrial Pkwy Northvale NJ 07647

WHALEY, FRANK, actor; b. Syracuse, N.Y., July 20, 1963. film appearances include: Ironweed, 1987, Field of Dreams, 1989, Little Monsters, 1989, Born on the Fourth of July, 1989, The Freshman, 1990, JFK, 1991, The Doors, 1991, Career Opportunities, 1991, Back in the U.S.S.R., 1992, A Midnight Clear, 1992, Hoffa, 1992, Swing Kids, 1993, Pulp Fiction, 1994, Swimming With Sharks, 1995; TV movies include: Unconquered, 1989, Flying Blind, 1990, To Dance with the White Dog, 1993, Fatal Deception: Mrs. Lee Harvey Oswald, 1993; stage appearances include: Tigers Wild, 1986, The Years, 1993. Office: c/o William Morris Agy 151 El Camino Beverly Hills CA 90212*

WHALEY, ROSS SAMUEL, academic administrator; b. Detroit, Nov. 7, 1937; s. Lyle John and Margaret Nielson (Semple) W.; m. Beverly Mae Heemstra, June 14, 1958; children—Heather Jean, Susan Lesli, Lindsay John. B.S., U. Mich., 1959, Ph.D., 1969; M.S., Colo. State U., 1961. Asst. prof., assoc. prof., prof. Utah State U., Logan, 1965-70, dept. head, 1967-70; assoc. dean Colo. State U., Ft. Collins, 1970-73; dept. head U. Mass., Amherst, 1973-76, dean, 1976-78; dir. econ. research USDA Forest Service, Washington, 1978-84; pres. SUNY Coll. Environ. Scis. and Forestry, Syracuse, 1984—; cons. UN FAO, Rome, 1983-84, UN, Budapest, Hungary, 1974, U.S. Peace Corps., South Am., 1972, Geddes, Brecher, Qualls & Cunningham, Denver, 1971-72. Contbr. articles to profl. jours. Bd. dirs. Hiwawatha coun. Boy Scouts Am., 1985—; bd. dirs. Pinchot Inst. Conservation, 1985—, ARC, 1994—, Au Sable Inst. Environ. Studies. Fellow Soc. Am. Foresters (pres. 1991). Mem. Christian Ref. Ch. Avocations: reading, swimming, hiking, fly fishing, cross-country skiing. Home: 2 Bradford Heights Rd Syracuse NY 13224-2158 Office: SUNY Office of Pres Coll Environ Sci & Forestry Syracuse NY 13210

WHALEY, STORM HAMMOND, retired government official, consultant; b. Sulphur Springs, Ark., Mar. 15, 1916; s. Storm Onus and Mabel Etta (Prater) W.; m. Jane Florence Bucy, Oct. 6, 1935; children: Carroll Jean Whaley Anderson, Ann Marie Whaley Adams, Rebecca Glenn Whaley Dyess. B.A., John Brown U., 1935; LL.D. (hon.), 1959; postgrad., Am. U. Law Sch., 1954; D.Sc. hon., U. Ark. for Med. Scis., 1983. Mgr. Sta. KUOA, Siloam Springs, Ark., 1935-53, Sta. KGER, Long Beach, 1948-53, KOME, Tulsa, 1951-53; asst. to Congressman J.W. Trimble, 1953-54; asst. to pres. U. Ark., 1954-59, acting pres., 1959-60, v.p. health scis., 1960-70; assoc. dir. communications NIH, Bethesda, Md., 1970-92; retired, 1992; mem. U.S. del. World Health Assembly, 1962, 63, 64; mem. nat. adv. health council USPHS, 1963-66; chmn. ad hoc com. Report to Pres. and Congress Regional Med. Programs, 1967; mem. U.S. Sr. Exec. Service, 1979. Author: They Call It, 1951. Del. Democratic Nat. Conv., 1940, 44, 48, 52. Recipient Superior Service award HEW, 1974, SES Performance award, 1982, Superior Service award USPHS, 1987. Fellow AAAS; mem. Broadcast Pioneers, Ark. Broadcasters Assn., Internat. Sci. Writers Assn., NIH Alumni Assn. (bd. dirs. 1992—, sec. 1995—), KT, Masons (33 deg.), Nat. Press Club, Omicron Delta Kappa, Lambda Chi Alpha. Home and Office: 4400 E West Hwy Bethesda MD 20814-4524

WHALEY, VERNON M., publisher, church musician, educator. Chmn. Music Commission of the Nat. Assn. of Free Will Baptists, Nashville, Tenn.; assoc. prof. ch. music Cedarville Coll., Ohio; pres. Integra Music Group, Inc.; composer, arranger Prism Music, Franklin, Tenn. Editor: REJOICE: The Free Will Baptist Hymn Book, 1988, The Rejoice Hymnal: for the Church at Worship, 1995, Understanding Music and Worship in the Local Church. Office: Integra Music Group Inc 7301 Cavalier Dr Nashville TN 37205

WHALLEY-KILMER, JOANNE, actress; b. Manchester, England, Aug. 25, 1964; m. Val Kilmer. Actress (theater) Bows and Arrows, 1982, Rita, Sue, and Bob Too, 1982, The Genius, 1983, Kate, 1983, The Crimes of Vautrin, 1983, The Pope's Wedding, 1984, Saved, 1984, As I Lay Dying, 1985, Women Beware Women, 1986, Three Sisters, 1987, What the Butler Saw, 1989 (Theatre World award 1989), (films) Pink Floyd-The Wall, 1982, Dance With a Stranger, 1985, The Good Father, 19886, No Surrender, 1986, Willow, 1988, Popielusko, (To Kill a Priest), 1989, Scandal, 1989, Kill Me Again, 1989, Navy SEALS, 1990, Crossing the Rapture, 1994, Trial By Jury, 1994, A Good Man in Africa, 1995 (TV) A Christmas Carol, 1984, A Kind of Loving, A Quiet Life, The Gentle Touch, Reilly, Save Your Kisses, Will You Love Me Tomorrow?, (TV mini-series) Edge of Darkness, 1986, The Singing Detective, 1988, Channel Crossings, 1988, Scarlett, 1994. Office: Creative Artists Agency 9830 Wilshire Blvd Beverly Hills CA 90212-1804*

WHALLON, EVAN ARTHUR, JR., orchestra conductor; b. Akron, Ind., July 24, 1923; s. Evan Arthur and Katharine (Kistler) W.; m. Jean Borgman, Aug. 28, 1948 (dec. 1977); children: Paul Evan, Eric Andrew; m. Rachael Shumate, Dec. 29, 1983 (div. 1992. MusB, Eastman Sch. Music, 1948, MusM, 1949; MusD (hon.), Denison U., 1963, Otterbein U., 1969, Ohio Dominican U., 1970. Debut with Phila. Orch., 1948; condr.: opera The Consul, 1949-50, Springfield (Ohio) Symphony, 1951-56, Columbus (Ohio) Symphony, 1956-82, guest condr., Spoleto (Italy) Festival, Phila. Orch., Cleve. Orch., San Francisco Symphony, Buffalo Philharmonic, Boston Arts Festival, N.Y.C. Opera, San Francisco Spring Opera, Balt. Symphony, Prague Symphony Orch., Budapest Mav Symphony, condr., mus. dir., Chatauqua (N.Y.) Opera Assn., 1966-81; mus. dir. Merola program and Western Opera Theater, San Francisco Opera, 1982-87, Ohio Light Opera, 1988-93. Lt. (j.g.) USNR, WWII. Recipient citation Columbus City Council, 1963, Ohio citation Ohioana Assn., 1983. Mem. Condrs. Guild (bd. dirs., pres. 1988-90). Home: 95 Orchard Dr Gaithersburg MD 20878-2223

WHALLON, WILLIAM, literature educator; b. Richmond, Ind., Sept. 24, 1928; s. Arthur J. and Adelaide (Wheeler) W.; m. Joanne Holland, Aug. 22, 1957; children: Andrew, Nicholas. B.A., McGill U., 1950; Ph.D., Yale U., 1957. Prof. Mich. State U., East Lansing, 1963—. Author: Formula, Character, and Context, 1969, Problem and Spectacle, 1980, Inconsistencies, 1983, (poetry) A Book of Time, 1990. Fellow Center for Hellenic Studies, 1962-63; Fulbright prof. comparative lit., U. Bayreuth, 1984-85. Home: 1655 Walnut Heights East Lansing MI 48823-2943

WHAM, DOROTHY STONECIPHER, state legislator; b. Centralia, Ill., Jan. 5, 1925; d. Ernest Joseph and Vera Thelma (Shafer) Stonecipher; m. Robert S. Wham, Jan. 26, 1947; children: Nancy S. Wham Mitchell, Jeanne Wham Ryan, Robert S. II. BA, MacMurray Coll., 1946; MA, U. Ill., 1949; D of Pub. Adminstrn. (hon.), MacMurray Coll., 1992. Counsellor Student Counselling Bur. U. Ill., Urbana, 1946-49; state dir. ACTION program, Colo./Wyo. U.S. Govt., Denver, 1972-82; mem. Colo. Ho. of Reps., 1986-87; mem. Colo. Senate, 1987—, chair jud. com., 1988—; with capital devel. com., health, environ, welfare, instns., fin. appropriations, legal svcs. Mem. LWV, Civil Rights Commn. Denver, 1972-80; bd. dirs. Denver Com. on Mental Health, 1985-88, Denver Symphony, 1985-88. Mem. Am. Psychol. Assn., Colo. Mental Health Assn. (bd. dirs. 1986-88), Colo. Hemophilia Soc. Republican. Methodist. Lodge: Civitan. Avocations: travel, furniture refinishing. Home: 2790 S High St Denver CO 80210-6352 Office: State Capitol Rm 342 Denver CO 80203

WHAM, GEORGE SIMS, publishing executive; b. Laurens, S.C., Jan. 27, 1920; s. George Sims and Nellie (Melette) W.; m. Beth Keeler, Sept. 13, 1947; children—Norman Brent, Bonnie Beth, Barry Keeler. B.S., Clemson U., 1941; M.S., U. Tenn., 1947; Ph.D., Pa. State U., 1951. Textile technologist USDA, 1947-49; research assoc. Sch. Chemistry and Physics, Pa. State U., 1949-51; prof., asst. dean Tex. Women's U., 1951-54; sr. editor Good Housekeeping mag., N.Y.C., 1954-60; v.p., tech. dir. Good Housekeeping mag., 1961-87; tech. cons., 1987—; disting. vis. prof. U. N.C., 1987-88; dir. R&D, Phillips Van Heusen, Inc., 1960-61; guest lectr. Purdue U., U. Md., Ariz. State U., U. Conn., U. Del., Clemson U., U. R.I., Mich. State U.; leader U.S. del. Internat. Standards Confs., 1968, 71, 86, 87. Contbr. articles to profl. jours. Pres. Governing Council, Hightstown, N.J., 1960-62; mem. Bd. Edn., Hightstown, 1959-61. Served to maj. AUS, 1941-46. Decorated Silver Star, Purple Heart. Mem. Am. Assn. Textile Chemists and Colorists (past pres., Harold C. Chapin award), Am. Nat. Standards Inst. (chmn. bd. dirs. 1986-88, chmn. textile standards bd. 1966-68, Howard Coonley medal 1985, George S. Wham Leadership medal 1990), Consumer Coun. (chmn. 1985), Sigma Xi, Phi Psi, Omicron Nu. Home: 201 E Ward St Hightstown NJ 08520-3313 Office: 959 8th Ave New York NY 10019-3767

WHAM, WILLIAM NEIL, publisher; b. N.Y.C., Dec. 28, 1934; s. William and Jessie (Neill) W.; m. Lynn McCorvie, Mar. 6, 1966; children: McCorvie, Avery. B.S., Syracuse U., 1956. Salesman Mut. N.Y., N.Y.C., 1959-61; regional sales mgr. Doubleday Pub. Co., N.Y.C., 1961-64, Reinhold Pub. Co., N.Y.C., 1964-68; sales mgr. United Bus. Publs., N.Y.C., 1968; pres., pub. jours. Internat. Scientific Communications, Inc., Shelton, Conn., 1968—. Founder: sci. jours. Am. Lab., Internat. Lab., Am. Biotech. Lab., Am. Clin. Lab., Internat. Biotech. Lab., Lab. Products Tech., Am. Lab. News, European Clin. Lab., Internat. Lab. News, Internat. Biotech. News, European Clin. Lab. News, Am. Environ. Lab. Served with AUS, 1956-58. Home: 157 Pinewood Trl Trumbull CT 06611-3312 Office: Internat Sci Communications Inc 30 Control Dr Shelton CT 06484-6111

WHANG, YUN CHOW, space science educator; b. Foochow, China, Dec. 13, 1931; came to U.S., 1955; s. Ta Chun and Wenlun (Lin) W.; m. Yeong-Ping Chu, Aug. 29, 1959; children: Ruth, Joyce, Kenneth. Ph.D., U. Minn., 1961. Asst. prof. U. Fla., 1961-62; asst. prof. The Cath. U. Am., 1962-63, assoc. prof., 1963-67, prof., 1968—, chmn. dept., 1971-83; sr. research assoc. Nat. Acad. Scis., 1967-68; vis. prof. Royal Inst. Tech., Stockholm, Sweden, 1972-73. Mem. Am. Geophys. Union, ASME. Research on slow shocks, solar wind theory, termination shock and heliopause, interaction solar wind with moon and planets. Home: 8003 Grand Teton Dr Potomac MD 20854-4073

WHARTON, BEVERLY ANN, utility company executive; b. St. Louis, Nov. 17, 1953; d. Lawrence A. and Helen M. Bextermueller; m. James R. Wharton, March 30, 1974; 1 child, Laura. BS, So. Ill. U., 1975; MBA, U. of S.D., 1980. Tax acct. supr. Iowa Pub. Service Co., Sioux City, Iowa, 1978-84; asst. sec. Iowa Pub. Service Co., Sioux City, 1981-84, sec., 1984-88, v.p. staff services, 1985-88, sr. v.p. support group, 1988-91; corp. sec. Midwest Energy Co., Sioux City, 1984-88, v.p., 1986-88, sr. v.p., 1988-90; gen. mgr. Midwest Gas, Sioux City, 1991-95, group v.p., gen. mgr., 1992-95; pres. Gas divsn. Mid-American Energy Co., Sioux City, 1995—; bd. dirs. Am. Gas Assn., Inst. Gas Tech. Bd. dirs. Security Nat. Bank, Marian Health Ctr., Briar Cliff Coll. Mem. Midwest Gas Assn. (bd. dirs. 1992—), Rotary (Sioux City club). Roman Catholic. Office: Mid American Energy Co 401 Douglas St Sioux City IA 51101-1443

WHARTON, CLIFTON REGINALD, JR., former university president, former government official, former insurance executive; b. Boston, Sept. 13, 1926; m. Dolores Duncan, 1950; children: Clifton, Bruce. BA, Harvard U., 1947; MA, Johns Hopkins U., 1948, U. Chgo., 1956; PhD in Econs., U. Chgo., 1958; LLD (hon.), Johns Hopkins U., 1970, U. Mich., 1970, Wayne State U., 1970, Hahneman Med. Sch., 1975, Georgetown U., 1976, Va. State U., 1977, CCNY, 1978, Wright State U., 1979, Lincoln U., 1979, Albany Law Sch., 1980, Duke U., 1981, Amherst Coll., 1983, U. Ill., 1984, U. Vt., 1987, Colgate U., 1987, Tuskegee U., 1987, Tufts U., 1988, Mich. State U., 1988, Claremont U. Ctr. and Grad. Sch., 1989, U. Notre Dame, 1989, Clark Atlanta U., 1990, Howard U., 1991, Shippensburg U., 1991, Miami U., Ohio, 1991, Washington U., 1991, Harvard U., 1992, Kenyon Coll., 1992, Ind. U. of Pa., 1992, Lehigh U., 1993; DPS (hon.), Ctrl. Mich. U., 1970, U. Pitts., 1989; LittD (hon.), N.C. Agrl. and Tech. State U., 1986, MacMurray Coll., 1993; LHD (hon.), Oakland U., 1971, No. Mich. U., 1975, Columbia U., 1978, Brandeis U., 1981, NYU, 1981, U. Conn., 1983, U. Mass., Boston, 1985, So. Ill. U., 1987, George Mason U., 1988, L.I. U., 1989, U. Ala., Birmingham, 1989, Va. Commonwealth U., 1990, SUNY, 1990, St. Paul's Coll., 1992, Johnson C. Smith U., 1994, Western Conn. State U., 1994, Northeastern U., 1994; DSc (hon.), Mercy Coll., 1989, Bryant Coll., 1990; PhD Internat. Rels. (hon.), Am. U., 1993; D. Mgmt. (hon.), GMI Inst. Engring. and Mgmt., 1992. Exec. trainee Am. Internat. Assn. Econ. and Social Devel., 1948-49, program analyst, 1949-51, head reports and analysis, 1951-53; rsch. asst. econs. U. Chgo., 1953-56, rsch. assoc., 1956-57; exec. assoc. Agrl. Devel. Coun., 1957-58, assoc., 1958-64, dir. Am. univs. rsch., 1964-67, v.p., 1967-69; pres. Mich. State U., 1970-78; chancellor SUNY System, 1978-87; chmn., CEO Tchrs. Ins. & Annuity Assn. Coll. Retirement Equities Fund, N.Y.C., 1987-93; dep. Sec. State U.S. Dept. State, Washington, 1993; bd. dirs. Ford Motor Co., Detroit, Tenneco, Harcourt Gen., N.Y. Stock Exch. Co-author: Patterns for Lifelong Learning, 1973; editor: Subsistence Agriculture and Economic Development, 1969; contbr. articles to profl. jours. Trustee Rockefeller Found., 1970-87, chmn., 1982-87; trustee Asia Soc., 1967-77, Overseas Devel. Coun., 1969-79, 94—, Carnegie Found., 1970-79, Agrl. Devel. Coun., 1973-80, Aspen Inst., 1980-93, Com. Econ. Devel., 1980-93, 94—, Coun. Fin. Aid to Edn., 1983-86, Coun. Fgn. Rels., 1983-93, Fgn. Policy Assn., 1983-87, MIT Corp., 1984-86, Acad. Ednl. Devel., 1985-86, Clark Found., 1991-93, Winrock Internat., 1994—; mem. Commn. on Intercollegiate Athletics, Knight Found., 1990-93, N.Y.C. Mayor's Coun. Econ. Advisors, 1990-93, Adv. Commn. on Trade Policy and Negotiations, 1990-92; bd. overseers Rockefeller Inst. of Govt., SUNY, 1994—. Mem. Am. Agrl. Econs. Assn., Assn. Asian Studies, Nat. Acad. Edn., Univ. Club (N.Y.C.), Country Club (Cooperstown, N.Y.). Office: TIAA-CREF 730 3rd Ave New York NY 10017-3206

WHARTON, DANNY CARROLL, zoo biologist; b. Ontario, Oreg., Mar. 13, 1947; s. Carroll Curtis and Norma (Grigg) W.; m. Marilyn Christine Hoyt, Sept. 22, 1973; children: Amanda, Catherine, Margaret, Arcadio. BA in Psychology, Coll. Idaho, 1969; MA in Internat. Adminstrn., Sch. for Internat. Tng., 1975; PhD in Biology, Fordham U., 1990. Rsch. assoc. Foresta Inst., Carson City, Nev., 1973-74; curatorial asst. Woodland Park Zool. Garden, Seattle, 1974-79; asst. curator N.Y. Zool. Soc./The Wildlife Conservation Soc., Bronx, 1979-85; assoc. curator N.Y. Zool. Soc., Bronx, 1985-89, curator, 1989—; dir. Ctrl. Pk. Wildlife Ctr., N.Y.C., 1994—; adjunct faculty Columbia U.; chmn. Internat. Advisors Internat. Snow Leopard Trust, Seattle, 1986; mem. US-USSR Environ. Agreement of U.S. Fish and Wildlife Svc., 1983. Contbr. articles to profl. jours. Vol. U.S. Peace Corps., Ecuador, 1969-71. Fulbright scholar, U. Münster, Fed. Republic Germany, 1976-77. Fellow Am. Assn. Zool. Parks and Aquariums (chmn. gorilla species survival plan 1992—, chmn. snow leopard species survival plan 1986—, co-chmn. marsupial and monotre,e taxon adv. group 1990-94; mem. Soc. for Conservation Biology, Internat. Union for Conservation of Nature/Species Survival Commn. (mem. captive breeding specialist group). Office: Wildlife Conservation Soc Ctrl Park Wildlife Ctr 830 5th Ave New York NY 10021-7001

WHARTON, KAY KAROLE, special education educator; b. Butler, Pa., Nov. 19, 1943; d. Clarence Henry Jr. and Alberta Elizabeth (Yost) Gilkey; m. David Burton Wharton, Nov. 28, 1975 (dec. May 1987). BS in Edn., Geneva Coll., 1965. Cert. spl. edn. tchr., Md. Tchr. 2d grade Butler Area Sch., 1965-71; resource tchr. Queen Anne County Bd. of Edn., Centreville, Md., 1971—; facilitator sch. improvement team Centreville Mid. Sch., 1992-95. Music dir. Diocese of Easton (Md.) Mid. Convocation Episcopal Cursillo, Old St. Paul's, Kent, 1989-91, St. Paul's, Hillsboro, 1993—; Sunday sch. supt. primary dept. St. Mark's Luth. Ch., 1966-71, St. Paul's Episcopal Ch., 1985-87; program dir. Queen Anne's County chpt. Am. Cancer Soc., Centreville, 1981-85; mem. PTA; Episcopal lay min. Meridian Nursing Home, 1978—. Mem. NEA, Queen Anne County Edn. Assn., Md. State Tchrs. Assn., Coun. for Exceptional Children, Internat. Reading Assn., Upper Shore Reading Assn. (sec. 1985-91, 93—), Learning Disabled Am., Guardians Learning Disabled (sec. 1991-92), Smithsonian Assocs., Order Ea. Star (worthy matron Centreville 1977, sec. 1982-93), Nat. Geographic Soc., Town and Country Women's Club (pres. 1977, 79), Delta Kappa Gamma (Nu chpt. pres. 1992—, rsch. com. chairperson Alpha Beta State 1993-95, membership chairperson 1995—). Republican. Avocations: piano, embroidery, handicrafts. Home: PO Box 237 Centreville MD 21617-0237 Office: Centreville Mid Sch 231 Ruthsburg Rd Centreville MD 21617-9702

WHARTON, LENNARD, engineering company executive; b. Boston, Dec. 10, 1933; s. Nathaniel Philip and Deeda (Levine) W.; m. Judith R. Gordon, Dec. 26, 1957; children: Ruth, Rebecca, Nathaniel. B.S. in Chem. Engring, MIT, 1955; B.A., Cambridge U., 1957, M.A., 1957; A.M., Harvard U.; A.M. (NSF fellow 1957-60), 1960, Ph.D. (Jr. fellow Soc. of Fellows 1960-63), 1963. Registered profl. engr., N.J., Ill. Prof. dept. chemistry U. Chgo., 1963-80; v.p. engring. ITE Imperial Corp., 1972-73; v.p. tech. Studebaker-Worthington, Barrington, Ill., 1978-79, McGraw Edison Co., Rolling Meadows, Ill., 1979-80; v.p. engring. and tech. Worthington group McGraw Edison Co., Mountainside, N.J., 1980-85; corp. v.p. tech. Material Research Corp., Pearl River, N.Y., 1985-87; v.p. Packer Engring. Inc., Naperville, Ill., 1987-95, chmn. bd., 1994-95; pres. Evidentia Engring. Inc., Short Hills, N.J., 1995—. Sloan fellow, 1964-66; named Outstanding Young Man of Chgo. Chgo. Jr. Assn. Commerce and Industry, 1968. Mem. IEEE (sr.), Nat. Fire Protection Assn., Am. Inst. Chem. Engrs. Office: 10 Park Pl Short Hills NJ 07078-2826

WHARTON, MARGARET AGNES, artist; b. Portsmouth, Va., 1943. BS, U. Md., 1965; MFA, Sch. of Art Inst. Chgo., 1975. vis. artist Sch. of Art Inst. of Chgo., 1978, 89, 90, Columbia Coll., Chgo., 1994. One women shows include Phyllis Kind Gallery, Chgo., 1976, 80, 85, 88, 91, N.Y.C., 1977, 78, 79, 81, 83, 87, 90, Mus. Contemporary Art, Chgo, 1981-82, Laguna Gloria Art Mus., Austin, Tex., 1981-82, Zolla/Lieberman Gallery, Inc., Chgo., 1992, 94, Evanston Art Ctr., 1994; exhibited in group shows at The Cinn. Art Mus., 1988-90, U. Wis. Art Mus., Milw., 1991, The Chgo. Cultural Ctr., 1992, Rockford (Ill.) Art Mus., 1994, and numerous others; represented in permanent collections Am. Med. Assn., Art Inst. of Chgo., Dallas Mus., Seattle Art Mus., State Ill. Collection, Whitney Mus. Am. Art, and others; comms. include Mus. of Contemporary Art, Chgo., 1985, Chgo. Pub. Libr., West Lawn Branch, Chgo., 1986. Founding mem. Artemesia Cooperative Gallery, Chgo., Ill. Recipient NEA grant 1979, 88, 93, Visual Arts award, 1984.

WHARTON, THOMAS WILLIAM, mining executive; b. St. Louis, Nov. 20, 1943; s. Thomas William and Elaine Margaret (Bassett) w.; divorced; children: Thomas William, Christopher John. BSc in Econs., U. Mo., 1967; M in Health Adminstrn., U. Ottawa, Ont., Can., 1978. Asst. to exec. dir. Ottawa Civic Hosp., 1978-80; exec. dir. Caribou Meml. Hosp., Williams Lake, B.C., Can., 1980-83; dir. clinic and rehab. services Workers' Compensation Bd., Vancouver, B.C., 1983-89; dir. Conquistador Gold Mines, Vancouver, 1989—; pres. Diagnostic and Health Cons., Vancouver, 1989—; dir. PHL Pinnacle Holdings, Ltd., Vancouver, B.C., Can., 1994—; ptnr., dir. Lynn Valley Med. Ctr., North Vancouver, B.C., 1993; bd. dirs. Corona Goldfields, Inc., Vancouver, Jackpine Mining Co. Inc., Vancouver, Internat. Topaz Bus. Devel. Corp. Recipient Founder award Cariboo Musical Soc., 1983; named Lord of the Manors of Wharton and Kirkby Stephen (Eng.), 1991. Avocations: music, art.

WHARTON, WILLIAM POLK, consulting psychologist, retired educator; b. Hopkinsville, Ky.; s. William Polk and Rowena Evelyn (Wall) W.; m. Lillian Marie Andersen, Mar. 11, 1944; 1 child, Christine Evelyn Wharton Leonard. BA, Yale U., 1934; MA, Tchrs. Coll., 1949; PhD, Columbia U., 1952. Diplomate Am. Bd. Profl. Psychology; lic. psychologist, Pa. Rsch. advt. promotion, advt. sales Esquire Inc., N.Y.C., 1934-40; dir. counseling, prof. edn., counseling psychologist Allegheny Coll., Meadville, Pa., 1952-74, emeritus dir. and prof. edn., 1974—; prof., dir. The Ednl. Guidance Clinic, Meadville, 1958-74; pvt. practice cons. psychologist Meadville, 1974—; cons. U.S. Army Edn. Ctr., Ft. Meade, Md., 1960-61; rsch. adv. coun. Ednl. Devel. Ctr., Berea, Ohio, 1971-72; cons. to pres. Alliance Coll., Cambridge Springs, Md., 1975-76. Mem. editorial bd. Psychotherapy, 1966-68; reviewer Jour. Coll. Student Personnel, 1984-88; contbr. articles to profl. jours. Chmn. MH/MR Bd. Crawford County Pa., Meadville, 1970-73; com. chmn., Drug and Alcohol Coun. Crawford County Pa., Meadville, 1973-76; ethics com. chmn. North West Pa. Psychol. Assn., 1975-78; del. Pa. Mental Health Assn. Crawford County, 1978-79. Served U.S. Army, 1940-46; lt. col. USAR, 1964. Psychotherapy Research Group vis. fellow, 1961-62; Romiett Stevens scholar, 1951. Fellow Pa. Psychol. Assn.; mem. Am. Psychol. Assn. (Disting. Contbn. award 1985), Am. Assn. for Counseling and Devel., Nat. Vocat. Guidance Assn., Pa. Coll. Personnel Assn. (chmn. 1956-57), Phi Beta Kappa, Phi Delta Kappa, Kappa Beta Pi, Pi Gamma Mu. Home and Office: 415 N Main St Meadville PA 16335-1510 also (summer): General Delivery Forest Dale VT 05745

WHATCOTT, MARSHA RASMUSSEN, elementary education educator; b. Fillmore, Utah, Mar. 29, 1941; d. William Hans and Evangelyn (Robison) Rasmussen; m. Robert LaGrand Whatcott, Sept. 14, 1961; children: Sherry, Cindy, Jay Robert, Justin William. Assoc., So. Utah State U., 1962; BS, Brigham Young U., 1968. Cert. tchr. early childhood, Utah. Tchr. 1st grade

Provost Elem. Sch., Provo, Utah, 1968-84, tchr. kindergarten, 1991—, kindergarten tchr., 1984-91, tchr. 3d grade, 1991—, music specialist, 93-94, art specialist, 1984-85, math. specialist, 1988-89; music specialist Provost Elem., 1984-87, 91-92, 93-94, art specialist, 1984-85, math. specialist, 1988-89, sci. specialist, 1994—; del. Utah Edn. Assn., 1989-90; bldg. rep. Provo Edn. Assn., 1993-94, 94-95. Mem. polit. action com. Provo Sch. Dist., 1982, 90, mem. profl. devel. com. Bonniville Uniserve (Provo, Alpine and Nebo Sch. Dist.), 1994-95. Recipient Millard County Utah PTA scholarship, 1959-62, Golden Apple award Provo City PTA, 1984, Recognition Disting. Svc. in Edn. award Utah State Legis., 1992; named Outstanding Educator in Utah Legis. Dist. # 64, 1992. Mem. Utah Edn. Asn. (del. 1989-90), Provo Edn. Assn. (bldg. rep. 1993-94, 94-95), Bonneville Uniserve (profl. devel. com.). Mem. LDS Ch. Avocations: music, gardening, art, drama, crafts. Office: Provost Elem Sch 629 S 1000 E Provo UT 84606-5204

WHEALEY, LOIS DEIMEL, humanities scholar; b. N.Y.C., June 20, 1932; d. Edgar Bertram Deimel and Lois Elizabeth (Hatch) Washburn; m. Robert Howard Whealey, July 2, 1954; children: Richard William, David John, Alice Ann Whealey Dediu. BA in History, Stanford U., 1951; MA in Edn., U. Mich., 1955; MA in Polit. Sci., Ohio U., 1975. Tchr. 5th grade Swayne Sch., Owyhee, Nev., 1952-53; tchr. 7th grade Ft. Knox (Ky.) Dependent's Sch., 1955-56; tchr. adult basic edn. USAF, Oxford, 1956-57; tchr. 6th grade Amerman Sch., Northville, Mich., 1957-58; tchr. 8th grade English, social studies Slauson Jr. High Sch., Ann Arbor, Mich., 1958-59; adminstrv. asst. humanities conf. Ohio U., Athens, 1974-76, 83; part-time instr. Ohio U., Athens, 1966-68, 75. Contbr. articles to profl. jours. Mem. Athens County Regional Planning Commn., 1974-78, treas., 1976-78; bd. dirs. Ohio Meadville Dist. Unitarian-Universalist Assn., 1975-81, Ohio Women Inc., 1995—; mem. Ohio coord. com. Internat. Women's Yr., 1977; v.p. Black Diamond Girl Scout Coun., 1980-86; chair New Day for Equal Rights Amendment, 1982; mem. Athens City Bd. Edn., 1984-90, v.p., 1984, pres., 1985; mem. Tri-County Vocat. Sch. Bd., Nelsonville, Ohio, 1984-90, v.p., 1988-89; mem. adv. com. Ohio River Valley Water Sanitation Commn., 1986-95; bd. dirs. Ohio Environ. Coun., 1984-90, sec., 1986-90; bd. dirs. Ohio Alliance for Environ., 1993—; coord. Southeast Ohio Collaborative on Women and Children, Ohio Dept. Edn., 1994—. Recipient Unsung UU award Ohio-Meadville Dist. Unitarian Universalist Assn., 1984, Thanks badge Black Diamond Girl Scout Coun., 1986, How to award Ednl. Press Assn. Am., 1990, Donna Chen Women's Equity award Ohio U., 1994; named Woman of Achievement, Black Diamond Girl Scout Coun., 1987. Mem. AAUW (pres. Athens br. 1969-70, 89-90, 93—, nat. pub. policy chair AAUW/Ohio 1995—), LWV (pres. 1975-77), Phi Lambda Theta (life). Democrat. Avocations: classical music, square dancing, choral singing. Home: 14 Oak St Athens OH 45701-2605

WHEAT, FRANCIS MILLSPAUGH, retired lawyer; b. L.A., Feb. 4, 1921; s. Carl Irving and Helen (Millspaugh) W.; m. Nancy Loring Warner, Oct. 14, 1944; children—Douglas Loring, Carl Irving, Gordon Warner. A.B., Pomona Coll., 1942; LL.B. cum laude, Harvard U., 1948. Bar: Calif. 1949. With firm Gibson, Dunn & Crutcher, Los Angeles, 1948-64; partner Gibson, Dunn & Crutcher, 1955-64, 69-89; commr. SEC, 1964-69. Contbr. articles to profl. jours. Trustee S.W. Mus., L.A., 1964, Pomona Coll., 1967—, vice chmn., 1972—, Ralph Parson Found., 1995—; bd. dirs. UN Assn. L.A., 1963-64, Assn. Governing Bds. Univs. and Colls., 1968-70, Ctr. for Law in Pub. Interest, 1974—, Alliance for Children's Rights (pres. 1992-94), Calif. Commn. on Campaign Fin. (co-chmn. 1985—), Sierra Club Legal Def. Fund, 1978—. Lt. USNR, 1942-45. Mem. Am. Law Inst., Los Angeles County Bar Assn. (chmn. com. corps. 1963-64, com. juvenile cts. 1957, trustee 1971-76, pres. 1975-76), Alumni Assn. Pomona Coll. (pres. 1964-65), Nat. Assn. Securities Dealers (bd. govs. 1973-76), Phi Beta Kappa. Democrat. Congregationalist (pres. 1961). Home: 2130 Lombardy Rd San Marino CA 91108-1302 Office: 333 S Grand Ave Fl 46 Los Angeles CA 90071-1504

WHEAT, JOE BEN, anthropologist; b. Van Horn, Tex., Apr. 21, 1916; s. Luther Peers and Elizabeth (Wellborn) W.; m. Frances Irene Moore, Apr. 6, 1947 (dec. Nov. 1987); m. Barbara K. Zernickow, Mar. 18, 1992. B.A., U. Calif.-Berkeley, 1937; M.A., U. Ariz., 1947, Ph.D. (Fund for Advancement Edn. fellow), 1953. Field dir. W.P.A. Archaeol. Project, Tech. Tech. Coll., Lubbock, 1939-41; archaeologist Smithsonian Instrn. River Basin Survey, Houston, 1947; fellow U. Ariz., Tucson, 1947-48; instr. anthropology U. Ariz., 1949-51; ranger, archaeologist Grand Canyon Nat. Park, U.S. Nat. Park Service, 1952-53; co-dir. Nubian Expdn., U. Colo., 1962-67; curator anthropology, prof. natural history Univ. Mus., 1953-87, prof. emeritus, 1987—; cons. to numerous profl. publs.; mem. anthropology rev. bd. NSF, 1978-79. Contbr. numerous articles to profl. jours. Served with USAAF, 1941-45. Recipient Colo. State Archeologists award, 1981, Robert L. Stearns award, 1982, Clarence T. Hurst award, 1990, Byron S. Cummings award, 1991; NSF grantee, 1968, 70-71; Graham Found. grantee, 1976-79; Smithsonian Instn. grantee, 1962-66, 70. Fellow Am. Anthrop. Assn., AAAS; mem. Soc. Am. Archaeology (pres. 1966-67, 50th Anniversary award), Council Mus. Anthropology (pres. 1977-78), Internat. Congress Americanists, Am. Ethnol. Soc. Club: Town and Gown. Home: 1515 Baseline Rd Boulder CO 80302-7650 Office: U Colo Museum Boulder CO 80309

WHEAT, MYRON WILLIAM, JR., cardiothoracic surgeon; b. Sapulpa, Okla., Mar. 24, 1924; s. Myron William and Mary Lee (Hudiburg) W.; m. Erlene Adele Plank, June 12, 1949 (div. June 1970); children: Penelope Louise, Myron William III, Pamela Lynn, Douglas Plank; m. Carol Ann Karmgard, June 18, 1970 (div. Apr. 1996); 1 child, Christopher West. AB, Washington U., St. Louis, 1949; MD cum laude, Washington U., 1951. Diplomate Am. Bd. Surgery, Am. Bd. Thoracic Surgery. Instr., clin. fellow Washington U., St. Louis, 1956-58; asst. prof. surgery U. Fla., Gainesville, 1958-65, prof. surgery, 1965-72; dir. profl. svcs., chief clin. physician U. Fla. Shands Teaching Hosp., Gainesville, 1968-72; prof. surgery, dir. thoracic and cardiothoracic surgery U. Louisville Sch. Medicine, 1972-75; clin. prof. surgery U. Louisville Sch. of Medicine, 1975—; cardiothoracic surgeon Cardiac Surg. Assocs., P.A., St. Petersburg, Fla., 1975-91; cons., thoracic surgery Bay Pine VA Hosp., St. Petersburg, Fla., 1994—; clin. prof. surgery U. So. Fla. Sch. Medicine, Tampa, 1995—; cardiothoracic surgeon Cardiac Surg. Assocs., P.A., Clearwater, Fla., 1978—; clin. prof. surger U. South Fla., 1995—; cons. Bay Pines VA Hosp., St. Petersburg, Fla., 1991—. Author (with others) 14 books; contbr. over 100 articles to profl. jours.; developed drug therapy for acute dissecting aneurysms of the aorta. 1st lt. USAF, 1943-46, ETO. Named First Howard W. Lillenthal Meml. lectr. Mt. Sinai Hosp., 1963. Fellow Am. Coll. Cardiology (chmn. bd. govs. 1968-69), Am. Coll. Surgeons (gov.); mem. Am. Surg. Assn., Am. Assn. for Thoracic Surgery, So. Surg. Assn., So. Thoracic Surg. Assn., Soc. Thoracic Surgeons, Soc. Thoracic Surgeons Great Britain and Ireland, Alpha Omega Alpha. Republican. Avocation: field trials-bird dogs. Home: 1772 Long Bow Ln Clearwater FL 34624-6402

WHEAT, WILLIS JAMES, retired university dean, management educator; b. Oklahoma City, Feb. 28, 1926; s. Willis R. and Aubyn (Roach) W.; m. Julia Francis Maguire, July 4, 1946; children—Willis J., Chatham James. B.S., Okla. State U.-Stillwater, 1949, M.S., 1950; DPA in Pub. Adminstrn., U. Pacific, 1968; LL.D., Tex. Wesleyan Coll., 1962; Dr. Comml. Sci., Oklahoma City U., 1980. Prof. mgmt., dean Sch. Bus., Oklahoma City U., 1954-64; exec. v.p., dir. mktg. Liberty Nat. Bank & Trust Co., Oklahoma City, 1964-87; mem. faculty Stonier Grad Sch. Banking, Rutgers U., New Brunswick, N.J., 1975-87; pres. Oklahoma City U., 1979-80, dean Meinders Sch. Bus., 1987-89, T.K. Hendricks prof. mktg. and mgmt, 1987-96; mem. faculty Essentials of Banking Sch., Norman, Okla., 1980-82, Grad. Sch. Banking of South, Baton Rouge, 1981-83. Contbr. articles to profl. jours. Chmn. Oklahoma City Plan Adv. Com., 1974-81, Okla. Employment Security Commn., Oklahoma City, 1981-89; trustee, mem. exec. com. Oklahoma City U., 1975-87; bd. dirs., chmn. United Bank Okla., 1987-95; bd. dirs. Pace Co., Baldor Electric Co. Served with U.S. Army, World War II. Recipient Disting. Service citation U.S. SBA, 1978; Disting. Service award Oklahoma City U., 1980, Okla. Council on Econ. Edn., 1982. Mem. Am. Bankers Assn., Soc. Advancement of Mgmt. (past pres.), Nat. Council for Small Bus. Mgmt. Devel., Okla. Polit. Sci. Assn., Okla. Council on Econ. Edn., Delta Sigma Pi, Beta Gamma Sigma. Methodist. Lodges: Masons, Shriners, Jesters. Office: PO Box 60804 Oklahoma City OK 73146

WHEATER, ASHLEY, dancer; b. Cutler, Scotland. Student, Royal Ballet Sch. Mem. Royal Ballet, London Festival Ballet, Australian Ballet, Joffrey Ballet; soloist San Francisco Ballet, 1989-90, prin. dancer, 1990—. Performances with the San Francisco Ballet include The Sleeping Beauty, Swan Lake, Romeo and Juliet, Menuetto, Valses Poeticos (Love Letters), Handel-a Celebration, Forevermore, Bugaku, Who Cares?, The Four Temperaments, Duo Concertant, Symphony in C, Company B, In G Major, In the Night, In the middle, somewhat elevated, New Sleep, Maelstrom, Tagore, The End, La Fille mal gardée, La Sylphide, Nutcracker, Forgotten Land, Pulcinella, Connotations, Job, The Son of Horus, The Wanderer Fantasy; with other cos. include La Fille mal gardée, Monotones II, The Dream, Wedding Bouquet, Romeo and Juliet, La Sylphide, Love Songs, Remembrances, Return to the Strange Land, Etudes, Echoing of Trumpets, Sphinx, Greening; performed at Reykjavik Arts Festivals, Iceland, 1990, Jacob's Pillow, 1990. Office: San Francisco Ballet 455 Franklin St San Francisco CA 94102-4438

WHEATLAND, RICHARD, II, fiduciary services executive, museum executive; b. Boston, Nov. 25, 1923; s. Stephen and Dorothy (Parker) W.; m. Cynthia McAdoo, Feb. 13, 1954; 1 child, Sarah Wheatland Fisher. AB, Harvard U., 1944, postgrad., 1946-47; JD, Columbia U., 1949. Various positions with Marshall Plan adminstrn. Office Spl. Rep. in Europe, Dept. State, Paris, 1950-53; v.p. N.Y. Airways, N.Y.C., 1953-68; pres. Acadia Mgmt. Co., Inc., Boston, 1968-93, chmn., 1993—; bd. dirs., v.p. Pingree Assocs., Bangor, Maine. Mem. Mayor's Com. Insl. Leaders for Youth, N.Y.C., 1963-66; mem. corp. New Eng. Forestry Found.; mem., former chmn. Fund for Preservation of Wild Life and Natural Areas, Boston, 1980-92, bd. dirs. 1980-91; trustee Penobscot Marine Mus., Searsport, Maine, 1968-90, hon. trustee, 1990—, ; bd. dirs. Friends of Pub. Garden, Boston, 1972-89, 90—, Beacon Hill Civic Assn., Boston, 1985-89, Boston Natural Areas Fund, 1987—, asst. treas., 1993-94, treas. 1994—; treas. Frank Hatch for Gov. com., Boston, 1977-78; chmn., bd. trustees & overseers Peabody Essex Mus., Salem, Mass., 1992—, trustee, 1972-92, pres., 1983-92. Lt. (j.g.) USN, 1943-46, PTO. Mem. Am. Assn. Mus. (bd. dirs. trustee com. 1976-86, govt. affairs com. 1985—), Mus. Trustee Assn. (founder, bd. dirs. 1986—, sec. 1986-92), City Club Corp. (former bd. mgrs., former treas.). Avocations: jogging, sailing, travel. Office: Acadia Mgmt Co Inc 31 Milk St Boston MA 02109-5104

WHEATLEY, BARNARESE P. (BONNIE WHEATLEY), health services consultant; b. New Iberia, La., Nov. 6, 1942; d. Ervin and Elizabeth (Pierce) Politte; m. Horace Wheatley, Oct. 9, 1967; children: Adrienne K., Alanna M. BS, Calif. State U., Hayward, 1989; MPH, San Jose State U., 1994. Project coord. Summit Med. Ctr., Oakland, Calif., 1989-93; health svc. cons. Alameda County, Oakland, 1993—. Co-author: Wellness Perspective, 1993. Treas. Leadership Am., 1992-93; coord. Nat. Black Leadership No. Calif., 1992—; bd. dirs. Susan B. Komen Found., 1994—, Breast Cancer Action, 1994—, Nat. Breast Cancer Coalition, 1993—; adv. com. Cancer Info. Svc., 1993—; active Calif. Breast Cancer Rsch. Coun., Healthy City Fund Bd. Recipient Community Svc. award Calif. Legislature, 1989, Outstanding Svc. award Nat. Assn. Bench and Bar Spouses, 1992. Mem. Women and Girls Against Tobacco (bd. dirs.). Democrat. Avocation: gardening. Home: 42 La Salle Ave Piedmont CA 94611-3549 Office: Alameda County Med Ctr 1411 E 31st St Oakland CA 94602-1018

WHEATLEY, GEORGE MILHOLLAND, medical administrator; b. Balt., Mar. 21, 1909; s. William Francis and Teresa Genevieve (Milholland) W.; m. Eleanor Dodge, June 28, 1933 (dec. June 1969); children: George Milholland, Jr., Mary Ellen Rausch, Sarah Grinnell Nichols, William Bradford; m. Virginia Connelly Garling, Feb. 21, 1970. BS, Cath. U., 1929; MD, Harvard U., 1933; MPH, Columbia U., 1942. Diplomate Am. Bd. Pediatrics, Am. Bd. Preventive Medicine. Intern Hartford Hosp., Conn., 1933-35; house officer pediatrics Johns Hopkins Hosp., Balt., 1935-36; rsch. fellow N.Y. Post. Grad. Hosp., N.Y.C., 1936-37; prin. pediatrician Health Dept., N.Y.C., 1937-40; asst. med. dir. Met. Life Ins. Co., N.Y.C., 1940-45, asst. v.p., 1945-69, v.p., chief med. dir., 1969-74; med. dir. Dept. Social Svcs., Hauppauge, N.Y., 1974-95; ret., 1995; founder, 1st chmn. com. for joint action with Am. Coll. Surgeons and Assn. Surgery of Trauma Nat. Safety Coun. Author: Health Observation of School Children, 3d edit., 1965; contbr. articles to profl. jours. Bd. dirs. Med. Alert Found. Internat., Calif., 1974-84. Recipient Disting. Svc. award Am. Heart Assn., 1968. Fellow Am. Acad. Pediatrics (pres. 1960-61, trustee Partnership for Child Health 1987—, Clifford Grulee award 1964, Injury and Poison Prevention award 1993); mem. Union League Club, Piping Rock Club. Avocations: civil war history, watercolor painting.

WHEATLEY, MELVIN ERNEST, JR., retired bishop; b. Lewisville, Pa., May 7, 1915; s. Melvin Ernest and Gertrude Elizabeth (Mitchell) W.; m. Lucile Elizabeth Maris, June 15, 1939; children: Paul Melvin, James Maris, John Sherwood. AB magna cum laude, Am. U., 1936, DD, 1958; BD summa cum laude, Drew U., 1939; DD, U. of Pacific, 1948. Ordained to ministry Meth. Ch., 1939. Pastor area Meth. ch., Lincoln, Del., 1939-41; assoc. pastor First Meth. Ch., Fresno, Calif., 1941-43; pastor Centenary Meth. Ch., Modesto, Calif., 1943-46, Cen. Meth. Ch., Stockton, Calif., 1946-54, Westwood Meth. Ch., L.A., 1954-72; bishop Denver Area, 1972-84, ret., 1984; instr. philosophy Modesto Jr. Coll., 1944; summer session instr. Hebrew-Christian heritage U. of Pacific; instr. Homiletics U. So. Calif., So. Calif. Sch. Theology, Clarement; lectr. St. Luke's Lectures, Houston, 1966; mem. Bd. of Ch. and Soc., Commn. on Status and Role of Women, United Meth. Ch., 1976-84; condr. European Christian Heritage tour, 1961, Alaska and Hawaii Missions, 1952, 54. Author: Going His Way, 1957, Our Man and the Church, 1968, The Power of Worship, 1970, Family Ministries Manual, 1970, Christmas Is for Celebrating, 1977; contbr. articles to profl. jours. Chmn. Community Rels. Conf. So. Calif., 1966-69; pres. So. Calif.-Ariz. Conf. Bd. Edn., 1960-68; hon. trustee Iliff Sch. Theology; hon. dir., active mem. Parents and Friends of Lesbians and Gays, 1980—. Recipient Disting. Alumnus award Am. U., 1979, Ball award Meth. Fedn. Social Action, 1984, Prophetic Leadership award The Consultation on Homosexuality, Tolerance and Roman Cath. Theology, 1985, Human Rights award Universal Fellowship of Met. Community Congregations, 1985. Home: 859A Ronda Mendoza Laguna Hills CA 92653-5964

WHEATLEY, WILLIAM ARTHUR, architect, musician; b. Knoxville, Tenn., Sept. 23, 1944; s. Arthur Cornwallis and Inda Mary (Benway) W.; m. Celeste Ann George, Mar. 25, 1970 (div.); children: Charles Arthur, James Harris Giddings; m. Rosaria Giovanna Cilia, June 10, 1995. Student, Rice U., 1962-66; BA, U. St. Thomas, 1972. Registered architect, Pa., Md., N.J. Design draftsman W.W. Alexander, Houston, 1966-70; chief of prodn. W.W. Scarborough, Houston, 1970-74; project architect Ronald H. Waldie & Assocs., Houston, 1972-74; pres. Wheatley & Assocs., Houston, 1974-81; project architect Brooks Assn., Houston, 1977-79; mgr. design Stone Bldg. Systems, Inc., Houston, 1979-81; project architect Bechtel, Houston, 1981-84; prin. Wheatley & Assocs., Houston, 1984-87; project mgr. STV/Sanders & Thomas, Pottstown, Pa., 1987-88, Day & Zimmerman, Inc., Phila., 1988—. Composer: piano solos, chorales, oratorio and cantata, 1961—; co-contbr. articles to profl. jours. Del. Tex. Rep. Convs., 1980, 82, 84. Mem. AIA (Phila. chpt.), Royal Archtl. Inst. of Can., Am. Arbitration Assn., Pa. Soc. Architects, Bldg. Ofcls. and Code Adminstrs. Internat., Forest Products Soc., The Mastersingers (bd. dirs. 1989-92, treas. 1990-91), Choral Soc. Montgomery County (bd. dirs. 1990—, pres. 1992-95). Episcopalian. Avocations: writing poetry and fiction, drawing, painting, sculpture. Also: Day & Zimmerman 280 King Of Prussia Rd Radnor PA 19087-5220

WHEATON, DAVID, professional tennis player; b. Mpls., Minn., June 2, 1969; s. Bruce and Mary Jane W. Student, Stanford U. 9th in U.S. Tennis Assn. rankings, 1992. Office: US Tennis Assn 70 W Red Oak Ln White Plains NY 10604-3602*

WHEATON, DAVID JOE, aerospace manufacturing company executive; b. Las Vegas, N.Mex., June 5, 1940; s. Joseph Charles and Estella Marie (Grubbs) W.; BS, U. Colo., 1962; m. Gail Ellen Moody, July 17, 1942; children: Deanna Lynn, Kimberly Gail, Joseph Charles II. Predesign engr., mktg. mgr. Convair div. Gen. Dynamics, San Diego, 1967-75, F-16 mktg. mgr. Fort Worth div., 1975-77, engrng. program mgr., 1977-79, dir. F-16 domestic mktg., 1979-80, v.p. mktg., 1980-88, corp. v.p. program devel. and planning, 1989-91, v.p. Ax program, 1991-93, New Bus. Devel., 1993—, v.p. joint strike fighter program mgr., 1995. Served with USN, 1962-67. Decorated Air medal (6). Mem. Air Force Assn., Am. Def. Preparedness Assn., Navy Tailhook Assn., Red River Fighter Pilots Assn., Nat. Mgmt. Assn., Sigma Tau, Scabbard and Blade, Tau Beta Phi. Republican. Office: Lockheed Martin Tactical Aircraft Systems PO Box 748 Fort Worth TX 76101-0748

WHEATON, PERRY LEE, management consultant; b. Corning, N.Y., Jan. 31, 1942; s. Raymond Elmer and Beatrice Estella (Rose) W.; A.B., Hamilton Coll., 1963; M.B.A., Rutgers U., 1964; m. Diane Lynn Mathewson, Sept. 18, 1971; children: James Gardner, William Bard, Lynley Mathewson. Mgr., mgmt. cons. services Coopers & Lybrand, Boston, 1964-76; prin., regional mgr. Theodore Barry & Assocs., 1976-81; sr. v.p., Putnam Fin. Services, Inc., 1981-85; dir. Theodore Barry & Assocs., 1985-90; mng. dir. Barrington Wellesley Group, Inc., 1990—. Served with N.G., 1965-71. C.P.A.; cert. mgmt. cons. Mem. AICPA, N.Y. Soc. C.P.A.s, Inst. Mgmt. Cons. Republican. Unitarian. Home: 23 Poor Rd New London NH 03257-4006 Office: Barrington Wellesley Group Inc PO Box 2390 New London NH 03257-2390

WHEDON, GEORGE DONALD, medical administrator, researcher; b. Geneva, N.Y., July 4, 1915; s. George Dunton and Elizabeth (Crockett) W.; m. Margaret Brunssen, May 12, 1942 (div. Sept. 1982); children: Karen Anne, David Marshall. AB, Hobart Coll., 1936, ScD (hon.), 1967; MD, U. Rochester, 1941, ScD (hon.), 1978. Diplomate Am. Bd. Internal Medicine, Am. Bd. Nutrition. Intern in medicine Mary Imogene Bassett Hosp., Cooperstown, N.Y., 1941-42; asst. in medicine U. Rochester Sch. Medicine; also asst. resident physician medicine Strong Meml. Hosp., Rochester, 1942-44; instr. medicine Cornell U. Med. Coll., 1944-50, asst. prof. medicine, 1950-52; chief metabolic diseases br. Nat. Inst. Arthritis, Diabetes, Digestive and Kidney Diseases, NIH, Bethesda, Md., 1952-65, asst. dir., 1956-62, dir., 1962-81, sr. sci. adv., 1981-82; sr. assoc., dir. conf. program Kroc Found., Santa Ynez, Calif., 1982-84; adj. prof. medicine (endocrinology) UCLA Sch. Medicine, 1982-84; dir. med. rsch. programs Shriners Hosps. for Crippled Children, Tampa, 1984-91; mem. subcom. on calcium, com. dietary allowances Food and Nutrition Bd., NRC, 1959-64; cons. to office manned space flight NASA, 1963-78, chmn. Am. Inst. Biol. Scis. med. program adv. panel to, 1971-75, chmn. NASA life scis. com., 1974-78, mem. space program adv. coun., NASA, 1974-78; cons. on endocrinology and metabolism adv. com. Bur. Drugs, FDA, 1977-82; mem. subcommn. on gravitational biology Com. on Space Rsch., Internat. Union Physiol. Scis., 1979-85; mem. rsch. adv. bd. Shriners Hosps., 1981-84; mem. subcom. spacecraft maximum allowable concentrations, com. toxicology, bd. on environ. studies and toxicology Commn. on Life Scis. NRC, 1989—; cons. in medicine Wadsworth Gen. Hosp. VA Ctr., L.A., 1982-84; mem. U.S. Del. of U.S.-Japan Coop. Med. Sci. Program, 1984-93; mem. Internat. Soc. Gravitational Physiol., 1991—. Mem. editorial bd. Jour. Clin. Endocrinology and Metabolism, 1960-67; adv. editor Calcified Tissue Rsch., 1967-76; contbr. articles to profl. publs. Mem. med. alumni coun. Sch. Medicine, mem. trustees' coun. U. Rochester, 1971-76, vice chmn. trustees' coun., 1973-74, chmn., 1974-75; trustee Dermatology Found., 1978-82; bd. dirs. Osteogenesis Imperfecta Found., 1991—, med. adv. coun., 1993—. Recipient Superior Svc. award USPHS, 1967, Alumni citation U. Rochester, 1971, Alumni citation Hobart Coll., 1986, Exceptional Sci. Achievement medal NASA, 1974. Fellow Royal Soc. Medicine; mem. AAAS, Am. Fedn. Clin. Rsch. Assn., Am. Physicians, Aerospace Med. Assn. (Arnold D. Tuttle Meml. award 1978), Internat. Bone and Mineral Soc., Internat. Soc. Gravitational Physiology, Md. Acad. Scis. (sci. coun. 1964-70, 81-82), Endocrine Soc. (Robert H. Williams Disting. Leadership award in endocrinology 1982, Ayerst award 1974), Am. Physiol. Soc., Am. Inst. Nutrition, Am. Acad. Orthopaedic Surgeons (hon.), Am. Bone and Mineral Rsch., Orthopaedic Rsch. Soc., Am. Soc. Gravitational/Space Biology (Founders award 1994), Theta Delta Chi. Episcopalian. Home: 880 Mandalay Ave Apt 1002S Clearwater FL 34630

WHEDON, MARGARET BRUNSSEN, television and radio producer; b. N.Y.C.; d. Henry and Anna Margaret (Nickel) Brunssen; m. G. Donald Whedon, 1942 (div. Sept. 1982); children: Karen Whedon Green, David Marshall. BA, U. Rochester, 1948; postgrad., CUNY-Hunter Coll., 1950. With ABC-TV and Radio News; asst. prodr. Coll. News Conf., 1952-60; prodr. This Week with David Brinkley, 1981-84. Prodr.: Issues and Answers, 1960-81, From the Capitol, ABC Radio, 1962-69; nres prodr. Pub. Affairs Satellite Sys., Inc., 1983—, Pubs at Pub. Affairs Satellite, Washington, 1986—; mem. Capitol Speakers, lectr., pub. speaker; commentator Flair Reports, 1962-64; music critic The Hill Rag; author: Always on Sunday, 1980, Dining in the Great Embassies, 1987. Recipient NCCJ award, 1968; nominee NATAS award, 1968. Mem. White House Corrs. Assn., Nat. Press Club, Am. Newspaper Women's Club (pres. 1983), Am. Women in Radio and TV, Radio-TV Corrs. Assn. Home: 4201 Cathedral Ave NW Apt 702E Washington DC 20016-4955 *Getting to know the leaders of the world, interviewing them in their capitols, and presenting their views to national and international TV and radio audiences were the fulfillment of my dreams since childhood. Next to my family, it has been the most important achievement of my life.*

WHEDON, RALPH GIBBS, manufacturing executive; b. Elizabeth, N.J., Aug. 10, 1949; s. Ralph Gibbs and Jane (MacMaster) W.; m. Lorna Jean Neebe, June 3, 1972; children: Deborah, David. Student, Clarkson Coll., 1968-70; BS, St. Lawrence U., 1972; student, Rensselaer Polytech. Inst., 1978; MBA, De Paul U., 1985. CPA, Ohio. Credit rep. Internat. Harvester Credit Corp., Albany, N.Y., 1972-75, ops. supr., 1975-79; mgr. export ops. Internat. Harvester Co., Chgo., 1979-86; treas. Pettibone Corp., Des Plaines, Ill., 1986-91; mgr. cash resources Bailey Controls Co., Wickliffe, Ohio, 1991—, acting dir. treas., 1992—, mgr. adminstrn., 1993—; dir. MIS HMI Industries, 1995—; sec. Tube Form, 1995—; v.p. fin., sec. Bliss Mgg., 1995—; sec. Newton Falls Holding Co., 1995—. Bd. dirs. Naperville (Ill.) Cmty. Chorus, 1985-87; trop leader Boy scouts Am., Naperville, 1985—; mem. adv. coun. United Way, 1993—; mem. adv. coun. Cleve. Treas. Club, 1992—, bd. dirs., 1994—; v.p. Brightwood Lakes Assn., 1996—; treas. S.J.E.C. Found., 1996—. Episcopalian. Avocations: sailing, flying. Home: 7066 Brightwood Dr Concord OH 44077-2167 also: Branchview Dr N Ellsworth ME 04605

WHEELAN, R(ICHELIEU) E(DWARD), lawyer; b. N.Y.C., July 10, 1945; s. Richard Fairfax and Margaret (Murray) W. BS, Springfield (Mass.) Coll., 1967; MS, Iona Coll., 1977; JD, Pace U., 1981. Bar: N.Y. 1982, Minn. 1983, Colo. 1989, Tex. 1990, U.S. Dist. Ct. (no dist.) Calif. 1982, (so. dist.) Tex. 1991, U.S. Internat. Trade 1982, U.S. Ct. Appeals (2d cir.) 1982, (9th cir.) 1983, (5th cir.) 1993, U.S. Supreme Ct. 1994; bd. cert. criminal law. Lt. of detectives White Plains (N.Y.) Police Dept., 1969-81; area counsel IBM, Armonk, N.Y., 1981-89; gen. counsel Kroll Assocs. (Asia), Hong Kong, 1989-91; pvt. practice, Houston, 1991—. Mem. ABA (mem. sentencing guidelines com.), Nat. Assn. Criminal Def. Lawyers (life mem., mem. death penalty com.), Houston Bar Assn., Coll. of State Bar Tex., Pro Bono Coll. State Bar Tex., Tex. Assn. Criminal Def. Lawyers, Harris County Criminal Def. Lawyers Assn. (treas. 1993). Office: 602 Sawyer St Ste 480 Houston TX 77007-7510

WHEELAND, D. A., church administrator. V.p. gen. svcs. The Christian and Missionary Alliance, Colorado Springs. Office: The Christian & Missionary Alliance PO Box 35000 Colorado Springs CO 80935-3500

WHEELER, ALBIN GRAY, U.S. Army career officer, educator, retail executive, law firm executive; b. Huntington, W.Va., Mar. 16, 1935; s. Harvey Gray and Hattie Benson (Weddle) W.; m. Beatrice Thomas, May 17, 1958; children: Dianne, Michelle, Patrice. BA, Marshall U., 1958; MBA, Pepperdine U., 1975; postgrad., Army War Coll., Carlisle Barracks, Pa., 1976, Harvard U., 1990. Enlisted U.S. Army, 1952, commd. 2nd lt., 1959, advanced through grades to maj. gen., 1985; comdr. divsn. spt. command, chief of staff 1st Inf. Divsn., Ft. Riley, Kans., 1978-80; dep. comdr. U.S. Army Logistics Ctr., Ft. Lee, Va., 1980-81; chief exec. officer Army AF Exch. Svc.-Europe, Munich, 1981-83; comdr. 2d Spt. Command, VII U.S. Corps, Germany, 1983-85; pres. Indsl. Coll. Armed Forces, Washington, 1985-89; dir. human resources Army Materiel Command, Washington, 1989-91; CEO Army and Air Force Exch. Svc., Dallas, 1991-93; ret. U.S. Army, 1993; exec. dir. Arent Fox Kitner Plotkin & Kahn, Washington, 1993-96. Mem. Yeager

Scholars Bd., Marshall U., 1986—. Decorated Def. and Army D.S.M., Bronze Star with two oak leaf clusters. Mem. Marshall U. Alumni Assn.

WHEELER, BEVERLY (BARNES), cardiology nurse specialist; b. St. Stephens, N.B., Can., Nov. 9, 1946; parents Am. citizens; d. Robert George and Elizabeth B. (Rideout) Barnes; divorced; children: Jeffrey, Tami. AA, Mohegan C.C., Norwich, Conn., 1981; BSN and cert. in gerontology, George Mason U., 1989, MSN, 1991. RN, Va.; cert. clin. nurse specialist; cert. ACLS. Various civilian adminstrv. positions U.S. Navy, Groton, Conn., Arlington, Va., 1974-87; vis. nurse Comprehensive Health Agy., Springfield, Va., 1984-86; nursing agy. pers. SRT Med.-Staff Internat., Springfield, 1982-88; legal asst. Office of Asst. Sec. of Navy for Rsch., Engring. and Sys., Washington, 1987-89; staff nurse Arlington Hosp., 1986-90, Fairfax Hosp., Falls Church, Va., 1991—; cardiology nurse specialist Nat. Naval Med. Ctr., Bethesda, Md., 1989—; textbook cons., 1994, 96. Contbr. articles to profl. nursing jours. Vol. Am. Heart Assn., 1994-96. Mem. ANA, NAFE, Va. Nurses Assn. Episcopalian. Avocations: aerobics, reading, gardening, crocheting. Home: 10302 Annaberg Ct Burke VA 22015-2833 Office: Nat Naval Med Ctr 8901 Wisconsin Ave Bethesda MD 20889

WHEELER, BURTON M., literature educator, higher education consultant, college dean; b. Mullins, S.C., Mar. 12, 1927; s. Paul and Elizabeth (Cleveland) W.; m. Jacquelyn Mulkey, Aug. 20, 1950; children—Paul, Geoffrey, Kristin. A.B., U. S.C., 1948, M.A., 1951; Ph.D., Harvard U., 1961. Teaching fellow Harvard U., Cambridge, Mass., 1953-56; mem. faculty Washington U., St. Louis, 1956—, prof., 1974-96; prof. emeritus, 1996—; dean Coll. Arts and Scis. Washington U., St. Louis, 1966-78, interim dean univ. librs., 1988-89; cons., panelist Danforth Found., St. Louis, 1958-82; mem. GPEP panel Assn. Am. Med. Colls., Washington, 1981-84; cons.-evaluator North Cen. Assn., Chgo. Contbr. articles to profl. jours. Eli Lilly Found. fellow, 1965-66. Mem. Soc. Values in Higher Edn., Kent Fellow, Phi Beta Kappa (senator, chmn. qualifications com.). Office: Washington U English Dept Saint Louis MO 63130

WHEELER, C. HERBERT, architect, consultant, educator; b. Merchantville, N.J., June 6, 1915; s. Clarence Herbert and Louise Emma (Pennell) W.; m. Cicely Pointer, Aug. 29, 1940; children—Pamela, Janet, Betsy. B.Arch., U. Pa., 1937; M.Arch., MIT, 1940, postgrad. in acoustics and creative engring., 1953, 56; postgrad. bus. program, Alexander Hamilton Inst., 1947. Registered architect N.Y., N.J., Pa., Mich.; cert. Nat. Council Archtl. Registration Bds. Archtl. designer Austin Co., N.Y.C., 1938-41; architect, then chief architect J.G. White Engring. Co., N.Y.C., 1941-55; mgr. engring. Stran Steel Corp., Detroit, 1955-58; mgr. environ. systems Curtiss-Wright Corp., Quehanna, Pa., 1958-64; prof. archtl. engring. Pa. State U., University Park, 1964-80, prof. emeritus, 1980—. author: Public Organizations and Public Architecture, 1987; co-author: Emerging Techniques of Architectural Practice, 1966, Emerging Techniques of Architectural Programming, 1969. Served to maj. C.E., U.S. Army, 1942-46. Decorated Commendation Ribbon U.S. Army CE, 1945. Fellow AIA (emeritus, internat. relations com. 1981-84, v.p. Central Pa. chtp. 1984), Union Internat. des Architects Paris (permanent sec. profl. devel. work group 1980-85, coll. dels. 1981-85), mem. Am. Soc. Engring. Edn. (emeritus, chmn. archtl. engring. div. 1970), constrn. Specifications Inst., Ret. Officers Assn., Theta Xi (v.p. St. Louis 1953-54). Republican. Episcopalian/Methodist. Avocations: travel; precanceled stamp collecting; geography; literature. Home: 638 Franklin St State College PA 16803-3459 Office: Pa State U 104 Engring A Unit University Park PA 16802

WHEELER, CLARENCE JOSEPH, JR., physician; b. Dallas, Sept. 25, 1917; s. Clarence Joseph Sr. and Sadie Alice (McKinney) W.; m. Alice Mary Freels, Dec. 6, 1942; deceased; m. Patsy Lester Butler, Sept. 2, 1995; children: Stephen Freels, C.J. III, Robert McKinney, Thomas Michael, David Ritchey. BS in Math., So. Meth. U., 1941, BA in Psychology, 1946; MD, John Hopkins U., 1950. Diplomate Am. Bd. Surgery; cert. provider ACLS and advanced trauma life support, Am. Heart Assn. Intern John Hopkins Hosp., Balti., 1950-51; resident in surgery Barnes Hosp., St. Louis, 1951-54; fellow thoracic surgery U. Wis. Hosp., Madison, 1954-56, instr. surgery, 1955-56; attending surgeon Welborne Clinic Baptist Hosp., Evansville, Ind., 1956-57; mem. consulting staff Tex. Children's Hosp., 1957-70; courtesy and consulting staffs Pasadena Hosp., Spring Br. Hosp., others, Houston, 1957-70; mem. active staff Hermann Hosp., Houston, 1957-70, St. Luke's Hosp., Houston, 1957-70, Meth. Hosp., Houston, 1957-70, St. Joseph's Hosp., Houston, 1957-70, Meml. Hosp., Houston, 1957-70, Ben Taub Gen. City/County Hosp., Houston, 1957-70, Diagnostic Hosp., &, 1957-70; attending surgeon Lindley Hosp., Duncan, Okla., 1970-71; sr. attending, chief surgery Gordon Hosp., Lewisburg, Tenn., 1971-73; chief thoracic surgery Lewisburg Community Hosp., 1973-75; mem. active med. staff, med. dir. Carver Family Health Clinic, 1975-82; dir. emergency dept. Meth. Med. Ctr. Ill., Peoria, 1975-82; mem. staff Contract Emergency Med. Care, Houston and Dallas, 1982-88; med. dir. substance abuse unit Terrell (Tex.) State Hosp., 1988-90; med. dir. Schick-Shadel Hosp., Dallas-Ft. Worth, 1991—; med. dir., chief of staff Schick-Shadel Hosp., Ft. Worth, 1991-93; med. dir. Skillman Med. Ctr., Dallas, 1993-95, Centers for Preventative Medicine, Dallas, 1995—; instr. surgery U. Wis. Med. Sch., 1955-56; clin. instr. Baylor Coll. Medicine, Houston, 1959-70; lectr. U. Tex. Postgrad. Sch., Houston, 1957-70; clin. asst. prof. U. Ill. Sch. Medicine, Peoria, 1977-82; sr. med. advisor Thue Tien Province, So. Vietnam, 1968-69; chief of surgery Bien Vien Hué So. Vietnam, 1968-69. Treas. Samuel Clark Red Sch. PTA, Houston, 1959-61; bd. dirs. Salvation Army Boys Club, Houston; mem. Am. Mus. of Nat. History, Met. Mus. Art, Smithsonian Inst., Dallas Symphony Assn., Dallas Opera Soc., Dallas Theatre Ctr., Theatre Three Assn. Capt. USMCR, 1942-45, PTO. Decorated DFC with three stars, Air medal with four stars, Pacific Combat Theatre Ribbon with three stars, Purple Heart, Vietnamese Medal of Health (1st class), Vietnamese Medal Social Welfare, Navy Commendation medal, Presdl. Unit citation medal, Meritorious Bronze Star. Fellow ACS, Am. Coll. Angiology, Am. Coll. Chest Physicians, Royal Soc. Medicine, Internat. Coll. Surgeons, Am. Coll. Gastroenterology, Southea. Surg. Congress, Southwestern Surg. Congress, Internat. Assn. Proctologists; mem. AAAS, AMA, Am. Thoracic Soc., Nat. Tb Assn., Am. Assn. History of Medicine, Am. Soc. Contemporary Medicine and Surgery, Am. Soc. Addiction Medicine (cert.), Am. Heart Assn., Am. Cancer Soc., Am. Soc. Abdominal Surgeons, Marine Corps Officer's Assn., Naval Res. Officer's Assn., Nat. Geog. Soc., Mil. Order of the World Wars, Navy League, Indsl. Med. Assn., So. Med. Assn., Tex. Med. Assn., Tex. Thoracic Soc., Tex. Heart Assn., Tex. Anti-Tb Assn., Postgrad. Med. Assembly So. Tex., St. Louis Med. Soc., Dallas County Med. Soc., Marshall County Med. Soc. (pres.), Harris County Med. Soc., Houston Heart Assn., Houston Gastroent. Soc., Houston Surg. Soc., Greater Dallas Res. Officers Assn., Sierra Club, Rotary, Kappa Sigma, Phi Eta Sigma, Kappa Mu Epsilon, Psi Chi. Episcopalian. Address: 7111 Chipperton Dr Dallas TX 75225-1708 Address: 7111 Chipperton Dr Dallas TX 75225-1708

WHEELER, CLAYTON EUGENE, JR., dermatologist, educator; b. Viroqua, Wis., June 30, 1917; s. Clayton Eugene and Vista Beulah (Heal) W.; m. Susie Brooks Overton, Oct. 11, 1952; children: Susan Brooks, Margaret Ann, Elizabeth Clayton. B.A., U. Wis., 1938, M.D., 1941. Diplomate Am. Bd. Internal Medicine, Am. Bd. Dermatology (vice pres. 1977-78, pres. 1978-79). Intern Cin. Gen. Hosp., 1941-42; resident in internal medicine U. Mich. Hosps., 1942-44, research fellow endocrinology and metabolism, 1947-48, resident in dermatology, 1948-51; from asst. prof. to prof. dermatology U. Va. Med. Sch., 1951-62; prof. dermatology U. N.C. Med. Sch., Chapel Hill, 1962—, chmn. div., 1962-72, chmn. dept., 1972-87, chmn., exec. com. Med. Faculty Practice Plan, 1986-90; Clayton E. Wheeler Jr. prof. dermatology Sch. Medicine, U. N.C., 1991. Author: Practical Dermatology, 3d edit, 1967, also articles. Served to maj. M.C. AUS, 1944-47. Mem. Soc. Investigative Dermatology (pres. 1974-75, Rothman award 1979, hon. mem. 1993), Assn. Profs. Dermatology (pres. 1975-76), Am. Dermatol. Assn. (pres. 1982-83), Am. Acad. Dermatology (past dir., pres.-elect 1983-84, pres. 1984-85, past pres. 1985-86, hon. mem. 1988, masters in dermatology 1993, Gold medal 1993), Phi Beta Kappa, Alpha Omega Alpha. Methodist. Home: 2120 N Lakeshore Dr Chapel Hill NC 27514-2027 Office: NC Meml Hosp Manning Dr Chapel Hill NC 27514

WHEELER, DANIEL SCOTT, publishing executive, editor; b. Richmond, Va., Apr. 23, 1947; s. Arthur Bruce Jr. and Lavinia (Akers) W.; m. Kathy E. Wheeler; children: Matthew, Beth Marie, Jennifer Lynne, Brandy, Jennifer Ann. Student, Va. Commonwealth U., 1966-69, Butler U., 1981, Ind. U., 1984-85. Spl. agt. Northwestern Mut. Life, Richmond, 1969-71; enlisted USN, 1971, resigned, 1979; editor Am. Legion Mag., Indpls., 1979-85, pub., editor-in-chief, 1985-95; exec. dir. The Am. Legion, 1995—; bd. dirs. HPC/PM Direct. pres. Citizens Flag Alliance, Inc. Mem. Am. Legion, Mensa. Republican. Avocation: oil painting. Home: 4518 Fairhope Dr Indianapolis IN 46237-2951 Office: The American Legion Mag PO Box 1055 Indianapolis IN 46206-1055

WHEELER, DAVID LAURIE, university dean; b. Saginaw, Mich., July 30, 1934; s. Clayton Final and Blanche Beatrice (Hunt) W.; m. Jane Louise Manchester, Sept. 6, 1958; children: Elizabeth, Anne. AB, U. Mich., 1956, AM, 1958, Ph.D., 1962. Asst. dean student service Ill. State U., Normal, 1967-68, assoc. dean, 1968-69, assoc. dean grad. sch., 1969-72; dean grad. sch. West Tex. State U., Canyon, 1972-79, Ball State U., Muncie, Ind., 1979—; cons. McGraw-Hill Pub. Co., N.Y.C., Van Nostrand Reinhold Pub. Co., N.Y.C. Editor: The Human Habitat: Contemporary Readings, 1971. Woodrow Wilson fellow, 1961. Mem. Assn. Am. Geographers, Nat. Coun. Univ. Rsch. Adminstrs., Western History Assn., Tex. State Hist. Assn., Sigma Xi, Phi Kappa Phi. Republican. Presbyterian. Home: 4205 W Riverside Ave Muncie IN 47304-3653 Office: Grad Sch Ball State U Muncie IN 47306

WHEELER, DOUGLAS PAUL, conservationist, government official, lawyer; b. Bklyn., Jan. 10, 1942; s. Robert S. and Lottie (Neubauer) W.; m. Heather A. Campbell, Aug. 28, 1965; children—Clay Campbell, Christopher Campbell. AB in Govt. with honors, Hamilton Coll., Clinton, N.Y., 1963; LLB, Duke U., 1966. Bar: N.C. 1966. Assoc. Levine, Goodman & Murchison, Charlotte, N.C., 1966-69; legis. atty. to asst. legis. counsel U.S. Dept. Interior, Washington, 1969-72, dep. asst. sec. Fish and Wildlife and Pks., 1972-77; exec. v.p. Nat. Trust for Hist. Preservation, Washington, 1977-80; pres. Am. Farmland Trust, Washington, 1980-85, now life mem.; exec. dir. Sierra Club, San Francisco, 1985-86; v.p. Land Heritage and Wildlife Conservation Found., Washington, 1986-88, exec. v.p., 1989-91; sec. for resources State of Calif., 1991—. Bd. visitors Duke U. Sch. of Law; bd. dirs. Calif. Nature Conservancy, Calif. Environ. Forum; mem. nat. coun. World Wildlife Fund, Am. Farmland Trust; candidate N.C. Ho. of Reps., 1968; mem. D.C. Rep. Ctrl. Com., 1984-85. Lt. JAGC, USNR, 1969-75. Recipient commendation U.S. Dept. Interior, 1976, Achievement award, 1980, Conservation award Gulf Oil Corp., 1985, Charles S. Murphy award for pub. svc, 1995, Presdl. award for sustainable devel., 1996. Mem. N.C. Bar Assn., Sierra Club (life). Episcopalian. Home: PO Box 3164 El Macero CA 95618-0764

WHEELER, ED RAY, mathematics educator; b. Bowling Green, Ky., June 13, 1947; m. Claire Mosteller; children: Aaron, Jodi. BA, Samford U., 1969; PhD, U. Va., 1973. Instr. Lynchburg (Va.) Coll., 1969-70; teaching asst. U. Va., Charlottesville, 1970-73; asst. prof. No. Ky. U., Highland Heights, 1973-77, assoc. prof., 1977-80; dept. head Meredith Coll., Raleigh, N.C., 1980-87, Armstrong State Coll., Savannah, Ga., 1987—. Author: (with others) Mathematics: An Every Day Language, 1979, Modern Mathematics, 1995, Activity Manual for Elementary School Teachers, 1995; contbr. articles to profl. jours. Woodrow Wilson Found. fellow, 1969. Mem. Maths. Assn. Am., Am. Math. Soc., Am. Sci. Affiliation. Baptist. Avocations: tennis, jogging, reading. Office: Armstrong State Coll 11935 Abercorn St Savannah GA 31419-1909

WHEELER, EDWARD KENDALL, lawyer; b. Butte, Mont., Oct. 23, 1913; s. Burton K. and Lulu M. (White) W.; children: Frederica Wheeler Smith, Kendall W. van Orman. AB, George Washington U., 1935; LLB, Harvard U., 1938; LLD (hon.), Mont. State U., 1994. Bar: D.C. 1939. Since practiced in Washington; ptnr. Wheeler & Wheeler, 1947—; bd. dirs. Wilmer Inst., Greater Mont. Found., Wheeler Ctr., Charlotte & Edward Wheeler Found.; pres., CEO Advantage Paging. Served as lt. USNR, 1943-46. Clubs: Chevy Chase; Met. (Washington), Burning Tree (Washington). Home: 6005 Highland Dr Chevy Chase MD 20815-6611 Office: Ste 400 808 17th St NW Washington DC 20006-3910

WHEELER, GEORGE CHARLES, materials and processes engineer; b. Balt., Oct. 9, 1923; s. George Charles and Julia Elizabeth (Watrous) W.; m. Dorothy W. Whittemore, Sept. 13, 1947; children: Scott, Craig, Mark, Matthew, Tracy, Bruce; m. Clare Frances Weiner, Jan. 21, 1978. BS in Metall. Engring., Lehigh U., 1944. Various engring. and supervisory positions GE, Mass. and N.Y., 1944-62; mgr. materials, welding and nondestructive test engring. Knolls Atomic Power Lab., G.E., Schenectady, N.Y., 1962-68; mgr. nondestructive testing G.E. Power Sys., Schenectady, N.Y., 1968-85; pres., chief exec. officer Wheeler Nondestructive Testing, Inc., Schenectady, 1985—; mgr. tech. svcs. Am. Soc. for Nondestructive Testing, Columbus, Ohio, 1993-94; cons. UN, N.Y.C., 1985—, Internat. Atomic Energy Agy., Vienna, Austria, 1985—, numerous others; guest lectr. Rensselaer Poly. Inst., Troy, N.Y., Union Coll., Schenectady, 1978-87; mem. math. sci. and tech. com. Schenectady County Community Coll., 1978-85, adj. prof., 1987—; U.S. del. Internat. Stds. Orgn., com. TC 135/SC7 NDT Pers. Qualification, 1987—, convenor working group #2, ISO-9712. Author: Guide to Developing Certification Exams, 1992; Guide to Personnel Cert., 1990; contbg. editor Jour. of ASNT; tech. editor Nondestructive Testing Handbook, 3d edit., vol. 3. Fellow Am. Soc. Nondestructive Testing (hon. life mem., bd. dirs. 1976-85, pres. 1983-84, chmn. cert. com. 1976-80, 86-89); mem. ASTM (com. internat. stds., com. nondestructive testing), NRA (life), Am. Soc. Metals, Nature Conservancy (life), Aircraft Owners and Pilots Assn. Avocations: mountaineering, flying, firearms, photography.

WHEELER, GEORGE WILLIAM, university provost, physicist, educator; b. Dedham, Mass., Dec. 23, 1924; s. John Brooks, Jr. and Alice (Chamberlin) W.; m. Margaret C. Pirie, Oct. 27, 1957; children: William Cameron, Alice Chamberlin. BS in Physics, Union Coll., Schenectady, 1949; PhD, Yale U., 1953. Research assoc. Woods Hole (Mass.) Oceanographic Inst., 1953-54; asst. prof. physics, sr. research asso. Yale U., 1954-64; physicist, div. head accelerator dept. Brookhaven Nat. Lab., Upton, N.Y., 1964-72; br. chief high energy physics program, div. phys. research AEC, Washington, 1972-74; dean natural and social sci., prof. physics Herbert H. Lehman Coll., CUNY, Bronx, 1974-79; prof. physics Temple U., Phila., 1979-83; dean Coll. Arts and Scis. Temple U., 1979-83; provost, prof. physics U. Tenn., Knoxville, 1984-90, ret., 1990; Trustee Southeastern Univs. Research Assn., 1984-92, chmn. 1985-89; dir. Oak Ridge Associated Univs., 1985-91; cons. in field; mem. bd. overseers Super Conducting Super Collider, 1988-91. Author papers on physics, particle accelerators. Mem. Branford (Conn.) Bd. Edn., 1961-64; trustee Village of Belle Terre, N.Y., 1967-69, bd. dirs. Southeastern Libraries Network, 1992-95; trustee Webb Sch. of Knoxville, 1985-94. Decorated Bronze Star. Mem. IEEE (sr.), AAAS, Am. Phys. Soc., Phi Beta Kappa, Sigma Xi. Home: 4909 Scenic Point Channel Louisville TN 37777-3221

WHEELER, HAROLD ALDEN, retired radio engineer; b. St. Paul, May 10, 1903; s. William Archie Wheeler and Harriet Maria Alden; m. Ruth Gregory, Aug. 25, 1926 (dec. Feb. 1986); children: Dorothy, Caroline, Alden Gregory. BS in Physics, George Washington U., 1925, DSc (hon.), 1972; DEngring. (hon.), Stevens Inst. Tech., 1978, Polytechnic U., 1992. Engr. Hazeltine Service Corp., N.Y.C. and Bayside, N.Y., 1929-39; v.p., chief cons. engr. Hazeltine Service Corp., Little Neck, N.Y., 1940-45; cons. radio physicist Great Neck, N.Y., 1946-59; pres. Wheeler Labs Inc., Great Neck, 1947-68; dir. Hazeltine Corp., Little Neck, 1959-70, v.p., 1959-65, chmn., 1965-70; dir. Hazeltine Corp., Greenlawn, N.Y., 1971-83, chmn., 1971-77, chmn. emeritus, 1977-87, chief scientist, 1971-87; cons. Office of Sec. of Def., Washington, 1950-53; mem. Def. Sci. Bd., Washington, 1961-64. About 180 patents in field, including diode automatic volume control, 1932; author: Wheeler Monographs, Vol. 1, 1953, Hazeltine the Professor, 1978, Early Days of Wheeler and Hazeltine Corporation, 1982, Hazeltine Corporation in World War II, 1993; numerous papers in, procs. and transactions of IRE and IEEE. Recipient Modern Pioneer award Nat. Assn. Mfrs., 1940. Fellow IEEE (medal of honor 1964), IRE (Morris Liebmann prize 1940), Radio Club Am. (Armstrong medal 1964); mem. Nat. Acad. Engring., Inst. Elec. Engrs. (U.K.), Sigma Xi, Tau Beta Pi, Gamma Alpha. Republican. Unitarian. Home: 4900 Telegraph Rd Apt 523 Ventura CA 93003-4125

WHEELER, HEWITT BROWNELL, surgeon, educator; b. Louisville, July 21, 1929; s. Arville and Lois (Vance) W.; m. Elizabeth Jane Maxwell, July 21, 1956; children: Stephen, Elizabeth, Jane, Mary. Student, Vanderbilt U., 1945-48; M.D., Harvard U., 1952. Diplomate Am. Bd. Surgery (bd. dirs. 1984-90). Cushing fellow Harvard Med. Sch., Boston, 1953, Peters fellow, 1956, research fellow, 1959-60, instr. surgery, 1961-64, clin. assoc. surgery, 1964-67, asst. clin. prof. surgery, 1967-70, assoc. prof. surgery, 1970-71; asst. in surgery Peter Bent Brigham Hosp., Boston, 1959-60, jr. assoc. surgery, 1961-64, assoc. surgery, 1964-69, sr. assoc. surgery, 1969-71; asst. chief surgery Roxbury VA Hosp., Boston, 1961-62, chief surgery, 1962-71, chief of staff, 1968-71; cons. surgery U. Mass. Med. Sch. at Worcester, 1966-71, prof., chmn. dept. surgery, 1971—, Harry M. Haidak disting. prof. surgery, 1985—; chief staff U. Mass. Hosp., 1974-76, surgeon-in-chief, 1976—; affiliate prof. biomed. engring. Worcester Poly. Inst., 1974—; lectr. surgery Harvard Med. Sch., 1974—; chief surgery St. Vincent Hosp., Worcester, 1971-75; cons. Meml. Hosp., Worcester City Hosp., 1970—, Worcester Hagnemann Hosp., 1974-94, Peter Bent Brigham Hosp., 1973—; chmn. surg. research program com. VA, Washington, 1965-67, nat. participant surg. cons., 1965-69, chmn. ad hoc adv. com. surgery, 1969-71. Trustee Cen. Mass. Health Care Found., 1975-77. Served to 1st lt., M.C. AUS, 1953-55. Mem. ACS (bd. govs. 1984-90, coun. Mass. chpt. 1973-76, pres. 1980), AAAS, AMA, Am. Surg. Assn., Soc. Univ. Surgeons, Internat. Cardiovascular Soc., Soc. Surg. Chairmen, New Eng. Surg. Soc. (treas. 1977-84, v.p. 1986-87, pres. 1989-91), Boston Surg. Soc. (pres. 1995), Worcester Surg. Soc. (pres. 1973-75), Transportation Soc., Mass. Med. Soc. (100th Shattuck lectr. 1990), Worcester Dist. Med. Soc., New Eng. Vascular Spc. (v.p. 1985-86, pres. 1988-89), Internat. Chirurg. Soc. Research exptl. transplantation, blood vessel surgery, method to detect blood clots. Home: 10 Old English Rd Worcester MA 01609-1306*

WHEELER, JACK COX, army officer; b. Canton, Ga., Feb. 2, 1939; s. Clinton Alfred and Juanita I. (Cox) W.; m. Marjorie Gunn, May 5, 1962; children: Leigh Ann, Clinton Alan. BA in History, North Ga. Coll., 1961; MA in Pub. Adminstrn., Shippensburg State U., 1979; postgrad., Harvard U., 1988. Commd. 2d lt. U.S. Army, 1961, advanced through grades to maj. gen., 1989; chief, officer mgmt. br. Mil. Assistance Command Vietnam, Tan Son Nat, 1969-70; pers. staff officer Dep. Chief of Staff for Pers., Washington, 1971-75; asst. to dir. army staff Office U.S. Army Chief of Staff, Washington, 1975-76; adj. gen. 1st Armored Div., Ansbach, Fed. Republic Germany, 1976-78; student Army War Coll., Carlisle Barracks, Pa., 1979; chief structure br. Dep. Chief of Staff for Pers., Washington, 1979-80, chief enlisted div., 1980-82, chief profl. devel., 1982-84; comdr. 8th Pers. Command-Korea, Youngsan, Seoul, 1984-86; dir. Enlisted Pers. Mgmt., Alexandria, Va., 1986-88; dep. comdg. gen. U.S. Army Recruiting Command, Ft. Sheridan, Ill., 1988-89, comdg. gen., 1989-93; sales dir. Citizen Newspapers, Fayetteville, Ga., 1995—. Decorated D.S.M., Legion of Merit, Bronze Star. Mem. Assn. U.S. Army. Methodist.

WHEELER, JACK R., medical educator. Office: 1111 S Main St Kokomo IN 46902-1607

WHEELER, JOCK R., dean. Dean Ea. Va. Med. Sch. Med. Coll. Hampton Rds. Office: Ea Va Med Sch Med Coll Norfolk Va PO Box 1980 Norfolk VA 23501

WHEELER, JOHN ARCHIBALD, physicist, educator; b. Jacksonville, Fla., July 9, 1911; s. Joseph Lewis and Mabel (Archibald) W.; m. Janette Hegner, June 10, 1935; children: Isabel Letitia Wheeler Ufford, James English, Alison Christie Wheeler Lahnston. PhD, Johns Hopkins U., 1933; ScD (hon.), Western Res. U., 1958, U. N.C., 1959, U. Pa., 1968, Middlebury Coll., 1969, Rutgers U., 1969, Yeshiva U., 1973, Yale U., 1974, U. Uppsala, 1975, U. Md., 1977, Gustavus Adolphus U., 1981, Cath. U. Am., 1982, U. Newcastle-upon-Tyne, 1983, Princeton U., 1986, U. Conn., 1989, U. Maine, 1992; ScD, Tufts U., 1992; LLD (hon.), Johns Hopkins U., 1977; LittD (hon.), Drexel U., 1987. NRC fellow N.Y., Copenhagen, 1933-35; asst. prof. physics U. N.C., 1935-38; asst. prof. physics Princeton U., 1938-42, assoc. prof., 1945-47, prof., 1947-76, Joseph Henry prof. physics, 1966-76, Joseph Henry prof. physics emeritus, 1976—; prof. physics and dir. Ctr. for Theoretical Physics, U. Tex., Austin, 1976-86; Ashbel Smith prof. U. Tex., Austin, 1979-86, Blumberg prof., 1981-86, Smith and Blumberg prof. emeritus, 1986—; cons. and physicist on atomic energy projects Princeton U., 1939-42, U. Chgo., 1942, E.I. duPont de Nemours & Co., Wilmington, Del., and Richland, Wash., 1943-45, Los Alamos, 1950-53; dir. project Matterhorn (H-bomb) Princeton U., 1951-53; Guggenheim fellow, Paris and Copenhagen, 1949-50; summer lectr. U. Mich., U. Chgo., Columbia U.; Lorentz prof. U. Leiden, 1956; Fulbright prof. Kyoto U., 1962; 1st vis. fellow Clare Coll. Cambridge U., 1964; Ritchie lectr. Edinburgh, 1958; vis. prof. U. Calif.-Berkeley, 1960; Battelle prof. U. Wash., 1975; I.I. Rabi visiting prof.,Columbia, U., 1983, sci. adviser U.S. Senate del. to 3d ann. conf. NATO Parliamentarians, Paris, 1957; mem. adv. com. Oak Ridge Nat. Lab., 1957-65, U. Calif., Los Alamos and Livermore, 1972-77; v.p. Internat. Union Physics, 1951-54; chmn. joint com. Am. Phys. Soc. and Am. Philos. Soc. on history theoretical physics in 20th Century, 1960-72; sci. adv. bd. USAF, 1961, 62; chmn. Dept. Def. Advanced Research Projects Agy. Project 137, (now Project Jason) 1958; mem. U.S. Gen. Adv. Com. Arms Control and Disarmament, 1969-72, 74-77. Author: Geometrodynamics, 1962, Gravitation Theory and Gravitational Collapse, 1965, Spacetime Physics, 1966, 2d edit. with E. Taylor, 1992, Einstein's Vision, 1968 (German), (with C.W. Misner and K.S. Thorne) Gravitation, 1973, (with M. Rees and R. Ruffini) Black Holes, Gravitation Waves and Cosmology, 1974, Frontiers of Time, 1979, (with W. Zurek) Quantum Theory and Measurement, 1983, A Journey into Gravity and Spacetime, 1990, transl. German, Japanese, Italian, Spanish At Home in the Universe, 1993, (with I. Ciufolini) Gravitation and Inertia, 1995; also translations, 1991-92; contbr. 375 articles to profl. jours. Trustee Battelle Meml. Inst., 1959-89, S.W. Rsch. Inst., San Antonio, 1977-92. Recipient A. Cressy Morrison prize N.Y. Acad. Sci. for work on nuclear physics, 1947, Albert Einstein prize Strauss Found., 1965, Enrico Fermi award AEC, 1968, Franklin medal Franklin Inst., 1969, Nat. medal of Sci., 1971, Herzfeld award, 1975, Outstanding Grad. Teaching award U. Tex., 1981, Niels Bohr Internat. Gold medal, 1982, Oersted medal Am. Assn. Physics Tchrs., 1983, J. Robert Oppenheimer meml. prize, 1984, Matteucci medal Nat. Acad. Sci. Rome, Soc. of the Forty, 1994. Fellow AAAS (dir. 1965-68), Am. Phys. Soc. (pres. 1966); mem. Am. Math. Soc., Internat. Astron. Union, Am. Acad. Arts and Scis., NAS, Am. Philos. Soc. (councillor 1963-66, 76-79, v.p. 1971-73, Franklin medal 1989), Philos. Soc. of Texas, Royal Acad. Sci. (Uppsala, Sweden), Tex. Philos. Soc., l'Academie Internationale de Philosophie des Sciences (v.p. 1987-90), Internat. Union Physics (v.p. 1951-54), Accademia Nazionale dei Lincei, Royal Soc. (London), Royal Danish Acad. Scis., Cenntury Assn. (N.Y.C.), Princeton Club (N.Y.C.), Phi Beta Kappa, Sigma Xi. Unitarian (trustee 1965). Office: Princeton U Dept Physics Princeton NJ 08544 *We will first understand how simple the universe is when we recognize how strange it is.*

WHEELER, JOHN CRAIG, astrophysicist, writer; b. Glendale, Calif., Apr. 5, 1943; s. G.L. and Peggy Wheeler; m. Hsueh Lie, Oct. 29, 1967; children: Diek Winters, J. Robinson. BS in Physics, MIT, 1965; PhD in Physics, U. Colo., 1969. Asst. prof. astronomy Harvard U., Cambridge, Mass., 1971-74; assoc. prof. U. Tex., Austin, 1974-80, prof., 1980—, Samuel T. and Fern Yanagisawa Regents prof. astronomy, 1985—, chmn. astronomy dept., 1986-90; vis. fellow Joint Inst. Lab. Astrophysics, Boulder, Colo., 1978-79, Japan Soc. for Promotion of Sci., 1983; 1st vis. prof. Assn. Univs. for Rsch. in Astronomy, 1990; mem. exec. com. astrophysics workshop Aspen (Colo.) Ctr. for Physics, Tex. Symposium on Relativistic Astrophysics. Author: The Krone Experiment, 1986; editor: Accretion Disks in Compact Stellar Systems, 1993. Recipient undergrad. teaching award Coll. Natural Scis., U. Tex., 1984, teaching award Bd. Visitors, Dept. Astronomy, U. Tex., 1986; Fulbright fellow, Italy, 1991. Mem. Internat. Astron. Union, Am. Astron. Soc., Sigma Xi. Avocations: running, writing, reading. Office: U Tex Dept Astronomy Austin TX 78712

WHEELER, JOHN HARVEY, political scientist; b. Waco, Tex., Oct. 17, 1918; m. Norene Burleigh; children: David Carroll, John Harvey III, Mark Jefferson. B.A., Ind. U., 1946, M.A., 1947; Ph.D., Harvard U., 1950. Instr. dept. govt., asst. dir. Summer Sch., Harvard U., 1950; asst. prof. Johns Hopkins U., 1950-54; assoc. prof. Washington and Lee U., 1954-56, prof. polit. sci., 1956-60; fellow in residence Ctr. for Study Dem. Instns., 1960-69, program dir., 1970-75; chmn., pres. Inst. Higher Studies, Carpinteria, Calif., 1975—; Martha Boaz rsch. prof. in acad. info. systems U. So. Calif. Libr. Systems, 1986—, Martha Boaz disting. rsch. prof., 1987—; cons. Fund for Republic, 1958-61; adj. prof. New Sch., 1986—, ISIM, 1989—; founder, bd. dirs. The Virtual Acad., 1987; mem. faculty Western Behavioral Scis. Inst., 1990—; mem. BESTnet, Nat. Rsch. and Edn. Network; pres. C-Mode Inst., 1992—; bd. dirs. Silicon Beach Comm. Author: The Conservative Crisis, 1958, (with Eugene Burdick) Fail-Safe, 1962, Democracy in a Revolutionary Era, 1968, The Politics of Revolution, 1971, The Virtual Library, 1987, The Virtual Society, 1988, 2d edit., 1992, (with E.M. Nathanson) The Rise of the Elders, 1996; editor, contbg. author: Beyond Punitive Society, 1973, Structure of Ancient Wisdom, 1983, Bioalgebra of Judgment, 1986, Fundamental Structures Human Reflexion, 1990; editor: (with George Boas) Lattimore, The Scholar, 1953; co-founder, joint chief editor: (with James Danielli) Jour. Social and Biol. Structures, 1973—; joint editor Goethe's Science, 1986; developed computer-mediated "Freshman Academy", 1993; contbr. articles to profl. jours. Served with AUS, 1941-46. Home: 7200 Casitas Pass Rd Carpinteria CA 93013-3120 Office: Inst Higher Studies PO Box 704 Carpinteria CA 93014-0704

WHEELER, JOHN OLIVER, geologist; b. Mussoorie, India, Dec. 19, 1924; s. Edward Oliver and Dorothea Sophie (Danielsen) W.; m. Nora Jean Hughes, May 17, 1952; children: Kathleen Anna Wheeler Hunter, Jennifer Margaret Wheeler Crompton. B.A.Sc. in Geol. Engring, U. B.C., 1947; Ph.D. in Geology, Columbia U., 1956. Geologist Geol. Survey Can., Ottawa, Ont., 1951-61, Vancouver, B.C., 1961-65; rsch. scientist Geol. Survey Can., 1965-70; rsch. mgr. Geol. Survey Can., Ottawa, 1970—; chief regional and econ. geology div. Geol. Survey Can., 1970-73, dep. dir. gen., 1973-79; rsch. scientist Geol. Survey Can. (Cordilleran div.), 1979-90, rsch. scientist emeritus, 1990—. Compiler of regional geol. maps of we. Can., Can. and no. N.Am. and Greenland; contbr. articles to profl. jours. Fellow Royal Soc. Can., Geol. Assn. Can. (pres. 1970-71, Logan medal 1983), Geol. Soc. Am. (councillor 1971-74), Can. Geosci. Council (pres. 1981); mem. Can. Inst. Mining and Metallurgy., Can. Geol. Found. (pres. 1974-79). Anglican. Clubs: Can. Alpine, Am. Alpine. Office: Geol Survey Can, 100 W Pender St, Vancouver, BC Canada V6B 1R8

WHEELER, JOHN WATSON, lawyer; b. Murfreesboro, Tenn., Sept. 11, 1938; s. James William and Grace (Fann) W.; m. Dorothy Anita Pressgrove, Aug. 5, 1959; children: Jeffrey William, John Harold. BS in Journalism, U. Tenn., 1960, JD, 1968. Bar: Tenn. 1968, U.S. Dist. Ct. (ea. dist.) Tenn. 1968, U.S. Supreme Ct. 1974, U.S. Ct. Appeals (6th cir.) 1975. Editor The Covington (Tenn.) Leader, 1963-65; adminstrv. asst. to lab. dir. UT-AEC Rsch. Lab., Oak Ridge, Tenn., 1965-68; assoc. Hodges, Doughty & Carson, Knoxville, Tenn., 1968-72; ptnr. Hodges, Doughty & Carson, Knoxville, 1972—; mem. commn. to study Apllellate Cts. in Tenn.; chair U.S. Magistrate Merit Selection Panel, Ea. Dist., Tenn., 1991; mem. Bankruptcy Judge Merit Selection Panel, Ea. Dist. Tenn., 1992-94; chmn. Hist. Soc., U.S. Dist. Ct. (ea. dist.) Tenn. Mem. organizing com. Tenn. Supreme Ct. Hist. Soc. Lt. U.S. Army, 1961-63, capt. Res. Fellow Am. Bar Found. (life), Tenn. Bar Found.; mem. ABA (ho. of dels. 1986—), Tenn. Bar Assn. (pres. 1989-90, bd. govs. 1981-91), Nat. Conf. Bar Pres., Am. Inns. of Ct. (master of bench), Internat. Assn. Def. Counsel, So. Conf. Bar Pres., Fox Den Country Club. Republican. Lutheran. Avocations: golf, travel. Home: 12009 N Fox Den Dr Knoxville TN 37922-2540 Office: Hodges Doughty & Carson PO Box 869 Knoxville TN 37901-0869

WHEELER, KATHERINE FRAZIER (KATE WHEELER), writer; b. Tulsa, July 27, 1955; d. Charles Bowen and Jan Nette (Moses) W. BA in English Fine Arts, Rice U., 1977; MA in Creative Writing, Stanford U., 1981. News reporter The Miami (Fla.) Herald, 1977-79; tchr. English composition Middlesex C.C., Lawrence, Mass., 1991; tchr. meditation Insight Meditation Soc., Barre, Mass., 1991—. Author: (short stories) Not Where I Started From, 1993; editor: (essays) In This Very Life, 1990; translator: (poems) Borrowed Time/Lo Esperady Lo Vivido, 1987; contg. editor: Tricycle Mag. Buddhist nun Mahasi Sasana Yeiktha, Rangoon, Burma, 1988; vol. Pet Share, Somerville (Mass.) Hosp., 1994. Recipient Pushcart Press prize, 1983-84, Best Am. Short Stories award Houghton Miflin, 1992, O'Henry award Doubleday, Inc., 1982, 93; nominee PEN/Faulkner award, 1994, Whiting Found. award, 1994; named one of Best 20 U.S. Novelists under 40, Granta Mmag., 1996; NEA grantee, 1994. Avocations: travel, dog training, sky gazing. Home: 72 Rev Nazareno Properzi Way Somerville MA 02143-3707

WHEELER, KENNETH WILLIAM, history educator; b. Amarillo, Tex., Mar. 7, 1929; s. Homer N. and Bertha (Campbell) W.; children: Amanda, Philip, David. B.A., U. Tex., 1951; diplome D'etudes Degré Superieur, Sorbonne, Paris, 1956; Ph.D., U. Rochester, 1963. Lectr., instr. history and city planning, asst. dean Grad. Sch. Ohio State U., 1960-66; asso. dean Met. Coll.; acting dean, dir. MetroCenter; assoc. prof. history Boston U., 1967-69; prof. history, dean Univ. Coll., Rutgers U., 1969-72, provost, 1972-87; sr. v.p. acad. affairs Rutgers U., 1987-91, Univ. prof. history, 1974—; mem. vis. com. Harvard U., 1972-80, adv. com. Lahey Clinic, 1989—, Planned Parenthood, 1988—. Author: To Wear a City's Crown, 1968, Women, The Arts, and The 1920's in New York and Paris, 1982; editor: For the Union, 1968. Trustee New Brunswick Tomorrow, George Street Theatre, Rutgers Prep. Sch. Served with AUS, 1951-53. Recipient award Am. Philos. Assn., 1966; fellow Am. Council Edn., 1966-67. Mem. Am. Hist. Assn., Orgn. Am. Historians, Soc. des amis des Univs. de Paris, Urban League, Phi Kappa Psi, Delta Sigma Pi. Clubs: Century Assn. (N.Y.C.), Palo Duro (Tex.). Office: Rutgers U 7 W 43d St New York NY 10036

WHEELER, LADD, psychology educator; b. Rosenberg, Tex., June 22, 1937; s. John DeWitt and Fredda (Stewart) W.; m. Clara McKee, June 20, 1961; 1 son, Scott; m. 2d Barbara Fox, Sept. 26, 1980; children: Karen, Robin; m. Helen Lee, Mar. 27, 1986; children: Natalie, Andrew. B.A., Stanford U., 1959; Ph.D., U. Minn., 1962. Research scientist Human Resources Research Office, Monterey, Calif., 1962-63, Nava. Med. Research Inst., Bethesda, Md., 1963-67; assoc. prof. Duke U., Durham, N.C., 1967-68, NYU, N.Y.C., 1968-71; prof. U. Rochester, (N.Y.), 1972—. Author: Interpersonal Influence, 1970, Interpersonal Influence, 2d edit., 1978, General Psychology, 1975; editor: Review of Personality and Social Psychology, Vols. 1-4, 1980-83. Fellow Am. Psychol. Assn., Am. Psychol. Soc., Soc. Personality and Social Psychology (pres. 1986). Home: 24 Locust Hill Dr Rochester NY 14618-5415 Office: Dept of Psychology U Rochester Rochester NY 14627

WHEELER, LAURENCE RANDOLPH, computer systems management; b. Austin, Tex., May 22, 1949; s. LeRoy T. and Phyllis A. (Smith) W.; m. Lou Ellen Currie, Dec. 23, 1971; children: Kevin Ross, Daniel Austin. B. U. Tex., 1971. Computer operator Tex. DPS, Austin, 1971-72, computer programmer analyst, 1972-74, systems programmer, 1974-77, systems programmer mgr., 1978-79; lead performance analyst Tex. Instruments-GSI, Austin, 1980-83; lead systems analyst IBM-Fed. Systems, Houston, 1983-86, mgr. system mgmt., 1986-94; mgr. system mgmt. Loral Space Info. Systems, Houston, 1994—; gen. chmn. Southwest Computer Measuremtne Group, 1980-81. Mem. Nat. Measurement Assn., Computer Measurement Group (editor, referee). Avocations: coaching youth sports, baseball, teaching Sunday sch. Office: Loral Space Info Systems 3700 Bay Area Blvd Houston TX 77058-1101

WHEELER, MALCOLM EDWARD, lawyer, law educator; b. Berkeley, Calif., Nov. 29, 1944; s. Malcolm Ross and Frances Dolores (Kane) W.; m. Donna Marie Stambaugh, July 21, 1981; children: Jessica Ross, M. Connor. SB, MIT, 1966; JD, Stanford U., 1969. Bar: Calif. 1970, Colo. 1992, U.S. Dist. Ct (cen. dist.) Calif. 1970, U.S. Ct. Appeals (9th cir.) 1970, U.S. Ct. Appeals (10th cir.) 1973, U.S. Dist. Ct. (no., so., ea. and cen. dists.) Calif. 1975, U.S. Ct. Appeals (11th cir.) 1987, U.S. Ct. Appeals (D.C. cir.) 1987, U.S. Supreme Ct. 1976, U.S. Ct. Appeals (3d cir.) 1989, (4th cir.) 1992. Assoc. Howard, Prim, Smith, Rice & Downs, San Francisco, 1969-71; assoc. prof. law U. Kans., Lawrence, 1971-74; assoc. Hughes Hubbard & Reed, Los Angeles, 1974-77, ptnr., 1977-81, 83-85, cons., 1981-83; ptnr. Skadden, Arps, Slate, Meagher & Flom, Los Angeles, 1985-91; dir. Parcel, Mauro, Hultin & Spaanstra P.C., Denver, 1991—; vis. prof. U. Iowa, 1978, prof., 1979; prof. U. Kans., Lawrence, 1981-83; chief counsel U.S. Senate Select Com. to Study Law Enforcement Undercover Activities, Washington, 1982-83. Mem. editorial bd. Jour. Products Liability, 1984—; bd. editors Fed. Litigation Guide Reporter, 1986—; contbr. articles to profl. jours. Mem. ABA, Calif. Bar Assn., Colo. Bar Assn., Am. Law Inst. Office: Parcel Mauro Hultin & Spaanstra PC 1801 California St Denver CO 80202-2658

WHEELER, MARK ANDREW, SR., lawyer; b. Pitts., Feb. 14, 1963; s. Andrew Mote Murdock and Anna Ruth (Whitfield) W.; m. Darla Jo Fusselman, May 10, 1993; children: Mark Andrew Jr., Lauren Anna. BA in Philosophy, Hampden-Sydney Coll., 1985; JD, W.Va. U., 1991. Bar: Pa. 1993, U.S. Dist. Ct. (we. dist.) Pa. 1993. Staff litigator W.Va. U. Coll. Law Legal Clinic, Morgantown, 1991-92; jud. clk. Mahoning County, Youngstown, Ohio, 1992-93; pvt. practice Reynoldsville, Pa., 1993—, Clarion, Pa., 1994—; legal cons. S.T. & E., Inc., Punxsutawney, Pa., 1993—, Jefferson County Gun Owners Assn., Brookville, Pa., 1994—, Crimestoppers of Jefferson County, Brookville, 1993-94, Five Star Homes, Inc., 1995—, Bembeng Cons., Inc., 1994—. Bd. dirs. Reynoldsville Area Indsl. Bd., 1993-96; mem. exec. dist. com. Boy Scouts Am., Dubois, Pa., 1993—; bd. dirs. Reynoldsville Pub. Libr. Assn., 1993-96; mem. Dubois Christian and Missionary Alliance Ch., mem. choir, 1995—. Mem. ABA, ATLA, Pa. Bar Assn. (young lawyers divsn., chair zone 7), Am. Ctr. for Law and Justice, Pa. Trial Lawyers Assn., Pa. Assn. Notaries, Jefferson County Bar Assn., Western Pa. Trial Lawyers Assn., Clarion County Bar Assn., Masons, Nat. Eagle Scout Assn. Republican. Avocations: songwriting, public speaking, home renovation, car restoration. Office: PO Box 176 512 Main St Reynoldsville PA 15851 also: 8 Grant St Clarion PA 16214

WHEELER, MARSHALL RALPH, zoologist, educator; b. Carlinville, Ill., Apr. 7, 1917; s. Ralph Adelbert and Hester May (Ward) W.; m. Edna Vivian Cronquist, July 3, 1944; 1 dau., Sandra Wheeler King; m. Linda Carol Lackner, May 10, 1966; children: Karen, Carson. Student, Blackburn Coll., 1935-37; B.A., Baylor U., 1939; postgrad., Tex. A&M U., 1939-41; Ph.D. (NRC fellow), U. Tex., 1947. Mem. faculty U. Tex., Austin, 1947—, assoc. prof. zoology, 1955-61, prof., 1961-78, emeritus prof., 1978—; Gosney fellow Calif. Inst. Tech.; former dir. Nat. Drosophila Species Resources Ctr.; mem. Nat. Wildflower Rsch. Ctr. Editor: Studies in Genetics, 1960-72. Served with USN, 1941-45. NSF grantee; NIH grantee. Mem. Entomol. Soc. Am. (editor Annals 1970-75), S.W. Assn. Naturalists (pres. 1961), Southwestern Entomol. Soc. (pres. 1978), Am. Hemerocallis Soc., Wilderness Soc., Nature Conservancy, Sierra Club. Home: 1313 Ardenwood Rd Austin TX 78722-1105 Office: U Tex Dept Zoology Austin TX 78712

WHEELER, ORVILLE EUGENE, university dean, civil and mechanical engineering educator; b. Memphis, Dec. 31, 1932; s. Eugene Lloyd and Sarah Josephine (Craig) W.; m. Mary Bea Rychlik, June 6, 1956; 1 dau., Lynnette Layne. B.Engring. cum laude, Vanderbilt U., 1954; M.S. in Civil Engring, U. Mo., 1956; Ph.D., Tex. A&M U., 1966. Registered profl. engr., Ala., Tenn., Wis. With Chance Vought Co., Dallas, 1959-60, Hayes Aircraft Co., Birmingham, Ala., 1960-61, Brown Engring. Co., Huntsville, Ala., 1961-62, NASA, Huntsville, 1962-66; design specialist Gen. Dynamics Co., Ft. Worth, 1966-72; chief structures engr. Bucyrus Erie Co., Milw., 1972-78; prof. civil and mech. engring., dean Herff Coll. Engring. Memphis State U., 1978-87, Herff prof. structural mechanics, 1987—. Served with USN, 1956-59. Mem. ASCE, ASTM, Assn. for Computing Machinery, Am. Inst. Steel Constrn., Memphis Engrs. Club. Methodist. Home: 3307 E Monticello Cir Memphis TN 38115-0640 Office: Dept of Engring U Memphis Memphis TN 38152

WHEELER, OTIS BULLARD, academic administrator, educator emeritus; b. Mansfield, Ark., Feb. 1, 1921; s. Clarence Charles and Georgia Elizabeth (Bullard) W.; m. Doris Louise Alexander, Jan. 17, 1943; children: Ann Carolyn, Ross Charles; m. Anne Carol Loveland, Mar. 23, 1991. B.A., U. Okla., 1942; M.A., U. Tex., 1947; Ph.D., U. Minn., 1951. Faculty La. State U., Baton Rouge, 1952—; prof. English La. State U., 1965-81, prof. emeritus, 1981—, chmn. dept., 1974, asst. dean grad. sch., 1962-67, vice chancellor for acad. affairs, 1974-80, acting chancellor, 1981; Fulbright-Hayes lectr. U. Innsbruck, Austria, 1968-69. Author: The Literary Career of Maurice Thompson, 1965; photographer religious architecture in La. (with R.W. Heck), 1995. Served with U.S. Army, 1942-46, 51-52. Decorated Bronze Star medal. Mem. Phi Kappa Phi, Omicron Delta Kappa. Democrat. Methodist. Home: 162 Clara Dr Baton Rouge LA 70808-4709

WHEELER, OTIS V., JR., public school principal; b. Silex, Mo., Oct. 1, 1925; s. Otis V. and Pearla F. (Howell) W.; m. Virginia Rogers, June 7, 1947; children: Jan Leigh, Mark Patrick. BBA, U. Mo., 1948, MEd, 1965, EdD, 1971. USN, 1948-52, Bus. mgr., 1952-61; sci. tchr. Columbia (Mo.) Pub. Schs., 1961-63, principal, 1963-91; supt. Boone County Sch. Dist., Mo., 1971; instr. U. Mo., Columbia, 1970-72, asst. prof. 1972-75, 78-79; cons. Midwest Ctr for Equal Ednl. Opportunities, 1972-75. Served to lt. USNR, 1943-85, World War II, Korea. Mem. Nat. Assn. Elem. Sch. Prins. (U.S. Dept. Edn., Nat. Disting. Prin. award 1985, Excellence in Edn. award 1986), Mo. Assn. Elem. Sch. Prins. (Disting. Service award 1984, editor jours. 1967-88), Mo. State Tchrs. Assn., Retired Officers Assn., U. Mo. Columbia Coll. Edn. Alumni (Citation of Merit award 1987), Phi Delta Kappa, Phi Delta Theta, Kappa Delta Pi. Methodist. Club: Lake Ozark Yachting Assn. (Mo.). Avocations: boating, dancing, travel, scuba diving. Home: 916 W Ash St Columbia MO 65203-2636 Office: Ridgeway IGE Sch 107 E Sexton Rd Columbia MO 65203-4082

WHEELER, PAUL JAMES, real estate executive; b. Mpls., Jan. 8, 1953; s. Philip James and Phyllis Lavonne (Holmquist) W.; m. Marianne Marie Stanton, June 3, 1978; children: Allison, Nathan, Kathryn. BA in Econs., DePauw U., 1975; MBA in Mgmt., Northwestern U., 1977. CPA, Ill. Acct. Deloitte, Haskins & Sells, Chgo., 1976-79; v.p. fin. Quinlan & Tyson, Inc., Evanston, Ill., 1979-82; sr. v.p. The Inland Group, Inc., Oakbrook, Ill., 1982—; bd. dirs. Westbank of Westchester, Inland Property Sales Inc., Inland Am. Ins. Co., Inland Securities Corp., Oak Brook, Ill. Mem. Ill. Soc. CPA's, Nat. Assn. Real Estate Investment Trusts, Nat. Multi Housing Coun., Investment Program Assn., Libertyville Sunrise Rotary. Republican. Evangelical Free. Home: 225 Ridgeway Ln Libertyville IL 60048-2457 Office: The Inland Group Inc 2901 Butterfield Rd Oak Brook IL 60521-1101

WHEELER, PETER MARTIN, federal agency administrator; b. Bronx, N.Y., Nov. 10, 1939; s. James and Mary A. (Doyle) W.; m. Mary Gaffey, Aug. 7, 1982; children: Bernadette, Peter, Mary Beth, James, Sam, Andrea. BA, Iona Coll., New Rochelle, N.Y., 1961; MPA, U. So. Calif., 1985, DPA (Dr. Pub. Adminstrn.), 1992. Claism rep., field rep. Social Security Adminstrn., Bronx, 1961-64; claims authorizer Social Security Adminstrn., Balt., 1964-65, comms. specialist, 1965-70, dep. assoc. commr., 1973-91, assoc. commr., 1992—; asst. exec. sec. Office of Sec. Dept. of Health, Edn. and Welfare, Washington, 1970-73; rep. Internat. Conf. on Social Welfare, Holland, 1972, Kenya, 1974; cons. Can. helath and Welfare Agy. Ottawa, 1989; adj. prof. George Washington U., Washington, 1994—. Mem. U.S. study team Benefits & Svcs. for Poor Children Eng., 1973. Recipient Nat. Inst. Pub. Affairs award U. So. Calif., 1969-70. Mem. Internat. Social Security Assn. (social security adminstrn. rep., mem. adv. com. rsch. Geneva, Vienna). Roman Catholic. Achievements include Social Security rsch., rebuilding Social Security Adminstrn.'s quality assurance systems. Home: 3238 Birchmede Dr Ellicott City MD 21042 Office: Social Security Adminstrn Rm 4-C-15 Ops 6401 Security Blvd Baltimore MD 21235

WHEELER, RAYMOND DAWSON, accountant; b. Sackville, N.B., Can., Oct. 26, 1946; s. James Allison and Hazel Hanna (MacElroy) W.; m. Jennifer Grace McKee, July 31, 1971. B Commerce, Mt. Alison U., Sackville, 1968; MBA, U. Toronto, Ont., Can., 1972. Chartered acct., N.S., B.C., Ont. Ptnr. in charge fin. svcs. Doane Raymond, Toronto. Fellow B.C. Inst. Chartered Accts., Ont. Inst. Chartered Accts., Oakville Curling Club, Islington Golf Club, Ont. Progressive Conservative Cornerstone Club, Strategic Leadership Forum (dir.). Office: Doane Raymond, 200 Bay St, Toronto, ON Canada M5J 2P9

WHEELER, RAYMOND LOUIS, lawyer; b. Ft. Sill, Okla., Feb. 10, 1945; s. Raymond Louis and Dorothy Marie (Hutcherson) W.; m. Priscilla Wheeler, July 1, 1966 (div. 1982); children: Jennifer, Hilary; m. Cynthia Lee Jackson, July 14, 1984 (div. 1994); children: Matthew Raymond, Madeline Elizabeth; m. Freddie Kay Park, June 10, 1995. BA, U. Tex., 1967; JD, Harvard U., 1970. Bar: Calif. 1972, U.S. Dist. Ct. (no., cen., ea. dists.) Calif., U.S. Ct. Appeals (9th cir.), U.S. Supreme Ct. Law clk. to hon. Irving L. Goldberg U.S. Ct. Appeals 5th cir., 1970-71; assoc. Morrison & Foerster, San Francisco, 1971-76, ptnr., 1976-90; ptnr. Morrison & Foerster, Palo Alto, Calif., 1990—; chmn. labor and employment law dept. Morrison & Foerster, San Francisco, 1984-88, 92—; lectr. labor and EEO law. Exec. editor Harvard Law Rev., 1969-70; editor in chief The Developing Labor Law; mem. nat. adv. bd. Indsl. Rels. Law Jour., 1980—; contbr. articles to law jours. Mem. ABA (chmn. com. on law devel. under labor rels. act 1990-93, coun. mem. sect. labor and employment 1994—). Republican. Office: Morrison & Foerster 755 Page Mill Rd Palo Alto CA 94304-1018

WHEELER, R(ICHARD) KENNETH, lawyer; b. Washington, July 25, 1934; s. Nathaniel Dudley and Ruth Lee (Matthews) W.; m. Christine Kandris, Jan. 11, 1990; children by previous marriage: Jennifer L., Ruth E. BA, Emory and Henry Coll., U. Richmond, 1957; LLB, U. Richmond, 1964. Bar: Va. 1963, D.C. 1977, U.S. Tax Ct. 1978. Assoc., then ptnr. Hunton, Williams, Gay, Powell & Gibson and successor firms, Richmond, 1963-88; sr. ptnr. Kane, Wheeler, Fenderson & Jeffries, Richmond, 1988-90; counsel Durrette, Irvin, Lemons & Fenderson, P.C., Richmond, 1990-94; sr. ptnr. Wallace, Harris & Wheeler, Richmond, 1994-95; adj. prof. law T.C. Williams Sch. Law, U. Richmond, 1966, 83, bd. dirs., 1977-79; adj. prof. law Va. Commonwealth U., 1970; lectr. trial practice U. Va., 1981-82, 85, 87; arbitrator Am. Arbitration Assn. Served to capt. USMCR, 1957-61. Williams scholar U. Richmond, 1961-63. Mem. ABA, Fed. Bar Assn., Nat. Assn. R.R. Trial Counsel, Am. Judicature Soc., Am. Law Inst., Va. State Bar (chmn. com. liaison with law schs. 1977-78, chmn. com. legal edn. and admission to bar 1978-80, spcl. com. on professionalism 1987-88), Va. Bar Assn., Bar Assn. D.C., Richmond Trial Lawyers Assn., Va. Trial Lawyers Assn., Richmond Bar Assn., Chesterfield-Colonial Heights Bar Assn., Henrico Bar Assn., Web Soc., McNeill Law Soc., Supreme Ct. Hist. Soc., Marine Corps League (life), Rector's Club (U. Richmond, life), Pi Sigma Alpha, Phi Delta Phi, Omicron Delta Kappa (hon.).

WHEELER, RICHARD WARREN, banker; b. Boston, Feb. 8, 1929; s. Wilfrid and Sybil Constance (Leckenby) W.; m. Betty Ann Owens, Sept. 9, 1950; children: Emily, Susan Knight, Thomas Adams, Alice Owens, Sarah Bennett. BA, Williams Coll., 1952; postgrad., Harvard U., 1962. With Citibank, N.A., 1952-82; assigned to Citibank, N.A., Hongkong, Manila and Tokyo, 1953-69, v.p., 1967-69, head Asia Pacific div., 1969-75, dep. overseas div., 1975-77; sr. v.p. Citibank, N.A., N.Y.C., 1969-82; head internat. relations unit Citibank, N.A., 1977-82; exec. v.p. Asia Soc., 1982-84; pres. Asia Internat. Bank, 1984-85; sr. v.p., gen. mgr. Bank of the Philippine Islands, N.Y.C., 1985-90; internat. fin. cons., 1991—. Chmn. Concord (Mss.) Bd. Assessors; bd. dirs., v.p. Am. Australian Assn., 1972-88; organizing dir. Nat. Coun. U.S.-China Trde; bd. dirs., chmn. exec. com. Presiding Bishop's Fund for World Relief, 1976-82; mem. standing com. on stewardship Episcopal Ch., 1978-84; mem. spl. refugee adv. panel Dept. Stte, 1982; mem. adf. bd. Ctr. for Contemporary Arab Studies, Georgetown U., 1977-79; chmn. adv. coun. Ctr. for Study World Religions, Harvard U., 1974-89, mem. adv. bd. Ctr. for East Asian Studies, 1971-76, mem. adv. bd. Ctr. for Strategic and Internat. Studies, 1970-80, v.p. exec. coun. Bus. Sch., 1971-75; chmn. bus. and industry adv. coun. to com. on capital markets and capitala movements OECD, 1980-82; mem. exec. com. ASEAN-U.S. Bus. Coun., 1976-82, Sudan-U.S. Bus. Coun., India-U.S. Bus. Coun., 1976-82, Philippine-Am. Found., 1987-92; chmn. adv. coun. Episc. Migration Ministries; pres., bd. dirs. U.S.-Korea Econ. Coun., mem. exec. com., 1978-82; trustee Cambridge Sch., Weston, Mass. With AUS, 1946-47. Mem. Japan Soc. (chmn. exec. com., bd. dirs. 1970-82), Nat. Planning Assn. (trustee, treas. 1976-82), Nat. Fgn. Trade Coun. (bd. dirs., mem. exec. com. 1976-82), Internat. C. of C. (vice chmn., trustee U.S. coun. 1976-82), Philippine Am. C. of C. (v.p., bd. dirs. 1987-92), U.S. Assn. for Internat. Migration (pres., bd. dirs., mem. exec. com. 1987-92), Univ. Club, Bronxville Field Club, Hodegaya Golf Club, Tokyo Law Tennis Club. Episcopalian. Home: 99 Sudbury Rd Concord MA 01742-2421 Office: Wheeler Realty Trust 150 Wheeler Rd Marstons Mills MA 02648-1110

WHEELER, SESSIONS SAMUEL, former foundation executive, author; b. Fernley, Nev., Apr. 27, 1911; s. Lister L. and Lythia Marie (Sessions) W.; m. Nevada Hazel Pedroli, Apr. 24, 1948. B.S., U. Nev., 1934, M.S., 1935. Forest technician U.S. Forest Service, summers 1930-35; Biologist Fernley High Sch., 1935-36, Reno schs., 1936-66; chmn. sci. dept. Reno High Sch., 1957-66; on leave as exec. dir. Nev. Fish and Game Commn., 1947-50; tchr. conservation edn. U. Nev., summers 1953-72, U. So. Calif., 1961; tchr. conservation natural resources U. Nev., 1966-74. Author: hist. novel Paiute, 1965, new edit., 1986; non-fiction The Desert Lake, 1967, The Nevada Desert, 1971, The Black Rock Desert, 1978, Gentleman in the Outdoors, 1985, Tahoe Heritage, 1992; ghost writer: Nevada Desert Sheepman, 1981; author also mag. articles; co-author: conservation textbooks Conservation and Nevada, 1949, Nevada Conservation Adventure, 1959. Trustee, adminstr. Max C. Fleischmann Found., Reno, 1951-80; Trustee Nev. State Museum, 1955-60; mem. Nev. Indian Affairs Commn., 1965-68; hon. trustee Ducks Unltd. Recipient Distinguished Nevadan award U. Nev., 1963; Conservation Edn. award Nat. Wildlife Fedn.-Sears Roebuck Found., 1965; Fire Prevention award U.S. Forest Service-Nat. Assn. State Foresters, 1965; Bd. Trustees ann. award Nev. Hist. Soc., 1978; named Outstanding Biology Tchr. Nev., Nat. Assn. Biology Tchrs., 1962, Nev. Conservationist of the Yr., Ducks Unltd., 1986; named to Nev. Writers Hall of Fame, Friends of the U. Libr., U. Nev.-Reno, 1989. Mem. Western Writers Am., Western History Assn., Westerners Internat. (pres. Nev. corral 1977-78), Explorers Club, Phi Kappa Phi, Sigma Nu. Roman Catholic. Home: 25 Moore Ln Reno NV 89509-3946

WHEELER, SUSIE WEEMS, retired educator; b. Cassville, Ga., Feb. 24, 1917; d. Percy Weems and Cora (Smith) Weems-Canty; m. Dan W. Wheeler Sr., June 7, 1941; 1 child, Dan Jr. BS, Fort Valley (Ga.) State U., 1945; MEd, Atlanta U., 1947, EdD, 1978; postgrad., U. Ky., 1959-60; EdS, U. Ga., 1977. Tchr. Bartow County Schs., Cartersville (Ga.) City Schs., 1938-44, Jeanes supr., 1946-58; supr., curriculum dir. Paulding Sch. Sys.-Stephens Sch., Calhoun City, 1958-64; summer sch. tchr. Atlanta U., 1961-63; curriculum dir. Bartow County Schs., Cartersville, 1963-79; pres., co-owner Wheeler-Morris Svc. Ctr., 1990—; mem. Ga. Commn. on Student Fin., 1985-95. Coord. Noble Hill-Wheeler Meml. Ctr. Project, 1983—. Recipient Oscar W. Canty Cmty. Svc. award, 1991, Woman in History award Fedn. Bus. and Profl. Women, 1994-95. Mem. AAUW (v.p. membership 1989-91, Ga. Achievement award 1993), Ga. Assn. Curriculum and Supervision (pres.-elect 1973-74, pres. 1974-75, Johnnye V. Cox award 1975), Delta Sigma Theta (pres. Rome alumnae chpt. 1978-80, mem. nat. bd. 1984, planning com. 1988—, Dynamic Delta award 1967, 78), Ga. Jeanes Assn. (pres. 1968-70). Home: 105 Fite St Cartersville GA 30120-3410

WHEELER, THOMAS BEARDSLEY, insurance company executive; b. Buffalo, Aug. 2, 1936; s. William Henry and Ruth (Matthews) W.; m. Anne Tuck Robertson, Nov. 25, 1961; children: Elizabeth Wheeler Soule, Wendy Bennett. BA, Yale U., 1958. CLU. Sales rep. IBM, White Plains, N.Y., 1961-62; sales rep., asst. gen. agt. Mass. Mut. Life Ins. Co., Boston, 1962, gen. agt., 1972-83; exec. v.p. Mass. Mut. Life Ins. Co., Springfield, 1983-86, pres., 1987-88, pres., chief exec. officer, 1988-96; chmn., CEO, 1996—; chmn. bd. dirs. Oppenheimer Acquisition Corp., DLB Acquisition Corp.; bd. dirs. Bank of Boston Corp., Textron, Inc.; pres. Jobs for Mass. Co-author: Managing Sales Professionals, 1984. Trustee Springfield Coll., 1985—, chmn., 1995—; trustee Am. Coll., Bryn Mawr, Pa., 1987-90, Baystate Health Systems, Inc., Springfield, 1983-92, Springfield Orch. Assn., Basketball Hall of Fame, Springfield; Mass. state chmn. U.S. Olympic Com. Lt. USNR, 1958-60. Mem. Springfield Life Underwriter's Assn., Am. Soc. C.L.U.'s (Pioneer Valley chpt., pres. Boston chpt. 1980-81), Boston Underwriter's Assn. (pres. 1972-73), Mass. Assn. Life Underwriters (pres. 1976-77), Health Ins. Assn. Am. (bd. dirs. 1990-93), Million Dollar Round Table, Yale Club of N.Y., Colony Club (Springfield), Longmeadow Country Club, Boca Grande, Chapoquoit Yacht Club (sec. 1973-75), The Links (N.Y.C.). Republican. Avocations: skiing, boating, art, antiques, music. Office: Mass Mut Life Ins Co 1295 State St Springfield MA 01111-0001

WHEELER, THOMAS EDGAR, communications technology executive; b. Redlands, Calif., Apr. 5, 1946; s. Charles Taylor and Martha (Edgar) W.; married; children: Nicole Pierce, David Maxwell. B.S., Ohio State U., 1968. Asst. dir. Ohio State U. Alumni Assn., Columbus, 1968-69; v.p. Grocery

Mfrs. Am., Inc., Washington, 1969-76; exec. v.p. Nat. Cable TV Assn., Washington, 1976-79, pres., chief exec. officer, 1979-85; pres., chief exec. officer NABU: The Home Computer Network, 1985-86; chmn., chief exec. officer NuCable Resources Corp., Washington, 1986-94; pres., dir. Media Enterprises Corp., 1982-95; pres., chief exec. officer Cellular Telecommunications Industry Assn., 1992—. Bd. trustees John F. Kennedy Ctr. for Performing Arts; bd. dirs. Vincent T. Lombardi Found., Cibernet Corp., Cellular Found., Inc., Youth Serve Am. Democrat. Office: Cellular Telecom Ind Assn 1250 Connecticut Ave NW Washington DC 20036-3390

WHEELER, VALERIE A. SYSLO, accountant; b. New Brunswick, N.J., Nov. 16, 1958; d. Joseph Jr. and Florence (Kulesa) Syslo; m. Ray J. Wheeler, Oct. 7, 1978. AAS in Acctg., Middlesex County Coll., 1979; BA in Acctg. and Econs., Rutgers U., 1993. Prodn. acctg. technician E. I. DuPont, Sayreville, N.J., 1981-86; import acctg. clk. Jeri-Jo Knitwear, Inc., Edison, N.J., 1986-87; cost acctg. clk. Neilson & Brainbridge, Edison, 1987-88; tax clk. Johnson & Johnson-CPI, Skillman, N.J., 1988-92; acct. mil. sales divsn. Johnson & Johnson-CPI, New Brunswick, 1992—. Fundraising chair Rugters U. Coll., 1990-91. Mem. Inst. Mgmt. Accts., Univ. Coll. Governing Assn. Roman Catholic. Avocations: travel, singing, dancing. Home: 12 Oxford Rd East Brunswick NJ 08816-4335

WHEELER, WARREN G(AGE), JR., retired publishing executive; b. Boston, Dec. 6, 1921; s. Warren Gage and Helen (Hoagl) W.; m. Jean Frances Moseley, Feb. 22, 1945; children: Richard, Michael, Ann, Duncan. B.S., Bowdoin Coll., 1943; B.J., U. Mo., 1947, M.A., 1948. With South Bend (Ind.) Tribune (name changed to Schurz Communications, Inc. 1976), 1948-82, gen. mgr., 1964-71, exec. v.p., 1971-75, pres., 1975-82. Campaign chmn. United Cmty. Svcs., South Bend, 1960, pres., 1964; treas. South Bend Urban League, 1962-63; trustee St. Joseph's Hosp., South Bend, 1969-77; gen. chmn. St. Joseph County (Ind.) Hosp. Devel., 1969-71; deacon, elder, pres. session 1st Presbyn. Ch., South Bend; chmn. bd. trustees United Ch. Marco Island, 1992-93, ch. pres., 1996. With USN, 1943-46. Protestant recipient Brotherhood award South Bend-Mishawaka chpt. NCCJ, 1970. Mem. Am. Newspaper Pubs. Assn., Am. Mgmt. Assn., Newspaper Personnel Relations Assn. (pres. 1955-56), Hoosier State Press Assn. (dir. 1967-70), Inland Daily Press Assn. (pres. 1972, pres. found. 1974-78), Sailing Assn. Marco Island, South Bend Press Club, Signal Point Club, Hideaway Beach Golf and Tennis Club, Sigma Delta Chi, Kappa Tau Alpha, Kappa Mu. Home: 6000 Royal Marco Way Apt 657 Marco Island FL 33937-1886

WHEELER, WESLEY DREER, marine engineer, naval architect, consultant; b. N.Y.C., Aug. 3, 1933; s. Wesley Lunn and Rosalie (Smith) W.; m. Dolores Janes-Wheeler, May 27, 1989; children: Wesley P., Jonathan H., Deborah B. BS in Mech. Engring., Worcester Poly. Inst., 1954; MSE in Naval Architecture and Marine Engring., U. Mich., 1958. Naval architect Am. Bulk Carriers, N.Y.C., 1966-68; port engr. Am. Trade and Prodn. Co., N.Y.C., 1968-69; pres. Techmarine, Inc., N.Y.C., 1969-71; asesor tecnico Astilleros Espanoles SA, Cadiz, Spain, 1971-72; tech. dir. Am. Bulk Carriers, N.Y.C., 1972-74; pres. Wesley D. Wheeler Assoc., Ltd., N.Y.C., 1974-83; v.p. J.J. Henry Co. Inc., N.Y.C., 1983; pres. Wheeler Assocs., N.Y.C., 1983—; Am. rep. Blohm & Voss, Astilleros Españoles, Dakar Marine, Shanghai Shipyards, 2 Mai Maugalia, M.C.I., Red Oak Mgmt. Cons. Elder and trustee Fifth Ave. Presbyn. Ch., N.Y.C., sec.; dir. Sutton Area Community, N.Y.C., Soc. Naval Architects and Marine Engrs., N.Y.C., 1990-92, treas.; chmn. Soc. Marine Cons., N.Y.C., 1987-94. Mem. Maritime Assn. Port of N.Y./N.J., Soc. Marine Port Engrs. N.Y., Soc. Maritime Arbitrators Inc., Royal Inst. Naval Architects, Inst. Marine Engrs., Asociacion Ingenieros Navales Madrid. Presbyterian. Avocations: boating, skiing, tennis, golf, travel. Home: 60 Sutton Pl S New York NY 10022-4168

WHEELER, W(ILLIAM) SCOTT, composer, conductor, music educator; b. Washington, Feb. 24, 1952; s. Malcolm Frederick and Aurora Dorothy (Anas) W.; m. Christen Struthers Frothingham, Jan. 5, 1985; children: Margaret Lee, Catherine Elizabeth. BA, Amherst Coll., 1973; MFA, Brandeis U., 1978, PhD, 1984. Artistic dir. Dinosaur Annex Music Ensemble, Boston, 1975—; dir. Cambridge (Mass.) Chorale, 1976-78; tchr. music, condr. Emerson Coll., Boston, 1978—. Composer (choral) A Babe is Born, , 1979, (theater) Winter Hills, 1987 (Somerville Arts Coun. Commn.), (symphony) Northern Lights, 1987 (Koussevitzky commn.), (opera) The Construction of Boston (libretto by Kenneth Koch), 1989, (choral) The Angle of the Sun, 1994 (Nat. Endowment for the Arts). Guggenheim fellow, 1988-89. Mem. Am. Music Ctr., ASCAP. Episcopalian. Home: 85 Haverhill St North Reading MA 01864-2816 Office: Emerson Coll Div Performing Arts 100 Beacon St Boston MA 02116-1501

WHEELER, WILMOT FITCH, JR., diversified manufacturing company executive; b. Southport, Conn., June 5, 1923; s. Wilmot Fitch and Hulda Day (Chapman) W.; m. Barbara Rutherfurd, Sept. 30, 1944 (dec. Sept. 1971); children: Wilmot Fitch III, James Alexander, John R. (dec.), Susan; m. Nonnye Landers, Dec. 20, 1973; children: Tracy Lynne, Alexa Margaret. BA, Yale U., 1945; postgrad., NYU, 1947-48. Staff engr. Stevenson, Jordan & Harrison, Inc. (mgmt. cons.), 1946-51; with Am. Chain & Cable Co., Inc., N.Y.C., 1951-76; pres., chmn., chief exec. officer Am. Chain & Cable Co., Inc., 1967-76; chmn., dir. Jelliff Corp., Southport, Conn., 1976—; prin. Case & Co. Inc. (mgmt. cons.), 1977-82; trustee Dollar Savs. Bank, 1974-83, chmn., chief exec. officer, 1982-83; chmn., trustee, chief exec. officer Dollar Dry Dock Savs. Bank, 1983-84; chmn. bd. dirs., CEO Manhattan Nat. Corp., 1986-87, vice-chmn. 1987-90; bd. dirs. People's Bank, Conn.; trustee People's Mut. Holdings, Bridgeport Hosp. Bd. dirs. William T. Morris Found., Wilmot Wheeler Found., Sormir Petroleum Inc. With AUS, 1943-46. Decorated Bronze Star. Episcopalian. Clubs: Yale (N.Y.C.), Sky (N.Y.C.); Country of Fairfield. Home: PO Box 429 Southport CT 06490-0429 Office: Jelliff Corp PO Box 758 354 Pequot Ave Southport CT 06490-1345

WHEELOCK, ARTHUR KINGSLAND, JR., art historian; b. Worcester, Mass., May 13, 1943; s. Arthur Kingsland and Anne (Kneass) W.; m. Susan Hoffman, June 13, 1964 (div. June 1988); children: Arthur Tobey, Laura, Matthew; m. Perry Carpenter Swain, Aug. 24, 1991. BA, Williams Coll., 1965; PhD, Harvard U., 1973. Instr. Bement Sch., Deerfield, Mass., 1965-66; asst. prof. art history U. Md., College Park, 1974-84, assoc. prof., 1984-88, prof., 1988—; David E. Finley fellow Nat. Gallery Art, Washington, 1971-74; research curator Nat. Gallery Art, 1974-75, curator Dutch and Flemish painting, 1976-84, curator No. Baroque painting, 1984—; cons. Centraal Laboratorium voor Onderzoek van Voorwerpen van Kunst en Wetenschap, Amsterdam, 1969-70. Author: Perspective; Optics and Delft Artists around 1650, 1977, Jan Vermeer, 1981, 2d rev. edit., 1988, Dutch Painting in the National Gallery of Art, 1984; co-author: Van Dyck 350, 1995, Jan Steen: Painter and Storyteller, 1996, exhbn. catalogue Gods, Saints and Heroes: Dutch Painting in the National Gallery of Art, 1987, Masterworks from Munich: Sixteenth-to-Eighteenth-Century Paintings from the Alte Pinakothek, 1988, Still Lifes of the Golden Age: Northern European Paintings from the Heinz Family Collection, 1989, Anthony Van Dyck, 1990; co-author/editor: Johannes Vermeer, 1995; co-editor: Dutch Paintings of the Seventheenth Century, 1995, Vermeer and the Art of Painting, 1995; contbr. exhbn. catalogue Leonardo's Last Supper: Precedents and Reflections, 1984, Images of Reality, Images of Arcadia: Seventeenth-century Netherlandish Paintings from Swiss Collectins, Art for the Nation: Gifts in Honor of the 50th Anniversary of the National Gallery of Art, 1989; contbr. articles and revs. to profl. jours. and encys. Decorated Knight officer Order Orange-Nassau (Netherlands); recipient Minda de Gunzburg prize, 1996, Johannes Vermeer prize, 1996; NDEA fellow, 1967-70, Nat. Gallery Art Curatorial fellow Ctr. Advanced Study Visual Arts, 1983-84, 87-88, Robert H. Smith Curatorial Rsch. fellow, 1990; Nat. Endowment Arts grantee, 1979-80. Decorated Knight officer Order Orange-Nassau (Netherlands); NDEA fellow, 1967-70; Nat. Endowment Arts grantee, 1979-80; Nat. Gallery Art curatorial fellow Ctr. Advanced Study Visual Arts, 1983-84, 87-88, Robert H. Smith curatorial rsch. fellow, 1990. Mem. Coll. Art Assn. Democrat. Episcopalian. Office: National Gallery Art Washington DC 20565

WHEELOCK, KEITH WARD, retired consulting company executive, educator; b. Phila., Oct. 17, 1933; s. Ward and Margot Trevor (Williams) W.; m. Susan Bowen Kimball, June 15, 1956 (div. Nov. 1975); children: Helen Fraser, James Voorhees; m. Bente Lorentzen Ott, July 1978 (div. June 1988). BA, Yale U., 1955; MA, U. Pa., 1957; MS, MIT, 1972. Fgn. svc. officer Dept. State, Washington, 1960-69; dir. programs and policy div. N.Y.C. Housing and Devel. Adminstrn., 1970-71; devel. officer Moody's Investors Svc., Inc., N.Y.C., 1972-74, v.p. internat. ops., 1974-75, exec. v.p., 1975-76; pres. The Fantus Co., Millburn, N.J., 1976-83; mem. Sr. Dun & Bradstreet Mgmt. Group, 1979-83; prin. Wheelock Cons., 1983-88; project dir. Mng. Growth in N.J., 1986-90; asst. prof. Raritan Valley C.C., 1992—. Mem. Montgomery (N.J.) Twp. Com., 1986-88. Author: Nasser's New Egypt, A Critical Analysis, 1960, New Jersey Growth Management, 1989. Sloan fellow MIT, 1972. Home: PO Box 339 Skillman NJ 08558-0339

WHEELOCK, LARRY ARTHUR, engineer, consultant; b. Chgo., Nov. 20, 1938; s. Preston J. and Rozella (Schonert) W.; m. Ruth E. Pruess (div. Sept. 1975); children: John P., J. Robert, William D., Thomas K.; m. Norma Jane Fair, Oct. 22, 1984. BSEE, U. Evansville, 1962. Registered profl. engr., Ind.; cert. instrument rated comml. pilot, airframe and powerplant mechanic, FAA. Co-op student engr. Naval Avionics Facility, Indpls., 1958-59; co-op student engr. Naval Weapons Support Ctr., Crane, Ind., 1959-62, elec. engr., 1963-78; elec. engr. Delco Electronics, Kokomo, Ind., 1962-63; sr. mfg. eng. Ford Aerospace & Comm., Bedford, Ind., 1979-80; plant engr. Ethyl Corp., Terre Haute, Ind., 1980-81; plant mgr. Tredegar Industries/Ethyl Corp., Terre Haute, 1981-91. Patentee in field. Bd. dirs. Hulman Regional Airport Authority, 1991-95, pres., 1992; pres. Greene County Airport Bd. Commrs., Bloomfield, Ind., 1972-81. Mem. IEEE, NSPE, Aircraft Owners & Pilots Assn., Exptl. Aircraft Assn., Antique Aircraft Assn., Internat. Flying Farmers, Flying Engrs. Internat. (pres. 1994, 95), Mensa, Internat. Assn. Flying Rotarians, Rotary Internat. Avocations: aviation, agriculture, mechanics, amateur radio, computers. Home: 7480 State Road 42 Terre Haute IN 47803-9778 also: PO Box 309 Raymondville TX 78580

WHEELOCK, MAJOR WILLIAM, JR., health care adminstrator; b. Fall River, Mass., Dec. 12, 1936; s. Major William and Mildred Mary (Rogers) W.; m. Rita Pauline Gauthier, Feb. 22, 1962; children: Major William III, Nancy Beth. B.S., Providence Coll., 1958. Budget examiner, spl. asst. to asst. sec. of Navy Washington, 1963-66; legis. analyst, budget examiner Bur. of Budget, Exec. Office of Pres., Washington, 1966-71; exec. asst. to the gov. State of N.H., 1971-73; supt. N.H. Hosp., Concord, 1973-77; preceptor George Washington U. Sch. Hosp. Adminstrn.; exec. dir. N.H. Charitable Fund, Concord, 1977-78; pres. Rumford Nat. Graphics, Inc., Concord, 1978-82; sr. v.p. N.H. Savs. Bank, 1982-85; exec. v.p. Franklin Pierce Coll., Rindge, N.H., 1985-95; pres. Crotched Mountain Found., Greenfield, N.H., 1995—; trustee N.H. Savs. Bank, 1981-83; bd. dirs. Yankee Pub. Co. Inc. Pres. Young Rep. Club, Fall River, Mass., 1957-58; bd. dirs. N.H. Indsl. Devel. Authority, 1972-75; bd. dirs. Community Health Care Assn., 1974-75, v.p., 1976; bd. dirs. N.H. Mental Health Assn., 1979-82, pres., 1980-82; bd. dirs. Crotched Mountain Found., 1980—; bd. dirs. N.H. Coun. for Humanities, 1980-86, chmn., 1984-86; bd. dirs. N.H. Social Welfare Coun., 1983, 90—, pres., 1986-90; bd. dirs. New Eng. Found. Humanities, 1990-95, Monadnock Family Svcs., 1990—, Monadnock Comm. Day Care Ctr., 1992—. Served with U.S. Army, 1959-61. Named N.H. Citizen of Yr., 1977; recipient Bancroft award N.H. Psychiat. Soc., 1977, Granite State award Plymouth State Coll., 1987. Mem. N.H. Hosp. Assn., Am. Coll. Hosp. Adminstrs., Concord Country (pres. 1976-77), Keene Country Club (v.p. 1993-94, pres. 1995—), Rotary (v.p. 1982-83, pres. 1983-84). Roman Catholic. Clubs: Concord Country (pres. 1976-77), Keene Country (pres. 1995-96); Lodge: Rotary (v.p. 1982-83, pres. 1983-84). Office: Crotched Mountain Foundation 1 Verney Dr Greenfield NH 03047 Office: College Rd Rindge NH 03461

WHEELON, ALBERT DEWELL, physicist; b. Moline, Ill., Jan. 18, 1929; s. Orville Albert and Alice Geltz (Dewell) W.; m. Nancy Helen Hermanson, Feb. 28, 1953 (dec. May 1980); children—Elizabeth Anne, Cynthia Helen; m. Cicely J. Evans, Feb. 4, 1984. B.Sc., Stanford U., 1949; Ph.D., Mass. Inst. Tech., 1952. Teaching fellow, then rsch. assoc. physics MIT, Boston, 1949-52; with Douglas Aircraft Co., 1952-53, Ramo-Wooldridge Corp., 1953-62; dep. dir. sci. and tech. CIA, Washington, 1962-66; with Hughes Aircraft Co., L.A., 1966-88, chmn., chief exec. officer, 1987-88; vis. prof. MIT, 1989; mem. Def. Sci. Bd., 1968-76; mem. Pres.'s Fgn. Intelligence, 1983-88; mem. Presdl. Commn. on Space Shuttle Challenger Accident, 1986; trustee Aerospace Corp., 1990-93, Calif. Inst. Tech., Rand Corp. Author 30 papers on radiowave propagation and guidance systems. Recipient R.V. Jones Intelligence award, 1994. Fellow IEEE, AIAA (Von Karman medal 1986); mem. NAE, Am. Phys. Soc., Sigma Chi. Republican. Episcopalian. Address: 181 Sheffield Dr Montecito CA 93108-2242

WHEELWRIGHT, STEVEN C., business educator; b. Salt Lake City, Sept. 13, 1943; s. Max and Deborah Ann (Coulam) W.; m. Margaret Steele, Dec. 21, 1965; children: Marianne, Melinda, Kristen, Matthew, Spencer. BS, U. Utah, 1966; MBA, Stanford U., 1969, PhD, 1970. Asst. prof. European Inst. Bus. Adminstrn., France, 1970-71; assoc. prof. Harvard U., Cambridge, Mass., 1971-73, 74-79; v.p. mktg. Wheelwright Lithographing, Utah, 1973-74; prof. Stanford (Calif.) U., 1979-88; prof. Harvard U., Cambridge, Mass., 1988—, also chn. MBA program; bd. dirs. TJ Internat., Heartport, Allegheny Ludlum Corp., Quantum Corp. Co-author: (with Spyros G. Makridakis) Computer-Aided Modeling for Managers, 1972, Forecasting Methods for Management, 1973, (with Spyros G. Makridakis and V. McGee) Forecasting Methods and Applications, 1988, (with Robert H. Hayes) Restoring Our Competitive Edge: Competing Through Manufacturing, 1984; (with Hayes and Kim B. Clark) Dynamic Manufacturing: Creating the Learning Organization, 1988, (with Kim B. Clark) Revolutionizing Product Development, 1992, Managing New Product and Process Development, 1993, Leading Product Development, 1995, (with Robert A. Burgelman and Modesto Maidique), Stategic Management of Technology and Innovation, 1995; co-editor: (with Spyros G. Makridakis) Handbook of Forecasting, 1987; assoc. editor various jours. Fellow Decision Scis. Inst. Office: Harvard U Bus Sch Dept of Business Boston MA 02163

WHELAN, ELIZABETH ANN MURPHY, epidemiologist; b. N.Y.C., Dec. 4, 1943; d. Joseph and Marion (Barrett) Murphy; m. Stephen T. Whelan, Apr. 3, 1971; 1 child, Christine B. BA, Conn. Coll., 1965; MPH, Yale U., 1967; MS, Harvard U., 1968, ScD, 1971. Coordinator County study Planned Parenthood, 1971-72; research assoc. Harvard Sch. Pub. Health, Boston, 1975-80; exec. dir. Am. Council Sci. and Health, N.Y.C., 1980-92, pres., 1992—; mem. com. on pesticides and toxics EPA; mem. U.S. Com. of Vital Stats., HHS; mem. Nat. Adv. Com. on Meat and Poultry Inspection USDA; guest lectr. Queen Elizabeth 2 (Cunard Line). Author: Sex and Sensibility, 1973, Making Sense Out of Sex, 1974, Panic in the Pantry, 1975, 92, A Baby?...Maybe, 1975, Boy or Girl?, 1976, The Pregnancy Experience, 1977, Preventing Cancer, 1978, The Nutrition Hoax, 1983, A Smoking Gun, 1984, Toxic Terror, 1984, 86, 93, Balanced Nutrition, 1988; contbr. articles to profl. jours. and consumer publs. Bd. dirs. Food and Drug Law Inst., Nat. Agrl. Legal Fund, Media Inst., N.Y. divsn. Am. Cancer Soc. Recipient Disting. Achievement medal Conn. Coll., 1979, award Am. Pub. Health Assn. Environ., 1992, Disting. Alumnus award Yale U., 1994-95, Ethics award Am. Inst. Chemists, 1996. Mem. APHA (Early Career award 1982, Homer Calver award 1992), Am. Inst. Nutrition, Am. Med. Writers Assn. (Walter Alvarez award 1986), U.S. Com. Vital Stats. Office: Am Council Sci and Health 1995 Broadway 2nd FL New York NY 10023-5882

WHELAN, GERALD P., surgeon; b. N.Y.C., May 6, 1944. MD, SUNY, 1970. Intern Brookdale Hosp. Ctr., Bklyn., 1970-71; resident in emergency medicine L.A. County-U. So. Calif. Med. Ctr., 1973-75, surgeon; assoc. prof. emergency medicine U. So. Calif., L.A. Office: LA County Med Ctr 1200 N State St rm 1011 Los Angeles CA 90033

WHELAN, JAMES ROBERT, communications executive, international trade and investment consultant, author, educator, mining executive, writer; b. Buffalo, July 27, 1933; s. Robert and Margaret (Southard) W.; children from previous marriage: Robert J., Heather Elizabeth; m. Guadalupe Aguirre, 1990. Student, U. Buffalo, 1951-53, U. R.I., 1955-57; BA, Fla. Internat. U., 1974. Staff corr., fgn. corr., country mgr., divsn. mgr. UPI, Buffalo, 1952-53; staff corr., fgn. corr., country mgr., div. mgr. UPI, Providence, 1955-57, Boston, 1957-58, Buenos Aires, Argentina, 1958-61, Caracas, Venezuela, 1961-66, San Juan, P.R., 1966, 68; regional dir. corp. rels., then v.p. ops. ITT World Directories, ITT, San Juan, 1968-70; Latin Am. corr. Scripps-Howard Newspaper Alliance, Washington, 1970-71; mng. editor Miami (Fla.) News, 1971-73; free-lance writer, 1973-74; freelance writer Hialeah (Fla.) Pub. Co., 1975-77; v.p., editl. dir. Panax Corp., Washington, 1977-80; v.p., editor Sacramento Union, 1980-82; editor, pub. Washington Times, 1982-84; mng. dir. CBN News, 1985-86; pres. Capital Comm. Internat., 1986—; editor-in-chief Conservative Digest, 1988-89; vice chmn. Inter-Am. Found., Arlington, Va., 1991-94; cons. external affairs advisor Inter-Am. Investment Corp., 1992-93; dir. strategic planning Cocetel Holding, Santiago, Chile, 1993-94; pres. Minera Silver Standard S.A., 1994—, Silver Std., Mex., 1995—; vis. prof. Polit. Sci. Inst., U. Chile, 1993-95; assoc. prof. Finis Terrae U., 1993—; adj. prof. U. Md., 1993; guest lectr. ednl. instns., including Boston U., U. Miami, Ctrl. U. Venezuela, Cath. U., Andrès Bello U., Chile, U. Chile, U. Tex., Austin, U. Concepcion, U. Santiago; guest prof. U. Fla., 1973. Author: Through the American Looking Glass; Central America's Crisis, 1980, Allende: Death of a Marxist Dream, 1981, Catastrophe in the Caribbean: The Failure of America's Human Rights Policy in Central America, 1984, The Soviet Assault on America's Southern Flank, 1988, Out of the Ashes: Life, Death and Transfiguration of Democracy in Chile, 1833-1988, 1989, Hunters in the Sky, 1991, Desde las Cenizas: Vida, Muerte y Transfiguracion de la Democracia en Chile, 1833-1988, 1993, 2nd edit., 1995. Bd. dirs. Christian Community Service Agy., Miami, 1973, Hialeah-Miami Springs (Fla.) C. of C., 1976-77, Wolf Trap Found., 1984-87; bd. dirs. Nat. Council for Better Edn.; chmn. print media div. United Way campaign, Sacramento, 1981; bd. govs. Council on Nat. Policy, Washington, 1981-87; del. Commn. of Californias, 1981; chmn. Council for Inter-Am. Security Ednl. Inst., 1986-90; mem. spl. task force on pub. safety Greater Washington Bd. Trade; mem. Nat. Commn. on Free and Responsible Media, 1983-84; bd. dirs. Nat. Bus. Consortium for Gifted and Talented Children, 1985-87; bd. govs. Internat. Policy Forum, 1985—; mem. Presdl. Bd. Fgn. Scholarships (Fulbright Commn.), 1986-92, exec. planning com., 1987-92. With Signal Corps U.S. Army, 1953-55. Nieman fellow Harvard U., 1966-67; recipient citation of excellence Overseas Press Club, 1971, Unity award Lincoln U., 1976, Golden Press award Am. Legion Aux., 1977, Freedom award Valley Forge Found., 1981, Bernardo O'Higgins award Chilean Govt., 1990, presented at Chilean Embassy by Amb. Octavio Errazuriz. Mem. Nat. Press Club, Overseas Press Club, Univ. Club (Washington), Georgetown Club, Cosmos Club, Harvard Club (N.Y.C.), Club de Ofcls. de Fuerza Aerea (Santiago), Club Militar Lo Curro (Santiago), Instituto O'Higginiano de Chile. Home: Cantarranas 21, Lomas de Bernardez, Guadalupe 98600, Mexico also: V Carranza 4120-13 D Europlaza Mall, 25230 Saltillo Coahuila Mexico

WHELAN, JOHN MARTIN, insurance executive; b. Phila., Aug. 22, 1944; s. John Martin and Catherine (Clarke) W.; m. Kathleen Rosamond, Apr. 11, 1970; children: Erika, Beth, Maura, John. BS, Drexel U., 1966; MBA, Columbia U., 1972. With corp. n. bus. devel. Continental Group, N.Y.C., 1970-71; mgr. mgmt. consulting Peat Marwick Mitchell & Co., Chgo., 1972-79; dir. Golden Rule Fin. Corp., Lawrenceville, Ill., 1983—, pres., chief operating officer, 1979-90, pres., chief exec. officer, 1990—, v.p., chief operating officer, chief operating officer, 1979-83, bd. dirs., pres., chief operating officer, 1983-90; pres., chief exec. officer, bd. dirs. Golden Rule Ins. Co., Lawrenceville, IL, 1990—; bd. dirs. Ad-Ventures, Indpls, 1985—; chmn. bd. dirs. All Savers Ins. Co. & Value Ins., Indpls, 1986—; pres., bd. dirs. Cen. States Securities Inc., Indpls., 1983—; bd. dirs., sec.-treas. Exec. Systems Inc., Indpls, 1983—; bd. dirs., v.p. M.A. Rooney, Indpls., 1984—. Bd. dirs. Vols. in Prevention, Probation & Prisons, Inc., Royal Oak, Mich., Greater Indpls. Progress Com., U.S. Bus. & Indsl. Coun., Washington; chmn. bd. Health & Hosp. Corp., Indpls. Capt. USAF, 1968-70. Named Sagamore of the Wabash, Gov. of Ind., 1990. Mem. Legatus. Roman Catholic. Avocations: golf, swimming. Office: Golden Rule Ins Co 7440 Woodland Dr Indianapolis IN 46278-1720*

WHELAN, JOHN WILLIAM, lawyer, law educator, consultant; b. Cleve., Apr. 23, 1922; s. Walter Edmund and Stacia Miriam W.; m. Maryrose Shields, May 29, 1947; children: Moira Ann Whelan Dykstra, Thomas M. AB, John Carroll U., 1943; JD, Georgetown U., 1948. Assoc. prof. law Columbus U., Washington, 1948-50; asst. prof. law U. Va., Charlottesville, 1955-56; asso. prof. law U. Wis., Madison, 1956-59; prof. law Georgetown U., Washington, 1959-67, U. Calif., Davis, 1967-75, Hastings Coll. Law U. Calif., San Francisco, 1975-91; prof. emeritus Hasting Coll. Law U. Calif., San Francisco, 1991—; vis. prof. Nihon U. Coll. Law, Tokyo, summer 1989; cons. to atty. gen. Trust Ty. Pacific Islands, 1976-78; mem. atomic energy com. Bd. Contract Appeals, 1965-73; hearing examiner Medi-Cal Fiscal Intermediary Contract, 1979-82; adminstrn. law judge constrn. contracts Trust Ter. Pacific Island, 1984-86; cons. on govt. contracts to Polish govt., 1992. Author: (with R.S. Pasley) Federal Government Contracts, 1975; (with K.H. York) Insurance, 1983, 2d edit., 1988, Federal Government Contracts, 1985, Supplement, 1989, 3d edit., 1996, Understanding Government Contracts, 1994; (with K.H. York, Leo Martinez) Insurance, 3d edit., 1994; editor: Yearbook of Procurement Articles, 1965-90; mem. editl. bd. Pub. Procurement Law Rev. (U.K. pub.), 1991—; contbr. articles to profl. jours. Served with inf. AUS, 1943-45; served with J.A.G., 1950-55. Decorated Bronze Star; Ford Found. grantee, 1958-59, 63-64, summer 1970. Mem. ABA, Fed. Bar Assn., D.C. Bar Assn., Nat. Contract Mgmt. Assn. Home: 306 Bristol Pl Mill Valley CA 94941-4005 Office: U Calif Hastings Coll Law 200 Mcallister St San Francisco CA 94102-4707

WHELAN, JOSEPH L., neurologist; b. Chisholm, Minn., Aug. 13, 1917; s. James Gorman and Johanna (Quilty) W.; m. Gloria Ann Rewoldt, June 12, 1948; children: Joe, Jennifer. Student, Hibbing Jr. Coll., 1935-38; BS, U. Minn., 1940, MB, 1942, MD, 1943. Diplomate Am. Bd. Psychiatry and Neurology. Intern Detroit Receiving Hosp., 1942-43; fellow neurology U. Pa. Hosp., Phila., 1946-47; resident neurology U. Minn. Hosps., Mpls., 1947-49; chief neurology svc. VA Hosp., Mpls., 1949; spl. fellow electroencephalography Mayo Clinic, Rochester, Minn., 1951; practice medicine specializing in neurology Detroit, 1949-73, Petoskey and Gaylord, Mich., 1973-87; asst. prof. Wayne State U., 1957-63; chief neurology svcs. Grace Hosp., St. John's Hosp., Bon Secour Hosp., Detroit; cons. neurologist No. Mich. Hosps., Charlevoix Area Hosp.; instr. Med. Sch. U. Minn., 1949; cons. USPHS, Detroit Bd. Edn. Contbr. articles to profl. jours. Founder, mem. ad hoc Com. to Force Lawyers Out of Govt. Fellow Am. Acad. Neurology (treas. 1955-57), Am. Electroencephalography Soc.; mem. AMA, AAAS, Assn. Rsch. Nervous and Mental Diseases, Soc. Clin. Neurologists, Mich. Neurol. Assn. (sec.-treas. 1967-76, Disting. Physician award 1988), Mich. Med. Soc., No. Mich. Med. Soc., Grosse Pointe (Mich.) Club. Address: 9797 N Twin Lake Rd Mancelona MI 49659-9203

WHELAN, KAREN MAE LEPPO, manufacturing executive; b. Lancaster, Pa., Mar. 20, 1947; children: Katherine, John. BA, U. Pitts., 1967; MS in Bus., Va. Commonwealth U., 1977. Sr. acct. Arthur Young, Richmond, Va., 1977-80; various positions, advanced to v.p. fin. reporting James River Corp., Richmond, 1980-92; v.p., treas. Universal Corp., Richmond, 1993—. Mem. AICPA (Elijah Watts Sells award 1976), Nat. Investor Rels. Inst., Fin. Execs. Inst., Va. Soc. CPAs (cert. CPA, gold medal award 1976). Office: Universal Corp 1501 N Hamilton St Richmond VA 23230-3925

WHELAN, RICHARD J., director special education and pediatrics programs, academic administrator; b. Emmett, Kans, June 23, 1931; s. Richard Joseph and Margaret Alma (Cox) W.; m. Carol Ann King, Nov. 21, 1959; children—Mark Richard, Cheryl Lynne. B.A., Washburn U., 1955; Ed.D., U. Kans., 1966. Dir. edn. Menninger Clinic, Topeka, Kans., 1959-62; dir. edn. children's rehab. unit U. Kans. Med. Ctr., Kansas City, Kans., 1966—; prof. spl. edn. and pediatrics, chmn. dept. spl. edn. U. Kans., Lawrence, 1966-72, 78-80, 83-88, assoc. dean grad. studies and outreach, 1988-94, Ralph L. Smith disting. prof. child devel., 1968—, dean sch. edn., 1992-94; div. dir. U.S. Office Edn., Washington, 1972-74; cons. colls. and univs., state and fed. agys.; chmn. policy bd. Evaluation Tng., Kalamazoo, 1975-81. Author, editor: Promising Practices..., 1983; cons. editor Ednl. Research Ency., 1982; contbr. articles to profl. jours., chpts. to books. Chmn. adv. bd. Kans. Bd. Edn., Topeka, 1982-92; mem. adv. bd. Shawnee Mission Sch. Dist., Kans., 1984-92; mem. Gov.'s Task Force on Early Childhood, 1984-92; hearing officer various sch. dists. Served with U.S. Army, 1952-54. Mem. Soc. for Learning Disabilities (pres. 1980-81), Council for Exceptional Children, Assn. for Persons with Severe Handicaps (bd. dirs. 1975-79), Kans. Council for Exceptional Children (pres. 1963-64, Service award 1978), Phi Kappa Phi. Avocations: reading, music, golf, running, flying. Home: 7204 High Dr Shawnee Mission KS 66208-3355 Office: U Kans Med Ctr 39th and Rainbow Sts Kansas City KS 66160-7335

WHELAN, ROGER MICHAEL, lawyer, educator; b. Montclair, N.J., Nov. 12, 1936; s. John Leslie and Helen Louise (Callahan) W.; m. Rosemary Bogdan, Aug. 26, 1961; children: Helen, Theresa, John, James, Kathleen (dec.), Julie, Jennifer. AB cum laude, Georgetown U., 1959, JD, 1962. Bar: D.C. 1962, U.S. Dist. Ct. D.C. 1962, U.S. Ct. Appeals (D.C. cir.) 1962, U.S. Supreme Ct. 1968, U.S. Dist. Ct. Md. 1985. Assoc. Fried, Rogers & Ritz, Washington, 1961-66; ptnr. Doctor & Whelan, Washington, 1967-72; judge U.S. Bankruptcy Ct., Washington, 1972-83; sr. mem. Verner, Liipfert, Bernhard, McPherson & Hand, Chartered, Washington, 1984-89; sr. counsel Shaw, Pittman, Potts & Trowbridge, Washington, 1989—; dir. Lincoln Ctr. for Legal Studies, Arlington, Va., 1974-84; disting. lectr. Columbus Sch. Law, Cath. U. Am., Washington, 1975—. Sec. local campaign com., Alexandria, Va., 1964; trustee YMCAA, Silver Spring, Md., 1972-74. Recipient award D.C. Cir. Jud. Conf., 1984. Fellow Am. Coll. Bankruptcy (bd. regents 1989-95, bd. dirs. 1995—); mem. FBA (chmn. bankruptcy subcom. 1988, exec. com. 1993—), Am. Bankruptcy Inst. (bd. dirs. 1991—, exec. com. 1993-95, chmn. legis. com. 1991—), Walter Chandler Inn of Ct. (master emeritus 1990—). Republican. Roman Catholic. Avocations: fishing, hunting, boating. Home: 17908 Ednor View Ter Ashton MD 20861-9757 Office: Shaw Pittman Potts & Trowbridge 2300 N St NW Washington DC 20037-1122

WHELAN, STEPHEN THOMAS, lawyer; b. Phila., July 28, 1947; s. Stephen Thomas and Virginia King (Ball) W.; m. Elizabeth Ann Murphy, Apr. 3, 1971; children: Christine Barrett. BA magna cum laude, Princeton U., 1968; JD, Harvard U., 1971. Bar: N.Y. 1972, U.S. Dist. Ct. (so. dist.) N.Y. 1975. Assoc. Mudge Rose Guthrie & Alexander, N.Y.C., 1971-75; assoc. Thacher Proffitt & Wood, N.Y.C., 1975-77, ptnr., 1978—; chmn. corp. dept. Thacher Proffitt & Wood, 1992—. Author: New York's Uniform Commercial Code Article 2-A, 1994; contbr. articles to profl. jours. Bd. dirs. Sons Revolution, N.Y., 1979—; active N.Y. County Rep. Com., 1985—; active Princeton U. Alumni Coun., 1993—. Fellow Am. Coll. Investment Counsel; mem. ABA (chmn. subcom. on leasing 1994—), N.Y. State Bar Assn., Equipment Leasing Assn. Am. (mem. fed. govt. rels. com. 1992—, legal com. 1995—). Roman Catholic. Avocations: road racing, secondary sch. students mentor, golf. Office: Thacher Proffitt & Wood 2 World Trade Ctr New York NY 10048-0203

WHELAN, WAYNE LOUIS, higher education administrator; b. Colonial Heights, Va., Jan. 10, 1939; s. Clarence Roscoe and Ruby Elizabeth (Farris) W.; m. Carlton Harville Whelan, Aug. 25, 1961; children: Karen Lynne Smith, Whitney Hoffman Whelan. BA in History, U. Va., 1960, M. in Edn. Adminstrn., 1967; EdD, Pacific States U., L.A., 1977. Tchr., administr. Hopewell (Va.) H.S., 1961-64; dir. guidance Colonial Heights (Va.) H.S., 1964-68; dir. evening and summer sessions Richard Bland Coll. Coll. William and Mary, 1968-72; assoc. dean evening and summer sessions Va. State U., 1972-78; dir. confs. and non-credit programs U. Tenn., 1978-86; assoc. v.p. continuing edn. and econ. devel. Trident Tech. Coll., Charleston, 1986—. Oustanding Young Man Colonial Heights, Va. Jaycees, 1977. Mem. Assn. Continuing Higher Edn. (exec. v.p., meritorious svc. award, 1989), N. Charleston Breakfast Rotary, Trident Metro C. of C. Avocations: sailing, naval history. Home: 553 Planter's Loop Mount Pleasant SC 29464 Office: Trident Tech Coll PO Box 118067 Charleston SC 29423-8067

WHELAN, WENDY, ballet dancer; b. Louisville; d. Rich and Kay Whelan. Student, Louisville Ballet Acad., Sch. Am. Ballet. Apprentice N.Y.C. Ballet, 1984-86, mem. corps de ballet, 1986-89, soloist, 1989-91, prin., 1991—. Appeared in feature roles in George Balanchine's ballets such as Apollo, Raymonda Variations, Swan Lake, Who Cares?, Symphony in Three Movements, Danses Concertantes, Episodes, Cortege Hongrois, The Four Temperaments, Brahms-Schoenberg Quartet, Divertimento # 15, A Midsummer Night's Dream, Bournonville Divertissements, The Nutcracker, Walpurgisnacht Ballet, Brahms-Schoenberg Quartet Pieces, Union Jack, The Cage; in Jerome Robbins' Antique Epigraphs and Glass Pieces; in Peter Martins' Ash, Jazz, Les Petits Riens, Sleeping Beauty; in William Forsythe's Behind the China Dogs and Herman Scherman; in Christopher D'Amboise's The Bounding Line in Richard Tanner's A Schubert Sonata; and performed in N.Y.C. Ballet's Balanchine Celebration, 1993. Office: NYC Ballet NY State Theater 20 Lincoln Center Plz New York NY 10023-6913

WHELPLEY, DENNIS PORTER, lawyer; b. Mpls., Feb. 16, 1951; s. John Olsen and Harriet Marie (Porter) W.; m. Patricia Jan Adamy, Nov. 27, 1976; children: Heather Nicolle, Christopher Eric. BA, U. Minn., 1973, JD magna cum laude, 1976. Bar: Minn. 1976. Assoc. Oppenheimer Wolff & Donnelly, St. Paul, 1976-83, ptnr., 1983—. Mem. Order of Coif (Minn. chpt.), Phi Beta Kappa (Alpha of Minn. chpt.), Psi Upsilon (Mu chpt.), Dellwood Hills Golf & Country Club. Avocations: golf, tennis, squash, bridge. Home: 49 Locust St Mahtomedi MN 55115-1542 Office: Oppenheimer Wolff & Donnelly 1700 First Bank Bldg Saint Paul MN 55101

WHETTEN, JOHN D., food products executive. Advt. and mktg. mgr. The Clorox Corp., Oakland, Calif., 1967-79; pres., CEO Challenge Dairy Products, Inc., Dublin, Calif., 1982—; CEO DairyAmerica, Inc., Dublin, Calif., 1995—. Mem. Am. Butter Inst. (v.p. 1995—), Dairy Export Incentive Program Coalition (pres. 1994—), Dairy Mktg. Coop. Fedn. (pres. 1992—). Office: Challenge Dairy Products Inc 11875 Dublin Blvd Ste B200 Dublin CA 94568-2842

WHETTEN, JOHN THEODORE, geologist; b. Willimantic, Conn., Mar. 16, 1935; s. Nathan Laselle and Theora Lucille (Johnson) W.; m. Carol Annette Jacobsen, July 14, 1960; children—Andrea, Krista, Michelle. A.B. with high honors, Princeton U., 1957; Ph.D., 1962; M.S., U. Calif.-, Berkeley, 1959. Mem. faculty U. Wash., Seattle, 1963-81; research instr. oceanography U. Wash., 1963-64, asst. prof., 1964-68, assoc. prof., 1968-72, prof. geol. scis. and oceanography, 1972-81, chmn. dept. geol. scis., 1969-74; assoc. dean Grad. Sch., 1968-69; geologist U.S. Geol. Survey, Seattle, 1975-80; asst. div. leader geoscis. div. Los Alamos Nat. Lab., 1980-81, dep. div. leader earth and space scis. div., 1981-84, div. leader earth and space scis. div., 1984-86, assoc. dir. energy and tech., 1986-92, assoc. dir. quality, policy and performance, 1992-93; lab. affiliate, 1994—; cons. in environ., safety and health and mfg. techs. Motorola Corp., 1994—. Contbr. articles to profl. jours. Fulbright fellow, 1962-63. Home: 154 Piedra Loop Los Alamos NM 87544-3837 Office: Los Alamos Nat Lab MS J-591 Los Alamos NM 87545

WHETTEN, LAWRENCE LESTER, international relations educator; b. Provo, Utah, June 12, 1932; s. Lester B. and Kate (Allred) W.; m. Gabriele Indra, Oct. 28, 1974 (dec. May 1985). B.A., Brigham U., 1954, M.A., 1955; Ph.D. with honors, NYU, 1963. Sr. polit. analyst Hdqrs. USAFE, Wiesbaden, Fed. Republic Germany, 1963-70; resident dir. grad. program in internat. relations U. So. Calif., Munich, Fed. Republic Germany, 1971-78, dir. studies USC/SIR grad. program in Germany, 1978-86; Erich Voegelin Gast prof. Munich U., 1987-88; lectr. Boston U., 1988—; lectr. Profl. Assoc. Ctr. Def. and Strategic Studies S.W. Mo. State U., Springfield, 1991—; cons. Fgn. Policy Inst., Phila., 1969-71, 76-79, R & D Assocs., Munich, 1977; prof. Hochschule für Politik, Munich U.; adj. prof., profl. assoc. Ctr. for Def. and Strategic Studies, S.W. Mo. State U., 1991—. Author: Germany's Ostpolitik, 1971, Contemporary American Foreign Policy, 1974, The Canal War: Four Power Conflict, 1974, Germany East and West, 1981. Author, editor: Present State Communist Internationalism, 1983, The Interaction of Political Reforms Within the East Block, 1989. Served to capt. USAF, 1960-63. Penfield fellow NYU, 1957-59; grantee Ford Found., 1970, Royal Inst. Internat. Affairs, London, 1970, Thyssen Found., Cologne, Germany, 1974-82, 89, Volkswagen Found., 1982-85. Mem. Am. Acad. Polit. and Social Scis., Internat. Inst. Strategic Studies, Am. Assn. Advancement of Soviet Studies, Gesellschaft für Auslandskunde, German Am. Assn. Home: Widenmayerstrasse 41, 80538 Munich Germany

WHICHARD, WILLIS PADGETT, state supreme court justice; b. Durham, N.C., May 24, 1940; s. Willis Guilford and Beulah (Padgett) W.; m. Leona Irene Paschal, June 4, 1961; children: Jennifer Diane, Ida Gilbert. AB, U. N.C., 1962, JD, 1965; LLM, U. Va., 1984, SJD, 1994. Bar: N.C. 1965. Law clk. N.C. Supreme Ct., Raleigh, 1965-66; ptnr. Powe, Porter, Alphin & Whichard, Durham, 1966-80; assoc. judge N.C. Ct. Appeals, Raleigh, 1980-86; assoc. justice N.C. Supreme Ct., Raleigh, 1986—; instr. grad. sch. bus. adminstrn. Duke U., 1978; vis. lectr. U. N.C. Sch. Law, 1986—. Contbr. articles to profl. jours. Rep. N.C. Ho. of Reps., Raleigh, 1970-74; senator N.C. Senate, 1974-80, chair numerous coms. and commns.; N.C. legis. rsch. commn., 1971-73, 75-77, land policy coun., 1975-79; bd. dirs. Sr. Citizens Coordinating Coun., 1972-74; chair local crusade Am. Cancer Soc., 1977, state crusade chair, 1980, chair pub. issues com., 1980-84; pres., bd. chmn. Downtown Durham Devel. Corp., 1980-84; bd. dirs. Durham County chpt. ARC, 1971-79; Durham county campaign dir. March of Dimes, 1968, 69, chmn., 1969-74, bd. dirs. Triangle chpt., 1974-79; bd. advisors Duke Hosp., 1982-85, U. N.C. Sch. Pub. Health, 1985—, U. N.C. Sch. Social Work, 1989—; bd. visitors N.C. Ctrl. U. Sch. Law, 1987—; mem. law sch. dean search com. U. N.C., 1978-79, 88-89, self-study com., 1985-86; pres. N.C. Inst. Justice, 1984-94; bd. dirs. N.C. Ctr. Crime and Punishment, 1984-94. Staff sgt. N.C. Army NG, 1966-72. Recipient Disting. Service award Durham Jaycees, 1971, Outstanding Legis. award N.C. Acad. Trial Lawyers, 1975, Outstanding Youth Service award N.C. Juvenile Correctional Assn., 1975, Citizen of Yr., Eno Valley Civitan Club, Durham, 1982, Faith Active in Pub. Life award N.C. Council of Churches, 1983, Outstanding Appellate Judge award N.C. Acad. Trial Lawyers, 1983, inducted Durham High Sch. Hall of Fame, 1987. Mem. ABA, N.C. Bar Assn. (v.p. 1983-84), Durham County Bar Assn., U. N.C. Law Alumni Assn. (pres. 1978-79, bd. dirs. 1979-82), Nat. Guard Assn. (judge advocate 1972-73, legis. com. 1974-76), Order of Golden Fleece, Order of Grail, Order of Old Well, Amphoterothen Soc., Order of Coif, Phi Alpha Theta, Phi Kappa Alpha. Democrat. Baptist. Clubs: Durham-Chapel Hill Torch (pres. 1984-85), Watauga (Raleigh, pres. 1994—). Home: 5608 Woodberry Rd Durham NC 27707-5335 Office: NC Supreme Ct 2 E Morgan St Raleigh NC 27601-1445

WHIDDEN, STANLEY JOHN, physiologist, physician; b. N.Y.C., Oct. 10, 1947; s. Stanley Graham and Maybell (Van Houten) W.; m. Jan Venable Whidden, 1987. AS, Delgado Coll., 1969; BS, Southeastern La. U., 1971, MS, 1973; PhD, Auburn U., 1979; MD, U. Auto. De Ciudad Juarex, Mex., 1984; postgrad. Hyperbaric Physicians Ctr., NOAA, Nat. Def. U., 1986, Naval War Coll., 1995. Asst. head ops. Nuclear Sci. Ctr., Auburn U., Ala., 1976-78; lectr. physiology U. Wis.-Madison, 1978-79; asst. prof. U. New Orleans, 1979-80; postdoctoral fellow shock physiology La. State U. Med. Ctr., New Orleans, 1980-82; rsch., med. staff JESM Baromed. Inst., New Orleans, 1984-86; asst. prof. rsch. physiology dept., La. State U. Med. Ctr., New Orleans, 1988-89; mgr. program Dept. of Justice, Nat. Inst. Justice; fellow Naval War Coll., Preventive Medicine U.S. Army Ctr. Health. Contbr. chpt. to books: Handbook of Shock and Trauma, 1983, Physiological Basis of Decompression Sickness, 1987, Active Duty Army Combat Operation "Just Cause" Panama, 1990. Lt. col. USAR, 1966—, Desert Storm/Shield, Saudia Action, 1991, Op. Provide Hope, Somalia, 1993. Decorated Bronze Star; recipient Meritorious Svc. medal, Acom medal, UN medal, 1994; named to Hon. Col., La. Gov. Staff, 1985; named one of Outstanding Young Men of Am., 1986; USAF fellow, Sch. Aero. Medicine, Brooks AFB, Tex., 1986, 87, NASA fellow, Johnson Space Ctr., 1987; named Outstanding Young Men in Am., 1986; recipient Md. Gov.'s Citation, 1991. Mem. AAUP, AAAS, Am. Physiology Soc., Soc. Neurosci. Am. Chem. Soc., Aerospace Med. Assn., Aerospace Physiol. Soc., Am. Vet. Physiology and Pharmacology Soc., Am. Burn Assn., N.Y. Acad. Sci., Shock Soc., Undersea Med. Soc. Republican. Club: Spl. Forces Assn. (New Orleans) (pres. 1983-84). Current work: Underlining preventive medical requirements during complex disaster with resources and from the government and non-goverment agencies. Subspecialties: Physiology (medicine); Space medicine. Office: US Army Ctr for Health Promotion & Preventive Medicine PO Box 1252 Temple Hills MD 20757-1252 also: Health Promotion & Preventive Medicine US Army Ctr Aberdeen Proving Ground MD 21010-5422

WHIDDON, CAROL PRICE, writer, editor, consultant; b. Gadsden, Ala., Nov. 18, 1947; d. Curtis Ray and Vivian (Dooly) Price; m. John Earl Caulking, Jan. 18, 1969 (div. July 1987); m. Ronald Alton Whiddon, Apr. 13, 1988. Student, McNeese State U., 1966-68; BA in English, George Mason U., 1984. Flute instr. Lake Charles, La., 1966-68; flutist Lake Charles Civic Symphony, 1966-69, Beaumont (Tex.) Symphony, 1967-68; freelance editor The Washington Lit. Rev., 1983-84, ARC Hdqrs., Washington, 1984; writer, editor Jaycor, Vienna, Va., 1985-87; writer, editor Jaycor, Albuquerque, 1987-90, publs. mgr., 1990-91; writer, editor Proteus Corp., Albuquerque, 1991-92; owner Whiddon Editorial Svcs., Albuquerque, 1989—; mem. S.W. Writer's Workshop, 1991—. Co-author: The Spirit That Wants Me: A New Mexico Anthology, 1991; contbr. various articles to Albuquerque Woman and mil. dependent pubs. in Fed. Rpublic Germany. Bd. dirs. Channel 27-Pub. Access TV, 1991-93, exec. bd. sec., 1992, v.p., 1993; dep. mgr. Fed. Women's Program, Ansbach, Fed. Republic Germany, 1980-81; pres. Ansbach German-Am. Club, 1980-82; sec. Am. Women's Activities, Fed. Republic Germany, 1980-81, chairwoman, 1981-82. Recipient cert. of appreciation from Am. amb. to Germany Arthur T. Burns, 1982, medal of appreciation from comdr. 1st Armored Div., Ansbach, Germany, 1982. Mem. NAFE, Women in Comm. (newsletter editor 1989-90, 91-92, 94-95, v.p. 1990-91, pres.-elect 1992-93, pres. 1993-94, chair programs com. Nat. Profl. Conf. 1994), Soc. Tech. Comm. (membership dir. 1993-94), Nat. Assn. Desktop Pubs., Am. Mktg. Assn., Greater Albuquerque C. of C., N.Mex. Cactus Soc. (historian 1989-94, sec. 1991, newsletter editor 1992—, various show ribbons 1989-91). Republican. Avocations: reading, writing, gardening, camping, music. Home: 1129 Turner Dr NE Albuquerque NM 87123-1917

WHIDDON, FREDERICK PALMER, university president; b. Newville, Ala., Mar. 2, 1930; s. Samuel Wilson and Mary (Palmer) W.; m. June Marie Ledyard, June 14, 1952; children: Charles Wilson, John Tracy, Karen Marie and Keith Frederick (twins). AB, Birmingham So. Coll., 1952; BD cum laude, Emory U., 1955, PhD in Philosophy, 1963, LittD (hon.), 1991. Asst. prof. philosophy, dean of students Athens (Ala.) Coll., 1957-59; dir. Mobile Ctr. U. Ala., 1960-63; pres. U. South Ala., Mobile, 1963—; mem. presdl. adv. com. Fed. Home Loan Bank, Atlanta. Contbr. articles to profl. jours. Chmn. Marine Environ Scis. Consortium. Named Outstanding Adminstr. in Ala., Am. Assn. Univ. Adminstrs., 1981. Mem. Am. Assn. Univ. Adminstrs., Phi Kappa Phi. Lodge: Kiwanis (Mobile). Office: U South Alabama Pres Office University Of South Alabama AL 36688

WHIFFEN, JAMES DOUGLASS, surgeon, educator; b. N.Y.C., Jan. 16, 1931; s. John Phillips and Lorna Elizabeth (Douglass) W.; child from a previous marriage, Gregory James; m. Sally Vilas Runge, Aug. 21, 1993. B.S., U. Wis., 1952, M.D., 1955. Diplomate: Am. Bd. Surgery. Intern Ohio State U. Hosp., 1955-56; resident U. Wis. Hosp., 1956-57, 59-61; instr. dept. surgery U. Wis. Med. Sch., 1962-64, asst. prof., 1964-67, asso. prof., 1967-71, prof., 1971—, vice chmn. dept., 1970-72, acting chmn., 1972-74; asst. dean Med. Sch., 1975—; mem. exam. council State of Wis. Emergency Med. Services, 1974-77. Bd. dirs. Wis. Heart Assn. Served to lt. comdr. USNR, 1957-59. John and Mary R. Markle scholar in acad. medicine, also; Research Career Devel. award NIH, 1965-75. Fellow A.C.S., Am. Soc. Artificial Internal Organs. Club: Maple Bluff Country. Research, publs. on biomaterials, thrombo-resistant surfaces and the physiology of heart-lung bypass procedures. Home: 17 Cambridge Ct Madison WI 53704-5906 Office: 600 Highland Ave Madison WI 53792-0001

WHIGHAM, MARK ANTHONY, computer scientist; b. Mobile, Ala., Jan. 14, 1959; s. Tommie Lee Sr. and Callie Mae (Molette) W. BS in Computer Sci., Ala. A&M U., 1983, MS in Computer Sci., 1990. Computer programmer U.S. Army Corps of Engrs., Huntsville, Ala., 1985-88; programmer analyst, coord. acad. computing Ala. A&M U., Normal, Ala., 1988-89; programmer analyst II, DEC systems coord., instr. part-time computer sci. dept. Ala. A&M U., 1989-91; systems engr. Advanced Bus. Cons. Inc.-La. div. Dow Chem. Co., 1991-93; owner Whigham's Computer Cons., 1990—; sys. engr. DOW Chem. Co.-USA La. Divsn., Plaquemine, La., 1991-93; instr. computer info. system Calhoun C.C., Decatur, Ala., 1993—; network specialist/cons. Ala. A&M U., Normal, 1994—; computer info. sys. instr. Calhoun C.C., Decatur, Ala., 1994—; instr. computer sci. dept. Ala. A&M U., 1989-91; network specialist, cons. Ala. A&M U., Normal, 1994—. Active Huntsville Interdenominational Ministerial Fellowship, Huntsville, 1984. Mem. Nat. Assn. Sys. Programmers, Ala. Coun. for Computer Edn., Assn. for Computing Machinery, Huntsville Jaycees, Nat. Soc. Black Engrs., So. Poetry Assn., Nat. Arts Soc., Internat. Black Writers and Artists Assn., Optimists, Sigma Tau Epsilon, Alpha Phi Omega. Baptist. Avocations: chess, skating, reading, playing piano. Home: PO Box 3032 Huntsville AL 35810-0032 Office: Calhoun CC Bus Divsn PO Box 2216 Decatur AL 35609-2216

WHILLOCK, CARL SIMPSON, electric cooperative executive, former academic administrator; b. Scotland, Ark., May 7, 1926; s. Joe and Johnnie (Simpson) W.; m. Margaret Moore Carter; children and stepchildren: Timothy, Tom, Sally Whillock Conduff, Susan Whillock Lipe, Sallie Overbey, Jenny Dakil, Melissa Campbell, Larry, Brennam, Benjamin. BS in Social Welfare, U. Ark., 1948, MA in History and Polit. Sci., 1951; JD, George Washington U., 1960. High sch. tchr., 1946-47, in family bus. livestock feeds, wholesale petroleum co., 1949-55; exec. asst. to Congressman J.W. Trimble, Berryville, Ark., 1955-63; pvt. practice law Clinton, Ark., 1963-66; pros. atty. 14th Jud. Dist., Ark., 1965-66; asst. to pres., dir. univ. rels., part-time instr. polit. sci. U. Ark., Fayetteville, 1966-71, v.p. govtl. rels. and pub. affairs, 1975-78; pres. Ark. State U., Jonesboro, 1978-80, Ark. Electric Coops. Inc., 1980—, Ark. Electric Coop. Corp., 1980—; bd. dirs. 1st Comml. Bank, Little Rock; campaign mgr. David Pryor for Gov. of Ark. Campaign, 1974-75; exec. sec. Gov. of Ark., 1975, mem., bd. of trustees Univ. of Ark. Mem. Ark. Ho. of Reps., two terms, 1953-56; chmn. Ark. Tax Reform Commn., 1987-88, mem. Pres.'s Ark. Adv. Coun. for Winrock, mem. bd. dirs. Winrock Internat. Inst. for Agrl. Devel.. Democrat. Home: PO Box 194208 Little Rock AR 72219-4208 *It is my belief that the success of any organization or effort depends on the caliber of the people involved in it. It is important that people be intelligent, imaginative, compassionate, willing to listen to others, courageous, conscientious, honest, and dependable. People who have these qualities have been the greatest inspiration to me.*

WHINNERY, JOHN ROY, electrical engineering educator; b. Read, Colo., July 26, 1916; s. Ralph V. and Edith Mable (Bent) W.; m. Patricia Barry, Sept. 17, 1944; children—Carol Joanne, Catherine, Barbara. B.S. in Elec. Engring, U. Calif. at Berkeley, 1937, Ph.D., 1948. With GE, 1937-46; part-time lectr. Union Coll., Schenectady, 1945-46; asso. prof. elec. engring. U. Calif., Berkeley, 1946-52, prof., vice chmn. div. elec. engring., 1952-56, chmn., 1956-59, dean Coll. Engring., 1959-63, prof. elec. engring., 1963-80, Univ. prof. Coll. Engring., 1980—; vis. mem. tech. staff. Bell Telephone Labs., 1963-64; research sci. electron tubes Hughes Aircraft Co., Culver City, 1951-52; disting. lectr. IEEE Microwave Theory and Technique Soc., 1989-92. Author: (with Simon Ramo) Fields and Waves in Modern Radio, 1944, 3d edit. (with Ramo and Van Duzar), 1994, (with D.O. Pederson and J.J. Studer) Introduction to Electronic Systems, Circuits and Devices; also tech. articles. Chmn. Commn. Engring. Edn., 1966-68; mem. sci. and tech. com. Manned Space Flight, NASA, 1963-69; mem. Pres.'s Com. on Nat. Sci. Medal, 1970-73, 79-80; standing com. controlled thermonuclear research AEC, 1970-73. Recipient Lamme medal Am. Soc. Engring. Edn., 1975, Centennial medal, 1993, Engring. Alumni award U. Calif.-Berkeley, 1980, Nat. Medal of Sci. NSF, 1992; named to Hall of Fame Modesto High Sch. (Calif.), 1983, ASEE Hall of Fame, 1993.; Guggenheim fellow, 1959. Fellow IRE (bd. dirs. 1956-59), IEEE (life, bd. dirs. 1969-71, sec. 1971, Edn. medal 1967, Centennial medal 1984, Medal of Honor 1985), Optical Soc. Am., Am. Acad. Arts and Scis.; mem. NAS, NAE (Founders award 1986), IEEE Microwave Theory and Techniques Soc. (Microwave Career award 1977), Phi Beta Kappa, Sigma Xi, Tau Beta Pi, Eta Kappa Nu. Congregationalist. Home: 1804 Wales Dr Walnut Creek CA 94595 Office: U Calif Dept Electrical Engineering Berkeley CA 94720

WHINSTON, ARTHUR LEWIS, lawyer; b. N.Y.C., Feb. 5, 1925; s. Charles Nathaniel and Charlotte (Nalen) W.; m. Melicent Ames Kingsbury, Mar. 19, 1949; children: Ann Kingsbury, James Pierce, Melicent Ames, Louise Ellen, Patricia Kingsbury. B.C.E., Cornell U., 1945; M.S.E., Princeton U., 1947; J.D., N.Y. U., 1957. Bar: N.Y. 1957, Oreg. 1964, U.S. Supreme Ct 1966, U.S. Patent Office 1958, U.S. Ct. Appeals (fed. cir.) 1959; registered profl. engr., N.Y., Oreg. Engr. Chas. N. & Selig Whinston, N.Y.C., 1947-50; lectr. Coll. City N.Y., 1950-51; structures engr. Republic Aviation Corp., Farmingdale, N.Y., 1951-57; practice in N.Y.C., 1957-64, Portland, Oreg., 1964—; patent lawyer Arthur, Dry & Kalish, 1957-64; partner Klarquist, Sparkman, Campbell, Leigh & Whinston, 1964—; chmn. Oreg. Bar com. on patent, trademark and copyright law, 1968-69, 77-78, mem. com. unauthorized practice law, 1970-73, chmn., 1972-73, com. on profl. responsibility, 1973-75. Served as ensign, C.E. USNR, 1945-46. Recipient Fuertes medal Cornell U. Sch. Civil Engring., 1945. Mem. ABA, Oreg. Bar Assn., N.Y. Bar Assn., Multnomah County Bar Assn., Am. Intellectual Property Law Assn., N.Y. Intellectual Property Law Assn., Oreg. Patent Law Assn. (pres. 1977-78), Profl. Engrs. Oreg. (past state legis. chmn.), Sigma Xi, Chi Epsilon, Phi Kappa Phi. Republican. Unitarian. Club: Multnomah Athletic. Home: 3824 SW 50th Ave Portland OR 97221-2112 Office: One World Trade Ctr Ste 1600 Portland OR 97204

WHIPPLE, DAVID DOTY, professional society administrator; b. Akron, Ohio, Dec. 26, 1923; s. Hugh Scott and Helene Eleanore (Doty) W.; m. Carolyn Terhune Decker, Feb. 28, 1953; children: Susan Casselman, Marc Evan, Tim Decker, Scott Adams Montgomery. BA, Dartmouth Coll., 1949; postgrad., Johns Hopkins U., 1949-50, The Nat. War Coll., Washington, 1966-67. From ops. officer to chief of various stations overseas CIA, Washington, 1950-85; with The Nat. Intelligence Officer for Counterterrorism, Washington, 1983-85; cons. internat. terrorism, 1985-89; exec. dir. Assn. Former Intelligence Officers, McLean, Va., 1989—; exec. v.p. Pagan Internat., Washington, 1987-89. Vol. Brit. 8th Army, 1944-45, Italy; sgt. U.S. Army, 1945-46, Italy, Philippines. Mem. Assn. Former Intelligence Officers (exec. dir. 1989—), Nat. War Coll. Alumni Assn., CIA Retirees Assn. Office: Assn Former Intel Officers 6723 Whittier Ave Ste 303A Mc Lean VA 22101

WHIPPLE, DEAN, federal judge; b. 1938. BS, Drury Coll., 1961; postgrad., U. Tulsa, 1961-62; JD, U. Mo., 1965, postgrad., 1965. Pvt. practice Lebanon, Mo., 1965-75; cir. judge div. II 26th Jud. Cir. Mo., 1975-87; dist. judge U.S. Dist. Ct., Kansas City, Mo., 1987—; prosecuting atty. Laclede County, Mo., 1967-71. Mem. Cen. United Meth. Ch., Kansas City. With Mo. N.G., 1956-61; USAR, 1961-66. Mem. Mo. Bar Assn. (mem. pub. info. com. 1971-72, mem. judiciary com. 1971-72, mem. bd. govs. 1975-87, mem. exec. com. 1983-84, 86-87, mem. planning com. for ann. meeting 1985, 87, chmn. 1986, mem. selection com. for Lon Hocker award 1986), Mo. Trial Judges Assn., 26th Jud. Bar Assn., Laclede County Bar Assn. (pres. 1968-69, 72-73), Kansas City Met. Bar Assn., Kansas City Inn of Ct. (instr. 1988-93), Mo. Hist. Soc., Phi Delta Phi. Office: US Dist Ct US Courthouse 811 Grand Ave Rm 613 Kansas City MO 64106-1909

WHIPPLE, FRED LAWRENCE, astronomer; b. Red Oak, Iowa, Nov. 5, 1906; s. Harry Lawrence and Celestia (MacFarl) W.; m. Dorothy Woods, 1928 (div. 1935); 1 son, Earle Raymond; m. Babette F. Samelson, Aug. 20, 1946; children: Dorothy Sandra, Laura. Student, Occidental Coll., 1923-24; AB, UCLA, 1927; PhD, U. Calif., 1931; AM (hon.), Harvard, 1945; ScD, Am. Internat. Coll., 1958; DLitt (hon.), Northeastern U., 1961; DSc (hon.), Temple U., 1961, U. Ariz., 1979; LLD (hon.), C.W. Post Coll., L.I. U., 1962. Teaching fellow U. Calif. at Berkeley, 1927-29, Lick Obs. fellow, 1930-31; instr. Stanford U., summer 1929, U. Calif., summer 1931; staff mem. Harvard Obs., 1931-77; instr. Harvard U., 1932-38, lectr., 1938-45; research asso. Radio Research Lab., 1942-45, asso. prof. astronomy, 1945-50, prof. astronomy, 1950-77, chmn. dept., 1949-56, Phillips prof. astronomy, 1968-77; dir. Smithsonian Astrophys. Obs., 1955-73, sr. scientist, 1973—; mem. Rocket Rsch. Panel U.S., 1946-57; U.S. subcom. NASA, 1946-52, U.S. Rsch. and Devel. Bd. Panel, 1947-52; chmn. Tech. Panel on Rocketry; mem. Tech. Panel on Earth Satellite Program, 1955-59; other coms. Internat. Geophys. Year, 1955-59; mem., past officer Internat. Astron. Union; cons. missions to U.K. and MTO, 1944; del. Inter-Am. Astrophys. Congress, Mexico, 1942; active leader project on Upper-Atmospheric Rsch. via Meteor Photog. sponsored by Bur. Ordnance, U.S. Navy, 1946-51; b. Bur. Ordnance, U.S. Navy (Office Naval Rsch.), 1951-57, USAF, 1948-62; mem. com. meteorology, space sci. bd., com. on atmospheric scis. Nat. Acad. Scis.-NRC, 1958-65; advisor Sci. Adv. Bd., USAF, 1963-67; spl. cons. com. Sci. and Astronautics U.S. Ho. Reps., 1960-73; chmn. Gordon Rsch. Confs., 1963; dir. Optical Satellite Tracking Project, NASA, 1958-73; project dir. Orbiting Astron. Obs., 1958-72; dir. Meteorite Photography and Recovery Program, 1962-73, cons. planetary atmospheres, 1962-69; mem. space scis. working group on Orbiting Astron. Observatories, 1959-70; chmn. sci. coun. geodetic uses artificial satellites Com. Space Rsch., 1965-70. Author: Earth, Moon and Planets, rev. edit, 1968, Orbiting The Sun: Planets and Satellites of The Solar System, The Mystery of Comets, 1985; co-author: Survey of the Universe; Contbr.: sci. papers on astron. and upper atmosphere to Ency. Brit; mags., other publs.; Asso. editor: Astronomical Jour, 1954-56, 64-71; editor: Smithsonian Contributions to Astrophysics, 1956-73, Planetary and

Space Science, 1958-83, hon. editor, 1983—, Science Revs, 1961-70; editorial bd.: Earth and Planetary Sci. Letters, 1966-73; inventor tanometer, meteor bumper; a developer window as radar countermeasure, 1944. Decorated comdr. Order of Merit for rsch. and invention, Esnault-Pelerie award France; recipient Donohue medals for ind. discovery of 6 new comets, Presdl. Cert. of Merit for sci. work during World War II, J. Lawrence Smith medal Nat. Acad. Scis. for rsch. on meteors, 1949, medal for astron. rsch. U. Liege, 1960, Space Flight award Am. Astronautical Soc., 1961, Disting. Fed. Civilian Svc. award, 1963; Space Pioneers medallion for contbns. to fed. space program, 1968, Pub. Svc. award for contbns. to OAO2 devel. NASA, 1969, Leonard medal Meteoritical Soc., 1970, Kepler medal AAAS, 1971, Career Svc. award Nat. Civil Svc. League, 1972, Henry medal Smithsonian Instn., 1973, Alumnus of Yr. Achievement award UCLA, 1976, Golden Plate award Am. Acad. Achievement, 1981, Gold medal Royal Aston. Soc., 1983, Bruce medal Astron. Soc. Pacific, 1986, Benjamin Franklin fellow Royal Soc. Arts, London, 1968—; depicted on postal stamp of Mauritania, 1986, St. Vincent, 1994. Fellow Am. Astron. Soc. (v.p. 1962-64, 1987 Russell lecturer), Am. Rocket Soc., Am. Geophys. Union (Fred L. Whipple yearly lectr. estab. in honor planetary div. 1990), Royal Astron. Soc. (assoc.); mem. AAAS, Nat. Acad. Scis., AIAA Astronautics (aerospace tech. panel space physics 1960-63), Astronautical Soc. Pacific, Solar Assos., Internat. Sci. Radio Union (U.S.A. . com. 1949-61), Am. Meteoritical Soc., Am. Standards Assn., Am. Acad. Arts and Scis., Am. Philos. Soc. (councillor sect. astronomy and earth scis. 1966-70), Royal Soc. Scis. Belgium (corr.), Internat. Acad. Astronautics (sci. advisory com. 1962-65), Internat. Astronautical Fedn., Am. Meteorol. Soc., Royal Astron. Soc. (assoc.), Phi Beta Kappa, Sigma Xi, Pi Mu Epsilon. Clubs: Examiner (Boston); Cosmos (Washington). Office: 60 Garden St Cambridge MA 02138-1516

WHIPPLE, HARRY M., newspaper publishing executive; b. Tulsa, June 30, 1947; m. Mary Jane Whipple; children: Garth, Erin. Student, Ind. U., 1965-68; U. Evansville, 1965-68, Ark Poly. Coll., 1965-68. Gen. mgr. Mt. Vernon (Ind.) Pub. Co., 1972-75; asst. pub. Pioneer Newspapers (formerly Scripps League Newspapers), Monongahela, Pa., 1975-77; advt. dir. Rockford (Ill.) Morning Star and Register Republic, 1977-81; pres., pub. Valley News Dispatch, The Herald, North Hills News Record, Tarentum, Pa., 1981-84; v.p., regional mgr. Midwest Gannett Media Sales/Gannett Nat. Sales, Chgo., 1984-87; pres. TNI Ptnrs., Tucson, 1987-92; pres., pub. The Cincinnati Enquirer, 1992—. Bd. trustees Cin. Symphony Orch., Jewish Hosp. Cin., Zool. Soc. Cin., NCCJ, Greater Cin. Region; co-chair, steering com. Nat. Underground R.R. Freedom Ctr.; bd. dirs. Greater Cin. Ctr. for Econ. Edn., Downtown Cin., Inc. Mem. Greater Cin. C. of C. (bd. trustees). Office: Cincinnati Enquirer 312 Elm St Cincinnati OH 45202-2739

WHIPPLE, JUDITH ROY, book editor; b. N.Y.C., May 14, 1935; d. Edwin Paul and Elizabeth (Levis) Roy; m. William Whipple, Oct. 26, 1963. AB, Mount Holyoke Coll., 1957. Head libr. Am. Sch. Lima (Peru), S.A., 1957-59; asst. editor children's books G.P. Putnam's Sons, N.Y.C., 1959-62; assoc. editor W.W. Norton & Co., Inc., N.Y.C., 1962-68; editor Four Winds Press, 1968-75; editor-in-chief Scholastic Gen. Book Divsn., 1975-77; pub. Four Winds Press subs. Scholastic Inc., N.Y.C., 1977-82; pub., v.p. Macmillan Pub. Co., N.Y.C., 1982-89, exec. editor, 1989-94; editl. dir. Benchmark Books and Cavendish Children's Books, Tarrytown, N.Y., 1994—. Mem. PEN, Children's Book Coun. (pres. 1977, bd. dirs. 1970-79), Women's Nat. Book Assn., Soc. Children's Book Writers and Illustrators. Avocations: gardening, swimming, piano, travel. Office: Marshall Cavendish Corp 99 White Plains Rd Tarrytown NY 10591-5502

WHIPPLE, KENNETH, automotive company executive; b. 1934. BS, MIT, 1958. With Ford Motor Co., Dearborn, Mich., 1958—, systems mgr. Ford Credit, 1966-69, mgr. mgmt. svcs. dept. fin. staff, 1969-71, systems analysis mgr. fin. staff, 1971-74, asst. contr. internat. fin. staff, 1974-75, v.p. fin. Ford Credit, 1975-77, exec. v.p. Ford Credit, 1977-80, pres. Ford Credit, 1980-84, v.p. corp. strategy, 1984-86; v.p. chmn. Ford of Europe, 1986-88; exec. v.p., pres. Ford Fin. Svcs. Group, Dearborn, 1988—. Office: Ford Motor Co The American Rd Dearborn MI 48121-1899*

WHIPPS, EDWARD FRANKLIN, lawyer; b. Columbus, Ohio, Dec. 17, 1936; s. Rusk Henry and Agnes Lucille (Green) W.; children: Edward Scott, Rusk Huot, Sylvia Louise, Rudyard Christian. B.A., Ohio Wesleyan U., 1958; J.D., Ohio State U., 1961. Bar: Ohio 1961, U.S. Dist. Ct. (so. dist.) Ohio 1962, U.S. Dist. Ct. (no. dist.) Ohio 1964, U.S. Ct. Claims 1963, U.S. Supreme Ct. 1963, Miss. 1965, U.S. Ct. Appeals (6th cir.) 1980. Assoc. George, Greek, King & McMahon, Columbus, 1961-66; ptnr. George, Greek, King, McMahon & McConnaughey, Columbus, 1966-79, McConnaughey, Stradley, Mone & Moul, Columbus, 1979-81, Thompson, Hine & Flory, Columbus, 1981-93; prin. Edward F. Whipps & Assocs., Columbus, 1993-94; ptnr. Whipps & Wistner, Columbus, 1995—; founder, trustee Creative Living, Inc., 1969—; trustee, v.p. Unverferth House, Inc., 1989. Host: TV programs Upper Arlington Plain Talk, 1979-82; TV program Briding Disability, 1981-82, Lawyers on Call, 1982—, U.A. Today, 1982-86, The Ohio Wesleyan Experience, 1984—. Mem. Ohio Bd. Psychology, 1992—; mem. Upper Arlington (Ohio) Bd. Edn., 1971-80, pres., 1978-79; mem. bd. alumni dirs. Ohio Wesleyan U., 1975-79; trustee Walden Ravines Assn., 1992—, pres. 1993—. Mem. ABA, Columbus Bar Assn., Ohio State Bar Assn., Assn. Trial Lawyers Am., Ohio Acad. Trial Lawyers, Franklin County Trial Lawyers Assn., Am. Judicature Soc., Columbus Bar Found., Ohio Bd. Psychology, Columbus C. of C., Upper Arlington Area C. of C. (trustee 1978—), Lawyers Club, Barrister Club, Columbus Athletic Club, Columbus Touchdown Club, Downtown Quarterback Club, Ohio State U. Faculty (Columbus) Club, Ohio State U. Golf Club, Highlands Country Club, Delta Tau Delta (nat. v.p. 1976-78). Republican. Home: 3111 Walden Ravines Columbus OH 43221-4640 Office: Whipps & Wistner 500 S Front St Columbus OH 43215-7619 *Personal philosophy: Commitment to personal growth, the development of interpersonal communication skills, the rule of law and a firm belief in the unique value of every individual are the primary factors seen in my approach to life.*

WHISENAND, JAMES DUDLEY, lawyer; b. Iowa City, Aug. 14, 1947; s. J.D. and Barbara Pauline (Huxford) W. BA in Mktg. cum laude, U. No. Iowa, 1970; MBA, Fla. State U., 1973, JD cum laude, 1973. Bar: Fla. 1973, U.S. Dist. Ct. (no., mid. and so. dists.) Fla. 1974, U.S. Tax Ct. 1974, U.S. Ct. Appeals (11th cir.) 1975, U.S. Supreme Ct. 1976. Law clk. U.S. Dept. Justice, Fla., 1972, Office of Fla. Atty. Gen., 1971-73; asst. atty. gen. Tax Div., 1973-74; head adminstr. law div., 1974-75; cabinet counsel Atty. Gen. Office, Fla., 1975; dep. atty. gen. Fla., 1975-78; ptnr. Sage, Gray, Todd & Sims, N.Y.C., Miami, 1979-81; of counsel Paul & Thomson, Miami, 1981-82; founding ptnr. Hornsby & Whisenand, Miami, 1982-90, Whisenand & Assocs., P.A., Miami, 1990-91; ptnr. Patton Boggs & Blow, Washington and Miami, 1991-93; founding ptnr. Whisenand & Turner, P.A., Miami, Fla., 1993—; pres. Americas Conf. Corp., 1994—. Publ.: The Cuba Report, 1992—; contbr. articles to profl. jours. Bd. advisors New World Sch. Arts, Miami, 1988; bd. dirs. Fla. State U. Sch. Law Alumni Assn., 1988-89; bd. trustees U. No. Iowa Found., 1993—; mem. bd. advisors Ctrl. European (Euromoney). Mem. Fla. Bar Assn., D.C. Bar Assn., Inter-Am. Bar Assn., Internat. Bar Assn., Greater Miami C. of C., European Forum. Avocations: polo, equestrian events, skiing, bicycling. Office: Whisenand & Turner PA 501 Brickell Key Dr Ste 200 Miami FL 33131-2608

WHISENHUNT, DONALD WAYNE, history educator; b. Meadow, Tex., May 16, 1938; s. William Alexander Whisenhunt and Beulah (Johnson) King; m. Betsy Ann Baker, Aug. 27, 1960; children: Donald Wayne Jr., William Benton. BA, McMurry Coll., 1960; MA, Tex. Tech U., 1962, PhD, 1966. Tchr. Elida (N.Mex.) High Sch., 1961-63; from asst. to assoc. prof. history Murray (Ky.) State U., 1966-69; assoc. prof., chmn. dept. Thiel Coll., Greenville, Pa., 1969-73; Dean Sch. Liberal Arts and Scis., Ea. N.Mex. U., Portales, 1973-77; v.p. acad. affairs U. Tex., Tyler, 1977-83; v.p., provost Wayne (Nebr.) State Coll., 1983-91, interim pres., 1985; prof. history, chmn. dept. Western Wash. U., Bellingham, 1991—; Fulbright lectr. Peoples Republic of China, 1995. Author: Environment and American Experience, 1974, Depression in the Southwest, 1979, Chronological History of Texas, Vol. 1, 1982, Vol.2, 1987, Texas: Sesquicentennial Celebration, 1984; editor: Encyclopedia USA, 1988—. Democrat. Methodist. Office: Western Wash U Dept History Bellingham WA 98225

WHISLER, JAMES STEVEN, lawyer, mining and manufacturing executive; b. Centerville, Iowa, Nov. 23, 1954; s. James Thomas and Betty Lou (Clark) W.; m. Ardyce Dawn Christensen, Jan. 20, 1979; children: James Kyle, Kristen Elyse. BS, U. Colo., Boulder, 1975; JD, U. Denver, 1978; MS, Colo. Sch. Mines, Golden, 1984. Bar: Colo. 1978; CPA, Ariz. Assoc. gen. counsel, sec. Western Nuclear, Inc., Denver, 1979-81; exploration counsel Phelps Dodge Corp., N.Y.C., 1981-85; legal and adminstrv. mgr. Phelps Dodge Corp., Phoenix, 1985-87, v.p., gen. counsel, 1987-88, sr. v.p., gen. counsel, 1988-91; pres. Phelps Dodge Mining Co., Phoenix, 1991—; bd. dirs. Phelps Dodge Corp., Unocal Corp., Burlington No. Santa Fe Corp., So. Peru Copper Corp. Trustee Heard Mus., Phoenix, 1989-94, Rocky Mountain Mineral Law Found., 1989-92; mem. Dean's Coun. of 100, Ariz. State U., 1992; mem. nat. bd. advs. Coll. Bus. and Pub. Adminstrn., U. Ariz., 1992—; bd. dirs. Met. Phoenix YMCA, 1989-92, Copper Bowl Found., Tucson, 1990-91, Ariz. Town Hall, 1991—, We. Rregional Coun., 1991—, Mont. Tech. Found., 1996—. Mem. AICPA, AIME, Soc. Mining Engrs., Colo. Bar Assn., Phoenix Thunderbirds, Phoenix Country Club. Office: Phelps Dodge Corp 2600 N Central Ave Phoenix AZ 85004-3050

WHISNAND, REX JAMES, housing association executive; b. Van Nuys, Calif., Jan. 2, 1948; s. Harold Theodore and Laura Fay (Brigham) Whisnand; m. Cathy Ladeane Bennett, Apr. 1, 1978; 1 child, Bryce James. BS in Agrl. Bus. Mgmt., Calif. Poly State U., San Luis Obispo, 1970; BSBA, Calif. State U., Sacramento, 1976; MPA in Housing Adminstrn., U. San Francisco, 1985; grad., U.S. Naval Submarine Sch., New London, Conn., 1972; C. of C. of U.S. grad. Inst. Orgn. Mgmt., Stanford U., 1994. Generalist W & W Hardware Store, Orcutt, Calif., 1964-70; state park ranger Calif. Dept. Parks and Recreation, Lompoc and Sacramento, 1969-75; exec. asst. Constrn. Industry Legis. Coun., Sacramento, 1974-75; dir. assn. svcs. Bldg. Industry Assn. Superior Calif., Sacramento, 1976-79; exec. v.p. West Bay divsn. Bldg. Industry Assn. No. Calif., Redwood City, 1980-84; exec. v.p. Bldg. Industry Assn., Tacoma/Pierce County, 1984-86; supr. Lumberjack Store, Lodi, Calif., 1988-90; exec. v.p. Rental Housing Owners Assn. of So. Alameda County, Hayward, Calif., 1990—; mem. com. Calif. Bldg. Industry Assn., Sacramento, 1976-84; mem. exec. officers coun., local govt. com., Calif. Apt. Assn., 1991—; mem. Alameda County Housing Rsch. Adv. Bd., Hayward, Calif., 1990-93; bd. dirs. Pacific Bay Fed. Credit Union, 1992—, Calif. Credit Union League, 1993—. Editor Pierce County Builder, 1984-86 (Assn. Achievement awards Nat. Assn. Home Builders 1984, 85). Active 20-30 Club Internat. # 1, Sacramento, 1977-80; mem. South Sacramento Area Comty. Planning Adv. Bd., 1978-79; grad. Pleasanton Leadership, 1995; chmn. Coastside Coalition for Safe Hwys., Half Moon Bay, 1983-84; bd. congregations Family Emergency Shelter Coalition, Hayward, 1995—; mem. Pleasanton Gen. Plan Econ./Fiscal Growth Com., 1994, Bay Area Indsl. Edn. Coun., 1995-96, Hayward Coalition for Youth, 1995-96; officer Half Moon Bay C. of C., 1982-84; cert. basketball coach Nat. Youth Sports Assn., 1994—. With USNR, 1970-76, U.S. Army N.G., 1990-92. Named Outstanding Young Man. in Am., Jr. C. of C., Foster City, Calif., 1983. Mem. Internat. Assn. Bus. Communicators (pres. Sacramento chpt. 1979, pres. Peninsula chpt. 1981), Am. Soc. Assn. Execs. (cert.), No. Calif. Soc. Assn. Execs. (bd. dirs. 1994—, com. chmn. 1993—), Pleasanton C. of C. (econ. devel. com. 1990—), Wash. State Home Builders Assn. (pres. exec. officers coun. 1985), Western Conf. Assn. Execs. (mem. com. 1995—), Hayward C. of C. (govt. rels. coun. 1990—), Calif. Vocat. Indsl. Clubs Am. (bd. dirs. 1977-80), Nat. Apt. Assn., Alpha Gamma Rho (charter, com. chair 1969—). Episcopalian. Avocations: YMCA Indian guides, little league baseball coach, dog training, genealogy. Home: 5435 Black Ave # 3 Pleasanton CA 94566 Office: Rental Housing Owners Assn of So Alameda County 1264 A St Hayward CA 94541-2926

WHISNANT, JACK PAGE, neurologist; b. Little Rock, Oct. 26, 1924; s. John Clifton and Zula I. (Page) W.; m. Patricia Anne Rimmey, May 12, 1944; children: Elizabeth Anne, John David, James Michael. B.S., U. Ark., 1948, M.D., 1951; M.S., U. Minn., 1955. Intern Balt. City Hosp., 1951-52; resident in medicine and neurology Mayo Grad. Sch. Medicine, Rochester, Minn., 1952-55; instr. neurology Mayo Grad. Sch. Medicine, 1956-60, asst. prof., 1960-64, asso. prof., 1964-69, prof., 1969—; Meyer prof. neurosci. Mayo Med. Sch.; chmn. dept. neurology Mayo Clinic, Mayo Med. Sch., Mayo Grad. Sch. Medicine, 1971-81; chmn. dept. health scis. research Mayo Clinic and Mayo Med. Sch., 1987-93; cons. neurology Mayo Clinic, 1955—, head sect. neurology, 1963-71; dir. Mayo Cerebrovascular Clin. Research Center, 1975—. Contbr. articles on neurology and cerebrovascular disease to med. jours. Trustee YMCA, Rochester. With USAAF, 1942-45. Decorated Air medal. NIH grantee, 1958, 75—. Fellow Am. Heart Assn., Am. Acad. Neurology (pres. 1993-95); mem. Am. Neurol. Assn. (pres. 1981-82), Am. Bd. Psychiatry and Neurology (bd. dirs. 1983-90, pres. 1989), Zumbro Valley Med. Soc., Minn. Med. Assn., Minn. Soc. Neurol. Scis., Ctrl. Soc. Neurol. Rsch., Nat. Adv. Neurol. Disease and Stroke Coun., Alumni Assn. Mayo Found. Presbyterian. Home: 1005 7th Ave NE Rochester MN 55906-7074 Office: Mayo Found Dept Health Scis Rsch 201 1st St SW Rochester MN 55902-3001

WHISNER, PEGGY JANELLE, administrator; b. Lovington, N.Mex., Aug. 28, 1966; d. Floyd Pleasant and Imogene (Gage) Green; m. Gregory David Hoskins, Aug. 13, 1988 (div. Apr. 1992); m. Charles Whisner, Jan. 27, 1995. Student, Wayland Bapt. U., 1984-86; BBA, Eastern N.Mex. U., 1988. Bookkeeper Gen. Welding Supply, Inc., Lovington, N.Mex., 1985, Manpower, Hobbs, N.Mex., 1987; cashier, bookkeeper Alco, Portales, N.Mex., 1989; bookkeeper Parson's Inc., Tatum, N.Mex., 1989-90; sales rep. Dunlaps, Hobbs, 1990-93; acctg. Lea County Treas., Lovington, 1993—. Mem. Nat. Trust Hist. Preservation, 1993—. Mem. NAFE, Delta Mu Delta. Republican. Baptist. Avocations: piano, crosstitch, collecting coins, travel.

WHISTLER, ROY LESTER, chemist, educator, industrialist; b. Morgantown, W.Va., Mar. 31, 1912; s. Park H. and Cloe (Martin) W.; m. Leila Anna Barbara Kaufman, Sept. 6, 1935; 1 child, William Harris. B.S., Heidelberg Coll., 1934, D.Sc. (hon.), 1957; M.S., Ohio State U., 1935; Ph.D., Iowa State U., 1938; D.Litt. (hon.), St. Thomas Inst., 1982; D.Agr., Purdue U., 1985. Instr. chemistry Iowa State U., 1935-38; research fellow Bur. Standards, 1938-40; sect. leader dept. agr. No. Regional Rsch. Lab., 1940-46; prof. biochemistry Purdue U., 1946-76, Hillenbrand distinguished prof., asst. dept. head, 1974-82; Hillenbrand disting. prof. emeritus Purdue U., Lafayette, Ind., 1982—; chmn. Inst. Agrl. Utilization Research, 1961-75; pres. Lafayette Applied Chemistry Inc., 1980—; vis. lectr. U. Witwatersrand, 1961, 65, 77, 85, Czechoslovakia and Hungary, 1968, 85, Japan, 1969, Taiwan, 1970, Argentina, 1971, New Zealand, Australia, 1967, 74, Acad. Sci., France, 1975, Vladivostock Acad. Sci., 1976, Brazil, 1977, Egypt, 1979; lectr. Bradley Polytech. Inst., 1941-42, People's Republic of China, 1985; adviser Whistler Ctr. for Carbohydrate Chemistry; indsl. cons. dir. Pfanstiehl Lab., Inc., Greenwich Pharm. Inc., FruteTec; mem. NRC subcom. nomenclature biochemistry; pres. Lafayette (Ind.) Applied Chemistry; bd. dirs. Banproco Corp. Author: Polysaccharide Chemistry, 1953, Industrial Gums, 1959, 2d rev. edit., 1976, 3d rev. edit., 1992; rev. edit.; Methods of Carbohydrate Chemistry, series, 1962—; co-author: Guar, 1979; editor: Starch-Chemistry and Technology, 2 vols., 1965, 67, rev. edit., 1984; editorial bd. Jour. Carbohydrate Research, 1960-91, Starchs Chemistry and Technology, 1985; bd. advisors: Advances in Carbohydrate Chemistry, 1950—, Organic Preparations and Procedures Internat., 1970—, Jour. Carbo-Nucleosides-Nucleotides, 1973-77, Starke, Starch, 1979—; contbr. 500 articles to profl. jours. Recipient Sigma Xi rsch. award Purdue U., 1953, Medal of Merit, Japanese Starch Tech. Soc., 1967, German Saare medal, 1974, Thomas Burr Osborne award Am. Assn. Cereal Chemists, 1974, Sterling Henricks award USDA, 1991, 93, Nicholas Appert award Inst. Food Technologists, 1994; Roy L. Whistler internat. award in carbohydrates named in his hon.; Fred W. Tanner lectr., Chgo., 1994. Fellow AAAS, Am. Chem. Soc. (chmn. Purdue sect. 1949-50, carbohydrate divsn. 1951, cellular divsn. 1962, nat. councilor 1953-87, bd. dirs. 5th dist. 1955-58, chmn. com. edn. and students, chmn. sub-com. polysaccharide nomenclature, symposium dedicated in his honor 1979, hon. fellow award cellulose divsn. 1983, Hudson award 1960, Anselme Payen award 1967, Carl Lucas Alsburg award 1970, Spencer award 1970, 75, Disting. Svc. award 1983, named one of 10 outstanding chemists Chgo. sect. 1948), Am. Inst. Chemists (pres. 1982-83, Gold medal 1992), Am. Assn. Cereal Chemists (pres. 1978), Internat. Carbohydrate Union (pres. 1972-74); mem. Lafayette Applied Chemistry (pres. 1970—), Argentine Chem. Soc. (life), Rotary (pres. 1966), Sigma Xi (pres. Purdue sect. 1957-59, nat. exec. com. 1958-62, hon. life mem. 1983—), Phi Lambda Upsilon, Rotary (pres. 1966).

WHISTON, RICHARD MICHAEL, lawyer; b. N.Y.C., Mar. 1, 1944; s. Michael W. and Dorothy M. (Kussman) W. BS in Econs. cum laude, U. Pa., 1964; JD, Harvard U., 1968. Bar: N.Y. 1968, Conn. 1978, Fla. 1979, D.C. 1992, U.S. Dist. Ct. (so. and ea. dists.) N.Y. 1977, U.S. Dist. Ct. Conn. 1978, U.S. Ct. Claims 1979, U.S. Tax Ct. 1977, U.S. Ct. Appeals (5th cir.) 1979, U.S. Supreme Ct. 1977. Assoc. Kelley, Drye, Warren, N.Y.C., 1970-77; dep. div. counsel Hamilton Standard, Windsor Locks, Conn., 1977-78; asst. gen. counsel United Techs. Corp., Hartford, Conn., 1980-82; div. counsel Latin Am. ops. Otis Elevator Co., West Palm Beach, Fla., 1978-80; div. counsel European ops. Otis Elevator Co., Paris, 1982-83; v.p. counsel No. Am. ops. Otis Elevator Co., Farmington, Conn., 1983-85, v.p., gen. counsel, sec., 1985-90; v.p., gen. counsel, sec. Carrier World Hdqtrs., Farmington, 1990-92; sr. v.p., gen. counsel United Tschs. Pratt & Whitney, East Hartford, Conn., 1993—. Served to capt. U.S. Army, 1968-70. Mem. Alpha Beta Psi, Beta Gamma Sigma. Episcopalian. Avocations: comml. pilot. Office: Pratt & Whitney M/S 101-10 400 Main St East Hartford CT 06108-1873

WHITACRE, CAROLINE CLEMENT, immunologist, researcher; b. Cin., Nov. 4, 1949; d. Richard Soteldo and Rosalyn (Wilson) W.; m. Michael Francis Para, June 28, 1975; 1 child, Alexander. BA, Ohio State U., 1971, PhD, 1975. Postdoctoral fellow Northwestern U., Chgo., 1975-78, instr., 1978-81; asst. prof. Ohio State U., Columbus, 1981-87, assoc. prof., 1987—. Contbr. articles to profl. pubs. Bd. dirs. Nat. Multiple Sclerosis Soc. (mid. Ohio chpt.), Columbus, 1984-85. NIMH grantee, 1988-91, Nat. Insts. for Allergy and Infectious Diseases grantee, 1987—, 90-91, NIH-Nat. Insts. for Neurol. Disorders and Stroke grantee, 1991—, Nat. Multiple Sclerosis grantee, 1991—. Mem. AAAS, NIH (spl. study sect. 1987-91, neurol. disorders com. 1991—), Am. Assn. Immunologists, N.Y. Acad. Scis. Presbyterian. Achievements include discovery that experimental autoimmune encephalomyelitis can be suppressed by the oral administration of myelin basic protein due to the anergy of myelin basic protein specific T lymphocytes; research on multiple sclerosis and the animal model, experimental autoimmune encephalomyelitis, human immunodeficiency virus specific T lymphocyte responses, and effects of stress on immune function. Office: Ohio State U Dept of Researcher Graves Hall 333 W 10th Ave Columbus OH 43210-1239

WHITACRE, EDWARD E., JR., telecommunications executive; b. Ennis, Tex., Nov. 4, 1941. BS in Indsl. Engring., Tex. Tech U., 1964. With Southwestern Bell Telephone Co., 1963-85; various positions in ops. depts. Tex., Ark., Kans.; pres. Kans. div. Topeka, 1984-85; group pres. Southwestern Bell Corp., 1985-86; v.p. revenues and pub. affairs, vice-chmn., chief fin. officer Southwestern Bell Corp., St. Louis, 1986-88, pres., chief oper. officer, 1988-89, chmn., chief exec. officer, 1990—, also bd. dirs.; bd. dirs. Anheuser-Busch Cos., Inc., May Dept. Stores Co., Emerson Electric Co., Burlington No., Inc. Bd. regents Tex. Tech. U. and Health Scis., Lubbock; mem. exec. bd. nat. coun. and so. region Boy Scouts Am. Presbyterian. Office: SBC Communications Inc PO Box 2933 175 E Houston St 6th Fl San Antonio TX 78205*

WHITACRE, JOHN, apparel executive; b. 1953. Student, U. Wash. With Nordstrom Inc., 1976—; co-chmn. Nordstrom Inc., Seattle, 1995—. Office: Nordstrom Inc 1501 5th Ave Seattle WA 98101-1603*

WHITAKER, A(LBERT) DUNCAN, lawyer; b. Ft. Wayne, Ind., Jan. 3, 1932; s. Robert Lynn and Rhoda Irene (Duncan) W.; m. Adelaide B. Saccone, Aug. 13, 1955; children: Brent Robert, Alene G., Karen E. B.A., Yale U., 1954; J.D., U. Mich., 1957. Bar: Mich. 1957, U.S. Ct. Appeals D.C. 1959, U.S. Supreme Ct. 1961. Atty. antitrust div. U.S. Dept. Justice, 1957-59; assoc. Howrey & Simon, Washington, 1959-65, ptnr., 1965—; lectr. George Washington U., George Mason U. Law Sch. Contbr. articles to profl. jours. Mem. ABA, Fed. Bar Assn., D.C. Bar Assn., Order of Coif, Phi Beta Kappa. Clubs: Metropolitan. Office: Howrey & Simon 1299 Pennsylvania Ave NW Washington DC 20004-2400

WHITAKER, BRUCE EZELL, college president; b. Cleveland County, N.C., June 27, 1921; m. Esther Adams, Aug. 22, 1947; children: Barry Eugene, Garry Bruce. BA, Wake Forest U., 1944; BD, So. Bapt. Theol. Sem., 1947, ThM, 1948, PhD, 1950; postgrad., George Peabody Coll., 1952; DL, Wake Forest U., 1987. Ordained to ministry Bapt. Ch., 1945; pastor Smithfield, Ky., 1945-49; instr. sociology and philosophy Ind. U., 1947-50; prof. religion Cumberland U., Lebanon, Tenn., 1950-51, Belmont Coll., Nashville, 1951-52; prof. sociology, asst. to pres. Shorter Coll., Rome, Ga., 1952-53; assoc. pastor, minister edn. Atlanta, 1953-54; state sec., student dept. Bapt. State Conv., N.C., 1954-57; pres. Chowan Coll., Murfreesboro, N.C., 1957-89, pres. emeritus, 1989—; mem. adv. com. to Nd. Higher Edn., 1962-66; to N.C. Commn. Higher Edn. Facilities, 1964—; pres. N.C. Conf. Social Svc., 1965-67, Assn. Governing Bds., 1973-82, Assn. So. Baptist Colls. and Schs., 1967-68, Assn. Eastern N.C. Colls., 1968-69; bd. dirs. Regional Edn. Lab. for Carolinas and Va. Pres. bd. trustees N.C. Found. Church-Related Colls., 1970-74; bd. dirs., v.p. Nat. Coun. Ind. Jr. Colls., 1974-75, pres., 1975-76; mem. adv. coun. presidents Assn. Governing Bds., from 1973; mem. N.C. Bd. Mental Health, from 1966; bd. dirs. Am. Assn. Cmty. and Jr. Colls., 1976-82; pres. N.C. Assn. Colls. and Univs., 1977-78; chmn. N.C. Commn. Mental Health/Mental Retardation Sers., 1978-81; mem. N.C. Commn. on Mental Health, Developmental Disabilities, and Alcohol and Drug Svcs., 1995—. V.p. Bapt. State Conv. N.C., 1989-91. Named Tarheel of Week Raleigh News and Observer, 1962, Boss of Year N.C. Jaycees, 1972; tribute paid in Congl. Record, 1962, 89; Whitaker Libr. at Chowan Coll. named for him; Whitaker Sch. at Butner, N.C. named for him; selected one of nation's 18 most effective coll. pres. in 1985, funded study Exxon Found.; featured in We the People of North Carolina, 1989. Mem. N.C. Lit. and Hist. Assn. (pres. 1970-71), Am. Acad. Polit. and Social Scis., NEA, Am. Assn. Community and Jr. Colls. (dir. 1976-82, Leadership Recognition award 1989), Nat. Assn. Ind. Colls. and Univs. (dir. 1977-78, 81-85), Am. Assn. Higher Edn., Am. Coun. Edn. (bd. dirs. 1985-89), Internat. Platform Assn., Omicron Delta Kappa. Clubs: Capital City (Raleigh, N.C.), Capitol Club (Raleigh); Rotary (chmn. dist. student exchange com. 1969-72, Paul Harris fellow); Optimist; Beechwood Country (Ahoskie, N.C.); Harbor (Norfolk, Va.). Office: PO Drawer 40 Murfreesboro NC 27855-0040

WHITAKER, CHARLES F., journalism educator; b. Chgo., Oct. 28, 1958; s. Andrew L. and Marjorie Whitaker; m. Stephanie J. Sanders, Oct. 1, 1988; children: Joshua, Christopher. BS in Journalism, Northwestern U., 1980, MS in Journalism, 1981. Suburban edn. writer N.E. Dade County Bur., Miami (Fla.) Herald, 1981-82, staff writer, 1982-84; staff writer Louisville Times, 1984-85; assoc. editor Ebony Mag., Chgo., 1985-87, sr. assoc. editor, 1987-89, sr. editor, 1989-92; mem. adj. faculty Northwestern U. Medill Sch. Journalism, Evanston, Ill., 1990-92, asst. prof. journalism, 1992—; dir. Gertrude Johnson Williams Lit. Contest, 1989—; assoc. fellow Joint Ctr. for Polit. and Econ. Studies, Urban Policy Inst., Chgo., 1992—; advisor, faculty editor Passport Africa, 1992. Contbr. to various pubs. Bd. dirs. Chocolate Chips Theatre Co., 1987—. Recipient 1st place award for mag. writing Nat.. Assn. Edn. Writers, 1982; 1st place award for feature writing Louisville Assn. Black Communicators, 1984, for commentary or criticism, 1984. Mem. Nat. Assn. Black Journalists, Chgo. Assn. Black Journalists (faculty Exposure satellite program 1988—), Phi Beta Sigma (editor-in-chief Crescent 1989-93). Office: Northwestern U Medill Sch Journalism 1845 Sheridan Rd Evanston IL 60208-2101

WHITAKER, CLEM, JR., advertising and public relations executive; b. Sacramento, Aug. 30, 1922; s. Clem and Harriett (Reynolds) W.; 1 child, Isabella Alexandra. Student, Sacramento Jr. Coll., 1942, U. Calif.-Berkeley, 1943. Reporter, Sacramento Union, 1938-40; staff mem. Campaigns, Inc.-Whitaker & Baxter, San Francisco, 1946-50; partner Campaigns, Inc.-Whitaker & Baxter, 1950-58, pres., 1958—; partner Whitaker & Baxter Advt. Agy., San Francisco, 1950-58; pres. Whitaker & Baxter Advt. Agy., 1958—; co-pub. Calif. Feature Svc., San Francisco, 1950—; chmn. Wye Energy Group. Bd. dirs. San Francisco Opera Assn. With USAAF, 1942-46, ETO. Mem. Cercle de L'Union. Home: 2040 Broadway St San Francisco CA 94115-1500 Office: Box 334 2443 Fillmore St San Francisco CA 94115-1825

WHITAKER, EILEEN MONAGHAN, artist; b. Holyoke, Mass., Nov. 22, 1911; d. Thomas F. and Mary (Doona) Monaghan; m. Frederic Whitaker. Ed., Mass. Coll. Art, Boston. Annual exhibits in nat. and regional watercolor shows; represented in permanent collections, Charles and Emma Frye Mus., Seattle, NAD, Hispanic Soc., N.Y.C., High Mus. Art, Atlanta, U. Mass., Norfolk (Va.) Mus., Springfield (Mass.) Mus. Art, Reading (Pa.) Art Mus., Nat. Acad. Design, U. Mass., Okla. Mus. Art, St. Lawrence U., Wichita State U., Retrospective show, Founders Gallery U. San Diego, 1988, invitational one-person show Charles and Emma Frye Art Mus., 1990; included in pvt. collections; featured in cover article of American Artist mag., Mar. 1987, in article Art of Calif. mag., July 1991; invitational Am. Realism Exhbn. Cir. Gallery, San Diego, 1992; author: Eileen Monaghan Whitaker Paints San Diego, 1986. Recipient numerous major awards, including Allied Artists Am., Am. Watercolor Soc., 1st prize Providence Water Color Club, Wong award Calif. Watercolor Soc., De Young award Soc. Western Artists, 1st award Springville (Utah) Mus., Ranger Fund purchase prize, Orbrig prize NAD, Walter Biggs Meml. award, 1987; silver medal Am. Watercolor Soc., Watercolor West; fellow Huntington Hartford Found., 1964. Academician NAD; mem. Am. Watercolor Soc. (Dolphin fellow), Watercolor West (hon.), San Diego Watercolor Soc. (hon.). Home and Studio: 1579 Alta La Jolla Dr La Jolla CA 92037-7101

WHITAKER, FOREST, actor; b. Longview, Tex., July 15, 1961. Student voice, U. So. Calif. Stage appearances (London) Swan, Romeo and Juliet, Hamlet, Ring Around the Moon, Craig's Wife, Whose Life Is It Anyway?, The Greeks; other stage appearances include Patchwork Shakespeare, Beggar's Opera, Jesus Christ Superstar; TV appearances include Amazing Stories, Hill Street Blues, Cagney and Lacey, Trapper John, M.D., The Fall Guy, Different Strokes; TV movies Hands of a Stranger, 1987, Criminal Justice, 1990, Last Light, 1993; mini-series North & South, Parts I and II; films: Fast Times at Ridgemont High, 1982, Vision Quest, 1985, The Color of Money, 1986, Platoon, 1986, Stakeout, 1987, Good Morning, Vietnam, 1987, Bloodsport, 1988, Bird, 1988 (best actor Cannes Festival 1988), Johnny Handsome, 1989, Downtown, 1990, (also co-prodr.) Rage in Harlem, 1991, Article 99, 1992, Diary of a Hit Man, 1992, Consenting Adults, 1992, Body Snatchers, 1993, The Crying Game, 1993, Blown Away, 1994, Jason's Lyric, 1994, Prêt-à-Porter, 1994, Species, 1995, Smoke, 1995. office: care ICM 8942 Wilshire Blvd Beverly Hills CA 90211*

WHITAKER, GILBERT RILEY, JR., academic administrator, business economist; b. Oklahoma City, Oct. 8, 1931; s. Gilbert Riley and Melodese (Kilpatrick) W.; m. Ruth Pauline Tonn, Dec. 18, 1953; children: Kathleen, David Edward, Thomas Gilbert. BA, Rice U., 1953; postgrad., So. Methodist U., 1956-57; MS in Econs., U. Wis., Madison, 1958, Ph.D. in Econs. (Ford Found. dissertation fellow), 1961. Instr., Sch. of Bus. Northwestern U., 1960-61, asst. prof. bus. econs., Sch. of Bus., 1961-64, asso. prof., Sch. of Bus., 1964-66, research assoc. Transp. Center, Sch. of Bus., 1962-66; asso. prof. Washington U., St. Louis, 1966-67; prof. Washington U., 1967-76, adj. prof. econs., 1968-76, asso. dean Sch. Bus. Adminstrn., 1969-76; dean, prof. bus. econs. M.J. Neeley Sch. Bus., Tex. Christian U., 1976-79; dean U. Mich., 1979-90; prof. Sch. Bus. Adminstrn. U. Mich., 1979—; provost, v.p. acad. affairs U. Mich., Ann Arbor, 1990-93, provost, exec. v.p. acad. affairs, 1993-95; sr. advisor Andrew W. Mellon Found., 1996—; dir. Am. Assembly of Collegiate Schs. of Bus., 1984-91, v.p., pres.-elect, 1988-89, pres., 1989-90, dir. Washington campus, 1980-89, chmn., 1985-88; bd. dirs. Lincoln Nat. Corp., Johnson Controls, Inc., Structural Dynamics Rsch. Corp., Handleman Co.; sr. economist banking and currency com. U.S. Ho. of Reps., 1964; mem. Grad. Mgmt. Admissions Coun., 1972-75, chmn., 1974-75; bd. dirs. Washtenaw County United Way, 1990-96. Author: (with Marshall Colberg and Dascomb Forbush) books including Business Economics, 6th edit., 1981, (with Roger Chisholm) Forecasting Methods, 1971. Bd. trustees, sec.-treas. JSTOR, 1995—. With USN, 1953-56. Mem. Am. Econ. Assn., Ft. Worth Boat Club. Home: 2360 Londonderry Rd Ann Arbor MI 48104-4014 Office: U Mich Sch Bus Adminstrn Ann Arbor MI 48109

WHITAKER, JOEL, publisher; b. Indpls., May 27, 1942; s. Quincy Myers and Sigur Elizabeth (Moore) W.; m. Donna Kay, Apr. 27, 1986. BS in Bus. Journalism, Ind. U., 1964, MA in Journalism, 1971; JD, Temple U., 1979. Reporter St. Petersburg (Fla.) Times, 1964, copy editor, 1966-68; copy editor Wall St. Journal, N.Y.C., 1968-73; bus. news editor Phila. Evening and Sunday Bull., 1973-78; law clk. Fellheimer, Krakower & Eicen, Phila., 1978-79; mng. editor Bank Letter, N.Y.C., 1979-80; editor, pres. Whitaker Newsletters Inc., Fanwood, N.J., 1980—. Chmn. Fanwood Planning Bd., 1981-85; mem. Downtown Redevel. Commn., Fanwood, 1983-85; chmn. Union County (N.J.) local adv. commn. on alcoholism and drug abuse, 1994-95, mem., 1993—. Major USAR, 1964-85. Mem. Newsletter Assn. (bd. dirs. 1983-92, found. trustee 1986—, treas. 1989-93), Soc. Profl. Journalists, Nat. Press Club (Washington), Rotary (bd. dirs. Fanwood-Scotch Plains club 1996—). Republican. Roman Catholic. Office: Whitaker Newsletters Inc 313 South Ave Fanwood NJ 07023-1350

WHITAKER, JOHN KING, economics educator; b. Burnley, Lancashire, Eng., Jan. 30, 1933; came to U.S., 1967; s. Ben and Mary (King) W.; m. Sally Bell Cross, Aug. 24, 1957; children: Ann Elizabeth, Jane Claire, David John. B.A. in Econs, U. Manchester, 1956; A.M., Johns Hopkins U., 1957; Ph.D., Cambridge U., 1962. Lectr. U. Bristol, Eng., 1960-66; prof., 1966-69; vis. prof. U. Va., Charlottesville, 1967-68; prof. econs. U. Va., 1969-86, chmn. dept. econs., 1979-82, Paul Goodloe McIntire prof. of econs., 1986-92; Georgia Bankard prof. of econs. U. Va., Charlottesville, 1992—. Author: The Early Economic Writings of Alfred Marshall, 1867-1890, 2 vols., 1975, The Correspondence of Alfred Marshall, Economist, 3 vols., 1996. Mem. Am. Econ. Assn., Royal Econ. Soc., Econometric Soc., History of Econs. Soc. Home: 1615 Yorktown Dr Charlottesville VA 22901-3046 Office: U Va Dept Econs Rouss Hall Charlottesville VA 22901

WHITAKER, LINDA M., principal; b. Blue Island, Ill., Apr. 2, 1950; d. William Martin and Evelyn Cecilia (Klucznik) Locke; m. David George Whitaker, June 10, 1972. BS in Edn. magna cum laude, No. Ill. U., 1972, MS in Edn., 1975, C.A.S., 1985. Cert. adminstrv. type 75, secondary type 9, elem. type 3. Tchr. High Sch. Dist. 218, Oak Lawn, Ill.; dean Hazelgreen Sch., Sch. Dist. 126, Alsip, Ill.; elem. sch. prin., dist. curriculum coord. Worth (Ill.) Sch. Dist. 127. Contbr. articles to profl. jours. Recipient Govs. Master Tchr. award, 1984, PTA State Life Membership award, 1988. Mem. ASCD, Ill. ASCD, Nat. Asns. Elem. Sch. Prins., Ill. Prins. Assn., Nat. Coun. for Social Studies, Mortar Board, Delta Kappa Gamma (chpt. 1st v.p.), Kappa Delta Pi, Phi Alpha Theta.

WHITAKER, LINTON ANDIN, plastic surgeon; b. Navasota, Tex., Nov. 16, 1936; s. Ira Andin and Lena Rivers (Stedman) W.; m. Renata Grasmanis, Dec. 20, 1963; children: Derek Andin (dec.), Ingrid Marlena, Brandon Andrew. BA, U. Tex., 1958; MD, Tulane U., 1962. Diplomate Am. Bd. Surgery, Am. Bd. Plastic Surgery. Intern Montreal Gen. Hosp., 1962-63; resident in gen. surgery Dartmouth Affiliated Hosps., Hanover, N.H., 1965-69; resident in plastic surgery U. Pa. Hosp., Phila., 1969-71; chief plastic surgery Grad. Hosp., 1971-77; chief plastic surgery U. Pa. Hosp., Phila., 87—, attending surgeon, 1971—; chief plastic surgery Children's Hosp. Phila., 1981—, attending surgeon, 1971—; v.p. med. staff Children's Hosp., Pitts., 1992-94, pres. med. staff, 1994-95; attending physician VA Hosp., 1971—, Phila. Gen. Hosp., 1971-77; assoc. in plastic surgery Sch. Medicine, U. Pa., Phila., 1971-73, asst. prof. in plastic surgery, 1973-76, assoc. prof., 1976-81, prof., 1981—; founder, dir. Ctr. Human Appearance U. Pa. Med. Ctr., Phila., 1988—; vis. prof. Walter Reed Army Med. Ctr., Washington, 1976, Ohio State U. Med. Ctr., Columbus, 1977, Cleve. Clinic, 1980, Wilmington Med. Ctr., 1980, South Australia Craniofacial Unit, Adelaide, Australia and New Zealand, 1981, U. Hawaii, 1983, Brown U., Providence, 1983, Mass. Gen. Hosp., Boston, 1984, U. Utah, Salt Lake City, 1984, U. B.C., Vancouver, 1986, U. Pitts., 1988, U. Calif., San Diego, 1992, Ohio Valley Soc. for Plastic and Reconstructive Surgery, 1992, N.Y. U., 1994; Curts vis. prof. Dartmouth U. Med. Ctr., Hanover, N.H., 1990, Kazanjian vis. prof. Mass. Gen. Hosp., Boston, 1990; First Seiichi Ohmori Meml. lectr. All Asiatic Congress on Aesthetic Surgery, Tokyo, 1988; vis. speaker Inst. Cosmotology and Inst. Stomatology, Moskow, Russia, 1985, vis. prof. Seoul Nat. U. and vis. speaker Korean Soc. for Plastic Surgeons, 1994; lectr., speaker at univs., assns. in field. Co-author: Atlas of Cranio-maxillofacial Surgery, 1982, Aesthetic Surgery of the Facial Skelton, 1992; editor: (with P. Randall) Symposium on the Reconstruction of Jaw Deformity, Clinics in Plastic Surgery, 1987, 91; co-editor: Yearbook of Plastic and Reconstructive Surgery, 1980—; mem. editorial bd. Jour. Cutaneous Aging and Cosmetic Dermatology, 1988—; contbr. articles to profl. jours. Capt. U.S. Army Med. Corps, 1963-65. Foederer fellow Foederer Fund for Excellence, 1985-88; NIH grantee, 1976-79, 81-87, 82-85, 89, Plastic Surgery Edn. Found. Rsch. grantee, 1980-82; recipient James IV Surg. Traveller award, 1979. Fellow Am. Coll. Surgeons, Am. Soc. Ophthalmic Plastic and Reconstructive Surgery (hon.); mem. AMA (mem. coun. sci. affairs, diagnostic and therapeutic tech. assessment reference panel 1982), Am. Assn. Plastic Surgeons (mem. program com. 1988, chmn. 1989, Rsch. grantee 1984-85), Am. Surg. Assn., Am. Alpine Workshop in Plastic Surgery (founding mem.), Am. Cleft Palate Assn. (chmn. com. classification craniofacial anomalies 1976-80, mem. program com. for 1978 mtg. 1977, mem. long-range planning com. 1980, mem. coun. 1981-84, chmn. internat. rels. com. 1981-83), Am. Cleft Palate Ednl. Found. (bd. dirs. 1975-84, chmn. rsch. com. 1975-78, chmn. instrl. courses 1980-81), Am. Soc. Aesthetic Plastic Surgery, Am. Soc. Craniofacial Surgery (mem. coun. 1992—), Am. Soc. Maxillofacial Surgeons, Am. Soc. Plastic and Reconstructive Surgeons (mem. pub. rels com. 1974-76, mem. plastic surgery speakers bur. 1977—), Am. Soc. Plastic and Reconstructive Surgeons Ednl. Found. (chmn. ednl. assessment com., maxillofacial truama and craniofacial anomalies 1975-78, mem. clin. symposia com. 1978-82, chmn. clin. symposia com. 1981-82), Internat. Cleft Palate & Related Craniofacial Anomalies Soc. (mem. program com. 1981, 89), Internat. Soc. Aesthetic Surgery, Internat. Soc. Craniofacial Surgeons (founding mem., organizer, mem. exec. com. 1987—, sec and treas. 1993-95, pres. 1995—), Phila. Med. Soc., Phila. Acad. Surgery, Coll. Physicians Phila., Assn. Acad. Suastern Soc. Plastic Surgeons N.Y. (chmn. program com. 1987, mem. programcom. 1988), Plastic Surgery Rsch. Coun., John Morgan Soc., Robert H. Ivy Soc., The Columbian Soc. Plastic, Maxillofacial and Hand Surgery (hon.), Academia Medica Lombarda (Italy, hon.). Sociedad Jamie Planas de Cirugia Plastica (Spain, hon.), Mt. Kenya Safari Club (hon.), Soc. Former Residents and Assocs. Plastic Surgery (hon.), Phila. Club, Merion Cricket Club. Avocations: mountaineering, skiing, wines. Office: U Pa Med Ctr 10 Penn Tower 3400 Spruce St Philadelphia PA 19104

WHITAKER, MARK THEIS, magazine editor; b. Lower Merion, Pa., Sept. 7, 1957; s. Cleophus Sylvester and Jeanne (Theis) W.; m. Alexis Lynn Gelber, May 5, 1985; children: Rachel Eva, Matthew Edward. BA summa cum laude, Harvard U., 1979; postgrad., Oxford (Eng.) U., 1979-81. Assoc. editor Newsweek mag., N.Y.C., 1981-83, gen. editor, 1983, sr. writer, 1984-86, sr. editor, bus. editor, 1987-91, asst. mng. editor, 1991-95, mng. editor, 1996—. Marshall scholar Brit. Marshall Fund, Oxford U., 1979-81. Mem. Am. Soc. Mag. Editors, Coun. on Fgn. Rels., Phi Beta Kappa. Office: Newsweek 251 W 57th St New York NY 10019-1894

WHITAKER, PERNELL (SWEET PEA WHITAKER), professional boxer. Olympic Gold Medalist, boxing, lightweight divsn. L.A., 1984; lightweight champion Internat. Boxing Fedn., 1989; jr. lightweight champion World Boxing Coun.; lightweight champion World Boxing Assn., 1990; welterweight champion World Boxing Coun., 1993—; middleweight champion World Boxing Assn., 1995. Recipient Gold medal boxing lightweight divsn. Olympics, 1984; named pound for pound best boxer in the world Ring Mag., 1995, winner record 6 world championship titles in 4 weight classes, 1995. Office: World Boxing Coun, Genova 33 Colonia Juarez, Cuauhtemoc Mexico City Mexico*

WHITAKER, SUSANNE KANIS, veterinary medical librarian; b. Clinton, Mass., Sept. 10, 1947; d. Harry and Elizabeth P. (Cantwell) Kanis; m. Daniel Brown Whitaker, Jan. 1, 1977. A.B. in Biology, Clark U., 1969; M.S. in Library Sci., Case Western Res. U., 1970. Regional reference librarian Yale Med. Library, New Haven, 1970-72; med. librarian Hartford Hosp., Conn., 1972-77; asst. librarian Cornell U., Ithaca, N.Y., 1977-78; vet. med. librarian Coll. Vet. Medicine, Cornell U., 1978—; sec. SUNY Council Head Librarians, 1981-83. Mem. Med. Libr. Assn. (sec.-treas. vet. med. librs. sect. 1983-84, chmn. 1984-85), Med. Libr. Assn. (upstate N.Y. and Ont. chpt.), Acad. Health Info. Profls. Home: 23 Wedgewood Dr Ithaca NY 14850 Office: Cornell U Coll Vet Medicine Flower-Sprecher Libr Ithaca NY 14853-6401

WHITAKER, THOMAS PATRICK, lawyer; b. Washington, Sept. 22, 1944; s. Thomas J. and Mary K. (Finn) W.; m. Donna Mae Brenish, Feb. 16, 1974; children: Laura, Kevin. BA, George Washington U., 1966, MPA, 1973, JD, 1979; postgrad., Naval War Coll., 1984. Bar: Va. 1979. Staff asst. Adminstrn. Office of U.S. Cts., Washington, 1972-73, analyst, 1975-77; cons. Planning Research Corp., McLean, Va., 1973-75; mgmt. analyst CAB, Washington, 1977-82; program analyst Social Security Adminstrn., Falls Church, Va., 1982—. Served to lt. (j.g.) USNR, 1966-71, Vietnam, capt. with Res. 1983—. Mem. ABA, Am. Soc. Pub. Adminstrn. (sect. chmn. 1974-76), U.S. Naval Inst., Naval Res. Assn., Res. Officers Assn. Home: 9817 Days Farm Dr Vienna VA 22182-7306

WHITAKER, THOMAS RUSSELL, English literature educator; b. Marquette, Mich., Aug. 7, 1925; s. Joe Russell and Sarah Genevieve (Houk) W.; m. Dorothy Vera Barnes, June 17, 1950; children: Thomas O'Hara, Sarah Mae, Mary Beth, Gwendolyn Anne. BA summa cum laude, Oberlin Coll., 1949; MA, Yale U., 1950, PhD, 1953. Instr. English Oberlin (Ohio) Coll., 1952-55, asst. prof., 1955-59, assoc. prof., 1959-63, prof., 1963-64; tchr. lit. Goddard Coll., Plainfield, Vt., 1964-66; prof. English U. Iowa, Iowa City, 1966-75; prof. English Yale U., New Haven, Conn., 1975-95, prof. theater studies, 1986-95, chmn. dept. English, 1979-85, Frederick W. Hilles prof. English, 1989-95; Frederick W. Hilles prof. emeritus English, 1995—. Author: Swan and Shadow: Yeats's Dialogue with History, 1964, 2d edit. with new preface, 1989, William Carlos Williams, 1968, rev. dit., 1989, Fields of Play in Modern Drama, 1977, Tom Stoppard, 1983, augmented edit., 1984; editor: Twentieth Century Interpretations of the Playboy of the Western World, 1969, Teaching in New Haven: The Common Challenge, 1991; editor Iowa Rev., 1974-77; chmn. editorial bd. On Common Ground, 1993—. Served with C.E. U.S. Army, 1944-46. Recipient Harbison award for gifted teaching Danforth Found., 1972; Am. Council Learned Socs. fellow, 1969-70; NEH-Huntington fellow, 1981. Mem. MLA. Home: 882 Moose Hill Rd Guilford CT 06437-2303

WHITAKER, VON BEST, nursing educator; b. New Bern, N.C.; d. Cleveland W. and Lillie (Bryant) Best; m. Roy Whitaker Jr., Aug. 9, 1981; 1 child, Roy Whitaker III. BS, Columbia Union Coll., 1972; MS, U. Md., 1974; MA, U. N.C., 1980, PhD, 1983. Lectr. U. N.C., Chapel Hill, 1981-82; asst. prof. U. Mo., Columbia, Mo., 1982-85; asst. prof. grad. sch. Boston Coll., Newton, Mass., 1985-86; asst. prof. U. Tex. Health Sci. Ctr., San Antonio, 1986-94; assoc. prof. Ga. So. U., Statesboro, 1994—; mem. cataract guideline panel Agy. for Health Care Policy Rsch., 1990-93; rsch. coord. glaucoma svc. Georgia Eye Inst., Savannah. Contbr. articles to profl. jours., chpts. to textbooks; presenter in field. Vol. to prevent blindness. Bush fellowship, 1979-81; recipient Cert. of Appreciation, Prevent Blindness South Tex., 1988, 89. Mem. ANA (cert. community health nurse), APHA, Am. Soc. Ophthalmic Nursing (chair rsch. com.), Assn. Black Faculty in Higher Edn., Nat. Black Nurses Assn., Sigma Theta Tau. Home: 1 Chelmsford Ln Savannah GA 31411

WHITBREAD, THOMAS BACON, English educator, author; b. Bronxville, N.Y., Aug. 22, 1931; s. Thomas Francis and Caroline Nancy (Bacon) W. B.A., Amherst Coll., 1952; A.M., Harvard U., 1953, Ph.D., 1959. Instr. English, U. Tex. at Austin, 1959-62, asst. prof., 1962-65, asso. prof., 1965-71, prof., 1971—; Vis. asso. prof. Rice U., 1969-70; mem. lit. adv. panel Tex. Commn. on Arts and Humanities, 1972-76. Author (poetry): Four Infinitives, 1964, Whomp and Moonshiver, 1982; contbg. author: Prize Stories, 1962, The O. Henry Awards, 1962; editor: Seven Contemporary Authors, 1966. Recipient third Aga Khan prize for fiction Paris Rev., 1960, Lit. Anthology Program award Nat. Endowment for Arts, 1968, Outstanding Freshman Tchr. award Phi Eta Sigma, 1972-73. Mem. MLA, AAUP, Tex. Inst. Letters (Poetry award 1965, 83), Nat., Am. amateur press assns., Phi Beta Kappa. Democrat. Home: 1014 E 38th St Austin TX 78705-1835 Office: U Tex Dept English Austin TX 78712

WHITBURN, GERALD, state agency administrator; b. Wakefield, Mich., July 12, 1944; s. Donald and Ruby E. (Nichols) W.; m. Charmaine M. Heise, May 3, 1969; children: Bree, Luke. BS, U. Wis., Oshkosh, 1966; MA, U. Wis., Madison, 1968; postgrad., Harvard U., 1988. Aide Gov. Warren P. Knowles, Wis., 1966-69; personal asst. USN sec. John H. Chafee, Washington, 1969-72; automoble dealer, real estate developer Merrill, Wis., 1973-80; exec. asst. to Senator Robert W. Kasten U.S. Senate, Washington, 1981-87; dep. sec. Wis. Dept. Adminstrn., Madison, 1987-89; sec. Wis. Dept. Industry, Labor and Human Rels., Madison, 1989-91, Wis. Dept. Health and Social Svcs., Madison, 1991-95; sec. exec. office of health and human svcs. Commonwealth of Mass., 1995—; Mem. U.S. Labor Sec.'s Commn. on Achieving Necessary Skills, Washington, 1990-92. Contbr. articles to newspapers. Del. Rep. Nat. Conv., 1988, 92. Recipient Disting. Alumni award U. Wis., Oshkosh, 1991. Home: 390 Main St Lynnfield MA 01940 Office: MA Exec Office Hlth & Human Svc 1 Ashburton Pl Rm 1109 Boston MA 02108

WHITBURN, MERRILL DUANE, English literature educator; b. Mpls., Apr. 29, 1938; s. George and Marie Ellen (Carlstedt) W.; m. Diane Robertson, June 15, 1960; children: Stephen, Mark, Elizabeth. AB, U. Mich., 1960, AM, 1968; PhD, U. Iowa, 1973. With Western Electric Co., N.Y.C. and Indpls., 1965-67; asst. prof. Tex. A&M U., College Station, 1973-77, assoc. prof., 1977-79; assoc. prof. English Rensselaer Poly. Inst., Troy, N.Y., 1979-83, prof., 1983-89, Louis Ellsworth Laflin prof., 1989—, chmn. dept., 1979-85, 88-95; co-owner Pride and Prejudice Books, Ballston Lake, N.Y., 1985—. Co-author: (booklet) Guide for Departments of English, 1985; contbr. articles to profl. publs. Recipient Disting. Svc. award Tex. A&M U., 1976, Disting. Teaching award, 1979, Jay R. Gould award for excellence in tchg. tech. comm. Soc. Tech. Comm., 1995; grantee Fund for the Improvement of Postsecondary Edn., 1983. Mem. MLA, Soc. for Tech. Communication, Nat. Coun. Tchrs. English (best article in tech. writing award 1981), Coun. for Programs in Tech. and Sci. Communication, Assn. Depts. English. Office: Rensselaer Poly Inst Troy NY 12180

WHITCHURCH, CHARLES AUGUSTUS, art gallery owner, humanities educator; b. Long Beach, Calif., Sept. 29, 1940; s. Charles Augustus and Frances Elizabeth (White) W.; m. Michèle Elizabeth Cartier, Aug. 17, 1968 (div. 1977); 1 child, Gialisa Elizabeth; m. Mary Susan Ornelas, Jan. 28, 1984; 1 child, Marisa Tatiana. BA in History, Santa Clara U., Irvine, 1962; MA in Comparative Lit., U. Calif., Irvine, 1970. Cert. grad. secondary teaching credential. Asst. ops. officer United Calif. Bank, Inglewood, 1965-66; tchr. English Laguna Beach (Calif.) High Sch., 1966-68; teaching assoc., fellow U. Calif., Irvine, 1968-70; prof. lit. and humanities Golden West Coll., Huntington Beach, Calif., 1971—; owner, dir. Charles Whitchurch Fine Arts, Huntington Beach, Calif., 1978—; cons. Pyo Gallery, Seoul, Dem. Peoples Rep. Korea, 1989-90, Gordon Gallery, Santa Monica, Calif., 1989-96; judge, spkr. in field. Author mus. catalogues; contbr. articles to profl. jours. Founding mem., mem. adv. coun. Modern Mus. Art, Santa Ana, Calif., 1987-92. NEA grantee; named One of Outstanding Young Men Am., 1977. Mem. Nat. Coun. Tchrs. English, Art Dealers Assn. of Calif. (bd. dirs. 1988—, sec. 1988-90, pres. 1990-92), Huntington Beach Art Assn. (founding mem. 1990), Robert Gumbiner Found. for the Arts (bd. dirs. 1994-96), The Libra Group (pres. 1994—), Santa Clara Alumni Assn., Alpha Sigma Nu, Phi Sigma Tau. Avocations: swimming, weight tng., writing, baseball coaching, reading.

WHITCOMB, CARL ERVIN, horticulturist, researcher; b. Independence, Kans., Oct. 26, 1939; s. Albion Carlyle and Marie V. (Burck) W.; m. LaJean C. Carpenter, June 2, 1963; children: Andrew Carl, Benjamin Dwight. BS, Kans. State U., Manhattan, 1964; MS, Iowa State U., 1966, PhD, 1969. Asst. prof. horticulture U. Fla., Gainesville, 1967-72; prof. horticulture Okla. State U., Stillwater, 1972-85; pres. Lacebark Inc, Stillwater, 1985—; cons. Sierra Chem. Co., Milpitas, Calif., 1987-90. Author: Know It and Grow It, 1975, rev., 1978, 80, 85, 95, Plant Production in Containers, 1984, rev., 1990, Establishment and Maintenance of Landscape Plants, 1989, Production of Landscape Plants, 1991. Recipient Chadwick award Am. Assn. Nurserymen, 1983, Wight award So. Nurserymens Assn., 1986. Fellow Internat. Plant Propagators Soc.; mem. Am. Soc. Hort. Sci., Am. Soc. Agronomy, Weed Sci. Soc. Am. Achievements include 12 patents on products relative to horticulture, numerous patents other countries; avocations: photography, fishing. Office: Lacebark Inc PO Box 2383 Stillwater OK 74076

WHITCOMB, JAMES HALL, geophysicist, foundation administrator; b. Sterling, Colo., Dec. 10, 1940; s. Clay Thane and Julia Melvina Whitcomb; m. Sandra Lynn McMurdo, July 13, 1965 (div. 1978); m. Teresa R. Idoni, Feb. 3, 1989; 1 child, Lisa M. Geophysics engring. degree, Colo. Sch. of Mines, 1962; MS in Oceanography, Geophysics, Oreg. State U., 1964; PhD in Geophysics, Calif. Inst. Tech., 1973. Grad. rsch. asst. dept. oceanography Oreg. State U., Corvallis, 1962-64; geophysicist ctr. astrogeology U.S. Geol. Survey, Flagstaff, Ariz., 1964-66; Fullbright-Hayes program rsch. fellow seismol. inst. U. Uppsala, Sweden, 1966-67; grad. rsch. asst. seismol. lab. Calif. Inst. Tech., Pasadena, 1967-73, sr. rsch. fellow seismol. lab., 1973-79; assoc. prof. attendant rank dept. geol. scis. U. Colo., Boulder, 1979-82, fellow Coop. Inst. Rsch. in Environ. Scis., 1979-84; v.p. technical applications and mktg. ISTAC, Inc., Pasadena, 1984-88; program dir. seismology NSF, Washington, 1989—; expert witness U.S. Ho. Reps. Com. on Sci. and Tech., 1977; mem. geodynamics rev. bd. Jet Propulsion Lab., 1980-82, com. on geodesy Nat. Acad. Scis., 1982-85; pres. Boulder Systems, Inc., Pasadena, 1987-88. Recipient Outstanding Achievement award U.S. Geol. Survey, 1964, Dir.'s award for mgmt. excellence NSF, 1995; scholar State of Colo., 1958-62, Mobil Oil Co., 1960; fellow Sweden-Am. Found., 1966. Mem. AAAS, Am. Geophysical Union, Seismol. Soc. Am., Soc. Exploration Geophysicists (scholar 1963), Tau Beta Pi, Phi Kappa Phi, Sigma Xi. Office: Nat Sci Found Geosciences 4201 Wilson Blvd Arlington VA 22230-0001

WHITCOMB, ROBERT BASSETT, journalist, editor; s. Robert B. and Alberta (Gillette) W.; m. Nancy Davison Spears, July 26, 1975; children: Lydia D., Elizabeth T. BA, Dartmouth Coll., 1970; MS, Columbia U., 1972. Cert. Am. Press Inst. Writer Boston Herald Traveler, 1970-71; editor, writer Wall Street Jour., N.Y.C., 1972-75; fin. editor Internat. Herald Tribune, Paris, 1983-87; news and bus. editor Providence Jour., 1976-82, news editor, 1987-89, editorial writer, 1989-92, editorial page editor, 1992—; mng. editor Brown World Bus. Adv., Providence, 1987-91; consulting editor, chmn. editorial adv. bd. Manisses Comm., Providence, 1987—; mem. exec. bd. Com. Fgn. Rels., Providence, 1989-92; trustee Am. Libr. Paris, 1984-87; co-moderator Truman Taylor Show, Providence, 1994—; columnist Primary Care Weekly, 1995—. Clapp-Poliak fellow Columbia U., 1972. Mem. Providence Art Club, Appalachian Mountain Club. Episcopalian. Office: Providence Jour Co 75 Fountain St Providence RI 02902-0050

WHITCRAFT, EDWARD C. R., investment banker; b. Lutherville, Md., 1914; s. Franklin Pierce and Louise Virginia (Regester) W. B.A., Yale, 1936. With Bank of New York, 1936-58, v.p. investment research, trust investment com., 1952-58; with Clark, Dodge & Co., N.Y.C., 1958-74; sr. v.p. Kidder, Peabody & Co., Inc., 1974-87; assoc. Shields & Co., 1987—. With USNR, 1944-46. Mem. N.Y. Soc. Security Analysts. Home: PO Box 486 Locust Valley NY 11560-0486 Office: 71 Broadway New York NY 10006-2601 also: 230 Birch Hill Rd Locust Valley NY 11560-1832

WHITE, ADRIAN MICHAEL STEPHEN, financial executive; b. Erith, Eng., Aug. 15, 1940; s. Malcolm Royston and Joan May (Richards) W.; m. Elaine M. Dorion, 1966; children: Malcolm, Catherine. Grad., McGill U., Montreal, 1964. Chartered accountant, Que., Ont. With Coopers & Lybrand, chartered accountants, 1962-66; acting treas. Rothesay Paper Corp., 1965; asst. treas. Genstar Ltd., 1967-71; treas. Brinco Ltd.; also Churchill Falls (Labrador) Corp., 1971-75; treas. Algoma Steel Corp., Ltd., Sault Ste. Marie, Ont., 1975-80; v.p., chief fin. officer Little Long Lac Gold Mines Ltd., Toronto, Ont., 1980-81; v.p. Bank of Montreal, Toronto, 1981-88; exec. v.p., CFO, bd. dirs. Curragh Inc., Toronto, 1988-93; also bd. dirs. Curragh Resources Group, Toronto; fin. columnist Indsl. Mgmt. mag.; Curragh Inc.; chmn. White-Maven Corp., 1993—; mng. ptnr. Hannival Group, 1993—; bd. dirs. Anvil Range Mining Corp., exec. v.p., CFP, 1994-96; bd. dirs. Doctors Hosp. Bd. dirs., chmn. Doctors Hosp. Found., 1986. Mem. Fin. Execs. Inst (past pres. Toronto chpt.), Can. Tax Found. Address: 72 Sir Williams Ln, Islington, ON Canada M9A 1V3

WHITE, ALBERT J., health products executive; b. 1933. BA, Tufts U., 1955; JD, Harvard U., 1958. Asst. sec. asst. gen. counsel Avis, Inc., 1959-63; v.p. sec. dir. Beecham, Inc., 1963—; v.p. sec., gen. counsel SmithKline

Beecham Corp., Phila., 1989—. Office: SmithKline Beecham Corp PO Box 7929 1 Franklin Plz Philadelphia PA 19101*

WHITE, ALICE ELIZABETH, physicist, researcher; b. Glen Ridge, N.J., Apr. 5, 1954; d. Alan David and Elizabeth Joyce (Jones) W.; m. Donald Paul Monroe, Oct. 13, 1990; children: Ellen Elizabeth White Monroe, Janet Clare White Monroe. BA in Physics, Middlebury (Vt.) Coll., 1976; MA in Physics, Harvard U., 1978, PhD in Physics, 1982. Postdoctoral mem. tech. staff AT&T Bell Labs., Murray Hill, N.J., 1982-84, mem. tech. staff, 1984-88, dept. head, 1988—. Contbr. over 100 articles to profl. pubs.; patentee in field. Recipient Alumni Achievement award Middlebury Coll., 1994. Fellow Am. Phys. Soc. (Maria Goeppert-Mayer award 1991); mem. Optical Soc. of Am., Materials Rsch. Soc., Phi Beta Kappa. Office: Bell Labs Lucent Technol RM 2D328 PO Box 636 New Providence NJ 07974

WHITE, ALVIN MURRAY, mathematics educator, consultant; b. N.Y.C., N.Y., June 21, 1925; s. Max and Beatrice White; m. Myra Goldstein, Dec. 4, 1946; children: Louis, Michael. BA, Columbia U., 1949; MA, UCLA, 1951; PhD, Stanford U., 1961. Acting instr. Stanford (Calif.) U., 1950-54; asst. prof. U. Santa Clara, Calif., 1954-61; prof. Harvey Mudd Coll., Claremont, Calif., 1962—; vis. scholar MIT, 1975; initiator-facilitator humanistic math. network of over 2000 mathematicians worldwide; cons. coop. learning tutorial program Claremont Unified Sch. Dist. Author: Interdisciplinary Teaching, 1981; pub., editor: Mathematics Network Jour.; contbr. articles to profl. jours. Served with USN, 1943-46, PTO. Grantee Fund for Improvement of Post-secondary Edn., Exxon Found. Mem. Am. Math. Soc., Math. Assn. Am., Nat. Coun. Tchrs. Math., Profl. Organizational Developers Network, Fedn. Am. Scientists, AAUP, Sigma Xi. Office: Harvey Mudd Coll 1250 N Dartmouth Ave Claremont CA 91711

WHITE, ALVIN SWAUGER, aerospace scientist, consultant; b. Berkeley, Calif., Dec. 9, 1918; s. Harold Hubbard and Ruth Amelia (Winkleman) W.; m. Betty Tomsett, Apr. 6, 1991; children: Stephen Alan, Cathie Lee, Leslie Ann. Student, U. Calif. at Davis, 1936-37, U. Calif. at Berkeley, 1937, 39-41; BME, U. Calif. at Berkeley, 1947. Engr., test pilot N.Am. Aviation, Inc., Los Angeles, 1954-61; chief test pilot N.Am. Aviation, Inc. (Los Angeles div.), 1961-66; mgr. flight ops., research and devel. Trans World Airlines, N.Y.C., 1967-69; aerospace cons. Tuscon, 1969—. Served with USAAF, 1941-46; with USAF, 1948-54. Decorated D.F.C., Air medal with 9 oak leaf clusters; recipient Warsaw Uprising Cross, Republic of Poland, 1944, Iven C. Kincheloe award Soc. Exptl. Test Pilots, 1965, Golden Plate award Am. Acad. Achievement, 1966, Harmon Internat. trophy, 1967, Richard Hansford Burroughs Jr. award Flight Safety Found., 1969, Aerospace Walk of Honor, 1994. Fellow Soc. Exptl. Test Pilots (pres. 1960-61); assoc. fellow AIAA (Octave Chanute award 1965); mem. Delta Upsilon. Republican. Episcopalian. Home and Office: 14441 N Sky Trail Tucson AZ 85737 *As I grow older I look more and more for honesty in my associates. Without it you don't have much. An honest person probably knows better than anyone else how much courage it takes to be honest in some situations; so when you find honesty you find courage and character as well. And since I look for that in other people, I try very hard to be honest myself; I said, I try very hard!.*

WHITE, ANN WELLS, community activist; b. Kansas City, Mo., Mar. 16, 1927; d. William Gates and Annie Loretta (Morton) Wells; m. Norman E. White, Oct. 2, 1949 (div. Dec. 1977); children: Thomas Wells, Norman Lee. BJ, U. Mo., 1948. Asst. to pres. Cities in Schs., 1978-79. Lobbyist Common Cause, Atlanta, 1972-73; vol. Jimmy Carter's Peanut Brigade, 1976, Carter/Mondale campaign, 1980; bd. dirs., vice chair Atlanta Area Svcs. for the Blind, 1973-81; Gov.'s Commn. on the Status of Women, Atlanta, 1974-76; office mgr. Carter/Mondale Transition Office, Atlanta, 1976; chair evaluation com. United Way Met. Atlanta, 1980-90; bd. dirs. Mems. Guild, The High Mus. of Art, Atlanta, 1982-83, Hillside Hosp., Atlanta, 1989-94, Ga. Forum, Atlanta, 1988-91; bd. dirs. Planned Parenthood of Atlanta area, 1975-89, pres., 1981-83; bd. dirs. Planned Parenthood Fedn. Am., N.Y.C., 1980-86, chair ann. meeting, New Orleans, 1986; legis. chair, lobbyist Ga. Women's Polit. Caucus, 1984-90; convenor, founding chair Georgians for Choice, 1989. Democrat. Presbyterian. Home: Colony House 1237 145 Fifteenth St Atlanta GA 30309

WHITE, ANNETTE JONES, early childhood education administrator; b. Albany, Ga., Aug. 29, 1939; d. Paul Lawrence and Delores Christine (Berry) Jones; m. Frank Irvin White, Nov. 13, 1964; children: Melanie Francine, Sharmian Lynell. BA, Spelman Coll., 1964; MEd, Va. State U., 1980. Tchr. Flint Ave Child Devel. Ctr., Albany, 1966-67; tchr., supr. Flintside Child Devel. Ctr., Albany, 1967-68; tchr., dir. Albany Ga. Community Sch., 1968-69; tchr. Martin Luther King Community Ctr., Atlanta, 1975-77, The Appleton Sch., Atlanta, 1977-78; sec., proofreader The Atlanta Daily World, 1978-80; tchr. kindergarten Spelman Coll., Atlanta, 1981-88, dir. nursery and kindergarten, lectr. in edn., 1988—; cons., presenter child devel. assoc. program Morris Brown Coll., Atlanta, 1991; presenter ann. child care conf. Waycross (Ga.) Coll., 1993. Contbr. articles to profl. jours. Mem. Peace Action, Washington, 1990—, Children's Def. Action Coun., Washington, 1990—; mem. Native Am. Rights Fund, Am. Indian Rights Coun. Mem. AAUW, ASCD, Acad. Am. Poets, Assn. Childhood Edn. Internat., Nat. Asn. Edn. Young Children, Nat. Black Child Devel. Inst., Ga. Assn. Young Children (cons., presenter 1992), Atlanta Hist. Soc., Mental Health Assn. Met. Atlanta, Nat. Coun. Negro Women, Atlanta Assn. Edn. Young Children, Sierra Club. Avocations: cane weaving, crocheting, cooking, drawing, reading, creative writing. Office: Spelman Coll Nursery-Kinder 350 Spelman Ln SW # 89 Atlanta GA 30314-4346

WHITE, ARTHUR CLINTON, physician; b. Williamsburg, Ky., Aug. 1, 1925; s. Herman Roya and Ethel Margaret (Goins) W.; m. Mary Katherine Pope, Dec. 27, 1949; children: Anne Litton White, Arthur Clinton Jr., Herman Roy II. BS, U. Ky., 1948; MD, Harvard U., 1952. Intern, then resident in medicine Vanderbilt U. Hosp., Nashville, 1952-57; asst. prof. medicine U. Louisville Med. Sch., 1958-63; assoc. prof. Med. Coll. Ga., 1963-67; prof. medicine, dir. infectious disease div. Ind. U. Med. Sch., 1967—; mem. drug efficacy study com. Nat. Acad. Scis., 1967. Contbr. articles med. publns. Served with USAAF, 1944-45. John and Mary R. Markle scholar, 1958-63. Mem. Infectious Disease Soc. Am., Cen. Soc. Clin. Rsch., Am. Clin. and Climatol. Assn., Med. Benevolence Found. (trustee 1986—), Meridian Hills Country Club, Skyline Club. Republican. Presbyterian. Home: 6363 Glen Coe Dr Indianapolis IN 46260-4736 Office: 1100 W Michigan St Indianapolis IN 46202-5208

WHITE, AUGUSTUS AARON, III, orthopedic surgeon; b. Memphis, June 4, 1936; s. Augustus Aaron and Vivian (Dandridge) W.; m. Anita Ottemo; children: Alissa Alexandra, Atina Andrea, Annica Akila. AB in Psychology cum laude, Brown U., 1957; MD, Stanford U., 1961; D in Med. Sci., Karolinska Inst., Sweden, 1969; Advanced Mgmt. Program, Harvard U., 1984; DHL (hon.), U. New Haven, 1987. Diplomate Nat. Bd. Examiners, Am. Bd. Orthopaedic Surgery. Intern U. Mich. Hosp., Ann Arbor, 1961-62; asst. resident in gen. surgery Presbyn. Med. Center, San Francisco, 1962-63; asst. resident in orthopaedic surgery Yale Med. Center, New Haven, 1963-65, sr. instr., resident orthopaedic surgery, 1965-66; asst. prof. orthopaedic surgery Yale Med. Sch., 1969-72, assoc. prof., 1972-76, prof., 1977-78, dir. biomech. research dept. orthopedics, 1978-89; prof. orthopedic surgery Harvard Med. Sch., 1978—; orthopedic surgeon-in-chief Beth Israel Hosp., Boston, 1978-91, chief spine surgery div., 1991-92; sr. assoc. orthopedic surgery Children's Hosp. Med. Ctr., Boston, 1979-89; assoc. in orthopedic surgery Brigham & Women's Hosp., Boston, 1980-89; cons. div. surgery Sidney Farber Cancer Inst., Boston, 1980—; rschr. biomechanics lab. Beth Israel Hosp.; chair sci. adv. bd., dir. OrthoLogic, Inc., Phoenix; bd. dirs. Am. Shared Hosp. Svcs., San Francisco; cons. orthopaedic surgery West Haven (Conn.) VA Hosp., 1970—, Hill Health Ctr., New Haven, 1970—; chief orthopedic surgery Conn. Health Care Plan, 1976-78; mem. adv. coun. Nat. Inst. Arthritis, Metabolism and Digestive Disease, NIH, 1979-82; mem. admission scom. Yale Med. Sch., 1970-72; presenter, moderator Symposium on Cervical Myelopathy, San Francisco, 1987; chmn. grant rev. com. NIH, 1985. Author: (monograph) Analysis of the Mechanics of the Thoracic Spine in Man, Leprosy, The Foot and The Orthopaedic Surgeon at Am. Acad. Orthopaedic Surgeons, 1970; book Clinical Biomechanics of the Spine, 1978, 2d edit., 1990; Symposium on Idiopathic Low Back Pain, 1982, Your Aching Back-A Doctor's Guide to Relief, 1983, rev. and updated edit., 1990, translated in German, 1992; prin. editor Time/Life Med. Video Back Pain; contbr. articles to profl. jours., chpts. to sci. books. Trustee Brown U., Providence, 1971-76, bd. fellows, 1981-92; trustee Northfield Mt. Hermon Sch., Northfield, Mass., 1976-81; chmn. corp. com. on minority affairs Brown U., Providence, 1981-86, chmn. corp. com. med. edn. med. sch.; mem. bd. dirs. The Partnership, Boston, 1984—. Capt. AUS, 1966-68. Decorated Bronze Star medal; named 1 of 10 Outstanding Young Men U.S. Jr. C. of C., 1969, Selected for Exceptional Black Scientist poster series CIBA-GEIGY Corp., 1982; recipient Martin Luther King, Jr. Med. Achievement award, 1972, Kappa Delta award, nat. prize for outstanding research in orthopaedics field, 1975; nat. award for spinal research Eastern Orthopaedic Assn., 1980; Disting. Service award Northfield Mt. Hermon Sch. Alumni Assn., 1983; William Rogers award Associated Alumni Brown U., 1984; Outstanding Achievement award Delta Upsilon, 1986; Am.-Brit.-Canadian Travelling fellow Am. Orthopedic Assn., 1975. Fellow Am. Acad. Orthopaedic Surgeons, Scoliosis Rsch. Soc.; mem. Orthopaedic Rsch. Soc., Cervical Spine Rsch. Soc., Internat. Soc. for Study Lumbar Spine, Internat. Soc. Orthopaedic Surgery and Traumatology, Nat. Med. Assn. (Orthopaedic Scholar award 1994), Cervical Spine Rsch. Soc. (pres. 1988), N.Am. Spine Soc., Acad. Orthopaedic Soc., Sigma Xi, Sigma Pi Phi.

WHITE, B. JOSEPH, university dean. Dean bus. administrn. U. Mich., Ann Arbor. Office: Dean School of Business Admin University of Michigan Ann Arbor Ann Arbor MI 48109

WHITE, BARRY A., lawyer; b. Chgo., May 26, 1948. BA, U. Wis., 1970; JD cum laude, Northwestern U., 1973. Bar: Ill. 1973. Ptnr. Mayer, Brown & Platt, Chgo. Mem. Phi Eta Sigma, Phi Kappa Phi. Office: Mayer Brown & Platt Ste 3900 190 S La Salle St Chicago IL 60603-3410*

WHITE, BARRY BENNETT, lawyer; b. Boston, Feb. 13, 1943; s. Harold and Rosalyn (Schneider) W.; m. Eleanor Greenberg; Joshua S., Adam J., Benjamin D. AB magna cum laude, Harvard U., 1964; JD magna cum laude, Harvard U., 1967. Bar: Mass. 1967, U.S. Dist. Ct. Mass.1967, U.S. Ct. Appeals, (1st cir.) 1967. Assoc. Foley Hoag & Eliot, Boston, 1969-74, ptnr., 1975—, mem. exec. com., 1981-92, 93—, chmn. exec. com., 1987-91, mng. ptnr., 1991-92, 93—, mem. exec. com. 1991—, sec. 1992-93; chmn. Lex Mundi, 1994. Secretary, General Counsel, Executive Committee, Greater Boston Chamber of Commerce. bd. dirs., exec. com. Mass. Assn. Mental Health, 1985—, pres., 1993—; bd. dirs. Boston Mcpl. Rsch. Bureau, Vol. Lawyers Project, 1987—, Support Ctr. ofMass., 1988—; mem. Jewish Family and Children's Services, Boston, 1979-87; bd. visitors Boston U. Grad. Sch. Dentistry, 1981—; bd. trustees Jewish Community Relations Council, 1988-92; chmn. com. for Clinton/Gore New Eng. Lawyers, 1992-96,chmn. Tsongas for Pres. Com., 1991—. With USPHS, 1967-69. Mem. ABA, Mass. BarAssn., Boston Bar Assn., Internat. Bar Assn., Am. Acad. Hosp. Attys., Am. Hosp.Assn. (adj. task force on health planning, 1982-84, contbg. editor hosp. law manual, 1981-84). Democrat. Clubs: Harvard of Boston, Badminton & Tennis. Editor: Harvard Law Rev., 1965-67. Office: Foley Hoag & Eliot 1 Post Office Sq Boston MA 02109-2103

WHITE, BENJAMIN BALLARD, JR., lawyer; b. Princeton, W.Va., Mar. 19, 1927; s. Benjamin Ballard and Zylpha Katherine (Karnes) W.; m. Gloria Lee Jones, Nov. 7, 1947 (dec. 1958); 1 child, Benjamin Ballard III; m. Wanda Ann Bowling, Sept. 2, 1959; children: Leigh Anne, Leonard Elbert. JD, Washington & Lee U., 1951. Bar: W.Va. 1951, U.S. Ct. Appeals (4th cir.) W.Va. 1956. Pvt. practice Princeton, 1951, 53-55; jr. ptnr. Ross & White, Bluefield, W.Va., 1952, Sanders & White, Princeton, 1956-60; pvt. practice Whites' Law Offices, Princeton, 1961-80; sr. ptnr. White & Ambrose, Princeton, 1981-83, Whites' Law Offices, Princeton, 1983—; v.p. New River Investments, Princeton, 1977—. Pres. Princeton Police Civil Svc. Commr., 1967-81. With U.S. Army, 1945-46. Mem. W.Va. State Bar, W.Va. Bar Assn., Mercer County Bar Assn. (pres. 1971), Def. Rsch. Inst., Internat. Assn. Def. Counsel, Elks, Moose. Republican. Presbyterian. Office: Whites' Law Offices 1426 E Main St Princeton WV 24740-3064

WHITE, BENJAMIN VROOM, III, lawyer; b. Hartford, Conn., Nov. 25, 1941; s. Benjamin Vroom and Charlotte (Conover) W.; m. Elizabeth Dodge, Sept. 6, 1969; children: Constance Atwood, Charles Conover. AB, Harvard U., 1964; MAT, Harvard Grad. Sch. of Edn., 1970; JD, Boston U., 1974. Law clk. to Hon. Alfred H. Joslin R.I. Supreme Ct., Providence, 1974-75; assoc., ptnr. Hinckley, Allen, Salisburg & Parsons, Providence, 1975-81; ptnr. Vetter & White, Providence, 1981—; mem. faculty MCLE and Nat. inst. Trial Advocacy, Boston, 1983—. Editor Note and Case, Boston U. Law Rev., 1993-94; contbr. articles to profl. jours. Bd. govs. Gordon Sch., East Providence, 1981-87, 1st v.p., 1984—; bd. dirs. Lipptt Hill Tutorial, Providence, 1978-82, Westport River Watershed Alliance, 1989-95. lt. USNR, 1964-68. Mem. ABA (litigation sect.), R.I. Bar Assn. (fed. ct. bench and bar com. 1982—, chmn. 1993—), Boston Bar Assn., R.I. Fed. Ct. Bd. of Bar Examiners, New Bedford Yacht Club, Harvard (R.I. and N.Y.C.) Club, Hope (Providence) Club, Acoaxet (Westport, Mass.) Club. Republican. Episcopalian. Office: Vetter & White Inc 20 Washington Pl Providence RI 02903-1328

WHITE, BETTY, actress, comedienne; b. Oak Park, Ill., Jan. 17, 1922; m. Allen Ludden, 1963 (dec.). Student pub. schs., Beverly Hills, Calif. Appearances on radio shows This Is Your FBI, Blondie, The Great Gildersleeve; actress: (TV series) including Hollywood on Television, The Betty White Show, 1954-58, Life With Elizabeth, 1953-55, A Date With The Angels, 1957-58, The Pet Set, 1971, Mary Tyler Moore Show, 1974-77, The Betty White Show, 1977, The Golden Girls, 1985-92 (Emmy award for best actress 1986), The Golden Palace, 1992-93, Maybe This Time, 1995—; (TV miniseries) The Best Place to be, 1979, The Gossip Columnist, 1980, (film) Advise and Consent, 1962; guest appearances on other programs; summer stock appearances Guys and Dolls, Take Me Along, The King and I, Who Was That Lady?, Critic's Choice, Bells are Ringing. Recipient Emmy award NATAS, 1975, 76, 86; L.A. Area Emmy award, 1952. Mem. AFTRA, Am. Humane Assn., Greater L.A. Zoo Assn. (dir.). Office: care William Morris Agy care Tony Fantozzi 151 S El Camino Dr Beverly Hills CA 90212-2704*

WHITE, BEVERLY J., cytogeneticist; b. Seattle, Oct. 9, 1938. Grad., U. Wash., 1959, MD, 1963. Diplomate Nat. Bd. Med. Examiners, Am. Bd. Pediatrics, Am. Bd. Med. Genetics; lic physician and surgeon, Wash., Va. Rsch. trainee dept. anatomy Sch. Medicine U. Wash., Seattle, 1960-62, pediatric resident dept. pediatrics, 1967-69; rotating intern Phila. Gen. Hosp., 1963-64; rsch. fellow med. ob-gyn. unit Cardiovascular Rsch. Inst. U. Calif. Med. Ctr., San Francisco, 1964-65; staff fellow lab. biomed. scis. Nat. Inst. Child Health and Human Devel. NIH, Bethesda, Md., 1965-67, sr. staff fellow, attending physician lab. exptl. pathology Nat. Inst. Arthritis, Metabolism and Digestive Diseases, 1969-74, acting chief sect. cytogenetics, 1975-76, rsch. med. officer, attending physician sect. cytogenetics lab. cellular biology and genetics, 1974-86, dir. cytogenetics unit, interinstitute med. genetics program clin. ctr., 1987-95; dir. cytogenetics Corning Clin. Labs., Teterboro, N.J., 1995—; vis. scientist dept. pediat. divsn. genetics U. Wash. Sch. Medicine, 1983-84; intramural cons. NIH, 1975-95; cons. to assoc. editor Jour. Nat. Cancer Inst., 1976; mem. staff cons. dept. ob-gyn. Naval Hosp., Bethesda, 1988-89; lectr., presenter in field. Recipient Mosby Book award, 1963, Women of Excellence award U. Wash. and Seattle Profl. chpt. Women in Comm., 1963, Reuben award Am. Soc. for Study Sterility, 1963. Fellow Am. Coll. Med. Genetics (founding), Am. Acad. Pediatrics; mem. AMA. Am. Soc. Human Genetics, Fed. Physicians Assn., Assn. Cytogenetic Technologists (program com. 1989). Home: 9916 Shrewsbury Ct Gaithersburg MD 20879 Office: Corning Clin Labs Dept Cytogenetics One Malcom Ave Teterboro NJ 07608-1070

WHITE, BURTON LEONARD, educational psychologist, author; b. Boston, June 27, 1929; s. Jack J. and Evelyn S. W.; m. Janet Hodgson-White; children—Laura, Emily, David, Daniel. B.S.M.E., Tufts Coll., 1949; B.A., Boston U., 1956, M.A., 1957; Ph.D., Brandeis U., 1960. Research assoc. Brandeis U., 1960-62, M.I.T., 1962-65; sr. research assoc. Harvard Grad. Sch. Edn., 1965-78; head Center Parent Edn., Newton, Mass., 1978—. Author: books including Human Infants, 1971, Experience and Environment, Vol. I, 1973, Vol. II, 1978, The First Three Years of Life, 1975, latest edit. 1995, The Origins of Competence, 1979, Educating the Infant and Toddler, 1988, Raising A Happy, Unspoiled Child, 1994, The New First Three Years of Life, 1995; contbr. articles to profl. jours. Served with AUS, 1951-53. Home: 115 Pine Ridge Rd Newton MA 02168-1616

WHITE, BYRON R., former United States supreme court justice; b. Ft. Collins, Colo., June 8, 1917; m. Marion Stearns; children: Charles, Nancy. Grad., U. Colo., 1938; Rhodes scholar, Oxford (Eng.) U.; grad., Yale Law Sch. Clk. to chief justice U.S., 1946-47; atty. firm Lewis, Grant & Davis, Denver, 1947-60; dep. atty. gen. U.S., 1961-62; assoc. justice Supreme Ct., U.S., 1962-93; ret., 1993. Served with USNR, World War II, Pacific. Mem. Phi Beta Kappa, Phi Gamma Delta, Order of Coif. Address: US Supreme Ct Supreme Ct Bldg 1 First St NE Washington DC 20543

WHITE, C. THOMAS, state supreme court justice; b. Humphrey, Nebr., Oct. 5, 1928; s. John Ambrose and Margaret Elizabeth (Costello) W.; m. Joan White, Oct. 9, 1971; children: Michaela, Thomas, Patrick. JD, Creighton U., 1952. Bar: Nebr. County atty. Platte County (Nebr.), Columbus, 1955-65; judge 21st Dist. Ct. Nebr., Columbus, 1965-77; justice Nebr. Supreme Ct., Lincoln, 1977—, chief justice, 1995—. Served with U.S. Army, 1946-47. Roman Catholic. Clubs: Elks, KC. Office: Nebr Supreme Ct 2214 State Capitol Bldg Lincoln NE 68509*

WHITE, CALVIN JOHN, zoo executive, financial manager, zoological association executive; b. Twillingate, Nfld., Can., Feb. 28, 1948; s. Harold and Meta Blanche (Abbott) W.; m. Lorna Joan Maclachlan; children: Chelsea Elizabeth, Evan Alexander. B in Commerce, U. Toronto, Ont., Can., 1971. Fin. analyst Can. GE Co. Ltd., Toronto, 1971-72, Ford Motor Co. Can., Oakville, Ont., 1972-74; sr. fin. analyst Municipality of Met. Toronto, 1974-77, asst. dir. budget and ops. analysis, 1977-81, dir. budget analysis and internal control, 1981-86; gen. mgr. Met. Toronto Zoo, 1986—; pres. Zool. Soc. Met. Toronto, 1994—; bd. dirs. Met. Toronto Conv. and Visitors Assn., Can. Assn. Zool. Parks and Aquariums. Fellow Am. Zoo and Aquarium Assn.; mem. Am. Assn. Zoo Keepers, Inst. Pub. Adminstrn. Can. (bd. dirs. 1989-91), Zool. Soc. Met. Toronto (bd. dirs. 1991—, pres. 1994—), World Conservation Union, Internat. Union Dirs. Zool. Gardens, Toronto Sportmen's Assn., Mensa. Office: Met Toronto Zoo, PO Box 280, Toronto, ON Canada M1E 4R5

WHITE, CHARLES ALBERT, JR., medical educator, obstetrician-gynecologist; b. San Diego, Aug. 1, 1922; s. Charles Albert and Helen (Hardy) W.; m. Suzan A. Alikadi, Dec. 6, 1960; children: Craig, Scott, Jennifer. D.V.M., Colo. State U., 1945; M.D., U. Utah, 1955. Diplomate: Am. Bd. Ob-Gyn. Intern Salt Lake County Hosp., 1955; resident in ob-gyn U. Iowa, 1959-61, mem. faculty ob-gyn, 1961-74; chmn. dept. ob-gyn W. Va. U., Morgantown, 1974-80; prof., chmn. dept. ob-gyn La. State U. Med. Ctr., New Orleans, 1980-92. Served to lt. comdr. USNR, 1957-59. Fellow ACS, Am. Gyn-Ob Soc.; mem. Am. Coll. Ob-Gyn, Central Assn. Ob-Gyn. Home and Office: 33 Chateau Du Jardin Kenner LA 70065

WHITE, CHARLES OLDS, aeronautical engineer; b. Beirut, Apr. 2, 1931; s. Frank Laurence and Dorothy Alice (Olds) W.; m. Mary Carolyn Liechty, Sept. 3, 1955; children—Charles Cameron, Bruce Blair. B.S. in Aero. Engring., MIT, 1953, M.S., 1954. Aero. engr. Douglas Aircraft Long Beach, 1954-60, aero. engr. Ford Aerospace & Communication Corp., Calif., 1960-79, sr. engr. specialist, 1979-80, staff office of gen. mgr. DIVAD div., 1980-81, tech. mgr. DIVAD Fuzes, 1981-82, supr. design and analysis DIVAD div., 1982-85; tech. mgr. Advanced Ordnance Programs, 1985-87, PREDATOR Missile, 1987-90, cons. 1990-93; engring. tech. prin. Aerojet Corp., 1993-94; tech. prin. OCSW Ammunition Olin Ordinance, 1994—. Mem. AIAA, Nat. Mgmt. Assn., Am. Aviation Hist. Soc., Sigma Gamma Tau. Republican. Presbyterian. Clubs: Masters Swimming, Newport Beach Tennis. Contbr. articles to profl. jours.

WHITE, CHRISTINE, physical education educator; b. Taunton, Mass., Apr. 1, 1905; d. Peregrine Hastings and Sara (Lawrence) W. Cert., Boston Sch. Phys. Edn.; BS, Boston U., 1935, MEd, 1939. Instr. Winthrop Coll., Rock Hill, S.C., 1927-29; instr., asst. prof. The Woman's Coll. U. N.C., Greensboro, N.C., 1929-41; assoc. prof., head dept. physical edn. Meredith Coll., Raleigh, N.C., 1941-43; assoc. prof., prof. chair dept. physical edn. Wheaton Coll., Norton, Mass., 1943-70, prof. emerita, 1970—. co-editor Taunton Architecture: A Reflection of the City's History, 1981, 89. Chmn. Hist. Dist. Study Com., 1975-78, Recreation Commn., 1972-81; mem. Hist. Dist. Commn., 1979—, sec., 1979-86, acting chair, 1992-94; mem. Park and Recreation Commn., 1982—; bd. dirs. Star Theatre for the Arts, Inc., 1993—. Fellow AAHPERD; mem. AAUP (pres. Wheaton Coll. chpt. 1960-61), AAUW, LWV, Nat. Assn. Phys. Edn. in Higher Edn., Pi Lambda Theta. Avocations: travelling, historic preservation, theatre, music. Home: 40 Highland Ter Taunton MA 02780-4729

WHITE, CLEVELAND STUART, JR., architect; b. Norwalk, Conn., Jan. 10, 1937; s. Cleveland Stuart and Helen Thurston (Stephenson) W.; m. Matilda Bowen Romaine, Sept. 14, 1963; children: Cleveland Stuart III, Laura Brewster. AB, Princeton U., 1959; BArch, Columbia U., 1963. Registered architect, Vt., N.H., N.Y., Mass., Conn. Draftsman, designer Hill & Assocs., Cambridge, Mass., 1964-68, Roy W. Banwell, Jr., Hanover, N.H., 1968-71; prin. Banwell White & Arnold, Hanover, N.H., 1968-84, Banwell White Arnold Hemberger & Ptnrs., Hanover, N.H., 1984—; cons. Brookhaven (N.Y.) Nat. Lab., 1979-83; adj. prof. environ. studies Dartmouth Coll., Hanover, 1981; lectr. MIT Summer Inst., Cambridge, 1979, 80, 81. Author, editor: Case Study: 424 W 33rd Street Apartment Conversion, 1981; prin. works include Dartmouth Coll. Boathouse, Madbury (N.H.) Elem. Sch., Pinckney Boathouse, Wolfeboro, N.H., Addition to Barton Hall-U. N.H., Durham, Soc. for Protection of N.H. Forests Conservation Ctr., Concord, Whitetail Ski and Summer Resort, Franklin County, Pa., Center Moriches (N.Y.) Free Pub. Libr. Recipient Merit award Am. Wood Coun., 1981, 2 Energy Innovation award U.S. Dept. Energy, 1984, 87, 1st Honor award New Eng. Reg. Coun. Architects, 1978, Internat. Solar Energy Soc./ Progressive Architecture Mag., 1982. Mem. AIA (chmn. environ. task force N.H. chpt. 1993-95, honor awards 1990, 92). Democrat. Avocations: sailing, skiing, music, gardening, art. Home: PO Box 40 Norwich VT 05055-0040 Office: Banwell White Arnold Hemberger & Ptnrs 2 W Wheelock St Hanover NH 03755-1709

WHITE, CONSTANCE BURNHAM, state official; b. Odgen, Utah, July 2, 1954; d. Owen W. and Colleen (Redd) Burnham; m. Wesley Robert White, Mar. 18, 1977. BA in English magna cum laude, U. Utah, 1976, postgrad., 1977; postgrad., Boston Coll., 1979; JD, Loyola U., 1981. Law clerk Kruse, Landa, Zimmerman & Maycock, Salt Lake City, 1979; law clerk legal dept. Bell & Howell, Lincolnwood, Ill., 1980; clerk, assoc. Parsons, Behle & Latimer, Salt Lake City, 1981-82; assoc. Reynolds, Vance, Deason & Smith, Salt Lake City, 1982-83; chief enforcement sect. Utah Securities Divsn., Salt Lake City, 1984-87, chief licensing sect., 1988, asst. dir., 1989-90; legal counsel Utah Dept. Commerce, Salt Lake City, 1990-92, exec. dir., 1993-95, commsr pub service div, 1995; mem. Gov.'s Securities Fraud Task Force, 1984; spl. asst. atty. gen., 1986-88; spl. asst. U.S. atty., 1986—. Mem. North Am. Securities Adminstrs. Assn. (vice chair market manipulation com. 1988-89, penny stock/telecom. fraud com. 1989-90, chair uniform examinations com. 1990-92, chair forms revision com. 1992), Utah State Bar (securities adv. com. 1991—, task force on community-based mediation 1991—, chair securities sect. 1992-93). Office: Utah Dept Commerce 160 E 300th S Salt Lake City UT 84103*

WHITE, DALE ANDREW, journalist; b. Jacksonville, Fla., Feb. 17, 1958; s. John Andrew and Jeannelle Corinne White. B in Journalism, U. Fla., 1983. Reporter UPI, Miami, Fla., 1980, Orlando (Fla.) Sentinel Star, 1981; corr. Fla. Times-Union, Gainesville, 1982; reporter, columnist, editorial writer Sarasota Herald-Tribune, Bradenton, Fla., 1983—. Contbr. short stories to profl. publs. Recipient Chmn.'s award N.Y. Times, 1987, 3d Pl. Editorial Writing award Fla. Soc. Newspaper Editors, 1993. Office: PO Box 1695 Bradenton FL 34206-1695

WHITE, DAVID CALVIN, electrical engineer, energy educator, consultant; b. Sunnyside, Wash., Feb. 18, 1922; s. David Calvin Sr. and Leafie Eloise (Scott) W.; m. Glorianna Guilii, July 30, 1949 (dec. Dec. 1965); 1 child, Julie Anne White Coman (dec.); m. Margot Ann Fuller, June 4, 1966; 1 child, Constance Anne. B.S., Stanford U., 1946, M.S., 1947, Ph.D., 1949. Registered profl. engr. Elec. engr. Kaiser Industries, Vancouver, Wash., 1941-42, 43-45; assoc. prof. elec. engring. U. Fla., Gainesville, 1949-52; asst. prof. elec. engring. MIT, Cambridge, 1952-54, assoc. prof., 1954-58, prof., 1958-62, Ford prof. engring., 1962-92, dir. energy lab., 1972-89, Ford prof. engring. emeritus, 1992—; pres., dir. Energy Conversion, Inc., 1961-64; cons. Gulf Oil, 1976-84, Johnson Controls, 1980—; sr. advisor and vis. prof. Birla Inst., India, 1968-70; mem. council U. Benin, Nigeria, 1972; trustee Lowell Tech. Inst., Mass., 1972-74; mem. corp. Woods Hole Oceanographic Inst., Mass., 1977-84; mem. research coordinating panel Gas Research Inst., Chgo., 1977-85; chmn. adv. council Electric Power Research Inst., Palo Alto, Calif., 1984-86, mem., 1980-87. Author: (with others) Electromechanical Energy Conversion, 1959. Commr. Electric Light Plant, Concord, Mass., 1959-64, Kalmia Woods Water Dist., Concord, 1960-63. Named hon. prof. Instituto Politecnico Nacional, Mex., 1961. Fellow IEEE; mem. Nat. Acad. Engring., Am. Acad. Arts and Scis., Am. Soc. Engring. Edn. (George Westinghouse award 1961), Phi Beta Kappa, Sigma Xi, Tau Beta Pi, Eta Kappa Nu. Republican. Clubs: New Seabury Country, Woodfield Country. Avocations: golf; boating. Home: 8 Chart Way Popponesset Island New Seabury MA 02649 also: 799 E Jeffery St Apt 314 Boca Raton FL 33487 Office: MIT 77 Massachusetts Ave Rm E40-473 Cambridge MA 02139

WHITE, DAVID CLEAVELAND, microbial ecologist, environmental toxicologist; b. Moline, Ill., May 18, 1929; s. Frederick Berryhill and Dorothy (Cleaveland) W.; m. Sandra Jean Shoults, July 7, 1957; children: Winifred Shoults, Christopher Cleaveland, Andrew Berryhill. AB magna cum laude, Dartmouth Coll., 1951; MD, Tufts U., 1955; PhD, Rockefeller U., 1962. Rotating intern Hosp. of U. Pa., 1955-56; asst. prof., assoc. prof., then prof. biochemistry U. Ky., Lexington, 1962-72; prof. biol. sci. Fla. State U., Tallahassee, 1972-86; disting. scientist U. Tenn./Oak Ridge Nat. Lab., Knoxville, 1986—; prof. microbiology, ecology U. Tenn., Knoxville, 1986—; prin. investigator Oak Ridge (Tenn.) Nat. Lab., 1988—; mem. adv. com. Ctr. Theol. Inquiry, Princeton (N.J.) U., 1986-91; former dir. Ctr. for Environ. Biotech., 1991—, Inst. Applied Microbiology, Knoxville, 1986-91; mem. sci. adv. panel Mich. State Ctr. Microbail Ecology, Lansing, 1989-92, Mont. State Ctr. for Biofilm Engring., Bozeman, Mont., 1991—; mem. sci. adv. bd. Nat. Water Rsch. Inst., 1993—; mem. Naval Rsch. Adv. Commn., 1995—; dir. Microbial Insights, Inc., Knoxville; Welcome vis. prof. U. Okla., Norman, 1984-85; spkr. profl. confs. Author: Sex, Drugs and Pollution, 1983, 2d edit., 1985; founding editor-in-chief Jour. Microbiol. Methods, 1985—; author 340 refereed sci. publs. Lt. M.C. USN, 1956-58. Recipient P.R. Edwards award S.E. br. Am. Soc. Microbiology, 1981, Proctor & Gamble Applied and Environ., Microbiology award Am. Soc. Microbiology, 1993, Applied and Environ. Microbiol. award ASM, 1993, Artarctic Svc. medal USN/NSF, 1984, Sci. and Tech. Achievement award EPA, 1987, Ari Clarke prize in water sci. and tech., Nat. Water Rsch. Inst., 1995. Presbyterian. Achievements include discovery of signature biomarker technique for microbial biomass, community structure and nutritional status from environmental samples, microbial ecology of deep subsurface, tropical and antarctic sediments, microbial biofilms in microbial influenced corrosion, biosensors environmental biotechnology. Office: Ctr for Environ Biotech 10515 Research Dr Ste 300 Knoxville TN 37932-2575

WHITE, DAVID HYWEL, physics educator; b. Cardiff, Wales, June 4, 1931; came to U.S., 1959, naturalized, 1966; s. William Richard and Bessie (Morgan) W.; m. Frances Mary Shearman, July 23, 1954; children: Richard Gerwyn, Christopher David. B.S., U. Wales, 1953; Ph.D., Birmingham U., 1956. Asst. lectr. Birmingham U., 1958-59; asst. prof. U. Pa., 1961-64; asso. prof. Cornell U., Ithaca, N.Y., 1964-69; prof. Cornell U., 1969-78; sr. physicist, head exptl. facilities div. Isabelle Project, Brookhaven Nat. Lab., Upton, L.I., N.Y., 1978-82; group leader nuclear and particle physics rsch. P divsn. Los Alamos (N.Mex.) Nat. Lab., 1986-94; cons., 1967-69, 76-78. Author: Elementary Electronics, 1967; Editor: Scintillation Counters, 1966. NSF sr. postdoctoral fellow, 1970; JSPS fellow, 1981. Fellow Am. Phys. Soc., AAAS. Home: 913 Calle Vistoso Santa Fe NM 87501-1031

WHITE, DAVID LEE, journalist; b. Cleve., Nov. 17, 1946; s. Royden Lee and Loretta Elizabeth (Wolf) W.; m. Sandra Jean Sweet, Aug. 25, 1983. Student, Cuyahoga C.C., 1965-67. Sports corr. The Cleve. Plain Dealer, 1966-67; sports reporter The Willoughby (Ohio) News Herald, 1968, asst. sports editor, 1968-69; editor sports makeup Cleve. Press, 1969-70, sports reporter, 1970-73, editor night news, 1973-78, asst. community weekly editor, 1978-80, asst. editor world news, 1980-81, editor page makeup, PM edits., 1981-82, weekend chief copy desk, 1981-82, editor weekend news, 1981-82, asst. Sunday editor, 1981-82; editor prodn. The Charlotte (N.C.) Observer/Charlotte News, 1982-84, asst. editor features/lifestyles, 1984-86, editor TV week, 1986—; asst. coverage Ky. Derby United Press Internat., 1970, 71, 72, 74, 75, U.S. Open Golf Tournament, 1971. Copy editor: (book) Cleveland-Yesterday, Today and Tomorrow, 1976. Office: Charlotte Observer/Knight Pub Co PO Box 32188 600 S Tryon St Charlotte NC 28232

WHITE, DAVID OLDS, researcher, former educator; b. Fenton, Mich., Dec. 18, 1921; s. Harold Bancroft and Doris Caroline (Olds) W.; m. Janice Ethel Russell, Sept. 17, 1923; children: John Russell, David Olds Jr., Benjamin Hill. BA, Amherst Coll., 1943; MS, U. Mass., 1950; PhD, U. Oreg., 1970. Tchr. human physiology Defiance (Ohio) Coll., summer 1950; sci. tchr. Roosevelt Jr. High Sch., Eugene, Oreg., 1951-52; prin. Glide (Oreg.) High Sch., 1952-56; tchr. Munich Am. Elem. Sch., 1957-69; prin. Wurzburg (Fed. Republic Germany) Am. High Sch., 1959-60, Wertheim (Fed. Republic Germany) Am. Elem. Sch., 1960-61; tchr. Dash Point Elem. Sch., Tacoma, 1961-63, Eugene (Oreg.) Pub. Schs., 1963-81; internat. rschr. in field. Contbr. articles to profl. publs.; patentee electronic model airplane. Staff sgt. U.S. Army, 1942-45, PTO. Fulbright grantee, 1956-57, 72-73. Mem. NEA, Fulbright Alumni Assn., Phi Delta Kappa. Avocations: skiing, camping, tennis, hunting, piano. Home: 4544 Fox Hollow Rd Eugene OR 97405-3904

WHITE, DAVID OLIVER, museum executive; b. Phila., Mar. 3, 1938; s. Thomas Morton and Bernice Lorraine (Twist) W.; B.A., Glassboro State Coll., 1969; M.A., U. Conn., 1970; m. Lorraine Carolyn Wilt, June 19, 1965; children—Kristin Leigh, Andrew David. Acctg. clk. Penn Mut. Life Ins. Co., Phila., 1955-65; mus. dir. Conn. Hist. Commn., Hartford, 1970-74, 1992—; dir. Mus. Conn. History, State Library, Hartford, 1974-92; liaison to Conn. Hist. Commn., 1977-86, Conn. Film Festival com., 1977-80. Vice pres. Tolland Hist. Soc., 1972, 73, 79, pres., 1974, 75, 80, bd. dirs., 1977-79, 84—. Served with U.S. Army, 1961-63. Mem. Conn. Humanities Coun., N.E. Mus. Assn., Assn. for Study of Conn. History, Conn. Hist. Soc. Methodist. Author: Connecticut's Black Soldiers 1775-83, 1973. Office: Conn Hist Comm 59 S Prospect St Hartford CT 06106-1901

WHITE, DEVON MARKES, professional baseball player; b. Kingston, Jamaica, Dec. 29, 1962. With Calif. Angels, 1981-90, Toronto Blue Jays, 1990—; player Am. League All Star Team, 1989, 93. Recipient Gold Glove award, 1988-89, 91-94; named Am. League leader put outs by outfielder, 1987, 91-92. Office: Toronto Blue Jays, One Blue Jay Way Ste 3200, Toronto, ON Canada M5V 3B3

WHITE, DIRK BRADFORD, printing company executive; b. St. Joseph, Mo., Aug. 18, 1955; s. John Paul and Sandra Sue (Dedmon) W.; m. Julie Maureen Eisenreich, June 30, 1979; children: Kristen Elizabeth, Paul Aaron. BS in Mktg., Southwest Mo. State U., 1977. Estimator I.J. Eagle Printing Co., Inc., Kansas City, Mo., 1978-83; customer svc. mgr. Eagle Lithographing Co., Kansas City, Mo., 1983-88, v.p. prodn., 1988-90, sr. v.p., gen. mgr., 1990-92; mgr. prodn. control Spangler Inc., Kansas City, Kans., 1992—. Mem. Printing Industries Am., Graphic Arts Tech. Found., Kappa Alpha. Avocations: fly fishing, bicycling, wilderness camping and hiking, mountaineering, photography. Home: 8309 Mullen Rd Lenexa KS 66215-4133

WHITE, DONALD HARVEY, retired physicist, educator; b. Berkeley, Calif., Apr. 30, 1931; s. Harvey Elliott and Adeline White; m. Beverly Evalina Jones, Aug. 8, 1953; children: Jeri, Brett, Holly, Scott, Erin. AB, U. Calif., Berkeley, 1953; PhD, Cornell U., 1960. Rsch. physicist Lawrence Livermore (Calif.) Nat. Lab., 1960-71, cons., 1971-90; prof. physics Western Oreg. State Coll., Monmouth, 1971-95; ret.; vis. rsch. scientist Inst. Laue-Langevin, Grenoble, France, 1977-78, 84-85, 91-92. Author: (with others) Physics, an Experimental Science, 1968, Physics and Music, 1980. Pres. Monmouth-Independence Cmty. Arts, 1983. DuPont scholar, 1958; Minna-Heineman Found. fellow, Hannover, Fed. Republic Germany, 1977. Mem. Am. Phys. Soc., Am. Assn. Physics Tchrs. (pres. Oreg. sect. 1974-75), Oreg. Acad. Sci. (pres. 1979-80), Phi Kappa Phi (pres. West Oreg. chpt. 1989-90). Democrat. Presbyterian. Home: 411 S Walnut Dr Monmouth OR 97361-1948

WHITE, DOUGLAS JAMES, JR., lawyer; b. N.Y.C., Mar. 20, 1934; s. Douglas James and Margaret (Stillman) W.; m. Denise Beale, May 28, 1960; children: Brian Douglas, James Roderick. BA, U. Oreg., 1955; LLB, Willamette U., 1958. Bar: Oreg. 1958. Law clk. to assoc. justice Oreg. Supreme Ct., Salem, 1958-59; assoc. Schwabe, Williamson & Wyatt (formerly known as Mautz, Souther, Spaulding, Kinsey & Williamson), Portland, Oreg., 1959-69; shareholder, gen. ptnr. Schwabe, Williamson & Wyatt, P.C. (formerly known as Schwabe, Williamson, Wyatt, Moore & Roberts), Portland, Oreg., 1969-79, sr. ptnr., 1979-93; shareholder, 1994—; bd. dirs. Portland Iron Works and Affiliates; gen. outside counsel Oreg. Grad. Inst. Sci. Tech., Beaverton. Trustee Jesuit H.S., Beaverton, 1991-94; bd. dirs. St. Vincent de Paul Child Devel. Ctr., Portland, 1979-90, Portland Coun., Soc. St. Vincent de Paul, 1989-92, Portland House of Umoja, 1995—; bd. dirs., officer Maryville Nursing Home, Beaverton, 1993—, St. Vincent de Paul Conf. of St. Thomas More, Portland, 1966—; active Saturday Acad. Beaverton, 1982—. Mem. ABA, Oreg. State Bar Assn. (real estate and land use sect. exec. com. 1984-85), Multnomah County Bar Assn., Multnomah Athletic Club (Portland), Arlington Club (Portland), Flyfisher Club of Oreg. Republican. Roman Catholic. Avocations: fly-fishing, cross-country skiing, bridge, hiking. Home: 6725 SW Preslynn Dr Portland OR 97225-2668 Office: Schwabe Williamson & Wyatt 1211 SW 5th Ave Portland OR 97204-3713

WHITE, DOUGLAS R., anthropology educator; b. Mpls., Mar. 13, 1942; s. Asher Abbott and Margaret McQuestin (Richie) W.; m. Jayne Chamberlain (div. Feb. 1971); m. Lilyan Amdur Brudner, Mar. 21, 1971; 1 child, Scott Douglas. BA, U. Minn., 1964, MA, 1967, PhD, 1969. Asst. prof. U. Pitts., 1967-72, assoc. prof., 1972-76; assoc. prof. U. Calif., Irvine, 1976-79, prof., 1979—; dep. dir. Lang. Attitudes Rsch. Project, Dublin, Ireland, 1971-73; vis. prof. U. Tex., Austin, 1974-75; chmn. Linkages: World Devel. Res. Coun., Md., 1986—, pres. 1986-90. Co-editor: Research Methods in Social Networks, 1989, Anthropology of Urban Environments, 1972; founder, gen. editor World Cultures Jour., 1985-90; author sci. software packages; contbr. articles to profl. jours. Fellow Ctr. for Advanced Studies, Western Behavioral Sci. Inst., La Jolla, Calif., 1981-84; recipient Sr. Scientist award Alexander von Humboldt Stiftung, Bonn, Germany, 1989-91, Bourse de Haute Niveau award Ministry of Rsch. and Tech., Paris, 1992. Mem. Social Sci. Computing Assn. (pres. elect 1991, pres. 1992.). Democrat. Home: 8888 N La Jolla Scenic Dr La Jolla CA 92037-1608 Office: U Calif Irvine School of Social Sci Irvine CA 92717

WHITE, DURIE NEUMANN, federal agency administrator; b. Westerly, R.I., June 19, 1950; d. Reed Maurice Neumann and Alice M. (Victoria) Quinn; m. Donald L. White, Oct. 6, 1979; 6 stepchildren. BA, U. R.I., 1972. Supply clk. USAF/Europe, Mainz Kastel, Germany, 1972-73; adminstrv. asst. Pearson's Travel, Providence, 1973; contracting officer GSA, Washington, 1973-77; contract specialist AID, Washington, 1977-80; procurement analyst A/SDBU Dept. State, Washington, 1980-91, ops. dir. A/SDBU, 1991—; mem. Interagy. Small Bus. Dirs. Group, Washington, 1993—, White House Conf. on Small Bus., 1995. Roman Catholic. Avocations: skiing, photography. Office: Small/Disadvantage Bus Dept State Rm 633, SA-6 Washington DC 20522-0602

WHITE, EDMUND WILLIAM, chemical engineer; b. Phila., July 8, 1920; s. Edmund Britten and Grace Salome (Faunce) W.; m. Kathrine Nathalie Cadwallader, Apr. 24, 1948; children: Christine Louise, William Cadwallader, Thomas Edmund, James Christopher. BA, Columbia Coll., 1940; BS, Columbia Sch. Engring., 1941, MChemE, 1942; PhD, Lehigh U., 1952. Registered profl. engr., Ohio. Jr. chemist Westvaco Chlorine Products Corp., South Charleston, W.Va., 1942-44; chem. engr. C.L. Mantel, N.Y.C., 1946-47, Diamond Alkali Co., Painesville, Ohio, 1947-49; grad. asst. Lehigh U., Bethlehem, Pa., 1949-51; sr. chemist Cities Svc. R & D Co., various cities, 1951-59, Athabasca Inc., Edmonton, Alberta, Canada, 1960-64; project mgr. U.S. Dept. Navy, Washington, 1965-66; rsch. chem. engr. Naval Surface Warfare Ctr., Annapolis, Md., 1966-95; ret., 1995; cons. in field. Contbr. articles to profl. jours. Treas., v.p., pres. sch. PTAs, Silver Spring, Md., 1968-79; den father, mem. troop com. Boy Scouts Am., Silver Spring, 1966-75. Lt. (j.g.) USN, 1944-46. Fellow ASTM (chairperson sect. subcom., com. 1967—, Award of Merit 1990, Scroll of Honor 1993); mem. AIChE (50 Yr. award), Am. Chem. Soc. (50 Yr. award), Potomac Curling Club (bd. dirs., pres. 1982-84), Internat. Assn. for Stability and Handling of Liquid Fuels (mem. steering com. 1985—), Sigma Xi. Republican. Achievements include 4 patents and 2 Canadian patents; research in consensus standardization, fuel stability testing, fuel stability, synthetic fuels, separation processes, wax oxidation, mixing and chlorine-caustic electrolytic cell. Home: 908 Crest Park Dr Silver Spring MD 20903-1307

WHITE, EDWARD ALFRED, lawyer; b. Elizabeth, N.J., Nov. 23, 1934. BS in Indsl. Engring., U. Mich., 1957, JD, 1963. Bar: Fla. 1963, U.S. Ct. Appeals (5th cir.) 1971, U.S. Supreme Ct. 1976, U.S. Ct. Appeals (11th cir.) 1981. Assoc. Jennings, Watts, Clarke & Hamilton, Jacksonville, Fla., 1963-66, ptnr., 1966-69; ptnr. Wayman & White, Jacksonville, 1969-72; pvt. practice, Jacksonville, 1972—; mem. aviation law com. Fla. Bar, 1972-94, chmn., 1979-81, bd. govs., 1984-88, admiralty com., 1984—, chmn., 1990-91, chmn. pub. relations com., 1986-88, exec. coun. trial lawyers sect., 1986-91. Mem. ABA (vice chmn. admiralty law com. 1995—), Fla. Bar Assn. (bd. cert. civil trial lawyer, 1984, bd cer Admiralty Lawyer, 1996—), Jacksonville Bar Assn. (chmn. legal ethics com. 1975-76, bd. govs. 1976-78, pres. 1979-80), Assn. Trial Lawyers Am. (sustaining mem. 1984—), Acad. Fla. Trial Lawyers (diplomate), Fla. Coun. Bar Assn. Pres.'s, Lawyer-Pilots Bar Assn., Am. Judicature Soc., Maritime Law Assn. (proctor in admirality), Southeastern Admiralty Law Inst. (bd. dirs. 1982-84, chmn./pres. 1994). Home: 1959 Largo Rd Jacksonville FL 32207-3926 Office: 610 Blackstone Bldg Jacksonville FL 32202

WHITE, EDWARD ALLEN, electronics company executive; b. Cambridge, Jan. 1, 1928; s. Joseph and Bessie (Allen) W.; m. Joan Dixon, Dec. 22, 1949 (div. Aug. 1978); children: Dixon Richard, Leslie Ann White Lollar; m. Nancy Rhoads, Oct. 6, 1979. B.S., Tufts U., 1947. Chmn. Bowmar Instrument Corp., Phoenix, Mass., 1951—, White Technology Inc., Phoenix, 1980-86; pres. Ariz. Digital Corp., Phoenix, 1975-91; chmn., chief exec. officer AHI, Inc., Ft. Wayne, Ind., 1970-88; mem. World Pres's. Orgn., Washington D.C., 1978—. Patentee in field. Bd. dirs. Gov.'s Council Children, Youth and Families, Phoenix, 1982-84, Planned Parenthood Fedn. Am., 1984-88; pres., bd. dirs. Planned Parenthood Central and No. Ariz., 1984-88; trustee Internat House, N.Y.C., 1973-75, Tufts U., 1973-83. Mem. Tau Beta Pi. Club: Paradise Valley Country. Home: 5786 N Echo Canyon Cir Phoenix AZ 85018-1242 Office: Bowmar Instrument Corp 5080 N 40th St Ste 475 Phoenix AZ 85018-2150

WHITE, ERSKINE NORMAN, JR., management company executive; b. N.Y.C., July 21, 1924; s. Erskine Norman and Catharine (Putman) W.; m. Eileen E. Lutz, Nov. 5, 1949; children: Erskine Norman III, Carol Putnam White Wolfe, Catharine Lutz. BE, Yale U., 1947; MS, MIT, 1949. Staff mem. rsch. devel. bd. Dept. Def., 1949; plant mgr. Gorham Mfg. Co. (became Gorham Corp. 1961, Gorham div. Textron Inc. 1968), Asheville, N.C., 1956-57, 1956-57, exec. v.p., 1964-68, pres., 1968-69, dir., 1960-69; group v.p. Textron Inc., Providence, 1969-71; exec. v.p. ops. Textron Inc., 1971-75, exec. v.p., 1975-79, exec. v.p. corp. affairs, 1979-81; pres. E.N. White Mgmt. Corp., Providence, 1981-95; v.p., treas. Cadwagan Assoc.; bd. dirs. Keyport Life Ins. Co., R.I. Hosp., Trust Nat. Bank, Carlisle Cos. Inc., 1983-95. Trustee Women and Infants Hosp., R.I., 1974-93, R.I. Sch. Design, 1966-72, 82-95, chmn. fin. com., 1988-95, treas., 1990-95; bd. dirs., exec. com. New Eng. Coun., 1979-81; chmn. NCCJ, 1987-89. With USN, 1944-46, PTO. Mem. NAM (bd. dir. 1974-80, regional v.p. 1975, div. vice chmn. 1978-80, exec. com.), Urban League (bd. dir. R.I. chpt. 1989—), Greater Providence C. of C. (bd. dir., pres. 1978), R.I. C. of C. Fedn. (pres. 1979), Sigma Xi, Tau Beta Pi. Office: 56 Pine St Ste 3A Providence RI 02903-2819

WHITE, EUGENE R., computer manufacturing company executive. With Gen. Electric Co., Fairfield, Conn., 1958-70, Fairchild Camera & Instrument Corp., 1970-74; chmn., chief exec. officer Amdahl Corp., Sunnyvale, Calif., from 1974, now vice chmn., also bd. dirs. Office: Amdahl Corp PO Box 3470 1250 E Arques Ave Sunnyvale CA 94088*

WHITE, EUGENE VADEN, pharmacist; b. Cape Charles, Va., Aug. 13, 1924; s. Paul Randolph and Louise (Townsend) W.; m. Laura Juanita LaFontaine, Aug. 28, 1948; children: Lynda Sue, Patricia Louise. BS in Pharmacy, Med. Coll. Va., 1950; PharM (hon.), Phila. Coll. Pharmacy and Sci., 1966. Pharmacist McKim & Huffman Drug Store, Luray, Va., 1950, Miller's Drug Store, Winchester, Va., 1950-53; pharmacist, ptnr. Shiner's Drug Store, Front Royal, Va., 1953-56; pharmacist, owner Eugene V. White, Pharmacist, P.C., Berryville, Va., 1956—; Sturmer lectr. Phila. Coll. Pharmacy and Sci., 1979; Lubin vis. prof. U. Tenn. Sch. Pharmacy, Memphis, 1974; mem. bd. visitors Sch. Pharmacy, U. Pitts., 1969. Author: The Office-Based Family Pharmacist, 1978; created first office practice in community pharmacy, 1960, developed patient medication profile record, 1960. 2d lt. USAAC, 1943-45. Recipient Nat. Leadership award Phi Lambda Sigma, 1979, Outstanding Pharmacy Alumnus award Med. Coll. Va. Sch. Pharmacy Alumni Assn., 1989. Fellow Am. Coll. Apothecaries (J. Leon Lascoff award 1973); mem. Am. Pharm Assn. (Daniel B. Smith award 1965, Remington Honor medal 1978), Va. Pharm. Assn. (Pharmacist of Yr. award 1966, Outstanding Pharmacist award 1992). Methodist. Avocations: reading, woodworking, computer. Office: 1 W Main St Berryville VA 22611-1340

WHITE, FAITH, sculptor; b. N.Y.C., Apr. 7, 1950; d. Edward and Faith-Hope (Green) Kahn. BA summa cum laude, L.I. U., 1971; studied woodcarving, with Nathaniel Burwash, Cambridge, Mass., 1976, with Joseph Wheelwright, Boston, 1977-94. Freelance sculptor Boston, 1971—, N.Y.C., 1995—; adminstrv. asst. to dean of students Grahm Jr. Coll., Boston, 1972-74; exec. sec. to New Eng. regional mgr. Bur. of Nat. Affairs, Inc., Boston, 1974-77; asst. to dir. New Eng. Aquarium, Boston, 1977-80, dir. pers., 1980-82; guest juror for travel grant Boston Visual Artists Union, 1994; show mgr. Sculpture and Large Works, The Copley Soc. of Boston, 1992; instr. woodcarving The Eliot Sch., Jamaica Plain, Mass., 1992-94; tchg. artist Very Spl. Arts program Mus. of Sci., Boston, 1992, 93; project coord. First Night, Boston, 1986, 87, 88; judge Sr. Panel Carving competition Belmont (Mass.) Hill Sch., 1985; docent Hands-On Sculpture show New Eng. Sculptors Assn. at Mus. of Sci., Boston, 1984. One-woman show at Mills Gallery, Boston, 1987; two-person invitational show at The Copley Soc. of Boston, 1994; other exhbns. include Boston Ctr. for Arts, 1984, 85, Boston Visual Artists Union Gallery, 1985, Concord Art Assn., 1985, Cambridge Art Assn., 1986, The Copley Soc. of Boston, 1984, 85, 88, 89, 91, 92, 93, 94, 95 (including holiday invitationals for award winners 1988, 91, 92), Fed. Res. Bank of Boston Gallery, 1989, with Copley Masters, 1984, Howard Yezerski Gallery, 1989, 90, 91, 92, 93, 94, 95, Libr. Ctr., Newport, Mass., 1990, Landau Gallery, Belmont Hill Sch., 1991, Attleboro (Mass.) Mus., 1992, Gallery NAGA, Boston, 1992, others; represented in permanent collection Sherrill House, Boston. Liaison between mission com. Trinity Ch., Boston and vol. program Sherrill House Nursing Home, 1987-94. Mem. Copley Soc. of Boston (Copley Master 1992), New Eng. Sculptors Assn. (bd. dirs., mem.-at-large 1985-86, 88-89), Nat. Sculpture Soc. Episcopalian. Avocations: fitness training, sailing. Studio: 115 E 34th St New York NY 10016-4629

WHITE, FLORENCE MAY, learning disabilities specialist; b. Ottawa, Kans., Sept. 1, 1936; d. O.C. Robert and Effie Lynne (Walker) Arnold; m. Donald L. White, June 1, 1958; children: Tab Vincent, Jacque Sue, Michelle May. BA, Ottawa U., 1958; MS, Kans. U., 1974; postgrad., Kans. U. Med. Ctr., 1975-76. Cert. reading specialist, learning disabilities specialist; cert. elem. and mid. sch. edn.: lang. arts, social studies, elem. curriculum. Classroom tchr. 2d grade Wellsville (Kans.) Elem., 1958-59; learning disabilities tchr. Olatha (Kans.) Spl. Edn. Coop., 1971-74; learning disabilities specialist, tchr. 7-9 Ottawa Mid. Sch., 1974-77; learning disabilities specialist, tchr. Paola Spl. Edn. Coop., Richmond, Kans., 1980-95; pub. rep., speaker on learning disabilities to civic groups and local orgns., 1972-75. Den mother Boy Scouts Am. and Brownies, Ottawa, 1968-70; chair state GOP women's polit. activities Rep. State Party, Topeka, 1964-67; chair scholarship contest DAR, Ottawa dist., 1984—; Sunday sch. tchr. Meth. Ch., Ottawa; crafts tchr. local 4-H, Ottawa; mem. Central Heights PTA (projects com. 1980-95). State of Kans. scholar State Spl. Edn. Dept., 1976. Mem. Internat. Reading Assn., Kans. Reading Assn., Franklin County Reading Coun. (exec. bd. 1993-94, v.p., pres.-elect 1989-91, pres. 1991-92), Alpha Delta Kappa (projects com. 1988—, environment com., planning asst. to asst. pastor). Roman Catholic. Avocations: oil painting, reading, travel, swimming, flower arranging, shopping.

WHITE, FREDERICK ANDREW, physics educator, physicist; b. Detroit, Mar. 11, 1918; s. Andrew Bracken and Mildred (Witzel) W.; m. Dorothy Janet Sibley, Nov. 7, 1942 (dec.); children: Wendell William, Lawrence Sibley, Eric Sibley, Roger Randolph (dec.). B.S., Wayne State U., 1940; M.S., U. Mich., 1941; postgrad., U. Rochester, 1943-46; Ph.D., U. Wis., 1959. Insp. U.S. Army Ordnance, Rochester, N.Y., 1941-43; research asst. Manhattan project U. Rochester, 1943-45, grad. instr. in research, 1946; research asst., research asso., cons. physicist Gen. Electric Co. Knolls Atomic Power Lab., Schenectady, 1947-62; adj. prof. nuclear sci. Rensselaer Poly. Inst., Troy, N.Y., 1961-62; prof. nuclear engring. and environmental engring., indsl. liaison scientist Rensselaer Poly. Inst., 1962-81, prof. emeritus, 1981—; mem. staff Bell Telephone Labs., 1969; research and liaison scientist Rochester Gas & Electric Co., N.Y., 1978—; adj. prof. physics SUNY, Albany, 1981-88; cons. NASA, 1965—; organist and acoustic cons., 1952—. Author: American Industrial Research Laboratories, 1961, Mass Spectrometry in Science and Technology, 1968, Our Acoustic Environment, 1975; Mass Spectrometry: Applications in Science and Engineering, 1986. Mem. AIAA, AAAS, IEEE, Am. Nuclear Soc., Am. Phys. Soc., Optical Soc. Am., Acoustical Soc. Am., Am. Chem. Soc., Am. Guild Organists, Soc. Applied Spectroscopy, Sigma Xi. Developer mass spectrometric instrumentation and its uses in measurements relating to nuclear and atomic physics; co-discoverer last naturally-occurring stable isotope. Home: 2456 Hilltop Rd Niskayuna NY 12309-2405 Office: Rensselaer Poly Inst Linac Lab Troy NY 12181

WHITE, GAYLE COLQUITT, religion writer, journalist; b. Lamar County, Ga., Nov. 4, 1950; d. Albert Candler and Ethel Eugenia (Moore) Colquitt; m. Robert Eugene White, Jr., Apr. 9, 1972; children: Margaret Candler, Robert Eugene III. AB in Journalism, U. Ga., 1972. Reporter Atlanta Jour. & Constn., 1972—. Named Templeton Reporter of Yr., Religion Newswriters Assn., 1992. Presbyterian. Office: Atlanta Journal & Constitution 72 Marietta St NW Atlanta GA 30303-2804

WHITE, GEORGE, government official, physical scientist; b. Bklyn., Dec. 19, 1937; s. Samuel Louis and Mollie (Telson) W.; m. Susan Jane Doppelhammer, Apr. 13, 1969; 1 child, Jeffrey Steven. B.S., CUNY, 1960; M.S., NYU, 1964; postgrad. Am. U., 1966-68. Research asst. Rockefeller Inst., N.Y.C., 1960, NYU, N.Y.C., 1961-64; research scientist Atlantic Research Corp., Alexandria, Va., 1965-72; sr. staff officer Nat. Acad. Scis., Washington, 1973-80; div. chief, asst. to dir. U.S. Bur. Mines, Dept. Interior, Washington, 1981—; lectr. chemistry, No. Va. Community Coll., Alexandria, Va., 1972-78, Bronx Community Coll., 1961-64; spl. asst. to congressman Ed Pastor, 1995—. Staff editor: Chemistry of Coal Utilization, 1980, Minerals and Materials, 1983—, Minerals Position of the U.S., 1985—. Named Presdl. Sci. Intern, Nat. Sci. Found., Dept. Transp., 1972; Legis. fellow U.S. Congress, 1992. Mem. Am. Chem. Soc., AAAS, Am. Inst. Mining Engrs., Washington Chem. Soc. Democrat. Jewish. Home: 3903 Forest Grove Dr Annandale VA 22003-1961 Office: Dept Interior US Bur Mines 810 7th St NW Washington DC 20241-0001

WHITE, GEORGE COOKE, theater director, foundation executive; b. New London, Conn., Aug. 16, 1935; s. Nelson Cooke and Aida (Rovetti) W.; m. Elizabeth Conant Darling, July 5, 1958; children: George Conant, Caleb Ensign, Juliette Darling. Student, U. Paris, 1956; BA, Yale U., 1957, MFA, 1961; student, Shakespeare Inst., 1959; ArtsD (hon.), Conn. Coll., 1994. Stage mgr. Imperial Japanese Azumakabuki Co., 1955; asst. mgr. Internat. Ballet Festival, Nervi, Italy, 1955; prodn. coordinator Talent Assos., 1961-63; adminstrv. v.p. score prodns. Paramount Pictures, 1963-65; founder, pres. Eugene O'Neill Meml. Theatre Found., 1965—; adviser, dir. Theatre One, Conn. Coll. Women, 1967-70; regional theater cons. Nat. Ednl. TV Network;

guest lectr. Wagner Coll., 1970; acting dir. Hunter Coll. Hunter Arts, 1972-73; adj. prof. U. N.C.; prof. theater adminstrn. program Yale U., 1978-91; co-chmn. Yale Drama Sch.; mem. exec. com. Theatre Library Assn., 1967; bd. govs. Am. Playwrights Theatre; mem. bd. ANTA, 1967-68; mem. Mayor N.Y.C.'s. Theatre Adv. Com.; advisory bd. Internat. Theatre Inst.; panel mem. Exptl. Theatre; U.S. State Dept. cultural exchange grantee to Australia; guest adminstr. Australian Nat. Playwrights Conf., 1973; U.S. del. Internat. Theatre Inst. Congress, Moscow, 1973; mem. Conn. Commn. on Arts, 1978-93, mem. exec. com., 1979-83, vice chair, 1992-93; co-founder Caribbean-U.S. Theatre Exchange; dir. Actors Theatre St. Paul, 1979, 80, 82, 83, 86, Hartman Repertory Theatre, 1980; guest dir. Chinese Theater Assn., Beijing, 1984, 87, Hedgerow Theatre, 1986; mem. nominating com. Antoinette Perry Awards, 1984-86, 88, 94; dir. Anna Christie Beijing Cen. Dramatic Theater, 1984, 87. Appeared in TV series Citizen Soldier, 1959-61; appeared in off-Broadway prodn. John Brown's Body. Trustee Goodspeed Opera House, 1966-68, Nat. Theatre Conf., 1973—, Eastern Conn. Symphony, Dance Arts Coun., Conn. Opera Assn., Conn. Pub. TV, 1973-83, Mitchell Coll., 1994—, Arts & Bus. Coun., 1994—; Trustee Conn. Edn. Telecommunications Corp., 1973-83, chmn., 1982; mem. planning bd. Op. Rescue; bd. dirs. Rehearsal Club, Centre for Inter-Am. Rels., Theater of Latin Am., Manhattan Theatre Club, 1970-80, Met. Opera Guild; Performance mag.; exec. com. Yale Drama Alumni, 1963-73; mem. Yale Alumni Bd.; bd. overseers drama dept. Brandeis U.; adv. bd. Am. Musical Theatre Program, Hartford Conservatory, Bd. Arts & Bus. Coun., Brandeis Creative Arts Award Jury, Theater and New Music Theatre Works Panel, NEA; mem. Waterford (Conn.) Rep. Town Meeting, 1975-77; presdl. appointment to Nat. Coun. NEA, 1992; mem. Coast Guard Auxillary, Crew mem. U.S. Coast Guard Barque Eagle. Served with AUS, 1957-59. Recipient spl. citation New Eng. Theatre Conf., 1968, Margo Jones award, 1968, Pub. Svc. award New London County Bar Assn., 1975, Disting. Citizen's award Town of Waterford, 1976, Disting. Service award Conn. mag., Contbns. to State award, 1981, Lifetime Contbn. to Theatre award Am. Theater Assn., Contbn. to Conn. Arts award Quinnipiac Coll., 1989; Internat. Communications Agy. cultural exch. grantee to People's Republic of China, 1980; Officer first class Royal Swedish Order of Polar Star; Chevalier des artes et des lettres (France). Fellow Royal Soc. Arts; mem. Chinese Theatre Assn. (hon.). Clubs: Century; Cosmos (Washington); Thames (New London); White's Point Yacht. Office: O'Neill Theater Ctr 305 Great Neck Rd Waterford CT 06385-3825

WHITE, GEORGE EDWARD, legal educator, lawyer; b. Northampton, Mass., Mar. 19, 1941; s. George LeRoy and Frances Dorothy (McCafferty) W.; m. Susan Valre Davis, Dec. 31, 1966; children: Alexandra V., Elisabeth McC. BA, Amherst Coll., 1963; MA, Yale U., 1964, PhD, 1967; J.D., Harvard U., 1970. Bar: D.C. 1970, Va. 1975, U.S. Supreme Ct. 1973. Vis. scholar Am. Bar Found., 1970-71; law clk. to Chief Justice Warren, U.S. Supreme Ct., 1971-72; asst. prof. law U. Va., 1972-74, assoc. prof., 1974-77, prof., 1977-86, John B. Minor prof. law and history, 1987-92, Disting. Univ. prof., John B. Minor prof. law and history, 1992—; vis. prof. Marshall-Wythe Law Sch. spring 1988, N.Y. Law Sch., fall 1988. Mem. Am. Acad. Arts and Scis., Am. Law Inst., Am. Soc. Legal History (bd. dirs. 1978-81), Soc. Am. Historians. Author books, including The American Judicial Tradition, 1976, 2d edit., 1988, Tort Law in America: An Intellectual History (Gavel award ABA 1981), 1980, Earl Warren: A Public Life (Gavel award ABA 1983), 1982, The Marshall Court and Cultural Change, 1988, 2d edit. 1991 (James Willard Hurst prize 1990), Justice Oliver Wendell Holmes: Law and the Inner Self, 1993 (Gavel award ABA 1994, Scribes award 1994, Littleton-Griswold prize 1994, Triennial Order of the Coif award 1996), Intervention and Detachment: Essays in Legal History and Jurisprudence, 1994; Oxford, U. Press, Creating the National Past Me: Baseball Transforms Itself, 1903-1953, 1996—,editor Studies in Legal History, 1980-86, Delegate in Law, 1986-96—. Office: U Va Law Sch Charlottesville VA 22903-1789

WHITE, GEORGE MALCOLM, architect; b. Cleve., Nov. 1, 1920; m. Susanne Neiley Daniels, Apr. 21, 1973; children: Stephanie, Jocelyn, Geoffrey, Pamela. B.S., MIT, 1942, M.S., 1942; M.B.A., Harvard, 1948; LL.B., Case Western Res. U., 1959. Design engr. Gen. Electric Co., Schenectady, 1942-47; practice architecture and law Cleve., 1948-71; Architect of Capitol, Washington, 1971-95; vice chmn., 1996—; bd. dirs. 3D Internat. Works include First Unitarian Ch., Cleve., 1959, Preformed Line Products Co. Office Bldg., Cleve., 1960, Mentor Harbor Yacht Club, 1968, restoration, Old Senate and Supreme Ct. Chambers, U.S. Capitol, 1975, Libr. of Congress James Madison Meml. Bldg., 1979, U.S. Capitol Power Plant Extension, 1979, master plan for U.S. Capitol, 1981, Hart Senate Office Bldg., 1982, restoration of the west cen. front U.S. Capitol Bldg., 1987, Thurgood Marshall Fed. Judiciary Bldg., 1992, U.S. Capitol west terr. restoration and courtyard addt., 1993. former mem. D.C. Zoning Commn., U.S. Capitol Police Bd., U.S. Capitol Guide Bd., U.S. Ho. of Reps. Page Bd., Adv. Coun. on Hist. Preservation, Internat. Ctr. Com., Nat. Conservation Adv. Coun., Nat. Capital Meml. Commn., art adv. com. Washington Met. Area Transit Auth.; former acting dir. U.S. Bot. Garden; former mem. bd. dirs., chmn. design com. Pennsylvania Ave. Devel. Corp.; former bd. dirs. Nat. Bldg. Mus.; former trustee Fed. City Coun.; mem. bd. regents Am. Archtl. Found; former chmn. archtl. adv. com. Restoration of Statue of Liberty; chmn. com. for Statue of Liberty Mus.; mem. nat. panel arbitrators Am. Arbitration Assn.; former mem. vis. com. dept. architecture and planning MIT; mem. bd. cons. Nubian monuments at Philae, Egypt; mem. internat. com. cons. for Egyptian Mus., Cairo; chmn. rev. com. Nat. Capital Devel. Commn. for Canberra, Australia. Recipient Gold medal Archtl. Soc. Ohio, 1971, Burton award for Disting. Pub. Svc. Cleve. Club, 1991. Fellow AIA (Thomas Jefferson award 1992), Nat. Soc. Profl. Engrs., ASCE (hon. fellow); mem. Sigma Xi, Eta Kappa Nu, Lambda Alpha, Tau Beta Pi. Office: Leo A Daly 1201 Connecticut Ave NW Washington DC 20036 Address: 3337 N St NW Washington DC 20007

WHITE, GEORGE W., federal judge; b. 1931. Student, Baldwin-Wallace Coll., 1948-51; J.D., Cleveland-Marshall Coll. Law, 1955. Sole practice law Cleve., 1956-68; judge Ct. Common Pleas, Ohio, 1968-80; judge U.S. Dist. Ct. (no. dist.) Ohio, 1980-95, chief judge, 1995—; referee Ct. Common Pleas, Cuyahoga County, 1957-62. Councilman, Cleve., 1963-68. Mem. ABA, Fed. Bar Assn., 6th Circuit Jud. Coun. (exec. com. 1995—). Office: US Dist Ct 135 US Courthouse 201 Superior Ave E Cleveland OH 44114-1201*

WHITE, GEORGE WENDELL, JR., lawyer; b. Washington, Nov. 9, 1915; s. George Wendell and Blanche E. (Berry) W.; m. Elnor L. Musson, Apr. 5, 1940; children: Randall C., Wendy Lou Gibson, Cynthia Lee Miller. AB, U. Md., College Park, 1937; LLB, U. Md., Balt., 1939. Bar: Md. 1939. Assoc. Weinberg & Green, Balt., 1940-50; sr. ptnr. White, Mindel, Clarke & Foard, Towson, Md., 1950—. Nat. campaign mgr. Nixon-Agnew, 1972, 76. Sgt. U.S. Army, 1942-45. Mem. ABA, Am. Coll. Trial Lawyers, Am. Bd. Trial Advocates, Md. Trial Lawyers Assn. (pres. 1988—), Elks, Optimists, Gamma Eta Gamma (nat. pres. 1939-42). Democrat. Methodist. Home: 5 Coldwater Ct Baltimore MD 21204-2044 Office: 40 W Chesapeake Ave Ste 300 Baltimore MD 21204-4803

WHITE, GERALD ANDREW, retired chemical company executive; b. L.I., N.Y., Aug. 2, 1934; s. Charles Eugene and Grace Mary (Trojan) W.; m. Mary Alice Turvey, June 8, 1957; children—Kevin, Patricia, Timothy, Megan. B in Chem. Engring., Villanova U., 1957; cert. advanced mgmt. program, Harvard Bus. Sch., 1975. Staff engr. Air Products and Chems., Inc., Allentown, Pa., 1962-65, mgr. systems devel., 1965-66, group controller, 1969-72, corp. controller, 1974-76, v.p. planning, 1977-82, v.p. fin., chief fin. officer, 1982-92, sr. v.p. fin., chief fin. officer, 1992-95. Pres. United Way in Lehigh County, 1981; bd. dirs. Pa. Coun. on Econ. Edn., 1981, Lord Corp., 1994; trustee, treas. Allentown Art Mus., 1984; trustee, chmn. bd. trustees Allentown Coll. St. Francis de Sales, Center Valley, 1983. Lt. USN, 1957-62. Recipient J. Stanley Morehouse Meml. award Villanova U. Coll. Engring., 1983. Mem. AICE, Fin. Execs. Inst. (pres. northeastern Pa. chpt. 1974-75), Fin. Execs. Rsch. Found. (trustee 1992), Tau Beta Pi. Avocation: squash.

WHITE, GILBERT F(OWLER), geographer, educator; b. Chgo., Nov. 26, 1911; s. Arthur E. and Mary (Guthrie) W.; m. Anne Elizabeth Underwood, Apr. 28, 1944; children: William D., Mary, Frances. BS, U. Chgo., 1932, SM, 1934, PhD, 1942; LLD (hon.), Hamilton Coll., 1951, Swarthmore Coll.; LL.D. (hon.), Earlham Coll., Richmond, Ind., Mich. State U., Augustana Coll.; ScD (hon.), Haverford Coll.; hon. degree, Northland Coll. Geographer Miss. Valley Com. of P.W.A., 1934, Nat. Resources Bd., 1934-35; sec. land and water com. Nat. Resources Com. and Nat. Resources Planning Bd., 1935-40; with Exec. Office Pres., Bur. Budget, 1941-42; asst. exec. sec. Am. Friends Service Com., 1945-46; relief adminstr. in France, 1942-43; interned Baden-Baden, 1943-44; sec. Am. Relief for India, 1945-46; pres. Haverford Coll., 1946-55; prof. geography U. Chgo., 1956-69; prof. geography, dir. Inst. Behavioral Sci., U. Colo., Boulder, 1970-78; Gustavson disting. prof. emeritus Inst. Behavioral Sci., U. Colo., 1979—; dir. Natural Hazards Info. Ctr., 1978-84, 92-94; exec. editor Environment mag., 1983-93; vis. prof. Oxford U., 1962-63; cons. Investigations Lower Mekong Basin, 1961-62, 70; U.S. mem. UNESCO adv. com. on arid zone research, 1954-55; mem. mission Am. Vol. Agys. Relief Germany, 1946; vice chmn. Pres.'s Water Resources Policy Commn., 1950; mem. com. natural resources Hoover Commn., 1948; chmn. UN Panel Integrated River Basin Devel., 1956-57; chmn. Task Force Fed. Flood Control Policy, 1965-66; sci. adv. to adminstr. UN Devel. Program, 1966-71; chmn. adv. bd. Energy Policy Project, 1972-74; chmn. Am. Friends Service Com., 1963-69; chmn. com. on man and environment IGU, 1969-76; chmn. steering com. High Sch. Geography com., 1964-70; mem. Tech. Assessment Adv. Council, 1974-76; chmn. environ. studies bd. NRC, 1975-77; pres. Sci. Com. on Problems of Environment, 1976-82; chmn. bd. Resources for Future, 1973-79; co-chmn. U.S.-Egypt Joint Consultative Com. on Sci. and Tech., 1981-86; mem. adv. group on greenhouse gases World Meteorol. Orgn., Internat. Council of Scientific Unions, UN Environ. Program., 1986-90; chmn. tech. rev. com. Nev. Nuclear Waste Project, 1987-93; mem. adv. group on water UN Environ. Program, 1989-93, working group for Action Plan for Aral Sea Basin, USSR, 1990-93; chmn. nat. rev. com. Status U.S. Floodplain Mgmt., 1989. Author: Human Adjustment to Floods, 1942, Science and Future of Arid Lands, 1960, Social and Economic Aspects of Natural Resources, 1962, Choice of Adjustment to Floods, 1964, Strategies of American Water Management, 1969; co-author: Drawers of Water, 1972, Assessment of Research on Natural Hazards, 1975, Flood Hazard in the United States, 1975, The Environment as Hazard, 1978, also various govt. reports, 1937-45; editor: Natural Hazards: Local, National and Global, 1974, Environmental Aspects of Complex River Development, 1977; co-editor: Environmental Issues, 1977, The World Environment, 1972-1982, 1982, Environmental Effects of Nuclear War, 1983. Reicpient Daly medal Am. Geog. Soc., 1971, Eben award Am. Water Resources Assn., 1972, Caulfield medal, 1989, Alumni medal U. Chgo., 1979, Outstanding Achievement award Nat. Coun. for Geog. Edn., 1981, Sasakawa UN Evniron. prize, 1985, Tyler prize, 1987, Laureat d'Honneur award Internat. Geog. Union, 1988, Vautrin Lud Internat. Geog. prize, 1992, Hubbard medal Nat. Geog. Soc., 1994, Volvo Environment prize, 1995. Mem. NAS (mem. commn. on natural resources 1973-80, chmn. 1977-80, chmn. com. on water 1964-68, Environ. award 1980), Assn. Am. Geographers (pres., Outstanding Achievement award 1955, 74, Anderson medal 1986), Internat. Coun. Sci. Unions (mem. steering com. on study of environ. consequences of nuclear war 1983-87, mem. adv. com. on environ. 1990—), Russian Geog. Soc. (hon.), Royal Geog. Soc. (hon.), Russian Acad. Scis. (fgn.), Am. Philos. Soc., Cosmos Club (Washington, award 1993), Sigma Xi,. Mem. Soc. Friends. Home: 624 Pearl St Apt 302 Boulder CO 80302-5072

WHITE, GLORIA WATERS, university administrator; b. St. Louis County, Mo., May 16, 1934; d. James Thomas and Thelma Celestine (Brown) W.; B.A., Harris Tchrs. Coll., 1956; M.A., Washington U., St. Louis, 1963, LLM, 1980; m. W. Glenn White, Jan. 1, 1955; 1 child, Terry Anita White Glover. Tchr., St. Louis Bd. Edn., 1956-63, counselor, 1963-67; dir. office spl. projects Washington U., 1967-76, asst. to assoc. vice chancellor personnel and affirmative action, 1975-88, vice chancellor for personnel, affirmative action officer, 1988-91, vice chancellor human resources, 1991—. Bd. dirs. Am. Assn. Affirmative Action, 1974-77; instl. chair Arts and Edn. Fund, 1975-88; mem. Eastern Dist. Mo. Desegregation and Adv. Com., 1981-82; bd. trustees, Blue Cross/Blue Shield of Mo., 1984—, chmn. 1994—; bd. trustees, The Caring Found., 1989—; adv. bd., Tchrs. Ins. Annuity Assn., 1988-91; bd. dirs., Bi state chpt. officer ARC, 1989—, chmn. 1994—; bd. dirs., Cath. Charities, 1993—, YWCA Met. St. Louis, 1993—, Goodwill Industries of Mo.; vice chmn., bd. dir. Caring Found. Accredited exec. in personnel, sr. profl. in human resources; cert. life counselor, life tchr. Recipient citations Urban League, Pres.'s Council Youth Opportunities, Disting. Alumni award Harris State Coll., 1987, Dollars and Sense award, 1992, Clara Barton Vol. Svc. award ARC, 1993.. Mem. Coll. and Univ. Personnel Assn. (bd. dirs. 1981-88, pres. 1986-87, 87-88, v.p. rsch. and publs. 1981-85, pres.-elect 1985-86, immediate past pres. 1987-88, v.p., Creativity award 1981, Disting. Service award 1988, Kathryn G. Hansen Publs. award 1989), Am. Soc. Personnel Adminstrn., Pers. Accreditation Inst. (bd. dirs.), St. Louis Symphony Soc., Delta Sigma Theta (v.p. St. Louis Alumnae chpt. 1989-91, nat. social action commr. 1988—, pres. St. Louis alumnae chpt. 1991—, chmn. exec. bd., chmn. Blitz Build habitat for humanity, 1994, chmn. 42nd convention, 1994, dir. leadership acad. 1994—). Author: Profiles of Success in the Human Resource Management Profession, 1991. Roman Catholic. Home: 545 Delprice Ct Saint Louis MO 63124-1912 Office: PO Box 1184 Saint Louis MO 63188-1184

WHITE, GORDON ELIOT, historian; b. Glen Ridge, N.J., Oct. 25, 1933; s. Maurice Brewster and Sarah Fullove (Gordon) W.; m. Nancy Johnson, 1955 (div. 1957); m. Mary Joan Briggs, Aug. 6, 1960 (dec. Nov. 1987); children: Sarah Elizabeth and Gordon O'Neal Brewster (twins), David McIntyre; m. Francis C. Barrineau, 1989. B.A., Cornell U., 1955; M.S. in Journalism, Columbia U., 1957. Lic. master mariner USCG; lic. pilot FAA. Stringer Nassau Daily Rev.-Star, Rockville Centre, L.I., N.Y., 1948-50; stringer Freeport (N.Y.) Leader, 1949-50; sports writer Morris County (N.J.) Citizen, 1950-51; stringer Ithaca (N.Y.) Evening News, 1951-55; photo editor, editorial writer Cornell Daily Sun, 1951-55; copy editor Am. Banker, N.Y.C., 1958; Washington corr. Chgo. Am., 1958-61; chief Washington bur. Deseret News, Salt Lake City, 1961-88; also corr. in Europe, U.S. and Antarctic for WJR, Detroit; KSL-KSL-TV, Salt Lake City, also KGMB, Honolulu; free lance writer with U.S. Navy, Army and Air Force, 1959; cons. Nat. Air and Space Mus.; auto racing, mil. aviation electronics historian. Author: Offenhauser, the Legendary American Racing Engine and the Men Who Built It, 1996. Advisor auto racing Nat. Mus. Am. History, Smithsonian Instn., 1989—. Recipient 1st prize for newsphoto Sigma Delta Chi, 1954; Raymond Clapper Meml. award White House Corrs. Assn., 1978; award for excellence in reporting Exec. Dept. and White House; award for excellence in reporting Nat. Press Club, 1979; award for investigative reporting Utah-Idaho-Spokane Regional AP; Nat. Sigma Delta Chi award for disting. work as Washington Corr., 1979; Roy W. Howard award for outstanding public service by a newspaper corr., 1979; award for disting. investigative reporting Investigative Reporters and Editors, 1980; Disting. Public Service Reporting Service Scripps Howard Found., 1980; Mark E. Peterson award, 1980; Reser-Tuthill award for writing on history of automobile racing, Indpls., 1985. Mem. Sigma Delta Chi, Pi Kappa Phi, Pi Delta Epsilon. Episcopalian. Club: Nat. Press (Washington). Home and Office: Box 3067 Alexandria VA 22302

WHITE, H. BLAIR, lawyer; b. Burlington, Iowa, Aug. 2, 1927; s. Harold B. and Harriet E. (St. Clair) W.; m. Joan Van Alstine, Oct. 2, 1954; children—Blair W., Brian J. B.A., U. Iowa, 1950, J.D., 1951. Bar: Ill. 1951. Assoc. Sidley & Austin and predecessor firms, 1951-61, ptnr., 1962-95; dir. DeKalb Energy Corp., 1967-95, Kimberly-Clark Corp., 1971-95, R.R. Donnelley & Sons Co., 1979—, Bankmont Fin. Corp., 1986-92, DeKalb Genetics Co., 1988—. Pres., bd. dirs. Cook County (Ill.) Sch. Nursing, 1966-71; bd. dirs. Rush-Presbyn.-St. Lukes Med. Ctr., 1986-93, life trustee; bd. dirs. Children's Meml. Hosp., Chgo., 1980—, chmn. bd. dirs., 1993—. Mem. ABA, Ill. Bar Assn., Chgo. Bar Assn., Am. Coll. Trial Lawyers, 7th Fed. Cir. Bar Assn., Commercial Club, Legal Club, Law Club, Chgo. Club, Econ. Club (Chgo.), Skokie Country Club, Old Elm Country Club, Lost Tree Club. Office: Sidley & Austin 1 First Nat Plz Chicago IL 60603

WHITE, HAROLD F., bankruptcy judge, retired federal judge; b. Hartford, Conn., Apr. 29, 1920; s. Harry and Maude C. (Strainge) W.; m. Edna Jeannette Murie, 1943; children: Francis James, Susan, Harold. BSc, Ohio U., 1946; JD, U. Akron, 1952. Bar: Ohio 1952. Chief police prosecutor City of Akron, Ohio, 1953; asst. prosecutor Summit County, Akron, 1957-58; bankruptcy referee, bankruptcy judge U.S. Cts., Akron, 1958-94; on recall as sr. bankruptcy judge U.S. Cts., 1994—. Trustee Summit County Kidney Found; elder Westminster Presbyn. Ch., Akron. Named Disting. Alumni Ohio U., 1979, Outstanding Alumni U. Akron Sch. Law, 1983; recipient John Quine adj. lectr. of law award U. Akron Sch. Law, 1991. Mem. Akron Bar Assn., Ohio State Bar Assn., Nat. Conf. Bankruptcy Judges (twice gov. 6th cir.), Commercial Law League, Am. Bankruptcy Inst. Office: US Bankruptcy Ct Fed Bldg Rm 240 2 S Main St Akron OH 44308-1813

WHITE, HAROLD TREDWAY, III, management consultant; b. Stamford, Conn., Nov. 3, 1947; m. Elizabeth Phillips. BA in History, Northwestern U., 1970; MBA, Darmouth U., 1974. Asst. to dir. urban affairs Am. Bankers Assn., Washington, 1972-73; sr. assoc. Cresap, McCormick & Paget Cons., 1974-75; dir. planning and devel. Tilton (N.H.) Sch., 1975-78; dir. alumni affairs Amos Tuck Sch. Dartmouth U., Hanover, N.H., 1978-82; chief devel. officer Manhattanville Coll., Purchase, N.Y., 1982-84; cons., 1985; pres. Resource Dynamics Group, White Plains, N.Y., 1987—; adj. asst. prof. Iona Coll., New Rochelle, N.Y., 1989-93; assoc. mem. cons. bd. Nat. Ctr. Nonprofit Bds., Washington, 1991—. Contbr. articles to profl. jours. Trustee, v.p., chmn. planning, devel. and mktg. coms. Tilton Sch., 1978—, pres. bd., 1992—; bd. dirs. Legal Awareness of Westchester, 1990—, Westchester Ctr. for Tng. and Devel., 1992—; pres. bd. Sci. Ctr. N.H., 1979-82, Nat. Coun. on Alcoholism and Other Drug Addictions/Westchester, 1985-89, Middle Patent Assn., 1988—; trustee Millbrook (N.Y.) Sch., 1981-87. Avocations: cross-country running, skiing, hiking, sailing. Office: Resource Dynamics Group 215 Katonah Ave Katonah NY 10536-2138

WHITE, HARRY EDWARD, JR., lawyer; b. Menominee, Mich., Apr. 26, 1939; s. Harry Edward and Verena Charlotte (Leisen) W.; m. Mary P.A. Sheaffer, June 7, 1980. BS in Fgn. Svc., Georgetown U., Washington, 1961; LLB, Columbia U., 1964. Bar: N.Y. 1965, U.S. Supreme Ct. 1970, U.S. Dist. Ct. (so. dist.) N.Y. 1979, U.S. Tax Ct. 1980. Assoc. Milbank, Tweed, Hadley & McCloy, N.Y.C., 1964-65, 67-73, ptnr., 1974—. Contbr. chpts. to books, articles to legal jours. Served with M.I., U.S. Army, 1965-66, Vietnam. Decorated Bronze Star. Mem. ABA, Internat. Bar Assn., N.Y. State Bar Assn. (chmn. taxation com. internat. law practice sect. 1987-90, co-chmn. exempt orgns. com. tax sect. 1987-88), Internat. Law Assn., Am. Soc. Internat. Law, Assn. Bar of City of N.Y., Internat. Fiscal Assn. Republican. Roman Catholic. Home: 333 E 55th St New York NY 10022-8316 Office: Milbank Tweed Hadley & McCloy 1 Chase Manhattan Plz New York NY 10005-1401

WHITE, HERBERT SPENCER, research library educator, university dean; b. Vienna, Austria, Sept. 5, 1927; came to U.S., 1938, naturalized, 1944; s. Leon and Ernestine (Lichteneger) Hochweis; m. Mary Virginia Dyer, Feb. 19, 1953; 1 son, Jerome. BS in Chemistry, CCNY, 1949; MSLS, Syracuse U., 1950. Intern Libr. of Congress, Washington, 1950, mem. tech. info. divsn., 1950-53; tech. libr. AEC, Oak Ridge, Tenn., 1953-54; organizer, mgr. corp. libr. Chance Vought Aircraft, Dallas, 1954-59; mgr. engring. libr. IBM Corp., Kingston, N.Y., 1959-62; mgr. tech. info. ctr. IBM Corp., Poughkeepsie, N.Y., 1962-64; exec. dir. NASA Sci. and Tech. Info. Facility, College Park, Md., 1964-68; v.p. info. mgmt. Leasco Systems & Rsch. Corp., Bethesda, Md., 1968-70; sr. v.p. Inst. Sci. Info., Phila., 1970-74, corp. dir., 1971-74; pres. Stechert-Macmillan, Inc., Pennsaucken, N.J., 1974-75; prof., dir. Rsch. Ctr. Grad. Libr. Sch. Ind. U., Bloomington, 1975-80, dean Sch. Libr. and Info. Scis., 1980-90, disting. prof., 1991-95; prof. emeritus, 1995—; adj. prof. U. Ariz. Sch. Libr. Scis., 1995—; vis. prof. Alberta, San Jose State, Hawaii; cons., lectr. Author books; contbr. articles to profl. publs.; columnist Libr. Jour. Mem. Pres.'s Adv. Com. for Adminstrn. Title II-B Higher Edn. Act, 1965-68, Libr. Rsch. Planning Com. for 1980s, U.S. Dept. Edn. With USAAF, 1946-47. Spl. honoree, U. of Essen (Germany) Conf., 1992. Fellow Spl. Libraries Assn. (pres. 1969-70, J.C. Dana award 1985, Hall of Fame 1994); mem. ALA (councillor 1988—, planning com. 1989-91, Dewey medal 1987), Am. Soc. Info. Sci. (pres. 1973-74, W. Davis award 1977, award of merit 1981, named Pioneer, 1987), Assn. Libr. and Info. Sci. Edn. (chmn. govtl. rels. com. 1980-88), Am. Fedn. Info. Processing Socs. (dir. 1972-78), Federation Internationale de Documentation (Netherlands, bd. dir. 1976-78, treas. 1978-82), Soc. for Scholarly Pub. (bd. dirs. 1981-82), Assn. Rsch. Libraries (com. on libr. edn, 1983-85), Coun. Libr. Resources (rsch. priorities task force 1984-88, Ind. Libr. Lifetime Achievement award 1990), Beta Phi Mu (Svc. award 1995). Address: 330 E El Viento Green Valley AZ 85614-2246

WHITE, HUBERT, architecture department director. Dir. sch. architecture U. Ill., Urbana. Office: Sch Architecture U Ill at Urbana Urbana IL 61801*

WHITE, HUGH VERNON, JR., lawyer; b. Suffolk, Va., July 24, 1933; s. Hugh Vernon and Mary Lois (Claud) W.; m. Mary Margaret Flowers, Nov. 25, 1961; children: Hunter, William, John. BS in Civil Engring., Va. Mil. Inst., 1954; LLB, Washington & Lee U., 1961. Bar: Va. 1961. Engr. E.I. DuPont de Nemours & Co., Parlin, N.J., 1954-55; exec. dir. Va. Legis. Study Commn., Richmond, Va., 1961-63; assoc. Hunton & Williams, Richmond, 1963-69, ptnr., 1969—; bd. dirs. Pulaski Furniture Corp., Pulaski, Va. Mem. Richmond First, 1966—, pres., 1971. Served to capt. USAF, 1955-58. Mem. ABA, Va. Bar Assn., Richmond Bar Assn., Phi Beta Kappa, Omicron Delta Kappa. Presbyterian. Clubs: Commonwealth, Country (Richmond). Home: 512 Gaskins Rd S Richmond VA 23233-5710 Office: Hunton & Williams Riverfront Plaza East Tower 951 E Byrd St Richmond VA 23219-4040

WHITE, JAMEELA ADAMS, family nurse practitioner; b. Rochester, Pa., Oct. 19, 1954; d. Elie James Adams and Alease Rebecca (Waldron) Adams Curry; m. William Harrison White Jr., June 5, 1982; children: William Maurice, Jamel John. BS in Nursing, Hampton U., 1976; MSN, Pace U., 1995. RN, Ohio, N.Y.; family nurse practitioner. Pvt. duty nurse Cleve., 1976-78; asst. head nurse ICU, coronary care unit Brentwood Hosp., Cleve., 1978-79; asst. dir. nursing Astor Gardens Nursing Home, Bronx, N.Y., 1983-84; pub. health nurse Westchester County Health Dept., White Plains, N.Y., 1979-86; mgr. patient service VNS-Home Care, Bronx, 1986-90; home care nurse coord., asst. dir. patient svcs. Wartburg Home LTHHCP, Mt. Vernon, N.Y., 1990-95; FNP United Cerebral Palsy N.Y.S., Inc., N.Y.C., 1995—. Chairperson policy com. Union Child Day Care, Greenburgh, N.Y., 1991-93, mem. edn. com., 1987, bd. dirs., 1991—; pres. nurses unit 1st Bapt. Ch., Elmsford, N.Y., 1987-90; mem. North Elmsford Civic Assn., 1988—, TransAfrica, 1989-92. Recipient N.Y. State Health Svcs. Corps. grant., 1993-95. Mem. NAACP, ANA, N.Y. State Nurses Assn., Nat. Black Child Devel. Assn., Hampton Alumni Assn. (bd. dirs. 1986-91), Chi Eta Phi, Sigma Theta Tau. Democrat. Office: United Cerebral Palsy NYS 330 W 34 St New York NY 10001-2488

WHITE, JAMES BARR, lawyer, real estate investor, consultant; b. Haverhill, Mass., June 13, 1941; s. Ned and Shirlee (Euster) W.; m. Carol Klein, June 23, 1963; children: Michael Andrew, Laurie Alison, Elizabeth Ellen. BS, Tufts U., 1962; LLB, Columbia U., 1965; MPA, Harvard U., 1988. Bar: Mass. 1965. Assoc. Goulston & Storrs, Boston, 1965-71, ptnr., 1971-74; ptnr. Palmer & Dodge, Boston, 1974-89; pvt. practice cons. Boston, 1989—; pres. ELAW Corp., Concord, Mass., 1992—; mem. adv. com. MIT Ctr. for Real Estate Devel., Cambridge, 1987-89; dir. Nat. Realty Com., Washington, 1987-89. Chmn., mem. Town of Wayland (Mass.) Planning Bd., 1974-78; mem. Route 128 Area Com., Lincoln, Mass., 1985-87; mem. Town of Lincoln Planning Bd., 1991—, Town of Lincoln Hist. Dist. Commn., 1992—; bd. overseers New Eng. Conservatory, 1995—. Mem. Boston Bar Assn., Handel and Haydn Soc. (gov. 1985-90, overseer 1990-94), Bostonian Soc. (bd. dirs. 1990—). Home: 38 Bedford Rd Lincoln MA 01773-2037 Office: ELAW Corp Office of Pres 175 Sudbury Rd Concord MA 01742-3419

WHITE, JAMES BOYD, law educator; b. Boston, July 28, 1938; s. Benjamin Vroom and Charlotte Green (Conover) W.; m. Mary Louise Fitch, Jan. 1, 1978; children: Emma Lillian, Henry Alfred; children by previous marriage: Catherine Conover, John Southworth. A.B., Amherst Coll., 1960; A.M., Harvard U., 1961, LL.B., 1964. Assoc. Foley, Hoag & Eliot, Boston, 1964-67; asst. prof. law U. Colo., 1967-69, assoc. prof., 1969-73, prof., 1973-75; prof. law U. Chgo., 1975-83; Hart Wright prof. law and English U. Mich., Ann Arbor, 1983—; vis. assoc. prof. Stanford U., 1972. Author: The Legal Imagination, 1973, (with Scarboro) Constitutional Criminal Procedure, 1976, When Words Lose Their Meaning, 1981, Heracles' Bow, 1985, Justice as Translation, 1990, "This Book of Starres", 1994, Acts of Hope, 1994. Sinclair Kennedy Traveling fellow, 1964-65; Nat. Endowment for Humanities fellow, 1979-80, 92; Guggenheim fellow, 1993. Mem. AAAS, Am. Law Inst. Office: U Mich Law Sch 625 S State St Ann Arbor MI 48109-1215

WHITE, JAMES CLAIBORNE, manufacturing engineer; b. Xenia, Ohio, May 6, 1962; s. John Delano and Janice Claire (Ingram) W.; m. Janna Unger, Aug. 24, 1985; children: Dakota James, Tristan Garrett, Colton Laramy. BS in Mech. Engring., Tenn. Tech. U., Cookeville, 1987; MS in Indsl. Engring., Purdue U., 1993. Registered profl. engr., Ky., Tenn. Quality assurance analsyt Johnson Controls, Inc., Greenfield, Ohio, 1987-88; mech. engr. Big Rivers Electric Corp., Henderson, Ky., 1988-95; sr. mfg. engr. Calsonic N.Am.-Tenn. Ops., Shelbyville, 1995—. Pres. Collegiate Bowling League, Cookeville, Tenn., 1984-85, U. Christian Student Ctr., Cookeville, 1984-85; fin. dir. local non-profit orgn., Evansville, Ind., 1993-95. Mem. ASME (assoc.), NSPE (engr. amb. 1989—, mathcounts co-chair 1989). Republican. Mem. Ch. of Christ. Achievements include design of modified sulfuric acid storage tanks; development and teaching of AutoCAD course at Henderson Community College; development of joint-venture contract between local electric utility and municipal wastewater treatment plant to provide water and waste services to newly located industry. Office: Calsonic NAm-Tenn Ops One Calsonic Way PO Box 350 Shelbyville TN 37160

WHITE, JAMES EDWARD, geophysicist; b. Cherokee, Tex., May 10, 1918; s. William Cleburne and Willie (Carter) W.; m. Courtenay Brumby, Feb. 1, 1941; children: Rebecca White Vanderslice, Peter McDuffie, Margaret Marie White Jamleson, Courtenay White Forte. B.A., U. Tex., 1941, M.A., 1946; Ph.D., MIT, 1949. Dir. Underwater Sound Lab., MIT, Cambridge, 1941-45; scientist Def. Research Lab., Austin, Tex., 1945-46; research assoc. MIT, 1946-49; group leader, field research lab. Mobil Oil Co., Dallas, 1949-55; mgr. physics dept. Denver Research Center, Marathon Oil Co., 1955-69; v.p. Globe Universal Scis., Midland, Tex., 1969-71; adj. prof. dept. geophysics Colo. Sch. Mines, Golden, 1972-73, C.H. Green prof., 1976-87, prof. emeritus, 1986—; L.A. Nelson prof. U. Tex., El Paso, 1973-76; Esso vis. prof. U. Sydney, Australia, 1975; vis. prof. MIT, 1982, U. Tex.-Austin, 1985, Macquarie U., Sydney, 1988; del. U.S.-USSR geophysics exchange Dept. State, 1965; mem. bd. Am. Geol. Inst., 1972; mem. space applications bd. Nat. Acad. Engring., 1972-77; exchange scientist Nat. Acad. Sci., 1973-74; del. conf. on oil exploration China Geophys. Soc.-Soc. Exploration Geophysicists, 1981; cons. world bank Chinese U. Devel. Project II, 1987. Author: Seismic Waves: Radiation, Transmission, Attenuation, 1965, Underground Sound: Application of Seismic Waves, 1983, (with R.L. Sengbush) Production Seismology, 1987; editor: Vertical Seismic Profiling (E.I. Galperin), 1974; contbr. articles to profl. jours.; patentee in field. Recipient Halliburton award, 1987. Fellow Acoustical Soc. Am.; mem. NAE, Soc. Exploration Geophysicists (hon., Maurice Ewing medal 1986), Cosmos Club, Sigma Xi. Unitarian. Office: Colo Sch Mines Dept Geophysics Golden CO 80401

WHITE, JAMES FLOYD, theology educator; b. Boston, Jan. 23, 1932; s. Edwin Turner and Madeline (Rinker) W.; m. Marilyn Atkinson, Aug. 23, 1959 (div. 1982); children: Louise, Robert, Ellen, Laura, Martin; m. Susan Jan Waller, Oct. 28, 1982 (div. 1993). Grad., Phillips Acad., Andover, Mass., 1949; AB, Harvard U., 1953; BD, Union Theol. Sem., 1956; PhD, Duke U., 1960. Ordained to ministry United Meth. Ch., 1955. Instr. Ohio Wesleyan U., Delaware, 1959-61, Meth. Theol. Sch. in Ohio, Delaware, 1960-61; prof. Perkins Sch. Theology, So. Meth. U., Dallas, 1961-83, U. Notre Dame, Ind., 1983—. Author: Cambridge Movement, 1962, New Forms of Worship, 1971, Introduction to Christian Worship, 1980, Protestant Worship, 1989, Roman Catholic Worship (1st place award Cath. Press Assn. 1995), also others; mem. editl. bd. Religious Book Club, 1980-93. Named one of 100 Most Influential People in Am. Religion, Christian Century mag., 1982; honored by book published in his honor: The Sunday Service of the Methodists: Studies in Honor of James F. White, 1996. Mem. N.Am. Acad. Liturgy (pres. 1979, Berakah award 1983), Am. Soc. Ch. History, Liturgical Conf., Societas Liturgica. Avocations: hiking, travel, book and antiques collecting. Office: U Notre Dame Dept Theology Notre Dame IN 46556

WHITE, JAMES JUSTESEN, legal educator; b. Omaha, Feb. 19, 1934; s. Leland Cobb and Vernie Marie (Bisgard) W.; m. Nancy Ann Coleman, Dec. 23, 1956; children: James, Patricia, Christopher. B.A., Amherst Coll., 1956; J.D., U. Mich., 1962. Bar: Mich. 1967. Assoc. Latham & Watkins, Los Angeles, 1962-64; prof. law U. Mich., Ann Arbor, 1964-78, 81-82, assoc. dean, 1978-81, Robert A. Sullivan prof. law, 1982—; exec. dir. Nat. Inst. Consumer Justice, 1972-74; chmn. Gov.'s Adv. Commn. on Regulation of Fin. Instn., 1976; bd. dirs. Southeast Mich. Legal Services, 1978—; pres. U. Mich. Credit Union, 1983. Author: (with Speidel and Summers) Commercial and Consumer Law, 4th edit., 1987, (with Summers) Handbook of the Law Under the Uniform Commercial Code, 3d edit., 1988, (with Symons) Banking Law Teaching Materials, 2d edit., 1984, (with Edwards) Negotiations Materials and Problems, 1976. Trustee Ann Arbor Bd. Edn., 1981-84. Served to 1st lt. USAF, 1956-59, 62. Mem. Am. Law Inst., Mich. Bar Assn., Order of Coif, Phi Beta Kappa. Republican. Congregationalist. Home: 1603 Granger Ave Ann Arbor MI 48104-4428 Office: U Mich Law Sch 625 S State St Ann Arbor MI 48109-1215*

WHITE, JAMES LINDSAY, polymer engineering educator; b. Bklyn., Jan. 3, 1938; s. Robert Lindsay and Margaret (Young) W. BS, Poly. Inst. Bklyn., 1959; MS, U. Del., 1962, PhD, 1965. Rsch. engr. Uniroyal Inc., Wayne, N.J., 1963-66, rsch. engr., group leader, 1966-67; assoc. prof. U. Tenn., Knoxville, 1967-70, prof., 1970-76, prof. in charge Polymer Sci. and Engring. Program, 1976-83; dir. Polymer Engring. Ctr. U. Akron, Ohio, 1983-89, dir. Inst. Polymer Engring., 1989—, head/chmn. Dept. Polymer Engring, 1983—; Author: Principles of Polymer Engineering Rheology, 1990, Twin Screw Extrusion: Technology and Principles, 1990, Rubber Processing: Technology of Materials and Principles, 1995; editor-in-chief Internat. Polymer Processing, 1990—; contbr. over 300 articles, papers. Recipient Internat. Edn. award Soc. Plastics Engrs., 1987, Internat. Rsch. award, 1992. Mem. Polymer Processing Soc. (pres. 1985-87, editor 1987-90, editor-in-chief 1990—), Soc. Rheology (editorial bd. 1967-92, Bingham medal 1981), Soc. Rheology Japan (Yuko-sho award 1984). Office: U Akron Inst Polymer Engring Akron OH 44325

WHITE, JAMES PATRICK, law educator; b. Iowa City, Sept. 29, 1931; s. Raymond Patrick and Besse (Kanak) W.; m. Anna R. Seim, July 2, 1964. BA, U. Iowa, 1953, JD, 1956; LLM, George Washington U., 1959; LLD (hon.), U. Pacific, 1964, John Marshall Law Sch., 1989, Weidner U., 1989, Campbell U., 1993; Jur D (hon.), Whittier Coll., 1992; LLD (hon.), Campbell U., 1993; Southwestern U., 1995; LLD (hon.), Quinnipiac U., 1995. Bar: Iowa 1956, D.C. 1959, U.S. Supreme Ct. 1959. Teaching fellow George Washington U. Law Sch., 1958-59; asst. prof. U. N.D. Law Sch., Grand Forks, 1959-62; asso. prof., acting dean U. N.D. Law Sch., 1962-63, prof., asst. dean, 1963-67; dir. agrl. law rsch. program, prof. law Ind. U. Law Sch., Indpls., 1967—, also dir. urban legal studies program, 1971-74; dean acad. devel. and planning, spl. asst. to chancellor Ind. Univ., Indpls., 1974-83; mem. for N.D., Commn. on Uniform State Laws, 1961-66; cons. legal edn. ABA, Indpls., 1974—. Contbr. papers to tech. lit. 1st lt. JAGC, USAF, 1956-58. Carnegie postdoctoral fellow U. Mich. Ctr. for Study Higher Edn., 1964-65. Fellow Am. Bar Found.; mem. ABA, Am. Law Inst., Order of Coif. Roman Catholic. Home: 7707 N Meridian St Indianapolis IN 46260-3651 Office: Ind U 550 W North St Indianapolis IN 46202-3162

WHITE, JAMES RICHARD, lawyer; b. McKinney, Tex., Jan. 22, 1948; s. James Ray and Maxine (Brown) W.; m. Marian Olivia Gates, Feb. 3, 1979; children: Nicole Olivia, Mandi Leigh, James Derek. BBA, So. Meth. U., 1969, MBA, 1970, JD, 1973, LLM, 1977. Bar: Tex. 1973, U.S. Tax Ct. 1975, U.S. Supreme Ct. 1989, U.S. Ct. Appeals (5th cir.) 1989); cert. Comml. Real Estate Law Tex. Bd. Legal Specialization. Assoc. Elliot, Meer, Vetter, Denton & Bates, Dallas, 1973-74, Atwell, Cain & Davenport, Dallas, 1974-75; atty. Sabine Corp., Dallas, 1975-77; assoc. Brice & Barron, Dallas, 1977-79; ptnr. Millard & Olson, Dallas, 1979-82, Johnson & Swanson, Dallas, 1982-83, Winstead, Sechrest & Minick P.C., Dallas, 1983—; mem. staff Southwestern Law Jour., Dallas, 1971-73; mem. So. Meth. U. Moot Ct. Bd., Order Barristers, Dallas, 1972-73; prof. North Lake Coll., Dallas, 1985; bd. dirs. Tex. Assn. Young Lawyers, Austin, 1980-82; sec. bd. dirs. Dallas Assn. Young Lawyers, 1976-80. Contbr. articles to profl. jours. Chmn. bd. dirs. Tex. Lawyers Credit Union, Austin, 1980-82; pres. North Tex. Premier Soccer Assocs., Dallas, 1979-81; v.p. Lake Highlands Soccer Assn., 1995—; mem. regional mobility task force Real Estate Coun., City of Dallas, 1991-92, mem. downtown revitalization com., 1995—; mem. Dallas Indsl. Devel. Bd., 1992-93, Dallas Higher Edn. Authority Bd., 1994—; spkr.'s bur. and accreditation divsn. World Cup USA '94. Mem. ABA (mem. survey, accreditation and opinion coms.), Tex. Bar Assn. (cert. 1973, mem. mortgage loan opinion com.), Tex. Coll. Real Estate Attys., Coll. State Bar Tex. Methodist. Avocations: soccer, golf, skiing, racquetball. Home: 8003 Hundley Ct Dallas TX 75231-4728 Office: Winstead Sechrest & Minick 5400 Renaissance Tower 1201 Elm St Dallas TX 75270

WHITE, JANE SEE, journalist; b. St. Louis, Aug. 26, 1950; d. Robert Mitchell and Barbara Whitney (Spurgeon) W.; 1 child, Laura Mitchell. BA in History and Am. Studies, Hollins Coll., 1972. Reporter Roanoke (Va.) Times, 1972-73, Kansas City (Mo.) City Star, 1973-76, AP, N.Y.C., Hartford, 1976-78; spl. writer AP, N.Y.C., 1978-81; sr. writer, chief news and bur., chief profl. div. Med. Econs. Mag., Oradell, N.J., 1981-87; dep. city editor, city editor Roanoke Times World News, 1987-91; asst. metro. editor Phoenix Gazette, 1991-93; asst. city editor Ariz. Rep., Phoenix, 1993, features editor, 1993—; asst. mng. editor adminstrn. Ariz. Rep., Pheonix, 1993-95. Editor: Medical Practice Management, 1985; contbr. articles to profl. jurs. Avocations: golf, reading, cooking. Home: 7143 N 15th Pl Phoenix AZ 85020-5416 Office: Ariz Rep PO Box 2243 Phoenix AZ 85002-2243

WHITE, JEAN TILLINGHAST, former state senator; b. Cambridge, Mass., Dec. 24, 1934; d. James Churchill Moulton and Clara Jean (Carter) Tillinghast; m. Peregrine White, June 6, 1970. B.A., Wellesley Coll., 1956. Supr., programmer Lumber Mut. Ins. Co., Cambridge, 1964-70; selectman, chmn. Town of Rindge (N.H.), 1975-80; clk. regulated revenues N.H. Ho. of Reps., Concord, 1978-80, vice chmn. regulated revenues, 1980-82; mem. N.H. Senate, 1982-88, chmn. fin. com.; v.p., treas. Perry White, Inc., Rindge, N.H., 1970—; dir. Peterborough Savings Bank (N.H.). Chmn., Rindge Friends of Library, 1972; pres. Nat. Order Women Legislators, 1990-91. Trustee Univ. System of N.H., 1989-92, Jaffrey/Rindge Sch. Bd., 1989—; commr. Cheshire County, 1995—. Republican. Unitarian. Office: Hampshire Rd Rindge NH 03461

WHITE, JEFFERY HOWELL, lawyer; b. Tyler, Tex., Aug. 4, 1959; s. Bluford D. and Tempie R. (Tunnell) W.; m. Michael Anne Mackley, May 21, 1989; children: Kristin, Alex. BS in History, So. Ark. U., 1983; JD, Oklahoma City U., 1986. Bar: Tex. 1987. Assoc. Dean White, Canton, Tex., 1986-90; asst. dist. atty. Van Zandt Co., Canton, 1991-94; ptnr. Elliott Elliott & White, Canton, 1994—. Mem. Van Zandt County Bar Assn., Tex. Criminal Def. Lawyers Assn. Democrat. United Methodist. Avocations: golf, tennis, spectator sports. Home: PO Box 102 Canton TX 75103-0102 Office: Elliott Elliott & White 166 N Buffalo St Canton TX 75103-1338

WHITE, JEFFREY GEORGE, healthcare consultant, educator; b. Lawrence, Mass., Apr. 16, 1944; s. Alfred James and Ruth Virginia (Maylum) W.; children: Jennifer L., Tracy E. AB in Econs., Bowdoin Coll., 1966; MBA, U. N.H., 1985. Asst. pers. dir., then asst. adminstr. Maine Med. Ctr., Portland, 1967-71; asst. adminstr. Regional Meml. Hosp., Brunswick, Maine, 1971, adminstr., 1971-74; assoc. dir. Elizabeth Ann Seton Hosp. (now Mid-Maine Med. Ctr.), Waterville, 1974-75; assoc. adminstr. Mid-Maine Med. Ctr., 1975-79, v.p. ops., 1979-83; asst. dir. Wentworth-Douglass Hosp., Dover, N.H., 1983-85; exec. v.p. Frisbie Meml. Hosp., Rochester, N.H., 1985-89, pres., 1989-92; sr. cons., prin. Helms & Co., Inc., Concord, N.H., 1992—; preceptor dept. health mgmt. and policy U. N.H., Durham, 1985-92, adj. asst. prof., 1991-93, asst. prof., 1993—; mem. instrnl. conf. coun. New Eng. Healthcare Assembly, 1992—. Vol. pub. TV sta.; bd. dirs. Greater Seacoast United Way, 1991-94, chmn. comty. campaign, 1993; pres. Greater Rochester C. of C., 1990. Fellow Am. Coll. Healthcare Execs. (past regent for N.H.); mem. N.H. Hosp. Assn. (trustee emeritus). Republican. Avocations: running, skiing, reading, travel. Home: 37 Mill Pond Rd Durham NH 03824-2722 Office: Helms & Co Inc 14 South St Concord NH 03301-3744

WHITE, JESSE MARC, actor; b. Buffalo, Jan. 3; s. Elias and Freda Weidenfeld; m. Cecelia Kahn, Jan. 18, 1942; children—Carole, Janet. Appeared in: 17 Broadway plays including Harvey, 1944; appeared in 64 movies; TV series Ann Sothern Show, 1956-62, Danny Thomas' Make Room for Daddy, 1952-58, Marlo Thomas Show, 1969-71; numerous dramatic and comedy TV shows, 1945—; TV spokesman, Maytag Co., 1967-89, Acura automobiles, 1990—. Mem. AFTRA, SAG, Actors Equity Assn. Club: Friars of Calif. Office: care Craig Wykoff Epstein & Samonna 280 S Beverly Dr Beverly Hills CA 90212 *At age seven I knew what I wanted in life-to bring a little laughter and joy to the world. I've been blessed twice-to be able to do the thing I know and do best and to make a decent and respectable living at it. I have had a good life in show business and feel sorry for people who are not in it.*

WHITE, JILL CAROLYN, lawyer; b. Santa Barbara, Calif., Mar. 20, 1934; d. Douglas Cameron and Gladys Louise (Ashley) W.; m. Walter Otto Weyrauch, Mar. 17, 1973. BA, Occidental Coll., L.A., 1955; JD, U. Calif., Berkeley, 1972. Bar: Fla. 1974, Calif. 1975, D.C. 1981, U.S. Dist. Ct. (no. and mid. dists.) Fla., U.S. Ct. Appeals (5th and 11th cirs.), U.S. Supreme Ct. Staff mem. U.S. Dept. State, U.S. Embassy, Rio de Janeiro, Brazil, 1956-58; with psychol. rsch. units Inst. Human Devel., Inst. Personality Assessment and Rsch., U. Calif., Berkeley, 1961-68; adj. prof. U. Fla. Criminal Justice Program, Gainesville, Fla., 1976-78; pvt. practice immigration and nationality law Gainesville, 1976—; appointed mem. Fla. Bar Inaugural Immigration and Nationality Law Certification Com., 1994—, bd. cert. in immigration and nationality law, 1995—. Contbr. articles to profl. jours. Mem. ABA, Am. Immigration Lawyers Assn. (bd. dirs. Ctrl. Fla. chpt. 1985-94, 95—, chair Ctrl. Fla. chpt. 1988-89, co-chmn. So. Regional Liaison com. 1990-92, nat. bd. dirs. 1988-89), Fla. Assn. Women Lawyers (8th jud. cir. chpt.), Bar Assn. 8th Jud. Cir. Fla., Gainesville Area C. of C., Gainesville Area Innovation Network, Altrusa Club Gainesville. Democrat. Office: 2830 NW 41st St Ste C Gainesville FL 32606-6667

WHITE, JOAN MICHELSON, artist; b. Hartford, Conn., Jan. 4, 1936; d. William Allen and Mitzi (Lurie) Michelson; m. Harvey Marshall White, June 28, 1958; children: Randi Lynn, Andrew Steven. BA, Ctrl. Conn. State U., 1958; postgrad., Wesleyan U., 1980. Cert. tchr., Conn. One woman shows include Canton (Conn.) Gallery on the Green, 1977, Saltbox Gallery, West Hartford, Conn., 1986, Key Gallery, N.Y.C., 1982, Hartford Jewish Cmty. Ctr., 1980; mem. Hartford Art Sch. Aux.; mem. adv. bd. U. Hartford Joseloff Gallery. Group shows include Silvermine Guild New Eng. Exhbn., 1977, 79, Springfield (Mass.) Art League Nat. Exhbn., 1980, 83, 86, The Galleries, Wellesley, Mass., 1983, Stephen Haller Fine Arts, N.Y.C., 1987, 88, Penrose Gallery, Nantucket, Mass., 1984, Conn. Artists Showcase, Conn. Commn. on the Arts, Hartford, 1986, Provincetown (Mass.) Art Assn. and Mus., 1986, Old Lyme (Conn.) Art Works, 1985, Greene Gallery, Guilford, Conn., 1986, Signature Gallery, West Hartford, Conn., 1986-94, Allan Stone Gallery, N.Y.C., 1984, Shippee Gallery, N.Y.C., 1984, Heritage State Park Mus., Holyoke, Mass., 1988, Southern Conn. State U., New Haven, 1989, Farmington Valley Arts Ctr., Avon, Conn., 1992, John Slade Ely House, New Haven, 1993, Ute Stebich Gallery, Lenox, Mass., 1994, North Coast Collage Soc., Seattle, 1994. Mem. Conn. Watercolor Soc. (bd. dirs. 1980-82), West Hartford Ctr. for Visual Arts, Conn. Women Artists, Conn. Acad. Fine Arts. Home: 73 Avondale Rd West Hartford CT 06117-1108

WHITE, JOE E., JR., lawyer; b. Roswell, N.Mex., Oct. 27, 1962. BA in Polit. Sci., Ctrl. State U., 1985; JD, U. Okla., 1988. Bar: Okla. Assoc. Hughes, White, Adams & Grant, Oklahoma City, Okla., 1985-93, ptnr., 1993-94; ptnr. White & Adams, Oklahoma City, Okla., 1995—; barrister Am. Inns of Ct., Oklahoma City, 1994—. Trustee Okla. Student Loan Assistanship, Oklahoma City, 1992—; vice chmn. U. Ctrl. Okla. Found. Bd., Edmond, 1992—. Democrat. Baptist. Office: White & Adams 25th Fl 204 N Robinson City Pl Bldg Oklahoma City OK 73102

WHITE, JOE LLOYD, soil scientist, educator; b. Pierce, Okla., Nov. 8, 1921; s. Claud Amos and Alta Maurice (Denney) W.; m. Wanita Irene Robertson, May 29, 1945; children—Lerrill, Darla, Ronna, Bren, Janeil. Student, Connors State Agrl. Coll., 1940-42; B.S., Okla. State U., 1944, M.S., 1945; Ph.D., U. Wis., 1947. Asst. prof. agronomy Purdue U., West Lafayette, Ind., 1947-51, assoc. prof., 1951-57, prof., 1957-88; cons. Bancroft Co., William H. Rorer Co., Chattem Chem. Co., Merck Sharp & Dohme Rsch. Lab. Patentee in field. Fellow NSF, 1965-66, Guggenheim Found., 1972-73; Fulbright scholar, 1973; recipient Sr. U.S. Scientist award Alexander von Humboldt Found., 1980-81. Fellow AAAS, Am. Soc. Agronomy, Am. Inst. Chemists, Soil Sci. Soc. Am., Mineral Soc. Am., Royal Soc. Chemistry; mem. Am. Chem. Soc., Clay Minerals Soc. (disting.), Am. Pharm. Assn., Coblentz Soc., Geochem. Soc., Internat. Soil Sci. Soc., Internat. Assn. Colloid and Interface Scientists, N.Y. Acad. Sci., Royal Soc. Chemists (chartered chemist), Soc. Petroleum Engrs. of AIME, Internat. Zeolite Assn., Soc. Applied Spectroscopy, Sigma Xi, Phi Kappa Phi, Phi Lambda Upsilon. Mem. Ch. of Christ. Achievements include patents for use of zeolites in ruminant nutrition, for stable dried aluminum hydroxide gel, for method and composition for treatment of hyperphosphatemia; establishment of the role of carbonate in inhibiting crystallization of aluminum hydroxide; definitive characterization of aluminum-containing adjuvants used in vaccines. Home: 2505 Roselawn Ave Lafayette IN 47904-2319 Office: Purdue U Dept Agronomy West Lafayette IN 47907

WHITE, JOHN, food marketing executive; b. 1953. BA, Washington U., 1975, MBA, 1976. With First Nat. Bank of St. Louis, Mo., 1976-80, Schneider Nat. Inc., Green Bay, Wis., 1980-86, Copeland Lumber Yards, Inc., Portland, Oreg., 1986-87; v.p., CFO United Grocers, Inc., Portland, Oreg., 1987—. Office: United Grocers Inc PO Box 22187 Milwaukie OR 97269-2187*

WHITE, JOHN ABIATHAR, pilot, consultant; b. Chgo., May 29, 1948; s. Abiathar Jr. and Gretchen Elizabeth (Zuber) W.; m. Therese Ann Denz, June 21, 1980; children: Kathryn Ann, Laura Ellen. Student, Art Ctr. Coll. of Design, 1969-70, Calif. Inst. Tech., 1966-67; BArch, U. Ill., 1972. Archtl. apprentice Farner Und Gründer Industriearchitekten, Zürich, Switzerland, 1972; archtl. draftsman Walter Carlson Assocs., Elk Grove, Ill., 1973; architectural job capt. Unteed Assocs., Palatine, Ill., 1974-75; flight instr. Planemasters, Inc., West Chicago, Ill., 1976; pilot Aero Am. Aviation, West Chicago, 1977, Beckett Aviation, Cleve., 1978; pilot Am. Airlines, Chgo. and L.A., 1979—, capt., 1988—; archtl. cons. Nat. Accelerator Lab., Batavia, Ill., 1980, Constrn. Collaborative, Park Ridge, Ill., 1982, L.K. White Assocs., San Diego, 1988-92. Nat. Coun. Tchrs. of English scholar, 1966. Mem. Nat. Assn. Flight Instrs. Unitarian. Avocations: skiing, photography, travel.

WHITE, JOHN ARNOLD, physics educator, research scientist; b. Chgo., Jan. 30, 1933; s. Maxwell Richard and Dorothy Edith (Arnold) W.; m. Rebecca Anne Cotten, June 20, 1964; children: Lauren, Thomas, Julia. B.A., Oberlin Coll., 1954; M.S., Yale U., 1955, Ph.D., 1959. Instr. physics Yale U., 1958-59, Harvard U., 1959-62; research assoc. Yale U., 1962-63; research physicist Nat. Bur. Standards, Washington, 1963-64; research assoc. U. Md., College Park, 1965-66; assoc. prof. Am. U., Washington, 1966-68; prof. Am. U., 1968—; cons. Nat. Bur. Standards, 1965-72; mem. tech. staff Bell Telephone Labs., summers 1954, 60-62; vis. scientist MIT, fall 1972, Nat. Bur. Standards, Washington, summer 1981; vis. prof. Inst. for Phys. Sci. and Tech., U. Md., College Park, fall 1993. Author sci. papers on atomic structure and fluorescence, magnetism, lasers, speed of light, thermodynamic fluctuations, critical point phenomena, extended renormalization group theory of fluids. Recipient (with Zoltan Bay) Boyden Premium Franklin Inst., Phila., 1980; honor scholar, 1950-54; Noyes Clark fellow, 1954-57; NSF fellow, 1957-58; grantee NSF, 1966, 67, 69, 71; grantee Office Naval Research, 1973, 74; Am. Soc. Engring. Edn. faculty fellow Naval Research Lab., Washington, summer 1985; Dept. Energy Office Basic Energy Scis. grantee, 1986, 88, 90. Fellow Am. Phys. Soc.; mem. AAUP, Washington Philos. Soc., Phi Beta Kappa, Sigma Xi. Home: 7107 Fairfax Rd Bethesda MD 20814-1234 Office: Am U Dept Physics Washington DC 20016-8058

WHITE, JOHN AUSTIN, JR., engineering educator, dean, consultant; b. Portland, Ark., Dec. 5, 1939; s. John Austin and Ella Mae (McDermott) W.; m. Mary Elizabeth Quarles, Apr. 13, 1963; children: Kimberly Elizabeth White Brakmann, John Austin III. BS in Indsl. Engring., U. Ark., 1962; MS in Indsl. Engring., Va. Poly. Inst., 1966; PhD, Ohio State U., 1969; PhD (hon.), Cath. U. of Leuven, Belgium, 1985, George Washington U., 1991. Registered profl. engr., Va. Indsl. engr. Tenn. Eastman Co., Kingsport, 1961-63, Ethyl Corp., Baton Rouge, 1965; instr. Va. Poly. Inst. and State U., Blacksburg, 1963-66, asst. prof., 1970-72, assoc. prof., 1972-75; teaching assoc. Ohio State U., Columbus, 1966-70; assoc. prof. Ga. Inst. Tech., Atlanta, 1975-77, prof., 1977-84, Regents' prof., 1984—, Gwaltney prof., 1988—, dean engring., 1991—; asst. dir. engring. NSF, 1988-91; founder, chmn. SysteCon Inc., Duluth, Ga., 1977-84; exec. cons. Coopers & Lybrand, N.Y.C., 1984-93; mem. mfg. studies bd. NRC, Washington, 1986-88; bd. dirs. CAPS Logistics, Russell Corp., Eastman Chem. Co., Motorola Corp.; pres. Nat. Consortium for Grad. Degrees for Minorities in Engring. and Sci., Inc., 1993-95; bd. dirs. Southeastern Consortium for Minorities in Engring., 1992—; apptd. U.S. del. to the Internat. Steering Com. of the Intelligent Mfg. System, 1995-97; mem. Nat. Sci. Bd., 1994—. Co-author: Facility Layout and Location: An Analytical Approach, 1974 (Book of Yr. award Inst. Indsl. Engrs. 1974), 2d edit., 1991, Analysis of Queueing Systems, 1975, Principles of Engineering Economic Analysis, 3d edit., 1989, Capital Investment Decision Analysis for Management and Engineering, 1980, 2d edit., 1996, Facilities Planning, 1984 (Book of Yr. award Inst. Indsl. Engrs. 1984), 2d edit., 1996; editor: Production Handbook, 1987; co-editor: Progress in Materials Handling and Logistics, Vol. 1, 1989; also numerous articles to profl. jours., chpts. to books and handbooks in field, conf. procs. Recipient Outstanding Tchr. award Ga. Inst. Tech., 1982, Disting. Alumnus award Ohio State U. Coll. Engring., 1984, Disting. Indsl. Engring. alumnus award Va. Polytech. Inst. and State U., 1993, Reed-Apple award Material Handling Edn. Found., 1985, Disting. Svc. award NSF, 1991, Rodney D. Chipp Meml. award Soc. Women Engrs., 1994. Fellow Am. Inst. Indsl. Engrs. (pres. 1983-84, facilities planning and design award 1980, outstanding indsl. engr. award region III 1974, region IV 1984, Albert G. Holzman disting. educator award 1988, outstanding pub. award 1988, David F. Baker disting. rsch. award 1990, Frank and Lillian Gilbreth award 1994), Am. Assn. Engring. Socs. (bd. govs., chmn. 1986, Kenneth Andrew Roe award 1989); mem. Nat. Acad. Engring., Ark. Acad. Indsl. Engring., Am. Soc. Engring. Edn. (Donald E. Marlowe award 1994), Coun. Logistics Mgmt. Internat. Material Mgmt. Soc. (material mgr. of yr. 1989), Soc. Mfg. Engrs. (mfg. educator award 1990), Nat. Soc. Profl. Engrs. Inst. for Ops. Rsch. and the Mgmt. Scis. (hon.), Golden Key, Sigma Xi, Alpha Pi Mu, Omicron Delta Kappa, Phi Kappa Phi, Tau Beta Pi, Omega Rho. Baptist. Avocations: reading, golf, writing. Office: Ga Inst Tech Coll Engring Office of Dean Atlanta GA 30332

WHITE, JOHN CHARLES, historian; b. Washington, Apr. 14, 1939; s. Bennett Sexton, Jr. and Mary Elizabeth (Wildman) W.; m. Carolyn R. West, July 6, 1963. A.B. magna cum laude with exceptl. distinction in History (Robert E. Lee scholar), Washington and Lee U., 1960; M.A. (So. fellow), Duke U., 1962, Ph.D. (So. fellow), 1964. Asst. prof. U. Ala., Huntsville, 1967-70, assoc. prof., 1970-76, prof., 1976-91, chmn. dept. history, 1970-91, dir., acting chmn. dept. langs. and lits., 1988-91, ret., 1991; dir., sec.-treas. Consortium on Revolutionary Europe, 1972-86; European travel cons., 1991—. Editor: Procs. Consortium on Revolutionary Europe, 1977, 81; contbr. articles on French adminstrv. history to profl. jours. Bd. dirs Ala. Preservation Alliance, 1989-95, Ala. com. humanitites NEH, 1979-82, mem. exec. com., 1980-81; vice chmn. bd. Ala. Constn. Hall, 1979-81, chmn. bd. dirs., 1982-84; bd. dirs. Ala. Humanities Found., 1985-89, vice chmn. bd. 1988-89; assoc. Ala. Humanities, 1982-85; pres. Alliance Francaise, 1970; active Huntsville Lit. Assn., Huntsville Mus. Assn. Served to capt. Recipient Chalons and Dunkirk City medals, 1964-65, Ala. Hist. Commn. award of merit, 1978, Multi-Cultural Svcs. Recognition award U. Ala., Huntsville, 1991, appreciation award U. Ala. Alumni Assn., 1991, cert. of appreciation Gov. of Ala., 1991, Ala. Senate, 1991, award of merit Ala. Preservation Alliance, 1994, others; Woodrow Wilson summer grantee, 1961-62, U. Ala. rsch. grantee, 1969, 70, 74. Mem. Ala. Assn. Historians (pres. 1978-80), Ala. Hist. Soc., Consortium on Revolutionary Europe, Phi Alpha Theta (Nat. Scholarship medal 1991), Phi Kappa Phi, Omicron Delta Kappa (Founder's Day Leadership award 1991), Phi Sigma Iota (Nat. Svc. award 1991). Club: Rotary. Home: 220 Longwood Dr Huntsville AL 35801

WHITE, JOHN DAVID, composer, theorist, cellist; b. Rochester, Minn., Nov. 28, 1931; s. Leslie David and Millie (Solum) W.; m. Marjorie Manuel, Dec. 27, 1952; children: Jeffrey Alan, Michele Kay, David Eliot. BA magna cum laude, U. Minn., 1953; MA, U. Rochester, 1954, PhD, 1960. Mem. faculty Kent (Ohio) State U., 1956-58, 60-63, 65-73, prof. music, asso. dean Grad. Sch., 1967-73; asst. prof. U. Mich., 1963-65; dean Sch. Music, Ithaca (N.Y.) Coll., 1973-74; vis. prof. U. Wis., 1975-78; chmn. music dept. Whitman Coll., 1978-80; prof. U. Fla., 1980—. Prin. cellist, Eastman Philharmonia, 1959, Akron Symphony Orch., 1969-73; cellist Fla. Baroque Ensemble, 1980—, Fla. Arts Trio, 1986-93; dir. Fla. Musica Nova, 1991—; author: (with A. Cohen) Anthology of Music for Analysis, 1965, Understanding and Enjoying Music, 1968 (pub. in Japanese 1978), Music in Western Culture, 1972, The Analysis of Music, 1976, 2d edit., 1984, Guidelines for College Teaching of Music Theory, 1981, Comprehensive Musical Analysis, 1994, Theories of Musical Texture in Western History, 1995; editor: Music and Man; editl. Jour. for Musicological Research, Jour. Music Theory Pedagogy; contbr. articles to profl. jours.; Composer: Symphony No. 2, 1960, Blake Songs, 1961, Divertimento for Flute, Violin and Viola, 1961; opera The Legend of Sleepy Hollow, 1962; Three Choruses From Goethe's Faust, 1965, Three Joyce Songs, 1966, Ode to Darkness, 1967, Cantos of the Year, 1969, Variations for Clarinet and Piano, 1971, Whitman Music, 1970, Three Madrigals for Chorus and Orchestra, 1971, Russian Songs for Voices and Winds, 1972, Prayer (Solzhenytsin), 1973, String Quartet 1, 1975, Variations for Piano, 1976, Ode on the Morning of Christ's Nativity (Donne), 1977, Music for Oriana for violin, cello and piano, 1978, Pied Beauty, 1980, Sonata for Cello and Piano, 1981, Zodiac, 1981, Music for Violin and Piano, 1982, The Soft Voice, 1983, Concerto for Flute and Wind Ensemble, 1983, Dialogues for Trombone and Piano, 1984, Symphony for Wind Band (3rd Symphony), 1985, Concerto da Camera for Cello and Orch., 1985, Symphony for a Saint (4th Symphony), 1986, The Heavens are Telling, 1988, Music for Cello and Percussion, 1988, Songs of the Shulamite, 1989, Mirrors for Piano and Orchestra, 1990, But God's Own Descent (5th Symphony), 1991, Music of the Open Road, 1993, Daylight and Moonlight, 1993, O Sing to the Lord a New Song, 1993, Illusions for Three, 1994, Music for Trumpet and Cello, 1994, Colors of Earth and Sky (6th Symphony), 1995, Summer Storm Madrigals, 1996; recs. on Advent, Mark, Capstone and Opus One Labels. Served with AUS, 1954-56. Recipient Benjamin award, 1960, award Nat. Fedn. Music Clubs, 1962, internat. composition award U. Wis.-Oriana Trio, 1979, composition award Am. Choral Dirs. Assn., 1984; grantee NEA; Fulbright rsch. fellow, 1995-96. Mem. ASCAP (awards 1965—), Soc. Composers (nat. coun. 1987-89, 93-96), Soc. Music Theory, Pi Kappa Lambda, Delta Omicron, Phi Mu Alpha, Phi Beta Delta. Home: 3102 NW 57th Terr Gainesville FL 32606

WHITE, JOHN FRANCIS, retired corporate executive; b. Madison, Wis., Dec. 2, 1929; s. Francis Bernard and Helen Margaret (Brown) W.; 1 dau., Susan Jeanne. B.S., U. Wis., 1951; grad., Harvard U. Advanced Mgmt. Program, 1974. With Kraft Inc., Glenview, Ill., v.p., dir. R&D, 1974-85, gen. mgr. spl. projects, retail venture group, 1985-87. Served with AUS, 1951-53. Mem. Inst. Food Technologists, Am. Chem. Soc., AAAS. Republican. Roman Catholic. Club: North Shore Country (Glenview). Home: 1439 Pebblecreek Dr Glenview IL 60025-2029

WHITE, JOHN JOSEPH, III, lawyer; b. Darby, Pa., Nov. 23, 1948; s. John J. Jr. and Catherine (Lafferty) W.; m. Catherine M Staley, Dec. 9, 1983. BS, U. Scranton, 1970; MPA, Marywood Coll., 1977; JD, Loyola U., New Orleans, 1983. Bar: Pa. 1983, U.S. Dist. Ct. (ea. dist.) Pa. 1983, N.J. 1984, U.S. Ct. Appeals (3d cir.) 1983, U.S. Dist. Ct. N.J. 1984, U.S. Tax Ct. 1984, D.C. 1985, U.S. Supreme Ct. 1987. Exec. dir. Scranton Theatre Libre, Inc., Scranton, Pa., 1973-77; pub. Libre Press Inc., Scranton, 1977-83; pvt. practice Phila., 1983—; pres. Washington Franklin Investment Corp., 1992—; N. Am. agt. Palacky U. Med. Sch., Czech Republic, 1995—; owner Mercury Transp. Co., Inc., Lansdowne, Pa., 1987—; N.Am. agt. Palacky U. Med. Sch., Olomouc, Czech Republic. Founder, pub. Metro Mag., 1977-83. Founder, Scranton Pub. Theatre, 1976; dir. Scranton Theatre Libre, Inc., 1973. Capt. USAF, 1970-73; lt. col. Res., 1973—. Mem. ABA, Pa. Trial Lawyers Assn., Phila. Bar Assn., Phila. Trial Lawyers Assn., Air Force Assn. (chpt. pres. 1975—), Phi Delta Phi Internat. Legal Frat. Democrat. Roman Catholic. Avocations: jogging, art collecting. Office: 1334 Walnut St Fl 5 Philadelphia PA 19107-5304

WHITE, JOHN LINDSEY, lawyer; b. Camden, N.J., Apr. 1, 1930; s. John R. and Jean L. (Lord) W.; m. Jane V. Evans, Dec. 27, 1952; children: Linda White McFadden, John Lindsey Jr., Douglas A., Karen R. Ulmer. AB, Franklin and Marshall Coll., 1952; LLB, Temple U., 1955. Bar: N.J. 1955, U.S. Dist. Ct. N.J. 1955, U.S. Supreme Ct. 1960, U.S. Ct. Appeals (3d cir.) 1984. Of counsel George, Korin, Quattrone & Blumberg, Woodbury, N.J. Mem. N.J. Assembly, Trenton, 1964-68, N.J. State Senate, Trenton, 1968-72; trustee Underwood-Meml. Hosp., Woodbury, chmn. bd., 1994—. Recipient Disting. Svc. award Woodbury Jaycees, 1966. Fellow Am. Bar Found., Am. Coll. Trial Lawyers; mem. ABA, N.J. Bar Assn. (pres. 1985-86), Internat. Assn. Def. Counsel, N.J. Def. Assn. (pres. 1992-93), Trial Attys. N.J. (Trial Bar award 1991), Gloucester County Bar Assn. (pres. 1979-80), Masons, Shriners. Republican. Presbyterian. Avocations: hunting, fishing, boating. Home: 193 Briar Hill Ln Woodbury NJ 08096-5916 Office: George Korin Quattrone Blumberg & Chant 307 S Evergreen Ave Woodbury NJ 08096-2753

WHITE, JOHN MICHAEL, chemistry educator; b. Danville, Ill., Nov. 26, 1938; married, 1960; 3 children. BS, Harding Coll., 1960; MS, U. Ill., 1962, PhD in Chemistry, 1966. From asst. to assoc. prof. U. Tex., Austin, 1966-77, prof. chemistry, 1977—, now Hackerman prof. chemistry, dir. Sci. and Tech. Ctr. Mem. Am. Chem. Soc., Am. Phys. Soc. Research in surface and materials chemistry. Office: U Tex Dept Chemistry Welch Hall # 310 Austin TX 78712

WHITE, JOHN PATRICK, lawyer; b. Boston, Oct. 14, 1946; s. John Marion and Margaret Patricia (Gannon) W.; m. Gemma Mary Flattly, Feb. 9, 1980; 1 son, John Myles. B.S. in Chem. Engring., Columbia U., 1968, M.A. in Biochemistry, 1971, M.Ph. in Molecular Biology, 1975; J.D., Fordham U., 1977. Bar: N.Y. 1978, U.S. dist. ct. (ea. and so. dists.) N.Y. 1978, U.S. Ct. Customs and Patent Appeals 1979, U.S. Ct. Appeals (Fed. cir.) 1982. Legis. dir. Community Council Greater N.Y., 1971-77; assoc. Cooper, Dunham, Clark, Griffin & Moran, N.Y.C., 1977-81, ptnr., 1981-88; ptnr. Cooper & Dunham, LLP, N.Y.C., 1988—; owner Shallow Brook Farm, Stillwater, N.J.; breeder Reg Angus Cattle, Ringneck Pheasants and Carriage Horses; dir. Oncogene Sci., Inc., BioTech. Gen. Corp.; instr. Practicing Law Inst. Democratic dist. leader, 1975-81; vice chmn. Dem. Com. N.Y. County, 1977-81; jud. del. 1st jud. dept., 1975, 76, 77, 79; adminstr. screening panel 2d Mcpl. Ct. Dist.; pub. mem. Columbia U. Recombinant DNA Biosafety Com. Columbia U. faculty fellow, 1969-71; NIH grantee, 1969-71. Mem. ABA, Am. Chem. Soc., Am. Intellectual Property Law Assn., N.Y. Intellectual Property Law Assn., Assn. Bar City N.Y., Fed. Bar Coun. (com. patents). Club: Columbia of N.Y.C. Contbr. articles to sci. and legal jours. Home: 824 Hudson St Hoboken NJ 07030-5004 Office: Cooper & Dunham 1185 Ave of Americas New York NY 10036

WHITE, JOHN SIMON, opera director; b. Vienna, Austria, Mar. 4, 1910; came to U.S., 1938, naturalized, 1943; s. Emil and Martha (Pollack) Schwarzkopf. PhD, U. Vienna, 1933; student, Sorbonne, U. Besançon, France, U. Perugia, Italy. Mem. faculty Schotten Realschule, Vienna, 1934, New Sch. Social Rsch., N.Y.C., Lycée Français, N.Y.C., 1942-43; cons. Ford Found., 1974—, Columbia Artists Mgmt., 1979; asst. stage dir., N.Y.C. Opera Assn., 1946-51, assoc. dir., 1952-68, mng. dir., 1968-81, artistic cons., 1981—; exec. dir., Vienna Burgtheater guest appearance in N.Y.C., 1968; dir. U.S. tour Spanish Riding Sch., 1980, 82, 84. Author: The Renaissance Cavalier, 1959, also rsch. papers. Co-founder Am. Dressage Inst. for Classical Horsemanship, Saratoga, N.Y., 1967; Bd. dirs. Gert von Gontard Found., 1968—. Served with AUS, 1942-45. Recipient 1st prize, scholarship Italian Cultural Inst., Vienna, 1935; elected to Friends of Lipizzans Vienna Hofburg, 1976. Office: NYC Opera Lincoln Ctr Pla New York NY 10023

WHITE, JOHN WESLEY, JR., university president; b. Nashville, Oct. 20, 1933; s. John W. and Ernestine (Engle) W.; m. Martha Ellen Bragg, June 24, 1956; children: Marcus Wesley, Michelle Suzanne. Student, Martin Jr. Coll., 1952-54; BA, Vanderbilt U., 1956, BD, 1959; MA, George Peabody Coll., 1966, PhD, 1968; LHD, U. Nebr., 1983; LLD, Kwansai Gakuin U., Japan, 1991. Dean admissions, dir. student affairs Martin Coll., 1960-65; asst. to acad. v.p. George Peabody Coll., 1965-67; assoc. dean for humanities Oklahoma City U., 1968-70, dean Coll. Arts and Scis., 1970-77, assoc. prof. English, 1968-73, prof., 1973-77; pres. Nebr. Wesleyan U., 1977—; cons., spkr. in field; bd. dirs. Norwest Bank, Woodmen Accident and Life Co.; mem. Nebr. Ednl. Telecomm. Commn. Immediate past pres. U. Senate, United Meth. Ch. Eli Lilly Sr. scholar Vanderbilt U., 1959. Mem. Nat. Assn. Ind. Colls. and Univs. (bd. dirs. 1989-93, 95—), Newcomen Soc. N.Am., Lincoln C. of C. (bd. dirs. 1990-93), Rotary (pres. West Oklahoma City sect. 1976), Kappa Delta Pi, Phi Kappa Phi, Alpha Mu Gamma, Blue Key. Office: Nebr Wesleyan U 5000 St Paul Ave Lincoln NE 68504-2760 *Two principles have been paramount in my life: One, related to the attitude toward myself, is that we can help to shape life, not simply endure it. We are "creative" creatures, not just "surviving" creatures. The second principle, related to the attitude toward others, is that communication is essential to coexistence; and only as we make a real effort to hear what is meant, rather than simply what is said or written, are we able to communicate effectively.*

WHITE, JOSEPH, financial advisor; b. Birmingham, Ala., Dec. 29, 1933; m. Lavada Vails, June 25, 1960; children: Leticia, Jarett, Everett. BS Mgmt., Canisius Coll., 1969. Cert. fin. planner; lic. Renaissance advisor. Postal clk. U.S. Postal Svc., Buffalo, N.Y., 1957-69; bus. devel. franchise officer Erie County CAO, Buffalo, 1969-71; personal fin. advisor Am. Express Fin. Advisors, Buffalo, 1971—. Bd. dirs., treas. Langston Hughes Inst., Buffalo, 1980-90; exec. com. Buffalo chpt. NAACP, 1994—. With USN, 1952-56. Recipient Bus. Week citation Iota Phi Lambda, Buffalo, 1989, Disting. Media award Langston Hughes Inst., 1988, Black Achievers in Industry, 1490 Community Ctr., Buffalo, 1989, Outstanding Black Leader of Erie County award Dennis T. Gorski Erie Co. Exec., Buffalo, 1989. Mem. Internat. Assn. Fin. Planning (sec. W.N.Y. chpt. 1988—, bd. dirs.), Inst. Cert. Fin. Planners, Kappa Alpha Psi. Roman Catholic. Avocations: bowling, golf. Office: Am Express Fin Advisors 325 Essjay Rd Ste 410 Williamsville NY 14221-8214

WHITE, JOSEPH B., reporter; b. N.Y.C., 1959. Attended, Harvard U. Reporter The Wall Street Journal. Author: (with Paul Ingrassia) Comeback: The Fall and Rise of the American Automobile Industry, 1994. Recipient Pulitzer Prize for beat reporting, 1993. Office: The Wall Street Journal Detroit Bureau 500 Woodward Ave Ste 1950 Detroit MI 48226*

WHITE, JOSEPH CHARLES, manufacturing and retailing company executive; b. Toronto, Ont., Can., Aug. 14, 1922; s. Joseph Cleveland and Edith Parker (Johnson) W.; m. G. Evelyn Vipond, July 15, 1944; children—Ronald, Richard, JoAnne. Chartered acct., Queens U., Kingston, Ont.; B.Commerce, U. Toronto. Vice-pres., dir. Agnew-Surpass, Inc., Brantford, Ont., Can., 1964-78; v.p., dir. Genesco Can., Inc., Cambridge, Ont., Can., 1978-82, exec. v.p., dir., 1982-87; pres., gen. mgr. retail op. Genesco Can., Inc., Cambridge, Ont., 1986-87; dir., v.p. Genesco Group Inc.; dir. Genesco Fin. Ltd. Chmn. Ross MacDonald Found., Brantford, Ont., 1983-86; pres. YMCA, Brantford, 1968-69; chmn. Brant County Post-Secondary Edn. Corp., Brantford, 1973-76. Served with Royal Can. Air Force, 1943-45. Mem. Ont. Inst. Chartered Accts., Can. Council Distbn. (pres. 1972-73), Brant County C. of C. (treas. 1966-68). Mem. United Ch. of Can. Avocations: downhill skiing; tennis. Home: 47 Golfdale Rd, Brantford, ON Canada N3T 5H6 Office: Genesco Can Inc, 401 Fountain St, Cambridge, ON Canada N3H 4V5

WHITE, JOYCE LOUISE, librarian; b. Phila., June 7, 1927; d. George William and Louisa (Adams) W. BA, U. Pa., 1949; MLS, Drexel U., 1963; MA in Religion, Episc. Sem. S.W., 1978. Head libr. Penniman Libr. Edn. U. Pa., Phila., 1960-76; archivist St. Francis Boys' Home, Salina, Kans., 1982-84; libr. Brown Mackie Coll., Salina, 1983-86; libr., dir. St. Thomas Theol. Sem., Denver, 1986-95; libr., dir. Archbishop Vehr Theol. Libr. Archdiocese of Denver, 1995—. Author: Biographical and Historial Yarnall Library, 1979; asst. editor: Women Religious History Sources, 1983; contbr. articles to profl. jours. and chpts. to books. Vol. libr. St. John's Cath., Denver, 1993—. Mem. Ch. and Synagogue Libr. Assn. (life, founding, pres. 1969-70, exec. sec. 1970-72, exec. bd. 1967-76, ann. conf. chair 1996). Avocations: gardening, cats, church libraries. Office: Archbishop Vehr Theol Libr 1300 S Steele St Denver CO 80210-2526

WHITE, KATE, editor-in-chief. Former editor-in-chief Child mag.; editor-in-chief Working Woman mag., N.Y.C., 1989-91, McCall's mag, N.Y.C., 1991-94, Redbook, N.Y.C., 1994—. Office: Redbook Hearst Magazines 224 W 57th St New York NY 10019-3299

WHITE, KATHLEEN MERRITT, geologist; b. Long Beach, Calif., Nov. 19, 1921; d. Edward Clendenning and Gladys Alice (Merritt) White; m. Alexander Kennedy Baird IV, Oct. 1, 1965 (dec. 1985); children: Pamela Roberts, Peter Madlem, Stephen Madlem, Mari Afify. Attended, Sch. Boston Mus. Fine Arts, 1939-40, Art Students League, 1940-42; BS in Geology, Pomona Coll., 1962; MS in Geochemistry, Claremont Grad. Sch., 1964. Rsch. asst. geology Pomona Coll., Claremont, Calif., 1962-66, rsch. assoc. geology, 1966-75; cons. geology Claremont, Calif., 1975-77; sr. scientist Jet Propulsion Lab./NASA, Pasadena, 1977-79, mem. tech. staff, 1979-86; ind. rschr. Claremont, 1986—; owner Kittie Tales, Claremont, 1992—. Contbr. Geosat Report, 1986; contbr. articles to profl. jours.; author, illustrator children's books. Grantee NASA, 1984, 85; Pomona Coll. scholar, 1963. Mem. Geol. Soc. Am. (invited paper 1994), Am. Geophys. Union, Pomona Coll. Alumni Assn. Republican. Avocations: painting, piano playing, weaving, hiking, swimming. Home: 265 W 11th St Claremont CA 91711-3804

WHITE, KENNETH RAY, health administration educator, consultant; b. Okmulgee, Okla., June 28, 1956; s. Miles Delano and Ollie Jane (Roberts) W. BS, Oral Roberts U., 1979; MPH, U. Okla., Oklahoma City, 1980; BS in Nursing, Va. Commonwealth U., 1995, MS in Nursing, 1995, PhD in Health Svcs. Orgn. and Rsch., 1996. Dir. planning Mercy Health Ctr., Oklahoma City, 1980-81, adminstrv. asst., 1981-86, v.p. mktg., 1987-89; v.p. ops. Harris Hosp.-HEB, Bedford, Tex., 1986-87; sr. cons. Mercy Internat., Farmington Hills, Mich., 1989-93; instr. health adminstrn. Va. Commonwealth U., Richmond, 1993-95, asst. prof., assoc. dir. profl. grad. programs dept. health, 1995—. Contbr. articles to profl. jours. Bd. dirs., officer March of Dimes, Oklahoma City, 1980-89, Am. Heart Assn., Oklahoma City, 1984-89. Named Outstanding Alumni, U. Okla., 1983. Fellow Am. Coll. Healthcare Execs., Sigma Theta Tau, Phi Kappa Phi. Avocations: travel, home renovation, foreign films. Office: Va Commonwealth U Med Coll Va PO Box 980203 Richmond VA 23298-0203

WHITE, KERR LACHLAN, physician, foundation director; b. Winnipeg, Man., Can., Jan. 23, 1917; s. John Alexander and Ruth Cecelia (Preston) W.; m. Isabel Anne Pennefather, Nov. 26, 1943; children: Susan Isabel, Margot Edith. BA with honors (Oliver Gold medal), McGill U., 1940, M.D., C.M., 1949; M.D. (hon.), U. Leuven, 1978; postgrad., London Sch. Hygiene and Tropical Medicine, 1960; DSc (hon.), McMaster U., 1983. Intern, resident in medicine Mary Hitchcock Meml. Hosp., Hanover, N.H., 1949-52; Hosmer fellow McGill U. and Royal Victoria Hosp., Montreal, Que., Can., 1952-53; asst. prof. medicine U. N.C. Sch. Medicine, Chapel Hill, 1953-57, assoc. prof. medicine and preventive medicine, 1957-62; Commonwealth advanced fellow Med. Rsch. Coun., Social Medicine Rsch. unit London Hosp., 1959-60; chmn., prof. epidemiology and community medicine U. Vt., Burlington, 1962-64; prof. Sch. Hygiene and Pub. Health Johns Hopkins U., Balt., 1965-76, chmn. dept. health care orgn., 1965-72; dir. Inst. Health Care Studies United Hosp. Fund N.Y., 1977-78; dep. dir. health scis. Rockefeller Found., N.Y.C., 1978—; chmn. U.S. Nat. Com. Vital and Health Stats., 1975-79; mem. health adv. panel Office of Tech. Assessment, U.S. Congress, 1975-82; cons. Nat. Ctr. Health Stats., 1967-83, WHO, 1967—. Editor: Manual for Examination of Patients, 1960, Medical Care Research, 1965, Health Care: An International Study, 1976, Epidemiology as a Fundamental Science, 1976, Task of Medicine, 1988, Healing the Schism, 1991; contbr. articles to profl. jours., chpts. to books in field; mem. editl. bd. Med. Care, 1962-73, Inquiry, 1967-79, Internat. Jour. Epidemiology, 1971-81, Internat. Jour. Health Svcs., 1971—. Bd. dirs. Found. for Child Devel., 1969-80; trustee Case-Western Res. U., 1974-79. With Can. Army, 1942-45. Recipient Pew Primary Care Achievement award, 1995. Fellow ACP, AAAS, NAS (Inst. Medicine coun. 1974-76, chmn. membership com. 1975-77), APHA (gov. coun. 1964-68, 71-73, coun. med. care sect. 1962-65), Am. Acad. Preventive Medicine, Am. Heart Assn., Royal Soc. Medicine (hon.); mem. AMA, Internat. Epidemiol. Assn. (hon. life, pres. 1974-77, treas., exec. com. 1964-71, 74-77, coun. 1971-81), Assn. Tchrs. Preventive Medicine (coun. 1963-68), Am. Hosp. Assn. (adv. coun. ednl. and rsch. trust 1965-68), Kerr L. White Inst. Health Svcs. Rsch. (hon. dir. 1995—), Cosmos Club (Washington), Century Club (N.Y.C.), Sigma Xi, Alpha Omega Alpha. Office: Rockefeller Found Div Health Scis 1133 Ave Of The Americas New York NY 10036-6710

WHITE, LAWRENCE J., economics educator; b. N.Y.C., June 1, 1943; s. Martin H. and Florence M. (Meiman) W. AB, Harvard U., 1964, PhD, 1969; MS in Econs., London Sch. Econs., 1965. Econ. adviser Harvard Devel. Adv. Svc., Pakistan and Indonesia, 1969-70; asst. prof. econs. Princeton U., N.J., 1970-76; mem. faculty Stern Sch. Bus., NYU, 1976—; prof. econs. Stern Sch. Bus., NYU, 1979—, chmn. dept., 1990-95; sr. staff economist U.S. Council Econ. Advisers, 1978-79; dir. econ. policy office, antitrust div. Dept. Justice, Washington, 1982-83; mem. Fed. Home Loan Bank Bd., 1986-89; cons. in field. Author: The Automobile Industry Since 1945, 1971, Industrial Concentration and Economic Power in Pakistan, 1974, Reforming Regulation: Processes and Problems, 1981, The Regulation: Processes and Problems, 1981, The Regulation of Air Pollutant Emissions from Motor Vehicles, 1982, The Public Library in the 1980s: The Problems of Choice, 1983, International Trade in Ocean Shipping Services: The U.S. and the World, 1988, The S&L Debacle: Public Policy Lessons for Bank and Thrift Regulation, 1991; N.Am. editor Jour. Indsl. Econs., 1984-87, 90-95. NSF fellow, 1965-69. Mem. Am. Econ. Assn., Phi Beta Kappa. Office: NYU Stern Sch Bus 44 W 4th St New York NY 10012-1126

WHITE, LEE CALVIN, lawyer; b. Omaha, Sept. 1, 1923; s. Herman Henry and Ann Ruth (Ackerman) W.; m. Cecile R. Zerinsky, Nov. 19, 1989 (dec. Apr. 1996); children: Bruce D., Rosalyn A., Murray L., Sheldon R., Laura H., Lori J. B.S. in Elec. Engring., U. Nebr., 1948, LL.B., 1950. Bar: Nebr. 1950, D.C. 1958. Atty. legal div. TVA, 1950-54; legis. asst. to Senator John F. Kennedy, 1954-57; asst. to Joseph P. Kennedy; mem. Hoover Commn., 1954-55; counsel U.S. Senate Small Bus. Com., 1957-58; adminstrv. asst. to Senator John S. Cooper, 1958-61; asst. spl. counsel to Pres. Kennedy, 1961-63; assoc. counsel to Pres. Johnson, 1963-65, spl. counsel, 1965-66; chmn. Fed. Power Commn., 1966-69; campaign mgr. R. Sargent Shriver (Democratic candidate v.p. U.S.), 1972; dir. Central Hudson Gas and Electric Corp., 1984-88. Bd. govs. N.Y. Merc. Exchange, 1980-84, 87-91. Served with AUS, 1943-46. Mem. D.C. Bar (gov. 1977-80). Home: 435 N St SW Washington DC 20024-3701 Office: Ste 1100 1350 New York Ave NW Washington DC 20005

WHITE, LEONARD, motion picture company executive. Pres., chief exec. officer Orion Pictures Corp. Office: Orion Pictures Corp 1888 Century Park E Ste 6 Los Angeles CA 90067-1702

WHITE, LESLIE MARY, epidemiologist; b. Huntington, N.Y., July 22, 1954; d. John B. and Inez M. (Montecalvo) W. BS, Mary Washington Coll., 1976; MPH, Johns Hopkins U., 1990; postgrad., U. Md., 1993-95. Microbiologist II Am. Type Culture Collection, Rockville, Md., 1980-83; analyst InterAm. Assocs., Rockville, Md., 1984-86; sr. assoc. Triton Corp., Washington, 1986-87; health analyst Row Scis., Inc., Rockville, 1987-88; rsch. analyst Nat. BioSystems, Rockville, 1988-90; sr. assoc. Clement Internat., Fairfax, Va., 1990-92; project dir. epidemiology Consultants in Epidemiology and Occupational Health, Washington, 1992-93; dir. epidemiology Scis. Internat., Inc., Alexandria, Va., 1993-94; pres. Epidemiology and Health Rsch., Inc., Bethesda, Md., 1994—, Dist. Nuskin/IDN Internat., Bethesda, 1996—. Mem. APHA, USTA, USTA Umpire Coun., Soc. Epidemiologic Rsch., Soc. Occupl. and Environ. Health, Bethesda Country Club. Avocations: tennis, ballet, reading, public health. Home: 7401 Westlake Ter Apt 512 Bethesda MD 20817-6566 Office: Epidemiology and Health Rsch Inc 7401 Westlake Ter Apt 512 Bethesda MD 20817-6566

WHITE, LINDA DIANE, lawyer; b. N.Y.C., Apr. 1, 1952; d. Bernard and Elaine (Simons) Schwartz; m. Thomas M. White, Aug. 16, 1975; 1 child, Alexandra Nicole. AB, U. Pa., 1973; JD, Northwestern U., 1976. Bar: Ill. 1976. Assoc. Walsh, Case, Coale & Brown, Chgo., 1976-77, Greenberger & Kaufmann (merged into Katten, Muchin), Chgo., 1977-82; ptnr. Greenberger & Kaufmann (merged into Katten, Muchin), 1982-85, Sonnenschein Nath & Rosenthal, Chgo., 1985—. Mem. ABA (real property fin. com., comml. leasing com., real property, probate and trust law sect. 1987—), Ill. Bar Assn., Chgo. Bar Assn., Internat. Assn. Corp. Real Estate Execs. Office: Sonnenschein Nath & Rosenthal 8000 Sears Tower 233 S Wacker Dr Chicago IL 60606-6306

WHITE, LORAY BETTY, public relations executive, writer, actress, producer; b. Houston, Nov. 27, 1934; d. Harold White and Joyce Mae (Jenkins) Mills; m. Sammy Davis Jr., 1957 (div. 1959); 1 child, Deborah R. DeHart. Student, UCLA, 1948-50, 90-91, Nichiren Shoshu Acad., 1988-92; AA in Bus., Sayer Bus. Sch., 1970; study div. mem. dept. L.A., Soka U., Japan, 1970-86. Editor entertainment writer L.A. Community News, 1970-81; exec. sec. guest rels. KNBC Prodns., Burbank, Calif., 1969-75; security specialist Xerox X10 Think Tank, L.A., 1975-80; exec. asst. Ralph Powell & Assocs., L.A., 1980-82; pres., owner, producer LBW & Assocs. Pub. Rels., L.A., 1980—; owner, producer, writer, host TV prodn. co. Pub. Pub. Rels., L.A., 1987—; dir., producer L.B.W. Prodn. "Yesterday, Today, Tomorrow, L.A., 1981—. Actress (film) Ten Commandments, 1956, (Broadway) Joy Ride; appeared in the following endorsements including Budweiser Beer, Old Gold Cigarettes, Salem Cigarettes, TV commls. including Cheer, Puffs Tissue, Coca Cola, Buffern, others; entertainment editor L.A. Community News, 1970-73; writer (column) Balance News, 1980-82. Vol. ARC, 1995. Recipient award ARC, 1955, Cert. of Honor, Internat. Orgn. Soka Gakkai Internat. of Japan, Cmty. Vols. of Am. award, 1994; named Performer of Yr. Cardella Demillo, 1976-77. Mem. ARC (planning, mktg., prodn. event com. 1995), ULCA Alumni Assn., Lupus Found. Am. (So. Calif. chpt.), Nat. Fedn. Blind, Myohoji-Hokkeko Internat. Buddhist. Avocations: singing, acting, TV, writing, producing. *Accepting challenges in life is a choice. The choice is always yours. I've chosen never to give up-to always give my best, to constantly keep a growing and open mind. Toremember to strengthen and reinforce the quality of my integrity no matter what- be a winner to yourself.*

WHITE, LOWELL E., JR., medical educator; b. Tacoma, Wash., Jan. 16, 1928; s. Lowell E. and Hazel (Conley) W.; m. Margie Mae Lamb, June 21, 1947; children: Henry, Leanna White Maynes, Inger-Britt. B.S. in Pharm., U. Wash., 1951, M.D., 1953. Diplomate Am. Bd. Neurol. Surgery. Intern. N.C. Meml. Hosp., Chapel Hill, 1953-54; resident neurosurgery, asst. to instr. U. Wash., 1954-60, asst. prof., 1960-64, asso. prof., 1964-70; asso. dean U. Wash. (Sch. Medicine), 1965-68; prof., chief div. neurol. surgery U. Fla., 1970-72; prof. U. South Ala., 1972-94, chmn. div. neurosci., 1972-77, ret., 1994; adj. prof. Ala. Sch. of Math. and Sci., 1993-94; chmn. nat. adv. com. Animal Resources NIH, 1966-70; cons. rsch. facilities and resources NIH; cons. divsn. hosp. and med. facilities USPHS; cons. grants adminstrn. policy U.S. Dept. HEW. Contbr. articles profl. jours. Bd. dirs. Mobile County Emergency Med. Svcs. Coun., 1973-82, Mobile cpt. Myasthenia Gravis Found. Am., 1974—, Mobile Mental Health Assn., 1979-89, Spl. Edn. Action Com., 1985—, pres. 1996. With USN, 1946-47, USNR, 1948-66. Guggenheim fellow, 1958-59. Mem. AMA, Am. Assn. Neurol. Surgeons, Am. Assn. Neuropathologists, Am. Acad. Neurol. Surgeons, Soc. for Neurosci., Assn. Am. Med. Colls., Am. Assn. Anatomists, Rsch. Soc. Neurol. Surgeons, Neurosurg. Soc. Ala. (pres. 1975), Skyline Country Club (pres. 1986), Cajal Club. Home: 5750 Huffman Dr N Mobile AL 36693-3013

WHITE, LUTHER WESLEY, lawyer; b. Norfolk, Va., Aug. 29, 1923; s. Luther Wesley White Jr. and Edith Prettyman; m. Patricia Bowers; children: Luther, John P., Nell White King, Mary Dix. BA, Randolph-Macon Coll., 1947, LLD (hon.), 1989; LLB, Washington & Lee U., 1949, LLD, 1969; LHD (hon.), Bridgewater Coll., 1979; HHD (hon.), Ky. Wesleyan Coll., 1988. Bar: Va. 1949. Pvt. practice law Norfolk, 1949-67; pres. Randolph-Macon Coll., Ashland, Va., 1967-1979, Ky. Wesleyan Coll., Owensboro, 1979-88; atty. Eggleston & Thelen, Lovingston, Va., 1989-95; pres. Nat. Assn. Colls. and Univs. of United Meth. Ch., 1977-78. Pres. Norfolk

Symphony Orch., 1966, Owensboro Symphony Orch., 1987. Lt. (j.g.) USN, 1943-46, PTO. Recipient Liberty Bell award Daviess County (Ky.) Bar Assn., Owensboro, 1983. Mem. Rotary (pres. Owensboro club 1982-83). Republican. Methodist. Avocations: music, tennis, gardening. Home: 31 Ashlawn Blvd Palmyra VA 22963-3329

WHITE, LYNNE M., public relations company executive. With Gilbert, Whitney & Johns, Whippany, N.J. Office: Gilbert Whitney & Johns Inc 110 S Jefferson Rd Whippany NJ 07981-1027

WHITE, MARGITA EKLUND, television association executive; b. Linköping, Sweden, June 27, 1937; came to U.S., 1948; d. Eyvind O. and Ella Maria (Erikkson) Eklund; m. Stuart Crawford White, June 24, 1961 (div. 1987); children: Suzanne Margareta Morgan, Stuart Crawford Jr. B.A. magna cum laude in Govt, U. Redlands, 1959, LL.D. (hon.), 1977; M.A. in Polit. Sci. (Woodrow Wilson fellow), Rutgers U., 1960. Asst. to press sec. Richard M. Nixon Presdl. Campaign, Washington, 1960; adminstrv. asst. Whitaker & Baxter Advt. Agy., Honolulu, 1961-62; minority news sec. Hawaii Ho. of Reps., 1963; research asst. to Senator Barry Goldwater and Republican Nat. Com., 1963-64; research asst., writer Free Society Assn., 1965-66; research asst. to syndicated columnist Raymond Moley, 1967; asst. to Herbert G. Klein, White House dir. communications, 1969-73; asst. dir. USIA, 1973-75; asst. press sec. to Pres. Gerald R. Ford, 1975; asst. press sec. to Pres., dir. White House Office of Communications, Washington, 1975-76; commr. FCC, 1976-79; dir. Radio Free Europe-Radio Liberty Inc., 1979-82, vice chmn., 1982; dir. Taft Broadcasting Co., 1980-87, Armtek Corp., 1987-88, Rayonier Forest Resources Co., 1985-93; pres. Assn. Maximum Svc. Television; bd. dirs. ITT Corp., ITT Edn. Svcs., Inc., Washington Mut. Investors Fund, Growth Fund Washington, Leitch Tech. Corp.; U.S. Del. Internat. Telecomm. Union Plenipotentiary Conf., Nairobi, 1982; coord. TV Operators Caucus, Inc., 1985-88/. Mem. George Foster Peabody Adv. Bd., 1979-86. Recipient Disting. svc. award U. Redlands Alumni Assn., 1974, Superior Honor award USIA, 1975, Dir.'s Choice award Nat. Women's Econ. Alliance, 1995, Disting. Svc. to Broadcasting award Broadcast Pioneers, 1995. Mem. Exec. Women in Govt. (founding mem., sec. 1975), Women's Forum of Washington. Home: 1533 28th St NW Washington DC 20007-3059 Office: 1776 Massachusetts Ave NW Washington DC 20036-1904

WHITE, MARILYN DOMAS, information science educator; b. Franklin, La., Aug. 16, 1940; d. George Julian and Norma Edwina (Melancon) Domas; m. Roger Stuart White, Aug. 31, 1968; 1 child, Joshua Stuart. BA, Our Lady of the Lake Coll., San Antonio, 1962; MS, U. Wis., 1963; PhD, U. Ill., 1971. Dir. Commerce Libr. U. Wis., Madison, 1963-65; head Social Sci./Bus. Libr. So. Ill. U., Edwardsville, 1965-67; cons. So. Ill. U./U.S. AID Adv. Team, South Vietnam, 1967; asst. prof. SUNY, Buffalo, 1972-74; lectr., vis. asst. prof. U. Md., College Park, 1976-77, asst. prof. info sci., 1977-82, assoc. prof. info. sci., 1982—; cons. USIA, Washington and abroad, 1977-83, Inst. for Def. Analyses, Bowie, Md.,Supercomputing Rsch. Ctr., 1990-91, Am. Health Care Assn., Washington, 1990-92, Am. Coun. on Edn., 1995. Contbr. articles to Libr. Quar., Drexel Libr. Quar., Reference Libr., others. James Lyman Whitney grantee ALA, 1983, Spl. Libr. Assn. rsch. grantee, 1993-94, Coun. Libr. Resources grantee, 1995-96. Mem. Am. Soc. for Info. Sci., Spl. Libr. Assn. Roman Catholic. Office: U Md Coll Libr and Info Svcs Hornbake 4117F South Wing College Park MD 20742

WHITE, MARTIN CHRISTOPHER, academic administrator; b. Anderson, S.C., Oct. 16, 1943; s. Jesse Martin and Christine Freida (Powell) W.; m. Linda Ann Fleming, July 31, 1965; children: Martin Lynn, Andrew Christopher. AB, Mercer U., 1965; MDiv, So. Bapt. Theol. Sem., 1968; PhD, Emory U., 1972. Prof. Elon Coll. (N.C.), 1972-76, dean acad. affairs, 1976-82, v.p. for acad. and student affairs, 1982-86; pres. Gardner-Webb U., Boiling Springs, N.C., 1986—; cons. So. Assn. Colls. and Schs., Atlanta, 1982—. Contbr. articles in field. Bd. dirs. United Way, Shelby, N.C., 1987. Woodrow Wilson fellow, 1971. Mem. Soc. Bibl. Lit., Nat. Assn. Bapt. Profs. of Religion, N.C. Ind. Coll. Assn., Alpha Chi, Omicron Delta Kappa. Democrat. Baptist. Lodge: Rotary (bd. dirs. Burlington, N.C. chpt. 1986). Avocations: golfing, tennis, music, traveling. Home: 303 W Marion St Shelby NC 28150-5335 Office: Gardner-Webb U Campus Mail Dept Boiling Springs NC 28017

WHITE, MARTIN F., lawyer; b. Warren, Ohio, Nov. 12, 1952; s. Benjamin and Bella Dorothy (Bernstein) W. BA, Ohio State U., 1973; JD, 1977. Bar: U.S. Dist. Ct. (no. dist.) Ohio, 1981, Pa., 1993. Atty. pvt. practice, Warren, Ohio, 1977—; spl. counsel Ohio Atty. Gen., Columbus, Ohio, 1991—. Mem. Am. Trial Lawyers Assn., Ohio Acad. Trial Lawyers, Mahoning-Trumbull Trial Lawyers Assn., Ohio Acad. Criminal Def. Attys., Ohio Bar Assn., Trumbull County Bar Assn. Office: PO Box 1150 Warren OH 44482-1150

WHITE, MARY LOU, fundraiser, writer, educator; b. Davenport, Iowa, Feb. 17, 1939; d. Edward Joseph and Madeleine (Levart) Briglia; m. Morton Bartho White, Dec. 6, 1965 (dec. Jan. 1973). Cert. d'etudes francaises, U. Grenoble, France, 1959; BA, Gettysburg Coll., 1960; postgrad., Sorbonne, Paris, 1961; MA, Middlebury Coll., 1962; MS, U. Bridgeport, 1972. Writer CIA, N.Y.C., 1962-64; tchr. French Miss Porter's Sch., Farmington, Conn., 1964-66; fundraiser N.Y. Philharm., N.Y.C., 1966-72; tchr. French Fairfield (Conn.) Country Day Sch., 1973-77, Greens Farms (Conn.) Acad., 1977-79; spl. events coord. N.Y. Philharm., N.Y.C., 1979-80; econ. devel. Broward C.C., Ft. Lauderdale, Fla., 1989-91; programming grants writer Broward Ctr. for the Performing Arts, Ft. Lauderdale, 1992—. Vol. Polit. Party, Ft. Lauderdale, 1990-93. Mem. Hereditary Register of U.S. Avocations: chess, piano, breeding dachshunds. Home: 888 Intracoastal Dr Fort Lauderdale FL 33304-3638

WHITE, MARY RUTH WATHEN, social services administrator; b. Athens, Tex., Dec. 27, 1927; d. Benedict Hudson and Sara Elizabeth (Evans) W.; m. Robert M. White, Nov. 10, 1946; children: Martha Elizabeth, Robert Miles, Jr., William Benedict, Mary Ruth, Jesse Wathen, Margaret Fay, Maureen Adele, Thomas Evan. BA, Stephen F. Austin State U., Nacogdoches, Tex., 1948. Chmn. Regional Drug Abuse Com., San Antonio, 1975-81, Met. Youth Council, San Antonio, 1976-78; state chmn. Citizens United for Rehab. Errants, San Antonio, 1978-91; sec. Bexar County Detention Ministries, San Antonio, 1979-88; chmn. Bexar County (Tex.) Jail Commn., 1980-82; chmn. com. on role of family in reducing recidivism Tex. Dept. Criminal Justice, Austin, 1985—; chmn. Met. Community Corrections Com., San Antonio, 1986-90; bd. dirs. Tex. Coalition for Juvenile Justice, 1975-93, Target 90 Youth Coordinating Coun., San Antonio, 1986-89; local chmn. vol. adv. bd. Tex. Youth Commn., 1986-87. Pres. San Antonio City Coun. PTA, 1976-78, Rep. Bus. Women Bexar County, San Antonio, 1984-86, North Urban Deanery, San Antonio Alliance Mental Illness, 1995-96, also legis. chmn.; bd. dirs. CURE, 1978-92; legis. chmn. Archdiocese of San Antonio Coun. Cath. Women; mem. allocation com. United Way, San Antonio, 1986-91. Named Today's Woman, San Antonio Light newspaper, 1985, Outstanding Rep. Woman, Rep. Bus. Women Bexar County, 1987; honoree Rep. Women Stars over Tex., 1992. Mem. Am. Corrections Assn., Assn. Criminal Justice Planners, LWV (pres. San Antonio chpt. 1984-86), Conservation Soc., Fedn. Women (bd. dirs. 1984-90), DAR (regent) Colonial Dames (pres.), Cath. Daus. Am. (registered parliamentarian, past regent Ct. of St. Anthony), Tex. Cath. Daus. Am. (state legis. chair.), San Antonio Alliance for Mentally Ill (pres. 1995-96). Home: 701 E Sunshine Dr San Antonio TX 78228-2516 Office: 5372 Fredericksburg Rd Ste 114 San Antonio TX 78229-3559

WHITE, MERIT PENNIMAN, engineering educator; b. Whately, Mass., Oct. 25, 1908; s. Henry and Jessie (Penniman) W.; m. Jarmila Jaskova, 1965; children: Mary Jessie, Irene Helen, Elisabeth Cecelia, Ellen Patricia. A.B. cum laude, Dartmouth Coll., 1930, C.E., 1931; M.S., Calif. Inst. Tech., 1932, Ph.D. magna cum laude, 1935. With U.S. Dept. Agr., 1935-37; postdoctoral fellow Harvard U., 1937-38; research asso. Calif. Inst. Tech., 1938-39; asst. prof. Ill. Inst. Tech., 1939-42; cons. OSRD, 1942-45, War and Navy Depts., 1945-47; prof., head civil engring. dept. U. Mass., 1948—, Commonwealth head of dept., 1961-77, Commonwealth prof., 1977-94, Commonwealth prof. emeritus, 1994—. Contbr. articles to engring. jours. Recipient Pres.'s certificate of merit, 1948. Fellow ASME; mem. ASCE (hon.), Instn. Mech. Engrs. (chartered), Rèunion Internat. Laboratoires d'Essais et Rechereches sur les Matériaux (founding), Boston Soc. Civil Engrs. (hon.), Phi Beta Kappa, Sigma Xi, Tau Beta Pi. Home: PO Box 42 101 Chestnut Plain Rd Whately MA 01093

WHITE, MICHAEL LEE, lawyer; b. Dilley, Tex., Mar. 27, 1953; s. Deryl and Ruby Alice (Gillis) W. BA, Tex. A&M U., 1975; JD, U. Houston, 1978. Bar: Tex. 1979. Briefing atty. 14th Ct. Appeals, Houston, 1979; contracts analyst Texaco Inc., Houston, 1979-80, legis. coord., 1980-82; mgr. state govt. rels. Pennzoil Co., Houston, 1982-85, mgr. employee comms., pub. affairs liaison, 1985-87, mgr. media comms., 1987-88; dir. govt. affairs Met. Transit Authority Harris County, Houston, 1988-90; v.p. C. of C. divsn. Greater Houston Partnership, 1990-94; legis. cons. Austin, Tex., 1994—. Fellow Houston Bar Found.; mem. ABA, State Bar Tex., Houston Bar Assn., Tex. Lyceum Assn. (bd. dirs., exec. com. 1984-89), Travis County Bar Assn. Avocations: golf, tennis, skiing, reading. Office: PO Box 1667 Austin TX 78767-1667

WHITE, MICHAEL REED, mayor; b. Cleve., Aug. 13, 1951; s. Robert and Audrey (Silver) W. BA, Ohio State U., 1973, MPA, 1974. Spl. asst. Columbus (Ohio) Mayor's Office, 1974-76; adminstrv. asst. Cleve. City Coun., 1976-77; sales mgr. Burks Electric Co., Cleve., 1978-84; state senator Ohio Senate, Columbus, 1984-89; mayor Cleve., 1990—; minority whip Ohio Senate Dems., 1987-89. City councilman City of Cleve., 1978-84; bd. dirs. Glenville Devel. Corp., Cleve., 1978—, Glenville Festival Found., Cleve., 1978—, United Black Fund, Cleve., 1986, Greater Cleve. Dome Corp., 1986. Named one of Outstanding Young Men Am., 1985, Outstanding Svc. award Cleve. chpt. Nat. Assn. Black Vets., 1985, Cmty. Svcs. award East Side Jaycees, Pres.'s award, 1993, named Black Profl. of Yr., 1993, Humanitarian award, 1994. Democrat. Home: 1057 East Blvd Cleveland OH 44108-2972 Office: Office of Mayor 601 Lakeside Ave E Cleveland OH 44114-1015

WHITE, MICHELLE JO, economics educator; b. Washington, Dec. 3, 1945; d. Harry L. and Irene (Silverman) Rich; m. Roger Hall Gordon, July 25, 1982. AB, Harvard U., 1967; MSc in Econs., London Sch. Econs., 1968; PhD, Princeton U., 1973. Asst. prof. U. Pa., Phila., 1973-78; from assoc. prof. to prof. NYU, N.Y.C., 1978-83; prof. econs. U. Mich., Ann Arbor, 1984—; dir. PhD program in econs. U. Mich., 1992-94; vis. asst. prof. Yale U., New Haven, 1978; vis. prof. People's U., Beijing, 1986, U. Warsaw, 1990, U. Wis., Madison, 1991, U. Munich, Germany, 1992, Tilburg U., The Netherlands, 1993, 95, U. Chgo., 1993, Copenhagen Bus. Sch., 1995; cons. Pension Benefit Guaranty Corp., Washington, 1987; chmn. adv. com. dept. econs. Princeton U., 1988-90. Editor: The Non-profit Sector in a Three Sector Economy, 1981; contbr. numerous articles to profl. jours. Bd. dirs. Com. on Status of Women in Econs. Profession, 1984-86. Resources for Future fellow, 1972-73; grantee NSF, 1979, 82, 88, 91, 93, Sloan Found., 1984, Fund for Rsch. in Dispute Resolution, 1989; Fulbright scholar, Poland, 1990. Mem. Am. Econ. Assn., Am. Law and Econ. Assn. (bd. dirs. 1991-92), Am. Real Estate and Urban Econs. Assn. (bd. dirs. 1992-95), Social Scis. Rsch. Coun. (bd. dirs. 1994—), Midwest Econs. Assn. (1st v.p. 1996—). Office: Univ Mich Dept Economics 611 Tappan St Ann Arbor MI 48109-1220

WHITE, MORTON GABRIEL, philosopher, author; b. N.Y.C., Apr. 29, 1917; s. Robert and Esther (Levine) Weisberger; m. Lucia Perry, Aug. 29, 1940; children: Nicholas Perry, Stephen Daniel. B.S., CCNY, 1936; L.H.D., CUNY, 1975; A.M., Columbia U., 1938, Ph.D., 1942. Instr. philosophy Columbia U., 1942-46; instr. physics CCNY, 1942-43; asst. prof. philosophy U. Pa., 1946-48; asst. prof. philosophy Harvard U., 1948-50, asso. prof., 1950-53, prof., 1953-70, chmn. dept., 1954-57, acting chmn. dept., 1967-69; prof. Inst. Advanced Study, 1970-87; prof. emeritus, 1987—; Guggenheim research fellow, 1950-51; vis. prof. Tokyo U., 1952, 60, 66, U. Oslo, 1977-78; Neesima lectr. Doshisha U., Kyoto, 1985, CUNY, 1968-69, Rutgers U., 1987-88, 88-89; mem. Inst. Advanced Study, 1953-54, 62-63, 67-68, 68-69. Author: The Origin of Dewey's Instrumentalism, 1943, Social Thought in America, 1949, The Age of Analysis, 1955, Toward Reunion in Philosophy, 1956, Religion, Politics, and the Higher Learning, 1959, (with Lucia White) The Intellectual Versus the City, 1962; Editor: (with Arthur M. Schlesinger, Jr.) Paths of American Thought, 1963, Foundations of Historical Knowledge, 1965, Science and Sentiment in America, 1972, Documents in the History of American Philosophy, 1972, Pragmatism and the American Mind, 1973, The Philosophy of the American Revolution, 1978, What Is and What Ought to Be Done, 1981, (with Lucia White) Journeys to the Japanese, 1952-79, 1986, Philosophy, The Federalist and the Constitution, 1987, The Question of Free Will, 1993. Fellow Center Advanced Study Behavioral Scis., 1959-60; fellow Am. Council Learned Socs., 1962-63. Mem. Am. Acad. Arts and Scis., Am. Antiquarian Soc., Am. Philos. Soc. Office: Inst for Advanced Study Princeton NJ 08540

WHITE, NATHAN EMMETT, JR., judge, lawyer; b. Dallas, Nov. 28, 1941; s. Nathan Emmett and Martha Eleanor (Scogin) W.; m. Wanda Joyce Cason, Feb. 28, 1964; children: Steven Kelly, Russell Bradley. BBA, So. Meth. U., 1964, JD, 1972; postgrad., George Washington U., 1969-71. Bar: Tex. 1972, U.S. Dist. Ct. (no. dist.) Tex. 1976. Sole practice, Plano, Tex., 1972-89; county judge, Collin County, McKinney, Tex., 1975-82, county treas., 1983-85; state dist. judge 366th dist. Ct., Collin County, Tex., 1989—. Chmn. Collin County Rep. Party, 1972-74; mem. exec. com. State Rep. Party, 1982-84. Served to lt. USNR, 1966-71. Named Citizen of Yr., Plano C. of C., 1982. Mem. State Bar Tex. (chmn. sch. law sect. 1981-82), Plano Bar Assn. (pres. 1988-89), Collin County Bar Assn. (pres. 1990-91). Mormon. Lodges: Rotary (pres. 1975-76, dist. gov. 1979-80), Masons. Home: 2406 Forest Ct Mc Kinney TX 75070 Office: PO Box 808 Mc Kinney TX 75070

WHITE, NICHOLAS J., retail company executive; b. Sacramento, 1945. Grad., Mo. So. State Coll. Exec. v.p. Wal-Mart Supercenter div. Wal-Mart Stores Inc. Home: 81 Champions Blvd Rogers AR 72758 Office: Wal-Mart Stores Inc 702 SW 8th St Bentonville AR 72712-6209*

WHITE, NICK, retail executive; b. Alameda, Calif., Mar. 12, 1945; s. Melvin J. and Dorothy May (Van Cleve) W.; m. Connie White, June 1, 1968; children: Nichole White Williams, Michele White Hudson. Student, Mo. So. Coll., 1968, Ctrl. Mo. State Coll., 1969-73. Store mgr. Wal*Mart, Bentonville, Ark., 1973-77; dist. mgr. Wal*Mart, Bentonville, 1977-80, regional mgr., 1980-81, v.p., 1981-86, sr. v.p., 1986-88, exec. v.p., 1988—; spkr. in field. With USMC, 1963-67, Viet Nam. Avocations: tennis, golf. Home: 81 Champions Blvd Rogers AR 72758 Office: Wal*Mart Stores 702 SW 8th St Bentonville AR 72716

WHITE, NORVAL CRAWFORD, architect; b. N.Y.C., June 12, 1926; s. William Crawford and Caroline Ruth (Taylor) W.; m. Joyce Leslie Lee, May 24, 1958 (div.); children: William Crawford, Thomas Taylor, Gordon Crawford, Alistair David; m. Camilla Cecilia Crowe, June 7, 1992. B.S., Mass. Inst. Tech., 1949; student, Sch. Fine Arts, Fontainbleau, 1954; M.F.A., Princeton, 1955. Designer, assoc. Lathrop Douglass (Architect), 1955-59; prin. Norval C. White (Architect), N.Y.C., 1959-62, 66-67; partner Rowan & White (Architects), N.Y.C., 1962-66, Gruzen & Partners, N.Y.C., 1967-70; prin. Norval C. White & Assos., N.Y.C., 1970-74; ptnr. Levien, Deliso & White, 1974-80, Levien Deliso White Songer, 1980-86; asst. prof. architecture Cooper Union, 1961-67; prof. architecture City Coll., CUNY, 1970-95, prof. emeritus, 1995—, chmn. dept. 1970-77. Author: (with E. Willensky) AIA Guide to New York City, 1968, 2d edit., 1978, 3d edit., 1988, The Architecture Book, 1976, New York: A Physical History, 1987, The Guide to the Architecture of Paris, 1991; prin. works include Seiden House, Tenafly, N.J., 1960, Essex Terrace (housing), Bklyn., 1970, N.Y.C. Police Hdqrs., 1973, Brookhaven Parks (L.I.) San Landfill, 1971, Forsgate Indsl. Park, South Brunswick, N.J., 1978-86, Del Vista Condominiums, Miami, 1981, 61 Christopher Street, Greenwich Village, 1987. Trustee Bklyn. Inst. Arts and Scis., 1973-82, Bklyn. Pub. Libr., 1993-96; gov. Bklyn. Mus., 1973-82, adv. com., 1982—; mem. N.Y.C. Art Commn., 1975-86, sec., 1975-77, v.p., 1978-80. Served with USNR, 1944-46. Fellow AIA; mem. Soc. Archtl. Historians, N.Y. State Assn. Architects. Democrat. Club: Century Assn. (N.Y.C.). Home and Office: 4 Bostwick St PO Box 1986 Lakeville CT 06039

WHITE, ONEIDA ELIZABETH, Daycare provider; b. Waco, Tex., Feb. 3, 1922; d. Oscar Eulali and Jim Lovey (Warner) W. BS, Bradley U., 1963; MA, Nova U., 1980; MA in Bibl. Studies, Bay Cities Sem., 1984. Libr. Peoria (Ill.) Jour. Star, 1965-67, tchr. primary sch., 1961-75, 67-71; asst. prin. Peoria Dist. 150, 1965-66; tchr. Oakland (Calif.) Unified Sch. Dist., 1971-86, substitute tchr., 1986—; pianist Sunday sch. Cuomosris Mission Union, 1983—; pres. pastor aid soc. Foothill Missionary Bapt. Ch., 1986—. Active Dem. Party, 1990. Baptist. Avocations: reading, missionary worker. Home: 540 21st St Apt 905 Oakland CA 94612-1638

WHITE, OWEN KENDALL, JR., sociologist, educator; b. Salt Lake City, Oct. 23, 1938; s. Owen Kendall and Thelma Clark White; m. Arlene Burraston; 1 child, C.A. Wood. BS in Sociology, U. Utah, 1964, MS in Sociology, 1967; PhD in Sociology, Vanderbilt U., 1975. Instr. part-time Vanderbilt U., Nashville, 1968; instr. sociology Washington and Lee U., Lexington, Va., 1969-75, asst. prof. sociology, 1975-80, assoc. prof. sociology, 1980-86, prof. sociology, 1986—, chair dept. sociology and anthropology, 1987—; vis. asst. prof. Inst. Urban Studies, U. Tex., summer 1978; referee Dialogue: A Jour. of Mormon Thought, 1989, Jour. of Urban Affairs, 1990—, Jour for Sci. Study of Religion, 1993—; lectr. in field. Author: Mormon Neo-Orthodoxy: A Crisis Theology, 1987, 2d printing, 1988; editor: Religion in the Contemporary South: Diversity Community and Identity, 1995; contbr. articles and book revs. to profl. publs. Recipient Glenn grant Washington and Lee U, 1970, 75, 81-93, Silver award The Silver Found., 1971, Mednick fellowship Va. Found. for Ind. Colls., 1985, 93. Mem. Am. Anthrop. Assn., Am. Sociol. Assn., Assn. for the Sociology of Religion, Soc. for Sociol. Study of Mormon Life (pres. 1991-93), So. Anthrop. Soc., So. Sociol. Soc., Religious Rsch. Assn., Va. Sociol. Sci. Assn. Office: Washington and Lee U Dept Sociology/Anthropology Lexington VA 24450

WHITE, PAMELA JANICE, lawyer; b. Elizabeth, N.J., July 13, 1952; d. Emmet Talmadge and June (Howlett) W. BA, Mary Washington Coll., 1974; JD, Washington and Lee U., 1977. Bar: Md. 1977, U.S. Dist. Ct. Md. 1978, D.C. 1979, U.S. Dist. Ct. D.C. 1979, U.S. Ct. Appeals (4th cir.) 1979, U.S. Ct. Appeals (D.C. cir.) 1981, U.S. Ct. Claims 1981, U.S. Ct. Appeals (2d cir.) 1983, N.Y. 1983, U.S. Dist. Ct. (so. dist.) N.Y. 1983, U.S. Ct. Appeals (9th cir.) 1988, U.S. Supreme Ct. 1981. Assoc. Ober, Kaler, Grimes & Shriver, Balt., 1977-84, ptnr., 1985—; mem. Md. Bd. Law Examiners, 1986-94; select com. on Gender Equality, 1989—; fed. dist. ct. adv. group, Civil Justice Reform Act, 1990. Note and comment editor Washington and Lee Law Rev. 1976-77, Washington and Lee Law Council 1983-87, emeritus mem., 1988—, pres. 1991-92. Mem. Fed. Ct. Bicentennial Com., 1988-90; vol. Profl. Gov.'s Drug-Free Workplace Initiative, 1990-93; bd. trustees Washington and Lee U., 1995—. Named Disting. Alumna, Washington and Lee U., 1994, Hon. mem. Order of the Coif, 1994. Fellow Am. Bar Found., Md. Bar Found.; mem. ABA, Fed. Bar Assn., Nat. Conf. Lawyers Corp. Fiduciaries, N.Y. State Bar Assn., Md. Bar Assn. (coun. legal edn. sect. 1987-96, chmn. 1992-93, labor sect. 1992-96, professionalism com. 1991—, chmn. 1994—, bd. govs. 1993-95, exec. com. 1994-95), D.C. Bar Assn., Balt. City Bar Assn. (exec. coun. 1995-96), Women's Bar Assn. Md. (treas. 1986-87, v.p. 1987-88, pres.-elect 1988-89, pres. 1989-90, bd. dirs. 1984-86), Md. Assn. Def. Counsel. Presbyterian. Avocations: hiking, softball, baseball. Office: Ober Kaler Grimes & Shriver 120 E Baltimore St Baltimore MD 21202-1674

WHITE, PATRICIA ANN, clinical nurse specialist; b. Indiana, Pa., Dec. 11, 1956; d. Darl J. and Virginia M. (Nealer) W. ADN, Erie C.C., 1978; BSN, U. Tex., Houston, 1989; MSN, U. Tex., 1991. Cert. critical care nurse, clin. nurse specialsit, ACLS instr., ABLS provider. Staff nurse M.D. Anderson, Houston, 1978-81; agy. nurse Kimberely Agy., San Francisco, 1981-82; staff nurse U. Calif., Davis, 1982-83; nurse Travel Nurse Corp., Malden, Mass., 1984-87; critical care instr. Hermann Hosp., Houston, 1987-91; clin. instr. U. Tex. Health Sci. Ctr., Houston, 1991-92; clin. edn. coord. Tampa (Fla.) Gen. Healthcare; presenter in field. Contbr. articles to profl. jours. Vol. St. Petersburg Free Clinic. Mem. ANA, Am. Coll. Cardiovascular Nursing (pres. 1993—), Am. Assn. Critical Care Nurses, Am. Heart Assn., Continuing Edn. League, Sigma Theta Tau. Presbyterian. Avocations: tennis, reading, dogs. Office: Tampa Gen Healthcare Davis Island CEDAR Tampa FL 33602

WHITE, PAUL DUNBAR, lawyer; b. LaGrange, Ky., Oct. 20, 1917; s. Isham Forrest and Florence (Harris) W.; m. Marion Loutenas Stallworth, Sept. 2, 1949; children: Paulette, Ronald. A.B., Ky. State Coll., 1940; LL.B., Western Res. U., 1950. Bar: Ohio 1950, U.S. Supreme Ct. 1972. Supr. Ind. State Boys Sch., 1940-41; group worker spl. projects Karamu, Cleve., 1941-43; visitor Cuyahoga County Agy., 1946-47; individual practice law Cleve., 1950-51; police prosecutor City of Cleve., 1951-59, 1st asst. prosecutor, 1960-63, dir. law, 1967-68; judge Cleve. Mcpl. Ct., 1964-67; assoc. Baker & Hostetler, Cleve., 1968-70; ptnr. Baker & Hostetler, 1970—; mem. State of Ohio Bd. Examiners, 1972-78. Trustee NCCJ, Cleve., 1972-86; trustee Ohio Law Opportunity Fund, 1975-87, Cleve. Urban League, 1975-78, Dyke Coll., Cleve., 1976-86; bd. commrs. Cleve. Met. Park, 1975-78. Served with U.S. Army, 1943-46. Mem. ABA, Ohio Bar Assn., Greater Cleve. Bar Assn. (trustee 1976-79, del. 8th Jud. Dist. Ohio conf. 1985—), Nat. Bar Assn., Soc. Benchers (Case Western Res. U.), Norman S. Minor Bar Assn. Home: 16210 Telfair Ave Cleveland OH 44128-3736 Office: Baker & Hostetler 3200 National City Ctr 1900 E 9th St Cleveland OH 44114-3401*

WHITE, PERRY MERRILL, JR., orthopedic surgeon; b. Texarkana, Ark., Oct. 11, 1925; s. Perry Merrill and Mary Gladys (Shelton) W.; m. Lucy Katherine Freeman, Dec. 23, 1947; children: Perry Merrill III, Georgia Lynette, Katherine Landis White Long, John David. B.S., Baylor U., 1948, M.D., 1953; postgrad., Vanderbilt U., 1948-49. Diplomate Am. Bd. Orthopedic Surgery. Intern VA Hosp., Houston, 1953-54; gen. practice medicine Spearman, Tex., 1955-57; resident orthopedic surgery Eugene Talmadge Meml. Hosp., Augusta, Ga., 1957-61; pvt. practice orthopedic surgery Atlanta, 1961-83; chief Ga. Adult Amputee Clinic, 1965-79; active staff Scottish Rite Hosp. for Crippled Children, Decatur, Ga., 1965-73; instr. orthopedic surgery residency program Ga. Bapt. Hosp., 1965-83; orthopedic panelist Ga. Dept. Vocat. Rehab.; cons. Ga. Crippled Children's Service, 1965-76. Former mem. bd. dirs. Haggai Inst., Atlanta, London, Singapore. Served with USNR, 1944-46. Fellow ACS, Am. Acad. Orthopedic Surgeons; mem. So., Ga., Atlanta med. assns., Eastern Orthopedic Assn., Ga., Atlanta orthopedic socs., Alpha Kappa Kappa. Republican. Baptist (deacon). Home: 1547 Cave Rd NW Atlanta GA 30327-3119

WHITE, PETER SHERWOOD, plant ecologist; b. Phila., Feb. 17, 1948; s. Courtland Yardley III and Helen (Schloss) W.; m. Carolyn Hervey; children: Sarah Linnaea Hickler, Matthew Trillium Hanlin. BA, Bennington Coll., 1971; PhD, Dartmouth Coll., 1976. Asst. prof. dept. biol. scis. Dartmouth Coll., 1976-77; postdoctoral fellow Mo. Bot. Garden, 1977-78; rsch. biologist Uplands Field Rsch. Lab. Gt. Smoky Mountains Nat. Park, 1978-86, acting rsch. coord., 1981-82; leader coop. park studies unit U. Tenn., Knoxville, 1985-86; dir. N.C. Bot. Garden U. N.C., Chapel Hill, 1986—, assoc. prof. dept. biology and curriculum in ecology, 1986—; adj. prof. grad. program in ecology U. Tenn., Knoxville, 1980—; Roger E. Wilson lectr. Miami U., Ohio, 1984; vice chmn. vegetation sect. Ecology Soc. Am., 1983-85; bd. dirs. Highlands Biol. Sta.; sci. adv. com. Tenn. Natural Heritage Program, 1980-86; mem. plant conservation bd. N.C. Dept. Agr., 1986—; nat. catalog steering com. Nat. Pk. Svc., 1982-85, adv. panel on ecol. inventory and monitoring, 1988-91; participant numerous workshops, symposia, and rev. panels. Mem. editl. bd. Ecology and Ecology Monographs, 1988-91, Jour. Vegetation Sci., 1993—, (spl. issue) Jour. Sustainable Forestry, 1994-95; editor: (with S.T.A. Pickett) The Ecology of Natural Disturbance and Patch Dynamics, 1985, also numerous procs.; contbr. articles to sci. jours. Recipient Spl. Achievement award Nat. Park Svc., 1981, 82, Grovenor award Mus. Sci., Boston, 1971; Kramer fellow Dartmouth Coll., 1971-76, NEA fellow Mo. Bot. Garden, 1977-78. Achievements include research in vegetation dynamics, vegetation-landscape relations, disturbance, plant strategies, biogeography, floristics, biological diversity, conservation biology. Office: U N C Chapel Hill Dept Biology Campus Box 3280 Coker Hall Chapel Hill NC 27599-3280

WHITE, PHILIP BUTLER, artist; b. Chgo., Jan. 23, 1935; s. Ralph Gerald and Mary (Butler) W.; m. Anita Malisani; children—David, Daniel. B.F.A., U. So. Calif., 1957. juror 71st annual exhbn. Nat. Water Soc., 1991, 24th ann. exhbn. Tenn. Watercolor Soc., 1995. One-man show, Oehlschlaeger Art Gallery, Chgo., 1976, 78, 80; exhibited in group shows 2d, 3d, ann. nat. art round-ups, Las Vegas, 1957, 58, Union League Club, Chgo., 1959, 63, 65, 67, 69, 72, 74, 76, Ill. State Fair, 1959, 60, 61, 62, 63, 64, 65, 66, 67, 68, Brotherhood Week Art Exhbn., Chgo., 1960, N. Miss. Valley Artists exhibit, Ill. State Mus., Springfield, 1961, 63, 65, 67, 69, 70, Magnificent Mile, Chgo., 1961, ann. midyear shows, Butler Inst. Am. Art, Youngstown, Ohio, 1962, 63, 64, ann. Chgo. Sun Times exhbns., 1962, 63, 21st ann. exhbn. Audubon Artists, N.Y.C., 1963, ann. exhbns., Nat. Acad. Design, N.Y.C., 1963, 64, 65, 67, 68, 69, 70, 74, 75, 76, Okla. Mus. Art, 1969, 70, Ball State U., 1970, Am. Watercolor Soc. ann., 1970-71, one-man show, Oak Park (Ill.) High Sch., 1968; rep., Art Inst. Chgo., various art fairs including, Oakbrook, Ill., 1963, Old Capitol at Springfield, 1963, 68, Oak Park, 1963, 78 subject of cover story, Am. Artist mag., 1978. Served with AUS, 1958-59. Recipient John Deluca medal Las Vegas, 1957, Henry Ward Ranger Fund Purchase prize NAt. Acad. Design, 1963, Julius Hallgarten award, 1964, 67, 69, Thomas B. Clark award, 1965, 68, 70, Helen H. Chambers Purchase prise Union League Club, 1959, 1st prize in oils Union League Club, 1963, 67, 1st prize in oils Ill. State Fair, 1960, 65, Emoly Goldsmith award, 1971, Mcpl. Art League Chgo. award of Excellence, 1995. Address: 710 Clinton Pl River Forest IL 60305-1914

WHITE, PHILLIP E., technology company executive; b. Paylorville, Ill., Dec. 24, 1943; s. Phillip Conrad and Lois Marion (Elliott) W.; m. Sheryl Faye Meyer (div. Feb. 1992); children: thler, Todd, Trevor. BA, Ill. Wesleyan, 1966; MBA, Ill. U., 1968. Dir. of planning IBM, White Plains, N.Y., 1968-84; exec. v.p. sales and mktg. Altos Computer System, San Jose, Calif., 1984-86; pres. Wyse Tech., San Jose, Calif., 1986-88; pres., chief exec. officer Informix Corp., Menlo Park, Calif., 1989—; bd. dirs. Intellicorp, Mountain View, Calif., 1989—, Informix Corp., Menlo Park, Calif., 1989—, Sam and Libby of Calif., San Carlos, 1992—. Bd. dirs. Santa Clara U., Calif., 1989—. Mem. Am. Electronics Assn. Republican. Methodist. Office: Informix Software 4100 Bohannon Dr Menlo Park CA 94025-1013*

WHITE, R. QUINCY, lawyer; b. Chgo., Jan. 16, 1933; s. Roger Q. and Carolyn Jane (Everett) W.; m. Joyce Caldwell, Aug. 4, 1962; children: Cleaver Layton, Annelia Everett. BA, Yale U., 1954; JD, Harvard U., 1960. Bar: Ill. 1960, U.S. Dist. Ct. (no. dist.) Ill. 1960, U.S. Ct. Appeals (9th cir.) 1989. Assoc. Leibman, Williams, Bennett, Baird & Minow, Chgo., 1960-67, ptnr., 1967-73; ptnr. Sidley & Austin, Chgo., 1973-93, of counsel, 1994—; sec., dir. W.F. McLaughlin Co., Chgo., 1964-68; hon. consul gen. Islamic Republic Pakistan, Chgo., 1978-92; designated mem. U.S. Trademark Assn., 1985-94. Bd. dirs. Off the Street Club, Chgo., 1974-84; sec. nat. governing bd. Ripon Soc., 1971-72; mem. exec. com. 43-44th ward Regular Rep. orgn., Chgo., 1970-73, mem. Coun. Fgn. and Domestic Affairs, 1970-76; v.p., bd. dirs. Juvenile Protective Assn., 1965-87. Recipient Sitara-i-Quaid-i-Azam Pakistan, 1982. Mem. ABA, Chgo. Coun. Lawyers, Chgo. Bar Assn., Harvard Law Soc. of Ill. (dir. 1988-93). Home: PO Box 178 10947 Marquette Rd New Buffalo MI 49117-0178 Office: Sidley & Austin 1 First Nat Plz Chicago IL 60603

WHITE, RALPH DALLAS, retired health insurance executive; b. Oklahoma City, Feb. 11, 1919; s. Ralph Allen and Ora Della (Lamberson) W.; m. Ramona Corrine Caffee, Aug. 29, 1943; children: Richard Dallas, Linda Diane. Grad., Okla. Sch. Bus., 1938; B.C.S., Okla. Sch. Accountancy, Law and Fin., 1941; postgrad., U. Tulsa, 1947, Mgmt. Inst., U. Mich., 1965-66. Discount clk. Gen. Motors Acceptance Corp., 1939-42; payroll supr. Douglas Aircraft Corp., 1942-45; with Blue Cross-Blue Shield of Okla., Tulsa, 1945-87, from acctg. supr., mgr. personnel and systems, office mgr., dir. adminstrn., sec.-treas., v.p. and sec.-treas., v.p., treas., to exec. v.p., treas., 1945-80, sr. v.p., 1980-81, cons. to pres., 1981-87, ret., 1987; v.p., treas. Mems. Service Life Ins. Co., 1977-79, dir., 1977-87. Mem. Internat. Com. Tulsa, Ark. Basin Devel. Assn. Named Boss of Yr. Am. Bus. Women's Assn., 1961; recipient Hall of Fame award Okla. Coll. of Bus., 1984. Mem. Nat. Office Mgmt. Assn., Adminstrv. Mgmt. Soc. (pres. 1957-58, Merit award key 1958, Diamond Merit award key 1968), Tulsa C. of C., Tulsa Farm Club, Downtown Kiwanis Club, Tulsa Computer Soc. Methodist. Home: 4709 E 22nd Pl Tulsa OK 74114-2127

WHITE, RALPH DAVID, retired editor and writer; b. Cleve., Mar. 10, 1931; s. Ralph Davis and Mildred Eva (Stein) W.; m. Lucy Margaret Sturm, Aug. 20, 1960; children: Randall, Eric, Karen, Kathleen. BA, Hamilton Coll., 1953; postgrad., SUNY, Buffalo. With Buffalo Evening News, 1956-89, reporter, 1956-61, successively copy editor, asst. city editor, feature editor, to, 1974, picture editor and dir. editorial art dept., 1974-83, gen. features editor, 1983-89, antiques columnist, 1983-89; guest lectr. SUNY, Buffalo. Served with U.S. Army, 1953-55, Far East. Recipient local awards Buffalo Newspaper Guild. Home: 1389 Whitehaven Rd Grand Island NY 14072-1915

WHITE, RALPH PAUL, automotive executive, consultant; b. Watertown, Mass., Aug. 1, 1926; s. Irving William and Margaret Sarah (McGowan) W.; m. Shirley Irene Christie, Nov. 22, 1947; children: Karin Ann, Eric John. BS in Indsl. Engring., Columbia U., 1951; postgrad., Yale U., 1958-59. Instr. engring. mechanics U. Conn., Torrington, 1956-57; mgr. data processing. B.F. Goodrich Co., Shelton, Conn., 1958-61; ptnr., mgmt. cons. Bavier, Bulger & Goodyear, New Haven, 1961-66; v.p. Davidson Rubber Co., Dover, N.H., 1966-69; pres. Davidson Rubber Co., Dover, 1969-80; group v.p. parent co. Ex-Cell-O, Troy, Mich., 1980-83; pres. Troy (N.H.) Mills Inc., 1983-86, chief exec. officer, 1983-89, chmn., 1987-89, also bd. dirs.; cons., 1989—; bd. dirs. J.A. Wright Co., Keene, N.H., J.D. Cahill Co., Hampton, N.H., Exeter Trust Co. Mem. N.H. Indsl. Devel. Authority, 1972-80, 85-88, Pease Devel. Authority, State of N.H., N.H. Bus. and Fin. Authority, 1992—; exec. bd. Whittemore Sch. Bus., U. N.H., Durham, 1984—. Mem. Am. Inst. Indsl. Engrs., Soc. Automotive Engrs., N.H. Bus. and Industry Assn. (bd. dirs. 1970-80, pres. 1972-73, vice chmn. 1984-86), Abenaqui Country Club, Rye Beach Club, Coral Beach Club. Democrat. Roman Catholic. Avocations: skiing, golf. Home: 70 Woodland Rd # 667 North Hampton NH 03862-2234

WHITE, RANDY, retired professional football player; b. Wilmington, Del., Jan. 15, 1953; s. Guy and Laverne W.; m. Vicci Hanes, 1978; 1 child, Jordan. Student, U. Md. Defensive tackle Dallas Cowboys, 1975-88; played in Super Bowl X, 1975, XII, 1977, XIII, 1978. Winner Outland Trophy for best coll. lineman, 1974, (with Harvey Martin) Most Valuable Player award Super Bowl XII, 1977; named to Pro Bowl team, 1977-85, Pro Football Hall of Fame, 1994.

WHITE, RAYMOND PETRIE, JR., dentist, educator; b. N.Y.C., Feb. 13, 1937; s. Raymond Petrie and Mabel Sarah (Shutze) W.; m. Betty Pritchett, Dec. 27, 1961; children—Karen Elizabeth, Michael Wood. Student, Washington and Lee U., 1955-58; D.D.S., Med. Coll. Va., 1962, Ph.D., 1967. Diplomate: Am. Bd. Oral and Maxillofacial Surgery. Postdoctoral fellow anatomy Med. Coll. Va., Richmond, 1962-67; resident in oral surgery Med. Coll. Va., 1964-67; asst. prof. U. Ky., Lexington, 1967-70; asso. prof. U. Ky., 1970-71, chmn. dept. oral surgery, 1969-71; prof., asst. dean adminstrn. Va. Commonwealth U., Richmond, 1971-74; prof. Sch. Dentistry U. N.C., Chapel Hill, 1974—, Dalton L. McMichael disting. prof., 1993—; dean Sch. Dentistry, U. N.C., Chapel Hill, 1974-81, assoc. dean Sch. Medicine, 1981-92; cons. Fayetteville VA Hosp.; mem. staff U.N.C. Hosps., mem. exec. com., 1974—, sec., 1977-78, assoc. chief staff, 1981-92; mem. adv. panel on dentistry U.S. Pharmacopeial Conv., 1985—; sr. program cons. The Robert Wood Johnson Found., 1982-90. Author: (with E.R. Costich) Fundamentals of Oral Surgery, 1971, (with Bell and Proffit) Surgical Correction of Dentofacial Deformities, 1980, (with W.R. Proffit) Surgical Orthodontic Treatment, 1990, (with M.R. Tucker, B.C. Terry, J.E. Van Sickels) Rigid Fixations for Maxillofacial Surgery, 1991; co-editor Internat. Jour. Adult Orthodontics and Orthodontic Surgery, 1985—; asst. editor Jour. Oral and Maxillofacial Surgery, 1993—; contbr. articles to profl. jours. Bd. dirs. Am. Fund for Dental Health, 1978-86, v.p., 1982-85. Recipient Outstanding Tchr. award U. Ky., 1971, Disting. Service award Am. Fund Dental Health, 1987. Mem. ADA, AAAS, N.C. Dental Soc., Internat. Assn. Dental Rsch. (pres. Ky. sect. 1970), Inst. Medicine of NAS, Chalmers J. Lyons Acad. Oral Surgery, Am. Assn. Oral and Maxillofacial Surgeons (gen. chmn. sci. sessions com. 1974-76, Outstanding Svc. award as committeeman 1976, chmn. strategic planning com. 1990-96), N.C. Soc. Oral and Maxillofacial Surgeons, Sigma Xi, Psi Omega, Delta Tau Delta, Alpha Sigma Chi, Sigma Zeta, Psi Omega (Scholarship award 1962), Omicron Kappa Upsilon. Roman Catholic. Home: 1506 Velma Rd Chapel Hill NC 27514-7601 Office: U NC Sch Dentistry Dept Oral/Maxillofacial Surgery Chapel Hill NC 27514-7450

WHITE, REGGIE (REGINALD HOWARD WHITE), professional football player; b. Chattanooga, Dec. 19, 1961; m. Sara Copeland; children: Jeremy, Jecolia. Student, U. Tenn. With Memphis Showboats, 1984-85, Phila. Eagles, 1985-93, Green Bay Packers, 1993—. Named to Sporting News Coll. All-Am. team, 1983, Sporting News United States Football League All-Star team, 1985, Pro Bowl team, 1986-95, Sporting News All-Pro team, 1987, 88, 91, 93. Holds NFL career record for sacks, 150. Office: Green Bay Packers 1265 Lombardi Ave Green Bay WI 54307-0628*

WHITE, RICHARD A., congressman; b. Bloomington, Ind., Nov. 6, 1953; m. Vikki; 4 children. BA in Govt., Dartmouth Coll., 1975; JD, Georgetown U., 1980. Law clk. to Hon. Charles Clark U.S. Ct. Appeals (5th dist.), 1980-81; assoc. Covington & Burling, 1981-83; assoc. Perkins Coie, 1983-88, ptnr., 1988—; mem. 104th Congress from 1st Wash. dist., 1994—. Del. to dist. county, State GOP Convs., 1984—; founder Farm Team; founder, trustee Books for Kids. Office: US House Reps 116 Cannon House Office Bldg Washington DC 20515-4701*

WHITE, RICHARD BOOTH, management consultant; b. N.Y.C., Aug. 26, 1930; s. Frank K. and Doris (Booth) W.; m. Mary Kane Russell, Dec. 9, 1961; children: Katherine Learned, Richard Booth (dec.), Anne Tristram, Leslie Russell. B.A., Yale U., 1952. Asst. account exec. Batten, Barton, Durstine & Osborn, N.Y.C., 1955; account exec. Batten, Barton, Durstine & Osborn, 1956-58, account supr., 1958-63, v.p., 1959-70, mgmt. supr., 1963-76, sr. v.p., 1970-76, exec. v.p., 1976-83, also dir., chmn. exec. com.; dir. BBDO Internat. Inc.; sr. dir., ptnr. Spencer Stuart & Assocs., N.Y.C., 1984—. Pres. bd. Waveny Care Ctr., New Canaan, Conn. 1st lt. USMCR, 1952-54. Mem. Beta Theta Pi. Presbyterian. Clubs: Yale, Racquet and Tennis (N.Y.C.); Country of New Canaan. Home: 774 Oenoke Rdg New Canaan CT 06840-3125 Office: Spencer Stuart & Assocs 695 E Main St Stamford CT 06901

WHITE, RICHARD CLARENCE, lawyer; b. Sioux City, Iowa, Oct. 31, 1933; m. Beverly Frances Fitzpatrick, Feb. 22, 1955; children—Anne, Richard, William, Christopher. B.A.; LL.B., Stanford U., 1962. Bar: Calif. 1963, U.S. Supreme Ct. 1970, N.Y. 1983. Assoc. O'Melveny & Myers, L.A., 1962-70, ptnr., 1970-94. Lectr. in field. Bd. dirs. Equal Employment Adv. Coun., Washington, 1976-80, 83, Performing Arts Ctr. of Orange County 1983-86. Capt. USMC, 1954-59; Mem. ABA (co-chmn. com. on practice and procedure labor and employment law sect. 1977-80, mem. equal opportunity law com. 1980-85, co-chmn. com. on insts. and meetings 1985-87, coun. 1987—). Contbr. articles to profl. publs.

WHITE, RICHARD DAVID, managing director; b. Flushing, N.Y., Dec. 8, 1953; s. Jerome and Marjorie White; m. Karen J. Newman, Nov. 18, 1979; children: Elizabeth Newman White, Alexandra Newman White. BA, Tufts U., 1976; MBA, Wharton Sch., 1978. CPA. Supr. cons. Coopers & Lybrand, N.Y.C., 1978-81; managing dir. Ardshiel Inc., N.Y.C., 1981-85, Oppenheimer & Co. Inc., N.Y.C., 1985—. Office: Oppenheimer & Co Inc Oppenheimer Tower World FInancial Ctr New York NY 10281

WHITE, RICHARD MANNING, electrical engineering educator; b. Denver, Apr. 25, 1930; s. Rolland Manning and Freeda Blanche (Behny) W.; m. Chissie Lee Chamberlain, Feb. 1, 1964 (div. 1975); children: Rolland Kenneth, William Brendan. AB, Harvard U., 1951, AM, 1952, PhD in Applied Physics, 1956. Rsch. assoc. Harvard U., Cambridge, Mass., 1956; mem. tech. staff GE Microwave Lab., Palo Alto, Calif., 1956-63; prof. elect. engring. U. Calif., Berkeley, 1963—; chmn. Grad. Group on Sci. and Math. Edn., U. Calif. at Berkeley, 1981-85; co-dir. Berkeley Sensor and Actuator Ctr., 1986—. Co-author: Solar Cells: From Basics to Advanced Systems, Microsensors, 1991; editor ElectroTechnology Rev.; patentee in field. Guggenheim fellow, 1968. Fellow AAAS, IEEE (Cledo Brunetto award 1986, Achievement award 1988, Disting. lectr. 1989); mem. Nat. Acad. Engring., Acoustical Soc. Am., Am. Phys. Soc., Phi Beta Kappa, Sigma Xi. Avocations: photography, hiking, skiing, running, music. Office: U Calif Sensor & Actuator Ctr Eecs Dept Berkeley CA 94720

WHITE, RICHARD NORMAN, civil and environmental engineering educator; b. Chetek, Wis., Dec. 21, 1933; s. Norman Lester and Lorna Elwilda (Robinson) W.; m. Margaret Claire Howell, Dec. 28, 1957; children—Barbara Ann, David Charles. BSCE, U. Wis.-Madison, 1956, MS, 1957, PhD, 1961. Registered profl. engr., N.Y. Staff assoc. Gulf Gen. Atomic, San Diego, 1967-68; assoc. prof. civil and environ. engring. Cornell U., 1965-72, prof. structural engring., 1972—, dir. Sch. Civil and Environ. Engring., 1978-84, assoc. dean for undergrad. programs, 1987-89, James A. Friend Family prof. engring., 1988—; vis. prof. U. Calif.-Berkeley, 1974-75, U. P.R., Mayaguez, 1982; cons. Def. Nuclear Agy., Washington, 1983-84, Sandia Nat. Lab., Albuquerque, 1981—, Stone & Webster Engring., 1983-87, SRI Internat., Palo Alto, Calif., 1979-83 , Bakhtar Assoc., 1988—, Kamtech, 1994—, numerous others. Author: Structural Engineering, vols. I and II, 1976, Vol. III, 1974; Structural Modeling and Experimental Techniques, 1982, Building Structural Design Handbook, 1987; contbr. numerous articles to tech. jours. Served with AUS, 1957. Fellow ASCE (Collingwood prize, 1967), Am. Concrete Inst. (Kelly award 1992, Wason medal 1993, Structural Rsch. award 1994, v.p. 1995-97); mem. NAE, NSPE, Precast/Prestressed Contrete Inst., Earthquake Engring. Rsch. Inst., Sigma Xi, Tau Beta Pi, Chi Epsilon. Republican. Presbyterian. Office: Hollister Hall Cornell U Ithaca NY 14853

WHITE, ROBERT, church administrator. Gen. overseer Ch. of God, Cleveland, Tenn. Author: Endued With Power, LifeBUILDERS, SpirtWalk. Office: Church of God PO Box 2430 Cleveland TN 37320-2430

WHITE, ROBERT BRUCE, keyboard instruments company acoustical consultant; b. Casper, Wyo., Aug. 16, 1937; s. Steel Bruce and Julia Doris (Mace) W.; m. Nancy Inez Christian, Sept. 3, 1961; children: Jane Marie, Richard Bruce. BS, Okla. State U., 1959. Field engr. GE, Charlotte, N.C., 1961-63; physics, electronics specialist Derring-Milliken Rsch., Spartanburg, S.C., 1963-66; engring. mgr. Consultants, Inc., Woodruff, S.C., 1966-67; div. mgr. Case Bros., Spartanburg, 1967—; acoustical cons. for religious bldgs.; tchr. Spartanburg Tech. Coll.,1965-66. Contbg. author cookbooks. With USAF, 1959-61. Mem. Inst. Radio Engring., Am. Soc. Engring. Technicians, Am. Guild Organ Technicians, Elks, Masons. Republican. Methodist. Avocations: woodworking, cooking. Home: 225 Singing Woods Ln Spartanburg SC 29301-2622 Office: Case Bros 906 S Pine St Spartanburg SC 29302-3311

WHITE, ROBERT FREDERICK, landscape architect; b. Pitts., June 18, 1912; s. Edward John and Sarah Ann (Romaine) W.; m. Florence Hilda Kusian, Aug. 21, 1937; children: Hans Willi, Ross (by adoption). BS in Landscape Architecture, Pa. State U., College Park, 1934; MA in Landscape Architecture, U. Mich., 1951. Park staff City of Pitts., 1934-35, 2 parks mgr., 1934-37, mem. planning dept., 1937-43, 45; assoc. Office of Ruth Z. London, Houston, 1946-47; asst. prof. Coll. of Architecture Tex. A&M U., College Station, 1947-58, prof., head landscape architecture dept., 1962-75, prof. emeritus Coll. of Architecture, 1975—; prin. Robert F. White Assoc., Houston, 1958-62; cons. LB Johnson Home Site Restoration, Stone Wall, Tex., 1965. Judge hwy. dept. contest award LB Johnson, Ranch, Tex., 1970, nat. contest ASLA Mag., Washington, 1978; mem. Action Group, Houston, 1960-61, Planning Com., College Station, 1967-68. With USAF, 1943-45. Recipient Citation award Ho. of Reps./State of Tex., 1975. Fellow Am. Soc. Landscape Architecture (S.W. chpt. emeritus); mem. Alpha Gamma Rho, Tau Sigma Delta. Avocations: gardening, traveling, birding, drawing, jewelry making.

WHITE, ROBERT GORDON, research director, biology educator; b. Lithgow, NSW, Australia, Jan. 17, 1938; s. Richard Robert and Francis Elsie (Schubert) W.; m. Sandra Elizabeth Ferrier, Dec. 9, 1961 (dec. May 1995); children: Robert Ian, Andrew Douglas. B. in Agrl. Sci., Melbourne U., Australia, 1962; M in Rural Sci./Physiology, U. New Eng., Australia, 1968, PhD, 1974. Rsch. asst. Melbourne U., 1962-63; demonstrator U. New Eng., Armidale, Australia, 1963-66, teaching fellow, 1966-69; asst. prof. zoophysiology and nutrition Inst. Arctic Biology, U. Alaska, Fairbanks, 1970-75; assoc. prof. U. Alaska, Fairbanks, 1975-81, prof., 1981—; acting dir. Inst. Arctic Biology, U. Alaska, Fairbanks, 1985, 92, dir., 1993—; dir. Large Animal Rsch. Sta., 1979—. Co-editor: (with Hudson) Bioenergetics of Wild Herbivores, 1985; editor: (proceedings, with Klein, Keller) First International Muskox Symposium, 1984 (proceedings, with Luick, Lent, Klein) First International Reindeer and Caribou Symposium, 1975; editorial bd.: Rangifer/Biol. Papers U. Alaska; contbr. over 100 papers to profl. jours. Pipe major Fairbanks Red Hackle Pipe Band, 1975-90; pres. Fairbanks Nordic Ski Club, 1973-75. NATO Rsch. fellow, Trondheim, Norway, 1975-76. Fellow AAAS (Alaska chmn. 1985, 94), Arctic Inst. N.Am.; mem. Am. Physiol. Soc., Wildlife Soc., Am. Soc. Mammologists, Australasian Soc. Wildlife Mgmt., Australian Soc. Animal Prodn., Australian Soc. Biochemistry and Molecular Biology, Sigma Xi. Avocations: cross country skiing, river boating, hunting, playing bagpipes. Office: U Alaska Inst Arctic Biology Fairbanks AK 99775

WHITE, ROBERT JAMES, newspaper columnist; b. Mpls., Nov. 6, 1927; s. Robert Howard and Claire Lillian (Horner) W.; m. Adrienne Hoffman, Sept. 24, 1955; children: Claire, Pamela, Sarah. BS, U.S. Naval Acad., 1950. V.p. White Investment Co., Mpls., 1957-67; editl. writer Mpls. Tribune, 1967-73, assoc. editor, 1973-82; editor editl. pages Mpls. Star Tribune, 1982-93, columnist, 1993-95, contbg. columnist, 1996—. Recipient cert. of excellence Overseas Press Club, 1981. Mem. Coun. Fgn. Rels., Refugee Policy Group (mem. bd. trustees), Mpls. Club. Presbyterian. Home: 4721 Girard Ave S Minneapolis MN 55409-2212

WHITE, ROBERT JOEL, lawyer; b. Chgo., Nov. 1, 1946; s. Melvin and Margaret (Hoffman) W.; m. Gail Janet Edenson, June 29, 1969 (div. Dec. 1982); m. Penelope K. Bloch, Dec. 22, 1985. BS in Accountancy, U. Ill., 1968; JD, U. Mich., 1972. Bar: Calif. 1972, N.Y. 1985, U.S. Dist. Ct. (cen., ea., so. dists.) Calif. 1972, U.S. Ct. Appeals (9th cir.) 1978, U.S. Ct. Appeals (5th cir.) 1983, U.S. Ct. Appeals (6th cir.) 1984, U.S. Supreme Ct. 1977. Staff auditor Haskin & Sells, Chgo., 1968-69; assoc. O'Melveny & Myers, L.A., 1972-79, ptnr., 1980—; vis. lectr. U. Mich. Law Sch., Ann Arbor, 1986; lectr. Profl. Edn. Sys., Inc., Dallas, 1987, L.A., 1987, 89, Phoenix, 1990, Practicing Law Inst., San Francisco and N.Y.C., 1989-93, Southwestern Legal Found., Dalalas, 1991, UCLA Bankruptcy Inst., 1993, UCLA, 1993; mem. L.A. Productivity Commn., 1993—; participant Nat. Bankruptcy Conf. Contbr. articles to profl. jours. Active Constl. Rights Found., 1980—; active Am. Cancer Soc., 1989—, mem. L.A. bd. dirs., 1995—; mem. Nat. Bankruptcy Conf. With U.S. Army, 1968-74. Fellow Am. Coll. Bankruptcy; mem. ABA (litigation sect., mem. comml. law and bankruptcy com. 1972—), L.A. County Bar Assn. (comml. law and bankruptcy sect., chmn. fed. cts. com. 1981-82, exec. com. 1982—), Assn. Bus. Trial Lawyers (bd. govs. 1983-85), Fin. Lawyers Conf. (bd. govs. 1986—, pres. 1990-91), Am. Bankruptcy Inst. Avocations: skiing, running, U.S. history. Office: O'Melveny & Myers 400 S Hope St Los Angeles CA 90071-2801

WHITE, ROBERT JOHN, journalist; b. Cin., Mar. 12, 1953; s. Robert John and Jean W.; m. Mary C. Cupito, Apr. 26, 1986. BA in English & Journalism, Miami U., 1975. Intern Cin. Enquirer, 1975-76; reporter, photographer Franklin (Ind.) Daily Jour., 1976-79; reporter Charleston (S.C.) News and Courier, 1979-80, Evansville (Ind.) Courier, 1981; reporter Cin. Post, 1981-83, asst. met. editor, 1983-86, statehouse bur. chief, 1986-92, editorial page editor, 1993—. Recipient Investigative Reporters and Editors, Inc. award, 1988, ABA cert. merit, 1988. Mem. Nat. Conf. Editorial Writers, Cin. Assn., Leadership Cin., Cin. Hist. Soc. Office: Cin Post 125 E Ct St Cincinnati OH 45202

WHITE, ROBERT LEE, electrical engineer, educator; b. Plainfield, N.J., Feb. 14, 1927; s. Claude and Ruby Hemsworth Emerson (Levick) W.; m. Phyllis Lillian Arlt, June 14, 1952; children: Lauren A., Kimberly A., Christopher L., Matthew P. BA in Physics, Columbia U., 1949, MA, 1951, PhD, 1954. Assoc. head atomic physics dept. Hughes Rsch. Labs., Malibu, Calif., 1954-61; head magnetics dept. Gen. Tel. and Electronics Rsch. Lab., Palo Alto, Calif., 1961-63; prof. elec. engring., materials sci. and engring. Stanford U., Palo Alto, 1963, chmn. elec. engring. dept., 1981-86; William E. Ayer prof. elec. engring. Stanford U., 1985-88; exec. dir. The Exploratorium, San Francisco, 1987-89; dir. Inst. for Electronics in Medicine, 1973-87, Stanford Ctr. for Rsch. on Info. Storage Materials, 1991—; initial ltd. ptnr. Mayfield Fund, Mayfield II and Alpha II Fund, Rainbow Co-Investment Ptnrs., Halo Ptnrs.; vis. prof. Tokyo U., 1975; cons. in field. Author: (with K.A. Wickersheim) Magnetism and Magnetic Materials, 1965, Basic Quantum Mechanics, 1967; Contbr. numerous articles to profl. jours. With USN, 1945-46. Fellow Guggenheim Oxford U., 1969-70, Canton Hosp., Swiss Fed. Inst. Tech., Zurich, 1977-78, Christensen fellow Oxford U., 1986; Sony sabbatical chair, 1994. Fellow Am. Phys. Soc., IEEE; mem. Sigma Xi, Phi Beta Kappa. Home: 450 El Escarpado Stanford CA 94305-8431 Office: Stanford U Dept Material Sci Engr Stanford CA 94305

WHITE, ROBERT M., II, newspaper executive, editor, columnist; b. Mexico, Mo., Apr. 6, 1915; s. L. Mitchell and Maude (See) W.; m. Barbara Whitney Spurgeon, Aug. 19, 1948 (dec. Feb., 1983); children: Barbara Whitney, Jane See, Laura L., Robert M. III; m. Linda Hess Grimsley, July 11, 1992. Grad., Mo. Mil. Acad., 1933; A.B., Washington and Lee U., 1938, LL.B. (hon.), 1972. Writer of newspaper articles Australia, Africa, S.Am., Europe, USSR, 1966, 86, People's Republic China, 1972, 77; reporter Mexico (Mo.) Eve. Ledger, 1938-39, editor, pub., 1945; vis. prof. Sch. Journalism, Mo. U., 1968-69; reporter UP Bur., Kansas City, 1939-40; pres. Ledger Newspapers, Inc., Mexico, Mo., 1945-86; spl. cons. to pub. Chgo. Sun-Times, 1956-58; pres. See TV Co., Mexico, 1966-81; editor, pres., bd. dirs. N.Y. Herald Tribune, 1959-61; juror Pulitizer prize journalism, 1964-65; bd. dirs. World Press Freedom Com. Co-author: A Study of the Printing and Publishing Business in the Soviet Union. President Gen. Douglas MacArthur Found., 1981—. Lt. col. AUS, 1940-45. Decorated Bronze Star; recipient nat. disting. service award for editorials Sigma Delta Chi, 1952, 68; editorial award N.Y. Silurians, 1959; Disting. Service to Journalism award U. Mo., 1967; Pres. award of merit Nat. Newspapers Assn., 1967; Ralph D. Casey Minn. award disting. service in journalism, 1983; finalist Journalist in Space 1986—. Mem. Am. Soc. Newspaper Editors (dir. 1968-69, chmn. freedom of info. com. 1970-72), Am. Newspaper Pubs. Assn. (nat. treas. 1963, dir. 1955-63, chmn. internat. group 1982-86), Washington Inst. Fgn. Affairs, Inland Daily Press Assn. (chmn. bd. 1958-59, pres., past sec., v.p.), Mo. Press Assn. (dir., v.p. 1981-83, pres. 1983-84), Mo. Press-Bar Commn. (chmn. 1972-74), Internat. Press Inst. (chmn. Am. com. 1982-85), Nat. Press Club, Bohemian Club, Dutch Treat Club, Burning Tree Club, Cosmos Club, Internat. Club, Masons, Rotary, Sigma Delta Chi (nat. pres. 1967, pres. found. 1968), Beta Theta Pi. Office: Ste 1036 4000 Massachusetts Ave NW Washington DC 20016

WHITE, ROBERT MARSHALL, physicist, government official, educator; b. Reading, Pa., Oct. 2, 1938; s. Carl M. and Miriam E. White; m. Sara Tolles; children: Victoria, Jonathan. BS in Physics, MIT, 1960; PhD, Stanford U., 1964. Vis. scientist Osaka U., Japan, 1963; NSF postdoctoral fellow U. Calif., Berkeley, 1965-66; asst. prof. physics Stanford U., 1966-70; NSF postdoctoral fellow, Cambridge, Eng., 1970-71; mgr. solid state research area Xerox PARC, 1971-78, mgr. storage technology, 1978-83, prin. scientist, 1983-84; v.p. research and tech. Control Data Corp. Data Storage Products Group, Mpls., 1984-86, chief tech. officer, v.p. research and engring, 1986-89; v.p., dir. advanced computer techs. Microelectronics & Computer Tech. Corp., Austin, Tex., 1989-90; under-sec. of commerce for tech., Dept. Commerce, Washington, 1990-93; prof., head dept. electrical and computer engring. Carnegie Mellon U., Pitts., 1993—; lectr. dept. applied physics Stanford U., 1971-81; vis. scientist Ecole Polytechnique, Paris, 1976-78, U. Pernambuco, Brazil, 1978; cons. prof. applied physics, prin. investigator Magnetic Thin Film Program, Stanford U., 1982-93; adj. prof. dept. physics U. Minn., 1987-89; guest Chinese Acad. Scis., 1982. Author: Quantum Theory of Magnetism, 1970 (Russian transl., 1972, Polish transl., 1979); Long Range Order in Solids, 1979 (Russian transl., 1982); Quantum Theory of Magnetism, 1983; Introduction to Magnetic Recording, 1985. Contbr. articles to profl. jours. Bd. advisors Inst. Tech. U. Minn., 1987; mem. State Minn. Com. on Sci. and Tech. Research and Devel., 1987-90; mem. adv. bd. U. Ill. Coll. Engring. Recipient Alexander von Humboldt Prize, Fed. Republic of Germany, 1981. Fellow AAAS, IEEE (disting. lectr. Magnetics Soc., mem. editorial bd. SPECTRUM, IEEE Disting. Pub. Svc.

award 1993), Am. Phys. Soc.; mem. NAE, NRC (mem. nat. materials adv. bd., chmn. com. magnetic materials 1984, material sci. and engring., nat. steering com. advanced steady state neutron source, vice chmn. IUPAP commn. on magnetism), Conf. Magnetism and Magnetic Materials (adv. com. 1976-78, 80-95, program com. 1973-75, chmn. 1981, chmn. Intermag Conf. 1991), Internat. Conf. Magnetism (program chmn. 1985), Found. Nat. Medals Sci. and Tech. (bd. dirs. 1993—), Ontrack Computer Systems (bd. dirs. 1994—), Zilog (bd. dirs. 1995—); mem. Panel on Advanced Computing of the Japanese Tech. Evaluation Ctr.; mem. Nat. Adv. Com. on Semiconductors, 1990-92, Mfg. Forum, 1991, Nat.Critical Techs. Panel, 1990-91. Office: Carnegie Mellon U Elec & Computer Engring Dept Pittsburgh PA 15213-3890

WHITE, ROBERT MAYER, meteorologist; b. Boston, Feb. 13, 1923; s. David and Mary (Winkeller) W.; m. Mavis Seagle, Apr. 18, 1948; children—Richard Harry, Edwina Janet. B.A., Harvard, 1944; M.S., Mass. Inst. Tech., 1949, Sc.D., 1950; D.Sc. (hon.), L.I. U., 1976, Rensselaer Poly. Inst., 1977, U. Wis., Milw., 1978; ScD (hon.), U. Bridgeport, 1984, U. R.I., 1986, Clarkson U.; PhD (hon.), Johns Hopkins U., 1982, Drexel U., 1985, Ill. Inst. Tech., 1994. Project scientist Air Force Cambridge Research Center, 1950-58, chief meteorol. devel. lab., 1958-59; asso. dir. research dept. Travelers Ins. Co., 1959-60; pres. Travelers Research Center, Inc., 1960-63; chief U.S. Weather Bur., 1963-65; adminstr. Environ. Sci. Services Adminstrn., 1965-70, NOAA, 1970-77; pres. Joint Oceanographic Inst., Inc., 1977-79; chmn. Climate Research Bd., exec. officer Nat. Acad. Scis., 1977-79; Washington; adminstr. Nat. Research Council, 1979-80; pres. Univ. Corp. Atmospheric Research, 1980-83, Nat. Acad. Eng., 1983-95; sr. fellow Univ. Corp. for Atmospheric Rsch., Washington, 1995—; Karl T. Compton lectr. MIT, Cambridge, 1995-96; sr. fellow Univ. Corp. Atmospheric Rsch., 1995—; bd. dirs. Charles Stark Draper Lab., Inc.; mem. adv. com. on oceans and internat. environ. and sci. affairs Dept. of State. Author articles in field; mem. editorial bd. Am. Soc. Engring. Edn. jour. Bd. overseers Harvard U., 1977—; vis. com. meteorology and planetary sci. Mass. Inst. Tech.; Mem. vis. com. Kennedy Sch. Govt., Harvard U.; bd. dirs. Resources for Future, 1980—. Served to capt. USAAF, World War II. Decorated Legion of Honor France; recipient Jesse L. Rosenberger medal U. Chgo., 1971; Cleveland Abbe award Am. Meteorol. Soc., 1969; Godfrey L. Cabot award Aero Club Boston, 1966; Rockefeller Pub. Service award, 1974; David B. Stone award New Eng. Aquarium, 1975; Neptune award Am. Oceanic Orgn., 1977; Matthew Fontaine Maury award Smithsonian Instn., 1976; Internat. Conservation award Nat. Wildlife Fedn., 1976; Internat. Meteorol. Orgn. prize, 1980, Tyler prize for Environ. Achievement U. Calif., 1992. Fellow AAAS, Am. Meterol. Soc. (coun. 1965-67, 77—, Charles Franklin Brooks award 1978, pres. 1980), Am. Geophys. Union, World Acad. Art and Scis., Australian Acad. Tech. Scis. and Engring., Am. Acad. Arts and Scis., UCAR (sr.); mem. NAE (coun. 1977, pres. 1983-95), Marine Tech. Soc., Coun. Fgn. Rels., Nat. Action Coun. Minorities in Engring. Inc., Finnish Acad. Tech. (fgn. mem. 1991—), Am. Philos. Soc., Nat. Commn. on the Environment World Wildlife Fund, Engring. Acad. Japan (fgn. assoc. 1988—), Internat. Acad. Astronautics (Paris), Russian Acad. Engring., Royal Acad. Engring. (U.K.) (hon.), Cosmos Club (Washington). Home: Somerset House II 5610 Wisconsin Ave Apt 1506 Bethesda MD 20815-4419 Office: Ste 410 1200 New York Ave NW Washington DC 20005

WHITE, ROBERT ROY, chemical engineer; b. Bklyn., Mar. 1, 1916; s. Laurance S. and Grace A. (Diffin) W.; m. Elizabeth R. Clark, July 2, 1940; children: Robert Roy, William Wesley, Elizabeth Ann, Margaret. B.S., Cooper Union Inst. Tech., 1936; student, Bklyn. Poly. Inst., 1936-37; M.S. (Horace H. Rackham predoctoral fellow 1938), U. Mich., 1938; Ph.D., 1941; student, DePaul U. Law Sch., 1940-41. Jr. chem. engr. Calco Chem. Co., Bound Brook, N.J., 1936-37; research chem. engr. Dow Chem. Co., 1937-38; chem. engr. Standard Oil Co. Calif., 1940, Universal Oil Products Co., 1940-42; mem. faculty U. Mich., 1942-60, prof. chem. engring., 1945-60, assoc. dean Horace H. Rackham Sch. Grad. Studies, 1958-60; assoc. dean Coll. Engring. U. Mich. (Coll. Engring.), 1958-60; dir. Inst. Sci. and Tech. U. Mich., 1959-60; v.p., gen. mgr. research and devel. Atlantic Refining Co., Phila., 1960-62; sr. staff mgmt. service div. Arthur D. Little, Inc., 1962; v.p. devel. Champion Papers, Inc., Hamilton, Ohio, 1962-66; pres. research div. W.R. Grace & Co., 1966-67; dean Sch. Mgmt., Case Western Res. U., Cleve., 1967-71; mng. dir. Karl Kroyer S.A., Denmark, 1970; spl. asst. to pres., dir. forum Nat. Acad. Sci., Washington, 1971-1981; adj. prof. chem. engring. U. Md., 1982-85, Cath. U. Am., Am. U.; v.p. JV Tech., 1986—; chem. engring. and mgmt. cons. Author: (with others) Unit Operations, 1950; Contbr. articles to profl. jours. Recipient Henry Russell award U. Mich., 1945; teaching award Phi Lambda Upsilon chpt. U. Mich., 1949; sesquicentennial award U. Mich., 1967; prof. award Cooper Union Inst., 1975; McCormack-Freud hon. lectr. Ill. Inst. Tech. Mem. AAAS, AIChE (jr. award 1945, presentation award 1951, profl. progress award 1956), SAR, Am. Chem. Soc., Am. Soc. Engring. Edn. (George Westinghouse award 1955), Soc. Profl. Engrs., Soc. Chem. Industry, St. Andrews Soc., Order Crown of Charlemagne, Baron Magna Charta, Cosmos Club, Sigma Xi, Alpha Chi Sigma, Phi Lambda Upsilon, Phi Kappa Phi, Tau Beta Pi, Iowa Alpha. Office: 2440 Virginia Ave NW Washington DC 20037-2601

WHITE, ROBERT STEPHEN, physics educator; b. Ellsworth, Kans., Dec. 28, 1920; s. Byron F. and Sebina (Leighty) W.; m. Freda Marie Bridgewater, Aug. 30, 1942; children: Nancy Lynn, Margaret Diane, John Stephen, David Bruce. AB, Southwestern Coll., 1942, DSc hon., 1971; MS, U. Ill., 1943; PhD, U. Calif., Berkeley, 1951. Physicist Lawrence Radiation Lab., Berkeley, Livermore, Calif., 1948-61; head dept. particles and fields Space Physics Lab. Aerospace Corp., El Segundo, Calif., 1962-67; physics prof. U. Calif., Riverside, 1967-92, dir. Inst. Geophysics and Planetary Physics, 1967-92, chmn. dept. physics, 1970-73, prof. emeritus physics dept., rsch. physicist, 1992—; lectr. U. Calif., Berkeley, 1953-54, 57-59. Author: Space Physics, 1970; contbr. articles to profl. jours. Officer USNR, 1944-46. Sr. Postdoctoral fellow NSF, 1961-62; grantee NASA, NSF, USAF, numerous others. Fellow AAAS, Am. Phys. Soc. (exec. com. 1972-74); mem. AAUP, Am. Geophys. Union, Am. Astron. Soc. Home: 5225 Austin Rd Santa Barbara CA 93111-2905 Office: U Calif Inst Geophysics & Planetary Physics Riverside CA 92521

WHITE, ROBERTA LEE, comptroller; b. Denver, Sept. 18, 1946; d. Harold Tindall and Araminta (Campbell) Bangs; m. Lewis Paul White, Jr., Jan. 23, 1973 (div. Sept. 1974). BA cum laude, Linfield Coll., 1976; postgrad., Lewis and Clark Coll. Office mgr. Multnomah County Auditor, Portland, Oreg., 1977-81; rsch. asst. Dan Goldy and Assocs., Portland, 1981-83; regional asst. Vocat. Rehab., Eugene, Oreg., 1983-85; internal auditor Multnomah County, Portland, 1985-89; cons. Portland, 1989-91; fin. analyst City of Portland, 1991-93; comptroller Wordsmith Svcs., Portland, 1993—; mem. Com. for Implementation of the ADA, Portland, 1991-93. Treas. Mary Wendy Roberts for Sec. of State, Portland, 1992, Re-Elect Mary Wendy Roberts, Portland, 1990, Elect Hank Miggins Com., 1994; mem. Oreg. Women's Polit. Caucus, Portland, 1982-85, City Club, Portland, 1978-81. Democrat. Mem. Disciples of Christ. Avocations: reading, hiking, opera, symphony, ballet. Home: 1620 NE Irving Apt 80 Portland OR 97232 Office: Wordsmith Svcs 1500 NE Irving Ste 350 Portland OR 97232

WHITE, RONALD LEON, financial management consultant; b. West York, Pa., July 14, 1930; s. Clarence William and Grace Elizabeth (Gingerich) W.; m. Estheranne Wieder, June 16, 1951; children: Bradford William, Clifford Allen, Erick David. BS in Econs, U. Pa., 1952, MBA, 1957. Cost analysis supr. Air Products & Chem. Corp., Allentown, Pa., 1957-60; cost control mgr. Mack Trucks, Inc., Allentown, 1960-64; mgmt. cons. Peat, Marwick, Mitchell & Co., Phila., 1964-66; mgr. profit planning Monroe, The Calculator Co. (div. Litton Industries), Orange, N.J., 1966-67, controller, 1967-68; v.p. fin. Bus. Systems Group of Litton Industries, Beverly Hills, Calif., 1968-70; pres. Royal Typewriter Co. div., Hartford, Conn., 1970-73; exec. v.p., chief operating officer, treas. Tenna Corp., Cleve., 1973-75, pres., dir., 1975-77; v.p. fin. Arby's, Inc., Youngstown, Ohio, 1978-79; exec. v.p., dir. Roxbury Am., Inc., 1979-81; v.p. fin., treas. Royal Crown Cos., Inc., Atlanta and Miami Beach, Fla., 1981-86, TDS Healthcare Systems Corp., Atlanta, 1987-88; v.p. Corp. Fin. Assocs., Atlanta, 1988-90; prin. The Janelle Co., Atlanta, 1991—; instr. acctg. Wharton Sch. U. Pa., 1952-53, instr. industry, 1953-54. Served to lt. USNR, 1954-57. Mem. Am. Mgmt. Assn., Nat. Assn. Accountants, Nat. Assn. Corp. Dirs., Fin. Execs. Inst., Acacia. Mem. United Ch. Christ (deacon). Lodges: Masons, Rotary. Home: 2362 Kingsgate Ct Atlanta GA 30338-5931 Office: The Janelle Co 2362 Kingsgate Ct Atlanta GA 30338-5931

WHITE, ROSANNE TERESA, educational association executive; b. Allentown, Pa., Aug. 29, 1954; d. Hugh Dennis and Helen Anne (McCoog) McClafferty; m. Thomas Alexander White, June 19, 1976; children: Maureen, Douglas. BS, Radford (Va.) U., 1976; MEd, George Mason U., 1982. Tchr. Child Devel. Ctr., Falls Church, Va., 1977-80; instr. adult edn. Fairfax County Pub. Schs., Fairfax, Va., 1981-83; exec. dir. Childbirth Edn. Assn., Annandale, Va., 1982-83; program mgr. George Mason U., Fairfax, 1983-85, asst. dir., 1985-87; exec. dir. Tech. Student Assn., Reston, Va., 1987—; chmn. Nat. Coordinating Coun. Vocat. Student Orgns., Reston, 1989—. Mem. Va. Rep. Com., 1989—. Recipient Chmn.'s award Vienna (Va.) C. of C., 1987; named Ky. Col., Gov. of Ky., 1990, Tenn. Col., Gov. of Tenn., 1990. Mem. Am. Soc. Assn. Execs., Am. Vocat. Assn., Fairfax County C. of C., AAUW. Roman Catholic. Office: Tech Student Assn 1914 Association Dr Reston VA 22091-1538

WHITE, ROY BERNARD, theater executive; b. Cin.; s. Maurice and Anna (Rudin) W.; m. Sally Lee Ostrom, June 17, 1951; children: Maurice Ostrom, Barbara Dee, Daniel Robert. B.A., U. Cin., 1949. Formerly mem. sales staff Twentieth Century Fox Films, Cin.; now pres. Mid-States Theatres; dir. Nat. Assn. Theatre Owners, nat. pres., exec. com., chmn. bd.; Mem. film adv. panel Ohio Arts Coun.; bd. dirs. Will Rogers Meml. Fund, Found. Motion Picture Pioneers, Inc.; mem. media arts panel Nat. Endowment for Arts. Served with USAAF, 1944-45. Named Exhibitor of Year Internat. Film Importers and Distbrs. Am. Mem. Nat. Assn. Theater Owners (pres.), Am. Film Inst. (trustee 1972-75, exec. com. 1972-75), Fedn. Motion Picture Pioneers (v.p.), Masons, Queen City Racquet, Crest Hills Country, Amberley Village (Ohio) Tennis Club (pres. 1972-73), Bankers Club, Quail Creek Country Club (Naples, Fla.), Alpha Epsilon Pi, Phi Eta Sigma. Home: 8171 Bay Colony Dr Apt 1904 Naples FL 33963-7567

WHITE, ROY MARTIN, engineering manager; b. Manchester, Conn., Sept. 10, 1947; s. Roy Henry and Elizabeth Mary (Mayer) W.; m. Jane Marie Pencek, Dec. 18, 1971; children: Rebecca Marie, Mary Elizabeth. BS, U.S. Air Force Acad., 1969; MPA, Golden Gate U., 1976. Commd. 2d lt. USAF, 1969, advanced through grades to lt. col., retired, 1989; systems engr. Systems Control Tech., Washington, 1989-94, sr. area mgr., engring., 1992—; bd. dirs. Vietnam Vets. of Am., No., Va.; mem. Advanced Automation Task Force, FAA, Washington, 1994. Author reports in field. Named to Outstanding Young Men of Am., 1976; decorated Disting. Flying Cross, USAF, Vietnam. Mem. AIAA, Air Force Acad. Soc., No. Va. Corvettes, K.C. Roman Catholic. Avocations: auto racing, zymurgist, mechanics, flying. Home: 13903 Quietway Ct Chantilly VA 22021-2829 Office: Nat Airspace Sys Implement Support Contract 400 Virginia Ave SW Washington DC 20024-2142

WHITE, RUTH LILLIAN, French language educator, researcher; b. Vancouver, B.C., Can., June 6, 1924; d. George Brooks and Olive (Wells) W. B.A., U. B.C.; A.R.C.T. in Piano, U. Toronto; Docteur, U. Paris, Sorbonne. Cert. profl. advanced phonetics Institut de Phonetique, Paris. Tchr. Vancouver Sch. Bd., 1946-66; head dept. lang. King Edward Continuing Edn. Ctr., B.C., 1962-65, Vancouver City Coll., 1965-66; prof. U. B.C., Vancouver, 1966-89, prof. edn. and arts, 1971-77, prof. arts, 1977-89; mem., chmn. numerous coms. B.C. Tchrs. Fedn., 1950-75; exec., chmn. Standing Com. on Lang., Acad. Coun., B.C., 1968-82; mem., chmn. exam and revision coms. Govt. of B.C., 1952-76; mem. adv. editl. Can. Modern Lang. Rev., Toronto 1971-79; mem. adv. bd. Can. Modern Lang. Rev., Toronto, 1979-90; scholar-in-residence Rockefeller Found., Bellagio Study and Conf. Ctr., Italy, 1979. Author: L'Avenir de La Mennais, 1974, Louis-Joseph Papineau et Lamennais, 1983, (with C.-L. Rogers) Relations Hugo-Lamennais, 1821-54, 1988, Verlaine et les musiciens, 1992, Paul Verlaine, poète des musiciens, musicien des poètes, 1996. Decorated chevalier Ordre des Palmes academiques (France), 1984; Can. Council fellow, 1978-79. Mem. Can. Assn. Univ. Tchrs., Association Internat. des Docteurs des Univs. de France, Soc. des Amis de Lamennais (Can. rep. 1971-89), Assn. des Ecrivains de Langue Française, Coll. and Univ. Tchrs. Assn., Coll. and Univ. Lang. Tchrs. Assn. Home: 206-1315 W 7th Ave, Vancouver, BC Canada V6H 1B8

WHITE, STANLEY ARCHIBALD, research electrical engineer; b. Providence, Sept. 25, 1931; s. Clarence Archibald White and Lou Ella (Givens) Arford; m. Edda María Castaño-Benítez, June 6, 1956; children: Dianne, Stanley Jr., Paul, John. BSEE, Purdue U., 1957, MSEE, 1959, PhD, 1965. Registered profl. engr., Ind., Calif. Engr. Rockwell Internat., Anaheim, Calif., 1959-68, mgr., 1968-84, sr. scientist, 1984-90; pres. Signal Processing and Controls Engring. Corp., 1990—; adj. prof. elec. engring. U. Calif., 1984—; cons. and lectr. in field; bd. dirs. Asilomar Signals, Systems and Computers Conf. Corp. Publisher, composer music; contbr. chpts. to books; articles to profl. jours.; patentee in field. Fellow N.Am. Aviation Sci. Engring., 1963-65; recipient Disting. Lectr. award Nat. Electronics Conf., Chgo., 1973, Engr. of Yr. award Orange County (Calif.) Engring. Coun., 1984, Engr. of Yr. award Rockwell Internat., 1985, Leonardo Da Vinci Medallion, 1986, Sci. Achievement award, 1987, Disting. Engring. Alumnus award Purdue U., 1988, Meritorious Inventor's award Rockwell Internat. Corp., 1989, Outstanding Elec. Engr. award Purdue U., 1992. Fellow AAAS, AIAA (Centennial medalist chair of ICASSP and ISCAS, Sigmal Processing Soc. disting. lect. and founding chmn. L.A. coun. chpt., Circuits and Sys. Soc. Tech. Achievement award 1996), Inst. for Advancement of Engring., N.Y. Acad. Scis.; mem. Choral Condrs. Guild and Saddleback Mastore Chorale; mem. Air Force Assn. (life), Am. Legion (life), Sigma Xi (founding pres. Orange County chpt.), Eta Kappa Nu (disting. fellow, internat. dir. emeritus), Tau Beta Pi. Avocation: choral music. Home: 433 E Avenida Cordoba San Clemente CA 92672-2350

WHITE, STEPHEN HALLEY, biophysicist, educator; b. Wewoka, Okla., May 14, 1940; s. James Halley and Gertrude June (Wyatt) W.; m. Buff Ertl, Aug. 20, 1961 (div. 1982); children: Saill, Shell, Storn, Sharr, Skye, Sunde; m. Jackie Marie Dooley, Apr. 14, 1984. BS in Physics, U. Colo., 1963; MS in Physics, U. Wash., 1965, PhD in Physiology and Biophysics, 1969. USPHS postdoctoral fellow biochemistry U. Va., Charlottesville, 1971-72; asst. prof. physiology and biophysics U. Calif., Irvine, 1972-75, assoc. prof. physiology and biophysics, 1975-78, prof. physiology and biophysics, 1978—, vice chmn. physiology and biophysics, 1974-75, chmn. physiology and biophysics, 1977-89; guest biophysicist Brookhaven Nat. Lab., Upton, L.I., N.Y., 1977—; bd. dirs. Brian Pharms., San Juan Capistrano. Contbr. numerous articles to profl. jours. Served to capt. USAR, 1969-71. Recipient Research Career Devel. award USPHS, 1975-80, Kaiser-Permanente award, 1975, 92; grantee NIH, 1971—, NSF, 1971—. Mem. NSF (adv. panel for molecular biology 1982-85, mem. nat. steering com. advanced neutron source 1992-95), Biophys. Soc. (chmn. membrane biophysics subgroup 1977-78, acting sec., treas. 1979-80, coun. 1981-84, exec. bd. 1981-83, program chmn. 1985, ann. meeting sec. 1987-95, pres.-elect 1995-96, pres. 1996—), Am. Physiol. Soc. (editl. bd. 1981-93, membership com. 1985-86, publ. com. 1987-91), Assn. Chmn. Depts. Physiology (rep. to coun. acad. scos. 1981-82, councilor 1982-83, pres. 1986-87), Soc. Gen. Physiologists (treas. 1985-88, The Protein Soc. (electronic pub. coord. 1993—). Avocations: skiing, cooking, travel. Office: Univ of Calif Dept of Physiology & Biophysics Irvine CA 92717

WHITE, SUSAN VICTORIA, nursing administrator; b. Ocala, Fla., Oct. 7, 1951; d. George and Agnes Victoria (Toffaletti) Spontak. BS in Nursing, U. Fla., 1973, MS in Nursing, 1982, postgrad., 1990—. Cert. critical care nurse. Asst. head nurse ICU Orlando (Fla.) Regional Med. Ctr., 1976-78, patient care coord., 1978-85; quality assurance mgr. Sand Lake Hosp., Orlando, 1985-88, assoc. exec. dir., dir. nursing, 1990-94; bus. sys. analyst Orlando Regional Healthcare Sys., 1995—. Mem. AACN, ANA (cert. nursing adminstrn.), Am. Hosp. Assn., Fla. Nurses Assn., Am. Orgn. of Nurse Execs., Fla. Orgn. Nurse Execs., Ctrl. Fla. Orgn. Nurse Execs., Nat. Quality Assurance Profession, Fla. Utilization Rev. Assn., Am. Coll. Healthcare Execs., Sigma Theta Tau (award for rsch.), Phi Kappa Phi. Home: PO Box 681133 Orlando FL 32868-1133

WHITE, SYLVIA FRANCES, gerontology home care nurse, consultant; b. Dayton, Ohio, May 2, 1952; d. Arthur Francis and Eleanor Ida (Beach) Scarpelli; m. Alan Bruce White, Nov. 28, 1981. BSN, Loyola U., 1975; MPH, U. Ill., Chgo., 1984. Cert. gerontol. nurse; lic. nursing home adminstrn., Ill. Staff nurse Vis. Nurse Assn., Chgo., 1975-80, team leader, 1980-81, supr., 1981-83, dist. adminstr., 1984-86, mgr. North side, 1986-87, dir. patient svcs., 1987; dir. clin. svcs. Kimberly Quality Care, Evanston, Ill., 1987-89; pub. health nurse City of Evanston, Ill., 1989-90; geriatric nurse assoc. City of Evanston, 1990—; cons. surveyor Joint Commn. on Accreditation of Healthcare Orgns., Oakbrook Terrace, Ill., 1988—; vol. Hospice, literacy. Trainer The Arthritis Found., Chgo., 1991-92; mem. Panel Rev. State of Ill. Continuing Edn.; mem. profl. edn. com. Arthritis Found.; hospice vol. Mem. APHA, Ill. Pub. Health Assn., Ill. Home Health Coun., Ill. Alliance for Aging, Zonta, Arthritis Profl. Edn. Com., Nat. Assn. Home Care. Roman Catholic. Avocations: reading, golf, racquetball, walking, quilting. Home: 222 Sunset Dr Wilmette IL 60091 Office: Evanston Health Dept 2100 Ridge Ave Evanston IL 60201-2796

WHITE, TERRENCE HAROLD, academic administrator, sociologist; b. Ottawa, Ont., Canada, Mar. 31, 1943; s. William Harold and Shirley Margaret (Ballantine) W.; m. Susan Elizabeth Hornaday; children: Christine Susan, Julie Pamela. Ph.D., U. Toronto, 1972. Head dept. sociology and anthropology U. Windsor, Ont., Can., 1973-75; prof., chmn. dept. sociology U. Alta., Edmonton, 1975-80, dean faculty of arts, 1980-88; pres. Brock U., St. Catharines, Ont., 1988—, T.H. White Orgn. Research Services Ltd., Edmonton, 1975—; dir. Labatt's Brewing Alta., Edmonton, 1981-88. Author: Power or Pawns: Boards of Directors, 1978, Human Resource Management, 1979; editor: Introduction to Work Science, 1981, QWL in Canada: Case Studies, 1983. Bd. dirs. Progressive Conservative Assn., Edmonton South, 1976-81, 1st v.p., 1981-85, pres., 1985-87; bd. dirs. Tri-Bach Festival Found., Edmonton, 1981-88, Alta. Ballet Co., 1985-88, Edmonton Conv. and Tourism Authority, Arch Enterprises, 1984-88, Niagara Symphony Soc., YMCA, St. Catharines, 1988-92; chair United Way Campaign St. Catharines, 1992, Fox Found., 1990—, Canada Summer Games 2001 Bid Com.; bd. dirs. Edmonton Symphony Soc., v.p., 1986-88; bd. govs. U. Alta., 1984-88, Brock U., 1988—, Ridley Coll., 1990—. Recipient Can. 125 Commemorative medal, Govt. of Can. Mem. St. Catharines Club, Garden Ct. Racquet Club, Rotary (pres. Edmonton South 1981-82), Delta Tau Kappa, Alpha Kappa Delta. Home: 15 Deer Park Cres, Fonthill, ON Canada L0S 1E1 Office: Brock U, Saint Catharines, ON Canada L2S 3A1

WHITE, THOMAS EDWARD, lawyer; b. N.Y.C., July 11, 1933; s. Thomas Aubrey and Gladys Mary (Piper) W.; m. Joan Carolyn Olsen, Dec. 2, 1967 (dec.); children: Charles Garret, Nancy Carolyn, Linda Marie, Penelope Lindsay, Elizabeth Ann. A.B., Princeton U., 1955; LL.B., Columbia U., 1960. Bar: N.Y. 1961. Atty. Seward & Kissel, N.Y.C., 1960-69; gen. counsel Howmet Corp., N.Y.C., 1969-70; v.p., gen. counsel, sec. Howmedica, Inc., N.Y.C., 1970-74; sr. v.p., dir. Howmedica, Inc., 1974-83; pvt. practice N.Y.C., 1983—; ptnr. Westmed Venture Ptnrs. (formerly Integrated Med. Venture Ptnrs.), N.Y.C., 1987—; chmn. Shoreside Cons. Ltd., Miami, Fla., 1987—. Mem. Mamaroneck Town Council, 1971-75; vestry Episcopalian Ch., 1987-90. Served to lt. U.S. Army, 1955-57. Republican. Clubs: Larchmont (N.Y.) Yacht; Princeton (N.Y.C.). Home: 260 Barnard Rd Larchmont NY 10538-1941 Office: 485 Madison Ave New York NY 10022-5803

WHITE, THOMAS EDWARD, government park official; b. Bozeman, Mont., Dec. 29, 1936; s. James Henry and Louesa (Coon) W.; m. Sylvia Moon Young, July 17, 1965 (dec. Aug. 1974); children—James Allen, Edward Paul; m. Patricia Lee Swanson, Mar. 1, 1975; 1 child, Andrew Todd. B.S., Mont. State U., 1959, M.S., 1963. Cert. tchr., Mont. Tchr. pub. schs. Mont., 1959-62; park historian Manassas Nat. Battlefield Park, Nat. Park Service, Va., 1964-66, Central Nat. Capital Parks, Nat. Park Service, Washington, 1966-68; supervisory park historian Fort Laramie Nat. Hist. Site, Nat. Park Service, Wyo., 1968-73; interpretive specialist So. Ariz. Group, Nat. Park Service, Phoenix, 1973-83; chief park interpreter Hawaii Volcanoes Nat. Park, 1983-87; interpretive planner Harpers Ferry (W.Va.) Ctr., Nat. Park Svc., 1987—; interpretive planner, internat. exchange assignment Can. Nat. Hist. Sites Service, Ottawa, Ont., 1969. Author: Garrison Life Trail: An Illustrated Guide to Fort Laramie, 1972 (Fed. Editors Assn. Blue Pencil award 1973). Adult adviser Order DeMolay, Mont., Va., Wyo., Ariz., 1960-83; Cub Scout and Boy Scout leader Theodore Roosevelt (Ariz.), Aloha (Hawaii), Shenandoah Area (W.Va.) coun. Boy Scouts Am., 1978—; adminstrv. bd. chmn. Hilo United Meth. Ch., 1985-87; scouting coord. New St. United Meth. Ch., 1988—. Recipient Chevalier Degree Order DeMolay, 1954, Legion of Honor award Order DeMolay, 1968; named Father of Yr., 1st Bapt. Ch., Scottsdale, Ariz., 1978, Statuette award Shenandoah Area coun. Boy Scouts Am., 1994, Cross and Flame Religious award for adult scout leaders Boy Scouts Am., 1995. Mem. Nat. Assn. Interpreters, Nat. Assn. United Meth. Scouters, NPS Employees and Alumni Assn., Sigma Nu. Lodge: Masons. Avocations: collecting stamps, hiking, model railroading, singing in church choir, genealogy. Office: Harpers Ferry Ctr NPS Div Interpretive Planning PO Box 50 Harpers Ferry WV 25410-0050

WHITE, THOMAS RAEBURN, III, law educator, consultant; b. Phila., Aug. 18, 1938; s. Thomas Raeburn Jr. and Charlotte (Gerhard) W.; m. Margaret Bardwell, Dec. 12, 1960 (div. June 1975); children: Elizabeth Krusenstjerma, Kathleen Harris, Thomas Ray IV; m. Maria Llanes, Oct. 19, 1975. BA, Williams Coll., 1960; LLB, U. Pa., 1963. Bar: Pa. 1964, Va. 1971. Assoc. White and Williams, Phila., 1963-65; atty.-advisor TLC U.S. Treasury Dept., Washington, 1965-67; assoc. prof. U. Va., Charlottesville, 1967-70, prof. law, 1970-96, John C. Stennis prof., 1996—; legis. atty. Joint Com. on Tax U.S. Congress, Washington, 1973-75; cons. adminstrn. conf. IRS Project, Washington, 1975-76; vis. prof. NYU Law Sch., N.Y.C., 1978-79. Mem. ABA (com. chmn. tax sect. 1987-87, 96-98), Am. Coll. Tax Counsel, Va. Bar Assn., Va. State Bar Assn., Phila. Bar Assn., Charlottesville-Albemarle Bar Assn. Home: 12 Deer Path Charlottesville VA 22903-4707 Office: U Va Sch Law 580 Massie Rd Charlottesville VA 22903-1789

WHITE, TIMOTHY DOUGLAS, biology educator; b. Los Angeles, Aug. 24, 1950; s. Robert Julian and Georgia Johnston (McDougall) W. B.S. in Biology, U. Calif., Riverside, 1972, B.S. in Anthropology, 1972; M.A., U. Mich., 1974, Ph.D., 1977. Paleontologist East Rudolf Research Project, N. Kenya, 1974-77, Laetolil Expdn., N. Tanzania, 1978, 88, Middle Awash Valley, Ethiopia, 1981—, Olduvai Gorge, 1985-86, Paleoanthropological Inventory of Ethiopia, 1988—; prof. U. Calif., Berkeley, 1977-95, prof. integrative biology, 1995—, co-dir. lab. for human evolutionary studies, 1995—. Grantee NSF, Nat. Geog. Soc. Fellow Calif. Acad. Sci.; mem. Soc. Vertebrate Paleontology, AAAS. An excavator earliest human ancestor footprints, Tanzania, 1978; co-discoverer earliest human ancestors A. afarensis 1978-79; A. ramidus 1994. Office: U of Calif Dept of Integrative Biology Berkeley CA 94720

WHITE, TIMOTHY OLIVER, newspaper editor; b. Albany, N.Y., June 29, 1948; s. Oliver C. and Yvonne (Letourneau) W.; 1 child, Eric B. BA in English, Siena Coll., 1971. Reporter Cape Cod Times, Hyannis, Mass., 1971-72, asst. Sunday editor, 1972-75, news editor, 1975-79, asst. editor, 1979-83, mng. editor, 1983—. Mem. AP Mng. Editors, New Eng. AP News Exec. Assn. (v.p. 1992, 93, pres. 1994), New Eng. Soc. Newspaper Editors. Avocations: community TV producer, photography, wilderness travel, bicycling, cooking, sailing. Home: PO Box 1187 56 Jolly's Crossing Rd Brewster MA 02631 Office: Cape Cod Times 319 Main St Hyannis MA 02601

WHITE, TIMOTHY PAUL, brokerage house executive; b. Ft. Sill, Okla., Jan. 9, 1963; s. Paul R. and Lucille (Mattison) W.; m. Susan Gertrude Foreman, Dec. 29, 1984; children: Jessica Lynn, Rebecca Anne, Kathleen Marie. BS in Fin., Pa. State U., 1985. Cert. fin. planner, Colo. Assoc. planner, agt. Pa. Fin. Group, Harrisburg, Pa., 1988-92; mgr. mktg. and sales Meridian Securities, Inc., Reading, Pa., 1992—. Contbg. editor Bank Securities Jour.; contbr. articles to profl. jours. Program cons. Jr. Achievement, Lancaster, Pa., 1990-91; pres. Adamstown Recreation Bd., 1996. 1st lt. U.S. Army, 1985-88, with Res. 1989-92. Recipient George C. Marshall award U.S. Army, 1985; decorated Commendation medal, Achievement medal; U.S. Army ROTC scholar, 1980-84. Mem. Inst. CFP, U.S. Cavalry Assn. (fundraising com. 1994-96), Ctrl. Pa. Soc. Inst. CFP (bd. dirs. 1996—). Republican. Lutheran. Avocations: military and political history, reading, gardening, wood-working. Office: Meridian Securities Inc 601 Penn St Reading PA 19603

WHITE, TIMOTHY THOMAS ANTHONY, writer, editor, broadcaster; b. Paterson, N.J., Jan. 25, 1952; s. John Alexander and Gloria Marie (Thomas) W.; m. Judith Anne Garlan, June 28, 1987; children: (twins) Alexander and Christopher. BA, Fordham U., 1972. Copyboy, sports and entertainment writer AP, N.Y.C., 1972-76; mng. editor Crawdaddy mag., N.Y.C., 1976-77, sr. editor, 1977-78; assoc. editor Rolling Stone mag., N.Y.C., 1978-79, sr. editor, 1979-82; host, co-producer Timothy White's Rock Stars/The Timothy White Sessions nationally syndicated radio series ABC Radio Network, 1986; LBS Radio Network, 1987, Westwood One Radio Network, 1988—; editor in chief Billboard mag., N.Y.C., 1991—. Author: Catch a Fire: The Life of Bob Marley, 1983, rev. enlarged edit., 1989, meml. edit., 1991, rev. edit., 1996 (Brit., Italian, German and Japanese edits.), Rock Stars, 1984, Rock Lives: Profiles and Interviews, 1990, rev. edit., 1996 (Brit. and Japanese edits.); co-author: Rolling Stone Visits Saturday Night Live, 1979, (with others) Roadside Food, 1986; contbg. author: The Best of the Music Makers, 1979, The 80s: A Look Back at the Tumultuous Decade, 1979, The Rolling Stone Interviews, 1981, Reggae International, 1982, Suddenly Poor! A Guide for Downwardly Mobile, 1983, Twenty Years of Rolling Stone, 1987, A & M Records: The First 25 Years, 1987, The Nearest Faraway Place: Brian Wilson, The Beach Boys and The Southern California Experience, 1995, rev. edit., 1995 (Brit. and Japanese edits.), Music To My Ears, 1996; contbr. articles to various mag. Recipient ASCAP-Deems Taylor award, 1991, 93. Democrat. Avocations: drums, dancing, Caribbean history, folklore, music. Office: Billboard Mag 1515 Broadway New York NY 10036

WHITE, TONY L., health and medical products executive. BA, We. Carolina U., 1969. Sales rep. Baxter Internat. Inc., 1970-74, dist. mgr., 1974-76, export mgr. Latin Am., 1976-82, v.p. AMPAC, pres. Travenol-Can., 1982-85, pres. Fenwal divsn., 1985-86, pres. scientific products, biomedical divsn., 1986; v.p. diagnostics Baxter Internat. Inc., Deerfield, Ill., 1986-92; exec. vp Baxter Internat. Inc., 1992-95; chmn., pres., CEO Pericon Elmer Corp., Norwalk, Conn., 1995—. With USAR, 1968-74. Office: Pericon Elmer Corp 761 Main Ave Norwalk CT 06851

WHITE, WARREN WURTELE, retailing executive; b. McKeesport, Pa., Feb. 29, 1932; s. Jay Leonard and Elizabeth Katherine (Fehr) W.; m. Marjorie Ada Shuman, Mar. 20, 1954; 1 dau., Laura Lynn. B.S., Duquesne U., 1954; M.Retailing, U. Pitts., 1957. With Strawbridge & Clothier, Phila., 1957—; buyer Strawbridge & Clothier, 1960-67, budget store divisional mdse. mgr., 1968-70, Clover Div. gen. mdse. mgr., 1970-76, v.p. for mdse. and sales promotion, 1977-79, exec. v.p., 1979—, also dir., 1981—; gen. mgr. Strawbridge & Clothier (Clover Div.), 1979-96—. Bd. dirs. Ea. Star Charity Found. N.J., 1978-83. Served to 1st lt. arty. U.S. Army, 1954-56. Mem. Internat. Mass Retail Assn. (officer 1987-93, bd. dirs. 1981-96—, chmn. bd. 1991-93), South Jersey C. of C. (bd. dirs. 199196—), Am. Lung Assn. (bd. dirs. Phila. chpt. 1991-94). Republican. Methodist. Club: Tavistock. Lodge: Masons. Home: 1 Heritage Rd Haddonfield NJ 08033-3405 Office: Strawbridge & Clothier Clover Divsn 801 Market St Philadelphia PA 19107-3109

WHITE, WILL WALTER, III, public relations consultant, writer; b. Glen Ridge, N.J., July 3, 1930; s. Will Walter and Miriam Chandler (Milburn) W.; m. Phyllis Marcia DuFlocq, Dec. 28, 1951 (div. 1971); children: Will Walter IV, Scott, Alan; m. Anne Elizabeth Levenson, Nov. 21, 1971 (div. 1992); children: Duncan, Christopher; stepchildren: Michael, Susan; m. Catherine Laur, Aug. 26, 1992. B.A., Cornell U., 1952. Supr. Union Carbide Corp., N.Y.C., 1954-59; account exec. Ketchum, MacLeod & Grove, N.Y.C., 1959-62; sr. v.p. Wilson, Haight & Welch, Hartford, Conn., 1962-72; chmn., chief exec. officer Lowengard & Brotherhood, Hartford, 1972-83; pres., chief exec. officer Harland & Tine & White, Hartford, 1983-87; chmn. Donahue Inc., Hartford, 1987-89; ptnr. Laur White & White, Sarasota, Fla., 1992—; exec. com. Conn. Dist. Export Council, 1979-88. Author: The Sunfish Book, 1983; contbg. editor Mid-Gulf Sailing mag., 1994-95. Mem. exec. com. Hartford Stage Co., 1982-86; pres. Vis. Nurse Assn., Hartford, 1979; fin. chmn. Vis. Nurse and Home Care, Inc., Hartford and Waterbury, 1982-91; mem. pub. rels. com. Fairfield County Rep. Com., 1961; chmn. S.W. Fla. Regional Harbor Bd., 1995—. 1st lt. U.S. Army, 1952-54. Nat. champion Sunfish Racing Class, 1966, 68. Mem. Pub. Rels. Soc. Am. (accredited, chmn. investor rels. sect. 1983, charter mem. Hall of Fame 1990), Bus. Profl. Advt. Assn. (cert. bus. communicator), Nat. Investor Rels. Inst., U.S. Sunfish Class Assn. (pres. 1985-88, charter mem. Hall of Fame 1991), Boaters Action and Info. League (vp. edn. 1992—), Hist. Soc. Sarasota County (bd. dirs. 1995—), Sarasota Sailing Squadron. Address: 7362 Palomino Ln Sarasota FL 34241-9779

WHITE, W(ILLIAM) ARTHUR, geologist; b. Sumner, Ill., Dec. 9, 1916; s. Millard Otto and Joy Olive (Atkins) W.; m. Alma Evelyn Simonton McCullough, June 21, 1941. B.S., U. Ill., 1940, M.S., 1947, Ph.D., 1955. With Ill. Geol. Survey, Urbana, 1943-79, geologist, 1955-58, head clay resources and clay mineral tech. sect., 1958-72, geologist, 1972-79, geologist emeritus, 1979—; pvt. cons. geologist Urbana, 1979-88; prof. geology Fed. U. Rio Grande do Sul, Brazil, 1970. Contbr. articles to profl. jours. Fellow Geol. Soc. Am., Mineral Soc. Am., AAAS; mem. Internat. Clay Mineral Soc., Am. Clay Mineral Soc., Ill. Acad. Sci., Mus. Natural History (assoc.), Nat. Geog. Soc., Am. Chem. Soc., Colloid Chem. Soc., Soc. Econ. Paleontologists and Mineralogists, Inter-Am. Soc., Farm Bur., AARP, Order United Comml. Travelers Am., U. Ill. Alumni Assn., Sigma Xi. Home: 603 E Colorado Ave Urbana IL 61801-5923

WHITE, WILLIAM BLAINE, geochemist, educator; b. Huntingdon, Pa., Jan. 5, 1934; s. William Bruce and Eleanor Mae (Barr) W.; m. Elizabeth Loczi, Mar. 27, 1959; children: Nikki Elizabeth White McCurry, William Brion (dec.). BS, Juniata Coll., 1954; PhD, Pa. State U., 1962. Rsch. assoc. Mellon Inst., Pitts., 1954-58; asst. prof. Pa. State U., University Park, 1963-67; asso. prof. Pa. State U., 1967-72, prof. geochemistry, 1972—, chmn. grad. program in materials, 1990-93. Assoc. editor: Am. Mineralogist, 1972-75, Materials Rsch. Bull., 1979-93, Jour. Am. Ceramic Soc., 1985-93, Water Resources Bull., 1992-93; editor earth scis. Nat. Speleol. Soc. Bull., 1964-94; author: Geomorphology and Hydrology of Karst Terrains, 1988, (with Elizabeth L. White) Karst Hydrology: Concepts from the Mammoth Cave Area, 1989, (with Susan Barger) Daguerreotype: Nineteenth-Century Technology and Modern Science, 1991; contbr. articles to profl. jours. Home: 542 Glenn Rd State College PA 16803-3472 Office: Pa State U Materials Rsch Lab University Park PA 16802

WHITE, WILLIAM DEKOVA (BILL WHITE), baseball league executive; b. Lakewood, Fla., Jan. 28, 1934; div.; 5 children. Student, Hiram Coll., 1952-53. With various minor league teams, 1953-55; with N.Y. Giants (later San Francisco Giants), 1956, 58, St. Louis Cardinals, 1959-65, 69, Phila. Phillies, 1966-68; broadcaster Sta. WPIX-TV, N.Y.C., 1970-88; pres. Nat. League, N.Y.C., 1989—. Recipient 7 Gold Glove awards; named to All-Star team 6 times. Office: Nat League Profl Baseball Clubs 350 Park Ave New York NY 10022-6022

WHITE, WILLIAM DUDLEY, safety engineer; b. Birmingham, Mich., June 11, 1958; s. Paul Richard and Annetta Carole (Manhart) W.; m. Tamara Jean Wishon, Mar. 13, 1992; 1 child, Stacy Michelle; 1 stepchild, Royce Edward Vorel. BS cum laude, U. Ctrl. Okla., 1994. Chief maintenance engr. First Union Mgmt., Oklahoma City, 1984-89; safety rep., chmn. safety and suggestion coms. E-Systems, Inc., Greenville, Tex., 1994—; creator curriculum for various safety programs, 1994. Pack master Boy Scouts Am., Edmond, Okla., 1991-92; CPR instr., std. first aid instr. ARC, Hunt County, Tex., 1993—. Mem. Am. Soc. Safety Engrs., Alpha Chi. Roman Catholic. Achievements include development of safety certification/O-J-T checklist tng. program to meet OSHA, AFOSH and DoD Stds. regarding task proficiency for aircraft servicing, maintenance and daily ops. powered aircraft ground and mobile equipment. Home: 2507 Hillcrest St Greenville TX 75402-8050 Office: E-Systems PO Box 6056 CBN072 Greenville TX 75403

WHITE, WILLIAM FREDRICK, lawyer; b. Elmhurst, Ill., Sept. 30, 1948; s. William Daniel and Carol Ruth (Laier) W.; m. Kathie Jean Nichols, May 27, 1979; children: Nicholas Roland, Andrew William. BA, U. Ill., 1970; JD, Antioch Sch. of Law, 1976. Bar: U.S. Ct. Appeals (D.C. cir.) 1976, Wis. 1982, U.S. Dist. Ct. (we. dist.) Wis. 1982, U.S. Dist. Ct. D.C. 1976, U.S. Ct. Claims 1978, U.S. Ct. Appeals (7th and 10th cirs.) 1982. With U.S. Dept. Labor, Washington, 1976; interim exec. dir. Common Cause, Washington, 1977; asst. counsel Nat. Treasury Employees Union, Washington, 1977-79, assoc. gen. counsel, 1979-81, dir. litigation, 1981-82; assoc. Michael, Best & Friedrich, Madison, Wis., 1982-88, ptnr., chmn. assoc. devel. com., 1988—; bd. dirs. Med. Physics Publ. Co. Treas. The Lufler com., Madison, 1984—; chmn. Pub. Health Commn., Madison, 1983-89; bd. dirs. exec com. Dane County Mediation Program, Madison, 1983-90, Perinatal Found., Madison, 1984—, Arthritis Found., Madison, 1986-92, chmn., 1991-92; bd. dirs. Dane County Natural Heritage Found., 1988-91; mem. Dane County Regional Airport Commn., 1991—, chmn. 1994—; chancellor Wis. Conf. United Meth. Ch., 1992—, gen. coun. Fin. and Adminstrn., 1991—, chmn. Legal Svcs. Com.; bd. dirs. Downtown Madison Inc.; mem. Dane County Transferrable Devel. Rights Task Force, Team Terrace Transp. Com., 1996—, chair. Mem. ABA, D.C. Bar Assn., Med. Physics Found. (bd. dirs. 1987—), Dane County Bar Assn., State Bar Assn. (sec. Health Law sect.). Democrat. Methodist. Avocations: cycling, skiing, volleyball, softball. Office: Michael Best & Friedrich 1 S Pinckney St Madison WI 53703-1806

WHITE, WILLIAM JAMES, information management and services company executive; b. Kenosha, Wis., May 30, 1938; s. William H. and Dorothy Caroline White; m. Jane Schulte, Aug. 13, 1960; children: James N., Thomas G., Maria, Gretchen S. BS, Northwestern U., 1961; MBA, Harvard U., 1963. Mech. planning engr. Procter & Gamble Corp., 1961-62; bd. dirs. TJ Internat., Boise, Idaho; corp. v.p. Hartmarx Corp., Chgo., 1963-74; group v.p. Mead Corp., Dayton, Ohio, 1974-81; pres., chief oper. officer, dir. Masonite Corp., Chgo., 1981-85; exec. v.p. and dir. USG Corp., 1985-88, pres., chief exec. officer Whitestar Enterprises, Inc., 1989-90; chmn., pres., chief exec. officer Bell & Howell Co., 1990-95; chmn. CEO Bell & Howell Holdings Co., 1995—. Author: (with Henderson et al) Creative Collective Bargaining, 1965. Vice chmn. adv. coun. McCormick Sch. Engring. and Applied Scis.; mem. bus. adv. coun. U. Ill., Chgo., 1981—; bd. dirs. TJ Internat., IMSA Fund for Advancement Edn., Aurora; past chmn. bd. Ill. div. Am. Cancer Soc. Mem. Econ. Club, The Chgo. Com., Chgo. Club, Glen View Country Club. Office: Bell & Howell Co 5215 Old Orchard Rd Skokie IL 60077-1035*

WHITE, WILLIAM NELSON, lawyer; b. Balt., Sept. 8, 1938; s. Nelson Cardwell and Ellen Atwell (Zoller) W.; m. Mary Kathleen Bitzel, Sept. 2, 1960 (div. 1971); children: Craig William, Jeffrey Alan, Colin Christopher; m. Christine Lewin Hanna, July 8, 1978. LLB, U. Md., 1968, JD, 1969. Bar: Md. 1972, U.S. Ct. Appeals (4th cir.) 1975, U.S. Dist. Ct. Md. 1976, U.S. Spreme Ct. 1976. Asst. state's atty. Balt., 1972; assoc. Brooks & Turnbull, Balt., 1973-76; pvt. practice Balt., 1977—; counsel St. Andrews Soc. Balt., 1989—; former cousnel, bd. dirs. St. George's Soc. Elder, former pres. of deacons Roland Park Presbyn. Ch. Mem. ABA, Md. Bar Assn., Baltimore County Bar Assn., U. Md. Alumni Assn. for Greater Balt. (pres. 1977), St. George's Soc. Balt. (former counsel, mem. bd. dirs.), Internat. Platform Assn. Avocations: history, philosophy, classical music, tennis, sailing. Office: Ste LL-3 305 W Chesapeake Ave Baltimore MD 21204

WHITE, WILLIAM NORTH, chemistry educator; b. Walton, N.Y., Sept. 16, 1925; s. George Fitch and Frances (Peck) W.; m. Hilda R. Sauter, Sept. 8, 1951; children: Carla Ann, Eric Jeffrey. A.B., Cornell U., 1950; M.A., Harvard U., 1951, Ph.D., 1953. NRC postdoctoral fellow Calif. Inst. Tech., Pasadena, 1953-54; asst. prof. Ohio State U., Columbus, 1954-59; asso. prof. Ohio State U., 1959-63; prof. chemistry U. Vt., Burlington, 1963-76, 77-95, prof. emeritus, 1995—; chmn. dept. U. Vt., 1963-70, acting chmn. dept., 1975-76; prof. chemistry U. Tex. at Arlington, 1976-77, chmn. dept., 1976-77; NSF sr. postdoctoral fellow Brookhaven Nat. Lab., Upton, N.Y., 1963-64, Harvard U., 1965; vis. scholar Brandeis U., 1974-75; chmn. arrangements com. Nat. Organic Chemistry Symposium, 1965-67. Contbr. articles on organic chemistry profl. jours. Selectman Town of Shelburne, Vt., 1968-74, water commr., 1973-74, justice of the peace, 1981—, sewer commr., 1991-93; mem. Chittenden County Regional Planning Commn., 1983-91. Served with AUS, 1943-46. Mem. Am. Chem. Soc. (chmn. Western Vt. sect. 1966-67), Royal Soc. Chemistry, New Eng. Assn. Chemistry Tchrs., AAAS, N.Y. Acad. Scis., Phi Beta Kappa, Sigma Xi, Phi Kappa Phi, Phi Lambda Upsilon. Home: Pierson Dr Shelburne VT 05482-7224 Office: U Vt Dept Chemistry Burlington VT 05405-0125

WHITE, WILLIAM SAMUEL, foundation executive; b. Cin., May 8, 1937; s. Nathaniel Ridgway and Mary (Loundes) W.; m. Claire Mott, July 1, 1961; children: Tiffany Loundes, Ridgway Harding. BA, Dartmouth Coll., 1959, MBA, 1960; LL.D. (hon.), Eastern Mich. U., 1975. With Barrett & Williams, N.Y.C., 1961-62; sr. assoc. Bruce Payne & Assos., N.Y.C., 1962-71; v.p. C. S. Mott Found., Flint, Mich., 1971-75; pres. C. S. Mott Found., 1976—, trustee, 1971—, also chmn. bd. dirs.; bd. dirs. Continental Water Corp; chmn. bd. dirs. U.S. Sugar Corp. Mem. exec. com. Daycroft Sch., Greenwich, Conn., 1966-70; bd. dirs. Flint Area Conf., 1971-84, Coun. on Founds., 1985-90, Independent Sector, 1994—, European Found. Centre, 1994—, Civicus, 1995—; mem. citizens adv. task force U. Mich., Flint, 1974-79; chmn. Coun. of Mich. Founds., 1979-81, Flint Area Focus Coun., 1988—; mem. Pres.'s Task Force on Pvt. Sector Initiatives, 1982; trustee GMI Engring. and Mgmt. Inst., 1982-86. Served with U.S. Army, 1960-62. Office: C S Mott Foundation 1200 Mott Foundation Bldg Flint MI 48502-1807

WHITE, WILLIS SHERIDAN, JR., retired utilities company executive; b. nr. Portsmouth, Va., Dec. 17, 1926; s. Willis Sheridan and Carrie (Culpepper) W.; m. LaVerne Behrends, Oct. 8, 1949; children: Willis Sheridan III, Marguerite Louise White Spangler, Cynthia D.W. Haight. B.S., Va. Poly. Inst., 1948; M.S., Mass. Inst. Tech., 1958. With Am. Electric Power Co., Inc., 1948-91; chmn., chief exec. officer Am. Electric Power Co., Inc. and its subs., N.Y.C., 1976-90, chmn., 1991, mem. bd. dirs., 1972-92; pres., bd. dirs. Ohio Valley Electric Corp., Ind.-KTV Electric Corp., 1977-91; bd. dirs. Bank of N.Y. Trustee Battellle Meml. Inst., Grant/Riverside Meth. Hosp., Columbus. With USNR, 1945-46. Sloan fellow, 1957-58. Mem. IEEE, NAE, Eta Kappa Nu, Omicron Delta Kappa. Methodist.

WHITE, WILLMON LEE, magazine editor; b. Lamesa, Tex., Mar. 10, 1932; s. Aubrey F. and Jewel (Henderson) W.; m. Carol A. Nelson, Nov. 2, 1957 (div.); children: Tracy, Wrenn, Gehrig, Bob; m. Barbara K. Kelly, Sept. 16, 1977; 1 child, Theresa. BA, McMurry Coll., Abilene, Tex., 1953; MA, U. Tex., 1956. Reporter Abilene Reporter-News, 1953-54; pub. rels. writer Tex. Ins. Adv. Assn., Austin, 1955-56; asst. editor Humble Way mag. Humble Oil & Refining Co. (Exxon), Houston, 1956-65; assoc. editor, news editor Together mag. Methodist Ch., Park Ridge, Ill., 1965-69; sr. editor World Book Ency., Chgo., 1969-70; asst. editor, then asso. editor Rotarian mag. (publ. Rotary Internat.), Evanston, Ill., 1970-74, editor, 1974—, mgr. communications and pub. rels. div., 1979-95; asst. gen. sec. Rotarian mag. (publ. Rotary Internat.), Evanston, 1995—; intern Newsweek mag., 1954. Mem. Am. Soc. Mag. Editors, Am. Soc. Assn. Execs., Rotary, Sigma Delta Chi. Office: Rotarian 1560 Sherman Ave Evanston IL 60201

WHITECOTTON, THOMAS EDWARD, III, construction company executive; b. Kansas City, Mo., Aug. 21, 1939. BSChemE, U. Mo., Rolla, 1962, BSCE, 1970, MSCE, 1971; grad., Command and Gen. Staff Coll., Ft. Leavenworth, Kans., 1978. Commd. 2d lt. U.S. Army, 1962, advanced through grades to brig. gen., 1993; platoon leader Co. B, 802d Engr. Bn., Korea, 1962-63; co. comdr. Co. A, 44th Engr. Bn., Korea, 19963-65; assigned to 401st Bn., Vietnam, 1968-69; adminstrv. officer Hdqs. 1st U.S. Army, Ft. Meade, Md., 1969; contract constrn. officer Am. Embassy, Seoul, 1969-74; staff officer U.S. Army John F. Kennedy Ctr. Spl. Warfare, Ft. Bragg, N.C., 1974-75; engr. mgmt. chief U.S. Army C.E., Ft. Leonard Wood, Mo., 1982-94; pres. Mid States Constrn. Svcs., Rolla. Decorated Bronze Star; honor medal (Republic of Vietnam); recipient Conspicuous Svc. medal State of Mo., 1986. Mem. U.S. Army Engr. Assn. (post pres. 1993-94, DeFluery medal 1994), Soc. Am. Mil. Engrs. (post pres. 1992-94), N.G. Assn. U.S., Assn. U.S. Army, Chi Sigma, Triangle. Democrat. Roman Catholic. Avocations: classical music, collcting antiques, reading, gardening. Home and Office: 210 Christy Dr Rolla MO 65401

WHITED, LINDA LEE, secondary school English language educator; b. Akron, Ohio, May 24, 1947; d. Robert Lee and Gloria Ann (Honeywill) Davis; m. Eugene Hearsel Whited, Mar. 4, 1972; children: Wendy Edna, Jefferson Eugene. BS in Secondary Edn., U. Akron, 1987, MS in Elem. Adminstrn., 1995. Sec. Goodyear Tire and Rubber Co., Akron, 1966-71, B.F. Goodrich Co., Akron, 1972-75; substitute tchr. area schs., Akron, 1987; intensive bus. tchr. Springfield H.S., Akron, 1987-92, English lang. tchr., 1992—; cheerleading advisor Springfield H.S., 1987-95, faculty mgr., 1991-95, mem. levy com., 1991-94, mem. Spartan Booster Club, 1992-95. Active local Parent, Tchr., Student Assn., 1981—, 2nd v.p., 1981-83, 93—. Mem. NEA, Ohio Edn. Assn., Springfield Local Assn. Classroom Tchrs., Nat. Coun. Tchrs. English, Kappa Delta Pi (Mabel Riedinger scholar 1983-84), Pi Lambda Theta. Avocations: reading, travel, volleyball, swimming. Home: 2079 Waterbury Dr Uniontown OH 44685-9770

WHITEFIELD, ANNE C., secondary school principal. Prin. Hum-Fogg High Sch., Nashville. Recipient Elem. Sch. Recognition award U.S. Dept. Edn., 1989-90. Office: Hum-Fogg High Sch 700 Broadway Nashville TN 37203-3937

WHITEFORD, ANDREW HUNTER, anthropologist; b. Winnipeg, Man., Can., 1913; came to U.S., 1923, naturalized, 1928; s. John and Janet Carduff (Hunter) W.; m. Marion Bonneville Salmon, Sept. 2, 1939; children: John Hunter, Michael Bonneville, Linda McMillan Whiteford Uzzell, Laurie Andrea Whiteford Richards. B.A., Beloit (Wis.) Coll., 1937, LL.D. (hon.), 1981; M.A., U. Chgo., 1943, Ph.D., 1950. Archaeologist N.Mex., 1938; supr. U. Tenn.-WPA, 1938-42; mem. faculty Beloit Coll., 1942-74, prof. anthropology, 1955-74, George L. Collie prof., 1955-74, chmn. dept., 1944-73, emeritus, 1974—; vis. prof. Mich. State U., 1975, 76, 79; vis. prof. art history U. N.Mex., 1980; Faye Laverne Bumpass lectr. Tex. Tech. U., 1981; rsch. fellow com. human rels. U. Chgo., 1945-46; dir. Logan Mus. Anthropology, Beloit Coll., 1946-74; urban rschr., Mex., Colombia, Spain; rsch. curator Indian Art Research Ctr., Sch. Am. Research, Santa Fe, 1980-84, 90—, interim adminstrv. dir., 1981-84 ; research assoc. Wheelwright Mus. Am. Indian, Santa Fe, 1980—, trustee, 1979-85; adv. bd. Florence H. Ellis Mus., Ghost Ranch Conf. Ctr., Abiquiu, N.Mex., 1979—; guest curator, rsch. assoc. N.Mex. Mus. of Indian Arts and Culture, 1987—. Author: Two Cities of Latin America, 1964, North American Indian Arts, 1970, An Andean City at Mid-Century, 1977, Southwestern Indian Baskets: Their History and Makers, 1988, (chpts.) The Thaw Collection of Indian Art, 1996; editl. adv. bd. Am. Indian Art mag.; contbr. articles to profl. jours., encys. and festschrifts. NSF faculty fellow, 1960-61; Social Sci. Rsch. Coun.-ACLS fellow, 1961-62; grantee Wenner Gren Found., Social Sci. Rsch. Coun., NSF, USPHS, Am. Philos. Soc.; recipient honor award Native Am. Art Studies Assn. Fellow Am. Anthrop. Assn.; mem. Coun. for Mus. Anthropology, Soc. for Latin Am. Anthropology, Phi Beta Kappa, Sigma Xi, Beta Theta Pi, Omicron Delta Kappa. Address: 447 Camino Monte Vis Santa Fe NM 87501-4585

WHITEHALL, WILLIAM, insurance executive. Sr. v.p. Sedgwick Noble Lowndes, N.Y.C. Office: Sedgwick Noble Lowndes 1285 Ave of Americas New York NY 10019

WHITEHEAD, BARBARA ANN, secondary school educator; b. Shreveport, La., Apr. 25, 1941; d. Clifton John and Leona Elizabeth (Lemoine) W. BA, McNeese State U., 1963, MEd, 1967; postgrad., Centenary Coll., 1982-83, La. Tech. U., 1983. Cert. secondary edn. tchr., La. Tchr. Calcasieu Parish Sch. System, Lake Charles, La., 1963-68, Caddo Parish Sch. System, Shreveport, 1968—; chair social studies dept. C.E. Byrd Math./Sci. Magnet High Sch., Shreveport, 1987—. Author: Teaching the Historical Origins of Nursery Rhymes and Folk Tales, 1982. Named La. Tchr. of Yr. DAR, 1983. Mem. NEA, La. Assn. Educators, Caddo Assn. Educators, Sigma Tau Delta. Roman Catholic. Avocations: writing, travel. Office: CE Byrd Math Sci Magnet High Sch 3201 Line Ave Shreveport LA 71104-4241

WHITEHEAD, DAVID BARRY, lawyer; b. San Francisco, Oct. 14, 1946; s. Barry and Fritzi-Beth (Bowman) W.; m. René Dayan, May 26, 1990. AB in History, Stanford U., 1968, JD, 1971. Bar: Calif. 1972, U.S. Dist. Ct. (no. dist.) Calif. 1972, U.S. Ct. Appeals (9th cir.) 1972, U.S. Dist. Ct. (cen. dist.) Calif. 1974. Assoc. Cullinan Hancock Rothert & Burns, San Francisco, 1972-74; assoc. Cullinan Burns & Helmer, San Francisco, 1975-77, ptnr., 1977-78; ptnr. Burns & Whitehead, San Francisco, 1979-85, Whitehead & Porter, San Francisco, 1986—; bd. dirs. Rainbow Music, Inc., San Francisco, ITP, Inc., Sunnyvale, Calif.; founding dir. A. Lincoln High Sch. San Francisco, 1989—. Mem. San Francisco Rep. Steering Com., 1984-89; bd. dirs. Enterprise for High Sch. Students, San Francisco, 1982-86, San Francisco chpt. Easter Seal Soc., 1986—, Opera West Found., San Francisco, 1986—, Traveler's Aid Soc., San Francisco, 1989—, Hosp. de la Familia, 1995—. 1st lt. USAR, 1968-71. Mem. ABA, Calif. Bar Assn., San Francisco Bar Assn., Calif. Scholarship Fedn. (life) Family Club San Francisco (bd. dirs. 1986-89, 93-95), Abraham Lincoln High Sch. San Francisco Alumni Assn. (founding dir.). Roman Catholic. Avocations: tenor, writer, director, actor. Home: 1896 Pacific Ave Apt 502 San Francisco CA 94109-2302 Office: Whitehead & Porter 1850 Montgomery St 18th fl San Francisco CA 94104

WHITEHEAD, DAVID LYNN, school counselor; b. Crockett, Tex., Mar. 24, 1950; s. Clifton Baine and Corene (Stowe) W.; m. Joyce Stalmach, June 23, 1973; children: Christopher, Kimberly, Allison. BA with honor, Sam Houston State U., Huntsville, Tex., 1972, MA, 1975. Cert. tchr., speech pathologist, learning disabilities, mental retardation, ednl. diagnostician, counseling, Tex. Speech pathologist Texas City Ind. Sch. Dist., 1972-73; speech pathologist Brenham (Tex.) Ind. Sch. Dist., 1973-75, ednl. diagnostician, 1975-86; ednl. diagnostician Austin County Edn. Coop., Sealy, Tex., 1986-88; sch. counselor Sealy (Tex.) Ind. Sch. Dist., 1988-92; counselor Alton Elem. Sch., Brenham, Tex., 1992—; ednl. cons., Austin County, Tex., 1987-88; reviewer spl. edn. program College Station (Tex.) Ind. Sch. Dist., 1983; feature artist Gov.'s Mansion, State of Tex., Austin, 1985. Pres. Whitehead Cemetery Assn., Grapeland, Tex., 1986-90. Mem. AACD, Tex. Assn. for Counseling and Devel., Ft. Bend County Counseling Assn., Region VI Educational Diagnosticians (pres. Bluebonnet chpt. 1977-78), Nat. Egg Art Guild (SW regional bd. dirs. 1986), Tex. Guild Egg Shell Artists (state pres. 1984-85). Mem. Brethren Ch. Avocations: gardening, reading, refinishing furniture. Home: RR 1 Box 74 New Ulm TX 78950-9729

WHITEHEAD, E. DOUGLAS, urology educator; b. Gajashiels, Scotland, Aug. 24, 1939; (div.); 1 child, Robin Stacey. BA, Vanderbilt U., 1961; MD, Ind. U., 1965; postgrad., U. London, 1972. Diplomate Am. Bd. Urology; med. lic. Ind., Ill., N.Y., Calif., N.J. Intern. surgery Mount Sinai Hosp., N.Y.C., 1965-66; resident in surgery Presbyn.-St. Luke's Hosp., Chgo., 1966-67; resident in urology N.Y.U. Med. Ctr., 1969-73; clin. assoc. urology Mount Sinai Sch. Medicine, N.Y.C., 1973-77, sr. clin. instr. urology, 1977-80, asst. clin. prof. urology, 1980-92; pvt. practice, N.Y.C., 1973—; assoc. clin. prof. urology Mount Sinai Sch. Medicine, 1992-96, Albert Einstein Coll. of Medicine, 1996—; assoc. attending Beth Israel Med. Ctr., N.Y.C.; mem. advisor Impotence Anonymous & Jr., Diabetes Self-Mgmt., 1983-85, Jour. Urol. Nursing; editl. adv. bd. The Female Patient, Med. Aspects of Human Sexuality; mem. med. adv. bd. Colostomy Soc., N.Y., Inc.; cons. and speaker in field. Editor: Current Operative Urology, 1975, 2d rev. edit., 1984, ann. edits., 1989-92, Mgmt. Impotence and Infertility, 1994, Sex Over Forty, 1990—, Atlas of Surgical Techniques in Urology, 1996; contbr. articles to profl. jours.; patentee in field. Grantee U.S.P.H., Clin. Research Ctr. Fellow ACS, Clin. Soc. Am. Diabetes Assn., N.Y. Diabetes Affiliate; mem. AMA, AAAS, Am. Urol. Assn., Soc. Internat. Urology (diplomate), Soc. for the Study of Impotence, Am. Assn. Clin. Urologists, N.Y. State Urol. Assn., Am. Acad. of Am. Acad. of Phalloplasty Surgeons (pres.-elect), Am. Acad. of Male Sexual Health, Internat. Soc. for Artificial Organs, Am. So. Nephrology, Med. Soc. State N.Y., Med. Soc. County N.Y., Am. Assn. Sex Educators, Counselors and Therapists, Soc. for the Sci. Study of Sex, Sex Info. and Edn. Coun. of the U.S. Coalition on Sexuality and Disability, Am. Cancer Soc., Nat. Kidney Found., Am. Geriatric Soc., N.Y. Acad. Sci., N.Y. Acad. Medicine, N.Y. Urodynamic Soc., Internat. Continence Soc. Home: 785 Park Ave New York NY 10021-3552 Office: Ste 2-1 24 E 12th St New York NY 10003

WHITEHEAD, GEORGE WILLIAM, retired mathematician; b. Bloomington, Ill., Aug. 2, 1918; s. George William and (Christine) Mary (Gutschlag) W.; m. Kathleen Ethelwyn Butcher, June 7, 1947. SB, U.

Chgo., 1937, SM, 1938, PhD, 1941. Instr. math. Purdue U., West Lafayette, Ind., 1941-45, Princeton (N.J.) U., 1945-47; asst. prof. Brown U., Providence, 1947-48, assoc. prof., 1948-49; asst. prof. MIT, Cambridge, 1949-51, assoc. prof., 1951-57, prof., 1957-85, prof. emeritus, 1985—. Author: Homotopy Theory, 1966, Elements of Homotopy Theory, 1978, Recent Advances in Homotopy Theory, 1970. Fellow Guggenheim Found., 1955-56, sr. post-doctoral fellow NSF, 1965-66; Fulbright Rsch. scholar, 1955-56. Fellow Am. Acad. Arts & Scis.; mem. NAS, Am. Math. Soc. (v.p.), Math. Soc. Am. Avocations: archeology, bridge, genealogy. Home: 25 Bellevue Rd Arlington MA 02174-7919

WHITEHEAD, IAN, insurance company executive. CEO, pres. London PCF Lf & Annuity Co., Raleigh, N.C. Office: London PCF Lf & Annuity Co 3109 Poplarwood Ct Raleigh NC 27604-1011*

WHITEHEAD, J. RENNIE, science consultant; s. William and Beatrice Cora (Fenning) W.; m. Nesta Doone James, Jan. 11, 1944; children—Valerie Lesley (dec.), Michael James Rennie. B.Sc. in Physics, Manchester U., Lancashire, Eng., 1939; Ph.D. in Phys. Chemistry, Cambridge U., Eng., 1949. Cert. profl. engr., Ont.; chartered engr., U.K. Sci. officer TRE (UK Radar), Eng., 1939-51; assoc. prof. McGill U., Montreal, P.Q., Can., 1951-55; dir. research RCA Victor Co Ltd., Montreal, 1955-65; prin. sci. adviser Govt. of Can., Ottawa, Ont., 1965-75; sr. v.p. Philip A. Lapp Ltd., Ottawa, 1975-82; pvt. practice sci. cons. Ottawa, 1982—; bd. dirs. Hancock-Lapp Assocs., Ottawa, 1986-89; bd. dirs. Found. for Internat. Tng., Toronto, 1976-86. Author: Superregenerative Receivers, 1949. Fellow Royal Soc. Can., Inst. Physics, Instn. Elec. Engrs., Can. Aeronautics and Space Inst., Can. Assn. for Club of Rome (chmn. 1976-81). Anglican. Avocations: automobiles; philately; carpentry; computers. Home and Office: 1368 Chattaway Ave, Ottawa, ON Canada K1H 7S3

WHITEHEAD, JAMES S., lawyer; b. Rockford, Ill., Dec. 22, 1948; s. John B. and Beverley (Williams) W.; m. Pamela A. Miller, June 26, 1970; children: Jennifer, John. BA, Yale U., 1970; JD, U. Chgo., 1974. Bar: Ill. 1974, U.S. Ct. Appeals (D.C., 2d, 3d, 6th, 7th, 8th, 11th cirs.), U.S. Supreme Ct., U.S. Dist. Ct. (no. and so. dists.) Ill., U.S. Dist. Ct. (ea. dist.) Mich. Assoc. Sidley & Austin, Chgo., 1975-80, ptnr., 1981—. Office: Sidley & Austin 1 First Nat Plz Chicago IL 60603*

WHITEHEAD, JOHN C., state judge; b. Loup City, Nebr., Mar. 4, 1939; s. Cyrus C. and Regina (Costello) W.; m. Linda L. Lykins, Sept. 11, 1965; children: Sarah, Amy. AB in History, Benedictine Coll., 1961; LLB, Washburn U., 1964, JD, 1964. Bar: Nebr. 1964, Kans. 1964. Mem. firm Snell & Whitehead, Columbus, Nebr., 1965-66, Walker Luckey & Whitehead, Columbus, 1966-71, Walker, Luckey, Whitehead & Sipple, Columbus, 1971-77; judge Nebr. State Dist. Ct., Columbus, 1977—; dep. county atty. Platte County, Nebr., 1965-67; atty. City of Columbus, 1967-72. Bd. dirs. Lower Loup Natural Resource Dist., 1971-74, vice chmn., 1975-76; bd. dirs. Columbus Family YMCA, 1974-80, pres., 1978-80; bd. dirs. Platte County Playhouse, 1972-74. Mem. ABA (regional rep. Nat. Assn. State Trial Judges 1994—), Nebr. Bar Assn., Platte County Bar Assn. (pres. 1976-77), Nebr. Dist. Judges Assn. (sec.-treas. 1988-90, v.p. 1990, pres. 1991-92), Columbus C. of C. (bd. dirs. 1977-81, pres. 1979), Elks, Optimists (pres. 1971-72, lt. gov. Nebr. dist. 1972-73), Toastmasters (pres. 1968—), Am. Vets. (comdr. 1994—, state judge advocate 1995—). Roman Catholic. Home: 3365 Pershing Rd Columbus NE 68601-8117 Office: State Dist Ct PO Box 445 Columbus NE 68602-0445 *What bothers me about America today is that we have become a nation of spectators, not just in sports, but in life itself. Life, like sports, provides the most rewards and enjoyment to the participant. The spectators only gain from the association, and when it's over find they have only the memories and no tangible benefits.*

WHITEHEAD, JOHN C., lawyer; b. Summit, N.J., June 19, 1946. BA, Harvard U., 1968; JD, U. Va., 1973. Mem. Morgan, Lewis & Bockius, N.Y. Office: Morgan Lewis & Bockius 101 Park Ave New York NY 10178

WHITEHEAD, JOHN CUNNINGHAM, investment executive; b. Evanston, Ill., Apr. 2, 1922; s. Eugene C. and Winifred W.; m. Helene E. Shannon, Sept. 28, 1946 (div. Dec. 1971); children: Anne Elizabeth, John Gregory; m. Jaan W. Chartener, Oct. 22, 1972 (div. 1986); 1 child, Sarah; m. Nancy Dickerson, 1989. BA, Haverford Coll., 1943; MBA, Harvard U., 1947; LLD (hon.), Pace. U., Rutgers U., Haverford Coll.; Harvard U.; LLD (hon.), Amherst Coll. With Goldman, Sachs & Co., N.Y.C., 1947-84, ptnr., 1956-76, sr. ptnr., co-chmn., 1976-84; dep. sec. Dept. State, Washington, 1985-89; now chmn. AEA Investors Inc., N.Y.C., 1989—; chmn. Fed. Res. Bank of N.Y. Trustee Haverford Coll., Rockefeller U., Lincoln Ctr. Theater, Outward Bound; past pres. bd. overseers Harvard U.; past chmn. trustees coun. Nat. Gallery Art; co-chmn. greater N.Y. coun. Boy Scouts Am.; chmn. Internat. Rescue Com., Andrew W. Mellon Found., UN Assn. U.S.A., Youth for Understanding, Internat. House; chmn. emeritus Brookings Inst. With USNR, 1943-46. Mem. Coun. on Fgn. Rels., Links Club, Univ. Club, F Street Club. Office: AEA Investors Inc 65 E 55th St New York NY 10022-3205

WHITEHEAD, JOHN JED, computer systems company executive; b. N.Y.C., June 1, 1945; s. Edwin Carl and Constance Rosemary (Raywid) W.; m. Christina Juillet, Sept. 24, 1985. B.A., Williams Coll., 1967; postgrad., Case Western Res. U., 1967-68. Dir. chem. mktg., chem. div. Technicon Corp., Tarrytown, N.Y., 1969-70; sr. v.p., gen. mgr. indsl. div. Technicon Corp., 1970-71, sr. v.p. clin. div., 1971-74, sr. v.p. corp. planning, 1974-75, sr. v.p. research and devel., 1975-81, sr. v.p. bus. devel. and market planning, 1981-83, pres. diagnostic systems div., 1983-85; pres., dir., CEO TDS Corp., 1985-92, chmn., CEO, dir., 1992-93; bd. dirs. Whitehead Assocs., 1980, Digene Diagnostics, Inc., Rsch. Am.; mem. adv. coun. Nat. Inst. Environ. Health Scis., NIH, 1971-73. Mem. Rockefeller adv. group to Pres.'s 1976 Bicentennial Planning Commn., 1971-72; bd. dirs. Westchester Urban League, 1973-74, Whitehead Biomed. Rsch. Inst., 1974—, Primary Care Network, 1985-87, Friends Nat. Libr. Medicine, 1992—, Sci. and Tech. Mus. of Atlanta (SciTrek), 1992—, Ams. Med. Progress, 1993—, Atlanta Internat. Sch. Atlanta, 1995—; trustee Nat. Mus. Health and Medicine Found., 1991—; dir. emeritus i-Stat Corp., 1995—. Home: Park Place on Peachtree 2660 Peachtree Rd NW Atlanta GA 30305-3673

WHITEHEAD, JOHN WAYNE, law educator, organization administrator, author; b. Pulaski, Tenn., July 14, 1946; s. John M. and Alatha (Wiser) W.; m. Virginia Carolyn Nichols, Aug. 26, 1967; children: Jayson Reau, Jonathan Mathew, Elisabeth Anne, Joel Christofer, Joshua Benjamen. BA, U. Ark., 1969, JD, 1974. Bar: Ark. 1974, U.S. Dist. Ct. (ea. and we. dists.) Ark. 1974, U.S. Supreme Ct. 1977, U.S. Ct. Appeals (9th cir.) 1980, Va. 1981, U.S. Ct. Appeals (7th cir.) 1981, U.S. Ct Appeals (4th and 5th cirs.). Spl. counsel Christian Legal Soc., Oak Park, Ill., 1977-78; assoc. Gibbs & Craze, Cleve., 1978-79; sole practice law Manassas, Va., 1979-82; pres. The Rutherford Inst., Charlottesville, Va., 1982—, also bd. dirs.; frequent lectr. colls., law schs.; past adj. prof. O.W. Coburn Sch. Law. Author: The Separation Illusion, 1977, Schools on Fire, 1980, The New Tyranny, 1982, The Second American Revolution, 1982, The Stealing of America, 1983, The Freedom of Religious Expression in Public High Schools, 1983, The End of Man, 1986, An American Dream, 1987, The Rights of Religious Persons in Public Education, 1991, Home Education: Rights and Reasons, 1993, Religious Apartheid, 1994, several others; contbr. numerous articles to profl. jours.; contbr. numerous chpts. to books. Served to 1st lt. U.S. Army, 1969-71. Named Christian Leader of Yr. Christian World Affairs Conf., Washington, 1986; recipient Bus. and Profl. award Religious Heritage Am., 1990, Hungarian Freedom medal, Budapest, 1991. Mem. ABA, Ark. Bar Assn., Va. Bar Assn. Office: The Rutherford Inst PO Box 7482 Charlottesville VA 22906-7482

WHITEHEAD, KENNETH DEAN, author, translator, retired federal government official; b. Rupert, Idaho, Dec. 14, 1930; s. Clarence Christian and May Bell (Allen) W.; m. Margaret Mary O'Donohue, Aug. 2, 1958; children: Paul Daniel, Steven Francis, Matthew Patrick, David Joseph. BA in French, U. Utah, 1955; postgrad., U. Paris, 1956-57; cert. in Arabic and Middle East studies, Fgn. Service Inst., Beirut, 1962. Instr. English U. Utah, Salt Lake City, 1955-56; fgn. service officer Dept. State, Rome, Beirut and Tripoli, Libya, 1957-65; chief Arabic service Voice of Am., Washington, 1965-67; dep. dir. fgn. currency program Smithsonian Instn., Washington, 1967-72; exec. v.p. Caths. United for Faith Inc., New Rochelle, N.Y., 1972-81; dir. Ctr. for Internat. Edn. U.S. Dept. Edn., Washington, 1982-86, dep. asst. sec. for higher edn. programs, 1986-88, asst. sec. for postsecondary edn., 1988-89. Author: Respectable Killing: The New Abortion Imperative, 1972, Agenda for the Sexual Revolution, 1981, Catholic Colleges and Federal Funding, 1988, DOA: The Ambush of the Universal Catechism, 1993; co-author: The Pope, The Council and the Mass, 1981, Flawed Expectations: The Reception of the Catechism of the Catholic Church, 1996; sr. editor: World Almanac Book of Dates, 1982, Macmillan Concise Dictionary of World History, 1983; translator 19 books from French, German, Italian, 1980—. Bd. dirs. Notre Dame Inst. for Advanced study, Arlington, Va., 1986-95. Fulbright scholar U.S. Dept. State, 1956-57. Mem. Fellowship Cath. Scholars (bd. dirs. 1990—), Brent Soc. Cath. Profls. (bd. dirs. 1992—), Cath. League for Religious and Civil Rights (bd. dirs. 1992—), KC. Republican. Home: 809 Ridge Pl Falls Church VA 22046-3631

WHITEHEAD, LUCY GRACE, health facility administrator; b. Jacksonville, Fla., Jan. 12, 1935; d. William Alexander and Hester Grace (Gray) Fisackerly; m. John Vernon Whitehead, Sept. 4, 1957; children: Marilyn Ruth, John Vernon Jr., James Andrew. BA, Fla. So. Coll., 1956; M of Christian Edn., Emory U., 1957; BSN, U. North Fla., 1990. RN, Fla. Staff nurse Venice (Fla.) Hosp., 1977, Med. Personnel Pool, Largo, Fla., 1978; charge nurse/nurse educator Gadsden Nursing Home, Quincy, Fla., 1979-85; primary nurse Meml. Regional Rehab. Hosp., Jacksonville, Fla., 1990-92; staff nurse, nurse mgr. Nassau Gen. Hosp., Fernandina Beach, Fla., 1992-94; clin. coord. Integrated Health Svcs., Ft. Pierce, Fla., 1994, dir. nursing, 1994-95. Mem. ANA, Fla. Nurses Assn., Order Ea. Star (worthy matron), Sigma Theta Tau. Methodist. Avocations: singing, theater/drama, clowning. Home: 1083 Tallavana Trail Havana FL 32333

WHITEHEAD, MARVIN DELBERT, plant pathologist; b. Paoli, Okla., Dec. 18, 1917; s. Chester Arthur and Lola Elizabeth (Donnell) W.; 1 child, James Mark. BS, Okla. State U., 1939, MS, 1946; PhD (fellow), U. Wis., 1949. Seed analyst Soil Conservation Svc. USDA, Stillwater, Okla., 1936-38; asst. in agronomy Okla. State U., 1939-40; sr. seed analyst Fed. State Seed Lab., Montgomery, Ala., 1940-42; asst. plant pathologist U. Wis., Madison, 1946-48; asst. prof. plant pathology Tex. A&M U., College Station, 1949-55; assoc. prof. U. Mo., Columbia, 1955-60; prof. botany Edinboro State Coll., Pa., 1960-63; prof. plant pathology Ga. So. Coll., Statesboro, Ga., 1963-68; prof. botany and plant pathology Ga. State U., Atlanta, 1968-75; owner, dir. Marvern Plant Health, Inc., Atlanta, 1978—; cons. control of plant diseases. Editor Ga. Jour.. Sci., 1969-75; contbr. 59 articles to rsch. jours. and publs.; developer fungicide Phyton 27 for control of Dutch Elm Disease. With USAAF, 1941-46, PTO. Mem. AAAS, VFW, Am. Phytopathol. Soc., Mycol. Soc. Am., Bot. Soc. Am., Am. Inst. Biol. Scis., Crop Sci. Soc. Am., Am. Soc. Agronomy, Ofcl. Seed Analysts N.Am., Ga. Acad. Sci., Wis. Acad. Sci., Druid Hills Golf Club (Atlanta). Democrat. Home and Office: Apt 5E 2211 Massachusetts Ave Lemon Grove CA 91945-3616

WHITEHEAD, MICHAEL ANTHONY, chemistry educator; b. London, June 30, 1935; emigrated to Can., 1962; s. Francis Henry and Edith Downes (Rotherham) W.; 1 son, Christopher Mark. B.Sc. in Chemistry with honors, Queen Mary Coll., U. London, 1956, Ph.D., 1960, D.Sc., 1974. Asst. lectr. Queen Mary Coll., U. London, 1958-60; postdoctoral fellow U. Cin., 1960, asst. prof., 1961; asst. prof. theoretical chemistry McGill U., Montreal, Que., Can., 1962-66; asso. prof. McGill U., 1966-74, prof., 1974—; vis. prof. U. Cambridge, Eng., 1971-72, U. Oxford, Eng., 1972-74; vis. professorial fellow Univ. Coll. Wales, Aberystwyth, 1980, U. Oxford, 1990-91; invited prof. U. Geneva, 1983-84; life guest prof. Nat. U. Def. Tech., Changsha, People's Republic of China; mem. Internat. Com. on Nuclear Quadrupole Resonance.; co-chmn. 7th Internat. Symposium on Nuclear Quadrapole Resonance, Kingston, Ont., Can., 1983. Research, over 200 publs. in field of quantum chemistry and radio spectroscopy. Fellow Royal Chem. Soc., Chem. Inst. Can., Royal Soc. Arts; mem. Am. Chem. Soc., Am. Phys. Soc., James McGill Soc. (pres. 1993-95), Sigma Xi (pres. McGill chpt. 1971-72, 81-82, 92-95), Phi Lambda Upsilon. Anglican. Office: McGill U Dept Chemistry, 801 Sherbrooke St W, Montreal, PQ Canada H3A 2K6 *My faith in God and belief in Christ.*

WHITEHEAD, RICHARD LEE, insurance company executive; b. Pitts., Feb. 26, 1927; m. Shirley Ann Fritz, Aug. 19, 1950; children: David Lee, Deborah Ann Head. A.B. in Polit. Sci., Otterbein Coll., 1950; student, U. Pa. Law Sch., 1950-52. Claims adjuster Lumberman's Mut. Casualty Ins. Co., Phila., 1951-52; dir. admissions Otterbein Coll., 1952-54; indsl. relations asst. Westinghouse Electric Corp., Pitts., 1954-56; personnel mgr. Home Life Ins. Co., N.Y.C., 1956-63; dir. employee relations, then v.p. personnel and co. relations Berkshire Life Ins. Co., Pittsfield, Mass., 1963-73; sr. v.p., sec. Berkshire Life Ins. Co., 1973-84, exec. v.p., sec., 1984-90, chmn. bd., chief adminstrv. officer, 1990-92, chmn. bd., 1992-95; guest speaker mgmt. edn. seminars. V.p., dir. Action for Opportunity, 1964-66; pres., dir. Berkshire County chpt. United Cerebral Palsy, 1966-67; v.p., bd. dirs. Pittsfield YMCA; bd. dirs., past pres. Pittsfield Urban Coalition; bd. dirs. North Adams Coll. Found.; chmn. Pittsfield Devel. Com., 1976-80, Berkshire Bus. Com. for Arts; trustee Berkshire C.C., 1992—; chmn. bd. trustees Berkshire Med. Ctr., 1992-94. With USAAF, 1945-47. Mem. Eastern Coll. Personnel Officers (hon.), Life Office Mgmt. Assn. (past dir.), Life Ins. Assn. Mass. (past chmn. exec. com.), Central Berkshire C. of C. (chmn. 1986), Silver Bay Assn. (past v.p. fin. devel.), Soc. Preservation and Encouragement Barbershop Quartet Singing Am. Methodist.

WHITEHEAD, ROBERT, theatrical producer; b. Montreal, Can., Mar. 3, 1916; s. William Thomas and Lena Mary (Labatt) S.; m. Zoe Caldwell, 1968. Student, Trinity Coll. Sch., Port Hope, Can. Comml. photographer, 1936-38, actor, 1938-42, producer, 1946—; Dir ANTA Am. Shakespeare Festival. Producer: plays include Medea (Robinson Jeffers), starring Judith Anderson, 1947, Crime and Punishment, starring John Gielgud, 1947, Member of the Wedding (Carson McCullers), 1950 (N.Y. Times Drama Critics Circle award), Waltz of the Toreadors, 1957 (N.Y. Times Drama Critics Circle award), Separate Tables (Terrence Rattigan), 1956-57, A Touch of the Poet (Eugene O'Neill), 1958, The Visit (Friedrich Durrenmatt), 1958 (N.Y. Times Drama Critics Circle award 1958), Much Ado About Nothing (Shakespeare), 1959, A Man for All Seasons (Robert Bolt), 1961-62 (Tony award 1962, N.Y. Times Drama Critics Circle award 1961), The Physicists (Durrenmatt), 1964, The Price (Arthur Miller), 1968, The Prime of Miss Jean Brodie (Jay Presson Allen), 1968, Sheep On The Runway, 1970, Bequest to the Nation, 1970, The Creation of the World and Other Business (Miller), 1972, Finishing Touches, 1973-74, A Matter of Gravity, 1976, A Texas Trilogy, 1976, No Man's Land (Harold Pinter), 1976, The Prince of Grand Street, 1979, Betrayal (Harold Pinter), 1979, Lunch Hour, 1980-81, The West Side Waltz, 1980-81, Death of a Salesman (Miller), 1983-84, The Petition, 1986, The Speed of Darkness, 1991, Park Your Car in Harvard Yard (Israel Horowitz), 1991-92, Broken Glass (Miller), 1994, Master Class (Terrence McNally), 1995; co-producer: Artist Descending a Staircase (Tom Stoppard), 1989; dir. plays: Medea, N.Y.C., 1982, Melbourne, Australia, 1984, Lillian, 1986. Served Am. Field Service AUS, 1942-45. Recipient Sam S. Shubert Found. award, 1973, Edwin Booth award, 1990, United Jewish Appeal/Fedn. Lifetime Achievement award, 1991. Clubs: Century (N.Y.C.), Players (N.Y.C.). Office: 1501 Broadway New York NY 10036

WHITEHEART, SIDNEY WALDO, medical educator. BS in Biology, Emory U., 1983, BA in Chemistry, 1983; PhD of Biol. Chemistry, Johns Hopkins U., 1989. Rsch. biochemist Merck, Sharp, and Dohme Rsch. Labs., West Point, Pa., 1989-90; postdoctoral fellow Princeton (N.J.) U., 1990-91, Sloan-Kettering Inst., 1991-94; asst. prof. biochemistry U. Ky., Lexington, 1994—; lectr. Marine Biology Labs., Woods Hole, Mass, 1994, U. Heidelberg, Germany, 1995, Washington U., St. Louis, 1995. Contbr. articles to profl. jours. Grantee Am. Heart Assn., 1995-98, Am. Cancer Soc., 1995-97. Mem. AAAS, Am. Soc. Cell Biology, Am. Heart Assn. Sci. Coun. Home: 3434 Fleetwood Dr Lexington KY 40502 Office: Univ Ky Coll Medicine 800 Rose St Lexington KY 40536-0084

WHITEHILL, CLIFFORD LANE, lawyer; b. Houston, Apr. 14, 1931; s. Clifford R. and Catalina (Yarza) W.; m. Daisy Mae Woodruff, Apr. 18, 1959; children: Clifford Scott, Alicia Anne, Stephen Lane. BA, Rice U., 1954; LLB, U. Tex., 1957; LLM, Harvard U., 1958. Bar: Tex. 1957, Minn. 1962. Assoc. Childress, Port and Crady, Houston, 1957-59; auditor Haskins and Sells, 1959; asst. gen. counsel Tex. Butadiene and Chem. Co., N.Y.C., 1959-62; with Gen. Mills, Inc., Mpls., 1962-94, gen. counsel, 1975-94, sr. v.p., gen. counsel, 1981—, sec., 1981-94; sr. v.p. gen. counsel, sec. Darden Restaurants, 1995—. Mem. Minn. Minority Corp. Counsel; mem. corp. adv. bd., mem. adv. com. Nat. Chamber Litigation Ctr.; trustee William Mitchell Coll. Law; assoc. bd. dirs. Minn. Opera; bd. dirs. Minn. Uruguay Ptnrs. Am., Nat. Hispanic Scholarship Fund, Fund Legal Aid Soc., Minn. Spl. Olympics, Greater Minn. Coun. Chs. Minn.; chmn. Better Bus. Bur.; chmn. coun. Better Bus. Burs.; mem. exec. com. Ctr. Pub. Resources. Mem. ABA, Minn. Bar Assn., Tex. Bar Assn., Am. Arbitration Assn. (bd. dirs.), Nat. Assn. Mfrs. (bd. dirs., state dir.), UN Assn. U.S., Assn. of Gen. Counsel, Harvard Club, Lafayette Club, Bay Hill Club. Republican. Roman Catholic. Avocations: boating, flying, skiing, tennis. Office: Darden Restaurants Inc PO Box 593330 5900 Lake Ellenor Dr Orlando FL 32809

WHITEHOUSE, ALTON WINSLOW, JR., retired oil company executive; b. Albany, N.Y., Aug. 1, 1927; s. Alton Winslow and Catherine (Lyda) W.; m. Helen MacDonald, Nov. 28, 1953; children: Alton, Sarah, Peter. B.S., U. Va., 1949, LL.B., 1952. Bar: Ohio 1953. Asso. partner firm McAfree, Hanning, Newcomer, Hazlett & Wheeler, Cleve., 1952-68; v.p., gen. counsel Standard Oil Co., Ohio, 1968- 69; sr. v.p. Standard Oil Co., 1969-70, pres., chief operating officer, 1970-77, vice chmn. bd., 1977-78, chmn. bd., chief exec. officer, 1978-86; bd. dirs. Timken Co., Canton, Ohio, McGean-Rohco, Cleve., Cleve.-Cliffs Inc., Orvis, Inc. Trustee Cleve. Clinic Found., Holden Arboretum; mem. Cleve. Mus. Art. Mem. Am. Petroleum Inst. Republican. Episcopalian. *

WHITEHOUSE, DAVID BRYN, museum director; b. Worksop, Nottinghamshire, Eng., Oct. 15, 1941; came to U.S., 1984; s. Brindley Charles and Alice Margaret (Dobson) W.; m. Ruth Delamain Ainger, 1963; children—Sarah, Susan, Peter; m. Elizabeth-Anne Ollemans, 1975; children—Julia, Simon, Nicola. B.A., Cambridge U., 1963, M.A., 1965, Ph.D., 1967. Wainwright fellow Oxford U., Eng., 1966-73; dir. Brit. Inst. Afghan Studies, Kabul, Afghanistan, 1973-74, Brit. Sch., Rome, 1974-84; chief curator Corning Mus. of Glass, N.Y., 1984-87, dep. dir., 1988-92, dir., 1992—; dir. Siraf expdn. Brit. Inst. Persian Studies, Tehran, Iran, 1966-73. Author: (with Ruth Whitehouse) Archaeological Atlas of the World, 1975; (with David Andrews and John Osborne) Aspects of Medieval Lazio, 1982, (with Donald B. Harden and others) Glass of the Caesars, 1987, Glass of the Roman Empire, 1988; (with Richard Hodges) Mohammed, Charlemagne and the Origins of Europe, 1983, Glass: A Pocket Dictionary, 1993, English Cameo Glass, 1994. Contbr. numerous articles and revs. to profl. jours. Fellow Soc. Antiquaries (London), Royal Geog. Soc., Pontificia Accademia Romana di Archeologia; mem. Accademia Fiorentina delle Arti del Disegno, Accademia di Archeologia, Lettere e Belle Arti, Deutsches Archaologisches Inst., Internat. Assn. for the History of Glass (pres. 1991-95). Club: Athenaeum (London). Office: Corning Mus of Glass One Museum Way Corning NY 14830-2253

WHITEHOUSE, DAVID REMPFER, physicist; b. Evanston, Ill., Nov. 13, 1929; s. Horace and Emma (Rempfer) W.; m. Ruth Agnes Walker, June 23, 1956; children—Walker Philip, Laura Lees, Sanford Davis. B.S., Northwestern U., 1952; M.S., M.I.T., 1954, Sc.D., 1958. Assoc. prof. elec. engring. M.I.T., 1958-65; prin. research scientist Raytheon Co., Waltham, Mass., 1965-67; mgr. laser center Raytheon Co., Burlington, Mass., 1967-85; pres. Whitehouse Assocs., Weston, Mass., 1985—; co-founder, dir. Magnion Inc., Burlington, 1960-63; co-founder, chm. bd. DYMED Corp., Marlboro, Mass., 1989-91. Bd. dirs. New Eng. Bapt. Hosp., Boston, 1976—. Fellow Laser Inst. Am. (pres. 1981, bd. dirs. 1977—); mem. IEEE, Am. Inst. Physics. Episcopalian. Patentee in plasma physics, laser engring. Home and Office: 99 South Ave Weston MA 02193-2324

WHITEHOUSE, FRED WAITE, endocrinologist, researcher; b. Chgo., May 6, 1926; s. Fred Trafton Waite and Grace Caroline (Peters) W.; m. Iris Jean Dawson, June 6, 1953; children: Martha, Amy, Sarah. BS, Northwestern U., 1947; MD, U. Ill., Chgo., 1949. Diplomate Am. Bd. Internal Medicine; cert. endocrinology and metabolism. Intern, then resident Henry Ford Hosp., Detroit, 1949-53, staff physician, 1955—, chief div. metabolism, 1962-88; chief div. endocrinology and metabolism Henry Ford Hosp., 1988-95; sr. staff physician, 1995—; fellow Joslin Clinic, Boston, 1954-55; cons. FDA, Washington, 1980—; mem. Coalition on Diabetes Edn. and Minority Health, 1989-91. Contbr. articles to profl. jours. Bd. dirs. Wheat Ridge Found., 1984-93. Lt. USNR, 1951-53. Fellow ACP; mem. NIH (nat. diabetes adv. bd. 1984-88), Am. Diabetes Assn. (pres. 1978-79, Banting medal 1979, Outstanding Clinician award 1989, Outstanding Physician Educators award 1994), Detroit Med. Club (pres. 1976), Detroit Acad. Medicine (pres. 1991-92). Lutheran. Avocations: bicycling, gardening. Home: 1265 Blairmoor Ct Grosse Pointe MI 48236-1230 Office: Henry Ford Hosp 2799 W Grand Blvd Detroit MI 48202-2608

WHITEHOUSE, JOHN HARLAN, JR., systems software consultant, diagnostician; b. Lakewood, Ohio, Sept. 12, 1951; s. John Harlan and Frances Elizabeth (Nation) W.; divorced; 1 child, John Harlan III. BA magma cum laude, Ohio Wesleyan U., 1973; MBA, Cleve. State U., 1976; PhD, Columbia Pacific U., San Rafael, Calif., 1988; postgrad., U. Chgo., 1974. Cert. computing profl.; cert. info. sys. auditor. Programmer San Antonio Express-News, 1977; programming mgr. S.W. Info. Mgmt. Systems, San Antonio, 1977, Utility Data Corp., Houston, 1978; sr. data systems auditor Nat. City Corp., Cleve., 1978-81; sys. programmer Standard Oil Co., Cleve., 1981-84; adv. systems engr. IBM, Cleve., 1984-92; pres. Semiotica Corp., 1992—; mem. exams. editorial coun. Inst. for Cert. Computer Profls., Des Plaines, 1990—. Author: CICS Problem Determination Workshop, 1990; co-author: ICCP Guidelines for Recertification, 1990, ICCP Official Study Guide, 1991-95; also numerous articles, columnist. Mem. Assn. for Computing Machinery (chmn. Greater Cleve. chpt. 1982-83, Svc. Recognition award 1984), Assn. of Inst. for Cert. Computer Profls. (regional dir. 1989-93, nominating com. 1991), Masons, Phillethes Soc., Scottish Rite, Phi Beta Kappa. Unitarian. Home: 22291 Berry Dr Rocky River OH 44116-2013 Office: Semiotica Corp 25935 Detroit Rd Ste 241 Westlake OH 44145-2426

WHITEHOUSE, PHYLLIS JEANNE, public relations executive; b. Chgo., Apr. 10, 1923; d. Philip Bernard II and Emily (Soravia) Stockhausen; m. Walter L. Forward Jr., Feb. 19, 1958 (div. 1963); m. Jack Pendleton Whitehouse, Mar. 6, 1964 (div. Nov. 1984); 1 child, Mark Philip. BS in Chemistry, U. Ill., 1944. Chemist Bell Tel. Labs., Murray Hill, N.J., 1944-46; flight attendant, then with sales dept. Am. Airlines, 1946-62; mem. sales staff, 1980—; pres. Whitehouse Enterprises, L.A. Mem. Internat. Visitors' Program. Mem. Who's Who Internat., Lahaina Yacht Club. Avocations: tennis, bridge, travel, symphony, opera. Home: 424 Kelton Ave Apt 310 Los Angeles CA 90024-2095

WHITEHURST, BROOKS MORRIS, chemical engineer; b. Reading, Pa., Apr. 9, 1930; s. David Brooks and Bessie Ann (Lowry) W.; B.S., Va. Poly. Inst. and State U., 1951; m. Carolyn Sue Boyer, July 4, 1951; children: Garnett, Anita, Robert. Sr. process asst. Am. Enka Corp., Lowland, Tenn., 1951-56; sr. process devel. engr. Va.-Carolina Chem. Corp., Richmond, Va., 1956-63; project engr. Texaco Inc., Richmond, 1963-66; mgr. engring. services Texasgulf, Inc., Aurora, N.C., 1967-80, mgr. spl. projects and long range planning, 1980-81; pres. Whitehurst Assocs., Inc., New Bern, N.C., 1981—; instr., lectr., cons. alternative sources of energy community colls. and univs.; presenter paper Solar World Forum, Brighton, Eng., 1981. Co-chmn. N.C. state supt. task force on secondary edn., 1974—; mem. N.C. Personnel Commn. for Public Sch. Employees; mem. N.C. state adv. com. on trade and indsl. edn., 1971-77; chmn. Gov.'s Task Force Vols. in the Workplace, 1981; chmn. State Adv. Council Career Edn., 1977—; gov.'s liaison for edn. and bus., 1978-79. Registered profl. engr., N.C. Recipient commendation Pres. U.S., 1981. Mem. Am. Inst. Chem. Engrs., Am. Inst. Chemists (dir. 1980-84, cert.), N.C. Inst. Chemists (pres. 1975-77), Nat. Soc. Profl. Engrs., N.C. Soc. Profl. Engrs., Royal Soc. Chemistry. Achievements include patents, and current work on biodegradable chelate systems, muncipal yard waste disposal, micronutrients for agriculture, waste rubber recycling. Home: 1983 Hoods Creek Rd New Bern NC 28562-9103 Office: PO Box 3335 New Bern NC 28564-3335

WHITEHURST, WILLIAM WILFRED, JR., management consultant; b. Balt., Mar. 4, 1937; s. William Wilfred and Elizabeth (Hogg) W.; B.A.,

Princeton, 1958; M.S., Carnegie Inst. Tech., 1963; m. Linda Joan Potter, July 1, 1961; children—Catherine Elizabeth, William Wilfred, III. Mathematician Nat. Security Agy., Fort George G. Meade, Md., 1961-63; mgmt. cons. McKinsey & Co., Inc., Washington, 1963-66; partner L.E. Peabody & Assos., Washington, 1966-69, exec. v.p., dir. L.E. Peabody & Assos., Inc., Lanham, Md., 1969-82, pres., dir., 1983-86, pres. W.W. Whitehurst & Assoc., Inc., Cockeysville, Md., 1986—. Contbr. to Code of Fed. Regulations 49 C.F.R. Sect. 1157. Served to comdr. USNR, 1958-65. Recipient Diploma De Honor 14th Pan Am. Rwy. Congress. Mem. Am. Railway Engring. Assn., Transportation Rsch. Forum, Assn. for Investment Mgmt. and Rsch., Ops. Rsch. Soc. Am., Inst. Mgmt. Scis., Washington Soc. Investment Analysts. Episcopalian. Clubs: University, Princeton (Washington); Princeton (N.J.) Quadrangle. Home and Office: 12421 Happy Hollow Rd Cockeysville Hunt Valley MD 21030-1711

WHITEKER, ROY ARCHIE, retired chemistry educator; b. Long Beach, Calif., Aug. 22, 1927; s. Ewing Harris and Mabel Mary (Williams) W.; m. Jean Fiske MacLean, June 3, 1960; 1 son, Scott MacLean. BS, UCLA, 1950, MS, 1952; PhD, Calif. Inst. Tech., 1956. Instr. chemistry M.I.T., 1955-57; asst. prof. Harvey Mudd Coll., Claremont, Calif., 1957-61; asso. prof. Harvey Mudd Coll., 1961-67, prof. chemistry, 1967-73; assoc. dir. fellowships Nat. Acad. Scis., Washington, 1967-68; dep. exec. sec. Council Internat. Exchange Scholar, Washington, 1971-72; exec. sec. Council Internat. Exchange Scholar, 1972-75; dir. Coun. Internat. Exchange Scholar, 1975-76; prof. chemistry U. Pacific, Stockton, Calif., 1976-92, dean Coll. Pacific, 1976-89. Bd. dirs. Stockton Symphony Assn., 1978-80; dir. cmty. adv. bd. Sta. KUOP, 1981-89; bd. dirs. Stockton Chorale, 1989—; pres. U. of the Pacific Emeriti Soc., 1992-94. With USNR, 1945-46. Recipient Dow Chem. Co. fellowship, 1953-54; DuPont Teaching fellowship, 1954-55; NSF Sci. Faculty fellowship Royal Inst. Tech., Stockholm, Sweden, 1963-64. Mem. Am. Chem. Soc., Alpha Chi Sigma, Phi Beta Kappa, Phi Kappa Phi, Sigma Xi. Home: 3734 Portsmouth Cir N Stockton CA 95219-3843

WHITELAW, JACQUELINE SUSAN, special education educator; b. Mt. Pleasant, Pa., Aug. 22, 1952; d. John Oliver and Cora Catherine (Daniels) Reed; m. Matthew Murray Whitelaw, Aug. 26, 1978; children: Kelly Moreen, Jonathan Murray. BS in Spl. Edn. and Elem. Edn., No. Ill. U., 1974, cert. in mentally impaired, visually impaired, social and emotionally disturbed, learning disabilities, 1987, cert. social/emotionally disturbed, 1994; MS in Elem. Edn., Purdue U., 1980. Cert. elem. edn. grades K-9, spl. edn. grades K-12, visually impaired. Tchr. N.W. Ind. Spl. Edn. Coop., Highland, 1974-75, South Met. Assn. for Low Incidence Handicaps, Flossmoor, Ill., 1975-95; cons. social/emotionally disturbed program Dist. 125, Alsip, Ill., 1994—. Developer/coord. (disability awareness program) Take A Look At Being Differently-Abled, 1986—. Tchr. Christ. Luth. Ch., Hammond, 1980—, ch. choir mem., 1984—, Sunday sch. supt., 1986-92, 94—; den mother, cub master pack 280 Boy Scouts Am., Hammond, 1992—. Mem. Gavit H.S. Band Boosters (hospitality chmn. 1991—), Jefferson Elem. PTA, Gavit Jr./Sr. H.S. PTA. Democrat. Avocations: camping, crafts, sign language, bicycling, cooking. Home: 7027 Baring Ave Hammond IN 46324-2203 Office: SMA Hamlin Upper Grade Ctr Dist 125 1215 S Hamlin Ave Alsip IL 60658-1218

WHITELEY, BENJAMIN ROBERT, insurance company executive; b. Des Moines, July 13, 1929; s. Hiram Everett and Martha Jane (Walker) W.; m. Elaine Marie Yunker, June 14, 1953; children—Stephen Robert, Benjamin Walker. B.S., Oreg. State U., 1951; M.S., U. Mich., 1952; postgrad. advanced mgmt. program, Harvard U. Clk. group dept. Standard Ins. Co., Portland, Oreg., 1956-69, asst. actuary group dept. then asst. actuary acturial dept., 1959-63, asst. v.p., asst. actuary, 1963-64, asst. v.p., assoc. actuary, 1964-70, v.p. group ins. adminstrn., 1970-72, v.p. group ins. div., 1972-80, exec. v.p. group ins., 1980-81, exec. v.p., 1981-83, pres., CEO, 1983-92, chmn. bd. dirs., CEO, 1993-94, chmn. bd. dirs., 1994—; bd. dirs. Gunderson, Inc., Portland, U.S. Bancorp., N.W. Natural Gas Co., Willamette Industries, Inc., Oreg. Natural Gas Devel. Corp., Canor Energy Ltd., The Greenbrier Cos. Past pres. Columbia Pacific coun. Boy Scouts Am.; past chmn. bd., trustee Pacific U., Forest Grove, Oreg.; bd. dirs. U.S. Bank of Oreg. 1st lt. USAF, 1952-55. Recipient Silver Beaver award Cascade Pacific coun. Boy Scouts Am., 1993, Harvey and Emiline Clark medal Pacific U., 1991, Alumni fellow award Oreg. State U., 1991, Aubrey R. Watzek award Lewis and Clark Coll., 1994, Lifetime Achievement award Bus. Youth Exch., Portland, Oreg., 1995. Fellow Soc. Actuaries; mem. Am. Acad. Actuaries (bd. dirs. 1984-86), Am. Council of Life Ins. (bd. dirs. 1986-89), Internat. Congress Actuaries, Portland C. of C. (bd. dirs. 1983-89). Republican. Methodist. Clubs: Arlington, Waverley Country, Multnomah Athletic (Portland, Oreg.). Office: Standard Ins Co PO Box 711 Portland OR 97207-0711

WHITELEY, SANDRA MARIE, librarian, editor; b. May 24, 1943; d. Samuel Smythe and Kathryn Marie (Voigt) Whiteley; m. R. Russell Maylone, Jan. 8, 1977; 1 child, Cybele Elizabeth. BA, Pa. State U., 1963; MLS, Columbia U., 1970; MA, U. Pa., 1975; postgrad., Northwestern U., 1985—. Tchr. Amerikan Kiz Koleji, Izmir, Turkey, 1967-69; reference libr. Yale U., New Haven, Conn., 1970-74; head reference dept. Northwestern U., Evanston, Ill., 1975-80; asst. editor Who's Who in Libr. and Info. ALA, Chgo., 1980-81, editor Reference Books Bull., 1985—; lectr. Grad. Libr. Sch. U. Chgo., 1982-83; assoc. exec. dir. Assn. Coll. and Rsch. Librs., Chgo., 1981-85. Author: Purchasing an Encyclopaedia, 5th edit., 1996, The American Library Association Guide to Information Access, 1994. Mem. ALA (various coms. 1977-81), Beta Phi Mu. Democrat. Congregationalist. Avocations: reading, hiking, travel. Home: 1205 Noyes St Evanston IL 60201-2635 Office: ALA 50 E Huron St Chicago IL 60611-2729

WHITEMAN, DOUGLAS E., publisher; b. Emporia, Kans., Mar. 4, 1961; s. Floyd E. and Phyllis E. (Troyer) W.; m. Susan R. Anderson, Sept. 14, 1985; 1 child, Aaron Anderson Douglas. BS in Bus. Adminstrn., U. Kans., 1983. With Putnam Pub. Group, Denver and N.Y.C., 1983—; dir. trade sales and mktg., internat. sales mgr. Putnam Pub. Group, N.Y.C., 1987-89, v.p. sales and mktg., 1989-94; sr. v.p., pub. Putnam and Grosset Book Group, 1994-95, pres., pub., 1995—. Methodist. Avocations: literature, tennis, golf, fantasy baseball. Office: Putnam Pub Group 200 Madison Ave New York NY 10016-3903

WHITEMAN, H(ORACE) CLIFTON, banker; b. Visalia, Calif., July 23, 1925; s. Horace Clifton and Henrietta Emma (Stewart) W.; m. Shirley Deyo, Nov. 28, 1953 (div. Apr. 1977); children: Susan Elizabeth, Pamela Stewart Ritz, Elizabeth Lyle Braun; m. Joan Coffin Leib, June 6, 1977. BA, Dartmouth Coll., 1950, MBA, 1951. V.p. Morgan Guaranty Trust Co., N.Y.C., 1951-68; sr. v.p., chief fin. officer Investors Diversified Services, Inc., Mpls., 1968-76; pres., trustee The Bowery Savs. Bank, N.Y.C., 1976-78; sr. v.p. The Irving Trust Co., N.Y.C., 1978-82; exec. v.p. The Bank of Tokyo Trust Co., N.Y.C., 1982-89; sr. dep. gen. mgr. The Bank of Tokyo, Ltd., N.Y.C., 1984-89; cons. The Bank of Tokyo Group, N.Y.C., 1989-92; bd. dirs. York Rsch. Corp., Keene Corp. Mem. Down Town Club (N.Y.C.), Piping Rock Club (Locust Valley, N.Y.). Repubican. Presbyterian. Home: 136 E 64th St New York NY 10021-7360 Office: 280 Park Ave New York NY 10017

WHITEMAN, JOHN O., rental company executive; s. Jack W. W. BA, Ariz. State U., 1962. With Empire Southwest Co., Mesa, Ariz., 1960—, officer, 1970—, exec. v.p., 1982—, also chmn. bd., pres. Empire Machinery Divsn., 1984—, now chmn, ceo. Office: Empire Southwest Co 1725 S Country Club Dr Mesa AZ 85210-6003*

WHITEMAN, JOSEPH DAVID, lawyer, manufacturing company executive; b. Sioux Falls, S.D., Sept. 12, 1933; s. Samuel D. and Margaret (Wallace) W.; m. Mary Kelly, Dec. 29, 1962; children: Anne Margaret, Mary Ellen, Joseph David, Sarah Kelly, Jane. B.A., U. Mich., 1955, J.D., 1960. Bar: D.C. 1960, Ohio 1976. Assoc. Cox, Langford, Stoddard & Cutler, Washington, 1959-64; sec., gen. counsel Studebaker group Studebaker Worthington, Inc., N.Y.C., 1964-71; asst. gen. counsel. United Telecommunications, Inc., Kansas City, Mo., 1971-74; v.p., gen. counsel, sec. Weatherhead Co., Cleve., 1974-77, Parker Hannifin Corp., Cleve., 1977—. Chmn. bd. dirs. St. Lukes Med. Ctr.; bd. dirs. Judson Retirement Community. Served as lt. USNR, 1955-57. Mem. ABA, Beta Theta Pi, Phi Delta Phi. Republican. Roman Catholic. Home: 23349 Shaker Blvd Cleveland OH 44122-2670 Office: Parker Hannifin Corp 17325 Euclid Ave Cleveland OH 44112-1209

WHITEMAN, RICHARD FRANK, architect; b. Mankato, Minn., Mar. 24, 1925; s. Lester Raymond and Mary Grace (Dawald) W.; m. Jean Frances Waite, June 20, 1948 (dec. May 1980); children: David, Sarah, Lynn, Ann, Carol, Frank, Marie, Steven; m. Mavis Patricia Knutsen, May 30, 1982. BArch, U. Minn., 1945; MArch, Harvard U., 1948. Registered architect, Minn. Designer Ellerbe Co., St. Paul, Minn., 1946; architect Thorshov and Cerny, Mpls., 1948-53; ptnr. Jyring and Whiteman, Hibbing, Minn., 1953-62; pres. AJWM Inc., Hibbing and Duluth, Minn., 1963-72, Architects Four, Duluth, 1972-83; owner Richard Whiteman, Duluth, 1983-95; sr. architect U. Minn., Duluth, 1993—; chmn. Architect Sect. Registration Bd., Minn., 1972-80. Prin. works include Washington Sch., Hibbing, 1957 (Minn. Soc. Architects Design award 1957), Whiteman Summer Home, Pengilly, Minn. (Minn. Soc. Architects Design award 1959), Bemidji State Coll. Phys. Edn. Bldg. (Minn. Soc. Architects Design award 1960), Whiteman Residence, Griggs Hall UMD, 1990. Pres. U. for Srs., 1993-94; bd. govs. St. Louis County Hist. Soc.; mem. adv. com. Glensheen, U. Minn. Duluth. With USN, 1943-46, PTO. Mem. Minn. Soc. Architects (pres. 1972), Northeast Minn. Architects (pres. 1962), Service Corps Retired Execs. (chmn. Northeast Minn. chpt. 1986), Minn. Designer Selection Bd. (chmn. 1990). Democrat. Roman Catholic. Club: Kitchi Gammi (Duluth). Lodge: Kiwanis. Avocations: photography, fishing, cross-country skiing, travel. Home: 3500 E 3rd St Duluth MN 55804-1812

WHITENER, WILLIAM GARNETT, dancer, choreographer; b. Seattle, Aug. 17, 1951; s. Warren G. and Virginia Louise (Garnett) W. Student, Cornish Sch. Allied Arts, Seattle, 1958-69. Dancer N.Y.C. Opera, 1969, Joffrey Ballet, N.Y.C., 1969-77, Twyla Tharp Dance, N.Y.C., 1978-87; asst. to choreographer Jerome Robbins for Robbins' Broadway, N.Y.C., 1988; artistic dir. Les Ballets Jazz de Montréal, 1991-93, Royal Winnipeg Ballet, 1993-95, State Ballet of Mo., 1996—; coord. dance dept. Concord Acad., Mass., 1988; vis. artist U. Wash., 1989-91; tchr. Harvard U. Summer Dance, 1989-90, NYU, 1985. Appeared in original Broadway cast Dancin', 1978; choreographer for Princeton Ballet, Joffrey II, John Curry Ice Theatre, Ballet Hispanico of N.Y., Boston Ballet Internat. Choreography Competition, Tommy Tune, Martine Van Hamel/Kevin McKenzie, Ann Reinking, Seattle Repertory Theatre, Am. Ballroom Theater, N.Y.C., Hartford (Conn.) Ballet, On the Boards, (with Bill Irwin) Alive From Off Center (PBS-TV), (opera ensemble of N.Y.) A Little Night Music, Pacific Northwest Ballet, (Seattle Opera) Rusalka, Aida; dancer (films) Amadeus, Zelig, (TV shows) The Catherine Wheel, Dance in America; performer Garden of Earthly Delights, 1988. Mem. Actor's Equity, Am. Guild Mus. Artists. Home: 484 W 43rd St Apt 44D New York NY 10036-6327 Office: State Ballet of Missouri 706 W 42nd St Kansas City MO 64111

WHITESELL, DALE EDWARD, retired association executive, natural resources consultant; b. Miamisburg, Ohio, Oct. 12, 1925; s. Harry Parker and Carmen Lucille (Holtzman) W.; m. Alma Irene Wells, Mar. 24, 1945; children: Catherine Elizabeth, Kimberly Lynn. B.S., Ohio State U., 1950, M.S. in Wildlife Mgmt., 1951. Game mgmt. supr. Ohio Div. Wildlife, Xenia, 1951-63, author farmer attitude survey, 1951-58; chief Ohio Div. Wildlife, Columbus, 1963-65; sr. exec. v.p. Ducks Unltd., Inc., Long Grove, Ill., 1965-87; ret. Ducks Unltd., Inc., 1987; bd. dirs. Safari Club Internat. Conservation Found., Tucson, 1982-83. Served as 2d lt. USAAF, 1943-46. Fellow Ohio State U., 1950; recipient Conservation award Gulf Oil Co., 1985. Mem. Ohio Wildlife Mgmt. Assn. (pres.), Internat. Assn. Fish, Game and Conservation Commrs. Office: Ducks Unltd Inc 1 Waterfowl Way Memphis TN 38120-2350 *Natural resource conservation means wise use—anything more or less will be manifested in additional zoos, museums, junk yards and the bone yards of fertilizer plants.*

WHITESELL, JOHN EDWIN, motion picture company executive; b. DuBois, Pa., Feb. 23, 1938; s. Guy Roosevelt and Grace Ethlyn (Brisbin) W.; m. Amy H. Jacobs, June 12, 1960; 1 child, Scott Howard; m. Martha Kathlyn Hall, Sept. 3, 1975; m. Phyllis Doyle, May 8, 1993. B.A., Pa. State U., 1962. Asst. mgr. non-theatrical div. Columbia Pictures Corp., N.Y.C., 1963-66; with Warner Bros., Inc., 1966—; nat. sales mgr. non-theatrical div. Warner Bros., Inc., Burbank, Calif., 1968-75; v.p. Warner Bros., Inc., 1975-76; v.p. internat. sales and adminstrn. Warner Bros. Internat. TV Distbn., 1976—; bd. dirs. Mastermedia Internat. Inc.; past bd. dirs. Found. Entertainment Programming in Higher Edn.; mem. self-study com. Nat. Entertainment Conf., 1974-75. Served with USNR, 1956-58. Recipient Outstanding Alumnus award Pa. State U. DuBois Campus, 1995, Founders award Nat. Entertainment Conf., 1975. Mem. Nat. Audio-Visual Assn. (motion picture coun. 1973-76, exec. com. film coun. 1969-76, ednl. materials producers coun. 1970-76), Acad. TV Arts and Scis., Nat. Assn. Media Educators (adv. com. 1973-76).

WHITESIDE, CAROL GORDON, state official, former mayor; b. Chgo., Dec. 15, 1942; d. Paul George and Helen Louise (Barre) G.; m. John Gregory Whiteside, Aug. 15, 1964; children: Brian Paul, Derek James. BA, U. Calif., Davis, 1964. Pers. mgr. Emporium Capwell Co., Santa Rosa, 1964-67; pers. asst. Levi Strauss & Co., San Francisco, 1967-69; project leader Interdatum, San Francisco, 1983-88; with City Coun. Modesto, 1983-87; mayor City of Modesto, 1987-91; asst. sec. for intergovtl. rels. The Resources Agy., State of Calif., Sacramento, 1991-93; dir. intergovtl. affairs Gov.'s Office, Sacramento, 1993—. Trustee Modesto City Schs., 1979-83; nat. pres. Rep. Mayors and Local Ofcls., 1990. Named Outstanding Woman of Yr. Women's Commn., Stanislaus County, Calif., 1988, Woman of Yr., 27th Assembly Dist., 1991. Republican. Lutheran. Office: Governor's Office 1400 10th St Sacramento CA 95814-5502

WHITESIDE, LOWELL STANLEY, seismologist; b. Trinidad, Colo., Jan. 7, 1946; s. Paul Edward and Carrie Belle (Burgess) W. BS, Hamline U., 1968; postgrad., Oswego State U. of N.Y., 1970-72; MS, U. Nebr., 1985; postgrad., Ga. Inst. of Tech., 1986-88, U. Colo., 1990-94. Instr. U.S. Peace Corps, Mhlume, Swaziland, 1968-71; rsch. assoc. CIRES, U. Colo., Boulder, 1988-90; geophysicist in charge of internat. earthquake data base NOAA, Nat. Geophys. Data Ctr., Boulder, 1990—. Scoutmaster Boy Scouts Am., St. Paul, Lincoln, Nebr., 1968-80, camp counselor, 1968-76. Recipient Eagle Scout award Boy Scouts Am., 1968, NGDC/DOAA Customer Svc. award, 1995. Mem. AAAS (chmn. 1986-87, vice chmn. 1985-86, Geology-Geography, Rocky Mountain sect., Outstanding Articles Referee 1992, Best Student Paper award 1984, 85), Seismol. Soc. of Am., Am. Geophys. Union, Sierra Club, Planetary Soc. Presbyterian. Avocations: hiking, camping, music, biking, running. Home: PO Box 3141 Eldorado Springs CO 80025-3141 Office: NOAA/NGDC/NESOIS 325 Broadway St Boulder CO 80303-3337

WHITESIDE, WILLIAM ANTHONY, JR., lawyer; b. Phila. Feb. 23, 1929; s. William Anthony and Ellen T. (Hensler) W.; m. Eileen Ann Ferrick, Feb. 27, 1954; children: William Anthony III, Michael P., Eileen A., Richard F., Christopher J., Mary P. BS Notre Dame U., 1951; LLB U. Pa., 1954. Bar: Pa. 1955. Assoc. Speiser, Satinsky, Gilliland & Packel, Phila., 1956-58, ptnr., 1958-61; ptnr. Fox, Rothschild, O'Brien & Frankel, Phila., 1961—. Served to 1st lt. USAF, 1954-56; chmn. bd. of trustees & chmn. exec. comm., Rochester Inst. Tech.; mem. pres. adv. coun. U. Notre Dame; bd. dirs. PAL, mem. exec. com.; emeritus trustee Germantown Acad (past pres.). Named Man of Yr., Notre Dame Club Phila., 1967. Mem. ABA, Pa. Bar Assn., Phila. Bar Assn., mem. Genesee Valley Club, Rochester, N.Y., Union League Club, Pyramid Club, Wissahickon Skating Club, Pa. Soc. (Phila.), Atlantic City (N.J.) Country Club. Republican. Roman Catholic. Home: 7808 Cobden Rd Laverock PA 19038 also: 901 Gardens Plz Ocean City NJ 08226-4719 Office: Fox Rothschild O'Brien 2000 Market St Fl 10 Philadelphia PA 19103-3231

WHITESIDES, GEORGE MCCLELLAND, chemistry educator; b. Louisville, Kty., Aug. 3, 1939; m. Barbara Breasted; children: George Thomas, Benjamin Haile. AB, Harvard U., 1960; PhD, Calif. Inst. Tech., 1964. Asst. prof. dept. chemistry MIT, Cambridge, 1963-69, assoc. prof., 1969-71, prof., 1971-75, Arthur C. Cope prof., 1975-80, Haslam and Dewey prof., 1980-82; prof. dept. chemistry Harvard U., Cambridge, 1982-86, Mallinckrodt prof., 1986—. Recipient Pure Chemistry award Am. Chem. Soc., 1975, Harrison Howe award Rochester sect., 1979, Arthur C. Cope award, 1995, James Flack Norris award, 1994, Remsen award, 1983, Arthur C. Cope scholar award, 1989, Disting. Alumni award Calif. Inst. Tech., 1980; Alfred P. Sloan fellow, 1968. Fellow AAAS; mem. NAS, Am. Acad. Arts and Scis. Office: Harvard U Dept of Chemistry 12 Oxford St Cambridge MA 02138-2902

WHITE-THOMSON, IAN LEONARD, mining company executive; b. Halstead, Eng., May 3, 1936; came to U.S., 1969; s. Walter Norman and Leonore (Turney) W-T.; m. Barbara Montgomery, Nov. 24, 1971. B.A. with 1st class honors, New Coll., Oxford U., 1960, M.A., 1969. Mgmt. trainee Borax Consol. Ltd., London, 1960-61; asst. to sales mgr. Borax Consol. Ltd., 1961-64, asst. to sales dir., 1964; comml. dir. Hardman & Holden Ltd., Manchester, Eng., 1965-67; joint mng. dir. Hardman & Holden Ltd., 1967-69; v.p. mktg. dept. U.S. Borax Inc., Los Angeles, 1969-73; exec. v.p. mktg. U.S. Borax Inc., 1973-88, pres., 1988—, also dir.; group exec. Pa. Glass Sand Corp., Ottawa Silica Co., U.S. Silica Co., 1985-87; bd. dirs. Canpotex Ltd., chmn. bd., 1974-76; bd. dirs. KCET. Served with Brit. Army, 1954-56. Mem. Can. POtash Prodrs. Assn. (v.p. 1976-77, dir. 1972-77), Chem. Industry Coun. of Calif. (bd. dirs. 1982-85, chmn. 1984), Am. Mining Congress (bd. dirs. 1989), RTZ Borax and Minerals (bd. dirs. 1992, chief exec. 1995—), Oryx Energy Co. (bd. dirs. 1993), Calif. Club. Home: 851 Lyndon St South Pasadena CA 91030-3712

WHITE-VOLK, ELLEN, mathematics educator; 1 child. BS in Home Econs., Stephen F. Austin State U., 1979, MEd in Early Childhood Edn., 1984; postgrad., U. Colo., 1989, U. wis., 1990, U. Tex., San Antonio, 1992. Tchr. Tanglewood Early Learning Ctr., 1980-84, Houston Ind. Sch. Dist., 1984-85, Natalia Ind. Sch. Dist., 1985-86, Harlandale Ind. Sch. Dist., 1986-95; dir. Jefferson Meth Learning Ctr., San Antonio, 1995—; presenter workshops in field. Vol. Am. Heart Assn.; mem. San Antonio Zool. Soc.; mem. nurture com. Jefferson United Meth. Ch.; bd. dirs. San Antonio Recycling Ctr. Recipient Pres.'s award for excellence in elem. sci. tchg., 1993. Mem. Nat. Assn. for Edn. of Young Children, Nat. Coun. Tchrs. Math., Nat. Sci. Tchrs. Assn., Soc. Elem. Presdl. Awardees, Kindergarten Tchrs. of Tex., Tex. Coun. Elem. Sci. Tchrs., Assn. Tex. Profl. Educators. Avocations: reading, nature walks, stitchery, traveling, storytelling. Office: Jefferson Meth Learning Ctr 758 Donaldson Ave San Antonio TX 78201

WHITE-WARE, GRACE ELIZABETH, secondary education educator; b. St. Louis, Oct. 5, 1921; d. James Eathel, Sr. and Madree (Penn) White; divorced; 1 son, James Otis Ware II (Oloye Kunle Adeyemon). BA in Edn., H.B. Stowe Tchrs. Coll., 1943. Mgr. advt. Superior Press, St. Louis, 1935-39; tri-owner, v.p. Carolina Oil Co., St. Louis, 1938-42; with pub. relations Triangle Press, St. Louis, 1939-47, sales promotion, 1939-47; account supr. overtime payroll Bell Tel. Labs., Inc., N.Y.C., 1943-46; tchr. Dunbar Elem. Sch., St. Louis, 1946-47, Garfield Elem. Sch., Chgo., 1948-49, Betsy Ross Elem. Sch., Chgo., 1950-51, Lincoln Sch., Richmond, Mo., 1951, Dunbar Sch., Kinlock, Mo., 1952, Gladstone Elem. Sch., Cleve., 1954-61, Quincy Elem. Sch., Cleve., 1961-78, W.H. Brett Elem. Sch., Euclid Park, Cleve., 1979-82; head tchr. Head Start program, 1965; adult edn. tchr. Cleve. Bd. Edn., 1965-82; program dir. Tutoring and Nutrition Project, Delta Sigma Theta, 1982-87; tchr. TV Tonight Sch., lessons for adults, Cleve., 1972; tri-owner, v.p., social editor Style mag., St. Louis, 1947-49; owner/mgr. Wentworth Record Distbrs., Chgo., 1947-51; supr. accounts receivable div. Spiegel, Inc., Chgo., 1947-52; radio panelist Calling All Americans, Cleve., 1957-58; sec. bd. dirs. Hough Pub. Co., also Hough Area Devel. Corp., Cleve., 1968-69. Mem. child devel. parent bd. Greater Cleve. Neighborhood Centers Assn.; mem. fund raising com. Food First Program, co-chmn. woman's aux. Black Econ. Union, Cleve.; vice chmn. Cleve. com. Youth for Understanding Teenage Program; mem. Cleve. Council Human Relations; mem. Cleve. chpt. CORE; charter mem., fin. sec. Tots and Teens, Inc.; treas. Jr. Women's Civic League; mem. Cleve. bd. Afro-Am. Cultural and Hist. Soc.; women's aux. bd. Talbert Clinic and Day Care Center, Cleve.; adv. bd. Langston Hughes Library; mem. Forest City Hosp. Aux. Bd., also Women's Aux. Com. Forest City Hosp.; scholarship com. Women's Allied Arts Assn. Greater Cleve., 1972-74; mem. spl. com. Lake Erie council Girl Scouts U.S.A., 1982-84; co-coordinator Cuyahoga County Child Watch Project, 1982-83. Named Most Outstanding Vol. of Year, N.Y. Fedn. Settlements, 1944, Leading Tchr. of Community, Cleve. Call and Post, weekly newspaper, 1958; recipient Martha Holden Jennings scholar award Martha Holden Jennings Found., Cleve., 1966-67, Spl. Outstanding Tchrs. award, 1973; Outstanding Service award Black Econ. Union, 1970; Cert. of Appreciation, City of Cleve., 1973; Ednl. Service to Community award Urban League, 1986 Mem. Ohio, Cleve. edn. assns., Nat. Assn. Public Sch. Adult Edn., Nat. Assn. Minority Polit. women (treas. 1985-87), NAACP, Phillis Wheatley Assn., Moreland Community Assn., Nat. Council Negro Women, Top Ladies of Distinction (pres. Cleve. 1980-82), Nat. Assn. Univ. Women, Phi Delta Kappa (1st v.p. Cleve. 1971-73, Outstanding Achievement award 1975), Delta Sigma Theta (pres. Cleve. 1969-73), Delta Kappa Gamma, Eta Phi Beta (chpt. treas. 1975-77, regional treas. 1980-84, nat. treas. 1984-88). Democrat. Clubs: Novelette Bridge (pres. Cleve. 1973-77), Arewa Du-Du Bridge (treas. 1980-91), Hooked on Bridge (pres. 1994—). Lodge: Kiwanis Internat. Home: 14701 Milverton Rd Cleveland OH 44120-4227

WHITFIELD, EDWARD (WAYNE WHITFIELD), congressman; b. Hopkinsville, Ky., May 25, 1943; m. Constance Harriman; 1 child, Kate. BS in Bus., U. Ky., 1965, JD, 1969. Mem. Ky. Ho. of Reps., 1973-74; pvt. practice law, 1973-79; govt. affairs counsel Seaboard Sys. R.R. subs. CSX Corp., 1979-82, counsel to pres., 1982-85; v.p. state rels. CSX Corp., 1986-88, v.p. fed. r.r. affairs, 1988-91; legal counsel to chmn. Interstate Commerce Commn., 1991-93; mem. 104th Congress from 1st Ky. dist., 1995—. 1st lt. USAR. Republican. Office: US Ho of Reps 1541 Longworth HOB Washington DC 20515

WHITFIELD, PRINCESS D., principal. Prin. Lemon G. Hine Jr. High Sch., Washington. Recipient Blue Ribbon award U.S. Dept. Edn., 1990-91. Office: Lemon G Hine Jr High Sch 8th And Pennsylvania Ave SE Washington DC 20003

WHITFORD, DENNIS JAMES, naval officer, meteorologist, oceanographer; b. York, Pa., Nov. 21, 1950; s. Richmond Ordway and Kathryn (Semantic) W.; m. Dorothy Lee Bundy, Aug. 7, 1976; children: Scott, Bradley. BS, U.S. Naval Acad., 1972; MS, Naval Postgrad. Sch., 1979, PhD, 1988. Commd. ensign USN, 1972, advanced through grades to capt., 1994; officer-in-chg., staff oceanographer Naval Oceanography CMD Detachment, Moffett Field, Calif., 1982-84; comdg. officer Oceanographic unit Four Aboard USNS Chauvenet, 1985; dir. numerical models dept. Fleet Numerical Oceanography Ctr., Monterey, Calif., 1988-89; comdg. officer Naval Oceanography Command Facility, San Diego, 1989-91; dir. Operational Oceanography Ctr., Stennis Space Ctr., Miss., 1991-93; exec. officer Naval Oceanographic Office, Stennis Space Ctr., Miss., 1993-95; chmn. dept. oceanography U.S. Naval Acad., Annapolis, Md., 1995—; Contbr. articles to profl. jours. Named to Outstanding Young Men of Am., 1982; Adam Burke PhD fellow, 1972. Mem. Am. Geophys. Union, Sigma Xi. Office: US Naval Academy 572 Holloway Rd Annapolis MD 21402

WHITHAM, GERALD BERESFORD, mathematics educator; b. Halifax, Eng., Dec. 13, 1927; came to U.S., 1956; s. Harry and Elizabeth (Howarth) W.; m. Nancy Lord, Sept. 1, 1951; children—Ruth H., Michael G., Susan C. BS, Manchester U., Eng., 1948, MS, 1949, PhD, 1953. Lectr. Manchester U., 1953-56; assoc. prof. NYU, N.Y.C., 1956-59; prof. math. MIT, Cambridge, 1959-62; prof. aeros. and math. Calif. Inst. Tech., Pasadena, 1962-67, prof. applied math., 1967-83, Charles Lee Powell prof. applied math., 1983—. Author: Linear and Nonlinear Waves, 1974; also research papers on applied math. and fluid dynamics. Recipient Wiener prize in applied math., 1980. Fellow Royal Soc., Am. Acad. Arts and Scis. Home: 1689 E Altadena Dr Altadena CA 91001-1855 Office: Calif Inst Tech Applied Math 217-50 Pasadena CA 91125

WHITHAM, KENNETH, science and technology consultant; b. Chesterfield, Derbyshire, Eng., Nov. 6, 1927; emigrated to Can., 1948; s. Joseph and Evelyn (Murphy) W.; m. Joan Dorothy Glasspool, Nov., 1953; children—Melanie Judith, Katherine Hilary, Stephanie Frances. B.A. with honors, Cambridge U., Eng., 1948, M.A., 1952; M.A., Toronto U., 1949, Ph.D., 1951. Research scientist Dominion Observatory, Ottawa, Ont., 1951-59, 60-64; mem. UN Tech. Assistance Adminstrn., Nairobi, Kenya, 1959-60;

dir. div. seismology and geothermal studies Earth Physics Br., Dept. Energy, Mines and Resources, Ottawa, 1964-73, dir. gen., 1973-80, asst. dep. minister conservation and non-petroleum energy, 1980-81, asst. dep. minister research and tech., 1981-87, chief sci. advisor, 1987; cons. in sci. and tech. Ottawa, 1987—. Contbr. articles to profl. jours. Recipient Outstanding Achievement award Public Service of Can., 1970. Fellow Royal Soc. Can. Anglican. Home and Office: 1367 Morley Blvd, Ottawa, ON Canada K2C 1R4

WHITING, ALBERT NATHANIEL, former university chancellor; b. Jersey City, July 3, 1917; s. Hezekiah Oliver and Hildegarde Freida (Lyons) W.; m. Charlotte Luck, June 10, 1950; 1 dau., Brooke Elizabeth. A.B., Amherst Coll., 1938; student, Columbia, summer 1938, U. Pitts., 1938-39; M.A. in Sociology, Fisk U., 1941, L.H.D. (hon.), 1980; Ph.D. in Sociology, Am. U., 1952; LL.D., Amherst Coll., 1968, Western Mich. U., 1974, Duke, 1974, Kyung Hee U., Seoul, Korea; L.H.D., N.C. Central U., 1983. Research and teaching asst. Fisk U., 1939-41; instr. sociology, dir. rural community study Bennett Coll., Greensboro, N.C., 1941-43, 46-47; asst. prof. sociology Atlanta U., 1948-53; dean coll., prof. sociology Morris Brown Coll., Atlanta, 1953-57; asst. dean coll. Morgan State Coll., Balt., 1957-59; dean of college Morgan State Coll., 1960-67; pres. N.C. Central U., Durham, 1967-72; chancellor N.C. Central U., 1972-83; mem. bd. regents U. Md. Sys., 1988-95. Contbr. articles profl. jours. Bd. dirs. Am. Coun. Edn., Ednl. Testing Svc.; bd. dirs., past pres. Assn. State Colls. and Univs.; v.p. Internat. Assn. Univ. Pres.; bd. dirs. Research Triangle (N.C.) Inst.; mem. Md. Higher Edn. Commn., 1995—. 1st lt. AUS, 1943-46. Episcopalian. Home: 11253B Slalom Ln Columbia MD 21044-2810

WHITING, ALLEN SUESS, political science educator, writer, consultant; b. Perth Amboy, N.J., Oct. 27, 1926; s. Leo Robert and Viola Allen (Suess) W.; m. Alice Marie Conroy, May 29, 1950; children: Deborah Jean, David Neal, Jeffrey Michael, Jennifer Hollister. B.A., Cornell U., 1948; M.A., Columbia U., 1950, cert. Russian Inst., 1950, Ph.D., 1952. Instr. polit. sci. Northwestern U., 1951-53; asst. prof. Mich. State U., East Lansing, 1955-57; social scientist The Rand Corp., Santa Monica, Calif., 1957-61; dir. Office Research and Analysis Far East U.S. Dept. State, Washington, 1962-66; dep. consul gen. Am. Consulate Gen., Hong Kong, 1966-68; prof. polit. sci. U. Mich., Ann Arbor, 1968-82; prof. U. Ariz., Tucson, 1982-93, Regents prof., 1993—, dir. Ctr. for East Asian Studies, 1982-93; cons. U.S. Dept. State, 1968-88; dir. Nat. Com. on U.S.-China Relations, N.Y.C., 1977-94; assoc. The China Council, 1978-88; pres. So. Ariz. China Coun., Tucson, 1983-95; fellow Woodrow Wilson Ctr., Washington, 1995-96. Author: Soviet Policies in China: 1917-1924, 1954, China Crosses the Yalu, 1968, Chinese Calculus of Deterrence, 1975, Siberian Development and East Asia, 1981, China Eyes Japan, 1989, others; contbr. articles to profl. jours.; spl. commentator McNeill-Lehrer Program; CBS and NBC Spls. on China. Served with U.S. Army, 1945. Social Sci. Rsch. Coun. fellow, 1950, 74-75; Ford Found. fellow, 1953-55; Rockefeller Found. fellow, 1978; Woodrow Wilson Ctr. fellow, 1995—. Mem. Assn. Asian Studies. Home: 125 E Canyon View Dr Tucson AZ 85704-5901 Office: U Ariz Dept Polit Sci Tucson AZ 85721

WHITING, GAYLORD PETER, communications executive; b. Aug. 2, 1950. CPA, Ill., Calif., Colo. Contr. Boulder (Colo.) Daily Camera, 1974-78, bus. mgr., 1978, v.p., gen. mgr., 1979; asst. to pres. Detroit Free Press, 1981-82, v.p. advt., 1982-84, reporter, editor, 1984-86; sr. v.p. fin. Dallas Times Herald, 1986-87; exec. v.p., chief fin. officer Media News Group, Dallas, 1987-88; v.p. fin. and systems Houston Post, 1988-90, sr. v.p. fin. and ops., 1990—. Mem. Am. Inst. CPA's.

WHITING, HENRY H., state supreme court justice. LLB, Univ. Va., 1949. Former judge 26th Jud. Cir. of Va.; sr. justice Va. Supreme Ct., Richmond, 1987—. Office: Va Supreme Ct Judicial Ctr 5 N Kent St Winchester VA 22601-5037*

WHITING, HUGH RICHARD, lawyer; b. East Chicago, Ind., Dec. 8, 1945; s. Harold C. and Nina (Hofstetter) W.; m. Sherry Ballast, July 2, 1965; 1 child, Kristin Anne. BA, U. Mich., 1967; JD, Ohio State U., 1974. Bar: Ohio 1974, Tex. 1981. Salesman, adminstr. Procter & Gamble, Cin., 1967-71; law clk. to Judge George Edwards U.S. Ct. Appeals (6th cir.) Ohio, Cin., 1974-75; assoc. Jones, Day, Reavis & Pogue, Cleve., 1975-81, ptnr., 1982—; chmn. Firmwide Profl. Svcs. Com.; mem. civil justice reform act adv. com. No. Dist. Ohio Adv. Com., Cleve., 1990—; mem. Ohio State U. Coll. Law Nat. Coun., Columbus, 1984—; speaker, presenter on legal practice and practice mgmt. various confs. and seminars. Co-chmn. Gen. Bus. Campaign Cleve. Orch., 1992. Mem. ABA (litigation sect., sect. bus. law), Tex. Bar Assn., Cleve. Bar Assn., Mayfield Country Club, Order of Coif. Avocations: golf, travel, reading. Office: Jones Day Reavis & Pogue 901 Lakeside Ave E Cleveland OH 44114-1116*

WHITING, JOHN RANDOLPH, publisher, writer, editor; b. N.Y.C., Apr. 22, 1914; s. John Clapp and Elizabeth Margaret (Zittel) W.; m. Helen Louise Gamertsfelder, June 3, 1937; children: Wendy Helen Whiting Livingston, Merry Natalie Whiting Coleman, Robin Elizabeth Whiting Uhr. AB in Journalism, Ohio U., 1936. Reporter newspapers Ohio and N.Y. State, 1935-36; assoc. editor Lit. Digest, 1936-37, True mag., 1937-38; free-lance writer for mags., 1938-40; mng. editor Click mag., 1940-41, Popular Photography mag., 1942-46; editor Sci. Illustrated mag., 1947-49; pub., editor Flower Grower mag., 1949-60; exec. v.p. Popular Sci. Pub. Co., 1961-66; pres. Communigraphics Cons., 1966-67; pub. Motor Boating and Sailing Mag., Hearst Mag. div., 1967-75, editor and pub. motor boating and sailing books, 1975-79; pub., editor Hearst Marine Books, 1979-81, cons. editor, 1981—; dir. Hastings Fed. Savs. & Loan Assn.; lectr. Colonial Williamsburg, univs., corps. and assns. on photo-journalism, illustrative photography. Author: Photography is a Language, 1946, You Can Sail, 1981, On Deck, 1985; editor and co-author books on photography, boating, picture books various subjects; contbr. to mags. on photography, scis. Trustee Community Hosp. Dobbs Ferry, N.Y. Recipient Editors' award Am. Seed Trade Assn., 1960. Mem. AAAS, Boating Writers Internat. (pres. 1973-79), Nat. Assn. Sci. Writers, Garden Writers Assn. (past pres.), Photog. Soc. Am., Phi Delta Theta, Sigma Delta Chi, Kappa Alpha Mu. Presbyterian. Clubs: N.Y. Yacht (N.Y.C.), Overseas Press (N.Y.C.); Cliffdwellers (Chgo.). Home: 44 Shady Ln Dobbs Ferry NY 10522-2019 *The computer, especially the word processor, is making "creativity" out of a technical tool—just as the camera did a century ago. The writer is freed from most of the dull copying work, just as the photographer was able to concentrate on seeing.*

WHITING, MARTHA COUNTEE, retired secondary education educator; b. Marshall, Tex., Mar. 24, 1912; s; d. Thomas and Mannie Selena (Yates) Countee; m. Samuel Whiting, June 8, 1937; children: Jacqueline Bostic, Sammie Ellis, Nan Broussard, Tommye Casey, Martha Goddard. BA in Sci., Bishop Coll., 1934; M of Secondary Edn., Tex. So. U., 1959; postgrad., U. Colo., 1963. Tchr., sci., math. Houston Ind. Sch. Dist., 1942-73; researcher, local history Houston, 1973—; lectr. in field. Mem. exec. com. Harris County Heritage Soc., Houston, 1984, Houston YWCA, 1976, adv. Preservation 4th Ward, Houston, 1991—; trustee Antioch Missionary Bapt. Ch., Houston, 1977; instrumental in getting the Antioch Missionary Bapt. Ch. in Christ Inc. on the National Register of Hist. Places, 1976; presented Queen Elizabeth with miniature history of Antioch Missionary Bapt. Ch. in Christ, 1991; author nomination form for Tex. hist. marker Antioch Missionary Bapt. Ch. in Christ, 1994. Named Woman Courage, Houston Radcliffe Club, 1985, Black Womens Hall Fame Mus. Africal Am. Life, Dallas, 1986; recipient Friend of the Soc. award Harris County Heritage Soc., 1994. Mem. Tex. Ret. Tchrs. Assn., Houston Mus. Fine Arts, Harris County Heritage Soc. (presenter gift of the John Henry), Bluebonnet Garden Club (pres., 1968), Jack & Jill Am. (pres. Houston chpt. 1955-57). Avocations: writing, gardening, travel, sewing, singing. Home: 3446 Southmore Blvd Houston TX 77004-6349

WHITING, PAUL L., holding company executive; b. 1943. BA in Econs., Ill. Benedictine Coll.; grad. courses, U. Ill. With Am. Nat. Bank & Trust Co. of Chgo., 1967-72, Lawrence Sys., Inc., Tampa, Fla., 1972-74; v.p. planning and control Questor Corp., 1978-81, v.p. fin., 1981-82; v.p. treas. E & S Holdings Corp. (Spauding Co. & Evenflo Co. Divsns.), Tampa, Fla., 1982-96, pres., ceo, 1996. Office: E & S Holdings Corp PO Box 30101 Tampa FL 33630-3101*

WHITING, RICHARD ALBERT, lawyer; b. Cambridge, Mass., Dec. 2, 1922; s. Albert S. and Jessie (Coleman) W.; m. Marvelene Nash, Feb. 22, 1948 (div. 1984); children—Richard A. Jr., Stephen C., Jeffrey D., Gary S., Kimberly G.; m. Joanne Sherry, Oct. 14, 1984. A.B., Dartmouth Coll., 1944; J.D., Yale U., 1949. Bar: D.C. 1949. Assoc. Steptoe & Johnson, Washington, 1949-55, ptnr., 1956-86, of counsel, 1987—; adj. prof. Vt. Law Sch., South Royalton, 1985-90; mem. exec. com. Yale Law Sch. Assn., New Haven, 1985-88; mem. adv. bd. The Antitrust Bull., N.Y.C., 1975—. Contbr. articles to profl. jours. Trustee Colby-Sawyer Coll., 1987—. Served to 1st lt. U.S. Army, 1945-46. Mem. ABA (council mem. Antitrust Law sect. 1977-85, del. to Ho. Dels. 1982-83, chmn. 1984-85). Presbyterian. Home: PO Box 749 Grantham NH 03753-0749 Office: 1330 Connecticut Ave NW Washington DC 20036-1704

WHITING, STEPHEN CLYDE, lawyer; b. Arlington, Va., Mar. 20, 1952; s. Richard A. Whiting; m. Patrice Quinn, May 24, 1980; children: Kelsey, Daniel, Seth, Samuel. BA magna cum laude, Dartmouth Coll., 1974; JD, U. Va., 1978. Bar: Maine 1978, U.S. Dist. Ct. Maine 1978. Ptnr. Douglas, Whiting, Denham & Rogers, Portland, Maine, 1978—. Co-author: Trying the Automobile Injury Case in Maine, 1993, Premises Liability: Preparation and Trial of a Difficult Case in Maine, 1994, Trying Soft Tissue Injury Cases in Maine, 1995. Mem. ATLA, Maine Bar Assn., Maine Trial Lawyers Assn., Phi Beta Kappa. Office: Douglas Whiting Denham & Rogers 103 Exchange St Portland ME 04101-5001

WHITIS, GRACE RUTH, nursing educator; b. San Antonio, Sept. 14, 1942; d. Allan and Jewel (Conlee) Richardson; m. Robert E. Whitis, Mar. 6, 1965; children: Jay, Jennifer. PhD, U. Tex., 1981; BS, U. Mary Hardin - Baylor, 1968; MS, Baylor U., 1970; MS in Nursing, U. Tex., 1972. Staff nurse Providence Hosp., Waco, Tex., 1965-67; faculty U. Mary Hardin-Baylor, Belton, Tex., 1970-79, prof., dean, 1979-83; prof. nursing Ark. State U., Jonesboro, 1993—, chmn. dept., 1985-93; vis. prof. La. Tech. U., Ruston, 1982-84. Contbr. articles to profl. jours. Mem. ANA, Nat. League for Nursing, Ark. Nurses Assn., Soc. Pediatric Nurses, Sigma Theta Tau. Home: 2403 Paula Dr Jonesboro AR 72404 Office: Ark State U PO Box 69 State University AR 72467-0069

WHITKO, JEAN PHILLIPS, academic administrator; b. Dover, Del., Oct. 31, 1940; d. Albert Leroy and Helen (Busch) Phillips; m. Donald A. Whitko, July 1, 1972; children: Lenore Ann, Wayne P., Donna J., Sheri L. BS, U. Del., 1962; MEd, Pa. State U., 1968, postgrad., 1968-72. Cert. tchr., Del., Pa. Tchr. Newcastle (Del.) Spl. Sch. Dist., 1962-68; rsch. asst. Pa. State U., University Park, 1969, instr. edn., grad. asst., 1969-72; substitute tchr. Jerusalem Lutheran Nursery Sch. and Day Care, Schwenksville, Pa., 1983-85; supr. student teaching Pa. State U., 1988—; evaluator fed. title I and III projects Pa. Dept. Edn., Harrisburg, 1970-72. Officer Women's Civ. Club Schwenksville, 1972—; vol. tchr. Perkiomen Valley Schs., Schwenksville, 1976-86; bd. dirs. Jerusalem Lutheran Nursery Sch. and Day Care, 1983-85. Named Friend of Edn., Perkiomen Valley Edn. Assn., 1983; recipient Commendation from Gov. Richard Thornburg, 1985. Mem. ASCD, Pa. Assn. Colls. and Tchr. Educators. Avocations: reading, photography. Home: 623 Main St Schwenksville PA 19473-1012 Office: Pa State Univ 179 Chambers Bldg University Park PA 16802-3205

WHITLEDGE, TERRY EUGENE, oceanographer; b. Keokuk, Iowa, May 18, 1943; s. Kenneth Elmer Whitledge and Lucille Gladys (Davidson) Malone; m. Sharon Rae Williams, Dec. 19, 1964; children—Gregory Warren, Lara Renee. B.S. in Chemistry, Western Ill. U., 1964, M.S. in chemistry, 1966; Ph.D. in Oceanography, U. Wash., 1972. Research assoc. U. Wash., Seattle, 1972-75; assoc. oceanographer Brookhaven Nat. Lab., Upton, N.Y., 1975-77, oceanographer, 1977—, acting head oceanographic scis. div., 1982-83; instl. rep. Univ. Nat. Oceanographic Lab. Systems, Seattle, 1976—; participant Conf. on Bioproductivity of Upwelling Ecosystems, USSR Acad. Scis., Moscow, 1979. Author: Automated Nutrient Analyses in Seawater, 1981; contbr. 35 articles to profl. jours., 9 chpts. to books, also profl. reports. Explorer post adviser Boy Scouts Am., Brookhaven Nat. Lab., 1981-83, scout master, Rocky Point, N.Y., 1983—. NSF grantee, 1972-86; NOAA grantee, 1978-86. Mem. Am. Soc. Limnology and Oceanography, AAAS, Am. Geophys. Union, Sigma Xi. Mem. Christian Ch. (Disciples of Christ). Office: Univ Texas at Austin Marine Sciences Inst Port Aransas TX 78373

WHITLEY, ARTHUR FRANCIS, retired international consulting company executive, engineer, lawyer; b. Bklyn., Apr. 14, 1927; s. John Boyd and Ellen (Walls) W.; m. Isabella Mary Passidomo, Apr. 9, 1950; children: Brent John, Scott Michael, Todd Joseph. B.E.E., Poly. Inst. N.Y., 1951; J.D., Seton Hall U., 1955; LL.M., Bklyn. Law Sch., 1958. Bar: N.J. 1960, U.S. Customs Ct. 1967, U.S. Patent Office 1972. Sales engr., atty. Pub. Service E&G, Newark, 1951-60; mgmt. cons. Nelson Walker Assocs., N.Y.C., 1961; atty. assoc. gen. counsel Engelhard Industries, Newark, 1962-75; v.p., group v.p. Engelhard Industries, Iselin, N.J., 1976-80, sr. v.p., 1981, exec. v.p., 1982-83; pres. Bro-Whit Assocs. Inc., 1983-89. Pres. World Trade Assn. N.J., 1965. Served with USN, 1945-46. Republican. Roman Catholic. Home: 24 Puddingstone Way Florham Park NJ 07932-2625

WHITLEY, DOUGLAS L., telecommunications industry executive. With Ill. Bell Telephone Co., 1993—, pres., chief exec. officer, 1993—; dir. Ill. Dept. Revenue. Office: Ill Bell Tel Co 225 W Randolph St Chicago IL 60606-1824*

WHITLEY, JOE DALLY, lawyer; b. Atlanta, Nov. 12, 1950; s. Thomas Youngie and Mary Jo (Dally) W.; m. Kathleen Pinion, Sept. 27, 1975; children: Lauren Jacqueline, Thomas McMillan. BA, U. Ga., 1972, JD, 1975. Bar: Ga. 1975, U.S. Supreme Ct. 1989. Assoc. Kelly, Denney, Pease & Allison, Columbus, Ga., 1975-78; asst. dist. atty. Chattahoochee Jud. Cir., Columbus, 1978-79; assoc. Hirsch, Beil & Partin, P.C., Columbus, 1979-81; U.S. atty. Dept. Justice, Macon, Ga., 1981-87; dep. asst. atty. gen., Criminal Div. Dept. Justice, Washington, 1987-88, dep. assoc. atty. gen., 1988-89, acting assoc. atty. gen., 1989; ptnr. Smith, Gambrell & Russell, Atlanta, 1989-90; U.S. atty. Dept. of Justice, Atlanta, 1990-93; ptnr. Kilpatrick & Cody, Atlanta, 1993—; mem. atty. gen.'s adv. com. Dept. Justice, Washington, 1982-85; chmn. organized crime and violent crime subcom. Atty. Gen.'s Adv. Com., 1990-93, mem. investigative subcom., 1990-93, chmn. white collar crime subcom., 1993. Treas. Muscogee County Young Reps., Columbus, 1979-80. Mem. Ga. Bar Assn., Macon Bar Assn., Young Lawyers Club (pres. Columbus chpt. 1980-81), Lawyers Club of Atlanta. Republican. Presbyterian. Home: 1100 Peachtree St Ste 2800 Atlanta GA 30309-4530 Office: Kilpatrick & Cody 1100 Peachtree St NE Ste 2800 Atlanta GA 30309-4530

WHITLEY, MICHAEL R., utilities executive; b. 1943. BA, Campbellsville Coll., 1963. Various positions Ky. Utilities Co., Lexington, Ky., 1964-78, corp. sec., 1978-87, sr. v.p., 1987-95, chmn, pres., 1995. Office: Ky Utilities Co 1 Quality St Lexington KY 40507-1428*

WHITLEY, NANCY O'NEIL, retired radiology educator; b. Winston-Salem, N.C., Feb. 21, 1932; d. Norris Lawrence and Thelma Mae (Hardy) O'Neil; m. J.E. Whitley, Dec. 20, 1958; children—John O'Neil, Catherine Anne. Student, Duke U., 1950-53; M.D., Bowman Gray Sch. Medicine, 1957. Fellow in cardiology Bowman Gray Sch. Medicine, Winston-Salem, 1958-60; intern Jefferson Davis Hosp., Houston, 1957-58; resident in radiology Bowman Gray Sch. Medicine, 1966-69, instr., 1969-70, asst. prof., 1970-74, assoc. prof., 1974-78; prof. radiology U. Md. Sch. Medicine, Balt., 1978-92; prof. oncology U. Md. Cancer Ctr., Balt., 1988-92; prof. radiology Med. U. S.C., Charleston, 1992-94; ret., 1994. Author: (with J.E. Whitley) Angiopgraphy, Techniques and Procedures, 1971.

WHITLEY, RALPH C., diversified financial services company executive; b. 1943. Grad., U. Calif., L.A., 1968. With Photo Reproductions, Inc., L.A., 1969-72; with CCH Computax, Inc., Torrance, Calif., 1972—, pres.; now exec v.p. CCH Computax, Inc., Ronwoods, IL. Office: CCH Computax Inc 2700 Lake Cook Rdlvd Ronwoods IL 60015*

WHITLOCK, BENNETT CLARKE, JR., retired association executive; b. Charleston, S.C., June 10, 1927; s. Bennett C. and Isabel Price (Beckman) W.; m. Elizabeth Darley Marshall, July 18, 1959; children: Mary Elizabeth, Bennett C. III. A.B., Presbyn. Coll., 1946; LL.B., U. S.C., 1949. With Am. Trucking Assns., Inc., Washington, 1949-89, asst. to mng. dir., 1961-70, asst. to pres., 1970-73, v.p., 1973-75, exec. v.p., chief oper. officer, 1975-76, pres., 1976-84, spl. adviser, pres., 1984-89; ret., 1989. Bd. dirs Braddock Road Boys Club; bd. visitors Mary Washington Coll., 1985-93, vice rector, 1986-88, rector, 1990-92. Mem. Hwy. Users Fedn. for Safety and Mobility (dir.), Country Club of Fairfax, Kiawah Island Club, Blue Key, Pi Kappa Alpha. Episcopalian.

WHITLOCK, CHARLES PRESTON, former university dean; b. Highland Park, N.J., June 19, 1919; s. Frank Boudinot and Rosena Craig (Foster) W.; m. Patricia Hamilton Hoey, Mar. 10, 1960; children: Carol Foster, Adam Hoey, Susan Boudinot, Matthew Fitzsimmons, Beth Brewer. BA, Rutgers U., 1941; MA, Harvard U., 1947. Asso. dir. Bur. Study Counsel Harvard U., 1948-52, Allston Burr sr. tutor, 1952-58, lectr. social psychology, 1955-72, asst. to pres., 1958-70, assoc. dean of coll., 1970-72, dean of coll., 1972-76, asso. dean faculty, 1976-82, master Dudley House, 1976-82; Dir. Cambridgeport Savs. Bank.; Mem. Mass. Higher Edn. Facilities Commn. Co-author: Harvard University Reading Films. Trustee Charity of Edward Hopkins, Lesley Coll.; bd. corporators New Eng. Deaconess Hosp. Col. USAF. Decorated Silver Star, D.F.C., Air medal. Home: 9 Barberry Heights Rd Gloucester MA 01930-1201 Office: Harvard U Cambridge MA 02138

WHITLOCK, DAVID C., retired military officer; b. Little Rock, Ark., Jan. 24, 1935; m. Rosemarie Binik (dec.); children: D. Patrick, David D. B Bus., U. Nebr., 1962; grad., Squadron Officer Sch., 1965; MA Speech and Drama, U. Colo., 1966, PhD Communication, 1970; grad., Air Command and Staff Coll., 1978, Air War Coll., 1983. With USAF, 1952-62, tech. sgt., 1962; audiovisual tng. officer, 2d lt., 1st lt. Hdqs. N. Am. Air Defense Command USAF, Colo., 1962-67; from English, speech instr., asst., dir. forensics, capt. to prof., major USAF Acad., 1967-74, prof. English, Speech, dir. Forensics, lt. col., 1979, pres. Tenure Coun., 1981-82; dir. Disting. Visitors Bureau Hdqs. USAF, Ramstein AFB, Germany, 1982-84; assoc. dean Civilian Inst. programs, col. AF Inst. Tech., Ohio, 1984-86; base comdr. 26th Combat Support Group Zweibrucken AFB, Germany, 1986-88; dean Civilian Inst. Programs Wright Patterson AFB, Ohio, 1989, commandant emeritus AF Inst. Tech. Air U., 1992-93. Recipient Legion of Merit, Meritorious Svc. medal with four oak leaf clusters, Air Force Commendation medal with two oak leaf clusters. Achievements include qualified parachutist. Home: 441 Green Vista Dr Enon OH 45323-1340 Office: Air Force Institute of Tech Dayton OH 45433

WHITLOCK, JOHN JOSEPH, museum director; b. South Bend, Ind., Jan. 7, 1935; s. Joseph Mark and Helen Marcella (Cramer) W.; m. Sue Ann Kirkman, June 10, 1956; children—Kelly Ann, Michele Lynn, Mark. BS in Art, Ball State U., 1957, MA in Art, 1963; EdD, Ind. U., 1971. Tchr. art Union City (Ind.) Pub. Schs., 1957-59; tchr. art, art dir. Madison (Ind.) City Schs., 1959-64; prof. art, dir. gallery Hanover (Ind.) Coll., 1964-69; dir. Burpee Art Mus., Rockford, Ill., 1970-72; prof. arts and humanities Elgin (Ill.) Community Coll., 1970-72; dir. Brooks Meml. Art Gallery, Memphis, 1972-78; prof. mus. studies Southwestern Coll., Memphis, 1973-78; adj. asst. prof. art and museology Memphis State U., 1976-78; dir. Univ. Mus., mem. grad. faculty So. Ill. U., Carbondale, 1978—, also dir. mus. studies, adj. assoc. prof. anthropology, 1978—, adj. assoc. prof. polit. sci., 1988—, adj. assoc. prof. history, 1994—, dir. mus. studies, 1989—, mem. ROTC acad. avc. coun., 1988—, mem. president's coun., 1988-93, adj. assoc. prof. art Univ. Mus., 1978-88; chmn. bd. Nat. Coal Mus.; mem. Newsfront adv. bd. NC Broadcast News, Washington; sr. cons. Marine Mil. Acad. Mus., 1988—, mem. bd. advisors, 1991—. Mem. Rockford Human Rels. Commn., 1971-72; mem. president's coun. Southwestern Coll., 1973-78. Mem. Am. Assn. Mus., Internat. Coun. Mus., Midwest Assn. Mus., Assn. Art Mus. Dirs., Marine Corps League (commandant Shawnee detachment 1994—, comdr. USCG Aux. 1994-95). Office: So Ill U Univ Mus Carbondale IL 62901-4508

WHITLOCK, JOHN L., lawyer; b. New Orleans, Oct. 24, 1946; s. John Bert and Virginia Katherine (Marzolf) W.; m. Dorothy Florence Oeste, Sept. 13, 1969; children: Sarah Katherine, Thomas John. AB, Harvard U., 1968, JD, 1973. Bar: Mass. 1973, U.S. Dist. Ct. Mass. 1974, U.S. Ct. Appeals (1st cir.) 1975. Assoc. Herrick & Smith, Boston, 1973-80, ptnr., 1981-86; ptnr. Palmer & Dodge, Boston, 1986—. Bd. dirs., sec. Harvard-Radcliffe Collegiate Mus. Found., Inc., 1978—; treas. The Cecilia Soc., 1974-85, bd. dirs., 1974-86, 94—, pres., 1994—. With U.S. Army, 1968-70. Lutheran. Avocation: singing. Office: Palmer & Dodge 1 Beacon St Boston MA 02108-3106

WHITLOCK, LUDER GRADICK, JR., seminary president; b. Jacksonville, Fla., June 20, 1940; s. Luder G. and Juanita O. (Nessmith) W.; m. Mary Louise Patton, Aug. 29, 1959; children: Frank Christopher, Alissa Ann, Beth LaVerne. BA, U. Fla., 1962; MDiv, Westminster Theol. Sem., 1966; D of Ministry, Vanderbilt U., 1973. Ordained to ministry Presbyn. Ch. in Am., 1966. Pastor Sharon Presbyn. Ch., Hialeah, Fla., 1966-69, West Hills Presbyn. Ch., Harriman, Tenn., 1969-75; prof. Reformed Theol. Sem., Jackson, Miss., 1975—, acting pres., 1978-79, pres., 1979—; bd. dirs. Ligonier Ministries, Orlando, Fla. Editorial adv. bd. Leadership, Wheaton, 1992—. Trustee Westminster Theol. Sem., Phila., 1973-76, Covenant Coll., Chattanooga, 1973-80; bd. dirs. Internat. Grad. Sch. Theology, Seoul, Republic of Korea, 1987—; dir. Greater Orlando Leadership Found., 1989-92, Found. for Reformation, Orlando, Fla., 1990—, Key Life, 1995—, World Evangelical Fellowship N.Am. Region, Wheaton, Ill., 1992—, Internat. Christian Leadership Univ., Campus Crusade for Christ, exec. com., 1992—, Internat. Reformed Fellowship, co-pres., 1993—. Mem. Evang. Theol. Soc., Nat. Assn. Evangs. (bd. adminstrn. 1992—, dir. 1995, chmn. theology com. 1994—, nat. commn. higher edn. 1995—), Assn. Theol. Schs. (nominating com., exec. com. 1994—), Fellowship of Evang. Sem. Pres. (chmn. 1990-93, 94—), Citrus Club. Republican. Office: Reformed Theol Sem 1015 Maitland Center Common Bl Maitland FL 32751-7130

WHITLOCK, WILLIAM ABEL, lawyer; b. Faribault, Minn., Feb. 6, 1929; s. William Abel and Alice Eleanor (Bartel) W.; m. Shirley Rae Olhausen; children: Anne, William, Justin, Jane, Thomas. BSL, U. Minn., 1951, LLB, 1953. Law clk. to justice Minn. Supreme Ct., St. Paul, 1952-53; law clk. to presiding justice U.S. Dist. Ct. Minn., 1953-54; assoc. Dorsey & Whitney, Mpls., 1957-62, ptnr., 1962-95, of counsel, 1995—. Served to capt. USAR, 1954-57. Mem. Order of the Coif. Office: Dorsey & Whitney 2200 Pillsbury Center S Minneapolis MN 55402*

WHITLOCK, WILLIE WALKER, lawyer; b. Mineral, Va., Nov. 16, 1925; s. Edward Jackson and Lottie Alma (Talley) W.; m. Eula Madeline Dymacek, July 15, 1950; children—John D., Jane Whitlock Sisk. B.S. in Bus., Coll. William and Mary, 1950, LL.B., Va. Coll. Law, 1953. Bar: Va. 1955, U.S. Dist. Ct. Va. 1957. Atty. Town of Mineral, 1965—, County of Louisa, 1976-79; mem. adv. bd. Jefferson Nat. Bank, Mineral, 1972—. Chmn. Louisa County Democratic Com., Louisa, Va., 1978-82, 32d Legis. Dist. Va., 1978-82. Served to sgt. U.S. Army, 1945-46. Mem. Va. State Bar, Piedmont Bar Assn. (pres. 1976), Louisa County Bar Assn. (pres. 1981—), Am. Legion. Baptist. Lodges: Lions, Masons.

WHITLOW, JAMES ADAMS, lawyer; b. Mayfield, Ky., Jan. 29, 1968; s. Charles William and June (Hawkens) W. BA, Transylvania U., 1990; JD, Harvard U., 1993. Bar: N.C. 1994. Assoc. Parker Poe Adams & Bernstein, L.L.P., Charlotte, N.C., 1993-95, Akin, Gump, Strauss, Hauer & Feld, L.L.P., Dallas, 1995—. Office: Akin Gump Strauss Hauer & Feld LLP 1700 Pacific Ave Ste 4100 Dallas TX 75201

WHITMAN, ALAN MORRIS, mechanical engineering educator; b. Phila., Jan. 26, 1937; s. Irwin Morris and Sybil (Garfinkel) W.; m. Matilda Sbar, June 21, 1959 (div. Mar. 1978); children: Karen Lynn Whitman Berman, Phyllis Ruth; m. Rachel Ariella Bregman, May 25, 1978; children:Noam Hillel, Roy Zipstein. BSME, U. Pa., 1958, MSME, 1959, PhD, 1965. Mech. engr. Air Proving Ground Ctr., Eglin AFB, Fla., 1959-62; sr. rsch. engr. power transmission divsn. GE Co., Phila., 1965-67; asst. prof. mech. engring U. Pa., Phila., 1967-72, assoc. prof. mech. engring, 1972-80; assoc. prof. interdisciplinary studies and mechanics Tel Aviv U., 1980-83, prof. interdisciplinary studies and mechanics, 1983-88, chmn. dept. interdisciplinary studies, 1986-88; prof., chmn. mech. engring Villanova (Pa.) U., 1988—; vis.

prof. Tel Aviv U., 1975-76, 78-79, Villanova U., 1984-85. Contbr. articles to profl. publs. Fellow Optical Soc. Am.; mem. ASME, Am. Soc. Engring. Edn., Sigma Xi, Tau Beta Pi, Sigma Tau. Office: Villanova U Dept Mech Engring Villanova PA 19010

WHITMAN, BRADFORD F., lawyer; b. N.Y.C., 1945. AB, Harvard U., 1966; JD, U. Pa., 1969. Bar: N.Y. 1969, D.C. 1974, Pa. 1979. Atty., asst. chief pollution control sect. U.S. Dept. Justice, 1971-79; ptnr. Reed Smith Shaw & McClay, Phila. Mem. Phila. Bar Assn. (former chair environ. law com.). Office: Reed Smith Shaw & McClay 2500 One Liberty Pl Philadelphia PA 19103*

WHITMAN, CHRISTINE TODD, governor; b. Sept. 26, 1946; d. Webster Bray and Eleanor Schley Todd; m. John Whitman, 1974; children: Kate, Taylor. BA in Govt., Wheaton Coll., 1968. Former freeholder Somerset County, N.J.; former pres. State Bd. Pub. Utilities; host radio talk show Sta. WKXW, Trenton, N.J.; gov. State of N.J., 1994—; chmn. Com. for an Affordable N.J. Columnist newspapers. Bd. freeholders Somerset County, N.J., 1982-87; bd. pub. utilities, 1988-89; Rep. candidate for senator State of N.J., 1990. First female governor in N.J.; delivered Republican response to President Clinton's 1995 State of the Union address. Office: State House CN 001 Office of Governor Trenton NJ 08625-0001*

WHITMAN, DALE ALAN, lawyer, university professor; b. Charleston, W.Va., Feb. 18, 1939; m. Marjorie Miller; 8 children. Student, Ohio State U., 1956-59; BES, Brigham Young U., 1963; LLB, Duke U., 1966. Bar: Calif. 1967, Utah 1974. Assoc. O'Melveny & Myers, Los Angeles, 1966-67; asst. prof., then assoc. prof. Sch. Law, U. N.C., Chapel Hill, 1967-70; vis. prof. law N.C. Cen. U., Durham, 1968, 69; vis. assoc. prof. law UCLA, 1970-71; dep. dir. Office Housing and Urban Affairs, Fed. Home Loan Bank Bd., Washington, 1971-72; sr. program analyst FHA, HUD, Washington, 1972-73; prof. law Brigham Young U., 1973-78, 92—; vis. prof. law U. Tulsa, 1976, U. Mo., Columbia, 1976; prof. law, assoc. dean U. Wash., Seattle, 1978-82; prof., dean U. Mo. Sch. Law, Columbia, 1982-88, prof., 1988-91; cons., lectr. in field. Co-author: Cases and Materials on Real Estate Finance and Development, 1976, Real Estate Finance Law, 1979, 3d edit., 1994, Cases and Materials on Real Estate Transfer, Finance and Development, 1981, 3d edit., 1992, Land Transactions and Finance, 1983, The Law of Property, 1984, 2d edit., 1993, Basic Property Law, 1989; contbr. articles to profl. jours. Fellow Am. Bar Found.; mem. Am. Law Inst., Am. Coll. Real Estate Lawyers. Home: 480 E 450 S Orem UT 84058-6449 Office: BYU Law Sch Provo UT 84602

WHITMAN, HOMER WILLIAM, JR., investment counseling company executive; b. Sarasota, Fla., Jan. 8, 1932; s. Homer William and Phoebe (Corr) W.; m. Anne Virginia Sarran, May 8, 1954; children: Burke William, Michael Wayne. BA in Econs. optime merens, U. South, 1953; grad., U.S. Naval Officer Candidate Sch., 1953; postgrad., Emory U., 1969. Served to group v.p. 1st Nat. Bank Atlanta, 1956-72; pres., dir. Palmer 1st Nat. Bank & Trust Co., Sarasota, 1973-74, Hamilton Bank & Trust Co., Atlanta, 1974-76; v.p. Lionel D. Edie & Co., Atlanta, 1976-78, Mfrs. Hanover Trust Co., Atlanta, 1978-85; sr. v.p. Montag & Caldwell, Inc., Atlanta, 1985—. Dir. Asolo State Theatre. Trustee Selby Found., 1973-74, West Paces Ferry Hosp., Ringling Sch. Art, St. Stephen's Sch.; bd. vis. Emory U.; mem. Leadership Atlanta. Lt. j.g. USNR, 1953-56. Named Hon. French Consul, Atlanta, Atlanta's Outstanding Young Man of Yr., 1963. Mem. Govt. Fin. Officer's Assn., Gla. Govt. Fin. Officers Assn., Ga. Govt. Fin. Officers Assn., Assn. Investment Mgmt. Sales Execs., Atlanta Soc. Fin. Analysts, Healthcare Fin. Mgmt. Assn., Fla. Pub. Pension Trustees Assn., Assn. Pvt. Pension and Welfare Plans (regional chmn.), Am. Cancer Soc. (dir. Atlanta city unit), Newcomen Soc., 300 Club, Atlanta C. of C. (life mem.), Piedmont Driving Club, Peachtree Golf Club, Commerce Club, Buckhead Club (bd. govs.), Union League Club (N.Y.), Breakfast Club, Sarasota U. Club (bd. dirs.), Rotary. Episcopalian. Home: 77 E Andrews Dr NW Apt 353 Atlanta GA 30305-1344 Office: Montag & Caldwell Inc 1100 Atlanta Fin Ctr 3343 Peachtree Rd NE Atlanta GA 30326-1022

WHITMAN, KATHY VELMA ROSE (ELK WOMAN WHITMAN), artist, sculptor, jeweler, painter, educator; b. Bismarck, N.D., Aug. 12, 1952; d. Carl Jr. and Edith Geneva (Lykken) W.; m. Robert Paul Luger, Feb. 21, 1971 (div. Jan. 1982); children: Shannon, Lakota, Cannupa, Palani; m. Dean P. Fox (div. 1985); 1 child, Otgadahe. Student, Standing Rock C.C., Ft. Yates, N.D., 1973-74, Sinte Gleska Coll., Rosebud, S.D., 1975-77, U. S.D., 1977, Ariz. State U., 1992-93. Instr. art Sinte Gleska Coll., 1975-77, Standing Rock C.C., 1977-78; co-mgr. Four Bears Motor Lodge, New Town, N.D., 1981-82; store owner Nux-Baga Lodge, New Town, 1982-85; artist-in-residence N.D. Coun. on Arts, Bismarck, 1983-84, bd. dirs., 1985; artist-in-residence Evanston Twp. H.S., Ill., 1996; cultural cons. movie prodn., Phoenix, Ariz., 1994. One woman shows include Mus. of Am. Indian, N.Y.C., 1983, Charleroi Internat. Fair, Belgium, 1984, Heard Mus., Phoenix, 1987-92, Phoenix Gallery, Nurnburg, Germany, 1990-96, Lovena Ohl Gallery, Phoenix, 1990-94, Phoenix Gallery, Coeur d'Alene, Idaho, 1992, Turquoise Tortoise Gallery, Tubac, Ariz., 1992-93, Yah-ta-hey Gallery, New London, Conn., 1992-93, Silver Sun Gallery, Santa Fe, N.Mex., 1992-96, Tribal Expessions Gallery, Arlington Heights, Ill., 1994-96, others; represented in permanent collections at Mus. of the Am. Indian, N.Y.C., Mesa (Ariz.) C.C. Bd. dirs. Ft. Berthold C.C., New Town, 1983-85; pres. Cannonball (N.D.) Pow-Wow Com., 1978; parent rep. Head Start, Ft. Yates, 1974. Recipient best craftsman spl. award Bullock's Indian Arts and Crafts, 1986, best of fine arts award No. Plains Tribal Arts, Sioux Falls, S.D., 1988, best of show award Pasadena Western Relic and Native Am. Show, 1991, 2 1st place awards Santa Fe Indian Market, 1993, 2 2nd place awards, 1994, 2 3rd place awards, 1994, 74th Ann. SWAIA Santa Fe Indian Mkt. 1st place award, 1995, 2d place award, 1995, 2 3rd place awards, 1995. Mem. Indian Arts and Crafts Assn., S.W. Assn. on Indian Affairs (life, 1st and 2nd place awards Santa Fe Indian Market 1995, 2 3rd place awards 1995). Avocations: native American crafts, furniture building, running and hiking, dancing, singing. Home and Studio: 3401 E Paradise Dr Phoenix AZ 85028

WHITMAN, MARINA VON NEUMANN, economist; b. N.Y.C., Mar. 6, 1935; d. John and Mariette (Kovesi) von Neumann; m. Robert Freeman Whitman, June 23, 1956; children: Malcolm Russell, Laura Mariette. BA summa cum laude, Radcliffe Coll., 1956; MA, Columbia U., 1959, PhD, 1962; LHD (hon.), Russell Sage Coll., 1972, U. Mass., 1975, N.Y. Poly Inst., 1975, Baruch Coll., 1980; LLD (hon.), Cedar Crest Coll., 1973, Hobart and William Smith Coll., 1973, Coe Coll., 1975, Marietta Coll., 1976, Rollins Coll., 1976, Wilson Coll., 1977, Allegheny Coll., 1977, Amherst Coll., 1978, Ripon Coll., 1980, Mt. Holyoke Coll., 1980; LittD (hon.), Williams Coll., 1980, Lehigh U., 1981, Denison U., 1983, Claremont U., 1984, Notre Dame U., 1984, Eastern Mich. U., 1992 . Mem. faculty U. Pitts., 1962-79, prof. econs., 1971-73, disting. pub. svc. prof. econs., 1973-79; v.p., chief economist Gen. Motors Corp., N.Y.C., 1979-85, group exec. v.p. pub. affairs, 1985-92; disting. vis. prof. bus. adminstrn. & pub. policy U. Mich., Ann Arbor, 1992-94, prof. bus. adminstrn. and pub. policy, 1994—; mem. U.S. Price Commn., 1971-72, Coun. Econ. Advisers, Exec. Office of Pres., 1972-73; bd. dirs. Chase Manhattan Corp., ALCOA, Procter & Gamble Co., Browning-Ferris Industries, UNOCAL; mem. Trilateral Commn., 1973-84, 88-95; mem. Pres. Adv. Com. on Trade Policy and Negotiations, 1987-93; mem. tech. assessment adv. coun. U.S. Congress Office of Tech. Assessment, 1990-95, Dept. Treasury, from 1977; mem. Consultative Group on Internat. Econs. and Monetary Affairs, from 1979; trustee Nat. Bur. Econ. Rsch., 1993—. Bd. dirs. Inst. for Internat. Econs, 1986, Eurasia Found, 1992-95; bd. overseers Harvard U., 1972-78, mem. vis. com. Kennedy Sch., 1992—; trustee Princeton U., 1980-90. Fellow Earhart Found., 1959-60, AAUW, 1960-61, NSF, 1968-70, also Social Security Rsch. Coun.; recipient Columbia medal for excellence, 1973; George Washington award Am. Hungarian Found., 1975. Mem. Am. Econ. Assn. (exec. com. 1977-80), Am. Acad. Arts & Scis., Coun. Fgn. Rels. (dir. 1977-87), Phi Beta Kappa. Author: Government Risk-Sharing in Foreign Investment, 1965; International and Interregional Payments Adjustment, 1967; Economic Goals and Policy Instruments, 1970; Reflections of Interdependence: Issues for Economic Theory and U.S. Policy, 1979; also articles; bd. editors Am. Econ. Rev., 1974-77; mem. editorial bd. Fgn. Policy. Office: U Mich Sch Pub Policy 411 Lorch Hall Ann Arbor MI 48109-1220

WHITMAN, NANCY IRENE, nursing educator; b. Hornell, N.Y., Nov. 27, 1947; d. Jack Almy and Miriam Sue (Brook) W.; m. Robert Earl Campbell, Dec. 24, 1988. BSN, Alfred U., 1969; MSN, U. Va., Charlottesville, 1978; PhD, U. Tex., 1988. Staff nurse adult medicine Tufts New Eng. Med. Ctr., Boston, 1969-70; staff nurse pediatrics N. Shore Children's Hosp., Salem, Mass., 1970-71, Tufts New Eng. Med. Ctr., Boston, 1971-72; staff nurse rsch. unit Children's Med. Ctr., Boston, 1972-73; asst. instr. Mass. Gen. Hosp. Sch. Nursing, Boston, 1973-74; instr. nursing U. Va., Charlottesville, 1978-81; asst. prof. nursing U. Va., 1981-91; assoc. prof., chmn. dept. Lynchburg (Va.) Coll., 1991—. Co-author: Teaching in Nursing Practice, 1988, 2d edit., 1992, Computers in Small Bytes, 1992; contbr. articles to profl. jours. Recipient New Investigator award Soc. for Rsch. in Nursing Edn., Nat. League for Nursing, 1989; HBO and Co. Nurse scholar, 1990. Mem. ANA, Va. Nurses Assn. (v.p. 1984-86), Nat. League Nursing, Assn. for Care Children's Health, Sigma Theta Tau (counselor 1988-90, Nancy Ballard award 1987), Phi Kappa Phi. Home: 5141 Cove Garden Rd Covesville VA 22931-9732 Office: Lynchburg Coll Lynchburg VA 24501

WHITMAN, ROBERT VAN DUYNE, civil engineer, educator; b. Pitts., Feb. 2, 1928; s. Edwin A. and Elsie (Van Duyne) W.; m. Elizabeth Cushman, June 19, 1954; children: Jill Martyne Whitman Marsee, Martha Allerton (dec.), Gweneth Giles Whitman Kaebnick. BS, Swarthmore Coll., 1948, DSc (hon.), 1990; SM, MIT, 1949, ScD, 1951. Mem. faculty MIT, 1953—, prof. civil engring., 1963-93, head structural engring., 1970-74, head soil mechanics div., 1970-72; prof. emeritus, 1993—; vis. scholar U. Cambridge, Eng., 1976-77; cons. to govt. and industry, 1953—; mem. adv. com. for nat. earthquake hazard reduction program Fed. Emergency Mgmt. Agy., 1991-94, mem. commn. engring. and tech. systems NRC, 1992—. Author: (with T. W. Lambe) Soil Mechanics. Mem. Town Meeting Lexington, Mass., 1962-76, 85—, mem. permanent bldg. com., 1968-75, mem. bd. appeals, 1979-81, 84—. Lt. (j.g.) USNR, 1954-56. Recipient U.S. Scientist award Humboldt Found., 1984-90; Norwegian Geotech. Inst. rsch. fellow, 1984. Mem. NAE, ASCE (Rsch. award 1962, Terzaghi Lecture 1981, Terzaghi award 1987, C. Martin Duke Lifeline Earthquake Engring. award 1992, James Croes medal 1994), Boston Soc. Civil Engrs. (Structural Sect. prize 1963, Desmond Fitzgerald medal 1973, Ralph W. Horne Fund award 1977), Internat. Soc. Soil Mechanics and Found. Engrs., Earthquake Engring. Rsch. Inst. (dir. 1978-81, 84-88, v.p. 1979-81, pres. 1985-87, Disting. lectr. 1994). Research in soil mechanics, soil dynamics and earthquake engring. Home: 5 Hancock Ave Lexington MA 02173-3412 Office: MIT Dept Civil & Environ Engring Cambridge MA 02139

WHITMAN, RUSSELL WILSON, lawyer; b. Phila., Feb. 20, 1940; s. Russell W. Whitman and Amelia M. (Schauer) Richard; m. Mary Carol Tyson, Sept. 16, 1961; children: Russell Whitman III, Douglas W. BS, Drexel Inst. Tech., 1964; LLB, U. Pa., 1967. Bar: N.Y. 1968, Pa. 1969, N.J. 1990. Ptnr. Dechert Price & Rhoads, Phila., 1969-93. Office: Ste 200 Box 5072 1322 Hooper Ave Toms River NJ 08754

WHITMAN, RUTH, poet, educator, translator; b. N.Y.C., May 28, 1922; d. Meyer David and Martha Harriet (Sherman) Bashein; m. Cedric Whitman, Oct. 13, 1941; children: Rachel Claudia, Leda Miriam; m. Firman Houghton, July 22, 1959; 1 child, David Will; m. Morton Sacks, Oct. 6, 1966. B.A., Radcliffe Coll., 1944; M.A., Harvard, 1947. Editor Harvard U. Press, 1947-60; dir. poetry workshop Cambridge Ctr. Adult Edn., 1964-68; fellow poetry and translation Bunting Inst., Radcliffe Coll., 1968-70; instr. Radcliffe Seminars, 1969—; faculty Harvard U., 1979-84; vis. poet Tufts U., 1972, 73; vis. poet in Israel, 1974, 77, 79, 81; poet-in-residence Hamden Sydney Coll., 1974, Trinity Coll., 1975, U. Denver, 1976, Holy Cross Coll., 1978, MIT, 1979, 1989, U. Mass., 1980, Centre Coll., Ky., 1980, 87, Ky. Arts Commn., 1981; founder, pres. Poets Who Teach, Inc., 1974—; dir. poetry writing program Mass. Council Arts, 1970-73; vis. prof. poetry MIT, 1989-92. Author: Selected Poems of Alain Bosquet, 1963, Anthology of Modern Yiddish Poetry, 1966, Blood and Milk Poems, 1963, Marriage Wig and other poems, 1968, Selected Poems of Jacob Glatstein, 1972, The Passion of Lizzie Borden: New and Selected Poems, 1973; editor: Poemmaking: Poets in Classrooms, 1975, Tamsen Donner: A Woman's Journey, 1977, Permanent Address: New Poems, 1973-80, 1980, Becoming a Poet: Source, Process and Practice, 1982, The Testing of Hanna Senesh, 1986, The Fiddle Rose, 1990, Laughing Gas: Poems New and Selected, 1963-90, 91, Hatshepsut, Speak to Me, 1992, An Anthology of Modern Yiddish Poetry, 3d edit., 1995. Recipient Alice Fay di Castagnola award, 1968, Kovner award, 1968, Chanin award, 1972, Guiness Internat. award, 1973; John Masefield award, 1976; grantee Nat. Found. Jewish Culture, 1968; Nat. Endowment Arts, 1974-75; Tananbaum Found. grantee, 1979, 80; R.I. Council grantee in lit., 1980; sr. Fulbright writer-in-residence fellow Hebrew U., Jerusalem, 1984-85. Mem. Authors League, P.E.N., Poetry Soc. Am., New Eng. Poetry Club, Phi Beta Kappa. Address: 40 Tuckerman Ave Middletown RI 02842-6044

WHITMER, FREDERICK LEE, lawyer; b. Terre Haute, Ind., Nov. 5, 1947; s. Lee Arthur and Ella (Diekhoff) W.; m. Valeri Cade; children: Caitlin Margaret, Meghan Connors, Christian Frederick. BA, Wabash Coll., 1969; JD, Columbia U., 1973. Bar: N.Y. 1975, U.S. Dist. Ct. (so. dist.) N.Y. 1975, N.J. 1976, U.S. Dist. Ct. N.J. 1976, U.S. Ct. Appeals (3d cir.) 1977, U.S. Ct. Appeals (fed. cir.) 1983, U.S. Ct. Appeals (2d cir.) 1987, U.S. Supreme Ct. 1988, U.S. Ct. Appeals (7th cir.) 1994. Assoc. Kaye, Scholer, Fierman, Hays & Handler, N.Y.C., 1973-76, Pitney, Hardin & Kipp, Morristown, 1976-78; ptnr. Pitney, Hardin, Kipp & Szuch, Morristown, 1979—. Mem. ABA, N.J. Bar Assn., Phi Beta Kappa. Republican. Lutheran. Home: 190 Hurlbutt St Wilton CT 06897-2706 Office: Pitney Hardin Kipp & Szuch Park Ave at Morris Co PO Box 1945 Morristown NJ 07962-1945

WHITMER, JOSEPH MORTON, benefits consulting firm executive, retired; b. Sacramento, Apr. 29, 1942; s. Carlos Raymond and Elizabeth Ellen (McDonald) W.; m. Judith Leigh Johnson, Aug. 11, 1963 (dec. Jan. 1985); children: Karen L., Brian D., Julia A.; m. Paula Ann Thurman, Mar. 19, 1986. BS in Acctg., U. Ky., 1964, JD, 1967. Ptnr. Veal & Whitmer, Nicholasville, Ky., 1967-68; v.p., sec., gen. counsel and dir. Consol. Mgmt. Svcs., Eagles Nat. Life Ins. Co., First Mut. Ins. Co., First. Mut. Life Ins. Co., Lexington, Ky., 1970-75; pvt. practice Lexington, 1975-89; exec. v.p., dir. Profl. Adminstrs. Ltd., Lexington, 1968-86, pres. chief exec. officer, 1987-90, dir., 1990-93. Mem. bd. overseers Duke U. Comprehensive Cancer Ctr., Durham, N.C., 1987—, co-chair Melanoma Consortium, 1987-90. Named one of Outstanding Young Men Am., 1975. Mem. ABA, Ky. Bar Assn. Democrat. Methodist. Avocation: computers.

WHITMER, KEVIN, newspaper sports editor. Sports editor The Daily News, N.Y.C. Office: NY News Inc 220 E 42nd St New York NY 10017-5806

WHITMIRE, JOHN LEE, daycare provider; b. Brevard, N.C., June 17, 1924; s. John Leander and Betty Burr (Owen) W.; m. Eva Lee Wilson, Aug. 13, 1950; 1 child, Bonita Dawn. Student, Brevard Coll., 1948-49; BS in Acctg., U. Balt., 1960. Asst. tchr. agr. pub. schs., Brevard, 1946-48; office mgr. Peninsula Poultry Co., Balt., 1955-59; auditor accounts receivable Ea. Products Corp., Balt., 1959-62; chief acct. Texize Corp., Mauldin, S.C., 1962-63; contr. Atlas Vending Co., Greenville, S.C., 1966-69; owner, dir. Twinkle Kiddie Kollege & Day Care, Greenville, 1969—; lobbyist state day care regulation, Columbia, S.C., 1977-81; mem. Adv. Com. on Regulation Child Day Care Facilities, Columbia, 1982-83; field counselor Day Care Child Trend, N.C., S.C., Ga., Ala., Miss., Tenn., Ark. Recipient 100% Dist. Leader Dog award Leader Dogs for the Blind, 1992, 100% Dist. Gov.'s award 1992. Mem. long range planning com. Grove Sch., East Gantt Sch., Greenville; precinct committeeman Greenville Dem. Com., 1970—. Sgt. AUS, 1944-46, ETO; with U.S. Army, 1950-52, Korea. Decorated Purple Heart. Recipient Model Sector Coord. award Campaign Sight First, 1993, Key Leader award, 1993, Leadership award, 1995. Mem. ASCD, Lions (1st v.p. Pleasantburg, L.C. 1985-86, pres. 1987-88, zone chmn. dist. 32-A 1988-89, region chmn. 1989-90, lt. gov. 1990-91, dist. gov. 1991-92, extension chmn., bd. dirs. S.C. Lions Sight Conservation Assn., contbr. Internat. Lions Mag., 1992, Palmetto Lion, 1993-94, Lion of Yr. award 1985, cert. of appreciation from internat. pres. 1989, 91, S.C. Eye Bank Vol. of Yr. award 1992). Baptist. Home: 13 Pecan Dr Greenville SC 29605-3729

WHITMIRE, MELBURN G., pharmaceutical distribution company executive; b. 1939. Student, Valley St. Coll. With Synergex Corp., Fresno, Calif., from 1958; pres. Drug Svcs., Inc., Fresno, Calif., 1980-85; with Amfac Distbn., Folsom, Calif., 1985-88; pres., c.e.o. MWC, Inc., Amfac Health Care (now known as Cardinal Health), Folsom, 1988-95; now vice chmn. With USAR, 1961-67. Office: Whitmire Distbn Co 81 Blue Ravine Rd Folsom CA 95630-4720*

WHITMORE, CHARLES HORACE, utility executive, lawyer, management consultant; b. Atlantic, Iowa, June 29, 1914; s. Tom Cornell and Adda Maria (Baldwin) W.; m. Millicent Stahly, May 3, 1935; children: Jacqueline, Tom Cornell. B.A., Grinnell Coll., 1935; J.D., State U. Iowa, 1940; LL.D., St. Ambrose Coll., 1960. Bar: Iowa bar 1937, Ill. bar 1939. Asst. counsel United Light & Power Co., 1937-41, exec. operating asst., 1942-43; asst. to pres. Iowa-Ill. Gas & Electric Co., Davenport, Iowa, 1946-47; gen. counsel Iowa-Ill. Gas & Electric Co., 1948-54, v.p., 1950-54, dir., 1950-80, pres., 1954-75, chmn. bd., 1956-79, chmn. exec. com., 1979-80; v.p., dir. Overseas Adv. Assos., Inc., Riyadh, Saudi Arabia, 1979-80; pres. Quad-City Devel. Group, 1971-73; chmn. Mid-Am. Interpool Network; also founding mem. Nat. Elec. Reliability Council, 1968-69. Served as lt., aviation supply officer USNR, 1944-45. Mem. Outing Club (Davenport), Rock Island Arsenal Golf Club (Ill.). Presbyterian. Home: Steepmeadow Rock Island IL 61201-4412 Office: 1800 Third Ave Rm 507 Rock Island IL 61201-8019

WHITMORE, DONALD CLARK, retired engineer; b. Seattle, Sept. 15, 1932; s. Floyd Robinson and Lois Mildred (Clark) W.; m. Alice Elinor Winter, Jan. 8, 1955; children: Catherine Ruth, William Owen, Matthew Clark, Nancy Lynn, Peggy Ann, Stuart John. BS, U. Wash., 1955. Prin. engr. The Boeing Co., Seattle, 1955-87, ret., 1987; developer, owner mobile home pk., Auburn, Wash., 1979—. Author: Towards Security, 1983, (monograph) SDI Software Feasibility, 1990, Characterization of the Nuclear Proliferation Threat, 1993, Rationale for Nuclear Disarmament, 1995. Activist for arms control, Auburn, Wash., 1962—; chmn. Seattle Coun. Orgns. for Internat. Affairs, 1973, Auburn Citizens for Schs., 1975; v.p. Boeing Employees Good Neighbor Fund, Seattle, 1977, Spl. Svc. award, 1977; bd. dirs. 8th Congl. Dist. Sane/Freeze, 1992—; pres., founder Third Millennium Found., 1994—. Avocations: hiking, travel, collecting. Home and Office: 16202 SE Lake Moneysmith Rd Auburn WA 98092-5274

WHITMORE, FRANK CLIFFORD, JR., geologist; b. Cambridge, Mass., Nov. 17, 1915; s. Frank Clifford and Marion Gertrude (Mason) W.; m. Martha Burling Kremers, June 24, 1939; children—Geoffrey, John, Katherine, Susan. B.A., Amherst Coll., 1938; M.S., Pa. State U., 1939; M.A., Harvard U., 1941, Ph.D., 1942. Teaching fellow Harvard U., Cambridge, Mass., 1940-42; instr. geology R.I. State Coll., Kingston, 1942-44; geologist U.S. Geol. Survey, Washington, 1944-84, scientist emeritus, 1984—; mem. com. on research and exploration Nat. Geog. Soc., 1970—, vice chmn., 1990—; research assoc. dept. Paleobiology Smithsonian Instn., Washington, 1967—; mem. adv. bd. Ctr. for Study of Early Man, U. Maine, Orono, 1985-90. Editor: Resources for 21st Century, 1982. Contbr. articles on geology and vertebrate paleontology to profl. jours. Bd. dirs. Prince Georges County Boys Clubs, Md., 1954-56; mem. program com. Nat. Capital council Girl Scouts U.S.A., Washington, 1967-69; pres. Thornton Soc., Washington, 1977-84. Recipient Medal of Freedom, U.S. Army, 1946; spl. achievement award, U.S. Geol. Survey, 1980; Meritorious Service award, U.S. Dept. Interior, 1981, Arnold Guyot Meml. award Nat. Geographic Soc., 1993. Fellow Geol. Soc. Am., AAAS; mem. Soc. Vertebrate Paleontology (hon. life, exec. com. 1960-62). Democrat. Clubs: Midriver, Harvard. Avocations: architectural history. Home: 20 Woodmoor Dr Silver Spring MD 20901-2447 Office: US Geol Survey Nat Mus Natural History MRC NHB 137 Washington DC 20560

WHITMORE, GEORGE MERLE, JR., management consulting executive; b. Tarrytown, N.Y., Jan. 1, 1928; s. George Merle and Elizabeth Helen (Knodel) W.; m. Priscilla Elizabeth Norman, Mar. 30, 1963; children: Elizabeth Whitmore Lippincott, George Norman, Stephen Bradford. BE, Yale U., 1949; MBA, Harvard U., 1951. Test engr. Gen. Electric Co., Bridgeport, Conn., Erie, Pa., 1949; rsch. assoc. Harvard Bus. Sch., Boston, 1951-52; assoc. Cresap, McCormick Paget Inc., N.Y.C., 1954-59, prin., 1959-61, ptnr., 1961-69, v.p., dir., 1969-79, mng. dir., CEO, 1979-81; mng. dir. Ayers, Whitmore & Co. Inc., N.Y.C., 1981-88, Ayers, Whitmore div. A.T. Kearney, Inc., N.Y.C., 1988-90; mng. dir. Whitmore & Co., Greenwich, Conn., 1990—; chmn. bd. The Advantage Ptnrs., Inc., Chatham, N.J., Philo Smith & Co., Inc., Stamford, Conn.; bd. dirs. Carroll Enterprises, Inc., Worcester, Mass., RTI Inc., Rockaway, N.J. Hon. trustee, former bd. pres. Hackley Sch., Tarrytown, N.Y.; former trustee, bd. chmn. Greenwich (Conn.) Acad.; former trustee, treas. Salisbury (Conn.) Sch. With USAF, 1952-53. Mem. Inst. Mgmt. Cons. (founding mem.), Newcomen Soc., Tau Beta Pi. Presbyterian. Clubs: Stanwich (former dir.) (Greenwich); Yale (N.Y.C.). Home and Office: 4 Cedarwood Dr Greenwich CT 06830-3905

WHITMORE, JAMES ALLEN, actor; b. White Plains, N.Y., Oct. 1, 1921; s. James Allen and Florence Belle (Crane) W.; m. Nancy Mygatt, Mar. 24, 1978 (div.); m. Audra Lindley; children: James, Steven, Daniel. B.A., Yale U., 1942; postgrad., Am. Wing Theatre Sch. Performances include: (Broadway plays) debut in Command Decision, 1947, Elba, Manhattan Theatre Club, Winesburg, Ohio, 1956, Inquest, 1970, Will Rogers U.S.A., Give 'Em Hell Harry, 1974, The Magnificent Yankee, Washington, 1976, Bully, 1977, Handy Dandy, 1985, (films) Battleground, 1949, Next Voice You Hear, 1950, Asphalt Jungle, 1950, Mrs. O'Malley and Mr. Malone, 1950, Outsiders, 1950, Please Believe Me, 1950, Across de Wide Missouri, 1951, It's a Big Country, 1951, Because You're Mine, 1952, Above and Beyond, 1952, Girl Who Had Everything, 1953, All the Brothers Were Valiant, 1953, Kiss Me Kate, 1953, The Command, 1954, Them!, 1954, Oklahoma, 1955, Battle Cry, 1955, McConnell Story, 1955, Eddy Duchin Story, 1956, Face of Fire, 1959, Who Was That Lady?, 1960, Black Like Me, 1964, Chuka, 1967, Waterhole 3, 1967, Nobody's Perfect, 1968, Planet of the Apes, 1968, Madigan, 1968, The Split, 1968, Guns of the Magnificent Seven, 1969, Chato's Land, 1972, Where the Red Fern Grows, 1974, Give 'Em Hell Harry, 1974 (Acad. award nomination 1975), Bully, 1978, The Serpent's Egg, 1978, First Deadly Sin, 1980, Nuts, 1987, The Shawshank Redemption, 1994, numerous others, (TV appearances) including The Law and Mr. Jones, 1960-61, My Friend Tony, 1969, Temperature Rising, 1972-73, Will Rogers U.S.A., 1973, (TV miniseries) Celebrity, 1986, Favorite Son, 1988. Served with USMCR, 1942-46. Nominated Acad. award, 1949; recipient Antoinette Perry award, 1947, Comedy award Am. Acad. Humor, Ace award, 1989; named Most Promising Newcomer, 1947.

WHITMORE, JON SCOTT, theater educator; b. Seattle, Mar. 22, 1945; s. Walter James and Eurma (Thody) W.; m. Jennifer Gean Gross, Aug. 17, 1985; children: Ian Scott, Amy Lee. BA in Speech and Theatre, Wash. State U., 1967, MA in Speech and Theatre, 1968; PhD in Dramatic Arts, U. Calif., Santa Barbara, 1974. Instr. theatre Highline Coll., Seattle, 1968-71; grad. asst. U. Calif., Santa Barbara, 1971-74; asst. prof. theatre W.Va. U., Morgantown, 1974-78, assoc. prof., 1978-82, prof., 1979-85, chmn. dept., 1979-84, interim dean, 1984-85; prof., dean Faculty Arts and Letters SUNY, Buffalo, 1985-90; dean Coll. of Fine Arts, U. Tex., Austin, 1990—. Dir. plays including Suddenly Last Summer, The Miracle Worker, Equus, Romeo and Juliet, Long Days Journey Into Night, The Sea Gull, The Comedy of Errors, The Glass Menagerie, Blithe Spirit, The Tavern, Black Comedy, You're a Good Man Charlie Brown, Vanities, The Effect of Gamma Rays on Man-In-The-Moon Marigolds, Epiphany, Endgame, The Miser, J.B., The Mousetrap, Knapp's Last Tape, Miss Julie, Servant of Two Masters, Before We Were; actor various classical, modern and contemporary plays, and performance pieces; author: Directing Postmodern Theater, 1994, William Saroyan, 1994. Mem. Erie County (N.Y.) Cultural Resources Adv. Bd., 1986-89, long range planning com. Studio Arena Theatre, Buffalo, 1986-90, trustee, 1987-90; mem. coun. fellows Am. Coun. Edn., 1984—; pres. W.Va. Theater Conf., 1978-80, pres.-elect, 1977-78, founding mem., bd. dirs., 1975-81. Recipient ACE Fellow award Am. Council Edn., 1983-84; fellow U. Calif., Santa Barbara, 1973-74, Lilly Found., 1976-77; Maynard Lee Daggy scholar Wash. State U., 1967. Mem. Internat. Council Fine Arts Deans, Am. Council Arts, Assn. Theatre in Higher Edn. (v.p. adminstrn. 1991—, chmn. nat. conf. planning com. chief adminstrs. program, 1987), Assn. Communication Adminstrn. (elected to exec. com. 1982-85, chmn. task force theatre adminstrn., 1982-84), Speech Communication Assn., Council Colls. Arts and Scis., Assn. Coll., Univ. and Community Arts Adminstrs., Nat. Assn. State Univs. and Land-Grant Colls. (chair elect commn. arts, 1990-92, chair 1992—). Home: 4503 Tortuga Cv Austin TX 78731-4541 Office: U Texas Coll Fine Arts Office of Dean Austin TX 78712

WHITMORE, KAY REX, retired photographic company executive; b. Salt Lake City, July 24, 1932; s. Rex Grange and Ferrol Terry (Smith) W.; m. Yvonne Schofield, June 6, 1956; children: Richard, Kimberly, Michele, Cynthia, Suzanne, Scott. Student, U. Utah, 1950-53, BS, 1957; MS, MIT, 1975. With Eastman Kodak Co., Rochester, N.Y., 1957-93, engr. film mfg., 1957-67; with factory start-up Eastman Kodak Co., Guadalajara, Mex., 1967-71; various mgmt. positions film mfg. Eastman Kodak Co., Rochester, 1971-74, asst. v.p., gen. mgr. Latin Am. Region, 1975-79, v.p., asst. gen. mgr. U.S. and Can. Photog. Div., 1979-80, exec. v.p. and gen. mgr., 1981-83, pres., 1983-90, chmn. bd., pres., chief exec. officer, 1990-93; bd. dirs. The Chase Manhattan Corp. Trustee U. Rochester. With U.S. Army, 1953-55. Mem. Am. Soc. for Quality Control, World Wildlife Fund. Mem. LDS Ch. Office: Eastman Kodak Co 343 State St Rochester NY 14650-0001*

WHITMORE, SHARP, lawyer; b. Price, Utah, Apr. 26, 1918; s. Leland and Anne (Sharp) W.; m. Frances Dorr, Aug. 15, 1940; children: Richard, William, Ann. A.B., Stanford U., 1939; J.D., U. Calif.-Berkeley, 1942; LL.D., U. Pacific, 1982. Bar: Calif. 1944. Asso. Gibson, Dunn & Crutcher, Los Angeles, 1946-50; partner Gibson, Dunn & Crutcher, 1951—; chmn. Calif. Com. Bar Examiners, 1956-58. Bd. dirs. Nat. Jud. Coll., 1989-92. Fellow Am. Bar Found. (chmn. 1982-83); mem. L.A. County Bar Assn. (pres. 1970-71), Nat. Conf. Bar Examiners (chmn. 1957-58), State Bar Calif. (bd. govs. 1962-65, v.p. treas. 1964-65), ABA (ho. of dels. 1957-58, 68-93, bd. govs. 1985-88, editl. bd. jour. 1994—), Order of Coif (hon.). Republican. Clubs: Bohemian, Sunset, Chancery (pres. 1962-63). Home: 2005 Gird Rd Fallbrook CA 92028-9685 Office: 750 B St Ste 3300 San Diego CA 92101-8105

WHITMORE, WILLIAM FRANCIS, physicist, retired missile scientist; b. Boston, Jan. 6, 1917; s. Charles Edward and Elizabeth Manning (Gardiner) W.; m. Elizabeth Sherman Arnold, Nov. 1, 1946; children: Charles, Edward, Thomas, Peter. SB, MIT, 1938; PhD (Univ. fellow), U. Calif., Berkeley, 1941. Math. physicist Naval Ordnance Lab., 1941-42; instr. physics MIT, 1942-46; sr. staff mem. ops. evaluation group USN, 1946-57, chief scientist spl. projects office, 1957-59; mem. chief scientist's staff missiles and space divsn. Lockheed Aircraft Corp., 1959-62; dep. chief scientist Lockheed Missiles & Space Co., Sunnyvale, Calif., 1962-64, asst. to pres., 1964-69, chief scientist (ocean systems), 1969-83, cons., 1984-88; ret., 1988; cons. evaluation bd. of USAAF, ETO, 1945; sci. analyst to comdg. gen. 1st Marine Wing, Korea, 1953; sci. analyst to asst. chief naval ops. for guided missiles, 1950-56; cons. adv. panel ordnance, transport and supply Dir. Def. Rsch. and Engring., 1958-62; mem. adv. bd. Naval Ordnance Labs., 1968-75, chmn., 1968-73; cons. marine bd. NRC, 1973-80. Mem. vis. com. math. dept. MIT, 1971-78. Recipient Navy Meritorious Pub. Svc. citation, 1961, Sec. of Navy cert. of commendations (3), 1960-66. Fellow AIAA (assoc.); mem. NRA (life), Am. Math. Soc., Math. Assn. Am., Optical Soc. Am., Ops. Rsch. Soc. Am., Cosmos Club, Phi Beta Kappa, Sigma Xi. Home: 801 Rose Ave Mountain View CA 94040-4040

WHITNEY, ALISON BURTON (WHITNEY BURTON MOVIUS), writer, educator, publisher, speaker; b. Billings, Mont., Apr. 4, 1945; d. William Robert and Alice Whitney (Burton) Movius; divorced; children: David Lindley, Elisabeth Whitney. BA in Humanities, U. Calif., Berkeley, 1967. Staff mem. Campus Crusade for Christ, various locations, 1967-78; dir. The Happy Place Nursery Sch., Ann Arbor, Mich., 1978-80; curriculum writer, children's songwriter, seminar spkr., 1976-85; founder, owner pub. co. Whitney Works!, La Jolla, Calif., 1992-96; writer, founder, pres. Abuse Edn. Network, La Jolla, 1992-96. Author: (workbook, lectures) The Challenge of Being a Women, 1976, Poems that Tell a Story, 1996, Poems for Battered Women, 1996, When There's Abuse, 1996, Making it Through the Hard Times, 1996, Happy Little Scripture Songs (for young children), 1996, Valued and Loved, 1996; writer 1500 children's songs. Named to Outstanding Young Women of Am., 1978. Avocations: running, reading, cooking, playing guitar, drawing. Office: Whitney Works! PO Box 13191 La Jolla CA 92039-3191

WHITNEY, BARRY LYN, religious studies educator; b. Cornwall, Ont., Can., Dec. 10, 1947; s. Earl Stanley Whitney and Gwendolyn Grace (Meldrum) Whitney. BA with honors, Carleton U., 1971; PhD in Religious Studies, McMaster U., Hamilton, Ont., 1977. Prof. religious studies U. Windsor, Ont., 1976—, rsch. prof., 1992-93; prof. pastoral edn. Southwestern Regional Ctr., Cedar Springs, Ont., 1977-79; mem. Anglican commn. Canterbury Coll., London and Windsor, 1977-79, tutor of admissions, Windsor, 1979-82, fellow, 1979-82; regional coord. Ctr. for Process Studies, 1979—. Author: Evil and the Process God, 1985, What Are They Saying About God and Evil?, 1989, Theodicy, 1993; contbr. articles to profl. jours. Scholar Carleton U., 1967-71, McMaster U., 1971-76, Can. Coun. scholar McMaster, U., 1972-75; rsch. grantee Social Scis. and Humanities Rsch. Coun., 1988-90. Mem. Soc. for Study Process Philosophies, Coll. Theology, Soc. Am. Acad. Religion, Coun. for Study Religion, others. Home: 601-1385 Riverside Dr W, Windsor, ON Canada N9B3R9 Office: U Windsor Religious Studies, 401 Sunset Ave, Windsor, ON Canada N9B 3P4 *Committed to the process vision of reality (Whitehead, Hartshorne) as a viable vision of God and a major advance in dealing with the terrible agony of suffering and injustice.*

WHITNEY, EDWARD BONNER, investment banker; b. Glen Cove, N.Y., June 6, 1945; s. Edward Farley and Millicent Bonner (Bowring) W.; m. Martha Congleton Howell, Aug. 17, 1974; children: William Howell, John Howell. B.A., Harvard U., 1966, M.B.A., 1969. Systems engr. IBM, Cambridge, Mass., 1966-67; assoc. Dillon, Read & Co. Inc., N.Y.C., 1969-74, v.p., 1975-79, sr. v.p., 1980-83, mng. dir., 1984—, also bd. dirs. Mem. Heights Casino Club (Bklyn.). Office: Dillon Read & Co Inc 535 Madison Ave New York NY 10022-4212

WHITNEY, JANE, foreign service officer; b. Champaign, Ill., July 15, 1941; d. Robert F. and Mussette (Cary) W. BA, Beloit Coll., 1963; CD, U. Aix, Marseille, France, 1962. Joined Fgn. Service, U.S. Dept. State, 1965, vice consul, Saigon, Vietnam, 1966-68, career counselor, 1968-70, spl. asst. Office of Dir. Gen., 1970-72, consul, Stuttgart, Fed. Republic Germany, 1972-74, Ankara, Turkey, 1974-76, spl. asst. Office of Asst. Sec. for Consular Affairs, 1976-77, mem. Bd. Examiners Fgn. Service, 1977-78, 79-81, consul, Munich, Germany, 1978-79, Buenos Aires, Argentina, 1981-82, ethics officer Office of Legal Adviser, 1982-85, advisor Office of Asst. Sec. for Diplomatic Security, 1985-86, dep. prin. officer, consul, Stuttgart, 1986-90, prin. officer, consul gen., Perth, Australia, 1990-91. Recipient awards U.S. Dept. State, 1968, 70, 81, 85, 87, 90. Mem. Presbyterian Ch.

WHITNEY, PAUL FRANCIS, gifted and talented education educator; b. N.Y.C., Sept. 28, 1947; s. William and Paula Ellen (Mehling) W.; m. Kathleen Travers, June 24, 1972. BA in History and Polit. Sci., Iona Coll., 1969, Profl. Diploma in Sch. Dist. Adminstrn., 1995; MA in Social Studies Tchg., CUNY, 1975, MS in Edn., 1981. Cert. social studies and English tchr., N.Y.; cert. sch. adminstrn. and supervision, sch. dist. adminstrn., N.Y. Guidance counselor, tchr.-mentor, dean, tchr. E.W. Stitt Jr. H.S., N.Y.C., 1970-86; coord., creator Alpha program Inwood Intermediate Sch., N.Y.C., 1994—; mem. Dist. 6 N.Y.C. Mentor Adv. Selection Com., 1988-94. Mem. Am. Fedn. Tchrs., United Fedn. Tchrs. (chpt. chairperson 1975-78), N.Y. State United Tchrs., Nat. Coun. Tchrs. English, Phi Delta Kappa. Democrat. Roman Catholic. Avocations: reading, traveling, golfing, fishing. Home: 204 Brittany Ct Valley Cottage NY 10989-2602 Office: Inwood IS 650 Academy St New York NY 10034-5004

WHITNEY, RALPH ROYAL, JR., financial executive; b. Phila., Dec. 10, 1934; s. Ralph Royal and Florence Elizabeth (Whitney) W.; m. Fay Wadsworth, Apr. 4, 1959; children: Lynn Marie, Paula Sue, Brian Ralph. BA, U. Rochester, 1957, MBA, 1972. Spl. agt. Prudential Ins. Co., Rochester, N.Y., 1958-59, divsn. mgr., 1959-63; gen. agt. Nat. Life Vt., Syracuse, 1963-64; contr. Wadsworth Mfg. Assocs. Inc., Syracuse, 1964-65, v.p., 1965-68, pres., 1968-71; pres. Warren (Pa.) Components Corp., 1968-72; pres., mng. prin. ptnr. Hammond Kennedy Whitney & Co., N.Y.C., 1972—; chmn. IFR Sys., Inc., Seneca Printing Inc., Control Devices Inc.; chmn., CEO Holbrook Patterson Inc., Globe Ticket & Label Co., Grobot File Co., Am. Maine Rubber Co., Miltco Inc.; bd. dirs. Excel Industries, Inc., Baldwin Tech. Corp., Selas Corp. Am., M. Mossberg & Son, Inc., Adage Inc., MedTek Inc. Mem. N.Y. Yacht Club, Lotus Club (N.Y.C.), Century Club (Syracuse), Merion Cricket Club, Princeton Club. Episcopalian. Home: 3441 Highway 34 Wheatland WY 82201-8714

WHITNEY, RICHARD BUCKNER, lawyer; b. Corpus Christi, Tex., Mar. 1, 1948; s. Franklyn Loren and Elizabeth Wolcott (Fish) W.; m. Chantal Marie Gindt, Aug. 18, 1972; children: Jennifer L., James R., Katherine E. BA in Polit. Sci., Union Coll., 1970; JD, Case Western Res. U., 1973. Bar: Ohio 1973, U.S. Dist. Ct. (no. dist.) Ohio 1974, U.S. Ct. Appeals (6th cir.) 1974, U.S. Ct. Appeals (3d cir.) 1987. From assoc. to ptnr. Jones, Day, Reavis & Pogue, Cleve., 1973—. Mem. ABA, Ohio Bar Assn., Cuyahoga County Bar Assn., Cleve. Bar Assn. (grievance com., unauthorized practice of law com.), Order of the Coif. Home: 2750 Southington Rd Cleveland OH 44120-1603 Office: Jones Day Reavis & Pogue 901 Lakeside Ave E Cleveland OH 44114-1116

WHITNEY, ROBERT MICHAEL, lawyer; b. Green Bay, Wis., Jan. 29, 1949; s. John Clarence and Helen (Mayer) W. Student, U. Wis., 1967-70, JD, 1974. Bar: Wis. 1974, U.S. Dist. Ct. (we. dist.) Wis. 1979, U.S. Ct. Appeals (7th cir.) 1980, U.S. Dist. Ct. (ea. dist.) Wis. 1984, U.S. Supreme Ct. 1990. Legal counsel Wis. State Election Bd., Madison, 1976-78; ptnr. Walsh, Walsh, Sweeney & Whitney, S.C., Madison, 1979-86, Foley & Lardner, Madison, 1986—; counsel Advocacy Assn. for Retarded Citizens, Madison, 1977-79. bd. dirs. Community TV, Inc., Madison, 1984-87. Mem. Assn. Trial Lawyers Am., Wis. Acad. Trial Lawyers, Wis. Bar Assn., Dane County Bar Assn., Rugby Club of Madison. Home: 5325 Lighthouse Bay Dr Madison WI 53704-1113 Office: Foley & Lardner First Wis Pla 1 S Pickney St PO Box 1497 Madison WI 53701

WHITNEY, RODGER FRANKLIN, associate directory, university housing; b. Dallas, Feb. 2, 1948; s. Roger Albert and Genevieve Mae (Mohr) W. Cert. higher studies, U. Lausanne, Switzerland, 1970; BA, So. Meth. U., 1971, M Liberal Arts, 1973; EdD, Harvard U., 1978. Dir. upperclass residences So. Meth. U., Dallas, 1971-73, mem. faculty, 1973-75; dir. Mohr Chevrolet Edn. Found., Dallas, 1975-77; dir. North Park East, Raymond D. Nasher Co., Dallas, 1977-79; dir. Stanford Housing Ctr., asst. dean student affairs Stanford (Calif.) U., 1979-91, assoc. dir. housing and dining, 1991—; dir. Camp Grady Spruce, YMCA, Dallas, 1971-76, bd. dirs., 1976-80. Bd. dirs. Kentfield Commons, Redwood City, Calif., 1989-91. Mem. APPA, Assn. Coll. and Univ. Housing Officers, Harvard Club San Francisco, Phi Beta Kappa. Avocations: swimming, travel, history, reading, music. Home: 861 Whitehall Ln Redwood City CA 94061-3685 Office: Stanford U Housing Ops 565 Cowell Ln Stanford CA 94305-8512

WHITNEY, RUTH REINKE, magazine editor; b. Oshkosh, Wis., July 23, 1928; d. Leonard G. and Helen (Diestler) Reinke; m. Daniel A. Whitney, Nov. 19, 1949; 1 son, Philip. BA, Northwestern U., 1949. Copywriter edn. dept. circulation div. Time, Inc., 1949-53; editor-in-chief Better Living mag., 1953-56; assoc. editor Seventeen magazine, 1956-62, exec. editor, 1962-67; editor-in-chief Glamour mag., N.Y.C., 1967—. Recipient Nat. Mag. award gen. excellence, 1981, 91, Pub. Interest, 1992, Cosmetic Executive Women Achiever award, 1993, honor award Women's City Club N.Y.; honoree Gala 11 Birmingham, So. Coll., 1993. Mem. Fashion Group, Am. Soc. Mag. Editors (pres. 1975-77, exec. com. 1989-92), Women in Communication (Matrix award 1980), Women in Media, U.S. Info. Agy. (mag. and print com. 1989-93), Alpha Chi Omega. Office: Glamour Condé Nast Bldg 350 Madison Ave New York NY 10017-3704*

WHITNEY, WILLIAM CHOWNING, retired banker, financial consultant; b. Fullerton, Nebr., June 28, 1920; s. Barlow N. and Lena C. (Price) W.; m. Joan F. Whitney; children—William H., David M., Terri Lynn, Sherri Lee, Jonathan P., Laura Louise. B.S. cum laude, Loyola U., Chgo., 1949. Asst. bank examiner Fed. Res. Bank, Chgo., 1938-41; asst. auditor South Side Bank and Trust Co., Chgo., 1946-49; comptroller Peoples Nat. Bank, Bay City, Mich., 1949-52; asst. v.p., comptroller Tex. Bank and Trust Co., Dallas, 1952-54; with Old Kent Bank and Trust Co., Grand Rapids, Mich., 1954-86; sr. v.p., CFO, sec. bd., dir. Old Kent Fin. Corp., 1965-86; cons. Amway Corp., 1986—. Chmn. Met. Hosp., 1986-93, Met. Health Corp., 1987-95; treas. Keswick United Meth. Ch. Capt. AUS, 1941-46. Mem. Fin. Execs. Inst. (past pres.), Mich. Banks Assn., Bank Adminstrn. Inst., Grand Rapids C. of C., Rotary, Peninsular Club, Cascade County Club, Univ. Club, Ada Lodge, Masons (fin. com. Grand Lodge), Econ. Club. Home: 742 Apple Tree Dr Suttons Bay MI 49682-9778

WHITNEY, WILLIAM ELLIOT, JR., advertising agency executive; b. Albany, N.Y., Feb. 22, 1933; s. William Elliot and Louise E. (Goldsmith) W.; m. Nancy B. Bivings, Mar. 1, 1958; children—Susan, James, Douglas. B.A. cum laude, Amherst Coll., 1954; M.B.A., Harvard U., 1956. Account exec. McCann-Erickson, N.Y.C., 1956-58, Marschalk Co., N.Y.C., 1958-60; v.p., then sr. v.p. Ogilvy & Mather, N.Y.C., 1960-80; sr. v.p., mng. dir. Ogilvy & Mather, Chgo., 1980-85, exec. v.p., 1985-87, pres., 1987-89, chmn., 1990-91; cons. ptnr. Redirections, Inc., 1991—; lectr. U. Chgo. Grad. Sch. Bus., 1991—. Bd. dirs., v.p. Chgo. Coun. Boy Scouts Am., 1978-81, 88—, Off-the-St. Club, Chgo., 1979—, pres., 1988-89; bd. dirs. Hinsdale (Ill.) Cmty. House, 1981, King-Bruwaert House, 1988—; v.p. civic adv. bd. Hinsdale Hosp., 1989-93; bd. dirs. Exec. Svc. Corps of Chgo., 1996—; trustee Village of Hinsdale, 1993—. Mem. Chgo. Advt. Club (pres.), Econs. Club, Hinsdale Golf Club. Home: 736 S Park Ave Hinsdale IL 60521-4646

WHITSEL, RICHARD HARRY, biologist, entomologist; b. Denver, Feb. 23, 1931; s. Richard Elstun and Edith Muriel (Harry) W.; children by previous marriages: Russell David, Robert Alan, Michael Dale, Steven Deane. BA, U. Calif., Berkeley, 1954; MA, San Jose State Coll., 1962. Sr. rsch. biologist San Mateo County Mosquito Abatement Dist., Burlingame, Calif., 1959-72; environ. program mgr., chief of watershed mgmt., chief of planning Calif. Regional Water Quality Control Bd., Oakland, 1972—; mem. grad. faculty water resource mgmt. U. San Francisco, 1987-89. Served with Med. Service Corps, U.S. Army, 1954-56. Mem. Entomol. Soc. Am., Entomol. Soc. Wash., Am. Mosquito Control Assn., Calif. Alumni Assn., The Benjamin Ide Wheeler Soc., Nat. Parks and Conservation Assn. (life), Sierra Club. Democrat. Episcopalian. Contbr. articles to profl. jours. Home: 4331 Blenheim Way Concord CA 94521-4258 Office: Calif Regional Water Quality Control Bd 2101 Webster St Oakland CA 94612-3027 *Any success that I have achieved probalby is the result of my fortune to have been exposed to some outstanding educators and scientists as well as being somewhat imaginative by nature. Working with young professional people keeps me young in spirit and seems to renew my enthusiasm in whatever I do.*

WHITSEL, ROBERT MALCOLM, retired insurance company executive; b. Lafayette, Ind., Dec. 30, 1929; s. Earl Newton and Elizabeth (Bader) W.; m. Marilyn Katherine House, Oct. 15, 1955; children—Rebecca Sue, Cynthia Ann. BS, Ind. U., 1951, MBA, 1954. With Lafayette Life Ins. Co., 1954-95, mem. exec. com., 1968-95, exec. v.p., 1973, pres., 1973-95, also bd. dirs., ret., 1995; mem. adv. bd. NBD, Bank. Elder, trustee, deacon Presbyn. Ch., 1965-74; dir., past pres. Jr. Achievement Greater Lafayette, Inc., 1976-77, Ctrl. Presbyn. Found., Edgelea PTA; past pres., bd. dirs., past campaign chmn. United Way Greater Lafayette; past v.p., bd. dirs. Wabash Sch. for Mentally Retarded; past mem. adv. bd. Purdue Ctr. for Econ. Edn.; past pres., bd. dirs. Capital Funds Found. Greater Lafayette; bd. dirs. Lafayette Home Hosp., 1972—, mem. fin. com., 1976—, past pres.; trustee YWCA Found.; past chmn. Greater Lafayette Progress Inc., North Ctrl. Health Svcs., Inc.; chmn. West Lafayette Found., Inc., Westminster Village Retirement Ctr.; past pres. Greater Lafayette Cmty. Found.; bd. dirs., mem. exec. com. purdue Rsch. Found. 1st lt. USAF, 1951-53. Recipient Nat. Bus. Leadership award, 1977. Mem. Soc. Residential Appraisers, Ind. Mortgage Bankers Assn. (past pres.), Am. Coun. Life Ins. (bd. dirs., chmn. Forum 500 sect.), Soc. Fin. Analysts, Assn. Ind. Life Ins. Cos. (past pres.), Ind. C. of C. (past dir.), Greater Lafayette C. of C. (past pres.), Ind. Soc. of Chgo., Lafayette Country Club (past pres., dir.), Sagamore of the Wabash (designated), Town and Gown Club, Masons, Beta Gamma Sigma. Republican. Home: 541 Old Farm Rd Lafayette IN 47905-3515 Office: Lafayette Life Ins Co 1905 Teal Rd # 7007 Lafayette IN 47905-2225

WHITSELL, DORIS BENNER, retired educator; b. Poplar Grove, Ill., Mar. 17, 1923; d. Ralph Erwin and Sarah McKay (Mulligan) Wheeler; m. Robert M. Benner, Dec. 1945 (div. 1955); 1 child, Geoffrey Mark Benner (dec.); m. Eugene B. Whitsell, Feb. 1969 (dec. 1972). BS, No. Ill. U., 1944, MS in Edn., 1967; postgrad., Rockford Coll., 1964. Tchr. English and home econs. Lee (Ill.) High Sch., 1944-45; tchr. English Ashton (Ill.) Community High Sch., 1945-46; tchr. Morris Kennedy Sch., Rockford, Ill., 1952-55, William Nashold Sch., Rockford, 1955-56; tchr. English, drama Jefferson Jr. High Sch., Rockford, 1956-69; tchr. English Richwoods High Sch., Peoria, Ill., 1969-71; tchr. Calvin Coolidge Sch., Peoria, 1972-81; mem. textbook selection com. Dist. 150, Peoria, 1973-75, curriculum planning com., 1974-75, tutor for homebound, 1982-83, cons. competency test seminar; cons. textbook divsn. Harcourt, Brace, Jovanovich, 1981-83; evaluator North Ctrl. Accreditation Team, Jefferson H.S., Rockford, 1980. Counselor Operation Sr. Security, Peoria, 1986-89; treas. Rockford Women's Club Fortnighty Dept., 1961-62; past deaconess 1st Federated Ch., Peoria; pres. Willow Heights Homeowner's Assn., Peoria, 1979-81; bldg. rep. Rockford Edn. Assn., 1954-56, 3d v.p., 1968-70; vol. Rockford Midway Village and Mus. Ctr., 1992, 95-96; bd. dirs. Forest Vale Estate Condominiums, Meadows Assn., Rockford, 1994, treas., 1995-96. Named for Significant Svc. to the Community, Ret. Sr. Vol. Program, Peoria, 1986. Mem. Ill. Ret. Tchrs. Assn. (life, sec. 1982-90, bd. dirs. Found. Inc., 1985-93, moderator conv. panel 1990, Outstanding Svc. award 1989), Peoria Area Ret. Tchrs. Assn. (2d v.p. 1987-88, pres. 1989-90, chmn. state bldg. fund. com. 1987-88), AAUW (program v.p. 1988-89), Nat. Ret. Tchrs. Assn. (life), No. Ill. U. Alumni Assn., Delta Kappa Gamma (chmn. ins. com. Beta Gamma chpt. 1956-60, v.p. 1962-64, pres. 1964-66, profl. affairs com. 1992-96, chmn. personal growth and svc. com. Nu chpt. 1988-90, program com. Lambda chpt. 1978-80). Avocations: reading, traveling, interior decorating, theatre. Home: 1283 Aarons Ct Rockford IL 61108-1536

WHITSELL, HELEN JO, lumber executive; b. Portland, Oreg., July 20, 1938; d. Joseph William and Helen (Cornwell) Copeland; m. William A. Whitsell, Sept. 2, 1960; 2 children. BA, U. So. Calif., 1960. With Copeland Lumber Yard Inc., Portland, 1960—, pres., chief exec. officer, 1973-84, chmn., chief exec. officer, 1984—; bd. dirs. First Interstate Bank of Orgn. Office: Copeland Lumber Yards Inc 901 NE Glisan St Portland OR 97232-2730

WHITSON, JAMES NORFLEET, JR., diversified company executive; b. Clinton, Okla., Mar. 14, 1935; s. James Norfleet and Georgia (Webb) W.; m. Lyda Lee Gibson, Apr. 19, 1956; 1 child, James Mark. BBA, Tex. Tech U., 1957. With LTV, Inc., Dallas, 1960-70; v.p. fin. Omega-Alpha, Inc., 1970-73; pres. Sammons Communications, Inc., Dallas, 1973-89; exec. v.p., chief operating officer Sammons Enterprises, Inc., Dallas, 1989—; bd. dirs. Sammons Enterprises, Inc., C-Span, Tri-Continental Corp. Mem. Alpha Tau Omega. Home: 6606 Forestshire Dr Dallas TX 75230-2856 Office: Sammons Enterprises Inc 300 Crescent Ct Dallas TX 75201-1876

WHITT, GREGORY SIDNEY, molecular phylogenetics, evolution educator; b. Detroit, June 13, 1938; s. Sidney Abram and Millicent (Ward) W.; m. Dixie Lee Dailey, Aug. 25, 1963. B.S., Colo. State U., 1962, M.S., 1965; Ph.D., Yale U., 1970. Asst. prof. zoology U. Ill., Urbana, 1969-72; asso. prof. genetics and devel. U. Ill., 1972-77, prof., 1977-87, prof. ecology, ethology and evolution, 1987—; affiliate Ill. Natural History Survey, 1981—; mem. NIH study sect., 1975-76. Co-editor: Isozymes: Current Topics in Biological and Medical Research, 1977-87; editor: Isozyme Bull., 1978-81; mem. editorial bd. Biochem. Genetics, 1975—, Devel. Genetics, 1978-83, Jour. Molecular Evolution, 1979—, Molecular Biology and Evolution, 1983-93, Molecular Phylogenetics and Evolution, 1992—; contbr. articles to profl. jours. Fellow AAAS; mem. Am. Genetics Assn., Am. Soc. Ichthyologists and Herpetologists, Soc. for Protection of Old Fishes, Internat. Soc. Molecular Evolution, Soc. Systematic Biologists. Home: 1510 Trails Dr Urbana IL 61801-7052 Office: U Ill Dept Ecol Ethol/Evol 515 Morrill Hall 505 S Goodwin Ave Urbana IL 61801-3707

WHITT, RICHARD ERNEST, reporter; b. Greenup County, Ky., Dec. 15, 1944; s. Walter Charles and Irene (Hayes) W.; children: Hayes Chadwick, Emily. Student, Ashland (Ky.) Community Coll., 1966-68; B.A. in Journalism, U. Ky., 1970. Reporter Middlesboro (Ky.) Daily News, 1970-71; asst. state editor Waterloo (Iowa) Courier, 1971-72; city editor Kingsport (Tenn.) Times, 1972-76; No. Ky. bur. chief Courier-Jour., Louisville, 1977; Frankfort bur. chief Courier-Jour., 1977-80, spl. projects reporter, 1980-89; investigative reporter Atlanta Jour. & Constn., 1989—. Served with USN, 1962-66. Decorated Air medal; recipient Pulitzer prize for coverage of Beverly Hills Supper Club fire, 1978; named Outstanding Ky. Journalist, 1978; recipient John Hancock award for excellence, 1983; named to U. Ky. Journalism Hall of Fame, 1995. Democrat. Office: Atlanta Jour & Constn 72 Marietta St NW Atlanta GA 30303-2804

WHITT, ROBERT AMPUDIA, III, advertising executive, marketing professional; b. San Antonio, Oct. 15, 1930; s. Robert and Alice (Whitt) Ampudia; m. Mary Jane Kothmann, June 2, 1951; children: April Whitt Horner, Robert IV, Roxanne Seaman. BA in Internat. Trade, U. of the Ams., Mexico City, 1955; postgrad., Am. Grad. Sch. Internat. Mgmt., Phoenix, 1991, 92. Sales mgr. Sinclair & Valentine Co., Cali, Colombia, 1956-59; CEO for L.Am. Vision, Inc., Mexico City, 1960-74; pres., CEO Tex. Parade, Inc., Austin, 1974-77; CEO world ops. Novedades Editores, Mexico City, 1977-82; chmn., CEO Mktg. Mercadeo Internat., Dallas, 1982—; bd. dirs. Robea, S.A., Mexico City, Poliform, S.A., Mexico City, Tex. Bus. Hall of Fame Foundation, Dallas; mem. Alliance for Progress Task Force, 1963-67. Co-author: How to Market and Distribute in Mexico, 1995; editor: (Spanish lang.) Dallas Cowboys mag., 1979, 80, 91 (Best Content award), Bienestar mag., 1978 (Best Content award); contbr. articles to profl. jours. Sgt. U.S. Airborne, 1950-53. Recipient Nat. Winner award Silver Microphone, 1991, Nat. Finalist award, 1991, Addy award Am. Advt. Fedn., 1992, Nat. Winner award Telly awards (4), 1993, 95; named Speaker of the Year Toastmasters Internat., 1980. Mem. Fgn. Corr. Club, 11th Airborne Div. Assn. (life), Brookhaven Country Club (Dallas), Univ. Club (Dallas), Univ. Club (Mexico City), Metropolitan Soc. of Clubs. Office: Mktg Mercadeo Internat 2929 Mossrock Ste 205 San Antonio TX 78230-5116 *Only oneself can truly measure one's achievements. My greatest achievement is that I have no regrets and wouldn't change a minute, day or year of my life...including the downtimes.*

WHITTEMORE, EDWARD REED, II, poet, retired educator; b. New Haven, Sept. 11, 1919; s. Edward Reed and Margaret Eleanor (Carr) W.; m. Helen Lundeen, Oct. 3, 1952; children: Catherine Carr, Edward Reed III, John Lundeen, Margaret Goodhue. A.B., Yale U., 1941; postgrad., Princeton U., 1945-46; Litt.D., Carleton Coll., 1971. Mem. faculty Carleton Coll., 1947-67, prof. English, 1962-67, chmn. dept., 1962-64; program assoc. Nat. Inst. Pub. Affairs, 1966-68; editor Carleton Miscellany, 1960-64; cons. in poetry Libr. of Congress, 1964-65, 84-85; Bain-Swiggett lectr. Princeton, 1967; prof. U. Md., 1968-84, prof. emeritus, 1984—; poet laureate State of Md., 1985-88; lit. editor New Republic, 1969-74. Author: Heroes and Heroines, 1947, An American Takes a Walk, 1956, The Self-Made Man, 1959, The Boy From Iowa, 1962, The Fascination of the Abomination, 1963, Poems, New and Selected, 1967, From Zero to the Absolute, 1967, 50 Poems 50, 1970, The Mother's Breast and the Father's House, 1974, William Carlos Williams: Poet from Jersey, 1975, The Poet as Journalist, 1976, The Feel of Rock, 1982, Pure Lives, 1988, Whole Lives, 1989, The Past, the Future, the Present, 1990, Six Literary Lives, 1993; editor: Furioso, 1939-53, Browning, 1960, Delos mag., 1988-91. Capt. USAAF, 1941-45. Recipient award merit AAAL, 1971. Home: 4526 Albion Rd College Park MD 20740-3610

WHITTEMORE, LAURENCE FREDERICK, private banker; b. Bangor, Maine, Mar. 7, 1929; s. John Cambridge and Elizabeth Payson (Prentiss) W.; m. Sarah Lee Arnold, Aug. 9, 1958; children—Arianna, Gioia, Lia, Nike. B.A., Yale U., 1951; M.B.A., Harvard U., 1953; student, Balliol Coll., Oxford U., Eng., 1950. Account mgr. Brown Bros. Harriman, N.Y.C., 1956-72; gen. mgr. Brown Bros. Harriman, 1972-74; ptnr. Brown Bros. Harriman & Co., 1974—; dir. Manhattan Life Ins. Co., N.Y.C., Otto Wolff US Holding Co., 1982-86, Hurricane Industries, Houston, 1982-85, Albany Ins. Co., N.Y.C., Atlas Assurance Co. of Am., N.Y.C., 1984-86; mem. investment adv. com. Union Investment GmbH, Frankfurt, West Germany, 1973—; mem. Chgo. Stock Exch., 1975—. Trustee Sarah Lawrence Coll., 1988—, Am. Inst. Contemporary German Studies, 1994—; mem. Nat. Com. on U.S. China Rels., N.Y.C., 1982—, Chgo. Coun. on Fgn. Rels., 1980—;

del. Assn. Yale Alumni, New Haven, 1982-86; chmn. Yale 35th Reunion Gift Drive, 1983-86. Served to comdr. USNR, 1953-56. Mem. Econ. Club of Chgo., N.Y. Soc. Security Analysts, Investment Analysts Soc. Chgo., Assn. for Investment Mgmt. and Rsch. Republican. Episcopalian. Clubs: Links, Yale, India House (N.Y.C.); Chicago; Minneapolis (Mpls.). Office: Brown Bros Harriman & Co 59 Wall St New York NY 10005-2818

WHITTEMORE, RONALD P., hospital administrator, retired army officer, nursing educator; b. Saco, Maine, Aug. 10, 1946; s. Ronald B. and Pauline L. (Larson) W.; m. Judy D. McDonald, Feb. 17, 1967; 1 child, Leicia Michelle. BGS, U. S.C., 1974, MEd, 1977; BSN, Med. Coll. Ga., 1975. Enlisted U.S. Army, 1968, advanced through ranks to maj., 1985, ret., 1991; adult/oncology nurse practitioner Martin Army Community Hosp.; asst. head nurse SICU, infection control practitioner Moncrief Army Community Hosp.; infection control practitioner U.S. Army Hosp., Seoul, Korea; chief nurse 2d Combat Support Hosp., Ft. Benning, Ga.; community health nurse Brooke Army Med. Ctr., Ft. Sam Houston, Tex.; comty. health nurse Giessen (Fed. Republic Germany) Mil. Comty.; clin. instr. Eisenhower Army Med. Ctr., Ft. Gordon, Ga.; chief nursing adminstrn. E/N Frankfurt (Germany) Army Med. Ctr.; adminstr., dir. quality improvement Gracewood (Ga.) State Sch. and Hosp., 1995—; instr. Augusta (Ga.) Tech. Inst.; nurse epidemiologist Med. Coll. Ga., Augusta. Mem. ANA, Ga. ANA (3d Dist. honoree, pres. 1983-85), Am. Holistic Nurses Assn., Nat. Assn. Health Care Quality Profls., Sigma Theta Tau. Home: 801 Bon Air Dr Augusta GA 30907 Office: Gracewood State Sch & Hosp Gracewood GA 30812

WHITTEN, CHARLES ALEXANDER, JR., physics educator; b. Harrisburg, Pa., Jan. 20, 1940; s. Charles Alexander and Helen (Shoop) W.; m. Joan Emann, Nov. 20, 1965; 1 son, Charles Alexander III. B.S. summa cum laude, Yale U., 1961; Ph.D. in Physics, Princeton U., 1966. Research asso. A.W. Wright Nuclear Structure Lab., Yale U., 1966-68; asst. prof. physics UCLA, 1968-74, assoc. prof., 1974-80, prof., 1980—, vice chmn. physics dept., 1982-86; vis. scientist Centre d'Etudes Nucléaires de Saclay-Moyenne Energie, 1980-81, 86-87. Contbr. articles to profl. jours. Mem. Am. Phys. Soc., Sigma Pi Sigma, Phi Beta Kappa. Home: 9844 Vicar St Los Angeles CA 90034-2719

WHITTEN, DAVID GEORGE, chemistry educator; b. Washington, Jan. 25, 1938; s. David Guy and Miriam Deland (Price) W.; m. Jo Wright, July 9, 1960; children: Jenifer Marie, Guy David. A.B., Johns Hopkins U., 1959; M.A., John Hopkins U., 1961, Ph.D., 1963. Asst. prof. chemistry U. N.C., Chapel Hill, 1966-70, assoc. prof., 1970-73, prof., 1973-80, M.A. Smith prof., 1980-83; C.E. Kenneth Mees prof. U. Rochester, N.Y., 1983—, chair dept. chemistry, 1988-91, 95—; dir. Ctr. for Photoinduced Charge Transfer U. Rochester, N.Y., 1989-95; mem. adv. com. for chemistry NSF; cons. Eastman Kodak Co.; Rochester, N.Y. Alfred P. Sloan fellow, 1970; John van Geuns fellow, 1973; recipient special U.S. scientist award Alexander von Humboldt Found., 1975; Japan Soc. for Promotion of Sci. fellow, 1982. Mem. AAAS, Am. Chem. Soc. (award in colloid and surface chemistry 1992), Internat. Union of Pure and Applied Chemistry (commn. on photochemistry), Interam. Photochem. Soc. (pres.). Democrat. Episcopalian. Home: 72 Canterbury Rd Rochester NY 14607-3405 Office: U Rochester Dept Chemistry 404 Hutchinson Hall Rochester NY 14627

WHITTEN, DOLPHUS, JR., former university administrator, educational consortium executive; b. Hope, Ark., June 20, 1916; s. Dolphus and Annie Tyree (Logan) W.; m. Marie Braden, May 1, 1939; 1 dau., Suzanne (Mrs. H. Robert Guy). B.A., Ouachita Coll., 1936; M.A., U. Tex., 1940, Ph.D., 1961; postgrad., Western Res. U.; LL.D., McMurry Coll., Abilene, Tex., 1964. High Sch. tchr. and prin., Ark. pub. schs., 1936-42; prin. Hope Jr.-Sr. High Sch., 1945-47; dir. extension and placement services, asso. prof. history Henderson State Tchrs. Coll., Arkadelphia, Ark., 1947-58; adminstrv. dean Oklahoma City U., 1958-61, adminstrv. v.p., 1961-70, acting pres., 1962-63, 69-70, pres., 1970-79, pres. emeritus, 1979—; adj. prof. history Elon Coll., 1979-80; exec. dir. Joint Ednl. Consortium, Arkadelphia, Ark., 1980-90. Bd. dirs. Ark. Humanities Coun., 1992—. Served with USAAF, 1942-45; lt. col. ret. Inducted into Okla. Hall of Fame, 1975. Mem. Am. Hist. Assn., Ark. Hist. Assn., Okla. Heritage Assn., Rotary (gov. local dist. 1991-92), Alpha Chi (past pres. region II), Pi Gamma Mu, Phi Alpha Theta, Sigma Alpha Iota. Methodist.

WHITTEN, JERRY LYNN, chemistry educator; b. Bartow, Fla., Aug. 13, 1937; s. John Graves and Dorothy Iola (Jordan) W.; m. Mary Hill (div. Sept. 1977); 1 child, Jerrard John; m. Adela Chrzeszczyk, June 21, 1980; 1 child, Christina. BS in Chemistry, Ga. Inst. Tech., 1960, PhD, 1964. Cert. chemist. Rsch. assoc. to instr. Princeton (N.J.) U., 1963-65; asst. prof. chemistry Mich. State U., East Lansing, 1965-67; asst. prof. chemistry SUNY, Stony Brook, 1967-68, assoc. prof., 1968-73, prof., 1973-89, chmn. chemistry dept., 1985-89; prof. chemistry, dean Coll. Phys. and Math. Scis. N.C. State U., Raleigh, 1989—; vis. prof. Centre Europèen de Calcul Atomique et Molèculaire, Orsay, France, 1974-75, Univ. Bonn and Wuppertal, Fed. Republic Germany, 1979-80, Eidgenossische Technische Hochschule, Zurich, Switzerland, 1984. Contbr. more than 140 articles to profl. jours. Bd. dirs. N.C. Sch. Sci. and Math Found. Recipient Alexander von Humboldt U.S. Sr. Scientist award, 1979; grantee Petroleum Rsch. Fund, 1966-67, 74-76, 77-81, NSF, 1967-72, U.S. Dept. Energy, 1977—; SDIO/ONR grantee, 1991-92; Alfred P. Sloan fellow, 1969-71. Mem. AAAS, Am. Phys. Soc., Am. Chem. Soc., N.Y. Acad. Scis., Burroughs Wellcome Fund (bd. dirs.), Sigma Xi. Democrat. Episcopalian. Avocations: boating, tennis, skiing. Office: NC State U Coll Dept Phy and Math Scis Box 8201 Raleigh NC 27695-8201

WHITTEN, LESLIE HUNTER, JR., author, newspaper reporter, poet; b. Jacksonville, Fla., Feb. 21, 1928; s. Leslie Hunter and Linnora (Harvey) W.; m. Phyllis Webber, Nov. 11, 1951; children: Leslie Hunter III, Andrew, Daniel, Deborah Wilson Gordon. B.A. in Journalism and English magna cum laude, Lehigh U., 1950, LHD, 1989. Newsman Radio Free Europe, 1952-57, I.N.S., 1957-58, U.P.I., 1958, Washington Post, 1958-63; with Hearst Newspapers, 1963-66; asst. bur. chief Hearst Newspapers, Washington, 1966-69; sr. investigator Jack Anderson's Washington Merry-Go-Round, 1969-92; pres. Athanor Inc., 1977-93; vis. assoc. prof. Lehigh U., 1967-69; adj. prof. So. Ill. U., 1984. Author: Progeny of the Adder, 1965, Moon of the Wolf, 1967, Pinion the Golden Eagle, 1968, The Abyss, 1970, F. Lee Bailey, 1971, The Alchemist, 1973, Conflict of Interest, 1976, Washington Cycle, 1979, Sometimes a Hero, 1979, A Killing Pace, 1983, A Day Without Sunshine, 1985, The Lost Disciple, 1989, The Fangs of Morning, 1994; contbr. numerous poems to anthologies and other publs. Served with AUS, 1946-48. Recipient hon. mention pub. service Washington Newspaper Guild, 1963, Edgerton award ACLU, 1974. Home and Office: 114 Eastmoor Dr Silver Spring MD 20901-1507

WHITTERS, JAMES PAYTON, III, lawyer, university administrator; b. Boston, Oct. 23, 1939; s. James P. Jr. and Norene (Jones) W.; m. Elizabeth Robertson, July 19, 1969; children: James P. IV, Catharine A. BA in History, Trinity Coll., Hartford, Conn., 1962; JD, Boston Coll., 1969; postgrad, U. Mass., Boston. Bar: Mass. 1969, U.S. Dist. Ct. Mass. 1970, U.S. Ct. Appeals (1st cir.) 1972. Assoc. Ely, Bartlett, Brown & Proctor, Boston, 1969-74; assoc. Gaston Snow & Ely Bartlett, Boston, 1974-79, ptnr., 1979-88; ptnr. Gaston & Snow, Boston, 1988-91; of counsel Peabody & Brown, Boston, 1991-95; dir. Office Career Svcs. Suffolk U. Law Sch., Boston, 1995—; adj. prof. Am. legal history Suffolk U. Law Sch., 1996—; bd. dirs., sec. Robertson Factories, Inc., Taunton, Mass., 1979—; bd. dirs., v.p. Alkalol Co., Taunton, 1976—; vis. tchr. Groton (Mass.) Sch., 1993-94; mem. Mass. Conflict Intervention Mediation Team, 1995—. Bd. dirs. New Eng. com. NAACP Legal Def. Fund, 1982—, Beacon Hill Nursery Sch., 1976-78; chmn. Mass. Outdoor Advt. Bd., Boston, 1975-81; vice chmn. Mass. Jud. Nominating Coun., Boston, 1983-87; trustee Trinity Coll., 1983-95; trustee, sec. Hurricane Island Outward Bound Sch., 1977-87; vice chmn., bd. dirs. Mass. affiliate Am. Heart Assn., 1979—, chmn., 1989-91; bd. dirs. Greater Boston Legal Svcs., 1982-84, 93—, Mass. Assn. Mediation Programs and Practitioners, 1993—. Lt. (j.g.) USN, 1962-65. Recipient Alumni Excellence award Trinity Coll., 1987. Mem. Boston Bar Assn., Mass. Bar Assn., ABA, The Country Club (Brookline, Mass.). Democrat. Unitarian. Avocations: reading history, mountain climbing & jogging. Home: 44 Mount Vernon St Boston MA 02108-1302

WHITTINGHAM, CHARLES ARTHUR, library administrator, publisher; b. Chgo., Feb. 11, 1930; s. Charles Arthur and Virginia (Hartke) W.; m. Jean Bragger Whittingham, June 4, 1955; children: Mary Elizabeth, Charles Arthur III, Philip Alexander, Leigh Ann. B.S. in English Lit. cum laude, Loyola U., Chgo., 1951. With McCall Corp., Chgo., 1956-59, Time, Inc., Chgo., 1959-62; pub.'s rep. Fortune mag., Time, Inc., N.Y.C., 1962-65; mgr. Fortune mag., Time, Inc. (San Francisco Office), 1965-69; asst. to pub. Fortune, N.Y.C., 1969-70, asst. pub., 1970-78; pub. Life mag., N.Y.C., 1978-88; sr. v.p. N.Y. Pub. Libr., 1989-92. Served to lt. (j.g.) USNR, 1951-55. Named to Athletic Hall of Fame Loyola U. Mem. Century Assn., Brook Club. Home and Office: 11 Woodmill Rd Chappaqua NY 10514-1128 also: 584 Bartram St Boca Raton FL 33433

WHITTINGHAM, CHARLES EDWARD, thoroughbred race horse owner and trainer; b. San Diego, Apr. 13, 1913; s. Edward and Ellen (Taylor) W.; m. Peggy Boone, Oct. 12, 1944; children: Michael Charles, Charlene. Trainer thoroughbred horses, Calif., 1930-42; asst. trainer Luro Pub. Stable, N.Y., 1945-49; owner, trainer Whittingham Pub. Stable, Sierra Madre, Calif., 1949—; winner Ky. Derby with Ferdinand, 1986, with Sunday Silence, 1989. Mem. Rep. Senatorial Inner-Circle, Washington, 1983—, nat. advisor bd. Am. Security Council, Washington, 1976—; campaigner mem. Rep. Nat. Com., Washington, 1976—. Served to master sgt. USMC, 1942-45, PTO. Recipient Eclipse awards Thoroughbred Race Track Assn./Daily Racing Form/Nat. Turf Writers Assn., 1971, 82, 89; named to Nat. Racing Hall of Fame, 1974, Brietbard Hall of Fame/Hall of Champions, San Diego, 1993. Mem. Horsemens Benevolent & Protective Assn. (v.p 1976—). Republican. Roman Catholic. Avocation: anything related to thoroughbred race horses. Home: 88 Lowell Ave Sierra Madre CA 91024-2510 Office: Charles Whittingham Inc 145 S Baldwin Ave Sierra Madre CA 91024-2556

WHITTINGHAM, HARRY EDWARD, JR., retired banker; b. Albany, N.Y., Dec. 25, 1918; s. Harry E. and Mary (Baer) W.; m. Gladys D. Willstaedt, Sept. 2, 1942; children: Jeffrey A., Neal E. Grad., Stonier Grad. Sch. Banking, 1961. With Schenectady Trust Co., 1947-84, pres., chief exec. officer, 1974-82, chmn., chief exec. officer, 1982-84. Author: (with Purdy, Schneider, Aldom) Automation in Banking, 1962. Served with AUS, 1941-46. Episcopalian (vestryman). Clubs: Mohawk Golf (Schenectady). Home: 2314 Brookshire Dr Niskayuna NY 12309-4838

WHITTINGHAM, M(ICHAEL) STANLEY, chemist; b. Nottingham, Eng., Dec. 22, 1941; came to U.S., 1968, naturalized, 1980; s. William Stanley and Dorothy Mary (Findlay) W.; B.A. in Chemistry, Oxford U., 1964, M.A. (Gas Council scholar 1964-67), D.Phil., 1968; m. Georgina Judith Andai, Mar. 23, 1969; children: Jenniffer Judith, Michael Stanley. Rsch. asso., head solid state electrochemistry group Materials Center, Stanford U., 1968-72; mem. staff Exxon Research Co., Linden, N.J., 1972—, group head solid state chem. physics, 1975-78, dir. solid state scis., 1978-80, mgr. chem. engring. tech., 1980-84; dir. phys. scis. Schlumberger Co., Ridgefield, Conn., 1984-88; prof. chemistry, dir. The Inst. for Materials Rsch., SUNY, 1988—, vice provost for rsch. SUNY, 1994—, vice-chair bd. dirs. Rsch. Found., 1995—; cons., lectr. in field. JSPS fellow U. Tokyo; mem. Electrochem. Soc. (Young Author award 1971, N.Y. chmn. 1980-81), Am. Chem. Soc. (chmn. solid state sect. 1987, chmn. Binghamton sect. 1991), Am. Phys. Soc., Materials Rsch. Soc. Author, editor papers in field; author 5 books. Achievements include patents in field; reversible (rechargeable) lithium batteries and methods for making intercalation batteries; method for making TiS_2 mixed material cathodes, high briteness luminescent displays. Home: 396 Meeker Rd Vestal NY 13850-3230 Office: SUNY Dept Chemistry Binghamton NY 13902

WHITTINGTON, BERNARD WILEY, electrical engineer, consultant; b. Charleston, W.Va., July 19, 1920; s. Owen Wiley and Ethel Parker (Thaxton) W.; m. Jean Wilhelm, Feb. 2, 1950; children: David Brian, Ann Leslie, Brenda Wiley. B.S. in Elec. Engring., W.Va. U., 1951. Registered profl. engr., W.Va. Elec. engr. Appalachian Power Co., Charleston, W.Va., 1951-56; mgr. sales Virginian Electric Co., Charleston, W.Va., 1956-59; engring. cons. Union Carbide Corp., Charleston, W.Va., 1959-82; pres. Whittington Engring., Inc., Charleston, W.Va., 1983—; chmn. bd. dirs. Bank of Sissonville, Pocatalico, W.Va.; pres. W.Va. Assn. Pub. Svc. Dists., 1983-86. Chmn. Water and Sewage Bd., Pocatalico, W.Va., 1958-89. Served to cpl. U.S. Army, 1942-45. Fellow IEEE (Standards Medallion award 1976, Outstanding Achievement award 1978, Centennial medal 1984, Richard Harold Kaufman award 1989); mem. Industry Applications Soc. (pres. 1982), Acad. Elec. Engring. Republican. Methodist. Lodge: Lions. Home and Office: 100 Whittingshire Ln Charleston WV 25312-9554

WHITTINGTON, FLOYD LEON, economist, business consultant, retired oil company executive, foreign service officer; b. Fairfield, Iowa, May 27, 1909; s. Thomas Clyde and Ora E. (Trail) W.; m. Winifred Carol McDonald, July 31, 1933; children: Susan Whittington West, Thomas Lee. A.B., Parsons Coll., 1931; M.A., U. Iowa, 1936; student, U. Minn., 1940, Northwestern U., 1941-42. Econs., speech instr. Fairfield High Sch., 1931-36, Superior (Wis.) High Sch., 1936-40; supr. tchr. tng. Superior State Tchrs. Coll., 1936-40; econs., finance instr. Carroll Coll., Waukesha, Wis., 1940-42; price exec. OPA, Wis. and Iowa, 1942-46; indsl. relations mgr. Armstrong Tire & Rubber Co., Des Moines, 1946-48; dir. price and distbn. div. SCAP, Tokyo, Japan, 1948-51; Far East economist ODM, Washington, 1951-52; asst. adviser to sec. on Japanese financial and econ. problems Dept. State, Washington, 1952-53; chief Far Eastern sect. Internat. Finance div.; bd. govs. FRS, Washington, 1953-56; officer charge econ. affairs Office S.E. Asian Affairs, Dept. State, 1956-57, dep. dir., 1957-58; became counselor of embassy Am. embassy, Bangkok, 1958; counselor, polit. officer Am. embassy, Djakarta, Indonesia, 1962-65; counselor of embassy for econ. affairs Seoul, Korea, 1965-66; v.p. Pacific Gulf Oil, Ltd., Seoul, 1966—; exec. v.p. S.E. Asia Gulf Co., Bangkok, 1967-72, Gulf Oil Co. Siam, Ltd., Bangkok, 1967-72; v.p. Gulf Oil Co.-South Asia, Singapore, 1970-72; now Asian bus. cons. Recipient Meritorious Civilian Service citation Dept. Army, 1950. Mem. Am. Econ. Assn., Am. Acad. Polit. Sci., World Affairs Council Seattle (pres.), Seattle Com. Fgn. Relations, Pi Kappa Delta, Theta Alpha Phi. Presbyterian. Clubs: Royal Bangkok (Thailand); Sports; Lakes (Sun City, Ariz.). Lodges: Masons; Shriners; Rotary. Home: 1 Towers Park Ln Apt 515 San Antonio TX 78209-6421

WHITTINGTON, FREDERICK BROWN, JR., business administration educator; b. Sept. 22, 1934; m. Marjorie Ann Babington; children: Frederick Brown III, Marjorie Ellen, Lisa Anne. SB, MIT, 1958; MBA, Tulane U., 1965; PhD, La. State U., 1969. Staff economist Miss. Rsch. Commn., Jackson, 1961-64; sr. assoc. econ. rsch. Gulf South Rsch. Inst., Baton Rouge, 1966-69; asst. prof. bus. adminstrn. Emory U., Atlanta, 1969-73, assoc. prof., 1973-79, prof. bus. adminstrn., 1979—, dir. customer bus. devel. track, 1991—; bd. dirs. Gwinnett Industries, Inc.; mem. forecasting panel Fed. Res. Bank Atlanta; vis. prof. Johannes Kepler U., Linz, Austria, 1983, 84, 89, 95, 96; guest lectr. Austrian Univs., Linz, Vienna, Innsbruck and Klagenfurt; presenter workshops; cons. in field. Contbr. articles and reports to profl. jours. Mktg. plan, mgmt. audit State of Miss., Park Commn.; past chmn., bd. deacons Decatur Presbyn. Ch.; mem. adv. bd. DeKalb/Rockdale Svc. Ctr., ARC. Capt. USNR, ret. Sears, Roebuck Found. fellow, 1965-66. Mem. Am. Mktg. Assn., Nat. Assn. Purchasing Mgmt., So. Mktg. Assn., Coun. for Logistics Mgmt., Warehousing Edn. and Rsch. Coun., Omicron Delta Kappa, Beta Gamma Sigma, Delta Tau Delta. Office: Goizueta Bus Sch Emory Univ Atlanta GA 30322

WHITTINGTON, ROBERT BRUCE, retired publishing company executive; b. Oakland, Calif., Mar. 5, 1927; s. Edward and Loretta (Edalgo) W.; m. Marie D. Sanguinetti, June 18, 1950; children: Mark, Lynn. Student, Stockton Jr. Coll., 1946-48; B.A. in Journalism and Polit. Sci. (Friend W. Richardson fellow), U. Calif., Berkeley, 1950. Reporter Stockton (Calif.) Record, 1950-60, exec. news editor, 1965-68, asso. pub., 1968-69, pub., 1969-72; v.p., dir. Speidel Newspapers, Reno, 1972-77; regional pres., dir. Gannett Co., Inc., Reno, 1977-82; publ. Reno (Nev.) newspapers, 1980-82; v.p., trustee Gannett Found., 1982-85; dir. Sierra Pacific Resources; pres. Speidel Newspapers Charitable Found. Served with USNR, 1944-46, PTO. Roman Catholic. Home: 2432 Pheasant Run Cir Stockton CA 95207-5212

WHITTINGTON, STUART GORDON, chemistry educator; b. Chesterfield, England, Apr. 16, 1942; came to Can., 1967; s. Frank and Eva May (Gretton) W.; m. Ann Fretwell, Aug. 3, 1964; children: Graeme, Megan. BA, U. Cambridge, Eng., 1963, PhD, 1972. Scientist Unilever Research, Welwyn, U.K., 1963-66, 68-70; postdoctoral fellow U. Calif., La Jolla, 1966-67; postdoctoral fellow U. Toronto, Can., 1967-68, asst. prof., 1970-75, assoc. prof., 1975-80, prof. chemistry, 1980—, chmn. dept. chemistry, 1985-88. Contbr. 150 articles to profl. jours. Mem. Am. Math. Soc., Internat. Soc. Math. Chemistry, Can. Assn. Theoretical Chemists. Mem. New Democratic Party. Avocations: music, natural history. Home: 173 Airdrie Rd, Toronto, ON Canada M4G 1M7 Office: U of Toronto, Dept Chemistry, Toronto, ON Canada M5S 1A1

WHITTLE, CHARLES EDWARD, JR., consultant, lecturer; b. Brownsville, Ky., Mar. 8, 1931; s. Charles Edward and Lillian (Skaggs) W.; m. Suzanne Lee Miller, June 22, 1952; children: Charles, Jane, Jessica, Gayl, Tamara, Thomas, David, Jeffrey, Mary, Michael. AB, Centre Coll., Ky., 1949; PhD, Washington U., St. Louis, 1953; postgrad., U. Leiden, Netherlands, 1953-54, U. Tenn., 1975. Registered land surveyor, Ky. Engr. Union Carbide Corp., N.Y.C., 1954-56; physicist Western Ky. U., Bowling Green, 1956-62; prof., dean Centre Coll., Danville, Ky., 1962-74; researcher Inst. Energy Analysis-Oak Ridge Associated Univs., 1974-85, divsn. dir., 1985-88; v.p. C & S Assocs., Oak Ridge, Tenn., 1988-93; dean Pikeville (Ky.) Coll., 1988-93; v.p. M.W. Garay Assocs., Oak Ridge, 1993—; bd. dirs. Ky. World Trade Ctr.; cons. and lectr. in field. Author: Nuclear Moratorium, 1977; contbr. articles to profl. jours. Life mem. Ky. Hist. Soc. Fulbright scholar, 1953-54; Danforth Found. grantee, 1970. Mem. Am. Phys. Soc., East Tenn. Hist. Soc., Oak Ridge C. of C. (indsl. recruitment com. 1984-89), Rotary (bd. dirs. Oak Ridge 1980-86, 89-90, pres. 1984-85, dist. 6780 group study exch. team leader to Mex. 1986, chmn. dist. group study exch. com. 1987-89, 95-96, gov. nominee 1996-97), Phi Beta Kappa, Sigma Xi. Avocation: genealogy. Home: 109 Trevose Ln Oak Ridge TN 37830-5454 Office: MW Garay Assocs Trevose Ln Oak Ridge TN 37830-5454

WHITTLE, JOHN JOSEPH, insurance company executive; b. Harrisburg, Pa., Mar. 3, 1936; s. Ernest James and Stephanie W.; m. Sarah A. Rausch, 1960; children: Jennifer, Jack, Lisabette. B.S., Pa. State U., 1958; grad. exec. devel. seminar, Cornell U., 1973; Masters, Am. Coll., 1986. C.L.U. Sales asst. Mut. Life Ins. Co. of N.Y., N.Y.C., 1958-65; mgr. Tacoma agy. Mut. Life Ins. Co. of N.Y., 1965-67, field sales dir. Eastern region, 1967-69, regional v.p. Central region, 1969-72, 2d v.p. for sales adminstrn., 1972-74, v.p. for sales service, 1974-76, v.p. for human resources/corp. services, 1976-79, v.p. for sales, 1979-80, sr. v.p. sales, 1980-83, sr. v.p. operating services, 1983-84, sr. v.p. Syracuse ops. MONY Fin. Services, 1984-89; pres., chief exec. officer Farmers & Traders Life Ins. Co., Cazenovia, N.Y., 1989-91, chmn., pres., chief exec. officer, 1991—; also bd. dirs. Farmers & Traders Life Ins. Co., Syracuse, N.Y.; bd. dirs. Syracuse div. Chase Manhattan Bank Adv. Bd. Bd. dirs. Cmty.-Gen. Hosp. and Found., Met. Devel. Assn. Syracuse and Ctrl. N.Y., Inc., Syracuse State, Wellness Coun., United Way, Everson Mus. Art. With USAFR, 1961-62. Mem. Gen. Agts. and Mgrs. Assn., C.L.U. Soc., Life Underwriters Assn., Am. Coun. Life Ins. (pub. rels. policy com., bd. govs.), Syracuse C. of C. (bd. dirs.), Life Ins. Coun. N.Y., Onondaga Golf and Country Club. Republican. Methodist. Office: Farmers & Traders Life Ins Co 960 James St Syracuse NY 13203-2503

WHITWAM, DAVID RAY, appliance manufacturing company executive; b. Stanley, Wis., Jan. 30, 1942; s. Donald R. and Lorraine (Stoye) W.; m. Barbara Lynne Peterson, Apr. 13, 1963; children: Mark, Laura, Thomas. B.S., U. Wis., 1967. Gen. mgr. sales So. Calif. div. Whirlpool Corp., Los Angeles, 1975-77; mdse. mgr. ranges Whirlpool Corp., Benton Harbor, Mich., 1977-79, dir. builder mktg., 1979-80, v.p. builder mktg., 1980-83, v.p. whirlpool sales, 1983-85, vice chmn., chief mktg. officer, 1985-87, chmn., pres., chief exec. officer, 1987—, also bd. dirs.; bd. dirs. Combustion Engring. Inc., Stamford, Conn. Pres. bd. dirs. The Soup Kitchen, Benton Harbor, 1980—; mem. Nat. Council Housing Industry, Washington. Served to capt. U.S. Army. Fellow Aspen Inst. Republican. Lutheran. Club: Point O'Woods (Benton Harbor). Office: Whirlpool Corp 2000 M63 North Benton Harbor MI 49022*

WHITWORTH, HALL BAKER, forest products company executive; b. St. Paul, N.C., Feb. 15, 1919; s. A. Frederick and Maude Ethel (Baker) W.; m. Mary Margaret Mease, May 18, 1946; children: Hall Baker, Laura Ellen, David Allen. Student, Miss. So. Coll., 1942, U. N.C., 1957. With Champion Internat., Canton, N.C., 1936-62; mgr. materials Champion Internat., Canton, 1956-62; dir. materials packages div. Champion Internat., Chgo., 1962-65; dir. purchase U.S. Plywood-Champion Papers, Inc. (now champion Internat. Corp.) Champion Internat., Hamilton, Ohio, 1965-68, dep. dir. corporate materials services, 1966, v.p., dir. purchase, 1968-75; v.p. materials Champion Internat., Stamford, Conn., 1975—, dir., 1975—, now ret.; v.p., dir. So. Agrl. Co., 1985—; pres., dir. H. Whitworth Enterprises, Cin., 1985—; dir. Pathfork-Harlan Coal Co. Served with U.S. Army, 1942-46. Recipient Thomas award Carolina-Va. Purchasing Agts. Assn., 1963. Mem. Am. Paper Inst. (chmn. energy subcom.), Am. Mgmt. Assn. (v.p. purchasing, transp. and phys. distbn. div. council). Methodist. Club: Canton Toastmakers (founder, 1st pres.). Lodges: Elks; Lions. Home and Office: 858 Lullwater Dr Oviedo FL 32765-8512

WHITWORTH, JOHN HARVEY, JR., lawyer; b. Pontotoc, Miss., Aug. 13, 1933; s. John Harvey Sr. and Clara Gladys (Tudor) W. BBA, U. Miss., 1955, JD, 1961; student, U. Delhi, India, 1958-59. Bar: Miss. 1961, N.Y. 1962, U.S. Supreme Ct.1965. Assoc. Dewey Ballantine, N.Y.C., 1961-69, ptnr., 1969-93. Editor in chief U. Miss. Law Jour., 1961. Mem. adv. bd. Nat. Arboretum, Washington, 1986-88; mem. vestry St. Peter's Ch. at Lithgow, Millbrook, N.Y., 1987—. Served with U.S. Army, 1955-57. Mem. Southwestern Legal Found. (trustee 1986—, chmn. Internat. and Comp. Law Ctr. 1984-85). Republican. Episcopalian. Clubs: Knickerbocker (N.Y.C.), Sandanona Hare Hounds (Millbrook, N.Y.). Avocations: landscape gardening, dogs. Home: PO Box 398 Millbrook NY 12545-0398 Office: Dewey Ballantine 1301 Avenue Of The Americas New York NY 10019-6022*

WHITWORTH, KATHRYNNE ANN, professional golfer; b. Monahans, Tex., Sept. 27, 1939; d. Morris Clark and Dama Ann (Robinson) W. Student, Odessa (Tex.) Jr. Coll., 1958. Joined tour Ladies Profl. Golf Assn., 1959—; mem. adv. staff Walter Hagen Golf Co., Wilson Sporting Goods Co. Named to Hall of Fame Ladies Profl. Golf Assn., Tex. Sports Hall of Fame, Tex. Golf Hall of Fame, World Golf Hall of Fame; Capt. of Solhiem Cup, 1990-92. Mem. Ladies Profl. Golf Assn. (sec. 1962-63, v.p. 1965, 73, 88, pres. 1967, 68, 71, 89, 1st mem. to win over $1,000,000). Office: care Ladies Profl Golf Assn 2570 Volusia Ave Daytona Beach FL 32114-1119

WHITWORTH, WILLIAM A., magazine editor; b. Hot Springs, Ark., Feb. 13, 1937; s. William C. and Lois Virginia (McNabb) W.; m. Carolyn Hubbard, Dec. 27, 1969; children—Matthew, Katherine. B.A., U. Okla., 1960. Reporter Ark. Gazette, Little Rock, 1960-63; reporter N.Y. Herald Tribune, 1963-65; staff writer The New Yorker, 1966-72, assoc. editor, 1973-80; editor-in-chief The Atlantic Monthly, Boston, 1981—. Office: Atlantic Monthly 745 Boylston St Boston MA 02116-2636

WHORISKEY, ROBERT DONALD, lawyer; b. Cambridge, Mass., May 9, 1929; s. John Joseph and Katherine Euphemia (MacDonald) W.; m. Martha Beebe Poutas, Apr. 16, 1966; children: Alexandra, Jonathan, Eliza. AB, Harvard U., 1952; JD, Boston Coll., 1958; LLM, NYU, 1960. Bar: Mass. 1958, N.Y. 1963, U.S. Tax Ct. 1961, U.S. Claims Ct. 1969, U.S. Dist. Ct. (so. dist.) N.Y. 1969, U.S. Ct. Customs 1971, U.S. Ct. Appeals (2d cir.) 1972, U.S. Ct. Appeals (3d cir.) 1983, U.S. Ct. Appeals (D.C. cir.) 1991, U.S. Supreme Ct. 1974. Sr. trial atty. Office Chief Counsel, IRS, N.Y.C., 1960-67; assoc. Curtis, Mallet-Prevost, Colt & Mosle, N.Y.C., 1967-70, ptnr., 1970—, mem. exec. com., 1978-82, chmn. tax dept., 1982-87; bd. dirs. Internat. Tax Inst., v.p., lectr., 1980-84, chmn. bd., pres., lectr., 1985-87; lectr. Practicing Law Inst., World Trade Inst., Tax Execs. Inst., Am. Mgmt. Assn., Coun. for Internat. Tax Edn.; bd. dirs. Life Ins. Co. of Boston and N.Y., Inc. Author: Foreign Trusts, 1977, Annual Institute on International Taxation, 1966, 80, 81, (with Sidney Pine, Ralph Seligman) Tax and Business Benefits of the Bahamas, 1986; contbg. author: International Boycotts, Bender's Federal Service, 1988, Third Party Information, John Wiley and Sons, Inc.'s Transfer Pricing, 1993, Transfer Pricing Under IRC & 482: Overview and

Planning, 1996. Trustee, treas. Montessori Sch. Westchester, 1974-77; mem. bd. ethics Village of Larchmont, N.Y., 1988—. Served with U.S. Army, 1952-54. Mem. ABA (com. on value added tax tax sect. 1994—), N.Y. State Bar Assn. (com. on practice and procedure tax sect. 1990—), Assn. of the Bar of the City of N.Y., Harvard Club, Larchmont Yacht Club. Democrat. Roman Catholic. Office: Curtis Mallet-Prevost Colt & Mosle 101 Park Ave New York NY 10178

WHORTON, M. DONALD, occupational and environmental health physician, epidemiologist; b. Las Vegas, N.Mex., Jan. 25, 1943; s. R.H. and Rachel (Siegal) W.; m. Diana L. Obrinsky, Apr. 9, 1972; children: Matthew Richard, Laura Elizabeth, Julie Hannah. Student, U.S. Naval Acad., 1961-62; B.Biology, N. Mex. Highlands U., 1964; M.D., U. N.Mex., 1968; M.P.H., Johns Hopkins U., 1973. Intern Boston City Hosp., 1968-69; resident in pathology U. N.Mex., Albuquerque, 1969-71; instr., resident in medicine Balt. City Hosp., 1972-74; instr. Johns Hopkins U., Balt.; assoc. dir. div. emergency medicine Balt. City Hosps., 1974-75; clin. asst. prof. div. ambulatory and community medicine Sch. Medicine, U. Calif.-San Francisco, 1975-77; lectr. sch. pub. health program Inst. Indsl. Relations, Ctr. for Labor Research and Edn., 1975-79, med. dir. labor occupational program, 1975-79, assoc. clin. prof. occupational medicine, 1979-88; prin. Environ. Health Assocs., Inc., Oakland, 1978-88; v.p. ENSR Health Scis., 1988-94; pvt. practice Alameda, Calif., 1994—; chmn. adv. com. for hazard evaluation service and info. system Indsl. Relations Dept. State of Calif., 1979-84; cons. in field. Contbr. articles to profl. jours. Recipient Upjohn Achievement award, 1968; Robert Wood Johnson Found. clin. scholar, 1972-74. Fellow Am. Coll. Epidemiology, Am. Coll. Occupational and Environ. Medicine; mem. Am. Pub. Health Assn., Soc. for Occupational and Environ. Health, Am. Coll. Emergency Physicians, Calif. Med. Assn., AAAS, Inst. Medicine, Nat. Acad. Sci., Alpha Omega Alpha. Office: 1135 Atlantic Ave Alameda CA 94501-1145

WHYBARK, DAVID CLAY, educational educator, researcher; b. Tacoma, Wash., Sept. 18, 1935; s. Clay Alfred and Irene (Stanton) W.; m. Neva Jo Richardson, July 6, 1957; children: Michael David, Suzanne Marie (dec.). BS, U. Washington, 1957; MBA, Cornell U., 1960; PhD, Stanford U., 1967. Rsch. assoc. Stanford (Calif.) U., 1962-67; asst. prof. Ariz. State U., Tempe, 1965-66; assoc. prof. Purdue U., West Lafayette, Ind., 1967-76; prof. Ind. U., Bloomington, 1976-90; Macon G. Patton disting. prof. U. N.C., Chapel Hill, 1990—; vis. prof. Shanghai Inst. Mech. Engring., 1986-87, Chinese U. of the Hong Kong, 1996, Victoria U., New Zealand, 1996, Canterbury U., New Zealand, 1996; adj. prof. Inst. for Mgmt. Devel., Lausanne, Switzerland, 1981-82, 85-90; dir., founder Global Mfg. Rsch. Group, 1990—; cons. in field. Author: Master Production Scheduling: Theory and Practice, 1979, Manufacturing Planning Control Systems, 1984, 2d edit., 1988, 3d edit., 1992, International Operations Management, 1989, Integrated Production and Inventory Management, 1993; editor: Global Manufacturing Practices, 1993; editor Internat. Jour. Prodn. Econs., 1991-95. Recipient Lilly Alumni MBA Teaching Excellence award, 1990. Fellow Decision Scis. Inst. (past pres., disting. svc. award 1984), Pan Pacific Bus. Assn. (mem. coun.); mem. Ops. Mgmt. Assn. (pres. 1992-93), Am. Prodn. Inventory Control Soc., Internat. Soc. Inventory Rsch. (mem. coun., chair mgmt. sect.), Coun. Logistics Mgmt., Assn. Mfg. Excellence. Avocations: travel, winemaking. Office: U NC Kenan-Flagler Sch Global Mfg Rsch Ctr Chapel Hill NC 27599-3490

WHYBROW, PETER CHARLES, psychiatrist, educator; b. Hertfordshire, Eng., June 13, 1939; came to U.S., 1964, naturalized, 1975; s. Charles Ernest and Doris Beatrice (Abbott) W.; m. Margaret Ruth Steele, Dec. 11, 1962 (div. 1988); children: Katherine, Helen. Student, Univ. Coll., London, 1956-59; M.B., B.S., Univ. Coll. Hosp. Med. Sch., 1962; diploma psychol. medicine, Conjoint Bd., London, 1968; M.A. (hon.), Dartmouth Coll., 1974, U. Pa., 1984. House officer endocrinology Univ. Coll. Hosp., 1962, sr. house physician psychiatry, 1963-64; house surgeon St. Helier Hosp., Surrey, Eng., 1963; house officer pediatrics Prince of Wales Hosp., London, 1964; resident psychiatry U. N.C. Hosp., 1965-67, instr., research fellow, 1967-68; mem. sci. staff neuropsychiat. research unit Charshalton, Surrey, 1968-69; dir. residency tng. psychiatry Dartmouth Med. Sch., Hanover, N.H., 1969-71; prof. psychiatry Dartmouth Med. Sch., 1970-84, chmn. dept., 1970-78, exec. dean, 1980-83; prof., chmn. dept. psychiatry U. Pa., Phila., 1984—, Ruth Meltzer prof. psychiatry, 1992; psychiatrist-in-chief Hosp. U. Pa., 1984—; dir. psychiatry Dartmouth Hitchcock Affiliated Hosp., 1970-78; vis. scientist NIMH, 1978-79; cons. VA, 1970—, NIMH, 1972— ; chmn. test com. Nat. Bd. Med. Examiners, 1977-84; researcher psychoendrocrinology. Author: Mood Disorders: Toward a New Psychobiology, 1984, The Hibernation Response, 1988; editor: Psychosomatic Medicine, 1977; mem. editl. bd. Cmty. Psychiatry, Psychiat. Times, Directions in Psychiatry, Neuropsychopharmacology; contbr. articles to profl. jours. Recipient Anclote Manor award psychiat. rsch. U. N.C., 1967, Sr. Investigator award nat. Alliance for Rsch. into Schizophrenia and Depression, 1989; Josiah Macy Jr. Found. scholar, 1978-79; fellow Cen. for Advanced Studies in Behavioral Sci., Stanford, 1993-94; recipient Lifetime Investigator award NDMDA, 1996; decorated Knight of Merit, Sovereign Order of St. John of Jerusalem, 1993. Fellow AAAS, Am. Psychiat. Assn., Royal Coll. Psychiatrist (founding mem.), Am. Coll. Psychiatrists, Ctr. Advanced Study of Behavioral Scis.; mem. Assn. Am. Med. Colls., Soc. Psychosomatic Rsch., Am. Assn. Chmn. Depts. Psychiatry (pres. 1977-78), Royal Soc. Medicine, Am. Psychopath Assn., Am. Coll. Neuropsychopharmacology, Soc. Biol. Psychiatry, N.Y. Acad. Scis., Soc. Neurosci., Sigma Xi, Alpha Omega Alpha, Cosmos Club (Washington). Club: Cosmos (Washington). Office: U Pa Dept Psychiatry 305 Blockley Hall Philadelphia PA 19104 also: 135 S 19th St Philadelphia PA 19103-4912

WHYTE, ANNE VERONICA, social science researcher, educator; b. Thorne, U.K., Apr. 14, 1942; arrived in Can., 1975; d. Philip and Grace Grant Mathieson (Tennant) Whyte; m. Robert Dewfall Auger; children from previous marriages: David Philip Kirkby, Clare Anne Kirkby, Joanna Catherine Whyte Burton. BA with honors, Cambridge U., Eng., 1963, MA, 1967; PhD, Johns Hopkins U., 1971. Geographer div. anthropology Smithsonian Inst., Washington, 1965-66; rsch. fellow Centre Latin-Am. Studies, U. Cambridge, 1967-68; rsch. assoc. depts. geography and psychology U. Bristol, Eng., 1968-74; univ. lectr. dept. geography U. Coll., U. London, 1974-75; assoc. prof. geography U. Toronto, Ont., Can., 1976-78, dir. undergrad. environ. studies Innis Coll., 1978-86; programme specialist MAB Programme Div. Ecol. Scis. UNESCO, Paris, 1984-86; dir. social scis. div. Internat. Devel. Rsch. Centre, Ottawa, Ont., Can., 1986-92, dir. gen., environment and natural resources div., 1992—; chairperson African Econ. Rsch. Consortium Inc., N.Y.C., 1987-90, Can. Nat. Com. UNESCO/MAB, Ottawa, 1989-93; Can. Global Change Program, Ottawa, 1990-92; mem. exec. bd. Can. Commn. for UNESCO, Ottawa, 1988-92; mem. internat. adv. com. Internat. Coun. Sci. Unions; active Ont. Roundtable for Environment and Economy, 1993-95; dir. LEAD Internat. Inc., 1994—. Author: Land and Water Resources in Oaxaca, Mexico, 1973, Field Studies in Environmental Perception, 1977, Environmental Risk Assessment, 1980, Building a New South Africa: Environment, Reconstruction and Development, 1995. Open Exhbn. and State scholar Girton Coll., Eng., 1961-63, Fulbright scholar Cambridge U., 1963-65. Fellow Royal Soc. Can., World Acad. Arts and Sci.; mem. Am. Assn. Geography, Can. Assn. Geographers (v.p.), Can. Assn. Geographers (v.p. 1993-94, pres. 1994—), Internat. Coun. Sci. Unions (mem. internat. adv. com.), Royal Canadian Geographical Soc. (gov. 1995—), Cambridge Club, Sigma Xi. Avocation, gardening. Home: White House Farm, RR 2, Russell, ON Canada K4R 1E5 Office: Internat Devel Rsch Centre, 250 Albert St PO Box 8500, Ottawa, ON Canada K1G 3H9

WHYTE, GEORGE KENNETH, JR., lawyer; b. Waukegan, Ill., Oct. 10, 1936; s. George K. and Ella Margaret (Osgood) W.; m. Ann B. Challoner, June 20, 1964; children: Mary, Douglas. AB in Polit. Sci., Duke U., 1958; LLB, U. Wis., 1965. Bar: Wis. 1965. Law clk. to chief justice Wis. Supreme Ct., Madison, 1965-66; assoc. Quarles & Brady, Milw., 1966-73, ptnr., 1973—. Lt. USN, 1958-62. Mem. ABA (employment law sect.), Wis. Bar Assn. (former chmn. labor and employment law sect.), Rotary. Congregationalist. Clubs: The Town, Milw. Athletic, Milw. Country. Home: 906 E Circle Dr Milwaukee WI 53217-5361 Office: Quarles & Brady 411 E Wisconsin Ave Milwaukee WI 53202-4409

WHYTE, JAMES PRIMROSE, JR., former law educator; b. Columbus, Miss., Aug. 25, 1921; s. James P. and Mary (Savage) W.; m. Martha Ann Jones, Sept. 11, 1948; children—James Jones, Stuart Ward, Wilson Scott. A.B., Bucknell U., 1943; M.A., Syracuse U., 1948; J.D., U. Colo., 1951. Bar: Okla. 1951, Mo. 1957, Va. 1961. With firm Gordon & Whyte, McAlester, Okla., 1951-55; county atty. Pittsburg County, Okla., 1955-56; atty. Great Lakes Pipe Line Co., Kansas City, Mo., 1957; prof. law Coll. William and Mary, 1958-82, asst. dean, 1958-68, asso. dean, 1969-70, dean, 1970-75; ad hoc arbitrator Fed. Mediation and Conciliation Svc., Va. Dept. Labor, also industry and govt. panels. Contbr. profl. jours.; Mem. editorial adv. bd.: John Marshall Papers, 1966-77. Mem. Bd. Zoning Appeals, Williamsburg, 1971-77, chmn., 1977; trustee, pres. Williamsburg Regional Libr., 1965; trustee Williamsburg Area Meml. Community Ctr., 1963-68, pres., 1966-67. Served with USNR, 1943-46. Mem. Nat. Acad. Arbitrators, Va. State Bar, Phi Beta Kappa, Tau Kappa Alpha, Sigma Tau Delta. Home and Office: 5626 Boatwright Cir Williamsburg VA 23185

WHYTE, MARTIN KING, sociology and Chinese studies educator; b. Oklahoma City, Nov. 4, 1942; s. William Foote and Kathleen (King) W.; m. Veronica Mueller, Nov. 5, 1966 (div. 1990); children: Adam, Tracy; m. Alice Hogan, Sept. 14, 1991; 1 child, Julia. A.B., Cornell U., 1964; M.A., Harvard U., 1966, Ph.D., 1971. From asst. prof. to prof. dept. sociology U. Mich., Ann Arbor, 1969-95; assoc. chmn. dept. sociology U. Mich., 1972-73, 79-81; dir. Univs. Service Ctr., Hong Kong, 1973-74; program dir.Sociology Program NSF, Washington, 1993-94; prof. dept. sociology George Washington U., Washington, 1995—; vis. prof. George Washington U., 1994-95; mem. joint com. on Chinese studies Am. Coun. of Learned Socs., 1978-81, 84-87; dir. Ctr. for Rsch. on Social Orgn., 1984-87, 90-92. Author: Small Groups and Political Rituals in China, 1974, The Status of Women in Preindustrial Societies, 1978; (with others) Village and Family in Contemporary China, 1978, Urban Life in Contemporary China, 1984, Dating, Mating and Marriage, 1990. Mem. Am. Sociol. Assn., Assn. Asian Studies, Phi Beta Kappa. Democrat. Avocation: tennis. Home: 10403 Muir Pl Kensington MD 20895-2929 Office: Dept Sociology The George Washington U 2129 G St NW Washington DC 20052-2746

WHYTE, MICHAEL PETER, medicine and pediatrics educator, research director; b. N.Y.C., Dec. 19, 1946; s. Michael Paul and Sophie (Dziuk) W.; m. Gloria Frances Golenda, Oct. 26, 1974; 1 child, Catherine Alexandra. BA in Chemistry, NYU, 1968; MD, SUNY, N.Y.C., 1972. Diplomate Am. Bd. Internal Medicine, Nat. Bd. Med. Examiners. Intern, 1st yr. resident dept. medicine NYU Sch. Medicine Bellevue Hosp., N.Y.C., 1972-74; clin. assoc. devel. and metabolic neurology br. Nat. Inst. Neurol. and Communicative Disorders and Stroke NIH, Bethesda, Md., 1974-76; fellow divsn. bone and mineral metabolism dept. medicine Wash. U. Sch. Medicine, 1976-79, instr. dept. medicine, 1979-80, asst. sci. dir. Clin. Rsch. Ctr., 1979—; asst. physician Barnes Hosp., 1979—; dir. Metabolism Clinic Shriners Hosp. Crippled Children, St. Louis, 1979—; staff physician St. Louis Children's Hosp., 1979—; NIH clin. assoc. physician Clin. Rsch. Ctr. Wash. U. Sch. Medicine, 1980-82, asst. prof. medicine dept. medicine, 1980-86, assoc. prof. medicine dept. medicine, 1986-91, asst. prof. pediatrics Edward Mallinckrodt dept. pediatrics, 1982-89, assoc. prof. pediatrics Edward Mallinckrodt dept. pediatrics, 1989-92, prof. medicine dept. medicine, 1991—, prof. pediatrics Edward Mallinckrodt dept. pediatrics, 1992—; med. dir. Metabolic Rsch. Unit Shriners Hosp. Crippled Children, St. Louis, 1982—, mem. staff., 1983—; assoc. attending physician Jewish Hosp. St. Louis, 1983—; staff cons. Shriners Hosp. Crippled Children, St. Louis, 1979-83, Mexico City, 1991—; editl. bd. Calcified Tissue Internat., 1995, Jour. Bone and Mineral Rsch., 1994—; med. adv. bd. Osteogenesis Imperfecta Found., 1986—, med. adv. panel Paget's Disease Found., 1986—; chmn. med. adv. coun., bd. dirs. Osteogenesis Found., 1995—. Assoc. editor: Primer on Metabolic Bone Diseases and Disorders of Mineral Metabolism, 1990, 93, 96; assoc. editor Calcified Tissue Internat., 1989—; contbr. chpts. to books, articles to profl. jours. Lt. comdr. USPHS, 1974-76. Mem. Am. Soc. Cell Biology, Am. Soc. Clin. Investigation, Am. Coll. Physicians (assoc.), Am. Fedn. Clin. Rsch., Am. Soc. Advancement Sci., Am. Soc. Bone and Mineral Rsch. (ednl. com. 1987—, Fuller Albright award 1987, Young Investigator award 1983), Am. Soc. Human Genetics, Endocrine Soc., Soc. Exptl. Biology and Medicine, Japanese Soc. Inherited Metabolic Disease (hon.). Office: Barnes-Jewish Hosp 216 S Kings Hwy Saint Louis MO 63110

WHYTE, RONALD M., federal judge; b. 1942. BA in Math., Wesleyan U., 1964; JD, U. So. Calif., 1967. Bar: Calif. 1967, U.S. Dist. Ct. (no. dist.) Calif. 1967, U.S. Dist. Ct. (cen. dist.) Calif. 1968, U.S. Ct. Appeals (9th cir.) 1986. Assoc. Hoge, Fenton Jones & Appel, Inc., San Jose, Calif., 1971-77, mem., 1977-89; judge Superior Ct. State of Calif., 1989-92, U.S. Dist. Ct. (no. dist.) Calif., San Jose, 1992—; judge pro-tempore Superior Ct. Calif., 1977-89; lectr. Calif. Continuing Edn. of Bar, Rutter Group, Santa Clara Bar Assn., State Bar Calif.; legal counsel Santa CLara County Bar Assn., 1986-89; mem. county select com. Criminal Conflicts Program, 1988. Bd. trustees Santa Clara County Bar Assn., 1978-79, 84-85. Lt. Judge Advocate Gen.'s Corps, USNR, 1968-71. Recipient Judge of Yr. award Santa Clara County Trial Lawyers Assn., 1992, Am. Jurisprudence award. Mem. Calif. Judges Assn., Assn. Bus. Trial Lawyers (bd. govs. 1991-93), Santa Clara Inn of Ct. (exec. com. 1993—), San Francisco Bay area Intellectual Property Inn of Ct. (exec. com. 1994—). Office: US Courthouse 280 S 1st St San Jose CA 95113-3095

WHYTE, WILLIAM FOOTE, industrial relations educator, author; b. Springfield, Mass., June 27, 1914; s. John and Isabel (VanSickle) W.; m. Kathleen King, May 28, 1938; children: Joyce, Martin, Lucy, John. A.B., Swarthmore Coll., 1936, L.H.D. (hon.), 1984; mem., Soc. of Fellows, Harvard U., 1936-40; Ph.D., U. Chgo., 1943. Asst. prof. sociology, acting chmn. dept. anthropology U. Okla., 1942-43; asst., then assoc. prof. sociology U. Chgo., 1944-48, exec. sec. Com. Human Relations in Industry, 1946-48; prof. indsl. relations N.Y. State Sch. Indsl. and Labor Relations, Cornell U., 1948-79; dir. Social Sci. Research Center, 1956-61; rsch. dir. Programs for Employment and Workplace Systems Sch. Indsl. and Labor Rels., 1984—; dir. O & O Investment Fund, 1983. Author: Street Corner Society, 1943, Human Relations in the Restaurant Industry, 1948, Pattern for Industrial Peace, 1951, Money and Motivation, 1955, Man and Organization, 1959, Men at Work, 1961, Organizational Behavior, 1969, Organizing for Agricultural Development, 1975, Learning from the Field, 1984, Participatory Action Research, 1990, Participant Observer: An Autobiography, 1994; co-author: Action Research for Management, 1965, Toward an Integrated Theory of Development, 1968, Dominación y Cambios en el Peru Rural, 1969, Power, Politics, and Progress, 1976, Worker Participation and Ownership, 1983, Higher Yielding Human Systems for Agriculture, 1983, Making Mondragón, 1988, 91, Social Theory for Action, 1991; editor: Industry and Society, 1946, Human Organization, 1956-61, 62-63, Street Corner Society (4th expanded edit. 50th anniversary), 1993. Trustee Found. Research Human Behavior, 1960-67; bd. dirs. Nat. Ctr. for Employee Ownership, 1981-88.. Fulbright fellow Peru, 1961-62; recipient Career Research award NIMH. Mem. Am. Sociol. Assn. (pres. 1981), Am. Acad. Arts and Scis., Soc. Applied Anthropology (pres. 1964), Indsl. Rels. Rsch. Assn. (pres. 1963). Home: 223 Savage Farm Dr Ithaca NY 14850-6501 *In social research, I have been as much concerned with practical applications as with scientific knowledge, and I have always sought to express findings in simple and clear prose.*

WIANT, SARAH KIRSTEN, law library administrator, educator; b. Waverly, Iowa, Nov. 20, 1946; s. James Allen and Eva (Jorgensen) W.; m. Robert E. Akins. BA, Western State Coll., 1968; MLS, U. North Tex., 1970; JD, Washington & Lee U., 1978. Asst. law librarian Tex. Tech. U., 1970-72; asst. law librarian Washington & Lee U., 1972—, dir., 1978—, asst. prof. law, 1978-83, assoc. prof. law, 1984-92, prof. law, 1993—. Co-author: Copyright Handbook, 1984, Libraries and Copyright: A Guide to Copyright Law in the 1990s, 1994 Legal Research In the District of Columbia, Maryland and Virginia, 1995; contbr. chpts. to books; mem. adv. bd. Westlaw, 1990-93. Mem. ABA (com. on libraries 1987-93), Am. Assn. Law Libraries (program chmn. for ann. meeting 1987, copyright office rep.), Am. Law Sch. (chmn. sec. on librs. 1990-92, accreditation com. 1991-94), Spl. Libraries Assn. (chair copyright com. 1990—), Maritime Law Assn., U.S. Trademark Assn. Office: Washington & Lee U Law Libr Lewis Hall Lexington VA 24450

WIATT, JAMES ANTHONY, theatrical agency executive; b. L.A., Oct. 18, 1946; s. Norman and Catherine (Sonners) W.; m. Randie Laine. BA, U. So. Calif., 1969. Campaign coord. Tunney for Senate, L.A., 1969-71; adminstrv. asst. Senator John V. Tunney, L.A., 1972-75; agt. FCA, L.A., 1976-78; lit. agt. Internat. Creative Mgmt., L.A., 1978-81, motion picture agt., 1981-83, head of motion picture dept., 1983-85, pres., COO, 1985—. *

WIBERG, LARS-ERIK, human resources consultant; b. Wakefield, Mass., June 1, 1928; s. Sverker Claesson and Ingrid (Heurlin) W.; m. Elizabeth Margaret Allenbrook, Oct. 18, 1957; children: Kirsten, Margaret, Brenda. BS in Geology, MIT, 1950; MA in Teaching, Harvard U., 1952. From engr. to dir. corp. communications EG&G Inc., Boston and Bedford, Mass., 1956-69; from asst. v.p. to v.p. compensation and orgnl. planning First Nat. Bank of Boston, 1969-81; cons. Rockport, Mass., 1981—; lectr. human resources mgmt. Boston U., 1988-92; lectr. job search and career planning U. Karlstad, Sweden, 1992. Author: It's Your Move, 1991; inventor in field. Mem. Gov. John A. Volpe's Mgmt. Engring. Task Force, 1965; mem. Planning Bd., Rockport, 1965-72, chmn., 1969-72; pres. ch. coun. Swedenborg Chapel, Cambridge, Mass., 1984—; dir. Mass. New Ch. Union, 1990—; mem. Zoning Bd. Appeals, Rockport, 1986—. 1st lt. USAF, 1953-55. Mem. Affiliated New Eng. Cons. (founder Lexington, Mass. 1985-95), Heritage Found., Internat. Platform Assn., Swedenborg Sci. Assn. Republican. Avocations: church work, home repairs, music, cooking, reading. Home and Office: 156 South St Rockport MA 01966-1916 *Most of us are well-motivated at heart. We really want to do good work. We are capable of strong, personal commitment. Nevertheless, indifferent motivation and weak commitment too often prevail. The main culprit is the wrong job!.*

WIBERLEY, STEPHEN EDWARD, chemistry educator, consultant; b. Troy, N.Y., May 31, 1919; s. Irving Charles and Ruth (Stanley) W.; m. Mary Elizabeth Bartle, Feb. 21, 1942; children: Stephen Edward, Sharon Elizabeth. B.A., Williams Coll., 1941; M.S., Rensselaer Poly. Inst., 1948, Ph.D., 1950. Sr. chemist Congoleum Nairn, Inc., Kearny, N.J., 1941-44; prof. chemistry Rensselaer Poly. Inst., Troy, N.Y., 1946—, chmn. dept. chemistry, 1984-88; dean Rensselaer Poly. Inst. (Grad. Sch.), 1964-79, vice provost, 1969-79; vis. sr. physicist Brookhaven Nat. Lab., Upton, N.Y., 1950; cons. Imperial Paper & Color Corp., Glens Falls, N.Y., 1957—, Socony Mobil Oil Co., Bklyn.; 1957—, Huyck Felt Co., Rensselaer, N.Y., 1958—, Schenectady Chems. Inc., 1961—, U.S. Gypsum Co., Buffalo, 1962—. Author: Instrumental Analysis, 1954, Laboratory Manual for General Chemistry, 1963, Introduction to Infrared and Raman Spectroscopy, 1964. Served with AUS, 1944-46. Mem. Am. Chem. Soc., AAUP, Sigma Xi, Phi Lambda Upsilon. Home: 1676 Tibbits Ave Troy NY 12180-3726

WIBORG, JAMES HOOKER, chemicals distribution company executive; b. Seattle, Aug. 26, 1924; s. John R. and Hazel (Hooker) W.; m. Ann Rogers, July 1948; children: Katherine Ann, Mary Ellen, Caroline Joan, John Stewart. B.A., U. Wash., 1946. Owner, Wiborg Mfg. Co., Tacoma, 1946-50; securities analyst Pacific N.W. Co., Seattle, 1950-53; founder Western Plastics Corp., Tacoma, 1953; pres. Western Plastics Corp., 1953-55, chmn. bd., dir., ret.; exec. v.p. Wash. Steel Products Co., Tacoma, 1955-58; mgmt. cons. Tacoma, 1958-60; v.p. United Pacific Corp., Seattle, 1960; pres. Pacific Small Bus. Investment Corp., Seattle, 1961-63; sr. v.p. indsl. div. United Pacific Corp., Seattle, 1963-65; pres., chief exec. officer, dir. United Pacific Corp., 1965; past pres., chief exec. officer, dir. Univar Corp. (formerly VWR United Corp.), Seattle, from 1966; chmn., chief exec. officer Univar Corp. (formerly VWR United Corp.), 1983-86, chief strategist, 1986-91, chmn., 1991—; dir., chmn., chief strategist VWR Corp., 1986—; dir. PACCAR Inc., Gensco Inc., Tacoma, Penwest Ltd., PrimeSource Corp. Clubs: Tacoma Country and Golf, Tacoma, Tacoma Yacht; Rainier (Seattle), Columbia Tower (Seattle), Mavi Country. Office: Univar Corp PO Box 34325 Seattle WA 98124-1325

WICAL, BARBARA LOU, elementary school educator; b. Kenton, Ohio, Aug. 27, 1949; d. William Harmon and Dorothy Margaret (Seiler) Woodard; m. Eldon Craig Wical, July 12, 1980; stepchildren: Shelden Wical, Kyle Wical. BS in Edn., Ohio No. U., 1971; MS in Ednl. Adminstrn., U. Dayton, 1981. Elem. tchr. Jackson Ctr. (Ohio) Local Sch., 1971—. Named Outstanding Educator, Bus. Adv. Coun. of Sidney/Shelby County, Ohio, 1993-94; The Martha Holden Jennings Found. scholar, 1986-87. Mem. Jackson Ctr. Jr. Am. Club (sec. 1987-88, pres. 1991-93, treas. 1993-94), Delta Kappa Gamma (ways and means chair 1986-90). Lutheran. Avocations: sewing, gardening, reading, crafts, watching sports. Home: 202 S Fork Jackson Center OH 45334 Office: Jackson Center Local School 204 S Linden Jackson Center OH 45334

WICH, PHILIP, wholesale distribution executive. CEO Les Schwab Tire Ctrs., Prineville, Oreg. Office: PO Box 667 Prineville OR 97754

WICHA, MAX S., oncologist, educator; b. N.Y.C., Mar. 24, 1949; m. Sheila Crowley; children: Jason, Allyson. BS in Biology summa cum laude with honors, SUNY, Stony Brook, 1970; MD, Stanford U., 1974. Diplomate Am. Bd. Internal Medicine; lic. physician, Mich., Ill. Intern in internal medicine U. Chgo. Hosps. and Clinics, 1974-75, jr., sr. resident in internal medicine, 1975-77; rsch. assoc. lab. pathophysiology Nat. Cancer Inst./NIH, Bethesda, Md., 1977-79, fellow in clin. oncology, 1978-80, investigator lab. pathophysiology, 1979-80; asst. prof. internal medicine divsn. hematology and oncology U. Mich., Ann Arbor, 1980-83, assoc. prof., 1983-88, prof., 1988—, mem. tumor metastasis, extracellular matrix, reproductive endocrinology programs, 1982—, dir. divsn. hematology and oncology, dir. Simpson Meml. Rsch. Inst., 1984-93, mem. program in cellular and molecular biology, 1984—, dir. Comprehensive Cancer Ctr., 1987—; mem. cancer rsch. com. U. Mich., 1981—, sci. adv. bd. dental rsch. inst., 1983—, dean's adv., 1988—, reproductive endocrinology selection com., breast care ctr. exec. com., 1988—, exec. dir.'s adv. coun., 1992—, chair instl. rev. com. gene therapy program project., 1992—, dean's adv. com. Howard Hughes Med. Inst., 1992—, strategic planning policy and organizational com. health scis. info. tech. and networking, 1992—; vis. prof. Mich. State U., 1985, Harvard U., Boston, 1986, Wash. State U., 1986, Boston U., 1986, Wayne State U./Harper Grace Hosps., 1987, U. Ill., 1987, Med. Coll. Wis., 1987., U. Chgo., 1987, Eppley Inst. for Rsch. in Cancer and Allied Diseases, Omaha, 1988, U. Nebr., Omaha, 1988, U. Minn./Minn. VA Hosp., 1988, MD Anderson Cancer Ctr., Houston., Mt. Sinai Med. Ctr., N.Y.C., Am. Cancer Soc., Kalamazoo, 1989, Gainesville, Fla., 1990, Orlando, Fla., 1990, Pezcoller Symposium, Rovereto, Italy, 1990, Prince Henry's Hosp., Melbourne, Australia, 1990, Northwestern U. Med. Ctr., Chgo., 1990, Meml. Sloan-Kettering Cancer Ctr., N.Y.C., 1990, Tex. S.W. U., Dallas, 1990, Mich. State U., 1991; lectr. U. Mich., 1990; mem. NIH Site Visit team U. Calif. Cancer Rsch. Lab., Berkeley, 1985; ad hoc mem. cell biology and physiology study sect. NIH, 1985, 86, study sect., Bethesda, 1991; mem. NCI Site Visit team Norris Cotton Dartmouth Cancer Ctr, 1989, Howard U., Wash., 1989, Howard U. Parent Com., 1989, MD Anderson Cancer Ctr., Houston, 1992; sci. advisor U. Colo. Cancer Ctr., Denver, 1990, Samuel Waxman Cancer Rsch. Found., Mt. Sinai Med. Ctr., N.Y.C., 1988-93; mem. NCI Adv. Panel, Bethesda, 1991; mem. sci. adv. com. U. Tex. San Antonio Cancer Ctr., U. Miami Sylvester Cancer Ctr., Mich. State U., East Lansing, Norris-Cotton Cancer Ctr., Dartmouth-Hitchcock Med. Ctr., Hanover, N.H., Mich. Cancer Found., Detroit, V. T. Lombardi Cancer Rsch. Ctr., Georgetown U., Washington, 1992—, MD Anderson Cancer Ctr., Houston, 1992—; mem. extramural sci. adv. bd. UCI Clin. Cancer Ctr., U. Calif. Irvine, Orange, 1992—; mem. NCI SPORE in Prostate Cancer Study Sect., 1992; chair NCI Cancer Ctr. Support Rev. Com., 1993; NCI Site Visit chair Jefferson Cancer Ctr., Phila., 1992, Worcester (Mass.) Cancer Found., 1993, Duke U. Cancer Ctr., Durham, N.C., 1993, Lineberger Comprehensive Ctr., Chapel Hill, N.C., 1993; mem. NCI Comprehensive Cancer Ctrs. Review, 1993, chmn. parent com. Cancer Ctr. Support Rev. Com., 1992—; cons. Warner Lambert Co., 1980—. Assoc. editor: Molecular and Cellular Differentation, 1993; co-editor: The Hematopoietic Microenvironment, 1993; mem. editorial bd. Blood, Molecular and Cellular Differentiation, Jour. Lab. and Clin. Medicine, Cancer Rsch., 1993—, Oncology, Cancer Prevention Internat.; reviewer Nature, Science, Proceedings of NAS, Jour. Clin. Investigation, Jour. Cell Biology, Exptl. Cell Rsch., Exptl. Hematology, Cancer., Clin. and Exptl. Metastasis, Jour. Nat. Cancer Inst., Tissue & Cell, Am. Inst. Biol. Scis., Am. Jour. Pathology, Jour Immunology, Jour. Med. Scis., NSF, Oncology Rsch., Lab. Investigatiosch. and Treatment; contbr. over 110 articles and to profl. jours., chpts. to books.; invited lectr. in field. With

USPHS, 1977-80. Recipient NSF RSch. award SUNY, 1969, Eli Luke and David Jacob Rsch. award Stanford U. Sch. Medicine, 1974, Upjohn Achievement Excellence in Medicine award, Outstanding Med. Resident award U. Chgo. Hosps., 1977, Jerome Conn Excellence in Rsch. award, 1983; grantee NIH, 1991—, 93—, Am. Cancer Soc., 1992—, Suntory Rsch. Inst., 1992-93. Mem. AAASN, Am. Assn. for Cancer Rsch. (state legis. com. 1992—, finance com. 1992—), Am. Fedn. for Clin. Rsch. (selections com. midwest sect. 1986—, comm. com., 1986—, awards com., 1986—), Am. Soc. for Cell Biology, Am. Soc. Hematology (com. on publs. 1991-93), Assn. Am. Cancer Insts. (bd. dirs. 1993—), Am. Soc. for Clin. Investigation, Am. Soc. Clin. Oncology (award selection com. 1992—), Ctrl. Soc. for Clin. Rsch., Mich. Soc. Hematology and Oncology, Southwest Oncology Group, Assn. Community Cancer Ctrs. Achievements include patents for antibodies to human mammary cell growth inhibitor and methods of production and use, human mammary cell growth inhibitor and methods of production and use; research in regulation of cell growth and differentiation, molecular mechanisms of tumor metastasis. Office: U Mich Simpson Meml Inst Med Rsch 102 Observatory St Ann Arbor MI 48109-2020

WICHERN, DEAN WILLIAM, business educator; b. Medford, Wis., Apr. 29, 1942; s. Arthur William and Rebecca Ann (Ambler) W.; m. Dorothy Jean Rutkowski, Dec. 7, 1968; children: Michael, Andrew. B.S. in Math., U. Wis., 1964, M.S. in Stats., 1965, Ph.D. in Stats., 1969. Instr. Sch. Bus. U. Wis.-Madison, 1967-69, asst. prof., 1969-72, assoc. prof., 1972-76, prof., 1976-84, chmn. quantitative analysis dept., 1975-78; prof. Coll. Bus. Adminstrn. Tex. A&M U., 1984—, head bus. analysis and research dept., 1984-88, assoc. dean, 1988-95, John E. Pearson prof. bus. adminstrn., 1985—; vis. prof. Math. Research Ctr., 1978-79. Co-author: Intermediate Business Statistics, 1977, Applied Multivariate Statistical Analysis, 3d edit., 1992; assoc. editor Jour. Bus. and Econ. Stats., 1983-91. Mem. Royal Statis. Soc., Am. Statis. Assn., Inst. Mgmt. Sci., Beta Gamma Sigma, Phi Kappa Phi. Home: 9217 Riverstone Ct College Station TX 77845-8333 Office: Tex A&M U Coll Bus Adminstrn Dept Bus Analysis College Station TX 77843

WICK, G. PHIL, retail executive; b. 1944. Sales & svc. Tire Ctr. Store, 1965-67, asst. mgr., 1967-69; mgr. Tire Ctrs., 1969-80; exec. v.p. retail ops., 1980-83; pres. Les Scwab Warehouse Ctr., Inc., Prineville, Oreg., 1984—. Office: Les Schwab Warehouse Ctr Inc 646 N Madras Hwy Prineville OR 97754-1409*

WICK, HILTON ADDISON, lawyer; b. Mt. Pleasant, Pa., Feb. 11, 1920; m. Barbara G. Shaw; children: James H., William S., B. Jane, Ann W. Julia A. BA, Maryville Coll., 1942; LLB, Harvard U., 1948. Bar: Vt. 1948. Practiced in Burlington; ptnr. Wick, Dinse & Allen, 1949-72; of counsel Dinse, Allen & Erdmann, Burlington, 1972-80, Wick & Maddocks, Burlington, 1980—; state senator Vt., 1989-91; COO Gifford Med. Ctr., Inc., Randolph, 1993-95; bd. dirs. Blue Cross/Blue Shield Vt., Beach Properties, Inc., Vt. Pub. Radio, chmn., 1990—. Trustee Middlebury Coll., 1969-85, Champlain Coll., 1974-94, Maryville Coll., 1981-86, Shelburne Mus., 1985-94, Ethan Allen Homestead, 1989—, Vt. Assn. for Blind and Visually Impaired, 1992—; bd. dirs. Intervale Found., 1995, bd. dirs. Vt. divsn. Am. Cancer Soc., 1979-93, Intervale Found., 1995—; pres. bd. trustees Vt. Law Sch., 1975-95; chmn. bd. trustees Vt. Cmty. Found., 1985-91; chancellor Vt. State Colls., 1984-85. Mem. ABA, Vt. Bar Assn. (pres. 1967-68), Chittenden County Bar Assn. (pres. 1963-64), Internat. Soc. Barristers, Am. Bankers Assn. (bd. dirs. 1975-76), Vt. Bankers Assn. (pres. 1973-74), Ethan Allen Club, Harvard Club (Boston and N.Y.C.), Phi Kappa Delta. Home: Two Appletree Point Ln Burlington VT 05401 Office: 308 College St Burlington VT 05401-8319

WICK, LAWRENCE SCOTT, lawyer; b. San Diego, Oct. 1, 1945; s. Kenneth Lawrence and Lorrayne (Scott) W.; m. Beverly Ann DeRoss, Aug. 26, 1972 (div.); children: Ryan Scott, Andrew Taylor, Hayley Lauren. BA, Northwestern U., Evanston, Ill., 1967; JD, Columbia U., 1970. Assoc. Leydig, Voit & Mayer Ltd., Chgo., 1978-84, ptnr., 1984-92, sr. ptnr., 1992—. Contbr. articles to profl. jours. and encys. Vice pres. Northwestern Young Reps., Evanston, 1965-66; bd. govs. Brand Names Edn. Found., 1994-95; exec. dir. Lefkowitz Internat. Trademark Moot Ct., 1994-95. Mem. ABA (young lawyers exec. coun. 1976-78), Internat. Intellectual Property Assn., Internat. Trademark Assn. (assoc. rep.), Copyright Soc. U.S., Pharm. Trade Marks Group, Chgo. Bar Assn. (bd. mgrs. 1981-83, chmn. young lawyers sect. 1975-76), Law Club Chgo., Winter Club Lake Forest (bd. dirs. 1988-92). Republican. Presbyterian. Avocations: international travel, swimming, cycling. Home: 317 Rothbury Ct Lake Bluff IL 60044-1927 Office: Leydig Voit & Mayer Ltd Two Prudential Plaza Ste 4900 Chicago IL 60601-6780

WICK, SISTER MARGARET, college administrator; b. Sibley, Iowa, June 30, 1942. BA in Sociology, Briar Cliff Coll., 1965; MA in Sociology, Loyola U., Chgo., 1971; PhD in Higher Edn., U. Denver, 1976. Instr. sociology Briar Cliff Coll., Sioux City, Iowa, 1966-71, dir. academic advising, 1971-72, v.p., acad. dean, 1972-74, 76-84, pres., 1987—; pres. Colls. of Mid-Am., 1985-87; bd. dirs. Boatmen's Bank, Sioux City. Bd. dirs. Mary J. Treglia Cmty. House, 1976-84, Marian Health Ctr., 1987—, Iowa Pub. TV, 1987-95. Mem. North Ctrl. Edn. Assn. (cons.-evaluator for accrediting teams 1980-84, 89—), Siouxland Initiative (adv. bd.), Assn. Cath. Colls. and Univs. (bd. dirs.), Quota Internat., Rotary. Home: 75 W Clifton Ave Apt 113 Sioux City IA 51104-2132 Office: Briar Cliff Coll Office of the President 3303 Rebecca St Sioux City IA 51104-2100

WICK, ROBERT THOMAS, retired supermarket executive; b. St. Louis, Nov. 26, 1927; s. Robert Berninger and Katherine (Burke) W.; m. Virginia Rose Allen, Sept. 6, 1952; children: Susan, Patrick, Nancy, Robert J. BS, St. Louis U., 1955; cert. in food distbn., Mich. State U., 1956. Sales mgr. Nat. Tea Co., St. Louis, 1966-68, asst. div. mgr., 1968-69; div. mgr. Nat. Tea Co., Sioux City, Iowa, 1969-71, Milw., 1971-73, Chgo., 1973-74; v.p., gen. mgr. A&P Food Stores, Indpls., 1975-77; div. v.p. Colonial Food Stores- Grand Union, Norfolk, Va., 1977-79; pres., chief exec. officer Bonnie Be-Lo Markets, Inc., Norfolk, 1979-90, ret., 1990. Bd. dirs. Virginia Beach (Va.) Community Svcs. Bd., 1985-89; mem. adv. bd. Straight, Inc., Chesapeake, Va., 1987-91; dir. Community Alternatives, Inc., Virginia Beach, 1991-92. Tech. sgt. U.S. Army, 1946-48. Recipient Citizen of Yr. award St. Louis Argus Newspaper, 1968. Mem. Food Mktg. Inst. (bd. dirs. 1982-89), Va. Food Dealers Assn. (bd. dirs. 1981-87), Tidewater Retail Mchts. Assn. (pres., bd. dirs. 1981-91). Republican. Roman Catholic. Avocations: travel, stamp collecting, golf, cycling. Home: 801 Winthrope Dr Virginia Beach VA 23452-3940

WICK, WILLIAM DAVID, lawyer; b. Dayton, Ohio, Aug. 18, 1949; s. Wilhelm Palmer and Esther (Brehm) W.; m. Barbara Helene Maco; children: Chelsea Maco, Jenna Maco. BA, Northwestern U., 1971; JD, Georgetown U., 1974. Bar: Calif. 1974. Legis. asst. U.S. Rep. Charles Whalen, Washington, 1971-75; assoc. McCutchen, Doyle, Brown & Enersen, San Francisco, 1975-78; atty. Office Regional Counsel U.S. EPA, San Francisco, 1978-85, chief hazardous waste br. Office Regional Counsel, 1985-91; ptnr. Crosby, Heafey, Roach & May, Oakland, Calif., 1991—; adj. prof. law Golden Gate U., San Francisco, 1981—. Editor Shepard's Calif. Environ. Law and Regulation Reporter, 1992-95. Mem. ABA, San Francisco Bar Assn. Office: Crosby Heafey Roach & May 1999 Harrison St Oakland CA 94612-3517

WICK, WILLIAM SHINN, clergyman, chaplain; b. West Chester, Pa.; s. William R. and Barbara (Shinn) W.; m. Debra R. Smith, Apr. 1, 1989; 1 child, Christopher R. BA, Trinity Coll., Deerfield, Ill., 1975; MDiv, Trinity Evang. Div. Sch., Deerfield, 1978. Ordained to ministry Evang. Free Ch. Am., 1978. Pastor Bradford (Vt.) Evang. Free Ch., 1978-85, Evang. Free Ch. Newport, Vt., 1985-89, Grace Evang. Free Ch., Northfield, Vt., 1989—; chaplain Norwich U., Northfield, 1989—; bd. dirs. Evang. Free Ch. Am., Mpls., 1991—. Avocations: alpine skiing, racquetball, tennis, scuba diving, sailing. Home: The Evang Free Ch Am 92 S Main Northfield VT 05663-1438 Office: Grace Evang Free Ch PO Box 245 Northfield VT 05663-0245

WICKBERG, JENS ERIK, industrial executive; b. Uppsala, Sweden, July 11, 1943; s. Nils Erik and Gerd Margareta (Andersson) W.; m. Karin Gunnarsson, Nov. 20, 1968; children: Eva, Anna. MBA, Stockholm Sch. Econs., 1967. Market analyst Exxon, Stockholm, 1967-70; fin. mgr. Fagersta AB, Sao Paulo, Brazil, 1970-73; mng. dir. Fagersta AB, Sao Paulo, 1973-76, AGA A/S, Copenhagen, 1976-78, AGA Gas AB, Sundbyberg, Sweden, 1978-81; corp. v.p. AGA AB, Lidingö, Sweden, 1981-89, sr. v.p., 1989-94; pres. Jekan AB, Stockholm, 1994—. Home: Sturegatan 64, S-114 36 Stockholm Sweden Office: Hogdala Gard, 27292 Simrishamn Sweden

WICKENS, DONALD LEE, engineer executive, consultant, rancher; b. Oklahoma City, Aug. 11, 1934; s. Claude Preston and Idora Bell (Wainscott) W.; m. Sylvia Ann Knopp, Aug. 25, 1957; children: Julia Ann, Donna Sue. BS, Okla. State U., 1957, MS, 1962. Engr. HTB Inc., Oklahoma City, 1961-65; chief structural engr. The Benham Group, Oklahoma City, 1965-70, prin. structural engr., 1970-75, sr. v.p. indsl., 1975-80; pres. Houston div. The Benham Group, 1980-82, pres. St. Louis div., 1982-88; pres. The Benham Group, Oklahoma City, 1988—, chmn., chief exec. officer, pres., 1991—; chmn., chief exec. officer, pres. The Benham Cos., Oklahoma City, Benham Real Estate & Devel., Oklahoma City, Benham Internat., Oklahoma City; chmn. bd. dirs. Roberts-Schornick & Assocs., Norman, Okla., Stewart and Bottomley, Tulsa, Benham-OPUS, Mexico City, Benham-Electrosynthesis, Oklahoma City, Benham Internat.-Far East, Benham Internat. U.K.; bd. dirs. Dynalogic, Detroit; chmn. Benham Internat. Eurasia Moscow, Stainless Equipment and Sys. Co., Atlanta, Benham Constructors; chmn. Gov.'s Internat. Team. Bd. visitors Sch. Arch., U. Okla. Mem. NSPE, ASCE, Am. Soc. Mil. Engrs., So. U.S. Japan Assn., Phi Delta Theta, Sigma Tau, Chi Epsilon. Republican. Lutheran. Home: 2604 Charleston Rd Edmond OK 73003-1623 Office: The Benham Group 9400 N Broadway Ext Oklahoma City OK 73114-7401

WICKER, DENNIS A., lieutenant governor; b. Sanford, N.C., 1952; s. J. Shelton and Clarice (Burns) W.; m. Alisa O'Quinn; children: Quinn Edward, Jackson Dennis, Harrison Lee. BA in Econs. with honors, U. N.C., 1974; JD, Wake Forest U., 1978. Atty. Love & Wicker, 1978-92; mem. N.C. Ho. of Reps., 1981-92; lt. gov. State of N.C., 1993—; chmn. law enorcement com., 1983, house com. cts. and adminstrn. justice, 1985, house jud. com., 1987; chmn. N.C. Small Bus. Coun., 1993—, N.C. State C.C. Bd., 1993—, N.C. State Health Purchasing Alliance Bd., 1993—, Gov.'s Task Force on Driving While Impaired, 1994—, N.C. Local Govt. Partnership Coun.; mem. N.C. Capitol Planning Com., 1993—, N.C. Coun. of State, 1993, N.C. Commn. on Bus. Laws and The Economy. Chmn. N.C. Local Govt. Partnership Coun.; chmn. Gov.'s Task Force on Driving While Impaired. Named Legis. of Yr., Children's Learning Disability Assn. N.C.; recipient Jane Alexander Pub. Svc. award MADD, 1993, Pres.'s award N.C. Assn. Educators, Legis. Leadership award Nat. Commn. Against Drunk Driving, 1994; listed among 10 most effective legis. N.C. Ctr. Pub. Policy Rsch. Mem. Phi Beta Kappa. Democrat. Methodist. Office: State Capitol Raleigh NC 27603-8006

WICKER, ROGER F., congressman; b. Pontotoc, Miss., July 5, 1951; m. Gayle Wicker; children: Margaret, Caroline, McDaniel. BA in Polit. Sci. and Journalism, U. Miss., 1973; JD, Ole Miss Law Sch., 1975. Judge advocate USAF, 1975-79; mem. staff rules com. Staff of U.S. Rep. Trent Lott, 1980-82; pvt. practice, 1982—; mem. Miss. State Senate, 1988-94, 104th Congress from 1st Miss. dist., 1995—. Republican. Office: US House Reps 206 Cannon Washington DC 20515

WICKER, THOMAS CAREY, JR., judge; b. New Orleans, Aug. 1, 1923; s. Thomas Carey and Mary (Taylor) W.; children: Thomas Carey III, Catherine Anne; m. Jane Anne Trepanier. BBA, Tulane U., 1944, LLB, 1949, JD, 1969. Bar: La. 1949. Law clk. La. Supreme Ct., New Orleans, 1949-50; asst. U.S. Atty., 1950-53; practiced in New Orleans, 1953-72; mem. firm Simon, Wicker & Wiedemann, 1953-67; partner firm Wicker, Wiedemann & Fransen, 1967-72; dist. judge Jefferson Parish (La.), 1972-85, judge, Court of Appeals 5th cir., 1985—, mem. faculty Nat. Jud. Coll., 1979-93, Tulane U. Sch. Law, 1978-83. Past bd. visitors Tulane U.; bd. dirs. La. Jud. Coll.; past pres. Sugar Bowl. Author: (with others) Judicial Ethics, 1982, (with others) Modern Judicial Ethics, 1992; editor Tulane Law Review, 1949. Lt. (j.g.), USNR, 1944-46. Mem. ABA (jud. div. council), La. (chmn. jr. bar sect. 1958-59, gov. 1958, mem. ho. of dels. 1960-72), Jefferson Parish, bar assns., Tulane U. Alumni Assn. (past pres.), Am. Judicature Soc., La. Dist. Judges Assn. (past pres.), Order of Coif, Beta Gamma Sigma, Pi Kappa Alpha. Republican. Episcopalian. Clubs: Rotary (pres. 1971-72), Metairie (La.) Country. Avocations: golf, photography, mil. history, duplicate bridge. Home: 500 Rue St Ann #127 Metairie LA 70005 Office: La Ct Appeal 5th Cir Gretna Courthouse Fl 4 Gretna LA 70053

WICKER, THOMAS GREY, retired journalist; b. Hamlet, N.C., June 18, 1926; s. Delancey David and Esta (Cameron) W.; m. Neva Jewett McLean, Aug. 20, 1949 (div. 1973); children: Cameron McLean, Thomas Grey; m. Pamela Abel Hill, Mar. 9, 1974. AB in Journalism, U. N.C., 1948. Exec dir. Southern Pines (N.C.) C. of C., 1948-49; editor Sandhill Citizen, Aberdeen, N.C., 1949; mng. editor The Robesonian, Lumberton, N.C., 1949-50; pub. info. dir. N.C. Bd. Pub. Welfare, 1950-51; copy editor Winston-Salem (N.C.) Jour., 1951-52, sports editor, 1954-55, Sunday feature editor, 1955-56, Washington corr., 1957, editorial writer, city hall corr., 1958-59; assoc. editor Nashville Tennesseean, 1959-60; mem. staff Washington bur. N.Y. Times, 1960-71, chief bur., 1964-68; assoc. editor N.Y. Times, 1968-85, columnist, 1966-91. Author: (novels) The Kingpin, 1953, The Devil Must, 1957, The Judgment, 1961, Facing the Lions, 1973, Unto This Hour, 1984, Donovan's Wife, 1992, (non-fiction) Kennedy without Tears, 1964, JFK and LBJ: The Influence of Personality upon Politics, 1968, A Time to Die, 1975, On Press, 1978, One of Us: Richard Nixon and the American Dream, 1991. Served to lt. (j.g.) USNR, 1952-54. Nieman fellow Harvard, 1957-58, fellow Joan Shorenstein Barone Ctr. on the Press, Politics and Pub. Policy Harvard, 1993. Mem. Soc. Nieman Fellows, Century Assn., Soc. Am. Historians.

WICKERHAM, RICHARD DENNIS, lawyer; b. Plainfield, N.J., Oct. 9, 1950; s. Richard Frame and Margaret Theresa (Waldron) W.; m. Margaret Ann Music, June 29, 1989. BS in Fgn. Svc., Georgetown U., 1972; JD, Fordham U., 1975. Bar: N.Y. 1976, U.S. Dist. Ct. (no. dist.) N.Y. 1977. Pvt. practice atty., counsellor at law Schenectady, N.Y., 1976—; law guardian Schenectady, 1976-85; atty., Office of Aging County of Schenectady, N.Y., 1981—; mem., Com. on Profl. Stds. N.Y. Supreme Ct., Appellate Divsn. (3rd. jud. dept.), Albany, N.Y., 1996—. Mem. St. Clare's Hosp. Found. Leadership, Schenectady, 1990—. Recipient Cert. of Appreciation and Merit, The Lawyers' Fund for Client Protection of the State of N.Y., Albany, 1994. Mem. Rotary Internat., Schenectady County C. of C. Roman Catholic. Avocations: rowing, salt water fishing. Home: 484 Hutchinson Rd Glenville NY 12302 Office: PO Box 1167 28 Jay St Schenectady NY 12301-1167

WICKES, GEORGE, English language educator, writer; b. Antwerp, Belgium, Jan. 6, 1923; came to U.S., 1923; s. Francis Cogswell and Germaine (Attout) W.; m. Louise Westling, Nov. 8, 1975; children by previous marriage: Gregory, Geoffrey, Madeleine (dec.), Thomas, Jonathan. BA, U. Toronto, Ont., Can., 1944; MA, Columbia U., 1949; PhD, U. Calif., Berkeley, 1954. Asst. sec. Belgian Am. Ednl. Found., N.Y.C., 1947-49; exec. dir. U.S. Ednl. Found. in Belgium, 1952-54; instr. Duke U., Durham, N.C., 1954-57; from asst. prof. to prof. Harvey Mudd Coll. and Claremont Grad. Sch., Calif., 1957-70; prof. English and comparative lit. U. Oreg., Eugene, 1970—; dir. comparative lit. U. Oreg., 1974-77, head English dept., 1976-83; lectr. USIS, Europe, 1969, Africa, 1978, 79; vis. prof. U. Rouen, France, 1970, U. Tübingen, Germany, 1981, U. Heidelberg, Germany, 1996. Editor: Lawrence Durrell and Henry Miller Correspondence, 1963, Henry Miller, Letters to Emil, 1989, Henry Miller and James Laughlin: Selected Letters, 1995; Author: Henry Miller, 1966, Americans in Paris, 1969, The Amazon of Letters, 1976: translator: The Memoirs of Frederic Mistral, 1986. Served with U.S. Army, 1943-46. Fulbright lectr. France, 1962-63, 66, 78; sr. fellow Ctr. for Twentieth Century Studies, U. Wis.-Milw., Milwaukee, 1971, Creative Writing fellow Nat. Endowment Arts, 1973, Camargo fellow, 1991. Mem. PEN. Office: U Oreg English Dept Eugene OR 97403

WICKES, R(ICHARD) PAUL, lawyer; b. Camden, N.J., June 11, 1948; s. Richard Gordon and Nancy Elizabeth (Roy) W.; m. Jane Avis Hunter, June 8, 1970, (div. Feb. 1978); m. Gail Thain Parker, Apr. 9, 1978. BA, Williams Coll., 1970; JD, Harvard U., 1973. Bar: Vt. 1973, U.S. Supreme Ct. 1976, Okla. 1982, Tex. 1985, N.Y. 1991. Ptnr. Williams & Wickes, Bennington, Vt., 1973-77; commr. Vt. Dept. Taxes, Montpelier, 1977-78; assoc. Gravel, Shea & Wright, Burlington, Vt., 1978-80; counsel to Gov. State of Vt., Montpelier, 1980-82; ptnr. Watson & McKenzie, Oklahoma City, 1982-84, Thompson & Knight, Dallas, 1984-90, Sherman & Sterling, N.Y.C., 1990—. Office: Shearman & Sterling 153 E 53rd St New York NY 10022-4602*

WICKESBERG, ALBERT KLUMB, retired management educator; b. Neenah, Wis., Apr. 2, 1921; s. Albert Henry and Lydia (Klumb) W.; m. Dorothy Louise Ahrensfeld, Oct. 28, 1944; children—Robert, William, James. B.A., Lawrence Coll., 1943; M.B.A., Stanford U., 1948; Ph.D., Ohio State U., 1955. Staff accountant S.C. Johnson & Son, Inc., Racine, Wis., 1948-50; asst. prof. Sacramento State Coll., 1950-51; prof. U. Minn., Mpls., 1953-86; prof. emeritus U. Minn., 1987—, chmn. dept. bus. adminstrn., 1959-62, dir. grad. studies, 1963-66, chmn. dept. mgmt. and transp., 1971-77. Author: Management Organization, 1966. Served with AUS, 1943-46, 51-52. Soc. Advancement Mgmt. fellow, 1972. Mem. Acad. Mgmt., Soc. Advancement Mgmt. (pres. Twin Cities chpt. 1961-62), Am. Assn. for Study Mental Imagery. Congregationalist. Home: 4501 Roanoke Rd Minneapolis MN 55422-5268 Office: U Minn Sch Mgmt Minneapolis MN 55455

WICKHAM, JOHN ADAMS, JR., retired army officer; b. Dobbs Ferry, N.Y., June 25, 1928; s. John Adams and Jean Gordon (Koch) W.; m. Ann Lindsley Prior, June 18, 1955; children: Lindsley, John Adams, Matthew. B.S., U.S. Mil. Acad., 1950; M.A., Harvard U., 1955, M.P.A., 1956; grad., Nat. War Coll., 1967. Commd. 2d lt. U.S. Army, 1950, advanced through grades to gen., 1979; asst. prof. social scis. U.S. Mil. Acad., 1956-60; bn. comdr. 1st Cavalry Div., Republic of Vietnam, 1967; brigade comdr., chief of staff 3d Inf. Div., Fed. Republic of Germany, 1969-70; army mem. chmn.'s staff group Office of Chmn. Joint Chiefs of Staff, Washington, 1970-71; dep. chief of staff for econ. affairs Mil. Assistance Command, Republic of Vietnam, 1971-73; dep. chief, negotiator U.S. del. Four Party Joint Mil. Commn., Republic of Vietnam, 1973; sr. mil. asst. to Sec. Def. Washington, 1973-76; comdr. 101st Airborne Div. (Air Assault), Ft. Campbell, Ky., 1976-78; dir. Joint Staff Orgn. Washington, 1978-79; comdr. in chief UN Command, Republic of Korea-U.S. Combined Forces Command, Korea, 1979-82; vice chief of staff U.S. Army, Washington, 1982-83, chief of staff, 1983-87, ret., 1987; pres., chief exec. officer Armed Forces Communications and Electronics Assn., Fairfax, Va., 1987-92; bd. dirs. Cooper Inst. for Aerobic Rsch., Xsirius, Inc., Honeywell Fed. Sys., Advanced Photonics, Nortel Inc. Decorated D.S.M. (8), Silver Star (2), Legion of Merit (4), Bronze Star with V device, Air medal (11), Purple Heart, Legion of Honor (France), Order of Mil. Merit (Rep. of Korea), Royal Order of Polar Star (Sweden). Mem. Assn. U.S. Army, 101st Airborne Assn. Home: 13590 N Fawnbrooke Dr Tucson AZ 85737

WICKHAM, KENNETH GREGORY, retired army officer, institute official; b. Hayti, Mo., Apr. 8, 1913; s. Charles Lawrence and Nell (Lively) W.; m. Helen Wickham, July 12, 1938 (dec.); 1 dau., Mary Harvey Wickham Anderson.; m. Norma A. Newcomb, Aug. 21, 1982. B.S., U.S. Mil. Acad., 1938; M.A., George Washington U., 1963; grad., Armed Forces Staff Coll., 1948, Army War Coll., 1956. Commd. 2d lt. U.S. Army, 1938, advanced through grades to maj. gen., 1964; assigned arty. U.S. and Hawaii, 1938-42; with inf. in PTO, ETO, 1942-45; various staff and command assignments, 1945-54; assigned Korea, 1954-55; comdt. (Adj. Gen.'s Sch.), 1959-61; comdg. gen. (Combat Service Support Group, Combat Devel. Command), 1964-66; adj. gen. U.S. Army, 1966-71; with Bus. Mgmt. Inst., Western Assn. Coll. and Univ. Bus. Officers, Stanford, Calif., 1975-80; Area dir. in Korea ARC campaign, 1955; bd. dirs. Army Emergency Relief Assn., U.S. Olympic Com., Army Mut. Aid Assn., Internat. Mil. Sports Council; pres., 1969-70; mem. exec. com. Council Internat. Mil. Sports, 1967-71; pres. Calif. Assn. Mil. Personnel, 1972-78, U.S. Mil. Sports Assn., 1982-84. Decorated D.S.M., Legion of Merit with 2 oak leaf clusters, Bronze Star with oak leaf cluster, Purple Heart, Commendation medal; Legion of Honor (France); 2 Croix de Guerre (France); Cross of Haakon VII (Norway); Ulchi Disting. Svc. medal (Korea). Home: 15 Sunkist Ln Los Altos CA 94022-2334

WICKISER, RALPH LEWANDA, painter, educator, author; b. Greenup, Ill., Mar. 20, 1910; s. Herk and Lydia (Denny) W.; m. Jane Bisson, June 1, 1936; children: Eric Lee, Lydia, Walter. Student, Chgo. Art Inst., 1928-31, Vanderbilt U., 1934-37; B.Ed., Eastern Ill. Coll., 1934, Ph.D. (hon.), 1956; A.M., Peabody Coll., 1935, Ph.D., 1938. Art writer also Peabody Reflector, 1934-35; instr. art La. State U., 1937-40, asst. prof., 1940, head fine arts dept., 1941, assoc. prof., 1944-49, prof., 1949-56; dir. art edn. div. SUNY Tchrs. Coll., New Paltz, 1956-59; chmn. art edn. dept. Pratt Inst., 1959-62, dir. grad. programs art and design, 1962-65, acting dean Sch. Art and Design, 1970-71, dir. grad. programs in art and design, 1971-75, emeritus prof., 1975—; lectr. art Vassar Coll., 1949; Mem. council National Com. Art Edn. One-man shows include Gallery 630B, New Orleans, 1990, Z Gallery, N.Y.C., 1990-91, Gallery at Park West, Kingston, N.Y., 1992, Walter Wickiser Gallery, 1993, 94 ; exhibited in group shows at Grand Central Galleries, N.Y.C., Tiffany Found. Group, 1934-35, A New So. Group, Gresham Gallery, New Orleans, travelling show, 1937-41, Pa. Acad. Fine Arts, 1946, Dallas Mus., 1947, The Arts Club, Washington, Library of Congress Annual Print Exhbn., U. Chattanooga, Assoc. Am. Artists Gallery, N.Y.C., Bklyn. Mus., Corcoran Gallery, Washington, Pa. Acad., Phila., Print Club, Phila., San Francisco Mus., Dayton (Ohio) Mus., Dallas Mus., Delgado Mus., Met. Mus., Whitney Mus., New Realism show Suffolk Mus., 1971, Lerner-Miraschi Gallery, N.Y.C., 1972, Pacem in Terris Gallery, UN, N.Y.C., 1975, Lotus Gallery, N.Y.C., 1976-77, Esta Robinson Gallery, N.Y.C., 1982, Ulster County Council for Arts, 1983, Princeton Gallery of Fine Art, N.J., 1987, The Thompson Gallery, N.Y.C., 1987, Z Squared Fine Art Gallery, N.Y.C., 1990-91, Woodstock Artists Assn., 1990, Pratt Schafler Gallery, 1990, Pratt Inst., 1991, Pratt Manhattan Gallery, 1991, 94, Woodstock Art Assn., 1993, Haenah-Kent Gallery, N.Y.C., 1993; retrospective exhbn., Eastern Ill. U., 1968, Rockefeller Ctr., N.Y.C., 1994, 95, 96; color lithographs for, Standard Oil Co., N.J., June 1947, water colors for, Ford Motor Co., 1948, creative painting, Woodstock, N.Y., 1948; cons., adv. bd., Unicorn Press for New Standard Ency. of Funk and Wagnalls; author: (with Capt. P. E. McDowell) Military Leadership, 1944, Introduction to Art Activities, 1947, An Introduction to Art Education, 1957; Editor: (with Caroline Durieux) Mardi Gras Day, 1948; contbg. editor: Ency. of the Arts, 1946; contbr.: Cath. Ency.; author: book rev. Sat. Rev, 1952, 53, 54. Served with USNR, 1945-46. Ford Found. grant advancement edn., 1952-53. Mem. Artists Equity, Am. Soc. Aesthetics, Coll. Art Assn., Phi Delta Kappa, Kappa Delta Pi. Home: PO Box 263 Bearsville NY 12409-0263 *It has been a mystery to me why it takes a lifetime to become fully aware of one's self, one's life. Even for the person who constantly studies there is not enough time to learn all one needs to know, to see all the marvelous things to be seen in nature and fully respond to a falling leaf. It is ironic that we begin to value life when it ebbs. I say all of this because my life has been a search for understanding, to discover the principles behind life and nature and the ideas that defined the principles. Art and education have both offered me a life of activity and quiet contemplation. They have, by diligent pursuit, given me a greater appreciation of things thought and seen, felt and intuited.*

WICKIZER, MARY ALICE See BURGESS, MARY ALICE

WICKLEIN, JOHN FREDERICK, journalist, educator; b. Reading, Pa., July 20, 1924; s. Raymond Roland and Parmilla Catherine (Miller) W.; m. Myra Jane Winchester, July 31, 1948; children: Elizabeth, Peter, Joanna. Litt.B., Rutgers U., 1947; M.S. in Journalism, Columbia, 1948. Reporter Newark (N.J.) Evening News, 1947-51; news mng. editor Elec. World (McGraw-Hill weekly), N.Y.C., 1951-54; reporter, editor N.Y. Times, 1954-62; news dir. Sta. WNET-TV, N.Y.C., 1962-64; exec. producer news Sta. WABC-TV, N.Y.C., 1964-67; exec. producer Washington Bur. chief Pub. Broadcast Lab. (Nat. Ednl. TV), 1967-70; mng. news and pub. affairs broadcasts Sta. WCBS-TV, N.Y.C., 1970-71; gen. mgr. Sta. WRVR, N.Y.C., 1971-74; prof. journalism and broadcasting Boston U., 1974-80; dean Sch. Public Communication Boston U., 1974-78; vis. prof. communication Meth. U., São Paulo, Brazil, 1979; program officer for news and pub. affairs programs Corp. for Pub. Broadcasting, 1980-84; Willard M. Kiplinger chair in pub. affairs reporting, dir. Kiplinger mid-career program for journalists Ohio State U., 1984-89; Fulbright rsch. scholar Charles Sturt Univ., Bathurst, NSW, Australia, 1990; lectr., cons. to Rutgers U. Media Resources Ctr., Warsaw, Poland, 1992; Ayers vis. prof. of Journalism, Jacksonville (Ala.) State U., 1992-93; producer news documentaries for public and comml. TV; ind. writing, reporting and editing coach for newspapers 1994—; lectr., cons. in field; coord. Working Group for Pub. Broadcasting, 1987-89; spl. com. on regulation of media Am. Civil Liberties Union, 1988-92; adj.

faculty, Poynter Inst. for Media Studies, 1988; adj. prof. journalism for rsch. Ohio State U., 1991-93; at-large mem., media ethics com. Nat. Coun. Chs., 1975—; fellow Inst. Democratic Communication Boston U., 1975-78; lectr. journalism Columbia Grad. Sch. Journalism, 1966-67; Danforth lectr. Barnard Coll., 1960-61; cons. Dept. Journalism, Jagiellonian U., Krakow, Poland, 1994. Author: (with Monroe Price) Cable Television: A Guide for Citizen Action, 1972, Electronic Nightmare: The New Communications and Freedom, 1981; editor: Investigative Reporting: The Lessons of Watergate, 1975; contgb. editor The Washington Monthly, 1969-72; contbr. to Am. Journalism Review, The Progressive, TV Quar., Atlantic Monthly, Columbia Journalism Rev., Archeology, Australian Journalism Rev., others. Recipient Polk award, 1963, documentary award Venice Film Festival, 1968, Dupont award, 1973, Brechner Freedom Info. prize, 1987. Mem. ACLU, Investigative Reporters and Editors, Amnesty Internat. U.S.A., Soc. Prof. Jours., Phi Beta Kappa. Democrat. Home and Office: 23200 Wilderness Walk Ct Gaithersburg MD 20882-2732

WICKLIFFE, JERRY L., lawyer; b. Dallas, Jan. 12, 1941; s. John A. and Ola (Kirk) W.; m. Lynda Hart, Aug. 26, 1961; children: Lisa Schmalhausen, Jeffrey, Mark. BBA, U. Tex., 1963, JD, 1965. Bar: Tex. 1965. Assoc. Fulbright & Jaworski, Houston, 1965-73, ptnr., 1973—. Office: Fulbright & Jaworski 1301 Mckinney St Fl 51 Houston TX 77010

WICKLINE, SAMUEL ALAN, cardiologist, educator; b. Huntington, W.Va., Oct. 23, 1952. BA in Philosophy cum laude, Pomona Coll., 1974; MD, U. Hawaii, 1980. Diplomate Am. Bd. Internal Medicine, Am. Bd. Cardiology. Intern, resident in internal medicine Barnes Hosp. Barnes/Washington U. Sch. Medicine, St. Louis, 1980-83, clin. fellow in cardiology, 1983-85, rsch. fellow in cardiology, 1985-87; asst. prof. medicine Sch. Medicine Washington U. Sch. Medicine, St. Louis, 1987-93, assoc. prof., 1993—, adj. asst. prof. physics, 1990, adj. assoc. prof. physics, 1994, attending cardiologist, dir. echocardiology Jewish Hosp., 1992—, dir. divsn. cardiology, 1993—. Reviewer Jour. Clin. Investigation, Circulation, Arteriosclerosis and Thrombosis, Hypertension, Ultrasound in Medicine and Biology; contbr. over 80 articles to med. and sci. jours., chpts. to books on topics related to basic rsch. in cardiovascular biophysics and acoustics/ultrasonics. Grantee NIH, 1990—, 92—, (two grants), 1995—, Whitaker Found., 1996. Fellow Am. Coll. Cardiology (reviewer jour.); mem. IEEE Soc. Ultrasonics, Ferroelectrics and Frequency Control (tech. program com. ultrasonics symposium), Am. Heart Assn. (coun. on radiology and clin. cardiology, Clinician-Scientist award 1988-93, Established Investigator award 1993—), Am. Soc. Clin. Investigation, Am. Inst. Ultrasound in Medicine, Acoustical Soc. Am., Alpha Omega Alpha. Home: 11211 Pointe Ct Saint Louis MO 63127-1741 Office: Jewish Hosp Cardiology 216 S Kingshighway Blvd Saint Louis MO 63110-1026

WICKMAN, JOHN EDWARD, librarian, historian; b. Villa Park, Ill., May 24, 1929; s. John Edward and Elsie (Voss) W.; m. Shirley Jean Swanson, Mar. 17, 1951; children—Lisa Annette, Eric John. A.B., Elmhurst Coll., 1953; A.M., Ind. U., 1958, Ph.D., 1964; LL.D., Lincoln Coll., 1973. Instr. history Hanover (Ind.) Coll., 1959-62, Southeast Campus, Ind. U., Jeffersonville, 1962; asst. prof. history Northwest Mo. State Coll., Maryville, 1962-64; asst. to Gov. William H. Avery of Kans., Topeka, 1964-65; asst. prof. history Regional Campus, Purdue U., Fort Wayne, Ind., 1965-66; dir. Dwight D. Eisenhower Libr., Abilene, Kans., 1966-89; ret., 1989. Contbr. articles on Am. West, archival mgmt., adminstrv. history, oral history to profl. publs. Served with U.S. Army, 1953-55. Nat. Ctr. for Edn. in Politics faculty fellow, 1964-65; Am. Polit. Sci. Assn. Congl. fellow, 1975-76. Mem. Oral History Assn. (v.p. 1971-72, pres. 1972-73), Western History Assn. (coun. 1972-75), Kans. Hist. Soc. (2d v.p. 1974-75, pres. 1976-77, dir.). Home: PO Box 325 Enterprise KS 67441-0325

WICKMANN, DAVID L., clergyman. V.p. and sec. ea. dist. Moravian Ch. Am. Office: Moravian Church in Am 1021 Center St PO Box 1245 Bethlehem PA 18016-1245

WICKS, EUGENE CLAUDE, college president, art educator; b. Coleharbor, N.D., Oct. 7, 1931; s. Claude Edward and Grace Ann (Wilkinson) W.; m. Lavonne Maureen Yineman, June 21, 1953; children: Christopher Edwin, Louis Eugene, James Edward. B.F.A., U. Colo., 1957, M.F.A., 1959. Mem. faculty U. Ill., Urbana, 1959-94; assoc. head U. Ill., 1961-76, head Sch. Art and Design, 1977-80, dir., 1981-89; also prof. art U. Ill. (Sch. Art and Design); pres. Burren Coll. Art, Newtown Castle, Ireland, 1994—; cons. in field. Represented in permanent collections at, Phila. Print Club, Art Inst. Chgo., Am. Fed. Arts, others. Served with USN, 1951-54. U. Ill. research grantee, 1960, 61, 67, 68, 69, 74, 75; Fulbright grantee, 1988-89. Mem. Coll. Art Assn., Nat. Assn. Schs. Art and Design (dir. commn. on accreditation 1978-81, v.p. 1981-84, pres. 1984-87). Home: Tigín, Ballyvaughan Ireland Office: Burren Coll Art, Newtown Castle, Ballyvaughan Ireland

WICKS, FREDERICK JOHN, research mineralogist, museum curator; b. Winnipeg, Can., Nov. 22, 1937; divorced; 1 child, Claire E. BSc, U. Manitoba (Can.), 1960, MSc, 1965. Geologist Giant Yellowknife Mines Ltd., 1960, 61; cons. mineralogist various govt. and pvt. industry cos., 1967; asst. curator Royal Ont. Mus., 1970-75, curator minerals, 1980—; assoc. prof. geology U. Toronto (Can.), 1980—. Fellow Geol. Assn. Can., Mineral Soc. Am., Clay Minerals Soc.; mem. Mineral Assn. Can. (sec. 1973-75, v.p. 1991-93, pres. 1994—). Office: Royal Ontario Mus/Dpt Mineralogy, 100 Queens Park, Toronto, ON Canada M5S 2C6*

WICKS, JOHN R., lawyer; b. Ottumwa, Iowa, Dec. 8, 1937; m. Nedra Morgan, Mar. 27, 1940; children: Catherine, John. BSC, U. Iowa, 1959, JD, 1964. Bar: Iowa 1964, Minn. 1966. Assoc. Dorsey & Whitney, Mpls., 1966-71; ptnr. Dorsey & Whitney, Rochester, Minn., 1972-92. Fellow Am. Coll. Trusts and Estates Counsel; mem. Minn. State Bar Assn. (probate and trusts law coun. 1989-92), Olmsted County Minn. Bar Assn. Office: Dorsey & Whitney 201 1st Ave SW Ste 340 Rochester MN 55902-3155

WICKS, WILLIAM WITHINGTON, retired public relations executive; b. Chgo., Dec. 20, 1923; s. William and Alice (Withington) W.; m. Frances M. Horner, Nov. 29, 1947; children: Barbara Anne, Christine Frances. BNS, U. Notre Dame, 1944, AB in Journalism magna cum laude, 1947. Staff corr. United Press Assn., Milw., 1947; pub. rels. mgr. Internat. Harvester Co., Louisville, 1948-58; mgr. field svcs. pub. rels. Standard Oil Co. (Ind.), Chgo., 1959-60; v.p. pub. rels. Griswold-Eshleman Co., Chgo., 1961-68; dir. pub. rels. G. D. Searle & Co., Chgo., 1968-74; dir. pub. rels./investor rels. Kimberly-Clark Corp., Neenah, Wis., 1974, staff v.p., 1974-80; v.p. Kimberly-Clark Corp., Neenah (hdqrs. relocated to Dallas in 1985), 1980-89; v.p. and asst. to chmn. bd. Kimberly-Clark Corp., Irving, Tex., 1989-92; chmn. pub. relations sect. Pharm. Mfrs. Assn., Washington, 1974. Pres. Jr. Achievement Neenah-Menasha, 1978-81. Served to lt. (j.g.) USNR, 1942-46, PTO. Recipient Silver Anvil award Pub. Rels. Soc. Am., 1963, 79. Mem. PRSA (founder, pres. Bluegrass chpt. 1957-58), Optimist (pres. South End Club in Louisville 1957), Publicity Club of Chgo. (pres. 1967-68). Republican. Roman Catholic. Home: 1312 S Travis Cir Irving TX 75038-6243

WICKSER, JOHN PHILIP, lawyer; b. Buffalo, Oct. 14, 1922; s. Philip John and Margaretta Melissa (Fryer) W.; m. Frances M. Halsey, July 2, 1949; children: Margaretta Melissa, Philip John, Gaius Halsey. B.A., Yale U., 1945; J.D., Columbia U., 1949. Bar: N.Y. 1949. Since practiced in Buffalo; mem. firm Palmer, Houck & Wickser, 1949-50; ptnr. Palmer, Heffernan Wickser & Beyer, 1950-94; of counsel Magavern, Magavern & Grimm, 1994; pres. Main-Pearl Corp., 1963-82; dir. Union-Am. Re-Ins. Co., 1975-77; pres. Kleinhans Music Hall Mgmt., Inc. Life mem. adv. bd. Salvation Army, Internat. Inst., 1951-54; council State Tchrs. Coll., Buffalo, 1954-55; bd. dirs. Greater Buffalo Devel. Found., Grosvenor Soc.; chmn. bd. trustees Buffalo and Erie County Pub. Library; bd. dirs. Buffalo Fine Arts Acad., 1954-77. Served to lt. (j.g.) USNR, World War II. Mem. Johnson Soc. London, Sons of Revolution, Buffalo Hist. Soc. (trustee), N.Y. State, Erie County bar assns., Am. Judicature Soc. Republican. Episcopalian. Clubs: Buffalo Country (Buffalo), Pack (Buffalo), Saturn (Buffalo); Yale (N.Y.C.); Elizabethan (New Haven); Pacific, Nantucket Yacht. Home: 22 Oakland Pl Buffalo NY 14222-2009 Office: Rand Bldg Buffalo NY 14203

WICKSTROM, JON ALAN, telecommunications executive, consultant; b. San Antonio, Apr. 17, 1949; s. Stanley Alan and Louise (MacMillan) W.; m. Mary Carmen Sparkman, Jan. 25, 1969 (div. Jan. 1978); children: Dana Marie, Jon Alan Jr.; m. Jane Bielby Slawson, June 19, 1988. BS, Tex. Tech. U., 1975. Ptnr. Hensley & Assocs., Albuquerque, 1976-78; dealer svcs. mgr. Gulf States Toyota, Houston, 1978-80; comms. mgr. Hughes Tool Co., Houston, 1980-85; network svcs. mgr. Tenneco Oil Co., Houston, 1986-89; comms. mgr. Clarke Am., San Antonio, 1989-94; USAA, San Antonio, 1994—; prin. Comm. Tech. Cons., Houston, 1980-89; cons. Comms. Consulting Group, Inc., San Antonio, 1989—. Author: (reference) 1976 Population Estimates for Bernallio County, New Mex., 1976. Rep. precinct chmn. Bexar County, Tex., 1992-94; cons. Houston Symphony Orch., 1988. Mem. Alamo Area Telecomms. Assn. (bd. dirs 1990-94, pres., 1992-93), S.W. Comms. Assn. (bd. dirs. 1981-85, pres. 1982-84), Tex. Telecomms. Assn. (bd. dirs. 1982-84, chmn. 1983). Avocations: sailing, golf, music, real estate investing. Office: USAA 9800 Fredericksburg Rd San Antonio TX 78288-0001

WICKSTROM, KARL YOUNGERT, publishing company executive; b. Moline, Ill., Sept. 20, 1935; s. George Washington and Harriet L. (Youngert) W.; m. Patricia Pinkerton, 1959 (div.); children: Eric, Blair, Drew, Holly; m. Sheila Zehner, June 9, 1979. B.S.J., U. Fla., 1957. Writer, editor Orlando (Fla.) Sentinel-Star, 1958-60; writer Miami (Fla.) Herald, 1960-67; adminstrv. asst. Fla. Senate, Tallahassee, 1968; founder, pres., publisher Wickstrom Pubs. Inc., mags., books, Miami, 1968—. Original pub.: Aloft Mag., for Nat. Airlines passengers, 1968-80; pub.: Fla. Sportsman, 1969—, Ryder World for Ryder System, Inc, 1980—. Bd. dirs. Nat. Coalition for Marine Conservation; v.p. Fla. Conservation Assn. Served with USAF, 1967-68. Recipient 1st Pl. award for pub. svc. Fla. AP, 1967; named Man of Yr., Am. Sportfishing Assn., 1995, Conservationist of Yr., Fla. Wildlife Fedn., 1995. Mem. Sigma Delta Chi (nat. 1st pl. award for investigative reporting Miami area crime, corruption 1967). Home: 745 S Alhambra Cir Miami FL 33146-3801 Office: Florida Sportsman 5901 SW 74th St Miami FL 33143-5165

WICKWIRE, PATRICIA JOANNE NELLOR, psychologist, educator; b. Sioux City, Iowa; d. William McKinley and Clara Rose (Pautsch) Nellor; m. Robert James Wickwire, Sept. 7, 1957; 1 child, William James. BA cum laude, U. No. Iowa, 1951; MA, U. Iowa, 1959; PhD, U. Tex., Austin, 1971; postgrad. U. So. Calif., UCLA, Calif. State U., Long Beach, 1951-66. Tchr., Ricketts Ind. Schs., Iowa, 1946-48; tchr., counselor Waverly-Shell Rock Ind. Schs., Iowa, 1951-55; reading cons., head dormitory counselor U. Iowa, Iowa City, 1955-57; tchr., sch. psychologist, adminstr. S. Bay Union High Sch. Dist., Redondo Beach, Calif., 1962-82, dir. student svcs. and spl. edn.; cons. mgmt. and edn.; pres. Nellor Wickwire Group, 1981—; mem. exec. bd. Calif. Interagency Mental Health Coun., 1968-72, Beach Cities Symphony Assn., 1970-82; chmn. Friends of Dominguez Hills (Calif.), 1981-85. Lic. ednl. psychologist, marriage, family and child counselor, Calif.; pres. Calif. Women's Caucus, 1993-95. Mem. APA, AAUW (exec. bd., chpt. pres. 1962-72), Nat. Career Devel. Assn. (media chair 1992—), Am. Assn. Career Edn. (pres. 1991—), L.A. County Dirs. Pupil Svcs. (chmn. 1974-79), L.A. County Personnel and Guidance Assn. (pres. 1977-78), Assn. Calif. Sch. Adminstrs. (dir. 1977-81), L.A. County SW Bd. Dist. Adminstrs. for Spl. Edn. (chmn. 1976-81), Calif. Assn. Sch. Psychologists (bd. dirs. 1981-83), Am. Assn. Sch. Adminstrs., Calif. Assn. for Measurement and Evaluation in Guidance (dir. 1981, pres. 1984-85), ACA (chmn. Coun. Newsletter Editors 1989-91, mem. com. on women 1989-92, mem. com. on rsch. and knowledge, 1994—, chmn. 1995—, chmn. 1996—), Assn. Measurement and Eval. in Guidance (Western regional editor 1985-87, conv. chair 1986, editor 1987-90, exec. bd. dirs. 1987-91), Calif. Assn. Counseling and Devel. (exec. bd. 1984—, pres. 1988-89, jour. editor 1990—), Internat. Career Assn. Network (chair 1985—), Pi Lambda Theta, Alpha Phi Gamma, Psi Chi, Kappa Delta Pi, Sigma Alpha Iota. Contbr. articles in field to profl. jours. Office: Calif Assn Counseling 2555 E Chapman Ave Ste 201 Fullerton CA 92631

WIDDEL, JOHN EARL, JR., lawyer; b. Minot, N.D., Nov. 17, 1936; s. John Earl Sr. and Angela Victoria (Gefroh) W.; m. Yvonne J. Haugen, Dec. 21, 1973; children: John P., James M., Susan N., Andrea K. B in Philosophy, BS in Bus. Adminstrn., U. N.D., 1966, BSBA, 1971. Bar: N.D. 1971, U.S. Dist. Ct. N.D., 1971, U.S. Ct. Appeals (8th cir.) 1989; accredited estate planner. Ptnr. Thorsen & Widdel, Grand Forks, N.D., 1971—; mcpl. judge City of Grand Forks, 1972—; ct. magistrate Grand Forks County, 1975. Mem. N.D. Foster Parent Program, 1974-87; bd. dirs. YMCA, Grand Forks, 1982; dist. chmn. Boy Scouts Am., 1987-88; corp. mem. United Hosp. Served with U.S. Army, 1960-62. Mem. State Bar Assn. N.D. (bd. govs. 1983-88, pres. 1986-87), Greater Grand Forks County Bar Assn. (pres. 1982), N.E. Cen. Jud. Dist. (pres. 1983), Grand Forks Cemetery Assn. (bd. dirs. 1984—, pres. 1989-94), Grand Forks Hist. Soc. (pres. 1983), Grand Forks Jaycees, Antique Automobile Club Am. (nat. bd. dirs. 1984—, v.p. 1985—), sec.-treas. 1989, pres. N.D. region 1977-78, 83-84), Sertoma (bd. dirs. 1994—), Elks (exalted ruler 1985-86), Masonic Bodies, Nat. Assn. Estate Planning Coun., Kem Temple Potentate. Roman Catholic. Home: Box 5624 Grand Forks ND 58206-5624 Office: Thorsen & Widdel 215A S 4th St Grand Forks ND 58206-5624

WIDDICOMBE, RICHARD PALMER, librarian; b. Paterson, N.J., Apr. 12, 1941; s. Robert Lord and Elvira Barbara (Guttilla) W.; m. Martha Elizabeth Bruyn, Feb. 26, 1972. B.A., Alfred U., 1963; M.S. L.S., Syracuse U., 1964. Asst. librarian Yonkers Pub. Library, N.Y., 1964-65; asst. librarian Cooper Union, N.Y.C., 1965-66; asst. librarian Stevens Inst., Hoboken, N.J., 1966-72, dir. library, 1973—. Episcopalian. Home: Castle Point Sta PO Box S-1342 Hoboken NJ 07030 Office: SC Williams Libr Stevens Inst Hoboken NJ 07030

WIDDRINGTON, PETER NIGEL TINLING, professional baseball team executive; b. Toronto, Ont., Can., June 2, 1930; s. Gerard and Margery (MacDonald) W.; m. Betty Ann Lawrence, Oct. 12, 1956; children: Lucinda Ann, Andrea Stacy. BA with honors, Queen's U., Kingston, Ont., 1953; MBA, Harvard, 1955. Salesman Labatt's Co., London, Ont., 1955-57; regional mgr. Ont. Labatt's Co., 1957-58, gen. mgr. Man., 1958-61, gen. mgr. B.C., 1962-65; gen. mgr. Kiewel & Pelissiers, Winnipeg, 1961-62; pres. Lucky Breweries Inc., San Francisco, 1968-71; v.p. corp. devel. John Labatt Ltd., 1971-73, sr. v.p., 1973-87, pres., chief exec. officer, 1973-89, chmn., 1987-91; chmn. Laidlaw Inc., 1990—; bd. dirs. Chief Execs. Orgn., Inc., CEC Resources Ltd., Cuddy Internat. Corp., Dialysis Ctrs. Am., Talisman Energy Inc., Can. Imperial Bank Commerce, Ellis-Don Inc., The SNC-Lavalin Group, Inc., Major League Baseball Properties, Inc., chmn. Office: 248 Pall Mall St Ste 400, London, ON Canada N6A 5P6

WIDEMAN, JOHN EDGAR, English literature educator, novelist; b. Washington, DC, June 14, 1941; married, 3 children. BA, U. Pa., 1963; BPhil, Oxford U., Eng., 1966; postgrad., U. Iowa Writers Workshop, 1967; DLitt (hon.), U. Pa., 1985, Rutgers U. Mem. faculty U. Wyo., Laramie; prof. English U. Wyo., 1974-85, U. Mass., Amherst, 1986—; USIS lectr. in Eastern Europe. Author: A Glance Away, 1967, Hurry Home, 1969, The Lynchers, 1973, Hiding Place, 1981, Damballah, 1981, Sent for You Yesterday, 1983 (PEN/Faulkner award for fiction 1984), Brothers and Keepers, 1984, Reuben, 1987, Fever, 1989, Philadelphia Fire, 1990 (PEN/Faulkner award for fiction 1991), The Homewood Books, 1992, The Stories of John Edgar Wideman, 1992, All Stories Are True, 1993, Fatheralong, 1994, The Cattle Killing, 1996; contbr. numerous articles and revs. to profl. jours., mags. Ben Franklin scholar; Lannan award, 1991; Kent fellow; Rhodes scholar; Nat. Endowment for Humanities grantee; MacArthur fellow 1993. Mem. Am. Assn. Rhodes Scholars (dir.), Am. Studies Assn. (council 1980-81), MLA, Am. Acad. Arts Scis. (elected), (Phi Beta Kappa). Office: Univ Mass Dept English Amherst MA 01003

WIDENER, HIRAM EMORY, JR., federal judge; b. Abingdon, Va., Apr. 30, 1923; s. Hiram Emory and Nita Douglas (Peck) W.; children: Molly Berentd, Hiram Emory III. Student, Va. Poly. Inst., 1940-41; B.S., U.S. Naval Acad., 1944; LL.B., Washington and Lee U., 1953, LL.D., 1977. Bar: Va. 1951. Pvt. practice law Bristol, Va., 1953-69; judge U.S. Dist. Ct. Western Dist. Va., Abingdon, 1969-71; chief judge U.S. Dist. Ct. Western Dist. Va., 1971-72; judge U.S. Ct. Appeals 4th Circuit, Abingdon, 1972—; U.S. commr. Western Dist. Va., 1963-66; mem. Va. Election Laws Study Commn., 1968-69. Chmn. Rep. party 9th Dist. Va., 1966-69; mem. Va. Rep. State Ctrl. Com., 1966-69, state exec. com., 1966-69. Served to lt. (j.g.) USN, 1944-49; to lt. USNR, 1951-52. Decorated Bronze Star with combat V. Mem. Am. Law Inst., Va. Bar Assn., Va. State Bar, Phi Alpha Delta. Republican. Presbyterian. Home and Office: 180 MAIN ST. RM 123 Abingdon VA 24210-0868

WIDENER, PERI ANN, business development executive; b. Wichita, Kans., May 1, 1956; d. Wayne Robert and LuAnne (Harris) W. BS, Wichita State U., 1978; MBA, Fla. Tech., 1992. Advt. intern Associated Advt., Wichita, 1978; pub. rels. asst. Fourth Nat. Bank, Wichita, 1978-79; mktg. communications rep. Boeing Co., Wichita, 1979-83, pub. rels. rep., Huntsville, Ala., 1983-85, pub. rels. mgr., 1985-92; sr. pub. rels. mgr. Boeing Mil. Airplanes, Seattle, 1992-95; bus. devel. mgr. Boeing Defense & Space Group, Washington, D.C., 1995—. mem. exec. devel. program Boeing Def. & Space Group, 1993—. Preston Huston scholar, Wichita State U., 1978; recipient Best Electronic Ad award Def. Electronics mag., 1982, Best Total Pub. Rels. Program award Huntsville Press Club, 1985, Huntsville Media awards, 1986, 87, 88, 89, 90, 91, Huntsville Advt. Fedn. Addys, 1988. Mem. Pub. Rels. Soc. Am. (Seattle chpt.), Women in Communications, Pub. Rels. Coun. Ala. (bd. dirs. 1985-92, state pres. 1992, officer Huntsville chpt. 1984-91, pres. No. Ala. chpt. 1989, Excellence award 1986-91, Achievement award 1986-91, Pres.'s award Huntsville chpt. 1985, State Practitioner of Yr. 1989, PRCA Medallion award excellence, numerous others), Internat. Assn. Bus. Communicators (D2 Silver Quills award 1985, 91, D6 Silver Quills 1993, 94), Pub. Rels. Soc. Am. (accredited 1989—), So. Pub. Rels. Fedn. (practitioner of yr. 1991, Excellence award 1986-91, Lantern award 1991), Huntsville-Madison County C. of C. (pub. rels. adv. com. 1987-92), Huntsville Press Club (bd. dirs. 1989-92), Sigma Delta Chi (pres.'s award 1991). Methodist. Office: The Boeing Co 1700 N Moore 20th Fl Arlington VA 22209

WIDERA, GEORG ERNST OTTO, mechanical engineering educator, consultant; b. Dortmund, Germany, Feb. 16, 1938; came to U.S., 1950; s. Otto and Gertrude (Yzermann) W.; m. Kristel Kornas, June 21, 1974; children: Erika, Nicholas. BS, U. Wis., 1960, MS, 1962, PhD, 1965. Asst. prof., then prof. materials engring. dept. U. Ill.-Chgo., 1965-82, prof. mech. engring., 1982-91, head dept., 1983-91, acting head indsl. systems engring. dept., 1985-86, dir. off-campus engring. programs, 1987-88; prof., chmn. mech. and indsl. engring. dept. Marquette U., Milw., 1991—; Gastdozent U. Stuttgart, Fed. Republic of Germany, 1968; vis. prof. U. Wis.-Milw., 1973-74, Marquette U., Milw., 1978-79; cons. Ladish Co., Cudahy, Wis., 1967-76, Howmedica, Inc., Chgo., 1972-75, Sargent & Lundy, 1970-88, Nat. Bur. Standards, 1980; vis. sci. Argonne Nat. Lab., Ill., 1968; bd. dirs. Wis. Ctr. for Mfg. Productivity. Editor: Procs. Innovations in Structural Engring., 1974, Pressure Vessel Design, 1982; assoc. editor: Pressure Vessel Tech., 1977-81, Applied Mechanics Revs., 1987-94, Manufacturing Review, 1991-95; editorial adv. bd. Acta Mechanica Sinica, 1990—; mem. editorial bd. Pressure Vessels and Piping Design Technology, 1982; tech. editor Pressure Vessel Technology, 1982-93; co-editor: SME Handbook of Metalforming, 1985, 94, Design and Analysis of Plates and Shells, 1986. Standard Oil Co. Calif. fellow, 1961-63; NASA fellow, 1966; NAS travel grantee, Russia, 1972; von Humboldt fellow, Fed. Republic Germany, 1968-69. Fellow ASME (v.p. materials and structures 1993-96, chmn. pressure vessel rsch. com. 1982-87, chmn. design and analysis com. pressure vessel and piping divsn. 1980-83, chmn. jr. awards com. applied mechanics divsn. 1973-76, chmn. machine design divsn. of Chgo. sect., 1967-68, editor newsletter Chgo. sect. 1971-73, exec. com. Chgo. sect. 1970-73, honors and awards chmn. Milw. sect. 1992-95, mem. exec. com. and program chmn. pressure vessel and piping divsn. 1985-89, vice-chmn., sec. pressure vessel and piping divsn., 1989-90, chmn. pressure vessel and piping divsn., 1990-91, historian, senate pressure vessel and piping divsn., 1991-92, pres. senate pressure vessel and piping divsn., 1992-93, bd. editors, 1983-93, mem. materials and structures group, 1990-91, mem. coun. on engring. 1993—, mem. bd. on pressure tech. codes and standards, 1989-94, soc. rep. to Fedn. Materials Socs. 1994-95, mem. tech. execs. com. 1993—, Pressure Vessel and Piping award 1995 and medal), ASCE (sec.-treas. structural divsn. of Ill. sect. 1972-73, chmn. divsn. 1976-77, chmn. peer review com., tech. coun. on rsch. 1984, coun. on structural plastics), Soc. Mfg. Engrs. (sr. mem.), Am. Soc. for Engring. Edn., French Pressure Vessel Assn., So. Plastics Engrs., Gesellschaft für Angewandte Mathematik und Mechanik, WRC (pressure vessel rsch. coun., chmn. subcom. on design procedures for shell intersections, 1983-87, chmn. com. on reinforced openings and external loads, 1987-91, vice chmn. com. on polymer pressure components 1991—, chmn. com. shells and ligaments 1994—), Internat. Coun. on Pressure Vessel Tech. (chmn. Am. regional com. 1988—, internat. chmn. 1992-96), 2nd China Nat. Standards Com. for Pressure Vessels (hon. cons.), Wis. Club. Research on mechanics of composite materials, plates and shells, asymptotic methods in elasticity, pressure vessels and piping, mechanics of deformation processing. Home: 19440 Killarney Way Brookfield WI 53045-4810 Office: Marquette U Dept Mech & Indsl Engring 1515 W Wisconsin Ave Milwaukee WI 53233-2222

WIDGOFF, MILDRED, physicist, educator; b. Buffalo, Aug. 24, 1924; d. Leo Widgoff and Rebecca Shulimson; children—Eve Widgoff Shapiro, Jonathan Bernard Widgoff Shapiro. B.A., U. Buffalo, 1944; Ph.D., Cornell U., 1952. Rsch. assoc. Brookhaven Nat. Lab., Yaphank, N.Y., 1952-54; rsch. fellow Harvard U., Cambridge, Mass., 1955-58; asst. prof. rsch. Brown U., Providence, 1959-66, assoc. prof. rsch., 1966-74, prof. physics, 1974-95; prof. rsch., 1995—. Fellow Am. Phys. Soc.; mem. Sigma Xi, Phi Beta Kappa, Phi Kappa Phi. Office: Brown U Dept Physics PO Box 1843 Providence RI 02912-1843

WIDISS, ALAN I., lawyer, educator; b. L.A., Sept. 28, 1938; s. Al and Rose H. (Sobole) W.; m. Ellen Louise Magaziner, June 28, 1964; children: Benjamin L., Deborah Anne, Rebecca Elizabeth. BS, U. So. Calif., 1960, LLB, 1963; LLM, Harvard U., 1964. Bar: Calif. 1963. Teaching fellow Harvard U., 1964-65; asst. prof. law U. Iowa, Iowa City, 1965-68; asso. prof. U. Iowa, 1968-69, prof., 1969-78, Josephine R. Witte prof., 1978—; vis. prof. U. So. Calif., U. San Diego; dir. CLRS Mass. No-Fault Automobile Ins. Study, 1971-76. Author: A Guide to Uninsured Motorist Coverage, 1969; (with others) No-Fault Automobile Insurance in Action: The Experiences in Massachusetts, Florida, Delaware and New York, 1977, Uninsured and Underinsured Motorist Insurance (3d edit.), Vol. 1, 1991, Vol. 2, 1992, Vol. 3, 1995; author, editor: (with others) Arbitration: Commercial Disputes, Insurance and Tort Claims, 1979; (with Judge Robert E. Keeton) Insurance Law, 1988 and Course Supplement, 1988; Insurance: Materials on the General Principles, Legal Doctrines and Regulatory Acts, 1989; contbr. articles to law jours. Bd. fellows U. Iowa Sch. Religion, 1976, v.p., 1991-93, pres., 1993-95; chmn. Johnson County Citizens Adv. Com. for Regional Transp. Study, 1971-75. Pres. Agudas Achim Synagogue, 1983-85, Iowa City Youth Orch., 1991-92. Mem. ABA, Am. Law Inst., Calif. Bar Assn., Assn. Am. Law Schs., Order of Coif, Phi Kappa Phi, Delta Sigma Rho. Avocations: tennis, theater. Home: 316 Kimball Rd Iowa City IA 52245-5825 Office: U Iowa Coll Law Iowa City IA 52242

WIDLUND, OLOF BERTIL, computer science educator; b. Stockholm, Feb. 11, 1938; s. Sten O. and Dagmar W.; m. Nadine H. Taub, June 13, 1972. M.S. in Engring., Royal Inst. Tech., Stockholm, 1960, Ph.D., 1964; Sc.D., Uppsala U., Sweden, 1966. Asst. prof. NYU, N.Y.C., 1968-72, assoc. prof., 1972-75, prof. computer sci., 1975—, chmn. dept. computer sci., 1980-86. Contbr. articles to various publs. Office: NYU Courant Inst 251 Mercer St New York NY 10012-1110

WIDLUS, HANNAH BEVERLY, lawyer; b. Montreal, Quebec, Can., Jan. 23, 1955; d. William Jayson and Martha (Klein) Widlus; m. Moses W. Gaynor, Dec. 20, 1986. BSBA cum laude, Miami U., Oxford, Ohio, 1976; JD with honors, George Washington U., 1979. Bar: Tex. 1979, N.Y. 1984, Ill. 1988, D.C. 1990. Assoc. Johnson & Gibbs (formerly Johnson, Swanson & Barbee), Dallas, 1979-82, Proskauer Rose Goetz & Mendelsohn, N.Y.C., 1982-83, Patterson, Belknap, Webb & Tyler, N.Y.C., 1983-86; assoc. Kirkland & Ellis, Chgo., 1987-88, ptnr., 1988-91; counsel benefits Waste Management, Inc., Oak Brook, Ill., 1991-94; assoc. D'Ancona & Pflaum, Chgo., 1994—; lectr. on pension and profit sharing plans, 1988-92; seminar on employment regulations in Ill., 1987-91, seminar on basic employee benefits, 1988-90, NYU 45th Ann. Inst. on Fed. Taxation, 1996, inst. for paralegal studies NYU Sch. Continuing Edn., 1984-86, tax seminar Dallas Gen. Agts. and Mgrs. Assn., 1980, 81, Corpus Christi chpt. Tex. Soc. CPAs, 1981, sect. taxation Dallas Bar Assn., 1980. Contbr. articles to profl. jours.

Mem. ABA (sect. taxation), State Bar Tex., State Bar N.Y., Ill. Bar, D.C. Bar. Jewish.

WIDMAN, GARY LEE, lawyer, former government official; b. Fremont, Nebr., June 1, 1936; s. Benjamin H. and Alice C. (Negley) W.; m. Mary Margaret Donnelly, Mar. 5, 1972(div. 1988); children: Andrew Scott, Natalie Claire. BS, U. Nebr., 1957; JD, Hastings Coll. Law U. Calif., 1962; LLM, U. Mich., 1966. Bar: Calif. 1962, D.C. 1982. Assoc. Thelen, Marrin, Johnson & Bridges, San Francisco, 1962-65; assoc. prof. law U. Denver, 1966-69; prof., dir. resource and environ. law program Hastings Coll. Law, U. Calif., San Francisco, 1969-80; gen. counsel Coun. Environ. Quality, Exec. Office Pres., Washington, 1974-76; lectr. U. Calif. at Davis, 1978, Boalt Hall, 1977-79; assoc. solicitor Dept. Interior, Washington, 1980-81; of counsel Fulbright & Jaworski, 1981-85; dir. staff attys. U.S. Ct. of Appeals (9th cir.), San Francisco, 1985-87; atty. Bronson, Bronson & McKinnon, San Francisco, 1988-95; chief counsel State Dept. Parks and Recreation, Sacramento, 1995—; trustee Rocky Mountain Mineral Law Found., 1969-74, 77-80; apptd. by gov. P. Wilson to Bay-Delta Oversight Coun., 1993-95. Author and project dir.: Legal Study of Oil Shale on Public Lands, 1969. Served with U.S. Army, 1957-59. Mem. ABA (council sect. natural resources 1975-77, spl. com. energy law 1977-82, council lawyers and scientists 1984-90), Fed. Bar Assn. (chmn. com. natural resources 1977), Calif. Bar Assn., D.C. Bar Assn., Trout Unlimited Calif. (pres. 1986-90). Home: 28 Marinero Cir Apt 31 Belvedere Tiburon CA 94920-1644 Office: State Dept Parks Recreation 1416 Ninth St Sacramento CA 95814

WIDMAN, RICHARD GUSTAVE, engineering and construction company executive; b. Detroit, Jan. 28, 1922; s. Edward J. and Lena E. (Hurrle) W.; m. Barbara Jean Roehm, Sept 7, 1946; children: Richard Thomas, Linda Widman Wyer, Jeanne Widman Overby. B.C.E., U. Mich., 1947. Various positions Arthur G. McKee & Co. and McKee Corp., 1948-65, gen. mgr. petroleum and chems. div., 1966-68, v.p., 1968-69, exec. v.p., dir., 1969, pres., 1970-71, pres., chief exec. officer, chmn. bd., 1971-79, also dir.; chmn. bd., dir. Am. Automobile Assn.; bd. dirs. Ohio Motorists Assn. Served with C.E. AUS, 1943-46. Mem. Tau Beta Pi. Clubs: Royal Poinciana Golf (Naples, Fla.). Lodges: Rotary, Shriners, Jesters. Home: 2901 Gulf Shore Blvd N Naples FL 33940-3937

WIDMANN, GLENN ROGER, electrical engineer; b. Newark, Jan. 8, 1957; s. Elmer and Ellen (Eccles) W. BSEE, Rutgers U., 1979; MSEE, Purdue U., 1981, PhDEE, 1988. Engr. N.J. Bell Telephone Co., Hopelawn, 1979; instr. Purdue U., West Lafayette, Ind., 1979-81, 83-88; prof. elec. engring. Colo. State U., Ft. Collins, 1989-91; engr. Hughes Aircraft Co., Canoga Park, Calif., 1980-83, scientist, project mgr., 1991-94; sr. sci. Hughes Rsch. Labs. Hughes Aircraft Co., Malibu, Calif., 1994-96; dept. mgr. Hughes Rsch. Laboratories, 1996—; cons. Bur. Reclamation, Denver, 1989, Benjamin Cummings Pub. Co., Ft. Collins, 1989; mem. program com. Internat. Symposium Robotics and Mfg., Santa Fe, N.Mex., 1991—. Contbr. articles to tech. jours.; patentee in robotics field. Recipient presentation award Am. Controls Conf., 1990. Mem. IEEE, Soc. Automotive Engrs., Tau Beta Pi, Eta Kappa Nu. Avocation: coin collecting. Home: 3434 Delilah St Simi Valley CA 93063-2720 Office: Hughes Aircraft Co Hughes Rsch Labs MS RL 71 3011 Malibu Canyon Rd Malibu CA 90265

WIDMANN, NANCY C., broadcast executive. Pres. radio div. CBS, N.Y.C., 1988—. Office: CBS Radio Networks 524 W 57th St New York NY 10019-2902

WIDMARK, RICHARD, actor; b. Sunrise, Minn., Dec. 26, 1914; s. Carl H. and Ethel Mae (Barr) W.; m. Ora Jean Hazlewood, Apr. 5, 1942; 1 dau., Anne Heath. B.A., Lake Forest (Ill.) Coll., 1936, D.F.A. (hon.), 1973. Instr. drama dept. Lake Forest Coll., 1936-38; Pres. Heath Prodns., 1955—; v.p. Widmark Cattle Enterprises, 1957—. Actor various radio networks, N.Y.C., 1938-47; Broadway appearances include Kiss and Tell, 1943, Get Away Old Man, 1943, Trio, 1944, Kiss Them for Me, 1944, Dunnigan's Daughter, 1945, Dream Girl, 1946-47; summer stock appearances include The Bo Tree, 1939, Joan of Lorraine, 1947; motion picture appearances include Kiss of Death, 1947, Street with No Name, 1948, Yellow Sky, 1948, Roadhouse, 1948, Down to the Sea in Ships, 1949, Night and the City, 1949, No Way Out, 1949, Panic in the Streets, 1950, Slattery's Hurricane, 1949, Halls of Montezuma, 1950, The Frogmen, 1950, Price of Gold, 1954, Co Blue, 1954, Broken Lance, 1954, Backlash, 1955, St. Joan, 1956, Time Limit, 1957, Warlock, 1958, The Alamo, 1959, Judgement at Nuremberg, 1961, Flight from Ashiya, 1962, How the West Was Won, 1962, The Long Ships, 1963, Cheyenne Autumn, 1963, Bedford Incident, 1964, Alvarez Kelly, 1965, The Way West, 1966, Madigan, 1967, Patch, 1968, Talent for Loving, 1968, The Moonshine War, 1969, When the Legends Die, 1971, Murder on the Orient Express, 1974, The Sellout, 1975, To the Devil, A Daughter, 1975, The Twilight's Last Gleaming, 1976, The Domino Principle, 1976, Roller Coaster, 1976, Coma, 1978, The Swarm, 1977, Hanky Panky, 1982, The Final Option, 1983, Against All Odds, 1984, True Colors, 1990; NBC TV appearance in Vanished, 1971, TV series Madigan, 1972; TV appearance in Benjamin Franklin, 1974, Mr. Horn, 1979, Bear Island, 1979, All God's Children, 1980, A Whale for the Killing, 1981, Blackout, 1985, A Gathering of Old Men, 1986, Once Upon a Texas Train, 1987, Cold Sassy Tree, 1989. True Colors, 1990. Bd. dirs. Hope for Hearing. Named Comdr. of Arts and Letters (France), 1987. Mem. Valley Club (Montecito, Calif.), Century Club (N.Y.C.).

WIDNALL, SHEILA EVANS, secreatry of the airforce, former aeronautical educator, former university official; b. Tacoma, July 13, 1938; d. Rolland John and Genievieve Alice (Krause) Evans; m. William Soule Widnall, June 11, 1960; children: William, Ann. BS in Aero. and Astronautics, MIT, 1960, MS in Aero. and Astronautics, 1961, DSc, 1964; PhD (hon.), New Eng. Coll., 1975, Lawrence U., 1987, Cedar Crest Coll., 1988, Smith Coll., 1990, Mt. Holyoke Coll., 1991, Ill. Inst. Tech., 1991, Columbia U., 1994, Simmons Coll., 1994, Suffolk U., 1994, Princeton U., 1994. Asst. prof. aeros. and astronautics MIT, Cambridge, 1964-70, assoc. prof., 1970-74, prof., 1974-93, head divsn. fluid mechanics, 1975-79; dir. Fluid Dynamics Rsch. Lab., MIT, Cambridge, 1979-90; chmn. faculty MIT, Cambridge, 1979-80, chairperson com. on acad. responsibility, 1991-92, assoc. provost, 1992-93; sec. USAF, 1993—; bd. dirs. Chemfab Inc., Bennington, Vt., Aerospace Corp., L.A., Draper Labs., Cambridge; past trustee Carnegie Corp., 1984-92, Charles Stark Draper Lab. Inc.; mem. Carnegie Commn. Sci., Tech. and Govt. Contbr. articles to profl. jours.; patentee in field; assoc. editor AIAA Jour. Aircraft, 1972-75, Physics of Fluids, 1981-88, Jour. Applied Mechanics, 1983-87; mem. editorial bd. Sci., 1984-86. Bd. visitors USAF Acad., Colorado Springs, Colo., 1978-84, bd. chairperson, 1980-82; trustee Boston Mus. Sci., 1989—. Recipient Washburn award Boston Mus. Sci., 1987. Fellow AAAS (bd. dirs. 1982-89, pres. 1987-88, chmn. 1988-89), AIAA (bd. dirs. 1975-77, Lawrence Sperry award 1972), Am. Phys. Soc. (exec. com. 1979-82); mem. ASME, NAE (coun. 1992—), NAS (panel on sci. responsibility), Am. Acad. Arts and Scis., Soc. Women Engrs. (Outstanding Achievement award 1975), Internat. Acad. Astronautics, Seattle Mountaineers. Office: USAF Office of Sec 1670 AF Pentagon Washington DC 20330-1670*

WIDNER, NELLE OUSLEY, retired elementary education educator; b. Loyston, Tenn., May 20, 1924; d. Jacob Milas and Myrtle (Longmire) Ousley; m. John DeLozier Widner; children: Stephen John, Beth Widner Jackson, David Earl. BA, Maryville (Tenn.) Coll., 1946; postgrad. U. Tenn. Cert. profl. educator. 1st grade tchr. Alcoa (Tenn.) City Schs., 1946-50, 74-87, tchr. remedial reading, 1966-74. Mem. AAUW, Alpha Delta Kappa (publicity chmn. 1982-84, chaplain 1984-86, sec. 1994-96), Order Ea. Star (worthy matron local chpt. 1941), Chilhowee Club, Epsilon Sigma Omicron (chmn. 1991-92), Passion Play Guild. Democrat. Methodist. Avocations: reading, sports. Home: 1629 Peppertree Dr Alcoa TN 37701-1514

WIDNER, RALPH RANDOLPH, civic executive; b. Phila., Oct. 21, 1930; s. Ralph Litteer and Viola (Cunningham) W.; m. Joan Sundelius Ziegler, July 9, 1955; children: Jennifer Anne, Wendy Rowe. BA, Duke U., 1952; student, Georgetown U., 1958; DHL (hon.), Union Coll., Ky., 1970, Capital U., Columbus, Ohio, 1971. Journalist Paterson (N.J.) Evening News, 1955-56, N.Y. Times, 1956-58; Congressional fellow Am. Polit. Sci. Assn., 1958; dir. pub. affairs Pa. Dept. Forests and Waters, 1959-60; asst. dir. Pa. Planning Bd., 1960-62; legis. asst. to U.S. Senator Clark, 1962-65; exec. dir. Appalachian Regional Commn., 1965-71; pres. Acad. for State and Local Govt., 1971-82; adj. prof. pub. adminstrn. and city planning Ohio State U., 1971-82; pres. Nat. Tng. and Devel. Service for State and Local Govt., 1979-81; staff v.p. Urban Land Inst., 1982-83; exec. dir. Greater Phila. First Corp., 1983-88; chmn., CEO Fairfax House Internat., Alexandria, Va., 1988—; mng. dir. Civic TN Network. Lt. (j.g.) USN, 1952-55. Fellow Nat. Acad. Pub. Administrn. Democrat. Methodist. Home: 2210 Belle Haven Rd Alexandria VA 22307-1100 Office: 21 Dupont Cir NW Washington DC 20036-1109

WIDOM, BENJAMIN, chemistry educator; b. Newark, Oct. 13, 1927; s. Morris and Rebecca (Hertz) W.; m. Joanne McCurdy, Dec. 21, 1953; children: Jonathan, Michael, Elisabeth. AB, Columbia U., 1949; PhD, Cornell U., 1953; DSc (hon.), U. Chgo., 1991. Rsch. assoc. U. N.C., Chapel Hill, 1952-54; instr. chemistry Cornell U., Ithaca, N.Y., 1954-55, asst. prof., 1955-59, assoc. prof., 1959-63, prof., 1963-83, Goldwin Smith prof., 1983—; van der Waals prof. U. Amsterdam, The Netherlands, 1972; vis. prof. Harvard U., Cambridge, Mass., 1975; IBM vis. prof. Oxford (Eng.) U., 1978; Lorentz prof. U. Leiden, The Netherlands, 1985; vis. prof. Cath. U. Louvain, Belgium, 1988. Author: (with J.S. Rowlinson) Molecular Theory of Capillarity, 1982. With U.S. Army, 1946-47. Recipient Clark disting. tchg. award Cornell U., 1973, Dickson prize for sci. Carnegie-Mellon U., 1986, Hirschfelder Prize in Theoretical Chemistry U. Wis., 1991, Bakhuis Roozeboom medal Royal Netherlands Acad. Arts & Scis., 1994, Onsager medal U. Trondheim, Norway, 1994. Fellow Am. Phys. Soc., Am. Acad. Arts and Scis., N.Y. Acad. Scis. (Boris Pregel award for chem. physics rsch. 1976); mem. NAS, Am. Philos. Soc., Am. Chem. Soc. (Langmuir award in chem. physics 1982, Hildebrand award in theoretical and exptl. chemistry of liquids 1992). Home: 204 The Parkway Ithaca NY 14850-2247 Office: Cornell U Chemistry Dept Ithaca NY 14853

WIEBE, BERNIE, conflict resolution studies educator; b. Altona, Man., Can., Jan. 30, 1935; s. Peter D. and Susanna (Hiebert) W.; m. Marge Dora Letkeman, July 8, 1956; Glen (dec.), Gayle, Gregory, Grant. BA, Goshen Coll., 1961; BD, Mennonite Biblical Sem., 1965; MA, U. N.D., 1972, PhD, 1974. Tchr. Mennonites in Man., Winnipeg, 1953-56, conf. min., 1965-71; pres. Freeman Jr. Coll., S.D., 1973-76; mng. editor Mennonite Med. Messenger, 1980-89; editor The Mennonite Gen. Conf. Mennonite Ch., 1976-86; prof. in CRS Menno Simons Coll., 1986—. Author: (book) Boblical Mutual Aid for the 1980's, 1987; contbr. chpts. to books, articles to profl. jours. lay min. Ft. Garry Mennonite Fellowship, 1977-80, exec. mem. Liberal Party, 1978-80, mem. edn. com. 1984-86, active spl. GC-MC inter-mennonite listening com. for homosexual concerns, 1990-92, mem. worship com. 1991-93; conf. moderator Mennonites in Man., 1979-82, 85-88, chair Can. program com. 1985-88, elected mem. divsn. gen. svcs. bd., 1989-92, mem. spl. com. to work with conflict in churches and to provide guidelines to CMM, 1992—, mem. GC Higher Edn. Coun., 1992—, appointee GC program com., 1992—, asst. moderator of Gen. Conf., 1992—; mem. NDP task force on environ. Province Manitoba, 1988-89. Mem. Gideons. Home: 46 Belair Rd, Winnipeg, MB Canada R3T 0S2 Office: Menno Simons Coll, 380 Spence St 3d fl, Winnipeg, MB Canada R3B 2E9

WIEBE, J. E. N., province official. Lt. gov. Govt. Saskatchewan, Regina, Can. Office: Office of the Lieutenant Gov, Govt House 4607 Dewdney Ave, Regina, SK Canada S4P 3V7*

WIEBE, LEONARD IRVING, radiopharmacist, educator; b. Swift Current, Sask., Can., Oct. 14, 1941; s. Cornelius C. and Margaret (Teichroeb) W.; m. Grace E. McIntyre, Sept. 5, 1964; children: Glenis, Kirsten, Megan. BSP, U. Sask., 1963, MS, 1966; PhD, U. Sydney, Australia, 1970. Pharmacist Swift Current Union Hosp., 1963-64; sessional lectr. U. Sask., Can., 1965-66; asst. prof. U. Alta., Can., 1970-73, assoc. prof., 1973-78, prof., 1978—, dir. Slowpoke Reactor Facility, 1975-89, asst. dean rsch., 1984-87; assoc. dean U. Alta., 1990—; sessional lectr. U. Sydney, Australia, 1973; pres. Internat. Bionucleonics Cons. Lts., 1991—; dir. BMH, Australian Nuclear Sci. Tech. Orgn., 1990, Noujaim Inst. Pharm. Oncology, 1994—; rsch. assoc. Cross Cancer Inst., Edmonton, 1978—, Med. Rsch. Coun. Can.; vis. prof. Royal P.A. Hosp., Sydney, 1983-84, Searle vis. prof., 1986; MRC vis. prof., Toronto, 1987; PMAC vis. prof., 1988; McCalla prof. U. Alta, 1993-94; radiopharmacy cons. Australian Atomic Energy Commn., Sydney, 1983-84; mem. MRC standing com. on sci. and rsch., 1995—. Editor: Liquid Scintillation: Science and Technology, 1976, Advances in Scintillation Counting, 1983; guest editor Jour. of Radioanalytical Chemistry, 1981; editor Internat. Jour. Applied Radiation Instrumentation Sect. A, 1988-90; regional editor Internat. Jour. Nuclear Biology and Medicine, 1992-95. Commonwealth Univs. Exchange grantee, 1966; Alexander von Humboldt fellow, 1976-79, 82. Mem. Pharm. Bd. of New South Wales, Sask. Pharm. Assn., Soc. Nuclear Medicine, Assn. Faculties of Pharmacy of Can. (McNeil Rsch. award 1988), Can. Radiation Protection Assn., Can. Assn. Radiopharm. Scientists, Am. Pharm. Assn., Am. Assn. Pharm. Sci., Australian Nuclear Sci. Tech. Orgn. (dir., biomedicine and health 1990), Internat. Assn. Radiopharmacy (exec. sec. 1991-95), Univ. Club (Edmonton) (pres. 1985). Mem. Mennonite Ch.

WIEBE, RICHARD HERBET, reproductive endocrinologist, educator; b. Herbert, Sask., Can., Dec. 28, 1937; came to U.S., 1971; s. Herbert and Olga Maragratha (Jahnke) W.; m. Jacquelyn Dee Yancy, Aug. 30, 1975; 1 child, Richard Herbert, Jr. MD, U. Sask., 1962. Resident Queen's Univ., Kingston, Ont., Can., 1970; asst. to assoc. prof. Duke U., Durham, N.C., 1972-81; assoc. prof. to prof. U. So. Ala., Mobile, 1981-88; chmn. and prof. Dept. Ob-Gyn. U. S.D., Sioux Falls, 1988-95; chmn., prof. dept. ob-gyn. East Tenn. State U., Johnson City, 1996—; editorial cons., Fertility/Sterility, Birmingham, Ala., 1978—; sec., Univ. Physicians, Sioux Falls, 1991—. Contbr. numerous articles to profl. jours. Recipient, Rsch. Grant, NIH, Ala., 1981-89, Edn./Svc. Grant, USPHS, S.D., 1989—. Mem. ACOG, Assn. Profs. of Ob-Gyn., Am. Soc. Primatologists, Soc. for Gynecol. Investigation, Soc. for Study of Reproduction, Am. Fertility Soc., Endocrine Soc. Home: 4319 Summerfield Dr Piney Flats TN 37686 Office: James H Quillen Sch Med East Tenn State U Dept Ob-Gyn Box 70569 Johnson City TN 37614

WIEBENSON, DORA LOUISE, architectural historian, educator, author; b. Cleve., July 29, 1926; d. Edward Ralph and Jeannette (Rodier) W. BA, Vassar Coll., 1946; MArch, Harvard U., 1951; MA, NYU, 1958, PhD, 1964. Architect N.Y., 1951-66; lectr. Columbia U., 1966-68; assoc. prof. U. Md., 1968-72, prof., 1972-77; vis. prof. Cornell U., 1974; prof. U. Va., Charlottesville, 1977-92, prof. emerita, 1992—, chmn. div. archtl. history, 1977-79, assoc. fellow U. Va. Ctr. Advanced Studies, 1982-83; pres. Archtl. Publs., N.Y.C., 1982—. Editor: Marsyas XI: 1962-64, 1965, Essays in Honor of Walter Friedlaender, 1965; Architectural Theory and Practice from Alberti to Ledoux, 1982, rev., 1983, Spanish transl., 1988; Guide to Graduate Degree Programs in Architectural History, 1982, rev., 1984, 86, 88, 90; author: Sources of Greek Revival Architecture, 1969, Tony Garnier: The Cité Industrielle, 1969, Japanese transl., 1983, The Picturesque Garden in France, 1978, Mark J. Millard Architectural Collection, Vol. I: French Books: Sixteenth through Nineteenth Centuries, 1993; contbr. articles to profl. jours. Student fellow Inst. Fine Arts, 1961-62, 62-63; grantee Am. Philos. Soc., 1964-65, 70, Samuel H. Kress Found., 1966, Gen. Rsch. Fund, U. Md., 1969, 74, 76, NEH, 1972-73, Samuel H. Kress Found., 1972-73, Am. Coun. Learned Socs., 1976, 81, 85, Ctr. Advanced Studies, U. Va., 1980, 81, Graham Found. Advanced Studies Fine Arts, 1982, 93; fellow Yale Ctr. Brit. Art, 1983; sr. rsch. fellow NEH, 1986-87. Mem. Soc. Archtl. Historians (bd. dirs. 1974-77, 80-83, chair edn. com. 1976-90), Coll. Art Assn., Am. Soc. Eighteenth Century (mem. exec. bd. 1991-94).

WIECEK, BARBARA HARRIET, advertising executive; b. Chgo., Mar. 30, 1956; d. Stanley Joseph and Irene (Zagajewski) W. AA, Am. Acad. of Art, Chgo., 1977. Illustrator Clinton E. Frank Advt., Chgo., 1977-78, art dir., 1978-80, assoc. creative dir., 1980-84, v.p.; instr. Am. Acad. of Art, Chgo., 1977-80; assoc. creative dir. Tatham, Laird & Kudner, 1984—; ptnr. Tatham, Laird & Kudner, Chgo., 1986—, creative dir., 1987—, sr. ptnr., 1995—, exec. creative dir., 1996. Recipient Silver Awd. Internat. Film Festival of N.Y., 1981, Gold Awd. Internat. Film Festival of N.Y., 1981. Roman Catholic. Avocations: painting, writing, gardening, remodeling, cycling. Office: Tatham Euro RSCG 980 N Michigan Ave Chicago IL 60611-4501

WIECEK, WILLIAM MICHAEL, law educator; b. Cleve., Jan. 31, 1938; s. Michael Frank and Mary (Kotecki) W.; m. Maryann Pickarski, June 17, 1961 (div. 1979); children: Michael, Sophie, Kristen. BA, Cath. U., 1959; LLB, Harvard U., 1962; PhD, U. Wis., 1968. Bar: N.H., 1962. Atty. Snierson & Chandler, Laconia, N.H., 1962-64; prof. history U. Mo., Columbia, 1968-84; prof. law. Syracuse (N.Y.) U., 1985—. Author: The Guarantee Clause of the U.S. Constitution, 1972, The Sources of Antislavery Constitutionalism in America, 1760-1848, 1977, Constitutional Development in a Modernizing Society: The United States, 1803-1917, 1985, (with Harold M. Hyman) Equal Justice Under Law: Constitutional Development, 1835-1875, 1982, (with Gerard H. Clarfield) Nuclear America: Military and Civilian Nuclear Power in the United States, 1940-1980, 1984, Liberty Under Law: The Supreme Court in American Life, 1988, (with Kermit Hall and Paul Finkelman) American Legal History: Cases and Materials, 1991 (with Kermit Hall, James Ely and Joel Grossman) The Oxford Companion to the Supreme Court of the United States, 1992; contbr. numerous articles, chpts. and papers on law to profl. books, jours. and confs. Vol. emergency med. technician, firefighter Fayetteville (N.Y.) Fire Dept. Mem. ABA, Am. Law Inst., Am. Soc. for Legal History (bd. dirs. 1987-90), Orgn. Am. Historians, Selden Soc., Am. Hist. Assn., Supreme Ct. Hist. Soc. (mem. editorial bd. 1984-86), Phi Beta Kappa. Democrat. Roman Catholic. Home: 137 Stanwood Ln Manlius NY 13104-1411 Office: Syracuse U Coll Of Law Syracuse NY 13244

WIECHA, JOSEPH AUGUSTINE, linguist, educator; b. Chorzów II, Poland, Sept. 20, 1926; came to U.S., 1955, naturalized, 1958; s. Karol and Gertruda (Rudzki) W.; m. Mary Ruth Moore, 1953; children: Joseph Damian, Charles Francis, John Moore. BA with 1st class honors, Nat. U. Ireland, 1950; PhD with highest distinction, NYU, 1963. Instr. fgn. langs. U.S. Third Air Force, London, 1951-55; instr. German and Spanish U. Md., London, 1951-55; tchr. Spanish and math. Bklyn. Friends Sch., 1955-56; instr. German N.Y. U., N.Y.C., summer, 1958; lectr. German and humanities Harvard U., Boston, 1959-63; lectr. German lit. Colby Coll., summer 1963; prof. German SUNY, Oswego, 1963-69; chmn. dept. fgn. langs. and lit. SUNY, 1963-69, chmn. dept. Germanic and Slavic langs. and lit., 1969-72, Disting. Teaching prof., 1973-92, disting. tchg. prof. emeritus, 1992—; chmn. SUNY (Fgn. Studies Center), 1972-73; lectr. and cons. methodology of tchg. fgn. langs., 1959—; condr. seminars tchg. methodology fgn. langs. Nat. U. of Pedro Enriquez Ureña, Santo Domingo, 1973, U. Pisa, Italy, 1974, Moscow State Pedagogical Inst.; Fgn. Langs., USSR, 1976; vis. prof. U. Wroctaw, Poland, 1977. Developed Wiecha Progressive-Reflex method of teaching fgn. langs. Served as officer 2d Polish Corps Brit. Army, 1944-47. Decorated Bronze medal Polish Army, also; Brit. Def. medal; French Star; Star of Italy; recipient diploma of spl. recognition Universidad Nacional de Pedro Enriquez Ureña, 1973; Galileo medal U. Pisa, 1974; Ogden Butler fellow, 1958-59; Fels fellow, 1956-59; Kosciuszko Found. fellow, 1959. Mem. MLA, N.Y. State Assn. Fgn. Lang. Tchrs. (dir. 1975-78, Disting. Tchr. award 1975, Disting. Bd. Dirs. award 1978, Spl. Contbn. to Teaching Fgn. Langs. award 1979), Am. Assn. Tchrs. of German, Polish Inst. Arts and Scis. in Am., Nat. Spanish Honors Soc. (hon.), Am. Coun. on Edn. (nat. honor roll), Delta Phi Alpha (hon.), Dobro Slovo (hon.). Home: 710 Copa De Oro Marathon FL 33050-5406 also: 22 Bayside Rd Northport ME 04849

WIECHERT, ALLEN LEROY, educational planning consultant, architect; b. Independence, Kans., Oct. 25, 1938; s. Norman Henry and Serena Johanna (Steinke) W.; BArch, Kans. State U., 1962; m. Sandra Swanson, Aug. 19, 1961; children: Kirstin Nan, Brendan Swanson, Megan Ann. Architect in tng. McVey, Peddie, Schmidt & Allen, Wichita, Kans., 1962-63; architect Kivett & Myers, Kansas City, Mo., 1963-68; asst. to vice chancellor plant planning and devel. U. Kans., Lawrence, 1968-74, asso. dir. facilities planning, 1974-78, univ. dir. facilities planning, 1978-92; univ. architect, 1993-95; campus planner Gould Evans Assocs., Lawrence, Kans., 1995-96; mem. long range phys. planning com. Kans. Bd. Regents, 1971-95; designer, archtl. programmer of ednl. facilities; bd. dirs. Kans. U. Fed. Credit Union, 1972-81, pres. bd., 1974. Chmn. horizons com. Lawrence Bicentennial Commn.; designer Kaw River Trail, 1976; mem. Action 80 Com., 1980-81, Lawrence-Douglas County Horizon 2020 Task Group, 1993-95; mem. standing com. Kans. Episcopal Diocese, 1976-80, pres. com., 1981, mem. diocesan council, 1982-84, chmn. coll. work com., 1982-84, commn. on ch. architecture and allied arts, 1986—, long range planning com., 1988; sr. warden Trinity Episc. Ch., Lawrence, 1978-80; trustee Kans. Sch. Religion, 1973-80, 82-95, v.p., 1984-85, pres., 1986-92, trustee friends of the dept. of relig. studies, 1995—; mem. adv. bd. Salvation Army, 1990—; bd. dirs. Trinity Group Care Home, 1973-79; advancement chmn. troop com. Boy Scouts Am., 1981-87, dist. com. Pelathe dist., 1984—, vice chmn., 1984; chmn., 1985-87, exec. bd. Heart of Am. council, 1985-87. Recipient Dist. Award of Merit Boy Scouts Am., 1988, Silver Beaver award, 1991. 1st lt. Kans. Air N.G., 1961-67. Lic. architect, Kans.; cert. Nat. Council Archtl. Registration Bds. Mem. AIA, Assn. Univ. Architects (sec./treas. 1986-87, v.p. 1987-88, pres. 1988-89), Nat. Hist. Trust, Kans. U. Endowment Assn. (sec. 1981-85, founder, exec. bd. Hist. Mt. Oread Fund. div.), Nat. Cathedral Assn. (regional co-chairperson 1993—). Editor, contbr. to Physical Development Planning Work Book, 1973. Home: 813 Highland Dr Lawrence KS 66044-2431 Office: U Kans Office Of Capital Prog Lawrence KS 66045

WIECHMANN, ERIC WATT, lawyer; b. Schenectady, N.Y., June 12, 1948; s. Richard Jerdone and Ann (Watt) W.; m. Merrill Metzger, May 22, 1971. BA, Hamilton Coll., 1970; JD, Cornell U., 1974. Bar: Conn. 1975, U.S. Dist. Ct. (so. and ea. dists.) N.Y. 1975, U.S. Dist. Ct. Conn. 1975, U.S. Ct. Appeals (2d cir.) 1975, U.S. Supreme Ct. 1978, U.S. Ct. Appeals (9th cir.) 1980, D.C. 1981, U.S. Dist. Ct. D.C. 1981, U.S. Ct. Appeals D.C. 1982, U.S. Ct. Appeals (5th cir.) 1986, U.S. Ct. Appeals (10th cir.) 1989. Assoc., Cummings & Lockwood, Stamford, 1974-82, ptnr., 1982—, ptnr. in charge, 1996—; spl. pretrial master U.S. Dist. Ct. Conn. 1984—; state atty. trial referee, 1986—, mem. law revision commn., evidence code drafting com.; faculty Def. Counsel Trial Acad.; mem. civil task force, civil jury instrn. com. Conn. Superior Ct. Contbr. articles to profl. jours. Mem. Zoning Bd. Appeals, New Canaan, Conn., 1984-85. Mem. ABA, Def. Rsch. Inst., Internat. Assn. Def. Counsel, Conn. Bar Assn. (exec. com. antitrust sect. 1982—, ct. rules adv. com., chmn. 1991-93), Fed. Bar Coun., Hartford Club, Golf Club Avon. Republican. Episcopalian. Home: 21 Foxcroft Run Avon CT 06001-2509

WIECZYNSKI, FRANK ROBERT, insurance brokerage executive; b. Balt., Jan. 14, 1939; s. Joseph John and Margaret Anna (Baranoswki) W.; m. Janice L. Furey; children: Dina, Steven. BS, Loyola Coll., Balt., 1961; postgrad. in law, U. Balt., 1964-68. Sr. revenue agt. IRS, Balt., 1961-69; sr. v.p. Alexander & Alexander Services, Inc., Balt., 1969-95; ret., 1995. Served to 1st lt. U.S. Army, 1962-64. Mem. Am. Soc. Corp. Secs. Republican.

WIED, GEORGE LUDWIG, physician; b. Carlsbad, Czechoslovakia, Feb. 7, 1921; came to U.S., 1953, naturalized, 1960; s. Ernst George and Anna (Travnicek) W.; m. Daga M. Graaz, Mar. 19, 1949 (dec. Aug. 1977); m. Kayoko Y. Yamauchi, Nov. 1, 1990. MD, Charles U., Prague, 1945, Hon. Med. Degree, 1995. Intern County Hosp., Carlsbad, Czechoslovakia, 1945; intern U. Chgo. Hosps., 1955; resident in ob-gyn U. Munich, Fed. Republic Germany, 1946-48; practice medicine specializing in ob-gyn West Berlin, 1948-53; asst. ob-gyn Free U., West Berlin, 1948-52; assoc. chmn. dept. ob-gyn Moabit Hosp., Free U., West Berlin, 1953; asst. prof., dir. cytology U. Chgo., 1954-59, assoc. prof., 1959-65, prof., 1965-91, mem. bd. adult edn., 1964-68, prof. pathology, 1967-91, Blum-Riese prof. ob-gyn, 1968-91, acting chmn. dept. ob-gyn, 1974-75. Editor-in-chief Jour. Reproductive Medicine, Acta Cytologica, Analytical and Quantitative Cytology, Clinical Cytology; editor: Introduction to Quantitative Cytochemistry, Automated Cell Identification and Cell Sorting, Compendium on Clinical Cytology, Compendium on the Computerized Cytology and Histology Laboratory, Compendium on Quality Assurance in Clinical Cytology; sr. editor Gen. and Diagnostic Pathology. Hon. dir. Chgo. Cancer Prevention Ctr., 1959-83; chmn. jury Maurice Goldblatt Cytology award, 1963-92. Recipient Cert. of Merit, U.S. Surgeon Gen., 1952, Maurice Goldblatt Cytology award, 1961, George N. Papanicolaou Cytology award, 1970. Mem. Am. Soc. Cytology (pres. 1965-66), Mex. Soc. Cytology (hon.), Spanish Soc. Cytology (hon.), Brazilian Soc. Cytology (fgn. corr.), Indian Acad. Cytology (hon.), Latin-Am. Soc. Cytology (hon.), Japanese Soc. Cytology (hon.), German Soc. Cytology (pres. 1977-80), Ctrl. Soc. Clin. Rsch., Chgo. Path. Soc., Chgo. Gynecol. Soc. (hon.), Am. Soc. Cell Biology, German Soc. Ob-Gyn, Bavarian Soc. Ob-Gyn, German Soc. Endocrinology, Russian Assn. Cytologists (hon.), Swedish Soc.

Medicine (hon.), Austrian Soc. Clin. Cytology (hon.), Sigma Xi. Home and Office: 1640 E 50th St Chicago IL 60615-3161

WIEDEMAN, GEOFFREY PAUL, physician, air force officer; b. London, Eng., Mar. 9, 1917; came to U.S., 1934, naturalized, 1942; s. Julius William Paul and Fanny (Poile) W.; m. Carolyn Sterling, Feb. 2, 1947; 1 son, Geoffrey Paul. BS, U. Vt., 1938, M.D., 1941. Diplomate: Am. Bd. Preventive Medicine. Commd 1st lt. USAAF, 1942; advanced through grades to brig. gen. USAF, 1970; surgeon Eastern Transport Air Force, McGuire AFB, N.J., 1958-61; comdr. USAF Hosp., Tachikawa, Japan; surgeon 315th Air Div., Japan; also surgeon Kanto Base Command, Japan, 1962-65; comdr. USAF Sch. Health Care Scis., 1965-69; command surgeon Air Tng. Command, Randolph AFB, Tex., 1969-74; retired USAF, 1974; physician Brooks AFB Clinic, Tex., retired, 1989. Decorated D.S.M., Legion of Merit, Bronze Star, Air medal, Air Force Commendation medal with oak leaf cluster, 1972. Fellow Am. Coll. Preventive Medicine; mem. Aerospace Medicine Assn., Assn. Mil. Surgeons, Am. Pub. Health Assn., Air Force Assn. Home: 6134 Windrock Dr San Antonio TX 78239-2707

WIEDEMANN, HERBERT PFEIL, physician; b. New Haven, Conn., May 9, 1951; s. Herbert Paul and Henrietta (Pfeil) W.; m. Patricia Barz, Feb. 12, 1983; children: Sarah, Andrew. BS, Yale U., 1973; MD, Cornell U., 1977. Diplomat Am. Bd. Internal Medicine, Am. Bd. Pulmonary Disease, Am. Bd. Critical Care Medicine. Med. resident U. Wash., Seattle, 1977-80; chief med. resident Harborview Med. Ctr., Seattle, 1980-81; postgrad. fellow in pulmonary and critical care medicine Yale U., New Haven, 1981-84; staff physician Cleve. Clinic Found., 1984—, chmn. dept. of pulmonary and critical care medicine, 1991—; pres. med. staff Cleve. Clinic Hosp., 1995—, bd. trustees, 1994—; prof. medicine Cleve. Clinic Found. Health Scis. Ctr. of Ohio State U., Cleve., 1993—; spkr. in field. Editor-in-chief Cleveland Clinic Jour. of Medicine, 1993—; editor: Ann. Rev. of Pulmonary and Critical Medicine, 7 edits., 1986-93. Grantee NIH, 1994—. Fellow ACP, Am. Coll. Chest Physicians, Am. Coll. of Critical Care Medicine; mem. Am. Thoracic Soc., Alpha Omega Alpha. Achievements include rsch. on surfactants decrease release of cytokines from stimulated macrophages. Home: 18040 S Woodland Shaker Heights OH 44120 Office: Cleve Clinic Found 9500 Euclid Ave Cleveland OH 44195

WIEDEMANN, JOSEPH ROBERT, insurance company executive; b. Chgo., June 18, 1928; s. Joseph Matthew and Ann Elizabeth (Zittman) W.; m. Ree McClure, Dec. 26, 1950; children: Sue Wiedemann Evans, Patti Wiedemann Podziomek, Jane Wiedemann Candela, Mary Wiedemann Darling, Julie Wiedemann Gotsch, Joseph, Thomas. BBA, Loyola U., Chgo., 1950. Sr. v.p. CNA Ins. Co., Chgo., 1952-77; v.p. Frank B. Hall Co., N.Y.C., 1977-79; pres., dir. Union Indemnity Ins. Co., N.Y.C., 1977-79, BCS Fin. Corp., Chgo., 1979-83; pres. C.V. Starr & Co., San Francisco, 1983-84, Lexington Ins. Co., Boston, 1985-87, Landmark Ins. Co., Los Angeles, 1986-87; pres. Am. Home Assurance Co., N.Y.C., 1987-92, chmn., 1992-93;, 1992-93; v.p. Am. Internat. Group, N.Y.C., 1986-93; sr. v.p. Starr Excess Liability Ins. Co. Ltd., 1993—. City parking commr. Reading, Pa., 1970-73. Served to sgt. U.S. Army, 1950-52, Korea. Mem. Riddell's Bay Golf and Country Club (Bermuda), Royal Bermuda Yacht Club. Republican. Roman Catholic. Home: 12 Smithfield Manor, 9 Riddell's Bay Rd, Warwick WK 04, Bermuda Office: Starr Excess Liability Ins Co Ltd, 29 Richmond Rd, Pembroke HM 08, Bermuda

WIEDENMAN, JERE WAYNE, lawyer; b. Madison, Wis., Oct. 22, 1950; s. William George and Janet Mae W.; m. Kathleen Louise Wescott, Jan. 30, 1971; 1 child, Karl Hans. BS, U. Wis., 1972; JD, Marquette U., 1976. Bar: Wis., U.S. Dist. Ct. (ea. and we. dists.) Wis., U.S. Dist. Ct. (we. dist.) Ky., U.S. Dist. Ct. (ea. dist.) Pa., U.S. Ct. Appeals (6th and 7th cirs.). Assoc. Foley and Lardner, Milw., 1976-83, ptnr., 1983—; associate Buchannon & Berry, Milwakee, WI. Editor: Employment Law for Wisconsin Employees, 1987. Active Zoning Bd. Appeals, Nashotah, Wis., 1986-88; trustee Village of Nashotah, 1988—. Mem. ABA (labor law sect., litigation sect.), Wis. Bar Assn. (dir. labor law sect. 1987—). *

WIEDENMAYER, CHRISTOPHER M., writing instrument manufacturer, distributor; b. Orange, N.J., May 16, 1941; s. Gustave E. and Margaret W.; m. Anne Iselin Morgan, June 18, 1966; children: Amanda, Elizabeth, Christopher. BA, Dartmouth Coll., 1963; MBA, Columbia U., 1968. Gen. mgr. Faber-Castell Corp., Parsippany, N.J., 1970-72, pres., chief exec. officer, 1972-84, chmn., chief exec. officer, 1984—; bd. dirs. DSG Internat. Ltd., Chem. Bank New Jersey N.A. Treas. Newark Mus., 1983—; bd. govs. Fairmount Cemetery Assn., Newark, 1978—; bd. dirs. Morristown YMCA, 1975-77. Mem. Writing Instrument Mfg. Assn. (bd. dirs. 1973—, v.p. 1989-93, pres. 1993-95). Office: Faber-Castell Corp Box 338P Bernardsville NJ 07924

WIEDMAN, TIMOTHY GERARD, management educator; b. Detroit, Nov. 3, 1951; s. Charles Albert and Doris Gertude (Kreager) W.; m. Lisa Kyle Mattimore, Mar. 24, 1987. BA, Oakland U., 1976; MS, Ctrl. Mich. U., 1978; cert. profl. fin. planning, Old Dominion U., 1995. Gen. mgr. Burger Chef Systems, Inc., Detroit, 1969-75; area mgr. Fotomat Corp., Cleve., Columbus, Ohio, 1978-85; instr. bus. mgmt. Ctrl. Ohio Tech. Coll., Newark, 1986-88, Ohio U., Lancaster, 1988-92; asst. prof. Thomas Nelson C. C., Hampton, Va., 1992-95; assoc. prof. Thomas Nelson C.C., Hampton, Va., 1995—; workshop leader Va. Peninsula Total Quality Inst., Hampton, 1994—; quality trainer Quality Union of Bus., Industry and Cmty. Program, Lancaster, 1991-92; invited spkr. USMCR, Hampton, 1994, Svc. Corps. Ret. Execs., Newark, 1988, USCGR Tng. Ctr., Yorktown, Va., 1994. Contbg. author: Great Ideas for Teaching Marketing, 1992, Great Ideas for Teaching Introduction to Business, 1994; contbr. articles to profl. jours.; author: (newsletter) The Quality Management Forum, 1993. Judge regional competition Future Bus. Leaders Am., Hampton, 1993—; judge team excellence competition Ohio Mfrs. Assn., Lancaster, 1991; county rep. UNICEF, Fairfield County, Ohio, 1988-91. Mem. Am. Soc. for Quality Control (invited speaker 1993), Soc. for Indsl. and Orgnl. Psychology, Va. Quality Network, Assn. Profl. Fin. Planners. Avocations: photography, travel, skiing, swimming, sailing. Office: Thomas Nelson CC 99 Thomas Nelson Dr Hampton VA 23670-1433

WIEDMAN, WAYNE RENTCHLER, retired association executive; b. Oklahoma City, Aug. 29, 1928; s. Lester Amon and Frieda Clara (Rentchler) W.; m. Nancy Jane Whitenight, Dec. 26, 1955; children: Kathryn Anne, Mary Francis. BA, U. Okla., 1950. Ind. credit mgr. Nat. Supply Co., Pitts., 1954-61; dist. sales rep. ARMCO Steel Corp., Chgo., 1961-71; automotive market mgr. Middletown, Ohio, 1972-74; dist. account mgr. ARMCO, Inc., Louisville, 1975-82; cons. mktg. Louisville, 1982-85; exec. dir. Nat. Soc. of SAR, Louisville, 1986-89, ret., 1990. Mayor City of Manor Creek, Ky., 1981-85; dist. commr. Jefferson County Preservation Commn., Louisville, 1985-86; bd. dirs. Friends of Ky. Pub. Archives, Frankfort, 1985-86. Named Eagle Scout, Boy Scouts Am., 1944. Mem. Jefferson Club, Blairwood Club. Episcopalian. Avocations: travel, history. Home: 211 Marksfield Cir Louisville KY 40222-5234

WIEGAND, BRUCE, lawyer; b. Dallas, Nov. 27, 1947; s. Frank Louis and Undine (Phillips) W.; m. Barbara Louise McKenna, July 18, 1970; children: Christy C., Laura C., Bruce Phillips. AB cum laude, Harvard U., 1969; JD, U. Pitts., 1973. Bar: Pa. 1973, U.S. Dist. Ct. (we. dist.) Pa. 1973, U.S. Ct. Appeals (3d cir.) 1973. Assoc. Kirkpatrick & Lockhart, Pitts., 1973-80, ptnr., 1980—; bd. dirs., pres. TWP, Inc. parent co. of T.W. Phillips, Butler, Pa.; bd. dirs., gen. counsel, sec. Phillips Resources, Inc., Butler, 1984—. Mem. ABA, Pa. Bar Assn., Allegheny County Bar Assn., Pa. Oil., Gas and Minerals, Duquesne Club, Rolling Rock Club, St. Clair Country Club, Rivers Club, Harvard U. Club, Yale U. Club, Princeton U. Club. Republican. Home: 94 Hoodridge Pittsburgh PA 15228-1805 Office: Kirkpatrick & Lockhart 1500 Oliver Bldg Pittsburgh PA 15222

WIEGAND, SYLVIA MARGARET, mathematician, educator; b. Cape Town, South Africa, Mar. 8, 1945; came to U.S., 1949; d. Laurence Chisholm and Joan Elizabeth (Dunnett) Young; m. Roger Allan Wiegand, Aug. 27, 1966; children: David Chisholm, Andrea Elizabeth. AB, Bryn Mawr Coll., 1966; MA, U. Wash., 1967; PhD, U. Wis., Madison, 1972. Mem. faculty U. Nebr., Lincoln, 1967—, now prof. math.; vis. assoc. prof. U. Conn., Storrs, 1978-79, U. Wis., Madison, 1985-86; vis. prof. Purdue U., 1992-93. Editor Communications in Algebra jour., 1990, Rocky Mountain Jour. Math., 1991—; contbr. rsch. articles to profl. jours. Troop leader Lincoln area Girl Scouts U.S., 1988-92. Grantee NSF, 1985-88, 90-93, Vis. Professorship for Women, 1992, Nat. Security Agy.. Mem. AAUP, Am. Math. Soc. (mem.-at-large, coun.), Assn. Women in Math (pres.-elect 1995, pres. 1996), London Math. Soc., Math. Assn. Am. Avocations: running, family activities. Office: U Nebr Dept Math Lincoln NE 68588-0323

WIEGEL, ROBERT LOUIS, consulting engineering executive; b. San Francisco, Oct. 17, 1922; s. Louis Henry and Antionette L. (Decker) W.; m. Anne Pearce, Dec. 10, 1948; children: John M., Carol E., Diana L. BS, U. Calif. at Berkeley, 1943, MS, 1949. Mem. faculty U. Calif. at Berkeley, 1946—, prof. civil engring., 1963-87, prof. emeritus, 1987—, asst. dean Coll. Engring., 1963-72, acting dean, 1972-73; dir. state tech. svcs. program for Calif. U. Calif., 1965-68, sec. acad. senate, 1988-89; vis. prof. Nat. U. Mex., summer 1965, Polish Acad. Sci., 1976, 88, U. Cairo, 1978; sr. Queen's fellow in marine sci. Australia, 1977; cons. to govt. and industry, 1946—; chmn. U.S. com. for internat. com. oceanic resources, mem. marine bd. Nat. Acad. Engring., 1975-81; pres. Internat. Engring. Com. on Oceanic Resources, 1972-75, hon. mem., 1988; mem. coastal engring. research bd. Dept. Army, 1974-85; mem. IDOE adv. panel NSF, 1974-77, Gov. Calif. Adv. Commn. Ocean Resources, 1967, Calif. Adv. Commn. on Marine and Coastal Resources, 1967-73, Tsunami Tech. Adv. Council, Hawaii, 1964-66; U.S. del. U.S.-Japan coop. sci. programs, 1964, 65. Author publs. in field; editor Shore and Beach jour.; patentee in field. V.p., bd. dirs. Am. Shore and Beach Preservation Assn., 1988-95, dir. emeritus, 1995—, editor jour. 1988-96; mem. Nat. Rsch. Coun. com. on Beach Nourishment and Protection, 1992-95. Recipient Outstanding Civilian Svc. medal Dept. Army, 1985, Berkeley citation U. Calif., 1987, Joe W. Johnson Outstanding Beach Preservation award Calif. Shore and Beach Preservation Assn., 1993, Coastal Zone Found. award, 1993, Morrough P. O'Brien award Am. Shore and Beach Preservation Assn., 1995. Fellow AAAS; mem. NAE, ASCE (hon., chmn. exec. com. waterways, harbors, coastal engring. div. 1974-75, vice chmn. coastal engring. rsch. coun. 1964-78, chmn. 1978-92, chmn. task com. wave forces on structures 1960-67, chmn. com. on coastal engring. 1970-71, Rsch. prize 1962, Moffatt-Nichol Coastal Engring. award 1978, Internat. Coastal Engring. award 1985), Sigma Xi. Home: 1030 Keeler Ave Berkeley CA 94708-1404

WIEGENSTEIN, JOHN GERALD, physician; b. Fredericktown, Mo., June 22, 1930; s. John Joseph and Dorothy Faye (Mulkey) W.; m. Dorothy Iris Scifers, Dec. 27, 1952; children: Mark, Barbara, Paula, Cynthia. BS, U. Mich., 1956, MD, 1960. Dir. dept. emergency medicine Mich. Capital Med. Ctr., Lansing, 1975—, pres. profl. staff, 1996—; prof., chief sect. emergency medicine Mich. State U., 1982—; founder Internat. Rsch. Inst. for Emergency Medicine, pres., 1983-85; pvt. practice, Lansing; founder Am. Bd. Emergency Medicine, 1982-83; pres. Physician Assocs., P.C., 1976-96; chmn. bd. Occupl. Medicine Assocs., P.C., 1989—; owner Health Care Info. Svcs., Inc., 1989—. With USAF, 1951-53; M.C., U.S. Army, 1960-63. Mem. AMA, Am. Coll. Emergency Physicians (founder, pres., chmn. bd. 1968-71, bd. dirs. 1968-76), Mich. State Med. Soc. (award 1971, 82), Ingham County Med. Soc., Galens Hon. Med. Soc., Soc. Acad. Emergency Medicine. Office: Mich Capital Med Ctr Dept Emergency Medicine 401 W Greenlawn Ave Lansing MI 48910-2819

WIEGERSMA, NAN, economics educator; b. Grafton, Mass., July 16, 1942; d. Oscar John and Esther Marie (Polson) Wiegersma; 1 child, Chandra Hancock. BS, U. Md., 1966, MA, 1969, PhD, 1976. Economist U.S. Dept. Agr., Washington, 1969-72; vis. asst. prof. econs. Antioch Coll., Yellow Springs, Ohio, 1972-73, San Diego State U., 1973-74; assoc. prof. econs. No. Va. Community Coll., Annandale, Va., 1974-79; prof. econs. Fitchburg (Mass.) State Coll., 1979—; cons. UN, 1987, FAO, 1994. Author: Vietnam: Peasant Land, Peasant Revolution, 1988; co-author: Agriculture in Vietnam's Economy, 1973; co-editor: The Women, Gender and Development Reader: Decades of Crisis and Change, 1996; editl. bd. Vietnam Generation, 1988-93; contbr. articles to profl. jours., chpts. to books. Recipient Disting. Svc. award USDA, 1973; Joiner Ctr. grantee, 1987; Grad. Assoc. Faculty rsch. fellow Fitchburg State Coll., 1989-90; Fulbright fellow, 1991. Mem. NEA, Am. Econs. Assn., New Eng. Women and Devel. Group, N.E. Feminist Scholars, Women's Work Project (coord. 1974-79), Mass. Tchrs. Assn. (chpt. treas. 1986-90, pres. 1992-94), Women for Economic Justice (econ. literacy compaign 1982-86). Democrat. Avocations: photography, hiking. Office: Fitchburg State Coll Pearl St Fitchburg MA 01420

WIEGLEY, ROGER DOUGLAS, lawyer; b. Buffalo, Dec. 8, 1948; s. Richard John and Georgianna (Eggleston) W.; m. Susan Carol Straus, Nov. 22, 1969; children: John William, Douglas James, Jennifer Jeanne. BA, SUNY, Buffalo, 1970; JD magna cum laude, U. Wis., 1977. Bar: Wis. 1977, Hawaii 1978, N.Y. 1982, D.C. 1982, Calif. 1986. Spl. asst. U.S. atty. U.S. Justice Dept., Honolulu, 1978-81; spl. asst. to gen. counsel Dept. of the Navy, Washington, 1981-82; assoc. Sullivan & Cromwell, Washington, 1982-85, 86-88; ptnr. Sidley & Austin, Washington, 1988-94, Winthrop, Stimson, Putnam & Roberts, Washington, 1994—; gen. counsel Benson, Inc. and Sentry, San Jose, Calif., 1985-86; arbitrator nat. panel Am. Arbitration Assn., 1988—. Contbg. editor The SEC Today, 1989—; contbr. numerous articles to profl. jours. Mem. pvt. sector study on cost control, Washington, 1982-83. Served with USN, 1973-82. Mem. ABA, Order of Coif. Office: Winthrop Stimson et al 1133 Connecticut Ave NW Washington DC 20036-4305

WIEGMAN, EUGENE WILLIAM, minister, former college administrator; b. Fort Wayne, Ind., Oct. 27, 1929; s. A. Henry and E. Catherine (McDonald) W.; m. Kathleen Wyatt, Apr. 26, 1952; children: Kathryn, Rose Marie, Mark, Jeanine, Gretchen, Matthew. BS, Concordia Coll., 1953; MS, U. Kans., 1956, EdD, 1962; grad., Pacific Luth. Theol. Sem., 1985. Tchr., coach Trinity Luth. Sch., Atchison, Kans., 1954-58; prin. tchr. St. John's Coll., Winfield, Kans., 1958-61; prof. Concordia Coll., Seward, Nebr., 1961-65; adminstrv. asst. to Rep. Clair Callan, Lincoln, Nebr., 1965-66; asst. to adminstr. fed. extension service Dept. Agr., Washington, 1966-67; dean community edn. Fed. City Coll., Washington, 1967-69; pres. Pacific Luth. U., Tacoma, 1969-75, Independent Colls. Wash., 1975-76; dir. Wash. Office Community Devel., 1977-78; commr. Dept. of Employment Security, 1978-81; exec. dir., pres., chief exec. officer Family Counseling Service of Tacoma and Pierce County, Wash., 1987—; assoc. pastor Luther Meml. Ch., Tacoma, 1987-90; pastor Gethsemane Luth. Ch., Tacoma, 1990—; dean clin. pastoral edn. Grad. Sch. of Korea, 1992—; mem. Wash. State Employment and Tng. Council; mem. cabinet Gov. of Wash., 1977-81; lectr., nat. public speaker, 1981—; pres. The Wiegman Inst., Tacoma, 1981—. Candidate for U.S. Congress from 6th dist. Wash., 1976; mem. Council on Washington's Future; exec. bd. dirs. Pacific Harbors Coun. Boy Scouts Am.; bd. dirs. Tacoma Area Urban Coalition; past chmn. Wash. Friends Higher Edn.; bd. dirs. Tacoma Urban League, Nat. Alliance Businessmen, Bellarmine Prep. Sch., Tacoma, Camp Brotherhood; trustee Tacoma Gen. Hosp., Pacific Sci. Center; mem. Commn. on Children for Tacoma and Pierce County, Coalition on Child Sexual Abuse, 1989—; mem. com. Faith Homes for Young Women; pres. Second City chamber of Tacoma. Recipient Disting. Teaching award City Winfield, Kans., 1960, Freedom Found. Teaching award, 1961, Disting. Eagle Scout award, 1982, Pres. award St. Martins Coll., 1980. Fellow Philosophy of Edn. Soc.; mem. Tacoma C. of C., N.W. Assn. Pvt. Colls., Assn. Higher Edn., Kiwanis, Phi Delta Kappa. Home: 405 N Stadium Way Tacoma WA 98403-3228

WIEGNER, ALLEN WALTER, biomedical engineering educator, researcher; b. Bethlehem, Pa., July 22, 1947; s. Howard Jay and Anna (Strouse) W.; m. Sandra A. Waddock, Aug. 26, 1978; 1 child, Benjamin Waddock. SB, SM, MIT, 1970, PhD, 1978. Rsch. assoc. Harvard U. Med. Sch., Boston, 1978-87, asst. prof. neurology (biomed. engring.), 1987—; asst. biomed. engr. Mass. Gen. Hosp., Boston, 1980—; cons. rsch. svc. VA Med. Ctr., 1984—, biomed. engr., 1987—. Contbr. articles, book chpts. to profl. publs. Lt. USPHS, 1970-72. Mem. IEEE (sr.), Biomed. Engring. Soc. (sr.), Soc. for Neurosci. Office: VA Med Ctr Spinal Cord Injury Svc 1400 Vfw Pky West Roxbury MA 02132-4927

WIEGNER, EDWARD ALEX, multi-industry executive; b. Waukesha, Wis., Dec. 13, 1939; s. Roy Edward and Margaret (Kuehnlein) W.; m. Cathryn J. Mullens, Oct. 16, 1970; children: Carlin, Ryan. BBA, U. Wis., 1961, MS in Econs., 1965, PhD in Econs., 1969. Asst. prof. bus. adminstrn. Marquette U., Milw., 1965-71; assoc. prof U. Wis., Madison, 1972-73; sec. Wis. Dept. Revenue, Madison, 1971-74; sr. v.p. fin., bd. dirs. Wis. Power and Light Co., Madison, 1974-76, sr. v.p. consumer, pub. and fin. affairs, dir., 1976-80, exec. v.p., bd. dirs., 1980-82; sr. v.p., chief fin. officer, bd. dirs. Am. Natural Resources Co., 1982-85, exec. v.p., chief adminstrv. officer, bd. dirs., 1985-86; sr. v.p. Coastal Corp., 1985-86; sr. v.p., chief fin. officer Household Internat., Inc., 1986-88; exec. v.p., chief fin. officer The Progressive Corp., Mayfield Heights, Ohio, 1988-91, pres. fin. svcs. div., 1989-93; gen. ptnr. Aurora Ptnrs., 1994—; vice chmn. 1st Am. Ins. Co., Kansas City, Mo., 1994—. Contbr. articles to Northwestern Law Rev., others. Mem. Grand Harbor Country Club. Home: 1330 N Saint Davids Ln Vero Beach FL 32967-7247

WIELAND, PAUL OTTO, environmental control systems engineer; b. Louisville, Apr. 9, 1954; s. Otto George and Flora Carolyn (Wolf) W. BS in Botany, U. Louisville, 1982, BS in Applied Sci., 1985, M. in Engring., 1987. Lic. profl. engr., Ala., Va.; cert. environ. insp. Paper carrier Courier-Jour., Louisville, 1976-77; youth program dir. UNICORN, Louisville, 1978; recreation worker Met. Parks Dept., Louisville, 1978-80; retail sales clk. Lose Bros. Lawn and Garden, Louisville, 1980-82; trainee engr. Sealand Svc., Inc., Elizabeth, N.J., 1982; engr. NASA Marshall Space Flight Ctr., Huntsville, Ala., 1983—. Author: Designing for Human Presence in Space: An Introduction to Environmental Control and Life Support Systems, 1994, Living Together in Space: The Design and Operation of the Life Support Systems on the International Space Station, 1996; contbr. articles to profl. jours. Vol. advocate R.A.P.E. Relief Ctr., Louisville, 1977-80; vol. tutor Adult Basic Edn. Program, Huntsville, 1988-89; vol. projectionist Film Co-op., Huntsville, 1990-91; vol. tech. advisor Am. Lung Assn. Health House '96, Huntsville. Mem. ASME, ASHRAE, AIAA (chmn. student chpt. 1984-85), NSPE (mathcounts vol. 1990-91), Environ. Assessment Assn., Inst. for Advanced Studies in Life Support (treas. 1990-92). Avocations: appreciation of nature, creating visual arts, dancing. Home: 4219 Hawthorne Ave SW Huntsville AL 35805-3423 Office: NASA/MSFC/ED62 Marshall Space Flight Ctr Huntsville AL 35812

WIELGOS, THADDEUS S(TANLEY), JR., research chemist; b. Chgo., Aug. 29, 1962; s. Thaddeus Stanley and Marylin Barbara (Kotlarz) W.; m. Melissa Lynne Leopold, June 1, 1985; children: Sherri Leanne, Brett Michael. BS in Chemistry, Loyola U., Chgo., 1984, MS in Chemistry, 1993. Rsch. asst. I Baxter Healthcare Corp., Morton Grove, Ill., 1984-85, rsch. asst. II, 1985-87; rsch. assoc. I Baxter Healthcare Corp., Round Lake, Ill., 1987-90, rsch. assoc. II, 1990-93, rsch. assoc. III, 1993-95, sr. rsch. assoc., 1995—; ISO 9000 internal auditor Baxter Healthcare Corp., Round Lake, 1994—, mem. safety com., 1987—. Organizer soccer marathon Chgo. Lung Assn., 1984. Mem. AAAS, Am. Chem. Soc., Assn. Analytical Chemists, Electrochem. Soc., Soc. Electroanalytical Chemists. Avocations: water skiing, soccer. Office: Baxter Healthcare Corp Rt 120 and Wilson Rd Round Lake IL 60073

WIELGUS, CHARLES JOSEPH, information services company executive; b. Hadley, Mass., Jan. 2, 1923; s. Joseph John and Anna Mary (Armata) W.; m. Irene Helen Graham, Jan. 1, 1949; children: Charles, Paul, Martha Jane. B.S. summa cum laude in Bus. Adminstrn, Bryant Coll., 1947, D.S. in Bus. Adminstrn. (hon.), 1977. With Bigelow-Sanford Carpet Co., Enfield, Conn. and N.Y.C., 1947-56; with Reuben H. Donnelley Corp. (subs. Dun & Bradstreet Corp.) Chicago and N.Y.C., 1956-71; v.p. personnel Dun & Bradstreet, Inc. (subs.), 1971-73; v.p. personnel Dun & Bradstreet Corp., 1973-76, sr. v.p. human resources, 1976-82, exec. v.p. human resources and communications, 1983-88, ret., 1988; nature photographer, 1989—; adj. faculty New Sch. Social Research, 1977-88, mem. adv. com. Masters program in human resources, 1977-88, ret., 1988; mem. adv. council on mgmt. edn. N.Y.C. C. of C., 1975-80; mem. bus. edn. adv. com. N.Y.C. Bd. Edn., 1977-88; dir. Nat. Ctr. Career Life Planning, 1986—; mem. adv. council on human resources mgmt. Nat. Conf. Bd., 1987-88. Bd. dirs. United Cerebral Palsy Assn. Westchester, 1966-75; trustee Operation Hope, Inc., 1966-75, active local and state Republican orgns., 1965-75. Served in USAF, 1943-46. Mem. Am. Arbitration Assn. (arbitrator 1988—), Nat. Alliance Bus. (dir., steering com.). Clubs: Univ, Larchmont Shore. Home: 151 Rockingstone Ave Larchmont NY 10538-1512 also: 7 Hummingbird Ct Hilton Head Island SC 29926-2551

WIEMAN, CARL E., physics educator; b. Corvallis, Oreg., Mar. 26, 1951; m. Sarah Gilbert. BS, MIT, 1973; PhD, Stanford U., 1977. Asst. rsch. physicist dept. physics U. Mich., Ann Arbor, 1977-79, asst. prof. physics, 1979-84; assoc. prof. physics U. Colo., Boulder, 1984-87, prof. physics, 1987—; fellow Joint Inst. for Lab. Astrophysics, Boulder, 1985—; Loeb lectr. Harvard U., 1990-91; Rosenthal Meml. lectr. Yale U., Columbia U., 1988. Recipient Ernest Orlando Lawrence Meml. award U.S. Dept. of Energy, 1993, Einstein medal for laser sci. Soc. Optical and Quantum Electronics, 1995, Richtmyer Lectr. award Am. Assn. Physics Tchrs., Fritz London prize for low temperature physics, 1996; fellow Guggenheim Found., 1990-91. Fellow Am. Phys. Soc. (Davisson-Germer prize 1994); mem. NAS (elected), Optical Soc. Am. Office: U Colo PO Box 390 Boulder CO 80309-0390

WIEMANN, JOHN MORITZ, communications educator, consultant; b. New Orleans, July 11, 1947; s. John M. and Mockie (Oosthuizen) W.; m. Mary Eileen O'Loghlin, June 7, 1969; children: Molly E., John M. BA, Loyola U., New Orleans, 1969; postgrad., NYU, 1970-71; MS, Purdue U., 1973, PhD, 1975. With employee comm. dept. IBM, East Fishkill, N.Y., 1969-71; asst. prof. comm. Rutgers U., New Brunswick, N.J., 1975-77; from asst. prof. to prof. U. Calif., Santa Barbara, 1977—, prof., 1988—, prof. comm. and Asian Am. studies, 1994—, acting vice chancellor instnl. advancement, 1994-95; vice chancellor instnl. advancement, 1995—; bd. dirs. Santa Barbara (Calif.) Econ. Forecast Project, Santa Barbara Industry-Edn. Coun., Santa Barbara Econ. Cmty. Project; multidisciplinary adv. bd. Ctrl. Coast Regional Tech. Alliance, 1996—. Editor: Nonverbal Interaction, 1983, Advancing Communication Science, 1988, Communication, Health and the Elderly, 1990, Miscommunication and the Problematic Talk, 1991, Strategic Interpersonal Communication, 1994, Interpersonal Communication in Older Adulthood, 1994; author: Competent Communication, 1995; series editor Sage Ann. Rev. Communication Rsch., 1988-94. Bd. dirs. Goleta Youth Basketball Assn., 1987-92; mem. sch. site coun. Foothill Elem. Sch., 1987-88; mem. budget adv. com. Goleta Union Sch. Dist., 1982-84. David Ross fellow Purdue U., 1975, W.K. Kellogg Found. fellow, 1980-83; Fulbright-Hayes sr. rsch. scholar U. Bristol, Eng., 1985. Mem. APA, Internat. Comm. Assn. (bd. dirs. 1988-90), Speech Comm. Assn. (bd. dirs. 1984-86), Western States Comm. Assn., Internat. Network on Personal Rels., Internat. Pragmatics Assn., Sigma Xi, Phi Kappa Phi. Democrat. Roman Catholic. Avocations: cooking, squash, swimming. Office: U Calif Instnl Advancement Santa Barbara CA 93106-2030

WIEMER, ROBERT ERNEST, film and television producer, writer, director; b. Highland Park, Mich., Jan. 30, 1938; s. Carl Ernest and Marion (Israelian) W.; m. Rhea Dale McGeath, June 14, 1958; children: Robert Marshall, Rhea Whitney. BA, Ohio Wesleyan U., 1959. Ind. producer, 1956-60; dir. documentary ops. WCBS-TV, N.Y.C., 1964-67; ind. producer of television, theatrical and bus. films N.Y.C., 1967-72; exec. producer motion pictures and TV, ITT, N.Y.C., 1973-84; pres. subs. Blue Marble Co., Inc., Telemontage, Inc., Alphaventure Music, Inc., Betaventure Music, Inc. ITT, 1973-84; founder, chmn., chief exec. officer Tigerfilm, Inc., 1984—; chmn., bd. dirs. Golden Tiger Pictures, Hollywood, Calif., 1988—; pres. CEO Tuxedo Pictures Corp., Hollywood, Calif., 1993—. Writer, prodr., dir.: (feature films) My Seventeenth Summer, Witch's Sister, Do Me a Favor, Anna to the Infinite Power, Somewhere, Tomorrow, Night Train to Kathmandu; exec. prodr.: (children's TV series) Big Blue Marble (Emmy and Peabody awards); dir. (TV episodes) seaQuest DSV, Star Trek: The Next Generation, Deep Space Nine, The Adventures of Superboy; composer (country-western ballad) Tell Me What To Do. Recipient CINE award, 1974, 76, 77, 79, 81, Emmy award, 1978. Mem. NATAS, ASCAP, Info. Film Producers Assn. (Outstanding Producer award), Nat. Assn. TV Programming Execs., Am. Women in Radio and TV, N.J. Broadcasters Assn., Dirs. Guild Am. Office: Golden Tiger Pictures 3896 Ruskin St Las Vegas NV 89117

WIEN, STUART LEWIS, retired supermarket chain executive; b. Milw., Sept. 11, 1923; s. Julius and Mildred (Rosenberg) W.; m. Charlotte Jean Milgram, June 4, 1949; children: Steven, John, William, Thomas.; m. Sheila B. Davis, July 25, 1982; stepchildren: Andrew, Stephen, Laurence, Geoffrey. B.S., UCLA, 1947. Chmn. bd. Milgram Food Stores, Inc., Kansas City, Mo., 1979-84; bd. dirs. UMB Funds. Trustee Menorah Med. Ctr.; bd. regents Rockhurst Coll. Mem. Oakwood Country Club.

WIENER, ANNABELLE, United Nations official; b. N.Y.C., Aug. 2, 1922; d. Philip and Bertha (Wrubel) Kalbfeld; ed. Hunter Coll.; married, Jan. 1, 1941; children: Marilyn Grunewald, Marjorie Petit, Mark. Chmn. UN Dept. Pub. Info., Nongovtl. Orgns. Exec. Com., spl. adviser to sec. gen. Internat. Women's Year Conf.; mem. exec. bd. Nongovtl. Orgns. Com. on Disarmament UN, UN Dept. Pub. Info's NGO Exec. Com.; bd. dirs. World Fedn. UN Assns., also founder, dir. art and philatelic program; bd. dirs. N.Y. chpt. UN Assn.-USA; bd. dirs., chmn. UN Day Programme, So. N.Y. State Div., v.p. North Shore chpt.; mem. UN Dept. Pub. Info.'s Non-Govtl. Orgn. Exec. Com.; mem., bd. dir. Non-Govtl. Orgn. for UNICEF at UN Hdqrs. Recipient Diplomatic World Bull. award for Distinction in politics and diplomacy and svc. to high ideals of UN, 1989; apptd. dep. sec.-gen. World Fedn. UN Assns., 1991. Mem. Am. Fedn. Arts, Mus. Modern Art, Musee Nat. Message Biblique Marc Chagall, Am. Philatelic Soc., UN Philatelic Soc., UN Assn. U.S., UNO Philatelie, Fed. Republic Germany. Address: Dep Sec-Gen World Fedn UN Assns DC1-1177 United Nations New York NY 10017

WIENER, DANIEL NORMAN, psychologist; b. Duluth, Minn., Feb. 6, 1921; s. Joseph Baxter and Fannie (Winer) W.; m. Phyllis Eileen Zager, Dec. 9, 1971; children: Jonathan Marc, Paul Aaron, Sara Ruth Wiener Pearson. BA, U. Minn., 1941, MA, 1942, PhD, 1950. Diplomate in Clin. Psychology Am. Bd. Profl. Psychology; lic. psychologist, Minn. Psychologist State of Conn., Hartford, 1943-44; chief psychologist VA Rehab. and Mental Hygiene Clinic, St. Paul and Mpls., 1944-76; Comty. Clinic, Two Harbors, Minn., 1968-89; pvt. practice psychology Mpls., 1952—; clin. prof. psychiatry and psychology U. Minn., Mpls., 1952—; cons. Hennepin County Dist. Ct., Mpls., 1982—. Author: Discipline, Achievement and Mental Health, 1960, Dimensions of Psychotherapy, 1965, Short-Term Psychotherapy and Structured Behavior Change, 1966, Training Children, 1968, Practical Guide to Psychotherapy, 1968, Classroom Management, 1972, Consumers Guide to Psychotherapy, 1975, Albert Ellis: Passionate Skeptic, 1988, B.F. Skinner: Benign Anarchist, 1996; book reviewer: Star-Tribune, Mpls. With USAF, 1942-43. Mem. Fellow APA, Am. Psychol. Soc.; mem. PEN, Minn. Psychol. Assn. (life, exec. coun.), Nat. Book Critics Cir. Avocations: tennis, squash. Home and Office: 1225 Lasalle Ave Apt 801 Minneapolis MN 55403-2329

WIENER, JACQUES LOEB, JR., federal judge; b. Shreveport, La., Oct. 2, 1934; s. Jacques L. and Betty (Eichenbaum) W.; children: Patricia Wiener Shifke, Jacques L. III, Betty Ellen Wiener Spomer, Donald B. BA, Tulane U., 1956, JD, 1961. Bar: La. 1961, U.S. Dist. Ct. (we. dist.) La. 1961. Ptnr. Wiener, Weiss, Madison & Howell, A.P.C., Shreveport, 1961-90; judge U.S. Ct. Appeals (5th cir.), Shreveport, 1990—; mem. coun. La. State Law Inst., 1965—; master of the bench Am. Inn of Ct., 1990—. Pres. United Way N.W. La., 1975, Shreveport Jewish Fedn., 1969-70. Fellow Am. Coll. Trust & Estates Counsel, Am. Bar Found., La. Bar Found.; mem. ABA, La. State Bar Assn., Shreveport Bar Assn. (pres. 1982), Am. Law Inst., Internat. Acad. Trust & Estate Law (academician). Avocations: fly fishing, upland game bird hunting, photography, travel. Office: US Ct Appeals 5th Cir US Ct House 300 Fannin St Ste 5101 Shreveport LA 71101-3070

WIENER, JERRY M., psychiatrist; b. Baytown, Tex., May 11, 1933; s. Isidore and Dora L. (Lerner) W.; m. Louise W. Weingarten, Apr. 13, 1964; children—Matthew, Ethan, Ross, Aaron. Student, Rice U., 1952; M.D., Baylor U., 1956; tng. in psychoanalysis, Columbia U. Psychoanalytic Center, 1968. Resident in psychiatry Mayo Clinic, Rochester, Minn., 1957-61, Columbia U. Coll. Physicians and Surgeons, N.Y.C., 1961-62; dir. child and adolescent psychiatry St. Luke's Hosp., N.Y.C., 1962-71; dir. child psychiatry Emory U., Atlanta, 1971-75; chmn. dept. psychiatry Children's Hosp., Washington, 1976-77; prof., chmn. dept. psychiatry George Washington U., 1977—; mem. faculty Washington Psychoanalytic Inst. Editor: Textbook of Child and Adolescent Psychology, 1991, 96, Psychopharmacology in Childhood and Adolescence, 1977, Diagnosis and Psychopharmacology in Childhood and Adolescence, 1995; contbr. articles to profl. jours., chpts. to books. Fellow Am. Psychiat. Assn. (past pres.), Am. Acad. Child Psychiatry (pres.-elect), Am. Coll. Psychiatrists; mem. Am. Psychoanalytic Assn. (past pres.), Am. Assn. Chmn. Depts. Psychiatry (past pres.), Am. Psychiat. Press, Inc. (chmn. bd. dirs.), Am. Acad. Child and Adolescent Psychiatry (past pres.). Office: 2150 Pennsylvania Ave NW Washington DC 20037-2396

WIENER, JON, history educator; b. St. Paul, May 16, 1944; s. Daniel N. and Gladys (Aronsohn) Spratt. BA, Princeton U., 1966; PhD, Harvard U., 1971. Vis. prof. U. Calif.-Santa Cruz, 1973; acting asst. prof. UCLA, 1973-74; asst. prof. history U. Calif.-Irvine, 1974-83, prof., 1984—; plaintiff Freedom of Info. Lawsuit against FBI for John Lennon Files, 1983—. Author: Social Origins of the New South, 1979; Come Together: John Lennon in His Time, 1984, Professors, Politics, and Pop, 1991; contbg. editor The Nation mag.; contbr. articles to profl. jours. including The New Republic and New York Times Book Review. Rockefeller Found. fellow, 1979, Am. Coun. Learned Socs.-Ford Found. fellow, 1985. Mem. Am. Hist. Assn., Nat. Book Critics Circle, Orgn. Am. Historians, Nat. Writers' Union, Liberty Hill Found. (cmty. funding bd.). Office: U Calif Dept History Irvine CA 92717

WIENER, JOSEPH, pathologist; b. Toronto, Can., Sept. 21, 1927; came to U.S., 1949, naturalized, 1960; s. Louis and Minnie (Salem) W.; m. Judith Hesta Ross, June 20, 1954; children: Carolyn L., Adam L. M.D., U. Toronto, 1953. Intern Detroit Receiving Hosp., 1953-54; resident to chief resident pathology Mallory Inst. Pathology, 1954-55; from asst. to assoc. prof. pathology Columbia U., N.Y.C., 1960-68, assoc. prof. pathology, 1960-68; prof. pathology N.Y. Med. Coll., N.Y.C., 1968-78; prof. pathology Wayne State U., Detroit, 1978—, chmn. dept., 1978-90; cons. NIH, 1970—. Served to capt. M.C. U.S. Army, 1955-57. Grantee: Heart, Lung and Blood Inst., 1971-93; named fellow Coun. for High Blood Pressure Rsch., 1982—. Mem. AAAS, Am. Soc. Investigative Pathology, Am. Soc. Cell Biology, Mich. Path. Soc., Internat. Acad. Pathology, Am. Heart Assn., U.S./Can. Acad. Pathology, Mich. Heart Assn., Alpha Omega Alpha. Research on exptl. cardiovascular pathology and hypertension. Office: 540 E Canfield St Detroit MI 48201-1928

WIENER, MALCOLM HEWITT, foundation executive; b. Tsingtao, China, July 3, 1935; (parents Am. citizens); s. Myron and Ethel (Zimmerman) W.; m. Carolyn Talbot Seely, June 8, 1990; children: Catherine Diktynna Talbot, Elizabeth Ariadne Seely. BA, Harvard U., 1957, JD, 1963. Bar: N.Y. 1964. Atty. N.Y.C., 1963-71, pvt. practice investing, 1971—; chmn. Millburn Corp., N.Y.C., 1977—, Millburn Ridgefield Corp., Ridgefield, Conn., 1982—, ShareInVest, Ridgefield, 1982—; chmn. bd. trustees Malcolm Hewitt Wiener Found., N.Y.C., 1984—; lectr. in field; fellow faculty of govt., John F. Kennedy Sch. Govt., Harvard U., 1985; advisor U.S. Dept. State on Internat. Conv. on Illicit Traffic in Antiquities, 1970-75. Columnist Newsday; contbr. articles to profl. publs. Co-dir. Aegean Bronze Age Colloquium, NYU Inst. Fine Arts, 1975—; founder, exec. dir. Inst. Aegean Prehistory, 1982-89, pres., 1990—; trustee Am. Classical Studies in Athens; founder Wiener Lab. Am. Sch. Classical Studies, Athens; co-chmn. vis. com. Dept. Egyptian Art, mem. vis. com. Dept. Painting Conservation, Prints and Drawings, Greek and Roman, chmn.'s coun.; vice chmn. bus. com. Met. Mus. Art; mem. adv. bd. Malcolm Wiener Ctr. for Social Policy, Kennedy Sch. Govt. Harvard U.; mem. vis. com., paintings Boston Mus. Fine Arts, 1985-91, drawings and prints Frick Collection; sponsor Malcolm and Carolyn Wiener Lab. for Aegean and Near East Dendochronology Cornell U. With USN, 1957-60. Fellow Archaeol. Inst. Am. (hon. life); mem. ABA, Coun. on Fgn. Rels. (ind. task force on non-lethal weapons). Office: 1270 Avenue Of The Americas New York NY 10020

WIENER, MARK SETH, health facility administrator; b. S.I., N.Y., July 7, 1956; s. Joseph and Audrey (Stone) W.; m. Marcie G. Gordon, Oct. 12, 1980; children: Aaron Lee, Jeffrey Daniel. BS, Wagner Coll., 1977; MA in Health Care Adminstrn., Wash. U., 1979. Exec. asst. Iowa Meth. Med. Ctr., Des Moines, 1979-82; asst. hosp. dir. U. Nebr. Med. Ctr., 1982-86; v.p. clin. svcs. Rsch. Med. Ctr., Kansas City, Mo., 1986-91; sr. v.p., COO Trinity Luth. Hosp., Kansas City, 1991—; bd. dirs. Shalom Geriatric Ctr., Hosp. Linen Svcs. Inc. Mem. healthcare adv. com. Presbyn. Metro Ministries Omaha, 1985; chmn. task force Cen. Iowa Assn. for Ind. Health Promotion, 1981-82; pres. Kansas City Assn. of Healthcare Execs., 1994. Fellow Am. Coll. Healthcare Execs.; mem. Am. Hosp. Assn., Mo. Hosp. Assn., Lions. Democrat. Jewish. Avocations: running, bicycling, tennis. Home: 9207 W 140 Terr Overland Park KS 66221-2025 Office: Trinity Luth Hosp 3030 Baltimore Ave Kansas City MO 64108-3404

WIENER, MARTIN JOEL, historian; b. Bklyn., June 1, 1941; s. Harold H. and Eva (Richter) W.; m. Carol Ann Zisowitz, Sept. 22, 1964 (div. 1977); children: Wendy, Julie; m. Meredith Anne Skura, May 17, 1981; children: Rebecca, Vivian. BA, Brandeis U., 1962; MA, Harvard U., 1963, PhD in History, 1967. Asst. prof. Rice U., 1967-72, assoc. prof., 1972-80, prof. history, 1980-82, Mary Gibbs Jones prof., 1982—; chair dept. history, 1990-94. Author: Between Two Worlds: The Political Thought of Graham Wallas, 1971, English Culture and the Decline of the Industrial Spirit, 1850-1980, 1981 (Schuyler prize Am. Hist. Assn. 1981), Reconstructing the Criminal, 1990. Research fellow NEH, 1973, 86, Am. Council Learned Socs., 1982. Fellow Royal Hist. Soc.; mem. Am. Hist. Assn., Am. Soc. Legal History, Coun. for European Studies (steering com. 1985-90), Conf. on Brit. Studies (nominating com. 1982-84, coun. 1992-96), Social History Soc. (U.K.), Am. Hist. Assn. (coun. 1987-90). Jewish. Home: 5510 Yarwell Dr Houston TX 77096-4012 Office: Rice U Dept of History 6100 S Main Houston TX 77005

WIENER, MARVIN S., rabbi, editor, executive; b. N.Y.C., Mar. 16, 1925; s. Max and Rebecca (Dodell) W.; m. Sylvia Bodek, Mar. 2, 1952; children: David Hillel, Judith Rachel. B.S., CCNY, 1944, M.S., 1945; B.H.L., Jewish Theol. Sem. Am., 1947, M.H.L., Rabbi, 1951, D.D. (hon.), 1977. Registrar, sec. faculty Rabbinical Sch., Jewish Theol. Sem. Am., 1951-57; cons. Frontiers of Faith TV Series, NBC, 1951-57; dir., instr. liturgy Cantors Inst.-Sem. Coll. Jewish Music, Jewish Theol. Sem. Am., 1954-58; faculty coordinator Sem. Sch. and Women's Inst., 1958-64; dir. Nat. Acad. for Adult Jewish Studies, United Synagogue Am., N.Y.C., 1958-78; editor Burning Bush Press, 1958-78, United Synagogue Rev., 1978-86; dir. com. congrl. standards United Synagogue Am., 1976-86, cons. community relations and social action, 1981-82, editor, exec. joint retirement bd., 1986—; mem. Joint Commn. on Rabbinic Placement, 1951-57, Joint Prayer Book Commn., 1957-62; mem. exec. coun. Rabbinical Assembly, 1958-86; editl. cons. N.Y. Bd. Rabbis, 1987-89; trustee joint retirement bd. Jewish Theol. Sem. Am. Rabbinical Assembly and United Synagogue Am., 1959-86, sec. 1968-76, 84-85, vice chmn., 1976-82, 85-86, chmn. 1982, treas., 1983-84; co-chmn. Jewish Bible Assn., 1960-64; chmn. bd. rev. Nat. Coun. Jewish Audio-Visual Materials, 1968-69; mem. exec. com. Nat. Coun. Adult Jewish Edn., 1966—; mem. exec. bd., editl. adv. bd., v.p. Jewish Book Couns., 1976-96; chmn. Internat. Conf. Adult Jewish Edn., Jerusalem, 1972. Editor: Nat. Acad. Adult Jewish Studies Bull., 1958-78, Past and Present: Selected Essays (Israel Friedlaender), 1961, Jewish Tract Series, 1964-78 (15 titles), Adult Jewish Edn., 1958-78, Talmudic Law and the Modern State (Moshe Silberg), 1973. Mem. Am. Acad. Jewish Research, Assn. Jewish Studies, N.Y. Bd. Rabbis, Rabbinical Assembly. Home: 67-66 108th St Apt D-46 Forest Hills NY 11375-2974 Office: Joint Retirement Bd 7 Penn Plz Ste 720 New York NY 10001-3900

WIENER, NORMAN JOSEPH, lawyer; b. Portland, Oreg., Sept. 10, 1919; s. Peter and Anna Wiener; m. Elizabeth Bentley, Jan. 26, 1945; children: Jane, Jon, Lisa. BA, U. Oreg., 1941, JD, 1947. Bar: Oreg. 1947. Assoc. King, Wood, Miller & Anderson, Portland, 1947-51; ptnr. Miller, Nash, Wiener, Hager & Carlsen, Portland, 1952—. Pres. United Way, Portland, 1977, Rehab. Inst. Oreg., Portland; trustee U. Oreg. Found. 1st lt. U.S. Army, 1942-46, World War II, 1951-52, Korea. Mem. ABA, Oreg. Bar Assn., Am. Bar Found. (life), Arlington Club (pres.), Portland Golf Club (pres.). Republican. Avocations: golf, swimming. Office: Miller Nash Wiener Hager & Carlsen 111 SW 5th Ave Ste 3500 Portland OR 97204-3638

WIENER, ROBERT ALVIN, accountant; b. N.Y.C., Jan. 9, 1918; s. George and Rose Vivian (Fink) W.; m. Annabelle Kalbfeld, Jan. 1, 1941; children—Marilyn Wiener Grunewald, Marjorie Wiener Petit, Mark. B.C.S., NYU, 1938. CPA, N.Y., Ill.; cert. insolvency and reorgn. acct. Sr. ptnr. Robert A. Wiener & Co. (CPAs), N.Y.C., 1946-71; ptnr. Grant Thornton & Co. (CPAs), N.Y.C., 1971-73; v.p., gen. auditor Seeburg Industries, Inc., N.Y.C., 1973-77; pvt. practice acctg., 1978—; asst. prof. Pace Coll., 1956-77; lectr. Baruch Coll., 1947-77; acctg. cons. Unistar Programme UN Devel. Programme, 1991. Author: Insolvency Accounting, 1977. Served with AUS, 1943-46. Decorated Bronze Star. Mem. AICPA, N.Y. State Soc. C.P.A.s, Accts. Club Am., Fin. Execs. Inst., Inst. Internal Auditors, Assn. Insolvency Accts., Am. Arbitration Assn. (arbitration panel), Pi Lambda Phi. Home: 30 Waterside Plz New York NY 10010-2622

WIENER, RONALD MARTIN, lawyer; b. Phila., June 1, 1939; s. William V. and Sylvia (Bookbinder) W.; m. Susan Cooper, June 16, 1963; children: Carol Jan, Alan Mark; m. 2d, Linda A. Fisher, Feb. 21, 1981. A.B., U. Pa., 1961; J.D. magna cum laude, Harvard U., 1964. Bar: D.C. 1965, Pa. 1966. Law clk., U.S. Tax Ct., 1964-66; assoc. Wolf, Block, Schorr and Solis-Cohen, Phila., 1966-72, ptnr., 1972—; mem. commr.'s adv. group IRS, 1992-93. Fellow Am. Coll. of Tax Counsel (regent 3d cir. 1996—); mem. ABA, Pa. Bar Assn., Phila. Bar Assn. (chair tax sect. 1989-90). Office: Wolf Block Schorr and Solis-Cohen 12th Floor Packard Bldg SE Corner 15 & Chestnut Sts Philadelphia PA 19102

WIENER, SOLOMON, author, consultant, former city official; b. N.Y.C., Mar. 5, 1915; s. Morris David and Anna (Pinchuk) W.; m. Gertrude Klings, Feb. 24, 1946; children: Marjorie Diane Wein, Willa Kay Ehrlich. BS, Cornell, 1936; MPA, NYU, 1946. Exam. asst. N.Y.C. Dept. Personnel, 1937-42, civil service examiner, 1946-55, asst. div. chief, 1955-59, div. chief, 1959-67, asst. dir. exams., 1967-70, dir. exams., 1970-72, asst. personnel dir. exams., 1972-75; author, cons., 1975—; tchr. Washington Irving Evening Adult Sch., N.Y.C., 1949-60, tchr.-in-charge, 1960-67. Served with AUS, 1942-46, PTO. Decorated Bronze Star. Mem. Am. Soc. Pub. Adminstrn., Internat. Personnel Mgmt. Assn., Authors Guild, Res. Officers Assn., Ret. Officers Assn., Assn. of U.S. Army, Am. Def. Preparedness Assn. Author: A Handy Book of Commonly Used American Idioms, rev. edit., 1981, Manual de Modismos Americanos Más Comunes, rev. edit., 1981, A Handy Guide to Irregular Verbs and the Use and Formation of Tenses, 1959, Guía Completa de Los Verbos Irregulares en Inglés y el Uso y Formación de los Tiempos, 1959, Questions and Answers on American Citizenship, rev. edit., 1982, Clear and Simple Guide to Business Letter Writing, rev. edit., 1978, The College Graduate Guide for Scoring High on Employment Tests, 1981, The High School Graduate Guide for Scoring High on Civil Service Tests, 1981, How to Take and Pass Simple Tests for Civil Service Jobs, 1981, Officer Candidate Tests, 3d edit., 1993, Military Flight Aptitude Tests, 2d edit., 1994; co-author Practice for the Armed Forces Test, ASVAB, 14th edit., 1994, Practica para el Examen de las Fuerzas Armadas, ASVAB En Español, 1989; contbr. to ARCO ROTC Coll. Guide, 1988. Home: 523 E 14th St New York NY 10009-2927

WIENER, THOMAS ELI, lawyer; b. Dallas, Nov. 29, 1940; s. Samson and Fan (Gardner) W.; m. Felice Gloria Goodwin, Jan. 24, 1970; children: Gary Allen, Debra Roslyn, Allison Beth, Todd David. B.A., U. Tex., 1962, J.D. with honors, 1968. Bar: Tex. 1968, D.C. 1969, Pa. 1972, U.S. Supreme Ct. 1972. Atty.-advisor office chief counsel IRS, Washington, 1968-72; assoc. Pepper Hamilton & Scheetz, Phila., 1972-74, Abrahams & Loewenstein, Phila., 1974-76, Goodis, Greenfield, Henry & Edelstein, Phila., 1976-77, Mesirov, Gelman, Jaffe, Cramer & Jamieson, Phila., 1977-78; prin. Franklin, Margulies & Huntington,, 1978-91, Riley & DeFalice, P.C., Phila., 1991-92, Wiener & Caplan, P.C., 1992-95; sole practitioner, 1995—; Dir. Lufkin (Tex.) Inds., Inc., Wiener Lumber Co., Dallas. Author: (with others) Tax Problems of Fiduciaries, 1977. Trustee Golden Slipper Club; pres. Main Line Reform Temple, 1992-94, pres. brotherhood 1981-83; pres. Rotary Gundaker Found., 1986-87; v.p. Nat. Fedn. Temple Brotherhoods, 1994—, N.Am. Bd. World Union Progressive Judaism, Phila. Fedn. Reform Synagogues, 1993—; chair Synagogue Fedn. Coun. of Phila., 1994—; bd. trustees Union of Am. Hebrew Congregation, 1995—. Mem. ABA, D.C. Bar Assn., Pa. Bar Assn., Tex. Bar Assn., Phila. Bar Assn., Am. Law Inst., Order of Coif. Lodges: Masons (32 degree K.C.C.H., past master), Rotary (pres. chpt. 1985-86). Home: 1233 Remington Rd Wynnewood PA 19096-2329 Office: One Belmont Ave Ste 605 Bala Cynwyd PA 19004-1609

WIENER, VALERIE, communications executive; b. Las Vegas, Nev., Oct. 30, 1948; d. Louis Isaac Wiener and Tui Ava Knight. BJ, U. Mo., 1971, MA, 1972; MA, Sangamon State U., 1974; postgrad., McGeorge Sch. Law, 1976-79. Producer TV show "Checkpoint" Sta. KOMU-TV, Columbia, Mo., 1972-73; v.p., owner Broadcast Assocs., Inc., Las Vegas, 1972-86; pub. affairs dir. First Ill. Cable TV, Springfield, 1973-74; editor Ill. State Register, Springfield, 1973-74; producer and talent "Nevada Realities" Sta. KLVX-TV, Las Vegas, 1974-75; account exec. Sta. KBMI (now KFMS), Las Vegas, 1975-79; nat. traffic dir. six radio stas., Las Vegas, Albuquerque and El Paso, Tex., 1979-80; exec. v.p., gen. mgr. Stas. KXKS and KKJY, Albuquerque, 1980-81; exec. adminstr. Stas. KSET AM/FM, KVEG, KFMS and KKJY, 1981-83; press sec. U.S. Congressman Harry Reid, Washington, 1983-87; adminstrv. asst Friends for Harry Reid, Nev., 1986; press sec. U.S. Senator Harry Reid, Washington, 1987-88; owner Wiener Comm. Group, Las Vegas, 1988—. Author: Power Communications: Positioning Yourself for High Visibility (Fortune Book Club main selection 1994), Gang Free: Friendship Choices for Today's Youth, 1995; contbg. writer The Pacesetter, ASAE's Comm. News. Sponsor Futures for Children, Las Vegas, Albuquerque, El Paso, 1979-83; mem. El Paso Exec. Women's Coun., 1981-83; mem. VIP bd. Easter Seals, El Paso, 1982; media chmn. Gov.'s Coun. Small Bus., 1989-93, Clark Coun. Sch. Dist. and Bus. Cmty. PAYBAC Spkrs. and Partnership Programs, 1989—; med. dir. 1990 Conf. on Women, Gov. of Nev.; media chmn. Congl. Awards Coun., 1989-93; vice chmn. Gov.'s Commn. on Post-secondary Edn., 1992—; bd. dirs. BBB So. Nev. Named Outstanding Vol., United Way, El Paso, 1983, SBA Nev. Small Bus. Media Adv. of Yr., 1992; recipient Woman of Achievement in Media award, 1992, Outstanding Achievement award Nat. Fedn. Press Women, 1991, Disting. Leader award Nat. Assn. for Cmty. Leadership, 1993, over 106 other comm. awards. Mem. Nev. Press Women (numerous 1st place media awards 1990—), Nat. Spkrs. Assn., Nat. Assn. Women Bus. Owners (media chmn., nat. rep. So. Nev. 1990-91, Nev. Adv. of Yr. award 1992), Dem. Press Secs. Assn., El Paso Assn. Radio Stas., U.S. Senate Staff Club, Las Vegas C. of C. (Circle of Excellence award 1993), Soc. Profl. Journalists. Democrat. Avocations: reading, writing, fitness training, pub. speaking, community involvement. Office: 1500 Foremaster Ln Ste 2 Las Vegas NV 89101-1103

WIENS, ARTHUR NICHOLAI, psychology educator; b. McPherson, Kans., Sept. 7, 1926; s. Jacob T. and Helen E. (Kroeker) W.; m. Ruth Helen Avery, June 11, 1949; children: Barbara, Bradley, Donald. B.A., U. Kans., 1948, M.A., 1952; Ph.D., U. Portland, 1956. Diplomate: Am. Bd. Examiners Profl. Psychology. Clin. psychologist Topeka State Hosp., 1949-53; sr. psychologist outpatient dept. Oreg. State Hosp., Salem, 1954-58; chief psychologist Oreg. State Hosp., 1958-61, dir. clin. psychology internship program, 1958-61; clin. instr. U. Oreg. Med. Sch., Portland, 1958-61; asst. prof. U. Oreg. Med. Sch., 1961-65, asso. prof., 1965-66, prof. med. psychology, 1966—; clin. asso. prof. psychology U. Portland, 1959-61; field assessment officer Peace Corps, 1965; cons. psychologist Portland Center for Hearing and Speech, 1964-67, Dammasch State Hosp., 1967-69, Raleigh Hills Hosp., 1968-84, Oreg. Vocat. Rehab. Div., 1973—, mem. state adv. com., 1976-93; cons. William Temple Rehab. House, Episcopal Laymen's Mission Soc., 1968-88; chmn. State Oreg. Bd. Social Protection, 1971-84, State Oreg. Bd. Psychologist Examiners, 1974-77; v.p. bd. dirs. Raleigh Hills Research Found., 1974-80. Contbr. articles to profl. jours. Fellow AAAS, APA (chmn. com. on vis. psychologist program 1972-76, chmn. accreditation com. 1978, mem. task force edn. and credentialing 1979-84); mem. Am. Assn. State Psychology Bds. (pres. 1978-79), Nat. Register Health Svc. Providers in Psychology (bd. dirs. 1985-92), Profl. Exam. Svc. (bd. dirs. 1982-88, 90—, chmn. 1986-88), Sigma Xi. Home: 74 Condolea Way Lake Oswego OR 97035-1010 Office: Oreg U-Health Sci Dept Sci Dept Portland OR 97201

WIENS, DUANE DATON, matrix-graphic design firm owner; b. Inman, Jan. 13, 1935; s. Jacob D. and Anna Marie (Dirks) W.; m. Barbara A. Hege, Nov. 5, 1959 (div. Nov. 1984); children: Brian V., David K.; m. Paula M. Streiff, Aug. 18, 1990; stepson, Luke Ouellette. Art sch. diploma, Colo. Inst. of Art, 1964. Graphic designer Hesdorfer Comml. Art, Denver, 1964-65, McCormick-Armstrong Printing, Wichita, Kans., 1965-67; co-founder, ptnr. Unit 1/ Graphic Design, Denver, 1967-78; founder, owner Matrix Internat. Assocs., Denver, 1978—. Works published in profl. jours. Inductee Hall of Fame, Colo. Inst. of Art, 1989, Nat. Hall of Fame, Nat. Assn. Trade and Tech. Schs., 1990. Mem. Art Dirs. Club of Denver. Avocations: bronze sculpting, sketching, skiing, mountain biking. Home: 7269 S Cook Cir Littleton CO 80122-1902 Office: Matrix Internat Assocs 50 S Steele St Ste 875 Denver CO 80209-2813

WIER, PATRICIA ANN, publishing executive, consultant; b. Coal Hill, Ark., Nov. 10, 1937; d. Horace L. and Bridget B. (McMahon) Norton; m. Richard A. Wier, Feb. 24, 1962; 1 child, Rebecca Ann. B.A., U. Mo., Kansas City, 1964; M.B.A., U. Chgo., 1978. Computer programmer AT&T, 1960-62; lead programmer City of Kansas City, Mo., 1963-65; with Playboy Enterprises, Chgo., 1965-71; mgr. systems and programming Playboy Enterprises, 1971; with Ency. Britannica, Inc., Chgo., 1971—; v.p. mgmt. svcs. Ency. Britannica USA, 1975-83, exec. v.p. adminstrn., 1983-84; v.p. planning and devel. Ency. Britannica, Inc., 1985, pres. Compton's Learning Co. div., 1985; pres. Ency. Britannica (USA), 1986-91, Ency. Britannica N.A., 1991-92; exec. v.p. Ency. Britannica, Inc., 1986-94; pres. Ency. Britannica N.Am., 1991-94; mgmt. cons. pvt. practice, Chgo., 1994—; lectr. mktg. U. Chgo. Grad. Sch. Bus., 1995—; cons. pvt. practice, Chgo., 1994—; bd. dirs. NICOR, Inc., Golden Rule Ins., Alcas Corp.; mem. coun. Northwestern U. Assocs. Mem. fin. Coun. Archdiocese of Chgo., Coun. of Grad. Sch. of Bus. U. of Chgo. Mem. Direct Selling Assn. (bd. dirs. 1984-93, chmn. 1987-88, named to Hall of Fame 1991), Women's Coun. U. Mo. Kansas City (hon. life) Com. 200, The Chgo. Network. Roman Catholic. Office: Patricia A Wier Inc 175 E Delaware Pl Apt 8305 Chicago IL 60611-1732

WIER, RICHARD ROYAL, JR., lawyer, inventor; b. Wilmington, Del., May 19, 1941; s. Richard Royal and Anne (Kurtz) W.; m. Anne E. Edwards, Nov. 25, 1978; children—Melissa Royal, Emma Kurtz; children from previous marriage: Richard Royal, III, Mimi Poole. BA in English, Hamilton Coll., 1963; LLB, U. Pa., 1966; postgrad. in labor law, Temple U., 1981-82. Bar: D.C. 1967, Del. 1967, Pa. 1980, U.S. Dist. Ct. Del., U.S. Ct. Appeals (3d cir.), U.S. Supreme Ct. Assoc. Connolly, Bove & Lodge, Wilmington, 1966-68; dep. atty. gen. State of Del., Wilmington, 1968-70; state prosecutor Del. Dept. Justice, Wilmington, 1970-74; atty. gen. State of Del., Wilmington, 1975-79; ptnr. Prickett, Jones, Elliott, Kristol & Schnee, Wilmington, 1979-92; sole practice lawyer Wilmington, 1993—; lectr. criminal and labor law various instns. Active United Way campaign, 1976, 77; mem. supervisory bd. Gov.'s Commn. on Criminal Justice; bd. dirs. Del. Coun. Crime and Justice, 1982-89; mem. adv. coun. Diabetes Control, 1990-92; dir. Project Assist, 1992-95. Recipient Law Enforcement award Newark Police Dept., 1974; Law Enforcement Commendation medal Nat. Soc. SAR, 1976; Ideal Citizen award Am. Found. for Sci. Creative Intelligence, 1976; Commendation Del. Gen. Assembly Senate, 1976, 77, 80; Outstanding Achievement award, 1976. Mem. ABA, Nat. Dist. Attys. Assn. (state dir.), Del. Bar Assn. (chmn. criminal law sect. 1987-91, co-chmn. on drug crisis 1993—, vice chmn. labor law sect. 1987-88, chmn. 1989-90), Pa. Bar Assn., D.C. Bar Assn., Nat. Assn. Attys. Gen. (hon. life, exec. com.), Am. Judicature Soc., Am. Del. Trial Lawyers Assn., Nat. Assn. Extradition Ofcls. (hon. life, regional v.p., exec. dir., Outstanding Achievement award), Italian Radio/TV Assn. (hon.), Internat. Platform Assn., Pi Delta Epsilon. Office: Richard R Wier Jr PA 1220 N Market St Ste 600 Wilmington DE 19801

WIERMAN, JOHN CHARLES, mathematician, educator; b. Prosser, Wash., June 30, 1949; s. John Nathaniel and Edith Elizabeth (Ashley) W.; m. Susan Shelley Graupmann, Aug. 13, 1971; 1 child, Adam Christopher. BS in Math., U. Wash., 1971, PhD in Math., 1976. Asst. prof. math. U. Minn., Mpls., 1976-81; asst. prof. Johns Hopkins U., Balt., 1981-82, assoc. prof., 1982-87, prof., 1987—, chmn. math. scis. dept., 1988—; sr. rsch. fellow Inst. Math. and Its Applications, Mpls., 1987-88. Co-author: First-Passage Percolation on the Square Lattice, 1978; contbr. articles to profl. jours.

Grad. fellow NSF, 1971-74; NSF rsch. grantee, 1976-93. Fellow Inst. Math. Stats. (organizer spl. session on percolation theory 1982, organizer spl. session on probability and math. stats. 1986); mem. Am. Soc. Quality Control, Bernoulli Soc., Am. Math. Soc., Am. Statis. Assn., Math. Assn. Am., Sigma Xi, Phi Beta Kappa. Office: Johns Hopkins U Dept Math Scis 34th & Charles Sts Baltimore MD 21218

WIERNICKI, LOUISE MARIE, special education educator; b. Little Falls, N.Y., Aug. 28; d. Joseph Paul and Ruth E. (Babcock) Pietrandrea; m. Kenneth Wiernicki; children: Ronald J., Anna Louise. BS, SUNY, Oswego, 1970; MS, SUNY, Cortland, 1975; postgrad., Syracuse U., 1975. Tchr. history Whitesboro (N.Y.) Ctrl. Sch., 1970-71; tchr. learning disabled Herkimer County B.O.C.E.S., Herkimer, N.Y., 1971-88; tchr. intermediate resource Frankfort-Sychule Schs., Frankfort, N.Y., 1988-89; tchr. intermediate learning disabled Little Falls (N.Y.) Ctrl. Sch., 1991—. Leader Girl Scouts U.S., Herkimer, cub scouts Boy Scouts Am., Herkimer; treas. Babe Ruth/Am. League Baseball, Herkimer. Democrat. Roman Catholic. Avocations: reading, sports, travel. Home: 204 Willis Ave Herkimer NY 13350-1026

WIERNIK, PETER HARRIS, oncologist, educator; b. Crocket, Tex., June 16, 1939; s. Harris and Molly (Emmerman) W.; m. Roberta Joan Fuller, Sept. 6, 1961; children: Julie Anne, Lisa Britt, Peter Harrison. B.A. with distinction, U. Va., 1961, M.D., 1965; Dr. h.c., U. of Republic, Montevideo, Uruguay, 1982. Diplomate Am. Bd. Internal Medicine, Am. Bd. Med. Oncology (mem. writing com. 1981-87). Intern Cleve. Met. Gen. Hosp., 1965-66, resident, 1969-70; resident Osler Svc. Johns Hopkins Hosp., Balt., 1970-71; sr. asst. surgeon USPHS, 1966, advanced through grades to med. dir., 1976; sr. staff assoc. Balt. Cancer Rsch. Ctr., 1966-71, chief sect. med. oncology, 1971-76, chief clin. oncology br., 1976-82, dir., 1976-82; assoc. dir. div. cancer treatment Nat. Cancer Inst., 1976-82; asst. prof. medicine U. Md. Sch. Medicine, Balt., 1971-74, assoc. prof., 1974-76, prof., 1976-82; Gutman prof., chmn. dept. oncology Montefiore Med. Ctr., 1982-94; head divsn. med. oncology Albert Einstein Coll., 1982-94; assoc. dir. for clin. rsch. Albert Einstein Cancer Ctr., 1982-94, 95—; prof. medicine Albert Einstein Coll. Medicine, 1982—; cons. hematology and med. oncology Union Meml. Hosp., Greater Balt. Med. Ctr., Franklin Sq. Hosp.; bd. dirs. Balt. City unit Am. Cancer Soc., 1971-78; chmn. patient care com., 1972-75, mem. profl. edn. and grants com., N.Y.C. divsn., 1983-90, mem. nat. clin. fellowship com., 1984—; mem. med. adv. com. Nat. Leukemia Assn., 1976-88, chmn. med. adv. com., 1989—; chmn. adult leukemia com. Cancer and Leukemia Group B, 1976-83; prin. investigator Ea. Coop. Oncology Group, 1982-94; chmn. gynecol. oncology com., 1986-88, chmn. leukemia com., 1988-94; sci. cons. Vt. Regional Cancer Ctr., 1987—. Editor: Controversies in Oncology, 1982, Supportive Care of the Cancer Patient, 1983, Neoplastic Diseases of the Blood, 1985, 2d edit., 1991, 3d edit. 1996; assoc. editor Medical Oncology and Tumor Pharmacotherapy, 1987-91, sr. editor, 1991—; assoc. editor onoclogy Am. Jour. Therapeutics, 1994—; co-editor: Year Book of Hematology, 1986—, Handbook of Hematologic and Oncologic Emergencies, 1988, Am. Jour. Med. Scis., 1976-81; N.Am. editor Jour. Cancer Rsch. and Clin. Oncology, 1986-89; mem. editorial bd. Cancer Treatment Reports, 1972-76, Leukemia Rsch., 1977-86, 91—, Leukemia, 1986—, Cancer Clin. Trials, 1977—, Jour. Therapeutic Rsch., 1994—, Hosp. Practice, 1979—, Jour. Clin. Oncology, 1989-91, PDQ Nat. Cancer Inst., 1987-94; sect. editor antineoplastic drugs Jour. Clin. Pharmacology, 1985—; editor-in-chief Medical Oncology, 1993—; also articles, chpt. in books. Recipient Z Soc. award U. Va., 1961, Byrd S. Leavell Hematology award U. Va. Sch. Medicine, 1965. Fellow AAAS, ACP, Am. Coll. Clin. Pharmacology, Internat. Soc. Hematology, Royal Soc. Medicine (London); mem. Am. Soc. Clin. Investigation, Am. Soc. Clin. Oncology (chmn. edn. and tng. com. 1976-79, 84, subcom. on clin. investigation 1980-82, program com. 1990, pub. issues com., 1990—), Am. Assn. Cancer Rsch., Am. Soc. Hematology, Am. Fedn. Clin. Rsch., Am. Acad. Clin. Toxicology, Internat. Soc. Exptl. Hematology, N.Y. Acad. Sci., Am. Soc. Hosp. Pharmacy, Am. Soc. Clin. Pharmacology and Therapeutics, Am. Radium Soc. (program com. 1987—, exec. com. 1988—, publ. com. 1988-92, sec. 1990-91, pres.-elect, 1992-93; pres. 1993-94, Janeway medalist, 1996), Polish Oncology Soc. (hon.), Harvey Soc., Uruguan Hematology Soc. (hon.), European Assn. Cancer Rsch., Phi Beta Kappa (assoc. 1991—), Sigma Xi, Alpha Omega Alpha, Phi Sigma (award 1961). Home: 43 Longview Ln Chappaqua NY 10514-1304 Office: Montefiore Med Ctr 111 E 210th St Bronx NY 10467-2490 *Always remember why you entered a profession in the first place. Leave the politics to those who have forgotten.*

WIERSBE, WARREN WENDELL, clergyman, author, lecturer; b. East Chicago, Ind., May 16, 1929; s. Fred and Gladys Anna (Forsberg) W.; m. Betty Lorraine Warren, June 20, 1953; children: David, Carolyn, Robert, Judy. B.Th., No. Baptist Sem., 1953; D.D. (hon.), Temple Sem., Chattanooga, 1965, Trinity Ev-Div. Sch., 1986; LittD (hon.), Cedarville Coll., 1987. Ordained to ministry Bapt. Ch., 1951; pastor Central Bapt. Ch., East Chicago, 1951-57; editorial dir. Youth for Christ Internat., Wheaton, Ill., 1957-61; pastor Calvary Bapt. Ch., Covington, Ky., 1961-71; sr. minister Moody Ch., Chgo., 1971-78; bd. dirs. Slavic Gospel Assn., Wheaton, 1973-87; columnist Moody Monthly, Chgo., 1971-77; author, conf. minister, 1978-80; vis. instr. pastoral theology Trinity Div. Sch., Deerfield, Ill.; gen. dir. Back to the Bible Radio Ministries, Lincoln, Nebr., 1984-89; writer-in-residence Cornerstone Coll., Grand Rapids, Mich.; disting. prof. preaching Grand Rapids Bapt. Sem.; sr. contbg. editor Baker Book House, Grand Rapids. Author: over 100 books including William Culbertson, A Man of God, 1974, Live Like a King, 1976, Walking with the Giants, 1976, Be Right, 1977, (with David Wiersbe) Making Sense of the Ministry, 1983, Why Us? Why Bad Things Happen to God's People, 1984, Real Worship: It Can Transform Your Life, 1986, Be Compassionate, 1988, The Integrity Crisis, 1988, Be What You Are, 1988, The New Pilgrim's Progress, 1989, Be Courageous, 1989. Home and Office: 441 Lakewood Dr Lincoln NE 68510-2419

WIERSMA, G. BRUCE, dean, forest resources educator; b. Paterson, N.J., Oct. 26, 1942; s. George and Marjorie (Zeedyk) W.; m. Ann Becker, Aug. 15, 1964; children: Heather, Robin, Jennifer, Joshua. BS, U. Maine, 1964; MF in Forestry, Yale U., 1965; PhD Coll. Environ. Sci. & Forestry, SUNY, 1968. Teaching asst., 1965-66; rsch. biologist Coll. Environ. Sci. and Forestry SUNY, 1968; combat devels. staff officer U.S. Army Inst. Land Combat, Alexandria, Va., 1968-70; head monitoring sect. U.S. EPA, Washington, 1970-72, chief ecol. monitoring branch, 1972-74; chief pollutant pathways br. U.S. EPA, Las Vegas, Nev., 1974-79, sr. ecologist, 1979-80; mgr. environ. earth scis. group, Idaho Nat. Engring. Lab. EG&G Idaho, Inc., 1980-87; instr. Idaho Falls Campus of Higher Edn. U. Idaho, 1981-90, affiliate grad. faculty Coll. Forestry Wildlife and Range Scis., 1988-90; mgr., dir. Ctr. Environ. Monitoring and Assesment Environ. Sci. and Tech. Group, 1989-90; dir. Ctr. Environ. Monitoring and Assesment Idaho Nat. Engring. Lab., EG&G Idaho, Inc., Idaho Falls, 1988-90; dean Coll. Forest Resources, assoc. dir. Maine Agrl. Experiment Sta., prof. Forest Resources U. Maine, Orono, 1991-93, dean Coll. Natural Resources, Forestry & Agrl., dir. Maine Agrl. and Forest Experiment Sta., prof. Forest Resources, 1993—; dir. Ctr. Environ. Monitoring and Assessment, Idaho Falls, Idaho, 1980-90; mem. ad-hoc task force to plan global environ. monitoring sys., 1993-95; trustee Nature Conservancy, 1993-95; mem. UN ad hoc task force to plan global terrestrial observing sys., 1993-95; bd. dirs. Maine Forest Products Coun., 1993—; U.S. Nat. Com. on Data for Sci. and Tech., 1990-92, others. Contbr. chpts. to books, articles to profl. jours; editor, founder Jour. Environ. Monitoring and Assesment. Capt. U.S. Army, 1968-70. Recipient numerous rsch. grants from various orgns. Mem. EPA (mem. sci. adv. bd. 1986-90), Nat. Rsch. Coun. (chair com. on databases, 1990-94, mem. com. on marine monitoring, 1986-90, Nat. Assn. Profl. Forestry Schs. (mem. exec. com. 1993—). Avocations: jogging, swimming, cross country skiing, backpacking, mountain climbing. Home: 30 Wildwood Dr East Holden ME 04429-9708 Office: Univ of Maine Coll Natural Res Forestry and Agrl 5782 Winslow Hall Orono ME 04469-5782

WIESCHAUS, ERIC F., molecular biologist, educator; b. June 8, 1947. BS, U. Notre Dame, 1969; PhD in Biology, Yale U., 1974. Rsch. fellow Zool. Inst., U. Zurich, Switzerland, 1975-78; group leader European Molecular Biol. Lab., Germany, 1978-81; from asst. prof. to assoc. prof. Princeton (N.J.) U., 1981-87, prof. biology, 1987—; fellow Lab. de Genetique Moleculaire, France, 1976; vis. rschr. Ctr. Pathobiology, U. Calif., Irvine, 1977; mem. sci. adv. coun. Damon Runyon-Walter Winchell Cancer Fund, 1987-92. Contbr. articles to profl. jours. Recipient Nobel Prize in Medicine, 1995. Fellow Am. Acad. Arts and Scis.; mem. NAS. Office: Princeton U Dept Molecular Biology Princeton NJ 08544*

WIESE, JOHN PAUL, federal judge; b. Bklyn., Apr. 19, 1934; s. Gustav and Margaret W.; m. Alice Mary Donoghue, June 1961; 1 child,John Patrick. BA cum laude, Hobart College, Geneva, NY, 1962; LLB, U. of Va., Charlottesville, 1965. With Cox, Langford & Brown, Washington, DC, 1967-1969, Hodson & Creyke, 1969-74; trial commr. U.S. Claims Court, Washington, DC, 1974-1986, judge, 1986—. Mem. Phi Beta Kappa. Office: US Ct of Federal Claims 717 Madison Pl NW Washington DC 20005-1011*

WIESE, NEVA, critical care nurse; b. Hunter, Kans., July 23, 1940; d. Amil H. and Minnie (Zemke) W. Diploma, Grace Hosp. Sch. Nursing, Hutchinson, Kans., 1962; BA in Social Sci., U. Denver, 1971; BSN, Met. State Coll., 1975; MS in Nursing, U. Colo., Denvr, 1978; postgrad., U. N.Mex., 1986—. RN, N.Mex.; CCRN. Cardiac ICU nurse U. N.Mex. Hosp., Albuquerque; coord. critical care edn. St. Vincent Hosp., Santa Fe, charge nurse CCU, clin. nurse III intensive and cardiac care. Recipient Mary Atherton Meml. award for clin. excellence St. Vincent Hosp., 1986. Mem. ANA (cert. med. surg. nurse), AACN (past pres., sec. N.Mex. chpt., Clin. Excellence award 1991), N.Mex. League Nursing (past v.p., bd. dirs., sec., membership com. 1992—).

WIESE, WOLFGANG LOTHAR, physicist; b. Tilsit, Fed. Republic Germany, Apr. 21, 1931; came to U.S., 1957; naturalized, 1965; s. Werner Max and Charlotte (Donath) W.; m. Gesa Ladehoff, Oct. 12, 1957; children: Margrit, Cosima. BS, U. Kiel, Fed. Republic Germany, 1954, PhD, 1957, PhD (hon.), 1993. Rsch. assoc. U. Md., College Park, 1958-59; rsch. physicist Nat. Bur. Standards, Gaithersburg, Md., 1960-62; chief plasma spectrosc. sect. Nat. Bur. Standards, Gaithersburg, 1962-77, chief atomic and plasma radiation div., 1978-91, chief atomic physics div., 1991—; lectr. U. Calif., 1963, 64. Author: Atomic Transition Probabilities, Vol. I., 1966, Vol. II, 1969, Vol. III, 1988, Vol. IV, 1988. Recipient Silver Medal award Dept. Commerce, 1962, Gold Medal award, 1971, Humboldt award, 1986, A.S. Fleming award U.S. C. of C., 1971, Disting. Career in Sci. award Wash. Acad. Sci., 1992; Guggenheim fellow, 1966. Fellow Am. Phys. Soc., Optical Soc. Am., Wash. Acad. Sci.; mem. Internat. Astron. Union, Sigma Xi. Lutheran. Home: 8229 Stone Trail Dr Bethesda MD 20817-4555 Office: Nat Inst Standards and Tech Gaithersburg MD 20899

WIESEHUEGEL, RICHARD ERWIN, science, engineering and mathematics educator; b. Columbus, Ohio, Dec. 18, 1935; s. Erwin George and Katherine Veach (Hale) W.; m. Katherine Lillian Dickson, Nov. 18, 1979 (div. Apr. 1990); m. Kay Stilz, July 14, 1990; children: William Vinson, Susan Hale, Robert Erwin. BS in Indsl. Engring., U. Tenn., 1957, MS in Indsl. Engring., 1967; PhD in Higher Edn. Adminstrn., George Peabody Coll. for Tchrs, 1978. Registered profl. engr., Tenn. Indsl. analyst Bethlehem Steel Co., Williamsport, Pa., 1957-63; sr. indsl. engr. Huyck Formex, Greenville, Tenn., 1963-68, mgr. quality assurance, 1968-70, mgr. mfg. svcs., 1970-73; coord. pub. svcs. and rsch. U. Tenn., Nashville, 1973-78; divsn. chmn. State Tech. Inst. at Knoxville, 1978-80; program dir. Oak Ridge (Tenn.) Assoc. Univs., 1980—; mem. adv. bd. Roane State C.C., Oak Ridge, 1990-95. Contbr. to Measuring Learning in Continuing Education for Engineers and Scientists, 1984. Chpt. pres. Am. Inst. Indsl. Engrs., Kingsport, Tenn., 1972; charter mem. Tenn. Alliance for Continuing Higher Edn., 1979; elder, deacon various Presbyn. chs., 1959—; vol. fireman Andersonville (Tenn.) Fire Dept., 1984. Mem. Am. Soc. for Engring. Edn., Am. Forest Found., Tenn. Forestry Assn. Avocations: forest management, jet skiing, computer, furniture refinishing, landscaping. Office: Oak Ridge Assoc Univs PO Box 117 Oak Ridge TN 37831-0117

WIESEL, ELIE, writer, educator; b. Sighet, Romania, Sept. 30, 1928; arrived in Paris, 1945; came to U.S., 1956, naturalized, 1963; s. Shlomo and Sarah (Feig) W.; m. Marion Erster, 1969; 1 child, Shlomo Elisha. Student, The Sorbonne, Paris, 1948-51; LittD (hon.), Jewish Theol. Sem., N.Y.C., 1967, Marquette U., 1975, Simmons Coll., 1976, Anna Maria Coll., 1980, Yale U., 1981, Wake Forest U., 1985, Haverford Coll., 1985, Capital U., 1986, L.I. U., 1986, U. Paris, 1987, U. Conn., 1988, U. Cen. Fla., 1988, Wittenberg U., 1989, Wheeling Jesuit Coll., 1989, Fairleigh Dickenson U., 1993; LHD (hon.), Hebrew Union Coll., 1968, Manhattanville Coll., 1972, Yeshiva U., 1973, Boston U., 1974, Coll. of St. Scholastica, 1978, Wesleyan U., 1979, Brandeis U., 1980, Kenyon Coll., 1982, Hobart/William Smith Coll., 1982, Emory U., 1983, Fla. Internat. U., 1983, Siena Heights Coll., 1983, Fairfield U., 1983, Dropsie Coll., 1983, Moravian Coll., 1983, Colgate U., 1984, SUNY, Binghamton, 1985, Lehigh U., 1985, Coll. of New Rochelle, 1986, Tufts U., 1986, Georgetown U., 1986, Hamilton Coll., 1986, Rockford Coll., 1986, Villanova U., 1987, Coll. of St. Thomas, 1987, U. Denver, 1987, Walsh Coll., 1987, Loyola Coll., 1987, Ohio U., 1988, Concordia Coll., 1990, N.Y.U., 1990, Fordham U., 1990, Conn. Coll., 1990, Upsala Coll., 1991, Duquesne U., 1991, Roosevelt U., 1991; PhD (hon.), Bar-Ilan U., 1973, U. Haifa, 1986, Ben Gurion U., 1988; LLD (hon.), Hofstra U., 1975, Talmudic U. Fla., 1979, U. Notre Dame, 1980, La Salle U., 1988, Bates Coll., 1995; HHD (hon.), U. Hartford, 1985, Lycoming Coll., 1987, U. Miami, 1988, Brigham Young U., 1989; D of Hebrew Letters, Spertus Coll. Judaica, 1973; DSc (hon.), U. Health Scis./Chgo. Med. Sch., 1989; ThD, U. Åbo Akadem, 1990; LHD (hon.), Hunter Coll., 1992, Susquehanna U., 1992, Am. U., 1992, Millersville U., 1993; hon. degree, U. Dayton, 1993, U. Mich., 1993; LHD (hon.), U. Bordeaux, 1993, Gustavus Adolphus Coll., 1994, McGill U., 1994, Mt. Sinai Med. Sch., 1994, Spelman Coll., 1995. Disting. prof. Judaic studies CCNY, 1972-76; prof. religious studies and univ. prof. Boston U., 1976—, prof. philosophy, 1988—; Disting. vis. prof. Henry Luce, 1982-83, Eckerd Coll., 1994; chmn. U.S. Pres.'s Commn. on the Holocaust, 1979-80, U.S. Holocaust Meml. Coun., 1980-86; founder Elie Wiesel Found. for Humanity, 1987; founding pres. Paris-based Universal Acad. Cultures; hon. chmn. Nat. Jewish Resource Ctr., N.Y.C. Holocaust Meml. Commn., Am. Friends of Ghetto Fighter's House; hon. pres. Am. Gathering of Jewish Holocaust Survivors; bd. dirs. Nat. Com. on Am. Fgn. Policy, 1983—, Elaine Kaufman Cultural Ctr., adv. bd. The Raoul Wallenberg Commn. of U.S., 1981—, Humanitas, Am. Assocs. Ben-Gurion U. of the Negev, Mut. of Am., France Libertés; v.p. Internat. Rescue Com., 1985—; bd. trustees Annenberg Rsch. Inst., 1983-89, Am. Jour. World Svc., 1985—; Haifa U., Tel-Aviv U.; bd. trustees Yeshiva U., 1977—; colleague Cathedral St. John the Divine, 1975—; mem. adv. bd. Boston U. Inst. for Philosophy & Religion, Nat. Inst. Against Prejudice & Violence, Internat. Ctr. in N.Y., Friends of Akim USA, Friends of LeChambon; mem. jury Neustadt Internat. Prize Lit., 1984; lectr. Andrew W. Mellon Ann. Lecture Series Boston U., 92d St. YMHA, YWHA Ann. Lectr. Series, ann. radio broadcast series Eternal Light for Jewish Theol. Sem. Am., advisory bd. Rena Costa Ctr. for Yiddish Studies at Bar-Ilan U., 1994, advisory Coun. Carnegie Commn. on Preventing Deadly Conflict, 1994. Author: Night, 1960, Dawn, 1961, The Accident, 1962, The Town Beyond the Wall, 1964, The Gates of the Forest, 1966, The Jews of Silence, 1966, Legends of Our Time, 1968, A Beggar in Jerusalem, 1970, One Generation After, 1970, Souls on Fire, 1972, The Oath, 1973, Ani Maamin, 1973, Zalmen, or the Madness of God, 1974, Messengers of God, 1976, A Jew Today, 1978, Four Hasidic Masters, 1978, The Trial of God, 1979, The Testament, 1980, Le Testament D'Un Poète Juif Assassiné (France's Prix Livre-Inter 1980, Bourse Goncourt, 1980, Prix des Bibliothécaires, 1981), 1985, Images from the Bible, 1980, Five Biblical Portraits, 1981, Somewhere A Master, 1982, Paroles d'Étranger, 1982, The Golem, 1983, The Fifth Son (Grand Prix de la Littérature, City of Paris), 1985, Signes d'Exode, 1985, Against Silence (3 vols., ed. Irving Abrahamson), 1985, Job ou Dieu dans la Tempête, 1986, A Song for Hope, 1987, The Nobel Address, 1987, Twilight, 1988; (essays) Silences et Mémoire d'hommes, 1989, L'Oublié, 1989, From the Kingdom of Memory, 1990, Célébration Talmudique, 1991, Sages and Dreamers, 1991, The Forgotten, 1992, (with John Cardinal O'Connor) A Journey of Faith, 1990, (with Albert Friedlander) The Six Days of Destruction, 1988, (dialogues with Philippe-Michaël Saint-Cheron) Evil and Exile, 1990; commentaries to A Passover Haggadah, 1993, All Rivers Run To The Sea (a memoir), 1994; editorial and adv. bds. Midstream, Religion and Lit. (U. Notre Dame), Sh'ma: Jour. of Responsibility, Hadassah Mag., Acad. of the Air for Jewish Studies, Holocaust and Genocide Studies: An Internat. Jour.; subject of 29 books; journalist Israeli, French and Am. newspapers. Chmn. adv. bd. World Union Jewish Students, 1985—; comité d'Honneur Ligue International Contre le Racisme et l'Antisemitisme, 1985—; founder Nat. Jewish Ctr. Learning and Leadership, 1974; mem. soc. fellows Ctr. Judaic Studies, U. Denver, 1980, bd. overseer Bar-Ilan U., 1970—. Recipient Prix Rivarol, 1963, Prix de l'Universite de la langue Francaise, 1963, Ingram Merrill award, 1964, Jewish Heritage award, Haifa U., 1975, Remembrance award, 1965, Prix du Souvenir, 1965, Nat. Jewish Book Council award, 1965, 73, Prix Médicis, 1968, Prix Bordin French Acad., 1972, Eleanor Roosevelt Meml. award, N.Y. United Jewish Appeal, 1972, Am. Liberties medallion Am. Jewish Com., 1972, Martin Luther King Jr. medallion, CCNY, 1973, Annual award for Disting. Service to Am. Jewry, Nat. Fedn. of Jewish Men's Clubs, 1973, Faculty Disting. Scholar award Hofstra U., 1974, Rambam award Am. Mizrachi Women, 1974, Meml. award N.Y. Soc. Clin. Psychologists, 1975, First Spertus Internat. award, 1976, Myrtle Wreath award Hadassah, 1977, King Solomon award, 1977, Liberty award HIAS, 1977, Jewish Heritage award, B'nai B'rith, 1966, Avodah award, Jewish Tchrs. Assn., 1972, Humanitarian award, B'rith Sholom, 1978, Joseph Prize for Human Rights, Anti-Defamation League, 1978, Zalman Shazar award State of Israel, 1979, Presdl. Citation, NYU, 1979, Inaugural award for Lit., Israel Bonds Prime Minister's Com., 1979, Jabotinsky medal, State of Israel, 1980, Rabbanit Sarah Herzog award Emunah Women of Am., 1981, Le Grand Prix Littéraire du Festival Internat. Deauville, 1983, Internat. Lit. prize for Peace, Royal Acad. Belgium, 1983, Lit. Lions award N.Y. Pub. Library, 1983, Jordan Davidson Humanitarian award Fla. Internat. U., 1983, Anatoly Scharansky Humanitarian award, 1983, Grand Officer, Legion of Honor, France, Congressional gold medal, 1985, Voice of Conscience award Am. Jewish Congress, 1985, Remembrance award, Israel Bonds, 1985, Anne Frank award, 1985, 4 Freedoms award FDR 4 Freedoms Found., 1985, Medal of Liberty award Statue of Liberty Presentation, 1986, Nobel Peace Prize, 1986, First Herzl Lit. award, First David Ben-Gurion award, Nat. UJA, Gov.'s award, Shaarei Tzedek, Internat. Kaplun Found. award Hebrew U. Jerusalem, Scopus award, 1974, Am.-Israeli Friendship award, Disting. Writers award Lincolnwood Library, 1984, First Chancellor Joseph H. Lookstein award Bar-Ilan U., 1984, Sam Levenson Meml. award Jewish Community Relations Council, 1985, Comenius award Moravian Coll., 1985, Henrietta Szold award Hadassah, 1985, Disting. Community Service award Mut. Am., 1985, Covenant Peace award Synagogue Council Am., 1985, Jacob Pat award World Congress Jewish Culture, 1985, Humanitarian award Internat. League Human Rights, 1985, Disting. Foreign-Born Am. award Internat. Ctr. N.Y., Inc., 1986, Freedom Cup award Women's League Israel, 1986, First Jacob Javits Humanitarian award UJA Young Leadership, 1986, Boston City Coun. Commendation, 1986, medal of Jerusalem, 1986, Freedom award Internat. Rescue Com., 1987, Achievement award Artist and Writers for Peace in the Middle East, 1987, La Grande Médaille de Vermeil de la Ville de Paris, 1987, La Médaille de la Chancellerie de l'Université de Paris, 1987, La Médaille de l'Université de Paris, 1987, First Eitinger Prize, U. Oslo, 1987, Lifetime Achievment award Present Tense mag., 1987, Spl. Christopher award The Christophers, 1987, Achievement award State Israel, 1987, Sem. medal Jewish Theol. Sem. Am., 1987, Metcalf Cup and Prize for Excellence in Teaching, Boston U., 1987, Spl. award Nat. Com. on Am. Fgn. Policy, 1987, Grã-Cruz da Ordem Nacional do Cruzeiro do Sul, Brazil's highest distinction, 1987, Profiles of Courage award B'nai B'rith, 1987, Centennial medal U. Scranton, 1987, Citation from Religious Edn. Assn., 1987, Golda Meir Sr. Humanitarian award, 1987, Presdl. medal Hofstra U., 1988, Human Rights Law award Internat. Human Rights Law Group, 1988, Bicentennial medal Georgetown U., 1988, Janus Korczak Humanitarian award NAHE, Kent State U., 1989, Count Sforza award in Philanthropy Interphil, 1989, Lily Edelman award for Excellence in Continuing Jewish Edn. B'nai B'rith Internat., 1989, George Washington award Am. Hungarian Found., 1989, Bicentennial medal N.Y.U., 1989, Humanitarian award Human Rights Campaign Fund, 1989, Internat. Brotherhood award C.O.R.E., 1990, Frank Weil award for Disting. Contbn. to Adv. of N.Am. Jewish Culture Jewish Community Ctrs. Assn. N.Am., 1990, 1st Raoul Wallenberg medal U. Mich., 1990, Award of Highest Honor Soka U., 1991, Facing History and Ourselves Humanity award, 1991, La Medaille de la Ville de Toulouse, 1991, 5th Centennial Christopher Columbus medal City of Genoa, 1992, 1st Primo Levi award, 1992, Lit. Arts award Nat. Found. for Jewish Culture, 1992, Ellis Island Medal of Honor, 1992, Guardian of the Children award AKIM USA, 1992, Bishop Francis J. Mugavero award for religious and racial harmony Cath. Newman Ctr. Queens Coll., 1994, Golden Slipper Humanitarian award, 1994, Interfaith Coun. on the Holocaust Humanitarian award, 1994, Crystal award Davos World Economic Forum, 1995, First Niebuhr award, Elmhurst Coll., 1995; named Humanitarian of the Century Coun. Jewish Orgns., Presdl. medal Freedom, 1992; Beth Hatefutsoth hon. fellow, 1988; honors established in his name: Elie Wiesel award for Holocaust Rsch., U. Haifa, Elie Wiesel Chair in Holocaust Studies, Bar-Ilan U., Elie Wiesel Endowment Fund for Jewish Culture, U. Denver, 1987, Elie Wiesel Disting. Svc. award, U. Fla., 1988, Elie Wiesel awards for Jewish Arts and Culture B'nai B'rith Hillel Founds., 1988, Elie Wiesel Chair in Judaic Studies Conn. Coll., 1990. Fellow Jewish Acad. Arts and Scis., Am. Acad. Arts & Scis., Timothy Dwight Coll., Yale U.; mem. Fgn. Press Assn. (hon. life), Amnesty Internat., PEN, Writers & Artists for Peace in Middle East, Writers Guild of Am. East, The Author's Guild,Royal Norwegian Soc. Scis. and Letters, Soc. des auteurs Paris, European Acad. of Arts, Sci. and Humanities, 1992; Phi Beta Kappa. Office: Boston U Univ Profs Program 745 Commonwealth Ave Boston MA 02215-1401

WIESEL, TORSTEN NILS, neurobiologist, educator; b. Upsala, Sweden, June 3, 1924; came to U.S., 1955; s. Fritz Samuel and Anna-Lisa Elisabet (Bentzer) W.; 1 dau., Sara Elisabet. MD, Karolinska Inst., Stockholm, 1954; D Medicine (hon.), Karolinska Inst, Stockholm, 1989; AM (hon.), Harvard U., 1967; ScD (hon.), NYU, 1987, U. Bergen, 1987. Instr. physiology Karolinska Inst., 1954-55; asst. dept. child psychiatry Karolinska Hosp., 1954-55; fellow in ophthalmology Johns Hopkins U., 1955-58, asst. prof. ophthalmic physiology, 1958-59; assoc. in neurophysiology and neuropharmacology Harvard U. Med. Sch., Boston, 1959-60; asst. prof. neurophysiology and neuropharmacology Harvard U. Med. Sch., 1960-64, asst. prof. neurophysiology, dept. psychiatry, 1964-67, prof. physiology, 1967-68, prof. neurobiology, 1968-74, Robert Winthrop prof. neurobiology, 1974-83, chmn. dept. neurobiology, 1973-82; Vincent and Brooke Astor prof. neurobiology, head lab. Rockefeller U., N.Y.C., 1983—, pres., 1992—; Ferrier lectr. Royal Soc. London, 1972; NIH lectr., 1975; Grass lectr. Soc. Neurosci., 1976; lectr. Coll. de France, 1977; Hitchcock prof. U. Calif.-Berkeley, 1980; Sharpey-Schafer lectr. Phys. Soc. London; George Cotzias lectr. Am. Acad. Neurology, 1983. Contbr. numerous articles to profl. jours. Recipient Jules Stein award Trustees for Prevention of Blindness, 1971, Lewis S. Rosenstiel prize Brandeis U., 1972, Friedenwald award Assn. Rsch. in Vision and Ophthalmology, 1975, Karl Spencer Lashley prize Am. Philos. Soc., 1977, Louisa Gross Horwitz prize Columbia U., 1978, Dickson prize U. Pitts., 1979, Nobel prize in physiology and medicine, 1981, W.H. Helmerich III award 1989. Mem. Am. Physiol. Soc., Am. Philos. Soc., AAAS, Am. Acad. Arts and Scis., Nat. Acad. Arts and Scis., Swedish Physiol. Soc., Soc. Neurosci. (pres. 1978-79), Royal Soc. (fgn. mem.), Physiol. Soc. (Eng.) (hon. mem.). Office: Rockefeller U Office Pres 1230 York Ave New York NY 10021-6307*

WIESEN, DONALD GUY, retired diversified manufacturing company executive; b. N.Y.C., July 4, 1928; s. Benjamin and Grace (Heath) W.; m. Patricia Ann Elfers, Apr. 29, 1950; children: Mara, Caitlin, Elizabeth, Anne, Megan. B.S., Columbia U., 1948, M.S., 1954. C.P.A., N.Y. Sr. tax specialist Price Waterhouse & Co., N.Y.C., 1950-58; with Chesebrough-Pond's Inc., Greenwich, Conn., 1958-87; gen. mgr. ops. Europe Chesebrough-Pond's Inc., 1965-70, treas., 1970-72, group v.p., chief fin. officer, 1972-77, group v.p., internat., 1977-82, sr. group v.p., 1982-84, vice chmn., chief fin. officer, 1984-87, also dir., ret., 1987; bd. dirs. Skandia Am. Corp., 1985-91. Trustee Greenwich Libr., 1974-80; bd. govs. St. Bernard Coll., Cullman, Ala., 1973-75; rep. Columbia U. Alumni, Geneva, 1968; bd. dirs. Inner-City Found. for Charity and Edn., Bridgeport, Conn., 1992-93. Capt. USMC, 1951-54. Mem. AICPA, Indian Harbor Yacht Club, Univ. Club (N.Y.). Roman Catholic.

WIESEN, RICHARD A., academic administrator, educator; b. Sharon, Pa., Sept. 23, 1937. BS in Edn., Clarion State U., 1959; MS, Syracuse U., 1964; EdD, SUNY, Buffalo, 1970. Asst. prof. Buffalo State Coll., 1967-67, assoc. prof., 1967-71, assoc. dean, 1976, prof., 1971-92, assoc.v.p., 1979-83, v.p., 1983-90, provost, v.p. for acad. affairs, 1990-92; sr. v.p. D'Youville Coll., Buffalo, 1992—. Recipient Disting. Alumni award SUNY-Buffalo, 1990, Outstanding Alumni award 1990. Mem. Am. Assn. U. Adminstrs., Am. Assn. for Higher Edn. Office: D'Youville Coll 320 Porter Ave Buffalo NY 14201-1032

WIESENBERG, RUSSEL JOHN, statistician; b. Kaukauna, Wis., Apr. 9, 1924; s. Emil Martin and Josephine (Appelbaker) W.; m. Jacqueline Leonardi, Nov. 23; children: James Wynne, Deborann Donna. BS, U. Wis., 1951; postgrad. Cornell U., 1960-61, U. Mich., 1969, George Washington U., 1976. Analyst, Gen. Electric Co., West Lynn, Mass., 1951-56; specialist Internat. Gen. Electric Co., Rio de Janeiro, Brazil, 1956-59; statistician Gen. Motors Corp., Lockport, N.Y., 1959-65, sr. statistician, Harrison Radiator div., 1965-78, sr. reliability engr., 1978-82, sr. reliability statistician, 1982-87 . Auditor, Community Chest Fund, 1952-55; umpire Little League Baseball, 1962-65; committeeman Buffalo Area council Boy Scouts Am., 1962—, Cub Scout committeeman, 1962-64, Webelos cubmaster, 1963-64; mem. Nat. Congress Parents and Tchrs., 1963—; heart fund Vol. Heart Assn., 1968; tournament dir. Am. Legion Baseball, 1975; vol. United Way campaign, 1983, nat. telethon March of Dimes, 1983-84. Served with AUS, 1943-46. Decorated Bronze Star. Mem. AAAS, Am. Statis. Assn., Nat. Register Sci. and Tech. Pers., U. Wis. Alumni Assn., Artus, Internat. Platform Assn., Phi Kappa Phi. Lutheran. com.). Contbr. articles to profl. jours. Home: 14 Norman Pl Buffalo NY 14226-4233

WIESENECK, ROBERT L., credit manager; b. 1938. Graduate, Roosevelt U., 1958; MBA, U. Chgo., 1963. With Sears Roebuck and Co., Chgo., 1963—; nowpres. SPS Syss., Inc., Deerfield, Ill. Office: SPS Payment Systems Inc 2500 Lake Cook Rd Riverwood IL 60015-3851*

WIESENFELD, JOHN RICHARD, chemistry educator; b. N.Y.C., July 26, 1944; s. Walter and Trude (Rosenberg) W. Stokes fellow, Pembroke Coll., Cambridge, Eng., 1971-72; BS with honors, CCNY, 1965; PhD, Case Inst. Tech., Cleve., 1969; MA, U. Cambridge, Eng., 1970. Asst. prof. Cornell U., Ithaca, N.Y., 1972-77, assoc. prof., 1978-84, prof., 1984-95, chair dept. chemistry, 1985-88, dep. v.p. for rsch., 1988-90, v.p. for plan, 1990-94; v.p. academic programs and planning, 1994-95; dean of sci. Fla. Atlantic U., Boca Raton, 1995—; vis. scholar Stanford U. Calif., 1978-79, U. Wash., 1988; cons. E.I. DuPont, Wilmington, Del., 1975, Phys. Dynamics, La Jolla, Calif., 1980-82, U.S. Dept. Energy, Pitts., 1982, NIH, 1994; bd. dirs. Associated Univs., 1989-92. Contbr. more than 100 sci. articles to profl. jours. Sloan Found. research fellow, 1975; recipient Tchr.-Scholar award, Dreyfus Found., 1975. Fellow AAAS; mem. Am. Chem. Soc., Coun. Chem. Rsch. (governing bd. 1987-90). Home: 3011 Jasmine Ct Delray Beach FL 33483 Office: Fla Atlantic U PO Box 3091 Boca Raton FL 33431

WIESENFELD, KURT ARN, physicist, educator; b. Roslyn Heights, N.Y., Feb. 12, 1958; s. David and Elaine Kaye (Dattner) W.; m. Karla Mari Jennings, Aug. 17, 1985. BS in Physics, MIT, 1979; MA in Physics, U. Calif., Berkeley, 1982, PhD in Physics, 1985. Lectr., rschr. physics U. Calif., Santa Cruz, 1984-85; rschr. Brookhaven Nat. Lab., Upton, N.Y., 1985-87; asst. prof. Ga. Inst. Tech., Atlanta, 1987-92, assoc. prof., 1992—. Contbr. over 70 articles to sci. jours. Office: Ga Inst Tech Sch Physics State St Atlanta GA 30332

WIESER, SIEGFRIED, planetarium executive director; b. Linz, Austria, Oct. 30, 1933; came to Can., 1955; s. Florian Wieser and Michaela Josepha (Kaufmann) Wieser-Burgstaller; m. Joan Xaven Quick, Sept. 8, 1962; children: Leonard Franz, Bernard Sidney. BS in Physics, U. Calgary, Alta., Can., 1966. Lead chorus singer, dancer Landes Theatre, Linz, 1949-53; project engr. EBG, Linz, 1952-54; with Griffith Farms Ltd., Eng., 1954-55; seismic computer operator Shell Can., Calgary, 1956-61; GTA systems analyst U. Calgary, 1961-66; planetarium dir. Centennial Planetarium, Calgary, 1966-84, exec. dir., 1984-91; exec. dir. emeritus Alberta Sci. Ctr., 1991—; cons. Electro Controls, Salt Lake City, 1978-79. Contbr. articles to profl. pubis. Recipient Violet Taylor award U. Calgary, 1964; Queen Elizabeth scholar Province Alta., 1961; Paul Harris fellow Rotary Internat. Mem. Calgary Region Arts Found., Alberta Coll. of Art Alumni Assn. (pres. 1991-92). Anglican. Club: Magic Circle (Calgary). Avocations: swimming, hiking, astronomy, lecturing.

WIESLER, JAMES BALLARD, retired banker; b. San Diego, July 25, 1927; s. Harry J. and Della B. (Ballard) W.; m. Mary Jane Hall, Oct. 3, 1953; children: Tom, Ann, Larry. B.S., U. Colo., 1949; postgrad., Stonier Sch. Banking, Rutgers U., 1962, Advanced Mgmt. Program, Harvard U., 1973. With Bank of Am., NT & SA, 1949-87; v.p., mgr. main office San Jose, Calif., 1964-69, regional v.p. Cen. Coast adminstrn., 1969-74; sr. v.p., head No. European Area office Frankfurt, Fed. Republic of Germany, 1974-78; exec. v.p., head Asia div. Tokyo, 1978-81; exec. v.p., head N.Am. div. Los Angeles, 1981-82; vice chmn., head retail banking San Francisco, 1982-87; ret., 1987; bd. dirs. Visa USA, Visa Internat., Sci. Applications Internat. Corp.; bd. dirs., chmn. Bank Adminstrn. Inst., 1986-87. Pres. Santa Clara County United Fund, 1969, 70, San Jose C. of C., 1968; fin. chmn. Santa Clara County Reps., 1967-74; bd. dirs. San Diego Armed Svcs., YMCA, Sidney Kimmell Cancer Ctr.; trustee Sharp Hosp.; hon. consul-gen. for Japan, 1990-95. With USN, 1945-46. Mem. San Diego Zool. Soc., Bohemian Club, DeAnza Country Club, San Diego Country Club, San Diego Yacht Club. Presbyterian. Home: 605 San Fernando St San Diego CA 92106-3312 Office: Bank Am Nat Trust & Savs 450 B St San Diego CA 92101-8001

WIESNER, JOHN JOSEPH, retail chain store executive; b. Kansas City, Mo., Mar. 31, 1938; s. Vincent A. and Jane Ann (Hagerty) W.; m. Georgiana Schild, Oct. 15, 1960; children: Susan, John V., Gretchen. BS in Bus. Adminstrn., Rockhurst Coll., 1960. Vice pres., contr. Fisher Foods, Cleve., 1970-77; asst. corp. contr. Richardson Vicks, N.Y.C., 1960-70; sr. exec. v.p. Pamida, Inc., Omaha, 1977-85, vice chmn., chief exec. officer, 1985-87; CEO C.R. Anthony Co., Oklahoma City, 1987—. Bd. dirs. Omaha Girls' Club, 1983—, Omaha Area Council on Alcohol and Drug Abuse, 1983—; bd. dirs. Fontenelle Forest, Omaha, chmn., 1983, 84, A Chance to Change Fedn.; mem. bd. regents Rockhurst Coll., Okla. City Golf & Country Club, Beacon Club, Oklahoma City, Kansas City, Mo. Named Bus. Assoc. of Yr., Am. Bus. Women's Assn., 1983. Mem. Nat. Assn. Accts. Republican. Roman Catholic.

WIESSLER, DAVID ALBERT, correspondent; b. Cambridge, Mass., July 20, 1942; s. Albert Francis and Vivian Mary (Thomas) W.; m. Mary Judith Burton, Dec. 28, 1968. AB, Princeton U., 1964; MA, U. Tex., 1968. Editor UPI, Dallas, N.Y.C., Washington, 1966-82; assoc. editor U.S. News & World Report, Washington, 1982-84; Washington Bur. chief UPI, Washington, 1984-90, sr. polit. editor, 1990-93; news editor Bloomberg News Svc., 1994-95; editor nat. news Reuters, Washington, 1995—. Recipient Best Feature Writer award Dallas Press Club, 1970. Mem. Washington Gridiron Club. Avocations: reading, travel, cooking.

WIEST, DIANNE, actress; b. Kansas City, Mo., Mar. 28, 1948. Student, U. Md. Appeared in numerous plays including Ashes (off-Broadway), 1976, Leave It to Beaver is Dead, The Art of Dining (Obie award, 1979, Theatre World award 1983), Bonjour La Bonjour, Three Sisters, Serenading Louie (Obie award, 1983), Othello, After the Fall, Heartbreak House, Our Town, and Hunting Cockroaches, 1987, In the Summer House, 1993, Blue Light, 1994; appeared in films including It's My Turn, 1980, I'm Dancing as Fast as I Can, 1982, Independence Day, 1982, Footloose, 1984, Falling in Love, 1984, The Purple Rose of Cairo, 1985, Hannah and Her Sisters, 1986 (Acad. award for Best Supporting Actress 1987), Radio Days, 1987, Lost Boys, 1987, September, 1987, Bright Lights, Big City, 1988, Parenthood, 1989 (Acad. award nominee), Cookie, 1989, Edward Scissorhands, 1990, Little Man Tate, 1991, Cops and Robbersons, 1994, The Scout, 1994, Bullets Over Broadway, 1994 (Golden Globe award Best Supporting Actress-Drama 1995, Acad. award for Best Supporting Actress 1995), Drunks, 1995, The Birdcage, 1996; TV appearances include The Wall, 1982, The Face of Rage, 1983. *

WIEST, WILLIAM MARVIN, education educator, psychologist; b. Loveland, Colo., May 8, 1933; s. William Walter and Katherine Elizabeth (Buxman) W.; m. Thelma Lee Bartel, Aug. 18, 1955; children: William Albert, Suzanne Kay, Cynthia May. BA in Psychology summa cum laude, Tabor Coll., 1955; MA, U. Kans., 1957; PhD, U. Calif., 1962. Rsch. asst. psychol. ecology U. Kans., 1955-57; rsch. asst. measurement cooperative behavior in dyads U. Calif., Berkeley, 1958-59; from asst. to assoc. prof. Reed Coll., Portland, Oreg., 1961-74, prof., 1974—; adj. investigator Ctr. Health Rsch., Portland, 1985—; project coord. WHO, Geneva, 1976-84; fgn. travel leader Assiniboine Travel, Winnipeg, Manitoba, Can., 1990-91, Willamette Internat. Travel, Portland, 1993-95; lectr. Fgn. Travel Club, Portland, 1990, 94; vis. scientist Oceanic Inst., Waimanalo, Hawaii, 1967-68; chmn. dept. psychology Reed Coll., Portland, 1973-75, 86; social sci. adv. com. Population Resource Ctr., N.Y.C., 1978—; vis. investigator Health Svcs. Rsch. Ctr., Portland, 1975-76, cons. 1976-80; com. protection human subjects Kaiser Permanente Med. Care Program, Portland, 1978-81; cons. WHO, 1980-81, U.S. Dept. Energy, 1980-83; mem. panel population study sect. HHS. Consulting editor Population and Environment, 1981—; jour. referee Health Psychology, Jour. Social Biology, Jour. Personality and Social Psychology, Memory and Cognition; contbr. articles to profl. jours. Sloan Found. Faculty Rsch. fellow, 1972-73, NSF fellow, 1975-76, USPSH fellow U. Calif., 1957-58, Woodrow Wilson Found. fellow U. Calif., 1960-61. Mem. AAAS, APHA, Am. Hist. Soc. Germans from Russia (conv. speaker 1991), Germans from Russia Heritage Soc., Am. Psychol. Assn., Population Assn. Am., Phi Beta Kappa, Sigma Xi. Home: 5009 SE 46th Ave Portland OR 97206-5048 Office: Reed Coll Psych Dept SE Woodstock Blvd Portland OR 97202

WIGDOR, LAWRENCE ALLEN, chemical company executive; b. N.Y.C., Sept. 7, 1941; s. Irving and Gertrude (Kuhlman) W.; divorced; children: Paul, Evan. BChemE, NYU, 1962; MBA, CUNY, 1964, PhD, 1969. Group v.p. chems. Tenneco, Saddle Brook, N.J., 1976-78, exec. v.p. chems. & plastics, 1978-82; exec. v.p., COO Nuodex, Piscataway, N.J., 1982-85, pres., CEO, 1985-87; pres., CEO Huls Am., Piscataway, 1987-90; CEO Kronos Inc., East Houston, Tex., 1990—; exec. v.p. NL Industries, 1992—; chmn. bd. dirs., CEO Rheox, Inc., 1990—; chmn. bd. dirs. MEMC, St. Louis, 1989-90; bd. dirs. Nuodex Mexicana, Guadalajara, Mex., Huls Can., Toronto. Contbr. articles to profl. jours. 2d lt. U.S. Army. Mem. Chem. Mfrs. Assn. (bd. dirs. 1989-91). Republican. Avocation: pvt. investments.

WIGELL, RAYMOND GEORGE, lawyer; b. Chgo., Apr. 18, 1949; s. Raymond Carl and Amanda D. (Santiago) W.; m. Barbara E. Buettner, June 28, 1980; children: Katherine, Elizabeth, Charles. BA, U. Ill., Chgo., 1971; JD, John Marshall Law Sch., 1975; LLM in Taxation, DePaul U., 1991. Bar: Ill. 1975, U.S. Dist. Ct. (no. dist.) Ill. 1975, U.S. Ct. Appeals (7th cir.) 1978, U.S. Supreme Ct. 1979, U.S. Tax Ct. 1987. Pvt. practice law Raymond G. Wigell, Ltd., Chgo., 1975-77; trial atty. Cook County Pub. Defender, Chgo., 1977-78; pres., owner, atty. Wigell & Assocs., Olympia Fields, Ill., 1978—; instr. MacCormac Jr. Coll., Chgo., 1976-77; lectr. in bus. law Oakton C.C., Des Plaines, Ill., 1976-84; adj. prof. Govs. State U., University Park, Ill., 1984-92. Commn. chair inquiry bd. Atty. Registration Disciplinary Commn. Supreme Ct. Ill., Chgo., 1985-90, commn. chair hearing bd., 1990-95. With USN, 1971-77. Mem. U. Ill. Alumni Assn. (life mem.). Roman Catholic. Office: Wigell & Assocs Atty at Law 418 Dixie Hwy Chicago Heights IL 60411

WIGGERS, CHARLOTTE SUZANNE WARD, magazine editor; b. Cleve., Dec. 14, 1943; d. Raymond Paul and Irene Mary (Knapp) W.; m. John Houston Black, Feb. 1975 (div. 1980). AB, Smith Coll., 1966. Asst. editor The Hudson Rev., N.Y.C., 1966-76; assoc. editor The Print Collector's Newsletter, N.Y.C., 1977-79; copy editor Electronics mag., McGraw-Hill, N.Y.C., 1979-81; sr. copy editor Spectrum mag., N.Y.C., 1981-85; mng. editor Essence mag., N.Y.C., 1985—. Avocations: swimming, writing, photography, tennis. Home: 50 W 85th St Apt 5 New York NY 10024-4572 Office: Essence Magazine 1500 Broadway New York NY 10036-4015

WIGGIN, KENDALL FRENCH, state librarian; b. Manchester, N.H., Aug. 21, 1951; s. Ralph M. Jr. and Frances (Miltimore) W.; m. Elaine M. Elliott, June 2, 1973 (div. Jan. 1989); children: Sara, Douglas; m. Laura A. Larson, May 26, 1990; children: Lindsey, Tess. BA, U. N.H., 1974; MS in LS, Simmons Coll., 1975. Libr. Litchfield (N.H.) Pub. Libr., 1975; dir. Merrimack (N.H.) Pub. Libr., 1975-83; coord. tech. svcs. Manchester City Libr., 1983-90; state libr. N.H. State Libr., Concord, 1990—. Mem. ALA,, New Eng. Libr. Assn., N.H. Libr. Assn., Chief Officers State Libr. Agys., Chief Officers State Libr. Agys. in N.E., N.H. Writers and Publishers Project. Republican. Presbyterian. Avocations: philately, gardening. Office: Cultural Affairs Dept 20 Park St Concord NH 03301-6314

WIGGINS, CHARLES EDWARD, judge; b. El Monte, Calif., Dec. 3, 1927; s. Louis J. and Margaret E. (Fanning) W.; m. Yvonne L. Boots, Dec. 30, 1946 (dec. Sept. 1971); children: Steven L., Scott D.; m. Betty J. Koontz, July 12, 1972. B.S., U. So. Calif., 1953, LL.B., 1956; LL.B. (hon.) Ohio Wesleyan, 1975, Han Yang. U., Seoul, Korea, 1976. Bar: Calif. 1957, D.C. 1978. Lawyer, Wood & Wiggins, El Monte, Calif., 1956-66, Musick, Peeler & Garrett, Los Angeles, 1979-81, Pierson, Ball & Dowd, Washington, 1982-84, Pillsbury, Madison & Sutro, San Francisco, 1984; mem. 90-95th congresses from 25th and 39th Calif. Dists.; judge U.S. Ct. Appeals 9th Circuit, 1984—. Mayor City of El Monte, Calif., 1964-66; mem. Planning Commn. City of El Monte, 1956-60; mem. Commn. on Bicentennial of U.S. Constitution, 1985—, mem. standing com. on rules of practice and procedure, 1987—. Served to 1st lt. U.S. Army, 1945-48, 50-52, Korea. Mem. ABA, State Bar Calif., D.C. Bar Assn. Republican. Lodge: Lions. Office: US Ct Appeals 9th Cir 50 W Liberty St Ste 950 Reno NV 89501-1949

WIGGINS, CHARLES HENRY, JR., lawyer; b. Balt., July 15, 1939; s. Charles Henry and Kathryn Wilson (Walker) W.; m. Wendy Jane Horn, June 20, 1964; children: Charles Hunter, Rebecca Rae, Melinda Marie. BSEE, U. Ill., Urbana, 1962; JD with honors, U. Ill., 1965. Bar: Ill. 1965, U.S. Dist. Ct. (no. dist.) Ill. 1970, U.S. Tax Ct. 1974, U.S. Ct. Appeals (7th cir.) 1983. Assoc. Vedder, Price, Kaufman & Kammholz, Chgo., 1969-73, ptnr., 1974—. Mem. zoning bd. appeals Village of Indian Head Pk., Ill., 1984-91. Capt. U.S. Army, 1965-68. Mem. Chgo. Bar Assn., University Club (Chgo.), Edgewood Valley Country Club (LaGrange, Ill., bd. dirs. 1991—), SAR. Avocations: golf, tennis, bridge. Office: Vedder Price Kaufman & Kammholz 222 N La Salle St Fl 26 Chicago IL 60601-1003

WIGGINS, JAMES BRYAN, religion educator; b. Mexia, Tex., Aug. 24, 1935; m. Kay Wiggins, Aug. 15, 1956; children: Bryan, Karis. BA, Tex. Wesleyan U., 1957; BD, So. Meth. U., 1959; PhD, Drew U., 1963; postgrad., Tübingen U., Fed. Republic Germany, 1968-69. Ordained to ministry Meth. Ch., 1959. Instr. humanities Union Jr. Coll., Cranford, N.J., 1960-63; asst. prof. religion Syracuse (N.Y.) U., 1963-69, assoc. prof., 1969-75, prof., 1975—, dir. grad. studies, 1975-80, chair dept., 1980—; exec. dir. Am. Acad. Religion, 1983-91, dir., 1973-75, 83-91; cons. in field; People to People del. leader to former Soviet Union, 1992. Author: The Embattled Saint, 1966, Foundations of Christianity, 1970; editor: Religion as Story, 1975, Christianity: A Cultural Perspective, 1987, In Praise of Religious Diversity, 1996; contbr. articles to profl. jours. Trustee Scholars Press, Atlanta, 1983-91, chmn., 1986-91. Rockefeller Found. fellow, 1962-63; Lilly Endowment rsch. grantee, 1992-93. Fellow Soc. for Arts (bd. dirs. 1976—), Religion and Culture; mem. AAUP, Am. Acad. Religion, Am. Soc. Ch. History. Democrat. Avocations: golf, tennis, music, reading, travel. Office: Syracuse U Dept Religion 501 Hall of Langs Syracuse NY 13244

WIGGINS, JAMES RUSSELL, newspaper editor; b. Luverne, Minn., Dec. 4, 1903; s. James and Edith (Binford) W.; m. Mabel E. Preston, Feb. 8, 1923 (widowed Oct. 1990); children: William James (dec.), Geraldine Wiggins Thomssen (dec.), Patricia Wiggins Schroth, John Russell. Grad. high sch., Luverne; LLD (hon.), Colby Coll., 1954, U. Maine, Bates Coll., 1968; DLitt (hon.), Anna Maria Coll., 1976, Clark U., 1977; LHD (hon.), Husson Coll., Bangor, Maine, 1979, U. New Eng., 1983; DSci (hon.), Maine Maritime Acad., 1987; LittD (hon.), Bowdoin Coll., 1988. Reporter Rock County Star, Luverne, 1922-25; editor, pub. Luverne Star, 1925-30; editorial writer Dispatch-Pioneer Press, St. Paul, 1930-33, Washington corr., 1933-38, mng. editor, 1938-45, editor, 1945-46; asst. to pub. N.Y. Times, 1946-47; mng. editor Washington Post, 1947-53, v.p., mng. editor, 1953-55; v.p., exec. editor Washington Post and Times Herald, 1955-60, editor, exec. v.p., 1960-68; U.S. amb. to UN, 1968-69; editor, pub. Ellsworth (Maine) Am., 1969-91, editor, 1969—. Author: Freedom or Secrecy, 1956. Served to maj. USAAF, 1943-45; air combat intelligence officer 1943-44, MTO. Mem. Am. Soc. Newspaper Editors (past pres.), Am. Antiquarian Soc. (pres. 1969-77), Sigma Delta Chi. Clubs: Nat. Press, Cosmos, Gridiron (past pres.) (Washington). Lodge: Masons. Home: Carlton Cove HCR 64 Box 506 Brooklin ME 04616-9709 Office: Ellsworth Maine America 63 Main St Ellsworth ME 04605-1902

WIGGINS, JEROME MEYER, apparel textile industry financial executive; b. Portsmouth, Ohio, July 28, 1940; s. Jerome M. and Mary Vallee (Harold) W.; m. Mary Lou Wetta, Aug. 3, 1963; children: Laura, Kelly, Kristin, Patrick. BA, U. Notre Dame, 1962; postgrad., Ohio State U., 1964-66. CPA, Ohio. Acct. Ernst & Young, Columbus, Ohio, 1965-72; v.p. fin. Greater Ohio Corp., Columbus, 1972-75; gen. auditor VF Corp., Reading, Pa., 1975-80, contr., 1980-81, v.p. fin., 1981-89; chief fin. officer Dyersburg (Tenn.) Corp., 1989-95, pres. ops., 1995—. Mem. Am. Inst. CPA's. Republican. Roman Catholic. Avocations: golf, sailing, bridge. Office: Dyersburg Corp Tenn Indsl Fin Exec Phillips St Dyersburg TN 38024

WIGGINS, NORMAN ADRIAN, university administrator, legal educator; b. Burlington, N.C., Feb. 6, 1924; s. Walter James and Margaret Ann (Chason) W.; m. Mildred Alice Harmon. AA, Campbell Coll., 1948; BA, Wake Forest Coll., 1950, LLB, 1952; LLM, Columbia U., 1956, JSD, 1964; Exec. Program, U. N.C., 1968-69; LLD, Gardner-Webb Coll., 1972. Deacon Wake Forest Baptist Ch., Winston-Salem, N.C., 1963-66, Buies Creek (N.C.) Bapt. Ch., 1973—; deacon, tchr. Sunday sch., 1952—, lay preacher, 1953—; pres. N.C. Found. of Ch.-Related Coll., 1969-70, Campbell U., Buies Creek, 1967—; prof. law Campbell U., 1976—. Author: Wills and Administration of Estates in North Carolina, 1964—, (with Gilbert T. Stephenson) Estates and Trusts, 1973; Editor: N.C. Will Manual, 1958—, Trust Functions and Services, 1978; Contbr. articles to legal jours. Chmn. Gov.'s Task Force Com. on Adjudication of the Com. on Law and Order, 1969-71; mem. Com. on Drafting Interstate Succession Act for N.C., 1957-59; mem. Com. for Revision of the Laws Relating to the Adminstrn. of Descs.' Estates, 1959-67, chmn., 1964-67; trustee Sunday Sch. Bd., So. Bapt. Conv., 1975—, chmn. bd. trustees, 1978—, nominations com., 1988—; pres. Bapt. State Conv. N.C., 1983-85; bd. dirs. N.C. Citizens for Bus. and Industry, 1982—. Recipient Outstanding Civilian Svc. award Dept. Army, 1985; Campbell Law Sch. renamed in his honor the Norman Adrian Wiggins Sch. of Law, 1989; recognized for outstanding svc. to high edn. and legal edn. Newcomen Soc. U.S., 1993; Comdr.'s award for Pub. Svc., 1995, Internat. Freedom of Mobility award, 1995. Mem. ABA, Nat. Assn. Coll. and Univ. Attys. (pres. 1972-73, Disting. Svc. award 1991), Am. Assn. Presidents Ind. Colls. and Univs. (pres. 1981-83), N.C. Assn. Colls. and Univs. (exec. com. 1980—, pres. 1984-85), N.C. Assn. Ind. Colls. and Univs. (pres. 1970-72, exec. com. 1980-81), N.C. Bar Assn., Harnett County Bar Assn., Nat. Fellowship Baptist Men (pres. 1987-90), Jay Waugh Evang. Assn. (dir./pres. 1970-72), Dunn Area C. of C., Wake Forest Alumni Assn., Rotary (hon. mem. Dunn club), Phi Alpha Delta, Phi Kappa Phi, Omicron Delta Kappa. Office: Campbell U PO Box 127 Buies Creek NC 27506-0127

WIGGINS, ROGER C., internist, educator, researcher; b. Tetbury, Eng., May 26, 1945. BA, Cambridge U., Eng., 1968; BChir, Middlesex Hosp. Med. Sch., London, 1971, MB, MA, 1972. House physician dept. medicine The Middlesex Hosp., London, 1971-72; house surgeon Ipswich (Eng.) and East Suffolk Hosps., 1972; sr. house officer Hammersmith Hosp., The Middlesex Hosp., Brompton Hosp., London, 1972-74; rsch. registrar The Middlesex Hosp. Med. Sch., London, 1975-76; postdoctoral fellow Scripps Clinic and Rsch. Found., La Jolla, Calif., 1976-78, rsch. assoc., 1978-79, asst. mem. 1, 1979-81; asst. prof. U. Mich., Ann Arbor, 1981-84, assoc. prof., 1984-90, prof., 1990—, chief nephrology, 1988—, dir. O'Brien Renal Ctr., 1988—, dir. NIH Nephrology Tng. Program, 1988—; lectr., speaker in field. Author chpts. to books; assoc. editor: Jour. Am. Soc. Nephrology, Clin. Sci.; contbr. articles to profl. jours. First Broderip scholar, 1971, Harold Boldero scholar, 1971, James McIntosh scholar, 1971, The Berkeley fellow Gonville and Caius Coll., 1976; recipient Leopold Hudson prize, 1971, The William Henry Rean prize, 1971, Disting. Rsch. Jerome W. Conn award, 1984. Fellow Royal Coll. Physicians (U.K.); mem. Am. Assn. Pathologists, Am. Assn. Immunologists, Am. Soc. Nephrology, Fedn. Clin. Rsch., Am. Soc. Clin. Investigation, Ctrl. Soc. Am. Fedn. Clin. Rsch., Assn. Am. Physicians. Home: 3142 Parkridge Dr Ann Arbor MI 48103-1741 Office: U Mich Nephrology Div 3914 Taubman Ctr Ann Arbor MI 48109-0364

WIGGINS, SAMUEL PAUL, education educator; b. Salisbury, N.C., Sept. 20, 1919; s. James Andrew and Mollie (Wilhelm) W.; m. Linda Jean Bessent, June 29, 1947; children: Stanley, David, Timothy, Mark. B.S., Ga. Tchrs. Coll., 1940; M.Ed., Duke U., 1942; Ph.D., Peabody Coll., 1952. Teaching prin. Alma, Ga., 1939-40; dir. lab. sch. Ga. Southwestern Coll., 1940-42; dir. student teaching Emory U., 1947-53; prof., adminstr. Peabody Coll., 1953-67; dean Coll. Edn., Cleve. State U., 1967-75, prof., 1975-85; prof. Norfolk State U., 1985—, co-dir. project nat. bd. tchr. certification, 1985-96; chief advisor ICA (AID), Korea Tchr. Edn. Project, 1961-62; Fulbright lectr., Colombia, S.Am., 1966, Lisbon, Portugal, 1978; pres. Am. Assn. Colls. Tchr. Edn., 1974-75; mem. forum of leaders Nat. Ednl. Orgns. USOE, 1975-77. Author: Successful High School Teaching, 1958, Student Teacher in Action, 1957, Southern High Schools and Jobless Youth, 1961, The Desegregation Era in Higher Education, 1966, Higher Education in the South, 1966, Battlefields in Teacher Education, 1964, Educating Personnel for Urban Schools, 1972, Improving Education for the Youth of Portugal, 1980, Revolution in Teacher Education: A Review of Reform Reports, 1985; co-author: Equity and Excellence for Minorities in T.Ed. (A.T.E.), 1988,. Served with USNR, 1942-47, comdr. Res. ret. Home: 609 Abbey Dr Virginia Beach VA 23455-6504

WIGGINS, TIMOTHY J., metal products executive; b. 1956. BA in Acctg., Mich. State U., 1979. CPA, 1981. Sr. mgr. Deloitte Haskins & Sells, Detroit, 1979-88; chief exec. officer Autodie Corp., Grand Rapids, Mich., 1988-93; cons. Glass & Assocs., Canton, Ohio, 1993; with Fruehauf Trailer Corp., Southfield, Mich., 1993—, exec. v.p. fin./adminstrn., chief fin. officer. Office: Fruehauf Trailer Corp 111 Monument Cir Ste 3200 Indianapolis IN 46204

WIGGS, EUGENE OVERBEY, ophthalmologist, educator; b. Louisville, Apr. 27, 1928; s. Eugene Overbey and Marie Helen (Martin) W.; children: Susan, Christopher, Karen, Mark. AB, Johns Hopkins U., 1950; MD, Duke U., 1955. Intern Denver Gen. Hosp., 1955-56; resident in ophthalmology Wilmer Inst. Johns Hopkins Hosp., 1956-59; ophthalmic plastic fellow Byron Smith, MD, N.Y.C., 1969; pvt. practice specializing in oculoplastic surgery Denver, 1961—; clin. prof. U. Colo. Med. Ctr.; lectr. ophthalmic plastic surgery various med. ctrs. Contbr. articles to med. jours. With USNR, 1959-61. Mem. AMA, Denver Med. Soc., Colo. Med. Soc., Am. Soc. Ophthalmic Plastic and Reconstructive Surgery, Am. Acad. Ophthalmology (svc. award 1982), Colo. Ophthalmology Soc. Republican. Roman Catholic. Office: 2005 Franklin St Denver CO 80205-5401

WIGHT, JANET HOWELL, nurse; b. Elmira, N.Y., May 29, 1936; d. Wallace John and Katie Lee (Simmons) Howell; m. Leland Walter Wight Jr., June 21, 1958; children: Stephen, Pamela W. (Mrs. James Kirkpatrick), Julia W. (Mrs. Jonathan Coyle). AA, Elmira Coll., 1956; BSN, Columbia U., 1959; cert. pediat. nurse practitioner, U. Conn., 1973; MS, So. Conn. State U., 1980; postgrad., Yale Div. Sch., 1981-82. Ordained deacon Episcopal Ch., 1986. Staff nurse Vis. Nurse Svc., Rochester, N.Y., 1959-61; office nurse Pediatric Group, Chapel Hill, N.C., 1962-64; nurse practitioner Pediatric Assocs., New Haven, 1973-75; instr. pediatrics So. Conn. State U., New Haven, 1975-82; counselor Episcopal Social Svc., New Haven, 1982-85; pastoral counselor Pastoral Ctr., New Haven, 1985-88; supr. nurses New Haven Nursing Ctr., 1984-86; staff nurse Vis. Nurse Assn., New Haven, 1990—; chaplain New Haven Nursing Ctr., 1984-88; visitor, mem. steering com. Interfaith Vol. Caregivers, New Haven, 1985-90; vol. chaplain Yale New Haven Hosp., 1981-86. Vol. ARC, New Haven, 1968-78, Columbus House Soup Kitchen, New Haven, 1982-90; tutor Lit. Vols. Am., New Haven, 1991-92; breast cancer group leader Am. Cancer Soc., New Haven, 1987-88. Roman Catholic. Avocations: aerobics, walking, reading, piano, painting, photography. Home: 332 Berwick Ln New Haven CT 06515-2509

WIGHT, NANCY ELIZABETH, neonatologist; b. N.Y.C., Aug. 27, 1947; d. John Joseph and Gisela (Landers) Probst; m. Robert C.S. Wight, Oct. 1, 1988; 1 child, Robert C.S. II. Student, Cornell U., 1965-67; AB in Psychology, U. Calif., Berkeley, 1968; postgrad., George Washington U., 1971-72; MD, U. N.C., 1976. Diplomate Am. Bd. Pediatrics. Resident in pediatrics U. N.C., Chapel Hill, 1976-79; fellow in neonatal/perinatal medicine U. Calif., San Diego, 1979-81; clin. instr. Dept. of Pediatrics La. State U. Sch. of Medicine, Baton Rouge, 1982-86; neonatologist The Baton Rouge Neonatology Group, 1981-86; co-dir. neonatology, med. dir.

respiratory therapy Woman's Hosp., Baton Rouge, 1981-85; med. dir. newborn svcs., neonatal respiratory therapy HCA West Side Hosp. Centennial Med. Ctr., Nashville, 1986-88; staff pediatrician, neonatologist Balboa Naval Hosp., San Diego, 1988-89; attending neonatologist Sharp Meml. Hosp., San Diego, 1990—, Children's Hosp.-San Diego, 1990—; asst. clin. prof. U. Calif. San Diego, 1991—; physician assoc. La Leche League. Contbr. articles to profl. jours. mem. exec. bd. Capital Area Plantation chpt. March of Dimes, Baton Rouge, 1981-86, chmn. health adv. com., 1982-86; mem. health com. Capital Area United Way, Baton Rouge, 1982-86; bd. mem. Baton Rouge Coun. for Child Protection, 1983-86, NICU Parents, Baton Rouge, 1981-86; mem. health adv. com. Nashville Area March of Dime, 1987-88. Recipient Am. Med. Women's Assn. award. Mem. AMA, Am. Acad. Pediatrics, Calif. Med. Assn., So. Med. Assn., San Diego County Med. Assn., Calif. Perinatal Assn., So. Perinatal Assn., Nat. Perinatal Assn., La. Perinatal Assn. (past 1st v.p. and pres.), Internat. Lactation Cons. Assn. (cert.), Hastings Soc. Home: 3226 Newell St San Diego CA 92106-1918 Office: Children's Assoc Med Group 8001 Frost St San Diego CA 92123-2746

WIGHTMAN, ALEC, lawyer; b. Cleve., Jan. 23, 1951; s. John and Betty Jane (Follis) W.; m. Kathleen A. Little, June 19, 1976; children: Nora, Emily. BA, Duke U., 1972; JD, Ohio State U., 1975. Bar: Ohio 1975, U.S. Tax Ct. 1982, U.S. Ct. Appeals (6th cir.) 1983. Assoc. Krupman, Fromson & Henson, Columbus, Ohio, 1975-77; ptnr. Krupman, Fromson, Bownas & Wightman, Columbus, 1978-82; assoc. Baker & Hostetler, Columbus, 1982-83, ptnr., 1984—. Mem. ABA, Ohio Bar Assn., Columbus Bar Assn. (com. bankruptcy law), Ohio Oil and Gas Assn. Avocation: tennis. Office: Baker & Hostetler 65 E State St Ste 2100 Columbus OH 43215-4213

WIGHTMAN, ARTHUR STRONG, physicist, educator; b. Rochester, N.Y., Mar. 30, 1922; s. Eugene Pinckney and Edith Victoria (Stephenson) W.; m. Anna-Greta Larsson, Apr. 28, 1945 (dec. Feb. 11, 1976); 1 dau., Robin Letitia; m. Ludmilla Popova, Jan. 14, 1977. B.A., Yale, 1942; Ph.D., Princeton, 1949; D.Sc., Swiss Fed. Inst. Tech., Zurich, 1968, Göttingen U., 1987. Instr. physics Yale, 1943-44; from instr. to asso. prof. physics Princeton, 1949-60, prof. math. physics, 1960-92; prof. emeritus, 1992—; Thomas D. Jones prof. math. physics Princeton, 1971—; vis. prof. Sorbonne, 1957, École Polytechnique, 1977-78. Served to lt. (j.g.) USNR, 1944-46. NRC postdoctoral fellow Inst. Teoretisk Fysik, Copenhagen, Denmark, 1951-52; NSF sr. postdoctoral fellow, 1956-57; recipient Dannie Heineman prize math. physics, 1969. Fellow Am. Acad. Arts and Scis., Royal Acad. Arts; mem. Nat. Acad. Scis., Am. Math. Soc., Am. Phys. Soc., AAAS. Office: Princeton U 350 Jadwin Hall Princeton NJ 08544

WIGHTMAN, GLENN CHARLES, environmental, health and safety administrator; b. Abington, Pa., Apr. 1, 1961; s. Glenn Clayton and Margaret Ann (Wilkinson) W.; m. Lauren Marie Saraceni, June 29, 1985; 1 child, Margaret Elizabeth. BSCE cum laude, Bucknell U., 1983; MBA, Lehigh U., 1991. Registered profl. engr., Pa. Student engr. Bechtel Nat., Inc., Middletown, Pa., 1982; occupl. engr. AT&T Corp., Allentown, Pa., 1984-87, Berkeley Heights, N.J., 1987-90; sr. engr. AT&T Corp., Basking Ridge, N.J., 1990-93; tech. mgr. AT&T Corp., Morristown, N.J., 1993—; mem. Toxic Substances Control Act course faculty Govt. Insts., Inc., Rockville, Md., 1990-92. Contbr. articles to profl. jours. Recipient ednl. award Kodak, 1981. Mem. Am. Electronics Assn. (environ. and occupl. health com. 1990-92), Phi Eta Sigma, Tau Beta Pi, Beta Gamma Sigma. Democrat. Roman Catholic. Avocations: fitness, trombone, personal finance. Office: AT&T Corp Rm 3S-3B, 475 South St Morristown NJ 07962-1976

WIGHTMAN, LUDMILLA G. POPOVA, language educator, foreign educator, translator; b. Sofia, Bulgaria, Sept. 29, 1933; came to U.S., 1977; d. Genko Mateev and Liliana (Kusseva) Popov; m. Ivan Todorov Todorov, Aug. 13, 1957 (div. 1976); 1 child, Todor; m. Arthur Strong Wightman, Jan. 14, 1977. MS, U. Sofia, 1956. Cons. Nat. Libr., Sofia, 1956-58; rsch. assoc. Joint Inst. for Nuclear Rsch., Moscow, 1958-65; lectr. Russian Rutgers U., New Brunswick, N.J., 1969-70; editor Bulgarian Ency., Sofia, 1973-77; tchr. lang. Princeton (N.J.) Lang. Group, 1977—; libr. Firestone Libr., Princeton U., 1983-87. Translator: Introduction to Axiomatic Field Theory, 1975, New Eng. Rev., Bread Loaf Quar., 1987, Mr. Cogito, 1989, N.Y. Rev. Books, 1990, Poetry East, 1990-91, Literary Rev., 1992, Partisan Rev., 1996, Shifting Borders: East European Poetries of the Eighties, 1993. Avocations: bird watching, music, photography, travel. Home and Office: 16 Balsam Ln Princeton NJ 08540-5327

WIGHTMAN, THOMAS VALENTINE, rancher, researcher; b. Sacramento, Oct. 7, 1921; s. Thomas Valentine and Pearl Mae (Cutbirth) W.; m. Lan Do Wightman. Student, U. Calif., Berkeley, 1945-46; B of Animal Husbandry, U. Calif., Davis, 1949; student, Cal. Poly. Inst., 1949-50. Jr. aircraft mechanic SAD (War Dept.), Sacramento, Calif., 1940-42; rancher Wightman Ranch, Elk Grove, Calif., 1950-59; machinest Craig Ship-Bldg. Co., Long Beach, Calif., 1959-70; rancher Wightman Ranch, Austin, Nev., 1970-88; dir. Wightman Found., Sacramento, 1988—. Dir. med. rsch. Staff sgt. U.S. Army, 1942-45. Recipient scholarship U.S. Fed. Govt., 1945-50. Fellow NRA, VFW, U. Calif. Alumni Assn., U. Calif. Davis Alumni Assn., Bowles Hall Assn.; mem. Confederate Air Force, The Oxford Club. Republican. Avocations: antique automobiles and aircraft. Home and Office: Wightman Found PO Box 278016 Sacramento CA 95827-8016

WIGINGTON, RONALD LEE, retired chemical information services executive; b. Topeka, May 11, 1932; s. Oscar and Virginia C. (Ritchie) W.; m. Margaret E. Willey, Aug. 17, 1951; children: Linda, Carol, David, Brian. BS in Engring. Physics, U. Kans., 1953; MEE, U. Md., 1959; PhD in Elec. Engring., U. Kans., 1964; postgrad. in advanced mgmt. program, Harvard Bus. Sch., 1976-77. Tech. staff mem. Bell Telephone Labs., Murray Hill, N.J., 1953-54; div. chief Dept. Def., Washington, 1956-68; dir. rsch. and devel. Chem. Abstracts Svc., Am. Chem. Soc., Columbus, Ohio, 1968-84; dir. Washington ops. Am. Chem. Soc., 1984-86; chief exec. officer, dir. Chem. Abstracts Svc., Am. Chem. Soc., Columbus, 1986-91; dir. info. tech. Am. Chem. Soc., Columbus, 1991-94; chmn. bd. Online Computer Libr. Ctr., Dublin, Ohio, 1985-87, trustee, 1978-92. Contbr. articles to profl. jours. Pres., various positions PTA Prince George's County, Md., 1966-68; moderator, treas. Cmty. Assn. Upper Arlington (Ohio) Schs., 1970-74; mem. Upper Arlington Civic Orch., 1970-84, pres., 1973, 76; bd. dirs. Nat. Fedn. Abstracting and Info. Svcs., 1979-84, pres. 1982-83, hon. fellow 1995—; bd. dirs. Ohio Ctr. of Sci. and Industry, 1988-93; trustee Health Coalition of Ctrl. Ohio, Columbus, 1991—, treas., 1994—. With U.S. Army, 1954-56. Summerfield scholar U. Kans., 1949; recipient Nat. Capital award D.C. Council Engring. and Archtl. Socs., 1967, Meritorious Civilian Service award Dept. Defense, 1967. Mem. IEEE (sr.), Am. Chem. Soc., Internat. Coun. Sci. and Tech. Info. (exec. bd. 1986-94, treas. 1992-94), Material Property Data Network (bd. dirs. 1987-94), Sigma Xi. Avocations: gardening, music. Home: 2470 Wimbledon Rd Columbus OH 43220-4212

WIGMORE, BARRIE ATHERTON, investment banker; b. Moose Jaw, Sask., Can., Apr. 11, 1941; came to U.S., 1970; s. Fred Henry and Pauline Elizabeth (Atherton) W.; m. Deedee Dawson, Aug. 24, 1964. B. Edn., U. Sask., Can., 1962, B.A., 1963; M.A., U. Oreg., 1964; B.A., Oxford U., Eng., 1966, M.A., 1971. Investment banker A.E. Ames & Co. Ltd., Toronto, Ont., Can., 1966-70; investment banker Goldman, Sachs & Co., N.Y.C., 1970—; bd. dirs. Potash Corp. Sask., Fibre Body Industries Inc. Author: The Crash and Its Aftermath, A History of U.S. Securities Markets 1929-33, 1985. Trustee Progressive Policy Inst., Dem. Leadership Coun., Am. Friends of Worcester Coll. (Oxford U.) Inc. Democrat. Avocations: politics, financial history. Home: 1 W 72nd St New York NY 10023 Office: Goldman Sachs & Co 85 Broad St New York NY 10004-2434

WIGMORE, JOHN GRANT, lawyer; b. L.A., Mar. 14, 1928; s. George Theodore and Mary (Grant) W.; m. Dina Burnaby, July 27, 1968 (dec. 1994); children: Alexander Trueblood, Adam Trueblood, John G. Jr., Mary. BS in Geology, Stanford U., 1949; JD, UCLA, 1958. Geologist Western Geophys., Calif., Colo., Mo., 1953-55; assoc. Lawler, Felix & Hall, L.A., 1958-62, ptnr., 1963-86; ptnr. Pillsbury, Madison & Sutro, L.A., 1986—; lectr. in field. Contbr. articles to profl. jours. Trustee, gov. L.A. County Mus. Natural History, 1970—; participant various local & state election campaigns, 1965-80. Officer USN, 1950-53. Fellow Am. Coll. Trial Lawyers, Am. Bar Found.; mem. ABA (chair litigation com. antitrust sect. 1970-74), Calif. State Bar (L.A. County bar del. 1965-75), L.A. County Bar Assn. (exec. com. trial sect. 1965-68), L.A. County Bus. Trial Lawyers (exec. com. 1984-87), Barristers (exec. com. 1960-65). Home: 114 Madison Ave PO Box 1328 Ketchem ID 83340 also: 870 Neptune Ave Encinitas CA 92024-2062 Office: Pillsbury Madison & Sutro Citicorp Plz 725 S Figueroa St Ste 1200 Los Angeles CA 90017-5443

WIGTON, PAUL NORTON, steel company consultant, former executive; b. Linesville, Pa., Aug. 13, 1932; s. Charles and Viola Grace (Dennis) W.; m. Janet Ohl, July 11, 1953; children: Bruce, Douglas. BS in Chemistry, Youngstown State U., 1957a; postgrad. exec. mgmt. program, MIT, 1974; hon. doctorate, Youngstown State U., 1980. Gen. supt. metal services Republic Steel Corp., Warren, Ohio, 1971-73, asst. to dist. mgr., 1973-75, dist. mgr., 1975-78; asst. v.p. ops. Republic Steel Corp., Cleve., 1978-80, v.p. steel ops., 1980-83, v.p., gen. mgr. flat rolled product group, 1983-84; pres. tubular products LTV Steel, 1984-91, ret., 1991; mem. Sr. Cons. Network Co., Inc., Beachwood, Ohio, 1991-92; prin. Paul N. Wigton & Assocs. Consultants, Sarasota, Fla., 1992—. Served to cpl. U.S. Army, 1953-54. Scholar Henry Roemer Found., 1957; scholar Am. Chem. Soc., 1957; named Industrialist of Yr. Mahoning Valley Econ. Devel. Corp., 1981, Mgr. of Yr., Mahoning Valley Econ. Devel. Corp., 1992. Mem. AIME, Am. Iron and Steel Inst., Assn. Iron and Steel Engrs. (nat. pres. 1988). Presbyterian. Clubs: Tournament Players (Prestancia-Sarasota, Fla.). Home: 3826 Torrey Pines Way Sarasota FL 34238-2839 Office: Paul N Wigton & Assocs Consultants 3826 Torrey Pines Way Sarasota FL 34238-2839

WIIG, ELISABETH HEMMERSAM, audiologist, educator; b. Esbjert, Denmark, May 22, 1935; came to U.S., 1957, naturalized, 1967; d. Svend Frederick and Ingeborg (Hemmersam) Nielsen; m. Karl Martin Wiig, June 10, 1958; children—Charlotte E., Erik D. B.A., Statsseminariet Emdrupborg, 1956; M.A., Western Res. U., 1960; Ph.D., Case Western Res. U., 1967; postgrad., U. Mich., 1967-68. Clin. audiologist Cleve. Hearing and Speech Center, 1959-60; instr. dept. phonetics Bergen (Norway) U., 1960-64; asst. prof., dir. aphasia rehab. program U. Mich., 1968-70; asst. prof. Boston U., 1970-73, asso. prof., chmn. dept., 1973-77, prof. dept. communication disorders, 1977-87, prof. emerita, 1987—; v.p. EDUCOM Assocs. Inc., 1992-93. Author: Language Disabilities in Children and Adolescents, 1976, Language Assessment and Intervention for the Learning Disabled, 1980, 84, CELF Screening Tests: Elementary and Secondary Levels, 1980, Clinical Evaluation of Language Fundamentals, rev. edit., 1987, Clinical Evaluation of Language Fundamentals 3, 1995, Test of Language Competence, 1985, expanded edit., 1989, Test of Word Knowledge, 1992, Clinical Evaluation of Language Fundamentals Preschool, 1992; editor: Human Communication Disorders: An Introduction, 1982, 86, 90, 94; contbr. articles to profl. jours. Recipient Metcalf Cup and Prize for excellence in teaching Boston U., 1967. Fellow Am. Speech and Hearing Assn. (cert. clin. competence in speech pathology and audiology); mem. Coun. for Learning Disabilities, Coun. for Exceptional Children, Internat. Assn. for Rsch. on Learning Disabilities, Am. Psychol. Soc. Address: 5211 Vicksburg Dr Arlington TX 76017-4941

WIIN-NIELSEN, AKSEL CHRISTOPHER, meteorologist educator; b. Juelsminde, Denmark, Dec. 17, 1924; emigrated to U.S., 1959; s. Aage Nielsen and Marie Christophersen; m. Bente Havsteen Zimsen, Dec. 5, 1953; children: Charlotte, Barbro Marianne, Karen Margrete. BS in Math, U. Copenhagen, Denmark, 1947, MS in Math, 1950; Fil. Lic. in Meteorology, U. Stockholm, Sweden, 1957, PhD in Meteorology, 1960; DSc (h.c.), U. Reading, 1981; DSc (honoris causa), U. Copenhagen, 1986. Staff meteorologist Danish Meteorol. Inst., 1952-55; research meteorologist Internat. Meteorol. Inst. U. Stockholm, 1955-58, asst. prof. Internat. Meteorol. Inst., 1957-58, exec. editor publ. Internat. Meteorol. Inst., Tellus, 1957-58; research meteorologist Air Weather Service, USAF; also staff mem. joint numerical weather prediction unit and lectr. George Washington U., 1959-61; research staff mem. Nat. Center Atmospheric Research, 1961-62, asst. dir., 1962-63; prof., chmn. dept. meteorology and oceanography U. Mich., 1963-71; prof. theoretical meteorology U. Bergen, Norway, 1971-72, U. Mich., 1972-74; dir. European Centre for Medium-Range Weather Forecasts, 1974-79; sec. gen. World Meteorol. Orgn., 1980-83; dir. Danish Meteorol. Inst., 1984-87; prof. U. Copenhagen, 1988-94; pres. Internat. Commn. for Dynamic Meteorology, 1971-79; chmn. working group on numerical experimentation, also mem. joint organizing com. Global Atmospheric Research Program, 1973-79; chmn. working group on earth scis., sci. adv. com. European Space Agy., 1977-79; sci. adv. com. Max Planck Inst. Meteorology, Hamburg, W. Ger.; v.p. Eumetsat Council, 1986-87; v.p. Council for European Ctr. for Medium-Range Weather Forecasts, 1985-86, pres., 1986-87; vis. scientist Nat. Ctr. Atmosphere Res., 1987; vis. prof. U. Mich., 1988; chmn. NATO-Panel on The Sci. of Global Environ. Changes, 1990-92. Recipient Ohridski medal Sofia (Bulgaria) U., 1980; Buys-Ballot medal Acad. Sci., Netherlands, 1981; Wihuri prize, Finland, 1983; Rossby prize Swedish Geophys. Soc., 1985, Friedman Rescue award, 1993. Fellow Am. Meteorol. Soc. (hon.); mem. Am. Geophys. Union, Swedish Acad. Sci., Royal Meteorol. Soc. (hon.), Finnish Acad. Arts and Scis., Euopean Geophys. Soc. (pres. 1988-90), Danish Acad. Tech. Scis. (v.p. 1989-92), Royal Danish Soc. Scis., N.Y. Acad. Scis., Tau Beta Pi. Home: Solbakken 6, 3230 Grasted Denmark

WIKANDER, LAWRENCE EINAR, librarian; b. Pitts., Dec. 16, 1915; s. Oscar Ragnar and Mary Edna (Gerdes) W.; m. Ethel Marie Whitlow, Nov. 23, 1940; children: Frederick Whitlow, Matthew Hays. B.A., Williams Coll., 1937; B.S. in Library Sci, Columbia U., 1939; M.A., U. Pa., 1949. Gen. asst. Carnegie Library, Pitts., 1939-40; supr. circulation Mt. Pleasant Br., D.C. Public Library, Washington, 1940-42; asst. librarian Temple U., Phila., 1946-50; librarian Forbes Library, Northampton, Mass., 1950-68; librarian Williams Coll., Williamstown, Mass., 1968-82, librarian emeritus, 1982—; curator Calvin Coolidge Meml. Room Forbes Library, Northampton, Mass., 1982-93. Author: Disposed to Learn, 1972, Completing a Century: History of the Northampton Social and Literary Club, 1962, Calvin Coolidge: A Chronological Summary, 1957; editor: The Hampshire History, 1962, The Northampton Book, 1954, A Guide to the Personal Files of Calvin Coolidge, 1986, (with Robert H. Ferrell) Grace Coolidge: An Autobiography, 1992. Pres. Northampton Community Chest, 1958-60; bd. dirs. Civil Liberties Union Mass., Hampshire, 1957-68; trustee Calvin Coolidge Meml. Found., 1969—; dir. South Mountain Concert Assn., 1975—; clk. Northampton Hist. Soc., 1955-68; dir. Hampshire Inter-Library Center, 1956-68. Served to capt. AUS, 1942-46. Mem. Am. Library Assn. (mem. council 1962-68), New Eng. Library Assn. (pres. 1967-68), Mass. Library Assn. (pres. 1960-61), Western Mass. Library Club (pres. 1953-55). Home: 21 Cluett Dr Williamstown MA 01267-2804

WIKSTEN, BARRY FRANK, communications executive; b. Seattle, June 23, 1935; s. Frank Alfred and Alice Gertrude (Ensor) W.; m. Madeleine Schmeil, Nov. 23, 1979; children: Karen Anne, Eric Marshal, Kurt Edward. BA, Miami U., Oxford, Ohio, 1960; MA, Fletcher Sch. Law and Diplomacy, 1961. Dir. econ. programs U.S. Council, Internat. C. of C., N.Y.C., 1962-63; with TWA, N.Y.C., 1964-79, dir. fin. relations, 1972, v.p. pub. affairs, 1973, v.p. pub. rels., 1973-76, sr. v.p. pub. affairs, mem. airline policy bd., 1976-79; v.p. corp. adminstrn. Trans World Corp., 1979-82, also sec. corp. policy com., mem. consumer affairs com. and corp. compensation com.; sr. v.p. communications CIGNA Corp., Phila., 1982-84, sr. v.p. pub. affairs, 1984—; bd. dirs. Sta. WHYY, Phila. Served with USMC, 1954-57. Mem. Bus. Roundtable (pub. info. com.), Conf. Bd. (pub. affairs rsch. coun.), Pub. Rels. Seminar, Wisemen, Ind. Hall Assn. (bd. dirs.), Union League Club (N.Y.), The Athenaeum (Phila.). Office: CIGNA Corp 1650 Market St 1 Liberty Pl Philadelphia PA 19192-1550

WILBANKS, JAN JOSEPH, philosopher; b. Lynchburg, Ohio, Dec. 17, 1928; s. James Odell and Bernice Elizabeth (Daugherty) W.; m. Alice Ramona Pacheco, Nov. 14, 1953; children—Elise, Anita, Jennifer. B.S., Cin. Coll. Pharmacy, 1951; Ph.D. in Philosophy, Ohio State U., 1964. Instr. Purdue U., 1961-64; mem. faculty Marietta (Ohio) Coll., 1964-89, prof. philosophy, 1973-89. Author: Hume's Theory of Imagination, 1968, also articles. With AUS, 1951-53. Home: 122 High St Marietta OH 45750-2636

WILBER, CHARLES GRADY, forensic science educator, consultant; b. Waukesha, Wis., June 18, 1916; s. Charles Bernard and Charlotte Agnes (Grady) W.; m. Ruth Mary Bodden, July 12, 1944 (dec. 1950); children: Maureen, Charles Bodden, Michael; m. Clare Marie O'Keefe, June 14, 1952; children: Thomas Grady (dec.), Kathleen, Aileen, John Joseph. BSc, Marquette U., 1938; MA, Johns Hopkins U., 1941, PhD, 1942. Asst. prof. physiology Fordham U., 1945-49; assoc. prof. physiology, dir. biol. labs. St. Louis U., 1949-52; leader Arctic expdns., 1943-44, 48, 50, 51; physiologist Chem. Corps, U.S. Army, 1952-61; assoc. physiology and pharmacology U. Pa., 1953-61, chief comparative physiology, 1956-61; profl. lectr. biol. scis. Loyola Coll., Balt., 1957-61; dir. Loyola Coll. (In-Service Inst. Sci. Tchrs.), 1958-61; prof. biol. scis., univ. rsch. coord., dean Grad. Sch. Kent State U., 1961-64; dir. marine laboratories U. Del., 1964-67; chmn., prof. dept. zoology Colo. State U., 1967-73, prof., 1967-87, emeritus prof. and chmn., 1987—, dir. forensic sci. lab., 1965—; dep. coroner Larimer County, Colo., 1968-78; pres. Manresa Co., 1978—; mem. Ctr. for Human Identification; expert witness fed. and state cts. on poisons, firearms, others; life mem. Marine Biol. Lab., Woods Hole, Mass., 1947—; mem. U.S. Army Panel Environ. Physiology, 1952-61; mem. study group Nat. Acad. Scis.-USAF, 1958-61; Wellcome vis. prof. basic med. scis. Ohio U. Med. Sch., 1983-84; vis. lectr. Am. Inst. Biol. Scis., 1957—. Author: Biological Aspects of Water Pollution, 2d edit, 1971, Japanese edit., 1970, Forensic Biology for the Law Enforcement Officer, 1975, Contemporary Violence, 1975, Ballistic Science for the Law Enforcement Officer, 1977, Medicolegal Investigation of The President John F. Kennedy Murder, 1978, Chemical Trauma from Pesticides, 1979, Forensic Toxicology, 1980, Beryllium, 1980, Agent Orange, 1980; Author: Turbidity, 1983, Selenium, 1983; contbr. articles to profl. jours.; exec. editor: Adaption to the Environment, vol. in series, 1962; editor: Am. Lecture Series in Environ. Studies; mem. editorial bd.: Am. Jour. Forensic Medicine and Pathology; contbr.: Harper Ency. Nat. Capt. USAAF, 1942-46; col. USAF, ret. Disting. scholar in criminal justice Albany State Coll., 1993. Fellow N.Y. Acad. Scis., Am. Acad. Forensic Sci.; mem. Am. Physiol. Soc., Cosmos Club (Washington), Phi Beta Kappa, Sigma Xi, Phi Sigma, Gamma Alpha. Republican. Roman Catholic. Home: 900 Edwards St Fort Collins CO 80524-3824 Office: Colo State U Dept Biology Fort Collins CO 80523 *The accident of history which has enabled me to study as I wished, work at what I enjoyed, and live as I chose is a mystery for which I must be eternally thankful.*

WILBER, DAVID JAMES, cardiologist; b. Ft. Atkinson, Wis., Apr. 1, 1951; s. Howard Spencer and Leona (Von Reuden) W.; m. Sandra Irene Reynertson, June 28, 1992. BS, U. Wis., 1973; MD, Northwestern U., 1977. Intern medicine Northwestern Meml. Hosps., 1977-80; fellow cardiology U. Mich., 1982-84; fellow electrophysiology Mass. Gen. Hosp., Boston, 1984-86; asst. prof. medicine Loyola U., Maywood, Ill., 1986-90, assoc. prof. medicine, 1990-94; prof. medicine U. Chgo., 1994—. Fellow Am. Coll. Cardiology, Am. Heart Assn. Office: Univ Chgo Hosps Sect Cardiology MC2080 5841 S Maryland Ave Chicago IL 60637

WILBER, ROBERT EDWIN, corporate executive; b. Boston, Dec. 15, 1932; s. Charles Edwin and Mary Charles (Gay) W.; m. Bonnie Marilyn Jones; children: Debra, Kathleen, Robert Jr., Thomas, Jeffrey, Mark, Matthew. BSBA in Acctg., Bowling Green State U., 1954. CPA, Mass., Tex. Sr. acct. Peat, Marwick, Mitchell and Co., Boston, 1954-58; gen. mgr. Door Controls Inc., Boston, 1958-59; asst. controller MKM Knitting Mills Inc., Manchester, N.H., 1959-63; internal audit supr. Raytheon Co., Lexington, Mass., 1963; asst. treas. Glens Falls (N.Y.) Ins. Co., 1963-66; controller Pnobscott Co., Boston, 1966-67; v.p. fin. and adminstrn. S.S. Pierce Co., Boston, 1967-73, Samson Ocean Systems Inc., Boston, 1973-79; v.p., chief acctg. officer Enserch Corp., Dallas, 1979-88; pres. Trade U.S.A., 1990—. Mem. Rep. Nat. Com. Mem. AICPAs, Nat. Assn. Trade Exchanges, Tex. Soc. CPAs, Mass. Soc. CPAs, , Fin. Execs. Inst., Inter City Assn., Pres.'s Club (Bowling Green, Ohio). Republican. Home: 5804 Goliad Ave Dallas TX 75206-6818 Office: 5740 Prospect Ave Dallas TX 75206-7286

WILBUR, BRAYTON, JR., distribution company executive; b. San Francisco, Oct. 2, 1935; s. Brayton and Matilda (Baker) W.; m. Judith Flood, June 29, 1963; children: Jennifer, Edward, Claire, Michael. B.A., Yale U., 1957; M.B.A., Stanford U., 1961. With Arthur Young & Co., San Francisco, 1962-63; v.p. Wilbur-Ellis Co., San Francisco, 1963-74, exec. v.p., 1974—, also dir.; dir. Chronicle Pub. Co., San Francisco, 1983-89; pres. Wilbur-Ellis Co., San Francisco, 1989—; bd. dir. Safeway Stores, 1977-86. Pres. San Francisco Symphony, 1980-87; v.p. Sponsors for Performing Arts Ctr., San Francisco, 1975—; trustee Fine Art Mus. of San Francisco, 1978-81, Asia Found., 1972—, chmn. 1990—. Served with USAR, 1958-63. Mem. Council on Fgn. Relations, Bohemian Club, Pacific Union Club, Cypress Point Club, Burlingame Country Club. Republican. Home: 821 Irwin Dr Burlingame CA 94010-6327 Office: Wilbur-Ellis Co 320 California St San Francisco CA 94104-1403*

WILBUR, COLBURN SLOAN, foundation administrator, chief executive officer; b. Palo Alto, Calif., Jan. 20, 1935; s. Blake Colburn and Mary (Sloan) W.; m. Maria Grace Verburg, Sept. 1, 1961; children: Marguerite Louise, Anne Noelle. BA in Polit. Sci., Stanford U., 1956, MBA, 1960. Asst. cashier United Calif. Bank, San Francisco, 1960-65; v.p. Standata, San Francisco, 1965-68; adminstrv. mgr. Tab Products, San Francisco, 1968-69; exec. dir. Sierra Club Found., San Francisco, 1969-76, David and Lucile Packard Found., Los Altos, Calif., 1976—; bd. dirs., mem. adv. bd. Coun. Founds., Washington, Found. Ctr., N.Y.C. Former bd. dirs., mem. adv bd. Global Fund Women, Palo Alto, Calif.; past bd. dirs. Big Bros. San Francisco, Calif. Confederation Arts, Peninsula Grantmakers, Women's Fund Santa Clara; former bd. dirs., pres. Big Bros. Peninsula, North Fork Assn., Peninsula Conservation Ctr.; past bd. dirs., chmn. No. Calif. Grantmakers; bd. dirs., mem. adv. bd. Sierra Club Found., Stanford Theater Found., Palo Alto, U. San Francisco/Inst. Nonprofit Orgn. Mgmt. With U.S. Army, 1957-58. Office: David and Lucile Packard Found 300 2nd St Los Altos CA 94022-3621

WILBUR, DWIGHT LOCKE, retired physician; b. Harrow-on-the-Hill, Eng., Sept. 18, 1903; came to U.S., 1904; s. Ray Lyman and Marguerite May (Blake) W.; m. Ruth Esther Jordan, Oct. 20, 1928; children—Dwight L., Jordan R., Gregory F. A.B., Stanford U., 1923; M.D., U. Pa., 1926; M.S. in Medicine, U. Minn.-Mpls., 1933; D.Sc. (hon.), Dartmouth Coll., 1973. Diplomate Am. Bd. Internal Medicine. Intern, U. Pa. Hosp., Phila., 1926-28; resident, Mayo Found., Rochester, Minn., 1929-31; staff Mayo Clinic, Rochester, 1931-37; clin. prof. medicine Stanford U., Calif., 1937-68; pvt. practice medicine, San Francisco, 1937-83; physician U.S. Naval Res., Oakland, Calif., 1942-46; clin. prof. medicine emeritus Stanford U., 1968—. Editor, Calif. Medicine, 1946-67. Author (with J.R. Gamble): Chemistry of Digestive Diseases, 1961, Current Concepts of Clinical Gastroenterology, 1965. Contbr. articles to profl. jours. Trustee Mayo Found., 1951-71, emeritus, 1971—. Served to comdr., USNR, 1942-46. Recipient Julius Friedenwald medal, Am. Gastroenterol. Assn., 1961; Spl. Commendation for Outstanding Achievement, U. Minn., 1964; Outstanding Civilian Service medal, Dept. Army, 1966; First Disting. Internist award, Am. Soc. Internal Medicine, 1970. Mem. Calif. Med. Assn. (hon. past pres.), Inst. Medicine Nat. Acad. Scis. (charter), ACP (charter, Alfred Stengel Meml. award 1964, pres. 1958-59, fellow), AMA (pres. 1968-69), Am. Gastroenterologic Assn. (pres. 1954-55). Republican. Club: Commonwealth, Bohemian. Home: 140 Sea Cliff Ave San Francisco CA 94121-1125

WILBUR, E. PACKER, investment company executive; b. Bridgeport, Conn., Sept. 9, 1936; s. E. Packer and Elizabeth (Wells) W.; m. Laura Mary Ferrier, Sept. 17, 1965; children—Alison Mary, Andrew Packer, Gillian Elizabeth. B.A., Yale U., 1959; M.B.A., Harvard U., 1965. Cons. McKinsey & Co. Inc., N.Y.C., 1964-67; dir. corp. planning Am. Express Co., N.Y.C., 1967-69; v.p. Van Alstyne Noel & Co., N.Y.C., 1969-70; exec. v.p., dir., mem. exec. com. Newburger Loeb & Co. Inc., N.Y.C., 1970-73; pres. E.P. Wilbur & Co., Inc., Southport, Conn., 1973—, Southport Fin. Corp., 1986—; chmn. bd. Criterion Mgmt., Inc., Lafayette, Ind., Trend Mgmt., Inc., Tampa, Fla., Fairfield Advisors, Inc., Southport, EPW Securities, Inc., Southport; gen. ptnr. Grandland Realty Assos., English Oaks Apts., Embankment Properties Ltd., London, Pepper Hill Townhouses, Kemar Townhouse Assos., Autumn Woods Assos., Country Villa Assos., others; former allied mem. N.Y. Stock Exchange. Contbr. articles to fin. jours. Bd. dirs. Harvard Inst. for Social and Econ. Policy in the Middle East, Inst. Govt. Assested Housing, Washington, Mus. Art, Sci., Industry, Bridgeport, Wakeman Meml. Boys' Club, Southport, Greater Bridgeport Jr. Hockey League, Pequot Library, Southport, Bridgeport U., Northfield-Mt. Hermon Sch. Served AUS, 1959-60. Clubs: Pequot Yacht (Southport),

Pequot Running (Southport) (chmn.); Country Club of Fairfield; Yale (N.Y.C.). Home: 648 Harbor Rd Southport CT 06490-1321 Office: 2507 Post Rd Southport CT 06490-1259

WILBUR, HENRY MILES, zoologist, educator; b. Bridgeport, Conn., Jan. 25, 1944; s. Robert Leonard and Martha (Miles) W.; m. Dorothy Spates, Jan. 27, 1967 (div. Dec. 1980); 1 child, Sarah; m. Rebecca Burchell, May 22, 1981; children: Helen, Lindsay. BS, Duke U., 1966; PhD, U. Mich., 1971. Asst. prof. Duke U., Durham, N.C., 1973-77, assoc. prof., 1977-81, prof., 1981-91, chmn., 1990-91; B.F.D. Runk prof. U. Va., Charlottesville, 1991—; dir. Mt. Lake Biol. Sta., Charlottesville, 1991—. Assoc. editor Ecol. Soc. Am., Soc. Study of Evolution, Soc. Am. Naturalists. Recipient Disting. Herpetologist Herpetologists League, 1990. Mem. Am. Soc. Icthyologists and Herpetologists, Am. Soc. Naturalists (treas., pres. 1996), Ecol. Soc. Am. (MacArthur award 1995), Soc. of Study of Evolution, Herpetologists League, Brit. Ecol. Soc. Office: U Va Dept Biology Gilmer Hall Charlottesville VA 22903-2477

WILBUR, JAMES BENJAMIN, III, philosopher, educator; b. Hartford, Conn., Feb. 21, 1924; s. James Benjamin, Jr. and Martha (Shekosky) W.; m. Margie Mattmiller, July 9, 1949; children: James Benjamin IV, Ann Elizabeth. B.A., U. Ky., 1948; postgrad., Harvard, 1948-50; M.A., Columbia, 1951, Ph.D., 1954. Mem. faculty Adelphi U., Garden City, N.Y., 1952-64; chmn. philosophy dept. Adelphi U., 1954-64, asst. prof., 1954-59, assoc. prof., 1959-64; assoc. prof. U. Akron, Ohio, 1964-66; prof. U. Akron, 1966-68, chmn. philosophy dept., 1964-68; prof. philosophy SUNY Coll. Arts and Sci., Geneseo, 1968-90; chmn. philosophy dept. SUNY Coll. Arts and Sci., 1968-78; founder, co-dir. Confs. on Value Inquiry, 1967-90; vis. prof. U. Kent, Canterbury, Eng., spring 1971; faculty adviser Empire State Coll., 1972-74. Author: (with H.J. Allen) The Worlds of Hume and Kant, 1967, 2d rev. edit., 1981, The Worlds of Plato and Aristotle, 1962, 2d rev. edit., 1979, The Worlds of the Early Greek Philosophers, 1979, The Moral Foundations of Business Practice, 1992; editor, contbr.; (with B. Magnus) Cartesian Essays (M. Nijhoff), 1969, Spinoza's Metaphysics (Van Gorcum), 1976; co-editor: (with E. Laszlo) Human Values and Natural Science, 1970, Values and the Mind of Man, 1971, Value Theory in Philosophy and Social Science (Gordon and Breach), 1971, Value and the Arts, 1978, The Dynamics of Value Change, 1978; editor: Human Value and Economic Activity, 1979, The Life Sciences and Human Values, 1979, Human Values and the law, 1980, Values in the Law, 1980, Ethics and Management, 1983, Integration of Ethics into Business Education, 1984, Integrating Ethics into Business Education, 1983; contbn. Self-interest Dictionary of Business Ethics, 1995, others. Served with AUS, 1943-45. SUNY grantee, 1969, 70; NEH grantee, 1981; Western Electric Fund awardee, 1983. Mem. AAUP, Am. Metaphys. Soc., L.I. Philos. Soc. (founder 1963), Creighton Club (pres. 1970-72), Rochester Oratorio Soc., Am. Soc. Value Inquiry (sec.-treas. 1971, pres. 1973-74, founder Jour. Value Inquiry 1967, exec. editor 1967-90, assoc. editor 1990—), Vt. Hist. Soc., Manchester Hist. Soc. (pres. 1991-94), Hudson (Ohio) Country Club (founding trustee, hon. life mem.), Ekwanok Country Club (Manchester), Harvard Club (N.Y.C.). Home: PO Box 376 Manchester VT 05254-0376

WILBUR, LESLIE CLIFFORD, mechanical engineering educator; b. Johnston, R.I., May 12, 1924; s. Clifford Elwood and Isabel (Winsor) W.; m. Gertrude Monica Widmer, Sept. 9, 1950; children—Clifford Leslie, Kenneth Charles, Ted Winsor, Christopher Francis. B.S. in Mech. Engring, U. R.I., 1948; M.S., Stevens Inst. Tech., 1949. Registered profl. engr., Mass. Instr., then asst. prof. Duke, 1949-57; mem. faculty Worcester Poly. Inst., 1957—, prof. mech. engring., 1961—, dir. nuclear reactor facility, 1959-86, prof. emeritus, 1987—; Mem. N.E. adv. council Atomic Indsl. Forum, 1972—. Editor-in-chief: Handbook of Energy Systems. Served with AUS, 1943-46, ETO. Mem. Am. Nuclear Soc. (mem. at large exec. com. Northeastern sect. 1961-62, 66-67, chmn. Northeastern sect. 1968-69), ASME (vice chmn. Eastern N.C. sect. 1956-57), Am. Soc. Engring. Edn., AAAS, Sigma Xi, Tau Beta Pi, Phi Kappa Phi, Pi Tau Sigma. Baptist (deacon 1962-65). Home: PO Box 105 Sebasco Estates ME 04565-0105 also (winter): 94 Parkway N Brewer ME 04412-1235 Office: Worcester Poly Inst Dept Mech Engring Ed Worcester MA 01609

WILBUR, LYMAN DWIGHT, consulting engineering executive; b. L.A., Apr. 27, 1900; s. Curtis Dwight and Olive (Doolittle) W.; m. Henrietta Shattuck, July 6, 1925 (dec.May 1984); 1 child, Olive Gamble Waugh; m. Pauline Jordan, Apr. 26, 1985 (dec. Mar. 1995). AB, Stanford U., 1921; LLD (hon.), Coll. Idaho, 1962; DSc (hon.), U. Idaho, 1967. Field engr. Hetch Hetchy Project, City of San Francisco, 1921-24; designer Merced (Calif.) Irrigation Dist., 1924-26; design engr. East Bay Mcpl. Utility Dist., Oakland, Calif., 1926-29; asst. to chief cons. engr. Mid. Asia Water Economy Svc., Tashkent, USSR, 1929-31; from engr. to dist. mgr. Morrison-Knudsen Co. Inc., L.A., 1932-47; chief engr. Morrison-Knudsen Co. Inc., Boise, 1947-52, v.p., 1950-70; constrn. mgr. Morrison-Knudsen-Ford Twaits Cos., Camp Roberts, Calif., 1939-40, Morrison-Knudsen-Peter Kiewit Cos., Camp White, Oreg., 1942; resident ptnr. Atlas Constructors, Casablanca, 1952-54, RMK-BRJ, Saigon, Republic of Vietnam, 1965-66; exec. v.p. Internat. Engring. Co. Inc., San Francisco, 1956-58, pres.-chmn., 1958-70; pvt. practice cons. engr., Boise, 1971—. Chmn. Blue Cross Idaho, Boise, 1977; pres. Good Samaritan League Inc., Boise, 1982-91; trustee Coll. of Idaho, Caldwell, 1981-92; bd. dirs. St. Alphonsus Med. Ctr. Found., Boise, 1980-88. Recipient Golden Beaver award The Beavers, L.A., 1962, Constrn. Man of Yr. award Engring. News Record, N.Y.C., 1966, John Fritz medal Five Founder Engring. Socs., 1973, Moles award The Moles, N.Y.C., 1974, Ann. award NSPE, 1975. Fellow ASCE (hon., chmn. exec. com. constrn. divsn. 1960, chmn. Pacific N.W. coun. 1973), Idaho Soc. Profl. Engrs. (sec./treas. 1972-74), Soc. Am. Mil. Engrs., Arid Club, Hillcrest Club, Rotary Internat. Republican. Presbyterian. Avocations: philately, photography. Address: 4502 Hillcrest Dr Boise ID 83705-2857

WILBUR, RICHARD PURDY, writer, educator; b. N.Y.C., Mar. 1, 1921; s. Lawrence L. and Helen (Purdy) W.; m. Mary Charlotte Hayes Ward, June 20, 1942; children: Ellen Dickinson, Christopher Hayes, Nathan Lord, Aaron Hammond. AB, Amherst Coll., 1942, AM, 1952, DLitt (hon.), 1967; AM, Harvard U., 1947; LHD (hon.), Lawrence Coll., Washington U., Williams Coll., U. Rochester, SUNY, Potsdam, 1986, Skidmore Coll., 1987, U. Lowell, 1990; DLitt (hon.), Clark U.; DLitt, Am. Internat. Coll., Marquette U., Wesleyan U., Carnegie-Mellon U.; D.Litt. (hon.), Lake Forest Coll., 1982; hon. degree, Smith Coll., 1996; LittD (hon.), Sewanee U., 1996. Jr. fellow Harvard U., Cambridge, Mass., 1947-50, Asst. prof. English, 1950-54; assoc. prof. Wellesley Coll., 1955-57; prof. Wesleyan U., 1957-77; writer in residence Smith Coll., 1977-86. Author: The Beautiful Changes, 1947, Ceremony, 1950, A Bestiary, 1955, reprint, 1993, Things of This World, 1956, Poems 1943-56, 1957, Advice to a Prophet, 1961, Poems of Richard Wilbur, 1963, Walking to Sleep, 1969, The Mind-Reader, 1976, Seven Poems, 1981, The Whale, 1982, New and Collected Poems, 1988 (Pulitzer prize for poetry 1989); (children's books) Loudmouse, 1963, Opposites, 1973, More Opposites, 1991, A Game of Catch, 1994, Runaway Opposites, 1995; (criticism) Responses, 1976; co-author: (comic opera, with Lillian Hellman) Candide, 1957, (cantata, with William Schuman) On Freedom's Ground, 1986; translator: (Moliere) The Misanthrope, 1955, Tartuffe, 1963 (co-recipient Bollingen Translation prize 1963), The School for Wives, 1971, The Learned Ladies, 1978, Four Comedies, 1982, (Racine) Andromache, 1982, Phaedra, 1986, Molière's The School for Husbands, 1992, Imaginary Cuckold, 1993, Molière's Amphitryon, 1995; editor: Complete Poems of Poe, 1959, Poems of Shakespeare, 1966, Selected Poems of Witter Bynner, 1978. Decorated chevalier Ordre des Palmes Academiques; recipient Harriet Monroe prize Poetry mag., 1948, Oscar Blumenthal prize, 1950, Prix de Rome, Am. Acad. Arts and Letters, 1954, Edna St. Vincent Millay Meml. award, 1957, Nat. Book award, 1957, Pulitzer prize, 1957, Sarah Josepha Hale award, 1968, Bollingen prize, 1971, Brandeis U. Creative Arts award, 1971, Prix Henri Desfeuilles, 1971, Shelley Meml. award, 1973, Harriet Monroe Poetry award, 1978, St. Botolph's Club Found. award, 1983, Drama Desk award, 1983, Aiken-Taylor award, 1988, Bunn award, 1988, Washington Coll. Lit. award, 1988, St. Louis Lit. award, 1989, Grand Master award Birmingham-So. Coll., 1989, Gold Medal for Poetry, Am. Acad. Inst. Arts and Letters, 1991, Edward MacDowell medal, 1992, Nat. Arts Club Medal of Honor for Lit., 1994, PEN/Manheim Medal for Translation, 1994, Milton Ctr. prize, 1995, Acad. Am. Achievement award, 1995, Robert Frost medal Poetry Soc. of Am., 1996; Guggenheim fellow, 1952-53, 63, Ford fellow, 1960-61, Camargo Found. fellow, 1985; named U.S. Poet Laureate, Libr. Congress, 1987, Nat. Medal of the Arts, 1994. Fellow MLA (hon.); mem. AAAL (pres. 1974-76, chancellor 1976-78, 80-81), ASCAP, PEN (Transl. award 1983), Am. Acad. Arts and Scis., Acad. Am. Poets (chancellor), Dramatists Guild, Century Club. Home: 87 Dodwells Rd Cummington MA 01026-9705 also: 715R Windsor Ln Key West FL 33040-6430

WILBUR, RICHARD SLOAN, physician, foundation executive; b. Boston, Apr. 8, 1924; s. Blake Colburn and Mary Caldwell (Sloan) W.; m. Betty Lou Fannin, Jan. 20, 1951; children: Andrew, Peter, Thomas. BA, Stanford U., 1943, MD, 1946; JD, John Marshall Law Sch., 1990. Intern San Francisco County Hosp., 1946-47; resident Stanford Hosp., 1949-51, U. Pa. Hosp., 1951-52; postgrad. tng. U. Mich. Hosp., 1957, Karolinska Sjukhuset, Stockholm, 1960; mem. staff Palo Alto (Calif.) Med. Clinic, 1952-69; dep. exec. v.p. AMA, Chgo., 1969-71, 73-74; asst. sec. for health and environment Dept. Def., 1971-73; sr. v.p. Baxter Labs., Inc., Deerfield, Ill., 1974-76; exec. v.p. Council Med. Splty. Socs., 1976-91, sec. accreditation council for continuing med. edn., 1979-91; asso. prof. medicine Georgetown U. Med. Sch., 1971-77, Stanford Med. Sch., 1952-69; pres. Nat. Resident Matching Plan, 1991-92; chmn. bd. Calif. Med. Assn., 1968-69, Calif. Blue Shield, 1966-68, Am. Medico-Legal Found., 1987—; chmn. bd., CEO Inst. for Clin. Info., 1994—; CEO Medic Alert, 1992-94; pres. Am. Bd. Med. Mgmt., 1992; mem. Am. Bd. Electrodiagnostic Medicine, 1993—. Contbr. articles to med. jours. Vice chmn. Rep. Cen. Com. Santa Clara County, Calif., 1966-89; bd. govs. ARC; chmn. bd. dirs. Medic Alert Found.; bd. dirs. Nat. Adv. Cancer Coun., Nat. Health Coun., 1993—; bd. visitors Drew U. Postgrad. Med. Sch.; chmn. Mid-Am. Blood Svcs. Bd., Lifesource Blood Bank, 1996. With USNR, 1942-49. Recipient Disting. Svc. medal Dept. Def., 1973, scroll of merit Nat. Med. Assn., 1971. Fellow ACP, Am. Coll. Legal Medicine (bd. dirs.), Am. Coll. Physician Execs. (bd. regents 1985-89, pres.-elect 1987, pres. 1988-89), Internat. Coll. Dentistry (hon.); mem. Inst. Medicine, Ill. Med. Assn., Lake County Med. Soc., Am. Gastroent. Assn., Pacific Interurban Clin. Club, Am. Soc. Internal Medicine, Santa Clara County Med. Soc. (hon.), Cedars Club (Soda Springs, Calif.), Union League Phila., Phi Beta Kappa, Alpha Omega Alpha. Home: 985 Hawthorne Pl Lake Forest IL 60045-2217 Office: 207 Westminster Rd Lake Forest IL 60045-1885

WILBURN, MARION TURNER, library and information scientist educator, consultant; b. Hamilton, Ont., Can., Aug. 30, 1946; d. Albert Gordon and Lilian (Heywood) Turner; m. Eugene Richard Wilburn, Nov. 27, 1971; 1 child, Trevor Michael. BA in English, History, McMaster U., 1969, MA in English, 1970; BEd in English and Theatre Arts, Queen's U., 1971; MEd in Adult Edn., Ont. Inst. Studies in Edn., 1977; MLS, U. Toronto, Ont., 1981. Cert. permanent high sch. specialist Eng., Ont.; permanent cert. theatre arts, Ont.; diploma life skills coaches. Asst. head English dept. W. Humber Collegiate Inst., Etobicoke, Ont., 1971-75; project leader asst. program for instrnl. devel. Coun. Ont. Univs., Toronto, 1977-80, dir. office tchg. and learning, 1980-81; sr. mktg. rep. Utlas Internat., Toronto, 1981-83; coord. libr. and info. technician program Sheridan Coll., Oakville, Ont., 1983—, ednl. techs. facilitator, 1994-96; v.p. Wilburn Comm. Ltd., Mississauga, Ont. Author: Automation in Libraries, various workbooks; author diploma course Libraries and the Info. Industry; contbr. articles to profl. jours.; presenter over 150 workshops, courses. Mem. Ont. Assn. Libr. Technician Instrs. (chair), Can. Libr. Assn., Ont. Libr. Assn., Spl. Librs. Assn., Can. Assn. Adult Edn., Ont. Genealogical Assn., Manchester and Lancashire Family Hist. Soc. Avocations: genealogy, microcomputers, bird watching, mystery fiction. Office: Sheridan Coll Applied Arts, 1430 Trafalgar Rd, Oakville, ON Canada L6H 2L1

WILBURN, MARY NELSON, lawyer, writer; b. Balt., Feb. 18, 1932; d. David Alfred and Phoebe Blanche (Novotny) Nelson; m. Adolph Yarbrough Wilburn, Mar. 5, 1957; children: Adolph II, Jason David. AB cum laude, Howard U., 1952; MA, U. Wis., 1955, JD, 1975. Bar: Wis. 1975, U.S. Supreme Ct 1981. Lectr. U. Wis. Law Sch., 1975-77, 83, 84, 85; atty. Bur. Prisons, Dept. Justice, 1977-82, 90—; chmn. Wis. State Parole Bd., Madison, 1986-87; gen. counsel D.C. Bd. Parole, 1987-89; commr. The Commn. to Restructure the Interstate Compact, 1988-89; mgr. Bethune Mus.-Archives, Inc., 1990; mem. Wis. Sentencing Commn., 1986-87. Mem. Madison Met. Sch. Dist. Bd. Edn., 1975-77; assoc. mem. Schutz Am. Sch. Bd., Alexandria, Egypt, 1983-85; commr. Nat. Coun. of Negro Women Commn. on Edn., 1986—; treas. Women's Strategies for 21st Century, Inc.; judge NAACP ACT-SO Competition, 1994—; mentoring mem. Women of Washington, 1996; vol. One Ch. One Addict, 1995—; mem. bd. edn. Cath. Archdiocese of Washington, 1995—. Mem. Internat. Assn. Paroling Authorities (exec. v.p. 1987-89), Nat. Assn. Black Women Attorneys (pres. Rolark chpt. 1989-93), Fedn. Internat. de Abogadas, Howard U. Alumni Assn., Links, Inc., Leadership Greater Washington (bd. dirs. 1992-94, v.p. 1995—), Women of Washington, Coun. Black Catholics, Alpha Kappa Alpha. Office: 320 1st St NW Rm 437 Washington DC 20534-0002

WILBURN, ROBERT CHARLES, institute executive; b. Latrobe, Pa., July 1, 1943; s. Robert Charles and Annabel Grace (McWherter) W.; m. Patricia Ellen Zuidema, May 18, 1968; children: Jason, Rae, Jesse, Benjamin. BS, U.S. Air Force Acad., 1965; MPA, Princeon U., 1967, PhD, 1970; LLD (hon.), U. Scranton, Pa., 1983, Hahneman U., 1984, Duquesne U., 1985. Econometrician Dept. of Def., Washington, 1967-69, policy analyst, 1970-72; economist The White House, Washington, 1969-70; v.p. Chase Manhattan Bank, N.Y.C., 1972-75; pres. Indiana U. of Pa., Indiana, 1975-79; sec. of budget Commonwealth of Pa., Harrisburg, 1979-83, sec. edn., 1983-84; pres. Carnegie Inst., Pitts., 1984-92, Colonial Williamsburg (Va.) Found., 1992—; bd. dirs. Harsco Corp., Wormleysburg, Pa. Trustee Carnegie Mellon U., 1985-92, Shadyside Hosp., Pitts., 1985-92; sec. Allegheny Conf. on Community Devel., Pitts. Capt. USAF, 1965-72. Named Man of Yr., Pitts. Vectors, 1992. Mem. ALA, Am. Mus. Assn. (bd. dirs. 1989-92), Urban Librs. Coun. Chgo. (pres. 1991-93), World Affairs Coun. (bd. dirs. 1988-92), Duquesne Club (bd. dirs. 1990-92), Pitts. Athletic Assn. Republican. Roman Catholic. Office: Colonial Williamsburg Found PO Box 1776 Williamsburg VA 23187-1776

WILBY, WILLIAM LANGFITT, global mutual fund manager, economist; b. New Orleans, May 10, 1944; s. Langfitt Bowditch and Routh (Trowbridge) W.; m. Cynthia Warren Pike, Mar. 19, 1982; 1 child, Molly. BS in Engring., U.S. Mil. Acad., 1967; MA in Econs., U. Colo., 1978, PhD in Econs., 1980. Commd. lt. U.S. Army, 1967, advanced through grades to capt., 1969, served in Europe, Vietnam, Washington, resigned, 1974; internat. economist Fed. Res. Bank Chgo., 1980-81; v.p., economist No. Trust Bank, Chgo., 1981-86; mng. dir. AIG Global Investors, N.Y.C., 1986-90; dir. Global Equities Oppenheimer Funds, N.Y.C., 1990—; vis. prof. Am. Grad. Sch. Internat. Mgmt., Glendale, Ariz., 1978-79, Kellogg Grad. Sch. Bus. Northwestern U., Evanston, Ill., 1981-84. Mem. Assn. Investment Mgmt. and Rsch. Office: Oppenheimer Funds Two World Trade Ctr 34th Fl New York NY 10048-0203

WILCHER, LARRY KEITH, lawyer; b. Lebanon, Ky., July 19, 1950; s. Dwain LaRue and Juanita (Tungate) W.; m. Mary Jo Hayden, Aug. 21, 1971; children: Emily Jane, Joseph Keith. BS in Pharmacy, St. Louis Coll. Pharmacy, 1973; JD, No. Ky. U., 1983; program of instrn. for lawyers, Harvard U., 1987, 91, 94. Pharmacist Wood Drugs, Princeton, Ky., 1973-74; pharmacist SuperX Drugs Corp., Cin., 1975-81, real estate supr., 1981-84; dir. real estate, real estate counsel Dollar Gen. Corp., Scottsville, Ky., 1984-85, gen. counsel, 1985—, asst. sec., 1988—; chmn., chief exec. officer John Doran & Assocs. Ltd., 1991—; bd. dirs. TransFin., Inc. Contbr. to book: Kentucky Business Organizations, 1989. Chmn. Warren County Young Reps., Bowling Green, Ky., 1977-79; sec., dir. Scottsville-Allen County Leasing Corp., 1992—; sec., dir. Scottsville-Allen County Indsl. Devel. Authority, Inc., 1991—; dir. Leadership Ky., 1994—. Named to Hon. Order Ky. Cols., 1968, One of Outstanding Young Men of Am., U.S. Jaycees, 1978; recipient Johnson & Johnson award St. Louis Coll. Pharmacy, 1973, Thurston B. Morton Leadership award Ky. Young Rep. Fedn., 1979. Mem. ABA, Nat. Assn. Corp. Dirs., Ky. Bar Assn. (recognition award 1987), Louisville Bar Assn., Def. Rsch. Inst., Am. Corp. Counsel Assn., The Federalist Soc. Republican. Baptist. Office: Dollar Gen Corp 427 Beech St Scottsville KY 42164-1670

WILCHER, SHIRLEY J., lawyer; b. Erie, Pa., July 28, 1951; d. James S. Wilcher and Jeanne (Evans) Cheatham. AB cum laude, Mt. Holyoke Coll., 1973; MA, New Sch. Social Research, 1976; JD, Harvard U., 1979. Bar: N.Y. 1980. Assoc. Proskauer Rose Goetz and Mendelsohn, N.Y.C., 1979-80; staff atty. Nat. Women's Law Ctr., Washington, 1980-85; assoc. counsel Com. on Edn. and Labor U.S. Ho. Reps., Washington, 1985-90; dir. state rels., gen. counsel Nat. Assn. Ind. Colls. and Univs., Washington, 1990-94; dep. asst. sec. Office Fed. Contract Compliance Programs, U.S. Dept. Labor, Washington, 1994—. Editor Harvard U. Civil Rights/Civil Liberties Law Rev., 1978-79; contbr. articles to profl. jours. Nat. bd. dirs. Nat. Polit. Congress of Black Women, Washington, 1985-87; convenor Black Women's Roundtable on Voter Participation, Washington, 1984-85. Mem. ABA, Nat. Bar Assn., Nat. Conf. Black Lawyers (local bd. dirs. 1980-87, nat. bd. dirs. 1986-87). Democrat. Buddhist. Avocations: music, Oriental art. Office: US Dept Labor Fed Contract Compliance Programs FPB 200 Constitution Ave NW Washington DC 20210-1531

WILCOCK, DONALD FREDERICK, mechanical engineer; b. Bklyn., Sept. 24, 1913; s. Frederick and Jennie Marie (Young) W.; m. Marjorie Ellen Ferris, Sept. 3, 1938; 1 son, Donald Everett. B.S. in Civil Engring, Harvard U., 1934; D.Engring. Sci., U. Cin., 1939. Research chemist Sherwin Williams Co., Chgo., 1939-42; with Gen. Electric Co., 1942-65; mgr. tribology dept. Mech. Tech., Inc., Latham, N.Y., 1965-78; pres. Tribolock Inc., Schenectady, 1978—, Inst. for Innovation Through Tribology, 1980-82. Author: Bearing Design and Application, 1957. Fellow ASME (Nat. Hersey award), Am. Soc. Lubrication Engrs. Patentee. Home and Office: 40 Autumn Dr Apt 200 Slingerlands NY 12159-9346

WILCOX, ARTHUR MANIGAULT, newspaper editor; b. Phila., May 2, 1922; s. John Walter and Caroline (Manigault) W.; m. Katharine Moore McMurray, Nov. 25, 1944; children: Margaret Moore, Arthur Manigault, Priscilla McMurray, Robert Manigault. B.S., Ga. Inst. Tech., 1943. Reporter Charleston (S.C.) Eve. Post, 1946-52, city editor, 1952-57, editor, 1968-74; asst. editor Charleston News and Courier, 1957-68, editor, 1974-90; sec., cons. Evening Post Pub. Co., pubs. Post-Courier, 1990—. Curator S.C. Hist. Soc., 1957-60; trustee Hist. Charleston Found., 1985-94; trustee Charleston Mus., 1967-96, trustee emeritus, 1996, pres. bd., 1971-81; mem. bd. visitors Winthrop Coll., Rock Hill, S.C., 1984-87; chmn. Nat. Com. to Save Ft. Sumter Flags, 1983-89; vestryman Protestant Episcopal Ch., 1954-59, 62-66, 68-72, 79-82, 96—, sr. warden, 1981. Lt. (j.g.) USN, 1943-46; rear adm. USNR. Mem. Am. Soc. Newspaper Editors, Nat. Conf. Editorial Writers, New Eng. Soc., St. Cecilia Soc., Soc. Colonial Wars (registrar 1991—), Caroline Art Assn., U.S. Naval Inst., Audubon Soc., Nat. Trust, Huguenot Soc. S.C. (v.p. 1990-91, pres. 1991—), Charleston Club, Carolina Yacht Club, Tennis Club, Army and Navy Club (Washington), Wild Dunes Club (Isle of Palms, S.C.), Rotary. Home: 26 St Augustine Dr Charleston SC 29407-6018 Office: 171 Church St Ste 300 Charleston SC 29401-3165

WILCOX, BENSON REID, cardiothoracic surgeon, educator; b. Charlotte, N.C., May 26, 1932; s. James Simpson and Louisa (Reid) W.; m. Lucinda Holderness, July 25, 1959; children: Adelaide, Alexandra, Melissa, Reid. BA, U. N.C., 1953, MD, 1957. Diplomate Am. Bd. Surgery, Am. Bd. Thoracic Surgery (chmn. 1991-93). Resident Barnes Hosp., St. Louis, 1958-59, N.C. Meml. Hosp., Chapel Hill, 1959-60, 62-64; clin. assoc. Nat. Heart Inst., Bethesda, Md., 1960-62; instr. U. N.C., Chapel Hill, 1963-65, asst. prof., 1965-68, assoc. prof., 1968-71, chief divsn. of cardiothoracic surgery, 1969—, prof., 1971—; cons. NIH Grant Com., Bethesda, 1986-89. Author: (with others) Atlas of the Heart, 1988, Surgical Anatomy of the Heart, 1992; contbr. articles to profl. jours. Pres. Atlantic Coast Conf., Greensboro, N.C., 1980-81; dir. Am. Bd. Thoracic Surgery, 1983-93, chmn., 1991-93. Markle scholar John and Mary Markle Found., 1967; recipient Hadassah Myrtle Wreath award, 1979. Mem. Am. Assn. Thoracic Surgery, Am. Surg. Assn., Soc. Thoracic Surgeons (treas. 1980-86, pres. 1994-95), Soc. Univ. Surgeons, So. Surg. Assn., Thoracic Surgery Dirs. Assn. (pres. 1985-87), Womack Soc. (pres. 1991-93). Democrat. Presbyterian. Avocations: medical history, tennis, golf, hiking. Office: U NC Med Sch Div Cardiothoracic Surgery 108 Burnett-Womack CB-7065 Chapel Hill NC 27599-7065

WILCOX, BRUCE GORDON, publisher; b. Boston, Sept. 3, 1947; s. Edward Teed and Maud (Eckert) W.; m. Greta Green, Apr. 7, 1974; children: Sarah M., Thor E., Hilary A. BA, Harvard U., 1969; postgrad., Peace Corps, Senegal, 1969-70, NYU, 1972-75. Asst. sales mgr. U. Wash. Press, Seattle, 1971-72, editor, 1975-82; program officer Franklin Book Programs, N.Y.C. and Dacca, Bangladesh, 1972-75; dir. U. Mass. Press, Amherst, 1983—; cons. NEH, Washington, 1983, 85, NEA, Washington, 1991. Mem. editl. adv. bd. Jour. Scholarly Publ., 1992—. Bd. dirs. Mass. Rev., 1987—. Mem. Assn. Am. Univ. Presses (del. to USSR and Ea. Europe 1977, to China 1985, to Estonia and CSFR 1992, bd. dirs. 1990—, pres. 1994-95). Home: 191 Lincoln Ave Amherst MA 01002-2009

WILCOX, CALVIN HAYDEN, mathematics educator; b. Cicero, N.Y., Jan. 29, 1924; s. Calvin and Vara (Place) W.; m. Frances I. Rosekrans, May 29, 1947; children: Annette Faye, Victor Hayden, Christopher Grant. Student, Syracuse U., 1947-48; A.B. magna cum laude, Harvard U., 1951, A.M., 1952, Ph.D., 1955. Mem. faculty Calif. Inst. Tech., Pasadena, 1955-61; asst. prof. math. Calif. Inst. Tech., 1957-60, asso. prof., 1960-61; prof. U. Wis.-Madison, 1961-66; prof., head dept. U. Ariz., Tucson, 1966-69; prof. U. Denver, 1969-70, U. Utah, Salt Lake City, 1971—; vis. prof. U. Geneva, 1970-71, U. Liege, Belgium, 1973, U. Stuttgart, Fed. Republic Germany, 1974, 76-77, Kyoto (Japan) U., 1975, Ecole Polytechnique Fédérale, Lausanne, Switzerland, 1979, U. Bonn (W. Ger.), 1980. Author: Lectures on Scattering Theory for the d'Alembert Equation in Exterior Domains, 1975; monograph Scattering Theory for Diffraction Gratings, 1983, Sound Propagation in Stratified Fluids, 1983; Editor: Asymptotic Solutions of Differential Equations and Their Applications, 1964, Perturbation Theory and its Application in Quantum Mechanics, 1966. Served with AUS, 1945-47. NSF predoctoral fellow, 1952-53; Sr. U.S. Scientist award Alexander von Humboldt Found., W. Ger., 1976-77. Mem. AAAS, Am. Math. Soc., Math. Assn. Am. Office: Univ Utah Dept Math Salt Lake City UT 84112

WILCOX, COLLIN M., author; b. Detroit, Sept. 21, 1924; s. Harlan Collin and Lucile Armina (Spangler) W.; m. Beverley Buchman, Dec. 20, 1954; children—Christopher, Jeffrey. B.A., Antioch Coll., 1948. Tchr., 1949-51, copywriter, 1951-53; partner Amthor & Co., 1953-54; propr. Collin Wilcox Lamps, San Francisco, 1955-72; mystery and suspense novelist, 1967—. Novelist (mystery and suspense) The Black Door, 1967, The Third Figure, 1968, The Lonely Hunter, 1969, The Disappearance, 1970, Dead Aim, 1971, Hiding Place, 1972, Long Way Down, 1972, Aftershock, 1973, The Faceless Man, 1974; pseudonym Carter Wick: works include The Third Victim, 1975, Doctor, Lawyer, 1975, The Watcher, 1976, (with Bill Pronzini) Twospot, 1977, Power Plays, 1978, Mankiller, 1980, Spellbinder, 1981, Stalking Horse, 1982, Swallow's Fall, 1983, Victims, 1985, Night Games, 1986, The Pariah, 1988, Bernhardt's Edge, 1988, A Death Before Dying, 1990, Silent Witness, 1990, Except for the bones, 1991, Hire a Hangman, 1991, Find Her a Grave, 1993, Switchback, 1993, Full Circle, 1994, Calculated Risk, 1995. Served with USAAF, 1943-44. Mem. Mystery Writers Am. (dir.), Sierra Club (com. 1975-76), Aircraft Owners and Pilots Assn. Democrat. Home: 4174 26th St San Francisco CA 94131-1915

WILCOX, DAVID ERIC, educational consultant; b. Cortland, N.Y., Sept. 4, 1939; s. James A. and Lucille (Fiske) C.; B.S. in Elec. Engring., U. Buffalo, 1961; postgrad. Syracuse U., 1965, Marist Coll.; M.S., U. Bridgeport, 1977; Ed.D. candidate Rutgers U.; m. Phyllipa Ann Wilcox, Jan. 23, 1977; children: Terri L., Cindy A., Jana L. Research engring. mgr. input/output devices Rome (N.Y.) Air Devel. Center, 1966-70; dir. sales Mercon Inc., Winsooki, Vt., 1970-73, dir., 1972—; pres. Wilcox Tng. Systems, Newburgh, N.Y., 1973—; prin. Exec. Effectiveness, Inc., N.Y.C.; instr. Dale Carnegie courses. Pres. N.Y. State Jaycees, 1972-73, chmn. bd., 1973-74; dir. U.S. Jaycees, 1970-71; bd. dirs., v.p. N.Y. State Spl. Olympics, 1972-73; bd. dirs., treas. Family Counseling Service, Inc.; mem. Orange County Pvt. Industry Coun.; mem. N.Y. State Excelsior Examiner, 1995. Served to lt. USAF, 1961-65. Registered profl. engr., N.Y. Mem. Soc. Info. Display, IEEE, N.Y., State Soc. Profl. Engrs., Internat. Transactional Analysis Assn., Internat. Platform Assn., Am. Soc. Quality Control. Methodist. Author: Information System Sciences, 1965; also articles. Patentee in field. Home: 511 River Rd Newburgh NY 12550-1304 Office: Rock Cut Rd Newburgh NY 12550 also: 30 W 60th St New York NY 10023-7902

WILCOX, EDWARD R., engineering executive; b. Youngstown, Ohio, Apr. 11, 1953; s. Edward R. And Dolores (Vanca) W. Enlisted USAF, 1976; maintenance technician USAF, Hickham AFB, Hawaii, 1977-81; maintenance instr. USAF, Norton AFB, Calif., 1982-84, technician, 1984-93, prodr. tng. films, 1987-91, quality assurance inspector, 1991-92, electro-optics rschr., 1990-93, non-destructive inspection technician, 1992-93; owner Wilcox Engring. & Rsch., Vacaville, Calif., 1993—; mem. mil. S.W.A.T. team 63 Security Police Squadron, San Bernardino, Calif., 1984-93. Night vision repair technician San Bernardino Sheriff's Dept., 1992-93, San Bernardino Police Dept., 1992-93. Roman Catholic. Achievements include patents in field; finding of repairability of MX-10160/UV. Avocation: helping people. Office: Wilcox Engring & Rsch PO Box 6503 Vacaville CA 95696-6503

WILCOX, HARRY HAMMOND, retired medical educator; b. Canton, Ohio, May 31, 1918; s. Harry Hammond and Hattie Estelle (Richner) W.; m. D. June Freed., June 21, 1941; children: Joyce L. Wilcox Graff, Margaret J. (Mrs. Grayson S. Smith), James Hammond. B.S., U. Mich., 1939, M.S., 1940, Ph.D., 1948. Asso. prof. biology Morningside Coll., Sioux City, Iowa, 1947-48; asso. in anatomy U. Pa., 1948-52; mem. faculty U. Tenn. Center for Health Scis., 1952-83, Goodman prof. anatomy, 1966-83, emeritus prof. anatomy, 1983—. Assoc. editor: Anat. Record, 1968-83. Served with AUS, 1945-46. Mem. AAAS, Am. Assn. Anatomists, Am. Soc. Zoologists, Sigma Xi. Home: 1031 Marcia Rd Memphis TN 38117-5513

WILCOX, HARRY WILBUR, JR., retired corporate executive; b. Phila., Feb. 13, 1925; s. Harry Wilbur and Justine Elizabeth (Doolittle) W.; m. Colleen Ann Cerra, Apr. 6, 1946; children: Justine, Harry Wilbur III. B.S., Yale U., 1949. With Gen. Electric Co., N.Y.C., 1949-50; mfg. supt. Sylvania Electric Products, 1951-67; v.p., gen. mgr. Granger Assocs. (electronics), Palo Alto, Calif., 1967-70; gen. mgr. ITT-Cannon Electric Co., Phoenix, 1970-72; pres. Hills McCanna Co., Carpentersville, Ill., 1972-75; pres. VSI, and group v.p. IU Internat. Corp., 1975-78; exec. v.p. ITT-Grinnell, 1978-85; pres. ITT Valve Div, Lancaster, Pa., 1985-88; dir. Meyer Industries, Nat. Temperature Control Centers, Paul N. Howard Co.; former chmn. VSI, VSI-UK. Mem. adv. com. Town of Sherborn, Mass. Served with U.S. Army, 1943-46. Decorated Bronze star. Mem. R.I. Country Club, Yale Club of Vero Beach, Grand Harbor Golf and Beach Club (Vero Beach), Bristol (R.I.) Yacht Club. Patentee in electroluminescence. Home: 31 Sea Breeze Ln Bristol RI 02809-1520 also: 4818 Wood Duck Cir Vero Beach FL 32967-7202

WILCOX, HARVEY JOHN, lawyer; b. Elyria, Ohio, Nov. 1, 1937; s. Hubbard Clyde and Sylvia (Wahter) W.; m. Leslie Louise Coleman, Apr. 11, 1970. BA cum laude, Amherst Coll., 1959; LLB, Yale U., 1962. Bar: Ohio 1962, Va. 1994. Mem. firm Wilcox & Wilcox, 1962-78; with office gen. counsel Dept. Navy, Washington, 1966-94; asst. to gen. counsel Dept. Navy, 1969-72, counsel Naval Air Systems Command, 1972-76, dep. gen. counsel, 1976-94; guest lectr. U.S. Army Logistics Mgmt. Center; mem. Navy Contract Adjustment Bd., 1968-72. Designed Arlington County (Va.) flag, 1983. Bd. dirs. Navy Fed. Credit Union, 1974-77, sec.-treas., 1974-75, 2d v.p., 1975-77; mem. Def. Adv. Panel on Streamlining Acquisition Laws, 1991-92. Lt. USNR, 1963-66. Recipient Meritorious Exec. rank 1990, Disting Exec. rank, 1981, 89, Navy Disting. Civilian Svc. award, 1989, Defense Disting. Civilian Svc. award, 1994. Mem. Ohio Bar Assn., Va. State Bar, Charlottesville-Albemarle Bar Assn., Nat. Trust Hist. Preservation, Nature Conservancy. Home: PO Box 338 Turner Mountain Rd Ivy VA 22945-0338

WILCOX, JERRY COOPER, architect; b. June 8, 1938; m. Nancy K. Wilcox; children: Lance Cooper, Kevin Morris. BArch, U. Ark., 1962. With Erhart, Eichenbaum, Rauch & Blass, 1964-76, Blass Chilcote Carter & Wilcox, 1976-89; pres. Wilcox Group, Little Rock, 1989—. Mem. adv. bd. U. Ark. Sch. Architecture; mem. adminstrv. bd. Asbury United Meth. Ch., Little Rock, 1983—, trustee, 1990—; mem. Little Rock Bicentennial Com., 1975-76; chmn. architects and engrs. divsn. United Way Campaign, 1981; mem. Pulaski County bd. dirs. Am. Heart Assn., 1986-91; bd. dirs. Camp Aldersgate, 1987-94. Capt. C.E., U.S. Army, 1962-64, USAR, 1964-66. Mem. AIA (bd. dirs. Ark. chpt. 1970-72, 77, treas. 1973, sec. 1974, v.p. 1975, pres. 1976; com. architecture for the arts and recreation 1973-80, chmn. 1977, ednl. endowment fund pres. 1985-94, steering com. 1978, nat. nominating com. 1980; co-chmn. Gulf States regional conv. 1979), Coun. Ednl. Facility Planners, U. Ark. Alumni Assn. (pres. Pulaski County chpt.), Little Rock C. of C. (econ. devel. com. 1979-85, bd. dirs. 1981-86), Rotary (Little Rock Downtown chpt.), Pi Kappa Alpha. Office: Wilcox Group Winrock Park 2222 Cottondale Ln Ste 100 Little Rock AR 72202-2037

WILCOX, JOHN CAVEN, lawyer, corporate consultant; b. N.Y.C., Nov. 12, 1942; s. Daniel A. and Jessie Alexandra (Caven) W.; m. Vanessa Guerrini-Maraldi, Sept. 30, 1983; children: Daniel D.G., William G.M., Julia G.M. BA magna cum laude, Harvard U., 1964, JD, 1968; MA, U. Calif., Berkeley, 1965; LLM, NYU, 1981. Bar: N.Y. 1973. Account exec. Georgeson & Co. Inc., N.Y.C., 1973-79, mng. dir., 1979-90, chmn. 1990—; trustee Family Dynamics, Inc., N.Y.C., 1979—. With U.S. Army, 1968-70, Vietnam. Woodrow Wilson fellow, 1965. Mem. ABA, NYSE (mem. shareholders comm. com. 1989—), N.Y. State Bar Assn., Am. Soc. Corp. Secs. (mem. securities industry com. 1987-95, securities law com. 1995—), Nat. Assn. Security Dealers (mem. issuer affairs com. 1990—), Downtown Assn., Harvard Club (N.Y.C.), Phi Beta Kappa. Democrat. Home: 580 W End Ave New York NY 10024-1723 Office: Georgeson & Co Inc Wall Street Plz New York NY 10005

WILCOX, JON P., justice; b. Berlin, Wis., Sept. 5, 1936; m. Jane Ann; children: Jeffrey, Jennifer. AB in Polit. Sci., Ripon Coll., 1958; JD, U. Wis., 1965. Pvt. practice Steele, Smyth, Klos and Flynn, LaCrosse, Wis., 1965-66, Hacker and Wilcox, Wautoma, Wis., 1966-69, Wilcox, Rudolph, Kubasta & Rathjen, Wautoma, 1969-79; elected judge Waushara County Cir. Ct., 1979-92; apptd. justice Wis. Supreme Ct., 1992—; commr. Family Ct., Waushara County, 1977-79; vice chmn., chmn. Wis. Sentencing Commn., 1984-92; chief judge 6th Jud. Dist., 1985-92; co-chair State-Fed. Jud. Coun., 1992, Jud. Coun. Wis., 1993; mem. Prison Overcrowding Task Force, 1988-90; mem. numerous coms. Wis. Judiciary; mem. faculty Wis. Jud. Coll., 1986—; chmn. Wis. Chief Judges Com., 1990-92; co-chair comm. on judiciary as co-equal br. of govt. Wis. State Bar; lectr. in field. Co-author: Wisconsin News Reporter's Legal Handbook: Wisconsin Courts and Court Procedures, 1987. Bd. visitors U. Wis. Law Sch, 1970-76. Lt. U.S. Army, 1959-61. Named Outstanding Jaycee Wautoma, 1974; recipient Disting. Alumni award Ripon Coll., 1993. Fellow Am. Bar Found.; mem. ABA (com. on continuing appellate edn.), Nat. Coun. Juvenile and Family Ct. Judges, Wis. Bar Assn. (bench bar com.), Wis. Law Found., Tri-County Bar Assn., Dane County Bar Assn., Trout Unltd., Ruffed Grouse Soc., Ducks Unltd., Rotary, Phi Alpha Delta. Office: Supreme Court State Capitol PO Box 1688 Madison WI 53701-1688

WILCOX, MARK DEAN, lawyer; b. Chgo., May 25, 1952; s. Fabian Joseph and Zeryle Lucille (Tase) W.; m. Catherine J. Wertjes, Mar. 12, 1983; children: Glenna Lynn, Joanna Tessie, Andrew Fabian Joseph. BBA, U. Notre Dame, 1973; JD, Northwestern U., 1976; CLU, Am. Coll., 1979, ChFC, 1992. Bar: Ill. 1976, U.S. Dist. Ct. (no. dist.) Ill. 1976, Trial Bar 1982, U.S. Ct. Appeals (7th cir.) 1987, U.S. Supreme Ct. 1989. Staff asst. Nat. Dist. Attys. Assn., Chgo., 1974-75; trial asst. Cook County States Atty., Chgo., 1975; intern U.S. Atty. No. Dist. Ill., Chgo., 1975-76; assoc. Lord, Bissell & Brook, Chgo., 1976-85, ptnr., 1986—. Bd. mgrs. YMCA Metropolitan Chgo., Internat. Spl. Olympics. Mem. ABA (tort and ins. practice sect.), Am. Soc. CLU and ChFC, Chgo. Bar Assn. (ins. law com.), Def. Rsch. Inst., Trial Lawyers Club Chgo., Notre Dame Nat. Monogram Club, Union League Club (Chgo.), Beta Gamma Sigma. Office: Lord Bissell & Brook 115 S La Salle St Chicago IL 60603-3801

WILCOX, MARY L., systems project analyst; b. Lewisville, Ark., Sept. 22, 1959; d. George Harold and Thelma Rene (Burton) Wise; m. Michael Darnell Wilcox, Dec. 24, 1978; 1 child, Melissa Christina. BS, Fla. State U., 1982. Pharmacy tech. Tallahassee Meml. Regional Med. Ctr., Fla., 1982-84; lab. tech. Dept. Health and Rehabilitative Svcs., State of Fla., Tallahassee, 1984-85, biological scientist, 1985-89, sr. human svcs. program specialist, 1989-92; systems project analyst Agency for Health Care Adminstrn., State of Fla., Tallahassee, 1992—. Home: 407 Great Lakes St Tallahassee FL 32310-0100 Office: Agency for Health Care Adminstrn State of Fla Bld 8 Rm 226 2730 Blairstone Rd Tallahassee FL 32301-5902

WILCOX, MAUD, editor; b. N.Y.C., Feb. 14, 1923; d. Thor Fredrik and Gerda (Ysberg) Eckert; m. Edward T. Wilcox, Feb. 9, 1944; children: Thor (dec.), Bruce, Eric, Karen. A.B. summa cum laude, Smith Coll., 1944; A.M., Harvard U., 1945. Teaching fellow Harvard U., 1945-46, 48-51; instr. English Smith Coll., Northampton, Mass., 1947-48, Wellesley Coll., Mass., 1951-52; exec. editor Harvard U. Press, 1958-66, humanities editor, 1966-73, editor-in-chief, 1973-89, ret.; freelance editorial cons. Cambridge, 1989—; cons., panelist NEH, Washington, 1974-76, 82-84; cons. Radcliffe Pub. Course, 1991. Mem. MLA (com. scholarly edits. 1982-86), Assn. Am. Univ. Presses (chair com. admissions and standards 1976-77, v.p. 1978-79, chair program com. 1981-82), Phi Beta Kappa. Democrat. Episcopalian. Home and Office: 63 Francis Ave Cambridge MA 02138-1911

WILCOX, MICHAEL WING, lawyer; b. Buffalo, July 21, 1941; s. Paul Wing and Barbara Ann (Bauter) W.; m. Diane Rose Dell, June 18, 1966; children: Timothy, Katherine, Matthew. AB, UCLA, 1963; JD, Marquette U., 1966. Bar: Wis. 1966, U.S. Ct. Appeals (7th cir.) 1967. Law clk. to judge U.S. Ct. Appeals (7th cir.), Chgo., 1966-67; with firm Boardman, Suhr, Curry & Field, Madison, Wis., 1967-83; ptnr. Quarles & Brady, Madison, Wis., 1983-90, Stolper, Koritzinsky, Brewster & Neider, Madison, 1990-94, Stolper, Wilcox & Hughes, Madison, 1995—; lectr. in field. Author: (with others) Marital Property Law in Wisconsin, 1986. Bd. dirs. Meriter Found. Mem. ABA (chmn. marital property com. of real property probate and trust law sect. 1986-89), Wis. State Bar Assn. (chmn. taxation sect. 1983-84), Am. Coll. Trust and Estate Counsel, Rotary (bd. dirs. Madison West chpt.). Club: The Madison. Home: 6318 Keelson Dr Madison WI 53705-4367 Office: Stolper Wilcox & Hughes 6510 Grand Teton Plz Madison WI 53719-1029

WILCOX, RHODA DAVIS, elementary education educator; b. Boyero, Colo., Nov. 4, 1918; d. Harold Francis and Louise Wilhelmina (Wilfert) Davis; m. Kenneth Edward Wilcox, Nov. 1945 (div. 1952); 1 child, Michele Ann. BA in Elem. Edn., U. No. Colo., 1941; postgrad., Colo. Coll., 1955-65. Life cert. tchr., Colo. Elem. tchr. Fruita (Colo.) Pub. Sch., 1938-40, Boise, Idaho, 1940-42; sec. civil service USAF, Ogden, Utah, 1942-43, Colorado Springs, Colo., 1943-44; sec. civil service hdqtrs. command USAF, Panama Canal Zone; sec. Tech. Libr., Eglin Field, Fla., 1945-46; elem. tchr. Colorado Springs Sch. Dist. 11, 1952-82, mem. curriculum devel. com., 1968-69; lectr. civic, profl. and edn. groups, Colo.; judge for Excellence in Literacy Coldwell Bankers Sch. Dist. 11, Colo. Coun. Internat. Reading. Assn. Author: Man on the Iron Horse, 1959, Colorado Slim and His Spectacklers, 1964, (with Jean Pierpoint) Changing Colorado (Social Studies), 1968-69, The Founding Fathers and Their Friends in Denver Posse of the Westerners Brand Bank, 1971, The Bells of Manitou, 1973, (with Len Froisland) In the Footsteps of the Founder, 1993. Mem. hist. adv. bd. State Colo., Denver, 1976; mem. Garden of the Gods master plan rev. com. City of Colorado Springs, 1987—; mem. cemetery adv. bd. City of Colorado Springs, 1988-91; mem. adv. bd. centennial com., 1971; mem. steering com. Spirit of Palmer Festival, 1986; judge Nat. Hist. Day, U. Colo., Colorado Springs, and Colo. Coll., Colorado Springs; hon. trustee Palmer Found., 1986—; mem. Am. the Beautiful Centennial Celebrations, Inc., 1992-93; active Friends of the Garden of the Gods, Friends of Winfield Scott Stratton, Friends of the Libr. Named Tchr. of the Yr., Colorado Springs Sch. Dist. 11, 1968. Mem. AAUW (Woman of Yr. 1987), Colo. Ret. Educators Assn., Colorado Springs Ret. Educators Assn., Helen Hunt Jackson Commemorative Coun., Women's Ednl. Soc. Colo. Coll. Avocations: lecturing, conducting tours and writing tour scripts, volunteering in Pioneers Mus. Archives, Ecumenical Social Ministries, Garden of the Gods, Rock Ledges Ranch. Home: 1620 E Cache La Poudre St Colorado Springs CO 80909-4612

WILCOX, RICHARD, grain company executive; b. 1952. BS, Phillips U., 1974. With Cargill Inc., Cin., 1974-80, Con Agra, Inc., St. Louis, 1980-82; v.p. Zen-Noh Grain Corp., Metairie, La., 1982-91; active with subsidiary, 1991—; with CGB Enterprises, Inc., Covington, La., 1993—, pres., chief exec. officer; also pres. Consolidated Grain at N. Bend, Cin. Office: CGB Enterprises Inc 1001 Service Rd E Covington LA 70433*

WILCOX, RICHARD HOAG, information scientist; b. Wooster, Ohio, Sept. 23, 1927; s. Raymond Boorman and Hazel (Hoag) W.; m. Jean Balderston, May 13, 1950; children: Linda, Kathryn. BS in Elec. Engring., Lafayette Coll., Easton, Pa., 1951, Elec. Engr., 1955; M Engring. Adminstrn., George Washington U., Washington, 1964. Enlisted USN, 1945-47; commd. ensign USNR, 1951, advanced through grades to comdr., 1969, ret., 1978; electronic scientist, ops. rsch. analyst U.S. Naval Rsch. Lab., Washington, 1951-58; ops. rsch. analyst, electronic engr. Office Naval Rsch., Washington, 1958-62, head info. systems br., acting dir. math. scis. div., 1961-68; head resource evaluation div. Exec. Office of Pres., Office Emergency Preparedness, Washington, 1968-69, head info. systems div., 1969-74; chief mil. affairs div. U.S. Arms Control and Disarmament Agy., Washington, 1974-75, chief arms transfer div., 1975-78, sr. scientist, 1978-93; pvt. cons. Info. Systems Mgmt. Sci., Temple Hills, Md., 1993—; ret. commdr., 1979; commr., dir. Commn. on Profls. in Sci. and Tech., Washington, 1967-92; asst. dir. computers and comm. Fed. Emergency Mgmt. Agy., Washington, 1981; vis. scholar Ctr. for Strategic and Internat. Studies, Georgetown U., Washington, 1983-84. Co-editor: Redundancy Techniques for Computing Systems, 1962, Computer and Information Sciences, 1964, Research Program Effectiveness, 1965; contbr. articles to profl. jours, chpts. to books. Recipient Superior Civiliam Svc. award Office Naval Rsch., 1966, Citation Pres. U.S., 1973, Superior Honor award U.S. Arms Control and Disarmament Agy., 1993. Mem. AAAS, George Washington U. Club, Herrington Harbour Sailing Assn., Sigma Xi, Tau Beta Pi. Achievements include patent for microwave multiplier device; devising info.-theoretic measure of randomness of human performance; mgmt. devel. and operation of first operational computer conferencing system; creation a variety of novel info. systems. Home: 5702 Cedar Bluff Pl Temple Hills MD 20748-4809 *The only decision available to us is what we are actually going to do in the circumstances presented to us in life. Not deciding actively or simply reacting to others, is a decision by default. Evaluating life's circumstances honestly requires a sense of humor, and acting so as to be at peace with our memories provides a good guide.*

WILCOX, RONALD BRUCE, biochemistry educator, researcher; b. Seattle, Sept. 23, 1934; s. Howard Bruce and Edna Jane (McKeown) W.; m. Susan Lenore Folkenberg, May 15, 1937; children: Deanna Marie, Lisa Suzanne. B.S., Pacific Union Coll., 1957; Ph.D., U. Utah, 1962. Research fellow Harvard Med. Sch., Boston, 1962-65; asst. prof. Loma Linda U., Calif., 1965-70, assoc. prof., 1970-73, prof., 1973—, chmn. dept. biochemistry, 1973-83. Mem. gen. plan rev. com. City of Loma Linda, 1981-92; bd. dirs. East Valley United Way, 1990—. Fellow Danforth Found., St. Louis, 1957; fellow Bank Am. Giannini Found. San Francisco, 1965. Mem. Am. Thyroid Assn., Endocrine Soc. Democrat. Seventh-day Adventist. Home: 25516 Lomas Verdes St Loma Linda CA 92354-2417 Office: Loma Linda U Dept Biochemistry Loma Linda CA 92350

WILCOXSON, ROY DELL, plant pathology educator and researcher; b. Columbia, Utah, Jan. 12, 1926; m. Iva Wall, 1949; children: Bonnie, Paul, Karren, John. BS, Utah State U., 1953; MS, U. Minn., 1955, PhD in Plant Pathlogy, 1957. Asst. prof., 1957-66; prof. plant pathology U. Minn., St. Paul, 1966—; spl. staff mem. Rockefeller Found.; vis. prof. Indian Agrl. Rsch. Inst., New Delhi; dir. Morocco project U. Minn., 1983-87; adj. prof. Inst. Agronomy and Vet. Medicine, Hassan II, Rabat, Morocco, 1985—. Fellow Am. Phytopath Soc., Indian NAS, Indian Phytopath Soc., AAAS. Research in diseases of forage crops and cereal crops; cereal rust diseases. Office: 1491 Raymond Ave Saint Paul MN 55108-1432 Address: Dept Plant Path U Minn Saint Paul MN 55101

WILCZEK, FRANK ANTHONY, physics educator; b. Mineola, N.Y., May 15, 1951; s. Frank John and Mary Rose (Cona) W.; m. Elizabeth Jordan Devine, July 3, 1973; children: Amity, Mira. BS in Math., U. Chgo., 1970; MA in Math., Princeton U., 1971, PhD in Physics, 1973. Instr. Princeton (N.J.) U., 1973-74, asst. prof., 1974-76, assoc. prof., 1978-79, prof., 1980-81; prof. Inst. for Theoretical Physics, Santa Barbara, Calif., 1981-88, Inst. for Advanced Study, Princeton, 1989—; vis. fellow Inst. for Advanced Study, Princeton, 1977-78; vis. prof. Harvard U., 1987-88. Author: Longing for the Harmonies, 1988, Fractional Statistics and Anyon Superconductivity, 1990; contbr. articles to profl. jours. Recipient J.J. Sakurai prize Am. Phys. Soc., 1986, Dirac medal UNESCO, 1994; A.P. Sloan fellow, 1975-77, MacArthur fellow, 1982-87, Huttenback prof. U. Calif., Santa Barbara, 1984-88. Mem. NAS, Am. Acad. Arts & Scis. Avocations: chess, music, logic puzzles. Home: 112 Mercer St Princeton NJ 08540-6827 Office: Inst Advanced Study Dept Natural Scis Olden Ln Princeton NJ 08540-4920

WILCZEK, JOHN FRANKLIN, history educator; b. San Francisco, Jan. 9, 1929; s. Leonard Matthew and Teresa Edith (Silvey) W.; m. Kuniko Akabane, Nov. 14, 1966; 1 child, Mary Theresa Shepherd. BA in History with honors, U. Calif., Berkeley, 1952; MA, U. Calif., 1953; PhD, Pacific Western U., Encino, Calif., 1978. Cert. secondary tchr., Calif. Instr. history and polit. sci. City Coll. San Francisco, 1956-94, instr. history of Japan, 1995; tchr. Japan History part-time City Coll. of San Francisco, 1996—; instr. Kobe (Japan) Women's Coll., 1979-81; instr. Seido Lang. Inst., Kobe, 1979-81; sec.-treas. Tokyo TV Broadcasting Corp., San Francisco, 1975—. Author: The Teaching of Japanese History on the Community College Level, 1978. Sgt. U.S. Army, 1953-55. Mem. U. Calif. Alumni Assn. Republican. Roman Catholic. Avocations: art, numismatics, philately, classical music, photography. Home: 5 Windsor Dr Daly City CA 94015-3257 Office: City Coll of San Francisco 50 Phelan Ave San Francisco CA 94112-1821

WILCZEK, JOSEPH, health facilities administrator. Sr. v.p., COO Caritas Christi Inc. Office: Caritas Christi Inc 125 Technology Dr Waltham MA 02154-8901*

WILCZEK, ROBERT JOSEPH, lawyer; b. Chgo., Jan. 8, 1944; s. Andrew J. and Anne (Danielczak) W.; m. Shirley Pfenning, Oct. 2, 1976; 1 child, Meghan R. BA, U. Dayton, 1965; LLB, U. Notre Dame, 1968. Bar: Ill. 1968, U.S. Supreme Ct. 1974. Ptnr., chmn. Gardner, Carton & Douglas, Chgo., 1971—; bd. dirs. Pacific Dunlop Holdings Inc., Chgo. Note and book rev. editor Notre Dame Law Rev., 1967-68; contbr. articles to profl. jours. Trustee St. Patrick High Sch., Chgo., Chgo. Cultural Found.; mem. adv. coun. Coll. Arts & Scis. U. Dayton. Capt. U.S. Army, 1968-70, Vietnam. Decorated Bronze Star. Mem. ABA, Chgo. Bar Assn., Law Club Chgo., Australian-Am. C. of C. (bd. dirs. Chgo. chpt.). Office: Gardner Carton & Douglas Quaker Tower Ste 3400 321 N Clark St Chicago IL 60610-4714

WILD, BONITA MARIE, hospital services company executive; b. Chgo., Jan. 14, 1949; d. Edward and Veronica (Hlad) Orzechowski; m. Forrest Wild; 1 child, Monica. Student, U. Chgo., 1973-75; BS, Roosevelt U., 1977; MA, U. Ariz., 1984. Sales rep. and dist. trainer Ortho Pharm. Corp., Raritan, N.J., 1978-82; v.p. and mktg. dir. Golden Era, Phoenix, 1982-84; sales rep. Surgikos, Arlington, Tex., 1984-88, Johnson & Johnson Med., Inc., Arlington, 1988-90; profl. products mgr. Johnson & Johnson Internat., Johnson & Johnson Poland, Warsaw, 1991-92; account bus. mgr. Johnson & Johnson Hosp. Svcs., New Brunswick, N.J., 1990-91, corp. bus. mgr., 1993—; corp. dir. Johnson & Johnson Health Care Sys., 1995—; counsellor Mariposa Women's Ctr., Orange, Calif., 1984-89. Mem. Toastmasters, Franklin Honor Soc. at Roosevelt U. Republican. Roman Catholic. Avocations: skiing, travel, hiking, golf, tennis. Home: 506 Nyes Pl Laguna Beach CA 92651-4145

WILD, HARRY E., engineering company executive; b. Province, R.I., Sept. 25, 1940; s. Harry Edward and Lula Elizabeth (Johnson) W.; m. Marjorie D. Dompe, Nov. 26, 1981; children: Elizabeth Ann, Eric Johnson. BCE, U. Fla., 1966, MS, 1967. Registered profl. engr. Fla., Ga., Maine. Draftsman, inspector, surveyor Briley Wild & Assocs., Ormond Beach, Fla., 1959-65; treatment plant operator U. Fla., Gainesville, 1965-66; design engr. Metcalf & Eddy, Boston, 1966-68, project engr., 1968-71; v.p. Briley, Wild & Assocs., Ormond Beach, 1971, pres., chief exec. officer, 1972—; peer reviewer in field. Contbr. articles to profl. jours. Served with U.S. Army. Recipient Harrison P. Eddy award, Water Pollution Control Fedn., 1972. Fellow Fla. Engring. Soc. (v.p. 1977-78, 81-83), Am. Cons. Engrs. Council; mem. ASCE, Am. Water Works Assn., Fla. Inst. Cons. Engrs. (officer 1974-80, pres. 1979-80, Ormond Beach C. of C. (bd. govs.). Presbyterian. Club: Halifax (Daytona Beach, Fla.). Home: 110 Knollwood Estate Dr Ormond Beach FL 32174-4223 Office: Briley Wild & Assocs Inc PO Box 1023 Ormond Beach FL 32175-1023

WILD, JAMES ROBERT, biochemistry and genetics educator; b. Sedalia, Mo., Nov. 24, 1945; s. Robert Lee and Frances Elleta (Wheeler) W.; m. Ann Lynn Brenner, Aug. 1, 1973; 1 child, Kalli Ann. BA in Zoology, U. Calif., Davis, Calif., 1967; PhD in Cell Biology, U. Calif., Riverside, 1971; post doctoral fellow, U. Calif., 1972. Rsch. microbiologist NMR Inst., Active Duty USN, Bethesda, Md., 1972-75; from asst. to assoc. prof. genetics and plant sci. Tex. A&M U., Coll. Sta., Tex., 1975-84; prof., chair genetics faculty Tex. A&M U., Coll. Sta., 1984-87, prof. biochemistry & genetics, 1984—, head biochemistry and biophysics dept., 1986-90; exec. assoc. dean Coll. Agriculture & Life Scs., Tex. A&M U., Coll. Sta., 1987-92; prof., head dept. biochemistry and biophysics, 1994—. Recipient Incentive in Excellence award Ctr. for Teaching Excellence, 1984-85, Outstanding Youth Educator, Tex. Conf., United Meth. Ch., 1984, So. Regional award for excellence in coll. and univ. teaching in food and agrl. scis. Higher Edn. program USDA, 1992. Methodist. Office: Tex A&M U Biochemistry Bldg Rm 339 College Station TX 77843-2128

WILD, JOHN JULIAN, surgeon, director medical research institute; b. Sydenham, Kent, Eng., Aug. 11, 1914; came to U.S., 1946; s. Ovid Frederick and Ellen Louise (Cuttance) W.; m. Nancy Wallace, Nov. 14, 1949 (div. 1966); children: John O., Douglas J.; m. Valerie Claudia Grosenick, Aug. 9, 1968; 1 child, Ellen Louise. BA, U. Cambridge, Eng., 1936, MA, 1940, MD, 1942, PhD, 1971. Intern, resident U. Coll. Hosp., London, 1938-42; intern U. College Hosp., London, 1938-42; staff surgeon Miller Gen., St. Charles and North Middlesex Hosps., London, 1942-44; venereologist Royal Army Med. Corps, 1944-45; rsch. fellow, instr. depts. surgery and elec. engring., prin. investigator U. Minn., Mpls., 1946-51; dir. rsch. Medico.-Technol. Rsch. Dept. St. Barnabas Hosp., Mpls., 1953-60; dir. Medico-Technol. Rsch. Unit Minn. Found., St. Paul, 1960-63; pvt. practice Mpls., 1966—; dir. Medico-Technol. Rsch. Inst. Mpls., St. Louis Park, Minn., 1965—; lectr. in field of medical instruments, ultrasound. Contbr. articles to profl. jours. Recipient Japan prize in Medical Imaging, Sci. and Tech. Found. Japan, 1991. Fellow Am. Inst. Ultrasound in Medicine (Pioneer award 1978); mem. AMA, World Fedn. Ultrasound in Medicine and Biology, Minn. State Med. Assn., Hennepin County Med. Soc., N.Am. Alvis Owners Club; hon. mem. British Inst. of Radiology, Japan Soc. of Ultrasound in Medicine. Achievements include patents in field; origination of ultrasonic medical imaging instruments and diagnostic techniques; origination of the field of pulse-echo ultrasonic diagnostic medicine. Avocations: automobile restoration, antique collecting and restoration. Home and Office: Medico-Technol Rsch Inst 4262 Alabama Ave S Minneapolis MN 55416-3105

WILD, NELSON HOPKINS, lawyer; b. Milw., July 16, 1933; s. Henry Goetseels and Virginia Douglas (Weller) W.; m. Joan Ruth Miles, Apr. 12, 1969; children: Mark, Eric. A.B., Princeton U., 1955; LL.B., U. Wis., 1961. Bar: Wis. 1962, Calif. 1967; cert. specialist in probate, estate planning and trust law State Bar of Calif. Research assoc. Wis. Legis. Council, Madison, 1955-56; assoc. Whyte, Hirschboeck, Minahan, Harding & Harland, Milw., 1961-67, Thelen, Marin, Johnson & Bridges, San Francisco, 1967-70; sole practice law San Francisco, 1970—; mem. State Bar Calif. Client Trust Fund Commn., 1983, mem. exec. com. conf. dels., 1985-88. Contbr. articles to legal jours. Bd. dirs. Neighborhood Legal Assistance Found., San Francisco, 1974-85, chmn. bd., 1978-81. Served with USAF, 1956-58. Mem. ABA, Calif. Bar Assn., San Francisco Bar Assn., Am. Bar Found., Lawyers of San Francisco Club (gov. 1975, treas. 1981, v.p. 1982, pres.-elect 1983, pres. 1984), Calif. Tennis Club (bd. dirs. 1995—). Office: 220 Montgomery St San Francisco CA 94104-3402

WILD, RICHARD P., lawyer; b. N.Y.C., Aug. 13, 1947; s. Alfred P. and Harriet C. (Hoffman) W.; m. Deirdre L. Felbin, June 15, 1969; children: Nicholas B., Daniel M. AB, Columbia U., 1968; JD, Yale U., 1971. Bar: Pa. 1971, U.S. Dist. Ct. (ea. dist.) Pa. 1971, U.S. Tax Ct. 1973, U.S. Claims Ct. 1977. Assoc. Dechert Price & Rhoads, Phila., 1971-78, ptnr., 1978—;

bd. dirs. Penn Fuel Gas, Inc. Mem. Phila. Bar Assn. (mem. tax sect.). Office: Dechert Price & Rhoads 4000 Bell Atlantic Tower 1717 Arch St Philadelphia PA 19103-2713

WILD, ROBERT ANTHONY, university president; b. Chgo., Mar. 30, 1940; s. John Hopkins and Mary Dorothy (Colnon) W. BA in Latin, Loyola U. Chgo., 1962, MA in Classical Lang., 1967; STL, Jesuit Sch. Theology, Chgo., 1970; PhD in Study of Religion, Harvard U., 1977. Joined S.J., Roman Cath. Ch., 1957, ordained priest, 1970. From asst. to assoc. prof. Marquette U., Milw., 1975-83; vis. prof. Pont. Istituto Biblico, Rome, 1983-84; dir. Jesuit philosophate program Loyola U. Chgo., 1984-85, assoc. prof. theology, 1985-92; provincial superior Chgo. Province S.J., Chgo., 1985-91; pres. Weston Jesuit Sch. Theology, Cambridge, Mass., 1992-96, Marquette U., Milw., 1996—; trustee Jesuit Sch. Theology, Berkeley, Calif., 1985-90, Weston Sch. Theology, Cambridge, Mass., 1985-96, Marquette U., 1990—, St. Louis U., 1994—. Author: Water in the Cultic Worship of Isis and Sarapis, 1981; co-editor: Sentences of Sextus, 1981; contbr. articles to profl. jours. Mem. Soc. Bibl. Lit., Cath. Bibl. Soc. Office: Marquette Univ O'Hara Hall PO Box 1881 Milwaukee WI 53201-1881

WILD, ROBERT LEE, physics educator; b. Sedalia, Mo., Oct. 9, 1921; s. Alwin Bernard and Nellie Marie (Nowlin) W.; m. Frances Elleta Wheeler, Oct. 7, 1943; children: James Robert, Janet Gayle, Margaret Nell. B.S., Central Mo. State U., 1943; M.A., U. Mo., 1948, Ph.D., 1950. Asst. prof. physics U. N.D., Grand Forks, 1950-52; prof. U. Calif., Riverside, 1953-88, prof. emeritus, 1988; Fulbright lectr. U. Philippines, 1981-82; mem. adv. com. Calif. Sci. Project, 1988—. Contbr. articles profl. jours. Served with AUS, 1943-45. NSF fellow, 1959-60; recipient Disting. Teaching award U. Calif., Riverside, 1973, Faculty of the Yr. award U. Calif.-Riverside Alumni, 1993. Pub. Svc. award Citizens U. Com., 1994. Mem. Am. Phys. Soc., Am. Assn. Physics Tchrs. (v.p. sect. 1983-84, pres. So. Calif. sect. 1985-86, pres., 1986-87, award 1966), Sigma Xi. Baptist. Home: 5709 Durango Rd Riverside CA 92506-3216 Office: U Calif Dept Physics Riverside CA 92521

WILD, ROBERT WARREN, lawyer; b. Syracuse, N.Y., Mar. 25, 1942; s. Robert Sumner and Evelyn I. (Yorman) W.; m. Elizabeth Trowbridge, Sept. 5, 1965; children: Robert Mason, Alexander Lewis, Elizabeth Anne. BS, MIT, 1964; JD, Cornell U., 1970. Bar: N.Y. 1971, D.C. 1973. Engr. Smithsonian Astrophysical Obs., Cambridge, Mass., 1965-67; atty., advisor U.S. Dept. Justice, Washington, 1970-72; law clk. to Hon. Justice William H. Rehnquist U.S. Supreme Ct., Washington, 1972-73; ptnr. Nixon, Hargrave, Devans & Doyle, Rochester, N.Y., 1973—. Trustee Rochester Police Benevolent Assn., 1994—. Mem. Monroe County Bar Assn. (trustee 1990-91, 92-94, treas. 1992-94, counsel 1994—). Office: Nixon Hargrave Devans & Doyle Clinton Sq PO Box 1051 Rochester NY 14603

WILDE, CARLTON D., lawyer; b. Houston, Apr. 11, 1935; s. Henry Dayton and Louise (Key) W.; m. Martha Cloyes, July 26, 1958; children: Carlton D. Jr., Jennifer. Student, Coll. of William and Mary, 1953-55; B.A., U. Tex., 1957, J.D., 1959. Assoc. Bracewell & Patterson, Houston, 1959-62, ptnr., 1962-67, 85—, mng. ptnr., 1967-85. Trustee Presbyn. Sch., So. Tex. Coll. Law. Fellow Am. Bar Found., Tex. Bar Found., Houston Bar Found.; mem. ABA, State Bar Tex., River Oaks Country Club, Coronado Club (Houston), Biltmore Forest Country Club (Asheville, N.C.). Republican. Home: 3105 Reba Dr Houston TX 77019-6209 Office: Bracewell & Patterson 2900 S Tower Pennzoil Pl 711 Louisiana St Ste 2900 Houston TX 77002-2721

WILDE, DANIEL UNDERWOOD, computer engineering educator; b. Wilmington, Ohio, Dec. 27, 1937; s. Arthur John and Ruby Dale (Underwood) W. BSEE, U. Ill., 1960; MS, M.I.T., 1962, Ph.D., 1966. Research instr. medicine Boston U. Med. Sch., 1964-66; asst. prof. info. adminstrn. U. Conn., 1966-69, assoc. prof., 1970-75, prof., 1976-85; assoc. dir. New Eng. Rsch. Application Ctr., Storrs, Conn., 1966-72, dir., 1973-85; dir. NASA Indsl. Application Ctr., 1972-91; pres. NERAC, Inc., Tolland, Conn., 1985—; trustee Engring. Index, Inc.; cons. Am. Soc. Metals, 1973—. Author: Introduction to Computing: Problem Solving, Algorithms and Data Structures, 1973; contbr. articles to profl. jours. Served with USAF. Recipient NASA Public Service award, 1975. Mem. IEEE, Am. Soc. Info. Sci., Assn. Computing Machinery, Assn. Info. and Dissemination Centers (sec.-treas. 1976-79, pres. 1979-81). Office: Nerac Inc 1 Technology Dr Tolland CT 06084-3902

WILDE, DAVID, publisher, writer; b. Hereford, Nov. 12, 1944; s. Elizabeth Lillian (Price-Slawson) W. Diploma, Kneller Hall, London, 1965; pvt. mus. studies with Carmello Pace, Malta, 1964-68; student, Cardiff (Wales) Coll. Music, 1970-71; diploma in art, Open U., Leicester, Eng., 1980; student, Lancaster (Eng.) U., 1980-81, U. N.Mex., 1984. With BBC Radio, Eng., 1975-79; resident mem. wind ensemble Loughborough (Eng.) U., 1976-79; oil field worker Western Oceanic Inc., North Sea, Scotland, 1983-84; tutor U. N.Mex., Albuquerque, 1986-88, tchr. dept. continuing edn., 1989-90; musician/composer Civic Orch., Albuquerque, 1988-89; legal rschr. Wilde & Sprague, Albuquerque, 1988-90; pub., author Wilde Pub., Albuquerque, 1989—; clerical officer Severn-Trent Water, Eng., 1972-74, Social Security, Eng., 1983. Author: In the South: The Five Year Diary of a Journey Across America, 1991, Route 66: The Five Year Diary of a Journey Across America, 1991, Wildeland: Prose, 1992, North Sea Saga, 1960s: Opera of Oil, 1993, Desert Meditations: A Fairy Tale of New Mexico, 1993, Black Innocence: The Immigrant, 1993, Poems, People, Places: Travels on My Own, 1994, Basic Horn Technique: Studies for the French Horn, 1994; editor 6 books; actor Geronimo prodn. Turner Network TV, 1993; extra various prodns., 1969-84. rschr. SRIC, Albuquerque, 1989-94; cons. N.Mex. Bd. Appraisers, Albuquerque, 1989-90. Roman Catholic. Avocations: travel, classical music, spirituality, history, mathematics. Office: 105 Stanford Dr SE Albuquerque NM 87106-3537 also: Wilde Pub PO Box 4524 Albuquerque NM 87196-4524

WILDE, EDWIN FREDERICK, mathematics educator; b. Lombard, Ill., Jan. 14, 1931; s. Edwin Frederick and Carrie Belle (Hammond) W.; m. Connie Mae Rawlings, Aug. 23, 1952; children—Brad Alan, Bruce Ramon, Elizabeth Lynn. B.S., Ill. State U., 1952, M.S., 1953; M.A., U. Ill., 1955, Ph.D., 1959; postgrad., U. Wis., part time, 1955-58, Stanford U., 1964-65. With Beloit (Wis.) Coll., 1955-76, prof. math., dean faculty, 1969-71, v.p. for planning, 1971-75; dean Roger Williams Coll., Bristol, R.I., 1976-80; provost, dean of faculty U. Tampa, Fla., 1980-86; vice chancellor U. S.C., Spartanburg, 1986-91, prof. math., 1991—; cons. AID insts., India, 1964, Insts. Internat. Edn., East Pakistan, 1969. NSF Sr. Sci. Faculty fellow, 1964-65. Mem. Math. Assn. Am. (bd. govs. 1968-69, 72-75). Home: 275 James Rd Gaffney SC 29341-4013 Office: U South Carolina Dept Ed Spartanburg SC 29303

WILDE, HAROLD RICHARD, college president; b. Wauwatosa, Wis., May 14, 1945; s. Harold Richard and Winifred (Wiley) W.; m. Benna Brecher, Feb. 4, 1970; children: Anna, Henry, Elizabeth Ty. BA, Amherst Coll., 1967; MA, PhD, Harvard U., Cambridge, Mass., 1973. Spl. asst. to gov. Office of Gov., State of Wis., Madison, 1972-75; ins. commr. Office of Commr. of Ins., State of Wis., Madison, 1975-79; spl. asst. to pres. U. Wis. System, Madison, 1979-81; v.p. for external affairs Beloit (Wis.) Coll., 1981-91; pres. North Ctrl. Coll., Naperville, Ill., 1991—. Bd. dirs. Ctr. for Pub. Representation, Inc., Madison, 1981-87, Beloit Community Found., 1988-91, Budget Funding Corp., 1993—. Mem. Phi Beta Kappa. Home: 329 S Brainard St Naperville IL 60540-5401 Office: North Ctrl Coll 30 N Brainard St Naperville IL 60540-4607

WILDE, JOHN, artist, educator; b. Milw., Dec. 12, 1919; s. Emil F. and Mathilda (Lotz) W.; m. Helen Ashman, July 1943 (dec. Dec. 1966); children: Jonathan, Phoebe; m. Shirley Miller, 1969. B.S., U. Wis., 1942, M.S., 1948. Mem. faculty U. Wis., 1948—, prof. art, 1960—, chmn. dept. art and art edn., 1960-62, Alfred Sessler Distinguished prof. art, 1969-82, prof. emeritus, 1982—; elected mem. Nat. Acad. Design, 1994. Works exhibited Met. Mus. Art, Mus. Modern Art, Whitney Mus. Am. Art, Corcoran Mus. Art, Mpls. Art Mus., San Francisco Mus. Art, Whitney Mus. Am. Art, 1978-80, Nat. Portrait Gallery, Smithsonian Instn., 1980, Nat. Gallery, Washington, 1988; retrospective Elvehjem Mus. Art, U. Wis., 1984-85; 3-man retrospective, Milw. Art Mus., 1982, others; represented in permanent collections, Pa. Acad. Art, Detroit Inst. Fine Art, Worcester Art Mus., Wadsworth Atheneum, Whitney Mus. Am. Art, Carnegie Inst., Nat. Collection Art, Smithsonian Instn., Yale U. Art Gallery, Butler Inst. Am. Art, Art Inst. Chgo., Sheldon Meml. Art Gallery, U. Nebr., Zimmerli Mus. Art, Rutgers U., N. Brunswick, N.J., Mus. Contemporary Art, Chgo., others, also extensive exhbns. abroad. Recipient numerous awards for painting and drawing in regional and nat. exhbns. including, Childe Hassam purchase award Am. Acad. and Inst. Arts and Letters, 1981, 87. Office: U Wis 6221 Humanities Bldg Madison WI 53706

WILDE, NORMAN TAYLOR, JR., investment banking company executive; b. Phila., Sept. 13, 1930; s. Norman Taylor and Elizabeth (Duthie) W.; m. Ruth Nancy Osterndorf, Sept. 26, 1959; children: Karen, Suzanne, Norman Taylor III. B.S., U. Pa., 1953. Vice pres. Janney, Montgomery, Scott, Inc., Phila., 1966-69; pres. Janney, Montgomery, Scott, Inc., Phila., 1969—; trustee Penn Mut. Life Ins. Co.; chmn. Pa. Trust Co., 1995—, Abington Meml. Hosp., 1995—. Served to lt. USN, 1953-55. Mem. Nat. Assn. Security Dealers (chmn. 1983—), Securities Industries Assn. (gov. 1979-82), Pine Valley Golf Club, Phila. Cricket Club. Office: Janney Montgomery Scott Inc 1801 Market St Philadelphia PA 19103-1628

WILDE, PATRICIA, artistic director; b. Ottawa, Ont., Can., July 16, 1928; m. George Bardyguine; children: Anya, Youri. Dancer Am. Concert Ballet, Marquis de Cuevas Ballet Internat., N.Y.C., 1944-45, Ballet Russe de Monte Carlo, N.Y.C., 1945-49, Roland Petit's Ballet Paris, Met. Ballet Britain, London, 1949-50; prin. ballerina N.Y.C. Ballet, 1950-65; dir. Harkness Sch. Ballet, N.Y.C., 1965-67; ballet mistress, tchr. Am. Ballet Theatre, N.Y.C., 1969-77; dir. Am. Ballet Theatre Sch., N.Y.C., 1977-82; artistic dir. Pitts. Ballet Theatre, 1982—; tchr. Am. Ballet Theatre, 1969-77, Joffrey scholarship program, N.Y.C. Ballet, 1968-69; established Sch. of Grand Theatre of Geneva, 1968-69; adjudicator Regional Ballet in Am. S.E. and S.W., 1969-82; choreographer N.Y. Philharmonic; guest tchr. various ballet cos. and colls.; trustee Dance U.S.A.; panelist Nat. Choreographic Project. Recipient Leadership award in Arts and Letters YWCA, 1990, Pitts. Woman of Yr. in Arts award, 1993. Office: Pitts Ballet Theatre 2900 Liberty Ave Pittsburgh PA 15201-1511

WILDE, PAUL K., computer company executive. BS in Acctg., Brigham Young U. With Prive Waterhouse and Co., L.A., 1974-78; chief fin. officer Infomatics, 1978-85; chief fin. officer, v.p. internat. ops. Candle Corp., 1985-89; chief fin. officer Viasoft, Inc., 1989-90; with Synon Corp., Larkspur, Calif., 1991—, v.p., sec., chief fin. officer. Office: Synon Corp 1100 Larkspur Landing Cir Larkspur CA 94939-1827*

WILDE, WILLIAM KEY, lawyer; b. Houston, May 3, 1933; s. Henry Dayton and Louise (Key) W.; m. Ann Jeannine Austin, Aug. 3, 1957; children—William Key, Austin, Adrienne, Michael. A.B., Coll. William and Mary, Williamsburg, Va., 1955; J.D., U. Tex., Austin, 1958. Bar: Tex. 1958. Assoc. Bracewell & Patterson, Houston, 1958-61, ptnr., 1961—; dir. Nat. Convenience Stores, Inc., 1959—. Bd. dirs. Goodwill Industries Houston, 1972—; elder 1st Presbyn. Ch.; trustee Presbyn. Found. U.S.A., Ky., 1983-391, Schriener Coll., 1991—. Fellow ABA, Am. Bar Found., Am. Coll. Trial Lawyers; mem. Tex. Bar Assn. (bd. dirs. 1984-87), Houston Bar Assn. (pres. 1982-83), Houston Club (pres. 1981-82), Houston Country Club (bd. dirs., pres. 1989-90). Republican. Avocations: golf; tennis; skiing; scuba diving. Home: 6206 Woods Bridge Way Houston TX 77007-7041 Office: Bracewell & Patterson 2900 S Tower Pennzoil Place Houston TX 77002

WILDE, WILLIAM RICHARD, lawyer; b. Markesan, Wis., Mar. 1, 1953; s. Leslie Maurice and Elaine Margaret (Schweder) W.; m. Carolyn Margaret Zieman, July 17, 1981 (div. 1987); 1 child, Leah Marie; m. Barbara Joan Rohlf, Jan. 6, 1990. BA, U. Wis., Milw., 1975; JD, Marquette U., 1980. Bar: Wis. 1980, U.S. Dist. Ct. (ea. and we. dists.) Wis. 1980. Dist. atty. Green Lake County, Green Lake, Wis., 1980-83, corp.counsel, 1981; ptnr. Curtis, Wilde and Neal, Oshkosh, Wis., 1983—. Mem. Assn. Trial Lawyers Am., Wis. Bar Assn., Wis. Acad. Trial Lawyers (Amicus Curiae Brief com. 1987-92, bd. dirs., assoc. editor The Verdict, treas. 1993, sec. 1994, v.p. 1995, pres.-elect 1996), Wis. Assn. Criminal Def. Lawyers (bd. dirs. 1987-91), Winnebbago County Bar Assn., Green Lake County Bar Assn., Lions. Home: PO Box 282 Markesan WI 53946-0282 Office: Curtis Wilde & Neal 1010 W 20th Ave Oshkosh WI 54901-6618

WILDE, WILSON, insurance company executive; b. Hartford, Conn., Sept. 24, 1927; s. Philip Alden and Alice Augusta (Wilson) W.; m. Joanne Gerta Menzel, June 19, 1953; children—Stephen W., David W., Elisabeth L., Richard A. Student, Swarthmore Coll., 1945-46; BA, Williams Coll., 1949. Sales agt. Conn. Gen. Life Ins. Co., Hartford, 1949-53; with Hartford Steam Boiler Inspection & Ins. Co., 1953—, exec. v.p., 1970-71, pres., CEO, 1971—, chmn., CEO, 1993-94, chmn. exec. com., 1994—; bd. dirs. Phoenix Home Life Mut. Ins. Co., PXRE Corp. Corporator Inst. Living, Hartford; hon. bd. dirs. Hartford Stage Co., 1973—, Jr. Achievement, Old State House Assn., 1976—; trustee Loomis-Chaffee Sch., 1974—, chmn. bd., 1988—. Served with USNR, 1945-47, 51-53. Club: Hartford (pres. 1974). Office: Hartford Steam Boiler 1 State St PO Box 5024 Hartford CT 06102-5024

WILDEBUSH, JOSEPH FREDERICK, economist; b. Bklyn., July 18, 1910; s. Harry Frederick and Elizabeth (Stolzenberg) W.; AB, Columbia, 1931, postgrad Law Sch., 1932; LLB, Bklyn. Law Sch., 1934, JD, 1967; m. Martha Janssens, July 18, 1935; children: Diane Elaine (Mrs. Solon Finkelstein), Joan Marilyn (Mrs. Bobby Sanford Berry); m. Edith Sorensen, May 30, 1964. Admitted to N.Y. State bar, 1934, Fed. bar, 1935; practice law, N.Y.C., 1934-41; labor relations dir. Botany Mills, Passaic, N.J., 1945-48; exec. v.p. Silk and Rayon Printers and Dyers Assn. Am., Inc., Paterson, N.J., 1948-70; exec. v.p. Textile Printers and Dyers Labor Rels. Inst., Paterson, 1954-70; mem. panel labor arbitrators Fed. Mediation and Conciliation Svc., N.Y. State Mediation Bd., N.J. State Mediation Bd., N.J. Pub. Employment Relations Commn., Am. Arbitration Assn.; co-adj. faculty Rutgers U., 1948-90; lectr. Pres. Pascack Valley Hosp., Westwood, N.J., 1950-64, chmn. bd., 1964-67, chmn. emeritus, 1967-80; dir. Group Health Ins. N.Y., 1950-56. Served as maj. Engrs. Corps, U.S. Army, 1941-43. Mem. N.Y. County Lawyers Assn., Am. Acad. Polit. and Social Sci., Indsl. Rels. Rsch. Assn., Ret. Officers Assn., Nat. Geog. Soc. Lutheran. Contbr. articles profl. jours. Home and Office: 37 James Ter Pompton Lakes NJ 07442-1921

WILDENTHAL, BRYAN HOBSON, university administrator; b. San Marcos, Tex., Nov. 4, 1937; s. Bryan and Doris (Kellam) W.; m. Joyce Lockhart; children: Rebecca, Bryan, Lora; m. Adele Sutton; children: Kerry, Andrea. BA, Sul Ross State Coll., 1958; PhD, U. Kans., 1964. Rsch. assoc. Rice U., Houston, 1964-66; AEC postdoctoral fellow Oak Ridge (Tenn.) Nat. Lab., 1966-68; asst. prof. physics Tex. A&M U., College Station, 1968-69; assoc. prof. physics Mich. State U., East Lansing, 1969-72, prof. physics, 1972-83; head physics and atmospheric sci. Drexel U., Phila., 1983-87; dean arts and scis. U. N.Mex., Albuquerque, 1987-92; v.p. acad. affairs U. Tex., Dallas, 1992-94; provost, v.p. acad. affairs, 1994—; cons. Los Alamos (N.Mex.) Nat. Lab., 1987-92; sr. U.S. prof. Humboldt Found., Germany, 1973. Fellow J.S. Guggenheim Found., 1977. Mem. Phi Beta Kappa. Home: 3002 Cross Timbers Ln Garland TX 75044-2008 Office: U Tex at Dallas Office Academic Affairs Richardson TX 75083

WILDENTHAL, C(LAUD) KERN, physician, educator; b. San Marcos, Tex., July 1, 1941; s. Bryan and Doris (Kellam) W.; m. Margaret Dehlinger, Oct. 15, 1964; children—Pamela, Catharine. B.A., Sul Ross Coll., 1960; M.D., U. Tex. Southwestern Med. Ctr., Dallas, 1964; Ph.D., U. Cambridge, Eng., 1970. Intern Bellevue Hosp., N.Y.C., 1964-65; resident in medicine, fellow cardiology Parkland Hosp., Dallas, 1965-67; research fellow Nat. Heart Inst., Bethesda, Md., 1967-68; vis. research fellow Strangeways Research Lab., Cambridge, 1968-70; asst. prof. to prof. internal medicine and physiology U. Tex. Southwestern Med. Ctr., Dallas, 1970-76, prof., dean grad. sch., 1976-80, prof., dean Southwestern Med. Sch., 1980-86, prof., pres., 1986—; hon. fellow Hughes Hall, U. Cambridge, 1994—; bd. dirs. Westcott Comm. Inc. Author: Regulation of Cardiac Metabolism, 1976, Degradative Processes in Heart and Skeletal Muscle, 1980; contbr. articles to profl. jours. Bd. dirs. Dallas Symphony, Dallas Opera, Dallas Mus. Art, S.W. Mus. Sci. and Tech., Dallas Citizen's Coun., Am. Friends Cambridge U. Recipient rsch. career devel. award NIH, 1972; spl. rsch. fellow USPHS, 1968-70; Guggenheim fellow, 1975-76. Mem. AMA, Am. Soc. Clin. Investigation, Am. Coll. Cardiology, Royal Soc. Medicine Gt. Britain, Am. Physiol. Soc., Internat. Soc. Heart Rsch. (past pres. Am. sect.), Am. Fedn. Clin. Rsch., Assn. Am. Med Colls., Assn. Am. Physicians, Am. Heart Assn. (past chmn. sci. policy com.), Assn. Acad. Health Ctrs. (past chmn. sci. policy com.). Home: 4001 Hanover Ave Dallas TX 75225-7010 Office: U Tex Southwestern Med Ctr 5323 Harry Hines Blvd Dallas TX 75235-7200

WILDER, BILLY, motion picture director, writer, producer; b. Vienna, Austria, June 22, 1906; came to U.S., 1934; m. Audrey Young. Reporter Berlin. Began: film writing with People On Sunday, produced in, Berlin; followed by Emil and the Detectives; now in, Mus. Modern Art, went to, Paris; writer, dir.: Mauvaise Graine; placed under contract as writer, Paramount Studios; writer: (in collaboration) screenplays Bluebeard's Eighth Wife, 1938, Midnight, 1939, Ninotchka, 1939, Arise My Love, 1940, Hold Back the Dawn, 1941; dir., writer: (in collaboration) Five Graves to Cairo, 1943, Double Indemnity, 1944, The Lost Weekend (Acad. award Best Dir.), 1945 (co-award with Charles Brackett for screenplay), The Emperor Waltz, 1948, A Foreign Affair, 1948, Sunset Boulevard, 1950 (Acad. award co-award best story, screenplay); producer, dir., writer: (in collaboration) The Big Carnival (Ace in the Hole), 1951, Stalag 17, 1953, Sabrina, 1954, Love in the Afternoon, 1957, Some Like It Hot, 1959, The Apartment, 1960 (Acad. awards best direction, best picture, co-award best story and screenplay); co-producer, dir., writer: (in collaboration) The Seven Year Itch, 1959; dir., collaborator: The Spirit of St. Louis, 1957, Witness for the Prosecution, 1957, Buddy, Buddy, 1981; producer, dir., writer: One, Two, Three, 1961, Irma La Douce, 1963, Kiss Me, Stupid, 1964, The Fortune Cookie, 1966, The Private Life of Sherlock Holmes, 1970, Avanti, 1972, Fedora, 1979; dir., author: screenplay The Front Page, 1974. Head film sect. Psychol. Warfare div. U.S. Army, 1945. Recipient Poses Creative Art medal for film Brandeis U., 1983, Irving G. Thalberg award Motion Picture Acad., 1988, D.W. Griffith Dirs. award, 6 Acad. awards, 2 Laurel awards Screen Writers Guild. Address: care Harold J Nelson Accty Corp 6345 Balboa Blvd Ste 382 Encino CA 91316

WILDER, DAVID RANDOLPH, materials engineer, consultant; b. Lorimor, Iowa, June 11, 1929; s. Rex Marshall and Ethel Marie (Busch) W.; m. Donna Jean Moore, June 17, 1951; children: Susan, Michael, Margaret, Bruce. BS, Iowa State U., 1951, MS, 1952, PhD, 1958. Registered profl. engr., Iowa. Engr. Ames Lab., 1951-81; faculty mem. dept. materials sci. and engring. Iowa State U., Ames, 1955—, prof. engring., chmn. dept., 1961-89, prof. engring., 1989-91, prof. emeritus, 1991—; cons. to various industries, fed. agys, 1955—. Contbr. numerous tech. paper to profl. lit.; patentee in field. Fellow Am. Ceramic Soc., Accreditation Bd. for Engring. and Tech.; mem. Nat. Inst. Ceramic Engrs., Am. Soc. for Engring. Edn., Keramos. Home: 1214 Ridgewood Ave Ames IA 50010-5208

WILDER, GENE, actor, director, writer; b. Milw., June 11, 1935; s. William J. and Jeanne (Baer) Silberman; m. Mary Joan Schutz, Oct. 27, 1967 (div. 1974); 1 child, Katharine Anastasia; m. Gilda Radner, 1984 (dec.); m. Karen Boyer, Sept. 8, 1991. BA, U. Iowa, 1955; postgrad., Bristol Old Vic Theatre Sch., 1955-56. Appeared in Broadway play: The Complaisant Lover, 1962 (Clarence Derwent award); appeared in motion pictures: Bonnie and Clyde, 1966, The Producers, 1967 (Acad. award nomination), Start the Revolution Without Me, 1968, Quackser Fortune Has a Cousin in the Bronx, 1969, Willy Wonka and the Chocolate Factory, 1970, Everything You Always Wanted to Know About Sex, 1971, Rhinoceros, 1972, Blazing Saddles, 1973, The Little Prince, 1974, Silver Streak, 1976, The Frisco Kid, 1979, Stir Crazy, 1980; Hanky Panky, 1982, See No Evil, Hear No Evil, 1989, Funny About Love, 1990, Another You, 1991; dir., writer, actor film: The Adventures of Sherlock Holmes' Smarter Brother, 1975, The World's Greatest Lover, 1977, Sunday Lovers, 1980, The Woman in Red, 1984, Haunted Honeymoon, 1986; actor, co-writer film: Young Frankenstein, 1974 (Acad. award nomination); TV appearances include: The Trouble With People, 1973, Marlo Thomas Spl., 1973, The Scarecrow, 1972, Thursday's Games, 1973, (series) Something Wilder, 1994—. Campaigned with Elaine May and Rene Taylor for Eugene McCarthy, Allard Lowenstein and Paul O'Dwyer, 1968. Served with U.S. Army, 1956-58. Office: Creative Artists 9830 Wilshire Blvd Beverly Hills CA 90212*

WILDER, JENNIFER ROSE, interior designer; b. Washington, Nov. 23, 1944; d. Winfield Scott and Blanche Irene (Taylor) Wilder; m. Scott Harris Smith, 1973 (div. 1987); children: Jason W., Adam S., Molly L., Whitney W. AA, Colo. Woman's Coll., Denver, 1965, BA, 1967. Interior designer Jamaica St. Interiors, Aurora, Colo., 1969-71; mgr./interior designer Interior Systems, Denver, 1971-73; owner/interior designer Jennifer Smith Designs, Denver, 1973-85, Inside Image Ltd., Castle Rock, Colo., 1985-86; interior designer Greenbaum Home Furnishings, Bellevue, Wash., 1986-94, Westbay Interiors, Gig Harbor, Wash., 1994—; instr. Tacoma C.C., Gig Harbor, Wash., 1995—. Recipient Design for Better Living award Am. Wood Coun., Seattle, 1987, Silver Mame awards Master Bldrs. Assn., 1992, 1st place Internat. Design Competition, Shintaku Daiwa, Hokaido, Japan,1 992. Mem. Am. Soc. Interior Design. Avocations: foreign languages, classical piano. Office: Westbay Interiors 5790 Soundview Dr Gig Harbor WA 98335

WILDER, JOHN SHELTON, lieutenant governor, president senate; b. Fayette City, TN, June 3, 1921; s. John Chamblee and Martha (Shelton) W.; m. Marcelle Morton, Dec. 31, 1941; children: John Shelton, David Morton. Student, U. Tenn.; LL.B., Memphis Law U., 1957. Bar: Tenn. 1957. Engaged in farming Longtown, Tenn., 1943—; supr. mgmt. Longtown Supply Co.; judge Fayette County Ct.; mem. Tenn. Senate, 1959—; lt. gov. Tenn., 1971—; past pres. Nat. Assn. Soil Conservation Dists., Tenn. Soil Conservation Assn., Tenn. Agrl. Council; exec. com. So. Legis. Conf., Conf. Lt. Govs.; dir. Oakland Deposit Bank, Tenn., Somerville Bank and Trust Co., Tenn. Served with U.S. Army, 1942-43. Mem. Tenn. Cotton Ginners Assn. (past pres.), Delta Theta Phi. Democrat. Methodist. Club: Shriners. Office: Legislative Plz Ste 1 Nashville TN 37243-0026*

WILDER, MICHAEL STEPHEN, insurance company executive; b. New Haven, Conn., Sept. 8, 1941. BA, Yale U., 1963; JD, Harvard U., 1966. Bar: Conn. 1966. Atty. Hartford (Conn.) Fire Ins. Co., 1967-69, asst. gen. counsel, 1969-71, assoc. gen. counsel, 1971-75, gen. coun., sec., 1975-87, sr. v.p., gen. counsel, sec., 1987-95; sr. v.p., gen. counsel ITT Hartford Group, Inc., 1995—. Mem. ABA, Conn. Bar Assn. Office: Hartford Fire Insurance Co Hartford Plz Hartford CT 06115

WILDER, PELHAM, JR., chemist, pharmacologist, educator; b. Americus, Ga., July 20, 1920; s. Pelham and Hattie (Wilder) W.; m. Alma Sterly Lebey, Mar. 20, 1945; children: Alma Ann, Pelham III, Sterly Lebey. A.B., Emory U., 1942, M.A., 1943; M.A., Harvard U., 1947, Ph.D., 1950. Teaching fellow Harvard U., 1943-44, 46-49; instr. chemistry Duke U., 1949-52, asst. prof., 1952-58, assoc. prof., 1958-62, prof., 1962-67, prof. chemistry and pharmacology, 1967-87, Univ. Disting. Svc. prof. chemistry and pharmacology, 1987-90, Univ. Disting. Svc. prof. emeritus, 1990—, univ. marshal, chief of protocol, 1977—; cons. NSF, Washington, 1960-68; Research Triangle Inst., Durham, 1965—, E.I. duPont deNemours & Co., 1966-69; mem. advanced placement com. Coll. Entrance Exam. Bd., N.Y., 1967-75, chmn. chemistry com., 1969-75, cons., 1975—; mem. exec. com. Gov. N.C. Sci. Advisory Com., 1962-64. Author: (with W.C. Vosburgh) Laboratory Manual of Fundamentals of Analytical Chemistry, 1956, Laboratory Manual of Physical Chemistry of Aqueous Solutions, 1967; Contbr. articles to profl. jours. Bd. dirs. Durham Acad., chmn., 1970-72; chmn. Exptl. Study of Religion and Soc., Raleigh, N.C., 1966-69. Served with USNR, 1944-46. Recipient 1st annual Alumni Distinguished Undergrad. Teaching award Duke, 1971, Disting. Pub. Svc. award USN, 1989. Mem. Am. Chem. Soc. (chmn. N.C. sect. 1956, com. on profl. tng.), Assn. Naval ROTC Colls. and Univs. (pres. 1982-88), Chem. Soc. London, Phi Beta Kappa (chpt. pres. 1974-75), Sigma Xi, Omicron Delta Kappa. Democrat. Presbyn. (ruling elder; exec. com. Ednl. Instns. Synod of N.C. 1966-72). Lodge: Rotary Club: Univ. (Durham, N.C.). Home: 2514 Wrightwood Ave Durham NC 27705-5830 Office: Duke U Dept Chemistry PO Box 90357 Durham NC 27708-0357

WILDER, ROBERT GEORGE, advertising and public relations executive; b. Hornell, N.Y., Mar. 27, 1920; s. George Reuben and Laura (Nolan) W.; m. Annabel D. Heritage, Feb. 21, 1953; children: Loraine Wilder Powell, Gordon Heritage. B.A., Coll. Wooster, 1942. Propr. Robert G. Wilder & Co., Inc. (public relations), Phila., 1945-50; dir. public relations Lewis &

Gilman (advt.-public relations), Phila., 1950-55; v.p. Lewis & Gilman (advt.-public relations), 1955-59, exec. v.p., 1959-64, pres., from 1964; chmn. Lewis, Gilman & Kynett ((merger with Foote, Cone & Belding)), 1983-90, chmn. emeritus, 1990—; bd. dirs. Rittenhouse Trust Co.; dir. emeritus Round Hill Devel. Co. Ltd., Montego Bay, Jamaica. Trustee emeritus Franklin Inst., Lankenau Hosp., Phila.; bd. dirs. Independence Hall Assn.; life trustee emeritus Coll. of Wooster, Ohio. Served to lt. comdr. USNR, 1942-46. Recipient award Charles M. Price Sch., 1971, Bus. and Industry award Opportunities Industrialization Ctr., 1971, Disting. Alumni award Coll. Wooster, 1971, Area Council Econ. Edn. Enterprise award, 1980, Gold Liberty Bell award TV, Radio & Advt. Club Phila., 1982, Vol. of Yr. award Leukemia Soc. Eastern Pa., 1983, Silver medal Phila. Club of Advt. Women, 1984, ann. achievers award Wheels, 1985, Good Scout award Phila. coun. Boy Scouts Am., 1986, Heart of Phila. award Am. Heart Assn., 1989, Great Am. award Poor Richard Club Phila., 1990; named to Bus./Profl. Advt. Assn. Hall of Fame, 1988; inducted into First Annual Hall of Fame of Broadcast Pioneers, Phila. chpt., 1992. Mem. Res. Officers Assn. (past pres. Pa.), Greater Phila. C. of C. (past chmn., bd. dirs., William Penn award 1991); Clubs: Union League (past pres.), Penn, Bachelors Barge (chmn.), Phila. Country, Merion Cricket, Sunday Breakfast. Home: Grays Ln House 100 Grays Ln Haverford PA 19041-1727 Office: Tierney & Ptnrs 200 S Broad St Philadelphia PA 19102-3803

WILDER, RONALD PARKER, economics educator; b. Freeport, Tex., Jan. 15, 1941; s. J. Barton and Lois (Parker) W.; m. Charlotte D. Pearson, Sept. 4, 1965; children: Erika, Rachel, David. BA, Rice U., 1963, MA, 1964; PhD, Vanderbilt U., 1969. Asst. prof. econs. U. S.C., Columbia, 1970-75, assoc. prof., 1975-80, prof., 1980—, chmn. dept. econs., 1987—. Co-author: Stock Life Insurance Profitability, 1986; mem. editorial bd. So. Econ. J., 1978-80; contbr. articles to profl. jours. Capt. U.S. Army, 1968-70. Fellow Ford Found., Vanderbilt U., 1964-65. Mem. Am. Econ. Assn., So. Econ. Assn., Omicron Delta Epsilon. United Methodist. Avocations: hiking, canoeing. Office: U of SC Dept of Econs Columbia SC 29208

WILDER, VALERIE, ballet company administrator; b. Pasadena, Calif., Aug. 5, 1947; d. Douglas Wilder and Helen Marie (Wilson) Morrill; m. Geoffrey Duer Perry, Nov. 24, 1973; children: Stuart Whittier, Sabina Woodman. Student, Butler U., Indpls., 1966-68, U. Toronto, 1969-75. Dancer Nat. Ballet Can., Toronto, 1970-78; ptnr. Perry & Wilder Inc., Toronto, 1976-83; artistic adminstr. Nat. Ballet Can., Toronto, 1983-86, assoc. artistic dir., 1986-87, co-artistic dir., 1987-89, assoc. dir., 1989-96, exec. dir., 1996—; adv. bd. Dancer Transition Ctr., Toronto, 1986—; dance adv. panel Can. Coun., 1984-89; dance adv. com. Ont. Arts. Coun., 1985-90. Bd. dirs. Toronto Arts Coun., 1990-94. Mem. Dance in Can. Assn., Can. Assn. Profl. Dance Orgns. (bd. dirs.). Avocations: competitive running, triathlon. Office: Nat Ballet of Can, 157 King St E, Toronto, ON Canada M5C 1G9

WILDERMUTH, GORDON LEE, architect; b. Lima, Ohio, Nov. 13, 1937; s. Oliver and Margery (Mason) W.; B.S. in Architecture, U. Cin., 1961; m. Patricia Williams, June 1, 1963 (dec. 1983); m. Hannelore Brauning, Aug. 10, 1993. With Skidmore, Owings & Merrill, Architects/Engrs., 1963—, assoc., 1967-70, assoc. ptnr., 1970-73, ptnr., 1973-87, ret. ptnr., 1987-90, cons. ptnr., 1991—. Bd. dirs. Police Athletic League N.Y., 1974-81, N.Y. Poly. Inst., 1975-77, Founders Council, Field Mus. Natural History. Served with Spl. Forces, U.S. Army, 1962-1963. Recipient Aga Khan award for architecture, 1983. Fellow AIA. Home: 175 E Delaware Pl Chicago IL 60611-1739 Office: Skidmore Owings & Merrill 224 S Michigan Ave Chicago IL 60604-2507

WILDES, LEON, lawyer, educator; b. Scranton, Pa., Mar. 4, 1933. BA magna cum laude, Yeshiva U., 1954; JD, NYU, 1957, LLM, 1959. Bar: N.Y. 1958, U.S. Dist. Ct. (so. dist.) N.Y. 1960, U.S. Supreme Ct. 1961. Ptnr. Wildes and Weinberg, N.Y.C., 1960—; adj. prof. law Benjamin N. Cardozo Sch. Law, N.Y.C., 1981—. Contbr. numerous articles to law revs. Mem. ABA, Assn. of Bar of City of N.Y. (com. immigration and nationality law 1975-78, 88-91, 95—), Am. Immigration Lawyers Assn. (nat. pres. 1970-71, bd. govs. 1971—, co-chair ethics com. 1993—, editor Immigration and Nationality Law Symposium 1983). Office: 515 Madison Ave New York NY 10022-5403

WILDHABER, MICHAEL RENE, accountant; b. Jefferson City, Mo., Aug. 4, 1952; s. Rainey A. and Velma W.; m. Paula M. Wildhaber, Sept. 28, 1974; 1 child, Wendy. AA, Florissant Valley Coll., 1972; BS, U. Mo., 1974. CPA, Mo.; cert. info. sys. auditor, cert. internal auditor, cert. tax preparer, assoc. ins. acctg. and fin., enrolled agt. Sr. auditor I.T.T. Fin., St. Louis, 1974-79; audit mgr. Navco, St. Louis, 1980-85; contr. Millers mutual, Alton, Ill., 1985-88; pres. R&M Tax and Acctg., St. Louis, 1988—. Tchr. Jr. Achievement, St. Louis, 1993-94; vol. Olympic Festival, St. Louis, 1994, 100 Neediest Cases, St. Louis, 1990-94, Old News Boy, St. Louis, 1992-94. Mem. AICPA, Mo. Soc. CPAs, Inst. Internal Auditors. Office: R&M Tax and Acctg 3805 S Kings Hwy Saint Louis MO 63109

WILDHACK, JOHN ROBERT, producer, broadcast executive; b. Buffalo, Oct. 23, 1958; s. Robert Henry and Beth Mae (Hankin) W. BA in TV/Radio, Syracuse U., 1980. Prodn. asst. Sta. ESPN-TV, Bristol, Conn., 1980-81; assoc. producer Sta. ESPN-TV, Bristol, 1981-82, sr. assoc. producer, 1982-84, producer, 1984-85, sr. producer, sr. v.p. programming, 1985—. Mem. Nat. Acad. Cable Programming. Republican. Roman Catholic. Avocations: golf, music.

WILDHACK, WILLIAM AUGUST, JR., lawyer; b. Takoma Park, Md., Nov. 28, 1935; s. William August and Martha Elizabeth (Parks) W.; m. Martha Moore Allston, Aug. 1, 1959; children: William A. III, Elizabeth L. B.S., Miami U., Oxford, Ohio, 1957; J.D., George Washington U., 1963. Bar: Va. 1963, D.C. 1965, Md. 1983, U.S. Supreme Ct. 1967. Agt. IRS, No. Va., 1957-65; assoc. Morris, Pearce, Gardner & Beitel, Washington, 1965-69; sole practice Washington, 1969; v.p., corp. counsel B.F. Saul Co. and affiliates, Chevy Chase, Md., 1969-87, Chevy Chase Bank, F.S.B. and affiliates, 1987-90; atty. pvt. practice, Arlington, Va., 1991—; sec. B.F. Saul Real Estate Investment Trust, Chevy Chase, 1972-87. Mem. Arlington Tenant Landlord Commn., 1976-91. Mem. ABA, Md. Bar Assn., D.C. Bar, Va. Bar, Arlington County Bar Assn., Nat. Acad. Elder Law Attys., Am. Soc. Corp. Secs., Phi Alpha Delta. Presbyterian.

WILDIN, MAURICE WILBERT, mechanical engineering educator; b. Hutchinson, Kans., June 24, 1935; s. John Frederick and Mildred Minerva (Dawson) W.; m. Mary Ann Brovan Christiansen, Aug. 9, 1958; children: Molly, Mildred. AA, Hutchinson Jr. Coll., 1955; BSME, U. Kans., 1958; MSME, Purdue U., 1959, PhD, 1963. Grad. asst. and instr. mech. engring. Purdue U., West Lafayette, Ind., 1958-61; from asst. prof. to assoc. prof. mech. engring. U. N.Mex., Albuquerque, 1961—, prof., 1973, dept. chair, 1968-73; mem. tech. staff Sandia Nat. Labs., Albuquerque, 1984-85; cons. several domestic and fgn. firms on stratified thermal storage, 1985—. Contbr. articles to profl. jours. Mem. ASME, ASHRAE, Am. Solar Energy Soc. Office: U NMex Dept Mech Engring Albuquerque NM 87131

WILDING, DIANE, marketing, financial and information systems executive; b. Chicago Heights, Ill., Nov. 7, 1942; d. Michael Edward and Katherine Surian; m. Manfred Georg Wilding, May 7, 1975 (div. 1980). BSBA in Acctg. magna cum laude, No. Ill. U., 1963; postgrad., U. Chgo., 1972-74; cert. in German lang., Goethe Inst., Rothenburg, Germany, 1984; cert. in internat. bus. German, Goethe Inst., Atlanta, 1994. Lic. cosmetologist. Systems engr. IBM, Chgo., 1963-68; data processing mgr. Am. Res. Corp., Chgo., 1969-72; system rsch. and devel. project mgr. Continental Bank, Chgo., 1972-75; fin. industry mktg. rep. IBM Can., Ltd., Toronto, Ont., 1976-79; regional telecommunications mktg. exec. Control Data Corp., Atlanta, 1980-84; gen. mgr. The Plant Plant, Atlanta, 1985-92; IBM; sys. engr. IBM, Atlanta, 1993—; pioneer installer on-line Automatic Teller Machines, Pos Equipment. Author: The Canadian Payment System: An International Perspective, 1977. Mem. Chgo. Coun. on Fgn. Rels.; bd. dirs. Easter House Adoption Agy., Chgo., 1974-76. Mem. Internat. Brass Soc., Goethe Inst., Mensa. Clubs: Ponte Verde (Fla.); Royal Ont. Yacht, Libertyville Racquet. Avocations: horticulture, travel, dancing, gourmet cooking, foreign languages. Home: 1948 Cobb Pky Apt 28J Smyrna GA 30080-2721

WILDING, JAMES ANTHONY, airport administrator; b. Washington, Dec. 22, 1937; s. Anthony Warwick and Dorothy (Lauten) W.; m. Marcella Anne Gibbons, Aug. 5, 1961; children: Matthew, William, Patricia, Marcella. B.S. in Civil Engring., Catholic U., 1959. With planning dept. Bur. Nat. Capital Airports, Washington, 1959-63, with civil engring. dept., 1963-72, acting dir., 1974; chief engring. staff Met. Washington Airports, 1972-75, dep. dir., 1975-79, dir., 1979-87; gen. mgr. Met. Washington Apts. Authority, Alexandria, Va., 1987—; chmn. Airports Coun. Internat. N.A., 1995. Recipient Sr. Exec. Service Performance award Dept. Transp., 1981, Meritorious Exec. award Pres. of U.S., 1982, Outstanding Achievement award Sec. Transp., 1985. Roman Catholic. Home: 1805 Crystal Ln Silver Spring MD 20906-2102 Office: Met Washington Airports Authority 44 Canal Center Plz Alexandria VA 22314-1563

WILDING, LAWRENCE PAUL, pedology educator, soil science consultant; b. Winner, S.D., Oct. 1, 1934; s. William Kasper and Ruth Inez (Root) W.; m. Gladys Dora Milne, Nov. 25, 1956; children: Linda Kay, Doris Bertha, Charles William, David Lawrence. BSc, S.D. State U., 1956, MSc, 1959; PhD, U. Ill., 1962. Asst. in agronomy S.D. State U., Brookings, 1956-59; rsch. fellow U. Ill., Urbana, 1959-62; prof. agronomy Ohio State U., Columbus, 1962-76; prof. pedology Tex. A&M U., College Station, 1976—; vis. prof. U. Guelph, Ont. Can., 1971-72; mem. NATO Advanced Rsch. Workshop on Expansive Soils, Cornell U., 1990-91. Author or/and editor 3 books; assoc. editor Catena Verlag, 1989, Geoderma, 1988-92; contbr. over 130 articles to profl. jours., chpts. to books. Sgt. S.D. N.G., 1956-59. Recipient Mem. award Sigma XI, 1988, Superior Svc. Group award sci. rsch. USDA, 1993; Campbell Soup fellow, 1959-62; grantee USDA, AID, 1986—. Fellow Am. Soc. Agronomy (cert.), Soil Sci. Soc. Am. (Soil Sci. Rsch. award 1987, opportunities in soil sci. com., chmn. subcommn. B 1989-92, chmn. divsn. S-5, bd. dirs. rep., mem. steering com. 1990-91, pres. elect 1992-93, pres. 1993-94, pst pres. 1994-95), Am. Inst. Chemists; mem. Soil Scientists Assn. Tex., Soil and Water Conservation Soc. Am., Tex. A&M Faculty Club, Gamma Sigma Delta. Democrat. Presbyterian. Avocations: golf, woodworking, travelling, sports, antiques. Office: Texas A&M U Dept Soil and Crop Scis College Station TX 77843

WILDMAN, GARY CECIL, chemist; b. Middlefield, Ohio, Nov. 25, 1942; s. Gerald Robert and Frances Jane (Swager) W.; m. Nancy Jackson, June 5, 1965; children: Debbie, Eric. A.B. in Chemistry, Thiel Coll., 1964; Ph.D. in Chemistry, Duke U., 1970. Research asst. B.F. Goodrich Research, Brecksville, Ohio, summer 1964; instr. Duke U., 1966-67; research chemist Hercules Research Center, Wilmington, Del., 1968-71; asso. prof. polymer sci. U. So. Miss., Hattiesburg, 1971-76; prof. U. So. Miss., 1976-83, chmn. dept., 1971-76, dean Coll. Sci. and Tech., 1976-83; v.p. research and devel. Schering Plough, Memphis, 1983—. Mem. Am. Chem. Soc., So. Soc. Coatings Tech., Soc. Plastics Engrs., Am. Crystallographic Assn., Phi Beta Kappa, Sigma Xi, Phi Lambda Upsilon, Sigma Pi Sigma, Omicron Delta Kappa. Republican. Methodist. Club: Rotary. Home: 8857 Aldershot Dr Memphis TN 38139-6522 Office: PO Box 377 Memphis TN 38151-0002

WILE, JULIUS, former corporate executive, educator; b. N.Y.C., Apr. 17, 1915; s. Irwin and Harriet (Brussel) W.; m. Ruth Miller, June 26, 1941 (dec. Feb. 1992); children: Barbara Miller Wile Schwarz, Andrew Brussel. B.S. in Mech. Engring. and Aeronautics, NYU, 1936; DFA (hon.), Culinary Inst. Am., 1994. With Julius Wile Sons & Co. Inc., N.Y.C., 1936-41, 45-76, v.p., 1955-66, sr. v.p., 1967-76; prodn. engr. Brewster Aero. Corp., L.I City, N.Y., 1942-44, Greer Hydraulics Inc., Bklyn., 1944-45; trustee Culinary Inst. Am., Hyde Park, N.Y., 1970-79, 81-90, chmn. bd. trustees, 1981-83; vis. lectr. Sch. Hotel Adminstrn. Cornell U., Ithaca, N.Y., 1953-82; wines and spirits lectr.; v.p. New Eng. Distillers Inc., Teterboro, N.J., 1955-72. Contbr. Brit. Book of Yr, 1957-75; editor: Frank Schoonmaker's Encyclopedia of Wine, 7th edit., 1978. V.p. Spain-U.S. C. of C., N.Y.C., 1972; bd. dirs. Scarsdale Family Counseling Service, N.Y., 1973-79; chmn. ann. drive ARC, Scarsdale, 1976. Decorated Ordre de l'Economie Nationale France, Ordre National du Merite France, Membre d'Honneur Academie du Vin de Bordeaux. Mem. Commanderie de Bordeaux (gov. 1959—, dep. grand maitre 1978-88, grand chancelier 1988—), Soc. Wine Educators (bd. dirs. 1980—, treas. 1986-93), Wine and Food Soc. N.Y. (bd. dirs. 1971-73, 77-83), Nat. Assn. Beverage Importers (chmn. table wine com. 1954-60, 65-76). Republican. Jewish. Clubs: Explorers, Quaker Ridge Golf (Scarsdale); Daniel Gray Fishing. Home and Office: 27 Grand Park Ave Scarsdale NY 10583-7611 *Fifteen years of Prohibition led to public ignorance of fine wines and spirits. Education of myself, employees, the trade and the public has been an important part of my career. It was and still is both a duty and a pleasure to pass on what I have learned and enjoyed. My tenet is that 'there is no premium for good taste.'*

WILEMAN, GEORGE ROBERT, lawyer; b. Ironton, Ohio, June 1, 1938; s. George Merchant and Marguerite (McCormack) W.; children: John Chandler, Julie Jo. AB, Duke U., 1960; JD, Georgetown U., 1963. Bar: Ohio 1968, Tex. 1977, U.S. Supreme Ct. 1993. Pvt. practice Dallas, 1977—. Mem. Coll. State Bar of Tex. Republican. Avocations: boating, running, horseback riding. Home: 5313 Paladium Dr Dallas TX 75240 Office: 5220 Spring Valley # 520 Dallas TX 75240

WILENSKY, ALVIN, real estate investment trust executive; b. Scranton, Pa., Nov. 3, 1921; s. Isaac and Sarah (Barnett) W.; m. Ruth L. Gross, June 3, 1945; children: I. David, Robert B. A.A., Keystone Jr. Coll., 1941; B.A., Pa. State U., 1943. C.P.A., Pa. Sr. acct. Alberts, Kahn & Levess, N.Y.C., 1945-48; prin. Alvin Wilensky, CPA, Scranton, Pa., 1948-72; v.p. fin. then pres. Century Village Inc., West Palm Beach, Fla., 1973-81; pres. CV Reit, Inc. (formerly Cenvill Investors, Inc.), N.Y. Stock Exch., West Palm Beach, Fla., 1981—; instr. Keystone Jr. Coll., La Plume, Pa., 1949-50. Mem. Dist. Dirs. IRS Profl. Adv. Com., Scranton, 1961-62; mem. Mayor's Tax Study Commn. City of Scranton, 1963-65; pres. Keystone Jr. Coll. Alumni Assn., 1966; v.p. Jewish Fedn. Palm Beach County, 1983-87, bd. dirs., 1987-94. 1st lt. USAF, 1943-45. Decorated Air medal with 5 oak leaf clusters, 1945; recipient Spl. award Jewish War Vets, 1960, Humanitarian award Mid-County Med. Ctr., West Palm Beach, 1981. Mem. AICPA, N.E. chpt. Pa. Inst. CPAs (pres. 1967-68, pres's award), Fla. Inst. CPAs, Nat. Assn. Real Estate Investment Trust (bd. govs. 1983-86). Republican. Jewish. Clubs: Forum of the Palm Beaches; President Country (West Palm Beach). Home: 2480 Presidential Way West Palm Beach FL 33401-1355 Office: CV Reit Inc 100 Century Blvd West Palm Beach FL 33417-2262

WILENSKY, GAIL ROGGIN, economist; b. Detroit, June 14, 1943; d. Albert Alan and Sophia (Blitz) Roggin; AB with honors, U. Mich., 1964, MA in Econs., 1965, PhD in Econs., 1968; hon. degree Hahnemann U., 1993; m. Robert Joel Wilensky, Aug. 4, 1963; children: Peter Benjamin, Sara Elizabeth. Economist, President's Commn. on Income Maintenance Programs, exec. dir. Md. Council of Econ. Advs., 1969-71; sr. researcher Urban Inst., Washington, 1971-73; assoc. research scientist, public policy and public health U. Mich., Ann Arbor 1973-75, vis. asst. prof. econs., 1973-75; sr. research mgr. Nat. Center for Health Services Research, Hyattsville, Md., 1975-83; assoc. profl. lectr. George Washington U., 1976-78; v.p. div. health affairs Project HOPE, Millwood, Va., 1983-90; adminstr. Health Care Fin. Adminstrn., Washington, 1990-92, dep. asst. to the pres. for policy devel., White House, 1992-93; sr. fellow Project Hope, Bethesda, Md., 1993—, chair phys. payment rev. com., 1995—. Vol. Am. Heart Assn., 1980-85; mem. health adv. com. Compt. Gen. U.S., 1987-90, 93—; bd. dirs. United Healthcare Corp., Adv.Tiss Sci., Coram, St. Jude Med., Syncor Internat., Capstone Pharmacy. Mem. vis. com. med. sch. U. Mich., 1993—; trustee United Mine Workers Am. Retirement Fund, 1993—. Flinn Found. disting. scholar, 1985; recipient Dean Conley award Am. Coll. Healthcare Execs, 1989. Mem. NAS (mem. inst. medicine 1989—), Am. Econ. Assn. (women's com. 1982-84), Fedn. Orgns. of Profl. Women (chmn. econ. task force 1981-83), Am. Statis. Assn., Nat. Tax Assn., Washington Women Economists, Assn. Health Svcs. Rsch. (dir. 1984-87), Found. Health Svcs. Rsch. (bd. dirs. 1987-90, commr. physician payment rev. com. 1989-90). Contbr. 90 articles in field to profl. jours. Mem. Cosmos Club (Washington). Home: 2807 Battery Pl NW Washington DC 20016-3439

WILENSKY, HAROLD L., political science and industrial relations educator; b. New Rochelle, N.Y., Mar. 3, 1923; s. Joseph and Mary Jane (Wainsten) W.; children: Stephen David, Michael Alan, Daniel Lewis. Student, Goddard Coll., 1940-42; AB, Antioch Coll., 1947; MA, U. Chgo., 1949, PhD, 1955. Asst. prof. sociology U. Chgo., 1951-53, asst. prof. indsl. relations, 1953-54; asst. prof. sociology U. Mich., Ann Arbor, 1954-57, assoc. prof., 1957-61, prof., 1961-62; prof. U. Calif., Berkeley, 1963-82, prof. polit. sci., 1982—, research sociologist Inst. Indsl. Relations, 1963—, project dir. Inst. Internat. Studies, 1970-90; project dir. Ctr. for German and European Studies, Berkeley, 1994—; mem. research career awards com. Nat. Inst. Mental Health, 1964-67; cons. in field. Author: Industrial Relations: A Guide to Reading and Research, 1954, Intellectuals in Labor Unions: Organizational Pressures on Professional Roles, 1956, Organizational Intelligence: Knowledge and Policy in Government and Industry, 1967, The Welfare State and Equality: Structural and Ideological Roots of Public Expenditures, 1975, The New Corporatism, Centralization, and the Welfare State, 1976, (with C.N. Lebeaux) Industrial Society and Social Welfare, 1965, (with others) Comparative Social Policy, 1985, (with L. Turner) Democratic Corporatism and Policy Linkages, 1987; editor: (with C. Arensberg and others) Research in Industrial Human Relations, 1957, (with P.F. Lazarsfeld and W. H. Sewell) The Uses of Sociology, 1967; contbr. articles to profl. jours. Recipient aux. award Social Sci. Rsch. Coun., 1962, Book award McKinsey Found., 1967; fellow Ctr. for Advanced Study in Behavioral Scis., 1956-57, 62-63, German Marshall Fund, 1978-79; Harry A. Millis rsch. awardee U. Chgo., 1950-51. Fellow AAAS; mem. Internat. Sociol. Assn., Internat. Polit. Sci. Assn., Indsl. Relations Research Assn. (exec. com. 1965-68), Soc. for Study Social Problems (chmn. editorial com.), Am. Polit. Sci. Assn., Am. Sociol. Assn. (exec. council 1969-72, chmn. com. on info. tech. and privacy 1970-72), Council European Studies (steering com. 1980-83), AAUP, ACLU. Democrat. Jewish. Avocations: music, trumpet, skiing. Office: U Calif Dept Polit Sci 210 Barrows Hall Berkeley CA 94720

WILENSKY, JULIUS M., publishing company executive; b. Stamford, Conn., Oct. 10, 1916; s. Joseph and Mary (Wainstein) W.; m. Dorothy T. Jobrack, July 2, 1939; children—Joseph L. (dec.), Nancy L. Jamie, Martha J. Hansen. Student, Rensselaer Poly. Inst., 1934-36. Methods engr. Yale & Towne Mfg. Co., Stamford, 1939-49; prodn. mgr. Yale & Towne Mfg. Co., 1953-57; dir. purchasing lock and hardware div. Eaton Yale & Towne, Rye, N.Y., 1957-67; mayor of Stamford, 1969-73; dir. materials, arms operations Winchester div. Olin Corp., New Haven, 1973-78; pres. Wescott Cove Pub. Co., 1978—; lectr. in field. Author guide books on cruising L.I. Sound, Cape Code, Windward Islands, Bay Islands of Honduras and Abacos; contbr. articles to boating mags. and newspapers; contbg. editor: Rudder, 1970-77; author cruising columns Ea. and So. edits. Sea mag., 1978-80, Rudder mag., 1981-83; editor cruising guides to Tahiti, French Soc. Islands, Maine (2 vols.), Turkey, Belize, Mexico's Caribbean Coast, I Don't Do Portholes, Lights and Legends, Beachcombing and Beachcrafting, Pacific Wanderer, Irma Quarterdeck Reports, Inside American Paradise, Beachcruising and Coastal Camping, Circumnagivation: Sail the Trade Winds (2 vols.), First Time Around. Bd. dirs. Stamford Ctr. for Arts, 1981-90; treas. Lifeline, 1983-85; first v.p. Met. Regional Coun., 1973; mem. Tri-State Regional Planning Commn., 1971-73, Stamford Bd. Fin., 1965-69, Stamford Planning Bd., 1963-65; chmn. Coun. Rep. Clubs, Stamford, 1961-62. With USAAF, 1943-46. Named Republican of Yr. Stamford Reps., 1962. Mem. Am. Mgmt. Assn., Stamford Power Squadron, Stamford Good Govt. Assn. (dir., treas. 1949-57), Stamford Chamber Residences (pres. 1953-55). Home: 51 Barrett Ave Stamford CT 06905-3212 *To be productive in fields or enterprises which are useful to other people has been my aspiration, and it's a high one. It's important to set goals early in life, then follow a plan to obtain the education and experience required to achieve these goals. Courage, honesty, objectivity, determination, hard work, and consideration for others will enable one to become outstanding in any field.*

WILENTZ, ROBERT NATHAN, retired state supreme court justice; b. Perth Amboy, N.J., Feb. 17, 1927; children: James Robert, Amy, Thomas Malino. Student, Princeton U., 1944-45; AB, Harvard U., 1949; LLB, Columbia U., 1952. Bar: N.J. 1952. Ptnr. Wilentz, Goldman & Spitzer, Perth Amboy, 1952-79; mem. N.J. legislature, 1966-69; chief justice N.J. Supreme Ct., 1979-96. With USN, 1945-46. Office: NJ Supreme Ct 257 Monmouth Rd Oakhurst NJ 07755-1502

WILENTZ, ROBERT SEAN, history educator, author; b. N.Y.C., Feb. 20, 1951; s. Elias and Jeanne Marie (Campbell) W.; m. Mary Christine Stansell, Jan. 30, 1980; children: James Thomas Farrell, Hannah Cady Rose. BA, Columbia U., 1972, Oxford U., 1974; PhD, Yale U., 1980. Asst. prof. history Princeton (N.J.) U., 1979-85, assoc. prof., 1985-87, prof., 1987—; dir. program in Am. studies, 1995—. Author: Chants Democratic, 1984; co-author: The Kingdom of Matthias, 1994; contbg. editor The New Republic, 1995—. John Simon Guggenheim Meml. Found. fellow, 1990; recipient A.J. Beveridge award Am. Hist. Assn., 1984, Ann. Book award Soc. for History of Early Republic, 1984, F.J. Turner award Orgn. Am. Historians, 1985. Home: 7 Edgehill St Princeton NJ 08540-6801 Office: Princeton U Dept History Princeton NJ 08544

WILES, CHARLES PRESTON, minister; b. Frederick, Md., Aug. 5, 1918; s. Charles Wesley and Nellie (Burgess) W.; m. Mary Margaret; children: Charles Preston, Wade Burgess. A.B., Washington Coll., 1939; postgrad., U. Va., 1940; M.A., Duke U., 1945, Ph.D. (Univ. fellow 1947-51, Kearns Honor fellow 1949-50), 1951; B.D., Va. Theol. Sem., 1947. Ordained to ministry Episc. Ch., 1947. Priest-in-charge St. Joseph's Ch., Durham, N.C., 1947-51; rector St. Mary's Episcopal Ch., Burlington, N.J., 1951-64; pres., trustee Burlington Coll., 1951-64, faculty cons., 1956-64; mem. faculty Phila. Div. Sch., 1959-62, lectr. ch. history, 1960-62; dean St. Matthew's Episcopal Cathedral, Dallas, 1964-87, dean emeritus, 1989; assoc. priest St. Luke's, Dallas, 1987—; dep. gen. Conv. from Diocese Dallas, 1967, 69, 70, 73, 76, 79; del. Provincial Synod from Diocese Dallas, 1966, 69, 72, 75, 78; mem. exec. council Diocese Dallas, 1967-77, 84-86, pres. mem. standing com., 1970-73, pres., 1971-73, mem. bd. missions, 1967-69, chmn. dept. coll. work, 1965-71, mem. bd. examing chaplains, 1965-71; mem. standing liturgical commn.; dean, warden Cathedral Center for Continuing Edn. and Pastoral Concern, 1971-87, Commn. Ministry, 1971-76; dean Dallas Deanery, 1965-69, 84-86, Bicentennial preacher, 1975; pres. convocation and clericus Diocese of N.J., 1961-64; examining chaplain, mem. bd. missions, mem. bd. Christina edn., dean Burlington-Trenton convocation; instr., dean Drew Conf. for Adults in N.J., 1952-56; retreat conductor St. Martin's House, Bernardsville, N.J., St. John Bapt. Convent, Mendhan, N.J.; dean Diocesan Sch. Religion, N.J., 1962-63; parish life lab. and weekend conductor Nat. Dept. Christian Edn., 1962; co-founder, dean Princeton (N.J.) Conf., 1956-64; mem. Goals for Dallas Com.; co-chmn. N.Am. Cathedral Deans' Conf., 1980-81. Author: Sacrament and Sacrifice, 2d edit., 1973, Lancelot Andrews, Caroline Divine, 1951, Lift Up Your Hearts, 1956, A Manual of Prayers, 1975, The Holy Eucharist: Word and Sacrament, 1993, The Gate of Heaven, 1993, A Centennial Narrative History of the Episcopal Diocese of Dallas, 1995. Trustee Gen. Theol. Sem., 1968-80; bd. dirs. Evergreen Home for Aging, St. Philip's Community Center, Overseas Mission Soc. Named Priest of Yr., 1969. Mem. Navy League, Ch. Hist. Soc. (dir. 1960-68), Kiwanian Club (Disting. Svc. award 1951, Disting. Citizen award Brunswick, Md. 1986), Dallas Athletic club, Chaparral, Vesper (Phila.) Club, Burlington County Country Club. Home: 7023 Northwood Rd Dallas TX 75225-2439

WILES, DAVID MCKEEN, chemist; b. Springhill, N.S., Can., Dec. 28, 1932; s. Roy McKeen and Olwen Gertrude (Jones) W.; m. Valerie Joan Rowlands, June 8, 1957; children: Gordon Stuart, Sandra Lorraine. B.Sc. with honors, McMaster U., 1954, M.Sc., 1955; Ph.D. in Chemistry, McGill U., 1957. Research officer chemistry div. Nat. Research Council of Can., Ottawa, 1959-66; head textile chemistry sect. chemistry div. Nat. Research Council of Can., 1966-75, dir. chemistry div., 1975-90; pres. Plastichem Cons., Victoria, B.C., Can., 1990—; chmn. Can. High Polymer Forum, 1967-69; v.p. N.Am. Chem. Congress, Mexico City, 1975. Contbr. articles to profl. jours.; mem. editorial adv. bd. numerous profl. jours. Can. Ramsay Meml. fellow, 1957-59. Fellow Chem. Inst. Can. (chmn. bd. dirs. 1972-74, pres. 1975-76, Dunlop Lectr. award 1981), Royal Soc. Chem. London, Royal Soc. Can.; mem. Am. Chem. Soc. (Polymer Chem. div.). Patentee in field. Home and Office: 3965 Juan de Fuca Terr, Victoria, BC Canada V8N 5W9

WILES, PAUL MARTIN, hospital administration executive; b. Takoma Park, Md., May 11, 1947; married. BA, St. Michael's Coll., 1969; MHA, Duke U., 1971. Adminstrv. asst. Fanny Allen Hosp., Winooski, Vt., 1968-69; adminstrv. resident Forsyth Meml. Hosp., Winston-Salem, N.C., 1970-71, asst. adminstr., 1971; asst. adminstr. USAF Hosp., Kincheloe AFB,

Mich., 1972-73; med. squad comdr. USAF Regional Hosp., Hampton, Va., 1973-74; asst. to pres. Forsyth County Hosp. Authority, Winston-Salem, 1974-75, v.p., 1975-79, sr. v.p., 1979-84; pres., CEO Carolina Medicorp Inc., Winston-Salem, 1985—; also adminstr. Forsyth Meml. Hosp., Winston-Salem. Contbr. articles to profl. jours. Mem. N.C. Hosp. Assn. (bd. dirs., chmn. regional adv. bd.). Office: Forsyth Meml Hosp 3333 Silas Creek Pky Winston Salem NC 27103-3013*

WILETS, LAWRENCE, physics educator; b. Oconomowoc, Wis., Jan. 4, 1927; s. Edward and Sophia (Finger) W.; m. Dulcy Elaine Margoles, Dec. 21, 1947; children—Ileen Sue, Edward E., James D.; m. Vivian C. Wolf, Feb. 8, 1976. BS, U. Wis., 1948; MA, Princeton, 1950, PhD, 1952. Research asso. Project Matterhorn, Princeton, N.J., 1951-53, U. Calif. Radiation Lab., Livermore, 1953; NSF postdoctoral fellow Inst. Theoretical Physics, Copenhagen, Denmark, 1953-55; staff mem. Los Alamos Sci. Lab., 1955-58; mem. Inst. Advanced Study, Princeton, 1957-58; mem. faculty U. Wash., Seattle, 1958—; prof. physics U. Wash., 1962-95; prof. emeritus U. Wash., Seattle, 1995—; cons. to pvt. and govt. labs.; vis. prof. Princeton, 1969, Calif. Inst. Tech., 1971. Author: Theories of Nuclear Fission, 1964, Nontopological Solitons, 1989; contbr. over 170 articles to profl. jours. Del. Dem. Nat. Conv., 1968. NSF sr. fellow Weizmann Inst. Sci., Rehovot, Israel, 1961-62; Nordita prof. and Guggenheim fellow Lund (Sweden) U., also Weizmann Inst., 1976—; Sir Thomas Lyle rsch. fellow U. Melbourne, Australia, 1989; recipient Alexander von Humboldt sr. U.S. scientist award, 1983. Fellow Am. Phys. Soc., AAAS; mem. Fedn. Am. Scientists, AAUP (pres. chpt. 1969-70, 73-75, pres. state conf. 1975-76), Phi Beta Kappa, Sigma Xi. Club: Explorers. Research on theory of nuclear structure and reactions, nuclear fission, atomic structure, atomic collisions, many body problems, subnuclear structure and elementary particles. Office: Univ Washington Dept Physics PO Box 351560 Seattle WA 98195-1560

WILEY, ALBERT LEE, JR., physician, engineer, educator; b. Forest City, N.C., June 9, 1936; s. Albert Lee and Mary Louise (Davis) W.; m. Janet Lee Pratt, June 18, 1960; children: Allison Lee, Susan Caroline, Mary Catherine, Heather Elizabeth. B in Nuclear Engring., N.C. State U., 1958, postgrad., 1958-59; MD, U. Rochester, N.Y., 1963; PhD, U. Wis., 1972. Diplomate Am. Bd. Nuclear Medicine, Am. Bd. Radiology, Am. Bd. Med. Physics. Nuclear engr. Lockheed Corp., Marietta, Ga., 1958; intern in surgery-medicine U. Va. Med. Sch., Charlottesville, 1963-64; resident in radiation therapy Sanford U., Palo Alto, Calif., 1964-65; resident and NCI postdoctoral fellow U. Wis. Hosp., Madison, 1965-68; med. dir. USN Radiol. Def. Lab., San Francisco, 1968-69; staff physician Balboa Hosp., USN, San Diego, 1969-70; asst. prof. radiotherapy M.D. Anderson Hosp. U. Tex., Houston, 1972-73; assoc. dir., clin. dir. radiation oncology U. Wis., Madison, prof. radiology, human oncology, med. physics, 1970-88; prof., chmn. radiation oncology, dir. cancer ctr. East Carolina U. Med. Sch., Greenville, N.C., 1988-93; cons. U.S. NRC, 1981-82, Nat. Cancer Inst., U.S. Dept. VA, 1990-93; advisor, cons. numerous univs. and govt. agys.; mem. Wis. Radioactive Waste Bd., Wis. Gov.'s Coun. on Biotech., Gov.'s Com. on UN. Author more than 140 articles and abstracts on med. physics, environ. health, nuclear medicine, biology and cancer treatment. Rep. candidate for U.S. Congress for 2d Wis. dist., 1982, 84; rep. primary candidate for gov., State of Wis., 1986; mem. Greenville Drug Task Force; bd. dirs. Greenville Salvation Army. Lt. comdr. USNR, ret. Oak Ridge Inst. Nuclear Studies fellow N.C. State U., 1958-59. Fellow Am. Coll. Radiology, Am. Coll. Preventive Medicine, N.C. Inst. Polit. Leadership; mem. IEEE, AMA, AAUP, Am. Assn. Physicists in Medicine, Am. Soc. Therapeutic Radiation Oncologists, Am. Assn. Physics Tchrs., Am. Bd. Sci. in Nuclear Medicine (sec.-treas.), Am. Acad. Health Physics, Am. Cancer Soc. (N.C. bd. dirs.), C. of C., VFW, Vietnam Vets. Am., Am. Legion, Masons, Rotary, Sigma Xi, Tau Beta Pi. Avocations: fishing, skiing, scuba diving, hiking. Home: Salter Path Rd Box 588 Indian Beach NC 28575 Office: Watson Clinic PO Box 95000 Lakeland FL 33805-5000

WILEY, BONNIE JEAN, journalism educator; b. Portland, Oreg.; d. Myron Eugene and Bonnie Jean (Galliher) W. BA, U. Wash., 1948; MS, Columbia U., 1957; PhD, So. Ill. U., 1965. Mng. editor Yakima (Wash.) Morning Herald; reporter, photographer Portland Oregonian; feature writer Seattle Times; war correspondent PTO AP; western feature editor AP, San Francisco; reporter Yakima Daily Republic; journalism tchr. U. Wash., Seattle, Cen. Wash. U., Ellensburg, U. Hawaii, Honolulu; mem. grad. faculty Bangkok U., Thailand, 1991; mem. faculty journalism program U. Hawaii, Honolulu, 1992—; Adminstr. Am. Samoa Coll., Pago Pago; news features advisor Xinhua News Agy., Beijing, Yunnan Normal U., Kumming, China, 1995. Mem. Women in Communications (Hawaii Headliner award 1985, Nat. Headliner award 1990), Theta Sigma Phi. Home: 1434 Punahou St Apt 1212 Honolulu HI 96822-4729

WILEY, CARL ROSS, timber company executive; b. Astoria, Oreg., Apr. 17, 1930; s. Hamilton Ross and Ada Ellen (Smith) W.; m. Dolores Eileen Brice, Dec. 19, 1953; children: Susan, Steven, Kenneth. BS in Indsl. Engring., Oreg. State U., 1958; grad. exec. tng. program, MIT, 1974. Quality control engr. Oreg. Metall. Corp., 1958-59; indsl. engr. Osborne Electronics Corp., Portland, Oreg., 1959-62; v.p. timber and mfg. Boise Cascade Corp., Idaho, 1962-80; exec. v.p. Roseburg (Oreg.) Lumber Co., 1980-85; chief exec. officer Puget Sound Plywood, Tacoma, 1986-93; pres., CEO Lane Plywood, Eugene, Oreg., 1993—. Bd. dirs. Boise YMCA, 1975-78. With AUS, 1951-53. Mem. Am. Plywood Assn. (trustee), Western Wood Products Assn. (bd. dirs., chmn. econ. svcs. 1974-80). Lutheran. Office: Lane Plywood 65 N Bertelsen Rd Eugene OR 97402-5310

WILEY, DEBORAH E., publishing executive; b. 1946. AA, Pine Manor Coll., 1966; BA, Boston U., 1968; Harvard U., 1983. Vice chmn. bd. John Wiley & Sons, Inc., 1977—. Office: John Wiley & Sons Inc 605 3rd Ave New York NY 10158

WILEY, DON CRAIG, biochemistry and biophysics educator; b. Akron, Ohio, Oct. 21, 1944; s. William Childs and Phyllis Rita (Norton) W.; m. Katrin Valgeirsdottir; children: William Valgeir, Lara; children from previous marriage: Kristen D., Craig S. BS in Physics and Chemistry, Tufts U., 1966; PhD in Biophysics, Harvard U., 1971; PhD (hon.), U. Leiden, The Netherlands, 1995; Doctorate (hon.), U. Leiden, Netherlands, 1995. Asst. prof. dept. biochemistry and molecular biology Harvard U., Cambridge, Mass., 1971-75, assoc. prof., 1975-79, prof. biochemistry and biophysics, 1979—, chmn. dept. molecular and cellular biology, 1992-95, investigator Howard Hughes Med. Inst., 1987—; mem. biophys. chemistry study sect. NIH, 1981-85; Shipley Symposium lectr. Harvard Med. Sch., 1985, Peter A. Leermakers Symposium lectr. Wesleyan U., 1986, K.F. Meyer lectr. U. Calif., San Francisco, 1986, John T. Edsall lectr. Harvard U., 1987, Washburn lectr. Boston Mus. Sci., 1987, Harvey lectr. N.Y. Acad. Sci., 1988, XVI Linus Pauling lectr. Stanford U., 1989; rsch. assoc. in medicine Children's Hosp., Boston, 1990—. Contbr. numerous articles to profl. jours. Recipient Ledlie prize Harvard U., 1982, Louisa Gross Horwitz prize Columbia U., 1990, William B. Coley award Cancer Rsch. Inst., 1992, V.D. Mattia award, 1992, Passano Found. Laureate award, 1993, Emil von Behring prize, 1993, Gairdner Found. Internat. award, 1994, Lasker award, 1995; European Molecular Biology fellow, 1976. Fellow NAS (lectr. 1988); mem. AAAS, Am. Acad. Arts and Scis., Am. Chem. Soc. (Nichol's Disting. Symposium lectr. N.E. sect. 1988), Am. Crystallographic Assn., Am. Soc. for Chemistry and Molecular Biology, Am. Soc. for Virology, Biophys. Soc. (Nat. lectr. 1989), Protein Soc. Achievements include research on amino acid sequences of haemagglutinins of influenza viruses of the H3 subtype isolated from horses, studies of infuenza haemagglutinin mediated membrane fusion. Office: Harvard U Dept Molecular and Cellular Biology 7 Divinity Ave Cambridge MA 02138-2019 also: Children's Hosp Lab of Molecular Medicine 320 Longwood Ave Boston MA 02115-5746

WILEY, EDWIN PACKARD, lawyer; b. Chgo., Dec. 10, 1929; s. Edwin Garnet and Marjorie Chastina (Packard) W.; m. Barbara Jean Miller, May 21, 1949; children: Edwin Miller, Clayton Alexander, Stephen Packard. BA, U. Chgo., 1949, JD, 1952. Bar: Wis. 1952, Ill. 1952, U.S. Dist. Ct. (ea. dist.) Wis. 1953, U.S. Supreme Ct. 1978. Assoc. Foley & Lardner, Milw., 1952-60, ptnr., 1960—; bd. dirs. Genetic Testing Inst., Inc., Nat. Rivet and Mfg. Co., Shaler Co., Waukesha Cutting Tools, other corps. and founds. Co-author: Bank Holding Companies: A Practical Guide to Bank Acquisitions and Mergers, 1988, Wisconsin Uniform Commercial Code Handbook, 1971; author: Promotional Arrangements: Discrimination in Advertising and Promotional Allowances, 1976; editor in chief U. Chgo. Law Rev., 1952; contbr. articles to legal jours. Bd. dirs. Blood Ctr. of Southeastern Wis., pres., 1978-82; pres. Blood Ctr. Rsch. Found., Inc., 1983-87; v.p. Friends of Schlitz Audubon Ctr., Inc., 1975-87; active United Performing Arts Fund of Milw.; pres. Wis. Conservatory of Music, 1968-74; pres. First Unitarian Soc. Milw., 1961-63; v.p. Mid-Am. Ballet Co., 1971-73, Milw. Ballet Co., 1973-74; pres. Florentine Opera Co., 1983-86; bd. dirs. Milw. Symphony Orch., pres., 1993-95; bd. dirs. Milw. Pub. Mus., Inc., sec. 1992—; bd. dirs. Wis. History Found. Mem. ABA, State Bar of Wis., Milw. Bar Assn., Am. Law Inst., Order of Coif, Milw. Club, Univ. Club, Phi Beta Kappa (pres. Greater Milw. assn. 1962-63). Unitarian-Universalist. Home: 929 N Astor St Unit 2101 Milwaukee WI 53202-3488 Office: Foley & Lardner Firstar Ctr 777 E Wisconsin Ave Milwaukee WI 53202-5302

WILEY, GREGORY ROBERT, publisher; b. Mpls., Sept. 21, 1951; s. William Joseph and Terese (Kunz) W.; m. Sheila Francis, May 25, 1979; children: Kathleen, Mary Glennon. BA in Personnel Adminstrn., U. Kans., 1972-74. Dist. sales mgr. Reader's Digest, St. Louis, 1976-80, regional sales dir., Chgo., 1980-82; nat. sales mgr. retail div. Rand McNally & Co., Chgo., 1982-83, nat. sales mgr. premium incentive div., 1983-86, nat. sales mgr. bookstore and mass market sales, 1986-88; book publisher, The Sporting News, St. Louis, 1988-90, v.p. mktg. Marketmakers Internat., St. louis, 1990-93; v.p. mktg. Sofsource Inc., 1993—. Mem Nat. Premium Sales Execs., Promotional Mktg. Assn. Am. Roman Catholic. Avocations: pvt. pilot., historic restoration, golf. Home: 1867 Ironstone Rd Saint Louis MO 63131-3804 Office: Sofsource Inc 14615 Manchester Rd Ste 203 Saint Louis MO 63105

WILEY, JASON LARUE, JR., neurosurgeon; b. Canandaigua, N.Y., Dec. 2, 1917; s. Jason LaRue and Eva Althea (Moore) W.; m. Alma Williams, Jan. 4, 1944 (div. Feb. 1956); children: Robert W., Richard L.; m. Ann Valentine Gerrish, Apr. 14, 1956 (div. July 1979); children: Martha V., Pamela M., Catherine A. Student, Antioch Coll., 1934-37; MD, Harvard U., 1941. Diplomate Am. Bd. Surgery, Am. Bd. Neurol. Surgery. Intern Kings County Hosp., Bklyn., 1941-42; asst. resident surgery Ellis Hosp., Schenectady, N.Y., 1948-49; from asst. to assoc. resident surgery Rochester (N.Y.) Gen. Hosp., 1949-51; from asst. to assoc. to chief resident neurosurgery Yale U. and Hartford Hosp., New Haven and Hartford Conn., 1951-54; practice medicine specializing in neurosurgery Kansa City, Mo., 1954-56, Rochester, 1956—; chief neurosurgery Rochester Gen. Hosp., 1959-71, emeritus neurosurgeon, 1989—; clin. asst. prof. neurosurgery U. Rochester, 1961-88. Mem. Bd. for Profl. Med. Conduct, N.Y. State Dept. Health, Albany, N.Y., 1985—. Served to lt. comdr. USN, 1942-47, PTO. Mem. Med. Soc. County Monroe, Med. Soc. State N.Y., N.Y. State Neurosurg. Soc. (bd. dirs.), Congress Neurol. Surgeons, Am. Assn. Neurol. Surgeons, Canandaigua Yacht Club. Republican. Episcopalian. Avocations: sailing, skiing, fishing, genealogy. Office: 1445 Portland Ave Rochester NY 14621-3008

WILEY, JAY D., lawyer; b. Anderson, Ind., June 13, 1945. BBA, U. Mich., 1967, JD, 1971. Bar: Ariz. 1972. Ptnr. Snell & Wilmer, Phoenix, 1971—; instr. legal writing Ariz. State U., 1971, 72. Mem. ABA. Office: Snell & Wilmer LLP One Arizona Ctr Phoenix AZ 85004

WILEY, MYRA, mental health nurse; b. Lexington, Ala., Jan. 20, 1938; d. Joseph Aaron and Annie Lura (Putnam) Haraway; m. Robert Harold Wiley, Sept. 17, 1960; children: Sonya, Robert, Marie. BSN, U. Ala., Huntsville, 1989. RN, Ala.; cert. in chem. dependency. Nursing asst., night-weekend coord. Upjohn Health Care, Huntsville, 1983-87; nursing asst. North Ala. Rehab. Hosp., Huntsville, 1987-89; staff nurse Humana Hosp., Huntsville, 1989-91; staff nurse counselor Bradford-Parkside, Madison, Ala., 1991-95; relief charge nurse for behavioral health Crestwood Hosp., Huntsville, 1995—. Mem. ANA, NCCDN, Ala. State Nurses Assn., Madison County Nurses Assn., Nat. Consortium of Chem. Dependency Nurses. Baptist. Avocations: reading, traveling, hiking, embroidery.

WILEY, RICHARD ARTHUR, lawyer; b. Bklyn., July 18, 1928; s. Arthur Ross and Anna Thorsen (Holder) W.; m. Carole Jean Smith, Aug. 13, 1955; children: Kendra Elizabeth, Stewart Alan, Garett Smith. AB, Bowdoin Coll., Brunswick, Maine, 1948; BCL, Oxford (Eng.) U., 1951; LLM, Harvard U., 1959; LLD, Bowdoin Coll., 1994. Bar: Mass. 1954, U.S. Ct. Mil. Appeals 1954, U.S. Dist. Ct. Mass. 1962, U.S. Supreme Ct. 1985. Atty. John Hancock Mut. Life Ins. Co., Boston, 1956-58; from atty. to mng. ptnr. Bingham, Dana & Gould, Boston, 1959-76; gen. counsel, asst. sec. Dept. Def., 1976-77; v.p., counsel First Nat. Bank Boston, 1977-78, exec. v.p., 1978-85; exec. v.p. Bank of Boston Corp., 1985; ptnr. Csaplar & Bok, Boston, 1986-90, mem. exec. com., 1987-90, chmn., 1989-90, of counsel, 1990; of counsel Gaston & Snow, Boston, 1990-91; dir. Powers and Hall P.C., Boston, 1991-94; of counsel, 1994-95, Hill & Barlow, Boston, 1995—; bd. dirs., chmn. Am. Student Assistance Corp.; bd. dirs. Nomadic Structures, Inc., Nypro, Inc., Carlo Gavazzi, Inc., R.F. Group Inc., Edn. Resources Inst., World Shelters, Inc., Mass. Higher Edn. Assistance Corp.; lectr. Boston U. Law Sch., 1961-64; past vice chmn. New Eng. Conf. on Doing Bus. Abroad; trustee New Eng. Legal Found., chmn., 1980-83; adj. lectr. govt. and legal studies Bowdoin Coll., 1995—. Author: Cases and Materials on Law of International Trade and Investment, 1961; contbr. articles to profl. jours. Bd. overseers Bowdoin Coll., 1966-81, pres., 1977-80, trustee, 1981-93, trustee emeritus, 1993—; mem. Mass. Edn. Financing Authority, 1986-91, chmn., 1987-91; mem. Wellesley (Mass.) Town Meeting, 1971-75, mem. fin. adv. com., 1973-74; chmn. Mass. Bd. Regents of Higher Edn., 1991; bd. regents Task Force on Student Fin. Aid, 1987; mem. Mass. Higher Edn. Coord. Coun., 1991-95, vice chmn., 1991-93, chmn., 1993-95; chmn. lawyers divsn. United Way Mass. Bay, 1975; mem. devel. com., trustees of donations Episcopal Diocese Mass., 1971-75; trustee, exec. com. North Conway Inst., mem., 1980-92, chmn., 1988-92; bd. trustees Internat. Coun. Trust, Boston; trustee, mem. exec. com., chmn. Mass. Taxpayers Found., 1989-92; chmn. bd. trustees World Peace Found., Boston, 1983-95; corporator Schepens Eye Rsch. Inst., 1991-95; dep. chmn. planning Mass. rep. state com., 1971, vice chmn. fin. com., 1971-72. Officer USAF, 1953-56. Decorated Air Force Commendation medal; recipient Dep. Def. Disting. Pub. Svc. medal, 1977; Rhodes scholar, 1949. Mem. ABA (vice chmn. fgn. and internat. bus. law com. 1967-69), Boston Bar Assn. (exec. com., antitrust com. 1965-68), Council on Fgn. Relations, Boston Com. on Fgn. Relations (mem. exec. com., chmn. 1980-83), Phi Beta Kappa.

WILEY, RICHARD EMERSON, lawyer; b. Peoria, Ill., July 20, 1934; s. Joseph Henry and Jean W. (Farrell) W.; m. Elizabeth J. Edwards, Aug. 6, 1960; children: Douglas S., Pamela L. B.S. with distinction, Northwestern U., 1955, J.D., 1958; LL.M., Georgetown U., 1962. Bar: Ill. 1958, D.C. 1972. Pvt. practice Chgo., 1962-70; gen. counsel FCC, Washington, 1970-72, mem., 1972-74, chmn., 1974-77, chmn. FCC's adv. com. on advanced TV svc., 1987—; mng. ptnr. Wiley, Rein & Fielding, Washington, 1983—; prof. law John Marshall Law Sch., U. Chgo., 1963-70. Chmn. adv. bd. Inst. for Tele-Info., Columbia U., 1989—. Capt. AUS, 1959-62. Fellow Am. Bar Found.; mem. ABA (mem. ho. of dels. 1969-71, 77-84, chmn. young lawyers sect., 1977-84, chmn. Forum com. on communications 1969, chmn. bd. editors ABA Jour. 1984-89, chmn. com. on scope and correlation of work 1989, chmn. adminstrv. law and regulatory practice 1993-94), Fed. Bar Assn. (pres. 1977), Fed. Communications Bar Assn. (pres. 1987), Ill. Bar Assn., Chgo. Bar Assn., Adminstrv. Conf. U.S. (coun., sr. fellow), Phi Delta Phi, Phi Delta Kappa. Methodist. Home: 3818 N Woodrow St Arlington VA 22207-4345 Office: Wiley Rein & Fielding 1776 K St NW Ste 1100 Washington DC 20006-2304

WILEY, RICHARD GORDON, electrical engineer; b. Wind Ridge, Pa., Aug. 25, 1937; s. Asa Gordon and Mildred Louise (Fisher) W.; m. Jane Bradley Wilmes, Oct. 15, 1960; children: Richard Bradley, John Gordon, Laura Jane, Timothy Scott, Martha Anne, James Robert. BS, Carnegie-Mellon U., 1959, MS, 1960; PhD, Syracuse U., 1975. Rsch. engr. Syracuse (N.Y.) Rsch. Corp., 1960-67, staff cons. engr., 1975-86; asst. dir. applied rsch. Lab. Microwave Systems, Inc., Syracuse, 1967-75; v.p., chief scientist Rsch. Assocs. Syracuse, Inc., 1986—. Author: Electronic Intelligence: The Analysis of Radar Signals, 1982, 2d edit. 1993, Electronic Intelligence: The Interception of Radar Signals, 1985; co-author: Radar Vulnerability to Jamming, 1990; co-inventor pulse train analysis using personal computer, 1987. 1st lt. U.S. Army, 1961-63. Fellow IEEE; mem. Assn. Old Crows. Republican. Episcopalian. Office: Rsch Assocs Syracuse Inc 510 Stewart Dr N Syracuse NY 13212-3451

WILEY, THOMAS GLEN, retired investment company executive; b. Salt Lake City, Feb. 1, 1928; s. Thomas J. and Juanita (Dean) W.; children: Jana Lynn, Jill, Tina Elizabeth, Tova Suzanne. B.B.A. cum laude, U. Wash., 1951, postgrad., 1954. With Shell Chem. Co., 1954-61; fin. analyst Shell Chem. Co., N.Y.C., 1960-63; mgr. fin. analysis and pricing Lear Siegler, Los Angeles, 1963-72; v.p. finance, treas. Electronic Memories & Magnetics Corp., Los Angeles, 1963-72; exec. v.p. Hale Bros. Assocs., San Francisco, 1972-80; pres. Computer Election Systems, Berkeley, Calif., 1980-84, Texport, Inc., Anaheim, Calif., 1988-89; dir. NetVantage, Santa Monica, Calif., 1994—, Osmotics, Denver, 1994—. 1st lt. AUS, 1951-53. Home: 1765 Broadway St San Francisco CA 94109-2425

WILEY, WILLIAM RODNEY, microbiologist, administrator; b. Oxford, Miss., Sept. 5, 1931; s. William Russell and Edna Alberta (Threlkeld) W.; m. Myrtle Louise Smith, Nov. 10, 1952; 1 child: Johari. B.S., Tougaloo Coll., Miss., 1954; M.S., U. Ill., Urbana, 1960; Ph.D., Wash. State U., Pullman, 1965. Instr. electronics and radar repair Keesler AFB-U.S. Air Force, 1956-58; Rockefeller Found. fellow U. Ill., 1958-59; research assoc. Wash. State U., Pullman, 1960-65; research scientist dept. biology Battelle-Pacific N.W. Labs., 1965-69, mgr. cellular and molecular biology sect. dept. biology, 1969-72, inst. coordinator, life scis. program, assoc. mgr. dept. biology, 1972-74, mgr. dept. biology, 1974-79, dir. research, 1979-84; dir. Pacific Northwest Lab., Richland, Wash., 1984-94; sr. v.p. for sci. & tech. policy Battelle Meml. Inst., Richland, Wash., 1994—; adj. assoc. prof. microbiology Wash. State U., Pullman, 1968—; found. assoc. Pacific Sci. Ctr., Seattle, 1989—; bd. dirs. Sta. KCTS Channel 9, Seattle, 1990-94; trustee Oreg. Grad. Ctr., 1990-95; cons. and lectr. in field. Contbr. chpts. to books, articles to profl. jours. Co-author book in microbiology. Bd. dirs. Wash. Tech. Ctr., 1984-88, sci. adv. panel Wash. Tech. Ctr., 1984-88, Fed. Res. Bank of San Francisco (Seattle br.) 1991—; mem. adv. com. U. Wash. Sch. Medicine, 1976-79; trustee Gonzaga U., 1981-89, bd. regents, 1968-81; bd. dirs. MESA program U. Wash., Seattle, 1984-90, United Way of Benton & Franklin Counties, Wash., 1984—, Tri-City Indsl. Devel. Coun., 1984-94; mem. Wash. Coun. Tech. Advancement, 1984-85; bd. dirs. Forward Wash., The Voice for Statewide Econ. Vitality, 1984-95, N.W. Coll. and Univ. Assn. for Sci., 1985—; mem. Tri-City Univ. Ctr. Citizens Adv. Coun., 1985—; apptd. Wash. State Higher Edn. Coord. Bd., 1985-89, Wash. State U. Found., 1986—; mem. Wash. State U. bd. Regents, 1989—, bd. dirs. Washington Roundtable, 1989—, Goodwill Games, 1989-90; mem. adv. coun. Mont. State Sci. and Tech., 1990-91; mem. bd. overseers Whitman Coll., 1990—; mem. external adv. bd. Clark Atlanta U., 1991—; mem. Ctrl. Wash. U. Inst. for Sci. and Soc. Bd. of Advisors, 1991—, Engring. exec. com. So. U., Baton Rouge, La., 1992—; mem. Coun. Govt. Univ. Industry Rsch. Roundtable, 1993—; trustee Fred Hutchinson Cancer Rsch. Ctr., 1992—; engring. exec. com. Southern U., 1992—. With U.S. Army, 1954-56. Named Black Engr. of Yr., 1994. Mem. AAAS, Am. Soc. Biol. Chemists, Am. Soc. Microbiology, Soc. Exptl. Biology and Medicine, Sigma Xi (pres.-elect 1995). Office: Battelle Meml Inst Pacific NW Divsn Battelle Blvd Richland WA 99352

WILFONG, BRENDA A., telecommunications executive; b. Ashland, Ohio, Jan. 2, 1963; d. Edward Eugene and Barbara Ann (Butterfield) Bush; m. Duane Hubert Wilfong, Oct. 22, 1984 (dec. Sept. 1994); children: Jessie Leona, Christina Elizabeth. BBA, Kent State U., 1989. Asst. editor Ohio dir. Harris Pub. Co., Twinsburg, Ohio, 1983-84; accounts payable clerk M. O'Neil's Co., Akron, Ohio, 1984-85; network mgmt. asst. Alltel Corp., Hudson, Ohio, 1985-86, treasury asst., 1986-87, assoc. analyst treasury, 1987-92, carrier svcs. coord., 1992-93; sr. staff asst. Alltel Corp., Twinsburg, 1993-95, adminstr. carrier svcs., 1995—; contracts adminstr. Alltel Corp., Hudson, Ohio, 1995—. Recipient Brownie Mother Vol. award Girl Scouts Am., Akron, 1994. Mem. Inst. Mgmt. Accts. (editor newsletter 1990-92, dir. ins. 1992-94). Baptist. Avocations: reading medical journals, swimming, hiking, classical music. Home: 1630 Goodyear Blvd Akron OH 44305-3505

WILFORD, BONNIE BAIRD, health policy specialist; b. Chgo., Jan. 11, 1946; d. George Martin and Ruth Eleanor (Anderson) Baird; m. David Edward Wilford, Oct. 2, 1967; children: Heather Lynn, Edward Baird. BA, Knox Coll., 1967; postgrad., Roosevelt U., 1969-71. Staff assoc. Am. Hosp. Assn., Chgo., 1967-70; mgr. plan devel. Blue Cross & Blue Shield Assn., Chgo., 1970-79; dir. dept. substance abuse AMA, Chgo., 1979-91, dir. divsn. clin. sci., 1988-91; ptnr. Wilford & Assocs., healthcare consultants, 1991—; exec. office of the Pres. The White House, 1991-92; cons. Pres.'s Commn. on Model State Drug Laws, 1993-94; dir. Pharm. Policy Project, George Washington U. Med. Ctr., Washington, 1992—. Author: Balancing the Response to Prescription Drug Abuse, 1990, Pharmaceutical Benefits for HIV/AIDS; editor Pharmaceutical Policy Rev., 1996—; contbr. articles to profl. jours. Recipient Outstanding Svc. award Fla. Task Force on Alcohol and Drug Abuse, 1986, Merit award State of Mo., 1985, Disting. Svc. award U.S. Dept. Health and Human Svcs., 1990. Mem. APHA, Internat. Narcotic Enforcement Officers Assn. (Award of Honor 1985), Assn. for Med. Edn. and Rsch. Substance Abuse, Informal Steering Com. Prescription Drug Abuse (bd. dirs.). Avocations: travel, gardening, needlework. Office: CHPR/George Washington U 2021 K St NW Ste 800 Washington DC 20006-1003

WILFORD, DAN SEWELL, hospital administrator; b. Memphis, June 11, 1940; married. BA, U. Miss., 1962; MA, Washington U., 1966. Adminstrv. resident Hillcrest Med. Ctr., Tulsa, 1965-66, asst. adminstr., 1966-69, sr. assoc. adminstr., 1969-74; adminstr. North Miss. Med. Ctr., Tupelo, Miss., 1974-82; pres. North Miss. Health Svcs., Tupelo, Miss., 1982-84, Meml. Healthcare System, Houston, 1984—. With Armed Forces, 1962-64. Home: 730 Chevy Chase Cir Sugar Land TX 77478-3600 Office: Meml Hosp System Meml Hosp SW 7600 Beechnut St Houston TX 77074-4302*

WILFORD, JOHN NOBLE, JR., news correspondent; b. Murray, Ky., Oct. 4, 1933; s. John Noble and Pauline (Hendricks) W.; m. Nancy Everett Watts, Dec. 25, 1966; 1 child, Nona. Student, Lambuth Coll., 1951-52; BS, U. Tenn., 1955; MA, Syracuse U., 1956; Internat. Reporting fellow, Columbia, 1961-62; DHL (hon.), R.I. Coll., 1987; DSc (hon.), Middlebury Coll., 1991. Reporter Comml. Appeal, Memphis, summers 1954-55; reporter Wall St. Jour., N.Y.C., 1956, 59-61; contbg. editor Time mag., N.Y.C., 1962-65; sci. reporter N.Y. Times, 1965-73, asst. nat. editor, 1973-75, dir. sci. news, 1975-79, sci. corr., 1979—; vis. journalist Duke U., 1984; McGraw lectr. Princeton U., 1985; Disting. prof. journalism, U. Tenn., Knoxville, 1989-90; mem. Am. Mus.-Mongolian Gobi Expdn., 1991, Dir.'s Visitor, Inst. for Advanced Study, 1995. Author: We Reach The Moon, 1969, The Mapmakers, 1981, The Riddle of the Dinosaur, 1985, Mars Beckons, 1990, The Mysterious History of Columbus, 1991; co-author: The New York Times Guide to the Return of Halley's Comet, 1985, (with William Stockton) Spaceliner, 1981; editor: Scientists at Work, 1979. With CIC AUS, 1957-59. Recipient Book award Aviation/Space Writers, 1970, Writing award Aviation/Space Writers, 1983, G.M. Loeb Achievement award U. Conn, 1972, Press award Nat. Sci. Club, 1974, AAAS-Westinghouse Sci. Writing award, 1983, Ralph Coats Roe medal ASME, 1995, Pulitzer prize nat. reporting, 1984, N.Y. Times Pulitzer Prize Winning Team, 1987. Mem. Nat. Assn. Sci. Writers, Authors Guild, Soc. Profl. Journalists, Am. Geog. Soc. (councilor 1994—), Century Assn., Sigma Chi, Phi Kappa Phi. Home: 232 W 10th St New York NY 10014-2976 Office: 229 W 43rd St New York NY 10036-3913

WILHARM, JOHN H., JR., lawyer; b. Pitts., May 19, 1932. BA, Amherst Coll., 1954; JD, Western Reserve U., 1960. Bar: Ohio 1960. Ptnr. Baker & Hostetler, Cleve.; mem. bd. bar examiners Supreme Ct., 1967-71. Editor: Western Reserve Law Review, 1959-60. Mem. bd. edn. Chagrin Falls Village, 1974-81. Mem. Phi Delta Phi. Office: Baker & Hostetler 3200 Nat City Ctr 1900 E 9th St Cleveland OH 44114-3401*

WILHELM, DAVID C., political organization administrator; m. Degee Wilhelm; 1 child, Luke. Grad., Ohio U., Harvard U. Campaign mgr. Senator Paul Simon, 1984, Senator Joseph Biden for Pres., Iowa, 1987, Richard M. Daley for Mayor, Chgo., 1989, 91, Gov. Bill Clinton for Pres., 1991-92; chmn. Nat. Dem. Com., 1993-94; sr. mng. dir. investment banking Kemper Securities, Inc., Chgo., 1994—. Exec. dir. Citizens for Tax Justice.

Mem. AFL-CIO (dir. pub. policy, pub. employee dept.). Office: Everen Securities Inc. Ste 2800 77 W Wacker Dr Chicago IL 60601-1629

WILHELM, GAYLE BRIAN, lawyer; b. Springfield, Mass., Sept. 1, 1936; s. William E. and Margaret (Koerber) W.; m. Emogene Chase, Sept. 1, 1957; children: Gayle Barrett, Erica Chase Fotta, Laura Elizabeth. BA, Harvard U., 1957, LLB, 1964. Bar: Conn. 1964. Sr. ptnr. Cummings & Lockwood, Stamford, Conn., 1964—. Author: Connecticut Estates Practice, 6 vols., 1970—, The Executor's Handbook, 1985, The Connecicut Living Trust, 1993. 1st lt. USAF, 1957-61, Japan. Fellow Am. Coll. Trust and Estate Counsel. Avocations: tennis, bicycling, fishing. Office: Cummings & Lockwood 4 Stamford Plaza Stamford CT 06901-3202

WILHELM, HARLEY A(LMEY), retired chemist, educator, mechanical engineer; b. Elliston, Iowa, Aug. 5, 1900; s. Bert C. and Anna B. (Glick) W.; m. Orpha E. Lutton, May 29, 1923; children: Lorna Wilhelm Livingston, Max Gene, Myrna Wilhelm Elliott, Gretchen. BA, Drake U., 1923, LLD, 1961; PhD, Iowa State U., 1931. Fellow in chemistry, 1924-25; postdoctoral work U. Mich., Ann Arbor, 1941; tchr. Mapleton (Iowa) H.S., 1923-24, Guthrie Center (Iowa) H.S., 1925-26; prof., coach Intermountain Union Coll., Helena, Mont., 1926-27; semi-pro baseball pitcher Ames (Iowa) Mchts. team, 1930-42; grad. asst. dept. chemistry Iowa State U., Ames, 1927-28, from instr. to prof. chemistry, 1928-45, prof. chemistry, 1945-71, prof. metallurgy, 1963-71; assoc. dir. Ames Lab. of U.S. AEC (now Dept. Energy), 1942-66; prof. emeritus Iowa State U., 1971-95; Manhattan Dist. engr., 1942-66, prin. scientist, 1966-95; AEC del. to Eng., 1949, to Eng. and Europe, 1953, to Argentina and Brazil, 1957; cons. desalinization of water Dept. Interior, 1967; cons. licensing of reactors AEC, Washington, 1968; vis. prof. U. Waterloo, Kitchener, Ont., Can., 1969; presenter, cons. in field. Author more than 100 published articles; holder more than 75 patents. Decorated Army-Navy E Flag with 4 stars; recipient Gold medal ASME, 1990, Alumni Disting. Svc. award Drake U., 1959, Double D. award Nat. D Club, 1968, Centennial award for svc. Drake U. Alumni Assn., 1981; named to Iowa H.S. Basketball Hall of Fame, 1988, Iowa Inventors Hall of Fame, 1993; metallurgy bldg. Harley A. Wilhelm Hall, Iowa State U., 1986, Centennial Recognition as one of 100 all time great athletes in Bulldog history Drake U., 1991, Chgo. Alumni award Iowa State U., 1949, faculty citation Iowa State U. Alumni, 1969. Fellow Am. Soc. Metals (nat. trustee 1957-60, William Hunt Eisenman award 1962); mem. SAR, Am. Chem. Soc. (gold medal Iowa sect. 1954), Iowa Acad. Sci. (Centennial citation 1975), Rotary Club (Paul Harris fellow 1995), Phi Beta Kappa, Sigma Xi, Phi Lambda Upsilon, Phi Kappa Phi. *Each of us should do our part to help make this world a better place than we found it. Died Oct. 7, 1995.*

WILHELM, KATE (KATY GERTRUDE), author; b. Toledo, June 8, 1928; d. Jesse Thomas and Ann (McDowell) Meredith; m. Joseph B. Wilhelm, May 24, 1947 (div. 1962); children: Douglas, Richard; m. Damon Knight, Feb. 23, 1963; 1 child, Jonathan. PhD in Humanities(hon.), Mich. State U., 1996. Writer, 1956—; co-dir. Milford Sci. Fiction Writers Conf., 1963-76; lectr. Clarion Fantasy Workshop Mich. State U., 1968-94. Author: (novels) More Bitter Than Death, 1962, (with Theodore L. Thomas) The Clone, 1965, The Nevermore Affair, 1966, The Killer Thing, 1967, Let the Fire Fall, 1969, (with Theodore L. Thomas) The Year of the Cloud, 1970, Abyss: Two Novellas, 1971, Margaret and I, 1971, City of Cain, 1971, The Clewiston Test, 1976, Where Late the Sweet Birds Sang, 1976, Fault Lines, 1976, Somerset Dreams and Other Fictions, 1978, Juniper Time, 1979, (with Damon Knight) Better Than One, 1980, A Sense of Shadow, 1981, Listen, Listen, 1981, Oh! Susannah, 1982, Welcome Chaos, 1983, Huysman's Pets, 1986, (with R. Wilhelm) The Hills Are Dancing, 1986, The Hamlet Trap, 1987, Crazy Time, 1988, Dark Door, 1988, Smart House, 1989, Children of the Wind: Five Novellas, 1989, Cambio Bay, 1990, Sweet, Sweet Poison, 1990, Death Qualified, 1991, And the Angels Sing, 1992, Seven Kinds of Death, 1992, Naming the Flowers, 1992, Justice for Some, 1993, The Best Defense, 1994, A Flush of Shadows, 1995, Malice Prepense, 1996, (multimedia space fantasy) Axoltl, U. Oreg. Art Mus., 1979, (radio play) The Hindenburg Effect, 1985; editor: Nebula Award Stories #9, 1974, Clarion SF, 1976; contbr. short stories to anthologies and periodicals. Mem. PEN, Nat. Writers Union, Mystery Writers Am., Sci. Fiction Writers Am., Authors Guild. Address: 1645 Horn Ln Eugene OR 97404-2957

WILHELM, LAWRENCE E., advertising sales manager; b. White Plains, N.Y., Apr. 25, 1949; s. John Renssen and Margaret (Maslin) W. BA with honors, Ohio U., 1972. Sales rep. William Morrow, Inc., N.Y.C., 1972-75; regional mgr. Viking Penguin, Inc., N.Y.C., 1975-79; pres. San Diego News, 1980-86; nat. sales mgr. Lodging, Washington, 1987—. Office: Am Hotel/Motel Assn 1201 New York Ave NW Washington DC 20005-3917

WILHELM, MARILYN, private school administrator. Founder-dir. The Wilhelm Sch., Houston. Office: The Wilhelm Sch 3003 Richmond Ave Houston TX 77098-3112

WILHELM, MORTON, surgery educator; b. Roanoke, Va., June 22, 1923; s. Walter LeRoy and Della Mae (Turner) W.; m. Jean Osborne, June 3, 1949; children: Melissa, Christina. BS, Va. Mil. Inst., 1944; MD, U. Va., 1947. Diplomate Am. Bd. Surgery. Intern, resident in surgery VA Mason Hosp., Seattle, 1947-51, 52-53; fellow, instr. surgery Med. Ctr. U. Va., Charlottesville, 53-54, 56-66, assoc. prof. surgery Med. Ctr., 1966-80, prof. surgery Med. Ctr., 1980-93, chief dept. surg. oncology Med. Ctr., 1990-93, Joseph Farrow prof. surg. oncology Med. Ctr., 1990-93. Pres. Va. div. Am. Cancer Soc., Meritorious Svc. award, Horsley award, Nat. Teresa Lasser award. Lt. U.S. Army, 1951-53. Fellow Am. Coll. Surgeons (vice chmn. commn. on cancer 1989-90, pres. Va. chpt.); mem. Am. Soc. Clin. Oncology, So. Surg. Assn., So. Soc. Clin. Surgeons, Soc. Surg. Oncology. Avocations: tennis, golf, woodworking. Office: U Va Med Ctr Box 334 Cancer Ctr Charlottesville VA 22908

WILHELM, PAUL J., steel company executive; b. Pitts., Feb. 5, 1942; s. Edward N. and Dorothy T. (Rectenwald) W.; m. Carol A. Wilhelm, May 15, 1965; children: Thomas E., Jay P. BSME, Carnegie Mellon U., 1964. With USX Corp., Pitts., also bd. dirs. Bd. dirs. Boy Scouts Am., Pitts., 1992—; trustee Carnegie Mellon U., Pitts., 1995—; chmn. Japan Am. Soc. Pa., Pitts., 1995—. Mem. Am. Iron and Steel Inst., Assn. Iron and Steel Engrs. Avocation: golf. Office: USX Corp 600 Grant St Rm 6144 Pittsburgh PA 15219-4776

WILHELM, RALPH VINCENT, JR., electronics company executive, ceramics engineer; b. Corpus Christi, Tex., Jan. 22, 1944; s. Ralph Vincent and Kathryn (Krug) W.; m. Katharine Elizabeth Foote, Aug. 26, 1967; children: Heidi, Peter. BSEE, Cornell U., 1967; PhD in Ceramic Engring., Rutgers U., 1972; postgrad., U. Ill., 1985; MBA, U. Mich., 1987. Project engr. Allis Chalmers Mfg. Corp., Boston, 1966-67; rsch. assoc. ceramics dept. Rutgers U., New Brunswick, N.J., 1967-71; sr. rsch. ceramist GM Rsch. Labs., GM, Warren, Mich., 1971-78; supr. thin film devel. AC Spark Plug div. GM, Flint, Mich., 1978-80, dept. head advanced devel., 1980-84; staff engr. advanced instrumentation GM-Delco Electronics Corp., Flint, 1984-87; staff engr. advanced instrumentation GM-Delco Electronics Corp., Kokomo, Ind., 1987-88, dir. tech. strategies, 1988-89, dir. advanced devel., 1989-94; v.p. dir. engring. GM-Delco Electronics Asia/Pacific Pte Ltd., Singapore, 1995—; trained visitor for ceramics Accreditation Bd. for Engring. and Tech., 1982-94; coord. univ. rels. team GM and Cornell U., Detroit and Ithaca, N.Y., 1985-93; mem. indsl. adv. bd. dept. elec. engring. Northwestern U., Evanston, Ill., 1989-94; mem. bd. mgrs. Mecel AB, Åmål, Sweden, 1990-94; lectr. in field. Contbr. numerous articles to profl. jours.; patentee in thin film materials and processes field. Mem. Delco Electronics-Kokomo Sch. Partnership, 1989-94; mem. coun. Cornell U., 1990-94. Fellow Am. Ceramic Soc.; mem. IEEE, Soc. Automotive Engrs. (Vincent Bendix Automotive Elec. Engring. award 1978, Arch. T. Colwell merit award 1978), Sigma Xi, Keramos. Presbyterian. Avocations: tennis, sailing, gardening. Office: Delco Electronics Asia/Pacific, 501 Orchard Rd, 18-00 Ln Crawford Pl Singapore 238880, Singapore

WILHELM, ROBERT OSCAR, lawyer, civil engineer, developer; b. Balt., July 7, 1918; s. Clarence Oscar and Agnes Virginia (Grimm) W.; m. Grace Sanborn Luckie, Apr. 4, 1959. B.S. in Civil Engring., Ga. Tech. Inst., 1947, M.S.I.M., 1948; J.D., Stanford U., 1951. Bar: Calif. 1952, U.S. Supreme Ct. Mem. Wilhelm, Thompson, Wentholt and Gibbs, Redwood City, Calif., 1952—; gen. counsel Bay Counties Gen. Contractors; pvt. practice civil engring., Redwood City, 1952—; pres. Bay Counties Builders Escrow, Inc., 1972-88. With C.E., AUS, 1942-46. Mem. Bay Counties Civil Engrs. (pres. 1957), Peninsula Builders Exchange (pres. 1958-71, dir.), Calif. State Builders Exchange (tres. 1971). Clubs: Mason, Odd Fellows, Eagle, Elks. Author: The Manual of Procedures for the Construction Industry, 1971, Manual of Procedures and Form Book for Construction Industry, 9th edit., 1995; columnist Law and You in Daily Pacific Builder, 1955—; author: Construction Law for Contractors, Architects and Engineers. Home: 134 Del Mesa Carmel Carmel CA 93923-7950 Office: 600 Allerton St Redwood City CA 94063-1504

WILHELM, SISTER PHYLLIS, principal; b. Toledo, Aug. 3, 1941; d. Edward John and Ellen Catherine (Sorg) W. BA, St. Francis Coll., 1964; MEd in Instruction, U. Wis., Superior, 1994. Cert. tchr., Wis., elem. tchr. spl. edn., Ill.; joined Sisters of St. Francis of Mary Immaculate. Tchr. primary St. Rita of Casica Sch., Aurora, Ill., 1963-65, St. Joseph Sch., Manhattan, Ill., 1965-74; tchr. primary Holy Family-St. Francis Sch., Bayfield, Wis., 1974-77, prin., tchr., 1979—, peace edn. instr. K-6, 1989—; tchr. spl. edn. Guardian Angel Sch., Joliet, Ill., 1977-79; instr. peace edn., 1988—. Mem. Superior Diocesan Prin. Assn. (treas. 1981-83, Educator of Yr. award 1991). Avocations: crafts, gardening, cooking. Home: RR 1 Box 92 Bayfield WI 54814-9724

WILHELM, WILLIAM JEAN, civil engineering educator; b. St. Louis, Oct. 5, 1935; s. Maurice Ferdinand and Eileen Winifred (McClintock) W.; m. Patricia Jane Zietz, Aug. 17, 1957; children—William, Robert, Andrew, Mary, David. BME, Auburn U., 1958, MS, 1963; PhD, N.C. State U., 1968. Registered profl. engr., Kans., W.Va. Structural engr. Palmer & Baker Engrs., Mobile, Ala., 1958-60; instr. engring. graphics Auburn U., 1960-64; asst. prof. civil engring. W.Va. U., Morgantown, 1967-72; assoc. prof. W.Va. U., 1972-76, prof., 1976-79, chmn., 1974-79; dean engring., prof. Wichita State U., 1979—, dir. Ctr. for Productivity Enhancement, 1984-86, exec. dir. Ctr. for Tech. Application, 1988-91; bd. dirs. Kans. Tech. Enterprise Corp., Orthopaedic Rsch. Inst. Via Christi Regional Med. Sys., Wichita Industries and Svcs. for the Blind, Inc. Contbr. articles to profl. jours. Served with C.E. U.S. Army, 1959, 62. Recipient Recognition award Wichita State U. Alumni Assn., 1993. Fellow ASCE, Am. Concrete Inst. (Joe W. Kelley award 1986, Henry L. Kennedy award 1994); mem. NSPE, Soc. Women Engrs. (sr.), Am. Soc. Engring. Edn., Kans. Engring. Soc. (pres. 1994-95, Outstanding Engr. of Yr. award 1989), Order of the Engr., Sigma Xi, Phi Kappa Phi, Tau Beta Pi, Pi Tau Sigma, Chi Epsilon (chpt. hon. W.Va. U. 1979). Roman Catholic. Home: 2500 Banbury Cir Wichita KS 67226-1046 Office: Wichita State U Coll Engring Wichita KS 67260-0044

WILHELMI, MARY CHARLOTTE, education educator, college official; b. Williamsburg, Iowa, Oct. 2, 1928; d. Charles E. and Loretto (Judge) Harris; m. Sylvester Lee Wilhelmi, May 26, 1951; children: Theresa Ann, Sylvia Marie, Thomas Lee, Kathryn Lyn, Nancy Louise. BS, Iowa State U., 1950; MA in Edn., Va. Poly. Inst. and State U., 1973, cert. advanced grad. studies, 1978. Edn. coord. Nova Ctr. U. Va., Falls Church, 1969-73; asst. adminstr. Consortium for Continuing Higher Edn. George Mason U., Fairfax, Va., 1973-78; adminstr., asst. prof. George Mason U., Fairfax, 1978-83; dir. coll. rels. and devel., assoc. prof. No. Va. C.C., Annandale, 1983—; bd. dirs. No. Va. C.C. Ednl. Found., Inc., Annandale, 1984—; v.p. mktg. Fairfax (Va.) Symphony, 1995—; chmn. Health Systems Agy. No. Va., Fairfax; mem. George Mason U. Inst. for Ednl. Transformation. Edtl. bd. Va. Forum, 1990-93; contbr. articles to profl. jours. Bd. dirs. Fairfax County chpt. ARC, 1981-86, Va. Inst. Polit. Leadership, 1996—, Fairfax Com. of 100, 1986-88, 90—, Hospice No. Va., 1983-88, No. Va. Mental Health Inst., Fairfax County, 1978-81, Fairfax Profl. Women's Network, 1981, Arts oun. Fairfax County, 1989—; vice chmn. Va. Commonwealth U. Ctr. on Aging, Richmond, 1978—; mem. supt.'s adv. coun. Fairfax County Pub. Schs., 1974-86, No. Va. Press Club, 1978—; pres. Fairfax Ext. Leadership Coun., 1995; mem. Leadership Fairfax Class of 1992. Named Woman of Distinction, Soroptomists, Fairfax, 1988, Bus. Woman of Yr., Falls Church Bus. and Profl. Women's Group, 1993; fellow Va. Inst. Polit. Leadership, 1995. Mem. State Coun. Higher Edn. Va. (pub. affairs adv. com. 1985—), Greater Washington Bd. Trade, Fairfax County C. of C. (legis. affairs com. 1984—) Va. Women Lobbyists, 1991—, No. Va. Bus. Roundtable, Internat. Platform Assn., Phi Delta Kappa (10-Yr. Continuous Svc. award 1991), Kappa Delta Alumni No. Va., Psi Chi, Phi Kappa Phi. Roman Catholic. Avocations: piano, organ, reading, hiking. Home: 4902 Ravensworth Rd Annandale VA 22003-5552 Office: No Va CC 4001 Wakefield Chapel Rd Annandale VA 22003-3744

WILHELMSEN, HAROLD JOHN, accountant, operations controller; b. Kansas City, Mo., July 13, 1928; s. Karl John and Cora Irene (Reynolds) W.; m. Audrey Loraine Woodard, Oct. 14, 1950. BBA, U. Wis., 1950. CPA, Wis. With S.C. Johnson & Son Inc., Racine, Wis., 1953-90, dir. fin. South Pacific., 1970-72, mgr. overseas fin. svcs., 1972-76, contr. U.S. ops., 1976-78, v.p., contr. internat. ops., 1978-90, ret., 1990. Pres. Racine Symphony Orch. Assn., 1957-60; trustee Carthage Coll., Kenosha, Wis., 1984-91, dir., sec. Pinnacle Peak Country Club Estates, 1992-95; dir., pres. Pinnacle Peak Country Club; treas. Christ the Lord Luth. Ch. Served with U.S. Army, 1950-52. Republican. Lutheran. Clubs: Pinnacle Peak Country (Scottsdale, Ariz.); Am. Nat. (Sydney, Australia). Avocations: golf, squash, bridge, reading, music.

WILHELMY, ODIN, JR., insurance agent; b. New Kensington, Pa., Oct. 9, 1920; s. Odin and May (Hazeltine) W.; m. Betty M. Rollins, Nov. 23, 1945; children: Ann Leslie, Margaret Linn, Janet Lee. BA with honors, U. Cin., 1941; PhD, Cornell U., 1950. CLU, ChFC. Asst. prof. Cornell U., Ithaca, N.Y., 1949-52; div. chief Battelle Meml. Inst., Columbus, Ohio, 1952-70; sr. agt. Prin. Mut. Life Ins. Co., Columbus, 1970—. Scoutmaster Boy Scouts Am., Ithaca, N.Y., Columbus, Ohio, 1946-74. Sgt. U.S. Army, 1942-46, Aleutian Islands. Recipient Silver Beaver award Boy Scouts Am. Mem. Phi Beta Kappa, Phi Kappa Phi, Pi Kappa Alpha, Omicron Delta Kappa. Presbyterian. Avocations: church work, scouting, gardening. Home: 2942 N Star Rd Columbus OH 43221-2961

WILHELMY, ROBERT MATTHEW, marketing agency financial executive; b. Bridgeport, Conn., Mar. 20, 1953; s. Robert Matthew and Rita (Argali) W.; m. Susan C. Wilhelmy, Nov. 24, 1974; children: Kelley S., Julie P., Katherine P., Christine E. BSBA, Babson Coll., 1975. CPA, N.Y., Conn. Sr. auditor Arthur Young & Co., N.Y.C., 1975-79; v.p fin. R&B Petroleum, White Plains, N.Y., 1979-84; exec. v.p., CFO Clarion Mktg. & Comm., Greenwich, Conn., 1984—. Mem. AICPA, Conn. Soc. CPAs. Republican. Avocations: flying, boating, biking. Home: 184 Godfrey Rd Weston CT 06883 Office: Clarion Mktg & Comm, Inc Greenwich Office Park 5 Greenwich CT 06831

WILHITE, CLAYTON EDWARD, advertising agency executive; b. Saginaw, Mich., Aug. 9, 1945; s. Clayton Robson and Ruth Margaret (Westendorf) W.; m. Ann Denise Douglass, June 27, 1970. BA in Polit. Sci., U. Mich., 1967, MBA, 1969. Account exec., account supr. Foote, Cone & Belding, Chgo. and Sydney, Australia, 1969-75; v.p., account supr. McCann-Erickson, N.Y.C., 1975-77; exec. v.p., dir. Ammirati & Puris Inc., N.Y.C., 1977-83; mktg. dir. Young & Rubicam Ltd., London, 1983-85; chief exec., mng. dir. D'Arcy, Masius, Benton & Bowles (formerly D'Arcy, MacManus, Masius, Inc.), St. Louis, 1985-88; pres. D'Arcy, Masius, Benton & Bowles/USA, N.Y.C., 1988-91, DMB&B/N.Am., N.Y.C., 1991-95; vice chmn. DMB&B Inc., N.Y.C., 1995—; bd. dirs. DMB&B Inc. Mem. Exec. Campaign 1976 In-House Advt. Agy. for Pres. Ford Re-election Com., Washington; pres. Nov. Co. Bush Re-election Advt. Agy., 1992, Young Pres Orgn., 1986—; bd. dirs. vis. com. White Burkett Miller Ctr., U.Va.; mem. pres.'s adv. group U. Mich. Mem. River Club (N.Y.C.), Phi Beta Kappa. Republican. Lutheran. Avocations: photography; overseas travel; rock climbing; tennis; skiing. Office: DMB&B Inc 1675 Broadway New York NY 10019-5820

WILHOIT, CAROL DIANE, special education educator; b. Rockford, Ill., June 2, 1950; d. Iris May (Zeigler) Cleeton; m. Jerry Dean Wilhoit, Aug. 15, 1971; children: David, Heather, Hilary, Erin. BSE, N.E. Mo. State U., 1972; MS in Edn., 1991. Cert. spl. edn. tchr., Mo. Tchr. emotionally handicapped Clarence Cannon Elem., Elsberry, Mo., 1972-73; EMH tchr. Bowling Green (Mo.) Elem., 1973-77, Clopton High Sch., Clarksville, Mo., 1979-82; tchr. learning disabilities Eugene Field Elem., Hannibal, Mo., 1982—; active Accelerated Sch., chair curriculum cadre, intervention cadre, steering com., 1992-93, mem. parent involvement com., 1994; del. Northeast Dist. Tchrs. Assn. Assembly, 1994. Mem. state due process subcom., 1994; PL-94-142 adv. com., 1992—. Mem. Coun. Exceptional Children (pres. 1986-88, bd. dirs. Mo. chpt. 1986, 1988-91, organizer local chpt. 1988, awards chmn., chair profl. devel. subcom., chair registration com. 1991-92, chair membership com. Mark Twain chpt. 1991—, spring conf. session leader, del. to internat. coun. assembly 1992-93, spring conf. chair 1994, del. to internat. conf. 1995), Mo. State Tchrs. Assn. (del. to state assembly 1989-90, superintendent's com. 1989-91, dist. prof. devel. com. 1990—, mentor tchr. 1990-92, state spl. edn. monitoring com. 1991-92), Hannibal Cmty. Tchrs. Assn. (bldg. rep. exec. com. 1987—, v.p. 1988, pres. 1989), Learning Disabilities Assn. Avocations: reading, crafts, sewing. Office: Eugene Field Elem 1405 Pearl St Hannibal MO 63401-4151

WILHOIT, GENE, state official. Edn. dir. Ark. Dept. Edn., Little Rock. Office: Ark Dept Edn Capitol Mall Bldg 4 Little Rock AR 72201

WILHOIT, HENRY RUPERT, JR., federal judge; b. Grayson, Ky., Feb. 11, 1935; s. H. Rupert and Kathryn (Reynolds) W.; m. Jane Horton, Apr. 7, 1956; children: Mary Jane, H. Rupert, William. LLB, U. Ky., 1960. Ptnr. Wilhoit & Wilhoit, 1960-81; city atty. City of Grayson, Ky., 1962-66; county atty. Carter County, Ky., 1966-70; judge U.S. Dist. Ct. (ea. dist.) Ky., 1981—. Recipient Disting. Service award U. Ky. Alumni Assn., 1980. Mem. ABA, Ky. Bar Assn. Office: US Dist Ct 320 Fed Bldg 1405 Greenup Ave Ashland KY 41101-7542*

WILKE, CHET, real estate executive; b. Chgo., Dec. 10, 1942; m. Beverly J. Galuska, July 31, 1981; children: Lisa Michelle, Rebecca Ann, Christa Leann. BA in Comm., Columbia Coll., L.A., 1970. Cert. real estate mktg. cons. Sta. mgr., dir. TV news, personality Armed Forces Radio & TV, 1965-69; acct. exec. Sta. KALI, L.A., 1970-72; sr. acct. exec. HR/Stone Radio Reps., L.A., 1972-75; gen. sales mgr. Sta. KYXY-FM, San Diego, 1975-77; pres., founder Wilke Enterprises Inc., San Diego and Houston, 1977-81; gen. sales mgr. Sta. KEYH, Houston, 1982; gen. sales mgr., acting mgr. Sta. KYST, Houston, 1982-85; mgr., mktg./creative dir. Advt. Concepts Inc., Houston, 1985-88; exec. v.p. First Hanover Real Estate/Mortgage, Houston and Sugar Land, Tex., 1988-89; pres., real estate broker Ameristar Group Corp., Plano, Tex., 1989—; CEO PRO, Profl. Realty Office Network, Inc., Plano, Tex., 1995—. With USAF, 1964-69. Mem. Nat. Assn. Realtors, Tex. Assn. Realtors, Greater Dallas Assn. Realtors, Collin County Assn. Realtors, Lions. Republican. Methodist. Home: 2312 Cardinal Dr Plano TX 75023-1470 Office: PRO Network 3033 W Parker Rd #106 Plano TX 75023

WILKE, LEROY, church administrator. Dir. dept. youth ministry Luth. Ch.-Mo. Synod, St. Louis, St. Louis. Office: 1333 S Kirkwood Rd Saint Louis MO 63122-7226

WILKEN, CLAUDIA ANN, judge; b. Mpls., Aug. 17, 1949; d. Claudius W. and Dolores Ann (Grass) W.; m. John M. True, 1984; 1 child, Peter Wilken True. BA with honors, Stanford U., 1971; JD, U. Calif., Berkeley, 1975. Bar: Calif. 1975, U.S. Dist. Ct. (no. dist.) Calif. 1975, U.S. Ct. Appeals (9th cir.) 1976, U.S. Supreme Ct. 1981. Asst. fed. pub. defender U.S. Dist. Ct. (no. dist.) Calif., San Francisco, 1975-78, U.S. magistrate judge, 1983-93, dist. judge, 1993—; ptnr. Wilkin & Leverett, Berkeley, Calif., 1978-84; adj. prof. U. Calif., Berkeley, 1978-84; prof. New Coll. Sch. Law, 1980-85; mem. jud. br. com. Jud. Conf. U.S.; mem. edn. com. Fed. Jud. Ctr. Magistrate Judges, 9th Cir. Magistrate Judges; chair 9th cir. Magistrates Conf., 1987-88. Mem. ABA (mem. jud. adminstrn. divsn.), Calif. State Bar Assn., Alameda County Bar Assn. (judge's membership), Fed. Magistrates Judges Assn. (sec.), Nat. Assn. Women Judges, Order of Coif, Phi Beta Kappa. Office: US Dist Ct No Dist 1301 Clay St Courtroom 2 Oakland CA 94612*

WILKENING, LAUREL LYNN, academic administrator, planetary scientist; b. Richland, Wash., Nov. 23, 1944; d. Marvin Hubert and Ruby Alma (Barks) W.; m. Godfrey Theodore Sill, May 18, 1974. BA, Reed Coll., 1966; PhD, U. Calif., San Diego, 1970. Asst. prof. to assoc. prof. U. Ariz., Tucson, 1973-80, dir. Lunar and Planetary Lab., head planetary scis., 1981-83, vice provost, prof. planetary scis., 1983-85, v.p. rsch., dean Grad. Coll., 1985-88; div. scientist NASA Hdqrs., Washington, 1980; prof. geol scis., adj. prof. astronomy, provost U. Washington, Seattle, 1988-93; chancellor U. Calif., Irvine, 1993—; dir. Seagate Tech., Inc., 1993—, Rsch. Corp., 1991—; vice chmn. Nat. Commn. on Space, Washington, 1984-86, Adv. Com. on the Future of U.S. Space Program, 1990; chair Space Policy Adv. Bd., Nat. Space Coun., 1991-92; co-chmn. primitive bodies mission study team NASA/European Space Agy., 1984-85; chmn. com. rendezvous sci. working group NASA, 1983-85; mem. panel on internat. cooperation and competition in space Congl. Office Tech. Assessment, 1982-83. Author: (monograph) Particle Track Studies and the Origin of Gas-Rich Meteorites, 1971; editor: Comets, 1982. U. Calif. Regents fellow, 1966-67, NASA trainee, 1967-70. Fellow Meteoritical Soc. (councilor 1976-80), Am. Assn. Advanced Sci.; mem. Am. Astron. Soc. (chmn. div. planetary scis. 1984-85), Am. Geophys. Union, AAAS, Planetary Soc. (dir. 1994—), Phi Beta Kappa. Democrat. Avocations: gardening, camping, swimming. Office: U Calif Chancellors Office 501 Adminstrn Bldg Irvine CA 92717

WILKENS, LEONARD RANDOLPH, JR. (LENNY WILKENS), professional basketball coach; b. Bklyn., Oct. 28, 1937; s. Leonard Randolph Sr. and Henrietta (Cross) W.; m. Marilyn J. Reed, July 28, 1962; children: Leesha Marie, Leonard Randolph III, Jamée McGregor. BS in Econs., Providence Coll., 1960, HHD (hon.), 1980. Counselor Jewish Employment Vocat. Services, 1962-63; salesman packaging div. Monsanto Co., 1966; profl. basketball player St. Louis Hawks, 1960-68; player-coach Seattle SuperSonics, 1969-72, head coach, 1977-85, gen. mgr., 1985-86; profl. basketball player Cleve. Cavaliers, 1972-74, player NBA All-Star Game, 1973, head coach, 1986-93; player-coach Portland (Oreg.) Trail Blazers, 1974-76; head coach Atlanta Hawks, 1993—; coach 4 NBA All-Star Teams including Ea. Conf. team All-Star game, Mpls., 1994, World Champion basketball team, 1979, IBM NBA Coach of the Year, 1994; winningest coach of all time, 1995, coach 1996 Olympic Basketball Team, asst. coach 1992 Olympic Basketball. Author: The Lenny Wilkens Story, 1974. Bd. regents Gonzaga U., Spokane; bd. dirs. Seattle Ctr., Big Bros. Seattle, Bellevue (Wash.) Boys Club, Seattle Opportunities Industrialization Ctr., Seattle U.; co-chmn. UN Internat. Yr. of Child program, 1979; organizer Lenny Wilkens Celebrity Golf Tournament for Spl. Olympics. 2d lt. U.S. Army, 1961-62. Recipient Whitney Young Jr. award N.Y. Urban League, 1979, Disting. Citizens award Boy Scouts Am., 1980; named MVP in NBA All-Star Game, 1971, Man of Yr., Boys High Alumni chpt. L.A., 1979, Sportsman of Yr., Seattle chpt. City of Hope, 1979, Congl. Black Caucus Coach of Yr., 1979, CBA Coach of Yr., 1979, Coach of Yr., Black Pubs. Assn., 1979, NBA Coach of Yr., 1994; named to NIT-NIKE Hall of Fame, 1988; named to 9 NBA All-Star Teams, elected to Naismith Memorial Basketball Hall of Fame, 1988.

WILKENS, ROBERT ALLEN, utilities executive, electrical engineer; b. Esmond, S.D., Jan. 3, 1929; s. William J. and Hazel C. (Girch) W.; m. Barbara M. Davis, Apr. 15, 1952; children—Bradley Alan, Beth Ann, Bonnie Sue, William Frank. B.S.E.E., S.D. State U., 1951. Dispatcher, engr. G.O., Northwestern Pub. Service Co., Huron, 1953-55, div. engr., Huron 1955-58, div. elec. supt., 1958-59, div. mgr., 1959-66, asst. to pres., 1966-69, vice pres. ops., G.O., 1969-80, pres., chief operating officer, 1980-90, pres., chief exec. officer, 1990-94, chmn. bd. dirs. 1994—, also dir.; v.p., past pres. N. Cen. Electric Assn., past dir. Midwest Gas Assn.; dir. Farmers & Mchts. Bank Huron; past adminstrv. chmn., treas. Mid-Continent Area Power Pool. Mem. Salvation Army Adv. Bd., 1962-87; S.D. State R.R. Bd., 1982-87; past pres. Huron United Way. Served to capt. USAF, 1951-53. Named Disting. Engr., S.D. State U., 1977. Mem. North Central Elec. Assn., Midwest Gas Assn., S.D. Engring. Soc., Huron C. of C. (pres. 1963). Republican. Methodist. Lodges: Kiwanis, Masons, Shriners. Office: Northwestern Pub Svc Co 33 3rd St SE Huron SD 57350-2015

WILKERSON, CHARLES EDWARD, architect; b. Essex County, Va., Apr. 1, 1921; s. John Pullen, Jr. and Eva Lee (Eubank) W.; m. Sallie Ray Bowers, Feb. 14, 1959; children: Judith Gardner, Ann Hunter, Edward

Ray. B.Arch., Va. Poly. Inst. and State U., 1943. Registered architect, Va. Bookkeeping clk. Crawford Mfg. Co., Richmond, Va., 1937-39; draftsman Dixon & Norman Architects, Richmond, 1946-47, John S. Efford Architect, Richmond, 1947-49; draftsman Walford & Wright Architects, Richmond, 1949-54, ptnr., 1955-60; ptnr. Wright, Jones & Wilkerson, Richmond, 1961-91. Pres., sec.-treas., bd. dirs. Va. Found. Architecture, 1964-86. Tech. sgt. C.E., U.S. Army, 1943-46, PTO. Fellow AIA (dir. Va. chpt., sec. Va. chpt. 1959-61, dir. James River chpt. 1979-82, William C. Noland award Va. Soc.). Baptist.

WILKERSON, JOHN LEE, telecommunications executive; b. Ft. Worth, Aug. 5, 1945; s. Leonard E. and Francis (Lee) W.; m. Muffie Daugherty, Aug. 3, 1984; children: John Jr., Mitchell, Leana, Tonia. BA, U. Tex., 1967. Gen. mgr. TeleMktg. Comm., Columbus, Ohio, 1981-86; midwest dir. ITT Comm., Secaucus, N.J., 1986-88; pres., CEO TeleCom Network Solutions, Inc., Orlando, Fla., 1988—; bd. dirs. Telecard Internat. Inc., Orlando, Fla., 1994—. Chmn. com. Columbus (Ohio) C. of C., 1982. Maj. USAR, ret. 1994. Mem. Nat. Interm Housing Network, Moose. Avocations: flying, men's senior baseball, bowling. Office: Telecom Network Inc 3660 Maguire Blvd Ste 210 Orlando FL 32803-3062

WILKERSON, KAREN LOUSIE, paralegal; b. Reidsville, N.C., June 28, 1957; d. William Henry and Jean Gloria (Tiller) W.; divorced. Student, N.C. State U., 1975-77, Western Carolina U., Cullowhee, N.C., 1978-80; diploma, Profl. Ctr. Paralegal Studies, Columbia, S.C., 1988. Paralegal Ken H. Lester, Esquire, Columbia, 1989—; spkr. Alumni Profl. Ctr. Paralegal Studies, Columbia, 1988-95. Mem. ATLA, S.C. Trial Lawyers Assn. (paralegal rep. 1993—). Democrat. Methodist. Office: Lester & Jones 1716 Main St Columbia SC 29201

WILKERSON, RITA LYNN, special education educator, consultant; b. Crescent, Okla., Apr. 22; Mem. ASCD, Coun. for Exceptional Children, OARC, OACLD, Phi Delta Kappa, Kappa Delta Pi. BA, Cen. State U., Edmond, Okla., 1963; MEd, Cen. State U., 1969; postgrad., U. Okla., 1975. Elem. tchr. music Hillsdale (Okla.) Pub. Sch., 1963-64; jr. high sch. music and spl. edn. Okarche (Okla.) Pub. Sch., 1965-71; cons. Title III Project, Woodward, Okla., 1971-72; dir. Regional Edn. Svc. Ctr., Guymon, Okla., 1972-81; dir., psychologist Project W.O.R.K., Guymon, 1981-90; tchr. behavioral disorders Unified Sch. Dist. 480, Liberal, Kans., 1990—; sch. psychologist Hardesty (Okla.) Schs., 1994; cons. Optima (Okla.) Pub. Schs., 1990, Felt (Okla.) Pub. Schs., 1990, Texhoma (Okla.) Schs., 1994, Balko (Okla.) Pub. Schs., 1996; spl. edn. cons. Optima Pub. Schs., 1992—, Goodwell (Okla.) Pub. Schs., 1992—; diagnostician Tyrone, Okla. Pub. Schs., 1992-95; home svcs. provider Dept. Human Svcs., Guymon, 1990; active Kans. Dept. Social and Rehab. Svcs., 1993—; adj. tchr. Seward County C.C., 1994—. Grantee Cen. State U., 1968-69, Oklahoma City Dept. Edn., 1988-89. Mem. ASCD, NAFE, NEA (liberal Kans. chpt.), AAUW, Coun. Exceptional Children, Okla. Assn. Retarded Citizens, Okla. Assn. for Children with Learning Disabilities, Phi Delta Kappa. Republican. Avocation: crafts. Home: 616 N Crumley St Guymon OK 73942-4341 Office: Unified Sch Dist 480 7th And Western Liberal KS 67901

WILKERSON, WILLIAM HOLTON, banker; b. Greenville, N.C., Feb. 16, 1947; s. Edwin Cisco and Agnes Holton (Gaskins) W.; m. Ellen Logan Tomskey, Oct. 27, 1973; 1 child, William Holton Jr. AB in Econs., U. N.C., 1970. Asst. v.p. First Union Nat. Bank, Greensboro, N.C., 1972-77; v.p. Peoples Bank & Trust Co., Rocky Mount, N.C., 1977-79; sr. v.p. Hibernia Nat. Bank, New Orleans, 1979-86; exec. v.p. Peoples Bank and Trust Co., 1987-89, pres., 1989-90; sr. exec. v.p., bd. dirs. Centura Banks, Inc., 1990—; chmn., Centura Ins. Svcs., Inc., 1995—; chmn. Centura Securities, Inc., 1995—, Carolinas Gateway Partnership, Inc., 1995—. Mem. Robert Morris Assoc., Rocky Mount C. of C. (bd. dirs. 1989—, vice chmn. 1992-94, chmn.-elect 1994, chmn. 1995), Benvenue Country Club, Kiwanis, Omicron Delta Epsilon, Chi Beta Phi, Phi Sigma Pi. Republican. Home: 336 Iron Horse Rd Rocky Mount NC 27804-2118

WILKES, BRENT AMES, management consultant; b. Melrose, Mass., Sept. 30, 1952; s. Gordon Borthwick and Frances (Ames) W.; 1 child, Erin. Bachelor, U. Mass., 1974; M of Pub. Affairs, U. Conn., 1977. Adminstrv. asst. Town of Tolland, Conn., 1975-76; mgmt. specialist Mass. Dept. Community Affairs, Boston, 1976-79; adminstrv.. asst. to mayor City of Gloucester, Mass., 1979-80; assoc. dir., dir. of field svcs. Mass. Mcpl. Assn., Boston, 1980-89; v.p., treas. Mass. Interlocal Ins. Assn., Boston, 1984-89; pres. MMA Consulting Group, Inc., Boston, 1989-94, MMA Mgmt. Svcs. Inc., Boston, 1995—; v.p., treas. Pub. Employer Risk Mgmt. Assn., Albany, N.Y., 1989—; adj. prof. Suffolk U. Grad. Sch. Mgmt., Boston, 1980-82; lectr. numerous regional and nat. trade assns. Author and editor: Managing Small Towns, 1986; contbr. articles to profl. jours. Mem. fin. com. Town of Acton, Mass., 1977-79; mem. town meeting Town of Reading, Mass., 1987-89; pres. Unitarian Universalist Ch. of Reading, 1990-93. Mem. Internat. City Mgmt. Assn. (cert. in mgmt.), Mass. Mcpl. Mgmt. Assn. Democrat. Unitarian Universalist. Avocations: golf, tennis, volleyball, reading. Office: MMA Mgmt Svcs Inc 60 Temple Pl Boston MA 02111-1306

WILKES, JOSEPH ALLEN, architect; b. N.Y.C., Aug. 14, 1919; s. Abraham P. and Rose W.; m. Margaret Wilcoxson, Dec. 7, 1946; children—Jeffrey, Roger. B.A., Dartmouth Coll., 1941; M.Arch., Columbia U., 1949. Registered architect, N.Y., Fla., Md., D.C., Va. Assoc. prof. architecture U. Fla., Gainesville, 1952-59; project dir. Bldg. Research Adv. Bd. Nat. Acad. Sci., Washington, 1959-62; assoc. architect Keyes, Lethbridge & Condon, Washington, 1962-66; ptnr. Wilkes & Faulkner, Washington, 1966-82, Wilkes Faulkner Jenkins & Bass, Washington, 1983-90; lectr. architecture U. Md., 1971-85. Editor: Ency. of Architecture, 5 vols., 1988-89; chmn. editorial rev. bd.: Architectural Graphic Standards, 7th edit., 1980; archtl. works include: bldgs. Nat. Zool. Park; (bldg. renovation) Fed. Res. Bd. Bldg., Washington. Pres. Nat. Ctr. for a Barrier Free Environment, Washington, 1978; mem. profl. adv. council Nat. Easter Seals Soc. for Crippled Children, 1977-80; mem. Pres. Com. for Employment of Handicapped, Washington, 1976-82. Served to capt. AC U.S. Army, 1942-45; ETO. Fellow AIA; mem. Alpha Rho Chi. Home: 1720 Winchester Rd Annapolis MD 21401-5851

WILKES, L. A., oil industry executive; b. 1937. BS in Chem. Engring., Ga. Inst. Tech., 1960. With Texaco Inc., 1960-88, regional mgr. USA's Tulsa region, 1985—; now v.p. manufacturing Texaco Corp.; v.p. ops. Star Enterprise, Houston, 1988—, pres., chief exec. officer. Office: Texaco Corp 1111 Bagby St Houston TX 77002*

WILKEY, MALCOLM RICHARD, retired ambassador, former federal judge; b. Murfreesboro, Tenn., Dec. 6, 1918; s. Malcolm Newton and Elizabeth (Gilbert) W.; m. Emma Secul Depolo, Dec. 21, 1959. AB, Harvard U., 1940, LLB, 1948; LLD (hon.), Rose-Hulman Inst. Tech., 1984. Bar: Tex. 1948, N.Y. 1963, U.S. Supreme Ct. 1952. U.S. atty. So. Dist. Tex., 1954-58; asst. atty. gen. U.S., 1958-61; ptnr. Butler Binion Rice & Cook, 1961-63; gen. counsel, sec. Kennecott Copper Corp., 1963-70; judge U.S. Ct. Appeals D.C. Circuit, 1970-85; U.S. amb. to Uruguay, 1985-90; official in charge fed. forces at Little Rock Sch. Crisis, Dept. Justice, 1958; mem. U.S.-Chile Arbitration Commn., 1991—; lectr. internat. constl. and adminstrv. law London Poly., 1979, 80; lectr. Tulane U. Law Summer Sch., Grenoble, France, 1981, 83, San Diego Law Summer Sch., Oxford, Eng., 1983, Brigham Young Law Sch., 1984, 93; vis. fellow Wolfson Coll., Cambridge U., 1985; chmn. Pres.'s Commn. on Revision Fed. Ethics Laws, 1989; spl. counsel to Atty. Gen. for inquiry into the House Banking Facility, 1992. Author: Is It Time For A Second Constitutional Convention, 1995. Del. Republican Nat. Conv., 1960. Served from 2d lt. to lt. col. AUS, 1941-45. Hon. fellow Wolfson Coll., Cambridge. Fellow Am. Bar Found.; mem. Am. Law Inst. (adv. com. restatement fgn. rels. law of U.S.), Jud. Conf. U.S. (com. on standards for admission to fed. cts. 1976-79), Phi Beta Kappa, Delta Sigma Rho, Phi Delta Phi (hon.). Address: Av El Bosque 379, Providencia, Santiago Chile

WILKIE, DONALD WALTER, biologist, aquarium museum director; b. Vancouver, B.C., Can., June 20, 1931; s. Otway James and Jessie Margaret (McLeod) W.; m. Patricia Ann Archer, May 18, 1980; children: Linda, Douglas, Susanne. B.A., U. B.C., 1960, M.Sc., 1966. Curator Vancouver Pub. Aquarium, 1961-63, Phila. Aquarama, 1963-65; exec. dir. aquarium-mus. Scripps Instn. Oceanography, La Jolla, Calif., 1965-93, ret., 1993; aquarium cons.; sci. writer and editor naturalist-marine edn. programs. Author books on aquaria and marine ednl. materials; contbr. numerous articles to profl. jours. Mem. Am. Soc. Ichthyologists and Herpetologists, San Diego Zool. Soc. (animal health and conservation com.). Home: 4548 Cather Ave San Diego CA 92122-2632 Office: U Calif San Diego Scripps Instn Oceanography Libr 9500 Gilman Dr La Jolla CA 92093-5003 *As a biologist and teacher my major goal has been to increase public interest in learning about our environment and promoting wise use of the earth's resources for the long term good of mankind and the plants and animals with which we share the planet.*

WILKIE, EVERETT CLEVELAND, JR., librarian; b. Kinston, N.C., June 27, 1947; s. Everett Cleveland, Sr. and Nancy Frances (Stroup) W.; m. Barbara Lande Turman, Feb., 1986; 1 child, Lauren Llewellyn. Student, Campbell Coll., 1965-67; BA in English, Wake Forest U., 1969, MA in English, 1970; PhD in Comparative Lit., U. S.C., 1977, M Librarianship, 1978. Instr. dept. English McDowell Tech. Inst., Marion, N.C., 1970-71, Anderson (S.C.) Coll., 1971-72; adminstrv. asst. office dean freshmen U. S.C., Columbia, 1973-76, adminstrv. asst. office dean Coll. Humanities and Social Scis., 1976-78; rsch. assoc. dept. comparative lit. Brown U., Providence, 1978-80, bibliographer John Carter Brown Libr., 1981-84; reference libr. Lilly Libr. Ind. U., Bloomington, 1980-81; head libr., Crofut curator rare books and manuscripts, editor Bulletin Conn. Hist. Soc., Hartford, 1985—; mem. publ. adv. com. Conn. Jewish Hsitory; mem. state Hist. Records Adv. Bd., 1994, subcom. on membership, 1994; mem. RBMS Security & Seminars Com.; presenter papers in field. Contbr. 29 articles to profl. jours. McClean fellow Libr. Co. Phila., 1989, Mellon fellow, 1992; Travel to Collections grantee NEH, 1992. Mem. ALA, Bibliographical Soc. Am., Am. Printing History Assn., Soc. Am. Archivists, New England Printing History Assn., New England Archivists. Office: Conn Hist Soc 1 Elizabeth St Hartford CT 06105-2213

WILKIE, VALLEAU, JR., foundation executive; b. Summit, N.J., July 3, 1923; s. Valleau and Amelia Wilkie (Parry) W.; m. Donna Hartwell, Oct. 28, 1985; children: Janice, Robert. A.B., Yale U., 1948; M.A., Harvard U., 1954. Instr. history Phillips Acad., 1948-59; headmaster Gov. Dummer Acad., Byfield, Mass., 1959-72; mem. bd. trustees Gov. Dummer Acad., 1960-72, dir. devel., 1972-73; exec. v.p. Sid W. Richardson Found., Ft. Worth, 1973—; bd. dirs. Nat. Charities Info. Bureau;. Bd. dirs. S.W. Ednl. Devel. Lab., 1976-82, pres. 1981-82; mem. Council on Founds., Inc., 1980—, bd. dirs., 1981-87, chmn. bd., 1985-87; bd. dirs. Conf. of S.W. Founds., 1977-82, pres., 1981-82; bd. dirs. Found. Ctr., 1982-91, Nat. Charities Info. Bur., 1991—. Served to 1st lt. USAAF, 1942-45. Mem. Headmasters Assn., N.E. Assn. Schs. and Colls. (chmn. commn. on ind. secondary schs. 1967-70, pres. 1972-73), Delta Kappa Epsilon. Episcopalian. Office: Sid W Richardson Found 309 Main St Fort Worth TX 76102-4006

WILKIN, MILES CLIFFORD, theatrical group executive; b. Norfolk, Va., Aug. 9, 1948; s. Winton Reynold and Elizabeth (Lawrence) W.; m. Kathleen Burke, June 13, 1968 (div. Aug. 1984); children: Miles Clifford II, Stephen Joseph; m. Constance Beth Weinstein, Feb. 4, 1991. BSBA, U. Fla., 1971. Asst. to dean of students U. Fla., Gainesville, 1971-78; dir. Orlando (Fla.) Centroplex, 1978-79; gen. mgr. Saenger Theatre, New Orleans, La., 1979-82; pres., chief exec. officer Pace Theatrical Group, Inc., Houston, N.Y.C., Miami, 1982—. Assoc. producer (plays) Jerome Robbins Broadway, 1989, Gypsy, 1990; producer (plays) Long Day's Journey into Night, 1986, South Pacific, 1987, Into The Woods, 1988, Starlight Express, 1989, Grand Hotel, 1991, Magic of David Copperfield, 1991, Bye Bye Birdie, 1991, Fiddler on the Roof, 1991 (Tony award). Pres. Story Theatre Prodn., Ft. Lauderdale, Fla.; mem. Performing Arts Ctr. Trust., Miami. Mem. League Am. Theatres & Producers (gov., mem. exec. com.). Avocation: scuba diving. Address: Pace Theatrical Group Inc 1515 Broadway Ste 3804 New York NY 10036-8901

WILKIN, RICHARD EDWIN, clergyman, religious organization executive; b. nr. Paulding, Ohio, Nov. 3, 1930; s. Gaylord D. and Beulah E. (Tarlton) W.; m. Barbara A. Zehender, Aug. 10, 1952; children—Richard Edward, James Lee, Deborah Ann. Student, Giffin Jr. Coll., 1948-49; B.S., Findlay Coll., 1952, D.D., 1975; postgrad., Ind. U., 1959-60. Ordained to ministry Churches of God Gen. Conf., 1953; pastor Neptune Ch. of God, Celina, Ohio, 1952-59, Wharton (Ohio) Ch. of God, 1959-64, Anthony Wayne Ch. of God, Ft. Wayne, Ind., 1964-70; adminstr., chief exec. Chs. of God Gen. Conf., Findlay, Ohio, 1970-87; supr. mission work India, Bangladesh, Haiti, 1970-85; dir. field edn. and Inst. for Biblical Studies, faculty mem. Winebrenner Theol. Sem., Findlay, 1987-92, adj. facult O.T., 1993—; interim sr. pastor Coll. 1st Ch. of God, Findlay, 1992-93, sr. pastor, 1992-93; Dir. summer youth camps, sec., mem. exec. com. Ohio Conf., 1952-59, state clk., pres., 1959-64; chmn. Commn. on Edn., mem. exec. com. Ind. Conf., 1964-70; adv. com. Am. Bible Soc.; steering com. U.S. Ch. Leaders, 1979; pres. Ft. Wayne Ministerial Assn.; bd. dirs. Associated Chs. of Ft. Wayne and Allen County, 1966-70; tchr. Center Twp. Jr. High Sch., Celina, Mendon (Ohio) Union High Sch., Van Del High Sch., Van Wert, Ohio, 1954-59; interim pastor Shawnee First Ch. of God, Lima, Ohio, 1987-88, ch. cons., 1987—. Vice pres. bd. trustees Winebrenner Haven, mem. adv. com. in race relations regarding sch. reorgn. and busing, Ft. Wayne, 1967-69; trustee Winebrenner Theol. Sem., 1980-87, sec. bd. trustees; trustee U. Findlay, 1985—, chmn. of com. on trustees of bd. of trustees; sec. Bd. of Pensions of Ch. of God, Gen. Conf., 1986—. Recipient Outstanding Tchr. award, 1958; Disting. Alumnus award Findlay Coll., 1973, Outstanding Leadership award Ohio Conf. Chs. of God, 1986, Disting. Assoc. award U. Findlay, 1992; named Hon. Alumnus Winebrenner Theol. Sem., 1978. Mem. NEA, Ohio Edn. Assn., NAACP, Farm Bur. Home: 1806 Greendale Ave Findlay OH 45840-6918

WILKINS, (GEORGE) BARRATT, librarian; b. Atlanta, Nov. 6, 1943; s. George Barratt and Mabel Blanche (Brooks) W. B.A., Emory U., 1965; M.A., Ga. State U., 1968, U. Wis., 1969. Reference libr. S.C. State Libr., Columbia, 1969-71; instl. libr. cons. Mo. State Libr., Jefferson City, 1971-73; asst. state libr. State Libr. Fla., Tallahassee, 1973-77; state libr. State Libr. Fla., 1977—; dir. Div. Libr. and Info. Svcs. State of Fla., Tallahassee, 1986—, acting asst. sec. state, 1987; abstractor Hist. Abstracts, 1967-71; dir. survey project Nat. Ctr. Edn. Statistics, 1976-77; del. The White House Conf. on Libr. and Info. Svcs., 1991; mem. planning com. Fla. Gov.'s Conf. on Libraries and Info. Svcs.; bd. dirs. Southeastern Libr. Network, Inc., 1979-82, treas., 1980-81, vice chmn., 1981-82; mem. adv. coun. U.S. Pub. Printer, 1983-86, Southeastern/Atlantic Regional Med. Libr. Svcs. 1986-89; mem. planning com., Fla. Automated Edn. Commn., 1989—; bd. dirs. Fla. Distance Learning Network, Inc., First Am. Found., Inc.; cons. in field. Contbr. articles to profl. jours. Mem. adv. com. statewide jail project Mo. Assn. Social Welfare, 1971-73, bd. dirs. central div., 1971-73; mem. State Univ. System Interinstl. Library Com., 1977—; bd. dirs. Fla. Ctr. Libr. Automation, 1984—, Fla. Ctr. for the Book, 1984—, Fla. Coll. Ctr. for Libr. Automation, 1990—. Recipient Exceptional Achievement award Assn. Specialized and Coop. Libr. Agys., 1991, Outstanding Pub. Svc. award Gov. of Fla., 1991; U. Wis. fellow, 1969. Mem. ALA (coun. 1981-85, legis. com. 1982-86, com. on orgn. 1988-90, planning com., 1993—), Assn. State Libr. Agys. (pres. 1976-77), Assn. Hosp. Instl. Librs. (bd. dirs. 1973-74), Am. Correctional Assn. (instn. libr. com.), Southeastern Libr. Assn. (pres. 1982-84), Chief Officers of State Libr. Agys. (bd. dirs. 1980-82, pres. 1990-92, chair legis. com. 1992—), Beta Phi Mu, Phi Alpha Theta. Democrat. Episcopalian. Office: Dept State Divsn Libr Svcs RA Gray Bldg Tallahassee FL 32399-0250

WILKINS, BURLEIGH TAYLOR, philosophy educator; b. Bridgetown, Va., July 1, 1932; s. Burleigh and Helen Marie (Taylor) W.; children: Brita Taylor, Carla Cowgill, Burleigh William. BA summa cum laude, Duke U., 1952; MA, Harvard U., 1954, Princeton U., 1963; PhD, Princeton U., 1965. Instr. MIT, Cambridge, 1957-60, Princeton U., 1960-61, 63; asst. prof. Rice U., Houston, 1965-66, assoc. prof., 1966-67; assoc. prof. U. Calif., Santa Barbara, 1967-68, prof., 1968—. Author: Carl Becker, 1961, The Problem of Burke's Political Philosophy, 1967, Hegel's Philosophy of History, 1974, Has History Any Meaning?, 1978, Terrorism and Collective Responsibility, 1992. Mem. Phi Beta Kappa. Office: Univ of Calif Dept of Philosophy Santa Barbara CA 93106

WILKINS, CAROLINE HANKE, consumer agency administrator, political worker; b. Corpus Christi, Tex., May 12, 1937; d. Louis Allen and Jean Guckian Hanke; m. B. Hughel Wilkins, 1957; 1 child, Brian Hughel. Student, Tex. Coll. Arts and Industries, 1956-57, Tex. Tech. U., 1957-58; BA, U. Tex., 1961; MA magna cum laude, U. Ams., 1964. Instr. history Oreg. State U., 1967-68; adminstr. Consumer Svcs. divsn. State of Oreg., 1977-80, Wilkins Assoc., 1980—; mem. PFMC Salmon Adv. subpanel, 1982-86. Author: (with B. H. Wilkins) Implications of the U.S.-Mexican Water Treaty for Interregional Water Transfer, 1968. Dem. precinct committeewoman, Benton County, Oreg., 1964-90; publicity chmn. Benton County Gen. Election, 1964; chmn. Get-Out-the-Vote Com., Benton County, 1966; vice chmn.Benton County Dem. Ctrl. Com., 1966-70; vice chmn. 1st Congl. Dist., Oreg., 1966-68, chmn., 1969-74; mem. exec. com. Western States Dem. Conf., 1970-72; vice chmn. Dem. Nat. Com., 1972-77, mem. arrangements com., 1972, 76, mem. Dem. Charter Commn., 1973-74; mem. Dem. Nat. Com., 1972-77, 85-89, mem. size and composition com., 1987-89, rules com., 1988; mem. Oreg. Govt. Ethics Commn., 1974-76; del., mem. rules com. Dem. Nat. Conv., 1988; 1st v.p. Nat. Fedn. Dem. Women, 1983-85, pres., 1985-87, parliamentarian, 1993-95; mem. Kerr Libr. bd. Oreg. State U., 1989-95, pres., 1994-95; mem. Corvallis-Benton County Libr. Found., 1991—, sec., 1993, v.p., 1994, pres., 1995; bd. dirs. Oreg. chpt. U.S. Lighthouse Soc. Named Outstanding Mem., Nat. Fedn. Dem. Women, 1992. Mem. Nat. Assn. Consumer Agy. Adminstrs., Soc. Consumer Affairs Profls., Oreg. State U. Folk Club (pres. faculty wives 1989-90), Zonta (vice area bd. dirs. dist. 8 1992-94, area dir., bd. dist. 8 1994—). Office: 3311 NW Roosevelt Dr Corvallis OR 97330-1169

WILKINS, CAROLYN NOREEN, early childhood educator; b. Fall River, Mass., Apr. 29, 1967; d. Thomas K. Jr. and Barbara A. (Messier) Porter; m. James A. Wilkins III, Feb. 22, 1992; 1 child, Zachary. BS in Edn., Lesley Coll., 1989. Cert. in elem. edn., Fla. 4-6th grade tchr. Paul Coffee Sch., Westport, Mass., 1989-90; prekindergarten tchr. Tender Loving Child Care Ctr., New Bedford, Mass., 1990-92, My Sch. Learning Ctr., Stuart, Fla., 1992-94, St. Michael's Ind. Sch., Stuart, 1994-95; tchr. White City Elem. Sch., Ft. Pierce, Fla., 1995-96; pvt. tutor, Westport, Stuart, 1989-95. Grantee Fla. Coun. Ind. Schs., 1995-96, Fla. Power & Light Co. Democrat. Roman Catholic. Avocations: reading, needlework. Office: 905 W 2d St Fort Pierce FL 34982

WILKINS, CHARLES L., chemistry educator; b. Los Angeles, Calif., Aug. 14, 1938; s. Richard and Lenore M. (McKean) W.; m. Susan J., Oct. 17, 1966; 1 child, Mark R. BS, Chapman Coll., 1961; PhD, U. Oreg., 1966. Prof. chemistry U. Nebr., Lincoln, 1967-81; prof. U. Calif., Riverside, 1981—. Office: Univ of Calif-Riverside Dept Of Chemistry Riverside CA 92521

WILKINS, CHRISTOPHER PUTNAM, conductor; b. Boston, May 28, 1957; s. Herbert Putnam and Angela (Middleton) W. BA, Harvard U., 1978; MusM, Yale U., 1981. Condr.-in-residence SUNY, Purchase, 1981-82; asst. condr. Oreg. Symphony, Portland, 1982-83, Cleve. Orch., 1983-86; assoc. condr. Utah Symphony, Salt Lake City, from 1986; condr. Colo. Springs Symphony Orch., 1989—; condr. Exxon Arts Endowment, 1982-86. Home: 168 Nashawtuc Rd Concord MA 01742-1617 Office: Colo Springs Symphony Orch PO Box 1692 Colorado Springs CO 80901-1692

WILKINS, DAVID GEORGE, fine arts educator; b. Battle Creek, Mich., Sept. 12, 1939; s. George Henry and Marjorie Ewing (Pierce) W.; m. Ann Thomas, June 25, 1966; children: Rebecca Louise, Katherine May. BA, Oberlin Coll., 1961; MA, U. Mich., 1963, PhD, 1969. Instr. U. N.H., Durham, 1963-64; prof. dept. history of art and arch. U. Pitts., 1967—, chair, 1989-92, dir. univ. art gallery, 1976-92; faculty mem. summer sessions Sarah Lawrence Coll.-U. Mich., Florence, Italy, 1975-81. Author: (with Bernard Schultz and Katheryn M. Linduff) Art Past/Art Present, 2d edit., 1994, (with Bonnie A. Bennett) Donatello, 1984, Maso di Banco, 1985, (with K.J. Arbitman) The Illustrated Bartsch, Vol. 53, Pre-Rembrandt Etchers, 1985, Paintings and Sculpture of the Duquesne Club, 1986 (with Mark M. Brown and Lu Donnelly) The History of the Duquesne Club, 1989; revising editor: Hartt History of Italian Renaissance Art, 4th edit., 1994. Bd. dirs. Pitts. Ctr. for Arts, 1979-93—; bd. dirs. Mendelssohn Choir of Pitts., 1979-84; mem. Pa. Humanities Coun., 1984-88; mus. adv. panel Pa. Coun. on Arts, 1985-87. William E. Suida fellow Kress Found., Kunsthistorisches Inst., Florence, 1966-67; recipient Chancellor's Disting. Teaching award U. Pitts., 1987. Mem. Coll. Art Assn., Italian Art Soc., Renaissance Soc. Am. Democrat. Home: 1217 Shady Ave Pittsburgh PA 15232-2811 Office: U Pitts Dept History Art & Arch 104 Frick Fine Arts Pittsburgh PA 15260-7601

WILKINS, (JACQUES) DOMINIQUE, professional basketball player; b. Paris, Jan. 12, 1960; s. John and Geraldine Wilkins; m. Nicole Berry, Sept. 26, 1992; 1 d.: Iyisha. Student, U. Ga., 1979-82. Basketball player Atlanta Hawks, 1982-94, Los Angeles Clippers, 1994, Boston Celtics, 1994-95, Panathinaikos-Athens, Athens, Greece, 1995—. Mem. NBA All-Star team, 1986-91, 93-94; NBA scoring leader, 1986; mem. All-NBA first team, 1986; mem. NBA All-Rookie team, 1983; Sporting News NCAA All-American, 1981, 82; mem. Dream Team II; slam dunk champion NBA, 1985, 90; mem. Panathinaikos-Athens european championship team, 1996. Holds single game record for most free throws without a miss-23, 1992. Office: Boston Celtics 151 Merrimac St Boston MA 02114-4714*

WILKINS, EARLE WAYNE, JR., surgery educator emeritus; b. Albany, N.Y., Aug. 17, 1919; s. Earle Wayne and Mildred Anna (Dana) W.; m. Suzanne Porter, Aug. 26, 1944; children: Clinton Porter, Wendy Dana Wilkins Hopkins, Wayne Lawrence. AB, Williams Coll., 1941; MD, Harvard U., 1944. Diplomate Am. Bd. Surgery, Am. Bd. Thoracic Surgery. Surg. resident Mass. Gen. Hosp., Boston, 1944-46, 48-51, mem. staff, 1952—, vis. surgeon, 1968—; mem. staff Harvard Med. Sch., Boston, 1953—, clin. prof. surgery, 1979-89, prof. emeritus, 1989—; Fulbright vis. prof. Allgemeines Krankenhaus, Vienna, Austria, 1964-65; vis. prof. Nat. Def. Med. Ctr., Taipei, Taiwan, 1989; surgeon Boston Bruins Hockey Club, 1969-85; physician tech. advisor div. of Emergency Med. Svcs., Washington, 1977-81, med. dir. Mass. Region IV, Boston, 1980-82; chmn. bd. Boston Med. Flight, 1985-87. Editor: Current Therapy in Cardiothoracic Surgery, 1989, Esophageal Cancer, 1988, Emergency Medicine: Scientific Foundations and Current Practice, 1989; contbr. numerous articles to profl. jours. Trustee Williams Coll., Williamstown, Mass., 1971-89, pres. Soc. of Alumni, 1967-69. Lt. (j.g.) USNR, 1946-48. Recipient Sports Illustrated Silver Anniversary award All-American Time Inc., N.Y.C., 1965, Commonwealth award Commonwealth Mass., 1986, Disting. Alumnus award Albany Acad., 1988, Rogerson Cup Williams Coll., 1991, Bicentenniel Medal Williams Coll., 1993. Fellow ACS, Am. Surg. Assn.; mem. AMA, Mass. Med. Soc., Boston Surg. Soc., Am. Assn. Thoracic Surgery (councillor 1984-88), Soc. Thoracic Surgeons, New Eng. Surg. Soc. (pres. 1980-81), Taconic Golf Club (pres. 1990-95). Republican. Avocations: golf, tennis, skiing, travel, stamps. Home: 240 South St Williamstown MA 01267-2822

WILKINS, FLOYD, JR., retired lawyer, consultant; b. Fowler, Calif., Sept. 8, 1925; s. Floyd and Kathryn (Springborg) W.; m. Holly Blee, June 18, 1949 (div. Jan. 1964); children: Douglas B., Janet H., Steven B., Kevin D.; m. Sybil Ann Perrault, Feb. 22, 1964. BS, U. Calif., Berkeley, 1946; LLB, Harvard U., 1952. Bar: N.Y. 1953, Calif. 1959. Assoc. Dwight, Royall, Harris, Koegel & Caskey, N.Y.C., 1952-58; v.p., trust officer San Diego Trust & Savs. Bank, 1958-63; assoc., then ptnr., prin. Seltzer Caplan Wilkins & McMahon, P.C. and predecessors, San Diego, 1963-91; lectr. U. So. Calif. Tax Inst., L.A., 1975, Title Ins. and Trust Co., L.A. and Santa Ana, Calif., 1973, 78, 83, Trust Svcs. of Am. Tax Forum, San Diego, U. Calif. Continuing Edn. of Bar, San Diego, 1977-91. Bd. dirs., pres. San Diego County Citizens Scholarship Found. Served with USNR, 1944-46. Mem. ABA, State Bar Calif., San Diego County Bar Assn. Republican. Avocations: travel, photography, wine, gardening. Home: 2005 Soledad Ave La Jolla CA 92037-3904

WILKINS, HERBERT PUTNAM, judge; b. Cambridge, Mass., Jan. 10, 1930; s. Raymond Sanger and Mary Louisa (Aldrich) W.; m. Angela Joy Middleton, June 21, 1952; children: Douglas H., Stephen M., Christopher P., Kate W. McManus. A.B., Harvard U., 1951, LL.B. magna cum laude, 1954; LL.D., Suffolk U., 1976; J.D., New Eng. Sch. Law, 1979. Bar: Mass. 1954.

Assoc. firm Palmer & Dodge, Boston, 1954-59; ptnr. Palmer & Dodge, 1960-72; assoc. justice Mass. Supreme Jud. Ct., 1972—. Editor: Harvard U. Law Rev, 1953-54. Bd. overseers Harvard U., 1977-83, pres. bd., 1981-83; trustee Milton Acad., 1971-76, Phillips Exeter Acad., 1972-78; mem. Concord (Mass.) Planning Bd., 1957-60; selectman Town of Concord, 1960-66, town counsel, 1969-72; town counsel Town of Acton, Mass., 1966-72. Mem. Am. Law Inst. (council), Am. Coll. Trial Lawyers (jud. fellow). Republican. Unitarian-Universalist. Office: Mass Supreme Jud Ct Pemberton Sq 1300 New Courthouse Boston MA 02108*

WILKINS, J. ERNEST, JR., mathematician; b. Chgo., Nov. 27, 1923; s. J. Ernest and Lucille B. (Robinson) W.; m. Gloria Louise Stewart, June 22, 1947 (dec.); children: Sharon Wilkins Hill, J. Ernest III; m. Maxine G. Malone, June 2, 1984. BS, U. Chgo., 1940, MS, 1941, PhD, 1942; BME, NYU, 1957, MME, 1960. Mathematician Am. Optical Co., Buffalo, 1946-50; mgr. R&D United Nuclear Corp., White Plains, N.Y., 1950-60; assoc. dir. lab. Gen. Atomic Co., San Diego, 1960-70; Disting. prof. applied math. physics Howard U., Washington, 1970-77; vis. scientist Argonne (Ill.) Nat. Lab., 1976-77, fellow, 1984-85; v.p., dep. gen. mgr. EG & G Idaho, Idaho Falls, 1977-84; Disting. prof. Clark Atlanta U., 1990—; chmn. Army Sci. Bd. Dept. Army, 1978-81; mem. Adv. Com. on Reactor Safeguards, Washington, 1990-94, chmn., 1993-94. Contbr. articles to profl. jours. With AUS, 1946-47. Recipient Outstanding Civilian Svc. medal U.S. Army, 1980. Mem. Am. Nuclear Soc. (pres. 1974-75, cons. 1987-90), Am. Math. Soc., Math. Assn. Am., Oak Ridge Assn. Univs. (coun. 1990—). Office: Clark Atlanta U Box J Atlanta GA 30314

WILKINS, JERRY L., lawyer, clergyman; b. Big Spring, Tex., June 1, 1936; s. Claude F. and Grace L. (Jones) W.; children by previous marriage: Gregory, Tammy, Scott, Brett; m. Valerie Ann Nuanez, Aug. 1, 1986. BA, Baylor U., 1958, LLB, 1960. Bar: Tex. 1960, U.S. Dist. Ct. (no. dist.) Tex. 1960, U.S. Ct. Appeals (5th cir.); ordained to ministry, 1977. Pvt. practice, Dallas, 1960—; capt. Air Am., Vietnam, 1967-68, Joint Church Aid, Biafra, 1969-70, TransInternat. Airlines, Oakland, Calif., 1977-79; gen. counsel First Tex. Petroleum, Dallas, 1982; owner Wooltex, Inc., Dallas, 1983—; owner, dir., legal counsel Intermountain Gas Inc., Dallas, 1983-84; legal counsel, dir. USA First (co-founder USA First Panama); co-founder Nederlandse Fin. Panama; founder, dir. Comanche Peak Reclamation Inc.; bd. dirs. Engineered Roof Cons., Continental Tex. Corp., Arlington, Landlord Rsch. Inc., Acklin Pain Rsch. Inst., Inc., Irving, Tex., Silver Leaf Metals Internat. Inc., Silver Leaf Mining Inc., Tex. Recycling Industries, Inc., Minerals Exploration Inc., Land Techs. Inc., Environ. Techs. Inc., Environ. Contractors Inc., Environ. Enterprises Inc., Desert Resources Inc.; founder, chmn. bd. dirs. Tex. Reclamation Industries, Inc.; founder Oxford Securities Funding Inc., Manchester Securieties Funding Inc., Cambridge Securities Funding Inc.; bd. dirs., v.p. for legal affairs, underwriter Lloyds U.S. Inc.; bd. dirs., co-founder R.O.A.S., Inc., Maritime Internat., Inc., Maritime Oil Recovery, Inc., Moriah Oil Recovery Barges, Inc., Megas Homes Internat., Urex Internat., Landlord Rsch. Co., Inc.; mem. legal counsel, bd. dirs. U.S. Fiduciary Co. Inc., U.S. Fiduciary Trust Co. Inc.; bd. dirs., legal counsel Lloyds U.S. Corp., Lloyds Link Inc., Lloyds Am. Inc., Image Security Co., Inc., Manchester Funding, Inc.; founder Kenai Cold Storage Inc., Kenai Pure Water Co., Arctic Pure Water Co., Arctic Cold Storage Inc., Shiloh Inc., Receivers, Inc., Internat. Equity Funding, Inc., C3 Plus Inc., UBO Sonoma Fin., UBO Caribbean Funding, Capstone Corp., Prowler Fouler Inc., Pacific Atlantic Funding Inc., Atlantic Funding, Inc.; bd. dirs., CEO Celex Nev., Inc.; bd. dirs. Minerals Exploration, Inc., Land Tech., Inc., Environ. Techs., Inc., Environ. Enterprises, Inc., Desert Gold Resources, Inc., Environ. Contractors, Inc.; co-founder USA First; cons. in field. Author: Gods Prosperity, 1980; So You Think You Have Prayed, 1980, Gods Hand in my Life, America, The Land of Sheep for Slaughter, I.R.S., America's Gestapo; Editor numerous books; contbr. articles to profl. jours. Bd. dirs., pres. Beasley For Children Found. Inc., Dallas, 1978—; mem. Rep. Presdl. Task Force, Washington, 1984—, Rep. Senatorial Inner Circle; bd. dirs., pilot Wings for Christians, Dallas, 1976—, Wings for Christ, Waco, Tex., 1976—. Recipient Cert. of Appreciation Parachute Club of Am., 1966; cert. of record holder for high altitude sky diving State of Tex., 1966, 67; Cert. of Achievement, Tex. State Guard, 1968. Mem. ABA, Nat. Lawyers Assn., Plaintiff Trial Lawyers Assn., Internat. Platform Assn., Tex. Trial Attys. Assn., Assn. Trial Lawyers Am., Quiet Birdmen, Tex. Outdoor Writers Assn., NRA, Tex. Rifle Assn., Parachute Assn. Am., P51 Mustang Pilots Assn., Phi Alpha Delta, U.S. Parachute Club (Monterey, Calif.). Avocations: shooting, hunting, fishing, flying, sports. Achievements: atty. (2 Tex. landmark cases) securing custody of female child for stepfather against natural parents (set the precedent which is now the standard visitation regarding children in divorce cases in Tex.), securing outside jail work program for convicted man, others. Office: PO Box 59462 Dallas TX 75229-1462

WILKINS, JOHN WARREN, physics educator; b. Des Moines, Mar. 11, 1936; s. Carl Daniel and Ruth Elizabeth (Warren) W. B.S. in Engring, Northwestern U., 1959; M.S., U. Ill., 1960, Ph.D., 1963; D.Tech. (hon.), Chalmers Tekniska Hogskola, Göteborg, 1990. NSF postdoctoral fellow U. Cambridge, Eng., 1963-64; asst. prof. physics Cornell U., 1964-68, assoc. prof., 1968-74, prof., 1974-88; Ohio Eminent scholar, prof. physics Ohio State U., 1988—; vis. prof. H.C. Ørsted Inst., Copenhagen, 1968, Nordita, Copenhagen, 1972-73, 75-76, 79-81; cons. Los Alamos Nat. Lab., 1984—. Assoc. editor Physica Scripta, 1977-85, Phys. Rev. Letters, 1982-85, Rev. Modern Physics, 1983-95; mem. editorial bd. Phys. Rev. B, 1991-94; coord. Comments on Condensed Matter Physics, 1985-90. Fellow AAAS, Am. Phys. Soc. (publs. oversight com. 1995—, chmn. 1995-96, councillor divsn. condensed matter physics 1989-93, exec. com. divsn. biol. physics 1973-77); mem. European Phys. Soc. Office: Ohio State U Dept Physics 174 W 18th Ave Columbus OH 43210-1106

WILKINS, LUCIEN SANDERS, gastroenterologist; b. Sanford, N.C., Mar. 30, 1942; s. Alexander Betts and Olive Elizabeth (Pittman) W.; m. Freda Barry Hartness, July 16, 1966; children: Lucien Sanders Jr., Elise Perryman. BA, Duke U., 1963; MD, Med. Coll. Va., 1967. Diplomate Am. Bd. Internal Medicine. Intern Medical Coll. Va., Richmond, 1967-68, resident in internal medicine, 1970-72, gastroenterology fellow, 1972-73; clin. gastroenterologist Wilmington (N.C.) Health Assoc., 1973—; vis. physician Hopital St. Croix, Leogane, Haiti, 1979-84; founder Divsn. Gastrointestinal Endoscopy Hopital St. Croix, Leogane, 1984, 1st Endoscopic Ambulatory Surgery Facility in State of N.C., 1990; chmn. dept. medicine New Hanover Regional Med. Ctr., Wilmington, N.C., 1990-92; asst. prof. clin. medicine U. N.C., Chapel Hill, 1974—; bd. dirs. Br. Banking and Trust, Wilmington, 1991—; physican adv. Nat. Found. Ileitis and Colitis, 1976-78. Author: Progeny, 1994. Bd. dirs. Cape Fear Coun. for the Arts, Wilmington, 1976-77, New Hanover Regional Med. Ctr. Found., Wilmington, 1993-95, exec. com., 1994-95, Com. of 100, Wilmington, 1992-95. Lt. comdr. M.C., USN, 1968-70. A. D. Williams rsch. fellow, 1965, Paul Harris fellow Rotary, 1986; winner GTP-L Al Holbert Meml. Race, Sebring, Fla., 1995. Mem. ACP, New Hanover-Pender County Med. Soc. (pres. 1980), Cape Fear Country Club, Surf Club, Hist. Stock Car Racing Group, Figure Eight Island Yacht Club (charter), Wrightsville Beach Ocean Racing Assn. (commodore). Presbyterian. Avocations: vintage automobile racing, tennis, sailing, skiing, outdoors. Home: 2215 Lynnwood Dr Wilmington NC 28403-8026 Office: Wilmington Health Assoc 1202 Medical Center Dr Wilmington NC 28401-7307 *Being a true physician means continually learning from your patients, about your patients, and on behalf of your patients.*

WILKINS, ORMSBY, music director, conductor, pianist; b. Sydney, Australia. Student, Sydney Conservatory Music, Melbourne (Australia) Conservatory Music. Joined Australian Ballet, 1973, condr., 1976-82, resident condr., 1982-83, guest condr. tour USSR and Eng., 1988, guest condr. tour Am., 1990; formerly condr. Sadler's Wells Royal Ballet (now Birmingham Royal Ballet); music dir., prin. condr. Nat. Ballet Can., Toronto, Ont., Can., 1990—; condr. Royal Swedish Ballet, Royal Opera House Orch. at Covent Garden, Opera Ballet de Lyon, Philharmonic Orch. London, Royal Philharm. Orch. Lodon, Hong Kong Philharmonic Orch., Winnipeg Symphony Orch. Performances include Swan Lake, Sleeping Beauty, Coppelia, Raymonda, Petrouchka, Rite of Spring, premiere of Hobson's Choice. Office: Nat Ballet Can, 157 King St East, Toronto, ON Canada M5C 1G9

WILKINS, PHILIP CHARLES, judge; b. Jan. 27, 1913; student Sacramento Jr. Coll.; LL.B., U. Calif., San Francisco, 1939; m. Sue Wilkins, Aug. 9, 1941. Bar: Calif. 1939. Mem. firm A.D. McDougall, Sacramento, 1940-42, Rowland & Craven, Sacramento, 1946-54; individual practice law, Sacramento, 1954-59; ptnr. firm Wilkins, Little & Mix, Sacramento, 1959-65, Wilkins & Mix, Sacramento, 1966-69; judge U.S. Dist. Ct., Eastern Dist. Calif., Sacramento, 1969—, now sr. judge. Served to lt. USNR, 1942-46. Office: US Dist Ct 4028 US Courthouse 650 Capitol Mall Sacramento CA 95814-4708*

WILKINS, RITA DENISE, researcher, multimedia design consultant; b. Detroit, June 21, 1951; d. William H. and Alice L. (Hayes) Smith. Student, George Peabody Coll., 1969-70, Cleveland (Tenn.) State Community Coll., 1973-75. Mgmt. coord., legal coord. Arlen Realty and Devel. Corp., Chattanooga, Tenn., 1973-76; asst. v.p., office mgr. Newburger Andes & Co., Atlanta, 1976-78, asst. v.p., project mgr., 1978-79; project mgr. Robinson-Humphrey, Atlanta, 1979-80; dept. head Office Properties Group Merrill Lynch Realty Comml. Svcs., Atlanta, 1980-83; acquisition devel. mgmt. rep. Cardinal Industries, Inc., Atlanta, 1983-86; pres., sr. cons. CPC/Foresite, Charleston, S.C., 1986—; guest lectr. Ga. State U. Contbr. articles to profl. jours. Mem. Indsl. Devel. Rsch. Coun. Office: CPC/Foresite 115 Dorris Ave Goodlettsville TN 37072-1306

WILKINS, ROBERT HENRY, neurosurgeon, editor; b. Pitts., Aug. 18, 1934; s. George H. and Mary M. (Lemon) W.; m. Gloria A. Kohl, Dec. 28, 1957; children: Michael I., Jeffrey K., Elizabeth A. BS, U. Pitts., 1955, MD, 1959. Diplomate Am. Bd. Neurol. Surgery. Intern, resident gen. surgery Duke U. Med. Ctr., Durham, N.C., 1959-61, resident neurosurgery, 1963-68, asst. prof. neurosurgery, 1968-72, prof., chief div. neurosurgery, 1976—; clin. assoc. surgery br. Nat. Cancer Inst., Bethesda, Md., 1961-63; chmn. dept. neurosurgery Scott and White Clinic, Temple, Tex., 1972-75; assoc. prof. neurosurgery U. Pitts., 1975-76; lectr. Cook County Grad. Sch. Medicine, Chgo., 1976—; attending neurosurgeon Durham VA Hosp., 1968-72, 78—; mem. Nat. Adv. Coun. Nat. Inst. Neurol. Disorders and Stroke, 1989-92. Co-editor: Neurosurgery, 2d edit., 3 vols., 1996, Neurosurgery Updates I and II, 1990, 91, Neurosurgery Operative Atlas, 1991—, Principles of Neurosurgery, 1994; editor Clin. Neurosurgery, 1972-75; assoc. editor Surg. Neurology, 1975-76; founding editor Neurosurgery, 1977-82; mem. editl. bd. Jour. Neurosurgery, 1987-96, chmn., 1996—; neurosurgery editor Key Neurology and Neurosurgery, 1993-96, Yr. Book of Neurology and Neurosurgery, 1994—. Recipient Travel award Copenhagen, Nat. Inst. Neurol. Diseases and Blindness, Royal Australasian Coll. Surgeons, Found. lectr. Adelaide 1986. Fellow ACS (gov. 1996—); mem. Congress Neurol. Surgeons (pres. 1979-80), Am. Assn. Neurol. Surgeons (treas. 1989-92), So. Neurosurg. Soc. (sec. 1988-91, pres. 1992-93), Soc. Neurol. Surgeons (v.p. 1995-96), Am. Bd. Neurol. Surgery (dir. 1991—, chmn. 1996—), Phi Beta Kappa, Alpha Omega Alpha. Democrat. Episcopalian. Avocations: medical writing and editing. Office: Duke U Med Ctr PO Box 3807 Durham NC 27710-3807

WILKINS, ROBERT PEARCE, lawyer; b. Jesup, Ga., Sept. 10, 1933; s. Ransom Little and Sarah (Pearce) W.; m. Rose Truesdale, Jan. 7, 1956; children: Robert Pearce, Chisolm Wallace (dec.), Sarah Ruth Weiss, Rose Anne Brooks. B.A., U. S.C., 1953, J.D., 1954; LL.M., Georgetown U., 1957. Bar: S.C. 1954; cert. mediator and arbitrator, S.C. Atty. Office Gen. Counsel, Sec. Army, Washington, 1956; trust officer First Nat. Bank S.C., Columbia, 1957-60; practice law Columbia, 1960-64; ptnr. McLain, Sherrill & Wilkins, Columbia, 1964-68, McKay, Sherrill, Walker, Townsend & Wilkins, Columbia, 1969-75; sole practice law Columbia and Lexington, S.C., 1975-88; of counsel Nelson, Mullins, Riley & Scarborough, Lexington, 1988—; pres. Sandlapper Press, Inc., 1967-72, pub. Sandlapper Mag. S.C., 1968-72; editor Sandlapper Mag. S.C., 1968-69, 89—; editor, pub. S.C. History Illustrated, 1970; pres. R.P.W. Pub. Corp.; mem., chmn. S.C. Splty. Adv. Bd. Estate Planning and Probate, 1982-85; lectr. in law U. S.C., 1971-78. Author: Draftin Wills and Trust Agreements in South Carolina, 1971, Drafting Wills and Trust Agreements in Michigan, 1978, Wills and Trust System (Arkansas), 1978, Drafting Wills and Trust Agreements: A Systems Approach, 1995, 3d edit., 1995, software edit.; (with others) Word Processing for a Law Office, 1979, also articles; editor: The Lawyer's Microcomputer, 1982-85, The Lawyer's PC, 1983—, What a Lawyer Needs to Know to Buy and Use a Computer, 1984, The Perfect Lawyer, 1990—, The Lawyers' Word, 1991, Shepard's Elder Care/Law Newsletter, 1991-95. Del., Spl. Liaison Tax Com. Southeastern Region, 1967-70; exec. com. Richland County Rep. Com., 1960-64; sec.-treas. Richland County Rep. Club, 1960; bd. dirs. Ctrl. Tb-RD Assn.; trustee Sch. Dist. 1, Lexington County, S.C., 1971-78, sec., 1972-75, chmn., 1975-78; mem. S.C. Commn. on Higher Edn., 1978-80, S.C. Commn. on Lawyer Competence, 1980-82; bd. dirs. Crime Stoppers of the Midlands, 1983-85, RPW Learning Ctr., 1987-94, Mt. Hope Cemetary, 1991—, also v.p., 1992—; v.p. 11th cir. Alumni Coun. U. S.C., 1993-95, mem. awards com., 1995—; mem. commn. Riverbanks Zoo, 1986—, sec., 1991-95, chmn., 1995—. With AUS, 1954-55. Fellow Am. Bar Found., Am. Coll. Trust and Estate Counsel (publs. com. 1984-87, bd. regents 1986-87, mem. tech. com. 1989—), Am. Coll. Tax Counsel, Coll. Law Practice Mgmt. (charter, trustee), S.C. Bar (tax coordinating com. 1968-70, chmn. legal econs. com. 1973-75, ho. of dels. 1978-80, editor S.C. Lawyer 1989-91, mem. alternative dispute resolution sect. 1993—), S.C. Bar Found. (life, bd. dirs. 1984-88, v.p. 1986-87, pres. 1987-88); mem. ABA (ho. of dels. 1986-87, chmn. valuation subcom., estate and gift tax com., taxation sect. 1967-73, vice chmn. svc. and assistance to law student div. com. gen. practice sect. 1971-72, vice chmn. corp. counsel com. gen. practice sect. 1972-74, editor econs. of law practice sect. legal econs. 1974-78, sect. 1977-78, vice chmn. 1978-79, chmn. 1980-81, mem. standing com. assn. comm. 1981-84, real property, probate and trust law, mem. publs. com. 1985-89, editor Probate and Property, 1986-89), Richland County Bar Assn. (chmn. probate sect. 1973-74, unauthorized practice of law com. 1976), Lexington County Bar (chmn. mediation com. 1994—), Columbia Jaycees (sec.-treas. 1958-59), Columbia Estate Planning Coun. (pres. 1964-65), Am. Y-Flyer Yacht Racing Assn. (area v.p. 1971, internat. dir. 1972-73), Omicron Delta Kappa, Sigma Chi. Clubs: Columbia Sailing (dir. 1968-71), Columbia Tip Off (dir. 1968-73), Columbia (pres. 1971-72). Home: PO Box 729 Lexington SC 29071-0729 Office: 334 Old Chapin Rd Lexington SC 29072-8801

WILKINS, ROGER CARSON, retired insurance company executive; b. Houlton, Maine, June 9, 1906; s. George W. and Amanda (Carson) W.; m. Evelyn McFadden, Aug. 23, 1933; 1 child, Susan J. Student, Ricker Classical Inst., 1919-24; B.A., U. Maine, 1929; LL.D., U. Hartford, 1966, Ricker Coll., 1970, Trinity Coll., 1973. With Travelers Ins. Companies, Hartford, from 1929; beginning as mgr. mortgage loan dept. for Travelers Ins. Companies, Tex., 1930; successively asst. mgr. home office, mgr., sec. v.p. Travelers Ins. Companies, 1953-65, sr. v.p., 1965-69, pres., 1969-71, chmn. bd., from 1971; also chief exec. officer; chmn. bd. Travelers Corp., 1971-73, chmn. exec. com., from 1974; former dir. Allis-Chalmers Corp., United Tech., Conn. Bank and Trust Co., Conn. Natural Gas Co.; former trustee Wells Fargo Mortgage Investor. Bd. dirs. U.S. C. of C. Corporator Hartford Hosp.; pres. Hartford Inst. Living; trustee St. Joseph Coll. Clubs: Hartford, Hartford Golf; Gulf Stream Golf (Fla.); Ekwanok Country (Manchester, Vt.).

WILKINS, WILLIAM WALTER, JR., federal judge; b. Anderson, S.C., Mar. 29, 1942; s. William Walter and Evelyn Louise (Horton) W.; m. Carolyn Louise Adams, Aug. 15, 1964; children: Lauren, Lyn, Walt. B.A., Davidson Coll., 1964; J.D., U. S.C., 1967. Bar: S.C., 1967, U.S. Dist. Ct. S.C. 1967, U.S. Ct. Appeals (4th cir.) 1969, U.S. Supreme Ct. 1970. Law clk. to judge U.S. Ct. Appeals 4th Cir., 1969; legal asst. to U.S. Senator Strom Thurmond, 1970; ptnr. Wilkins & Wilkins, Greenville, S.C., 1971-75; solicitor 13th Jud. Cir., 1974-81; judge U.S. Dist. Ct., Greenville, 1981-86, U.S. Ct. Appeals (4th cir.), 1986—; lectr. Greenville Tech. Coll.; chmn. U.S. Sentencing Commn., 1985-94. Editor-in-chief S.C. Law Rev., 1967; contbr. articles to legal jours. Served with U.S. Army, 1967-69. Named Outstanding Grad. of Yr. U. S.C. Sch. Law, 1967. Mem. S.C. Bar Assn., Wig and Robe. Republican. Baptist. Office: US Cir Ct 4th Ct PO Box 10857 Greenville SC 29603-0857

WILKINSON, ALBERT MIMS, JR., lawyer; b. Nashville, June 29, 1925; s. Albert Mims and Mary Nelle (Derryberry) W.; m. Edythe Bush, Mar. 27, 1953 (div.); children: William Terry, Elizabeth Ann, David Bush; m. Dolores Jean Attard, Oct. 22, 1971 (div.); 1 child, Mary Dolores. Student, Emory U., 1942-43; JD, U. Ga., 1949. Bar: Ga. 1948. Pvt. practice law Atlanta, 1950-85; gen. counsel GEC-Marconi Avionics Inc., Atlanta, 1985—; hon. legal adviser to Brit. Consul Gen. at Atlanta. Author: The Winning of the Revolutionary War in the South, 1976, The Rights of Unsecured Creditors-The Law in Georgia, 1979. Mem. DeKalb County Bd. Elections, 1966-72; chmn. 4th Congl. Dist. Republican Exec. Com., 1968-70, Ga. State Rep. Exec. Com., 1968-74; 1st vice chmn. Ga. Rep. Party, 1972-74, asst. gen. counsel, 1974-75; vice chmn., trustee Atlanta Counseling Center, Inc., 1960-83. Served with USCGR, 1943-46. Decorated Order Brit. Empire. Fellow Comml. Law Found.; mem. BA, Ga. Bar Assn., Atlanta Bar Assn., Ga. Soc. (pres. 1962-63), SAR, Southeastern Mem.'s Assn. (pres. 1960-61), Comml. Law League Am., Ga. Soc. Colonial Wars, Old Guard of Gate City Guard (comdt. 1986), N.C. Soc. of Cincinnati, Sphinx Club, Gridiron Club, Commerce Club, Civitan, Masons, Blue Key, Omicron Delta Kappa. Baptist. Home and Office: 333 Sky Vly Dillard GA 30537-9507 *By precept and example my parents pointed out the upward way in life, on a foundation of religious faith. "To do justly, to love mercy, to walk humbly with thy God." Later a beloved teacher taught the lines from Ulysses as he prepared to set sail, "To strive, to seek, to find and never yield." Their inspiration has continued throughout my life.*

WILKINSON, BEN, chancellor, evangelist, ministry organizer, writer; b. Gloster, Miss., July 6, 1932; s. Thomas Lamar and Evie (Quackenbush) W.; m. Mary Pittman; children: Evangeline Patricia Wilkinson Light, William Dwight, Manford Leighton, Glen Calvin. BA in Pub. Speaking, U. So. Miss., 1954; MDiv, Columbia Theol. Sem., Decatur, Ga., 1957, postgrad., 1964-65; DD, Whitefield Theol. Sem., 1992. Pastor Trinity Presbyn. Ch., Huntsville, Ala., 1955-62; pastor Ga. Ave Presbyn. Ch., Atlanta, 1962-66, evangelist, 1966—, exec. dir., 1973-95; founder, dir. Synod of the City-PEF Planting Bibl. Chs. in the Inner City, 1993—; with Presbyn. Evangelistic fellowship, Decatur, Ga.; bd. dirs. Atlanta Sch. Bibl. Studies, Westminster Bibl. Missions, World Harvest Missions, Lords Day Alliance; founder, dean, president Atlanta Sch. Bibl. Studies, 1971-85, chancelor, 1986—. Editor: Come...Follow, 1973-95. Avocations: sports, writing, reading, family life. Home: 214 Inman Dr Decatur GA 30030-3833 Office: Presbyn Evangelistic Fellowship 4211 Flat Shoals Pky Decatur GA 30034-4203

WILKINSON, DAVID TODD, physics educator; b. Hillsdale, Mich., May 13, 1935; s. Harold Arba and Thelma Ellen (Todd) W.; m. Sharon E. Harper, June 14, 1958 (div. June 1979); children: Wendy, Kenton; m. Eunice H. Dowell, Oct. 13, 1984. BS in Engring. Physics, U. Mich., 1957, MS in Nuclear Engring., 1959, PhD in Physics, 1962. Lectr. physics U. Mich., Ann Arbor, 1962-63; instr. Princeton U., N.J., 1963-65; asst. prof. Princeton U., 1965-68, assoc. prof., 1968-71; prof. Princeton U., N.J., 1971—, chmn. dept., 1987-90; cons. NASA, mem. COBE satellite team. Contbr. articles to profl. jours. Alfred P. Sloane fellow, 1965-67, John Simon Guggenheim fellow, 1977-78. Mem. NAS. Office: Princeton U Jadwin Hall PO Box 708 Dept Princeton NJ 08544

WILKINSON, DORIS Y., medical sociology educator; b. Lexington, Ky., June 13, 1936; d. Howard Thomas and Regina Wilkinson. BA, U. Ky., 1958; MA, Case Western Res. U., 1960, PhD, 1968; MPH, Johns Hopkins U., 1985. Asst. prof. U. Ky., Lexington, 1968-70; assoc. prof., then prof. Macalester Coll., St. Paul, 1970-77; exec. assoc. Am. Sociol. Assn., Washington, 1977-80; prof. med. sociology Howard U., Washington, 1980-84; vis. prof. U. Va., 1984-85; prof. sociology U. Ky., Lexington, 1985—; chmn. panel women in sci. program NSF, Washington, 1976; rev. panelist Nat. Inst. Drug Abuse, Washington, 1978-79; mem. bd. sci. counselors Nat. Cancer Inst., Bethesda, Md., 1980-84; vis. scholar Harvard U., Cambridge, Mass., 1989-90, vis. prof., summers 1992, 93, 94; Rapoport vis. prof. social theory Smith Coll., summer 1995. Author: Wookbook for Introductory Sociology, 1968; editor: Black Revolt: Strategies of Protest, 1969; co-editor: The Black Male in America, 1977, Alternative Health Maintenance and Healing Systems, 1987, Race, Gender and the Life Cycle, 1991; social history photographic exhbn. "The African American Presence in Medicine" Harvard Med. Libr., 1991, Pearson Mus.- So. Ill. U. Med. Sch., 1992, N.J. Coll. Medicine and Dentistry, 1993, Louisville Mus. History and Sci., 1994, U. Cin. Med. Sch. Libr., 1994, Albert Einstein Coll. of Medicine, 1995; contbr. articles to profl. jours. Bd. overseers Case Western Res. U., Cleve., 1982-87. Recipient Pub. Humanities award U. Ky., 1990, Midway Coll. Women's History Month award, 1991, Gt. Tchr. award Nat. Alumni Assn. U. Ky., Disting. Scholar award Assn. Black Sociologists, 1993; inducted into Hall of Disting. Alumni, U. Ky., 1989; fellow Woodrow Wilson Found., 1959-61, Ford Found., 1989-90; grantee Social Sci. Rsch. Coun., 1975, Nat. Inst. Edn., 1978-80, Nat. Cancer Inst., 1986-88, Ky. Humanities Coun., 1988, Am. Coun. Learned Soc., 1989-90, NEH, 1991; Disting. Prof. in Coll. Arts and Scis., U. Ky., 1992-93. Mem. So. Sociol. Soc. (honors com. 1993-94), Am. Sociol. Assn. (exec. assoc., budget com. 1985-88, v.p. 1991-92, mem. coun. 1994—, Dubois-Johnson-Frazier award 1988), D.C. Sociol. Soc. (pres. 1982-83), Soc. for Study of Social Problems (v.p. 1984-85, pres. 1987-88), Ea. Sociol. Soc. (v.p. 1983-84, pres. 1992-93, I. Peter Gellman award 1987), Phi Beta Kappa (valedictorian), Alpha Kappa Delta. Unitarian.

WILKINSON, EDWARD ANDERSON, JR., retired naval officer, business executive; b. Selma, Ala., Sept. 21, 1933; s. Edward Anderson and Alice Margaret (Moorer) W.; m. Barbara Anne Parker, June 4, 1955 (dec. June 1991); children: Daryl Edward, Daniel Bryan, Edward Anderson III, David Park; m. Sondra Marie Moore, Oct. 2, 1994. B.S., U.S. Naval Acad., 1955; M.S. in Mech. Engring., 1964; grad., Nat. War Coll., 1972. Commd. ensign U.S. Navy, 1955, advanced through grades to rear adm., 1979; dir. Anti-Submarine Warfare Systems Program Office, Washington, 1978-79; dep. dir. Def. Mapping Agy., Washington, 1979-81; cmdr. Patrol Wings, U.S. Atlanta Fleet, Brunswick, Maine, 1981-83; dir. Def. Mapping Agy., Washington, 1983-85; ret., 1985; exec. v.p. Internat. Fed. Systems Intergraph Corp., Reston, Va. Decorated Legion Merit, D.S.M. (Dept. Def.). Methodist. Home: 1555 Regatta Ln Reston VA 22094 Office: Intergraph Corp Reston VA

WILKINSON, EUGENE PARKS, nuclear engineer; b. Long Beach, Calif., Aug. 10, 1918; s. Dennis William and Daisy Amelia (Parks) W.; m. Janice Edith Thuli, Mar. 28, 1942; children: Dennis Eugene, Stephen James, Marian Lynn, Rodney David. AB in Chemistry, San Diego State U., 1938. Instr. chemistry San Diego State U., 1938-39; commd. ensign U.S. Navy, 1940, advanced through grades to vice adm., 1970; served various locations including 1st comdg. officer USS Nautilus (1st nuclear-powered submarine), 1953-57; 1st comdg. officer USS Long Beach, 1959-63, 1st nuclear-powered surface ship; ret., 1974; exec. v.p. Data Design Labs., Cucamonga, Calif., 1977-80; pres., chief exec. officer Inst. Nuclear Power Ops., Atlanta, 1980-84, pres. emeritus, 1984—; bd. dirs. Data Design Labs. Decorated Legion of Merit, Silver Star, D.S.M. with three oak leaf clusters, others, Second Order Sacred Treasure Japan; recipient George Westinghouse Gold medal ASME, 1983, Oliver Townsend medal Atomic Indsl. Forum, 1984, Gold medal Uranium Inst., 1989. Mem. Am. Soc. Naval Engrs., Am. Nuclear Soc. (Henry DeWolf Smyth Nuclear Statesman medal 1994), Navy League, Submarine League, Nat. Acad. Engring. Avocations: tennis, bridge. Home: 1449 Crest Rd Del Mar CA 92014-2530

WILKINSON, G. THOMAS, gas and oil industry executive; b. 1937. BSE, St. Louis U., 1959. With AMOCO, ARCO, Seagull Energy S&P; pres. Ashland Exploration, Inc., 1990—; v.p. Ashland Oil, Inc., 1990-91, sr. v.p., 1992—. Office: Ashland Exploration Inc 14701 Saint Marys Ln Ste 700 Houston TX 77079-2905*

WILKINSON, GARY, management consultant. Treas. Bain & Co., Boston. Office: Brin & Co 2 Copley Pl Boston MA 02116

WILKINSON, HAROLD ARTHUR, neurosurgeon; b. Wake Forest, N.C., June 17, 1935; s. Charles T. and Ursula (Bernstein) W.; m. Alice D. Speas, June 22, 1957; children: Arthur, Edward. BS, Wake Forest Coll., 1955; MD, Duke U., 1959, PhD, 1962. NIH postdoctoral rsch. fellow Duke U. Med. Ctr., Durham, N.C., 1959-61, intern, 1961-62; resident in neurosurgery Mass. Gen. Hosp., Boston, 1962-66; mem. faculty Harvard U. Med. Ctr., Cambridge, Mass., 1966-78; mem. staff Boston City Hosp., 1966-71, Beth Israel Hosp., Boston, 1971-78; prof. neurosurgery, chmn. div. U. Mass. Med. Ctr., Worcester, 1979—, prof. anatomy cell biology program, 1985—, residency program dir., 1991—. Contbr. articles to profl. jours.; inventor intracranial pressure monitoring cup catheter. Med. Found. fellow, 1966-69. Mem. AMA, ACS, Am. Assn. Neurol. Surgery, Congress of Neurosurgery, New Eng. Neurol. Soc. Office: U Mass Med Ctr Div Neurosurgery 55 Lake Ave N Worcester MA 01655-0002

WILKINSON, HARRY EDWARD, management educator and consultant; b. Richmond Heights, Mo., June 30, 1930; s. Harry Edward and Virginia Flo (Shelton) W.; m. Sara Beth Kikendall, Aug. 30, 1958; children: Linda Beth, Cheryl Susan. BA in Physics, Princeton U., 1952; MBA, Washington U., St. Louis, 1957; D Bus. Adminstrn., Harvard U., 1960. Lic. psychologist, Mass. Staff engr. Southwestern Bell Tel. Co., St. Louis, 1954-57; traffic engr. New Eng. Tel. & Telegraph Co., Boston, 1957-60; sr. mgmt. cons. Harbridge House Inc., Boston, 1961-65; dean bus. adminstrn., dir. Mgmt. Inst., Northeastern U., Boston, 1965-67; pres., chmn. bd. Univ. Affiliates Inc., North Port, Fla., 1967—; vis. prof. mgmt. Rice U., Houston, 1990-94, dir. office of exec. devel., 1994—; cons. to various industries and govt., 1961—. Author: Influencing People in Organizations, 1993; contbr. articles to mgmt. jours. Lt. (j.g.) USN, 1952-54, Korea. Mem. APA, Acad. Mgmt., N.Am. Case Rsch. Assn., S.W. Case Rsch. Assn., Harvard Bus. Sch. Assn. Office: Jones Grad Sch Rice U 6100 Main St Houston TX 77005-1892

WILKINSON, HARRY J., technical company executive; b. Phila., Nov. 15, 1937; s. Frank and Annie Wilkinson; children: Tracey, Todd, Betsey. BS in Indsl. Engring., Temple U., 1965. Mktg. mgr. aerospace div. SPS Techs., Jenkintown, Pa., 1969-75; mng. dir. Unbrako, Ltd. div. SPS Techs., Coventry, Eng., 1975-79; pres. Unbrako, Ltd. div. SPS Techs., Jenkintown, 1979-82; pres. aerospace and indsl. products div., group v.p. domestic ops. SPS Techs., Newtown, Pa., 1984-86, pres., chief operating officer, 1986—, also bd. dirs.; bd. dirs. Drexelbrook Engring., Horsham, Pa., Flexible Cirs., Inc., Warrington, Pa. Served to lt. U.S. Army, 1957-59. Office: SPS Technologies 301 Highland Ave Jenkintown PA 19046-2630

WILKINSON, JAMES ALLAN, lawyer, healthcare executive; b. Cumberland, Md., Feb. 10, 1945; s. John Robinson and Dorothy Jane (Kelley) W.; m. Elizabeth Susanne Quinlan, Apr. 14, 1973; 1 child, Kathryn Barrett. BS in Fgn. Service, Georgetown U., 1967; JD, Duquesne U., 1978. Bar: Pa., U.S. Dist. Ct. (we. dist.) Pa. Legis. analyst Office of Mgmt. and Budget, Washington, 1972-73; dep. exec. sec. Cost of Living Council, Washington, 1973-74; sr. fin. analyst U.S. Steel Corp., Pitts., 1974-82; ptnr. Buchanan Ingersoll, Pitts., 1982-88; CFO, gen. counsel Meritcare, Pitts., 1988—; sr. v.p. Culwell Health Inc., 1991—; adj. prof. U. Pitts. Sch. Law, 1988-91. Author: Financing and Refinancing Under Prospective Payment, 1985; contbr. articles to profl. jours. Chmn. Oversight Com. on Organ Transplantation, Pitts., 1986—; sec.-treas. bd. dirs. Pitts. Symphony Soc., 1986—, Western Pa. Com. of Prevention of Child Abuse, 1987-90, Comprehensive Safety Compliance, 1988-91, Buchanan Ingersoll Profl. corp., 1988-90, Parental Stress Ctr., 1990-94; sec. Ross Mountain Club, 1995—. Mem. ABA, Am. Acad. Hosp. Attys., Am. Soc. of Law and Medicine, Nat. Assn. of Bond Lawyers, Nat. Health Lawyers Assn., Healthcare Fin. Mgrs. Assn. Republican. Episcopalian. Clubs: Duquesne (Pitts.), Pitts. Athletic Assn. Home: 1005 Elmhurst Rd Pittsburgh PA 15215-1819 Office: Meritcare Inc 1 Ppg Pl Ste 2260 Pittsburgh PA 15222-5401

WILKINSON, JAMES HARVIE, III, federal judge; b. N.Y.C., Sept. 29, 1944; s. James Harvie and Letitia (Nelson) W.; m. Lossie Grist Noell, June 30, 1973; children: James Nelson, Porter Noell. B.A., Yale U., 1963-67; J.D., U. Va., 1972. Bar: Va. 1972. Law clk. to U.S. Supreme Ct. Justice Lewis F. Powell, Jr., Washington, 1972-73; asst. prof. law U. Va., 1973-75, assoc. prof., 1975-78; editor Norfolk (Va.) Virginian-Pilot, 1978-81; prof. law U. Va., 1981-82, 83-84; dep. asst. atty. gen. Civil Rights div. Dept. Justice, 1982-83; judge U.S. Ct. Appeals (4th cir.), 1984—. Author: Harry Byrd and the Changing Face of Virginia Politics, 1968, Serving Justice: A Supreme Court Clerk's View, 1974, From Brown to Bakke: The Supreme Court and School Integration, 1979. Bd. visitors U. Va., 1970-73; Republican candidate for Congress from 3d Dist. Va., 1970. Served with U.S. Army, 1968-69. Mem. Va. State Bar, Va. Bar Assn., Am. Law Inst. Episcopalian. Home: 1713 Yorktown Dr Charlottesville VA 22901-3035 Office: US Ct Appeals 255 W Main St Rm 230 Charlottesville VA 22901-5058

WILKINSON, JOEL, oil company executive. Office: LL & E Petroleum Mktg 909 Poydras St New Orleans LA 70112-4000

WILKINSON, JOHN BURKE, former government official, novelist, biographer; b. N.Y.C., Aug. 24, 1913; s. Henry and Edith (Burke) W.; m. Frances I. Proctor, June 11, 1938; children: Eileen B. Wilkinson Wirta, Charles P. Student, St. George's Sch.; B.A. magna cum laude, Harvard U., 1935; Lionel Harvard studentship, Cambridge (Eng.) U., 1936. Copy writer Lord & Thomas (advt.), 1936-38; asst. advt. mgr. Reynal & Hitchcock, 1938-39; advt. mgr. Little, Brown & Co., 1939-41; free lance writer, 1946-50, 52-54, spl. asst. to asst. sec. state for pub. affairs, 1954-56, dep. asst. sec. state pub. affairs, 1956-58; pub. affairs adviser SHAPE, Paris, 1958-62; dir. U.S. Nat. Tennis Hall of Fame, v.p., 1962-81. Author: Proceed at Will, 1948, Run, Mongoose, 1950, Last Clear Chance, 1954, By Sea and By Stealth, 1956, Night of the Short Knives, 1964, The Helmet of Navarre, 1965, Cardinal in Armor, 1966, The Adventures of Geoffrey Mildmay (trilogy of 1st 3 novels), 1969, Cry Spy!: Anthology, 1970, Young Louis XIV, 1970, Francis in All His Glory, 1972, Cry Sabotage!, 1972, The Zeal of the Convert, 1976, re-issued, 1985, Uncommon Clay, the Life and Works of Augustus Saint Gaudens, 1985 (Pulitzer Prize nominee, Trustees' medal of St. Gaudens Hist. Site, 1994); Contbr. to: nat. mags. Christian Sci. Monitor. Trustee Corcoran Gallery of Art, 1973-88. Comdr. USNR, 1941-46, 51-52. Decorated Commendation Ribbon; commendatore Italian Order of Merit. Mem. Public Members Assn. of Fgn. Service (pres. 1979-83), Phi Beta Kappa; hon. mem. Internat. Lawn Tennis Club France Gt. Britain (chmn. Prentice Cup com. 1956-57). Clubs: Metropolitan (Washington), National Press (Washington); Chevy Chase (Md.), Tavern (Boston). Home: 3210 Scott Pl NW Washington DC 20007-2946 *My life as a writer has been a running battle with the English language. My own 14 books have been in the nature of experimentation in style and language, and this has also held true in doing reviews and magazine articles. Whether novel or article or biography, the purpose has been the same: to try to make the style carry the content as effectively and as clearly as possible. I don't know how well I have succeeded so far, but as Hemingway truly said authors are apprentices all their lives.*

WILKINSON, JOHN HART, lawyer; b. Newton, Mass., Dec. 31, 1940; s. Roger Melvin and Margaret (Carter) W.; children: Heather, Carter. BA, Williams Coll., 1962; LLB, Fordham U., 1965. Bar: N.Y. 1965, U.S. Dist. Ct. (so. and ea. dists.) 1968, U.S. Ct. Appeals (2d cir.) 1981, U.S. Ct. Appeals (11th cir.) 1982, U.S. Ct. Appeals (3d cir.) 1984, U.S. Ct. Appeals (5th cir.) 1987. Assoc. Donovan, Leisure, Newton & Irvine, N.Y.C., 1965, 67-73, ptnr., 1973—, editor, contbg. author to firm's ADR Practice Book, 1990; law clk. to presiding justice U.S. Dist. Ct. N.Y. (so. dist.), 1967-68; frequent speaker on litigation. Contbr. numerous articles to profl. jours. Bd. dirs., pres. Childfind of Am., Inc., 1993-94; v.p. bd. dirs. Pelham (N.Y. Family Svc., 1982-85; vol. learning disabled children Chelsea Neighborhood, N.Y.C., 1965-67; bd. dirs. Catskill Ctr. for Conservation and Devel., 1993—. Recipient Am. Jurisprudence award Fordham U. Mem. ABA (alt. dispute resolution com. 1989—), N.Y. State Bar Assn. (alt. dispute resolution com. 1989-93), Fed. Bar Coun., Assn. Bar City N.Y. (profl. responsibility com. 1987-89, pub. assistance com. 1991-94). Avocation: woodworking, flyfishing, biking, camping. Office: Donovan Leisure Newton & Irvine 30 Rockefeller Plz New York NY 10112

WILKINSON, LOUISE CHERRY, psychology educator, dean; b. Phila., May 15, 1948; m. Alex Cherry Wilkinson; 1 child, Jennifer Cherry. B.A. magna cum laude with honors, Oberlin Coll., 1970; Ed.M., Ed.D., Harvard U., 1974. Prof., chmn. dept. ednl. psychology U. Wis., Madison, 1976-85; prof., exec. officer Grad. Sch. Ph.D. Program CUNY, N.Y.C., 1984-86; prof. II, dean Grad. Sch. Edn. Rutgers U., 1986—; mem. Nat. rev. bd. Nat. Inst. Edn., 1977, 85, 87; cons. Nat. Ctr. for Bilingual Rsch., 1982, 84, U.S. Dept. Edn., 1995-96; adv. bd. Nat. Reading Rsch. Ctr., 1992—. Co-author: Communicating for Learning, 1991; editor: Communicating in Classroom, 1982, Social Context of Instruction, 1984, Gender Influences in the Classroom; mem. editorial bds. and contbr. articles to profl. jours. Fellow Am. Psychol. Assn., Am. Psychol. Soc.; mem. Internat. Assn. for Study Child Lang., Am. Ednl. Rsch. Assn. (v.p. 1990-92, program chair 1997). Home: 3 Andrews Ln Princeton NJ 08540-7633 Office: Rutgers U Grad Sch Edn 10 Seminary Pl New Brunswick NJ 08901-1108

WILKINSON, MICHAEL KENNERLY, physicist; b. Palatka, Fla., Feb. 9, 1921; s. Robert Ridley and Henrietta Lucille (Kennerly) W.; m. Virginia Sleap, June 18, 1944; children: Robert Warren, William Michael, Lucille Elizabeth. B.S., The Citadel, 1942; Ph.D., M.I.T., 1950. Research asso. M.I.T., 1948-50; research scientist Oak Ridge Nat. Lab., 1950-64, assoc. dir. Solid State div., 1964-72, dir. Solid State div., 1972-86, sr. advisor Solid State div., 1986-91; cons., 1991—; vis. prof. physics Ga. Inst. Tech., 1961-62, adj. prof., 1962-91; mem. adv. com. div. materials research NSF.; mem. council on materials sci. Dept. Energy. Contbr. articles on solid state physics to profl. jours. Served with AUS, 1942-46. Fellow Am. Phys. Soc., AAAS; mem. Am. Crystallog. Assn., Tenn. Acad. Sci., Sigma Xi, Sigma Pi Sigma. Episcopalian. Home: 124 Morningside Dr Oak Ridge TN 37830-8320 Office: Oak Ridge Nat Lab Oak Ridge TN 37831

WILKINSON, REBECCA ELAINE, human resources systems analyst; b. Dallas, Nov. 11, 1960; d. John Cephas and Mary Magdeline (Rhea) Bishop; m. Billy Don Wilkinson, July 31, 1982; children: Eric Tyler, Kristen Rhea. BEd, U. Dallas, 1982, MBA, 1995. Human resources/payroll systems analyst IBM, Irving, Tex., 1982-85; equal opportunity coord. IBM, Irving, 1985-90; human resources data analyst IBM, Roanoke, Tex., 1990-94; systems analyst specialist Westinghouse Security Systems, Irving, 1994—. Mem. NOW, Greenpeace, Sigma Iota Epsilon. Democrat. Episcopalian. Avocations: needlework, rollerblading, reading.

WILKINSON, ROBERT EUGENE, plant physiologist; b. Oilton, Okla., Oct. 24, 1926; s. Olney Samuel and Grace Elma (Curry) W.; m. Evalyn Dolores Smith, Jan. 31, 1951; children: Olney Thomas, Randall David. BS in Botany, U. Ill., Champaign, 1950; MS in Plant Physiology, U. Okla., 1952; PhD in Plant Physiology, U. Calif., Davis, 1956. Plant physiologist USDA, Clarkdale, Ark., 1957-62, Los Lunas, N.Mex., 1962-65; assoc. agronomist U. Ga. Agrl. Ext. Sta., 1965-74; agronomist U. Ga., 1974-94; ret., 1994; cons. U. Sao Paulo, Piricicaba, Brazil, 1978. Contbr. articles to profl. jours. With USNR, 1944-45; to lt. USAFR, 1950-58. Sr. Fulbright grantee, Turku, Finland, 1974-75, Teaching Rsch. Fulbright grantee, Nova Sad, Yugoslavia, 1975. Fellow Am. Inst. Chemistry; mem. Weeds Sci. Soc. Am., Am. Soc. Plant Physiologists, Kiwanis. Home: 665 Laura Dr Griffin GA 30223-5315

WILKINSON, SIGNE, cartoonist; b. Phila.. BA in English, 1972. Reporter West Chester (Pa.) Daily Local News, Academy of Natural Scis., Phila.; organizer for housing project Cyprus, 1974; freelance cartoonist Phila. and N.Y. publs.; cartoonist San Jose (Calif.) Mercury News, 1982-85, Phila. Daily News, 1985—. Recipient Pulitzer Prize for editorial cartooning, 1992. Mem. Assn. Am. Editl. Cartoonists (pres. 1994-95). Avocation: gardening. Office: Phila Daily News PO Box 8263 400 N Broad St Philadelphia PA 19101*

WILKINSON, STANLEY RALPH, agronomist; b. West Amboy, N.Y., Mar. 28, 1931; s. Ralph Ward and Eva Goldie (Perkins) W.; m. Jean Saye; children: Rachael, Stanley R. Jr., Augusta J. BS, Cornell U., 1954; MS, Purdue U., 1956, PhD, 1961. Soil scientist U.S. Regional Pasture Rsch. Lab., University Park, Pa., 1960-64, So. Piedmont Conservation Rsch. Ctr., Watkinsville, Ga., 1965—. Past advance chmn. Boy Scouts Am. Served to capt. USAF, 1955-57. Recipient 3d prize Freedoms Found., 1956. Fellow Soil and Water Conservation Soc. Am., Am. Soc. Agronomy; mem. Am. Soc. Agronomy, Soil Sci. Soc. Am., Soil and Water Conservation Soc., Sigma Xi. Methodist. Contbr. 18 chpts. to books and 140 tech. articles to profl. jours.

WILKINSON, SUZANNE, human services executive director; b. Dallas, Feb. 15, 1940; d. Jay F. and Iola Murphy; m. Ernest B. Wilkinson, July 23, 1960; children: Audree Clark II, Mike Elizabeth Wilkinson Kirkpatric. A. North Tex. U., 1960; Lic. Vocat. Nurse, Frank Phillips Coll., Borger, Tex., 1967; BS in Health Mgmt., Kennedy Western U., Augora Hills, Calif., 1990, MS in Health Adminstrn., 1991. Cert. I.V. therapy, case mgr. Nurse med. staff Higland Gen. Hosp., Pampa, Tex.; dir. fl. Pampa Nursing Home; exec. dir. Agape Health Svcs., Amarillo, Tex.; adminstr., exec. dir. case mgmt., owner, pvt. duty nursing staff Shepard's Crook Nursing Agy., Pampa, Amarillo, Borger, Wheeler and Shamrock, Tex.; pres. bd. dirs. Gray County Retarded Adults, Highland Hosp. Chmn. food bank dr.; mem. St. Matthew Episc. Ch; tchr. Sunday Sch.; mem. Alter Guides. Lt. Civil Air Patrol, 1980. Mem. Lic. Vocat. Assn. State Bd. Vocat. Nurse Examiners (pres. divsn. 14), Alzheimers Support Group (divsn. 14. L.V.N. Assoc.), AARP (chpt. pres.), Am. Heart Assn. (pres. bd. dirs.), Gold Coats of the Pampa C. of C.

WILKINSON, WARREN SCRIPPS, manufacturing company executive; b. Detroit, Feb. 2, 1920; s. Almadus DeGrasse and Harriet Gertrude (Whitcomb) W.; m. Joan Todd, June 14, 1941; m. Mireille De Bary, Dec. 17, 1966. Grad., Hotchkiss Sch., Lakeville, Conn., 1937; BS in Math, Harvard U., 1941; student, Calif. Inst. Tech., 1941-42. With U.S. Rubber Co., Detroit, 1942-43, Hanson Van Winkle-Munning Co., Matawan, N.J., 1946-64; pres. Hanson Van Winkle-Munning Co., 1961-64; v.p., gen. mgr. Hanson-Van Winkle-Munning div. M & Chems. Inc., 1964-66; chmn. RPI Designs, Marlette, Mich., 1966—. Pres. Detroit Hist. Commn., 1994. Home: 2 Woodland Pl Grosse Pointe MI 48230-1920

WILKINSON, WILLIAM DURFEE, museum director; b. Utica, N.Y., Sept. 2, 1924; s. Winfred Durfee and Edith (Lockwood) W.; m. Dorothy May Spencer, Apr. 2, 1966. B.S., Harvard U., 1949; postgrad., Munson Inst. Am. Maritime History, Mystic, Conn., 1961-62. Group ins. underwriter Home Life Ins. Co., N.Y.C., 1949-59; adminstr., marine curator Mus. City of New York, 1960-63; registrar Met. Mus. Art, N.Y.C., 1963-71; assoc. dir. Mariners Mus., Newport News, Va., 1971-73, dir., 1973-94, dir. emeritus, 1994—; ret., 1994. Mem. Sec. of Navy Adv. Com. on Naval History, 1986-88, 91-96, chmn. 1991-95; mem. Exec. Coun. Internat. Congress Maritime Mus., 1989-93; bd. dirs. Coun. Am. Maritime Mus., 1975-79, pres., 1978-79; bd. dirs. Mus. Computer Network, Inc., 1972-83, Assn. for Rescue at Sea, Inc., Coast Guard Acad. Foun., Inc., 1981-87, U.S. Life Saving Svc. Heritage Assn. With C.E. AUS, 1943-45. Mem. Am. Assn. Mus., Nat. Trust Hist. Preservation (maritime preservation com. 1978-80), Explorers Club, Harvard-Radcliffe Club Phila. Office: 747 W Springfield Rd Springfield PA 19064-1337

WILKINSON, WILLIAM SHERWOOD, lawyer; b. Williston, N.D., Sept. 6, 1933; s. John Thomas and Evelyn (Landon) W.; m. Carol Ann Burns, Aug. 20, 1960; children—Leslie Ann, Richard Sherwood, Greta Diann. B.S. in Bus, U. Idaho, 1955; J.D., U. Denver, 1960. Bar: Colo. bar 1960, Mich. bar 1966. Practiced in Canon City, Colo., 1960-66; asst. dist. atty. 11th Jud. Dist., Colo., 1961-65; gen. counsel, sec. Mich. Farm Bur. Family Cos., Lansing, 1966-96; Lectr. Pre-Parole Release Center, Colo. State Penitentiary, 1961-65; instr. adult edn., Canon City, 1965; counsel Canon City Recreation Dist., 1964-65. Mem. lay adv. bd. St. Thomas More Hosp., Canon City, 1963-66; Del., county, dist. and congl. convs. Republican party, 1964. Served to capt. USAF, 1955-58. Recipient Cmty. Disting. Svc. award Canon City Jr. C. of C., 1964. Mem. ABA, Colo. Bar Assn., Mich. Bar Assn., Am. Judicature Soc., Am. Corp. Counsel Assn., Nat. Coun. Farmer Coops. (legal, tax and acctg. com.), Phi Delta Phi, Tau Kappa Epsilon. Methodist (lay leader, mem. ch. ofcl. bd.). Home: 1707 Foxcroft Rd East Lansing MI 48823-2131

WILKNISS, PETER E., foundation administrator, researcher; b. Berlin, Germany, Sept. 28, 1934; U.S. citizen.; s. Fritz and Else (Stueber) W.; m. Edith P. Koester, May 25, 1963; children: Peter F., Sandra M. MS in Chemistry, Tech. U., Munich, Ger., 1958, PhD in Radio and Nuclear Chemistry, 1961. Rsch. chemist, radiological protection officer U.S. Naval Ordnance Sta., 1961-64, head nuclear chemistry branch, 1964-66; rsch. oceanographer U.S. Naval Rsch. Lab., 1966-70, head chemical oceanography branch, 1970-75; mgr. Nat. Ctr. Atmospheric Rsch. Program NSF, Washington, 1975-76, mgr. Internat. Phase of Ocean Drilling/Ocean Sediment Coring Program, 1976-80, mgr. Ocean Drilling Project Team, AAEO Directorate, 1980, dir. divsn. Ocean Drilling Programs, 1980-81, sr. sci. assoc. Office of Dir., 1981-82, dep. asst. dir. Sci, Tech., Internat. Affairs Directorate, 1982-84, dir. divsn. Polar Programs, 1984-93, sr. sci. assoc. Geoscis. Directorate, 1993—; liaison mem. NRC, NAS, Marine Bd., 1978-81, Polar Rsch. Bd., 1984-93; mem. atmospheric chemistry and radioactivity com. Am. Meteorological Soc., 1975-78; mem. interagy. com. atmospheric scis., 1975-76, space station adv. com., NASA, 1988-93. Contbr. 61 articles to sci., tech. jours., USN reports; over 100 formal presentations nat., internat. sci. confs., symposia, meetings; participant 16 nat., internat. workshops. Presdl. citation AIA, 1993; Wilkniss mountain Antarctic named in his honor Sec. Interior, U.S. Bd. Geographic Names, 1992. Mem. AAAS, Am. Geophysical Union, Antarctican Soc., Sigma Xi. Episcopalian. Avocations: soccer, swimming, skiing. Home: 8814 Stockton Pky Alexandria VA 22308-2360 Office: Nat Sci Found 4201 Wilson Blvd Arlington VA 22230-0001

WILKS, ALAN DELBERT, chemical research and technology executive, researcher; b. Liberal, Kans., Sept. 4, 1943; s. Delbert Elvado and Mabel Ida (Howell) W.; m. Irvana Sue Keagy, June 11, 1967; 1 child, Jolin Rai. BS in Chemistry, U. Kans., 1965; PhD in Analytical Chemistry, U. Iowa, 1970. Chemist UOP Rsch. Ctr., Des Plaines, Ill., 1969-76, group leader catalysis div., 1976-77, mgr. catalysis rsch., 1977-84; dir. phys. chemistry and surface sci. Allied-Signal Inc., Des Plaines, 1984-88, v.p. rsch. & tech., 1988-93, v.p., dir. rsch. & tech., 1993-94; pres. The Wilks Group, Inc., Mount Prospect, Ill., 1994—; cons. Los Alamos (N.Mex.) Nat. Lab., 1990-94. Contbr. articles to profl. jours.; holder 5 patents. Mem. Am. Chem. Soc., Am. Vacuum Soc., Rsch. Dirs. Assn. Chgo., Chgo. Catalyst Club, Alpha Chi Omega. Office: The Wilks Group Inc 1201 W Cleven Dr Mount Prospect IL 60056-2909

WILKS, IVOR GORDON HUGHES, historian, educator; b. Coventry, Warwickshire, Eng., July 19, 1928; came to U.S., 1965; s. Gordon Wilfred and Lilian Mary (Hughes Bates) W.; m. Grace O. Amanor, 1956 (div. 1972); children: Sebastian Amanor-Wilks, Anne Amanor-Wilks, Compton Amanor-Wilks, Margaret Amanor-Wilks; m. Nancy Ellen Lawler, 1989. BA with 1st class honors, U. Wales, 1951, MA, 1958; PhD, U. Cambridge, Eng., 1971. Lectr. in philosophy U. Gold Coast, Ghana, 1953-55; resident tutor Inst. Extra-Mural Studies U. Ghana, Africa, 1955-61, prof., dep. dir. Inst. African Studies, 1961-66; prof. history Northwestern U., Evanston, Ill., 1970-93, Herskovits prof. African studies, 1984-93, prof. emeritus, 1994—; asst. dir. research Faculty History, U. Cambridge, Eng., 1968-70; vis. prof. Ind. U., Bloomington, 1965-66, U. Wales, Lampeter, 1989, hon. prof. history and Welsh history, Aberystwyth, 1993—; cons. Ency. Brit., 1972—. Author: Asante in the 19th Century, 1975, 2d edit., 1989, South Wales and the Rising of 1839, 1984, Wa and the Wala, 1989, Forests of Gold, 1993; sr. author: Chronicles from Gonja, 1986; contbr. articles to profl. jours. Served to lt. Brit. Army, 1946-48. Recipient Herskovits award African Studies Assn., 1976, Non-fiction prize Welsh Arts Council, 1985. Office: Northwestern U Dept History 306N Harris Evanston IL 60201-5032

WILKS, R(ALPH) KENNETH, JR., government planner; b. Springfield, Mo., Sept. 25, 1956; s. Ralph Kenneth and Virginia Lacy (Phillips) W.; s. Melinda Sue Maxwell, July 21, 1984. BA, Evangel Coll., 1978; MPA, U. Mo., Kansas City, 1980. Adminstrv. aide City of Leawood (Kans.), 1979-80; theater mgr. Crown Cinema Corp., Jefferson City, Mo., 1981-84; rsch. analyst II Mo. Dept. Social Svcs., Jefferson City, 1984-86, planner II, 1986-93; planner III Mo. Dept. Corrections, Jefferson City, 1993—; legis. intern U.S. Sen. Robert Dole, Washington, 1978; lectr. in field. Contbr. articles to profl. jours. Mem. Am. Soc. Pub. Adminstrn., Am. Corrections Assn., Mo. Inst. Pub. Adminstrn., Social Sci. Honor Soc. (life). Avocations: photography, biking, hiking, gardening, reading. Home: 4802 Rainbow Hills Rd Jefferson City MO 65109

WILL, CLIFFORD MARTIN, physicist, educator; b. Hamilton, Ont., Can., Nov. 13, 1946; m. Leslie Saxe, June 26, 1970; children: Elizabeth, Rosalie. BS, McMaster U., Hamilton, 1968; PhD, Calif. Inst. Tech., 1971. Enrico Fermi fellow U. Chgo., 1972-74; asst. prof. physics Stanford U., Palo Alto, Calif., 1974-81; assoc. prof. physics Washington U., St. Louis, 1981-85, prof. physics, 1985—, chmn. dept. physics, 1991—; chmn. com. on time transfer in satellite systems Air Force Studies Bd., Washington, 1984-86. Assoc. editor Physical Rev. Letters, 1989-92; author: Theory and Experiment in Gravitational Physics, 1981, rev. edit., 1993, Was Einstein Right?, 1986, rev. edit., 1993. Alfred P. Sloan Found. fellow, 1975-79, J.S. Guggenheim Found. fellow, 1996—, J.W. Fulbright fellow, 1996—; recipient Sci. Writing award Am. Inst. Physics, 1987. Fellow Am. Phys. Soc. (exec. com. astrophysics div. 1988-90); mem. Am. Astron. Soc., Am. Assn. Physics Tchrs. (Richtmyer Meml. Lectr. 1987), Internat. Soc. Gen. Relativity and Gravitation. Office: Washington U Dept Physics Campus Box 1105 1 Brookings Dr Saint Louis MO 63130-4862

WILL, ERIC JOHN, state senator; b. Omaha, Nebr., Apr. 16, 1959; s. John Babcock and Patricia Elaine (Propst) W. BA in Polit. Sci., U. So. Calif., 1981; postgrad., Creighton U., 1993—. Legis. researcher Nebr. State Legis., Omaha, 1981-90, senator, 1991—; chmn. enrollment and rev. com., 1991-93, rules com., 1993—; vice chmn. gen. affairs com., 1991—; mem. revenue and urban affairs com., 1991—. Mem. Phi Beta Kappa. Democrat. Presbyterian. Avocations: softball, bowling, volleyball. Home: 6029 Pinkney St Omaha NE 68104-4333 Office: Nebr State Capitol District 8 Lincoln NE 68509

WILL, GEORGE FREDERICK, editor, political columnist, news commentator; b. Champaign, Ill., May 4, 1941; s. Frederick L. and Louise (Hendrickson) W.; children: Jonathan, Geoffrey, Victoria. BA, Trinity Coll., 1962, Oxford (Eng.) U., 1964; MA, Ph.D., Princeton U., 1967; LLD (hon.), U. San Diego, 1977; LittD (hon.), Dickinson Coll. and Georgetown U., 1978; hon. degree, U. Ill., 1988. Prof. polit. philosophy Mich. State U., 1967-68, U. Toronto, 1968-70; mem. staff of Sen. Gordon Allott U.S. Senate, Washington, Can., 1970-72; editor The Nat. Rev., Washington, 1973-76; contbg. editor Newsweek mag., 1976—; syndicated columnist Washington Post, 1974—; TV news analyst ABC-Capitol Cities, 1981—; bd. dirs. Ctr. for Strategic Internat. Studies, Washington, Balt. Orioles. Author: The Pursuit of Happiness and Other Sobering Thoughts, 1979, The Pursuit of Virtue and Other Tory Notions, 1982, Statecraft as Soulcraft: What Government Does, 1983, The Morning After: American Successes and Excesses, 1986, The New Season: A Spectator's Guide to the 1988 Election, 1987, Men at Work, 1990, Suddenly: The American Idea at Home and Abroad 1988-89, 1990, Restoration: Congress, Term Limits and the Recovery of Deliberate Democracy, 1992, The Leveling Wind: Politics, the Culture and Other News, 1994; participant This Week With David Brinkley, ABC-TV, 1981—; commentator World News Tonight, 1984—. Recipient Pulitzer prize for Commentary, 1977; named Young Leader Am. Time mag., 1974. Mem. Coun. Fgn. Rels., The Trilateral Commn., The Emil Verban Soc. Avocation: baseball. Office: The Washington Post 1150 15th St NW Washington DC 20071-0001

WILL, JAMES FREDRICK, steel company executive; b. Pitts., Oct. 12, 1938; s. Fred F. and Mary Agnes (Ganter) W.; m. Mary Ellen Bowser, Dec. 19, 1964; children: Mary Beth, Kerry Ann. BSEE, Pa. State U., 1961; MBA, Duquesne U., 1972. Works mgr. Kaiser Steel Corp., Fontana, Calif., 1976-78, v.p. ops., 1978-80, v.p. planning, 1980-81, exec. v.p., 1981, pres., 1981-82; exec. v.p., pres. indsl. group Cyclops Corp., Pitts, 1982-86; pres., chief operating officer Cyclops Corp., Pitts., 1986-88, pres., chief exec. officer, 1989-92; pres., chief oper. officer Armco, Inc., Parsippany, NJ, 1992-93; pres., chief exec. officer Armco, Inc., Pitts., 1994-96; chmn., pres., CEO Armco, Inc., 1996—; vice-chmn. 1994, chmn. 1995, Specialty Steel Industry of N.Am. Office: Armco Inc 1 Oxford Ctr Pittsburgh PA 15219-1415

WILL, JANE ANNE, psychologist; b. Evansville, Ind., Feb. 6, 1945; d. Edwin Francis and Frances Elizabeth (Patry) W. BA in Edn., St. Benedict's Coll., Ferdinand, Ind., 1968; MA in Edn., MS in Clin. Psychology, U. Evansville, 1973, 1987; MA in Christian Spirituality, Creighton U., 1979; D Psychology, Fla. Tech., Melbourne, 1991. Lic. psychologist, Ind.; joined Sisters of St. Benedict, Inc., Roman Cath. Ch. Tchr. Ireland (Ind.) Jr. H.S., 1969-76, Meml. H.S., Evansville, Ind., 1976-77; dir. recruitment and tng. Sisters of St. Benedict, Inc., Ferdinand, Ind., 1978-84, cons. admissions bd., 1984—; tchr. Mater Dei H.S., Evansville, 1984-88; therapist Osceola Ctr., Kissimme, Fla., 1989-90, Charter Hosp., Kissimme, Fla., 1989-90; intern VA Med. Ctr., St. Louis, 1990-91; clin. psychologist St. Mary's Health Care

Svcs., Evansville, 1991—; adj. prof. Bresica Coll., Owensboro, Ky., 1978-80, St. Mary's of the Woods Coll., Terre Haute, Ind., 1980-84. Author jour. Ind. Reading Quarterly, 1973. Bd. dirs. Nat. Formation Dirs., Washington, 1982-84; chairperson region VII Formation Conf., Mich. and Ind., 1982-84. Luise Whiting Bell scholar, 1986. Mem. APA, Ind. Psychol. Assn., Southwestern Ind. Psychol. Assn. (treas. 1992, sec. 1993, v.p. 1994, pres. 1995), Vanderburgh County Mental Health Assn. (bd. dirs. 1994—, v.p. 1996). Roman Catholic. Avocations: hiking, crocheting, music, reading. Home: 725 Wedeking Ave Evansville IN 47711-3861

WILL, JOANNE MARIE, food and consumer services executive, communications consultant, writer; b. Mpls., Mar. 18, 1937; d. Lester John and Dorothea Amelia (Kuenzel) W. BS in Home Econs. and Journalism, Iowa State U., 1959. Food writer, editor food guide Chgo. Tribune, 1959-67; account supr., home econs. coordinator J. Walter Thompson Co., Chgo., 1967-73; assoc. food editor, then food editor Chgo. Tribune, 1973-81; dir. food and consumer services Hill and Knowlton, Inc., Chgo., 1981-87; dir., group mgr. food and consumer svcs. Selz/Seabolt Comms., Inc., Chgo. Mem. bd. govs. Iowa State U. Found., past mem. home econs. adv. bd.; past bd. dirs., officer Sr. Ctrs. Met. Chgo. Recipient Alumnae Recognition medal Iowa State U., 1994; named Outstanding Young Alumnus Iowa State U., 1968. Mem. Home Econs. in Bus., Am. Home Econs. Assn., Ill. Home Econs. Assn. (past bd. dirs.), Chgo. Nutrition Assn. (pres.-elect 1993-94, pres. 1994-95), Am. Assn. Family and Consumer Scis., Ill. Assn. Family and Consumer Scis., Dames d'Escoffier (bd. dirs. Chgo. chpt., past v.p.).

WILL, MARI MASENG, communications consultant; b. Chgo., Mar. 15, 1954; d. Leif Eric and Betty (Hagen) Maseng; m. George F. Will. B.A., U. S.C., 1975. Reporter Charleston Evening Post, S.C., 1976-78; press sec. Re-elect Thurmond Com., Columbia, S.C., 1978; staff dir. Dole for Pres. Com., Alexandria, Va., 1979-80; spl. asst. to chmn. Reagan-Bush Com., Arlington, Va., 1980; press officer Office of Pres.-Elect, Washington, 1980-81; presdl. speechwriter The White House, Washington, 1981-83; asst. sec. for pub. affairs Dept. Transp., Washington, 1983-85; v.p., dir. corp. rels. Beatrice Cos. Inc., Chgo., 1985-86; dep. asst to the pres., dir. Office of Public Liaison The White House, Washington, 1986-87; press sec. Dole for Pres. Campaign, Washington, 1987-88; pub. affairs cons. Washington, 1988; asst. to Pres. for communications White House, 1988-89; prin. Maseng Communications, cons., Washington, 1989—. Active Nat. Coun. on Vocat. Edn., 1989-91, Def. Adv. Com. on Women in Svcs., 1992—. Recipient Alumna Achievement award U. S.C., Columbia, 1984. Mem. Soc. Profl. Journalists, U. S.C. Alumni Assn., Nat. Press Club, Chi Omega. Republican. Presbyterian. Avocation: photography.

WILL, ROBERT ERWIN, economics educator; b. Dousman, Wis., Mar. 8, 1928; s. Erwin and Gena (Luedtke) W.; m. Barbara Anne Couture, Dec. 22, 1956; children: Jonathan (dec.), Leslie Anne, Jennifer. B.A. cum magna laude, Carleton Coll., 1950; M.A., Yale U., 1951, Ph.D., 1965. Mem. faculty Yale, 1951-54, U. Mass., 1954-57; mem. faculty econs. Carleton Coll., Northfield, Minn., 1957—; prof. Carleton Coll., 1968-73, W.A. Williams prof., 1973-82, Plank prof., 1982—, chmn. dept. econs., dir. First Bank System execs. seminars, 1971-80; vis. prof. U. Minn., 1965; vis. fellow Inst. Devel. Studies, U. Sussex, Eng., 1970-71, H.H. Humphrey Inst., 1981-82; John de Quedville Briggs lectr., St. Paul Acad., 1966-70; dir. Kings' Coll. seminar in econs. Cambridge (Eng.) U., 1990. Author: Poverty in Affluence: The Social, Political and Economic Dimensions of Poverty in the United States, 1965, Scalar Economies and Urban Service Requirements, 1965, also articles and research on manpower, tourism, and devel. Mem. Minn. Dept. Manpower Svcs. Adv. Coun., 1966-80, Wilton Pk., Brit. Fgn. Office Study Ctr., 1970—; dir., chief fin. officer Cmty. Electronics Corp., Mpls., 1968-91; dir. Minn. World Affairs Ctr., 1972-90, Minn. Internat. Ctr., 1979-86; pres.-elect Minn. Trade Conf., 1995—; mem. policy com. United Shareowners Am., 1960-80; mem. Northfield Heritage Preservation Commn., 1982—, Northfield Sister Cities Commn., 1991-94, Mpls. Inst. Art, Walker Art Ctr., Northfield Arts Guild; bd. visitors Am. Grad. Sch. Internat. Mgmt., 1980-90; bd. dirs. Northfield United Way, 1983-86, Minn. UN Rally Bd., 1973—, Lutheran Home Cannon Valley, Northfield Manor, Northfield Parkview, 1993—; exec. dir. Northfield Retirement Ctr. Found., 1995—. Ford Found. Faculty fellow, 1962-63, NSF Faculty fellow, 1970-71; Interuniv. Ctr. for European Studies fellow, 1975-85; Mellon grantee, Mex., 1976, Spain, 1981; Devel. Fund grantee, France, 1985, World Tourism grantee, Eng., 1990. Mem. World Future Soc., Assn. for 3d World Studies, Soc. for Internat. Devel., Bus. and Econ. History Soc., Assn. Cultural Econs., Assn. Comparative Econ. Studies, Am. Friends Wilton Pk, Assn. for Pvt. Enterprise Edn., Nat. Assn. Bus. Economists, Assn. Evolutionary Econs., History Econ. Assn., Caribbean Studies Assn., N.Am. Econ. and Fin. Assn., Population Action Coun. (nat. com.), Minn. Econ. Ass., Chactonbury Ring Club (Sussex), Rotary (Rotary Found. Svc. award 1995), Phi Beta Kappa. Democrat. Episcopalian. Home: 708 3rd St E Northfield MN 55057-2311

WILL, TREVOR JONATHAN, lawyer; b. Ashland, Wis., Aug. 11, 1953; s. William Taylor and Geraldine Sue (Trevor) W.; m. Margaret Ann Johnson, Aug. 28, 1976; children: Tyler William, Alexandra Marie, Jennifer Catherine. BA summa cum laude, Augustana Coll., 1975; JD cum laude, Harvard U., 1978. Bar: Wis. 1978, U.S. Dist. Ct. (ea. dist.) Wis. 1978, U.S. DIst. Ct. (we. dist.) Wis. 1980, U.S. Ct. Appeals (7th cir.) 1983, U.S. Supreme Ct. 1984, U.S. Dist. Ct. (ea. dist.) Mich. 1985. Assoc. Foley & Lardner, Milw., 1978-87, ptnr., 1987—; adj. law prof. Marquette U. Law Sch., 1994. Mem. ABA, State Bar Wis., Milw. Bar Assn., Def. Rsch. Inst. Home: 10011 N Waterleaf Dr Thiensville WI 53092-6146 Office: Foley & Lardner 777 E Wisconsin Ave Milwaukee WI 53202-5302

WILLANS, JEAN STONE, religious organization executive; b. Hillsboro, Ohio, Oct. 3, 1924; d. Homer and Ella (Keys) Hammond; student San Diego Jr. Coll.; D.D. (hon.) Ch. of the East, 1996; m. Richard James Willans, Mar. 28, 1966; 1 dau., Suzanne Jeanne. Asst. to v.p. Family Loan Co., Miami, Fla., 1946-49; civilian supr. USAF, Washington, 1953-55; founder, dir. Blessed Trinity Soc., editor Trinity mag., Los Angeles, 1960-66; co-founder, exec. v.p., dir. Soc. of Stephen, Altadena, Calif., 1967—, exec. dir., Hong Kong, 1975-81; lectr. in field. Republican. Episcopalian. Author: The Acts of the Green Apples, 1974, rev. edit 1995; co-editor: Charisma in Hong Kong, 1970; Spiritual Songs, 1970; The People Who Walked in Darkness, 1977; The People Who Walked in Darkness II, 1992. Recipient Achievement award Nat. Assn. Pentecostal Women, 1964, Hong Kong Govt. Commemorative plaque Kowloon Walled City Park, 1996. Address: PO Box 6225 Altadena CA 91003-6225 *I am interested in telling as many people as possible about the experience with the Holy Spirit which brings a language unknown to the speaker. I believe this experience is the source of the power of the early church and that anyone who appropriates it receives the power to change many things, not the least of these being himself.*

WILLARD, A. KEITH, chemicals executive; b. 1941. With Sun Life Assurance Co. Can., 1964-81, Wardair Internat., 1981-88, ICI Can. Inc., 1988-93; with Zeneca Holdings, Inc., Wilmington, Del., 1993—, now chmn. bd. Office: Zeneca Holdings Inc 1800 Concord Pike Wilmington DE 19803-2902*

WILLARD, LOUIS CHARLES, librarian; b. Tallahassee, Fla., Sept. 28, 1937; s. Bert and Rose (De Milly) W.; m. Nancy Booth, June 22, 1963. BA, U. Fla., 1959; BD, Yale, 1965, MA, 1967, PhD, 1970. Tchr. Tripoli (Lebanon) Boys' Sch., 1959-62; ordained to ministry Presbyn. Ch., 1965; acting librarian Princeton Theol. Sem., 1968-69, librarian, 1969-86; librarian, mem. faculty Harvard Div. Sch., 1986—. Mem. A.L.A., Theol. Library Assn., Soc. Bibl. Lit., Am. Acad. Religion, Phi Beta Kappa, Chi Phi. Home: 24 Concord Greene Unit 8 PO Box 1250 Concord MA 01742-1250 Office: Andover-Harvard Theol Libr Divinity Sch 45 Francis Ave Cambridge MA 02138-1911

WILLARD, NANCY MARGARET, writer, educator; b. Ann Arbor, Mich.; d. Hobart Hurd and Margaret (Sheppard) W.; m. Eric Lindbloom, Aug. 15, 1964; 1 child, James Anatole. B.A., U. Mich., 1958, Ph.D., 1963; M.A., Stanford U., 1960. Lectr. English Vassar Coll., Poughkeepsie, N.Y., 1965—. Author: (poems) In His Country: Poems, 1966; Skin of Grace, 1967; A New Herball: Poems, 1968, Testimony of the Invisible Man: William Carlos Williams, Francis Ponge, Rainer Maria Rilke, Pablo Neruda, 1970, Nineteen Masks for the Naked Poet: Poems, 1971, The Carpenter of the Sun: Poems, 1974, A Visit to William Blake's Inn: Poems for Innocent and Experienced Travelers, 1981 (Newbery Medal 1982), Household Tales of Moon and Water, 1983, Water Walker, 1989, The Ballad of Biddy Early, 1989; (short stories) The Lively Anatomy of God, 1968, Childhood of the Magician, 1973; (juveniles) Sailing to Cythera and Other Anatole Stories, 1974, All on a May Morning, 1975, The Snow Rabbit, 1975, Shoes Without Leather, 1976, T0e Well-Mannered Balloon, 1976, Night Story, 1986, Simple Pictures are Best, 1977, Stranger's Bread, 1977, The Highest Hit, 1978, Papa's Panda, 1979, The Island of the Grass King, 1979, The Marzipan Moon 1981, Uncle Terrible, 1982, (adult) Angel in the Parlor: Five Stories and Eight Essays, 1983, The Nightgown of the Sullen Moon, 1983, Night Story, 1986, The Voyage of the Ludgate Hill, 1987, The Mountains of Quilt, 1987, Firebrat, 1988; (novel) Things Invisible To See, 1984, Sister Water, 1993; (play) East of the Sun, West of the Moon, 1989, The High Rise Glorious Skittle Skat Roarious Sky Pie Angel Food Cake, 1991, A Nancy Willard Reader, 1991, Pish Posh said Hieronymus Bosch, 1991, Beauty and the Beast, 1992; illustrator: The Letter of John to James, Another Letter of John to James, 1982, The Octopus Who Wanted to Juggle (Robert Pack), 1990, (novel) Sister Water, 1993, (essays) Telling Time, 1993, (juvenile) A Starlit Somersault Downhill, 1993, (juvenile) The Sorcerer's Apprentice, 1993; author, illustrator: An Alphabet of Angels, 1994; (juvenile) Gutenberg's Gift, 1995; (poems, with Jane Yolen) Among Angels, 1995. Recipient Hopwood award, 1958, Devins Meml. award, 1967, John Newbery award, 1981, Empire State award, 1996; Woodrow Wilson fellow, 1960; NEA grantee, 1987. Mem. The Lewis Carroll Soc., The George MacDonald Soc. Office: Vassar Coll Dept English Raymond Ave Poughkeepsie NY 12601

WILLARD, RALPH LAWRENCE, surgery educator, physician, former college president; b. Manchester, Iowa, Apr. 6, 1922; s. Hosea B. and Ruth A. (Hazelrigg) W.; m. Margaret Dyer Dennis, Sept. 26, 1969; children: Laurie, Jane, Ann, H. Thomas. Student, Cornell Coll., 1940-42, Coe Coll., 1945; D.O., Kirksville Coll. Osteo. Medicine, 1949; EdD (hon.), U. North Tex., 1985; ScD (hon.), W.Va. Sch. Osteo. Medicine, 1993. Intern Kirksville Osteo. Hosp., 1949-50, resident in surgery, 1954-57; chmn. dept. surgery Davenport Osteo. Hosp., 1957-68; dean, prof. surgery Kirksville Coll. Osteo. Medicine, 1969-73; asso. dean acad. affairs, prof. surgery Mich. State U. Coll. Osteo. Medicine, 1974-75; dean Tex. Coll. Osteopathic Medicine, 1975-76, pres., 1981-85, prof. surgery, 1985-87; v.p. med. affairs North Tex. State U., Denton, 1976-81; assoc. dean W.Va. Sch. Osteo. Medicine, Lewisburg, 1988-91; mem. Nat. Adv. Council Edn. for Health Professions, 1971-73, Iowa Gov.'s Council Hosps. and Health Related Facilities, 1965-68; chmn. council deans Am. Assn. Colls. Osteo. Medicine, 1970-73, pres., 1979-80. Served with USAAF, 1942-45; Served with USAF, 1952-53; col. USAFR, ret. Decorated D.F.C., Air medal with 4 oak leaf clusters, Meritorious Svc. medal, Legion of Merit; recipient Robert A. Kistner Educator award Am. Assn. Colls. Osteo. Medicine, 1989. Fellow Am. Coll. Physician Execs., Am. Coll. Osteo. Surgeons; mem. Am. Osteo. Assn. (Disting. Svc. cert. 1992), Tex. Osteo. Assn., W.Va. Soc. Osteo. Medicine, Am. Acad. Osteopathy, Acad. Osteo. Dirs. Med. Edn., Aerospace Med. Assn., Flying Physicians Assn., Quiet Birdmen, Davis-Monthan Officers Club, Masons, Shriners, Lewisburg Rotary, Internat. Comanche Soc., Order of Daedalians. Democrat. Episcopalian. Home: PO Box 749 Lewisburg WV 24901-0749 Office: WVa Sch Osteo Medicine 400 N Lee St Lewisburg WV 24901-1128 *The wise man has faith, the fool is he who betrays that faith.*

WILLARD, RICHARD KENNON, lawyer; b. Houston, Sept. 1, 1948; s. Fair McDaniel Willard and Elsbeth Rowe (Kennon) Willard Armistead; m. Leslie Harral Hopkins, July 10, 1976; children: Stephen Hopkins, Lauren Suzanne. B.A., Emory U., 1969; J.D., Harvard U., 1975. Bar: D.C. 1988, Tex. 1978, Ga. 1975. Law clk. U.S. Ct. Appeals, San Francisco, 1975-76, U.S. Supreme Ct., Washington, 1976-77; atty. Baker & Botts, Houston, 1977-81; counsel for intelligence policy U.S. Dept. Justice, Washington, 1981-82, dep. asst. atty. gen. civil div., 1982-83, asst. atty. gen., 1983-88; ptnr. Steptoe & Johnson, Washington, 1988—; adj. prof. Georgetown U. Law Ctr., 1991—. Note editor: Harvard U. Law Rev., 1974-75. Gen. counsel Republican Party of Tex., Austin, 1980-81. Served to 1st lt. U.S. Army, 1969-72. Epsicopalian. Office: 1330 Connecticut Ave NW Washington DC 20036-1704

WILLARD, ROBERT EDGAR, lawyer; b. Bronxville, N.Y., Dec. 13, 1929; s. William Edgar and Ethel Marie (Van Ness) W.; m. Shirley Fay Cooper, May 29, 1954; children: Laura Marie, Linda Ann, John Judson. B.A. in Econs., Wash. State U., 1954; J.D., Harvard U., 1958. Bar: Calif. 1959. Law clk. to U.S. dist. judge, 1958-59; pvt. practice L.A., 1959-82; assoc. firm Flint & Mackay, 1959-61; pvt. practice, 1962-64; mem. firm Willard & Baltaxe, 1964-65, Baird, Holley, Baird & Galen, 1966-69, Baird, Holley, Galen & Willard, 1970-74, Holley, Galen & Willard, 1975-82, Galvin & Willard, Newport Beach, Calif., 1982-86; pvt. practice Newport Beach, 1987-89; mem. firm Davis, Punelli Keathley & Willard, Newport Beach, 1990—; Dir. various corps. Served with AUS, 1946-48, 50-51. Mem. ABA, Los Angeles County Bar Assn., State Bar Calif., Assn. Trial Lawyers Am., Am. Judicature Soc., Acacia Frat. Congregationalist. Club: Calcutta Saddle and Cycle. Home: 1840 Oriole Dr Costa Mesa CA 92626-4758 Office: 610 Newport Center Dr Ste 1000 Newport Beach CA 92660-6451

WILLAUER, WHITING RUSSELL, consultant; b. Boston, May 24, 1931; s. Whiting and Louise Knapp (Russell) W.; m. Julie Matheson Arnold, July 11, 1959 (div.); children—Whiting Russell, Jr., William Arnold. B.S., Princeton U., 1955, M.S., 1959; Ph.D., Georgetown U., 1964. Research assoc. joint research com. Dept. Def., 1951-52; ops. mgr. Civil Air Transport Airline Taiwan, 1952-53; scientist Analytic Services, Inc., 1958-61; asst. prof. astronomy Georgetown U., 1965-68; mgr. TRW Systems Group support to chief Naval ops., McLean, Va., 1968-73, TRW Antisubmarine projects, 1973-79, TRW Ship Acquisition project, 1979-85; advanced systems mgr. TRW Systems Integration Group, 1985-90, cost estimating mgr., 1990-95; sr. cons., 1995—; cons. Nat. Geog. Soc., 1961-65, U. Tex., 1962, NSF, 1963, Booz-Allen & Hamilton, 1966-67. Mng. editor: Jour. Astronautical Scis, 1969-71; Designer: Orrery (planetarium) on permanent exhibit, New Explorers Hall, Nat. Geog. Soc. Asst. chief steward Alpine Venue XIII Olympic Winter Games, Lake Placid, 1980; mem. U.S. Olympic Com., bd. dirs., 1987-94, sec. nat. governing bodies, 1989-92, mem. membership svcs. com., 1988-92, mem. athletic devel. com., 1992—; chef de mission Winter Pan Am. Games, Las Lenas, Argentina, 1990; asst. chief de mission XVI Winter Olympics, Albertville, France, 1992; U.S. Olympic Com. liaison to VI Paralympic Winter Games, Lillehammer, Norway, 1994. Research fellow Georgetown U., 1961-65. Fellow AAAS (coun.); mem. Am. Astronautical Soc. (v.p. fin.), Blue Ridge Ski Coun. (pres. 1976-78), U.S. Ski Assn. (pres. 1982-87, Julius Blegan award 1988), U.S. Skiing (vice chmn. 1994-96), Internat. Ski Fedn. (chmn. U.S. del. 1983, 85, chmn. recreational skiing com. 1987—, eligibility com. 1988—), Ea. Ski Assn. (treas. 1980-82), Pan Am Sports Orgn. (winter games adv. com. 1988—), Sigma Xi, Chevy Chase Club (Md.), Nantucket Yacht Club (Mass.) (commodore 1981-83, bd. govs. 1957-59, 68—). Home: 4201 Cathedral Ave NW Apt 701W Washington DC 20016-4946

WILLCOTT, MARK ROBERT, III, chemist, educator, researcher; b. Muskogee, Okla., July 23, 1933; s. Mark Robert Willcott Jr. and Josephine Oliver; m. Earline Faye Hinkle, June 4, 1955; children: Julie, June Elinor, Mark Robert IV, Ashley. BA, Rice U., 1955; MS, Yale U., 1959, PhD, 1963. Asst. prof. chemistry Emory U., Atlanta, 1962-64; asst. prof. chemistry U. Houston, 1965-68, assoc. prof., 1968-73, prof., 1973-83; head biomed. Nuc. Magnetic Resonance lab. Baylor Coll. Medicine, Houston, 1982-83; pres., chmn. bd. Nuc. Magnegic Resonance Imaging, Inc., Houston, 1983-88; prof. chemistry and radiology Vanderbilt U., Nashville, 1989-94; prof., dir. of rsch. U. Tex. Med. Br., Galveston, 1994—; cons. Codman & Shurtleff, Inc., Rendolph, Msas., 1991—,. Advanced NMR Systems, Andover, Mass., 1994—, Cooper and Dunham, N.Y.C., 1994—; adj. prof. chemistry Rice U., Houston, 1995—; adj. prof. medicine Baylor Coll. Medicine, 1996—. Author patents for magnetic resonance imaging, 1988-94. Bd. dirs. Bay Oaks Cmty. Assn., Houston, 1996—. Lt. (j.g.) USN, 1955-58. John Simon Guggenheim fellow Guggenheim Found., 1972; recipient Alexander von Humboldt Sr. Scientist prize Humboldt Found., 1978. Mem. Am. Chem. Soc., Am. Assn. Physicists in Medicine, Soc. Magnetic Resonance. Democrat. Presbyterian. Avocations: mountaineering, photography, philately. Home: 1807 Orchard Country Ln Houston TX 77062-2338 Office: U Tex Med Br Dept Radiology Houston TX 77555-0793

WILLCOX, CHRISTOPHER P., magazine editor; b. Chgo., Nov. 2, 1946; s. James Christopher and Rita (Donovan) W.; m. Emily Turner, July 6, 1996; 1 child, Kathleen. BA, U. Notre Dame, 1968. Editl. writer Detroit News, 1980-82, dep. editl. page editor, 1982-84; program advisor Radio Free Europe/Radio Liberty, Munich, Germany, 1984-88; sr. editor Reader's Digest, Pleasantville, N.Y., 1988-90, sr. staff editor, 1990-91, exec. editor, 1991—; adj. prof. journalism Columbia U., N.Y.C., 1993-96. Mem. Am. Soc. Mag. Editors, Deadline Club. Office: Readers Digest Assn Readers Digest Rd Pleasantville NY 10570

WILLCOX, FREDERICK PRESTON, engineer; b. L.A., Aug. 1, 1910; s. Frederick William and Kate Lillian (Preston) W.; m. Velma Rose Gander, 1935; 1 child, Ann Louise. Grad. high sch. Pvt. practice rsch. and devel. engr. and cons., 1939-51, govt. cons., 1949-50, 61-65; tech. v.p. Fairchild Camera & Instrument Corp., 1951-60; inventor R&D lab. New Canaan, Conn., 1960—. Patentee in field of photog. sci. and data communications; photography work exhibited Smithsonian Gallery. Maj. U.S. Army, 1940-45. Recipient Sherman Fairchild Photogrammetric award Am. Soc. Photogrammetry, 1951. Fellow AAAS; mem. ASME, AIAA (sr. mem.), Am. Soc. Photogrammetry and Remote Sensing, Soc. Photographic Scientists and Engrs., Optical Soc. Am., Am. Def. Preparedness Assn. Avocations: machine sculpture, photography. Home and Office: 565 Oenoke Rdg New Canaan CT 06840-3613

WILLE, KARIN L., lawyer; b. Northfield, Minn., Dec. 14, 1949; d. James Virginia Wille. BA summa cum laude, Macalester Coll., 1971; JD cum laude, U. Minn., 1974. Bar: Minn. 1974, U.S. Dist. Ct. Minn. 1974. Atty. Dresselhuis & Assoc., Mpls., 1974-75; assoc. Dorsey & Whitney, Mpls., 1975-76; atty. Dayton-Hudson Corp., Mpls., 1976-84; gen. counsel B. Dalton Booksellers, Edina, Minn., 1985-87; assoc. Briggs & Morgan, Mpls., 1987-88; shareholder Briggs and Briggs, 1988—; co-chair Upper Midwest Employment Law Inst., 1983-94. Mem. ABA, Minn. State Bar Assn. (labor and employment sect., corp. counsel sect., dir. 1989-91), Hennepin County Bar Assn. (labor and employment sect.), Minn. Women Lawyers, Phi Beta Kappa. Office: Briggs & Morgan 2400 IDS Ctr Minneapolis MN 55402

WILLE, LOIS JEAN, retired newspaper editor; b. Chgo., Sept. 19, 1931; d. Walter and Adele S. (Taege) Kroeber; m. Wayne M. Wille, June 6, 1954. B.S., Northwestern U., 1953, M.S., 1954; Litt.D. (hon.), Columbia Coll., Chgo., 1980, Northwestern U., 1990, Rosary Coll., 1990. Reporter Chgo. Daily News, 1958-74, nat. corr., 1975-76, assoc. editor charge editorial page, 1977; assoc. editor charge editorial and opinion pages Chgo. Sun-Times, 1978-83; assoc. editor editorial page Chgo. Tribune, 1984-87, editor editorial page, 1987-91, ret., 1991. Author: Forever Open, Clear and Free: the Historic Struggle for Chicago's Lakefront, 1972. Recipient Pulitzer prize for public svc., 1963, Pulitzer prize for editorial writing, 1989, William Allen White Found. award for excellence in editorial writing, 1978, numerous awards Chgo. Newspaper Guild, numerous awards Chgo. Headline Club, numerous awards Nat. Assn. Edn. Writers, numerous awards Ill. AP, numerous awards Ill. UPI. Home: 120 Charmont Dr Radford VA 24141-4205

WILLE, WAYNE MARTIN, retired editor; b. Des Plaines, Ill., Nov. 17, 1930; s. Clarence Louis and Lois Naomi (Martin) W.; m. Lois Jean Kroeber, June 6, 1954. B.S.J., Northwestern U., 1952, M.S.J., 1953. Reporter Chgo. Sun Times, 1956-57; dir. press info. WBBM-TV and CBS-TV, Chgo., 1957-58; feature editor Sci. and Mechanics mag., 1958-60, mng. editor, 1960-62; news editor Nat. Safety Council, Chgo., 1962-64, asst. dir. pub. info., 1964-67; mng. editor World Book Year Book, Chgo., 1967-69; exec. editor World Book Yr. Book, 1969-83; mng. editor World Book Yr. Book and Sci. Yr. and Health & Med. Ann., 1983-91. Served with AUS, 1953-55. Mem. Chgo. Headline Club (pres. 1967-68), Soc. Profl. Journalists. Clubs: La Salle Street Rod and Gun.

WILLEMS, CONSTANCE CHARLES, lawyer; b. Zuilen, Utrecht, Netherlands, Oct. 31, 1942; came to U.S., 1967, naturalized, 1977; d. Anton Henri and Maria (Van der Meys) Charles; m. Cornelis Franciscus Willems, May 25, 1965; 1 son, Maurice. B.A. in Sociology magna cum laude, U. New Orleans, 1974; J.D. with honors, Tulane U., 1977. Bar: La. 1977, U.S. Dist. Ct. (ea. dist.) La. 1977, U.S. Ct. Appeals (5th cir.) 1977, U.S. Supreme Ct. 1983. Assoc. McGlinchey, Stafford, Mintz, Cellini, and Lang, New Orleans, 1977-81, ptnr., 1982—; instr. law office mgmt. Loyola U. Sch. Law, 1986-90; instr. European law Tulane U. Sch. Law, New Orleans, 1994, 96. Mem. Task Force on Municipalization; hon. consul for The Netherlands, 1989—; bd. dirs. United Way Agy. REls. Com., 1987-91, Coun. Internat. Visitors, 1992-94, Com. of 21, 1994—, New Orleans Opera Assn., 1995—; sec./treas. Consular Corps; bd. visitors Coll. Liberal Arts U. New Orleans, 1995—. Recipient Disting. Alumni award U. New Orleans, 1989. Mem. ABA, La. Assn. Women Attys. (pres. 1983-85, 86-87), La. State Bar Assn. (mem. ho. of dels. 1984-85, chair internat. law sect. 1994—). Office: McGlinchey Stafford Lang 643 Magazine St New Orleans LA 70130-3405

WILLENBECHER, JOHN, artist; b. Macungie, Pa., May 5, 1936; s. John George and Geneva (Bacon) W. B.A., Brown U., 1958; postgrad., N.Y. U., Inst. Fine Arts, 1958-61. sculptor-mem. N.Y.C. Art Commn., 1980-92; mem. commn. for plaza and pavillion, Mpls. Inst. Arts, 1991. Exhibited in one-man shows including Hamilton Gallery Contemporary Art, N.Y.C., 1977, 80, U. Mass. Art Gallery, Amherst, 1977, Wright State U. Art Gallery, Dayton, Ohio, 1977, Jaffe-Friede Gallery, Dartmouth Coll., Hanover, N.H., 1977, Fine Arts Ctr. U. R.I., Kingston, 1978, Neuberger Mus., SUNY at Purchase, 1979, Allentown (Pa.) Art Mus., 1979, Mpls. Inst. Arts, 1993, U. N.Mex. Art Gallery, Albuquerque, 1996; exhibited in numerous group shoes including Albright-Knox Art Gallery, Buffalo, 1963, Whitney Mus. Am. Art, N.Y.C., 1964-68; represented in permanent collections including Solomon R. Guggenheim Mus., N.Y.C., Met. Mus., N.Y.C., Whitney Mus. Am. Art, Albright-Knox Art Gallery, Phila. Mus. Art, Centre d'Art et Culture Georges Pompidou, Paris, Hirshhorn Mus. and Sculpture Garden, Washington, Art Inst. Chgo. Nat. Endowment for Arts grantee, 1977, Esther and Adolph Gottlieb Found. grantee, 1994. Subject of profl. articles and catalogues.

WILLENS, ALAN RUSH, management consultant; b. Detroit, Jan. 14, 1936; s. Gerald Lionel Willens and Gertrude Virginia Rush; m. Harriet Lois Sinclair (June 30, 1958 (div. 1985); children: Beth Willens Hollander, Scott Sinclair Willens, Lori Helen Willens. BBA, U. Mich., 1957, MBA, 1958. Project dir. United Rsch., Inc., Cambridge, Mass., 1958-61; sr. assoc. Systems Analysis and Rsch. Corp., Boston, 1961-64; sr. cons. Regional and Urban Planning Implementation, Inc., Cambridge, 1964-65; v.p. Charles River Assocs., Inc., Boston, 1965-87, exec. v.p., 1987-92, pres., 1992-95, exec. v.p., 1992-95, sr. advisor, 1996—. Chmn. com. Ellis Neighborhood Assn., Boston, 1985-88; trustee Dartmouth Sq. Condo. Assn., Boston, 1992-96, chmn., 1994. Mem. Profl. Svcs. Mgmt. Assn. (bd. dirs. 1977-80, treas. 1978-80, First Fellow 1979). Avocations: sailing, skiing, photography, personal computers, tennis. Home: 130 Appleton St Apt 1G Boston MA 02116-6045 Office: Charles River Assocs Inc John Hancock Tower 200 Clarendon St T-33 Boston MA 02116

WILLERDING, MARGARET FRANCES, mathematician; b. St. Louis, Apr. 26, 1919; d. Herman J. and Mildred F. (Icenhower) W. A.B., Harris Tchrs. Coll., 1940; M.A., St. Louis U., 1943, Ph.D., 1947. Tchr. (Pub. Schs.), St. Louis, 1940-46; instr. math. Washington U., St. Louis, 1947-48; asst. prof. Harris Tchrs. Coll., St. Louis, 1948-56; mem. faculty San Diego State Coll., 1956—, asso. prof., 1959-65, prof. math., 1966-76, prof. emeritus, 1976—. Author: Intermediate Algebra, 1969, Elementary Mathematics, 1971, College Algebra, 1971, College Algebra and Trigonometry, 1971, Arithmetic, 1968, Probability: The Science of Chance, 1969, Mathematics Around the Clock, 1969, Mathematical Concepts, 1967, From Fingers to Computers, 1969, Probability Primer, 1968, Mathematics: The Alphabet of Science, 1972, 74, 77, A First Course in College Mathematics, 1973, 77, 80, Mathematics Worktext, 1973, 77, Business and Consumer Mathematics for College Students, 1976, The Numbers Game, 1977. Mem. Nat. Council Tchrs. Math., Assn. Tchrs. Sci. and Math., Am. Math. Soc., Math. Assn. Am., Greater San Diego Math. Council (dir. 1963-65), Sigma Xi, Pi Mu Epsilon. Home: 10241 Vivera Dr La Mesa CA 91941-4370 Office: Dept Math San Diego State Coll San Diego CA 92085

WILLERMAN, LEE, psychologist, educator; b. Chgo., July 26, 1939; s. Israel and Anna Willerman; m. Benne Secter, Jan. 21, 1962; children: Raquel, Amiel. BA, Roosevelt U., Chgo., 1961, MA, 1964; PhD, Wayne State U., 1967. Research psychologist NIH, Bethesda, Md., 1967-70; NIH postdoctoral fellow dept. human genetics U. Mich. Med. Sch., Ann Arbor, 1970-71; asst. prof. psychology U. Tex., Austin, 1971-74, assoc. prof., 1974-81, prof., 1981—, Sarah M. and Charles E. Seay Regents prof. clin. psychology, 1985—; vis. Scheinfeld prof. Hebrew U. Jerusalem, 1983. Author: Psychology of Individual and Group Differences, 1979; co-author: Psychopathology, 1990. Fellow Am. Psychol. Assn., Internat. Soc. Twin Studies; mem. AAAS, Soc. Study Social Biology, Behavior Genetics Assn. Jewish. Home: 3415 Ledgestone Dr Austin TX 78731-5124 Office: U Tex at Austin Dept Psychology Austin TX 78712-1189

WILLERTSEN, STEVEN, food products executive. With Cargill Corp., Wayzata, Minn.; pres. Rocco Turkeys, Inc., Dayton, Va. Office: Rocco Turkeys Inc Huffman Dr RR 42 Dayton VA 22821*

WILLES, MARK HINCKLEY, media industry executive; b. Salt Lake City, July 16, 1941; s. Joseph Simmons and Ruth (Hinckley) W.; m. Laura Fayone, June 7, 1961; children: Wendy Anne, Susan Kay, Keith Mark, Stephen Joseph, Matthew Bryant. AB, Columbia U., 1963, PhD, 1967. Mem. staff banking and currency com. Ho. of Reps., Washington, 1966-67; asst. prof. fin. U. Pa., Phila., 1967-69; economist Fed. Res. Bank, Phila., 1967, sr. economist, 1969-70, dir. research, 1970-71, v.p., dir. research, 1971, 1st v.p., 1971-77; pres. Fed. Res. Bank of Mpls., 1977-80; exec. v.p., chief fin. officer Gen. Mills, Inc., Mpls., 1980-85, pres., chief oper. officer, 1985-92, vice chmn., 1992-95; chmn., pres., CEO Times Mirror Co., L.A., 1995—. Office: Times Mirror Co Times Mirror Sq Los Angeles CA 90053 *My success is based on adherence to principles I learned in the home, which is the most basic and important organizational unit in the world. Three of those principles stand out in my mind: Be just, honest and moral—do things not only because they are required, but because they are right. Have mercy—care enough about others to be fair and kind. Be humble—you can get more done effectively with the help of others than you can do on your own.*

WILLETT, EDWARD FARRAND, JR., lawyer; b. Takoma Park, Md., Jan. 30, 1933; s. Edward Farrand and Fern Leona (Hawkins) W.; m. Anita Joan McComas, Dec. 26, 1954; children—Jeffrey Dean, Gary Louis, Deborah Ann. B.A., Andrews U., Berrien Springs, Mich., 1954; J.D., George Washington U., 1957. Bar: D.C. 1958. Atty. advisor U.S. Civil Service Commn., Washington, 1958-69, legis. counsel, 1969-70; asst. law revision counsel U.S. Ho. of Reps., Washington, 1970-73, law revision counsel, 1973—. Editor: U.S. Codes, 1973—. Mem. ABA, D.C. Bar Assn. Home: 11320 Country Club Rd New Market MD 21774-6700 Office: Law Revision Counsel 304 Ford House Office Bldg Washington DC 20515

WILLETT, THOMAS EDWARD, lawyer; b. N.Y.C., Nov. 8, 1947; s. Oscar Edward and Alice (Fleming) W.; m. Marilyn Kenney, Dec. 28, 1969; children: Thomas Justin, Christopher Joseph. BS, USAF Acad., Colo., 1969; JD with distinction, Cornell U., 1972. Bar: N.Y. 1973, U.S. Ct. Claims 1973, U.S. Supreme Ct. 1977. Judge advocate USAF, Syracuse, N.Y., 1973-75, Kincheloe AFB, Mich., 1975-77; judge advocate USAF Hdqs., Washington, 1977-79; assoc. Harris, Beach & Wilcox, Rochester, N.Y., 1979-84, ptnr., 1985—. Pres. Monroe County Legal Assistance Corp., Rochester, 1983-89. Capt. USAF, 1969-79. Mem. ABA, N.Y. State Bar Assn., Monroe County Bar Assn., Order of Coif. Office: Harris Beach & Wilcox Granite Bldg 130 Main St E Rochester NY 14604-1620

WILLEY, FRANK PATRICK, financial company executive, lawyer; b. Albany, N.Y., July 15, 1953. BS in Acctg., LeMoyne Coll., 1975; JD, Union U., 1978. Bar: Ariz. 1978. Assoc. T. M. Shumway, Scottsdale, Ariz., 1978-80, Foley, Clark & Nye, Phoenix, 1980-83; gen. counsel, v.p. Land Resources Corp., Scottsdale, 1983-84; gen. counsel, exec. v.p. Fidelity Nat. Title Ins., Irvine, Calif., 1984—; pres. Fidelity Nat. Fin., Inc., 1995—.

WILLEY, GORDON RANDOLPH, retired anthropologist, archaeologist, educator; b. Chariton, Iowa, Mar. 7, 1913; s. Frank and Agnes Caroline (Wilson) W.; m. Katharine W. Whaley, Sept. 17, 1938; children: Alexandra, Winston. AB, U. Ariz., 1935, AM, 1936, LittD (hon.), 1981; PhD, Columbia U., 1942; A.M. honoris causa, Harvard U., 1950; Litt.D. honoris causa, Cambridge U., 1977, U. N.Mex., 1984. Archaeol. asst. Nat. Pk. Svc., Macon, Ga., 1936-38; archaeologist La. State U., 1938-39; archaeol. field supr. Peru, 1941-42; instr. anthropology Columbia U., 1942-43; anthropologist Bur. Am. Ethnology, Smithsonian Instn., 1943-50; Bowditch prof. archaeology Harvard U., 1950-83, sr. prof. anthropology, 1983-87, chmn. dept. anthropology, 1954-57; vis. prof. Am. archaeology Cambridge (Eng.) U., 1962-63; mem. expdns. to Peru, Panama, 1941-52, Brit. Honduras, 1953-56, Guatemala, 1958, 60, 62, 64, 65, 66, 67, 68, Nicaragua, 1959, 61, Honduras, 1973, 75-77. Author: Excavations in the Chancay Valley, Peru, 1943, Archaeology of the Florida Gulf Coast, 1949, Prehistoric Settlement Patterns in the Viru Valley, Peru, 1953, Introduction to American Archaeology, 2 vols, 1966-71, The Artifacts of Altar de Sacrificios, 1972, Excavations of Altarde Sacrificious, Guatemala: Summary and Conclusions, 1973, Das Alte Amerika, 1974, The Artifacts of Seibal, Guatemala, 1978, Essays in Maya Archaeology, 1987, Portraits in American Archaeology, 1988, New World Archaeology and Culture History, 1990, Excavations at Seibal: Summary and Conclusions, 1990; co-author: Early Ancon and Early Supe Cultures, 1954, The Monagrillo Culture of Panama, 1954, Method and Theory in American Archaeology, 1958, Prehistoric Maya Settlements in the Belize Valley, 1965, The Ruins of Altar de Sacrificios, Department of Peten, Guatemala: An Introduction, 1969, the Maya Collapse: An Appraisal, 1973, A History of American Archaeology, 1974, 3d edit., 1993, The Origins of Maya Civilization, 1977, Lowland Maya Settlement Patterns: A Summary View, 1981, the Copan Residential Zone, 1994; co-editor: Courses Toward Urban Life, 1962, Precolumbian Archaeology, 1980, A Consideration of the Early Classic Period in the Maya Lowlands, 1985; editor: Prehistoric Settlement Patterns of the New World, 1956, Archaeological Researches in Retrospect, 1974. Overseas fellow Churchill Coll., Cambridge U., 1968-69; decorated Order of Quetzal Guatemala; recipient Viking Fund medal, 1953; Gold medal Archaeol. Inst. Am., 1973; Alfred V. Kidder medal for achievement in Am. Archaeology, 1974; Huxley medal Royal Anthrop. Inst., London, 1979; Walker prize Boston Mus. Sci., 1981; Drexel medal for archaeology Univ. Mus., Phila., 1981, Golden Plate award Am. Acad. Achievement, 1987. Fellow Am. Anthrop. Assn. (pres. 1961), Am. Acad. Arts and Sci., London Soc. Antiquaries, Soc. Am. Archaeology (pres. 1968, Disting. Svc. award 1980); mem. Nat. Acad. Sci., Am. Philos. Soc., Royal Anthrop. Inst. Gt. Britain and Ireland, Cosmos Club (Washington), Tavern Club (Boston), Phi Beta Kappa, Brit. Acad. (corr.).

WILLEY, JOHN DOUGLAS, retired newspaper executive; b. Melrose, Mass., June 4, 1917; s. Arthur Peach and Lillian (Holden) W.; m. Marilynn Miller, July 3, 1943; children: Margery Lynn Willey Marshall (dec.), John Douglas, James Campbell, David Spencer, Peter Whitney. LLD (hon.), U. Toledo, 1972. Sec. Boston & Maine R.R., Boston, 1935-40, Jones & Lamson Machine Co., Springfield, Vt., 1940-41; reporter The Blade, Toledo, 1946-49, asst. to pub., 1949-51, city editor, 1952-54, asst. mng. editor, 1954-56, dir. pub. rels., 1956-58, treas., 1962-69, assoc. pub., 1965-81, pres., 1969-81, also bd. dirs.; pres. Clear Water, Inc., 1966-89; bd. dirs. Buckeye Cablevision, Inc., Monterey Peninsula Herald; v.p., dir. Lima Communications Corp., 1971-81, Red Bank Register, 1975-81; mem. Ohio adv. bd. Liberty Mut. Ins. Co., 1976-82. Mem. exec. com. of bd. trustees, treas. Toledo Area Med. Coll. and Edn. Found., 1960-75, hon. trustee, 1975—; mem. adv. bd. St. Vincent Hosp., 1961-75; trustee Maumee Valley Country Day Sch., 1974-77, Med. Coll. Ohio, 1982-91; treas. Amateur Athletic Union Task Force Com., 1976-82, Ohio chmn. U.S. Olympic Commn. 1979-80; mem. Inter-Univ. Coun., Ohio, 1988-91. Capt. A.C., U.S. Army, 1942-46. Recipient Disting. Citizen award Med. Coll. Ohio, 1994. Mem. Belmont Country Club, Med. Coll. Ohio Faculty Club, Sigma Delta Chi. Home: 3534 River Rd Toledo OH 43614-4326

WILLGING, PAUL RAYMOND, trade association executive; b. New Rochelle, N.Y., Feb. 14, 1942; s. Herbert Martin and Pauline Mary (Mast) W.; m. Monika Guenther, Aug. 25, 1967; children: Kirsten, Birgit. BA, U. St. Thomas, 1963; M in Internat. Affairs, Columbia U., 1966, PhD, 1973. Assoc. adminstr. Health Services Adminstrn., Parklawn, Md., 1973-75; dep. commr. Med. Services Adminstrn., Washington, 1975-80; dep. adminstr. Health Care Fin. Adminstrn., Balt., 1980-82; asst. v.p. Blue Cross/Blue Shield Greater N.Y., N.Y.C., 1982-83; exec. v.p. Am. Health Care Assn., Washington, 1983—. Contbr. articles to profl. jours. Bd. dirs. Nat. Health Coun., Washington, 1986—, Howard County Gen. Hosp., Columbia, 1987—. Fulbright scholar, 1964; fellow Woodrow Wilson Found., 1965, Ford Found., 1966. Avocations: skiing, jogging. Home: 10366 Crossbeam Ct Columbia MD 21044-3819 Office: Am Health Care Association 1201 L St NW Washington DC 20005-4024

WILLHAM, RICHARD LEWIS, animal science educator; b. Hutchinson, Kans., May 4, 1932; s. Oliver S. and Susan E. (Hurt) W.; m. Esther B. Burkhart, June 1, 1954; children: Karen Nell, Oliver Lee. B.S., Okla. State U., 1954; M.S., Iowa State U., 1955, Ph.D., 1960. Asst. prof. Iowa State U., Ames, 1959-63, assoc. prof., 1966-71, prof. dept. animal sci., 1971-78, Disting. prof., 1978—; assoc. prof. Okla. State U., Stillwater, 1963-66; cons. in field; tchr. livestock history; guest curator exhbn. Art About Livestock, 1990. Author: A Heritage of Leadership - The First 100 Years of Animal Science at Iowa State University, 1996. Recipient Svc. award Beef Improvement Fedn., 1974, Edn. and Rsch. award Am. Polled Herefore Assn., 1979, Rsch. award Nat. Cattlemen's Assn., 1986, 91, Disting. Alumnus award Okla. State U., 1978, Regents Faculty Excellence award Iowa State U., 1993; named to Hall of Fame Am. Hereford Assn., 1982, Am. Angus Assn., 1988. Fellow Am. Soc. Animal Sci. (animal breeding and genetics award 1978, industry service award 1986). Home: 316 E 20th St Ames IA 50010-5563 Office: Iowa State U Dept Animal Sci Ames IA 50011

WILLIAM, DAVID, director, actor; b. London, Eng., June 24, 1926; arrived in Can., 1986; s. Eric Hugh and Olwen (Roose) W. BA, U. Coll., Oxford, Eng., 1950. Artistic dir. Glasgow Citizen's Theatre, The Nottingham Playhouse, The New Shakespeare Co., London, The National Theatre of Israel, Stratford Festival, Can., 1989-93; instr. U.S., Can., Britain; founder, 1st artistic dir. Ludlow Festival. Theatre directing credits include: Bacchae, The Importance of Being Earnest, The Tempest, Entertaining Mr. Sloane, Love Letters, Treasure Island, Hamlet, Love for Love, The Shoemaker's Holiday, Murder in the Cathedral, Troilus and Cressida, The Winter's Tale, She Stoops to Conquer, Antigone, Separate Tables, Romeo and Juliet, Othello, King Lear, Volpone, Albert Herring, The Merry Wives of Windosr, Twelfth Night; directing world premiers of operas include: Therese, Royal Opera House Covent Garden, The Lighthouse, Edinburgh festival, Red Emma; other operas directed include Iphigenie en Tauride, The Fairy Queen, Lisbon, La Traviata, Scottish Opera, Il Re Pastore, Camden Festival, Albert Herring, Aldeburgh Festival; appeared in Uncle Vanya as Serebryakov, As You Like It as Jaques, Twelfth Night as Malvolio, Hamlet as Rosencrantz to Richard Burton's (Hamlet); appeared in numerous TV prodns. most notably as Richard the Second in the BBC series An Age of Kings; compiled, directed and acted in My Shakespeare, Stratford Festival and CBC Radio. Home: 194 Langarth St E, London, ON Canada N6C 1Z5

WILLIAMS, AENEAS DEMETRIUS, professional football player; b. New Orleans, Jan. 29, 1968. Degree in acctg., So. Univ. La., 1990. Cornerback Ariz. Cardinals, 1991. Selected to Pro Bowl, 1994; tied for NFL lead in interceptions (9), 1994. Office: c/o Ariz Cardinals 8701 S Hardy Tempe AZ 85284*

WILLIAMS, ALAN DAVISON, publishing company executive; b. Duluth, Minn., Oct. 25, 1925; s. Curtis Gilbert and Marjorie Barton (Townsend) W.; m. Beverly Alexander, Apr. 1, 1951 (div. May 1988); children: Wistar W. Rawls, Anne Alexander, Marjorie Williams Noah; m. Rosina Rue, June 25, 1988; 1 child, Rosina Barton. Grad., Phillips Exeter Acad., 1944; B.A., Yale U., 1949. Advt. mgr. McGraw-Hill Book Co., 1949-53; publicity mgr., editor J.B. Lippincott Co., 1953-58; N.Y. editor Little, Brown & Co., 1959-65; mng. editor, editorial dir., v.p. Viking Press, Inc., N.Y.C., 1965-84; v.p. editorial Viking-Penguin Inc., 1975-84; exec. editor, v.p. G.P. Putnam Co., N.Y.C., 1985-87; pub., editor in chief Arbor House/William Morrow, N.Y.C., 1987-89; pub. Grove Weidenfeld Inc., N.Y.C., 1990-92; Mem. adv. council English dept. Princeton, 1972-86. Editor: Fifty Years-A Farrar, Straus and Giroux Reader, 1996. Bd. dirs. Friends of Princeton Art Mus., 1980-85; trustee Princeton U. Press, 1991-95. Served with USAAF, 1944-45. Woodrow Wilson vis. fellow. Club: Century Assn. (N.Y.C.). Home: 560 Palisade Ave Jersey City NJ 07307-1125

WILLIAMS, ALUN GWYN, publishing company executive; b. Newtown, Powys, Wales, Oct. 31, 1953; s. Edgar Pugh and Pamela Beresford (Jones) W.; m. Deborah Elaine Smith, May 1, 1982; children: Megan Elizabeth, Gareth Huw. BA in Math., Worcester Coll., Oxford (Eng.) U., 1975, MA, 1980. Chartered acct. Audit mgr. Touche Ross, London, 1980-83; group fin. contr. October Pub., London, 1986-88; comml. dir. Reed Consumer Books, London, 1988-92; v.p. fin. Reed Reference Pub., New Providence, N.J., 1992-95, exec. v.p. fin. and ops., 1995—. Mem. Inst. Chartered Accts. Eng. and Wales (Strachan prize 1980). Home: 771 Amsterdam Rd Bridgewater NJ 08807 Office: Reed Reference Pub 121 Chanlon Rd New Providence NJ 07974

WILLIAMS, ANDY, entertainer; b. Wall Lake, Iowa, Dec. 3, 1930; s. Jay Emerson and Florence (Finley) W.; m. Claudine Longet, Dec. 15, 1961 (div.); children: Noelle, Christian, Robert; m. Debbie Haas, May 3, 1991. pres. Barnaby Records, Barnaby Prodns., Barnaby Sports; owner Moon River Enterprises; host Andy Williams San Diego Golf Open, 1969-89. Worked with 3 brothers as Williams Brothers Quartet, on radio stations in Des Moines, Chgo., Cin. and Los Angeles, 1938-47, Williams Brothers, (teamed with Kay Thompson); worked for night clubs, U.S. and Europe, 1947-52; regular performer: Steve Allen Tonight TV show, 1953-55; star: Andy Williams TV Show, 1962-71; night club and concert entertainer, rec. artist for Columbia Records; recordings include Moon River, Love Story, theme from The Godfather, Can't Get Used to Losing You, Days of Wine and Roses, Born Free, Hawaiian Wedding Song, Butterfly. Named Number One Male Vocalist Top Artist on Campus Poll, 1968; recipient 17 gold albums, 3 Emmy awards, 6 Grammy awards. Office: Moon River Theatre 2500 W Highway 76 Branson MO 65616-2164

WILLIAMS, ANITA JEAN, elementary educator educator; b. Little Rock, July 14; d. Hoover and Clara Mae (Lewis) W. BS in Edn., Ark. State U., 1983, MS in Edn., 1989. Tchr. Carver Washington YMCA Day Care, Little Rock, 1978-79, Annie Nannies Day Care, Memphis, 1986-87; elem. tchr. Parkin (Ark.) Sch. Dist., 1983-84; tchr. kindergarten Hughes (Ark.) Pub. Schs., 1984-86; receipt and ctrl. clk. IRS, Memphis, 1987-90; elem. tchr. English, kindergarten and 3d and 4th grade tchr. Earle (Ark.) Sch. Dist., 1988—; sec., bookkeeper Lewis and Son Rice Processing Mill, Earle, 1977—; wedding dir. and coord., Earle, 1992—. coach/sponsor Cheerleading Squad. Recipient Ednl. award Nacerima Club, Forrest City, Ark., 1977, 83, 89, award Bulter Chapel Christian Meth. Episcopal Ch., Earle, 1991, 92, 93. Mem. NEA, Ark. Edn. Assn., Ark. Cheerleading Coaches Assn., Nat. Cheerleading Assn., (5 trophies for safety, most spirited, and most improved team award), Order Eastern Star, Kappa Delta Pi. Methodist. Avocations: playing piano, listening to music, directing weddings, singing gospel music. Home: 01197 Street Hwy 149 South Earle AR 72331-9745 Office: Earle Sch Dist PO Box 637 Earle AR 72331-0637

WILLIAMS, ANN CLAIRE, federal judge; b. 1949; m. David J. Stewart. BS, Wayne State U., 1970; MA, U. Mich., 1972; JD, U. Notre Dame, 1975. Law clk. to hon. Robert A. Sprecher, 1975-76; asst. U.S. atty. U.S. Dist. Ct. (no. dist.) Ill., Chgo., 1976-85; faculty mem. Nat. Inst. for Trial Advocacy, 1979—; judge U.S. Dist. Ct. (no. dist.) Ill., Chgo., 1985—; chief Crime Drug Enforcement Task Force North Ctrl. Region, 1983-85; chair ct. adminstrn. and case mgmt. com. Jud. Conf. U.S., 1993—. Trustee U. Chgo. Lab Sch.; sec. bd. trustees U. Notre Dame, Mus. Sci. and Industry. Mem. Fed. Bar Assn., Fed. Judges Assn. (treas.), Women's Bar Assn. of Ill. Office: US Dist Ct 219 S Dearborn St Chicago IL 60604-1702

WILLIAMS, ANNA M., social worker; b. Ft. Meade, Md., Sept. 5, 1956; d. William Arthur and Jacqueline Rae (Hall) W. BSW, B in African Studies, U. Md., 1978; MSW, U. Pitts., 1981. Lic. social worker. Investigator child abuse Dept. Social Svcs., Balt., 1978-80; counselor, program coord., supr. girls unit Ward Home for Children, Pitts., 1981-86; mental health therapist Pace Sch., Pitts., 1986-89; program coord. Justice Resources Inc., Balt., 1989-94; therapist Union Meml. Hosp., Balt., 1993-94; v.p. resdl. svcs. Children's Home Wyoming Conf., Binghamton, N.Y., 1994-95; dir. Casey Family Svcs., Balt., 1996—; cons. Youth Advocacy Program, Balt., 1992-94. Bd. dirs. Ward Home for Children, Pitts., 1986-88, South Balt. Youth Ctr., 1993-94; speaker Meth. Women; adv. bd. WSKG Pub. Broadcasting, 1994—. Mem. NASW, Nat. Girls Caucus (charter), Kiwanis Internat., Alpha Kappa Alpha (Lambda Phi chpt.). Democrat. Avocations: reading, cooking, gardening, interior decorating. Office: Casey Family Svcs 1809 Ashland Ave Baltimore MD 21205

WILLIAMS, ANTHONY, lawyer; b. N.Y.C., Jan. 12, 1946; s. Patrick and Palma (Leone) W. AB in Govt. cum laude, Harvard U., 1968; JD, NYU, 1973. Bar: N.Y. 1974, U.S. Supreme Ct. 1976, Calif. 1977. Assoc. Coudert Bros., N.Y.C., 1973-75, San Francisco, 1976-79; ptnr. Coudert Bros., N.Y.C., 1981—, adminstrv. ptnr., 1982-85; chmn. exec. com. Coudert Bros., 1993—. Served with U.S. Army, 1968-70. Mem. ABA, N.Y. Bar Assn., Assn. Bar of City of N.Y., Calif. Bar Assn. Avocations: reading, baseball, golf. Office: Coudert Bros 1114 Avenue Of The Americas New York NY 10036-7703*

WILLIAMS, ANTHONY A., federal official; m. Diana Lynn Simmons; 1 child. BA in Polit. Sci. magna cum laude, Yale U., 1982; JD, M of Pub. Policy, Harvard U., 1987. Law clk. to Hon. David Nelson U.S. Dist. Ct., Boston, 1987-88; asst. dir. Boston Redevel. Authority, 1988-89; exec. dir. Cmty. Devel. Agy., St. Louis, 1989-91; dep. comptr. State of Conn., Boston, 1991-93; CFO Dept. Agrl., 1993—; exec. dir. Cmty. Devel. Agy., St. Louis, 1989-91; dept. contr. State of Conn., 1991-93; CFO Dept. Agr., Washington, 1993—; adj. prof. pub. affairs Columbia U., N.Y.C., 1992-93. Pres. pro tempore, chmn. cmty. devel. com. Conn. Bd. Alderman, 1980-83; dir. comm. Conn. Spkr. House and Assembly Dem., 1983. Kellogg Found. Nat. fellow, 1991. Office: Dept of Agrl Chief Fin Officer 14th & Independence Ave SW Washington DC 20250*

WILLIAMS, ANTHONY JEROME, lawyer; b. Lubbock, Tex., Jan. 11, 1963; s. Vera Lee Williams. BA magna cum laude, Tex. Tech U., 1985, JD, 1990. Bar: Tex. 1991. Atty. I, Office City Atty., Lubbock, 1991-94; assoc. Fadduol and Glasheen, Lubbock, 1994; pvt. practice Law Office Anthony Williams, Lubbock, 1994—; instr. South Plains Coll., Lubbock, 1993-94. Bd. dirs. Dunbar Neighborhood Assn., Lubbock, 1995. Fellow Sloan Found., 1985; Martin Luther King scholar Tex. Tech U. Sch. Law, 1990. Avocations: gourmet cooking, gardening. Home: 1804 E 25th St Lubbock TX 79404 Office: 1114 10th St Lubbock TX 79401-2740

WILLIAMS, ARTHUR BENJAMIN, JR., bishop; b. Providence, R.I., June 25, 1935; m. Lynette Rhodes, 1985. AB, Brown U., 1957; MDiv, Gen. Theol. Sem., 1964; MA, U. Mich., 1974; DD, Gen. Theol. Sem., 1986. Clarence Horner fellow Grace Ch., Providence, 1964-65; asst. St. Mark, Riverside, R.I., 1965-67; sub-dean St. John Cathedral, Providence, 1967-68; assoc. & interim rector Grace Ch., Detroit, 1968-70; asst. to bishop Diocese of Mich., 1970-77; archdeacon Ohio Cleve., 1977-85; suffragan bishop Episcopal Diocese of Ohio, Cleve., 1986—; v.p. House of Bishops, 1995—; chair Com. on Justice, Peace and Integrity of Creation, 1995—. Chair editl. com. Lift Every Voice and Sing II, 1993. Office: Diocese of Ohio 2230 Euclid Ave Cleveland OH 44115-2405

WILLIAMS, ARTHUR COZAD, broadcasting executive; b. Forty Fort, Pa., Feb. 12, 1926; s. John Bedford and Emily Irene (Poyck) W.; m. Ann Cale Bragan, Oct. 1, 1955; children: Emily Williams Van Hoorickx, Douglas, Craig. Student, Wilkes U., 1943-44; B.A. cum laude, U. So. Calif., 1949. With Kaiser Aluminum, 1949, Sta. KPMC, 1950-51; v.p., mgr. KFBK and KFBK-FM Radio Stas., Sacramento, 1951-80; with public relations dept. Sacramento Bee, McClatchy Newspapers, 1981-86; dir.-treas. Norkal Opportunities, Inc.; pres. Sacramento Bee Credit Union. Served with AUS, 1944-46. Mem. Sigma Delta Chi. Clubs: Rotary, Sutter, Valley Hi Country, Masons, Shriners. Home: 1209 Nevis Ct Sacramento CA 95822-2532 Office: 1125 Brownwyk Dr Sacramento CA 95822-1028

WILLIAMS, ARTHUR E., federal agency administrator; b. Watertown, N.Y.; m. Carole Waite; children: Scott, Christina, Cheryl. BA in Math., St. Lawrence U., Canton, N.Y., 1960; BSCE, Rensselaer Poly. Inst., 1962; M in Civil Engring./Econ. Planning, Stanford U., 1969; grad., U.S. Army Comd. and Gen. Staff Coll., U.S. Naval War Coll.; D in Engring. (hon.), Rensselaer U., 1994. Registered profl. engr., Minn. Comdr. various assigments U.S. Army Corps Engrs.; chief engrs., comdr. U.S. Army Corps Engrs., Washington, 1992—. Office: Dept of the Army Chief of Engineers 20 Massachusetts Ave NW Washington DC 20314-0001

WILLIAMS, ARTHUR T., JR., gas, oil industry executive; b. 1927. With Winston Salem (N.C.) Tobacco Bd. of Trade, 1949-57, Taylor Oil Co., Inc., Winston Salem, N.C., 1957-63; with A T Williams, Winston Salem, N.C., 1963—, now CEO. Office: A T Williams Oil Co 5446 University Pky Winston Salem NC 27105-1366*

WILLIAMS, AUBREY WILLIS, anthropology educator; b. Madison, Wis., July 31, 1924; s. Aubrey Willis and Anita (Schreck) W.; m. Alice Rebecca Williams, Sept. 20, 1950 (div. June 1972); children: Jonathan Goree, Nancy Clark; m. Graceanne Adamo, Dec. 21, 1974 (div. June 1992); 1 child, Aubrey Philip Rhys. BA, U. N.C., 1955, MA, 1957; PhD, U. Ariz., 1964. Circulation mgr. So. Farmer Inc., Montgomery, Ala., 1950-53, pub. rep., 1953-55; research asst. dept. anthropology U. N.C., Chapel Hill, 1956; field camp dir. Am. Friends Service Com., San Salvador el Verde, Puebla, Mex., 1957-58; teaching asst. U. Ariz., Tucson, 1958-60; ethnologist Navajo Tribe, Window Rock, Ariz., 1961-62; asst. prof. U. Md., College Park, 1962-66, assoc. prof., dir. div. of anthropology, 1967-71, full prof., 1971—; research assoc. Smithsonian Instn., Washington, 1966-67; Fulbright prof., USSR, 1982, Fulbright-Hays prof., Mex., 1984, USIA prof. Tampere (Finland) U., 1990-91. Mem. Am. Anthrop. Assn., Soc. for Applied Anthropology. Democrat. Office: U Md Dept Anthropology College Park MD 20472

WILLIAMS, B. JOHN, JR., lawyer, former federal judge; b. Lancaster, Pa., Dec. 13, 1949; s. Bernard John and Sarah Elizabeth (Sykes) W.; m. Martha Caroline Roberts, Aug. 6, 1977; children: Robert, Sarah, Anne, Bernard. BA, George Washington U., 1971, JD, 1974. Bar: D.C., Pa., U.S. Ct. Appeals (fed. cir.). Law clk. to judge U.S. Tax Ct., Washington, 1974-76; assoc. Ballard, Spahr, Andrews & Ingersoll, Phila., 1976-81; spl. asst. to chief counsel IRS, Washington, 1981-83; dep. asst. atty. gen. Tax Div. Dept. Justice, Washington, 1983-84; ptnr. Morgan, Lewis & Bockius, Washington, 1984-85; judge U.S. Tax Ct., Washington, 1985-90; ptnr. Morgan, Lewis & Bockius, Washington, 1990—; mem. adv. com. U.S. Ct. Appeals, Fed. Cir. Fellow Am. Coll. Tax Counsel; mem. ABA, Am. Law Inst., Phi Beta Kappa, Omicron Delta Kappa. Republican. Office: Morgan Lewis & Bockius 1800 M St NW Washington DC 20036-5802

WILLIAMS, BARBARA JEAN MAY, state official; b. Alphoretta, Ky., June 5, 1927; d. Andrew Jackson and Bess (Salisbury) May. A.B. in Spanish, Centre Coll., 1949; postgrad., Columbia U., 1957; M.S. in L.S., U. Ky., 1963. Librarian Midway Jr. Coll., 1960-62, Ky. Dept. Libraries, Frankfort, 1965-68; planning librarian Ky. Program Devel. Office, Frankfort, 1968-71, Ky. Exec. Dept. for Fin. and Adminstrn., Frankfort, 1972-76; asst. state librarian Ky. Dept. Libraries and Archives, Frankfort, 1976; state librarian Ky. Dept. Libraries and Archives, 1977-80; adminstr. Ky. suggestion system program Dept. Personnel, div. employee services State of Ky., Frankfort, 1980-91; retired; mem. Depository Library Council to Public Printer. Mem. ALA, Southeastern Libr. Assn., Ky. Libr. Assn. (sec. spl. libr. sect. 1976, chmn. sect. 1976), Chief Officers State Libr. Agys. (liaison com. office Edn. 1979-80), Assn. State Libr. Agys. (Index State Libr. Activities 1979-80), Coun. Planning Libr. (treas.), Ky. Coun. Archivists, Ky. Hist. Soc., J.B. Speed Mus. Guild, Dem. Woman's Club, Filson Club, La Jardinere Club, Garden Club. Episcopalian.

WILLIAMS, BARBARA JUNE, lawyer; b. Lansing, Mich., Jan. 6, 1948; d. Ben Allan and Virginia Jane (Searing) W.; m. John Paul Halvorsen, Oct. 21, 1971. AA, Stephens Coll., 1968; BA, U. Ill.-Champaign, 1970; JD, Rutgers U., 1974. Bar: N.J. 1974, N.Y. 1981. Assoc., Bookbinder, Coulagori & Bookbinder, Burlington, N.J., 1974-76, Law Offices of Cyrus Bloom,

Newark, 1976-78, Warren, Goldberg, Berman & Lubitz, Princeton, N.J., 1978-84; staff atty. Rutgers U. Sch. of Law, Newark, 1984-85; assoc. Strauss & Hall, Princeton, 1985-87; of counsel Weg & Myers, P.C., New York, 1987—. Assoc. editor Rutgers Camden Law Jour., 1973-74; contbr. articles to profl. jours. Mem. Nat. Sch. Bds. Assn. (bd. dir. nat. coun. sch. attys. 1981-86), ABA, N.J. Bar Assn. (dir. govt. law sect. 1981-84), Mercer County Bar Assn., Princeton Bar Assn., Assn. Trial Lawyers Am., NOW, Lawrence Arts Assn., Lawrence Twp. Home: 90 Denow Rd Trenton NJ 08648-2047

WILLIAMS, BEN FRANKLIN, JR., mayor, lawyer; b. El Paso, Tex., Aug. 12, 1929; s. Ben Franklin and Dorothy (Whitaker) W.; m. Daisy Federighi, June 2, 1951; children: Elizabeth Lee, Diane Marie, Katherine Ann, Benjamin Franklin III. BA, U. Ariz., 1951, JD, 1956. Bar: Ariz. 1956. With Bd. Immigration Appeals, Dept. Justice, 1957, ICC, 1959; pvt. practice Tucson, Ariz., 1956—; city atty. Douglas and Tombstone, 1962; atty. Mexican consul, 1960; mayor of Douglas, 1980-88; bd. dirs. Ariz. Pub. Service Co. Pres. Ariz. League Cities and Towns, pres. Douglas Sch. Bd., 1963, 69, 70; mem. bd. Ariz. Dept. Econ. Planning and Devel.; bd. dirs. Ariz.-Mex. Commn., Ariz. Acad. (Town Hall), Merabank & Ariz. Pub. Service Co.; ward committeeman Douglas Republican Com., 1962. Served to 1st lt. AUS, 1951-53. Mem. ABA, Internat. Bar Assn., Ariz. Bar Assn. (treas. 1963), Cochise County Bar Assn. (pres. 1959), Pima County Bar Assn., Am. Judicature Soc., U. Ariz. Law Coll. Assn. (dir.), Ariz. Hist. Soc. (dir.), Sigma Nu, Phi Delta Phi, Blue Key. Episcopalian. Lodge: Elks. Home: 6555 N St Andrews Dr Tucson AZ 85718-2615 Office: 3773 E Broadway Blvd Tucson AZ 85716-5409

WILLIAMS, BENJAMIN TALLIFARO, pathologist, educator; b. Bartlesville, Okla., Jan. 25, 1931; s. Benjamin Tallifaro and Edna Jane (Potter) W.; m. Elizabeth Ann Klein, Sept. 23, 1957; children: Monica, Marcia, Marie, Mark, Grace, Mary, Sarah, Richard. BS, Washington U., St. Louis, 1952; MD, U. Okla., 1955; cert. in anatomic and clin. pathology, St. Louis U. Hosps., 1959; postgrad. in combinatorial math., microelectronic engring., U. Calif., San Diego, 1961. Diplomate Am. Bd. Pathology. Pathologist Scripps Hosp., La Jolla, Calif., 1961-62; dir. labs. Mercy Hosp., Urbana, Ill., 1962-88; pres. Univ. Pk. Pathology Assocs., Urbana, 1971—, Cognitive Systems, Ltd., Urbana, 1979—; chmn. bd. Regional Health Resource Ctr., Urbana, 1971-91; prof. med. info. sci. U. Ill. Coll. Medicine, Urbana, 1986—, head. dept. pathology, 1986—; pres. Life Span Rsch. Inst., Englewood, Fla., 1987—; pres. Soc. for Advanced Med. Systems, Washington, 1979-81; pres. Internat. Health Evaluation Assn., 1990-92. Author: Computer Aids to Clinical Decisions, 1982; contbr. articles to profl. jours. Pres. Model Community Coord. Coun., Champaign, Ill., 1973-75. Lt. USN, 1959-61. Fellow Coll. Am. Pathologists, Am. Soc. Clin. Pathologists, Am. Coll. Med. Info. (founding fellow); mem. Am. Med. Informatics Assn., Rotary, Serra Internat. (pres. Champaign 1987-88), Alpha Omega Alpha. Roman Catholic. Avocations: investment analysis, travel. Office: Univ Park Pathology Assocs 1408 W University Ave Urbana IL 61801-2341

WILLIAMS, BERNABE FIGUEROA, professional baseball player; b. San Juan, P.R., Sept. 13, 1968. Outfielder New York Yankees, 1991—. Office: New York Yankees Yankee Stadium E 161 St and River Ave Bronx NY 10451*

WILLIAMS, BETTY LOURENE, volunteer, manager, consultant; b. Topeka, Oct. 3, 1934; d. Jim and Catherine (Sears) Lewis; m. Herman Williams, Sept. 22, 1950; children: Herm Jr., Danny Clay, Iris Angela, John Joseph, Steve Arnold. AA, Compton Coll., 1988. Lic. real estate agt., Calif. Lumbleau Real Estate Sch. Kindergarten, music tchr. St. Catherine Cath. Mission Sch., Guthrie, Okla., 1956-57; real estate agt. Diamond Realty, Compton, Calif., 1964-65; office mgr. J & H Clin. Lab., Inglewood, Calif., 1967-71; exam clk. typist Fed. Office of Personnel Mgmt., L.A., 1981, consulting adminstrv. coord., designer of office ops. system, 1983; vol. Harbor Chpt. AAKP, Long Beach, Calif., 1979—; office orgn., cons. Inglewood Chpt., 1989—; kidney peer patient counseling. Author: (book of poems) Expressions, 1988. Mem. NAACP, Compton, Calif. Br., 1992; mem. Congl. hearing com. Nat. Urologic and Kidney Diseases Adv. Bd. for West Coast, L.A., 1988; organizer Tng. Seminar for So. Calif. State Rehab. Dept., 1988. Recipient Shirley Berman Nat. Outstanding Vol. of Yr. award, 1992, Award for 20 Yrs. of Outstanding Svc., Am. Assn. for Kidney Patients; grantee McDonald Douglas to purchase van for patients, 1993. Mem. Am. Assn. Kidney Patients, Normal Bridge Club (sec. 1986-87), Am. Bridge Assn. (L.A. unit 1986—). Democrat. Avocations: piano playing, duplicate bridge, singing, collector of Black history, poetry writing, scenery painting.

WILLIAMS, BEVERLY, health services administrator; b. Kalamazoo, Oct. 29, 1942; d. Sheldon Burkholder and Arline Marie (Decko) Burnett; m. Douglas Earl Williams, June 19, 1971; children: Jennifer Sharline, Jeffrey Sheldon. Student, Presbyn. Hosp. Sch. Nursing, 1963; BSN, Calif. State U., 1966, MS, 1977. RN, Calif. Health ctr. adminstr. deputy Whittier Health Ctr. and La Puente Health Ctr., L.A., 1977-80; adminstrv. asst. Edward R. Royba Comprehensive Health Ctr., L.A., 1980-82; emergency med. systems program head L.A. Dept. of Health Svcs., 1982-93, nurse mgr., comprehensive perinatal svcs. program, 1993—. Capt. USAF, 1966-68. Mem. Women in Health Adminstrn. of South Calif., Health Svcs. Mgmt. Forum. Home: 14237 Christine Dr Whittier CA 90605-1531

WILLIAMS, BILL, academic administrator. Pres. Grand Canyon U. Office: Grand Canyon U 3300 W Camelback Rd Phoenix AZ 85017-3030

WILLIAMS, BILLY DEE, actor; b. N.Y.C., Apr. 6, 1937. Student (Hallgarten scholar), Nat. Acad. Fine Arts and Design; student acting, Paul Mann, Sidney Poitier, Actor's Workshop in Harlem. Child actor; Broadway adult debut The Cool World, 1961; other stage appearances include A Taste of Honey, 1961, I Have a Dream, 1976, Hallelujah, Baby, Fences, 1988; films The Last Angry Man, 1959, The Out-of-Towners, 1970, The Final Comedown, Lady Sings the Blues, 1972, Hit!, 1973, Mahogany, 1975, The Bingo Long Travelling All-Stars and Motor Kings, 1976, Scott Joplin, 1977, The Empire Strikes Back, 1980, Nighthawks, 1981, Return of the Jedi, 1983, Marvin and Tige, 1983, Fear City, 1985, Number One with a Bullet, 1987, Batman, 1989, Driving Me Crazy, 1991; TV films Carter's Army, 1970, Brian's Song, 1971, The Glass House (Emmy nomination), The Hostage Tower, 1980, Children of Divorce, 1980, Shooting Stars, 1983, Chiefs, 1983, Time Bomb, 1984, Dangerous Passion, 1990, The Jacksons: An American Dream, 1992, Marked for Murder, 1993; guest appearances: TV series The Jeffersons, The Interns, The FBI, Mission Impossible, Mod Squad, Police Woman, Dynasty, In Living Color; appeared in TV movie Scott Joplin: King of Ragtime, 1978. Office: David Shapiro and Assocs 15301 Ventura Blvd Ste 345 Sherman Oaks CA 91403-3129*

WILLIAMS, BILLY LEO, professional baseball coach; b. Whistler, Ala., June 15, 1938; m. Shirley Ann Williams; children: Valarie, Nina, Julia, Sandra. Profl. baseball player Chgo. Cubs, Nat. League, 1959-74, coaching staff, 1978-82, hitting instr., from 1986; profl. baseball player Oakland (Calif.) Athletics, Am. League, 1975-76, coaching staff, 1983-85. Named to Nat. League All-Star Team, 1962, 64-65, 68, 72-73, to Baseball Hall of Fame, 1987, Ala. Sport Hall of Fame, Mobile Sport Hall of Fame; named Nat. League Rookie of Yr., 1961, Nat. League and Maj. Leagues Player of Yr., Sporting News, 1972, Nat. Batting Champ., 1972. Mem. Chgo. Sports Hall of Fame. Nat. League record holder for consecutive games played, 1963-70; maj. league record holder for most games by an outfielder in a season, 1965. Office: Chicago Cubs Wrigley Field 1060 W Addison St Chicago IL 60613-4397*

WILLIAMS, BOBBY See EVERHART, ROBERT PHILLIP

WILLIAMS, BROWN F, television media services company executive; b. Evanston, Ill., Dec. 22, 1940; s. Jack Kermit Williams and Virginia Helen (Benjamin) Likar; m. Linda Francee Ludt, Sept. 1961 (div. 1968); 1 child, Eden Carol Williams McCarthy; m. Martha Amidon Powers, 1970 (div. 1974); m. Sandra Ann Matkowski, Jan. 1984; 1 child, Bronwyn Emily. AB in Math. and Physics, U. Calif., Riverside, 1962, MA in Physics, 1964, PhD in Physics, 1966. Mgr. Electro-Optics Lab., Princeton, N.J., 1969-75; dir. RCA Labs., Princeton, 1976-82, v.p., 1982-87; pres. Williams Cons. Group, Princeton, 1988-90; pres. Princeton Video Image, 1990—. Fellow IEEE; mem. AAAS, Am. Phys. Soc., Sigma Xi. Avocations: skiing, ocean sailing, tennis. Office: 47 Hulfish St Princeton NJ 08542-3709

WILLIAMS, BRYAN, university dean, medical educator; b. Longview, Tex., July 28; s. Lewis Bryan and Margaret Louise (Smart) W.; m. Frances Montgomery, Mar. 31, 1950; children: Harrison, Amy, Philip, Nickolas, Margaret, Lincoln. MD, Southwestern Med. Sch., 1947. Diplomate Am. Bd. Internal Medicine. Pvt. practice Dallas, 1957-70; prof. internal medicine, assoc. dean student affairs Southwestern Med. Sch., 1970-90; retired. Fellow ACP; mem. Inst. Medicine Nat. Acad. Scis. (charter). Home: 3712 Beverly Dr Dallas TX 75205-2806

WILLIAMS, CAMILLA, soprano, voice educator; b. Danville, Va.; d. Booker and Fannie (Cary) W.; m. Charles T. Beavers, Aug. 28, 1950. BS, Va. State Coll., 1941; postgrad., U. Pa., 1942; studies with, Mme. Marian Szekely-Freschl, 1943-44, 1952, Berkowitz and Cesare Sodero, 1944-46, Rose Dirman, 1948-52, Sergius Kagen, 1958-62; MusD (hon.), Va. State U., 1986, D. (hon.), 1985. Prof. voice Bronx Coll., N.Y.C., 1970, Bklyn. Coll., 1970-73, Queens Coll., N.Y.C., 1974, Ind. U., Bloomington, 1977—; 1st black prof. voice Cen. Conservatory Music, Beijing, People's Republic China, 1983. Created role of Madame Butterfly as 1st black contract singer, N.Y.C. Ctr., 1946, 1st Aida, 1948; 1st N.Y. performance of Mozart's Idomeneo with Little Orch. Soc., 1950; 1st Viennese performance Menotti's Saint of Bleecker Street, 1955; 1st N.Y. performance of Handel's Orlando, 1971; other roles include Nedda in Pagliacci, Mimi in La Boheme, Marguerite in Faust; major tours include Alaska, 1950, London, 1954, Am. Festival in Belgium, 1955, tour of 14 African countries for U.S. Dept. State, 1958-59, Israel, 1959, concert for Crown Prince of Japan as guest of Gen. Eisenhower, 1960, tour of Formosa, Australia, New Zealand, Korea, Japan, Philippines, Laos, South Vietnam, 1971, Poland, 1974; appearances with orchs. including Royal Philharm., Vienna Symphony, Berlin Philharm., Chgo. Symphony, Phila. Orch., BBC Orch., Stuttgart Orch., many others; contract with RCA Victor as exclusive Victor Red Seal rec. artist, 1944—. Recipient Marian Anderson award (1st winner), 1943, 44, Newspaper Guild award as First Lady of Am. Opera, 1947, Va. State Coll. 75th anniv. cert. of merit, 1957, NYU Presdl. Citation, 1959, Gold medal Emperor of Ethiopia and Key to City of Taiwan during Pres. Johnson's Cultural Exchange Program, 1962, Art, Culture and Civic Guild award, 1962, Negro Musician's Assn. plaque, 1963, Harlem Opera and World Fellowship Soc. award, 1963; named Disting. Virginian Gov. of Va., 1972; inducted Danville (Va.) Mus. Fine Arts and History Hall of Fame, 1974; Camilla Williams Park designated in her honor, Danville, 1974; honored by Ind. U. Sch. Music Black Music Students' Orgn., 1979; named to Hon. Order Ky. Cols., 1979; honored by Phila. Pro Arte Soc., 1982; Disting. award of Ctr. for Leadership and Devel., 1983; Taylor-Williams student residence hall at Va. State U. named in Billy Taylor's and her honor, 1985. Mem. NAACP (hon. life), Internat. Platform Assn., Alpha Kappa Alpha. Office: Ind U Sch Music Bloomington IN 47401 *Years of travel have given me the chance to meet people of every race, kind, and condition. I have been a witness to the brotherhood and sisterhood of mankind, for we are all children of God. The most important lesson of my life is the value of giving. When you give of yourself you receive the blessings of your talents.*

WILLIAMS, CARL CHANSON, oil company executive; b. Cin., Oct. 16, 1937; s. Charles J. and Alcie (Brazile) W.; m. Clare Bathé, May 26, 1985; 1 child, Michelle. A.S., U. Cin., 1965; B.S., SUNY-Brockport, 1974; M.B.A., U. Rochester, 1975. Mgr. fin. systems Xerox Corp., Rochester, N.Y., 1972-77; dir. info. mgmt. Am. Can Co., Greenwich, Conn., 1977-79, mng. dir. info. mgmt., 1979-80, mng. dir. ops. control, 1980-82; sr. v.p., dir. mgmt. info. systems DDB Needham Worldwide, N.Y.C., 1982-90; pres. The Intertechnology Group, Inc., N.Y.C., 1990-91; v.p. infosystems and tech. Macmillan Pub. Co., N.Y.C., 1991-93; gen. mgr. info. tech. Amoco Corp., Chgo., 1993-94, v.p. info. tech., 1994—; cons. Stamford (Conn.) Bd. Edn., 1981-82; lectr. U. Rochester, N.Y., 1975-77; adj. prof. Fordham U., 1991—. Exec. dir. Concerned Assn. Rochester, N.Y., 1971-75; bd. dirs. Stamford Cmty. Arts Coun., 1983-84; trustee Roosevelt U., 1995. Mem. Soc. Info. Mgmr. (exec. coun. 1980-83, pres. 1985, pres. coun. 1986—), Exec. Leadership Coun. Office: Amoco Corp 200 E Randolph St Chicago IL 60601-6436

WILLIAMS, CARL E., SR., bishop. Presiding bishop Ch. of God in Christ, Internat., N.Y.C., 1978—. Office: Ch of God in Christ Internat 170 Adelphi St Brooklyn NY 11205-3302

WILLIAMS, CARL HARWELL, utilities executive; b. Mansfield, Ga., Oct. 22, 1915; s. John Horace and Mary Ruby (Harwell) W.; m. Diane Barnes, June 25, 1967; children: Edward Vincent, Lesa Anne. Student, U. Fla., 1934-35; B.S., Ga. Sch. Tech., 1939; postgrad., Harvard Advanced Mgmt. Program, U. Hawaii, 1956. Registered profl. engr., Hawaii. Engr. Fla. Power & Light Co., Miami, 1939-41; with Hawaiian Electric Co., Inc., Honolulu, 1945-80; mgr. engring. Hawaiian Electric Co., Inc., 1955-62, v.p., 1962-71, exec. v.p., 1971-72, pres., 1972-80, dir., 1970-85, chmn. exec. com., 1980-85; chmn. bd., dir. Maui Electric Co. (subsidiary), 1972-80, Hawaii Electric Light Co. (subsidiary), 1972-80; dir. Bank of Hawaii., Hawaiian Electric Industries, Inc., Bancorp Hawaii, Inc. Bd. dirs. Aloha United Way, 1973-79; bd. dirs. Oahu Devel. Conf., 1972-81, chmn., 1979-80; bd. visitors Coll. Bus. Adminstrn., Hawaii, mem. adv. com. advanced mgmt. program, 1969-75, mem. adv. com. Hawaii geothermal project, 1973-78; mem. State Energy Policy Task Force, 1974-78, Hawaii Energy Conservation Council, 1978-80, Gov.'s Com. Alt. Energy Devel., 1978-80; bd. dirs. Am.-Samoa Power Authority, 1981-83. Served to lt. col., Signal Corps AUS, 1941-45. Decorated Legion of Merit. Fellow IEEE; mem. Hawaii C. of C., Engring. Assn. Hawaii, Nat. Soc. Profl. Engrs. (past dir.), Hawaii Soc. Profl. Engrs. (past dir., pres.), Pacific Coast Elec. Assn. (dir. 1972-81, pres. 1979-80), AIEE (past chmn. Hawaii sect.). Clubs: Pacific, Outrigger Canoe. Home: 2969 Kalakaua Ave Apt 501 Honolulu HI 96815-4620

WILLIAMS, CAROLE ANN, cytotechnologist; b. Duquesne, Pa., Apr. 14, 1934; d. Theodore Wylie and Dorothy Belle (Mehrmann) Williams; BS, Chatham Coll., 1956; postgrad. Case-Western Res. U., 1956-57; MS Calif. State U., 1989. Cytotechnologist, Clin. Path. Lab. of Paul Gross, Pitts., 1957-59; chief cytotechnologist, teaching supr. Presbyn. U. Hosp., Pitts., 1959-63; staff Pathology Lab. of Drs. Armanini & Wegner, Stockton, Calif., 1964; chief cytotechnologist, teaching supr. Hosp. of Good Samaritan, Los Angeles, 1964-89; dir. cytotechnology tng. program UCLA Med. Ctr., 1989—; conductor workshops in field. Mem. Am. Soc. Clin. Pathologists (cytotech. exam. com. bd. registry 1978, mem. bd. govs. 1990-95), Calif. Assn. Cytotechnologists (pres. 1967-68, 72-73), Internat. Acad. Cytology, Am. Soc. Cytopathology (Technologist of Yr. award 1981). Republican. Presbyterian. Home: 2460 Stoner Ave Los Angeles CA 90064-1326 Office: 10833 Le Conte Ave Los Angeles CA 90024

WILLIAMS, CAROLYN ELIZABETH, manufacturing executive; b. L.A., Jan. 24, 1943; d. George Kissam and Mary Eloise (Chamberlain) W.; m. Richard Terrill White, Apr. 9, 1972; children: Sarah Anne, William Daniel. BS, Ga. Inst. Tech., 1969; MM, Northwestern U., 1988. Saleswoman Ea. Airlines, Atlanta, Montreal (Can.) and Seattle, 1964-69; job analyst Allied Products Corp., Atlanta, 1969-70; mgr. Allied Products Corp., Frankfort, Mich., 1970-71; planning analyst, sr. planning analyst Allied Products Corp., Chgo., 1972-74, dir. planning, 1974-76, staff v.p. planning, 1976-79, v.p. planning and bus. research, 1979-86, v.p. corp. devel., chief planning officer, 1986-93; pres. White, Williams & Daniels, 1993—. Mem. adv. bd. Ga. Inst. Tech. Mem. Winnteka Yacht Club (dir. jr. sailing), Midwest Youth Sailing Assn. (bd. dirs., treas.).

WILLIAMS, CHARLES D., bishop. Bishop of Alaska Ch. of God in Christ, Anchorage. Office: Ch of God in Christ 2212 Vanderbilt Cir Anchorage AK 99508-4563

WILLIAMS, CHARLES DAVID, oil and steel company executive; b. Mineola, Tex., July 16, 1935; s. Floyd L. and Audie N. (Hall) W.; m. Shirley R. Dodd, Jan. 23, 1954; children: Jan, Charles David. BS in Petroleum Engring., Tex. A&M U., 1957, MS in Petroleum Engring., 1959; MBA in Fin., So. Meth. U., 1971. Asst. to exec. v.p. Atlantic Richfield Co., N.Y.C., 1971-72; dir. planning Atlantic Richfield Co., Dallas, 1972-76; mgr. investor relations Atlantic Richfield Co., L.A., 1976-79; v.p. investor affairs Tex. Oil and Gas Corp., Dallas, 1979-86; v.p. investor relations USX Corp., Pitts., 1986—. Mem. Soc. Petroleum Engrs., N.Y. Soc. Security Analysts, Petroleum Investor Relations Assn., Sigma Xi, Beta Gamma Sigma. Republican. Baptist. Avocations: golf, fishing. Office: USX Corp 600 Grant St Pittsburgh PA 15219-2702

WILLIAMS, C(HARLES) K(ENNETH), poet, literature and writing educator; b. Newark, N.J., Nov. 4, 1936; s. Paul Bernard and Dossie (Kasdin) W.; m. Sarah Dean Jones, June, 1966 (div. 1975); 1 child, Jessica Anne; m. Catherine Justine Mauger, Apr. 15, 1975; 1 child, Jed Mauger. BA, U. Pa., 1958. Vis. prof. lit. Beaver Coll., Jenkintown, Pa., 1975, Drexel U., Phila., 1976, U. Calif., Irvine, 1978, Boston U., 1979-80, Bklyn. Coll., 1982-83; Mellon vis. prof. lit. Franklin and Marshall Coll., Lancaster, Pa., 1977; prof. writing Columbia U., N.Y.C., 1981-85; prof. lit. George Mason U., Fairfax, Va., 1992-95; Halloway lectr. U. Calif., Berkeley, 1986, Princeton U., 1995—. Author: A Day for Anne Frank, 1968, Lies, 1969, I Am the Bitter Name, 1972, With Ignorance, 1977, The Lark, The Thrush, The Starling, 1983, Tar, 1983, Flesh and Blood, 1987, Poems, 1963-1983, 1988, The Bacchae of Euripides, 1990, Helen, 1991, A Dream of Mind: Poems, 1992, Selected Poems, 1994; contbr. editor Am. Poetry Rev., 1972—; translator: Women of Trachis (Sophocles), 1978. Sponsor People's Fund, Phila., 1967—. Recipient Nat. Book Critics Circle award in poetry, 1987, Morton Dauwen Zabel prize Am. Acad. of Arts and Letters, 1989, Harriet Monroe prize, 1993; fellow Guggenheim Found., 1975, Nat. Endowment for Arts, 1985, 93; Lila Wallace-Reader's Digest grantee, 1993—. Mem. PEN, Poetry Soc. Am. Avocations: piano, guitar, drawing. Home: 82 Rue d'Hauteville, 75010 Paris France

WILLIAMS, CHARLES LAVAL, JR., physician, international organization official; b. New Orleans, Jan. 19, 1916; s. Charles Laval and Lewise (McLaurine) W.; m. Ellen Clendenin Ustick, Dec. 14, 1946; children: Ellen Clendenin, Katherine McLaurine. Student, U. Va., 1933-35; M.D., Tulane U., 1940; M.P.H., U. Mich., 1945. Diplomate: Am. Bd. Preventive Medicine and Pub. Health. Intern U.S. Marine Hosp., New Orleans, 1941; with USPHS, 1941-67; assigned N.C. State Health Dept., 1941-44, USPHS States Relations div., 1944, U. Mich., 1944-45, Am. Acad. Pediatrics Nat. Study Child Health Services, 1945-47; chief planning unit, asst. chief div. commd. officers, 1947-51; with US/AID Div. Pub. Health, 1951-62; chief pub. health adviser AID Mission to Peru, 1959-62; asso. dir. internat. relations Office Internat. Health, 1962-64; chief Office Internat. Research, NIH, Bethesda, Md., 1965-66; dep. dir., then dir. Office Internat. Health, Office Surgeon General, USPHS, Washington, 1966-67; dep. dir. Pan Am. Health Orgn., 1967-79; ret.; exec. v.p. Am. Assn. World Health, 1980-84. Fellow Am. Pub. Health Assn.; mem. U.S.-Mexico Border Pub. Health Assn., Phi Kappa Phi, Delta Omega. Home: 5600 Wisconsin Ave 1009 Chevy Chase MD 20815-4411

WILLIAMS, CHARLES LINWOOD (BUCK WILLIAMS), professional basketball player; b. Rocky Mount, N.C., Mar. 8, 1960; s. Moses and Betty Williams. Student, U. Md. Basketball player New Jersey Nets, NBA, 1981-89, Portland Trail Blazers, 1989—. Mem. U.S. Olympic Team, 1980, NBA All-Rookie Team, 1982; player NBA All-Star Games, 1982, 83, 86; named NBA Rookie of Yr., 1982; named to NBA All-Defensive Team, 1990, 91. Office: Portland Trail Blazers Port of Portland Bldg 700 NE Multnomah St Ste 600 Portland OR 97232-4106*

WILLIAMS, CHARLES MARVIN, commercial banking educator; b. Romney, W. Va., Apr. 20, 1917; s. W. Marvin and Lula H. (Taylor) W.; m. Elizabeth Huffman, Oct. 19, 1946; children: Holland H., Andrea L. AB, Washington and Lee U., 1937; MBA, Harvard U., 1939, DCS, 1951; LLD, Washington and Lee U., 1966. Credit trainee Mfrs. Trust Co., N.Y.C., 1939-41; asst. prof. finance Harvard Grad. Sch. Bus. Adminstrn., 1947-51, assoc. prof., 1951-56, prof. bus. adminstrn., 1956-60, Edmund Cogswell Converse prof. banking and finance, 1960-66, George Gund prof. comml. banking, 1966-86, prof. emeritus, 1986—; pres. Charles M. Williams Assocs.; bd. dirs. Horace Mann Educators Corp. Author: Cumulative Voting for Directors, 1951, (P. Hunt) Case Problems in Finance, 1949, (with P. Hunt and G. Donaldson) Basic Business Finance, 1958. Served to lt. comdr., Supply Corps USNR, 1941-47. Mem. Inst. Fin. Mgmt. (bd. dirs.), Phi Beta Kappa, Kappa Alpha. Clubs: Harvard (N.Y.C.); Weston Golf. Home: 50 Cherry Brook Rd Weston MA 02193-1306 Office: Soldiers Field Boston MA 02163

WILLIAMS, CHARLES MURRAY, computer information systems educator, consultant; b. Ft. Bliss, Tex., Dec. 26, 1931; s. Robert Parvin and Barbara (Murray) W.; m. Stanley Bright, Dec. 31, 1956; children: Margaret Allen Williams Becker, Robert Parvin, Mary Linton Williams Bondurant. BS, Va. Mil. Inst., 1953; MS, Stanford U., 1964; PhD, U. Tex., 1967. Physicist USAF, Kirtland AFB, N.Mex., 1956-58; staff mem. Sandia Labs., Albuquerque, 1958-62; programmer analyst Control Data Corp., Palo Alto, Calif., 1962-63; mathematician Panoramic Rsch., Inc., Palo Alto, 1963-64; mem. tech. staff Thomas Bede Found., Los Altos, Calif., 1964-65; rsch. scientist assoc. U. Tex., Austin, 1965-67; asst. prof. Computer Sci. Pa. State U., State College, 1967-72, Va. Poly. Inst. and State U., Blacksburg, 1972-75; assoc. prof. Computer Info. Systems Ga. State U., Atlanta, 1975-83, prof. Computer Info. Systems, 1983—; cons. Visicon Inc., State Coll., 1970-72, Broomall (Pa.) Industries Inc., 1973-79, Bausch & Lomb Inc., Rochester, N.Y. 1981, Bell South Media Techs. Inc., Atlanta, 1987-90; mem. tech. staff Bell Labs., Whippany, N.J., 1979; textbook reviewer various publs. including Harper & Row, Prentice Hall, Simon & Schuster, 1976—. Contbr. articles to profl. computer graphics and image processing publs. Bd. dirs. Ga. Striders, 1993—; presenter Walking and Running to the Fountain of Youth Seminar, 26 municipalities in 6 states, 1992—. Grantee Xerox Corp., 1985, Ga. Rsch. Alliance Telemedicine Project, 1993; recipient Silver medals in 1500-meter and 3000 meter runs 60-64 age divsn. Athletic Congress (now U.S.A. Track & Field) Nat. Masters Indoor Track and Field Championships, 1992, Gold medals in 5000-meter and 10,000-meter runs, Bronze medal in 1500-meter run, 1992, Gold medals in 1500-meter and 3000-meter runs U.S.A. Track & Field Indoor Championships, 1993, Gold medals in 5000-meter and 10,000 meter runs, Bronze medal in 1500-meter run U.S. Track and Field Outdoor Championships, 1993, Bronze medal in 5000-meter run and 10,000-meter runs U.S.A. Track & Field Outdoor Championships, 1994, Gold medal in 3000-meter run U.S.A. Track & Field Indoor Championships, 1994; ranked 3d nationally in road racing Running Times, 1992; ranked 5th, (2nd honorable mention) 1993. Mem. Nat. Computer Graphics Assn. (hon., Ga. bd. dirs. 1979-85, bd. dirs. Ga. chpt. 1985-89, sec. 1988-89), Computer Graphics Pioneers, Upsilon Pi Epsilon, Omicron Delta Kappa. Republican. Episcopalian. Avocation: competitive road running (recipient numerous gold and silver medals). Home: 316 Argonne Dr NW Atlanta GA 30305-2814 Office: Ga State U Dept of Computer Info Sys University Pla Atlanta GA 30303 *Throughout life, gain inspiration from the actions of your elders. Emulate them by focusing your energies so that your own actions may inspire the young. You are never too old to begin new ventures.*

WILLIAMS, CHARLES WESLEY, technical executive, researcher; b. Palestine, Ark.; s. Fredrick Charles and Fannie Rochet (Southall) W.; m. Nancy Sue Rhea, Sept. 5, 1959; children: Brent L., Brian E. B.S.E.E., U. Tenn.-Knoxville, 1959, M.S., 1963. Registered profl. engr., Ohio. Devel. engr. Mead Research Lab., Chillicothe, Ohio, 1959-60, Oak Ridge Nat. Lab., 1960-63; tech. mgr. EG & G Ortec, Oak Ridge, 1963-76, tech. dir. phys. and life sci., 1976-81; mgr. Assay Inst. EG & Ortec, Oak Ridge, 1981-85; pres. Autograffix Inc., Knoxville, Tenn., 1985—. Contbr. articles to tech. jours., chpt. to book. Fellow IEEE (v.p. Nuclear and Plasma Sci. Soc. 1979); mem. Tau Beta Pi, Eta Kappa Nu. Baptist.

WILLIAMS, CHARLOTTE EVELYN FORRESTER, civic worker; b. Kansas City, Mo., Aug. 7, 1905; d. John Dougal and Georgia (Lowerre) Forrester; student Kans. U., 1924-25; m. Walker Alonzo Williams, Sept. 25, 1926; children: Walker Forrester, John Haviland. Trustee, Detroit Grand Opera Assn., 1960-87 , dir., 1955-60; chmn. Grinnell Opera Scholarship, 1958-66; founder, dir., chmn. adv. bd. Cranbrook Music Guild, Inc., 1952-59, life mem.; bd. dirs. Detroit Opera Theater, 1959-61, Severo Ballet, 1959-61; Detroit dist. chmn. Met. Opera Regional Auditions, 1958-66; mem. Children's Mus., Boca Raton, Friends of Children's Mus. at Singing Pines, Boca Raton Hist. Soc., Fla. Atlantic U. Found.; past pres. Friends of Caldwell Playhouse, Boca Raton. Mem. Debbie-Rand Meml. Svc. League (life), DAR, English-Speaking Union, Vol. League Fla. Atlantic U., PEO,

Order Eastern Star. Home: 2679 S Ocean Blvd Apt 5C Boca Raton FL 33432-8353

WILLIAMS, CHERYL, educator; b. Neosho, Mo., July 7, 1957; d. Allen and Travestine Williams. BS in Math., East Tex. State U., 1978, postgrad., 1978-79; postgrad., Rose State Coll., 1980-81, Sheppard Tech. Tng. Ctr., 1980-81; MS in Math., Spl. Edn., U. Tex., 1996. Computer scientist Tinker AFB, Oklahoma City, 1980-81, Defense Comm. Agy., Washington, 1986; tchr. Parent Child Inc., San Antonio, 1989; asst. sec. Antioch Bapt. Ch., San Antonio, 1989-92; substitute tchr. San Antonio Ind. Sch. Dist., 1990-93; instrnl. asst. spl. edn. Northside Ind. Sch. Dist., San Antonio, 1993-94, asst. tchr., 1994—; asst. mgr. Fashion Place, San Antonio, 1994-95. Counselor YMCA, San Antonio, 1989-91; active Girl Scouts U.S., 1964-86; mem. choir, asst. sec. area ch., 1972, tutor, 1970—, tchr. Sunday Sch., 1973—; mem. Dorcas Circle, Lupus Found. Am., Biomed. Rsch. U. Tex., 1995—; mem. Epilepsy Found. Am., Tex. Head Injury Assn., Nat. Head Injury Assn., Smithsonian Instn. Mem. NEA, Tex. Edn. Assn., Mu. Alpha Theta. Avocations: jigsaw puzzles, bowling.

WILLIAMS, CHESTER ARTHUR, JR., insurance educator; b. Blakely, Pa., Mar. 6, 1924; s. C. Arthur and Alice (Robinson) W.; m. Roberta Riegel, Sept. 1, 1951; children—Robert Arthur, Bruce Allan. A.B., Columbia U., 1947; A.M., 1949, Ph.D., 1952. Lectr. ins. U. Buffalo, N.Y., 1950-52; asst. prof. U. Minn., 1952-55, asso. prof., 1955-58, Ford Found. faculty fellow, 1957-58, prof., 1958-80, acting dean, 1970-71, asso. dean, 1971-72, dean, 1972-78, Minn. Ins. Industry chair prof., 1980-92, prof. emeritus, 1992—; vis. prof. U. Pa., 1960-61, Keio U., Tokyo, 1984. Author: Price Discrimination in Property and Liability Insurance, 1959, Economic and Social Security, 1957, Risk Management and Insurance, 1964, Insurance Arrangements under Workmen's Compensation, 1969, Insurance Principles and Practices: Property and Liability, 1976, Principles of Risk Management and Insurance, 1978, Insurance and Risk Management, 1980, Ocean Marine Insurance, 1988, An International Comparison of Workers' Compensation, 1991; editor Jour. of Risk and Ins., 1981-86. Contbr. articles to profl. jours. Bd. dirs. State Capitol Credit Union, 1965-68, pres., 1967-68; bd. dirs. Consumers Union, 1972-75; bd. dirs. Minn. State Coun. on Econ. Edn., 1973-78, chmn., 1975-77; bd. dirs. St. Paul Cos., Inc., 1975-90. Served to 1st lt. USAF, 1943-46. Recipient Gold medal Internat Ins. Soc., 1993, Elizur Wright award Am. Risk and Ins. Assocs., 1993; laureate Ins. Hall of Fame. Mem. Am. Risk Ins. Assn. (dir. 1960-65, 81-86, pres. 1965), Am. Acad. Actuaries, Decision Sci. Inst., Am. Statis. Assn., Am. Finance Assn., AAUP, Phi Beta Kappa, Beta Gamma Sigma. Episcopalian. Home: 1984 Shryer Ave W Saint Paul MN 55113-5415

WILLIAMS, CHRISTOPHER PEELE, architect; b. Denver, Apr. 21, 1947; s. Arnold H. and Margaret A. (Keith) W.; m. Ann Hulley, Oct. 26, 1975; 1 child, Mae H. BArch, Carnegie Mellon U., 1972. Registered architect, N.H., Maine, Mass., Vt. Architect WM Design Group, Center Harbor, N.H., 1975-84; prin. arch. Christopher P. Williams Architects, Meredith, N.H., 1984—. Bd. dirs. Lakes Region Planning Commn., Meredith, 1980-88, Percent for Arts Program, Concord, 1979-84; bd. dirs. Ctr. Harbor Planning Bd., 1976-83; bd. dirs., vice chmn. Ctr. Harbor Bd. Adjustment, 1983—; bd. dirs., chair Waukewan Shore Owners Assn., Meredith, 1989—; chmn. bd. dirs. Inherit N.H., Cooncord, 1985—. Recipient Builder's Gold award N.H. Home Builder's Assn., 1991, 93, 94, 95, Citation Urban Design award Progressive Arch., 1980. Mem. AIA (N.H. chpt., v.p. 1984, bd. dirs. 1990—, Excellence in Arch. award 1990, 94, 95, Internat. Illumination Design award 1995), New Eng. Solar Energy Assn., Nat. Trust for Hist. Preservation, N.H. Coun. Sch. Archs. Avocations: hiking, music, reading, travel. Office: PO Box 703 Meredith NH 03253-0656

WILLIAMS, CLARENCE LEON, management, sociology and public policy company executive, educator; b. Longview, Tex., Aug. 9, 1937; s. Ruby Marlene (McLemore) W.; m. Kathleen Susan Robbins, June 7, 1975; children: Clarence Leon 2d, Thomas Chatterton. BA, Prairie View A&M U., 1959; MA in Sociology, Calif. State U., 1973; postgrad., U. Oreg., 1973-75. Exec. dir. Galveston County (Tex.) Community Action Coun., 1966-68, San Diego County (Calif.) Econ. Opportunity Commn., 1969-70; from assoc. dep. dir. program and contract dept. to dir. budgeting, planning, rsch. and evaluation dept. Econ. and Youth Opportunities Agy., Inc., L.A., 1970-71; dir. Rocky Mtn. Forum Internat. Issues, Denver, 1976-77; cons., adminstr. Regional Ctr. for Health Planning and Rsch. Svcs., Inc., Phila., 1977-78; with Albany (N.Y.) Interracial Coun., Inc., 1978-80; pres. Williams Academic and Pub. Policy Svcs., Fanwood, N.J., 1981—; vis. asst. prof., assoc. prof. Grad. Sch. Internat. Studies, U. Denver, 1976-77; asst. prof., dir. Black Edn. Program Ea. Wash. State Coll., 1975-76; policy analyst, speaker, guest panelist various colls., univs., instns. nationally and internationally including U. Iowa, U. Krakow (Poland), U. Lodz (Poland), Warsaw (Poland) U., U. Erlangen (Fed. Republic Germany), Polish Inst. Sociology, Bergen County (N.J.) Ethical Culture Soc., 1965-92; policy analyst, mgmt. cons. Nat. Rural Ctr., Washington, 1976-79, Computerland and Computer Showcase Inc., N.J., 1987-88. Policy analyst, adv. mem. numerous task forces, govtl. confs. including Kettering Found. programs and confs. on econ. devel. in Asia, Africa, Latin Am., on trans-national dialog in Senegal, Mali, West Africa, 1976-80, Nat. Alliance of Businessmen, 1973-75, White House Conf. on Aging, 1967, White House Conf. on Hunger, Nutrition, Health and Poverty, 1969, Pres.' Adv. Coun. on Reorganization of OEO, 1971; regional race rels./intergroup rels. officer Home and Housing Fin. Agy., Washington, 1964-66; mem. Citizen Amb. Program, Russia and Ea. Europe, 1992. With USAF, 1961-64. Recipient Das Family Acad. Rsch. award, 1992; rsch. grantee Woodrow Wilson Nat. Found.; fellow Ford Found., Martin Luther King, Jr., Woodrow Wilson Found., U. Oreg., 1973-75; named U.S. Rep. to U.N. Human Rights 30th Anniversary Commemorative Programs, Europe, 1979-80. Mem. Alpha Kappa Delta, Phi Kappa Phi. Home and Office: 222 N Martine Ave Fanwood NJ 07023-1337

WILLIAMS, CLYDE E., JR., lawyer; b. Niagara Falls, N.Y., Dec. 17, 1919; s. Clyde E. and Martha (Barlow) W.; m. Ruth Van Aken, Oct. 16, 1948; children: Clyde E. III (dec.), Mark Van Aken, Sara. AB, Denison U., Granville, Ohio, 1942; LLB, Harvard U., 1945. Bar: Ohio 1945. Practice corp. and real estate law, 1945—; v.p. Spieth, Bell, McCurdy & newell Co., L.P.A., Cleve., 1964—; also bd. dirs. Spieth, Bell, McCurdy & Newell Co., Cleve.; gen. counsel Growth Cos., Inc., Phila., 1950-55; pres., dir. Williams Investment Co., Cleve., 1954—; sec., dir. Williams Internat. Corp., Walled Lake, Mich., 1954—; dir., gen. Counsel Techno-fund, Inc., Columbus, Ohio, 1960-67; dir. rAdio Seaway, Inc. (Sta. WCLV-FM), 1962—; mem. faculty Fenn Coll. and Cleve. Coll. divsn. Western Res. U., 1945-50. Trustee, mem. exec. com., v.p. Cleve. Soc. for Blind, 1979—, pres., 1985-87, mem. adv. council, 1987—. Mem. ABA, Ohio Bar Assn., Cleve. Bar Assn., Union Club, Skating Club. Office: Spieth Bell McCurdy et al 2000 Huntington Bldg 925 Euclid Ave Cleveland OH 44115-1496

WILLIAMS, DARRYL MARLOWE, medical educator; b. Denver, Apr. 3, 1938; s. Archie Malvin and Dorothy Merle (Grapes) W.; m. Susan Arlene Moore, June 24, 1966; children: Carol Ruth, Peter Todd, Sarah Elizabeth. Student, U. Colo., 1956-58; BS, Colo. State U., 1993; MD, MS in Anatomy, Baylor U., 1964. Diplomate Am. Bd. Internal Medicine, Am. Bd. Hematology. Intern and resident Baylor Affiliated Hosps., Houston, 1964-66, 67-68; resident U. Utah, Salt Lake City, 1966-67, fellow in hematology, 1968-73, asst. prof., 1973-77; assoc. prof. La State U., Shreveport, 1977-81, prof., 1981-90, chief hematology sect., 1977-85, asst. dean/rsch., 1981-85, dean Sch. Medicine, 1985-90; prof. medicine, dean Sch. Medicine Tex. Tech U. Health Scis. Ctr., Lubbock, 1990-95; prof. medicine office border health and area health edn. Tex. Tech. Health Scis. Ctr., El Paso, 1995—, also bd. dirs., 1995—; dir. med. edn. Cmty. Partnership Tex. Tech. Health Sci. Ctr., El Paso, 1995—; mem. hemophilia adv. com. La. Legislature, Baton Rouge, 1977-83; vice chair La. Lung and Cancer Bd., New Orleans, 1984-90; pres. N.W. La. AIDS Task Force, Shreveport, 1987. Mem. Am. Heart Assn., Lubbock chpt., Shreveport Biracial Commn., 1988, Lubbock Indigent Health Care Coalition Task Force, 1991-92, Health Professions Edn. Adv. Com., Lubbock Friends of Pub. Radio; vice chair health profls. edn. adv. com. Tex. Coord. Bd. Higher Edn., 1992-95. Recipient award Nat. Ski Patrol System, Salt Lake City, 1975. Fellow ACP, Am. Coll. Nutrition; mem. AMA, Am. Soc. Hematology, Am. Inst. Nutrition, Am. Soc. Clin. Nutrition, Tex. Med. Assn. (physicians oncology edn. com.), Royal Soc. Medicine, Alpha Omega Alpha. Office: Tex Tech Health Sci Ctr Health Scis Ctr Tex Tech U El Paso TX 79905

WILLIAMS, DAVE HARRELL, investment executive; b. Beaumont, Tex., Oct. 5, 1932; s. George Davis and Mary (Hardin) W.; m. Reba White, Mar. 15, 1975. B.S. in Chem. Engring, U. Tex., 1956; M.B.A. (Baker scholar, Teagle fellow), Harvard U., 1961. Chartered fin. analyst. Chem. engr. Exxon Corp., Baton Rouge, 1959; security analyst deVegh & Co., N.Y.C., 1961-64; dir. research Waddell & Reed, Kansas City, Mo., 1964-67; exec. v.p. Mitchell Hutchins, Inc., N.Y.C., 1967-77; chmn. bd. Alliance Capital Mgmt. Corp., N.Y.C., 1977—; bd. dirs. The Equitable Cos., Inc. Contbr.: articles to Fin. Analysts Jour. Trustee Am. Fedn. of Art, Fgn. Policy Assn, Metropolitan Mus. of Art. Served with USNR, 1956-59. Mem. Fin. Analysts Fedn. (past officer, dir.), N.Y. Soc. Security Analysts (past pres.), Bond Club N.Y., Econ. Club N.Y., Knickerbocker Club, Down Town Assn., Century Assn., Grolier Club. Presbyterian. Office: Alliance Capital Mgmt Corp 1345 Avenue Of The Americas New York NY 10105

WILLIAMS, DAVID A., lawyer, educator; b. Rochester, N.Y., July 1, 1942; s. Charles E. and Lorraine C. (Fitzgerald) W.; m. Margaret E. Ryan, May 30, 1970. BA, Williams Coll., 1964; postgrad., U. Mich., 1965; JD, U. Pa., 1968. Bar: N.Y. 1968, Vt. 1972, U.S. Dist. Ct. Vt. 1972, U.S. Ct. (we. dist.) 1990. Assoc. Law Offices of Fred G. Blum, Rochester, 1968-72; ptnr. Wolchik & Williams, Morrisville, Vt., 1972-80; sole practice Morrisville, 1980-89; ptnr. Williams and Green, P.C., Morrisville, Vt., 1989—; adj. prof. Rochester Inst. Tech., 1969-72, Community Coll. Vt., Johnson, 1972-80, Johnson State Coll., 1973—. Author: Guide to Service of Civil Process by Vt. Sheriffs, 1980. Justice of Peace Town of Johnson, 1976-92, moderator, 1992; pres. Village of Johnson, 1978—; bd. dirs. Johnson Town Sch. Dist., 1992—. Mem. Vt. Bar Assn., Lamoille County Bar Assn. (pres. 1986-92), Sigma Phi Ednl. Found (bd. dir. 1986—). Office: P O Box 800 Morrisville VT 05661-0800

WILLIAMS, DAVID ARTHUR, marketing professional; b. Lima, Ohio, Jan. 22, 1953; s. Arthur Henry and Jane Elenor (Davisson) W. AA Bus., Coll. DuPage, 1973; BA Mktg., Columbia Coll., Chgo., 1976. Dir. mktg. Breckenridge (Colo.) Ski Corp., 1976-81; pres. Williams & Assocs., Denver, 1981-84; dir. real estate advt. Kohler (Wis.) Co., 1984-89; v.p. mktg. Kahn Realty Cos., Inc., Glencoe, Ill., 1989-95; v.p.mktg. The Kahn Realty Cos., Glencoe, Ill., 1996—. Office: The Kahn Realty Cos 640 Vernon Ave Glencoe IL 60022

WILLIAMS, DAVID FULTON, industrial distribution company executive; b. Columbus, Ohio, Oct. 28, 1926; s. William Wallace and Marion Fulton W.; m. Velma Sater, June 30, 1951; children—William S., Patricia Williams French, Elizabeth. BS, Ohio State U., 1950. Chmn., W. W. Williams Co., Columbus, 1963—, also dir.; bd. dirs. Bank One of Columbus, 1978—. Bd. dirs. Riverside Meth. Hosp., Columbus. Served with USAAF, 1944-45. Methodist. Home: 3750 Hillview Dr Columbus OH 43220-4734 Office: W W Williams Co 835 Goodale Blvd Columbus OH 43212-3824

WILLIAMS, DAVID HOWARD, lawyer; b. Las Vegas, Nev., Sept. 21, 1945; s. Howard Cummins and Alice Emma (Taufenbach) W.; m. Kathleen Graham, Sept. 2, 1967; children: David Howard Jr., Jonathan Graham. BA in History cum laude, Denison U., 1967; MA in Polit. Sci., Columbia U., 1969; JD cum laude, Ohio State U., 1973. Bar: Ohio 1973, Ga. 1980. Assoc. Vorys, Sater, Seymour & Pease, Columbus, Ohio, 1973-79; from assoc. to ptnr. Powell, Goldstein, Frazer & Murphy, Atlanta; ptnr. Hunton & Williams, Atlanta; adj. prof. U. Ga. Sch. Law, 1994—; lectr. workshop ann. conv. Ohio League of Savs. Assns., others. Former mem. profl. adv. bd. Ohio Assn. for Children with Learning Disabilities; bd. dirs. Northside Youth Orgn., Atlanta, 1985—; active Peachtree Presbyn. Ch., Atlanta, 1982—. Served to 1st lt. Ohio NG, 1969-75. Mem. ABA (exec. compensation com. corp. sect., taxation and employee benefits sects.), Ga. Bar Assn. (taxation sect.), Atlanta Bar Assn., So. Pension Conf., Midwest Pension Conf. (cen. Ohio chpt. organizer, former vice chmn.). Republican. Office: Hunton & Williams NationsBank Plz 600 Peachtree St NE Atlanta GA 30308*

WILLIAMS, DAVID PERRY, manufacturing company executive; b. Detroit, Nov. 16, 1934; s. M.S. Perry and Virginia (Hayes) W.; m. Jill Schneider, July 27, 1972; children: Tracy, Perry, David, William, Nell. B.A., Mich. State U., 1956, M.B.A., 1964. V.p. sales Automotive div. Kelsey Hayes Co., Romulus, Mich., 1958-71; v.p., mgr. automotive product line ITT, N.Y.C., 1971-76; v.p., dir. Budd Co., Troy, Mich., 1976-79, sr. v.p. ops., dir., 1979-80, sr. v.p., chief ops. officer, 1980-86, pres., chief operating officer, dir., 1986—; dir. Standard Fed. Bank, Troy, Mich., 1990—, SPX Corp., Muskegon, Mich., 1992—, Budd Canada, Inc., Kitchener, Ont., 1981—, Thyssen Prodn. Systems, 1994. Served to 1st lt. USAF, 1956-58. Mem. Soc. Automotive Engrs., Engring. Soc. Detroit, Soc. Jfg. Engrs., Bloomfield Hills Country Club, Country of Detroit, Yondotega, PGA Nat. Club (Fla.), Tournament Players Club (Mich.), Question Club, Royal and Ancient Golf Club of St. Andrews (Scotland), Beta Gamma Sigma. Republican. Episcopalian. Home: 333 Lincoln Rd Grosse Pointe MI 48230-1604 Office: Budd Co PO Box 2601 3155 Big Beaver Rd Troy MI 48084

WILLIAMS, DAVID ROGERSON, JR., engineer, business executive; b. Tulsa, Oct. 20, 1921; s. David Rogerson and Martha Reynolds (Hill) W.; m. Pauline Bolton, May 28, 1944 (dec. Feb. 4, 1988); children: Pauline B. Williams Lampshire, David Rogerson III, Rachel K. Williams Zebrowski; m. Anne W. Kerr, Jan. 5, 1990. B.S., Yale U., 1943. Constrn. foreman, supt. Williams Bros. Corp., 1939-49; co-founder, v.p. Williams Bros. Co., 1949-56, exec. v.p., 1956-66, chmn. exec. com., 1966-70; chmn. bd. Resource Scis. Corp., Tulsa, 1970-83, Williams Techs. Inc., Carbon Resources, Inc.; chmn. Integrated Carbons Corp., Tulsa; co-founder, dir. Patagonia Corp., Tucson; dir. The Williams Cos., Tulsa. Trustee Hudson Inst., Indpls. Served to capt. USAAF, World War II. Fellow ASCE; mem. Am. Petroleum Inst., Alta. Assn. Profl. Engrs., Am. Gas Assn., Yale Engring. Assn., Ind. Natural Gas Assn., Royal Soc. Arts, Duke of Edinburgh's World Fellowship, Springdale Hall (Camden, S.C.), Racquet and Tennis Club, Yale Club N.Y., So. Hills (Tulsa). Office: 320 S Boston Ave Ste 831 Tulsa OK 74103-3728

WILLIAMS, DAVID RUSSELL, music educator; b. Indpls., Oct. 21, 1932; s. H. Russell and Mary Dean (Whitmer) W.; m. Elsa Bühlmann, Jan. 30, 1960. AB, Columbia U., 1954, MA, 1956; PhD, U. Rochester, 1965. Dir. music Windham Coll., Putney, Vt., 1959-62; opera coach Eastman Sch. Music, Rochester, N.Y., 1962-65, assoc. prof. theory, adminstr. of MusM program, 1965-80; prof., chmn. dept. music Memphis State U., 1980-87, prof. music, 1980—; bd. dirs. Memphis Youth Symphony, Memphis Symphony, 1984-90; mem. exec. bd. Opera Memphis, 1980-87, Salute to Memphis Music, 1980-87. Author: Bibliography of the History of Music Theory, 1971, Conversations with Howard Hanson, 1988, Music Theory from Zarlino to Schenker: A Bibliography and Guide, 1990; producer: Highwater Records album 8201 featuring John Stover, classical guitar, 1983; composer Suite for Oboe, Clarinet and Piano, 1968, Five States of Mind, 1970. Bd. dirs., sec. Rochester Philharm. Orch., 1976-78; v.p., bd. dirs. Rochester Chamber Orch., 1974-78; pres., bd. dirs. Opera Theatre of Rochester, 1973-74; bd. dirs., chmn. Am. Ritual Theatre, 1979-80; bd. sponsors Met. Opera Mid. South Region, Memphis, 1983—. Served as cpl. U.S. Army, 1957-59. Recipient Eastman Sch. Music Pub. award, 1970. Mem. NARAS (treas. Memphis chpt. 1984-86), Coll. Music Soc. (sec. 1973-83), Music Tchrs. Nat. Assn. Sci. (state chmn. 1971-74), Nat. Assn. Schs. of Music (chmn. region 8 1989-92), Tenn. Assn. Music Execs. in Colls. and Univs. (pres. 1986-87), Southeastern Composers League (composer mem.), Pi Kappa Lambda (pres. Memphis State U. chpt. 1988-90), Phi Beta Kappa, Phi Mu Alpha (hon.), Sigma Alpha Iota (hon.). Clubs: Rochester, Univ., Summit. Avocations: stock market study, language study, word puzzles. Home: 273 W Central Park St Apt 1 Memphis TN 38111-4570 Office: U Memphis Dept Music Memphis TN 38152 *Having had a family background that was superior in so many ways has helped me to sharpen my purpose in life, in that it has made me realize to what an extent affirmative action is necessary in order to provide a milieu in which truly equal opportunity can exist. Many doors of opportunity have been held open for me; those of disadvantaged access are often not aware that these doors exist. The more individuals I can lead to these portals, the more I will have achieved in my lifetime.*

WILLIAMS, DAVID SAMUEL, insurance company executive; b. Purcell, Okla., Oct. 16, 1926; s. David Skelton and Mattie Carolyn (Kimberlin) W.; m. Gloria Jean Trudgeon, Jan. 14, 1951; children: Mellanie K., David R., Gary B., Kimberly R. BA, U. Okla., 1950; LLB, LaSalle U., 1968. With U.S. Fidelity & Guaranty Cos., various locations, 1952-74; asst. mgr. U.S. Fidelity & Guaranty Cos., Albuquerque, 1963-66; mgr. U.S. Fidelity & Guaranty Cos., San Jose, Calif., 1966-74; v.p. Eldorado Ins. Co., Palo Alto, Calif., 1974-77, exec. v.p., chief operating officer, 1977-78; v.p. Eldorado Mgmt. Co., Palo Alto, Calif., 1973-78, chief operating officer, exec. v.p., 1978; mng. dir. Eldorado Service Corp., 1974-76, exec. v.p., 1976-78; ptnr. Williams Ranch Co., 1977—; owner David S. Williams and Assocs. L.C., 1988—; chmn. bd., pres. Homeland Gen. Corp., Homeland Ins. Co. and Homeland Indsl. Corp., San Jose, Calif., 1978-87; pres. Homeland Mgmt. Corp. (Cayman) Ltd., 1980-87, Homeland Internat. (Bermuda) Ltd., 1982-87; chmn. bd. On Line Ins. Systems, Inc., 1982-92; underwriting mem. Lloyds of London, 1979—; adv. bd. Pacific Valley Bank, 1975-87; tchr. Albuquerque U., 1957-58, N.Mex. U., 1958-59, bd. dirs. Fin. Guardian Group, Inc., Kansas City, Mo., Kestrel Aircraft Co. Mem. indsl. panel Stanford Research Inst., 1968; mgmt. cons. County Santa Clara Edn. Dept., 1968-73; mem. Calif. adv. com. Ins. Services Office; bd. dirs. ins. council City of Hope, Los Angeles; committeeman pioneer council Boy Scouts Am., 1968; pres. Immanuel Luth. Ch., Saratoga, Calif., 1989-90. Served to lt. col. AC U.S. Army, 1944-46, 50-52. Recipient Outstanding Fieldman's award for N.Mex., N.Mex. Insurors Assn., 1959. Mem. Internat. Bar Assn., Cen. Coast Fieldmen's Assn., Assn. Calif. Ins. Cos. (dir.), Sigma Alpha Epsilon. Lutheran. Clubs: San Jose Athletic, Rotary (pres. 1974, Paul Harris fellow 1976); Univ. San Jose, British-Am., Center., San Francisco Comml. Home: 4220 Ridgeline Cir Norman OK 73072-1731

WILLIAMS, DAVID VANDERGRIFT, organizational psychologist; b. Balt., Feb. 5, 1943; s. Laurence Leighton and Mary Duke (Warfield) W.; m. Diane M. Gayeski, Aug. 23, 1980; 1 child, Evan David Williams. BA, Gettysburg (Pa.) Coll., 1965; MA, Temple U., 1967; PhD, U. Pa., 1971. Asst. prof. psychology Ithaca (N.Y.) Coll., 1970-75, assoc. prof. psychology, 1975—; ptnr. OmniCom Assocs., Ithaca, 1979—; co-dir. Inst. Behavior-Econs., Ithaca, 1993—; cons. and speaker in field. Co-author: Interactive Media, 1985, (multimedia comms.), interactive multimedia software, 1979—; contbr. to books and articles to profl. jours. Bd. dirs. Ctr. for Religion, Ethics and Social Policy, Cornell U., 1975-77, Eco-Justice Task Force, Ithaca, 1975-78; trustee Montessori Sch. Ithaca, 1993—; Alternatives Fed. Credit Union, Ithaca, 1994—. Rsch. fellow U.S. Office of Edn., 1967-70; recipient various grants. Mem. APA, Nat. Soc. for Performance and Instrn., Am. Montessori Soc., Welsh Nat. Gymanfa Ganu Assn., Ithaca Yacht Club, Tau Kappa Epsilon. Avocations: singing, sailing, sign language, geneology, travel. Office: OmniCom Assocs 407 Coddington Rd Ithaca NY 14850-6011

WILLIAMS, DAVID WELFORD, federal judge; b. Atlanta, Mar. 20, 1910; s. William W. and Maude (Lee) W.; m. Ouida Maie White, June 11, 1939; children: David Welford, Vaughn Charles. A.A., Los Angeles Jr. Coll., 1932; A.B., UCLA, 1934; LL.B., U. So. Calif., 1937. Bar: Calif. 1937. Practiced in Los Angeles, 1937-55; judge Mcpl. Ct., Los Angeles, 1956-62, Superior Ct., Los Angeles, 1962-69, U.S. Dist. Ct. (cen. dist.) Calif., Los Angeles, 1969—; now sr. judge U.S. Dist. Ct. (cen. dist.) Calif.; judge Los Angeles County Grand Jury, 1965. Recipient Russwurm award Nat. Assn. Newspapers, 1958; Profl. Achievement award UCLA Alumni Assn., 1966. Office: US Dist Ct 255 E Temple St Rm 7100 Los Angeles CA 90012-3334

WILLIAMS, DEBBIE KAYE, optometrist; b. Benham, Ky., Mar. 13, 1960; d. Charles Hughes and Bernice (Knotts) W.; m. Gregory Allen Collins, July 2, 1983 (div. July 1989); re-married, Dec. 28, 1990; 1 child, Arianna Courtney, 1994. AS, U. Louisville, 1980-82, BS, 1985; DO, Ill. Coll. Optometry, 1989. Pvt. practice Whitesburg, Ky., 1989—; cons. LKLP Head Start, Whitesburg, 1991—. Mem. Letcher County Bd. Health, 1993. Mem. Am. Optometric Assn., Ky. Optometric Assn., U. Louisville Alumni Assn., Ill. Coll. of Optometry Alumni Assn., Retinitis Pigmetosa Found. (Letcher county chpt. v.p. 1990-91), Beta Simga Kappa. Democrat. Baptist. Avocations: travel, walking, reading, painting. Home and Office: Dr DK Williams OD PSC 120 River Rd Whitesburg KY 41858-1178

WILLIAMS, DEBRA ARNEICE, computer engineer; b. Toledo, July 14, 1953; d. Albert M. and Doretha (Walls) Carter; m. Clarence Williams, Jr., Feb. 5, 1988; children: Latisha Doretha, El Christopher. Cert. Computer Sci., Davis Bus. Coll., Toledo; Cert. Computer Technology, Control Data Inst., Toledo. Clk. Toledo County Pub. Libr., 1979-85; computer engr. IBM/TSS, Toledo, 1988—. Methodist. Avocations: doll collecting, reading. Office: DC Enterprise Ste 103 39 W Alexis Rd Toledo OH 43612-3601

WILLIAMS, DELWYN CHARLES, telephone company executive; b. Idaho Falls, Idaho, Apr. 27, 1936; s. Charles H. and Vonda (Wood) W.; m. Marlene Grace Nordland, Feb. 29, 1964; children—Stephen, Kirstin, Nicole. B.S. in Bus., U. Idaho, 1959. C.P.A., Calif. Accountant Peat, Marwick, Mitchell & Co. (C.P.A.s), San Francisco, 1960-65; treas. Dohrmann Instruments Co., Mountain View, Calif., 1965-68; with Continental Telephone Co. of Calif., Bakersfield, 1968-84; controller Continental Telephone Co. of Calif., 1969-70, v.p., treas., 1970-77, v.p., gen. mgr., 1977-79, pres., 1977-84, also dir.; pres. J.H. Evans, Inc., and subs., 1984-95; CEO J.H. Evans, Inc., and sbus., 1995—. Mem. Am. Inst. C.P.A.s, Calif. Soc. C.P.A.s. Home: 10052 Oak Branch Cir Carmel CA 93923-8000 Office: 4918 Taylor Ct Turlock CA 95382-9579

WILLIAMS, DIANE ANITA, computer scientist, systems analyst; b. St. Louis, Aug. 1, 1961; d. Samuel and Wanda Anita (Greenwood) W.; m. Quintin Todd Agnew, May 5, 1982; children: Quintin Todd Agnew II, Amber Iman Williams, Mariah Williams. BS in Computer Sci., U. Mo., St. Louis, 1984; postgrad., Washington U., St. Louis, 1990—. Programmer U. Mo., 1983-85, AT&T Network Systems, Ballwin, Mo., 1985-87; system developer AT&T Bell Labs., Naperville, Ill., 1988-90; systems analyst Southwestern Bell Telephone, St. Louis, 1990—; cons. Metro Ministries, St. Louis, 1985-86; cons. sci. fair Chgo. Pub. Schs., 1988-90. Mentor, tchr. Jr. Achievement, St. Louis, 1992—. Recipient Nova Achievement award, 1994. Mem. Nat. Tech. Assn., Sisters in the Spirit, Phi Beta Kappa, Delta Sigma Theta, Phi Theta Kappa. Roman Catholic. Avocations: golf, tennis, writing, sewing. Office: Southwestern Bell Telephone 25 D5 One Bell Ctr Saint Louis MO 63101

WILLIAMS, DONALD CLYDE, lawyer; b. Oxnard, Calif., Oct. 12, 1939; s. Leslie Allen and Elizabeth Esther (Orton) W.; m. Miriam Arline, Oct. 5, 1966; children—Erin K., Nikki Dawn. B.A. in Gen. Bus, Fresno State Coll., 1963; J.D., Willamette U., 1967. Bar: Oreg. 1967. Practice in Grants Pass, 1967-70; ptnr. Myrick, Seagraves, Williams & Nealy, 1968-70, Carlsmith, Ball, Wichman, Murray & Ichiki, 1977—; asst. atty. gen. Am. Samoa, 1970-71, atty. gen., 1971-75; assoc. justice High Ct. Trust Ter. of Pacific Islands, 1975-77. Served with USCGR, 1958-59. Mem. ABA, Calif. Bar Assn., Oreg. Bar Assn., Am. Samoa Bar Assn., Guam Bar Assn., Hawaii Bar Assn., Commonwealth No. Mariana Islands Bar Assn., Fed. States of Micronesia Bar Assn., Guam C. of C., Long Beach C. of C. Office: Carlsmith Ball Wichman & Ichiki 555 S Flower 25th Fl Los Angeles CA 90071-2326

WILLIAMS, DONALD HERBERT, psychiatric educator; b. Chgo., Oct. 29, 1936; s. Herbert George and Theresa Elizabeth (Pratt) W.; m. Beverly Joann Wagner, Oct. 11, 1968 (div. 1981); 1 child, David; m. Sharon Rebecca Hobbs, June 18, 1983; children: Jonathan, Rebecca. BA cum laude, U. Ill., Urbana, 1957; MD, U. Ill., Chgo., 1962. Intern U. Ill. Research and Ednl. Hosps., Chgo., 1962-63, resident in anesthesiology, 1963-64, resident in psychiatry, 1964-67; instr., then asst. prof. psychiatry U. Chgo., Chgo., 1967-71; asst. prof. psychiatry Yale U., New Haven, Conn., 1971-77, assoc. prof., 1977-84; prof. Mich. State U., East Lansing, 1984—, chmn. dept. psychiatry, 1984-89; chief mental health sect. Woodlawn Mental Health Ctr., Chgo., 1967-70; chief inpatient service Hill-West Haven div. Conn. Mental Health Ctr., New Haven, 1971-73, head med. evaluation com., 1973-78, chief community support services, 1973-79, asst. dir. out-patient div., 1979-84; staff, liason psychiat. services West Haven VA Hosp. 1971-80; head liason team Conn. Valley Hosp., 1973-79; med. dir. Eaton, Clinton and Ingham Community Mental Health Ctr., Lansing, 1984-87; cons. psychiatry edm br., faculty NIMH, Rockville, Md., 1971-81; mem. task panel Pres.' Commn. on Mental Health, Washington, 1978; speaker in field. Referee Archives Gen.

Psychiatry, Am. Jour. Psychiatry, Soc. Psychiatry, Hosp. and Community Psychiatry; contbr. articles to profl. jours. Served to capt. M.C. U.S Army, 1963-68. Recipient Ill. Psychiat. Soc. award, 1968. Fellow Am Psychiat. Assn.; mem. Black Psychiatrists Am. (treas. 1978-80), Am. Orthopsychiat. Assn., Nat. Med. Assn., AMA, Omega Beta Pi. Democrat. Episcopalian. Office: Mich State U Dept Psychiatry East Fee Hall East Lansing MI 48824

WILLIAMS, DONALD JOHN, research physicist; b. Fitchburg, Mass., Dec. 25, 1933; s. Toivo John and Ina (Kokkinen) W.; m. Priscilla Mary Gagnon, July 4, 1953; children: Steven John, Craig Mitchell, Eino Stenroos. B.S., Yale U., 1955, M.S., 1958, Ph.D., 1962. Sr. staff physicist Applied Physics Lab., Johns Hopkins U., 1961-65; head particle physics br. Goddard Space Flight Center, NASA, 1965-70; dir. Space Environ. Lab., NOAA, Boulder, Colo., 1970-82; prin. investigator Energetic Particles expt. NASA Galileo Mission, 1977—; prin. staff physicist Johns Hopkins U. Applied Physics Lab., 1982-89, dir. Milton S. Eisenhower Rsch. Ctr., 1990—; mem. nat. and internat. sci. planning coms.; chmn. NAS com. on solar-terrestrial rsch., 1989-93; mem. sci. adv. bd. USAF, 1993—. Author: (with L.R. Lyons) Quantitative Aspects of Magnetospheric Physics, 1983; assoc. editor: Jour. Geophys. Research, 1967-69, Revs. of Geophysics and Space Research, 1984-86; editor: (with G.D. Mead) Physics of the Magnetosphere, 1969, Physics of Solar-Planetary Environments, 1976; mem. editorial bd.: Space Sci. Revs., 1975-85; contbr. articles to profl. jours. Mem. USAF Sci. Adv. Bd., 1994—. Lt. USAF, 1955-57. Recipient Sci. Research award, 1974; Disting. Authorship award, 1976, 85. Fellow Am. Geophys. Soc.; mem. Am. Phys. Soc., Internat. Assn. Geomagnetism and Aeronomy (pres. 1991-95), Sigma Xi. Home: 14870 Triadelphia Rd Glenelg MD 21737

WILLIAMS, DONALD MAXEY, dancer, singer, actor; b. Chgo., June 23, 1959; s. Arlandus Maxey and Florida (Jelks) W. Student, pub. schs., Chgo. Prin. dancer Dancer Theatre of Harlem, N.Y.C., 1977—. Dancer in movie Cotton Club, 1983-84. Mem. Am. Guild Mus. Artists, Screen Actors Guild. Baptist. Club: The Sevens (co-founder). Avocations: basketball; bowling; table tennis. Office: Dance Theatre of Harlem 466 W 152nd St New York NY 10031-1814

WILLIAMS, DONALD SPENCER, scientist; b. Pasadena, Calif., May 28, 1939; s. Charles Gardner and Delia Ruth (Spencer) W. BS, Harvey Mudd Coll., 1961; MS, Carnegie Inst. Tech., 1962; PhD, Carnegie-Mellon U., 1969. Asst. project dir. Learning Rsch. & Devel. Ctr., Pitts., 1965-67; cons. system design, Pitts., 1967-69; mem. tech. staff RCA Corp., Palo Alto, Calif., 1969-72; prin. investigator robot vision Jet Propulsion Lab., Calif. Inst. Tech., Pasadena, 1972-80; chief engr. oper. TRW, Inc., Redondo Beach, 1980—; cons. system design, 1984—. Japan Econ. Found. grantee, 1981. Mem. AAAS, Assn. Computing Machinery, Audio Engring. Soc., Nat. Fire Protection Assn., IEEE, Soc. Motion Picture & TV Engrs., Town Hall Calif. Contbr. articles to profl. jours. Home: PO Box 40700 Pasadena CA 91114-7700 Office: TRW Inc 1 Space Park Dr Redondo Beach CA 90278-1001

WILLIAMS, DOYLE Z., university dean, educator; b. Shreveport, La., Dec. 18, 1939; s. Nuell O. and Lurline (Isbell) W.; m. Maynette Derr, Aug. 20, 1967; children: Zane Derr, Elizabeth Marie. B.S., Northwestern State U., 1960; M.S. in Acctg., La. State U., 1962, Ph.D., 1965. CPA, Tex. Mgr. spl. edn. projects AICPA, N.Y.C., 1967-69; assoc. prof. Tex. Tech. U., Lubbock, 1969-71, prof. acctg., 1972-73, prof. area acctg., coord., 1973-78; prof. acctg. U. So. Calif., L.A., 1978-93, dean Sch. Acctg., 1979-87, interim dean Sch. Bus., 1986-88; dean U. Ark. Coll. Bus. Adminstrn., Fayetteville, 1993—; vis. prof. U. Hawaii, Honolulu, 1971-72. Author over 40 jour. articles and books. Chmn. Acctg. Edn. Change Commn., 1989-93. Named Mem. of Yr. N.Y. chpt. Nat. Assn. Accts., 1967, Outstanding Acctg. Educator Beta Alpha Psi, 1982; recipient Disting. Faculty award Calif. CPA Found., 1983, Nat. Leadership award Acad. Bus. Adminstrs., 1995. Mem. AICPA (coun. 1983-91, v.p. 1987-88, bd. dirs. 1987-91, Outstanding Educator award 1990), Am. Acctg. Assn. (dir. edn. 1973-75, pres. 1984-85), Fedn. Schs. Accountancy (pres. 1982, Faculty Merit award 1993), Adminstrs. Acctg. Programs (pres. 1977-78). Home: 2447 Boston Mountain Vw Fayetteville AR 72701-2802 Office: Coll Bus Adminstrn U Ark Fayetteville AR 72701

WILLIAMS, DREW DAVIS, surgeon; b. San Augustine, Tex., Jan. 18, 1935; s. Floyd Everett and Villamae (Morehead) W.; m. Marilyn Raus, June 27, 1958; children: Leslie, Cynthia, Matthew, Jennifer, Amelia. BS, Tex. A&M Coll., 1957; MD, U. Tex., 1960; grad., naval flight surgeon, U.S. Naval Sch. Aviation Medicine, Jan.-June, 1963. Diplomate Am. Bd. Surgery, Am. Bd. Quality Assurance and Utilization Rev. Physicians. Intern USPHS Hosp., Seattle, 1960-61; resident in gen. surgery U. Tex. Med. Br., Galveston, 1961-62, 64-68; resident pulmonary svc. M.D. Anderson Hosp., Houston, 3 months, 1968; pvt. practice gen. surgery Baytown, Tex., 1968—; active staff San Jacinto (Tex.) Meth. Hosp., 1968-95, chief of surgery, 1972, 73, pres. med. staff, 1976; mem. courtesy staff Bay Coast Hosp., Baytown, 1968-95; cons. staff Baytown Med. Ctr. Hosp., 1972-95; 1st chmn. dept. surgery in devel. of family practice residency program affiliated with Tex. Med. Sch., Houston, 1977; mem. Tex. State Bd. Med. Examiners, 1983-89, sec.-treas., 1984-88, pres., 1988-89; unit med. dir., clin. instr. dept. preventive medicine and cmty. health U. Tex. Med. Br., Galveston, 1995—. Contbr. articles to med. publs. Flight surgeon USN, 1962-64; lt. comdr. USNR, ret., 1967. Am. Cancer Soc. clin. fellow, 1966-67. Fellow ACS, AMA (Physicians Recognition award), Tex. Med. Assn.; mem. Tex. Med. Found. (fed. peer rev. group), Houston Surg. Soc. (pres. 1994), Southwestern Surg. Congress, Tex. Surg. Soc., Singleton Surg. Soc. (past pres.), Harris County Med. Soc. (chmn. coun. med. splty., mem. exec. bd. 1994), East Harris County Med. Soc. (pres. 1982), Baytown Surg. Soc., Sir William Osler Soc., Am. Cancer Soc. (pres. Baytown chpt. 1970-71), Sons of Republic Tex. (at large life), SAR (past pres. local chpt.), Soc. Descendents of Colonial Clergy, Magna Carta Barons (Somerset chpt.), Colonial Order of the Crown, Sovereign Colonial Soc.-Ams. of Royal Descent, Masons (32 degree), Shriners, KT, Gideons Internat., Phi Beta Pi. Democrat. Mem. Ch. of Christ. Avocations: gardening, hunting, fishing, genealogy, golf. Home and Office: 1217 Kilgore Rd Baytown TX 77520-3912

WILLIAMS, EARLE CARTER, retired professional services company executive; b. Selma, Ala., Oct. 15, 1929; s. Henry Earle and Nora Elizabeth (Carter) W.; m. June Esther Anson, Sept. 7, 1951; children: Gayle Marie, Carol Patrice, Sharon Elaine. B.E.E., Auburn U., 1951; postgrad., U. N.Mex., 1959-62; DSc (hon.), Auburn U., 1991. Registered profl. engr., N.Mex. Utilities design engr. Standard Oil Co. Ind., Whiting, 1954-56; mem. tech. staff Sandia Corp., Albuquerque, 1956-62; sr. engr. BDM Internat., Inc., El Paso, Tex., 1962-64, spl. projects dir., 1964-66, dir. ops., 1966-68; v.p., gen. mgr. BDM Internat., Inc., Vienna, Va., 1968-72; pres., CEO, BDM Internat., Inc., Vienna and McLean, Va., 1972-92, bd. dirs., 1972—; ret. as CEO, BDM Internat. Inc., Vienna and McLean, Va., 1992; bd. dirs. Parsons Corp., Nortel Fed. Sys., Inc., GTS Duratek, Inc., Gamma-A Techs., Inc.; mem. Naval Rsch. Adv. Com., 1984-90, chmn., 1986-90; dir. Am. Bus. Conf., 1985-88. Exec. com., steering com. El Paso C.C., 1968-69, trustee, 1969-70; commr. Fairfax County Econ. Devel. Authority, 1976-80, chmn., 1978-80; mem. Va. State Bd. for C.C., 1980-87; bd. dirs. Ctrl. Va. Ednl. TV Corp., 1978-87, The Atlantic Coun. of the U.S., 1987—; chmn. George Mason Inst. Indsl. Policy Bd., 1982-91; bd. dirs. Wolf Trap Found., 1984-92, vice chmn., 1985-87, chmn., 1988-90, emeritus dir., 1992—; trustee Va. Found. for Ind. Colls., 1984-87, 90-94, Flint Hill Sch., Oakton, Va., 1990-95, George Mason U. Found., 1987—, Auburn U. Found., 1991—; bd. dirs. Potomac KnowledgeWay Project, 1995—; mem. Va. Bus. Higher Edn. Coun., 1995—. With AUS, 1951-53. Recipient Engr. of Yr. award Va. Soc. Profl. Engrs., 1989, Superior Pub. Svc. award Dept. Navy, 1990; named to Ala. Engring. Hall of Fame, 1994. Mem. NSPE, Profl. Svcs. Coun. (bd. dirs. 1974-92, emeritus bd. dirs. 1992—, pres. 1976-79), Armed Force Comm. and Electronics Assn. (bd. dirs. 1978-82, 86-87, permanent dir. 1990, internat. v.p. 1979-82, 84-85, chmn. 1988-90, Disting. Svc. award 1987), Coun. on Fgn. Rels., Fairfax County C. of C. (bd. dirs. 1978-86), City Club (D.C.), Met. Club (D.C.), Tower Club (Vienna, Va.), Bay Colony Club (Naples, Fla.), Eta Kappa Nu. Presbyterian.

WILLIAMS, EDDIE NATHAN, research institution executive; b. Memphis, Aug. 18, 1932; s. Ed and Georgia Lee (Barr) W.; m. Jearline F. Reddick, July 18, 1981; children: Traci Lynne, Edward Lawrence, Terence Reddick. BS, U. Ill., 1954; postgrad., Atlanta U., 1957, Howard U., 1960; LLD (hon.), U. D.C., 1986; DHL, Bowie State Coll., 1980, Chgo. State U., 1994. Reporter Atlanta Daily World Newspaper, 1957-58; staff asst. U.S. Senate Com. on Fgn. Relations, Washington, 1959-60; fgn. service res. officer U.S. Dept. State, Washington, 1961-68; v.p. U. Chgo., 1968-72; pres. Joint Ctr. for Polit. and Econ. Studies, Washington, 1972—; vice chmn. Black Leadership Forum, 1996; bd. dirs. Harrah's Entertainment, Inc., The Riggs Nat. Bank Washington, Blue Cross Blue Shield Nat. Capital Area, LeMoyne-Owen Coll.; advisor Ctrs. for Disease Control, 1992—. Editorial columnist: Chgo. Sun Times, 1970-72; contbr. articles to profl. jours. Bd. dirs. Nat. Opinion Rsch. Ctr., 1992—; chmn. Pew Partnerships for Civic Change, 1993—. Am. Polit. Sci. Assn. fellow, 1958, MacArthur Found. fellow, 1988, Nat. Acad. Pub. Adminstrn. fellow, 1993; recipient Adam Clayton Powell Award Congl. Black Caucus, 1981, Washingtonian of Yr. award Washingtonian Mag., 1991, Nation Builder award Nat. Black Caucus of State Legislators, 1993, Outstanding Leadership award Korean Am. Alliance, 1994. Mem. Coun. Fgn. Rels., Kappa Tau Alpha, Omega Psi Phi, Sigma Pi Phi. Office: Joint Ctr Polit & Econ Studies 1090 Vermont Ave NW Ste 1100 Washington DC 20005-4905

WILLIAMS, EDGAR GENE, university administrator; b. Posey County, Ind., May 4, 1922; s. Noley Wesley and Anna Lena (Wilsey) W.; m. Joyce Ellen Grigsby, May 7, 1944; children: Cynthia Ellen Williams Mahigian, Thomas Gene. A.B., Evansville Coll., 1947; M.B.A., Ind. U., 1948, D.B.A., 1952. Instr. Ind. U., Bloomington, 1948-52; asst. prof. Ind. U., 1952-55, assoc. prof., 1955-58, prof. bus. adminstrn., 1958—, assoc. dean, 1965-69, v.p., 1974-88, now emeritus. Bd. dirs. Found. for Sch. of Bus., Ind. U., Bloomington, 1966—, Bloomington Community Found.. Served with U.S. Army, 1943-46. Mem. Beta Gamma Sigma. Democrat. Methodist. Clubs: Masons, Bloomington Country. Home: 1126 E 1st St Bloomington IN 47401-5076

WILLIAMS, EDNA DORIS, retired educational administrator; b. Bronson, Iowa, July 26, 1908; d. Franklin James and Sarah Jane (Hunt) W. BA, U. No. Iowa, 1939; MA, U. Minn., 1947; postgrad., U. S.D., 1955-60, U. Iowa, 1957, 59, 60, U. Minn., 1951, 67, 69. Cert. adminstr., guidance counselor. Rural sch. tchr. Eurikia # 8, Sac County Rural Schs., Schaller, Iowa, 1929-30; tchr. grades 5 and 6 Bronson (Iowa) Consolidated Sch., 1931-38; normal tng. and English tchr. Rockwell City (Iowa) High Sch., 1939-44; history and debate tchr. Ames (Iowa) High Sch., 1944-47; dramatics and English tchr. East High, Sioux City (Iowa) Community Sch. Dist., 1947-51; dean of girls Central High, Sioux City Community Sch. Dist., 1951-52, East High, Sioux City Community Sch. Dist., 1952-67; asst. prin. East Sioux City Community Sch. Dist., 1967-72, asst. prin. North, 1972-73; cons., chmn. course of study in Am. history Iowa State Dept. Pub. Instrn., Des Moines, 1947-48; demonstration tchr. State Dept. Pub. Instrn., 1957; demonstration tchr. Woodbury County Supt., 1958; student coun. workshop adviser, mem. staff Iowa Assn. Student Couns., Cedar Falls, 1960-63; rep. of dist. Coll. Entrance Exam. Bd., 1950-73; advisor N.W. Coun. Student Coun., 1960-64; mem. exec. bd. N.W. Guidance Coun., 1965-66. Editor: (course book and handbook, high schs.) Ednl. Opportunities, 1968-69; author, editor: Food for Thought Yesterday Today and Tomorrow, 1987; author choral reading plays. Tax aide vol. IRS, Sioux City, 1979-86, 87-91; vol. Iowa Commn. for the Blind; chmn. of com. Sioux City Women's Club, pres. Sioux City Adminstrn. Club, 1957-58; circle chmn. United Meth. Women, 1978. Named one of 100 Counselors in U.S. Selected as a Guest, MIT, 1958, 1 of 30 Counselors as Guest of 6 Minn. Colls., 1966; recipient Cert. of Appreciation, Dir. Student Couns. in Iowa, 1963, Gov.'s Vol. award State of Iowa, 1989, Cert. Dedicated Svc. Am. Assn. Retired Persons, 1990. Mem. NEA (life), Iowa Assn. Women Deans and Counselors (state pres. 1961-62), Iowa State Edn. Assn. (life), Nat. Ret. Tchrs. Assn. (award from Iowa div., Cert. of Appreciation 1986), Sioux City Ret. Educators (life, pres. 1985-88), AAUW (life, treas. 1981-82, v.p. 1984-85, Cert. for Significant Svc. to Ednl. Found. 1981-82, 82-83, chair career women study group), Northern Iowa Alumni Assn., U. Minn. Alumni Assn. (life mem.). Methodist. Avocations: writing, making visual aids, sewing, gardening, reading.

WILLIAMS, EDSON POE, retired automotive company executive; b. Mpls., July 31, 1923; s. Homer A. and Florence C. Williams; m. Irene Mae Streed, June 16, 1950; children: Thomas, Louise, Steven, Linnea, Elisa. B.S.M.E. cum laude, U. Minn., 1950. Spl. purpose machinery operator, 1946-50; mfg. mgr., project engr. Crestliner div. Bigelow Sanford Inc., 1950-53, v.p., mgr. mfg. and engring., 1953-58, pres., 1958-63; with Ford Motor Co., 1963-87, mgr. customer svc. div., 1973; gen. mgr. Ford Motor Co. (Ford Mexico), 1973-75; pres. Ford Motor Co. (Ford Mid-East & Africa), 1975-79, Ford Motor Co. (Ford Asia-Pacific Inc.), 1979-87; v.p. Ford Motor Co., 1979-82, v.p.-gen. mgr. N.Am. truck ops., 1982-86, v.p. Ford Diversified Products ops., 1986-87. Served with USAAF, 1942-46. Mem. Naples Yacht and Sailing Club. Home: 688 21st Ave S Naples FL 33940-7610

WILLIAMS, EDWARD, textile executive; b. 1943. With E & B Carpet Mills, 1964-70; western divsnl. mgr. Galaxy Carpet Mills, 1970-73; pres., owner N.Am. Carpet Corp. (acquired by Galaxy Carpet Mills in 1986), 1973-89; officer Galaxy Carpet Mills, Chatsworth, Ga., 1986—, pres., chief operating officer. Office: Mohawk Industries PO Box 12069 Calhoun GA 30703

WILLIAMS, EDWARD DAVID, consulting executive; b. Scranton, Pa., June 20, 1932; s. David Thomas and Mabel (Sims) W. m. Natalie Imnadze, Oct. 18, 1952; children: Denise, Claudia. BBA, Hofstra U., 1960; postgrad. in Bus. Adminstrn., Fairleigh Dickenson U., 1979. Cons. Cresap, McCormick and Paget, N.Y.C., 1964-65; sr. mgmt. cons. Union Carbide Corp., N.Y.C., 1965-67; asst. contr. data processing Western Union, N.Y.C., 1967-69; v.p. mgmt. info. systems ABC, Hackensack, N.J., 1970-86; v.p., chief info. officer Blue Cross Blue Shield of N.J., Newark, 1986-88; v.p. Chantico Pub. Co., Carrellton, Tex., 1989-90; pres. SMC-BIS Inc., Basking Ridge, N.J., 1990-93; pres., CEO Strategic Outsourcing Svcs. Inc., Mountain Lakes, N.J., 1993—; speaker in field. Mem. adv. bd. YMCA. With U.S. Army, 1948-52. Decorated Silver Star with oak leaf cluster, Bronze Star with V, Purple Heart with 2 oak leaf clusters. Mem. Soc. Mgmt. Info. Systems, N.J. C. of C., Profit Oriented Systems Planning Bd. (bd. dirs.), Masons. Republican. Office: Strategic Outsourcing Svcs 49 Old Bloomfield Ave Mountain Lakes NJ 07046-1449

WILLIAMS, EDWARD EARL, JR., entrepreneur, educator; b. Houston, Aug. 21, 1945; s. Edward Earl and Doris Jewel (Jones) W.; m. Susan M. Warren, June 28, 1983; children: Laura Michelle, David Brian. BS, U. Pa., 1966; PhD, U. Tex., 1968. Asst. prof. econs. Rutgers U., New Brunswick, N.J., 1968-70; assoc. prof. fin. McGill U., Montreal, Que., Can., 1970-73; v.p., economist Service Corp. Internat., Houston, 1973-77; prof. adminstrv. sci. Rice U., Houston, 1978-82, Henry Gardiner Symonds prof., 1982—, prof. stats., 1995—; chmn. bd. Edward E. Williams & Co., Houston, 1976-92; chmn. bd., pres. Tex. Capital Investment Co., 1979—; chmn. bd. First Tex. Venture Capital Corp., 1983-92; mng. dir. First Tex. Venture Capital, LLC, 1992—; dir. Video Rental of Pa. Inc., Svc. Corp. Internat, EQUUS II, Inc. Benjamin Franklin scholar, Jesse Jones scholar, U. Pa., 1966, Tex. Savs. and Loan League fellow, NDEA fellow, U. Tex., 1968. Mem. Am. Statis. Assn., Coll. Innovation Mgmt. and Entrepreneurship, Fin. Mgmt. Assn., Beta Gamma Sigma, Alpha Kappa Psi. Author: Prospects for the Savins and Loan Industry, 1968, An Integrated Analysis for Managerial Finance, 1970, Investment Analysis, 1974, Business Planning for the Entrepreneur, 1983, The Economics of Production and Productivity: A Modeling Approach, 1996; contbr. articles to profl. jours. Home: 7602 Wilton Park Dr Spring TX 77379-4672 Office: Rice U Jesse H Jones Grad Sch Adminstrn Houston TX 77251

WILLIAMS, EDWARD F(OSTER), III, environmental engineer; b. N.Y.C., Jan. 3, 1935; s. E. Foster Jr. and Ida Frances (Richards) W.; m. Sue Carol Osenbaugh, June 5, 1960; children: Cecile Elizabeth, Alexander Harmon. BS in Engring., Auburn U., 1956; MA in History, U. Memphis, 1974. Registered profl. engr., Tenn. Engr. Buckeye Cellulose Corp. (subs. of Procter & Gamble), Memphis, 1957, process safety engr., 1960; resident constrn. engr. Buckeye Cellulose Corp. (subs. of Procter & Gamble), Perry, Fla., 1960-61; staff engr. Buckeye Cellulose Corp. (subs. of Procter & Gamble), Memphis, 1961-70; chief engr., v.p. Enviro-trol, Inc., Memphis, 1970-73; v.p., then pres. Ramcon Environ. Corp., Memphis, 1973-80; pres. E.F. Williams & Assocs., Inc., Memphis, 1980—, EFW Comml. Ventures Inc., 1990—; bd. dirs. Mobile Process Tech. Inc., Memphis; v.p. Environ. Testing and Cons., Inc., Memphis, 1985-94; environ. coord. Shelby County, Tenn., 1995-96. Author: Fustest with the Mostest, 1968, Early Memphis and Its River Rivals, 1969; editor Environ. Control News for So. Industry, 1971—. State rep. Tenn. Gen. Assembly, 1970-78; mem. Shelby County Bd. Commrs., Memphis, 1978-94, chmn., 1987-88, 90-92; mem. Shelby County Records Commn., 1978—, chmn., 1993—; environ. coord. Shelby County Mayor's staff, 1995-96; trustee Bolton Coll., 1982—, chmn., 1987-88, 90-92; del. Rep. Nat. Conv., 1988, 92, 96, Rep. state exec. com., 1994—; state chmn. Nat. Conf. Rep. County Ofcls., 1993—; vice-chmn. Memphis-Shelby local Emergency Planning Com., 1986—; bd. dirs. Better Bus. Bur., Memphis, 1995—. Capt. USAF, 1957-60. Named Tenn. Water Conservationist of Yr., Tenn. Conservation League, 1973, Tenn. Legis. Conservationist of Yr., Nat. Wildlife Fedn., 1974, Memphis Outstanding Engr., Memphis Joint Engrs. Coun., 1980; recipient Shelby County Environ. Improvement award, 1983, Tenn. Lifetime Environ. award Tenn. Dept. Environ. and Conservation, 1995. Mem. NSPE, ASME, Am. Acad. Environ. Engrs. (diplomate), Water Environ. Fedn., Am. Indsl. Hygiene Assn. (chpt. pres.), Am. Soc. Safety Engrs. (outstanding achievement award 1995-96), Air and Waste Mgmt. Assn., Engrs. Club Memphis (bd. dirs. 1979-80), Rotary, C. of C. (environ. coun. chmn. 1988—), Tenn. Hist. Soc. (v.p. 1972), Tenn. Hist. Commn. (vice chmn. 1987—), West Tenn. Hist. Soc. (pres. 1983-85), Am. Hist. Assn. Republican. Presbyterian. Avocation: history. Home: 148 Perkins Ext Memphis TN 38117-3127 Office: EF Williams & Assocs 751 E Brookhaven Cir Memphis TN 38117-4501 also: PO Box 241813 Memphis TN 38124-1813 *It has been my observation that history does not repeat itself, but human nature does. Knowledge of this principle can be put to use in politics, business, and other endeavors if one knows history.*

WILLIAMS, EDWARD GILMAN, retired banker; b. Ware, Mass., Apr. 11, 1926; s. Carl Emmons and Susan Helen (Gilman) W.; m. Barbara Thompson Russell, June 19, 1959; children: Thomas Clarke, Susan Gilman. B.A., Trinity Coll., Conn., 1950. With Union Trust Co., New Haven, 1951-89; asst. trust officer Union & New Haven Trust Co., 1956-59, trust officer, 1959-64, v.p., 1964-65, v.p., sr. adminstrv. officer, 1965-69; sr. v.p. Union Trust Co., 1969-72, exec. v.p., 1972-89; v.p. Northeast Bancorp., Inc., 1972-89. Former treas. Leila Day Nurseries, Inc., New Haven; treas., pres. Ridge Rd. Sch. PTA, Hamden Hall Country Day Sch. Parents Assn.; bd. dirs. Vis. Nurse Assn., New Haven, 1963-86, pres., treas., 1970-75; trustee New Eng. Sch. Banking, 1971-74, 81-88, vice chmn., 1985-86, chmn. 1986-88; trustee Shubert Performing Arts Ctr., New Haven, 1985-90; bd. dirs. New Haven Colony Hist. Soc., 1987-89; trustee, deacon, chmn. music com. Ch. of Redeemer, New Haven; bd. dirs., treas. Edgerton Garden Ctr., 1992—; bd. dirs. Easter Seals Goodwill Rehab. Ctr., New Haven, 1993—. Mem. English-Speaking Union (treas. New Haven chpt. 1994—), New Haven Lawn Club (pres. 1979-82), Masons. Home: 900 Mix Ave Apt 17 Hamden CT 06514-5107 Office: 3074 Whitney Ave # 3-10 Hamden CT 06518-2324

WILLIAMS, EDWARD JOSEPH, banker; b. Chgo., May 5, 1942; s. Joseph and Lillian (Watkins) W.; children from previous marriage: Elaine, Paul; m. Ana J. Ortiz, Apr. 20, 1996. BBA, Roosevelt U., 1973. Owner Mut. Home Delivery, Chgo., 1961-63; exec. v.p. Harris Trust and Savs. Bank, Chgo., 1964—; mem. Consumer Adv. Council, Washington, 1986—. Trustee Adler Planetarium, Chgo., 1982, Roosevelt U., Chgo.; chmn. Provident Med. Ctr., Chgo., 1986; bd. dirs. Voices for Ill. Children, Chgo. Coun. on Urban Affairs; pres. Neighborhood Housing Svcs. Recipient Disting. Alumni award Clark Coll., Atlanta, 1985. Mem. Nat. Bankers Assn., Urban Bankers Forum (Pioneer award 1986), Econ. Club. Chgo. Clubs: Metropolitan, Plaza (Chgo.). Office: Harris Trust & Savs Bank 111 W Monroe St Chicago IL 60603-4003

WILLIAMS, EDWARD VINSON, music history educator; b. Orlando, Fla., July 12, 1935. B.M., Fla. State U., 1957; M.M., Ind. U., 1962; M.A., Yale U., 1966, Ph.D., 1968. Prof. music history dept. music U. Kans., Lawrence, 1969-90, chmn. dept. music history, 1975-84; assoc. dean rsch. and grad. studies Coll. Arts and Architecture, prof. music Pa. State U., University Park, Pa., 1990—. Author: The Bells of Russia: History and Technology, 1985. Served with U.S. Army, 1957-60. Recipient Chancellor's award for Excellence in Teaching, U. Kans., 1975; Kennan Inst. fellow Wilson Ctr., Washington, 1985; fellow Nat. Humanities Ctr., Research Triangle Park, N.C., 1980-81. Mem. Am. Musicological Soc., Am. Assn. for Advancement Slavic Studies, Assn. Bell Art (Moscow). Home: 330 Toftrees Ave Apt 149 State College PA 16803-2043 Office: Pa State U Coll Arts and Architecture 115 Arts Bldg University Park PA 16802-2900

WILLIAMS, EDWIN NEEL, newspaper editor; b. Rives, Mo., Jan. 14, 1942; s. Carl Edwin and Vina Marie (Edmonston) W.; m. Marylyn Lentine, 1973; 1 child, Jonathan Lentine. BA in History, U. Miss., 1965. Reporter Clarksdale (Miss) Press-Register, 1965; reporter, editor Delta Dem.-Times, Greenville, Miss., 1967-72; Nieman fellow Harvard U., Cambridge, Mass., 1972-73; writer, researcher Ford Found., N.Y.C., 1973; editorial writer Charlotte (N.C.) Observer, 1973-76, editor of editorial pages, 1976-80, 87—. Chmn. KinderMourn, Charlotte, 1988, N.C. Harvest, 1993-94; bd. dirs. N.C. Ctr. for Pub. Policy Rsch., Raleigh, 1992-95. With U.S. Army, 1965-67. Baptist. Home: 916 Mount Vernon Ave Charlotte NC 28203-4845 Office: Charlotte Observer PO Box 30308 Charlotte NC 28230-0308

WILLIAMS, EDWIN WILLIAM, publisher; b. N.Y.C., May 3, 1912; s. William and Amelia W.; m. Doris O. Smith, June 3, 1953 (div.); children: Edwina, Andrew; m. Alma Davies Kaye, June 22, 1985. Student, Columbia U., 1930. Publisher Quick Frozen Foods Internat. mag., N.Y.C., 1938—, Pvt. Label mag., 1979—, PL Internat. and PL Directories and Newsletter; pres. Pioneer Assocs., Inc., North Bergen, N.J., 1972—, E.W. Publns. Co., N.Y.C., 1940—, Williams Electric Co., Shelby, N.C., 1970—; owner Columbia Pub. Co. N.Y., 1995—; organizer frozen food industry directories and convs., speaker in field. Author: Frozen Foods, Biography of an Industry, 1969; co-author: Private Labels. Chmn. Dept. Commerce mission to Eastern countries. Recipient award ICA, 1956, award Internat. Assn. Refrigerated Warehouses, 1960, Presdl. E award 1962, Man of Yr. award Food Divsn. Nat. Conf. Christians and Jews, 1995. Mem. Am. Frozen Food Inst., Pvt. Label Mfrs. Assn. (founder), Advt. Club N.Y.C., Oversees Press Club (N.Y.C.), Princeton Club. Republican. Home: 8200 Boulevard E North Bergen NJ 07047-6039 Office: 2125 Center Ave Fort Lee NJ 07024-5859 *If a man early in his career carves his dream like a sculptor on the unyielding stone of life, with many a sharp incision, he is bound to reach his goal; he has caught the angel vision.*

WILLIAMS, ELEANOR JOYCE, government air traffic control specialist; b. College Station, Tex., Dec. 21, 1936; d. Robert Ira and Viola (Ford) Toliver; m. Tollie Williams, Dec. 30, 1955 (div. July 1978); children: Rodrick, Viola Williams Smith, Darryl, Eric, Dana Williams Jones, Sheila Williams Watkins, Kenneth. Student Prairie View A&M Coll., 1955-56, Anchorage Community Coll., 1964-65, U. Alaska-Anchorage, 1976. Clk./stenographer FAA, Anchorage, 1965-66, adminstrv. clk., 1966-67, pers. staffing asst., 1967-68, air traffic control specialist, 1968-79, air traffic contr. supr., San Juan, P.R., 1979-80, Anchorage, 1983-85, airspace specialist, Atlanta, 1980-83 ; with FAA, Washington, 1985-87; area mgr. Kansas City Air Rt. Traffic Control Ctr., Olathe, Kans., 1987-89, asst. mgr. quality Assurance, 1989-91, supr. traffic mgmt., 1991, supr. system effectiveness section, 1991-93, asst. air traffic mgr., 1993-94, air traffic mgr. Cleve. Air Route Traffic Control Ctr., Oberlin, Ohio, 1994—, acting mgr. sys. mgmt. br., Des Plaines, Ill., 1995-96, mem. human resource reform team task force, Washington, 1996—. Sec. Fairview Neighborhood Coun., Anchorage, 1967-69; mem. Anchorage Bicentennial Commn., 1975-76; bd. dirs. Mt. Patmos Youth Dept., Decatur, Ga., 1981-82; mem. NAACP; del. to USSR Women in Mgmt., 1990; mem. citizens amb. program People to People Internat. Recipient Mary K. Goddard award Anchorage Fed. Exec. Assn. and Fed. Women's Program, 1985, Sec.'s award Dept. transp., 1985, Pres. VIP award, 1988, C. Alfred Anderson award, 1991, Disting. Svc. award Nat. Black Coalition of Fed. Aviation Employees, 1991, Paul K. Bohr award FAA, 1994, Nat. Performance Rev. Hammer award from V.P. Al Gore, 1996; A salute to Her Name in the Congl. Record 104th Congress, 1995. Mem. Nat. Assn Negro Bus. and Profl. Women (North to the Future club, charter pres. 1975-76), Blacks in Govt., Nat. Black Coalition of Fed. Aviation Employees (pres. cen. region chpt. 1987-92, Over Achievers award, 1987, Disting. Svc.

award 1988), Profl. Women Contrs. Orgn., Air Traffic Contrs. Assn., Fed. Mgrs. Assn., Internat. Platform Assn., Women in Mgmt. (del. Soviet Union), Gamma Phi Delta. Democrat. Baptist. Avocations: singing; sewing. Home: 5770-D2 Great Northern Blvd North Olmsted OH 44070 Office: FAA 326 E Lorain St Oberlin OH 44074-1216

WILLIAMS, ELIZABETH YAHN, author, lecturer, lawyer; b. Columbus, Ohio, July 20, 1942; d. Wilbert Henry and Elizabeth Dulson (Brophy) Yahn. BA cum laude, Loyola Marymount U., 1964; secondary teaching credential, UCLA, 1965; JD, Loyola U., 1971. Cert. tchr. h.s. and jr. coll. law, English and history. Writer West Covina, Calif., 1964—; designer West Covina, 1966-68; tchr. jr./sr. h.s. L.A. City Schs., Santa Monica, Calif., 1964-65, La Puente (Calif.) H.S. Dist., 1965-67; legal intern, lawyer Garvey, Ingram, Baker & Uhler, Covina, Calif., 1969-72; lawyer, corp. counsel Avco Fin. Svcs., Inc., Newport Beach, Calif., 1972-74; sole practitioner and arbitrator Santa Ana, Calif., 1974-80, Newport Beach, 1980-87; mem. faculty continuing edn. State Bar of Calif., 1979; adj. prof. Western State U. Sch. Law, Fullerton, Calif., 1980; mem. fed. cts. com. Calif. State Bar, San Francisco, 1977-80. Author: (1-act plays) Acting-Out Acts, 1990, Grading Graciela, 1992, Boundaries in the Dirt, 1993; author, lyricist: (1-act children's musical) Peter and the Worry Wrens, 1995; contbr. articles to profl. jours.; panelist TV show Action Now, 1971; interviewee TV show Women, 1987; scriptwriter, dir. TV show Four/Four, 1994, (3-act adaptation) Saved in Sedona, 1995; scriptwriter, prodr., host TV show Guidelights to Success, 1996. Mem. alumni bd. Loyola-Marymount U., L.A., 1980-84; mem. adv. bd. Rancho Santiago Coll., Santa Ana, 1983-84; speaker Commn. on Status on Women, Santa Ana, 1979. Grantee Ford Found., 1964-65; French scholar Ohio State U., 1959, acad. scholar Loyola-Marymount U., 1960-64; Editor's Choice award, 1995, Telly award finalist, 1996; award Nat. Libr. of Poetry. Mem. Calif. Women Lawyers (co-founder, life, bd. dirs. 1975-76), Orange County Bar Assn. (faculty Orange County Coll. Trial Advocacy 1982, chmn. human and individual rights com. 1974-75, comml. law and bankruptcy com. 1978-79, corp. and bus. law sect. 1980-81), So. Calif. Book Writers and Illustrators, Phi Delta Delta, Phi Alpha Delta, Phi Theta Kappa (hon. life mem.). Avocation: directing and producing ensemble and liturgical dramas and musicals. Address: PO Box 146 San Luis Rey CA 92068-0146

WILLIAMS, EMILY ALLEN, English language educator; b. Nottoway, Va., Aug. 14, 1955; d. Joseph Robert and Cornelia (Scott) Allen; m. Kenneth Jerome Williams, Feb. 29, 1992. BA, St. Paul's Coll., 1977; MA, Va. Commonwealth U., 1979; DAH, Clark Atlanta U., 1996. Instr. adult edn. Med. Coll. Va./Va. Commonwealth U., Richmond, 1977-79; instr. English Richmond Bus. Coll., 1979-80; regional grants coord. Va. Com. for Arts, Richmond, 1980-85; grants program coord. Ga. Coun. for Arts, Atlanta, 1986-87; grants dir. City of Atlanta Bur. Cultural Affairs, 1987-91; prof. English Clark Atlanta U., 1991-92, Morehouse Coll., Atlanta, 1992—, Spelman Coll., 1995—; adj. instr. English Reynolds C.C., Richmond, 1983-85; site reviewer NEA, Washington, 1990-91; panelist Nat. Black Arts Festival, Atlanta, 1991, Ga. Coun. Arts, Atlanta, 1987-90; cons. Fulton County Arts Coun., Atlanta, 1991-92, African Am. Philharmonic Orch., Atlanta, 1991-92. Contbr. numerous articles to profl. publs. Advisor student newspaper Morehouse Coll., 1992-93, grant com. chmn. English dept., 1992-93; speaker arts sem. Va. Commonwealth U., Richmond, 1982; cons. The APEX Mus., Atlanta, 1992-93. E. Bradlee Watson scholar, St. Paul's Coll., 1976. Mem. Popular Culture Assn., Coll. Lang. Assn., Delta Sigma Theta, Alpha Kappa Mu. Home: 6196 Spring Lake Walk Lithonia GA 30038-3467 Office: Morehouse Coll 830 Westview Dr SW Atlanta GA 30314-3773

WILLIAMS, EMORY, former retail company executive, banker; b. Falco, Ala., Oct. 26, 1911; s. William Emory and Nelle (Turner) W.; m. Janet Hatcher Allcorn, May 15, 1943; children: Nelle (Mrs. Gilbert Brown), Janet (Mrs. Edwin Harrison), Bliss (Mrs. Howell Browne), Carol (Mrs. James Schroeder), Emory III. A.B., Emory U., 1932. With Sears, Roebuck & Co., 1933-75; pres. Sears, Roebuck (S.A.), Brazil, 1958-60, Homart Devel. Co., 1960-67; treas. parent co., 1962-64, v.p., treas., 1964-75; chmn. bd., chief exec. officer Sears Bank & Trust Co., 1975-81, also dir.; chmn. bd. dirs., pres. Chgo. Milw. Corp., 1981-85; ptnr. Williams Realdy Co.; chmn. Williams & Nichols Co., SureBlock Co., Am. Investors in China. Div. chmn. Chgo. Crusade of Mercy, 1962-64, gen. chmn., 1966, pres, 1976-78; chmn. Ill. Health Edn. Commn., 1968-70; pres. Adler Planetarium, 1972-75, Ravinia Festival Assn., 1972-78; ptrs. bd. dirs. Community Fund, 1970-73; trustee Emory U., Chgo. Community Trust, Northwestern Meml. Hosps., Episcopal Diocesan Found., Kellstadt Found.; chmn. Chgo. Chamber Musicians. Lt. col. C.E., U.S. Army, World War II, CBI. Mem. Piedmont Driving Club (Atlanta); Chgo. Club, Old Elm Club (Chgo.), Commercial Club; Indian Hill Club (Winnetka, Ill.), Loblolly Bay Yacht Club, Loblolly Pines Golf Club (Hobe Sound, Fla.), Seminole Golf Club (North Palm Beach). Home: 1630 Sheridan Rd Wilmette IL 60091 Also: 7760 SE Lake Shore Dr Hobe Sound FL 33455-3833

WILLIAMS, ERIK GEORGE, professional football player; b. Phila., Sept. 7, 1968. Student, Ctrl. State U. Offensive tackle Dallas Cowboys, 1991—; mem. Superbowl Championship team, 1993, 94. Named to Pro Bowl Team, 1993; named offensive tackle on The Sporting News NFL All-Pro Team, 1993. Office: Dallas Cowboys 1 Cowboys Pky Irving TX 75063-4945

WILLIAMS, ERNEST GOING, retired paper company executive; b. Macon, Miss., Sept. 24, 1915; s. Augustus Gaines and Mary (Sanford) W.; m. Cecil Louise Butler, Aug. 18, 1951; children: Ernest Sanford, Turner Butler, Elizabeth Cecil. BS in Commerce and Bus. Adminstrn., U. Ala., 1938, LLD, 1987. Asst. to treas. U. Ala., 1938-42, 45-48, treas., 1948-56; v.p. First Nat. Bank Tuscaloosa, Ala., 1956-58; dir. First Nat. Bank Tuscaloosa, 1956-84; v.p., dir. Gulf States Paper Corp., Tuscaloosa, 1958-77; chmn. bd., dir. Affiliated Paper Cos., Inc., Tuscaloosa, 1977-94; bd. dirs., chmn. Southland Nat. Ins. Corp.; past pres. Associated Industries Ala. Trustee emeritus U. Ala., David Warner Found.; past pres. YMCA, United Way of Tuscaloosa County; past chmn. Tuscaloosa County chpt. ARC; past pres. DCH Found.; mem. Tuscaloosa Indsl. Devel. Bd. With USNR, 1942-45. Named Tuscaloosa Citizen of Year Civitan Club, 1974. Mem. Greater Tuscaloosa C. of C., Newcomen Soc. N.Am., Ala. Acad. of Honor, Univ. Club, River Club, Indian Hills Country Club, North River Yacht Club (vice commodore), Exch. Club (past pres.), Kappa Alpha, Omicron Delta Kappa, Beta Gamma Sigma. Presbyterian. Home: 156 The Highlands Tuscaloosa AL 35404-2900 Office: Affiliated Paper Co Inc 1806 6th St Tuscaloosa AL 35401-1721

WILLIAMS, ERNEST WILLIAM, JR., economist, educator; b. Scranton, Pa., Oct. 27, 1916; s. Ernest William and Kathryn (Winterstein) W.; m. Thelma Foxwell Klohr, Dec. 7, 1957 (dec. 1984). B.S., Columbia U., 1938, M.S., 1939, Ph.D., 1951. Economist Nat. Resources Planning Bd., 1940-42, WPB, 1942-44; chief transp. div. U.S. Strategic Bombing Survey, 1944-45; fiscal analyst U.S. Bur. Budget, 1945-46; lectr. transp. Grad. Sch. Bus. Columbia, 1947-52, assoc. prof., 1952-58, prof. transp., 1958-86, prof. emeritus, 1987—, vice dean, 1977-79; vis. prof. mgmt. U. Ariz., 1972, 74; cons. ODM, 1951-60; dir. transp. study Dept. Commerce, 1959-60; dir. ACF Industries, Inc., N.Y.C., 1960-84; mem. N.Y.-N.J. Met. Rapid Transit Commn., 1955-58; mem. task force Pres.'s Adv. Com. Transp. Policy and Orgn., 1954-55; mem. task force on regulatory agencies First Hoover Commn., 1948. Author: (with Marvin L. Fair) Economics of Transportation, rev. edit, 1959, The Regulation of Rail-Motor Rate Competition, 1958, Freight Transportation in the Soviet Union, 1962, The Future of American Transportation, 1971, Economics of Transportation and Logistics, 1974, rev. edit., 1981, (with G.K. Sletmo) Liner Conferences in the Container Age, 1981; contbr. articles to profl. publs. Trustee TAA Research Fund, 1962-65; bd. visitors U.S. Army Transp. Sch., 1963-66. Recipient Medal for Freedom. Mem. Am. Econ. Assn., Am. Soc. Transp. and Logistics. Home: 415 Janes Ln Stamford CT 06903-4818

WILLIAMS, ERNESTINE, substance abuse counselor; b. Fayetteville, N.C., July 11, 1937; d. Ernest and Melarez (Drye) McDonald; m. Donald Douglas Williams, Sept. 27, 1958; children: Daral, Trina. BA, Coll. New Rochelle, 1984. Credentialed substance abuse counselor, N.Y. Paraprofl. Bd. Edn., Bklyn., 1969-72, parent program asst., 1972-88, substance abuse counselor, 1988—; substance abuse supr. Bd. Edn. Dist. 23, Bklyn., 1991—; coord. parental workshops Bd. Edn., Bklyn., 1978—, coord. Substance Abuse Conf., 1988-93. Recipient awards for leadership. Mem. Coalition of Labor Union Women, Bd. Edn. Employees Local 372 (exec. bd. sec.-treas. 1993—, sec. dist. coun. 1988-93), Goodie award 1989), Coalition Black Trade Unionists. Baptist. Avocations: reading, music, arts and crafts. Office: Bd Edn Employees Dist Coun 37 125 Barclay St New York NY 10007-2199

WILLIAMS, ERVIN EUGENE, religious organization administrator; b. Corning, N.Y., Feb. 25, 1923; s. Douglas Lewis and Mina P. (Barnes) W.; m. Ruth Evelyn Snyder, June 12, 1945; children: Roger Eugene, Virginia Ruth. Student, Toccoa Falls (Ga.) Bible Coll., 1939, Cornell U., 1942; BA, Pa. State U., 1949; MA, Mich. State U., 1961, PhD in Communications, 1971. Ordained to ministry Ind. Bapt. Ch., 1950. Acad. dean Greensburg (Pa.) Bible Inst., 1949-51; min. Bapt. Ch., New Kensington, Pa., 1951-53; instr. Pa. State U., 1953-55; sr. min. East Lansing (Mich.) Trinity Ch., 1955-71; vis. prof. Trinity Evang. Div. Sch., Deerfield, Ill., 1968-71, prof. communication and practical theology, 1971-77, dir. D Ministry program, 1975-76; gen. dir. Am. Missionary Fellowship, Villanova, Pa., 1977-92; exec. min. Ch. of the Apostles, Atlanta, 1993-95; ch. and instl. cons. Smyrna, Ga., 1995—; chaplain Mich. State U., East Lansing, 1955-71; cons. Haggai Inst. for Advanced Leadership Tng., Atlanta, 1969—; lectr. Calvary Bapt. Coll., Kansas City, Mo., 1962, Haggai Inst. Third World Leaders, Singapore, 1970—; Staley lectr. Robert Wesleyan Coll., North Chili, N.Y., 1973, Judson Coll., Elgin, Ill., 1977-79; cons. to mission bds., 1967-76; assoc. dir. Camp of Woods, Speculator, N.Y., 1971-77. Author: 3 books; contbr. numerous articles to religious periodicals, also monographs. Trustee Dorothy H. Theis Meml. Found., Sierra Vista, Ariz., 1987—; trustee Gospel Vols., Speculator, N.Y., 1963-93; mem. bd. regents Owosso (Mich.) Coll., 1971-73. Pilot USAAF, 1942-45, prisoner of war, ETO, 1945. Mem. Nat. Sunday Sch. Assn., Christian Assn. Psychol. Studies, Mich. Acad. Arts and Scis., Aircraft Owners and Pilots Assn., Phi Beta Kappa, Pi Gamma Mu, Phi Kappa Phi, Alpha Kappa Delta. *It is much more difficult to conceal ignorance and prejudice than it is to acquire knowledge and fairness.*

WILLIAMS, FORMAN ARTHUR, engineering science educator, combustion theorist; b. New Brunswick, N.J., Jan. 12, 1934; s. Forman J. and Alice (Pooley) W.; m. Elsie Vivian Kara, June 15, 1955 (div. 1978); children: F. Gary, Glen A., Nancy L., Susan D., Michael S., Michelle K.; m. Elizabeth Acevedo, Aug. 19, 1978. BSE, Princeton U., 1955; PhD, Calif. Inst. Tech., 1958. Asst. prof. Harvard U., Cambridge, Mass., 1958-64; prof. U. Calif.-San Diego, 1964-81; Robert H. Goddard prof. Princeton U., N.J., 1981-88; prof. dept. applied mechs. and engring. scis. U. Calif., San Diego, 1988—; predsidential chair in Energy and Combustion Rsch U. Calif., San Diego, Ca., 1994—. Author: Combustion Theory, 1965, 2d edit., 1985; contbr. articles to profl. jours. Fellow NSF, 1962; fellow Guggenheim Found., 1970; recipient U.S. Sr. Scientist award Alexander von Humboldt Found., 1982, Silver medal Combustion Inst., 1978, Bernard Lewis Gold medal Combustion Inst., 1990, Pendray Aerospace Literature award Am. Inst. of Aeronautics and Astronautics, 1993. Fellow AIAA; mem. Am. Phys. Soc., Combustion Inst., Soc. for Indsl. and Applied Math., Nat. Acad. Engring., Nat. Acad. Engring Mex. (fgn. corr. mem.), Sigma Xi. Home: 8002 La Jolla Shores Dr La Jolla CA 92037-3230 Office: U Calif San Diego Ctr Energy & Combustion Rsch 9500 Gilman Dr La Jolla CA 92093-0411

WILLIAMS, FRANCIS LEON, engineering executive; b. McGill, Nev., Sept. 19, 1918; s. Leon Alfred and Mazie Arabella (Blanchard) W.; m. Ailsa Bailey, Oct. 1944 (div.); children: Rhonda, Grapham, Alison; m. Marita I. Furry, Feb. 23, 1974. Student, Calif. Inst. Tech., 1940-41, UCLA, 1946-47, Am. TV Labs., 1948; BME, Sydney U., Australia, 1952; postgrad., San Jose State Coll., 1958-60, Foothill Coll., 1961, Regional Vocat. Ctr., San Jose, Calif., 1962, Alexander Hamilton Inst., 1971-72, Lane Community Coll., 1978-85. Project engr., prodn. supr. Crompton, Parkinson, Australia Pty., Ltd., Sydney, 1949-50; field and sales engr. Perkins Australia Pty., Ltd., Sydney, 1951-54; chief mech. engr. Vicon Corp., San Carlos, Calif., 1955-60; design engr., group leader Lockheed Missiles and Space Co., Sunnyvale, Calif., 1960-70; prin. Astro-Tech Cons. Co., Los Altos, Calif., 1971-72; mech. designer Morvue and Morden Machines, Portland, Oreg., 1973-74; sr. mech. design engr. Chip-N-Saw div. Can-Car of Can., Eugene, Oreg., 1974-75; sales mgr. Indsl. Constrn. Co., Eugene, 1975-76, gen. mgr., 1977-78; ops. mgr. Steel Structures, Eugene, 1976-77; mech. design and project engr. Carothers Co., Eugene, 1978-80; chief engr. Bio Solar and Woodex Corps., Eugene and Brownsville, Oreg., 1980-83; cons. and design engr. Am. Fabricators, Woodburn, Oreg., 1983-84; design engr., draftsman Peterson Pacific Corp., Pleasant Hill, Oreg., 1984-85, Jensen Drilling Co., Glenwood, Oreg., 1985; design engr. Judco & Ball Flight Dryers, Inc., Harbor City, Calif., 1985-86; sr. v.p. The Richelsen Co., also cons.; chief engr. Peterson Pacific Corp., Eugene, 1984-93, mgr. new product devel. R&D, 1993—; owner, designer Williams Machine Design, Eugene, 1995—; also cons.; advisor solid waste recovery County Bd. Commr.'s Office, Eugene, 1984-85. Contbr. articles to profl. jours.; patentee in field. Chmn. bldg. and grounds Westminster Presbyn. Ch., Eugene, 1984-86. Served with USAF, 1941-45. Democrat. Lodge: Elks. Avocation: writing. Home: 2324 Lillian St Eugene OR 97401-4916

WILLIAMS, FRANK JAMES, JR., department store chain executive, lawyer; b. St. Louis, July 2, 1938; s. Frank James and Alberta Klaus Williams; children by previous marriage: Kimberly, Andrew, Renee; m. Sandra M. Garbe, Feb. 13, 1988. B.S.B.A., Washington U., St. Louis, 1960; J.D., Washington U., 1963; postgrad., U. Mo., 1960-61. Bar: Mo. 1963. Asst. gen. counsel May Dept. Stores, St. Louis, 1963-66, v.p.-labor relations, 1970-75, v.p.-labor relations and govt. affairs, 1975-80, v.p.-pub. affairs, 1980—; atty. Pet, Inc., St. Louis, 1966-67; lectr. various trade, profl. orgns. Treas. May Dept. Stores Polit. Action Com., St. Louis, 1981—. Mem. Mo. Bar Assn., Nat. Retail Mchts. Assn. (chmn. employee rels. com. 1977-78, silver plaque), Am. Retail Fedn. (chmn. employee rels. com. 1973-76), Nat. Retail Fedn. Roman Catholic. Club: Mo. Athletic (1st v.p. and treas. 1980-81) (St. Louis). Home: 2907 Bayberry Ridge Dr Saint Louis MO 63129-6422 Office: May Dept Stores 611 Olive St Saint Louis MO 63101-1721

WILLIAMS, FRANKLIN CADMUS, JR., bibliographer; b. Palestine, Tex., July 30, 1941; s. Franklin Cadmus and Cathryn Lucille (Pessoney) W. BA, Baylor U., 1963; MA, Stephen F. Austin State U., 1965; PhD, U. Wis., 1975. Cert. in secondary edn. English and History. Teaching fellow Stephen F. Austin State U., Nacogdoches, Tex., 1964-65, U. Wis., Madison, 1965-68; instr. English Austin Peay State U., Clarksville, Tenn., 1970-71; adj. asst. prof. East Tex. State U., Commerce, 1975; asst. prof. English Jarvis Christian Coll., Hawkins, Tex., 1976-78, 79-81; ind. scholar Palestine, Tex., 1981—; owner, bibliographer Goldsmith Archive, Palestine, 1981—; cons. Diocese of Galveston-Houston, 1977-84, Tex. State Hist. Assn., Austin, 1988; speaker, editor Jarvis Christian Coll., Hawkins, Tex., 1976-78, 79-81; nat. teaching fellow Office Edn., Washington, 1976-77; del. to Baylor U., U. Wis. System, Madison, 1981. Contbr. articles to profl. jours. Mem. Modern Lang. Assn., Tex. State Hist. Assn., Tex. Cath. Hist. Soc., Baylor Alumni Assn. (life), Wis. Alumni Assn. (life), Sigma Tau Delta. Avocations: reading, record collecting, historical genealogy, tennis, swimming. Office: PO Box 96 Palestine TX 75802-0096

WILLIAMS, FREDERICK, statistics educator; b. Middlesbrough, Eng., Feb. 9, 1922; came to U.S., 1926; s. Frederick William and Violet (Taylor) W.; m. Frances Marian Sacks, July 7, 1945. B.S.E., U. Mich., 1947, M.B.A. with distinction, 1948; Ph.D., Northwestern U., 1958. Teaching asst. statistics U. Mich., 1947-48; instr. statistics Northwestern U., 1948-54; instr., then asst. prof. statistics U. Ill., 1954-58; asso. prof. statistics U. Mo., 1958-61, prof., 1961—, chmn. dept., 1966-71, 1973-76, acting chmn., 1980-81, tchr. exec. devel. program, 1959-65, dir. grad. studies statistics, 1971-72; prof. emeritus, 1992—; cons., lectr. in field. Co-author: An Introduction to Probability, 1965. Served with USNR, 1943-46. Mem. Am. Statis. Assn. (pres. Mid-Mo. chpt. 1982, 93-94, past pres. 1995, mem. nat. coun. 1982-83, 85-96), Ops. Rsch. Soc. Am., Beta Gamma Sigma, Phi Kappa Phi. Home: 2501 N Leisurely Way Columbia MO 65202-2204

WILLIAMS, GARY, collegiate basketball team coach. B.Bus., U. Md., 1968. Asst. coach U. Md., College Park, 1969; asst. coach Woodrow Wilson H.S., Camden, N.J., head coach; asst. coach Lafayette Coll., head soccer coach; asst. coach, head coach Boston Coll., 1978-79, 83-87, American U., Washington, 1979-83; head coach Ohio State U., Columbus, U. Md., College Park, 1989—. Named Dist. Coach of Yr., 1981. Office: University of Maryland PO Box 295 College Park MD 20741-0295

WILLIAMS, GARY MURRAY, medical researcher, pathology educator; b. Regina, Sask., Can., May 7, 1940; s. Murray Austin and Selma Ruby (Domstad) W.; m. Julia Christine Lundberg; children: Walter, Jeffrey, Ingrid. BA, Washington and Jefferson Coll., 1963; MD, U. Pitts, 1967. Diplomate Am. Bd. Pathology, Am. Bd. Toxicology. Assoc. prof. pathology Temple U., Phila., 1971-75; mem. Fels Rsch. Inst., Phila., 1971-75; rsch. prof. N.Y. Med. Coll., Valhalla, 1975—; dir. med. scis., chief. pathology and toxicology div. Am. Health Found., Valhalla, 1975—; mem. toxicology study sect. NIH, Bethesda, Md., 1985-87; mem. working groups Internat. Agy. Rsch. on Cancer, Lyon, France, 1976, 80, 82, 83, 85, 86, 87, 89, 91, 96. Editor: Sweeteners; Health Effects, 1988; co-editor: Cellular System for Toxicity Testing, 1983; founding editor: Cell Biology and Toxicology, 1984—, Antioxidants: Chemical, Physiological, Nutritional and Toxicological Aspects, 1993; mem. editl. bd. Nutrition and Cancer, 1981—, Toxicologic Pathology, 1983—, Archives of Toxicology, 1988—, European Jour. Cancer Prevention, 1991—, Drug and Chem. Toxicology, 1994—; contbr. more than 380 sci. papers to profl. publs. Lt. comdr. USPHS, 1969-71. Recipient Sheard-Sanford award Am. Soc. Clin. Pathologists U. Pitts., 1967. Mem. Am. Assn. Cancer Rsch., Soc. Toxicology (Arthur J. Lehman award 1982, Lectr. award 1996), Soc. Toxicol. Pathology, Phi Beta Kappa, Alpha Omega Alpha. Home: 8 Elm Rd Scarsdale NY 10583-1410 Office: Am Health Found 1 Dana Rd Valhalla NY 10595-1549

WILLIAMS, GEORGE EARNEST, engineer, retired business executive; b. Bartow, Fla., Nov. 27, 1923; s. Earnest Roscoe and Ruby Barnett (Mathews) W.; m. Muriel Theodorsen, June 9, 1949. BS in Engring. with honors, USCG Acad., 1944; postgrad., Harvard U., 1945-46; SM in Mgmt., MIT, 1949. Registered profl. engr. 2 states. Project engr., bus. cons. Ebasco, N.Y.C.; design engr., prodn. supr. Minute Maid Corp., Orlando, Fla.; asst. contr., div. contr., group contr., corp. dir. fin. planning and analysis United Technologies Corp., Hartford, 1957-76, v.p., 1977-82; sr. v.p. Kensington Mgmt. Cons., 1982-84; sr. v.p. fin. Otis Elevator Co., N.Y.C., 1976-77; Mem. exec. com. Conn. Commn. Services and Expenditures, 1971. Contbr. articles to fin. jours., chpts. to books. Served with USCG, 1941-47. Mem. AIAA, Fin. Execs. Inst., Army and Navy Club (Washington), Naples Yacht Club, Port Royal Club. Originator pricing system purchase of Fla. oranges for concentrate mfg.; avocation: yachtsman. Home: 1325 7th St S Naples FL 33940-7316

WILLIAMS, GEORGE HOWARD, lawyer, association executive; b. Hempstead, N.Y., Feb. 12, 1918; s. George R. and Marcella (Hogan) W.; m. Mary Celeste Madden, Nov. 23, 1946; children—Mary Beth Williams Barritt, Stephen, Kevin, Jeanne Marie. A.B., Hofstra Coll., 1939, LL.D. (hon.), 1969; J.D., N.Y. U., 1946, LL.D. (hon.), 1969; postgrad., Inst. Advanced Legal Studies, U. London, 1959. Bar: N.Y. 1946. Adminstrv. asst. to dean NYU Law Sch., N.Y.C., 1946-48, instr. law, 1948-50, asst. prof., 1950-52, assoc. prof., 1952-55, prof., 1956-62, v.p. univ. devel., 1962-66, exec. v.p. planning and devel., 1966-68; pres. Am. U., Washington, 1968-75; exec. v.p., dir. Am. Judicature Soc., Chgo., 1976-87. Author: (with A.T. Vanderbilt and L.L. Pelletier) Report on Liberal Adult Education, 1955; (with K. Sampson) Handbook for Judges, 1984. Bd. dirs. Nat. Ctr. Edn. Politics, 1948-58, trustee, 1958-65; trustee Hofstra U., 1961-64; chmn. bd. trustees Trinity Coll., Vt., 1978-86; bd. dirs. Ctr. for Conflict Resolution, 1988—, Univ. Support Svcs. Served to lt. col., inf. AUS, World War II. Decorated Legion of Merit, Silver Star. Mem. Am. Polit. Sci. Assn., ABA Assn. Bar City N.Y., Alpha Kappa Delta, Phi Delta Phi. Clubs: N.Y. U. (N.Y.C.); Nat. Lawyers (Washington). Home: 1322 Judson Ave Evanston IL 60201-4720 Office: Am Judicature Soc 25 E Washington St Ste 1600 Chicago IL 60602-1805

WILLIAMS, GEORGE HUNTSTON, church historian, educator; b. Huntsburg, Ohio, Apr. 7, 1914; s. David Rhys and Lucy Adams (Pease) W.; m. Marjorie Louise Derr, July 27, 1941; children: Portia, Jeremy, Jonathan, Roger. Student, U. Munich, 1934-35; AB, St. Lawrence U., 1936; BDiv, U. Chgo., 1939, LittD (hon.), 1965; postgrad., U. Strasbourg, 1939-40, U. Calif., 1943-45; ThD, Union Theol. Sem., 1946; DD (hon.), Meadville Theological Sch., 1954; DHL (hon.), Loyola U., 1980, St. Anselm Coll., 1984; DCnL (hon.), King's Coll. U., 1986; DD, U. Edinburgh, Scotland, 1987. Ordained to ministry Unitarian and Congl. Chs., 1940. Asst. minister Ch. of Christian Union, Rockford, Ill., 1940-41; mem. faculty Starr King Sch. for Ministry, Pacific Sch. Religion, Berkeley, Calif., 1941-47; asso. prof. ch. history Starr King Sch. for Ministry, Pacific Sch. Religion, 1946-47; lectr. ch. history, head dept. Harvard Div. Sch., 1947-53, asso. prof., acting dean, 1953-55, prof., 1955—, Winn prof. ecclesiastical history, 1956, Hollis prof. div., 1963-81, emeritus, 1981—; Fulbright lectr. U. Strasbourg, 1960-61; Gunning lectr. U. Edinburgh, Scotland, 1987. Author: The Church and the Democratic State and the Crisis in Religious Education, 1948, An Examination of the Thought of Frederic Henry Hedge, 1949, The Norman Anonymous of ca. 1100, 1951, Public Aid to Parochial Education, 1951, Christology and ChurchState Relations in the Fourth Century, 1951, Church History in the U.S 1900-1950, 1951, Church, State and Society in John Paul II, 1983; editor, contbr. Harvard Divinity School History, 1954, Ministry in the Patristic Period, 1956, Golden Priesthood and the Leaden Statel, 1957, Anabaptist and Spiritual Writers, 1957, Anselm, 1960, The Radical Reformation, 1962 (enlarged Spanish edit. 1983, 2d English edit. 1992), Wilderness and Paradise, 1962, Camillo Renato, 1965, Georges Florovsky, 1965, Sacred Condominium in American Debate on Abortion, 1970, The Last Catholic Modernist, 1973, Two Social Strands Italian Anabaptism, 1973, The Stancarist Schism, 1980; co-editor: Writings of Thomas Hooker before 1633, 1976, Polish Brethren, 1601-85, 1980, Protestantism in The Ukraine, 1550-1701, 1978, The Mind of John Paul II, 1981; translator, editor Lubieniecki's History of the Polish Reformation, 1995, Divinings: Religion at Harvard, 1636-1992, 1993; mem. editorial bd. or co-editor: Harvard Theol. Rev. and Studies, Church History, Greek, Roman, and Byzantine Studies, Jour. Church and State, Studies in Romanticism, Mennonite Quar. Rev., Reflections, Bibliotheca Unitariorum. Decorated knight Order of St. Gregory the Great (John Paul II); Guggenheim fellow and IREX scholar U. Lublin, Poland, 1972-73; NEH 1980. Fellow Deputizaione di Storia Patria per le Venezie (hon.); mem. Am. Soc. Reformation Rsch. (pres. 1967), Patristic Soc., Am. Acad. Arts and Scis., Medieval Acad. Am., Am. Soc. Ch. History (pres. 1958), Cath. Hist. Assn., European Soc. Culture, Civil Liberties Union Mass. (adv. com.), Americans United for Life (pres. 1971-77), Mass. Hist. Soc., Phi Beta Kappa. Honored by jubilee vol. Continuity in Church History, 1979. Home: 58 Pinehurst Rd Belmont MA 02178-1504 Office: Widener Libr K Cambridge MA 02138

WILLIAMS, GEORGE LEO, retired secondary education educator; b. N.Y.C., June 29, 1931; s. Leo Dominick and Cathryn Margaret (Schellderfer) W.; m. Adelia Gilda Musa, Feb. 26, 1958; children: Adelia, Marina, Gilda. BA, CUNY, 1953, MA, 1955; PhD, NYU, 1966. Tchr. Port Washington (N.Y.) Pub. Schs., 1953, chairperson integrated studies, 1960-65, coord. Amherst project, 1968-69, chairperson English dept., 1970-90; adminstrv. asst. secondary and higher edn. dept. NYU, N.Y.C., 1965-66; adj. prof. NYU, 1966-74, Adelphi U., Garden City, N.Y. 1967-69, Hofstra U., Hempstead, N.Y., 1967-74; chmn. profl. growth and devel. com. Port Washington Pub. Schs., 1973-90, chmn. bicentennial com. 1989-90, mem. policy bd. Port Washington Tchr. Ctr., 1987-90. Co-author: (play) The Triumph of the Constitution, 1988; author: Fascist Thought and Totalitarianism in Italy's Secondary Schools: Theory and Practice, 1922-1943, 1993, Port Washington in The Twentieth Century: Places and People, 1995, (play) Remembrances of the First Colonial Settlement, 1993; editor Port Arrow Community Newsletter, 1973-84, Cow Neck Peninsula Hist. Soc. Newsletter, 1974-77; contbg. editor L.I. Forum, 1985—. Chairperson landmarks com. Cow Neck Peninsula Hist. Soc., Port Washington, 1980—, trustee, 1974-77; commr. landmarks com. Village of Port Washington North, 1983—, chmn., 1991; chair Hist. Landmark Preservation Commn., North Hempstead, N.Y., 1984—; Port Washington Continuing Edn. Adv. Coun.; co-chair 1895 Roslyn Clock Tower Com., 1994-96. Recipient environ. award Residents for a More Beautiful Port Washington, 1994. Mem. ASCD, Nat. Coun. Tchrs. English, Soc. for Preservation L.I. Antiquities, Port Washington Tchrs. Assn. (v.p. 1963-64, bd. dirs. 1966-74, founder ret. tchrs. chpt. 1991, newsletter editor 1990-92), Am. Hist. Assn. (cert. recognition 1988), Friends for L.I.'s Heritage, Roslyn Landmark Soc., N.Y. Geneal./Biog. Soc., N.Y. State Hist. Assn., Fulbright Assn., Hofstra Univ. Club, Residents for a More Beautiful

Port Washington (1994 Environ. award), Phi Beta Kappa, Phi Alpha Theta, Pi Sigma Alpha. Home: 84 Radcliff Ave Port Washington NY 11050-1600

WILLIAMS, G(EORGE) MELVILLE, surgeon, medical educator; b. Soochow, China, Nov. 16, 1930; came to U.S., 1940; s. Melville Owens and Annie Lee (Young) W.; m. Lee Logan, June 12, 1955 (div. 1985); children: Curtiss John, Steven Hoyt, Lucy Roxanna, Elizabeth; m. Elizabeth Hopkins, Feb. 14, 1986; m. Elizabeth Hopkins, Feb. 14, 1986 (div.); m. Linda Parsons, Apr. 14, 1996. BA, Oberlin Coll., 1953; MD, Harvard U., 1957. Diplomate Am. Bd. Surgery. Spl. fellow NIH, Melbourne, Australia, 1963-64; instr. surgery Med. Coll. Va., Richmond, 1964-65, asst. prof. surgery, 1965-66, assoc. prof. surgery, 1966-67, prof. surgery, 1967-69; prof. surgery The Johns Hopkins U. Sch. Medicine, Balt., 1969—. Editor: Transplant Rejection. United Network Organ Sharing (pres. 1984-85). Capt. U.S. Army, 1960-62. Grantee NIH, 1969, 82, Am. Heart Assn., 1991. Mem. Am. Surg Assn., The Halsted Soc. (pres. 1983), Am. Soc. Transplant Surgeons (pres. 1982-83), So. Assn. for Vascular Surgery (pres. 1991). Democrat. Methodist. Avocations: carpentry, fishing, boating. Office: Johns Hopkins Hosp 600 N Wolfe St Baltimore MD 21205-2110

WILLIAMS, GEORGE RAINEY, surgeon, educator; b. Atlanta, Oct. 25, 1926; s. George Rainey and Hildred (Russell) W.; m. Martha Vose, June 16, 1950; children: Bruce, Alden, Margaret, Rainey. Student, U. Tex., 1944-46; B.S., Northwestern U., 1948; M.B., 1950, M.D., 1950. Intern Johns Hopkins Hosp., 1950-51, William Stewart Halsted fellow surgery, 1951-52, asst. resident surgery, 1952-53, asst. resident surgeon, 1955-57, resident surgeon, 1957-58; practice medicine specializing in gen. and thoracic surgery Oklahoma City, 1958—; asst. prof. surgery U. Okla. Health Scis. Center, Oklahoma City, 1958-61; assoc. prof. U. Okla. Health Scis. Center, 1961-63; prof. surgery U. Okla. Health Scis. Center Coll. of Medicine, 1963—, chmn. dept. surgery, 1974—; interim dean U. Okla. Coll. Medicine, 1981-82, 85-86, 88-89; dir. Am. Bd. Surgery, 1975-81, vice chmn., 1979-81. Contbr. articles on gen. and thoracic surgery to profl. jours. Served lt., MC, 3d Inf. Div. AUS, 1953-55. Recipient Disting. Service citation U. Okla., 1982; named to Okla. Hall of Fame, 1986. Fellow ACS (sec. bd. govs. 1985-87, 1st v.p. 1989-90), Soc. Univ. Surgeons, Am. Assn. Thoracic Surgery, So. Surg. Assn., Am. Surg. Assn., Phi Beta Kappa, Delta Kappa Epsilon, Phi Beta Pi, Alpha Epsilon Delta, Alpha Omega Alpha, Pi Kappa Epsilon. Home: 6722 Country Club Dr Oklahoma City OK 73116-4706 Office: U Okla Dept Surgery PO Box 26307 Oklahoma City OK 73126-0307

WILLIAMS, GEORGE WALTON, English educator; b. Charleston, S.C., Oct. 10, 1922; s. Ellison Adger and Elizabeth Simonton (Dillingham) W.; m. Harriet Porcher Simons, Nov. 28, 1953; children: George Walton Jr., Ellison Adger II, Harriet Porcher Stoney. B.A., Yale U., 1947; M.A., U. Va., 1949, Ph.D., 1957. Asst. cashier Carolina Savs. Bank, Charleston, 1949-54; asst. prof. English, Duke U., 1957-63, asso. prof., 1963-67, prof., 1967, chmn. dept. English, 1982-86, prof. emeritus, 1993—; dir. summer inst. Commn. on English, Coll. Entrance Exam. Bd., 1962; pres. Durham Savoyards, Ltd., 1966-68, 81-82; sr. fellow Coop. Program in Humanities, Duke-U. N.C., 1969; Historiographer, Diocese of S.C., 1960-78; vis. prof. U.S. Mil. Acad., 1982-83. Author: St. Michael's, Charleston, 1751-1951, 1951, Image and Symbol in the Sacred Poetry of Richard Crashaw, 1963, The Craft of Printing and the Publication of Shakespeare's Plays, 1985; editor: Romeo and Juliet, 1964, Complete Poetry of Richard Crashaw, 1970, Jacob Eckhard's Choirmaster's Book, 1971, Shakespeare's Speech-Headings, 1996; contbg. editor Dramatic Works of Beaumont and Fletcher, 1966-96; assoc. editor Arden Shakespeare, 1996—. Served with inf. U.S. Army, 1943-45, ETO. Decorated Combat Inf. badge; recipient Outstanding Civilian Service medal Dept. Army, 1983; Guggenheim Found. fellow, 1977-78; Huntington Library fellow, 1981. Mem. MLA (com. on new variorum 1980-92, chmn. Shakespeare divsn. 1990), South Atlantic MLA (pres. 1980-81), Southeastern Renaissance Conf. (editor 1960-70, 91-95, pres. 1973), Bibliog. Soc., Royal Soc. Arts London, S.C. Hist. Soc., Carolina Yacht Club (Charleston), St. Cecilia Soc. (Charleston), Elizabethan Club Yale U., Phi Beta Kappa, Phi Kappa Phi. Home: 6 Sylvan Rd Durham NC 27701-2849 Office: Duke U Dept English Box 90015 Durham NC 27708

WILLIAMS, GLEN MORGAN, federal judge; b. Jonesville, Va., Feb. 17, 1920; s. Hughy May and Hattie Mae W.; m. Jane Slemp, Nov. 17, 1962; children: Susan, Judy, Rebecca, Melinda. A.B. magna cum laude, Milligan Coll., 1940; J.D., U. Va., 1948. Bar: Va. 1947. Pvt. practice law Jonesville, 1948-76; judge U.S. Dist. Ct. (we. dist.) Va., 1976-88, sr. judge, 1988—; commonwealth's atty. Lee County, Va., 1948-51; mem. Va. Senate, 1953-55. Mem. editorial bd.: Va. Law Rev, 1946-47. Mem. Lee County Sch. Bd., 1972-76; trustee, elder First Christian Ch., Pennington Gap, Va. Lt. USN, 1942-46, MTO. Recipient Citation of Merit Va. Def. Lawyers Assn., Oustanding Alumnus award Milligan Coll., 1980. Mem. ABA, Va. State Bar (citation of merit), Va. Bar Assn. (citation of merit), Fed. Bar Assn., Va. Trial Lawyers Assn. (Meritorious Svc. award 1986, Disting. Svc. award), Am. Legion, 40 and 8. Clubs: Lions, Masons, Shriners. Office: US Dist Ct Fed Bldg PO Box 339 Abingdon VA 24212

WILLIAMS, GORDON BRETNELL, construction company executive; b. Phila., Apr. 3, 1929; s. Thomas W. and Helen (Berryman) W.; m. Susan M. Cunningham, June 20, 1953 (div. 1980); children: Lucy Chase, Marcus Bretnell. B.S., Yale, 1951. Registered profl. engr., Mich., Ohio, Tex. Chief indsl. engr. Chrysler Corp., Detroit, 1954-57; pres., dir. Cunningham-Limp Co., Birmingham, Mich., 1957-76; v.p.-mktg. H.K. Ferguson Co., Cleve., 1976-78; pres. H.K. Ferguson Co., 1979-85, vice chmn., 1986-91; exec. v.p. indsl. mfg. divsn. Morrison Kindsen Corp., 1992—. Bd. dirs. St. Vincent Charity Hosp. and Health Ctr., Cleve.; adv. bd. engring. sch. U. Akron. Served as ensign, ordnance USNR, 1952-54. Mem. Phi Gamma Delta. Clubs: Union (Cleve.); Yale of Ohio. Home: 12700 Lake Ave Cleveland OH 44107-1576 Office: MK-Ferguson Co 1500 W 3rd St Cleveland OH 44113-1453

WILLIAMS, GORDON HAROLD, internist, medical educator, researcher; b. Denver, Colo., May 23, 1937; s. Freeman Royal and Vonda Larcine (Olsen) W.; m. Dorrell Deen Ward, June 11, 1963; children: Jeffrey Scott, Christopher Shawn, Jonathan Sylvan, TarrynSue, Megan Suzanne, Brenya Shannon. BA, Harvard U., 1959, MD, 1963. Diplomate Am. Bd. Internal Medicine, 1970, endocrinology, 1975, 93. Intern U. Chicago Hosps., 1963-64; resident Peter Bent Brigham Hosp., Boston, Mass., 1966-67; fellow, endocrinology, 1967-70; sr. physician Brigham Women's Hosp., Boston, Mass., 1981—; asst. prof. medicine Harvard U., Boston, 1970-73, assoc. prof., 1973-80, prof., 1980—; dir. endocrine and hypertension unit Brigham and Women's Hosp., Boston, 1973—, chief svc., 1980—. Lt. USN, 1964-66. Fellow ACP, Coun. High Blood Pressure Rsch.; mem. Endocrine Soc., Am. Soc. Clin. Investigation, Am. Physiol. Soc., Am. Assn. Physicians. Mem. LDS Ch. Office: Brigham and Womens Hosp Dept Endocrinology/ Hypertension 221 Longwood Ave Boston MA 02115-5817

WILLIAMS, GORDON L., aircraft manufacturing executive; b. 1932. BS, U. Colo. Dir. aircraft components program Martin Marietta Corp., Balt., 1959-85; group v.p. LTV Aerospace and Defense Co., Inc., Dallas, 1985-92; pres. Aircraft Products Group, Dallas, 1989; pres., CEO Vought Aircraft Co., Dallas, 1992—. Office: Vought Aircraft Co 9314 W Jefferson Blvd Dallas TX 75211-9302*

WILLIAMS, GREGORY HOWARD, lawyer, educator; b. Muncie, Ind., Nov. 12, 1943; s. James Anthony Williams; m. Sara Catherine Whitney, Aug. 29, 1969; children: Natalia Dora, Zachary Benjamin, Anthony Bladimir, Carlos Gregory. B.A., Ball State U., 1966; M.A., U. Md., 1969; Ph.D., George Washington U., 1982, M.Ph., 1977, J.D., 1971. Bar: Va. 1971, D.C. 1972. Dep. sheriff Delaware County, Muncie, Ind., 1963-66; tchr. Falls Ch. Public Sch., Va., 1966-70; legis. asst. U.S. Senate, Washington, 1971-73; dir. exptl. programs George Washington U., 1973-77; prof. law U. Iowa Coll. Law, Iowa City, 1977-93; assoc. v.p. Acad. Affairs U. Iowa, 1991-93; dean, prof. law Ohio State U., Columbus, 1993—. Author: Law and Politics of Police Discretion, 1984, Iowa Guide to Search and Seizure, 1986, Life on the Color Line: The True Story of a White Boy Who Discovered He Was Black, 1995. Mem. Iowa Adv. Commn. to U.S. Commn. on Civil Rights, Washington, 1978-86; chmn., mem. Iowa Law Enforcement Acad., Camp Dodge, 1979-85. Recipient Cert. of Appreciation Black Law Students Assn., 1984, GW Edn. Opportunity Program, 1977, Disting. Alumnus award George Washington U., Nat. Law Ctr., 1994, L.A. Times Book prize Current Interest Category, 1995. Office: Ohio State U Coll of Law 55 W 12th Ave Columbus OH 43210-1338

WILLIAMS, HANK, JR., country music singer, songwriter; b. Shreveport, La., May 26, 1949; s. Hank and Audrey W.; 1 son, Shelton Hank; m. 2d Beck White (div.); children: Hilary, Holly; m. Mary Jane Thomas, July 1990. Performer throughout U.S.; recorded song Ain't Misbehavin'; latest albums include: Montana Cafe, 1986, Hank Live, 1987, Born to Boogie, 1987, Wild Streak, 1988, Greatest Hits III, Lone Wolf, 1990, Pure Hank, 1991, (with Clink Black) Maverick, 1992, Out of Left Field, 1993, A Tribute to My Father, 1993, (with Waylon Jennings and Ray Charles) Greatest Hits, vol. 2, 1994; composer All My Roudy Friends, 1993. Recipient 18 Gold albums, 5 Platinum/1 Double Platinum album; voted Entertainer of Yr., Acad. Country Music, 1987, 88, 89, Entertainer of Yr., Country Music Assn., 1987, 88, Video of Yr. award Acad. Country Music, 1987-88, best music video Acad. Country Music, 1989, Album of Yr. Acad. Country Music, 1989, Music Video of Yr. Country Music Assn., 1987, Grammy award, 1990. Office: Hank Williams Jr Enterprises PO Box 850 Paris TN 38242-0850 Office: Warner/Curb Records 10585 Santa Monica Blvd # 300 Los Angeles CA 90025-4921

WILLIAMS, HAROLD, geology educator; b. St. John's, Nfld., Can., Mar. 14, 1934; s. Alexander and Catherine (Snow) W.; m. Emily Jean King, Sept. 19, 1958; children—Alexander, David, Steven. B.Sc., Meml. U., 1956, diploma in engring., 1956, M.Sc., 1958; Ph.D., U. Toronto, 1961. Research scientist Geol. Survey Can., Ottawa, Ont., 1961-68; prof. geology Meml. U., St. John's, 1968—, Alexander Murray prof., 1990—. Contbr. numerous articles and geol. maps to profl. jours. Killam scholar Can. Council, 1977-81, Miller medal Royal Soc. Can., 1987, Gov. Gen.'s medal Meml. U. Fellow Royal Soc. Can., Geol. Assn. Can. (Past Pres. medal 1976, Logan medal 1988), Geol. Soc. Am., Can. Soc. Petroleum Geologists (Douglas medal 1981). Avocation: folk musician. Office: Meml Univ Dept Earth Sci, SJ Carew Bldg, Saint John's, NF Canada A1B 3X5

WILLIAMS, HAROLD ANTHONY, retired newspaper editor; b. Milw., Apr. 22, 1916; s. Harold Ambrose and Helen Theresa (Schmitt) W.; m. Ruth Edna Smith, Oct. 17, 1942; children—Anne Meredith Williams Gibson, Mary Helen Williams Winter, Sara B. Williams Cherner, Julie C. Williams Stewart. A.B., U. Notre Dame, 1938. Editor Towson (Md.) Union News, 1938-40; mem. staff Balt. Sunpapers, 1940-81; fgn. corr. Balt. Sunpapers, Europe, 1949-50; asst. to exec. editor, then city desk editor Balt. Sunpapers, 1950-54, Sunday editor, 1954-79, asst. mng. editor, 1979-81; sr. instr. Towson (Md.) State U., 1982-89; chmn. Newspaper Comics Coun., 1970-72, mem. exec. com., 1972-81; chmn. curriculum com., lectr. Renaissance Inst., Coll. Notre Dame of Md., 1989-92; discussion leader Am. Press Inst.; lectr. Towson State U. Elderhostel, 1993—. Author: A History of the Western Maryland Railway, 1952, Baltimore Afire, 3d edit, 1990, Guide to Baltimore and Annapolis, 1957, History of the Hibernian Society of Baltimore, 1957, A History of Eudowood, 1964, Robert Garrett and Sons, 1965, Bodine, A Legend in His Time, 1971; The Baltimore Sun, 1837-1987. Chmn. Friends Coun., Albin O. Kuhn Libr. and Gallery, U. Md., Balt. County, 1990-94; mem. adv. coun. Friends of the Johns Hopkins U. Librs., 1990—, pres., 1993-95. With CIC, AUS, 1942-46. Named Marylander of Yr., Md. Colonial Soc., 1989. Mem. Am. Assn. Sunday and Feature Editors, Wine and Food Soc. Balt. (pres. 1979-81), Balt. Bibliophiles (pres. 1978-79, exec. com.), Md. Hist. Soc., 14 W Hamilton St. Club (Balt.), Johns Hopkins Club. Democrat. Roman Catholic. Home: 307 Cedarcroft Rd Baltimore MD 21212-2520

WILLIAMS, HAROLD MARVIN, foundation official, former government official, former university dean, former corporate executive; b. Phila., Jan. 5, 1928; s. Louis W. and Sophie (Fox) W.; m. Nancy Englander; children: Ralph A., Susan J., Derek M. AB, UCLA, 1946; JD, Harvard U., 1949; postgrad. U. So. Calif. Grad. Sch. Law, 1955-56; DHL (hon.), Johns Hopkins U., 1987. Bar: Calif. 1950; practiced in Los Angeles, 1950, 53-55; with Hunt Foods and Industries, Inc., Los Angeles, 1955-68, v.p. 1958-60, exec. v.p., 1960-68, pres., 1968; gen., mgr. Hunt-Wesson Foods, 1964-66, pres., 1966-68; chmn. finance com. Norton Simon, Inc., 1968-70, chmn. bd., 1969-70, dir., 1959-77; dir. Times-Mirror Corp., SunAmerica; prof. mgmt., dean Grad. Sch. Mgmt., UCLA, 1970-77; pres., dir. Special Investments & Securities Inc., 1961-66; chmn. SEC, Washington, 1977-81; pres., chief exec. officer J. Paul Getty Trust, 1981—; regent U. Calif., 1983-94. Mem. Commn. for Econ. Devel. State of Calif., 1973-77; energy coordinator City of Los Angeles, 1973-74; public mem. Nat. Advt. Review Bd., 1971-75; co-chmn. Public Commn. on Los Angeles County Govt.; mem. Coun. on Fgn. Rels., Com. for Econ. Devel.; commn. to rev. Master Plan for Higher Edn., State of Calif., 1985-87; trustee Nat. Humanities Ctr., 1987-93; dir. Ethics Resource Ctr.; mem. Pres.' Com. on Arts and Humanities; mem. Commn. on the Acad. Presidency. Served as 1st lt. AUS, 1950- 53. Mem. State Bar Calif. Office: J Paul Getty Trust 401 Wilshire Blvd Ste 900 Santa Monica CA 90401

WILLIAMS, HAROLD ROGER, economist, educator; b. Arcade, N.Y., Aug. 22, 1935; s. Harry Alfred and Gertrude Anna (Scharf) W.; m. Lucia Dorothy Preuschoff, Apr. 23, 1955; children: Theresa Lynn, Mark Roger. B.A., Harpur Coll., SUNY, Binghamton, 1961; M.A., Pa. State U., 1963; Ph.D., U. Nebr., 1966; postgrad., Harvard U., 1969-70. Instr., Pa. State U., 1962-63; Instr. U. Nebr., 1965-66; mem. faculty Kent (Ohio) State U., 1966—, prof. econs. and internat. bus., 1972—, chmn. dept., 1974-81, dir. Internat. Bus. Program, Grad. Sch. Mgmt., 1980-86, chmn. faculty senate, 1988-89; assoc. dean Grad. Sch. Mgmt., 1994—; econ. cons. and adv. to numerous govt., bus. and internat. orgns. Author over 100 books and articles in field. Served with AUS, 1954-57. Grantee NSF. Mem. Am. Econ. Assn., Internat. Econs. Assn., Acad. Internat. Bus., Midwest Econ. Assn. (v.p. 1969-70), So. Econ. Assn., Phi Gamma Mu, Omicron Delta Epsilon, Beta Gamma Sigma, Phi Beta Delta. Home: 415 Suzanne Dr Kent OH 44240-1933 Office: Dept Econs Kent State U Kent OH 44242

WILLIAMS, HARRIET CLARKE, retired academic administrator, artist; b. Bklyn., Sept. 5, 1922; d. Herbert Edward and Emma Clarke (Gibbs) W. AA, Bklyn. Coll., 1958; student, Art Career Sch., N.Y.C., 1960; cert., Hunter Coll., 1965, CPU Inst. Data Processing, 1967; student, Chineses Cultural Ctr., N.Y.C., 1973; hon. certs., St. Labre Sch./St. Joseph's, Ind. Sch., Mont., 1990. Adminstr. Baruch Coll., N.Y.C., 1959-85; mktg. researcher 1st Presbyn. Arts and Crafts Shop, Jamaica, N.Y., 1986—; tutor in art St. John's U., Jamaica, 1986—; founder, curator Internat. Art Gallery, Queens, N.Y., 1991—. Exhibited in group shows at Union Carbide Art Exhibit, N.Y.C., 1975, Queens Day Exhbn., N.Y.C., 1980, 1st Presbyn. Arts and Crafts Shop, N.Y.C., 1986, others; contbr. articles to profl. publs. Vol. reading tchr. Mabel Deen Vocat. High Sch., N.Y.C., 1965-67; mem. polit. action com. dist. council 37, N.Y.C., 1973-77; mem. negotiating team adminstrv. contracts, N.Y.C., 1975-78; mem. Com. To Save CCNY, 1976-77, Statue Liberty Ellis Island Found., Woodrow Wilson Internat. Ctr. Scholars, Wilson Ctr. Assocs., Washington, St. Labre Indian Sch., Ashland, Mont. Appreciation award Dist. Coun. 37, 1979; recipient Plaque Appreciation Svcs., Baruch Coll., Key award St. Joseph's Indian Sch., 1990, Key award in Edn. and Art, 1990, others. Mem. NAFE, AAUW, Women in Mil. Svc., Assn. Am. Indian Affairs, Nat. Mus. of Am. Indian, Artist Equity Assn. N.Y., Lakota Devel. Coun., Am. Film Inst., Bklyn. Coll. Alumni, Nat. Geographic Soc., Nat. Mus. Woman in the Arts, Statue of Liberty Ellis Island Found., Inc., Alliance of Queens Artists, U.S. Naval Inst., El Museo Del Barrio, Am. Mus. Natural History, Internat. Ctr. for Scholars-Wilson Ctr. Assocs., Arrow Club-St. Labre Indian Sch., Mus. of Television and Radio, Women in Military Meml. Found., Nat. Mus. of Am. Indian, U.S. Holocaust Mus., Navy Meml. (adv. coun.). Roman Catholic. Avocations: aerobics, vol. work, world travel, music. Office: Baruch Coll 17 Lexington Ave New York NY 10010-5526

WILLIAMS, HENRY STRATTON, radiologist, educator; b. N.Y.C., Aug. 26, 1929; m. Frances S. Williams; children: Mark I, Paul S., Bart H. BS, CCNY, 1950; MD, Howard U., 1955. Diplomate Nat. Bd. Med. Examiners. Intern Brooke Army Hosp., San Antonio, 1956; resident in radiology Letterman Army Hosp., San Francisco, 1957-60; pvt. practice radiology L.A., 1963—; assoc. clin. prof. radiology Charles R. Drew Med. Sch., L.A.; chmn. bd. Charles Drew U. Medicine and Sci. Found.; interim pres. Charles R. Drew U. of Medicine and Sci. Mem. ad hoc adv. com. Joint Commn. Accreditation Hosps. Served to maj. U.S. Army, 1960-63. Fellow Am. Coll. Radiology; mem. Calif. Physicians Service (bd. dirs. 1971-77), Calif. Med. Assn. (counselor, mem. appeals bd., del., chmn. urban health com.), Los Angeles County Med. Assn.

WILLIAMS, HENRY THOMAS, retired banker, real estate agent; b. Worton, Md., Mar. 27, 1932; s. Henry Thomas W. and Ivy Lorraine (Urie) Francis; m. Marion Dwyer, Aug. 1953 (div. 1954); m. Laura Lynne Davis, Sept. 13, 1958; children: Lisa C. Ross, Henry Thomas III, Davis F. Student, Washington Coll., 1951-52; grad., ABA Nat. Installment Credit Sch. at U. Chgo., 1968, Va.-Md. Sch. Bank Mgmt. at U. Va., 1972. Grad. Realtors Inst. Teller Chestertown Bank Md., 1960-61, note teller, 1961-63, asst. cashier, 1963-68, mgr. installment loans, 1968-73, v.p., sr. loan officer, sec., 1973-85; v.p., br. mgr. Chestertown Bank Md., Rock Hall, 1985-88; now assoc. broker-realtor The Hogans Agy., Inc., Chestertown; mem. Queen Anne's County Real Estate Bd. Past dir. United Way Kent County, Chestertown; past vestryman, past chmn. budget com. St. Paul's Ch., Chestertown. Mem. Bank Adminstrn. Inst. (past sec., past chmn. Ea. Shore Chpt.), Md. Bankers Assn. (past v.p., past chmn. group 5), Md. Young Bankers Com., Chester River Yacht and Country Club, Lions (bd. dirs., past sec., past v.p.). Democrat. Home: 21139 Green Ln Rock Hall MD 21661-1634 Office: The Hogans Agy Inc Rt 213 N 515 Washington Ave Chestertown MD 21620

WILLIAMS, HERBERT J., bishop. Bishop of N. Cen. Mich. Ch. of God in Christ, Saginaw. Office: Ch of God in Christ 1600 Cedar St Saginaw MI 48601-2837

WILLIAMS, HERMAN, JR., protective services offical. Fire chief Balt. Fire Dept., 1994—. Office: Balt Fire Dept Hdqrs 414 N Calvert St Baltimore MD 21202

WILLIAMS, HIBBARD EARL, medical educator, physician; b. Utica, N.Y., Sept. 28, 1932; s. Hibbard G. and Beatrice M. W.; m. Sharon Towne, Sept. 3, 1982; children: Robin, Hans. AB, Cornell U., 1954, MD, 1958. Diplomate Am. Bd. Internal Medicine. Intern Mass. Gen. Hosp., Boston, 1958-59, resident in medicine, 1959-60, 62-64, asst. physician, 1964-65; clin. assoc. Nat. Inst. Arthritis and Metabolic Diseases, NIH, Bethesda, MD, 1960-62; instr. medicine Harvard U., Boston, 1964-65; asst. prof. medicine U. Calif., San Francisco, 1965-68, assoc. prof., 1968-72, prof., 1972-78, chief divsn. med. genetics, 1968-70, vice chmn. dept. medicine, 1970-78; prof., chmn. dept. medicine Cornell U. Med. Coll., N.Y.C., 1978-80; physician-in-chief N.Y. Hosp.-Cornell Med. Ctr., N.Y.C., 1978-80; dean Sch. Medicine U. Calif., Davis, 1980-92, prof. internal medicine, 1980—; mem. program project com. NIH, Nat. Inst. Arthritis and Metabolic Diseases, 1971-73. Editor med. staff confs. Calif. Medicine, 1966-70; mem. editl. bd. Clin. Rsch., 1968-71, Am. Jour. Medicine, 1978-88; cons. editor Medicine, 1978-86; assoc. editor Metabolism, 1970-80; mem. adv. bd. physiology in medicine New Eng. Jour. Medicine, 1970-75; contbr. articles to med. jours. With USPHS, 1960-62. Recipient Career Devel. award USPHS, 1968; recipient award for excellence in teaching Kaiser Found., 1970, Disting. Faculty award U. Calif. Alumni-Faculty Assn., 1978; John and Mary R. Markle scholar in medicine, 1968. Fellow ACP; mem. AAAS, Am. Fedn. Clin. Rsch., Am. Soc. Clin. Investigation (sec.-treas. 1974-77), Assn. Am. Physicians, Assn. Am. Med. Colls. (adminstrv. bd., coun. deans 1989-92, exec. coun. 1990-92), Calif. Acad. Medicine (pres. 1984), San Francisco Diabetes Assn. (bd. dirs. 1971-72), Western Assn. Physicians (v.p. 1977-78), Western Soc. Clin. Rsch., Calif. Med. Assn. (chmn. coun. sci. affairs 1990-95, bd. dirs. 1990-95), Giannini Found. (sci. adv. bd. 1990—), St. Francis Yacht Club, Alpha Omega Alpha. Office: U Calif Sch Medicine TB150 Davis CA 95616

WILLIAMS, HIRAM DRAPER, artist, educator; b. Indpls., Feb. 11, 1917; s. Earl Boring and Inez Mary (Draper) W.; m. Avonell Baumunk, July 7, 1941; children—Curtis Earl, Kim Avonell. B.S., Pa. State U., 1950, M.Ed., 1951. Tchr. art U. So. Calif., 1953-54, UCLA, summer 1959, U. Tex., 1954-60; mem. faculty and pres's. coun. U. Fla., Gainesville, 1960—; Disting. Service prof. U. Fla., until 1982, prof. emeritus, 1982; Mem. chancellor's council U. Tex. System. Exhibited, Pa. Acad. Fine Arts anns., Whitney Mus. Am. Art bi-anns., Corcoran Gallery Bi-anns., U. Ill. bi-anns., Mus. Modern Art exhbns., also Nordness Gallery, N.Y.C.; represented in permanent exhbns., Mus. Modern Art, Wilmington Art Center, Whitney Mus. of Am. Art, N.Y.C., Sheldon Meml. Art Mus., Milw. Art Center, Guggenheim Mus., Smithsonian Inst., Harn Art Mus., U. Fla., Yale; also pvt. collections.; author: Notes for a Young Painter, 1963, rev., 1985; contbr. articles to mags. Served to capt. C.E. U.S. Army, World War II, ETO. Tex. Rsch. grantee, 1958; Guggenheim fellow, 1962-63; inducted into Fla. Artists Hall of Fame, 1994. Address: 2804 NW 30th Ter Gainesville FL 32605-2727 *My desire as a painter is to animate material with imagery that strikes conjunctions of art and life.*

WILLIAMS, HOWARD RUSSELL, lawyer, educator; b. Evansville, Ind., Sept. 26, 1915; s. Clyde Alfred and Grace (Preston) W.; m. Virginia Merle Thompson, Nov. 3, 1942; 1 son, Frederick S.T. AB, Washington U., St. Louis, 1937; LLB, Columbia U., 1940. Bar: N.Y. 1941. With firm Root, Clark, Buckner & Ballantine, N.Y.C., 1940-41; prof. law, asst. dean U. Tex. Law Sch., Austin, 1946-51; prof. law Columbia U. Law Sch., N.Y.C., 1951-63; Dwight prof. Columbia Law Sch., 1959-63; prof. law Stanford U., 1963-85, Stella W. and Ira S. Lillick prof., 1968-82, prof. emeritus, 1982, Robert E. Paradise prof. natural resources, 1983-85, prof. emeritus, 1985—; Oil and gas cons. President's Materials Policy Commn., 1951; mem. Calif. Law Revision Commn., 1971-79, vice chmn., 1976-77, chmn., 1978-79. Author or co-author: Cases on Property, 1954, Cases on Oil and Gas, 1956, 5th edit., 1987, Decedents' Estates and Trusts, 1968, Future Interests, 1970, Oil and Gas Law, 8 vols., 1959-64 (with ann. supplements/rev. 1964-95), abridged edit., 1973, Manual of Oil and Gas Terms, 1957, 9th edit., 1994. Bd. regents Berkeley Bapt. Divsn. Sch., 1966-67; trustee Rocky Mountain Mineral Law Found., 1964-66, 68-85. With U.S. Army, 1941-46. Recipient Clyde O. Martz Tchg. award Rocky Mountain Mineral Law Found., 1994. Mem. Phi Beta Kappa. Democrat. Home: 360 Everett Ave Apt 4B Palo Alto CA 94301-1422 Office: Stanford U Sch Law Nathan Abbott Way Stanford CA 94305

WILLIAMS, HUGH ALEXANDER, JR., retired mechanical engineer, consultant; b. Spencer, N.C., Aug. 18, 1926; s. Hugh Alexander and Mattie Blanche (Megginson) W.; BS in Mech. Engring., N.C. State U., 1948, MS in Diesel Engring. (Norfolk So. R.R. fellow), 1950; postgrad. Ill. Benedictine Coll. Inst. Mgmt., 1980; m. Ruth Ann Gray, Feb. 21, 1950; children: David Gray, Martha Blanche Williams Heidengren. Jr. engr.-field service engr. Baldwin-Lima Hamilton Corp., Hamilton, Ohio, 1950-52, project engr., 1953-55; project engr. Electro-Motive div. Gen. Motors Corp., La Grange, Ill., 1955-58, sr. project engr., 1958-63, supr. product devel. engine design sect., 1963-86, staff engr., advanced mech. tech., 1986-87. Trustee Downers Grove (Ill.) San. Dist., 1965-92, pres., 1974-91, v.p., 1991-92; pres. Ill. Assn. San. Dists., 1976-77, bd. dirs., 1977-89; mem. statewide policy adv. com. Ill. EPA, 1977-79; mem. DuPage County Intergovtl. Task Force Com., 1988-92; elder Presbyn. Ch. Served with USAAC, 1945. Registered profl. engr., Ill. Recipient Trustee Svc. award Ill. Assn. San. Dists., 1986, Citizens award Downers Grove Evening chpt. Kiwanis, 1991. Fellow ASME (chmn. honors and awards com. 1993—, Diesel and Gas Engine Power Div. Speaker awards 1968, 84, Div. citation 1977, Internal Combustion Engine award 1987, exec. com. Internal Combustion Engine div. 1981-87, 88-92, chmn. 1985-86, sec. 1988-92); mem. Soc. Automotive Engrs. (life), ASME (chmn. Soichiro Honda medal com. 1987-92), Ill. Assn. Wastewater Agys. (Outstanding Mem. award 1990, hon. mem. 1992), Raleigh Host Lions Club (pres. 1996—), Masons (32 degree), Sigma Pi. Republican. Editor: So. Engr., 1947-48; contbr. articles to profl. jours. Patentee in field. Home: 2108 Weybridge Dr Raleigh NC 27615-5562

WILLIAMS, HUGH HARRISON, physics educator; b. Boston, Dec. 1, 1944; married; two children. BS, Haverford Coll., 1966; PHD, Stanford U., 1972. From rsch. assoc. physics to assoc. physicist Brookhaven Nat. Lab., 1971-74; from asst. prof. to prof. physics U. Pa., 1974—; adv. com. Fermilab Physics, 1982-86, chmn., 1984-86; chmn. SSC Detector Rsch. & Devel. Com., 1987-91, policy adv. com., 1990—. Mem. Am. Phys. Soc. Office: U

Penn/ High Energy Phys & Elem Particle Rsch Program 33rd & Walnut Sts Philadelphia PA 19104*

WILLIAMS, HULEN BROWN, former university dean; b. Lauratown, Ark., Oct. 8, 1920; s. Ernest Burdett and Ann Jeanette (Miller) W.; m. Virginia Anne Rice, June 20, 1942 (dec. June 1970); children: James Browning, Virginia Jean; m. Michaela Galasso, Mar. 20, 1971. BA, Hendrix Coll., 1941; MS, La. State U., 1943, PhD, 1948; postgrad., Cornell U., summer 1950, U. Calif., Berkeley, 1953. Instr. through asso. prof. La. State U., Baton Rouge, 1947-56; prof., head chemistry dept. La. State U., 1956-68, dean Coll. Chemistry and Physics, 1968-82; ret., 1982; Cons. to chem. and legal professions. Co-author books on chemistry; contbr. articles to profl. jours. Served to lt. (j.g.) USNR, 1944-46. Mem. Am. Chem. Soc., Sigma Xi, Sigma Pi Sigma, Phi Lambda Upslion, Phi Kappa Phi, Omicron Delta Kappa. Home: 470 Castle Kirk Dr Baton Rouge LA 70808-6011

WILLIAMS, IDA JONES, consumer and home economics educator, writer; b. Coatesville, Pa., Dec. 1, 1911; d. William Oscar and Ida Ella (Ruth) Jones; m. Charles Nathaniel Williams, Mar. 17, 1940 (dec. July 1971). BS, Hampton Inst., 1935; MA, U. Conn., 1965; cert. recognition, Famous Writers Sch., Westport, Conn., 1976, 78. Cert. high sch. tchr., English, sci., home econs., Va., Pa. Sci. and home econs. tchr. Richmond County High Sch., Ivondale, Va., 1935-36; English and home econs. tchr. Northampton County High Sch., Chesaepeake, Va., 1936-40; consumer and home econs. tchr. Northampton County High Sch., Machipongo, Va., 1940-71, Northampton Jr. High Sch., Machipongo, 1971-76. Author: Starting Anew After Seventy, 1980 (plaque 1980), News and Views of Northampton County High Principals and Alumni, 1981; editor: Fifty Year Book 1935-1985 - Hampton Institute Class, 1985, Favorite Recipes of Ruth Family & Friends, 1986. V.p. Ea. Lit. Coun., Melfa, Va., 1987-89; mem. Ea. Shore Coll. Found., Inc.,Melfa, 1988-94; mem. Gov.'s Adv. Bd. on Aging, Richmond, Va., 1992-94; instr. Ladies Community Bible Class, 1976-80 (Plaque 1980); sec., treas., v.p. Hospice Support of Ea. Shore, 1980-94; mem. Northampton/ Accomack Adv. Counc., 1992-94; marshall 28th anniv. commencement Ea. Shore Cmty. Coll., 1996. Recipient Nat. Sojourner Truth Meritorious Svc. award Nat. Assn. Negro Bus. and Profl. Women's Clubs, Gavel Ea. Shore Ret. Tchrs. Assn., 1994, Jefferson award Am. Inst. Pub. Svc., Wavy-TV-Bell Atlantic and Mattress Discounters, 1991, Gov.'s award for Vol. Excellence, 1994; named Home Econs. Tchr. of Yr., Am. Home Econs. Assn. and Family Cir., 1975. Mem. Progressive Women of Ea. Shore (pres. 1985-93, Gold Necklace 1993), C. of C., Univ. Women (v.p. Portsmouth br. 1985-87), Ea. Shore Ret. Tchrs. (pres. 1977-84), Dist. L Ret. Tchrs. (pres. 1989-91), Va. State Fedn. Colored Women's Club (pres. 1990-94, editor history com. 1996—), Am. Assn. Ret. Persons (Va. state legis. com. 1995—). Mem. Ch. of Christ. Avocations: crafts, travel, writing, lecturing. Home and Office: PO Box 236 14213 Lankford Hwy Eastville VA 23347-0236

WILLIAMS, J. BRYAN, lawyer; b. Detroit, July 23, 1947; s. Walter J. and Maureen June (Kay) W.; m. Jane Elizabeth Eisele, Aug. 24, 1974; children: Kyle Joseph, Ryan Patrick. AB, U. Notre Dame, 1969; JD, U. Mich., 1972. Bar: Mich. 1972, U.S. Dist. Ct. (ea. dist.) Mich. 1972. Exec. ptnr. Dickinson, Wright, Moon, Van Dusen & Freeman, Detroit, 1972—. Mem. Mich. Bar Assn., Detroit Bar Assn., Notre Dame Club of Detroit (pres. 1984), Oakland Hills Country Club, Nat. Club Assn. (bd. dirs., sec. 1995-96), Greater Detroit C. of C. (bd. dirs.). Roman Catholic. Home: 993 Suffield Ave Birmingham MI 48009-1242 Office: 500 Woodward Ave Ste 4000 Detroit MI 48226-3423

WILLIAMS, J. VERNON, lawyer; b. Honolulu, Apr. 26, 1921; s. Urban and W. Amelia (Olson) W.; m. Malvina H. Hitchcock, Oct. 4, 1947 (dec. May 1970); children—Carl H., Karin, Frances E., Scott S.; m. Mary McLellan, Sept. 6, 1980. Student, Phillips Andover Acad., 1937-39; B.A. cum laude, Amherst Coll., 1943; LL.B., Yale, 1948. Bar: Wash. 1948. Assoc. Riddell, Riddell & Hemphill, 1948-50; ptnr. Riddell, Williams, Bullitt & Walkinshaw (and predecessor firms), 1950-95; prin. Graham & James L.L.P./Riddell Williams, P.S., Seattle, 1996—; sec., dir. Airborne Freight Corp., 1968-79, gen. counsel, 1968-96. Chmn. March of Dimes, Seattle, 1954-55; Mem. Mayor's City Charter Rev. Com., 1969-69; chmn. Seattle Bd. Park Commrs., 1966-68; co-chmn. parks and open space com. Forward Thrust, 1966-69; dir. bd. and commrs. br. Nat. Recreation and Parks Assn., 1968-69; chmn. Gov.'s adv. com. Social and Health Services, 1972-75; Bd. dirs. Seattle Met. YMCA, 1965—, pres., 1976-79; trustee Lakeside Sch., 1971-79; mem. alumni council Phillps Andover Acad., 1970-73, Yale Law Sch., 1969-77; chancellor St. Mark's Cathedral, Seattle, 1964—. Served with USAAF, 1943-45. Mem. Univ. Club, Seattle Tennis Club, Birnam Wood Golf Club. Home: 1100 38th Ave E Seattle WA 98112-4434 Office: 4500 1001 4th Ave Seattle WA 98154-1065

WILLIAMS, JACK MARVIN, research chemist; b. Delta, Colo., Sept. 26, 1938; s. John Davis and Ruth Emma (Gallup) W. B.S. with honors, Lewis and Clark Coll., 1960; M.S., Wash. State U., 1964, Ph.D., 1966. Postdoctoral fellow Argonne (Ill.), Nat. Lab., 1966-68, asst. chemist, 1968-70, assoc. chemist, 1970-72, chemist, 1972-77, sr. chemist, group leader, 1977—; vis. guest prof. U. Mo., Columbia, 1980, 81, 82, U. Copenhagen, 1980, 83, 85; chair Gordon Rsch. Conf. (Inorganic Chemistry), 1980. Bd. editors: Inorganic Chemistry, 1979—, assoc. editor, 1982-93. Crown-Zellerbach scholar, 1959-60; NDEA fellow, 1960-63; recipient Disting. Performance at Argonne Nat. Labs. award U. Chgo., 1987, Centennial Disting. Alumni award Wash. State U., 1990. Mem. Am. Crystallographic Assn., Am. Chem. Soc. (treas. inorganic div. 1982-84), Am. Phys. Soc., AAAS. Office: Chemistry Div 9700 Cass Ave Lemont IL 60439-4803

WILLIAMS, JAMES A., principal. Prin. Gulliver Prep. Sch., Miami, Fla. Recipient Blue Ribbon award U.S. Dept. Edn., 1990-91. Office: Gulliver Prep Sch 6575 N Kendall Dr Miami FL 33156-1872

WILLIAMS, JAMES ALEXANDER, lawyer; b. Pine Bluff, Ark., Oct. 30, 1929; s. Absalom Alexander and Kyle (Baggarly) W.; m. Janet L. Bray, Nov. 27, 1953; children: Laura Kay, Victoria Lynn, Diana Leigh. Student, U. Ark., 1948; B.A., So. Methodist U., 1951, J.D., 1952, M.L.A., 1971. Bar: Tex. 1952. Since practiced in Dallas; mem. firm Touchstone, Bernays & Johnston, 1955-57; partner firm Bailey and Williams, 1957—. Bd. dirs. Spl. Care Sch.; bd. mgmt. YMCA; chmn. adminstrv. bd. Univ. Park United Meth. Ch., 1973; bd. dirs. Dallas Opera. Lt. USNR, 1952-55. Mem. ABA, Dallas Bar Assn., State Bar Tex., Dallas, Tex. Assn. Def. Counsel, Internat. Assn. Def. Counsel, Fedn. Ins. and Corp. Counsel, Am. Bd. Trial Advocates, Acad. Hosp. Attys., Trial Attys. Am., So. Meth. U. Law Alumni Assn. (pres. 1970-72), Exch. Club (pres. 1967), Dallas Club, Northwood Club, Crescent Club, Giraud Club (San Antonio), Chapperal Club (Dallas), Lambda Chi Alpha, Phi Alpha Delta. Democrat. Home: 4630 Northaven Rd Dallas TX 75229-4225 Office: Maxus Energy Bldg 717 N Harwood St Ste 1650 Dallas TX 75201-6508 *Honesty and fair dealing with one's fellow man are essential to real success.*

WILLIAMS, JAMES ARTHUR, retired army officer, information systems company executive; b. Paterson, N.J., Mar. 29, 1932; s. Charles M. and Elsie (Kretszchmar) W.; m. Barbara Widnall, June 26, 1959; children: Steven, Karen. BS, U.S. Mil. Acad.; MA in Latin Am. Studies, U. N.Mex. Commd. 2d lt. U.S. Army, 1954, advanced through grades to lt. gen.; asst. army attache U.S. Def. Attache Office, Caracas, Venezuela, 1966-72; exch. officer State-Def. Exch. Program Office of Sec. Def., Washington, 1972-74; comdr. 650th MI Group, Shape, 1974-76; dep. dir. estimates Def. Intelligence Agy., Washington, 1977-80; dep. chief staff for intelligence U.S. Army, Europe, 1980-81; dir. Def. Intelligence Agy., Washington, 1981-85; ret., 1985; v.p. PSC Corp., 1986; pres. Direct Info. Access Corp., Annandale, Va., 1987—. Decorated Legion of Merit, Bronze Star with oak leaf cluster, Air medals, D.S.M., Nat. Intelligence D.S.M., Army Commendation medal, French Legion of Honor; Dist. Mem. Mil. Intelligence Hall of Fame. Mem. Assn. U.S. Army, Nat. Mil. Intelligence Assn. (chmn. bd. 1987—). Methodist. Home: 8928 Maurice Ln Annandale VA 22003-3914 Office: Direct Info Access Corp PO Box 721 Annandale VA 22003-0721

WILLIAMS, JAMES BRYAN, banker; b. Sewanee, Tenn., Mar. 21, 1933; s. Eugene G. and Ellen (Bryan) W.; m. Betty G. Williams, July 11, 1980; children: Ellen, Elizabeth, Bryan. AB, Emory U., 1955. Chmn., CEO SunTrust Banks, Inc., Atlanta, 1991—; bd. dirs. The Coca-Cola Co., Atlanta, Genuine Parts Co., Atlanta, Rollins, Inc., Ga.-Pacific Corp., Atlanta, RPC, Inc., Atlanta, Sonat Inc., Birmingham, Ala. Trustee Emory U.; chmn. bd. trustees Robert W. Woodruff Health Scis. Ctr. Lt. USAF, 1955-57. Mem. Bankers Roundtable. Presbyterian. Clubs: Piedmont Driving (Atlanta), Capital City (Atlanta), Commerce (Atlanta), Peachtree Golf (Atlanta), Augusta Country. Office: SunTrust Banks Inc 25 Park Pl NE Atlanta GA 30303

WILLIAMS, JAMES CASE, metallurgist; b. Salina, Kans., Dec. 7, 1938; s. Luther Owen and Clarice (Case) W.; m. Joanne Rufener, Sept. 17, 1960; children: Teresa A., Patrick J. B.S. in Metall. Engring, U. Wash., 1962, M.S., 1964, Ph.D., 1968. Rsch. engr., lead engr. Boeing Co., Seattle, 1961-67; tech. staff N.Am. Rockwell Corp., Thousand Oaks, Calif., 1968-74; mgr. interdivisional tech. program N.Am. Aerospace group, 1974, program devel. mgr. structural materials, 1974-75; prof. metallurgy, co-dir. Ctr. for Joining of Materials, Carnegie-Mellon U., Pitts., 1975-81; pres. Mellon Inst., Pitts., 1981-83; dean Carnegie Inst. Tech., Carnegie-Mellon U., Pitts., 1983-88; gen. mgr. materials dept. GE Aircraft Engines, 1988—; Mem bd. NRC, com. on Engrin. and Tech. Systems, 1996—; chmn. Nat. Materials Adv. Bd., 1988-95, materials and structures com. NASA Aero. Adv. Com. 1992—; mem. Materials Sci. and Engring. Study, 1986-88; bd. govs. Inst. for Mechs. and Materials, U. Calif., San Diego, 1989-95. Co-editor: Scientific and Technological Aspects of Titanium and Titanium Alloys, 1976; contbr. numerous articles to tech. jours. Trustee Oreg. Grad. Inst. Sci. and Tech., 1988-94; cons. Cubmaster Boy Scouts Am., 1976-77. Recipient Ladd award Carnegie Inst. Tech.; Adams award Am. Welding Soc.; Boeing doctoral fellow. Fellow Am. Soc. Metals (Gold medal 1992); mem. NAE, ASM, AIME (Leadership award 1993), ARPA Materials Rsch. Coun., Alpha Sigma Mu. Republican. Episcopalian. Home: 3307 Brinton Trl Cincinnati OH 45241-4814 Office: GE Aircraft Engines Gen Mgr Material Dept MD H85 Cincinnati OH 45215

WILLIAMS, JAMES E., food products manufacturing company executive; married. With Golden State foods Corp., 1961—; chief exec. officer Golden State foods Corp., Pasadena, Calif., 1978—. Office: Golden State Foods Corp 18301 Von Karman Ave Ste 1100 Irvine CA 92715-1009*

WILLIAMS, JAMES EUGENE, JR., management consultant; b. Macon, Ga., June 23, 1927; s. James Eugene and Margaret Elizabeth (Tinker) W.; m. Linda K. Magnuson, June 23, 1984; children: Paul David, Lisa Jane Williams Robertson, Philip Alan, Gail Ellen Williams Feeney, Amanda Allen Thompson, Jason Douglas Allen, Joel Winston Allen. BS in Aero. Engring., Iowa State Coll., 1950. Engr. Robins AFB, Ga., 1950-54, Hdqrs. USAF, Washington, 1954-61; dep. asst. sec. Office Asst. Sec. Air Force, Washington, 1961-85; dir. govt. bus. policy Northrop Corp., Washington, 1986-88; mgmt. cons. Tempe, Ariz., 1988—. Recipient Presdl. Meritorious Exec. award, 1981, Presdl. Disting. Exec. award, 1982. Home: 3223 S College Ave Tempe AZ 85282-3773

WILLIAMS, JAMES FRANCIS, JR., religious organization administrator; b. Coffeyville, Kans., June 20, 1938; s. James Francis and Sarah Kathryn (Tavenner) W.; m. Alice Carol Kinney, June 1, 1963; children: James F. III, Todd Alexander, Leslie. BA, So. Meth. U., 1960; ThM, Dallas Theol. Sem., 1964; HHD, U. Tex., 1988. Campus dir. Campus Crusade for Christ, Dallas, 1961-64; area dir. Campus Crusade for Christ, various North Tex. locations, 1964-68; regional dir. Campus Crusade for Christ, Southwestern U.S., 1968-71; nat. dir. tng. Campus Crusade for Christ, U.S., 1971-72; founder, pres. Probe Ministries, Internat., Dallas, 1973—; dir. music Campus Crusade for Christ, Arrowhead, Calif., 1967-71. soloist, chorus Dallas Opera, 1982-84. Named one of Outstanding Young Men in Am. Dallas Jaycees, 1965. Evangelical Christian. Office: Probe Ministries 1900 Firman Dr Ste 100 Richardson TX 75081-1869

WILLIAMS, JAMES FRANKLIN, II, university dean, librarian; b. Montgomery, Ala., Jan. 22, 1944; s. James Franklin and Anne (Wester) W.; m. Madeline McClellan, Jan. 1966 (div. May 1988); 1 child, Madeline Marie; m. Nancy Allen, Aug. 1989; 1 child, Audrey Grace. BA, Morehouse Coll., 1966; MLS, Atlanta U., 1967. Reference libr. Wayne State U. Sci. Libr., Detroit, 1968-69; document delivery libr. Wayne State U. Med. Libr., Detroit, 1969-70, head of reference, 1971-72, dir. med. libr. and regional med. libr. network, 1972-81, regional dir., 1975-82; assoc. dir. of librs. Wayne State U., 1981-88; dean librs. U. Colo., Boulder, 1988—; bd. regents Nat. Libr. Medicine, Bethesda, Md., 1978-81. Mem. editl. bd. ACRL Publications in Librarianship, College and Research Libraries; contbr. articles to profl. jours., chpts. to books; book editor and author. Subject of feature interview in centennial issue Am. Librs. jour., 1976. Mem. ALA (Visionary Leader award 1988), Coll. and Rsch. Librs. (editl. bd.), Assn. Rsch. Librs. (bd. dirs. 1994—). Avocations: cycling, travel, fishing. Office: U Colo Office of Dean Librs Campus Box 184 Boulder CO 80309-0184

WILLIAMS, JAMES HENRY, JR., mechanical engineer, educator, consultant; b. Newport News, Va., Apr. 4, 1941; s. James H. Williams and Margaret L. (Holt) Mitchell; children: James Henry III, Sky Margaret Melodie. Mech. designer (Homer L. Ferguson scholar), Newport News Apprentice Sch., 1965; S.B., MIT, 1967, S.M., 1968; Ph.D., Trinity Coll., Cambridge U., 1970. Sr. design engr. Newport News Shipyard, 1960-70; asst. prof. mech. engring. M.I.T., 1970-74, assoc. prof., 1974-81, prof., 1981—, duPont prof., 1973, Edgerton prof., 1974-76; cons. engring. to numerous cos. Contbr. numerous articles on stress analysis, vibration, fracture mechanics, composite materials and nondestructive testing to profl. jours. Recipient Charles F. Bailey Bronze medal, 1961, Charles F. Bailey Silver medal, 1962, Charles F. Bailey Gold medal, 1963, Baker award M.I.T., 1973, Den Hartog Disting. Educator award, 1981; named prof. teaching excellence Sch. Engring., 1991; C.F. Hopewell faculty fellow, 1993—. Mem. ASME, Am. Soc. Nondestructive Testing, Nat. Tech. Assn. Subspecialties: Theoretical and applied mechanics; Composite materials. Office: MIT Room 3-360 77 Massachusetts Ave Cambridge MA 02139

WILLIAMS, JAMES JOSEPH, environmental scientist, researcher; b. Akron, Ohio, Jan. 12, 1954; s. Joseph Chester and Fawnabelle (Taylor) W. BS in Biology, U. Cin., 1976, MS in Environ. Sci., 1990; Exec. MBA, Ohio U., 1995. Chemist, plant operator Delaware (Ohio) WWTP, 1977-81; chemist CLC Lab., Columbus, Ohio, 1979-80; lab. supr. Burgess & Niple Ltd., Columbus, 1981-83; chemist, supr. Nestle QAL, Marysville, 1983-85; rsch. assoc. Roxanne Labs., Columbus, 1985-87; mgr. O&M manual div. OCS, Inc., Mason, Ohio, 1987-91; R & D assoc. Martin Marietta Energy Systems, Piketon, Ohio, 1991-93; supr. organic analytical svcs. Lockheed Marietta Utility Svcs., Piketon, 1993—. Leader 4-H Club, Mechanicsburg, Ohio, 1965-74; singer, soloist Cantari Singers, Columbus, 1983-87; tenor soloist Trinity Episcopal Ch., Columbus, 1987-92; soloist Opera Columbus, 1981-90, Second Ch. of Christ Scientist, 1992—. Recipient Leadership award Nat. 4-H Found., 1972; U. Cin. grad. minority scholar, 1988, 89. Mem. Am. Chem. Soc., Water Pollution Control Fedn., Am. Water Works Assn., Sigma Xi (assoc.). Democrat. Baptist. Home: 550 Terrace Ln Chillicothe OH 45601-2948

WILLIAMS, JAMES KELLEY, diversified resources company executive; b. Bentonia, Miss., Mar. 29, 1934; s. James C. and Katheryn (Kelley) W.; m. Jean Pittman, June 16, 1956; children: James Kelley Jr., George P., Clifford C. B.S. in Chem. Enging, Ga. Inst. Tech., 1956; M.B.A., Harvard U., 1962. Asst. to pres. Tyrone Hydraulics, Corinth, Miss., 1962-67; mgr. corp. planning and devel. First Miss. Corp., Jackson, 1967-69, v.p., 1969-71, pres., CEO, 1971-88, chmn., pres., CEO, 1988—, also chmn. exec. com., bd. dirs.; chmn. B.C. Rogers Poultry, Inc., Morton, Miss., 1981—; mem. adv. coun. Degussa Corp.; dir. Deposit Guaranty Corp., Deposit Guaranty Nat. Bank. Dirs. Miss. Econ. Coun., Com. for Econ. Devel., Washington; deacon Northminster Bapt. Ch.; trustee Miss. Found. Ind. Colls., Nature Conservancy; chmn. Inst. Tech. Devel. for Miss. With USAR, 1957-60. Mem. Fertilizer Inst., Chief Execs. Orgn., Mfg. Chemists Assn., Agribus Promotion Coun., World Bus. Coun., Hundred of Jackson. Clubs: Jackson Country, River Hills, Hundred of Jackson. Office: First Miss Corp PO Box 1249 700 North St Jackson MS 39215-1249 also: BC Rogers Poultry Inc 121 Old Hwy 80 E Morton MS 39117*

WILLIAMS, JAMES KENDRICK, bishop. Ed., St. Mary's Coll., St. Mary's, Ky., St. Maur's Sch. Theology, South Union, Ky. Ordained priest Roman Catholic Ch., 1963; ordained titular bishop Catula and aux. bishop of Covington, 1984; ordained first bishop of Lexington, Ky., installed 1988. Office: Bishop of Lexington PO Box 12350 1310 Leestown Rd Lexington KY 40582-2350*

WILLIAMS, JAMES LEE, financial industries executive; b. Tampa, Fla., Nov. 5, 1941; s. Donald Clark and Nell (Medlin) W.; m. Linda Taylor, Dec. 28, 1968; children: Donald Clark II, Taylor Lee. AA, St. Petersburg (Fla.) Jr. Coll., 1965; BS, Fla. State U., 1967. Mgmt. Ryder Truck Lines, Jacksonville, Fla., 1967-69; dist. mgr. underwriting div. U.S. Leasing Corp., Dallas, 1969-73; area v.p. Mfrs. Hanover Leasing Corp., Houston and London, 1973-79; v.p. corp. fin. Underwood Neuhause & Co. Inc., Houston, 1979-81; chmn., chief exec. officer 1st City Leasing Corp., Houston, 1981-85; mng. dir. capital markets 1st City Bancorp., Houston, 1985-89; mng. dir. fin. svcs. M.P.S.I. Systems Inc., Dallas, 1989-90; pres., chief exec. officer Strategic Decisions Holdings Corp., Dallas, 1990-92; sr. mng. dir. Williams and Assocs., 1992; pres. Global Svcs. Capital Corp., Houston, 1993—. Served with USN, 1959-62. Mem. Equipment Leasing Assn. (fed. govt. rels. com. 1984-88, 95—), Tex. Assn. Equipment Lessors (bd. dirs. 1985-89), Greater Houston Partnership. Republican. Presbyterian. Clubs: Houston Ctr. (bd. dirs. 1985-89), Lakeside Racquet (athletic com. 1986-89), Forum (Houston). Avocations: golf, jogging, swimming. Office: Global Svcs Capital Corp 2902 W 12th St Houston TX 77008-6114

WILLIAMS, JAMES ORRIN, university administrator, educator; b. New Orleans, Jan. 8, 1937; married, 1956; 3 children. BS, Auburn U., 1960, MEd, 1963, EdD, 1967; postgrad., Tchrs. Coll., Columbia U., summer 1964. Tchr. social sci., coach Columbus High Sch. Ga., 1960-61; tchr., coach Eufaula High Sch. Ala., 1961-63; prin. Troy Jr. High Sch., 1963-65; grad. asst. Sch. Edn. Auburn U., 1965-66, interim dir. field service, 1966-67; asst. prof. edn. adminstrn. U. Fla., 1967-68; asst. prof. Columbus Coll., 1968-69; assoc. prof., chmn. div. Auburn U., Montgomery, 1969-73, vice chancellor acad. affairs, 1973-80, chancellor, 1980—. Contbr. articles to profl. jours. Phi Delta Kappa grantee, 1967. Mem. Am. Assn. State Colls. and Univs., Am. Assn. Coll. Tchr. Edn., Assn. Tchr. Edn., So. Regional Council Edn. Adminstrn., Phi Delta Kappa (v.p. 1965), Phi Kappa Phi. Office: Auburn U-Montgomery Office of Chancellor 7300 University Dr Montgomery AL 36117-3531

WILLIAMS, JAMES RICHARD, human factors engineering psychologist; b. Chgo., Apr. 16, 1932; s. James Henry and Margaret Lucille (Keefer) W.; m. Jonetta Rae Gilbert, Dec. 19, 1959; children: Janise Rebecca, Jason Richard. BS in Psychology, Purdue U., 1958, MS in Human Factors/Indsl. Psychology, 1960; PhD in Edn., NYU, 1971. Bd. cert. in profl. ergonomics. Technical asst. Sci. Rsch. Assocs., Chgo., 1960-61; sr. systems cons. System Devel. Corp., Paramus, N.J., 1961-64; human factors engr. Kollsman Instrument Corp., Elmhurst, N.Y., 1964-66; project mgr. System Devel. Corp., Paramus, 1966-69; supr. tng. and standards Bell Labs., Piscataway, N.J., 1969-74; dist. mgr. AT&T, Basking Ridge, N.J., 1975-80; mem. technical staff Bell Labs., Piscataway, 1981-83; learning technologist Bell Communications Rsch., Piscataway, 1984—; cons. NYU, N.Y.C., 1968-70; chair U.S. Tech. Adv. Group, to internat. orgn. for standardization in ergonomics of human system interaction, 1988—. Editor: International Standards for Menu Dialogues, Command Dialogues and Form-fill Dialogues with Computer Systems. Cub master Boy Scouts, Watchung, N.Y., 1973-74, asst. scout master, 1975-78. With USAF, 1951-55. Mem. Am. Psychol. Soc. (charter), Assn. for Computing Machinery (spl. interest group on computer-human interaction), Human Factors and Ergonomics Soc. (rep. 1986—), Delta Rho Kappa, Kappa Delta Pi. Avocations: winemaking-co-owner Del Vista Vineyards, astronomy, body bldg. Home: 137 County Rd 513 Frenchtown NJ 08825-3727 Office: Bell Comm Rsch 6 Corporate Pl Piscataway NJ 08854-4120

WILLIAMS, JERALD ARTHUR, mechanical engineer; b. Miller, S.D., Dec. 22, 1942; s. Willard Arthur and Mildred Irene Williams; m. Judy Deannia Allsip, May 30, 1966; children: Todd, Monique, Heather. BSME, Wash. State U., 1966; MS in Mech. Engring., U. Wash., 1967. Mech. engr. Mobile Oil Co., Bakersfield, Calif., 1966; assoc. rsch. engr. Boeing Airplane Co., Seattle, 1968; mech. engr. Boeing Airplane Co., Renton, Wash., 1971-72; exec. v.p. Bouillon, Christofferson & Schairer, Seattle, 1972—. Contbr. articles to profl. jours. Cub scout pack leader Boy Scouts Am., Issaquah, Wash., 1979-80. Capt. U.S. Army, 1968-71, Viet Nam. Mem. Cons. Engrs. Coun. Wash. (dir. 1986-90, chair various coms. 1982-94), Am. Cons. Engrs. Coun. (naval fac. engring. command liaison com. 1985-95, chmn. 1989-95), Seattle Rotary, Phi Eta Sigma, Phi Kappa Phi, Sigma Tau, Tau Beta Pi. Avocations: fishing, hunting, hiking, beach combing, antiques. Home: 16151 SE 42nd St Bellevue WA 98006-1809 Office: Bouillon Christofferson & Schairer 1201 3rd Ave Ste 800 Seattle WA 98101-3000

WILLIAMS, JESSIE WILLMON, church worker, retired librarian; b. Boynton, Okla., Feb. 23, 1907; d. Thomas Woodard and Eliza Jane (Adams) Willmon; m. Austin Guest, Aug. 13, 1932 (div. 1945); m. Thomas Washington Williams, Dec. 12, 1946 (dec.). BA, East Tex. State U., 1930, MA, 1944. cert. English and Spanish tchr., Tex. Libr. Gladewater (Tex.) Pub. Libr., 1935-46; med. libr. VA Hosp., North Little Rock, Ark., 1946-58; base libr. Little Rock AFB, 1958-68; ret., 1968; lay worker 1st Bapt. Ch., Pecan Gap, Tex., 1988—. Mem. Delta Kappa Gamma, Phi Beta Kappa. Democrat. Mem. So. Bapt. Conv. Home: PO Box 43 Pecan Gap TX 75469-0043 *Proverbs 30: 8-9 summarizes the good life for me! "Remove far from me vanity and lies; give me neither poverty nor riches; feed me with food convenient for me; lest I be full and deny thee and say 'Who is the Lord?' or lest I be poor and steal, and take the name of my God in vain.*

WILLIAMS, JOBETH, actress; b. Houston, 1953; m. John Pasquin; children: Nick, Will. Student, Brown U. Appeared in plays A Coupla White Chicks Sitting Around Talking, 1980, Gardenia, 1982, Idiot's Delight, 1986, Cat on a Hot Tin Roof, 1993; films include Kramer vs. Kramer, 1979, The Dogs of War, 1980, Stir Crazy, 1980, Poltergeist, 1982, Endangered Species, 1982, The Big Chill, 1983, American Dreamer, 1984, Teachers, 1984, Desert Bloom, 1986, Poltergeist II, 1986, Memories of Me, 1988, Welcome Home, 1989, Switch, 1991, Dutch, 1991, Stop! Or My Mom Will Shoot, 1992, Me, Myself and I, 1993, Wyatt Earp, 1994; TV movies include Fun and Games, 1980, The Big Black Pill, 1981, Adam, 1983 (Emmy award nominee, Golden Globe award nominee), The Day After, 1983, Kids Don't Tell, 1985, Adam: His Song Continues, 1986, Murder Ordained, 1987, Baby M, 1988 (Emmy award nominee, Golden Globe award nominee), My Name is Bill W., 1989, Child in the Night, 1990, Victim of Love, 1991, Jonathan: The Boy Nobody Wanted, 1992, Sex, Love and Cold Hard Cash, 1993, Chantilly Lace, 1993, Voices from Within, 1994, Lemon Grove, 1994, Parallel Lives, 1994, Voices from Within, 1994, Season of Hope, 1994; TV series include The Guiding Light, Somerset, John Grisham's The Client; contbr. voice to Fish Police; co-exec. prodr.: (TV movie) Bump in the Night, 1991; dir. film: On Hope, 1994 (Acad. award nominee for Best Live Action Short Film 1995). Office: William Morris Agy Inc 151 S El Camino Dr Beverly Hills CA 90212-2704*

WILLIAMS, JOCELYN JONES, reading educator; b. Greenville, N.C., Sept. 24, 1948; d. William Edward and Elinor Suejette (Albritton) Jones; m. Robert Alexander Simpkins Jr., Sept. 7, 1969 (div. May 1972); m. Oscar James Williams Jr., July 12, 1985 (div. Mar. 1989). BS, Bennett Coll., 1970; MEd, N.C. Cen. U., 1988; MS, N.C. Agrl. & Tech. State U., 1992. Kindergarten/1st grade tchr. Greenville City Schs., 1970-74; elem./reading tchr. Orange County Schs., Hillsborough, N.C., 1974—; mem. N.C. Reading Recovery Adv. Bd., 1994—, Reading Recovery Coun. N.Am., 1994—. Mem. NEA, ASCD, Internat. Reading Assn., Nat. Assn. Edn. Young Children, N.C. Assn. Educators, Phi Delta Kappa, Alpha Kappa Alpha, Progressive Sertoma Club. Democrat. Baptist. Avocations: reading, singing, sewing, cooking. Home: 47 Celtic Dr Durham NC 27703-2894

WILLIAMS, JOE, jazz and blues singer; b. Cordele, Ga., Dec. 12, 1918. Founder singing group, The Jubilee Boys, Chgo., 1930's, numerous nightclub appearances, Chgo.; appeared with Jimmie Noone Band, Les Hite Band, Coleman Hawkins Band, Lionel Hampton Band, Red Saunders Band, blues singer, Count Basie Orch., 1954-61, also appeared, with Duke and Mercer Ellington Orchs.; appeared in concerts with Buddy Rich, Harry Edison, Junior Mance and frequent reunions with Count Basie Orch., numerous jazz festivals including regular appearances Newport Jazz Festival;

film Moonshine War, 1969; video Joe Williams: A Song Is Born with George Shearing, 1992; recs. include Joe Williams and his Count Basie Orch., 1993, (with the Robert Farnon Orch.) Here's To Life, 1994; actor Bill Cosby Show, 1987. Winner Downbeat Readers Poll, 1955-56. Downbeat Internat. Critics Poll, 1955, 74, 75, 76, 77, 78, D.J. Poll, Billboard mag., 1959; recipient Top award Rhythm and Blues Mag., 1956, Grammy award for Best Jazz Vocal, 1984. Office: Thomas Cassidy Inc 366 Horseshoe Dr Basalt CO 81621-9104

WILLIAMS, JOHN A. (JACK WILLIAMS), newspaper publishing executive; b. Springfield, Ill., May 1, 1950; m. Judy Williams; children: Suzanne, Michel. BBA, U. Ill., 1972. Part-time employee Ill. State Jour. & Register, Springfield, 1968-72; bus. mgr. San Francisco Progress, 1972-74; gen. mgr. Yakima (Wash.) Herald Republic, 1975-80, Modesto (Calif.) Bee, 1980-85; v.p. sales & mktg. Seattle Times Co., 1985-89, exec. v.p., 1989—; dir., 1st v.p. Direct Mktg. Puget Sound, Inc., Times Communications Co., Inc, Times Distribution, Inc., Times Info. Svcs., Inc.; v.p., dir. Yakima Herald-Republic, Inc., Rotary Offset Press, Inc., Times Community Newspapers, Inc. Chmn. bd. Leadership Tomorrow, bd. dirs., 1987—; mem. strategic planning com. United Way, 1991—; bd. dirs. Corp. Coun. Arts, 1989—. Mem. Newspaper Assn. Am. (dir.), Newspapers First (dir., exec. com.), Glendale Country Club, The Lakes Club, The Rainier Club, Washington Athletic Club, Bellevue Athletic Club. Office: Seattle Times Co PO Box 70 Fairview Ave N & John Seattle WA 98111-0070

WILLIAMS, JOHN ALAN, secondary education educator, coach; b. Watertown, N.Y., May 30, 1949; s. John F. and Doris (Fuess) W.; m. Ana Maria Delima Moniz, Feb. 22, 1977; children: Timothy John, Katherine Evelyn. BS in Oceanography, U.S. Naval Acad., 1971; MS in Sci. Edn., Syracuse U., 1978; postgrad., SUNY, Oswego, 1989-90. Sci. tchr., coach Liverpool (N.Y.) High Sch., 1977-80, sci. tchr., coach, dir. sci. and tech. fair, 1981—, advisor, coach Olympiad Team, 1987—; application engr. Hoffman Air & Filtration, Syracuse, N.Y., 1980-81. Coach wrestling team Liverpool High Sch., 1982—; coach local Pee Wee wrestling team, 1982—; bd. dirs. sci. fair com. Syracuse Discovery Ctr., 1986—. Lt. USN, 1971-76, Vietnam. Named Ctrl. N.Y. Sci. Tchr. of Yr. Syracuse Discovery Ctr., 1986-87, Onondaga High Sch. League-North Wrestling Coach of Yr., 1984-85, 88-89, 92-93. Mem. Nat. Earth Sci. Tchrs. Assn., United Liverpool Faculty Assn., N.Y. State Sci. Tchrs. Assn. (10 Yr. award 1990), Assn. Sci. Tech. Ctrs. (Honor Roll Tchrs. 1987), Syracuse Tech. Club (Outstanding Tchr. award 1990), NFL (Tchr. of Yr. 1990), Sigma Xi (Outstanding Sci. Tchr. award 1989). Home: 4320 Luna Crse Liverpool NY 13090-2050 Office: Liverpool High Sch 4338 Wetzel Rd Liverpool NY 13090-2011

WILLIAMS, JOHN ALFRED, educator, author; b. Jackson, Miss., 1925; m. Lorrain Isaac; 1 son, Adam; children by previous marriage: Gregory, Dennis. Grad., Syracuse U., Nat. Inst. Arts and Letters, 1962; LL.D., U. Mass., Dartmouth, 1978; Lit.D, Syracuse U., 1995. With Am. Com. on Africa, N.Y.C.; Disting. prof. English La Guardia Community Coll., 1973-74, 74-75; prof. English Rutgers U., 1979—, Paul Robeson prof. English, 1990—; Bard Ctr. fellow Bard Coll., 1994-95; lectr. CCNY; guest writer Sarah Lawrence Coll.; Regents lectr. U. Calif., Santa Barbara, 1972, U. Hawaii, 1974, Nat. Endowment for the Arts, 1977; vis. prof. Boston U., 1978-79, NYU, 1986-87. Started writing poetry during World War II, in Pacific; Author: (novels) The Angry Ones, 1960; novels Night Song, 1961, Sissie, 1963, The Man Who Cried I Am, 1967, Sons of Darkness, Sons of Light, 1969, Captain Blackman, 1972, Mothersill and the Foxes, 1975, The Junior Bachelor Society, 1976, (plays) Last Flight from Ambo Ber, 1981, The Berhama Account, 1985, Jacob's Ladder, 1987, also 8 vols. of non-fiction, vol. of poems; !Click Song, 1982 (Before Columbus Found. Am. Book award 1983); 7 anthologies. Recipient Centennial medal for outstanding achievement Syracuse U., 1970, Lindback award for Disting. Teaching Rutgers U., 1982. Home: 693 Forest Ave Teaneck NJ 07666-2042 *I've tried to adhere to the philosophies of W.E.B. DuBois. He never quit.*

WILLIAMS, JOHN ANDREW, physiology educator, consultant; b. Des Moines, Aug. 3, 1941; s. Harold Southall and Marjorie (Larsen) W.; m. Christa A. Smith, Dec. 26, 1965; children: Rachel Jo, Matthew Dallas. BA, Cen. Wash. State Coll., 1963; MD, U. Wash., Seattle, 1968, PhD, 1968. Staff fellow NIH, Bethesda, Md., 1969-71; research fellow U. Cambridge, Eng., 1971-72; from asst. to prof. physiology U. Calif., San Francisco, 1973-87; prof. physiology, chair dept. physiology, prof. internal medicine U. Mich., Ann Arbor, 1987—; mem. gen. medicine study sect. NIH, Bethesda, 1985-88, DDK-C study sect., 1991-95. Contbr. numerous articles to profl. jours.; editor Am. Jour. Physiology: Gastrointestinal Physiology, 1985-91. Trustee Friends Sch. in Detroit, 1992—. NIH grantee, 1973—. Mem. Am. Physiol. Soc. (Hoffman LaRoche prize 1985, mem. coun. 1996-99), Am. Soc. Cell Biology, Am. Soc. Clin. Investigation, Am. Gastroenterology Assn., Am. Pancreatic Assn. (pres. 1985-86). Democrat. Home: 1115 Woodlawn Ave Ann Arbor MI 48104-3956 Office: Dept Physiology Univ of Mich Med Sch Ann Arbor MI 48109

WILLIAMS, JOHN CHRISTOPHER RICHARD, bishop; b. Sale, Cheshire, Eng., May 22, 1936; arrived in Can., 1960; s. Frank Harold and Ceridwen Roberts (Hughes) W.; m. Rona Macrae Aitken, Mar. 18, 1964; children: Andrew David, Judith Ann. BA in Commerce, Manchester U., Eng., 1958; diploma in theology, Cranmer Hall, Durham, Eng., 1960. Ordained deacon Anglican Ch. of Can., 1960, priest, 1962. Missionary in charge Anglican Ch. Can., Sugluk, Que., Can., 1961-72, Cape Dorset, N.W.T., Can., 1972-75, Baker Lake, N.W.T., 1975-78; archdeacon of the Keewatim Anglican Ch. Can., 1975-87; rector Holy Trinity Anglican Ch. Can., Yellowknife, N.W.T., 1978-87; bishop suffagan Diocese of the Arctic, Can., 1987-90, diocesan bishop, 1990—; trustee Can. Churchman, Anglican Ch. Can., 1976-82, mem. nat. exec. com., 1976-79, 92—. Coord., trans. into Eskimo Inukkitut New Testament, 1992. Avocations: reading, skiing, swimming.

WILLIAMS, JOHN COBB, lawyer; b. Chgo., June 11, 1930; s. Ralph Milton and Mary Mason (Cobb) W.; m. Helen Gilbert, Aug. 19, 1955; children: Holly Montague, Nancy Morrison, Sarah M. B.A., Wesleyan U., 1951; LL.B., Yale U., 1954. Bar: Ill. 1955, Fla. 1974. Assoc. firm. Sidley & Austin, Chgo., 1954-63; ptnr. Sidley & Austin, 1964—; off counsel Sidley & Austin, Chicago, Il. Trustee Village of Northbrook, Ill., 1965-69, village pres., 1969-73, mem. plan commn. zoning bd. appeals, 1965-69; mem. police pension fund bd. Village of Glencoe, Ill., 1980-82; chmn. pub. safety commn. Village of Gencoe, 1982—; bd. dirs. North Suburban Assn. Health Resources, 1973, pres., 1974-75; bd. dirs. North Suburban Blood Ctr., 1973-75. Fellow Am. Coll. Probate Counsel; mem. ABA, Ill. Bar Assn. (chmn. on legis. 1975-76, chmn. estate planning, probate and trust sec. council 1984-85), Chgo. Bar Assn. (chmn. legis. com. 1969-71, chmn. com. on probate practice 1972-73). Clubs: Skokie Country (Glencoe); University, Econ, Law, Legal (Chgo.). Home: 486 Greenleaf Ave Glencoe IL 60022-1768 Office: Sidley & Austin 1 First Nat Plz Chicago IL 60603*

WILLIAMS, JOHN CORNELIUS, lawyer; b. Lee Valley, Tenn., Jan. 24, 1903; s. Hugh and Kitty (Lawrence) W.; 1 son by former marriage, John Cornelius; m. Darthey I. Black, Aug. 12, 1954; 1 dau., Kitty. A.B., Wofford Coll., 1927; LL.B., U. S.C., 1931. Bar: S.C. bar 1931. Prin. Campobello High Sch., Spartanburg County, S.C., 1927-28; practiced in Spartanburg, 1931-61; U.S. atty. Western Dist. S.C., 1951-54, 61-68; partner law firm Williams and Williams, Spartanburg, 1968—; Mem. S. C. Legislature, 1931-32, 49-50. Served to col. U.S. Army, 1940-46. Mem. S.C. Bar Assn., Spartanburg County Bar Assn. (past pres.), 4th U.S. Jud. Conf., V.F.W. (past comdr. S.C.), Am. Legion, 40 and 8, Blue Key, Pi Kappa Delta, Phi Kappa Sigma, Phi Alpha Delta. Democrat. Baptist. Club: Masons (32 degree). Home: 318 S Park Dr Spartanburg SC 29302-3244

WILLIAMS, JOHN EDWARD, lawyer; b. Atlanta, May 21, 1946; s. Edward Carl and Mary E. (Griffin) W.; m. Kristin Forsberg, May 22, 1976; children: Alexandra, Courtney, Charles. BA, Yale U., 1968; JD, U. Va., 1974; LLM in Taxation, Georgetown U., 1977. Bar: Va. 1974, D.C. 1975, U.S. Dist. Ct. D.C. 1975, U.S. Tax Ct. 1975, U.S. Ct. Appeals (D.C. cir.) 1975, U.S. Supreme Ct. 1977. Law clk. to Judge Charles R. Richey U.S. Dist. Ct. (D.C. dist.), 1974-75; assoc. Patton, Boggs & Blow, Washington, 1975-78, Cadwalader, Wickersham & Taft, Washington, 1978-81; asst. to the commr. IRS, Washington, 1981-84; tax counsel Ropes & Gray, Washington, 1984-86; ptnr. David & Hagner, P.C., Washington, 1986-90, Winston & Strawn, Washington, 1990—; mem. Jud. Conf. of D.C. Circuit, 1978, 82, 85, 87, 92. With U.S. Army, 1968-74. Mem. ABA (tax sect., chmn. tech. subcom., adminstrv. practice com. 1986-88), Met., Yale N.Y.C., Chevy Chase Club. Home: 4526 36th St NW Washington DC 20008-4250 Office: Winston & Strawn 1400 L St NW Washington DC 20005-3509

WILLIAMS, JOHN EDWIN, psychology educator; b. Bluefield, W.Va., June 12, 1928; s. Marvin Glenn and Kathleen Virginia (Stinson) W.; m. Doris Jean Crawford, July 6, 1948 (div. 1971); children: Kathleen Diane, James Taylor, Thomas Crawford, Jeannette Kiser; m. Kathryn Lee Bond, June 19, 1971 (div. 1995); stepchildren: Kimberly Lyn Himan, Brock Eugene Himan; m. Sarah Jane Noland, Apr. 3, 1995; stepchildren: Charlotte A. Matthis, Ginger G. Matthis. Student, Bluefield Coll., 1945-46, 48-49; B.A., U. Richmond, 1951; M.A., U. Iowa, 1953, Ph.D., 1954. Instr. Yale U., 1954-55; asst. prof., then assoc. prof. U. Richmond, 1955-59; prof. psychology Wake Forest U., 1959—, Disting. prof., 1992-95, chmn. dept., 1969-94; prof. emeritus, 1996—; editor Jour. of Cross-Cultural Psychology, 1991-95. Author: (with J.K. Morland) Race, Color and the Young Child, 1976, (with D.L. Best) Measuring Sex Stereotypes—A 30-Nation Study, 1982, Sex and Psyche: Gender and Self Viewed Cross-Culturally, 1990; contbr. articles to profl. jours. Served with AUS, 1946-48. Recipient research grants Nat. Inst. Child Health and Human Devel., 1967-73, research grants NIMH, 1977-79. Fellow APA, Am. Psychol. Soc., N.C. Psychol. Assn. (pres. 1964-65); mem. AAUP, Soc. Exptl. Social Psychology, Southeastern Psychol. Assn. (pres. 1991-92), Internat. Assn. Cross-Cultural Psychology, Coun. Grad. Depts. of Psychology (chair 1984-85), Phi Beta Kappa, Sigma Xi, Phi Theta Kappa, Psi Chi.

WILLIAMS, JOHN HORTER, civil engineer, oil, gas, telecommunications and allied products distribution company executive; b. Havana, Cuba, Aug. 17, 1918; s. Charles P. and Alice Magruder (Dyer) W.; m. Emily Alice Ijams, June 6, 1942 (dec.); children—John H., Burch I., S. Miller; m. Joanne Harwell Simpson., Feb. 1, 1975. B.S., Yale U., 1940. Registered profl. engr., Okla., Minn. With The Williams Cos. Inc., Tulsa, 1940-42, 46-50, pres., dir., 1950-70, chmn., chief exec. officer, 1971-78, now hon. dir.; bd. dirs. Apco Argentina, Inc., Unit Corp. Served with USNR, 1942-46. Decorated Order of Condor of Andes (Bolivia); named Okla. Hall of Fame, 1977; recipient Outstanding Okla. Oil Man awad Okla.-Kans. Oil and Gas Assn., 1982, Disting. Svc. award Nat. Petroleum Hall of Fame, 1985; inducted into Okla. Commerce and Industry Hall of Honor, 1986, Tulsa Hall of Fame, 1993. Mem. ASCE, Yale Engring. Assn. Office: The Williams Cos Inc 1 Williams Ctr Fl 49 Tulsa OK 74172-0165

WILLIAMS, JOHN JAMES, JR., architect; b. Denver, July 13, 1949; s. John James and Virginia Lee (Thompson) W.; m. Mary Serene Morck, July 29, 1972. BArch, U. Colo., 1974. Registered architect, Colo., Calif., Idaho, Va., Utah, Nev. Project architect Gensler Assoc. Architects, Denver, 1976, Heinzman Assoc. Architects, Boulder, Colo., 1977, EZTH Architects, Boulder, 1978-79; prin. Knudson/Williams PC, Boulder, 1980-82, Faber, Williams & Brown, Boulder, 1982-86, John Williams & Assocs., Denver, 1986—; panel chmn. U. Colo. World Affairs Conf.; vis. faculty U. Colo. Sch. Architecture and Planning, Coll. Environ. Design, 1986-91. Author (with others) State of Colorado architect licensing law, 1986. Commr. Downtown Boulder Mall Commn., 1985-88; bd. dirs. U. Colo. Fairway Club, 1986-88; mem. Gov's. Natural Hazard Mitigation Coun., State of Colo., 1990. Recipient Teaching Honorarium, U. Colo. Coll. Architecture and Planning, 1977, 78, 79, 80, 88, Excellence in Design and Planning award City of Boulder, 1981, 82, Citation for Excellenc, WOOD Inc., 1982, 93, Disting. Profl. Svc. award Coll. Environ. Design U. Colo., 1988. Mem. AIA (sec. 1988, bd. dirs. Colo. North chpt. 1985-86, chair Colo. govtl. affairs com., Design award 1993, pres. 1990, v.p. 1989, sec. 1987, sec. Colo. chpt. 1988, ednl. fund Fisher I traveling scholar 1988, state design conf. chair 1991, North chpt. Design award 1993), Architects and Planners of Boulder (v.p. 1982), Nat. Coun. Architect Registration Bd., Nat. Golf Found. (sponsor), Kappa Sigma (chpt. pres. 1970). Avocations: golf, polit. history, fitness and health. Home: 1031 Turnberry Cir Louisville CO 80027-9594 Office: John Williams & Assocs 821 17th St Ste 502 Denver CO 80202

WILLIAMS, JOHN LEE, lawyer; b. Nashville, Dec. 23, 1942; s. Leslie Elwood and Gladys Mae (Ridings) W.; m. Norma Jean Givens, May 27, 1967; 1 child, Jacob Andrew. BA, Tenn. Technol. U., 1964; JD, U. Tenn., 1967. Bar: Tenn 1967. Ptnr. Porch, Peeler & Williams, Waverly, Tenn., 1967-78, Porch, Peeler, Williams Thomason, Waverly, 1978—; asst. dist. atty. 21st Jud. Cir. Ct. Tenn., 1972-74; judge Ct. Gen. Sessions of Humphreys County, Tenn., 1978-82; county atty. Humphreys County, 1968-72, 82-86, 94—; city atty. City of Waverly, 1978—, City of McEwen, Tenn., 1978—, City of Lobelville, Tenn., 1985-89; gen. counsel Meriwether Lewis Elec. Coop., Centerville, Tenn., 1980—; cmty. dir. NationsBank, Humphreys County, 1984-95. State legal counsel Tenn. Jaycees, 1970; treas., sec. Humphreys County Dem. Exec. Com., 1978—; chmn. Humphreys County Election Commn., 1968-72. Col. Tenn. Army Nat. Guard. Mem. ABA, Am. Judicature Soc., Tenn. Bar Assn. (ho. of dels.), Humphreys County Bar Assn. (pres. 1978—), Masons (master 1985). Home: 102 South Court Sq Waverly TN 37185

WILLIAMS, JOHN TAYLOR, lawyer; b. Cambridge, Mass., June 19, 1938; s. Paul Merchant Taylor and Audrey Arlene Dowling; m. Leonora Hall; children: Caleb, Jared, Nathaniel. AB, Harvard U., 1960; LLB, U. Pa., 1965. Bar: Mass. 1965, U.S. Dist. Ct. Mass., U.S. Ct. Appeals (1st cir.), U.S. Supreme Ct. Corp. loans officer State St. Bank & Trust Co., Boston, 1960-62; from assoc. to ptnr. Haussermann, Davison & Shattuck, Boston, 1965-83; ptnr. Palmer & Dodge, Boston, 1983—; bd. dirs. Blackwell Sci. Inc.; lectr. on 1st amendment, copyright, pub. and intellectual property law for Practicing Law Inst., Mass. CLE/New Eng. Law Inst., Nat. Assn. Archivists, Boston Patent Lawyers Assn., others; apptd. mem. U.S. Courthouse Arts Comm., U.S. Publ. Del. to China, 1993; mem. lit. panel Nat. Endowment for the Arts, 1990, 91, 94. Author: (screenplay) Rolf in the Woods, 1987, (screenplay) Toussaint L'Overture, 1989, (with E. Gabriel Perle) The Publishing Law Handbook, 2 vols. (revised annually); contbg. author: Legal Problems in Book Publishing, 1981, 84, 86; contbg. editor: Small Voices and Great Trumpets: Minorities and the Media, 1980. Bd. dirs. City of Cambridge Arts Coun., 1973-83, chmn., 1981-83; bd. dirs. Ploughshares Inc., 1988-89; trustee Arthur Fiedler Meml. Inc., 1983—, Boston Philharm Orch., 1983-85, Petra Found., 1988—; trustee, gen. counsel Inst. Contemporary Art, 1970-92; mem. corp. Mass. Gen. Hosp., 1985—; mem. Patent and Tech Conflicts Coms., 1985-91; clk. John F. Kennedy Meml. Commn. Inc., 1986—; mem. adv. bd. Provincetown Fine Arts Work Ctr., 1992—. Mrm. ABA (sect. patent, trademark, copyright law, chmn. com. on authors 1978-81, communications and entertainment law forum coms.), Boston Bar Assn. (former chmn. com. on delivery of legal svcs. to indigent), Lawyers' Com. for Civil Rights under Law (chmn. steering com. 1988-91), Mass. Bar Assn. (bus. law and computer law sects.), Nat. Lawyers' Com. for Civil Rights (bd. dirs. 1989—), Tavern Club (Boston). Home: 9 Orchard St Cambridge MA 02140-1321 Office: Palmer & Dodge 1 Beacon St Boston MA 02108-3106

WILLIAMS, J(OHN) TILMAN, insurance executive, real estate broker, city official; b. Detroit, Feb. 26, 1925; s. Aubrey and Martha (Lou) W.; m. Sally Jane Robinson, Aug. 22, 1947; children: Leslie Ann, Martha Lou. B.S. in Agr. Mich. State U., 1951. Pres. Satellite Ins. Brokerage, Garden Grove, Calif., 1959—; pres. Satellite Real Estate, Satellite Mortgage & Loan Co. Mayor Garden Grove, 1976-78, re-elected, 1987, mem. coun., 1980-92, apptd. vice mayor, 1989—; mem. Ad Hoc Com. on Property Tax to Limit Govt. Spending with Spirit of 13 Initiative; past pres. Garden Grove High Sch. Band Boosters. With USAAF, World War II, PTO. Mem. Bd. Realtors, Ind. Ins. Agts. Assn., Orange County Esperanto Assn. (pres. 1985—), Am. Legion, VFW. Democrat. Methodist. Clubs: Toastmasters (Anaheim, Calif.); Fifty-Plus Sr. Citizens of Garden Grove (pres. 1986—). Lodges: Lions, Elks. Home: 11241 Chapman Ave Garden Grove CA 92640-3301 Office: 12311 Harbor Blvd Garden Grove CA 92640-3809 *Service to one's fellowman and community is the greatest avocation and pleasure one can follow.*

WILLIAMS, JOHN TOWNER, composer, conductor; b. Flushing, N.Y., Feb. 8, 1932. Student, UCLA; pvt. studies with Mario Castelnuovo-Tedesco, Los Angeles; student, Juilliard Sch.; pvt. studies with, Madame Rosina Lhevinne, N.Y.C.; hon. degree, Berklee Coll. Music, Boston, Northeastern U., Boston, Tufts U., U. So. Calif., Boston U., New Eng. Conservatory Music, Providence Coll.; others. Condr. Boston Pops Orch., 1980—. Works include: composer (film scores) I Passed for White, 1960, Because They're Young, 1960, The Secret Ways, 1961, Bachelor Flat, 1962, Diamond Head, 1962, Gidget Goes to Rome, 1963, The Killers, 1964, John Goldfarb, Please Come Home, 1964, None But the Brave, 1965, How to Steal a Million, 1966, The Rare Breed, 1966, Not With My Wife, You Don't, 1966, The Plainsman, 1966, Penelope, 1966, A Guide for the Married Man, 1967, Valley of the Dolls, 1967 (Acad. award nominee), Fitzwilly, 1968, Sergeant Ryker, 1968, The Reivers, 1969 (Acad. award nominee), Daddy's Gone A-Hunting, 1969, Goodbye, Mr. Chips, 1969 (Acad. award nominee), The Story of A Woman, 1970, Fiddler on the Roof, 1971 (Acad. award for musical adaptation 1971), The Cowboys, 1972, The Poseidon Adventure, 1972 (Acad. award nominee), Images, 1972 (Acad. award nominee), Pete 'n' Tillie, 1972, The Paper Chase, 1973, The Long Goodbye, 1973, The Man Who Loved Cat Dancing, 1973, Cinderella Liberty, 1973 (Acad. award nominee), Tom Sawyer, 1973 (Acad. award nominee), Sugarland Express, 1974, Earthquake, 1974, The Towering Inferno, 1974 (Acad. award nominee), Conrack, 1974, Jaws, 1975 (Acad. award 1976, Grammy award, Golden Globe award), The Eiger Sanction, 1976, Family Plot, 1976, Midway, 1976, The Missouri Breaks, 1976, Raggedy Ann and Andy, 1977, Black Sunday, 1977, Star Wars, 1977 (Acad. award, 3 Grammy awards, Golden Globe award), Close Encounters of the Third Kind, 1977 (2 Grammy awards, Acad. award nominee), The Fury, 1978, Jaws II, 1978, Superman, 1978 (2 Grammy awards), Meteor, 1979, Quintet, 1979, Dracula, 1979, "1941", 1979, The Empire Strikes Back, 1980 (2 Grammy awards, Acad. award nominee), Raiders of the Lost Ark, 1981 (Grammy award, Acad. award nominee), Heartbeeps, 1981, E.T., 1982 (Acad. award for best original score, 3 Grammy awards, Golden Globe award), Monsignor, 1982, Yes, Giorgio, 1982 (Acad. award nominee), Superman III, 1983, Return of the Jedi, 1983 (Acad. award nominee), Indiana Jones and the Temple of Doom, 1984 (Acad. award nominee), The River, 1984 (Acad. award nominee), Space Camp, 1986, Emma's War, 1986, The Witches of Eastwick, 1987 (Acad. award nominee), Empire of the Sun, 1987 (Acad. award nominee), Jaws: The Revenge, 1987, Superman IV: The Quest for Peace, 1987, The Secret of My Success, 1987, The Accidental Tourist, 1988 (Acad. award nominee, Indiana Jones and the Last Crusade, 1989 (Acad. award nominee), Always, 1989, Born On The Fourth of July, 1989 (Acad. award nominee), Stanley and Iris, 1990, Presumed Innocent, 1990, Home Alone, 1990 (Acad. award nominee), Hook, 1991 (Acad. award nominee), JFK, 1991 (Acad. award nominee), Far and Away, 1992, Home Alone II, 1992, Jurassic Park, 1993, Schindler's List, 1993 (Acad. award for best original score 1993), Sabrina, 1995 (Acad. award nominee for best original score 1996, Nixon, 1995 (Acad. award nominee for best dramatic score 1996); composer music for songs including: (from Sabrina, lyrics by Alan and Marilyn Bergman) Moonlight, 1995 (Acad. award nominee for best original song 1996); composer: (TV programs) Heidi, 1969 (Emmy award), Jane Eyre, 1971 (Emmy award), others; composer numerous concert pieces and symphonies including Jubilee 350 Fanfare for the Boston Pops, 1980, theme to the 1984 Summer Olympic Games, Liberty Fanfare, 1987; recorded numerous albums with Boston Pops Orch. including Pops in Space, That's Entertainment (Pops on Broadway), Pops on the March, Pops Around the World (Digital Overtures), Aisle Seat, Pops Out of This World, Boston Pops on Stage, America, the Dream Goes On; collaborator (with Jessye Norman) With A Song in My Heart, Swing, Swing, Swing, Unforgettable; guest condr. major orchs. including London Symphony Orch., Cleve. Orch., Phila. Orch., Toronto Orch., Montreal Orch. Served with USAF. Recipient several gold and platinum records Rec. Industry Assn. Am. Office: Gorfaine & Schwartz care of Michael Gorfaine 3301 Barham Blvd Ste 201 Los Angeles CA 90068-1477

WILLIAMS, JOHN TROY, librarian, educator; b. Oak Park, Ill., Mar. 11, 1924; s. Michael Daniel and Donna Marie (Shaffer) W.; B.A., Central Mich. U., 1949; M.A. in Libr. Sci., U. Mich., 1951, M.A., 1954; Ph.D., Mich. State U., 1973. Reference libr. U. Mich., Ann Arbor, 1955-59; instr. Bowling Green (Ohio) State U., 1959-60; reference librarian Mich. State U., East Lansing, 1960-62; 1st asst. reference dept. Flint (Mich.) Pub. Library, 1962-65; head reference svcs., Purdue U., West Lafayette, Ind., 1965-72; head pub. svcs. No. Ill. U., Dekalb, 1972-75; asst. dean, asst. univ. libr. Wright State U., Dayton, Ohio, 1975-80; vis. scholar U. Mich., Ann Arbor, 1980—; cons. in field. Served with U.S. Army, 1943-46. Mich. State fellow, 1963-64; HEW fellow, 1971-72. Mem. Am. Libr. Assn., Spl. Libraries Assn., Am. Soc. for Info. Scis., Am. Sociol. Assn., AAUP, Coun. on Fgn. Rels. Contbr. articles to profl. jours. Home: PO Box 7531 Ann Arbor MI 48107-7531

WILLIAMS, JOHN WESLEY, fine arts educator; b. Memphis, Feb. 25, 1928; s. Wesley Alfred and Anna Belle (Curtis) W.; m. Mary Ellen Schmidt, Dec. 26, 1955; children: Maxwell, Katherine, Sarah, Cyril, Elena, Amelia. Student, Duke U., 1948-50; B.A., Yale U., 1952; M.A., U. Mich., 1953, Ph.D., 1960. Instr., assoc. prof. Swarthmore Coll., Pa., 1960-72; prof. fine arts U. Pitts., 1972—, Disting. Svc. prof., 1993—; dir. Internat. Center Medieval Art, N.Y.C., 1982-85. Author: Early Spanish Illum, 1977, Apocalypse in Spain, 1991, The Illustrated Beatus, 1994. Served with USMC, 1946-48. Guggenheim fellow, 1984-85, Inst. for Advanced Study member, 1991-92. Home: 749 S Linden Ave Pittsburgh PA 15208-2814 Office: Univ Pitts Dept of Ed Pittsburgh PA 15260

WILLIAMS, JOHN YOUNG, merchant banker; b. Cordele, Ga., Apr. 13, 1943; s. George Wilmer and Minnie Converse (Roberts) W.; m. Julian Perdue Boykin; m. Joyce, Isabel. BS in Indsl. Engring., Ga. Inst. Tech., 1965; MBA in Fin., Harvard U., 1969. CFA, Ga. Assoc. Kuhn, Loeb & Co., N.Y.C., 1969-71; asst. v.p. Stone & Webster Securities Corp., N.Y.C., 1971-74, Chem. Bank, N.Y.C., 1974-75; mng. dir. Dean Witter Reynolds, Inc., Atlanta, 1975-84; sr. v.p., ltd. ptnr. Bear Stearns & Co., Atlanta, 1984-85; mng. dir. Robinson Humphrey Co., Atlanta, 1985-87; mng. dir., co-founder Grubb & Williams, Ltd., Atlanta, 1987—, Equity South Ptnrs., 1995—; bd. dirs. Tech Data Corp., Clearwater, Fla., Law Cos. Group, Inc., Atlanta, Frisco Furniture Co., High Point, N.C., co-chmn. 1st lt. U.S. Army, 1965-67, Korea. Fellow Soc. Internat. Bus. Fellows (sec. 1988-89); mem. Assn. for Investment Mgmt. and Rsch. (CFA), Assn. for Corp. Growth (pres. 1983-84), Harvard Bus. Sch. Club (pres. 1982-83), Phi Delta Theta (alumni pres. 1980-81). Episcopalian. Avocation: military history. Home: 750 Arden Close NW Atlanta GA 30327-1275 Office: Equity South Advisors, LLC 3399 Peachtree Rd NE Ste 1790 Atlanta GA 30326-1151

WILLIAMS, JOSEPH DALTON, pharmaceutical company executive; b. Washington, Pa., Aug. 15, 1926; s. Joseph Dalton and Jane (Day) W.; m. Mildred E. Bellaire, June 28, 1973; children: Terri, Daniel. BS in Pharmacy, U. Nebr., 1950; DSc (hon.), Union U., 1991, U. Nebr., 1989; LHD (hon.), Albany Coll. Pharmacy, Union U., 1980, Rutgers U., 1987, Long Island U., 1988; DSc (hon.), Phila. Coll. Pharmacy and Sci., 1988, Long Island U., 1988, Albany Coll. Pharmacy of Union U., 1991; D Human Svcs. (hon.), Caldwell Coll., 1989; LLD (hon.), Bethune-Cookman Coll., 1990, Coll. St. Elizabeth, 1990, Seton Hall U., 1990, U. Md., 1991, St. Augustine Coll., 1992. Pres. Parke-Davis Co., Detroit, 1973-76; pres. pharm. group Warner-Lambert Co., Morris Plains, N.J., 1976-77; pres. Internat. Group, 1977-79; pres., dir. Warner-Lambert Corp., 1979-80, pres., chief operating officer, 1980-84, chmn., CEO, 1985-91, chmn. exec. com., 1991—; bd. dirs. AT&T, J.C. Penney & Co., Exxon Corp., Rockefeller Fin. Svcs., Inc., Rockefeller and Co., Inc., Thrift Drug Inc. Bd. dirs. People to People Health Found., United Negro Coll. Fund; trustee Columbia U.; chmn. Commn. on Higher Edn. for State of N.J. With USNR, 1943-46. Mem. Am. Pharm. Assn., N.J. Pharm. Assn., Somerset Hills Country Club, Links Club, Pine Valley Golf Club, Baltusrol Golf Club, Mid Ocean Club, Robert Trent Jones Internat. Golf Club. Office: Warner-Lambert Co 182 Tabor Rd Morris Plains NJ 07950-2614

WILLIAMS, JOSEPH HILL, retired diversified industry executive; b. Tulsa, June 2, 1933; s. David Rogerson and Martha Reynolds (Hill) W.; children: Joseph Hill Jr., Peter B., James C.; m. Terese T. Ross, May 7, 1977; stepchildren: Margot Ross, Jennifer Ross. Diploma, St. Paul's Sch., 1952; B.A., Yale U., 1956, M.A. (hon.), 1977; postgrad., Sch. Pipeline Tech. U. Tex., 1960. Field employee div. domestic constrn. The Williams Cos., Inc., Tulsa, 1958-60; project coord. div. engring. The Williams Cos. Inc., Tulsa, 1960-61; project supt. Iran, 1961-62, asst. resident mgr., 1962-64; project mgr., 1964-65, resident mgr., 1965-67; exec. v.p. Tulsa, 1968—, pres., chief operating officer, 1971-78; chmn., chief exec. officer The Williams Cos., Inc., Tulsa, 1979-93; chmn. bd. The Williams Cos., Inc., 1994; now chmn. & CEO The Williams Co., Inc., Tulsa, O.K.; dir. The Williams Co., Inc., Tulsa, 1995—. Former fellow, trustee Yale Corp. Served with AUS, 1956-58. Mem. (hon.) Am. Petroleum Inst. (hon. bd. dirs.), Met. Tulsa C. of C. (past chmn.), Okla. State C. of C. and Industry (past. chmn.), Bus. Coun., Nature Conservancy (chmn. bd. govs.). Episcopalian. Clubs: Southern Hills Country, Tulsa; Springdale Hall (Camden, S.C.); Augusta (Ga.); Grandfather Golf and Country (Linville, N.C.); Old Baldy Club, (Saratoga, Wyo). Office: Williams Cos Inc 1 Williams Ctr PO Box 2400 Tulsa OK 74102-2400*

WILLIAMS, JOSEPH THEODORE, oil and gas company executive; b. Oklahoma City, June 19, 1937; s. Roland Leslie and Mary Virginia (Maloy) W.; m. Marilyn Kay Hansen, Sept. 3, 1948; children: Joseph Kent, John Kevin, Katharine Ann, Jennifer Lyn. BS in Petroleum Engring., U. Tex., 1960. Engr. Chevron Corp., New Orleans and Brookhaven, Miss., 1960-65; engr. mgr. Arabian Am. Oil Co., Dhahran, Saudi Arabia, 1965-70, Chevron Corp., Denver and San Francisco, 1970-74; gen. mgr. ops. Chevron Petroleum (U.K.) Ltd., London, 1974-78; sr. v.p. Mitchell Energy and Devel. Corp., Houston, 1978-81; pres., chmn. Sovran Energy Corp., Houston, 1981-83; v.p. Lear Petroleum Corp., Dallas, 1983-85, pres., chief exec. officer, 1985-89, also chmn. bd. dirs.; pres., CEO DALEN Resources Corp. (formerly PG&E Resources Co.), Dallas, 1989-95; vice chmn., CEO Enserch Exploration, Inc., 1995-96; pvt. practice Dallas, 1996—. Mem. AIME, Soc. Petroleum Engrs., Tex. Ind. Producers and Royalty Owners Assn., Ind. Petroleum Assn. Am., Domestic Petroleum Coun., Dallas Petroleum Club, Northwood Club. Avocations: golf, tennis, bridge, music.

WILLIAMS, JULIE BELLE, psychiatric social worker; b. Algona, Iowa, July 29, 1950; d. George Howard and Leta Maribelle (Durschmidt) W. BA, U. Iowa, 1972, MSW, 1973. Lic. psychologist, ind. clin. social worker, marriage and family therapist, Minn.; lic. social worker, Iowa. Social worker Psychopathic Hosp., Iowa City, 1971-72; OEO counselor YOUR, Webster City, Iowa, 1972; social worker Child Devel. Clinic, Iowa City, 1973; therapist Mid-Eastern Iowa Community Mental Health Ctr., Iowa City, 1973; psychiat. social worker Mental Health Ctr. No. Iowa, Mason City, 1974-79, chief psychiat. social worker, 1979-80; asst. dir. Community Counseling Ctr., White Bear Lake, Minn., 1980-85, dir., 1985—; lectr., cons. in field. NIMH grantee, 1972-73. Mem. NASW (Acad. Cert. Social Workers, Qualified Clin. Social Workers, diplomate), NOW, Am. Orthopsychiat. Assn., Am. Assn. Sex Educators, Counselors and Therapists, Minn. Women Psychologists, Minn. Lic. Psychologists, Phi Beta Kappa. Democrat. Office: 1280 N Birch Lake Blvd White Bear Lake MN 55110

WILLIAMS, JULIE FORD, mutual fund specialist; b. Long Beach, Calif., Aug. 7, 1948; d. Julious Hunter and Bessie May (Wood) Ford; m. Walter Edward Williams, Oct. 20, 1984; 1 child, Andrew Ford. BA in Econs., Occidental Coll., 1970. Legal sec. Kadison, Pfaelzer, Woodard, Quinn & Rossi, L.A., 1970-71, 74-77; legal sec. Fried, Frank, Harris, Shriver & Jacobson, N.Y.C., 1971-72, Pallot, Poppell, Goodman & Shapo, Miami, Fla., 1973-74; adminstrv. asst. Capital Research-Mgmt., Los Angeles, 1978-82; corp. officer Cash Mgmt. Trust Am., 1982—, Bond Fund Am., 1982—, Tax-Exempt Bond Fund Am., 1982—, AMCAP Fund, 1984—, Am. Funds Income Series, 1985—, Am. Funds Tax-Exempt Series II, 1986—, Capital World Bond Fund, 1987—, Am. High-Income Trust, 1987—, Intermediate Bond Fund Am., 1987—, Tax-Exempt Money Fund Am., 1989—, U.S. Treasury Money Fund Am., 1991—, Fundamental Investors, 1992—, Ltd. Term Tax-Exempt Bond Fund Am., 1993—, Am. High-Income Mcpl. Bond Fund, 1994—; v.p. fund bus. mgmt. group Capital Rsch. Mgmt., 1986—. V.p. regions Alumni Bd. Govs. Occidental Coll., 1994—. Democrat. Episcopalian. Avocations: scuba diving, RVing, theatre. Office: Capital Rsch and Mgmt Co 333 S Hope St Los Angeles CA 90071-1406

WILLIAMS, JUSTIN W., government official; b. N.Y.C., Jan. 4, 1942; s. Louis P. and Edith W. Williams. BA, Columbia U., 1963; LLB, U. Va., 1967. Bar: Va. 1967. Atty. Dept. Justice, 1967-68; asst. commonwealth atty. Arlington County, Va., 1968-70; asst. U.S. atty. Ea. Dist. Va., 1970-78, 1st asst. U.S. atty., 1978-79; U.S. atty. Alexandria, Va., 1979-81; asst. U.S. atty., 1981-86; U.S. atty. Ea. dist. Va., 1986; asst. U.S. atty., chief criminal divsn. Ea. dist. Va., Alexandria, Va., 1986—. Episcopalian. Office: US Atty's Office 2100 Jamieson Ave Alexandria VA 22314*

WILLIAMS, KAREN HASTIE, lawyer, think tank executive; b. Washington, Sept. 30, 1944; d. William Henry and Beryl (Lockhart) Hastie; m. Wesley S. Williams, Jr.; children: Amanda Pedersen, Wesley Hastie, Bailey Lockhart. Cert., U. Neuchatel, Switzerland, 1965; BA, Bates Coll., 1966; MA, Tufts U., 1967; JD, Cath. U. Am., 1973. Bar: D.C. 1973. Staff asst. internat. gov. relations dept. Mobil Oil Corp., N.Y.C., 1967-69; staff asst. com. Dist. Columbia U.S. Senate, 1970, chief counsel com. on the budget, 1977-80; law clk. to judge Spottswood Robinson III U.S. Ct. Appeals (D.C. Cir.), Washington, 1973-74; law clk. to assoc. justice Thurgood Marshall U.S. Supreme Ct., Washington, 1974-75; assoc. Fried, Frank, Harris, Shriver & Kampelman, Washington, 1975-77, 1975-77; adminstr. Office Mgmt. and Budget, Washington, 1980-81; of counsel Crowell & Moring, Washington, 1982, ptnr., 1982—; Bd. dirs. Crestar Fin. Services Corp., Fannie Mae, Washington Gas Light Co., Continental Airlines, SunAmerica, Inc. Chair, trustee Greater Washington Research Ctr., chair. Mem. ABA (pub. contract law sect., past chair), Nat. Bar Assn., Washington Bar Assn., Nat. Contract Mgmt. Assn., NAACP (bd. dirs. legal defense fund). Office: Crowell & Moring Ste 1200W 1001 Pennsylvania Ave NW Washington DC 20004-2595

WILLIAMS, KAREN JOHNSON, federal judge; b. Orangeburg, S.C., Aug. 4, 1951; d. James G. Johnson and Marcia (Reynolds) Johnson Dantzler; m. Charles H. Williams, Dec. 27, 1968; children: Marian, Ashley, Charlie, David. BA, Columbia Coll., 1972; postgrad., U. S.C., 1973, JD cum laude, 1980. Bar: S.C. 1980, U.S. Dist. Ct. S.C. 1980, U.S. Ct. Appeals (4th cir.) 1981. Tchr. Irmo (S.C.) Mid. Sch., 1972-74, O-W High Sch., Orangeburg, 1974-76; assoc. Charles H. Williams P.A., Orangeburg, 1980-92; circuit judge U.S. Ct. Appeals (4th cir.), 1992—; mem. exec. bd. grievance commn. S.C. Supreme Ct., Columbia, 1983-92. Mem. child devel. bd. First Bapt. Ch., Orangeburg; bd. dirs. Orangeburg County Mental Retardation Bd., 1986-94, Orangeburg-Calhoun Hosp. Found.; bd. visitors Columbia Coll., 1988-92; dir. Reg. Med. Ctr. Hosp. Found., 1988-92; mem. adv. bd. Orangeburg-Calhoun Tech. Coll., 1987-92. Mem. ABA, Am. Judicature Soc., Fed. Judges Assn., S.C. Bar Assn., Orangeburg County Bar Assn. (co-chair Law Day 1981), S.C. Trial Lawyers Assn., Bus. and profl. Women Assn., Rotary, Order of Wig and Robe, Order of Coif. Home: 2503 Five Chop Rd Orangeburg SC 29115 Office: 1021 Middleton St Orangeburg SC 29115

WILLIAMS, KATHRYN SANDERS, middle school educator; b. Lexington, Ky., May 18, 1961; d. Gerald Louis and Donna Lee (Freeman) Sanders; m. R. Duane Williams, Jr., May 21, 1983; children: Bryan, Brad. BS in Elem. Edn., U. Louisville, 1983, M in Elem. Curriculum, 1990, rank I in ednl. adminstrn., 1995. Tchr. elem. sch. Indpls. Pub. Schs., 1984-85; tchr. mid. sch. Jefferson County Pub. Schs., Louisville, 1985—. Vol. Talent Ctr. grantee, Louisville, 1990. Mem. ASCD, NEA, Ky. Assn. for Supervision and Curriculum Devel., Ky. Edn. Assn., Jefferson County Tchrs. Assn., Nat. Assn. for Yr.-Round Edn. Democrat. Roman Catholic. Avocations: reading, skating, sporting events. Home: 4319 Saratoga Hill Rd Jeffersontown KY 40299-8306 Office: Newburg Mid Sch 5008 Indian Trail Louisville KY 40218

WILLIAMS, KENNETH JAMES, retired county official; b. Eureka, Calif., Apr. 28, 1924; s. E. J. and Thelma (Hall) W.; student Humboldt State Coll., 1942-43; B.S., U. Oreg., 1949, M.Ed., 1952; m. Mary Patricia Warring, Sept. 3, 1949; children—James Clayton, Susan May, Christopher Kenneth. Engaged as mountain triangulation observer with U.S. Coast and Geodetic Survey, 1942; instr. bus. and geography Boise (Idaho) Jr. Coll., 1949-51; tchr. Prospect High Sch., 1952-54; prin. Oakland (Oreg.) High Sch., 1954-58; supt. prin. Coburg Public Schs., 1958-64; supt. Yoncalla (Oreg.) Public Schs., 1964-66, Amity (Oreg.) Public Schs., 1966-72; adminstr. Yamhill County, McMinnville, Oreg., 1974-85; cons., 1985—; county liaison officer Land and Water Conservation Fund, 1977-85. Dist. lay leader Oreg.-Idaho ann. conf. United Methodist Ch., 1968-80, bd. dirs. western dist. Ch. Extension Soc., 1976; mem. Mid-Willamette Manpower Council, 1974-85; bd. dirs. Lafayette Noble Homes, 1970-72; mem. adv. com. local budget law sect. State of Oreg. Served with AUS, 1943-46. Decorated Purple Heart. Mem. NEA, Oreg. Edn. Assn., Oreg. Assn. Secondary Prins., Nat. Assn. Secondary Prins., AAUP, Oreg., Am. Assn. Sch. Adminstrs., Assn. Supervision and Curriculum Devel., Nat. Sch. Pub. Relations Assn., Phi Delta Kappa. Mason (Shriner), Lion. Home: 21801 SE Webfoot Rd Dayton OR 97114-8832

WILLIAMS, KENNETH OGDEN, farmer; b. Clarksdale, Miss., Jan. 18, 1924; s. Peter Fairley and Robbie (Casey) W.; m. Frances Dyer Lott, June 14, 1969; 1 child, Frances. BS, Vanderbilt U., 1949. Ptnr. P.F. Williams and Sons, Clarksdale, 1949-88, Swan Lake Farms, Clarksdale, 1989—. Mem. Miss. Ho. of Reps., Jackson, 1960-84, Miss. Senate, 1988-92. Sgt. U.S. Army, 1942-46. Decorated Bronze Star. Republican. Baptist. Home: 1505 Holly St Clarksdale MS 38614-2912

WILLIAMS, KENNETH SCOTT, entertainment company executive; b. Tulsa, Okla., Dec. 31, 1955; s. David Vorhees Williams and Mary Louise (Newell) Rose; m. Jann Catherine Wolfe, May 20, 1989; children: Catherine Eloise, Michael Holbrook. BA, Harvard Coll., 1978; MS, Columbia U., 1985. Bank officer Chase Manhattan Bank, N.Y.C., 1978-82; asst. treas. Columbia Pictures Entertainment, N.Y.C., 1982-84, v.p., treas., 1984-89; sr. v.p. fin. and adminstrn. Columbia Pictures Entertainment, Burbank, Calif., 1990-91; sr. v.p. corp. ops. Sony Pictures Entertainment, Culver City, Calif., 1991-95; exec. v.p. Sony Pictures Entertainment, Culver City, 1995—. Mem. Blue Hill Troupe, N.Y.C., 1979—; vice chmn. Graphic Arts Coun., L.A. County Mus., 1993—; bd. dirs. L.A. Conservatory. Mem. N.Y. Soc. Securities Analysts, Fin. Execs. Inst., Harvard Club. So. Calif. (bd. dirs.), Beta Gamma Sigma. Home: 966 Stone Canyon Rd Los Angeles CA 90077-2914 Office: Sony Pictures Entertainment 10202 Washington Blvd Culver City CA 90232-3119

WILLIAMS, KENT HARLAN, coast guard officer; b. Forty Fort, Pa., Aug. 18, 1943; m. Geraldine M. Boyle, 1965; children: Deborah, Rebecca, Jessica. BS in Engring., USCG Acad., 1965; postgrad., Naval Postgrad. Sch., 1969-70, Naval War Coll., 1978-79, MIT, 1983-84. Commd. ensign USCG, 1965, advanced through grades to vice adm., 1994; resource dir., comptr. USCG, Washington, 1990-91, chief, office acquisition, 1991-93; dist. comdr. USCG, Boston, 1993-94, chief of staff, 1994-96. Decorated D.S.M., Legion of Merit with three oak leaf clusters, Bronze Star with combat V; Sloan medal MIT, 1983-84. Mem. Am. Soc. Mil. Comptr., Coast Guard Acad. Alumni Assn., MIT Club. Office: USCG 2100 2d St SW Washington DC 20593-0001

WILLIAMS, LARRY BILL, academic administrator; b. Cushing, Okla., June 9, 1945; s. Louis Albert and Morene Ruth (Cox) W.; m. Pam Bryan, May 1, 1993; children: Natalie Michelle, Nicole Diane, Louis Bradley, Sharla Dianne Bryan, Vanessa Joy Bryan. BS, Cen. State U., Edmond, Okla., 1967, MBA, 1972; PhD, U. Okla., 1985. Office mgr. Okla. State U., Stillwater, 1967-69; asst. comptroller Cen. State U., Edmond, 1969-71, dir. affirmative action, 1971-72, assoc. dir. univ. personnel services, 1971-72, dir. affirmative action, 1972-80, dir. univ. personnel services, 1972-80, asst. v.p. adminstrn., 1980-84, v.p. adminstrn., 1984-87; interim pres. Southeastern Okla. State U., Durant, 1987, pres., 1987—; managerial cons. various municipalities; mktg. cons. State of Okla.; arbitrator Met. Fraternal Order of Police; bd. dirs. Okla. Small Bus. Devel. Ctr., 1987—, Okla. Acad. State Goals, 1992—, southeast region chmn. 1995. Bd. dirs. Bryan County Econ. Devel. Corp., 1989—, Bryan County United Way, 1988-94; mem. adv. bd. Med. Ctr. Southeastern Okla., 1987-92; bd. dirs. Bryan County Ret. Sr. Vol. Program, 1990-92, Leadership Okla. Class IV, 1991, mem. adv. bd., 1991-95; mem. exec. bd. Boy Scouts Am., 1991; com. mem. Okla. Ctr. for Advancement Sci. and Tech. Long Range Planning Task Force, Most Eminent Scholars and Rsch. Equipment, 1990-91; mem. higher edn. alumni coun. Okla. State Regent for Higher Edn. Tuition Com., budget com., outreach com., quality initiative com., capital com., chmn. legis. affairs com., 1995; mem. adv. coun. Ea. Okla. Schs., 1987—; trustee Southeastern Found., 1990—; past pres. Kickingbird Golf Course Mgmt., Edmond; bd. dirs. Edmond C. of C., 1984; mem. Okla. State Regents for Higher Edn. Coun. of Pres., 1987—, chair, 1994; Chocktaw Nation of Okla. JTPA Adv. Coun., 1987—; mem. Okla. Regional Pres.' Coun., 1987—, chair, 1994; vice chmn. Diamond Jubilee Commn., Edmond; mem. found. bd. trustees Ctrl. State U., Edmond; mem. adv. com. Durant Airport. With USNG, 1962-70. Named One of Outstanding Young Men of Am., Edmond Jaycees, 1971, 74, 79; recipient Presdl. Leadership award Nat. U.S. Jaycee Pres., 1971, Presdl. Leadership, Achievement and Honor awards Nat. Jaycees, 1972, Nat. Presdl. award of Honor Nat. Coll. and Univ. Pers. Assn., 1973, Disting. Svc. award City of Edmond, 1974, Dwight F. Whelan Meml. award for Outstanding Leadership, Edmond, 1972; named to Cushing Alumni Hall of Fame, 1988, recipient Nat. Order Omega (charter hon. mem), 1991. Mem. Okla. Assn. Coll. and Univ. Pers. Adminstrs. (founder, bd. dirs., chmn.), Nat. Coll. and Univ. Pers. Assn., Nat. Coll. and Univ. Bus. Officers Assn., Okla. Assn. Affirmative Action (co-founder, pres., bd. dirs.), Okla. City Pers. Assn. , Am. Assn. State Colls. and Univs., Okla. Assn. Coll. and Univ. Bus. Officers (bd. dirs., pres.), Acad. Cert. Adminstrv. Mgrs., Okla. Small Bus. Devel. Ctr. (bd. dirs. 1987—), Industry Ednl. Coun. McCurtain County, Okla. Acad. for State Goals (bd. dirs. 1992—, vice chair S.E. region 1995), Okla. Advocates for Arts and Humanities (steering com. 1995), Durant C. of C. (past pres., bd. dirs.), Okla. State C. of C. (bd. dirs. 1991—), Blue Key, Rotary. Democrat. Presbyterian. Lodge: Rotary (sec. Edmond club 1986-87). Avocation: golf. Office: Southeastern Okla State U Office of Pres Durant OK 74701

WILLIAMS, LAWRENCE FLOYD, conservation organization official; b. Eugene, Oreg., Mar. 26, 1937; s. Carroll Parven and Catherene (Dorris) W.; m. Patricia Ann Pride, Feb. 25, 1978. Student, Portland State U. Advt. staff asst. Omark Industries, Portland, Oreg., 1963-67; internat. advt. liaison Hyster Co., Portland, 1968; exec. dir. Oreg. Environ. Coun., Portland, 1969-78; policy analyst pub. land mgmt. White House Coun. on Environ. Quality, Washington, 1978-81; spl. cons. Sierra Club, Portland, 1969, Washington rep. Sierra Club, 1981-85; dir. internat. program Sierra Club, Washington, 1985—; Former mem. dist. adv. bd. Bur. Land Mgmt.; former mem. Adv. Com. on Forest Mgmt. Policy; former cons. Coun. on Econ. Priorities; former mem. acv. com. Bonneville Power Adminstrn.; mgr. N.W. Workshops for Conservation Found. on Implementation Clean Air Act, 1972, Clean Water Act, 1975, U.S. Energy Policy, 1976; former mem. Western Forst Environ.-Industry Policy Discussion Group. Author: (with Raymond Mikesell) International Banks and the Environment, from Growth to Sustainability: An Unfinished Agenda, 1992; mng. editor: Bankrolling Disasters, International Development Banks and the Global Environment, 1986. Past mem. bd. dirs. Inst. for Transp. and Devel. Policy, N.W. Environ. Def. Ctr.; past chmn. Nat. Coalition for Clean Water, Pacific N.W. chpt. Sierra Club; founder, past 1st chmn. Portland Sierra Club; past v.p. Fedn. Western Outdoor Clubs; past pres. Trails Club Oreg.; past assembly pres. Inst. Ecology; organizer, past chmn. Com. for Volcanic Cascades Study, People Against Nerve Gas; organizer Oreg. League Conservation Voters; mem. steering com. Biodiversity Action Network, 1993; mem. adv. bd. Global Forest Policy Project, 1994. With USAF, 1956-70. Recipient Richard L. Neuberger award Oreg. Environ. Coun., 1988. Democrat. Home: 4607 Van Ness St NW Washington DC 20016-5631 Office: Sierra Club 408 C St NE Washington DC 20002-5818

WILLIAMS, LEA EVERARD, history educator; b. Milw., July 25, 1924; s. William Everard and Paula Herndon (Pratt) W.; m. Daisy Shen, Sept. 15, 1949; children—Adrienne Paula Covington, William Herndon. B.A., Cornell U., 1950; M.A., Harvard U., 1952, Ph.D., 1956. With U.S. Fgn. Service, Chungking, China, 1944-45; Am. vice consul U.S. Fgn. Service, Shanghai, 1945-48; with Brown U., 1956—, prof. Asian history, 1969-76, prof. history, 1976-89, prof. history emeritus, 1989—; dir. East Asia Lang. and Area Ctr., 1969-84; vis. prof. history U. Singapore, 1961-63; vis. prof. Asian affairs Fletcher Sch., 1964-65; lectr. Fgn. Svcs. Inst., U.S. Dept. State, staff lectr. spl. expeditions, 1993—. Author: Overseas Chinese Nationalism, 1960, The Future of the Overseas Chinese in Southeast Asia, 1966, Southeast Asia: A History, 1976; editor, transl.: The Origins of the Modern Chinese Movement in Indonesia, 1969. Served with U.S. Army, 1943. Social Sci. Research fellow, 1957; Fulbright-Hays fellow, 1966-67; Am. Council Learned Socs. fellow, 1969; Nat. Sci. Council vis. scholar Taiwan, 1980; Gulbenkian Found. travel grantee, 1980, 82, 85, 89. Mem. The South Seas Soc., Assn. Asian Studies, Royal Asiatic Soc. (Malayan br.), Koninklijk Instiuut voor Taal, Land-en Volkenkunde, Hakluyt Soc., Providence Athenaeum, Phi Beta Kappa. Clubs: Bristol Yacht (R.I.); Catboat Assn., Am. Club (Singapore); Royal Singapore Yacht, U.S. Coast Guard Aux. Home: 73 Transit St Providence RI 02906-1022 Office: Brown U History Dept Providence RI 02912

WILLIAMS, LEAMON DALE, feed and grain company executive, consultant; b. Flippin, Ark., Sept. 28, 1935; s. Johnny Boyd and Ruby Ann (Treat) W.; m. Joyce Lea Jenkins; children: John I., Wendy L., Leamon D. Jr. BS, U. Ark., 1958, MS, 1961; PhD, Mich. State U., 1964. Chemist Anderson Clayton Foods, Sherman, Tex., 1963-67; research sect. leader CPC Internat., Argo, Ill., 1967-69; dir. research Cen. Soya Co. Inc., Chgo., 1969-78; v.p. research Cen. Soya Co. Inc., Ft. Wayne, Ind., 1978-85, v.p. chemurgy, 1985-91; sr. v.p. Oilseed Products Group, 1987-91; cons. Internat. Agribusiness, Fort Wayne, Ind., 1991—. Recipient outstanding alumni award Alpha Gamma Rho, U. Ark., 1973, outstanding alumni award Mich. State U. Food Sci. Dept., 1980, outstanding alumni in agriculture U. Ark., 1993. Mem. Am. Oil Chemists Soc. (outstanding grad. student award 1962), Inst. Food Technologists, Am. Mgmt. Assn. Office: Internat Agribusiness 4646 W Jefferson Blvd Ste 175 Fort Wayne IN 46804-6832

WILLIAMS, LESLIE PEARCE, history educator; b. Harmon-on Hudson, N.Y., Sept. 8, 1927; s. George and Addie Adelia (Williams) Greenberg; m. Sylvia Irene Alessandrini, Sept. 3, 1949; children: David Rhys, Alison Ruth, Adam Jonathan, Sarah Lucille. BA, Cornell U., 1949, PhD, 1952. Instr. history Yale U., 1952-56; assoc. historian Nat. Found. for Infantile Paralysis, N.Y.C., 1956-57; asst. prof. U. Del., 1956-59; asst. prof. history Cornell U., 1960-62, assoc. prof., 1962-65, prof., 1965-71, John Stambaugh prof. history of sci., 1971-94, prof. emeritus, 1994—, chmn. dept. history, 1969-74, dir. program in history and philosophy sci. and tech., 1984-91. Author: Michael Faraday, A Biography, 1965, The Origins of Field Theory, 1967, Album of Science: The Nineteenth Century, 1978, (with Henry John Steffens) A History of Science in Western Civilization, 3 vols, 1978; editor: The Selected Correspondence of Michael Faraday, 2 vols, 1972, Relativity Theory: Its Origin and Impact on Modern Thought, 1968, (with B. Tierney and D. Kagan) Great Issues in Western Civilization, 2 vols., 1968; cons. editor Italian jour. Physis, Rivista della Storia della Scienza. With USNR, 1945-46. NSF fellow, 1959-60; 1st degree black belt Hayashi-ha Shito-ryu Karate. Mem. History of Sci. Soc., Internat. Acad. History of Sci., French Acad. Scis. (mem. com. Lavoisier), Phi Beta Kappa. Home and Office: 207 Iradell Rd Ithaca NY 14850-9207 Office: Cornell Univ Dept Sci and Tech Studies Ithaca NY 14853

WILLIAMS, LISLE EDWARD, civil and structural engineer; b. Indiana, Pa., Feb. 10, 1945; s. Lisle Edward and Marguerite Lighte (Roadarmel) W.; m. Pamela Jayne Long, Aug. 12, 1972; children: April, Andrew, Amy. Assoc. Degree, Gateway Tech. Inst., Pitts., 1967; Cert., Carnegie-Mellon U., 1970, U. Pitts., 1974, Pa. State U., 1982. Registered profl. engr., Pa.; profl. land surveyor; fallout shelter analysis lic. Numerous managerial and tech. positions Pa. Dept. Transp., Pitts., 1964-90; program mgr. transp. HDR Engring., Inc., Pitts., 1991-92; asst. v.p. Parsons Brinckerhoff, Inc., Pitts., 1992-93; dep. dir. ops. Buchart-Horn, Inc., Pitts., 1993—; bd. dirs. TRB Com., Washington, Planning & Design Divsn. ARTBA, Washington; pres. Constrn. Legis. Coun., 1988. Author, editor newsletter Cross-Sect., 1968-95, Pitts. Profl. Engr., 1974-95; contbr. numerous tech. articles to PE Reporter and Scanner mag. Elder, deacon, chmn. Plum Creek Presbyn. Ch., Pitts., 1972-95; instl. rep. Boy Scouts Am., Troop #77, Pitts., 1980-90; mem. Plum PTSA, Plum Area Soccer League, Pitts., 1983-95. Named Pitts. Outstanding Young Civil Engr. of Yr., ASCE, 1983; recipient Svc. to People award ASCE, 1988, citation Pa. Senate, 1991, Pa. House of Reps., 1991; Resolution in his honor, City of Pitts., 1995, Proclamation, County of Allegheny, 1995. Mem. Am. Soc. Hwy. Engrs. (life, nat. bd. dirs. 1964-98, pres. 1983-84, testimonial 1987, Pres.'s award 1983, 84, Disting. Svc. award 1984), Pa. Soc. Profl. Engrs. (v.p., pres.-elect, pres., bd. dirs. 1970-97, Young Engr. of Yr. award 1980, L.W. Hornfeck award 1984, President's Four Star award, 1986), Pa. Engring. Found. (trustee 1991-95), Internat. Bridge Conf. (gen. chmn. 1992-93, chmn. 1993); chmn. CEC/Pa. Trans. subcom. 1992-96, Greater Pitts. C. of C., 1992-96, Western Pa. Conservancy, 1992-96. Democrat. Presbyterian. Home: 15 Plumcrest Dr Pittsburgh PA 15239-1503 Office: Buchart Horn Inc Conestoga Bldg 7 Wood St 2d Fl Pittsburgh PA 15222-1920

WILLIAMS, LOUIS CLAIR, JR., public relations executive; b. Huntington, Ind., Nov. 7, 1940; s. Louis Clair and Marian Eileen (Bowers) W.; children—Terri Lynn, L. Bradley, Lisa C.; m. Mary Clare Moster. B.A., Eastern Mich. U., 1963. Copywriter, Rochester (N.Y.) Gas and Electric Co., 1963-65, editor RG&E News, 1965-66; employee info. specialist Gen. Ry. Signal Co., Rochester, 1966-67, supr. employment and employee rels., 1967-69; supr. pub. rels. Heublein, Inc., Hartford, Conn., 1969-70; dir. corp. communications Jewel Cos., Inc., Chgo., 1970-71; account exec. Ruder & Finn of Mid-Am., Chgo., 1971-73, v.p., 1973-76, sr. v.p., 1976-78; cons. Towers, Perrin, Forster & Crosby, Los Angeles, 1978-79; exec. v.p., gen. mgr. Harshe-Rotman & Druck, Inc., Chgo., 1979, pres. midwest region, 1979-80; v.p. Hill & Knowlton, Inc., Chgo., 1980-81, sr. v.p., 1981-83; pres. Savlin Williams Assocs., Evanston, Ill., 1983-85, L.C. Williams & Assocs., Chgo., 1985—. Recipient Clarion award Women in Communications, 1978, award of Excellence, Internat. Coun. Indsl. Editors, 1969, Bronze Oscar-of-Ind., Fin. World, 1974. Mem. Internat. Assn. Bus. Communicators (pres. 1979-80), Chgo. Assn. Bus. Communicators (pres.), Publicity Club Chgo., Pub. Rels. Soc. Am.

WILLIAMS, LOUIS STANTON, glass and chemical manufacturing executive; b. Honolulu, Oct. 7, 1919; s. Urban and Amelia (Olson) W.; m. Dorothy Webster Reed, June 12, 1943; children: Eric Reed, Timothy Howell, Steven Neil, Deborah Reed Sawin. A.B., Amherst Coll., 1941, LL.D., 1981; M.B.A., Harvard U., 1943; D.H.L., Thiel Coll., 1985. With PPG Industries (formerly Pitts. Plate Glass Co.), 1946-84, various acctg. positions, 1946-56, became controller, 1956, v.p. finance, 1963-75, dir., 1975-90, exec. v.p., 1975-76, vice chmn., 1976-78, chmn., chief exec. officer, 1979-84; chmn. Fed. Home Loan Bank, Pitts., 1971-73; bd. dirs. Duplate Can., 1976-84, Rubbermaid Inc., 1977-90, Dravo Corp., 1978-91, Prudential Ins. Co. Am., 1981-89, Mellon Bank Corp, 1981-92, Texaco Inc., 1988-92. Trustee Family and Children's Service, Pitts., 1955-61; bd. dirs. YMCA, Pitts., 1959-93, pres., 1975-77, mem. YMCA nat. bd., 1973-88, chmn., 1983-85; trustee YMCA Retirement Fund, 1989-94; pres. exec. com. Allegheny Conf. on Community Devel., 1982-83, chmn., 1983-85; bd. dirs. Pa. Economy League, 1978-83, Community Chest Allegheny County, 1961-67, Pitts. Symphony Soc., 1978-90; chmn. United Way Campaign of Southwestern Pa., 1981; bd. dirs. United Way of Allegheny County, 1978—, pres., 1984-86; trustee St. Margaret's Meml. Hosp., Pitts., 1969-83, Carnegie-Mellon U., 1978-95, Carnegie Inst., 1977-95, Com. Econ. Devel., 1981-84, Tax Found., 1980-84, Pitts. Cultural Trust, 1984-93. Lt. USNR, 1943-46. Mem. Financial Execs. Inst. (pres. Pitts. 1965-66, nat. dir. 1968-73, nat. v.p. 1972-73), Bus. Roundtable (Policy Com. 1982-84), Phi Beta Kappa. Presbyn. Clubs: Duquesne, Fox Chapel Golf (Pitts.); Laurel Valley Golf, Rolling Rock (Ligonier, Pa.); Iron City Fishing (Can.); John's Island, Bent Pine Golf (Fla.). Home: 5 The Trillium Pittsburgh PA 15238-1928 Office: PPG Industries 1 PPG Pl Pittsburgh PA 15272

WILLIAMS, LOWELL CRAIG, lawyer, employee relations executive; b. Tehachapi, Calif., Dec. 3, 1947; s. Lyndon Williams and Gertrude (White) Sievert; m. Marsha Mendelssohn; children: John S., Jeffrey A. Bescheinigungsechichte, Georg August U., Germany, 1968; BA, U. Calif., Santa Barbara, 1969; JD, Columbia U., 1972. Bar: N.Y. 1973, U.S. Ct. Appeals (2nd cir.) 1974, U.S. Supreme Ct. 1974. Assoc. Sullivan & Cromwell, N.Y.C., 1972-75; sr. v.p. Elf Aquitaine, Inc., N.Y.C., 1976-95; v.p. Compagnie des Machines Bull, N.Y.C., 1995—; bd. dirs. Am. Natural Soda Ash Co. Pres. Scarsdale Synagogue. Mem. Internat. Bar Assn., German Law Assn. (dir.). Home: 37 Paddington Rd Scarsdale NY 10583-2321 Office: Bull Info Sys 1211 Ave of the Americas New York NY 10018

WILLIAMS, LUCINDA, country musician; b. Lake Charles, La., 1953; d. Miller W.; m. Greg Sowders (div.). Albums include: Ramblin' On My Mind, 1979, Happy Woman Blues, 1980, Lucinda Williams, 1988, Passionate Kisses, 1989 (Grammy award Best Country Song 1994), (EP, Sweet Old World, 1992; contbr. songs to: Sweet Relief, 1993, Born to Choose, 1993.

WILLIAMS, LULA AGNES, retired writer, retired educator; b. Bentonville, Ark., May 11, 1904; d. Thomas Andrew and Nellie Louella (Mason) Nichols; m. Esmond Leonidas Williams, June 12, 1927 (dec. Jan. 1961). BA, U. Ark., 1956. Cert. secondary tchr., cert. to teach English and social studies. Stenographer Benton County Hardware Co., Bentonville, Ark., 1922-25; tchr. country sch. Cross Lanes, Bentonville, 1925-26; stenographer-sec. Skelly Oil Co., El Dorado, Kans., 1926-27; asst. adminstr. Benton County Home, Bentonville, 1935-40; acting postmaster U.S. Post Office, Bentonville, 1944-45; tchr. Bentonville Schs., 1956-70; acting postmaster U.S. Post Office, Bentonville, 1961-62; writer Bentonville, 1985-88. Author, pub.: Hills Are for Climbing, 1988. Pres. Bates Meml. Hosp. Aux., 1972, Qui Vive, Gen. Fedn. Women's Clubs, Bentonville, 1973, Benton County Ret. Tchrs. Assn., 1976-77; worthy matron Order of Eastern Star, Bentonville, 1936. Named Woman of Yr., Bus. and Profl. Women's Club, Bentonville, 1981-82; recipient Svc. award AAUW, Bentonville, 1981, gift named in her honor AAUW 1987. Mem. Nat. Retired Tchrs. Assn. (life), Ark. Retired Tchrs. Assn. (life), U. Ark. Alumni Assn. (life). Democrat. Mem. Christian Ch. (Disciples of Christ). Avocations: reading, walking. Home: 425 SE A St Bentonville AR 72712-5933

WILLIAMS, LUTHER STEWARD, science foundation administrator; b. Sawyerville, Ala., Aug. 19, 1940; s. Roosevelt and Mattie B. (Wallace) W.; m. Constance Marie Marion, Aug. 23, 1963; children: Mark Steward, Monique Marie. BA magna cum laude, Miles Coll., 1961; MS, Atlanta U., 1963; PhD, Purdue U., 1968, DSc (hon.), 1987; DSc (hon.), U. Louisville, 1992. NSF lab. asst. Spelman Coll., 1961-62; NSF lab. asst. Atlanta U., 1962-63, instr. biology, faculty rsch. grantee, 1963-64, asst. prof. biology, 1969-70, prof. biology, 1984-87, pres., 1984-87; grad. tchg. asst. Purdue U., West Lafayette, Ind., 1964-65, grad. rsch. asst., 1965-66, asst. prof. biology, 1970-73, assoc. prof., 1973-79, prof., 1979-80, NIH Career Devel. awardee, 1971-75, asst. provost, 1976-80; dean Grad. Sch., prof. biology Washington U., St. Louis, 1980-83; v.p. acad. affairs, dean Grad. Sch. U. Colo., Boulder, 1983-84; Am. Cancer Soc. postdoctoral fellow SUNY-Stony Brook, 1968-69; assoc. prof. biology MIT, 1973-74; spl. asst. to dir. Nat. Inst. Gen. Med. Scis., NIH, Bethesda, Md., 1987-88; dep. dir. Nat. Inst. Gen. Med. Scis. NIH, Bethesda, 1988-89; sr. sci. advisor to dir. NSF, Washington, 1989-90, asst. dir. for edn. and human resources, 1990—; chmn. rev. com. MARC Program, Nat. Inst. Gen. Med. Scis., NIH, 1972-76; grant reviewer NIH, 1971-73, 76, NSF, 1973, 76-80, Med. Research Council of N.Z., 1976; mem. life scis. sreening com. recombinant DNA adv. com. HEW, 1979-81; mem. nat. adv. gen. med. sci. council NIH, 1980-85; mem. adv. com. Office Tech. Assessment, Washington, 1984-87; chmn. fellowship adv. com. NRC Ford Found., 1984-85; mem.-at-large Grad. Record Exam. Bd., 1981-85, chmn. minority grad. edn. com., 1983-85; mem. health, safety and environ. affairs. com. Nat. Labs., U. Calif., 1981-87; mem. adv. panel Office Tech. Assessment, U.S. Congress, 1985-86; mem. fed. task force on women, minorities and the handicapped in sci. and tech., 1987-91; mem. adv. panel to dir. sci. and tech. ctrs. devel. NSF, 1987-88; mem. nat. adv. com. White House Initiative on Historically Black Colls. and Univs. on Sci. and Tech., 1986-89; numerous other adv. bds. and coms. Contbr. sci. articles to profl. jours. Vice chmn. bd. advisors Atlanta Neighborhood Justice Ctr., 1984-87; bd. dirs. Met. Atlanta United Way, 1986-87, Butler St. YMCA, Atlanta, 1985-87; trustee Atlanta Zool. Assn., 1985-87, Miles Coll., 1984-87, Atlanta U., 1984-87, 90-96; mem. nominating com. Dana Found. NIH predoctoral fellow Purdue U., 1966-68. Fellow AAAS, Am. Acad. Microbiology; mem. Am. Soc. Microbiology, Am. Chem. Soc., Am. Soc. Biol. Chemists (mem. ednl. affairs com. 1979-82, com. on equal opportunities for minorities 1972-84), AAAS, N.Y. Acad. Scis. Home: 11608 Split Rail Ct Rockville MD 20852-4423 Office: NSF Education & Human Resources 4201 Wilson Blvd Arlington VA 22203-1803

WILLIAMS, LYNN RUSSELL, former labor union official; b. Springfield, Ont., Can., July 21, 1924; came to U.S., 1977; s. Waldemar and Emma Elizabeth (Fisher) W.; m. Audrey Hansuld, Sept. 12, 1946; children—Judith Williams Hocking, David, Barbara, Brian. BA, McMaster U., Hamilton, Ont., 1944, LLD (hon.), 1978; LittD, Brock U., St. Catherines, Ont., 1985. Organizer Can. Congress of Labour (now Can. Labour Congress), 1947-55; staff rep. United Steelworkers Am., Toronto, Ont., Can., 1956-57; area supr. United Steelworkers Am., Niagara Peninsula, 1958-62; asst. dir. Dist. 6 United Steelworkers Am., Toronto, 1963-73, dir. Dist. 6, 1973-77; internat. sec. United Steelworkers Am., Pitts., 1977-83, internat. pres., 1983—; mem. exec. council AFL-CIO, Washington, 1983, mem. exec. council Ind. Union Dept., 1983; mem. exec. com. Metalworkers Fedn., Geneva, 1983; dir. Am. Arbitration Assn., 1983; bd. dirs. African-Am. Labor Ctr., Am. Productivity Ctr., Citizen/Labor Energy Coalition, Com. for Nat. Health Ins., Work in Am. Inst.; trustee Am. Inst. for Free Labor Devel.; mem. exec. com. Can.-Am. Com.; mem. panel Econ. Policy Council; mem. adv. com. Labor Desk, USYC; trustee Labor Heritage Found.; v.p. Labor-Industry Coalition for Internat. Trade; mem. ad hoc com. Nat. Planning Assn.; mem. adv. bd. Niagara Inst.; visiting fellow, Inst of Politics. Vice pres. Ams. for Democratic Action; bd. dirs. Am. Open U., 1983—; mem. steering group Council on Fgn. Relations; bd. dirs. Pitts. Symphony Soc., 1978—, United Way of Allegheny County, 1984—, World Affairs Council of Pitts.; bd. govs. United Way, 1984—; mem. Aspen Inst., 1983—, Econ. Policy Council of UN, USA, 1982—; trustee Brother Brothers Found., 1983—; mem. Can.-Am. Commn., 1983—. Served with Can. Navy, 1944-45. Avocations: running; jogging; reading; skiing. Office: Institute of Politics 79 JFK St Cambridge MA 02138*

WILLIAMS, MARGARET, federal official. Asst. to Pres., chief of staff to First Lady The White House, Washington, 1993—. Office: Office of the First Lady The White House 1600 Pennsylvania Ave NW Washington DC 20500

WILLIAMS, MARGARET LU WERTHA HIETT, nurse; b. Midland, Tex., Aug. 30, 1938; d. Cotter Craven and Mollie Jo (Tarter) Hiett; m. James Troy Lary, Nov. 16, 1960 (div. Jan. 1963); 1 child, James Cotter; m. Tuck Williams, Aug. 11, 1985. BS, Tex. Woman's U., 1960; MA, Tchrs. Coll., N.Y.C., 1964, EdM, 1974, doctoral studies, 1981; postgrad., U. Tex., 1991-92, U. Wis.; cert. completion, U. Wis., Scotland. Cert. clin. nurse specialist, advanced practice nurse; cert. psychiat./mental health nurse, nursing continuing edn. and staff devel. Nurse Midland Meml. Hosp., 1960-63; instr. Odessa (Tex.) Coll., 1963-67; dir. ADNP Laredo (Tex.) Jr. Coll., 1967-70; asst. prof. Pan Am. U., Edinburgh, Tex., 1970-72; rsch. asst. Tchrs. Coll., 1973-74; nursing practitioner St. Luke's Hosp., N.Y.C., 1975-79; sgt. Burns Security, Midland, 1979-81; with Area Builders, Odessa, 1981-83; field supr. We Care Home Health Agy., Midland, 1983-87; clin. educator, supr. Glenwood, A Psychiat. Hosp., Midland, 1987-92; dir. nursing Charter Healthcare Systems, Corpus Christi, Tex., 1992-93; nurse examiner Nurse Aid Competency Evalution Svc. Tex. Nurses Found., Austin, 1994—; RN III Brown Sch., San Marcos, Tex., 1993—; co-owner, operator MTW Med. Legal Cons.; adj. prof. Pace U., 1974-75, S.W. Tex. State U., 1995. Mem. Gov. Richards' Exec. Leadership Coun., 1991-95, re-election steering com., 1994. Recipient Isabelle Hampton-Robb award Nat. League for Nursing, 1976, Achievement award Community Leaders of Am., 1989, Ladies 1st of Midland, 1974. Mem. NAFE, ANA, Tex. Nurses Assn. (pres. dist. 21 1962-65, dist. 32 1970-72), Am. Psychiat. Nurses Assn., Parkland Meml. Hosp. Nurses Alumnae Assn., Tex. Women's U. Alumnae Assn., Midland H.S. Alumni, Bus. and Profl. Women's Club, Mensa, Lockhart Breakfast Lions Club. Democrat. Avocations: songwriting, public speaking, singing, travel. Office: PO Box 324 Lockhart TX 78644

WILLIAMS, MARIE CLONEY, rehabilitation nurse administrator, owner business; b. Abilene, Tex., Oct. 20, 1944; d. Morton Earl and Emily Marie (Stepanek) Phillips; m. Richard Morgan Cloney, Aug. 25, 1965 (div. Nov., 1989); children: Kellen Frances, Shannon Cooper.; m. Clifton John Williams, Jr., May 17, 1992. BSN, U. N.C., 1966, MPH, 1967. RN, Pa.; cert. nurse adminstr. Rsch. assoc. U. N.C. Sch. of Pub. Health, Chapel Hill, N.C., 1967-68; head nurse Comty. Dr. Nursing Ctr., Manhasset, N.Y., 1968; staff nurse Hackettstown (N.J.), 1973-74; dir. nursing Welkind Neurol. Hosp., Chester, N.J., 1974-78; dir. nursing svcs. Healthbank Rehab. Ctr., Columbia, Pa., 1978-81; adminstr. for nursing svcs. Pa. State U.- Elizabethtown (Pa.) Rehab., 1981-83; assoc. adminstr. nursing svcs. Rehab. Hosp. York, Pa., 1983-85; adminstr., CEO Rehab. Hosp. York, 1985-88; v.p. ops. Rehab. Systems Co., Camp Hill, Pa., 1988-93; owner, ptnr. Interactive Health Co., Mechanicsburg, Pa., 1993—; mem. profl. adv. com. VNA of York, Pa., 1985-88; asst. sec., bd. dirs. York County Health Corp., York, 1986-88; bd. dirs. Mt. View Regional Rehab. Hosp., Morgantown, W. Va., 1990-92; owner, mgr., cons. Marie Williams Assocs., Mechanicsburg, Pa., 1993—. Contbr. articles to profl. jours. Com. mem. Country and Town Bapt. Ch., Mechanicsburg, Pa., 1989—. Mem. Assn. Rehab. Nurses, Ctrl. Pa. Tech. Coun., Am. Electronics Assn., Nat. Disting. Svc. Registry: Med. Rehab., Sigma Theta Tau, Delta Omicron. Republican. Avocations: tennis, piano. Home: 26 Cumberland Estates Dr Mechanicsburg PA 17055-1719 Office: Interactive Health Co 2415-A Old Gettysburg Rd Camp Hill PA 17011

WILLIAMS, MARK, food products executive; b. 1949. With Safeway Corp., L.A., 1966-67, Fred Meyer Corp., Seattle, 1967-75; exec. v.p., COO Carr-Gottstein Foods Co., Anchorage, 1975—, now pres., CEO. Office: Carr-Gottstein Foods Co 6411 A St Anchorage AK 99518-1824*

WILLIAMS, MARK H., marketing communications agency executive; b. Omaha, Apr. 30, 1959; s. Perry T. and Donna M. (Hodges) W. BA in Comm. and Bus., Loyola U., Chgo., 1981. Asst. account exec. Bozell & Jacobs, Omaha, 1981-82, account exec., 1982-86; account supr. Bozell, Jacobs, Kenyon & Eckhardt, Omaha, 1986-88, v.p., 1987—; sr. v.p. client svcs. and devel. Bozell Worldwide, Chgo., 1988—; speaker Creighton U., 1985-87, U. Nebr., 1985, Harvard U., 1989-90, Northwestern U., 1990-95. Contbr. articles to profl. jours. Mem. Am. Advt. Fedn., and numerous trade assns. Home: 910 Lake Shore Dr Chicago IL 60611-1540 Office: Bozell Worldwide Inc 625 N Michigan Ave Chicago IL 60611-3110

WILLIAMS, MARSHALL HENRY, JR., physician, educator; b. New Haven, July 15, 1924; s. Marshall Henry and Henrietta (English) W.; m. Mary Butler, Aug. 27, 1948; children: Stuart, Patricia, Marshall, Frances, Richard. Grad., Pomfret Sch., 1942; B.S., Yale, 1945, M.D., 1947. Diplomate Nat. Bd. Med. Examiners, Am. Bd. Internal Medicine. Intern Presbyn. Hosp., N.Y.C., 1947-48; asst. resident medicine Presbyn. Hosp., 1948-49; asst. resident medicine New Haven Hosp., 1949-50, asst. in medicine, 1950; trainee Nat. Heart Inst., 1950; practice medicine, specializing in internal medicine Bronx, N.Y.; chief respiratory sect., dept. cardiorespiratory diseases Army Med. Service Grad. Sch., Walter Reed Army Med. Center, 1953-55; dir. cardiorespiratory lab. Grasslands Hosp., Valhalla, N.Y., 1955-59; dir. chest svc. Bronx Mcpl. Hosp. Ctr., 1959-94; vis. asst. prof. physiology Albert Einstein Coll. Medicine, Bronx, 1955-59, assoc. prof. medicine and physiology, 1959-66, prof. medicine, 1966—; dir. pulmonary div. Montefiore Med. Ctr., Albert Einstein Coll. Medicine, 1981-94. Author: Clinical Applications of Cardiopulmonary Physiology, 1960, Essentials of Pulmonary Medicine, 1982, Consultation in Chest Medicine, 1985; contbr. articles to profl. jours. Served from 1st lt. to capt. U.S. Army, 1950-52. Mem. Am. Physiol. Soc., AAAS, Am. Heart Assn., Westchester Heart Assn (past pres.), Am. Thoracic Soc., Am. Fedn. Clin. Research, N.Y. Acad. Sci., N.Y. Trudeau Soc. (past pres.), Am. Soc. Clin. Investigation, Soc. Urban Physicians (past pres.), N.Y. Tb. and Health Assn. (past dir.), Alpha Omega Alpha. Home: 103 Fox Meadow Rd Scarsdale NY 10583-2301 Office: Albert Einstein Coll Medicine Bronx NY 10461

WILLIAMS, MARTHA ETHELYN, information science educator; b. Chgo., Sept. 21, 1934; d. Harold Milton and Alice Rosemond (Fox) W. B.A., Barat Coll., 1955; M.A., Loyola U., 1957. With IIT Rsch.Inst., Chgo., 1957-72, mgr. info. scis., 1962-72, mgr. computer search ctr., 1968-72; adj. assoc. prof. sci. info. Ill. Inst. Tech., Chgo., 1965-73, lectr. chemistry dept., 1968-70, rsch. prof. info. sci., coordinated sci. lab. Coll. engring.; also dir. info. retrieval research lab. U. Ill., Urbana, 1972—, prof. info. sci. grad. sch. of libr. info. sci., 1974—, affiliate, computer sci. dept., 1979—; chmn. large data base conf. Nat. Acad. Sci./NRC, 1974, mem. ad hoc panel on info. storage and retrieval, 1977, numerical data adv. bd., 1979-82, computer sci. and tech. bd., nat. rsch. network rev. com., 1987-88, chmn. utility sub-com., 1987-88; mem. task force on sci. info. activities NSF, 1977; U.S. rep. review com. for project on broad system of ordering, UNESCO, Hague, Netherlands, 1974; vice chmn. Gordon Rshc. Conf. on Sci. Info. Problems in Rsch., 1978, chmn., 1980; mem. panel on intellectual property rights in age of electronics and info. U.S. Congress, Office of Tech. Assessment; program chmn. Nat. Online Meeting, 1980—; cons. to numerous cos., govt. agys. and rsch. founds.; invited lectr. Commn. European Communities, Industrial R&D adv. com., Brussels, 1992. Editor in chief Computer-Readable Databases Directory and Data Sourcebook, 1976-89, founding editor, 1989-92; editor Ann. Rev. Info. Sci. and Tech., 1976—, Online Rev., 1979-92, Online and CDROM Rev., 1993—, procs. nat. online meeting, 1981—; contbg. editor column on databases to Bull. Am. Soc. Info. Sci., 1974-78; mem. editorial adv. bd. Database, 1978-88; mem. editorial bd. Info. Processing and Mgmt., 1982-89, The Reference Libr.; contbr. more than 200 articles to profl. jours. Trustee Engirng. Info., Inc., 1974-87, bd. dirs., 1976-91, chmn. bd. dirs., 1982-91, v.p., 1978-79, pres., 1980-81; regent Nat. Libr. Medicine, 1978-82, chmn. bd. regents, 1981; mem. task force on sci. info. activities NSF, 1977-78; mem. nat. adv. com. ACCESS ERIC, 1989-91. Recipient best paper of year award H. W. Wilson Co., 1975; NSF travel grantee Luxembourg, 1972; NSF travel grantee Honolulu, 1973; NSF travel grantee Tokyo, 1973; NSF travel grantee Mexico City, 1975; NSF travel grantee Scotland, 1976. Fellow AAAS (computers, info. and comm. mem.-at-large 1978-81, nominating com. 1983, 85), Inst. Info. Sci. (hon.); mem. NAS (joint com. with NRC on chem. info. 1971-73), Am. Chem. Soc., Am. Soc. Info. Sci. (councilor 1971-72, 87-89, chmn. networks com. 1973-74, spl. interest group of SDI 1974-75, pres.-elect 1986-87, pres. 1987-88, past pres., mem. planning com. 1988-89, publs. com. 1974—, chmn. 1989, mem. nominations com. 1989, chmn. budget and fin. com. 1987-89, award of merit 1984, Pioneer Info. Sci. award 1987, Watson Davis award 1995), Assn. for Computing Machinery (pub. bd. 1972-76), Assn. Sci. Info. Dissemination Ctrs. (v.p. 1971-73, pres. 1975-77), Internat. Fedn. for Documentation (U.S. nat. com.). Home: 2134 Sandra Ln Monticello IL 61856-9801 Office: U Ill 1308 W Main St Urbana IL 61801-2307

WILLIAMS, MARTHA SPRING, psychologist; b. Dallas, Oct. 5, 1951; d. Thomas Ayers and Emma Martha (Felmet) Spring; m. James Walter Williams, June 30, 1979; children: Dane Ayers, Jake Austin. BA, East Tex. State U., 1972, MEd, 1974, EdD, 1978. Cert. and lic. psychologist, Tex.; lic. profl. counselor, marriage and family therapist. Tchr. Dallas Ind. Sch.; grad. asst. to dean Coll. Edn. East Tex. State U., 1975-77; intern Terrell State Hosp. Outreach Clinic and Hunt County Clinic, Greenville, Tex., 1975-76, Univ. Counseling Ctr., East Tex. State U., 1976-77; learning dir. Man and His Environ. Program, 1978-85; pvt. practice psychology Dallas, 1981—; adolescent group therapist in-patient psychiat. facility, 1986-91; mem. staff Baylor/Richardson (Tex.) Med. Ctr., clin. dir. allied mental health profls., 1992-94; v.p. for provider rels. Advanced Behavioral Health Care Sys., Inc., 1995—; mem. staff Green Oaks, St. Paul, Seany Behavioral Hosps. Author: (with others) The Role Innovative Woman and Her Positive Impact on Family Functioning, 1981, Women and Intimacy, 1982, Permenstral Syndrome: A Family Affair, 1984, The Expanding Horizons of Traditional Private Pracitce: High Tech High/Touch, 1986, Adolescent Suicide: Consequences of an Anti-Child Society, 1986, Therapist as a Partner, 1987. Nat. del. Dem. Conv., San Francisco, 1984; Dem. county chair Kaufman County, 1993—; mem. state Dem. Exec. Com. 1993—. Mem. APA, Am. Assn. Marriage and Family Therapists, Am. Soc. Clin. Hypnosis. Lutheran. Avocations: snow skiing, travel, politics, tap dancing. Home: PO Box 1119 Terrell TX 75160-1119 Office: Ste 825 4835 Lyndon B Johnson Fwy Dallas TX 75244-6005 *In this increasingly complex, mobile, and hurried world, it is vital that people seek out and nurture healthy relationships to maintain a sense of connection which in times past flowed more naturally from extended family and communities.*

WILLIAMS, MARY ALICE, journalist; b. Mpls.; m. Mark Haefeli; children: Alice Ann, Sara Mary and Laura Abigail (twins). BA in English and Mass Communications, Creighton U. Reporter, news producer Sta. KSTP-TV, Mpls.; exec. producer, news mgr. Sta. WPIX-TV, N.Y.C.; reporter, anchor Sta. WNBC-TV, N.Y.C., from 1974; with Cable News Network, 1979-89, prime-time anchor, v.p., 1982-89; with NBC News, N.Y.C., 1989—, co-anchor Yesterday, Today and Tomorrow, 1989, co-anchor Sunday Today, 1990—. Recipient By Line award N.Y. Press Club, 1977, Headliner award, 1986; named Woman of Yr., Women in Cable, 1988.

WILLIAMS, MARY ELEANOR NICOLE, writer; b. Atlanta, May 14, 1938; d. Edward King Merrell and Bernice I. (Pitts) Smith; m. Charlie Lloyd Williams, July 25, 1993; children: Mary Palmer, Susan Gober, Traci Cox. Student, Fla. Jr. Coll., 1974. Lic. real estate broker, Fla. Editor, writer, former owner Southwestern Advt. and Pub., Carrollton, Ga., 1991-94; freelance writer children's stories, 1992—. Author, editor: West Georgia Area Guide, 1991-93. Mem. Carroll County C. of C. Avocations: writing, music, travel, walking, art. Home: 103 Ferndale Rd Carrollton GA 30117-4312

WILLIAMS, MARY ELIZABETH, elementary school educator; b. Gary, Ind., Nov. 14, 1943; d. Morris O. and Mary C. (Hall) Douglas; m. Timothy Williams Jr., July 30, 1966; children: Donna M., Brian T., Derrick A. BS, Purdue U., 1965; MS, Ind. U., Gary, 1973, reading endorsement, 1990, lic. adminstr., 1994. Tchr. Hammond (Ind.) Schs., 1965-66, Gary Cmty. Sch., 1966—. Author: Building Public Confidence Through Communication, 1983. Deaconess, Sunday sch. tchr. St. John Bapt. Ch., Gary, 1967—; founder, coord. Boys and Girls Club, 1994-95. Recipient Outstanding Svc. award Kappa Delta Pi, 1991, Svc. award Nobel Sch. PTA, 1993, Adult Vol. Literacy award Gary Pub. Libr., 1991, Women of Distinction award YWCA, 1995. Mem. Am. Fedn. Tchrs., Gary Reading Coun. (sec. 1993, v.p. 1994—, pres. 1995), Ind. State Reading Assn. (mem. family involvement in reading com. 1993-95), N.W. Ind. Alliance Black Sch. Educators, Alpha Kappa Alpha (sec. 1987-90), Afrocentric Curriculum Cadre, Phi Delta Kappa (v.p. Krinon Club 1991). Democrat. Avocations: reading, sewing, cooking, photography, gardening. Home: 8535 Lakewood Ave Gary IN 46403-2250

WILLIAMS, MARY PEARL, judge, lawyer; b. Brownsville, Tex., Jan. 12, 1928; d. Marvin Redman and Theo Mae (Kethley) Hall; m. Jerre Stockton Williams, May 28, 1950; children—Jerre Stockton, Shelley Hall, Stephanie Kethley. B.A., U. Tex., 1948, J.D., 1949. Bar: Tex. 1949, U.S. Supreme Ct. 1955, U.S. Dist. Ct. (we. dist.) Tex., 1987. Asst. atty. gen. State of Tex. Austin, 1949-50, relief judge Municipal Ct., summer 1964; asst. instr. dept. govt. U. Tex., Austin, 1966-67; atty. Office of Emergency Preparedness, Exec. Office of Pres., Washington, 1968-70; labor arbitrator, mem. arbitration panel Am. Arbitration Assn., 1972-73; judge County Ct. at Law 2, Travis County, Tex., 1973-80, 53d Judicial Dist. Ct., 1981—; cons. Dept. HEW, 1966-67. Mem. adv. com. Juvenile Bd. of Travis County, 1964-67; trustee United Way, 1974-78. Named Outstanding Woman, Austin Am.-Statesman, 1974, Austin Citizen, 1978; named Woman of Yr., Austin Dist. Bus. and Profl. Women, 1977; elected to Austin H.S. Hall of Fame, 1996. Mem. ABA, State Bar Tex., Coll. State Bar Tex., Tex. Bar Found., Am. Bar Found., Travis County Bar Assn., Am. Law Inst., Am. Judicature Soc., Inst. Jud. Adminstrn., Jr. League Austin, Kappa Alpha Theta, Delta Kappa Gamma (hon.). Democrat. Methodist. Office: Travis County Courthouse PO Box 1748 Austin TX 78767-1748

WILLIAMS, MATT (MATTHEW DERRICK WILLIAMS), professional baseball player; b. Bishop, Calif., Nov. 28, 1965. Student, U. Nev., Las Vegas. With San Francisco Giants, 1986—; player Nat. League All-Star Team, 1990, 94. Recipient Gold Glove award, 1991, 93, 94, Silver Slugger award, 1990, 93-94; named to Sporting News Nat. League All-Star team, 1990, 93-94, Coll. All-Am. team Sporting News, 1986; Nat. League RBI Leader, 1990. Office: San Francisco Giants Candlestick Park San Francisco CA 94124

WILLIAMS, MAURICE JACOUTOT, development organization executive; b. New Brunswick, Can., Nov. 13, 1920; s. Alfred Jacoutot and Yvonne (Theberge) W.; m. Betty Jane Bath, Dec. 18, 1943; children: Jon, Peter, Stephen. Student, Northwestern U., 1940-42, U. Manchester, Eng., 1945; M.A., U. Chgo., 1949. Research fellow London Sch. Econs., summer 1948; Dir. U.S. student program U. Fribourg, Switzerland, 1946; prin. examiner Chgo. Civil Service Commn., 1949; economist Office Internat. Trade Policy, Dept. State, Washington, 1950-53; econ. officer Am. embassy, London, 1953-55; chief Econ. Def. Coordination, 1955-58; asst. dir. U.S. Operations Mission to Iran, ICA, 1958-60, dep. dir., 1961-63; dep. dir. USAID/Pakistan, 1963-65, dir., 1965-67; chief program div. Near East-South Asia, 1961; asst. adminstr. Nr. East-South Asia AID/W, 1967-70; dep. adminstr. AID, 1970-74; chmn. Devel. Assistance Com. OECD, Paris, 1974-78; exec. dir. UN World Food Council, 1978-86; sec.-gen., pres. emeritus Soc. Internat. Devel., 1986—; Presdl. coordinator Fgn. Disaster Relief, Bangladesh, Peru, Philippines, Managua, Sahel, 1971-74; chief U.S. del. U.S.-N. Vietnam Joint Econ. Commn., 1974—. Recipient Nat. Civil Service award, 1971, AID Distinguished Honor award, 1974, Rockefeller Pub. Service award, 1974. Club: Cosmos. Address: Overseas Devel Council 1875 Connecticut Ave NW Washington DC 20009-5728 *The principles guiding me have been those of middle-America at mid-century, namely that integrity and concentrated efforts yield their own reward. Implicit are beliefs in democratic values, equity in opportunities for social and economic progress, and the need to build up institutions for their realization. The challenge of our time has been to extend these goals worldwide. They are best pursued in cooperative endeavors through the United Nations. A decent standard of food, health and personal security is possible for all people and nations. Endeavors to these ends have been personally rewarding.*

WILLIAMS, MELVIN JOHN, sociologist, educator; b. Stovall, N.C., Feb. 13, 1915; s. John Presley and Mary Jenera (Wilkerson) W.; m. Frances Clark, Oct. 15, 1936; children—Kay Frances (Mrs. Bradley Yount), Dorothy Virginia (dec.), Melvin John, Deborah Susan (Mrs. Monte F. Little), Steven Clark, Eric Stanton. A.B., Duke, 1936, B.D., 1939, Ph.D., 1941. From instr. to asst. prof. sociology Albion (Mich.) Coll., 1941-44; prof. sociology, head dept. Wesleyan Coll., Macon, Ga., 1944-47; asso. prof. sociology Fla. State U., Tallahassee, 1947-52; prof. sociology, head dept. Stetson U., De Land, Fla., 1952-60; prof. sociology, chmn. social work Stetson U., 1960-63; prof. sociology. East Carolina U., Greenville, 1963—; chmn. dept. sociology East Carolina U., 1963-71; vis. prof. summers Mich. State Normal Coll., 1943, Whittier Coll., 1957, U. N.C., 1970; With Duke Found., summer 1936. Author: with others Contemporary Social Theory, 1940, Catholic Social Thought, Its Approach to Contemporary Problems, 1950, Social Norms of Adolescents, A Study in Social Guidance, 1959, Moral and Spiritual Values in Education, 1955; Contbr. articles to profl. publs. Co-dir. Addison project Kresge Found., 1942-44; dir. YWCA Community Survey, Macon, Ga., 1944; dir., family counselor Children's Center, Macon, 1946-47; dir. Adolescent Research project Wesleyan Coll., 1944-46, East Carolina U., 1963; research and sociol. cons., 1946—; dir. NSF Inst. in Sociology, 1967. Fellow Am. Sociol. Assn.; mem. AAAS, AAUP, Am. Acad. Polit. and Social Sci., So. Sociol. Soc. (sec. treas. 1953-55, 1st v.p. 1955-56), Groves Conf., Nat. Council Family Relations, S.A.R., Omicron Delta Kappa, Alpha Kappa Delta, Pi Gamma Mu. Methodist. Club: Lion (pres. DeLand, Fla. 1960). Home: 103 Poplar Dr Greenville NC 27834-6435

WILLIAMS, MICHAEL ANTHONY, lawyer; b. Mandan, N.D., Sept. 14, 1932; s. Melvin Douglas and Lucille Ann (Gavin) W.; m. Marjorie Ann Harrer, Aug. 25, 1962 (div. 1989); children: Ann Margaret, Douglas Raymond, David Michael; m. Dorothy Ruth Hand, 1989. B.A., Coll. of St. Thomas, 1954; LL.B., Harvard U., 1959. Bar: Colo. 1959, N.D. 1959, U.S. Dist. Ct. Colo. 1959, U.S. Ct. Appeals (10th cir.) 1959, U.S. Supreme Ct. 1967. Assoc. Sherman & Howard and predecessor Dawson, Nagel, Sherman & Howard, Denver, 1959-65, ptnr., 1965-91; pres. Williams, Youle & Koenigs, P.C., Denver, 1991—. Served as 1st lt. USAF, 1955-57. Mem. Am. Coll. Trial Lawyers, Am. Bd. Trial Advs., Colo. Bar Found., Am. Law Inst., ABA, Colo. Bar Assn., Denver Bar Assn., Arapahoe County Bar Assn. Office: Williams Youle & Koenigs PC 1200 17th St Ste 1420 Denver CO 80202-5814

WILLIAMS, MICHAEL ROY, marketing research, management educator; b. Altus, Okla., Apr. 14, 1946; s. Roy L. and Goldie L. (Smith) W.; m. Marilyn Kay Henry, Oct. 5, 1968; children: Aimee Lynn, Kerri Nicole. BBA, U. Okla., 1968, MBA, 1970; PhD, Okla. State U., 1992. Teaching assoc. Coll. Bus. U. Okla., Norman, 1968-69, dean's rsch. assoc., 1969-70; nat. rsch. dir. Doric Corp., Oklahoma City, 1970-71, asst. to pres., 1971-73; gen. mgr. A&W Sales and Leasing Corp., Lawton, Okla., 1973-78, pres., 1978-87; rsch. assoc. Bus. Devel. Svcs., Inc., Lawton, 1978—, Sales Promotion Cons., Inc., Englewood, Colo., 1986-90, Ctr. for Values Rsch., Dallas; prof. Cameron U., Lawton, 1987-91, Ill. State U., Normal, 1991—; mem. undergrad. curriculum com. Ill. State U., 1992-93; rsch. assoc. Ctr. for Values Rsch. Internat., Inc., Dallas; co-dir. Bur. for Market Driven Quality; reviewer for nat. conf. in sales and sales mgmt.; lectr. Internat. Bus. Inst., 1994, 95; cons. in field. Author: Project Evaluation, 1988, The Political

Futures Game, 1993, The Professional Selling Skills Workbook, 1996, other manuscripts; reviewer European Jour. Mktg., 1994, So. Mktg. Assn., 1995, Am. Mktg. Assn. Nat. Educators Conf., 1995, Acad. Mktg. Sci., 1995; editor Proceedings of the Nat. Conf. in Sales Mgmt., 1996; mem. editl rev. bd. Jour. Personal Selling and Sales Mgmt., 1995, 96. Mem. adminstrv. bd. Centenary Meth. Ch., Lawton, 1985-90; mktg. advisor Comanche Indian Nation, Lawton, 1986-88; advisor Leadership Lawton Found., 1990; mem. undergrad. curriculum com. Coll. of Bus., Ill. State U.; chair Acad. of Mktg. Sci. Jane K. Fenyo award, 1996. Grantee Kellogg Found., 1987, Ill. State U., 1992, 93, 94, 95, Old Republic Rsch. Program, 1993, 94; Nat. Consortium fellow, 1990; Richard D. Irwin Found. fellow, 1991, IBM-U. Toronto Inst. Market Driven Quality Rsch. Consortium, 1993; Old Republic Corp. rsch. scholar, 1993, 94, 95; recipient Outstanding Manuscript award S.W. Bus. Symposium, 1990, Hon. Mention award Mktg. Sci. Inst., Alden G. Clayton Competition, 1992, Innovation in Leadership of Bus. Edn. award MidContinent Am. Assembly Collegiate Schs. of Bus., 1993, Outstanding Rsch. Manuscript award Nat. Conf. Sales Mgmt., 1994, 95. Fellow Alpha Mu Alpha, Beta Gamma Sigma, Phi Kappa Phi; mem. Am. Mktg. Assn. (Nat. Faculty Consortium fellow 1992, 94), So. Mktg. Assn., Acad. Mktg. Sci. (presentor spl. panel 1993, 94; discussant 1994), Small Bus. Adminstrn., Kiwanis (pres. Lawton chpt. 1983), Beta Theta Pi, Pi Sigma Epsilon (charter mem., faculty adv.), Phi Kappa Phi. Republican. Avocations: flying, scuba diving instructing, writing. Home: 5 Hayloft Rd Bloomington IL 61704-1276 Office: Ill State U Dept Mktg Williams Hall Normal IL 61761

WILLIAMS, MILLER, poet, translator; b. Hoxie, Ark., Apr. 8, 1930; s. Ernest Burdette and Ann Jeanette (Miller) W.; m. Lucille Day, Dec. 29, 1951 (div.); m. Rebecca Jordan Hall, Apr. 11, 1969; children: Lucinda, Robert, Karyn. BS, Ark. State Coll., 1951; MS, U. Ark., 1952; postgrad., La. State U., 1951, U. Miss., 1957; HHD (hon.), Lander Coll., 1983; DHL, Hendrix Coll., 1995. Instr. in English La. State U., 1962-63, asst. prof., 1964-66; vis. prof. U. Chile, Santiago, 1963-64; assoc. prof. Loyola U., New Orleans, 1966-70; Fulbright prof. Nat. U. Mex., Mexico City, 1970; co-dir. grad. program in creative writing U. Ark., 1970-84, assoc. prof., 1971-73, prof. English and fgn. langs., dir. program in transl., 1973-87, univ. prof., 1987—, dir. poetry-in-the prisons programs div. continuing edn., 1974-79, chmn. program in comparative lit., 1978-80; dir. U. Ark. Press, 1980—, Bank of Elkins, Ark. 1988—; fellow Am. Acad. in Rome, 1976—, mem. adv. coun. Sch. Classical Studies, 1985-91; first U.S. del. Pan Am. Conf. Univ. Artists and Writers, Concepcion, Chile, 1964; invited del. Internat. Assembly Univ. Press Dirs., Guadalajara, Mex., 1991; mem. poetry staff Bread Loaf Writers Conf., 1967-72; founder, exec. dir. Ark. Poetry Ctr., 1975; participant Assn. Am. Univ. Presses Soviet Mission, 1989. Author: (poems) A Circle of Stone, 1964, Recital, 1965, So Long At the Fair, 1968, The Only World There Is, 1971; (criticism) The Achievement of John Ciardi, 1968, The Poetry of John Crowe Ransom, 1971; (with John Ciardi) (criticism) How Does a Poem Mean?, 1974; (poems) Halfway From Hoxie: New & Selected Poems, 1973, Why God Permits Evil, 1977, Distractions, 1981, The Boys on Their Bony Mules, 1983; translator: (poems) Poems & Antipoems (Nicanor Parra), 1967, Emergency Poems (Nicanor Parra), 1972, Sonnets of Giuseppe Belli, 1981; editor: (poems) 19 Poetas de Hoy en Los Estados Unidos, 1966, (with John William Corrington) Southern Writing in the Sixties: Poetry, 1967, Southern Writing in the Sixties: Fiction, 1966, Chile: An Anthology of New Writing, 1968, Contemporary Poetry in America, 1972, (with James A. McPherson) Railroad: Trains and Train People in American Culture, 1976, A Roman Collection: An Anthology of Writing about Rome and Italy, 1980, Ozark, Ozark: A Hillside Reader, 1981, (criticism) Patterns of Poetry, 1986, (poetry) Imperfect Love, 1986, Living on the Surface: New and Selected Poems, 1989, Adjusting to the Light, 1992, Points of Departure, 1995; poetry editor La. State U. Press, 1966-68; contbr. articles to profl. publs. Mem. ACLU. Recipient Henry Bellaman Poetry award, 1957, award in poetry Arts Fund, 1973, Prix de Rome, Am. Acad. Arts and Letters, 1976, Nat. Poets prize, 1990, Charity Randall citation Internat. Poetry Forum, 1993, John William Corrington award for excellence in lit., Centenary Coll., Shreveport, La., 1994, Acad. Lit. award AAAL, 1995; named Bread Loaf fellow in poetry, 1963. Mem. MLA, PEN, AAUP, South Ctrl. MLA, Am. Lit. Translators Assn. (v.p. 1978-79, pres. 1979-81), Authors' Guild, Soc. Benemerito dell'Assn. Centro Romanesco Trilussa (Rome). Home: 1111 Valley View Dr Fayetteville AR 72701-1603 Office: U Ark Press 201 Ozark Ave Fayetteville AR 72701-4041

WILLIAMS, MILTON A., bishop. Bishop 12th Episcopal dist. A.M.E. Zion Ch., Greensboro, N.C. Office: AME Zion Ch PO Box 7441 Greensboro NC 27417-0441

WILLIAMS, MILTON LAWRENCE, judge, educator; b. Augusta, Ga., Nov. 14, 1932; s. Richard and Helen (Riley) W.; m. Rose King, Oct. 22, 1960; children: Milton Lawrence, Darrie T. BS, NYU, 1960; LLB, N.Y. Law Sch., 1963. Bar: N.Y. 1965, U.S. Dist. Ct. (so. and ea. dists.) N.Y. 1967, U.S. Supreme Ct. 1968, U.S. Customs Ct. 1971. Regional counsel SBA, N.Y.C., 1966-68; assoc. gen. counsel Knapp Commn., N.Y.C., 1970-71; exec. dir. McKay Commn., N.Y.C., 1972; judge N.Y.C. Criminal Ct., 1977-84; acting justice N.Y. State Supreme Ct., N.Y.C., 1978-84, adminstrv. judge Criminal Term, N.Y. State Supreme Ct., 1st Jud. Dist., 1983-85, justice, 1985—; dep. chief adminstrv. judge N.Y.C. Cts., 1985-93; assoc. justice appellate divsn. 1st Dept., 1994—; mem. N.Y. State Commn. on Sentencing Guidelines, N.Y.C., 1983-86, bd. trustees Edwin Gould Found. for Children, St. Patrick's Cathedral, Inner City Scholarship Fund, Cath. Charities of N.Y., New York Law Sch. With USN, 1951-55. Fellow Am. Bar Found.; mem. Assn. of Bar of City of N.Y., Am. Bar Assn. (bd. dirs.), Sigma Pi Phi, Zeta Boule, Knight of Malta. Roman Catholic. Office: Assoc Justice Appellate Divsn First Dept 27 Madison Ave New York NY 10010-2201

WILLIAMS, MORGAN LLOYD, retired investment banker; b. N.Y.C., Mar. 30, 1935; s. John Lloyd and Adelaide Veronica (Patchell) W.; m. Margaret Patricia Rooney, May 13, 1961; children: Morgan Lloyd Jr., John Graham, Christine Joyce. BS in Econs., Wharton Sch., U. Pa., 1957; MBA, Columbia U., 1961. V.p., stockholder Kidder, Peabody & Co., N.Y.C., 1970-90, mng. dir., 1985-87. Trustee Inc. Village of Plandome, N.Y., 1982-86, mayor, 1986-87. Lt. USN, 1957-59. Mem. Nassau Country Club (Glen Cove, N.Y.). Republican. Roman Catholic. Home: 2040 Broadway St Apt 403 San Francisco CA 94115-1587

WILLIAMS, NANCY CAROLE, nursing researcher; b. Conover, N.C., Dec. 22, 1953; d. Howard G. and Edith (Hager) W. Diploma nursing, Gaston Coll., Dallas, N.C., 1981; student, U. N.C., 1990—. Charge nurse critical care unit Lincoln County Hosp., Lincolnton, N.C., 1981-83; primary charge nurse N.C. Meml. Hosp., Chapel Hill, N.C., 1983-85; charge nurse U. N.C. Clin. Rsch., Chapel Hill, 1985—. Mem. Nat. Assn. Rsch. Nurses and Dietitians, Am. Nurses Assn., N.C. Nurses Assn.

WILLIAMS, NATHANIEL, JR., elementary education educator; b. Jacksonville, Fla., June 7, 1940; s. Nathaniel Sr. and Alice Elizabeth (Dusom) W.; m. Carol Ann Odom, Sept. 6, 1969; children: Monica C., Nathaniel Joshua. BS in Chemistry and Math., Bethune-Cookman Coll., Daytona Beach, Fla., 1965; M in Teaching Elem., U. Pitts., 1973. Chemist Pitts. Plate Glass Coating and Resin, Springdale, Pa., 1966-67; ins. agt. Can. Life Assurance Co., Pitts., 1967-70; tutorial tchr. Model Cities Program, Pitts., 1968-69; employment adminstr. South Oakland Citizen Coun., Pitts., 1969-70; substitute tchr. Bd. Edn., Pitts., 1970-72; elem. tchr. Penn Hills (Pa.) Sch. Dist., 1973—; dir. edn. Pitts. Challenge, Wilkinsburg, Pa., 1974-79; bd. dirs. East End Family Ctr., Pitts., 1982-84; elem. evaluator Pa. Dept. Edn., Harrisburg, 1992—. Editor newsletter Ethnic Minority News, 1989—; coord. sci. program Invent Am., 1993. Ch. trustee, deacon Lincoln Ave. Ch. of God, Pitts., 1980-90, 94, mem. scholarship com., 1990-94. Recipient 1st place Mural award WQED/MacDonald, Pitts., 1992, plaque Ethnic Minority Caucus, Gettysburg, Pa., 1993. Mem. NEA, Pa. State Edn. Assn. (Western region com. chair 1988-94, bd. dirs. 1989-91), Penn Hills Edn. Assn. (com. chair 1983-94). Democrat. Avocations: reading, science projects, plays. Home: 218 Hawkins Ave Braddock PA 15104-2117 Office: Dibble Elem Sch 1079 Jefferson Rd Pittsburgh PA 15235

WILLIAMS, NEIL, JR., lawyer; b. Charlotte, N.C., Mar. 22, 1936; s. Lyman Neil and Thelma (Peterson) W.; m. Sue Sigmon, Aug. 23, 1958; children: Fred R., Susan S. AB, Duke U., 1958, JD, 1961. Bar: Ga. 1962, U.S. Dist. Ct. (no. dist.) Ga. 1977, U.S. Ct. Appeals (11th cir.) 1977. Assoc. Alston & Bird (and predecessor firm), Atlanta, 1961-65, ptnr., 1966—, mng. ptnr., 1984—; bd. dirs. Nat. Data Corp., Atlanta, Printpack, Inc., Atlanta, Atty's Liability Assurance Soc., Inc., Chgo. Chmn. bd. trustees Duke U., 1983-88, trustee, 1980-93; chmn. bd. trustees Vasser Woolley Found., Atlanta, 1975—, Leadership Atlanta, 1976-80; trustee Brevard Music Ctr., 1977-86, 91—, Presbyn. Ch. USA Found., Jeffersonville, Ind., 1983-90, Research Triangle Inst., 1983-88; bd. dirs. Atlanta Symphony Orch., 1970-76, 84-93, 95—, pres. 1988-90; Woodruff Arts Ctr., 1987—; bd. counsellors The Carter Ctr., Atlanta, 1987—; Cen. Atlanta Progress, 1984—; bd. dirs. Am. Symphony Orch. League, Washington, 1990—, chmn., 1995—. Recipient Disting. Alumni award Duke U., 1991, Rhyne award, 1996. Mem. ABA, Am. Bar Found., State Bar Ga., Am. Law Inst., Atlanta C. of C. (bd. dirs., 1994—, vice chmn. 1994-95), Phi Beta Kappa, Omicron Delta Kappa. Clubs: Piedmont Driving, Commerce (Atlanta); University (N.Y.C.). Home: 3 Nacoochee Pl NW Atlanta GA 30305-4164 Office: Alston & Bird 1 Atlantic Ctr 1201 W Peachtree St NW Atlanta GA 30309-3424

WILLIAMS, NEVILLE, international development organization executive; b. Muncie, Ind., Mar. 28, 1943; s. Donald Charles and Rose Eileen (Boughton) W. Student, U. Colo., 1964-66, U. Neuchatel, Switzerland, 1967. Freelance corr. Vietnam, 1968-69; freelance journalist Montreal, Que., Can., 1970-71, London, 1971-73; writer, producer Sta. WNBC-TV News, N.Y.C., 1973-74; freelance writer Telluride, Colo., 1975-79; media liaison Office of Solar Energy U.S. Dept. Energy, Washington, 1979-80; dir. of mktg. Telluride Ski Resort, Inc., 1981-83; owner, operator Hist. Sheridan Opera Ho., Telluride, 1983-85; nat. media dir. Greenpeace U.S.A., Washington, 1987-89; founder, pres., chmn. Solar Electric Light Fund, Washington, 1990—; also, bd. dirs.; pres. Williams & Assocs., Telluride and Washington, 1983-90. Author: The New Exiles, 1971, (monograph) Great Telluride Strike, 1977; contbr. articles to N.Y. Times mag., Penthouse, Outside, New Times, The Nation, The New Republic, Nature, others. Apptd. mem. Adv. Com. for Commerce and Devel., State of Colo., 1980-85; apptd. mem. Gov.'s Motion Picture & TV Commn., 1981-85. Fellow Am. Solar Energy Soc., Internat. Solar Energy Soc. Avocations: mountaineering, hiking, history, metaphysics. Office: Solar Electric Light Fund 1734 20th St NW Washington DC 20009-1105

WILLIAMS, NORMAN DALE, geneticist, researcher; b. Roca, Nebr., Nov. 4, 1924; s. John Alva and L. Carrie (Crawford) W.; m. Elaine Elizabeth Kuster, Aug. 7, 1947; children: David N., Curtis A. BS, U. Nebr., 1951, MS, 1954, PhD, 1956. Assoc. trainee Argonne Nat. Lab., Lemont, Ill., 1954-56, rsch. assoc., 1956; rsch. geneticist USDA Agrl. Rsch. Svc., Fargo, N.D., 1956-72, rsch. leader, 1972—; adj. prof. N.D. State U., Fargo, 1961—. Contbr. articles to profl. jours. With U.S. Army, 1945-47. Fellow AAAS, Am. Soc. Agronomy, Crop Sci. Soc. Am.; mem. Am. Genetics Assn., Genetics Soc. Am., Coun. for Agrl. Sci. and Tech., Masons, Sigma Xi (pres., pres.-elect N.D. chpt. 1976-78). Presbyterian. Avocations: golf, fishing, bowling, woodworking, gardening. Home: 809 South Dr Fargo ND 58103-4933 Office: USDA Agrl Rsch Svcs State University Sta PO Box 5677 Fargo ND 58105-5677

WILLIAMS, NORMAN FRANCIS, geologist, researcher; b. Norman, Okla., Oct. 3, 1916; s. Arthur James and Carolyn Maria (Hill) W.; m. Geneva West, July 20, 1942; children: Norman F. Jr., Geneva, Carolyn Sue. BS in Geol. Engring., U. Okla., 1939. Geology instr. U. Okla., Norman, 1946-47; field geologist Geology div. Ark. Resources and Devel. Commn., Little Rock, 1947-51, state geologist, 1951-56; state geologist Ark. Geol. and Conservation Commn., Little Rock, 1956-63, Ark. Geol. Commn., Little Rock, 1963-95; Ark. State geologist emeritus Ark. State Senate, 1995. Lt. col. U.S. Army, 1940-46. Home: 8490 N Rodney Parham Rd Little Rock AR 72205-2423 Office: Ark Geol Commn 3815 W Roosevelt Rd Little Rock AR 72204-6369

WILLIAMS, NORRIS HAGAN, JR., biologist, educator, curator; b. Birmingham, Ala., Mar. 31, 1943; s. Norris Hagan Sr. and Ernestyne Edna (Brown) W.; m. Nancy Jane Fraser, June 26, 1970; children: Matthew Ian, Luke Fraser. BS, U. Ala., 1964, MS, 1967; PhD, U. Miami, 1971. Asst. prof. Fla. State U., Tallahassee, 1973-78, assoc. prof., 1978-81; assoc. curator U. Fla., Gainesville, 1981-83, curator, 1983—, dept. chmn., 1985-94. Co-author: Orchid Genera of Costa Rica, 1986, Identification Manual for Wetland Plant Species of Florida, 1987; author: (chpt.) Orchid Biology II, 1982, Handbook of Experimental Pollination Biology, 1983; contbr. article to Biol. Bull., 1983. Mem. Assn. for Tropical Biology, Bot. Soc. Am., Soc. for Study Evolution, Linnean Soc. of London. Democrat. Office: U Fla Fla Mus Natural History Gainesville FL 32611

WILLIAMS, OMER S. J., lawyer; b. Rushville, Ind., June 20, 1940; s. John Thomas and Dorothy June (Jackson) W.; m. Gail Duff Shute, July 17, 1965; children: James Jackson, John Wesley. BA, Yale U., 1962, LLB, 1965. Assoc. Thacher Proffitt & Wood, N.Y.C., 1965-71, ptnr., 1971—, chmn. exec. com., mng. ptnr., 1992—. Dir. Greater N.Y. Coun. Boy Scouts Am., coun. commr.; dir. Downtown Lower Manhattan Assn. Mem. ABA (coms. new devels. bus. financing, banking law), N.Y. State Bar Assn., Assn. of the Bar of the City of N.Y. (coms. savings instns., banking law), The Downtown Assn. Club. Mem. Christian Ch. Avocations: tennis, genealogy, civil war history. Home: 206 N Franklin Tpke Ho Ho Kus NJ 07423-1425 Office: Thacher Proffitt & Wood 2 World Trade Ctr New York NY 10048-0203

WILLIAMS, PAT, congressman; b. Helena, Mont., Oct. 30, 1937; m. Carol Griffith, 1965; children: Griff, Erin, Whitney. Student, U. Mont., 1956-57, William Jewell U.; BA, U. Denver, 1961; postgrad., Western Mont. Coll.; LLD (hon.), Carroll Coll., Montana Coll. of Mineral Sci. and Tech. Mem. Mont. Ho. of Reps., 1967, 69; exec. dir. Hubert Humphrey Presdl. campaign, Mont., 1968; exec. asst. to U.S. Rep. John Melcher, 1969-71; mem. Gov.'s Employment and Tng. Council, 1972-78, Mont. Legis. Reapportionment Commn., 1973; co-chmn. Jimmy Carter Presdl. campaign, Mont., 1976; mem. 96th-102nd Congresses from 1st Mont. dist., 1979—; ranking mem. postsecondary edn. subcom. Coordinator Mont. Family Edn. Program, 1971-78. Served with U.S. Army, 1960-61; Served with Army N.G., 1962-69. Mem. Mont. Fedn. Tchrs. Democrat. Lodge: Elks. Office: House of Representatives 2329 Rayburn Ho Office Bldg Washington DC 20515*

WILLIAMS, PATRICK MOODY, composer; b. Bonne Terre, Mo., Apr. 23, 1939; s. Wilson Moody and Jean (Murphy) W.; m. Catherine Greer, Apr. 7, 1962; children: Elizabeth, Greer, Patrick. B.A., Duke U., 1961; hon. doctorate, U. Colo., 1983. vis. prof. U. Utah, 1970-71, U. Colo., 1975-77. Composer, N.Y.C., 1961-68, Los Angeles, 1968—; composer 60 film scores, music for TV series; artist 11 record albums; works include An American Concerto, 1977, (for jazz quartet and symphony orch.) Rhapsody (for concert band, jazz ensemble), 1975, (for solo cello and orch.) The Silent Spring, 1974, (for narrator and orch.) Gulliver, 1985 (for symphony orch. and narrator) Romances, (jazz soloist, orch.) 1986, Theme For Earth Day, 1990, An Overture To A Time, 1990. Served with U.S. Army. Acad. award nominee, 1980, nominee for Grammy 10 times, winner, 1974, 86, Pulitzer prize music nominee, 1977, nominee for Emmy 19 times, winner, 1979, 81, 93, nominee for Cable ACE award 2 times, winner 1994. Mem. Acad. Motion Picture Arts and Scis., Acad. TV Arts and Scis., Acad. Recording Arts and Scis., Broadcast Music, Inc. Democrat. *I am a convinced believer in the apprenticeship system of learning. There were a few people in my life that taught me many things, and I will be forever grateful that I had the opportunity to know them and learn from them. What they knew about music was invaluable to me, and what they were as people was even better.*

WILLIAMS, PAUL, federal agency administrator; b. Jacksonville, Ill., Aug. 6, 1929; s. Russell and Bernice (Wheeler) W.; m. Ora B. Mosby; 1 child, Reva Williams. BA, Ill. Coll., 1956, LHD, 1980. Dir. fin. City of Chgo., 1956-63; assoc. dir. fin. United Planning Orgn., Washington, 1964-65; internat. adminstrv. officer Dept. State, Washington, 1965-68; dir. of office mgmt. Dept. Housing and Urban Devel., Washington, 1968-93, gen. deputy dept. fair housing and equal opportunity, 1993-94, dep. ops. and mgmt., 1994—. Author: Questionnaire on Execution of Urban Renewal Programs, 1959. Pres. Bel Pre Civic Assn., Wheaton, Md., 1978; bd. dirs. Bel Pre Civic Assn., Wheaton, Md., 1971, 79; pres. Bel Pre PTA, Wheaton, Md., 1973. Served as sgt. U.S. Army, 1948-52. Recipient Cert. Superior Svc., Dept. Housing and Urban Devel., 1979, Sr. Exec. Svc. Performance award, 1983, 93-94, 95, Cert. Spl. Achievement, Com. Fraud Waste and Mismanagement Dept. Housing and Urban Devel., 1984, Cert. Recognition, Nat. Assn. Black and Minority C. of C., 1987. Methodist. Avocations: racquetball, jogging. Home: 14009 Blazer Ln Silver Spring MD 20906-2321 Office: Dept Housing and Urban Devel 451 7th St SW Rm 5100 Washington DC 20410-0001

WILLIAMS, PAUL HAMILTON, composer, singer; b. Omaha, Sept. 19, 1940; s. Paul Hamilton and Bertha Mae (Burnside) W.; m. Hilda Keenan Wynn, Apr. 16, 1993. Grad. high sch. asso. A & M Records, 1970—; pres. Hobbitron Enterprises, 1973—. Songwriter: (with Roger Nichols) Out in the Country, 1969, Talk it Over in the Morning, 1970, We've Only Just Begun, 1970, (with Craig Doerge) Cried Like A Baby, 1970, (with Jack S. Conrad) Family of Man, 1971, Rainy Days and Mondays, 1971, An Old Fashioned Love Song, 1972, Family of Man, 1972, Let Me Be the One, 1972, (with John Williams) You're So Nice to Be Around, 1973 (Acad. award nomination best song), The Hell of It, 1974, (with Barbara Streisand) Evergreen, 1976 (Acad. award best song, 1976, Golden Globe award 1977, Grammy award 1977), (with Michael Colombier) Wings, 1977, (with Charles Fox) My Fair Share, 1977, (with Kenny Ascher) The Rainbow Connection, 1979; film appearances include The Loved One, 1964, The Chase, 1966, Planet of the Apes, 1967, Watermelon Man, 1970, The Phantom of the Paradise, 1974 (also score 1974, Acad. award nomination best score 1974), Smokey and the Bandit, 1977, The Cheap Detective, 1978, The Muppet Movie, 1979, Stone Cold Dead, 1980, Smokey and the Bandit II, 1980, Smokey and the Bandit III, 1983, The Chill Factor, 1990, The Doors, 1991, A Million to Juan, 1994, Headless Body in Topless Bar, 1995; wrote songs for: The Getaway, 1972, (with John Williams) The Man Who Loved Cat Dancing, 1972, (with Williams) Cinderella Liberty, 1973, (with John Barry) The Day of The Locust, 1975; wrote scores for: (with Ascher) A Star is Born, 1976 (Golden Globe award best score 1976), Bugsy Malone, 1976, One on One, 1977, The End, 1978, (with Ascher) The Muppet Movie, 1979, Agatha, 1979, (with Jerry Goldsmith) The Secret of Nihm, 1982, Ishtar, 1987, The Muppet Christmas Carol, 1992; TV scores include (series) The McLean Stevenson Show, 1976-77, (with Charles Fox) The Love Boat, 1977-86, Sugar Time!, 1977-78, It Takes Two, 1982-83, (movies) No Place to Run, 1972, Emmet Otter's Jug Band Christmas, 1980; numerous TV appearances including 4 NBC Midnight spls; co-host on: numerous TV appearances including Mike Douglas show; other TV appearances including, Merv Griffin, Jonathan Winters, others; albums include Simeday Man: Just An Old-Fashioned Love Song, 1971, Life Goes On, 1972, A Little Bit of Love, 1974, Here Comes Inspiration, 1974, Ordinary Fools, 1975, Classics, 1977, A Little on the Windy Side, 1979, Crazy For Loving You, 1981. Co-recipient Best Songwriter Grammy award, 1977. Mem. ASCAP, Nat. Acad. Rec. Arts and Scis. (trustee). Office: 8545 Franklin Ave Los Angeles CA 90069 also: Tugboat Prodns Lazy Creek Prodns 4508 Noeline Ave Encino CA 91436-3336

WILLIAMS, PAULETTE W., state agency administrator; b. Moulton, Ala., Oct. 21, 1944; d. Paul Price and Sallie Davis (Bass) Wiley; m. Robert Thomas Williams, Oct. 11, 1968; 1 child, Shannon Thomas. Student, Florence State Coll., 1963-64. Planning and ops. officer civil def Decatur (Ill.)/Morgan Co., 1964-74, planning and ops. officer emergency mgmt., 1975-77; planning and ops. officer, dep. dir. emergency mgmt. Mobile (Ala.) Co., 1977-89; emergency mgmt. area coord. I State of Ala., Clanton, 1989-95; dir. Ala. Emergency Mgmt. Agy., Clanton, 1994-95; observer nuc. power plant Dept. Def., Romania, 1994; mem. gov. cabinet State of Ala., Clanton, 1994-95. Mem. cmty. advisor coun. Occidental Chem. Co., Muscle Shoals, Ala., 1993—; mem. state disaster svcs. com. ARC, Ala., 1993—. Recipient Spl. Recognition award Ala. Police Acad., 1986, Appreciation cert. Mobile (Ala.) Police Acad., 1986, Outstanding Svc. and Dedication cert. and flag, 1988, Hon. Adm. cert. Mayor of Decatur, 1988, Outstanding Svc. and Contbns. Appreciation cert. Nat. Coordinating Coun. on Emergency Mgmt., 1988, Appreciation plaque Greater Mobile Indsl. Assn., 1989, Appreciation for Profl. Assistance plaque Kerr McGee Chem. Corp., 1989, Appreciation cert. State of Ala., 1989, Meritorious Svc. cert. City of Mobile, 1989, Appreciation for Help and Support plaque City of Mobile Police Dept. Hazardous Materials Unit, 1989, Outstanding Dedication and Svc. plaque Mobile County Local Emergency Planning Com., 1989, Appreciation cert. FEMA-Floods of 1990, 1990, Pub. Svc. award U.S. Dept. Commerce, NOAA, 1994. Mem. Ala. Emergency Mgmt. Coun. (pres., Sec.-treas. plaque 1986, Appreciation cert. 1986, Legis. Chmn. plaque 1987), Nat. Emergency Mgmt. Assn. (mem. recovery com.). Episcopal. Home: 2224 Marietta Ave Muscle Shoals AL 35661-2620 Office: Alabama Emergency Mgmt PO Drawer 2160 Clanton AL 35045

WILLIAMS, PAULINE ELIZABETH, special education educator; b. Spanish Town, Jamaica, Nov. 11, 1949; came to U.S., 1972; d. Limwell and Julia Ann (Thomas) Cranston; m. Boswell Frank Williams, May 18, 1975; children: Boswell Frank Jr., Latesha, Conrad. Student, Church Tchrs. Coll., Mandeville, Jamaica, 1969; BS in Edn., Northeastern U., 1975; MA in Pre-Sch. Handicapped, Chgo. State U., 1983; postgrad., U. Fla., 1990. Cert. English for speaker of other lang. tchr., Fla. Tchr. McAuley's Primary Sch., Jamaica, 1970-72; tchr. spl. edn. Chgo. Bd. Edn., 1975-85; varying exceptional tchr. College Park Elem. Sch., Ocala, Fla., 1985-86, Wyomina Park Elem. Sch., Ocala, 1986-87, Fessenden Elem. Sch., Ocala, 1987—. Dir. Vacation Bible Sch., Silver Springs Shores 7th-day Adventist Ch., Ocala, 1986-94. Tchr. mini-grantee Marion County Pub. Schs. Found., 1990-91. Mem. NEA, Marion Edn. Assn. (bldg. rep.), Fla. Teaching Profession. Avocations: swimming, choir, arts and crafts. Office: Fessenden Elem Sch 4200 NW 90th St Ocala FL 34482-1542

WILLIAMS, PERCY DON, lawyer; b. Dallas, Sept. 19, 1922; s. Percy Don and Frances (Worrill) W.; m. Helen Lucille Brunsdale, Aug. 4, 1954; children—Anne Lucy, Margaret Frances, Elizabeth Helen. B.A. with honors, So. Methodist U., 1942, M.A., 1943; LL.B. magna cum laude, Harvard U., 1946. Bar: Tex. 1951. Instr. So. Meth. U. Law Sch., 1946-47; asst. prof., then assoc. prof. U. Tex. Law Sch., Austin, 1947-49; lectr. U. Va. Law Sch., 1951; law clk. to Justice Tom C. Clark U.S. Supreme Ct., 1949-51; pvt. practice Houston, 1952—; master dist. ct. Harris County, Tex., 1980-95. Contbr. articles to legal jours. Decorated Order of Sacred Treasure Gold Rays, Rosette, Japan. Fellow Tex. Bar Found.; mem. ABA, State Bar Tex. (col.), Fed. Bar Assn., Houston Bar Assn., Am. Law Inst., Am. Judicature Soc., Order of Coif, Phi Beta Kappa, Phi Eta Sigma, Pi Sigma Alpha, Tau Kappa Alpha, Kappa Sigma. Clubs: Houston, Houstonian. Home: 31 Briar Hollow Ln Houston TX 77027-9301 Office: 5685 1st Interst Bank Plz Houston TX 77002

WILLIAMS, PETRA SCHATZ, antiquarian; b. Poughkeepsie, N.Y., Sept. 2, 1913; d. Grover Henry and Mayme Nickerson (Bullock) Schatz; m. J. Calvert Williams, Nov. 26, 1946; children: Miranda, Frederica, Valerie. AB, Skidmore Coll., 1936; JD, Fordham U., 1940. Founder Fountain House, Phoenix, 1953, Fountain House East, Jeffersontown, Ky., 1966. Author: Flow Blue China, An Aid to Identification, 1971, Flow Blue China II, 1973, Flow Blue China and Mulberry Ware, 1975, Staffordshire Romantic Transfer Patterns, 1979, Staffordshire II Romantic Transfer Patterns, 1986. Past pres. Meml. Hosp. Aux., Phoenix, Heard Mus. Guild, Phoenix; bd. dirs. Ky. Humane Soc. Mem. Nat. Soc. Interior Designers (nat. dir. for Ariz. 1957-58, Ky. 1968, pres. Ky. 1967-68), DAR, Ky. Hist. Soc., Flow Blue Internat. Collectors Club (hon.). Mem. Soc. of Friends. Club: Filson. Address: PO Box 99298 Jeffersontown KY 40269-0298

WILLIAMS, PHILLIP L., newspaper publishing executive; married. BA, Harvard U., MBA. Mgr. Mach devel. Owens-Corning Fiberglas Corp., 1948-60; dir. spl. ventures Starwood Corp., 1960-62; pres., treas., dir. Westland Capital Corp., 1962-64; chmn. bd., treas., dir. Grove Mortgage Corp., 1964-65; v.p., asst. to pres. Beneficial Standard Corp., 1965-68; formerly v.p. corp. programs, v.p. fin., group v.p. newspapers and TV Times Mirror Co., L.A., sr. v.p. newspapers and TV, exec. v.p., from 1980, now vice chmn. bd., also bd. dirs. Lt. comdr. USN. Mem. L.A. C. of C. (bd. dirs.). Office: Times Mirror Co Times Mirror Sq Los Angeles CA 90053

WILLIAMS, PHYLLIS CUTFORTH, retired realtor; b. Moreland, Idaho, June 6, 1917; d. William Claude and Kathleen Jessie (Jenkins) Cutforth; m. Joseph Marsden Williams, Jan. 21, 1938 (dec. 1986); children: Joseph Marlis, Bonnie L. Williams Thompson, Nancy K. Williams Stewart, Marjorie Williams Karren, Douglas Claude, Thomas Marsden, Wendy K. Williams Clark, Shannon I. Williams Ostler. Grad., Ricks Coll., 1935. Lic. realtor, Idaho.

Tchr. Grace (Idaho) Elem. Sch., 1935-38; realtor Williams Realty, Idaho Falls, Idaho, 1972-77; mem. Idaho Senate, Boise, 1977; owner, mgr. river property. Compiler: Idaho Legisladies Cookbook, Cookin' Together, 1981. With MicroFilm Ctr., LDS Ch. Mission, Salt Lake City, 1989-90; block chmn. March of Dimes Soc.; active Idaho State Legisladies Club, 1966-84, v.p., 1982-84. Republican. Avocations: genealogy, cooking, music, politics, photography, travel. Home: 1950 Carmel Dr Idaho Falls ID 83402-3020

WILLIAMS, PRESTON NOAH, theology educator; b. Alcolu, S.C., May 23, 1926; s. Anderson James and Bertha Bell (McRae) W.; m. Constance Marie Willard, June 4, 1956; children—Mark Gordon, David Bruce. A.B., Washington and Jefferson Coll., 1947, M.A., 1948; B.D., Johnson C. Smith U., 1950; S.T.M., Yale, 1954; Ph.D., Harvard, 1967. Ordained to ministry Presbyn. Ch., 1950. Martin Luther King, Jr. prof. social ethics Boston U. Sch. Theology, 1970-71; Houghton prof. theology and contemporary change Harvard U. Div. Sch., Cambridge, Mass., 1971—; acting dean Harvard U. Div. Sch., 1974-75; acting dir. W.E.B. DuBois Inst., 1975-77. Editor-at-large: Christian Century, 1972—; contbr. articles to profl. jours. Mem. Am. Acad. Religion (pres. 1975—), Am. Soc. Christian Ethics (dir., pres. 1974-75), Phi Beta Kappa. Home: 36 Fairmont St Belmont MA 02178-2919 Office: 45 Francis Ave Cambridge MA 02138-1911

WILLIAMS, QUENTIN CHRISTOPHER, geophysicist, educator; b. Wilmington, Del., Jan. 1, 1964; s. Ferd Elton and Anne Katherine (Lindberg) W.; m. Elise Barbara Knittle, Dec. 19, 1987; children: Byron Frederick, Alanna Katherine. AB, Princeton U., 1983; PhD, U. Calif., Berkeley, 1988. Rsch. geophysicist Inst. of Tectonics, U. Calif., Santa Cruz, 1988-91; asst. prof. dept. earth sci. U. Calif., Santa Cruz, 1991-95, assoc. prof. dept. earth sci., 1995—. Contbr. articles to profl. jours. Presdl. Faculty fellow, 1993—. Mem. Am. Geophys. Union, Am. Phys. Soc. Office: U Calif Santa Cruz Dept Earth Sciences Santa Cruz CA 95064

WILLIAMS, QUINN PATRICK, lawyer; b. Evergreen Park, Ill., May 6, 1949; s. William Albert and Jeanne Marie (Quinlan) W.; children: Michael Ryan, Mark Reed, Kelly Elizabeth. BBA, U. Wis., 1972; JD, U. Ariz., 1974. Bar: Ariz. 1975, N.Y. 1984, U.S. Dist. Ct. Ariz. 1976. Vice pres., sec., gen. counsel Combined Comm. Corp., Phoenix, 1975-80; v.p., sec., gen. counsel Swensen's Ice Cream Co., Phoenix, 1980-83; sr. v.p. legal and adminstrn. Swensen's Inc., Phoenix, 1983-86; of counsel Winston & Strawn, Phoenix, 1985-87, ptnr., 1987-89, ptnr. Snell & Wilmer, Phoenix, 1989—. Vice chmn., treas. Combined Comm. Polit. Action Com., Phoenix, 1976-80; chmn. Ariz. Tech. Inventor, Ariz. Tech. Incubator, Ariz. Venture Capital Conf.; co-chair Gov. Small Bus. Advocate Exec. Coun., 1993—. Served with USAR, 1967-73. Mem. ABA, Maricopa County Bar Assn., N.Y. Bar Assn., State Bar Ariz., Internat. Franchise Assn., Paradise Valley Country Club, Phi Alpha Delta. Republican. Roman Catholic. Home: 8131 N 75th St Scottsdale AZ 85258-2781 Office: Snell & Wilmer One Arizona Ctr Phoenix AZ 85004

WILLIAMS, RALPH CHESTER, JR., physician, educator; b. Washington, Feb. 17, 1928; s. Ralph Chester and Annie (Perry) W.; m. Mary Elizabeth Adams, June 23, 1951; children—Cathy, Frederick, John (dec.), Michael, Ann. AB with distinction, Cornell U., 1950, MD, 1954; MD (hon.), U. Lund, Sweden, 1991. Diplomate: Am. Bd. Internal Medicine. Intern Mass. Gen. Hosp., Boston, 1954-55; asst. resident internal medicine Mass. Gen. Hosp., 1955-56; resident internal medicine N.Y. Hosp., 1956-57; chief resident Mass. Gen. Hosp., Boston, 1959-60; guest investigator Rockefeller Inst., N.Y.C., 1961-63; practice medicine specializing in internal medicine (subspecialty rheumatology), 1963—; asso. prof. U. Minn. at Mpls., 1963-68, prof., 1968-69; prof., chmn. dept. medicine U. N.Mex., Albuquerque, 1969-88; Schott prof. rheumatology and medicine U. Fla., Gaineville, 1988—; Diplomate Am. Bd. Internal Medicine. Asso. editor: Jour. Lab. and Clin. Medicine, 1966-69; editorial bd.: Arthritis and Rheumatism, 1968—; Contbr. numerous articles to profl. jours. Served to capt. USAF, 1957-59. Master Am. Coll. Rheumatology; fellow ACP; mem. Am. Assn. Immunology, Assn. Am. Physicians, Am. Fedn. Clin. Rsch., Am. Soc. Clin. Investigation, Ctrl. Soc. Clin. Rsch., Western Soc. Clin. Rsch., Phi Beta Kappa, Alpha Omega Alpha. Research in immunologic processes and connective tissue diseases. Home: 2516 NW 20th St Gainesville FL 32605-2981

WILLIAMS, RALPH WATSON, JR., retired securities company executive; b. Atlanta, July 2, 1933; s. Ralph Watson and Minnie Covington (Hicks) W.; m. Nancy Jo Morgan, Mar. 19, 1955 (dec. Dec. 1989); children: Ralph Watson III, Nancy Jane, John Martin Hicks; m. Almonese Brown Clifton, Nov. 24, 1990. Student, Davidson Coll., 1951; B.B.A., U. Ga., 1955. Trainee banking Trust Co. Ga., Atlanta, 1955; mcpl. sales staff Courts & Co., Atlanta, 1955-57; v.p., salesman securities First Southeastern Corp., Atlanta, 1957-60; br. mgr. Francis I. duPont & Co., 1960-69; spl. partner duPont Glore Forgan Inc., N.Y.C., 1969-70; gen. partner Glore Forgan Inc., 1970, exec. v.p., 1971—, sr. v.p., 1972—; also dir.; sr. v.p., dir., mem. exec. com. duPont-Walston Inc., 1973-74; sr. v.p. E.F. Hutton & Co. Inc., 1974-81; exec. v.p., dir. E.F. Hutton & Co., Inc., 1981-88; exec. v.p. Shearson Lehman Hutton Inc., Atlanta, 1988-89; ret., 1989. Mem. Nat. Assn. Security Dealers (chmn. dist. com. 7), Benedicts Atlanta, Phi Delta Theta. Methodist. Clubs: Commerce (Atlanta), Capital City (Atlanta), Piedmont Driving (Atlanta). Home: 3504 Dumbarton Rd NW Atlanta GA 30327-2614

WILLIAMS, RAYMOND F., regigious organization executive. Gen. sec. of evangelism, missions and human concerns Christian Meth. Episcopal Ch.

WILLIAMS, REDFORD BROWN, medical educator; b. Raleigh, N.C., Dec. 14, 1940; s. Redford Brown Sr. and Annie Virginia (Betts) W.; m. Virginia Carter Parrott, August 9, 1940; children: Jennifer Betts, Lloyd Carter. AB, Harvard U., 1963; MD, Yale U., 1967. Diplomate Am. Bd. Internal Medicine. Intern, then resident Yale-New Haven Med. Ctr., 1967-70; sr. surgeon USPHS, Bethesda, Md., 1970-72; asst. prof. Duke U. Med. Ctr., Durham, N.C., 1972, prof. psychiatry, 1977—, prof. psychology, 1990—, dir. behavioral medicine rsch. ctr., 1985—; cons. NIH rev. coms., Bethesda, 1977—. Author: The Trusting Heart, 1989, Anger Kills, 1993; contbr. articles to profl. jours. Dir. N.C. Heart Assn., Chapel Hill, 1980-83. Recipient Rsch. Scientist award NIMH, 1974—; NIH grantee, 1986—. Fellow Soc. Behavioral Medicine (pres. 1984-85, Upjohn Disting. Scientist award 1992), Acad. Behavioral Medicine Rsch. (pres. 1995—); mem. Am. Psychosomatic Soc. (bd. dirs. 1978-81, pres. 1992). Unitarian Universalist. Avocation: tennis. Office: Duke U Med Ctr Box 3926 Durham NC 27710

WILLIAMS, RHYS, minister; b. San Francisco, Feb. 27, 1929; s. Albert Rhys and Lucita (Squier) W.; m. Eleanor Hoyle Barnhart, Sept. 22, 1956; children: Rhys Hoyle, Eleanor Pierce. AB, St. Lawrence U., 1951, BD, MDiv, 1953, DD, 1966; postgrad., Union Sem., summer 1956; LLD (hon.), Emerson Coll., 1962. Ordained to ministry Unitarian Ch., 1954. Min. Unitarian Ch., Charleston, S.C., 1953-60, 1st and 2d Ch., Boston, 1960—; mem. faculty, field edn. supr. Harvard U., 1969—; Russell lectr. Tufts U., 1965, Minns lectr., 1986. Pres. Edward Everett Hale House, 1987—, Soc. of Cincinnati, State of N.H., 1986-89; v.p. Franklin Inst., 1960—, sec., 1990-96; v.p. Benevolent Frat. Unitarian Universalist Chs., 1982-93; pres. Unitarian Universalist Urban Ministries, 1991—; sec. bd. trustees Emerson Coll., 1961-94, trustee, 1994—; chaplain Gen. Soc. Cin., Washington, 1977—, New Eng. coun. Navy League, 1980—, Founders and Patriots of Mass., SR; chmn. Festival Fund, Inc., Am.-Soviet Cultural Exch., 1989-91; trustee Opera Co. Boston, 1970—; trustee Meadville Lombard Theol. Sch., Chgo., 1971-77, mem. ministerial fellowship com., 1961-69, chmn., 1968-69; fin. chmn. Ch. Larger Fellowship, 1968-86; bd. dirs. Peter Faneuil Housing Corp., 1992—, AIDS Housing, 1995; trustee Franklin Square House, 1993—. Mem. Unitarian Universalist Mins. Assn. (pres. 1968-70), Unitarian Hist. Soc. (pres. 1960-75), Evang. Missionary Soc. (pres. 1965-80, v.p. 1980—), Soc. for Propagation Gospel Among Indians and Others in N.Am. (v.p. 1975—), Unitarian Svc. Pension Soc. (pres. 1973—), Soc. Ministerial Relief (pres. 1973—, mem. com. for ch. staff fin.), Mass. Hist. Soc., Colonial Soc. Mass., Union Club (Boston), Union Boat Club (Boston), Beta Theta Pi (pres. New Eng. 1964-66). Office: 1st and 2d Church in Boston 66 Marlborough St Boston MA 02116-2007

WILLIAMS, RICHARD, collegiate basketball team coach; b. Oceanside, Calif., Aug. 22, 1945; s. Richard T. and Ruth (Sager) W.; m. Diann McEwen. BS, Miss. State U., 1967; M in Sch. Adminstrn., Miss. Coll., 1970. Head basketball coach Montebello Jr. H.S., Natchez, Miss., 1967-68, St. Andrew's Episc. Jr. H.S., Jackson, Miss., 1968-70; asst. basketball coach South Natchez H.S., 1970-72, head basketball coach, 1972-79; head basketball coach Copiah-Lincoln Jr. Coll., Wesson, Miss., 1979-84; asst. basketball coach Miss. State (Miss.) U., 1984-86, head basketball coach, 1986—. Named SEC Coach of Yr., 1995, 1991. Office: Miss State Univ PO Drawer 5327 Mississippi State MS 39762

WILLIAMS, RICHARD CHARLES, computer programmer, consultant; b. Boston, Dec. 25, 1955; s. Richard Clayton and Nancy Karolyn (Kerr) W.; m. Jean Elizabeth Daniels, Oct. 21, 1989. BA, SUNY, New Paltz, 1991. Cert. in software engring. Programmer/cons. Shared Ednl. Computing, Poughkeepsie, N.Y., 1976-78; systems programmer, comms. mgr. Cornell U. Med. Sch., N.Y.C., 1978-79; staff programmer IBM Corp. Hdqrs., White Plains, N.Y., 1979-84; systems programmer IBM Data Systems Div., Poughkeepsie, 1984-86; adv. programmer IBM Network Systems, White Plains, 1986-89; open systems cons. IBM Large Systems, Kingston, N.Y., 1989-95; architect IBM-SAP Competency Ctr., 1996—; cons. IBM Hudson Valley Fed. Credit Union, Poughkeepsie, 1986—, C-Net, Broomfield, Colo., 1988-89, Toastmasters Bd. Dirs., Santa Ana, Calif., 1987, Landmark Edn., N.Y.C., 1989—. Author: Lasting Legacy, 1987; co-author: Migrating to TSO from VSPC, 1986; inventor, patentee. Bd. dirs. Hudson Valley FCU, 1995—, 2d vice chair, 1996—; bd. dirs. SUNY Alumni Bd. Named one of Outstanding Young Men of Am., 1985, Vol. of Yr., NACUSAC, 1995. Mem. IEEE, ACM, SUNY Alumni Assn. (bd. dirs. 1994—), Poughkeepsie Toastmasters Internat. (chpt. pres. 1982, dist. gov. 1985, Toastmaster of Yr. 1984), Open Online Transactional Programming Users Group (mem. planning bd.). Democrat. Methodist. Avocations: skiing, community organizing, travel. Home: 2 Jansen Rd New Paltz NY 12561-3810 Office: IBM 522 South Rd Poughkeepsie NY 12602

WILLIAMS, RICHARD CLARENCE, retired librarian; b. Guide Rock, Nebr., Apr. 9, 1923; s. Lyall Wesley and Elsie Marie (Guy) W. Student, Southwestern U., Georgetown, Tex., 1944-45; student, U. Tex., Austin, 1945-46; BA, U. Idaho, Moscow, 1948; BA in Librarianship, U. Wash., Seattle, 1949; MLS, U. Mich., Ann Arbor, 1952. Sec. Schaefer-Hitchcock Co., Sandpoint, Idaho, 1941-42; asst. librarian Willamette U. Library, Salem, Oreg., 1949-51; cataloger U. Mich. Library, Ann Arbor, 1951-59; serials cataloger N.Y.C. Pub. Library, 1959-66, asst. dir. for cataloging, 1967-88, Astor fellow for library research, 1988-89; mem. subcom. on cataloging standards Research Libraries Group, Palo Alto, Calif., 1978-88. Contbr. poetry to coll. publs., 1944-48; bibliographer for Mexicon, 1986—. Bd. dirs. Eugene James Dance Co., N.Y.C., 1978—. Served with USN, 1943-46. Mem. ALA, Soc. Am. Archaeology, Am. Anthrop. Assn., Archeol. Inst. Am., John Bartram Assn., Bot. Soc. Am., Coun. on Botanical and Horticultural Librs., Pre-Columbian Art Rsch. Inst., Phi Beta Kappa (U. Idaho chpt.). Avocations: New World archeology, Black studies, botany.

WILLIAMS, RICHARD DAVID, III, naval officer; b. Memphis, May 4, 1942; s. Richard David Jr. and Lucille Sue (Sequin) W.; m. Sherryl Cooper; children: Deborah Lea, Richard David IV. BS in Naval Sci., U.S. Naval Acad., 1964; MS in Physics, Naval Postgrad. Sch., 1972. Commd. ensign USN, 1964, advanced through grades to rear adm., 1992; comdg. officer USS Clark (FFG 11), 1982-84, USS California (CGN 36), 1985-88, Naval Ship Weapon Sys. Engring. Sta., Port Hueneme, Calif., 1990-92; DUINS Surface Warfare Officers Sch. Command, 1985; DUINS naval reactors activity Dept. Energy, Washington, 1985; chief staff for Surface Combatants Directorate, Naval Sea Sys. Command, 1988-90; dir. warfare sys. architecture and engring. Space and Naval Warfare Sys. Command, 1992; program exec. officer for mine warfare Office Asst. Sec. Navy, Arlington, Va., 1992—. Mem. edn. partnership com. Oxnard (Calif.) Sch. Dist., 1990-92. Decorated Legion of Merit with two gold stars. Avocations: rare books, sports memorabilia. Home: Quarters Washington Navy Yd Washington DC 20374 Office: 2531 Jefferson Davis Hwy Arlington VA 22242-5167*

WILLIAMS, RICHARD DONALD, retired wholesale food company executive; b. Audubon, Iowa, Feb. 19, 1926; s. Walter Edward and Olga M. (Christensen) W.; m. Carol Francis, June 17, 1950; children: Gayle, Todd, Scott. B.A., Ohio Wesleyan U., 1948; M.B.A., Northwestern U., 1949. Dir. indsl. and pub. rels. Gardner div. Diamond Nat. Corp., Middletown, Ohio, 1949-61; with Fleming Cos., Inc., 1961-89; v.p. pers. Fleming Cos., Inc., Oklahoma City, 1972-76; sr. v.p. human resources Fleming Cos., Inc., 1976-80, exec. v.p. human resources, 1980-89, ret., 1989. Pres. Jr. Achievement, Topeka, Kans., 1972; v.p. Last Frontier council Boy Scouts Am., Oklahoma City, 1980; campaign chmn. United Way Greater Oklahoma City, 1980, pres., 1985-87; bd. dirs. Community Council Central Okla., Oklahoma City chpt. ARC, Support Ctr. Okla., Better Bus. Bur., Okla. City Beautiful. Served with USN, 1944-46. Mem. Am. Soc. Personnel Adminstrn., Soc. Advancement Mgmt., Am. Mgmt. Assn., Phi Gamma Delta. Clubs: Quail Creek Country (Oklahoma City), Petroleum (Oklahoma City); Baille 'd Oklahoma (hon.), La Chaine des Rotisseurs. Home: 2940 Brush Creek Rd Oklahoma City OK 73120-1858

WILLIAMS, RICHARD DWAYNE, physician, educator; b. Wichita, Kans., Oct. 7, 1944; s. Errol Wayne and Roseanna Jane (Page) W.; m. Beverly Sue Ferguson, Aug. 29, 1964; 1 child, Wendy Elizabeth. BS, Abilene Christian U., 1966; MD, Kans. U., 1970. Diplomate Am. Bd. Urology, Nat. Bd. Med. Examiners. Intern, then resident in gen. surgery U. Minn., Mpls., 1970-72, resident in urology, 1972-76, asst. prof., 1976-79; asst. prof. U. Calif., San Francisco, 1979-84; prof., chmn. dept. urology U. Iowa, Iowa City, 1984—; chief urology VA Med. Ctr., San Francisco, 1979-84, VA Med. Ctr., Iowa City, 1984-88; mem. task force on bd. exams Am. Bd. Urology, 1981-85, guest examiner Oral exams, 1984—, trustee, 1994—; Rubin H. Flocks chair in urology U. Iowa, 1994; mem. nat. adv. coun. NIDDK, NIH. Author: (with others) Advances in Urologic Oncology, 1987, Genitourinary Cancer: Basic and Clinical Aspects, 1987, Adult and Pediatric Urology, 1987, General Urology, 1988, Textbook of Medicine, 1988, also others; editor: Advances in Urologic Oncology, 1987; guest editor Seminars in Urology, 1985, Problems in Urology: Prostate Cancer, 1989; bd. editors Jour. Urology, 1980-88; mem. editorial bd. Urology, Jour. Urology; also articles. Bd. dirs. Iowa chpt. Nat. Kidney Found., bd. sci. advisors 1989—. Major USAR, 1971-77. Bordeau scholar Kans. U. Med. Ctr., 1968-69; NIH, VA, Am. Cancer Soc. grantee. Fellow ACS (chmn. urology sect. No. Calif. chpt. 1980-82, chmn. ann. meeting programs 1988, mem. residency rev. com. urology 1993—, vice chair 1995); mem. AAAS, Iowa Med. Soc., Iowa Urologic Soc., Am. Urologic Assn. (dir. seminar on residency evaluation 1987, bd. editors alt. 1988—, rep. North Ctrl. sect., prodr. slide presentations 1988, recipient prizes 1982, 87, mem. various coms. 1987—), Am. Assn. for Cancer Rsch., Am. Soc. Clin. Oncology, Am. Assn. GU Surgeons, Clin. Soc. Genitourinary Surgeons, Soc. Internat. D'Urologie (U.S. sect.), Soc. Univ. Urologists (chmn. com. on residency evaluation 1986-88, councillor 1987—, pres. 1993), Soc. Surg. Oncology, Soc. Urologic Oncology (chmn. membership com. 1987-90, sec. 1990-91, 91-94, pres.-elect 1995), Johnson County Med. Soc., Flock's Soc., Western Urologic Forum, Nat. Urologic Forum, Surgeons Club, Alpha Omega Alpha. Republican. Office: U Iowa Dept Urology 200 Hawkins Dr Iowa City IA 52242-1009

WILLIAMS, RICHARD FRANCIS, banker; b. Oak Park, Ill., Sept. 9, 1941; s. Harvey B. and Marie (Gallery) W.; m. Barbara Ann Zdon, Aug. 8, 1964; children: Ann Marie, Richard Lewis. Grad., DePaul U., 1964. Various positions CNA Ins., Chgo., 1964-80; 2asst. v.p. Zurich Ins. Co., Chgo., 1980-84; pres., CEO, Empire Fire & Marine, Omaha, 1984-93, Fidelity & Deposit Co. Md., Balt., 1993—. Republican. Roman Catholic. Home: 15404 Duncan Hill Rd Sparks MD 21152-9765 Office: Fidelity & Deposit Co Md 300 St Paul Pl Baltimore MD 21202-2120

WILLIAMS, RICHARD LEROY, federal judge; b. Morrisville, Va., Apr. 6, 1923; s. Wilcie Edward and Minnie Mae (Brinkley) W.; m. Eugenia Kellogg, Sept. 11, 1948; children: Nancy Williams Davies, R. Gregory, Walter L., Gwendolyn Mason. LLB, U. Va., 1951. Bar: Va. 1951. Ptnr. McGuire, Woods & Battle and predecessor firms, 1951-72; judge Cir. Ct. City of Richmond, 1972-76; ptnr. McGuire, Woods & Battle, 1976-80; dist. judge U.S. Dist. Ct., Richmond, Va., 1980—, sr. judge, 1992—. Served to 2d lt., USAAF, 1940-45. Fellow Am. Coll. Trial Lawyers; mem. Va. State Bar, Va. Bar Assn., Richmond Bar Assn. Office: Louis F Powell Court House 1000 E Main St Ste 307 Richmond VA 23219-3525

WILLIAMS, RICHARD LUCAS, III, electronics company executive, lawyer; b. Evanston, Ill., Oct. 30, 1940; s. Richard Lucas Jr. and Ellen Gene (Munster) W.; m. Karen Louise Carmody, Nov. 11, 1967. AB, Princeton U., 1962; LLB, U. Va., 1965. Bar: Ill. 1965, D.C. 1968, U.S. Supreme Ct. 1968. Assoc. Winston & Strawn, Chgo., 1968-74; ptnr. Winston & Strawn, 1974-79; sr. v.p., gen. counsel Gould Inc., Rolling Meadows, Ill., 1979-81; sr. v.p., adminstrn., gen. counsel Gould Inc., 1981-90, also bd. dir., 1985-88; ptnr. Smith Williams and Lodge, Chgo., 1990-95, Vedder, Price, Kaufman & Kammholz, Chgo., 1995—; bd. dirs. GNB Batteries, Inc., 1984-86, ULINE Inc., Lake Bluff, Ill, Branca, Inc., Chgo. Bd. dirs. Internat. Tennis Hall of Fame, Newport, R.I.; v.p. Chgo. Dist. Tennis Assn., 1968-70; vice chmn. Am. Cancer Soc., Chgo., 1984; bd. dirs., pres. Lake Shore Found. for Animals, Chgo., 1990-94. With JAGC USNR, 1965-68. Mem. ABA, Ill. Bar Assn., Chgo. Bar Assn., Execs. Club Chgo. (co-chmn. Western Europe internat. com.), Law Club (Chgo.), Meadow Club (Rolling Meadows, gov. 1979—, chmn. 1985-90). Home: 1200 N Lake Shore Dr Chicago IL 60610-2370 Office: Vedder Price 222 N LaSalle St Ste 2500 Chicago IL 60601

WILLIAMS, RICHARD THOMAS, lawyer; b. Evergreen Park, Ill., Jan. 14, 1945; s. Raymond Theodore and Elizabeth Dorothy (Williams) W. AB with honors, Stanford U., 1967, MBA, JD, 1972. Bar: Calif. 1972, U.S. Supreme Ct. 1977. Assoc., then ptnr. Kadison Pfaelzer Woodard Quinn & Rossi, L.A., 1972-87; ptnr. Whitman & Ransom, 1987-93, Whitman Breed Abbott & Morgan, L.A., 1993—. Contbg. editor Oil and Gas Analyst, 1978-84. Mem. ABA, L.A. County Bar Assn. Office: Whitman Breed Abbott & Morgan 633 W 5th St Los Angeles CA 90071-2005

WILLIAMS, RICHMOND DEAN, library appraiser, consultant; b. Reading, Mass., Dec. 10, 1925; s. Theodore Ryder and Anabel Lee (Hutchison) W.; m. Eleanor Davidson Washbourne, Sept. 26, 1953; children—Richmond Lyttleton, Eleanor Davidson, Anne Ryder. AB cum laude, Williams Coll., 1950; MA, U. Pa., 1952, PhD, 1959. Instr., asst. dean Williams Coll., Williamstown, Mass., 1954-56; dir. Wyo. Hist. and Geol. Soc., Wilkes-Barre, Pa., 1956-60; asst. dir. Am. Assn. State and Local History, Madison, Wis., 1960-61; dir. libraries Eleutherian Mills-Hagley Found., Wilmington, Del., 1962-87; cons. archivist M.S. Hershey Found., Pa., 1981—, Md. Dept. Housing and Community Devel., 1993-94; bd. dirs. Scholarly Resources Inc. Co-author: A Look at Ourselves, 1962; author: They Also Served, 1965; compiler: Directory of Historical Records in Delaware, 1995. Sec., U. Del. Library Assocs., Wilmington, 1972-86; mem. adv. bd. Del. Hist. Records, Dover, 1982—; mem. Del. Humanities Forum, Wilmington, 1984-91; trustee Conservation Ctr. Phila., 1984-86. Served to lt. AUS, 1943-47. Pennfield fellow U. Pa., 1953. Mem. Econ. History Assn (sec.-treas. 1975-88), Mid-Atlantic Regional Archives Com., Am. Assn. State and Local History (pres. 1974-76), Am. Antiquarian Soc., Phi Beta Kappa. Avocations: golf; sailing; book collecting. Home and Office: 202 Brecks Ln Wilmington DE 19807-3011

WILLIAMS, ROBERT AUGUSTUS, manufacturing company executive; b. Macon, Ga., June 11, 1936; s. John Herbert and Mary Dean (Pritchett) W.; m. Antionette Caruso, Feb. 14, 1959; children: Robert A. Jr., Ronald M. Student, Syracuse (N.Y.) U. Salesperson Mobile Paint Mfg. Co. Inc., Theodore, Ala., 1954-70, sales mgr., 1970-75, v.p. sales, 1975-78, exec. v.p., 1978-84, pres., 1984—; pres. Spetromatic Assocs., Ill., 1974-76, Nat. Paint Distbrs., Park Ridge, Ill., 1984-86. Chmn. Goodwill Industries, Mobile, Ala., 1987—; bd. dirs. Vols. of Am., Mobile, 1986-87, Jr. Achievement, Mobile, Better Bus. Bur., Mobile. Mem. Sales and Mktg. Execs. of Mobile (past pres.). Democrat. Baptist. Club: Country Club of Mobile. Lodge: Rotary (past pres.). Avocation: golf. Home: 601 Shenandoah Rd W Mobile AL 36608-3354 Office: Mobile Paint Mfg Co Inc PO Box 717 Theodore AL 36590-0717

WILLIAMS, ROBERT BENJAMIN, convention center executive; b. Newton, Miss., Jan. 19, 1935; s. Lee W. and Bessie L. (Dowdell) W.; m. Cornelia I. Holiday, June 4, 1963 (div. Jan. 15, 1991); children: Robert Jr., Vincent, Andrea, Lisa, John. BA in Polit. Sci., U. Dayton, 1958; MA in Polit. Sci., Villanova (Pa.) U., 1964; grad., Nat. War Coll., 1979. Commd. 2d lt. U.S. Army, 1958, advanced through grades to col.; prof. mil. sci. Ga. Inst. Tech., 1970-72; chief pers. svc. divsn. U.S. Army, 1973-75, comdr. inf. battalion, 1975-76, strategic policy planner Joint Chiefs of Staff, 1976-78; dep. chief Joint Chiefs of Staff Nuclear Negotiation Divsn., Washington, 1979-82; sr. mil. adviser U.S. delegation to START U.S. Army, Geneva, 1982-83; ret. U.S. Army, 1983; v.p. for student affairs Morehouse Coll., Atlanta, 1983-84; exec. dir. human resources com. of cabinet Commonwealth of Pa., Harrisburg, 1984-87; dir. of adminstrn. Pa. Convention Ctr. Authority, Phila., 1987—. Vice chmn. Urban Edn. Found., Phila., 1989—; bd. dirs. Mercy Douglas Human Svcs. Camp, Phila., 1990—; chmn. Housing and Devel. Corp., Phila., 1993—, Trevors Campaign for the Homeless, 1988-93. Republican. Baptist. Office: Pa Conv Ctr Authority 1101 Arch St Philadelphia PA 19107-2208

WILLIAMS, ROBERT BRICKLEY, lawyer; b. Moon Run, Pa., July 3, 1944; s. David Emanuel and Margaret E. (Brickley) W.; m. Teresa Maria Kutzavitch, Aug. 26, 1967; children: R. Benjamin, Lizabeth A., Matthew M. BA, Swarthmore Coll., 1966; JD, Georgetown U., 1969. Bar: Pa. 1969, U.S. Tax Ct. 1974, U.S. Claims Ct. 1978. Sr. ptnr. Eckert Seamans Cherin & Mellott, Pitts., 1969-95, Williams, Coulson, Johnson, Lloyd, Parker & Tedesco, LLC, Pitts., 1995—. Trustee Union Cemetary Assn., 1974-96; chmn. Allegheny Tax Soc., Pitts., 1976, Pa. State Tax Conf., 1978, Family Firm Inst., Pitts., 1993, United Way Endowment, Pitts., 1995; pres. Union Ch., Gayly, Pa., 1988-92; dir. Estate Planning Coun., Pitts., 1989, Pitts. (Pa.) Presbyn. Found., 1995, YMCA Pitts., Cancer Support Network, Neighborhood Elder Care. Fellow Am. Coll. Trusts and Estates Counsel; mem. ABA, Pa. Bar Assn., Allegheny County Bar Assn., Pitts. Rotary (found. chair 1990-96, citation of merit 1993), Pitts. Tax Club. Republican. Avocations: family, travel, charitable and church activities. Office: Williams Coulson Johnson Lloyd Parker & Tedesco LLC 1550 Two Chatham Ctr Pittsburgh PA 15219

WILLIAMS, ROBERT C., paper company executive; b. 1930. BSME, U. Cin.; MBA, Xavier U.; postgrad., Inst. Paper Chemistry, Rochester Inst. Tech. Various tech. and supervisory positions Gardner div. Diamond International Corp., 1947-59; with research and devel. dept. Albermarle Paper Co., 1963-68; co-founder James River Corp. of Va., Richmond, 1969—, formerly pres., COO, chmn., pres., CEO; now chmn. emeritus James River Corp Va Richmond; bd. dirs. Sovran Fin. Corp. Office: James River Corp Va 120 Tredegar St Richmond VA 23219*

WILLIAMS, ROBERT CHADWELL, history educator; b. Boston, Oct. 14, 1938; s. Charles Reagan and Dorothy (Chadwell) W.; m. Ann Bennett Kingman, Aug. 27, 1960; children: Peter, Margaret, Katharine. B.A., Wesleyan U., 1960; A.M., Harvard U., 1962, Ph.D., 1966. Asst. prof. history Williams Coll., Williamstown, Mass., 1965-70; prof. history Washington U., St. Louis, 1970-86; dean of faculty Davidson Coll., N.C., 1986—; pres. Central Slavic Conf., 1971-72; v.p. History Assocs. Inc., Gaithersburg, Md., 1980—; sr. research assoc. St. Antony's Coll., Oxford, 1985. Author: Culture in Exile, 1972, Artists in Revolution, 1976, Russian Art and American Money, 1980 (Pulitzer nominee), The Other Bolsheviks, 1986, Klaus Fuchs, Atom Spy, 1987; co-author: Crisis Contained, 1982; mem. editorial bd.: Slavic Rev., 1979-82. Fellow Kennan Inst., 1976-77; fellow Am. Council Learned Socs., 1973-74, W. Wilson Found., 1960-61. Mem. Am. Assn. for Advancement of Slavic Studies, Phi Beta Kappa, Sigma Xi. Presbyterian. Office: Davidson Coll Office VP Acad Affairs Davidson NC 28036

WILLIAMS, ROBERT EUGENE, astronomer; b. Dunsmuir, Calif., Oct. 14, 1940; s. Francis Henry and Lois Evangeline (Youde) W.; m. Elaine Carolyn Eckwall, Dec. 29, 1961; 1 child, Scott Francis. AB, U. Calif., Berkeley, 1962; PhD, U. Wis., 1965. Rsch. asst. U. Calif., Berkeley, 1960-62; Wis. Alumni Rsch. Found. fellow U. Wis., 1962-65; from asst. prof. to assoc. prof. U. Ariz., Tucson, 1965-78, prof., 1978-83; vis. rsch. assoc. European So. Obs., Garching, 1983-84; NRC sr. rsch. fellow NASA-Ames Rsch. Ctr., 1984-85; dir. Cerro Tololo Inter-Am. Obs., La Serena, Chile, 1985-93, Space Telescope Sci. Inst., 1993—; mem. NRC Spl. Studies Bd., 1995—; mem.

exec. com. Aspen (Colo.) Ctr. for Physics, 1983-88, trustee/treas., 1982-88; adj. prof. The Johns Hopkins U., 1993—; sr. Fulbright prof. Univ. Coll. London, 1972-73; mem. NSF Minority Grad. Fellowship Panel, 1982-85, CTID Users Com., 1978-81, Kitt Peak Nat. Observatory Telescope Allocation Com., 1978-80, Cerro Tololo Inter-Am. Observatory Telescope Allocation Com., 1976-78; chmn. U.S. Nat. Fulbright Com., Astronomy, 1974-78. Author 100 profl. papers. Recipient Alexander von Humboldt award German Govt., 1991, Dorothy Klumpke Roberts prize, 1962; Fulbright prof. U. London, 1971-72; Heinz Pagels Meml. lectr., 1995, Stanford Bunyan lectr., 1995. Mem. Internat. Astron. Union (U.S. nat. commn. 1990-92), Am. Astron. Soc. (com. on astronomy and pub. policy 1994-96, edn. adv. bd. 1981-83), Astron. Soc. of the Pacific. Avocations: running, biking. Office: Space Telescope Science Institute 3700 San Martin Dr Baltimore MD 21218-2410

WILLIAMS, ROBERT HENRY, oil company executive; b. El Paso, Jan. 12, 1946; s. William Frederick and Mary (Page) W.; m. Joanne Marie Mudd, Oct. 22, 1967; children: Lara, Michael, Suzanne, Jennifer. BS in Physics, U. Tex., El Paso, 1968; PhD in Physics, U. Tex., Austin, 1973; MS in Physics, Va. Poly. Inst., 1971. Dir. Gulf Oil R&D, Houston, 1978-81; tech. mgr. Gulf Oil Internat., Houston, 1981-83; exploration mgr. Gulf Oil Co., Houston, 1983-85; mgr. geophys. rsch. Tenneco Oil Co., Houston, 1985-87, mgr., chief geophysicist, 1987-88; founder, mng. dir. Dover Energy, Houston, 1988—; exec. v.p. Tatham Offshore Inc. Houston, 1989-95, also bd. dirs.; chmn., CEO Dover Tech. Inc., Houston, 1989—; cons. Tenneco Inc., Houston, 1989—; DeepTech Internat., 1992-95; Ukraine Acad. Sci., 1993; bd. dirs., exec. v.p. DeepTech Inc., 1991-95; founder, pres. Westway tech. Assocs., 1986—; co-founder, chmn. CEO Castaway Graphite Rods, Inc., 1990—; owner, CEO Team Tex. Inc., 1993—; Bulldog Lures, Inc., 1994—; founder, CEO Houston Books Inc., 1994—; founder, CEO, chmn. Dover Energy Exploration, 1995—; pres. Westway Interests, 1995—; bd. dirs. Tatham Offshore. Contbr. articles to profl. jours. Mem. coun. Boy Scouts Am., Houston, 1989—; patron Mus. Fine Arts, Houston, 1990-96, Houston Zool. Soc., 1994-96; leader Girl Scouts U.S., Houston, 1989—. Mem. Soc. Exploration Geophysics, Am. Assn. Petroleum Geologists, Am. Geophys. Union. Republican. Avocations: scuba diving, book collecting, fishing. Office: Dover Tech Ste 1000 11767 Katy Frwy Ste 1000 Houston TX 77079

WILLIAMS, ROBERT JENE, lawyer, rail car company executive; b. Darby, Pa., Oct. 30, 1931; s. Joslyn Justus and Dolores Marie (Dugan) W.; m. Shirley Geraldine Fiedler, Aug. 8, 1953; children: Robin Jeanne, Sara Ann. B.S., Ursinus Coll., 1953; J.D., U. Pa., 1956. Bar: N.J. 1957, Pa. 1959, Ill. 1973. Asso. firm Bleakly, Stockwell & Zink, Camden, N.J., 1956-58; atty., asst. gen. atty. Reading Co., Phila., 1958-69; gen. counsel, sec. Trailer Train Co., Phila., 1969-71, Trailer Train Co. (now TTX Co.), Chgo., 1971-94; v.p. Trailer Train Co., 1975-94; ret., 1994. Mem. Ill. Bar Assn. Home: 1349 Woodland Dr Deerfield IL 60015-2017

WILLIAMS, ROBERT JOSEPH, museum director, educator; b. Bennington, Vt., June 21, 1944; s. Joseph and Ruthe Allison (Moody) W. BS in Edn., U. Vt., 1970; MA in Interdisciplinary Social Sci., San Francisco State U., 1981. Tchr. adult edn. Mt. Anthony Union High Sch., Bennington, Vt., 1972-74; columnist Bennington Banner, 1972-77; tchr. San Francisco State U., 1976-79; founder, dir. NORRAD Drug Rehab. Ctr., San Francisco, 1986-88; museum curator Shaftsbury (Vt.) Historical Soc., 1989—; founder, dir. Bennington Tutorial Ctr., 1971-74. Author: Toward Humanness in Education, 1981; Chalice of Leaves: Selected Essays and Poems, 1988, Modern Salvation: Guidelines from Cosmology, 1994; author: (with others) Intimacy, 1985. Recipient Edmunds Essay medal Vt. Historical Soc., Montpelier, 1961, award of the League of Vt. Writers, 1972, Golden Poet award World of Poetry, Sacramento, Calif., 1990. Democrat. Avocation: cosmology. Home: 102 Putnam St Bennington VT 05201-2348 Office: Shaftsbury Hist Soc PO Box 401 Shaftsbury VT 05262-0401 *I sought the truth, and sought to live by it.*

WILLIAMS, ROBERT L., pharmaceutical executive; b. 1946. Undergrad. degree, Ind. U., 1968, JD, 1971. With Price Waterhouse, N.Y.C., 1971-75; with Pfizer, Inc., N.Y.C., 1975—, treas., 1993—. Office: Pfizer Corp 235 E 42nd St New York NY 10017-5703*

WILLIAMS, ROBERT LEON, psychiatrist, neurologist, educator; b. Buffalo, July 22, 1922; s. Leon R. and L. Paulyne (Ingraham) W.; m. Shirley Glynn Miller, Feb. 5, 1949; Karen, Kevin. B.A., Alfred U., 1944; M.D., Albany Med. Coll., Union U., 1946. Chief neurology and psychiatry Lackland AFB Hosp., USAF, San Antonio, 1952-55; cons. neurology and psychiatry to USAF Surgeon Gen., 1955-58; faculty Coll. Medicine, U. Fla., Gainesville, 1958-72, prof., chmn. dept. psychiatry, 1964-72; prof. psychiatry Baylor Coll. Medicine, Houston, 1972-92, chmn. dept., 1972-90, prof. neurology, 1976-92, acting chmn. dept., 1976-77, prof. emeritus psychiatry and neurology, 1992—; mem. faculty various univs., part time 1949-58 including Albany Med. Coll. at Union U., Columbia Coll. Physicians and Surgeons, Boston U., U. Tex., Georgetown U. Author: (with W.B. Webb) Sleep Therapy: A. Bibliography and Commentary, 1966, (with others) EEG of Human Sleep: Clinical Applications, 1974; editor: (with Ismet Karacan and Carolyn J. Hursch) Psychopharmacology of Sleep, 1976, Sleep Disorders: Diagnosis and Treatment, 1978, 2d edit., 1988; (with others) Phenomenology and Treatment of Anxiety, 1979, of Alcoholism, 1980, of Psychophysiological Disorders, 1982, of Psychosexual Disorders, 1983, of Psychiatric Emergencies, 1984. Served from 1st lt. to lt. col. USAF, 1949-58; col. Res., ret. Recipient Cert. Profl. Achievement USAF Surgeon Gen., 1967. Mem. Am. Psychiat. Assn., Am. Electroencephalographic Soc., Am. Coll. Psychiatrists (pres. 1982-83), Am. Acad. Neurology, AMA, Group for Advancement of Psychiatry, Benjamin Rush Soc. (pres. 1986-88), Accreditation Coun. for grad. Med. Edn. (residency rev. com. for psychiatry 1985-93), Alpha Omega Alpha. Research and publs. on basic psychophysiology of human sleep.

WILLIAMS, ROBERT LUTHER, city planning consultant; b. Porterville, Calif., June 24, 1923; s. Luther Esco and Mary (Lyon) W.; children: Jeffrey Robert, Derrick Paul, Gail Diane. Student, Utah State Coll., 1944; A.B., U. Calif.-Berkeley, 1949, M.C.P., 1951. Asst. planning dir. Stockton, Calif., 1951-54; planning dir. Alameda, Calif., 1954-57, Alameda County, 1957-63; exec. dir. Am. Inst. Planners, Washington, 1963-69; v.p. Hill Devel. Corp., Middletown, Conn., 1969-71; dir. land mgmt. dept. Gulf Oil Corp., Reston, Va., 1971-74; pres. Coleman-Williams, Inc., Greenbrae, Calif., 1975-78, Robert Williams Assocs., Inc., San Rafael, Calif., 1978-87; mem. community affairs panel KQED-TV, San Francisco, 1991-94; lectr. U. Calif. at Berkeley extension, 1956-59; tech. adviser regional planning Assn. Bay Area Govts., Calif., 1961-63; vis. prof. U. R.I., 1969-71; pres. G.I.F.T. Inst., Inc., 1991-94. Bd. dirs. Planning Found. Am., 1965-70, Communities Found., Inc., 1973-77. Served to 1st lt. AUS, 1943-46, 52, ETO. Named Young Man of Year Alameda, 1956. Mem. Am. Inst. Cert. Planners (pres. Calif. chpt. 1960), Am. Planning Assn., World Future Soc., Lambda Alpha, Lambda Chi Alpha. Presbyterian. Home: RR #2 Box 379 Pitcher Pond Rd Lincolnville ME 04849

WILLIAMS, ROBERT LYLE, corporate executive, consultant; b. Nowata, Okla., June 22, 1942; s. Clifford Lyle and Eula Mae (Barnes) W.; m. Lorene Linnet Dillahunty, June 12, 1965; 1 child, Eleanor Lynn. B.S., Okla. State U., 1964; M.B.A., Baylor U., 1965. Acctg. supr. Southwestern Bell Telephone Co., Houston, 1965-66; fin. exec. Ford Motor Co., Dearborn, Mich., 1969-80; treas. Ford Brasil, Sao Paulo, 1976-79, Agrico Chem. Co., Tulsa, 1980-82; v.p., chief fin. officer Texas City Refining, Inc., Tex., 1983-88; sr. v.p. Furnishings 2000, Inc., San Diego, 1988-89; pvt. cons. Houston, 1990—; chmn. Galveston County Taxpayers Research Council, 1987-88. Served to lt. USN, 1966-69. Republican. Presbyterian. Avocation: travel. Office: Ste #200 2500 E TC Jester Houston TX 77008

WILLIAMS, ROBERT MARTIN, economist, consultant; b. N.Y.C., May 4, 1913; s. Joseph Tuttle and Mary Adeline (Johnson) W.; m. Vera Jean Bobsene, July 31, 1956; 1 son, Kenneth Martin. B.A., Pomona Coll., 1934; M.A., UCLA, 1942; Ph.D., Harvard U., 1950. Teaching fellow physics Dartmouth Coll., 1935-36; mgmt. trainee Western Electric Co., Inc., Los Angeles, 1936-40; lectr. UCLA, 1947-51, asst. prof., 1951-56, asso. prof., 1956-63, prof. bus. econs. and statis. Grad. Sch. Mgmt., 1963-83, prof. emeritus, 1983—, vice chmn. dept. mgmt., 1961-67, dir. bus. forecasting project, 1952-81, consulting, 1981—; dir. Imperial Corp. Am., 1975-86, emeritus dir., 1986—; dir. Am. Savs. and Loan Assn. Kans., 1982-86, Silver State Savs. and Loan Assn. Colo., 1982-86; mem. exec. com., dir. Imperial Savs. and Loan Assn. Calif., 1978-82; econ. cons. Fed. Res. Bank Kansas City, Lockheed Aircraft Corp., others, also state and fed. agys. Editor, contbr. The UCLA Business Forecast for the Nation and California, 1961-88; contbr. numerous articles on bus. forecasting and regional econ. devel. Served to lt. comdr. USNR, 1942-46. Resources for Future, Inc. Research grantee, 1962; NSF grantee, 1965. Mem. Am. Econ. Assn., Am. Statis. Assn., Nat. Assn. Bus. Economists, World Future Soc., Centre for Internat. Rsch. on Econ. Tendency Surveys, Ostomy Assn. L.A. (exec. v.p. 1989—). Home: 750 Enchanted Way Pacific Palisades CA 90272-2818 Office: UCLA John E Anderson Grad Sch Mgmt Bus Forecasting Project Los Angeles CA 90095

WILLIAMS, ROBERT ROY, trade association administrator; b. Lima, Ohio, Aug. 31, 1909; s. Forrest Clyde and Minnie May (McKee) W.; m. Alyce Hogarth, Aug. 14, 1937 (dec. Mar. 1996); children: Cheryl Elizabeth Williams Lucks, Robert Roy Williams, Jr. Student, Miami U., Oxford, Ohio, 1929-33; LHD (hon.), Urbana U., 1996. Exec. v.p. Ohio State Restaurant Assn., Columbus, 1938-53, Nat. Food Svc. Assn., Columbus, 1953—; lectr. trade assn. mgmt., Ohio State U., Columbus, 1947-53. Benefactor Cuyahoga Falls Schs. Found. Mem. Am. Soc. Assn. Execs. (Distinguished Svc. award, 1986), Nat. Rep. Assn. (pres. 1992—), Nat. Rep. Found. (life), Am. Legion (life), Navy League U.S. (life), Sigma Chi (Constantine award, 1994), Rotary Club (Paul Harris fellow, 1986), Masons. Methodist. Developer continental cadre sys. for Nat. Rep. Found., creator term food service. Avocations: world travel, photography, genealogical research. Home: 3010 Sunset Blvd Columbus OH 43202-1954 Office: Nat Food Svc Assn PO Box 1932 Columbus OH 43216-1932

WILLIAMS, ROBERT WALTER, physics educator; b. Palo Alto, Calif., June 3, 1920; s. Philip S. and Louise (Brown) W.; m. Erica Lehman, Sept. 23, 1946; children: Paul, David, Eric. AB, Stanford U., 1941; MA, Princeton U., 1943; PhD, MIT, 1948. Assoc. physicist Los Alamos Lab., 1943-46; rsch. assoc. MIT, 1946-48, asst. prof., 1948-52, assoc. prof., 1952-59; prof. physics U. Wash., Seattle, 1959-90, prof. emeritus, 1990—; cons. Boeing Co., Seattle, 1961-64; vis. scientist CERN (European Orgn. Nuclear Rsch.) Lab., Geneva, 1967, 74, 81, 88—; trustee Univs. Rsch. Assn., 1978-84. Contbr. articles to profl. jours. Fellow Am. Phys. Soc., Am. Acad. Arts and Scis. Research on properties of fundamental particles. Home: 3413 E Laurelhurst Dr NE Seattle WA 98105-5357 Office: Univ Wash Dept Physics Box 351560 Seattle WA 98195-1560

WILLIAMS, ROBERTA GAY, pediatric cardiologist, educator; b. Rocky Mount, N.C., Oct. 23, 1941. BS, Duke U., 1963; MD, U. N.C., 1968. Diplomate Am. Bd. Pediats. (mem. com. ofcl. examiners 1985—, bd. dirs. and rep. sub-bd. chmn. com. 1992—, mem. exec. com. 1993—), Am. Bd. Pediat. Cardiology (chmn. 1991-92, cons. 1993). Med.-pediat. intern N.C. Meml. Hosp., Chapel Hill, 1968-69; pediat. resident Columbia Presbyn. Med. Ctr., N.Y., 1969-70; fellow in cardiology Children's Hosp. Med. Ctr., Boston, 1970-73, from asst. in cardiology to assoc. in cardiology, 1973-75, sr. assoc. in cardiology, 1976-82; from instr. pediats. to asst. prof. pediats. Harvard Med. Sch.-Children's Hosp., Boston, 1973-82; assoc. prof. pediats. UCLA Med. Ctr., 1982-86, chief divsn. pediat. cardiology, 1982-95, prof. pediats., 1986-95; chair pediatrics U. N.C. Sch. Medicine, Chapel Hill, 1995—; attending physician Cardiac Med. Svcs., Children's Hosp. Med. Ctr., Boston, 1974, cardiology cons. Cardiothoracic Surgery Svc., 1974, med. dir. Cardiovasc. Surgery ICU, 1974-79, dir. Cardiac Graphic Lab. and Cost Ctr., 1977-82, mem. com. neonatal ICU, 1978-79, v.p. med. staff, 1980-81; guest lectr., invited spkr., seminar leader in field. Mem. editl. bd.: Pediat. Cardiology, 1979, Circulation, 1983-91, Am. Jour. Cardiology, 1984-91, Jour. Applied Cardiology, 1985, Clin. Cardiology, 1988, Internat. Jour. Cardiology, 1992-95, Archives of Pediats. and Adolescent Medicine, 1994—; editl. cons. Jour. of Am. Coll. of Cardiology, 1992-94. Mem. exec. coun. cardiovasc. disease in the young Am. Heart Assn., 1979-85, mem. subcom. congenital cardiac defects, 1980-82, subcom. nominating com., 1982-83; mem. Am. Heart Assn.-Greater L.A. affiliate, 1983—, exec. com. and rsch. com., 1984—, judge young investigator competition, 1984, mem. program com., 1986-90, v.p. med.-exec. com., 1991-92, pres.-elect, 1992-93, and numerous other coms. Fellow Am. Coll. Cardiology (allied health profls. com. 1984-87, mem. physician workforce adv. com. 1988-94, mem. manpower adv. com. 1988—, mem. extramural continuing edn. com. Heart House 1990—, co-chmn. Bethesda conf. 1993, gov. So. Calif. chpt. 1994—, pres. Calif. chpt. 1994—), Am. Acad. Pediats. (sec. exec. com. sect. on cardiology 1985-87, mem. com. on fetus and newborn 1985-88, mem. exec. com. sect. on cardiology 1985—, chmn. program com. 1988-89, mem. subcom. Am. Heart Assn. task force on assessment of diagnosis and therapeutic cardiovascular procedures 1989, chairperson sec. cardiology 1989, mem. credentials com. 1991—, mem. coun. on sects. mgmt. com. 1995—); mem. Soc. for Pediat. Rsch., Am. Pediat. Soc., Am. Soc. Echocardiography (mem. exec. com. 1975-78, com. on guidelines for technician tng. 1975-78, bd. dirs. 1976-80, treas. exec. coun. com. 1981-83). Avocations: photography, hiking. Office: U NC Dept Pediatrics CB 7220 509 Burnett-Womack Chapel Hill NC 27599

WILLIAMS, ROBIN, actor, comedian; b. Chgo., July 21, 1951; s. Mr. and Mrs. Robert W.; m. Valerie Velardi, June 4, 1978 (div.); 1 child, Zachary; m. Marsha Garces, Apr. 30, 1989; children: Zelda, Cody. Attended, Claremont Men's Coll., Marin Coll., Juilliard Sch., N.Y.C. Started as stand-up comedian in San Francisco clubs, including Holy City Zoo, The Boardinghouse; later became regular at Comedy Store, Los Angeles; appeared in TV series Laugh-In, The Richard Pryor Show, America 2-Night, Happy Days, Homicide: Life on the Streets, 1993 (Emmy nomination, Guest Actor - Drama Series, 1994); star of TV series Mork and Mindy, 1978-82 (People's Choice award), (cable) Robin Williams: An Evening at the Met, 1986 (Grammy award), host of HBO's Shakespeare: The Animated Tales, 1993 (CableAce Award, Best Entertainment Host); film appearances include: Popeye, 1980, The World According to Garp, 1982, The Survivors, 1983, Moscow on the Hudson, 1984, Club Paradise, 1986, Good Morning Vietnam, 1987 (Golden Globe award 1988, Acad. Award nominee for best actor), The Adventures of Baron Munchausen, 1989, Dead Poets Society, 1989 (Best Actor nomination Golden Globe award, 1994, nominated best actor Acad. award), Cadillac Man, 1990, The Fisher King, 1991 (Golden Globe award, Acad. award nominee for best actor 1991), Dead Again, 1991, Hook, 1991, Aladdin (voice) (Spl. Achievement award Hollywood Fgn. Press, Nat. Bd. Rev. 1992), 1992, Toys, 1992, Mrs. Doubtfire, 1993 (Best Picture, Best Actor in a Musical or Comedy, Golden Globe, 1994, Best Picture, Best Actor, People's Choice award), Nine Months, 1995, Jumanji, 1995; theatre: Waiting for Godot, 1988; recorded albums: Reality, What a Concept, 1979 (Grammy award), Throbbing Python of Love, A Night at the Met (Grammy award); host Comic Relief, 1986; appeared in TV variety programs, ABC Presents a Royal Gala, 1988 (Emmy award, 1988), Carol, Carl, Whoopi & Robin, 1987 (Emmy award). Recipient Golden Apple award Hollywood Women's Press Club; Golden Globe award; ACE award; Am. Comedy award, 1987, 88; Grammy award for best comedy rec., 1987. Office: PO Box 480909 Los Angeles CA 90048-9509

WILLIAMS, ROGER LAWRENCE, historian, educator; b. Boulder, Colo., June 22, 1923; s. Raymond Ustick and Mabel (Woolf) W. BA, Colo. Coll., 1947; MA, U. Mich., 1948, PhD, 1951. Asst. prof. Minn. State Coll., Mankato, 1950-52, MIT, Cambridge, 1952-55; vis. prof. Mich. State U., East Lansing, 1955-56; assoc. prof. Antioch Coll., Yellow Springs, Ohio, 1956-65; prof. U. Calif., Santa Barbara, 1965-71; prof. U. Wyo., Laramie, 1971-78, Disting. prof., 1978-88. Author: French Revolution of 1870-71, 1969, The Mortal Napoleon III, 1971, The Horror of Life, 1980, Aven Nelson of Wyoming, 1984, Gérard and Jaume: Two Neglected Figures in the History of the Jussiaean Classification, 1988, Napoleon III and the Stoffel Affair, 1993; co-author: How Modernity Came to a Provençal Town, 1988, Handbook of Rocky Mountain Plants, 1992; mem. editorial bd. Antioch Rev., 1958-64. Vol. Rocky Mountain Nat. Park, Estes Park, Colo., 1986-87. Mem. French Hist. Studies (life), History Sci. Soc. (life), Nat. Coun. for History Edn., N.Y. Bot. Soc., Denver Bot. Soc. Home: 1701 S 17th St Laramie WY 82070-5406

WILLIAMS, ROGER STEWART, physician; b. San Diego, Feb. 15, 1941; s. Manley Samuel and Ethelyn Mae W.; children: Roger S., Karen E., David G., Sarah E. MD cum laude, Emory U., 1966. Diplomate Am. Bd. Psychiatry and Neurology. Intern, Grady Hosp., Atlanta, 1966-67. Med. resident Emory U., Atlanta, 1966-68; resident neurology Mass. Gen. Hosp., Boston, 1970-73, assoc. neurologist, 1973-87; assoc. prof. neurology Harvard Med. Sch., Boston, 1977-87; neurologist Billings (Mont.) Clinic, 1987—; adj. prof. Mont. State U., Bozeman. Contbr. articles to profl. jours. Served to lt. comdr. USN, 1968-70. Kennedy fellow Kennedy Found., Washington, 1973-75; NIMH grantee, Bethesda, Md., 1979-87. Mem. Am. Acad. Neurology, Mont. Med. Assn., AMA, Alpha Omega Alpha.

WILLIAMS, ROGER WRIGHT, public health educator; b. Great Falls, Mont., Jan. 24, 1918; s. Elmer Howard and Mary (Stuart-Davidson) W.; m. Marjorie Madeline Jones, May 9, 1943; children: Barbara, Stuart Roger. B.S., U. Ill., 1939, M.S., 1941; postgrad., Cornell U., U. N.C. Sch. Pub. Health; Ph.D., Columbia Sch. Pub. Health, 1947; cert. applied parasitology and entomology, U. London, 1957. Mem. faculty Columbia Sch. Pub. Health, N.Y.C., 1944-83, prof. med. entomology, 1966-82, prof. emeritus, 1983, acting head div. tropical medicine, 1970; cons. USPHS, Alaska, 1949, Newton, Ga., 1952, Therapeutic Research Found. of Phila. Inc., 1949, Jackson Hole Preserve Inc., Govt. V.I., U.S. Nat. Park Service, 1959-61, Rockefeller Found., Trinidad, W.I. and Brazil, 1963; filariasis research project WHO, Rangoon, Burma, 1966-70; mem. arbovirus field staff Rockefeller Found., Nigeria, 1964-65; mem. Corp. Bermuda Biol. Sta. for Rsch., 1955-80. Contbr. articles on arthropods of med. importance and diseases they transmit to profl. jours. and books. Mem. Tenafly (N.J.) Cmty. Orch., 1960-63; mem. Tenafly Town-Wide Com., 1970; mem. Boys Activities Com., 1968-72, trustee, 1969-72, pres., 1970-72; chmn. dads' com. troop 140 Boy Scouts Am., Tenafly, 1968-69, merit badge councilor, 1965-83, 88-92; mem. Ocean County Coun., 1991-92; dist. coord. Manchester Township, N.J., 1989-91; trustee Tenafly Nature Ctr., 1967-71, v.p., 1968-71; adv. bd. Am. Christian Coll., 1971-78; deacon Tenafly Presbyn. Ch., 1968-74, elder, 1974-79, 81-82; deacon Lakehurst Presbyn. Ch., 1984-87, elder, 1988-93, chmn. Vesper com., mem. chapel com. and exec. com. Crestwood Manor, 1993—; vol. Meals on Wheels program, 1989-92. Officer USNR, 1943-46. Recipient commendation Boy Scouts Am., 1990; Rockefeller traveling fellow, 1947; Childs Frick fellow Bermuda, 1955, 57; NSF sr. postdoctoral fellow U. London (Eng.) Sch. Hygiene and Tropical Medicine, 1956-57; La. State U. Sch. Medicine fellow in tropical medicine Central Am., 1957. Fellow AAAS; mem. Internat. Coll. Tropical Medicine, Internat. Filariasis Assn., Am. Wash. Entomol. Socs., Am. Mosquito Control Assn., Am. Soc. Parasitologists, Am. Royal Socs. Tropical Medicine and Hygiene, Elisha Mitchel Sci. Soc., N.Y. Soc. Tropical Medicine (pres. 1969-70), Tenafly Swim Club (trustee 1972-74, v.p. 1973, pres. 1974), Travel Club of Leisure Village West (bd. dirs. 1983-89, v.p. 1988), Nature Club (pres. 1989), Kiwanis (pres. elect Leisure Village West chpt. 1985-86, pres. 1986-87, Disting. past pres. 1987-88), Mens Club Crestwood Manor, 1993—, Phi Sigma. Achievements include discovery of a Filariasis model for laboratory research on human filariasis; the first filariid parasite to be demonstrated to be transmitted by a mite; co-discoverer West African Arbovirus, Dugbe virus. Home: 50 Lacey Rd Ste B105 Whiting NJ 08759-2954 *Success is living in peace and contentment with one's self. I have attempted to achieve this by leading what I consider to be a Christian Life and helping others to do the same, by giving some of my time to help improve the world around us for others, and by giving a little more effort to a task than the minimum necessary to just get it done.*

WILLIAMS, RONALD BOAL, JR., financial consulting company executive, software designer, consutant; b. Lake Forest, Ill., Dec. 23, 1938; s. Ronald Boal Sr. and Dorothy (Herreman) W.; m. Sue Ellen White, Dec. 23, 1961; children: Elizabeth, Anna, Abigail. BA, U. Wis., 1961; MBA, Northwestern U., Evanston, Ill., 1969. Cert. mgmt. cons. Fin. analyst The Richardson Co., Melrose Park, Ill., 1965-68; from exec. coord. to dir. corp. planning Beatrice Foods Co., Chgo., 1968-82; exec. v.p. Systema Corp., Chgo., 1980-82; pres. RW Assocs., Hinsdale, Ill., 1982-84; exec. v.p. Fin. Tng. Resources, Lombard, Ill., 1983—. Contbr. articles to profl. jours. Lt. USN, 1961-65. Avocations: marathon running. Home: 4825 Seeley Ave Downers Grove IL 60515-3411 Office: Fin Tng Resources 905 Parkview Blvd Lombard IL 60148-3267

WILLIAMS, RONALD DEAN, minister, religious organization executive; b. Decatur, Ill., Oct. 23, 1940; s. Henry Lawrence and Ella Loudica Williams; m. Carole Jeanette Lane, June 16, 1962; children: Scott Allan, Mark Lawrence, Derek James. BTh, LIFE Bible Coll., L.A., 1965; DD, Internat. Ch. Foursquare Gospel, L.A., 1992. Ordained to ministry Internat. Ch. Foursquare Gospel, 1966. Pastor Foursquare Gospel Ch., Surrey, B.C., Can., 1965-69; missionary Foursquare Gospel Ch., Hong Kong, 1969-85; prof. LIFE Bible Coll., 1985-95; mng. editor Foursquare World ADVANCE, 1993—; comm. officer Internat. Ch. of Foursquare Gospel, 1988—; bd. dirs. Foursquare Gospel Ch.; pres. exec. bd. Internat. Pentecostal Press Assn., Oklahoma City, 1990—; comm. officer Pentecostal/Charismatic Chs. North Am., Memphis, 1994—; coord. E. Coun. Foursquare Miss., 1979-82. Editor: The Vine and The Branches, 1992; mng. editor Foursquare World ADVANCE mag., 1985. With USAF, 1958-61. Avocations: writing, golf, reading, music. Office: Internat Ch Foursquare Gospel 1910 W Sunset Blvd Ste 200 Los Angeles CA 90026-3247

WILLIAMS, RONALD L., pharmaceutical association executive; b. Akron, Ohio, July 30, 1935; s. Reuben and Thelma W. BS in Pharmacy, Ohio No. U., 1957. Pharmacist, pharmacy owner Akron, 1957-66; exec. sec. Student Am. Pharm. Assn., Washington, 1968-71, 77-81; asst. exec. sec. Am. Pharm. Assn. Acad. Pharm. Practice, Washington, 1971-72; exec. sec. Am. Pharm. Assn. Acad. Pharm. Practice, 1972-83, Am. Pharm. Assn. Acad. Pharm. Sci., 1978-83; dir. liaison and state relations Am. Pharm. Assn., 1983-85, dir. profl. affairs, 1985-86, dir. communications, 1986-90, exec. dir. planning, exec. officer ops., 1990-95, dir. comm., strategic planning, 1995—, coord. pharm. recovery program, 1984-95; nat. high blood pressure coord. com., 1977-86, Interdisciplinary Task Force on Provider Roles, 1979-80, U.S. Drug Enforcement Adminstrn./Pharmacy Working Com., 1974-86; co-chmn. Nat. Conf. on High Blood Pressure Control, 1979-80; ann. meeting planning com. Nat. Coun. on Patient Info. and Edn., 1985-86; mem. Medic Alert Nat. Pharmacy Task Group, 1985-92, Poison Prevention Week Coun., 1988—; informal steering com. Com. on Prescription Drug Abuse, 1982-86; leader pharmacists sect. U. Utah Sch. Alcohol and Other Drug Dependencies, 1984-95; adv. bd. Ohio No. U. Coll. Pharmacy, 1987-94, Campbell U. Coll. Pharmacy, 1993—; planning com. Nat. Conf. on Impaired Health Profl., 1986-88. Editor: Pharmacy Practice, 1971-86, Pharmacy Student, 1977-82, Acad. Reporter, 1978-83. Named Distiguished Person of Yr., Pharmacist Planning Svc., Inc., 1996; recipient Ewart A. Swinyard award U. Utah Sch. on Alcoholism and Other Drug Dependencies, 1996. Mem. AMA (affiliate), Am. Pharm. Assn., Washington Pharm. Assn., Strategic Leadership Forum, Am. Soc. Assn. Execs., Soc. for Profl. Well-Being, Cuyahoga Falls Schs., Found., Am. Legion, Kappa Psi. Democrat. Methodist. Office: Am Pharm Assn 2215 Constitution Ave NW Washington DC 20037-2975

WILLIAMS, RONALD OSCAR, systems engineer; b. Denver, May 10, 1940; s. Oscar H. and Evelyn (Johnson) W. BS in Applied Math., U. Colo. Coll. Engring., 1964, postgrad. U. Colo., U. Denver, George Washington U. Computer programmer Apollo Systems dept., missile and space divsn. Gen. Electric Co., Kennedy Space Ctr., Fla., 1965-67, Manned Spacecraft Ctr., Houston, 1967-68; computer programmer U. Colo., Boulder, 1968-73; computer programmer analyst def. systems divsn. System Devel. Corp. for NORAD, Colorado Springs, 1974-75; engr. def. systems and command-and-info. systems Martin Marietta Aerospace, Denver, 1976-80; systems engr. space and comm. group, def. info. systems divsn. Hughes Aircraft Co., Aurora, Colo., 1980-89; rsch. analyst, 1990—. Vol. fireman Clear Lake City (Tex.) Fire Dept., 1968; officer Boulder Emergency Squad, 1969-76, rescue squadman, 1969-76, liaison to cadets, 1971, pers. officer, 1971-76, exec. bd., 1971-76, award of merit, 1971, 72, emergency med. technician 1973—; spl. police officer Boulder Police Dept., 1970-75; spl. dep. sheriff Boulder County Sheriff's Dept., 1970-71; nat. adv. bd. Am. Security Coun., 1979-91, Coalition of Peace through Strength, 1979-91. Served with USMCR, 1958-66. Decorated Organized Res. medal; recipient Cost Improvement Program award Hughes Aircraft Co., 1982, Systems Improvement award, 1982, Top Cost Improvement Program award, 1983. Mem. AAAS, AIAA, Math. Assn. Am., Am. Math. Soc., Soc. Indsl. and Applied Math., Math. Study Unit of the Am. Topical Assn., Armed Forces Comm. and Electronics Assn., Assn. Old Crows, Am. Def. Preparedness Assn., Marine Corps Assn., Air Force

Assn., U.S. Naval Inst., Nat. Geog. Soc., Smithsonian Instn., Soc. Amateur Radio Astronomers, Met. Opera Guild, Colo. Hist. Soc., Hist. Denver, Inc., Historic Boulder, Inc., Hawaiian Hist. Soc., Denver Botanic Gardens, Denver Mus. Natural History, Denver Zool. Found., Inc., Mensa. Lutheran.

WILLIAMS, RONALD PAUL, lawyer; b. Tulsa, June 28, 1947; s. Donald Paul and Reon Bessie (Thomason) W.; m. Judy Ann Seivers, May 25, 1968 (div. Apr. 1984); children: Heather Ann, Brian Paul; m. Barbara Susan Wehby, Nov. 9, 1984; children: Amy Katherine Williams, Marianne Christine Williams. BA in Polit. Sci., Southwestern Coll., Winfield, Kans., 1974; JD, Washburn U., 1977. Bar: Kans. 1977, U.S. Dist. Ct. Kans. 1977, U.S. Dist. Ct. (we dist.) Mo. 1986, U.S. Ct. Appeals (10th cir.) 1980. Assoc. Shaw, Hergenreter, Quarnstrom & Wright, Topeka, 1977-80, McDonald, Tinker, Skaer, Quinn & Herrington, Wichita, Kans., 1980-84, Morrison & Hecker, Wichita, 1984—; instr. Nat. Inst. for Trial Advocacy, 1982—, Kans. Coll. Advocacy, Topeka, 1980—. Served with USAF, 1965-69. Mem. Nat. Transp. and Safety Bd. Bar Assn. (regional v.p. 1986—), Def. Rsch. Inst., Kans. Bar Assn. (pres. aviation sect. 1984, 85), Kans. Assn. Def. Counsel (pres. 1988-89). Republican. Avocations: flying, golf. Home: 9408 Wyncroft St Wichita KS 67205-1404 Office: Morrison & Hecker 150 N Main St Ste 600 Wichita KS 67202-1320

WILLIAMS, ROSS EDWARD, physicist; b. Carlinville, Ill., June 28, 1922; s. Cyrus Hillis and Mildred Denby (Ross) W.; m. Carolyn Chenoweth Williams, July 5, 1958 (div. June 12, 1986); children: Robert H. (dec.), Katherine J., Ross E. Jr. BS in Physics and Math., Bowdoin Coll., Brunswick, Maine, 1940-43; MS in Physics, Columbia U., 1947; PhD in Physics, 1955. Instr. in Physics Bowdoin Coll., Brunswick, Maine, 1942-43; project engr. Spl. Devices Ctr. ONR, Sands Point, L.I., 1946; sr. rsch. engr. Sperry Products, Inc., Danbury, Conn., 1947-49; cons., govt. and indsl. pvt. practice, 1953-60; sr. rsch. assoc. Hudson Labs Columbia U., Dobbs Ferry, N.Y., 1960-65; assoc. dir., 1965-68; prof. Engring. and Applied Sci. Columbia U., N.Y.C., 1968-74; pres., CEO Ocean and Atmospheric Scis., Inc., Dobbs Ferry, N.Y., 1974—; cons. Nat. Acad. Scis., Washington, 1967—, Naval Rsch. Lab., Washington, 1968-78; dir. Ocean and Atmospheric Sci. Inc., Dobbs Ferry, N.Y., 1968—, Optimum Applied Systems, Inc., Dobbs Ferry, N.Y., 1974—, Valleywood Realty, Inc., Yonkers, N.Y., 1991—, Esthetic Challenges, Inc., Exeter, N.H., 1993—. Lay leader, 1976-79, trustee, 1985-94, Asbury United Meth. Ch., Tuckahoe, N.Y., 1976-79. Lt. USNR, 1943-46. Fellow Acoustical Soc. Am., 1994. Mem. Am. Phys. Soc., Phi Beta Kappa, Sigma Xi. Avocations: hiking, ice skating. Home: 23 Alta Pl Yonkers NY 10710-2601 Office: Ocean & Atmospheric Science Inc 145 Palisade St Dobbs Ferry NY 10522-1617

WILLIAMS, ROY, university athletic coach. Head coach U. Kansas Jayhawks, 1988—. Named Nat. Rookie Coach of Yr., Basketball Times, 1989, Coach of Yr., Basketball Writers Assn., 1990, Big 8 Coach of Yr., AP and UPI, 1990, Big 8 Coach of Yr., AP, 1992, Nat. Coach of Yr., 1992. 1991 NCAA Tournament runner-up. Office: Univ Kansas Allen Fieldhouse Lawrence KS 66045

WILLIAMS, RUSSELL, II, production sound mixer; b. Oct. 14, 1952. BA in Film Prodn., Art History, Lit., Am. U., Washington, 1974; student, Rec. Inst. Am., Silver Spring, Md., 1974; student in Basic Electronics, U. Sound Arts, Hollywood, Calif., 1979. Studio engr. rec. lab. Libr. Congress, Washington, 1971-73; vol. co-dir. Spirits Radio Workshop, WAMU-FM radio, Am. U., Washington, 1972-79; engr. WRC/NBC TV, Washington, 1973, 77; documetnary sound recordist, transfer engr. WMAL TV, Washington, 1974-76; workshop leader radio vol. activity com. Corp. for Pub. Broadcasting, Washington, 1976; engr., editor WMAL/ABC radio, Washington, 1978-79; motion picture sound mixer, 1979—; founder, owner Sound Is Ready, 1979—; guest lectr. U. D.C., 1973, 77; vis. prof. dept. film and TV, UCLA, 1991. Productions include (feature films) The Distinguished Gentleman, Boomerang, Mo Money, True Identity, Jungle Fever, Dances with Wolves (Acad. award 1991, Brit. Acad. nomination 1992), Glory (Acad. award 1990), Field of Dreams, (movies for TV) Heatwave, The Women of Brewster Place, Inherit the Wind, Billionaire Boys Club, Terrorist on Trial (Prime Time Emmy award), (documentary and indsl. films) Eyes on the Prize I, The Making of JoJo Dancer, Return to Iwo Jima. Mem. IATSE, Acad. Motion Picture Arts and Scis., Acad. Television Arts and Scis., Cinema Audio Soc. (3 awards).

WILLIAMS, RUTH ELIZABETH (BETTY WILLIAMS), retired educator; b. Newport News, Va., July 31, 1938; d. Lloyd Haynes and Erma Ruth (Goodrich) W. BA, Mary Washington Coll., 1960; cert. d'etudes, Converse Coll., 1961, U. Oreg., 1962. Cert. tchr., Va. French tchr. York High Sch., York County Pub. Schs., Yorktown, Va., 1960-65; French resource tchr. Newport News Pub. Schs., 1966-74, tchr. French and photography, 1974-81, tchr. French, Spanish, German and Latin, 1981-91, ret., 1991; pres. Cresset Publs., Williamsburg, Va., 1977—; lectr. Sch. Edn., Coll. Williamand Mary, Williamsburg, 1962-65; French tchr., coord. fgn. langs. York County Pub. Schs., 1962-65; workshop leader dept. pub. instrn. State of Del., Dover, 1965; cons. Health de Rochemont Co., Boston, 1962-71. Driver Meals on Wheels, Williamsburg, 1989-90; contbr. Va. Spl. Olympics, Richmond, 1987—; charter mem. Capitol Soc. Colonial Williamsburg Found., Inc., 1994; mem. Altar Guild, Bruton Parish Ch., Williamsburg, 1960—. Grantee Nat. Def. Edn. Act, 1961, 1962. Mem. AAAU, Fgn. Lang. Assn. Va., AARP (ret. tchrs. divsn.), Heritage Soc., Mary Washington Coll. Alumni Assn., Va. Hist. Soc., Am. Assn. Tchrs. French, Mortar Bd., Women in the Arts, Alpha Phi Sigma, Phi Sigma Iota. Episcopalian. Avocations: photography, coin and stamp collecting, geology, walking, sailing. Home and Office: 471 Catesby Ln Williamsburg VA 23185-4732

WILLIAMS, RUTH LEE, clinical social worker; b. Dallas, June 24, 1944; d. Carl Woodley and Nancy Ruth (Gardner) W. BA, So. Meth. U., 1966; M Sci.in Social Work, U. Tex., Austin, 1969. Milieu coordinator Starr Commonwealth, Albion, Mich., 1969-70; clin. social worker Katherine Hamilton Mental Health Care, Terre Haute, Ind., 1973-74; clin. social worker, supr. Pikes Peak Mental Health Ctr., Colorado Springs, Colo., 1974-78; pvt. practice social work Colorado Springs, 1978—; pres. Hearthstone Inn, Inc., Colorado Springs, 1978—; practitioner Jin Shin Jyutsu, Colorado Springs, 1978—; pres., v.p. bd. dirs. Premier Care (formerly Colorado Springs Mental Health Care Providers Inc.), 1986-87, chmn. quality assurance com., 1987-89, v.p. bd. dirs., 1992-93. Author, editor: From the Kitchen of The Hearthstone Inn, 1981, 2d rev. edit., 1986, 3d rev. edit., 1992. Mem. Am. Bd. Examiners in Clin. Social Work (charter mem., cert.), Colo. Soc. Clin. Social Work (editor 1976), Nat. Assn. Soc. Workers (diplomate), Nat. Bd. Social Work Examiners (cert.), Nat. Assn. Ind. Innkeepers, So. Meth. U. Alumni Assn. (life). Avocations: gardening, hiking, sailing. Home: 11555 Howells Rd Colorado Springs CO 80908-3735 Office: 536 E Uintah St Colorado Springs CO 80903-2515

WILLIAMS, S. LINN, lawyer; b. St. Louis, July 1, 1946; s. Sidney Duane and Elizabeth Gertrude (Relfe) W.; m. Noriko Kurosawa, Sept. 13, 1975. B.A., Princeton U., 1968, J.D., Harvard U., 1971, postgrad. Cambridge U., 1972-74. Bar: Mass. 1971, D.C. 1972, Pa. 1987. Law clk. to Hon. I.L. Goldberg, U.S. Ct. Appeals 5th Cir., Dallas, 1971-72; assoc. Blakemore & Mitsuki, Tokyo, 1974; assoc., then ptnr. Leva, Hawes, Symington, Martin & Oppenheimer, Washington, 1975-81; v.p., gen. counsel Overseas Pvt. Investment Corp., Washington, 1981-84; v.p., gen. counsel Sears World Trade, Inc., 1984-85; ptnr. Gibson Dunn and Crutcher, Washington and Tokyo, 1985-89, 92-93, Jones Day Reavis & Pogue, Washington, 1993-94; sr. v.p., gen. counsel Edison Mission Energy, Irvine, Calif., 1995—; Japanese fgn. legal cons. Tokyo Dainibengoshikai, 1987-89; dep. U.S. trade rep., amb., Washington, 1989-91; mem. bd. adv. Coun. Competitiveness, CEO Inst., Inst. Asian Law and Policy Studies Georgetown U., Washington, U.S. Com. of Pacific Econ. Coop. Coun., European Inst.; sr. fellow Ctr. Strategic and Internat. Studies, Washington. Fulbright scholar, 1972, NEH fellow, 1972, McConnell fellow, 1967, Ford Found. fellow, 1972. Mem. Inst. Internat. Commercial Law (trustee), United Oxford & Cambridge Club (London), Met. Club (Washington). Author: Developing an Export Trading Business, 1989; contbr. chpts. in book, also numerous articles on trade and investments. Office: Mission Energy Co 18101 Von Karman Ave Irvine CA 92715-1010

WILLIAMS, SALLY BROADRICK, infection control nurse and consultant; b. Dalton, Ga., Dec. 25, 1943; d. Columbus N. and Anne M. (McHan) Broadrick; m. Joe P. Williams, Aug. 30, 1969; children: Michael J., Andrew B. Diploma in Nursing, Grady Meml. Hosp., Atlanta, 1969; BS in Health Arts, Coll. of St. Francis, Joliet, Ill., 1981. Cert. in infection control. Emergency dept. nurse Hamilton Med. Ctr., Dalton, 1963-69; patient care coord. Wesley Woods Health Ctr., Atlanta, 1969-70; critical care nurse DeKalb Gen. Hosp., Decatur, Ga., 1970-71, emergency dept. nurse, 1971-73, infection control and employee health nurse, 1973-75; infection control dir. DeKalb Med. Ctr., Decatur, 1973-94; infection control/employee health dir. R.T. Jones Hosp.(formerly Promina R.T. Jones Hosp.), Canton, 1994—; tng. cons. CDC, Atlanta, 1984-89; bloodborne pathogen cons. Merck, 1992, 93. Author: Infection Control for Emergency Medical Technicians, 1990, Infection Control for Pre-Hospital Care Givers, 1989, Infection Control for Pre-Hospital Care Givers and Emergency Departments, 1994. Observer/reporter Cherokee LWV, Cherokee County, Ga., 1993-94; vol. Am. Cancer Soc.; fin. chairperson Cherokee County Relay for Life; mem. adv. com. Boy Scouts Am. Med. Explorer Post #23, Canton, Ga. Mem. Ga. Infection Control Network (pres. 1981-84, 90, 95, dist. 3 liaison 1981-84, 90, dist. 1 liaison 1995-96, Infection Control Practitioner of Yr. award 1984, 89, Outstanding Contbr. award 1985, 87, 91), Assn. Practitioners in Infection Control (pres. 1978, Outstanding Practitioner award 1990), Assn. for Profls. in Infection Control and Epidemiology (nominating chmn. 1993, pres.-elect 1995, pres. Greater Atlanta chpt. 1996), Internat. Assn. for AIDS Educators, Southeastern Assn. Microbiologists. Democrat. Methodist. Avocations: reading, travel. Home: 1454 White Columns Blvd Canton GA 30115 Office: Promina RT Jones Hosp 201 Hospital Dr Canton GA 30114

WILLIAMS, SANDRA, insurance company executive; b. 1947. Law degree, U. Conn. With Farmington Casualty Co., Hartford, 1979—, sec. Office: Farmington Casualty Co 151 Farmington Ave Hartford CT 06156-0001*

WILLIAMS, SANDRA CASTALDO, elementary school educator; b. Rahway, N.J., Sept. 19, 1941; d. Neil and Loretta Margaret (Gleason) Castaldo; m. Arthur Williams III, 1962; children: Arthur IV, Melinda S., Thomas N. Student, Syracuse U., 1959-61; AB, Kean Coll., 1969, MA magna cum laude, 1978. Cert. tchr. K-8, early childhood, N.J. Preschool tchr. St. Andrew's Nursery & Kindergarten, New Providence, N.J., 1973-82; kindergartern tchr. Walnut Ave. Sch. Cranford (N.J.) Sch. Dist., 1978-79; adjunct prof. Farleigh Dickinson Coll., Rutherford, Teaneck, N.J., 1983-86; tchr. 4th grade The Peck Sch., Morristown, N.J., 1986-89; dir. Summit Child Care Ctr., 1990-91; tchr. 1st grade Oak Knoll Sch. of Holy Child Jesus, Summit, N.J., 1992—, tchr. Confraternity of Christian Doctrine, 1995—; bd. dirs. Summit Child Care Ctr., 1970-71, cons., 1991; cert. instr. Jacki Soresen Aerobic Dancing, Inc., Summit, 1990, Westfield, 1992-95. Co-chair United Way, Summit, 1991; Eucharistic min. St. Teresa's Ch., Summit, 1994—. Mem. ASCD, Internat. Reading Assn., Phi Kappa Phi, Alpha Sigma Lambda, Kappa Kappa Gamma. Republican. Roman Catholic. Avocations: needle work, gardening, church, physical fitness. Home: 8 Sunset Dr Summit NJ 07901-2323 Office: Oak Knoll Sch Holy Child Jesus 44 Blackburn Rd Summit NJ 07901-2408

WILLIAMS, SANDRA KELLER, postal service executive; b. Bethesda, Md., Oct. 3, 1944; d. Park Dudley and Julia Mildred (Hunter) Keller; m. Tommy Allen Williams, Dec. 24, 1970; children: Chris Allen, Wakenna, Barbara. BA, U. Colo., 1966; MBA, U. Mo., Kansas City, 1971; MS, Ga. Inst. Tech., 1973. Mathematician Colo. State U., Ft. Collins, 1966; sr. scientist Booz-Allen Applied Rsch., Kansas City, Mo., 1967-68; computer sci. instr. Mo. Western Coll., St. Joseph, 1968-71; systems planning analyst Decatur (Ga.) Fed. Savs. and Loan Assn., 1972-73; planning analyst Fed. Res. Bank, Atlanta, 1974-75; indsl. engr. so. region hdqrs. U.S. Postal Svc., Memphis, 1975-79; nat. mgr. quality control U.S. Postal Svc., Washington, 1979-86; dir. city ops. so. Md. div. U.S. Postal Svc., Capital Heights, 1986-87, dir., oper. supt. so. Md. div., 1987-88; postmaster U.S. Postal Svc., Reading, Pa., 1988—; cons. Personal Bus., St. Joseph, 1968-69; grad. teaching asst. Ga. Inst. Tech., Atlanta, 1971-73; adj. faculty Dekalb C.C., Clarkston, Ga., 1973-75, Memphis State U., 1976-78; owner Custom Florals, 1995—. Chmn. Combined Fed. Campaign, Reading, 1988-96, U.S. Postal Svc.-Berks County Savs. Bond Program, 1988-95, United Way's Govt. divsn., 1989-90; bd. dirs. YWCA, Reading and Berks County, treas., 1990, pres., 1991. Mem. Nat. League Postmasters (legis. officer 1988-91), Berks County Women's Network (bd. dirs. 1994-95, treas. 1995). Republican. Avocations: interior design, gardening, investment portfolio management. Home: 1514 Hill Rd Reading PA 19602-1410

WILLIAMS, SANKEY VAUGHAN, health services researcher, internist; b. San Antonio, Apr. 15, 1944; s. James Sankey and Helen (Long) W.; m. Constance Hess, June 27, 1972; children: Elizabeth Helen, Jennifer Lee. AB, Princeton U., 1966; MD, Harvard U., 1970. Diplomate Am. Bd. Internal Medicine. Intern Hosp. of U. Pa., 1970-71, jr. resident, 1971-72, chief med. resident, 1974-75; assoc. dir. clin. rsch. Ctr. for Study of Aging, U. Pa., 1982-86; assoc. dir. for med. affairs Leonard Davis Inst. for Health Econs., U. Pa., 1978-90; dir. clin. scholars program U. Pa., Phila., 1988-96; prof. health care systems Wharton Sch., U. Pa., Phila., 1989—; prof. medicine U. Pa., Phila., 1989—, chief div. gen. internal medicine, 1992—, Sol Katz prof. medicine, 1992—; commr. Prospective Payment Assessment Commn., U.S. Congress, Washington, 1988-91; chairman health svcs. rsch. devel. grants study sect. Agy. for Health Care Policy and Rsch., 1991-94; counselor for med. affiars to the pres. U. Pa., 1990-92. Co-editor: The Physician's Practice, 1980; author 14 revs, chpt. or editorials; contbr. 35 articles to various sci. jours. Lt. comdr. USPHS, 1972-74. Recipient Career Devel. award Henry S. Kaiser Family Found., 1981-86. Mem. ACP (diplomate, chmn. clin. privileges com. 1989-93, Am. Fedn. Clin. Rsch. (program chmn. health svcs. rsch. 1985), Soc. for Med. Decision Making (pres. 1985-86), Soc. for Gen. Internal Medicine (coun. 1979-84, editor Jour. Gen. Internal Medicine 1995-2000). Office: Hosp Univ of Pa Divsn Gen Internal Medicine Silverstein 3 Philadelphia PA 19104

WILLIAMS, SHARRON ELAINE, gifted education specialist, legal consultant; b. Cin., July 6, 1951; d. Robert and Mary (Smith) Sawyer; 1 child, Wesley. BS, Kent State U., 1973; MS, Cleve. State U., 1988; JD, U. Akron, 1979. Tchr. Akron (Ohio) Pub. Schs., 1973-79; bus. law instr. Lorain (Ohio) Cmty. Coll., 1980; law clk. Roberty Sawyer, Cleve., 1981; gifted edn. tchr. Cleveland Heights (Ohio) Schs., 1983-88; resource tchr. Coventry Sch., Cleve., 1989-90; gifted edn. specialist Shaker Heights (Ohio) Schs., 1991—; workshop coord. Cleve. Alliance of Educators, 1994; Gestalt trainer Cleveland Heights Schs., 1990; instr. Gov.'s Summer Inst., Cleve., 1989; presenter in field. Contbg. author: Windows of Opportunity, 1994 (NCTM award 1994). Recipient grant Marth Holden Jennings Found., 1979, grant Shaker Heights Schs., 1994. Mem. Nat. Alliance of Black Educators, Heights Alliance of Black Educators, Delta Sigma Theta, Phi Delta Kappa (svc. coord. 1991—), Phi Alpha Delta. Avocations: foreign travel, decorating. Office: Shaker Heights City Schs 17917 Lomond Blvd Shaker Heights OH 44122

WILLIAMS, SOLOMON, Indian organization executive; b. Mekoryuk, Alaska, Aug. 29, 1943; s. Jack Uyohitch and Susie (Brown) W.; m. Alice Marie Mathlaw, Oct. 29, 1969; children: Claudine Jo Williams Davis, Patricia Renee. Grad. edn. diploma, Juneau (Alaska)-Douglas C.C., 1971. Notary pub., Alaska. Warehouseman Native Village of Mekoryuk, 1957-66; store mgr., 1972-73; acctg. clk. Bur. Indian Affairs, Juneau, 1966-72; realty specialist Bur. Indian Affairs, Bethel, Alaska, 1974-81; land law examiner Bur. Indian Affairs, Anchorage, 1987-89; mgr. Bering Sea Reindeer Products, Mekoryuk, 1981-84; city clk. City of Mekoryuk, 1984-85; pres.-supt. Indian Reorgn. Act Coun., Meyoryuk, 1989-95, exec. officer, 1995—. Recipient 10-Yr. Svc. award Bur. Indian Affairs, 1985. Avocations: hunting, commercial fishing. Office: Indian Reorgn Act Coun 1st Chase St Mekoryuk AK 99630

WILLIAMS, SPENCER MORTIMER, federal judge; b. Reading, Mass., Feb. 24, 1922; s. Theodore Ryder and Anabel (Hutchison) W.; m. Kathryn Bramlage, Aug. 20, 1943; children: Carol Marcia (Mrs. James B. Garvey), Peter, Spencer, Clark, Janice, Diane (Mrs. Sean Quinn). AB, UCLA, 1943; postgrad., Hastings Coll. Law, 1946; JD, U. Calif., Berkeley, 1948. Bar: Calif. 1949, U.S. Supreme Ct. 1952. Assoc. Beresford & Adams, San Jose, Calif., 1949, Rankin, O'Neal, Center, Luckhardt, Bonney, Marlais & Lund, San Jose, Evans, Jackson & Kennedy, Sacramento; county counsel Santa Clara County, 1955-67; adminstr. Calif. Health and Welfare Agy., Sacramento, 1967-69; judge U.S. Dist. Ct. (no. dist.) Calif., San Francisco, from 1971, now sr. judge; County exec. pro tem, Santa Clara County; adminstr. Calif. Youth and Adult Corrections Agy., Sacramento; sec. Calif. Human Relations Agy., Sacramento, 1967-70. Chmn. San Jose Christmas Seals Drive, 1953, San Jose Muscular Dystrophy Drive, 1953, 54; team capt. fund raising drive San Jose YMCA, 1960; co-chmn. indsl. sect. fund raising drive Alexian Bros. Hosp., San Jose, 1964; team capt. fund raising drive San Jose Hosp.; mem. com. on youth and govt. YMCA, 1967-68; Candidate for Calif. Assembly, 1954, Calif. Atty. Gen., 1966, 70; Bd. dirs. San Jose Better Bus. Bur., 1955-66, Boys City Boys' Club, San Jose, 1965-67; pres. trustees Santa Clara County Law Library, 1955-66. Served with USNR, 1943-46; to lt. comdr. JAG Corps USNR, 1950-52, PTO. Named San Jose Man of Year, 1954. Mem. ABA, Calif. Bar Assn. (vice chmn. com. on publicly employed attys. 1962-63), Santa Clara County Bar Assn., Sacramento Bar Assn., Internat. Assn. Trial Judges (pres. 1995-96), Calif. Dist. Attys. Assn. (pres. 1963-64), Nat. Assn. County Civil Attys. (pres. 1963-64), 9th Cir. Dist. Judges Assn. (pres. 1981-83), Fed. Judges Assn. (pres. 1982-87), Kiwanis, Theta Delta Chi. Office: US Dist Ct 280 S 1st St San Jose CA 95113-3002

WILLIAMS, STANLEY, ballet dancer and teacher; b. Chappel, Eng., 1925. guest tchr. Sch. Am. Ballet, N.Y.C. Ballet Co., 1960-62; mem. faculty Sch. Am. Ballet, N.Y.C., 1964—, now co-chmn. faculty; guest instr. Royal Danish Ballet, 1966-80; sr. faculty chair The Brown Found., Inc., 1987. Staged: Bournonville Divertissement for, N.Y.C. Ballet (Dance Mag. award 1981); studied at school, Royal Danish Ballet, also in, Paris; accepted into the company, 1943, became solo dancer, 1949, tchr., 1950—, guest artist, Iceland, 1947, Brussels and Stockholm, 1948, ballet master, leading dancer with, George Kirsta's Ballet Comique in Eng., 1953-54; repertoire in Denmark includes leading roles in Coppelia, others. Knighted by King of Denmark; recipient Mae L. Wien award, 1992. Address: Sch Am Ballet 70 Lincoln Center Plz New York NY 10023-6548

WILLIAMS, STEPHEN, anthropologist, educator; b. Mpls., Aug. 28, 1926; s. Clyde Garfield and Lois (Simmons) W.; m. Eunice Ford, Jan. 6, 1962; children: Stephen John, Timothy. BA, Yale U., 1949, PhD, 1954; MA, U. Mich., 1950; MA (hon.), Harvard, 1962. Asst. anthropology dept. Peabody Mus., Yale U., 1950-52; mem. faculty Harvard U., Cambridge, Mass., 1958—, prof. anthropology, 1967-72, Peabody prof., 1972-93, prof. emeritus, chmn. dept., 1967-69; rsch. fellow Peabody Mus., Harvard U., Cambridge, Mass., 1954-57, mem. staff, 1954—, dir. mus., 1967-77; curator N.Am. Archaeology, 1962-93, hon. curator 1993—; dir. rsch. of Peabody Mus.'s Lower Miss. Survey, 1958-93. Author books and articles on N.Am. archaeology and "Fantastic" archaeology. Home: 1017 Foothills Trl Santa Fe NM 87505-4537 Office: PO Box 22354 Santa Fe NM 87502-2354

WILLIAMS, STEPHEN FAIN, federal judge; b. N.Y.C., N.Y., Sept. 23, 1936; s. Charles Dickerman and Virginia (Fain) W.; m. Faith Morrow, June 11, 1966; children: Susan, Geoffrey Fain, Sarah Margot Nu, Timothy Dwight, Nicholas Morrow. B.A., Yale U., 1958; J.D., Harvard U., 1961. Bar: N.Y. 1962, Colo. 1977. Assoc. Debevoise, Plimpton, Lyons & Gates, N.Y.C., 1962-66; asst. U.S. atty. So. Dist. N.Y., 1966-69; asst. prof. law U. Colo., Boulder, 1969-77; prof. U. Colo., 1977-86; judge U.S. Ct. Appeals (D.C. cir.), Washington, 1986—; vis. prof. UCLA, 1975-76; vis. prof., fellow in law and econs. U. Chgo., 1979-80; vis. William L. Hutchison prof. energy law So. Meth. U., 1983-84; cons. Adminstrv. Conf. U.S., 1974-76, FTC, 1983-85; mem. Boulder Area Growth Study Commn., 1972-73. Contbr. articles to law revs., mags. Served with U.S. Army, 1961-62. Mem. Am. Law Inst. Office: US Courthouse 3rd Constitution Ave NW Washington DC 20001

WILLIAMS, STERLING LEE, electronics executive; b. Spokane, Wash., July 29, 1943; s. Henry Sterling and Alma (Whitaker) W.; m. Sharolyn Snow, Aug. 23, 1963 (div. Nov. 5, 1971); children: Brett, Lance; m. Barbara Gattis, Nov. 22, 1971; 1 child, Tiffany Nicole. BS, East Central U., Ada, Okla., 1967; postgrad. studies, Tex. Christian U., 1967-69. Sales rep. RCA computer systems div., Dallas, 1969-71; gen. mgr. computer services div. University Computing Co., Dallas, 1971-78; v.p. domestic ops. Inforex, Burlington, Mass., 1978-79; pres. numerical control div. Mfg. Data Systems Inc., Ann Arbor, Mich., 1979-81; pres., chief exec. officer Sterling Software Inc., Dallas, 1981—, also bd. dirs. Mem. Assn. Data Processing Services Orgns., Sigma Pi Sigma. Republican. Avocations: reading, traveling. Office: Sterling Software Inc 8080 N Cen Expressway St #1100 LB53 Dallas TX 75206*

WILLIAMS, STEVEN A., hospital administrator. With Livingston County Hosp., Salem, Ky., 1972-79, Norton-Children's Hosp., Louisville, 1977-79, Caldwell County Hosp., Princeton, Ky., 1979-84; officer N.K.C. Mgmt., Inc., Louisville, 1984-85; with Alliant Hosp., Inc., Louisville, 1986—, pres., chief exec. officer. Office: Alliant Hosp Inc 200 E Chestnut St Louisville KY 40202-1822*

WILLIAMS, SUE DARDEN, library director; b. Miami, Fla., Aug. 13, 1943; d. Archie Yelverton and Bobbie (Jones) Eagles; m. Richard Williams, Sept. 30, 1989. B.A., Barton Coll., Wilson, N.C., 1965; M.L.S., U. Tex., Austin, 1970. Cert. librarian, N.C., Va. Instr. Chowan Coll., Murfreesboro, N.C., 1966-68; libr.'s asst. Albemarle Regional Libr., Winston, N.C., 1968-69; br. libr. Multnomah County Pub. Libr., Portland, Oreg., 1971-72; asst. dir. Stanly County Pub. Libr., Albemarle, N.C., 1973-76; dir. Stanly County Pub. Libr., 1976-80; asst. dir. Norfolk (Va.) Pub. Libr., 1980-83; dir., 1983-94, Rockingham County Pub. Libr., Eden, N.C., 1996—. Mem. ALA (orientation com. 1990-92, chair 1991), Libr. Adminstrv. and Mgmt. Assn. (pub. rels. sec. 1985-87), Southeastern Libr. Assn. (staff devel. com. 1986-88, Rothrock award com. 1984-86, sec. pub. libr. sect. 1982-84), Va. Libr. Assn. (SELA rep. 1993-96, coun. 1984, 88-91, 93-96, ad hoc conf. guidelines com. 1985-86, chmn. conf. program 1984, awards and recognition com. 1983), Pub. Libr. Assn. (bd. dirs.-at-large Met. area 1986-89), Va. State Libr. (coop edn. com. 88-89). Home: 817A Carter St Eden NC 27288-5923 Office: Rockingham County Pub Libr 527 Boone Rd Eden NC 27288

WILLIAMS, SUE WINKLE, educator, administrator; b. Checotah, Okla., June 19, 1943; d. Herman Dalton and Faye Louise (Davidson) Winkle; m. James W. Williams, Aug. 14, 1965; 1 child, Joshua. BS, Okla. State U., 1965, EdD, 1980. Tchr. Jefferson County Pub. Schs., Wheat Ridge, Colo., 1965-66, Chicopee (Mass.) Pub. Schs., 1966-70; child devel. specialist Okla. State Dept. Health, Oklahoma City, 1972-75; child devel. specialist, child devel. assoc. pilot project Oscar Rose Jr. Coll., Midwest City, Okla., 1975-76; lectr. Cen. State U., Edmond, Okla., 1976-79; vis. asst. prof. U. Okla., Norman, 1980-81; asst. prof. U. Akron, Ohio, 1981-85; prof. Southwest Tex. State U., San Marcos, 1985—; presenter in field. Outside manuscript reviewer Home Econs. Rsch. Jour., 1984-87, A Child's World, 1988; contbr. articles to profl. jours. Tex. Dept. Human Svcs. grantee, 1986-93; secured numerous rsch. and pilot program grants. Mem. Nat. Assn. Edn. Young Children, Southwestern Psychol. Assn., Soc. Rsch. in Child Devel., Omicron Nu, Phi Kappa Phi. Unitarian. Office: Southwest Tex State U Dept Home Econs San Marcos TX 78666

WILLIAMS, SYLVESTER EMANUAL, III, educator, consultant; b. Chgo., Feb. 4, 1937; s. Sylvester Emanual and Carita (Brown) W.; children: Sylvia, Sylvester, Sydnee, Steven. BS, No. Ill. U., 1958; MA, Chgo. State U., 1968; PhD, U. S.C., 1992. Cert. tchr., S.C., N.C., Ill. From asst. to supt. Washington D.C. Pub. Schs., 1968-69; tchr. Chgo. Pub. Schs., 1958-68; program officer Dept. Edn., Washington, 1971-86; prof. Lander U., Greenwood, S.C., 1986-89, U. S.C., Akin, 1990-91; tchr., coach Charlotte (N.C.) Mecklenburg Pub. Schs., 1992—; bd. dirs. John de Home Sch., McCormick, S.C., 1986—. Mem. Phi Delta Kappa. Republican. Baptist. Avocation: motion picture prodn. Home: 205 Briggs Ave Greenwood SC 29649-1603

WILLIAMS, TED (THEODORE SAMUEL WILLIAMS), former baseball player, former manager, consultant; b. San Diego, Aug. 30, 1918; s. Samuel Steward and May W.; m. Doris Soule; 3 children. Played with Boston Red Sox, 1939-42, 46-60; now cons. and spring tng. instr.; mgr. Washington Senators, 1969-71, Tex. Rangers, 1972; sports cons. Sears, Roebuck & Co. Author: (with John Underwood) My Turn at Bat: The Story of My Life, 1968, The Science of Hitting, 1972. Served to 2d lt. USMCR, 1942-45.

Named to Am. League All-Star Team, 1940-42, 46-51, 54-60; named Sporting News Player of Year, 1941, 42, 47, 49, 57, Am. League Most Valuable Player, 1946, 49, Am. League Mgr. of Year, 1969; inducted to Baseball Hall of Fame, 1966.

WILLIAMS, TEMPLE WEATHERLY, JR., internist, educator; b. Wichita Falls, Tex., Apr. 19, 1934; s. Temple Weatherly and Dorothy (Coleman) W.; married; children: Holly Clare, Temple Weatherly III; m. Joan Loos, Apr. 6, 1991. Student, Midwestern U., 1951-53; B.S., So. Meth. U., 1955; M.D., Baylor U., 1959. Intern, resident in internal medicine Duke U. Hosp., Durham, N.C., 1959-60, 62-63; fellow in infectious disease Baylor U., 1960-62; clin. assoc. infectious disease NIH, Bethesda, Md.; prof. medicine and microbiology/immunology Baylor Coll. Medicine, Houston, 1974—. Contbr. 100 articles on infectious diseases to profl. jours., chpts. to books. Served with USPHS, 1963-65. Fellow ACP, Infectious Disease Soc. Am.; mem. AMA. Republican. Methodist. Office: 6565 Fannin MS 910 Houston TX 77030

WILLIAMS, THEODORE EARLE, industrial distribution company executive; b. Cleve., May 9, 1920; s. Stanley S. and Blanche (Albaum) W.; m. Rita Cohen, Aug. 28, 1952; children: Lezlie, Richard Atlas, Shelley, William Atlas, Wayne, Marsha, Patti Blake, Jeff Blake. Student, Wayne U., 1937-38; BS in Engring, U. Mich., 1942, postgrad. in bus. adminstrn, 1942. Pres. Wayne Products Co., Detroit, 1942-43, L.A., 1947-49; pres. Williams Metal Products Co., Inglewood, Calif., 1950-69; chmn. bd., pres., chief exec. officer Bell Industries, L.A., 1970—; instr. U. Mich., 1942. Patentee in field. Served to 1st lt. AUS, 1943-46. Recipient Humanitarian award City of L.A., 1977. Democrat. Home: 435 N Layton Way Los Angeles CA 90049-2022 Office: Bell Industries Inc 11812 San Vicente Blvd Los Angeles CA 90049-5022 *It seems to me that many of our current problems in this world originate from the drift away from concern for other people to the emphasis on self. We are reluctant to get involved, and as this spaceship gets smaller, we become more interdependent all the time. If we don't learn to live together, I'm afraid we may all perish together.*

WILLIAMS, THEODORE JOSEPH, engineering educator; b. Black Lick, Pa., Sept. 2, 1923; s. Theodore Finley and Mary Ellen (Shields) W.; m. Isabel Annette McAnulty, July 18, 1946; children: Theodore Joseph, Mary Margaret, Charles Augustus, Elizabeth Ann. B.S.Ch.E., Pa. State U., 1949, M.S.Ch.E., 1950, Ph.D., 1955; M.S. in Elec. Engring., Ohio State U., 1956. Research fellow Pa. State U., University Park, 1947-51; asst. prof. Air Force Inst. Tech., 1953-56; technologist Monsanto Co., 1956-57, sr. engring. supr., 1957-65; prof. engring. Purdue U., Lafayette, Ind., 1965-94, prof. emeritus, 1995—, dir. control and info. systems lab., 1965-66; dir. Purdue Lab. Applied Indsl. Control, 1966-94, dir. emeritus, 1995—; cons., 1964—; vis. prof. Washington U., St. Louis, 1962-65. Author: Systems Engineering for the Process Industries, 1961, Automatic Control of Chemical and Petroleum Processes, 1961, Progress in Direct Digital Control, 1969, Interfaces with the Process Control Computer, 1971, Modeling and Control of Kraft Production Systems, 1975, Modelling, Estimation and Control of the Soaking Pit, 1983, The Use of Digital Computers in Process Control, 1983, Analysis and Design of Hierarchical Control Systems - With Special Reference to Steel Plant Operations, 1985, A Reference Model for Computer Integrated Manufacturing (CIM) - A Description from the Viewpoint of Industrial Automation, 1989, The Purdue Enterprise Reference Architecture, 1992; editor: Computer Applications in Shipping and Shipbuilding, 6 vols., 1973-79, Proceedings Advanced Control Confs., 19 vols., 1974-93. Served to 1st lt. USAAF, 1942-45; to capt. USAF, 1951-56. Decorated Air medal with 2 oak leaf clusters. Fellow AAAS, AIChE, Instrument Soc. Am. (hon. mem., pres. 1968-69, Albert F. Sperry gold medal 1990, Lifetime Achievement award 1995), Am. Inst. Chemists, Inst. Measurement and Control (London, sr. Harold Hartley silver medal 1975); mem. IEEE (sr.), Soc. for Computer Simulation (hon.), Am. Chem. Soc., Am. Automatic Control Coun. (pres. 1965-67), Am. Fedn. Info. Processing Socs. (pres. 1976-78), Sigma Xi, Tau Beta Pi, Phi Kappa Phi, Phi Lambda Upsilon. Home: 208 Chippewa St West Lafayette IN 47906-2123 Office: Purdue U Potter Rsch Ctr Inst Interdisciplinary Engring Studies West Lafayette IN 47907-1293

WILLIAMS, THOMAS A., data processing executive. V.p., corp. controller Oracle Corp., Redwood, Calif. Office: Oracle Corp 500 Oracle Pkwy Redwood CA 94065

WILLIAMS, THOMAS ALLISON, lawyer; b. Port Chester, N.Y., Dec. 19, 1936; s. Howard Hunter and Mary Katharine (Covell) W.; m. Anne Lamson Bell, Sept. 7, 1961; children: Thomas Allison, Laura L., James C., David D. BA in Econs., Yale U., 1959, LLB, 1962. Bar: N.Y. 1963. Assoc. Milbank, Tweed, Hadley & McCloy, N.Y.C., 1962-70, ptnr., 1971-94, pres., dir., The Depository Trust Co., N.Y.C., 1994—. Trustee Rye Free Reading Room (N.Y.), 1965-85, pres., 1978-85; trustee Rye Presbyn. Ch., 1972-75; trustee, chmn. planning com. United Hosp., Port Chester, N.Y., 1978-86, chmn. bd., 1986-96; trustee Westchester Libr. System, Westchester, N.Y., 1968-73, pres., 1972-73. Mem. ABA, N.Y. State Bar Assn., Assn. of Bar of City of N.Y., Am. Yacht Club (vice commodore), N.Y. Yacht Club, Apawamis Club. Republican. Presbyterian. Office: The Depository Trust Co 55 Water St New York NY 10041

WILLIAMS, THOMAS ARTHUR, biomedical computing consultant, psychiatrist; b. Racine, Wis., May 11, 1936; s. Robert Klinkert and Marion Anne (Wisneski) W.; m. Rexanne Louise Smith, Aug. 8, 1988; children: Jennifer, Thomas, Ted, Susan. BA, Harvard Coll., 1958; MD, Columbia U., 1963; postgrad., NIH, 1967-68. Diplomate Nat. Bd. Med. Examiners, Am. Bd. Psychiatry and Neurology. Intern in surgery Presbyn. Hosp., N.Y.C., 1963-64; resident in psychiatry N.Y. State Psychiat. Inst., N.Y.C., 1964-67; chief depression sect. NIMH, Bethesda, Rockville, Md., 1967-71; asst. prof. U. Pitts., 1969-70; assoc. prof. U. Utah, Salt Lake City, 1971-77; prof., chmn. dept. psychiatry Eastern Va. Med. Sch., Norfolk, Va., 1977-78; clin. dir. Sheppard & Enoch Pratt Hosp., Towson, Md., 1978-80; prof. U. South Fla., Tampa, 1980-83; practitioner psychiat. medicine, med. dir. St. Augustine (Fla.) Psychiat. Ctr., 1983-89, 89-90; prin. Williams & Assocs., Tampa, 1990—. Chief editor: Psychobiology of Depression, 1972, Mental Health in the 21st Century, 1979; contbr. numerous articles to profl. jours. and chpts. to books. Mem. Gov.'s Adv. Com. on Mental Health, Salt Lake City, 1971-77, Gov.'s Adv. Com. on Penal Code, Richmond, Va., 1978, Dist. Mental Health Bd., Tampa, 1980-83; sponsor, coach Forest Hills Little League Baseball, Tampa, 1980-83. Sr. surgeon USPHS, 1958-67. Recipient Predoctoral fellowship NIMH, 1960-61, Alumni Rsch. award N.Y. State Psychiat. Inst., 1964, Rush Bronze Medal award Am. Psychiat. Assn., 1973, Rsch. grants VA, 1971-77. Mem. AMA, Fla. Med. Assn., Hillsborough County Med. Assn., Columbia U. Alumni Club (dir. 1995—). Avocations: personal computing, classical music, opera, profl. basketball. Home: 831 S Delaware Ave Tampa FL 33606 Office: Williams & Assocs 831 S Delaware Ave Tampa FL 33606-2914

WILLIAMS, THOMAS FFRANCON, chemist, educator; b. Colwyn Bay, Wales, Jan. 30, 1928; came to U.S., 1961; s. David and Margaret (Williams) W.; m. Astra Silvia Birins, Jan. 31, 1959; children: Ifor Rainis, Gwyn David. B.Sc., Univ. Coll., London, Eng., 1949; Ph.D., U. London, 1960. Sci. officer U.K. Atomic Energy Authority, Harwell, Eng., 1949-55; sr. sci. officer U.K. Atomic Energy Authority, 1955-61, prin. sci. officer, 1961; research scientist Ill. Inst. Tech. Research Inst., Chgo., 1961; asst. prof. chemistry U. Tenn., Knoxville, 1961-63; assoc. prof. U. Tenn., 1963-67, prof., 1967—, Alumni Distinguished Service prof., 1974—; teaching, research assoc. Northwestern U., Evanston, Ill., 1957-58; NSF vis. scientist Kyoto (Japan) U., 1965-66; coordinator U.S.-Japan Sci. Sem., Hakone, Japan, 1969; chmn. Gordon Research Conf. on Radiation Chemistry, New Hampton, N.H., 1971, Gordon Research Conf. Radical Ions, Wolfeboro, N.H., 1984; John Simon Guggenheim Meml. Found. fellow, Swedish Research Councils' Lab., Studsvik, Nykoping, 1972-73; vis. scientist Royal Inst. Tech., Stockholm, Sweden, 1972-73; chmn. 10th Southeastern Magnetic Resonance Conf., 1978; mem. chemistry div. rev. com. Argonne (Ill.) Nat. Lab., 1988, 91, 95. Contbg. author: Fundamental Processes in Radiation Chemistry, 1968, Radiation Chemistry of Macromolecules, 1972; mem. editorial bd. Radiation Rsch., 1993-97; contbr. numerous articles on chem. effects of high energy radiation to profl. jours. AEC, ERDA, Dept. Energy grantee, 1962—. Mem. Am. Chem. Soc. (program chmn. sect. 1968-69, exec. com. 1986-88), Brit. Chem. Soc., Radiation Rsch. Soc., Phi Beta Kappa (hon.), Sigma Xi (pres. U. Tenn. chpt. 1993-94). Home: 3117 Montlake Dr Knoxville TN 37920-2836 Office: U Tenn Dept Of Chemistry Knoxville TN 37996

WILLIAMS, THOMAS FRANKLIN, architect; b. Atlanta, Aug. 14, 1944; s. George and Annie Grace (Stansell) Feckoury; m. Sandra Jean Harris Williams, July 12, 1966; children: Leigh Ann, Andrew Thomas. A in Engring., So. Tech. Coll., Marietta, Ga., 1966. Registered architect; cert. Nat. Coun. Archtl. Registration Bds. Architect Philip B. Windsor Co., Atlanta, 1964-75; v.p. Diedrich Architects & Assocs., Atlanta, 1976—. Trustee Christian City, Union City, Ga., 1992—. Served with U.S. Army, 1966-68.. Mem. AIA, Constrn. Specifications Inst. (Dan Bodin Meml. award Atlanta chpt. 1981, Citation S.E. Region 1980, Cert. of Appreciation Atlanta chpt. 1983). Avocations: hunting, fishing. Home: 6326 Saddlewood Dr Lithonia GA 30058-6122 Office: Diedrich Architects & Assocs Inc 3399 Peachtree Rd NE Ste 820 Atlanta GA 30326-1149

WILLIAMS, THOMAS FRANKLIN, physician, educator; b. Belmont, N.C., Nov. 26, 1921; s. T.F. and Mary L. (Deaton) W.; m. Catharine Carter Catlett, Dec. 15, 1951; children: Mary Wright, Thomas Nelson. BS, U. N.C., 1942; MA, Columbia U., 1943; MD, Harvard U., 1950; DSc (hon.), Med. Coll. Ohio, 1987, U. N.C., 1992. Diplomate Am. Bd. Internal Medicine. Intern Johns Hopkins, Balt., 1950-51; asst. resident physician Johns Hopkins, 1951-53; resident physician Boston VA Hosp., 1953-54; research fellow U. N.C., Chapel Hill, 1954-56; instr. dept. medicine and preventive medicine U. N.C., 1956-57, asst. prof., 1957-61, assoc. prof., 1961-68, prof., 1968; attending physician Strong Meml. Hosp., Rochester, N.Y., 1968—; cons. physician Genesee Hosp., Rochester, N.Y., 1973—, St. Mary's Hosp., Rochester, N.Y., 1974-83, Highland Hosp., Rochester, N.Y., 1973; prof. medicine, preventive medicine and community health U. Rochester, 1968-92, also prof. radiation biology and biophysics, 1968-91, on leave, 1983-91, prof. emeritus, 1992—; mem. adv. bd. U. Rochester (Sch. Medicine and Dentistry), 1968-83; clin. prof. medicine U. Va., 1983-89; lectr. medicine Johns Hopkins U., 1983-89; clin. prof. depts family medicine and medicine Georgetown U., 1983-89; dir. Nat. Inst. on Aging NIH, 1983-91; asst. surgeon gen. USPHS, 1983-91, ret., 1991; attending physician Monroe Community Hosp., Rochester, 1991—, vice chmn. Cmty. Coalition for Long Term Care, 1991—; disting. physician VA Med. Ctr., Canandigua, N.Y., 1995—; med. dir. Monroe Cmty. Hosp., Rochester, 1968-83; mem. rev. coms. Nat. Ctr. for Health Svcs. Rsch.; mem. adv. bd. St. Ann's Home; mem. gov. bd. NRC, 1981-83; sci. dir. Am Fedn. Aging Rsch., 1992—; bd. dirs. Kirkhaven, Nat. Coun. on Aging. Contbr. articles on endocrine disorders, diabetes, health care delivery in chronic illness and aging to profl. publs. Served with USNR, 1943-46. USPHS fellow, 1966-67; Markle scholar, 1957-61. Fellow Am. Pub. Health Assn., ACP; mem. AAAS, Inst. Medicine, NAS (coun. 1980-83, governing bd. 1981-83), Assn. Am. Physicians, N.Y. State Med. Soc., Monroe County Med. Soc., Am. Diabetes Assn. (bd. dir. 1974-80), Am. Fedn. Clin. Rsch., Soc. Exptl. Biology and Medicine, Am. Geriatrics Soc., Am. Gerontol. Soc., Rochester Regional Diabetes Assn. (pres. 1977-79), N.C. Coun. for Human Rels. (chmn. 1963-66), Am. Clin. Climatol. Assn. Episcopalian. Home: 287 Dartmouth St Rochester NY 14607-3202 Office: Monroe Community Hosp Office Med Dir Rochester NY 14620

WILLIAMS, THOMAS RAYMOND, lawyer; b. Meridian, Miss., Aug. 26, 1940. BS, U. Ala., 1962, LLB, 1964. Bar: Ala. 1964, Tex. 1979, U.S. Supreme Ct. 1980, D.C. 1983. Ptnr. McDermott, Will & Emery, Washington. Mem. D.C. Bar Assn., Ala. State Bar Assn., State Bar Tex. Office: McDermott Will & Emery 1850 K St NW Washington DC 20006-2213

WILLIAMS, THOMAS RHYS, educator, anthropologist; b. Martins Ferry, Ohio, June 13, 1928; s. Harold K. and Dorothy (Lehew) W.; m. Margaret Martin, July 12, 1952; children: Rhys M., Ian T., Tom R. B.A., Miami U., Oxford, Ohio, 1951; M.A., U. Ariz., 1956; Ph.D., Syracuse U., 1956. Asst. prof., asso. prof. anthropology Calif. State U., Sacramento, 1956-65; vis. asso. prof. anthropology U. Calif. Berkeley, 1962; vis. prof. anthropology Stanford U., 1976; prof. anthropology Ohio State U., Columbus, 1965-78; chmn. dept Ohio State U., 1967-71, mem. grad. council, 1969-72, mem. univ. athletic council, 1968-74, chmn. univ. athletic council, 1973-74, exec. com. Coll. Social and Behavior Scis., 1967-71; dean Grad. Sch. George Mason U., Fairfax, Va., 1978-81, prof. anthropology, 1981—; dir. Ctr. for Rsch. and Advanced Studies George Mason U., 1978-81, fed. liaison officer, 1978-81, chmn. faculty adv. bd. grad. degree program in conflict resolution, 1980-86. Author: The Dusun: A North Borneo Society, 1965, Field Methods in the Study of Culture, 1967, A Borneo Childhood: Enculturation in Dusun Society, 1969, Introduction to Socialization: Human Culture Transmitted, 1972, Socialization, 1983; editor, contbg. author: Psychological Anthropology, 1975, Socialization and Communication in Primary Groups, 1975, Cultural Anthropology, 1990; contbr. articles to profl. jours. Mem. United Democrats for Humphrey, 1968, Citizens for Humphrey, 1968. Served with USN, 1946-48. Research grantee NSF, 1958, 62, Am. Council Learned Socs.-Social Sci. Research Council, 1959, 63; Ford Found. S.E. Asia, 1974, 76; recipient Disting. Faculty award Calif. State U., Sacramento, 1961, George Mason U., 1983; Disting. Teaching awards Ohio State U., 1968, 76. Fellow Am. Anthrop. Assn., Royal Anthrop. Inst. Gt. Britain; assoc. mem. Current Anthropology; mem. AAAS, Sigma Xi. Office: George Mason U Robinson Hall B-315 4400 University Dr Fairfax VA 22030-4443

WILLIAMS, THRESIA WAYNE MATTHEWS, occupational health nurse; b. Moultrie, Ga., Oct. 20, 1945; d. James Wayne and Ola (Cone) Matthews; m. William Ensey Williams, Dec. 31, 1966; children: Darren Ensey, April Thresia Williams McIntosh. ADN, Abraham Baldwin Coll., Tifton, Ga., 1966. Nat. cert. occupls. health nurse, Ga.; specialist COHN-S. Supr. Floyd Med. Ctr., Rome, Ga., 1967-71, 74-75; instr. Coosa Valley Vocat. H.S., Rome, 1972-73; med. dept. supr. Riegel Textile Corp., Trion, Ga., 1975-78, CBS Records, Carrollton, Ga., 1980-83, Carriage Industries, Inc., Calhoun, Ga., 1984-94, Galey & Lord, Inc., Shannon, Ga., 1994—; specialist and spokesperson disaster health svcs. ARC, Rome, 1993—, chair disaster health svcs. cluster com., 1993—, mem. disaster action team, 1993—, vol. local, state and nat. disasters, 1991—, instr. HIV-AIDS, CPR/first aid, blood borne pathogens, freedom from smoking, 1996. Mem. Nat. Assn. Occupational Health Nurses, Am. Lung Assn., Ga. Assn. Occupational Health Nurses (scholarship com. 1991—, chair com. 1994—, dir. 1995, proctor Atlanta 1994, cert. facilitator freedom from smoking), N.W. Ga. Assn. Occupational Health Nurses (v.p. 1990-94, Ga. rep. 1993, 95, newsletter editor 1991-94), Jane Delano Soc. Methodist. Avocations: cross stitch, camping, backpacking, antique knife collecting, flower/herb gardening. Home: PO Box 86 208 Floyd Springs Rd Armuchee GA 30105 Office: Galey & Lord Inc PO Box 972 401 Burlington Dr Shannon GA 30172

WILLIAMS, THURMON, retail company executive. Pres. Mex. Corp. Sears. Office: Sears Roebuck & Co Sears Towers Chicago IL 60684*

WILLIAMS, TIMOTHY JAMES, sanctuary administrator, naturalist; b. Covington, Ky., Sept. 22, 1950; s. Carl Henry and Marcella Virginia (Neff) W.; m. Deborah Louise LeForce, Feb. 15, 1975. B.S. in Biology, No. Ky. State U., 1974. Waiter various restaurants in No. Ky.; park aide Mammoth Cave Nat. Park, 1971; sanctuary mgr. Nat. Audubon Soc.'s Clyde E. Buckley Wildlife Sanctuary, Frankfort, Ky., 1975—. Mem. Nat. Audubon Soc., Assn. of Interpretive Naturalists, Ky. Assn. Environ. Edn. (bd. dirs.).

WILLIAMS, TONDA, entrepreneur, consultant; b. N.Y.C., Nov. 21, 1949; d. William and Juanita (Rainey) W.; 1 child, Tywana. Student, Collegiate Inst., N.Y.C., 1975-78, C.W. Post Coll., 1981-83; BA in Bus. Mgmt., Am. Nat. U., Phoenix, 1983. Notary pub. N.Y. Asst. controller Acad. Ednl. Devel., N.Y.C., 1971-81; mgr. office Chapman-Apex Constrn. Co., Bayshore, N.Y., 1982-84; specialist computer RGM Liquid Waste Removal, Deerpark, N.Y., 1985-87; contr. LaMar Lighting Co., Freeport, N.Y., 1987—; owner, pres. Omni-Star, Bklyn., 1981—. Author: Tonda's Songs in Poetry, 1978, The Magic of Life, 1991; co-author: Computer Management of Liquid Waste Industry, 1986. Recipient Golden Poet award World of Poetry, 1992. Mem. Am. Mus. Natural History, Am. Soc. Notary Pubs. Avocations: bowling, chess, singing. Home: 74 Cedar Dr Bay Shore NY 11706-2419

WILLIAMS, TONY, jazz drummer; b. Chgo., Dec. 12, 1945. Played with Sam Rivers, Boston, Jackie McLean, N.Y.C., 1962, mem. Miles Davis quintet, 1963-69, founder group Lifetime (with John McLaughlin and Larry Young), re-formed Lifetime (with Miles Davis), 1975; albums include: Nefertiti, Believe It, Emergency, Turn It Over, Ego, Million Dollar Legs, The Joy of Flying, Foreign Intrigue, Old Burn's Rush, Miles Smiles, Sorcerer, Nefertiti, Civilization, 1987, Angel Street, 1988, Native Heart, 1990; albums include (with Gil Evans) There Comes a Time, Spring, 1985, Tokyo Live, 1993.

WILLIAMS, TREAT (RICHARD TREAT WILLIAMS), actor; b. Stamford, Conn., Dec. 1, 1951; s. Richard Norman and Marian (Andrew) W. BA, Franklin and Marshall Coll., 1973. Appeared in Broadway plays Over There, Grease; films include Deadly Hero, Eagle Has Landed, Hair, 1941, 1978, Why Would I Lie, 1979, Pursuit, 1980, Prince of the City, 1980, Once Upon a Time in America, 1982, Flashpoint, 1984, Men's Club, 1985, Sweet Lies 1986, Smooth Talk, 1986, The Heart of Dixie, 1989, Russicum, 1989, Where the Rivers Run North, 1994; repertory plays Servant of Two Masters, Ohio, Claptrap, Cambridge, Mass., 1985, Pirates of Penzance at N.Y. Shakespeare Festival, Glass Menagerie, Long Wharf, New Haven, 1986, Bobby Gould in Hell, 1989; TV movies Jack Dempsey Story, 1982, Streetcar Named Desire, 1983, Some Men Need Help, 1983, Hoover, Sweet Lies, 1986, Things To Do in Denver When You're Dead, 1995; TV appearances Faerie Tale Theatre, 1984, Men's Club, 1985, Third Degree Burn, 1989, Max and Helen, 1990, Drug Wars: The Enrico Camerena Story, 1990, Bonds of Love, 1993, Eddie Dodd, 1992; TV series include Good Advice, 1993-94. Mem. AFTRA, SAG, Actors Equity Assn. Episcopalian. Office: UTA 9560 Wilshire Blvd 5th Fl Beverly Hills CA 90212*

WILLIAMS, TRUDY ANNE, English language educator, college administrator; b. Winnipeg, Man., Can., Mar. 4, 1946; d. Herbert Francis and Melita French (Russell) Sly; m. Harry G. Williams, June 17, 1980; 1 child, David Langdon Jr. BA, U. Southwestern La., 1969, MA, 1970. Teaching asst. U. Southwestern La., Lafayette, 1968-72; instr. Gaston Coll., Dallas, N.C., 1980-83; asst. prof. English, St. Petersburg (Fla.) Jr. Coll., 1983—, also acting program dir., comm., program dir. acad. svcs.; program dir. acad. svcs. St. Petersburg (Fla.) Jr. Coll., Tarpon Springs Campus; adj. prof., cons. St. James Sch. Theology, Tarpon Springs, Fla., 1992—. Founding mem. Episcopal Synod of Am.; dir. Christian edn. St. Anne of Grace Episcopal Ch., Seminole, Fla. Mem. MLA, Nat. Coun. Tchrs. English, Southeastern Conf. on English in 2-Yr. Colls., Fla. Assn. Community Colls., Fla. Devel. Edn. Assn., Fla. Coll. English Assn., Pinellas County Tchrs. of English, South Atlantic Modern Lang. Assn., Fla. Coun. Instructional Affairs. Home: 8021 Bayhaven Dr Largo FL 34646-3320

WILLIAMS, UNA JOYCE, psychiatric social worker; b. Youngstown, Ohio, June 24, 1934; d. Samuel Wilfred and Frances Josephine (Woods) Ellis; children: Wendy Louise, Christopher Ellis, Sharon Elizabeth. BA, U. Ala., 1957; MSW, Adelphi U., 1963. Diplomate CSW, Am. Bd. Examiners in Clin. Social Work, Internat. Acad. Behavioral Medicine, Counseling, Psychotherapy. Dir. Huntington Program for Sr. Citizens; psychiat. social worker-supr. N.Y. State Dept. Mental Hygiene, Suffolk Psychiat. Hosp., Central Islip; info.-referral counselor Mental Health Assn. Nassau County, Hempstead, N.Y.; therapist Madonna Heights Family Clinic, Dix Hills, N.Y.; med. and psychiat. social worker Northport (N.Y.) VA Med. Ctr., psychiat. social worker acute psychiat. treatment svs.; med. social worker dialysis svcs. Northport (N.Y.) Va. Med. Ctr.; cons. on programs for aging Luth. Social Svcs. Mt. N.Y., 1959, sr. citizens cons. Port Jefferson-L.I. Bd. Edn., 1963. Chmn. Huntington Twp. Com. Human Rels., 1970; sec. bd. trustess Unitarian Universalist Fellowship Huntington, 1984. Named Mem. of Yr. Germany Philetelic Soc. Mem. NASW (cert., diplomte), Am. Assn. Family Counselors and Mediators, Germany Philetelic Soc. (pres. chpt. 30, 1990). Avocations: oil painting, stamp collecting, music (voice & piano), family geneology. Home: 316 Lenox Rd Huntington Station NY 11746-2640

WILLIAMS, VANESSA, recording artist, actress; b. Millwood, N.Y., 1963; m. Ramon Hervey II, 1988; children: Melanie, Jillian, Devin. Recording artist, 1988—. Stage appearances include: (Broadway) Kiss of the Spider Woman, 1994; film appearances include Another You, 1991, Harley Davidson and the Marlboro Man, 1991, The Drop Squad, 1994; albums: The Right Stuff, 1988, The Comfort Zone, 1991, The Sweetest Days, 1994; # 1 hit single Save the Best for Last. Recipient 8 Grammy award nominations; named one of 50 Most Beautiful People, People Mag. First Black to be named Miss America, 1983 (resigned title 1983). Office: Polygram Records Worldwide Plaza 825 8th Ave New York NY 10019-7416

WILLIAMS, VAUGHN CHARLES, lawyer; b. L.A., Mar. 2, 1945; s. David Welford and Ovida M. (White) W.; m. Joan M. Maddox, May 1, 1971 (div. June 1975). AB, Harvard U., 1966; JD, Stanford U., 1967. Bar: Calif. 1969, Washington 1971, N.Y. 1977, U.S. Supreme Ct. 1981. Law clk. to Hon. Carl McGowan U.S. Ct. of Appeals (D.C. cir.), Washington, 1969-70; counsel U.S. Senate, Dist. Col. Comm., Washington, 1970-71; assoc. Wilmer Cutler & Pickering, Washington, 1971-74; gen. counsel U.S. Coun. on Wage-Price Stability, Washington, 1975-76; assoc. Skadden Arps Slate Meagher & Flom, N.Y.C., 1977-79, ptnr., 1979—; dir. N.Y.C. Campaign Fin. Bd. Dir. Lincoln Ctr. for Performing Arts, N.Y.C., Bklyn. Acad. Music; vice chmn. Fund for the City of N.Y. Mem. Assn. Bar of City of N.Y. (Bainbridge-Smith com., com. for future), University Club. Office: Skadden Arps Slate Meagher & Flom 919 3rd Ave New York NY 10022*

WILLIAMS, VERGIL LEWIS, criminal justice educator; b. Crosbyton, Tex., Sept. 29, 1935; s. Albert Lewis W. and Neola Belle (Bass) Pinkston; m. Vergnel Campbell, June 8, 1956 (div. 1967); 1 son, Delwin Victor; m. Velma Arlene Minor, Dec. 23, 1974; 1 stepdau., Colleen Angela Jeffries. B.A. in Econs., West Tex. State J., 1966; Ph.D. in Bus. Adminstrn., U. Ala.-Tuscaloosa, 1972. Patrolman Amarillo Police Dept., Tex., 1960-64, police patrol sgt., 1964-66; instr. fin. U. Ala., University, 1968-71, asst. prof. Sch. Social Work, 1971-75, assoc. prof., 1975-77, prof., chmn. dept. criminal justice, 1977—; rsch. cons. Police Dept., Birmingham, Ala., 1977-79. Co-author: Convicts, Codes and Contraband, 1974, Introduction Criminal Justice, 1982; author: Dictionary American Penology, 1979 (Outstanding Reference Book ALA 1979). Mem. Ala. Assn. Criminal Justice Educators (pres. 1981-82), Nat. Assn. Vols. in Criminal Justice (bd. gids. 1983—). Bahai. Home: 2633 47th Ave E Tuscaloosa AL 35404-5234 Office: Dept Criminal Justice U Ala PO Box 870320 Tuscaloosa AL 35487-0320

WILLIAMS, VICKI, mortgage company executive; b. 1949. With Colonial Mortgage, Montgomery, Ala., 1970-76, Bank Boston, Montgomery, 1976-83, Window Fashions, Montgomery, 1983-84, Aronov Realty, Montgomery, 1984-86, Century Mortgage, Montgomery, 1986-88; with Anchor Mortgage Svcs Inc, Montgomery, 1988—, pres. Office: Anchor Mortgage Svcs Inc 4260 Carmichael Ct N Montgomery AL 36106-2874*

WILLIAMS, W. CLYDE, religious organization administrator. Exec. sec. Christian Meth. Episcopal Ch., Atlanta, 1987—. Office: Christian Meth Episcopal Ch 2805 Shoreland Dr SW Atlanta GA 30331-6714 Office: 201 Ashby St NW Ste 212 Atlanta GA 30314-3422

WILLIAMS, WALTER BAKER, mortgage banker; b. Seattle, May 12, 1921; s. William Walter and Anna Leland (Baker) W.; m. Marie Davis Wilson, July 6, 1945; children: Kathryn Williams-Mullins, Marcia Frances Williams Swanson, Bruce Wilson, Wendy Susan. BA, U. Wash., 1943; JD, Harvard U., 1948. With Bogle & Gates, Seattle, 1948-63, ptnr., 1960-63; pres. Continental Inc., Seattle, 1963-91, chmn., 1991—; bd. dirs. United Graphics Inc., Seattle, 1973-86, Fed. Nat. Mortgage Assn., 1976-77; chmn. Continental Savings Bank, 1991—. Rep. Wash. State Ho. of Reps., Olympia, 1961-63; sen. Wash. State Senate, Olympia, 1963-71; chmn. Econ. Devel. Council of Puget Sound, Seattle, 1981-82; pres. Japan-Am. Soc. of Seattle, 1971-72; chmn. Woodland Park Zoo Commn., Seattle, 1984-85. Served to capt. USMC, 1942-46, PTO. Recipient Brotherhood Citation, NCCJ, Seattle, 1980. Mem. Mortgage Bankers Assn. Am. (pres. 1973-74), Wash. Mortgage Bankers Assn., Fed. Home Loan Mortgage Corp. (adv. com.), Wash. Savs. League (bd. dirs., chmn. 1991-92), Rotary (pres. local club 1984-85), Rainier Club Seattle (pres. 1987-88). Republican. Congregationalist. Office: Continental Inc 2000 Two Union Sq Seattle WA 98101

WILLIAMS, WALTER DAVID, aerospace executive, consultant; b. Chgo., July 22, 1931; s. Walter William and Theresa Barbara (Gilman) W.; m. Joan Haven Armstrong, Oct. 22, 1960; children: Latham Lloyd, Clayton Chapell, William Haven. BS, Ohio U., 1951; MBA, Harvard U., 1955; MS, MIT, 1972. Supr. fin. policy and systems Hughes Aircraft Co., Culver City, Calif., 1955-57; staff mem. Rand Corp. and SDC, Santa Monica, Calif., 1957-60; mgr. adminstrn. and fin. Microwave Div. TRW Inc., Canoga Park, Calif., 1960-63; exec. asst. Space Labs. Northrop Corp., Hawthorne, Calif., 1963-66; fin. mgr. comml. group Aircraft Div. Northrop Corp., Hawthorne, Calif., 1966-72; dir. internat. plans Northrop Corp., L.A., 1972-74, dir. internat. mkt. devel., 1974-77, exec. dir. internat., 1977-93; pres. Williams Internat. Assocs., L.A., 1994—; export advisor U.S. Sec. Commerce, Washington, 1986—. Author (study/lect. series) Internat. Def. Mktg., 1982. Dir. KCET Men's Coun., L.A., 1970; pres. Westwood Rep. Club, L.A., 1970; assoc. mem. Rep. State Ctrl. Com., Calif., 1968; div. chmn. Rep. Ctrl. Com., L.A. County, 1968. Served to capt. U.S. Army, 1951-53. Recipient fellowship Alfred P. Sloan Found., 1971-72. Mem. AIAA, Soc. Sloan Fellows, MIT Club, Harvard Bus. Sch. Assn., Newcomen Soc., Chaine des Rotisseurs, L.A. Country Club, Harvard Club, Soc. Bacchus Am., Delta Sigma Pi. Avocations: golf, tennis, paddle tennis. Office: Williams Internat Assocs PO Box 491178 Los Angeles CA 90049-9178

WILLIAMS, WALTER FRED, steel company executive; b. Upland, Pa., Feb. 7, 1929; s. Walter James and Florence (Stott) W.; m. Joan B. Carey, Aug. 26, 1950; children: Jeffrey F., Richard C., Douglas E. B. in Civil Engring. summa cum laude, U. Del., 1951; postgrad., Harvard, 1969; D (hon.), Allentown Coll., 1983, Leigh U., 1990. With Bethlehem Steel Corp., Pa., 1951—, asst. chief engr. on staff v.p. operations, 1965-66, chief engr. constrn., 1966-67, chief engr. projects group engring. dept., then mgr. engring. in charge projects, design and constrn., 1967-68, asst. to v.p. engring., 1968, asst. v.p. shipbldg., 1968-70, v.p. shipbldg., 1970-75, v.p. steel operations, 1975-77, sr. v.p. steel operations, 1978-80, pres., chief operating officer, 1980-85, chmn., chief exec. officer, 1986-92, also dir.; bd. dirs. Gen. Re Corp., Wilmington Trust of Fla. 1st lt. U.S. Army, 1951-53. Mem. Bus. Coun., Saucon Valley Country Club, Hobe Sound Golf Club. Methodist.

WILLIAMS, WALTER JACKSON, JR., electrical engineer, consultant; b. Elkhart, Ind., Jan. 17, 1925; s. Walter Jackson and Mary (Delcamp) W.; m. Helen L. Evans, July 20, 1944 (dec. Aug. 1980); children: David, Eileen, Valerie; m. Evelyn M. Bowyer, May 26, 1984 (dec. Oct. 1990); m. Margaret M. McLaughlin, Aug. 26, 1995. BSEE, Purdue U., 1948, MS, 1950; PhD, 1954. From grad. asst. to instr. Purdue U., Layfayette, Ind., 1948-54; jr. engr. Argonne (Ill.) Nat. Lab., Ill., 1950, Naval Ordnance Plant, Indpls., 1951; engr. Internat. Tel. & Tel. Co., Ft. Wayne, Ind., 1954-60, cons., 1961-63, sr. tech. advisor Aerospace Optical divsn., 1975-80, tech. dir., 1980-87, ret., 1987, cons., 1987—; chmn. dept. elec. engring. Ind. Inst. Tech., Ft. Wayne, 1961-65, dean engring., 1963-67, v.p., acad. dean, 1967-75, interim pres., 1970-72; cons. in field, 1960—. Patentee in field. Bd. dirs. Assoc. Chs., Ft. Wayne, 1965-67. With AUS, 1943-46. Mem. IEEE (mem. com. on accreditation activities com. 1984-89), NSPE, Am. Soc. Engring. Edn., Accreditation Bd. for Engring. and Tech. (mem. engring. accreditation commn. 1990-95), Ind. Soc. Profl. Engrs. (bd. dirs. Ft. Wayne chpt. 1968-70), Ft. Wayne Engrs. Club (pres. 1967-68, bd. dirs. 1969-71), Sigma Xi, Tau Beta Pi, Eta Kappa Nu. Home: 8707 Stellhorn Rd Fort Wayne IN 46815

WILLIAMS, WALTER JOSEPH, lawyer; b. Detroit, Oct. 5, 1918; s. Joseph Louis and Emma Geraldine (Hewitt) W.; m. Maureen June Kay, Jan. 15, 1944; 1 child, John Bryan. Student, Bowling Green State U., 1935-36; B.S.B.A., Ohio State U., 1940; J.D., LL.B., U. Detroit, 1942. Bar: Mich. bar 1942. Title atty. Abstract & Title Guaranty Co., 1946-47; corp. atty. Ford Motor Co., 1947-51, Studebaker-Packard Corp., 1951-56; asst. sec., house counsel Am. Motors Corp., Am. Motors Sales Corp., Am. Motors Pan-Am. Corp., Evart Products Co., Ltd., 1956-65, corp. sec. house counsel, 1965-72; asst. corp. sec., dir. Am. Motors (Can.) Ltd.; dir. Evart Products Co., 1959-72; dir., corporate sec., house counsel Jeep Corp., Jeep Sales Corp., Jeep Internat. Corp., 1968-72; partner Gilman and Williams, Southfield, Mich., 1972-74; atty. Detroit Edison Co., 1974-75; asst. sec., sr. staff atty. Burroughs Corp. (and subsidiaries), 1975-84; pvt. practice, pres. Walter J. Williams P.C., Bloomfield Hills, Mich., 1984—. Charter commr., city of Dearborn Heights, Mich., 1960-63; dir. Detroit Met. Indsl. Devel. Corp., 1962-72, also asst. sec. Served to capt. U.S. Army, 1942-46. Mem. ABA, Detroit Bar Assn. (chmn. corp. gen. counsel com. 1965-68), Fed. Bar Assn., State Bar Mich., Ohio State U. Alumni Assn. (pres. Detroit 1961-63), U. Detroit Law Alumni, Delta Theta Phi. Club: Oakland Hills Country. Home and Office: 3644 Darcy Dr Bloomfield Hills MI 48301-2125

WILLIAMS, WALTER WAYLON, lawyer, pecan grower; b. Gause, Tex., Nov. 12, 1933; s. Jesse Nathaniel and Lola Fay (Matthews) W.; m. Velmalene Von Gonten, Mar. 6, 1953; children—Diana Lee, Virginia Marie. B.B.A. with honors, U. Tex., 1959, J.D. with honors, 1960. Bar: Tex. bar 1960. Since practiced in Houston; mem. firm Fulbright, Crooker, Freeman, Bates & Jaworski, 1960-63, Bates & Brock, 1964-66, Brock, Williams & Boyd, 1966-79, Williams & Boyd, 1979-88; pres. Nat. Pecan Growers Coun., 1976-78, Tex. Pecan Growers Assn., 1976-78. Served with AUS, 1953-55. Named Outstanding Soldier of Second Army, 1955. Mem. ABA, Houston Bar Assn., State Bar Tex., Tex. Trial Lawyers Assn. (dir. 1972-76), Houston Trial Lawyers Assn. (dir. 1969), Assn. Trial Lawyers Am., Chancellors, Beta Gamma Sigma, Phi Delta Phi. Home: RR 3 Box 101 Yoakum TX 77995-9711

WILLIAMS, WAYNE DE ARMOND, lawyer; b. Denver, Sept. 24, 1914; s. Wayne Cullen and Lena Belle (Day) W.; m. Virginia Brinton Deal, Sept. 9, 1937; children: Marcia Lee, Daniel Deal; m. Thelma Ralston, Apr. 8, 1995. A.B., U. Denver, 1936; J.D., Columbia U., 1938. Bar: Colo. 1938. Pvt. practice Denver, 1938-43, 46-58; ptnr. firm Williams & Erickson (and predecessors), Denver, 1958-77; gen. counsel Denver Water Dept., 1977-91; asst. city atty. Denver, 1939-43, spl. asst. city atty., 1946-49; chmn. Denver County Ct. Nominating Commn., 1968-69; mem. Denver Dist. Ct. Nominating Commn., 1969-75; lectr. in field U. Denver, 1947-60. Contbr. articles to legal jours. Chmn. Denver Mcpl. Airport Adv. Commn., 1963-65; chancellor Rocky Mountain Meth. Ann. Conf., 1978-86; former mem. governing bd. Colo. chpt. English Speaking Union, Colo. Tuberculosis Assn., Colo. Soc. for Prevention Blindness; mem. adv. bd. Anchor Ctr. for Blind Children. Capt. JAGD U.S. Army, 1943-46. Mem. ABA (Ross Essay prize 1944), Colo. Bar Assn. (gov. 1974-77), Denver Bar Assn. (pres. 1974-75), Sigma Alpha Epsilon, Phi Delta Phi, Omicron Delta Kappa. Democrat. Methodist. Clubs: Lions, Masons. Home: 625 S Alton Way Apt 3A Denver CO 80231-1752

WILLIAMS, WESLEY SAMUEL, JR., lawyer; b. Phila., Nov. 13, 1942; s. Wesley Samuel and Bathrus Amanda (Bailey) W.; m. Karen Roberta Hastie, Aug. 17, 1968; children: Amanda Pedersen, Wesley Hastie, Bailey Lockhart. BA in French Lit. magna cum laude, Harvard U., 1963, JD, 1967; MA (Woodrow Wilson fellow), Fletcher Sch. Law and Diplomacy, 1964; LLM, Columbia U., 1969. Bar: D.C., U.S. Supreme Ct., N.Y. Spl. counsel D.C. City Council, 1967-69; assoc.-in-law Columbia U. Law Sch., 1968-69; legal counsel Com. on D.C. U.S. Senate, 1969-70; assoc. Covington & Burling, Washington, 1970-75, ptnr., 1975—; trustee Penn Mut. Life Ins. Co., Phila., 1978—; bd. dirs. Broadcast Capital Cos., 1979-92, chmn., 1989-92, Carr Realty, Co., Inc., 1993—; mem. Pres.'s U.S. Circuit Judge Nominating Commn., 1977-80; gen. counsel D.C. Bar, 1979-81; adj. prof. Georgetown U. Law Sch., 1971-73; mem. exec. com. Washington Lawyers Com. Civil Rights Under Law, 1972—; mem. editorial bd. D.C. Real Estate Reporter; vice chmn., bd. dirs. Lockhart Cos., St. Thomas, U.S. Virgin Islands, 1987—, co-chief exec. officer, 1989—; vice chmn., bd. dirs. Blackstar Communications, Cos., 1987—. Author legal articles, texts. Pres. bd. trustee Nat. Child Rsch. Ctr., 1980-82; bd. overseers Harvard U., 1985-91, chmn. vis. com. Harvard U. Div. Sch., 1986-91; bd. dirs. World Affairs Coun. Washington, D.C., Inc., 1980—, Nat. Symphony Orch. Assn., 1977-92; bd. dirs. Family and Child Svcs. Washington, 1970—, pres., 1973-76; exec. com. community adv. com. Jr. League Washington, 1977-86; pres. standing com. Episc. Diocese of Washington, 1983-88; sec. bd. trustees Protestant Episc. Cathedral Found., 1982-90; bd. regents Smithsonian Inst., 1993—. Fellow Am. Bar Found.; mem. ABA, Am. Law Inst., Nat. Bar Assn., Fed. Bar Assn., D.C. Bar Assn., Washington Bar Assn., Harvard Law Sch. Assn. (pres.), Order Hosp. St. John Jerusalem, Harvard Club, City Tavern Club, Met. Club, Chevy Chase Club, Univ. Club, Alpha Phi Alpha, Sigma Pi Phi. Office: Covington & Burling PO Box 7566 1201 Pennsylvania Ave NW Washington DC 20044

WILLIAMS, WILLIAM ARNOLD, agronomy educator; b. Johnson City, N.Y., Aug. 2, 1922; s. William Truesdall and Nellie Viola (Tompkins) W.; m. Madeline Patricia Moore, Nov. 27, 1943; children—David, Kathleen, Andrew. B.S., Cornell U., 1947, M.S., 1948, Ph.D., 1951. Prof. emeritus U. Calif., Davis, 1993—. Editor agr. sect. McGraw-Hill Ency. Sci. & Tech.; contbr. articles to profl. jours. Mem. Nat. Alliance for Mentally Ill. Served to lt. U.S. Army, 1943-46. Grantee NSF, 1965-82, Kellogg Found., 1963-67; Fulbright scholar, Australia, 1960, Rockefeller Found. scholar, Costa Rica, 1966. Fellow AAAS, Am. Soc. Agronomy, Crop Sci. Soc. Am.; mem. Soil Sci. Soc. Am., Soc. Range Mgmt., Am. Statis. Assn., Assn. for Tropical Biology, Fedn. Am. Scientists, Am. Math. Soc., Math Assn. Am. Democrat. Home: 718 Oeste Dr Davis CA 95616-3531 Office: Univ California Dept Agronomy And Rang Davis CA 95616

WILLIAMS, WILLIAM COREY, Old Testament educator, consultant; b. Wilkes-Barre, Pa., July 12, 1937; s. Edward Douglas and Elizabeth Irene (Schooley) W.; m. Alma Simmenroth Williams, June 27, 1959; 1 child, Linda. Diploma in Ministerial Studies, NE Bible Inst., 1962; BA in Bibl. Studies, Cen. Bible Coll., 1963, MA in Religion, 1964; MA in Hebrew and Near Ea. Studies, NYU, 1966, PhD in Hebrew Lang. and Lit., 1975; postgrad., Hebrew U., 1977-78, Inst. Holyland Studies, 1986. Ref. libr. Hebraic section Libr. of Congress, Washington, 1967-69; prof. Old Testament So. Calif. Coll., Costa Mesa, 1969—; adj. prof. Old Testament Melodyland Sch. Theology, Anaheim, Calif., 1975-77; vis. prof. Old Testament Fuller Theol. Sem., Pasadena, Calif., 1978-81, 84, Asian Theol. Ctr. for Evangelism and Missions, Singapore and Sabah, E. Malaysia, 1985, Continental Bible Coll., Saint Pieters-Leeuw, Belgium, 1985, Mattersey Bible Coll., Eng., 1985, Inst. Holy Land Studies, Jerusalem, 1986, Regent U., 1994; transl. cons. and reviser New Am. Std. Bible, 1969-94; transl. cons. The New Internat. Version, 1975-76, New Century Version, 1991, A New Translation, 1992—, New Internat. Version, Reader's Version, 1993-94; transl. cons. and editor Internat. Children's Version, 1985-86. Author: (books, tapes) Hebrew I: A Study Guide, 1986, Hebrew II: A Study Guide, 1986; transl. editor: Everyday Bible, 1990; contbr. articles to International Standard Bible Encyclopedia, New International Dictionary of Old Testment Theology and Evangelical Dictionary of Biblical Theology; contbr. articles to profl. jours.; contbr. notes to Spirit Filled Life Study Bible. Nat. Def. Fgn. Lang. fellow NYU, 1964-67; Alumni scholar N.E. Bible Inst., 1960-61; NEH fellow, summer 1992. Mem. Soc. Bibl. Lit., Evang. Theol. Soc. (exec. office 1974-77), Am. Acad. Religion, Nat. Assn. Profs. of Hebrew, Inst. Bibl. Rsch., The Lockman Found. (hon. mem. bd. dirs. 1992-94, mem. editorial bd. 1974-94). Home: 1817 Peninsula Pl Costa Mesa CA 92627-4591 Office: So Calif Coll 55 Fair Dr Costa Mesa CA 92626-6520

WILLIAMS, WILLIAM H., food products executive, retail executive; b. 1948. BS, Okla. State U., 1970. Pres., CEO Neiman-Marcus Inc., Dallas, 1970-88; pres. Bear Creek Corp., Medford, Oreg., 1988—; pres., CEO Harry & David Co., Medford, Jackson & Perkins Co., Medford. Office: Bear Creek Corp 2518 S Pacific Hwy Medford OR 97501-8724*

WILLIAMS, WILLIAM HARRISON, retired librarian; b. Seattle, Apr. 18, 1924; s. William E. and Letah M. (Hollenback) W.; m. Mary Helen Sims, Apr. 19, 1945; children: Linda Lee, Dee Ann. B.S., Brigham Young U., 1969, M.L.S., 1970. Dir. Provo Pub. Library, Utah, 1969-70; Wyo. State Librarian, 1970-78; dir. Wyo. state Archives and Hist. dept., 1971-78; exec. sec. Wyo. Hist. Soc., 1971-78; sr. research analyst Wyo. Taxpayers Assn., 1978-84. Served to lt. col. USAAF, 1943-64. Decorated USAF commendation with oak leaf cluster. Mem. Beta Phi Mu, Phi Alpha Theta. Home: 21607 N 123rd Dr Sun City West AZ 85375-1950

WILLIAMS, WILLIAM JOHN, JR., lawyer; b. New Rochelle, N.Y., Feb. 6, 1937; s. William John and Jane (Gormley) W.; m. Barbara Reuter. BA, Holy Cross Coll., Worcester, Mass., 1958; LLB, NYU, 1961. Bar: N.Y. 1961. Practiced in N.Y.C., 1962—; ptnr. firm Sullivan & Cromwell, 1969—. Trustee NYU Law Sch. Found., 1977—, Holy Cross Coll., 1988—. Fellow Am. Bar Found.; mem. ABA, Am. Law Inst., N.Y. State Bar Assn., Assn. of Bar of City of N.Y., U.S. Golf Assn. (mem. exec. com. 1978-87, sec. 1980-81, v.p. 1982-85, pres. 1986-87). Democrat. Roman Catholic.

WILLIAMS, WILLIAM JOSEPH, insurance company executive; b. Cin., Dec. 19, 1915; s. Charles Finn and Elizabeth (Ryan) W.; m. Helen DeCourcy, May 26, 1941; children—Mary Frances Williams Clauder, William Joseph, Richard Francis, Carol Ann Williams Jodar, Sharon Mary Williams Frisbie, Thomas Luke. AB, Georgetown U., 1937; postgrad. in bus., Harvard U., 1938. With Western-So. Life Ins. Co., Cin., 1939-54, chmn. bd., 1979-84, pres., chief operating officer, 1984-88; pres., chief exec. officer, 1988-89, chmn. bd., pres., chief exec. officer, 1989, chmn. bd., chief exec. officer, 1989—; bd. dirs. Western-So. Life Ins. Co., Cin.; pres. N.Am. Mgmt. & Devel. Co., Cin., 1954-84; chmn. Cin. Reds Baseball Club, 1966-85; dir. Cin. Bengals, Columbus Life Ins., Ohio. Chmn. bd. Good Samaritan Hosp., Cin., 1984-86, Taft Mus., Cin., 1984-87; trustee, v.p. Cin. Art Mus.; trustee Cin. Inst. Fine Arts; bd. dirs. Georgetown U. Served to capt. U.S. Army, 1941-45. Decorated knight Order Knights of Malta, knight comdr. Holy Sepulchre; honored by NCCJ, 1979. Roman Catholic. Clubs: Queen City (pres. 1982-84), Commercial (pres. 1983), Cin. Country (Cin.); Camargo; Royal Poinciana Golf (Naples, Fla.). Home: 7801 Ayers Rd Cincinnati OH 45255-4610 Office: Western & So Life Ins Co 400 Broadway St Cincinnati OH 45202-3312*

WILLIAMS, WILLIAM JOSEPH, physician, educator; b. Bridgeton, N.J., Dec. 8, 1926; s. Edward Carlaw and Mary Hood (English) W.; m. Margaret Myrick Lyman, Aug. 12, 1950 (dec. Aug., 1985) ; children: Susan Lyman, William Prescott, Sarah Robb; m. Karen A. Hughes, Feb. 18, 1989. Student, Bucknell U., 1943-45; MD, U. Pa., 1949. Diplomate: Am. Bd. Internal Medicine. (hematology com. 1976-80). Intern U. Pa., 1949-50, Am. Cancer Soc. research fellow in Biochemistry, 1950-52, resident medicine, 1954-55, assoc. to asst. prof. medicine, 1955-58, assoc. prof. to prof. medicine, chief hematology, 1961-69; sr. instr. microbiology Case Western Res. U., 1952; asst. prof. medicine Washington U., St. Louis, 1959-60; research fellow Oxford U., Eng., 1960-61; mem. hematology tng. com. Nat. Inst. Arthritis and Metabolic Disease, 1964-68, research career program com., 1968-72; chmn. dept. medicine SUNY Health Sci. Ctr., Syracuse, N.Y., 1969-92, prof. medicine, 1969—; interim dean Coll. Medicine SUNY Health Sci. Ctr., Syracuse, 1991-92; vis. scientist Walter and Eliza Hall Inst., Melbourne, Australia, 1980; vis. prof. Monash U., Melbourne, 1980; mem. thrombosis adv. com. Nat. Heart and Lung Inst., 1969-73, chmn., 1971-73; adv. coun. Nat. Arthritis, Metabolism and Digestive Diseases, 1975-79; mem. residency rev. com. internal medicine Accreditation Coun. Grad. Med. Edn., 1983-89, mem. bd. appeals panel for internal medicine, 1989—; mem. N.Y. State Coun. Grad. Med. Edn., 1987-89. Editor-in-chief: Hematology, 1972, 4th edit., 1989, Williams Hematology Companion Handbook, 1996; contbr. articles to med. lit. Trustee Everson Mus. Art, 1975-81, 83-89. With USNR, 1944-46, 52-54. Recipient Research Career Devel. award Nat. Heart Inst., 1963-68; Daland fellow Am. Philos. Soc., 1955-57; Markle scholar, 1957-62. Mem. AMA, ACP (gov. Upstate N.Y. 1976-81), Am. Soc. Biol. Chemists, Am. Soc. Clin. Investigation, Assn. Am. Physicians, Am. Clin. and Climatol. Assn., Am. Heart Assn. (council on thrombosis exec. com. 1977-81), Internat. Soc. Thrombosis and Haemostasis, Assn. Profs. Medicine, Am. Soc. Hematology, Interurban Clin. Club (sec. 1964-70), Internat. Hematology Soc., Alpha Omega Alpha. Mem. Soc. Friends. Home: 5160 Peck Hill Rd Jamesville NY 13078-9724 Office: 750 E Adams St Syracuse NY 13210-2306

WILLIAMS, WILLIAM LANE, university administrator, anatomist; b. Rock Hill, S.C., Dec. 23, 1914; s. Oscar Kell and Cora Robertson (Mobley) W. B.S., Wofford Coll., 1935; M.A., Duke U., 1939; Ph.D., Yale U., 1941. Instr. anatomy U. Rochester, N.Y., 1941-42, Yale U., 1942-43; asst. prof. anatomy La. State U., New Orleans, 1943-45; asst. prof. U. Minn., Mpls., 1945-49; asso. prof. U. Minn., 1949-58; prof. U. Miss. Med. Center, Jackson, 1958-80; chmn. dept. anatomy U. Miss. Med. Center, 1958-79, asst. vice chancellor, 1975-80, emeritus, 1980—. Asso. editor: Anat. Record, 1959-75. Donner Found. fellow, 1942-43; NIH grantee, 1949-73. Mem. Am. Assn. Pathologists, Am. Physiol. Soc., Endocrine Soc., Histochem. Soc., Soc. Exptl. Biology and Medicine, Inst. Nutrition, Am. Assn. Anatomists. Presbyterian. Home: 3975 I55N Apt J2 Jackson MS 39216

WILLIAMS, WILLIAM MAGAVERN, headmaster; b. Niles, Mich., Dec. 22, 1931; s. Errol Edwin and Mary Elizabeth (Magavern) W.; m. Linda Carol Grush, June 15, 1958; children: Diana, William Jr., Sarah. BA, Williams Coll., 1953, LHD (hon.), 1984; postgrad. in Philosophy, Columbia U., 1954-58, MA in Ednl. Psychology, 1966. Tchr. elem. English, history, phys. edn. McTernan Sch., Waterbury, Conn., 1953-54; head guidance, boarding, and humanities depts., instr. English, coach varsity wrestling Riverdale Country Sch., Bronx, N.Y., 1955-66; headmaster Doane Acad., Burlington, N.J., 1966-70, Poly. Prep. Country Day Sch., Bklyn., 1970—. Trustee Bklyn Inst. Arts and Scis., 1972-79, Bklyn. Ctrl. YMCA, 1974-78, Profl. Children's Sch., 1976-79, Bklyn. Children's Mus., 1979-82, Plymouth Ch. Pilgrims, 1979-86, N.Y. State Assn. Ind. Schs., 1980-86. Mem. Headmasters' Assn., Country Day Sch. Headmasters' Assn., Cum Laude Soc. (regent dist. III 1971-87, dep. pres. gen. 1981-87, pres. gen. 1987-96), Guild Ind. Schs. N.Y. (pres. 1986-88). Avocations: skiing, chess, travel, Civil War history. Home: 195 Amity St Brooklyn NY 11201-6203 Office: Poly Prep Country Day Sch 92d St and 7th Ave Brooklyn NY 11228

WILLIAMS, WILLIAM RALSTON, retired bank and trust company executive; b. Hattiesburg, Miss., Jan. 20, 1910; s. William Ralston and Beulah (Smith) W.; m. Mary E. Marsh, May 8, 1936; chiildren—Mary J. (Mrs. Charles W. Cargill, Jr.), Julie D. Sher. Student, Central State Coll., Edmond, Okla., 1929-32, Okla. State U., 1933. Dist. mgr. Oklahoma City area Internat. Harvester Co., 1935-43; owner Stipes-Williams Co., Altus, Okla., 1943-55, Williams Investment and Ins. Co., Altus, 1955-69; sr. v.p. Fidelity Nat. Bank & Trust Co., Oklahoma City, 1968-83; ret., 1983; Regent A. and M. Colls. Okla., 1952-69, chmn., 1957-64; v.p. Am. Assn. Gov. Bds. Colls. and Univs. Am., 1958. Mem. Altus City Council, 1948-52. Served to lt. USNR, 1944-46. Mem. Oklahoma City C. of C., Am. Legion, Beta Theta Pi. Democrat. Episcopalian. Clubs: Kiwanis (pres. Altus 1947, lt. gov. 1952), Masons (33 deg., K.T., Jester), Elks; Quail Creek Country (Oklahoma City). Home: 3012 Thorn Ridge Rd Oklahoma City OK 73120-1924

WILLIAMS, WILLIAM STANLEY COSSOM, physics educator and researcher; b. Margate, Kent, England, Aug. 4, 1929; s. Stanley Charles and Winifred Florence (Cossom) W.; m. Renée Emilienne Maria Duval-Destin, Sept. 5, 1956; children: Claire, Matthieu. BSc, U. Coll. London, 1950, PhD, 1953. Univ. lectr. U. Glasgow, 1955-61; sr. rsch. officer dept. nuclear physics U. Oxford, 1961-90, re-designated lectr. physics, 1990—; fellow and tutor St. Edmund Hall, Oxford, 1963—. Author: Introduction to Elementary Particle Physics, 1961, 2d edit. 1971, Nuclear and Particle Physics, 1991; contbr. articles to profl. jours. Mem. Inst. Physics London, Am. Phys. Soc. Office: Nuclear and Astrophys Lab Dept Physics, 1 Keble Rd, Oxford OX1 3RH, England

WILLIAMS, WILLIAM THOMAS, artist, educator; b. Cross Creek, N.C., July 17, 1942; s. William Thomas and Hazel (Davis) W.; m. Patricia Ayn Deweese; children—Nila Winona, Aaron Thomas. B.F.A., Pratt Inst., 1966; M.F.A., Yale U., 1968. Mem. faculty Sch. Visual Arts, Pratt Inst., 1969-70; mem. faculty dept. art Bklyn. Coll., City U., N.Y., 1970—; prof. art Bklyn. Coll., City U., 1977—. Home: 654 Broadway New York NY 10012-2327

WILLIAMS, WILLIE, protective services official; b. 1943; m. Evelina; children: Lisa, Willie Jr., Eric. AS, Phila. Coll. Textiles and Sci., 1982; postgrad., St. Joseph U., 1991. Police officer City of Phila., 1964-72, police detective, 1972-74, police sgt., 1974-76, police lt. juvenile aid div., 1976-84, police capt. 22nd and 23rd dists., 1984-86, police inspector, head tng. bur., civil affairs div., North police div., 1986-88, dep. commr. adminstrn., 1988, police commr., 1988-92; chief of police L.A. Police Dept., 1992—; lecture, instr. Temple U., Univ. Pa., Univ. Del. Former scoutmaster Boy Scouts Am.; mem. Pa. Juvenile Officers' Assn., Southeastern Pa. Chiefs of Police, West Angeles Ch. of God in Christ; past bd. dirs. Rebuild L.A. Mem. Nat. Orgn. Black Law Enforcement Execs. (past nat. pres.), Internat. Assn. Chiefs of Police, Alpha Sigma Lambda. Office: Office of Police Chief 150 N Los Angeles St Los Angeles CA 90012-3750*

WILLIAMS, WILLIE, JR., physicist, educator; b. Independence, La., Mar. 24, 1947; s. Willie Sr. and Lee Anner (Booker) W.; 1 child, Willie Williams III. B.S., So. U., 1970; M.S., Iowa State U., 1972, Ph.D., 1974. Mem. faculty Lincoln U., Lincoln University, Pa., 1974—, assoc. prof. physics, 1979-84; prof. physics Lincoln U., Lincoln University, 1984—, chmn. dept., 1976—, chmn. sci. and math. div., 1978-80, 83—, founder, dir. Lincoln Advance Sci. and Engring. Reinforcement (LASER) Program, 1980—, dir. pre-engring., 1976—, dir., prin. investigator Early Alert-Young Scholars Program, 1992—; bd. dirs. women tech. program Lincoln U. Urban Ctr., Phila.; vis. prof. Ctr. for Teaching Innovation, Drexel U., 1975; liaison officer Nat. Assn. for Equal Opportunity in Higher Edn., Dept. Def. Program, 1987—; mem. steering com. NSF Comprehensive Ctr. for Minorities, Phila.; bd. dirs. Prime Inc., Phila. Contbr. articles to profl. jours. Chmn. Cheyney Lincoln Temple Cluster, 1974-78; pres. The Men Fedn., So. U., 1968-69. Recipient Lindback award for Outstanding Teaching, 1976, Outstanding Scientist award White House Initiative, 1988; named one of Outstanding Young Men of Am., 1979; fellow NASA, 1979, Mobil Oil Corp., 1977, Nat. Bur. Standards, 1979, Dept. Def., 1980-81, Navy fellow, 1982. Mem. AAAS, AAUP, Am. Assn. Physics, N.Y. Acad. Scis., Math. Assn. Am., Am. Phys. Soc., Nat. Soc. Black Physicists, Nat. Geog. Soc., Iowa State Alumna Assn., Sigma Xi, Sigma Pi Sigma. Baptist. Home: 1454 Church Hill Pl Reston VA 22094-1228 Office: Lincoln U Dept Physics Lincoln University PA 19352 *Throughout my life I have always striven to achieve the very best and have held on to the belief that wherever possible improve upon today, so that everyone might have a better tomorrow! I have been guided by the principle of being selective in my endeavors, having specific objectives, followed by detailed analysis, concise actions and intense work with continous review.*

WILLIAMS, WINTON HUGH, civil engineer; b. Tampa, Fla., Feb. 14, 1920; s. Herbert DeMain and Alice (Grant) W.; m. Elizabeth Walser Seelye, Dec. 18, 1949; children: Jan, Dick, Bill, Ann. Grad. Adj Gens. Sch., Gainesville, Fla., 1943; student U. Tampa, 1948; grad. Transp. Sch., Ft. Eustis, Va., 1949; BCE, U. Fla., 1959; grad. Command and Gen. Staff Coll., Ft. Levenworth, Kans., 1964, Engrs. Sch., Ft. Belvoir, 1965, Indsl. Coll. Armed Forces, Washington, 1966, Logistics Mgmt. Center, Ft. Lee, Va., 1972. Registered profl. engr., Fla., N.C. Constrn. engr. air fields C.E., U.S. Army, McCoy AFB, Fla., 1959-61, Homestead AFB, Miami, Fla., 1961-62; civil engr. C.E., Jacksonville (Fla.) Dist. Office, 1962-64, chief master planning and layout sect., mil. br., engring. div., 1964-70; chief master planning and real estate div. Hdqrs. U.S. Army So. Command, Ft. Amador, C.Z., 1970-75, spl. asst. planning and mil. constrn. programming Marine Corps Air Bases Eastern Area, Marine Corps Air Sta., Cherry Point, N.C., 1975-82; cons. engr., Morehead City, N.C., 1982—. Mem. Morehead City Planning Bd., 1982-94; mem. Carteret County N.C. Health Bd., 1990—, chmn. 1995—; active Boy Scouts, C.Z.; mem. nat. council U. Tampa. Served with AUS, World War II, ETO, Korean War; col. Res. Decorated Breast Order of Yun Hi (Republic of China); presdl. citation, Meritorious Service medal (Republic of Korea); eagle scout with gold palm. Fellow ASCE (life); mem. NSPE (life), Res. Officers Assn. (life, v.p. C.Am. and S.Am.), Profl. Engrs. N.C., Am. Soc. Photogrammetry, Prestressed Concrete Inst. (profl.), Soc. Am. Mil. Engrs. (life, engr.), Nat. Eagle Scout Assn., Nat. Rifle Assn. Am., Am. Legion (life), Order Arrow, Theta Chi. Presbyterian. Home and Office: 4322 Coral Point Dr Morehead City NC 28557-2745

WILLIAMS-ASHMAN, HOWARD GUY, biochemistry educator; b. London, Eng., Sept. 3, 1925; came to U.S., 1950, naturalized, 1962; s. Edward Harold and Violet Rosamund (Sturge) Williams-A.; m. Elisabeth Bächli, Jan. 25, 1959; children—Anne Clare, Christian, Charlotte, Geraldine. B.A., U. Cambridge, 1946; Ph.D., U. London, 1949. From asst. prof. to prof. biochemistry U. Chgo., 1953-64; prof. pharmacology and exptl. therapeutics, also prof. reproductive biology Johns Hopkins Sch. Medicine, 1964-69; prof. biochemistry Ben May Inst., U. Chgo., 1969—, Maurice Goldblatt prof., 1973-91, prof. emeritus, 1991. Contbr. numerous articles in field to publs. Recipient Research Career award USPHS, 1962-64. Fellow Am. Acad. Arts and Scis. (Amory prize 1975); mem. Am. Soc. Biochemistry and Molecular Biology. Home: 5421 S Cornell Ave Chicago IL 60615-5608 Office: U Chgo Ben May Inst Chicago IL 60637

WILLIAMS-BRIDGERS, JACQUELYN, federal government official. Inspector gen. Dept. State, 1995—. Office: Office Inspector Gen Dept State 2201 C St NW Washington DC 20520-7512

WILLIAMS JONES, ELIZABETH, financial planner, business consultant; b. San Francisco, Jan. 16, 1948; d. John and Myrtle Mary (Thierry) W.; children: Brian, Jonathan; m. Archie W. Jones Jr. Cert. in bus., U. Calif., 1979. Cert. computers loan processing. Manpower coord., fed. programs U.S. Govt., San Francisco; patient svc. rep. Health Care Svc., Oakland, Calif.; ins. and real estate cons.; pres. Investments Unlimited, Oakland, EWJ & Assocs. Mktg. Firm; v.p. A&E Catering Svcs.; CEO Ultimate Vacations Inc. Mem. NAACP. Recipient Pub. Speaking award; European Investment fellow. Mem. AAUW, NAFE, Nat. Real Estate Owners Assn., Nat. Notary Assn., Order Ea. Star, Heroines Jericho, Daus. Isis, Toastmistress Club.

WILLIAMS-MONEGAIN, LOUISE JOEL, science educator, administrator; b. Chgo., June 13, 1941; d. Sylvester Emanuel Jr. and Carita Bell (Brown) Williams; m. Martin Monegain, Aug. 19, 1961; children: Michael Martin, Martin Marion II. BS, Shaw U., 1975; JD, Antioch Sch. of Law, Washington, 1979; cert. adminstrn., Roosevelt U., 1988; PhD, U. Ill., 1994. Tchr. Chgo. Archdiocese, 1968-73; assoc. dir. pub. affairs Warren Regional Planning Commn., Soul City, N.C., 1973-74; comm. specialist Coun. of the Great City Schs., Washington, 1974-76; lawyer Equal Employment Opportunity Commn., Washington, 1979-80; tchr. Olive Harvey City Coll., Chgo., 1981-83; mgr. Joy Travel Agt., Chgo., 1981-83; owner, pres. MJS Your Travel Agt., Chgo., 1983-86; sci. tchr. Chgo. Pub. Schs., 1986-91; program leader, evaluator Argonne (Ill.) Nat. Lab., 1991—; program leader, evaluation rep. Nat. Cancer Program, Accra and Jumasi, Ghana, West Africa, 1995. Vol. Art Inst., Chgo., 1994; green team adv. bd. Lincoln Park Zool. Soc., Chgo., 1992—. Scholarship State of Ill., 1987. Mem. ASCD, Am. Edn. Rsch. Assn., Nat. Sci. Tchrs. Assn., Assn. for Coll. and Univ. Women, Phi Delta Kappa. Avocations: attending opera, dance performances, plays, galleries. Office: Argonne Nat Lab 9700 Cass Ave Argonne IL 60439-4803

WILLIAMSON, ALAN BACHER, English literature educator, poet, writer; b. Chgo., Jan. 24, 1944; s. George and Jehanne (Bacher) W.; m. Anne Winters, Oct. 12, 1968 (div. Feb. 1988); 1 child, Elizabeth Kilner. BA, Haverford Coll., 1964; MA, Harvard U., 1965, PhD, 1969. Asst. prof. U. Va., Charlottesville, 1969-75; Briggs-Copeland lectr. Harvard U., Cambridge, Mass., 1977-80; Fannie Hurst lectr. Brandeis U., Waltham, Mass., 1980-82; prof. English, U. Calif., Davis, 1982—; poetry panelist Nat. Endowment for Arts, 1989. Author: (criticism) Pity the Monsters, 1974, Introspection and Contemporary Poetry, 1984, Eloquence and Mere Life, 1994, (poetry) Presence, 1983, The Muse of Distance, 1988, Love and the Soul, 1995. Poetry fellow Nat. Endowment for Arts, 1973; Guggenheim fellow, 1991. Mem. MLA (exec. com. div. on poetry 1987-91). Democrat. Zen Buddhist. Office: U Calif Dept English Davis CA 95616

WILLIAMSON, CARL AUGUSTUS, engineering executive; b. Newport News, Va., Sept. 7, 1950; s. Marvis Harrison Sr. and Annie Lucille (Amos) W.; m. Bonnie Bernel Mitchell, Sept. 21, 1973; 1 child, Carl Michael; 1 stepson, Leon Mitchell. BS, Norfolk State Coll., 1972; MBA, Northeastern U., 1982; DEng, MIT, 1987. Cert. secondary edn. tchr. Electrical estimator Stone & Webster, Boston, 1973-74; instr. D.C. Pub. Schs., Washington, 1974-76; sales engr. Westinghouse, Framingham, Mass., 1976-78; cost engr. Gilbert Commonwealth, Jackson, Mich., 1978-80; instr. Boston Pub. Schs., Boston, 1980-82; cons. Gilbert Commonwealth, Washington, 1983—. Col. U.S. Army, 1968-72. Mem. NRA, MBA Assn., Washington Tchrs. Union. Baptist. Avocations: sports, arts, dance. Home and Office: 3108 Brightseat Rd Hyattsville MD 20785-2817

WILLIAMSON, CLARENCE KELLY, microbiologist, educator; b. McKeesport, Pa., Jan. 19, 1924; s. James Frederick and Loretta (McDermott) W.; m. Dorothy Birgit Ohlsson, Aug. 18, 1951; children: Lisa Ann, Erik James. B.S., U. Pitts., 1949, M.S., 1951, Ph.D., 1955. Bacteriologist E.S. Magee Hosp., Pitts., 1951; instr. bacteriology U. Pitts., 1951-55, Pa. State U., summer 1953; mem. faculty Miami U., Oxford, Ohio, 1955—, chmn. dept. microbiology, 1962-72, prof., 1963-85, dean Coll. Arts and Sci., 1971-82, prof. emeritus, 1985—, exec. v.p. acad. affairs, provost, 1982-85, provost, exec. v.p. acad. affairs emeritus, 1985—; cons. Warren-Teed Products Co., Columbus, Ohio, 1953-62; cons. editor microbiology World Pub. Co., Cleve., 1965-68. Sec.-treas. McCullough-Hyde Meml. Hosp., 1968-70, trustee, bd. dirs., 1967-77, vice chmn., 1970-71, 72-74, chmn., 1974-76; trustee Hospice of the Miami Valley, 1984-92, United Campus Ministry, 1992-96; mem. commn. on arts and scis. Nat. Assn. State Univs. and Land-Grant Colls., 1974-80; bd. govs. Am. Inst. Biol. Scis., 1977-83; bd. dirs. Coun. Colls. of Arts and Scis., 1975-79, pres., 1977-78; trustee S.W. Ohio and No. Ky. chpt. Nat. Multiple Sclerosis Soc., 1981-89; trustee Lakeside Assn., Chautauqua, Lakeside, Ohio, 1990—. With USNR, 1943-46. Recipient Benjamin Harrison medallion, 1982. Fellow Am. Acad. Microbiology, Ohio Acad. Sci. (v.p. med. sci. sect. 1970-71); mem. Am. Soc. Microbiology, Sigma Xi, Beta Gamma Sigma, Phi Kappa Phi, Omicron Delta Kappa, Rho Chi, Phi Sigma (nat. v.p. 1975-77, pres. 1977-83). Club: Torch (pres. Butler County 1969-70). Lodge: Rotary (pres. Oxford 1967-68). Spl. research poststreptococcal glomerulonephritis, classification of viridans streptococci, dissociation of Pseudomonas aeruginosa. Home: 104 Mckee Ave Oxford OH 45056-9025

WILLIAMSON, DON, newspaper columnist; b. St. Louis. Attended, Wichita State U. Editor, pub. 67214 Mag., Wichita, Kans., 1973-74; prodr., cons. As We See It Series Chgo. Pub. TV, 1974-76; gen. assigment reporter Wichita (Kans.) Eagle-Beacon, 1977-78, news, pub. affairs dir., 1978-79, editorial writer, columnist, 1979-83; edn. writer San Diego Union, 1983-85; assoc. editor, columnist, editorial pages Phila. Daily News, 1985-89; columnist, editorial bd. Seattle Times, 1989—; instr. Journalism Edn.; dir. Urban Newspaper Workshop High Sch. Students; minority profl. in-residence program Am. Soc. Newspaper Editors. Recipient William Allen White Found. Kans. News Enterprise award, AP Sports Editors Investigative Reporting award, Outstanding Reporting award Nat. Headliners, Washington Gov.'s Child Abuse Prevention award, Outstanding Govtl. News Reporting award Seattle Mcpl. League, Journalism award Kans. NAACP, Investigative Reporting award Kans. Press Women, Proficiency in Eng. Program Vol. award, Seattle Pub. Schs. Vol. award, Community Svc. award Royal Esquire Club Seattle, Community Svc. award Atlantic St. Ctr., Benefit Guild Seattle Children's Svc. award; John S. Knight Stanford U. fellow. Mem. Nat. Conf. Editorial Writers, Nat. Assn. Black Journalists (Leadership award, Region 10 Mem. of Yr. award), Soc. Profl. Journalists, Sigma Delta Chi. Office: The Seattle Times PO Box 70 Fairview Ave N & John St Seattle WA 98111

WILLIAMSON, DONALD RAY, retired career Army officer; b. Amarillo, Tex., Oct. 13, 1943; s. Floy Edwin and Dorothy Lorene (Orr) W.; m. Beverly Ann Howard, Aug. 31, 1963; children: Rebecca Ann, Catherine Paige. BS in Econs., W. Tex. State U., 1966; MA in Bus., Cen. Mich. U., 1977; degree, Dept. Def. Program Mgrs., 1982, U.S. Army Command and Gen. Staff Coll., 1980. Commd. 2d lt. U.S. Army, 1966, advanced through grades to lt. col., 1982, retired, 1986; comdg. officer combat support co. U.S. Army, Ft. Hood, Tex., 1973-74; comdg. officer 2d aviation co. U.S. Army, Ft. Hood, 1974-75; dep. insp. gen. U.S. Army, Ft. Leavenworth, Kans., 1975-78; comdg. officer 213th aviation co. U.S. Army, Rep. of Korea, 1978-79; asst. program mgr. advanced scout helicopter program U.S. Army, 1981-86; owner Witan Group, Chesterfield, Mo., 1986-88; pres. Sys. Test Evaluation Inc., St. Louis, Mo., 1988—. Contbr. articles to profl. jours. Decorated Bronze Star, 37 Air medals with "V" device, D.F.C. with oak leaf cluster, Legion of Merit. Mem. Army Aviation Assn. Am., Assn. U.S. Army, Lansing Jaycees (past pres.), Mensa. Avocations: flying, reading, tennis. Home: 50 Orange Hills Dr Chesterfield MO 63017-3248 Office: 4433 Woodson Rd Saint Louis MO 63134-3713

WILLIAMSON, DONNA MARIA, pastoral counselor; b. Oswego, N.Y., Feb. 26, 1944; d. Donald Carl and Helen Mary (Saber) Townsley; m. Patrick H. Williamson, July 7, 1962; children: Kevin Patrick, Michael Brian, Timothy Daniel. Grad. pub. schs., Fulton, N.Y. Cert. in clin. pastoral edn., pastoral care, Onondaga Pastoral Counseling Ctr.; weight loss counselor. Chaplain Loretto Geriatric Ctr., Syracuse, 1981-82; hosp. chaplain St. Rose of Lima Parish, Syracuse, 1982-84, pastoral counselor, 1984—; weight loss counselor Nutri-System, Syracuse, 1988-91. Founding mem. Fulton Community Nursery Sch., 1967, Commn. on Women in Ch. and Society, Syracuse, 1984; mem. Alethea, Ctr. on Death and Dying, Inc., Syracuse, 1978, Syracuse Area Domestic Violence Coalition's Religious Task Force, 1993—. Mem. Menninger Found. Roman Catholic. Avocations: flower arranging, vocalist. Office: St Rose of Lima Parish 409 S Main St North Syracuse NY 13212

WILLIAMSON, DOUGLAS FRANKLIN, JR., lawyer; b. Anniston, Ala., Mar. 23, 1930; s. Douglas Franklin and Elizabeth Louise (Connor) W.; m. Barbara Tuerk, Dec. 28, 1957; children: Mary Leyden, Douglas Franklin III, Bruce Reynolds. AB summa cum laude, Amherst Coll., 1952; LLB, Yale U., 1955. Bar: N.Y. 1958, Fla. 1976. Assoc. Breed, Abbott & Morgan, N.Y.C., 1957-63, ptnr., 1963-72; ptnr. Williamson & Hess and predecessor firm, N.Y.C., 1972-79; of counsel Winthrop, Stimson, Putnam & Roberts, N.Y.C., 1979-81, ptnr., 1982-95, sr. counsel, 1996—. Bd. dirs. World Wildlife Fund, Washington, 1979-88, treas., 1986-88, mem. nat. coun., 1988—; bd. dirs. Conservation Found., Washington, 1985-88, treas., 1986-88; bd. dirs. Lower Hudson chpt. Nature Conservancy, Mt. Kisco, N.Y., 1976-87, 93—, sec., 1976-87, hon. dir., 1987—, chmn., 1993-94; bd. dirs. Oblong Land Conservancy, Pawling, N.Y., 1990—, chmn. 1996—; bd. dirs. Quaker Hill Civic Assn., Pawling, 1974—, past pres.; chmn. Pawling Assessment Rev. Bd., 1976—. With U.S. Army, 1955-57. Fellow Am. Coll. Trust and Estate Counsel, N.Y. State Bar Found.; mem. ABA, N.Y. State Bar Assn., Assn. of Bar of City of N.Y. (mem. com. on trusts, estates and surrogate cts. 1973-78, chmn. 1975-78), Everglades Club, Quaker Hill Country Club (pres. 1980-81), Old Guard Soc. of Palm Beach Golfers, Phi Beta Kappa, Phi Beta Kappa Assocs. (sec. 1975-77, v.p. 1977-79). Address: PO Box 350 Pawling NY 12564-0350 Office: Winthrop Stimson Putnam & Roberts One Battery Park Plz New York NY 10004

WILLIAMSON, EDWIN DARGAN, lawyer, former federal official; b. Florence, S.C., Sept. 23, 1939; s. Benjamin F. and Sara (Dargan) W.; m. Kathe Gates, July 12, 1969; children: Samuel Gates, Edwin Dargan Jr., Sara Elizabeth. BA cum laude, U. of the South, 1961, DCL (hon.), 1992; JD, NYU, 1964. Bar: N.Y. 1965, D.C. 1988. Assoc. Sullivan & Cromwell, N.Y.C., 1964-70, ptnr., 1971-76; ptnr. Sullivan & Cromwell, London, 1976-79, N.Y.C., 1979-88, Washington, 1988-90, 93—; legal adviser U.S. Dept. State, Washington, 1990-93, Permanent Ct. of Arbitration, 1991—; bd. dirs. Triton Energy Corp., 1994—. Regent U. of the South, Sewanee, Tenn., 1981-87, chmn., 1985-87; bd. dirs. Nat. Dance Inst., N.Y.C., 1984-88, Episcopal Ch. Found., N.Y.C., 1986-94; vestryman St. James Episcopal Ch., N.Y.C., 1984-88. Mem. ABA (coun. internat. law sect. 1993—), Coun. Fgn. Rels., Assn. Bar City N.Y. (com. internat. security affairs 1993—), U.S. Coun. Internat. Bus. and Bus. Industry Adv. Coun. to OECD (vice chmn. coms. on multinat. enterprises and investment 1993—, chmn. BIAC, group on multinat. agy. inv. 1996—), Internat. Rep. Inst. (rule of law adv. bd. 1993), Racquet and Tennis Club (N.Y.C.) Met. Club. Republican.

WILLIAMSON, ERNEST LAVONE, petroleum company executive; b. Perryton, Tex., Sept. 10, 1924; s. Ernest and Mabel Robert (Donnell) W.; m. Gertrude Florence Watkins, Dec. 2, 1950; children: Richard Dean, Judith Watkins, Mary Nan, David Ernest. BSEE, U. Okla., 1950; student, Hill's Bus. Coll., 1943. Sales and svc. rep. Hughes Tool Co., 1950-52; with land dept. Phillips Petroleum Co., 1952-54; with La. Land & Exploration Co., New Orleans, 1954—, exec. v.p., 1967-74, pres., 1974-84, COO, 1982-83, CEO, 1984-88, chmn., 1985-88, also dir.; bd. dirs. Hibernia Nat. Bank, New Orleans, Halliburton Co., Cen. La. Electric Co. Mem. adv. bd. Salvation Army, 1971—; bd. visitors U. Okla.; bd. dirs. New Orleans Jr. Achievement. With U.S. Army, 1943-46. Mem. Am. Assn. Petroleum Landmen, Ind. Petroleum Assn. Am., Mid-Continent Oil and Gas Assn. (chmn. 1980-81), Am. Petroleum Inst., Petroleum Club, Tchefuncta Country Club. Presbyterian. Office: La Land & Exploration Co 909 Poydras St PO Box 60350 New Orleans LA 70160

WILLIAMSON, FLETCHER PHILLIPS, real estate broker; b. Cambridge, Md., Dec. 16, 1923; s. William Fletcher and Florence M. (Phillips) W.; student U. Md., 1941, 42; m. Betty June (Stoker), Apr. 6, 1943; 1 son, Jeffrey Phillips; m. 2d, Helen M. Stumberg, Aug. 28, 1972. Test engr. Engring. Lab., Glen Martin Co., 1942-43; salesman Corkran Ice Cream Co., Cambridge, 1946-50; real estate broker, 1950—; chmn. bd. Williamson Real Estate, Dorchester Corp., 1963-72; bd. dirs. WCEM, Inc., 1966-75; vice chmn. bd., dir. Nat. Bank of Cambridge, 1979—; dir. Cam-Storage Inc., Dorchester Indsl. Devel. Corp., Delmarva Bank Data Processing Ctr.; co-receiver White & Nelson, Inc. Bd. dirs. Delmarva council Boy Scouts Am.; past pres. Cambridge Hosp., United Fund of Dorchester County; bd. dirs. Del. Mus. Natural History, Dorchester County Pub. Library; bd. dirs., v.p. Game Conservation Internat.; v.p. Del. Mus. Natural History. Served as ordnance tech. intelligence engr. AUS, 1943-46; ETO. Mem. Md. Real Estate Assn. (gov. 1956-66), Outdoor Writers Assn., Nat. Rifle Assn., Nat. Def. Preparedness Assn., Cambridge Dorchester C. of C. (dir. 1955—), Power Squadron (comdr. 1954-56), Dorchester County Bd. Realtors (pres.), Scandinavian Atlantic Salmon Group, Explorers Club, Soc. of S. Pole. Methodist. Clubs: Rolling Rock, Shikar Safari, Anglers, Chesapeake Bay Yacht, Camp Fire, Md., Georgetown. Lodges: Masons, Shriners.

WILLIAMSON, FREDERICK BEASLEY, III, rubber company executive; b. Balt., June 21, 1918; s. Frederick Beasley and Virginia Ogden (Ranson) W.; m. Katherine Stryker, Apr. 19, 1941; children—Katherine L., Frederick Beasley IV, Marsha R. Student, Princeton, 1937-40. With Goodall Rubber Co., Trenton, N.J., 1940-41, 46-88, pres., chmn. bd., 1957-85, dir., 1950-89; bd. dirs. N.J. Nat. Bank. Bd. dirs. Mercer Med. Center, Trenton, N.J., 1965-89, New Jobs, 1962-91 ; campaign chmn. Delaware Valley United Way, 1964. Served to capt., 5th Armored Div. U.S. Army, 1942-46. Mem. Rubber Mfrs. Assn. (dir. 1958-86), Nat. Assn. Mfrs. (bd. dirs. 1981-82), N.J. Mfrs. Ins. Co. (bd. dirs. 1965-90, dir. emeritus 1990—, chmn. 1977-79), N.J. Bus. Industry Assn. (dir. emeritus 1990—). Clubs: Princeton (N.Y.C.); Trenton Country; Hartwood (Port Jervis, N.Y.); Pine Valley Golf. Home: 1265 Eagle Rd New Hope PA 18938-9221

WILLIAMSON, HENRY GASTON, JR., banker; b. Whiteville, N.C., Aug. 18, 1947; s. Henry Gaston and Elizabeth Lee (Brittain) W.; m. Nancy Thomas Williamson, Aug. 30, 1969; children: Leigh, Clay. BSBA, East Carolina U., 1969, MBA, 1972; grad. bus. adminstrn., U. N.C., 1979. Mgr. bus. loans Branch Banking & Trust Co., Fayetteville, N.C., 1973-77; v.p., regional loan adminstr. Branch Banking & Trust Co., Wilson, N.C., 1977-80; v.p., city exec. Branch Banking & Trust Co., Tarboro, N.C., 1980; exec. v.p., mgr. ops./human resources div. Branch Banking & Trust Co., Wilson, N.C., 1981-83, sr. exec. v.p., adminstrv. group mgr., 1983-89, pres., 1989—, COO, 1991—; bd. dirs. BB&T Fin. Corp., BB&T; bd. dirs. BB&T Ctr. for Leadership Devel. Author: American Antiques: A Case Study, 1973 (First Place award Robert Morris Assocs.). Bd. dirs. Wilson County chpt. ARC, 1984—, East Carolina U. 1985—, N.C. Med. Soc. Found., Inc., 1991; mem. exec. com., bd. dirs. East Carolina coun. Boy Scouts Am., 1985—; bd. dirs. Wilson Heart Fund Assn., 1983-87, pres., 1985-86. East Carolina faculty scholar, 1969; recipient Outstanding Alumni award East Carolina U., 1988. Mem. Omicron Delta Epsilon, Beta Gamma Sigma. Club: Wilson Country. Lodge: Kiwanis (pres. Wilson club 1984-85). Avocation: skiing. Home: 1210 Cambridge Rd NW Wilson NC 27896-1458 Office: BB&T Fin Corp PO Box 1250 Winston Salem NC 27102*

WILLIAMSON, JACK (JOHN STEWART WILLIAMSON), writer; b. Bisbee, Ariz., Apr. 29, 1908; s. Asa Lee and Lucy Betty (Hunt) W.; m. Blanche Slaten Harp, Aug. 15, 1947 (dec. Jan. 1985); stepchildren: Keign Harp (dec.), Adele Harp Lovorn. BA, MA, Eastern N.Mex. U., 1957, LHD (hon.), 1981; PhD, U. Colo., 1964. Prof. English Eastern N.Mex. U., Portales, 1960-77. Author numerous sci. fiction books including The Legion of Space, 1947, Darker Than You Think, 1948, The Humanoids, 1949, The Green Girl, 1950, The Cometeers, 1950, One Against the Legion, 1950, Seetee Scock, 1950, Seetee Ship, 1950, Dragon's Island, 1951, The Legion of Time, 1952, (with Frederik Phhl) Star Bridge, 1955, Dome Around America, 1955, The Trial of Terra, 1962, Golden Blood, 1964, The Reign of Wizardry, 1965, Bright New Universe, 1967, Trapped in Space, 1968, The Pandora Effect, 1969, People Machines, 1971, The Moon Children, 1972, H.G. Wells: Critic of Progress, 1973, Teaching SF, 1975, The Early Williamson, 1975, The Power of Blackness, 1976, The Best of Jack Williamson, 1978, Brother to Demons, Brother To Gods, 1979, Teaching Science Fiction: Education for Tomorrow, 1980, The Alien Intelligence, 1980, The Humanoid Touch, 1980, Manseed, 1982, The Queen of a Legion, 1983, Wonder's Child: My Life in Science Fiction, 1984 (Hugo award 1985), Lifeburst, 1984, Firechild, 1986, Mazeway, 1990: (with Fredrick Pohl) Undersea Quest, 1954, Undersea Fleet, 1955, Undersea City, 1956, The Reefs of Sapce, 1964, Starchild, 1965, Rogue Star, 1969, The Farthest Star, 1975, Wall Around a Star, 1983, Land's End, 1988, Mazeway, 1990. (with Frederik Phol) The Singers Of Time, 1991, Beachhead, 1992, Demon Moon, 1994, The Black Sun, 1996; (with Miles J. Breuer) The Birth of an New Republic, 1981. Served as staff sgt. USAAF, 1942-45. Mem. Sci. Fiction Writers Am. (pres. 1978-80, Grand Master Nebula award 1976), Sci. Fiction Research Assn. (Pilgrim award 1968), World Sci. Fiction, Planetary Soc. Avocations: travel, astronomy, photography. Home: PO Box 761 Portales NM 88130-0761 Office: Ea NMex U Golden Libr Portales NM 88130

WILLIAMSON, JOEL RUDOLPH, humanities educator; b. Anderson County, S.C., Oct. 27, 1929; s. James Henry and Carrie Mae (Swaney) W.; m. Marie Ahern, Nov. 17, 1953 (div. May 1983); children: Joelle, William, Alethea; m. Anna Woodson, Oct. 18, 1986. AB, U. S.C., 1949, MA, 1951; PhD, U. Calif., 1964. Instr. dept. history U. N.C., Chapel Hill, 1960-64, asst. prof., 1964-66, assoc. prof., 1966-69, prof., 1969-85, Lineberger prof. in humanities, 1985—; resident fellow Rockefeller Ctr., Bellagio, Italy, 1988; Eudora Welty prof. in so. studies Millsaps Coll., 1984; disting. vis. prof. Rhodes Coll., 1984; vis. prof. dept. history, assoc. Lowell House Harvard U., 1981-82. Author: After Slavery: The Negro in South Carolina During Reconstruction, 1986-1877, 1965, The Origins of Segregation, 1968, New People: Miscegenation and Mulattoes in the United Staes, 1980, The Crucible of Race, 1984 (Francis Parkman prize Soc. Am. Historians, Ralph Waldo Emerson award Phi Beta Kappa, Mayflower Cup, Frank L. and Harriet C. Owsley award 1985, Robert Francis Kennedy Book award, Pulitzer prize in History nomination 1985, 94), A Rage for Order, 1986, William Faulkner and Southern History, 1993 (Pulitzer prize in History nomination, Mayflower Cup), also articles. Lt. USN, 1951-55. Fellow Guggenheim Found., 1970-71, NEH, 1987-88, Ctr. for Advanced Study in Behavioral Scis., Stanford, Calif., 1977-78, summer 1979, 80, 81, So. fellow, 1961-62, Charles Warren Ctr., 1981-82. Avocation: travel. Home: 211 Hillsborough St Chapel Hill NC 27514 Office: U NC Dept History 567 Hamilton Chapel Hill NC 27599-3195

WILLIAMSON, JOEL V., lawyer; b. Akron, Ohio, May 26, 1945. BA, Davidson Coll., 1967; JD, U. Ky., 1970. Bar: Ky. 1970, Ill. 1986, U.S. Supreme Ct., U.S. Ct. Appeals (6th, 7th, 8th, 9th and 11th cirs.), U.S. Dist. Ct. (no. dist.) Ill., U.S. Tax Ct., U.S. Ct. Fed. Claims. Ptnr. Mayer, Brown & Platt, Chgo. Mem. Ky. Bar Assn., Chgo. Bar Assn., Internat. Fiscal Assn. Office: Mayer Brown & Platt 190 S La Salle St Chicago IL 60603-3410*

WILLIAMSON, JOHN PRITCHARD, utility executive; b. Cleve., Feb. 22, 1922; s. John and Jane (Pritchard) W.; m. Helen Morgan, Aug. 3, 1945; children: John Morgan, James Russell, Wayne Arthur. BBA, Kent State U., 1945; postgrad., U. Toledo, 1953-56, U. Mich., 1956. CPA, Ohio. Sr. acct. Arthur Andersen & Co., Detroit and Cleve., 1945-51; dir. methods and procs. Toledo Edison Co., 1951-59, asst. treas., 1959-60, sec., 1960-62, sec.-treas., 1962-65, v.p. finance, 1965-68, sr. v.p., 1968-72, pres., chief exec. officer, 1972-79, chmn., chief exec. officer, 1979-86; chmn. Centerior Energy Corp., 1985-86; chmn. emeritus Toledo Edison Co., Centerior Energy Corp., 1986—; dir. emeritus, chmn. 1st Nat. Bank of Toledo, 1974-75; chmn. N.Am. Electric Reliability Coun., 1984-87; founder, chmn. Nat. Electric Security Com., 1987-88. Pres. Ohio Electric Utility Inst., 1972; chmn. East Cen. Area Power Coordination Pool, 1971-72, mem. exec. com. Edison Electric Inst., 1981-85; trustee Assn. Edison Illuminating Cos., 1982-84; pres. Toledo C. of C., 1970; chmn. Ohio C. of C., 1979-81, life dir.; trustee Toledo Symphony Orch., pres., 1985-86; hon. trustee Toledo Mus. Art, Toledo Hosp.; trustee U. Toledo Found., 1980-87, Kent State U. Found.; vice chmn. Greater Toledo Corp., 1984-86; trustee, treas. Rio Verde Cmty. Ch., 1989-92; elder Presbyn. Ch.; pres. Toledo Cmty. Chest, 1972; chmn. Greater Toledo Area United Way, 1971. Named Toledo Outstanding Citizen, 1976; recipient Kent State U. medallion, 1992;Williamson Alumni Ctr. named in his honor, 1991. Mem. Fin. Analysts Soc. Toledo (pres. 1968-69), Systems and Procs. Assn. (internat. treas. 1960), Inst. Pub. Utilities (chmn. exec. com. 1969-70), Toledo Boys Club (Echo award 1974), Kent State U. Alumni Assn. (pres. 1971-72, Outstanding Alumnus 1974), Belmont Country Club, Rio Verde Country Club, Inverness Club (gov. 1967-76), Rio Verde Saddle Club (past pres.), Kiwanis (past pres. Toledo, Disting. Svc. award 1977), Blue Key, Delta Sigma Pi, Beta Alpha Psi, Delta Upsilon. Republican. Home: 10661 Cardiff Rd Perrysburg OH 43551-3404 also: 18524 E Poco Vista Rio Verde AZ 85263-7125

WILLIAMSON, LAIRD, stage director, actor; b. Chgo., Dec. 13, 1937; s. Walter B. and Florence M. (Hemwell) W. B.S. in Speech, Northwestern U., 1960; M.F.A. in Drama, U. Tex., 1965. Dir. Am. Conservatory Theatre, San Francisco, 1974—; stage dir. A Christmas Carol, 1976-81, The Matchmaker (tour of Soviet Union), 1976, A Month in the Country, 1978, The Visit, 1979, Pantagleize, 1980, Sunday in the Park, 1986, End of the World, 1988, Imaginary Invalid, 1990; dir. Oreg. Shakespearean Festival, Ashland, 1972-74, Western Opera Theatre, San Francisco, 1976-77, Theater Fest, Santa Maria, Calif., 1971-84, Denver Theater Ctr., 1981, Bklyn. Acad. Music, 1981, Denver Ctr. Theatre Co., 1985-94, Seattle Repertory Theatre, 1990, Old Globe Theatre, San Diego, 1977, 92, 94; artistic dir. Theater Fest, Solvang, Calif., 1981-83, Intiman Theatre, 1986, 88, Seattle Repertory Theatre, 1990, Berkeley Shakespeare Festival, 1990, Guthrie Theatre, 1991, 93, The Shakespeare Theatre, Washington, 1995, 96; actor in Othello, 1973, Twelfth Night, 1974, Cyrano, 1974, Enrico IV, 1977, Judas, 1978, Hamlet, 1979, The Bacchae, 1981. Mem. Soc. Stage Dirs. Actors Equity Assn., Screen Actors Guild. *Learn from the multitude of wonderful teachers that life provides. Keep it fun, and work from your heart.*

WILLIAMSON, MARILYN LAMMERT, English educator, university adminstrator; b. Chgo., Sept. 6, 1927; d. Raymond Ferdinand and Edith Louise (Eisenbies) Lammert; m. Robert M. Williamson, Oct. 28, 1950 (div. Apr. 1973); 1 child, Timothy L.; m. James H. McKay, Aug. 15, 1974. BA, Vassar Coll., 1949; MA, U. Wis., 1950; PhD, Duke U., 1956. Instr. Duke U., Durham, N.C., 1955-56, 58-59; lectr. N.C. State U., Raleigh, 1957-58, 61-62; asst. prof. Oakland U., Rochester, Mich., 1965-68, assoc. prof., 1968-72; prof. English Wayne State U., Detroit, 1972-90, Disting. prof. English, 1990—, chmn. dept. English, 1972-74, 81-83, assoc. dean Coll. Liberal Arts, 1974-79; dir. women's studies Wayne State U., 1976-87; dep. provost Wayne State U., Detroit, 1987-91, sr. v.p. for acad. affairs, provost, 1991-95; pres. Assn. Depts. English, 1976-77. Author: Infinite Variety, 1974, Patriarchy of Shakespeare's Comedies, 1986, British Women Writers 1650-1750, 1990; editor: Renaissance Studies, 1972, Female Poets of Great Britain, 1981; contbr. articles to profl. jours. Pres. LWV, Rochester, 1963-65. Recipient Detroit Disting. Svc. award, 1986, Faculty Recognition award Bd. Govs., Wayne State U., 1991; Bunting Inst. fellow, 1969-70, AAUW fellow, 1982-83, J.N. Keal fellow, 1985-86. Mem. MLA (exec. coun. 1977-80, mem. editorial bd. 1992-94), Renaissance Soc. Am., Coll. English Assn., Mich. Acad. (pres. 1978-79), Shakespeare Assn. Am., Mich. Coun. Humanities (chair 1991-93), Fed. State Humanities Coun. (bd. dirs. 1994—). Democrat. Home: 2275 Oakway Dr West Bloomfield MI 48324-1855 Office: Wayne State Univ Dept of English Detroit MI 48202

WILLIAMSON, MYRNA HENNRICH, retired army officer, lecturer, consultant; b. Gregory, S.D., Jan. 27, 1937; d. Walter Ferdinand and Alma Lillian (Rajewich) H. BS with highest honors, S.D. State U., 1960; MA, U. Okla., 1973; grad., U.S. Army Command and Gen. Staff Coll., 1977, Nat. War Coll., 1980. Commd. 2d lt. U.S. Army, 1960, advanced through grades to brig. gen., 1985; bn. comdr. Mil. Police Sch. U.S. Army, Fort McClellan, Ala., 1977-79; chief plans policy and service div. Jl 8th Army U.S. Army, Korea, 1980-81; chief mgmt. support Office Dep. Chief Staff for Research, Devel. and Acquisition U.S. Army, Washington, 1981-82; brigade comdr. U.S. Army, Fort Benjamin Harrison, Ind., 1983-84; comdg. gen. 3d ROTC Region U.S. Army, Fort Riley, Kans., 1984-87; dep. dir. mil. personnel mgmt. U.S. Army, Washington, 1987-89, ret., 1989; U.S. del. com. on women in NATO Forces, 1986-89. Pres., bd. dirs. S.D. State U. Found., 1988-96; bd. dirs. Women in Mil. Svc. to Am. Found.. Recipient Disting. Alumnus award S.D. State U., 1984. Mem. Internat. Platform Assn., Assn. U.S. Army (trustee), United Svcs. Automobile Assn. (bd. dirs.), The Internat. Alliance, Phi Kappa Phi.

WILLIAMSON, NORMA BETH, adult education educator; b. Hamilton, Tex., Nov. 2, 1939; d. Joseph Lawrence and Gladys (Wilkins) Drake; m. Stuart Williamson, Mar. 14, 1981. BA, Baylor U., 1962; MA, Tex. A&I U., 1969; postgrad., Tex. Tech. U., 1976-80, CIDOC, Cuernavaca, Mex., 1973, 75. Instr. English, Tex. Southmost Coll., Brownsville; coll. prep. tchr. Tex. Dept. Corrections; lectr. Spanish Sam Houston State U., Huntsville, SD; lectr. in Spanish, Sam Houston State U. Music chmn. Huntsville Unitarian Universalist Ch.; pres. S.W. Dist., 1982-86. Mem. Delta Kappa Gamma (pres. Upsilon chpt.). Home: RR 1 Box 349 Bedias TX 77831-9625

WILLIAMSON, OLIVER EATON, economics and law educator; b. Superior, Wis., Sept. 27, 1932; s. Scott Gilbert and Lucille S. (Dunn) W.; m. Dolores Jean Celeni, Sept. 28, 1957; children: Scott, Tamara, Karen, Oliver, Dean. SB, MIT, 1955; MBA, Stanford U., 1960; PhD, Carnegie-Mellon U., 1963; PhD (hon.), Norwegian Sch. Econs. and Bus. Adminstrn., 1986; PhD in Econ. Sci. (hon.), Hochschule St. Gallen, Switzerland, 1987, Groningen U., 1989, Turku Sch. Econs. & Bus. Admin, 1995. Project. engr. U.S. Govt., 1955-58; asst. prof. econs. U. Calif., Berkeley, 1963-65; assoc. prof. U. Pa., Phila., 1965-68, prof., 1968-83, Charles and William L. Day prof. econs. and social sci., 1977-83; Gordon B. Tweedy prof. econs. law and orgn. Yale U., 1983-88; Transam. prof. of bus., econs. and law U. Calif., Berkeley, 1988-94, Edgar F. Kaiser prof. bus. adminstrn., prof. econs. and law, 1994—; spl. econ. asst. to asst. atty. gen. for antitrust Dept. Justice, 1966-67; dir. Ctr. for Study Orgnl. Innovation, U. Pa., 1976-83; Edgar F. Kaiser prof. bus., econs. and law U. Calif., Berkeley, 1988—; cons. in field. Author: The Economics of Discretionary Behavior, 1964, Corporate Control and Business Behavior, 1970, Markets and Hierarchies, 1975, The Economic Institutions of Capitalism, 1985, Economic Organization, 1986, Antitrust Economics, 1987, The Mechanisms of Governance, 1996; assoc. editor Bell. Jour. Econs., 1973-74, editor, 1975-82; co-editor Jour. Law, Econs. and Orgn., 1983—. Fellow Ctr. for Advanced Study in Behavioral Scis., 1977-78; Guggenheim fellow, 1977-78; Am. Acad. Arts and Scis. fellow, 1983; recipient Alexander Henderson award Carnegie-Mellon U., 1962, Alexander von Humboldt Rsch. prize, 1987, Irwin award Acad. of Mgmt., 1988. Fellow Econometric Soc.; mem. Nat. Acad. Scis., Am. Econ. Assn. Office: U Calif Dept Econs Berkeley CA 94720

WILLIAMSON, PETER DAVID, lawyer; b. Houston, Oct. 13, 1944; s. Sam and Sophie Ann (Kaplan) W.; m. Patricia Golemon; children: Heather, Amber, Asia, Ginger. B.A., U. Ill., 1966; J.D., U. Tex., 1969. Bar: Tex. 1969, U.S. Supreme Ct. 1974, U.S. Ct. Appeals (4th, 9th, 5th, 8th, 10th, 11th and D.C. cirs.); lic. comml. pilot. Pvt. practice Houston, 1971—; founder IMMLAW, The Nat. Consortium of Immigration Law Firms. Mem. Am. Immigration Lawyers Assn. (pres. 1994-95). Home: 2417 Branard St Houston TX 77098-2213 Office: 1111 Fannin St Ste 1360 Houston TX 77002-6923 *I do not believe in the existence of national boundaries. The philosophy of my practice of the law is to help my clients achieve the ability to pass freely through such artificial political barriers.*

WILLIAMSON, PHILIP, apparel executive. CEO Williamson-Dickie Mfg. Co., Ft. Worth. Office: Williamson-Dickie Mfg Co PO Box 1779 Fort Worth TX 76101

WILLIAMSON, RICHARD CARDINAL, physicist; b. Minocqua, Wis., Sept. 10, 1939; s. Lyman Olaf and Edna (Cardinal) W.; m. Christine Bauer, Sept. 2, 1961; children—Kari, Meagan, Heidi, Ryan. B.S. in Physics, MIT, 1961, Ph.D. in Physics, 1966. Staff physicist NASA Electronics Research Ctr., Cambridge, Mass., 1965-70; staff mem. and assoc. group leader MIT Lincoln Lab., Lexington, Mass., 1970-80, group leader applied physics, electrooptic device rsch., 1980-95, sr. staff electro-optical devices and materials group, 1995—. Contbr. articles to jours., chpts. to books; patentee in field. Fellow IEEE (Centennial award 1984, Sonics and Ultrasonics Achievement award 1985); mem. IEEE, Am. Phys. Soc., Optical Soc. Am., Sigma Xi. Methodist. Home: 21 Pendleton Rd Sudbury MA 01776-1612 Office: MIT Lincoln Lab 244 Wood St Rm C-317 Lexington MA 02173-9108

WILLIAMSON, RICHARD HALL, association executive; b. Canton, N.C., July 29, 1940; s. James Eustace and Gwendolyn (Nevada) H.; m. Julia Draper Brown, Nov. 7, 1965 (div. Jan. 1981); children: Shawn Nicol, Kevin Carson. BS in Physics, N.C. State U., 1962, MS in Nuclear Engring., 1970, PhD in Econs., 1972. Instr. N.C. State U., Raleigh, 1968-72; chief, energy systems analysis AEC, Washington, 1972-75; asst. dir., energy analysis U.S. Energy R & D Adminstrn., Washington, 1975-77; dir., program analysis U.S. Dept. Energy, Washington, 1977-80, dir., policy devel., 1980-84, dep. asst. sec. for internat. affairs, 1984-94; dep. exec. dir. U.S. Energy Assn., Washington, 1995—. Author: A Group Strategy for Energy Research, Development and Demonstration, 1980; contbr. articles to jours. in field. Football ofcl. Atlantic Coast Conf., Greensboro, N.C., 1980—, Rose Bowl, Pasadena, Calif., 1995. 1st lt. U.S. Army, 1962-64; col. USAR, 1964-93. NSF fellow, 1964-65; AEC fellow, 1965-68; recipient Outstanding alumnus award IFC, N.C. State U., 1971, Presdl. Rank award U.S. Dept. Energy, 1990. Mem. Sigma Alpha Mu (nat. pres. 1984-86), Tau Beta Pi, Phi Kappa Phi, Omicron Delta Kappa, Sigma Pi Sigma, Pi Mu Epsilon. Republican. Methodist. Avocations: stamp collecting, tennis, golf, skiing. Home: Apr 1107-S 3705 S George Mason Dr Falls Church VA 22041-3720 Office: US Energy Assn 1620 I St NW Ste 1000 Washington DC 20006

WILLIAMSON, RICHARD SALISBURY, lawyer; b. Evanston, Ill., May 9, 1949; s. Donald G. and Marion (Salisbury) W.; m. Jane Thatcher, Aug. 25, 1973; children: Elizabeth Jean, Craig Salisbury, Richard Middleton. A.B. with honors, Princeton U., 1971; J.D., U. Va., 1974. Bar: Ill. bar 1974, D.C. bar 1975. Legis. counsel, adminstrv. asst. to Congressman Philip M. Crane of Ill., 1974-76; assoc. firm Winston & Strawn, Washington, 1977-80; ptnr. Winston & Strawn, 1980; asst. to Pres. for intergovtl. affairs, Washington, also assoc. dir. President's Task Force on Regulatory Relief, 1981-83; U.S. ambassador Vienna, Austria, 1983-85; sr. v.p., corp. and internat. relations Beatrice Cos., Inc., Chgo., 1985-86; ptnr. Mayer, Brown & Platt, Chgo., 1986-88, 89—; asst. sec. of state internat. orgn. affairs Dept. of State, Washington, 1988-89; rep. UN Orgns., Vienna, 1983-85; dep. ref. with rank of ambassador IAEA. Editor: Trade & Economic Growth, 1993, United States Foreign Policy and the United Nations System, 1996; co-editor: (with Paul Laxalt) A Changing America: Conservatives View the 80's From the United States Senate, 1980, Reagan's Federalism: His Efforts to Decentralize Government, 1990, The United Nations: A Place of Promise and of Mischief, 1991. Republican. Office: Mayer Brown & Platt 190 S La Salle St Chicago IL 60603-3410

WILLIAMSON, RICHARD THOMAS, lawyer, real estate broker; b. New Orleans, La., Sept. 24, 1958; s. Thomas Mose and Catherine Anne (Arnold) W. AA, Long Beach (Calif.) C.C., 1982; BS, U. So. Calif., 1986; postgrad., Calif. State U., Long Beach, 1988; JD, Southwestern U., L.A., 1992. Bar: Calif.; cert. real estate appraiser. Pres., CEO Campus Systems, L.A., 1982-86; bus. cons. Intelligent Solutions, Long Beach, Calif., 1986-87; real estate broker Coldwell Banker, Long Beach, 1987—; assoc. Landis & Assocs., Long Beach, Calif., 1992—; cons. TVO Med. Group, Long Beach, 1986, Leather 'N More, Fountain Valley, Calif., 1988-90; mem. adv. bd. Coldwell Banker, Long Beach, Calif., 1988-90. Bd. dirs. Homeless Relief Program, Long Beach, 1987-91. With USAF, 1976-78. Grantee, scholar Haynes Found., L.A., 1982-86. Mem. ABA, ATLA, Calif. Assn. Realtors. Office: Landis & Assocs 5580 E 2d St # 209 Long Beach CA 90803

WILLIAMSON, ROBERT CHARLES, marketing executive; b. West Chester, Pa., Jan. 3, 1925; s. Herman Gideon and Grace (Faddis) W.; m. Frances Yvonne Ishmael, Apr. 10, 1945 (div. July 1969); children: Robert C. Jr., Edward H., Richard F., Kathryn G.; m. Mary Elizabeth Bogle, Oct. 1, 1983. BS, Naval Sci. Sch., Monterey, Calif., 1959; postgrad. in Internat. Rels., Naval War Coll., Newport, R.I., 1960. Commd. ensign, designated naval aviator USN, 1944, advanced through grades to comdr., 1963, ret., 1966; gen. mgr. Springfield (Va.) Assocs., 1966-69; v.p. CCC Corp., Rosslyn, Va., 1969-70; pres. WILCO Assocs., Mt. Vernon, Va., 1970-73; dir. mktg. Documail Systems, Lenexa, Kans., 1973-80; N.Am. mktg. mgr. Leigh Instruments, Waterloo, Ont., Can., 1981-83; v.p. Tabs Assocs., Abingdon, Md., 1983-87; pres. WILLMAR Assocs. Internat., Brandon, Fla., 1987—. Mem. Nat. Assn. Presort Mailers (exec. dir. 1984—), Ret. Officers' Assn., Assn. Former Intelligence Officers, Assn. Naval Aviation. Club: Army and Navy. Home and Office: 3906 Butternut Ct Brandon FL 33511-7961

WILLIAMSON, SAMUEL RUTHVEN, JR., historian, university administrator; b. Bogalusa, La., Nov. 10, 1935; s. Samuel Ruthven and Frances Mitchell (Page) W.; m. Joan Chaffe Andress, Dec. 30, 1961; children: George Samuel, Treeby Andress, Thaddeus Miller. BA, Tulane U., 1958; AM, Harvard U., 1960, PhD, 1966, grad. advanced mgmt. program, 1986; hon. degrees, Furman U. Va. Theol. Sem. Asst. prof. U.S. Mil. Acad., 1963-66; instr. history Harvard U., 1966-68, asst. prof., 1968-72, Allston Burr sr. tutor, 1968-72, asst. to dean of Harvard Coll., 1969-70; rsch. assoc. Inst. Politics, faculty asso. Ctr. for Internat. Affairs, 1971-72; mem. faculty J.F. Kennedy Sch. Govt., 1971-72; assoc. prof. history U. N.C., Chapel Hill, 1972-74; prof. U. N.C., 1974-88, dean Coll. Arts and Scis., 1977-85, provost univ., 1984-88; pres., vice chancellor The U. of the South, Sewanee, Tenn., 1988—; cons. Historian's Office, Office of Sec. Def., 1974-76; vis. fellow Churchill Coll., 1976-77; mem. vis. com. Harvard Coll., 1986-92; dir. Research Triangle Inst., 1984-88; trustee N.C. Sch. Sci. and Math., 1985-88, Day Found., 1990-93; mem. bd. visitors Air U., 1994—. Author: The Politics of Grand Strategy: Britain and France Prepare for War, 1904-1914, 1969, 2d edit., 1990; co-author: The Origins of U.S. Nuclear Strategy, 1945-53, 1993; editor: The Origins of a Tragedy: July 1914, 1981; co-editor: Essays on World War I: Origins and Prisoners of War, 1983, Austria-Hungary and the Origins of the First World War, 1991; Am. editor: War and Soc. Newsletter, 1973-88. Mem. cen. com. Morehead Found., 1978-93; vice chmn. bd. visitors Air U., 1996—. Capt. U.S. Army, 1963-66. Fulbright scholar U. Edinburgh, 1958-59; Woodrow Wilson fellow, 1958-63; Danforth fellow, 1958-63; Nat. Endowment Humanities fellow, 1976-77; Ford Found. grantee, 1976; fellow Nat. Humanities Ctr., 1983; recipient George Louis Beer prize for best book on internat. history Am. Hist. Assn., 1970. Mem. Am. Hist. Assn., Internat. Inst. Strategic Studies, Nat. Assn. Ind. Colls. and Univs. (chairperson bd. dirs. 1994-95). Democrat. Episcopalian. Home: PO Box 837 Sewanee TN 37375-0837 Office: U of the South Office of Pres Sewanee TN 37375-4013

WILLIAMSON, THOMAS GARNETT, nuclear engineering and engineering physics educator; b. Quincy, Mass., Jan. 27, 1934; s. Robert Burwell and Elizabeth B. (McNeer) W.; m. Kaye Darlan Love, Aug. 16, 1961; children: Allen, Sarah, David. BS, Va. Mil. Inst., 1955; MS, Rensselaer Poly. Inst., 1957; PhD, U. Va., 1960. Asst. prof. nuclear engring. and engring. physics dept. U. Va., Charlottesville, 1960-62, assoc. prof., 1962-69, prof., 1969-90, prof. emeritus, 1990—, chmn. dept., 1977-90; sr. scientist Westinghouse Savannah River Labs., Aiken, S.C., 1990—; with Gen. Atomic (Calif.), 1965, Combustion Engring., Windsor, Conn., 1970-71, Los Alamos Sci. Lab., 1969, Nat. Bur. Standards, Gaithersburg, Md., 1984-85; cons. Philippine Atomic Energy Commn., 1963, Va. Power Co., 1975-90, Babcock & Wilcox, Lynchburg, Va., 1975-90. Vestryman Ch. of Our Savior, Charlottesville, St. Thaddeus, Alken, S.C. Fellow Am. Nuclear Soc.; mem. AAAS, Am. Soc. Engring. Edn., Sigma Xi, Tau Beta Pi. Episcopalian. Home: 217 Colleton Ave Aiken SC 29801 Office: Westinghouse Savannah River Labs Aiken SC 29806

WILLIAMSON, THOMAS SAMUEL, JR., lawyer; b. Plainfield, N.J., July 14, 1946; s. Thomas Samuel and Winifred (Hall) W.; married; 2 children. BA, Harvard U., 1968; postgrad., Oxford U., Eng., 1968-69; JD, U. Calif., Berkeley, 1974. Bar: D.C. 1975, Calif. 1975, U.S. Dist. Ct. D.C. 1977. Dir. tng. div. Alem Pub. Relations, Addis Ababa, Ethiopia, 1970-71; assoc. Covington & Burling, Washington, 1974-78, 81-82, ptnr., 1982-93; dep. inspector gen. U.S. Dept. Energy, Washington, 1978-81; solicitor U.S. Dept. Labor, Washington; ptnr. Covington & Burling, Washington; mem. exec. com. Washington Lawyers for Civil Rights Under Law, 1983-93, co-chair, 1990-92. Mem. vis. com. to dept. of athletics Harvard U., 1985-87. Rhodes scholar, 1968. Mem. ABA, Nat. Bar Assn., Coun. on Fgn. Rels., Washington Coun. Lawyers (bd. dirs. 1975-90). Avocations: camping, cycling. Home: 1663 Primrose Rd NW Washington DC 20012-1117 Office: US Dept Labor Solicitor Office 200 Constitution Ave NW Washington DC 20210-0001

WILLIAMSON, WILLIAM ALLEN, optometrist; b. Dossville, Miss., July 29, 1933; s. Donald Wodsworth and Ruth Beatrice (Doss) W.; m. Martha Pearl Taylor, Mar. 28, 1959; children: Lamar Arthur, William Allen, Donna Taylor. AA, Northwest Jr. Coll., Senatobia, Miss., 1952; OD, So. Coll. Optometry, Memphis, 1956. Pvt. practice optometry Greenville, Miss., 1959—; chmn. Adv. Com. to Medicaid, Miss., 1972-75. Mem. Miss. Blind & Deaf Bd. Trustees, 1974-76; charter mem. Optomist Club, Greenville, Miss., 1964; pres. Wash. County Assn. Retarded Citizens, Greenville, 1981-83, S.O.S. Retarded Workshop, Inc., Greenville, 1985-87, Christian Mission Concerns of Miss., Greenville, 1987-89. 1st lt. U.S. Army, 1956-59. Mem. Am. Optometric Assn. (legis. keyman 1971-72), Miss. Optometric Assn. (legis. chmn. 1973-74), Masons (32 degree), Shriners, Elks. Presbyterian. Avocations: The Bible, history, genealogy research, politics, fishing. Office: Eye Clinic of Optometry 239 S Washington Ave Greenville MS 38701-4234

WILLIAMSON, WILLIAM FLOYD, JR., architect; b. Baton Rouge, Dec. 20, 1924; s. William Floyd and Georgie (Perkins) W.; m. Adele Redditt, Aug. 24, 1946; children: Adele Redditt Williamson Scielzo, Nancy Scott Williamson Cadwallader. B.S. in Architecture, Tulane U., 1947. Lic. architect, La. Treas., gen. mgr. La. Agrl. Supply Co., Inc., Baton Rouge, 1947-69; owner W.F. Williamson, Jr., Architect, Baton Rouge, 1970-74; pres., ptnr. Williamson-Carroll Architect, Inc., Baton Rouge, 1974—; chmn. Polit. Com. for Design Profls., La., 1975-83; chmn. Benefit Ins. Trust, 1981-82; trustee, vice-chmn. Architects Nat. Employers Trust, 1986—. Architect chmn. United Givers Fund Drive, Baton Rouge, 1978; bd. dirs. First United Meth. Ch., 1968-82. With USN, 1943-45. Fellow AIA (pres. Baton Rouge chpt. 1978, chmn. chpt. govt. affairs com. 1973-75, nat. trustee Benefit Ins. Trust 1978-83); mem. La. Inst. Bldg. Scis. (founding), La. Architects Assn. (pres. 1981, chmn. govtl. affairs com. 1973-78 commendation outstanding service), Delta Tau Delta. Republican. Club: Baton Rouge Country. Home: 920 N Foster Dr Baton Rouge LA 70806-1807 Office: Williamson & Carroll Architects PO Box 843 Baton Rouge LA 70821-0843

WILLIAMSON, WILLIAM PAUL, JR., journalist; b. Des Moines, Mar. 30, 1929; s. William Paul and Florence Alice (Dawson) W.; m. Vania Torres Neirinha, Nov. 27, 1959; children—Mary Liz (Mrs. Omar Fernandez), Jon Thadeus, Margaret Ann(Mrs. Cesar Rocha). Student, Mex. City Coll., 1952, U. Havanna, 1955; B.A., U. No. Iowa, 1953; M.A., U. Iowa, 1954. Editor Brazilian Bus., Rio de Janeiro, 1958-60; mng. ptnr. Editora Mory Ltd., Rio de Janeiro, 1960-79; editor Brazil Herald, Rio de Janeiro, 1960-80; exec. dir. Inter Am. Press Assn., Miami, Fla., 1981-94, hon. life mem., mem. adv. coun., 1994—; dir. Inter Am. Press Assn., 1966-80, chmn. awards com., 1975-80; solo navigator 1st passage Madeira Island, Portugal-Madeira Island, Brazil, 1994-95. Editor for Brazil, Fodor's South America, 1970-79; contbr. articles to various newspapers and mags. Pres. Am. Soc., Rio de Janeiro, 1968; bd. dirs. Instituto Brasil-Estados Unidos, Rio de Janeiro, 1977-80, Am. C. of C. for Brazil, Rio de Janeiro, 1964-68. Served with USMC, 1946-48. Decorated Order of Rio Branco (Brazil); recipient Citizen of Rio de Janeiro award State Legislature, 1975; Hon. Carioca award O Globo Newspaper, Rio de Janeiro, 1972; Ralph Greenbuerg award Am. Soc. Rio de Janeiro, 1977; Outstanding Svc. to Freedom of Expression and Newspapers award Internat. Fedn. of Newspaper Pubs. and Internat. Assn. of Broadcasting, 1994; Benemeritous Citizen award Mcpl. Legislature, Itaquai, Brazil, 1995. Mem. Am. Soc. Assn. Execs., South Fla. Soc. Assn. Execs. (pres. 1987), Soc. Profl. Journalists, Overseas Press Club Am., Rio Yacht Club, Ilha da Madeira Yacht Club, Kappa Tau Alpha. Home: 2600 Castilla Is Fort Lauderdale FL 33301-1594 Office: Inter Am Press Assn 2911 NW 39th St Miami FL 33142-5148

WILLIAMS-THOMAS, JOAN LORENA, biology educator, genetics counselor, administrator b. Washington; d. Ernest Young and Matilda (Herbert) Williams; BS, Howard U., 1959, MS (Am. Heart Assn. grad. fellow 1963-64), 1964, PhD (NDEA fellow 1971-73), 1973; Cert. and lic. genetic counselor, clin. lab. scientist; CPR, ACLS, EMT instr.; children: Charles Anthony, Carlton Alexei. Tchr. biology D.C. Pub. Schs., 1965-74; assoc. prof. biotechnology, Washington Tech. Inst., 1974-80; chmn. dept. biotech., 1975-80, prof. biology, U. D.C., 1980—, coord. biotech. and genetics programs, 1980-88, coord. med. tech. programs, 1983-95, genetic counselor, 1979—; bd. dirs. Health Sci. Acad.; cons. N.C. Health Manpower Program, 1978-81, D.C. Pub. Schs., Howard U. Hosp. Dept. Radiation Therapy, 1992; mem. Adminstrn. Developmental Disabilities/U.S. Dept. Health and Human Svcs., commr.'s multicultural com., 1994; coord. Emergency Med. Svcs. program, 1985—, dir., instr. Emergency Med. Technician programs, 1985—, Health Career Opportunity program, 1983—; CPR and ACLS instr., 1989; med. technologist, 1980; legislative chair Delegation to People's Rep. of China, 1988; del. Internat. Congress on Genetics, 1973, 78. Bd. trustees Am. Med. Tedh. Inst. for Edn., v.p., 1992-94; mem. D.C. Commn. Pub. Health; chair Healthy People 2000, adv. bd.; congressional judge D.C. Sci. Fair, 1977—, Mongomery County Sci. Fair, 1990—; sec. bd. dirs. Ebony Industries, 1977—; trustee Maret Sch., 1978-79; sec.-treas. Nat. Capital Parliamentarians, 1978—; faculty rep. Barry M. Goldwater Scholarship & Excellence Edn. Founs., 1990-94; bd. dirs. D.C./Md./Del. State Soc., Am. Med. Technologists, 1989-93, 95—; chair Employment Svc., 1987-89. Recipient Exceptional Svc. award Am. Med. Technologists, 1995, Disting. Achievement award,1991; named Tchr. of the Year Nat. Soc. Allied Health, 1994. Mem. AAAS, Am. Inst. Biol. Sci., Fedn. Am. Scientists, Am. Genetic Assn., Genetic Soc. Am., Am. Soc. Human Genetics, Nat. Soc. Allied Health (treas. 1988-94), Sigma Xi, Beta Kappa Chi. Contbr. articles to profl. jours. Office: 4200 Connecticut Ave NW Washington DC 20008-1174

WILLIAMS-WENNELL, KATHI, human resources officer; b. Danville, Pa., Sept. 22, 1955; d. Raymond Gerald and Julia Dolores (Higgins) Williams; m. Mark Kevin Wennell, Apr. 3, 1982; children: Ryan Christopher, Lauren Ashley. BA, Immaculata Coll., 1977; MEd, Pa. State U., State College, 1978. Cert. rehabilitation counselor, Pa. From project dir. to coord. devel. activities Community Interactions, Blue Bell, Pa., 1978-83; from mgmt. trainee to coord. coll. recruiting and rels. Meridian Bancorp, Inc., Reading, Pa., 1983-86, mgmt. recruiter, compensation analyst, 1986-88, 89-93; recruiter, 1993—; cons. Norristown (Pa.) Life Ctr., 1981; instr. Immaculata (Pa.) Coll., 1981-83, Alvernia Coll., Reading, 1988-89. Meridian campaign coord. United Way Berks County, Reading, 1985. Named Recruiter of Yr. LaSalle U., Phila., 1986; recipient Excellence in Programming award Nat. Assn. Bank Women, Pa., 1986. Mem. Soc. Human Resources Mgmt. Republican. Roman Catholic. Avocations: walking, racquetball, golf, tennis, reading. Home: 69 S Hampton Dr Wyomissing PA 19610-3108 Office: Meridian Bancorp Inc Meridian Ctr at Springridge 1 Meridian Blvd Wyomissing PA 19610-3200

WILLIE, CHARLES VERT, sociology educator; b. Dallas, Oct. 8, 1927; s. Louis James and Carrie (Sykes) W.; m. Mary Susannah Conklin, Mar. 31, 1962; children: Sarah Susannah, Martin Charles, James Theodore. BA, Morehouse Coll., 1948, DHL (hon.), 1983; MA, Atlanta U., 1949; PhD, Syracuse U., 1957, DHL (hon.), 1992; DD (hon.), Gen. Sem., 1974; DHL (hon.), Berkeley Div. Sch., Yale U., 1972, R.I. Coll., 1983, Johnson C. Smith U., Charlotte, N.C., 1991; MA (hon.), Harvard U., 1974; DL (hon.), Framingham (Mass.) State Coll., 1992; DHL (hon.), Franklin Pierce Coll., Rindge, N.H., 1996. Instr. to asst. prof. sociology Syracuse (N.Y.) U., 1952-63, assoc. prof., 1964-67, prof., 1968-74, chmn. dept. sociology, 1967-71, v.p., 1972-74; prof. edn. and urban studies Grad. Sch. Edn. Harvard U., 1974—; instr. dept. preventive medicine SUNY Upstate Med. Center, Syracuse, 1955-60; research dir. Washington Action for Youth delinquency prevention project, Pres.' Com. on Juvenile Delinquency and Youth Crime, Washington, 1962-64; vis. lectr. Lab. Community Psychiatry, Harvard U. Med. Sch., Boston, Mass., 1966-67; vis. lectr. ch. and soc. Episcopal Div. Sch., Cambridge, Mass., 1966-67; commr. Pres.'s Commn. on Mental Health, 1977-78; mem. tech. adv. bd. Maurice Falk Med. Fund, 1968—; bd. dirs. Social Sci. Rsch. Coun., 1969-75; master Boston Sch. Desegregation case, Fed. Dist. Ct., 1975. Author: Church Action in the World, 1969, Black Students at White Colleges, 1972, Race Mixing in the Public Schools, 1973, Oreo, 1975, A New Look at Black Families, 1976, 2d edit., 1981, 3d edit., 1988, 4th edit., 1991, The Sociology of Urban Education, 1978, The Caste and Class Controversy on Race and Poverty, 1979, 2d edit., 1989, The Ivory and Ebony Towers, 1981, Race, Ethnicity and Socioeconomic Status, 1983, School Desegregation Plans That Work, 1984, Black and White Families, 1985, Five Black Scholars, 1986, (with Michael Grady) Metropolitan School Desegregation, 1986, Effective Education, 1987, (with Michael Grady and Richard Hope) African-Americans and the Doctoral Experience, 1991, Theories of Human Social Action, 1994; editor: The Family Life of Black People, 1970, (with B. Brown and B. Kramer) Racism and Mental Health, 1973, Black/Brown/White Relations, 1977, (with R. Edmonds) Black Colleges in America, 1978, (with S. Greenblatt) Community Politics and Educational Change, 1981, (with Inabeth Miller) Social Goals and Educational Reforms, 1988, (with A. Garibaldi and W. Reed), The Education of African-Americans, 1991, (with P. Rieker, B. Kramer and B. Brown) Mental Health, Racism and Sexism, 1995. Hon. trustee Episcopal Div. Sch., Cambridge, Mass.; mem. United Negro Coll. Fund, 1983-90; mem. nat. exec. coun. Episcopal ch., 1967-74, v.p. gen. conv., 1970-74; host Inner City Beat nat. pub. affairs weekly television program, monitor channel, 1991-92; mem. Maxwell Sch. Adv. bd. of Syracuse U., 1992—. Recipient faculty svc. award Nat. Univ. Ext. Assn., 1969, 50th Anniversary Disting. Alumnus award Syracuse U. Maxwell Sch., 1974; Lee-Founders award Soc. for Study Social Problems, 1983, Disting. Family Scholar award, 1986; Disting. Career Contbn. award com. on role and status minorities in ednl. R & D, Am. Ednl. Rsch. Assn., 1990, Benjamin E. Mays Svc. award Morehouse Coll., 1994, Father John LaFarge, S.J. award Fairfield U., 1995. Mem. am. Ednl. Rsch. Assn., Am. Sociol. Assn. (coun. 1980-83, 95-98, v.p. 1996-97, DuBois-Johnson-Frazier award 1994), Phi Beta Kappa, Alpha Phi Alpha. Episcopalian. Home: 41 Hillcrest Rd Concord MA 01742-4615 Office: Harvard U Grad Sch Edn 457 Gutman Libr 6 Appian Way Cambridge MA 02138-3704

WILLIFORD, DONALD BRATTON, accounting company executive; b. York, S.C., Sept. 20, 1936; s. Thomas Leslie and Florence Odessa (Brown) W.; m. Linda Craven, June 12, 1959; 1 child, Linda Sharon. BSBA, U. S.C., 1958. CPA, N.C. Jr. acct. J. P. Stevens, Charlotte, N.C., 1959; staff acct. Haskins & Sells, CPAs, Charlotte, 1959-62; with audit and tax div. Belk Stores Svcs., Inc., Charlotte, 1962-69; corp. sec. Ruddick Corp., Charlotte, 1969—. Mem. AICPA, N.C. Assn. CPA, Am. Soc. Corp. Secs., Risk and Ins. Mgmt. Soc., Employee Stock Ownership Plans Assn. (chair 1991-93), River Hills Country Club. Avocation: golf. Office: Ruddick Corp 2000 Two 1st Union Ctr Charlotte NC 28282

WILLIFORD, RICHARD ALLEN, oil executive, flight simulator company executive; b. Galveston, Tex., Dec. 24, 1934; s. Walter Hamilton and Marian Lela (Heartfield) W.; m. Mollie Marie Blansett, Feb. 16, 1957; children: Richard Allen Jr., Monica Marie Williford Powell. BS in Petroleum Engring., Tex. A&M U., 1956, BS in Geol. Engring., 1956. Registered profl. engr., Tex. Petroleum/reservoir engr. Gulf Oil Co., La., Tex., 1956-61; mgr. prodn. Tenneco Oil Co., Lafayette, La., and Denver, 1961-73; exec. v.p. Samson Resources Co., Tulsa, 1973-79; owner, chmn. Williford Energy Co., 1979—; chmn., CEO Safety Tng. Systems, Inc., Tulsa, 1984—, Williford Bldg. Corp., Tulsa, 1990—; chmn. Engineered Equipment Systems, Tulsa, 1989—; past bd. dirs. Samson Resources Co., Tulsa, Tilco, Inc., Tulsa, Intersci. Capital Mgmt. Corp., Tulsa, W-R Leasing Co., Fourth Nat. Bank Tulsa, Sun Belt Bank & Trust Tulsa, Union Nat. Bank Tulsa. Patentee in field. Bd. dirs. OIPA, 12th Man Found., College Station, Tex., 1983-85, Tulsa Opera, Inc., 1985—, Thomas Gilcrease Mus. Assn., Tulsa, 1987-93, Tex. A&M Assn. Former Students, College Station, 1985-91, pres., 1989; bd. dirs. Inst. Nautical Archaeology, 1993—, chmn., 1996; trustee River Parks Authority, Tulsa, 1987-93, chmn. bd. trustees, 1993-94; trustee, chmn. Tex. A&M Devel. Found., 1991—, Verde Valley Sch., Sedona, Ariz., 1983-86; pres. exec. bd. Indian Nations coun. INA (pres. 1996)., Boy Scouts Am. Recipient Disting. Achievement medal Geoscis. and Resource Coun., Tex. A&M U., 1991, Humanitarian award Nat. Jewish Ctr. for Immunology, 1994. Mem. Ind. Petroleum Assn. Am., Soc. Petroleum Engrs., Okla. Ind. Producers Assn., Tex. Ind. Producers and Royalty Owners Assn., Masons, Shriners, Royal Order Jesters, So. Hills Country Club, The Golf Club Okla., Philcrest Tennis Club, The Summit Club, Tex. A&M Faculty Club, Tau Beta Pi. Republican. Methodist. Avocations: golf, hunting, fishing, flying, scuba diving. Home: 6730 S Evanston Ave Tulsa OK 74136-4509 Office: Williford Companies 1323 E 71st St Ste 323 Tulsa OK 74136

WILLIG, KARL VICTOR, computer firm executive; b. Idaho Falls, Idaho, June 4, 1944; s. Louis Victor and Ethel (McCarty) W.; m. Julianne Erickson, June 10, 1972; 1 son, Ray. BA magna cum laude, Coll. of Idaho, 1968; MBA (Dean Donald Kirk David fellow), Harvard U., 1970. Pres. Ariz. Beef, Inc., Phoenix, 1971-73; group v.p. Ariz.-Colo. Land & Cattle Co., Phoenix, 1973-76; v.p. Rufenacht, Bromagen & Hertz, Inc., Chgo., 1976-77; pres. Sambo's Restaurants, Inc., Santa Barbara, Calif., 1977-79; ptnr. Santa Barbara Capital, 1979-85; pres. EURUSA Equities Corp., 1985-86; pres., chief exec. officer InfoGenesis, 1986—; trustee Am. Bapt. Sem. of West, 1977-85. Named one of Outstanding Young Men of Am., 1972; recipient Assn. of U.S. Army award, 1964.

WILLIG, ROBERT DANIEL, economics educator; b. Bklyn., Jan. 16, 1947; s. Jack David and Meg W.; m. Virginia Mason, July 8, 1973; children: Jared Mason, Scott Mason, Brent Mason, Alexandra Mason. BA, Harvard U., 1967; MS in Ops. Rsch., Stanford U., 1968, PhD in Econs, 1973. Lectr. Stanford U., Palo Alto, Calif., 1971-73; mem. tech. staff Bell Labs., Holmdel, N.J., 1973-77; supr. dept. econs. rsch. Bell Labs., 1977-78; prof. econs. and pub. affairs Princeton U., 1978—; mem. Aspen Inst. Task Force on Future of Postal Svc., 1978-80; dep. asst. atty. gen. U.S. Dept. Justice, Washington, 1989-91; cons. in field; rsch. fellow U. Warwick, Eng., 1977; mem. organizing com. Telecom Policy Rsch. Conf., 1977-78; mem. rsch. adv. bd. Am. Enterprise Inst., 1980-88; mem. N.J. Gov.'s Task Force on Market-Based Pricing of Electricity, 1987; bd. dirs. Consultants in Industry Econs., Inc., 1983—; mem. Def. Sci. Bd. Task Force on Antitrust for the Def. Industry, 1993-94, Transp. Rsch. Bd. Task Force, 1995-96. Author: Welfare Analysis of Policies Affecting Prices and Products, 1973, Contestable Markets and the Theory of Industry Structure, 1982; editor: Handbook of Industrial Organization, 1986; contbr. articles to profl. jours. mem. editorial bd.: M.I.T. Press Series on Govt. Regulation, 1978—, Am. Econ. Rev., 1980-83, Jour. Indsl. Econs., 1985-89, Utility Policy, 1989—. Mem. adv. bd. B'nai B'rith Hillel Found., Princeton U., 1978—. NSF grantee, 1979-85. Fellow Econometric Soc. (program com. 1978-81); mem. Am. Econ. Assn. (nominating com. 1980-81). Office: Princeton Univ Economics Dept Princeton NJ 08540

WILLIMON, WILLIAM HENRY, minister, educator; b. Greenville, S.C., May 15, 1946; s. Robert Charles and Ruby (Steer) W.; m. Patricia Parker, June 7, 1969; children: William Parker, Harriet Patricia. BA, Wofford Coll., 1968, DLitt (hon.), 1994; MDiv, Yale U., 1970; STD, Emory U., 1972; DD (hon.), Westminster Coll., New Wilmington, Pa., 1990; DLitt, Wofford Coll., 1993; LHD, Lehigh U., 1995. Ordained to ministry United Meth. Ch., 1972. Pastor Level Creek/Trinity United Meth. Chs., Buford, Ga., 1970-71; assoc. pastor Broad St. United Meth. Ch., Clinton, S.C., 1971-73; pastor Trinity United Meth. Ch., North Myrtle Beach, S.C., 1973-76; assoc. prof. Duke Divinity Sch., Durham, N.C., 1976-80; pastor Northside United Meth. Ch., Greenville, S.C., 1980-84; minister to univ., prof. Duke U., Durham, 1984-89, dean of chapel, prof., 1989—. Author: Why I Am a United Methodist, 1990, Clergy and Laity Burnout, 1988, Acts of the Apostles, Interpretation, A Commentary for Teaching and Preaching, 1988, The Promise of Marriage, 1988, Preaching About Conflict in the Local Church, 1987, Rekindling the Flame, 1987, With Glad and Generous Hearts, 1986, The Laugh Shall Be First, 1986, Sighing for Eden, 1985, What's Right With the Church, 1984, Handbook on Preaching and Worship, 1984, On A Wild and Windy Mountain, 1984, many other books. 1st lt. U.S. Army, 1969-70. Fellow N.Am. Acad. of Liturgy; mem. Phi Beta Kappa. Home: 3104 Doubleday Pl Durham NC 27705-5412 Office: Duke Univ Dean Chapel Durham NC 27706

WILLINGHAM, CLARK SUTTLES, lawyer; b. Houston, Nov. 29, 1944; s. Paul Suttles and Elsie Dell (Clark) W.; m. Jane Joyce Hitch, Aug. 16, 1969; children: Meredith Moores, James Barrett. BBA, Tex. Tech U., 1967; JD, So. Meth. U., 1971, LLM, 1984. Bar: Tex. 1971. Ptnr. Kasmir, Willingham & Krage, Dallas, 1972-86, Finley, Kumble et al, Dallas, 1986-87, Hill, Held & Metzger and predecessor, Dallas, 1988—; mem. Tex. Bd. Vet. Med. Examiners, 1991-95, pres., 1994. Contbr. articles to profl. jours. Mem. exec. com. Dallas Summer Musicals, 1979-93, pres., 1994-95. Mem. ABA (chmn. agrl. com. tax sect. 1984-86), State Bar Tex. (chmn. agrl. tax com. 1985-87), Am. Law Inst., Nat. Cattlemen's Beef Assn. (bd. dirs., v.p. Region IV 1990-92, 1st v.p. 1996), U.S. Meat Export Fedn. (exec. com. 1991-93), Beef Industry Coun. (exec. com. 1990-91, promotion chmn. 1992-94), Tex. Cattle Feeders Assn. (bd. dirs., pres. 1987-88), Dallas Bar Assn., Dallas County Club. Republican. Episcopalian. Home: 3824 Shenandoah St Dallas TX 75205-1702 Office: Hill Held & Metzger 1 Turtle Creek Village Dallas TX 75219

WILLINGHAM, EDWARD BACON, JR., ecumenical minister, administrator; b. St. Louis, July 27, 1934; s. Edward and Harriet (Sharon) W.; m. Angeline Walton Pettit, June 14, 1957; children: Katie, Carol. BS in Physics, U. Richmond, 1956; postgrad., U. Rochester, 1958-59; MDiv., Colgate Rochester Div. Sch., 1960. Ordained to ministry Am. Bapt. Ch., 1960. Min. Christian edn. Delaware Ave. Bapt. Ch., Buffalo, N.Y., 1960-62; dir. radio and TV Met. Detroit Coun. Chs., 1962-75; exec. dir. Christian Communication Coun. Met. Detroit Chs., 1976—; bus. mgr. N.Am. Broadcast sect. WACC, 1972—, chmn., 1970-71; broadcast cons. Mich. Coun. Chs., 1965-75; guest cons. religious broadcasting Germany, 1968; mem. coord. com. Mich. Ecumenical Forum, 1986, 90-92, chmn., 1991-92. Bd. mgrs. Broadcasting and Film Commn., Nat. Coun. Chs., 1965-73; mem. Muslim-Christian-Jewish Leadership Forum, 1987—; bd. deacons 1st Bapt. Ch. Birmingham, chmn., 1994. Recipient Gabriel award Cath. Broadcasting Assn., 1972, 1st Ann. Ecumenical award Am. Bapt. Chs. of Mich., 1992, Race Rels. award Booker T. Washington Bus. Assn. of Detroit, 1983. Mem. Assn. Regional Religious Communicators (pres. 1969-71), World Assn. Christian Comm. (ctrl. com. 1973-78), Phi Gamma Delta, Sigma Pi Sigma. Office: 1300 Mutual Bldg Detroit MI 48226

WILLINGHAM, JEANNE MAGGART, dance educator, ballet company executive; b. Fresno, Calif., May 8, 1923; d. Harold F. and Gladys (Ellis) Maggart. student Tex. Woman's U., 1942; student profl. dancing schs., worldwide. dance tchr. Beaux Arts Dance Studio, Pampa, Tex., 1948—; artistic dir. Pampa Civic Ballet, 1972—. Mem. Tex. Arts and Humanities, Tex. Arts Alliance, Pampa C. of C. (fine arts com.), Pampa Fine Arts Assn. Office: Pampa Civic Ballet Beaux Arts Dance Studio 315 N Nelson St Pampa TX 79065-6013

WILLINGHAM, MARY MAXINE, fashion retailer; b. Childress, Tex., Sept. 12, 1928; d. Charles Bryan and Mary (Bohannon) McCollum; m. Welborn Kiefer Willingham, Aug. 14, 1950; children: Sharon, Douglas, Sheila. BA, Tex. Tech U., 1949. Interviewer Univ. Placement Svc., Tex. Tech U., Lubbock, 1964-69; owner, mgr., buyer Maxine's Accent, Lubbock, 1969—; speaker in field. Leader Campfire Girls, Lubbock, 1964-65; sec. Community Theatre, Lubbock, 1962-64. Named Outstanding Mcht., Fashion Retailor mag., 1971, Outstanding Retailer; recipient Golden Sun award Dallas Market, May 1985. Mem. Lubbock Symphony Guild, Ranch and Heritage Ctr. Club: Faculty Women's. Office: 16 Briercroft Shopping Ctr Lubbock TX 79412-3022

WILLINGHAM, WARREN WILLCOX, psychologist, testing service executive; b. Rome, Ga., Mar. 1, 1930; s. Calder Baynard and Eleanor (Willcox) W.; m. Anna Michal, Mar. 17, 1954; children: Sherry, Judith, Daniel. Student, Ga. Inst. Tech., 1952; PhD, U. Tenn., 1955. Rsch. assoc. World Book Co., N.Y.C., 1959-60; dir. evaluation studies Ga. Inst. Tech., Atlanta, 1960-64; dir. rsch. Coll. Bd., N.Y.C., 1964-68; dir. access rsch. office Coll. Bd., Palo Alto, Calif., 1968-72; asst. v.p., disting. rsch. scientist Ednl. Testing Svc., Princeton, N.J., 1972—; vis. prof. U. Minn., 1988; mem. adv. bd. on ednl. requirements on Sec. Navy, 1968; cons. to numerous schs., colls. U.S. Office Edn. Author: Free Access Higher Education, 1970, Source Book for Higher Education, 1973, College Placement and Exemption, 1974, Assessing Experimental Learning, 1977, Selective Admissions in Higher Education, 1977, Personal Qualities and College Admissions, 1982, Success in College, 1985, Testing Handicapped People, 1988, Predicting College Grades, 1990, Gender and Fair Assessment, 1996; editor: Measurement in Education, 1969-72; mem. editl. bd. Jour. Ednl. Measurement, 1971-75, Alternate Higher Edn., 1976-80, Am. Ednl. Rsch. Jour., 1968-71; contbr. articles, tech. reports to profl. jours. Served to lt. USNR, 1955-59. Recipient Ann. award So. Soc. Philosophy and Psychology, 1958. Fellow Am. Psychol. Assn., AAAS; mem. Nat. Council on Measurement in Edn. (dir.), Am. Ednl. Research Assn., Sigma Xi. Office: Edn Testing Svc Princeton NJ 08540

WILLIS, BEVERLY ANN, architect; b. Tulsa, Feb. 17, 1928; d. Ralph William and Margaret Amanda (Porter) W. BFA, U. Hawaii, 1954; PhD in Fine Arts (hon.), Mt. Holyoke Coll., 1983. Registered architect, Calif. Prin. Willis Atelier, Honolulu, 1954-66, Willis & Assocs., Inc., San Francisco, 1966-80, Beverly Willis Architects, N.Y.C., 1990—; dir., Architecture Rsch. Inst., Inc., N.Y.C. 1993—. Prin. works include Union St. Stores (merit award San Francisco chpt. AIA, award of distinction State of Calif.), Nob Hill Cts. (merit award AIA), 1970, Margaret Hayward Park (grand and merit awards Pacific Coast Bldg. Con., hon. award Design Internat.), 1983, San Francisco Ballet Bldg., 1984, Manhattan Village Acad. Loft H.S., N.Y.C., 1995; contbr. articles to profl. jours., chpts. to books. Trustee Nat. Bldg. Mus., Washington, 1976—; bldng. rsch. adv. bd. Nat. Acad. Sci., 1971-79, chair Fed. Construction Coun., 1976-79. Recipient Phoebe Hearst Gold Medal award, 1969. Fellow AIA; mem. Achievement Rewards for Coll. Scientists, Internat. Women's Forum, Lambda Alpha Internat. (pres. San Francisco chpt. 1981-82). Club: Villa Taverna (San Francisco). Avocations: poetry, sketching, walking. Office: 119 East 35th St New York NY 10016 also: 19 Hillside Rd Northampton MA 01060

WILLIS, BRUCE WALTER, actor, singer; b. Fed. Republic of Germany, Mar. 19, 1955; came to U.S., 1957; s. David and Marlene Willis; m. Demi Moore; children: Rumer Glenn, Scout Larve, Tallulah Belle. Student, Montclair State Coll.; studied with Stella Adler. mem. First Amendment Comedy Theatre. Actor: (off-Broadway prodns.) Heaven and Earth, 1977, Fool for Love, 1984, The Bullpen, The Bayside Boys, The Ballad of Railroad William, (TV film) Trackdown, (feature films) Prince of the City, 1981, The Verdict, 1982, Blind Date, 1987, Sunset, 1988, Die Hard, 1988, In Country, 1989 (Golden Globe nomination 1990), Look Who's Talking (voice), 1989, Die Hard 2: Die Harder, 1990, Bonfire of the Vanities, 1990, Mortal Thoughts, 1991, Hudson Hawk, 1991, Billy Bathgate, 1991, The Last Boy Scout, 1991, Death Becomes Her, 1992, Striking Distance, 1993, Color of Night, 1994, North, 1994, Pulp Fiction, 1994, Nobody's Fool, 1994, Color of Night, 1994, Die Hard With a Vengeance, 1995, 12 Monkeys, 1995, Four Rooms, 1995, Last Man Standing, 1996; guest star (TV series) Miami Vice, The Twilight Zone; regular (TV series) Moonlighting, 1985-89 (People's Choice award 1986, Emmy award 1987, Golden Globe award 1987), musician (TV spl.) The Return of Bruno, 1986; rec. artist (album) The Return of Bruno, 1987, If It Don't Kill You, It Just Makes You Stronger, 1989; appeared in numerous commls. Named Internat. Broadcasting Man of Yr. Hollywood Radio and TV Soc.

WILLIS, CARL BERTRAM, pathologist; b. Charlottetown, Can., Nov. 27, 1937; married L. Gayle MacWilliams, 1962; children: Rodney G., Jeffrey W. BS, McGill U., 1959; PhD in Plant Pathology, U. Wis., 1962. Rsch. scientist plant pathology Agr. Can., Charlottetown, PEI, 1962-85, rsch. coord., 1985-88, dir. gen., rsch. coord., 1988-91, dir. rsch. sta., 1991—. Fellow Agr. Inst. Can.; mem. Can. Phytopath. Soc. Can. Soc. Agronomy, Can. Soc. Horticulture Sci. Office: Agriculture Canada Research Stn, 440 University Ave PO Box 1210, Charlottetown, PE Canada C1A 7M8*

WILLIS, CLAYTON, broadcaster, corporation executive, former government official, educator, arts consultant, photojournalist, lecturer; b. Washington, Aug. 11, 1933; s. William H. and Elizabeth Carl (Keferstein) W. Student, The Sorbonne, Paris, 1953-54; BA, George Washington U., 1957; student, U. Oslo, 1953; grad., N.Y. Inst. Fin., 1966, Assn. Commodities Exch. Firms Inc., 1966. Spl. assignment Am. Embassy, London, 1957; writer NBC Network radio show Tex and Jinx, 1958; spl. corr. NBC News, La Paz, Bolivia, 1959; spl. Washington corr. Fin. News TV Network (now CNBC), N.Y.C., 1988; contbr., corr. Saudi Arabian TV, Newsweek mag., Philips News Svc. The Hope (Ark.) Star, Christian Sci. Monitor, L.A. Times-Mirror Syndicate, The Palm Beach (Fla.) Post, The Greenwich (Conn.) Time, The Bar Harbor (Maine) Times, Info-Exploi Mining Jour., Rouyn-Noranda, Que., Can., Fin. News TV Network, New York, The Mainichi, Tokyo, The China Post, Taipei, Taiwan, Chattanooga Times, The Nashville Tennesseean, the Daily Nation of Kenya, The Khartoum Echo, Sudan, The Washington Daily News, Washington Post, Cape Argus of Capetown, South Africa, Bangkok Post, Irish Times, Dublin; reporter, movie, art critic Albuquerque Tribune, 1959-61; asst. editor Newsweek Mag., N.Y.C., 1961-62; TV broadcaster-writer UPI Newsfilm, N.Y.C., 1962; White House, Washington corr., chief bur., anchor World Radio News, Houston; White House, Washington corr. WAVA Radio Sta., Washington, 1963-65; editorial writer, corr. Hearst Newspapers, N.Y.C., 1965; press officer UN, N.Y.C., 1965-66; spl. assignment Am. Embassy, Reykjavik, Iceland, 1967; editorial writer, critic, reporter N.Y. Amsterdam News, N.Y.C., 1967-68; cons. Ford Found., N.Y.C., 1968-69; dir. pub. affairs U.S. EEOC, Washington, 1969-70; cons. OEO, Washington, 1970, Pres.'s Nat. Coun. on Indian Opportunity, Washington, 1970-71, Community Rels. Svc., U.S. Dept. Justice, Washington, 1970-73, Cabinet Com. on Opportunities for Spanish-Speaking People, 1971-72, Fed. Energy Adminstrn., Washington, 1973-74; dir. pub. affairs Office Petroleum Allocation U.S. Dept. Interior, 1973-74; dir. Congl. rels., dir. pub. affairs Pres.'s Nat. Commn. on Fire Prevention and Control, 1971-73; pub., editor, owner Four Corners Chieftain, Ignacio and Durango, Colo., 1972-73; lectr. Sch. of Bus., U. D.C., Washington, 1973-74; owner, White House corr., photojournalist Willis News Svc., Washington, 1974—; pub. affairs dir. Inaugural Vets. Com., 1976-77; White House corr., photojournalist Washington Life mag., 1993—; anchor Channel 33, Arlington, Va., 1991—; adviser to Fernando E.C. de Baca, spl. asst. to the Pres., White House, 1974-76; lectr. nat., internat. affairs, Haiti, art, communications, strategic and precious metals, diamond, nickel, copper, and cobalt mining, energy; corr.-broadcaster Sta. KTEN-TV, Ada, Okla., 1985; mem. staff presdl. transition office U.S. Pres. Bush, 1988-89, 90; anchor, pres. 30 minutes with Clayton Willis, 2000 Today With Clayton Willis; pres., anchor, exec. producer TV show 30 Minutes with Clayton Willis, PBS, 1990; dir. L. Clayton Willis Art Collection, Washington; anchor, corr. Channel 33 Arlington, Va., 1991—; pres., White House corr., congressional corr., photojournalist, Evening News Broadcasting Co., Collector Watch TV Show Ltd. with Clayton Willis, Alexandria, 1991—, 30 Mins. with Clayton Willis, and Willis News Service; prodr., anchor documentary programs Saudi Arabian TV, 1992—; exec. prodr., anchor Glimpses of the World documentaries, 1993; White House corr., photojournalist Hope (Ark.) Star, 1994—. Contbg. author: Capital Fare; contbr. articles to Daily Mail, London, London Sunday Express, Umtali Post, Zimbabwe, Gwelo (Zimbabwe) Times, To the Point news mag., Johannesburg, The Citizen, Johannesburg, Hartford Courant, Sacramento Union, Chattanooga Times, UPI Radio Networks, Washington Post, The Hope (Ark.) Star, Phillips News Svc., also other mags. and newspapers. Broadcaster with Bush/Quayle Nat. Campaign Hdqrs., Won, 1988; adviser Presdl. Transition Office of Pres. George Bush, 1988-89; loaned Haitian paintings for spl. exhbn. to Haitian Embassy, Washington, 1991, Milw. Art Mus., 1992. Recipient Outstanding Svc. award Harlem Prep. Sch., Johannes Gutenberg medal, 1984, Letters of Cert. Appreciation Pres. of U.S., 1989. Mem. Blue Ridge Summit, Penna. Club: Overseas Press of Am.; Monterey Country Club, Blue Ridge Summit, Pa. Covered Vietnam, Congo, Mid. East, Rhodesian and South African wars; visited 150 countries; specialist gold, diamond, energy, silver, platinum, nickel, copper, and cobalt mining and strategic minerals; covered Clarence Thomas and Robert Gates U.S. Senate confirmation hearings, 1991. Home and Office: Evening News Broadcasting Co PO Box 25615 Washington DC 20007

WILLIS, CLIFFORD LEON, geologist; b. Chanute, Kans., Feb. 20, 1913; s. Arthur Edward and Flossie Duckworth (Fouts) W.; m. Serreta Margaret Thiel, Aug. 21, 1947 (dec.); 1 child, David Gerard. BS in Mining Engring., U. Kans., 1939; PhD, U. Wash., 1950. Geophysicist The Carter Oil Co. (Exxon), Tulsa, 1939-42; instr. U. Wash., Seattle, 1946-50, asst. prof., 1950-54; cons. geologist Harza Engring. Co., Chgo., 1952-54, 80-82, chief geologist, 1954-57, assoc. and chief geologist, 1957-67, v.p., chief geologist, 1967-80; pvt. practice cons. geologist Tucson, Ariz., 1982—; cons. on major dam projects in Iran, Iraq, Pakistan, Greece, Turkey, Ethiopia, Argentina, Venezuela, Colombia, Honduras, El Salvador, Iceland, U.S. Lt. USCG, 1942-46. Recipient Haworth Disting. Alumnus award U. Kans., 1963. Fellow Geol. Soc. Am., Geol. Soc. London; mem. Am. Assn. Petroleum Geologists, Soc. Mining, Metallurgy and Exploration Inc., Assn. Engring. Geologists, Sigma Xi, Tau Beta Pi, Sigma Tau. Republican. Roman Catholic. Avocations: travel, reading. Home: 4795 E Quail Creek Dr Tucson AZ 85718-2630

WILLIS, CONNIE (CONSTANCE E. WILLIS), author; b. 1945. Tchr. elem. and jr. high schs. Branford, Conn., 1967-69. Author: (short stories/novels) Letter from the Clearys (Nebula award 1982, Hugo award 1983), Lincoln's Dreams, 1987, Doomsday Book (Nebula award 1992, Hugo award 1993), Impossible Things, 1993, Uncharted Territory, 1994, Even the Queen (Nebula award 1992, Hugo award 1993), (novelette) Fire Watch (Nebula award 1982, Hugo award 1983), At the Rialto (Nebula award 1990), The Last of the Winnebagos (Nebula award 1988, Hugo award 1989), Death on the Nile (Hugo award 1994), (novel) Uncharted Territory, 1994, Remake, 1995, Bellwether, 1996; (with Cynthia Felice) Water Witch, 1982, Light Raid, 1989. Address: 1716 13th Ave Greeley CO 80631-5418

WILLIS, CRAIG DEAN, academic administrator; b. Cambridge, Ohio, Mar. 21, 1935; s. John Russell and Glenna (Stevens) W.; m. Marilyn Elaine Foster, June 9, 1956; Mark Craig, Bruce Dean, Todd Laine, Garth John. B.A., Ohio Wesleyan U, 1957; M.A., Ohio State U., 1960, Ph.D., 1969. Registrar Ohio Wesleyan U., 1964-69; dir. admissions Wright State U., 1970-72, dean, 1971-77; v.p. acad. affairs Concord Coll., 1977-82; pres. Lock Haven U. Pa., 1982—; chmn. Internat. Affairs com. Am. Assn. State Colls. and Univs.; vice chmn. Clinton region Mellon Bank Ctr., 1987, chmn., 1988, also bd. dirs. Lock Haven U., Lock Haven Hosp.; chmn. Lock Haven Hosp. Health Fund; cons. Ellis Assocs., Princeton, W.Va., 1980-82. Chmn. bd. Kirkmont Preschool, Beavercreek, Ohio, 1974-77, Beavercreek Library, 1976-77, Regional Edn. Service Agy., Beckley, W.Va., 1978-82; mem. N.E.-Midwest leadership Coun., 1989—. Recipient Disting. Alumnus award dept. edn. Ohio Wesleyan U., 1991; scholar Sohio Oil, 1953, Govt. of France, Paris, 1964, Shell Oil Co, 1967. Mem. Commn. State Coll. and Univ. Pres., Assn. State Colls. annd Univs., Rotary (Citizen of Yr. award Lock Haven 1989), Ohio Wesleyan U. Alumni Assn. (Disting. Sesquicentennial Alumnus of the Edn. 1992), Phi Kappa Phi, Kappa Kappa Psi, Phi Delta Kappa, Kappa Delta Pi. Presbyterian. Office: Lock Haven U North Fairview St Lock Haven PA 17745

WILLIS, DAVID EDWIN, retired geophysicist; b. Cleve., Mar. 13, 1926; s. Russell E. and Eleanor Marie (Himebaugh) W.; m. Martha Louise Mumma, Jan. 3, 1948; children: Karen, Mark, Marta, Seth. B.S., Case Western Res. U., 1950; M.S. (U. Mich. Engring. Research Inst. fellow), U. Mich., 1957, Ph.D., 1968. Party chief, asst. supr. Keystone Exploration Co., Houston, 1950-55; research geophysicist, geophysics lab. head U. Mich., Ann Arbor, 1955-70; asso. prof. U. Mich., 1968-70; prof. dept. geol. scis. U. Wis., Milw., 1970-82; chmn. dept. U. Wis., 1972-76; v.p. Geo-Aid Corp., 1975-80; sr. geophysicist UNOCAL, L.A., 1982-92; geophysical cons. Richmond, Tex., 1992-96. Contbr. articles to profl. jours. Served with USNR, 1944-46. NSF grantee, 1964-79; Air Force Office Sci. Research grantee, 1958-76; AEC grantee, 1971-74; ERDA grantee, 1974-77. Fellow Geol. Soc. Am.; mem. Seismol. Soc. Am., Soc. Exploration Geophysicists, Am. Assn. Petroleum Geologists, L.A. Basin Geol. Soc., Phi Beta Kappa, Sigma Xi, Phi Kappa Phi. Home: 1311 Woodfair Dr Richmond TX 77469-6650

WILLIS, DAVID LEE, radiation biology educator; b. Pasadena, Calif., Mar. 15, 1927; s. Olan Garnet and Ida May (Lott) W.; m. Earline L. Fleischman, Dec. 26, 1950; children: David Lee, Paul J., Daniel N. B.Th., Biola Sem., Los Angeles, 1949; B.A., Biola U., 1951; B.S., Wheaton (Ill.) Coll., 1952; M.A., Calif. State U., Long Beach, 1954; Ph.D., Oreg. State U., 1963. Tchr. sci. various high schs., Calif., 1952-57; instr. biology Fullerton (Calif.) Coll., 1957-61; mem. faculty Oreg. State U., Corvallis, 1962—, prof. radiation biology, 1971-87, prof. emeritus, 1987—, chmn. dept. gen. sci., 1969-85; mem. Hanford Health Effects Panel, 1986; cons. in radioecology. Co-author: Radiotracer Methodology in Biological Science, 1965, Life in the Laboratory, 1965, Radiotracer Methodology in the Biological, Environmental and Physical Sciences, 1975. Mem. Am. Sci. Affiliation (pres. 1975), Health Physics Soc., Radiation Research Soc. Republican. Baptist. Home: 3135 NW McKinley Dr Corvallis OR 97330-1139 Office: Oreg State Univ Radiation Ctr Corvallis OR 97331-5901

WILLIS, DEBRA RUBUSH, public speaker; b. Haines City, Fla., May 14, 1955; d. Jack Everette and Shirley Ann (Carmichael) Rubush. Student, Polk C.C., Winter Haven, Fla., 1973-74. Cert. in crime and rape prevention, children's safety, neuro-linguistics programming tng., chem. def. sprays. Motivational speaker and singer Willis and Hill, Orlando, Fla., 1981-84; children's safety educator Citizens Against Crime, Winter Park, 1989—, crime and rape prevention educator, 1990—; mgmt. team Citizens Against Crime, Orlando, Jacksonville, 1990—, regional trainer, 1991—. Mem. Stop Turning Out Prisoners, Orlando, 1993. Recipient Nat. Pioneer award for Children's Safety, Divsn. of Citizens Against Crime, 1990; inducted into Spkrs. Hall of Fame for Citizens Against Crime, 1992. Mem. Winter Park C. of C., Orlando C. of C., Nat. Victim Ctr., Nat. Orgn. for Victim Assistance, NAFE, Cen. Fla. Am. Soc. for Tng. and Devel. Methodist. Avocations: singing, writing, travel. Office: Citizens Against Crime Ste 1201-3 931 N State Road 434 Altamonte Springs FL 32714-7022

WILLIS, DOLLIE P., adult education educator; b. West Union, Ohio, Nov. 13, 1957; d. Arbra Edgar and Mallie Mae (Erwin) Plymail; m. Orland Willis, Aug. 14, 1983; children: Emerson, Thomas. Student, So. State Coll., Fincastle, Ohio, 1977; BS in Edn., Morehead (Ky.) State U., 1979; MEd, Coll. Mt. St. Joseph, Ohio, 1991. Cert. tchr. vocat. home econs., reading; cert. reading supr.; cert. Irlen screener. Substitute tchr. Ohio Valley Local Schs., West Union, 1983—, Highland County Schs., Hillsboro, Ohio, 1983—; pvt. tutor/owner Eclectic Reading Svc., Hillsboro, 1989—; tchr. jr. high sci. Lynchburg-Clay (Ohio) Schs., 1990-91, alternative classroom tchr., 1993—. Treas. Folsom (Ohio) United Meth. Ch., 1983—. Mem. ASCD, Ohio Reading Assn., Internat. Reading Assn. Republican. Avocations: ceramics, horses, gardening, needlepoint. Home: 7360 Oakridge Rd Hillsboro OH 45133-9682

WILLIS, DOUGLAS M., secondary education educator, consultant; b. Ironton, Ohio, Oct. 11, 1945; s. Brady C. and Mary T. (Dodson) W.; m. Karen K. Cory, June 8, 1969; children:: Andrew M., Matthew D. BS in Indsl. Arts, Morehead (Ky.) State U., 1968; MS in Indsl. Edn., Ctrl. Mo. State U., 1973. Cert. permanent K-12 tchr., Ohio. Tchr. indsl. arts Dawson-Bryant H.S., Coal Grove, Ohio, 1968-71, Little Miami H.S., Morrow, Ohio, 1971-72; grad. asst. Ctrl. Mo. State U., Warrensburg, 1972-73; tchr. indsl. arts Ankeney Jr. H.S., Beavercreek, Ohio, 1973-75, tchr. unified arts, 1975-80, tchr. tech., dept. chmn., 1980—; mem. Greene County Tech. Edn. Curriculum Com., Xenia, Ohio, 1980—, Beavercreek Tech. Study Com., 1992—; western reg. State Stds. Task Force, Columbus, Ohio, 1991—. Mem. Xenia Twp. Vol. Fire Dept., 1974-89, pres., 1980-82. Recipient cert. of accomplishment Ohio Ho. of Reps., 1995. Mem. Internat. Tech. Edn. Assn., Ohio Tech. Edn. Assn., Western Ohio Tech. Edn. Assn., Ohio Tech. Edn. Leadership Coun. (pres. 1993-94). Avocation: custom woodworking. Home: 985 Jane Ave Xenia OH 45385-1517 Office: Ankeney Jr HS 4085 Shakertown Rd Beavercreek OH 45430-1034

WILLIS, DOYLE HENRY, state legislator, lawyer; b. Kaufman, Tex., Aug. 18, 1908; s. Alvin and Eliza Jane (Phillips) W.; m. Evelyn McDavid, 1942; children: Doyle Jr., Dan, Dina, Dale. BS, BA, U. Tex., 1934; LLB, Georgetown U., 1938. Bar: D.C. 1937, Tex. 1938, U.S. Supreme Ct. 1942. Mem. coun. City of Fort Worth, 1963-64; mem. Tex. Ho. of Reps., Austin, 1946-52, 1969—, Tex. State Senate, Austin, 1952-62. Maj. USAF, 1941-46, PTO. Decorated Bronze Star, 4 battle stars, USAF. Mem. KP (life), Masons (life), Shriners (life), Ind. Order Odd Fellows., Lions Club. Democrat. Methodist. Avocations: golf, fishing, reading. Home: 3316 Browning Ct E Fort Worth TX 76111-5021 Office: Sinclair Bldg Fort Worth TX 76102

WILLIS, EDWARD CHARLES, legislator; b. Barstow, Calif., Nov. 29, 1923; s. Charlie Brice and Mary Elizabeth (Indihar) W.; m. Joyce Houtz, June 23, 1949; children: Steve (dec.), Rodney, Charles, Linda, Marla. Student, San Bernadino C.C., 1941-42. Lessee, operator svc. sta. Barstow, 1948-49; power plant engr. Dept. of Army, Alaska, 1950-74; maintenance worker State of Alaska, 1979-84. Rep. Alaska Ho. of Reps., 1993—; senator Alaska State Senate, 1975-78; assemblyman Anchorage

Borough Assembly, 1966-74, pres., 1973-74, 69-70; mem. Chugiak (Alaska) Adv. Sch. Bd., 1961-63; co-chair Operation Chugiak High Sch., 1961-63. With USCG/Merchant Marines, 1944-47, PTO. Decorated Mcht. Marine emblem Pacific War Zone Bar; recipient Bear Paw award Chugiak-Eagle River C. of C., 1970, Appreciation honor Alaskan VFW, 1993. Mem. NRA, Mothers Against Drunk Driving, Alaska Retarded Citizens Assn., Am. Legion (life; Alaska Legionnaire of Yr. 1994), Alpine Alternatives (bd. dirs. 1990), Am. Assn. Ret. Persons, Ret. Officers Assn. (hon.), Elks. Office: 11940 Business Blvd Eagle River AK 99577-7742

WILLIS, EVERETT IRVING, lawyer; b. Canadian, Tex., Oct. 28, 1908; s. Newton Percy and Lena (Powers) W.; m. Margaret Virginia Wilson, Dec. 25, 1935; children: Everett Irving, Robert Frampton. Student, Austin Coll., Sherman, Tex., 1924-26; AB, U. Mo., 1928; LLB magna cum laude, Harvard U., 1932. Bar: N.Y. 1933. With firm Dewey Ballantine (and predecessors), N.Y.C., 1932—, ptnr., 1944—. Mem. Bd. of Edn., Rye, N.Y., 1946-52, pres., 1951-52. Recipient drug industry Man of Year award, 1964. Mem. ABA (coun. pub. utilities sect. 1966-69), N.Y. State Bar Assn., Assn. Bar City N.Y., N.Y. County Lawyers Assn., Univ. Club (N.Y.C.), City Midday Club (N.Y.c.), Apawamis Club (Rye, N.Y.), Phi Beta Kappa, Sigma Nu, Alpha Pi Zeta. Republican. Presbyterian. Home: 59 Hillandale Rd Rye Brook NY 10573-1704 Office: 1301 Avenue Of The Americas New York NY 10019-6022

WILLIS, FRANK EDWARD, retired air force officer; b. Clinton, Ill., June 19, 1939; s. William Edward and Bernardine (Saveley) W.; m. Clarice Marie Hull, June 7, 1961; children: Michael, Steven, William. BS in Engring., USAF Acad., Colorado Springs, Colo., 1961; MA in Bus. Mgmt., U. Nebr., 1973. Commd. 2d lt. USAF, 1961, advanced through grades to maj. gen., 1989; dep. comdr. 314th Tactical Airlift Group, Little Rock AFB, 1978-79, comdr., 1979-80; vice comdr. 374th Tactical Airlift Wing, Clark Air Base, The Philippines, 1980-81, comdr., 1981-83; comdr. 317th Tactical Airlift Wing, Pope AFB, N.C., 1983-84; vice comdr. Air Force Manpower and Pers. Ctr., Randolph AFB, Tex., 1984-85; comdt. Air Command and Staff Coll., Maxwell AFB, Ala., 1985-88; vice comdr. 22d Air Force, Travis AFB, Calif., 1988-89; dir. and dep. chief of staff for requirements Air Mobility and Mil. Airlift Command, Scott AFB, Ill., 1989-93; ret., 1993; co-owner retail hobby shop Tinker Town, Inc., St. Louis, 1994—. Decorated D.S.M. (2), Legion of Merit (2), Air medal (7), Meritorious Svc. medal (2). Presbyterian. Avocations: electronics, computers, model railroading. Home: 1901 Mistflower Glen Ct Chesterfield MO 63005-4713

WILLIS, FRANK ROY, history educator; b. Prescot, Lancashire, Eng., July 25, 1930; s. Harry and Gladys Reid (Birchall) W.; children from previous marriage, Jane, Clare, Geoffrey. BA, Cambridge (Eng.) U., 1952, cert. in edn., 1955, diploma in devel. econs., 1974; PhD, Stanford U., 1959. Instr. Stanford (Calif.) U., 1959-60; from instr. to assoc. prof. history U. Wash., Seattle, 1960-64; assoc. prof. then prof. U. Calif., Davis, 1964—. Author: The French in Germany, 1962, France, Germany and the New Europe, 1945-1967, 1968, Europe in the Global Age, 1968, Italy Chooses Europe, 1971, Western Civilization: An Urban Perspective, 1973, World Civilizations, 1982, The French Paradox, 1982, Western Civilization: A Brief Introduction, 1987. Fellow Rockefeller Found., Paris, 1962-63, Guggenheim Found., 1966-67, Social Scis. Research Council, Cambridge, 1973-74. Avocation: travel. Office: Univ of Calif Davis Dept Of History Davis CA 95616

WILLIS, GORDON, cinematographer; m. Helen Willis. Cinematographer: (films) including End of the Road, 1970, Loving, 1970, The Landlord, 1970, Little Murders, 1970, Klute, 1971, The Godfather, 1972, Up the Sandbox, 1972, Bad Company, 1972, The Paper Chase, 1973, The Godfather, Part II, 1974, The Parallax View, 1974, The Drowning Pool, 1975, All the President's Men, 1976, Sept 30, 1955, 1977, Annie Hall, 1977, Comes a Horseman, 1978, Interiors, 1978, Manhattan, 1979, Stardust Memories, 1980, Pennies from Heaven, 1981, A Midsummer Night's Sex Comedy, 1982, Zelig, 1983, Broadway Danny Rose, 1984, Purple Rose of Cairo, 1985, Perfect, 1985, The Money Pit, 1986, The Pick-Up Artist, 1987, Bright Lights, Big City, 1988, Presumed Innocent, 1989, The Godfather, Part III, 1990, Damages, 1992; cinematographer, dir.: (film) Windows, 1980. Office: care Ron Taft 18 W 55th St New York NY 10019-5315

WILLIS, GUYE HENRY, JR., soil chemist; b. L.A., July 1, 1937; s. Guye Henry and Esther Mae (Bloomer) W.; m. Phyllis Joy Payne, Dec. 27, 1960; children: Michael Guye, Mark Charles. BS, Okla. State U., 1961; MS, Auburn U., 1963, PhD, 1965. Soil chemist USDA Agrl. Rsch. Svc., Baton Rouge, 1965—. Contbr. articles to profl. jours. Mem. Am. Soc. Agronomy, Am. Chem. Soc., Am. Soc. Agrl. Engrs. Achievements include discovery that less than 5% of applied pesticides are lost in surface runoff; volatile loss to atmosphere is pathway of greatest loss of surface applied pesticides; rainfall amount more important than rainfall intensity in washing pesticides from plant foliar surfaces. Office: USDA Agrl Rsch Svc 4115 Gourrier Ave Baton Rouge LA 70808-4443

WILLIS, HAROLD WENDT, SR., real estate developer; b. Marion, Ala., Oct. 7, 1927; s. Robert James and Della (Wendt) W.; student Loma Linda U., 1950, various courses San Bernardino Valley Coll.; m. Patsy Gay Bacon, Aug. 2, 1947 (div. Jan. 1975); children: Harold Wendt II, Timothy Gay, April Ann, Brian Tad, Suzanne Gail; m. Vernette Jacobson Osborne, Mar. 30, 1980 (div. 1984); m. Ofelia Alvarez, Sept. 23, 1984; children: Ryan Robert, Samantha Ofelia. Ptnr., Victoria Guernsey, San Bernardino, Calif., 1950-63, co-pres., 1963-74, pres., 1974—; owner Quik-Save, 9th & Waterman shopping ctr., 1966—, Ninth and Waterman Shopping Ctr., San Bernardino, 1969—; pres. Energy Delivery Systems, Food and Fuel, Inc. San Bernardino City water commr., 1965—, pres. bd. water commrs., 1994—. Bd. councillors Loma Linda (Calif.) U., 1968-85, pres., 1971-74; mem. So. Calif. Strider's Relay Team (set indoor Am. record in 4x800 1992, set distance medley relay U.S. and World record for 60 yr. old 1992). Served as officer U.S. Mcht. Marine, 1945-46. Mem. Calif. Dairy Industries Assn. (pres. 1963, 64), Liga Internat. (2d v.p. 1978, pres. 1982, 83). Seventh-day Adventist (deacon 1950-67). Lic. pvt. pilot; rated multi engr. in 601 P aerostar. Office: PO Box 5607 San Bernardino CA 92412-5607

WILLIS, ISAAC, dermatologist, educator; b. Albany, Ga., July 13, 1940; s. R.L. and Susie M. (Miller) W.; m. Alliene Horne, June 12, 1965; children: Isaac Horne, Alliric Isaac. BS, Morehouse Coll., 1961, DSc (hon.), 1989; MD, Howard U., 1965. Diplomate Am. Bd. Dermatology. Intern Phila. Gen. Hosp., 1965-66; fellow Howard U., Washington, 1966-67; resident, fellow U. Pa., Phila., 1967-69, assoc. in dermatology, 1969-70; instr. dept. dermatology U. Calif., San Francisco, 1970-72; asst. prof. Johns Hopkins U. and Johns Hopkins Hosp., Balt., 1972-73, Emory U., Atlanta, 1973-77, assoc. prof., 1977-82; prof. Morehouse Sch. Medicine, Atlanta, 1982—, chief dermatology, 1991—; dep. commdr. of 3297th USA Hosp. (1000B), 1990—; attending staff Phila. Gen. Hosp., 1969-70, Moffit Hosp., U. Calif., 1970-72, Johns Hopkins Hosp., Balt. City Hosp., Good Samaritan Hosp., 1972-74, Crawford W. Long Meml. Hosp., Atlanta, 1974—, West Paces Ferry Hosp., 1974—, others; mem. grants rev. panel EPA, 1986—; mem. gen. medicine group IA study sect. NIH, 1985—, mem. nat. adv. bd. Arthritis and Musculoskeletal and Skin Diseases, 1991—; chmn. instl. rev. bd., mem. pharmacy and therapeutic com.; mem. nat. adv. coun. U. Pa. Sch. Medicine, 1995—, charter mem. nat. alumni coun., 1995—; bd. mem. Comml. Bank Gwinnett; West Paces Med. Ctr.; mem. gov.'s commn. on effectiveness and economy in govt. State of Ga. Human Resources Task Force, 1991—; charter mem. Nat. Alumni Adv. Coun. U. Pa. Med. Ctr., 1995—; mem. com. adv. bd. sch. pub. health Emory U., 1994—; cons. in field. Bd. dirs. Heritage Bank, Comml. Bank of Ga., chmn. audit rev. com., 1988—; chmn. State of Ga. Dermatology Found., 1995. Served to col. USAR, 1983—. EPA grantee, 1985—. Author: Textbook of Dermatology, 1971—; Contbr. articles to profl. jours. Chmn. bd. med. dirs. Lupus Erythematrosus Found., Atlanta, 1975-83; bd. dirs. Jacquelyn McClure Lupus Erythematrosus Clinic, 1982—; bd. med. dirs. Skin Cancer Found., 1980—; trustee Friendship Bapt. Ch., Atlanta, 1980-82 . Nat. Cancer Inst. grantee, 1974-77, 78—; EPA grantee, 1980—. Fellow Am. Acad. Dermatolgy, Am. Dermtol. Assn.; mem. AAAS, Soc. Investigative Dermatology, Am. Fedn. Clin. Research, Am. Soc. Photobiology, Am. Med. Assn., Nat. Med. Assn., Internat. Soc. Tropical Dermatology, Pan Am. Med. Assn., Phi Beta Kappa, Omicron Delta Kappa. Clubs: Frontiers Internat., Sportsman Internat. Subspecialties: dermatology; cancer research (medicine). Home: 1141 Regency Rd NW Atlanta GA 30327-2719 Office: NW Med Ctr 3280 Howell Mill Rd NW Ste 342 Atlanta GA 30327-4109

WILLIS, JOHN ALVIN, editor; b. Morristown, Tenn., Oct. 16, 1916; s. John Bradford and George Ann (Myers) W.; m. Claire Olivier, Sept. 25, 1960 (div.); m. Marina Sarda, Jan. 26, 1978 (div.). BA cum laude, Milligan Coll., 1938; MA, U. Tenn., 1941; postgrad., Ind U., Harvard U. Asst. editor Theatre World, N.Y.C., 1945-65, editor, 1965—; asst. editor Screen World, N.Y.C., 1948-65, editor, 1965—; tchr. pub. high schs., N.Y.C., 1950-76; editor Dance World, 1966-80; asst. editor Opera World, 1952-54, Great Stars of Am. Stage, 1952, Pictorial History of Silent Screen, 1953, Pictorial History of Opera in America, 1959, Pictorial History of the American Theatre, 1950, 60, 70, 80, 85; mem. Tony Theatre Awards Com. Nat. bd. dirs. U. Tenn. Theatre; mem. com. to select recipients for Mus. Theatre Hall of Fame, NYU. Lt. USNR, 1943-45. Recipient Lucille Lortel Lifetime Achievement award, 1993, Drama Desk Lifetime Achievement award, 1994; high sch. auditorium renamed John Willis Performing Arts Ctr. in his honor, Morristown, 1993. Mem. Actors Equity Assn., Nat. Bd. Rev. Motion Pictures (past bd. dirs.). Home and Office: 190 Riverside Dr New York NY 10024-1008

WILLIS, JOHN T., state official; b. Nov. 1, 1946; m. Kathy S. Mangan; children: Karen M., James T. BA in Econs. cum laude, Bucknell U., 1968; JD, Harvard Law Sch., 1971. Clk. Army Ct. of Mil. Rev., 1971-74; legal asstance officer Aberdeen Proving Grounds, 1974-75; pvt. practice atty. Westminster, Balt. City, Md., 1975-90; chief of staff County Exec. of Prince George's County, 1990-94; apptd. sec. of state State of Md., 1995—; adj. prof. Western Md. Coll., 1979—; chmn. Gov.'s Commn. on Md. Mil. Monuments; adv. bd. U. Balt.'s Schaefer Ctr. for Pub. Policy. Author: Presidential Elections in Maryland, 1984; contbg. author: Western Maryland: A Profile, 1980, Justice and the Military, 1972; contbr. articles to profl. jours.; editor: The Advocate, 1973-74. Vice-chmn. Md. Dem. Party, 1987-89, mem. various coms. and del. to Dem. Nat. Convs., 1976-96; chair Dem. Secs. of State, 1995—. Judge advocate gen. corps U.S. Army, 1968-75. Mem. Md. Bar Assn., Carroll County Bar Assn., Md. Hist. Soc., Carroll County Arts Coun. (past pres.). Office: Office of Sec of State State House Annapolis MD 21401

WILLIS, KEVIN ALVIN, professional basketball player; b. L.A., Sept. 6, 1962. Student, Jackson C.C., Mich., Mich. State U. Basketball player Atlanta Hawks, 1984-94; with MiamiHeat, 1994—. Named NBA All-Star, 1992. Office: Miami Heat The Miami Arena Miami FL 33136*

WILLIS, PAUL ALLEN, librarian; b. Floyd County, Ind., Oct. 1, 1941; s. Clarence Charles and Dorothy Jane (Harritt) W.; m. Barbara Marcum, June 15, 1963; children: Mark, Sally. A.B., U. Ky., 1963, J.D., 1969; M.L.S., U. Md., 1966. Cataloger, Library of Congress, Washington, 1963; head descriptive cataloging br. Sci. and Tech. Info. Facility NASA, College Park, Md., 1963-66; law librarian, prof. law U. Ky., Lexington, 1966-73; dir. libraries U. Ky., 1973—, acting dean Coll. Library Sci., 1975-76, 88; exec. sec. Ky. Jud. Retirement and Removal Commn., 1977-81; mem. adv. com. Center for Jud. Conduct Orgns., Am. Judicature Soc., Chgo., 1979-81; bd. dirs. Southeastern Library Network, Atlanta, 1980-83; mem. exec. com. Ky. Hist. Soc., 1984-88; mem. Ky. Adv. Coun. on Libraries, 1985—, adv. com. Online Computer Library Ctr., 1986-90; cons. S.E. Consortium for Internat. Devel., U. Sriwijaya, Palembang, Sumatera, Indonesia, 1987-88. Sr. fellow UCLA, summer 1982. Mem. Assn. Southeastern Research Libraries (chair 1986-88). Home: 2055 Bridgeport Dr Lexington KY 40502-2615 Office: U Ky Libr Office of Dir Lexington KY 40506

WILLIS, RALPH HOUSTON, mathematics educator; b. McMinnville, Tenn., Dec. 26, 1942; s. Carl Houston and Carrie Lee (Hill) W.; m. Gayle Catherine Celestin, June 29, 1973 (div. Apr. 1985); m. Velma Inez Church, Aug. 10, 1985; stepchild, Bobbie Lynn White. BS in Math., Mid. Tenn. State U., 1964, MA in Math., 1966. Cert. secondary edn. Instr. math. dept. Western Carolina U., Cullowhee, N.C., 1968-73, asst. prof. math. dept., 1973-83, assoc. prof. math. dept., 1983—. Editor: (newsletters) Abelian Grapevine-Secondary Math, 1970-88, The Child of Mathematics-Elementary-Middle Grade Math., 1972-78; mem. editl. bd. The Centroid, 1995—; contbr. articles to profl. jours. Dir., coord. Western Carolina U. High Sch. Math. Contest, Cullowhee, 1970—; solicitor-coord. Math. Contest Scholarship Program, Cullowhee, 1971-82; initiator-coord. Math. Dept.'s Vis. Speaker Program, Western Carolina U., Cullowhee, 1974-77; faculty sponsor N.C. Coun. Tchrs. Math. Student Affiliate, Cullowhee, 1988—. 1st lt. U.S. Army, 1966-68. Recipient Paul A. Reid Disting. Svc. award Western Carolina U., 1991, hon. mention N.C. Gov.'s Award for Excellence, 1991, Innovator award N.C. Coun. Tchrs. in Math., 1994. Mem. Nat. Coun. Tchrs. Math. (Innovator award 1994), N.C. Coun. Tchrs. Math. (historian 1993—, Innovator award 1994. editl. bd. Centroid 1995—), Phi Kappa Phi, Kappa Mu Epsilon. Avocations: genealogy, gardening, military history, model building, carpentry. Office: Western Carolina U Math Dept Stillwell Bldg Cullowhee NC 28723

WILLIS, RAYMOND EDSON, strategic management and organization educator; b. Winthrop, Mass., June 9, 1930; s. Raymond Edson and Mollie (Murtagh) W.; m. Elizabeth Frances Monaghan, Aug. 24, 1957; children: Peter, Brian, Kevin, Garth. BS in Physics, Rensselaer Poly. Inst., 1951; MBA, Boston U., 1956; PhD in Econs., MIT, 1964. Prof. strategic mgmt. and orgn. U. Minn., Mpls., 1959—, chmn. dept. mgmt., 1984-87, prof. emeritus, 1995—. Co-author: Statistical Analysis and Modeling for Management Decision Making, 1974; author: A Guide to Forecasting for Planners and Managers, 1987; contbr. articles to profl. jours. Served to lt. (j.g.) USN, 1951-54, PTO. Fulbright-Hays fellow, 1981. Mem. Alliance Francais. Avocations: bicycling, cross country skiing, bookbinding. Home: 2267 Commonwealth Ave Saint Paul MN 55108-1602 Office: U Minn Carlson Sch Mgmt 271 19th Ave S Minneapolis MN 55455-0430

WILLIS, SELENE LOWE, electrical engineer, software consultant; b. Birmingham, Ala., Mar. 4, 1958; d. Lewis Russell and Bernice (Wilson) Lowe; m. André Maurice Willis, June 12, 1987. BSEE, Tuskegee (Ala.) U., 1980; postgrad. in Computer Programing, UCLA, 1993-94. Component engr. Hughes Aircraft Corp., El Segundo, Calif., 1980-82; reliability and lead engr. Aero Jet Electro Systems Corp., Azusa, Calif., 1982-84; sr. component engr. Rockwell Internat. Corp., Anaheim, Calif., 1984, Gen. Data Comm. Corp., Danbury, Conn., 1984-85; design engr. Lockheed Missile & Space Co., Sunnyvale, Calif., 1985-86; property mgr. Penmar Mgmt. Co., L.A., 1987-88; aircraft mechanic McDonnell Douglas Corp., Long Beach, 1989-93; Unix system adminstrn. Santa Cruz Ops., 1994; mem. tech. staff Space Applications Corp., El Segunda, Calif., 1995; bus. ops. mgr., cons. New Start, Santa Monica, Calif., 1995; cons., software designer Kern & Wooley, attys., Westwood, Calif., 1995; software developer Nat. Advancement Corp., Santa Ana, Calif., 1995—. Vol. Mercy Hosp. and Children's Hosp., Birmingham, 1972-74; mrm. L.A. Gospel Messengers, 1982-84, West Angeles Ch. of God and Christ, L.A., 1990; cons., mgr. bus. ops. New Start/Santa Monica (Calif.) Bay Area Drug Abuse Coun., 1995. Scholar Bell Labs., 1976-80. Mem. IEEE, ASME, Aerospace and Aircraft Engrs., So. Calif. Profl. Engring. Assn., Tuskegee U. Alumni Assn., UCLA Alumni Assn. (scholarship and adv. com.), Eta Kappa Nu. Mem. Christian Ch. Avocations: piano, computers, softball, real estate.

WILLIS, THOMAS DELENA, health insurance company executive; b. Barstow, Calif., May 26, 1955; s. William Thomas and Delena (Curtis) W.; m. Olena Ann Seaton, Jan. 1, 1977 (div. Mar. 1981); 1 child, Amber LaShelle. Student, South Plains Coll., Levelland, Tex., 1973-74, 76, Mid. Tenn. State U., 1975-76. Computer technician NCR, Lubbock, Tex., 1976-77; loan officer Southwestern Investment Co., Lubbock, 1977-78; agt., sales mgr. Am. Nat. Ins. Co., Lubbock, 1978-81; owner, mgr. Willis Ins., Lubbock, 1981-86; regional sales mgr. Time Ins. Co., Dallas, 1986-90; pres., CEO Gt. S.W. Brokerage, Dallas, 1990—; instr. Life Underwriters Tng. Coun., Dallas, 1991—. Fouding mem. Heritage Bapt. Ch., Lubbock, 1984, Am. Men's Bus. Club, Lubbock, 1984-85; mem. president's cabinet Nat. Farm Life, 1985; vol. United Way, ARC, Dallas and Milw., 1986—. With USMC, 1973-75. Mem. Nat. Assn. Health Underwriters (chmn. health ins. tng. coun. 1988-90), Nat. Assn. Life Underwriters (chmn. membership com. 1989-90, industry awards 1990-91). Republican. Avocations: golf, snorkling, snow skiing. Office: 15400 Knoll Trail Dr Ste 204 Dallas TX 75248-3465

WILLIS, THORNTON WILSON, painter; b. Pensacola, Fla., May 25, 1936; s. Willard Wilson and Edna Mae (Hall) W.; m. Peggy Jean Whisenhant, June, 1960; 1 son, David Shaw.; m. Vered Lieb, 1983; 1 dau., Rachel Elizabeth. B.S., U. So. Miss., 1962; M.A., U. Ala., 1966. vis. artist-in-residence La. State U., New Orleans, 1971-72. Represented in U.S. by André Zarre Gallery, N.Y.C., in Europe by Galerie Nordenhake, Stockholm.; assoc. editor: Re-View, 1978—; one-man exhbns. include: Henri Gallery, Washington, 1968, Paley and Lowe, N.Y.C., 1970, New Orleans Mus. Art, 1972, 55 Mercer St. Gallery, 1979, Galerie Nordenhake, Sweden, 1980, Oscarsson Hood Gallery, N.Y.C., 1980-84, Gloria Luria Gallery, Miami, 1985, Pensacola Mus. retrospective, 1988, Galerie Nordenhake retrospective, Stockholm, 1988, 89, Twining Gallery retrospective, 1990, André Zarre Gallery, N.Y.C., 1993; group exhbns. include: Phila. Civic Center, 1970, Whitney Mus., 1971, Contemporary Art Mus., Houston, 1980, 81, Sidney Janis Gallery, N.Y.C., 1980, 81, Johnson Mus., Ithaca, N.Y., 1981, Mus. Modern Art, N.Y.C., 1981, 84, 85-86, Galerie Arnesen, Copenhagen, 1981, ARS '83, Helsinki, André Emmerich Gallery, N.Y.C., 1992, Anita Shapolsky Gallery, N.Y.C., 1993; represented in permanent collections, Whitney Mus., N.Y.C., Mus. Modern Art, N.Y.C., New Orleans Mus. Art, Denver Mus. Fine Art, Rochester Meml. Gallery, Albright-Knox Mus., Phillips Collection, Washington, Herbert F. Johnson Mus., Cornell U., Chase Manhattan Collection, William Paley Collection, CBS, Power Collection, Sidney, Australia, Solomon R. Guggenheim Mus., N.Y.C., various collections, museums Europe, Scandanavia. With USMC, 1954-57. Recipient award Adolph & Esther Gottlieb Found., 1991; John Simon Guggenheim fellow, 1978-79; Nat. Endowment Arts grantee, 1980-81. Mem. U.S. Golf Assn. Avocation: golf. Home: 85 Mercer St New York NY 10012-4438 Office: 87 Mercer St New York NY 10012-4402

WILLIS, WESLEY ROBERT, college administrator; b. Rahway, N.J., Mar. 16, 1941; s. Meachen William and Mildred (Sisco) W.; m. Elaine Stanislaw, May 22, 1965; children: Mark, Kevin, Nathan. BS, Phila. Coll. Bible, 1963; ThM, Dallas Theol. Sem., 1967; EdD, Ind. U., 1978. Prof., dept. chmn. Washington Bible Coll., 1967-70; minister edn. Forcey Meml. Ch., Washington, 1967-71; prof., acad. v.p. Ft. Wayne (Ind.) Bible Coll., 1971-78; exec. v.p. Scripture Press Ministries, Wheaton, Ill., 1978-80; sr. v.p. Scripture Press Publs., Inc., Wheaton, 1980-90; v.p. acad. affairs Phila. Coll. Bible, Langhorne, Pa., 1990—; bd. dirs. Scripture Press Publs., Ltd., Whitby, Ont., Can.; bd. dirs., chmn. bd. Christian Svc. Brigade, Wheaton, 1972-88. Author: 200 Years and Still Counting, 1981, Make Your Teaching Count, 1984, Developing the Teacher in You, 1990, also 6 others; contbr. over 150 articles to religious publs. Sunday sch. tchr., elder Coll. Ch., Wheaton; bd. regents Dallas Theol. Sem., 1987—. Recipient Disting. Edn. Alumnus award Phila. Coll. Bible, 1988, Gold Medallion award Evang. Pubs. Assn., 1990. Mem. Nat. Assn. Profs. Christian Edn., Nat. Assn. Dirs. Christian Edn., Evang. Theol. Soc. Office: Phila Coll Bible 200 Manor Ave Langhorne PA 19047-2942

WILLIS, WILLIAM DARRELL, JR., neurophysiologist, educator; b. Dallas, July 19, 1934; s. William Darrell and Dorcas (Chamberlain) W.; m. Jean Colette Schini, May 28, 1960; 1 child, Thomas Darrell. BS, BA, Tex. A&M U., 1956; MD, U. Tex. Southwestern Med. Sch., 1960; PhD, Australian Nat. U., 1963. Postdoctoral research fellow Nat. Inst. Neurol. Diseases and Blindness, Australian Nat. U., 1960-62, Istituto di Fisiologia, U. Pisa, Italy, 1962-63; from asst. prof. to prof. anatomy, chmn. dept. U. Tex. Southwestern Med. Sch., Dallas, 1963-70; chief lab. comparative neurobiology Marine Biomed. Inst., prof. anatomy and physiology U. Tex. Med. Br., Galveston, 1970—, dir. Marine Biomed. Inst., 1978—, chmn. dept. anatomy and neurosci., 1986—, Ashbel Smith prof., 1986-95, Cecil and Ida Green prof., 1995—; mem. neurology B study sect. NIH, 1968-72, chmn., 1970-72, mem. neurol. disorders Program Project rev. com., 1972-76, Nat. Adv. Neurol. and Communicative Disorders and Stroke Coun., 1987-90; tng. grant com. Nat. Inst. of Neurol. Disorders and Stroke, 1994—. Mem. editl. bd. Neurosci., Exptl. Neurology, 1970-90, Archives Italienne Biologie, Neurosci. Letters, 1976-92; chief editor Jour. Neurophysiology, 1978-83, Pain, 1986-89; assoc. editor Jour. Neurosci., 1986-89, editor-in-chief, 1993-94; sect. editor Exptl. Brain Rsch., 1990-92, 95—. Mem. AAAS, Am. Assn. Anatomists (exec. com. 1980-86), Am. Pain Soc. (pres. 1982-83), Internat. Assn. Study Pain (coun. 1984-90), Am. Physiol. Soc., Soc. Exptl. Biol. Medicine, Soc. Neurosci. (pres. 1984-85), Internat. Brain Rsch. Orgn., Cajal Club, Sigma Xi, Alpha Omega Alpha. Home: 2925 Beluche Dr Galveston TX 77551-1511 Office: U Tex Med Br Marine Biomed Inst 301 University Blvd Galveston TX 77555-1069

WILLIS, WILLIAM ERVIN, lawyer; b. Huntington, W.Va., Oct. 11, 1926; s. Asa Hannon and Mae (Davis) W.; m. Joyce Litteral, Sept. 1, 1949; children: Kathryn Cunningham, Anne Dresser, William. Student, Ind. U., 1944, NYU, 1945; AB, Marshall U., 1948; JD, Harvard, 1951. Bar: N.Y. 1952. Pvt. practice N.Y.C., 1951—; ptnr. Sullivan & Cromwell, 1960—; lectr. Practising Law Inst., 1963—; trustee Fed. Bar Council, 1968-72; mem. 2d Circuit Commn. on Reduction Burdens and Costs Civil Litigation, 1977-82. Co-author Doing Business in America; contbr. Edn. Civil Practice Law Rev. Forms and Guidance for Lawyers, also articles to legal jours. Mem. panel arbitrators Pub. Resources; trustee Tenafly (N.J.) Nature Ctr., 1994—; dir. Soc. Yeager Scholars, Marshall U., Huntington, 1995—. With AUS, 1944-46. Fellow Am. Coll. Trial Lawyers, Am. Bar Found.; mem. ABA (standing com. on fed. judiciary 1987-95, chair 1992-93, 94-95), N.Y. Bar Assn. (chmn. antitrust sect. 1976-77, exec. com. 1976-83), Assn. Bar City of N.Y. (chmn. profl. discipline com. 1983-86), Fed. Bar Coun. (trustee 1969-72), Am. Judicatured Soc., Am. Arbitration Assn. (panel arbitrators), N.Y. Law Inst., N.Y. County Lawyers, Ins. Judicial Adminstrn., India House, World Trade Ctr. Home: 190 Tekening Dr Tenafly NJ 07670-1219 Also: Otterhole Rd West Milford NJ 07480 Office: Sullivan & Cromwell 125 Broad St New York NY 10004-2400

WILLIS, WILLIAM HAROLD, JR., management consultant, executive search specialist; b. Harrisburg, Pa., Dec. 19, 1927; s. William Harold and Elizabeth Tilford (Keferstein) W.; BA, Yale U., 1949; m. Pauline Sabin Smith, Oct. 15, 1955; children: Wendell Willis Livingston, Christopher, Gregory. Mktg. mgr. Owens-Corning Fiberglas Corp., N.Y.C., 1956-62; div. mgr. AMF, Inc., Greenwich, Conn., 1962-65; ptnr. Devine, Baldwin & Willis, N.Y.C., 1965-70; pres. William Willis Worldwide Inc., Greenwich, Conn., 1970—. Bd. dirs. Girls Inc. (formerly Girls Clubs Am., Inc.), N.Y.C., 1962-80, treas., chmn. fin. com., 1961-76, chmn. devel. com., 1976-77; expdn. leader Am. Mus. Nat. History Davison-Willis Expdn. to Madagascar; vestryman St. Barnabas Episcopal Ch., Greenwich, Conn., 1978-81; bd. dirs. Greenwich Hosp. Corp.; human resources com. YMCA of Greater N.Y.; del. People to People Citizen Amb. Program, del. traveling to Peoples Republic of China. With U.S. Army, 1950-52. Named to Exec. Search Hall of Fame, 1992. Mem. Assn. Exec. Search Cons. (dir. 1979-82), Internat. Assoc. of Corp. and Profl. Recruiters, Inc., Yale Club. Republican. Home: 55 Zaccheus Mead Ln Greenwich CT 06831-3716 Office: 164 Mason St Greenwich CT 06830-6611

WILLIS, WILLIAM HENRY, marketing executive; b. Canton, Ohio, Mar. 15, 1951; s. William Lincoln and Gwendolyn Ann (Wasem) W.; m. Rebecca Ann Klinker, June 16, 1973; children: Kristen Ann, Patrick Michael, Susan Kathleen. BSBA, Ohio State U., 1973; M of Mgmt., Northwestern U., 1974. Assoc. product mgr. H.J. Heinz Co., Pitts., 1974-76; product mgr. Pillsbury Co., Mpls., 1976-77, mktg. mgr., 1977-79, group mktg. mgr., 1979-81; dir. bus. planning Pepsico, Inc., Purchase, N.Y., 1981-82, dir. mktg., 1982-85; exec. v.p. mktg. Ogden Svcs. Corp., N.Y.C., 1985-87, exec. v.p. indsl. svcs., 1987-93; pres. spl. mkts. divn. Reader's Digest Inc., Pleasantville, N.Y., 1994-95; pres. Pacific region Reader's Digest Inc., Pleasantville, 1995—. Exec. fundraiser Minn. Orch. Guaranty Fund, Mpls., 1979; United Way chmn. Pillsbury Co., Mpls., 1980. Named Advertiser of Yr. Aviation mag., 1986. Republican. Roman Catholic. Avocations: real estate management, renovating old homes. Office: Reader's Digest Inc Reader's Digest Rd Pleasantville NY 10570

WILLISCROFT, BEVERLY RUTH, lawyer; b. Conrad, Mont., Feb. 24, 1945; d. Paul A. and Gladys L. (Buck) W.; m. Kent J. Barcus, Oct. 1984. BA in Music, So. Calif. Coll., 1967; JD, John F. Kennedy U., 1977. Bar: Calif., 1977. Elem. tchr., Sunnyvale, Calif., 1968-72; legal sec., legal asst. various law firms, Bay Area, 1972-77; assoc. Neil D. Reid, Inc., San Francisco, 1977-79; sole practice, Concord, Calif., 1979—; exam. grader

Calif. Bar, 1979—; real estate broker, 1980-88; tchr. real estate King Coll., Concord, 1979-80; lectr. in field; judge pro-tem Mcpl. Ct., 1981—. Bd dirs. Contra Costa Musical Theatre, Inc., 1978-82, v.p. adminstrn., 1980-81, v.p. prodn., 1981-82; mem. community devel. adv. com. City of Concord, 1981-83, vice chmn., 1982-83, mem. status of women com., 1980-81, mem. redevel. adv. com., 1984-86, planning commnr. 1986-92, chmn., 1990; mem. exec. bd. Mt. Diablo coun. Boy Scouts Am., 1981-85; bd. dirs. Pregnancy Ctrs. Contra Costa County, 1991—, chmn., 1993—. Recipient award of merit Bus. and Profl. Women, Bay Valley Dist., 1981. Mem. Concord C. of C. (bd. dir., chmn. govt. affairs com. 1981-83, v.p. 1985-87, pres. 1988-89, Bus. Person of Yr. 1986), Calif. State Bar (chmn. adoptions subcom. north, 1994), Contra Costa County Bar Assn., Todos Santos Bus. and Profl. Women (co-founder, pres. 1983-84, pub. rels. chmn. 1982-83, Woman of Achievement 1980, 81), Soroptimists (fin. sec. 1980-81). Office: 3018 Willow Pass Rd Ste 205 Concord CA 94519-2570

WILLITS, EILEEN MARIE, medical, surgical nurse, health facility administrator; b. Euclid, Ohio, 1953; d. John Francis and Geraldine Alice (Denoyer) Donohoe; m. Gary Eugene W., May 24, 1986; 1 child, William. Diploma, Providence Hosp. Sch. Nursing, 1974; BS in Human Svcs., U. Detroit, 1979; MS in Nursing Adminstrn., U. Mich., 1984. Diplomate Am. Coll. Healthcare Execs. From nurse to head nurse, then to adminstrv. asst. St. John Hosp., Detroit, 1974-84; v.p. patient svcs. E.L. Bixby Med. Ctr., Adrian, Mich., 1984-89; v.p. nursing Grandview Hosp. and Med. Ctr., Dayton, Ohio, 1989—. Mem. Am. Orgn. Nurse Execs., Ohio Orgn. Nurse Execs., Am. Coll. Healthcare Execs., Am. Hosp. Assn. Office: Grandview Hosp & Med Ctr 405 W Grand Ave Dayton OH 45405-4720

WILLKE, THOMAS ALOYS, university official, statistics educator; b. Rome City, Ind., Apr. 22, 1932; s. Gerard Thomas and Marie Margaret (Wuennemann) W.; m. Geraldine Ann Page, Dec. 28, 1954; children: Richard, Susan, Donald, Jeanne, Mary, Kathleen. AB, Xavier U., 1954; MS, Ohio State U., 1956, PhD, 1960. Sr. engr. N.Am. Aviation, Columbus, Ohio, 1959-60; instr. math. Ohio State U., Columbus, 1960-61, assoc. prof., 1966-70, assoc. prof. statistics, 1970-72, prof., 1972—, dir. stats. lab., 1971-73, vice provost Arts and Scis., 1973-86, acting dean Univ. Coll., 1983-85, dean undergrad. studies Arts and Scis., 1987; prof. math. scis. Otterbein coll., Westerville, Ohio, 1987—, chmn. dept. math. scis., 1988-96; rsch. mathematician U.S. Nat. Bur. Standards, Washington, 1961-66; asst. prof. math. U. Md., College Park, 1963-66. Contbr. articles on statis. non parametric methods and robustness to profl. jours. Mem. Am. Statis. Assn., Math. Assn. Am. Roman Catholic. Home: 4375 Mumford Dr Columbus OH 43220-4438 Office: Otterbein Coll Dept Of Math Scis Westerville OH 43081

WILLKIE, WENDELL LEWIS, II, lawyer; b. Indpls., Oct. 29, 1951; s. Philip Herman Willkie and Rosalie (Heffelfinger) Hall; m. Carlotta Fendig, June 27, 1987; children: Alexandra Elizabeth, Diana Fendig. AB, Harvard U., 1973; BA, Oxford (Eng.) U., 1975, MA, 1983; JD, U. Chgo., 1978. Bar: N.Y. 1979. Assoc. Simpson Thacher and Bartlett, N.Y.C., 1978-82; gen. counsel NEH, Washington, 1982-84; assoc. counsel to Pres. The White House, Washington, 1984-85; chief of staff, counselor to Sec. U.S. Dept. Edn., Washington, 1985, gen. counsel, 1985-88; counsel Office of the Pres.-elect, Washington, 1988-89; gen. counsel Dept. of Commerce, Washington, 1989-93; v.p. Westvaco Corp., N.Y.C., 1995-96, sr. v.p., gen. counsel, 1996—; vis. fellow Am. Enterprise Inst., Washington, 1993-94. Co-author, editor: (with J.R. Lilley) Beyond MFN: Trade with China and American Interests, 1994. Harvard U. scholar, 1969-73, Rhodes scholar, 1973-75. Republican. Episcopalian. Home: 155 Christie Hill Rd Darien CT 06820 Office: Westvaco Corp 299 Park Ave New York NY 10171

WILLMAN, ARTHUR CHARLES, healthcare executive; b. N.Y.C., Oct. 25, 1938; s. Arthur Charles Willman and Irene (Lamb) Meyer; m. Mary McHugh, Dec. 30. 1961; children: Jean, Susan, Brian, Kevin. BS in Pharmacy, St. Johns U., 1960; MS, Columbia U., 1968. Staff pharmacist St. Vincent's Hosp., S.I., N.Y., 1960-61, Valentine Pharmacy, S.I., 1961; commd. ensign USPHS, 1962, advanced through grades to capt., 1982; chief pharmacist USPHS Hosp., Kotzebue, Alaska, 1962-63, adminstr., 1963-66; svc. unit dir. USPHS Hosp., Sitka, Alaska, 1971-86; ret. USPHS Hosp., 1991; adminstrv. resident So. Nassau Communities Hosp., Oceanside, N.Y., 1967-68; exec. officer Gallup (N.Mex.) Indian Med. Ctr., 1968-71; dir. Phys. Asst. Tng. Program, Gallup, N.Mex., 1971; v.p. S.E. Alaska Regional Health Corp., Sitka, 1986—; chmn. bd. dirs. S.E. Alaska Health Systems Agy., Ketchikan, 1980-83; instr. mgmt. U. Alaska, Sitka, 1975-85. Active Ad hoc Com. on Diversification, Sitka, 1993. Fellow APHA, Am. Coll. Healthcare Execs.; mem. Sitka Rotary Club (v.p., chmn.). Roman Catholic. Avocations: boating, running, mechanics, computers. Home: 1203 Seward Ave Sitka AK 99835-9418 Office: SE Alaska Regional Health Corp 222 Tongass Dr Sitka AK 99835-9416

WILLMAN, JOHN NORMAN, management consultant; b. St. Joseph, Mo., Jan. 19, 1915; s. John N. and Frances (Potter) W.; m. Victoria King, May 9, 1941; 1 dau., Victoria. Student, St. Benedict's Coll., 1936; B.A., St. Louis U., 1979. With Am. Hosp. Supply Corp., 1940-59, v.p., 1954-59; with Brunswick Corp., St. Louis, 1959-68; v.p. Brunswick Corp., 1961-68, pres. Health and Sci. div., 1961-68; v.p. Sherwood Med. Industries, Inc., St. Louis, 1961-67; pres. Sherwood Med. Industries, Inc., 1967-72, vice chmn. bd., 1972-73, also dir.; pres., chief exec. officer, dir. IPCO Corp., White Plains, N.Y., 1973-78; mgmt. cons., 1978—. Mem. Old Warson Country Club (St. Louis), St. Louis Club, Noonday Club (St. Louis), Univ. Club (St. Louis). Home: 530 N Spoede Rd Saint Louis MO 63141-7754

WILLMAN, VALLEE LOUIS, physician, surgery educator; b. Greenville, Ill., May 4, 1925; s. Philip L. and Marie A. (Dall) W.; m. Melba L. Carr, Feb. 2, 1952; children: Philip, Elizabeth, Susan, Stephen, Mark, Timothy, Jane, Vallee, Sarah. Student, U. Ill., 1942-43, 45-47; MD, St. Louis U., 1951. Diplomate Am. Bd. Surgery (sr. examiner 1976—), Am. Bd. Thoracic Surgery. Intern Phila. Gen. Hosp., 1951-52; intern, resident St. Louis U. Group Hosps., 1952-56; Ellen McBride fellow in surgery St. Louis U., 1956-57, sr. instr. surgery, 1957-58, asst. prof. surgery, 1958-61, assoc. prof., 1961-63, prof., 1963—, C. Rollins Hanlon prof. surgery, chmn. dept., 1969—, vice chmn. dept., 1967-69; attending physician St. Louis U. Hosp., 1969—; chief of surgery, 1969—; mem. staff Cardinal Glennon Children's Hosp., 1969—; cons. St. Louis VA Hosp., 1969—. Mem. editorial bd. Jour. Thoracic and Cardiovascular Surgery, 1976-86, Archives of Surgery, 1977-87, Jour. Cardiovascular Surgery, 1982-87, N.Am. editor, 1987—; contbr. over 250 articles to profl. jours. With USN, 1943-45. Recipient Merit award St. Louis Med. Soc., 1973, Health Care Leadership award Hosp. Assn. Met. St. Louis, 1988. Fellow Am. Surg. Assn., Am. Assn. Thoracic Surgery, Cen. Surg. Assn. (pres., mem. ad hoc com. on coronary artery surgery 1971-72); mem. ACS (Disting. Svc. award 1987), Soc. for Vascular Surgery, Internat. Soc. for Cardiovascular Surgery (pres. N.Am. chpt. 1985-87), Phi Beta Kappa, Phi Eta Sigma, Alpha Omega Alpha. Roman Catholic. Office: St Louis U Hosp 3635 Vista Ave Saint Louis MO 63110-2539

WILLMARTH, WILLIAM WALTER, aerospace engineering educator; b. Highland Park, Ill., Mar. 25, 1924; s. Sinclair Anson and Dorothy (Cox) W.; m. Nancy Robinson, Nov. 20, 1959; children—Robert, Deborah, Elizabeth, Kathleen. B.S. in Mech. Engring, Purdue U., 1949; M.S. in Aero. Engring, Calif. Inst. Tech., 1950, Ph.D., 1954. Research fellow, then sr. research fellow Calif. Inst. Tech., 1954-58; mem. faculty U. Mich., Ann Arbor, 1958—; prof. aerospace engring. U. Mich., 1961-90, prof. emeritus aerospace engring., 1990—; cons. to industry, 1952—. Author papers, reports. Served with AUS, 1943-46. Vis. fellow Joint Inst. Lab. Astrophysics, Boulder, Colo., 1963-64; fellow Max Planck Inst. für Stromungsforschung, Göttingen, Fed. Republic Germany, summer 1975. Fellow AIAA, Am. Phys. Soc. (Fluid Dynamics prize 1989); mem. AAUP, Sigma Xi, Tau Beta Pi, Tau Sigma. Home: 765 Country Club Rd Ann Arbor MI 48105-1034

WILLMORE, ROBERT LOUIS, lawyer; b. Ramstein AFB, Fed. Republic Germany, July 16, 1955; s. Wendell James and Theresia (Galler) W. BS in Econs., MIT, 1977; JD, Yale U., 1980. Bar: D.C. 1981, U.S. Ct. Appeals (D.C. cir.) 1985. Legis. asst. Senator Carl T. Curtis, Washington, 1977-78; law clk. to presiding judge U.S. Dist. Ct. (no. dist.) Tex., Dallas, 1980-81; assoc. Shaw, Pittman, Potts & Trowbridge, Washington, 1981-82; asst. gen. counsel Office of Mgmt. and Budget, Exec. Office of the Pres., Washington, 1982-85; dep. asst. atty. gen. civil div. U.S. Dept. Justice, Washington, 1985-88; of counsel Arent, Fox, Kintner, Plotkin & Kahn, Washington, 1988-93, Crowell & Moring, Washington, 1993—; exec. sec. Cabinet Council Tort Policy Working Group, Washington, 1985-88; chmn. task force on liability ins. availability, Washington, 1985-88. Editor Yale Law Jour., 1979-80. Mem. ABA, D.C. Bar Assn. Republican. Roman Catholic. Home: 6879 St Albans Rd Mc Lean VA 22101-2810 Office: Crowell & Moring 1001 Pennsylvania Ave NW Washington DC 20004-2505

WILLNER, ALAN ELI, electrical engineer, educator; b. Bklyn., Nov. 16, 1962; s. Gerald and Sondra (Bernstein) W.; m. Michelle Frida Green, June 25, 1991. BA, Yeshiva U., 1982; MS, Columbia U., 1984, PhD, 1988. Summer tech. staff David Sarnoff Rsch. Ctr., Princeton, N.J., 1983, 84; grad. rsch. asst. dept. elec. engring. Columbia U., N.Y.C., 1984-88; postdoctoral mem. tech. staff AT&T Bell Labs., Holmdel, N.J., 1988-90; mem. tech. staff Bell Communications Rsch., Red Bank, N.J., 1990-91; assoc. prof. U. So. Calif., L.A., 1992—, assoc. dir. Ctr. Photonic Tech., 1994—; head del. Harvard Model UN Yeshiva U., 1982; instr. Columbia U., 1987; rev. panel mem. NSF, Washington, 1992, 93, 94; invited optical comm. workshop NSF, Washington, 1994, chair panel on optical info. and comm., 1994. Author 1 book; contbr. articles to IEEE Photonics Tech. Letters, Jour Lightwave Tech., Jour. Optical Engring., Jour. Electrochem. Soc., Electronics Letters, Applied Physics Letters, Applied Optics; assoc. editor Jour. Lighwave Tech., guest editor. Mem. faculty adv. bd. U. So. Calif. Hillel Orgn., 1992. Grantee NSF, Advanced Rsch. Projects Agy., Packard Found., Powell Found., Ballistic Missile Def. Orgn.; fellow Semiconductor Rsch. Corp., 1986, NATO/NSF, 1985, Sci. and Engring. fellow David and Lucile Packard Found., 1993, presdl. faculty fellow NSF, 1994; recipient Armstrong Found. prize Columbia U., 1984, young investigator award NSF, 1992. Mem. IEEE (sr. mem.), IEEE Lasers and Electro-Optics Soc. (v.p. tech. affairs, mem. optical comm. tech. com., bd. govs., chmn. optical commn. tech. com., chmn. optical comm. subcom. ann. mtg. 1994, mem. optical networks tech. com.), Optical Soc. Am. (vice-chair optical comm. group, symposium organizer ann. mtg. 1992, 95, panel organizer ann. mtg. 1993, 95, program com. for conf. on optical fiber commn. 1996, 97), Soc. Photo-Instrumentation Engring. (program chair telecomm. engring. photonics west 1995, chmn. conf. on emerging technologies for all-optical networks, photonics west, 1995, program com. for Conf. on Optical Fiber Comm., 1996, conf. program com. components for WDM), Sigma Xi. Achievements include patents for localized photochemical etching of multilayered semiconductor body, optical star coupler utilizing fiber amplifier technology, and one-to-many simultaneous optical WDM 2-dim. plane interconnections. Home: 1200 S Shenandoah St Apt 201 Los Angeles CA 90035-2265 Office: U So Calif Dept Elec Engring EEB 538 Los Angeles CA 90089-2565

WILLNER, ANN RUTH, political scientist, educator; b. N.Y.C., Sept. 2, 1924; d. Norbert and Bella (Richman) W. B.A. cum laude, Hunter Coll., 1945; M.A., Yale U., 1946; Ph.D., U. Chgo., 1961. Lectr. U. Chgo., 1946-47, research assoc. Ctr. for Econ. Devel. and Cultural Change, 1954-56, 61-62; advisor on orgn. and tng. Indonesian Ministry for Fgn. Affairs, Jakarta, 1952-53; expert for small scale indsl. planning Indonesian Nat. Planning Bur., Jakarta, 1953-54; fgn. affairs analyst Congl. Reference Service, Library of Congress, 1960; asst. prof. polit. sci. Harpur Coll., Binghamton, N.Y., 1962-63; postdoctoral fellow polit. sci. and Southeast Asian studies Yale U., New Haven, 1963-64; research assoc. Ctr. Internat. Studies, Princeton U., 1964-69; assoc. prof. polit. sci. U. Kans., Lawrence, 1969-70, prof., 1970—; vis. prof. polit. sci. CUNY, 1975; cons. govt. agys. and pvt. industry. Polit. sci. editor: Ency. of the Social Scis., 1961; mem. editorial bd. Econ. Devel. and Cultural Change, 1954-57, Jour. Comparative Adminstrn., 1969-74, Comparative Politics, 1977—; author: The Neotraditional Accomodation to Political Independence, 1966, Charismatic Political Leadership: A Theory, 1968, The Spellbinders, 1984; also monographs, articles, chpts. to books. Grantee Rockefeller Found., 1965, Social Sci. Research and Am. Council Learned Socs., 1966. Mem. Am. Polit. Sci. Assn. (gov. council 1979-81). Home: 2112 Terrace Rd Lawrence KS 66049-2733

WILLNER, DOROTHY, anthropologist, educator; b. N.Y.C., Aug. 26, 1927; d. Norbert and Bella (Richman) W. Ph.B., U. Chgo., 1947, M.A., 1953, Ph.D., 1961; postgrad., Ecole Pratique des Hautes Etudes, U. Paris, France, 1953-54. Anthropologist Jewish Agy., Israel, 1955-58; tech. asst., adminstrn. expert in community devel. UN, Mexico, 1958; asst. prof. dept. sociology and anthropology U. Iowa, Iowa City, 1959-60; research assoc. U. Chgo., 1961-62; asst. prof. dept. sociology and anthropology U. N.C., Chapel Hill, 1962-63, Hunter Coll., N.Y.C., 1964-65; assoc. prof. dept. anthropology U. Kans., Lawrence, 1967-70; prof. U. Kans., 1970-90; professorial lectr. Johns Hopkins U. Sch. Advanced Internat. Studies, 1992. Author: Community Leadership, 1960, Nation-Building and Community in Israel, 1969. Contbr. numerous articles to profl. publs. Fellow Am. Anthrop. Assn., Soc. Applied Anthropology, Royal Anthrop. Inst.; mem. Cen. States Anthrop. Soc. (past pres.), Assn. Polit. and Legal Anthropology (past pres.). Home: 5480 Wisconsin Ave Bethesda MD 20815-3530

WILLNOW, RONALD DALE, editor; b. Adrian, Mich., Mar. 12, 1933; s. Wilbur A. and Irene L. (Sword) W.; m. Onnalee Thompson, Aug. 24, 1957; childrn: Lindle, Randall, Evan. AB, Adrian Coll., 1954; MA, U. Mich., 1959. Reporter St. Louis Post-Dispatch, 1959-66, asst. city editor, 1966-71, city editor, 1971-76, news editor, 1976-81, asst. mng. editor, 1981-90, dep. mng. editor, 1990—. With U.S. Army, 1954-56. Mem. Mid-Am. Press Inst. (bd. dirs. 1978—, past pres.), Mo. Associated Press Editors Assn. (pres. 1995—), St. Louis Journalism Found. (chmn. 1973-79), Press Club St. Louis (pres. 1983-86). Unitarian. Home: 7432 Cornell Saint Louis MO 63130 Office: St Louis Post-Dispatch 900 N Tucker Saint Louis MO 63101

WILLOCKS, ROBERT MAX, retired librarian; b. Maryville, Tenn., Oct. 1, 1924; s. Willis Lemuel and Hannah (Emert) W.; m. Neysa Nerene Ferguson, May 23, 1947; children—Margret Sharon, Samuel David, Mark Timothy, Robert Daniel, Kent Max. B.A., Maryville Coll., 1949; B.D., Golden Gate Bapt. Theol. Sem., 1951, Th.M., 1962; M.A. in Library Sci, Peabody Coll., 1962. Ordained to ministry Bapt. Ch., 1950; pastor in Calif., 1950-56; missionary to Korea So. Bapt. Fgn. Mission Bd., Taejon, 1956- 65; assoc. dir. library Heidelberg Coll., Tiffin, Ohio, 1965-67; dir. library Columbia (S.C.) Coll., 1967-70; asst. dir. libraries Syracuse (N.Y.) U., 1970-76; assoc. dir. libraries U. Fla., Gainesville, 1976-83, acting dir. libraries, 1983-84, dep. dir. libraries, 1984-89, ret., 1989; pastor Northwood Bapt. Ch., Gainesville, 1981-92; libr. Bapt. Theol. Sem., Lusaka, Zambia, 1994-95; ret., 1995; cons. Choong Chung Nam Province Library Assn., Korea, 1962-65; dir. Korea Bapt. Press, 1959-61; prof. ch. history Korea Bapt. Sem., 1957-65, acting pres., 1958-59, librarian, 1959-65; Vice chmn. Korea Bapt. Mission, 1962-64; del. Fla. Gov.'s Conf. on Libraries, 1978. Editor: Korean translations Thus it is Written, 1963, The Progress of Worldwide Missions, 1965. Chmn. trustees Wallace Meml. Bapt. Hosp., Pusan, Korea, 1964-65; pres. bd. dirs. Phoenix Homeowners Assn., 1980-88. With USNR, 1943-46. Mem. ALA (chmn. telefacsimile com. 1976-78, tech. com. 1980-84, chmn. standards com. 1985-88), Fla. Libr. Assn., Southeastern Library Assn., AAUP, Peabody Coll. Alumni Assn. (pres. S.C. 1968-69). Home: 1930 NW 12th Rd Gainesville FL 32605-5338

WILLOUGHBY, CARROLL VERNON, retired motel chain executive; b. Toms River, N.J., Nov. 8, 1913; s. Cleveland Carroll and Margaret Vernia (Ely) W.; m. Jo Evelyn Williams, Aug. 3, 1944; children: Charles Carroll, Jon Michael (dec.). Cert. in aero. engring, Balt. Vocat. Sch., 1933; student, Johns Hopkins U., 1939-42. Asso. Booz Allen & Hamilton, 1952-58; v.p., gen. mgr. Lawrence L. Frank Enterprises, 1958-60; real estate broker, v.p. Felger Constrn. Co., 1960-66; asst. to chmn. bd. Ky. Fried Chicken, Inc., 1966-70; sr. group v.p. Ramada Inns, Inc., Phoenix, 1970-81, also bd. dirs.; bd. dirs. Aztar Corp. Elder Presbyterian Ch. Served to capt. USAAF, 1942-45. Mem. San Fernando Valley Symphony Assn. (pres. 1962-66). Republican. Home: 4801 N 72nd Way Scottsdale AZ 85251-1301

WILLOUGHBY, JOHN WALLACE, former college dean, provost; b. Brumanna, Lebanon, July 30, 1932; s. James Wallace and Ida Cecilia (Frost) W.; m. Joanne Arnoldt DeWitt, Sept. 2, 1959; children—James Wallace, David Frost. B.A., Yale U., 1952; B.A., M.A., Oxford U., Eng., 1954; Ph.D., U. Rochester, 1959. Instr. English U. N.Mex., Albuquerque, 1959-60; instr. U. Chgo., 1960-63; from asst. prof. to prof., dean faculty Southampton Coll. Long Island, N.Y., 1963-73; v.p. for acad. affairs S.W. Minn. State Coll., Marshall, 1973-74, St. Francis Coll., Loretto, Pa., 1974-83; provost, dean of faculty, dir. continuing edn. Southwestern Coll., Winfield, Kans., 1983-92; distributor Success Motivation Inst., 1988—. Editor: English: Selected Readings, 1963; asst. editor Brownings Correspondence Wedgestone Press, 1993—; dcontbr. articles to profl. jours. Treas. Cambria-Somerset Coun. for Health Edn., Johnstown, Pa., 1976-83; v.p. for scouting Penns Woods Coun. Boy Scouts Am., 1978-82; mem. com. on preparation fro ministry South Kans. Presbytery, 1989-95; staff devel. and history writer Ctr. for Improvement of Human Functioning, Wichita, 1991—; pres. Winfield (Kans.) Lions Club, 1996-97. Rhodes scholar, Oxford, 1952-54. Mem. Am. Assn. Rhodes Scholars. Democrat. Presbyterian. Avocations: bicycling; camping; philately; gardening; singing. Home: 518 E 15th Ave Winfield KS 67156-4403

WILLOUGHBY, RODNEY ERWIN, retired oil company executive; b. Dallas, July 24, 1925; s. Charles V. and Juanita (Jones) W.; m. Marie J. Johnston, Feb. 27, 1954; five children. B.B.A., Tulane U., 1945; M.B.A., Harvard U., 1947. Mem. dean's staff Harvard Bus. Sch., 1947-48; with ECA, Paris, France, 1948-49; petroleum attache Am. embassy, London, Eng., 1949-52; concession mgr. Gulf Oil Corp., N.Y.C., 1952-55; mem. fgn. staff Standard Oil Co. Calif., San Francisco, 1955-65; pres. Refineria Conchan Chevron, Peru, 1965-69, Chevron Oil Co. Latin Am., 1969-71; v.p., treas. Chevron Corp. (formerly Standard Oil Co.), Calif., San Francisco, 1971-84; v.p. fgn. Chevron Corp. (formerly Standard Oil Co.), 1984-89. Trustee U. San Francisco, Fine Arts Mus. San Francisco. Served to lt. (j.g.) USNR, 1943-46. Clubs: Pacific Union, Burlingame Country. Office: 55 Newplace Rd Hillsborough CA 94010-6446

WILLOUGHBY, STEPHEN SCHUYLER, mathematics educator; b. Madison, Wis., Sept. 27, 1932; s. Alfred and Elizabeth Frances (Cassell) W.; m. Helen Sali Shapiro, Aug. 29, 1954; children: Wendy Valentine (Mrs. Peter Gallen), Todd Alan. AB (scholar), Harvard U., 1953, AM in Teaching, 1955; EdD (Clifford Brewster Upton fellow), Columbia U., 1961. Tchr. Newton (Mass.) Pub. Schs., 1954-57, Greenwich (Conn.) Pub. Schs., 1957-59; instr. U. Wis., Madison, 1960-61, asst. prof. math. edn. and math., 1961-65; prof. math. edn. and math. NYU, 1965-87, dir. math. edn. dept., 1967-83, chmn. math., sci. and stats. edn. dept., 1970-80, 86-87, chmn. Univ. Faculty Council, 1981-82; prof. math. U. Ariz., Tucson, 1987—; mem. nat. bd. advisor Sq. One TV, 1983-94, U.S. Commn. on Math. Instrn., 1984-95, chmn., 1991-95; math. adv. com. Nat. Tchr. Exam. Successor (Praxis), 1989-94; edn. panel New Am. Schs. Devel. Corp., 1991—; U.S. Nat. rep. Internat. Commn. on Math. Instrn., 1991-95. Author: Contemporary Teaching of Secondary School Mathematics, 1967, Probability and Statistics, 1968, Teaching Mathematics: What Is Basic, 1981, Mathematics Education for a Changing World, 1990, Real Math, 1981, 85, 87, 91—; contbr. articles to profl. jours. and encys., chpts. to yearbooks and anthologies. Recipient Leadership in Math. Edn. Lifetime Achievement medal, 1995. Mem. Nat. Coun. Tchrs. Math. (dir. 1968-71, pres. 1982-84), Coun. Sci. Soc. Pres. (exec. bd. 1984, 85, 86, 87, chmn. 1988). Home: 5435 E Gleneagles Dr Tucson AZ 85718-1805 Office: U Ariz Dept Math Tucson AZ 85721

WILLOUGHBY, WILLIAM, II, retired nuclear engineer; b. Birmingham, Ala., Jan. 14, 1933; s. William and Marion Louise (Hart) W.; m. Doris Jean Lindsey, Oct. 16, 1954; 1 child, William III. BSChemE, MIT, 1954; MS in Nuclear Engring., U. Calif., Berkeley, 1960. Registered profl. engr., S.C. Physicist U. Calif. Lawrence Livermore (Calif.) Lab., 1957-61; tech. support supr. Carolina Va. Nuclear Power Assocs., Parr, S.C., 1962-67; mgr. nuclear engr. S.C. Elec. & Gas, Columbia, 1967-76; sr. project mgr., consulting engr. Stone & Webster Engring., N.Y.C., 1976-93; ret., 1993; mem. S.C. Nuclear Adv. Coun., Columbia, 1974-76; instr. Bridgeport Engring. Inst., Fairfield, Conn., 1994, Midlands Tech. Coll., Columbia, S.C., 1994-96. Contbr. articles to profl. jours. Commodore Columbia Sailing Club, 1974. 1st lt. U.S. Army, 1955-57. Mem. AAAS, Am. Nuclear Soc., Sigma Xi, Tau Beta Pi. Episcopalian. Home: 506 Killington Ct Columbia SC 29212

WILLOUGHBY, WILLIAM FRANKLIN, II, physician, researcher; b. Washington, Feb. 4, 1936; s. William Westel and Patricia (DeZychlinska) W.; m. Mary Scott Fishburne, 1963 (div. 1974); children: Westel Woodbury, William Franklin III, Laura Fishburne, Mary Scott; m. Judith Eleanor Barbaras, Oct. 25, 1975; 1 child, Robert Alexander Willoughby. AB, Johns Hopkins U., 1957, MD, 1965, PhD in Microbiology, 1965; grad. with distinction, USAF War Coll., 1985. Diplomate Am. Bd. Pathology. Intern then resident in pathology Johns Hopkins Hosp., 1965-67; asst. prof. depts. pathology and microbiology Case Western Res. U., Cleve.; dir. Virginia Mason Rsch. Ctr., Seattle, 1972-75; assoc. prof. dept. pathology Sch. Medicine, Johns Hopkins U., Balt., 1975-87; prof., chmn. dept. pathology Sch. Medicine, U. S.C., Columbia, 1987-92; prof. dept. pathology Rush U. Coll. Medicine, 1994—; dir. labs. Cook County Hosp., Chgo., 1992—, interim med. dir., 1994-96; prof. dept. pathology Rush Med. Coll., Chgo., 1994—; cons. NIH, Bethesda, Md., 1979—, mem. pathology A study sect., 1982-86; cons. NRC, Washington, 1981-84; mem. Res. Component Med. Coun., Dept. Def., Pentagon, 1991-93; dep. surgeon gen. for res. affairs USAF, Bolling AFB, D.C., 1993-95; asst. surg. gen. USAF, Desert Storm/Desert Shield, 1990-91. Mem. editorial bd. Am. Rev. Respiratory Disease, 1978-84; contbr. articles to profl. jours., reviewer numerous sci. manuscripts. Vestryman Trinity Episcopal Ch., Long Green, Md., 1984-87; bd. dirs. Ctrl. S.C. chpt. ARC, Columbia, 1989-92; bd. fellow Norwich U., 1992-95. Maj. USAFR, 1975-95, advanced through grades to maj. gen., 1992-95. Decorated Legion of Merit, D.S.M., Meritorious Svc. medal; recipient Edwin E. Osgood prize Va. Mason Rsch. Ctr., 1973; Arthritis Found. fellow Scripps Clinic and Rsch. Found., 1967-69; Poncine scholar Poncine Found., 1972-74; NIH rsch. grantee, 1976-91. Fellow Coll. Am. Pathologists; mem. AAAS, Am. Soc. Investigative Pathology, Am. Assn. Immunologists, Am. Soc. Cell Biologists, Internat. Acad. Pathology, Assn. Pathology Chmns., Aerospace Med. Assn., Soc. USAF Flight Surgeons (bd. govs. 1993—), Soc. Cons. to Armed Forces, Am. Thoracic Soc., Assn. Mil. Surgeons U.S. Avocations: aviation, music, tennis. Home: 1416A S Plymouth Ct Chicago IL 60605-2710 Office: Cook County Hosp Hektoen Inst 627 S Wood St Chicago IL 60612-3810

WILLRICH, MASON, executive, consultant; b. L.A., 1933; m. Patricia Rowe, June 11, 1960; children: Christopher, Stephen, Michael, Katharine. BA magna cum laude, Yale U., 1954; JD, U. Calif., Berkeley, 1960. Atty. Pillsbury Madison and Sutro, San Francisco, 1960-62; asst. gen. coun. U.S. Arms Control and Disarmament Agy., 1962-65; assoc. prof. law U. Va., 1965-68, prof. law, 1968-75, John Stennis prof. law, 1975-79; dir. internat. rels. Rockefeller Found., N.Y.C., 1976-79; v.p. Pacific Gas & Electric, San Francisco, 1979-84, sr. v.p., 1984-88, exec. v.p., 1988-89; CEO, pres. PG&E Enterprises, San Francisco, 1989-94; exec. Pacific Gas and Electric Co., San Francisco, 1979-94; chmn. EnergyWorks, 1995—; cons., 1994—. Author: Non-Proliferation Treaty, 1969, Global Politics of Nuclear Energy, 1971, (with T.B. Taylor) Nuclear Theft, 1974, Administration of Energy Shortages, 1976 (with R.K. Lester) Radioactive Waste Management and Regulation, 1977. Trustee, past chmn. bd. dirs. World Affairs Coun. No. Calif.; pres. Midland Sch.; dir. Resources for the Future, Atlantic Coun. Guggenheim Meml. fellow, 1973. Mem. Phi Beta Kappa, Order of Coif. Office: PO Box 50907 Palo Alto CA 94303

WILLS, CHARLES FRANCIS, former church executive, retired career officer; b. Avalon, N.J., July 26, 1914; s. Charles H. and Anna Margaret (Diemand) W.; m. Charlotte Emily Robson, Aug. 22, 1936; children: C. Frederic, Emily, Sally and Larry (twins). B.S., Wheaton (Ill.) Coll., 1935; B.D., Eastern Bapt. Theol. Sem., 1938, Th.M., 1941; grad., Air War Coll., 1961. Commd. 1st lt. U.S. Army, 1941; advanced through grades to col. U.S. Air Force, 1963; chaplain AUS, 1941-49, U.S. Air Force, 1949-67; ret., 1967; exec. dir. chaplaincy services Am. Bapt. Chs., Valley Forge, Pa., 1969-75; exec. dir. profl. services Am. Bapt. Chs., 1975-78; assoc. sec. Bapt. World Alliance, Washington, 1978-80; treas. Bapt. World Alliance, 1980-81; mem. Commn. on Doctrine and Interchurch Cooperation, 1980-90. Decorated Legion of Merit, Bronze Star, Purple Heart. Mem. Mil. Chaplains Assn., Mil. Order of Purple Heart.

WILLS, DAVID WOOD, minister, educator; b. Portland, Ind., Jan. 25, 1942; s. Theodore Oscar Mitchell and Elizabeth Lochore (Wood) W.; m. Carolyn Reynolds Montgomery, Aug. 22, 1964; children: John Brookings, Theodore Worcester, Thomas Churchill. BA, Yale U., 1962; BD, Princeton

Theol. Sem., 1966; PhD, Harvard U., 1975. Ordained to ministry Presbyn. Ch., 1970. Asst. prof. Sch. of Religion, U. So. Calif., 1970-72; asst. prof. dept. of religion Amherst Coll., Mass., 1972-78, assoc. prof., 1978-83, prof., 1983-90, prof. religion and Black studies, 1990-94, Winthrop H. Smith '16 prof. Am. history and Am. studies, dept. religion and Black studies, 1994—, also dir. Luce Program in Comparative Religious Ethics 1978-88. Editor (with Richard Newman) Black Apostles at Home and Abroad, 1982, (with Albert Raboteau) Afro-American Religion: A Documentary History Project, 1987—. Kent fellow Danforth Found., 1966-70, 75, Ford Found. fellow, 1972, Inst. for Ecumenical and Cultural Rsch. fellow, 1972, Nat. Humanities Ctr. fellow, 1980-81, 94, NEH fellow for Coll. Tchrs., 1988-89, W. E. B. DuBois Inst. for Afro-Am. Rsch. fellow, 1989-91. Mem. Am. Acad. Religion (chair Afro-Am. religious history group 1975-78), Am. Hist. Assn., Am. Soc. Ch. History, Am. Studies Assn., Orgn. Am. Historians, So. Hist. Assn., Phi Beta Kappa. Home: 100 Woodside Ave Amherst MA 01002-2526 Office: Amherst Coll Dept Religion Amherst MA 01002

WILLS, EDGAR W. (BILL WILLS), newspaper editor; b. Urbana, Ill., Oct. 27, 1943; s. Edgar and Laura Loretta (McDermott) W.; m. Phyllis A. Robinson, Jan. 21, 1962; children: Teresa, Richard, Michael. Graduate, Mahomet H.S. From reporter to mng. editor/editorial The Pantagraph, Bloomington, Ill., 1962—. Dir. Four Seasons Assn., Bloomington, 1990-91; advisor Students for Free Enterprise Ill. State U., Normal, 1990-91; mem. adv. bd. Centrilio Girl Scout Coun., Bloomington, 1990-94; v.p. St. Joseph Med. Ctr. Cmty. Bd., Bloomington, 1987—; dir. McLean County Assn. for Retarded Citizens; sec. cabinet McLean County United Way, 1995. Mem. AP Mng. Editors, Ill. AP Editors (bd. dirs., former pres.), Mid-Am. Press Inst. (dir.), Nat. Conf. Editors and Writers, Bloomington Rotary Club. Avocation: woodworking. Home: 2404 Clarkson Ln Bloomington IL 61704 Office: The Pantagraph 301 W Washington St Bloomington IL 61701-3827

WILLS, GARRY, journalist, educator; b. Atlanta, May 22, 1934; s. John and Mayno (Collins) W.; m. Natalie Cavallo, May 30, 1959; children: John, Garry, Lydia. BA, St. Louis U., 1957; MA, Xavier U., Cin., 1958, Yale U., 1959; PhD, Yale U., 1961; LittD (hon.), Coll. Holy Cross, 1982, Columbia Coll., 1982, Beloit Coll., 1988, Xavier U., 1993, St. Xavier U., 1993, Union Coll., 1993, Macalester Coll., 1995, Bates Coll., 1995. Fellow Center Hellenic Studies, 1961-62; assoc. prof. classics Johns Hopkins U., 1962-67, adj. prof., 1968-80; Henry R. Luce prof. Am. culture and public policy Northwestern U., 1980-88, adj. prof., 1988—; newspaper columnist Universal Press Syndicate, 1970—. Author: Chesterton, 1961, Politics and Catholic Freedom, 1964, Roman Culture, 1966, Jack Ruby, 1967, Second Civil War, 1968, Nixon Agonistes, 1970, Bare Ruined Choirs, 1972, Inventing America, 1978, At Button's, 1979, Confessions of a Conservative, 1979, Explaining America, 1980, The Kennedy Imprisonment, 1982, Lead Time, 1983, Cincinnatus, 1984, Reagan's America, 1987, Under God, 1990, Lincoln at Gettysburg, 1992 (Pulitzer Prize for gen. non-fiction 1993), Certain Trumpets: The Call of Leaders, 1994, Witches and Jesuits: Shakespeare's Macbeth, 1994. Recipient Pulitzer prize, 1993, Merle Curti award Orgn. Am. Historians, Nat. Book Critics Circle award (2), Wilbur Cross medal Yale U., Peabody award. Mem. AAAL, Am. Acad. Arts and Scis., Am. Antiquarian Soc., Mass. Hist. Soc. Roman Catholic. Office: Northwestern U Dept History Evanston IL 60201

WILLS, J. ROBERT, academic administrator, drama educator, writer; b. Akron, Ohio, May 5, 1940; s. J. Robert and Helen Elizabeth (Lapham) W.; m. Barbara T. Salisbury, Aug. 4, 1984. B.A., Coll. of Wooster, 1962; M.A., U. Ill., 1963; Ph.D., Case-Western Res. U., 1971; cert. in arts adminstrn, Harvard U., 1976. Instr. to asst. prof., dir. theatre Wittenberg U., Springfield, Ohio, 1963-72; assoc. prof., dir. grad. studies, chmn. dept. theatre U. Ky., Lexington, 1972-77; prof. theatre, dean U. Ky. (Coll. Fine Arts), 1977-81; prof. drama, dean Coll. Fine Arts, U. Tex., Austin, 1981-89, Effie Marie Cain Regents chair in Fine Arts, 1986-89; provost, prof. theatre Pacific Luth. U., Tacoma, Wash., 1989-94; prof. theatre, dean coll. fine arts Ariz. State U., Tempe, 1994—; cons. colls., univs., arts orgns., govt. agencies. Author: The Director in a Changing Theatre, 1976, Directing in the Theatre: A Casebook, 1980, rev. edit., 1994; dir. 92 plays; contbr. articles to profl. jours. Bd. dirs. various art orgns., Ky., Tex., Wash., Ariz. Recipient grants public and pvt. agencies. Mem. Nat. Assn. State Univs. and Land-Grant Colls.(chmn. commn. on arts 1981-83), Coun. Fine Arts Deans (exec. com. 1984-89, sec./treas. 1986-89), Univ. and Coll. Theatre Assn. (pres. 1981-82), Assn. for Communication Adminstrn. (pres. 1986-87), Ky. Theatre Assn. (pres. 1976). Office: Ariz State U Coll Fine Arts Tempe AZ 85287-2101

WILLS, JOHN ELLIOT, JR., history educator, writer; b. Urbana, Ill., Aug. 8, 1936; s. John Elliot and George Anne (Hicks) W.; m. Carolin Connell, July 19, 1958; children: Catherine, Christopher John, Jeffrey David, Joanne, Lucinda. BA in Philosophy, U. Ill., 1956; MA in East Asian Studies, Harvard U., 1960, PhD in History and Far Ea. Langs., 1967. History instr. Stanford (Calif.) U., 1964-65; history instr. U. So. Calif., L.A., 1965-67, asst. prof., 1967-72, assoc. prof., 1972-84, prof., 1984—, acting chair East Asian Langs. and Cultures, 1987-89; dir. East Asian Studies Ctr. USC-UCLA Joint East Asian Studies Ctr., L.A., 1990-94; rsch. abroad in The Netherlands, Taiwan, China, Japan, Macao, Philippines, Indonesia, India, Italy, Spain, Portugal, Eng. Author: Pepper, Guns, and Parleys: The Dutch East India Company and China, 1662-1681, 1974, Embassies and Illusions: Dutch and Portuguese Envoys to K'ang-hsi, 1666-1687, 1984, Mountain of Fame: Portraits in Chinese History, 1994; co-editor: (with Jonathan D. Spence) From Ming to Ch'ing: Conquest, Region, and Continuity in Seventeenth-Century China, 1979; contbr. articles to profl. jours. Grantee Nat. Acad. Scis., 1985, Am. Coun. Learned Soc., 1979-80; Younger Humanist fellow NEH, 1972-73. Mem. Assn. for Asian Studies, Am. Hist. Assn., Phi Beta Kappa, Phi Kappa Phi (Recognition award 1986, 95). Avocation: travel. Office: U So Calif Dept History Los Angeles CA 90089-0034

WILLS, MICHAEL RALPH, medical educator; b. Bath, Somerset, Eng., May 4, 1931; came to U.S., 1977; s. Ralph Herbert and Una Read (Hearse) W.; m. Margaret Christine Lewis, Sept. 12, 1955; children: Matthew, Catherine, Sarah, Benjamin, Thomas. M.B., Ch.B., U. Bristol, Eng., 1954, M.D., 1964, Ph.D., 1978. Intern Bristol Royal Infirmary, 1954-55, fellow, resident, 1957-64; sr. lectr. Royal Free Hosp. and Med. Sch., London, 1964-70, reader, 1970-74, prof., 1974-77; dir. clin. labs. U. Va., Charlottesville, 1977—. Author books, films; contbr. articles to profl. jours. Lt. comdr. Royal Naval Res., Eng. NIH rsch. fellow, 1967-68. Fellow ACP, Royal Coll. Physicians, Royal Coll. Pathologists. Roman Catholic. Avocations: reading, wood carving, gardening, military modelling. Home: 236 Rookwood Dr Charlottesville VA 22903-4644 Office: U Va Dept Pathology Charlottesville VA 22908

WILLS, ROBERT HAMILTON, retired newspaper executive; b. Colfax, Ill., June 21, 1926; s. Robert Orson and Ressie Mae (Hamilton) W.; m. Sherilyn Lou Niersheimer, Jan. 16, 1949; children: Robert L., Michael H., Kendall J. B.S., M.S., Northwestern U., 1950. Reporter Duluth (Minn.) Herald & News-Tribune, 1950-51; reporter Milw. Jour., 1951-59, asst. city editor, 1959-62; city editor Milw. Sentinel, 1962-75, editor, 1975-91; exec. v.p. Jour./Sentinel, Inc., Milw., 1991-92, pres., 1992-93; vice-chmn., 1993; also bd. dirs. Jour./Sentinel, Inc., Milw.; pub. Milw. Jour.; sr. v.p., bd. dirs. Jour. Communications; pres. Wis. Freedom of Info. Council, 1979-86; Pulitzer Prize juror, 1982, 83, 90. Mem. media-law rels. com. State Bar Wis.; mem. privacy coun. Wis. Pub. Svc. Commn., 1996, chmn., 1994-95. Recipient Leadership award Women's Ct. and Civic Conf. Greater Milw., 1987, Freedom of Info. award, 1988; named Wis. Newsman of Yr. Milw. chpt., 1973. Mem. Wis. Newspaper Assn. (pres. 1985-86, Disting. Svc. award 1992), Wis. AP (pres. 1975-76, Dion Henderson award Svc. 1993), Am. Soc. Newspaper Editors, Internat. Press Inst., Milw. Press Club (Media Hall Fame 1993), Soc. Profl. Journalists (prs. Milw. chpt. 1979-80, nat. pres. 1986-87), Sigma Delta Chi Found. (bd. dirs. 1993—). Home: 2030 Allen Blvd Apt 3 Middleton WI 53562-3469

WILLS, WALTER JOE, agricultural marketing educator; b. Beecher City, Ill., Oct. 8, 1915; s. Joe J. and Lillian L. (Buzzard) W.; m. Mary E. Triffet, May 22, 1942 (dec. 1981); m. Martha Jane Smith Peck, June 12, 1982. Student, Blackburn Coll., Carlinville, Ill., 1934; B.S. in Agr, U. Ill., 1936, M.S. in Agrl. Econs, 1937, Ph.D., 1952. Credit examiner Prodn. Credit Corp., St. Louis, 1937-47; asst. prof. U. Ill., 1947-52; dir. farm relations Am. Trucking Assn., 1953-54; extension marketing specialist Wash. State Coll., 1954-56; prof. agrl. marketing So. Ill. U., Carbondale, 1956-83, chmn. agrl. industries dept., 1957-72, cons., 1983—; Fulbright lectr. Ege U., Izmir, Turkey, 1969-70. Author: Introduction to Grain Marketing, 1972, Introduction to Agribusiness Management, 1973, (with Michael E. Newman) Agribusiness Management and Entrepreneurship, 3d edit., 1993, Introduction to Agricultural Sales, 1982. Served to capt., ordnance dept. U.S. Army, 1941-46. Recipient Outstanding Coop. Educator award Am. Inst. Cooperation, 1978; Great Tchr. award So. Ill. U., 1984, Disting. Svc. award, 1992. Mem. Goldern Key, Phi Kappa Phi, Gamma Sigma Delta, Alpha Zeta. Club: Rotarian. Home: 904 S Valley Rd Carbondale IL 62901-2421

WILLS, WILLIAM RIDLEY, II, former insurance company executive, historian; b. Nashville, June 19, 1934; s. Jesse Ely and Ellen (Buckner) W.; m. Irene Weaver Jackson, July 21, 1962; children: William Ridley III, Morgan Jackson, Thomas Weaver. BA, Vanderbilt U., 1956. Agt., staff mgr. Nat. Life & Accident Ins. Co., Nashville, 1958-62, supr., 1962-64, asst. sec., 1964-67, asst. v.p., 1967-70, 2d v.p., 1970-75, v.p., 1975-81, sr. v.p., 1981-83; sr. v.p. Am. General Services Co., 1982-83; dir. Nat. Life & Accident Ins. Co., Nashville, 1976-83; pres. Tenn. Hist. Soc., 1985-87; bd. dirs. Nat. Trust for Hist. Preservation, 1988-91. Author: History of Belle Meade: Mansion, Plantation and Stud, 1991, Old Enough to Die: A Tennessee Confederate Family, 1996. Nat. chmn. Living Endowment Drive Vanderbilt U., 1974; pres. Cumberland Mus. and Sci. Ctr., Nashville, 1977; gen. chmn. campaign United Way, Nashville and Middle Tenn., 1978; pres. YMCA of Met. Nashville, 1984; trustee Ladies Hermitage Assn., 1981-90; mem. Tenn. Hist. Commn.; chmn. bd. Montgomery Bell Acad., 1988—; bd. dirs. Vanderbilt U., 1988—. Lt. USN, 1956-58. Recipient awards YMCA, 1977, 1983, United Way De Tocqueville award, 1989, Tenn. History Book award Tenn. Lib. Assn. and Tenn. Hist. Comm., 1991. Fellow Life Office Mgmt. Assn.; mem. Assn. Preservation Tenn. Antiques (pres. Nashville chpt. 1987-89), Belle Meade Country Club, YMCA Athletic Club, Coffee House Club, Round Table Literary Club. Presbyterian.

WILLSE, JAMES PATRICK, newspaper editor; b. N.Y.C., Mar. 17, 1944; s. Sherman Stokes and Katherine (Mackey) W.; m. Sharon Margaret Stack, Sept. 15, 1973; 1 child, Elizabeth Ruth. BA, Hamilton Coll., 1967; MS, Columbia U., 1968. Nat. editor AP, N.Y.C., 1969-74; news editor AP, San Francisco, 1975-78; city editor San Francisco Examiner, 1978-82, mng. editor, 1982-84; mng. editor N.Y. Daily News, 1984-89, editor, pub., 1989-95; editor Star Ledger, Newark, 1995—. Fellow Stanford U., 1975. Mem. Am. Soc. Newspaper Editors, AP Mng. Editors. Office: Star Ledger 1 Star Ledger Plz Newark NJ 07102-1200*

WILLSON, C. GRANT, chemistry educator, engineering educator; b. Vallejo, Calif., Mar. 30, 1939; s. Carlton P. and Margaret Ann (Cosner) W.; m. Deborah Jeanne Merritt, Dec. 13, 1975; children: William, Andrew. BS in Chemistry, U. Calif., Berkeley, 1962, PhD in Organic Chemistry, 1973; MS in Organic Chemistry, San Diego State U., 1969. With propellent rsch. Aerojet Gen. Corp., Sacramento, 1962-64; tchr., coach Fairfax High Sch., L.A., 1964-67; prof. Calif. State U., Long Beach, 1973-74, U. Calif., San Diego, 1974-78; mgr. polymer sci. and tech. IBM Almaden Rsch. Ctr., San Jose, Calif., 1978-93; prof. chemistry, chem. engring. U. Tex., Austin, 1993—. Contbr. articles to profl. jours.; patentee in field. Mem. NAE, AAAS, Soc. Photographic and Instrumentation Engrs., Am. Phys. Soc., Am. Chem. Soc. (Arthur K. Doolittle award 1986, award Chemistry of Materials 1991, Carouthers award 1992, Coop. Rsch. award in Polymer Sci. 1993), St. Francis Yacht Club, Sigma Xi. Avocations: sailing, skiing. Office: U Tex Dept Chem Engring CPE3 474 Austin TX 78712

WILLSON, CHARLES EMERY, school system administrator; b. Bunkerhill, Kans., Jan. 16, 1936; s. Emery J. and Clara Louise (Marsh) W.; m. Margaret Sue Caldwell, Sept. 23, 1960; children: Nanci Sue, Wade Hunter, Amy Louise. BS in Edn., Emporia State U., 1960; MS in Edn., Ft. Hays State U., 1965; postgrad., Kans. U., Iowa State U. Cert. tchr., adminstr., Kans. Classroom tchr., coach Unified Sch. Dist. 208, WaKeeney, Kans., 1960-63; classroom tchr. USD 489, Hays, Kans., 1963-64; classroom tchr., coach R-1 Jefferson County Schs., Lakewood, Colo., 1964-67, bldg. adminstr., 1967-74; bldg. adminstr. Unified Sch. Dist. 407, Russell, Kans., 1974-78, adminstr., 1985-87; banking, ins. exec. Home State Bank, Russell, 1978-85; asst. supt. Unified Sch. Dist. 234, Ft. Scott, Kans., 1987-91; supt. schs. Unified Sch. Dist 449, Easton, Kans., 1991—; tchr./trainer Tchr. Effectiveness and Student Achievement, Ft. Scott, 1988—; presenter, coord. Outcomes Based Edn./Effective Schs., Kans., 1987—. Cast mem. Russell Arts Coun., 1981; mem. sch. bd. Unified Sch. Dist. 407, 1980; chmn. bd. trustees Trinity United Meth. Ch., Russell, 1976-86; mgr., coach Am. Legion Baseball, Russell, 1985-86; mem. Leadership Ft. Scott, 1988. Mem. ASCD, Am. Assn. Sch. Adminstrs., United Sch. Adminstrs. Kans., Kans. Assn. Sch. Adminstrs., Kans. Assn. Supervision and Curriculum Devel., Kans. State Bd. Edn. (coun. supts. 1993-95), Greater Kansas City Assn. Supervision and Curriculum Devel., Kansas City Learning Exch., Masons, Phi Delta Kappa (coord. 1988). Avocations: golf, hunting, classical music. Home: 19321 Santa Fe Trail Leavenworth KS 66048 Office: Unified Sch Dist 449 32502 Easton Rd Easton KS 66020

WILLSON, JAMES DOUGLAS, aerospace executive; b. Edinburgh, Scotland, May 24, 1915; came to U.S., 1921; s. George William and Margaret (Douglas) W.; m. Genevieve Best, Nov. 11, 1939; children: James Douglas, Stephen J., Wendy. B.S. with honors, Ohio State U., 1937, M.B.A., 1938. C.P.A., N.Y. Sr. auditor Arthur Andersen & Co. (C.P.A.'s), N.Y.C., 1938-42; controller Stinson div. Consol. Vultee Aircraft Corp., 1946-48, Plaskon div. Libbey-Ownes-Ford Glass Co., 1948-53; treas. Affiliated Gas Equipment Co., Cleve., 1953; v.p. finance, treas. Norris-Thermador Corp., Los Angeles, 1957-59; controller, mgr. finance Tidewater Oil Co., Los Angeles, 1959-60; v.p. finance Tidewater Oil Co., 1960-66, Northrop Corp., Los Angeles, 1966-70; sr. v.p. finance, treas. Northrop Corp., 1970-80, also dir. Author: Controllership, 1952, 63, 81, 90, 95, Business Budgeting and Control, 1956, 57, Internal Auditing Manual, 1983, 89, Budgeting and Profit Planning, 1983, 89, 92, Financial Information Systems, 1986. Served to lt. comdr. USNR, 1942-46. Mem. Nat. Assn. Accts. (Lybrand Gold medal 1960), Am. Inst. C.P.A.s, Controllers Inst. Am. Home: 1715 Chevy Chase Dr Beverly Hills CA 90210-2709

WILLSON, JOHN MICHAEL, mining company executive; b. Sheffield, England, Feb. 21, 1940; s. Jack Desmond and Cicely Rosamond (Long Price) W.; m. Susan Mary Partridge, Aug. 26, 1942; children: Marcus J., Carolyn A. BSc in Mining Engring. with honors, Imperial Coll., London, 1962, MSc in Mining Engring., 1985. With Cominco Ltd., 1966-74; v.p. No. Group Cominco Ltd., Vancouver, B.C., Can., 1981-84; pres. Garaventa (Canada) Ltd., Vancouver, 1974-81; pres., CEO Western Can. Steel Ltd., Vancouver, 1985-88, Pegasus Gold Inc., Spokane, Wash., 1989-92, Placer Dome, Inc., Vancouver, B.C., Can., 1993—; chmn. bd. dirs. Placer Pacific Ltd., Sydney, Australia, Placer Dome U.S., San Francisco, Placer Dome Can. Ltd., Placer Dome Latin Am. Pres. N.W.T. Chamber Mines, Yellowknife, Can., 1982-84; chmn. bd. dirs. Western Pub. Lands Coalition, Pueblo, Colo., 1990-91; bd. dirs. World Gold Coun. Mem. AIME, Can. Inst. Mining and Metallurgy, Inst. Mining and Metallurgy (London), Assn. Profl. Engrs. B.C., Assn. Profl. Engrs. and Geologists N.W.T., N.W. Mining Assn. (bd. dirs. Corp. Leadership award 1991), World Gold Coun. (bd. dirs.). Avocations: cycling, tennis, squash, sailing, skiing. Home: 4722 Drummond Dr, Vancouver, BC Canada V6T 1B4 Office: Placer Dome Inc, 1055 W Dunsmuir St Ste 1600, Vancouver, BC Canada V7X 1P1

WILLSON, MARY F., ecology researcher, educator; b. Madison, Wis., July 28, 1938; d. Gordon L. and Sarah (Loomans) W.; m. R.A. von Neumann, May 29, 1972 (dec.). B.A. with honors, Grinnell Coll., 1960; Ph.D., U. Wash., 1964. Asst. prof. U. Ill., Urbana, 1965-71, assoc. prof., 1971-76, prof. ecology, 1976-90; rsch. ecologist Forestry Scis. Lab., Juneau, Alaska, 1989—; adj. prof. zoology Wash. State U., Pullman; prin. rsch. scientist, affiliate prof. biology Inst. Arctic Biology U. Alaska, Fairbanks; faculty assoc. divsn. biol. scis. U. Mont., Missoula. Author: Plant Reproductive Ecology, 1983, Vertebrate Natural History, 1984; co-author: Mate Choice in Plants, 1983. Fellow AAAS, Am. Ornithologists Union; mem. Soc. for Study Evolution, Am. Soc. Naturalists (hon. mem.), Ecol. Soc. Am., Brit. Ecol. Soc. Office: Forestry Scis Lab 2770 Sherwood Ln Juneau AK 99801-8545

WILLSON, PRENTISS, JR., lawyer; b. Durham, N.C., Sept. 20, 1943; s. Prentiss and Lucille (Giles) W.; m. Ellen Borgersen, May 22, 1982. AB, Occidental Coll., 1965; JD, Harvard U., 1968. Bar: Calif. 1969, U.S. Dist. Ct. (no. dist.) Calif. 1971, U.S. Ct. Appeals (9th cir.) 1971, U.S. Tax Ct. 1971, U.S. Supreme Ct. 1975. Instr. law Miles Coll., Birmingham, Ala., 1968-70; ptnr. Morrison & Foerster, San Francisco, 1970—; prof. Golden Gate U., 1971-84; lectr. Stanford U. Sch. Law, 1985-88. Contbr. articles to legal publs. Mem. ABA, Calif. Bar Assn. Democrat. Office: Morrison & Foerster 345 California St San Francisco CA 94104-2635

WILLSON, ROBERT (WILLIAM), glass sculpture and watercolor artist; b. Mertzon, Tex., May 28, 1912; s. James Thomas and Birdie Alice (Blanks) W.; m. Virginia Lambert, Aug. 12, 1941 (div. 1977); 1 child, Mark Joseph; m. Margaret Pace, May 30, 1981. BA, U. Tex., 1934; MFA, U. Bellas Artes, Mex., 1941. Pub. sch. tchr. various small Tex. towns, 1936-40; chmn. art dept. Tex. Wesleyan Coll., Ft. Worth, 1940-48; owner Nob Hill Tourist Resort, Winslow, Ark., 1948-52; prof. art U. Miami, 1952-77, ret., 1977; represented by Sol Del Rio Gallery, San Antonio, Galleria d'Arte Moderna Ravagnan, Venice, Italy, Lyons-Matrix Gallery, Austin, Tex., Sandra Ainsley Gallery, Toronto, Stein Gallery, Portland, Maine, Judy Youens Gallery, Houston, Painted Horse Gallery, Aspen, Colo., Parchman-Stremmel Gallery, San Antonio; tchr. U. Mex., 1935; dir. Nob Hill Art Gallery, Ark. Ozarks, 1948-52; dir. Tex. Wesleyan Coll. Art Gallery, 1940-48; cons.-dir. Peoria Art Mus., Ill., 1969. One-man shows include U. Tex., Austin, 1980, McNay Art Mus., San Antonio, 1982, Art Inst. of the Permian Basin, Odessa, Tex. 1985, Tulane U., New Orleans, 1986, San Antonio Mus. Art, 1986, San Angelo (Tex.) Mus. of Art, 1989, Lyons-Matrix Gallery, Austin, 1989, 92, 95, Mus. of Modern Art, Venice, Italy, 1984, Galleria d'Arte Sant'Apollonia, 1989, Galleria d'Arte Moderna, San Marco, Vencie, 1984-89, Martin Mus. of Art, Baylor U., Waco, Tex., 1991-92, N.Mex. Mus. of Fine Art, Santa Fe, 1993; exhibited in group shows at Internat. Glass Art 982 Show, Venice, Italy, 1994; juried shows include San Francisco Mus. Art, 1971, Mus. Modern Art, Mexico City, Adria Gallery, N.Y.C., Harmon Gallery, Naples, Fla., Lowe Art Mus., Fucina degli Angeli Internat. Glass Scuplture Exhbns., Venice, 1966-88, La Biennale di Venizia, 1972; permanent collections include Museo Correr, Venice, Victoria and Albert Mus., London, Nat. Italian Glass Mus., Murano, Italy, Auckland Nat. Art Mus., New Zealand, U. Tex., Austin, Corning Mus. Glass, N.Y., Witte Art Mus., San Antonio, San Antonio Mus. Art, Phila. Mus. Art, Little Rock Ctr., Ark., Ft. Lauderdale (Fla.) Art Mus., Peoria Art Mus., Lowe Art Mus., Miami, Fla., Columbus (Ga.) Art Mus., Duke U. Art Mus., N.C., Oxford (Eng.)-Wilson-Willson Glass Collection, New Orleans Mus. Art, New Mex. Mus. Fine Art, Santa Fe, others; contbr. articles to profl. jours. Capt. USMCR, 1942-45. Tex. Regents scholarship U. Tex., 1930-34, Farmer Internat. fellowship to Mex., 1935; Nat. study grant Corning Mus. of Glass, 1956, rsch. grant U. Miami, 1964, 66, Feldman Found., 1976, Internat. rsch. grant U.S. Office of Edn., 1966-68, Coll. grants Shell Co. Found., 1971, 73. Mem. AAUP, Coun. of Ozark Artists and Craftsmen (founder), Fla. Craftsmen, Coll. Art Assn., Am. Assn. Mus., Fla. Sculptors, Tex. Sculptors, Tex. Watercolor Soc., others. Avocations: collecting ancient glass, Indian poetry. Home: 207 Terrell Rd San Antonio TX 78209-5915

WILLUMSON, GLENN GARDNER, curator, art historian; b. Glendale, Calif., June 22, 1949; s. Donald Herbert and Aileen Ann (Gardner) W.; m. Margaret Julia Moore, June 20, 1970; children: Erik Ryan, Ashley Aileen. BA, St. Mary's Coll., 1971; MA, U. Calif., Davis, 1984; PhD in Art History, U. Calif., Santa Barbara, 1988. Asst. curator Nelson Art Gallery, Davis, Calif., 1982-83; with collection devel. Getty Ctr. for History of Art and Humanities, Santa Monica, Calif., 1988-92; curator Palmer Mus. of Art, University Park, Pa., 1992—; fellow Nat. Writing Project, 1987; vis. prof. U. Calif., Irvine, 1990; adj. prof. art history Pa. State U., University Park, 1994—. Author: W. Eugene Smith and the Photo-Essay, 1992 (grantee J. Paul Getty Trust 1991), Collecting With a Passion, 1993; mem. editl. bd. History of Photography mag., London, 1991-94, Cambridge Univ. Press., N.Y.C., 1993—. Mem. Am. Studies Assn. (Annette K. Baxter prize 1987), Coll. Art Assn., Soc. Photog. Edn. (mem. governing bd. Mid-Atlantic region), Assn. Historians Am. Art. Office: Palmer Mus Art Curtin Rd University Park PA 16802

WILMERDING, JOHN, art history educator, museum curator; b. Boston, Apr. 28, 1938; s. John Currie and Lila Vanderbilt (Webb) W. A.B., Harvard U., 1960, A.M., 1961, Ph.D., 1965. Asst. prof. art Dartmouth Coll., 1965-68, asso. prof., 1968-73, Leon E. Williams prof., 1973-77, chmn. dept. art, 1968-72, chmn. humanities div., 1971-72; sr. curator Am. art Nat. Gallery of Art, 1977-83, dep. dir., 1983-88; Sarofim prof. Am. art Princeton (N.J.) U., 1988—, chmn. dept. art and archeology, 1992—; vis. lectr. history of art Yale U., 1972; vis. prof. fine arts Harvard U., 1976; vis. prof. art U. Md., 1979; vis. prof. art history U. Del., 1982; hon. curator painting Peabody Mus., Salem, Mass.; vis. curator Met. Mus., 1988—. Author: Fitz Hugh Lane, American Marine Painter, 1964, A History of American Marine Painting, 1968, Pittura Americana dell' Ottocento, 1969, Robert Salmon, Painter of Ship and Shore, 1971, Fitz Hugh Lane, 1971, Winslow Homer, 1972, Audubon, Homer, Whistler and 19th Century America, 1972, The Genius of American Painting, 1973, American Art, 1976, American Light, The Luminist Movement, 1980, American Masterpieces from the National Gallery of Art, 1980, An American Perspective, 1981, Important Information Inside, 1982, Andrew Wyeth, The Helga Pictures, 1987, American Marine Paintings, 2d edit., 1987, Paintings by Fitz Hugh Lane, 1988; American Views: Essays on American Art, 1991, The Artist's Mount Desert: American Painters on the Maine Coast, 1994. Trustee Shelburne Mus., Vt., Guggenheim Mus., N.Y.C., Lewis Walpole Libr., Hartford, Conn., N.E. Harbor Libr., Maine, Wendell Gilley Mus., S.W. Harbor, Maine, Wyeth Endowment for Am. Art, Wilmington, Del. Guggenheim fellow, 1973-74. Fellow Phila. Atheneum (hon.); Mem. Coll. Art Assn., Am. Studies Assn. Office: Princeton U Dept Art and Archaeology 105 McCormick Hall Princeton NJ 08544-1018

WILMERS, ROBERT GEORGE, banker; b. N.Y.C., Apr. 20, 1934; s. Charles K. and Cecilia (Eitingon) W.; children: Robert George, Christopher C. B.A., Harvard U., 1956; postgrad., Harvard Bus. Sch., 1958-59. Dep. fin. adminstr. City of N.Y., 1966-70; v.p. Morgan Guaranty Trust Co., N.Y.C. and Belgium, 1970-80; chmn., pres., chief exec. officer, dir. First Empire State Corp., Buffalo, 1982—; chmn. bd., pres., chief exec. officer, dir. Mfrs. & Traders Trust Co., Buffalo, 1983—; bd. dirs. Fed. Res. Bank N.Y., The Bus. Coun. N.Y. State, A/Knox Art Gallery, ENY Savs. Bank, Greater Buffalo Partnership; mem. gov. coun. N.Y. State Bankers Assn. Bd. dirs. Buffalo Found., 1986. Decorated officer de l'Ordre de la Couronne (Belgium). Mem. Coun. Fgn. Rels. Home: 800 W Ferry St Buffalo NY 14222-1660 also: 1 W 64th St New York NY 10023-6731 Office: Mfrs & Traders Trust Co 1 M&T Plz Buffalo NY 14211-1638

WILMETH, DON BURTON, theater arts educator, theater historian, administrator, editor; b. Houston, Dec. 15, 1939; s. Perry Davis and Pauline Wilmeth; m. Judy Eslie Hansgen, June 10, 1963; 1 child, Michael Tyler. BA, Abilene Christian U., 1961; MA, U. Ark., 1962; PhD, U. Ill., 1964; MA Ad Eundem (hon.), Brown U., 1970. Teaching asst. U. Ark., Fayetteville, 1961-62, U. Ill., Urbana, 1962-64; asst. prof., head drama dept. Eastern N.Mex. U., Portales, 1964-67; from asst. to prof. theatre arts, dept. chmn. Brown U., Providence, 1967—; curator H. Adrian Smith Collection of Conjuring Books and Magicana, 1988—; cons. Internat. Exchange of Scholars (Fulbright), Washington, 1982-84, Am. memory Libr. Congress, 1992-95, Am. Theatre series Sta. WNET-TV, N.Y.C.; bd. dirs. Inst. Am. Theatre Studies, Bloomington, Ind., 1981-84; juror George Freedley Theatre Book Award com., 1971-93, 94-96, Barnard Hewitt Book Award com., 1985-89; mem. Theatre Hall of Fame Com. Hist. Figures, 1993—; O.R. and Eva Mitchell Vis. Disting. prof. Trinity U., San Antonio, 1995. Dir. numerous theatrical prodns. including (Brown U. prodns.) Carousel (Rodgers and Hammerstein), 1968, The Devils, 1969, The Night of the Iguana (Tennesee Williams), 1970, Much Ado About Nothing (Shakespeare), 1971, Too True to be Good, 1972, Dial "M" for Murder, 1972, The Beggar's Opera (John Gay), 1973, Company (Stephen Sondheim), 1974, Look Homeward, Angel, 1975, Secret Service, 1976, Romeo and Juliet (Shakespeare), 1977, The Hostage (Brendan Behan), 1978, The Seagull (Chekhov), 1979, The Importance of Being Earnest (Oscar Wilde), 1980, The Playboy of the Western World (J.M. Synge), 1982, The Rivals (Sheridan), 1983, Our Town (Thornton Wilder), 1985, Philadelphia Story, 1987, Mrs. Warren's Profession (Shaw), 1989, The Duchess of Malfi (John Webster), 1992, The Illusion, 1994, also numerous prodns. at other venues; acting roles include Twelfth Night (Colo. Shakespeare Festival 1960), The Tempest (Champlain Shakespeare Festival 1962), The Passion of Dracula, 1979, The Runner Stumbles, 1984, Follies, 1991; author: The American Stage to World War I, 1978, American and English Popular Entertainment, 1980, George Frederick Cooke, 1980 (Hewitt award 1981), The Language of American Popular Entertainment, 1981, Variety Entertainment and Outdoor Amusements, 1982; co-author: Theatre in the United States: A Documentary History, Vol. 1, 1750-1915, 1996; co-editor: Plays by Augustin Daly, 1984, Plays by William Hooker Gillette, 1983, Mud Show, American Tent Circus Life, 1988, Cambridge Guide to America Theatre, 1993, sole edit., 1996; editor (book series) Cambridge Studies Am. Theatre and Drama, 1992—; contbg. editor: Cambridge Guide to World Theatre, 1988, 95; contbr. articles to profl. jours., chpts. to books and reviewer of books; adv. editor of 6 jours; contbr. articles to World Book Encyclopedia, Dictionary of Am. Biography, Encyclopedia of New York City, and other reference material. Corp. mem. Providence Pub. Library, 1983—; bd. mgrs. The Players of Providence, 1968-80; mem. adv. bd. East Lynne Theatre Co., Secaucus, N.J., 1981—, Langston Hughes Cultural Arts Ctr., Providence, 1982-92, Actors Theatre of Louisville, 1987—; grants panelist R.I. State Council on the Arts, Providence, 1981—; cons. Libr. of Congress, 1992—. John Simon Guggenheim fellow, 1982. Fellow Am. Theatre Assn. (chmn. pubs. 1975-77); mem. Theatre Library Assn. (v.p. 1981-84), Internat. Fed. Theatre Research (exec. bd. 1995—), Theatre Hist. Soc., Am. Soc. Theatre Research (exec. com. 1976-78, 80-83, 85-88, 94—, pres. 1991-94, sec. 1995—), Soc. for Advancement of Edn.-N.Y.C. (bd. trustees 1977-91), Coll. Fellows of Am. Theatre (bd. dirs. 1995-96, dean 1996), Nat. Theatre Conf. Avocations: reading, collecting theatre books and memorabilia, bookbinding. Home: 525 Hope St Providence RI 02906-1630 Office: Brown U Dept Theatre Speech and Dance PO Box 1897 Providence RI 02912-1897

WILMORE, DOUGLAS WAYNE, physician, surgeon; b. Newton, Kans., July 22, 1938; s. Waldo Wayne and Hilda Gard (Adrian) W.; m. Judith Kay Shabert; 1 child, Carol Kristann. BA, Washburn U., 1960; MD, Kans. U., 1964; MS (hon.), Harvard U., 1979; PhD (hon.), Washburn U., 1995. Diplomate Am. Bd. Surgery. Intern Hosp. U. Pa., Phila., 1964-65, resident, fellow, 1965-71; chief clin. rsch. and staff surgeon U.S. Army Inst. Surg. Rsch., Ft. Sam Houston, 1971-79; staff surgeon Brigham and Women's Hosp., Boston, 1979—. Editor: Scientific American Surgery, 1988. Lt. Col. U.S. Army, 1971-74. Achievements include development of safe modern techniques for providing parenteral nutrition to critically-ill patients.

WILMOT, IRVIN GORSAGE, former hospital administrator, educator, consultant; b. Nanking, China, June 30, 1922; s. Frank Alonzo and Ethel (Ranney) W.; m. Dorothy Agnes Mohlfeld, Feb. 6, 1943; children: Marcia Beth, David Michael. BS, Northwestern U., 1955; MBA, U. Chgo., 1957. With Internat. Register Co., Chgo., 1946-47; buyer U. Chgo., 1947-49; adminstrv. asst., then asst. supt. U. Chgo. Clinics, 1949-61; adminstr. NYU Med. Center-Univ. Hosp., 1961-68, exec. v.p., 1968-81; exec. v.p. Blue Cross-Blue Shield Greater N.Y., 1981-83, dir., 1977-81; exec. v.p., chief operating officer Montefiore Hosp. and Med. Ctr., N.Y.C., 1984-85; healthcare cons., 1985—; instr. then asst. prof. U. Chgo., 1957-61; asso. prof. NYU, 1961-68; prof., 1968—; assoc. dir. U. Chgo. Grad. Program Hosp. Adminstrn., 1959-61; mem. hosp. rev. and planning council State of N.Y., 1979-87. Bd. dirs. N.Y. Blood Center, 1978-81. With USN, 1940-46. Fellow Am. Coll. Hosp. Adminstrs. (chmn. central. com. insts. 1959-65, regent N.Y. State and P.R. 1974—); mem. Assn. U. Programs Hosp. Adminstrs. (exec. sec. 1959-61), Am. Hosp. Assn. (mem. council research and planning 1965-68, council on mgmt. 1979-80, council on fin. 1981-84, trustee 1979-81), Assn. Am. Med. Colls. (chmn. council teaching hosps. 1970-71), Greater N.Y. Hosp. Assn. (bd. govs., pres. 1973-74), Hosp. Assn. N.Y. State (trustee, chmn. 1976-77). Home: 34 Helen Ave Rye NY 10580-2447 Office: PO Box 672 Rye NY 10580-0672

WILMOT, LOUISE C., retired naval commander, charitable organization executive; b. Wayne, N.J., Dec. 31, 1942; d. W.J. Currie and Dorothy Murphy; m. James E. Wilmot. BA in History, Coll. St. Elizabeth, Convent Sta., N.J., 1964; student, Naval War Coll., Newport, R.I., 1977; M in Legis. Affairs, George Washington U., 1978. Commd. ensign USN, 1964; advanced through grades to rear adm., 1991; comm. watch officer, registered publs. custodian, women's barracks officer Naval Air Sta., Pensacola, Fla.; with NATO staff Allied Forces, So. Europe, 1966-68; officer recruiter Recruiting Area Seven, Dallas; Naval Senate liaison officer Office Legis. Affairs, Washington; head women's equal opportunity br. Bur. Naval Pers., 1974-76; exec. officer Navy Recruiting Dist., Montgomery, Ala., 1977-79; command of Navy Recruiting Dist., Omaha, 1979-82; dep. dir accession policy Asst. Sec. Def. for Manpower, Installations, and Logistics, Washington, 1982-85; comdr. Navy Recruiting Area Five, Gt. Lakes, Ill., 1985-87; exec. asst., Naval aide Asst. Sec. Navy for Manpower and Reserve Affairs, Washington, 1987-89; comdr. Naval Tng. Ctr., Orlando, Fla., 1989-91; vice chief Naval Edn. and Tng., Pensacola, 1991-93; comdr. Naval Base, Phila., 1993-94; ret. U.S. Navy, 1994; dep. exec. dir. Cath. Relief Svcs., Balt., 1994—. Decorated DSM, Def. Superior Svc. medal, Legion of Merit with 3 gold stars. Office: Cath Relief Svcs Baltimore MD 21201-3443

WILMOUTH, ROBERT K., commodities executive; b. Worcester, Mass., Nov. 9, 1928; s. Alfred F. and Aileen E. (Kearney) W.; m. Ellen M. Boyle, Sept. 10, 1955; children: Robert J., John J., James P., Thomas G., Anne Marie. BA, Holy Cross Coll., 1949; MA, U. Notre Dame, 1950, LLD, 1984. Exec. v.p., dir. 1st Nat. Bank Chgo., 1972-75; pres., chief adminstrv. officer Crocker Nat. Bank, San Francisco, 1975-77; pres., chief exec. officer Chgo. Bd. Trade, 1977-82; chmn. LaSalle Nat. Bank, 1982—; pres., chief exec. officer Nat. Futures Assn., 1982—; dir. Pvt. Export Funding Corp. Trustee U. Notre Dame, chmn. investment com.; mem. adv. coun. Kellogg Grad. Sch. Mgmt., Northwestern U. 2d lt. USAF, 1951-53. Mem. Chgo. Club, Barrington Hill Country Club, Econ. Club. Home: 429 Caesar Dr Barrington IL 60010-4029 Office: Nat Futures Assn 200 W Madison St Ste 1600 Chicago IL 60606-3415

WILNER, JUDITH, journalist; b. Framingham, Mass., Mar. 30, 1943; d. John C. and Marjorie E. (Devonshire) Earley; m. David Alan Wilner, Aug. 27, 1964 (div. Aug. 1968); 1 child, Erica Susan; m. Fred Karp, July 28, 1991; 1 child, Shai Shalom Karp. BA in Letters, U. Okla., 1964. Wire editor, copy editor The Norman (Okla.) Transcript, 1967-72; news editor Loveland (Colo.) Reporter-Herald, 1972-73; editor of editl. page The Albuquerque Tribune, 1974-76, city editor, 1974-76; copy editor The Denver Post, 1976-77, copy desk chief, 1977-80, mgr. editl. sys., 1980-84; dep. tech. editor N.Y. Times, 1984-86, tech. editor, 1986—; women's editor The Norman Transcript, 1964-66. Mem. Newspaper Assn. of Am. (tech. com., chmn. wire svc. guidelines com. 1992—).

WILNER, MORTON HARRISON, retired lawyer; b. Balt., May 28, 1908; s. Joseph A. and Ida (Berkow) W.; m. Zelda Dunkelman, Nov. 3, 1940; children: James D., Thomas B., Lawrence J., Theodora. B.S. in Econs, U. Pa., 1930; J.D., Georgetown U., 1934. Bar: D.C. 1933. Gen. counsel emeritus Armed Forces Benefit Assn.; vice chmn. AFBA Indsl. Bank; bd. dirs. Armed Forces Benefit Svcs., Inc.; mem. emeritus Giant Food, Inc. Past pres. Jewish Community Center of Greater Washington.; Emeritus life trustee U. Pa.; past pres. Nat. Child Research Center; bd. govs. St. Albans Sch., 1968-72. Served to maj. USAAF; dep. dir. aircraft div. WPB 1942-45. Decorated Legion of Merit; recipient Ourisman Meml. award for civic achievement, 1970; Ben Franklin award U. Pa., 1973; alumni award of merit, 1975; Friar of Yr. award U. Pa., 1976; Wharton Sch. Club Joseph Wharton award, 1980. Mem. Fed. Bar Assn., ABA (ho. dels. 1971-73), D.C. Bar Assn., Internat. Bar Assn., Fed. Communications Bar Assn. (pres. 1969-70). Clubs: Army and Navy, Woodmont Country. Home: 2701 Chesapeake St NW Washington DC 20008-1042 Office: AFBA 909 N Washington St Alexandria VA 22314-1555

WILNER, PAUL ANDREW, journalist; b. N.Y.C., Feb. 12, 1950; s. Norman and Sylvia (Rubenstein) W.; m. Alyson Paula Bromberg, June 3, 1980; children: Anne Charlotte, Daniel Joseph. Student, U. Calif., Berkeley, 1968; BA, CUNY, 1976. Copy clk. N.Y. Times, 1976-80; reporter L.A. Herald Examiner, 1980-85; mng. editor Hollywood Reporter, L.A., 1985-87; asst. mng. editor features San Francisco Examiner, 1987—; sr. instr. U. So. Calif., L.A., 1983-85. Author: (poetry) Serious Business, The Paris Rev., 1977. Office: SF Examiner Mag 110 5th St San Francisco CA 94103-2918

WILNER, THOMAS BERNARD, lawyer; b. Toronto, Ont., Can., July 7, 1944; came to U.S., 1944; s. Morton H. and Zelda (Dunkelman) W.; m. Jane Ten Broeck; children: Amanda, Adam, David. BA, Yale U., 1966; LLB, U. Pa., 1969. Clk. U.S. Ct. Appeals, Phila., 1969-70; assoc. Debevoise Plimpton, N.Y.C., 1970-72; counsel Amtrak, Washington, 1972-73; ptnr. Arnold & Porter, Washington, 1973-89, Shearman & Sterling, Washington and Tokyo, 1989—.

WILOCK, ROBERT A., advertising and marketing executive; b. Niskayuna, N.Y., Apr. 11, 1944; s. Henry S. and Helen B. (Gorzynski) W.; m. Linda Leitz, Sept. 3, 1966; children: Rob, David. BS, Va. Poly. Inst. and State U., 1965; MA, Emory U., 1967. Staff asst. Procter & Gamble, Cin., 1969-72; product mgr. Gen. Foods, White Plains, N.Y., 1972-77; group product mgr. Morton Frozen Foods, Charlottesville, Va., 1977-79; dir. mktg. Hostess Cake, Rye, N.Y., 1979-84; sr. v.p. group dir. Ketchum Advt., N.Y.C., 1984-93; sr. v.p. mgmt. supr. Jordan, McGrath, Case & Taylor, N.Y.C., 1993—; creative advt. seminar Assn. Nat. Advertisers, N.Y.C., 1974, mktg. mgmt. seminar Harvard Grad. Sch. Bus., Cambridge, Mass., 1975. 1st lt. U.S. Army, 1967-69. Recipient Silver award Mag. Week, 1991, Gold award Am. Mktg. Assn., 1993. Avocations: biking, swimming, reading. Office: Jordan McGrath Case & Taylor 445 Park Ave New York NY 10022

WILPON, ALLEN GARY, designer; b. Miami, Fla., Dec. 24, 1960; m. Maria Isabel Leal, Nov. 25, 1989. BArch, U. Fla., 1982; M in Indsl. Design, Pratt Inst., Bklyn., 1985; MArch, Domus Acad., Milan, Italy, 1986. Designer Morris Lapidus Assocs., Miami Beach, Fla., 1979-80, Arquitectonica Internat., Miami, Fla., 1981-85; sr. designer Sottsass Associati Srl, Milan, 1986, Tihany Internat., N.Y.C., 1987-88, Donovan & Green, N.Y.C., 1988-95; design dir. Estée Lauder Inc., N.Y.C., 1995—; cons. Prescriptives, N.Y.C., 1992-93; profl. magician, N.Y.C. Designer water pitcher. Recipient Design Excellence award Soc. Environ. Graphic Designers, 1992. Mem. Univ. Club N.Y. Office: Estée Lauder Inc 767 Fifth Ave New York NY 10153

WILSKE, KENNETH RAY, internist, rheumatologist, researcher; b. American Falls, Idaho, Jan. 4, 1935; s. Emil and Emelia (Levi) W.; m. Edna Janean Walsh, June 23, 1958; children: Lisa Janean, Ashley Renee, Kendell Colleen. BA in Biology, Coll. Idaho, 1955; MD with honors, U. Wash., Seattle, 1959. Diplomate Am. Bd. Internal Medicine, Am. Bd. Rheumatology. Intern in medicine Columbia Presbyn. Hosp., N.Y.C., 1959-60, asst. resident in medicine, 1960-61; asst. resident in medicine U. Wash., Seattle, 1961-62, postdoctoral rsch. fellow in arthritis, 1962-64; with Virginia Mason Clinic, Seattle, 1968—, chmn. continuing med. edn. com., 1968-78, head section allergy, immunology and rheumatic diseases, 1969—, dep. chief of medicine, staff physician, 1976—, mem. clin. pharmacology com., 1983—, co-chmn. ad hoc com. on establishment Ctr. for Asian & Internat. Memdine, 1984—; pres. bd. trustees and chmn. exec. com. Virgina Mason Rsch. Ctr., 1978-82, mem. long range planning com., other coms., 1979—; mem. pub. rels. and devel. com. Virgina Mason Med. Found., 1978—, bd. dirs., 1979—, v.p., 1984-86; clin. assoc. prof. medicine U. Wash., 1970; cons. arthritis Pub. Health Svc. Hosp., Seattle, VA Hosp., Seattle; cons. staff physician Univ. Hosp., Seattle; staff physician Harborview Hosp., St. Francis Xavier Hosp., Drs. Hosp., all Seattle; clin. prof. medicine U. Wash.; mem. nat. teaching faculty Merck, Sharp & Dohme, 1984-86; mem. arthritis adv. com. FDA, 1979; speaker, presenter, vis. lectr. numerous profl. orgns., symposia, confs. and hosps. U.S.A., Can., Buenos Aries, Prague, Czechoslovakia, Eng., Indonesia, Japan. Author: (with L.A. Healy, B.H. Hansen) Beyond the Copper Bracelet, 1972, (with Healey), Systemic Manifestation of Temporal Arteritis, 1978; contbr. numerous articles, revs. to profl. jours. Recipient Physicians Recognition award AMA, 1969. Fellow ACP, Am. Coll. Rheumatologists; mem. N.W. Soc. Clin. Rsch. (pres. 1972), N.W. Rheumatism Soc. (pres. 1970), N.W. Med. Assn., N. Pacific Soc. Internal Medicine (prgram com. 1977-79), Am. Rheumatism Assn. (program com., chmn. local arrangements Western sect. 1983, mem. nat. exec. com. 1974-76), Am. Group Practice Assn. (continuing med. edn. com. 1971-76), Am. Soc. Clin. Rheumatology, Am. Soc. Rheumatology, Wash. State Med. Assn. (various coms. 1974-78, liaison sub-com. Bd. Med. Axaminers 1978, Aesculapius award 1967), Seattle Acad. Internal Medicine, King County Med. Soc. (trustee 1979-81, jud. coun. 1984), Arthritis Found. (bd. dirs. and exec. com. 1974-76, bd. dirs. Western Wash. chpt. 1965—, mem. med. and sci. com. 1965—, Disting. Svc. award 1966), Pacific Interurban Clin. Club, U. Wash. Med. Alumni Assn. (sec./treas. 1977, exec. com. 1977-79, pres. 1978). Home: 6529 NE Windermere Rd Seattle WA 98105-2057 Office: Virginia Mason Clinic 1000 9th Ave Seattle WA 98104-1227

WILSNACK, ROGER E., medical association administrator. Dir. Becton Dickinson Rsch. Ctr., Research Triangle Park, N.C. Office: Becton Dickinson & Co Becton Dickinson Rsch Ctr PO Box 12016 Research Triangle Park NC 27709-2016*

WILSON, AARON MARTIN, religious studies educator, college executive; b. Bazette, Tex., Sept. 30, 1926; s. John Albert and Myrtle (Hulsey) W.; m. Marthel Shoults, Jan. 31, 1947; children: Gloria Dallis, John Bert. BA, So. Bible Coll., 1963, DD (hon.), 1980; MA, Pitts. State U., 1972; PhD, Valley Christian U., 1980. Pastor various chs., 1947-58, Pentecostal Ch. of God, Houston, 1958-64, Pentacostal Ch. of God, Modesto, Calif., 1985-88; nat. dir. Christian edn. Pentecostal Ch. of God, Joplin, Mo., 1964-79, 88-93; pres. Evang. Christian Ch., Fresno, Calif., 1979-85; v.p. devel. Messenger Coll., Joplin, 1993-95; editor The Pentecostal Messenger, Joplin, 1995—; treas. Evang. Curriculum Commn., 1988-93; prof. So. Bible Coll., Houston, 1962-64. Author: Basic Bible Truth, 1988, Studies on Stewardship, 1989, My Church Can Grow, 1996. Republican. Home: 4701 Connecticut Ave Joplin MO 64804-5147 Office: Messenger Publ House PO Box 850 Joplin MO 64802-0850

WILSON, ADDISON GRAVES (JOE WILSON), lawyer, state senator; b. Charleston, S.C., July 31, 1947; s. Hugh deVeaux and Wray Smart (Graves) W.; m. Roxanne Dusenbury McCrory, Dec. 30, 1977; children—Michael Alan, Addison Graves, Julian Dusenbury, Hunter Taylor. B.A., Washington and Lee U., 1969; J.D., U. S.C.-Columbia, 1972. Bar: S.C. 1972. Staff mem. Sen. Strom Thurmond, Washington, 1967, Congressman Floyd Spence, Columbia, S.C., 1970-72; ptnr. Kirkland, Wilson, Moore, Allen, Taylor & O'Day and predecessor, West Columbia, S.C., 1972—; dep. gen. counsel U.S. Energy Sec. Jim Edwards, Washington, 1981-82; bd. dirs. NationsBank, Lexington, S.C.; senator State of S.C., Columbia, 1984—; presdl. appointee to Intergovtl. Adv. Coun. on Edn., 1990-91; mem. Internat. Observation Del. for 1990 Bulgarian parliamentary election. Campaign mgr. Congressman Floyd Spence, Columbia, 1974, 78, 80, 82; dist. campaign mgr. Gov. Carroll Campbell, 1986; vice chmn. S.C. Republican Party, 1972-74. Served to lt. col. USNG, 1975—. Presbyterian. Lodges: Rotary, Masons, Shriners. Home: 2825 Wilton Rd Springdale SC 29170 Office: Kirkland Wilson Moore Allen Taylor & O'Day 1700 Sunset Blvd West Columbia SC 29169-5940 also: PO Box 5709 West Columbia SC 29171-5709

WILSON, ALICE BLAND, real estate consultant; b. Rainelle, W.Va., Apr. 1, 1938; d. Brady Floyd and Mildred Martha (George) Bland; m. Louis William Groves, Jr., Apr. 20, 1957 (div. 1981); children: Martha Rachel, Leonora Jayne; m. Glen Parten Wilson, Dec. 11, 1982. AB, W.Va. U., 1959, postgrad. in microbiology, 1975-78. Contract adminstr. Washington Plate Glass Co., Washington, 1979-80; mem. acctg. staff Forbes Co., Washington, 1981; customer relations rep. Stern's Co., Washington, 1982; real estate assoc. Prudential Preferred Properties, Washington, 1985—. Contbr. articles to Jour. Parasitology. Vol. coord. John Glenn for Pres. campaign, Washington, 1983-84; co-chmn. hospitality com. Women's Nat. Dem. Club, Washington, 1985—; mem. internat. adv. coun. ARC, Washington, 1985—; mem. exec. com. Nat. Symphony Orch., 1990—. Mem. Washington Assn. Realtors (mem. residential sales com. 1985—), Leading Edge Soc., Million Dollar Club. Avocations: flying, aerobatics, nature study. Home: Box 25297 Washington DC 20007 Office: Pardoe Real Estate, Inc 2828 Pennsylvania Ave NW Washington DC 20007

WILSON, ALLAN BYRON, graphics company executive; b. Jackson, Miss., Aug. 19, 1948; s. Allen Bernice Wilson and Mary Pickering (Levereault) W.; m. Ines Ghinato, May 19, 1975; 1 child, Lucas Ghinato. B.S., Rice U., 1970, M.S. in Elec. Engring., 1971. Systems adminstr. Max Planck Institut für Kohlenforschung, Mülheim Ruhr, Fed. Republic Germany, 1971; systems programmer Digital Equipment Corp., Maynard, Mass., 1972-74, mktg. specialist, 1974-75, mktg. mgr., 1976-79; internat. ops. dir. Intergraph Corp., Huntsville, Ala., 1980-82, v.p. corp. and internat. ops., 1982-83, exec. v.p., 1983—. Contbr. articles to profl. jours. Mem. Assn. for Computing Machinery, IEEE. Home: 52 Revere Way Huntsville AL 35801-2846 Office: Intergraph Corp Huntsville AL 35894-0001

WILSON, ALMA, state supreme court justice; b. Pauls Valley, Okla.; d. William R. and Anna L. (Schuppert) Bell; m. William A. Wilson, May 30, 1948 (dec. Mar. 1994); 1 child, Lee Anne. AB, U. Okla., 1939, JD, 1941, LLD (hon.), 1992. Bar: Okla. 1941. Sole practice Muskogee, Okla., 1941-43; sole practice Oklahoma City, 1943-47, Pauls Valley, 1948-69; judge Pauls Valley Mcpl. Ct., 1967-68; apptd. spl. judge Dist. Ct. 21, Norman, Okla., 1969-75, dist. judge, 1975-79; justice Okla. Supreme Ct., Oklahoma City, 1982—, now chief justice. Mem. alumni bd. dirs. U. Okla.; mem. Assistance League; trustee Okla. Meml. Union. Recipient Guy Brown award, 1974, Woman of Yr. award Norman Bus. and Profl. Women, 1975, Okla. Women's Hall of Fame award, 1983, Pioneer Woman award, 1985, Disting. Svc. Citation U. Okla., 1985. Mem. AAUW, Garvin County Bar Assn. (past pres.), Okla. Bar Assn. (co-chmn. law and citizenship edn. com.), Okla. Trial Lawyers Assn. (Appellate Judge of Yr. 1986, 89), Altrusa, Am. Legion Aux. Office: Okla Supreme Ct State Capitol Rm 245 Oklahoma City OK 73105*

WILSON, ALMON CHAPMAN, surgeon, physician, retired naval officer; b. Hudson Falls, N.Y., July 13, 1924; s. Almon Chapman and Edith May (Truesdale) W.; m. Sofia M. Bogdons, Jan. 24, 1945; 1 child, Geoffrey Peter. B.A., Union Coll., Schenectady, 1946; M.D., Albany Med. Coll., 1952; M.S., George Washington U., 1969; student, Naval War Coll., Newport, R.I., 1968-69. Diplomate: Am. Bd. Surgery. Served as enlisted man and officer U.S. Navy, 1943-46, lt. j.g., M.C., 1952, advanced through grades to rear adm., 1976; intern U.S. Naval Hosp., Bremerton, Wash., 1952-53; resident VA Hosp., Salt Lake City, 1954-58; chief of surgery Sta. Hosp. Naval Sta., Subic Bay, Philippines, 1959-61; staff surgeon Naval Hosp., San Diego, 1961-64; asst. chief surgery Naval Hosp., Chelsea, Mass., 1964-65; comdg. officer 3d Med. Bn., 3d Marine Div. Fleet Marine Force, Pacific, Vietnam, 1965-66; chief surgery Naval Hosp., Yososuka, Japan, 1966-68; assigned Naval War Coll., 1968-69; fleet med. officer, comdr. in chief U.S. Naval Forces, Europe; sr. med. officer Naval Activities London, 1969-71; dep. dir. planning div. Bur. Medicine and Surgery Navy Dept., Washington, 1971-72; dir. planning div. Navy Dept., 1972-74; with additional duty as med. adv. to dep. chief naval ops. (logistics) and personal physician to chmn. Joint Chiefs of Staff, 1972-74; comdg. officer Naval Hosp., Great Lakes, Ill., 1974-76; asst. chief for material resources Bur. Medicine and Surgery Navy Dept., Washington, 1976-79; comdg. officer (Navy Health Scis. Edn. and Tng. Command), 1979-80; the med. officer U.S. Marine Corps., 1980-81, project mgr. Fleet Hosp. Programs, 1981-82; dir. Resources Div., 1982-83; dep. dir. naval medicine, dep. surgeon gen. Dept. Navy, 1983-84; ret., 1984; mem. grad. med. edn. adv. com. Dept. Def. Decorated Legion of Merit with gold V (2 stars), Meritorious Service medal, Joint Service Commendation medal. Fellow ACS (gov.); mem. Assn. Mil. Surgeons U.S.

WILSON, ALPHUS DAN, plant pathologist, researcher; b. Ft. Worth, Tex., Sept. 27, 1958; s. Alphus James and Essie Morris (Nugent) W.; m. Lisa Beth Forse, July 11, 1992; 1 child, Jon Colter. BS in Bioenviron. Sci., Tex. A&M U., 1981, MS in Plant Pathology, 1983; PhD in Plant Pathology, Wash. State U., 1988. Grad. rsch. asst. Tex. A&M U., College Station, 1981-83, Wash. State U., Pullman, 1984-88; postdoctoral plant pathologist USDA-Agrl. Rsch. Svc., Pullman, 1989-90, rsch. plant pathologist, 1990-91; rsch. plant pathologist USDA-Forest Svc., Stoneville, Miss., 1991—; tech. cons. Tex. Oak Wilt Suppression Adv. Bd., Austin, 1992—, Tex. Forest Svc. Strategic Plan Team, Austin, 1994—. Author: (chpt.) Systematics, Ecology, and Evolution of Endophytic fungi in Grasses and Woody Plants, 1995; contbr. articles to profl. jours. Project judge Delta Regional Sci. Fair, Greenville, Miss., 1992; sci. demonstrator Delta Schs. Sci. Awareness Day, Stoneville, 1993. Recipient fellowship Chevron Chem. Corp., 1981-83, Rsch. fellowship Wash. State U., 1984-88. Mem. AAAS, N.Y. Acad. Scis., Am. Phytopathological Soc., Mycol. Soc. Am., Soc. Am. Foresters, Alpha Zeta. Republican. Methodist. Achievements include discovery of genetic system controlling mating incompatibility in the Indian paint fungus, E. tinctorium; discovery of endosymbiotic Acremonium endophytes in wild Hordeum cereal grass species; development of Giemsa protocol for permanent nuclear staining of fungi; discovery of genetic system controlling sexual incompatibility in the chickpea blight fungas, D. rabiei. Avocations: fly fishing, backpacking, exploring wilderness areas, snow skiing, photography, hunting. Home: 2202 Highway 1 N Greenville MS 38703-9471 Office: USDA Forest Svc So Hardwoods Lab PO box 227 Stoneville MS 38776

WILSON, ANN ALLBRITTON, science and home economics educator; b. Urania, La., Feb. 22, 1943; d. Walter Roy and Emaline (Glidewell) Allbritton; m. Richard Joseph Wilson, Mar. 21, 1964 (div. Mar. 1991); children: James Michael, Richard Gardner, Kathleen JoAnn. BS, La. Tech. U., 1965; cert. sci., N.E. La. U., 1991. Cert. home econs. tchr., sci. secondary tchr., La.; lic. realtor, La. Tchr. clothing Jefferson Parish, Morrero, La., 1965-68; tchr. home econs., head dept. St. Mary Parish, Morgan City, La., 1968-70; tchr. home econs. St. Mary Parish, Morgan City, 1971-73; receptionist Office of Dr. C.C. Gaddis, Jena, La., 1977; pvt. practice Jena, 1978-85; tchr. bus. edn. LaSalle Parish, Jena, 1979; asst. interior decorator Justiss Interiors, Jena, 1980-82; realtor Carol Traver Real Estate, Alexandria, La., 1986-90; tchr. biology, chemistry, home econs. Catahoula Parish, Enterprise, La., 1987-93, dept. head., FHA advisor, 1987-93; tchr. biology Rapides Parish, Alexandria (La.) Sr. H.S., 1993—; cons. La. State Dept. Edn. Curriculum Guides, Baton Rouge, 1990-91. Mem. Morgan City Panhellenic Orgn., 1969-73, LaSalle Gen. Hosp. Ladies Aux., Jena, 1982-84; judge, asst. Miss Patterson (La.) Contest, 1971-75, Miss LaSalle Contest, Jena, 1971-75; den. mother Cub Scouts, Morgan City, Jena, 1973-74, 78; others. Named Parish Secondary Tchr. of Yr., 1991. Mem. NEA, Am. Home Econs. Assn., La. Real Estate Assn., La. Sci. Tchrs. Assn., La. Edn. Assn., Alpha Tau Delta, Phi Kappa Phi, Phi Mu. Methodist. Avocations: gardening, watercolor, reading. Home: 1109 Ola St Alexandria LA 71303-2347 Office: Alexandria Sr HS 800 Ola St Alexandria LA 71303-2340

WILSON, ANNE GAWTHROP, artist, educator; b. Detroit, Apr. 16, 1949; d. Gerald Shepard and Nancy Craighead (Gawthrop) Wilson; m. Michael Andreas Nagelbach. Student, U. Mich. Sch. of Art, 1967-69; BFA, Cranbrook Acad. Art, Bloomfield Hills, Mich., 1972; MFA, Calif. Coll. Arts and Crafts, 1976. Chair textile dept. The De Young Mus. Art Sch., San Francisco, 1973-78; prof. fiber dept. Sch. of the Art Inst., Chgo., 1979—; adj. instr. Calif. Coll. Arts and Crafts, Oakland, Calif., 1975-78; panelist Nat. Endowment for Arts, Washington, 1986, Chgo. Artists' Coalition at Artemisia Gallery, 1993, Western States Arts Fedn./Nat. Endowment for Arts Regional Fellowships for Visual Artists, Santa Fe, 1995; co-curator Artemisia Gallery, Chgo., 1988; juror Fiber Nat. '90, Adams Art Gallery, Dunkirk, N.Y., 1990; co-moderator Women's Caucus for Art, Chgo., 1992; panelist, workshop instr. Internat. Symposium '92, Toyama, Japan, 1992; panelist The Textile Mus., Washington, 1994; bd. trustees Haystack Sch., Deer Isle, Maine, 1990-95; artists adv. bd. Kohler Arts Ctr., Sheboygan, Wis., 1994—; lectr. No. Ill. U., DeKalb, 1989, Fla. State U., Tallahassee, 1990, Evanston (Ill.) Art Ctr., 1993, Columbia Coll., Chgo., 1994, others. One person shows include Chgo. Pub. Libr. Cultural Ctr., Randolph Gallery, 1988, Roy Boyd Gallery, Chgo., 1994, Halsey Gallery, Sch. of Arts, Coll. Charleston, S.C., 1992, Madison (Wis.) Art Ctr., 1993-94, Ill. Wesleyan U., Bloomington, Ill., 1995; exhibited in group shows Netherlands Textile Mus., 1989, Musee Cantonal des Beaux-Arts, Palais de Rumine, Lausanne, Switzerland, 1989, Gallery and Mus., Fla. State U., Tallahassee, 1990, Gallery of Contemporary Art, Colorado Springs, 1990, Newhouse Ctr. for Contemporary Art, Snug Harbor Cultural Ctr., S.I., N.Y., 1991, Rockford (Ill.) Art Mus., 1992, Calif. Coll. Arts and Crafts, Oakland, Calif., 1992, John Michael Kohler Arts Ctr., Sheboygan, Wis., 1992-93, Tarble Arts Ctr., Ea. Ill. U., Charleston, 1993, Art Inst. of Chgo., 1993, Textile Mus., Washington, 1994, Gallery 2, Chgo., 1994, Hyde Park Art Ctr., Chgo., 1994, Cranbrook Acad. Art Mus., Bloomfield Hills, 1994-95; represented in permanent collections Randall Fleming and Assocs., Archs., Oakland, Calif. Poly. State U., San Luis Obispo, Calif., Robert L. Kidd Assocs., Inc., Birmingham, Mich., Sandoz Crop Protection Corp., Chgo., M. H. De Young

Meml. Mus., San Francisco, Art Inst. Chgo., Cranbrook Acad. Art Mus., Bloomfield Hills; contbr. articles and revs. to profl. jours. Recipient Louis Comfort Tiffany Found. award, 1989; Nat. Endowment for Arts curatorial fellow in decorative arts and mus. edn. Fine Arts Mus. San Francisco, 1978; Nat. Endowment for Arts Visual Artists Fellowship grantee, 1982, 88, Chgo. Artists Abroad grantee, 1988, 89, Ill. Arts Coun. Individual Artist grantee, 1983, 84, 87, 93. Office: Sch of the Art Inst Fiber Dept 37 S Wabash Chicago IL 60603

WILSON, ANTHONY VINCENT, business executive, mechanical engineer; b. Harrow, Eng., June 30, 1936; came to U.S., 1966; s. Maurice William and Betty (Hodgson) W.; m. Jennifer Margaret Braund, Dec. 12, 1959; children: Claire Margaret, Neil Geoffrey. B.S.M.E., London U., 1957; M.S.M.E., Purdue U., 1973; AMP, Harvard U., 1985. Engring. mgr. Rolls Royce, 1957-66; program mgr. Cummins Engine, Columbus, Ind., 1966-76; dir. research, design and devel. Onan Corp., Mpls., 1978-80, v.p. tech. and new product mgmt., 1980-82, v.p., div. gen. mgr., 1982-86; pres., chief oper. officer Churchill Inds., 1987-91; pres., chief exec. officer LB White Co., 1992—. Mem. Soc. Automotive Engrs., ASME, Inst. Mech. Engrs. Home: 5250 Brackenwood Ct La Crosse WI 54601 Office: LB White Co W6636 L B White Rd Onalaska WI 54650-9082

WILSON, ARCHIE FREDRIC, medical educator; b. L.A., May 7, 1931; s. Louis H. and Ruth (Kert) W.; m. Tamar Braverman, Feb. 11, 1937; children: Lee A., Daniel B. BA, UCLA, 1953, PhD, 1967; MD, U. Calif., San Francisco, 1957. Intern L.A. County Gen. Hosp., 1957-58; resident U. Calif., San Francisco, 1958-61; fellow in chest disease dept. medicine UCLA, 1966-67, asst. prof., 1967-70; asst. prof. U. Calif., Irvine, 1970-73, assoc. prof., 1973-79, prof., 1979—. Editor: Pulmonary Function Test: Interpretation, 1986; contbr. articles to profl. jours. Bd. mem. Am. Lung Assn., Orange County, 1970-90, Am. Heart Assn., Calif., 1990—. Capt. USMC, 1961-63. Mem. Am. Fedn. Clin. Rsch., Western Soc. Clin. Investigation. Office: Univ Calif 101 The City Dr S Orange CA 92668-3201

WILSON, ARTHUR JESS, psychologist; b. Yonkers, N.Y., Oct. 25, 1910; s. Samuel Louis and Anna (Gilbert) W.; B.S., N.Y.U., 1935, M.A., 1949, Ph.D., 1961; LL.B., St. Lawrence U., 1940; J.D., Bklyn. Law Sch., 1967; m. Lillian Moss, Sept. 16, 1941; children—Warren David, Anton Francis. Tchr., Yonkers Pub. Schs., 1935-40; dir. adult edn. Yonkers, 1940-42; supr. vocat. rehab. N.Y. State Dept. Edn., 1942-44; personnel exec. Abraham & Straus, Bklyn., 1946-47; rehab. field sec. N.Y. Tb and Health Assn., 1947-48; dir. rehab. Westchester County Med. Center, Valhalla, N.Y., 1948-67; dir. Manhattan Narcotic Rehab. Center, N.Y. State Drug Abuse Control Commn., 1967-68; clin. psychologist VA Hosp., Montrose, N.Y., 1968-73; pvt. practice clin. psychology, Yonkers, 1973—; cons. N.Y. State Dept. Edn., HEW; spl. lectr. Sch. Pub. Health and Adminstrv. Medicine, Columbia U. and Grad. Sch., N.Y. U.; instr. Westchester Community Coll., Valhalla, N.Y.; selected participant Clin. Study Tour of China, 1980. Served in USN, 1944-46. Mem. Internat. Mark Twain Soc. (hon.), N.Y. Acad. Scis., Am. Psychol. Assn., N.Y. State Psychol. Assn., Kappa Delta Pi, Phi Delta Kappa, Epsilon Pi Tau. Author: The Emotional Life of the Ill and Injured, 1950; A Guide to the Genius of Cardozo, 1939; The Wilson Teaching Inventory, 1941; also articles. Honored as Westchester Author, Westchester County Hist. Soc., 1957. Home and Office: 4121 NW 88th Ave Apt 204 Coral Springs FL 33065-1820

WILSON, AUGUST, playwright; b. Pitts., 1945; s. David Bedford (stepfather) and Daisy Wilson; 1 child, Sakina Ansari. Founder Black Horizons Theatre Co., Pitts., 1968; script writer Sci. Mus. of Minn., 1979. Author: (playwright) The Homecoming, 1979, The Coldest Day of the Year, 1979, Fullerton Street, 1980, Black Bart and the Sacred Hills, 1981, Jitney, 1982, Ma Rainey's Black Bottom, 1984 (N.Y. Drama Critics Circle award for best play 1985, Tony award nomination for best play 1985, Whiting Writers' award 1986), Fences, 1985 (Am. Theatre Critics Outstanding Play award 1986, Drama Desk award for outstanding new play 1986, N.Y. Drama Critics' Circle award for best play 1986, Pulitzer Prize for drama 1987, Tony award for best play 1987, Outer Critics' Circle award for best play 1987), Joe Turner's Come and Gone, 1986 (N.Y. Drama Critics Circle award for best play 1988, Tony award nomination for best play 1988), The Piano Lesson, 1987 (Drama Desk award for outstanding new play 1990, N.Y. Drama Critics' Circle award for best play 1990, Pulitzer Prize for drama 1990, Tony award nomination for best play 1990, Am. Theatre Critics Outstanding Play award 1990), Two Trains Running, 1990 (Am. Theatre Critics Assn. award 1992, Tony award nomination for best play 1992), Seven Guitars, 1995 (N.Y. Drama Critics Cir. award 1996, Tony nomination Best Play 1996). Recipient John Gassner Best Am. Playwright award Outer Critics Circle, 1987; named Artist of Yr., Chgo. Tribune, 1987, Literary Lion award N.Y. Pub. Libr., 1988. Mem. AAAL. Office: care John Breglio Paul Weiss Rifkind Wharton & Garrison 1285 Avenue Of The Americas New York NY 10019-6028*

WILSON, BARBARA LOUISE, communications executive; b. Bremerton, Wash., Aug. 3, 1952; d. Algernon Frances and Dorothy Virginia (Martin) W.; m. Ashby A. Riley III, Feb. 7, 1979 (div. Dec. 1983). BA in Fin. and Econs., U. Puget Sound, 1974; MBA, U. Wash., Seattle, 1985. With Pacific N.W. Bell, Seattle and Portland, Oreg., 1974-86, divsn. mgr. pub. comm., 1983-85, asst. v.p., exec. dir. number svcs. mktg., 1985-86; v.p. implementation planning US West, Inc., Englewood, Colo., 1986-87; pres. US West Info. Systems, Englewood, 1987-89; v.p. govt. and edn. svcs. US West Comm., Englewood, 1989; v.p. human resources U.S. West Comm., Denver, 1989-92; v.p., chief exec. officer Idaho state U.S. West Communications, Boise, 1992—; bd. dirs. U.S. West New Vector Group, Bellevue, Wash., 1988-90, U.S. Bank Idaho, Idaho Bus. Coun.; audit com. chair U.S. Bank; chair nat. adv. com. Tel. Pioneers Am., N.Y.C., 1989; chair adv. bd. Coll. Bus. and Boise State U. Bd. dirs., mem. exec. com. Wash. Coun. for Edn., Seattle, 1985-86; team capt. major gifts com. Boys and Girls Club, Seattle, 1986; chairperson co. campaign United Way, Seattle, 1985; bd. dirs. Denver Arts Ctr. Found., 1989-91; bd. advisors U. Wash. Exec. MBA Program, 1991-93; mem. adv. bd. Boise State U. Sch. Bus.; mem. bd. Boise State U. Found. Bd. dirs., mem. exec. com. Wash. Coun. for Edn., Seattle, 1985-86; team capt. major gifts com. Boys and Girls Club, Seattle, 1986; chair co. campaign United Way, Seattle, 1985; bd. dirs. Denver Arts Ctr. Found., 1989-91; bd. advisors U. Wash. Exec. MBA Program, 1991-93; mem. adv. bd. Boise State U. Sch. Bus.; bd. mem. Mountain States Med. Rsch. Inst.; bd. dirs. Boise State U. Found.; bd. mem. U.S. Bank; bd. dirs. Bishop Kelly Found.; mem. Gov.'s Econ. Stimulus Com. Mem. Idaho Bus. Coun. (bd. dirs., chair-elect), Idaho Assn. Commerce and Industry (vice chmn. bd. dirs. 1992—), Boise C. of C. (bd. dirs. 1992—), Arid Club Boise. Roman Catholic. Avocations: golf, snow skiing, travel, boating. Office: US West Communications 999 Main St Fl 11 Boise ID 83702-9001

WILSON, BARBARA T., physical education educator; b. Pisgah, Ala., June 5, 1944; d. Jesse Leroy and Lillie Belle (Long) Tinker; m. Jimmy Dale Wilson, June 30, 1963; childern: Eric Dale, Christopher, Chadwick, Jeremy Lance. BS in Heatlh Phys. Edn., Biology, Jacksonville State U., 1967; MS in Health Phys. Edn., U. Ala., 1969, EdS Heatlh Edn., 1980. Cert. tchr. Tchr. Calhoun County Bd. Edn., Anniston, Ala., 1967-74, Jacksonville (Ala.) State U., 1974—. Author: Aqua Robics, 1991; co-author: Curriculum Voices, 1986; editor Jacksonville State U. H.P.E.R. Alumni newsletter, 1993-95. Mem. AAHPERD, NEA, Coll. Assn. Health, Phys. Edn., Recreation and Dance (sec., treas. 1986-87, 84-85, pres. elect 1994-95, pres. 1995—), Ala. Assn. Health, Phys. Edn., Recreation and Dance, Ala. Edn. Assn., Delta Kappa Gamma (past pres. Beta Phi chpt., dist. II dir.). Avocations: jogging, ceramics, gardening, cooking, traveling. Office: Jacksonville State U Pete Mathews Coliseum Jacksonville AL 36265

WILSON, BARRY WILLIAM, biology educator; b. Bklyn., Aug. 20, 1931; s. Albert Abraham Wilson and Ethel (Lubart) Bedsow; m. Joyce Ann Sisson, June 7, 1957; 1 child, Sean. BA, U. Chgo., 1950; BS, MS, Ill. Inst. Tech., 1957; PhD, UCLA, 1962. Asst. prof. biology U. Calif., Davis, 1962-1972, prof. avian sci. and environ. toxicology, 1972—, chmn. dept. Avian scis., 1991—; mem. drug task force Muscular Dystrophy Assn., N.Y.C., 1980—; councilor NeuroToxicology subsect. Soc. Toxicology, Washington, 1985-86; pres. Calif. br. Tissue Culture Assn., Washington, 1978; mem. editorial bd. NeuroToxicology, Little Rock, 1986-91; ad hoc mem. NIH Toxicology Study Sect., Washington, 1985; mem. EPA sci. adv. panel Cholinesterase, 1989—; chair EPA Cholinesterase Methodologies Workshop, 1991. Editor: Birds: Readings From Science American, 1980; assoc. editor Bulletin Environ. Contamination and Toxicology, 1990—; contbr. numerous articles to profl. jours. Mem. Am. Physiol. Soc., Am. Soc. Cell Biology, Am. Ornithologists Union, Soc. Neurosci., Soc. Toxicology, Soc. Environ. Toxicology and Chemistry, Tissue Culture Assn., Soc. Devel. Biology, Am. Chem. Soc., Soc. for In Vitro Biology. Avocations: bird watching, photography, music. Office: U Calif Dept Avian Scis Davis CA 95616

WILSON, BARY WALLACE, neuroendocrinologist; b. Moscow, Idaho, Dec. 12, 1945; s. Arlin Chadwick and June (Rawlings) W.; m. Martha Ericka Ruf, Aug. 21, 1967; children: Melanie, Mark, Meaghan, Miranda, Brandon, Benjiman. BS, U. Wash., Seattle, 1972; PhD, U. London, 1977; post doctoral assoc., MIT, 1977-78. Engr. Varian Mat, Bremen, Germany, 1973-74; biochemist St. Bartholomew's Med. Sch., London, 1974-76; sr. rsch. scientist, staff scientist Battelle Northwest, Richland, Wash., 1978—; founder, prin. Tecna Corp., San Bernardino, Calif., 1983—; founder Columbia Magnetics Inc., Kennewick, Wash., 1993—; founder, chief scientist Gulf Tech. Ctr., Abu Dhabi, U.A.E., 1994—; cons. SCA Assocs., McLean, Va., 1990-93, Univ. Petroleum & Minerals RI, Dhahran, Saudi Arabia, 1986-87; mem. EPA sci. adv. bd. NIEMF com., Washington, 1990—; bd. dirs. Bioelectromagnetics Soc., Falls Church, Md. Author, editor Extremely LF EMF: The Question of Cancer, 1990; patentee: Microbial Solubilization of Coal, 1990, Methods and Treatment of NIDDM, 1989; contbr. articles to profl. jours. Sgt. USMCR, 1965-72. Recipient Mentor award Internat. Sci. and Engring. Fair, 1991. Avocations: snow skiing, writing. Home: 4727 Tripple Vista Dr Kennewick WA 99337 Office: Pacific Northwest Lab 617 Battelle Blvd Richland WA 99352

WILSON, BEN, elementary school principal. Prin. Ingleside Sch., Athens, Tenn. Recipient Elem. Sch. Recognition award U.S. Dept. Edn., 1989-90. Office: Ingleside Sch Guille St Athens TN 37303

WILSON, BETTY MAY, resort company executive; b. Moberly, Mo., Mar. 13, 1947; d. Arthur Bunyon and Martha Elizabeth (Denham) Stephens; m. Ralph Felix Martin, Aug. 22, 1970 (div. May 1982); m. Gerald Robert Wilson Sr., Mar. 3, 1984; stepchildren: Gerald Robert Jr., Heather Lynn, Jeffrey Michael. BS in Acctg. and Bus. Adminstrn., Colo. State U., 1969. CPA, Mo. Tax mgr. Arthur Andersen and Co., St. Louis, 1969-75; v.p., asst. sec., dir. taxes ITT Fin. Corp., St. Louis, 1975-95; v.p. taxes Caesar's World, Inc., Las Vegas, Nev., 1995—; sr. v.p., bd. dirs. Lyndon Ins. Co., St. Louis, 1977-95, ITT Lyndon Life Ins. Co., ITT Lyndon Property Ins. Co., St. Louis, 1977-95. Mem. AICPA, Mo. Soc. CPAs (chmn. family issues com.), Am. Fin. Svcs. Assn. (chmn. tax com. 1987-88), Tax Execs. Inst. Inc. (chair corp. tax mgmt. com. 1993-95, regional v.p. 1995-96, exec. com. 1995-96, bd. dirs. St. Louis chpt., past sec., past pres.), Mo. Girls Racing Assn. (pres. 1977-82). Baptist. Avocations: country western dancing, horses. Office: Cesar's World Inc Ste 1600 3800 Howard Hughes Pkwy Las Vegas NV 89109

WILSON, BLENDA JACQUELINE, academic administrator; b. Woodbridge, N.J., Jan. 28, 1941; d. Horace and Margaret (Brogsdale) Wilson; m. Louis Fair Jr. AB, Cedar Crest Coll., 1962; AM, Seton Hall U., 1965; PhD, Boston Coll., 1979; DHL (hon.), Cedar Crest Coll., 1987, Loretto Heights Coll., 1988, Colo. Tech. Coll., 1988, U. Detroit, 1989; LLD (hon.), Rutgers U., 1989, Ea. Mich. U., 1990, Cambridge Coll., 1991, Schoolcraft Coll., 1992. Tchr. Woodbridge Twp. Pub. Schs., 1962-66; exec. dir. Middlesex County Econ. Opportunity Corp., New Brunswick, N.J., 1966-69; exec. asst. to pres. Rutgers U., New Brunswick, N.J., 1969-72; sr. assoc. dean Grad. Sch. Edn. Harvard U., Cambridge, Mass., 1972-82; v.p. effective sector mgmt. Ind. Sector, Washington, 1982-84; exec. dir. Colo. Commn. Higher Edn., Denver, 1984-88; chancellor and prof. pub. adminstrn. & edn. U. Mich., Dearborn, 1988-92; pres. Calif. State U., Northridge, 1992—; Am. del. U.S./U.K. Dialogue About Quality Judgments in Higher Edn.; adv. bd. Mich. Consolidated Gas Co., Stanford Inst. Higher Edn. Rsch., U. So. Col. Dist. 60 Nat. Alliance, Nat. Ctr. for Rsch. to Improve Postsecondary Teaching and Learning, 1988-90; bd. dirs. Alpha Capital Mgmt.; mem. higher edn. colloquium Am. Coun. Edn., vis. com. Divsn. Continuing Edn. in Faculty of Arts & Scis., Harvard Coll., Pew Forum on K-12 Edn. Reform in U.S.; trustee Children's TV Workshop. Dir. U. Detroit Jesuit High Sch., Northridge Hosp. Med. Ctr., Arab Cmty. Ctr. for Econ. and Social Svcs., Union Bank, J. Paul Getty Trust, James Irvine Found., Internat. Found. Edn. and Self-Help, Achievement Coun., L.A.; dir., vice chair Met. Affairs Corp.; exec. bd. Detroit area coun. Boy Scouts Am.; bd. dirs. Commonwealth Fund, Henry Ford Hosp.-Fairlane Ctr., Henry Ford Health System, Met. Ctr. for High Tech., United Way Southeastern Mich.; mem. Nat. Coalition 100 Black Women, Detroit, Race Rels. Coun. Met. Detroit, Women & Founds., Greater Detroit Interfaith Round Table NCCJ, Adv. Bd. Valley Cultural Ctr., Woodland Hills; trustee assoc. Boston Coll.; trustee emeritus Cambridge Coll.; trustee emeritus, bd. dirs. Found. Ctr.; trustee Henry Ford Mus. & Greenfield Village, Sammy Davis Jr. Nat. Liver Inst. Mem. AAUW, Assn. Governing Bds. (adv. coun. of pres.'s), Edn. Commn. of the States (student minority task force), Am. Assn. Higher Edn. (chair-elect), Am. Assn. State Colls. & Univs. (com. on policies & purposes, acad. leadership fellows selection com.), Assn. Black Profls. and Adminstrs., Assn. Black Women in Higher Edn., Women Execs. State Govt., Internat. Women's Forum, Mich. Women's Forum, Women's Econ. Club Detroit, Econ. Club, Rotary. Office: Calif State Univ Office of President 18111 Nordhoff St Northridge CA 91330-0001

WILSON, BRIAN DOUGLAS, recording artist, composer, record producer; b. Inglewood, Calif., June 20, 1942; s. Murry Gage and Audree Neva (Korthof) W.; m. Marilyn Sandra Rovell, Dec. 7, 1964; children: Carnie, Wendy. Student, El Camino Coll. Mem. musical group, The Beach Boys, 1961—; also composer; albums include Surfin Safari, 1962, Surfin' USA, 1963, Surfer Girl, 1963, Little Deuce Coupe, 1963, All Summer Long, 1964, Christmas Album, 1964, Beach Boys Party, 1965, Pet Sounds, 1966; solo album: Brian Wilson, 1988, Sire, 1988, Sweet Insanity, 1991; author: (autobiography) Wouldn't It Be Nice, 1991. Named to Rock and Roll Hall of Fame, 1988. also: 151 S El Camino Dr Beverly Hills CA 90212-2704

WILSON, BRUCE BRIGHTON, transportation executive; b. Boston, Feb. 6, 1936; s. Robert Lee and Jane (Schlotterer) W.; m. Elizabeth Ann MacFarland, Dec. 31, 1958; children: Mabeth, Mary, Bruce Robert, Caroline Daly. AB, Princeton U., 1958; LLB, U. Pa., 1961. Bar: Pa. 1962. Assoc. Montgomery, McCracken, Walker & Rhoads, Phila., 1962-69; atty. U.S. Dept. Justice, Washington, 1969-79; dep. asst. atty. gen. antitrust div. U.S. Dept. Justice, 1971-76; spl. counsel Consol. Rail Corp., Phila., 1979-81, gen. counsel litigation and antitrust, 1981-82, v.p., gen. counsel, 1982-84, v.p. law, 1984-87, sr. v.p. law, 1987—; bd. dirs. Concord Resources Group, Inc., Princeton, N.J., Phila. Indsl. Devel. Corp.; mem. mgmt. com. Concord Resources Group, 1989-91. Fellow Salzburg Seminar in Am. Studies (Austria), 1965; fellow Felz Inst. State and Local Govt., 1967. Mem. ABA, Phila. Bar Assn. Clubs: Corinthian Yacht, Pyramid. Home: 224 Chamounix Rd Wayne PA 19087-3606 Office: Consol Rail Corp PO Box 41417 2001 Market St 17th Flr Philadelphia PA 19101-1417

WILSON, BRUCE G., lawyer; b. Iowa City, Dec. 17, 1949. BS, Iowa State U., 1972; MBA with distinction, U. Mich., 1974; JD with distinction, U. Iowa, 1977. Bar: Ill. 1977. Ptnr. Jenner & Block, Chgo. Mem. ABA, Ill. State Bar Assn. Office: Jenner & Block 1 E Ibm Plz Chicago IL 60611*

WILSON, BRUCE KEITH, men's health nurse; b. Alton, Ill., Aug. 18, 1946; s. Lewis Philip and Ruth Caroline Wilson; m. Karen Loughrey, Aug. 14, 1977; children: Sarah Ann, Andrew James. BSN, U. Tex., San Antonio, 1975, MSN, 1977; PhD, North Tex. State U., Denton, 1987. Cert. in nursing informatics. Coord. Pan Am. U., Edinburg, Tex., 1982-83; house supr. HCA Rio Grande Regional Hosp., McAllen, Tex., 1986-87; program dir. Tex. Southmost Coll., Brownsville, 1983-86; mem. faculty U. Tex.-Pan Am., Edinburg, 1986—. Author: Logical Nursing Math., 1987. With U.S. Army, 1966-68. Mem. ANA, Nat. League for Nursing, Am. Assembly for Men in Nursing, Tex. League for Nursing (bd. dirs. 1993—). Avocations: photography, computer. Home: 1702 Ivy Ln Edinburg TX 78539-5367 Office: Dept Nursing U Tex-Pan Am Edinburg TX 78539

WILSON, C. DANIEL, JR., library director; b. Middletown, Conn., Nov. 8, 1941; s. Clyde D. and Dorothy M. (Neal) W.; m. M. April Jackson, Apr. 1986; children: Christine, Cindy, Clyde, Ben. BA, Elmhurst Coll., 1967; MA, Rosary Coll., 1968; MPA, U. New Orleans, 1995. Trainee Chgo. Pub. Libr., 1967-68; instr. U. Ill., 1968-70; asst. dir. Perrot Meml. Libr., Greenwich, Conn., 1970-76; dir. Wilton Pub. Libr., Wilton, Conn., 1976-79; assoc. dir. Birmingham Pub. Libr., Birmingham, Ala., 1979-83; dir. Davenport Pub. Libr., Davenport, Iowa, 1983-85, New Orleans Pub. Libr., 1985--. With USMC, 1962-65. Mem. Am. Libr. Assn., La. Libr. Assn., Am. Soc. Pub. Adminstrs., Pi Gamma Mu, Rotary. Episcopalian. Office: New Orleans Pub Libr Simon Heinsheim & Fisk Libe 219 Loyola Ave New Orleans LA 70112-2007

WILSON, C. NICK, health educator, consultant, researcher, lecturer; b. Balt., Feb. 18, 1942; s. Anna May (Gallion) W.; m. Nancy Ann King, Sept. 17, 1966 (div. Apr. 1976); children: Anna Nicole, Tara Stacia; m. Linda Persons, Feb. 25, 1984; children: Melissa Anne, Kristin Marie. BS, U. Hartford, 1966; MHA, George Washington U., 1972; PhD, U. Miss., 1983. Dir. ops. Health Am., Louisville, 1976-79, So. Health Svcs., Marks, Miss., 1979-81; rsch. and teaching asst. U. Miss., Oxford, 1981-83; asst. prof. U. Tex., Galveston, 1983-85, U. Okla., Oklahoma City, 1987-91; pres. Shriners Burn Hosp., Galveston, 1985-87; assoc. prof. health, cons., sr. lectr. U. North Fla., Jacksonville, 1991—; cons., Jacksonville, 1991—. Author: Health Care Management, 1983; also over 125 articles. Bd. dirs., treas. First Coast Healthcare Execs. Group, Jacksonville, 1991—. Lt. USAF, 1966-69. Fellow Am. Coll. Healthcare Execs. (various offices, faculty advisor student chpt. Jacksonville 1991—), Royal Soc. Health; mem. APHA (various offices), Am. Hosp. Assn. (various offices). Republican. Episcopalian. Avocations: golf, tennis, hunting, fishing, sailing. Office: U North Fla Coll Health 4567 Saint Johns Bluff Rd S Jacksonville FL 32224-2646

WILSON, CARL ARTHUR, real estate broker; b. Manhasset, N.Y., Sept. 29, 1947; s. Archie and Florence (Hefner) W.; divorced; children: Melissa Starr, Clay Alan. Student UCLA, 1966-68, 70-71. Tournament bridge dir. North Hollywood (Calif.) Bridge Club, 1967-68, 70-71; computer operator IBM, L.A., 1967-68, 70-71; bus. devel. mgr. Walker & Lee Real Estate, Anaheim, Calif., 1972-76; v.p. sales and mktg. The Estes Co., Phoenix, 1976-82, Continental Homes Inc., 1982-84; pres. Roadrunner Homes Corp., Phoenix, 1984-86, Lexington Homes, Inc., 1986, Barrington Homes, 1986-90; gen. mgr. Starr Homes, 1991—; pres. Offsite Utilities, Inc., 1992—; adv. dir. Liberty Bank. Mem. Glendale (Ariz.) Citizens Bond Coun., 1986-87, Ariz. Housing Study Commn., 1988-89, Valley Leadership, 1988—; pres.'s coun. Am. Grad. Sch. Internat. Mgmt., 1985-89; vice-chmn. Glendale Planning and Zoning Commn., 1986-87, chmn., 1987-91; mem. bd. trustees Valley of Sun United Way, 1987-92, chmn. com. Community Problem Solving and Fund Distbn., 1988-89; mem. City of Glendale RTC Task Force, 1990, Maricopa County Citizens Jud. Reform Com., 1990-92, Maricopa County Citizens Jud. Adv. Coun., 1990-91; co-founder, bd. dirs. Leadership West, Inc., 1993—; mem. Maricopa County Trial Ct. Appointment Commn., 1993—. Mem. Nat. Assn. Homebuilders (bd. dirs. 1985-93, nat. rep. Ariz. 1990-92), Cen. Ariz. Homebuilders Assn. (adv. com. 1979-82, treas. 1986, sec. 1987, v.p. 1987-89, chmn. 1989-90, bd. dirs. 1985—, life dir. 1994—); mem. bd. adjustments City of Glendale, 1976-81, chmn., 1980-81, mem. bond coun., 1981-82; mem. real estate edn. adv. coun. State Bd. Community Coll., 1981-82; precinct committeeman, dep. registrar, 1980-81. With U.S. Army, 1968-70. Mem. Glendale C. of C. (dir. 1980-83, 89-91), Sales and Mktg. Coun. (chmn. edn. com. 1980, chmn. coun. 1981-82, Mame grand award 1981). Home: PO Box 39985 Phoenix AZ 85069-0985 Office: Starr Homes Inc Offsite Utilities Inc 2432 W Peoria Ave Ste 1190 Phoenix AZ 85029-4736

WILSON, CARL WELDON, JR., construction company executive, civil engineer; b. Norfolk, Va., Sept. 4, 1933; s. Carl Weldon and Janie Marie (Ludford) W.; m. Jean Roberts, Feb. 13, 1960; children: Lisa Ann, Carl Weldon III. BCE, Tex. A&M U., 1954. Registered profl. engr., Tex. Engr. Magnolia Petroleum Co., Morgan City, La., 1954-55, Brown & Root, Houston, 1957-60; project mgr. Claude Everett Constrn. Co., Houston, 1960-62; pres. Falcon Constrn. Co., Houston, 1962-63; pres., owner Wilson Engring. and Constrn. Co., Houston, 1963-68; v.p. Divcon, Inc., Houston, 1968-71, Wilson Industries, Inc., Houston, 1971-81; pres., prin. owner BS&B Engring. Co., Inc., Houston, 1981-86; chmn., majority shareholder Task Internat., Inc., Houston, 1986—. Served to 1st lt. U.S. Army, 1955-57. Republican. Episcopalian. Avocations: tennis, running, painting. Home: 750 Bison Dr Houston TX 77079-4401 Office: Task Internat Inc PO Box 218327 Houston TX 77218-8327

WILSON, CATHERINE PHILLIPS, elementary education educator; b. Calif., July 19, 1935; d. Harry Leland and Catherine (Waterbury) Phillips; m. Henry S. Wilson Jr., Apr. 12, 1958 (dec. Jan. 1979); children: Lee, Janell, Carey, Kimberly, Blake. Student, U. of the Pacific, 1953-54; BA in Edn. and Psychology, Calif. State Coll., San Jose, 1957; postgrad., Portland State U., 1981-89, Chapman U., Danville, Calif., 1990-93. Cert. tchr., Oreg. Sales coord. The Donatello Hotel, San Francisco, 1981-82; ind. mgmt. cons. A. Cal Rossi, Inc., San Francisco, 1983-84; tchr. 5th grade Portland (Oreg.) Pub. Schs., 1985, tchr. Glencoe Sch., 1987-89; tchr. 1st grade Oakland (Calif.) Unified Dist., 1989-90; tchr. 2d grade Martin Luther King Elem. Sch. Portland Pub. Schs., 1990-93, tchr. 2d grade Lent Elem. Sch., 1993—. Author: Soaring to Success, 1986, Escape to Freedom, 1987, Journey Through the Galazies, 1988. Named Oreg. Tchr. of Yr., U.S. West, 1991, Spirit of the N.W., KATU Channel 2, Portland, 1992; recipient Tchrs. Making a Difference award Nationwide Ins., 1994, Impact II award Reading in a Castle of Dreams, 1994, KEX-Fred Meyer Tchr. award, 1994. Mem. Oreg. Edn. Assn., Kiwanis Early Risers, Kappa Alpha Theta, Alpha Delta Kappa. Republican. Roman Catholic. Avocations: reading, writing, collecting, speaking to groups. Office: Lent Elem Sch 5105 SE 97th Ave Portland OR 97266-3747

WILSON, CHARLES (CHARLIE WILSON), congressman; b. Trinity, Tex., June 1, 1933. Student, Sam Houston State U., Huntsville, Tex., 1951-52; B.S., U.S. Naval Acad., 1956. Commd. ensign U.S. Navy, 1956, advanced through grades to lt.; ret., 1960; mem. Tex. Ho. of Reps., 1960-66, Tex. Senate, 1966-72, 93nd-104th Congresses from 2nd Tex. dist., Washington, D.C., 1973-96; ranking minority mem. appropriations subcom. on fgn. ops., export financing & related programs; mgr. lumber yard, 1962-72. Democrat. Office: US Ho of Reps 2256 Rayburn Bldg Ofc B Washington DC 20515-0005

WILSON, CHARLES B., neurosurgeon, educator; b. Neosho, Mo., Aug. 31, 1929; married; 3 children. BS, Tulane U., 1951, MD, 1954. Resident pathologist Tulane U., 1955-56, instr. neurosurgery, 1960-61; resident Ochsner Clinic, 1956-60; instr. La. State U., 1961-63; from asst. prof. to prof. U. Ky., 1963-68; prof. neurosurgery U. Calif., San Francisco, 1968—. Mem. Am. Assn. Neurol. Surgery, Soc. Neurol. Surgery. Achievements include research in brain and pituitary tumors. Office: U Calif Sch Medicine Box 0350 San Francisco CA 94143

WILSON, CHARLES BANKS, artist; b. Springdale, Ark., Aug. 6, 1918; s. Charles Bertram and Bertha Juanita (Banks) W.; m. Edna Frances McKibben, Oct. 10, 1941; children—Geoffrey Banks, Carrie Vee. Student, Art Inst. Chgo., 1936-41. Mag. and book illustrator, 1943-60; head art dept. N.E. Okla. A. & M. Coll., Miami, Okla., 1947-61; painter, printmaker. Executed mural, Okla. State Capitol, 1975; represented in permanent collections, Met. Mus., N.Y.C., Library of Congress, Washington, U.S. Capitol Bldg., D.C. Corcoran Gallery, Smithsonian Inst., Will Rogers Meml. Mus., Philbrook Art Center, Tulsa, Nat. Cowboy Hall of Fame, Oklahoma City; Illustrator numerous books. Bd. dirs. Thomas Gilcrease Mus. History and Art, Tulsa, 1957-61; chmn. Pub. Libr. Bd., Miami, Okla., 1954-59. Named to Okla. Hall of Fame; recipient Western Heritage award Cowboy Hall of Fame, D.S.C., U. Okla.; subject of books The Lithographs of Charles Banks Wilson, 1989, Search for the Purebloods, 1989, An Oklahoma Portrait, 1989. Mem. Internat. Inst. Arts and Letters (Geneva). Office: 1611 Mission Blvd Fayetteville AR 72703-3043

WILSON, CHARLES GLEN, zoo administrator; b. Clinton, Okla., Aug. 24, 1948; s. Claude Lee and Alva Dean (Gaskins) W.; m. Susan Elizabeth Mosher, Nov. 21, 1975; children: Erica Dean, Grant Mosher. BS, Okla.

State U., 1972, MS, 1980. Dir. Memphis Zool. Gardens and Aquarium, 1976—. Contbr. articles to profl. jours. Served with U.S. Army, 1968-70. Recipient Ark. Traveler award, 1977. Profl. fellow Am. Zool. Parks and Aquariums. Office: Memphis Zoo & Aquarium 2000 Galloway Ave Memphis TN 38112-9990

WILSON, CHARLES HAVEN, lawyer; b. Waltham, Mass., July 27, 1936; s. Charles Haven Sr. and Kathryn (Sullivan) W.; children: Kathryn Wilson Self, Charles H. Jr. AB in Govt. magna cum laude, Tufts U., 1958; MS in Journalism, Columbia U., 1959; JD, U. Calif., Berkeley, 1967. Bar: D.C. 1968, U.S. Supreme Ct. 1972. Sr. law clk. to Chief Justice Earl Warren, 1967-68; from assoc. to counsel Williams & Connolly, Washington, 1968-90; sr. lawyer ACLU of Nat. Capital Area, Washington, 1992—; adj. prof. constitutional law Georgetown U. Law Ctr., 1971, 72. With U.S. Army, 1959-62. Mem. ABA (litigation sect. coun. 1976-79, dir publs. 1975-90, founding editor jour. Litigation 1974, bd. editors ABA Jour. 1985-91), Order of Coif. Democrat. Roman Catholic. Avocation: reading. Office: ACLU of Nat Capital Area S 119 1400 20th St NW Washington DC 20036

WILSON, CHARLES REGINALD, real estate executive; b. Bear Lake, Pa., Nov. 7, 1904; s. Earl Ayling and Edith (Finch) W.; m. Josephine Harrison, Sept. 8, 1927; children—Charles Reginald, Jacquelyn Ann. Student, U. Pitts., 1927. Asst. dean men U. Pitts., 1927-29; bus. promotion mgr. Hotel Schenley, Pitts., 1929-35; sales mgr. William Penn Hotel, Pitts., 1935-39; v.p., gen. mgr. William Penn Hotel, 1952; mgr. Roosevelt Hotel, Pitts., 1939-52; sr. v.p. Union Nat. Bank of Pitts. (formerly Commonwealth Bank & Trust Company), 1952-71, Realty Growth Corp., Pitts., 1972—; pres. Commonwealth Real Estate Co., 1957-64. Pres. Panther Found., U. Pitts.; exec. com. Pitts. Conv. and Visitors Bur. Mem. Pitts. Athletic Assn., Soc. Indsl. Realtors, Delta Tau Delta, Omicron Delta Kappa. Clubs: Mason, Pittsburgh Field, Duquesne. Home: 4601 5th Ave Pittsburgh PA 15213-3666 Office: Roosevelt Bldg Sixth St and Penn Ave Pittsburgh PA 15222

WILSON, CHARLES VINCENT, human resources executive; b. Rockledge, Fla., May 7, 1949; s, Phillip J. and Etta R. (Talley) W.; m. Priscilla A. Johnson, Mar. 22, 1976; children: Stephanie Brooke, Rachel Marie. BSBA, Pa. State U., 1971. Dir. human resources Kendall Co., Boston, 1971-84; zone E.R. mgr. Frito-Lay, Dallas, 1984-86, group human resources mgr.-sales, 1986-87, group human resources mgr.-hdqrs., 1987-89; dir. mgmt. planning & devel. Pearle, Inc., Dallas, 1989; v.p. cultural diversity & pers. devel. Grand Met. Food Sector, Mpls., 1989-91, v.p., dir. human resources tech., 1991-94; v.p. for human resources U. Md. Med. System, Balt., 1994—; mem. tech. adv. coun. Olympus Corp., Inc., 1993-94; chmn. Univ. Med. System/Frederick Douglas H.S. Partnership Steering Com.; mem. Univ. Hosp. Consortium Human Resources Officers Coun.; bd. dirs. Big Bros. & Big Sisters Ctrl. Md. Bd. dirs. Big Brothers/Big Sisters of Ctrl. Md. Recipient Black Achiever award Chgo. YMCA, 1975; Nat. Merit scholar, 1967. Mem. Nat. Black Human Resources Soc., Soc. for Human Resource Mgmt. Democrat. Baptist. Avocations: fitness workouts, golf, reading, travel, music. Office: U Md Med Sys Corp 22 S Greene St Baltimore MD 21201

WILSON, CHARLES ZACHARY, JR., newspaper publisher; b. Greenwood, Miss., Apr. 21, 1929; s. Charles Zachary and Ora Lee (Means) W.; m. Doris J. Wilson, Aug. 18, 1951 (dec. Nov. 1974); children: Charles III, Joyce Lynne, Joanne Catherine, Gary Thomas, Jonathan Keith; m. Kelly Freeman, Apr. 21, 1986; children: Amanda Fox, Walter Bremond. BS in Econs., U. Ill., 1952, PhD in Econs. and Stats., 1956. Asst. to v.p. Commonwealth Edison Co., Chgo., 1956-59; asst. prof. econs. De Paul U., Chgo., 1959-61; assoc. prof. bus. SUNY, Binghamton, 1961-67, prof. econs. and bus., 1967-68; prof. mgmt. and edn. UCLA, 1968-84, vice chancellor acad. programs, 1985-87; CEO, pub., pres. Cen. News-Wave Publs., L.A., 1987—; pres. Czand Assocs., Pacific Palisades, Calif., 1994—; mem. adv. council Fed. Res. Bank, San Francisco, 1986-88, 2001 com. Office of Mayor of Los Angeles, 1986-89. Author: Organizational Decision-Making, 1967; contbr. articles on bus. to jours. Bd. dirs. Los Angeles County Mus. Art, 1972-84; com. on Los Angeles City Revenue, 1975-76, United Nations Assn. panel for advancement of U. and Japan Relations, N.Y.C. 1972-74; chmn. Mayor's task force on Africa, 1979-82. Fellow John Hay Whitney, U. Ill., 1955-56, Ford Found., 1960-61, 81-82, 84, Am. Council of Edn., UCLA, 1967-68, Aspen Inst. for Human Studies; named one of Young Men of Yr., Jaycees, 1965. Mem. AAAS, Am. Econ. Assn., Nat. Newspaper Pub. Assn., Am. Mgmt. Assn., Alpha Phi Alpha (pres., pledgemaster 1952-54), Phi Kappa Phi, Order of Artus (pres.). Avocations: tennis, jogging, collecting old bus. texts. Home: 1053 Tellem Dr Pacific Palisades CA 90272-2243 Office: Cen Newspaper Publs 2621 W 54th St Los Angeles CA 90043-2614

WILSON, CLARENCE IVAN, banker; b. Kerrville, Tex., Sept. 16, 1927; s. Jesse Leroy and Ruby Jewel (Longley) W.; m. Lola Jean Tiner, Jan. 30, 1954; children: Alan, Dale, Greg, Mark. Student, Freed Hardeman Coll., 1944-46, Abilene Christian U., 1947-48; BS in Math., S.W. Tex. State U., 1949; banking degree, So. Meth. U., 1967. Bank systems specialist Burroughs Corp., San Antonio, 1954-64; v.p., cashier First City Tex., Corpus Christi, 1964-70, pres., 1971-75, chief exec. officer, 1975-91, chmn. bd., 1975-92; chmn., chief exec. officer First City Tex., Alice, 1988-90, Houston, 1991-92; chmn., chief exec. officer 1st City Bankcorp. Tex., Inc., Houston, 1991-95; vice chair First City Fin. Corp., Houston, 1995—. Trustee Driscoll Found., Corpus Christi, 1982—; pres. United Way Coastal Bend, Corpus Christi, 1972; pres. bd. regents Del Mar Coll., 1982-83; bd. dirs. Univ. System South Tex., 1986-89. Sgt. USAF, 1950-53. Named civic salesman of yr. Sales and Mktg. Club Corpus Christi, 1974; recipient Eleanor Roosevelt award for humanitarian service State of Israel, 1977, brotherhood award NCCJ, 1980. Mem. Am. Bankers Assn. (chmn. edn. policyand devel. coun., Tex. rep. to govt. rels. com.), Conf. State Bank Suprs. (state rep. 1981-91), Tex. Bankers Assn. (chmn. 1989, chmn. govt. rels. com. 1986, past chmn. state bank divsn., past chmn. com. bank taxation task force), Corpus Christi Bankers Assn. (pres. 1981), Tex. Assn. Taxpayers (area v.p. 1976, pres.-elect 1983, pres. 1985), Tex. Rsch. League (bd. dirs. 1981, exec. com.), Corpus Christi C. of C. (pres. 1974). Lodges: Rotary; Kiwanis (pres. 1972). Office: First City Bancorp of Texas 1021 Main St Ste 2600 Houston TX 77002-6606

WILSON, CLAUDE RAYMOND, JR., lawyer; b. Dallas, Feb. 22, 1933; s. Claude Raymond and Lottie (Watts) W.; m. Emilynn; 1 dau., Deidre Nicole Frazier. BBA, So. Meth. U., 1954, JD, 1956. Bar: Tex. 1956; CPA, Calif., Tex. Asso. firm Cervin & Melton, Dallas, 1956-58; atty. Tex. & Pacific R.R. Co., Dallas, 1958-60; atty. office regional counsel IRS, San Francisco, 1960-63; sr. trial atty. office chief counsel IRS, Washington, 1963-65; ptnr. Wilson, White & Copeland, Dallas, 1965—; chmn., Dallas dist. dir. IRS Adv. Commn., 1990-91. Mem. ABA, AICPA (coun. 1989-93), State Bar Tex., Dallas Bar Assn. (pres. sect. taxation 1969-70), Tex. Soc. CPAs (pres. 1989-90, pres. Dallas chpt. 1983-84), Greater Dallas C. of C. (chmn. appropriations and tax com. 1990-91), Dallas Gun Club, Crescent Club, Park City Club, Montaigne Club, Masons, Shriners, Jesters, Delta Sigma Phi, Delta Theta Phi. Republican. Episcopalian. Office: 3500 Bank One Ctr 1717 Main St Dallas TX 75201

WILSON, CLEALYN BULLOCK, elementary education educator; b. Phila., Mar. 25, 1950; d. Clinton Nathaniel Bullock and Odaris (Wilson) Jeter; s. Thomas A. Jeter Jr. (stepfather); m. Cecil Charles Wilson, Mar. 19, 1989. BS in Elem. Edn., Morgan State U., 1972; postgrad., We. Wash. U., 1976, Berry Coll., 1978; MEd in Early Childhood Edn., West Ga. Coll., 1980; postgrad., U. New Orleans, 1981, Wilmington Coll., 1991—. Cert. tchr. elem. and early childhood, Del.; cert. elem. tchr. La., Ga., Md. Tchr. 2nd grade Schaeffer Elem. Sch., Pitts., 1972-74; tchr. 1st grade Friends Lower Sch., Balt., 1974-75; follow through tchr. 1st grade Roosevelt Elem., Tacoma, Wash.; open space tchr. 2nd grade Boze. Elem Sch., Tacoma, 1976-77; title 1 tchr. reading resource North Heights Elem. Sch., Rome, Ga., 1977-80; tchr. 2nd grade Main Elem. Sch., Rome, 1980-81; tchr. 4th grade Nelson Elem. Sch., New Orleans, 1981; tchr. 1st and 3rd grades, resource tchr. lang. and early acad. program. Joseph A. Craig Elem. Sch., New Orleans, 1981-88; tchr. 1st grade, 1st and 2nd grade split Towne Point Elem. Sch., Dover, Del., 1988-90; tchr. first grade Willards (Md.) Elem. Sch., 1990-91, East Dover Elem. Sch., 1991—; tchr. homework Community Edn. Program, New Orleans, 1982, high potential tchr., 1983-84; team tchr. Capital Sch. Dist. Summer Reading Camp, Dover, 1992, coord., 1993; creator art projects The Edn. Ctr., Inc., 1992; cons. district-wide writing workshops; mem. district-wide English Lang. Arts Review and Selection Com.; chairperson Del. Tchrs. Forum. Youth coord., MYF co-leader, coun. on ministries, chancel choir, active aerobics programs, altar guild, tchr. Sunday sch. Whatcoat United Meth. Ch., chair Christian Edn., 1992—; layspeaker United Meth. Comm. Com.; active United Meth. Women.; counselor Camp Pe-Co-Meth, Centreville, Md., 1969, mgr. dining room, 1971; mem. choir, brownie leader, nominating com., chair Women's Day observance, instr. aerobics program Bethany United Meth. Ch., New Orleans; program aide Nat. Youth Sports Program; counselor Camp George. Recipient Tchr. of Yr. award State of Del., 1992-93, Capital Sch. Dist., Dover, 1992-93, Appreciation award Whatcoat United Meth. Ch. Winterim Summer Day Camp; named High Potential Tchr., Orleans Parish Cmty. Ctr., 1983-84. Mem. NEA, ASCD, Assn. for Childhood Learning Internat., Del. State Edn. Assn., Diamond State Reading Assn., Capital Educators Assn., Kent Coun. for Reading, Alpha Kappa Alpha (sub-debutantes, assist with youth awareness activities, project lead), Phi Delta Kappa, Kappa Delta Pi, Alpha Delta Kappa. Democrat. Avocations: aerobics, dance, cooking, doll collecting, writing poetry. Home: 130 Brandywine Dr Dover DE 19904-2287 Office: East Dover Elem Sch 852 S Little Creek Rd Dover DE 19901-4722

WILSON, COLIN HENRY, writer; b. Leicester, Eng., June 26, 1931; s. Arthur and Anetta W.; m. Joy Stewart; children: Sally, Damon, Rowan; 1 child from previous marriage, Roderick. writer in residence Hollins (Va.) Coll., 1966-67; vis. prof. U. Wash., Seattle, 1967, Rutgers U., New Brunswick, N.J., 1974. Author (numerous books including novels): The Glass Cage, 1967, The Occult, 1971, The Black Room, 1971, The Space Vampires, 1975, Mysteries, 1978; 6 critical studies in the Outsider series; non-fiction: Access to Inner Worlds, 1982, The Criminal History of Mankind, 1983, (with Donald Seaman) Modern Encyclopedia of Murder, 1983, The Essential Colin Wilson, 1984, The Personality Surgeon, 1986, (with Damon Wilson) Encyclopedia of Unsolved Mysteries, 1987, Spiderworld, 1987, The Misfits, 1988, Beyond The Occult, 1988, Written in Blood, 1989, (with Donald Seaman) The Serial Killers, 1990; (play) Mozart's Journey to Prague, 1991, Spiderworld: The Magician, 1992, The Strange Life of P.D. Ouspensky, 1993, Unsolved Mysteries Past and Present (with Damon Wilson), 1993. Club: Savage.

WILSON, DARRYL CEDRIC, lawyer, law educator, consultant; b. Chgo., Nov. 5, 1961. BFA, BBA, So. Meth. U., 1982; JD, U. Fla., 1984; LLM, John Marshall Law Sch., 1989. Bar: Ill. 1986, Fla. 1995, U.S. Ct. Appeals (7th cir.), U.S. Supreme Ct. 1995. Law clk. Ctr. for Govtl. Responsibility, Gainesville, Fla., 1984-85; Reginald Heber Smith law fellow Cook County Legal Assistance, Harvey, Ill., 1985-86, staff atty. property specialist, 1986-87; pro bono coord. Cook County Legal Assistance, Oak Park, Ill., 1987; corp. atty. intellectual property divsn. Soft Sheen Products Corp., Chgo., 1987; real estate atty. UAW, Ford Legal Svcs., Lansing, Ill., 1988-89; of counsel Steck & Spataro, Chgo., 1989-93; pvt. practice Wilson and Assocs., Chgo., 1989—; prof. law Detroit Coll. Law, 1992-94; mng. ptnr., gen. counsel Freico Diversified Svcs., 1988—; prof. law Stetson U. Sch. Law, 1994—; cons. Pvt. Minority Small Bus. Assocs., Chgo., 1992, Detroit, 1992. Contbr. articles to profl. and acad. jours. Mem. ABA, Am. Intellectual Property Lawyers Assn., Black Entertainment and Sports Lawyers Assn., Internat. Trademark Assn., Ill. Bar Assn., Fla. Bar Assn., Sports Lawyers Assn., Lawyers for Creative Arts. Avocations: music, sports, history. Office: Stetson U Coll Law Saint Petersburg FL 33711 also: Wilson & Assoc Box 27023 Saint Petersburg FL 33711

WILSON, DAVID EUGENE, magistrate judge; b. Columbia, S.C., Jan. 12, 1940; s. David W. and Emma (Moseley) W.; m. Nancy Ireland, Sept. 5, 1964; children: Amy R., Cara S. BA, U. S.C., 1963, JD, 1966; MA, Boston U., 1971. Bar: Vt. 1972, D.C. 1973, Wash. 1980, U.S. Dist. Ct. Vt. 1972, U.S. Dist. Ct. (we. dist.) Wash. 1976. Asst. atty. gen. State of Vt., Montpelier, 1972-73; asst. U.S. atty. U.S. Dist. Ct. D.C., Washington, 1973-76; asst. U.S. atty. U.S. Dist. Ct. (we. dist.) Wash., Seattle, 1976-89, U.S. atty., 1989, asst. U.S. atty., chief criminal div., 1989-92; U.S. magistrate judge Seattle, 1992—; mem. faculty Atty. Gen.'s Advocacy Inst., Washington, 1979—, Nat. Inst. Trial Advocacy, Seattle, 1987—. Capt. U.S. Army, 1966-71, col. USAR. Recipient Disting. Community Svc. award B'nai Brith, 1987. Fellow Am. Coll. Trial Lawyers; mem. Fed. Bar Assn., Wash. State Bar, Seattle-King County Bar. Avocations: hunting, fishing, skiing, books. Office: 304 US Courthouse Seattle WA 98104

WILSON, DAVID GORDON, mechanical engineering educator; b. Sutton Coldfield, Warwick., Eng., Feb. 11, 1928; s. William and Florence Ida (Boulton) W.; m. Anne Ware Sears, July 18, 1963 (div. May 1988); children: John M.B., Erica Sears; m. Ellen Cecilia Warner, Dec. 20, 1988; 1 child, Susan Speck. Postgrad., MIT, Harvard U., 1955-57; BS with honors, U. Birmingham, UK, 1948; PhD, U. Nottingham, UK, 1953. Brush fellow, rsch. asst. Nottingham U., 1950-53; ship's 7th engr. officer Donaldson Line, Glasgow, UK, 1953; engr. Brush Elec. Engring. Co., Ltd., UK, 1953-55; sr. gas-turbine designer Ruston & Hornsby, Lincoln, UK, 1957-58; sr. lectr., mech. engring. U. Ibadan, Zaria, Nigeria, 1958-60; v.p., tech. dir. No. Rsch. and Engring. Corp., Cambridge, Mass., also U.K., 1960-66; assoc. prof. mech. engring. MIT, Cambridge, 1966-71, prof., 1971-94; prof. emeritus, 1994—; vis. engr., Boeing Airplane Co., 1956-57; vis. fellow MIT and Harvard U., 1955-56; cons., lectr. in field. Author: The Design of Gas-Turbine Engines, 1991, The Design of High-Efficiency Turbomachinery and Gas Turbines, 1984; co-author: (with Frank Rowland Whitt) Bicycling Science, 1974, 2d edit., 1982, (with Richard Wilson et al) The Health Effects of Fossil-Fuel Burning, 1981, (with Douglas Stephen Beck) Gas-Turbine Regenerators, 1996; co-editor: (with Allan V. Abbott) Human-Powered Vehicles, 1995; editor: Solid-Waste-Management Handbook, 1977, The Treatment and Management of Urban Solid Waste, 1972. Recipient T. Bernard Hall prize Inst. Mech. Engrs., 1954, Lord Weir 1st prize Inst. Mech. Engrs., 1955, Indsl. Rsch. IR-100 award, 1974, Reclamation Industries Internat. prize, 1974; Power-Jets-Sch. scholar, 1954; Commonwealth Fund fellow MIT and Harvard U., 1955-57. Avocations: human power, biking, hiking, tennis, music. Office: MIT/Mech Engring Rm 3-455 Cambridge MA 02139

WILSON, DAVID JAMES, chemistry researcher, educator; b. Ames, Ia., June 25, 1930; s. James Calmar and Alice Winona (Olmsted) W.; m. Martha Carolyn Mayers, Sept. 6, 1952; children: John Wesley, Charles Steven, William David, Andrew Lyman, Joyce Ballin. BS in Chemistry, Stanford U., 1952; postgrad., 1952-53, 55-57; PhD, Calif. Inst. Tech., 1958. Mem. faculty U. Rochester, N.Y., 1957-69, assoc. prof., 1963-67, prof. phys. chemistry, 1967-69; prof. Vanderbilt U., Nashville, 1969—, prof. chemistry and environ. engring., 1977-95, prof. emeritus, 1995—, Alexander Heard disting. service prof., 1983-84; sr. rsch. assoc. Eckenfelder, Inc., Nashville, 1988-95, sr. rsch. fellow, 1995—; vis. sr. lectr. chemistry U. Ife, Nigeria, 1964-65; vis. prof. U. Málaga, Spain, 1993-94; mem. Rochester Com. for Sci. Info., 1960-69, v.p., 1966-69; chmn. Nashville Com. for Sci. Info., 1971-74. Pres. Tenn. Environ. Coun., 1985-87. With AUS, 1953-55. Recipient award Monroe County Conservation Coun., 1967, Tenn. Conservation League, 1971; Alfred P. Sloan Found. fellow, 1964-66. Mem. AAAS, Am. Chem. Soc., Tenn. Acad. Sci., Sigma Xi, Phi Beta Kappa. Home: 3600 Wilbur Pl Nashville TN 37204-3829

WILSON, DAVID LEE, clinical psychologist; b. Mooresville, N.C., July 5, 1941; s. William John Mack and Joyce Evelyn (Evans) W.; m. Barbara Ann Klepfer, Apr. 22, 1960 (div. Jan. 1982); children: Cheryl, Lisa, David; m. Cheryl Andersen, May 22, 1983 (div. Jan. 1992). Student, Auburn U., 1959-60; AB in Psychology, Davidson Coll., 1963; PhD in Clin. Psychology, U. N.C., 1967. Teaching fellow U. N.C., Chapel Hill, 1964; psychology intern Letterman Hosp., San Francisco, 1966-67, supr., 1967-70; sr. psychologist Kaiser Hosp., Hayward, Calif., 1970-72; pvt. practice psychology San Francisco, 1970-72; mem. staff Far No. Regional Ctr., Redding, Calif., 1970-74; dir. Redding Psychotherapy Group, 1974—, Vietnam Vets. Readjustment Program, Shasta and Tehama, 1984-—; cons. in field. Author: play The Moon Cannot Be Stolen, 1985; contbr. articles to profl. jours. Chmn. Shasta Dam P.U.D. Com., Shasta County, 1981-82, Shasta County Headstart Bd., 1982-85, Criminal Justice Adv. Bd. Shasta County, 1982-87, Youth and Family Counseling Ctr., Shasta County, 1986-89. Capt. U.S. Army, 1965-70. Recipient Danforth award Danforth Found., 1959; Woodrow Wilson Found. fellow, 1963; Smith Fund grantee, 1966; Dana scholar, 1960-63. Fellow Am. Bd. Med. Psychotherapy; mem. APA, Calif. State Psychol. Assn.(chpt. rep. 1990-95, bd. dirs. 1990-95, chair membership com. 1993-95, exec. com. 1993-95, chair publs. com. 1994-95, chair divsn. VI 1996—, chair-elect divsn. I 1996—, Silver PSI award 1995), Shasta Cascade Psychol. Assn.(pres. 1990-91, mem. bd. dirs. 1990—, Outstanding Psychologist 1993), Am. Assn. Advancement of Behavior Therapy, Eye Movement Desensitization and Reprocessing Network (Outstanding Rsch. award 1994), EMDRIA (bd. dirs. 1995—, chair 1996—). Democrat. Avocations: fly fishing, backpacking, camping, white water rafting. Office: Redding Psychotherapy Group 616 Azalea Ave Redding CA 96002-0217

WILSON, DEANNE MARIE, lawyer; b. L.A., Apr. 5, 1944; d. William Wayne and Marie Antoinette (Arnerich) W.; m. Phillip Bradford Plank, Nov. 21, 1970 (div. Jan. 1990); 1 child, Bartlett Alfred Plank; m. Laurence Bernard Orloff, Apr. 26, 1992. AB in Sociology, Stanford U., 1966; JD, Seton Hall U., 1980. Bar: N.J. 1980, U.S. Dist. Vt. N.J. 1980, U.S. Ct. Appeals (3d cir.) 1984, N.Y. 1988, U.S. Tax Ct. 1988, U.S Supreme Ct. 1990. Law clk. Schenck Price Smith Knig, Morristown, N.J., 1979-80, N.J. Supreme Ct., Morristown, 1980-81; assoc. Lowenstein, Sandler, Brochin, Kohl, Fisher, Boylan, Roseland, N.J., 1981-83, Orloff Lowenbach Stifelman & Siegel, Roseland, N.J., 1983-87, Ellenport & Holsinger, Roseland, N.J., 1988; ptnr. Greenberg Margolis, Roseland, N.J., 1989-93; mng. atty. Mound Cotton & Wollan, East Hanover, N.J., 1993—; Bd. dirs. N.J. Inst. Continuing Edn., East Brunswick; mem. Supreme Ct. Civil Practice Commn., Trenton, N.J., 1985-93, Superior Ct. Commn. Women in Cts., Trenton, 1991-94. Fundraiser People for Whitman, Clark, N.J., 1992-94, Stanford (Calif.) U., 1988-91; master Arthur T. Vanderbilt Inns of Ct., Montclair, N.J., 1994—. Mem. ABA, N.J. State Bar Assn. (trustee 1993—), Essex County Bar Assn. (chair equity jurisprudence 1990—), Morris COunty Bar Assn. Republican. Roman Catholic. Avocations: scuba diving, travel, cooking, dog training. Office: Mound Cotton & Wollan Box 78 72 Eagle Rock Ave Bldg 2 East Hanover NJ 07936

WILSON, DEBORAH SUE, elementary education educator; b. Ft. Riley, Kans., Feb. 16, 1966; d. George Nathaniel and Barbara Sue (Deavers) W. BA in History and Edn., Agnes Scott Coll., 1988; MEd, Ga. State U., 1993. Cert. tchr., Ga. Tchr. Atlanta Pub. Schs., 1989—. Active ch. neighborhood ctr. Peachtree Presbyn. Ch., Atlanta, 1991—. Mem. Nat. Assn. Edn. Young Children, PEO, Kappa Delta Pi. Avocations: reading, hiking, travel. Home: 11 Hampshire Ct Atlanta GA 30002

WILSON, DEBRA, oil, gas industry executive. Mgr. devel., adminstr. United Aviation Fuels Corp., Arlington Heights, Ill., 1985—, mgr. elect. purchasing. Office: United Aviation Fuels Corp 1200 E Algonquin Rd Arlington Heights IL 60005-4712*

WILSON, DELANO DEE, consultant; b. Great Falls, Mont., Apr. 15, 1934; s. William McKinley and Alvina Henrietta (Beck) W.; m. Marilyn Ann Harant, Nov. 14, 1959; children: Robin David, Leslie Ann Wilson, Christian William. BSEE, Mont. State U., 1959. Analytical engr. GE, Schenectady, N.Y., 1960-69, sr. engr., 1964-69, mgr. alternating current studies, 1969-72; mgr. engring. projects GE, Phila., 1972-74; prin. engr. Power Techs., Inc., Schenectady, 1974-82; v.p., prin. engr. Power Techs., Inc.-Tech. Assessment Group, Schenectady, 1980-85; pres., CEO Power Techs. Inc., Schenectady, 1986-95, chmn. bd. dirs., 1989-95; expert eyewitness, cons. Internat. Conf. on High Voltage Systems, Paris, 1974-90. U.S. rep., 1986-92. Author, co-author 6 books; contbr. numerous tech. papers to profl. jours.; patentee in field. Bd. dirs. Ellis Hosp., Schenectady, 1987—; trustee Capital Dist. YMCA, 1989—. With U.S. Army, 1954-56. Fellow IEEE (mem. transp. and dist. com., exec. bd. Power Engring. Soc. 1988-94, Disting. Svc. award 1988); mem. Am. Nat. Standards Inst., Nat. Fedn. Indsl. Bus., Schenectady C. of C. (bd. dirs.), Bone Marrow Resource Found. (bd. dirs.), Rotary. Avocations: skiing, fishing, amateur auto rebuilding. Office: Power Techs Inc 1482 Erie Blvd PO Box 1058 Schenectady NY 12301

WILSON, DELBERT RAY, publisher, author; b. Riverdale, Calif., Jan. 16, 1926; s. Elmer Ray and Hanna Marie (Pelto) W.; m. Beatrice Joy Daffer, Oct. 5, 1947; children: Jeri Rae, Vicky Joy, Julianne, Margaret Erin. A.A., A.S., Elgin (Ill.) Community Coll., 1975; B.S., No. Ill. U., 1980; Litt.D. (hon.), Judson Coll., 1985. Editor The Reporter, McCook, Nebr., 1949-50; co-pub. The Reporter, Times-Republican (Hayes Center, Nebr.), Pioneer-Press (Palisade, Nebr.), News (Haigler, Nebr.), 1951-52; advt. mgr. Daily Telegram, Norton, Kans., 1952-53; mgr. The Star, Dos Palos, Calif., 1953-54; gen. mgr. Tribune, Holtville, Calif., 1954-57; bus. mgr. Desert Newspapers, Glendale, Ariz., 1957-59; advt. sales rep. Union Tribune Pub. Co., San Diego, 1959-60, merchandising mgr., 1961-65; gen. advt. mgr. Union Tribune Pub. Co., 1966; editor, pub. Evening Star-News, Culver City, Calif., 1966-70, Daily Courier-News, Elgin, Ill., also, Daily Jour., Wheaton, Ill., 1970-91; CEO Crossroads Communications, Carpentersville, Ill., 1991—, AmTec Learning Corp., Elgin, Ill., 1992—. Author: The Folks, 1974, Fort Kearny on the Platte, 1980, Episode on Hill 616, 1981, Nebraska Hist. Guide, 1983, Wyoming Hist. Guide, 1984, Iowa Hist. Tour Guide, 1985, Kansas Hist. Guide, 1987, Missouri Hist. Tour Guide, 1987, Greater Chicago Hist. Tour Guide, 1989, Colorado Hist. Tour Guide, 1989, Illinois Hist. Tour Guide, 1990; editor Oklahoma Hist. Tour Guide, 1991, Indiana Hist. Tour Guide, 1993, Organizing the Organization, 1993; editor: Valley Voices A Radio History, 1996. Founder, chmn. bd. VIP Friendship Council, Inc. of Ill., 1972—, DuPage County Heritage Gallery, Wheaton, 1976—; bd. govs. State Colls. and Univs., Ill., 1981-91; trustee Judson Coll., Elgin, 1971—, Elgin Acad., 1973-78; chmn. bd. Elgin Sesquicentennial Inc.; bd. mgrs. Sherman Hosp., Elgin, 1971—; active Boy Scouts Am. (Silver Beaver award 1977); chmn. bd. Christian Coll. So. Africa, Harare, Zimbabwe, 1983-87; bd. govs. Luth. Social Services of Ill., 1983-89; mem. Ill. Vets. Adv. Council, 1983—; bd. dirs. Cornerstone Found., 1984—, Wheaton Eye Found., 1985-93, Elgin Community Coll. Found., 1986—, Summit Sch. Found., 1987—, Ill. C.C. Coll. System Found., 1992—, Elgin United Way, 1988—; bd. dirs. western div. Jr. Achievement Chgo., 1991—; mem. No. Star Publs. Bd. No. Ill. U., 1988—; pres. Council on America's Mil. Past, Dept. Ill.; mem. nat. adv. com. Ednl. Assistance, Ltd., Glen Ellyn, Ill., 1989—; bd. dirs. Sherman Health Systems, Elgin, 1989, Elgin Symphony, 1989—, Elgin Devel., Inc., 1989-91; chmn. nat. adv. bd. Lincoln Train Project, Ill. Benedictine Coll., Lisle, 1991—; consulting dir., Sister Cities Assn. of Elgin, Russian dept., 1992—, v.p., bd. dirs. Ill. Chpt. Sister Cities Internat., 1993—; mem. ch. coun. Metro Synod Evang. Luth. Ch. in Am., 1993—. With USN, 1943-45, USAF, 1946-49. Mem. Am. Soc. Newspaper Editors, Nebr. Hist. Soc. (life mem.), DAV (Man of Yr. 1978, comdr. Ill. 1980-82, editor and pub. Ill. DAV News 1977-87), Am. Legion, Sigma Delta Chi. Republican. Lutheran. Home: 1507 Laurel Ct Dundee IL 60118-1708 Office: 35 N Western Ave Carpentersville IL 60110-1730

WILSON, DON WHITMAN, archivist, historian; b. Clay Center, Kans., Dec. 17, 1942; s. Donald J. Wilson and Lois M. (Sutton) Walker; m. Patricia Ann Sherrod, July 9, 1983; children—Todd, Jeffrey, Michael, Denise. AB, Washburn U., Topeka, 1964; MA, U. Cin., 1965, PhD, 1972, LittD (hon.), 1988. Archivist Kans. State Hist. Soc., Topeka, 1967-69; instr. history Washburn U., 1967-69; historian, dept. dir. Dwight D. Eisenhower Library, Abilene, Kans., 1969-78; assoc. dir. State Hist. Soc. Wis., Madison, 1978-81; dir. Gerald R. Ford Library and Mus., Ann Arbor, Mich., 1981-87; lectr. history U. Mich., 1982-87; Archivist of the U.S. Washington, 1987-93; rsch. prof. Tex. A&M U., College Station, 1993—, exec. dir. George Bush libr. ctr., 1993—. Author: Governor Charles Robinson of Kansas, 1975; editor: D-Day: The Normandy Invasion, 1971. Mem. Abilene Library Bd., 1973-76; mem. Abilene City Commn., 1976-78; pres. Dickinson County Hist. Soc., Abilene, 1976-77. NDEA fellow, 1964-67; recipient Pub. Service award Gen. Services Adminstrn., 1973. Mem. Am. Hist. Assn. (mem. Beveridge Book Prize com. 1979-82), Am. Assn. State and Local History, Kans. Hist. Soc. (bd. dirs. 1987—), Am. Antiquarian Soc. Republican. Baptist. Home: 209 Chimney Hill Cir College Station TX 77840-1829 Office: Tex A&M U George Bush Libr Ctr College Station TX 77843-1145

WILSON, DONALD EDWARD, physician, educator; b. Worcester, Mass., Aug. 28, 1936; s. Rivers Rivo and Licine (Bradshaw) W.; m. Patricia C. Littell, Aug. 27, 1977; children: Jeffrey D.E., Sean D., Monique, Sheila L. A.B., Harvard U., 1958; M.D., Tufts U., 1962. Diplomate Am. Bd. Internal Medicine. Intern St. Elizabeth Hosp., Boston, 1962-63; resident in medicine, research fellow in gastroenterology VA Hosp. and Lemuel Shattuck Hosp., Boston, 1963-66; assoc. chief gastroenterology Bklyn. Hosp.,

1968-71; instr. medicine SUNY Downstate Med. Center, Bklyn., 1968-71; asst. prof. medicine U. Ill., Chgo., 1971-73; asso. prof. U. Ill., 1973-75, prof., 1975-80, acting head dept. medicine, 1976-77; dir. div. gastroenterology U. Ill. Hosp., Chgo., 1971-80; chief of gastroenterology U. Ill. Hosp., 1973-80, physician-in-chief, 1976-77; prof., chmn. dept. medicine SUNY Downstate Med. Center, Bklyn., 1980-91; physician-in-chief State U. and Kings County Hosp., 1980-91; dean, prof. medicine U. Md.Sch. Medicine, Balt., 1991—; vis. prof. medicine U. London, Kings Coll. Med. Sch., 1977-78; mem. gastrointestinal drugs adv. bd. FDA, 1985-87, chmn., 1986-87; mem. Part II test com. Nat. Bd. Med. Examiners, 1985-88; mem. nat. digestive adv. bd. NIH, 1985-87, chmn., 1986-87; mem. gen. clin. rsch. ctrs. com. NIH, 1987—; mem. nat. adv. com. Agy. for Health Care Policy and Rsch., Dept. HHS, 1991—, chmn., 1992—; mem. residency rev. com. for internal medicine Acque, 1993—; mem. nat. com. fgn. med. edn. and accreditation U.S. Dept. Edn., 1994—. Contbr. articles to med. jours. Bd. vis. Harvard Sch. of Pub. Health, 1992-94. Served to capt. M.C., USAF, 1966-68. Recipient Rsch. award HEW, 1971, 74, Rsch. award John A. Hartford Found., Inc., 1972-79, Rsch. award Distilled Spirits Coun. U.S., 1972-74, Rsch. award VA, 1974. Master ACP; mem. NAS, AAAS, Am. Gastroent. Assn., Am. Fedn. Clin. Rsch., Am. Assn. Study Liver Disease, Accreditation Coun. Grad. Med. Edn. (rev. com. internal medicine), Central Soc. Clin. Rsch., Central Rsch. Club, Chgo. Soc. Gastroenterology (pres. 1978-79), Digestive Disease Found., Midwest Gut Club, Soc. Exptl. Biology and Medicine, N.Y. Acad. Scis., N.Y. Acad. Medicine, N.Y. Soc. Gastroenterology, Chgo. Soc. Gastrointestinal Endoscopy (pres. 1979-80), Assn. Am. Physicians, Assn. for Acad. Minority Physicians (sec./treas. 1986—), Nat. Med. Assn., Am. Clin. and Climatological Assn., 1994—, Assn. Profs. Medicine (sec.-treas. 1990-91), Inst. of Medicine, Med. Club Bklyn., Sigma Pi Phi (grand boule). Club: Harvard (Chgo., N.Y.C.), 14 West Hamilton St. Club (Balt.), The Ctr. Club, (Balt.). Office: U Md Sch Medicine 655 W Baltimore St Baltimore MD 21201-1509

WILSON, DONALD GREY, management consultant; b. Bridgeport, Conn., Sept. 20, 1917; s. William Gray and Jeannetta McAvoy (Kerr) W.; m. Elizabeth Jean Lanning, Apr. 24, 1943 (dec. Mar. 1971); children: Kirk Lanning, Craig Gardner, William Grey. B.S. in Elec. Engring, Rensselaer Poly. Inst., 1938; S.M., Harvard U., 1939, M.E.S., 1947, Ph.D., 1948. Mgr. automatic fire alarm div. Sealand Corp., Bridgeport, Conn., 1939-40; instr. elec. engring. Rensselaer Poly. Inst., 1940-42; staff mem. Radiation Lab. Mass. Inst. Tech., 1942-45; prof. elec. engring. U. Kan., Lawrence, 1947-50; prof. U. Kan., 1950-55, chmn. dept., 1948-55; dir. Phila. Brass & Bronze, 1962-64, Mallory-Xerox Corp., 1964-65; cons. U.S. Naval Ordance Test Sta., China Lake, Calif., 1953-54; assoc. dir. rsch. dept. Stromberg-Carlson Co., San Diego, 1955-59, gen. mgr., 1959, asst. v.p., 1959-60; v.p. rsch. P.R. Mallory & Co., Indpls., 1960, v.p. rsch. and engring., 1961-71, v.p. rsch., engring. and environ. affairs, 1971-75; alt. dir. Mallory Metal. Products, Eng., 1967; pres. Contemporary Custom Cabinets, San Diego, 1975-76; v.p. Continental Resources and Minerals Corp., Dayton, Ohio, 1978-79; sr. v.p. Tanzi Mergers/Acquisitions, San Diego, 1983-86; mgmt. cons., 1976—; sr. lectr. U. Rochester, 1956-57; lectr. dept. elec. engring. San Diego State U., 1981-92, asst. dean coll. engring., 1987, prof. emeritus, 1992—; mng. dir., exec. bd. nat. Bur. Prof. Cons., 1988-94, sr. counsel, 1994—. Contbr. articles to profl. jours. Bd. dirs. Speech and Hearing Clinic, Indpls., 1960-66; Bd. dirs. Washington Twp. Sch. Dist., 1964-68, pres., 1966-67. Recipient Outstanding Acad. Advisor award San Diego State U., 1992. Fellow AAAS; mem. IEEE (sr.), Affiliation Profl. Cons. Orgns. (chmn. bd. govs. 1991-93, Internat. Outstanding Br. Counselor award 1992), Mensa, Intertel, Sigma Xi, Sigma Phi Epsilon, Tau Beta Pi, Eta Kappa Nu. Home: 3110 Levante St Carlsbad CA 92009-8332

WILSON, DONALD MALCOLM, publishing executive; b. Glen Ridge, N.J., June 27, 1925; s. Robert and Adelaide (Streubel) W.; m. Susan M. Neuberger, Apr. 6, 1957; children: Dwight Malcolm, Katherine Loudon, Penelope. Grad., Deerfield (Mass.) Acad., 1943; B.A., Yale U., 1948. Reporter Life mag., 1949-53, chief Far Ea. corr., 1953-56, chief Washington corr., 1956-60, asso. pub., 1968-69; gen. mgr. Time- Life Internat., 1965-68; v.p. corporate and pub. affairs Time, Inc., 1969-81, corp. v.p. pub. affairs, 1981-89; pu. Business News N.J., New Brunswick, 1989—; dep. dir. USIA, 1961-65; mem. adv. council Edward R. Murrow Ctr., Tufts U., The Nat. Council of La Raza, 1985-89; mem. Pub. Broadcasting Authority of N.J., 1969-73, 76-79. Trustee Vassar Coll., 1971-79, The Brearley Sch., 1977-86; bd. dirs. Solomon R. Guggenheim Mus., The Schumann Fund for N.J., Ctr. for Analysis of Pub. Issues. Decorated Air medal. Mem. Council on Fgn. Relations. Clubs: Federal City (Washington); Century Assn. (N.Y.C.). Home: 4574 Province Line Rd Princeton NJ 08540-2212 Office: Business News NJ 391 George St New Brunswick NJ 08901-2017

WILSON, DONALD WALLIN, academic administrator, communications educator; b. Poona, India, Jan. 9, 1938; s. Nathaniel Carter and Hannah Myrtle Wilson; m. Kathleen, Dec. 28, 1965; children: Carrie, Jennifer, Gregory, Andrew. B.A., So. Missionary Coll., 1959; M.A., Andrews U., 1961; Ph.D., Mich. State U., 1966. Dean applied arts and tech. Ont. (Can.) Colls., North Bay, 1968-73; acad. dean Olivet Coll., 1973-76; pres. Castleton State Coll., 1976-79; pres. Southampton Coll., 1979-83, prof. communications and history, 1973-83; pres., prof. Pittsburg State U. (Kans.), 1983-95; pres. Kilang Nusantara Pacific, 1995—. Author: The Untapped Source of Power in the Church, 1961, Long Range Planning, 1979, The Long Road From Turmoil to Self Sufficiency, 1989, The Next Twenty-Five Years: Indonesias Journey Into The Future, 1992, The Indispensable Man: Sudomo, 1992. Mem. Kans. Adv. Coun. of C.C.'s; bd. dirs. Internat. U. Thailand; pres. Internat. Univ. Found. Named Alumnus of Achievement Andrews U., 1981; recipient Outstanding Alumni award Mich. State U., 1984. Mem. Speech Communication Assn., Assn. Asian Studies, Internat. Univ. Found. (pres.), Rotary. Methodist. Home: 824-B Hugh St Frontenac KS 66763 Office: Kilang Nusantara Pacific Office of Pres Frontenac KS 66763

WILSON, DONNA MAE, foreign language educator, administrator; b. Columbus, Ohio, Feb. 25, 1947; d. Everett John and Hazel Margaret (Bruck) Palmer; m. Steven L. Wilson, Nov. 16, 1968. BA, Ohio State U., 1973, MA, 1976; postgrad studies, U. Wash., Seattle Pacific U., 1980-93; cert., U. Salamanca, Spain, 1985. Tchg. assoc. Ohio State U., Columbus, 1974-76; lectr. U. Wash., Seattle, 1977-78; grants officer Seattle U., 1978-82; adj. prof. Shoreline Coll., Seattle, 1982-84; coord. fgn. langs., prof. Spanish Bellevue (Wash.) Coll., 1984-87; prof. Spanish Highline Coll., Des Moines, Wash., 1987—, chair fgn. lang. dept., 1990-94; chair arts and humanities Highline Coll., Des Moines, 1994—; bd. dirs. Wash. C.C.s, Olympia, 1991—; spkr. at lang. orgns., confs. regional and nat., 1985—. Editor: (book) Fronteras: En Contacto, 1992-93; (jours.) Modern Lang. Jour., 1991, 92, 94, Hispania, 1993; text editor D. C. Heath and Co., Harcourt, Brace and Jovanovich, Houghton Mifflin, Prentice Hall; contbr. articles to profl. jours., chpt. to book. Recipient cert. of excellence Phi Theta Kappa, 1990, Pathfinder award Phi Beta Kappa, 1995; fellowshp grant Coun. Internat. Edn. Exchange, Santiago, Chile, 1992. Mem. Am. Assn. Tchrs. of Spanish (v.p. Wash.), Am. Coun. Tchrs. of Fgn. Langs. (cert. oral proficiency), Assn. Dept of Fgn. Langs. (exec. bd. 1994—), Pacific N.W. Coun. Fgn. Langs., 1986—, Nat. Assn. Fgn. Lang. Suprs., Sigma Delta Mu. (nat. exec. sec. 1992—). Avocations: travel, rsch. on 2d lang., outdoors. Home: 8720 229th Pl SW Edmonds WA 98026-8438 Office: Highline Coll 240th & Pacific Hwy S Des Moines WA 98198

WILSON, DOROTHY CLARKE, author; b. Gardiner, Maine, May 9, 1904; d. Lewis Herbert and Flora Eva (Cross) Clarke; m. Elwin L. Wilson, Aug. 31, 1925; adopted children: Joan S., Harold Elwin (dec.). A.B., Bates Coll., 1925, Litt.D., 1947; L.H.D., U. Maine, 1984. Author of: about seventy religious plays, vol. religious plays Twelve Months of Drama for the Average Church, 1934; novels The Brother, 1944, The Herdsman, 1946, Prince of Egypt, 1949 (winner Westminster $7500 award for best religious novel), House of Earth, 1952, Fly With Me to India, 1954, Jezebel, 1955, The Gifts, 1957, Dr. Ida: A Biography Dr. Ida S. Scudder of India, 1959, The Journey, 1962, Take My Hands: Biography Dr. Mary Verghese, 1963, The Three Gifts, 1963, Ten Fingers for God: Biography Dr. Paul Brand, 1965, Handicap Race: The Story of Roger Arnett, 1967, Palace of Healing, The Story of Dr. Clara Swain, 1968, Lone Woman: Biography of Dr. Elizabeth Blackwell, 1970, The Big-Little World of Doc Pritham, 1971, Hilary, The Brave World of Hilary Pole, 1973, Bright Eyes, the Story of Susette La Flesche-an Omaha Indian, 1974, Stranger and Traveler, The Story of Dorothea Dix, American Reformer, 1975, Climb Every Mountain, 1976, Granny Brand, Her Story, 1976, Twelve Who Cared: My Adventures with Christian Courage, 1977, Apostle of Sight, Story of Dr. Victor Rambo, 1980, Lincoln's Mothers: A Story of Nancy and Sally Lincoln, 1981, Lady Washington, 1984, Queen Dolley: A Story of Dolley Madison, 1987, Alice and Edith: The Wives of Theodore Roosevelt, 1989, Union in Diversity: The Story of Our Marriage, 1993, Leaves in the Wind: A Lifetime in Verse, 1994; lectr. on India, Middle East. Trustee Bates Coll. Recipient Woman of Distinction award Alpha Delta Kappa, 1971, New Eng. United Meth. award, 1975, Distinguished Achievement award U. Maine, 1977, achievement citation award AAUW, 1988, MaryAnn Hartman award U. Maine, 1989, Deborah Morton award Westbrook Coll., 1989. Mem. Phi Beta Kappa. Home: 117 Bennoch Rd Orono ME 04473-1121

WILSON, DOUGLAS LAWSON, research center director; b. St. James, Minn., Nov. 10, 1935; s. Charles Edward and Mae (Lawson) W.; m. Sharon Elaine Sheldon, June 8, 1957; children—Cynthia Ann, Timothy Charles. A.B., Doane Coll., 1957; A.M., U. Pa., 1959, Ph.D., 1964. Instr. English Knox Coll., Galesburg, Ill., 1961-64; asst. prof. Knox Coll., 1964-69, assoc. prof., 1969-79, prof., 1979-96, dir. library, 1972-91; dir. Internat. Ctr. for Jefferson Studies at Monticello, 1994—. Editor: The Genteel Tradition, 1967, Jefferson's Literary Commonplace Book, 1989, Thomas Jefferson's Library, 1989; author: Jefferson's Books, 1996; contbr. articles on Am. lit., Thomas Jefferson and Abraham Lincoln to Atlantic Mo., Am. Heritage and profl. jours. Grantee Am. Philos. Soc., 1980, Am. Coun. Learned Socs., 1981, 85-86; rsch. fellow Huntington Libr., 1981, 91-92, 92-93, NEH, 1982-83; Lester J. Cappon rsch. assoc. Newberry Libr., 1985-86. Mem. Am. Antique Soc. Democrat. Methodist.

WILSON, DWIGHT LISTON, former military officer, investment advisor; b. Hereford, Tex., Oct. 30, 1931; s. Liston Oscar and Pauline (Smart) W.; m. Barbara Ann Alderman, Sept. 4, 1955; children: Terri Ann, Ron Alan, Diana Kay. B.A. in Govt., Okla. U., 1953; M.A. in Public Adminstrn., Shippensburg (Pa.) U., 1973. Commd. 2d lt. U.S. Army, 1953, advanced through grades to maj. gen., 1980; service in Vietnam, W.Ger.; dir. force mgmt. (Hdqrs. Dept. Army), Washington, 1979-80; ret., 1980; fin. cons., resident mgr. Merrill Lynch, Pierce, Fenner and Smith, Punta Gorda, Fla., 1981-95. Decorated D.S.M., Legion of Merit, Bronze Star, Meritorious Service medal, Army Commendation medal (3), Air medal (10). Mem. Assn. U.S. Army. Methodist.

WILSON, EARLE LAWRENCE, church administrator; b. Rensselaer, N.Y., Dec. 8, 1934; s. Lawrence Wilbur Wilson and Wilhelamina Knapp; m. Sylvia M. Beck; children: Deborah, Stephen, Colleen. B in Theology, United Wesleyan Coll., 1956, BS, 1961; M of Divinity, Evang. Sch. of Theology, 1965; M of Theology, Princeton Theol. Sem., 1967; D of Divinity, Houghton Coll., 1974. Sr. pastor Wesleyan Church, Gloversville, N.Y., 1956-61; gen. supt. Wesleyan Ch., Indpls., 1984—; sr. pastor First Wesleyan Church, Bethlehem, Pa., 1961-72; pres. United Wesleyan Coll., Allentown, Pa., 1972-84. Author: When You Get Where You're Going, 1966, Within a Hair's Breadth, 1989. Mem, chaplain Rotary. Republican. Home: 11697 Pompano Dr Indianapolis IN 46236-8819 Office: Wesleyan Ch PO Box 50434 Indianapolis IN 46250-0434

WILSON, EDWARD CONVERSE, JR., oil and natural gas production company executive; b. Cambridge, Mass., Jan. 1, 1928; s. Edward Converse and Jean (McLean) W.; m. Patricia Ann Cairns, Sept. 10, 1953; children—Amy Cairns, Sarah Converse. A.B., Harvard U., 1949. Brokerage trainee Estabrook & Co., Boston, 1951; Midwest Stock Exchange clk. Paul H. Davis & Co., Chgo., 1951-52; mem. Chgo. Bd. Trade, 1952-78, dir., 1966-67, chmn., 1970-71; partner Nolan & Wilson Co. (specialists on Midwest Stock Exchange), 1965-72; sr. partner Wilson Prodn. Co., Ft. Smith, Ark., 1972-74; dir. Rutledge Assos., Wakefield, Mass., 1965-74, Paul H. Robinson Inc., Chgo., 1972-81. Mem. devel. com. Chgo. chpt. Nat. Multiple Sclerosis Soc., 1970; mem. vis. com. on univ. resources Harvard, 1971-74, 76-81; Bd. dirs. Franklin Blvd. Community Hosp., 1970-74. Served with USAAF, 1946-47. Mem. Racquet Club (Chgo.). Home: 11114 Wickwood Dr Houston TX 77024-7523 Office: 1770 Saint James Pl Houston TX 77056-3405

WILSON, EDWARD COX, minister; b. Danville, Va., Sept. 30, 1938; s. James Thomas and Sallie Estelle (Cox) W.; m. Nancy Alva Hudson, Aug. 9, 1960; children: Michael Edward, Suzanne Adams. AB magna cum laude, Elon Coll., 1960; MDiv, Union Sem., 1965. Ordained to ministry Presbyn. Ch. (U.S.A.), 1965. Pastor Meadowbrook Presbyn. Ch., Greenville, N.C., 1965-67, Indian Trail (N.C.) Presbyn. Ch., 1971-86, Locust (N.C.) Presbyn. Ch., 1987-92; assoc. pastor Selwyn Ave Presbyn. Ch., Charlotte, N.C., 1968-71; pastor Williams Meml. Presbyn. Ch., Charlotte, 1992—; commr. Gen. Assembly, Presbyn. Ch. (U.S.A.), 1973, 79, 86; mem. com. on ministry, nomination com., mem. coun. Presbytery, also moderator, 1976-77. Author: Broken--But Not Beyond Repair, 1992, Play Ball! Reflections on Coaching Young Folk, 1994; contbr. articles, sermons and prayers to religious jours. Union Theol. Sem. fellow, 1965. Mem. Alban Inst. Democrat. Home: 8618 Appaloosa Way Ln Charlotte NC 28216-8732 Office: 4700 Beatties Ford Rd Charlotte NC 28216-2845 *In my life I am discovering that love is the primary law and the basic creed.*

WILSON, EDWARD NATHAN, mathematician, educator; b. Warsaw, N.Y., Dec. 2, 1941; s. Hugh Monroe and Margaret Jane (Northrup) W.; m. Mary Katherine Schooling, Aug. 19, 1976; children: Nathan Edward, Emily Katherine. BA, Cornell U., 1963; MS, Stanford U., 1965; PhD, Washington U., St. Louis, 1971. Instr. Ft. Valley (Ga.) State Coll., 1965-67, Washington U., St. Louis, 1968-69, U. Calif., Irvine, 1970-71, Brandeis U., Waltham, Mass., 1971-73; asst. prof. Washington U., St. Louis, 1973-77, assoc. prof., 1977-87, dean grad. sch., 1983-93, dean univ. coll., 1986-88, prof., 1987—, chair dept. math., 1995—; mem. Grad. Record Exams. Bd., Princeton, N.J., 1986-90; sec.-treas. Assn. Grad. Schs. Contbr. articles to profl. jours. Mem. Brentwood Sch. Bd., Mo., 1984. Woodrow Wilson fellow, 1963; NSF fellow, 1963-65; NDEA fellow, 1967-70. Mem. Am. Math. Soc., Math. Assn. of Am. Democrat. Office: Washington U Campus Box 1146 1 Brookings Dr Saint Louis MO 63130-4862

WILSON, EDWARD OSBORNE, biologist, educator, author; b. Birmingham, Ala., June 10, 1929; s. Edward Osborne and Inez (Freeman) W.; m. Irene Kelley, Oct. 30, 1955; 1 dau., Catherine Irene.; BS, U. Ala., 1949, MS, 1950; PhD, Harvard U., 1955; DS (hon.), Duke U., Grinnell Coll., Lawrence U., U. West Fla., Oxford U., Fitchburg State Coll., Ohio U., Ripon Coll., Macalester Coll., U. Mass., U. Conn., Bate Coll., Ohio U.; DPhil, Uppsala U.; LHD (hon.), U. Ala., U. Ala., Hofstra U., Pa. State U.; LLD (hon.), Simon Fraser U., Pa. State U.; D.h.c., U. Madrid Complutense, 1995. Jr. fellow Soc. Fellows, Harvard U., 1953-56, mem. faculty, 1956—, Baird prof. sci., 1976-94, Pellegrino U. prof., 1994—, curator entomology, 1971—; fellow Guggenheim Found., 1978, mem. selection com., 1982-89; bd. dirs. World Wildlife Fund, 1983-94, Orgn. Tropical Studies, 1984-91, N.Y. Bot. Gardens, 1991-95, Am. Mus. Natural History, 1992—, Am. Acad. Liberal Edn., 1993—, Nature Conservancy, 1994—. Author: The Insect Societies, 1971, Sociobiology: The New Synthesis, 1975, On Human Nature, 1978 (Pulitzer prize for non-fiction 1979), (with C.J. Lumsden) Promethean Fire, 1983, Biophilia, 1984, (with Bert Holldobler) The Ants, 1990 (Pulitzer prize for non-fiction 1991), Success and Dominance in Ecosystems, 1990, The Diversity of Life, 1991 (Nat. Wildlife Assn. award Sir Peter Kent Conservation prize), (with Bert Holldobler) Journey to the Ants, 1994 (Phi Beta Kappa prize sci. 1995), Naturalist, 1994 (L.A. Times Book prize sci. 1995). Recipient Cleve.-AAAS rsch. prize, 1967, Nat. Medal Sci., 1976, Leidy medal Acad. Natural Sci., Phila., 1979, Disting. Svc. award Am. Inst. Biol. Scis., 1976, Mercer award Ecol. Soc. Am., 1971, Founders Meml. award and L.O. Howard award Entomol. Soc. Am., 1972, 85, Archie Carr medal U. Fla., 1978, Disting. Svc. award Am. Humanist Soc., 1982, Tyler ecology prize, 1984, Silver medal Nat. Zool. Park, German Ecol. Inst. prize, 1987, Weaver award scholarly letters Ingersoll Found., 1989, Crafoord prize Royal Swedish Acad. Scis., 1990, Prix d'Inst. de la Vie, Paris, 1990, Revelle medal, 1990, Gold medal Worldwide Fund for Nature, 1990, Achievement award Nat. Wildlife Fedn., 1992, Shaw medal Mo. Bot. Garden, 1993, Internat. prize Biology Govt. of Japan, 1993, Eminent Ecologist award, 1994, Audubon medal Audubon Soc., 1995, AAAS Pub. Understanding Sci. award, 1995, John Hay award Orion Audubon Soc., 1995, Schubert prize, Germany, 1996, numerous others. Fellow Am. Acad. Arts and Scis., Am. Phil. Soc., Deutsche Akad. Naturforsch; mem. NAS, Am. Genetics Assn. (hon. life), Brit. Ecol. Soc. (hon. life), Entomol. Soc. Am. (hon. life), Zool. Soc. London (hon. life), Am. Humanist Soc. (hon. life), Acad. Humanism (hon. life), Netherlands Entomol. Soc. (hon. life), Royal Soc. London, Finnish Acad. Sci. and Letters, Russian Acad. Nat. Sci., Royal Soc. Sci. Uppsala (Sweden), others. Home: 9 Foster Rd Lexington MA 02173-5505 Office: Harvard U Mus Comparative Zoology Cambridge MA 02138

WILSON, EDWIN GRAVES, university official. BA, Wake Forest U.; AM, Harvard U., PhD; Litt.D., U. N.C. Mem. faculty dept. English Wake Forest U., Winston-Salem, N.C., 1951—, prof. English, 1959—, asst. dean, 1957-58, acting dean, 1958-60, dean, 1960-67, provost, 1967-90; v.p. spl. projects Wake Forest U., 1990—. Author: (with David B. Green) Keats, Shelley, Byron, Hunt and Their Circles, 1964. Bd. trustees Belmont Abbey Coll., 1979—; mem. N.C. Humanities Coun., 1977-80; bd. visitors Winston-Salem State U., 1989—. With USN, 1943-46. Mem. Phi Beta Kappa, Omicron Delta Kappa, Alpha Phi Omega, Kappa Sigma. Office: Wake Forest U Office of Provost Winston Salem NC 27109

WILSON, EMERY ALLEN, university dean, obstetrician-gynecologist, educator; b. Frankfort, Ky., Apr. 8, 1942; s. Emery Lee and Mary Catheryne (Cooper) W.; m. Clara Bullock, June 18, 1966; children: Emily, Bryan. BA, Emory U., 1964; MD, U. Ky., 1968. Diplomate Am. Bd. Ob-Gyn (examiner 1979-89), Am. Bd. Reproductive Endocrinology. Intern, resident U. Ky., 1968-72; instr. Harvard U. Med. Sch., Boston, 1974-76; asst. prof. ob-gyn U. Ky. Coll. Medicine, Lexington, 1976-79, assoc. prof., 1979-81, prof., 1981—, dean, 1987—, dir. Ctr. for Reproductive Medicine, 1983-87; vice chancellor for clin. profession svcs. U. Ky., 1987—; cons. Nat. Inst. Occupational Safety and Health, Cin., 1980-82; dir. Florence Crittendon House, Lexington, 1986-89. Editor: Nutrition in Pregnancy, 1980, Endometriosis, 1987, Professional Management and Practice Management, 1989; author over 100 articles, book chpts., abstracts; reviewer several profl. jours. Maj. USAF, 1972-74. Recipient Acad. Tng. award Ortho Pharms., 1972. Fellow Am. Coll. Obstetricians and Gynecologists; mem. Am. Fertility Soc., Soc. Gynecologic Investigation, Alpha Omega Alpha, Omicron Delta Kappa. Mem. Disciples of Christ Ch. Home: 967 Edgewater Dr Lexington KY 40502-3159 Office: U Ky Coll Medicine 800 Rose St Lexington KY 40536-0001

WILSON, ESTHER ELINORE, technical college educator; b. Uehling, Nebr., Nov. 4, 1921; d. Lorenz John and Dorothea Emma Rosena (Schmidt) Paulsen; m. Billy LeRoy Wilson, Nov. 14, 1919; 1 child, Frances Ann Wilson Dellar. BS, Morningside Coll., 1950; postgrad., U. Nebr., 1947-80, U. S.D., 1954-83; MS, U. Minn., 1963. Cert. postsecondary tchr., Iowa. Tchr. Irvington (Nebr.) Pub. Schs., 1942-44, Immanuel Luth. Schs., Wichita, Kans., 1944-45, Winnebago (Nebr.) Pub. Schs., 1946-50, Nat. Bus. Coll., Sioux City, Iowa, 1950-51; tchr., asst. prin. Liberty Consol. Sch., Merrill, Iowa, 1951-55; mktg. tchr. coord. South Sioux City (Nebr.) Community Schs., 1955-86; adj. faculty prof. adult basic edn. Western Iowa Tech. Coll., Sioux City, 1989-94; mgr. rental properties Sioux City, 1950—; real estate assoc. State Nat., Dakota City, Nebr., 1988-92, Century 21 Marketplace, Sioux City, 1987-88; advt. sales mgr. Auto Hotline, South Sioux City, 1986-87. Author: I Said I Would, 1995. Vol. tchr. N.E. Nebr. C.C., South Sioux City, 1987-90; supt. St. Paul's Luth. Sunday Sch., Sioux City, 1972-76; treas. Hope Luth. Ch., 1989-95; SBA counselor SCORE, 1995—; co-pres. Friends of Libr., South Sioux City, 1986-88; fundraiser South Sioux City Pub. Libr., 1984-85; pres. Am. Cancer Soc., Dakota County, Nebr., 1979-88; state pres. Nebr. Bus. Edn. Assn., 1979, Distributive Edn. Tchrs. Assn., 1980. Recipient Outstanding Svc. to State Orgns., Nebr. Vocat. Edn. Assn., 1976, Woman of the Yr. Am. Bus. Women Assn., 1972. Mem. Nebr. State Edn. Assn. (sec., treas., v.p., pres., Dedicated Svc. award 1986), NEA, South Sioux City Chamberettes (sec., v.p., pres. 1972-89), Am. Federated Women's Club (sec., v.p., pres.). Avocations: reading, political and economic studies, gardening, evangelism. Home and Office: 435 Dixon Path South Sioux City NE 68776

WILSON, EUGENE ROLLAND, foundation executive; b. Findlay, Ohio, Jan. 14, 1938; s. Clair and Ethel Bernice (Cryer) W.; m. Mary Ann Dalton; children: Jeff, Andy. B.A., Bowling Green State U., 1960; M.S., Syracuse U., 1961. Dir. devel., asst. to pres. Bowling Green (Ohio) State U., 1966-70; mgr. radio-TV advt. Columbia Gas of Ohio, Inc., Columbus, 1964-66; assoc. dir. devel. Calif. Inst. Tech., Pasadena, 1971-77, v.p. for inst. relations, 1979-80; assoc. dir. ARCO Found., Los Angeles, 1977-79, exec. dir., 1980-83, pres., 1984-94; pres. youth devel. Ewing Marion Kauffman Found., Kansas City, Mo., 1995—; chmn. contbns. coun. Conf. Bd.; mem. corp. grant makers com. Coun. of Founds. Nat. bd. of visitors Ctr. on Philanthropy; founding trustee Arcadia (Calif.) Edn. Found.; elder trustee Presbyn. Ch. Named Outstanding Young Man Bowling Green Jaycees, 1967; recipient hon. service award Hugo Reid Sch. PTA, 1977, Corp. Social Responsibility award Mex.-Am. Legal Def. and Edn. Fund, 1989, Nat. Leadership award in edn. Inst. for Ednl. Leadership, 1992. Mem. Bowling Green State U. Alumni Assn. (pres. 1965), Gnome and Athenaeum Clubs of Caltech, Omicron Delta Kappa. Home: 14117 W 56th Ct Shawnee KS 66216 Office: 4900 Oak St Kansas City MO 64112-2776 *Our values and judgments are shaped by our roots. The special relationships developed in small-town rural America, and the many opportunities to enjoy a variety of leadership experiences, prove invaluable later in life to cope with the broader, more vexing problems of pluralistic society. Later sophistication—tempered by the humility of those early roots—then becomes more meaningful.*

WILSON, EWEN MACLELLAN, economist; b. Nairobi, Kenya, July 29, 1944; came to U.S., 1969; s. Walter Maclellan and Barbara (Gange) Maclellan W.; m. Kay Stephens, May 31, 1969; children: Libby, Cindy, Riara. BS, U. London, 1965; MS, W.Va. U., 1970; PhD, N.C. State U., 1973. With conservation and extension dept. Ministry of Agrl., Banket, Rhodesia, 1965-68; research fellow U. Rhodesia, Salisbury, 1973-74; asst. prof. Va. Tech. Inst., Blacksburg, 1975-77; dir. econs. and stats. Am. Meat Inst., Arlington, Va., 1977-83, v.p., 1983-85; apptd. dep. asst. sec. U.S. Dept. Agrl., Washington, 1985-87, asst. sec., 1987-89; pres. Wilson Agribus. Analysis, 1989-90; exec. dir. Commodity Futures Trading Commn., Washington, 1990-94; chief agriculture and fin. statistics div. Bur. of Census, Washington, 1994—; bd. dirs. Nat. Cooperative Bank, 1988-90, Commodity Credit Corp, 1987-89. Mem. Am. Agrl. Econs. Assn. Republican. Episcopalian. Office: Bur of Census 437 Iverson AGFS Washington DC 20233

WILSON, FRANCES EDNA, protective services official; b. Keokuk, Iowa, Aug. 4, 1955; d. David Eugene and Anna Bell (Hootman) W. BA, St. Ambrose Coll., 1982; MA, Western Ill., 1990; cert. massage therapist, Shocks Ctr. for Edn., Moline, Ill., 1993. Lic. massage therapist, Iowa. Trainer, defensive tactics Davenport (Iowa) Police, 1990—, police corporal, 1985-94; police sgt. Iowa Assn. Women Police, Davenport, 1994—, apptd. recs. bur. comdr., 1996—, pres., 1989-92; cons., def. tactics Scott C.C., Bettendorf, Iowa, 1993—; owner Wilson Enterprises Ltd., Davenport, 1995—; spkr. workshops. Bd. dirs. Scott County Family YMCA, Davenport, 1990-95, instr., 1989—, The Family Connection, Ltd.; instr. Davenport Cmty. Adult Edn., 1991-94; mem. Iowa SAFE KIDS Coalition, 1992—; mem. First Presbyn. Ch., Davenport, 1986—, bd. deacons, 1995; vol. asst. Davenport Police Dept.'s Sgts. Planning Com. on Tng., 1991, K-9 Unit, 1990-94. Mem. Am. Soc. Law Enforcement Trainers, Law Enforcement Alliance Am., Am. Women Self Def. Assn., Iowa Assn. Women Police (pres. 1989-92, Officer of Yr. 1995), Iowa State Police Assn., Internat. Platform Assn., Internat. Assn. Women Police. Avocations: photography, reading, education, massage therapy, enjoying life. Office: Davenport Police Dept 420 N Harrison st Davenport IA 52801-1310

WILSON, F(RANCIS) PAUL, novelist; b. Jersey City, May 17, 1946; s. Frank P. and Mary (Sullivan) W.; m. Mary Murphy, Aug. 23, 1969. BS, Georgetown U., 1968. With Cedar Bridge Med. Group, Bricktown, N.Y., 1974—. Author: Healer, 1976, 2d edit., 1992, Wheels Within Wheels, 1978, 2d edit., 1992, An Enemy of the State, 1980, 2d edit., 1992, The Keep, 1981 (N.Y. Times bestseller list), 2d edit., 1982, The Tomb, 1984 (N.Y. Times bestseller list, Porgie award West Coast Rev. Books 1984), The Touch, 1986, Black Wind, 1988, Soft and Others, 1989, Dydeetown World, 1989, The Tery, 1990, Reborn, 1990, Reprisal, 1991, Sibs, 1991, Nightworld, 1991; editor: Freak Show, 1992, The Select, 1994, Implant, 1995; also numerous short stories. Office: care Albert Zuckerman Writers House 21 W 26th St New York NY 10010-1003

WILSON, FRANK HENRY, electrical engineer; b. Dinuba, Calif., Dec. 4, 1935; s. Frank Henry and Lurene (Copley) W.; m. Carol B. Greening, Mar. 28, 1964; children: Frank, Scott E. BS, Oreg. State U., 1957. Electronic engr. Varian Assoc., Palo Alto, Calif., 1960-61, Stanford U. Med. Sch., Palo Alto, 1961-68, U. Calif. Med. Sch., Davis, 1968-77, Litronix, Cupertino, Calif., 1978-81, Quantel, Santa Clara, Calif., 1981-87, Heraeus Lasersonics, Milpitas, Calif., 1987-91, Continuum Electro-Optics, Santa Clara, Calif., 1992—. 1st lt. Signal Corps U.S. Army, 1958-60. Mem. IEEE. Home: 3826 Nathan Way Palo Alto CA 94303-4519 Office: Continuum 3150 Central Expy Santa Clara CA 95051-0801

WILSON, FRANKLIN D., sociology educator; b. Birmingham, Ala., Sept. 3, 1942; s. Ernest and Ollie Lee (Carter) W.; children—Rachel, Chareese. B.A., Miles Coll., 1964; postgrad., Atlanta U., 1964-65; M.A., Wash. State U., 1971, Ph.D., 1973. Instr. Grambling U., La., 1965-66; prof. sociology U. Wis.-Madison, 1973—; cons. Madison Pub. Schs. 1976—; cons. planning dept. City of Madison, Wis., 1984—. Author: Residential Consumption, Economic Opportunities and Race, 1979. Served with U.S. Army, 1966-69; Vietnam. Decorated Purple Heart, Silver Star, Vietnam medal of Valor. Mem. Am. Statis. Assn., Population Assn. Am., Am. Sociol. Assn. Unitarian. Avocation: swimming. Office: U Wis Ctr for Demography and Ecology Social Sci Bldg Madison WI 53713

WILSON, FRANKLIN LEONDUS, III, political science educator; b. L.A., Feb. 7, 1941; s. Franklin Leondus II and Ruth (Elieson) W.; m. Carol Ann West, Feb. 16, 1968; children: Erin, Sara, John, Marc. BA in Internat. Rels., UCLA, 1964, MA in Polit. Sci., 1965, PhD in Polit. Sci., 1969; postgrad., Harvard U., 1996. Teaching asst. UCLA, 1966-67, lect., 1969-70; asst. prof. Iowa State U., Ames, 1970-71; assoc. prof. Purdue U., West Lafayette, Ind., 1971-83, prof., head dept. polit. sci., 1987—; vis. scholar Ctr. for European Studies, Harvard U., 1993; vis. asst. prof. Calif. State Coll., Long Beach, 1969-70; vis. prof. UCLA, summers 1984-86, Brigham Young U., Provo, Utah, 1986; chmn. advanced placement test devel. in govt. and politics Coll. Bd., N.Y.C., 1988-93. Author: French Political Parties under the Fifth Republic, 1982, Interest Group Politics in France, 1987, (co-author) Comparative Politics, 1986, 3rd edit., 1995, The Failure of West European Communism, 1993, West European Politics Today, 2nd edit., 1994, Concepts and Issues in Comparative Politics, 1995. Ct. apptd. spl. advocate Tippecanoe County Superior Ct. No. 3, Lafayette, Ind., 1988—&. Named Frederick Hovde Outstanding Faculty Fellow, Purdue U., 1989; Spencer Found. grantee, Chgo., 1989; Japan Found. grantee, N.Y.C., 1990-93. Fellow Am. Philos. Soc.; mem. Am. Polit. Sci. Assn., Midwest Polit. Sci. Assn., French Politics and Soc. (exec. com.), Coun. European Studies, Phi Beta Kappa (pres. Purdue chpt. 1991-92). Home: 423 Jennings St West Lafayette IN 47906-1147 Office: Purdue U Dept Polit Sci 1363 LAEB West Lafayette IN 47907-1363

WILSON, FRED C., manufacturing company executive; b. 1932. MBA, U. Chgo., 1976. With Caterpillar Tractor Co., East Peoria, Ill., 1950-53, 56-60; with Ingersoll Milling Machine Co., Rockford, Ill., 1960—, project mgr., 1965, chief engr., 1967-71, dir. mktg., 1971-80, gen. mgr. prodn. machinery, 1980-81, v.p., gen. mgr. prodn. machinery, 1981-84, pres., CEO, 1984—. Office: Ingersoll Milling Machine Co 707 Fulton Ave Rockford IL 61103-4069*

WILSON, FRED M., II, ophthalmologist, educator; b. Indpls., Dec. 10, 1940; s. Fred Madison and Elizabeth (Fredrick) W.; m. Karen Joy Lyman, Sept. 10, 1959 (div. June 1962); 1 child, Teresa Wilson Kulick; m. Claytonia Leigh Pemberton, Aug. 28, 1964; children: Yvonne Wilson Hacker, Jennifer, Benjamin James. AB in Med. Scis., Ind. U., 1962, MD, 1965. Cert. Am. Bd. Ophthalmology. Intern Sacred Heart Hosp., Spokane, Wash., 1965-66; resident in ophthalmology Ind. U., Indpls., 1968-71, fellow in ophthalmology, 1971-72; fellow in ophthalmology F.I. Proctor Found., San Francisco, 1972-73; from asst. prof. to assoc. prof. ophthalmology Ind. U., Indpls., 1972-76, prof. ophthalmology, 1981—; med. dir. Ind. Lions Eye Bank, Inc., Indpls., 1973—; cons. surgeon Ind. U., Indpls., 1973—. Author or editor numerous sci. articles, book chpts. and books on ophthalmology. Lt. comdr. USNR, 1966-68, PTO. Mem. Am. Acad. Ophthalmology (assoc. sec. 1988-93, Sr. Teaching award 1989), Assn. Proctor Fellows, Soc. Heed Fellows, Am. Ophthalmol. Soc., Am. Bd. Ophthalmology (bd. dirs. 1993—), Ill. Soc. Ophthalmology (hon.), Mont. Acad. Ophthalmology (hon.), Pacific-Coast Ophthalmol. Soc. (hon.). Republican. Avocations: photography, guitar, history, language, natural history. Home: 12262 Crestwood Dr Carmel IN 46033-4323 Office: Ind U Sch Medicine Dept Ophthalmolgy 702 Rotary Cir Indianapolis IN 46202-5133

WILSON, FREDERICK ALLEN, medical educator, medical center administrator, gastroenterologist; b. Winchester, Mass., Aug. 22, 1937; s. Warren Archibald and Alice Jane (Springall) W.; m. Lynne Stewart Cantley, Feb. 24, 1962; children: Douglas, Victoria. A.B., Colgate U., 1959; M.D., Albany Med. Coll., 1963. Intern Hartford Hosp., Conn., 1963-64, resident in medicine, 1964-66; fellow in gastroenterology Albany Med. Coll., N.Y., 1966-67; USPHS postdoctoral fellow in gastroenterology U. Tex. Southwestern Med. Sch., Dallas, 1969-72; asst. prof. medicine Vanderbilt U. Sch. Medicine, Nashville, 1972-76, assoc. prof., 1976-82, mem. adv. com. clin. research ctr., 1978-81; prof. medicine, chief div. gastroenterology Milton S. Hershey Med. Ctr., Pa. State U., Hershey, 1982-90; prof. medicine, dir. div. gastroenterology Med. U. S.C., Charleston, 1990-94; mem. ACP Med. Knowledge Self-Assessment Program VI, 1980-81; mem. gastroenterology and clin. nutrition rev. group Nat. Inst. ARthritis, Diabetes, Digestive and Kidney Disease, NIH, Bethesda, Md., 1985-89; pre=reviewer Am. Coun. Grad. Med. Edn., 1994-95. Contbr. numerous articles, abstracts, chpts. to profl. publs.; reviewer for sci. jours. Served to maj. M.C., U.S. Army, 1967-69. Recipient Clin. Investigator award VA Med. Ctr., Nashville, 1972-75; recipient Investigator award Howard Hughes Med. Inst., Vanderbilt U., 1975-78; NIH Fogarty Internat. Ctr. sr. internat. fellow Max Planck Inst. for Biophysics, Frankfurt, W.Ger., 1979-80. Mem. Am. Fedn. Clin. Research, Central Soc. Clin. Research, Am. Gastroenterology Assn., Am. Assn. Study Liver Diseases, Am. Soc. Clin. Investigation, N.Y. Acad. Scis., Eastern Gut Club, Pa. Soc. Gastroenterology. Office: Med U SC Div Gastroenterology 171 Ashley Ave Charleston SC 29425-0001

WILSON, GAHAN, cartoonist, author; b. Evanston, Ill., Feb. 18, 1930; s. Allen Barnum and Marion (Gahan) W.; m. Nancy Dee Midyette ((Nancy Winters)), Dec. 30, 1966; stepchildren—Randy Winters, Paul Winters. Graduate, Art Inst. Chgo., 1952. Commentator, Nat. Public Radio. Collections include Gahan Wilson's Graveyard Manner, 1965, The Man In the Cannibal Pot, 1967, I Paint What I See, 1971, Weird World of Gahan Wilson, 1975, Gahan Wilson's Cracked Cosmos, 1975, First World Fantasy Collection Anthology, 1977, Gahan Wilson's Favorite Tales of Horror, 1977, And Then We'll Get Him, 1978, Nuts, 1979, Chog: A Gothic Fable, 1980, Is Nothing Sacred, 1982, Wilson's America, 1985, Eddy Deco's First Case, 1987, Playboy's Gahan Wilson, 1980, Eddy Deco's Last Caper, 1989, Still Weird, 1994; juvenile works: Harry, The Fat Bear Spy, 1973, The Bang Bang Family, 1974, Harry and the Sea Serpent, 1976, Harry and the Snow Melting Ray, 1980; editor: First World Fantasy Awards, 1977, The Raven & Other Poems, 1990; illustrator: Matthew Looney & the Space Pirates, 1972, Catch Your Breath: A Book of Shivery Poems, 1973, Granny's Fish Story, 1975, Maria Looney & The Cosmic Circus, 1978, Maria Looney & The Remarkable Robot, 1979, Bob Fulton's Amazing Soda-Pop Stretcher, 1982, Plots & Pans, 1989, How To Be A Guilty Parent, Murder For Christmas, Passport to World Band Radio, 1992, The Keep of Two Moons, 1992, The Keep of Two Moons, 1992, A Night in the Lonesome October, 1993, Credo!: The Game of Dueling Dogmas, 1993, A Night in the Lonesome October, 1993, Spooky Stories For A Dark & Stormy Night, 1994; co-editor: Animals, Animals, Animals, 1979; co-author: The Upside-Down Man, 1977, Hairticklers, 1989, The Devil's Dictionary & Other Works; author: Everybody's Favorite Duck, 1989; animator (movie): Gahan Wilson's Diner, 1993; contbr. to Nat. Lampoon, New Yorker, Collier's, Look, Playboy, Punch, Esquire, Fantasy and Sci. Fiction, Paris Match, Pardon. Mem. Mystery Writers Am., Sci. Fiction Writers Am., Soc. Illustrators, Wolfe Pack, Cartoonists Assn. Commentator, Horror Writers Am. (Life Achievement award 1992), Writers Guild East, Authors Guild, Nat. Public Radio. Office: HMH Pubs care Readers Svc 919 N Michigan Ave Chicago IL 60611-1601

WILSON, GARY DEAN, lawyer; b. Wichita, Kans., June 7, 1943; s. Glenn E. and Roe Zella (Mills) W.; m. Diane Kay Williams, Dec. 29, 1965; children: Mark R., Matthew C., Christopher G. BA, Stanford U., 1965, LLB, 1968. Bar: D.C. 1970, U.S. Dist. Ct. D.C. 1970, U.S. Ct. Appeals (D.C. cir.) 1972, U.S. Ct. Appeals (7th cir.) 1979, U.S. Ct. Appeals (2d cir.) 1983. Law clk. U.S. Ct. Appeals, 2d cir., N.Y.C., 1968-69, U.S. Supreme Ct., Washington, 1969-70; assoc. Wilmer, Cutler & Pickering, Washington, 1970-75, ptnr., 1976—; acting prof. law Stanford (Calif.) Law Sch., 1981-82. Bd. visitors Stanford Law Sch., 1990-92. Democrat. Home: 4636 30th St NW Washington DC 20008-2127 Office: Wilmer Cutler & Pickering 2445 M St NW Washington DC 20037-1435

WILSON, GARY LEE, airline company executive; b. Alliance, Ohio, Jan. 16, 1940; s. Elvin John and Fern Helen (Donaldson) W.; children: Derek, Christopher. BA, Duke U., 1962; MBA, U. Pa., 1963. V.p. fin., dir. Trans-Philippines Investment Co., Manila, 1964-70; exec. v.p., dir. Checchi & Co., Washington, 1971-73; exec. v.p. Marriott Corp., Washington, 1973-85; exec. v.p., chief exec. officer, dir. The Walt Disney Co., Burbank, Calif., 1985-89, dir., 1990; co-chmn. bd. Northwest Airlines, Inc., St. Paul, Minn., 1990—. *

WILSON, GENEVA JUNE, gerontology nurse, consultant; b. Albany, Tex., July 30, 1931; d. Alford Addison and Francis Aliene (Smith) Alexander; children: Carla, Jeff, Susan, Laura. AA with honors, Ranger (Tex.) Jr. Coll., 1951; BSN, Tex. Christian U., 1957; diploma with honors, LNHA Wayland Bapt. U., Plainview, Tex., 1989. Cert. CPR; lic. nursing home adminstr. Dir. nursing svc. Univ. Hosp., Lubbock, Tex.; assoc. dir. nursing edn., instr. Sch. Nursing Meth. Hosp., Lubbock; discharge planner Lubbock Gen. Hosp.; nursing cons. ARA Living Ctrs., Houston; quality assurance profl. Beverly Enterprises, Austin, Tex.; adminstr. Lubbock Health Care & Rehab. Ctr./Beverly Enterprises; owner Big Country Home Health Agy., Abilene, Tex. Mem. Am. Bus. Women's Assn., Harris Coll. Nursing-Tex. Christian U. Alumni Assn.

WILSON, GEORGE LARRY, computer software company executive; b. Greensboro, N.C., July 31, 1946; s. George Thomas and Charlcie (Worrell) W.; m. Patricia Ervin, Jan. 19, 1966; children: Christopher Chadwick, Elizabeth Burns. BS, U. S.C., 1968, MBA, 1970. CPCU; cert. data processor. Sr. v.p. Seibels, Bruce & Co., Columbia, S.C., 1966-81, bd. dirs., 1975—; pres. Policy Mgmt. Systems Corp., Columbia, 1981-85, chmn., 1985—, also bd. dirs.; bd. dirs. LEGENT Corp., Vienna, Va. Bd. dirs. Gov.'s Sch. for Arts, Greenville, S.C., 1988—, Cen. Carolina Community Found., Columbia, 1990—, Cities in Schs., Columbia, 1990—; chmn. Enterprise Devel., Inc., Columbia, 1991—; mem. bd. visitors Heathwood Hall, 1980-85. Recipient Disting. Alumnus award U. S.C. Coll. Bus. Adminstrn., 1985, 5 ann. awards as one of top 3 chief exec. officers in computer software and svcs. industry Wall Street Transcript. Mem. Soc. CPCU's, Summit Club. Republican. Methodist. Avocations: sport fishing, vintage cars. Office: Policy Mgmt Systems Corp PO Box 10 Columbia SC 29202-0010*

WILSON, GEORGE PETER, international organization executive; b. Perth, Scotland, July 6, 1935; came to U.S., 1985; s. Alan Johnson and Doris L. (Allan) W.; m. Sandra Graham, Feb. 6, 1960 (div. 1984); 1 child, Iain; m. Robbyn Dee LaCroix, Nov. 17, 1984; 1 stepchild, Orion. Diploma in Hotel Mgmt., Scottish Coll. Commerce, Glasgow, 1954. Chartered acct., 1965, cert. internal auditor, 1985. Hotel mgr., auditor Can. Nat. Rys., Ottawa and Montreal, 1956-65; fin. officer Treasury Bd. Can., asst. sec. to Cabinet, dir. Pub. Service Commn., counsellor external affairs Govt. of Can., Ottawa, Geneva, 1965-78; dir. gen. audit UN, N.Y.C., 1978-80; dep. auditor gen. of Can. Govt. of Can., Ottawa, 1980-85; pres. Inst. Internal Auditors, Orlando, Fla., 1985-92; dir. audit FAO UN, Rome, 1992—. Contbr. articles to profl. jours. Mem. Can. Inst. Chartered Accts. (com. mem.), Inst. Internal Auditors (com. mem.), Can. Comprehensive Audit Found. (gov. 1985-88), Internat. Consortium on Govt. Fin. Mgmt. (bd. dirs. 1983-92), Inst. for Fin. Crime Prevention. Home: Via Giulia 98 # 9, 00186 Rome Italy Office: FAO HQ, Viale delle Terme di, Caracalla, 00100 Rome Italy

WILSON, GEORGE WHARTON, newspaper editor; b. Phila., Feb. 22, 1923; s. Joshua Wharton and Eva (Frear) W.; m. Neva Jean Gossett, Nov. 18, 1950; children: Guy Richard, Lee Robert. B.A., Western Md. Coll., 1947; postgrad., U. Pa., 1948. Reporter, city editor News-Chronicle, Shippensburg, Pa., 1945-46; asst. news dir. Sta. WILM-Radio, Wilmington, Del., 1947-48; sports editor Evening Chronicle, Uhrichsville, Ohio, 1948-49, editor, 1949-50; editor Daily Record, Morristown, N.J., 1950-54; chief editorial writer Standard-Times, New Bedford, Mass., 1954-59; editorial writer Phila. Inquirer, 1959-64, chief editorial writer, 1964-87. Author: Yesterday's Philadelphia, 1975, Stephen Girard: America's First Tycoon, 1995. Served with USAAF, 1942-45. Recipient George Washington honor medal Freedoms Found., 1961, 67, 72; Phila. Press Assn. award editorial writing, 1967, 68; award for editorial writing Pa. Press Assn., 1972, 79; award for editorial writing U.S. Indsl. Council, 1975, 77; Disting. Service award Sigma Delta Chi, 1977; Disting. Journalism award Citizens Com. on Public Edn. in Phila., 1978; Public Service award Phila. Convention and Visitors Bur., 1980; award for column writing N.J. Soc. Profl. Journalists, 1981; Elm award Fishtown Civic Assn., 1982. Mem. Am. Acad. Polit. and Social Sci., Franklin Inst., Acad. Natural Sci., Hist. Soc. Pa., Soc. Profl. Journalists, Phila. Mus. Art, Phila. Maritime Mus., Phila. Writers Orgn., Phila. Zool. Soc., Pa. Soc., Friends of Independence Nat. Hist. Park, Huguenot Hist. Soc., Pa. Acad. Fine Arts, Pen and Pencil Club (Phila.), Elks, Am. Legion. Republican. Congregationalist. Club: Pen and Pencil (Phila.). Home: PO Box 617 Albrightsville PA 18210-0617

WILSON, GEORGE WILTON, economics educator; b. Winnipeg, Man., Can., Feb. 15, 1928; came to U.S., 1952, naturalized, 1970; s. Walter and Ida (Wilton) W.; m. I. Marie McKinney, Sept. 6, 1952 (dec. July 1986); children: Ronald Leslie, Douglas Scott, Suzanne Rita; m. Joan Murdock, May 16, 1988. B.Commerce, Carleton U., Ottawa, Can., 1947-50; M.A., U. Ky., 1951; Ph.D., Cornell U., 1955. Economist Bd. Transp. Commrs., Ottawa, 1951-52; teaching fellow Cornell U., 1952-55; asst. prof. econs. Middlebury (Vt.) Coll., 1955-57; prof. transp. Ind. U., Bloomington, 1957-66; prof. bus. econs., chmn. dept. Ind. U., 1966-70, dean Coll. Arts and Scis., 1970-73, disting. prof. bus. econs., 1978-92, disting. prof. emeritus bus. econs., prof. emeritus econs., 1992; Collaborator study South Asia 20th Century Fund, 1962-65, dir. research Can.'s needs and resources, 1964-65; dir. case studies role transp. in econ. devel. Brookings Instn., 1964, study transport and econ. devel. of Indochina, 1974; mem. Presdl. Task Force Transp., 1964, 68; dir. Transp. Res. Ctr., Ind. U., 1990-92. Author: Essays on Some Unsettled Questions in the Economics of Transportation, 1962, Economic Analysis of Intercity Freight Transportation, 1980, Inflation: Causes, Consequences and Cures, 1982, U.S. Intercity Passenger Transportation Policy, 1930-91, An Interpretive Essay, 1992; co-author: Mathematical Models and Methods in Marketing, 1961, Canada: An Appraisal of Its Needs and Resources, 1965, The Impact of Highway Investment on Development, 1966, Growth and Change at Indiana U, 1966, Transportation on the Prairies, 1968, Asian Drama, 1968, Essays in Economic Analysis and Policy, 1970, Southeast Asian Regional Transport Survey, 1972, Regional Study of the Impact of the Energy Situation on Transport Development, 1983; Editor: Classics of Economic Theory, 1964, Technological Development and Economic Growth, 1971. Recipient A. Davidson Dunton Alumni award Carleton U., Salzberg Hon. Medallion Syracuse U., 1992. Mem. Am. Econ. Assn. (Disting. Mem. award 1986), Transp. Rsch. Forum (pres. 1969, Transp. Rsch. award 1990), Gamma Sigma. Address: RD 3 Box 1132 Butternut Ridge Rd Middlebury VT 05753-8744

WILSON, GERALD, I, insurance executive; b. 1938. BS, Lafayette Coll., 1960. Formerly with Conn. Gen. Life Ins. Co.; with Hewitt Assocs., Inc., 1962—, ptnr., chmn. exec. com., 1966—. Fellow Soc. Actuaries. Office: 100 Half Day Rd Lincolnshire IL 60069

WILSON, GERALD EINAR, mechanical and industrial engineer, business executive; b. Newhill, Alta., Can., Mar. 20, 1922; s. Robert E. and Cecelia (Stephenson) W.; m. Helen M. Martens, June 9, 1945. B.A.Sc., U. Toronto, 1950. Registered profl. engr., 8 provinces. Asst. brewmaster John Labatt Ltd., London, Ont., Can., 1950-62; v.p. prodn. Labatt Ont. Breweries, 1962-64; v.p. engring. John Labatt Ltd., 1964-69, v.p. engring. services, 1969-85, v.p., 1986-87, retired; pres. Carpools Environ. Protection Services Ltd., 1977—. Patentee solar quilt, continuous separator, others. Bd. dirs. Ont.a Environ. Assessment Bd., 1977-83; chmn. Boys and Girls Club Found., London; bd. dirs. Boys and Girls Clubs, Can., Heritage London Found. Served to 1st lt. RCAF, 1942-45. Decorated D.F.C., others. Mem. Assn. Profl. Engrs., Engring. Inst. Can., Master Brewers Assn., Internat. C. of C. Conservative. Anglican. Clubs: London Hunt (London); Union (Victoria , B.C.). Lodge: Royal Can. Legion (pres. 1981-82). Home: Sir Adam Beck Suite, 240 Sydenham St, London, ON Canada N6A 1W5

WILSON, GLEN PARTEN, professional society administrator; b. Waco, Tex., Dec. 10, 1922; s. Glen P. and Hazel (Parnell) W.; m. Alice B. Groves, Dec. 11, 1982. BS in Aero. Engring., U. Tex., Austin, 1943, MA in Psychology, 1948, PhD in Psychology, 1952. Engr. Lockheed Aircraft Co., Burbank, Calif., 1943-44; teaching fellow, rsch. asst., instr. U. Tex., Austin, 1946-52; rsch. psychologist USAF, Lackland AFB, Tex., 1952-53; gen. mgr. Tex. Ednl. Devices Co., Austin, 1953-54; asst. to Senator Lyndon B. Johnson Washington, 1955-57; staff Senate Preparedness Investigating Subcom. and Senate Spl. Com. on Space and Astronautics, Washington, 1957-59; chief clk., profl. staff mem. Senate Com. on Aero. and Space Scis., Washington, 1959-77; cons. Washington, 1977-79; spl. asst. for student activities NASA, Washington, 1979-80, acting dir. acad. affairs div., 1980-82; pres. Marie D. and Glen P. Wilson Found., Washington, 1982-87; exec. dir. Nat. Space Soc., Washington, 1984-88, exec. dir. emeritus, 1988—; lectr. on aero. and space programs, Senate orgn., sci. policy, tech. assessment, student activities, space activism. Participant as staff passage of Nat. Aeros. and Space Act, 1958, Communications Satellite Act, 1962, NASA Authorization Acts, 1958-77; editor Policy Planning for Aeronautical Rsch. and Devel., Senate Document 90, 89th Congress, 1966; developer NASA shuttle student involvement program, 1980, space edn. orgn., 1984—. With USN, 1944-46. Recipient Exceptional Svc. medal NASA, 1981; Nat. Space Soc. Hdqrs. renamed The Glen P. Wilson Internat. Space Ctr., 1988. Mem. AIAA (spl. presdl. citation 1976), Am. Astro. Soc., AAAS, Nat. Space Soc., Internat. Acad. of Astronautics, Sigma Xi, Nat. Space Club, Cosmos Club. Home: 433 New Jersey Ave SE Washington DC 20003-4034 Office: 922 Pennsylvania Ave SE Washington DC 20003-2140

WILSON, GLENN, economist, educator; b. East St. Louis, Ill., Feb. 4, 1929; s. Herschel and Regina (Hayes) W.; m. Helen Janice O'Dell, Jan. 28, 1951; children—David, Thomas, Ann. B.A., U. Okla., 1951; M.A., 1952. Adminstr., Welfare and Retirement Fund United Mine Workers, Pitts., Knoxville, Tenn., 1952-58; dir. med. care research Nationwide Ins. Co., Columbus, 1958-62; exec. dir. Community Health Found., Cleve., 1962-68; exec. v.p. Kaiser Community Health Found., Cleve., 1968-69; assoc. dean U. N.C. Med. Sch., Chapel Hill, 1970-88, prof. dept. social medicine, 1977—, chmn. dept., 1977-89; cons. Sault Ste. Marie and Dist. Group Health Assn.; health adv. Mayor Stokes, Cleve., 1967-69. Contbr. articles to profl. jours. Home: 214 Glandon Dr Chapel Hill NC 27514-3816 Office: U NC Med Sc Dept Social Medicine Chapel Hill NC 27514

WILSON, GRAHAM MCGREGOR, energy company executive; b. Kilwinning, Scotland, Aug. 2, 1944; s. Peter and Jessie (Scott) W.; m. Josee Perrault; children: Stefanie, Richard, Patrick. BS, McGill U., Montreal, Que., Can., 1967; MBA, U. Western Ont., London, Can., 1969. Investment analyst Greenshields Inc., 1969-72; asst. treas. Genstar, 1972-74; various fin. positions, v.p. fin. MacMillan Bloedel Ltd., Vancouver, B.C., Can., 1974-83; v.p. fin. and adminstrn. Petro-Can. Inc., Calgary, Alta., 1983-88; exec. v.p., CFO Westcoast Energy Inc., Vancouver, 1988—; bd. dirs. Foothills Pipe Lines Ltd., Calgary, Pacific No. Gas Ltd., Vancouver, Pacific Coast Energy Corp., Vancouver, Westcoast Power Inc., Vancouver, Westcoast Gas Svcs., Calgary, Centra Gas Inc., Toronto, Ont., Centra Gas Alta., Inc., Leduc Centra Gas B.C. Inc., Victoria, Itron Inc., Spokane, Wash., Union Gas Ltd., Chatham, Ont., Union Energy Inc., Chatham, Westcoast Energy Internat. Inc., Lake Superior Power Inc., Sta. KCTS-VT, Seattle. Avocations: squash, golf. Office: Westcoast Energy Inc Park Pl, 666 Burrard St Ste 3400, Vancouver, BC Canada V6C 3M8

WILSON, H. DAVID, dean; b. West Frankfort, Ill., Sept. 13, 1939; m. Jeannette Wilson; children: Jennifer, Jacqueline, Mary Jeanne. AB in Zoology, Wabash Coll., 1961; MD, St. Louis Sch. Medicine, 1966. Diplomate Nat. Bd. Med. Examiners, Am. Bd. Pediatrics. Intern pediatrics Cardinal Glennon Meml. Hosp. for Children, St. Louis U., 1966-67; resident dept. pediatrics U. Ky. Med. Ctr., Lexington, 1967-68, chief resident, 1968-69; NIH rsch. fellow U. Tex. Health Scis. Ctr., Dallas, 1971-73; fellowship Am. Coun. on Edn., 1988-89; dir. admissions Coll. of Medicine, U. Ky., 1986-88; assoc. dean for acad. affairs, prof. Coll. Medicine, U. Ky., 1989-95; dean, prof. U. N.D. Sch. of Medicine, Grand Forks, 1995—; Author: (TV series) For Kids Sake, 1987-88; dir. pediatric infectious diseases U. Ky. Med. Ctr., Lexington, 1973-95, dir. cystic fibrosis care and tchg. ctr., 1975-80, med. dir., clin. virology lab., 1982-95; staff United Hosp., Grand Forks, 1995—; elected univ. senate U. Ky., 1993-96, bd. trustees Gluck Equine Rsch. Found., 1991-95, rules and elections univ. senate standing com., 1991-92, steering com. for U.K. self-study, 1990-95, co-chmn. steering com., 1990-95, chmn. review and search com. for chmn. dept. obstetrics and gynecology, 1990, chmn. curriculum com. Coll. of Medicine, 1989-95; elected acad. coun. of med. ctr. U. Ky. Med. Ctr., 1989-92; lectr. in field. Contbr. numerous articles to profl. jours. Fellow Pediatric Infectious Dieseases Soc.; mem. AMA, Am. Soc. of Microbiology, Am. Thoracic Soc., Am. Acad. Pediatrics, Pan Am. Group for Rapid Viral Diagnosis. Home: 10 Shadyridge Estates Grand Forks ND 58201 Office: U ND Sch of Medicine Rm 1925 501 N Columbia Rd Box 9037 Grand Forks ND 58202-9037

WILSON, H(AROLD) FRED(ERICK), chemist, research scientist; b. Columbiana, Ohio, Aug. 15, 1922; s. Lloyd Ralph and Erma Rebecca (Frederick) W.; m. Alice Marjorie Steer, Aug. 20, 1949; children: Janice, Deborah, James, Kathleen. B.A., Oberlin Coll., 1947; Ph.D., U. Rochester, 1950. With Rohm & Haas Co., Phila., 1950-83; beginning as rsch. scientist, successively lab. head, rsch. supr., asst. dir., assoc. dir., dir. rsch. Rohm & Haas Co., 1950-74, v.p., 1974-83, chief sci. officer, from 1981; now with Wilson Assocs., Cape May, N.J.; mem. U.S. nat. com. IUPAC, 1977-84, vice chmn., 1980-82, chmn., 1982-84, fin. com., 1979-89, chmn., 1981-89; chmn. I.R.I. Research Corp., 1980-82, dir., 1979-82. Served to 1st lt. USAAF, 1942-46. Decorated Air Medal. Mem. Am. Chem. Soc., AAAS, Soc. Chem. Industry, Dirs. Indsl. Research. Patentee in field. Home: 214 Gilmore Ave Merchantville NJ 08109-2531 Office: Wilson Assocs 24 Congress St Cape May NJ 08204-5308

WILSON, HARRY B., retired public relations company executive; b. St. Louis, May 17, 1917; s. H. Burgoyne and Margaret (Drew) W.; m. Helen Cain, July 27, 1940 (dec. Oct. 1983); children: Margaret Wilson Pennington, Harry B., Andrew B., Daniel B., Josephine Wilson Havlak, Julie Wilson Sakellariadis, Ellen Wilson Shumway; m. Mary Virginia Peisch, Apr. 7, 1984. Ph.B., St. Louis U., 1938. Mng. editor Sedalia (Mo.) Capital, 1939-40; reporter Kansas City Star; also state capital bur. chief St. Louis Globe-Democrat, 1940-42, polit. writer, columnist, 1946-52; corr. Business Week mag., 1948-52; with Fleishman-Hillard Inc., St. Louis, 1953; sr. ptnr. Fleishman-Hillard Inc., 1964-70, pres., 1970-74, chmn. bd., 1974-88, sr. ptnr., 1989-92. Bd. dirs. St. Louis Family Support Network, Friends of the New Cathedral. With USNR, 1942-46. Home: # 901 625 S Skinker Saint Louis MO 63105-2301

WILSON, HARRY COCHRANE, clergyman; b. St. John, N.B., Can., May 31, 1945; s. Harry Shepherd and Gertrude (Cochrane) W.; m. Gloria Lea Trites, Oct. 8, 1965; children: Troy Spurgeon, Kristi Lea. BA, Bethany Bible Coll., 1972, DD (hon.), 1988; DD (hon.), Cen. Wesleyan Coll., S.C., 1989. Br. exec. Can. Permanent Trust Co., Monton, N.B., 1965-70; pastor Wesleyan Ch., Blacks Harbor, N.B., 1971-74, Dartmouth, N.S., Can., 1974-80; dist. supt. Delta dist. Wesleyan Ch., Jackson, Miss., 1981-88; bd. adminstr. Wesleyan Ch., Indpls., 1984—; dir. Sunday schs. Wesleyan Ch. World Hdqrs., Marion, Ind., 1980-81; gen. supt. Wesleyan Ch. Internat. Ctr., Indpls., 1988—. Author: The Wesleyan Advocate, 1992, Seize the Day-Your Church Can Thrive, 1992. Active A.D. 2000, Heritage USA. Recipient Pastor's award Atlantic Dist., 1975, 77. Mem. Nat. Assn. Evangs., World Meth. Coun. Office: Internat Ctr Wesleyan Ch 6060 Castleway West Dr Indianapolis IN 46250-1969

WILSON, HARRY L., lawyer; b. Hutchinson, Kans., Dec. 13, 1942. BA summa cum laude, Mich. State U., 1970; JD, U. Mich., 1973. Bar: Ill. 1973. Ptnr. Clausen Miller Gorman Caffrey & Witous P.C., Chgo. Office: Clausen Miller Gorman Caffrey & Witous PC 10 S La Salle St Chicago IL 60603-1002*

WILSON, HERMAN T., JR., agricultural products supplier; b. 1941. Food divsn. mgr. Granada Corp., Houston, 1986-88; chmn., co-founder Western Farm Svc. Inc., Fresno, Calif., 1988—. Office: Western Farm Svc Inc 2001 Kirby Dr Ste 712 Houston TX 77019

WILSON, HERSCHEL MANUEL (PETE WILSON), retired journalism educator; b. Candler, N.C., July 17, 1930; s. Shuford Arnold and Ida Camilla (Landreth) W.; m. Ruby Jean Herring, Aug. 10, 1952. AB in Journalism, San Diego State U., 1956; MS in Journalism, Ohio U., Athens, 1959; postgrad., U. So. Calif., 1966-70. Reporter, copy editor, picture editor The San Diego Union, 1955-58; reporter, wire editor Long Beach (Calif.) Ind., 1959-65; prof. journalism Calif. State U., Northridge, 1965-71; fgn. desk copy editor L.A. Times, 1966-71; prof. and former chmn. journalism Humboldt State U., Arcata, Calif., 1971-91; ret., 1991; cons. KVIQ-TV News Dept., Eureka, Calif., 1985-87. Contbr. articles to profl. jours. Publicity dir. Simi Valley (Calif.) Fair Housing Coun., 1967; bd. dirs., publicity dir. NAACP, Eureka, Calif., 1978-80. With USN, 1948-52, Korea. Named Nat. Outstanding Advisor, Theta Sigma Phi, 1970. Mem. Soc. Profl. Journalists. (named Disting. Campus Advisor 1982), San Fernando Valley Press Club (v.p. 1969-70), Beau Pre Men's Golf Club (McKinleyville, Calif., pub. rels. dir., treas. 1978). Democrat. Methodist. Avocations: golf, walking, gardening, reading. Home: 115 Bent Creek Ranch Rd Asheville NC 28806-9521

WILSON, HUGH STEVEN, lawyer; b. Paducah, Ky., Nov. 27, 1947; s. Hugh Gipson and Rebekah (Dunn) W.; m. Clare Maloney, Apr. 28, 1973; children: Morgan Elizabeth, Zachary Hunter, Samuel Gipson. BS, Ind. U., 1968; JD, U. Chgo., 1971; LLM, Harvard U., 1972. Bar: Calif. 1972, U.S. Dist. Ct. (cen. dist.) Calif. 1972, U.S. Dist. Ct. (so. dist.) Calif. 1973, U.S. Ct. Appeals (9th cir.) 1975, U.S. Dist. Ct. (no. dist.) Calif. 1977, U.S. Dist. Ct. (ea. dist.) 1980. Assoc. Latham & Watkins, Los Angeles, 1972-78, ptnr., 1978—. Recipient Jerome N. Frank prize U. Chgo. Law Sch., 1971. Mem. ABA, Los Angeles County Bar Assn., Order of Coif, Calif. Club. Republican. Avocations: lit., zoology.

WILSON, I. DODD, dean; b. St. Peter, Minn., July 10, 1936. AB summa cum laude, Dartmouth Coll., 1958; MD, Harvard U., 1961. Diplomate Am. Bd. Internal Medicine. Intern dept. medicine U. Minn. Hosps., Mpls., 1961-62; med. fellow Dept. of Medicine, 1962-63, 65-66; instr. dept. of medicine U. Minn. Med. Sch., Mpls., 1967-68, asst. prof., 1968-71, assoc. prof., 1971-76, dir. sect. of gastroenterology, 1972-83, vice chmn. dept. of medicine, 1983-86, prof. medicine, 1976-86; dean, prof. medicine U. Ark. Coll. of Medicine, Little Rock, 1986—; exec. vice chancellor U. Ark. Med. Scis., 1994—; mem. Univ. Hosp. Consortium Rsch. Task Force, 1994; adv. bd. UALR Donaghey Project, 1994—; mem. State Crime Lab. Bd., 1992—, chmn. 1991-92; bd. dirs. First Comml. Nat. Bank, Ark. Children's Hosp. Rsch. Inst., Inc.; mem. Ark. Rice Depot Bd., 1988-94; mem. State Med. Examiner's Commn., 1986-90; med. bd. Univ. Hosp., 1986—; mem. chancellor's cabinet U. Ark. for Med. Scis., 1986—; chmn. U. Minn. Clin. Assocs., ad hoc com. for fin matters, 1986; vice chmn. U. Minn. Clin. Assocs., 1986, clin. assoc. exec. com., 1985; mem. univ. com. Univ. Press, 1985-86; clin. assoc. planning and mktg. com. U. Minn., 1985; mem. Hosp. Quality Assurance Steering com., 1984-96, chmn. hosp. utilization mgmt. com., 1985; mem. Univ. Bookstore com., 1985; mem. Univ. Senate, 1985-86; chmn. dept. medicine search com. for Dir. of Gen. Internal Medicine, 1985; chmn. med. sch. search com. head of dept. dermatology U. Minn., 1984, chmn. dept. medicine search com. for dir. pulmonary sect. 1984, mem. hosp. bd. govs. com. on planning and devel., 1983-86, med.=surg. hosp. facilities com., 1982-83, mem. steering com. of self-study task force U. of Minn. Med. Sch., 1982-83, many more coms. Contbr. numerous articles to profl. jours. Lt. USNR, 1963-65. Fellow ACP; mem. AMA, Am. Fedn. for Clin. Rsch., Am. Gastroenterol. Assn., Ctrl. Soc. for Clin. Rsch., Am. Assn. for the Study of Liver Disease, Ark. Med. Soc. (editl. bd. 1988-93, ex-officio mem., coun. 1987—), Pulaski County Med. Soc., Assn. of Am. Med. Colls. (coun. of deans, chair 1995-96, mgmt. edn. program planning com. 1993—, adv. panel on strategic positioning for health care reform 1992—, exec. coun. 1992—, adminstrv. bd. 1992—, DEANS-VA coordinating com. 1990-94, ad hoc com. on nursing svcs. and the tchg. hosp. 1989, adv. com. on medicare regulations for payment of physicians in tchg. hosps. 1989), So. Med. Phi Beta Kappa, Alpha Omega Alpha. Office: Univ Ark for Med Scis Mail Slot #550 4301 W Markham Little Rock AR 72205

WILSON, IAN EDWIN, cultural organization administrator, archivist; b. Montreal, Que., Can., Apr. 2, 1943; s. Andrew and Marion (Mundy) W.; m. Ruth Dyck, Mar. 24, 1979. BA, Queen's U., Kingston, Ont., 1968, MA History, 1974. Archivist Queen's U., Kingston, Ont., Can., 1966-76; provincial archivist Sask. (Can.) Archives, 1976-86; archivist of Ont. Ont. Govt., Toronto, 1986—; dir. gen. info. resource mgmt. divsn. Ministry Culture, Tourism and Recreation, Toronto, 1990-93; sec. Kingston Hist. Soc., 1967-72, v.p., 1972-76; chair cons. group Social Sci. and Humanities Rsch. Coun. Can., Ottawa, 1979-80; adj. prof. Faculty Info. Studies U. Toronto, 1993—; spkr. in field. Author: (with J. Douglas Stewart) Heritage Kingston, 1973; editor: Kingston City Hall, 1975; producer: (with J. William Brennan) Regina Before Yesterday, 1978; contbr. articles to profl. jours. Chmn. congregation Mennonite Ch., Regina, 1981-84; mem. Sask. award merit selection com., 1985-86; chair Sask. Heritage adv. bd., 1978-83, mem., 1983-86; Ont. dir. Forum for Young Canadians, 1995—. Recipient Queen Elizabeth II silver jubilee medal, 1977, W.G. Leland cert. commendation Soc. Am. Archivists, 1981, W. Kaye Lamb prize Assn. Can. Archivists, 1983; Woodrow Wilson hon. fellow, 1967. Mem. Assn. Can. Archivists (various coms., editl. bd. 1986-88), Ont. Hist. Soc. (exec. coun. 1970-73, v.p. 1973-75, pres. 1975-76), Can. Hist. Assn. (past chmn., vice chmn., pres. archives sect. 1972-74), Champlain Soc. (bd. dirs., v.p. 1989-95, pres. 1995—), Sask. Mus. Assn., Sask. History and Folkore Soc., Sask. Geneal. Soc., Soc. Hist. de Sask. (bd. dirs., spkr.). Home: 30 Holly St #604, Toronto, ON Canada M4S 3C2 Office: Archives of Ontario, 77 Grenville St, Toronto, ON Canada M7A 2R9

WILSON, IAN HOLROYDE, management consultant, futurist; b. Harrow, England, June 16, 1925; came to U.S., 1954; s. William Brash and Dorothy (Holroyde) W.; m. Page Tuttle Hedden, Mar. 17, 1951 (div. Dec. 1983); children: Rebecca, Dorothy, Ellen, Holly, Alexandra; m. Adrianne Marcus, July 12, 1992. MA, Oxford U., 1948. Orgn. cons. Imperial Chem. Industries, London, 1948-54; various staff exec. positions in strategic planning, mgmt. devel. Gen. Electric Co., Fairfield, Conn., 1954-80; sr. cons. to maj. U.S. and internat. cos. SRI Internat., Menlo Park, Calif., 1980-93; prin. Wolf Enterprises, San Rafael, Calif., 1993—; exec. in residence Va. Commonwealth U., Richmond, 1976. Author: Planning for Major Change, 1976, The Power of Strategic Vision, 1991, Rewriting the Corporate Social Charter, 1992, Managing Strategically in the 1990s, 1993, Executive Leadership, 1995; mem. editl. bd. Planning Rev., 1973-81; Am. editor Long Range Planning Jour., London, 1981-89; sr. editor Strategy and Leadership, 1993—. Mem. adv. bd. Technol. Forecasting and Social Change, 1989—; chmn. Citizen's Long Range Ednl. Goals Com., Westport, Conn., 1967-70; mem. strategic process com. United Way of Am., Alexandria, Va., 1985-94. Capt. Brit. Army, 1943-45, ETO. Mem. AAAS, Strategic Leadership Forum, World Future Soc. Unitarian. Avocations: camping, writing, photography. Office: 79 Twin Oaks Ave San Rafael CA 94901-1915

WILSON, IAN ROBERT, food company executive; b. Pietermaritzburg, South Africa, Sept. 22, 1929; s. Brian J. and Edna C. W.; m. Susan Diana Lasch, Jan. 14, 1970; children: Timothy Robert, Christopher James, Diana Louise, Jason Luke. B.Commerce, U. Natal, South Africa, 1952; postgrad., Harvard U. Bus. Sch., 1968. With Coca-Cola Export Corp., Johannesburg, South Africa, 1956-74; mgr. Coca-Cola Export Corp., 1969-72, v.p., regional mgr., 1972-73, area mgr., 1973; pres., chief exec. officer Coca-Cola Ltd., Toronto, Ont., Can., 1974-76; chmn. bd., dir. Coca-Cola Ltd., 1976-81; exec. v.p. Coca-Cola Co., Atlanta, 1976-79; vice chmn. Coca-Cola Co., 1979-81, pres. Pacific group; dir. Coca-Cola Export Corp., Atlanta, 1976-81; pres., chief exec. officer, dir. Castle & Cooke, Inc., San Francisco, 1983-84, Wyndham Foods, Inc., 1985-89; chmn. bd., chief exec. officer Windmill Corp., San Francisco, 1989-94; mng. ptnr. Dartford Partnership and Induna Ptnrs., San Francisco, 1993—; also bd. dirs. Dartford Partnership and Induna Ptnrs.; bd. dirs. Novell Inc., Golden State Foods, Inc., Egoli Ptnrs., New Age Beverages Ltd., U.S./Asean Coun., East-West Ctr.; chmn. bd. dirs. Windy Hill Pet Foods and Van de Kamp Inc. Mem. Church of Eng. Clubs: Durban Country and Johannesburg Country, Inanda Hunt and Polo, Atlantic Salmon, San Francisco Golf, Pacific Union, Burlingame Country. Home: 945 Green St San Francisco CA 94133-3639 Office: Dartford Partnership 801 Montgomery St Ste 400 San Francisco CA 94133-5164

WILSON, IRA LEE, middle school educator; b. Taylor, La., Dec. 20, 1927; d. Henry and Sadie Mae (Milbon) Parker; m. Odie D. Wilson, Jr., May 11, 1946; children: Ervin Charles, Annie Jo, Carrido Michelle. BS, Grambling State U., 1954; postgrad., Pepperdine U., 1974, Pepperdine U., 1976; MEd, La Verne Coll., 1976. Tchr. Willowbrook Sch. Dist., Los Angeles, 1955-67, Compton (Calif.) Unified Sch. Dist., 1968—; grade level chairperson Roosevelt Middle Sch. P.T.A., Compton, 1988—; corr. sec., 1988—, sch. site leadership resource team; mem. associated student body coun. advisor Roosevelt Middle Sch., 1993-95, mem. discipline com., 1994-95. Asst. sec. Los Angeles Police Dept. Sweethearts Area Club, Los Angeles, 1988-95; mem. planning activities com. L.A. Football Classic Found., 1989; chairperson higher edn. Travelers Rest Bapt. Ch., 1992—. Recipient Perfect Attendance award Compton Unified Sch. Dist., 1987-88, S.W. Area Sweethearts for Outstanding Svcs. Los Angeles Police Dept., 1988, Disting. Svc. award Compton Edn. Assn., 1987-88, 83, Cert. of Achievement Roosevelt Jr. High Sch., 1984-85, Perfect Attendance award Roosevelt Middle Sch., 1984, Cert. of Achievement Mayo Elem. Sch., 1973-74, Roosevelt Mid. Sch., 1989, Disting. Svc. award Compton Edn. Assn., 1987-88, Key of Success award Am. Biog. Inst., Inc., 1990. Mem. NEA, Calif. Tchr. Assn., Grambling State U. Alumni Assn. (life, asst. activity chairperson 1987—), Black Women's Forum, Block Club. Democrat. Baptist. Avocations: reading, horticulture, attending sports events. Home: 828 W 126th St Los Angeles CA 90044-3818

WILSON, J. PARRISH, religious organization administrator. Chmn. Education Bd. of the Nat. Baptist Convention, USA, Saginaw, Mich. Office: Education Bd 19 Commons West Ct Saginaw MI 48603

WILSON, J. STEVEN, lumber company executive; b. 1943. BS, U. N.C., 1966; MBA, Ga. State U., 1970. With First Nat. Bank, Atlanta, 1968-73; with The Charter Co., Inc., 1973-80; pres., chmn. CEO Riverside Group Inc., 1979—; pres. Wilson Fin. Co., 1980—; CEO Wickes Lumber, Vernon Hills, Ill., 1991—. Office: Wickes Lumber 706 N Deerpath Dr Vernon Hills IL 60061-1802*

WILSON, J. TYLEE, business executive; b. Teaneck, N.J., June 18, 1931; s. Eric J. and Florence Q. W.; m. Patricia F. Harrington, July 17, 1970; children: Jeffrey J., Debra L., Christopher F. A.B., Lafayette Coll., 1953. Group v.p., dir. Chesebrough-Pond's Inc., 1960-74; pres., chief exec. officer RJR Foods, Inc., 1974-76; chmn., chief exec. officer R.J. Reynolds Tobacco Internat. Inc., Winston-Salem, N.C., 1976-78; exec. v.p. RJR Nabisco, Inc. (formerly R.J. Reynolds Industries Co., Inc.), Winston-Salem, N.C., 1976-79; pres. RJR Nabisco, Inc., Winston-Salem, 1979-83; chmn., chief exec. officer RJR Nabisco, Inc. (formerly R.J. Reynolds Industries Inc.), Winston-Salem, 1984-87; bd. dirs. Bell South Corp., Carolina Power & Light Co. With U.S. Army, 1954-56. Mem. Piedmont Club, Old Town Club, Marsh Landing Country, Epping Forest Yacht Club, Ponte Vedra Club, Elk River Club. Office: PO Box 2057 Ponte Vedra Beach FL 32004-2057

WILSON, JACK, aeronautical engineer; b. Sheffield, Yorkshire, Eng., Jan. 5, 1933; came to U.S., 1956; s. George and Nellie (Place) W.; m. Marjorie Reynolds, June 3, 1961 (div. Jan. 1991); children: Tanya Ruth, Cara. BS in Engring., Imperial Coll., London, 1954; MS in Aero. Engring., Cornell U., 1958, PhD in Aero. Engring., 1962. Sr. scientific officer Royal Aircraft Establishment, Farnborough, Eng., 1962-63; prin. rsch. sci. Avco-Everett Rsch. Lab., Everett, Mass., 1963-72; vis. prof. Inst. de Mecanique des Fluides, Marseille, France, 1972-73; sr. scientist U. Rochester (N.Y.), 1973-80; sr. rsch. assoc. Sohio/BP Am., Cleve., 1980-90; sr. engring. specialist Sverdrup Tech. Inc., Cleve., 1990-93, NYMA, Brook Park, 1994—. Author: (chpt.) "Gas Lasers" of Applied Optics in Engineering VI, 1980, "Laser Sources" of Techniques in Chemistry XVII, 1982; contbr. articles to profl. jours. Mem. AIAA (sr., mem. tech. com. 1991-92). Achievements include first to demonstrate gas-dynamic laser; patent in application of high speed flow to gas laser media; patent in devel. of antimony dopant sources; measurement of air ionization rate at very high speeds. Office: NYMA 2001 Aerospace Pky Brookpark OH 44142-1002

WILSON, JACK FREDRICK, retired federal government official; b. Salt Lake City, Apr. 2, 1920; s. John Lorimer and Mayme J. (James) W.; m. Gwendolyn Gwynn, Nov. 20, 1947; children—Wendy, Elaine, Barbara Ann, Laurel, John F. Jr., James C. B.S., Brigham Young U., 1942; postgrad., Mont. State U., 1962, Pa. State U., 1965. Range conservationist Bur. Land Mgmt., Rawlins, Wyo., 1949-57; dist. mgr. Bur. Land Mgmt., Burley, Idaho, 1957-67; dist. and land office mgr. Bur. Land Mgmt., Riverside, Calif., 1967-72; dir. Boise Interagy. Fire Ctr., Idaho, 1972-81; dir. Office Aircraft Services U.S. Dept. Interior, Boise, 1981-87; dir. Boise Interagy. Fire Ctr., 1987-92; ret., 1992. Contbr. articles to profl. jours. Dir. county disaster com. ARC, 1982-88. Maj. USAF, 1942-47. Recipient Meritorious award U.S. Dept. Interior, 1976, Disting. Service award, 1981, EEO Performance award, 1985; Outstanding Contbn. to Fire Mgmt. award U.S. Dept. Agr. Forest Service, 1976. Mem. Soc. Am. Foresters (chmn. fire com. 1980-82), Am. Soc. Range Mgmt. (sec. pres. 1967), So. Calif. Assn. Foresters and Fire Wardens, Lions (sec. 1954-57), Rotary. Mem. Ch. of Jesus Christ of Latter-day Saints. Avocations: long range weather forecasting, genealogy, reading, golf. Home: 1820 Sunrise Rim Rd Boise ID 83705-5138

WILSON, JACK MARTIN, dean, scientific association executive, physics educator; b. Camp Atterbury, Ind., June 29, 1945; s. Jack Maurer and Ruth L. (Leiseder) W., m. Judi Chang, Aug. 18, 1990; children: John, Jessica; children from previous marriage: Erika, Gretchen. A.B., Thiel Coll., Greenville, Pa., 1967; M.A., Kent State U., 1970, Ph.D., 1972. Assoc. prof. physics Sam Houston State U., Huntsville, Tex., 1972-80; chmn. dept. physics Sam Houston State U., Huntsville, 1980-81, chmn. div. chemistry and physics, 1981-82; prof. physics U. Md., College Park, 1984-90, co-dir. univ. project in physics and ednl. tech.; dir. Anderson Ctr. for Innovation in Undergrad. Edn. Rensselaer Poly. Inst., Troy, N.Y., 1990-95, dean undergrad. and continuing edn., 1995—; mem. U.S. com. Internat. Union Pure and Applied Physics, Washington, 1984-90, IBM consulting scholar, 1992—; dir. U.S. team in Internat. Physics Olympia, 1985-90. Editor: Teacher Institutes and Workshops, 1984, The Education of the Physicist, 1985; also articles in field. Recipient Computers in Physics award Dept. Edn., Washington, 1985; Physics Teaching Resource Agents award NSF, 1985; Developing Student Confidence award Exxon Edn. Found., 1983; grantee various fed. agys. and pvt. founds. Mem. AAAS, Am. Assn. Physics Tchrs. (exec. officer 1982-90), Am. Phys. Soc. (edn. com. 1982—), Am. Inst. Physics (governing bd. 1984-91), Am. Soc. for Engring. Edn. (Theodore Hesburgh award 1995, Boeing Outstanding Engring. Educator award 1995), Sigma Xi (del., rsch. award 1972). Office: Rensselaer Poly Inst Undergrad & Continuing Edn 212 Pittsburgh Bldg Troy NY 12180

WILSON, JAMES ERNEST, petroleum consultant, writer; b. McKinney, Tex., Apr. 19, 1915; s. James Ernest and Agnes (Neill) W.; m. Elloie Barkely, Apr. 4, 1940; children: Judith Wilson Grant, Elizabeth Wilson. BS, Tex. A&M U., 1937. Surface geologist Shell Oil Co., Tex., 1938-41, various positions, 1945-59, v.p., Houston, New Orleans and Denver, 1959-73; cons., Denver, 1973—. Trustee and chmn. Am. Assn. Petroleum Geologists Found., 1975-79; trustee children's Hosp. Denver, 1970-83, Denver Symphony, 1968-82, Inst. Internat. Edn., Denver, 1968-82; mem. bd. University Park Meth. Ch., 1968—. Maj. U.S. Army, 1941-45; ETO. Recipient Geosciences and Earth Resources medal Tex. A&M, 1986, Disting. Alumnus, 1991. Fellow Geol. Soc. Am., Soc. Petroleum Engrs., Am. Assn. Petroleum Geologists (hon., recipient Sidney Powers Meml. medal, 1988). Republican. Methodist. Clubs: Cherry Hill Country (Denver); Confrerie des Chevaliers du Tastevin (pres. 1983-93, grand officier honoraire). Home: 4248 S Hudson Pky Englewood CO 80110-5015

WILSON, JAMES HARGROVE, JR., lawyer; b. Oliver, Ga., Nov. 26, 1920; s. James Hargrove and Louise (Sealy) W.; m. Frances Audra Schaffer, Dec. 24, 1942 (dec. Nov. 1990); children: Susan Frances, James Hargrove. A.B. with honors, Emory U., 1940; LL.B. summa cum laude, Harvard U., 1947. Bar: Ga. 1947, D.C. 1951. Assoc. firm Sutherland, Tuttle & Brennan (now Sutherland, Asbill & Brennan), Atlanta and Washington, 1947-53, ptnr., 1953—; lectr. Emory U., 1959, chmn. bd. visitors, 1967-68; trustee The Northwestern Mut. Life Ins. Co., Milw., 1972-91; mem. advisory group Commr. of Internal Revenue, 1963-64. Pres.: Harvard Law Review, 1946-47. Chmn. bd. trustees Met. Atlanta Crime Commn., 1970-71; mem. Harvard U. Overseers Com. to Visit Law Sch., 1959-65; trustee Emory U., 1983-90, trustee emeritus, 1990—. Served to lt. comdr. USNR, 1942-46. Fellow Am. Bar Found., Am. Coll. Tax Counsel; mem. ABA, State Bar Ga., D.C. Bar, Atlanta Bar Assn., Am. Law Inst. (coun. 1974—), Lawyers Club Atlanta (pres. 1960-61), Am. Judicature Soc., Harvard Law Sch. Assn. (coun. 1981-85), Emory U. Alumni Assn. (pres. 1966-67), Capital City Club, Piedmont Driving Club, Commerce Club, Peachtree Club, Phi Beta Kappa, Omicron Delta Kappa, Kappa Alpha. Methodist. Home: 3171 Marne Dr NW Atlanta GA 30305-1931 Office: Sutherland Asbill & Brennan 999 Peachtree St NE Ste 2300 Atlanta GA 30309-3964

WILSON, JAMES L., superintendent. Supt. Cape Henlopen Sch. Dist., Lewes, Del. Recipient State Finalist for Nat. Supt. of Yr. award, 1992. Office: Cape Henlopen Sch Dist Adminstrv Office 1270 Kings Hwy Lewes DE 19958-1735

WILSON, JAMES LAWRENCE, chemical company executive; b. Rosedale, Miss., Mar. 2, 1936; s. James Lawrence and Mary Margaret (Klingman) W.; m. Barbara Louise Burroughs, Aug. 30, 1958; children: Lawrence Burroughs, Alexander Elliott. B.Mech. Engring., Vanderbilt U., 1958; M.B.A., Harvard, 1963. Vice pres. Nyala Properties, Inc., Phila., 1963-65; staff assoc. Rohm & Haas Co., Phila., 1965-67; exec. asst. to pres. Rohm & Haas Co., 1971-72, treas., 1972-74; regional dir. Rohm & Haas Co., Europe, 1974-77; group v.p. Rohm & Haas Co., 1977-86, vice-chmn., 1986-88, chmn., CEO, 1988—; treas. Warren-Teed Pharms., Inc., Columbus, Ohio, 1967-68, v.p., 1969; pres. Consol. Biomed. Labs., Inc., Dublin, Ohio, 1970-71; bd. dirs. Rohm and Haas Co., Vanguard Group Investment Cos., Cummins Engine Co., Inc. Co-author: Creative Collective Bargaining, 1964. Trustee Vanderbilt U., 1987—, Culver Ednl. Found., 1988—; chmn. Phila. High Sch. Acads., 1989—. Mem. Chem. Mfrs. Assn. (bd. dirs. 1988—, chmn. 1996). Office: Rohm & Haas Co 100 Independence Mall W Philadelphia PA 19106

WILSON, JAMES LEE, retired geology educator, consultant; b. Waxahachie, Tex., Dec. 1, 1920; s. James Burney and Hallie Christine (Hawkins) W.; m. Della I. Moore, May 8, 1944; children: James Lee Jr., Burney Grant, Dale Ross (dec.). Student, Rice U., 1938-40; BA, U. Tex., 1942, MA, 1944; PhD, Yale U., 1949. Geologist Carter Oil Co., Tulsa, 1943-44; asst. and assoc. prof. U. Tex., Austin, 1949-52; rsch. geologist Shell Devel. Co., Houston, 1952-66; prof. Rice U., Houston, 1966-79, U. Mich., Ann Arbor, 1979-86; geol. cons. New Braunfels, Tex., 1986—; cons. Erico Corp., London, 1985-88, Masera Corp., Tulsa, 1988—, Coyote Geol. Svcs., Boulder, Col., 1990—; adj. prof. Rice U., 1986—. Author: Carbonate Facies in Geologic History, 1975; contbr. articles to tech. jours. With C.E., U.S. Army, 1944-46, Italy. Grantee NSF. Mem. Am. Assn. Petroleum Geologists (hon., Disting. Educator award), Internat. Sedimentological Soc., Soc. Econ. Paleontology and Minerology (pres. 1972-73, field trip guide books 1989), Paleontological Soc., West Tex. Geol. Soc., South Tex. Geol. Soc., Can. Soc. Petroleum Geologists. Avocations: piano, languages. Home and Office: 1316 Patio Dr New Braunfels TX 78130-8505

WILSON, JAMES MONROE, computer science educator; b. Knoxville, Tenn., Mar. 27, 1941; s. Jesse James Wilson and Ada Louise Hendrix Cone; m. Margaret Irene Vesely, Nov. 21, 1992. AAS in Instr. Tech., C.C. of Air Force, 1977; BS in Occupl. Edn., So. Ill. U., 1977; MA in Mgmt. and Human Rels., Webster U., St. Louis, 1978; PhD in Mgmt. Info. Sys., Kennedy Western U., Boise, Idaho, 1994. Cert. master instr. USAF. Dir. safety and security Meml. Hosp., Belleville, Ill., 1980-81; engring. recruiter Kendall & Davis, St. Louis, 1981-82; mgr./trainer Bankers Life & Casualty Co., Chgo., 1982-87; sys. analyst/instr. SIMA, St. Louis, 1987-93; course designer/instr. Saudi Aramco, Dhahran, Saudi Arabia, 1993-94; dir. computer programming Vatterott Coll., St. Ann, Mo., 1994—; adj. prof. computer sci. McKendre Coll., Lebanon, Ill., 1991—; edn./MIS cons. Wilson & Assocs., St. Louis, 1989—; evening prof. computer sci. Lewis & Clark C.C., Godfrey, Ill., 1989-92; adj. prof. Tarkio Coll., St. Louis, 1988-90; adult edn. instr. Parkway Sch. Dist., St. Louis, 1994; lectr. in field. Contbr. articles to profl. jours. Vice pres. Carmelwoods Homeowners Assn., Ellisville, Mo., 1994. Master sgt. USAF, 1960-80. Decorated Air Force Commendation medal (2). Mem. ACM, Am. Soc. for Human Resource Mgmt., Soc. Am. Mil. Engrs., Am. Legion, Toastmasters (1st place award humorous speech contest 1993). Republican. Baptist. Avocations: travel, building wooden model ships, bowling, theater, public speaking. Home: PO Box 6052 Chesterfield MO 63006-6052 Office: Wilson & Assocs PO Box 6052 Chesterfield MO 63006-6052

WILSON, JAMES QUINN, government, management educator; married; 2 children. Henry Lee Shattuck prof. govt. Harvard U., 1961-86; now James Collins prof. mgmt., UCLA; bd. dirs. Am. Enterprise Inst., New Eng. Electric Sys., Rand Corp., State Farm Ins. Author: Negro Politics, 1960, Political Organizations, 1961, Varieties of Police Behavior, 1968, The Amateur Democrat, 1973, The Investigators, 1978, Thinking About Crime, 1983; (with R.J. Herrnstein) Crime and Human Nature, 1985, (with Roberta Wilson) Watching Fishes, 1985; Bureaucracy: What Government Agencies Do and Why They Do It., 1989, American Government: Institutions and Policies, 1991, The Moral Sense, 1993, On Character, 1994. Former chmn. Nat. Adv. Coun. for Drug Abuse Prevention, Police Found.; former mem. com. on rsch. on law enforcement and the adminstrn. of justice NRC, Pres.'s Fgn. Intelligence Adv. Bd.; former mem. U.S. Atty. Gen.'s Task Force on Violent Crime; former mem. Commn. on Presdl. Scholars, Sloan Commn. on Cable Comms.; former dir. Joint Ctr. for Urban Studies MIT and Harvard. Fellow Am. Acad. Arts and Scis.; mem. Am. Philos. Soc., Am. Polit. Sci. Assn. (pres., James Madison award). Office: UCLA Grad Sch Mgmt 405 Hilgard Ave Los Angeles CA 90024-1301

WILSON, JAMES RAY, international business educator; b. Hamilton, Ohio, Mar. 7, 1930; s. Ray Crawford and Ruth Lee (Walthers) W.; B.A. (U.S. Navy Coll. Tng. Program scholar), Miami U., Oxford, Ohio, 1952, postgrad., 1967-68; M.A., Ohio State U., 1956; Ph.D., U. Minn., 1984; m. Carolyn Dempsey, Feb. 1, 1952; children—Robin E., Victoria, Mark, Jamie. Grad. asst. Ohio State U., 1955-56; grain mcht. Cargill Inc., Balt., 1956-58; pres. Granexport Corp., Manila, Philippines, 1959-66; mng. dir. Tradax Graanhandel B.V., Amsterdam, 1966-67; instr. in geography Miami U., 1967-68; pres. Cargill Agricola S.A., Sao Paulo, Brazil, 1968-78; dir. indsl. div. Tradax Geneve S.A., Geneva, 1978-80; corp. v.p. Cargill Inc., Mpls., 1980-83; pres. Cargill Southeast Asia, Ltd., Singapore, 1984-88; internat. bus. prof. Miami U., Oxford, Ohio, 1988-92, prof. mgmt. dept., 1994-95; chmn. Cargill Tech. Svcs., Ltd., Thame, Eng., 1992-94. Served with USN, 1952-55. Fellow Royal Geog. Soc.; mem. Assn. Am. Geographers. Congregationalist. Home: 6533 Buckley Rd Oxford OH 45056-9727

WILSON, JAMES RIGG, aircraft manufacturing company executive; b. 1941. BA, Coll. Wooster, 1963; MBA, Harvard U., 1965. V.p. Textron, Providence, 1967-76; with Fairchild Industries Inc., Chantilly, Va., 1977-80, 82-87, chief fin. officer, 1977—, v.p., 1977-80, sr. v.p., 1982-85, exec. v.p., 1985—; chief fin. officer, sr. v.p. Wickes Cos., San Diego, 1980-82; exec. v.p., CFO Thiokol Corp., Ogden, Utah, 1989-93, pres., CEO, 1993—. Office: Thiokol Corp 2475 Washington Blvd Ogden UT 84401-2300*

WILSON, JAMES ROBERT, lawyer; b. Meade, Kans., Dec. 3, 1927; s. Robert J. and Bess O. (Osborne) W.; m. Marguerite Jean Reiter, Nov. 27, 1960; 1 son, John Ramsey. B.A., Kans. U., 1950, LL.B., 1953. Bar: Kans. 1953, Nebr. 1961, Colo. 1981. Pvt. practice Meade, Kans., 1953-57, Lakewood, Colo., 1989-93; county atty. Meade County, 1954-57; city atty. Meade, 1954-57; asst. gen. counsel Kans. Corp. Commn., 1957-59, gen. counsel, 1959-61, mem., 1961; atty. KN Energy, Inc., 1961-75, personnel dir., 1964-67, v.p., treas., 1968-75, exec. v.p., 1975-78, pres., chief operating officer, 1978-82, pres., chief exec. officer, 1982-85, chmn., pres., chief exec. officer, 1985-88, chmn., 1988-89; bd. dirs. Alliance Ins. Cos. With USNR, 1945-46. Mem. Phi Kappa Sigma. Home: 1725 Foothills Dr S Golden CO 80401-9167

WILSON, JAMES WILLIAM, lawyer; b. Spartanburg, S.C., June 19, 1928; s. James William and Ruth (Greenwaldt) W.; m. Elizabeth Clair Pickett, May 23, 1952; children: Susan Alexandra Wilson Albright, James William. Student, Tulane U., 1945-46; BA, U. Tex., Austin, 1950, LLB, 1951. Bar: Tex. 1951. Practiced in Austin, 1951-79; ptnr. McGinnis, Lochridge & Kilgore (and predecessors), 1960-76; of counsel Stubbeman, McRae, Sealy, Laughlin & Browder, 1976-79; sr. v.p. and gen. counsel Brown & Root, Inc., Houston, 1980-93, also dir.; of counsel Sewell & Riggs, Houston, 1993-95; asst. atty. gen., 1957-58; legis. asst. to senate majority leader Lyndon B. Johnson, 1959-60; adj. prof. U. tex. Law Sch., 1962-63, 95-96. Lt. (j.g.) USNR, 1952-55. Fellow Tex. Bar Found., Houston Bar Found.; mem. ABA, Tex. Bar Assn., Am. Law Inst., Order of Coif, Phi Beta Kappa. Home: 3412 Timberwood Cir Austin TX 78703-1013

WILSON, JANE, artist; b. Seymour, Iowa, Apr. 29, 1924; d. Wayne and Cleone (Marquis) W.; m. John Gruen, Mar. 28, 1948; 1 child, Julia. BA, U. Iowa, 1945, MA, 1947. Mem. fine arts faculty Parsons Sch. Design, 1973-83, 89-90; vis. artist U. Iowa, 1974; adj. assoc. prof. painting and drawing Columbia U., 1975-85, assoc. prof., 1985-86, prof., 1986-88, acting chair, 1986-88; Andrew Mellon vis. prof. painting Cooper Union, 1977-78. One-woman shows include Hansa Gallery, N.Y.C., 1953, 55, 57, Stuttman Gallery, N.Y.C., 1958, 59, Tibor de Nagy Gallery, N.Y.C., annually, 1960-66, Graham Gallery, N.Y.C., 1968, 69, 71, 73, 75, Fischbach Gallery, N.Y.C., 1978, 81, 84, 88, 90, 91, 93, 95, Munson-Williams-Proctor Inst., Utica, N.Y., 1980, Cornell U., Ithaca, N.Y., 1982, Compass Rose Gallery, Chgo., 1988, Am. U., Washington, 1989, U. Richmond, Va., 1990, Earl McGrath Gallery, L.A., 1990-91, 93, Dartmouth Coll., Hanover, N.H., 1991, Arnot Mus., Elmira, N.Y., 1993-94, Parish Mus., Southampton, N.Y., 1996, Glenn Horowitz Gallery, East Hampton, N.Y., 1996; represented in permanent collections Met. Mus., Mus. Modern Art, Whitney Mus., Wadsworth Atheneum, Heron Art Mus., NYU Rockefeller Inst., Vassar Coll., Pa. Acad. Fine Arts, Hirschorn Mus., Washington, Nelson-Atkins Mus., Kansas City, Mo., San Francisco Mus. Modern Art. Recipient Purchase prize Childe Hassam Fund, 1971, 73, Ranger Fund Purchase prize 1977; Ingram-Merrill grantee, 1963, Louis Comfort Tiffany grantee, 1967, Eloise Spaeth award The Guild Hall, East Hampton, N.Y., 1988. Mem. Am. Acad. Arts and Letters (treas. 1992-95, Award in Art 1981), Nat. Acad. Design (pres. 1992-94), Phi Beta Kappa.

WILSON, JANIE MENCHACA, nursing educator, researcher; b. Lytle, Tex., Mar. 15, 1936; m. Patrick W. Wilson; 1 child, Kathryn Lynn Kohlleppel. BSN, Incarnate Word Coll., San Antonio, 1958; MSN, U. Tex., San Antonio, 1973; PhD in Nursing, U. Tex., Austin, 1978. RN. Oper. rm. nurse Santa Rosa Hosp., San Antonio, 1958-59; instr. Brackenridge Hosp. Sch. Nursing, Austin, 1963-66; staff nurse Med. Coll. Ga., Augusta, 1967-68; instr. dept. nursing San Antonio Coll., 1968-72, prof. dept. nursing edn., 1976—; counselor Project GAIN Tex. Nurses Assn., Austin, 1973-76; rsch. assoc. Ctr. for Health Care Rsch. and Evaluation, U. Tex. System, Austin, 1974-75; cons. Nurse Aide Competency Evaluation Program, San Antonio, 1989—; mem. manuscript rev. panel Nursing Rsch., N.Y.C., 1989-91. Contbr. chpts. to books, articles to profl. jours. Bd. dirs. Ctr. for Health Policy Devel., San Antonio, 1988-92; mem. Nat. Adv. Coun. on Nurse Edn. and Practice, 1995—. 1st lt. USAF, 1960-63. Mem. AAUP, ANA (coun. nurse rschrs., coun. cultural diversity, fellow program for ethnic minorities 1975-77), Am. Acad. Nursing, Nat. League Nursing, Nat. Assn. Hispanic Nurses, Sigma Theta Tau. Roman Catholic. Avocations: music, reading, fishing, dancing, sewing. Home: 4126 Longvale Dr San Antonio TX 78217-3525 Office: San Antonio Coll 1300 San Pedro Ave San Antonio TX 78212-4201

WILSON, JEAN DONALD, endocrinologist, educator; b. Wellington, Tex., Aug. 26, 1932; s. J.D. and Maggie E. (Hill) W. BA in Chemistry, U. Tex., 1951, MD, 1955. Diplomate: Am. Bd. Internal Medicine. Intern, then resident in internal medicine Parkland Meml. Hosp., Dallas, 1955-58; clin. assoc. Nat. Heart Inst., Bethesda, Md., 1958-60; instr. internal medicine U. Tex. Southwestern Med. Sch., Dallas, 1960-61; prof. U. Tex. Southwestern Med. Sch., 1968—. Editor: Jour. Clin. Investigation, 1972-77. Served as sr. asst. surgeon USPHS, 1958-60. Recipient Amory prize Am. Acad. Arts and Scis., 1977, Fuller prize Am. Urol. Assn., 1983, Lita Annenberg Hazen award, 1986, Dale medal Soc. for Endocrinology, 1991, Pincus medal Worchester Found., 1992. Fellow Royal Coll. Physicians; mem. NAS, Am. Acad. Arts and Scis., Inst. Medicine, Am. Fedn. Clin. Rsch., Am. Soc. Clin. Investigation, Assn. Am. Physicians, Soc. Exptl. Biology and Medicine, Am. Soc. Biochemistry and Molecular Biology, Endocrine Soc. (Oppenheimer award 1972, Koch award 1993). Office: U Tex Southwestern Med Ctr Dept Internal Medicine 5323 Harry Hines Blvd Dallas TX 75235-8857

WILSON, JIM, Canadian provincial official; b. Alliston, Ont., Can., 1963. Grad., U. Toronto. Constituency asst. to former chair Mgmt. Bd. of Cabinet, Mem. Parliament; spl. asst. Local MP; mem. Ont. Legislature, 1990—; min. of health Province of Ont., 1995—. Conservative. Office: Hepburn Block, Queen's Park 8th Fl, Toronto, ON Canada M7A 2C4*

WILSON, JIMMY, computer service company executive. CFO Fisery Basis, Inc., Atlanta, 1990—. *

WILSON, JOHN, artist; b. Boston, Apr. 14, 1922; s. Reginald and Violet (Caesar) W.; m. Julia Kowitch, June 25, 1950; children—Rebecca, Roy, Erica. Diploma with highest honors, Boston Mus. Sch. (Paige fellow for European study), 1944; B.S. in Edn, Tufts U., 1947; student, Fernand Leger's Sch., Paris, France, 1948-49; student (John Hay Whitney fellow), Esmeralda Sch. of Art, Mex. Instr. Boston Mus. Sch., 1949-50, Bd. Edn., N.Y.C., 1959-64; prof. Boston U., 1964-86, prof. emeritus, 1986—. Exhibited at, Atlanta U., Smith Coll., Carnegie Inst. Annual Art Show, Library of Congress Print Nationals, Mus. Modern Art, at N.Y.C. Met. Mus. Art, N.Y.C., Rose Art Mus., Brandeis U., Detroit Inst. Arts, Mus. Fine Arts, Boston; represented in permanent collections, Boston Pub. Library, Smith Coll., Mus. Modern Art, Atlanta U., Carnegie Inst., Bezalel Mus., Jerusalem, Rose Art Mus., Brandeis U., Howard U., Tufts U., Dept. Fine Arts, French govt., Mus. Nat. Ctr. Afro-Am. Artists, Boston; winner competitions for monument, Statue of Martin Luther King, Jr., Buffalo, 1983, U.S. Capitol, Washington, 1986, monument, Roxbury Community Coll., Boston, 1985. Illustrator: children's books Spring Comes to the Ocean (Jean Craighead George), 1965, Becky (Julia Wilson), 1970, Striped Ice Cream (Joan Lexau), 1968, Malcolm X (Arnold Adoff), 1970. Bd. dirs. Elma Lewis Sch. Fine Arts, Boston, 1970-75. Sculpture fellow Mass. Arts and Humanities Found., 1976. Home: 44 Harris St Brookline MA 02146-4933

WILSON, JOHN ABRAHAM ROSS, academic administrator; b. Trout Lake, B.C., Can., Aug. 25, 1911; s. Henry and Grace Ellen (Ross) W.; m. Nora Margaret (Mains) June 28, 1940; children: John Richard Meredith, Douglas Gordon. BA, U. B.C., 1932, MA, 1939; EdD, Oreg. State U., 1951; LLD with honors, U. Santa Barbara, 1979. Tchr., counselor various schs., B.C., 1934-51; prof. U. Calif., Santa Barbara, 1951-79; prof., adminstr. U. Santa Barbara, 1979—; chmn. bd. Acoustic Mktg. of Can. Ltd., Vancouver, Can., 1979—. Author: (with others) Psychological Foundation of Learning and Teaching, 1969, Kind Evaluation of Learning Potential, 2d edit. 1967, Psychology of Reading, 1974; editor; Diagnosis of Learning Difficulties, 1971. Mem. Calif. Ednl. Research Assn. (pres. 1968-69), Nat. Edn. Assn., Nat. Assn. for Study Edn., Phi Delta Kappa. Club: Cosmopolitan (Santa Barbara). Home: 2550 Treasure Dr # H1 Santa Barbara CA 93105-4148

WILSON, JOHN D., retired academic administrator; b. Lapeer, Mich., Aug. 17, 1931; s. Myron John and Helen (O'Conner) W.; m. Anne Veronica Yeomans, Sept. 21, 1957; children: Stephen, Anthony, Patrick, Sara. BA, Mich. State U., 1953, PhD, 1965; BA with honors, Oxford (Eng.) U., 1955, MA with honors, 1955. Asst. to v.p. acad. affairs Mich. State U., East Lansing, 1958-59, assoc. dir. Honors Coll., 1963-65, dir. Honors Coll., 1965-67, dir. undergrad. edn., 1967-68; asst. to pres. SUNY, 1959-63; pres. Wells Coll., Aurora, N.Y., 1969-75; v.p. acad. affairs Va. Poly. Inst. and State U., Blacksburg, 1975-83, univ. provost, 1976-83; pres. Washington and Lee U., Lexington, Va., 1983-95. Served with USAF, 1955-57. Mem. Assn. Am. Rhodes Scholars, Phi Beta Kappa, Phi Kappa Phi. Home: 2 University Pl Lexington VA 24450-2114

WILSON, JOHN DONALD, banker, economist; b. McKeesport, Pa., Feb. 8, 1913; s. John Johnston and Katherine A. (Hollerman) W.; m. Myriam Rohr, Mar. 10, 1942 (div. Feb. 18, 1950); 1 dau., Nina Marie; m. Danesi Matthews Hilton, Nov. 3, 1951; children: John Douglas, David Matthews, Mary Danesi. B.A. magna cum laude, U. Colo., 1935; M.A. in Econs. (Braker teaching fellow), Tufts Coll., 1937; M.A. in Econs., Harvard U., 1940. Instr. econs. Harvard U., 1937-40; editor Survey of Current Bus., U.S. Dept. Commerce, 1940-42; economist Editor and Publisher McGraw-Hill Pub. Co., 1946-50; established McGraw-Hill Am. Letter; mem. research and devel. staff N.Y. Life Ins. Co., 1950-51; v.p. charge ops. Inst. Internat. Edn., 1951-53; with Chase Manhattan Bank, 1953-81, successively bus. cons., v.p. and dir. econ. research, group exec. econ. research, pub. relations and market research, 1961-63, sr. v.p., dir. bank's corp. plans, 1963-69, sr. v.p., dir. econ. group, 1969-72, sr. v.p., chief economist, dir. econs., 1972-81, econ. cons., 1981-84; cons. U.S. Govt. Intelligence Svcs., 1984-92; dir. Chase Econometric Assos., 1971-81, chmn., 1971-75. Author: The Chase—The Chase Manhattan Bank, N.A., 1945-1985, 1986. Bd. dirs. United Neighborhood Houses, N.Y.C., 1955-68; treas., organizing trustee Found. Libr. Ctr., 1956-63; dir. Associated Alumni U. Colo., 1959-63; trustee Inst. Internat. Edn., N.Y.C., 1964-85. Lt. (j.g.) USNR, 1943-46, OSS. Mem. Council Fgn. Relations, Internat. C. of C. (exec. com. U.S. council internat. bus. 1969—, sr. trustee), Am. Econ. Assn., Am. Statis. Assn., Phi Beta Kappa, Sigma Chi. Presbyn. Club: Harvard (N.Y.C.), Field (Bronxville, N.Y.). Home: 6 Sunset Ave Bronxville NY 10708

WILSON, JOHN DOUGLAS, economics educator; b. Bronxville, N.Y., Sept. 30, 1952; s. John Donald and Danesi (Hilton) W.; m. Patricia Furlong, July 19, 1986; 1 child, Elizabeth Danesi. AB magna cum laude, Brown U., 1975; PhD, MIT, 1979. Asst. prof. Columbia U., N.Y.C., 1979-84; assoc. prof. Ind. U., Bloomington, 1985-90, prof., 1990—, chair econs. dept., 1992—; vis. asst. prof. U. Wis., Madison, 1984-85. Co-editor: Income Taxation and International Personal Mobility, 1989; mem. editorial bd. Jour. Urban Econs., 1991—; assoc. editor Econs. & Politics, 1990—; co-editor Jour. Internat. Econs., 1992-95; mem. bd. editors Am. Econ. Rev., 1989-94; contbr. articles to profl. jours. NSF Rsch. grantee, 1993-94. Mem. Phi Beta Kappa. Presbyterian. Avocation: running. Office: Ind U Econs Dept Wylie Hall Bloomington IN 47405

WILSON, JOHN ERIC, biochemistry educator; b. Champaign, Ill., Dec. 13, 1919; s. William Courtney and Marie Winette (Lytle) W.; m. Marion Ruth Heaton, June 7, 1947; children—Kenneth Heaton, Douglas Courtney, Richard Mosher. S.B., U. Chgo., 1941; M.S., U. Ill., Urbana, 1944; Ph.D., Cornell U., 1948. Research asst. Pyroxylin Products, Inc., Chgo., summers 1941-42, Gen. Foods Corp., Hoboken, N.J., summer, 1943; asst. in chemistry U. Ill., 1941-44; asst. in biochemistry Cornell U. Med. Coll., N.Y.C., 1944-48, research asso., 1948-50; asst. prof. biochemistry U. N.C., Chapel Hill, 1950-60, asso. prof., 1960-65, prof., 1965-90, prof. emeritus, 1990—, dir. grad. studies, dept. biochemistry, 1965-71, acting dir. neurobiology program, 1968-69, asso. dir., 1969-72, dir., 1972-73; Kenan prof. U. Utrecht, Netherlands, 1978. Mem. editl. bd. Jour. Neurochemistry, 1987-94; contbr. numerous articles on biochemistry and neurochemistry to profl. publs. Scoutmaster Occoneechee council Boy Scouts Am., 1959-66; mem. Chapel Hill Twp. Adv. Council, 1978-85, Orange County (N.C.) Planning Bd., 1979-85. Fellow AAAS; mem. Am. Chem. Soc., Am. Soc. for Biochemistry and Molecular Biology, Am. Soc. Neurochemistry, N.C. Acad. Sci., Internat. Soc. for Neurochemistry, Internat. Brain Rsch. Orgn., Soc. Neurosci. (coun. 1969-70, chmn. fin. com. 1973-78, organizer and mem. exec. com. N.C. chpt. 1974-75), Harvey Soc., Sigma Xi, Phi Lambda Upsilon, Alpha Chi Sigma, Beta Theta Pi. Home: 214 Spring Ln Chapel Hill NC 27514-3540 Office: U NC Sch Medicine Dept Biochemistry Chapel Hill NC 27599-7260

WILSON, JOHN FRANCIS, educational administrator; b. Springfield, Mo., Nov. 4, 1937; s. Frederick Marion and Jesse Ferrel (Latimer) W.; m. L. Claudette Faulk, June 9, 1961; children: Laura, Amy, Emily. BA, Harding U., Searcy, Ark., 1959; MA, Harding U., Memphis, 1961; PhD, U. Iowa, 1967. Dir. Christian Student Ctr., Springfield, 1959-73; prof. religious studies S.W. Mo. State U., Springfield, 1961-83; prof. of religion, dean Seaver Coll. Arts, Letters and Scis. Pepperdine U., Malibu, Calif., 1983—. Author: Religion: A Preface, 1982, 2d edit., 1989; co-author: Discovering the Bible, 1986, Excavations at Capernaum, 1989; contbr. articles, revs. to profl. publs. Mem. Archaeol. Inst. Am., Am. Schs. of Oriental Rsch., Soc. Bib. Lit., Am. Numismatic Soc., Am. Coun. Acad. Deans. Mem. Ch. of Christ. Office: Pepperdine U Seaver Coll 24255 Pacific Coast Hwy Malibu CA 90263-0001

WILSON, JOHN GROVER, securities trader; b. Chattanooga, June 7, 1945; s. Minos Fletcher and Marguerite (Church) W.; m. Michele Harbrook, Apr. 12, 1946; children: Christopher J., Brooke E., Ashley R.; stepchildren: Bradley B. Lance, Meredith B. Lance. BS, U. Tenn., 1967; MPA, U. No. Colo., 1977. Registered rep. and reg. investment advisor. Commd. 2d lt. USAFR, 1968; advanced through grades to lt. col. USAF, resigned, 1977; broker Merrill Lynch Pierce Fenner and Smith, Knoxville, Tenn., 1977-78; broker, v.p., mem. Pacesetter coun. PaineWebber, Knoxville, 1978-82; 1st v.p., broker, mem. chmn.'s coun. Shearson Lehman, Knoxville, 1982-88; sr. v.p. investments, mem. Pres.'s Coun. Prudential Securities, Inc., Knoxville, 1988—. Pres. bd. dirs. Knoxville Cerebral Palsy Ctr., 1984-88; scoutmaster handicapped troop Boy Scouts Am., Knoxville, 1979-84. With USAFR, 1977-93, lt. col. ret. Decorated D.F.C., Air medal with 1 oak leaf cluster. Mem. Sigma Phi Epsilon. Republican. Methodist. Home: 501 Augusta National Way Knoxville TN 37922-1534 Office: Prudential Securities Inc Plaza Tower 800 S Gay St Ste 2605 Knoxville TN 37929-9701

WILSON, JOHN I., accounting firm executive; b. 1945. BS in Acctg., U. Balt., 1967. CPA, Md.; CFP. Pvt. practice CPA Balt., 1967-71; with C.W. Amos & Co., 1971—, audit mem., 1978—, pntr., mng. mem., 1978—; mem. adv. bd. acctg. dept. U. Balt. Bd. dirs. League: Serving People with Phys. Disabilities. Mem. AICPA (adv. group B), Md. Assn. CPA's (quality rev. com.), Balt. City C. of C. (bd. dirs.). Office: C W Amos & Co 2 N Charles St Baltimore MD 21201-3754 Office: 2 N Charles St Baltimore MD 21201*

WILSON, JOHN LEWIS, university official; b. Columbus, Ohio, Mar. 18, 1943; s. John Robert and Betty Marie (Barker) W.; m. Linda Patricia Kiernan, Apr. 23, 1966; 1 child, Heidi Annette. BA in Internat. Rels., Am. U., 1963, MA in Econs., 1973, PhD, 1977. Staff asst. Congressman Paul N. McCloskey, Washington, 1968-72; sr. assoc. Govt. Affairs Inst., Washington, 1973-77; pres. Experience Devel., Inc., Tucson, 1978-85; from asst. to assoc. dean faculty sci. U. Ariz., Tucson, 1985-93, acting asst. to sr. v.p. adminstrn. and fin., 1988-89, dir. decision and planning support, 1994—; instr. U. Phoenix, Tucson, 1980-83. Author: (with others) Managing Planned Agricultural Development, 1976. 1st lt. U.S. Army, Vietnam, 1964-68. Decorated Bronze Star with oak leaf cluster and V device. Mem. Am. Econ. Assn., Am. Soc. Quality Control, Assn. for Instnl. Rsch., Tucson Met. C. of C. Democrat. Avocations: walking, computers, reading, bicycle racing. Home: 8030 E Garland Rd Tucson AZ 85750-2830 Office: U Ariz Administration 116 Tucson AZ 85721

WILSON, JOHN OLIVER, economist, educator, banker; b. St. James, Mo., May 22, 1938; s. John Riffie and Jacquetta Ruth (Linck) W.; B.A. in Math., Northwestern U., 1960; Ph.D. in Econs., U. Mich., 1967; m. Beclee Newcomer, Jan. 28, 1961; children—Beth Anne, Benjamin Duncan. Asst. prof. Yale U., 1967-70; asst. dir. Office Econ. Opportunity, Washington, 1969-71; asst. sec. HEW, 1972; dir. North Star Research Inst., Mpls., 1972-74; exec. v.p., chief economist Bank of Am., San Francisco 1975—, chief economist, 1982—; prof. Grad. Sch. Pub. Policy and Haas Sch. Bus. U. Calif., Berkeley, 1979-92. bd. dirs. Nat. Bur. Econ. Rsch., Cambridge, Mass. Bd. visitors Joint Center for Urban Studies, Harvard U.-M.I.T., 1978-87; trustee Grad. Theol. Union, Berkeley, Calif. Served with U.S. Navy, 1960-63. Ford Found. fellow, 1966-67. Mem. Am. Econ. Assn., Western Econ. Assn., Nat. Assn. Bus. Economists. Republican. Presbyterian. Author: After Affluence, Economics to Meet Human Needs 1980, Middle Class Crisis: The American and Japanese Experience, 1983, The Power Economy, Building An Economy That Works, 1985; contbr. articles to profl. jours. Office: Bank of America Ctr 555 California St San Francisco CA 94104-1502

WILSON, JOHN ROSS, retired law educator; b. Memphis, Aug. 8, 1920; s. Charles Monroe and Lida Scott (Christenberry) W.; m. Anne Woodruff Talley, Feb. 7, 1944; children—Margaret Anne, Andrew Ross. B.B.A., So. Meth. U., 1943, LL.B., 1948; student, U. Tex., Austin, 1939-41. Bar: Tex. bar 1948. Mem. faculty Baylor U. Law Sch., Waco, Tex., 1948-86; assoc. prof. law Baylor U. Law Sch., 1951-55, prof., 1955-86, prof. emeritus, 1986; cons. on bankruptcy and judicial remedies. Author: Cases and Materials on Judicial Remedies, 1966; contbr. articles to profl. jours. Served to lt. USNR, 1943-46. Mem. Am. Judicature Soc., Tex. Bar Assn., Am. Bar Assn., Waco-McLennan County Bar Assn., Tex. Trial Lawyers Assn., Delta Theta Phi, Sigma Alpha Epsilon. Republican. Methodist. Office: Baylor Univ Law Sch Waco TX 76703

WILSON, JOSEPH CHARLES, IV, ambassador; b. Bridgeport, Conn., Nov. 6, 1949; s. Joseph Charles III and Phyllis (Finnell) W.; m. Susan Dale Otchis, Apr. 27, 1973 (div. 1986); children: Sabrina Cecile, Joseph Charles; m. Jacqueline Marylene Giorgi, July 1, 1986. BA in History, U. Calif., Santa Barbara, 1972. Fgn. svc. officer Dept. of State, Washington, 1976—; congl. fellow Am. Polit. Sci. Assn., Washington, 1985-86; dep. chief of mission Am. Embassy, Bujumbura, Burundi, 1982-85, Brazzaville, Congo, 1986-88, Baghdad, Iraq, 1988-91; amb. Dept. of State Am. Embassy, Libreville, Gabon, Sao Tome and Principe, 1992-95; polit. adv. to Commdr. in Chief U.S. Armed Forces Europe, 1995—. Recipient Disting. Alumni award U. Calif. Santa Barbara, 1991; named hon. adm. County Commr., El Paso, Tex., 1991. Mem. Am. Polit. Sci. Assn., Am. Fgn. Svc. Assn. (William R. Rivkin award 1987), U. Calif. Santa Barbara Alumni Assn. (Disting. Alumni award 1991), San Onofre Surfing Club. Avocations: golf, bicycling, weight lifting. Home and Office: HQ USEUComm Box 1458 Unit 30400 APO AE 09128

WILSON, JOSEPH MORRIS, III, lawyer; b. Milw., July 26, 1945; s. Joseph Morris Jr. and Phyllis Elizabeth (Cresson) W.; children: Elizabeth J., Eric M.; m. Dixie Lee Brock, Mar. 23, 1984. BA, Calif. State U., Chico, 1967; MA, U. Washington, 1968; JD summa cum laude, Ohio State U., 1976. Bar: Alaska 1976, U.S. Dist. Ct. Alaska 1976, U.S. Ct. Appeals (9th cir.) 1986. Recruiter and vol. U.S. Peace Corps, People's Republic of Benin, 1969-73; legal intern U.S. Ho. of Reps., Washington, 1975; ptnr. Guess & Rudd P.C., Anchorage, 1976-83, chmn. comml. dept., 1981-82, ptnr. compensation com., 1982-84; mgr. Alaska taxes, sr. tax atty. BP Exploration Inc., Alaska, 1990—; bus. law instr. U. Alaska, Anchorage, 1977-78. Counsel Tanaina Child Devel. Ctr., Anchorage, 1982-84, Alaska Child Passenger Safety Assn., Anchorage, 1983-86; bd. dirs. Alaska Alcohol Safety Action Program, Anchorage, 1977-79. Mem. ABA, Alaska Bar Assn. (taxation sect.), Anchorage Bar Assn. Democrat. Club: UAA Basketball Boosters, World Affairs Coun. Avocations: music, sports, travel. Home: 1779 Morningtide Ct Anchorage AK 99501-5722 Office: MB6-4 PO Box 196193 Anchorage AK 99519-6193

WILSON, KAREN LEE, museum director; b. Somerville, N.J., Apr. 2, 1949; d. Jon Milton and Laura Virginia (Van Dyke) W.; m. Paul Ernest Walker, 1980; 1 child, Jeremy Nathaniel. AB, Harvard U., 1971; MA, NYU, 1973, PhD, 1985. Rsch. assoc., dir. excavation at Mendes, Egypt Inst. Fine Arts, NYU, 1979-81; coord. exhbn. The Jewish Mus., N.Y.C., 1981-82, adminstrv. cataloguer, 1982-83, coord. curatorial affairs, 1984-86; curator Oriental Inst. Mus. U. Chgo., 1988-96, mus. dir., 1996—. Author, editor: Mendes, 1982; contbr. articles to profl. jours. Mem. Am. Oriental Soc., Am. Rsch. Ctr. in Egypt. Office: Oriental Institute Museum 1155 E 58th St Chicago IL 60637-1540

WILSON, KATHRYN TERESE, food service director; b. Milw., Mar. 7, 1959; d. George Charles and Mary Kathryn (Fink) Schuld; m. Russel Harold Wilson, Dec. 21, 1985; children: Thomas Lawrence, James Charles. BS in Dietetics, U. Wis.-Stout, Menomonie, 1981, MS in Food Sci. and Nutrition, 1984. Lic. food svc. dir./adminstr. Resident housing-bldg. dir. U. Wis.-Stout, Menomonie, 1983-85, substitute teaching staff, 1984-85; asst. food svc. dir. Onalaska (Wis.) Pub. Schs., 1987-90; food svc. dir. West Salem (Wis.) Schs., 1990—; cons. outreach Wis. Dept. Pub. Instrn., Madison, 1993—. Recipient Silver Penguin award Nat. Frozen Food Assn., 1995-96; named Dir. of Yr., Wis. Sch. Food Svc., 1995-96; nutriton edn. grantee Wis. Dept. Pub. Instrn., Madison, 1992. Mem. Am. Sch. Food Svc. Assn. (legis. del. 1991-92, 93, 94, 95, midwest rep. dirs./suprs. com. 1995-98), Wis. Sch. Food Svc. Assn. (chpt. pres. 1991-93, v.p. 1992-93, pres.-elect 1993-94, state pres. 1994-95, legis. com., dist. rep. 1990-93, cons. program of excellence 1992—, legis. com. chair 1996-98, Gold awards 1991-93). Avocations: crafts, cross country skiing, camping, reading to my sons. Home: N2130 Sunset Ln Rt 2 La Crosse WI 54601

WILSON, KEITH DUDLEY, media and music educator; b. Windermere, July 13, 1936; s. Charles Alexander and Fanny (Shaw) W.; 1 child, Nicholas. BA with honors, Kings Coll., Cambridge, 1957, MA, 1960. Lectr. Brit. Coun./Zagreb Univ., Croatia, 1957-58; assoc. prof., dir. TV Brit. Coun. Tehran U., Iran, 1958-64; reader Brit. Coun. Osmania U., Hyderabad, India, 1964-66; head of liberal edn. Salford Coll. of Tech., U.K., 1967-72, head of humanities, 1972-85; head of performing arts and media U. Coll. Salford, 1985-90; dir. ctr. for media performance and comm. U. Salford, 1990—, founding dir. internat. media ctr., 1993—; dean faculty of media, music and performance Salford U., 1996—; dir. Aspects Prodn. Assocs., TVUK, Adelphi Prodns., Salford, 1988—; chair PRS John Lennon awards, London, 1990-93; co-chair NYNEX Cable TV, Manchester, 1993-95; vis. acad. The Brit. Coun., Korea, 1992; founder over 20 higher edn. courses in music and recording. Contbr. articles to profl. jours.; concert tours to Brazil, Belgium, Holland, Iceland, Norway, Denmark, Greece, Ecuador, Russia and Hungary; residencies at Edinburgh Internat. Festival, broadcasts and recordings, 1986-96. Mem. U. Salford Centenary Com., 1994-96, City of Salford LS Lowry Centenary, 1988, City of Salford Millenium Lowry Centre for performing and visual arts and Nat. Indsl. Ctr. for Virtual Reality, 1994—; founder Salford U. Brass Band, Wind Band, Big Band, Soundworks, Jazz Ensembles, Groove Machine, Aspects Theatre; mem. City Pride Initiative, Manchester, 1993—, Fellowship Great Britain Sasakawa Found., Japan, 1991. Fellow Royal Soc. of Arts (IMC assoc.); mem. Royal TV Soc., British Film Inst., British Acad. of Film and TV. Avocations: nordic culture, wines of the world, fellwalking. Office: Internat Media Centre, Adelphi House The Crescent Salford, Manchester M3 6EN, England

WILSON, KENNETH GEDDES, physics research administrator, educator; b. Waltham, Mass., June 8, 1936; s. E. Bright and Emily Fisher (Buckingham) W.; m. Alison Brown, 1982. A.B., Harvard U., 1956, DSc hon., 1981; Ph.D., Calif. Tech. Inst., 1961; Ph.D. (hon.), U. Chgo., 1976. From asst. prof. to prof. physics Cornell U., Ithaca, N.Y., 1963-88, James A. Weeks prof. in phys. sci., 1974-87; Hazel C. Youngberg Trustees Disting prof. The Ohio State U., Columbus, 1988—. Co-author: Redesigning Education, 1974. Recipient Nobel prize in physics, 1982, Dannie Heinemann prize, 1973, Boltzmann medal, 1975, Wolf prize, 1980, A.C. Eringen medal, 1984, Franklin medal, 1982, Aneesur Rahman prize, 1993. Mem. NAS, Am. Philos. Soc., Am. Phys. Soc., Am. Acad. Arts and Scis.

WILSON, KENNETH JAY, writer; b. Oklahoma City, Aug. 25, 1944; s. Kenneth J. and Betty Wallace (Bleakmore) W. B.A. magna cum laude, Yale U., 1966, M.Phil., 1969; postgrad. Queen's Coll., Oxford U., Eng., 1969-70; Ph.D., Yale U., 1973. From instr. to assoc. prof. English U. Rochester, N.Y., 1970-83; assoc. Clare Hall, Cambridge U., Eng., 1977; vis. assoc. prof. English Coll. William and Mary, Williamsburg, Va., 1983; editor in chief Peter Lang Pub., N.Y.C., 1983-87; dir. of rights and permissions Princeton U. Press, 1987-88; commissioning editor polit. sci. and psychology Routledge, N.Y.C., 1988-90; adminstrv. dir. HIV Clin. Rsch. Ctr. Mt. Zion Med. Ctr./U. Calif., San Francisco, 1994-95; cons. USIA, 1985. Editor: Letters of Sir Thomas Elyot, 1976, English Works of Thomas More, 1978; author: Incomplete Fictions, 1985, Pope John Paul II, 1992; contbr. articles to profl. jours. Woodrow Wilson fellow, 1966, 83; sr. fellow Folger Shakespeare Library, Washington, 1976; Am. Philos. Soc. grantee, 1976; Am. Council Learned Soc. fellow, 1977. Mem. Mory's Club, Elizabethan Club (New Haven), Yale Club (N.Y.C.), Palm-Aire Country Club, Phi Beta Kappa. Democrat. Roman Catholic. Home and Office: 5570 Country Club Way Sarasota FL 34243-3759

WILSON, KIRK GEORGE, medical service executive; b. Great Falls, Mont., Apr. 1, 1951; s. Floyd Daniel and Lorna (Stark) W.; m. Monica Jane

Moline, Aug. 17, 1975; 1 child, Bret Michael. BABS, Concordia Coll., Moorhead, Minn., 1972; MA in Hosp. Adminstrn., U. Iowa, 1975. Adminstrv. asst. Columbus Hosp., Great Falls, 1975-78, asst. adminstr., 1978-80; asst. adminstr., profl. services St. Anthony Hosp., Oklahoma City, Okla., 1981-83, St. Vincent Med. Ctr., Portland, Oreg., 1983-86; adminstr. Meml. Women's/Childrens Hosp., Meml. Med. Ctr., Long Beach, Calif., 1987-88; pres., chief exec. officer Mont. Deaconess Med. Ctr., Great Falls, 1988—; Bd. dirs. Mountain States VHA Regional Bd., Denver, Bank of Mont. Co-author: (monograph) Mental Health Care Systems, 1975. Bd. dirs. Symphony Assn. Bd., Great Falls, 1988—; mem. pres.'s coun. Coll. Great of Falls. Fellow Am. Coll. Healthcare Execs., Mont. Hosp. Assn. (bd. dirs. Dist. II), Mont. Amb., Great Falls C. of C. (bd. dirs., Leadership award 1981), Rotary. Republican. Congregationalist. Home: 520 Fox Ct Great Falls MT 59404-3874 Office: Mont Deaconess Med Ct PO Box 5014 Great Falls MT 59403-5014

WILSON, LANFORD, playwright; b. Lebanon, Mo., Apr. 13, 1937; s. Ralph E(ugene) and Violetta (Tate) W. Student, San Diego State Coll., 1955-56; PhD in Humanities, U. Mo., 1985, Grinnell Coll., 1994; PhD in Literature, Southampton Coll., 1995. Playwright, 1962—; resident playwright, dir. Circle Repertory Co., N.Y.C., 1969-95. Author: (plays) So Long at the Fair, 1963, Home Free, 1964, No Trespassing, 1964, Sandcastle, 1964, The Madness of Lady Bright, 1964, Ludlow Fair, 1965, Balm in Gilead, 1965, This is the Rill Speaking, 1965, Days Ahead, 1965, Sex in Between Two People, 1965, The Gingham Dong, 1966, The Rimers of Eldritch, 1966, Wandering, 1966, Days Ahead, 1967, Lemon Sky, 1969, Serenading Louie, 1970, The Great Nebula in Orion, 1970, The Hot L Baltimore, 1972, The Family Continues, 1972, The Mound Builders, 1975, Fifth of July, 1978, Brontasaurus, 1978, Talley's Folly, 1979, A Tale Told, 1981, Angels Fall, 1983, A Betrothal, 1984, Talley & Son, 1985, Burn This, 1987, A Poster of the Cosmos, 1987, The Moonshot Tape, 1990, Redwood Curtain, 1991, Trinity, 1993, I'm Not the Ocean, 1995, Sympathetic Magic, 1995, Virgil is Still the Frogboy, 1996; translator Three Sisters, 1984; author: (books) Balm in Gilead and Other Plays, 1966, The Rimers of Eldritch and Other Plays, 1968, The Gingham Dog, 1969, Lemon Sky, 1970, The Hot L Baltimore, 1973, The Mound Builders, 1976, Fifth of July, 1979, Talley's Folly, 1980, Angels Fall, 1983, Serenading Louie, 1985, Talley & Son, 1986, Burn This, 1988, Redwood Curtain, 1992, 21 Short Plays, 1994, By the Sea, 1996. ABC Yale fellow, 1969; Rockefeller grantee, 1967, 73, Guggenheim grantee, 1970, NEA grantee, 1990; recipient Vernon Rice award, 1966-67, Inst. Arts and Letters award, 1970, Obie award, 1972, 75, 84, Outer Critics Circle award, 1973, Drama Critics Circle award, 1973, 80, Pulitzer prize, 1980, Brandeis award, 1981, John Steinbeck award, 1990, Edward Albee Last Frontier award, 1994, Am. Acad. of Achievement award, 1995. Mem. Dramatists Guild Council.

WILSON, LAUREN ROSS, academic administrator; b. Yates Center, Kans., May 4, 1936; s. Roscoe C. and Margaret D. W.; m. Janie Haskin, Jan. 25, 1959; children—Lance Kevin, Keela Lynn. B.S., Baker U., Baldwin, Kans., 1958; Ph.D., U. Kans., 1963. Mem. faculty Ohio Wesleyan U., Delaware, 1963-87; prof. chemistry Ohio Wesleyan U., 1971-87, Homer Lucas U. prof., dean acad. affairs, 1978-86, acting provost, 1985-86, asst. to pres., 1986, 87; vice chancellor for acad. affairs U. N.C., Asheville, 1987-95, prof. chemistry, 1987-95, interim chancellor, 1993-94; pres., prof. chemistry Marietta Coll., 1995—; vis. prof. Ohio State U., 1968, 74; vis. research assoc. Oak Ridge Nat. Lab., 1972-73. Recipient Outstanding Tchr. award Ohio Wesleyan U., 1968. Mem. AAAS, AAUP, Am. Chem. Soc., Am. Assn. Higher Edn., Coun. Undergrad. Rsch., Sigma Xi. Office: Marietta Coll 215 5th St Marietta OH 45750

WILSON, LAWRENCE ALEXANDER, construction company executive; b. Nashville, 1935. Grad., Vanderbilt U., 1957. With H.C. Beck Co., Inc., Dallas, 1959-80, pres., COO, 1976-80; chmn., CEO Beck Co., Inc., Dallas, 1980—; pres., CEO HCB Contractors, Dallas, 1980—. Office: HCB Contractors 1700 Pacific Ave Ste 3800 Dallas TX 75201*

WILSON, LAWRENCE FRANK (LARRY WILSON), professional football team executive; b. Rigby, Idaho, Mar. 24, 1938; m. Nancy Drew, Apr. 15, 1980. Student, U. Utah, 1956-60. Defensive back St. Louis Cardinals, NFL, 1960-72, dir. profl. scouting, 1973-76, dir. profl. pers., 1977-88; v.p., former gen. mgr. Ariz. Cardinals, NFL, 1988—. Mem. All-NFL Team, 1963, 66, 67, 68, 69; player Pro Bowl, 1962-63, 65-70; inducted Pro Football Hall of Fame, 1978; led in interceptions NFL, 1966. *

WILSON, LELAND EARL, petroleum engineering consultant; b. Ft. Recovery, Ohio, Oct. 28, 1925; s. John Huffman and Matilda Caroline (Sunderhaus) W.; m. Marian Ruthetta Trygstad, Nov. 27, 1948; children: Kathleen Ann, Linda Kay, Mary Lee, John Russell. BS in Petroleum Engring., Tulsa U., 1950. Registered profl. engr., Alaska, Tex. Drilling engr. Atlantic Refining Co., Tex., Ark., and La., 1950-56; drilling supr. Atlantic Refining Co., La., Tex., 1956-65; drilling supt. Atlantic Richfield, Anchorage, 1965-67, prodn. and drilling supt., 1967-72; ops. mgr. ARCO Oil Prodn. Co., London, 1972-75; resident mgr. ARCO Greenland, Copenhagen, 1975-78; pres. ARCO Indonesia, Inc., Jakarta, 1978-82; v.p. ARCO China, Hong Kong, 1982-85; petroleum cons. Lindale, Tex., 1985—; bd. dirs. Houma Oil Treaters, Inc., DPM Non-Destructive Testing, Odessa, Tex. Author family history Dear John; contbr. articles to profl. jours.; inventor in field. Aviation cadet AAF, 1943-45. Mem. NSPE, Tex. Soc. Profl. Engrs., Tyler Petroleum Club, Soc. Petroleum Engrs., Petroleum Club (pres. Anchorage 1971-72), Indonesian Petroleum Assn. (pres. 1981-82). Republican. Roman Catholic. Avocations: geneaology, golf, travel. Home: PO Box 893 428 Lonestar Ln Lindale TX 75771 Office: PO Box 893 2715 S Main Lindale TX 75771

WILSON, LEONARD GILCHRIST, history of medicine educator; b. Orillia, Ont., Can., June 11, 1928; s. George Edward and Mary Agnes (MacPhee) W.; m. Adelia Katherine Hans, June 7, 1969; 1 child, George Edward Hans. B.A., U. Toronto, Can., 1949; M.Sc., U. London, 1955; Ph.D., U. Wis., Madison, 1958. Lectr. Mount Allison U., Sackville, N.B., Can., 1950-53; vis. instr. U. Calif., Berkeley, 1958-59; asst. prof. Cornell U., Ithaca, N.Y., 1959-60; asst. prof. Yale U., New Haven, 1960-65, assoc. prof., 1965-67; prof., head dept. history of medicine U. Minn., Mpls., 1967—. Author: Charles Lyell: The Years to 1841: The Revolution in Geology, 1972, Medical Revolution in Minnesota, 1989; editor: Benjamin Silliman and His Circle, 1979, Sir Charles Lyell's Scientific Journals on the Species Question, 1971; editor Jour. History Medicine and Allied Scis., 1973-82; co-editor: Readings in History of Physiology, 1966; mem. bd. mgrs. Jour. Hist. Medicine, 1962—. Fellow AAAS; mem. Am. Assn. History of Medicine, Am. Hist. Assn., History of Sci. Soc., Minn. Acad. Medicine (pres. 1984-85, sec.-treas. 1989—), Brit. Soc. for the History of Sci., Soc. for the History of natural History. Home: 797 Goodrich Ave Saint Paul MN 55105-3344 Office: U Minn Dept History of Medicine 420 Delaware St SE Minneapolis MN 55455-0374

WILSON, LEROY, retired glass manufacturing company executive; b. Indpls., July 15, 1928; s. Paul Allison and Lula (Berry) W.; m. Claudie Leenaert, Aug. 9, 1968; children: Paul Neil, Daniel Stuart, Benjamin, Antoine, Virginie. B.S. in Mech. Engring, Purdue U., 1950. With Corning Glass Works, N.Y., 1950-87; v.p. gen. mgr. electronic products div. Corning Glass Works, 1975-80; pres. Corning Europe Inc., Neuilly, France, 1980-87. Mem. dean's adv. council Krannert Sch., Purdue U. Served with AUS, 1954-56. Named Disting. Engring. Alumnus, Purdue U., 1981. Fellow Inst. Dirs.; mem. Royal Automobile Club (London). Ch. of Eng. Home: Egypt House, Rushlake Green, Heathfield, East Sussex TN21 9QT, England

WILSON, LESLIE, biochemist, cell biologist, biology educator; b. Boston, June 29, 1941; s. Samuel Paul Wilson and Lee (Melniker) Kamerling; m. Carla Helena Van Wingerden, Sept. 9, 1989; children from previous marriage: Sebastian A. Michael, Naomi Beth. BS, Mass. Coll. Pharmacy and Allied Health Scis., 1963; PhD, Tufts U., 1967; postdoctoral study, U. Calif. at Berkeley, 1967-69. Asst. prof. dept. pharmacology Stanford U. Sch. Medicine, 1969-74; assoc. prof. dept. biol. scis. U. Calif., Santa Barbara, 1975-78, prof. biochemistry, 1979—, chmn. dept. biol. scis., 1987-91, head divsn. molecular, cellular, devel. biol., 1992-93; sci. adv. panel mem. cell and devel. biology Am. Cancer Soc., Atlanta, 1984-88; cons. Eli Lilly & Co., Indpls., 1980—. Editor: (book series) Methods in Cell Biology, 1987—; assoc. editor Biochemistry; contbr. numerous rsch. papers to profl. publs. Bd. dirs. Cancer Found. Santa Barbara. Rsch. grantee NIH, 1970—, Am. Cancer Soc., 1986—. Mem. AAAS, Am. Soc. Cell Biology (chmn. sci. program 1977), Am. Soc. Biol. Chemistry and Molecular Biology, Am. Soc. Pharmacology and Exptl. Therapeutics. Democrat. Office: Univ Calif Dept Molec, Cell, Devel Bio Santa Barbara CA 93106

WILSON, LINDA, librarian; b. Rochester, Minn., Nov. 17, 1945; d. Eunice Gloria Irene Wilson. BA, U. Minn., Morris, 1967; MA, U. Minn., 1968. Libr. rsch. svcs. U. Calif., Riverside, 1968-69, head dept. phys. scis. catalog, 1969-71; city libr. Belle Glade (Fla). Mcpl. Libr., 1972-74; instr. part-time Palm Beach Jr. Coll., Belle Glade, 1973; head adult-young adult ext. Kern County Libr. Sys., Bakersfield, Calif., 1974-80; dir. dist. libr. Lake Agassiz Regional Libr. System, Crookston, Minn., 1980-85; supervising libr. San Diego County Libr., 1985-87; county libr. Merced (Calif.) County Libr., 1987-93; learning network mgr. Merced Coll., 1994-95; libr. dir. Monterey Park (Calif.) Bruggemeyer Meml. Libr., 1995—. Active Leadership Merced, 1987-88; mem. East Site Based Coordinating Coun., Merced, 1990-92, Merced Gen. Plan Citizens Adv. Com., 1992-95, Sister City Com., Merced, 1992-95, East L.A. Bus. and Profl. Women, 1996—, Monterey Pk. Rotary, 1996—. Recipient Libr. award Eagles Aux., 1984, Woman of Achievement award Commn. on the Status of Women, 1990, Libr. award Calif. Libr. Trustees and Commrs., 1990, Woman of Yr. award Merced Bus. and Profl. Women, 1987. Mem. ALA (sec. pub. libr. sys. sect. 1988-89), Calif. Libr. Assn. (sec. govt. rels. com. 1991-92, continuing edn. com. 1993-96), Minn. Libr. Assn. (pres. pub. libr. divsn. 1985), Merced County Mgmt. Coun. (pres. 1989), Merced Bus. and Profl. Women (pres. 1988-89). Democrat. Lutheran. Avocations: travel, walking, reading, swimming, stamp collecting. Home: 1000 E Newmark Ave # 22 Monterey Park CA 91755

WILSON, LINDA SMITH, academic administrator; b. Washington, Nov. 10, 1936; d. Fred M. and Virginia D. (Thompson) Smith; m. Paul A. Wilson, Jan. 22, 1970; 1 dau. by previous marriage: Helen K. Whatley, a stepdau., Beth A. Wilson. B.A., Newcomb Coll., Tulane U., 1957; Ph.D., U. Wis., 1962; HLD (hon.), Tulane U., 1993; DLitt. (hon.), U. Md., 1993. Postdoctoral rsch. assoc. U. Md., College Park, 1962-64, rsch. asst. prof., 1964-67; vis. asst. prof. U. Mo.-St. Louis, 1967-68; asst. to vice chancellor for rsch., asst. vice chancellor for rsch., assoc. vice chancellor for rsch. Washington U. St. Louis, 1968-75; assoc. vice chancellor for rsch. U. Ill., Urbana, 1975-85; assoc. dean Grad. Coll., U. Ill., Urbana, 1978-85; v.p. for rsch. U. Mich., Ann Arbor, 1985-89; pres. Radcliffe Coll., Cambridge, Mass., 1989—; chmn. adv. com. office sci. and engring. pers. NRC, 1990—; mem. dir.'s adv. coun. NSF, Washington, 1980-89, adv. com. edn. and human resources, 1990-95; mem. Nat. Commn. on Rsch., Washington, 1978-80; mem. com. on govt.-univ. relationships NAS, 1981-83, mem. coun. for govt.-univ.-industry rsch. roundtable, 1984-89; mem. rsch. resources adv. coun. NIH, Bethesda, Md., 1978-82, energy rsch. adv. bd. DOE, 1987-90; mem. sci., tech. and states task force Carnegie Commn. on Sci., Tech. and Govt., 1991-92; trustee com. on econ. devel., 1995—, overseer Mus. of Sci., Boston, 1992—. Author book chpts.; contbr. articles to profl. jours. Bd. govs. YMCA, Champaign-Urbana, Ill., 1980-83; mem. adv. bd. Nat. Coalition for Sci. and Tech., Washington, 1983-87; trustee Mass. Gen. Hosp., 1992—; dir. Citizen's Fin. Corp., 1996—. Recipient Centennial award Newcomb Coll., 1986; named One of 100 Emerging Leaders Am. Coun. Edn. and Change, 1978. Fellow AAAS (bd. dirs. 1984-88); mem. NAS (coord. coun. for edn. 1991-93), Am. Chem. Soc. (bd. coun. com. on chemistry and pub. affairs 1978-80), Soc. Rsch. Adminstrs. (Disting. Contbn. to Rsch. Adminstrn. award 1984), Nat. Coun. Univ. Rsch. Adminstrs., Assn. for Biomed. Rsch. (bd. dirs. 1983-86), Inst. Medicine (mem. coun. 1986-89), Am. Coun. Edn. (commn. on women in higher edn. 1991-93, chair 1993), Phi Beta Kappa, Sigma Xi, Alpha Lambda Delta, Phi Delta Kappa, Phi Kappa Phi. Home: 76 Brattle St Cambridge MA 02138-3452 Office: Radcliffe Coll Office of Pres Fay House 10 Garden St Cambridge MA 02138

WILSON, LLOYD LEE, organization administrator; b. Elkton, Md., Sept. 14, 1947; s. Clifton Laws and Betty Raye (Bare) W.; m. Susan Sieg Wilson, 1992; children: Asa, Ryan, Morgan, Daniel. BS in Mgmt., MIT, 1969, MS in Mgmt., 1977. Bus. mgr. med. clinics Mass. Gen. Hosp., Boston, 1970-73; ptnr. Willow Co., mgmt. cons., Cambridge, Mass., 1974-77; dir. community relations Wilson Neuropsychiat. Hosp., Charlottesville, Va., 1977-78; exec. dir. Jefferson Area United Transp. Inc., Charlottesville, Va., 1978-80, Va. Mountain Housing Inc., Blacksburg, 1980-82; gen. sec. Friends Gen. Conf. Religious Soc. Friends, Phila., 1982-85; dir. rsch. and devel. Va. Mountain Housing, Inc., Christiansburg, 1985-88, dir. multifamily housing, 1989-91, regional dir., 1991-92; pres. Friendly Mgmt. Svcs. Corp., Norfolk, Va., 1992-95, Not-for-Profit Mgmt., Inc., Norfolk, Va., 1995—; pres., dir. Va. Housing Coalition, Inc., 1981-82; treas., bd. dirs. Fiddle Hill Farm, Inc., Barboursville, Va., 1982-89; bd. mgrs. Bible Assn. Friends in Am., Phila., 1983-85; mem. com. rec. ministers Balt. Yearly Meeting Friends, Sandy Spring, Md., 1984-86; asst. sec.-treas. Friends Meeting House Fund, Inc., Phila., 1984-85; asst. presiding clk. Communications Commn. of Friends United Meeting, Richmond, Ind., 1987-88; recorded minister of the gospel, Soc. of Friends, 1989— (presiding clk. Va. Beach monthly meeting 1990-92); dir. coordinating cabinet Va. Coun. Chs., 1988; presiding clk. N.C. Yearly Meeting of Friends, 1991-92. Author: Essays on the Quaker Vision of Gospel Order, 1993; contbr. articles to profl. jours. Treas., bd. dirs. Norfolk (Va.) Quaker House, Inc., 1995—; bd. dirs. New Dominion Housing, Inc., Norfolk, 1992-94; vice chmn. Montgomery County Cmty. Svc. Commn., Christianburg, Va., 1980-82; mem. ednl. coun. MIT, 19777-89; bd. dirs. Am. Friends Svc. Com., Inc., Phila., 1980-83; bd. dirs. Interfaith Housing Corp. Cambridge, Inc., 1975-77, treas., 1976-77, also numerous others. Home: 536 Carnaby Ct Virginia Beach VA 23454-3473 Office: Not for Profit Mgmt Inc PO Box 7891 Norfolk VA 23509-0891

WILSON, LOIS M., minister; b. Winnipeg, Man., Can., Apr. 8, 1927; d. Edwin Gardiner Dunn and Ada Minnie (Davis) Freeman; m. Roy F. Wilson, June 9, 1950; children: Ruth, Jean, Neil, Bruce. BA, United Coll., Winnipeg, 1947, BDiv, 1969; Diploma in TV prodn., Ryerson Tech. Inst., 1974; DDiv (hon.), Victoria U., Toronto, 1978, United Theol. Coll., Montreal, 1978, Wycliff Coll., 1983, Queens U., Kingston, 1984, U. Winnipeg, 1986, Mt. Allison U., 1988; LLD (hon.), Trent U., Peterborough, 1984, Dalhousie U., 1989, Dalhousie U., 1989, Ripon Coll., Wis., 1992; DCL (hon.), Acadia U., 1984; DHuml (hon.), Mt. St. Vincent, Halifax, 1984. Ordained to ministry United Church of Can., 1965. Minister Thunder Bay, 1965-69, Hamilton, 1969-78, Kingston, 1978-80; moderator United Church of Can., Kingston, 1980-82; McGeachy sr. scholar United Church of Can., 1989-91; pres. Can. Council of Chs., Toronto, Ont., 1976-79; co-dir. Ecumenical Forum Can., Toronto, Ont., 1983-89; pres. World Council of Chs., Geneva, 1983-91; chancellor Lakehead U., Thurder Bay, Ont., 1990—; chmn. contemporary theology Lafayette-Orinda (Calif.) Presbyn. Ch., 1995; mem. adv. coun. internt. devel. studies U. Toronto, 1987-93; spokesperson Project Ploughshares, 1st and 2d UN Conf. on Disarmament, N.Y.C., 1978-82; lectr. Vancouver Sch. Theology, 1980, Queens Theol. Coll., 1982-83, 92, Chancellor's lectr., 1992; officer Human Rights Commn., Ont., 1973; mem. bd. regents Victoria U., 1990—; chief Can. Fact finding Mission to Sri Lanka, 1992; team mem. Ctrl. Am. Monitoring Group to El Salvador and Guatemala, 1993. Author: Like a Mighty River, 1980, Turning the World Upside Down, 1989, Miriam, Mary and Me, 1992, Telling Her Story, 1992; mem. adv. bd. Can. Woman Studies Jour., York U., 1993—; contbr. articles to profl. publs. Pres. Social Planning Coun., Thunder Bay, 1967-68, Can. Com. for Scientists and Scholars, Toronto, 1982; bd. dirs. Elizabeth Fry Soc., Hamilton, 1976-79, Amnesty Internat., 1978-90, Can. Inst. for Internat. Peace and Security, 1984-88, Energy Probe, 1981-86; active Refugee Status Adv. Com., 1985-89; bd. dirs. Can. Univ. Svc. Overseas, 1983-85; chmn. Urban Rural Mission, Can., 1990—; mem. Environ. Assessment Panel Govt. Can., Nuclear Fuel Waste Mgmt. and Disposal Concept, 1989—; trustee Nelson Mandela Fund, 1990-92. Decorated Order of Can., 1984, Order of Ont., 1991; recipient Queens Jubilee medal, Commemorative medal for 125th Anniversary of Confederation of Can., 1992, World Federalist Peace award, 1985, Pearson Peace medal UN Assn. of Can., 1985; named hon. pres. Student Christian Movement of Can., Toronto, 1976. Mem. CAW (pub. rev. bd. 1986—), Can. Assn. Adult Edn. (bd. dirs. 1986-90), Friends Can. Broadcasting (bd. dirs. 1986—, v.p.), Civil Liberties Assn. (v.p. 1986—), UNIFEM (nat. v.p. 1993-95, mem. CCIC team to monitor El Salvador election 1994), Parliament of World's Religions (del. 1993), Christian-Jewish Dialogue Jerusalem (keynote speaker 1994). Home and Office: 40 Glen Rd Apt 310, Toronto, ON Canada M4W 2V1

WILSON, LORRAINE M., medical and surgical nurse, nursing educator; b. Mich., Nov. 18, 1931; d. Bert and Frances Fern (White) McCarty; m. Harold A. Wilson, June 9, 1953; children: David Scott, Ann Elizabeth. Diploma in Nursing, Bronson Meth. Sch. Nursing, Kalamazoo, Mich., 1953; BS in Chemistry, Siena Heights Coll., 1969; MSN, U. Mich., 1972; PhD, Wayne State U., Detroit, 1985. RN, Mich. Staff nurse U. Mich. Med. Ctr., Ann Arbor, 1953-54, Herrick Meml. Hosp., Tecumseh, Mich., 1954-69; asst. prof. nursing U. Mich., Ann Arbor, 1972-78, Wayne State U., Detroit, 1978-79; assoc. prof. nursing Sch. of Nursing Oakland U., Rochester, Mich., 1986-89; prof. nursing Ea. Mich. U., Ypsilanti, Mich., 1989—; researcher in field; bd. advs. Profl. Fitness Systems, Warren, Mich., 1986—; cons. wellness and exercise program General Motors CPC Hdqs., Warren, 1986; cons. and faculty liaison nurse extern program in critical care Ea. Mich. U. Catherine McAuley Health Ctr., 1989—. Co-author: (with Sylvia Price) Pathophysiology: Clinical Concepts of Disease Processes, 5th edit., 1986; contbr. articles to profl. jours. Vol. Community Health Screening Drives, Tecumseh, 1960-70, leader Girl Scouts U.S., Tecumseh, 1960; sunday sch. tchr. Gloria Dei Luth. Ch., Tecumseh, 1960; mem. PTA. Grantee Mich. Heart Assn., 1984, 88, R.C. Mahon Found., 1988. Mem. ANA (various offices and com. chairs), Midwest Nursing Rsch. Soc. (v.p., sec.-treas., bd. dirs.), Mich. Nurses Assn. (del.), Nat. League Nursing, Nat. Orgn. Women, Sigma Theta Tau. Lutheran. Avocations: traveling, theatre, jogging. Home: 1010 Red Mill Dr Tecumseh MI 49286-1145 Office: Ea Mich U 53 W Michigan Ave Ypsilanti MI 48197-5436

WILSON, LOUISE ASTELL MORSE, educator, home economist; b. Corning, N.Y., Oct. 26, 1937; d. James Leland and Hazel Irene (Bratt) Morse; m. Robert Louis Wilson, Dec. 26, 1965 (dec. June 1981); 1 child, Patricia Louise. BS, SUNY, Buffalo, 1960; MS, Elmira Coll., 1971. Cert. home economist, N.Y. Tchr. Corning City Sch. Dist., 1960—; com. mem. Corning Sch. Dist., 1991—. Mem. Internat. Fed. Home Econs. (area rep. 1991—), Am. Home Econs. Assn., Am. Vocat. Assn., N.Y. Home Econs. Assn. (treas. 1989-91), N.Y. State Home Econs. Tchrs. Assn. (area coord. 1988-89, Tchr. of Yr. 1993-94), Am. Coun. consumer Interests, Corning Tchrs. Assn. (exec. coun. 1981-91, 93—), Order Ea. Star (past matron), Corning Country Club. Republican. Methodist. Avocations: photography, sports, needlework, glassware, coins. Home: PO Box 2 Coopers Plains NY 14827-0002

WILSON, LYNTON RONALD, telecommunications company executive; b. Port Colborne, Ont., Can., Apr. 3, 1940; s. Ronald Alfred and Blanche Evelyn (Matthews) W.; m. Brenda Jean Black, Dec. 23, 1968; children: Edward Ronald, Margot Jean, Jennifer Lyn. BA, McMaster U., 1962, LLD, 1995; MA, Cornell U., 1967; D honoris causa, U. Montreal, 1995. Dep. minister Ministry Industry and Tourism, Ont., 1978-81; pres., chief exec. officer Redpath Industries, Ltd., Toronto, Ont., 1981-88; mng. dir. N.Am. Tate & Lyle, PLC, 1986-89; chmn. bd. Redpath Industries, Ltd., 1988-89; vice chmn. Bank of Nova Scotia, 1989-90; pres., chief operating officer BCE, Inc., Montreal, 1990-92; pres., CEO BCE Inc., Montreal, Can., 1992-93, chmn., pres. CEO, 1993-96, chmn., CEO, 1996—; bd. dirs. Tate & Lyle plc, London, Stelco Inc., BCE, Inc., Bell Can., No. Telecom, Teleglobe Inc., C.W. Howe Inst., Bell Can. Internat., BCE Mobile Comm., Inc., Chrysler Can. Ltd., Chrysler Corp., Bell-No. Rsch. Ltd.; mem. internat. coun. J.P. Morgan and Co., N.Y.C. Bd. govs. Olympic Trust Can., McGill U., 1992—; mem. policy com. Bus. Coun. on Nat. Issues; mem. The Trilateral Commn.; trustee Montreal Mus. of Fine Arts Found. Mem. The Mount Royal Club of Montreal, York Club, Toronto Club, Toronto Golf Club, Rideau Club, Univ. Club of Montreal, Royal Montreal Golf Club, Mount Bruno Country Club. Home: 1321 Sherbrooke St W Apt A-110, Montreal, PQ Canada H3G 1J4 Office: BCE Inc / Ste 3700, 1000 Rue de la Gauchetière O, Montreal, PQ Canada H3B 4Y7

WILSON, M. ROY, medical educator; b. Yokohama, Japan, Nov. 28, 1953. BS, Allegheny Coll., 1976; MD, Harvard Med. Sch., 1980; MS in Epidemiology, UCLA, 1990. Diplomate Nat. Bd. Medicine, Am. Bd. Ophthalmology. Intern Harlem Hosp. Ctr., N.Y.C., 1980-81; resident in ophthalmology Mass. Eye & Ear Infirmary/Harvard Med. Sch., Boston, 1981-84, glaucoma, 1984-85; clin. fellow in ophthalmology Harvard Med. Sch., 1980-85, clin. asst. ophthalmology, 1985-86; clin. instr. dept. surgery, Divsn. Ophthalmology Howard U. Sch. Medicine, Washington, 1985-86; asst. prof. ophthalmology UCLA, 1986-91; asst. prof., chief Divsn. Ophthalmology Charles R. Drew U. of Medicine and Sci., L.A., 1986-90, assoc. prof., chief Divsn. Ophthalmology, 1991-94, acad. dean, 1993-95, 94—, dean, 1995—, prof., 1994—; prof. UCLA, 1994—; asst. in ophthalmology Mass. Eye and Ear Infirmary, 1985-86; cons. ophthalmologist, Victoria Hosp., Castries, St. Lucia, 1985-86; hosp. appointment, UCLA; chief physician Martin Luther King, Jr. Hosp., L.A., 1986—; project dir. Internat. Eye Found., Ministry of Health, 1985-86; biology lab instr., Allegheny coll., 1975; instr. in biochemistry Harvard U. Summer Sch., 1977-78; instr. Harvard Med. Sch., 1980-85, others; cons. and presenter in field; participant coms. in field. Mem. AMA, Assn. Rsch. in Vision and Ophthalmology, Chandler-Grant Glaucoma Soc., Nat. Med. Assn., Am. Acad. Ophthalmology, Soc. Eye Surgeons Internat. Eye Found., Mass. Eye and Ear Infirmary Alumni Assn., So. Calif. Glaucoma Soc., West Coast Glaucoma Study Club, Assn. Univ. Profs. in Ophthalmology, L.A. Eye Soc., Calif. Med. Assn., Am. Glaucoma Soc., Soc. Epidemiol. Rsch., Am. Pub. Health Assn. Office: 1621 E 120th St Los Angeles CA 90059

WILSON, MABLE JEAN, paralegal; b. Pine Bluff, Ark., July 17, 1948; d. James Arthur and Ruthia Mae (Dansby) Watson; children: Dana Eileen, Dana Kent Fuller. Student, U.So. Calif., 1983-86. Dep. sheriff L.A. County, 1971-80; ind. paralegal Wilson's Divorce Clinic, L.A., 1980—. Participant Dist. Atty. Victim Witness Program, L.A., 1991; active Brotherhood Crusade, L.A., 1992. Recipient Merit award L.A. County Bar Assn., 1993. Mem. Assn. Family and Conciliation Cts., Folk Power Inc. (bd. dirs. 1993—), Alpha Svc. Co. (v.p. 1993—). Avocations: interior decorating, making stained glass windows, ceramics, painting, writing poetry. Office: 3860 Crenshaw Blvd Ste 201 Los Angeles CA 90008-1816

WILSON, MARC FRASER, art museum administrator and curator; b. Akron, Ohio, Sept. 12, 1941; s. Fraser Eugene and Pauline Christine (Hoff) W.; m. Elizabeth Marie Fulder, Aug. 2, 1975. BA, Yale U., 1963, MA, 1967. Departmental asst. Cleve. Mus. Art, 1964; translator, project cons. Nat. Palace Mus., Taipei, Taiwan, 1968-71; assoc. curator of Chinese art Nelson Gallery-Atkins Mus., Kansas City, Mo., 1971-73, curator of Oriental art, 1973—, interim dir., 1982, dir. and curator Oriental art, 1982—; mem., rapporteur Indo-US Subcom. on Edn. and Culture, Washington, 1976-79; mem. adv. com. Asia Soc. Galleries, N.Y.C., 1984—, China Inst. in Am., 1985—. Mem. adv. com. Muni-Art Commn. on Urban Sculpture, Kansas City, 1984-87; com. mem. Kansas City-Xi'an, China, Sister City program, 1986—; mem. humanities coun. Joynson County Cmty. Coll., 1976-79; commr. Japan-U.S. Friendship Commn., Washington, 1986-88; panelist Japan-U.S. Cultural and Edn. Cooperation, Washington, 1986-88; mem. mayor's task force on race relations, 1996—; mem. indemnity adv. panel, 1995—; v.p. Brush Creek Ptnrs. 1995—. Recipient The William Yates Medallion Civic Svc. award William Jewell Coll., 1995. Mem. Assn. Art Mus. Dirs. (treas., trustee 1988-90, chmn. works of art com. 1986-90), Mo. China Coun., Fed. Coun. Arts and Humanities (chmn. arts and artifacts indemnity adv. panel 1986-89). Office: Nelson-Atkins Mus Art 4525 Oak St Kansas City MO 64111-1818

WILSON, MARGARET BUSH, lawyer, civil rights leader; b. St. Louis, Jan. 30, 1919; married; 1 child, Robert Edmund. B.A. cum laude, Talladega Coll., 1940; LL.B., Lincoln U., 1943. Ptnr. Wilson & Wilson, St. Louis, 1947-65; now with firm Wilson & Assocs.; asst. dir. St. Louis Lawyers for Housing, 1969-72; asst. atty. gen. Mo., 1961-62; atty. Rural Electrification Adminstrn., Dept. Agr., St. Louis, 1943-45; instr. civil procedure St. Louis U. Sch. Law, 1971; chmn. St. Louis Land Reutilization Authority, 1975-76; mem. Mo. Coun. Criminal Justice, 1972—; chmn. Intergroup Corp., 1985-87; bd. dirs. Mut. of N.Y. Mem. gen. adv. com. ACDA, 1978-81; trustee emeritus Washington U., St. Louis; chmn. bd. trustees Talladega Coll., Ala., 1988-92; nat. bd. dirs. ARC, 1975-81, United Way, 1978-84, Police Found., 1976-93; treas. NAACP Nat. Housing Corp., 1971-84, chmn. nat. bd., 1975-84; dep. dir./acting dir. St. Louis Model City Agy., 1968-69; adminstr. Mo. Commn. Svc. and Continuing Edn., 1967-68. Recipient Bishop's award Episcopal Diocese Mo., 1962; Juliette Derricotte fellow, 1939-40. Mem.

ABA (chmn. youth edn. for citizenship 1991-94), Nat. Bar Assn., Mo. Bar Assn., Mound City Bar Assn., St. Louis Bar Assn., Alpha Kappa Alpha. Office: Wilson & Assocs 4054 Lindell Blvd Saint Louis MO 63108-3202

WILSON, MARGARET DAULER, philosophy educator; b. Pitts., Jan. 29, 1939; d. Lee Van Voorhis and Margaret (Hodge) D.; m. Emmett Wilson, Jr., June 12, 1962. A.B., Vassar Coll., 1960; A.M., Harvard U., 1963, Ph.D., 1965; postgrad., Oxford U., 1963-64. Asst. prof. philosophy Columbia U., 1965-67; asst. prof. Rockefeller U., 1967-70; asso. prof. philosophy Princeton (N.J.) U., 1970-75, prof., 1975—, acting chmn. dept. philosophy, 1987-88; dir. Summer Inst. Early Modern Philosophy, Bristol, R.I., 1974; vis. asst. prof. Barnard Coll., part-time 1969-70. Author: Descartes, 1978; editor: The Essential Descartes, 1969. Mem. Planning Bd. Franklin Twp., N.J., 1988-92, Environ. Commn., 1988-95. Recipient Centennial medal Harvard Grad. Sch. Arts and Scis., 1989, Behrman prize for distinction in humanities Princeton U., 1994; Japan Soc. for Promotion of Sci. fellow, 1990, Guggenheim fellow, 1977-79, Am. Coun. Learned Socs. fellow, 1982-83; visitor Inst. Advanced Study, spring 1973. Fellow Am. Acad. Arts and Scis.; mem. Am. Philos. Assn. (v.p. ea. divsn. 1993-94, pres. ea. divsn. 1994-95), Leibniz Soc. N.Am. (pres. 1986-90), Internat. Berkeley Soc. Home: 943 Canal Rd Princeton NJ 08540-8509 Office: Princeton U Dept Philosophy 1879 Hall Princeton NJ 08544

WILSON, MARGARET EILEEN, retired physical education educator; b. Kansas City, Mo., Aug. 4, 1925; d. Edward Leslie and Bertha Mae (Coe) W. BS in Edn., U. Ark., 1944, MS, 1949; PhD, U. Iowa, 1960. Cert. secondary tchr., Ark. Recreation dir. Pine Bluff (Ark.) Arsenal, 1944-45; instr. Ctrl. High Sch., Muskogee, Okla., 1945-48; grad. asst. U. Ark., Fayetteville, 1948-49; instr. Fayetteville High Sch., 1949-52; from instr. to asst. prof. Ark. Poly. Coll., Russellville, 1952-57, assoc. prof., 1959-65; grad. asst. U. Iowa, Iowa City, 1957-59; prof. Tex. Tech. U., Lubbock, 1965-90, dept. chair health, phys. edn. and recreation for women, 1967-76, prof. emerita, 1990—; mem. Tex. Tech. Faculty Senate, 1978-90, pres., 1978-79, 85-86. Active Lubbock County Dem. Ctrl. Com., 1993, 94, 96. Recipient AMOCO Found. Disting. Tchg. award, 1978, Disting. Faculty award in Tex. Tech. Moms and Dads Assn., 1987. Mem. AAHPERD (life), Tex. Assn. for Health, Phy. Edn., Recreation and Dance (Honor award 1979, David K. Bruce award 1992), Tex. Tech. Faculty Legal Action Assn. (pres. 1990-96), Lubbock Ret. Tchrs. Assn. (cmty. svc. chair 1994-96, co-treas. 1996—), Double T Connection (chair membership 1991-94), Delta Gamma (house corp. treas. 1982-91, Cable award 1978), Delta Kappa Gamma (chpt. pres. 1972-74, Chpt. Achievement award 1976, state corr. sec. 1979-81, state conv. chair 1979-80, state nominations com. 1985-87, state pers. com. 1987-89, State Achievement award 1987, state necrology com. 1993-95, state fin. com. 1995—). Presbyterian. Avocations: gardening, needlepoint, reading. Home: 5411 46th St Lubbock TX 79414-1513 Office: Tex Tech U Womens Gymnasium Lubbock TX 79409

WILSON, MARJORIE PRICE, physician, medical commission executive. Student, Bryn Mawr Coll., 1942-45; M.D., U. Pitts., 1949. Intern U. Pitts. Med. Ctr. Hosps., 1949-50; resident Children's Hosp. U. Pitts., 1950-51, Jackson Meml. Hosp., U. Miami Sch. Medicine, 1954-56; chief residency and internship div. edn. svc. Office of Rsch. and Edn., VA, Washington, 1956, chief profl. tng. div., 1956-60, asst. dir. edn. svc., 1960; chief tng. br. Nat. Inst. Arthritis and Metabolic Disease NIH, Bethesda, Md., 1960-63, asst. to assoc. dir. for tng. Office of Dir., 1963-64, assoc. dir. program devel. OPPD, 1967-69, asst. dir. program planning and evaluation, 1969-70; assoc. dir. extramural programs Nat. Libr. Medicine, 1964-67; dir. dept. instl. devel. Assn. Am. Med. Colls., Washington, 1970-81; sr. assoc. dean U. Md. Sch. Medicine, Balt., 1981-86, vice dean, 1986-88, acting dean, 1984; pres., CEO, Ednl. Commn. Fgn. Med. Grads., Phila., 1988-95, emeritus, 1995—; mem. Inst. Medicine Nat. Acad. Scis.,1974—; bd. visitors U. Pitts. Sch. Medicine, 1974—; mem. Nat. Bd. Med. Examiners, 1980-87, 89—; mem. adv. bd. Fogarty Internat. Ctr., 1991—. Contbr. articles to profl. jours. Mem. adv. bd. Robert Wood Johnson Health Policy Fellowships, 1975-87; trustee Analytic Services, Inc., Falls Church, Va., 1976—. Fellow Am. Coll. Physician Execs., AAAS; mem. Assn. Am. Med. Colls., Am. Fedn. Clin. Research, IEEE. Office: Ste 475 2401 Pennsylvania Ave NW Washington DC 20037

WILSON, MARY ELIZABETH, physician, educator; b. Indpls., Nov. 19, 1942; d. Ralph Richard and Catheryn Rebecca (Kurtz) Lausch; m. Harvey Vernon Fineberg, May 16, 1975. AB, Ind. U., 1963; MD, U. Wis., 1971. Diplomate Am. Bd. Internal Medicine, Am. Bd. Infectious Diseases. Tchr. of French and English Marquette Sch., Madison, Wis., 1963-66; intern in medicine Beth Israel Hosp., Boston, 1971-72, resident in medicine, 1972-73, fellow in infectious diseases, 1973-75; physician Albert Schweitzer Hosp., Deschapelles, Haiti, 1974-75, Harvard Health Svcs., Cambridge, Mass., 1974-75; asst. physician Cambridge Hosp., 1975-78; hosp. epidemiologist Mt. Auburn Hosp., Cambridge, 1975-79, chief of infectious diseases, 1978—; adv. com. immunization practices Ctrs. for Disease Control, Atlanta, 1988-92; acad. adv. com. Nat. Inst. Pub. Health, Mex., 1989-91; cons. Ford Found., 1988; instr. in medicine Harvard Med. Sch., Boston, 1975-93, asst. clin. prof., 1994—; asst. prof. depts. epidemiology and population and internat. health Harvard Sch. Pub. Health, 1994—; lectr. Sultan Qaboos U., Oman, 1991; chair Woods Hole Workshop, Emerging Infectious Diseases. Author: A World Guide to Infections: Diseases, Distribution, Diagnosis, 1991; co-editor: (with Richard Levins and Andrew Spielman) Disease in Evolution: Global Changes and Emergence of Infectious Diseases, 1994; mem. editl. bd. Current Issues in Pub. Health; edtl. bd., travel medicine & tropical diseases sect. editor Infectious Diseases in Clinical Practice. Mem. Cambridge Task Force on AIDS, 1987—, Earthwatch, Watertown, Mass., Cultural Survival, Inc., Cambridge; bd. dirs. Horizon Communications, West Cornwall, Conn., 1990. Recipient Lewis E. and Edith Phillips award U. Wis. Med. Sch., 1969, Cora M. and Edward Van Liere award, 1971, Mosby Scholarship Book award, 1971. Fellow ACP, Infectious Diseases Soc. Am., Royal Soc. Tropical Medicine and Hygiene; mem. Am. Soc. Microbiology, N.Y. Acad. Scis., Am. Soc. Tropical Medicine and Hygiene, Mass. Infectious Diseases Soc., Peabody Soc., Internat. Soc. Travel Medicine, Wilderness Med. Soc., Soc. for Vector Ecology, Internat. Union Against Tuberculosis and Lung Disease, Soc. for Epidemiol. Rsch., Sigma Sigma, Phi Sigma Iota, Alpha Omega Alpha. Avocations: playing the flute, hiking, reading, travel. Office: Mt Auburn Hosp 330 Mount Auburn St Cambridge MA 02138-5502

WILSON, MARY LOUISE, learning systems company executive; b. Chgo., June 29, 1940; d. John Baptiste and Marion Margaret (Coveney) Sweig; m. John Paul Wilson, June 7, 1969; 1 son, Devin Sweig. Student, U. Toronto, 1960-61; B.A., Smith Coll., 1962; M.A., Emerson Coll., 1965; Ph.D., Northwestern U., 1968. Assoc. prof. speech pathology California (Pa.) State Coll., 1968-69; prof. communication scis. and disorders U. Vt., Burlingon, 1969-94, prof. emerita, 1994—, dir. program in communication sci. and disorders, 1971-77, acting chmn., 1977-80; dir. E. M. Luse Center for Communication Disorders, 1971-81; disting. vis. scholar Worcester State Coll., Mass., 1984; pres. Laureate Learning Systems, Inc., 1982—; mem. Vt. State Adv. Com. on Spl. Edn., 1974; project dir. Bur. Edn. of Handicapped, 1971-83. Author: Wilson Initial Syntax Program, 1972, Wilson Expanded Syntax Program, 1976, Syntax Remediation: A Generative Grammar Approach to Language Development, 1977, Prescriptive Analysis of Language Disorders, 1979, Expressive Syntax Assessment, 1979, Sequential Software for Language Intervention, 1991; co-author: First Words, 1982, 3d edit., 1989, Speak Up, 1983, First Categories, 1983, Microcomputer Language Assessment and Development System, 1984, 2d edit., 1988, First Verbs, 1985, 2d edit., 1989, Fast Access Scan Talker, 1985, First Words II, 1986, 2d edit., 1989, Twenty Categories, 1986, 2d edit., 1989, Talking Series, 1987, Creature Antics, 1987, Creature Chorus, 1987, Creature Capers, 1988, Words and Concepts, 1989, Concentrate! On Words and Concepts, 1989, Early Emergins Rules, 1990, Creature Features, 1992, Exploring Vocabulary, 1994, Simple Sentence Structure, 1994. Mem. Am. Speech and Hearing Assn., Am. Assn. Mental Retardation (pres. region X), Coun. Exceptional Children, Vt. Speech and Hearing Assn. Home: RR 2 Box 355 Hinesburg VT 05461-9409 Office: Laureate Learning Systems Inc 110 E Spring St Winooski VT 05404-1837

WILSON, MATTHEW FREDERICK, newspaper editor; b. San Francisco, May 10, 1956; s. Kenneth E. and Verna Lee (Hunter) W. BA in Philosophy, U. Calif., Berkeley, 1978. Copy person San Francisco Chronicle, summers 1975, 76, 77, copy editor, 1978-82, editorial systems coord., 1982-84; budget analyst San Francisco Newspaper Agy., 1984085; asst. news editor San Francisco Chronicle, 1985-87, asst. to exec. editor, 1987-88, mng. editor, 1988-95, exec. editor, 1995—. Mem. Am. Soc. Newspaper Editors, AP Mng. Editors, Calif. Soc. Newspaper Editors. Office: San Francisco Chronicle 901 Mission St San Francisco CA 94103-2905

WILSON, MELVIN EDMOND, civil engineer; b. Bremerton, Wash., Aug. 3, 1935; s. Edmond Curt and Madeline Rose (Deal) W.; m. Deanna May Stevens, Nov. 22, 1957 (div. Mar. 1971); children: Kathleen, Debra Wilson Frank. BSCE, U. Wash., 1957, MSCE, 1958. Registered profl. engr., Wash. Asst. civil engr. City of Seattle, 1958-60, assoc. civil engr., 1960-64, sr. civil engr., 1964-66, supervising civil engr., 1966-75, sr. civil engr., 1975-77, mgr. X, 1977-88; owner Wilson Cons. Svcs., Seattle, 1988-89; transp. systems dir. City of Renton, Wash., 1989—; owner Mel Wilson Photographer, Seattle, 1975-84. Contbr. reports to profl. jours. Rep. Renton transp. work group King County (Wash.) Growth Mgmt. Policy Com.; rep. Renton tech. adv. com. South County Area Transp. Bd., King County, 1992—, developer svc. policy (adopted by Puget Sound Govtl. Conf.) to encourage travel by transit. successfuly led effort to make Renton first suburban city to receive direct transit svc. under Met. King County Plan, 1994. Mem. ASCE, Am. Pub. Works Assn., Inst. Transp. Engrs., Tau Beta Pi, Sigma Xi. Avocations: pphotography, weight lifting, hiking. Office: City of Renton 200 Mill Ave S Renton WA 98055-2132

WILSON, MICHAEL ALAN, health facility administrator; b. Springfield, Mo., Aug. 18, 1947; s. Allen and Hazel (Hudson) W.; m. Alla L. Sachowicz, Feb. 14, 1985; children: Shawn, Cara. B, Baylor U., 1970; M, Chapman Coll., 1973; MBA, S.W. Mo. State U., 1975. Asst. adminstr. Nicollet Clinic, Mpls., 1976-80; exec. dir. Colorado Springs (Colo.) Med. Ctr., 1980-84; exec. v.p. LaSalle Clinic, Neenah, Wis., 1984-90; pres., chief adminstrv. officer Dean Med. Ctr., Madison, Wis., 1990—; bd. dirs. Dean Med. Ctr. and Dean Care HMO, Madison, Physician Ins. Co. Wis., Madison. Bd. dirs. Edgewood High Sch., Madison, 1991-93, Physician Ins. Co. of Wis., 1991—, SMS Holdings, 1990-91; mem. cabinet United Way, Madison, 1991—, chmn. ptnrs. in prevention, 1992—. With USN, 1970-76. Mem. Wis. Med. Group Mgmt. Assn. (pres. 1989-90), Med. Group Mgmt. Assn. (2d v.p. Midwest sect. 1991-92, 1st v.p. Midwest sect. 1992-93, pres. Midwest sect. 1994-95, nat. 1st v.p. 1996), Rotary Club. Presbyterian. Avocations: golf, literature, sports. Office: Dean Med Ctr 1313 Fish Hatchery Rd Madison WI 53715-1911

WILSON, MICHAEL GREGG, film producer, writer; b. N.Y.C., Jan. 21, 1942; s. Lewis Gilbert Wilson and Dana (Natol) Broccoli; m. Coila Jane Hurley; children: David, Gregg. BS, Harvey Mudd Coll., 1963; JD, Stanford U., 1966. Bar: D.C., Calif., N.Y. Legal advisor FAA-DOT, Washington, 1966-67; assoc. Surrey, Karasik, Gould, Green, Washington, 1967-71; ptnr. Surrey and Morse, Washington and N.Y.C., 1971-74; legal advisor Eon Prodns., London, 1974-78, producer, mng. dir., 1978—. Writer/prodr.: For Your Eyes Only, 1981, Octopussy, 1983, View to a Kill, 1985, The Living Daylights, 1987, Licence to Kill, 1989; prodr.: Goldeneye, 1995; author: Pictorialism in California, Getty Museum, 1994. Avocation: 19th and 20th century photograph collecting.

WILSON, MILNER BRADLEY, III, retired banker; b. Spartanburg, S.C., Nov. 17, 1933; s. Milner Bradley and Margaret (Nash) W.; m. Nancy Brock, Aug. 18, 1956; children—Margaret, Julia, Bradley. A.B., Duke U., 1955; LL.B., U. S.C., 1961; A.M.P., Harvard U., 1973. CLU. With Citizens & So. Nat. Bank S.C., Charleston, 1961-84, gen. trust officer, 1971-72, exec. v.p., 1972-84; v.p. Barnett Banks Trust Co. N.A., Hallandale, Fla., 1984-86; regional v.p. Barnett Banks Trust Co. N.A., Tampa, Fla., 1986-87; sr. v.p. Barnett Banks Trust Co. N.A., Jacksonville, Fla., 1987-89; v.p. No. Trust Bank of Fla., Miami, 1989-95. Served with USMC, 1955-58. Mem. ABA. Home: 1603 Hunters Rd Huntersville NC 28078

WILSON, MINTER LOWTHER, JR., retired officers association executive; b. Morgantown, W.Va., Aug. 19, 1925; s. Minter Lowther and Mary Mildred (Friend) W.; m. Helen Hope Sauerwein, June 18, 1946; children—Mary Florence, Barbara Ann, Karen Lee, Stephen David. B.S. in Mil. Sci. and Engring., U.S. Mil. Acad., 1946; M.S. in Journalism, U. Wis., Madison, 1963; diploma, NATO Def. Coll., Rome, 1969, U.S. Army War Coll., 1971. Commd. officer U.S. Army, 1946, advanced through grades to col., comdg. officer 1st Brigade, 1st Armored Div., 1968-69; chief of pub. info. Supreme Hdqrs. Allied Powers, Europe, 1969-72; editor Ret. Officer Mag., Alexandria, Va., 1972-88; dir. communications Ret. Officers Assn., Alexandria, 1972-88. Contbr. articles to profl. jours. Chmn. bd. deacons Ch. of the Covenant, Arlington, 1974-77, elder, 1977-80, 88-93, clk. of session, 1991-94, chmn. bd. trustees, 1982-86; mem. troop com. Boy Scouts Am., 1972-78. Decorated Commendation medal, Legion of Merit (2); recipient George Washington Honor medal Freedoms Found., 1975, 76, 77, George Washington Honor medal encased Freedoms Found., 1979, Honor cert. Freedoms Found., 1973, 74, 78. Mem. West Point Soc. of D.C. (life, bd. govs. 1978-81), Army Distaff Found. (bd. dirs. 1980-83), Assn. U.S. Army, Ret. Officers Assn. (life). Presbyterian. Club: Army Navy Country. Avocations: photography; golf; skiing; tennis; racquetball. Home: 3116 N Thomas St Arlington VA 22207-4120

WILSON, MIRIAM GEISENDORFER, physician, educator; b. Yakima, Wash., Dec. 3, 1922; d. Emil and Frances Geisendorfer; m. Howard G. Wilson, June 21, 1947; children—Claire, Paula, Geoffrey, Nicola, Marla. B.S., U. Wash., Seattle, 1944, M.S., 1945; M.D., U. Calif., San Francisco, 1950. Mem. faculty U. So. Calif. Sch. Medicine, L.A., 1965—, prof. pediatrics, 1969—. Office: U So Calif Med Ctr 1129 N State St Los Angeles CA 90033-1069

WILSON, MITCHELL B., fraternal organization administrator; b. Berea, Ky., Jan. 27, 1956; s. William Paul and Shirley Ann (Rose) W.; m. Joan Gentry, May 25, 1985; 1 child, Theodore Mitchell. BA, U. Ky., Lexington, 1980. Chpt. cons. Kappa Sigma Frat., Charlottsville, Va., 1980-82, exec. asst., 1982-83, dir. chpt. ops., 1983-85, dir. pub. rels., 1985-87, exec. dir., 1987—. Editor: The Caducens Mag., 1987—. Mem. Am. Soc. Assoc. Execs., Frat. Execs. Assn. Home: 506 Nottingham Rd Charlottesville VA 22901-1239 Office: Kappa Sigma PO Box 5066 Charlottesville VA 22905-5066

WILSON, MYRON ROBERT, JR., retired psychiatrist; b. Helena, Mont., Sept. 21, 1932; s. Myron Robert Sr. and Constance Ernestine (Bultman) W. BA, Stanford U., 1954, MD, 1957. Diplomate Am. Bd. Psychiatry and Neurology. Dir. adolescent psychiatry Mayo Clinc, Rochester, Minn., 1965-71; pres. and psychiatrist in chief Wilson Ctr., Faribault, Minn., 1971-86; ret., 1986; chmn. Wilson Ctr., 1986-90; ret., 1990; assoc. clin. prof. psychiatry UCLA, 1985—. Contbr. articles to profl. jours. Chmn., chief exec. officer C.B. Wilson Found., L.A., 1986—; mem. bd. dirs. Pasadena Symphony Orchestra Assn., Calif., 1987. Served to lt. comdr., 1958-60. Fellow Mayo Grad. Sch. Medicine, Rochester, 1960-65. Fellow Am. Psychiat. Assn., Am. Soc. for Adolescent Psychiatry, Internat. Soc. for Adolescent Psychiatry (founder, treas. 1985-88, sec. 1985-88, treas. 1988-92); mem. Soc. Sigma Xi (Mayo Found. chpt.). Episcopalian. Office: Wilson Found 8033 W Sunset Blvd # 4019 West Hollywood CA 90069-1925

WILSON, NANCY, singer; b. Chillicothe, Ohio, Feb. 20, 1937; d. Olden and Lillian (Ryan) W.; m. Kenneth C. Dennis (div. 1969); 1 child, Kenneth C.; m. Wiley Burton, 1974; children: Samantha, Sheryl. Ed., Columbus (Ohio) schs. Began career as singer with local groups, then joined Rusty Bryant band, 1956, toured Midwest and Can., until 1958, singing independently, 1959—, rec. artist Capitol Records, EMI Records, Japan, Nippon Columbia, Japan, Interface, Japan, Columbia Records, USA, Epic/Sony Japan; ablums include (with Heart): Dreamboat Annie, 1976, Little Queen, 1977, Magazine, 1978, Dog and Butterfly, 1978, Beb La Strange, 1980, Greatest Hits Live, 1980, Private Audition, 1982, Passionwroks, 1983, Heart, 1985, Bad Animals, 1987; recs. include I'll Be a Song, Just To Keep You Satisfied, Forbidden Lover, Nancy Now, Lady With A Song, With My Lover Beside Me, 1991; internat. concert tours, U.S., Japan, Europe, Indonesia, Australia; rec. artist; TV appearances include Police Story, Hawaii Five-O, It's A Living; hostess: TV series Nancy Wilson Show, Sta. KNBC, L.A., 1974-75, Red Hot & Cool (syndicated), 1990—; appeared in film: The Big Score. Recipient Grammy award for Best R&B Vocal Nat. Acad. Rec. Arts and Scis., Best Female Vocalist award Playboy and Down Beat Jazz Polls, Image award NAACP, 1986, award Nat. Med. Assn., Equitable (17th Black Achievement) award, Urban Network Lifetime Achievement award, 1990, Whitney Young awd., Los Angeles Urban League, Essence awd., Essence Magazine, 1992; Star on Hollywood Walk of Fame, 1990.

WILSON, NANCY JEANNE, laboratory director, medical technologist; b. Neptune, N.J., Apr. 17, 1951; d. Harry E. Sr. and Kathryn E. (O'Shea) W. BS, Monmouth Coll., 1975; MPA, Fairleigh Dickinson U., 1988. Clin. intern med. tech., staff med. technologist Riverview Med. Ctr., 1975; staff med. technologist Rush Clin. Labs., Red Bank, N.J., 1975; staff med. technologist Kimball Med. Ctr., Lakewood, N.J., 1975-76, clin. lab. supr., 1976-86; infection control practice Jersey Shore Med. Ctr., Neptune, N.J., 1990; dir. lab. and diagnostic svcs. Carrier Found., Belle Meade, N.J., 1991—. Mem. Am. Soc. Clin. Pathologists (diplomate lab. mgmt.), Am. Assn. Clin. Chemistry, Am. Soc. Microbiology, Clin. Lab. Mgmt. Assn., Am. Soc. Clinics Lab. Sci., Pi Alpha Alpha. Avocations: golf, walking, relaxing. Home: 42 Monument St Freehold NJ 07728 Office: Carrier Found Rt 601 PO Box 147 Belle Mead NJ 08502

WILSON, NANCY LINDA, church officer; b. Mineola, N.Y., July 13, 1950. Grad., Allegheny Coll.; student, Boston U.; MDiv, SS, Cyril and Methodius Sem. Ordained to ministry Universal Fellowship of Met. Cmty. Chs. Dist. coord. N.E. dist. Universal Fellowship of Met. Cmty. Chs.; clk. bd. of elders Fellowship hdqrs. Universal Fellowship of Met. Cmty. Chs., L.A., 1979-86; sr. pastor Met. Comty. Ch. UFMCC, L.A., 1986—, vice-moderator, 1993—; bd. trustees Samaritan Coll.; founder, chief ecumenical officer Ecumenical Witness and Ministry. Author: Our Tribe: Queen Folks, God, Jesus and the Bible, 1995; co-author: Amazing Grace; prodr.: (brochure) Our Story Too. Rockefeller scholar. Office: Met Cmty Ch PO Box 46609 Los Angeles CA 90046

WILSON, NORMAN GLENN, church administrator, writer; b. Rensselaer, N.Y., Nov. 3, 1936; s. Lawrence Wilbur and Wilhelmena Augusta (Knapp) W.; m. Nancy Ann Deyo, Nov. 17, 1956; children: Beth, Lawrence, Jonathon. BRE in Religious Edn., United Wesleyan Coll., 1958, DD (hon.), 1986; MA in Biblical Studies, Winona Lake Sch. Theology, 1968. Pastor The Wesleyan Ch., 1958-76, Gloversville, N.Y., 1963-66, North Lakeport, Mich., 1966-70, Owosso, Mich., 1970-76; dir. comm. The Wesleyan Ch., Indpls., 1992—; program prodr., speaker The Wesleyan Hour, Indpls., 1975—; mem. gen. bd. adminstrn. The Wesleyan Ch., Indpls., 1992—; disting. lectr. Staley Found., 1986. Author: How to Have a Happy Home, 1976, Christianity in Shoe Leather, 1978, The Constitution of the Kingdom, 1989, People Just Like Us, 1994; editor The Wesleyan Advocate, 1992—. Mem. Nat. Religious Broadcasters (bd. dirs. 1984—, Merit award 1984). Avocations: oil painting, antique cars. Home: 304 Scarborough Way Noblesville IN 46060-3881

WILSON, NORMAN LOUIS, psychiatrist, educator; b. Buffalo, Oct. 4, 1937; s. Norman Louis and Martha (Aiken) W.; m. Phien Ly Thi, Aug. 22, 1988; 1 child, Daniel. BS in Biophysics summa cum laude, Yale U., 1959; MD, Harvard U., Boston, 1963. Diplomate Am. Bd. Psychiatry and Neurology, Am. Coll. Forensic Examiners, Am. Bd. Forensic Medicine, Am. Acad. Experts in Traumatic Stress, Nat. Registry Group Therapists. Med. intern Rush-Presbyn.-St. Luke's Med. Ctr., Chgo., 1963-64; resident in psychiatry, tchg. fellow Mass. Mental Health Ctr.-Harvard U., Boston, 1964-66, Peter Bent Brigham Hosp.-Harvard U., 1966-67; pvt. practice, Washington, 1969—; condr. workshops on use of hypnosis in treatment of multiple personality disorder, mood disorders, psychopharmacology; asst. clin. prof. dept. psychiatry and behavioral sci. George Washington U. Sch. Medicine, Washington, 1973—; founding mem., mem. faculty Washington Psychotherapy Tng. Inst., 1989—; staff psychiatrist Cmty. Psychiat. Clinic, Bethesda, Md., 1969-71, D.C. Forensic Psychiat. Adminstrn., 1974-89; psychiatrist NIH Employee Health Svc., 1971-74, John Howard Pavilion, St. Elizabeth's Hosp., Washington, 1987-89; cons. Clin. Ctr., NIH, 1974-80, Mental Health Assocs., Adelphi, Md., 1983-92, Luth. Social Svcs., Washington, 1990-93, occupl. med. svc. NIH, 1989-93; chmn. dept. psychiatry Washington Hosp. Ctr., 1987-92, admitting privileges; admitting privileges George Washington U. Hosp., Psychiat. Inst. Washington, Dominion Hosp.; mem. mktg. com. Nat. Capital Reciprocal Ins. Co. Capt. M.C., USAF, 1967-69. Fellow Am. Psychiat. Assn.; mem. Am. Group Therapy Assn., Am. Coll. Forensic Examiners, Am. Acad. Psychiat. and Law, Internat. Soc. for Study Dissociation, Washington Psychiat. Soc. (former mem. coms. on liaison with non-psychiatry mental health works, forensic psychiatry, pub. rels.), Med. Soc. D.C. (past mem. alcohol com. and mental health com.), Amnesty Internat., Physicians for Social Responsibility, Am. Coalition for Abuse Awareness, Phi Beta Kappa. Avocations: scuba diving, backpacking, canoe tripping, movies, classical and folk music. Office: 4025 Connecticut Ave NW Washington DC 20008-1148 *I quote Spinoza: "Learn as if yo will live forever, live as if you will die tomorrow." Work to achieve balance in your life.*

WILSON, OWEN MEREDITH, JR., lawyer; b. Oakland, Calif., Dec. 22, 1939; s. O. Meredith and Marian Wilson; m. Sandra A. Wilson (div.); children: Ann, Melissa, Jennifer; m. Teddi Anne Wilson; children: Amanda, Lisa. Student, U. Utah, 1957-59; AB, Harvard U., 1961; LLB, U. Minn., 1965. Bar: Oreg. 1965, Wash. 1985. Ptnr. Lane Powell Spears Lubersky, Portland, Oreg., 1965—; mem. mediation panel U.S. Dist. Ct., 1986—. Mem. bd. visitors Law Sch. U. Minn., 1990—. Mem. ABA, Oreg. State Bar Assn., Wash. State Bar, Multnomah Bar Assn. Office: 520 SW Yamhill St Ste 800 Portland OR 97204-1331

WILSON, P. CRAIG, program director, marketing professional, consultant; b. Erie, Pa., Nov. 2, 1943; s. Percy Walter and Jean Marie (Orton) W.; m. Darlene Anne Ford; children: Allen, Dain. BA in Polit. Sci., Gannon U., Erie, 1965; MA in Founds. of Edn., Troy (Ala.) State U., 1971; EdS in Higher Edn. Adminstrn., George Washington U., 1978, EdD in Higher Edn. Adminstrn., 1991. Commd. USAF, 1966, advanced through grades to maj., ret., 1986; benefits mgr. Coll. William and Mary, Williamsburg, Va., 1986-87; mktg. cons., pres. Career Transition Inc., Hampton, Va., 1987—; mktg. program mgr. George Washington U., Hampton, 1987—; asst. prof. George Washington U., Washington, 1989—; adj. faculty St. Leo Coll., Hampton, 1976-84, Golden Gate U., Hampton, 1976-84. Contbr. articles to profl. jours. Pres. Willow Oaks Civic Assn., Hampton, 1990, membership chmn., 1989; bd. dirs. Big Bros., Big Sisters, Hampton, 1984. Named Pers. Office of the Yr. USAF, 1979. Mem. NRA, Learning Resources Network, Assn. Continuing Higher Edn., S.E. Va. Live Steamers (pres. 1991—), Kiwanis (v.p. 1987—). Republican. Lutheran. Avocations: live steam locomotive technology, woodcraft, hunting. Office: George Washington Univ One Enterprise Pky Hampton VA 23666

WILSON, PAMELA SUSAN, advertising executive; b. Pasadena, Calif., Dec. 15, 1961; d. Edward Leroy and Mary Ellen (Lovemark) W. BA in English, Stanford U., 1984; postgrad., U. So. Calif., 1986. Account exec. Cable Guide, Mountain View, Calif., 1985; asst. media planner Dailey & Assocs., L.A., 1985-86, jr. media planner, 1986-87, media planner, 1987-88, sr. media planner, 1988-89, media supr., 1989-90, asst. media dir., 1990-91, assoc. media dir., 1991-94, group media dir., 1995—; panel mem. Mktg. and Media Decisions, L.A., 1990—. Active Tournament of Roses Assn., Pasadena, 1985—. Mem. Cum Laude Soc. Republican. Avocations: Italian language, reading, golf, tennis, travel. Home: 287 S Oak Knoll Ave Apt 1 Pasadena CA 91101-2982 Office: Dailey & Assocs 3055 Wilshire Blvd Los Angeles CA 90010-1108

WILSON, PATRICIA POTTER, library science and reading educator, educational and library consultant; b. Jennings, La., May 3, 1946; d. Ralph Harold and Wilda Ruth (Smith) Potter; m. Wendell Merlin Wilson, Aug. 24, 1968. BS, La. State U., 1967; MS, U. Houston-Clear Lake, 1979; EdD, U. Houston, 1985. Cert. tchr., learning resources specialist (librarian), Tex. Tchr., England AFB (La.) Elem. Sch., 1967-68, Edward White Elem. Sch., Clear Creek Ind. Schs., Seabrook, Tex., 1972-77; librarian C.D. Landolt Elem. Sch., Friendswood, Tex., 1979-81; instr./lectr. children's lit. U. Houston 1983-86; with U. Houston/Clear Lake, 1984-87, asst. prof. libr. sci. and reading, 1988-94, assoc. prof. learning resources and reading edn., 1994—, mem. faculty senate, 1992-93; cons. Hermann Hosp., Baywood Hosp., 1986-87, Bedford Meadows Hosp., 1989-90, Wetcher Clinic, 1989;

v.p., sec. Potter Farms, Inc., 1994—. Trustee, Freeman Meml. Library, Houston, 1982-87, v.p., 1985-86, pres., 1986-87; trustee Evelyn Meador Libr., 1993-94; adv. bd. Evelyn Meador Libr., 1994—; mem. adv. bd. Bay Area Soc. Prevention Cruelty Animals, 1994—; mem. Armand Bayou Nature Ctr., Houston, 1980—, bd. dirs. 1989-94; bd. dirs. Sta. KUHT-TV, 1984-87; mem. Bay Area Houston Symphony League. Editor A Rev. Sampler, 1985-86, 89-90; dir. Learning Resources Book Rev. Ctr., 1989-90. Author: HAPPENINGS: Developing Successful Programs for School Libraries, 1987, The Professional Collection for Elementary Educators, 1996; contbg. editor Tex. Library Jour., 1988-94; contbr. articles to profl. jours. Recipient Rsch. award Tex. State Reading Assn., 1993, Pres. award Tex. Coun. Tchrs. of English; grantee Tex. Libr. Assn., 1993. Mem. ALA, Am. Assn. Sch. Librarians, Internat. Reading Assn., Nat. Coun. Tchrs. English, (Books for You review com. 1985-88, Your Reading review com., 1993-96), Tex. Coun. Tchrs. English, Antarctican Soc., Phi Delta Kappa. Methodist. Home: 629 Bay Vista Dr Seabrook TX 77586-3001 Office: U Houston Clear Lake 2700 Bay Area Blvd Houston TX 77058-1002

WILSON, PATRICK CHARLES, chemist; b. Brooklyn, Aug. 21, 1950; s. Elbert and Mary Madgeline (Williams) W. AA in Sci., Borough of Manhattan C.C., N.Y.C., 1974; BS, CCNY, 1976; postgrad., NYU, 1990, U. Buffalo, 1995—. Analyst HHS/FDA-N.Y. Regional Lab., Brooklyn, 1978-87, supervisory drug chemist, 1987-91, supervisory food chemist, 1991; dir. lab. HHS/FDA-Buffalo Dist., 1991—; mem. people's adv. com. HHS/FDA-Buffalo Dist., Buffalo and Washington, 1989-90; mem. field lab instrument com. tech. advisor HHS/FDA-Buffalo Dist., N.Y.C. and Washington, 1993; mem. lab. dir.'s steering com. adv. com. HHS/FDA-Buffalo Dist., Washington, 1993; mem. adv. com. FDA/Commr.'s Office, Washington, 1981-91. Contbr. articles to profl. jours. Kairos ministry Koinonian Cmty., Western N.Y. and Ont., Can., 1995—; mentor N.Y. State Dep. Spkr.'s Mentor 2000, 1992; bd. dirs. Fed. Credit Union, N.Y., 1990-91; history practitioner, bd. mem. Buffalo Quarters Hist. Soc. Mem. Am. Mgmt. Assn., Nat. Orgn. Black Chemists and Engrs., N.Y. Acad. Sci. Office: HHS/FDA Buffalo Dist 599 Delaware Ave Buffalo NY 14201

WILSON, PAUL EDWIN, lawyer, educator; b. Quenemo, Kans., Nov. 2, 1913; s. Dale Edwin and Clara (Jacobs) W.; m. Harriet Eileen Stephens, June 16, 1941; children: Elizabeth, Mary Paulette, Eileen, David. BA, U. Kans., 1937, MA, 1938; LLB, Washburn U., 1940. Bar: Kans. 1940, U.S. Supreme Ct. 1952, U.S. Ct. Appeals 1950. Pvt. practice law Ashland, Kans., 1941-42, Lyndon, Kans., 1946-50; atty. County of Osage, Kans., 1947-50; gen. counsel dept. social welfare State of Kans., 1950-51, asst. atty. gen., 1951-53, 1st asst. atty. gen., 1953-57; assoc. prof. law U. of Kans., 1957-62, prof., 1962-68, Kane prof., 1968-81, prof. emeritus, 1981—; assoc. dir. Inst. Judicial Adminstrn., 1964-65; vis. prof. The Menninger Found., 1972; cons. in field. Author: (with Reams) Segregation and the Fourteenth Amendment in the States, 1975, Pattern Rules of Court and Code Provisions, 1975, Judicial Education in the United States, 1965, A Time to Lose, 1995; editor: American Criminal Law Quar. 1963-70; contbr. articles in field to profl. jours. Mem. Lawrence (Kans.) Planning Commn., 1962-65; chmn. Bd. Zoning Appeals, Lawrence, 1966-67; mem. Kans. Hist. Sites Bd. Rev., 1973-77; trustee Ft. Burgwin (N.Mex.) Rsch. Ctr., 1976-79, Task Force for Hist. Preservation, Lawrence, Kans. (Disting. Svc. citation 1991), 1987-89. With U.S. Army, 1942-46. Recipient Justice award Kans. Supreme Ct., 1992; cited for Disting. Svc. to Bar and Pub., Kans. Bar Assn., 1987, Gov. Kans., Ho. Reps., Kans.; Disting. Svc. award S.W.Kans. Bar Assn., 1995. Mem. Am. Bar Assn., Kans. Bar Assn. (chmn. com. criminal law 1960-68), Am. Law Inst., Am. Bar Found., Selden Soc., Nat. Trust Historic Preservation (bd. advisors 1972-78), Kans. State Hist. Soc. (v.p. 1987-89, pres. elect 1990, pres. 1990-91f, Phi Alpha Delta. Republican. Methodist. Office: U Kans 301 Green Hall Lawrence KS 66045 *Few things in my life have happened according to a preconceived plan. My admonition to the young is "Don't plan, just live." Perhaps I should add "also let live," by which I mean a concern for humanity, contemporary and prospective.*

WILSON, PAUL HOLLIDAY, JR., lawyer; b. Schenectady, N.Y., Sept. 4, 1942; s. Paul H. and Sarah Elizabeth (MacLean) W.; m. Elaine Hawley Griffin, May 30, 1964; children: Hollace, Paul, Kirsten, Katherine. AB, Brown U., 1964; LLB, MBA, Columbia U., 1967. Bar: N.Y. 1967, U.S. Dist. Ct. (so. dist.) 1968. Law clk. U.S. Dist. Ct. (so. dist.) N.Y., N.Y.C., 1967-68; assoc. Debevoise & Plimpton, N.Y.C., 1968-75, ptnr., 1976—, fin. ptnr., 1980-88, 91-93, dep. presiding ptnr., 1993—. Vice-chmn., trustee St. Michael's Montessori Sch., N.Y.C., 1977-79, chmn. bd. trustees, 1979-81. Mem. ABA, Assn. Bar City N.Y. (mem. commn. on securities regulations 1985-88). Club: Vineyard Haven Yacht (Mass.) (vice-commodore 1985, commodore 1986-87). Avocations: sailing, reading, music. Office: Debevoise & Plimpton 875 3rd Ave New York NY 10022-6225

WILSON, PEGGY DELORIS, executive secretary, cosmetologist; b. Warsaw, Ind., Apr. 12, 1943; d. Orin Leo and Roxie Mae (Sausaman) Pike; m. Bernard Hal Wilson Sept. 30, 1961 (div. July 1986); children: Bernadine Wilson Waikel, Lori Wilson, Jodie Wilson Hall, Sean Wilson. Diploma in Cosmetology/Hairstyling, Warner's. Beautician and frame stylist Hair Hut & Dr. Carman, Warsaw, 1986; mgr. Elizabeth Ardens Uhlmans, Warsaw, 1986-87; receptionist Creighton Bros., Warsaw, 1987-88; receiving clerk Zimmers, Warsaw, 1988-89; exec. sec. Kimble Glass, Warsaw, 1989—; transcriber NLRB, South Bend, Ind., 1994; typist Union Local 614 Contract, Warsaw, 1993. leader 4H Club, 1965; vol. Cancer Drive, 1970-74, Hosp. Auxillary, 1979. Recipient Telephone Techniques award Fred Pryor, 1986, Secretarial award Keye, 1989, Exceptional Asst. award Fred Pryor, 1994. Mem. NAFE, Onized Club (sec. 1993—), Claypool Alumni (sec. 1991-92). Avocations: bridge, walking, biking, reading. Home: 1416 Fox Farm Rd Warsaw IN 46580-2133 Office: Kimble Glass Inc PO Box 798 Center St Warsaw IN 46580

WILSON, PEGGY HENICAN, city official; b. New Orleans, June 24, 1937; d. C. Ellis and Elizabeth (Cleveland) Henican; m. Gordon Francis Wilson Jr., Dec. 10, 1932; children: Gordon, Alice, Peter, Carter. BA cum laude, Barat Coll., Lake Forest, Ill., 1959; postgrad., Tulane and Dominican Coll., 1960-75. Cert. tchr. Tchr. Mercy Acad., New Orleans, 1961-62, Acad. Sacred Heart, New Orleans, 1959-72; mgr. polit. campaigns Campaign Specialists, 1978-80; ptnr. Mason, Glickman, Wilson, New Orleans, 1981-82; owner Trolley Tours, 1975-85; pres. Peggy Wilson & Assocs., New Orleans, 1980-87; mem. City Coun., New Orleans, 1986—, pres., 1994—; chmn. fin. com. S&WB, mem. bd. liquidations. Author: Trolley Tours, 1982. Chmn. Alcoholic Beverage Control Bd., 1984-86; sec.-treas. Warehouse Dist. Devel. Assn., 1982-84, pres., 1984; bd. dirs. Carrollton-Hollygrove Community Ctr.; bd. dirs. YWCA, 1984-87; bd. dirs. City Park, New Orleans Mus. Art, Preservation Action; mem. mktg. com. City of New Orleans; mem. Cox Cable Com.; chmn. Hist. Dist. Landmarks Commn., 1981, 82; mem. bd., exec. com. St. George's Episcopal Sch., 1980-82; mem. Housing Task Force, 1978-80; mem. Police Chief Selection Com., 1978-79. Inst. Politics fellow Loyola U., 1978. Mem. Alliance for Good Govt., LWV, Upper St. Charles Civic Assn., Warehouse Dist. Devel. Assn., AARP. Office: Office City Council City Hall Rm 2E09 1300 Perdido St New Orleans LA 70112-2114

WILSON, PETE, governor of California; b. Lake Forest, Ill., Aug. 23, 1933; s. James Boone and Margaret (Callaghan) W.; m. Betty Robertson (div.); m. Gayle Edlund, May 29, 1983. B.A. in English Lit., Yale U., 1955; J.D., U. Calif., Berkeley, 1962; LL.D., Grove City Coll., 1983, U. Calif., San Diego, 1983, U. San Diego, 1984. Bar: Calif. 1962. Mem. Calif. Legislature, Sacramento, 1966-71; mayor City of San Diego, 1971-83; U.S. Senator from Calif., 1983-91; gov. State of Calif., 1991—. Trustee Conservation Found.; mem. exec. bd. San Diego County council Boy Scouts Am.; hon. trustee So. Calif. Council Soviet Jews; adv. mem. Urban Land Inst., 1985-86; founding dir. Retinitis Pigmentosa Internat.; hon. dir. Alzheimer's Family Ctr., Inc., 1985; hon. bd. dirs. Shakespeare-San Francisco, 1985. Recipient Golden Bulldog award, 1984, 85, 86, Guardian of Small Bus. award, 1984, Cuauhtemoc plaque for disting. svc. to farm workers in Calif., 1991, Julius award for outstanding pub. leadership U. So. Calif., 1992, award of appreciation Nat. Head Start, 1992; named Legislator of Yr., League Calif. Cities, 1985, Man of Yr. N.G. Assn. Calif., 1986, Man of Yr. citation U. Calif. Boalt Hall, 1986; ROTC scholar Yale U., 1951-55. Mem. Nat. Mil. Family Assn. (adv. bd.), Phi Delta Phi, Zeta Psi. Republican. Episcopalian. Office: State Capitol Office Of Governor Sacramento CA 95814*

WILSON, PHILIP DUNCAN, JR., orthopedic surgeon; b. Boston, Feb. 14, 1920; s. Philip Duncan and Germaine Wilson; m. Katherine Stern. Grad., Harvard U.; MD, Columbia U., 1944. Diplomate Am. Bd. Orthopaedic Surgery. Surg. intern, then resident Mass. Gen. Hosp., Boston, 1944-46; resident in orthopaedic surgery Hosp. for Spl. Surgery, N.Y.C., 1948-50, attending surgeon, 1951-72, surgeon in chief, 1972-89, surgeon in chief emeritus, trustee, 1989—; resident orthopaedic surgery San Francisco Med. Ctr., U. Calif., 1950-51; attending orthopaedic surgeon N.Y. Hosp., 1951—; prof. surgery Med. Ctr., Cornell U., N.Y.C., 1951—; cons. dept. surgery VA Hosp., Bronx, N.Y., 1972-89, North Shore U. Hosp., Manhasset, N.Y., 1975—, Meml. Hosp., N.Y.C., 1978—, Jamaica Hosp., Queens, N.Y., 1989—; orthopaedic cons. Cho Ray Hosp.-Cholon, South Vietnam, 1962; mem. adv. panel on total hip replacements FDA, Washington, 1969, adv. panel on prophylactic antibitotic in surgery, 1977; chmn. consensus devel. panel on total hip replacements NIH, Bethesda, Md., 1982; mem., sec. Adv. Coun. on Orthopaedic Resident Edn., 1981-93. Bd. dirs. M.E. Muller Found., 1989—. Capt. U.S. Army, 1946-48. Fellow ACS; mem. AMA, Am. Acad. Orthopaedic Surgeons (pres. 1972-73), U.S. Hip Soc. (pres. 1980-81), Orthopaedic Rsch. Soc., Assn. Authoritative Hip and Knee Surgery, Am. Orthopaedis Assn., Internat. Hip. Soc., Internat. Soc. Orthopaedic Surgery and Traumatology, N.Y. Acad. Medicine (chmn. orthopaedic sect. 1962-63, chmn. biochem. sect. 1969-70), Orthopaedic Rsch. and Edn. Found. (trustee 1981-83), N.Y. State Soc. Orthopaedic Surgeons, N.Y. Clin. Soc. Office: Hosp Spl Surgery 535 E 70th St New York NY 10021-4892

WILSON, R. DALE, marketing educator, consultant; b. Ironton, Ohio, July 16, 1949; s. Robert J. and Treva L. (Shively) W.; m. Emily J. Ray, June 19, 1971; 1 child, Travis Ray. BBA cum laude, Ohio U., 1971; MBA, U. Toledo, 1972; PhD, U. Iowa, 1977. Asst. prof. mktg. Pa. State U., University Park, 1976-80; v.p., dir. mktg. scis. Batten, Barton, Durstine & Osborn, Inc., N.Y.C., 1980-83; vis. prof. Cornell U., Ithaca, N.Y., 1983-84; assoc. prof. Mich. State U., East Lansing, 1984-87, prof., 1987—; cons. in field. Contbr. articles to profl. jours. Youth baseball and basketball coach, East Lansing, 1989—. Faculty research grantee Pa. State U., Mich. State U. Mem. Am. Acad. Advt., Am. Mktg. Assn., Inst. Ops. Rsch. and Mgmt. Scis. (assoc. editor Interfaces, cert. recognition 1983), Assn. Consumer Rsch., Product Devel. and Mgmt. Assn., Beta Gamma Sigma. Home: 859 Audubon Rd East Lansing MI 48823-3003 Office: Mich State U Eli Broad Grad Sch Mgmt Dept Mktg and Logistics N322 N Business Complex East Lansing MI 48824-1122

WILSON, R. MERINDA D., lawyer; b. Pitts., Feb. 24, 1952. BA magna cum laude, U. Pa., 1973; JD, Harvard U., 1976. Bar: Ga. 1976, D.C. 1978. Ptnr. Sidley & Austin, Washington; chair bd. trustees Pub. Defender Svc., Washington, 1985-89. Mem. Nat. Bar Assn. (chair legal edn. com. 1989-91). Office: Sidley & Austin 1722 I St NW Washington DC 20006-3705*

WILSON, RACHEL SARA, accountant; b. Bridgeport, Conn., Feb. 5, 1959; d. John Allan and Arline Rose (Delaney) McCague; m. Frank Wilson, Dec. 2, 1983; 1 child, Brittany Ayn. Grad. jr. accountancy program, Butler Bus. Coll., 1978; student, Contra Costa Coll.; ed. tax preparation program, H & R Block, Walnut Creek, Calif., 1984; student, U. Calif., Berkeley, 1987—. Office clk. Kombi Ltd., Norwalk, Conn., 1978-79; sr. acctg. clk. Brinks, Inc., Darien, Conn., 1979-81; bookkeeper Safeway Tire Co., Inc., Stamford, Conn., 1977-81, Mil Corp., San Francisco, 1982-83; acct./mgr. office of med. dir. Elkhart (Ind.) Gen. Hosp., 1990-92; office adminstr. Frank Wilson, MD, Inc., Richmond, Calif., 1983-85, v.p., sec., 1985—. Active Calhoun County Women's Aux. Mem. NAFE. Republican. Roman Catholic. Avocations: golf, horseback riding, fitness, backpacking, reading. Home and Office: 329 Jonesville Rd Coldwater MI 49036-9210

WILSON, RALPH EDWIN, lawyer, justice; b. Osceola, Ark., Sept. 28, 1921; s. Emmett A. and Lillie (Simmons) W.; m. Mary Ann Murray, Apr. 23, 1949; children: Ralph Edwin, Teresa Ann, Don Alan. Student, U.S. Naval Acad., 1943; A.B., Union U., 1946; J.D., Vanderbilt U., 1949. Bar: Tenn. 1948, Ark. 1948. Practice in Osceola, 1949—, city atty. Osceola, 1949; dep. pros. atty. 2d Jud. Dist. Ark., 1950-53; spl. asst. to atty. gen. Ark., 1956-60, spl. assoc. justice Supreme Ct. Ark., 1984; pres. Liberal State Bank, Gt. Eastern Assurance Co., North Little Rock; sec. Farmers Agri Export, Inc.; dir. Allied Cos., Inc., Does-More Products Corp., Allied Real Estate Investment Trust, Osceola Land Devel. Co.; Mem. adv. council Nat. Pub. Works Week, 1964. Alderman Osceola City Council, 1958-61. Served as lt. U.S. Mcht. Marines USNR, 1943-45. Recipient Ark. House and Senate Concurrent Resolutions Commendation, 1971. Mem. Ark. Bar Assn. (past mem. exec. com.), Osceola Bar Assn. (pres.), Am. Trial Lawyers Assn., U.S. Bar (Supreme Ct.), Am. Legion, Phi Alpha Delta, Alpha Tau Omega, Tau Kappa Alpha. Democrat. Methodist. Club: Kiwanian (internat. v.p. 1970-71, trustee 1966-70, life fellow internat. found.). Home: 903 W Hale Ave Osceola AR 72370-2428 Office: 109 N Maple St Osceola AR 72370-2537 *I believe it is man's highest achievement to reach far and find truth. The adversary system in law is this searching and finding truth. The drama of the courtroom involves all that is precious—life, liberty, property, dominion over children. These interacting forces play against each other, but if all facts are before the court, truth invariably prevails.*

WILSON, RAMON B., educator, administrator; b. Ogden, Utah, Sept. 22, 1922; s. Benjamin Andrew and Hannah Josephine (Browning) W.; m. Ruth G. Worlton, July 27, 1945; children: Lynn, William Scott, Bruce Ramon, JoAnne, Kathleen. B.S., Utah State U., 1947; M.S., Purdue U., 1948, Ph.D., 1950; postgrad., U. Calif., Berkeley, 1972, Georgetown U., 1976. Extension economist Utah State U., Logan, 1950-53; mktg. economist Calif. Dept. Agr., Sacramento, 1953-55; asst. prof. Purdue U., West Lafayette, Ind., 1955-57; assoc. prof. Purdue U., 1957-63, prof. agrl. econs., 1963-78, prof. emeritus, 1978—, market service dir., 1960-68; asst. dir. Ind. Coop. Extension Service, 1963-74, assoc. dir. agrl. expt. sta., asst. to dean agr., 1968-74; from asst. to assoc. dir. Benson Agrl. Food Inst. Brigham Young U., Provo, Utah, 1979-82; asst. to sec. U.S. Dept. Agr., Washington, 1974-76; cons., lectr. in field. Served with U.S. Army, 1943-46. Home: 435 E 2200 N Provo UT 84604-1725

WILSON, RAYMOND CLARK, former hospital executive; b. Birmingham, Ala., July 8, 1915; s. Raymond Clyde and Lida (Gay) W.; m. Sara Elizabeth Paris, Feb. 17, 1940; children: Margery Jo, Richard Clark, Sara Elizabeth, Raymond Paul. Student, Oglethorpe U., 1933-34, U. Ga., 1934-37, Tulane U., 1948; D.Bus. Adminstrn. (hon.), William Carey Coll. Office mgr. firm C.R. Justi (contractor), Atlanta, 1933-42; paymaster J.A. Jones Constrn. Co., Brunswick, Ga., 1942-45; asst. supt. So. Bapt. Hosp., New Orleans, 1946-53; adminstr. So. Bapt. Hosp., 1953-68, exec. dir., 1969-77; pres. Affiliated Bapt. Hosps., Inc., 1977-80, Health Care Cons. & Mgmt. Services, Inc., 1977-80; ret., 1980; exec. dir. Bapt. Meml. Hosp., Jacksonville, Fla., 1973-77; dir., chmn. La. Health and Indemnity Co.; dir. New Orleans Area Health Planning Council, 1969-74. Bd. dirs. Bapt. Hosp. Found., 1970-78; bd. trustees Crosby Meml. Hosp., 1992-94, chmn., 1993-94. With USAAF, 1945-46. Paul Harris fellow Rotary Found. Fellow Am. Coll. Healthcare Execs. (bd. regents 1972-75); mem. Hosp. Svc. Assn. (bd. dirs., treas. 1953-74), Am. Hosp. Assn. (ho. dels. 1972-75), La. Hosp. Assn. (pres. 1956), New Orleans Hosp. Coun. (pres. 1954-55), Southeastern Hosp. Conf. (pres. 1963), Bapt. Hosp. Assn. (pres. 1964-65). Baptist (trustee, deacon). Home: 200 W Sunnybrook Rd Carriere MS 39426-7831

WILSON, RAYMOND P., communications systems marketing professional; b. 1954. BA, MA, Merrimack Coll., 1981; MA, MBA, Bentley Coll., 1986. With Chaffin Co., Cambridge, Mass., 1975-79, Lexidata Corp., Billerica, Mass., 1979-85; with Scitex Am Corp., Bedford, Mass., 1985—, now v.p. fin., treas., CFO; now v.p. mktg. & sales. Office: Scitex Am Corp 8 Oak Park Dr Bedford MA 01730-1414*

WILSON, REBECCA LYNN, lawyer; b. Glen Ellyn, Ill., July 22, 1965; d. Wayne Robert Wilson and Rosemary Phylis (Stoecklin) Maglio. BA, U. Wis., 1987; JD, William Mitchell Coll., 1990; cert. mediation, Lakewood (Minn.) C.C., 1994. Bar: Minn. 1990, U.S. Dist. Ct. Minn. 1992. Law clk., assoc. Jack S. Jaycox Law Offices, Bloomington, Minn., 1988-93; assoc. Steffens, Wilkerson & Lang, Edina, Minn., 1993, Wilkerson, Lang & Hegna, Bloomington, 1993-95, Wilkerson, Hegna & Walsten, Bloomington, 1996—. Mem. ABA, Minn. State Bar Assn., Hennepin County Bar Assn. Office: Wilkerson Hegna & Walsten Ste 1100 3800 W 80th St Bloomington MN 55431-4426

WILSON, RICHARD ALEXANDER, career officer; b. San Francisco, Apr. 5, 1941; s. William Alexander and Myrlin Francis (Ralph) W.; m. Elizabeth Ray Esleeck, Feb. 24, 1962; children: Richard Scott, David Alexander. BS in Naval Sci., U.S. Naval Academy, 1963; MS in Systems Acquisition, Navy Postgrad. Sch., 1975; grad., USN Test Pilot Sch. Commd. ensign USN, advanced through grades to rear adm.; commdg. officer Fighter Squadron 154, Miramar, Calif., 1976-78; comdr. Carrier Airwing 14, Miramar, 1981-82; chief of staff Comfitaewing PAC, Miramar, 1982-84; commdg. officer USS Camden, Bremerton, Wash., 1984-86; with OPNAV Staff, Pentagon, Washington, 1986-87; commdg. officer USS Midway, Yokosuka, Japan, 1987-89; with Joint Staff, Pentagon, Washington, 1989-91; comdr. Carrier Group 7, San Diego, 1991-92; dep. chief staff ops. and plans CINCPACFLT, Pearl Harbor, Hawaii, 1993-95; dep. dir.-space electronic warfare OPNAUPARENS, Washington D.C., 1995—. Named Outstanding Young Man of Am., Jaycees, 1970. Mem. Naval Inst. Procs. (life), Assn. Naval Aviation (life), Naval Aviation Mus. Found. (life), U.S. Naval Acad. Alumni Assn. (life), Order Daedalians. *

WILSON, RICHARD ALLAN, landscape architect; b. Chgo., Feb. 5, 1927; s. Edgar Allan and Lois Helena (Hearn) W.; m. Lisabet Julie Horchler, May 31, 1958; children: Gary Allan, Carl Bruce. BS, U. Calif., Berkeley, 1952. Engrng. draftsman Freeland Evanson & Christenson, San Diego, 1952-53; designer, estimator Blue Pacific Nursery & Landscape Co., San Diego, 1955-59; prin. Richard A. Wilson, FASLA and Assocs., San Diego, 1959—; sec. Calif. Coun. Landscape Architects, 1982-85; expert witness for law firms, 1983—. Designer Phil Swing Meml. Fountain, 1967. Mem. landscape com. Clairemont Town Coun., San Diego, 1955. With U.S. Army, 1944-46, Korea. Recipient First Pl. award for landscape So. Calif. Expdn., Del Mar, 1963. Fellow Am. Soc. Landscape Architects (del. coun. 1982-85), Am. Inst. Landscape Architects (treas. 1970, 2d v.p. 1971). Republican. Home and Office: 2570 Tokalon Ct San Diego CA 92110-2232

WILSON, RICHARD CHRISTIAN, engineering firm executive; b. Bethlehem, Pa., July 17, 1921; s. Christian and Laura Barrows (Langham) W.; m. Jean M. Avis, July 16, 1949; children—Richard A., Christy. B.S., Carnegie-Mellon U., 1943; M.S., Lehigh U., 1947; Ph.D., U. Mich., 1961. Mfg. engr. Westinghouse Electric Corp., East Pittsburgh, 1943; instr. mech. engrng. Carnegie-Mellon U., Pitts., 1943-44; vacuum test engr. Kellex Corp., N.Y.C., 1944; area supr. Carbide & Carbon Chem. Co., Oak Ridge, 1945-46; apparatus engr. Westinghouse Electric Corp., Jackson, Mich., 1947-55; instr. indsl. and operation engrng. U. Mich., 1955-61, asst. prof., 1961-63, assoc. prof., 1963-66, prof., 1966-85, chmn. dept., 1973-77, assoc. dean Coll. Engring., 1968-72; pres. Techware, Inc., 1985-86, ret., 1986; dir. Cascade Data Corp., 1969-72. Contbr. articles to profl. jours. Bd. dirs. Ecumenical Assn. Internat. Understanding, 1970-87, pres., 1975-76, 86-87. Mem. IEEE, Inst. Mgmt. Sci., Am. Inst. Indsl. Engrs., Ops. Research Soc. Am., Sigma Xi, Beta Theta Pi, Phi Kappa Phi. Club: Rotary. Home: 805 Mt Pleasant Ave Ann Arbor MI 48103-4776 Office: U Mich Dept Indsl Engrng Ann Arbor MI 48109

WILSON, RICHARD DALE, executive training, consulting company; b. L.A., July 22, 1933; s. Wayne Merle and June Lillian (Buys) W.; m. Nancy Irene Colby, 1974; children: Christopher, Jennifer, Janie, Matthew, Dixie, Tracey, Mark, Mysti, Tiffany. BA, San Jose Coll., 1964, MTH; LLB, Blackstone Law Sch., 1974; postgrad., Harvard U., 1987; PhD, Kennedy Western U., 1993. Cert. profl. cons. TV news anchor, overseas correspondent, investigative reporter numerous TV stas., 1964-75; legis. services dir. Utah State Legis., Salt Lake City, 1976; pres. Nat. Inst. for Tng. and Consulting, Salt Lake City, 1977—; sr. cons. The Co. Cons., 1981—; pres. Nat. Inst. for Sales Tng. and Cons. Author: Handwriting 12 Keys to Every Personality, 1968, 10 Basic Habits Superstar Salesperson, 1986, 10 Critical Steps to Building a Powerful and Profitable Sales Organization, 1987, 10 Basic Habits of A Superstar Sales Manager, 1989, Do It Right The First Time: Finding, Assessing and Selecting the Best Sales Force Force For The 90's, 1991; editor, pub. The Co. Cons. Newsletter, 1985—; contbr. articles to profl. jours. Media planner Rep. Conv., N.D., 1972; organizer Rep. Conv., Calif., 1964; del. Utah State Conv., 1976. Sgt. USMC, 195-57, Korea. Recipient Gavel award ABA, 1973; named Regional Dir. Yr. Westworld Services, Inc., 1981. Mem. Soc. Profl. Cons., Am. Handwriting Analysis Found., Nat. Assn. Realtors, Realtors Nat. Mktg. Inst., Nat. Speakers Assn. Mormon. Avocation: certified handwriting expert. Home: 1736 S 320 W Orem UT 84058-7597 Office: Nat Inst Tng & Consulting Inc PO Box 0817 2696 N University Ave Provo UT 84603-0817

WILSON, RICHARD FERROL, plant physiologist, educator; b. Macomb, Ill., July 6, 1947; s. Elmer Ferrol and Velma Lucille (Swartzbaugh) W.; m. Pamela Ann Magerl, Aug. 28, 1971. BS, Western Ill. U., 1970; MS, U. Ill., 1973, PhD, 1975. Plant physiologist USDA Agrl. Rsch. Svc., Raleigh, N.C., 1975—; prof. crop sci. N.C. State U., Raleigh, 1975—. Recipient Arthur S. Fleming award Downtown Jaycees, D.C., 1986, Alumni Achievement award Western Ill. U., 1989, Merit award Gamma Sigma Delta, 1989, Disting. Svc. award USDA, 1989, Utilization Rsch. award Am. Soybean Assn., 1990, Soybean Team Rsch. award Am. Soybean Assn., 1991; named Disting. Scientist of Yr., USDA Agrl. Rsch. Svc., 1987. Fellow Am. Soc. Agronomy, Crop Sci. Soc. Am.; mem. Am. Oil Chemists Soc., Am. Soc. Crop Sci., N.Y. Acad. Sci., Am. Soc. Plant Physiologists, Kiwanis, Sigma Xi, Alpha Zeta (chancellor 1969-70, Outstanding Alumni award 1991). Republican. Methodist. Avocations: bicycling, bowling, golf. Home: 110 Chattel Close Cary NC 27511-9745 Office: USDA Agrl Rsch Svc PO Box 7620 Raleigh NC 27695

WILSON, RICHARD HAROLD, government official; b. Waterloo, Iowa, July 15, 1930; s. Clarence Hough and Mary (Dillon) W.; m. Elaine Elizabeth Aniol., June 14, 1957; children: Elizabeth Aniol Wilson Adams, Andrew Edward. B.A., U. Ill., 1952; M.P.A., U. Kans., 1958. Lic. real estate broker, Tex.; cert. econs. devel. specialist Nat. Devel. Coun.; police. ct. clk., Kans. Adminstrv. asst. to city mgr. San Antonio, 1956-58; budget analyst Kansas City, Mo., 1959; research asso. Internat. Union Local Authorities, The Hague, 1959-60; city mgr. Nevada, Mo., 1960-65; asst. to city mgr. Ft. Worth, 1965-67; asst. city mgr. Albuquerque, 1967-68, city mgr., 1968-72; dir. housing and urban rehab. Dallas, 1972-82; sr. v.p. Metroplex R&D Cons., Dallas, 1982-83; regional dir. comty. planning and devel. HUD Region V, Chgo., 1983-94; sr. advisor HUD, Chgo., 1994—; lectr. real estate U. Tex.-Arlington; instr. govt. Dallas County Community Coll. Dist.; exec. v.p. Designs for Worship, Inc., Dallas, 1982-83. Bd. dirs. Neighborhood Housing Svcs. Am., Inc., 1974-82; chmn. Housing Tax Force of North Cen. Tex. Coun. Govts., 1974-80, chmn. human resources com., 1981-82; active Boy Scouts Am.; docent Prairie Ave. House Mus., 1995—; bd. dirs. Marina Towers Condominium Assn., 1991-96. Fulbright fellow Leiden (The Netherlands) U., 1959-60, Kennedy Sch., Harvard U., 1981, Fed. Exec. Inst., 1995, NEH, U. Calif., Santa Barbara, 1978, Urban Execs. Exch. Program, Internat. City-County Mgmt. Assn., 1979-80. Mem. Nat. Assn. Housing and Redevel. Ofcls. (v.p. Tex. chpt. 1975-80, mem. S.W. regional coun. 1975-82), Internat. City-Coun. Mgmt. Assn. (fellow 1979-80), Am. Soc. Pub. Adminstrn. (pres. N.Mex. 1968-69, v.p. North Tex. 1976-77, pres. North Tex. 1977-78, mem. nat. coun. 1979-82, Greater Chgo. chpt. coun. 1987-93, 96—), Naval Res. Assn., Chgo. Arch. Found. (docent 1990—), Fed. Exec. Inst. Alumni Assn., Phi Gamma Delta, Pi Sigma Alpha, Alpha Phi Omega. Episcopalian. Club: Rotary (Chicago). Home: 300 N State St Apt 2833 Chicago IL 60610-4805 Office: HUD 77 W Jackson Blvd 24th Floor Chicago IL 60604-3507

WILSON, RICK KEITH, political science educator; b. New Underwood, S.D., Sept. 19, 1953; s. Richard K. and Darlene J. (Klosterman) W.; m. Patricia M. Dupras. BA, Creighton U., 1975, MA in History, 1977; PhD in Polit. Sci., Ind. U., 1982. Vis. lectr. Washington U., St. Louis, 1982-83; asst. prof. Rice U., Houston, 1983-88, assoc. prof., 1990-95, chmn. polit. sci. dept., 1991-94, prof., 1995—; vis. prof. Calif. Inst. Tech., Pasadena, 1989, Ind. U., Bloomington, 1989-90. Author: (book) Congressional Dynamics, 1994; contbr. articles to Legislative Studies Quarterly, 1989—. Pres. Willow Meadows Civic Assn., Houston, 1991-93. Grantee NSF, Bloomington, Ind., 1981-83, Houston, Tex., 1988-90. Mem. Am. Polit. Sci. Assn., Econ. Sci. Assn., Midwest Polit. Sci. Assn. Democrat. Avocations: biking, baseball, computer programming. Home: 4327 McDermed Houston TX 77035 Office: Rice Univ Dept Polit Sci PO Box 1892 Houston TX 77251

WILSON, ROBERT ALLEN, religion educator; b. Geff, Ill., Oct. 7, 1936; s. Perry Arthur and Eva Mae (Dye) W.; m. Patsy Ann Jarrett, June 1, 1957; children: Elizabeth Ann, Angela Dawn, Christine Joy. AB, Lincoln (Ill.) Christian Coll., 1958, Hanover Coll., 1961; MRE, So. Bapt. Seminary, 1965, EdD, 1972. Ordained to ministry Ch. of Christ, 1958. Minister Fowler (Ind.) Christian Ch., 1955-59, Zoah Christian Ch., Scottsburg, Ind., 1959-64; minister of edn. and youth Shively Christian Ch., Louisville, 1964-69; prof. Christian edn. and family life Lincoln (Ill.) Christian Seminary, 1969—; pres. Christian Marriage and Family Enrichment Services, Lincoln, 1980—. Contbr. articles to profl. jours. Mem. Nat. Assn. Profs. Christian Edn. (editor newsletter 1975-79, pres. 1979-80), Religious Edn. Assn. Lodge: Rotary (bd. dirs. Lincoln chpt. 1988—, pres. 1993-94). Home: 330 Campus View Dr Lincoln IL 62656-2106 Office: Lincoln Christian Coll & Seminary 100 Campus View Dr # 178 Lincoln IL 62656-2167

WILSON, ROBERT BURTON, veterinary and medical educator; b. Salt Lake City, June 29, 1936; s. Stanley Burton and Jessie Adelia (Hassell) W.; m. Janet Diane McMurdie, June 1, 1962; children: Robert Burton Jr., Janet Diane. BS, Utah State U., 1958; DVM with highest honors, Wash. State U., 1961; PhD, U. Toronto, Ont., Can., 1967. Lic. veterinarian, Mass., Wash., Utah. Intern Angell Meml. Animal Hosp., Boston, 1962-63; asst. prof. Brigham Young U., Provo, Utah, 1963-64; asst. scientist Hosp. for Sick Children, Toronto, 1964-69; assoc. prof. MIT, Cambridge, 1969-73; prof. vet. medicine U. Mo., Columbia, 1973-76; prof., chmn. vet. micro. and pathology Wash. State U., Pullman, 1976-83, dean coll. vet. medicine, 1983-88; vet. cons. Forsyth Dental Inst., Boston, 1972-73; mem., chmn. adv. com. NIH, Bethesda, Md., 1976-80, 89-93. Contbr. over 100 articles to profl. jours. Recipient Mary Mitchell award Mass. Soc. Prevention Cruelty to Animals, 1964, Tchr. of Yr. award MIT, 1971, Tchr. of Yr. award W.A.M.I. Med. Program, 1992, 94, 95. Fellow Am. Heart Assn. (coun. of arteriosclerosis); mem. Am. Vet. Med. Assn., Am. Inst. Nutrition. Mem. LDS Ch. Avocations: genealogy, history, golf, fishing. Home: 505 SE Crestview St Pullman WA 99163-2212 Office: Wash State U Coll Vet Medicine Bustad Hall Pullman WA 99164-7040

WILSON, ROBERT FOSTER, lawyer; b. Windsor, Colo., Apr. 6, 1926; s. Foster W. and Anne Lucille (Svedman) W.; m. Mary Elizabeth Clark, Mar. 4, 1951 (div. Feb. 1972); children: Robert F., Katharine A.; m. Sally Anne Nemec, June 8, 1982. BA in Econs., U. Iowa, 1950, JD, 1951. Bar: Iowa 1951, U.S. Dist. Ct. (no. and so. dists.) Iowa 1956, U.S. Ct. Appeals (8th cir.) 1967. Atty., FTC, Chgo., 1951-55; sole practice, Cedar Rapids, Iowa, 1955—; pres. Lawyer Forms, Inc.; dir. Lawyers Forms, Inc. Democratic state rep. Iowa Legislature, Linn County, 1959-60; mem. Iowa Reapportionment Com., 1968; pres. Linn County Day Care, Cedar Repids, 1968-70; del. to U.S. and Japan Bilateral Session on Legal and Econ. Rels. Conf., Tokyo, 1988, Moscow Conf. on Law and Bilateral Rels., Moscow, 1990; U.S. del. to Moscow conf. on legal and econ. rels., 1990. Served to sgt. U.S. Army, 1944-46. Mem. ATLA, Am. Arbitration Assn. (panel arbitrators), Am. Legion (judge advocate 1970-75, 1987-93), Iowa Trial Lawyers Assn., Iowa Bar Assn., Linn County Bar Assn., Delta Theta Phi. Club: Cedar View Country. Lodges: Elks, Eagles. Home: 100 1st Ave NE Cedar Rapids IA 52401 Office: 810 Dows Bldg Cedar Rapids IA 52401

WILSON, ROBERT GODFREY, radiologist; b. Montgomery, Ala., Mar. 18, 1937; s. Robert Woodridge and Lucille (Godfrey) W.; B.A., Huntingdon Coll., 1957; M.D., Med. Coll. Ala., 1961; m. Dorothy June Waters, Aug. 31, 1957; children—Amy Lucille, Robert Darwin, Robert Woodridge II, Lucy Elizabeth. Intern, Letterman Gen. Hosp., San Francisco, 1961-62; resident in radiology U. Okla. Med. Center, Oklahoma City, 1965-68, clin. instr. in radiology, 1968—; practice medicine specializing in diagnostic and therapeutic radiology, nuclear medicine, Shawnee, Okla., 1968—; mem. med. staff Shawnee Med. Center, Mission Hill Meml. Hosp., Shawnee, 1968—. Served to capt. M.C., USAF, 1960-65. Diplomate Nat. Bd. Med. Examiners, Am. Bd. Radiology, Am. Bd. Nuclear Medicine. Mem. AMA, Okla., Pottawatomie County med. socs., Okla., Greater Oklahoma City radiol. socs., Am. Coll. Radiology, Soc. Nuclear Medicine, Radiol. Soc. N.Am. Methodist. Home: 26 Sequoyah St Shawnee OK 74801-5570 Office: 1110 N Harrison St Shawnee OK 74801

WILSON, ROBERT GOULD, management consultant; b. Springfield, Mass., July 29, 1929; s. George Winthrop Wilson and Clara Margret (Smyth) Turnbull; m. Jane Seaman, Sept. 14, 1952; children: Roberta Wilson DiBlasi, Richard Jan. BA in Eng., Bates Coll., 1951. Various positions Gen. Electric Co., Bridgeport, Conn., 1953-64; v.p. planning Warnco, Inc., Bridgeport, 1964-76; pres. Hathaway Can., Prescott, Ont., 1976-79; sr. mgmt. cons. Arthur D. Little, Cambridge, Mass., 1979-84; pres. Northeast Cons., Boston, 1984—, now chmn. Co-author: Business Strategy, 1983. Trustee Bates Coll., Lewiston, Maine, 1984-89. Office: NE Cons Resources Inc One Liberty Sq11th Fl Boston MA 02109*

WILSON, ROBERT JAMES MONTGOMERY, investment company executive; b. Millbrook, N.Y., Feb. 8, 1920; s. Albert James Montgomery and Charlotte (Kaye) W.; m. Yvette Laneres, May 10, 1952; children—Robert James Montgomery, Olivia Laneres Wilson Welbourn, Geoffrey Laneres. Grad., Choate Sch., 1938; A.B., Yale U., 1942. Securities analyst buying dept. Union Securities Corp., N.Y.C., 1946-49; securities analyst Union Service Corp., N.Y.C., 1949-59; v.p. Union Service Corp., 1959-63; pres., dir. Surveyor Fund, Inc. (formerly Gen. Public Service Corp.), N.Y.C., 1963-71; with Rockefeller Family and Assos., 1972-75; pres. Adams Express Co., N.Y.C., 1975-86, also bd. dirs., 1975—; pres. Petroleum & Resources Corp. (formerly Petroleum Corp. Am.), N.Y.C., 1975-86, also bd. dirs., 1975—; mem. adv. investment com. Md. State Retirement Systems, 1979-82; bd. dirs. Assn. Publicly Traded Investment Cos., 1968-71, chmn., 1969-71. Mem. 1940 Fahnestock Expdn. of Am. Mus. Natural History to South Seas. Served to capt. AUS, World War II. Mem. Md. Club, Sea Oaks Beach and Tennis Club.

WILSON, ROBERT M., theatre artist; b. Waco, Tex., Oct. 4, 1941; s. D.M. and Loree Velma (Hamilton) W. Student, U. Tex., 1962; BFA, Pratt Inst., 1966, DFA (hon.), 1991. Artistic dir. Byrd Hoffman Found., N.Y.C., 1969—; lectr. Internat. Sch., Paris, 1971, Atelje Festival, Belgrade, Yugoslavia, Internat. Theater Inst. of UNESCO, Durdan, France, 1971, Skowhegan Art Sch., Maine, 1977, Harvard U., 1982; condr. seminars U. Calif.-Berkeley, 1970, George Sch., New Hope, Pa., 1970, U. Iowa, 1970, Newark State Coll., 1971; condr. workshops Royaumont, France, 1972, Boulder, Colo., 1973, Ohio State U., 1973, Centre de Development du Potential Humain, Paris, 1973, 74, NEA, Seattle, 1982, UCLA, 1985. Theatrical and operatic performances U.S. and Europe include: Deafman Glance, 1970 (Best Fgn. Play award Le Syndicat de la Critique Dramatique et Musicale, Paris 1970, Drama Desk award for best direction 1971), The Life and Times of Joseph Stalin (Obie Spl. Citation award for direction 1974), A Mad Man A Mad Giant A Mad Dog A Mad Urge A Mad Face, 1974, The Life and Times of Dave Clark, 1974, A Letter for Queen Victoria, 1974 (Maharam Found. award for scenic design 1975, nominee Tony award for best score and libretto 1975, Best Lyric Theatre award Le Syndicat de la Critique Dramatique et Musicale Paris, 1977), The $ Value of Man, 1974, Dialog, 1974, Einstein on the Beach, 1976, 84 (Best Play award Theatre of Nations, Belgrade, Yugoslavia, 1977, Lumen award, 1977), I Was Sitting on my Patio This Guy Appeared I Thought I Was Hallucinating, 1977, Dialog/Network, 1978, Death, Destruction and Detroit, 1979 (German Critics award 1979, German Press award 1979), Edison, 1979, Dialog/Curious George, 1980, The Man in the Raincoat, 1981, Prologue to Fourth Act of Deafman Glance, 1982, Medea, 1984, Great Day in the Morning, 1982, The Golden Windows, 1982, 85 (Der Rosenstrauss award 1982), The Civil Wars, 1983-85 (Pulitzer prize nominee for drama 1986), Hamletmachine, 1986 (Obie award for direction Village Voice 1986), Alceste, 1986, Salome, 1987, Parzival, 1987, Quartett, 1987, Death, Destruction and Detroit II, 1987, The Martyrdom of St. Sebastian, 1988, Cosmopolitan Greetings, 1988, The Forest, 1988, DeMaterie, 1989, Doktor Faustus, 1989 (Best Prodn. award Italian Theatre Critics, 1989), Swan Song, 1989, Orlando, 1989, The Black Rider, 1990, (German Theater Critics award for Best Prodn. of Yr.), King Lear, 1990, When We Dead Awaken, 1991, Parsifal, 1991, The Magic Flute, 1991, Lohengrin, 1992, Dr. Faustus Lights the Lights, 1992, Alice, 1993, Alice in Bed, 1993, Madame Butterfly, 1993, The Black Rider, 1993, Orlando, 1993, Der Mond im Gras, 1994, Hanjo/Hagoromo, 1994, T.S.E., 1994, The Meek Girl, 1994, The Death of Moliere, 1994, Hamlet: A Monologue, Bluebeard's Castle and Erwartung, 1995, Four Saints in Three Acts, Time Rocker, 1996;; author (plays): Two Conversations with Edwin Denby, 1973, A Letter for Queen Victoria, 1974, I Was Sitting on my Patio This Guy Appeared I Thought I Was Hallucinating, 1977, Death, Destruction and Detroit, 1979, The Golden Windows, 1981, The Civil Wars, 1983, Death, Destruction and Detroit II, 1987; contbg. author: (anthology) New American Plays Vol. III, 1970; films include: Overture for a Deafman, Murder; video works include: Spaceman, 1976, 84, Video 50, 1978, Deafman Glance, 1981, Stations, 1982, La Femme a la Cafeterie, 1989 (Grand Prize Biennale Festival of Cinema Art, Barcelona), The Death of King Lear, 1989, Mr. Bojangles' Memory, 1991, La Mort de Moliere, 1993; exhibited drawings and sculpture one-man shows: Iolas Gallery, N.Y.C., Palazzi Gallery, Milan, Galerie Fred Lanzenberg, Brussels, Paula Cooper Gallery, N.Y.C., Musée Galliera, Paris, 1972, 74, Multiples/Goodman Gallery, 1977, 79, Neuberger Mus., Purchase, N.Y., 1980, Contemporary Art Ctr., Cin., 1980, Castelli Feigen Corcoran, N.Y.C., Portia Harcus Gallery, Cambridge, Mass., Alpha Gallery, Cambridge, Richard Kunlenschmidt Gallery, Los Angeles, Hewlet Gallery, Pitts., Lehman Coll. Arts Gallery, Bronx, Walker Art Ctr., Mpls., 1984, Rhona Hoffman Gallery, 1986, Galerie der Stadt Stuttgart, 1987, Galerie Herald Behm, Hamburg, 1988, AnneMarie Verna Galerie, Zurich, 1989, Galerie Ha Galerie Yvon Lambert, 1989, Feigen Gallery, Chgo., 1990, Mus. Fine Arts, Boston, 1991, Centre Georges Pompidou, Paris, 1991, Galerie Fred Jahn, Munich, 1991, Hiram Butler Gallery, Houston, 1992, Laura Carpenter Gallery, Sante Fe, 1992, IVAM, Valencia, 1992, Produzenentengalerie, Hamburg, 1992, Deichtorhallen, Hamburg, 1993, Mus. Boymans-van Beuningen, Rotterdam, 1993, Akira Ikeda Gallery, N.Y.C., 1994; exhibited numerous other maj. galleries, U.S. and abroad, including: Willard Gallery, N.Y.C., 1971, Marian Goodman Gallery, 1982, Pavillion des Arts, Paris, 1983, Otis-Parsons, Los Angeles, 1984, Inst. Contemporary Art, Boston, 1985, Galeria Gamarra y Garrigues, Madrid, 1992, Kamakura Gallery, Tokyo, 1992, Galerie van Rijsbergen, Rotterdam, 1993; works represented in permanent collections: Mus. Modern Art, N.Y.C., Boston Mus. Fine Arts, Australian Nat. Gallery, Canberra, Kunst Mus., Bern, Lannan Mus., L.A., Mus. Modern Art, Paris, Mus. Art, R.I. Sch. Design, Providence, The French Govt., Paris, Mus. Contemporary Art, Los Angeles, Boymans Mus., Rotterdam, Stedelijk Mus., Amsterdam, Menil Mus., Houston, Tex., Centre Georges Pompidou, Paris, Art Inst., Chgo., Huntington Art Mus. U. Tex., Austin, Met. Mus. Art, N.Y.C., Phila. Mus. Art. Recipient Chgo. Art Inst. Skowhegan medal for drawing Skowhegan Sch. Painting, 1987, Inst. Honor award AIA, 1988, Mondello award, Palermo, 1988, Brandeis Univ. Poses Creative Arts award, 1991, Golden Lion award in sculpture, Venice Bienniale, 1993, Tex. Artist of the Yr., 1995; named Most Outstanding Theater Designer of the Seventies, U.S. Inst. Theater Tech., Washington, 1977; Rockefeller grantee, 1970, 77-80; Guggenheim fellow, 1971, 80. Mem. Nat. Inst. Music Theatre (trustee), Am. Repertory Theatre (hon. bd. dirs.), The Dramatists Guild, Soc. des Auteurs et Compositeurs Dramatiques, Soc. Stage Dirs. and Choreographers, PEN Am. Ctr., I.C.A. Boston (bd. overseers). Office: RW Work Ltd 131 Varick St Rm 908 New York NY 10013-1410

WILSON, ROBERT NATHAN, health care company executive; b. Covington, Ky., Aug. 7, 1940; s. Robert Thomas and Ruth (Pearce) W.; m. Anne Wright, Mar. 29, 1969; children: Julie Anne, Jonathan Robert. BA in Bus., Georgetown (Ky.) Coll., 1962; grad. exec. program Grad. Sch. Bus. Adminstrn., Columbia U., 1975; LLD (hon.), Phila. Coll. Pharmacy and Sci., 1991. Sales rep. Ortho Pharm. Corp., Raritan, N.J., 1964; various exec. and mgr. positions, 1964-77; pres. Johnson & Johnson Dental Products Co., East Windsor, N.J., 1977-79; co. group chmn. Johnson & Johnson, New Brunswick, N.J., 1981-83, mem. exec. com., 1983—, apptd. vice chmn. exec. com., 1994—, vice chmn., bd. dirs., 1989—; pres. Ortho Pharm. Corp., Raritan, N.J., 1979-83; chmn. Ortho Pharm. Ltd. Can., 1979-83; bd. dirs. Alliance for Aging Rsch., Washington, 1989—, U.S. Trust Corp. 1991—, James Black Found., London; sci. adv. bd. Ctr. Advanced Biotechnology amd Medicine. Trustee Mus. Am. Folk Art, N.Y.C., 1981—, Found. of U. Medicine and Dentistry N.J., Newark, 1984-93; bd. dirs. World Wildlife Fund, 1995—, Georgetown Coll. Found., World Bus. Coun. for Sustainable Devel., Pharm. Rsch. and Mfrs. Am. Found., 1994—; mem. Trilateral Commn. Recipient Alumni Achievement award Georgetown Coll., 1987. Mem. Pharm. Rsch. and Mfrs. Am. (bd. dirs. 1984—, exec. com. 1988—, policy analysis and planning com. 1989—). Presbyterian. Office: Johnson & Johnson 1 Johnson Johnson Plz New Brunswick NJ 08933

WILSON, ROBERT NEAL, sociologist, educator; b. Syracuse, N.Y., Nov. 15, 1924; s. Robert Marchant and May Eloise (Neal) W.; m. Arleene Eleanor Smith, Aug. 21, 1948 (div. 1973); children—Lynda Lee, Deborah Eloise; m. Joan Wallace, Aug. 1, 1973. B.A., Union Coll., 1948; Ph.D., Harvard U., 1952. Research assoc. Cornell U., Ithaca, N.Y., 1951-53; staff Social Sci. Research Council, Washington, 1953-56; lectr. Harvard U., Cambridge, Mass., 1957-60; assoc. prof. Yale U., New Haven, 1960-63; prof. sociology U. N.C., Chapel Hill, 1963—; trustee Easter Seal Research Found., Chgo., 1966-72; cons. NIMH, Washington, 1968-72, Nat. Inst. Child Health and Human Devel., Washington, 1970-77; reviewer NEH, Washington, 1977—. Author: Man Made Plain, 1958, Sociology of Health, 1970, The Writer as Social Seer, 1979, Experiencing Creativity, 1986; author, editor: The Arts in Soc., 1964. Served to sgt. U.S. Army, 1943-46, ETO. Ctr. for Advanced Study Behavioral Scis. fellow, 1956-57; Fulbright scholar, 1975. Fellow Am. Sociol. Assn., Am. Pub. Health Assn., So. Sociol. Soc. Democrat. Episcopalian. Avocation: poetry. Home: 103 Springvalley Rd Carrboro NC 27510-1246 Office: Univ NC Chapel Hill NC 27514

WILSON, ROBERT RATHBUN, retired physicist; b. Frontier, Wyo., Mar. 4, 1914; s. Platt Elvin and Edith (Rathbun) W.; m. Jane Inez Scheyer., Aug. 20, 1940; children—Daniel, Jonathan, and Rand. AB, U. of Calif., 1936; PhD, 1940; DSc (hon.), Notre Dame U., U. Bonn, Harvard U., 1986, Wesleyan U., 1987. Instr. Princeton U., 1940-42, asst. prof., 1942-45; head rsch. divsn. Los Alamos Lab., 1944-45, 1944-45; assoc. prof. physics Harvard, 1946-47; prof. physics and dir. Lab Nuclear Studies Cornell U., 1947-67; prof. physics U. Chgo., 1967-78, Peter B. Ritzma prof., 1978-80; dir. Fermi Nat. Accelerator Lab., Batavia, Ill., 1967-78; Michael Pupin prof. Columbia U., 1980-83; now ret. Contbr. articles to Physics Rev. Recipient Elliott Cresson medal Franklin Inst., 1964, Nat. medal sci., 1973, Enrico Fermi award, 1984, The Wright prize, 1986, del Regato medal, 1989, Gemant award, 1995. Fellow NAS, Am. Phys. Soc. (pres. 1985), Am. Acad. Arts and Scis., Fedn. Am. Scientists (chmn. 1946, 63), Am. Philos. Soc., Sigma Xi. Address: 916 Stewart Ave Ithaca NY 14850-2123

WILSON, ROBERT SPENCER, magazine editor; b. Bolling Field, D.C., Feb. 21, 1951; s. Joseph Griswold and Helen (Hodnett) W.; m. Martha Elaine Ritchie, Oct. 19, 1974; children—Matthew Spencer, Cole Ritchie, Robert Samuel. B.A., Washington and Lee U., 1973; M.A., U. Va., 1977. Lectr. U. Va., Charlottesville, 1977-80; asst. editor Washington Post, 1977-83; book editor, book columnist USA Today, Washington, 1983-94; lit. editor Civilization mag., Washington, 1994-95; editor Historic Preservation mag., Manassas, Va., 1996—. Home and Office: 9301 Grant Ave Manassas VA 22110-5040

WILSON, ROBERT WILLIAM, defense systems company executive; b. Green Island, N.Y., July 26, 1935; s. William James and Margaret Ann (Ayotte) W.; m. Dolores Ann Kirchert; children: Kirk, Kathy Doherty, Karen McBride. BS in Chemistry, St. Michael's Coll., Winooski, Vt., 1956; MS in Physics, Boston U., 1964; MS in Mgmt., MIT, 1972. Program mgr., v.p. Avco Systems div., Wilmington, Mass., 1960-82; dir. TAC E/O systems Honeywell Corp., Lexington, Mass., 1982-84; v.p., asst. gen. mgr. Avco Everett (Mass.) Rsch. Lab., 1984-87, Textron Def. Systems, Wilmington, 1987—. With USAF, 1956-60. Recipient Firepower award Am. Def. Preparedness, 1986. Mem. AIAA, Nat. Security Indsl. Assn., Air Force Assn. Roman Catholic. Avocation: piloting. Home: 69 Marble Rd Gloucester MA 01930-4312 Office: Textron Def Systems Div 201 Lowell St Wilmington MA 01887-4113

WILSON, ROBERT WOODROW, radio astronomer; b. Houston, Tex., Jan. 10, 1936; s. Ralph Woodrow and Fannie May (Willis) W.; m. Elizabeth Rhoads Sawin, Sept. 4, 1958; children—Philip Garrett, Suzanne Katherine, Randal Woodrow. B.A. with honors in Physics, Rice U., 1957; Ph.D., Calif. Inst. Tech., 1962. Research fellow Calif. Inst. Tech., Pasadena, 1962-63; mem. tech. staff AT&T Bell Labs., Holmdel, N.J., 1963-76; head wireless tech. rsch. dept. AT&T Bell Labs., 1976-94; sr. sci. Harvard-Smithsonian Ctr. for Astrophysics, Cambridge, Mass., 1994—. Discoverer 3 deg. k microwave background radiation, 1965; discoverer CO and other molecules in interstellar space using their millimeter wavelength radiation. Recipient Henry Draper medal Royal Astron. Soc., London, 1977, Herschel medal Nat. Acad. Scis., 1977; named Fairchild Disting. scholar Caltech., 1987; Nobel prize in physics, 1978; NSF fellow, 1958-61, Cole fellow, 1957-58. Mem. Am. Astron. Soc., Internat. Astron. Union, Am. Phys. Soc., Internat. Sci. Radio Union, Nat. Acad. Scis., Phi Beta Kappa, Sigma Xi. Home: 9 Valley Point Dr Holmdel NJ 07733-1320 Office: Harvard-Smithsonian Ctr Astrophysics 60 Garden St # 42 Cambridge MA 02138-1516

WILSON, ROBIN SCOTT, university president, writer; b. Columbus, Ohio, Sept. 19, 1928; s. John Harold and Helen Louise (Walker) W.; m. Patricia Ann Van Kirk, Jan. 20, 1951; children: Kelpie, Leslie, Kari, Andrew. B.A., Ohio State U., 1950; M.A., U. Ill., 1951, Ph.D., 1959. Fgn. intelligence officer CIA, Washington, 1959-67; prof. English Clarion State Coll., (Pa.), 1967-70; assoc. dir. Com. Instnl. Cooperation, Evanston, Ill., 1970-77; assoc. provost instrn. Ohio State U., Columbus, 1977-80; univ. pres. Calif. State U., Chico, 1980-93, pres. emeritus, 1993—. Author: Those Who Can, 1973, Death By Degrees, 1995; short stories, criticism, articles on edn. Lt. USN, 1953-57. Mem. AAAS, Phi Kappa Phi.

WILSON, ROBLEY CONANT, JR., English educator, editor, author; b. Brunswick, Maine, June 15, 1930; s. Robley Conant and Dorothy May (Stimpson) W.; m. Charlotte A. Lehon, Aug. 20, 1955 (div. 1991); children: Stephen, Philip; m. Susan Hubbard, June 17, 1995. B.A., Bowdoin Coll., 1957, D.Litt (hon.), 1987; M.F.A., U. Iowa, 1968. Reporter Raymondville Chronicle, Tex., 1950-1951; asst. publicity dir. N.Y. State Fair Syracuse, 1956; instr. Valparaiso U., Ind., 1958-63; asst. prof. English U. No. Iowa, Cedar Falls, 1963-69, assoc. prof., 1969-75, prof., 1975—, editor N.Am. Rev., 1969—. Author: The Pleasures of Manhood, 1977, Living Alone, 1978, Dancing for Men, 1983 (Drue Heinz Lit. prize 1982), Kingdoms of the Ordinary, 1987 (Agnes Lynch Starrett award 1986), Terrible Kisses, 1989, A Pleasure Tree, 1990 (soc. Midland Authors Poetry award 1990), The Victim's Daughter, 1991, A Walk Through the Human Heart, 1996. Bd. dirs. Associated Writing Programs, Norfolk, Va., 1983-86; pres. Iowa Woman Endeavors, Inc., 1986-90. With USAF, 1951-55. Guggenheim fellow, 1983-84, Nicholl Screenwriting fellow, 1996. Mem. Am. Soc. Mag. Editors, Authors' Guild. Home: PO Box 527 Cedar Falls IA 50613-0527 Office: Univ Northern Iowa North Am Review Cedar Falls IA 50614

WILSON, ROGER B., lieutenant governor, school administrator; b. Columbia, Mo., Oct. 10, 1948; m. Patricia O' Brien; children: Erin, Drew. BA, Ctrl. Methodist Coll.; MA in Edn., U. Mo.; grad., Harvard U., 1990. Asst. prin. Russell Blvd. Elem. Sch., Columbia, Mo.; real estate broker; collector Boone County, Mo., 1976-79; mem. Mo. State Senate from Dist. 19, 1979-92; lt. gov. State of Mo., 1993—; chmn. senate appropriations com., apportionment com., vice chmn. tourism commn.; mem. Mo. bus. and edn. partnership commn., transportation devel. commn., gov.'s adv. coun. physical fitness. Bd. dirs. United Way, Columbia; mem. Mo. Assn. Community Arts Agencies, Boone County Hist. Soc.; mem. com. Mo. Parents as Tchrs. Recipient Everett award MSTA, Boss of the Yr. award Am. Businesswomen's Assn., Disting. Legis. award NCSL, Horace Mann award MNEA, Outstanding Legis. of Yr. award MSTA, 1991 Pub. Official of Yr. award Mo. Assn. Homes for Aging, M.U. Alumni award, 1991. Mem. Columbia C. of C., Cosmopolitan Internat. Office: State Capitol Bldg # 121 Jefferson City MO 65101*

WILSON, ROGER GOODWIN, lawyer; b. Evanston, Ill., Sept. 3, 1950; s. G. Turner Jr. and Lois (Shay) W.; m. Giovinella Gonthier, Mar. 7, 1975. AB, Dartmouth Coll., 1972; JD, Harvard U., 1975. Bar: Ill. 1975, U.S. Dist. Ct. (no. dist.) Ill. 1976, U.S. Ct. Appeals (7th cir.) 1977, U.S. Dist. Ct. (no. dist.) Ind. 1985. Assoc. Kirkland & Ellis, Chgo., 1975-81, ptnr., 1981-86; sr. v.p., gen. counsel, corp. sec. Blue Cross/Blue Shield, 1986—; speaker Nat. Healthcare Inst., U. Mich., 1987-93, Am. Law Inst.-ABA Conf. on Mng. and Resolving Domestic and Internat. Bus. Disputes, N.Y.C., 1988, Washington, 1990; cert. health cons. program Purdue U., 1993-94, Inst. for Bus. Strategy Devel., Northwestern U., 1993-94, The Health Care Antitrust Forum, Chgo., 1995. Advisor Constl. Rights Found., Chgo., 1982-87; mem. So. Poverty Law Ctr., Montgomery, Ala., 1981—. Mem. ABA, Nat. Health Lawyers Assn. (spkr. 1984), Chgo. Coun. Lawyers (bd. govs. 1988-92), Sinfonietta (bd. dirs. 1987—), Univ. Club, Phi Beta Kappa. Avocations: French lang. and culture. Home: 2800 N Lake Shore Dr Apt 1917 Chicago IL 60657-6246 Office: Blue Cross/Blue Shield 676 N Saint Clair St Chicago IL 60611

WILSON, RONALD D., soft drink bottling company executive; b. Mesa, Ariz., May 16, 1949; s. William Wayne and Theresa (Mallin) W.; m. Kathleen Jean Wilson, May 10, 1975; children: Christopher, Erin. BA in History U., Rutgers U., New Brunswick, N.J., 1971, postgrad., 1973-74; postgrad., Rutgers U., Camden, N.J., 1971-72. Route. mgr. Pepsi-Cola Met. Bottling Co., North Brunswick, N.J., 1974-75; ter. mgr. Pepsi-Cola Met. Bottling Co., Boston, 1975-77; fin. analyst N.J. div. Coca-Cola Bottling Co. N.Y., N.Y.C., 1977, div. mgr. Conn. div., 1977-79, v.p., gen. mgr. No. New Eng. div., 1979-81, v.p., gen. mgr. N.J.-Upstate N.Y. div., 1981-84; exec. v.p., gen. mgr. Phila. Coca-Cola Bottling Co., 1984-85, pres., COO, 1985—; bd. dirs. Coca-Cola Co. Trustee Suburban Gen. Hosp., Norristown, Pa., mem. adv. bd., 1994-95; bd. dirs. United Negro Coll. Fund, Phila., Chestnut Hill Acad., Phila.; mem. adv. bd. Rutgers U. Sch. Bus., Camden. Recipient chmn.'s award United Negro Coll. Fund, 1992, bd. recognition Suburban Gen. Hosp., 1992, Chestnut Hill Acad., 1994. Mem. Pa. and N.J. Soft Drink Assn., Cedarbrook Country Club. Republican. Roman Catholic. Avocations: basketball, golf, reading. Office: Phila Coca-Cola Bottling Co 725 E Erie Ave & G St Philadelphia PA 19134

WILSON, RONALD JAMES, geologist; b. San Antonio, Dec. 24, 1948; s. James Robert and Robbie Lee (Bell) W.; m. Beverly Ann Engelhorn, June 23, 1970 (div. May 1980); children: Jennifer, Jason; m. June Guynette Nolin, Aug. 5, 1983; 1 child, Heather. BA, Rice U., 1971. Sr. logging engr. Schlumberger, Houston, 1971-75; sr. petrophysicist Delta Drilling Co., Tyler, Tex., 1975-78; sr. log analyst Dresser Industries, Houston, 1978-81; mgr., geology and petrophysics Intercomp, Houston, 1981-83; cons. geologist C G & A, Ft. Worth, 1983-90; exec. v.p. Alpha Bio Internat., Ltd., Dallas, 1990-91; pres. Integrated Energy Solutions, Ft. Worth, 1991-94, Lahd Energy, Inc., Granbury, Tex., 1994—; bd. dirs. Tex. Energy Resources, Arlington, 1994—. Author: Practical Log Analysis, 1981, Quick-Look Techniques, 1981; contbr. articles to jour. Prodn. Log Analyst, Log Analyst. Mem. nat. edn. bd. Luth. Ch. Am., Denver, 1975; elder Richland Hills Ch. of Christ, Ft. Worth, 1991; edn. com. Action United Meth. Ch., Acton, Tex., 1994-95; bd. trustees The White Lake Sch., 1995—. Mem. Am. Assn. Petroleum Geologists (cert.), Soc. Profl. Well Log Analysts (pres. 1987-88), Soc. Petroleum Engrs. (bd. edn. 1976—), Divsn. Environ. Geoscientists (charter). Republican. Methodist. Avocations: reading, crafts, wood-working, golfing. Home: 301 Willow Ridge Rd Fort Worth TX 76103 Office: Lahd Energy Inc 307 W 7th St Ste 1717 Fort Worth TX 76102

WILSON, RONALD LAWRENCE, professional hockey coach; b. Windsor, Ont., Can., May 28, 1955. BA in Econs., Providence Coll. Profl. hockey player Toronto Maple Leafs, 1975-85, Minn. North Stars, 1986-88; asst. coach Milw., Vancouver Canucks, 1989-90, Vancouver Canucks, 1990-93; interim coach Milw. North Stars, 1990; head coach Anaheim (Calif.) Mighty Ducks, 1993—. Named to NCAA All-Am. East 1st team, 1974-76. Office: Mighty Ducks PO Box 61077 2695 E Katella Ave Anaheim CA 92803-6177

WILSON, ROOSEVELT LEDELL, secondary education educator; b. Baton Rouge, La., Aug. 8, 1941; m. Barbara Batiste; 1 child, Janile. BS, So. U., 1964, MEd, 1970; MS, U. Okla., 1973; PhD, U. Iowa, 1975. Cert. tchr. math. and sci., La. Tchr. East Baton Rouge Parish Sch. Bd., 1964-75, 81—; teaching asst. U. Iowa, Iowa City, 1974; asst. prof. Jackson (Miss.) State U., 1976-81; tchr. earth and physical sci., dean of students Baton Rouge Prep. Acad., 1994—; club sponsors, dept. chairperson McKinley Mid. Magnet, Baton Rouge, 1981—; dir. workshops E. Baton Rouge Parish Schs., 1983,

85; coord. after-sch. tutorial program Jordan United Meth. Ch., Baton Rouge, 1992—; participant adminstrv. internship program E. Baton Rouge Parish, 1993-94. Contbr. articles to profl. jours. Mem. male chorus Jordan United Meth. Ch., Baton Rouge. Fellow Nat. Fellowship Fund; grantee NSF. Mem. NEA, Nat. Sci. Tchrs. Assn., La. Assn. Educators, Phi Delta Kappa. Methodist. Avocations: golf, tennis, fishing. Home: 21253 Old Scenic Hwy Zachary LA 70791 Office: Baton Rouge Prep Acad 5959 Cadillac St Baton Rouge LA 70811

WILSON, ROY GARDINER, real estate developer; b. Coronation, Alta., Can., May 4, 1932; s. Forest Archibald and Florence Mabel (Gardiner) W.; m. Leila Erma Graham, 1956; children: Keith, Shannon. Salesman, broker, 1951-71; dir. Carma Developers Ltd., Calgary, Alta., 1958—, pres., 1971-85, chmn., 1985-86; dir., pres. Devstar Properties Ltd., Calgary, 1987-90; dir. URBCO Inc., 1988—, chmn., 1990—; dir., chmn. Mortgage Properties Inc., 1991-93. Chmn. Residential Devel. Council, 1977, 78; Mem. Legis. Assembly Alta., 1971-75; mem. Calgary Police Commn., 1976-80. Named to Hall of Fame Olds Coll., 1988.

WILSON, ROY KENNETH, retired education association executive, consultant; b. Charleston, Ill., July 9, 1913; s. George William and Ruth (Woody) W.; m. Ruth June Royce, Aug. 19, 1939; 1 child, Robert Royce (dec.). B.Ed., Eastern Ill. State Coll., 1936; A.M., U. Ill., 1943; Litt. D. (hon.), Glassboro (N.J.) State Coll., 1959. Asso. editor Nat. Printer Journalist, The Printing Industry, Springfield, Ill., 1935-37; dir. pub. relations Eastern Ill. U., Charleston, 1937-42; asst. dir. div. press and radio relations N.E.A., Washington, 1946-57; dir. div. press, radio and TV relations N.E.A., 1957-68; sec-treas., staff dir. Nat. Sch. Pub. Relations Assn., 1950-68, exec. dir., 1968-76; cons. Ednl. Research Service, 1977—. Editorial dir.: Edn. U.S.A, 1958-76. Served to lt. comdr. USNR, World War II. Mem. NEA, Pub. Rels. Soc. Am., Nat. Sch. Pub. Rels. Assn., Am. Assn. Sch. Adminstrs., Houndslake and Woodside Plantation (S.C). Methodist. Home: Brandon Wilde # 414 4275 Owens Rd Evans GA 30809-8600 Office: 2000 Clarendon Blvd Arlington VA 22201-2908

WILSON, RUBY LEILA, nurse, educator; b. Punxsutawney, Pa., May 29, 1931; d. Clark H. and Alda E. (Armstrong) W. BS in Nursing Edn., U. Pitts., 1954; MSN, Case Western Res. U., 1959; EdD, Duke U., 1969. Staff nurse, asst. head nurse Allegheny Gen. Hosp., Pitts., 1951-52; night clin. instr., adminstrv. supr. Allegheny Gen. Hosp., 1951-55; staff nurse, asst. head nurse Fort Miley VA Hosp., San Francisco, 1957-58; instr. nursing Duke U. Sch. Nursing, Durham, N.C., 1955-57; asst. prof. med. surg. nursing Duke U. Sch. Nursing, 1959-66, assoc. in medicine, 1963-66, prof. nursing, 1971—, dean sch. nursing., 1971-84, asst. to chancellor for health affairs, 1984—; asst. prof. dept. community and family medicine Duke U. Sch. Medicine, 1971—; cons., vis. prof. Rockefeller Found., Thailand, 1968-71; vis. prof. Case Western Res. U., 1982-84; mem. Gov.'s Commn. on Health Care Reform in N.C., 1994. Contbr. articles to profl. jours. Active N.C. Med. Care Commn., Gov.'s Commn. on N.C. Health Care Reform, 1994—. Fellow Am. Acad. Nursing, Inst. Medicine; mem. ANA, Am. Assn. Colls. Nursing, Am. Assn. Higher Edn., Nat. League Nursing, Assn. for Acad. Health Ctrs. (mem. inst. planning com.), Women's Forum N.C. (bd. dirs. 1984-88, 95—), N.C. Found. for Nursing (pres. 1990-94). Office: Duke U Med Ctr PO Box 3243 Durham NC 27715-3243

WILSON, SAM N., transportation services consultant; b. 1935. Grad., North Tex. State U., 1958. Mgr. internat. distbn. Tex. Instruments, Inc., Dallas, 1958-75; v.p. Circle Airfreight Corp., DFW Internat. Airport, Dallas, 1975-80; chmn., CEO Intertrans Corp., Irving, Tex., 1978—; now cons. San Francisco, CA. Office: Intertrans Corp 706 Miseco ST San Francisco CA 94103*

WILSON, SAMUEL GRAYSON, federal judge; b. 1949. BS, U. Richmond, 1971; JD cum laude, Wake Forest U., 1974. Asst. commonwealth atty. City of Roanoke, Va., 1974-76; asst. U.S. atty. Western Dist. Va., 1976; U.S. magistrate U.S. Dist. Ct. for Western Dist. Va., 1976-81; mem. Woods, Rogers & Hazlegrove, Roanoke, 1981-90; dist. judge U.S. Dist. Ct. for Western Dist. Va., Abingdon, Va., 1990—. Mem. staff Wake Forest Law Rev., 1973-74. Mem. law bd. visitors Wake Forest U. Mem. Va. State Bar, Fed. Bar Assn., Va. Bar Assn., Roanoke Bar Assn., Supreme Ct. Hist. Soc. Methodist. Office: US Dist Ct PO Box 749 180 W Main St Abingdon VA 24210-0749*

WILSON, SAMUEL V., academic administrator. Pres. Hampden-Sydney (Va.) Coll. Office: Hampden-Sydney Coll Office of Pres PO Box 128 Hampden Sydney VA 23943-0128

WILSON, SARAH JANE, nursing educator; b. Erie, Pa., Nov. 25, 1942; d. Russell R. and A. Glendine (Link) Leo; m. William R. Wilson, Dec. 14, 1963; children: Russell William, Michael David. Grad., Hamot Hosp. Sch. Nursing, Erie, 1963; BS, Gannon U., 1988, MS in Counseling Psychology, 1995. RN, Pa.; cert. psychiat. mental health nurse ANCC. Nurse instr. staff devel. Warren (Pa.) State Hosp., 1989—, instr., coord. CPR, presenter cmty. mental health programs, 1990—. Mem. Warren County AIDS Network. Mem. ANA, Pa. Nurses Assn., Am. Psychiat. Nurses Assn. Office: 33 Main Dr North Warren PA 16365

WILSON, SHERRY DENISE, speech and language pathologist; b. Rutherford, N.C., Jan. 10, 1963; d. Morris William and Betty Jean (Hudgins) Wilson. AA, Isothermal Community Coll., 1981; BS, Cen. Mo. State U., 1985, MS, 1988. Lic. speech-lang. pathologist, N.C. Speech pathologist DePaul Hosp. Home Health, Cheyenne, Wyo., 1987, 89; coord. handicap svcs., staff speech-lang. pathologist Laramie County Head Start, Cheyenne, 1987-89; speech pathologist, supr., coord., dir. inclusive pre-sch. Ednl. Svcs. Unit # 13, Scottsbluff, 1989-95, project dir. The Early Intervention Demonstration Project, 1991-95; dir. rehab. svc. Brentwood Hills Nursing Ctr. (Beverly Enterprises), Asheville, N.C., 1995—; planning region chair Interagy. coord. Coun. Presch. Spl. Edn., Scottsbluff, Nebr., 1989-93, mem. 1993-95; mem. health adv. bd. Head Start, Gering, Nebr., 1989-91; cons. trainer in field. Founding mem. S.E. Wyo. AIDS Project, Cheyenne, 1989; Odyssey of the Mind coach Gering Jr. H.S., 1989-93; project dir., mem. exec. bd. Cmty. Devel. Coalition, 1994. Named Outstanding Speech Pathologist of Yr., Sigma Alpha Eta, 1985. Mem. NEA, Am. Speech-Lang.-Hearing Assn. (cert. clin. competence, Cert. Excellence 1993), N.C. Speech-Lang.-Hearing Assn., Nebr. State Edn. Assn., Coun. for Exceptional Children (early childhood div.). Avocations: travel, visual arts, photography. Office: Brentwood Hills Nursing Ctr Asheville NC 28804

WILSON, SHERYL A., pharmacist; b. Nashville, Apr. 6, 1957; d. Robert Lewis and Norma Anne (Cox) W. BS in Biology, David Lipscomb U., 1979; BS in Pharmacy, Auburn U., 1985. Lic. pharmacist, Tenn. Student extern/intern East Alabama Med. Ctr., Opelika, Ala., 1982-86; staff pharmacist Metro Nashville Gen. Hosp., 1987-95, PharmaThera, Inc., Nashville, 1995—. Flutist Nashville Community Concert Band, 1973—; preschool tchr. Donelson Ch. of Christ, 1988—. Mem. Am. Pharm. Assn., Am. Soc. Health Sys. Pharmacists, Am. Soc. Parenteral and Enteral Nutrition, Tenn. Soc. Hosp. Pharmacists, Nashville Area Pharmacists Assn. Democrat. Avocations: art, music, reading, cooking, sewing. Home: 1439 Mcgavock Pike Nashville TN 37216-3231 Office: PharmaThera Inc 1410 Donelson Pike Ste B-3 Nashville TN 37217

WILSON, SHERYL J., state agency administrator; b. Shelton, Wash., May 23, 1936; d. Kenneth F. and Bernice (Angell) Sturdevant; m. Daniel I. Stuckey, Sept. 8, 1956 (div. June 1967); children: Mark, Ann, David, Noni; m. Donald R. Wilson, Aug. 9, 1968. Student, Wash. State U., 1954-57; BA, Evergreen State Coll., 1985. Rsch. analyst Wash. Pub. Pension Commn., Olympia, 1967-75; budget analyst Wash. State Senate, Olympia, 1975-80; retirement and ins. officer U. Wash., Seattle, 1980-83; asst. dir. Wash. Dept. Retirement Sys., Olympia, 1983-89, dir., 1993—; exec. dir. Oreg. Pub. Employees Retirement Sys., Portland, 1989-93; mem. exec. com. Nat. Coun. Tchr. Retirement, Astin, 1992—, mem. com. on deferred compensation, 1995—; pres., mem. exec. com. Nat. Preretirement Edn. Assn., 1985-91; chair Wash. State Investment Bd., Olympia, 1995—; mem. steering com. cert. employee benefit specialist program U. Wash., 1983—; mem. vis. com. U. Wash. Ext., 1996—. Chair Interagy. Com. Status of Women, Olympia, 1987-88. Mem. Nat. Assn. State Retirement Adminstrs. (legis. com. 1989—), Women in Pub. Adminstrn. (founder Oreg. chpt. 1990), Govt. Fin. Officers (retirement and benefits adminstrn. com. 1992—), Zonta Internat. Avocations: photography, travel, hiking, snorkeling.

WILSON, SLOAN, author, lecturer; b. Norwalk, Conn., May 8, 1920; s. Albert F. and Ruth (Danenhower) W.; m. Elise Pickhardt, Feb. 4, 1941 (div.); children—Lisa, Rebecca, David Sloan; m. Betty Stephens; 1 dau., Jessica. Grad., Fla. Adirondack Sch., 1938; AB, Harvard, 1942; LHD (hon.), Rollins Coll., 1982. Writer, contbr. New Yorker and other mags.; with Providence Jour., 1946-47, Time, Inc., 1947-49, Nat. Citizens Commn. for Pub. Schs., 1949-53; dir. information services, asst. prof. English Buffalo U., 1953-55; asst. dir. White House Conf. on Edn., 1955-56; Disting. writer-in-residence Rollins Coll., Winter Park, Fla., 1981-82; dir. Winter Park Artists Workshop, 1983-85; cons. Philip Crosby Assocs., Winter Park, 1984-87; lectr. Va. Commwealth U., 1990. Author: Voyage to Somewhere, 1946, The Man in the Gray Flannel Suit, 1955, A Summer Place, 1958, A Sense of Values, 1960, Georgie Winthrop, 1962, Janus Island, 1966, Away From It All, 1969, All The Best People, 1970, What Shall We Wear to This Party, 1976, Small Town, 1978, Ice Brothers, 1979, The Greatest Crime, 1980, Pacific Interlude, 1982, The Man in the Gray Flannel Suit II, 1983. Served to lt. USCGR, World War II. *Although some of my books have been widely read, I of course am not as successful as a writer as I would like to be. Almost all writers, after all, must, if they are honest, suspect that their triumphs are temporary. This is no cause for lament, for the same happens to almost everybody in all walks of life. I am lucky to have a wife who makes my private life a joy and three daughters and a son who with my ten grandchildren give me a kind of immortality. Much like the characters in most of my books, I find my family the only part of my life which does not disappoint. My children and my wife always give me excellent reviews which never yellow in a scrapbook. I sometimes lecture on the topic of "Success." Nowadays that word seems to me to be much more complex than it did when I was young. As I grow old I love life more and more.*

WILSON, SONJA MARY, secondary education educator, consultant, poet; b. Lake Charles, La., Mar. 28, 1938; d. Albert Ronald and Annelia (DeVille) Molless; m. Willie McKinley Williams, Apr. 28, 1956 (div. May 1969); children: William P., Dwayne L., Rachelle A., Devon A., Lisa M., Ricardo Soto; m. Howard Brooks Wilson, Nov. 12, 1982; stepchildren: Howard N. Wilson, Yvonne Wilson. AA in Social and Behavioral Scis., Mt. St. Jacinto Jr. Coll., 1992; Designated Subjects Credential, U. Calif., San Bernardino, 1983; student, Calif. State Poly. U., 1986, Laverne U., 1984-85; BS in Edn., So. Ill. U., 1995; student, Riverside (Calif.) City Coll., 1988-89, 94. Prin.'s sec. Elsinore (Calif.) H.S., Elsinore Jr. H.S., 1974-83, tchr. bus. and adult vocat. edn. coord., 1979-88, notary pub., 1981-85, class adviser, 1983-88; long-term substitute tchr. Perris H.S. Dist., 1991-94. V.p., pres., clk. Lake Elsinore Unified Sch. Dist. Bd., 1988—; pres., clk., mem. Lake Elsinore Elem. Sch. Bd., 1979-88; pres., sec. treas., v.p. Riverside County Sch. Bds. Assn., 1979—; assoc. sponsor, advisor Black Student Union/Future Leaders of Am., 1984-90; svc. unit rep., leader Girl Scouts U.S.; den mother Boy Scouts Am.; mem. Ctrl. Dem. Com., 1989-91; del. PTSA, 1991-93. Tribute in her honor Black Student Union/Future Leaders Am., 1989; recipient Excellence in Edn. award Hilltop Community Ctr. Club, 1989, Leadership award Black Art and Social Club, 1989, Svc. award Sojourner Truth Media Network, 1989, Proclamation award City of Elsinore, 1989, County of Riverside, 1984; named Outstanding Poet, Nat. Libr. of Congress, 1994, 95. Mem. NAACP (Lake Elsinore affiliate, plaque), Calif. Sch. Bds. Assn. (regional dir. 1988-92, conf. planning com. 1989, legis. com. 1981—, nominations com. 1988, media com., dir. at large black 1993-95, audit com. 1993, dir./del. trainer 1993, alt. del., sgt. at arms 1994, 95, Fed. Rels. Network del. 1992, 95), Calif. Elected Women Ofcls. Assn., Calif. Sch. Employees Assn. (pres., treas., regional rep. asst., state negotiation com., del. to conf.), Internat. Soc. Poets, Lake Elsinore C. of C., Calif. Coalition Black Sch. Bd. Mems. (v.p. 1989, pres. 1990, program liaison 1989), Nat. Sch. Bds. Assn. (alt. del. 1994, 95), Nat. Coalition Black Sch. Bd. Mems. (dir. 1989-94, v.p. 1995—), Nat. Coun. Negro Women (charter, Willa Mae Taylor sect.), Black Art and Social Club, Hilltop Cmty. Club (plaque), Sojourner Truth Media Network (plaque), Eta Phi Beta (treas., sec. Gamma Alpha chpt., plaque, pres. 1992-94). Avocations: travel, writing poetry, winemaking, childcare, reading. Home: 21330 Waite St Lake Elsinore CA 92530-9503

WILSON, STANLEY P., retired lawyer; b. Hamlin, Tex., Sept. 1, 1922; s. Milton Young and Ethel M. (Patterson) W.; m. Claudie Park, Sept. 23, 1944; children: Stanley P., Russell Park, Marianne. BS, U. North Tex., Denton, 1943; LLB, U. Tex., Austin, 1948. Bar: Tex. 1948. Ptnr. McMahon, Smart, Wilson, Surovik & Suttle, Abilene, Tex., 1948-81; sr. v.p., gen. counsel Central and S.W. Corp., Dallas, 1981-86; exec. v.p., gen. counsel Central and S.W. Corp., 1986-88, ret., 1988. Lt. (j.g.) USN, 1943-46, PTO. Mem. ABA, State Bar Tex., Am. Coll. Trial Lawyers, Abilene Bar Assn., Abilene Country Club, Preston Trail Club. Methodist. Home: 1921 Elmwood Dr Abilene TX 79605-4802 Office: Ste 800 First Nat Bank Bldg Abilene TX 79601

WILSON, STEPHEN VICTOR, federal judge; b. N.Y.C., Mar. 26, 1942; s. Harry and Rae (Ross) W. B.A. in Econs., Lehigh U., 1963; J.D., Bklyn. Law Sch., 1967; LL.M., George Washington U., 1973. Bars: N.Y. 1967, D.C. 1971, Calif. 1972, U.S. Ct. Appeals (9th cir.) U.S. Dist. Ct. (so., cen. and no. dists.) Calif. Trial atty. Tax div. U.S. Dept. Justice, 1968-71; asst. U.S. atty., L.A., 1971-77, chief spl. prosecutions, 1973-77; ptnr. Hochman, Salkin & Deroy, Beverly Hills, Calif., from 1977; judge U.S. Dist. Ct. (cen. dist.) Calif., L.A., 1985—; adj. prof. law Loyola U. Law Sch., 1976-79; U.S. Dept. State rep. to govt. W.Ger. on 20th anniversary of Marshall Plan, 1967; del. jud. conf. U.S. Ct. Appeals (9th cir.), 1982-86. Recipient Spl. Commendation award U.S. Dept. Justice, 1977. Mem. ABA, L.A. County Bar Assn., Beverly Hills Bar Assn. (chmn. criminal law com.), Fed. Bar Assn. Jewish. Contbr. articles to profl. jours. Home: 9100 Wilshire Blvd Beverly Hills CA 90212-3415 Office: US Dist Ct 312 N Spring St Los Angeles CA 90012-4701*

WILSON, STEVEN J., metal products executive; b. 1943. BSME, Northwestern U., Evanston, Ill., 1966; MBA, U. Chgo., 1973. With Vapor Corp., Niles, Ill., 1966-69; with Electro Products Co., Niles, 1969-71, Signode Corp., Lincolnshire, Ill., 1971-89; with Duo-Fast Corp., Franklin Park, Ill., 1991—, v.p. engring. and tool mfg. Office: Duo-Fast Corp 3702 River Rd Franklin Park IL 60131-2121

WILSON, TERRENCE RAYMOND, manufacturing executive; b. St. Louis, July 1, 1943; s. Raymond Lemuel and Eula Ellen (Sutton) W.; m. Judy Marie Coleman, May 23, 1964; children: John Scott, Dustin Marint. Student, Drury Coll., 1961-62, St. Louis Jr. Coll., 1962-64, Mo. U., 1965-67. Program control planning adminstr. McDonnell Aircraft, St. Louis, 1962-65, 67; mgmt. control mgr. Vitro Labs., Silver Spring, Md., 1966; mgr. customer svc. Teledyne Wis. Motor, Milw., 1968-69, dir. ops., 1970-71, dir. mktg., 1972-73; gen. mgr. Teledyne Still-Man, Cookeville, Tenn., 1973-74; pres. multiplant div. Teledyne Still-Man, Cookeville, 1975-78; group exec. Teledyne, Inc., 1979-84; pres. Teledyne Indsl. Engines, 1984-87; pres., chief exec. officer Morgan Corp., Morgantown, Pa., 1987-92; pres. Magnatech Internat. Inc., Sinking Spring, Pa., 1992—. Bd. dirs. Tenn. Tech. U. Coll. Bus. Found.; mem. exec. bd. Hawk Mountain Coun. Boy Scouts Am.; bd. trustees Cmty Gen. Hosp., Kutztown U. Found., mem. pres. adv. com. Mem. Beta Gamma Sigma. Roman Catholic. Home: 411 Green Ln Reading PA 19601-1009 Office: Magnatech Internat Inc 796 Fritztown Rd Sinking Spring PA 19608-1522

WILSON, THEDA MORRIS, school board administrator, educator; b. Newark, Jan. 15, 1922; d. William Boen and Maggie (Hall) Morris; m. Donald Octavio Wilson, June 26, 1947; children: Milagros Wilson Williams, Sylvia Wilson Collins, Juana Wilson Brown. BS in Elem. Edn., N.J. State Tchrs., 1943; MA in Guidance and Pers. Adminstrn., NYU, 1946. Elem. tchr. Oakwood Ave. Sch., Orange, N.J., 1944-48, Sumner Ave Sch. and Forest Pk., Springfield, Mass., 1948-51, Elbert Elem. Sch., Wilmington, Del., 1951-54; elem. prin. Elbert Elem. Sch., N.E. Elem. Sch., Wilmington, 1954-64; prin. Sch. # 138, Sch. #97 Collington Sq., Balt., 1964-74; regional supt. Cen. and N.E. Balt. Regions, 1974-84; instr. Johns Hopkins U., Balt., 1975-80; vice-chmn. Flagler County Sch. Bd., Fla., 1988-90, chmn., 1990—; founder Edn. Opportunities Found., Balt., 1984-90. Co-author: World of Language, 1969, rev. edit., 1974. Bd. dirs. Citrus coun. Girl Scouts U.S.A., Winter Park, Fla., 1991—, YWCA, Springfield, Mass., Wilmington, Del., Balt. Recipient Balt.'s Best award Mayor and City Coun., 1983. Mem. AAUW (v.p. 1992-94, pres. 1994—), Girl Friends Inc. (pres. Orlando, Fla. chpt. 1991—), Les Amies des Arts, Phi Delta Kappa. Episcopalian. Avocations: quilting, photography. Home and Office: PO Box 350768 Palm Coast FL 32135-0768

WILSON, THEODORE HENRY, retired electronics company executive, aerospace engineer; b. Eufaula, Okla., Apr. 23, 1940; s. Theodore V. and Maggie E. (Buie) W.; m. Barbara Ann Tassara, May 16, 1958 (div. 1982); children: Debbie Marie, Nita Leigh, Wilson Axten, Pamela Ann, Brenda Louise, Theodore Henry II, Thomas John; m. Colleen Fagan, Jan. 1, 1983 (div. 1987); m. Karen L. Lerohl, Sept. 26, 1987. BSME, U. Calif., Berkeley, 1962; MSME, U. So. Calif., 1964, MBA, 1970, MSBA, 1971. Sr. rsch. engr. N.Am. Aviation Co. div. Rockwell Internat., Downey, Calif., 1962-65; propulsion analyst, supr. div. applied tech. TRW, Redondo Beach, Calif., 1965-67, mem. devel. staff systems group, 1967-71; sr. fin. analyst worldwide automotive dept. TRW, Cleve., 1971-72; contr. systems and energy group TRW, Redondo Beach, 1972-79; dir. fin. control equipment group TRW, Cleve., 1979-82, v.p. fin. control indsl. and energy group, 1982-85; mem. space and def. group TRW, Redondo Beach, 1985-93, ret., 1993; lectr., mem. com. acctg. curriculum UCLA Extension, 1974-79. Mem. Fin. Execs. Inst. (com. govt. bus.), Machinery and Allied Products Inst. (govt. contracts coun.), Nat. Contract Mgmt. Assn. (bd. advisors), Aerospace Industries Assn. (procurement and fin. coun.), UCLA Chancellors Assocs., Tau Beta Pi, Beta Gamma Sigma, Pi Tau Sigma. Republican. Avocations: golf, bridge. Home: 3617 Via La Selva Palos Verdes Peninsula CA 90274-1115

WILSON, THOMAS ARTHUR, economics educator; b. Vancouver, B.C., Canada, Aug. 5, 1935; s. Victor and Edith Christina (Grange) W.; m. Julia Ann Dillon, Feb. 8, 1958; children: Christine Diana, Arthur Dillon. B.A., U. B.C., 1957; Ph.D., Harvard U., 1961. Instr. Harvard U., 1961-62, asst. prof., 1962-67; assoc. prof. U. Toronto, 1967-68, prof., 1968—, dir. Inst. for Policy Analysis, 1969-75, dir. econs., 1979-82, chmn. econs. dept., 1982-85, dir. policy and econ. analysis program, 1987—, area coord. bus. econs. Faculty of Mgmt., 1989—; cons. various govtl. depts. Author: Advertising and Market Power, 1974, Canadian Competition Policy, 1979, Fiscal Policy in Canada, 1993, The Future of Telecommunications Policy in Canada, 1995. Fellow Royal Soc. Can.; mem. Am. Econs. Assn., Canadian Econ. Assn. (pres. 1984-85). Office: 140 St George St, Toronto, ON Canada M5S 1A1

WILSON, THOMAS LEON, physicist; b. Alpine, Tex., May 21, 1942; s. Homer Marvin and Ogarita Maude (Bailey) W.; m. Joyce Ann Krevosky, May 7, 1978; children: Kenneth Edward Byron, Bailey Elizabeth Victoria. BA, Rice U., 1964, BS, 1965, MA, 1974, PhD, 1976. With NASA, Houston, 1965—, astronaut instr., 1965-74, high-energy theoretical physicist, 1969—. Author of two books on cosmic dust and astrophysics; contbr. articles in field to profl. jours. Recipient Hugo Gernsback award IEEE, 1964; NASA fellow, 1969-76. Mem. AAAS, Am. Phys. Soc., N.Y. Acad. Scis., Am. Assn. Physicists in Medicine. Research on grand unified field theory, relativistic quantum field theory, quantum chromodynamics, quantum probability theory, supergravity, quantum cosmology, astrophysics, deep inelastic scattering, neutrino astronomy, authority on neutrino tomography, discoverer classical uncertainty principle; subspecialty: relativity and gravitation. Patentee in field; contributor to design of NASA's proposed lunar base; originator olive branch as symbol of man's 1st landing on moon (on Susan B. Anthony and Eisenhower dollars); manual Saturn takeover for Apollo moon program. Home: 206 Woodcombe Dr Houston TX 77062-2538 Office: NASA Johnson Space Ctr Houston TX 77058

WILSON, THOMAS WILLIAM, lawyer; b. Bklyn., Sept. 14, 1935; s. Matthew and Alice (McCrory) W.; m. Eileen Marie McGann, June 4, 1960; children—Jeanne Alice, Thomas William, David Matthew, A.B., Columbia U., 1957, LL.B., 1960. Bar: N.Y. 1962, U.S. Dist. Ct. (so. and ea. dists.) N.Y. 1962, D.C. 1972. Assoc. Mendes and Mount, N.Y.C., 1961-65, Haller & Small, N.Y.C., 1965-66; gen. counsel Prudential of Gt. Brit., N.Y.C., 1966-68; mng. ptnr. Wilson, Elser, Moskowitz, Edelman & Dicker, N.Y.C., 1968—. Contbr. articles to profl. jours. Served with U.S. Army, 1960-65. Mem. ABA, N.Y. State Bar Assn., Def. Research Inst. (editorial bd. profl. liability reporter). Office: Wilson Elser Moskowitz Edelman & Dicker 150 E 42nd St New York NY 10017-5612

WILSON, TOM, cartoonist, greeting card company executive; b. Grant Town, W.Va., Aug. 1, 1931; s. Charles Albert and Hazel Marie W.; m. Carol; children: Tom, Ava. Grad., Art Inst. Pitts., 1955. Advt. layout man Uniontown Newspapers Inc., Uniontown, PA, 1950-53; designer Am. Greetings Corp., Cleveland, OH, 1955-56; creative dir. Am. Greetings Corp., 1957-78, v.p. creative devel., 1978-81; pres. Those Characters from Cleve., 1981—; former mem. faculty Cooper Sch. Art. Cartoonist: Ziggy, 1971—, syndicated in newspapers across U.S. by Universal Press Syndicate, Kansas City; collections include: Life is Just a Bunch of Ziggys, 1973, It's a Ziggy World, 1974, Ziggy Coloring Book, 1974, Never Get Too Personally Involved with Your Own Life, 1975, Promises to Myself: Ziggy's Thirty-Day Ledger of I Owe Me's, 1975, Plants are Some of My Favorite People, 1976, Ziggys of the World Unite!, 1976, Pets Are Friends You Like Who Like You Right Back, 1977, The Ziggy Treasury, 1977, This Book is for the Birds, 1978, Encore! Encore!, 1979, Ziggy's Love Notes, 1979, Ziggy's Thinking of You Notebook, 1979, Ziggy's Fleeting Thoughts Notebook, 1979, A Ziggy Christmas, 1980, Ziggy's Door Openers, 1980, Ziggy Faces Life, 1981, One Thing You Can Say About Living Alone...There's Never Any Question About Who Didn't Jiggle the Handle on the John, 1981, Short People Arise, 1981, A Word to the Wide is Sufficient, 1981, Ziggy's Sunday Funnies, 1981, Ziggy & Friends, 1982, Ziggy Faces Life...Again!, 1982, Ziggy's For You With Love, 1982, Ziggy's Gift, 1982, Ziggy's Big Little Book, 1983, Ziggy and Friends, 1983, Ziggy's Funday Sunnies, 1983, Alphabet Soup Isn't Supposed to Make Sense, 1984, Ziggy Weighs In, 1984, Ziggy's Ship Comes In, 1984, Ug! The Original Hunk, 1985, Ziggy In the Rough, 1985, Ziggy's Ins and Outs, 1985, Ziggy's Ups and Downs, 1985, Ziggy In the Fast Lane, 1987, Ziggy's Follies, 1988, Ziggy's Star Performances, 1989, Ziggy's School of Hard Knocks, 1989, Ziggy On the Outside Looking In, 1990, (also illustrator) Ziggy's Christmas Book Levels 1, 2, 1991, (also illustrator) Ziggy's Play Today Guitar Method, 1991, Look Out World...Here I Come! Ziggy's Own Down-to-Earth Humor: A Look At the Environment and Ourselves, 1991, Ziggy...A Rumor in His Own Time, 1992, The Ziggy Cookbook: Great Food From Mom's Diner, 1993, A Day in the Life of Ziggy, 1993, One-Eight Hundred-Ziggy, 1994, My Life As a Cartoon: A Ziggy Collection, 1995, Ziggy's Place. Served with U.S. Army, 1953-55. Recipient Purchase award Butler Mus. Nat. Painting Competition, Emmy award for best animated spl., 1982. Developer Soft Touch line of greeting cards. Office: Universal Press Syndicate PO Box 419149 Kansas City MO 64141-6149 *My objective and chief motivation has always been . . . "to bring something about that wasn't there before.".*

WILSON, VICTORIA JANE SIMPSON, former nurse, farmer; b. Floresville, Tex., Nov. 30, 1952; d. Joseph Eugene and Eva Gertrude (Ferguson) Simpson; m. Richard Royce Wilson, May 15, 1976; children: Sarah Beth, Nathan Lawrence. BSN, U. Cen. Ark., 1977; MS in Nursing, Northwestern State U., 1981. Charge nurse surg. St. Vincent Infirmary, Little Rock; staff nurse ICU La. State U. Med. Ctr., Shreveport, La.; patient edn. coord. White River Med. Ctr., Batesville, Ark.; co-owner, chief exec. officer Health Plus, Stuttgart, Ark.; co-owner, mgr. Wilson & Son Fish Farm. Mem. Catfish Farmers Am., Catfish Farmers Ark., Sigma Theta Tau. Home: PO Box 310 Humphrey AR 72073-0310

WILSON, W. STANLEY, federal agency administrator. BS, Coll. William and Mary, 1959, MA, 1964; PhD, Johns Hopkins U., 1972. Marine biol. collector Va. Inst. Marine Scis., 1959-64; computer systems analyst Johns Hopkins U., Balt., 1964-72; from scientific officer to program mgr. phys. oceanography Office of Naval Rsch., 1972-79; chief oceanic processes br. NASA, 1979-89, program scientist earth observing system, 1989-92; asst. adminstr. Nat. Ocean Svc., 1992—. Recipient award Remote Sensing Soc., 1992, Disting. achievement award Compass, 1989. Mem. Oceanography Soc. (former coun. mem., chair meetings com.), Am. Geophys. Union, Am. Meteorol. Soc., Coastal Soc., Sigma Xi, Omicron Delta Kappa. Office: Dept of Commerce Nat Ocean Service SSMC Bldg 4 1305 E-W Highway Silver Spring MD 20910

WILSON, WALLACE, art educator, artist; b. Dallas, June 10, 1947; s. William Wallace and Zoe (Naylor) W.; m. Mary Claire Straw, Apr. 3, 1982; 1 child, Erin Rebecca. Student, Tex. Tech. U., 1965-67; B.A., U. Tex., 1970; MFA, Sch. of Art Inst. Chgo., 1975. Asst. prof. U. Ky., Lexington, 1970-75, U. Del., Newark, 1975-79; assoc. prof. U. Fla., Gainesville, 1979-90, prof., 1990-94; prof., chmn. art dept. U. South Fla., Tampa, 1994—; vis. prof. U. Gothenburg, Sweden, 1984, 86, London Study Ctr. Fla. State U., 1988. One-man shows O.K. Harris Gallery, N.Y.C., 1977, 87, Photopia, Mancini Gallery, Phila., 1977, Balt. Mus. Art, 1977, Images Gallery, New Orleans, 1979, U. Ala., Birmingham, 1983, Francesca Anderson Gallery, Boston, 1986, Marcuse Pfeifer Gallery, N.Y.C., 1987, 89, Tartt Gallery, Washington, 1987, 90, 92, The Photographers Gallery, London, 1989, Robert Klein Gallery, Boston, 1991, Southeast Mus. Photography, Fla., 1993; group exhbns. include U. Nebr., Lincoln, 1972, Galerie Zabriskie, Paris, 1978, Boston Visual Arts Union, 1981, Santa Barbara Mus. Art, Calif., 1982, Robert Freidus Gallery, N.Y.C., 1983, N.Mex. State U. Gallery, Las Cruces, 1987, Spl. Photographers Co., London, 1989, Douglas Drake Gallery, N.Y.C., 1992, Art Network, Atlanta, 1993, The Art Inst. Chgo., 1994; represented in permanent collections Mus. Modern Art, N.Y.C., Art. Inst. Chgo., Oakland Mus., Calif., New Orleans Mus. Art, Balt. Mus. Art, City Mus. Munich, Houston Mus. Fine Arts, The Bklyn. Mus. Recognized in various publs. including Village Voice, N.Y.C., 1977, 87, 89, Le Figaro, Paris, 1978, Art Voices, Palm Beach, Fla., 1981, Art Papers, Atlanta, 1982, Miami Herald, 1989, 90, The Sunday Times, 1989, Photo Metro, San Francisco, 93, Washington Post, 1987, 92; recipient U. Del. Faculty research award, 1978, 20x24 Camera award Polaroid, 1985; fellow Swedish Found., Stockholm, 1986; U. Fla. Faculty research grantee, 1980, 88, 93; Individual Artist fellow State of Fla. Div. Cultural Affairs, 1982, 88. Mem. Soc. for Photog. Edn. (vice chmn. S.E. region 1982-85). Office: U South Fla Art Dept Tampa FL 33620-7350

WILSON, WALTER CLINTON, gas, oil industry executive; b. Brownwood, Tex., Sept. 21, 1942; s. Henry Eliga and Lottie Mae (Palmore) W.; m. Debra M. Thompson, Aug. 26, 1965; children: Walter Scott, Aimée Renee. BS cum laude, Howard Payne U., 1965. CPA, Tex. Fin. mgmt. Exxon Co. USA, Kingsville, Corpus Christi, Houston, Tex., 1965-81; asst. contr., fin. cons. The Superior Oil Co., Houston, 1982-85; v.p. Enron Oil and Gas Co., Houston, 1985-87, contr., 1987-88, sr. v.p., CFO, 1988—. Chmn. deacons First Bapt. Ch., Houston, 1994-96, chmn. pers. com., 1985-87. Lt. USNR, 1966-69, Vietnam. Mem. AICPA, Fin. Execs. Inst., Ind. Petroleum Assn. Am., Tex. Soc. CPA (Houston chpt.), Club Corp. Am.-Houston Soc., Petroleum Club Houston, Kingwood Country Club. Republican. Office: Enron Oil & Gas Co PO Box 4362 1400 Smith St Ste 2360 Houston TX 77210-4362

WILSON, WARNER RUSHING, psychology educator; b. Jackson, Miss., July 27, 1935; s. William Enouch and Ruby (Goyne) W. A.B., U. Chgo., 1956; M.A., U. Ark., 1958; Ph.D., Northwestern U., 1960. Teaching asst. Northwestern U., 1957-60; research psychologist E.I. duPont de Nemours & Co., Wilmington, Del., 1960; asst. prof. U. Hawaii, 1960-65; assoc. prof. U. Ala., 1965-73; prof. Wright State U., Dayton, Ohio, 1973-93; pvt. practice Las Vegas, Nev., 1993—; Cons. Bryce State Hosp., Tuscaloosa, Ala., 1966, Ednl. Testing Service, 1968, Tuscaloosa VA Hosp., 1968-74, H.R.B. Singer Co., 1972; Trainee Downey (Ill.) VA Hosp., summer 1959. Contbr. articles to profl. jours. spl. summer fellow in evaluation research Northwestern U., 1973-74, NSF grantee, 1976-78, Johnson Assocs. Postdoctoral Clin. fellow, 1981-82; Research grantee DuPont Co., 1961-62; Research grantee NIMH, 1965, 68-70; Research grantee NSF, 1966-68; Named Outstanding Psychology student U. Ark., 1956-57. Mem. Soc. Exptl. Social Psychology. Home: 2117 Flower Ave N Las Vegas NV 89109 Office: 3376 S Eastern Ave Las Vegas NV 89109-3367

WILSON, WARREN SAMUEL, clergyman, bishop; b. New Orleans, May 15, 1927; s. Charlie Price and Warnie (Heart) W.; m. Lillie Pearl Harvey, Mar. 31, 1949; 1 child, Barbara LaJoyce. BA, So. U., Baton Rouge, 1950; DDiv, Moody Coll., Chgo., 1952; DDiv (hon.), Trinity Hall Coll. and Sem., Springfield, Ill., 1975. Ordained to ministry Ch. of God in Christ, 1952, crowned bishop, apptd. state bishop, Calif., 1970. Min. St. Bernard St. Church of God in Christ, New Orleans, until 1960, Fresno (Calif.) Temple Ch. of God in Christ, 1960—. Served with USN, 1942-46, PTO. Mem. NAACP (life). Avocations: bass fishing, boating. Office: Fresno Temple Ch of God in Christ 1137 F St Fresno CA 93706-3314

WILSON, WENDY MELGARD, elementary and special education educator; b. Fargo, N.D., Jan. 13, 1952; d. Howard A. Melgard and Grace B. (Alphson) Watkins; m. Henry Milton Wilson II, July 31, 1982; children: Andrew J., Aaron C. BA/BS in Edn., U. N.D., 1972-77; postgrad., Drake U., 1984-86, Simpson Coll., 1992-94. Secondary spl. edn. tchr. Ctrl. Decatur Community Schs., Leon, Iowa, 1978-80; work experience instr. Green Valley AEA, Creston, Iowa, 1980-82; elem. spl. edn. tchr. Stuart (Iowa) Menlo Community Schs., 1983-86; elem. spl. edn. tchr. Greenfield (Iowa) Community Schs., 1986-93, kindergarten tchr., 1993—; pres., bd. dirs. Little Lambs Presch., Greenfield, 1991-92; sec., v.p. bd. Sunshine Daycare Ctr., Greenfield, 1987-90; co-chairperson S.W. Iowa Very Spl. Art Festival, Creston, 1981; innkeeper, co-owner Wilson Home Bed & Breakfast, 1986-95. com. mem. Greenfield Tourism Com., 1988-94; mem. Greenfield Mother's Club, 1987—, sec., 1991; mem. Adair County Meml. Hosp. Aux., 1987—. Mem. NEA, PEO, Greenfield Edn. Assn. (pres., v.p., com. ch. 1989-91), Nat. Assn. for Educating Young Children, Iowa State Edn. Assn., Iowa Bed and Breakfast Innkeepers Assn. (sec. 1990-92), Greenfield C. of C., Winterset C. of C., Greenfield Bus. Women, Iowa Aviation Preservation Soc. Home: 401 NE Grant Greenfield IA 50849-9757

WILSON, WILLIAM JULIUS, sociologist, educator; b. Derry Twp., Pa., Dec. 20, 1935; s. Esco and Pauline (Bracy) W.; m. Mildred Marie Hood, Aug. 31, 1957; children: Colleen, Lisa; m. Beverly Ann Huebner, Aug. 30, 1970; children—Carter, Paula. BA, Wilberforce U., 1958; MA, Bowling Green State U., 1961; PhD, Wash. State U., 1966; LHD (hon.), U. Mass., 1982, L.I. U., 1982, Columbia Coll., Santa Clara U., Loyola Coll., 1988, De Paul U., 1989; LLD (hon.), Marquette U., Mt. Holyoke Coll., 1989; LHD (hon.), New Sch. for Social Rsch., 1991, Bard Coll., 1992, John Jay Sch. Criminal Justice, 1992, U. Pa., 1993, So. Ill. U., 1993, Northwestern U., 1993, Bowling Green State U., 1994, SUNY, Binghamton, 1994, Princeton U., 1994, Columbia U., Rutgers U., Haverford Coll., Johns Hopkins U. Asst. prof. U. Mass., Amherst, 1965-69; assoc. prof. U. Mass., 1969-71; vis. asso. prof. U. Chgo., 1971-72, assoc. prof. dept. sociology, 1972-75, prof., 1975—, chmn. dept. sociology, 1978—, Lucy Flower prof. urban sociology, 1980-84, Lucy Flower disting. service prof., 1984—; Lucy Flower Univ. prof., 1990-96; Malcolm Eiener Prof. of social policy Harvard U., 1996—; mem. bd. univ. publs. U. Chgo. Press, 1975-79; bd. dirs. Ctr. for Nat. Policy, 1988—, Ctr. for Advanced Study of Behavioral Scis., 1988—, Twentieth Century Fund, 1992—, Jerome Levy Inst., 1992—, Manpower Demonstration Rsch. Corp., 1993—; mem. domestic strategy group Aspen Inst., 1992—; bd. dirs. Pub./Private Ventures, Phila. Author: Power, Racism and Privilege, 1973, Through Different Eyes, 1973, The Declining Significance of Race, 1978, The Truly Disadvantaged, 1987, The Ghetto Underclass, 1993, Sociology and the Public Agenda, 1993, When Work Disppears, 1996. Bd. dirs. Social Sci. Rsch. Coun., 1979-84, Chgo. Urban League, 1983—, Spencer Found., George M. Pullman Found., Russell Sage Found., 1989—, Ctr. for the Advanced Study of the Behaviorial Scis., 1989—, Nat. Humanities Ctr., 1990; mem. Environment, Devel., and Public Policy, 1980—; nat. bd. dirs. A. Philip Randolph Inst., Inst. Rsch. on Poverty, 1983—; trustee Spelman Coll., 1989—; mem. Pres. Commn. on White House Fellowships, 1994—; mem. Pres. Com. Nat. Medal Sci., 1994—; trustee Wilberforce U. With U.S. Army, 1958-60. Recipient Disting. Tchr. of Year award U. Mass., Amherst, 1970, Regents Disting. Alumnus award Wash. State U., 1988, Burton Gordon Feldman award Brandeis U., 1991, Frank E. Seidman Disting. award in polit. econ., 1994; MacArthur Prize fellow, 1987. Fellow AAAS, Am. Acad. Arts and Scis.; mem. NAS, Am. Philos. Soc., Am. Sociol. Assn. (pres. 1989-90, Sydney M. Spivack award 1977, DuBois, Johnson, Frazier award 1990), Soc. for Study Social Problems (C. Wright Mills award 1988), Sociol. Rsch. Assn. (pres. 1987-88), Consortium Of Social Sci. Assn. (pres. 1993-94), Internat. Sociol. Assn., Chgo. Urban League (Beautiful People award 1979). Democrat. Home: PO Box 197 Lincoln NM 88338-0197 Office: John F Kennedy Sch Govt Harvard Univ 79 John F Kennedy St Cambridge MA 02138

WILSON, WILLIAM PRESTON, psychiatrist, emeritus educator; b. Fayetteville, N.C., Nov. 6, 1922; s. Preston Puckett and Rosa Mae (VanHook) W.; m. Dorothy Elizabeth Taylor, Aug. 21, 1950; children: William Preston, Benjamin V., Karen E., Tammy E., Robert E. B.S., Duke U., 1943, M.D., 1947. Diplomate: Am. Bd. Psychiatry and Neurology (examiner). Intern Gorgas Hosp., Ancon, C.Z.; then resident psychiatry Duke U. Med. Center, later resident neurology, 1949-54; asst. prof. psychiatry Duke U. Med. Sch., 1955-58; asso. prof. psychiatry, dir. psychiat. research U. Tex. Med. Br., Galveston, 1958-60; asso. prof. psychiatry Duke U. Med. Center, 1961-64, head div. clin. neurophysiology, 1961-83, prof. psychiatry, head div. biol. psychiatry, 1964-84, emeritus prof. psychiatry, 1985—; dir. Inst. Christian Growth, Burlington, N.C., 1985—; chief neurophysiol. labs. VA Hosp., Durham, N.C., 1961-76; sec. Am. Bd. Qualification in Electroencephalography, 1971-77; mem. N.C. Gov.'s Task force on Diagnosis and Treatment; mem. med. adv. com. N.C. Found. Mental Health Rsch.; bd. dirs. nat. div. Contact Teleminstry USA, also mem. internat. commn. healing; cons. numerous area hosps.; Finch lectr. Fuller Theol. Sem., Pasadena, Calif., 1974; vis. prof. psychiatry Marshall U. Sch. Medicine, Huntington, W.Va., 1985-89. Co-author: The Grace to Grow; editor: Applications of Electroencephalography in Psychiatry; co-editor: EEG and Evoked Potentials in Psychiatry and Behavioral Neurology; Contbr. med. jours. Mem. ofcl. bd. Asbury United Methodist Ch., Durham; mem. program and curriculum com. United Meth. Ch., 1973-81; trustee Meth. Retirement Home, Durham, N.C.; pres. United Meth. Renewal Services, Inc., 1978-82. Served with AUS, 1943-46. Recipient Ephraim McDowell award Christian Med. Found., 1982, Pioneer in Christian Psychiatry award Congress on Christian Counseling, 1988; named Educator of Yr., Christian Med. and Dental Soc., 1996; EEG Montreal Neurol. Inst. fellow, 1954-55, postdoctoral fellow NIMH. Mem. Am. Psychiatric Assn., So. Psychiatric Assn. (pres. 1977-78), AMA, So. Med. Assn. (chmn. sect. neurology and psychiatry 1970), Med. Soc. N.C., Durham-Orange County Med. Soc. (chmn. student recruitment com. 1965), Soc. Biol. Psychiatry, Am. EEG Soc. (councillor), So. EEG Soc. (pres. 1964), Assn. Research Nervous and Mental Diseases, Am. Epilepsy Soc., AAAS, Am. Acad. Neurology, Sigma Xi, Alpha Omega Alpha. Republican. Club: U.S. Power Squadron (comdr. Durham 1971). Home: 1209 Virginia Ave Durham NC 27705-3263 Office: PO Box 2347 Burlington NC 27216-2347

WILSON, WILLIAM R., JR., judge; b. 1939. Student, U. Ark., 1957-58; BA, Hendrix Coll., 1962; JD, Vanderbilt U., 1965. Atty. Autrey & Goodson, Texarkana, Ark., 1965-66, Wright, Lindsey & Jennings, Little Rock, 1969-72, Wilson & Hodge, Little Rock, 1972-74; prin. William R. Wilson Jr., P.A., Little Rock, 1974-80, Wilson & Engstrom, Little Rock, 1980-83, Wilson, Engstrom & Vowell, Little Rock, 1984, Wilson, Engstrom, Corum & Dudley, Little Rock, 1984-93; judge U.S. Dist. Ct. (ea. dist.) Ark., Little Rock, 1993—; chair Ark. Supreme Ct. Com. on Model Criminal Jury Instrns., 1978—; active Ark. Supreme Ct. Com. on Civil Practice, 1982—. Lt. USN, 1966-69. Named Disting. Alumnus, Hendrix Coll., 1993, Outstanding Lawyer, Pulaski County Bar Assn., 1993. Mem. ABA, ATLA, Am. Bd. Trial Advocates (Nat. Civil Justice award 1992), Am. Coll. Trial Lawyers, Internat. Acad. Trial Lawyers, Internat. Soc. Barristers, Ark. Bar Assn. (Outstanding Lawyer 1991), S.W. Ark. Bar Assn., Ark. Trial Lawyers Assn. (pres. 1982, Outstanding Trial Lawyer 1988-89). Office: US Dist Ct Ark 600 W Capitol Ave Rm 153 Little Rock AR 72201-3329*

WILSON, WILLIAM STANLEY, oceanographer; b. Alexander City, Ala., June 5, 1938; s. Norman W. and Helen C. (Hackemack) W.; m. Anne M. Stout; children: Lauren, Jonathan (dec.). BS, William & Mary Coll., 1959, MA, 1965; PhD, Johns Hopkins U., 1972. Marine biol. collector Va. Inst. Marine Sci., Gloucester Point, 1959-62, computer systems analyst, 1964-65; computer systems analyst Chesapeake Bay Inst., Balt., 1965-66; phys. oceanography program mgr. Office of Naval Rsch., Washington, 1972-78; chief oceanic processes program NASA, Washington, 1979-89, program scientist earth observing system, 1989-92; asst. adminstr. for ocean svcs. and coastal zone mgmt. NOAA, Washington, 1992—. Recipient Antarctica Svc. medal NSF, 1961, Superior Civilian Svc. award USN, 1979, Exceptional Sci. Achievement medal NASA, 1981, Disting. Achievement award MTS and Compass Publs., 1989, award Remote Sensing Soc., 1992, medal French Space Agy., 1994. Mem. Am. Meteorol. Soc., Am. Geophys. Union (Ocean Scis. award 1984), Oceanography Soc. (com. chmn. 1989-92), The Coastal Soc., Sigma Xi. Avocations: bicycling, scuba diving, gardening. Home: 219 Tunbridge Rd Baltimore MD 21212-3423 Office: N SSMC4 Sta 13632 1305 E West Hwy Silver Spring MD 20910-3278

WILSON-COKER, PATRICIA ANNE, social service administrator, educator; b. Willimantic, Conn., Aug. 26, 1950; d. Bertram W. and Mary Evelyn (Spurlock) Wilson; m. Edward H. Coker (div. 1973). BA, U. Conn., 1977, MSW, JD, 1981. Bar: Conn. 1981. Asst. prof. social work, dir. Ctr. for Child Welfare Studies St. Joseph Coll., West Hartford, Conn., 1981-86; assoc. prof. social work, chair social work & child welfare St. Joseph Coll., West Hartford, 1986-88; exec. asst. to commr., statewide dir. divsn. children protective svcs. Conn. Dept. Children and Youth Svcs., Hartford, 1988-91, mediation panelist Office Atty. Gen., 1990-91; monitoring panelist dept children and youth svcs. Fed. Dist. Ct., New Haven, 1991-92; dir. social svc. planning & interdisciplinary program devel. Dept. Social Svcs., Middletown, Conn., 1992-93; dir. adminstrv. hearings and appeals Dept. Social Svcs., Middletown, 1993-95; regional administr. north ctrl. region Dept. Social Svcs., 1995—; instr. U. Conn., Storrs, summer 1977, social rsch. asst. philosophy dept., summer 1978; legal social work intern juvenile unit Hartford (Conn.) Legal Aid Soc., 1978-79, legal rschr. juvenile unit, summer 1979, legal rschr., fall 1979; instr. Ea. Conn. State U., Willimantic, spring 1980; cons. New Eng. Clin. Assocs., West Hartford, 1985-86, Office of Policy & Mgmt., State Conn., Hartford, 1988, Perisky and Daniels, Hartford, 1988; apptd. Juvenile Justice Adv. Com. to the Office of Policy and Mgmt., State Conn., 1983-89, Conn. Task Force on Family Violence, 1985-86, Criminal Sanctions Task Force, 1987, Child Support Task Force, 1987-88, Conn. Children's Commn., 1988-91; instr. St. Joseph Coll., West Hartford, 1988—, So. Conn. State Coll., New Haven, 1990—; trustee, chair ednl. policies St. Joseph Coll.; lectr. and presenter in field. Contbr. articles to profl. jours. Recipient Judge Thomas Gill award Conn. Children in Placement Program, 1991, Annual award Conn. Coun. on Adoption, 1991; named Educator of Yr., Conn. Girl Scout Coun., 1987. Office: Dept Social Svcs 3580 Main St Hartford CT 06120

WILSON-SIMPSON, DOROTHY ANDREA, healthcare facility executive; b. Bremerton, Wash., July 27, 1945; d. Merritt Hampden Wilson and Eva Jane (Quaring) Daniell; m. Marion Ray Simpson, Mar. 11,1983; children: Kimberly Simpson Walter, Chad Mitchell. BA cum laude, La. Coll., 1967; MS, La. State U., 1970. Instl. counselor, social svcs. dept. Cen. La. State Hosp., Pineville, 1967-68, 70-74; psychiat. social worker dept. child psychiatry Western Mo. Mental Health Ctr., Kansas City, 1974-76; dir. child care, then dir. treatment The Spofford Home, Kansas City, 1976-82; interim exec. dir. The Spofford Home, 1983, pres., chief exec. officer, 1983—; mem. Spofford Ozanam Svcs., Inc., bd. dirs.; mem. adv. coun. Health Edn. Coalition; bd. dirs. Gillis Ozanam Spofford Consortium, Inc.; subcom. chair Gov.'s Com. on Children and Youth, Mo., 1980-81; mem. Western Mo. Psychiat. Adv. Coun., 1986, ad hoc com. Jackson County, Mo. Mental Health Levy Bd., 1991, Mo. State Task Force for Investigation of Instl. Abuse, 1991; treas. children, youth, and family sect. United Meth. Assn. Health and Welfare Ministries, Dayton, Ohio, 1988-90. Contbr. to various publs. Community adviser Kansas City Jr. League, 1988. Mem. Child Welfare League Am., Nat. Fellowship Child Care Execs., Mo. Child Care Assn. (bd. dirs. 1982—, sec. 1982-85, treas. 1985-87, pres.-elect 1987-89, pres. 1989-90, past pres. 1990), Greater Kansas City Assn. United Way Agys., Rotary (treas. Kansas City South Club 1991, v.p. 1993), Alpha Chi, Phi Kappa Phi. Democrat. Baptist. Office: Spofford Home 9700 Grandview Rd Kansas City MO 64137-1135

WILSON-SMITH, BARBARA ANN, reading specialist; b. Enterprise, Ala., Sept. 10, 1945; d. William Franklin and Opal Elizabeth (Jones) W. BA, Stetson U., 1970, MEd, 1979, EdS in Ednl. Leadership, 1994. Cert. early childhood, elem., reading, specific learning disabilities, emotionally handicapped tchr., ednl. leadership, Fla. Ednl. cons. Macmillan Pub. Co., N.Y.C., 1984-89; tchr. Lake County Bd. Edn., Tavares, Fla., 1970-76, Chpt. I rsch. tchr., 1976-79, primary specialist, 1979-84, Chpt. I reading program specialist, 1989—; nat. math. cons. Macmillan Pub. Co., N.Y.C., 1989. Mem. ASCD, Reading Suprs. Fla., Fla. Reading Assn., Internat. Reading Assn. Avocations: reading, swimming, tennis. Home: 2453 Broadvue Ave Eustis FL 32726-7626 Office: Lake County Bd Edn 201 W Burleigh Blvd Tavares FL 32778-2418

WILSON-WEBB, NANCY LOU, adult educational administrator; b. Maypearl, Tex., Jan. 20, 1932; d. Madison Grady and Mary Nancy Pearson (Haney) Wilson; m. John Crawford Webb, July 29, 1972. BS magna cum laude, Abilene (Tex.) Christian U., 1953; MEd with high honors, Tex. Christian U., 1985. Cert. tchr., adult edn. dir., Tex. Tchr. elem. grades Ft. Worth Ind. Sch. Dist., 1953-67, tchr., 1970-73; dir. adult edn. coop. for 38 sch. dists. Tex. Edn. Agy., 1973—; pres. Nat. Commn. on Adult Basic Edn., 1994-95; pres. Tex. Adult Edn. Adminstrn., 1994-95; apptd. mem. Tex. State Literacy Coun., 1987-94; mem. exec. bd. Tex. Coun. Co-op Dirs., 1989—; apptd. Tex. State Sch. Bd. Commn., 1994-95. Cons. to textbook: On Your Mark?, 1994. Pres. Jr. Woman's Club, Ft. Worth, 1969, Fine Arts Guild, Tex. Christian U., Ft. Worth, 1970-72, Ft. Worth Women's Civic Club Coun., 1970, Nat. Commn. Literacy/Adult Edn.; mem. Exec. Libr. Bd., Ft. Worth, 1990—; apptd. bd. dirs. Literacy Plus in North Tex., 1988, Greater Ft. Worth Literacy Coun.; commr. Ed-16 Task Forces Tex. Edn. Agy., 1985-92, Gen. Dynamics Literacy Task Force; bd. dirs. Friends of Libr., 1967—, Opera Guild of Ft. Worth, 1965—, Johnson County (Tex.) Corrs. Recipient Bevy award City of Ft. Worth, 1968, award for leadership literacy Nat. DAR, 1995, Proclamation Commrs. Ct. Outstanding 40 Yr. Literacy Svc. to Tarrant County, 1994, Tarrant County Woman of Yr. award, 1995, Outstanding Leadership award Ft. Worth ISD Sch. Bd., 1984, 91; named one of Most Outstanding Educators in U.S. Nat. Assn. Adult Edn., 1983, Most Outstanding Woman of Edn., Fort Worth Star Telegram, 1991, Woman of Yr., 1995, others; named to Tex. Hall of Fame for Women, 1991; scholar Fed. Republic of Germany, 1983. Mem. NEA, DAR (Nat. Most Outstanding Literacy award 1995), AAUW, Am. Assn. Adult and Continuing Edn. (v.p. 1987-89, chair 1993 internat. conv. 1992, co-chair 1993), Internat. Reading Assn. (literacy award 1995), Tex. Assn. Adult and Continuing Edn. (pres. 1985-86, Most Outstanding Adult Adminstr. in Tex. award 1984), Tex. Coun. Adult Edn. Dirs. (pres.), Coun. World Affairs (bd. dirs. 1980-95), Am. Bus. Women's Assn. (pres. commn. of adult basic edn.), Ft. Worth C. of C., Lecture Found., Internat. Reading Assn. (literacy challenge award 1991), Ft. Worth Adminstrv. Assn., Zonta, Ft. Worth Garden Club, Woman's Club of Ft. Worth, Petroleum Club, Carousel Dance Assn., Optimist Club (Ft. Worth), Met. Dinner and Dance Club, Ridglea Country Club, Crescent Club, Phi Beta Kappa, Alpha Delta Kappa, Phi Delta Kappa. Democrat. Home: 3716 Fox Hollow St Fort Worth TX 76109-2616 Office: 100 N University Dr Fort Worth TX 76107-1360

WILT, ALAN FREESE, history educator; b. Nappanee, Ind., May 14, 1937; s. Lisle and Helen (Freese) W.; m. Maureen Gilmore, Aug. 3, 1963; children: Karen, Rachel. BA, DePauw U., 1959; MA, U. Mich., 1960, PhD, 1969. Part-time instr. history Midwestern U., Wichita Falls, Tex., 1961-62; from instr. to prof. Iowa State U., Ames, 1967-81, prof., 1981—; vis. prof. mil. history Air War Coll., Maxwell AFB, Ala., 1982-83. Author: The Atlantic Wall: Hitler's Defenses in the West, 1941-44, 1975, The French Riviera Campaign of August 1944, 1981, War from the Top: German and British Military Decision Making during World War II, 1990, Nazi Germany, 1994. 1st lt. USAF, 1960-63, Korea. Mem. Am. Hist. Assn., Soc. for Military History, German Studies Assn. Democrat. Presbyterian. Home: 4203 Arizona Cir Ames IA 50014-3612 Office: Iowa State U Dept History 643 Ross Hall Ames IA 50011

WILT, JEFFREY LYNN, pulmonary and critical care physician; b. Fairmont, W.Va., Nov. 15, 1963; s. Paul Lynn and Linda (Amos) W. BA, U. Mich., 1986, MD, 1988. Diplomate Am. Bd. Internat. Medicine, subspecialty pulmonary diseases and critical care medicine, Am. Bd. Med. Examiners; cert. ACLS. Resident in internal medicine Blodgett/St. Mary's Hosp., Grand Rapids, Mich., 1988-91, chief med. resident in internal medicine, 1990-91; asst. dir. internal medicine residency St. Mary's Hosp., Grand Rapids, 1992; fellow sect. pulmonary and critical care W.Va. U., Morgantown, 1992-95. Mem. ACP (Nat. Clin. Vignette winner 1991), AMA, Am. Thoracic Soc. (assoc.), Am. Coll Chest Physicians (Young Investigators award 1993). Republican. Avocations: bicycling, karate, magic, reading, swimming. Home: 3410 Winterberry Ct SE Grand Rapids MI 49546 Office: Ste 150 1900 Wealthy SE Grand Rapids MI 49506

WILT, LAWRENCE J.M., librarian; b. Buffalo, June 2, 1948; s. Cecil J.W. and Bernice M. (Yaeck) W.; m. Jane Maienschein, Mar. 10, 1974 (div. 1981); m. Pamela Gail Nase, May 15, 1982; 1 child, Tori Lauren. BA in Humanities, SUNY, Binghamton, 1970; MA in Philosophy, Ind. U., 1974, MLS, 1977, PhD in Philosophy, 1980. Assoc. faculty Ind. U./Purdue U., Indpls., 1976-77; asst. prof. libr. resources Dickinson Coll., Carlisle, Pa., 1977-79, head reference dept., 1979-81; collection mgmt. libr. U. Md. Baltimore County, Catonsville, 1981-86, assoc. dir for collections and info. svcs., 1986-90, dir libr., 1990—. Contbr. articles to profl. jours. Mem. ALA (chair Assn. of Coll. and Rsch. Libraries publs. com. 1979-81, mem. Assn. of Coll. and Rsch. Libraries acad. status com. 1988-91). Home: 4 N Beechwood Ave Catonsville MD 21228-4925 Office: U Md Baltimore County Albin O Kuhn Libr & Gallery Catonsville MD 21228

WILT, VALERIE RAE, lawyer; b. Springfield, Ohio, June 8, 1963; m. Gregory L. Wilt, July 11, 1987; children: Arianne Rae, Samantha Moore. BA, Miami U., Oxford, Ohio, 1985; JD cum laude, U. Dayton, 1988. Bar: Ohio 1988, U.S. Dist. Ct. (so. and we. dists.) Ohio 1988, U.S. Ct. Appeals (6th cir.) 1994. Assoc. Bieser, Greer & Landis, Dayton, Ohio, 1988-90; ptnr. Juergens & Wilt, Springfield, 1991—; spkr. on risk mgmt. for vol. workshops; spkr. to Springfield Legal Secs. Assn. on Case Mgmt. Mem. Rep. Nat. Com., 1994; vol. spkr. career day United Way. Named Lawyer of Yr. Greater Dayton Area Lawyers Vol. Projects, 1989. Mem. Ohio State Bar Assn., Springfield Bar Assn., Springfield Law Libr. Assn., Springfield-Clark County C. of C. Republican. Roman Catholic. Avocations: reading, athletics, speaking. Office: Juergens & Wilt 200 N Fountain Ave Springfield OH 45504

WILTBANK, JOSEPH KELLEY, lawyer, university counsel, sports association executive; b. Albuquerque, June 5, 1950; s. William J. and Joyce I. (Jones) W.; m. Antonia Louise Urquidi, Aug. 5, 1978; children: Mitch, Drew, Jay, Neeley. BA in History, U. Fla., 1972; JD, Gonzaga U., 1977; BA in French with high honors, Idaho State U., 1990. Bar: Idaho 1977, U.S. Dist. Ct. Idaho 1977, U.S. Ct. Appeals (9th cir.) 1979. Adminstrv. asst. to mayor Mountain Home, Idaho, 1977-79; dep. prosecuting atty. Ada County, Boise, Idaho, 1979-83; univ. counsel, counsel to pres. Idaho State U., Pocatello, 1983-94, gen. counsel, dir. Intercollegiate Athletics., 1995—; interim dir. athletics Idaho State U., 1989-90. Editor: The Practical Aspects of Technology Transfer, 1990. Ex officio bd. dirs. Idaho State U. Found., 1983—; bd. dirs. First Security Games of Idaho, 1991—, pres. 1992-94, Bannock Boys Baseball, Pocatello, 1989-91, Real Dairy Bowl (formerly Centennial Bowl), 1987-94, exec. dir., 1991-94; advisor Mortar Bd. Idaho State U., 1988-91. Mem. Nat. Assn. Coll. and Univ. Attys. (bd. dirs. 1990-93), Rotary (bd. dirs. 1994—). Avocations: sports, music.

WILTROUT, ANN ELIZABETH, foreign language educator; b. Elkhart, Ind., Aug. 3, 1939; d. F. LeRoy and Margaret Elizabeth (Williams0 W. BA, Hanover Coll., 1961; MA, Ind. U., 1964, PhD, 1968. Vis. asst. prof. Ind. U., Bloomington, 1968-69; asst. prof. Miss. State U., Mississippi State, 1969-71, assoc. prof., 1971-87, prof., 1987—; NEH fellow in residence Duke U., 1977-78. Author: A Patron and a Playwright in Renaissance Spain, 1987; contbr. articles to profl. publs. Recipient Disting. Svc. cert. Inst. Internat. Edn., 1986. Mem. AAUP, MLA (del. to assembly 1975-78), Assn. Internat. Hispanitas, Cervantes Soc. Am., Am. Assn. Tchrs. of Spanish and Portuguese, Assn. Hispanic Classical Theater, Soc. Scholars in Arts and Scis., Phi Kappa Phi, Sigma Delta Pi. Avocations: Shakespeare, travel, reading, roses. Office: Miss State U Dept Fgn Langs Drawer FL Mississippi State MS 39762

WILTSE, JAMES CLARK, civil engineer; b. Dearborn, Mich., Apr. 14, 1927; s. Cecil C. and Mary G. (Brashear) W.; m. Marlyn R. Glatus, Feb. 14, 1953; children: Richard, Mary, Michael. BSCE, U. Mich., 1953. Registered profl. engr., Mass. Civil engr. U.S. Army C.E., Detroit, 1954-67; project engr. USAF Civil Engring., London, 1968-72; civil engr. USN Facilities Engring. Command, Norfolk, Va., 1973-75; chief engr. USN Resident Office,

Keflavik, Iceland, 1976-81; staff civil engr. USAF Electronic Systems Div., Kaiserslautern, Germany, 1982-91; spl. asst. ROICC Norfolk, Lantnavfac Eng Com, Norfolk, Va., 1992-93; quality assurance engr. HQ Lantnavfac, 1993-94; ret., 1994. Sgt. U.S. Army, 1946-47, Japan. Fellow ASCE; mem. Soc. Am. Mil. Engrs. Home: 8555 Lawson Ave Norfolk VA 23503-5220

WILTSHIRE, RICHARD WATKINS, SR., insurance company executive; b. Richmond, Va., July 17, 1921; s. William Ernest and Essie (Watkins) W.; m. Jean Watkins Betts, Sept. 5, 1942; children: Mrs. Henry M. Massie, Jr., Richard Watkins, Jr., William Betts, Virginia Betts McGurn. B.A., U. Va., 1943. With Home Beneficial Life Ins. Co., Richmond, Va., 1946—; dir. agy. tng. Home Beneficial Life Ins. Co., 1947, asst. supr. agys., 1947-50, asst. v.p., 1950-52, dir., 1949—, v.p., 1952-66, exec. v.p., gen. mgr., 1966-68, pres., 1968—, chmn., 1983—. Trustee The Collegiate Schs., Richmond Meml. Hosp., Children's Hosp.; bd. dirs. Union Theol. Sem. Served with USMCR, 1942-45. Presbyterian (elder). Office: Home Beneficial Life Ins Co 3901 W Broad St Richmond VA 23230-3962

WILVER, WAYNE R., electronics executive; b. 1933. BA, Rutgers U., 1955. Various positions, then chief fin. exec. GE, Lynchburg, Va., 1955-83; mem. U.S. Com. Energy Awareness, Washington, 1983-86; v.p., CFO, sec., treas. Comdial Corp., Charlottesville, Va., 1986—. Office: Comdial Corp 1180 Seminole Trl Charlottesville VA 22901-2829*

WIMBERLY, EVELYN LOUISE RUSSELL, nursing coordinator; b. Tallulah, La., Feb. 7, 1941; d. Luther Franklin and Marion Gertrude (Martin) Russell; m. William Lary Wimberly, Mar. 29, 1963; children: Collin, Holly, Allison. BSN, Northwestern State U., 1963; MSN, Northwestern State U. La., 1994. Head nurse Hanna Hosp., Coushatta, La.; dir. nurses Sr. Citizen Ctrs., Coushatta; evening supr. Riverside Med. Ctr., Bossier City, La.; house supr. La. State U. Hosp., Shreveport, coord. nursing quality improvement and policy and procedure. Mem. ANA, La. Nurses Assn., Sigma Theta Tau (Beta Chi chpt.). Home: PO Box 145 Hall Summit LA 71034-0145

WIMMER, MAUREEN KATHRYN, chemical engineer; b. Quakertown, Pa., Oct. 25, 1969; d. Ronald Homer and Jane (Astheimer) W. BSChemE, Lehigh U., 1992. Engring. intern Gen. Chem., Claymont, Del., 1991; process control engr. Johnson Matthey CSD, Wayne, Pa., 1992-94, washcoat engr., 1994—. Mem. AIChE. Republican. Lutheran. Avocations: music, movies. Home: 123 Roskeen Ct Phoenixville PA 19460

WIMMER, NANCY T., lawyer; b. Newark, Jan. 13, 1951; d. Harold and Gilda (Schwartz) Tainow; m. Howard A. Wimmer, Sept. 1, 1974; 2 children. BS magna cum laude, Temple U., 1973; JD, Temple U. Sch. Law, 1994. Bar: Pa. 1995. Staff atty. Cmty. Health Law Project, Camden, N.J., 1993—; legal cons. elder law project Temple U., Phila., 1994; mng. atty., dir. Cancer Patient Legal Advocacy Network, Pa., 1994—. Mem. Pa. Bar Assn., Phila. Bar Assn.

WIMPRESS, GORDON DUNCAN, JR., corporate consultant, foundation executive; b. Riverside, Calif., Apr. 10, 1922; s. Gordon Duncan and Maude A. (Waldo) W.; m. Jean Margaret Skerry, Nov. 30, 1946; children—Wendy Jo, Victoria Jean, Gordon Duncan III. B.A., U. Oreg., Eugene, 1946, M.A., 1951; Ph.D., U. Denver, 1958; LL.D., Monmouth Coll., Ill., 1970; L.H.D., Tusculum Coll., Greenville, Tenn., 1971. Lic. comml. pilot. Dir. pub. relations, instr. journalism Whittier (Calif.) Coll., 1946-51; asst. to pres. Colo. Sch. Mines, Golden, 1951-59; pres. Monticello Coll., Alton, Ill., 1959-64, Monmouth Coll., Ill., 1964-70, Trinity U., San Antonio, 1970-77; vice chmn. S.W. Found. for Biomed. Rsch., San Antonio, 1977-82, pres., 1982-92, also bd. govs.; pres. Duncan Wimpress & Assocs., Inc., San Antonio, 1992—; commr. Burlington No. R.R. scholarship selection com.; chmn. Valero Energy Corp. scholarship commn.; bd. dirs. Southwest Rsch. Inst. Author: American Journalism Comes of Age, 1950. Bd. dirs. Am. Inst. Character Edn., ARC, Am. Heart Assn., Cancer Therapy and Rsch. Found.; trustee San Antonio Med. Found., Eisenhower Med. Ctr., Rancho Mirage, Calif.; mem. San Antonio Fiesta Commn.; ruling elder United Presbyn. Ch., U.S.A.; mem. adv. bd. Alamo Area chpt. Am. Diabetes Assn. 1st lt. AUS, 1942-45, ETO. Decorated Bronze Star. Mem. Aircraft Owners and Pilots Assn., Am. Acad. Polit. and Social Sci., Am. Assn. Higher Edn., MENSA, Nat. Pilots Assn., Pilots Internat. Assn., Inc., Quiet Birdmen, Greater San Antonio C. of C. (bd. dirs.), North San Antonio C. of C. (bd. dirs.), Assn. Former Intelligence Officers, Confederate Air Force, Pi Gamma Mu, Sigma Delta Chi, Sigma Delta Pi, Sigma Phi Epsilon (trustee found.), Sigma Upsilon, Newcomen Soc. N.Am. Clubs: Argyle, St. Anthony, San Antonio Country, the Dominion (bd. govs.), City , Plaza, San Antonio Golf Assn. Lodge: Rotary (dist. gov. 1983-84, San Antonio). Avocations: golf, skiing, flying. Office: PO Box 780818 San Antonio TX 78278-0818

WIN, KHIN SWE, anesthesiologist; b. Rangoon, Burma, Sept. 27, 1934; came to U.S., 1962; d. U Mg and Daw Aye (Kyin) Maung; m. M. Shein Win, May 28, 1959; children: Tha Shein, Thwe Shein, Maw Shein, Thet Shein, Htoo Shein. Intermediate of Sci. Degree, U. Rangoon, 1954, MB, BS, 1962. Intern Waltham (Mass.) Hosp., 1962-63; resident anesthesiology Boston City Hosp., 1963-65; fellow pediatric anesthesiology New Eng. Med. Ctr. Hosps., Boston, 1965-66; fellow anesthesiology Martin Luther King Jr. Gen. Hosp., L.A., 1978-79; pvt. practice anesthesiology Apple Valley, Calif., 1984—; asst. prof. anesthesiology Martin Luther King Jr./Charles R. Drew Med. Ctr., L.A., 1979-84. Republican. Buddhist. Avocations: gardening, meditation. Home: 13850 Pamlico Rd Apple Valley CA 92307-5400 Office: St Mary Desert Valley Hosp Dept Anesthesiology 18300 Us Highway 18 Apple Valley CA 92307-2206

WINAHRADSKY, MICHAEL FRANCIS, drug company executive; b. Syracuse, N.Y., Oct. 21, 1948; s. Frank F. and Genelle M. (Charmley) W.; m. Linda L. Peters, Oct. 10, 1981; children: Kevin M., Kari M. Distbn. ctr. supr. Fay's Inc., Liverpool, N.Y., 1967-76, distbn. ctr. mgr., 1976-81; asst. v.p. distbn. Fay's Drug Co. Inc., Liverpool, N.Y., 1981-82, v.p. distbn., 1982—; guest speaker Syracuse (N.Y.) U., 1984. Participant Cen. N.Y. chpt. Cystic Fibrosis Bowl for Breath, 1987-93. Mem. Warehouse Edn. and Rsch. Coun., Nat. Fire Protection Assn., Boat Owners U.S., Moose, Elks, Lakeshore Yacht & Country Club, Nat. Assn. Chain Drug Stores (co-chmn. distbn. and logistics com. 1995). Avocations: power boating, fishing, cross-country skiing, cruising, golf. Home: 4320 Lazybrook Cir Liverpool NY 13088 Office: Fay's Inc 7245 Henry Clay Blvd Liverpool NY 13088-3523

WINAWER, SIDNEY JEROME, physician, clinical investigator, educator; b. N.Y.C.; s. Nathan and Sally Winawer; children: Daniel, Jonathan, Joanna. BA, NYU, 1952; MD, SUNY, N.Y.C., 1956. Asst. in medicine Harvard Med. Sch., Boston, 1962-66; asst. physician Harvard Med. Svc. Boston City Hosp., 1964-66; with Meml. Sloan-Kettering Cancer Ctr., N.Y.C., 1978—, head lab for gastroent. cancer rsch., 1988—, chief gastroent. and nutrition svc., 1988—, mem. with tenure of title, 1988—, Paul Sherlock chair, 1991—; prof. medicine Cornell U. Coll. Medicine, N.Y.C., 1980—; head Ctr. for Prevention Colon Cancer WHO, Geneva, 1985; liason rep. Nat. Cancer Adv. Bd., Washington, 1984-89; mem. adv. com. on cancer prevention Am. Cancer Soc., 1988-90; mem. sci. adv. bd. ICRF; cons. various rev. coms., Nat. Cancer Inst., Washington. Editor: Prevention Colorectal Cancer, 1980, Basic and Clinical Perspectives of Colorectal Polyps and Cancer, 1988, Lar Bowel Cancers: Policy, Prevention, Research and Treatment, 1991, Management of Gastrointestinal Disease, 1992, Gastrointestinal Cancer, 1992, Cancer of the Colon, Rectum and Anus, 1994, Cancer Free, 1995; contbr. chpts. to books, articles to profl. jours. Capt. USAF, 1959-61. Nat. Cancer Inst. grantee 1974, 77, 80 (2), 85, 88 , 90. Fellow ACP, Am. Coll. Gastroenterology (pres. 1979-80, Disting. Sci. Achievement award 1982, Baker Presdl. lectr. 1992, Master 1993); mem. Am. Soc. Gastrointestinal Endoscopy (bd. dirs. 1974-78, disting. lectr. 1985, Schindler award 1994), Am. Gastroent. Assn. (nat. chmn. cancer sect. 1989-91), Am. Soc. Clin. Oncology, Am. Assn. Cancer Rsch., N.Y. Soc. Gastrointestinal Endoscopy (founder, pres. 1978-79, ann. lectr. 1985). Jewish. Avocations: opera, modern art, biking, cross-country skiing, sailing. Office: Meml Sloan-Kettering Cancer Ctr 1275 York Ave New York NY 10021-6094

WINCENC, CAROL, concertizing flutist, educator; b. Buffalo, June 29, 1949; d. Joseph and Margaret (Miller) Wincenc; m. Douglas Webster; 1 child, Nicola Wincenc-Webster. Grad., Santa Cecilia Acad., Rome, 1967, Chigiana Acad., Siena, Italy, 1968; MusB, Manhattan Sch. Music, N.Y.C., 1971; MusM, Juilliard Sch. Music, N.Y.C., 1972. Concertizing flutist recs. with Deutsche, Gramaphon, Nonesuch, New World, Music Masters, and Decca records; soloist with major symphony orchs.; artist faculty Juilliard Sch., 1988—. Bd. dirs., v.p. Chamber Music Am., N.Y.C., 1990-91, 91—. Recipient Naumburg award, 1978. Mem. Nat. Flute Assn. (life, bd. dirs.). Home: 875 W End Ave Apt 14E New York NY 10025-4954 Office: The Juilliard Sch Lincoln Ctr New York NY 10023

WINCER, SIMON, film director. Films include Harlequin, 1980, The Day After Halloween, 1981, Phar Lap, 1984, D.A.R.Y.L., 1985, The Lighthorsemen, 1987, Quigley Down Under, 1990, Harley Davidson and the Marlboro Man, 1991, Free Willy, 1993, Operation Dumbo Drop, 1995; exec. prodr.: The Man From Snowy River, 1982, One Night Stand, 1983; TV dir.: Prisoner: Cell Block H, 1980, The Girl Who Spelled Freedom, 1986, The Last Frontier, 1986, Bluegrass, Lonesome Dove, 1989 (Outstanding Direction Emmy award 1989); cons. The Adventures of the Black Stallion, 1990. Office: c/o Creative Artists Agency 9830 Wilshire Blvd Beverly Hills CA 90212-1804

WINCE-SMITH, DEBORAH L., federal agency administrator; m. Michael B. Smith; 2 children. Grad. magna cum laude, Vassar Coll., 1972; Master's, Cambridge (Eng.) U., 1974. Former program mgr. internat. programs NSF; asst. dir. internat. affairs and global competitiveness Office of Sci. and Tech. Policy The White House, 1984-89; asst. sec. tech. policy Dept. Commerce, Washington, 1989-93; sr. fellow Coun. on Competitiveness, Washington, 1993—; sr. fellow Congl. Econ. Leadership Inst., Washington, 1993—. Office: Coun on Competitiveness 1401 H St NW Ste 650 Washington DC 20005

WINCHELL, MARGARET WEBSTER ST. CLAIR, realtor; b. Clinton, Tenn., Jan. 26, 1923; d. Robert Love and Mayme Jane (Warwick) Webster; student Denison U., 1940, Miami U., Oxford (Ohio), 1947, 48; m. Charles M. Winchell, June 7, 1941; children—David Alan (dec.), Margaret Winchell Boyle; m. 2d, Robert George Sterrett, July 15, 1977 (dec. 1982). Saleswoman Fred K.A. Schmidt & Shirmer real estate, Cin., 1960-66, Cline Realtors, Cin., 1966-70; owner, broker Winchell's Showplace Realtors, Cin., 1972—; ins. agt. United Liberty Life Ins. Co., 1966—, dist. mgr., 1967-70, 77-82, regional mgr., 1982—; stockbroker Waddell & Reed, Columbus, Ohio, 1972—, Security Counselors; ins. broker, 1984, gen. agent; dir. Fin. Consultants, 1984, 85, 86, 87, owner; instr. evening coll. Treas., v.p. Parents without Partners, 1969, sec., 1968; pres. PTA; dir. Children's Bible Fellowship Ohio, 1953-76; dir. Child Evangelism Cin.; nat. speaker Child Evangelism Fellowship and Nat. Sunday Sch. Convs., 1955-57; pres. Christian Solos, 1974, Hamilton Fairfield Singles; chaplain Bethesda N. Hosp.; leader singles groups Hyde Park Community United Meth. Ch.; dir. Financial Cons., Sr. Ctr. Dance Leader and Coord. Mem. Nat. Assn. Real Estate Bds. West Shell Realtors (v.p.), Womens Council Real Estate Bd. (treas.). Clubs: Alfonta, Travel go go, Guys and Gals Singles (founder, 1st pres.), Hamilton Singles (pres.). Home and Office: 8221 Margaret Ln Cincinnati OH 45242-5309

WINCOR, MICHAEL Z., psychopharmacology educator, clinician, researcher; b. Chgo., Feb. 9, 1946; s. Emanuel and Rose (Kershner) W.; m. Emily E.M. Smythe; children: Meghan Heather, Katherine Rose. SB in Zoology, U. Chgo., 1966; PharmD, U. So. Calif., 1978. Rsch. project specialist U. Chgo. Sleep Lab., 1968-75; psychiat. pharmacist Brotman Med. Ctr., Culver City, Calif., 1979-83; asst. prof. U. So. Calif., L.A., 1983—; cons. Fed. Bur. Prisons Drug Abuse Program, Terminal Island, Calif., 1978-81, Nat. Inst. Drug Abuse, Bethesda, Md., 1981, The Upjohn Co., Kalamazoo, 1982-87, 91-92, Area XXIV Profl. Stds. Rev. Orgn., L.A., 1983, Brotman Med. Ctr., Culver City, Calif., 1983-88, SmithKline Beecham Pharms., Phila., 1990-93, Tokyo Coll. of Pharmacy, 1991, G. D. Searle & Co., Chgo., 1992—. Contbr. over 30 articles to profl. jours., chpts. to books, papers presented at nat. and internat. meetings and reviewer. Mem. adv. coun. Franklin Avenue Sch., 1986-89; trustee Sequoyah Sch., 1992-93; mem. tech. com. Ivanhoe Sch., 1993-96. Recipient Cert. Appreciation, Mayor of L.A., 1981, Bristol Labs Award, 1978; Faculty scholar U. So. Calif. Sch. Pharmacy, 1978. Mem. Am. Coll. Clin. Pharmacy (chmn. constn. and bylaws com. 1983-84, mem. credentials com. 1991-93, 95-96, ednl. affairs com. 1994)0, Am. Assn. Colls. Pharmacy (focus group on liberalization profl. curriculum), Am. Soc. Hosp. Pharmacists (chmn. edn. and tng. adv. working group 1985-88, com. on acedemia 1996-97), Am. Pharm. Assn. (del. ann. meeting ho. of dels. 1989), Sleep Rsch. Soc., Am. Sleep Disorders Assn., Calif. Pharmacists Assn. (DuPont Pharma Innovative Pharmacy Practice award 1995), U. So. Calif. Sch. Pharmacy Alumni Assn. (bd. dirs. 1979—), Rho Chi. Avocation: photography. Office: U So Calif 1985 Zonal Ave Los Angeles CA 90033-1058

WINCZOWSKI, MARILYN DIANNE, women's health nurse; b. Middlesboro, Ky., Sept. 19, 1945; d. Clarence E. and Ruby Christina (England) Turner; m. Edward Stephen Winczowski Sr., Dec. 14, 1968; children: Ginnifer Marie, Edward Stephen Jr. Cert., Appalachian Sch. Practical Nursing, 1964; ADN, Ill. Valley C.C., 1980; BSN, Pa. State U., 1988. Cert. in inpatient obstetrics, childbirth edn. Staff nurse obs-gyn. St. Mary's Hosp., Streator, Ill., 1981-82, Jeannette (Pa.) Dist. Meml. Hosp., 1982-85; supr., perinatal educator Monsour Med. Ctr., JEannette, 1986—; mem. craft adv. com. Ctrl. Westmoreland Career Tech. Ctr., New Stanton, 1991-96. Mem. Western Pa. chpt. March of Dimes, 1990-96, chmn. Walkathon, Greensburg, 1991-96, Canine Walk, 1993, 95, mem. health prof. adv. com. western chpt., Pitts., 1992-96. Mem. Monsour Med. Ctr. Ladies Aux., Phi Theta Kappa. Roman Catholic. Avocations: reading, family.

WIND, HERBERT WARREN, writer; b. Brockton, Mass., Aug. 11, 1916; s. Max E. and Dora O. Wind. BA, Yale U., 1937; MA, Cambridge U., Eng., 1939. Staff writer New Yorker mag., N.Y.C., 1947-54, 62-90, Sporting Scene; editor, writer Sports Illustrated mag., N.Y.C., 1954-60; cons., writer, assoc. producer TV series Shell's Wonderful World of Golf, 1961-62; tchr. seminar on lit. of sports, Yale U., 1973. Author: The Story of American Golf, 1948, revised 1956, 75, (with Ben Hogan) The Modern Fundamentals of Golf, 1957, (with Jack Nicklaus) The Greatest Game of All, 1969, Game, Set, and Match, collection of tennis articles, 1979, Following Through, collection of golf articles, 1985; editor The Classics of Golf reprint series, 1983—. With USAAF, 1942-46, PTO. Mem. Oxford and Cambridge Golfing Soc., Yale Golf Assn., Royal and Ancient Golf Club of St. Andrews. Home: 32 Jericho Rd Weston MA 02193-1210

WINDELS, PAUL, JR., lawyer; b. Bklyn., Nov. 13, 1921; s. Paul and Louise E. (Gross) W.; m. Patricia Ripley, Sept. 10, 1955; children: Paul III, Mary H., James H.R., Patrick D. AB, Princeton U., 1943; LLB, Harvard U., 1948. Bar: N.Y. 1949. Spl. asst. counsel N.Y. State Crime Commn., 1951; asst. U.S. atty. Ea. Dist. N.Y., 1953-56; N.Y. regional adminstr. SEC, 1956-61, also spl. asst. U.S. atty. for prosecution securities frauds, 1956-58; lectr. law Am. Inst. Banking, 1950-57; mem. Windels, Marx, Davies & Ives and predecessor firms, 1961-88, of counsel, 1988—. Author: Our Securities Markets-Some SEC Problems and Techniques, 1962. Trustee, chmn. Bklyn. Law Sch., Lycée Francais N.Y.; trustee Princeton U. Rowing Assn., Knox Sch., Gerta Charitable trust; past pres. Fed. Bar Coun.; mem. adv. bd. NYU Inst. French Studies, SUNY Marine Scis. Rsch. Sta.; bd. dirs. Horticulture Soc. N.Y. Capt. F.A., AUS, 1943-46, ETO; maj. USAR. Recipient Flemming award for fed. svc.; decorated chevalier Order French Acad. Palms; officer Nat. Order Merit France. Fellow Am. Bar Found.; mem. ABA, N.Y. State Bar Assn., Assn. of Bar of City of N.Y. Republican. Presbyterian. Office: Windels Marx Davies & Ives 156 W 56th St New York NY 10019-3800

WINDER, ALVIN ELIOT, public health educator, clinical psychologist; b. N.Y.C., Feb. 17, 1923; s. Martin Winder and Frances (Erdrick) Isaacson; m. Barbara Ina Dietz, July 19, 1949; children: Mark, Joshua, Sarah, Susan. BA, CUNY, 1947; MS, U. Ill., 1948; PhD, U. Chgo., 1952; MPH, U. Calif., Berkeley, 1980. Lic. clin. psychologist, Mass. Chief psychologist VA Hosp., Downey, Ill., 1953-56; rsch. asst., asst. prof. Clark U., Worcester, Mass., 1956-58; chief psychologist VA Clinic, Springfield, Mass., 1958-61; assoc. prof. psychology Springfield Coll., 1961-63; chmn. psychology dept. Westfield (Mass.) State Coll., 1963-65; assoc. prof. counseling edn. Sch. Edn., U. Mass., Amherst, 1965-69, prof., dir. grad. program div. nursing, 1969-78, prof. Sch. Pub. Health, 1978-93; dir. planning, cons. Springfield (Mass.) Pub. Health Dept., 1993-95; adj. prof. Sch. Pub. Health, Boston U., 1995—; assoc. to exec. sec. Asian Pacific Assn. for Control of Tobacco, 1988—. Author: Introduction to Health Education, 1984, Solid Waste Education Recycling Directory, 1989; editor: Adolescence Contemporary Studies, 1974; guest editor Jour. Applied Behavior, 1970; co-editor: Internat. Quar. of Cmty. Health Edn., 1992—. Sr. selectman Town of Leverett, Mass., 1988-90; Lilly Found. mentor U. Mass., 1989. Grantee U.S. Childrens Bur., 1966, 67, Dexter Found., 1969, NIMH, 1974, Nat. Cancer Inst., 1986-91. Mem. APHA, APA. Avocations: dressage, handball, tennis. Home and Office: 84 Booth Rd Dedham MA 02026-5702

WINDER, CLARENCE LELAND, psychologist, educator; b. Osborne County, Kans., June 16, 1921; s. Clarence McKinley and Edna (Ikenberry) W.; m. Elizabeth Jane Jacobs, Aug. 14, 1943; children—David William, Christina Louise. Student, Santa Barbara State Coll., 1941; A.B. with honors, U. Calif. at Los Angeles, 1943; M.A., Stanford U., 1946, Ph.D., 1949. From instr. to asso. prof. Stanford, 1949-61; dir. Psychol. Clinic, 1953-61; prof., dir. Psychol. Clinic, Mich. State U., 1961-62, prof. psychology, 1961-91, prof. emeritus, 1991—, chmn. dept., 1963-67; dean Coll. Social Sci. Mich. State U., 1967-74, assoc. provost, 1974-77, provost, 1977-86, provost emeritus, 1991—; prof., dir. Psychol. Services Center, U. So. Calif., 1962-63; spl. research psychol. aspects schizophrenia, parent-child rels., personality devel., and higher edn. adminstrn. Served to 1st lt. USAAF, 1943-45. Decorated Air medal with 7 clusters, D.F.C. Fellow APA, AAAS; mem. Sigma Xi. Home: 1776 Hitching Post Rd East Lansing MI 48823-2144

WINDER, DAVID KENT, federal judge; b. Salt Lake City, June 8, 1932; s. Edwin Kent and Alma Eliza (Cannon) W.; m. Pamela Martin, June 24, 1955; children: Ann, Kay, James. BA, U. Utah, 1955; LLB, Stanford U., 1958. Bar: Utah 1958, Calif. 1958. Assoc. firm Clyde, Mecham & Pratt Salt Lake City, 1958-66; law clk. to chief justice Utah Supreme Ct., 1958-59; dep. county atty. Salt Lake County, 1959-63; chief dep. dist. atty., 1965-66; asst. U.S. atty. Salt Lake City, 1963-65; partner firm Strong & Hanni, Salt Lake City, 1966-77; judge State of Utah Dist. Ct., Salt Lake City, 1977-79; U.S. Dist. judge Utah, 1979-93, chief U.S. Dist. judge, 1993—; examiner Utah Bar Examiners, 1975-79, chmn., 1977-79. Served with USAF, 1951-52. Mem. Am. Bd. Trial Advocates, Utah State Bar (Judge of Yr. award 1978), Salt Lake County Bar Assn., Calif. State Bar. Democrat. Office: US Dist Ct 235 US Courthouse 350 S Main St Salt Lake City UT 84101-2106

WINDER, RICHARD EARNEST, legal foundation administrator, writer, consultant; b. Vernal, Utah, Sept. 23, 1950; s. William Wallace and Winnifred (Jenkins) W.; m. Janice Fay Walker, Apr. 19, 1975; children: Scott Christian, Eric John, Brian Geoffrey, Laura Jeanne, Amy Elizabeth. BA magna cum laude, Brigham Young U., 1974, JD cum laude, 1978; MBA with honors, U. Michigan, Flint, 1988. Bar: Utah 1978, U.S. Dist. Ct. Utah 1978, Mich. 1979, U.S. Dist. Ct. (ea. and we. dists.) Mich. 1979. Tchg. asst., grad. instr. Brigham Young U., Provo, Utah, 1976-78; law clk. Willingham & Coté, E. Lansing, Mich., 1978-79, atty., 1979-87; exec. v.p. Mgmt. Leasing, Inc., Battle Creek, Mich., 1987-88, Mgmt. Options, Inc., Lansing, Mich., 1988-91; fin. mgr. Mich. State Bar Found., Lansing, Mich., 1991-94, dep. dir., fin. mgr., 1994—; panelist 9th Nat. Legis. Conf. Small Bus., San Antonio, 1987; adj. prof. Davenport Coll. Bus., Lansing, 1990-92, mgmt. adv. com., 1993—; mem. founding steering com. Capital Quality Initiative, Lansing, 1992—; co-founder, rsch. prin. Quality Dynamics Rsch. Inst., Haslett, Mich., 1994—. Author: (with others) Value Sharing: Value Building, 1990, Corporate Orienteering, 1995; contbr., bd. editors: Summary of Utah Real Property Law, 1978. Vol. leader Boy Scouts Am., Chief Okemos Coun., Lansing, 1978—. Mem. ABA, Am. Soc. Quality Control (chmn. Lansing-Jackson sect. 1994-95, spkr. and writer 1992—), Mich. Bar Assn., Utah Bar Assn., Lansing Regional C. of C. (small bus. coun., MBA task force Bus. and Edn. com. 1988-92, recipient Chmn.'s award 1992), Beta Gamma Sigma. Republican. Mem. LDS Ch. Avocations: writing, speaking, computer technology, research, teaching. Office: Michigan State Bar Found 306 Townsend St Lansing MI 48933

WINDER, ROBERT OWEN, retired mathematician, computer engineer executive; b. Boston, Oct. 9, 1934; s. Claude V. and Harriet O. W.; m. Kathleen C. Winder; children by previous marriage: Katherine, Amy. A.B., U. Chgo., 1954; B.S., U. Mich., 1956; M.S., Princeton U., 1958, Ph.D., 1962. With RCA, 1957-78; group head RCA, Princeton and Somerville, N.J., 1969-75; dir. microprocessors RCA, 1975-77, dir. systems, 1977-78; mgr. workstation devel. Exxon Enterprises, Inc., Princeton, 1978-85; v.p. Syntex Computer Systems Inc., Bordentown, N.J., 1985-88; mgr. product engring., Princeton Operation Intel Corp., 1988-93; mgr. engring. ops. Video Products Div., Intel, Chandler, Ariz., 1993-95; ret., 1995. Contbr. articles to profl. jours.; patentee in field. NSF fellow, 1956-57. Recipient David Sarnoff award RCA, 1975. Fellow IEEE.

WINDHAGER, ERICH ERNST, physiologist, educator; b. Vienna, Austria, Nov. 4, 1928; came to U.S., 1954; s. Maximilian and Bertha (Feitzinger) W.; m. Helga A. Rapant, June 18, 1956; children: Evelyn Ann, Karen Alice. MD, U. Vienna, 1954. Research fellow in biophysics Harvard Med. Sch., Boston, 1956-58; instr. in physiology Cornell U. Med. Coll., N.Y.C., 1958-61; vis. scientist U. Copenhagen, 1961-63; asst. to prof. physiology Cornell U. Med. Coll., N.Y.C., 1963—, Maxwell M. Upson prof. physiology and biophysics, 1978—, chmn. dept. physiology, 1973—. Recipient Homer W. Smith award N.Y. Heart Assn., 1978. Office: Cornell U Med Coll Dept Physiology 1300 York Ave New York NY 10021-4805

WINDHAM, CUYLER LARUE, state narcotics agent; b. Lamar, S.C., Nov. 29, 1936; s. Raymond Baxter and Zeloise (Parnell) W.; m. Mary Frances Dowling, Aug, 24, 1955; children: Cuyler LaRue Jr., David Baxter. Student, Ben Franklin U., 1956. With fingerprint divsn. FBI, Washington, 1955-57; night security clk. Charlotte (N.C.) divsn. FBI, 1957-62; condr. investigations resident agy. FBI, Fayetteville, N.C., 1962-67; spl. agt. N.C. State Bur. Investigation, Fayetteville & Kannapolis, 1967-72; supr. inter-agy. narcotics squad N.C. State Bur. Investigation, Fayetteville, 1968-72; asst. supr. Fayetteville divsn. N.C. State Bur. Investigation, 1972-73, asst. dir., 1974-85; sr. asst. dir. N.C. State Bur. Investigation, Fayetteville, 1985-94; ret., 1994; maj., chief of detectives Cumberland County Sheriff's Office, Fayetteville, 1994-95; chief dep. Cumberland County Sheriff's Office, Fayetteville, N.C., 1995—; speaker on law enforcement, violent crimes and narcotics problems, N.C. and southeastern U.S.; chmn. drug subcom. Law Enforcement Coord. Com., Ea. Dist. N.C. Pres. Christian Peace Officers Assn., Cumberland County chpt., Fayetteville, 1991-92; deacon Southview Bapt. Ch., Hope Mills, N.C. Named Outstanding Young Law Enforcement Officer Cumberland County, Cape Fear Jaycees, 1970-71; recipient 1st place award for outstanding young law enforcement officer N.C., N.C. Jaycees, 1971. Mem. Law Enforcement Officers Assn. (com. mem. statewide violent crimes task force, violent crimes com.), Law Enforcement Officers Alumni Assn. (pres. nat. tng. inst. drug enforcement adminstrn. 1977), Gamecock Club. Democrat. Baptist. Home: 112 Bledsoe St Hope Mills NC 28348-9701

WINDHORST, JOHN WILLIAM, JR., lawyer; b. Mpls., July 6, 1940; s. John William and Ardus Ruth (Bottge) W.; m. Diana Margarita Aranda, Feb. 15, 1975; 1 child, Diana Elizabeth. AB, Harvard U., 1962; LLB, U. Minn., 1965. Bar: Minn. 1965, U.S. Tax Ct., U.S. Ct. Appeals (8th cir.) 1965, U.S. Dist. Ct. Minn. 1967, U.S. Supreme Ct. 1975. Law clk. to Hon. H.A. Blackmun U.S. Cir. Ct., Rochester, Minn., 1965-66; assoc. Dorsey & Whitney, Mpls., 1966-70; with office of Revisor of Statutes State of Minn., 1967, 69; ptnr. Dorsey & Whitney, 1971—. Bd. dirs. St. Paul Chamber Orch., 1980-86. Mem. ABA (com. on state and local taxes), Minn. State Bar Assn., Hennepin County Bar Assn., Mpls. Athletic Club, Skylight Club, Harvard Club of Minn. (pres. 1977-78). Home: 4907 Lakeview Dr Minneapolis MN 55424-1525 Office: Dorsey & Whitney LLP Pillsbury Ctr S 220 S 6th St Minneapolis MN 55402-1498

WINDLE, JOSEPH RAYMOND, bishop; b. Ashdad, Ont., Can., Aug. 28, 1917; s. James David and Bridget (Scollard) W. Student, St. Alexander's Coll., Limbour, Que., 1936-39; D.D., Grand Sem., Montreal, 1943; D.C.L., Lateran U., Rome, 1953. Ordained priest Roman Catholic Ch., 1943; asst. priest, later parish priest and vice-chancellor Pembroke Diocese, 1943-61;

titular bishop of Ugita and aux. bishop of Ottawa, 1961-69; coadjutor bishop of Pembroke, 1969-71; bishop, 1971—. Club: K.C. Office: Chancery Office, 188 Renfrew St PO Box 7, Pembroke, ON Canada K8A 6X1

WINDMAN, ARNOLD LEWIS, retired mechanical engineer; b. N.Y.C., Oct. 17, 1926; s. Raphael and Anna (Wexler) W.; m. Patricia Foley, Dec. 13, 1967; children—Richard, Marjorie, Kevin, Colleen, Sean, JoAnn, Brian, William. B.M.E., Coll. City N.Y., 1947. Bar: registered profl. engr., N.Y., 13 other states. Project engr. F.E. Sutton, N.Y.C., 1947-50; with Syska & Hennessy, Inc., N.Y.C., 1950-90, pres., 1976-86, vice chmn., 1986-90, also bd. dirs.; pres. Am. Cons. Engrs. Coun., 1985-86; chmn. N.Y. State Bd. Engring. and Land Surveying, 1982-84; bd. dirs. Sea Pines Plantation. Bd. dirs. Phelps Meml. Hosp., Tarrytown, N.Y., 1974-82; planning commn. Hilton Head Island. Mem. Am. Soc. Heating, Refrigerating and Air Conditioning Engrs., chpt. pres. (1965), N.Y. Assn. Cons. Engrs. (pres. 1981-82, dir. 1977), ASME, Tau Beta Pi, Pi Tau Sigma. Democrat. Jewish. Home: 1919 S Beach Club Vl Hilton Head Island SC 29928-4068 *Professional integrity, enthusiasm, and a continuing effort to train younger people for advancement are three key ingredients of a successful career.*

WINDMULLER, JOHN PHILIP, industrial relations educator, consultant; b. Dortmund, Germany, Dec. 4, 1923; came to U.S., 1942; s. Solomon and Bertha (Kahn) W.; m. Ruth Heilbrun, Aug. 15, 1947; children: Betsey, Thomas. B.A., U. Ill., 1948; Ph.D., Cornell U., Ithaca, N.Y., 1951; postgrad., Grad. Inst. Internat. Studies, U. Geneva, 1957-58. Elections examiner NLRB, St. Louis, 1949; asst. prof. indsl. and labor relations Cornell U., 1951-54, assoc. prof., 1954-61, prof., 1961-83, dir. internat. activities N.Y. State Sch. Indsl. and Labor Relations, 1961-64, assoc. dean sch., 1975-77, Martin P. Catherwood prof. indsl. and labor relations, 1983-87; prof. emeritus, 1987—; vis. prof. Free U., Amsterdam, Netherlands, 1964-65; sr. staff mem. ILO, Geneva, 1971-72, ILO Dir. Gen.'s rep. in Netherlands, 1984; vis. lectr. Dept. State, Germany, Austria, Netherlands, 1957-58, U. Istanbul, Turkey, 1958, Dept. State, Germany, 1964-65. Author: American Labor and the International Labor Movement, 1954, Labor Relations in the Netherlands, 1970, Collective Bargaining in Industrialized Market Economies: A Reappraisal, 1987, The International Trade Secretariats, 1991, rev., 1995; co-author: Convergence and Diversity in International and Comparative Industrial Relations, 1995; editor: Industrial Democracy in International Perspective, 1977; co-editor: Employers Associations and Industrial Relations, 1984; mem. editl. bd. Indsl. and Labor Relations Rev., 1953—; bd. editors Cornell U. Press, 1981-84, Labour (Rome), 1987-94. Recipient Silver medal Gov. Netherlands Minister Social Affairs, 1970; Fulbright sr. research fellow U.S. Commn. on Internat. Exchange, Netherlands, 1964-65; Ford Found. internat. relations fellow, 1957-58. Mem. Indsl. Relations Research Assn., Conseil Scientifique Institut de Travail, U. Bordeaux, Phi Beta Kappa, Phi Kappa Phi. Office: Cornell U NY State Indsl & Labor Rels Ithaca NY 14853-3901

WINDOM, HERBERT LYNN, oceanographer, environmental scientist; b. Macon, Ga., Apr. 23, 1941; m. Patricia Woodruff, 1963; children: Kevin, Elizabeth. BS, Fla. State U., 1963; MS, U. Calif., San Diego, 1965, PhD in Earth Sci., 1968. Prof. oceanography Skidaway Inst. Oceanography and Ga. Inst. Technology, Savannah, Ga., 1968-93, acting dir., 1994—. Mem. Am. Soc. Limnol. and Oceanography, Internat. Coun. ExplorSea, Am. Geophys. Union, Oceanography Soc. Office: Skidaway Inst of Oceanography 10 Ocean Science Circle Savannah GA 31411

WINDOM, STEPHEN RALPH, lawyer; b. Florence, S.C., Nov. 6, 1949; s. Ralph and Connie (Hinds) W.; children: Robert Stephen, Thomas Patrick. BS, U. Ala., 1971, JD, 1974. Bar: Ala. 1974, U.S. Supreme Ct. 1980. Assoc. McDermott, Slepian, Kittrell & Fleming, Mobile, Ala., 1974-77; ptnr. McDermott, Slepian, Windom & Reed, Mobile, Ala., 1974-86, Sirote & Permutt, P.C., 1984—; mem. Ala. State Senate, 1989—; lectr. in field, 1985—. Pres. Greater Gulf State Fair, Mobile, 1981, Cystic Fibrosis Found., Mobile, 1981. Capt. USAFR, 1971-82. Mem. Ala. State Bar Assn., Mobile Bar Assn., Am. Bankruptcy Inst., Comml. Law League, Jaycees, Shriners, Masons, Phi Delta Phi. Democrat. Avocations: hunting, water sports. Office: Sirote Permutt PO Box 2025 Mobile AL 36652-2025

WINDSOR, JAMES THOMAS, JR., printing company executive, newspaper publisher; b. Blakely, Ga., July 30, 1924; s. James Thomas and Mary Alice (Blitch) W. Student, Emory Jr. Coll., Valdosta, Ga., 1941-42, Cardiff (Wales) U., 1945-46; BA, Emory U., 1947. Insp./scientist U.S. Argl. Rsch. Adminstrn., San Augustine, Tex., 1948; pres. J.T. Windsor & Co., McRae, Ga., 1949-65; v.p. McRae Industries, Inc., 1963-64; pers. dir. Sunbeam Corp., McRae, 1965-71; editor, pub. The Laurens County News, 1973-74; editor, publisher The Soperton (Ga.) News, 1971—, The Wheeler County Eagle, Alamo, Ga., 1975—, The Montgomery Monitor, Mt. Vernon, Ga., 1987—; pres. The Mulberry Bush, Inc., Soperton, 1985-89, Suburban Printing Corp., Higgston, Ga., 1972—. Editor: Blueprint for Progress, 1963 (Washington Model award), also cookbooks and hist. books; area newspaper columnist, 1971—. Mayor City of McRae, 1962-70; adminstr. Telfair County, McRae, 1965; pres. Telfair Redevel. Corp., 1963-64; former coun. bd. dirs. Boy Scouts Am., Macon, Ga.; bd. dirs. Million Pines Festival, Soperton, 1973-87, Ga. Mcpl. Assn., Atlanta, 1963-66; dir. Eastman (Ga.) Planning and Devel. Commn., 1965-70; supt. sch. McRae Meth. Ch., 1951-71; active Eagle Scouts Am. With AUS, 1943-46, ETO. Recipient 20 yrs. perfect attendance award McRae Meth. Ch. Sch. Mem. Ga. Press Assn. (numerous awards 1972—), Nat. Newspaper Assn., Montgomery County C. of C., Soperton-Treutlen C. of C., Telfair County C. of C. (pres.), Wheeler county C. of C., Jaycees (editor jour. 1959, 1st place Jour. in Nation award, Rebel Corps col. 1991—, One of 5 Ga. Outstanding Young Men award 1961), VFW, Am. Legion (post comdr. 1957-58), Treutlen County Sportsman Club, McRae Rotary Club (pres.), Toastmasters, Lions (pres. Soperton 1975-76, 15 yrs. perfect attendance award). Avocations: photography, reading, walking, writing, graphic arts. Home: 308 3rd St # 537 Soperton GA 30457 Office: Suburban Printing Corp RR 1 Ailey GA 30410-9801

WINDSOR, LAURENCE CHARLES, JR., publishing executive; b. Bronxville, N.Y., July 4, 1935; s. Laurence Charles and Margaret (Phalen) W.; m. Ruth Ester Lindstrom, 1977. Disting. grad., St. John's Mil. Acad., 1953; student, Grinnell Coll., 1953-55, U.S. Mil. Acad., 1957-58. V.p., dir. promotion Conover-Mast, 1960-67; assoc. promotion dir. Life mag., N.Y.C., 1967-70; merchandising dir. Life mag., 1970—; v.p., dir. advt. and pub. relations Sterling Communications subsidiary Time-Life; exec. v.p. Calderhead, Jackson, Inc., 1974-78; sr. v.p., dir. promotion Young and Rubicam Army Group, N.Y.C., 1978—; pub. relations cons. Penobscot Charitable Trust, 1966.; spl. asst. to postmaster gen. U.S., 1972-74. Appeared in motion picture The D.I., 1957. Mem. pub. edn. com. N.Y. Gov.'s Conf. on Alcohol Problems; mem. coun. Episcopal Ch. Found., pres.'s coun. Phoenix House; mem. adv. bd. Army ROTC. With USMC, 1955-61. Decorated Commemorative War Cross Royal Yugoslav Army; recipient citation of merit Wis. Res. Officers Assn., Am. Spirit Honor medal Citizen's Com. for Army, Navy, and Air Force, Inc., 1956. Mem. U.S. Sales Promotion Exec. Assn. (dir., named Promotion Exec. of Yr. 1969), Marine Corps Combat Corr. Assn. (sec.), West Point Soc. N.Y. (gov. 1967—), Publicity Club N.Y., Publicity Club Chgo., Nat. Acad. TV Arts and Scis., Internat. Radio and TV Soc., Am. Inst. Plant Engrs., Order Vet. Corps Arty. (lt. col., aide-de-camp, comdg. gen., coun. of adminstrn., Disting. Expert pistol award, 1st Provincial Regtl. medal, Order Centennial Legion), 7th Regt. Rifle Club, Marine Corps Pub. Affairs Unit, U.S. Darting Assn., Nat. Sci. Tchrs. Assn., Assn. U.S. Army (v.p. N.Y. chpt.), Am. Def. Preparedness Assn., Kosciuszko Assn., Marine Corps League, Employer Support of the Guard and Res. (N.Y. State Exec. Com.), Army-Navy Union, NRA, Conn. AAU of U.S., Nat. Jogging Assn., New Eng. Soc., Ends of Earth Assn. (chaplain), English Speaking Union, Sovereign Mil. Order of the Temple of Jerusalem, Time-Life Alumni Soc., Nat. Com. for Responsible Patriotism, St. Georges Soc., Nat. Eagle Scout Assn., Old Boys Assn., Nat. Fedn. Breeders of Giant Flemish Rabbits, Soc. Colonial Wars, Soc. Colonial Clergy, Order Descs. Colonial Govs., Order Colonial Acorn, SAR, Soc. Descs. Founders of Hartford, Order of St. Vincent, Soc. of 1812, Order Crown of Charlemagne in U.S.A., Order Lafayette, Sons and Daus. of Pilgrims, The Pilgrims, Sons of Colonial New England, N.Y. Geneal. and Biog. Soc., Met. Squash Racquets Assn., Church Club N.Y., Union League (v.p., bd. govs., chmn. pub. and mil. affairs), Manhattan Club, Bedford Bicycle Polo Club, Bombay Bicycle Club, Squadron A Club, Soldiers, Sailors and Airmens Club (bd. advisors), Road Runners Club, Alpha Phi Omega. Republican. Episcopalian (vestryman, lay reader). Office: Union League Club Box 7 38 E 37th St New York NY 10016-3095

WINDSOR, MARGARET EDEN, writer; b. Flemington, Mo., Aug. 10, 1917; d. John Denny and Rhoda Belle (Morgan) Head; m. Eugene B. Windsor, Jan. 10, 1987. Ret. med. technologist, 1982. Author: Murder in St. James, 1990, The Outhouse, 1996; editor: From Pandora's Box, 1993. Cpl. USAF, 1944-45. Mem. Columbia Chpt. Mo. Writers Guild (v.p. 1989-90). Democrat. Roman Catholic. Avocations: music, theatre, reading, television. Home: 2404 Iris Dr Columbia MO 65202-1265

WINDSOR, PATRICIA (KATONAH SUMMERTREE), author, educator, lecturer; b. N.Y.C., Sept. 21, 1938; d. Bernhard Edward and Antoinette (Gaus) Seelinger; m. Laurence Charles Windsor, Jr., Apr. 3, 1959 (div. 1978); children: Patience Wells, Laurence Edward; m. Stephen E. Altman, Sept. 21, 1986 (div. 1989). Student, Bennington Coll., 1956-58, Westchester Community Coll.; A.A., NYU. V.p. Windsor-Morehead Assocs. N.Y.C., 1960-63; info. mgr. Family Planning Assn., London, 1974-76; faculty mem. Inst. Children's Lit., Redding Ridge, Conn., 1976-94; editor-in-chief AT&T, Washington, 1978-80; instr. U. Md. Writers Inst., Open Univ., Washington, 1980-82; creative developer, faculty mem. Long Ridge Writer's Group, Danbury, Conn., 1988—; dir. Summertree Studios, Savannah, Ga., 1992—; dir. Wordspring Lit. Cons., 1989—; dir. Devel. Writing Workshops, Katonah, N.Y., 1976-78; judge Internat. Assn. Bus. Communicators, Washington, 1979, 89; lectr. L.I. U., Jersey City State Coll., Skidmore Coll., others, 1987—; instr. Coastal Ga. Ctr. for Continuing Edn., 1996—. Author: The Summer Before, 1973 (ALA Best Book award 1973, transl. 1980 Austrian State prize 1980, also Brit., Norwegian, German edits.), Something's Waiting for You, Baker D, 1974 (starred selection Libr. Jour., Brit., Japanese edits.), Home Is Where Your Feet Are Standing, 1975, Diving for Roses, 1976 (N.Y. Times Outstanding Book for Young Adults award, starred selection Libr. Jour.), Mad Martin, 1976, Killing Time, 1980, Demon Tree, 1983 (pen name Colin Daniel), The Sandman's Eyes, 1985 (Edgar Allan Poe Best Juvenile Mystery award Mystery Writers Am.), How a Weirdo and a Ghost Can Change Your Life, 1986, The Hero, 1988 (highest rating Voice of Youth Advocate), Just Like the Movies, 1990, The Christmas Killer, 1991 (Edgar nominee, Brit., Danish, French edits.), Two Weirdos and a Ghost, 1991, A Weird and Moogly Christmas, 1991, The Blooding, 1996, The House of Death, 1996; columnist The Blood Rev., 1990-92, Savannah Parent, 1990-92; also short stories in anthologies and mags.; actress: The Haunting of Hill House, City Lights Theatre Co., 1991. Mem. City Lights Theatre Co., Savannah, Ga., 1991. Mem. Children's Book Guild, Authors Guild, Poetry Soc. Ga., Savannah Storytellers. Avocations: skiing, painting, modern dance. Office: Writers House 21 W 26th St New York NY 10010

WINDSOR, WILLIAM E., consulting engineer, sales representative; b. Evansville, Ind., Jan. 24, 1927; s. Charles H. and Lora E. (Archey) W.; divorced; children: Kim, William, Robert. Student, Purdue U., 1946-50. Field engr. Philco Corp., Phila., 1950-53; studio ops. engr. Sta. WFBM, Indpls., 1953-55; field engr. RCA Svc. Co., Cherry Hill, N.J., 1955-56; audio facilities engr. ABC, N.Y.C., 1956-62; rsch. engr. Fine Recording, Inc., N.Y.C., 1962-66; chief engr. A & R Recording, Inc., N.Y.C., 1966-68; chief engr., corp. sec. DB Audio Corp., N.Y.C., 1968-70; pres. Studio Cons., Inc., N.Y.C., 1970-72; sr. v.p., v.p., gen. mgr. Quad Eight Electronics-Quad Eight/Westrex, San Fernando, Calif., 1972-85; sr. mktg. exec. Mitsubishi Pro Audio Group, San Fernando, Calif., 1985-89; pres., CEO Quad Eight Electronics, Inc., Valencia, Calif., 1989-90; ind. cons., Valencia, 1991—. Inventor monitor mixer for multitrack audio consoles, 1967, update function for audio console automation, 1973; designer of new architecture for film scoring and film re-recording sound mixing consoles, 1974. Served with USNR, 1945-50. Fellow Audio Engring. Soc.; mem. Soc. Motion Picture & TV Engrs. Avocations: photography, foreign travel, art collecting. Home and Office: 23112 Yvette Ln Valencia CA 91355-3060

WINE, DONALD ARTHUR, lawyer; b. Oelwein, Iowa, Oct. 8, 1922; s. George A. and Gladys E. (Lisle) W.; m. Mary L. Schneider, Dec. 27, 1947; children: Mark, Marcia, James. B.A., Drake U., 1946; JD, State U. Iowa, 1949. Bar: Iowa 1949, D.C. 1968. Pvt. practice in Newport and Wine, 1949-61; U.S. atty. So. Dist. Iowa, 1961-65; of counsel Davis, Brown, Koehn, Shors & Roberts. Bd. dirs. Des Moines YMCA, 1963-75; bd. dirs. Salvation Army, 1969—, chmn., 1971; bd. dirs. Davenport YMCA, 1961; bd. dirs. Internat. Assn. Y's Men, 1957-59, area v.p., 1961; bd. dirs. Polk County Assn. Retarded Persons, 1991-95; mem. internat. com. YMCA's U.S. and Can., 1961-75; v.p. Iowa Council Chs.; pres. Des Moines Area Religious Coun. Found., 1992—; chmn. bd. trustees First Bapt. Ch., 1975; trustee U. Osteo. Medicine and Health Scis., 1980-95; Organizer Young Dems., Iowa, 1946; co-chmn. Scott County Citizens for Kennedy, 1960. Served to capt., navigator USAAF, 1943-45. Decorated D.F.C. Mem. ABA (chmn. com. jud. adminstrn. jr. bar sect. 1958), Iowa Bar Assn. (pres. jr. bar sect. 1957), Polk County Bar Assn. (sec. 1973-74), Des Moines C. of C. (chmn. city-state tax com. 1978-79, chmn. legis. com. 1979-84, bd. dirs. 1981), Des Moines Club, Masons, Kiwanis (pres. Downtown club 1969), Order of Coif, Sigma Alpha Epsilon. Office: 2500 Financial Ctr 666 Walnut St Des Moines IA 50309-3904

WINE, L. MARK, lawyer; b. Norfolk, Va., Apr. 16, 1945; s. Melvin Leon and Mildred Sylvia (Weiss) W.; m. Blanche Weintraub, June 8, 1969; children—Kim, Lara, Dana. B.A. with high honors, U. Va., 1967; J.D., U. Chgo., 1970. Bar: D.C. 1970, U.S. Supreme Ct. 1977. Assoc., Kirkland, Ellis & Rowe, Washington, 1970-72; trial atty. land and natural resources div. Dept. of Justice, Washington, 1972-78; ptnr. Kirkland & Ellis, Washington, 1978—. Mem. ABA. Office: Kirkland & Ellis 655 15th St NW Ste 1200 Washington DC 20005-5701

WINE, MARK PHILIP, lawyer; b. Iowa City, Jan. 6, 1949; s. Donald Arthur and Mary Lepha (Schneider) W.; children: Nicholas, Meredith Kathryn; m. Kathryn Bouquet Arneson, May 31, 1986. AB, Princeton U., 1971; JD, U. Iowa, 1974. Bar: Iowa 1974, Minn. 1976, U.S. Dist. Ct. Minn. 1976, U.S. Ct. Appeals (8th cir.) 1976, U.S. Supreme Ct. 1984, U.S. Ct. Appeals (4th cir.) 1985, U.S. Ct. Appeals (7th and Fed. cirs.) 1992. Law clk. to judge U.S. Ct. Appeals (8th cir.), St. Louis, 1974-76; ptnr. Oppenheimer Wolff & Donnelly, Mpls., 1976—. Mem. ABA, Minn. Bar Assn., Internat. Assn. Def. Counsel, Princeton Club N.W. Democrat. Congregationalist. Avocations: cooking, reading, biking, golf. Home: 5404 Larada Ln Edina MN 55436-1025 Office: Oppenheimer Wolff & Donnelly 3400 Plaza VII 45 S 7th St Minneapolis MN 55402-1614

WINE, SHERWIN THEODORE, rabbi; b. Detroit, Jan. 25, 1928; s. William Harry and Tillie (Israel) W. B.A., U. Mich., 1950, A.M., 1952; B.H.L., Hebrew Union Coll., Cin., M.H.L., 1956, rabbi, 1956. Rabbi Temple Beth El, Detroit, 1956-60, Windsor, Ont., Can., 1960-64; Rabbi Birmingham (Mich.) Temple, 1964—; cons. editor Humanistic Judaism, 1966—. Author: A Philosophy of Humanistic Judaism, 1965, Meditation Services for Humanistic Judaism, 1977, Humanistic Judaism-What Is It?, 1977, Humanist Haggadah, 1980, High Holidays for Humanists, 1980, Judaism Beyond God, 1985, Celebration, 1988. Bd. dirs. Ctr. for New Thinking, Birmingham, 1977—; founder Soc. Humanistic Judaism, 1969; pres. N.Am. Com. for Humanism, 1982-93. Chaplain U.S. Army, 1956-58. Mem. Conf. Liberal Religion (chmn. 1985—), Leadership Conf. Secular and Humanistic Jews (chmn. 1983-93), Internat. Inst. Secular Humanistic Judaism (co-chmn. 1986—), Internat. Assn. Humanist Educators, Counselors and Leaders (pres. 1988-93), Internat. Fedn. Secular Humanistic Jews (co-chmn. 1993—). Home: 362 Southfield Rd Birmingham MI 48009-3739 Office: 28611 W 12 Mile Rd Farmington MI 48334-4225

WINE-BANKS, JILL SUSAN, lawyer; b. Chgo., May 5, 1943; d. Bert S. and Sylvia Dawn (Simon) Wine; m. Ian David Volner, Aug. 21, 1965; m. Michael A. Banks, Jan. 12, 1980. BS, U. Ill.-Champaign-Urbana, 1964; JD, Columbia U., 1968; LLD (hon.), Hood Coll., 1975. Bar: N.Y. 1969, U.S. Ct. Appeals (4th cir.) 1969, U.S. Ct. Appeals (6th and 9th cirs.) 1973, U.S. Supreme Ct. 1974, D.C. 1976, Ill. 1980. Asst. press. and pub. rels. dir. Assembly of Captive European Nations, N.Y.C., 1965-66; trial atty. criminal div. organized crime and racketeering sect. and labor racketeering sect. U.S. Dept. Justice, 1969-73; asst. spl. prosecutor Watergate Spl. Prosecutor's Office, 1973-75; lectr. law seminar on trial practice Columbia U. Sch. Law, N.Y.C., 1975-77; assoc. Fried, Frank, Harris, Shriver & Kampelman, Washington, 1975-77; gen. counsel Dept. Army, Pentagon, Washington, 1977-79; ptnr. Jenner & Block, Chgo., 1980-84; solicitor gen. State of Ill. Office of Atty. Gen., 1984-86, dep. atty. gen., 1986-87; exec. v.p., chief oper. officer ABA, Chgo., 1987-90; pvt. practice law, 1990-92; bd. dirs. Cenvill Devel. Corp., 1991-92; v.p. Motorola Internat. Network Ventures Inc. and dir. strategic transaction and alliance group Network Ventures Divsn., Motorola, 1992—; mem. EEC disting. vis. program European Parliament, 1987; bd. dirs. Cenvill Devel. Corp., 1991-92; chmn. bd. dirs. St. Petersburg Telecom, Russia, 1994—, Omni Capital Ptnrs., Inc., 1994—; mem. bd. assocs. program for the study of cultural values & ethics U. Ill. Recipient Spl. Achievement award U.S. Dept. Justice, 1972, Meritorious award, 1973, Cert. Outstanding Svc., 1975; decoration for Disting. Civilian Svc., Dept. Army, 1979; named Disting. Visitor to European Econ. Community. Mem. Internat. Women's Forum, The Chgo. Network, Econ. Club. Address: 425 N Martingale Rd Ste 18 Schaumburg IL 60173-2219

WINEBRENNER, BETH ANN, social worker, college student affairs specialist; b. South Bend, Ind., Feb. 25, 1950; d. Jack Joseph and Marina Louise (Hudson) W.; m. Louis Attila Pierre Balázs, May 27, 1984. BS, Ball State U., 1972; MSW, Ind. U., Indpls., 1978; MS, Purdue U., 1991. Cert. clin. social worker; lic. sch. social worker. Case worker Clay County Dept. Pub. Welfare, Brazil, Ind., 1973, Monroe County Dept. Pub. Welfare, Bloomington, Ind., 1973-76; med. social worker Bloomington Hosp., 1978-79; assessment counselor Employment Devel. Systems, Inc., Frankfort, Ind., 1979-88; fin. planner Waddell & Reed, Inc., Lafayette, Ind., 1988-90; case worker Family Svcs. Inc., Lafayette, Ind., 1989-90; med. social worker Vis. Nurse Home Health Svc., Lafayette area, 1992; spl. asst. to dir. internat. student svcs. Purdue U., West Lafayette, Ind., 1992-93; program mgr./psychotherapist partial hospitalization program Charter Hosp. Lafayette, 1993-94, psychotherapist adolescent outpatient program, 1994—; asst. exec. dir. Lion and Lamb Journeys, Inc., West Lafayette, 1995—; tchr. Hong Kong Coll. Langs., Kowloon, summer 1977; asst. to v.p. Ind. Hosp. Assn., Indpls., summer 1978. Chmn. Com. Human Rights in USSR of Greater Lafayette, 1982-91; mem. Speaker's Corps Mayor's Commn. on Status of Women, Columbus, Ind., 1972, Internat. Awareness Task Force Greater Lafayette, 1991. Mem. ACA, NASW (student rep. to state bd. 1977), Assn. Specialists in Group Work, Am. Coll. Counseling Assn., Acad. Cert. Social Workers, Pi Gamma Mu, Kappa Delta Pi. Democrat. Roman Catholic. Avocations: foreign languages, vegetarian cooking, gardening, reading, swimming. Home: 218 Trace 2 West Lafayette IN 47906-1869

WINECKI, WILLIAM, food products executive; b. 1944. With Cargill Inc., Mpls., 1968-78; with Premier Edible Oils Corp., Portland, Oreg., 1978—, exec. v.p. sales/trading. Office: Premier Edible Oils Corp 10400 N Burgard Way Portland OR 97203*

WINEGAR, ALBERT LEE, computer systems company executive; b. Beloit, Wis., Apr. 23, 1931; s. Albert Richard and Theo Rayneta (Hubbell) W.; m. Phyllis M. Everill, June 21, 1953; children: Bradford, Steven, Kristine, Kathleen. B.B.A., U. Wis., 1954; Stanford Sloan Exec. fellow, Stanford U., 1970. With IBM Corp., 1956-79, div. dir. mgmt. services, 1977-79; v.p. corp. planning, then group v.p. field ops. Olivetti Corp., Tarrytown, N.Y., 1979-80; pres. Olivetti Corp., 1980-81; v.p. field ops. NBI Inc., Boulder, Colo., 1981-84; pres., chief exec. officer Sensory, Inc., Santa Clara, Calif., 1984-85; pres., chief exec. officer VICOM Systems, Inc., Fremont, Calif., 1985-91, ret., 1991; bd. dirs. JRL Systems, Inc. V.p. bd. trustees Valley Hosp., Ridgewood, N.J., 1978-81; pres. N.J. Bus. Arts Found., 1977-78, Estates of Barton Creek Homeowners Assn., 1992-94. Capt. AUS, 1954-56. Mem. Computer and Bus. Equipment Mfrs. Assn. (dir. 1980-81), Barton Creek Country Club, Beta Theta Pi. Republican. Home: 8401 Hickory Creek Dr Austin TX 78735-1530

WINEGRAD, GERALD WILLIAM, lawyer, state senator, educator; b. Balt., Sept. 9, 1944; s. Benjamin Bernard and Eleanor D. (Messick) W.; m. Madeline Frost Powers, Dec. 10, 1970; children: Pamela Leah, Susan Frost, Rebecca Ann. B.A., Western Md. Coll., 1966; J.D., U. Md., 1969. Bar: Md. 1969. Assoc. revisor Gov.'s Commn. to revise the code, Annapolis, Md., 1974-78; cons. Friends of the Earth, Washington; mem. Md. Senate, 1982—; instr. pub. policy, environ. Grad. Sch. U. Md., 1988. Bd. dirs. Md. Environ. Trust, Balt., 1983—; mem. Chesapeake Bay Commn.; mem. Md. Ho. of Dels., 1978-82; del. Dem. Nat. Conv., 1984. Lt. JAGC, USN, 1970-74, comdr. Res. Recipient Outstanding Conservation Legislator award Md. Wildlife Fedn., 1981, Cert. of Merit, Common Cause of Md., 1984, Outstanding Conservation Legislator award Clean Water Action Project, 1985, Outstanding Environmentalist award Sierra Club, 1985. Mem. Nat. Conf. State Legislators (energy com.), Sierra Club, of Md., Am. Legion, Optimists. Democrat. Roman Catholic.

WINEKE, WILLIAM ROBERT, reporter, clergyman; b. Madison, Wis., Apr. 4, 1942; s. Edward Ervin and Jennie Mae (Lanigan) W.; m. Susan L. Detering, Dec. 9, 1964 (div. June 1975); children: Gregory, Andrew; m. Jacqueline Cone, Mar. 18, 1990. BS, U. Wis., 1965; BDiv, chgo. Theol. Sem., 1969. Reporter Wis. State Jour., Madison, 1963-65; writer United Ch. of Christ, N.Y.C., 1966-68; pub. rels. dir. Chgo. (Ill.) Theol. Sem., Chgo., 1968-69; reporter Wis. State Jour., Madison, 1969—; chaplain Wis. Rescue Mission, Madison, 1977—; bd. rev. Wis. Health Policy Network, Madison, 1994—. Fellow Religions Pub. Rels. Soc., 1974; recipient Disting. Svc. award State Med. Soc. Wis., 1992, Disting. Svc. award LWV, Madison, 1994. Democrat. Home: 1024 Ridgewood Dr Stoughton WI 53589-4125 Office: Wis State Jour 1901 Fish Hatchery Rd Madison WI 53713

WINER, WARD OTIS, mechanical engineer, educator; b. Grand Rapids, Mich., June 27, 1936; s. Mervin Augustus and Ina Katherine (Wood) W.; m. Mary Jo Wielinga, June 15, 1957; children: Mathew Owen, James Edward, Paul Andrew, Mary Margaret. Asso., Grand Rapids Jr. Coll., 1956; B.S., U. Mich., 1958, M.S., 1959, Ph.D., 1961; Ph.D. (Cavendish Lab. fellow), Cambridge (Eng.) U., 1961-63. Asst. prof. dept. mech. engring. U. Mich., Ann Arbor, 1963-66, assoc. prof., 1966-69; assoc. prof. mech. engring. Ga. Inst. Tech., 1969-71, prof., 1971-84, Regents' prof., 1984—, dir. George W. Woodruff Sch. Mech. Engring., 1988—, mem. exec. bd., 1983-88, chmn., 1984-86; chmn. Gordon Research Conf. on Friction, Lubrication and Wear, 1980; mem. NRC, 1980-88; chmn. Com. on Recommendations for U.S. Army Basic Sci. Research, 1985-87; mem. div. mech., structural, materials engring. adv. bd. NSF Engring. Directorate, 1984-89. Co-editor: Wear Control Handbook, 1980; tech. editor: Jour. Lubrication Tech., 1980-84, Jour. of Tribology, 1984-87; contbr. articles to profl. jours. Democratic precinct chmn., 1967-68; Mem. exec. bd. Horace H. Rackham Sch. Grad. Studies, U. Mich., 1968. Recipient Disting. Faculty Svc. award Coll. Engring. U. Mich., 1967, Cert. Recognition, NASA, 1977, Clarence E. Earle Meml. award Nat. Grease Lubricating Inst., 1979, Disting. Prof. award Ga. Inst. Tech., 1987. Fellow AAAS, ASME (bd. comms. 1987-81, v.p. rsch. 1989-93, Melville medal 1975, Centennial medallion 1980, Mayor D. Hersey award 1986, Charles Russ Richards Meml. award 1988), Soc. Tribologists and Lubrication Engrs. (bd. dirs. 1983-86), Brit. Tribology Trust (gold medal 1987); mem. Am. Soc. Engring. Educators (Benjamin Garver Lamme award 1995, Donald Marlowe award 1996), NAE, Metro Atlanta Engring. Soc. (Engr. of Yr. 1989), Am. Acad. Mechanics, Soc. Rheology, Soc. Engring. Sci. (dir. 1980-84), AAUP (pres. Ga. Tech. chpt. 1972-74, v.p. state conf. 1973-75), Sigma Xi (chpt. pres. 1982-83, Sustained Rsch. in Engring. award 1975), Tau Beta Pi, Pi Tau Sigma, Phi Kappa Phi. Home: 1025 Mountain Creek Trl NW Atlanta GA 30328-3535

WINER, WARREN JAMES, insurance executive; b. Wichita, Kans., June 16, 1946; s. Henry Charles and Isabel (Ginsburg) W.; m. Mary Jean Kovacs, June 23, 1968 (div. Feb. 1973); m. Jo Lynn Sondag, May 3, 1975; children: Adam, Lauren. BS in Math., Stanford U., 1968. With Gen. Am. Life Ins. Co., St. Louis, 1968-73, dir. retirement plans, 1973-76, 2d v.p., 1976-80; v.p., sr. actuary Powers, Carpenter & Hall, St. Louis, 1980-84, sr. v.p., dir. pension div., 1984-85, pres., chief operating officer, 1985-86, lobbyist, commentator, 1985—, pres., chief exec. officer, 1986—; pres. W F Corroon, 1988-93; prin. William M. Mercer, 1993—, mng. dir., 1994-95; exec. v.p. Gen. Am. Life Ins. Co., St. Louis, 1995—; mem. Actuarial Exam. Com., Chgo., 1973-74. Contbr. articles to profl. jours. Bd. dirs. Lucky Lane Nursery Sch. Assn., St. Louis, 1978-93, pilot divsn. United Way, 1986-87;

co-pres. Conway Sch. Parent Assn., 1986-87; bd. dirs. Paraquad, 1991—, chmn., 1994—; bd. dirs. ATD, 1992—. Fellow Soc. Actuaries; mem. Am. Acad. Actuaries, Enrollment of Actuaries (joint bd.), Am. Life Ins. Assn. (small case task force 1979-80), Life Office Mgmt. Assn. (ICPAC com. 1975-80), St. Louis Actuaries Club. Jewish. Clubs: St. Louis, Clayton (St. Louis). Avocations: bridge, wine tasting, swimming, weight tng. Office: Gen Am Life Ins Co 13045 Tesson Ferry Rd Saint Louis MO 63128

WINES, LAWRENCE EUGENE, lawyer, corporate executive; b. St. Louis, Jan. 17, 1957; s. Frank Peter and Audrey Margret (Murphy) W. BA, U. Mo., 1984; JD, St. Louis U., 1987. Bar: Mo., U.S. Dist. Ct. (we. dist.) Mo. Mem. staff Gephardt for President, Washington, 1987-88; sole practice Ferguson, Mo., 1989-90; ptnr. Progressive Consulting, Ferguson, 1988-93, Wines & Stein attys., P.C., Ferguson, 1990-95; Wines Law Office, L.C., 1995—; pres. Catewood Industries, Inc., Wines Properties, Inc., Wines Enterprises, Inc.; prin. Wines Law Offices, L.C., 1995—. Cons. fundraising Missourias for Mike Wolff, St. Louis, 1988-92, John Shear Election Com., St. Louis, 1988-95, Congresswoman Joan Kelly Horn, St. Louis, 1990-92, Quinn for Sec. State, St. Louis, 1991-92; Ferguson Com. man St. Louis County Dem. Com., 1987-92; vol. Congressman Richard Gephardt, St. Louis and Washington, 1984—. Recipient: Presdl. Svc. award U. Mo. St. Louis Alumni Assn., 1989-90, Disting. Svc. award Disabled Student Union, 1991, Disting. Vol. award U. Mo. St. Louis, 1987; named Outstanding Male Young Dem. Mo. Young Dems., 1986. Mem. Mo. Bar Assn., Mo. Assn. Trial Attys. Roman Catholic. Avocations: weighlifting, shooting, archery. Office: 111 Church St Ste 214 Saint Louis MO 63135-2458

WINETT, SAMUEL JOSEPH, manufacturing company executive; b. Chgo., June 15, 1934; s. Maurice and Ruby (Caplan) W.; m. Susan Carol Finkel, Apr. 24, 1957; children: Bradley, William, James. BS in Acctg., U. Ill., 1956; MBA, U. Chgo., 1970. CPA, Ill. Staff auditor Arthur Young & Co., Chgo., 1958-63; with Outboard Marine Corp., Waukegan, Ill., 1963-91, asst. controller, 1974-78, controller ops., 1978-86, v.p. fin., 1986-91; cons. QED Ptnrs., Chgo., 1993—. Served as 1st lt. U.S. Army, 1956-58. Mem. AICPA, Ill. CPA Soc., Fin. Execs. Inst., Assn. for Corp. Growth. Home: 3128 Mapleleaf Dr Glenview IL 60025-1123

WINFIELD, DAVID MARK, former professional baseball player, commentator; b. St. Paul, Oct. 3, 1951. Student, U. Minn.; LL.D.(hon.), Syracuse U., 1987. Player San Diego Padres (Nat. League), 1973-80, N.Y. Yankees (Am. League), 1980-90, Calif. Angels (Am. League), 1990-91; with Toronto Blue Jays (Am. League), 1991-92, Minnesota Twins (Am. League), 1992-94, Cleve. Indians, 1995; commentator Fox Broadcasting Co., Beverly Hills, Calif., 1996—; mem. Nat. League All-Star team, 1977-80, Am. League All-Star team, 1981-88; led Nat. League in total bases, 1979; played in World Series, 1981. Author (with Tom Parker) autobiography Winfield: A Player's Life, 1988. Recipient Golden glove, 1979-80, 82-85, 87, Silver Slugger award, 1981-85, 92; named top Sporting News All-Star Team, 1979, 82-84, 92; named Sporting News Am. League Comeback Player of Yr., 1990. Office: Fox Broadcasting Co PO Box 900 Beverly Hills CA 90213*

WINFIELD, JOHN BUCKNER, rheumatologist, educator; b. Kentfield, Calif., Mar. 19, 1942; s. R. Buckner and Margaret G. (Katterfelt) W.; m. Patricia Nichols (div. 1968); 1 child, Ann Gibson; m. Teresa Lee McGrath, 1969; children: John Buckner III, Virginia Lee. BA, Williams Coll., 1964; MD, Cornell U., 1968. Diplomate Am. Bd. Internal Medicine. Intern in medicine N.Y. Hosp., N.Y.C., 1968-69; staff assoc. LI/Nat. Inst. Allergy and Infectious Diseases NIH, Bethesda, Md., 1969-71; resident in medicine, fellow in rheumatology U. Va. Sch. Medicine, Charlottesville, 1971-73; fellow in immunology Rockefeller U., N.Y.C., 1973-75; asst. prof. medicine U. Va. Sch. Medicine, Charlottesville, 1975-76, assoc. prof. medicine, 1976-78; assoc. prof. medicine U. N.C., Chapel Hill, 1978-81, prof. medicine, 1981—, chief div. rheumatology and immunology, 1978—; dir. Thurston Arthritis Rsch. Ctr. U. N.C. Sch. Medicine, Chapel Hill, 1982—; Smith prof. medicine U. N.C. Sch. Med., Chapel Hill, 1987—; adv. coun. Nat. Inst. Arthritis and Musculoskeletal and Skin Diseases, NIH, 1988-92; chmn. edn. com. Am. Rheumatism Assn., Atlanta, 1980-84; immunol. scis. study sect. NIH, 1979-83, Arthritis Musculoskeletal and Skin study sect., 1992—; vice-chair fellowship com. Arthritis Found., 1982; med. coun. Lupus Found. Am., 1987—. Author more than 100 med. and sci. articles in peer reviewer rheumatology and immunology jours.; mem. editl. bd. Arthritis and Rheumatism, Bull. Rheumatic Diseases, Rheumatology Internat., Clin. Exptl. Rheumatology, Am. Jour. Medicine. Sr. asst. surgeon with USPHS, NIH, Bethesda, Md., 1968-71. Recipient Borden prize Cornell U. Med. Coll., 1964, numerous rsch. grants NIH and Arthritis Found., 1975—, Sr. Investigator award Arthritis Found., 1976-79, Kenan award U. N.C., 1985, NIH merit award, 1992. Fellow ACP; mem. Am. Assn. Immunologists, Am. Coll. Rheumatology, Am. Fedn. Clin. Rsch., Am. Soc. Clin. Investigation, Assn. Am. Physicians, Am. Clin. Climatol. Assn., Chapel Hill Country Club. Republican. Episcopalian. Avocations: golf, off-road motorcycling, scuba diving instructor. Home: 801 Kings Mill Rd Chapel Hill NC 27514-4920 Office: U NC Sch Medicine Thurston Arthritis Rsch Ctr CB 7280 Rm 3310 Chapel Hill NC 27599

WINFIELD, MICHAEL D., engineering company executive; b. 1939. BS in Chem. Engring., Ohio State U.; MBA, U. Chgo. Chem. engr. UOP, Des Plaines, Ill., 1962-74, mgr. refinery projects, 1974-76, asst. dir. tech. svcs., 1976-81, dir. bus. devel., 1981-83, v.p. tech. svcs., 1983-84, v.p. process svcs., 1984-92, pres., CEO, 1992—. Office: UOP 25 E Algonquin Rd Des Plaines IL 60016-6101

WINFIELD, PAUL EDWARD, actor; b. Los Angeles, May 22, 1941. Student, U. Portland, 1957-59, Stanford U., 1959, Los Angeles City Coll., 1959-63, UCLA, 1962-64. artist-in-residence Stanford U., 1964-65, U. Hawaii, 1965, U. Calif., Santa Barbara, 1970-71. Films include Gordons War, 1973, Huckleberry Finn, 1974, Conrack, 1974, Guess Who's Minding the Mint, 1969, Sounder, 1972 (Acad. Award nomination 1973), Hustle, 1975, Twilights Last Gleaming, 1976, A Hero Ain't Nothing But A Sandwich, 1978, Carbon Copy, 1981, White Dog, 1981, Star Trek II, 1982, Mike's Murder, 1982, On the Run, 1982, The Terminator, 1985, Blue City, 1986, Death Before Dishonor, 1987, The Serpent and the Rainbow, 1988, Presumed Innocent, 1990, Cliff Hanger, 1993, Dennis the Menace (The Movie), 1993, Kingdom of The Blind, 1994, The Mike Tyson Story, 1994, Fluke, 1994; TV appearances include Green Eyes, 1976, All Deliberate Speed, 1976, King, 1978 (Emmy nomination), Backstairs at the White House, 1979, The Blue and the Gray, 1982, Star Trek: Next Generation, 1992; guest star: TV appearances include Roots II (Emmy nomination), Angel City, 1980, Sisters, 1981, Sophisticated Gents, 1981, Go Tell It on the Mountain, 1983, Queen (miniseries), 1993, Scarlett (miniseries), 1994, Picket Fences, 1994 (Guest Actor in a Drama Emmy award); theatrical appearances include Checkmates, 1988, nat. tour A Few Good Men, 1992, Othello, Guthrie Theatre, 1993. Office: 5750 Wilshire Blvd Ste 590 Los Angeles CA 90036-3697

WINFREE, ARTHUR TAYLOR, biologist, educator; b. St. Petersburg, Fla., May 15, 1942; s. Charles Van and Dorothy Rose (Scheb) W.; m. Ji-Yun Yang, June 18, 1983; children: Rachael, Erik from previous marriage. B.Engring. in Physics, Cornell U., 1965; Ph.D. in Biology, Princeton U., 1970. Lic. pvt. pilot. Asst. prof. theoretical biology U. Chgo., 1969-72; assoc. prof. biology Purdue U., West Lafayette, Ind., 1972-79; prof. Purdue U., 1979-86; prof. ecology and evolutionary biology U. Ariz., Tucson, 1986-88, Regents' prof., 1989—; pres., dir. research Inst. Natural Philosophy, Inc., 1979-88. Author: The Geometry of Biological Time, 1980, When Time Breaks Down, 1986, The Timing of Biological Clocks, 1987. Recipient Career Devel. award NIH, 1973-78, The Einthoven award Einthoven Found. and Netherlands Royal Acad. Scis., 1989; NSF grantee, 1966—; MacArthur fellow, 1984-89, John Simon Guggenheim Meml. fellow, 1982. Home: 1210 E Placita De Graciela Tucson AZ 85718-2834 Office: U Ariz 326 BSW Tucson AZ 85721

WINFREY, CAREY WELLS, journalist, magazine editor; b. N.Y.C., Aug. 1, 1941; s. William Colin and Mary (Robinson) W.; m. Laurie Beardsley Platt, July 30, 1972 (div. 1980); m. Jane Elizabeth Keeney, Feb. 13, 1982; children: Graham William, Wells Millar. AB, Columbia U., N.Y.C., 1963, MS in Journalism, 1967. With Pub. Broadcasting Lab., NET; assoc. editor Time Inc., N.Y.C., 1968-71; exec. producer Ednl. Broadcast Corp., N.Y.C., 1971-77; reporter, fgn. corr. for Africa N.Y. Times, N.Y.C., 1977-80; mag. editor CBS Mags., N.Y.C., 1981-90, dir. video devel., 1981-83, editor Cuisine mag., 1983-84, v.p., editorial dir., 1985-87; v.p. Diamandis Comm., Inc. (formerly mag. divsn. CBS), N.Y.C., 1987-90, editor-in-chief Memories mag., 1987-90; editor-in-chief Am. Health mag. Reader's Digest Publs., N.Y.C., 9190-96; dir. Delacorte Ctr. for Mag. Journalism, N.Y.c., 1996—; cons. Ford Found., N.Y.C., 1976. Author: Starts and Finishes, 1975; exec. producer: (TV programs) Behind the Lines, 1971-75 (Emmy award 1973-74, NYU Don Hollenback award 1974), Assignment America, 1975, WNET Reports, 1976-77; columnist: "Eye on Books" for Book of the Month Club News, 1980, Parenting mag., 1986-89; producer Mixed Bag, twice-weekly video arts mag. for CBS Cable; contbr. articles to numerous publs. including The N.Y. Times Mag., Harpers, N.Y. Mag. Served to capt. USMC, 1963-66. Pulitzer Travelling fellow, 1967; recipient Meyer Berger award for Disting. Reporting Columbia U., 1978. Home: 340 Riverside Dr New York NY 10025-3423 also: Dutchess County NY Office: Columbia U Grad Sch Journalism New York NY 10027

WINFREY, DIANA LEE, lawyer; b. Kansas City, Mo., July 17, 1955; d. James William and Louise Augusta (Harrison) W. BA in Spanish, U. Mo., 1978, JD, 1984. Bar: Mo. 1984, Calif. 1985. Tchr. Pan-Am. Workshop, Mexico City, 1979; law clk. Mo. Ct. of Appeals, Kansas City, 1984-85; assoc. Early, Maslach, Leavy & Nutt, L.A., 1985-87, Wilson, Elser, et al, L.A., 1987-88, Wood, Lucksinger & Epstein, L.A., 1988-90, Coony & Bihr, Beverly Hills, Calif., 1990-95; sole practitioner Woodland Hills, Calif., 1995—. Asst. editor The Urban Lawyer Jour., 1983-84. Member Heal the Bay, Santa Monica, Calif., 1991—. Recipient Outstanding Achievement and Svc. award U. Mo., 1978. Mem. ABA, Calif. Bar Assn., Mo. Bar Assn., L.A. County Bar Assn., Beverly Hills Bar Assn., Am. Bd. Trial Attys., Inns of Ct. Democrat. Office: 21112 Ventura Blvd Woodland Hills CA 91364-2103

WINFREY, JOHN CRAWFORD, economist, educator; b. Somerville, Tenn., July 2, 1935; s. Arthur Peter and Frances (Crawford) W.; m. Barbara Ann Strickland, July 20, 1957; 1 child, Mae Millicent. A.B., Davidson Coll., 1957; Ph.D., Duke U., 1965. Asst. dir. data processing Hanes Hosiery, Winston Salem, N.C., 1959-62; research asst. in econs. Duke U., Durham, N.C., 1963-64; asst. prof. econs. Washington and Lee U., Lexington, Va., 1965-68, assoc. prof., 1969-73, prof., 1974—; vis. prof. Vanderbilt U., Nashville, 1966, Tufts U., Boston, 1975, UCLA, 1978, U. Ill., 1982, U. Va., 1986, Duke U., 1989, 95, U. Calif., Berkeley, 1993, U. Utrecht, The Netherlands, 1995. Co-author: The Motion Commotion, 1972; author: Public Finance, Public Choice and the Public Sector, 1973. Bd. dirs. Lexington Tennis Clinic, Va., 1968-72, Rockridge Area Conservation Council, 1982-84; pres. Rockbridge Arts Guild, 1986-88. Recipient Comunity Svc. Lexington Jaycees, 1971; NEH fellow, 1975, 78, 82, 86, 89, 93; vis. fellow U. Coll. Oxford U., Eng., 1979, 95. Fellow Soc. for Values in Higher Edn.; mem. Am. Econ. Assn., So. Econ. Assn., History of Econs. Soc., Eastern Econ. Assn. Democrat. Presbyterian. Club: High Wheelers (Lexington). Home: 628 Stonewall St Lexington VA 24450-1933 Office: Washington and Lee U Dept Econs Lexington VA 24450

WINFREY, MARION LEE, television critic; b. Knoxville, Tenn., July 7, 1932; s. Charles Houston and Norma Elsa (Wesenberg) W.; m. Mary Anne Hight, Sept. 5, 1958 (div. 1977); 1 son, David Dylan; m. Kiki Olson, Aug. 24, 1978 (div. 1982). B.S., U. Tenn., 1966; M.F.A., U. Iowa, 1968. Reporter Nashville Tennessean, 1957-58, Knoxville News-Sentinel, 1958-60, Miami bur. UPI, 1960-62, Miami Herald, 1962-63, Washington bur. Knight Newspapers, 1963-66, Detroit Free Press, 1968-71; reporter Phila. Inquirer, 1972-74, TV critic, 1974—; instr. journalism U. Iowa, 1966-68; Bernard Kilgore journalism counselor DePauw U., 1971. Author: Kent State Report, The President's Commission on Campus Unrest, 1970; included in Best Sports Stories (edited by Marsh and Ehre), 1963. Served with U.S. Army, 1954-56. Nieman fellow Harvard U., 1971-72. Mem. TV Critics Assn. (founding pres. 1978-79), Sigma Delta Chi, Phi Gamma Delta. Baptist. Clubs: Harvard (Phila.); Pen and Pencil; Nat. Press (Washington). Home: 1700 Benjamin Franklin Pky Philadelphia PA 19103-1210 Office: 400 N Broad St Philadelphia PA 19130-4015

WINFREY, OPRAH, television talk show host, actress, producer; b. Kosciusko, Miss., Jan. 29, 1954; d. Vernon Winfrey and Vernita Lee. BA in Speech and Drama, Tenn. State U. News reporter Sta. WVOL Radio, Nashville, 1971-72; reporter, news anchorperson Sta. WTVF-TV, Nashville, 1973-76; news anchorperson Sta. WJZ-TV, Balt., 1976-77, host morning talk show People Are Talking, 1977-83; host talk show A.M. Chgo. Sta. WLS-TV, 1984; host The Oprah Winfrey Show, Chgo., 1985—; nationally syndicated, 1986—; host series of celebrity interview spls. Oprah: Behind the Scenes, 1992—; owner, prodr. Harpo Prodns., 1986—. Appeared in films The Color Purple, 1985 (nominated Acad. award and Golden Globe award), Native Son, 1986, Throw Momma From the Train, 1988, Listen Up: The Lives of Quincy Jones, 1990; prodr., actress ABC-TV mini-series The Women of Brewster Place, 1989, also series Brewster Place, 1990, movie There Are No Children Here, 1993; exec. prodr. (ABC Movie of the Week) Overexposed, 1992; host, supervising prodr. celebrity interview series Oprah: Behind the Scenes, 1992, ABC Aftersch. Spls., 1991-93; host, exec. prodr. Michael Jackson Talks...to Oprah-90 Prime-Time Minutes with the King of Pop, 1993. Recipient Woman of Achievement award NOW, 1986, Emmy award for Best Daytime Talk Show Host, 1987, 91, 92, 94, 95, America's Hope award, 1990, Industry Achievement award Broadcast Promotion Mktg. Execs./Broadcast Design Assn., 1991, Image awards NAACP, 1989, 90, 91, 92, Entertainer of Yr. award NAACP, 1989, CEBA awards, 1989, 90, 91; named Broadcaster of Yr. Internat. Radio and TV Soc., 1988. Office: Harpo Prodns 110 N Carpenter St Chicago IL 60607-2101

WING, ADRIEN KATHERINE, law educator; b. Oceanside, Calif., Aug. 7, 1956; d. John Ellison and Katherine (Pruitt) Wing; children: Che-Cabral, Nolan Felipe. A.B. magna cum laude, Princeton U., 1978; M.A., UCLA, 1979; J.D., Stanford Law Sch., 1982. Bar: N.Y. 1983, U.S. Dist. Ct. (so. and ea. dists.) N.Y. 1983, U.S. Ct. Appeals (5th and 9th cirs.). Assoc. Curtis, Mallet-Prevost, Colt & Mosle, N.Y.C., 1982-86, Rabinowitz, Boudin, Standard, Krinsky & Lieberman, 1986-87; assoc. prof. law U. Iowa, Iowa City, 1987-93, prof. law, 1993—; mem. alumni council Princeton U., 1983-85, trustee Class of '78 Alumni Found., 1984-87, v.p. Princeton Class of 1978 Alumni, 1993—; mem. bd. visitors Stanford Law Sch., 1993-96. Mem. bd. editors Am. Jour. Comp. Law, 1993—. Mem. ABA (exec. com. young lawyers sect. 1985-87), Nat. Conf. Black Lawyers (UN rep., chmn. internat. affairs sect. 1982-95), Internat. Assn. Dem. Lawyers (UN rep. 1984-87), Am. Soc. Internat. Law (exec. council 1986-89, group chair S. Africa 1996—, nom. com. 1991, 93), Black Alumni of Princeton U. (bd. dirs. 1982-87), Transafrica Scholars Forum Coun. (bd. dirs 1993—), Iowa City Foreign Rels. Coun. (bd. dirs. 1989-94), Iowa Peace Inst. (bd. dirs. 1993-95), Council on Fgn. Rels., Internat. Third World Legal Studies Assn. (bd. dirs. 1996—). Democrat. Avocations: photography, jogging, writing, poetry. Office: U Iowa Sch Law Boyd Law Bldg Iowa City IA 52242

WING, ELIZABETH SCHWARZ, museum curator, educator; b. Cambridge, Mass., Mar. 5, 1932; d. Henry F. and Maria Lisa Schwarz; m. James E. Wing, Apr. 18, 1957; children: Mary Elizabeth Wing-Berman, Stephen R. BA, Mt. Holyoke Coll., 1955; MS, U. Fla., 1957, PhD, 1962. Interim asst. curator Fla. Mus. Natural History, U. Fla., Gainesville, 1961-69, asst. curator, 1969-73, assoc. curator, 1973-78, curator, 1978—; U. Fla., Fla. Mus. Natural History, Gainesville, 1990-92; U.S. rep. Internat. Congress Archaeozoology, 1981—. Author: (with A.B. Brown) Paleonutrition, 1979; editor (with J.C. Wheeler) Economic Prehistory of the Central Andes, 1988; contbr. articles to profl. jours. Recipient Fryxell award Soc. Am. Archaeology, 1996; NSF grantee, 1961-64, 68-73, 79-80, 84-85, 89-91, 95-96. Mem. Soc. Ethnobiology (pres. 1989-91, trustee 1991—). Office: U Fla Fla Mus Natural History PO Box 117800 Museum Rd Gainesville FL 32611-7800

WING, JOHN ADAMS, financial services executive; b. Elmira, N.Y., Nov. 9, 1935; s. Herbert Charles and Clara Louise (Stewart) W.; m. Joan Cook Montgomery, June 19, 1964; children: Lloyd Montgomery, Elizabeth Montgomery, Mary Ellen. B.A. in Econs., Union Coll., 1958; LL.B., George Washington U., 1963. Bar: Va. 1963, D.C. 1965, Ill. 1968. Fin. analyst SEC, Washington, 1960-63; trial atty. SEC, 1963-66; asst. to pres. Investors Diversified Services, Inc., Mpls., 1966-67; v.p., gen. counsel A.G. Becker & Co., Chgo., 1968-71, sr. v.p., 1971-74, pres., 1974-80, also dir.; pres., chief exec. officer Chgo. Corp., 1981—, now chmn. bd. dirs.; bd. dirs. Chgo. Bd. Options Exch., Am. Mut. Life. Bd. dirs. Ill. Inst. Tech., Risk Mgmt. Ctr. Chgo. With U.S. Army, 1958-60. Mem. Ill. Bar Assn., Va. Bar Assn., Ill. State C. of C. (bd. dirs. capital fund). Episcopalian. Clubs: Chgo., Economics, Civic, Mid-Day, Bond, Saddle & Cycle. Office: Chgo Corp 208 S La Salle St Chicago IL 60604-1003*

WING, JOHN RUSSELL, lawyer; b. Mt. Vernon, N.Y., Jan. 20, 1937; s. John R. and Elinore (Smith) W.; m. Mary Zeller, Aug. 24, 1963 (div. June 1975); children: Ethan Lincoln, Catherine Dorothy; m. Audrey Strauss, Aug. 12, 1979; children: Carlin Elinore, Matthew Lawrence. BA, Yale U., 1960; JD, U. Chgo., 1963. Bar: N.Y. 1964. Assoc. Sherman & Sterling, N.Y.C., 1963-66; asst. U.S. atty. So. Dist. N.Y., N.Y.C., 1966-78; chief fraud unit U.S. Dist. Atty. So. Dist. N.Y., 1971-78; ptnr. Weil, Gotshal & Manges, N.Y.C., 1978—. Contbr. articles to profl. jours. Fellow Am. Coll. Trial Lawyers; mem. ABA (white collar crime com. criminal justice sect. 1978—, environ. task force com. 1983-85), Assn. Bar of City of N.Y. (criminal advocacy com. 1985-88), Fed. Bar Coun. (2d cir. cts. com. 1982-84), N.Y. Coun. Def. Lawyers (bd. dirs. 1986-90). Republican. Episcopalian. Avocation: sailing. Home: 52 Livingston St Brooklyn NY 11201-4813 Office: Weil Gotshal & Manges 767 5th Ave New York NY 10153

WINGARD, JOHANN HENDRICK, engineering company executive, ostrich farmer; b. Bloemfontein, South Africa, Mar. 19, 1936; s. Stephen Michael and Johanna Dorothea (Becker) W.; m. Aletta Gerbrecht Magdalena, Aug. 20, 1960; children: Hein, Martha-Marie. Student, U. Pretoria, South Africa, 1955; PMD, U. Cape Town, South Africa, 1970. Tech. officer Internat. Red Locust Control, Zambia/Tanzania, 1956-59; coexec. Acrow Engrs., South Africa, 1960-64, Rootes Tempair, South Africa, 1964-69, African Oxygen Ltd., South Africa, 1969-74; chmn. Gassentraal, South Africa, 1974-76; co. exec. ELB Group, South Africa, 1976-94; chmn. Gasal Mgmt. Systems, South Africa, 1988—; exec. dir. Bateman Project Holdings Ltd., South Africa, 1987—; exec. dir. Bateman Davy Engring. Ltd., 1987-92, Tajikistan Indsl. Devel. Corp., London, 1993—; chmn. Bateman Engring. Ltd., 1987-91, Indsl. & Petrochem. Cons., Johannesburg, South Africa, 1988-93, Rainbow Indsl. Minerals Corp., Johannesburg, 1992-93. Author: Technology Transfer, 1985; patentee in field. Cons. AVSTIG, Pretoria, 1990—; Chmn. Found. for Performing Arts., S. Africa, 1993-94. Mem. ASME, Ostrich Producers' Assn. (chair volkstaat coun. 1994—).Governor Sacada, 1996—. Mem. Dutch Reformed Ch. Avocations: farming, golf.

WINGARD, RAYMOND RANDOLPH, transportation products executive; b. Goshen, Ala., Nov. 6, 1930; s. Raymond T. and Mary (Sanders) W.; student So. Meth. U., 1948-49, Birmingham-So. Coll., 1949-50, Harvard, 1973; m. Gainnell Harris, June 2, 1951; children: Renee, Kay, Beckie, Robin, Randy. With Koppers Co. Inc., 1951-62, area mgr., Montgomery, Ala., 1963-64, mgr. R.R. sales and plannning Western region, Chgo., 1964-71, div. mgr., asst. v.p. R.R. sales and planning, 1971-74, asst. v.p., mktg. mgr., Pitts., 1974-75, v.p., mgr. human resources, 1975-80, v.p., mgr. mktg. dept., 1981-85, v.p., mgr. adminstrv. svcs. and corp. planning, 1985-88; agy. mgr. Ala. Farm Bur. Svc., Andalusia, 1962-63; exec. dir. Railway Tie Assn., 1988-96; chmn. Telemed techs., Internat., 1996—. Chmn., R-1 Sch. Dist. Adv. Coun., Independence, Mo., 1960; pres. Independence Suburban Community Improvement League, 1959-60; mem. dist. 58 Bd. Edn., 1969-71; trustee Pitts. Coun. Internat. Visitors, 1978-84, pres., 1982-83; pres. Minority Engring. Edn. Effect, Inc., 1977-80; bd. dirs. Allegheny coun. Boy Scouts Am., Blue Cross of Pa., vice-chmn., 1986-89; bd. dirs. Diversified Benefits Svc., Inc., 1990—, Children's Make-A-Wish Found., 1995—, Baldwin Anti-Violence Ctr., 1996—. With AUS, 1950-51. Mem. Am. Wood Preservers Assn., Japan Mgmt. Assn., Railway Tie Assn., Western Ry. Club. Methodist. Duquesne Club, Harvard Club Mobile. Home: 15300 State Hwy 180 Gulf Shores AL 36542-8242 Office: PO Box 1039 140 Cove Ave Gulf Shores AL 36547

WINGATE, C. KEITH, law educator; b. Darlington, S.C., May 12, 1953; s. Clarence L. and Lilly (Frazier) W.; m. Gloria Farley. BA in Polit. Sci., U. Ill., 1974, JD cum laude, 1978. Bar: Calif., 1978. Assoc. litigation dept. Morrison & Foerster, San Francisco, 1978-80; from asst. to assoc. prof. law U. Calif.-Hastings, San Francisco, 1980-86, prof., 1986—; dir. Coun. Legal Edn. Opportunity Region I Inst., 1989; vis. prof. law Stanford (Calif) Law Sch., fall 1990, 94; chair Minority Law Tchrs.' Conf. Com., 1990; mem. acad. assistance work group, law sch. admissions coun., 1991. Author: (with David I. Levine and William R. Slomanson) Cases and Materials on California Civil Procedure, 1991, (with William R. Slomanson) California Civil Procedure in a Nutshell, 1992, (with Donald L. Doernberg) Federal Courts, Federalism and Separation of Powers, 1994. Bd. dirs. Community Housing Devel. Corp., North Richmond. Recipient 10 Outstanding Persons award U. Ill. Black Alumni Assn., 1980; Harno fellow U. Ill., Coll. of Law, 1976. Mem. Assn. Am. Law Schs. (chair sect. minority groups 1990, exec. com. mem. sect. civil proceedure 1991), Charles Housting Bar Assn., Phi Sigma Alpha. Office: U Calif Hastings Coll Law 200 Mcallister St San Francisco CA 94102-4707

WINGATE, DAVID AARON, manufacturing company executive; b. Tel Aviv, Jan. 6, 1921; came to U.S., 1950, naturalized, 1955; s. Israel Winograd and Hanna Glick; m. Shoshanna L. Abrams, June 16, 1943; children—Bathsheva Wingate Ostrow, Ealan J. Student, Grad. Sch. Law and Econs., Tel Aviv, 1938-42. Mem. War Supply Bd., Jerusalem, 1943-47; pres. Yale Mfg. Co., Tel Aviv, 1947-50, Corona Internat. Corp., N.Y.C., 1951-55; v.p. Reynolds Atlantic Corp., N.Y.C., 1956-58; pres., chief exec. Midwood Industries, Inc., North Hills, N.Y., 1959-77; chmn., chief exec. officer Hi-Shear Industries Inc., North Hills, 1977—. Clubs: Glen Oaks (Old Westbury); Mission Hills Country (Palm Springs, Calif.); Govs. and Palm Beach Country (Palm Beach, Fla.). Home: 33 Applegreen Dr Old Westbury NY 11568-1202 Office: Hi-Shear Industries Inc 3333 New Hyde Park Rd New Hyde Park NY 11042-1205

WINGATE, HENRY TAYLOR, JR., foundation administrator, fundraiser; b. Opelika, Ala., Mar. 2, 1929; s. Henry T. and Dorothy Inez (Mathews) W.; m. Mary Frances Grimes, Sept. 17, 1949; children: Frances, Kenneth, Mathew. BS in Agrl. Sci., Auburn U., 1950. Field rep. agrl. chems. div. Swift Co., Birmingham, Ala., 1953-57; regional dir. Muscular Dystrophy Assn. Am., Birmingham, 1958-64; dir. state crusade Am. Cancer Soc., Atlanta, 1964-65; regional fund raising rep. Nat. Assn. Retarded Citizens, Atlanta, 1965-69; regional dir. Nat. Multiple Sclerosis Soc., Atlanta, 1969-77; asst. dir. field services Epilepsy Found. Am., Washington, 1977-78; group v.p. fin. devel. Nat. Arthritis Found., Atlanta, 1978-89. Vol. counselor Svc. Corp. Retired Execs., 1991—. 1st lt. U.S. Army, 1951-53. Named to Gov.'s com. on employment of handicapped Gov. of Ga., 1977, Col. Aide de Camp, Gov. of Tenn., 1982, 86. Mem. Nat. Soc. Fund Raising Execs. (bd. dirs. 1971-72, cert.), Arthritis Found. Staff Assn., Nat. Vol. Health Agys. (chmn. 1981-82), Combined Health Appeals Am. (bd. dirs. 1985-88). Republican. Baptist. Avocations: photography, fishing. Home: 4860 Mountain West Ct Stone Mountain GA 30087-1038

WINGATE, HENRY TRAVILLION, federal judge; b. Jackson, Miss., Jan. 6, 1947; s. J.T. and Eloise (Anderson) W.; m. Turner Arnita Ward, Aug. 10, 1974. BA, Grinnell Coll., 1969; JD, Yale U., 1973; LLD (hon.), Grinnell Coll., 1986. Bar: Miss. 1973, U.S. Dist. Ct. (so. dist.) Miss. 1973, U.S. Ct. Appeals (5th cir.) 1973, U.S. Mil. Ct. 1973. Law clk. New Haven (Conn.) Legal Assistance, 1971-72, Community Legal Aid, Jackson, 1972-73; spl. asst. atty. gen. State of Miss., Jackson, 1976-80; asst. dist. atty. (7th cir.), Jackson, 1980-84; asst. U.S. atty. U.S. Dist. Ct. (so. dist.), Jackson, 1984-85; judge U.S. Dist. Ct. (so. dist.) Miss., Jackson, 1985—; lectr. Miss. Prosecutors Coll., 1980-84, Law Enforcement Tng. Acad., Pearl, Miss., 1980-84, Miss. Jud. Coll., 1980-84, Nat. Coll. Dist. Attys., 1984-85; adj. prof. law Golden Gate U., Norfolk, Va, 1975-76, Tidewater Community Coll., 1976, Miss. Coll. Sch. Law, 1978-84. Former mem. adv. bd. Jackson Parks and Recreation Dept.; former mem. bd. dirs. SCAN Am. of Miss., Inc., Jackson Arts Alliance, Drug Rsch. and Edn. Assn. in Miss., Inc., United Way Jackson; mem. exec. com. Yale U. Law sch., 1989—; chmn. bd. dirs. YMCA, 1978-80. Racquetball State Singles Champion Jr. Vets. Div., 1981, State Singles Champion Srs. Div., 1982, Outstanding Legal Service award NAACP

(Jackson br. and Miss. br.), 1982, Civil Liberties award Elks, 1983, Community Service award Women for Progress Orgn., 1984. Mem. ABA (co-chmn. sect. litigation liaison with judiciary 1989-91), Miss. Bar Assn., Hinds County Bar Assn., Fed. Bar Assn., Yale Club Miss. Avocations: reading, theater, racquetball, jogging, bowling. Home: 6018 Huntview Dr Jackson MS 39206-2130 Office: James O Eastland Courthouse 245 E Capitol St Ste 109 Jackson MS 39201-2409*

WINGATE, ROBERT LEE, JR., internist; b. Columbia, S.C., May 28, 1936; s. Robert Lee and Helen (Owen) W.; m. Ritanne Cooper, Apr. 19, 1962 (div. 1965); 1 child, Elizabeth Butterfield-Wingate; m. Jeannette De-Latte, Mar. 27, 1968 (div. 1980); children: Laura Owen, Charlotte Cramer. BS, U. S.C., 1957; MD, Med. Coll. S.C., 1961. Intern Cin. Gen. Hosp., 1961-62, jr. resident internal medicine, 1964-65; asst. resident in internal medicine Med. Coll. of Va., Richmond, 1965-66; resident in internal medicine Charity Hosp. of La., New Orleans, 1966-67, resident in neurology, 1967-68; pvt. practice Columbia, 1968-78; PruCare physician Memphis, 1983-85; med. dir. M. Lowennstein and Celanese Corps., Rock Hill, S.C., 1978-80; med. dir. nursing home care unit Dorn VA Hosp., Columbia, 1980-82; med. cons. disability determination div. Vocat. Rehab. S.C., Columbia, 1982-83; cons. Student Health Ctr. U. S.C., Columbia, 1985-86; cons. Urgent Care Ctrs. S.C., 1986-87; pvt. practice Pelion, S.C., 1987-92; staff internist, cons. internal medicine Western Mental Health Inst., Western Institute, Tenn., 1992—; med. dir. Forest Hills Nursing Ctr., Columbia, 1968-78; med. cons. S.C. Commn. for Blind, Columbia, 1970-78, Mid-Carolina Coun. on Alcoholism, Columbia, 1970-74; instr. internal medicine U. S.C. Sch. Medicine, 1980-82; cons. internal medicine and urgent care Pelion Cmty. Care Ctr., 1989-92; instr. Sch. Nursing, Med. Coll. S.C., Winthrop divsn., 1978-80; lectr. in field. Contbr. articles to newspapers. Ofcl. physician Peanut Party S.C., 1990-92. Lt. comdr. M.C., USNR, 1958-66. Grantee Burroughs-Wellcome Co., 1958, Med. Coll. S.C., 1960, Congress of U.S., 1987. Mem. ACP, AMA (physician's recognition award 1969, 74, 79, 85, 86, 94-96, 96—), Am. Soc. Internal Medicine, Am. Occupational Med. Assn., So. Med. Assn., S.C. Med. Assn., Lexington County Med. Assn., Soc. of 1824, Ruritan, Phi Rho Sigma. Avocations: chess, hunting, fishing, movie making, collecting stamps and coins. Office: Western Mental Health Inst Western Institute TN 38074

WINGATE, THOMAS MARIE JOSEPH, headmaster; b. Guildford, Surrey, England, May 23, 1959; came to the U.S., 1993; s. Peter Henry and Therese M. (Vachon) W.; m. Maria Elena Espinosa de los Reyes Bolanos, July 10, 1982; children: Elenita, Juliet, Thomas Philip. BA in English, History, Theory Art, U. Kent, Canterbury, Kent, U.K., 1981; postgrad. cert. in edn. in English, U. Leeds, U.K., 1982; MEd, Ga. State U., 1996. English tchr. St. George's Coll., Weybridge, Surrey, 1985-86; English tchr. Brit. Internat. Sch., Mexico City, 1986-89, head English, 1989-91, head intermediate sch., 1991-93; lang. arts tchr. Wesleyan Sch., Atlanta, 1993-94, prin., 1994-96, asst. headmaster, 1996—. Author: The Chapel on the Heath, 1985. Vol. Saint Vincent de Paul Soc., Atlanta, 1994. Grantee Ga. State U., Atlanta, 1993-94, Wesleyan Sch. Governing Bd., Atlanta, 1994. Mem. ASCD, Kappa Delta Pi. Roman Catholic. Avocations: photography, mountain climbing, cricket, coin collecting. Office: Wesleyan Sch 85 Mount Vernon Hwy NW Atlanta GA 30328-3825

WINGENBACH, GREGORY CHARLES, minister, religious-ecumenical agency director; b. Washington, Feb. 1, 1938; s. Charles Edward and Pearl Adeline (Stanton) W.; m. MaryAnn Pearce, Sept. 16, 1961; children: Mary-Adele, Karl Eduard, John Clair, Evgenia Kisa Maria. Student, Georgetown U., 1958-62; BA, Goddard Coll., 1972; postgrad., U. Thessalonike, Greece, 1973-74; MDiv, Louisville Presbyn. Theol. Sem., 1976, D of Ministry in Pastoral and Ecumenical Theology, 1982. Ordained to ministry Greek Orthodox Archdiocese North and South Am. as deacon, 1971, assoc. priest, 1973. Editl. asst., mem. staff Washington Star and N.Y. Herald-Tribune, 1957-62; rsch. and legis. asst. U.S. Senator Clair Engle, Calif., 1962-63; cmty. rels. programs mgr. U.S. Exec. OEO, Washington, 1965-69; regional program devel. officer AEC-Oak Ridge (Tenn.) Assn. Univs., 1970-73; assoc. St. George's Ch., Knoxville, Tenn., 1971-73; chaplain St. John Chrysostomos Ch. and Vlatadon Monastery, Thessalonike, 1973-74; named steward/oikonomos, preacher Met. Archdiocese of Thessalonike, 1974; pastor Assumption of Virgin Mary Ch., Louisville, 1974-79, Holy Trinity Ch., Nashville, 1979-82; named protopresbyter of Greek Orthodox Archiocese and Ecumenical Patriarchate Greek Orthodox Archdiocese, 1980; pastor St. Spyridon's Ch., Monessen, Pa., 1983-86; nat. dir. family life/pastoral ministries Greek Orthodox Archdiocese North and South Am., N.Y.C. and Brookline (Mass.), 1986-90; exec. dir. Kentuckiana Interfaith Community, Louisville, 1990—; Orthodox del. Louisville Area Interch. Coun. and Ecumedia Com., 1974-79; pres., exec. adminstr. LAIOS-Kentuckiana Interfaith Coun., 1977-79; diocesan rep. Archdiocese Nat. Presbyters Coun., 1982-85; archdiocese del. Nat. Coun. Chs., Orthodox/Luth. Dialogues Consultation, 1986—, Orthodox Nat. Missions Bd., 1981-90. Author: The Peace Corps, 1961, Guide to the Peace Corps, 1965, Broken...Yet Never Sundered: The Ecumenical Tradition, 1987; editorial researcher: Richard Nixon, 1959, Duel at the Brink, 1960, The Floating Revolution, 1962. Mem. Fellowship St. Alban and St. Sergius, Orthodox Theol. Soc. Am. (exec. bd.), N.Am. Acad. Ecumenists (exec. bd.). Office: Kentuckiana Interfaith Community 1115 S 4th St Louisville KY 40203-3175

WINGER, DEBRA, actress; b. Cleve., 1955; d. Robert and Ruth W.; m. Timothy Hutton, March 16, 1986 (div.); 1 child, Emanuel Noah. Student, Calif. State U., Northridge. Made 1st profl. appearance in Wonder Woman TV series, 1976-77; appeared TV film Spl. Olympics, 1977; appeared in films Thank God It's Friday, 1978, French Postcards, 1979, Urban Cowboy, 1980, Cannery Row, 1982, An Officer and a Gentleman, 1982, Terms of Endearment, 1983, Mike's Murder, 1984, Legal Eagles, 1986, Black Widow, 1987, Made in Heaven, 1987, Betrayed, 1988, Everybody Wins, 1990, The Sheltering Sky, 1990, Leap of Faith, 1992, Wilder Napalm, 1992, Shadowlands, 1993 (Academy award nominee, Best Actress, 1993), A Dangerous Woman, 1993, Forget Paris, 1995. Office: care Creative Artists Agency 9830 Wilshire Blvd Beverly Hills CA 90212*

WINGER, RALPH O., lawyer; b. Keokuk, Iowa, July 8, 1919; s. Ralph O. and Mary Ellen (Lee) W.; m. Irene L. Sutton, Apr. 5, 1941; children: Ralph O. (dec.), Allen, Louise, Robert. BA, State U. Iowa, 1940; LLB, Harvard U., 1947. Bar: N.Y. 1948. Assoc. Cahill Gordon & Reindel and predecessor firms, N.Y.C., 1947-60, ptnr., 1960-91, sr. counsel, 1992—. Lt. USNR, 1942-46, PTO. Mem. ABA, N.Y. State Bar Assn. (chmn. tax sect. 1973-74, ho. of dels. 1974-75), Bay Terrace Country Club (N.Y.). Republican. Home: 20908 28th Rd Flushing NY 11360-2413 Office: Cahill Gordon & Reindel 80 Pine St New York NY 10005-1702

WINGER, ROGER ELSON, church administrator; b. Fisherville, Ont., Can., Dec. 25, 1933; s. Elson Clare and Bertha Caroline (Schweyer) W.; m. Della Bertha Lebien, June 7, 1958; children: Jeffrey, Karen Mohr, David, Thomas, Susan. AA, Concordia Jr. Coll., Ft. Wayne, Ind., 1953; BA, Concordia Sem., St. Louis, 1955, theol. diploma, 1958; DD (hon.), Concordia Luth. Sem., Edmonton, Alta., Can., 1991. Ordained to ministry, Luth. Ch., 1958. Pastor Holy Trinity Luth. Ch., London, 1958-64, Good Shepherd Luth. Ch., Coventry, Eng., 1964-69, Luth. Mission, Liverpool, Eng., 1969-72, Faith Luth. Ch., Dunnville, Ont., 1972-78, St. Matthew Luth. Ch., Smithville, Ont., 1972-78, St. Paul's Luth. Ch., Kitchener, Ont., 1978-91; pres. ea. dist. Luth. Ch.-Can., Kitchener, 1991—; v.p. Ont. dist. Luth. Ch.-Can., 1982-88; sec. Luth. Ch.-Can., Winnipeg, Man., 1988-91; mem. bd. regents Concordia Luth. Sem., Edmonton, Alta., 1984-88, Concordia Luth. Sem., St. Catharines Ont., 1991—. Avocations: photography, golf, woodworking. Home: 76 Deerwood Crescent, Kitchener, ON Canada N2N 1R3 Office: Luth Ch Can East Dist, 275 Lawrence Ave, Kitchener, ON Canada N2M 1Y3

WINGLE, JAMES MATHEW, bishop; b. Pembroke, Ont., Can., Sept. 23, 1946; s. James Mathew and Elizabeth Anne (Coyne) W. BA, U. Windsor, 1966-69, MA, 1971-75; STL, Alfonsiano Acad., 1979-82. Ordained priest Roman Cath. Ch., 1977. Probation officer Ministry Correctional Svcs., Ont., 1970-75; priest (parish ministry) Diocese of Pembroke, Mattawa, Ont., 1977-79; asst. prof. St. Augustine's Sem., Toronto, Ont., 1987-93, pres., rector, 1987-93; consecrated bishop, 1993; bishop Diocese of Yarmouth, N.S., 1993—; sec. Toronto Sch. of Theology, 1985-87, bd. dirs. 1987-93; bd. dirs. Villa St. Joseph, Yarmouth, 1993—. Cons. and bd. dirs. Big Sisters Assn., Windsor, Ont., 1972-75. Avocations: cycling, skiing, music (organ), poetry, gardening. Office: Diocese of Yarmouth, PO Box 278, Yarmouth, NS Canada B5A 4B2

WINHAM, GEORGE KEETH, retired mental health nurse; b. Plain Dealing, La., Nov. 25, 1934; s. Henderson and Lula Mae (Kelly) W.; m. Patricia Annie Weise, Nov. 7, 1959; children: Adrian Keeth, George Kevin, Karla Ann. ADN, La. State U., 1974; BS in Health Care, Carolina Christian U., 1986. Cert. chem. dependency nurse specialist; RN, La. Staff nurse preceptor ward 10 VAMC, Shreveport, La., 1972-76, staff nurse ward 10, 1976-88; ret. Overton Brooks VA Med. Ctr., Shreveport, 1996; guest speaker in field. With USAFR, 1982-95. Mem. Drug and Alcohol Nurses Assn., Am. Soc. Pain Mgmt. Nurses, Nat. Fedn. Federal Employees (local treas. 1956, nurse of yr. 1989), Air Force Sgts. Assn., Nat. Consortium Chem. Dependency Nurses, Consol. Assn. Nurses in Substance Abuse, Masons. Baptist. Avocations: repairing antique furnitures, framing pictures. Home: 106 Lancashire Dr Bossier City LA 71111-2023

WINHAM, GILBERT RATHBONE, political science educator; b. Flushing, N.Y., May 11, 1938; s. Alfred Rathbone and Margery Rankin (Post) W.; m. Linda Joyce Tanner, June 11, 1960; children: Nina Gail, Russell Post, Karla Joyce. A.B., Bowdoin Coll., 1959; diploma in internat. law, U. Manchester, Eng., 1964; Ph.D., U. N.C., 1967. Asst. prof., then assoc. prof. polit. sci. McMaster U., Hamilton, Ont., Can., 1967-75; assoc. prof., then prof. polit. sci. Dalhousie U., Halifax, N.S., Can., 1975-92; Eric Dennis Meml. prof. govt. and polit. Sci. Dalhousie U., Halifax, N.S., 1992—, dir. Centre Fgn. Policy Studies, 1975-82, chmn. dept., 1985-88; Claude T. Bissell prof. Can.-Am. studies U. Toronto, Ont., 1990-91; cons. GATT/WTO, numerous govt. agys. in Can. and U.S.; guest scholar Brookings Instn., 1972; vis. scholar Ctr. Internat. Affairs Harvard U., 1979-80; external faculty Internat. Peace Acad., N.Y.C., 1981-85; chmn. N.S. Adjustment Adv. Coun., 1988—; mem. internat. trade adv. com. Govt. Can., 1988—, dispute settlement panels for Can.-U.S. Free Trade Agreement, NAFTA and World Trade Orgn., 1989—. Author: International Trade and the Tokyo Round Negotiation, 1986, Trading with Canada: The Canada-U.S. Free Trade Agreement, 1988, The Evolution of International Trade Agreements, 1992; editor: New Issues in International Crisis Management, 1988; mem. editorial bd. Internat. Jour., Negotiation Jour.; contbr. articles to profl. jours. Served to lt. USNR, 1959-62. Can. Coun. leave fellow, 1973-74, 82-83, Rockefeller fellow in internat. rels., 1979-80, Killam rsch. fellow, 1988—. Fellow Royal Soc. of Canada; Mem. Can. Polit. Sci. Assn. (dir. 1974-76), Am. Polit. Sci. Assn., Can. Civil Liberties Assn., Can. Inst. Internat. Affairs (chmn. Halifax br. 1978-82), Bedford Basin Yacht Club. Home: 120 Shore Dr, Bedford, NS Canada B4A 2E1 Office: Dalhousie U, Dept Polit Sci, Halifax, NS Canada B3H 4H6

WINICK, MYRON, educator, physician; b. N.Y.C., May 4, 1929; s. Charles B. and Ruth E. (Gesser) W.; m. Elaine L. Lasky, Sept. 19, 1964; children: Jonathan, Stephen. A.B., Columbia U., 1951; M.S., U. Ill., 1952; M.D., SUNY, 1956. Intern U. Pa., Phila., 1956-57; asst. resident pediatrics Cornell U. Med. Coll., N.Y.C., 1957-59; chief resident Cornell U. Med. Coll., 1959-60; attending pediatrician Stanford U. Hosp., 1963-64; asst. prof. pediatrics Cornell U. Med. Coll., N.Y.C., 1964-68, assoc. prof. pediatrics and nutrition, 1968-70, prof., 1970-71; dir. Inst. Human Nutrition Columbia U. Inst. Human Nutrition, 1972-87, prof. pediatrics, 1972-89, R.R. Williams prof. nutrition, 1973-89, R.R. Williams prof. emeritus, 1990—; pres. U. Health Scis./Chgo. Med. Sch., North Chgo., Ill., 1990-93; dir. Ctr. for Nutrition, Genetics and Human Devel., 1975-87; vis. prof. pediatrics U. Chile, Santiago, 1967; asst. attending pediatrician N.Y. Hosp., N.Y.C., 1964-68, asso. attending pediatrician, 1968-70, attending pediatrician, 1970-71; attending pediatrician Presbyn. Hosp., N.Y.C., 1972-89; cons. Pan Am. Health Orgn., 1966—. Author: Malnutrition and Brain Development, 1976; textbook Nutrition in Health and Disease, 1980; Growing Up Healthy; A Parent's Guide to Good Nutrition, 1982; For Mothers and Daughters: A Guide to Good Nutrition for Women, 1983; Your Personalized Health Profile: Choosing the Diet That's Right for You, 1985; Nutrition, Pregnancy and Early Infancy, 1989; The Fiber Prescription, 1992; editor: textbook Current Concepts in Nutrition, 1972—, Nutrition: Pre- and Postnatal Development, Vol. I, Human Nutrition: A Comprehensive Treatise, 1979, Columbia Ency. of Nutrition, 1988; contbg. editor Nutrition Revs., 1969-76; mem. editorial bd. Jour. Nutrition, 1972-76, 82-86, The Year in Metabolism (now Contemporary Metabolism), 1975—; assoc. editor Growth, 1984—; nutrition editor Cancer Prevention, 1994—. Trustee Found. for Internat. Child Health; mem. nutrition interdisciplinary cluster Pres.' Biomed. Research Panel, 1975; mem. panel on infants and children Pres.' Commn. on Mental Health, 1977; cons. Office of Tech. Assessment, U.S. Congress, 1976-78; mem. Food and Nutrition Bd. NRC, 1982-88. With USNR, 1960-62. Bank of Am.-Gianini Found. fellow Stanford, 1962; NIH Spl. fellow, 1963; recipient NIH Career Devel. award, 1968-71; E. Mead Johnson award pediatric research, 1970; Osborne and Mendel award Am. Inst. Nutrition, 1976; Agnes Higgins award March of Dimes Found., 1983. Fellow Royal Soc. Health, Am. Acad. Pediatrics; mem. AAAS, Am. Soc. Cell Biology, Soc. Developmental Biology, Harvey Soc., Soc. Pediatric Research, Royal Soc. Medicine, Brit. Nutrition Soc., Am. Inst. Nutrition, Am. Soc. Clin. Nutrition, N.Y. Acad. Scis., N.Y. Acad. Medicine, (cons.), Soc. for Exptl. Biology and Medicine, Soc. for Neurosci., Internat. Soc. for Devel. Neurosci. HOME: 112 Lakeshore Dr Putnam Valley NY 06790 Office: Columbia U Inst Human Nutrition New York NY 10027

WINIK, JAY B., writer, political scientist, consultant; b. New Haven, Feb. 8, 1957; s. Herbert Edward Winik and Marilyn Joan (Fishman) Abrams; m. Lyric Wallwork, Nov. 17, 1991. BA in Psychology cum laude, Yale U., 1980, PhD in Polit. Sci., 1993; MS in Internat. Rels. with distinction, London Sch. Econs., 1981. Arms control cons. Rand Corp., Santa Monica, Calif., 1983; chief speechwriter Ambassador Benjamin Netanyahu, N.Y.C., 1984; sr. profl. staff mem. House Com. on Armed Svcs., Washington, 1985-88; vis. fellow Ctr. for Strategic and Internat. Studies, Washington, 1988; dep. exec. dir. Def. Sec.'s Commn. on Base Realignment and Closure, Washington, 1988; legis. asst. for def. and fgn. policy Office of Sen. Charls S. Robb & Senate Com. on Fgn. Rels., Washington, 1989-91; sr. fellow Sch. Pub. Affairs U. Md., College Park, 1991—; advisor to Sec. Defense, 1993; prin. advisor for def. and fgn. policy, 1986 policy commn. Dem. Nat. Com.; assoc. staff mem. select com to investigate covert arms transactions with Iran, 1987. Author: On the Brink, 1996; editl. contbr. Wall Street Jour., N.Y. Times, Washington Post, others pubs., 1981—; dep. editor Millenium, Jour. Internat. Studies, 1981; contbr. articles to profl. jours. Grantee U.S. Inst. Peace, 1987; fellow Bradley Found. Fellow Ctr. for Strategic and Internat. Studies (adj.); mem. Coun. on Fgn. Rels. (term mem.), Coalition for Dem. Majority (bd. dirs.). Jewish. Avocation: tennis. Home: 4628 Hunt Ave Chevy Chase MD 20815-5425 Office: U Md CISSM Sch Pub Affairs College Park MD 20740

WINKEL, JUDY KAY, lawyer; b. Sibley, Iowa, Mar. 14, 1947; d. Harold Ralph and Hazel (Johnson) W. BBA, U. Iowa, 1969, JD, 1972. Bar: Iowa 1972. Govt. affairs counsel Assocs. Corp. N.Am., South Bend, Ind., 1972-76; asst. v.p. govt. affairs Assocs. Corp. N.Am., Dallas, 1976-79, v.p., 1979-89, sr. v.p., 1989—. Methodist. Avocations: piano, theatre. Office: Assocs Corp N Am PO Box 660237 250 Carpenter Frwy Dallas TX 75266-0237*

WINKEL, PAUL PATTON, JR., retired army officer, research historian; b. Chgo., July 10, 1931; s. Paul Patton and Doris Elizabeth (Menely) W.; m. Nance Jane Porter, Jan. 26, 1961 (div. Mar. 1975); children: Paul Patton III, Heather Anne Porter; m. Donice Kate Miller Durrer, Aug. 15, 1975 (div. Sept. 1983); m. Rita Louise Hoffman, Nov. 28, 1992; stepchildren: Christina Marciniak Tompkins, Julie Marciniak Mallon. BS in Mil. Sci. and Engring., U.S. Mil. Acad., 1956; MA in Pers. Adminstrn., George Washington U., 1967; MA in Internat. Studies, Am. U., 1973; grad., U.S. Army War Coll., Carlisle, Pa., 1978. Enlisted U.S. Army, 1950-52, commd. 2d lt., 1956, advanced through grades to col., 1978; plans chief, divsn. hdqs. U.S. Army Europe, Heidelberg, Germany, 1975-77, exec. officer, 1977-78; chief command and control (Allied Command Europe) Hdqs. Ctrl. Army Group, NATO, Heidelberg, 1978-80; command, control & comm. evaluation officer Orgn. Joint Chiefs Staff Dept. Def., Washington, 1980-83; chief internat. programs Dept. Army Office Dep. Chief Staff for R & D and Acquisition, Washington, 1983-84; dir. for policy and strategies Dept. Army Office Dep. Chief Staff for Info. Mgmt., Washington, 1984-85; spl. asst. to dep. dir. U.S. Army Concepts Analysis Agy., Bethesda, Md., 1985-86; ret., 1986; fin. planner MANNA Fin. Svcs. Corp., Merrifield, Va., 1986-87; project leader European programs Grumman Space Sta. Support Contract to NASA, Reston, Va., 1987-88, mgr. adminstrv. support for tech. integration, 1988-90; rsch. historian, Sterling, Va., 1993—; cons. bd. on army sci. and tech. NAS, Washington, 1991; cons. Am. Mil. U., Manassas, Va., 1993. Vice chmn. Explorer scouting Transatlantic coun. Boy Scouts Am., 1976-80; divsn. rep. Fairfax County Volleyball, 1992—; mem. Loudoun County (Va.) Rep. Com., 1992—; vol. Fairfax County Recreation, 1993—. Decorated DFC, Bronze Star medal; recipient Silver Beaver award Boy Scouts Am., 1980. Mem. Vietnam Helicopter Pilots Assn., Assn. U.S. Army, Army Aviation Assn. Am., Assn. Grads. U.S. Mil. Acad., Ia Drang Battles Vets. Assn., Army and Navy Club, Masons (3d degree). Episcopalian. Avocation: volleyball. Home and Office: 46467 Saffron Ct Sterling VA 20165

WINKEL, RAYMOND NORMAN, avionics manufacturing executive, retired naval officer; b. Flint, Mich., Dec. 8, 1928; s. Norman Martin and Evelyn Matilda (Hylen) W.; m. Ellen Stefula, Dec. 29, 1955; children: Raymond Norman, Ann, Maryellen. B.S., U.S. Naval Postgrad. Sch., Monterey, Calif., 1964; M.S., Villanova (Pa.) U., 1967; grad., Advanced Mgmt. Program, Harvard U., 1973. Enlisted in U.S. Navy, 1948, commd. ensign, designated naval aviator, 1951, advanced through grades to rear adm., 1979; service in Far East; comdg. officer Naval Electronics Systems Test and Evaluation Facility St. Inigoes, Md., 1969-71; dir. avionics U.S. Navy, 1973-76; project mgr. Navy/Marine Corps heavy lift helicopter, 1976-78; gen. mgr. Navy/industry team to develop new ship/aircraft weapon system for anti-submarine warfare LAMPS Mark III, 1978-81; ret. U.S. Navy, 1981; v.p. Washington ops. Telephonics Corp., Huntington, N.Y., 1981-82; v.p. programs and contracts Astronautics Corp. Am., Milw., 1982-94; aerospace industry cons. Heathsville, Va., 1994—. Decorated Legion of Merit, Meritorious Service medal, Air medal, Navy Achievement medal. Mem. Am. Helicopter Soc., Armed Forces Comms. and Electronics Assn., Navy Helicopter Assn., Exptl. Aircraft Assn., U.S. Naval Inst., Assn. Naval Aviation, Ret. Officers Assn., Kiwanis, Rappahannock River Yacht Club, U.S. Power Squadron. Republican. Roman Catholic. Home and Office: Island Point Rd RR 2 Box 123 Heathsville VA 22473

WINKELMAN, JAMES WARREN, hospital administrator, pathology educator; b. Bklyn., Oct. 29, 1935; s. Charles Winkelman and Augusta Spiselman; m. Sidra Levi, Sept. 1, 1957 (div. Sept. 1972); children: Elizabeth, Claudia, Recha; m. Rina Lavie, Sept. 20, 1977; 1 child, Zev. AB, U. Chgo., 1955; MD, Johns Hopkins U., 1959; MA (hon.), Harvard U., 1990. Diplomate Am. Bd. Pathology. Intern in medicine Johns Hopkins Hosp., 1959-60; resident in pathology NYU Hosp., Bellevue Hosp., 1962-65; asst. prof. pathology NYU, 1965-67; assoc. clin. prof. UCLA, 1969-80; asst. dir. Bio-Sci. Labs., Van Nuys, Calif., 1967-70, v.p., 1970-72, pres., 1972-77, bd. dirs., 1970-77; exec. v.p. Nat. Health Labs., La Jolla, Calif., 1977-80; prof. pathology SUNY Health Sci. Ctr., Syracuse, 1980-86, Harvard U. Med. Sch., Boston, 1986—; v.p., dir. clin. labs. Brigham and Women's Hosp., Boston, 1986—; cons. to numerous govt. agys. and industry; vis. prof. Soroka Med. Ctr., Beersheva, Israel, 1982. Author: Clinical Chemistry, 1974; also over 100 articles; patentee in field lab. sci. Capt. USPHS, 1960-62. Mem. Coll. Am. Pathologists, Acad. Clin. Lab. Scientists, Am. Soc. Clin. Pathology, Clin. Lab. Mgmt. Assn., Alpha Omega Alpha. Republican. Jewish. Avocations: tennis, golf, travel, classical music. Office: Brigham and Women's Hosp 75 Francis St Boston MA 02115-6110

WINKELMAN, MARY LYNN, middle school educator; b. May 22, 1950; children: Candice, Joseph. Student, U. Wis., 1968-70, BS, 1975. Cert. tchr. 1-8, Wis. 6th grade tchr. St. Williams Sch., Waukesha, Wis., 1979-90; 7th grade tchr. Waukesha Cath. Sch. Sys., St. Joseph's Middle Sch., Waukesha, 1990—. Mem. Phi Kappa Phi. Avocations: reading, softball. Office: Waukesha Cath Sch Sys St Josephs 822 N East Ave Waukesha WI 53186-4808

WINKELSTEIN, WARREN, JR, physician, educator; b. Syracuse, N.Y., July 1, 1922; s. Warren and Evelyn (Neiman) W.; children: Rebecca Winkelstein Yamin, Joshua, Shoshana; m. Veva Kerrigan, Feb. 14, 1976. BA, U. N.C., 1942; MD cum laude, Syracuse U., 1947; MPH, Columbia U., 1950. Diplomate Am. Bd. Preventive Medicine. Intern Charity Hosp., New Orleans, 1947-48; with ICA (Vietnam), 1951-53; from dir. div. communicable disease control to 1st dep. comdr. local, environ. health svcs. Erie County Health Dept., 1953-62; from assoc. prof. to prof. SUNY, Buffalo, 1962-68; prof. epidemiology, dean pub. health U. Calif., 1972—. Author: Basic Readings in Epidemiology, 1972; contbr. articles profl. jours. With AUS, 1944-46. Mem. APHA, AAAS, Internat. Am. Epidemiol. Socs., Am. Heart Assn. Home: 4239 Terrace St Oakland CA 94611-5127

WINKLE, SHARON LOUISE, library administrator; b. Cin., Nov. 29, 1950; d. John F. and Marguerite T. (Platt) W.; m. Clifford J. Smith, June 16, 1979. BS, Findlay Coll., 1972; MLS, U. Ky., 1973; MPA, U. Denver, 1984. Libr. Findlay (Ohio)-Hancock County Pub. Libr., 1973-74; deputy dir. Sandusky (Ohio) Libr., 1974-76, dir., 1976-79; libr. dir. Englewood (Colo.) Pub. Libr., 1979-89; dir. libr. and recreation svcs. City of Englewood, 1989-90; libr. dir. Mead Pub. Libr., Sheboygan, Wis., 1991—. Ohio State U. scholar, 1972; named Mktg. Student of Yr., Findlay Coll., 1972, Outstanding MPA Student U. Denver, 1984, Woman of Yr. Englewood Bus and Profl. Women, 1989. Mem. ALA, Wis. Libr. Assn., Sheboygan Rotary, Altrusa Club Sheboygan, Sheboygan C. of C. Home: 1810 N 5th St Sheboygan WI 53081-2840 Office: Mead Pub Library 710 N 8th St Sheboygan WI 53081-4505

WINKLE, SUSAN RENEE, elementary education educator; b. Rochester, Pa., May 28, 1952; d. Allen Jordan and Patricia Ielene (Whittingham) Wachob; m. Raymond Frank Winkle, Aug. 17, 1974; children: Timothy Frank, Joseph Allen. BS in Edn., Edinboro (Pa.) State U., 1974; MS in Edn., Old Dominion U., Norfolk, Va., 1992. Cert. tchr., Pa., Va. Substitute tchr. Norfolk City Schs., 1975; children's shoes clk. Kauffmann's Store, Rochester, Pa., 1982-84; tutor Rochester, 1984; kindergarten tchr. Kinder-care Day Care, Newport News, Va., 1984-86, daycare dir., 1986; transitional 1st grade tchr. Newport News Schs., 1986-93, REACH reading tchr., 1993—; mentor Christopher Newport U., Newport News, 1992; workshop facilitator. Contbg. author: K/T-1 Cross Reference Curriculum Guide, 1990. Active Apostles Luth. Ch., Gloucester, Va., 1987—. Primary Block grantee, 1994. Mem. ASCD, Odyssey of the Mind (judge, ofcl.), Va. Reading Coun., Newport News Reading Coun., So. Early Childhood Assn., Tidewater Assn. Early Childhood Edn. (2d v.p. 1994), Sch. Improvement Team. Avocations: gardening, reading. Home: 1787 Chiskiake St Gloucester Point VA 23062-2403 Office: Richneck Elem Sch 205 Tyner Dr Newport News VA 23602-1660

WINKLE, WILLIAM ALLAN, music educator; b. Rapid City, S.D., Oct. 10, 1940; s. Curis Powell and June Ada (Alexander) W.; m. Carola Kay Croll, June 16, 1968; children: Brenda, Rachelle. MusB, Huron U., 1962; MA, U. Vt., 1971; ArtsD, U. Northern Colo., 1976; postgrad., North Tex. State U. Dir. choral and band Arlington (S.D.) High Sch., 1962-64; band dir. DeSmet (S.D.) High Sch., 1964-67; coord. music Huron (S.D.) Pub. Schs., 1967-69; head of instrumental music Huron Coll., 1969-71; dir. bands, prof. music Chadron (Nebr.) State Coll., 1971—; instr. tuba music camp S.D. State U., Brooking, 1969-71, Internat. Music Camp, Dunseith, Nebr., 1977—, high sch. sessions U. Vt., Burlington, 1964-71; tubist, bassoonist Huron Symphony/Huron Mcpl., 1957-69, Nebr. Panhandle Symphony & Symphonia, Chadron, 1971—; tubist Blue Jean Philharmonic, Estes Park, Colo., 1960-64, Internat. Brass Quintet, 1985—; conductor, tour dir. Am. Youth Symphony and Chorus, European Tours, 1967-78; performing artist, clinician Yamaha Music Corp. USA, 1977—. Author: List of Tuba/Euphonium Solos, 1984; co-author: Art of Tuba, 1992; contbr. articles to mags. Moderator, trustee, deacon, conf. bd. dirs. United Ch. of Christ, 1974-90. Recipient Freedom Found. award, 1972, Chadron State Coll. Rsch. Inst. 5 awards, 1974-78. Mem. Chadron C. of C., Nebr. State Bandmasters (dist. VI and coll. rep. 1978-84), Internat. Music Camp (bd. dirs. 1980-86, Disting. Svc. award 1987), Tubist Universal Brotherhood Assn. (internat. rep. 1971—, Nat. Sem. award 1975, 77), Music Educators Nat. Conf., Internat. Assn. Jazz Educators, Concert Bands Am., Nat. Band Assn., Coll. Band Dirs. Nat. Assn., Phi Beta Mu, Kappa Kappa Psi, Kappa Delta Pi.

Republican. Avocation: cycling. Home: 318 Ann St Chadron NE 69337-2412 Office: Chadron State Coll 10th Main Chadron NE 69337

WINKLER, ALLAN MICHAEL, history educator; b. Cin., Jan. 7, 1945; s. Henry Ralph and Clare (Sapadin) W.; div.; children: Jennifer, David; m. Sara Penhale, May 2, 1992. BA, Harvard U., 1966; MA, Columbia U., 1967; PhD, Yale U., 1974. Vol. Peace Corps, The Philippines, 1967-69; instr., asst. prof. history Yale U., New Haven, 1973-78; asst. prof., assoc. prof. U. Oreg., Eugene, 1979-86; prof. history Miami U., Oxford, Ohio, 1986—, chmn. dept., 1986-95; prof. Helsinki (Finland) U., 1978-79, U. Amsterdam (Netherlands), 1984-85, U. Nairobi (Kenya), 1995-96. Author: The Politics of Propaganda, 1978, Modern America, 1985, Home Front, U.S.A., 1986, The American People, 1986, The Recent Past, 1989, Life Under a Cloud, 1993, America: Pathways to the Present, 1994, Cassie's War, 1994. Fulbright grantee, 1978-79, 84-85, 95-96, NEH grantee, 1981-82. Mem. Am. Hist. Assn., Orgn. Am. Historians, Am. Studies Assn., Harvard Club (Cin.). Avocations: running, bicycling, squash, tennis, golf. Home: 925 Cedar Dr Oxford OH 45056-2416 Office: Miami U Dept History Oxford OH 45056

WINKLER, DOLORES EUGENIA, retired hospital administrator; b. Milw., Aug. 10, 1929; d. Charles Peter and Eugenia Anne (Zamka) Kowalski; m. Donald James Winkler, Aug. 18, 1951; 1 child, David John. Grad., Milw. Bus. Inst., 1949. Acct. Curative Rehab. Ctr., Milw., 1949-60; staff acct. West Allis (Wis.) Meml. Hosp., 1968-70, chief acct., 1970-78, reimbursement analyst, 1978-85, dir. budgets and reimbursement, 1985-95; ret., 1995; mem. adv. coun./fin. com. Tau Home Health Care Agy., Milw., 1981-83. Mem. Healthcare Fin. Mgmt. Assn. (pres. 1989-90, Follmer Bronze award 1980, Reeves Silver award 1986, Muncie Gold award 1989, medal of honor 1993), Inst. Mgmt. Accts. (pres. 1983-84, nat. dir. 1986-88, pres. Mid Am. Regional Coun. 1988-89, award of excellence 1989), Beta Chi Rho (pres. 1948). Avocations: travel, photography, golf. Home: 12805 W Honey Ln New Berlin WI 53151-2652

WINKLER, GUNTHER, biotechnology executive, drug development expert; b. Laa Thaya, Noe, Austria, Aug. 20, 1957; came to U.S., 1986; s. Kurt and Irmgard (Lahner) W.; m. Maria Toifl, Sept. 11, 1979; children: Claudia, Marc. MS in Biochemistry, U. Vienna, Austria, 1983, PhD in Biochemistry, 1986. Rsch. assoc. Inst. Virology U. Vienna, 1982-86; postdoctoral fellow U. Medicine and Dentistry of N.J., Piscataway, 1986-88; rsch. scientist Biogen, Inc., Cambridge, Mass., 1988-91, dir. med. ops., 1991—; program exec. Biogen, Inc., Cambridge, 1995—; contbr. to sci. confs.; expert presentations on drug devel. strategies and mgmt. of clin. studies, chair clin. confs. Contbr. articles to profl. jours. Recipient Outstanding Achievement award Austrian Soc. Microbiology, 1986. Mem. Am. Mgmt. Assn., Drug Info. Assn., Assocs. Clin. Pharmacology. Achievement include research in virology dealing with structure function relationship of proteins, HIV, flaviviruses; industrial research in CD4, CD4-toxins, complement proteins; 3 patent applications; international clinical development of Hirulog and Beta-Interferon from phase I to phase III and preparations for FDA and internat. market approvals; pre-clinical and clinical development of anti-inflammatory drugs. Home: 8 Churchill Rd Winchester MA 01890-1008 Office: Biogen Inc 14 Cambridge Ctr Cambridge MA 02142

WINKLER, HENRY FRANKLIN, actor; b. N.Y.C., Oct. 30, 1945; s. Harry Irving and Ilse Anna Maria (Hadra) W.; m. Stacey Weitzman, May 5, 1978; 1 dau., Zoe Emily. Student, Emerson Coll., 1963-67, D.H.L., 1978; student, Yale Sch. Drama, 1967-70. With Yale Repertory Theatre, 1970-71; founder New Haven Free Theatre, 1968, Off The Wall N.Y., improvisation co., 1972; tchr. drama UCLA Adult Extension. Off-Broadway shows, 1972-73, Cin. Playhouse, 1973; films include The Lords of Flatbush, 1972, Crazy Joe, 1974, Heroes, 1977, The One and Only, 1977, Night Shift, 1983; starred in TV series Happy Days, 1973-84, Monty, 1994, Mr. Sunshine; appeared in TV movie An American Christmas Carol, 1979 (ABC), Absolute Strangers, 1991 (CBS), The Only Way Out, 1994 (ABC), Truman Capote's One Christmas, 1994 (NBC), The Dog Heinut, 1995 (CBS); prodr. Sightings; exec. producer TV program Who Are the Debolts and Where Did They Get Nineteen Kids, TV series for ABC Ryan's Four, 1983, TV movie Scandal Sheet, 1984, MacGyver, 1985, producer, host home video Strong Kids, Safe Kids, 1985, PBS animated spl. Happy Ever After, 1985, Two Daddies to Love Me, 1988; producer ABC After Sch. Spl. Losing a Sister, 1988; pres. Fair Dinkum Prodns., Hollywood, Calif., 1979—, Winkler-Daniels Prodns., Hollywood, 1987-91; producer TV program Run, Don't Walk for own co. JZM Prodns., 1981; dir. TV movie A Smokey Mountain Christmas, 1986, feature film Memories of Me, 1988, Cop and a Half, 1992. Named Best Actor in Comedy Series, Photoplay mag. 1976-77, recipient Golden Globe award 1976, 77, 78; named King of Baccus, Mardi Gras, New Orleans 1977, Emmy nominee 1975, 76, 77; recipient Golden Plate award Am. Acad. Achievement 1980, Daytime Emmy nomination best dir. All The Kids Do It, produced for JZM Prodns., 1985; Sorrisi e Canzoni Telegatto award (Italian TV award) 1980; nat. spokesperson United Friends of the Children, 1982—. Recipient Humanitarian award Women in Film, 1988; named hon. youth chmn. Epilepsy Found.; chmn. Toys for Tots, 1977. Mem. AFTRA, Screen Actors Guild, Actors Equity. Office: care Richard Grant & Assoc 8484 Wilshire Blvd Ste 500 Beverly Hills CA 90211-3220

WINKLER, HENRY RALPH, retired academic administrator, historian; b. Waterbury, Conn., Oct. 27, 1916; s. Jacob and Ethel (Rieger) W.; m. Clare Sapadin, Aug. 18, 1940; children—Allan Michael, Karen Jean; m. Beatrice Ross, Jan. 28, 1973. A.B., U. Cin., 1938, M.A., 1940; Ph.D., U. Chgo., 1947; hon. degrees, Lehigh U., 1974, Rutgers U., 1977, No. Ky. U., 1978, St. Thomas Inst., 1979, Hebrew Union Coll., 1980, Xavier U., 1981, U. Akron, 1984, U. Cin., 1987, Thomas More Coll., 1989. Instr. U. Cin., 1939-40; asst. prof. Roosevelt Coll., 1946-47; mem. faculty Rutgers U., 1947-77, prof. history, 1958-77, chmn. dept., 1960-64; dean Faculty Liberal Arts, 1967, vice provost, 1968-70, acting provost, 1970, v.p. for acad. affairs, 1970-72, sr. v.p. for acad. affairs, 1972-76, exec. v.p., 1976-77; exec. v.p. U. Cin., 1977, pres., 1977-84, pres. emeritus, 1984—, Univ. prof. history, 1977-86, prof. emeritus, 1986—; mng. editor Am. Hist. Rev., 1964-68; vis. prof. Bryn Mawr Coll., 1959-60, Harvard, summer 1964, Columbia, summer 1967; faculty John Hay Fellows Inst. Humanities, 1960-65; bd. overseers Hebrew Union Coll., 1984—. Author: The League of Nations Movement in Great Britain, 1914-19, 1952, Great Britain in the Twentieth Century, 1960, 2d edit., 1966; editor: (with K.M. Setton) Great Problems in European Civilization, 1954, 2d edit., 1966, Twentieth-Century Britain, 1977, Paths Not Taken: British Labour and International Policy in the Nineteen Twenties, 1994; mem. editorial bd. Historian, 1958-64, Liberal Edn., 1986—; mem. adv. bd. Partisan Rev., 1972-79; contbr. articles to jours., revs. Nat. chmn. European history advanced placement com. Coll. Entrance Exam. Bd., 1960-64; mem. Nat. Commn. on Humanities in Schs., 1967-68, Am. specialist Eastern Asia, 1968; exec. com. Conf. on Brit. Studies, 1968-75; chmn. bd. Nat. Humanities Faculty, 1970-73; chmn. adv. com. on history Coll. Entrance Exam. Bd., 1977-80; mem. council on acad. affairs, mem. bd. trustees, chmn., 1982-84; pres. Highland Park (N.J.) Bd. Edn., 1962-63; mem. exec. com. Nat. Assn. State Univs. and Land-Grant Colls., 1978-81, mem. Cin. Lit. Club, 1978, pres., 1993—; bd. dirs. Am. Council on Edn., 1979-81; trustee Seasengood Good Govt. Found., 1979—, pres., 1991-93; trustee Thomas More Coll., 1986-93; mem. Ohio Indsl. Tech. and Enterprise Bd., 1983-89; bd. dirs. Nat. Civic League, 1986—, Planning Accreditation Bd., 1988—; mem. adv coun. Clin. Valley State Coll., Ohio Humanities Coun., 1994— With USNR, 1943-46. Recipient Lifetime Achievement award N.Am. Conf. on Brit. Studies, 1995. Mem. Am. Hist. Assn., Phi Beta Kappa, Tau Kappa Alpha, Phi Alpha Theta. Clubs: Comml., Bankers, Cin., Lit. Office: U Cin 571 Langsam Library Cincinnati OH 45221

WINKLER, HOWARD LESLIE, investment banker, stockbroker, business consultant; b. N.Y.C., Aug. 16, 1950; s. Martin and Magda (Stark) W.; m. Robin Lynn Richards, Sept. 12, 1976; 1 child, David Menachem. AA in Mktg., Los Angeles City Coll., 1973, AA in Bus. Data Processing, 1977, AA in Bus. Mgmt., 1981. Sr. cons. Fin. Cons. Inc., Los Angeles, 1972-81; asst. v.p. Merrill Lynch, Inc., Los Angeles, 1981-83; v.p. Drexel, Burnham, Lambert, Inc., Beverly Hills, Calif., 1983-84; pres. Howard Winkler Investments, Beverly Hills, Calif., 1984-90, Landmark Fin. Group, L.A., 1990—; ptnr. N.W.B. Assocs., L.A., 1988-91; chmn. bd. United Cmty. and Housing Devel. Corp., L.A., 1986—; bd. dirs. Earth Products Internat., Inc., Kansas City, Kans., 1992, Fed. Home Loan Bank of San Francisco, 1991-93. Nat. polit. editor B'nai B'rith Messenger, 1986-95. Mem. Calif. Rep. Cent. Com., 1985-93; mem. L.A. County Rep. Cent. Com., 1985-92, chmn. 45th Assembly Dist., 1985-90; mem. Rep. Senatorial Inner Circle, 1986—, Rep. Presdl. Task Force, 1985— (Legion of Merit award 1992); mem. Rep. Eagles, 1988-92; Nat. Rep. Senatorial Com., 1986—, Golden Circle Calif., 1986-92, GOP Platform Planning Com. at Large del., 1992, 96; del. to GOP nat conv., Houston, 1992; Calif. chmn. Jack Kemp for Pres., 1988, mem. nat. steering com. Bush-Quayle '88, 1987, nat. exec. com. Bush-Quayle '92, 1991; mil. adminstrv. supr. CID US Army, 1969-72, SE Asia; legis. and civic action Agudath Israel Calif., 1985—; mem. L.A. County Narcotics and Dangerous Drugs Commn., 1988—; trustee, sec.-treas. Minority Health Professions Edn. Found., 1989-94; program chmn. Calif. Lincoln Clubs Polit. Action Com., 1987-88; state co-chmn. Pete Wilson for Gov. Campaign, 1989, John Seymour for Lt. Gov. Campaign, 1989-90; chpt. pres. Calif. Congress of Reps., 1989-93; chmn. Claude Parrish for Bd. of Equalization, 1989-90; founder, dir. Community Rsch. & Info. Ctr.; mem. fin. com. John Seymour for Senate '92, 1991. Decorated Legion of Merit; recipient Cmty. Svc. award Agudath Israel Calif., 1986, Pres.'s Cmty. Leadership award, 1986, Disting. Cmty. Svc. U.S. Senator Pete Wilson, 1986, Calif. Gov.'s Leadership award, 1986, Cmty. Svc. award U.S. Congresswoman Bobbi Fiedler, 1986, Resolution of Commendation Calif. State Assembly, 1986, Outstanding Cmty. Svc. Commendation Los Angeles County Bd. Suprs., 1986, 90, Outstanding Citizenship award City of Los Angeles, 1986, 90, Cmty. Leadership award Iranian-Jewish Community L.A., 1990, Resolution of Commendation, State of Calif., 1992, Cmty. Svc. Commendation, 1993, Rep. Senatorial Medal of Freedom award, Sentorial Inner Circle, 1994, Commendation L.A. County Bd. Suprs., 1994. Mem. Calif. Young Reps., Calif. Rep. Assembly, VFW, Jewish War Veterans. Jewish. Avocations: philanthropy, family time. Office: PO Box 480454 Los Angeles CA 90048-1454

WINKLER, IRWIN, motion picture producer; b. N.Y.C., May 28, 1931; s. Sol and Anna Winkler. BA, NYU, 1955. Mailroom messenger William Morris Agy., N.Y.C., 1955-62; motion picture producer, owner Winkler Films, Culver City, Calif., 1982—; pres., Chartoff-Winkler Prodns., 1966—. Producer: Rocky, 1976 (10 Acad. award nominations, winner 3 including Best Picture, Los Angeles Film Critics award for best picture), They Shoot Horses Don't They, 1969 (9 Acad. award nominations), Nickelodeon, 1976, The Gambler, 1974, Up the Sandbox, 1972, The New Centurions, 1972, Point Blank, 1967, Double Trouble, 1967, Leo the Last, 1970 (Best Dir. award Cannes Film Festival, Belgrade Film Festival), The Strawberry Statement, 1970 (Jury prize Cannes Film Festival), The Split, 1968, Breakout, 1975, Believe in Me, 1971, The Gang That Couldn't Shoot Straight, 1971, The Mechanic, 1972, Busting, 1974, S.P.Y.S, 1974, Peeper, 1975, New York, New York, 1977, Valentino, 1977, Uncle Joe Shannon, 1978, Comes a Horseman, 1978, Rocky II, 1979, Raging Bull, 1980 (8 Acad. award nominations, winner 2, Los Angeles Film Critics award for best picture), Rocky III, 1981, True Confessions, 1981, Author, Author, 1982, The Right Stuff, 1983 (8 Acad. award nominations), Rocky IV, 1984, Revolution, 1985, 'Round Midnight, 1986 (2 Acad. award nomiations, Acad. award Best Original Score), Betrayed, 1988 (Chgo. Film Festival Lifetime Irwin Achievement award 1987), Goodfellas, 1990 (6 Acad. award nominationThe Net, 1995, The Juror, 1996; dir, writer: The Net, 1995, Guilty by Suspicion,1991.s, winner 1, Brit. Acad. award Best Picture, N.Y. Film Critics Best Picture, L.A. Film Critics Best Picture), Rocky V, 1990, Music Box, 1990 (Golden Bear award for best film Berlin Film Festival); writer/dir.: Guilty by Suspicion, 1991 (U.S. selection Cannes Film Festival); producer/dir.: Night and the City, 1992 (N.Y. Film Festival, London Film Festival), The Net, 1995; retrospectives Brit. Film Inst., 1989, Chgo. Film Festival, 1989, Mus. Modern Art, N.Y.C., 1990, L.A. County Mus. Art, 1992. Served with U.S. Army, 1951-53. Named Commander d'Artes et de Lettres, French Govt. Minister of Culture, 1985. Mem. Am. Film Inst. (bd. govs.), Prodrs. Guild Am. (bd. dirs.). Office: Winkler Films 211 S Beverly Dr Ste 200 Beverly Hills CA 90212-3828*

WINKLER, JOANN MARY, secondary school educator; b. Savanna, Ill., Dec. 17, 1955; d. Donald Edgar and Genevieve Eleanor (Withhart) Winkler; m. Russell Arthur Ehlers, May 25, 1990. BS in Art Edn., No. Ill. U., 1979; MA in Art Edn., N.E. Mo. State U., 1984. Tchr. art, chmn. dept. art Clinton (Iowa) H.S., 1979—; Coll. for Kids instr. Area Edn. Agy. #9, Clinton, summers, 1986—, Davenport, summers, 1987—; instr. St. Ambrose U., Clinton, 1990, Mt. St. Clare Coll., Clinton, 1993—. Costume designer Utah Mus. Theatre, "Two by Two," 1987; exhibited in group shows at Clinton Art Assn., 1990-93. Judge Art in the Park, Clinton, 1988, 93; co. mgr. Utah Mus. Theager, Ogden, 1987; founding bd. dirs. Art's Alive, Clinton, 1985-86; bd. dirs. Gateway Contemporary Ballet, Clinton, 1987-89; founding com. mem. Louis Sullivan's Van Allen Bldg. Jr. Mus., Clinton, 1991-93. Recipient Gold Key Group award Clinton Sch. Bd., 1990, Gold Key Individual award, 1989; R.I. Sch. Design scholar, 1989, Alliance for Ind. Colls. of Art scholar, summers 1988. Mem. NEA, Ill. Art Edn. Assn., Chgo. Art Inst., Clinton Art Assn., Art Educators of Iowa, Nat. Art Edn. Assn., PEO. Avocations: swimming, travel, theater. Home: 722 Melrose Ct Clinton IA 52732-5508 Office: Clinton High Sch 817 8th Ave S Clinton IA 52732-5616

WINKLER, JOSEPH CONRAD, former recreational products manufacturing executive; b. Newark, May 20, 1916; s. Charles and Mollie (Abrams) W.; m. Geraldine M. Borok, Sept. 20, 1953; children: Charles H., David J. B.S., NYU, 1941. Gen. mgr. Indsl. Washing Machine Corp., New Brunswick, N.J., 1941-48; controller Mojud Corp., N.Y.C., 1948-52; controller, asst. treas. Barbizon Corp., N.Y.C., 1952-57; controller Ideal Toy Corp., N.Y.C., 1957-58; dir. fin. and adminstrn. Ideal Toy Corp., 1960-62, v.p. fin., 1962-68, sr. v.p. fin., 1968-78, exec. v.p., chief operating officer, dir., 1978-81, pres., dir., 1981-83; exec. in residence, mem. bus. adv. coun. Sch. Bus. Adminstrn., Montclair (N.J.) State U., 1983-90; controller McGregor-Doniger, Inc., N.Y.C., 1958-59; dir. Ideal of Australia Ltd., Melbourne, 1963-82, Ideal of Canada Ltd., Toronto, 1963-82, Ideal of Japan Ltd., Tokyo and Kiowa, 1963-80, Ideal Toy Co. Ltd., High Wycombe and Wokingham, Eng., 1966-82, Arxon Spiel & Freizeit GmbH, Rotgau, Germany, 1968-82, Perfekta Ltd. and Hollis Industries Ltd., Hong Kong, 1970-74, Ideal Loisirs S.A., Paris, 1972-82. Mem. editorial rev. bd. Issues in Internat. Bus., 1985—. Committeeman, troop treas. Boy Scouts Am., Tenafly, N.J., 1965-71; bd. dirs. N.Y. League Hard of Hearing, 1982-88; active Nat. Roster Sci. and Splized. Pers., War Manpower Commn., 1941-46. Served with Office Statis. Control USAAF, 1945. Mem. Fin. Execs. Inst. Home: 3546 S Ocean Blvd Apt 605 Palm Beach FL 33480-5720

WINKLER, LEE B., business consultant; b. Buffalo, Dec. 31, 1925; s. Jack W. and Caroline (Marienthal) W.; children: James, Cristina Ehrlich, Richard Ehrlich Jr.; m. Maria Mal Verde. B.S. cum laude, NYU, 1945, M.S. cum laude, 1947. Mgr. LBW, Inc. (formerly Winkler Assocs. Ltd.), N.Y.C., 1948-58; pres. Winkler Assocs. Ltd., Beverly Hills, Calif., and N.Y.C., 1958—; exec. dir. Global Bus. Mgmt. Inc., Beverly Hills, 1967—; v.p. Bayly Martin & Fay Inc., N.Y.C., 1965-68, John C. Paige & Co., N.Y.C., 1968-71; cons. Albert G. Ruben Co., Beverly Hills, 1971—. Served with AUS, 1943-45. Decorated chevalier comdr. Order Holy Cross Jerusalem, also spl. exec. asst., charge d'affaires, 1970; chevalier comdr. Sovereign Order Cyprus, 1970. Mem. Nat. Acad. TV Arts and Scis., Nat. Acad. Recording Arts and Scis., Beverly Hills C. of C., Phi Beta Kappa, Beta Gamma Sigma, Mu Gamma Tau, Psi Chi Omega. Office: 15250 Ventura Blvd Sherman Oaks CA 91403 *In the final analysis, the bottom line, if you will—the only thing that truly matters in life are those friends and family that hold you dear to them. Success, and its attendant monies, rise and fall like the tides, and even vanish at times, but earned love is as constant as the earth's rotation is independent of the tides.*

WINKLER, PAUL FRANK, JR., astrophysicist, educator; b. Nashville, Nov. 10, 1942; s. Paul Frank and Estelle (Pye) W.; m. Geraldine Huck, Aug. 20, 1966 (div. 1979); children: Katharine Estelle, Johanna Pye; m. Janet Pippit Beers, June 25, 1983; stepchildren: Sarah Creighton Beers, Nathan Pippitt Beers. B.S., Calif. Inst. Tech., 1964; A.M., Harvard U., 1965, Ph.D., 1970. From instr. to prof. physics Middlebury Coll., Vt., 1969—, chmn. dept., 1980-88, William R. Kenan Jr. prof. physics, 1984-87, chmn. nat. scis. div., 1988-93, asst. to pres. for sci. planning, 1993—; vis. scientist MIT, Cambridge, 1973-74, 78-80; sr. vis. fellow Inst. Astronomy U. Cambridge, 1985-86; vis. resident astronomer Cerro Tololo InterAm. Observatory, La Serena, Chile, 1990-91; vis. fellow Joint Inst. for Laboratory Astrophysics, U. Colo., Boulder, 1991. Contbr. articles to profl. jours. NSF fellow, 1965-69, Alfred P. Sloan Found. fellow, 1976-80. Mem. Am. Phys. Soc., Am. Astron. Soc., Internat. Astron. Union, Coun. on Undergraduate Rsch. Office: Middlebury Coll Dept Physics Middlebury VT 05753

WINKLER, SHELDON, dentist, educator; b. N.Y.C., Jan. 25, 1932; s. Ben and Lillian (Barsh) W.; m. Sandra M. Cohen, Aug. 13, 1961; children: Mitchell, Lori. BA, Washington Sq. Coll., 1953; DDS, NYU, 1956. Asst. prof. denture prosthesis NYU Coll. Dentistry, N.Y.C., 1958-61, 66-68, rsch. asst. prof., 1962-63; dir. materials rsch. Consol. Metal Products Industries Inc., Albany, N.Y., 1963-65, cons. materials rsch., 1966-68; asst. prof. removable prosthodontics sch. dentistry SUNY, Buffalo, 1968-70; assoc. prof. SUNY, 1970-79; prof., chmn. dept. prosthodontics Temple U. Sch. Dentistry, Phila., 1979-86, 94—, asst. dean for advanced studies, continuing edn./rsch., 1987-89, acting asst. dean, 1993-95; asst. dir., vis. dentist, dental dept. N.Y. U. Med. Center, Goldwater Meml. Hosp., N.Y.C., 1966-68; attending in prosthodontics E.J. Meyer Meml. Hosp., Buffalo, 1975-79; postgrad. instr. First Dist. Dental Soc. N.Y., N.Y.C., 1963—; cons. Coe Labs., Chgo., 1967-87, Harkness Center, Buffalo, Rosa Coplon Home and Infirmary, Buffalo, 1970-79, Erie Community Coll., Buffalo, 1979—, Lever Bros. Co., N.Y.C., 1981—, VA Hosp., Phila., 1989—; lectr. dept. dental hygiene N.Y.C. Community Coll., 1967-68. Author: (with A. Davidoff and M.H.M. Lee) Dentistry for the Special Patient: The Aged, Chronically Ill and Handicapped, 1972, Essentials of Complete Denture Prosthodontics, 1979, 2d edit., 1988; editor: Resins in Dentistry, 1975, Complete Dentures, 1977, Removable Prosthodontics, 1984; editor Jour. Implant Dentistry, 1990—; contbr. articles to profl. lit.; co-designer McGowan-Winkler complete denture trays. Served as capt. AUS, 1956-58, 61-62. Recipient Outstanding Layman award Vocat. Tech. Alumni and Student Assn., SUNY, Buffalo, 1974, Internat. Edn. award Internat. Congress Oral Implantologists, 1992, journalism award Internat. Coll. Dentists, 1993. Fellow Am. Coll. Dentists, Greater N.Y. Acad. Prosthodontics; mem. ADA, Internat. Assn. Dental Rsch., Am. Assn. Dental Schs., Am. Acad. Implant Prosthodontics, Sci. Rsch. Soc. Am., Acad. Plastics Rsch., Am. Prosthodontic Soc., Am. Soc. Geriatric Dentistry, Internat. Congress of Oral Implantologists, Sigma Xi, Sigma Epsilon Delta, Omicron Kappa Upsilon. Home: 1224 Liberty Bell Dr Cherry Hill NJ 08003-2759 Office: Sch Dentistry Temple U Philadelphia PA 19140

WINKS, ROBIN WILLIAM, history educator; b. West Lafayette, Ind., Dec. 5, 1930; s. Evert McKinley and Jewell (Sampson) W.; m. Avril Flockton, Sept. 27, 1952; children: Honor Leigh, Eliot Myles. BA magna cum laude, U. Colo., 1952, MA, 1953; PhD with distinction, Johns Hopkins U., 1957; MA (hon.), Yale U., 1967; DLitt (hon.), U. Nebr., 1976, U. Colo., 1987; MA (hon.), Oxford U., 1992; DPhil, Westminster Coll., 1995. From instr. to Randolph W. Townsend prof. history Yale U., New Haven, 1957—, dir. office of spl. projects and founds., 1974-76, master Berkeley Coll., 1977-90; Eastman prof. Oxford U., 1992-93, chair studies in environment, 1993-96, chair dept. history, 1996—. Author: Canada and the U.S., 1960, The Cold War, 1964, Historiography of the British Empire-Commonwealth, 1966, History of Malaysia, 1967, Age of Imperialism, 1969, Pastmasters, 1969; The Historian as Detective, 1969, A Forty-Year Minuet, 1970, The Blacks in Canada, 1971, Slavery, 1972, An American's Guide to Britain, 1977, Other Voices, Other Views, 1978, Relevance of Canadian History, 1979, Western Civilization, 1979, Detective Fiction, 1980, Modus Operandi, 1982, History of Civilization, 1984, Cloak and Gown, 1987, Asia in Western Fiction, 1990, Frederick Billings, 1991, The Imperial Revolution, 1994. Cultural attache U.S. Embassy, London, 1969-71; chair Nat. Park System Adv. Bd., Washington, 1981-83, bicentennial com. for Internat. Confs. of Americanists Dept. State, 1974-77. Smith-Mundt prof. U. Malaya, 1962; Inst. Commonwealth Studies at U. London fellow, 1966-67; Guggenheim fellow, 1976-77; grantee Social Sci. Rsch. Coun., 1959, 75; Resident scholar Sch. Am. Rsch., 1985, 91, 94. Fellow Royal Hist. Soc., Explorers Club; mem. Am. Hist. Assn., Can. Hist. Assn., Royal Commonwealth Soc. (life), Yale Club (N.Y.C.), Athenaeum, Spl. Forces Club. Office: Yale U Dept History PO Box 1504 A New Haven CT 06506-1504

WINN, ALBERT CURRY, clergyman; b. Ocala, Fla., Aug. 16, 1921; s. James Anderson and Elizabeth (Curry) W.; m. Grace Neely Walker, Aug. 29, 1944; children: Grace Walker (Mrs. Stewart E. Ellis), James Anderson, Albert Bruce Curry, Randolph Axson. A.B., Davidson Coll., 1942, LL.D., 1968; B.D., Union Theol. Sem., Va., 1945, Th.D., 1956; Th.M., Princeton Theol. Sem., 1949; LL.D., Stillman Coll., 1975. Ordained to ministry Presbyn. Ch., 1945; asst. prof. Davidson Coll., 1946-47; pastor Potomac Rural Parish, Va., 1948-53; prof. Bible Stillman Coll., 1953-60; prof. theology Louisville Presbyn. Theol. Sem., 1960-73, pres., 1966-73; pastor 2d Presbyn. Ch., Richmond, Va., 1974-81, N. Decatur Presbyn. Ch., Decatur, Ga., 1981-86; Moderator Presbyn. Synod Ala., 1958, Presbyn. Synod Ky., 1969, Gen. Assembly, Presbyn. Ch. in U.S., 1979; vis. prof. Union Theol. Sem. in Va., 1987, Columbia Theol. Sem., 1987, Louisville Presbyn. Theol. Sem., 1988; interim pastor Cen. Presbyn. Ch., Atlanta, 1989-90, St. Andrews Presbyn. Ch., Tucker, Ga., 1993-94. Author: Layman's Bible Commentary on Acts, 1960, The Worry and Wonder of Being Human, 1966, Where Do I Go From Here, 1972, Proclamation Two: Epiphany, 1980, A Sense of Mission, 1981, Christ the Peacemaker, 1982, Plain Talk about the Apostles' Creed, 1985, The Christian Primer, 1990, Ain't Gonna Study War No More, 1993. Chmn. trustees Stillman Coll., 1965-70. Served as chaplain USNR, 1945-46. Mem. Phi Beta Kappa, Beta Theta Pi, Omicron Delta Kappa. Office: 2425 Harrington Dr Decatur GA 30033-4903

WINN, EDWARD BURTON, lawyer; b. Dallas, Sept. 23, 1920; s. Edward Frost and Verdie Catherine (Robbins) W.; m. Conchita Elisa Hassell, June 1, 1945; children—Edward Arthur, David Burton, William Hassell, Richard Wellington, Alan Randolph. B.A., U. Tex., 1942; LL.B., Yale, 1948. Bar: Tex. bar 1948. Since practiced in Dallas; ptnr. Lane, Savage, Counts & Winn., 1958-81, Winn, Beaudry & Virden, 1981-91, Winn, Beaudry & Winn, L.L.P., 1992—; Pres. Dallas Jr. Bar Assn., 1951, Jr. Bar Tex., 1953, Dallas Estate Council, 1954-55; adv. council Dallas Community Chest Trust Fund, 1965-68; mem. staff armed forces preparedness subcom U.S. Senate, 1951; chmn. Inst. on Wills and Probate, Southwestern Legal Found., 1966—. Coauthor: Texas Estate Administration, How to Live and Die with Texas Probate, 1985; Contbr. articles to profl. jours. Chmn. Dallas County Profl. and Bus. Men for Kennedy-Johnson, 1960; vice chmn. Dallas County Democratic Exec. Com., 1964-66; Bd. dirs. Operation LIFT, 1962-82; trustee Nat. Pollution Control Found., Southwestern Legal Found., 1986—. Served to lt. USNR, 1942-46, ETO. Decorated with the Admirals' Commendations, 1943; recipient William W. Treat award Nat. Coll. Probate Judges, 1985. Fellow Am. Coll. Probate Counsel (pres. 1974-75), Am. Coll. of Trust and Estate Council; mem. ABA (bd. govs. 1985-88, council 1955-84, sect. chmn. 1963-64, sect. real property probate and trust law, ho. of dels. 1965-66, 78-84, 85-90, conf. of sect. and div. dels. 1982-84), Dallas Bar Assn. (dir. 1959-61), Dallas UN Assn. (pres.), UN Assn. of U.S. (gov. 1980-84, dir., pres. Tex. div. 1967-71), State Bar Tex. (chmn. sect. real estate, probate and trust law 1962-63), Am. Bar Found., Tex. Bar Found., Dallas Council World Affairs (pres. young execs. group 1959-60, bd. dirs. 1958-73), Yale Law Sch. Alumni Assn. N. Tex. (pres. 1962-66, regional rep. 1966-72), U. Tex. Ex-Students Assn. Dallas (pres. 1963-64), Dallas Club, Dallas Knife and Fork Club (pres. elect 1994-95, bd. dirs.), Calyx Club, Rotary (Park Cities club, pres. elect 1995—), Phi Kappa Sigma (pres. Sigma chpt. 1941-42), Phi Eta Sigma. Home: 6712 Prestonshire Ln Dallas TX 75225-2712 Office: Winn Beaudry & Winn Thanksgiving Tower 1601 Elm St Ste 4200 Dallas TX 75201-7203

WINN, ELWOOD F., consumer product company executive; b. 1951; married. BS, Wayne State U., 1977; MBA, De Paul U., 1990. With Deloitte, Haskins & Sells, Detroit, 1977-82; divsn. contr. Allied Super Markets, Detroit, 1982-85; sec., treas., CFO Certified Grocers Midwest, Inc., Hodgkins, Ill., 1985—, pres., CEO, 1992—. With USAF, 1970-74. Office: Certified Grocers Midwest Inc 1 Certified Dr Hodgkins IL 60525-4836*

WINN, H. RICHARD, surgeon. MD, U. Pa., 1968. Diplomate Am Bd. Neurological Surgeons. Intern U. Hosp., Cleve., 1968-69, resident surgery, 1969-70; resident neurolog. surgery U. Hosp. Va., Charlottesville, 1970-74; neurol. surgeon U. Wash. Hosp., Seattle, 1983—; prof., chmn. neurol. surgery U. Wash., Seattle, 1983—. Mem. AMA, Coll. Neurol. Surgery, Am. Assn. Neurol. Surgeons. Office: U Wash Dept Neurosurg 325 9th Ave Box 359766 Seattle WA 98104-2499

WINN, JAMES JULIUS, JR., lawyer; b. Colon, Panama, Nov. 7, 1941; came to U.S., 1941; s. James Julius and Molly (Brown) W.; m. Elizabeth Kokernot Lacy, Aug. 15, 1970; children: Mary Ann, Elizabeth Lacy, James Julius VI. AB, Princeton U., 1964; JD cum laude, Washington and Lee U., 1970. Bar: Md. 1970, U.S. Dist. Ct. Md. 1971, U.S. Dist. Ct. D.C. 1982. Assoc. Piper & Marbury L.L.P., Balt., 1970-78, ptnr., 1978—. Assoc. editor, contbr. author Washington & Lee U. Law Rev., 1968-70. Counselor St. John's Ch., Western Run Parish, Glyndon, Md., 1974—; mem. com. on canons and other bus., investment com. Episc. Diocese Md., 1986—; dir. Ctr. for Ethics and Corp. Policy, 1988-95, chmn., 1991-95; dir. Ctr. Stage, 1986—; dir. Oldfields Sch., 1991-96; v.p., dir. Ruxton Country Sch., 1988-91. Mem. ABA (chmn. subcom. on publs. of com. on law and acctg. of sect. of bus. law), Md. State Bar Assn. (com. on corp. law of sect. of bus. law). Office: Piper & Marbury LLP 36 S Charles St Baltimore MD 21201-3018

WINN, KENNETH HUGH, archivist, historian; b. Seattle, June 27, 1953; s. John Hugh and Elaine (Spoor) W.; m. Karen Anderson, June 13, 1981; children: Alice Anderson, David Dysart. BA, Colo. State U., 1975, MA, 1977; AM, Washington U., 1979, PhD, 1985. Resident historian Mo. Hist. Soc., St. Louis, 1987-90, jour. editor, 1987-91, dir. publications, 1989-91; state archivist Sec. State, Jefferson City, Mo., 1991—; vis. asst. prof. Washington U., St. Louis, 1984-87, adj. asst. prof., 1987-90, adj. prof., 1991—; cons. St. Louis Art Mus., 1989-90; dep. coord. Mo. Hist. Records adv. bd., 1991—; adv. bd. Mo. Ctr. for Book, 1993—; bd. dirs. Mo. Conf. History, 1991—, pres., 1994-95; vice chair Mo. Bd. Geog. Place Names, 1995—. Author: Exiles in a Land of Liberty, 1989; co-author Differing Visions, 1994; contbr. chpt. to ency. Charlotte W. Newcombe fellow Woodrow Wilson Found., 1981-82; grantee Richard S. Brownlee Fund, 1992-93, 93-94. Mem. Nat. Assn. Govt. Archives and Records Adminstrs. (pubs. com. 1996—), Am. Hist. Assn., Orgn. Am. Historians, Coun. State Hist. Records Coords. (steering com. 1996—), Soc. Historians Early Am. Republic. Home: 814 Primrose Ln Jefferson City MO 65109-1888 Office: Mo State Archives 600 W Main St Jefferson City MO 65101-1532

WINN, PAUL T., electronics executive; b. 1944. With IBM, Stamford, Conn.; pres., CEO, dir. Genicom Corp., Chantilly, Va., 1990. Office: Genicom Corp Ste 400, Westfield 14800 Conference Center Dr Chantilly VA 22021-3806*

WINN, STEVEN JAY, critic; b. Phila., Apr. 25, 1951; s. Willis Jay and Lois (Gengelbach) W.; m. Katharine Weber, Sept. 15, 1979 (div. Dec. 1985); m. Sally Ann Noble, July 22, 1989; 1 child, Phoebe Ann. BA, U. Pa., 1973; MA, U. Wash., 1975. Staff writer, editor Seattle Weekly, 1975-79; staff critic San Francisco Chronicle, 1980—. Co-author: Ted Bundy: The Killer Next Door, 1980; contbr. articles to various publs. Wallace Stegner fellow Stanford U., 1979-80. Office: San Francisco Chronicle 901 Mission St San Francisco CA 94109

WINNEKER, CRAIG ANTHONY, journalist; b. Chgo., Dec. 19, 1966; s. Allan Seymour and Betty Sue (Stone) W.; m. Karen Elizabeth Hoehn, Apr. 21, 1990. BA, Tex. Christian U., 1987. Rschr. Capitol Jour./PBS, Washington, 1986; asst. prodr. The McLaughlin Group/PBS, Washington, 1987-89; staff writer Roll Call Newspaper, Washington, 1989-91, assoc. editor, 1991-93, sr. editor, 1993-95, mng. editor, 1995—; guest lectr. Close Up Found., Washington, 1991—; treas. exec. com. of corr. Periodical Press Gallery, U.S. Congress, Washington, 1994—. Recipient Disting. Alumni award The Washington Ctr. for Internships and Acad. Seminars, 1995. Office: Roll Call Newspaper 900 2d St NE Washington DC 20002

WINNER, KARIN, newspaper editor. Editor San Diego Union-Tribune. Office: Copley Press Inc 350 Camino De La Reina San Diego CA 92108-3003

WINNER, LESLIE JANE, state legislator, lawyer; b. Asheville, N.C., Oct. 24, 1950; d. Harry and Julienne (Marder) W.; m. Kenneth L. Schorr, Dec. 20, 1987; 1 child, Lilian I. AB, Brown U., 1972; JD, Northeastern U., Boston, 1976. Bar: N.C. 1976, U.S. Dist. Ct. (we. dist.) N.C. 1976, U.S. Ct. Appeals (4th cir.) 1976, U.S. Dist. Ct. (ea. and mid. dists.) 1981, U.S. Supreme Ct. 1985. Clk. to presiding judge U.S. Dist. Ct., Charlotte, N.C., 1976-77; mng. atty. Legal Services of So. Piedmont, Charlotte, 1977-81; ptnr. Ferguson, Stein, Watt, Wallas, Adkins and Gresham, P.A., Charlotte, 1981-92; mem. N.C. Senate, Raleigh, 1993—; mem. adv. com. U.S. Ct. Appeals (4th cir.), N.C. rep., 1989-95. Pres. N.C. Women's Employment Law Ctr., 1989-90; past chmn. Mecklenburg County Dispute Resolution Ctr., Charlotte, 1985-86; coun. mem. So. Regional Coun., Atlanta, 1989-94; trustee Temple Israel, Charlotte, 1988-89; pres. Elizabeth Cmty. Assn., Charlotte, 1980-81. Mem. N.C. Assn. Women Attys. (pres. 1982-83, pub. svc. award 1985), N.C. Acad. Trial Lawyers (legis. com.), N.C. Bar Assn. (litigation sect. coun.), Mecklenburg County Bar Assn. (grievance com.). Democrat. Jewish. Avocations: hiking, jogging, cooking. Office: NC Senate Legis Office Bldg Rm 409 Raleigh NC 27611-2808

WINNER, MICHAEL ROBERT, film director, writer, producer; b. London, Oct. 30, 1935; s. George Joseph and Helen (Zloty) W. Degree in law and econs. with honors, Cambridge (Eng.) U., 1956. Writer Fleet St. (newspapers), London, 1956-58; columnist London Sunday Times, 1990—, London News of the World, 1995—. Engaged in film prodn., 1956—; dir. films Play it Cool, 1962, West 11, 1963, The Mechanic, 1972, Death Wish II, 1981; dir., writer The Cool Mikado, 1962, You Must be Joking, 1965, The Wicked Lady, 1982; producer, dir. The System, 1963, I'll Never Forget What's 'isname, 1967, The Games, 1969, Lawman, 1970, The Nightcomers, 1971, Chato's Land, 1971, Scorpio, 1972, The Stone Killer, 1973, Death Wish, 1974, Won Ton Ton The Dog Who Saved Hollywood, 1975, Firepower, 1978, Scream for Help, 1983, Death Wish III, 1985; producer, writer, dir. films The Jokers, 1966, Hannibal Brooks, 1968, The Sentinel, 1976, The Big Sleep, 1977, Appointment With Death, 1987, A Chorus of Disapproval, 1988, Bullseye!, 1989, Dirty Weekend, 1992; producer plays Nights at the Comedy, Comedy Theatre, London, 1960, The Silence of St. Just, Gardner Centre, Brighton, 1971, The Tempest, Wyndhams Theatre, London, 1974, A Day in Hollywood, A Night in the Ukraine, Mayfair Theatre, London, 1978, (TV series London Weekend TV) Michael Winner's True Crimes, 1990, 91, 92, 93, 94. Founder, chmn. Police Meml. Trust, 1984. Mem. Dirs. Guild Gt. Britain (coun., trustee, chief censorship officer 1983). Office: Scimitar Films Ltd, 6-8 Sackville St, London W1X 1DD, England

WINNER, THOMAS GUSTAV, foreign literature educator; b. Prague, Czechoslovakia, May 4, 1917; came to U.S., 1939, naturalized, 1950; s. Julius and Franziska (Grünhutová) Wiener; m. Irene Portis, Sept. 25, 1942; children: Ellen, Lucy Franziska. Student, Charles U., Prague, 1936-38, U. Lille, France, 1936; B.A., Harvard U., 1942, M.A., 1943; Ph.D., Columbia U., 1950; M.A. (hon.), Brown U., 1966; PhD (hon.), Masaryk U., 1995. With OWI, 1943-46; vis. fellow Johns Hopkins, 1947-48; from instr. Russian to asso. prof. Duke, 1948-58; asso. prof., then prof. Slavic langs. and lits. U. Mich., 1958-65; prof. Slavic langs. and comparative lit. Brown U., 1965-82, chmn. dept. Slavic langs., 1968-72, prof. emeritus, 1982—; dir. Center for Research in Semiotics, 1977-83; dir. Program in Semiotic Studies Boston U., 1984—; Fulbright lectr. Sorbonne, Paris, 1956-57, Ruhr Univ., Bochum, Fed. Republic Germany, 1989; exchange prof. U. Warsaw, 1972-73, U. Zagreb, spring 1973; mem. seminar theory lit. Columbia, 1968—. Author: Oral Art and Literature of the Kazakhs of Russian Central Asia, 1958, Chekhov and his Prose, 1965; editor: Brown U. Slavic Reprints; editor Am. Jour. Semiotics, 1980-85; spl. interests Russian lit., Czech lit., semiotics and poetics. Ford Found. sr. fellow, 1951-52, NEH sr. fellow, 1972, 92-93; Rockefeller grantee, 1977, IREX grantee, 1972, 78, 79, 90, 92, Fulbright-Hayes, 1973. Mem. MLA, Am. Com. Slavists, Internt. Assn. for Semiotic Studies, Semiotics Soc. Am. (pres. 1977-78), Czech. Semiotic Soc. (hon.), Am. Soc. Tchrs. Slavic and East European Langs., Czechoslovak Soc. for Arts and Scis. (v.p. 1982-85), Comparative Lit. Assn., Itnernat. Assn. Slavists, Am. Assn. Advancement of Slavic Studies, Karel Teige Soc. (Czech Republic), F.X. Salda Soc. (Czech Republic). Address: 986 Memorial Dr Apt 404 Cambridge MA 02138-5739

WINNIE, ALON PALM, anesthesiologist, educator; b. Milw., May 16, 1932; s. Russell Griffith and Evelyn Dorothy (Olson) W.; m. June Patton Bethune, July 16, 1960 (div.); children: Alon Palm Jr., Russell, Debra. B.A., Princeton U., 1954; M.D., Northwestern U., 1958. Diplomate Am. Bd. Anesthesiology. Mem. teaching staff Cook County Hosp., Chgo., 1963-72; assoc. dir. anesthesia Cook County Hosp., 1968-72; prof. anesthesiology, head dept. U. Ill. Coll. Medicine, 1972-89; dir. Pain Control Ctr., U. Ill. Hosp., Chgo., 1989-92; chmn. dept. anesthesiology & pain mgmt. Cook County Hosp., Chgo., 1992—. Author: Plexus Anesthesia (Book of Yr. award Anesthesia Found. 1983). Served as 1st lt. M.C. USAF. Recipient Humanitarian award Mil. Soc. Anesthesiologists, 1980, Gillespie award Faculty of Anesthetists of Royal Australasian Coll. Surgery, 1986, Nils Lofgren award Astra Pharmm. Products inc., 1987. Fellow Am. Coll. Anesthesiologists, Australian and New Zealand Coll. Anesthetists, Royal Coll. Anesthetists; mem. AMA, Am. Soc. Regional Anesthesia (pres. 1976-80, Gaston Labat award 1982), Am. Soc. Anesthesiologists, Ill. Soc. Anesthesiologists (pres. 1971-72, Disting. Svc. award 1974, McQuiston award 1983), Ill. Med. Soc., Chgo. Soc. Anesthesiologists (pres. 1968-74). Republican. Episcopalian. Office: 1835 W Harrison St Chicago IL 60612-3701

WINNINGHAM, MARE, actress; b. Northridge, Calif., May 6, 1959. Appeared in films including One Trick Pony, 1980, Threshold, 1981, St. Elmo's Fire, 1985, Nobody's Fool, 1986, Shy People, 1987, Made in Heaven, 1987, Turner & Hooch, 1989, Miracle Mile, 1989, Hard Promises, 1991, Sexual Healing, 1993, Wyatt Earp, 1994, The War, 1994, Teresa's Tattoo, 1994, Georgia, 1995 (Oscar Best Supporting Actress nominee); appeared in TV movies including Special Olympics, 1978, The Death of Ocean View Park, 1979, The Women's Room, 1980, Off the Minnesota Strip, 1980, Amber Waves, 1980, Freedom, 1981, A Few Days in Weasel Creek, 1981, Missing Children: A Mother's Story, 1982, One Too Many, 1983, Single Bars, Single Women, 1984, Helen Keller: The Miracle Continues, 1984, Love is Never Silent, 1985, A Winner Never Quits, 1986, Who is Julia?, 1986, Eye on the Sparrow, 1987, God Bless the Child, 1988, Love and Lies, 1990, Crossing to Freedom, 1990, She Stood Alone, 1991, Fatal Exposure, 1991, Those Secrets, 1992, Intruders, 1992, Better Off Dead, 1993, Betrayed by Love, 1994, Letter to My Killer, 1995, The Boys Next Door, 1996; appeared in TV mini-series including The Thorn Birds, 1983. Office: c/o Ames Cushins Agy Inc 151 El Camino Dr Beverly Hills CA 90212 also: William Morris Agy Beverly Hills CA 90212*

WINNOWSKI, THADDEUS RICHARD (TED WINNOWSKI), bank executive; b. Albany, N.Y., Feb. 20, 1942; s. Thaddeus Walter and Harriet Frances (Witko) W.; m. Sheila Margaret Neary, June 15, 1968; children: Dona, Paul. BS in Econs., Siena Coll., 1963. Adminstrv. v.p. Key Bank N.A., Albany, 1978-80; pres. Key Bank L.I., Sayville, N.Y., 1980-85; pres., CEO Key Bank of Oreg., Woodburn, 1985-86, chmn., CEO, Portland, 1986-95, chmn., 1995—, exex. v.p., group exec. N.W. region, Seattle, 1995—. Bd. dirs. Blue Cross/Blue Shield Oreg, Benchmark, 1996—; bd. regents U. Portland, Oreg. 1st lt. U.S. Army, 1964-66. Mem. Oreg. SBA (mem. adv. coun.), Oreg. Bankers Assn. (mem. exec. coun.), Seattle C. of C. (bd. dirs. 1996—), Portland Met. C. of C. (hon. bd. dirs.). Roman Catholic. Home: 4220 E Lynn St Unit One Seattle WA 98112

WINOGRAD, AUDREY LESSER, advertising executive; b. N.Y.C., Oct. 6, 1933; d. Jack J. and Theresa Lorraine (Elkind) Lesser; m. Melvin H. Winograd, Apr. 29, 1956; 1 child, Hope Elise. BA, U. Conn., 1953. Asst. advt. mgr. T. Baumritter Co., Inc., N.Y.C., 1953-54; asst. dir. pub. rels. and creative merchandising Kirby, Block & Co., Inc., N.Y.C., 1954-56; divsn. mdse. mgr., dir. advt. and sales promotion Winograd's Dept. Store, Inc., Point Pleasant, N.J., 1956-73, v.p., 1960-73, exec. v.p., 1973-86; pres. AMW Assocs., Ocean Twp., N.J., 1976—. Editor bus. newsletters. Bd. dirs. Temple Beth Am, Lakewood, N.J., 1970-72. Mem. NAFE, Jersey Pub. Rels. and Advt. Assn. (past pres., bd. dirs.), Retail Advt. and Mktg. Assn. Internat., Monmouth Ocean Devel. Coun., Monmouth County Bus. Assn. (bd. dirs. 1985—, pres. 1988-90, Woman of Yr. 1992-93, Person of Yr. 1995), N.J. Assn. Women Bus. Owners, Am. Soc. Advt. and Promotion, Ocean C. of C. (bd. dirs. 1994—, award 1993, 94), Retail Advt. Conf. (Career Achievements & Contbns. to Soc. award 1993), Soc. Prevention Cruelty to Animals, Animal Protection Inst. Am., Human Soc., United Animal Nation U.S., Internat. Fund Animal Welfare, World Wildlife Fund, Friends of Animals, Animal Protection Inst., Defenders of Wildlife, Nat. Humane Edn. Soc. Avocations: collecting animal collectibles, gourmet cooking, skiing exercise. Office: AMW Assocs 10 Pine Ln Ocean NJ 07712-7242

WINOGRAD, BERNARD, financial adviser; b. Detroit, Dec. 31, 1950; s. Daniel and Lillian (Walder) W.; m. Carol Leslie Snodgrass, Mar. 8, 1974; children: Simon James Bartholomew, Christina Lynn. B.A., U. Chgo., 1970. Pub. affairs mgr. Bendix Corp., Southfield, Mich., 1975; exec. asst. to W.M. Blumenthal, 1975-77, dir. corp. communications, 1977-79, treas., 1979-83; exec. v.p. Taubman Investments, 1983-84; pres. Taubman Investment Co., 1984—, now exec. v.p., CFO; exec. asst. to W. Michael Blumenthal, U.S. Sec. Treasury, Washington, 1977. Mem. Fin. Mgmt. Assn., Fin. Execs. Inst., Econ. Club of Detroit. Home: 841 N Glengarry Rd Bloomfield Hills MI 48301-2227 Office: Taubman Investment Co 200 E Long Lake Rd Bloomfield Hills MI 48304-2360*

WINOGRAD, NICHOLAS, chemist; b. New London, Conn., Dec. 27, 1945; s. Arthur Selig Winograd and Winifred (Schaefer) Winograd Mayes; m. Barbara J. Garrison. BS, Rensselaer Poly. Inst., 1967; PhD, Case Western Reserve U., 1970. Asst. prof. chemistry Purdue U., West Lafayette, Ind., 1970-75, assoc. prof. chemistry, 1975-79; prof. chemistry Pa. State U., University Park, 1979-85, Evan Pugh prof. chemistry, 1985—; cons. Shell Devel. Co., Houston, 1975—; mem. chemistry adv. bd. NSF, Washington, 1987-90, analytical chemistry adv. bd., 1986-89. Contbr. articles to profl. jours. A.P. Sloan Found. fellow, 1974; Guggenheim Found. fellow, 1977; recipient Founder's prize Tex. Instruments Found., 1984, Faculty Scholar's Pa. State U., 1985, Bennedetti Pichler award Am. Microchem. Soc., 1991, Outstanding Alumnus award Case Western Res. U., 1991. Fellow AAAS (Sect. award); mem. Am. Chem. Soc. Home: 415 Nimitz Ave State College PA 16801-6412 Office: Pa State U Dept of Chemistry 152 Davey Lab University Park PA 16802-6300

WINOGRAD, SESSILE SARAH, psychotherapist, consultant; b. Providence, June 18, 1928; d. Benjamin and Freda (Shaulson) Mayberg; m. Seymore Winograd, May 27, 1956; children: Yeuhda Leib, Jeffrey Asher. BA in Psychology summa cum laude, U. R.I., 1974, cert. in drug counseling, 1976; MS, Barry U., 1979. Diplomate Am. Bd. Med. Psychotherapists; lic. mental health counselor; nat. cert. counselor; cert. clin. mental health counselor. Field interviewer Brown U., Providence, 1968-69, med. coder, 1969-71; student counselor continuing edn. for women U. R.I. Ext., Providence, 1970-74; student counselor The Talmudic Coll. Fla., Miami Beach, 1979-84; drug counselor Aleph Inst., Miami Beach, 1979-86; dir. social svcs. Jewish Outreach Project Greater Miami, Inc., Miami, Fla., 1992-93; coord. cancer activities Ctr. for Psychol. Growth, Miami, 1992—; coord. women's cancer recovery program family workshop Miami Heart Inst., Miami Beach, 1992-94; pvt. practice Miami Beach, 1979—, Bklyn., 1994—; cons. Reaching Out for Emergency Help, Brookline, Mass., 1980—, Caring and Sharing, Bklyn., 1984—; lectr. and workshop presenter in field, 1985—; mem. instnl. rev. bd. Guidelines, Inc., Miami, 1991—. Author: Get Help, Get Positive, Get Well: The Aggressive Approach to Cancer Therapy, A Resource Book, 1992, (chpt.) Times of Challenge, 1988. Vice pres. Beth Yeshaye Charities of Miami, Miami Beach, 1980—; cons. Jewish Community Coun. for Russian Immigrants, Miami Beach, 1988—; bd. dirs. Jewish Outreach of Greater Miami, Inc., Miami Beach, 1991—; mem. Neshei Chabad Miami Beach, 1981—. Recipient Pulitzer prize nomination, 1992; named to Barry U. Alumni Hall of Fame, 1994. Mem. ACA, Am. Mental Health Counselor Assn., Gestault-in-Action, Alumni Assn. Barry U., Phi Kappa Phi. Avocations: spending time with grandchildren, charitable activities, pro bono counseling, cancer consulting. Home and Office: 900 Bay Dr Apt 627 Miami FL 33141-5631

WINOGRAD, SHMUEL, mathematician; b. Tel Aviv, Jan. 4, 1936; came to U.S., 1956, naturalized, 1965; s. Pinchas Mordechai and Rachel Winograd; m. Elaine Ruth Tates, Jan 5, 1958; children: Daniel H., Sharon A. BSEE, MIT, MSEE; PhD in Math., NYU, 1968. Mem. research staff IBM, Yorktown Heights, N.Y., 1961-70, dir. math. sci. dept., 1970-74, 81-94; IBM fellow, 1972—; permanent vis. prof. Technion, Israel. Author: (with J.D. Cowan) Reliable Computations in the Presence of Noise; research on complexity of computations and algorithms for signal processing. Fellow IEEE (W. Wallace McDowell award 1974), Assn. Computing Machinery, N.Y. Acad. Scis.; mem. NAS, Am. Math. Soc., Math. Assn. Am., Am. Philos. Soc., Soc. Indsl. and Applied Math., Am. Acad. Arts & Scis. Home: 235 Glendale Rd Scarsdale NY 10583-1533 Office: IBM Research PO Box 218 Yorktown Heights NY 10598-0218

WINOGRADE, AUDREY, lawyer; b. N.Y.C., Jan. 14, 1937; d. Joseph and Mildred (Weisbart) Weiner; m. Richard Earl Winograde, Dec. 7, 1960 (div. Jan. 1971); children: Leslie Jo, Jana; m. Paul Lewis Levinson, Sept. 19, 1989. BBA, CUNY, 1957; teaching credential, UCLA/Calif. State U., Northridge, 1960; JD cum laude, Southwestern U., L.A., 1986. Bar:Calif. 1986, U.S. Dist. Ct. (cen. dist.) Calif. 1986, U.S. Ct. Appeals (9th cir.) 1986. Tchr. L.A. City Schs., 1958-62, 71-78; advt. salesperson The Hollywood Reporter, L.A., 1966-70; regional sales mgr. Carol Little, L.A., 1978-80; nat. sales mgr. Bijou, L.A., 1980-81; owner, adminstr. James Reva Having Fun, L.A., 1981-83; law clk. Chaleff & English, Santa Monica, Calif., 1984-86, assoc., 1986-92, ptnr., 1993—; adj. prof. juvenile law Southwestern U. Sch. Law, L.A., 1993; spkr. in field. Fundraiser Kathleen Brown for Gov.; criminal law advisor Com. to Elect Gray Davis, L.A., 1994; judge pro-tem L.A. Mcpl. Ct., 1993—; bd. dirs. Camp Pacific Heartland; vol. lawyer Sybil Brand Inst., 1990—. Recipient Bradley Scholarships Southwestern U. Sch. Law, L.A., 1984-86. Mem. ABA (sentencing and corrections com. 1990—), Women Lawyers L.A. (bd. dirs. 1988-96, sec.-treas. 1991-92), Calif. State Bar Assn. (del. from Los Angeles County 1988-94), Southwestern U. Sch. Law Alumni Assn. (pres. 1993-95, bd. trustees 1993—), Am.-Jewish Congress (rel. rights com. 1996—). Avocations: reading, exercising, movies, theatre. Office: Chaleff & English 1337 Ocean Ave Santa Monica CA 90401-1009

WINOKUR, GEORGE, psychiatrist, educator; b. Phila., Feb. 10, 1925; s. Louis and Vera P. Winokur; m. Betty Stricklin, Sept. 15, 1951; children: Thomas, Kenneth, Patricia. A.B., Johns Hopkins U., 1944; M.D., U. Md., 1947. Intern Church Home and Hosp., Balt., 1947-48; asst. resident Seton Inst., Balt., 1948-50; assoc. in neuropsychiatry Washington U., St. Louis, 1950-51; resident in neuropsychiatry Barnes Hosp., St. Louis, 1950-51; asst. prof. psychiatry Washington U., St. Louis, 1955-59, assoc. prof., 1959-66, prof., 1966-71; assoc. psychiatrist Barnes Hosp., 1963-71; cons. in psychiatry Homer G. Phillips Hosp., 1954-64; instr. psychiatry Meharry Med. Coll., Nashville, 1954-55; prof. U. Iowa, Iowa City, 1971—, head dept. psychiatry, 1971-90; dir. Iowa Psychiat. Hosp. Author: Manic Depressive Illness, 1969, Depression: The Facts, 1981, Mania and Depression, A Classification of Syndrome and Disease, 1991, The Natural History of Mania, Depression and Schizophrenia, 1996; mng. editor European Archives of Psychiatry and Neurol. Scis.; chief Am. editor Jour. Affective Disorders, 1979—; mem. editl. bd. 8 profl. jours.; contbr. numerous articles on clin. genetics of affective disorders, alcoholism and schizophrenia to profl. jours. Served to capt. M.C. USAF, 1952-54. Recipient Anna-Monika 1st prize award, 1973, Hofheimer prize, 1972, Samuel W. Hamilton award, 1977, Leonard Crammer Meml. award, 1980, Paul Hoch award, 1981, Vol. Svc. award Nat. Coun. Alcoholism, 1974, Achievement award Am. Acad. Clin. Psychiatrists, 1987, Nelson Urban Rsch. award Mental Health Assn., Iowa, 1988, Lifetime Rsch. award Nat. Depressive and Manic Depressive Assn., 1990, Lifetime Achievement award Internat. Soc. Psychiat. Genetics, 1993, Regents award U. Iowa, 1994, Paul Huston award Iowa Psychiat. Soc., 1994, Gold medal Soc. Biol. Psychiatry, 1984, Lapinlahti medal Helsinki Finland Lapinlahti Hosp. Fellow Am. Psychiat. Assn. (life), Royal Coll. Psychiatrists (hon.); mem. Am. Psychopath. Assn. (pres. 1975-77, Joseph Zubin award 1992), Am. Soc. Human Genetics, Assn. Am. Physicians (hon.), Internat. Group Study of Affective Disorders, Psychiat. Rsch. Soc., Am. Fedn. Clin. Rsch., Assn. Rsch. in Nervous and Mental Disorders, Am. Coll. Neuropsychopharmacology, Societat Catalana de Psiquiatra, Sigma Xi, Tudor and Stewart Club (Balt.). Office: U Iowa Psychiatry Rsch MEB Iowa City IA 52242-1000

WINOKUR, ROBERT M., lawyer; b. N.Y.C., Oct. 28, 1924; s. Harry S. and Katherine S. W.; m. Diane R. Kramer, June 21, 1953; children: Hugh R., Andrew S., Douglas B. B.S., CUNY, 1947; S.J.D., Columbia U., 1949. Bar: Calif., N.Y., U.S. Supreme Ct. Sr. partner firm Winokur, Maier & Zang (and predecessors), San Francisco, 1954-85; of counsel Crosby, Heafey, Roach & May, Oakland, 1985—; guest lectr. Hastings Coll. Law, U. Calif., NYU Tax Inst., U. So. Calif. Tax Inst., Practising Law Inst.; mem. adv. group to U.S. Commr. Internal Revenue, 1967-68. Contbr. articles to legal jours. Served to lt. U.S. Army, 1943-46. Decorated Bronze Star. Mem. Am., Calif., San Francisco bar assns., Am. Law Inst., San Francisco Tax and City Club. Democrat. Home: 645 Stockton St Apt 1100 San Francisco CA 94108-2353 Office: 1999 Harrison St Oakland CA 94612-3517

WINOKUR, ROBERT S., federal agency administrator. BS, Rensselaer Polytech Inst.; MS, Am. U. Tech. dir. Office of Oceanographer USN, Washington, 1985-93; asst. adminstr. Satellite and Info. Svcs. Nat. Oceanic and Atmospheric Adminstrn., Washington, 1993—. Vice chmn. Interagy. Task Force on Observations and Data Mgmt. Recipient Presdl. Disting. Exec., Meritorious Rank award. Fellow Acoustical Soc. Am.; mem. Marine Tech. Soc. (v.p. tech. affairs), Internat. Global Climate Observing Sys. (vice chmn. joint sci. and tech. com.). Office: Dept Commerce-Nat Enviromental Satellite Data & Info Srv Federal Bldg 4 Washington DC 20233

WINSETT-YOUNG, VICTORIA LOUISE, advertising executive, public relations consultant; b. Dallas, Feb. 6, 1950; d. Milo Asa and Louise Love (Metcalfe) Winsett; m. Robert Miles Young, May 27, 1983; 1 son, Christopher Asa. A.A. in Merchandising, Wade's Coll., Dallas, 1970; student So. Methodist U., 1974-78. Copywriter Sugarman Internat., Dallas, 1969-71; promotion dir. Quandrangle, Dallas, 1971-74; account exec. Tracy-Locke, Dallas, 1974-78, account supr., 1978-80, mgr. pub. relations Tracy-Locke/BBDO, 1980-82; dir. pub. relations Cunningham & Walsh, Dallas, 1982-86; owner The Young Co., Dallas, 1986—; cons. pub. rels. Haggar Apparel Co., Big Fish Films, The Container Store, The Dallas Morning News, NorthPark Shopping Ctr., Mary Kay Cosmetics; vol. YMCA, OPEN, Inc., Assn. Retarded Citizens, Boys Clubs Am., Dallas Children's Adv. Ctr., Dallas Assn. Homeless. Mem. NAFE, Pub. Rels. Soc. Am. (assoc.), Tex. Pub. Rels. Assn., Women in Comm. (profl.). Episcopalian. Address: 10806 Colbert Way Dallas TX 75218-1807

WINSHIP, BLAINE H., lawyer; b. Ithaca, N.Y., Apr. 3, 1951; s. Hershell F. and June M. (Nickless) W.; m. Karin M. Byrne, Dec. 21, 1979. AB magna cum laude, Dartmouth Coll., 1973; JD, Cornell U., 1976. Bar: Ill. 1976, Fla. 1982. Assoc. Sonnenschein, Nath & Rosenthal, Chgo., 1976-82; ptnr. Winship & Byrne, Miami, Fla., 1983—. Contbg. author: ABA Criminal Antitrust Manual, 1982. Mem. bd. trustees StageWorks, Tampa, Fla., 1984-86, pres., 1986. Rufus Choate scholar Dartmouth Coll., 1972-73. Mem. Miami City Club, Phi Beta Kappa. Home: 1014 Hardee Rd Coral Gables FL 33146-3330 Office: Winship & Byrne 200 S Biscayne Blvd Ste 2710 Miami FL 33131-2310

WINSHIP, DANIEL HOLCOMB, medicine educator, university dean; b. Houston, July 4, 1933; m. Winnifred Jeneanne Rowold; children: Charles Dwayne, Nancy Ellen, David Rhoads, Rebecca Susan, Molly Beth. BA, Rice U., 1954; MD, U. Tex., Galveston, 1958. Diplomate Am. Bd. Internal Medicine. Intern in internal medicine Ochsner Found. Hosp., New Orleans, 1958-59; asst. resident U. Utah Coll. Medicine, Salt Lake City, 1959-61; fellow in gastroenterology Yale U. Sch. Medicine, New Haven, 1961-63; rsch. fellow med. ethics, fellow law, sci.-medicine program Yale U. Divinity Sch., Yale U. Law Sch., New Haven, 1977; asst. prof., then assoc. prof. medicine Marquette U. Sch. Medicine, Milw., 1963-69; assoc. prof., then prof. U. Mo. Sch. Medicine, Columbia, 1969-84, assoc. dean for VA affairs, 1982-84; prof. U. Kans. Sch. Medicine, Kansas City, 1984-87; assoc. dep. chief med. dir. dept. medicine and surgery VA Ctrl. Office, Washington, 1987-90; prof. medicine, dean Loyola U. Stritch Sch. Medicine, Maywood, Ill., 1990—; gastroenterologist Harry S. Truman Meml. Vets. Hosp., Columbia, 1974-79, chief med. svc., 1979-82, chief staff, 1982-84; chief staff VA Med. Ctr., Kansas City, 1984-86, dir., 1986-87; attending physician Loyola U. Med. Ctr., 1990—, Edward Hines (Ill.) Med. Ctr., 1990—; mem. adv. bd. Greater Chgo. Alliance for Mentally Ill, 1991; pres., bd. dirs. gastroenterology adv. com. VA, 1982-85, chmn. clin. and programs adv. coun., 1988-90; mem. rev. com. Mo. Dept. Mental Health, 1981-82; numerous others. Mem. editl. bd. Clin. Rsch., 1970-73, Annals Clin. Gastroenterology, 1978-83, Gastroenterology: A Weekly Update, 1978-81; assoc. editor Jour. Lab. and Clin. Medicine, 1980-83; contbr. numerous articles and abstracts to med. jours.

Bd. dirs. John H. Walters Hospice Ctrl. Mo., 1982-84, chmn., 1983-84. Recipient Outstanding Clin. Tchr. in Medicine award Milwaukee County Hosp. Housestaff, 1964, Golden Apple award Student AMA, 1972, Disting. Svc. medal and award VA, 1990, Ashbel Smith Disting. Alumnus award U. Tex. Med. Br., 1992. Mem. Am. Gastroent. Assn. (com. on rsch. 1975-78, com. on tng. and edn. 1978-81, dir. clin. tchg. project 1990-82, program chmn. motility sect. 1987), Gastroenterology Rsch. Group, Ctrl. Soc. for Clin. Rsch., So. Soc. for Clin. Investigation, Am. Fedn. for Clin. Rsch., Midwest Gut Club (presiding pres. 1980-83), Soc. for Health and Human Values, Inst. Society, Ethics and Life Scis., Sigma Xi, Alpha Omega Alpha (vis. prof. U. Mo. Sch. Medicine 1991, Med. Coll. Wis. 1993). Office: Loyola U Med Ctr 2160 S 1st Ave Maywood IL 60153-3304

WINSHIP, FREDERICK MOERY, journalist; b. Franklin, Ohio, Sept. 24, 1924; s. Wilbur William and Edna B. (Moery) W.; m. Joanne Tree Thompson, Aug. 29, 1967. A.B., DePauw U., 1945; M.S., Columbia, 1946. Corr. UPI, 1946—; assigned UN, 1947-49; editorial staff N.Y.C., 1950-60, cultural affairs editor, 1960-72, sr. editor, 1972-75, asst. mng. editor, 1975-80; sr. editor arts/theater N.Y.C., 1980—; Broadway critic, 1985—. Contbr. articles mags. Pres. Letters Abroad, Inc., 1962-83; chmn. Easter Seal Soc., N.Y.C., 1964-73, Oratorio Soc. N.Y., 1965-75, N.Y. Conf. Patriotic Socs., 1967-72; Bd. dirs. Odell House-Rochambeau Hdgrs., 1965-75, N.Y. State Easter Seal Soc., 1969-72, Mus. of City of N.Y., 1974—, Am. Philharm. Orch., 1981-82, Friends of the Am. Theater Wing, 1990—. Recipient Am. Legion Journalism award, 1955; Whitelaw Reid Journalism fellow India, 1958; Creative Club Journalism award, 1962. Mem. S.A.R. (sec. N.Y. chpt. 1963-68), St. Nicholas, Founders and Patriots, Mayflower Descs., Soc. Colonial Wars (bd. dirs.), S.R., Soc. Cincinnati, Sigma Delta Chi. Republican. Episcopalian. Home: 417 Park Ave New York NY 10022-4401 Office: UPI 2 Penn Plz New York NY 10121

WINSKI, NORMAN, financial trader; b. Frankfort, Ind., Feb. 17, 1951; s. Herbert and Nell (Silverstein) W.; m. Patricia Downes, Jan. 30, 1985; 1 child, William. BS in Fin., Ind. State U., 1975. Market maker Chgo. Bd. Options Exch., 1975; prin. Norman Winski & Assocs.; founder Astro-Cyclical Exch., 1980; appeared various TV interviews; lectr. in field. Office: Norman Winski & Associates 117 Colonade Cir Naples FL 33940-8714

WINSLET, KATE, actress; b. Reading, Eng., Oct. 5, 1975. Appeared in plays including Peter Pan, What the Butler Saw (Manchester Evening News award for Best Supporting Actress), A Game of Soldiers, (musical) Adrian Mole; appeared in TV shows including Anglo-Saxon Attitudes, Shrinks, Dark Season, Casualty, Get Back; appeared in films including Heavenly Creatures, 1994 (Best Fgn. Actress award New Zealand Film and TV Awards), Sense and Sensibility, 1995 (SAG award, Brit. Acad. of Film and TV award for Best Supporting Actress, Golden Globe nominee, Am. Acad. of Motion Picture Arts and Scis. nominee), A Kid in King Arthur's Court, 1995, Jude, 1996, Hamlet, 1996; appeared in various TV commls. Office: The William Morris Agy 151 El Camino Dr Beverly Hills CA 90212

WINSLOW, ALFRED AKERS, retired government official; b. Gary, Ind., June 16, 1923; s. Harry Wendell and Lenora (Allen) W.; AA, Wilson Jr. Coll., 1964; BBA, Northwestern U., 1969; m. Patricia Ann Freeman, Aug. 22, 1992. With Chgo. Post Office, 1947-66; with U.S. Postal Svc., Chgo. Cen. Region, 1967-83, dir. Office Employee Rels., 1973-83; mgr. mktg. Afro-Am. Distbg. Co., 1986-93; fin. sec. St. Bartholomew Episcopal Ch.; ptnr., Winslow's Apparel Shop, Chgo., 1954-66; v.p., bd. dirs. Univ. Park Condominiums, 1986-88. Mem. adv. com. on human rels. City of Chgo., 1969-73; pres. Cheryl Condominium, Chgo., 1965-67, Evans-Langley Neighborhood Club, Chgo., 1960-64; chmn. Post Office Bd. U.S. Civil Svc. Examiners Ill., Mich., 1967-71; bd. dirs. NAACP, 1968-83. With USCGR, 1943-46. Recipient Outstanding Achievement award, Chgo. Assn. Commerce and Industry, 1969, 70, 68; Great Guy award, Radio Sta. WGRT, 1969. Mem. Bus. Honor Soc. Northwestern U., Soc. Personnel Adminstrn., Indsl. Rels. Assn. Chgo., Am. Legion, Field Mus. Natural History, Chgo. Art Inst., Lyric Opera, Chgo. Ednl. TV Assn., Northwestern U. Alumni Assn.

WINSLOW, DAVID ALLEN, chaplain, naval officer; b. Dexter, Iowa, July 12, 1944; s. Franklin E. and Inez Maude (McPherson) W.; m. Frances Lavinia Edwards, June 6, 1970; children: Frances, David. BA, Bethany Nazarene Coll., 1968; MDiv, Drew U., 1971, STM, 1973. Ordained to ministry United Meth. Ch., 1969; cert. FEMA instr. Clergyman, 1969—; assoc. minister All Sts. Episcopal. Ch., Millington, N.J., 1969-70; asst. minister Marble Collegiate Ch., N.Y.C., 1970-71; min. No. N.J. Conf., 1971-75; joined chaplain corps USN, 1974, advanced through grades to lt. comdr., 1980, ret., 1995; exec. dir. Marina Ministries, 1995—. Author: The Utmost for the Highest, 1993, Epiphany: God Still Speaks, 1994, Be Thou My Vision, 1994, Evening Prayers At Sea, 1995, Wiseman Still Adore Him, 1995, God's Power At Work, 1996; (with Walsh) A Year of Promise: A Year of Meditations, 1995, God's Power at Work: Sermons, 1995-96; editor: The Road to Bethlehem: Advent, 1993, Preparation for Resurrecton: Lent, 1994, God's Promise: Advent, 1994, The Way of the Cross: Lent, 1995; contbr. articles to profl. jours. Bd. dirs. disaster svcs. and family svcs. ARC, Santa Ana, Calif., 1988-91, Santa Clara Valley chpt., Child Abuse Prevention Ctr., Orange, Calif., 1990-91; bd. dirs. Santa Clara County Coun. Chs., 1993-94, del., 1995—; bd. dirs. The Salvation Army Adult Rehab. Ctr. Adv. Coun., San Jose, Calif. Mem. ACA, USN League (hon.), Sunrise Exch. Club (chaplain 1989-91), Dick Richards Breakfast Club (chaplain 1988-91), Masons (charter), Shriners, Scottish Rite. Avocations: golf, skiing, sailing. Home: 20405 Via Volante Cupertino CA 95014-6318

WINSLOW, JOHN FRANKLIN, lawyer; b. Houston, Nov. 15, 1933; s. Franklin Jarnigan and Jane (Shipley) W. BA, U. Tex., 1957, LLB, 1960. Bar: Tex. 1959, D.C. 1961. Atty., Hispanic law div. Library Congress, Washington, 1965-68; counsel, com. on the judiciary Ho. of Reps., Washington, 1968-71; atty., editor Matthew Bender & Co., Washington, 1973-79; atty. FERC, Washington, 1979-84; sole practice Washington, 1984—; researcher Hispanic Law Research, Washington, 1979—. Author: Conglomerates Unlimited: The Failure of Regulation, 1974; editor: Fed. Power Service, 1974-79; contbr. articles to Washington Monthly, Nation, 1975—. Mem. Tex. Bar Assn., D.C. Bar Assn.

WINSLOW, PAUL DAVID, architect; b. Phoenix, June 12, 1941; s. Fred D. and Thelma E. (Ward) W.; m. Carole Lynn Walker, June 13, 1964; 1 child, Kirk David. B.Arch., Ariz. State U., 1964. Lic. architect, Ariz., Calif., Nev. Ptnr. The Orcutt/Winslow Partnership, Phoenix, 1972—; speaker solar energy workshops, Phoenix, 1986-89; adj. prof. Ariz. State Univ., 1991; mem. faculty Advanced Mgmt. Inst., San Francisco. Mem. profl. adv. council Ariz. State U. Coll. Architecture, Tempe, 1970—, bd. dirs. Architecture Found., 1972-76; mem. adv. com. City of Phoenix Bldg. Safety Bd., 1981. Bd. dirs. Central Ariz. Project Assn., Phoenix, 1971-74, Ariz. Ctr. for Law in the Pub. Interest, Phoenix, 1979-86, Phoenix Cmty. Alliance; chmn. Encanto Village Planning Com., Phoenix, 1981-86; mem. council City of Phoenix, chmn. adv. com. Indian Sch. Citizens adv. com. Ind. Sch. Land Use Planning Team; lectr. on planning Ariz. State Univ. planning dept., 1989, city of Presott, Phoenix and Tempe, 1988-89; active Coun. Ednl. Facilities Planners Internat. Mem. AIA (bd. dirs. Central Ariz. chpt. also sec., treas. and pres.), Ariz. Soc. Architects (bd. dirs. 1970-71, 78-82), Bldg. Owners and Mgrs. Assn. Greater Phoenix (pres. 1989-90, 90-91), Boar Valley Forward Assn.. (exec. com. 1994—). Methodist. Club: Plaza (Phoenix). Home: 816 E Circle Rd Phoenix AZ 85020-4144 Office: The Orcutt.Winslow Partnership 1130 N 2nd St Phoenix AZ 85004-1806

WINSLOW, WALTER WILLIAM, psychiatrist; b. Lacombe, Alta., Can., Nov. 23, 1925; came to U.S., 1959, naturalized, 1964; s. Floyd Raymond and Lily Evangeline (Palmer) W.; m. Barbara Ann Spiker; children: Colleen Denise, Dwight Walter, Barbara Jean, Wendi Jae. BS, La Sierra Coll., 1949; MD, Loma Linda U., 1952. Diplomate: Am. Bd. Psychiatry and Neurology. Intern Vancouver Gen. Hosp., 1952; psychiat. resident Provincial Mental Hosp., Essondale, B.C., 1957-59, Harding Hosp., Worthington, Ohio, 1959-60; instr. dept. psychiatry and indsl. medicine U. Cin., 1960-66, dept. preventive medicine, 1964-66; asst. prof. psychiatry U. N.Mex., Albuquerque, 1966-68, assoc. prof. psychiatry, 1969-74, prof., chmn. dept. psychiatry, 1974-91, dir. mental health programs, 1976-91; med. dir. Charter Hosp. of Albuquerque, 1991—; assoc. prof. psychiatry Georgetown U., Washington, 1968-69; dir. bernalillo County Mental Health/Mental Retardation Ctr., 1970-78, 81-91. Contbr. articles to profl. jours. Recipient N.Mex. Gov.'s Commendation for 10 yrs. service in mental health, 1979. Fellow Am. Psychiat. Assn. (life, area VII rep. 1981-85, Assembly Speaker's award 1984), Am. Coll. of Psychiatrists, Am. Assn. Community Psychiatrists (hon.); mem. AMA, Am. Assn. Psychiatry and the Law, N.Mex. Psychiat. Assn. (pres. 1974-75). Republican. Office: Ste 215 101 Hospital Loop NE Albuquerque NM 87109-3073

WINSOR, KATHLEEN, writer; b. Olivia, Minn., Oct. 13, 1919; d. Harold Lee and Myrtle Belle (Crowder) W.; m. Robert John Herwig, 1936 (div. 1946); m. Arty Shaw (div.); m. Paul A. Porter, June 26, 1956 (dec. Nov. 1975); m. Arnold Robert Krakower. AB, U. Calif., 1938. Author: Forever Amber, 1944, Star Money, 1950, The Lovers, 1952, America, With Love, 1957, Wanderers Eastward, Wanderers West, 1965, Calais, 1979, Jacintha, 1984, Robert and Arabella, 1986; story cons.: (TV series) Dreams in the Dust, 1971. Mem. Authors Guild. Democrat. Presbyterian. Office: care Roslyn Targ Lit Agy Inc 115 E 67th St Apt 8C New York NY 10021*

WINSPEAR, WILLIAM W., home improvement company executive; b. Edmonton, Alta., Can., Oct. 1933; s. Francis George and Bessie Brooks (Watchorn) W.; B.Commerce, U. Alta., 1954; m. Margot Macleod, May 30, 1955; children—Deborah Jean, Donald William, Malcolm George, Barbara Louise, Robert Lloyd. Partner, Winspear, Higgins, Stevenson & Co., Edmonton, 1958-64; pres. TPL Industries Ltd., Vancouver, B.C., Can., 1964-70; pres. Lake Ont. Steel Co. Ltd., Whitby, Ont., 1970-75; pres., chief exec. officer Chaparral Steel Co., Midlothian, Tex., 1975-82; chief exec. officer Associated Materials Inc., Dallas, 1983—. Pres. Tex. Arts Alliance; trustee Dallas Opera, 1982-84, chmn., 1984-86; pres. Dallas Civic Music Assn.; trustee, exec. com. Dallas Arboretum. Home: 4815 Brookview Dr Dallas TX 75220-3915 Office: Assoc Materials Inc 2200 Ross Ave Ste 4100E Dallas TX 75201-6711*

WINSTEAD, CLINT, financial publisher; b. Stanford, Ky., Jan. 31, 1956; m. Catherine R. Venturini; 1 child, Alexander Clay. BA, Columbia U., 1983, MBA, 1986. Dir. publs. Loan Pricing Corp., N.Y.C., 1986-87; v.p., editor-in-chief Investment Dealers' Digest Inc., N.Y.C., 1987-96; v.p., gen. mgr. IDD Enterprises, N.Y.C., 1996—. Home: 593 S Maple Ave Glen Rock NJ 07452-1853 Office: IDD Enterprises LP 2 World Trade Ctr Fl 18 New York NY 10048-1899

WINSTEAD, DANIEL KEITH, psychiatrist; b. Cin., Dec. 30, 1944; s. Daniel Sebastian and Betty Jane (Kirsch) W.; m. Jennifer Reiner, June 15, 1968; children: Laura Suzanne, Nathaniel Scott. BA, U. Cin., 1966; MD, Vanderbilt U., 1970. Diplomate Am. Bd. Psychiatry and Neurology. Resident U. Cin., 1970-72, fellow, 1972-73; chief VA Med. Ctr. psychiat. svc. Tulane U., New Orleans, 1976-79, dir., consultation/liaison psychiat. tng., 1979-83, dir. psychiatric edn. and residency tng., 1983-87, assoc. prof., 1979-84, prof., 1984—, chmn. dept. psychiatry and neurology, 1987—; chief psychiat. svc. VA Med. Ctr., New Orleans, 1976-80; assoc. chief staff for edn. VA Med Ctr., New Orleans, 1979-87; staff psychiatrist VA Med. Ctr., New Orleans, 1987—; med. dir. Jefferson Parish Substance Abuse Clinic, 1980-81; cons. E.R. Squibb and Sons, 1985-86; vis. physician psychiatry Charity Hosp., New Orleans, 1979-90. Contbr. articles to profl. jours. Maj. U.S. Army, 1973-76. Mem. AMA, Am. Coll. Psychiatrists, Am. Acad. Psychiatry and Law, Am. Psychiat. Assn., La. State Med. Soc., So. Assn. for Rsch. in Psychiatry, Acad. Psychosomatic Medicine, Am. Assn. Chairmen Depts. Psychiatry, Am. Assn. Dirs. Psychiat. Residency Tng., Assn. Acad. Psychiatry, La. Psychiat. Assn. (pres. 1991-92), Soc. Biol. Psychiatry, New Orleans Area Psychiat. Assn., New Orleans Neurol. Soc., Orleans Parish Med. Soc. Republican. Presbyterian. Avocations: oenology, travel. Home: 5348 Bellaire Dr New Orleans LA 70124-1033 Office: Tulane Med Sch 1430 Tulane Ave New Orleans LA 70112-2699

WINSTEAD, JOY, journalist, consultant; b. Washington, May 31, 1934; d. Purnell Judson and Mellie Richardson (Winstead) W.; m. David Boyd Propert, Jul. 28, 1956 (div. June 1980); children: Kathleen Joy, David Bruce. BA in pol. sci., U. Richmond, 1955. Reporter Richmond (Va.) Times-Dispatch, 1955-56; staff writer, pub. rels. U. Pa., Phila., 1956-58; dir. publicity Children's Hosp., Washington, 1958-59; staff writer Richmond News Leader, 1972-77; features editor Columbia (S.C.) Record, 1977-81; asst. editor lifestyles Richmond Times-Dispatch, 1981-83, fashion editor, 1983-92; coord. pub. rels. Sci. Mus. Va., Richmond, 1992-93; dir. communications Medical Soc. Va., Richmond, 1993—; guest lectr. U. Richmond, Va. Commonwealth U., U. S.C.; book reviewer Richmond Times-Dispatch. Contbg. author: Richmond Reader; contbg. editor: A Gem of a Coll. History of Westhampton Coll.; author (introduction): University of Richmond, A Portrait. Co-chmn. alumni weekend U. Richmond, 1968, chmn. alumnae fund, 1989, chmn. lectr. series, 1992-94, mem. 75th Anniversary Com. Recipient 1st pl. award for spl. articles Nat. Fedn. Press Women, 1975, Va. Press Women, 1975, 95, Va. Press Assn., 1978. Mem. Soc. Profl. Journalists (bd. dirs. 1975), Va. Press Women (hospitality chmn. 1993), Soc. Profl. Journalists Found. (bd. dirs. 1987-91), Va. Assn. Med. Soc. Execs. (assoc.), Am. Assn. Med. Soc. Execs., Richmond Pub. Rels. Assn., Fashion Editors and Reporters Assn. (bd. dirs. 1985-91, nominating com. chmn. 1991). Presbyterian. Avocations: theater, music, travel. Home: 109 N Crenshaw Ave Richmond VA 23221-2705 Office: Medical Soc Va 4205 Dover Rd Richmond VA 23221-3267

WINSTEAD, NASH NICKS, university administrator, phytopathologist; b. Durham County,, N.C., June 12, 1925; s. Nash L. and Lizzy (Featherston) W.; m. Geraldine Larkin Kelly, Sept. 17, 1949; 1 dau., Karen Jewell. B.S., N.C. State U., 1948, M.S., 1951; Ph.D., U. Wis., 1953. Asst. prof. plant pathology Raleigh, 1953-58; assoc. prof. N.C. State U., Raleigh, 1958-61; prof. N.C. State U., 1961-90, prof. emeritus, 1991—, dir. inst. biol. scis., 1965-67, asst. dir. agrl. exptl. sta., 1965-67, asst. provost, 1967-73, assoc. provost, 1973-74, provost and vice chancellor, 1974-90, acting chancellor, 1981-82; Phillip Found. intern acad. adminstrn. Ind. U., 1965-66; bd. trustees N.C. Sch. Sci. and Math., 1985-90. Contbr. articles profl. jours. Mem. N.C. Council on Higher Edn. for Adults, 1967-75; inst. rep. So. Assn. for Colls. and Schs., 1967-74; mem. Cooperating Raleigh Colls., 1968-90, pres., 1971-73, 83-85; chmn. interaction between protoplasm and toxicants com. So. Regional Edn. Bd., 1964-65; Bd. dirs. N.C. State U. YMCA, 1963-65; trustee Meth. Home for Children, 1980-88, pres., 1983-84, N.C. Wesleyan Coll., 1987—. Served with USAAF, 1943-46. Recipient Sigma Xi research award, 1960. Fellow AAAS; Mem. Am. Phytopath. Soc. (chmn. disease, pathogen physiology com.), Am. Inst. Biol. Scis., N.C. Assn. Colls. and Univs. (exec. com. 1974-80, pres. 1978-79), Nat. Assn. State Univs. and Land Grant Colls. (edn. telecommunications com. 1980-85, equal opportunity com. 1985-88), Acad. Deans for So. States, N.C. Assn. of Acad. Officers (exec. com. 1986-89, v.p., pres. 1987-88), Sigma Xi, Phi Kappa Phi, Omicron Delta Kappa. Club: Torch Internat. (sec.). Home: 1109 Glendale Dr Raleigh NC 27612-4709 Office: NC State U Box 7111 Raleigh NC 27695-7101

WINSTEN, ARCHER, retired newspaper and movie critic; b. Seattle, Sept. 18, 1904; s. Harry Jerome and Nell (Archer) W.; m. Sheila Raleigh, Feb. 6, 1931 (div.); children: Kezia, Stephen, Martha. Student, Augusta Mil. Acad., 1916-18, Univ. Sch., Cleve., 1918-22; A.B., Princeton U., 1926. Reporter Phila. Evening Pub. Ledger, 1928, New Yorker mag., 1930; columnist (In the Wake of the News) New York Post, 1933-35, motion picture critic, 1936-86, also ski editor, 1947-86; motion picture documentary script writer Princeton Film Center, 1944-48, for R.K.O. Pathe, 1946; lectr., asso. in journalism Columbia U., 1946, 47. Recipient 1st prize Harper's 1st Intercollegiate Short Story prize contest, 1926. Mem. Am. Newspaper guild. Home: 150 Old West Rd Gansevoort NY 12831 *Having learned in the course of more than seven decades of varied living that I am neither a physical marvel nor a mental giant, I have adjusted to my limitations but have resisted complete rejection of either competition in sports, which I enjoy, or independent thinking, which keeps my mind out of total desuetude. I try to do unto others as I would be done by, at the same time resisting the temptation to control others (for their good) or be controlled (for my good). This has enabled me to regard life, in success or failure, as rather fascinating. The past is remembered, the future a suspense story proceeding to a known destination. I am moderately content. Postscript: Approaching 90, I sleepless nights, which provide a necessary re-evaluation of my life downward. It started so well athletically and literarily, but ended a flap.*

WINSTEN, SAUL NATHAN, lawyer; b. Providence, Feb. 23, 1953; s. Harold H. and Anita E. Winsten; m. Patricia J. Miller, Aug. 7, 1977; children: David A., J. Benjamin, Jennifer M. BA with honors, Beloit Coll., 1976; JD, Drake U., 1980. Ptnr. Michael, Best & Friedrich, Milw., 1988—. Contbr. articles to profl. jours. Mem. legal com. Jewish Cmty. Ctr., Milw., 1983—; mem. devel. com. Milw. Sch. Engring. Mem. ABA (chmn. com. young lawyers divsn. 1989-90, governing coun., mem. antitrust law sect.), Wis. Bar Assn., Internat. Bar Assn., Japan-Am. Soc. Wis. (pres. 1993-94, co-founder 1990, sec. 1990-92), Nat. Assn. Japan-Am. Socs. (bd. dirs. 1991—, mem. exec. com. 1993—), Am. Soc. Assn. Execs. (legal sect.), Wis. Found. Ind. Colls. (bd. dirs., strategic planning com.), Order of Barristers. Office: Michael Best & Friedrich 100 E Wisconsin Ave Milwaukee WI 53202-4107

WINSTON, BENTE, academic administrator. Dir. Sussex Sch. Office: Sussex Sch 1800 S 2nd St W # D Missoula MT 59801-1532

WINSTON, GEORGE, keyboardist, recording company executive; b. Hart, Mich., 1949. Ind. musician, 1966—; founder Dancing Cat Productions, Santa Cruz, CA, 1983—. Premier rec. artst for Windham Hill Records, 1980—; albums include Ballads and Blues, 1972, Autumn, 1980, Winter Into Spring, 1982, December, 1982, Summer, 1991, Forest, 1995; audiobook soundtracks: (with Meryl Streep) The Velveteen Rabbit, 1985, (with Liv Ullmann) Sadako and the Thousand Paper Cranes, 1995; prodr. albums of the masters of traditional Hawaiian slack key guitar. Office: care Dancing Cat Productions PO Box 639 Santa Cruz CA 95061-0639

WINSTON, HAROLD RONALD, lawyer; b. Atlantic, Iowa, Feb. 7, 1932; s. Louis D. and Leta B. (Carter) W.; m. Carol J. Sundeen, June 11, 1955; children: Leslie Winston Yannetti, Lisa, Laura L. BA, U. Iowa, 1954, JD, 1958. Bar: Iowa 1958, U.S. District Ct. (no. and so. dists.) Iowa 1962, U.S. Tax Ct. 1962, U.S. Ct. Appeals (8th cir.) 1970, U.S. Supreme Ct. 1969. Trust Officer United Home Bank & Trust Co., Mason City, Iowa, 1958-59; mem. Breese & Cornwell, 1960-62, Breese, Cornwell, Winston & Reuber, 1963-73, Winston, Schroeder & Reuber, 1974-79, Winston, Reuber, Swanson & Byrne, P.C., Mason City, 1980-92, Winston, Reuber & Byrne, 1992-96. Police judge, Mason City, 1961-73. Contbr. articles to profl. publs. Past pres. Family YMCA, Mason City, Cerro Gordo County Estate Planning Coun.; active numerous local charitable orgns. Capt. USAF, 1955-57. Fellow Am. Coll. Trust and Estate Counsel, Am. Bar Found. (life), Iowa Bar Found. (life); mem. ABA, Iowa Bar Assn. (gov., lectr. ann. meeting 1977, 78, 79), 2d Jud. Dist. Bar Assn. (lectr. meeting 1981, 82), Cerro Gordo County Bar Assn. (past pres.), Am. Judicature Soc., Assn. Trial Lawyers Am., Euchre and Cycle Club, Mason City Country Club, Kiwanis, Masons. Republican. Presbyterian (elder). Office: Winston Reuber & Byrne 119 2nd St NW Mason City IA 50401-3105

WINSTON, JUDITH ANN, lawyer; b. Atlantic City, Nov. 23, 1943; d. Edward Carlton and Margaret Ann (Goodman) Marianno; B.A. magna cum laude, Howard U., Washington, 1966; J.D., Georgetown U., 1977; m. Michael Russell Winston, Aug. 10, 1963; children: Lisa Marie, Cynthia Eileen. Dir. EEO Project, Council Great City Schs., Washington, 1971-74; legal asst. Lawyers Com. for Civil Rights Under Law, Washington, 1975-77; admitted to D.C. bar, 1977, U.S. Supreme Ct. bar; spl. asst. to dir. Office for Civil Rights, HEW, Washington, 1977-79; exec. asst., legal counsel to chair U.S. EEO Commn., Washington, 1979-80; asst. gen. counsel U.S. Dept. Edn., 1980-86; dep. dir. Lawyers Com. for Civil Rights Under Law, 1986-88; dep. dir. pub. policy Women's Legal Def. Fund, Washington, 1988-90, chair employment discrimination com., 1979-88; ednl. cons., 1974-77; asst. prof. law Washington Coll. Law of Am. U., 1990-93, assoc. prof. law, 1993-95; gen. counsel U.S. Dept. Edn., Washington, 1993—. Pres. bd. dirs. Higher Achievement Program. Fellow ABA Found.; mem. ACLU (pres. Nat. Capital Area, bd. dirs.), Fed. Bar Assn. (chair gen. counsels sect. 1993—), D.C. Bar Assn., Washington Council Lawyers, Washington Bar Assn., Nat. Bar Assn., Lawyers' Com. for Civil Rights Under Law (treas., bd. dirs.), Links Inc., Alpha Kappa Alpha, Phi Beta Kappa, Delta Theta Phi. Democrat. Episcopalian. Author: Desegregating Schools in the Great Cities: Philadelphia, 1970, Chronicle of a Decade 1961-1970, 1970, Desegregating Urban Schools: Educational Equality/Quality, 1970; contbr. articles to profl. jours. Home: 1371 Kalmia Rd NW Washington DC 20012-1444 Office: Dept Edn 600 Independence Ave SW Washington DC 20202-0004

WINSTON, KARI JOHNSON, broadcast executive. V.p., gen. mgr. KRO AM, KIRO FM, KNWX AM, Seattle. Office: Bonneville Broadcast Group 1820 eAstlake Ave E Seattle WA 98102

WINSTON, KRISHNA RICARDA, foreign language professional; b. Greenfield, Mass., June 7, 1944; d. Richard and Clara (Brussel) W.; 1 child, Danielle Billingsley. BA, Smith Coll., 1965; MPhil, Yale U., 1969, PhD, 1974. Instr. Wesleyan U., Middletown, Conn., 1970-74, asst. prof., 1974-77; assoc. prof. Wesleyan U., Middletown, 1977-84, prof., 1984—, acting dean, 1993-94; coord. Mellon Minority Undergrad. Program, 1993—. Author: O. v. Horváth: Close Readings of Six Plays, 1975; translator: O. Schlemmer, Letters and Diaries, 1972, S. Lenz, The Heritage, 1981, G. Grass, Two States, One Nation, 1990, C. Hein, The Distant Lover, 1989, G. Mann, Reminiscences and Reflections, 1990, W. v. Goethe, Wilhelm Meister's Journeyman Years, 1989, C. v. Krockow, The Hour of the Women, 1991, E. Heller, With the Next Man Everything Will be Different, 1992, R.W. Fassbinder, The Anarchy of the Imagination, 1992, G. Reuth, Goebbels, 1994, E. Lappin, editor, Jewish Voices, German Words, 1994, P. Handke, Essay on the Jukebox, 1994. Vol. Planned Parenthood, Middletown, 1972-77; mem. Recycling Task Force, Middletown, 1986-87; chmn. Resource Recycling Adv. Coun., Middletown, 1989—. Recipient Schlegel-Tieck prize for translation, 1994; German Acad. Exch. Svc. fellow. Mem. MLA, NEMLA, Soc. for Exile Studies, Am. Lit. Translators' Assn., Am. Assn. Tchrs. German, PEN, Phi Beta Kappa (pres. Wesleyan chpt. 1987-90). Home: 655 Bow Ln Middletown CT 06457-4808 Office: Wesleyan Univ German Studies Dept Middletown CT 06459

WINSTON, MICHAEL RUSSELL, foundation executive, historian; b. N.Y.C., May 26, 1941; s. Charles Russell and Jocelyn Anita Prem Das Winston; m. Judith Ann Marianno, Aug. 10, 1963; children: Lisa Marie, Cynthia Eileen. BA magna cum laude, Howard U., 1962; MA, U. Calif.-Berkeley, 1964, PhD, 1974. Instr. dept. history Howard U., Washington, 1964-66, asst. dean Coll. Liberal Arts, 1968-69, asst. prof. dept. history, 1970-73, v.p. acad. affairs, 1983-90, prof. emeritus, 1990—; assoc. dir. Inst. Svcs. to Edn., Washington, 1966; fellow Haus. Hof-und Staatsarchiv, Vienna, Austria, 1969; dir. Moorland Spingarn Rsch. Ctr., 1973-83; v.p., bd. dirs. Alfred Harcourt Found., Silver Spring, Md., 1992-93, pres., 1993—; cons. Smithsonian Instn., 1979—, nat. Inst. Edn., 1978-85, NSF, 1985—. Author: (with R.W. Logan) The Negro in the United States, 1970, The Howard University Department of History, 1913-73, 1973; editor: (with R.W. Logan) Dictionary of American Negro Biography, 1982, (with G.R. McNeil) Historical Judgements Reconsidered, 1988; mem. editorial bd. Washington History, 1993—. Trustee spl. contbn. fund NAACP, 1980-82; trustee D.C. Pub. Defender Svc., 1985-88; mem. exec. bd. Nat. Capital Area coun. Boy Scouts Am., 1988-90; bd. mgrs. Hist. Soc. Washington; bd. dirs. Harcourt Brace Jovanovich, 1980-91, D.C. Pub. Libr. Found., 1994—, pres., 1995—, Nat. Coun. for History Standards; mem. Commn. on Coll. and Univ. Nonprofit Studies, ABA; mem. Nat. Ctr. for History in the Schs., UCLA/NEH; mem. nat. adv. com. and coun. of scholars Libr. of Congress, nat. adv. bd. Protect Historic Am. Moten fellow U. Edinburgh, 1962, Wilson fellow U. Calif., 1962, Ford fellow, 1969-70, Woodrow Wilson Internat. Ctr. Scholars fellow, 1979-80. Mem. Am. Hist. Assn., Orgn. Am. Historians, Am. Antiquarian Soc., Hist. Soc. Washington, Atlantic Coun. of U.S., Coun. on Fgn. Rels., Nat. Coun. for History Standards, Epsilon Boule, Sigma Pi Phi. Democrat. Episcopalian. Club: Cosmos (Washington). Home: 1371 Kalmia Rd NW Washington DC 20012-1444 Office: Alfred Harcourt Found 8401 Colesville Rd Silver Spring MD 20910-3352

WINSTON, MORTON MANUEL, equipment executive; b. N.Y.C., Dec. 9, 1930; s. Myron Hugh and Minna (Schneller) W.; m. Katherine Tupper Winn, Feb. 3, 1979; 1 child, Kate Winston; children by previous marriages: Gregory Winston, Livia Winston; stepchildren—Wesley Hudson, Laura Hudson. A.B., U. Vt., 1951; M.A., U. Conn., 1953; LL.B. magna cum laude, Harvard U., 1958. Bar: D.C. 1961. Law clk. to Justice Frankfurter, Supreme Ct. U.S., 1959-60; asso. firm Cleary, Gottlieb, Steen & Hamilton,

N.Y.C., Washington, 1960-67; v.p. Tosco Corp., N.Y.C., 1964-67; exec. v.p. Tosco Corp., 1967-71, pres., 1971-83, chief exec. officer, 1976-83, chmn., 1983-84, dir., 1984-86; pres., chmn. Stamet, Inc., Gardena, Calif., 1987—; chmn. Norad Corp., 1986—; dir. Stamet, Inc. and Norad Corp, 1986—; bd. dir. Baker Hughes Corp. trustee George C. Marshall Research Found., Lexington, Va., Mus. Contemporary Art, L.A.; chmn. Station KLON-FM, Long Beach, Calif.; trustee Calif. State Summer Sch. for the Arts Found. Served to lt. (j.g.) USCGR, 1953-55. Office: Stamet Inc 17244 S Main St Gardena CA 90248-3101

WINSTON, ROLAND, physicist, educator; b. Moscow, USSR, Feb. 12, 1936; s. Joseph and Claudia (Goretskaya) W.; m. Patricia Louise LeGette, June 10, 1957; children—Joseph, John, Gregory. A.B., Shimer Coll., 1953; B.S., U. Chgo., 1956, M.S., 1957, Ph.D., 1963. Asst. prof. physics U. Pa., 1963-64; mem. faculty U. Chgo., 1964—, prof. physics, 1975-95, chmn. physics dept., 1989-95. Recipient Kraus medal Franklin Inst., 1996. Fellow AAAS, Am. Phys. Soc., Am. Optical Soc.; mem. Internat. Solar Energy Soc. (Abbot award 1987). Achievements include patent for ideal light collector for solar concentrators. Home: 5217 S University Ave # C Chicago IL 60615-4405 Office: Physics Dept U Chgo 5630 S Ellis Ave Chicago IL 60637-1433

WINT, DENNIS MICHAEL, museum director; b. Macon, Ga., Mar. 17, 1943; s. Paul Kenneth and Mary (McClure) W.; m. Patricia McLaughlin, Dec. 27, 1970; 1 child, Laurel Julia. B.S., U. Mich., 1965; tchr.'s cert., Lake Erie Coll., 1970; Ph.D., Case Western Res. U., 1977. Dir. environ. edn. Wiloughby Eastlake City Schs., 1968-70; dir. Ctr. Devel. Environment Curiculum, 1970-75; cons. Ohio Dept. Edn., 1975-77; dir. mus. and edn. Acad. Natural Scis., Phila., 1977-79; v.p., dir. natural history mus. Acad. Natural Scis., 1979-82; dir. Cranbrook Inst. Sci., Bloomfield Hills, Mich., 1982-86; pres. St. Louis Sci. Ctr., 1986-95; pres., CEO The Franklin Inst., Phila., 1995—; adj. asst. prof. Temple U.; past chmn. edn. and human resources adv. com. NSF, 1991-92; immediate past pres. St. Louis Area Mus. Collaborative, 1991-92, mem. exec. com. Grantee in field. Mem. Am. Assn. Mus. (mem. accreditation commn., ethics com.), Assn. Sci.-Tech. Ctrs. (mem. nominating com., v.p. 1993-95, pres. 1995—), Greater Phila. Cultural Alliance. Home: 8205 Ardmore Ave Wyndmoor PA 19038

WINTER, ALAN, retired publishing company executive; b. Rogate, Sussex, Eng., Oct. 14, 1937; came to U.S., 1982; s. George Adolph and Muriel (Burton) W.; m. Anne Claire, Sept. 22, 1962; children: Mark, Paul. B.S., U. Wales, 1959, Ph.D., 1963; M.A., U. Cambridge, Eng., 1972. Instr. Harvard U., Cambridge, Mass., 1964-65; lectr. U. York, Eng., 1965-68; editor Cambridge U. Press, 1968-82; dir. Cambridge U. Press, N.Y.C., 1982-93. Contbr. numerous articles to sci. jours. Chmn. Govs. of Newnham Croft Sch., Cambridge, Eng., 1975-81. Clubs: Athenaeum (London); Century Assn. (N.Y.C.).

WINTER, ARCH REESE, architect; b. Mobile, Ala., Sept. 13, 1913; s. Augustus Reese and Winona (Battson). BArch, Auburn U., 1935; MArch, Cath. U. Am., 1937; postgrad., Cranbrook Acad. Art, Bloomfield Hills, Mich., 1939-41. Cons. Nat. Resources Planning Bd., Washington, 1941-43; practice architecture city planning firm as Arch R. Winter, Mobile, 1945-84. City plans include Natchez and Gulfport, Miss., Shreveport and Monroe, La., Old Louisville, Ky., restoration area archtl. includes YWCA Youth Center and Residence, Isle Dauphine Country Club, Dauphin Island (Gulf States region AIA Honor award, 1957). Cons. Mobile Planning Commn. Recipient medal of merit Tenn. Soc. Architects, 1971, Thomas Jefferson medal selection com U. Va. Sch. Architecture, 1976-79, cert. of commendation Mobile Historic Devel. Commn., 1981. Fellow AIA (pres. Ala. chpt. 1955, nat. AIA engrs. joint coun. 1957-59, urban design com. 1959-64, chmn., del to commn. d'Urbanisme, 1962, design com. 1972-78, bd. dirs. 1968-71, chmn. Honor award, 1969, chmn. environ. commn. 1970-71, Citation for Excellence in Community Architecture 1965); mem. Am. Planning Assn. (Disting Svc. Plaque Ala. chpt. 1984). Address: 9 Bienville Ave Mobile AL 36606-1463

WINTER, CHESTER CALDWELL, physician, surgery educator; b. Cazenovia, N.Y., June 2, 1922; s. Chester Caldwell and Cora Evelyn (Martin) W.; m. Mary Antonia Merullo, Oct. 22, 1983; children by previous marriage: Paul, Ann, Jane. B.A., U. Iowa, 1943, M.D., 1946. Diplomate: Am. Bd. Urology. Intern Meth. Hosp., Indpls., 1946-47; med. resident St. Luke's Hosp., Cedar Rapids, Iowa, 1947; resident gen. surgery VA Hosp., Los Angeles, 1952-53; resident urology VA Hosp.-U. Calif. at Los Angeles Med. Center, 1953-57; physician Mentone, Calif., 1950-51; clin. asst. surgery UCLA, 1954-57, instr. surgery and urology, 1957-58, asst. prof. surgery and urology, 1958-59, asst. prof. Step II, 1959-60; prof. surgery and urology Ohio State U., 1960-88, prof. emeritus surgery and urology, 1988—, Louis Levy prof. urology, 1980-88; dir. urology Ohio State U. Hosp., Columbus, 1960-78; cons. urology VA, Air Force hosps., Dayton. Author: Radioisotope Renography, 1963, Correctable Renal Hypertension, 1964, Nursing Care of Patients with Urologic Diseases, 4th edit, 1977, Practical Urology, 1969, Vesicoureteral Reflux, 1969; Editorial cons.: Exerpta Medica: Nuclear Medicine, Jour. AMA; editorial bd.: Andrology, Jour. Urology; Contbr. articles to med. jours. Served to capt. M.C. U.S. Army, 1943-46, 48-49. Fellow Am. Acad. Pediatricians, Am. Coll. Surgeons; mem. Am. Assn. Genitourinary Surgeons, Am. Urol. Assn., Soc. Univ. Surgeons, Soc. Pediatric Urology, Soc. Univ. Urologists, Internat. Soc. Urology, Urol. Investigators Forum, Ohio State Med. Assn., Columbus Surg. Soc., Central Ohio Urology Soc., Columbus Acad. Medicine, Ohio State U. Med. Soc., York Country Club (Worthington, Ohio), Kiwanis. Home: 6425 Evening St Worthington OH 43085-3054

WINTER, DAVID FERDINAND, electrical engineering educator, consultant; b. St. Louis, Nov. 9, 1920; s. Ferdinand Conrad and Annie (Schaffer) W.; m. Bettie Jeanne Turner; children: Suzanne, Sharie Winter Chappeau. BSEE, Washington U., St.Louis, 1942; MSEE, MIT, 1948. Registered profl. engr., Mo. Staff mem. radiation lab. MIT, Cambridge, 1942-45, rsch. assoc. electronics lab., 1945-48; prof. elec. engring. Washington U., 1948-55, affiliate prof. elec. engring., 1955-67; v.p. engring. and rsch. Moloney Elec. Co., St. Louis, 1955-74; v.p. rsch. and engring. Blackburn div. IT&T, St. Louis, 1974-82, dir. advanced tech. devel., 1982-86; pvt. practice cons. St. Louis, 1986—; tech. expert on effects of stray voltage on dairy cattle for Wis. Pub. Svc. Commn.; cons. Naval Ordanance Lab. of Ind., Indpls., 1950-53, other industries, St. Louis, 1979—. Contbr. articles to profl. jours.; holder 28 patents. Elder, pastor Maplewood Bible Chapel, St. Louis. Fellow IEEE (life), Inst. Radio Engrs.; mem. NSPE, Am. Soc. Agrl. Engrs., Mo. Soc. Profl. Engrs., Sigma Xi, Tau Beta Pi, Eta Kappa Nu. Avocations: cabinet maker, photography, music instruments. Home and Office: 629 Meadowridge Ln Saint Louis MO 63122-3021

WINTER, DAVID LOUIS, systems engineer, human factors scientist, retired; b. Pitts., July 30, 1930; s. Louis A. and Gladys M. (Quinn) W.; m. Nancy L. Tear, July 1, 1952; children: Leeson, Blaise, Gregory, Lauren. BA, U. Pitts., 1952; MA, Columbia U., 1960; cert. computer sci., Northeastern U., 1971. Assoc. rsch. scientist Am. Insts. Rsch., Washington, 1961-66; sr. rsch. scientist Am. Insts. Rsch., Bedford, Mass., 1966-71, prin. rsch. scientist, 1976-94, retired, 1995; sr. systems analyst RCA Corp.-Sarnoff Labs., Princeton, N.J., 1971-73; mgr. systems engring. Codon Corp., Bedford, 1973-76; computer systems cons. Mass. Dept. Mental Health, 1971-73. Pres. Mayo Peninsula Civic Assn., Edgewater, Md., 1964-65; v.p. Bedford Human Rels. Coun., 1992-94. Capt. USAF, 1952-64. Mem. Am. Acad. Polit. Sci., Human Factors Soc., Soc. Ednl. Tech. Democrat. Roman Catholic. Achievements include design and human factors test for 8 USAF electronic, intelligence and backscatter radar systems; design of 4 computer-assisted training systems for USAF E3 AWACS radar, computer displays, communications and navigation subsystems; cons. engr. for design and test of E6 Joint Stars battlefield surveillance system. Office: MicroVentures Ltd 27 Gould Rd Bedford MA 01730

WINTER, DONALD FRANCIS, lawyer; b. Hackensack, N.J., June 11, 1941; s. Frank Joseph and Ina Beulah (Swanson) W.; m. Katherine C. Blodgett, Nov. 30, 1963 (div. 1974); children: Andrew Blodgett, Matthew Francis, Anthony Reed. AB, Harvard U., 1963, JD, 1966. Bar: Mass. 1966, U.S. Dist. Ct.Mass. 1966. Assoc. Palmer & Dodge, Boston, 1966-73, ptnr., 1973—; bd. dirs. Ellis Meml. Assn. Chmn. Back Bay Archtl. Commn., 1969-82; trustee Boston Ballet Co., 1969—; mem. Park Pla. Civic Adv. Com., 1980—. Mem. ABA, Mass. Bar Assn., Boston Bar Assn., Nat. Assn. Bond Lawyers, Somerset Club, Harvard Club. Lutheran. Home: 2 Clarendon St Boston MA 02116-6137 Office: Palmer & Dodge 1 Beacon St Boston MA 02108-3106

WINTER, DOUGLAS E., lawyer, writer; b. St. Louis, Oct. 30, 1950; s. William E. and Dorothy E. (Schuster) W.; m. Lynne G. Turner, July 9, 1977; step-children: John, Stephen. BS, U. Ill., 1971, MS, 1972; JD, Harvard U., 1975; postgrad., Judge Advocate Gen.'s Sch., 1977. Bar: Mo. 1975, Ill. 1976, D.C. 1976. Clk. to Hon. William H. Webster U.S. Ct. Appeals (8th cir.), St. Louis, 1975-76; assoc. Covington & Burling, Washington, 1976-84; ptnr. Bryan Cave LLP, Washington, 1985—; vis. prof. U. Iowa, Iowa City, 1980-81. Author: Stephen King, 1982, Shadowings: The Reader's Guide to Horror Fiction, 1983, Stephen King: The Art of Darkness, 1984, Faces of Fear, 1985, Black Wine, 1986, Splatter: A Cautionary Tale, 1987, Prime Evil, 1988, Darkness Absolute, 1991, Black Sun, 1994, American Zombie, 1996, Millennium, 1996; contbr. articles and short stories to popular mags. and newspapers. Capt. U.S. Army, 1973-77. Recipient world fantasy award World Fantasy Conv., 1986, award Internat. Horror Critics Guild, 1995, 96. Mem. Nat. Book Critics Circle, Horror Writers Assn. (chmn. grievance com. 1989—). Office: Bryan Cave LLP 700 13th St NW Washington DC 20005-3960

WINTER, FREDERICK ELLIOT, fine arts educator; b. Barbados, W.I., June 19, 1922; s. Edward Elliot and Constance Mabel (Gill) W.; m. Joan Elizabeth Hay, June 9, 1951; children: Elizabeth, Penelope, Mary, Michael. B.A., McGill U., 1945; Ph.D., U. Toronto, 1957. Instr. U. Toronto, 1947-49, 50-51, lectr., 1951-57, asst. prof., 1957-61, asso. prof., 1961-68, prof., 1968-90, prof. emeritus, 1990—, chmn. dept. fine art, 1971-77, grad. coordinator history of art, 1978-81; chmn. U. Toronto Assn. Teaching Staff, 1968-69; mem. mng. com. Am. Sch. Classical Studies, Athens, Greece; mem. programme com. Can. Archaeol. Inst. at Athens, 1990-94; dir. Can. Acad. Inst., Athens, 1994—. Author: (with G.S. Vickers, P.H. Brieger) Art and Man, Vol. I, 1963, Greek Fortifications, 1971; contbr. articles Jour. Classical Assn. Can., Am. Jour. of Archaeology, Echos du Moude Classique/Classical Views. Recipient Gold medal in classics McGill U., 1945; Flavelle fellow U. Toronto, 1947-48; White fellow Am. Sch., Athens, 1949-50; spl. research fellow, 1977-78, 87-88; sr. assoc. fellow, 1982, 83-84, 86, 91; Am. Philos. Soc. grantee, 1957; grantee Soc. Scis. Humanities Rsch. Coun. Can., 1962, 68, 71, 75, 77-78, 82, 83-84, 86, 87-88, 91; grantee U. Toronto Humanities and Social Scis. Rsch. Com., 1993. Mem. Classical Assn. Can., Archeol. Inst. Am. (editorial adv. bd. Am. Jour. Archaeology 1981-85). Home: 164 Highgate Ave, Willowdale, ON Canada M2N 5G8 Office: Dept Fine Art, U Toronto, Toronto, ON Canada

WINTER, HARVEY JOHN, government official; b. New Albion, N.Y., Apr. 6, 1915; s. George J. and Irene (Harvey) W.; m. Virginia M. Shaw, Sept. 2, 1939; 1 child, Jeffrey S. B.A. magna cum laude, U. Buffalo, 1938, M.A., 1939; teaching fellow, George Washington U., 1939-40. Historian U.S. Nat. Park Service, 1940-42; archivist U.S. Nat. Archives, 1942-43; with U.S. Office Alien Property Custodian, 1943-51, chief reports and stats. sect., 1948- 51; with State Dept., 1951—, chief internat. bus. practices div., 1959-61, asst. chief, 1961-70, chief bus. practices div., 1970-71, dir. office bus. protection, 1971-73, dir. office bus. practices, 1973-90; dir. office intellectual property and competition, 1991-92; U.S. del. European Productivity Agy. cartel meetings, Paris, 1958-60; mem. U.S. del. diplomatic confs. Internat. Design Agreement, The Hague, 1960, 17th session GATT, Geneva, Switzerland, 1960; U.S. alt. rep. 5th session Intergovtl. Copyright Com., London, 1960, 6th session, Madrid, 1961, 7th session, New Delhi, 1963; U.S. alt. rep. Interunion Coordinating Com., Geneva, 1963-69; U.S. observer African Seminar on Indsl. Property, Brazzaville, Congo, 1963; U.S. alt. observer Latin Am. Indsl. Property Seminar, Bogota, Colombia, 1964, Asian Indsl. Property Seminar, Colombo, Ceylon, 1966, Com. of Experts on Inventors' Certificates, Geneva, 1965, Com. of Experts on Adminstrv. Agreement, Geneva, 1965, Intellectual Property Diplomatic Conf., Stockholm, 1967, Diplomatic Conf. on Agreement for Classification of Indsl. Designs, Locarno, Switzerland, 1968, Diplomatic Conf. on Patent Cooperation Treaty, Washington, 1970, Diplomatic Conf. on Agreement for Internat. Patent Classification, Strasbourg, France, 1971, Diplomatic Conf. on Universal Copyright Conv., Paris, 1971; U.S. alt. rep. Diplomatic Conf. on Phonogram Conv., Geneva, 1971, Diplomatic Conf. on Indsl. Property, Vienna, 1973; U.S. rep. Com. Experts on Type Face Agreement, Geneva, 1972, Com. Experts on Communications Satellites Problems, Nairobi, Kenya, 1973; U.S. del. Diplomatic Conf. on Communications Satellites Conv., Brussels, 1974, Diplomatic Conf. on Treaty for Deposit Microorganisms, Budapest, Hungary, 1977, Diplomatic Conf. on Plant Protection Conv., Geneva, 1978, World Intellectual Property Orgn. Governing Bodies, Geneva, 1979-82; alt. del. World Intellectual Property Orgn. Governing Bodies, 1983-91; alt. U.S. del. Diplomatic Conf. on Revision of Paris Conv., Geneva, 1980, 82, 83, 84 Nairobi, 1981; U.S. del. UNESCO Experts on Rental of Videograms, Paris, 1984, Com. Govtl. Experts on Audiovisual Works and Phonograms, Paris, 1986, Com. Govtl. Experts on Internat. Register of Audiovisual Works, Geneva, 1988, Diplomatic Conf. on Treaty for Internat. Registration of Audiovisual Works, Geneva, 1989, Com. Experts on Disputes Steelement Treaty on Intellectual Property, 1990; chmn. Internat. Patent Classification Assembly, 1992. Recipient Superior Honor award Dept. State, 1971, 75, 89, 92, 50-Yr. Svc. award, 1990, Jefferson meda. N.J. Patent Law Assn., 1982; honoree Copyright Soc. U.S.A., 1989. Mem. Phi Beta Kappa. Episcopalian (vestry). Home: 1019 22nd St S Arlington VA 22202-2137 Office: Dept of State Washington DC 20520

WINTER, JOHN DAWSON, III, blues guitarist, singer; b. Beaumont, Tex., Feb. 23, 1944; s. John Dawson II and Edwina (Holland) W. Grad. high sch. Organizer, performer numerous rock and blues bands, rec. artist, CBS Records, Inc., 1969—, TV and concert appearances through, U.S. and Europe, 1969—; albums include Johnny Winter, 1969, Second Winter, 1969, Johnny Winter-And, 1970, Live, 1971 (Gold Record award 1974), Still Alive and Well, 1973, Saints and Sinners, 1974, John Dawson Winter III, 1974, Nothin' But the Blues, 1977, White Hot and Blue, 1978, The Johnny Winter Story, 1980, Raisin' Cain, Serious Business, 1985, 3rd Degree, 1986, The Winter of '88, 1988, Winter Scene, 1990, Let Me In, 1991, Scorchin' Blues, 1992, A Rock n' Roll Collection, 1994; producer recs. by Muddy Waters: albums include Still Hard (Artist of Yr., Rolling Stone mag. 1969). Mem. Broadcast Music Inc., Musicians Union.

WINTER, MIRIAM THERESE (GLORIA FRANCES WINTER), nun, religious education educator; b. Passaic, N.J., June 14, 1938; d. Mathias William and Irene Theresa (Marton) W. BMus, Cath. U. Am., 1964; M in Religious Edn., McMaster Divinity Coll., Hamilton, Ont., Can., 1976; PhD in Liturgical Studies, Princeton Theol. Sem., 1983; LHD (hon.), Albertus Magnus Coll., 1991, St. Joseph Coll., 1993. Joined Med. Mission Sisters, Roman Cath. Ch., 1955. Dir. liturgy and liturgical music Med. Mission Sisters, Phila., 1960-76, pub. rels. dir., coord., 1963-72; assoc. prof. liturgy, worship and spirituality Hartford (Conn.) Sem., 1980-85, prof., 1985—, prof. liturgy, worship, spirituality, and feminist studies, 1994—; mem. faculty St. Therese's Inst., Phila., 1964-68, acad. dir., 1968-72, Immaculate Conception Sem. Summer Program, Mo., 1969, Cath. U. Summer Grad. Program, Washington, 1970, Hope Ecumenical Inst., Jerusalem, summer 1974, 75, 76, McMaster Divinity Coll. Grad. Program, 1976, Continuing Edn. Program, 1976, N.Y. Archdiocesan Sch. Liturgical Music, summer 1980, 82, Vancouver Sch. Theology, summer 1982, USN Chaplains through Auburn Theol. Sem., 1990; mem. adj. faculty Union Inst., Cin., 1992-94; with emergency relief work Internat. Rescue Com., Cambodia, 1979-80, Malteser-Hilfsdienst Auslandsdienst, Germany, 1984, Med. Mission Sisters, Ethiopia, 1985; lectr., instr., performer, worship leader, song leader for various groups by invitation, nat. and internat., 1967—. Author: Preparing the Way of the Lord, 1978, God-With-Us: Resources for Prayer and Praise, 1979, An Anthology of Scripture Songs, 1982, Why Sing? Toward a Theology of Catholic Church Music, 1984, WomanPrayer, Woman Song: Resources for Ritual, 1987, WomanWord: A Feminist Lectionary and Psalter, 1990, WomanWisdom: A Feminist Lectionary and Psalter, Women of the Hebrew Scriptures, Part I, 1992 (First Place award for books on liturgy Cath. Press. Assn. 1992), WomanWitness: A Feminist Lectionary and Psalter, Women of the Hebrew Scriptures, Part II, 1992 (First Place award for books on liturgy Cath. Press Assn. 1993), The Gospel According to Mary: A New Testament for Women, 1993; co-author: Defecting in Place: Women Claiming Responsibility for Their Own Spiritual Lives, 1994, (Second place awardfor books on gender studies Cath. Press Assn. 1995;), The Chronicles of Noah and Her Sisters: Genesis and Exodus According to Women, 1995; songlines: hymes, songs, rounds, and refrains, 1996; author numerous songs included in albums EarthSong, Woman Song, Remember Me, Sandstone, Songs of Promise, RSVP: Let Us Pray, Gold, Incense and Myrrh, In Love, Seasons (Christian Oscar award Nat. Evang. Film Found. 1971), Knock, Knock, Praise the Lord in Many Voices (live recording of Mass of A Pilgrim People premired at Carnegie Hall, 1967), I Know the Secret, Joy is Like the Rain (Gold album in USA and Australia), Mass of A Pilgrim People (live recording premiered at Carnegie Hall 1967); contbr. articles to profl. jours. Bd. dirs. Capitol Region Conf. Chs., 1984-91, v.p., 1986-88. pres. bd. dirs., 1988-90, past pres., 1990-91, Archdiocesan Office Urban Affairs, 1986-95; mem. Christian Conf. ann. event WINFEST, 1986, 87; mem. small christian communities design team Archdiocese of Hartford, 1987-91; mem. major events design team RENEW, 1986; subcommn. chair Archdiocesan Office of Synod, 1991; mem. New Eng. team Ministry of Money, 1984-90, 93; mem. The New Century Hymnal editl. com. United Ch. of Christ, 1993-95; active Ho. of Bread, Pediats. AIDS Unit Yale-New Haven Hosp., Covenant to Care, Voices of Joy Gospel Choir women imprisioned at Niantic. Grantee Lilly Endowment, 1989-90, 91-93; recipient Ho. of Reps. citation Commonwealth of Pa., 1968, Women in Leadership Edn. award YWCA Conn., 1989, Covenant to Care award for ministry to children, 1993; named to McMaster U. Alumni Gallery, 1982, Celebration of 120 Women in Leadership, 1987, Bayley-Ellard H.S. Hall of Fame, 1993. Mem. ASCAP (Popular Awards list 1968—), AAUW (Excellence in Equity awardn. cpht. 1995), Nat. Assn. Pastoral Musicians, N.Am. Acad. of Liturgy, Societas Liturgica. Avocations: photography, calligraphy. Office: Hartford Sem 77 Sherman St Hartford CT 06105-2260

WINTER, PAUL THEODORE, musician; b. Altoona, Pa., Aug. 31, 1939; s. Paul Theodore and Beaulah (Harnish) W.; m. Cherry Liley, 1991. B.A., Northwestern U., 1961. Leader: Paul Winter Sextet, 1961-65, Winter Consort, 1967—; performed concerts in 26 countries and throughout U.S., 1st jazz group to perform at White House, 1962, recorded numerous albums; founder Living Music Records, Inc., 1980. Founder Living Music Found., 1976. Fellow Lindisfarne Assn., 1977; recipient Global 500 award UN, 7 Grammy nominations, Best New Age Album Grammy Award, 1994 for Spanish Angel, 1995 for Prayer for the Wild Things. Address: Living Music Records Inc PO Box 72 Litchfield CT 06759-0072

WINTER, PETER MICHAEL, physician, anesthesiologist, educator; b. Sverdlovsk, Russia, Aug. 5, 1934; came to U.S., 1938, naturalized, 1944; s. George and Anne Winter; m. Michelle Yakopec, Dec. 28, 1991; children: Karin Anne, Christopher George, Lia Lynn. BA, Cornell U., 1958; MD, U. Rochester, 1962. Intern U. Utah, Salt Lake City, 1962-63; resident in anesthesiology, pharmacology and respiratory physiology Mass. Gen. Hosp., Boston, 1963-65; USPHS fellow Harvard U. Med. Sch., 1964-66; Buswell fellow dept. physiology, asst. prof. SUNY, Buffalo, 1966-69; assoc. prof. dept. anesthesiology Sch. Medicine, U. Wash., Seattle, 1969-74; prof. Sch. Medicine, U. Wash., 1974-79; prof., chmn. dept. anesthesiology and critical care medicine U. Pitts. Sch. Medicine, 1979—, Peter and Eva Safar prof. anesthesiology/critical care med.; anesthesiologist in chief Univ. Health Ctr. Hosps., Pitts. Editorial cons. Anesthesiology; contbr. chpts. to books, papers and abstracts on anesthesia, environ. phys. pharmacology and med. edn. to publs. Served with U.S. Army, 1953-56. Recipient NIH career devel. award, 1971. Mem. AMA, Am. Coll. Chest Physicians, Am. Soc. Anesthesiologists, Royal Soc. Medicine, N.Y. Acad. Scis., Undersea Med. Soc. Internat. Anesthesia Research Soc., Soc. Acad. Anesthesia Chairmen, Assn. Univ. Anesthetists. Club: Am. Alpine. Office: U Pitts Sch Medicine 1385 Scaife Hall Pittsburgh PA 15261-2013

WINTER, RALPH KARL, JR., federal judge; b. Waterbury, Conn., July 30, 1935; married. B.A., Yale U., 1957, J.D., 1960. Bar: Conn. 1973. Research assoc., lectr. Yale U., 1962-64, asst. prof. to assoc. prof. law, 1964-68, prof. law, 1968-82; spl. cons. subcom. on separation of powers U.S. Senate Com. on Judiciary, 1968-72; sr. fellow Brookings Inst., 1968-70; adj. scholar Am. Enterprise Inst., 1972-82; judge U.S. Ct. Appeals (2d cir.), New Haven, 1982—; vis. prof. law U. Chgo., 1966; mem. adv. com. civil rules Jud. Conf. U.S., 1987-92, chair adv. com. rules evidence, 1993. Contbr. articles to profl. jours. Office: Second Circuit 55 WHITNEY AVE. New Haven CT 06510-1300

WINTER, RICHARD LAWRENCE, financial and health care consulting company executive; b. St. Louis, Dec. 17, 1945; s. Melvin Lawrence and Kathleen Jane (O'Leary) W.; children from previous marriage: Leigh Ellen, Jessica Marie, George Bradford; m. Kathryn Ann Geppert, Dec. 4, 1993. B.S in Math., St. Louis U., 1967, M.S. in Math. (fellow), 1969; M.B.A., U. Mo., St. Louis, 1976. Rsch. analyst Mo. Pacific R.R., St. Louis, 1971-73; dir. fin. relations Linclay Corp., St. Louis, 1973-74; asst. v.p. 1st Nat. Bank in St. Louis (name now Centerre Bank, N.A.) subs. Boatmen's Nat. Bank, 1974-79; v.p. fin. UDE Corp., St. Louis, 1979-81; pres. Health Care Investments, Ltd., St. Louis, 1981—, Larus Corp., St. Louis, 1981—, Garden View Care Ctr., Inc., O'Fallon, Mo., 1987—; mem. exec. bd. Duchesne Bank, St. Peters, Mo., 1989—; lectr. math. U. Mo.-St. Louis, 1972-74, St. Louis U., 1982-90. Active various fund raising activities including St. Louis Symphony, Jr. Achievement, United Way St. Louis, Arts and Edn. Fund, St. Louis, 1974-79. Served with U.S. Army, 1969-71. Mem. Nat. Health Lawyers Assn., Pi Mu Epsilon. Roman Catholic. Club: Mo. Athletic (St. Louis). Home: 1321 Green Tree Ln Saint Louis MO 63122-4744 Office: Ste 175 12412 Powerscourt Dr Saint Louis MO 63131

WINTER, ROGER PAUL, government official; b. Hartford, Conn., July 13, 1942; s. Raymond Gustav and Marion Nellie (Stafford) W.; m. Delorise Allen, Aug. 22, 1966; children: Jonathan, Raymond Todd, Nicole. B.A. in Psychology, Wheaton Coll., 1964; LLD (hon.), Holy Family Coll., 1993. Asst. sec. Md. Dept. Human Resources, Balt., 1970-79, Md. Dept. Budget and Fiscal Planning, Annapolis, 1979-80; dir. Office of Refugee Resettlement, HHS, Washington, 1980-81, U.S. Com. for Refugees, Washington, 1981—; exec. dir. Immigration and Refugee Svcs. Am., Washington, 1994—; cons. on refugee affairs Women's Refugee Project, Washington, 1981-84; adv. bd. Refugee Policy Group, 1981-86; mem. bd. Refugee Voices, 1988—; mem. exec. com. Coun. Washington Reps. on UN, 1989-91. Recipient Disting. Service Cambodian Assn. Am., 1982, Disting. Service award Indochina Resource Action Ctr., 1988. Mem. Nat. Ry. Hist. Soc.-Balt., Sudan Relief and Rehab. Assn. (bd. dirs., sec. 1991-93). Lodge: Eagles. Home: 6328 Departed Sunset Columbia MD 21044-6009 Office: US Com for Refugees 1717 Massachusetts Ave NW Washington DC 20036-2001

WINTER, RUTH GROSMAN (MRS. ARTHUR WINTER), journalist; b. Newark, May 29, 1930; d. Robert Delmas and Rose (Rich) Grosman; m. Arthur Winter, June 16, 1955; children: Robin, Craig, Grant. B.A., Upsala Coll., 1951; MS, Pace U., 1989. With Houston Press, 1955-56; gen. assignment Newark Star Ledger, 1951-55, sci. editor, 1956-69; columnist L.A. Times Syndicate, 1973-78, Register and Tribune, syndicate, 1981-85; contbr. to consumer mags.; instr. St. Peters Coll., Jersey City.; vis. lectr. mag. writing Rutgers U. Author: Poisons in Your Food, rev. edits., 1971, 91, How to Reduce Your Medical Bills, 1970, A Consumer's Dictionary of Food Additives, 1972, 3d rev. edit. 1994, Vitamin E, The Miracle Worker, 1972, So You Have Sinus Trouble, 1973, Ageless Aging, 1973, So You Have a Pain in the Neck, 1974, A Consumer's Dictionary of Cosmetic Ingredients, 1974, 4th rev. edit., 1994, Don't Panic, 1975, The Fragile Bond: Marriage in the 70's, 1976, Triumph Over Tension, 1976 (N.J. Press Women's Book award), Scent Talks Among Animals, 1977, Cancer Causing Agents: A Preventive Guide, 1979, The Great Self-Improvement Sourcebook, 1980, The Scientific Case Against Smoking, 1980, People's Guide to Allergies and Allergens, 1984, A Consumer's Guide to Medicines in Food, 1995; co-author: The Lean Line One Month Lighter Program, 1985, Thin Kids Program, 1985, Build Your Brain Power, 1986, Eat Right: Be Bright, 1988, A Consumer's Dictionary of Medicines: Prescription, Over-the-Counter and Hebral, 1994, Super Soy,: The Miracle Bean, 1996. Recipient award of merit ADA, 1966, Cecil award Arthritis Found., 1967, Am. Soc. Anesthesiologists award, 1969, Arthritis Found. award, 1978; named Alumnus of Year Upsala Coll., 1971, Woman of Year N.J. Daily Newspaper Women, 1971, Woman of Achievement Millburn Short Hills Profl. and Bus. Women's Assn., 1991. Mem. Soc. Mag. Writers, Authors League, Nat. Assn. Sci. Writers, Am. Med. Writers

Assn. (Eric Martin Meml. award), N.J. Daily Newspaper Women (awards news series 1958, 70, named Woman of Achievement 1971, 83), Am. Soc. Journalists and Authors (pres. 1977-78, spl. service award 1983), N.J. Press Women (pres. 1982-84). Home and Office: 44 Holly Dr Short Hills NJ 07078-1318

WINTER, THOMAS SWANSON, editor, newspaper executive; b. Teaneck, N.J., Dec. 28, 1937; s. Frank J. and Beulah (Swanson) W.; m. Dawne Cina, Mar. 28, 1978; children—Victoria Ruth, Abigail Swanson. A.B., Harvard U., 1959, M.B.A., 1961. Asst. editor Human Events newspaper Human Events, Inc., Washington, 1961-64, editor, 1964—, co-owner, pres., 1966—; pres. Fund for Objective News Reporting. Treas. Conservative Victory Fund, Washington, 1975—; 1st vice chmn. Am. Conservative Union, 1972—. Lutheran. Clubs: Nat. Press, Capitol Hill. Home: 16 4th St SE Washington DC 20003-3804 Office: Human Events 422 1st St SE Washington DC 20003-1803

WINTER, WILBURN JACKSON, JR., financial executive; b. Savannah, Ga., June 23, 1944. BSBA, U. N.C., 1966. Asst. v.p. Nations Bank, Charlotte, N.C., 1969-74; v.p. 1st Nat. Bank Chgo., Atlanta, 1974-86; prin. Acorn Fin. Svcs., Inc., Atlanta, 1986-88; v.p. Greyhound Fin. Corp., Atlanta, 1988-89; mng. dir. LBO Capital Corp., Atlanta, 1989-90; sr. v.p., CFO, Rosser Internat., Inc., Atlanta, 1990—. Lt. USN, 1966-69; capt. USNR, 1969—. Mem. Assn. for Corp. Growth, Soc. Am. Mil. Engrs., Constrn. Fin. Mgmt. Assn., Atlanta Venture Forum, S.R. Home: No 8 3050 Margaret Mitchell Dr Atlanta GA 30327

WINTER, WILLIAM EARL, mayor, retired beverage company executive; b. Granite City, Ill., Sept. 21, 1920; s. William M. and Ada M. (Compton) W.; m. Dorothy E. Schuster, Feb. 20, 1944 (dec. 1976); children: William C., Douglas E.; m. Mildred E. Stiebel, Mar. 18, 1977. AB, U. Ill., 1942. With Seven-Up Co., St. Louis, 1946-81; v.p., dir. mktg. Seven-Up Co., 1969-71, exec. v.p., 1971-74, pres., chief operating officer, 1974-76, pres., chief exec. officer, 1976-79, chmn. bd., 1979-81, also former dir., cons.; mayor City of Creve Coeur, Mo.; cons. Cadbury Beverages N.Am. Bd. dirs. Combined Health Appeals Am., YMCA Greater St. Louis, U. Ill. Found., Deaconess Hosp. Found.; mem. exec. bd. St. Louis Area coun. Boy Scouts Am. Capt. U.S. Army, 1942-46. Named to Promotion Mktg. Hall of Fame, 1979, Beverage World Hall of Fame, 1986. Mem. Am. Mktg. Assn., Sales and Mktg. Execs. St. Louis, Promotion Mktg. Assn. Am. (chmn. bd. 1971-72), Phi Beta Kappa, Phi Eta Sigma, Omicron Delta Gamma. Home: 12310 Boothbay Ct Saint Louis MO 63141-8119 Office: Cadbury Beverage Co 8900 Page Ave Saint Louis MO 63114-6108

WINTER, WILLIAM F., federal agency administrator; b. Grenada, Miss.; m. Elise Varner, 3 children. BA, U. Miss., LLB; LLD (hon.), Millsaps Coll., William Carey Coll., Troy State U. State rep., state treas., lt. gov. State of Miss., gov., 1980-84; chmn. MDC, Inc., Nat. Adv. Commn. Intergovt. Rels., Washington, 1994—; Eudora Welty prof. Millsaps Coll., 1989, Jamie Whitten prof. law and govt. U. Miss. Sch. Law, 1989. Contbg. author: History of Mississippi, Yesterday's Constitution Today, Mississippi Heroes. With U.S. Army, WWII, Korean War. Office: Adv Commn Intergovtl Rels South Bldg 800 K St NW Washington DC 20575

WINTER, WILLIAM FORREST, former governor, lawyer; b. Grenada, Miss., Feb. 21, 1923; s. William Aylmer and Inez (Parker) W.; m. Elise Varner, Oct. 10, 1950; children: Anne, Elise, Eleanor. BA, U. Miss., 1943, LLB, 1949; LLD, William Carey Coll., 1980, Millsaps Coll., 1983, Troy State U., 1988. Bar: Miss. 1949. Practice in Grenada, 1949-58; practice in Jackson, Miss., 1968—; ptnr. Watkins, Pyle, Ludlam, Winter and Stennis, 1968-80; sr. ptnr. Watkins, Ludlam & Stennis, 1985—; mem. Miss. Ho. of Reps., 1948-56; state tax collector, 1956-64, state treas., 1964-68; lt. gov. State of Miss., 1972-76; gov., 1980-84; Eudora Welty prof. So. studies Millsaps Coll., 1989, Jamie Whitten prof. law U. Miss., 1989; chmn. So. Growth Policies Bd., 1981, So. Regional Edn. Bd., 1982, Adv. Commn. on Intergovtl. Rels., 1993—; bd. dirs. MDC, Inc. Pres. bd. trustees Miss. Dept. Archives and History; chmn. Kettering Found., 1990-93, Appalachian Regional Commn., 1983, Commn. on Future of South, 1986, Nat. Civic League, 1987-88, Nat. Commn. on State and Local Pub. Svc., Stennis Ctr. for Pub. Svc., Found. for the Mid South. With AUS, 1943-46, 51. Harvard U. Inst. Politics fellow, 1985. Mem. Am., Miss., Hinds County bar assns., U. Miss. Alumni Assn. (pres. 1979), Phi Delta Phi, Omicron Delta Kappa, Phi Delta Theta. Democrat. Presbyterian. Club: Univ. (Jackson). Office: 633 N State St Jackson MS 39202-3300

WINTER, WINTON ALLEN, JR., lawyer, state senator; b. Ft. Knox, Ky., Apr. 19, 1953; s. Winton A. and Nancy (Morsbach) W.; m. Mary Boyd, July 28, 1978; children: Katie, Molly, Elizabeth. BA, U. Kans., 1975, JD, 1978. Bar: Kans. 1978. Ptnr. law firm Stevens, Brand, Golden, Winter & Skepnek, Lawrence, Kans., 1978—; pres. Corp. for Change; mem. Kans. Senate, 1982-92. Bd. dirs. Lawrence United Fund, Boys Club of Lawrence. Mem. ABA, Kans. Bar Assn., Douglas County Bar Assn. Kans. U. Law Soc. Republican. Roman Catholic. Club: Rotary. Note and comment editor Kans. Law Rev., 1977-78. Office: PO Box 189 502 Mercantile Bank Tower Lawrence KS 66044-0189

WINTERER, PHILIP STEELE, lawyer; b. San Francisco, July 8, 1931; s. Steele Leland and Esther (Hardy) W.; m. Patricia Dowling, June 15, 1955; children: Edward J., Amey C. BA, Amherst Coll., 1953; LLB, Harvard U., 1956. Bar: N.Y. 1957, Republic of Korea 1958. Assoc. Debevoise & Plimpton, N.Y.C., 1956-65, ptnr., 1966-93, of counsel, 1994—; dir. Am. Savs. Bank, 1972-92. Contbr. articles to profl. publs. Trustee Amherst Coll.; chmn. emeritus Sch. of Am. Ballet; mem. Com. on the Folger Shakespeare Libr.; past pres. Am. Italy Soc.; chmn. exec. com. Phipps Houses; chn. Austen Riggs Ctr.; vice chmn. N.Y. State Bd. Nature Conservancy; bd. dirs. Phi Beta Kappa Assocs. Recipient Amherst Coll. medal for Eminent Service, 1980. Mem. Assn. of Bar of City of N.Y., Coun. on Fgn. Rels., Am. Law Inst. (tax adv. group), Citizens Housing and Planning Coun. N.Y., N.Y. Sci. Policy Assn., N.Y. Acad. Scis., Tax Forum, Am. Coll. Tax Counsel. Home: 1165 5th Ave New York NY 10029-6931 also: East Hill Rd Keene NY 12942 Office: Debevoise & Plimpton 875 3rd Ave New York NY 10022-6225

WINTERMANS, JOSEPH JACK GERARD FRANCIS, financial services executive; b. Eindhoven, North Brabant, The Netherlands, Oct. 4, 1946; arrived in Can., 1973; s. Joseph J.F.G. and Catherine (Van Dijk) W.; m. Eileen Simon, Oct. 30, 1972. LLB, Leyden, The Netherlands, 1967, LLM, 1972; MBA, Queens, Kingston, Ont., Can., 1972. V.p. Bristol Myers Can., Toronto, Ont., 1981-82; sr. v.p. Am. Express Can., Markham, Ont., 1982-87; pres. Can. Tire Acceptance Ltd., Welland, Ont., 1988—; sr. v.p. diversified bus. Can. Tire Corp., 1995—. Hon. fellow Ryerson Poly. Univ., Toronto, 1993. Mem. Am. Mktg. Assn. (pres. Toronto chpt. 1981-82). Office: Can Tire Acceptance Ltd, 555 Prince Charles Dr, Welland, ON Canada L3C 6B5

WINTERMUTE, MARJORIE MCLEAN, architect, educator; b. Great Falls, Mont., Sept. 15, 1919; d. Allan Edward and Gladys Pearl (Pelton) McLean; m. Charles Richard Wintermute, June 14, 1947 (div.); children: Lynne Wintermute, Lane. BA, U. Oreg., 1941; postgrad. Portland State U., 1969-72. Registered architect, Oreg. Archtl. draftsman Def. Projects, Portland and San Francisco, 1941-43; architect Pietro Belluschi, Portland, 1943-47; free-lance architect, Portland, 1948—; architect-in-residence Edn. Service Dist., Portland, 1978-91, ret.; instr. Portland State U., 1973—; architect-in-residence Dept. Def. Dependents Sch., Asian Region Hdqrs. Japan, 1981-83; with Upshur Group Collaborative, 1976-87; architect-in-residence program coord. Oreg. Arts Commn., 1987—, AIA; leader archtl. tours to Europe, 1969, 71, 73, Greece and Turkey, 1989, 91. Author: Students, Structures, Spaces, 1983, Blueprints: A Built Environment Education Program, 1984, Architecture As A Basic Curriculum Builder, 1987-90; editor: Pitter Patter (Gold medal 1965), 1960-69. Prin. archtl. works include comml. and residential bldgs. and restoration and mus. installation Timberline Lodge, Oreg., 1983, 2d Timberline Restoration project, 1993. Bd. dirs. Oreg. Heart Assn., Portland, 1960-70, pres. 1968-69; bd. dirs. Friends of Timberline, Creative Arts Community, pres. 1993—; program devel. cons. Am. Heritage Assn., Lake Oswego, Oreg., 1969-83, Mt. Angel Abbey, St. Benedict, Oreg., 1970-73; bd. dirs., com. chmn. Environ. Edn. Assn., Portland, 1978-85. Recipient Disting. Citizen award Environ. Edn. Assn., 1983; role model award area coun. Girl Scouts, 1994; Woman of Achievement award Inst. Profl. and Managerial Women, 1984; Woman of Distinction award Women in Arch., 1993, named Disting. Citizen Portland Hist. Landmarks Commn., 1988, fellowship in The Am. Inst. of Architects, 1978. Fellow AIA (pub. edn. com. 1970-80, chair 1972-73); mem. Women's Archtl. League (bd. dirs., com. chmn. 1980—), Fashion Group Internat. (facilitator 1983-84), Ednl. Futures Inc. (Western rep. 1978-83), Oreg. State Dept. Edn. (adv. bd. 1980-83). Republican. Presbyterian. Home: 6740 SW Canyon Ln # 1 Portland OR 97225-3606

WINTER-NEIGHBORS, GWEN CAROLE, special education educator; b. Greenville, S.C., July 14, 1938; d. James Edward and Evelyn (Lee) Walters; m. David M. Winter Jr., Aug., 1963 (dec. Feb. 1982); children: Robin Carole Winter, Charles G. McCuen; m. Thomas Frederick Neighbors, Mar. 24, 1989. BA in Edn. & Art, Furman U., 1960, MA in Psychology, 1967; cert. in guidance/pers., Clemson U., 1981; EdD in Youth & Mid. Childhood Edn., Nova Southeastern U., 1988; postgrad., U. S.C., Spartanburg, 1981-89; cert. clear specialist instruction, Calif. State U., Northridge, 1991; postgrad., Calif. State U., L.A., 1990—, 1996—. Cert. tchr. art, elem. edn., psychology, secondary guidance, S.C. Tchr. 7th grade Greenville Jr. H.S., 1960-63; art tchr. Wade Hampton H.S., Greenville, 1963-67; prin. adult edn. Woodmont H.S., Piedmont, S.C., 1983-85, Mauldin H.S., Greenville and Mauldin, S.C., 1981; tchr. ednl. psychology edn. dept. Allen U., Columbia, S.C., 1969; activity therapist edn. dept. S.C. Dept. of Corrections, Columbia, 1973-76; art specialist gifted edn. Westcliffe Elem. Sch., Greenville, 1976-89; tchr. self-contained spl. day class Elysian Heights Elem. Sch., Echo Park and L.A., Calif., 1989-91; art tchr. medh. drawing Sch. Dist. Greenville County Blue Ridge Mid. Sch., Greer, S.C., 1991—; participant nat. conf. U.S. Dept. Edn./So. Bell, Columbia, 1989; com. mem. nat. exec. com. Nova Southeastern U., 1988-89. Illustrator: Mozart Book, 1988; author: (drama) Let's Sing a Song About America, 1988 (1st pl. Nat. Music award 1990). Life mem. Rep. Presdl. Task Force, 1970—; mem. voter registration com. Lexington County Rep. Party, 1970-80; grand jury participant 13th Jud. Ct. Sys., Greenville, 1987-88, guardian ad litem, 1988-89. Tchr. Incentive grantee Sch. Dist. Greenville County, 1986-88, Project Earth grantee Bell South, 1988-89, 94-95, Edn. Improvement Act/Nat. Dissimination Network grantee S.C. State Dept. Edn., 1987-88, Targett 2,000 Arts in Curricular grantee, 1994-95, Alliance grantee Bus. Cmty. Greenville, 1992-95, Greer Art Rsch. grantee, 1993-94, S.C. Govs. Sch. Study grantee, 1994, Edn. Improvement Act Competitive Tchr. grantee, 1994-95, Alliance grant, 1995-96. Mem. NEA, Nat. Art Edn. Assn., Nat. Mus. Women in Arts, S.C. Arts Alliance, S.C. Art Edn. Assn., Phi Delta Kappa (com. mem. 1976-90), Upstate IBM-PC Users Group. Baptist/Lutheran. Avocations: computers, art, writing, music composition, law. Home: 26 Charterhouse Ave Piedmont SC 29673-9139 Office: Neighbors Enterprises 3075 Foothill Blvd Apt 138 La Crescenta CA 91214-2742

WINTEROWD, WALTER ROSS, English educator; b. Salt Lake City, Jan. 24, 1930; s. Harold Ross and Henrietta Ethel (Fike) W.; m. Norma Graham, Aug. 2, 1952; children: Geoffrey Ross, Anthony Gordon. B.S., Utah State U., 1952; Ph.D., U. Utah, 1962. Asst. prof. U. Mont., Missoula, 1962-66; assoc. prof. U. So. Calif., Los Angeles, 1966-71, prof. English, 1971-79; McElderry prof. English U. So. Calif., 1979—. Author: Rhetoric: A Synthesis, 1967, Contemporary Rhetoric, 1975, The Contemporary Writer, 1975, Composition/Rhetoric: A Synthesis, 1986, The Culture and Politics of Literacy, 1989, The Rhetoric of the "Other" Literature, 1990, (with Geoffrey Winterowd) The Critical Reader, Thinker, and Writer, 1992. Served with U.S. Army, 1953-55. Mem. Nat. Council Tchrs. English, AAUP. Democrat. Home: 17551 San Roque Ln Huntington Beach CA 92647-6641 Office: Dept English U So Calif Los Angeles CA 90089-0354

WINTERROND, WILLIAM J., bishop. Bishop Diocese of Colo., Denver, 1991—. Office: Diocese of Colo PO Box M 1300 Washington Denver CO 80203

WINTERS, ARTHUR RALPH, JR., chemical and cryogenic engineer, consultant; b. Mercer, Pa., May 17, 1926; s. Arthur Ralph and Rebecca Grace (McLaughry) W.; m. Elizabeth Colt Burgess, Oct. 4, 1952; children: Philip, Andrew, Paul. BSChemE summa cum laude, Lafayette Coll., Easton, Pa., 1948; SM, MIT, 1952. Registered profl. engr., Pa. Devel. engr. Allied Chem. Corp., Morristown, N.J., 1948-50; process engr. Monsanto Co., Boston and St. Louis, 1952-55; specialist Gen. Electric Co., Hudson Falls, N.Y., 1955-62; process mgr. Air Products and Chems. Inc., Trexlertown, Pa., 1963-86; sr. cons. CCI Cyrogenics Inc., Allentown, Pa., 1986—. Contbr. articles to profl. jours. Pres. Saucon Assn. for a Viable Environ., Coopersburg, Pa., 1981-86, other offices, 1976-92. Mem. NSPE, AIChE (chairperson 1980-81), Am. Chem. Soc., Phi Beta Kappa, Tau Beta Pi. Republican. Presbyterian. Achievements include patents; design and construction of nuclear off-gas clean-up systems for use in some 50 nuclear plants worldwide. Home: 4584 Pleasant View Dr Coopersburg PA 18036-9350 Office: CCI Cryogenics Inc 1176 N Irving St Allentown PA 18103-1320

WINTERS, BARBARA JO, musician; b. Salt Lake City; d. Louis McClain and Gwendolyn (Bradley) W. AB cum laude, UCLA, 1960, postgrad., 1961; postgrad., Yale, 1960. Mem. oboe sect. L.A. Philharm., 1961-94, prin. oboist, 1972-94; ret.; clinician oboe, English horn, Oboe d'amore. Recs. movie, TV sound tracks. Avocation: painting in oils and mixed media. Home: 3529 Coldwater Canyon Ave Studio City CA 91604-4060 Office: 135 N Grand Ave Los Angeles CA 90012-3013

WINTERS, DONALD, finance company executive. Pres. Farm Cr. Svcs. Mid. Am. An. Acad., Louisville, 1970—. Office: Farm Cr Svcs Mid Am An Aca PO Box 34390 Louisville KY 40232*

WINTERS, HAROLD FRANKLIN, physicist; b. Renton, Wash., May 19, 1932; s. Walter Wade and Ruth Elizabeth (Meyer) W.; m. Marjorie Ann Neiswender, June 9, 1956; children: Kathie Moe, David Winters, John Winters, Janice Assadi, Judy Ahlquist. Attended, Biola Coll., 1950-51; BS, Whitworth Coll., 1958; PhD, Washington State U., 1963. Rsch. staff mem. IBM Almaden Rsch. Ctr., San Jose, Calif., 1963-93; emeritus IBM Almaden Rsch. Ctr., San Jose, 1993—; vis. prof. Odense U., Denmark, 1979-80; past N.Am. rep. Subcom. on Plasma Chemistry, Internat. Union Pure and Applied Chemistry; past lectr. numerous major nat. and internat. confs. throughout the world. Past mem. editorial bd. Plasma Materials Interactions; contbr. numerous articles to sci. jours. Corp. U.S. Army, 1952-54. Recipient (with John Coburn) Thinkers award Tegal Corp., 1983, Disting. Alumni Achievement award Wash. State U., 1992, John A. Thornton Meml. award and lectr. Am. Vacuum Soc., 1993, honored by plasma sci. divsn. of Am. Vacuum Soc. with naming of John Coburn and Harold Winters Student Award, 1994. Mem. AAAS, Am. Vacuum Soc., Am. Sci. Affiliation. Achievements include patents for plasma processing, ion sources and ion pumps; scientific contributions in the fields of plasma science, surface science, thin films, ion bombardment of solids, dissociation of gases by electron impact. Home: 632 Lanfair Dr San Jose CA 95136-1947 Office: IBM Almaden Rsch Ctr 650 Harry Rd San Jose CA 95120-6001 *My conversion to evangelical Christianity in high school led to a change in my attitude, lifesyle, behavior, and study habits. I changed from a poor student with a bad attitude to an excellent student with a great love for science. These changes led to a successful and enjoyable scientific career. I find no contradiction or conflict between science and my Christian faith; on the contrary science has increased my respect for God.*

WINTERS, J. OTIS, oil industry consultant; b. Tulsa, Nov. 6, 1932; s. John McAfee, Jr. and Marian Dunn (McClintock) W.; m. Ann Allene Varnadow, Oct. 18, 1958; children: John, Richard, David, Paul. MS in Petroleum Engring., Stanford U., 1955; MBA, Harvard U., 1962. Registered profl. engr., Okla. V.p. Warren Am. Oil Co., Tulsa, 1962-65; pres. Ednl. Devel. Corp., Tulsa, 1965-73; exec. v.p., dir. Williams Cos., Tulsa, 1973-77, First Nat. Bank of Tulsa, 1978-79; pres. Avanti Energy Corp., Tulsa, 1980-87, Zephyr Corp., Tulsa, 1980-90; chmn. Pate Winters & Stone Inc., 1990—; bd. dirs. Triton Energy Corp., NGC Corp., Hat Brands, Inc., Liberty Bancorp Inc., United Medicorp Inc. Chmn. bd. First United Meth. Ch., 1977-79; pres. Downtown Tulsa Unltd., 1977; former vice chmn. bd. Oral Roberts U.; bd. dirs. Jr. Achievement; commr. Tulsa Urban Renewal Authority; 1st v.p. Ark. Basin Devel. Assn. Served as 1st lt., C.E. U.S. Army, 1955-57. Recipient various pub. service awards. Mem. Tulsa C. of C. (bd. dirs.), So. Hills Country Club (Tulsa), Pine Valley Golf Club, Augusta Nat. Golf Club, Cypress Point Club, Royal and Ancient Club, St. Andrews. Home: 4616 Christopher Pl Dallas TX 75204-1611 Office: Pate Winters & Stone Inc 5956 Sherry Ln Ste 2001 Dallas TX 75225-8301

WINTERS, J. SAM, lawyer, federal official; b. Amarillo, Tex., July 7, 1922; m. Dorothy Jean Rushing, Dec. 21, 1947; 1 child, Leila Winters Mischer. BA, U. Tex., 1944, JD, 1948. Bar: Tex. 1948. Briefing atty. Supreme Ct. Tex., Austin, 1948-49; chief Charter div. Sec. of State, State of Tex., Austin, 1949-50; ptnr. Bagby & Winters, Austin, 1950-57; shareholder Clark, Thomas, & Winters, Austin, 1957—; bd. govs. U.S. Postal Svc., Washington, 1991-95, chmn. bd. govs., 1994-95, vice chair, 1995—; mem. stds. com. Nat. Flood Inst. Program, Washington, 1990-93, dir., 1990-94. Bd. dirs. Tex. Assn. Taxpayers; mem. devel. bd. U. Tex., Austin, 1988—, mem. Pres.'s Assocs., 1981—; mem. chancellor's coun. U. Tex. Sys., 1983—; mem. symposium planning com. Lyndon B. Johnson Sch. Pub. Affairs, Austin, 1987—. Mem. ABA (chair, sect. pub. utility comm. and transp. law, chair sect. pub. utility, comms. and transp. law), State Bar Tex., Travis County Bar Assn., Tex. Bar Found., Internat. Assn. Def. Counsel, Tex. Assn. Def. Counsel, Fedn. Ins. and Corp. Counsel, Tex. Rsch. League (past chair), Tex. Coun. Econ. Edn., Tex. Hist. Soc., Panhandle Plains Hist. Soc., SAR. Democrat. Episcopalian. Office: Clark Thomas & Winters PO Box 1148 Austin TX 78767-1148

WINTERS, JONATHAN, actor; b. Dayton, Ohio, Nov. 11, 1925; s. Jonathan H. and Alice Kilgore (Rodgers) W.; m. Eileen Ann Schauder, Sept. 11, 1948; children: Jonathan IV, Lucinda Kelley. Student, Kenyon Coll., 1946; B.F.A., Dayton Art Inst., 1950. With radio sta. WING, Dayton, 1949; disc jockey sta. WBNS-TV, Columbus, Ohio, 1950-53. Appeared on: Garry Moore Show, 1954-63, Steve Allen Show, 1954-61, Omnibus, 1954, NBC Comedy Hour, 1956, Jonathan Winters Show, 1956-57, Jack Paar Show, 1963-64, Andy Williams Show, 1966-67, Dean Martin Show, 1966-67, Jonathan Winters Show, CBS-TV, 1968-69, Wacky World of Jonathan Winters, 1972-73; numerous appearances NBC Monitor show, 1963—, Hollywood Squares, 1975—; TV series include Mork & Mindy, 1982-83, Davis Rules, (Emmy award for best supporting actor) 1991-92, 5 spls. Showtime Cable TV; night club appearances, 1953-60; motion picture appearances: It's a Mad, Mad, Mad World, 1963, The Loved One, 1964, The Russians Are Coming, The Russians Are Coming, 1966, Penelope, 1967, The Midnight Oil, 1967, 8 On the Lam, 1967, Oh Dad, Poor Dad, 1968, Viva Max, 1969, The Fish That Saved Pittsburgh, 1979, The Longshot, 1986, Say Yes, 1986, Moon Over Parador, 1988, The Flintstones, 1994, The Shadow, 1994; rec. artist, Columbia Records.; author: Mouse Breath, Conformity and Other Social Ills, 1965, Winter's Tales, 1987, Hang-Ups, 1990; voice numerous cartoon characters. Served with USMCR, 1943-46, PTO. Named to Comedy Hall of Fame U.S., 1993, Comedy Hall of Fame Can., 1994; recipient Grammy for Comedy Album of Yr., 1996.

WINTERS, NOLA FRANCES, food company executive; b. Achilles, Kans., Aug. 27, 1925; d. Edward Earl and Mary Ruby (Mikesell) Ginther; divorced. Student, U. Kans., 1943-45; BA, U. Colo., 1972. Exec. sec. Holly Sugar Corp., Colorado Springs, Colo., 1953-66, asst. sec., 1966-84, dir. corp. rels., asst. sec., 1981-84, dir. corp. and pub. rels., asst. sec., 1984-90; asst. sec. HSC Export Corp., Colorado Springs, 1980-90, Imperial Holly Corp., Colorado Springs, 1988-90. Mem. Phi Beta Kappa. Republican. Methodist.

WINTERS, RALPH E., film editor. Films include Gaslight, Little Women, King Solomon's Mines, Quo Vadis (Acad. award nomination), Kiss Me Kate, Executive Suite, Seven Brides for Seven Brothers (Acad. award nomination), High Society, Jailhouse Rock, Ben-hur (Acad. award), Butterfield 8, Soldier in the Rain, The Pink Panther, The Great Race (Acad. award nomination), Fitzwilly, How to Succeed in Business without Really Trying, The Party, The Thomas Crown Affair, The Hawaiians, Kotch (Acad. award nomination), The Front Page, Mr. Majestyk, King Kong, 10, S.O.B., Victor Victoria, Curse of the Pink Panther, Big Trouble, Let's Get Harry, Moving, Tagget. Office: The Mirisch Agy 10100 Santa Monica Blvd Ste 70 Los Angeles CA 90067-4003

WINTERS, ROBERT CUSHING, insurance company executive; b. Hartford, Conn., Dec. 8, 1931; s. George Warren and Hazel Keith (Cushing) W.; m. Patricia Ann Martini, Feb. 10, 1962; children: Sally, Beth. BA, Yale U., 1953; MBA, Boston U., 1963; LHD, Montclair State Coll., 1991, St. Peter's Coll., 1993. With Prudential Ins. Co. Am., 1953—, v.p. actuary, 1969-75, sr. v.p. Cen. Atlantic home office, 1975-78, exec. v.p., Newark, 1978-84, vice chmn., 1984-86, chmn., CEO, 1987-94; chmn. emeritus Prudential Ins. Co. Am., Newark, 1995—; bd. dirs. Allied-Signal Inc. Trustee Mayo Found. With U.S. Army, 1954-56. Fellow Soc. Actuaries; mem. Am. Acad. Actuaries (past pres.), Am. Coun. Life Ins. (chmn. bd. dirs. 1990-91), Bus. Coun., Trilateral Commn., Sigma Xi. Office: Prudential Ins Co Am 751 Broad St Newark NJ 07102-3777

WINTERS, ROBERT W., medical educator, pediatrician; b. Evansville, Ind., May 23, 1926; s. Frank and Clara (Flentke) W.; m. Madoris Seiler, Sept. 5, 1948 (div. Feb. 1992); children: Henry N., R. George; m. Agnete Thomsen, Feb. 11, 1992; children: Charlotte, Anne. AB magna cum laude, Indiana U., 1948; MD cum laude, Yale U., 1952. Diplomate Am. Bd. Pediatrics. Intern, resident, and fellow U. N.C., Chapel Hill, 1954-58; asst. prof. U. Pa., Phila., 1959-61; prof. Columbia U., N.Y.C., 1962-81; CEO HNS-Healthdyne, Parsippany, N.J., 1985-89; chmn. Nat. Alliance Infusion Therapy, 1990-92; pres. Winters Assocs., Inc., 1989—. Contbr. to profl. jour.; author 5 books. 2nd lt. cav. U.S. Army, 1944-46. Recipient Mead Johnson award Am. Acad. Pediatrics, 1966, Borden award, 1972. Office: HNS-Healthdyne 959 Rt 46 E Parsippany NJ 07054

WINTERS, SHELLEY (SHIRLEY SCHRIFT), actress; b. St. Louis, Aug. 18, 1922; m. Vittorio Gassman (div.); 1 child, Vittoria; m. Anthony Franciosa, 1957 (div. Nov. 1960). Student, Wayne U. Began acting career in vaudeville, later played roles on legitimate stage; motion pictures include The Diary of Anne Frank, 1958 (Acad. award best supporting actress), Odds Against Tomorrow, Let No Man Write My Epitaph, Matter of Convictions, Lolita, 1962, Wives and Lovers, 1963, The Balcony, 1964, A House Is Not a Home, 1964, Patch of Blue, 1966 (Acad. award best supporting actress), Time of Indifference, 1965, Alfie, 1965, The Moving Target, 1965, Harper, 1966, Enter Laughing, 1967, The Scalp Hunters, 1968, Buona Sera Mrs. Campbell, 1968, Wild in the Streets, 1968, The Mad Room, 1969, How Do I Love Thee, 1971, What's the Matter with Helen, 1971, The Poseidon Adventure, 1972, Blume in Love, 1973, Cleopatra Jones, 1973, Something to Hide, 1973, Diamonds, 1975, Next Stop Greenwich Village, 1976, The Tenant, 1976, An Average Man, 1977, Tentacles, 1977, Pete's Dragon, 1977, King of the Gypsies, 1978, The Visitor, 1980, Looping, 1981, S.O.B., 1981, My Mother, My Daughter, 1981, Over the Brooklyn Bridge, Ellie, Deja Vu, 1985, The Delta Force, 1986, Marilyn Monroe: Beyond the Legend, 1987, Purple People Eater, 1988, An Unremarkable Life, 1989, Touch of a Stranger, 1990, Stepping Out, 1991, The Pickle, 1993; appeared in: TV films Revenge!, 1971, The Devil's Daughter, 1973, Double Indemnity, 1974, The Sex Symbol, 1974, Elvis, 1978, Alice in Wonderland; plays A Hatfull of Rain, 1955, Girls of Summer, 1957, Night of the Iguana, Cages, Who's Afraid of Virginia Wolf?, Minnie's Boys; TV miniseries The French Atlantic Affair, 1979; Author: play One Night Stands of a Noisy Passenger, 1971; autobiography Shelley: Also Known As Shirley, 1980, Shelley II: The Middle of My Century, 1989. Recipient Emmy award Best Actress, 1964, Monte Carlo Golden Nymph award, 1964, Internat. TV award as best actress Cannes Festival, 1965. *

WINTERSHEIMER, DONALD CARL, state supreme court justice; b. Covington, Ky., Apr. 21, 1932; s. Carl E. and Marie A. (Kohl) W.; m. Alice T. Rabe, June 24, 1961; children: Mark D., Lisa Ann, Craig P., Amy T., Blaise Q. BA, Thomas More Coll., 1953; MA, Xavier U., 1956; JD, U. Cin., 1959. Bar: Ky. 1960, Ohio 1960. Pvt. practice Covington, Ky., 1960—; city solicitor City of Covington, 1962-76; judge Ky. Ct. Appeals, Frankfort, 1976-83; justice Ky. Supreme Ct., Frankfort, 1983—, chmn. criminal rules com., 1988-94, chmn. continuing jud. edn. com., 1983—, chmn. rules com., 1994—; del. Foster Parent Rev. Bd., 1985—; mem. adv. bd. Sta. WNKU-FM, 1984-94, Am. Soc. Writers on Legal Subjects. Trustee Sta. WNKU-FM. Recipient Cmty. Svc. award Thomas More Coll., 1968; recipient Disting. Alumnus award Thomas More Coll., 1982; named Disting. Jurist Chase

Coll. Law, 1983, Outstanding Jurist Phi Alpha Delta Law Frat., 1990. Mem. ABA, Am. Judicature Soc., Ky. Bar Assn., Ohio Bar Assn., Cin. Bar Assn., Inst. Jud. Adminstrn. Democrat. Roman Catholic. Home: 224 Adams Ave Covington KY 41014-1712 Office: Ky Supreme Ct Capitol Building Rm 201 Frankfort KY 40601

WINTERS-MALONEY, CAROL EMERSON, nursing educator, academic administrator; b. Logan, W.Va., Sept. 2, 1949; d. Carmi Emerson and Mary Louise (Stallings) W.; children: Heather, Chapin, Claire. BA cum laude, Greensboro Coll., 1971; BSN magna cum laude, U. N.C. Greensboro, 1974, MSN with honors, 1978; PhD, U. Pitts., 1985. Dir. religious edn. Elon (N.C.) Coll. and Elon Coll. Community Ch., 1971-72; primary nurse Moses H. Cone Meml., Greensboro, 1974-81, Children's Hosp. Pitts., 1981; asst. prof. Allegheny Community Coll., Pitts., 1981-82, U. Pitts., 1982-85, U. Rochester, N.Y., 1986; instr. U. N.C., Greensboro, 1978-81, asst. prof., 1986-90; asst. dir. nursing and health care studies Hawaii Loa Coll, Kaneohe, 1990; prof. dean Nursing and Acad. Adminstrn. Hawaii Loa Campus/Hawaii Pacific U., Kaneohe, 1990—. Contbr. articles to nursing jours. Active PTA, Kaneohe, 1990—. Mem. ANA (Hawaii cabinet on profl. nursing edn., Hawaii cabinet on nursing rsch. 1992), Am. Orgn. Nurse Execs., Epilepsy Found. Am. (bd. dirs.), Sigma Theta Tau (charter mem., 1st pres. Gamma Zi chpt. 1976-78, counselor 1987-89, rsch. com. Gamma Psi chpt. at large 1993—). Mem. Soc. of Friends. Avocations: Scottish country dance, hula, ukelele and guitar, reading, sailing. Office: Hawaii Pacific U Hawaii Loa Campus 45-045 Kamehameha Hwy Kaneohe HI 96744-5221

WINTERSTEIN, JAMES FREDRICK, academic administrator; b. Copperas Cove, Tex., Apr. 8, 1943; s. Arno Fredrick Herman and Ada Amanda Johanna (Wagnr) W.; m. Diane Marie Bochmann, July 13, 1963; children: Russell, Lisa, Steven, Amy. Student, U. N.M., 1962; D of Chiropractic cum laude, Nat. Coll. Chiropractic, 1968; cert., Harvard Inst. for Ednl. Mgmt., 1988. Diplomate Am. Chiropractic Bd. Radiology; lic. chiropractic, Ill., Fla., S.D., Md. Night supr. x-ray dept. DuPage Meml. Hosp., Elmhurst, Ill., 1964-66; x-ray technologist Lombard (Ill.) Chiropractic Clinic, 1966-68, asst. dir., 1968-71; chmn. dept. diagnostic imaging Nat. Coll. Chiropractic, Lombard, Ill., 1971-73, chief of staff, 1985-86, pres., 1986—; pvt. practice West Chicago, Ill., 1968-73, Fla., 1973-85; faculty Nat.-Lincoln Sch. Postgrad. Edn., 1967—; chmn. x-ray test com. Nat. Bd. Chiropractic Examiners, 1971-73; govs. adv. panel on coal worker's pneumoconiosis and chiropractic State of Pa., 1979; v.p. Am. Chiropractic Coll. Radiology, 1981-83; mem. adv. coun. on radiation protection Dept. Health and Rehabilitative Svcs. State of Fla., 1984-85; cons. to bd. examiners State of S.C., 1983-84, State of Fla., 1980-85; cons. to peer review bd. State of Fla., 1980-84; trustee Chiropractic Centennial Found., 1989-90; speaker in field. Pub. Outreach, monthly Nat. Coll. Chiropractic; author numerous monographs on chiropractic edn. and practice; inventor composite shielding and mounting means for x-ray machines; contbr. articles to profl. jours. Chmn., bd. dirs. Trinity Luth. Ch., West Chgo., 1970-72, Luth. High Sch., Pinellas County, Fla., 1979-82, St. John Luth. Ch., Lombard, 1988; chmn. bd. edn. First Luth. Sch., 1975-79; chmn. First Luth. Congregation, Clearwater, Fla., 1979-82; chmn. bldg. planning com. Grace Luth. Ch. and Sch., St. Petersburg, Fla., 1984-85; bldg. planning com. ch. expansion, new elem. sch., First Luth. Sch., 1975-79; stewardship adv. coun. Fla./Ga. dist. Luth. Ch. Mo. Synod, 1983-85; trustee West Suburban Regional Acad. Consortium, 1993—. With U.S. Army, 1961-64. Recipient Cert. Meritorious Svc. Am. Chiropractic Registry of Radiologic Technologists, Cert. Recognition for Inspiration, Guidance, and Support Delta Tau Alpha, 1989, Cert. Appreciation Chiropractic Assn. South Africa, 1988. Mem. Am. Chiropractic Assn., Am. Chiropractic Coll. Radiology (pres. 1983-85, exec. com. 1985-86), Am. Chiropractic Coun. on Diagnostic Imaging, Am. Chiropractic Coun. on Diagnosis and Internal Disorders, Am. Chiropractic Coun. on Nutrition, Nat. Coll. Alumni Assn., Am. Pub. Health Assn., Assn. Chiropractic Colls. (sec.-treas. 1986-91), Coun. Chiropractic Edn. (sec.-treas. 1988-90, v.p. 1990-92, pres. 1992-94, immediate past pres. 1994), Fla. Chiropractic Assn. (chmn. radiol. health com. 1977-. Republican. Lutheran. Avocations: racket ball, reading, automobile rehabilitation. Home: 276 E Edward St Lombard IL 60148-3905

WINTER-SWITZ, CHERYL DONNA, travel company executive; b. Jacksonville, Fla., Dec. 6, 1947; d. Jacqueline Marie (Carroll) Winter; m. Frank C. Snedaker, June 24, 1974 (div. May 1976); m. Robert William Switz, July 1, 1981. AA, City Coll. of San Francisco, 1986; BS, Golden Gate U., 1990, MBA, 1992. Bookkeeper, agt. McQuade Tours, Ft. Lauderdale, Fla., 1967-69; mgr. Boca Raton (Fla.) Travel, 1969-76; owner, mgr. Ocean Travel, Boca Raton, 1976-79; ind. contractor Far Horizons Travel, Boca Raton, 1979-80; mgr. Tara/BPF Travel, San Francisco, 1981-84; mgr. travel. dept. Ernst & Whinney/Lifeco Travel, San Francisco, 1984-86; travel cons. Siemer & Hand Travel, San Francisco, 1989—; instr. Golden Gate U., 1986—, U. San Francisco. Mem. Amateur Trapshooting Assn., Hotel and Restaurant Mgmt. Club. Republican. Episcopalian. Avocations: trap shooting, gardening, cooking, travelling, reading. Home: 642 Brussels St San Francisco CA 94134-1902 Office: Siemer & Hand Travel 101 California St Ste 1750 San Francisco CA 94111-5862

WINTHROP, JOHN, investment company executive; b. Boston, June 22, 1936; s. Nathaniel Thayer and Serita Bartlett (Harwood) W.; m. Elizabeth Goltra; children: John, H. Grenville, Bayard, Edward Field Winthrop. BA, Harvard U., 1958; MBA, Columbia U., 1962. With Wood, Struthers & Winthrop, N.Y.C., 1964-79; former chmn. Mgmt. Co. (subs. DJL); pres. de Vegh Fund, 1973-79, dir., 1973—; founder, pres. John Winthrop & Co., S.C.; dir. Alliance Capital Reserves, N.Y.C., Nat. Utilities & Industries, N.J., Ivanhoe Plantation, Inc., S.C., Pioneer Funds, Boston; bd. dirs. Am. Farmland Trust, Washington. founder, pres. John Winthrop & Co., S.C.; dir. Home Acct. Network, Inc., Charleston, S.C., Nat. Utilities and Industries, N.J., Ivanhoe Plantation, Inc., S.C., Pioneer Funds, Boston; bd. dirs. Am. Farmland Trust, Washington. Former bd. govs. Investment Co. Inst., Washington. With USNR, 1958-60. Mem. N.Y. Soc. Security Analysts, Mass. Hist. Soc., Harvard Alumni Assn. (bd. dirs.), Pilgrims. Republican. Clubs: Harvard (past bd. mgrs. N.Y.C. club), Knickerbocker (N.Y.C.). Home: 9 Ladson St Charleston SC 29401-2703 Office: One North Adger's Wharf Charleston SC 29401-2571

WINTHROP, JOHN, real estate company officer/executive; b. Salt Lake City, Apr. 20, 1947; m. Marilyn MacDonald, May 17, 1975; children: Grant Gordon, Clayton Hanford. AB cum laude, Yale U., 1969; JD magna cum laude, U. Tex., 1972. Bar: Calif. 1972. Law clk. 9th cir. U.S. Ct. Appeals, L.A., 1972-73; conseil juridique Coudert Freres, Paris, 1973-75; v.p. gen. counsel MacDonald Group, Ltd., L.A., 1976-82; pres., CEO MacDonald Mgmt. Corp. and MacDonald Group Ltd., L.A., 1982-86; pres., chief exec. officer MacDonald Corp. (gen. contractors), L.A., 1982-86; chmn., CEO Comstock Mgmt. Co., L.A., 1986—; pres., CEO Winthrop Investment Properties, Los Angeles, 1986—; CEO Veritas Imports, L.A., 1995—; bd. dirs. Plus Prods., Tiger's Milk Prods., Irvine, Calif., 1977-80. Bd. dirs., sec. L.A. Sheriff's Dept. Found.; bd. dirs. L.A. Opera. Mem. Calif. Bus. Properties Assn. (mem. bd. advisors 1981-87), Internat. Coun. Shopping Ctrs., Nat. Eagle Scout Assn. (life), French-Am. C. of C. (bd. dirs. 1982-87), Urban Land Inst., Nat. Realty Bd., Regency Club, Yale Club N.Y., Calif. Club, The Beach Club, Elizabethan Club. Republican. Office: Comstock Mgmt Co Penthouse 9460 Wilshire Blvd Beverly Hills CA 90212

WINTHROP, LAWRENCE FREDRICK, lawyer; b. L.A., Apr. 18, 1952; s. Murray and Vauneta (Cardwell) W.; BA with honors, Whittier Coll., 1974; JD magna cum laude, Calif. Western Sch., 1977. Bar: Ariz. 1977, Calif. 1977, U.S. Dist. Ct. Ariz. 1977, U.S. Dist. Ct. (so. dist.) Calif. 1981, U.S. Ct. Appeals (9th cir.) 1981, U.S. Dist. Ct. (cen. dist.) Calif. 1983, U.S. Supreme Ct. 1983. Assoc. Snell and Wilmer, Phoenix, 1977-83, ptnr., 1984-93, Doyle, Winthrop, Oberbillig & West, P.C., Phoenix, 1993—. judge pro tem Maricopa County Superior Ct., 1987—, Ariz. Ct. Appeals, 1992—; lectr. Ariz. personal injury law and practice and state and local tax law Tax Exec. Inst., Nat. Bus. Inst., Profl. Edn. Systems, Inc., Ariz. Trial Lawyers Assn., Maricopa County Bar Assn.; bd. dirs. Valley of the Sun Sch., 1989—, chmn., 1994—; mem. Vol. Lawyers Program, Phoenix, 1980—. Fellow Ariz. Bar Found., Maricopa Bar Found.; mem. ABA, Calif. Bar Assn., Ariz. Bar Assn. (mem. com. on exam, 1995—), Ariz. Tax Rsch. Assn. (bd. dirs. 1989-93), Maricopa County Bar Assn., Ariz. Assn. Def. Counsel (bd. dirs., pres. 1988-89, chmn. med.-malpractice com. 1993—). Republican. Methodist. Clubs: Aspen Valley, LaMancha Racquet. Avocations: music, golf, tennis. Editor-in-chief Calif. Western Law Rev., 1976-77. Home: 6031 N 2nd St Phoenix AZ 85012-1210 Office: Doyle Winthrop Oberbillig & West PC PO Box 10417 2800 N Central Ave Ste 1550 Phoenix AZ 85016-4666

WINTON, HOWARD PHILLIP, optometrist; b. Springfield, Mo., June 23, 1925; s. George Lecoumpt and Emma Pearl (Schoonover) W.; m. Frances Jeanne Zellweger, June 29, 1946; children: Susan, James, Stephen, Gary, Carolyn. Student, Northern Ill. Coll. of Optometry, Midwest Sch. of Optics; LHD, Ill. Coll. of Optometry, 1965. Pvt. practice optometry Melbourne, Fla.; nat. cons. to Surgeon Gen. USAF, 1979. Pres. Melbourne C. of C.; pres., chmn. bd. dirs. Brevard Econ. Devel. Coun., Brevard County, 1970-79. With USN, 1943-46, PTO. Named Optometrist of the Yr., Fla. Optometric Assn., 1972. Fellow Am. Acad. Optometry; mem. Fla. Optometric Assn. (pres. 1965), Am. Optometric Assn. (pres. 1975-76, mem. coun.), So. Coun. Optometrics (pres. 1968), Brevard Optometric Assn. (founder, pres. 1973), Rotary Internat. (founder Interact Club 1962, pres. Melbourne 1962).

WINTON, JAMES C., lawyer; b. Ft. Worth, Oct. 8, 1952. AB cum laude, U. So. Calif., 1974; JD magna cum laude, Southwestern U., 1977. Bar: Calif. 1977, U.S. Ct. Military Appeals 1979, D.C. 1980, U.S. Dist. Ct. (no. dist.) Calif. 1980, U.S. Dist. Ct. (ctrl. dist.) Calif. 1981, U.S. Dist. Ct. (so. dist.) Calif. 1983, U.S. Ct. Appeals (9th cir.) 1985, Tex. 1988, U.S. Dist. Ct. (so. dist.) Tex. 1989, U.S. Ct. Appeals (5th cir.) 1991, U.S. Dist. Ct. (no. dist.) Tex. 1992. Ptnr. Baker & Hostetler, Houston. Mem. ABA, State Bar Calif., D.C. Bar, State Bar Tex., Maritime Law Assn. U.S., Houston Bar Assn. Office: Baker & Hostetler 1000 Louisiana St Ste 2000 Houston TX 77002-5009*

WINTOUR, ANNA, editor; b. Eng., Nov. 3, 1949; came to U.S., 1976; d. Charles and Elinor W.; m. David Shaffer, Sept. 1984; children: Charles, Kate. Student, Queens Coll., 1963-67. Deputy fashion editor Harper's and Queen Mag., London, 1970-76; fashion editor Harper's Bazaar, New York, 1976-77; fashion and beauty editor Viva Mag., New York, 1977-78; contbg. editor fashion and style Savvy Mag., New York, 1980-81; sr. editor N.Y. Mag., 1981-83; creative dir. U.S. Vogue, N.Y., 1983-86; editor-in-chief British Vogue, London, 1986-87, House and Garden, N.Y., 1987-88, Vogue, N.Y., 1988—. Office: Vogue Mag Conde Nast Bldg 350 Madison Ave New York NY 10017-3704*

WINTRODE, RALPH CHARLES, lawyer; b. Hollywood, Calif., Dec. 21, 1942; s. Ralph Osborne and Maureen (Kavanagh) W.; m. Leslie Ann O'Rourke, July 2, 1966 (div. Feb. 1994); children: R. Christopher, Patrick L., Ryan B. BS in Acctg., U. So. Calif., 1966, JD, 1967. Bar: Calif. 1967, N.Y. 1984, Japan 1989, Washington 1990. From assoc. to ptnr. Gibson, Dunn & Crutcher, Tokyo, L.A., Newport Beach and Irvine, Calif., 1967—. Sec. Music Ctr. Los Angeles County, 1986-88; bd. dirs. Coro Found., L.A. County, 1986-87. Mem. Newport Harbor Club, Am. Club Tokyo. Avocations: sailboat racing, car racing, flying. Office: Gibson Dunn & Crutcher 4 Park Plz Irvine CA 92714-8560 also: Gibson Dunn & Crutcher 333 S Grand Ave Los Angeles CA 90071-1504

WINTROL, JOHN PATRICK, lawyer; b. Wichita, Kans., Feb. 13, 1941; s. Clarence Joseph and Margaret (Gill) W.; m. Janet Lee Mitchell; children: John Howard, Joanna Lee. BA, Rockhurst Coll., 1963; JD, Georgetown U., 1969. Bar. D.C. 1969, U.S. Ct. Appeals (5th, 10th and 11th cirs.) 1981, U.S. Dist. Ct. Md. 1984. Law clk. to Hon. Howard Corcoran U.S. Dist. Ct., Washington, 1969-71; assoc. Howrey & Simon, Washington, 1971-77; mng. ptnr. Perito, Duerk & Pinco, Washington, 1978-85; ptnr. Finley Kumble, Washington, 1985-87, Laxalt, Washington, Perito & Dubuc, Washington, 1987-91, McDermott, Will & Emery, Washington, 1991—; mem. jud. conf. U.S. Ct. Appeals (D.C. cir.). Mem. ABA, D.C. Bar Assn. Democrat. Roman Catholic. Office: McDermott Will & Emery 1850 K St NW Washington DC 20006-2213

WINTROUB, BRUCE URICH, dermatologist, educator, researcher; b. Milw., Nov. 8, 1943; s. Ernest Bernard and Janet (Zien) W.; m. Marya Kraus, Jan. 20, 1973; children: Annie, Ben, Molly. BA, Amherst Coll., 1965; MD, Washington U., St. Louis, 1969. Diplomate Am. Bd. Internal Medicine, Am. Bd. Dermatology. Intern in medicine Peter Bent Brigham Hosp., Boston, 1969-70, jr. asst. resident in medicine, 1970-71, jr. assoc. in medicine, 1976-80, asst. then attending physician, 1976-81; resident in dermatology Harvard Med. Sch., Boston, 1974-76, instr., 1976-78, asst. prof., 1978-82; assoc. prof. dermatology Sch. Medicine, U. Calif., San Francisco, 1982-85, attending physician med. ctr., 1982—, prof., mem. exec. com. dept. dermatology, 1985-95; chmn. exec. com. dept. dermatology U. Calif., San Francisco, 1985-95; mem. dean's adv. com., governing bd. continuing med. edn., other coms. Sch. Medicine, U. Calif., San Francisco, 1986—; exec. vice dean Sch. Medicine U. Calif., San Francisco, 1995—; assoc.dean Sch. Medicine, U. Calif., Mount Zion, 1990—; dir. Dermatology Assocs., San Francisco, 1982-85; cons. in dermatology Mass. Gen. Hosp., Boston, 1976-82, Beth Israel Hosp. and Children's Hosp. Med. Ctr., Boston, 1978-82, Parker Hill Med. Ctr., Boston, 1980-82; attending physician Robert B. Brigham Hosp. div. Brigham and Women's Hosp., Boston, 1980-81, assoc., 1980-82; chief dermatology svc. Brockton (Mass.) VA Med. Ctr., 1980-82; asst. chief dermatology VA Med. Ctr., San Francisco, 1982-85, mem. space com., 1984-85, dean's adv. com., 1985—, chmn. budget com., 1987—; clin. investigator Nat. Inst. Allergy, Metabolism and Digestive Disease, NIH, 1978. Author: (with others) Biochemistry of the Acute Allergic Reactions, Fifth International Symposium, 1988; contbr. numerous articles, abstracts to profl. jours. NIH clin. fellow and grantee, 1967-69. Fellow Am. Acad. Dermatology (com. evaluations 1985—, coun. govt. liaison 1987—, congress on tech. plannning commn. 1988—, assoc. editor Dialogues in Dermatology jour. 1982-85, Stellwagon prize 1976); mem. Soc. Investigative Dermatology (chmn. pub. rels. com. 1987-88), Assn. Profs. Dermatology (chmn. program com. 1987—, bd. dirs.), Pacific Dermatol. Assn. (chmn. program com. 1987—), San Francisco Dermatol. Soc., Am. Fedn. Clin. Rsch. (chmn. dermatology program 1988-89), Am. Assn. Immunology, Dystrophic Epidermolysis Bullosa Rsch. Am. (bd. dirs. 1981), Internat. Soc. Dermatology, Internat. Soc. Cutaneous Pharmacology (founding mem.), Am. Soc. Clin. Investigation, Skin Pharmacology Soc., Calif. Med. Soc., San Francisco Med. Soc., Clin. Immunology Soc., Dermatology Found., (bd. dirs., exec. com.), AAAS, Am. Assn. Physicians, Calif. Acad. Medicine, Am. Dermatol. Assn., Sigma Xi, Alpha Omega Alpha. Avocation: golf. Office: Deans Office Sch Medicine U Calif San Francisco 513 Parnassus Ave Rm S224 San Francisco CA 94143-0410

WINWOOD, STEPHEN LAWRENCE, musician, composer; b. Birmingham, Eng., May 12, 1948; s. Lawrence Samuel and Lillian Mary (Saunders) W.; m. Eugenia Crafton, Jan. 17, 1987; children: Mary Clare, Elizabeth Dawn, Stephen Calhoun, Lillian Eugenia. Rec. artist Spencer Davis Group, 1964-67, Blind Faith, 1970, Traffic, 1967-74; solo artist N.Y.C. and in England, 1974—; dir. F.S. Ltd. Albums include: Arc of a Diver, 1980, Talking Back to the Night, 1982, Back in the High Life, 1986, Roll With It, 1988 (Grammy 1989), Chronicles, Refugees of the Heart, 1991, Traffic: Far From Home, 1994. Recipient 14 Gold Record awards, 4 Platinum Record awards, 2 Grammy awards.

WINZELER, JUDITH KAY, foundation administrator; b. Canton, Ohio, Dec. 17, 1942; d. Charles and Pauline Doris (Werstler) Wenzlawski; m. Robert Lee Winzeler, Nov. 4, 1961; children: Elizabeth Ann, Alice Louise Winzeler Smith. BA, U. Nev., 1971, MA, 1981. Instr. anthropology Western Nev. C.C., Reno, 1976-77; program developer Nev. Humanities Com., Reno, 1977-78, asst. dir., 1978-80, assoc. dir., 1980-84, exec. dir., 1984—; panelist NEH, 1991; mem. Hilliard Found. Com., Reno, 1984—; mem. program com. Fedn. of State Humanities Couns., Washington, 1989; mem. selections com. Grace A. Griffen Chair in History, Reno, 1992. Mem. Nev. Commn. on Bicentennial of U.S. Constn., 1985-91; pres. Luth. Ch. of Good Shepherd, Reno, 1987-89; mem. nominating com. Evang. Luth. Ch. Am., Sierra Synod, Oakland, Calif., 1991-94; bd. dirs., officer Reno/Sparks Metro Min., Reno, 1987—; active Nev. Hist. Soc., Nev. State Mus., Nev. Mus. Art, Western Folklife Ctr., Friends of Washoe County Libr. Mem. Asian Pacific Assn. of No. Nev., Sierra Art Found., Reno Rotary Club, Nev. Corral, Westerners Internat. Avocation: traveling. Home: 1579 Belford Rd Reno NV 89509-3907 Office: Nev Humanities Com 1034 N Sierra St Reno NV 89503-3721

WINZENRIED, JESSE DAVID, retired petroleum executive; b. Byron, Wyo., June 13, 1922; s. Fritz and Margaret Smith W.; m. Marion Suzan Jacobson, Mar. 15, 1945 (dec. 1984); children: Suzan Winzenried Carlston, Jay Albert, Keith Frederic; m. Lela Madsen, Mar. 12, 1988. B.S., U. Wyo., 1945; M.S., U. Denver, 1946; Ph.D., NYU, 1955. Dir. research Tax Found., N.Y.C., 1947-56; sr. v.p. Husky Oil Ltd., Cody, Wyo., 1956-65, Calgary, Alta., Can., 1965-67; v.p. firm Booz, Allen & Hamilton, Cleve., 1968-69; v.p. Coastal States Gas Corp., Houston, 1969-74; group v.p., dir. Crown Central Petroleum Corp., Balt., 1974-81; vice chmn., dir. Securities Investor Protection Corp., Washington, 1988-95; lectr. mgmt. NYU, 1955-56. Contbr. articles to profl. jours. Served with US Air Corps, 1942-43. Republican. Mem. Ch. Jesus Christ of Latter-day Saints.

WION, J. MIKE, oil industry executive; b. 1944. With Shell Oil Co., Inc., Anacortes, Wash., 1968-93; with Atlas Processing Co., Shreveport, La., 1993—, pres. Office: Atlas Processing Co 3333 Midway St Shreveport LA 71109-5719*

WIOT, JEROME FRANCIS, radiologist; b. Cin., Aug. 24, 1927; s. Daniel and Elvera (Weisgerber) W.; m. Andrea Kockritz, July 29, 1972; children—J. Geoffrey, Jason. M.D., U. Cin., 1953. Diplomate: Am. Bd. Radiology (trustee, pres.). Intern Cin. Gen. Hosp., 1953-54, resident, 1954-55, 58-59; gen. practice medicine Wyoming, Ohio, 1955-57; mem. faculty U. Cin., 1959-67, 68—, prof., chmn. radiology, 1973-93, acting sr. v.p., provost for med. affairs, 1985-86; practice medicine specializing in radiology Tampa, Fla., 1967-68. Contbr. articles to med. jours. Bd. dirs. Ruth Lyons Fund. Served with USN, 1945-46. Fellow Am. Coll. Radiology (pres. 1983-84, chmn. commn. on diagnostic radiology); mem. Radiol. Soc. N.Am., Am. Roentgen Ray Soc. (pres. 1986-87), Am. Bd. Radiology (pres. 1982-84), Ohio Med. Assn., Cin. Acad. Medicine, Radiol. Soc. Greater Cin., Ohio Radiol. Soc., Am. Thoracic Soc., Ohio Thoracic Soc., Fleischner Soc., Soc. Gastrointestinal Radiologists. Office: U Cin Med Ctr 234 Goodman St Cincinnati OH 45267-0001

WIPKE, W. TODD, chemistry educator; b. St. Charles, Mo., Dec. 16, 1940; BS, U. Mo., Columbia, 1962; PhD, U. Calif., Berkeley, 1965. Research chemist Esso Research and Engring. Co., Baton Rouge, 1962; postdoctoral research fellow Harvard U., 1967-69; asst. prof. Princeton U., 1969-75; assoc. prof. chemistry, U. Calif., Santa Cruz, 1975-81, prof. chemistry, 1981—; founder, cons. Molecular Design Ltd., San Leandro, Calif., 1978-91, Ciba-Geigy, Basle, Switzerland, 1978-82, BASF, Ludwigshafen, Fed. REpublic Germany, 1974-78, Squibb, Princeton, N.J., 1976-81; adv. EPA, 1984—. Editor: Computer Representation and Manipulation of Chemical Information, 1973, Computer-Assisted Organic Synthesis, 1977 ; editor in chief: (jour.) Tetrahedron Computer Methodology, 1987-92; editor Tetrahedron and Tetrahedron Letters, 1987-92; contbr. articles to profl. jours. Served to capt. U.S. Army, 1966-67. Recipient Eastman Kodak Research award, 1964, Texaco Outstanding Research award, 1962; Alexander von Humboldt Sr. Scientist award, 1987; Merck Career Devel. grantee, 1970; NIH, fellow, 1964-65. Mem. NAS, Am. Chem. Soc. (assoc., Computers in Chemistry award 1987, Herman Skolnik award 1991), Assn. Computing Machinery, Chem. Soc., Am. Assn. Artificial Intelligence (charter), Chemical Structure Assn. (charter), Internat. Soc. Study Xenobiotics. Office: U Calif Dept Chemistry Santa Cruz CA 95064

WIRE, WILLIAM SHIDAKER, II, retired apparel and footwear manufacturing company executive; b. Cin., Jan. 5, 1932; s. William Shidaker and Gladys (Buckmaster) W.; m. Alice Dumas Jones, Aug. 31, 1957; children: Alice Wire Freeman, Deborah Wire Suber. Student, U. of South, 1950; AB, U. Ala., 1954, JD, 1956; LLM, NYU, 1957. Bar: Ala. 1956. Atty. Hamilton, Denniston, Butler & Riddick, Mobile, 1959-60; with Talladega Ins. Agy., Ala., 1961-62; with Genesco, Inc., Nashville, 1962-94, former chmn. and CEO; bd. dirs. Genesco Inc., 1st Am. Corp., 1st Am. Nat. Bank Nashville, Dollar Gen. Corp. Mem. Belle Meade Country Club (Nashville), University Club (N.Y.), Shoal Creek (Ala.) Club, Golf Club Tenn., Kappa Alpha. Presbyterian. Home: 6119 Stonehaven Dr Nashville TN 37215-5613

WIREMAN, BILLY OVERTON, college president; b. Jackson, Ky., Oct. 7, 1932; s. William and Emily (Bach) W.; m. Katie Marie Coomer, Mar. 3, 1955; children: J. Gary, Emily Kay Crigler. B.A., Georgetown Coll. (Ky.), 1954, LHD, 1987; M.A., U. Ky., 1957; Ed.D., Peabody Coll., Vanderbilt U., 1960; L.H.D., U. Tampa, 1970, Eckerd Coll., 1977, Georgetown Coll., 1987. Mem. faculty Eckerd Coll., St. Petersburg, Fla., 1960-63, v.p. devel., 1963-68, pres., 1968-77; pres. Queens Coll., Charlotte, N.C., 1978—; guest lectr. People's U. Beijing (China), 1982, also Hong Kong, Taiwan, Philippines; pub. interviews with polit. leaders in Phillipines and South Korea, 1988, 89; rsch. work in USSR, 1989; spkr. fundraising panel, evaluator, accrediting agy. So. Assn. Colls. and Schs., 1989; past v.p. Ormond Beach Pier, Inc., Fla. Co-author: Getting It All Together: The New American Imperative, 1973, Dangerous Grace, 1992, The Peninsula Plot, 1995; contbr. over 150 articles to profl. publs. Chmn. edn. divsn. St. Petersburg United Fund, 1966-67; del. White House Conf. children and Youth, 1970, White House Conf. You, 1971; trustee, chmn. devel. cabinet United Bd. Christian Higher Edn. in Asia, 1974-83; chmn., trustee Bd. for Need-Based Med. Student Loans, State of N.C., 1982; past bd. dirs. Coll. Fund Pinellas County; mem. internat. adv. bd. Han Nam U., Korea, 1987-92, OALS Coll. Bd.; rep. Charlotte C. of C. in China; chair Charlotte-Mecklenburg Cmty. Rels. Com., 1989-95, bd. dirs. Friendship Trays, Charlotte World Affairs Coun.; vice chair Multiple Sclerosis Dinner of Champions Hope Award event, 1988; chmn. Charlotte-Mecklenburg Cmty. Rels. Com. Bd., co-chair Common Ground; mem. steering com. Wildacres Inititiative; bd. dirs. Johnson C. Smith U.; bd. visitors Charlotte Country Day Sch.; mem. Billy Graham Crusade Com., 1996; chmn. selection com. Wilderacres Leadership Initiative. Recipient Liberty Bell award St. Petersburg Bar Assn., 1971, Univ. Medal of Honor Han Nam U., South Korea, 1988, Dinner of Champions Hope award Multiple Sclerosis Soc., Charlotte, 1989. Mem. AAUP, Am. acad. Polit. and Socil Sci., Am. Mgmt. Assn. (dir.), Club of Rome, Am. Coun. Edn. (Internat. Commn.), Young Pres. Orgn., Univ. Club of N.Y.C., N.C. Soc. of N.Y., Charlotte Squires, Tower Club, City Club of Charlotte, Goodfellows, N.C. Trade Assn. (bd. dirs.), British Am. Bus. Assn. (bd. dirs.), Friday Fellows. Office: Queens Coll 1900 Selwyn Ave Charlotte NC 28274-0001

WIRKEN, JAMES CHARLES, lawyer; b. Lansing, Mich., July 3, 1944; s. Frank and Mary (Brosnahan) W.; m. Mary Morse, June 12, 1971; children: Christopher, Erika, Kurt, Gretchen, Jeffrey, Matthew. BA in English, Rockhurst Coll., 1967; JD, St. Louis U., 1970. Bar: Mo. 1970, U.S. Dist. Ct. (we. dist.) Mo. 1970. Asst. prosecuter Jackson County, Kansas City, Mo., 1970-72; assoc. Morris, Larson, King, Stamper & Bold, Kansas City, Mo., 1972-75; dir. Spradley, Wirken, Reismeyer & King, Kansas City, Mo., 1976-88, Wirken & King, Kansas City, Mo., 1988-93; pres. The Waken Group, Kansas City, Mo., 1993—; adj. prof. law U. Mo., Kansas City, 1984—. Author: Managing a Practice and Avoiding Malpractice, 1983; co-author Missouri Civil Procedure Form Book, 1984; mem. editorial bd. Mo. Law Weekly, 1989—, Lender Liability News, 1990—. Mem. ABA, Nat. Conf. Bar Pres. (coun. 1993—), Met. Bar Caucus (pres. 1992-93), Am. Trial Lawyers Assn., Mo. Bar Assn. (bd. govs. 1976-78, chmn. econs. and methods practice com. 1982-84, quality and methods of practice com. 1989-91, vice chmn. young lawyers sect. 1976-78), Mo. Assn. Trial Attys. (bd. govs. 1983-85), Kansas City Met. Bar Assn. (pres. young lawyers sect. 1975, chair legal assistance com. 1977-78, chair tort law com. 1982, pres. 1990), L.P. Gas Group (founder, chair 1991—). Home: 47 W 53rd Kansas City MO 64112 Office: Wirken Group PC 4717 Grand Ave Ste 620 Kansas City MO 64112-2206

WIRKLER, NORMAN EDWARD, architectural, engineering, construction management firm executive; b. Garnavillo, Iowa, Apr. 1, 1937; s. Herbert J. and Irene (Kregel) W.; m. Margaret Anne Gift, Oct. 16, 1959; children: Chris Edward, Scott Norman, Elizabeth Anne. BArch, Iowa State U., 1959. Designer The Durrant Group Inc., Dubuque, Iowa, 1959-64, assoc., 1964-67, prin., 1967-82; pres. The Durrant Group Inc., Denver, 1982—; co-owner Wirkler Property Mgmt. Snowmass Co., 1993; pres. Foresite Capital Facilities Corp., Denver County, 1993—; commr., mem. exec. com. Commn. on Accreditation on Corrections, 1985-91; archtl. cons. to Am. Correctional Assn. Standards Program; mem. Am. Correctional Assn. Standards Com., 1992-98; v.p. Garnavillo (Iowa) Bank Corp. Co-author: Design Guide for Secure Adult Correctional Facilities, 1983;. Bd. dirs. United Way, Dubuque,

1984. Fellow AIA (pres. Iowa chpt. 1977; mem. nat. com. on arch. for justice 1974—, chmn. 1979; chmn. AIA Ins. Trust 1985-87, mem. Colo. chpt. 1987—); mem. ASTM (detention component standards com. 1982-84), Dubuque C. of C. (legis. com. 1978-83, chmn. 1979; v.p. 1984, exec. com. 1982-85), Iowa State U. Devel. Coun. Club. Republican. Avocations: flying, skiing, jogging, golf, hunting. Office: The Durrant Group Inc Ste 240 3773 Cherry Creek North Dr Denver CO 80209-3812

WIRSCHING, CHARLES PHILIPP, JR., brokerage house executive, investor; b. Chgo., Oct. 26, 1935; s. Charles Philipp and Mamie Ethel (York) W.; m. Beverly Ann Bryan, May 28, 1966. BA, U. N.C., 1957. Sales rep. Adams-Millis Corp., Chgo., 1963-67; ptnr. Schwartz-Wirsching, Chgo., 1968-70; sec., dir. Edwin H. Mann, Inc., Chgo., 1971-74; stockbroker Paine Webber, Inc., Chgo., 1975-85, account v.p., 1986-95; ret., 1995; ind. cons. Paine Webber, Inc., Chgo., 1996—. Mem. adv. coun. John Nuveen & Co., Inc., 1993-95; trustee Wirsching Charitable Trust, 1987—. Republican. Episcopalian. Avocation: foreign travel. Home and Office: 434 Clinton Pl River Forest IL 60305-2249

WIRSIG, WOODROW, magazine editor, trade organization executive, business executive; b. Spokane, Wash., June 28, 1916; s. Otto Alan and Beulah Juliet (Marohn) W.; m. Jane Barbara Dealy, Dec. 11, 1942; children: Alan Robert, Guy Rodney, Paul Harold. Student, Kearney (Nebr.) State Tchrs. Coll., Los Angeles City Coll., UCLA, 1933-39; B.A., Occidental Coll., 1941; M.S., Columbia Grad. Sch. Journalism, 1942. Dir. Occidental Coll. News Bur., 1939-41; radio newswriter WQXR, N.Y.C., 1941-42; news writer, propaganda analyst CBS, 1942-43; rewrite man Los Angeles Times, 1943-44; asst. editor This Week mag., 1944-45; staff writer Look mag., 1946, asst. mng. editor, 1946-49, exec. editor, 1950-52; mng. editor Quick mag., 1949-50; asso. editor Newsweek mag., Ladies' Home Jour., 1952; editor Woman's Home Companion, 1952-56; editorial cons. Ednl. Testing Service, Princeton, 1957-67; TV cons. NBC-TV, ABC-TV; creator Nat. Daytime Radio Programs, 1957-60; radio documentary Companion; pres. communications firm Wirsig, Gordon and O'Connor, Inc., 1956-58; editor Printers' Ink mag., N.Y.C., 1958-65, Salesweek mag., 1959-60; editorial dir. Overseas Press Club ann. mag. Dateline, 1961, 62; creator, editorial dir. Calif. Life mag.; pres. Better Bus. Bur. Met. N.Y., Inc., 1966-77; also pres. Edn. Research Found.; pres. Bus. Advocacy Center, Inc., 1977—; creator Corp. Social Accountability Audit and Customer Services/Consumer Affairs Audit.; Cons. to Office Sec. HEW, 1965-66. Author: I Love You, Too., 1990; editor, contbr.: Your Diabetes (Dr. Herbert Pollack), 1951; editor: Advertising: Today-Yesterday-Tomorrow; New Products Marketing; cons. editor: Principles of Advertising; contbr. nat. mags.; lectr.; syndicated columnist: other newspapers L.A. Times, 1964-65. Recipient gold medal Benjamin Franklin Mag. Awards, 1956. Mem. Soc. Consumer Affairs Profls. (pres. 1983), Newcomen Soc., Archons, Players Club, Overseas Press Club, Nat. Press Club, N.Y. Advt. Club, N.Y.C. Club, Springdale Country Club, Evergreen Country Club (v.p.), Nassau Club, Century Assn., Families for Alzheimers Rights Assn. (pres. 1994—), Univ. Club, Sigma Delta Chi, Phi Gamma Delta, Gamma Delta Upsilon. Democrat. Presbyterian. Home and Office: Sandhill Cove 1459 SW Shoreline Dr Palm City FL 34990-4533

WIRSZUP, IZAAK, mathematician, educator; b. Wilno, Poland, Jan. 5, 1915; came to U.S., 1949, naturalized, 1955; s. Samuel and Pera (Golomb) W.; m. Pola Ofman, July 19, 1940 (dec. 1943); 1 son Vladimir (dec. 1943); m. Pera Poswianska, Apr. 23, 1949; 1 dau., Marina (Mrs. Arnold M. Tatar). Magister of Philosophy in Math, U. Wilno, 1939; Ph.D. in Math, U. Chgo., 1955. Lectr. math. Tech. Inst. Wilno, 1939-41; dir. Bur. d'Études et de Statistiques Spéciales, Société Centrale d'Achat-Société Anonyme des Monoprix, Paris, 1946-49; mem. faculty U. Chgo., 1949—, prof. math., 1965-85, prof. math. emeritus, 1985—, prin. investigator U. Chgo. Sch. Math. Project (sponsored by Amoco Found., also dir. resource devel. component), 1983—, dir. Internat. Math. Edn. Resource Ctr., 1988—; dir. NSF Survey Applied Soviet Rsch. in Math. Edn., 1985-91; cons. Ford Found., Colombia, Peru, 1965-66, Sch. Math Study Group, 1960, 61, 66-68; participant, writer tchr. tng. material African Math. Program, Entebbe, Uganda, summer 1964, Mombasa, Kenya, summers 1965-66; assoc. dir. Survey Recent Ea. European Math. Lit., 1956-68, dir., 1968-84; dir. NSF program application computers to mgmt., 1976-83; cons. NSF-AID Sci. Edn. Program, India, 1969; mem. U.S. Commn. on Math. Instn., 1969-73. Contbr. articles to profl. jours.; Editor Math. books, transls., adaptions from Russian.; Adviser math.: Ency. Brit., 1971—. Recipient Lewellyn John and Harriet Manchester Quantrell award U. Chgo., 1958, Univ. Alumni Svc. medal, U. Chgo., 1994; resident master Woodward Ct., U. Chgo., 1971-85; endowed Wirszup Lecture Series, U. Chgo., 1986. Mem. N.Y. Acad. Scis., Am. Math. Soc., Math. Assn. Am., AAAS, Nat. Council Tchrs. Math. (chmn. com. internat. math. edn. 1967-69, lifetime achievement medal for leadership, tchg., and svc. in maths. edn. 1996). Home: 5750 S Kenwood Ave Chicago IL 60637-1744 Office: U Chgo Dept Math 5734 S University Ave Chicago IL 60637-1514

WIRT, FREDERICK MARSHALL, political scientist; b. Radford, Va., July 27, 1924; s. Harry Johnson, Sr. and Goldie (Turpin) W.; m. Elizabeth Cook, Sept. 6, 1947; children: Leslie Lee, Sandra Sue, Wendy Ann. B.A., DePauw U., 1948; M.A., Ohio State U., 1949, Ph.D., 1956. Instr. to prof. polit. sci. Denison U., Granville, Ohio, 1952-66; vis. prof., lectr. U. Calif., Berkeley, 1966-68, 69-72; dir. policy sci. grad. program U. Md. Balt. County, 1972-75; prof. polit. sci. U. Ill., Urbana, 1975—; dir. Inst. for Desegregation Problems, U. Calif.-Berkeley, 1970-72; cons. Motion Picture Assn. Am., Rand Corp., Nat. Inst. Edn., SUNY Sch. Edn. Albany; vis. prof. U. Rochester, Nova U., U. Melbourne; acad. visitor London Sch. Econs. Author: Politics of Southern Equality, 1970 (honorable mention for best book 1972), Power in the City, 1974; (with others) The Polity of the School, 1975, Political Science and School Politics, 1977, Education, Recession, and the World Village, 1986, (with others) Culture and Education Policy in the American States, 1992. Mem. Granville City Charter Commn., 1964. Am. Philos. Soc. grantee, Denison Rsch. Assn. grantee, U. Ill. Rsch. Bd. grantee, NEH grantee, Ford Found. grantee, Ctr. Advanced Studies grantee; U. Ill. fellow, Dept. Edn. fellow, Spencer Found. fellow; recipient Lifetime Achievement awards Am. Ednl. Rsch. Assn., 1975, Am. Polit. Sci. Assn., 1994. Mem. Am. Polit. Sci. Assn. (nat. council, Career Achievement award 1993), Midwestern Polit. Sci. Assn., Am. Ednl. Rsch. Assn., Policy Studies Orgn. Home: 2007B Eagle Ridge Ct Urbana IL 61801-8617 Office: U Ill Dept of Polit Sci Urbana IL 61801

WIRT, MICHAEL JAMES, library director; b. Sault Ste. Marie, Mich., May 21, 1947; s. Arthur James and Blanche Marian (Carruth) W.; m. Barbara Ann Hallesy, Aug. 12, 1972; 1 child, Brendan. BA, Mich. State U., 1969; MLS, U. Mich., 1971; postgrad. U. Wash., 1990. Cert. librarian, Wash. Acting librarian Univ. Mich., Ctr. for Research on Econ. Devel., Ann Arbor, 1971-72; instnl. services librarian Spokane County Library Dist., Wash., 1972-76, asst. dir., 1976-79, acting dir., 1979, dir., 1980—. Mem. Adv. com. Partnership for Rural Improvement, Spokane, 1982-85, Wash. State Libr. Planning and Devel. Com., 1984-85, Ea. Wash. U. Young Writers Project Adv. Bd., 1988-89; mem. issues selection com. Citizens League of Greater Spokane, 1991-93, City of Spokane Indian Trail Specific Plan Task Force, 1992-95; mem. comm. com. United Way Spokane County, 1994. Mem. Wash. Libr. Assn. (2d v.p. 1984-86, Merit award 1984, dir. 1989-91, legis. planning com., 1991—, pub. rels. com. 1993—), Wash. Libr. Network (rep. Computer Svc. Coun. 1983-86, v.p., treas. State Users Group 1986-87), Am. Libr. Assn. (Pub. Libr. Affiliates Network 1990-93, PLA Bus. Coun. 1990-94, chmn. 1991-94), Spokane Valley C. of C. (local govt. affairs com. 1987—), Spokane Area C. of C. (local govt. com. 1990-94, human svcs. com. 1990-92, chmn. 1991-92, govt. reorgn. task force 1995), Spokane Civic Theatre (bd. dirs. 1996—), Momentum (local govt. strategy com. 1992-94). Office: Spokane Ct Libr Dist 4322 N Argonne Rd Spokane WA 99212-1853

WIRTH, FREMONT PHILIP, neurosurgeon, educator; b. Nashville, July 23, 1940; s. Fremont P. and Willa (Dean) W.; m. Penelope Simpson, July 25, 1964; children: Fremont Philip II, Andrew Simpson, Carolyn Howe. BA with honors in History, Williams Coll., 1962; MD, Vanderbilt U., 1966. Diplomate Am. Bd. Neurol. Surgery (guest examiner 1989, bd. dirs. 1992—), Nat. Bd. Med. Examiners; cert. advanced trauma life support ACS. Surg. intern Johns Hopkins Hosp., Balt., 1966-67, resident and fellow in surgery, 1967-68; asst. resident in neurosurgery Barnes Hosp., Washington U., St. Louis, 1970-72, fellow in neurosurgery, 1972-74; pvt. practice, Savannah, Ga., 1974—; asst. clin. prof. neurosurgery Med. Coll. Ga., Augusta, 1991—, vis. prof., 1978, 79, 86, 87; mem. staff, neurosurg. ICU, St. Joseph's Hosp., 1974—, dir. 1978—; mem. staff Meml. Med. Ctr., 1974—, dir. rehab., 1983; mem. staff Candler Gen. Hosp., 1974—; med. dir. Head and Spinal Cord Injury Prevention Project for Ga., 1984—; presenter in field, 1970—; vis. prof. U. Md., Balt., 1981, Tufts New Eng. Med. Ctr., Boston, 1982. Series editor (with R.A. Ratcheson) Concepts in Neurosurgery, 1986-93; editor: (with Ratcheson) Neurosurgical Critical Care, Concepts in Neurological Surgery, Vol. 1, 1987, Ruptured Cerebral Aneurysms, Concepts in Neurological Surgery, Vol. 6, 1994; contbr. articles and book revs. to med. jours., chpts. to books. Elder Skidaway Island Presbyn. Ch., 1981-83; mem. pack 57 com. Cub Scouts Am., Savannah, 1979-84; mem. troop 57 com. Boy Scouts Am., Savannah, 1980-85, mem. fin. com. Coastal Empire coun., 1987-90, mem. adv. bd., 1990—; chmn. physicians' solicitation United Way Coastal Empire, 1987; bd. dirs. Think First Found., 1990—. With USPHS, 1968-70. Fellow ACS (bd. govs. 1984-90, sr. mem. trauma com. 1991—); mem. AMA (physician's recognition award 1973-76, 77-79, 80-82, 83-85, 88-91, 91-94, 95—), Congress Neurol. Surgeons (profl. conduct com. 1989—, Disting. Svc. award 1989), Neurol. Soc. Am., Am. Assn. Neurologic Surgeons, Brain Surgery Soc., Ga. Med. Soc., Med. Assn. Ga. (editl. bd. 1987-93), pres. 1995, Ga. Neurosurg. Soc. (exec. com. 1981-88, pres. 1988-89), So. Neurosurg. Soc. (exec. com. 1982-91, pres. 1988-89), Am. Heart Assn. (fellow stroke coun.). Avocations: golf, fly fishing, hunting. Office: Neurol Inst Savannah 4 E Jackson Blvd Savannah GA 31405-5810

WIRTH, LAWRENCE, chemicals executive; b. 1935. With prodn. Reynolds Consumer Products, Appleton, Wis., 1964-73, v.p.prodn., 1973-83, pres., CEO, 1983—. Office: Reynolds Consumer Products 670 N Perkins St Appleton WI 54914-3133*

WIRTH, PETER, lawyer; b. Halgehausen, Germany, July 17, 1950; came to U.S., 1956; BA, U. Wis., 1972; JD, Harvard U., 1975. Bar: Mass. 1975. Assoc. Palmer & Dodge, Boston, 1975-81, ptnr., 1982—; sr.v.p., gen. counsel Genzyme Corp., 1996—; lectr. grad. tax program Boston U., 1982-85. Mem. ABA, Mass. Bar Assn., Boston Bar Assn., Phi Beta Kappa. Office: Palmer & Dodge 1 Beacon St Boston MA 02108-3106 Office: Genzyme Corp One Kendall Square Cambridge MA 02139

WIRTH, TIMOTHY ENDICOTT, federal official, former senator; b. Santa Fe, Sept. 22, 1939; s. Cecil and Virginia Maude (Davis) W.; m. Wren Winslow, Nov. 26, 1965; children: Christopher, Kelsey. B.A., Harvard U., 1961, M.Ed., 1964; Ph.D., Stanford U., 1973. White House fellow, spl. asst. to sec. HEW, Washington, 1967; asst. to chmn. Nat. Urban Coalition, Washington, 1968; dep. asst. sec. for edn. HEW, Washington, 1969; v.p. Great Western United Corp., Denver, 1970; mgr. Rocky Mountain office Arthur D. Little, Inc. (cons. firm), Denver, 1971-73; mem. 94th-99th Congresses from 2d Colo. Dist., 1975-87, mem. energy and commerce com., sci. and tech. com., budget com., chmn. subcom. telecommunications, fin. and consumer protection; U.S. senator from Colo., 1987-93, mem. armed services com., energy and natural resources com., budget com., banking com., housing and urban affairs com.; counselor U.S. Dept. State, Washington, 1993-94, Under Sec. of State for global affairs, 1994—. Mem. Gov.'s Task Force on Returned Vietnam Vets., 1970-73; mem. bd. visitors U.S. Air Force Acad., 1978—; advisor Pres.'s Commn. on the 80's, 1979-80; trustee Planned Parenthood, Denver Head Start. Recipient Disting. Service award HEW, 1969; Ford Found. fellow, 1964-66. Mem. White House Fellows Assn. (pres. 1968-69), Denver Council Fgn. Relations (exec. com. 1974-75). Office: Dept of State Under Sec State Global Affr 2201 C St NW Washington DC 20520-0001

WIRTHLIN, DAVID BITNER, hospital administrator; b. Salt Lake City, Sept. 19, 1935; s. Joseph L. and Madeline (Bitner) W.; m. Anne Goalen, Apr. 25, 1961; children: Kimberly, Jennifer, David, Deborah, John, Marianne. BSBA cum laude, U. Utah, 1960; MHA, U. Minn., 1963. Asst. adminstr. Idaho Falls (Idaho) Latter Day Saints Hosp., 1963-66; asst. to adminstr. Latter Day Saints Hosp., Salt Lake City, 1966-67; 1st asst. adminstr. Latter Day Saints Hosp., 1967-70, assoc. adminstr., 1970-73, adminstr., 1973-85; adminstr. Primary Children's Med. Ctr., 1973-75; regional v.p. IHC Hosps., Inc., 1985-89; trustee Utah State Hosps.; mem. rev. com. Great Salt Lake Health Planning Agy., 1974; mem. Comprehensive Health Planning Rev. Com., 1975; chmn. Met. Hosp. Coun., 1975; mem. bd. Utah Profl. Rev., 1985-89; adv. com. Robert Wood Johnson Found.'s Hosp.-based Rural Health Care Program. Active with Mission for the LDS Ch., 1989-92, exec. dir. Inc Fund Devel., 1992—, exec. dir. LDS desert Hosp. Found., 1992; exec. dir. Altaview Cohon Wood Found. Fellow Am. Coll. Hosp. Adminstrs. (regent, mem. editl. bd. 1989); mem. Am. Hosp. Assn., Utah Hosp. Assn. (past pres.), Western Assn. Hosps. (del. from Utah Hosp. Assn.), Coun. Tchg. Hosps., Rotary, Timpanogos Club, Bonneville Knife and Fork Club. Republican. Home: 2757 St Marys Way Salt Lake City UT 84108-2071 Office: Intermountain Health Care Ste 2200 36 S State St Salt Lake City UT 84111

WIRTHLIN, JOSEPH B., church official; b. Salt Lake City, June 11, 1917; s. Joseph L. and Madeline (Bitner) W.; m. Elisa Young Rogers, May 26, 1941; 8 children. Degree in Bus. Adminstrn., U. Utah. Ordained apostle LDS Ch., 1986. Served a mission to Germany, Austria and Switzerland LDS Ch., 1930s, served in stake and ward aux. positions, counselor, bishop to mem. stake presidency, until 1971, 1st counselor Sunday Sch. Presidency, 1971-75, asst. to coun. of 12 apostles, 1975-76, gen. authority area supr. Europe area, 1975-78, mem. 1st Quorum of Seventy, 1976-86, exec. adminstr. to S.E. area U.S. and Caribbean Islands, 1978-82, mng. dir. Melchizedek Priesthood Com., Relief Soc. and Mil. Rels. Com., 1978-84; exec. adminstr. LDS Ch., Brazil, 1982-84; pres. Europe area of ch. LDS Ch., 1984-86, mem. presidency of 1st Quorum of Seventy, exec. dir. curriculum dept., editor ch. mags., 1986, apostle, 1986—, mem. missionary exec. coun., mem. gen. welfare svcs. com., ch. bd. edn. and bd. trustees, 1986—. Office: LDS Ch Joseph Smith Meml Bldg 15 E South Temple Salt Lake City UT 84150-1005

WIRTHS, THEODORE WILLIAM, public policy consultant; b. Ansonia, Conn., June 23, 1924; s. Theodore Eugene and Elizabeth (McLean) W.; m. Claudine Turner Gibson, Dec. 28, 1945; children: William M., David G. B.A., Yale, 1947; M.A., U. Ky., 1949; postgrad., U. N.C., 1948-51. Teaching fellow U. N.C., 1949-50, field dir. urban studies, 1951-53; with AEC, 1953-66; chief reports and emergency planning Savannah River Ops., Aiken, S.C., 1960-62; real estate officer Washington, 1962-64; planning officer, 1964-65, Congl. fellow, 1965-66; congl. liaison officer NSF, Washington, 1966-70, dep. for govt. liaison, 1970-73, dir. Office of Govt. and Pub. Programs, 1973-76, dir. Office Small Bus. R&D, 1976-83; cons. in sci. and pub. policy, 1983—. Author: (with Chapin, Gould and Denton) In the Shadow of a Defense Plant, 1954. Chmn. Aiken Zoning Bd. Adjustment, 1956-62; vol. Hospice of Frederick County, 1986— (Hospice Vol. of Yr. 1994, 95). With AUS, 1943-45, ETO. Recipient Meritorious Service award NSF, 1970, Disting. Service award NSF, 1983. Mem. AAAS. Episcopalian. Home: 6608 Jefferson Blvd PO Box 335 Braddock Heights MD 21714

WIRTZ, ARTHUR MICHAEL, JR., professional hockey team executive; m. Sunny Wirtz; children: Laura, Arthur III, Jimmy. BS, U. Pa. V.p. Chgo. Black Hawks, 1958—. Office: Consol Enterprises 680 N Lake Shore Dr Fl 19 Chicago IL 60611-4402 also: Chgo Black Hawks 1901 W Madison St Chicago IL 60612*

WIRTZ, VIRGINIA HAYNES, nursing educator. Diploma in nursing, St. Anthony Hosp., Louisville, 1951; BSN, Spalding Coll., 1962; MSN, U. Fla., 1967; EdD, E. Tex. State U., 1976. RN, Mass., Ky., Fla., Tex., Okla., Ill., La., Md., Wis.; cert. advanced adminstrn. ANCC. Nurse various med. orgns. and instns., Ky., Ill., and Mass., 1951-66; nursing educator various hosps. and univs., Ky., Fla., La., and Tex., 1952-75; DON women's clinic, prof. nursing Johns Hopkins Hosp. Coll. of Medicine, Balt., 1975-77; prof., chair baccalaureate nursing Ea. Ky. U., Richmond, 1977-78; asst. adminstr. patient care Prince Georges Hosp., Cheverly, Md., 1978-79, Suburban Hosp., Bethesda, Md., 1979-80, Citizens Meml. Hosp., Victoria, Tex., 1980-81; prof. grad. program U. Okla. Coll. Nursing, Oklahoma City, 1981-86; mgmt. cons. The ALPHA Group, 1986-89; prof., chair dept. nursing Assumption Coll., Worcester, Mass., 1989-93; prof., asst. dir. nursing U. So. Miss., 1993-95; prof., chair dept. nursing Edgewood Coll., Madison, Wis., 1995—; cons., lectr. in field, 1982—; mem. Nat. Commn. on Nursing Implementation Projects, 1985-86. Author: (book) Introduction to Budgeting: A Self-Paced Program, 1989, Advanced Budgeting: A Self-Paced Program, 1989; contbr. articles to profl. jours. Active Phoenix Players of Worcester. Grantee Internat. Edn. in Gynecology and Obstetrics, 1975, HHS. Mem. Nat. League for Nursing, New Eng. Orgn. Nursing, Mass. Assn. Colls. Nursing, Mass. Orgn. BS Programs for RNs, Mass. League for Nursing, R.I. League for Nursing (bd. dirs.), Wis. League for Nursing, Excellence in Nursing for Worcester, Phi Delta Kappa, Sigma Theta Tau. Baptist. Office: Edgewood Coll 855 Woodrow St Madison WI 53711

WIRTZ, WILLEM KINDLER, garden and lighting designer, public relations consultant; b. N.Y.C., Jan. 8, 1912; s. Carel Augustus Marie and Wilhelmina Johanetta (Kindler) W. Ed., Ethical Culture Sch., N.Y.C., also Inst. Musical Art, N.Y.C. Dir. exhibits svc. Pa. Art Program, 1937-42, pub. rels. dir., 1937-42; ptnr. Campbell-Wirtz Assos., Phila., 1942-51; pres. Willem Wirtz Assos., Phila., 1952—; founder, 1961, since pres. Willem Wirtz Garden Assos., Inc., and Willem Wirtz Assocs., mfrs. of Ribbonlite; design assoc. Am. Soc. Interior Decorators; dir. Am. Jour. Nursing Co.; also chmn. Pa. bull. award com., 1964; guest lectr. Charles Morris Price Sch., Phila.; pres. Phila. chpt. Am. Pub. Relations Assn., 1954-56, nat. sec., 1955-57, Eastern v.p., 1960. Inventor (with Isaiah Roossine): Ribbonlite. Mem. Nat. Assn. Pub. Rels. Counsel (dir.), Pub. Rels. Soc. Am. (v.p. 1961, assembly del. 1961-63), Pa. Hort. Soc., Phila. Art Alliance, Zool. Soc. Palm Beaches (sec. 1971), Netherlands-Am. Soc., Poinciana Club (Palm Beach, Fla.). Office: 228 Phipps Plz Palm Beach FL 33480-4241

WIRTZ, WILLIAM WADSWORTH, real estate and sports executive; b. Chgo., Oct. 5, 1929; s. Arthur Michael and Virginia (Wadsworth) W.; m. Joan Roney, Dec. 15, 1950 (dec. May 1983); children: William R., Gail W., Karen K., Peter R., Alison M.; m. Alice Pirie Hargrave, Dec. 1, 1987. A.B., Brown U., 1950. Pres. Chgo. Blackhawk Hockey Team, Inc., 1966—, Chgo. Stadium Corp., 1966—, Consol. Enterprises, Inc., Chgo., 1966—, Forman Realty Corp., Chgo., 1965—, 333 Bldg. Corp., Chgo., 1966—, Wirtz Corp., Chgo., 1964—; chmn. bd. govs. Nat. Hockey League. Inducted into NHL Hall of Fame, 1976; recipient Lester Patrick trophy, 1978. Clubs: Saddle and Cycle (Chgo.), Racquet (Chgo.), Mid-America (Chgo.); Fin and Feather (Elgin, Ill.); Sunset Ridge Country (Northbrook, Ill.). Office: Wirtz 680 N Lake Shore Dr Fl 19 Chicago IL 60611-4402 also: Chgo Stadium 1800 W Madison St Chicago IL 60612-2620 also: Nat Hockey Leage, 1155 Metcalfe St Ste 960, Montreal, PQ Canada H3B 2W2*

WIRTZ, WILLIAM WILLARD, lawyer; b. DeKalb, Ill., Mar. 14, 1912; s. William Wilbur and Alfa Belle (White) W.; m. Mary Jane Quisenberry, Sept. 8, 1936; children—Richard, Philip. Ed., No. Ill. State Teachers Coll., DeKalb, Ill., 1928-30, U. Calif. at Berkeley, 1930-31; A.B., Beloit Coll., 1933; LL.B., Harvard, 1937. Instr. Kewanee (Ill.) High Sch., 1933-34, U. Iowa, 1937-39; asst. prof. Sch. Law, Northwestern U., 1939-42; asst. gen. counsel Bd. Econ. Warfare, 1942-43; with War Labor Bd., 1943-45, gen. counsel and pub. mem., 1945; chmn. Nat. Wage Stblzn. Bd., 1946; prof. law Northwestern U., 1946-54; engaged law practice, 1955-61; sec. of labor Dept. Labor, 1962-69; prof. law U. San Diego;. Mem. Ill. Liquor Control Commn., 1950-56. Mem. Am., D.C., Ill. bar assns., Phi Beta Kappa, Beta Theta Pi, Delta Sigma Rho. Office: 1211 Connecticut Ave NW Washington DC 20036-2701

WIRZ, GEORGE O., bishop; b. Monroe, Wis., Jan. 17, 1929. Student, St. Francis Sem., Milw., Marquette U., Milw., Cath. U. Ordained priest Roman Cath. Ch., 1952. Appointed titular bishop of Municipa Roman Cath. Ch., Madison, Wis., 1978—; aux. bishop Roman Cath. Ch., Madison, 1978—. Office: St Patrick Church 404 E Main St Madison WI 53703-2891 Office: Box 11 15 E Wilson St Madison WI 53701*

WISBAUM, WAYNE DAVID, lawyer; b. Niagara Falls, N.Y., May 29, 1935; s. Franklin C. and Elizabeth (Boff) W.; m. Janet Katz, July 3, 1960; children—Karen, Wendy, Deborah. B.A., Cornell U., 1956; LL.B., Harvard U., 1959. Bar: N.Y. 1960. Assoc. Kavinoky & Cook, Buffalo, 1960-66; sr. ptnr. Kavinoky & Cook, 1966—; mem. adv. com. Ticor Title Co.; bd. dirs., pres., chmn. bd. Kleinhans Music Hall Mgmt. Inc. Pres. Buffalo Coun. on World Affairs, 1968-70; mem. Young Leadership Cabinet Nat. United Jewish Appeal, 1967-73; mem. com. on leadership devel. Nat. Coun. Jewish Fedn. and Welfare Funds, 1967—; mem. Mayor's Com. on Youth Opportunity; bd. dirs. Anti-Defamation League; mem. Coun. Internat. Studies, SUNY, Buffalo; chmn. Buffalo chpt. Am. Jewish Com.; treas. Buffalo Fedn. Jewish Philanthropies; bd. govs. United Jewish Fedn., Buffalo; chmn. bd. dirs. Buffalo Philharm. Orch. Soc.; bd. dirs., mem. exec. com. Burchfield Art Ctr.; bd. dirs., pres. Jewish Family Service of Erie County. Served to capt. U.S. Army, 1964. Recipient United Jewish Fedn. Buffalo Leadership award, 1967, Community Relations award Am. Jewish Com., 1985, Abram Pugash award Jewish Family Service, 1985; named Harvard Alumnus of Yr., 1990. Mem. ABA, N.Y. State Bar Assn. (chmn. com. lawyers title guaranty funds), Erie County Bar Assn., Am. Law Inst., Harvard Law Sch. Assn. Western N.Y. (sec.), Zool. Soc. Buffalo (dir., mem. exec. com.), Harvard Club (pres. Buffalo chpt., mem. N.Y.C. chpt.), Buffalo Club, Cornell Club (N.Y.C. chpt.), Zeta Beta Tau. Home: 180 Greenaway Rd Buffalo NY 14226-4166 Office: Kavinoky & Cook 120 Delaware Ave Buffalo NY 14202-2704

WISDOM, JOHN MINOR, federal judge; b. New Orleans, May 17, 1905; s. Mortimer Norton and Adelaide (Labatt) W.; m. Bonnie Stewart Mathews, Oct. 24, 1931; children: John Minor (dec.), Kathleen Mathews, Penelope Stewart Wisdom Tose. AB, Washington and Lee U., 1925; LLB, Tulane U., 1929, LLD (hon.), 1976; LLD (hon.), Oberlin Coll., 1963, San Diego U., 1979, Haverford Coll., 1982, Middlebury Coll., 1987, Harvard U., 1987, So. Meth. U., 1994. Bar: La. 1929. Mem. Wisdom, Stone, Pigman & Benjamin, New Orleans, 1929-57; judge U.S. Ct. Appeals (5th cir.), 1957—, now sr. judge; mem. Multi-Dist. Litigation Panel, 1968-78, chmn., 1975-78; mem. Spl. Ct. Regional Reorgn. of R.R.s, 1975-86, presiding judge, 1986—; adj. prof. law Tulane U., 1938-57; faculty IJA Appellate Judges Seminar, 1961-70; vis. coms. law schs. U. Chgo., Harvard U., U. San Diego. Mem. Pres.'s Com. on Govt. Contracts, 1953-57; past pres. New Orleans Council Social Agys.; Republican nat. committeeman for La., 1952-57; trustee Washington and Lee U., 1953—. Served from capt. to lt. col. USAAF, 1942-46. Decorated Legion of Merit, Army Commendation medal; recipient 1st Disting. Jurist award La. Bar Found., 1986, St. Thomas More Medallion, Loyola U. of La., 1987, Devitt Disting. Svc. to Justice award, 1989, Tulane Disting. Alumnus award, 1989, Alfred E. Clay award Children's Bur., 1992, Strength in Aging award (with Mrs. Wisdom) LSU Geriatric Ctr., 1992, LPB Living Legends award, 1993, Trumpet award Turner Broadcasting, 1994. Mem. ABA (chmn. appellate judges conf. 1966-67, 1st recipient John Minor Wisdom pub. svc. and profl. award sect. litigation 1990, Am. Inns of Ct. Lewis F. Powell Jr. award 1991, Fellows award young lawyers div. 1991, Pres.'s medal of Freedom 1993), Am. Acad. Arts and Scis., La. Bar Assn., New Orleans Bar Assn., La. Bar Found., Am. Law Inst. (coun. mem. 1961), La. Law Inst., Am. Judicature Soc., Order of Coif, Delta Kappa Epsilon, Phi Alpha Delta (Tom C. Clark Equal Justice under Law award 1982), Omicron Delta Kappa. Episcopalian. Clubs: Boston (New Orleans), Louisiana (New Orleans); Metropolitan (Washington). Office: John Minor Wisdom 200 John Minor Wisdom Bldg 600 Camp St New Orleans LA 70130-3425*

WISE, BARBARA SUE, counselor educator; b. Stillwater, Okla., Apr. 20, 1940; d. Horace Maynard and Joanna Maureen (Rose) Haws; m. Robert Lawrence Wise, Aug. 21, 1959 (div. Dec. 1989); children: Robert Todd, Christopher Anthony, Matthew Tate, Traci Elizabeth. BS, U. Ctrl. Okla., 1971, MEd, 1972; postgrad., Menningers Hosp., Topeka, 1988, Pacifica Grad. Inst., 1994. Lic. profl. counselor; cert. counselor substance abuse; cert. elem. tchr., mental retardation and learning disabilities. Coll. tchr. Southwestern Okla. State U., Weatherford, Okla., 1973-80; counselor Family Life Ctr., Oklahoma City, 1981-87; owner, mgr. Wise Couseling Inc., Oklahoma City, 1987—; program facilitator, counselor for adolescent dept. Laureate Pscyhiat. Hosp., Tulsa, 1992-94; counselor adolescents, case mgr. CPC Southwinds Hosp., Oklahoma City, Okla., 1995—; cons. Addiction Mgmt., Santa Fe, 1989-90; cons., writer Morter Health System, Rogers, Ark., 1993-94. Mem. ACA. Avocation: home decorating. Home: 820 N Macarthur Blvd Oklahoma City OK 73127-5608 Office: CPC Southwinds Hosp Oklahoma City OK 73159

WISE, CHARLES CONRAD, JR., educator, past government official, author; b. Washington, Apr. 1, 1913; s. Charles Conrad and Lorena May (Sweeney) W.; m. Ruth Miles Baxter, Nov. 19, 1938; children: Gregory Baxter, Charles Conrad III, Jenifer; m. Norma Lee Clasbey, Apr. 28, 1984. A.B., George Washington U., 1938, J.D., 1936; M. Fiscal Adminstrn., Columbus U., 1943. Bar: D.C. 1935. Clk. U.S. Dept. Agr., 1933-36; adminstrv. asst. Bur. Accounts, Treasury Dept., 1936-39; atty. R.R. Retirement Bd., 1939-41; claims atty. Q.M.C., C.E., U.S. War Dept., 1941-43; asst. counsel Office Gen. Counsel, U.S. Navy Dept., 1946-47; gen. counsel War Contracts Price Adjustment Bd., 1948-51, mem., 1950-51; legislative counsel R.F.C., 1951-53; exec. sec. Subversive Activities Control Bd., 1953-61; dept. counsel indsl. plant security Dept. Def., 1962-71, chief dept. counsel, 1971-73; instr. thanatology, religion and philosophy Blue Ridge C.C., 1973-89; assoc. English dept. George Washington U., 1960, Am. U., 1961. Author: Windows on the Passion, 1967, Windows on the Master, 1968, Ruth and Naomi, 1971, Mind Is It: Meditation, Prayer, Healing and the Psychic, 1978, Picture Windows on the Christ, 1979, The Magian Gospel, 1979, Thus Saith the Lord: The Autobiography of God, 1984, The Holy Families, 1990; various articles for mags. Served as lt. USNR, 1944-46. Mem. Fed. Bar Assn., Delta Theta Phi, Phi Beta Kappa. Home: PO Box 117 Penn Laird VA 22846-0117

WISE, DAVID, author, journalist; b. N.Y.C., May 10, 1930; s. Raymond L. and Karena (Post) W.; m. Joan Sylvester, Dec. 16, 1962; children: Christopher James, Jonathan William. BA, Columbia Coll., 1951. Reporter N.Y. Herald Tribune, 1951-66, N.Y. city hall bur. chief, 1953-57; bur. chief N.Y. Herald Tribune, Albany, N.Y., 1956-57; mem. Washington bur. N.Y. Herald Tribune, 1958-66, chief Washington bur., 1963-66; fellow Woodrow Wilson Internat. Center for Scholars, 1970-71; lectr. in polit. sci. U. Calif. at Santa Barbara, 1977-79. Author: The Politics of Lying: Government Deception, Secrecy, and Power, 1973, The American Police State: The Government Against the People, 1976, Spectrum, 1981, The Children's Game, 1983, The Samarkand Dimension, 1987, The Spy Who Got Away, 1988, Molehunt: The Secret Search for Traitors that Shattered the CIA, 1992, Nightmover: How Aldrich Ames Sold the CIA to the KGB for $4.6 Million, 1995; co-author: (with Thomas B. Ross) The U-2 Affair, 1962, The Invisible Government, 1964, The Espionage Establishment, 1967 (with Milton C. Cummings, Jr.), Democracy Under Pressure: An Introduction to the American Political System, 1971, 7th edit., 1993; contbg. author: The Kennedy Circle, 1961, None of Your Business, 1974, The CIA File, 1976; contbr. articles to nat. mags. Recipient Page One award Newspaper Guild N.Y., 1969. Mem. Washington Ind. Writers, Am. Polit. Sci. Assn. Clubs: Fed. City (Washington), Gridiron (Washington). Office: c/o Sterling Lord Literistic Inc 65 Bleecker St New York NY 10012

WISE, GEORGE EDWARD, lawyer; b. Chgo., Feb. 26, 1924; s. George E. and Helen L. (Gray) W.; m. Patricia E. Finn, Aug. 3, 1945; children: Erich, Peter, Abbe, Raoul, John. J.D., U. Chgo. Bar: Calif. 1949, U.S. Dist. Ct. (no. dist.) Calif. 1948, U.S. Ct. Appeals (9th cir.) 1948, U.S. Dist. Ct. (cen. dist.) 1950, U.S. Supreme CT. 1955. Law clk. Calif. Supreme Ct., 1948-49; sr. ptnr. Wise, Wiezorek, Timmons & Wise, Long Beach, 1949—. With USNR, 1943-45. Fellow Am. Coll. Trial Lawyers; mem. ABA, Los Angeles County Bar Assn., Long Beach Bar Assn. (pres. 1970, Atty. of Yr. 1990), Calif. State Bar. Home: 5401 E El Cedral St Long Beach CA 90815-4112 Office: Wise Wiezorek Timmons & Wise 3700 Santa Fe Ave Ste 300 Long Beach CA 90810-2171

WISE, HAROLD B., internist, educator; b. Hamilton, Ont., Can., Feb. 14, 1937. MD, U. Toronto, 1961. Physician Prince Albert Clin., Sask., Can., 1962-63; resident Kaiser Found. Hosp., San Francisco, 1963-64, Montefiore Hosp. and Med. Ctr., Bronx, 1964-65; acting dir. ambulatory svc. and home care Morrisania City Hosp., 1965-66; dir. health ctr. Dr. Martin Luther King Jr. Health Ctr., 1966-71; assoc. prof. comty. health Albert Einstein Coll. Medicine, 1970—; Milbank Meml. Fund fellow; dir. internship and residency program social medicine Montefiore Hosp. and Med. Ctr., 1969—, dir. inst. health team devel., 1972; dir. Family Ctr. Health. Mem. Inst. Medicine-NAS, N.Y. Chiropractic Assn. (bd. mem. 1972—).

WISE, JOHN AUGUSTUS, lawyer; b. Detroit, Mar. 30, 1938; s. John Augustus and Mary Blanche (Parent) W.; m. Helga M. Bessin, Nov. 27, 1965; children: Monique Elizabeth, John Eric. Student, U. Vienna, 1957-58; AB cum laude, Coll. Holy Cross, 1959; JD, U. Mich., 1962; postgrad., U. Munich, 1962-63. Bar: Mich. 1963, D.C. 1966. Assoc. Dykema, Gossett, Detroit, 1962-64; asst. to pres. Internat. Econ. Policy Assn., Washington, 1964-66; assoc. Parsons, Tennent, Hammond, Hardig & Ziegelman, Detroit, 1967-70; pres. Wise & Marsac P.C., 1970—; dir. Peltzer & Ehlers Am. Corp., 1975-80, Colombian Am. Friends Inc., 1974-89. Mem. Detroit Com. on Fgn. Rels.; bd. dirs. Huyde Park Coop., 1974-77; trustee Friends Sch., Detroit, 1977-81, Brighton Health Svcs. Corp., 1991-94; chmn. bd. trustees Brighton Hosp., 1995—. Ford Found. grantee U. Munich, 1962-63. Mem. ABA, Mich. Bar Assn., Detroit Bar Assn., Internat. Bar Assn., Detroit Athletic Club, Detroit Club, Detroit Econ. Club. Roman Catholic. Home: 1221 Yorkshire Rd Grosse Pointe MI 48230-1105 Office: BUHL Bldg 11th Fl Detroit MI 48226

WISE, JOHN JAMES, oil company executive; b. Cambridge, Mass., Feb. 28, 1932; s. Daniel and Alice E. (Donlon) W.; m. Rosemary S. Bishop, Mar. 4, 1967; children: Susannah, Jean. BS, Tufts U., 1953; PhD, MIT, 1966. Rsch. scientist Mobil R & D Corp., Paulsboro, N.J., 1953-76, mgr. process R & D, 1976-77, sect. mgr., 1976-77; v.p. planning Mobil R & D Corp., N.Y.C., 1977-81; mgr. exploration and producing rsch. Mobil R & D Corp., Dallas, 1981-82; v.p. planning Mobil R & D Corp., N.Y.C., 1982-84; mgr. process and products R & D Mobil R & D Corp., Paulsboro, N.J., 1984-87, v.p. rsch., 1987—. Patentee in field (25); contbr. articles to profl. jours. Mem. NAE, Am. Inst. Chem. Engrs., Indsl. Rsch. Inst. (Achievement award 1995), World Petroleum Congress, Sigma Xi. Office: Mobil R & D Corp PO Box 1031 Princeton NJ 08543-1031

WISE, KELLY, private school educator, photographer, critic; b. New Castle, Ind., Dec. 1, 1932; s. John Kenneth W. and Geraldine (Kelly) Edwards Wise; m. Sybil Anahid Zulalian, Aug. 15, 1959; children: Jocelyn Anne, Adam Kelly, Lydia Louise. B.S., Purdue U., 1955; M.A., Columbia U., 1959. Instr. English Mt. Hermon Sch., Gill, Mass., 1960-66; instr. English Phillips Acad., Andover, Mass., 1966—, chmn. dept., 1978-82, acting dean faculty, 1982-83, dean faculty, 1985-90; founder, dir. Inst. for Recruitment of Tchrs., Andover, Mass., 1989—; photography critic The Boston Globe, 1982-93; art commentator Nat. Pub. Radio, 1987-89; photography and English cons. Nat. Humanities Faculty, Concord, Mass., 1970-83; mem. Pub. Art Adv. Bd. of Mass. Coun.; cons. editor Addison House Pubs., Danbury, N.J., 1974-79. Author: (with Kalkstein and Regan) English Competence Handbook, 1972; editor: The Photographers' Choice, 1975, Lotte Jacobi, 1978, Portrait: Theory, 1981, Photo Facts and Opinions, 1981; author, photographer: Still Points, 1977, A Church, A People, 1979; editor photographer: City Limits, 1987; assoc. editor: Views, Jour. Photography, 1980-81; works included in anthologies, one-man shows, Portland Museum Art, Maine, 1974, Silver Image Gallery, Columbus, Ohio, 1975, Canon Photo Gallery, Amsterdam, Holland, 1977, Focus Gallery, San Francisco, 1977, Art Mus., U. Mass., Amherst, 1978, Neikrug Gallery, N.Y.C., 1979, Sheldon Gallery, U. Nebr., Lincoln, 1980, Yuen Lui Gallery, Seattle, 1980, Rose Art Mus., Brandeis U., Waltham, Mass., 1981, Blixt Gallery, Ann Arbor, Mich., 1981, Snite Art Gallery, U. Notre Dame, 1981, Jeb Gallery, Providence, 1981, Currier Gallery Art, Manchester, N.H., 1985, Addison Gallery Am. Art, Andover, Mass., 1985, Art Ctr., DePauw U., 1986, Art Gallery, Conn. Coll., 1986, Yuen Lui Gallery, Seattle, 1986, Kresge Art Mus., Mich. State U., 1987, Brockton Art Mus., 1987; group shows include Inst. Contemporary Art, Boston, 1972, Mus. Fine Arts, Boston, 1974, Fogg Art Mus., Cambridge, 1976, Sidney Janis Gallery, N.Y.C., 1977, The Photographer's Gallery, London, 1979, Il Diaframma, Milan, Italy, 1979, Iisalmen Kamera, Helsinki, Finland, 1984, Archive Gallery, N.Y., 1987, Mass. Coll. Art, 1988, Martin Schweig Gallery, St. Louis, 1988, Satellite Gallery, Cultural Affairs Dept., Los Angeles; works included in book Flesh and Blood: Photographers' Images of Their Own Families. Served with USN, 1955-57, PTO. Recipient Disting. Alumnus award Purdue U., 1996. Office: Phillips Acad Andover MA 01810

WISE, MARVIN JAY, lawyer; b. San Antonio, Apr. 6, 1926; s. Philip and Anna Edith (Corman) W.; m. Gloria Marian Johnston, Sept. 19, 1954; children: Philip Johnston, Jennifer Lea, Amelia Ann. B.A. magna cum laude, U. Tex., 1945; LL.B. cum laude, Harvard U., 1949; diploma comparative legal studies, U. Cambridge, Eng., 1950. Bar: Tex. 1949. Assoc. Thompson & Knight, Dallas, 1950-57; ptnr. Wise and Stuhl, Dallas, 1957-88; of counsel Novakov, Davidson & Flynn, Dallas, 1988—. Bd. dirs. Dallas Assn. Mental Health, Isthmus Inst., Dallas Home Jewish Aged, Dallas Civic Ballet Soc., Walden Prep. Sch. Served with AUS, 1945-46. Fulbright scholar, 1949-50. Fellow Tex. Bar Found.; mem. ABA, Tex. Bar Assn., Dallas Bar Assn. (chmn. probate, trusts and estates sect. 1981-82), Am. Coll. Probate Counsel, UN Assn. (dir. Dallas chpt.), Phi Beta Kappa, Alpha Phi Omega, Phi Eta Sigma, Pi Sigma Alpha. Jewish. Club: Crescent. Home: 3444 University Blvd Dallas TX 75205-1834 Office: 2000 St Paul Pl 750 N Saint Paul St Dallas TX 75201-7105

WISE, PATRICIA, lyric coloratura; b. Wichita, Kans.; d. Melvin R. and Genevieve F. (Dotson) W.; 1 child, Jennifer. B. Music Edn., U. Kans., Lawrence, 1966. Debut as Susanna in Marriage of Figaro, Kansas City, 1966; prin. roles include Lucia, Gilda, Micaela, Juliette, Zerbinetta, Pamina, Musetta, Lulu, Violetta, Nedda, numerous others; appeared with leading Am. opera cos. including, Chgo., Santa Fe, N.Y.C., San Francisco, Houston, San Diego, Miami, Balt., Phila., Pitts.; European appearances, 1971-76, London Royal Opera, Glyndebourne Festival, Vienna Volksoper, Geneva Opera; guest artist with Vienna, Hamburg, Munich, Cologne, Frankfurt, and Berlin State Operas; guest appearances in Madrid, Barcelona, Rome, La Scala Milan, Nice, Paris Chatelet, Zurich, Dresden, Salzburg Festival, Theatro Colon, Buenos Aires; appeared with orchs. including, Chgo. Symphony Orch., Los Angeles Symphony Orch., N.Y. Handel Soc., Israel Philharm. Orch., Vienna Philharm. Orch., N.Y. Philharm., Cleve. Orch., Berlin Symphonic Orch., BBC Orch., Nat. Orch. France; Angel Recordings; internat. TV, film appearances. Recipient Morton Baum award N.Y.C. Ctr., 1971, Dealey Meml. award Dallas Symphony, 1966, Naftzger young Artist award Wichita Symphony, 1966, Midland Young Artist award Midland (Tex.) Symphony Orch., 1966; M.B. Rockefeller Fund grantee, 1967-70; Sullivan Found. grantee, 1967-68; named Kammersänger Vienna Staatsoper, 1989.

WISE, PAUL SCHUYLER, insurance company executive; b. Pratt, Kans., July 16, 1920; s. George Warren and Bess Grace (Cossairt) W.; m. Frances H. Christie, Oct. 26, 1975; children by previous marriage: Schuyler, David, Betsy. Student, U. Kans., 1938-40; BA, Washburn U., 1942, JD, 1947; student, U. Mich., 1945-46. Bar: Kans. Atty. Kans. Ins. Dept., 1947, asst. commr. ins., 1948-51, commr. workmen's compensation, 1951-52; atty.-ins. legislation Alliance of Am. Insurers, Chgo., 1952-56, mgr. legis. bur., 1956-61, asst. mgr., 1961-62, gen. mgr., 1962-68, pres., chief exec. officer, 1968-84, chmn. bd., 1984-85; dir. Ins. Inst. for Hwy. Safety, Coll. of Ins.; bd. overseers Inst. for Civil Justice; lectr. in field; bd. dirs. United Funds, Kansas City, Mo., Potash Corp. of Sask., Can. Contbr. articles to profl. jours. Co-founder, bd. dirs. Hospice of North Shore; bd. dirs. Sr. Net. Lt. USN. Recipient Man of Yr. award Fedn. Ins. Counsel, 1982; inducted into Hall of Fame, Kans. Ins. Ednl. Found., 1983. Home: 8648 Silver Saddle Dr PO Box 5248 Carefree AZ 85377-5248

WISE, ROBERT, film producer, director; b. Winchester, Ind., Sept. 10, 1914. Student, Franklin Coll., D.F.A. (hon.), 1968. Staff cutting dept. R.K.O., 1933, became sound cutter, asst. editor, film editor, 1939-43, dir., 1943-49; with 20th Century-Fox, 1949-52, M.G.M., 1954-57; free-lance, 1958—, ptnr. ind. film co., 1970—; Past mem. Nat. Council of Arts. Ind. producer/dir. various studios; motion pictures include The Curse of the Cat People, 1944, Mademoiselle Fifi, 1944, The Body Snatcher, 1945, A Game of Death, 1945, Criminal Court, 1946, Born to Kill, 1947, Mystery in Mexico, 1948, Blood on the Moon, 1948, The Set-Up, 1949, Two Flags West, 1950, Three Secrets, 1950, The House on Telegraph Hill, 1951, The Day the Earth Stood Still, 1951, The Captive City, 1952, Something For the Birds, 1952, The Desert Rats, 1953, Destination Gobi, 1953, So Big, 1953, Executive Suite, 1954, Helen of Troy, 1955, Tribute to a Bad Man, 1956, Somebody Up There Likes Me, 1957, This Could Be the Night, 1957, Until They Sail, 1957, Run Silent, Run Deep, 1958, I Want to Live, 1958, Odds Against Tomorrow, 1959, West Side Story (Acad. awards best dir. with Jerome Robbins, and best picture), 1961, Two For the Seasaw, 1962, The Haunting, 1963, The Sound of Music, 1965 (Acad. award best dir., best picture), The Sand Pebbles, 1966, Star!, 1968, The Andromeda Strain, 1971, Two People, 1973, The Hindenburg, 1975, Audrey Rose, 1977, Star Trek-The Motion Picture, 1979, Rooftops, 1989. Recipient Nat. Medal of Arts award, 1992. Mem. Dirs. Guild (pres. 1971-74), Acad. Motion Picture Arts and Scis. (pres. 1985-87). Office: Robert Wise Prodns 315 S Beverly Dr Ste 214 Beverly Hills CA 90212-4310

WISE, ROBERT EDWARD, radiologist; b. Pitts., May 21, 1918; s. Joseph Frank and Victoria Rose (Conley) W.; m. Yvonne Burkhard, Mar. 27, 1943; children: Lynne Dailey, Robert Edward, John Burkhard. B.S., U. Pitts., 1941; M.D., U. Md., 1943. Intern U.S. Naval Hosp., Phila., 1943-44; fellow in radiology Cleve. Clin. Found., 1947-49; radiologist Cleve. Clinic, 1949-52; practice medicine specializing in radiology Pitts., 1952-53; radiologist Lahey Clinic Found., Boston, 1953—, CEO, chmn. bd. govs., 1975-91; chmn. bd. Lahey Clinic Found., 1986—; instr. radiology U. Pitts., 1952-53; clin. prof. radiology Sch. Medicine, Boston U.; dir. Bay State Skills Corp., Boston. Author: Intravenous Cholangiography, 1962, Accessory Digestive Organs, 1973, Radiology, Gallbladder and Bile Ducts. Trustee Eleanor Naylor Dana Charitable Trust, Lahey Clinic Hosp., Boston Ballet Co., Lahey Clinic Found.; bd. dirs. Boston Pub. Libr. Found.; corporator New Eng. Deaconess Hosp., Boston Opera Assn., Lahey-Hitchcock Clinic; chmn. Robert E. Wise M.D. Rsch. and Edn. Inst. of Lahey Clinic Found. Lt. Med. Corp USN, 1943-47. Mem. Am. Coll. Radiology (pres. 1975), Radiol. Soc. N.Am. (pres. 1974), New Eng. Roentgen Ray Soc. (pres. 1963), AMA, Mass. Med. Soc. Mass. Radiol. Soc. (pres. 1973), Eastern Radiol. Soc. (pres. 1965), N. Suburban C. of C. (dir.). Roman Catholic. Clubs: Algonquin (Boston) (dir); Brae Burn Country (West Newton, Mass.); Webhannet Golf (Kennebunk Beach, Maine), Kennebunk River (Kennebunkport), Atlantis Golf (Atlantis, Fla.), La Coquille (Manalapan, Fla.), Beach (Palm Beach). Home: PO Box 41 Kennebunkport ME 04046-0041 also: Marshalls Point Rd Kennebunkport ME 04014 Office: Lahey Clinic Found 31 Mall Rd Burlington MA 01805-0001

WISE, ROBERT ELLSWORTH, JR. (BOB ELLSWORTH), congressman; b. Washington, D.C., Jan. 6, 1948; m. Sandra Casber, 1984. BA, Duke U., 1970; JD, Tulane U., 1975. Bar: W.Va., 1975. Sole practice Charleston, W.Va., 1975-80; atty., legis. council for judiciary com. W.Va. Ho. of Dels., 1977-78; mem. W.Va. Senate, 1980-82, 97th-103rd Congresses from 2nd W.Va. dist., Washington, D.C., 1982—; whip at large Congress from W.Va., 1986—. Dir. West Virginians for Fair and Equitable Assessment of Taxes, Inc. Mem. ABA, W.Va. State Bar Assn. Democrat. Avocations: physical fitness, bluegrass music. Office: US Ho of Reps 2434 Rayburn House Office Bldg Washington DC 20515-4802

WISE, ROBERT F., JR., lawyer; b. Bronxville, N.Y., Oct. 1, 1947; m. Alison Bell; children: Katherine B., Robert A. BA, U. Va., 1969; JD, Yale U., 1972. Bar: N.Y. 1973, U.S. Dist. Ct. (so. and ea. dists.) N.Y. 1973, U.S. Ct. Appeals (2d cir.) 1973, U.S. Supreme Ct. 1980. Ptnr. Davis Polk & Wardwell, N.Y.C., 1972—. Pres. Purchase (N.Y.) Environ. Protective Assn., 1988-92. 1st lt. USAFR, 1969-73. Mem. ABA, Fed. Bar Coun., N.Y. Bar Assn. (chmn. fed. procedure com. 1991—), N.Y.C. Bar Assn., Westchester Country Club (bd. govs. 1993—). Office: Davis Polk & Wardwell 450 Lexington Ave New York NY 10017-3911

WISE, ROBERT LESTER, utilities executive; b. Curwensville, Pa., Oct. 4, 1943; s. Robert Lester Wise and Kathryn Elizabeth (Riddle) Husak; m. Sandra Lee Leonard, June 12, 1965; 1 child: Robert L. III. BSME, Lafayette Coll., 1965. Registered profl. engr., Pa. Cadet engr., jr. engr. Pa. Electric Co., Johnstown, 1965-68, stat. supr. prodn., sta. supt. ops., 1968-71, sta. supt., mgr. generating stas., 1971-79, asst. v.p. ops., 1979-82, v.p. generation engring. and support, 1982-83, v.p. ops., 1984-86, pres., bd. dirs., 1986-94; pres. fossil generation GPU Svc. Corp., Johnstown, Pa., 1994-96; pres. GPU Generation Corp., Johnstown, 1996—; bd. dirs. GPU Svc. Corp., GPU Nuclear Corp., El Power, Inc., Parsippany, U.S. Nat. Bank, USBANCORP, Inc., USBANCORP Trust Co., Johnstown Area Regional Industries, Greater Johnstown/Cambria county C. of C.; mem. Pa. Bus. Roundtable, 1990; mem. Edison Electric Inst. Policy com. on environ. affairs, 1995. Bd. dirs. Johnstown Symphony Orch., 1988; mem. adv. coun. of exec. bd. Penn's Woods coun. Boy Scouts Am., 1980—; mem. exec. com. Greater Johnstown Com., 1987, Pa. Electric Assn., Harrisburg, 1987, Cambria-Somerset Labor Mgmt. Com., 1987; mem. exec. adv. com. Johnstown Bus. Coun. on Health Care, 1987; trustee United Way Greater Johnstown, 1991. Mem. Sunnehanna Country Club. Republican. Avocations: sailing, racquet sports, golf. Office: GPU Generation Corp 1001 Broad St Johnstown PA 15906-2437

WISE, WARREN ROBERTS, lawyer; b. Beaver City, Nebr., Oct. 8, 1929; s. Harold Edward and Doris Lorene (Roberts) W.; m. Marcia Hench, Oct. 14, 1961; children: Debra, David, Susan. BS, U. Nebr., 1950, LLB, 1953; LLM, Georgetown U., 1960. Atty. U.S. Dept. Justice Lands Div., Washington, 1955-61, U.S. Dept. Justice Tax Div., Washington, 1961-63; assoc. counsel Mass. Mut. Life Ins. Co., Springfield, 1963-67, asst. gen. counsel, 1967-72, 2d v.p., assoc. gen. counsel, 1972-74, v.p., assoc. gen. counsel, 1974-85, sr. v.p., assoc. gen. counsel, 1985-88, exec. v.p., gen. counsel, 1988-93; ret., 1993. Author: Business Insurance Agreements, 1970, 80, 91; editor; Massachusetts Life Insurance Law, 1980. Chmn. bd. East Coast Conf., Evang. Covenant Ch., 1987-89, chmn. pension bd., 1984-86, exec. bd., 1995—; bd. dirs. Mass. Family Inst., 1994—, vol. policy analyst, 1994—. Mem. ABA (chmn. life ins. law com. torts and ins. sect. 1992-93), Assn. Life Inst. Counsel (bd. dirs. 1987-92, pres. 1992-93), Colony Club, Longmeadow Country Club. Republican. Avocation: golf. Home: 37 W Colonial Rd Wilbraham MA 01095-2117

WISE, WILLIAM ALLAN, oil company executive, lawyer; b. Davenport, Iowa, July 10, 1945; s. A. Walter and Mary Virginia (Kuhl) W.; m. Marie Figge, Sept. 27, 1969; children—Vivian Marie, Genevieve Marie, Mary Elizabeth. B.A., Vanderbilt U.; J.D., U. Colo. Bar: Colo. 1970. Prin. counsel El Paso Natural Gas, Tex., 1970-80, sr. v.p. mktg., 1985-87, exec. v.p. mktg., 1987-89; pres., chief oper. officer El Paso Natural Gas, 1989-90, pres., chief exec. officer, 1990-93, chmn, pres. & CEO, 1994-96; asst. gen. counsel in Houston The El Paso Co., 1980-82, v.p., gen. counsel, 1983, sr. v.p., gen. counsel and sec., 1983-85; chmn., pres. & CEO El Paso Energy Corp. (formerly El Paso Natural Gas Co.), 1996—; also bd. dirs. El Paso Energy Corp.; bd. dirs. Am. Gas Assn., Arlington, Va., The El Paso Co., Mojave Pipeline Oper. Co., Bakersfield, Calif., Tex. Commerce Bank, El Paso, Tex. Commerce Bancshres, Inc., Houston, Interstate Natural Gas Assn. Am., Washington; mem. N.Y. Merc. Exch., Tri-Regional Com. Contbr. articles to profl. jours. Bd. dirs. Battle Mountain Gold Co., U. Colo. Found., Boulder, Gas Industry Stds., Natural Gas Coun., Tex. Gov.'s Bus. Coun.; mem. bus. adv. coun. and devel. bd. U. Tex., El Paso; bd. visitors M.D. Anderson Cancer Ctr. Mem. Nat. Petroleum Coun. (bd. dirs.), Colo. Bar Assn., Tex. C. of C. (bd. dirs.), El Paso Country Club, George Town Club (Washington), River Oaks Country Club (Houston), Old Baldy Club (Saratoga, Wyo.). Republican. Roman Catholic. Avocations: golf, running. Home: 5605 Westside Dr El Paso TX 79932-2921 Office: El Paso Energy Corp. 100 N Stanton One Paul Kayser Cen El Paso TX 79901

WISE, WILLIAM JERRARD, lawyer; b. Chgo., May 27, 1934; s. Gerald Paul and Harriet Muriel (Rosenblum) W.; m. Peggy Spero, Sept. 3, 1959; children: Deborah, Stephen, Betsy, Lynne. B.B.A., U. Mich., 1955, M.B.A., 1958, J.D. with distinction, 1958. Bar: Ill. 1959. Spl. atty. Office Regional Counsel, IRS, Milw., 1959-63; with firm McDermott, Will & Emery, Chgo., 1963-70, Coles & Wise, Ltd., 1971-81, Wise & Stracks, Ltd., 1982—; Lectr., contbr. Ill. Inst. Continuing Legal Edn.; arbitrator Cir. Ct. Cook County Ill., 1990—. Mem. Village of Winnetka (Ill.) Caucus, 1974-75; Bd. dirs. Blind Service Assn., Chgo., 1964-74; dir., treas. Suzuki Orff Sch. for Young Musicians, Chgo., 1981-91. Served with AUS, 1958-59. Mem. Chgo. Bar Assn. Home: 1401 Tower Rd Winnetka IL 60093-1628 Office: Wise & Stracks Ltd 20 N Clark St Ste 1000 Chicago IL 60602-4111 *I believe that one succeeds best in our society if one gives as little thought as possible to one's personal well being.*

WISEHART, ARTHUR MCKEE, lawyer; b. Evanston, Ill., July 3, 1928; s. Arthur J. and Dorothy H. (Rice) W.; m. Mary Elizabeth Dodson, 1953; children: William, Ellen, Arthur, Charles. B.A., Miami U., Oxford, Ohio, 1950; M.P.A., Wayne State U., 1953; J.D., U. Mich., 1954. Bar: N.Y. 1955. With firm Chadbourne, Parke, Whiteside & Wolff, N.Y.C., 1954-59; with Am. Airlines, Inc., 1959-69, corp. sec., asst. gen. counsel, 1968-69; sr. v.p., gen. counsel, sec. REA Express, 1969-74; dir., sec. REA Holding Corp., 1969-74; sr. partner Law Offices of Arthur M. Wisehart, 1974-75, Wisehart & Koch, 1975—, 1981—; dir. Hoover Co., 1975-76. Author articles. Mem. ABA, Assn. of Bar of City of N.Y., Order of Coif, Delta Chi. Presbyterian. Clubs: Princeton. Office: Wisehart & Koch 19 W 44th St Ste 412 New York NY 10036-5902

WISEHART, MARY RUTH, academic administrator; b. Myrtle, Mo., Nov. 2, 1932; d. William Henry and Ora (Harbison) W. BA, Free Will Baptist Bible Coll., 1955; BA, George Peabody Coll. Tchrs., 1959, MA, 1960, PhD, 1976. Tchr. Free Will Bapt. Bible Coll., Nashville, 1956-60, chmn. English dept., 1961-85; exec. sec.-treas. Free Will Bapt. Women Nat. Active for Christ, 1985—. Author: Sparks Into Flame, 1985; contbr. poetry to jours. Mem. Nat. Coun. Tchrs. English, Christian Mgmt. Assn., Religious Conf. Mgmt. Assn., Scribbler's Club. Avocations: photography, music, drama. Office: Women Nat Active for Christ Free Will Bapt PO Box 5002 Antioch TN 37011-5002

WISEMAN, ALAN M(ITCHELL), lawyer; b. Long Branch, N.J., July 6, 1944; s. Lincoln B. and Gertrude (Gorcey) W.; m. Paula Wiseman, July 8, 1965; children—Steven, David, Julie. B.A., Johns Hopkins U., 1965; J.D., Georgetown U., 1968. Bar: Md. 1968, Ill. 1970, D.C. 1973. Law clk. to Hon. William J. McWilliams Md. Ct. Appeals, 1968-69; assoc. Schiff Hardin & Waite, Chgo., 1970-74; ptnr. Howrey & Simon, Washington, 1976—. Editor Georgetown Law Jour., 1967-68. Mem. U.S. C. of C. (council on antitrust policy). Office: 1299 Pennsylvania Ave NW Washington DC 20004-2400

WISEMAN, DENNIS GENE, college dean; b. Anderson, Ind., Sept. 25, 1947; s. Harold Leslie and Lillian Loetta (Woods) W.; m. Susan Jean Reidenbach, June 10, 1971; children: Matthew Benjamin, Andrew Joseph. BA, U. Indpls., 1969; MA, U. Ill., 1970, PhD, 1974; postgrad., Ind. U., 1970-71. Tchr. Indpls. Pub. Schs., 1970-71; rsch. asst. U. Ill., Urbana, 1971-74, clinician, supr., 1972-74, coord. Office for Profl. Svc., 1973-74; dir., tchr. Champaign (Ill.) pub. schs., 1972-73; asst. prof. U. S.C. Coastal Carolina Coll., Conway, 1974-77, assoc. prof., 1977-84, prof., 1984—, dean Sch. Edn., 1982-93; dean Sch. Edn. and Grad. Studies, Coastal Carolina U., 1993—; field disseminator Social Sci. Edn. Consortium, Boulder, Colo., 1979-81; reviewer Ethnic Heritage Studies Program, U.S. Office Edn., Washington, 1980-81; cons. S.C. State Dept. Edn., Columbia, 1986—; dir. Oxford program U. S.C. Coastal Carolina Coll., summer, 1990; evaluator So. Assn. Colls. and Schs., Atlanta, 1991. Co-author: Effective Teaching, 1st edit., 1984, 2d edit. 1991, Wondering about Thinking, 1988; contbr. articles to jours. in field. Mem. Horry County Human Rels. Coun., Conway, 1990-93; mem. curriculum frameworks rev. panel S.C. Dept. Edn., 1993—. Named Tchr. of Yr., U. S.C. Coastal Carolina Coll., 1980; S.C. Com. for the Humanities grantee, 1984, S.C. Com. on Higher Edn. grantee, 1985, 86; Japan Study Program scholar U.S. Office Edn., 1980. Mem. S.C. Assn. Colls. for Tchr. Edn. (pres. elect 1989, pres. 1989-91), Coun. Edn. Deans (pres. 1986-90), Nat. Coun. for the Social Studies, Am. Assn. Colls. for Tchr. Edn. (instl. rep. 1980—), Assn. Tchr. Educators, Phi Delta Kappa (pres. Coastal Carolina chpt. 1984-85). Methodist. Avocations: reading, travel, tennis, writing. Office: Coastal Carolina U Office Dean & Grad Studies PO Box 1954 Conway SC 29526-1954

WISEMAN, FREDERICK, filmmaker; b. Boston, Jan. 1, 1930; s. Jacob Leo and Gertrude Leah (Kotzen) W.; m. Zipporah Batshaw, May 29, 1955; children: David B., Eric T. BA, Williams Coll., 1951; LLB, Yale U., 1954; LHD (hon.), U. Cin., 1973, Williams Coll., 1976, John Jay Coll. Crim. Justice, 1994; DFA (hon.), Lake Forest Coll., 1991, Princeton U., 1994. Bar: Mass. 1955. Lectr. law Boston U. Law Sch., 1958-61; research assoc. Brandeis U., Waltham, Mass., 1962-66; treas. Orgn. for Social and Tech. Innovation, 1966-70; filmmaker Zipporah Films, Cambridge, Mass., 1970—;

vis. lectr. numerous schs. Filmmaker: Titicut Follies, 1967, High School, 1968, Law and Order, 1969, Hospital, 1970, Basic Training, 1971, Essene, 1972, Juvenile Court, 1973, Primate, 1974, Welfare, 1975, Meat, 1976, Canal Zone, 1977, Sinai Field Mission, 1978, Manoeuvre, 1979, Model, 1980, Seraphita's Diary, 1982, The Store, 1983, Racetrack, 1985, Deaf, 1986, Blind, 1986, Multi-Handicapped, 1986, Adjustment and Work, 1986, Missile, 1987, Near Death, 1989, Central Park, 1989, Aspen, 1991, Zoo, 1993, High School II, 1994, Ballet, 1995, La Comedie Française, 1996; dir. theatre Tonight We Improvise, 1986-87, Life and Fate, 1988, Hate, 1991, Am. Repertory Theatre, Welfare: The Opera, Am. Music Theater Festival, 1992. Served with U.S. Army, 1955-56. Fellow Russell Sage Found., 1961-62, NATAS fellow, 1991; Guggenheim Found., 1980-81; recipient MacArthur prize, 1982-87, The Peabody award, Personal award, 1991. Fellow Am. Acad. Arts and Scis. Office: 1 Richdale Ave # 4 Cambridge MA 02140-2627

WISEMAN, JAMES RICHARD, classicist, archaeologist, educator; b. North Little Rock, Ark., Aug. 29, 1934; s. James Morgan and Bertie Lou (Sullivan) W.; m. Margaret Lucille Mayhue, Aug. 20, 1954; children: James Alexander, Stephen Michael. BA, U. Mo., Columbia, 1957; MA, U. Chgo., 1960, PhD, 1966; postgrad., Am. Sch. Classical Studies, Athens, Greece, 1959-60. Instr. U. Tex., Austin, 1960-64; asst. prof. classics U. Tex., 1964-66, asso. prof., 1966-70, prof., 1970-73; dir. archaeol. excavations at Ancient Corinth, Greece, 1965-72; chmn. archaeol. studies program, 1969-73; prof. classics Boston U., 1973—, prof. art history, 1975—, prof. archeology, 1980—, chmn. dept. classical studies, 1974-82, chmn. dept. archeology, 1982-96, dir. archaeol. studies program, 1975-76, 79-82, dir. Ctr. Archeol. Studies, 1980—; dir. summer program Greece, 1976-77, 81, 91-94; vis. assoc. prof. classics U. Colo., Boulder, 1970; Am. prin. investigator, co-dir. Am.-Yugoslav Archaeol. Excavations at Stobi, Yugoslavia, 1970-81; project supr. Boston U. Archaeol. Excavations in Temple, N.H., 1975-76; vis. research prof. Am. Sch. Classical Studies, Athens, 1978-79; cons. archaeology; chmn. exec. com. Ctr. Remote Sensing; dir. Boston U. Nikopolis Project in N.W. Greece. Author: Stobi, A Guide to the Excavations, 1973, The Land of the Ancient Corinthians, 1978, (with Thomas Sever) Remote Sensing and Archaeology: Potential for the Future, 1985; contbr. numerous articles on ancient history, epigraphy, classical studies, archaeology to profl. jours.; editor, contbg. author: Studies in the Antiquities of Stobi I, 1973, II, 1975, III, 1981; founding editor: Jour. Field Archaeology, 1974—. Trustee Am. Schs. Oriental Research, 1985-89. Served with USN, 1952-55. Recipient Bromberg award U. Tex., 1964, Bronze Plaque award City of Titov Veles, SR Makedonija, Yugoslavia; disting. alumnus award Coll. Arts and Sci. U. Mo. Columbia, 1989; Am. Council Learned Socs. fellow, 1967-68, 78-79, 90-91; Guggenheim fellow, 1971-72; U. Tex. Research Inst. grantee, summers 1961, 66, 67, and 1967-68, 71-72; NEH grantee, 1968, 69, 76-80; Ford Found. grantee, 1968-72; Smithsonian Instn. grantee, 1970-75, 79-81; Dumbarton Oaks fellow, 1983-84; NGS grantee, 1984, 92; NASA grantee, 1984, 91; W.M. Keck Found. grantee, 1985, 86, 88, 92; NEH fellow, 1990; Mellon fellow Inst. Advanced Study, Princeton U., 1990-91. Fellow Soc. Antiquaries of London, Explorers Club; mem. Archaeol. Inst. Am. (nat. pres. 1985-88, exec. com. 1973-77, 81-92, trustee 1993—, pres. Ctrl. Tex. Soc. 1962-64, pres. Boston Soc. 1979-81, Gold Seal award 1989, Chase Eliot Norton lectr.), Am. Philol. Assn., Am. Sch. Classical Studies at Athens (exec. com. 1973-76), Am. Acad. at Rome, Assn. Ancient Historians, Assn. Field Archaeology (exec. com. 1970-85), Am. Inst. Nautical Archaeology, Internat. Assn. Archaeology, Ctr. Materials Rsch. in Archaeology and Ethnology (exec. com. 1975-78, 79-83), Soc. Am. Archaeology, Soc. Hist. Archaeology, Am. Coun. Learned Soc. (del. 1985-89), German Archeol. Inst. (corr.). Democrat. Office: Boston U Dept Archaeology 675 Commonwealth Ave Boston MA 02215-1406

WISEMAN, JAY DONALD, photographer, mechanical designer and contractor; b. Salt Lake City, Dec. 23, 1952; s. Donald Thomas and Reva (Stewart) W.; m. Barbara Helen Taylor, June 25, 1977; children: Jill Reva, Steve Jay. Ed. Utah State U., Logan, U. Utah. Cert. profl. photographer. Pvt. practice photography; owner, pres. JB&W Corp. Recipient Grand prize Utah State Fair, 1986, Kodak Crystal for Photographic Excellence, 1986, 87, Master of Photography degree, 1989, Best of Show award, 1991-92; Profl. Photographer Mag. cover photo, 1988; numerous photos inducted for permanent collection Internat. Photographic Hall of Fame, 1989; photo named one of World's Greatest, Kodak, 1987-88; 2 photos named among World's Best, Walt Disney World and Profl. Photographers Assn., 1988, 2 prints tied for Best of Show award RMPPA Regional contest, 1991; recipient Gold Medallion award Best in Show (world wide). Mem. Profl. Photographers Assn. Am. (one of top 10 scores internat. photo contest), Rocky Mountain Profl. Photographers (Best of Show, highest score ever 1987, Master Photographer of Yr. 1991, Ct. of Honour 1981-91), Inter-Mountain Profl. Photographers Assn. (Master's Trophy Best of Show 1982, 86, 88, Photographer of Yr. award 1986, Ct. of Honour 1981-91), Photographers Soc. Am (Best of Show award Utah chpt. 1986). Latter Day Saints. Represented in Salt Lake City Internat. Airport permanent photo exhibit, various traveling loan collections, U.S. and Europe, 1988, loan collection Epcot Ctr., 1988-91; photographs published numerous profl. jours.

WISEMAN, LAURENCE DONALD, foundation executive; b. Washington, Feb. 24, 1947; s. Leon Robert and Marion (Zuckerman) W.; m. Robin Lynn Jeweler, May 29, 1978; children: Justin J., David B. AB with highest distinction, Dartmouth Coll., 1969; M in Pub. Affairs, Princeton U., 1971. Exec. producer Sta. WQED-TV (pub. broadcasting), Pitts., 1971-75; prin. Moses, Epstein and Wiseman, Washington, 1975-78; v.p. Yankelovich, Skelly and White, N.Y.C., 1978-81; v.p. Am. Forest Council, Washington, 1981-84, pres., 1984—; pres. Am. Forest Coun., 1984-92, Am. Forest Found., 1993—. Author: Coalition Building, 1977. Bd. dirs. Cystic Fibrosis Found., N.Y.C., 1979-80, Urban Philharmonic, Washington, 1980-83, Sasha Bruce House, Washington, 1980-82; adv. com. Soc. for Profl. Journalists, Washington, 1984; hon. trustee Nat. Arbor Day Found., Nebraska City, Nebr., 1984—. Mem. Am. Forestry Assn., Soc. Am. Foresters, Pub. Rels. Soc. Am. Home: 10621 Democracy Ln Potomac MD 20854-4016 Office: Am Forest Found 1111 19th St NW Washington DC 20036-3603

WISEMAN, THOMAS ANDERTON, JR., federal judge; b. Tullahoma, Tenn., Nov. 3, 1930; s. Thomas Anderton and Vera Seleta (Poe) W.; m. Emily Barbara Matlack, Mar. 30, 1957; children: Thomas Anderton III, Mary Alice, Sarah Emily. B.A., Vanderbilt U., 1952, LL.B., 1954; LLM, U. Va., 1990. Bar: Tenn. Pvt. practice Tullahoma, 1956-63; ptnr. Haynes, Wiseman & Hull, Tullahoma and Winchester, Tenn., 1963-71; treas. State of Tenn., 1971-74; ptnr. Chambers & Wiseman, 1974-78; judge U.S. Dist. Ct. (mid. dist.) Tenn., Nashville, 1978—, chief judge, 1984-91, sr. chief judge, 1995—; mem. Tenn. Ho. of Reps., 1964-68; adj. prof. law Vanderbilt U. Sch. Law. Asso. editor: Vanderbilt Law Rev, 1953-54. Democratic candidate for gov., Tenn., 1974; Chmn. Tenn. Heart Fund, 1973, Middle Tenn. Heart Fund, 1972. Served with U.S. Army, 1954-56. Fellow Tenn. Bar Found.; mem. Masons (33 deg.), Shriners, Amateur Chefs Soc. Presbyterian. Office: US Dist Ct 736 US Courthouse 801 Broadway Nashville TN 37203-3816

WISER, JAMES LOUIS, political science educator; b. Detroit, Mar. 4, 1945; s. Louis Bernard and Nita Pauline (Neff) W.; m. Bethany Marie Goodall, Dec. 27, 1967; children: Steven Louis, Michael James. B.A., U. Notre Dame, 1967; M.A., Duke U., 1968, Ph.D., 1971. Asst. prof. Loyola U., Chgo., 1971-74, assoc. prof., 1974-81, prof., 1981—, chmn. dept. polit. sci., 1980-84, dean Coll. Arts and Scis., 1987-89, sr. v.p., dean of faculties, 1989—. Author: Political Philosophy: A History of the Search for Order, 1983; Political Theory: A Thematic Inquiry, 1986. Bd. dirs. Am. Cancer Soc., Chgo., 1982-84. Recipient dissertation award Woodrow Wilson Found., 1970; Fulbright-Hayes grantee, 1969; NEH grantee, 1979. Mem. Am. Polit. Sci. Assn., Conf. for Study of Polit. Thought (chmn. 1975-77), Internat. Seminar for Philosophy and Polit. Theory. Democrat. Roman Catholic. Home: 6725 N Wildwood Ave Chicago IL 60646-1306 Office: Loyola U 820 N Michigan Ave Chicago IL 60611-2103

WISHARD, DELLA MAE, state legislator; b. Bison, S.D., Oct. 21, 1934; d. Ervin E. and Alma J. (Albertson) Preszler; m. Glenn L. Wishard, Oct. 18, 1953; children: Glenda Lee, Pamela A., Glen Ervin. Grad. high sch., Bison. Mem. S.D. Ho. of Reps., Pierre, 1984—. Columnist County Farm Bur., 1970—. Committeewoman state Rep. Cen. Com., Perkins County, S.D., 1980-84. Mem. Am. Legis. Exch. Coun. (state coord. 1985-91, state chmn. 1991—), Fed. Rep. Women (chmn. Perkins County chpt. 1978-84), S.D. Farm Bur. (state officer 1982). Lutheran. Avocations: writing, gardening. Home and office: HC 1 Box 139 Prairie City SD 57649-9714

WISHARD, GORDON DAVIS, lawyer; b. Indpls., Jan. 7, 1945; s. William Niles Jr. and Caroline (Davis) W.; m. Anne Emison; children: Claire Clark, Gordon Davis Jr. BA, Williams Coll., 1966; JD, Ind. U., 1969. Bar: Ind. 1969, U.S. Dist. Ct. (so. dist.) Ind. 1969, U.S. Ct. Appeals (7th cir.) 1976, U.S. Supreme Ct. 1980, U.S. Tax Ct. 1983. Ptnr. Ice Miller Donadio & Ryan, Indpls. Mem. Am. Coll. Trust and Estate Coun. (Ind. chmn. 1990-95). Avocations: hunting, fishing. Office: Ice Miller Donadio & Ryan 1 American Sq Indianapolis IN 46282-0001

WISHART, ALFRED WILBUR, JR., foundation administrator; b. Pitts., Dec. 21, 1931; s. Alfred W. and Corrinne C. (Bell) W.; m. Barbara J. Scott, June 30, 1956; children: Scott S., Kathryn A., Craig C. BA, Coll. Wooster, 1953; MDiv, Union Theol. Seminary, 1956; DHL (hon.), Waynesburg U., 1976; DD (hon.), Washington and Jefferson Coll., 1983. Asst. min. Shadyside Presbyn. Ch., Pitts., 1956-60; sr. min. Arlington Ave. Presbyn. Ch., East Orange, N.J., 1961-70; exec. dir. Howard Heinz Endowment, Pitts., 1970-92, Vira I. Heinz Endowment, Pitts., 1985-92; sec. H.J. II Charitable and Family Trust, Pitts., 1970-89; exec. sec. Pitcairn-Crabbe Found., Pitts., 1970—; pres., CEO Pitts. Edn. Found., Pitts., 1970—. Mem. Duquesne Club (bd. dirs. 1983-86), Fox Chapel Golf Club, Rolling Rock Club. Republican. Avocations: tennis, golf, squash, shooting, fishing. Home: 408 Buckingham Rd Pittsburgh PA 15215-1555 also: Pitts Found One PPG Pl 30th Fl Pittsburgh PA 15222

WISHART, LEONARD PLUMER, III, army officer; b. Newark, Sept. 24, 1934; s. Leonard Plumer and Mabel Dorothea (Womsley) W.; m. Sandra Frances De Vito, Apr. 12, 1958; children: Leonard Plumer IV, Scott Brian. Student, Va. Mil. Inst., 1952-53; BS in Engring., U.S. Mil. Acad., 1957; MS in Nuclear Physics, U. Va., 1966. Commd. 2d lt. U.S. Army, 1957, advanced through grades to lt. gen., 1988; served in Germany and Vietnam; tactical officer U.S. Mil. Acad., West Point, N.Y., 1971-73; sr. mil. asst. to Sec. of Army, 1975-76; comdr. 1st Brigade, 24th Inf. Div., Ft. Stewart, Ga., 1977-78; chief of staff 24th Inf. Div., 1979, VII Corps in Germany, 1979-81; asst. div. comdr. 1st Armored Div., 1981-83; dep. comdr. CACDA, Ft. Leavenworth, Kans., 1983-86; comdr. 1st Inf. Div., Ft. Riley, Kans., 1986-88, Combined Arms Command, Ft. Leavenworth, Kans., 1988-91; dep. comdr. TRADOC, Ft. Leavenworth, Kans., 1988-91, ret., 1991; assoc. Burdeshaw Assocs. Ltd., Bethesda, Md., 1991-92; apptd. 1st dir. non-legis. and fin. svcs. U.S. Ho. of Reps., Washington, 1992-94, resigned, 1994; assoc. Burdeshow Assocs., Ltd., Bethesda, Md., 1994—. Active in cmty. activities. Decorated Disting. Service Medal (2), Legion of Merit (2), D.F.C., Bronze Star medal (2), Army Commendation medal, Air medals. Mem. Assn. U.S. Army, Assn. Grads. U.S. Mil. Acad., Alumni Assn. U. Va., VFW, Soc. of the First Divsn. Methodist. Office: Burdeshaw Assocs Ltd 4701 Sangamore Rd Bethesda MD 20816-2508

WISHART, RONALD SINCLAIR, retired chemical company executive; b. Bklyn., Mar. 1, 1925; s. Ronald Sinclair and Elizabeth Lathrop (Phillips) W.; m. Betty B. Burnup, Sept. 14, 1951 (dec. Dec. 1973); children: Michael Sinclair, James Ronald; m. Eleanor Dorothy Parrish Dooley, Jan. 11, 1975; stepchildren: Donna Dooley Willix, Arthur D. Dooley. BChemE, Rensselaer Poly. Inst., 1948. Engr., chemist Linde air div. Union Carbide Corp., Tonawanda, N.Y., 1948-51; sales rep. Chgo., Cleve., 1951-56; region mgr. Chgo., 1956-57; product mgr., mktg. mgr. Silicones div. N.Y.C., 1957-64, gen. mgr., pres., 1964-66, pres. devel. and coating materials divs., 1966-71, corp. dir. energy and transp. policy, 1972-82, v.p. fed. govt. regulations, 1983-85; v.p. pub. affairs Danbury, Conn., 1985-90; chief of staff to chmn. of corp. Union Carbide, N.Y.C., 1984-85; mem. adv. coun. Gas Rsch. Inst., Energy Modeling Ctr., Stanford U., 1979-83, Environ. and Energy Policy Ctr., John F. Kennedy Sch. Pub. Policy, Harvard U., 1980-87; energy com. Aspen Inst., 1976-88; chmn., exec. dir. Electricity Consumers Resource Coun., Washington, 1976-79. Author: The Marketing Factor, 1966; contbr. chpts. to books and articles to profl. jours.; patentee silicone formulas. Vol. Am. Field Svc., Burma, 1944-45; pres., trustee, elder White Plains (N.Y.) Presbyn. Ch., 1987-90; elder Plam City Presbyn. Ch., 1996—; treas., bd. dirs. St. Christopher's Jenni Clarkson Home, 1968-91; mem. exec. bd. Westchester Putnam coun. Boy Scouts Am., White Plains, 1985-91; v.p. Carbide Retiree Corps. Mem. NAM (mem. energy com.), Am. Mgmt. Assn. (v.p. 1966-69), Chem. Mfrs. Assn. (chmn. energy com. 1974-78), Nat. Petroleum Refiners Assn. (v.p. 1972-76, chmn. issues com. 1985-89), Internat. Fedn. Ind. Energy Users (chmn. 1978), Am. Chem. Soc., Soc. Chem. Industry, U.S. C. of C. (mem. energy com.), Met. Club Washington, Harbor Ridge Yacht and Country Club. Republican. Presbyterian. Avocations: golf, skiing, reading. Home: 1329 NW Lancewood Ter Palm City FL 34990-8050

WISHNER, MAYNARD IRA, finance company executive, lawyer; b. Chgo., Sept. 17, 1923; s. Hyman L. and Frances (Fisher) W.; m. Elaine Loewenberg, July 4, 1954; children: Ellen (Mrs. Tom Kenemore), Jane, Miriam. B.A., U. Chgo., 1944, J.D., 1947. Bar: Ill. 1947. Exec. dir. Chgo. Commn. on Human Relations, 1947-52; chief ordinance enforcement div. Law Dept., City of Chgo., 1952-55; mem. law firm Cole, Wishner, Epstein & Manilow, Chgo., 1955-63; with Walter E. Heller & Co., Chgo., 1963-86, pres., 1974-86; of counsel Rosenthal and Schanfield, Chgo., 1986-95; dir. Walter E. Heller Internat. Corp., Am. Nat. Bank & Trust Co., and br. cos., Chgo. Pres. Jewish Fedn. Met. Chgo., 1987-89; chair adv. coun. Nat. Jewish Community Rels., 1992-94, pres. Coun. Jewish Fedn., 1993—; chmn. nat. exec. coun. Am. Jewish Com., 1973-76, chmn. bd. govs., 1977-80, nat. pres. 1980-83, hon. pres., recipient Human Rights medallion, 1975; bd. dirs. Nat. Found. for Jewish Culture; chmn. Ill. Humanities Coun.; commr. Nat. Hillel Found.; mem. vis. com. U. Chgo. Sch. Social Svc. Adminstrn.; chair Ill. Humanities Coun., 1991-93. Served with AUS, 1943. Home: 1410 Sheridan Rd Wilmette IL 60091-1840 Office: Rosenthal & Schanfield 55 E Monroe St Chicago IL 60603-5702

WISHNER, STEVEN R., retail executive; b. N.Y.C., Mar. 21, 1950; s. Jerome and Florence (Wanger) W.; m. Lauri Ruth Berkson, June 5, 1977; children: Andrew R., Sara M. BA, Colgate U., 1972; MBA, Cornell U., 1976. 2nd v.p. Chase Manhattan Bank, N.Y.C., 1976-78; functional v.p. Chase Manhattan Bank, 1978; dir. fin. svcs. Gen. Instrument Corp., Clifton, N.J., 1978-79; asst. to treas. Gen. Instrument Corp., 1979-81; dir. fin. svcs. Viacom Internat. Inc., N.Y.C., 1981-82; asst. treas. Viacom Internat. Inc., 1982-86; v.p., treas. Zayre Corp., Framingham, Mass., 1987-89; v.p. fin., treas. The TJX Cos., Inc., Framingham, 1987—; mem. ea. adv. bd. Protection Mut. Ins. Co., 1987-91. Vice chmn. fin. com. Town of Sudbury, Mass. Mem. Fin. Execs. Inst., Nat. Assn. Corp. Treas., Nat. Investor Rels. Inst., Cornell U. Alumni Assn. (co-chmn. admissions com., alumni exec. coun. 1987-90), Masons. Home: 92 Fox Run Rd Sudbury MA 01776-2768 Office: The TJX Companies Inc 770 Cochituate Rd Framingham MA 01701-4657

WISKIND, MILTON I., wholesale distribution executive, chemicals executive; b. 1925. BS, Wharton Sch. Commerce, 1947. With Myers Industries, Inc., Akron, Ohio, 1957—, v.p., 1963; v.p., sec. Myers Industries, Inc., Akron, 1971, now sr. v.p., sec. With USN, USNR, 1947-67. Office: Myers Industries Inc 1293 S Main St Akron OH 44301-1302*

WISLER, CHARLES CLIFTON, JR., retired cotton oil company executive; b. Oklahoma City, June 6, 1926; s. Charles Clifton and Lucille Sunshine (McCormick) W.; m. Frances Joan Higgins, Sept. 21, 1946; children: Karen Lynn Collins-Eiland, Gary Clifton, David Charles. Student, Oklahoma City U., 1945-47. Bookkeeper Magnolia Petroleum Co., Oklahoma City, 1947-51; cotton buyer C.S. Higgins Co., Lubbock, Tex., 1951-52; office mgr. Sharp & Glover, Harlingen, Tex., 1952; with Toyo Cotton Co., Dallas, 1952-81, pres., 1972-81; pres. Chickasha Cotton Oil Co., Ft. Worth, 1981-86, chmn., 1986-88; advisor to bd. dirs. Nat. Cotton Coun., 1985-91. Bd. dirs. Nat. Kidney Found., Dallas, 1976-83, Granbury Opera House Assn., 1992-94; mem. Agr. Policy Adv. Com. for Trade Negotiations, Washington, 1975-77. With USAAF, 1944-45. Mem. Tex. Cotton Assn. (dir. 1971-75, 79-80, pres. 1974), Am. Cotton Shippers Assn. (dir. 1972, 74-75, 77). Republican. Methodist. Home: 6115 Belvidere Cir Granbury TX 76049 *I have always believed in living a disciplined life and the practice of Christian principles in business.*

WISLER, WILLARD EUGENE, health care management executive; b. Cliffside Park, N.J., May 31, 1933; s. Willard Walter and Doris Alice (McGlone) W.; m. Carol M. Askey, Aug. 19, 1966; children: Diana Marie, Jennifer Lee. BBA, U. Fla., 1955; MBA, The George Washington U., 1963. Asst. adminstr. Halifax Dist. Hosp., Daytona Beach, Fla., 1963-64; CFO Waterman Meml. Hosp., Eustis, Fla., 1964-67, COO, 1967-72; COO Suburban Hosp., Louisville, 1972-73; exec. dir. Gen. Hosp. of Fort Walton Beach, Fla., 1973-77; pres. Winter Pk. (Fla.) Meml. Hosp., 1977-91, Park Health Corp., Winter Pk., 1985-91, The Tampa Bay Hosp. Assn., St. Petersburg, Fla., 1991—; bd. dirs. Village on the Green, Longwood, Fla., 1983-88; mem. ho. of dels. Am. Hsp. Assn., Chgo., 1985-88; regent State of Fla. Am. Coll. Healthcare Execs., Chgo., 1988-93. Adv. council mem. Hamilton Holt Sch., Rollins Coll., Winter Pk., 1986-89, Orlando Bus. Jour., 1989, Pioneer Savings Bank, Winter Pk., 1986-88. Sgt. U.S. Army, 1955-59. Fellow Am. Coll. Healthcare Execs., Citrus Club, Winter Park Racquet, Interlachen Country. Democrat. Home: 3414 W Mullen Ave Tampa FL 33609-4632 Office: The Tampa Bay Hosp Assn 9455 Koger Blvd N Ste 118 Saint Petersburg FL 33702-2431

WISMER, PATRICIA ANN, secondary education educator; b. York, Pa., Mar. 23, 1936; d. John Bernhardt and Frances Elizabeth Loreen Marie (Fry) Feiser; m. Lawrence Howard Wismer, Aug. 4, 1961. BA in English, Mt. Holyoke Coll., 1958; MA in Speech/Drama, U. Wis., 1960; postgrad., U. Oreg., 1962, Calif. State U., Chico, 1963-64, U. So. Calif., 1973-74. Tchr., co-dir. drama program William Penn Sr. High Sch., York, 1960-61; instr. English, dir. drama York Jr. Coll., 1961-62; assoc. church editor San Francisco Examiner, 1962-63; reporter, publicist News Bur. Calif. State U., Chico, 1963-64; chmn. English Dept. Chico Sr. H.S., 1966-96; mentor tchr. Chico Sr. High Sch., Chico Unified Sch. Dist., 1983-93; judge writing awards Nat. Coun. Tchr. English, 1970—; cons. No. Calif. Writing Project, 1977—; curriculum cons., freelance writer and photographer, 1996—. Mem. Educators for Social Responsibility, Calif. Assn. for Gifted, Upper Calif. Coun. Tchrs. English (bd. dirs. 1966-85, pres. 1970-71), Calif. Assn. Tchrs. English, Nat. Coun. Tchrs. English, NEA, Calif. Tchrs. Assn., Chico Unified Tchrs. Assn. Democrat. Lutheran. Avocations: photography, play prodn., video prodn. Home: 623 Arcadian Ave Chico CA 95926-4504 Office: PO Box 1250 Cannon Beach OR 97110

WISNE, ANTHONY E., metal products executive; b. 1918. With Prog Tool & Indsl. Co., Southfield, Mich., 1939—, now chmn. Office: Prog Tool & Inds Co 21000 Telegraph Rd Southfield MI 48034-4280*

WISNE, LAWRENCE A., metal products executive; b. 1947; s. Anthony E. W. With Prog Tool & Indsl. Co., Southfield, Mich., v.p., 1977-79, pres., 1979—. Office: Prog Tool & Inds Co 21000 Telegraph Rd Southfield MI 48034-4280*

WISNER, FRANK GEORGE, ambassador; b. N.Y.C., July 2, 1938; s. Frank Gardiner W. and Mary Knowles (Fritchey) W.; m. Genevieve de Virel, July, 1969 (dec. 1974); 1 dau., Sabrina; m. Christine de Ganay, June, 1976; 1 son, David; stepchildren: Caroline Sarkozy, Olivier Sarkozy. BA, Princeton U., 1961. With Fgn. Svc. Dept. Dept. State, Algiers, Morocco, 1962-64; from staff aide to sr. advisor Vietnamese province Tuyen Duc Agy. Internat. Devel., Vietnam, 1964-68; officer-in-charge Tunisian affairs Dept. State, Washington, 1968-71; chief econ.-comml. sect. Am. Embassy, Tunis, Tunisia, 1971-73; chief polit. sect. Am. Embassy, Dacca, Bangladesh, 1973-74; dir. plans and mgmt. Bur. Pub. Affairs, Washington, 1974-75; spl. asst. to dir., then dep. dir. Pres.' Interagy. Task Force Refugee Resettlement, Washington, 1975; spl. asst. to undersec. polit. affairs, 1975-76; dir. office So. African affairs Dept. State, Washington, 1976-77, dep. exec. sec., 1977-79; U.S. amb. to Zambia Lusaka, 1977-82; dep. asst. sec. African affairs Dept. State, Washington, 1982-86; U.S. amb. to Egypt Cairo, 1986-91; U.S. amb. to Philippines Manila, 1991-92; under sec. of state for internat. security affairs Washington, 1992-93; under sec. of def. for policy Dept. Def., Washington, 1993-94; U.S. amb. to India, 1994—. Recipient meritorious honor award Dept. State, 1973, superior honor award, 1992; recipient Mil. Medal of Honor Govt. Vietnam, 1968, Social Welfare medal of honor, 1968. Mem. Council on Fgn. Relations, Metropolitan Club (Washington), Ivy Club (Princeton, N.J.), Knickerbocker Club (N.Y.). Episcopalian. Office: Am Embassy New Delhi State Dept Washington DC 20521-9000

WISNER, ROSCOE WILLIAM, JR., retired human resources executive; b. Beatrice, Nebr., Mar. 17, 1926; s. Roscoe William Sr. and Genevieve M. (McVey) W.; m. Louise Jackson, Mar. 15, 1952; children: Jacqueline Louise, Valerie Joyce. BA, Lincoln U., Oxford, Pa., 1950; MEd, Temple U., 1963. Accredited profl. in human resource mgmt. Sr. personnel examiner Phila. Personnel Dept., 1954-64; supr. testing and rsch. Port Authority of N.Y. and N.J., N.Y.C., 1964-76, coord. spl. programs for people with disabilities, 1976-91; ret.; instr., adj. faculty LaGuardia C.C. Author: Performance Test Procedures and Problems, 1964; contbr. articles to profl. jours. Adv. coun. Industry-Labor Coun., Albertson, N.Y., 1976-91, Kessler's Rehab. Inst., East and West Orange, N.J., 1979-91, Rusk Rehab. Inst., N.Y.C., 1980-91, Mayor's Office People with Disabilities, N.Y.C., 1980, Internat. Ctr. for Disabled, N.Y.C., 1980-91, N.Y.C. Bd. Edn. Spl. Edn. Project Future, 1986-91; exec. dir. Cmty. Action Program, Westbury, 1965; mem. Watchful Eye Civic Assn., Roosvelt, N.Y., 1983—; life mem. NAACP. Sgt. U.S. Army, 1944-46. Recipient Exec. Dir. Unit citation Port Authority N.Y. and N.J., 1984, Disting. Svc. award, 1990, Profl. Achievement award Ea. Region/Pub. Pers. Assn. Conf., 1969. Mem. APA (assoc.), ASPA, NAACP (life), Internat. Pers. Mgmt. Assn., Soc. Human Resource Mgmt. (life), Masons, Alpha Phi Alpha (life). Home: 266 E Greenwich Ave Roosevelt NY 11575-1205

WISNESKI, MARY JO ELIZABETH, reading specialist, educator; b. Saginaw, Mich., Dec. 18, 1938; d. Walter Frank and Hedwig Josephine (Borowicz) W. BS, Cen. Mich. U., 1961; MS, So. Ill. U., 1969; EdD, U. No. Colo., 1979; postdoctoral, U. Calif., Berkeley, 1980-81. Cert. elem. educator, elem. adminstr., reading specialist, Calif.; reading recovery tchr. Elem. educator various schs., 1960-75; instr. U. No. Colo., Greeley, 1976-78, 79; reading specialist Vacaville (Calif.) Unified Sch. Dist., 1980—; lectr. San Francisco State U., 1983-86; prof. Chapman Coll., Travis AFB, Calif., 1986-90; med. transcriptionist, office mgr. collections, 1991-94; cons. in field. Author: Clifford Books Teacher Manual, 1991, Reading Recovery Position Paper, 1995. Vol. ARC, Travis Air Mus., Travis AFB; bd. dirs. Polish Arts and Culture Found., San Francisco, 1988-91, Vistula Dancers; mem. Reading Del. to Vietnam, People-to-People Internat. Amb. Program, 1995. Recipient Tchr. in Space Certificate NASA, 1986, Outstanding Tchr. Commendation Dept. of Defense, 1973. Mem. AAUW, Nat. Women's Polit. Caucus, Nat. Reading Conf., Internat. Reading Assn., Western Coll. Reading Assn., Calif. Profs. Reading (v.p., treas.), Calif. Edn. Assn., Solano County Reading Assn. (pres., v.p., sec.), Lowiczanie Folk Dance Ensemble (pres. pro tem, treas.), Polish Am. Congress, Phi Delta Kappa, Phi Kappa Phi, Kappa Delta Pi, Pi Lambda Theta. Avocations: modeling, travel, skiing, gardening, nature. Home: 314 Creekview Ct Vacaville CA 95688-5318

WISNIEWSKI, HELENA STASIA, telecommunications and information systems company executive, mathematician; b. Englewood, N.J., Dec. 8, 1949; d. Julius George and Katherine Rose (Godlewski) W.; m. Phillip B. Chesson, Jan. 1, 1978; 1 child, Alexis Wisniewski-Chesson. BS in Maths., William Patterson Coll., 1971; MS in Maths., Stevens Inst. Tech., 1973; PhD in Maths., CUNY, 1980. Cert. secondary tchr., N.J. Prof. computer and decision scis. Seton Hall U., South Orange, N.J., 1980-81, dept. chair, 1981-82, dir. div. rsch., 1983-84; prof. maths. Rochester (N.Y.) Inst. Tech., 1982-83; project officer CIA, Washington, 1984-85; founding dir. maths. program Def. Advanced Rsch. Projects Agy., Washington, 1985-88; corp. dir.hdqrs. Lockheed Corp., Calabasas, Calif., 1988-92; v.p. VITA, Arlington, Va., 1992-93; dir. advanced program devel. Titan Corp., Reston, Va., 1993-94, v.p. advanced programs, 1995—; rev. panel Computational Fluid Dynamics Office of the Under Sec. Def., Washington, 1987-88; chair adv. bd. So. Ill. U. Neuro-Engr. Rsch. Ctr., Carbondale, Ill., 1990—; founding bd. dirs. Calif. Coalition for Maths., 1991—. Founding editor: Technology Acceleration, 1991—; editl. bd. Jour. Applied Numerical Maths., 1987-91; co-chair Lockheed Horizons editl. bd., 1991-92; editor SPIE Proceedings, Springer Verlag, vol. 1771; contbr. articles to jour. SPIE, Visual Info. Processing, Chaoes & Comm., NATO ASI Series-Springer Verlag, Transactions of the Am. Math. Soc., Internat. Symposium Dynamical Systems, Proceedings Rio de Janiero, Springer Verlag. Sci. fair judge Westlake High Sch., Westlake Village, Calif., 1990; organizer career exploration program Calabasas High Sch., 1990; mem. math. coun. L.A. Ednl. Partnership, 1991. Recipient Teaching Excellence award Va. Poly. Inst. and State U., 1976, Spl. Achievement award, CIA 1986, Spl. Recognition award DARPA, 1988, Dedicated Svc. award George Washington U. Adv. Bd., 1995. Mem. AIAA (sr.), N.Y. Acad. Scis., Soc. Indsl. and Applied Maths., Security Affairs Support Assn., Armed Forces Comm. & Electronics Assn., Lockheed Mgmt. Assn. (v.p. 1989-90, pres. 1990-91, adv. bd. George Washington U. 1995—, Recognition of Extraordinary Leadership, Mgmt. & Svc. Honor award 1992), Pi Mu Epsilon, Kappa Delta Pi. Office: Titan Corp 1900 Campus Commons Dr Ste 400 Reston VA 22091

WISNIEWSKI, HENRY GEORGE, wholesale distribution executive; b. Chgo., Feb. 26, 1940; s. Henry John and Jeanette A. (Wawrylska) W.; m. Joyce Anne Kennedy, May 28, 1966; children: Mark, Paul. BSc, Loyola U., Chgo., 1961; MBA, Northwestern U., 1981. CPA, Ill. Ptnr. Arthur Andersen & Co., Chgo., 1961-76; pres. JMPH Enterprises, Chgo., 1977-82, Robank & Co., Chgo., 1982-89; exec. v.p., CFO Tash Inc., Des Plaines, Ill., 1989-92; sr. v.p. fin. Tuthill Corp., Hinsdale, Ill., 1992—; bd. dirs. Quality Control Corp., Chgo., Paragon Die Casting, Chgo. Bd. dirs. Chgo. Youth Ctrs., 1966—, past pres., 1971. Sgt. USMCR, 1962-67. Mem. AICPAs, Ill. Soc. CPAs, Fin. Execs. Inst. Roman Catholic. Office: Tuthill Corp 908 N Elm St Hinsdale IL 60521-3635*

WISNIEWSKI, HENRYK MIROSLAW, pathology and neuropathology educator, research facility administrator, research scientist; b. Luszkowko, Poland, Feb. 27, 1931; came to U.S., 1966; s. Alexander and Ewa (Korthals) W.; m. Krystyna Wylon, Feb. 14, 1954; children: Alexander (dec.), Thomas. MD, Med. Sch., Gdansk, Poland, 1955; PhD in Exptl. Neuropathology, Med. Sch., Warsaw, Poland, 1960; DSc (hon.), Med. Sch., Gdansk, Poland, 1991, Coll. of Staten Island, 1992. From asst. to assoc. prof., head. lab. exptl. neuropathology, assoc. dir. Inst. Neuropathology Polish Acad. Sci., Warsaw, 1958-66; rsch. assoc., from asst. prof. to prof. Albert Einstein Coll. Medicine, N.Y.C., 1966-75; dir. MRC Demyelinating Diseases Unit, Newcastle upon Tyne, Eng., 1974-76; prof. neuropathology SUNY Health Sci. Ctr., Bklyn., 1976—; dir. N.Y. State Inst. Basic Rsch. in Devel. Disabilities, S.I., 1976—; vis. neuropathologist U. Toronto, Ont., Can., 1961-62; vis. scientist Lab. of Neuropathology Nat. Inst. Neurol. and Communicative Diseases and Stroke, NIH, 1962-63; docent Med. Sch., Warsaw, 1965; past mem. Neuology B study sect. NIH; past mem. mental retardation rsch. com. Nat. Inst. Child Health and Human Devel. Mem. editl. bd. Acta Neuropathologica, Neurotoxicology, Jour. Neuropathology and Exptl. Neurology, Devel. Neurosci., Internat. Jour. Geriatric Psychiatry, Alzheimer Disease and Assoc. Disorders Internat. Jour., Brain Sysfunction, Dementia; mem. editl. adv. bd. Neurobiology of Aging; contbr. over 625 articles to profl. jours. and symposia procs. Recipient N.Y.C. Chpt. award Assn. for Help of Retarded Children, 1984, Welfare League award letchworth Village chpt. Assn. for Help of Retarded Children, 1985, Staten Island Chpt. award Benevolent Soc. for Retarded Children, 1986; named Career Scientist, Health Rsch. Coun. of City of N.Y., Honoris Causa Doctor of Sci., Med. Sch., Gdansk, Poland, 1992, Honoris Causa, Doctor of Sci., Coll. of Staten Island, 1992. Fellow AAAS; mem. Am. Assn. Neuropathologists (pres. 1984, Weil award 1969, Moore award 1972), British Soc. Neuropathology, Can. Assn. Neuropathologists, Am. Assn. Retarded Citizens, Assn. Rsch. in Nervous and Mental Disease, Am. Assn. Mental Deficiency, Internat. Soc. Devel. Neurosci., Soc. Exptl. Neuropathology, World Fedn. Neurology, Sigma Xi. Roman Catholic. Achievements include research of developmental disabilities, aging, Alzheimer disease, Down syndrome, amyloidosis, neuronal fibrous protein pathology; demyelinating diseases. Office: NY State Inst Basic Rsch Devel Disabilities 1050 Forest Hill Rd Staten Island NY 10314-6330

WISNIEWSKI, JOHN WILLIAM, mining engineer, bank engineering executive; b. Portage, Pa., Jan. 22, 1932; s. John and Agnes (Ease) W.; m. Joan Smith, Aug. 24, 1957; children: John Andrew, Jean Marie, Maria. BS in Mining Engring., U. Pitts., 1954, postgrad., 1967-68. Mining engr. Bethlehem Mines Corp., Johnstown, Pa., 1956-61, Fairmont, W.Va., 1961-62; mining and gen. engr. IRS, Pitts., 1962-69; mining engr., then coordinating engr. IRS, Washington, 1969-72, supervisory gen. engr., chief rsch., planning and studies sect., 1972-76; mining engr., then dep. chief engr. Export-Import Bank U.S., Washington, 1976-82, chief engr., 1982, v.p. engring., 1982-94; v.p. engring. and environ. div., 1994-95, ret., 1995. With U.S. Army, 1954-56; Korea. AIME scholar U. Pitts., 1950. Home: 9308 Ironhorse Ln Gaithersburg MD 20879-2161

WISNIEWSKI, STEPHEN ADAM, professional football player; b. Rutland, Vt., Apr. 7, 1967. Student, Pa. State U. Offensive guard L.A. Raiders, 1989—. Named All-Pro Team Guard by Sporting News, 1990-93, Coll. All-Am. Team, 1987, 88. Played in Pro Bowl, 1990-91, 93. Office: L A Raiders 332 Center St El Segundo CA 90245-4047

WISNIEWSKI, THOMAS JOSEPH, music educator; b. Chgo., Sept. 17, 1926; s. George Wisniewski and Rose (Jelewski) W.; children: Dieter, Lisa Ann, Ericka. B.Mus., Am. Conservatory of Music, Chgo., 1948; M.Mus., No. Ill. U., 1964. Instr. string instrument Sch. Dist. 89, Maywood, Ill., 1950-55; orch. dir. Sch. Dist. 44, Lombard, Ill., 1955-67; dir. orchs. Glenbard East High Sch., Lombard, 1959-67; prof. music U. Ill., Urbana, 1967-94, emeritus prof., 1994—, chair music edn. div., 1988-92; music cons. Webster Internat. Illustrated Dictionary, 1993. Prodr. films Playing the String Bass, 1967, Playing the Cello, 1968; developer computer software program Visualized Vibrato, 1995. Author: Learning Unlimited String Program, Vol. 1, 1975, Vol. 2, 1976; editor Orch. Publs., 1990; music editor Webster International Illustrated Dictionary, 1994. Mem. Am. String Tchrs. Assn. Assn. (Disting. Svc. award Ill. unit 1991, Disting. Svc. award Tenn. unit 1993), Ill. Music Educators Assn. (Pres.'s award 1996), Music Educators Nat. Conf., Ill. String Tchrs. Assn. (editor 1967, 87, pres. 1970), Nat. Jazz Educators Assn. (nat. orch. chmn. 1976), Pi Kappa Lambda, Phi Mu Alpha. Office: U Ill 1114 W Nevada St Urbana IL 61801-3859

WISOTSKY, SERGE S., SR., engineering executive; b. Chelsea, Mass., Oct. 19, 1919; s. Sidor Radionovich and Anna Epatiovna (Fariba) W.; m. Marion Ellen Ramsdell, Aug. 10, 1952; children: Serge S. Jr. (dec.), Tanya Lloyd, Stephan, John and Alexander (twins), Phillip. Student, Boston Trade Sch., 1933-37, Lowell Inst. Sch., 1937-43; BS in Physics, MIT, 1950; MS in Physics, Brown U., 1952. Registered profl. engr., Mass., Okla.; lic. electrician, Mass. Elec. motor mech./armature winder United Motor Corp., Boston, 1937-40; machinist apprentice, mfg. methods steam turbine test GE River Works, Lynn, Mass., 1940-44; engr. R & D Ultrasonics Corp., Cambridge, Mass., 1952-53; instrument engr. Control Engring. Corp., Canton and Norwood, Mass., 1953-57; staff engr. MIT/Draper Lab., Cambridge, Mass., 1957-59; hydroacoustic transducer sect. head Raytheon/Submarine Signal Divsn., Portsmouth, R.I., 1959-70; MSR engr. Raytheon Equipment Divsn. North Dighton, Mass. and Kwajalein Atoll, 1958; v.p. engring. ORB Inc., Sharon, Mass. and Tulsa, 1970—; chief engr. Indsl. Vehicles, Internat., Tulsa, 1974-84; cons. Amoco Prodn. Rsch. ctr., Tulsa, 1985-86, 93. Contbr. articles to profl. jours. including Jour. Underwater Acoustics, Jour. Geophys. Rsch., Jour. Inst. Navigation, ONR, Jour. Acoustical Soc. Am., Offshore Tech. Conf., Soc. Exptl. Geophys., Sea Tech.; appeared on Dave Garroway's morning TV show, 1953. Brass band clarinetist Stoughton VFW, 1937-42, Bklyn. Armed Guard Ctr., 1945, Brockton Cosmopolitan, 1951-65, Aleppo Shrine, 1965—, Lawrence Colonial, 1989—, Canton/Am. Legion, 1992—. With USNR, 1944-46. Mem. ASME, Acoustical Soc. Am., ASM, Masons. Russian Orthodox, Congregationalist and Baptist. Achievements include patents for Electro/Syn Pressure Gauge, Electro/HydroSonic Transducer, 6 Water Hammer Piledrivers, and WastePile, also numerous foreign patents. Home and Office: 89 Bullard St Sharon MA 02067-1007

WISS, MARCIA A., lawyer; b. Columbus, Ohio, May 15, 1947; d. John William and Margaret Ann (Cook) W.; m. Donald Gordon MacDonald, Nov. 18, 1921; children: Christopher C. Wiss, Joan Merle. BS in Fgn. Svc., Georgetown U., 1969, JD, 1972. Bar: D.C. 1972. Econ. analyst World Bank, Washington, 1969; atty. U.S. Dept. Justice, Washington, 1972-73; atty. office gen. counsel Overseas Pvt. Investment Corp., Washington, 1973-78; assoc. Stroock & Stroock & Lavan, Washington, 1978-79; gen counsel-designate Inst. for Sci. and Tech. Cooperation, Washington, 1979; affiliate Curtis, Mallet-Prevost, Colt & Mosle, Washington, 1979-80; ptnr. Anderson & Pendleton, Chartered Attys., Washington, 1980-87, Kaplan Russin & Vecchi, Washington, 1987-92, Whitman & Ransom, 1992-93, Whitman, Breed, Abbott & Morgan, Washington, 1993—; gen. counsel Washington chpt., Soc. Internat. Devel., 1980—; gen. counsel, Assn. for Women in Devel., 1982—; bd. advisers, Procedural Aspects of Internat. Law Inst., 1985—. editor Georgetown Law Ctr. Jour. Law and Policy in Internat. Bus., 1971-72. Chairperson Holy Trinity Parish Coun., Washington, 1976; mem. bd. advisers Trees for Life, Wichita, Kans., 1984—. Mem. Am. Fedn. Govt. Employees (chmn. 1975-76), D.C. Bar (steering com. divsn. 12, 1985-88, co-chmn. fin. and banking com. 1985), Am. Soc. Internat. Law (v.p. 1991-94, coun. 1987-90), Washington Fgn. Law Soc. (pres. 1983-84). Roman Catholic. Office: Whitman Breed Abbott & Morgan 1215 17th St NW Washington DC 20036-3008

WISSBRUN, KURT FALKE, chemist, consultant; b. Brackwede, Westphalia, Germany, Mar. 19, 1930; came to the U.S., 1939; s. Hermann and Bertha (Falke) W. BS, U. Pa., 1952; PhD, Yale U., 1956. Rsch. chemist Hoechst-Celanese (formerly Celanese Corp.), Summit, N.J., 1957-60; group leader Hoechst-Celanese, Summit, N.J., 1960-62; rsch. assoc. Hoerst-Celanese (formerly Celanese Corp.), Summit, N.J., 1966-70, sr. rsch. assoc., 1970-90; polymer cons. Summit, 1990—. Author: Melt Rheology and Plastics Processing, 1989, (with others) Blow Molding Handbook, 1988; contbr. articles to profl. jours.; patentee, inventor in field. Mem. Am. Chem. Soc., Soc. Rheology (pres. 1995-97, Bingham medal 1992), British Soc. Rheology, Sigma Xi. Jewish. Avocations: golf, opera, travel. Home: 1 Euclid Ave Apt 4E Summit NJ 07901-2164

WISSMAN, DONALD JOHN, economic consulting firm executive; b. Marine City, Mich., Sept. 26, 1937; s. Edwin c. and Helen M. (Crawford) W.; m. Janice R. Wanklyn, June 28, 1969; children: Scott Donald, Sean David. BS in Agrl. Econ., Mich. State U., 1959, MS in Agrl. Econ., 1965; PhD in Econs., Kans. State U., 1983. Youth exch. del. Internat. Farm Youth Exch., Australia, 1959-60; economist Agri Rsch. Inc., Manhattan, Kans., 1965-67, sr. economist, 1967-72; sr. economist Devel. Planning and Rsch. Lab., Manhattan, 1972-74, v.p., 1974-80; sr. v.p. DPRA Inc., Manhattan, 1980-86, chmn., 1987—; bd. dirs. Kans. State U. Rsch. Found., Manhattan, Security Nat. Bank, Mid Am. Comm. Corp. Contbr. more than 70 articles and reports to profl. publs. Chmn. Manhattan Arts Coun., 1983-85; pres. McCain Devel. Bd., Manhattan, 1989-90; dir. Coronado Area coun. Boy Scouts, 1989—. Capt. USAF, 1969-63. Recipient Disting. Alumni award Gamma Sigma Delta, 1994. Mem. Manhattan C. of C. (chmn. 1994), Manhattan Rotary Club (bd. dirs. 1986-89, pres. 1988-89, Paul Harris fellow). Baptist. Avocations: hiking, travel, birding, sports. Home: 313 Fordham Rd Manhattan KS 66503 Office: DPRA Inc 200 Research Dr 200 Research Dr Manhattan KS 66503

WISSNER, GARY CHARLES, motion picture art director, production designer; b. N.Y.C., Feb. 9, 1964; s. Sidney and Penina (Gologor) W.; m. Tambre Hemstreet, Nov. 13, 1993. BFA, NYU, 1986. Scenic artist Cape Code Melody Tent, Hyannas, Mass., 1983; prodn. technician Imero Fiorentino Assocs., N.Y.C., 1984-86; asst. scenic designer Radio City Music Hall, N.Y.C., 1986; art dir. MTV Networks, N.Y.C., 1987-88; asst. art dir. Country Music Awards, L.A., 1987; asst. art dir. TV show Young and the Restless, L.A., 1987; asst. art dir. Patty Hearst Atlantic Entertainment, L.A., 1987. Art dir.: (commls.) Chrysler, Laser Tag, Michelob, (theme parks/indsls.) Tomorrowland, 1990, Korean World Expo, 1991, AT&T Futurecom, 1993, (TV) Road to Daytona (MTV segment), 1987, Superbowl in San Diego (MTV spl.), 1988, Family of Spies (CBS mini-series), 1989, In Living Color, 1991, (feature films) Teenage Mutant Ninja Turtles, 1989, Another 48 Hours, 1990, Hoffa, 1992, Wyatt Earp, 1993, Junior, 1994, Seven, 1995; prodn. designer: (comml.) Balance Health Foods, 1993, (television) Millenium, 1996, (feature film) Stephen King's Graveyard Shift, 1990, Last Man Standing, 1995, Steel, 1996; asst. art dir.: (feature films) Warlock, 1988, The Abyss, 1988. Mem. Acad. Motion Picture Arts and Scis. (voting mem.), Soc. Motion Picture Art Dirs. (voting mem.), United Scenic Artists (voting mem.). Avocations: computers, sculpture, sports, fitness. Office: care Art Directors Guild 11365 Ventura Blvd Ste 315 Studio City CA 91604-3148

WISSNER, JOHN KARL, lawyer; b. Evansville, Ind., Nov. 11, 1951; s. Gustave A. and Emma K. (Winiger) W.; m. Maridawn Dempsey, June 23, 1973; children: John Andrew, Matthew Karl, Ryan Patrick. BS in Acctg., Ind. U., 1973, JD, 1976. Assoc. Clark, Statham & McCray, Evansville, Ind., 1976-78; ptnr. Scales, Wissner & Krantz, Boonville, Ind., 1978—; counsel Warrick County, 1995—. Mem. Boonville Kiwanis, Ducks Unltd. (treas. Pigeon Creek chpt. 1992-95), Outboard Boating Club Evansville (commodore). Avocations: boating, hunting. Office: PO Box 288 Boonville IN 47601

WIST, ABUND OTTOKAR, biomedical engineer, radiation physicist, educator; b. Vienna, Austria, May 23, 1926; s. Engelbert Johannes and Augusta Barbara (Ungewitter) W.; m. Suzanne Gregson Smiley, Nov. 30, 1963; children: John Joseph, Abund Charles. BS, Tech U. Graz, 1947; MEd, U. Vienna, 1950, PhD, 1951. Research and devel. engr. Hornyphon AG, Vienna, 1952-54, Siemens & Halske AG, Munich, Germany, 1954-58; dir. research and devel. Brinkman Instruments Co., Westbury, N.Y., 1958-64; sr. scientist Fisher Sci. Inc., Pitts., 1964-69; mem. faculty U. Pitts., 1970-73; asst. prof. computer sci. Va. Commonwealth U., 1973-76, asst. prof. biophysics, 1976-82, asst. prof. physiology and biophysics, 1982-84, assoc. prof. radiology, 1984-92, adj. prof. radiology, 1992—; founder, gen. chmn. Symposium Computer Applications in Med. Care, Washington, 1977-79, chmn. Biomedical Optics Conf., Clin. Application of Modern Imaging Tech. I and II, L.A., 1993, 94; session chmn., lectr. European Radiology Conf., Vienna, 1993, Advanced Laser Dentistry Conf., St. Petersburg, Russia, 1994; session chmn., lectr. Biomedical Optics Europe Conf., Lille, France, 1994. Author: Electronic Design of Microprocessor Based Instrumentation and Control Systems, 1986; contbr. numerous articles and chpts. to profl. jours. and books; patentee in electronic and lab. instrumentation (10). NASA/Am. Soc. Engring. Edn. faculty fellow, summer 1975; U.S. biomed. engring. del. People's Republic China, 1987, 93, Russia, 1993; lectr. in field; bd. regents Liberty U., Lynchburg, Va., 1991—. Mem. AAAS, IEEE (sr., sec. cen. Va.), ASTM, SPIE (editor proceedings, 1993, 94), Am. Chem. Soc., N.Y. Acad. Scis., Am. Coll. Radiology (assoc.), Richmond Computer Club (founder, pres. 1977-79), Biomed. Engring. Soc., Am. Assn. Physics in Medicine, Sigma Xi. Roman Catholic. Home: 9304 Farmington Dr Richmond VA 23229-5336 Office: Med Coll Va/VCA 1101 E Marshall St Richmond VA 23298-0072

WISTISEN, MARTIN J., agricultural business executive; b. Bancroft, Idaho, May 30, 1938; s. Raoul and Cora (Johnson) W.; m. Katherine Callister, Dec. 28, 1960; children: Kevin, Diane, Kaeleen, Janette, Richard, Michelle, R. Brent, N. Greg. BS, Brigham Young U., 1962; MBA, Northwestern U., 1964; PhD, Columbia U., 1976. Fin. analyst Esso Internat., Inc., N.Y.C., 1964-65; dir. fin. analysis, mgr. econ. analysis TWA, N.Y.C., 1967-70; dir. bus. and econs., prof. bus. mgmt. and bus. econs., dir. MBA program, asst. dean Grad. Sch. Mgmt. Brigham Young U., Provo, Utah, 1971-80; v.p. sales and mktg. U & I, Inc., Kennewick, Wash., 1980-82; exec. v.p., chief oper. officer UI Group, Kennewick, 1982-86; pres., chief exec. officer AgriNorthwest, Kennewick, 1986—. Pres. Blue Mountain Coun. Boy Scouts Am., Kennewick, 1987-89; bd. dirs. Wash. State Potato Commn., Moses Lake, 1990-93; mem. strategy comm. Wash. State Energy Adv. Bd., 1991-92. Mem. Assn. Wash. Bus. (bd. dirs. 1987—), Tri City Cmty. Hosp. Physician Orgn. (pres. 1995—), Beta Gamma Sigma, Phi Kappa Phi. Republican. Mem. LDS Ch. Office: AgriNorthwest 2810 W Clearwater Ave Kennewick WA 99336-2963

WISWALL, FRANK LAWRENCE, JR., lawyer, educator; b. Albany, N.Y., Sept. 21, 1939; s. Frank Lawrence and Clara Elizabeth (Chapman) W.; m. Elizabeth Curtiss Nelson, Aug. 9, 1975; children by previous marriage: Anne W. Kowalski, Frank Lawrence III. BA, Colby Coll., 1962; JD, Cornell U., 1965; PhD in Law, Cambridge U., 1967. Bar: Maine 1965, N.Y. 1968, U.S. Supreme Ct. 1968, D.C. 1975; lic. master near coastal steam and motor vessels, 1960—. Assoc. Burlingham, Underwood, Barron, Wright & White, N.Y.C., 1967-73; maritime legal adviser Rep. of Liberia, 1968-88; mem. legal com. Internat. Maritime Orgn., London, 1972-74, vice chmn. 1974-79, chmn., 1980-84; tutorial supr. internat. law Clare Coll., Cambridge, Eng., 1966-67; vis. lectr. Cornell Law Sch., 1969-76, 82; lectr. U. Va. Law Sch. and Ctr. for Oceans Law and Policy, 1978-82; prof. law Cornell U., 1984; Johnsen prof. maritime law Tulane U., 1985; adj. prof. law World Maritime U., Malmo, Sweden, 1986—; prof. Internat. Maritime Law Inst., Malta, 1991—, mem. governing bd., 1992—; prof. admiralty law Maine Maritime Acad., 1993-94; del. Internat. Conf. Marine Pollution, London, 1973; del., chmn. drafting com. Internat. Conf. Carriage of Passengers and Luggage by Sea, Athens, 1974; del. Internat. Conf. on Safety of Life at Sea, London, 1974, 3d UN Conf. on Law of Sea, Caracas, Venezuela, 1974, 3d UN Conf. on Law of Sea (all subsequent sessions); del., chmn. com. final clauses Internat. Conf. on Limitation of Liability for Maritime Claims, London, 1976; del. UN Conf. Carriage of Goods by Sea, Hamburg, 1978, XIII Diplomatic Conf. on Maritime Law, Brussels, 1979; chmn. com. of the whole Internat. Conf. Carriage of Hazardous Substances by Sea, 1984; del. internat. conf. on Maritime Terrorism, Rome, 1988; counsel various marine casualty bds. of investigation, 1970—, harbormaster, Port of Castine, 1960-62; ofcl. prin. Diocese of the Mid-Atlantic States Anglican Cath. Ch., 1988—, chancellor, Missionary Diocese of N.E., 1993—. Author: The Development of Admiralty Jurisdiction and Practice Since 1800, 1970; editor-in-chief Benedict on Admiralty, Vols. 6, 6A-6C (treaties and convs.), 1992—; contbr. articles to profl. jours. Spkr. assembly laity Anglican Cath. Ch., 1995—. Recipient Yorke prize U. Cambridge, 1968-69. Fellow Royal Hist. Soc.; mem. Nat. Lawyers Assn., Titulaire of the Comité Maritime Internat. (exec. councillor 1989—), Maritime Law Assn. U.S. (chmn. com. on intergovtl. orgns. 1983-87, chmn. com. on CMI 1987-95), Ecclesiastical Law Soc., Selden Soc., Am. Soc. Legal History, U.K. Assn. Average Adjusters, U.S. Assn. Average Adjusters, Maine State Bar Assn., Assn. Bar City N.Y., United Oxford and Cambridge U. Club (London), Century Assn., Alpha Delta Phi, Phi Delta Phi. Office: PO Box 201 Castine ME 04421-0201

WIT, DANIEL, international consultant; b. N.Y.C., June 8, 1923; s. Benjamin and Stella (Bloom) W.; m. Phyllis J. Citron, June 15, 1947; children: Pamela S., Frederick W. AB, Union Coll., N.Y., 1943; postgrad., Yale U. Italian program, Paris, 1943-44, Inst. d'Etudes Politiques, Paris, 1945-46; AM, Princeton U., 1948, PhD, 1950. Mem. dept. polit. sci. Ohio State U., 1948-50, U. Cin., 1950-54, U. Mich., 1954-56, Ind. U., 1956-58; mem. dept. polit. sci. George Washington U., 1959-61; head dept. polit. sci. No. Ill. U., Dekalb, 1961-69; dir. internat. programs No. Ill. U., 1969-77, dean internat. and spl. programs, 1977-92, acting v.p., provost, 1986-87; internat. mgmt. cons., 1992—; co-dir. Ctr. S.E. Asian Studies and Tng., 1962-69; Fulbright prof. pub. adminstrn., master's degree dir. Inst. social Studies, The Hague, The Netherlands, 1966-67; vis. prof. pub. adminstrn., adv. Ind. U.-ICA program, Thailand, 1956-58; dir. internat. studies Govtl. Affairs Inst., Washington, 1959-61; project dir. Thai Labor Law and Practice, 1960, Brazailan Labor-A Mgmt. Survey, 1960, Indonesian Labor-A Mgmt. Survey, 1961; cons. tng. program Peace Corps S.E. Asia, Thai Dept. Interior; prof. fgn. affairs Nat. War Coll., 1963-64. Author: Comparative Political Institutions, 1953, A Comparative Survey of Local Government and Administration, 1958, Local Government in Thailand, 1958, Manpower Problems in Southeast Asia, 1960, Labor Conditions in Thailand, 1960, Labor Law and Practice in Thailand, 1964, Thailand: Another Vietnam?, 1968; co-author: Our American Government and Political System, 1972, 77, 82; contbr. articles to profl. jours. Inst. Am. Univs. fellow, France, 1981. Mem. Am. Polit. Sci. Assn. (nat. coun. 1967-69), Phi Beta Kappa. Home: 222 Fairmont Dr De Kalb IL 60115-2332

WIT, HAROLD MAURICE, investment banker, lawyer, investor; b. Boston, Sept. 6, 1928; s. Maurice and Martha (Bassist) W.; m. Judith Haworth, Apr. 1989; children from previous marriage: David Edmund, Hannah Edna. A.B. magna cum laude, Harvard, 1949; J.D. (editor law jour.), Yale, 1954. Bar: N.Y. 1954. Assoc. Cravath, Swaine & Moore, N.Y.C., 1954-58; asst. sec. One William St. Fund, Inc., N.Y.C., 1958-59; v.p., sec. One William St. Fund, Inc., 1959-60; assoc. Allen & Co., 1960-70; assoc Allen & Co., Inc., 1965—, v.p., 1965-70, exec. v.p., 1970—, mng. dir., mem. exec. com.; dir., mem. exec. com., chmn. audit com., chmn. nominating com. Toys-R-Us, Inc.; dir. Allen Investments, Inc. Trustee The Nature Conservancy, South Folk-Shelter Island chpt.; co-founder Group for South Fork; mem. Panel on Future of Govt. in N.Y., 1979-80; mem. vis. coms. Harvard U. Div. Sch.; mem. nat. adv. bd. Project on Being with Dying Upaya Found. With Mass. N.G., 1947-50; lt. (j.g.) USNR, 1951-53, Korea. Mem. VFW, Am. Legion, Korean War Vets. Assn., University Club (N.Y.C.), Harvard Club (N.Y.C.), Phi Beta Kappa, Phi Delta Phi. Home: 150 E 69th St New York NY 10021 also: Cross Hwy PO Box 348 East Hampton NY 11937 Office: Allen & Co Inc 711 5th Ave New York NY 10022-3109

WITCHER, DANIEL DOUGHERTY, retired pharmaceutical company executive; b. Atlanta, May 17, 1924; s. Julius Gordon and Myrtice Eleanor (Daniel) W.; divorced; children: Beth S., Daniel Dougherty Jr., J. Wright, Benjamin G.; m. Betty Lou Middaugh, Oct. 30, 1982. Student, Mercer U., 1946-47, Am. Grad. Sch. Internat. Mgmt., 1949-50. Regional dir. Sterling Drug Co., Rio de Janeiro and Sao Paulo, Brazil, 1951-56; gen. mgr. Mead Johnson & Co., Sao Paulo, 1956-60; area mgr. Upjohn Internat., Inc., Sao Paulo, 1960-64; v.p. Upjohn Internat., Inc., Kalamazoo, 1964-70, group v.p., 1970-73; pres., gen. mgr. Upjohn Internat., 1973-86; v.p. Upjohn Co., 1973-86, sr. v.p., 1986-89, asst. to pres., 1988-89; chmn. Upjohn Healthcare Svcs., 1982-87; ret., 1989; bd. dirs. Upjohn Co.; trustee Am. Grad. Sch. Internat. Mgmt., 1981—. With USNR, 1943-46. Mem. Pharm. Mfrs. Assn. (chmn. internat. sect. 1981-82, 85-86), Am. Grad. Sch. Internat. Mgmt. Alumni Assn. (pres. 1989-91). Republican. Episcopalian. Avocations: tennis, golf.

WITCHER, ROBERT CAMPBELL, bishop; b. New Orleans, Oct. 5, 1926; s. Charles Swanson and Lily Sebastian (Campbell) W.; m. Elisabeth Alice Cole, June 4, 1957; 2 children. BA, Tulane U., 1949; MDiv, Seabury-Western Theol. Sem., 1952, DD, 1974; MA, La. State U., 1960, PhD, 1968; DCL (hon.), Nashotah House, 1989. Ordained priest Episc. Ch., 1953; consecrated bishop, 1975. Priest-in-charge St. Andrew Ch., Linton, La. and St. Patrick Ch., Zachary, La., 1953-56; priest-in-charge St. Augustine Ch., Baton Rouge, La., 1953-54; rector St. Augustine Ch., 1954-61; canon pastor Christ Ch. Cathedral, New Orleans, 1961-62; rector St. James Ch., Baton Rouge, 1962-75; coadjutor bishop L.I., 1975-77; bishop, 1977-91; prof. ch. history Mercer Sch. Theology, 1975-91; interim bishop of Armed Forces, 1989-90; bishop in residence Baton Rouge, New Orleans, 1991-92; pres. Mercer Scholarship Fund; trustee Ch. Pension Fund, 1991-92; pres. bd. trustees estate belonging to Diocese of L.I., 1975-91; pres. Anglican Soc. N.Am., 1980-83; chmn. pastoral com. House of Bishops, 1980-90, Com. to Revise Title III, 1980-90; chmn. Com. on Developing Guidelines for Theol. Edn.; cons. Episc. Health Fund L.I. Author: The Episcopal Church in Louisiana, 1801-1861. Trustee U. of South, 1963-69, Seabury-Western Theol. Sem., 1963-82, Gen. Theol. Sem., 1979-88, Ch. Pension Fund, 1985-91, Bch. Reins. Corp.; pres. Episc. Health Svcs.; bd. dirs. Nat. Coun. Alcoholism, L.I. Coun. Alcoholism, Alcohol and Drug Abuse Coun., Baton Rouge, St. Mary's Hosp. for Children, Baton Rouge Green, La. Urban Forestry Coun., United Way; bd. dirs., trustee St. James Place; active NCCJ (Baton Rouge chpt.). Capt. USNR, ret. Mem. N.Y. State Coun. Chs., L.I. Coun. Chs. (com. social justice), Am. Legion, Mil. Order of World Wars. Address: 1934 Steele Blvd Baton Rouge LA 70808-1673

WITCOFF, SHELDON WILLIAM, lawyer; b. Washington, July 10, 1925; s. Joseph and Zina (Ceppos) W.; m. Margot Gail Hoffner, Sept. 6, 1953; children: Lauren Jill, David Lawrence, Lisa Ann, Julie Beth. B.S. in Elec. Engring, U. Md., 1949; J.D., George Washington U., 1953. Bar: D.C. 1953, N.Y. 1955, Ill. 1956. Patent examiner Patent Office, Dept. Commerce, 1949-53; patent lawyer Bell Telephone Labs., Murray Hill, N.J., 1953-55; ptnr. Bair, Freeman & Molinare, Chgo., 1955-69, Allegretti, Newitt, Witcoff & McAndrews, Chgo., 1970-88, Allegretti & Witcoff, LTD, Chgo., 1988—; v.p. Art Splty. Co., Chgo., 1967—; v.p. Caspian Fur Trading Co., N.Y.C.; dir. Child Abuse Unit for Studies, Edn. and Svcs., Chgo. Fire and police commr., Skokie, Ill., 1960-63. Served with USNR, 1943-46. Mem. Am. Bar Assn., Bar Assn. 7th Circuit, Intellectual Property Assn. of Chgo., Order of Coif, Tau Epsilon Phi, Phi Delta Phi., B'nai B'rith. Home: 235 Maple Hill Rd Glencoe IL 60022-1257 Office: 10 S Wacker Dr Chicago IL 60606-7407

WITCOVER, JULES JOSEPH, newspaper columnist, author; b. Union City, N.J., July 16, 1927; s. Samuel and Sarah (Carpenter) W.; m. Marian Laverty, June 14, 1952 (div. Oct. 1990); children: Paul, Amy, Julie,

Peter. AB, Columbia Coll., 1949, MS in Journalism, 1951. Reporter Hackensack (N.J.) Star-Telegram, 1949-50, Providence Jour., 1951-52, Newark Star-Ledger, 1953, Washington br. Newhouse Newspapers, 1954-69, L.A. Times, Washington, 1970-72, Washington Post, 1973-76; columnist Washington Star and Tribune Media Svcs., 1977-81, Balt. Sun, Washington, 1981—. Author: 85 Days: The Last Campaign of Robert Kennedy, 1969, The Resurrection of Richard Nixon, 1970, White Knight: The Rise of Spiro Agnew, 1972, (with Richard M. Cohen) A Heartbeat Away: The Investigation and Resignation of Vice President Spiro T. Agnew, 1974, Marathon: The Pursuit of the Presidency, 1972-76, 1977, (novel) The Main Chance, 1978, (with Jack W. Germond) Blue Smoke and Mirrors: How Reagan Won and Why Carter Lost the Election of 1980, 1981, (with Germond) Wake Us When It's Over: Presidential Politics of 1984, 1985, (with Germond) Whose Broad Stripes and Bright Stars?: The Trivial Pursuit of the Presidency 1988, 1989, Sabotage at Black Tom: Imperial Germany's Secret War in America, 1914-1917, 1989, Crapshoot: Rolling the Dice on the Vice Presidency, 1992, (with Germond) Mad as Hell: Revolt at the Ballot Box 1992, 1993. With USN, 1945-46. Recipient Washington Corr. award Sigma Delta Chi, 1963, Alumni award Columbia Grad. Sch. Journalism, 1972; Reid Found. fellow, Europe, 1958. Roman Catholic. Home: 3042 Q St NW Washington DC 20007-3080 Office: Washington Bur Balt Sun 1627 K St NW Washington DC 20006-1702

WITEK, JAMES EUGENE, public relations executive; b. LaPorte, Ind., Sept. 14, 1932; s. Stanley and Victoria (Peret) W.; m. Mary Carolyn Hood, June 18, 1955; children: James Jay, Janet Marie, Jeffrey Patrick, Jean Theresa. A.B., Ind. U., 1954; M.A., U. Mo., 1970. Joined U.S. Army, 1954, commd. 2d lt., 1954, advanced through grades to lt. col., 1968; editor, pub. Infantry Mag., Fort Benning, Ga., 1968-70; advisor to Vietnamese Mil. Region IV Ranger Comdr., 1970-71; plans officer CINCPAC, Hawaii, 1971-75; exec. editor Soldiers, Washington, 1975-77; editor in chief Soldiers, 1977-79; dir. public affairs Nat. Com. for Employer Support Guard and Res., Arlington, Va., 1979-82, ret., 1982; dep. dir. pub. relations Am. Legion, Washington, 1982-86; mgr. pub. rels. Dowty Aerospace, Sterling, Va., 1986—. Decorated Legion of Merit, Bronze Star, Air Medal, Purple Heart, Vietnamese Cross of Gallantry with Silver Star. Mem. Assn. U.S. Army, Am. Legion, Ret. Officers Assn., Phi Beta Kappa, Tau Kappa Alpha, Pi Kappa Phi. Roman Catholic. Home: 3240 Atlanta St Fairfax VA 22030-2128 Office: Dowty Aerospace PO Box 5000 Sterling VA 20167-1050

WITH, GERDA BECKER, artist; b. Hamburg, Germany, Mar. 4, 1910; came to U.S., 1939; d. Ludwig and Martha (De Bruycker) Becker; m. Karl E. With, July 17, 1939 (dec. Dec. 1980); children: Christopher B., Nela W. Dwyer. M in Decorative Arts, Charlottenburg, Berlin, 1938. One woman shows include Otis Art Inst., Mus. St. Barbara, also pvt. galleries throughout Europe and U.S., 1958—; illustrator: (book) The Man Who Stole the Word "Beautiful", 1991, others. Avocations: reading, traveling, friends and family. Home: 3045 Kelton Ave Los Angeles CA 90034-3021

WITHERINGTON, JENNIFER LEE, sales and marketing executive; b. Albuquerque, Sept. 8, 1960; d. Terrence Lee and Pamela Ann (Hoerter) W. BA in Polit. Sci., James Madison U., 1982. Asst. press sec. U.S. Senate, Washington, 1983-85; nat. sales mgr. Madison Hotels, Washington, 1986-88; dir. sales Madison Air Charter Svcs., Washington, 1987-88; nat. sales mgr. Ritz-Carlton Hotels, Palm Springs, Calif., 1988-90; dir. sales and mktg. Cappa and Graham, Inc., San Francisco, 1990-95; gen. mgr. USA Hosts, San Francisco, 1995—; spkr. in field. Contbr. articles to profl. jours. Vol. San Francisco Emergency Rescue Team, Yerba Buena Ctr. for Arts. Mem. Am. Soc. Assn. Execs., Profl. Conv. Mgmt. Assn., Hospitality Sales and Mktg. Assn. Internat. (pres. San Francisco chpt. 1994—), Meeting Profls. Internat. Republican. Roman Catholic. Avocations: painting, golf, gourmet food. Home: 1565 Green St Apt 304 San Francisco CA 94123-5129 Office: USA Hosts 177 Post St Ste 550 San Francisco CA 94108

WITHEROW, JIMMIE DAVID, secondary school educator; b. Dalton, Ga., Nov. 13, 1961; s. Jimmie W. and Jimmie Lou (Nixon) W. BA in English, Emory U., 1983; MEd in Secondary Edn., Ga. State U., 1989. Cert. English tchr., Ga. Tchr. SE Whitfield High Sch., Whitfield County Bd. Edn., Dalton, 1983-92, Murray County High Sch., Chatsworth, Ga., 1992—. Contbr. article to profl. jour. Mem. NEA, Nat. Coun. Tchrs. English, Ga. Edn. Assn., Ga. Coun. Tchrs. English, Kappa Delta Pi. Home: PO Box 891 Chatsworth GA 30705-0891

WITHERS, HUBERT RODNEY, radiotherapist, radiobiologist, educator; b. Queensland, Australia, Sept. 21, 1932; came to the U.S., 1966; s. Hubert and Gertrude Ethel (Tremayne) W.; m. Janet Macfie, Oct. 9, 1959; 1 child, Genevieve. MBBS, U. Queensland, Brisbane, Australia, 1956; PhD, U. London, 1965, DSc, 1982. Bd. cert. Ednl. Coun. for Fgn. Med. Grads. Intern Royal Brisbane (Australia) and Associated Hosps., 1957; resident in radiotherapy and pathology Queensland Radium Inst. and Royal Brisbane (Australia) Hosp., 1958-63; Univ. Queensland Gaggin fellow Gray Lab., Mt. Vernon Hosp., Northwood, Middlesex, Eng., 1963-65, Royal Brisbane (Australia) Hosp., 1966; radiotherapist Prince of Wales Hosp., Randwick, Sydney, Australia, 1966; vis. rsch. scientist Lab. Physiology, Nat. Cancer Inst., Bethesda, Md., 1966-68; assoc. prof. radiotherapy sect. exptl. radiotherapy U. Tex. Sys. Cancer Ctr. M.D. Anderson Hsop. & Tumor Inst., Houston, 1968-71, prof. radiotherapy, chief sect. sect. exptl. radiotherapy, 1971-80; prof. dir. exptl. radiation oncology dept. radiation oncology UCLA, 1980-89, prof., vice-chair dir. exptl. radiation oncology dept. radiation oncology, 1991-94, Am. Cancer Soc. Clin. Rsch. prof. dept. radiation oncology, 1992—, interim dir. Jonsson Comprehensive Cancer Ctr., chmn. radiation oncology, 1994-95; assoc. grad. faculty U. Tex., Grad. Sch. Biomed. Scis, Houston, 1969-73, mem. grad. faculty, 1973-80; prof. dept. radiotherapy Med. Sch., U. Tex. Health Sci. Ctr., Houston, U. Tex. Med. Sch., Houston, 1975-80; prof., dir. Inst. Oncology, The Prince of Wales Hosp., U. NSW, Sydney, Australia, 1989-91; mem. com. mortality mil. pers. present-at-atmosphere tests of nuclear weapons Inst. Medicine, 1993-94; mem. radiation effects rsch. bd. NRC, 1993—; mem. com. neutron dose reporting Internat. Commn. Radiation Units and Measurements, 1982—, mem. report com. clin. dosimetry for neutrons, 1993—; mem. task force non-stochastic effects radiation Internat. Com. Radiation Protection, 1980-84, mem. com. 1, 1993—; mem. radiobiology com. Radiation Therapy Oncology Group, 1979—, mem. dose-time com., 1980-89, mem. gastroenterology com., 1982-89; mem. edn. bd. Royal Australian Coll. Radiology, 1989-91; mem. cancer rsch. coord. com. U. Calif., 1991-95, mem. standing curriculum com. UCLA biomed. physics grad. program, 1983-84; cons. exptl. radiotherapy U. Tex. System Cancer Ctr., 1980—. Mem. Am. editl. bd.: Internat. Jour. Radiat. Oncol. Biol. Phys., 1982-89, 94—, internat. editl. bd., 1989-91; cons. editor: The European Jour. Cancer, 1990-95; editl. bd. dirs.: Endocurietherapy/Hyperthermia Oncology, 1991—, Radiation Oncology Investigations, 1992—; assoc. editor: Cancer Rsch., 1993-94, editl. bd. 1995-97. Mem. Kettering selection com. Gen. Motors Cancer Rsch. Found., 1988-89, chmn., 1989, awards assembly, 1990-94. Recipient Medicine prize Polish Acad. Sci., 1989, Second H.S. Kaplan Disting. Scientist award Internat. Assn. for Radiation Rsch., 1991, Gray medal Internat. Commn. Radiation Units, 1995; named Gilbert H. Fletcher lectr. U. Tex. Sys. Cancer Ctr., 1989, Clifford Ash lectr. Ont. Cancer Inst., Princess Margaret Hosp., 1987, Erskine lectr. Radiol. Soc. N.Am., 1988, Ruvelson lectr. U. Minn., 1988, Milford Schultz lectr. Mass. Gen. Hosp., 1989, Del Regato Found. lectr. Hahnemann U., 1990, Bruce Cain Meml. lectr. New Zealand Soc. Oncology, 1990, others. Fellow Royal Australasian Coll. Radiologists (bd. cert.), Am. Coll. Radiology (bd. cert. therapeutic radiology, adv. com. patterns of care study 1988—, radiation oncology advisory group 1993—, others), Am. Radium Soc. (mem. and credential com. 1986-89, 93-94, treas. 1993-94, pres.-elect 1995-96, others), Am. Soc. Therapeutic Radiology and Oncology (awards com. 1993, publs. com. 1993-96, keynote address 1990, 96, Gold medal 1991, others); mem. Nat. Cancer Inst. (various ad-hoc rev. coms. 1970—, radiation study sect. 1971-75, cons. U.S.-Japan Coop. Study high LET Radiotherapy 1975-77, cancer rsch. empha. com. 1976, clin. cancer ctr. rev. com. 1976-79, toxicology working group 1977-78, reviewer outstanding investigator grants 1984-93, bd. sci. counselors, 1986-88), Nat. Cancer Inst. Can. (adv. com. rsch. 1992-95), Pacific N.W. Radiol. Soc. (hon.), Tex. Radiol. Soc. (hon.), So. Calif. Radiation Oncology Soc. (sec., treas., 1992-94, pres. 1996—), European Soc. Therapeutic Radiology and Oncology (hon.), Polish Oncology Soc. (hon.) Austrian Radiation Oncology Soc. (hon.), Phila. Roentgen Ray Soc. (hon.), Radiation Rsch. Soc. (pres. 1982-83, honors and awards com. 1984-88, ad hoc com. funds utilization 1987-89, adv. com. Radiation Rsch. Jour., 1988—, Failla award 1988). Office: UCLA Med Ctr 10833 LeConte Ave Los Angeles CA 90095-1714

WITHERS, RAMSEY MUIR, government consultant, former government official; b. Toronto, Ont., Can., July 28, 1930; s. William Muir and Alice Smith Hope (Hannah) W.; m. Jean Alison Saunders, May 8, 1954; children—James Scott, Leslie Susan, Deidre Ann. BSc, Royal Mil. Coll. Can., Kingston, Ont., 1952, DEng (hon.), 1994; BSc in Elec. Engring., Queen's U., Kingston, 1954; D Mil. Sci. honoris causa, Royal Roads Mil. Coll., Victoria, B.C., 1992. Registered profl. engr., Ont. Commd. officer Can. Army, 1948, advanced through grades to gen., 1980; sta. in Can., Republic of Korea, Fed. Republic of Germany and U.K., 1952-76; comdr. Can. Forces Europe, Fed. Republic of Germany, 1976-77; vice chief def. staff Can. Forces, 1977-80, chief def. staff, 1980-83, ret., 1983; dep. minister transport Dept. of Transp., Ottawa, Ont., 1983-88; pres., chief oper. officer Govt. Cons. Internat., Ottawa, 1988-93; dir. Can. Inst. Strategic Studies, 1990—, ATS Aerospace Inc., 1993—; chmn. Industry Govt. Rels. Group Inc. (IGRG Inc.), Ottawa, 1993—. V.p., sec. nat. coun. Boy Scouts Can., 1977-84, internat. commr., 1985-90, hon. v.p., 1990—; chmn. Can. War Mus. Com., 1988-95; trustee Can. Mus. Civilization, 1990-95. Decorated comdr. Order of Mil. Merit, comdr. Order of St. John, Can. Forces Decoration with two bars; Georgian Coll. fellow, 1987; recipient Outstanding Achievement Pub. Svc. award, 1986, Silver Wolf award Boy Scouts Can., 1990, Alumni Achievement award Queen's U., Kingston, 1995. Mem. Assn. Profl. Engrs. Ont., Rideau Club. Avocations: boating; cycling. Home: 150 Waverly St Apt 2C, Ottawa, ON Canada K2P OV4

WITHERS, W. RUSSELL, JR., broadcast executive; b. Cape Girardeau, Mo., Dec. 10, 1936; s. Waldo Russell Sr. and Dorothy Ruth (Harrelson) W.; 1 child, Dana Ruth. BA, S.E. Mo. State U., 1958. Disc jockey Sta. KGMO Radio, Cape Girardeau, 1955-58; account exec. Sta. WGGH Radio, Marion, Ill., 1961-62; v.p. LIN Broadcasting Corp., Nashville, 1962-69; exec. v.p., dir. Laser Link Corp., Woodbury, N.Y., 1970-72; owner Withers Broadcasting of Hawaii, 1975-79, Withers Broadcasting of Minn., 1974-79, Withers Broadcasting Cos., Iowa, 1981—, Mood Music Ill., Mt. Vernon, 1973—, Mood Music, Inc., Cape Girardeau, 1972—, Royal Hawaiian Radio Co., Inc., others; owner various radio and TV stas., including KREX-TV, Grand Junction, Colo., KREY-TV, Montrose, Colo., KREG-TV, Glenwood Springs, Colo., KREZ-TV, Durango, Colo., KAVU-TV, Victoria, Tex., Page Ins. and Real Estate, Mt. Vernon, Ill.; chmn. bd., CEO Withers Beverage Corp., Mobile Ala., 1973-79; chmn. adv. bd. Mut. Network; bd. dirs. Theatrevision, Inc., Turneffe Island Lodge, Ltd., Belize, Sta. WDTV, Clarksburg, W.Va., WMIX-AM-TV, Mt. Vernon, KGMO-KAPE, Cape Girardeau, KOKX AM-FM, Keokuk, Iowa, KVSR, Santa Fe, KNAL, Victoria, KMPL and KSTG, Sikeston, Mo.; pres. Ill. Pub. Airports assn.; co-chmn. TARPAC. Bd. dirs., chmn. bd. Mt. Vernon Tourism and Conv. Bur.; chmn. Mt. Vernon Airport Authority; gen. trustee Lincoln Acad. With U.S. Army, 1957-58. Mem. Mt. Vernon c. of C. (bd. dirs.), Nat. Assn. Broadcasters, Ill. Broadcasters Assn., Stadium club, Mo. Athletic Club, Elks, Moose, AmVets, Masons, Sigma Chi. Christian Scientist. Home: 1 Sleepy Hollow Ln Mount Vernon IL 62864-2852 Office: PO Box 1508 Mount Vernon IL 62864-1508

WITHERS, W. WAYNE, lawyer; b. Enid, Okla., Nov. 4, 1940; s. Walter O. and Ruby (Mackey) W.; m. Patricia Ann Peppers, Dec. 12, 1974; children: Jennifer Lynn, Whitney Lee. BA, U. Okla., 1962; JD, Northwestern U., 1965. Bar: Okla. 1965, Mo. 1970, U.S. Ct. Appeals (8th cir.), 1972, U.S. Supreme Ct. 1972, U.S. Ct. Appeals (fed. cir.) 1984, U.S. Ct. Appeals (D.C. cir.) 1985, U.S. Ct. Claims, 1988. Staff atty. FTC, Washington, 1965-68; co. atty. Monsanto Co., St. Louis, 1968-78, asst. gen. counsel, 1978-85; gen. counsel Monsanto Agrl. Co., St. Louis, 1985-87, v.p., gen. counsel, 1987-89; sr. v.p., sec., gen. counsel Emerson Electric Co., St. Louis, 1989—; v.p. Internat. Food Biotech. Coun., Washington, 1989-90; bd. dirs. Internat. Life Scis. Inst., Washington, 1989-90. Contbr. articles to profl. jours. Mem. ABA (sec. corp. law dept.), Am. Law Inst., Assn. Gen. Counsel, Bar Assn. Met. St. Louis, Indsl. Biotech. Assn. (chmn. law com.), Environ. Law Inst. (assoc.), Nat. Agrl. Chem. Assn. (chmn. law com. 1983-85), The Conf. Bd. Coun. for Gen. Counsel (vice chmn. 1992—), MAPI Law Coun. Home: 608 Claymont Estate Dr Chesterfield MO 63017-7060 Office: Emerson Electric Co 8000 W Florissant Ave Saint Louis MO 63136-8506

WITHERSPOON, CAROLYN BRACK, lawyer; b. Little Rock, Mar. 29, 1950; d. Gordon Paisley and Mildred Louise (Lemon) Brack; m. Joseph Roger Armbrust, July 25, 1970 (div. 1976); 1 child, Catherine Paisley; m. John Leslie Witherspoon, June 15, 1979. Student, U. Ark., 1968-70, So. Meth. U., 1970; BA, U. Ark., 1974, JD with honors, 1978. Bar: Ark. 1978, U.S. Dist. Ct. (ea. and we. dists) Ark. 1978, U.S. Ct. Appeals (8th cir.) 1979, U.S. Supreme Ct. 1981. Asst. atty. City of Little Rock, 1978, chief dep. atty., acting city atty., 1984-85; assoc. House, Wallace & Jewell, Little Rock, 1985-87, ptnr., 1987-90; dir. McGlinchey Stafford Lang, Little Rock, 1990—; co-chmn. Fed. Ct. Orientation Seminar, 1983-85; mem. com. Fed. Ct., 1988-91, Ark. Supreme Ct., 1989—; chair adv. com. Civil Justice Reform Act, 1993-95. Contbr. articles to profl. jours. Commr. Ark. Real Estate Commn., 1978-81; chmn. Little Rock Housing Authority Bd. of Comm., past pres., bd. dirs. Advs. for Battered Women; past bd. dirs., pub. rels. chmn. LWV; past pres. Ark. Women's History Inst.; del. Dem. Committeewoman for Pulaski County; vol. PTA, United Way, March of Dimes, Heart Found., Am. Cancer Soc. Recipient Am. Jurisprudence labor law award, 1977. Mem. Am. Law Inst., Ark. Bar Assn. (exec. coun., ho. of dels., jud. nominating com., chmn. civil procedure com., chair labor law sect., pres.-elect 1994-95, pres. 1995-96, Golden Gavel award 1989, 93, Ark. Inst. for Continuing Legal Edn. award 1991), Ark. Assn. Women Lawyers (pres. 1982-83), Pulaski County Bar Assn. (pres. 1989-90), Nat. Inst. Mcpl. Law Officers (state chmn. 1985-87, v.p. 1987-89), William R. Overton Inn of Ct. (pres. 1992-93). Avocations: hunting, fishing, reading, traveling.

WITHERSPOON, JERE WARTHEN, foundation executive; b. Shepherdstown, W.Va., June 24, 1932; m. Ellen L. Wheby, Oct. 5, 1957; children: Jere W. Jr., Jean Katherine, James A. BS, Davidson Coll., 1954; MHA, Washington U., 1961. Adminstrv. asst. Meml. Mission Hosp., Asheville, N.C., 1960-63; asst. adminstr. Meml. Hosp., Charleston, W.Va., 1963-67; adminstr. Cape Fear Valley Hosp., Fayetteville, N.C., 1967-69; dir. mgmt. svc. The Duke Endowment, Charlotte, N.C., 1969-77, assoc. dir., 1977-89, asst. to exec. dir., 1989-90, dep. exec. dir., 1990-92, exec. dir., 1992—. Bd. deacons, chmn., elder, chmn. endowment coun. Myers Park Presbyn. Ch.; pres., bd. dirs. Hospice at Charlotte; v.p., bd. dirs. Hospice of N.C.; mem. study com. on AIDS United Way; com. chmn. Mecklenburg County Area Mental Health Bd.; trustee Southeastern Coun. Founds.; bd. dirs. Grantmakers in Health, Presbyn. Home at Charlotte; bd. vis. Davidson Coll.; adv. bd. Kate B. Reynolds Charitable Trust; mem. N.C. Med. Care Commn. With USAF, 1954-58. Fellow Am. Coll. Healthcare Execs.; mem. Am. Hosp. Assn. (life). Office: Duke Endowment 100 N Tryon St Ste 3500 Charlotte NC 28202-4000

WITHERSPOON, JOHN KNOX, JR., investment banking executive; b. Chattanooga, May 3, 1928; s. John Knox and Helen (Newell) W.; m. Norma Cofer, Sept. 28, 1957; children: Laura, Alice, Mark, Eric, Cary, Clay. BA, Princeton U., 1950. CLU. Pension analyst Provident Life and Accident Ins. Co., Chattanooga, 1953-57, asst. mgr. pension div., 1957-60, agy. sec., 1960-64, asst. v.p., 1964-69, v.p., 1969-84, sr. v.p., 1984-90; mng. dir. Crownpoint Fin. Group, Chattanooga, 1990-92; v.p. Porter, White & Co., Inc., Chattanooga, 1993—. Chmn. Hamilton County Bd. Edn., Chattanooga, 1984-85; pres. Met. Council Community Services, Chattanooga, 1977; v.p. Family and Children's Services, Chattanooga, 1978-80. Served as cpl. U.S. Army, Korea. Mem. Am. Soc. CLUs, Assn. for Corp. Growth, Phi Beta Kappa. Republican. Presbyterian. Lodge: Kiwanis. Office: Porter White & Co 651 E 4th St Ste 100 Chattanooga TN 37403-1924

WITHERSPOON, WILLIAM, investment economist; b. St. Louis, Nov. 21, 1909; s. William Conner and Mary Louise (Houston) W.; student Washington U. Evening Sch., 1928-47; m. Margaret Telford Johanson, June 25, 1938; children: James Tomlin, Jane Telford, Elizabeth Witherspoon Vodra. Rsch. dept. A. G. Edwards & Sons, 1928-31; pres. Witherspoon Investment Co., 1931-34; head rsch. dept. Newhard Cook & Co., 1934-43; chief price analysis St. Louis Ordnance Dist., 1943-45; head rsch. dept. Newhard Cook & Co., 1945-53; owner Witherspoon Investment Counsel, 1953-64; ltd. ptnr. Newhard Cook & Co., economist, investment analyst, 1965-68; v.p. rsch. Stifel, Nicolaus & Co., 1968-81; lectr. on investments Washington U., 1948-67. Mem. Clayton Bd. of Edn., 1955-68, treas., 1956-68, pres., 1966-67; mem. Clayton Park and Recreation Commn., 1959-60; trustee Ednl. TV, KETC, 1963-64; mem. investment com. Gen. Assembly Mission Bd. Presbyn. Ch. (USA), Atlanta, 1976-79, mem. permanent com. ordination exams, 1979-85; cons. to investment com. Ctr. Theol. Inquiry, Princeton, N.J., 1995—. Served as civilian Ordnance Dept., AUS, 1943-45. Chartered fin. analyst. Mem. St. Louis Soc. Fin. Analysts (pres. 1949-50). Club: Mo. Athletic (St. Louis). Home: 6401 Ellenwood Ave Saint Louis MO 63105-2228 *Many of the current social and ethical problems of today might be partially resolved if theology would be influenced by the 4th dimension of spacetime plus the 5th dimension of the mind, the 6th dimension of the spirit and the 7th dimension of God the Father.*

WITHERWAX, CHARLES HALSEY, lawyer, arbitrator, mediator; b. Schroon Lake, N.Y., July 24, 1934; s. Halsey Jerome and Elizabeth Daisy (Bingham) W.; m. Marianne Jehander, June 24, 1980. BS in Marine Transp., N.Y. State Maritime Coll., 1956; LLB, Union U., 1959. Bar: N.Y. 1962, U.S. Dist. Ct. (so. dist.) N.Y. 1962, U.S. Supreme Ct. 1968, Hawaii 1971, U.S. Dist. Ct. Hawaii 1971, U.S. Ct. Appeals (9th cir.) 1984, U.S. Tax Ct. 1984, Nev. 1991, D.C. 1993. Assoc. prof. N.Y. State Maritime Coll., Fort Schuyler, N.Y., 1963-64; asst. v.p., bond claims atty. Chubb Ins. Group, N.Y.C., 1961-70; v.p., gen. counsel Hawaiian Ins. Group, Honolulu, 1970-74; ptnr. Davis, Witherwax, Playdon & Gerson, Honolulu, 1974-78; prin. atty. Witherwax, Pottenger & Nishioka, Honolulu, 1978-91; of counsel D'Amato & Lynch, N.Y.C., 1992—. Author: (manual) Hawaii Construction Law, Mechanics Liens and Bond Claims, 1985, co-author, 1987. Bronx county chmn. N.Y. State Conservative Party, 1962-67; state sec. N.Y. State Conservative Party, 1967-70. Lt. comdr. USNR, 1959-79. Mem. ABA (vice chair fidelity and surety com. 1978-83), Internat. Assn. Def. Counsel. Roman Catholic. Avocations: sailing, travel, golf. Office: D'Amato & Lynch 37th Flr 70 Pine St New York NY 10270

WITHROW, LUCILLE MONNOT, nursing home administrator; b. Alliance, Ohio, July 28, 1923; d. Charles Edward Monnot and Freda Aldine (Guy) Monnot Cameron; m. Alvin Robert Withrow, June 6, 1945 (dec. 1984); children: Cindi Withrow Johnson, Nancy Withrow Townley, Sharon Withrow Hodgkins, Wendel Alvin. AA in Health Adminstrn., Eastfield Coll., 1976. Lic. nursing home adminstr., Tex.; cert. nursing home ombudsman. Held various clerical positions Dallas, 1950-72; office mgr., asst. adminstr. Christian Care Ctr. Nursing Home, Mesquite, Tex., 1972-76; head adminstr. Christian Care Ctr. Nursing Home and Retirement Complex, Mesquite, 1976-91; nursing home ombudsman Tex. Dept. Aging and Tex. Dept. Health, Dallas, 1991-93; legal asst. Law Offices of Wendel A. Withrow, Carrollton, Tex., 1993—; mem. con. on geriatric curriculum devel. Eastfield Coll., Mesquite, 1979, 87; mem. ombudsman adv. com. Sr. Citizens Greater Dallas; nursing home cons.; notary pub., 1995—. Vol. Dallas Arboretum and Bot. Soc., Dallas Summer Musicals Guild; mem. Ombudsman adv. com. Sr. Citizens of Greater Dallas, Health Svcs. Speakers Bur.; charter mem. Stage Show Prodns. Recipient Volunteerism awards Tex. Atty. Gen., 1987, Tex. Gov., 1992. Mem. Tex. Assn. Homes for Aging, Am. Assn. Homes for Aging, Health Svcs. Speakers Bur., White Rock Kiwanis. Republican. Mem. Ch. of Christ. Avocations: reading, travel, theater. Home: 11344 Lippitt Ave Dallas TX 75218-1922 Office: Law Office of W A Withrow 1120 Metrocrest Dr Ste 200 Carrollton TX 75006-5787

WITHROW, MARY ELLEN, treasurer of United States; b. Marion, Ohio, Oct. 2, 1930; d. Clyde Welsh and Mildred (Stump) Hinamon; m. Norman David Withrow, Sept. 4, 1948; children: Linda Rizzo, Leslie Legge, Norma, Rebecca. Mem. Elgin Local Bd. Edn., Marion, Ohio, 1969-73, pres., 1972; safety programs dir. ARC, Marion, 1968-72; dep. registrar State of Ohio, Marion, 1972-75; dep. county auditor Marion County, Ohio, 1975-77, county treas., 1977-83; treas. State of Ohio, Columbus, 1983-94; treas. of the U.S. Dept. Treasury, Washington, 1994—; chmn. Ohio Bd. Deposits, 1983—, Anthony Commn. on Pub. Fin. Mem. exec. com. Ohio Dem. Com., mem. exec. com. women's caucus; mem. Dem. Nat. Com.; mem. Met. Women's Ctr.; pres. Marion County Dem. Club, 1976; participant Harvard U. Strategic Leadership Conf., 1990.; mem. Dem. Leadership Coun. Recipient Donald L. Scantlebury Meml. award, 1991, Women of Achievement award YWCA of Met. Columbus, 1993, Outstanding Govt. Svc. award Am. Numis. Assn., 1995; inducted Ohio Women's Hall of Fame, 1986; named Outstanding Elected Dem. Woman Holding Pub. Office, Nat. Fedn. Dem. Women, 1987, Advocate of Yr., SBA, 1988, Most Valuable State Pub. Ofcl., City and State newspaper, 1990; Women Execs. in State Govt. fellow Harvard U., 1987. Mem. LWV (dem. leadership coun.), State Assn. County Treas. (legis. com. 1979-83, treas. 1982), Nat. Assn. State Treas. (pres. 1992, Jesse Unruh award 1993, chair long range planning com., mem. exec. com.), Nat. Assn. State Auditors Comtps. and Treas. (pres. 1990, strategic planning com., intergov. rels. com., chair state and mcpl. bonds com.), Coun. State Govts. (exec. com., internat. affairs com., orgnl. planning and coord. com., strategic planning task force), Women Execs. in State Govt. (chair fund devel. com.). Club: Bus. and Profl. Women's. Office: Dept Treasury 1500 Pennsylvania Ave NW Washington DC 20005-1007

WITIAK, DONALD THEODORE, medicinal chemistry educator; b. Milw., Nov. 16, 1935; s. Theodore and Elvi (Dahlbacka) W.; m. Deanne Beth Knapton, Dec. 16, 1958; children—Mark Donald, Elizabeth Jane. B.S. in Pharmacy, U. Wis.-Madison, 1958, postgrad., 1959-60, Ph.D. in Medicinal Chemistry, 1961; postgrad., U. Kans., 1960-61. Asst. prof. U. Iowa, Iowa City, 1961-66, assoc. prof., 1966-67; assoc. prof. Ohio State U., Columbus, 1967-71, prof. medicinal chemistry, 1971-93, chmn. div. medicinal chemistry, 1973-82, dir. basic rsch. univ. Comprehensive Cancer Ctr., 1987-93, prof. emeritus, 1993—; prof. med. chemistry U. Wis., Madison, 1993—, Dean Sch. Pharmacy, 1993-95; mem. study sect. NIH, 1980-83; U.S. rep. to provisional sect. com. Internat. Union Pure and Applied Chemistry, 1986-88; mem. Can. Govt. internat. multidisciplinary peer-rev. com. for networks of Ctr. Excellence; mem. drug. devel., hematology and pathology study sect. Am. Cancer Soc., 1995—. Editor: Calcium Regulation, 1982, Antilipidemic Drugs Medicinal, Chemical and Biochemical Aspects, vol. 17, 1991; assoc. editor Current Medicinal Chemistry, 1995; mem. editl. bd. Jour. Medicinal Chemistry, 1971-75, European Jour. Med. Chemistry, 1986—, Pharmacochemistry Libr., 1987—; assoc. editor Current Medicinal Chemistry, 1994—; contbr. numerous articles to profl. jours., chpts. to books; holder 15 patents in field. Mem. Columbus Biotech. Adv. Com., 1985, Columbus Tech. Roundtable, 1983. Served with USNR, 1955-63. Recipient Kimberly prof. rsch. award, 1985, Apha Found./Acad. Pharm. Scis. Rsch. Achievement award, 1985, Taito O. Soine Meml. award U. Minn., 1988; grantee NIH 1971—, EPA, 1984—. Fellow Am. Pharm. Assn., Acad. Pharm. Scis., Am. Assn. Pharm. Scis.; mem. Am. Chem. Soc. (com. nomenclature 1984-85, chmn. com. to rev. Jour. Medicinal Chemistry 1983, councilor div. med. chem. 1990-92), Am. Cancer Soc. (supported rsch. com. Ohio div. 1988, bd. dirs. 1991-93). Home: 3046 Bosshard Dr Madison WI 53711-5860 Office: U Wis 425 N Charter St Madison WI 53706-1508

WITKE, DAVID RODNEY, newspaper editor; b. Council Bluffs, Iowa, Mar. 24, 1937; s. Arnold and Rosamond Louise (Storer) W.; m. Priscilla Bill Smith, Oct. 8, 1960; 1 son, Carl. B.S. in Journalism, Northwestern U., 1959. Reporter, editor The Courier, Champaign-Urbana, Ill., 1962-66; copy editor The Register, Des Moines, 1966-70, city editor, 1970-73, asst. mng. editor adminstrn., 1973-74, asst. mng. editor electronics, 1974-75, mng. editor, 1975-83, dir. ops., 1983-85, dep. editor, 1985-87, exec. sports editor, 1987—; rep. Iowa Freedom of Info. Coun., Des Moines, 1973—, pres., 1986-88; vis. lectr. Drake U., 1986—, Iowa State U., 1990—; juror Pulitzer Prize, 1989-91. Served to lt. (j.g.) USN, 1959-62, PTO. Mem. Assoc. Press Mng. Editors Assn., Mid-Am. Newspaper Assn., AP Sports Editors Assn., The Prairie Club, Sigma Delta Chi. Unitarian. Home: 2521 48th Pl Des Moines IA 50310-2506 Office: Des Moines Register and Tribune Co 715 Locust St Des Moines IA 50309-3724

WITKIN, ERIC DOUGLAS, lawyer; b. Trenton, N.J., May 14, 1948; s. Nathan and Norma Shirley (Stein) W.; m. Regina Ann Bilotta, June 8, 1980; children: Daniel Robert, Sarah Ann. AB magna cum laude, Columbia U., 1969; JD, Harvard U., 1972. Bar: N.Y. 1973, D.C. 1989, U.S. Dist. Ct. (so. and ea. dists.) N.Y. 1974, U.S. Ct. Appeals (2d and D.C. cirs.) 1974, U.S. Supreme Ct. 1977, U.S. Dist. Ct. D.C. 1989. Assoc. Poletti, Freidin, Prashker & Gartner, N.Y.C., 1972-80, ptnr., 1980-85; sr. atty. labor Kaye,

Scholer, Fierman, Hays & Handler, N.Y.C., 1985-88; of counsel Akin, Gump, Strauss, Hauer & Feld, Washington, 1988-90; counsel Benetar, Bernstein, Schair & Stein, N.Y.C., 1990—. treas., founder Property Owners Against Unfair Taxation, N.Y.C., 1983-90. Lawrence Chamberlain scholar Columbia U., N.Y.C., 1968; recipient Alumni medal Alumni Fedn. Columbia U., 1982. Mem. ABA (labor and employment law sect.), N.Y. State Bar Assn. (labor and employment law sect.), Assn. of Bar of City of N.Y. (spl. com. on sex and law, com. on labor and employment law), Westchester County Bar Assn., Columbia Coll. Alumni Assn. (pres. 1988-90, bd. dirs. 1974—, Robert Lincoln Carey prize, Alumni prize 1969, Lions award 1990), Alumni Fedn. Columbia U. (v.p. 1995—, alumni trustee nominating com. 1990—), Am. Soc. Pers. Adminstrn. (contbr. monthly newsletter 1986-88), Soc. Human Resource Mgmt., Soc. Columbia Grads. (bd. dirs. 1994—), Phi Beta Kappa. Club: Harvard (N.Y.C.). Avocations: piano, sailing. Home: 103 Wendover Rd Rye NY 10580-1939 Office: Benetar Bernstein Schair & Stein 330 Madison Ave New York NY 10017-5001

WITKIN, EVELYN MAISEL, geneticist; b. N.Y.C., Mar. 9, 1921; d. Joseph and Mary (Levin) Maisel; m. Herman A. Witkin, July 9, 1943 (dec. July 1979); children—Joseph, Andrew. AB, NYU, 1941; MA, Columbia U., 1943, PhD, 1947; DSc honoris causa, N.Y. Med. Coll., 1978, Rutgers U., 1995. Mem. staff genetics dept. Carnegie Inst., Washington, 1950-55; mem. faculty State U. N.Y. Downstate Med. Center, Bklyn., 1955-71; prof. medicine State U. N.Y. Downstate Med. Center, 1968-71; prof. biol. scis. Douglass Coll., Rutgers U., 1971-79, Barbara McClintock prof. genetics, 1979-83; Barbara McClintock prof. genetics Waksman Inst. Microbiology, 1983-91; Barbara McClintock prof. emerita Waksman Inst. Microbiology, Rutgers U., 1991—. Author articles; mem. editorial bds. profl. jours. Postdoctoral fellow Am. Cancer Soc., 1947-49; fellow Carnegie Instn., 1957; Selman A. Waksman lectr., 1960; Phi Beta Kappa vis. scholar, 1980-81; grantee NIH, 1956-89; recipient Prix Charles Leopold Mayer French Acad. Scis., 1977, Lindback award, 1979. Fellow AAAS, Am. Acad. Microbiology; mem. NAS, Am. Acad. Arts and Scis., Environ. Mutagen Soc., Am. Genetics Soc., Am. Soc. Microbiology. Home: 1 Firestone Ct Princeton NJ 08540-5220 Office: Rutgers U Waksman Inst Microbiology Piscataway NJ 08854

WITKIN, ISAAC, sculptor; b. Johannesburg, South Africa, May 10, 1936; children: Tamar, Nadine. Student, St. Martin's Sch. Art, London, 1957-60. Asst. to Henry Moore, 1961-63; tchr. St. Martin's Sch. Art, London, 1963-65; artist in residence Bennington (Vt.) Coll., 1965-79; tchr. Parson's Sch. Design, N.Y.C., 1975-78; vis. prof. Middlebury Coll., Vt., 1981; mem. Yale U. Adv. Com. to the Art Sch., 1987-90; mem. Bennington Coll. Art Collection Com., 1987-91; bd. mem. Internat. Sculpture Ctr., 1990—. One-person shows include Hamilton Gallery Contemporary Art, N.Y.C., 1981, Mattingly Baker Gallery, Dallas, 1982, McIntosh/Drysdale Gallery, Washington, 1982, 1986, Hirschl & Adler Modern, N.Y.C., 1985, 1988, Jan Turner Gallery, L.A., Patricia Hamilton, N.Y.C., Locks Gallery, Phila., 1991, 93, Walker Hill Art Ctr., Seoul, Korea, 1992, others; exhibited in group shows at Hamilton Gallery, N.Y.C., 1981, Freeman Gallery, Albright Coll., 1982, Fuller Goldeen Gallery, San Francisco, 1982, The Berkshire Mus., Pittsfield, Mass., 1982, Washington Square Plaza, Washington, 1983, Wave Hill, Bronx, N.Y., 1983, Pratt Inst. Gallery, N.Y.C., 1984, Sonoma State U., Calif., 1984, N.J. State Mus., Trenton, 1984, Number One Penn Plaza, N.Y.C., 1984, Williams Coll. Mus. Art, Williamstown, Mass., 1984, N.J. Ctr. for the Visual Arts, Summit, 1987, Zone Arts Ctr., Springfield, Mass., 1988, James A. Michener Fine Arts Ctr., Doylestown, Pa., 1989, Robeson Ctr. Gallery, Rutgers U., Trenton, 1989, Locks Gallery, Phila., 1990-91, Robert Morrison Gallery, N.Y.C., 1993, Marc de Montebello Gallery, N.Y.C., 19995, Atlantic Found., Hamilton, N.J., 1995, Hunterdon Art Ctr., Clinton, N.J., 1995, others; represented in permanent collections Alcoa Co., Pitts., Am. Rep. Ins. Co., Des Moines, Arts Coun. Gt. Brit., London, Atlantic Found., Princeton, Carnegie Inst., Pitts., Chase Manhattan Bank, N.Y.C., CIGNA Corp., Phila., Columbus (Ohio) Mus. Fine Art, Denver (Colo.) Mus. Art, Fine Arts Mus., U. Sydney, Australia, MIT, Boston, Nat. Mus. Am. Art, Washington, numerous others. Recipient First prize Paris Biennale, 1965, Guggenheim fellowship, 1981; grantee N.J. State Coun. on the Arts, 1985, Adolph and Esther Gottlieb Found., 1994. Studio: 137 Scrapetown Rd Pemberton NJ 08068

WITKIN, JOEL-PETER, photographer; b. Bklyn., Sept. 13, 1939; s. Max and Mary (Pellegrino) W.; m. Cynthia Jean Bency, June 30, 1978; one child, Kersen Ahanu. B.F.A., Cooper Union, 1974; M.F.A., U. N.Mex., 1986; student (fellow), Columbia U., 1973-74. Exhibited in Projects Studio One, N.Y.C., 1980, Galerie Texbraun, Paris, 1982, Kansas Ctiy Art Inst., 1983, Stedelijk Mus., Amsterdam, 1983, Fraenkel Gallery, 1983-84, 87, 91, 93, 95, Pace/MacGill Gallery, N.Y.C., 1983, 84, 87, 89, 91, 93, 95, San Francisco Mus. Modern Art, 1985, Bklyn. Mus., 1986, Galerie Baudoin Lebon, Paris, 1987, 89, 91, 95, Centro de Arte Reina Sofia Mus., Madrid, 1988, Palais de Tokyo, Paris, 1989, Fahey/Klein Gallery, L.A., 1989, 92, 93, Mus. Modern Art, Haifa, Israel, 1991, Photo Picture Space Gallery, Osaka, Japan, 1993, Guggenheim Mus., N.Y.C., 1995, Interkamera, Prague, 1995, Il Castello de Rivoli Mus., Turin, 1995, Taipei Photo Gallery, Taiwan; group shows: Mus. Moder Art, N.Y.C., 1959, San Francisco Mus. Moder Art, 1981, Whitney Biennial, 1985, Palais de Tokyo, Paris, 1986; represented in permanent collections, Mus. Modern Art, N.Y.C., San Francisco Mus. Modern Art, 1980, Nat. Gallery Art, Washington, Victoria and Albert Mus., London, George Eastman House, N.Y., The Getty Collection, Moder Museet, Stockholm, Sweden, Whitney Mus., N.Y.C., The Guggenheim Mus., N.Y.C.; represented by Pace/MacGill, N.Y.C., Fraenkel Gallery, San Francisco, Baudoin Lebon Gallery, Paris; subject of monographs: Joel-Peter Witkin, 1985, 88-89, 91, 93, 95-96; editor: Masterpeices of Medical Photography, 1987, Harms Way, 1994. Served with U.S. Army, 1961-64. Decorated Chevalier Des Arts et de Letters (France), 1990, The Augustus Saint Gaudens medal The Cooper Union, 1996; recipient Disting. Alumni award The Cooper Union, 1986, Internat. Ctr. Photography award, 1988; Ford Found. grantee, 1977, 78, Nat. Endowment in Photography grantee, 1980, 81, 86, 92. Address: 1707 Five Points Rd SW Albuquerque NM 87105-3017 *My need is to understand existence. That need becomes art when it reaches into the extreme limit of the possible.*

WITKIN, MILDRED HOPE FISHER, psychotherapist, educator; b. N.Y.C.; d. Samuel and Sadie (Goldschmidt) Fisher; children: Georgia Hope, Roy Thomas, Laurie Phillips, Kimberly, Nicole, Scott, Joshua, Jennifer; m. Jorge Radovic, Aug. 26, 1983. AB, Hunter Coll., MA, Columbia U., 1968; PhD, NYU, 1973. Diplomate Am. Bd. Sexology, Am. Bd. Sexuality; cert. supr. Head counselor Camp White Lake, Camp Emanuel, Long Beach, N.J.; tchr. econs., polit. sci. Hunter Coll. High Sch.; dir., group leader follow-up program Jewish Vacation Assn., N.Y.C.; investigator N.Y.C. Housing Authority; psychol. counselor Montclair State Coll., Upper Montclair, N.J., 1967-68; mem., lectr. Creative Problem-Solving Inst., U. Buffalo, 1968; psychol. counselor Fairleigh Dickinson U., Teaneck, N.J., 1968, dir. Counseling Center, 1969-74; pvt. practice psychotherapy, N.Y.C., also Westport, Conn.; sr. faculty supr., family therapist and psychotherapist Payne Whitney Psychiat. Clinic, N.Y. Hosp., 1973—; clin. asst. prof. dept. psychiatry Cornell U. Med. Coll., 1974—; assoc. dir. sex therapy and edn. program Cornell-N.Y. Hosp. Med. Ctr., 1974—; sr. cons. Kaplan Inst. for Evaluation and Treatment of Sexual Disorders, 1981—; supr. master's and doctoral candidates, NYU, 1975-82; pvt. practice psychotherapy and sex therapy, N.Y.C., also Westport, Conn.; cons. counselor edn. tng. programs N.Y.C. Bd. Edn., 1971-75; cons. Health Info. Systems, 1972-79; vis. prof. numerous colls. and univs.; chmn. sci. com. 1st Internat. Symposium on Female Sexuality, Buenos Aires, 1984. Exhibited in group shows at Scarsdale (N.Y.) Art Show, 1959, Red Shutter Art Studio, Long Beach, 1968. Edn. legislation chmn. PTA, Yonkers, 1955; publicity chmn. United Jewish Appeal, Scarsdale, 1959-65; Scarsdale chmn. mothers com. Boy Scouts Am., 1961-64; mem. Morrow Assn. on Correction N.J., 1969-91; bd. dirs. Girl Scouts of Am. Recipient Bronze medal for svcs. Hunter Coll.; United Jewish Appeal plaque, 1962; Founders Day award N.Y. U., 1973, citation N.Y. Hosp./Cornell U. Med. Ctr., 1990. Fellow Internat. Coun. Sex Edn. and Parenthood of Am. U., Am. Acad. Clin. Sexologists; mem. AAUW, APA, ACA, Assn. Counseling Supervision, Am. Coll. Personnel Assn., Internat. Assn. Marriage and Family Counselors, Am. Coll. Sexuality (cert.), Women's Med. Assn. N.Y.C., N.Y. Acad. Sci., Am. Coll. Pers. Assn. (nat. mem. commn. II 1973-76), Nat. Assn. Women Deans and Counselors, Am. Assn. Sex Educators, Counselors and Therapists (regional bd., nat. accreditation bd., cert. internat. supr.), Soc. for Sci. Study Sex Therapy and Rsch., Eastern Assn. Sex Therapists, Am. Assn. Marriage and Family Counselors, N.J. Assn. Marriage and Family Counselors, Ackerman Family Inst., Am. Personnel and Guidance Assn., Am., N.Y., N.J. psychol. assns., Creative Edn. Found., Am. Assn. Higher Edn., Assn. Counselor Supervision and Edn., Profl. Women's Caucus, LWV, Am. Assn. counseling and Devel., Am. Women's Med. Assn., Nat. Coun. on Women in Medicine, Argentine Soc. Human Sexuality (hon.), Am. Assn. Sexology (diplomate), Conn. Assn. Marriage and Family Therapy, Pi Lambda Theta, Kappa Delta Pi, Alpha Chi Alpha. Author: 45-And Single Again, 1985, Single Again, 1994; contbr. articles to profl. jours. and textbooks; lectr. internat. and nat. workshops, radio and TV. Home: 9 Sturges Commons Westport CT 06880-2832 Office: 35 Park Ave New York NY 10016-3838

WITKOP, BERNHARD, chemist; b. Freiburg, Baden, Germany, May 9, 1917; came to U.S., 1947, naturalized, 1953; s. Philipp W. and Hedwig M. (Hirschhorn) W.; m. Marlene Prinz, Aug. 8, 1945; children: Cornelia Johanna, Phyllis, Thomas. Diploma, U. Munich, 1938, PhD, 1940, Golden Dr. Diploma, 1990; ScD, Privat-Dozent, 1947. Matthew T. Mellon research fellow Harvard U., 1947-48, mem. faculty, 1948-50; spl. USPHS fellow Nat. Heart Inst., NIH, 1950-52; vis. scientist Nat. Inst. Arthritis and Metabolic Diseases, 1953, chemist, 1954-55, chief sect. metabolites, 1956-87, chief lab. chemistry, 1957-87, scholar, 1987-92, hon. scholar emeritus, 1993; vis. prof. U. Kyoto, Japan, 1961, U. Freiburg, Fed. Repubic Germany, 1962; adj. prof. U. Md. Med. Sch., Balt.; Nobel symposium lectr. Stockholm-Karlskoga, 1981; mem. bd. Internat. Sci. Exchange, 1974; mem. exec. com. NRC, 1975; mem. Com. Internat. Exchange, 1977, Paul Ehrlich Award Com., Frankfurt, 1980. Editor: Fedn. European Biochem. Soc. Letters, 1979-90. Recipient Superior Service award USPHS, 1967; Paul Karrer gold medal U. Zurich, 1971; Kun-ni-to (medal of sci. and culture 2d class) Emperor of Japan, 1975; Alexander von Humboldt award for sr. U.S. scientists, 1978. Mem. NAS, Am. Chem. Soc. (Hillebrand award 1958), Am. Acad. Arts and Sci., Acad. Leopoldina (fgn.), Pharm. Soc. Japan (hon.), Chem. Soc. Japan (hon.), Japanese Biochem. Soc. (hon.). Office: NIH-Dept Health Edn & Welfare Rm B1A-11 Bethesda MD 20892 *A career between two worlds and two wars, spanning 50 years of research aims changing from structural to dynamic aspects, may be considered epigonal in the sense that my teacher H. Wieland (Nobel Prize 1928) always considered biochemistry as a neglected area of organic chemistry. In a small way I tried to follow his example and interests, such as oxidation mechanisms, natural products and highly active toxins.*

WITKOWSKI, KIM LOUISE, counselor; b. Winchester, Mass., June 24, 1949; d. Sam R. and Glorya (Sheehan) Macaione; m. Walter Joseph Witkowski, Feb. 7, 1981. BA, U. Mass., 1971; MEd, U. S.C., 1982; MA, Webster U., 1991; PhD, Walden U., 1993. Tchr. Horry County Sch. Dist., Conway, S.C., 1976-79; English resource tchr. Georgetown (S.C.) County Sch. Dist., 1980; tchr. profoundly mentally handicapped Horry County Sch. Dist., 1981-82, spl. edn. resource tchr., 1982-86; dir. edn., staff psychologist Coastal Carolina Psychiatric Hosp., Conway, 1986-90; intern individual and family therapy Navy Family Svcs., Charleston, S.C., 1991; sch. psychologist Horry County Sch. Dist., 1990-93; pvt. practice in family and individual therapy Myrtle Beach, S.C., 1991—; adj. faculty Coastal Carolina U., Conway, 1993; adj. prof. Webster U.; hosp. credentialing com. Coastal Carolina Hosp., quality assurance com., clin. adv. com., accreditation com., fire and safety com., master treatment plan com., child and adolescent program devel. com., mktg. com., infection control com.; multicultural com. Horry County Sch. Dist., 1993, homebound instruction policies and procedures com., 1990, Coastal Carolina Hosp. rep., 1990, Myrtle Beach primary sch. discipline com., 1986, Spl. Edn. Dept. Head, 1985-86. Edn. chair Horry Human Rels. Coun., exec. dir. Afro-Fest; mem. Horry County Dept. Social Svcs. Multidisciplinary Case Adv. Team, Children's Protective Svcs.,/1989-91; v.p., bd. dirs. South Horry Med. Ctr. Rural Health Initiative, 1984-87; treas., bd. dirs. Community Vol Svcs., 1979-81; past S.C. Guardian Ad Litem Program, 1985—; governing bd. Horry Human Rels. Coun., 1994. Mem. AACD, Coun. for Exceptional Children, Assn. Children with Learning Disabilities, S.C. Assn. Sch. Psychologists, Orton Dyslexia Soc., Assn. Edn. Therapists. Avocations: reading, travel. Home: Briarcliffe Acres 12 S Gate Rd Myrtle Beach SC 29572-5621

WITKOWSKY, GIZELLA, dancer; b. Toronto, Ont., Can.. Student, Nat. Ballet Sch. With Nat. Ballet Can., 1975—, 2nd soloist, 1977, 1st soloist, 1978, prin. dancer, 1985—; dancer David Allan's Italian Tour, 1985. Performances include Swan Queen/Black Queen in Swan Lake, Snow Queen/Sugar Plum Fairy in Nutcracker, Queen of the Wilis in Giselle, Swanild in Coppélia, Hanna in Merry Widow, Tatiana in Onegin, others; lead roles in Sphinx, Alice, Voluntaries, Rite of Spring; other roles include Serenade, Four Temperaments, Les Sylphides, Paquita, La Bayadere Act II, Offenbach in the Underworld, Elite Syncopations; created roles Pastorale, Compenents, L'Ile Inconnue, Oiseaux Exotiques, Concerto for the Elements, Lostin Twilights; guest performances include inaugural Huntsville Festival of Arts, 1993, Hungarian Nat. Ballet, Budapest, 1992, Bermuda Festival, 1991, 93, Annual Nijinsky Gala, Hamburg, 1991, Stars and Soloists of Can. Ballet, Italy, 1985. Office: National Ballet of Canada, 157 King St East, Toronto, ON Canada M5C 1G9

WITMAN, FRANK MCCONNELL, clergyman, educator; b. Altoona, Pa., Dec. 1, 1931; s. Edwin Henry and Mary Frances (Grose) W.; m. Elsie Ellen McLaughlin, Mar. 28, 1953; children: Mark Allan, Paul David.. BA, Calif. State U., L.A., 1956; ThM, Sch. Theology at Claremont, Calif., 1959, D Ministry, 1977; cert. supervising pastor, Fuller Theol. Sem. Ordained elder United Meth. Ch., 1961; cert. L.A. Police Dept. Acad., Advanced Police Chaplain Sch. Assoc. pastor Trinity United Meth. Ch., Pomona, Calif., 1959-62; sr. pastor Rialto (Calif.) United Meth. Ch., 1962-69, United Meth. Ch., Simi Valley, Calif., 1969—; bd. dirs. United Meth. Fed. Credit Union, Montclair, Calif., 1964—, chmn. bd., 1976—; mem. adj. faculty Sch. Theology at Claremont, 1992, trustee, 1966-69; mem. CKW Partnership, adminstrn. and fin. cons., Vista, Calif., 1988—. Co-author: Christian Response in a Hungry World, 1978, Church Administration and Finance, 1995. Chaplain Simi Valley Police Dept., 1978—; guest chaplain U.S. Ho. of Reps., Washington, 1990. Sgt. U.S. Army, 1953-55. Named Young Man of Yr., Rialto Jr. C. of C., 1965, Citizen of Yr., Rialto C. of C., 1969; recipient Disting. Ministry award Sch. Theology at Claremont, 1993, Walter Teagle fellow, 1976-77. Mem. Sch. Theology at Claremont Alumni Assn. (pres. 1965-69), Rotary (bd. dirs. Rialto 1064-65, Simi Valley 1973-74, Paul Harris fellow 1985). Republican. Avocations: camping, leading youth and adult camps, travel. Home: 2794 Harrington Rd Simi Valley CA 93065-2296 Office: United Meth Ch 2394 Erringer Rd Simi Valley CA 93065-2296

WITMER, G. ROBERT, retired state supreme court justice; b. Webster, N.Y., Dec. 26, 1904; s. George H. and Lillian (Woodhull) W.; m. Marian P. Costello, June 27, 1936; children: George Robert, John R., Thomas W., Sylvia Witmer Bissell. A.B., U. Rochester, N.Y., 1926; LL.B., Harvard U., 1929. Bar: N.Y. 1929. Pvt. practice Rochester, 1929-45; ptnr. Easton & Witmer, 1931-45; surrogate Monroe County, 1946-53; justice N.Y. State Supreme Ct., 1954-81, assoc. justice appellate div. 1st dept., 1963-67, appellate div. 4th dept., 1968-81; jud. adminstrv. officer, appellate div. N.Y. State Supreme Ct. (4th dept.), 1981-94; adminstrv. judge N.Y. State Supreme Ct. (7th Jud. Dist.), 1962-68; ret., 1994; town atty., Webster, 1934-35; served on N.Y. State Ct. Appeals, 1974. Co-author: N.Y. Pattern Jury Instructions-Civil, Vol. 1, 1965, rev. edit., 1974, Vol. 11, 1968; co-chmn. pub. com. Practitioner's Handbook for Appeals Appellate Divs. N.Y., 1979, Practitioner's Handbook for Appeals to the Court of Appeals of New York, 1981. Supr. Town of Webster and County of Monroe, 1936-45; chmn. Webster Republican Com., 1933-45, mem. exec. com. of Monroe County Republican Com., 1933-45. Mem. Am., N.Y. State, Monroe County Bar Assns., Am. Law Inst., Webster Grange, Univ. Club (Rochester), Masons, Theta Chi. Home: 45 Corning Park Webster NY 14580-3503

WITMER, GEORGE ROBERT, JR., lawyer; b. Rochester, N.Y., Mar. 23, 1937; s. George Robert and Marian Pauline (Costello) W.; m. Nancy Rosetta Wenner, Dec. 28, 1968; children: Wendy Lynn, Heidi Dawn, George Robert, III, Frank David. A.B., U. Rochester, 1959; LL.B., Harvard U., 1962. Bar: N.Y. 1962, U.S. Dist. Ct. (we. dist.) N.Y. 1963, U.S. Supreme Ct. 1967, U.S Dist. Ct. (no. dist.) N.Y. 1977. Assoc. Nixon, Hargrave, Devans & Doyle, Rochester, 1962-70; ptnr. Nixon, Hargrave, Devans & Doyle, 1970—; instr. in bus. law U. Rochester, 1965-66; mem. com. to advise and cons. Jud. Conf. State N.Y. on Civil Practice Law and Rules, 1970-77. Mem. N.Y. State Rep. Com., 1976-93; trustee Eastman Dental Ctr. Rochester, 1977—, pres. bd. trustees, 1989-90; trustee U. Rochester, 1979—, chmn. exec. com., 1992—. Fellow N.Y. Bar Found. (dir. 1991—), ABA Found.; mem. ABA, Monroe County (N.Y.) Bar Assn., N.Y. State Bar Assn. (ho. of dels. 1978—, v.p. 1984-88, sec. 1989-90, pres.-elect 1993-94, pres. 1994-95, exec. com. environ. law sect. 1981-96, environ. law sect. Disting. Svc. award), Am. Law Inst., Rochester Rotary Club (dir. local club 1977-79), Masons (master 1971), Phi Beta Kappa. Republican. Lutheran. Home: 892 Lake Rd Webster NY 14580-9008 Office: Nixon Hargrave Devans & Doyle PO Box 1051 Clinton Sq Rochester NY 14604-1729

WITMER, JOHN ALBERT, librarian; b. Lancaster, Pa., Nov. 29, 1920; s. Albert Franklin and Mary Esther (Conrad) W.; m. Doris May Ferry, June 10, 1943; children: Marilyn May Witmer Custis, John Richard, Deborah Witmer Redd. AB, Wheaton Coll., 1942, AM, 1946; ThM, Dallas Theol. Sem., 1946, ThD, 1953; MS in L.S., E. Tex. State U., 1969; cert. Archival Adminstrn., U. Tex., Arlington, 1988. Grad. fellow Wheaton Coll., 1942-44; mng. editor Child Evanglism mag., Dallas, 1944-46; instr. Child Evangelism Inst., Dallas and Chgo., 1945-47; instr. systematic theology Dallas Theol. Sem., 1947-54, asst. prof., 1954-86, assoc. prof., 1986-87, assoc. prof. emeritus, 1987—; librarian Mosher Library, 1964-86, archivist, 1987—; cert. instr. Dale Carnegie Course, 1956-92, instr. emeritus, 1992—. Contbr. articles to profl. jours., essays; editor: The Christian Librarian, 1972-74. Treas. Evang. Communications Research Found., 1970-73; bd. dirs. Dallas Bible Coll., 1972-83, chmn., 1974-77, sec., 1979-82; bd. dirs. Evang. Projects, 1975-92. Mem. Assn. Christian Librs., Evang. Philos. Soc., Evan. Theol. Soc., Soc. Am. Archivists, Soc. Southwest Archivists, Grace Evang. Soc. Home: 6630 Westlake Ave Dallas TX 75214-3441

WITMER, JOHN HARPER, JR., lawyer; b. Phila., May 5, 1940; s. John Harper and Jane Carolyn (Lentz) Witmer; m. Arlene Marie Rosipal, June 9, 1962; 1 dau., Tara Leah. BA, Pa. State U., 1962; JD, George Washington U., 1969. Bar: Md. 1969, D.C. 1970, Ill. 1979, Colo. 1991. Mgmt. analyst Nat. Security Agy., Ft. Meade, Md., 1963-66; mem. Sidley & Austin, Washington, 1969-78; sr. v.p., gen. counsel DEKALB Energy Co., 1978-95, DEKALB Genetics Corp., 1978—. Mem. ABA, Ill. State Bar Assn., Md. State Bar Assn., D.C. Bar Assn. Home: 2575 Greenwood Acres Dr De Kalb IL 60115-4916 Office: DEKALB Genetics Corp 3100 Sycamore Rd De Kalb IL 60115-9621

WITMEYER, JOHN JACOB, III, lawyer; b. New Orleans, Dec. 18, 1946; s. John J. and Thais Audrey (Dolese) W. B.S., Tulane U., 1968; J.D. with distinction, Duke U., 1971. Bar: N.Y. Assoc. Mudge Rose Guthrie & Alexander, N.Y.C., 1971-76; ptnr. Ford Marrin Esposito & Witmeyer (now Ford, Marrin, Esposito, Witmeyer & Gleser, L.L.P.), N.Y.C., 1976—. Col. USAR. Office: Ford Marrin Esposito Witmeyer & Gleser LLP Wall St Plz New York NY 10005-1875

WITSCHEY, WALTER ROBERT THURMOND, science museum administrator, archaeologist, computer systems consultant; b. Charleston, W.Va., June 19, 1941; s. Robert E. and Sarah Elizabeth (Thurmond) W.; m. Joan DuRelle Vincent, July 19, 1980; children: Anne Elizabeth, Schon Roberts Parris, Sarah C. Brauner, Walter Robert Thurmond II, Benjamin Hart Vincent. BA in Physics, Princeton U., 1963; MBA in Ops. Rsch., U. Va., 1965; MA in Anthropology-Maya Archaeology, Tulane U., 1989, PhD in Anthropology-Maya Archaeology, 1993. Systems engr. IBM Corp., Richmond, Va., 1965-67, mktg. rep., 1967-69; v.p. The Computer Co., Richmond, Va., 1969-70, pres., CEO, 1970-84; cons., pub., proprietorship Gatewood Co., Richmond, Va., 1978—; dir., CEO Sci. Mus. Va., Richmond, Va., 1992—; bd. dirs. Highland Data Svcs., 1982-85; vis. instr. computer systems U. Va., 1985-86; instr. word processing, Delgado Community Coll., 1989; lectr. microcomputer applications, Our Lady Of Holy Cross Coll., 1989-92; lectr. dept. Anthropology, Tulane U., 1987—, asst. to the dir., 1987-88, lectr., curriculum cons., 1988-92, adj. instr. A.B. Freeman Sch., 1991; adj. faculty dept. Sociology, Anthropology and Mathematical Scis., Va. Commonwealth U., 1992—. Contbr. articles to profl. jours. Dir. Assn. Sci.-Tech. Ctrs., 1995—, Sci. Mus. Va. Found., Richmond, 1981-90, La. Sci. Ctr., New Orleans, 1985-90; pres., dir. Richmond-on-the-James, 1984-85; sec., dir. Richmond Cmty. H.S. Policy Bd.; cons. Federated Arts Coun., Richmond. Tinker Found. archaeol. rsch. grantee (3), Middle Am. Rsch. Inst. archaeol. grantee, Mesoam. Ecology Inst. archaeol. rsch. grantee (3), Middle Am. Rsch. Inst. archaeol. rsch. grantee (3), pvt. archaeol. rsch. grantee. Mem. AAAS, Am. Assn. Mus., Am. Anthrop. Assn., Assn. Sci.-Tech. Ctrs., Soc. Am. Archaeology, Va. Acad. Sci., Va. Assn. Mus., Va. Space Grant Consortium, Assn. Computing Machinery, Sigma Xi. Presbyterian. Avocation: field archaeology. Office: Sci Mus Va 2500 W Broad St Richmond VA 23220-2057

WITT, ANNE CLEINO, musician, education educator; b. Winston-Salem, N.C., May 14, 1945; d. Edward Henry and Elizabeth Anne (White) Cleino; m. Robert Ernest Witt, Nov. 23, 1977; children: Peter Ivy, Karen Ivy. BS in Music Edn., U. Ala., 1967; MMus, U. Tex., 1974, PhD in Music Edn., 1983. Choral dir. Lee H.S., Huntsville, Ala., 1967-70; profl. cellist Austin (Tex.) Symphony Orch., 1974-95; pvt. cello tchr. Austin, 1990-93; orch. dir. and string tchr. Lamar Mid. Sch. and McCallum H.S., Austin, 1974-80, 83-90; lectr. edn. U. Tex., Austin, 1990-93; dir. U. Tex. String Project, Austin, 1993-95; clinician conv. sessions, insvc. tng., 1980—. Author: Recruiting for the School Orchestra, 1984, 2d edit. 1987; editor: Teaching Stringed Instruments, 1991, Strategies for Teaching Strings and Orchestra, 1996. Mem. Am. String Tchrs. Assn. (past pres., Citation for Exceptional Leadership and Merit 1988, 96, nat. pres. 1992-94), Tex. Orch. Dirs. Assn. (pres. 1991-92), Music Educators Nat. Conf. (life), Tex. Music Educators Assn., Suzuki Assn. of Americas. Episcopalian. Home: 2329 Table Rock Arlington TX 76006 Office: Univ of Texas School of Music Arlington TX 76019

WITT, BUFORD RANDOLPH, air force officer; b. Memphis, June 6, 1946; s. Buford Witt; m. Margaret Ann Murphy, Aug. 9, 1969; children: Ann, Randolph. Commd. USAF, 1968, advanced through grades to brig. gen., 1993; comdr. Comm. Squadron 509th Bomb Wing, Pease AFB, N.H., 1980-82; comms. staff officer hdqs. USAF, Washington, 1982-84; exec. officer to comdr. Air Force Comms. Command, Scott AFB, Ill., 1984-86; comdr. 3d Combat Comms. Group, Tinker AFB, Okla., 1986-88; dep. chief of staff C4 Sys. Hdqs. 9th AF and U.S. Cen. Command, Shaw AFB, S.C., 1989-92; asst. dep. dir. Unified and Command Support, Joint Staff Pentagon, Washington, 1992-93; dir. plans, policy, dep. chief of staff C4 Hdqs. USAF, Washington, 1993-94; dir. command, control comm. sys. Hdqs. U.S. European Command, Stuttgart, Germany, 1994—. Editor: AF Tactical Communications in War, 1991. Mem. Armed Forces Comms. Electronics Assn., Washington Citadel Club (pres. 1993-94). Avocation: flying. Home: Box 741 HQ USEUCOM Unit 30400 APO AE 09128 Office: HQ USEUCOM/ECJ6 Unit 30400 Box 1000 APO AE 09128

WITT, DAVID L., curator, writer; b. Kansas City, Mo., Nov. 3, 1951; s. Lloyd Vernon and Dean W. B.S. in Polit. Sci., Kans. State U., 1974. Naturalist Naish Nature Ctr., Edwardsville, Kans., summers 1967-70; asst. curator Seton Mus., Cimarron, N.Mex., summers 1972-74; curatorial asst. Riley County Hist. Mus., Manhattan, Kans., 1973-74; mus. asst. Millicent Rogers Mus., Taos, N.Mex., 1976-77; curator The Gaspard House Mus., Taos, N.Mex., 1978-79, The Harwood Found., Taos; 1979—; Author: The Taos Artists, 1984, Taos Moderns: Art of the New, 1992 (Southwest Book award Border Regional Libr. Assn. 1993); contbr. articles to profl. jours. Organizer first N.Mex. Art History Conf., 1986; founder Southwest Art History Coun., 1990. Mem. PEN, Mountain-Plains Mus. Assn. (council mem. 1983-85), N.Mex. Assn. Mus. (pres. 1986-88). Democrat. Home: PO Box 317 Taos NM 87571-0317 Office: PO Box 4081 Taos NM 87571

WITT, ELIZABETH NOWLIN (BETH WITT), special education educator; b. Columbus, Miss., Apr. 11, 1941; d. Mervyn Davis and Elizabeth (Moody) Smith; m. Lawrence V. Witt Jr., Feb. 10, 1963; children: Lawrence V. III, Ben, John, Catherine, Elizabeth. BS in Journalism and English, Miss. U. for Women, Columbus, 1963; MA in Spl. Edn., La. Tech. U., Ruston, 1979; postgrad., La. State U., 1990—. Cert. in English, learning disabilities, mental retardation, presch. handicapped severe/profound, also prin., ednl. cons., ednl. diagnostician, La. Tchr. spl. edn. Caddo-Bossier Assn. for Retarded Citizens, Shreveport, La., 1976-79; tchr presch. handicapped

Bossier Parish Schs., Bossier City, La., 1979-83; ednl. diagnostician Caddo Parish Schs., Shreveport, 1983—; ednl. cons. Ruston (La.) State Sch., summer 1981; instr. La. Tech. U., 1990-95; mem. author adv. bd. Comm. Skill Builders, Tucson, 1986-88; ex officio mem. Region VII Infant Coun., Shreveport, 1990-92; bd. dirs. Childcare of N.W. La., Shreveport, 1986-90, Head Start, Shreveport, 1984-85. Mem. editorial adv. bd. JCCD, DCCD; author lang. activity kits and programs. Vol. edn. cons. Lighthouse Presch. Program, Vols. of Am., Shreveport, 1986—; elder First Presbyn. Ch., Bossier City, 1989-91. Mem. Am. Speech and Hearing Assn., Coun. for Exceptional Children (editor newsletter La. Fedn. 1988-90, pres. La. div. early childhood 1989-90, pres. La. div. mental retardation 1986-87, coun. for children with commun. disorders 1986—). Avocations: reading, anthropology, country decorating, travel. Office: Caddo Parish Sch Spl Edn Ctr 5948 Union Ave Shreveport LA 71108-3928

WITT, HUGH ERNEST, technology consultant; b. Winchester, Ky., Nov. 18, 1921; s. Hugh E. and Louella (Milliken) W.; m. Janie Bryan (dec. Oct. 1990); m. Evelyn Chapman, Apr. 22, 1993. Student, Transylvania U., 1941-43; BS, U. Ky., 1945; MS, MIT, 1957. Asst. to dep. asst. sec. Dept. of Air Force, Washington, 1954-61, dep. asst. sec., 1961-70; dep. asst. sec. Dept. of Navy, Washington, 1970-73; prin. dep. asst. Sec. of Def., Washington, 1973-74; fed. procurement policy adminstr. Office Mgmt. and Budget, Washington, 1974-77; dir., govt. liaison United Techs. Corp., Washington, 1977-81, v.p., govt. liaison, 1981-87, cons. to United Techs. Corp., 1987—. Pres. Old Town Civic Assn., Alexandria, Va., 1961-63; bd. dirs. Alexandria Hist. Found.; mem. Alexandria Bd. Archtl. Rev., 1964-77; trustee Alexandria Hosp. Found., 1992-94. Alfred P. Sloan fellow MIT, Cambridge, Mass., 1956-57. Fellow Nat. Contract Mgmt. Assn.; mem. Aerospace Industries Assn., Nat. Security Indsl. Assn., MIT Alumni Assn., Soc. Sloan Fellows, Kappa Alpha.

WITT, JAMES LEE, federal agency administrator; b. Dardanelle, Ark., 1944; m. Lea; children: Jimmy, Michael. Founder Witt Constrn. Co.; county judge Yell County, Ark.; state dir. Office Emergency Svcs., Ark.; dir. Fed. Emergency Mgmt. Agy., Washington, 1993—. Chmn. bd. Child Devel., Inc., charter; Gov.'s rep. state disasters, Presdl. disasters. Recognized for outstanding efforts Nat. Assn. Counties. Office: Federal Emergency Mgmt Agency Office of Dir 500 C St SW Washington DC 20472-0001

WITT, RAY, automotive manufacturing executive. CEO CMI Internat., Southfield, Mich. Office: 30333 Southfield Rd Southfield MI 48076

WITT, RAYMOND BUCKNER, JR., lawyer; b. Lenoir City, Tenn., Apr. 20, 1915; s. Raymond Buckner and Gertrude (Jackson) W.; m. Florence Elder Bagley, Sept. 14, 1943; children—Florence Elder, Mary Alice, George Evans. A.B., U. Chattanooga, 1937; LL.B., U. N.C., 1939. Bar: Tenn. 1939. Since practiced in Chattanooga; with Witt, Gaither, Whitaker and predecessor firms, 1945—, partner, 1946—; dir., gen. counsel Dixie Yarns, Inc., 1947-92. Pres. Met. Council Community Services, 1966-68; mem. Chattanooga Bd. Edn., 1953-65, vice chmn., 1963-65; chmn. Chattanooga Bicentennial Religious Com., 1976; chmn. bd. Chattanooga-Hamilton County Bicentennial Library, 1976-78; trustee Westend Found.; mem. U. Chatanooga Found. Inc., 1969—, trustee, sec., gen. counsel , chmn. 1988-90; pres. Chattanooga YMCA, 1986-87; chmn. United Way Fund campaign, 1987; chmn. bd. trustees 1st Centenary United Methodist, 1989, chmn. adminstrv. bd., 1993, 94. Served to lt. comdr. USNR, 1942-45, PTO. Recipient Distinguished Service award Chattanooga Kiwanis, 1963, Tenn. Sch. Bds. Assn., 1963. Mem. ABA, Tenn. Bar Assn. Methodist (chmn. commn. on Christian edn. 1953-55, ch. sch. supt. 1955-60). Home: 1615 Minnekahda Rd Chattanooga TN 37405-2411 Office: American Nat Bank Bldg Sun Trust Bldg Chattanooga TN 37402

WITT, ROBERT E., marketing educator; b. Sept. 16, 1940; m. Anne Witt; children: Peter, Karen. BA in Econs., Bates Coll., 1962; MBA, Dartmouth Coll., 1964; PhD in Bus. Adminstrn., Pa. State U., 1968. Rsch. asst. Amos Tuck Sch., Dartmouth Coll., Hanover, N.H., 1964-65; instr. mktg. Pa. State U., 1967-68; asst. prof. Coll. and Grad. Sch. Bus., U. Tex., Austin, 1968-71, assoc. prof., 1971-75, chmn. dept. mktg., 1973-83, prof., 1975-83, Zale Corp. centennial prof. bus., 1983-85, Betty and Glenn Mortimer centennial prof. bus., 1985-95, centennial chairperson bus. edn. leadership, 1986-95, acting dean, then dean, 1985—; interim pres. U. Tex., Arlington, 1995-96, pres., 1996—; mem. budget coun. dept. mktg. adminstrn. U. Tex., Austin, 1969-85, mem. faculty exec. devel. program 1969—, mem. dean's coun., 1986—; mem. athletes adv. com. NCAA, 1986—; mem. acad. adv. bd. World Mgmt. Coun., 1988; mem. future directions coun. U. Tex. Ex-Students Assn., 1978-88, mem. exec. coun., 1981-83, 87-89; mem. adv. bd. dirs. Post Oak Bank, 1993—, Frost Nat. Bank, 1993—; mem. Acctg. Edn. Change Commn., 1992—; bd. dirs. Life Ptnrs. Group. Assoc. editor Social Sci. Quar., 1970-72; mem. editl. rev. bd. Jour. Mktg., 1971-73, 82-85; contbr. articles to profl. jours. Bd. dirs. Austin Symphony, 1991—, Univ. Coop. Soc., 1978-82. Recipient Top Hand award U. Tex. Ex-Students Assn., 1988. Mem. Am. Mktg. Assn. (fellow doctoral consortium 1967, progran chmn. doctoral consortium 1972, reviewer, presenter), Assn. for Consumer Rsch. (treas. 1976, mem. exec. com. 1975-76, reviewer, conf. session chmn.), Am. Assembly Collegiate Schs. of Bus. (bd. dirs. 1991—, mem. visitation com. 1991, mem. govtl. rels. com. 1986-89, chmn. govtl. rels. com. 1987-89), So. Mktg. Assn. (conf. trach chmn., presenter), Beta Gamma Sigma (v.p. U. Tex. chpt. 1973-74, pres. chpt. 1974-75), Phi Kappa Phi. Office: U Tex Arlington UTA Box 19125 Arlington TX 76019

WITT, ROBERT LOUIS, materials manufacturing and sales company executive, lawyer; b. Vallejo, Calif., Feb. 22, 1940; s. Charles Louis and Encie Lyndell (Bates) W.; m. Myrna Doreen Harvey; 1 child, Mark Louis. A.A., Solano Coll., 1959; student, Oreg. State U., 1959-61; J.D., San Francisco Law Sch., 1968. Sec., corp. counsel Hexcel Corp., San Francisco, 1969-76, v.p., sec., 1976-80, v.p. adminstrn., 1980-82, sr. v.p. internat., 1982-84, exec. v.p., 1984-85, CEO, 1986-93; prin. WWS Assocs., San Francisco, 1993—.

WITT, ROBERT WAYNE, English educator; b. Scottsville, Ky., Mar. 26, 1937; s. Aubrey G. Witt and Nina Loyce (Cook) Jackson. BA, Georgetown Coll., 1959; MA, U. Miss., 1961, PhD, 1970. Instr. U. Miss., Oxford, 1965-70; asst. prof. Ea. Ky. U., Richmond, 1970-75, assoc. prof., 1975-80, prof., 1980—. Author: Mirrow-within, 1975, Shakespeare's Sonnets, 1979, Rocking Chair, 1987, Combining Modes, 1992, Hour in Paradise, 1993, Toxic, 1995. Mem. MLA, South Atlantic Modern Lang., Dramatists Guild, Automatic Musical Instruments Collectors. Avocations: playing piano, collecting antique automatic musical instruments. Home: PO Box 419 Richmond KY 40476-0419

WITT, THOMAS POWELL, lawyer; b. Pitts., Nov. 11, 1946; s. Fabian J. and Blanche (Powell) W.; m. Loretta Jean Cooper, June 27, 1970; children: John, Christopher, Susan. BA magna cum laude, LaSalle U., Phila., 1968; MA, Harvard U., 1969; JD cum laude, Temple U., 1975. Bar: Pa. 1975, U.S. Dist. Ct. (ea. dist.) Pa. 1976. Adminstrv. asst. Phila. Housing Devel. Corp., 1969-72; supr. loan processing Firstrust Savs. Bank, Phila., 1972-75; atty. Morgan, Lewis & Bockius, Phila., 1975-83; ptnr. Wolf, Block, Schorr & Solis-Cohen, Phila., 1983—. Dir., pres. S. W. Germantown Assn. Fed. Credit Union, Phila., 1982-89, bd. dirs. Women Against Abuse, Inc., Phila., 1988-89, Juvenile Justice Ctr. Pa., Phila, 1989—, Regional Housing Legal Svcs., 1989—, The Pa. Prison Soc., 1994—. Fellow Woodrow Wilson Found., Princeton, N.J., 1968. Mem. Bicycle Club Phila. (pres. 1992-95). Democrat. Avocation: bicycle touring. Home: 5127 Pulaski Ave Philadelphia PA 19144-4021 Office: Wolf Block Schorr et al 12th Fl Packard Bldg SE Corner 15 & Chestnut Sts Philadelphia PA 19102

WITT, TOM, economics researcher, educator; b. Borger, Tex., Apr. 22, 1944; s. Eugene Thomason and Helen C. (Hathaway) W.; m. Grethe A. Myles, Mar. 4, 1976. BA, Okla. State U., 1966; MA, Washington U., St. Louis, 1968, PhD, 1974. Asst. prof. Dept. Econs., W.V. U., Morgantown, 1970-75, assoc. prof., 1975-80; acting asst. dean Grad. Sch., W.V. U., Morgantown, 1977-78; exec. dir. Bureau of Bus. Rsch., W.V. U., Morgantown, 1985—; dir. Ctr. Econs. Rsch., W.Va. U., Morgantown, 1985—; acting assoc. dean Coll. Bus. and Econs., W.V. U., Morgantown, 1985-86; assoc. dean rsch. and outreach Coll. Bus. and Econs. W.Va. U., Morgantown, 1994—; cons. Nat. Regulatory Rsch. Inst., Columbia, Ohio, 1980-81; cons., expert witness W.Va. Human Rights Commn., Charleston, 1984; expert witness W.Va. Atty. Gen., 1987-88, Ashland Oil, 1992-93. Author: (monograph) Guidelines for Attracting Private Capital to Corps of Engineers Projects, 1977; The Cost of Doing Business in West Virginia, 1988; (book) Power from the Appalachians, 1989; co-editor: (book) West Virginia in the Nineties: Policies for Econ. Progress; contbr. articles to profl. jours. Pres. Cheat Canyon Park Homeowners, Morgantwon, 1979-87, Monongalia Arts Ctr., 1980-81; bd. dirs., treas. Friends of W.Va. Pub. Radio, Charleston, 1985-93, chmn., 1989-91; sec.-treas. Cheat Neck Pub. Svc. Dist., 1989-95, Main Street Morgantown, 1994—; mem. Monongalia County Econ. Devel. Authority, 1994—; assoc. dean. rsch. and outreach Coll. of Bus. and Econ. W.Va. U., 1995—. Mem. Am. Econ. Assn., Am. Statis. Assn., Regional Sci. Assn., So. Econ. Assn., Rotary. Home: 3202 Deerfield Ct Morgantown WV 26505-8612 Office: Bureau of Bus Rsch WV U PO Box 6025 Morgantown WV 26506-6052

WITT, WALTER FRANCIS, JR., lawyer; b. Richmond, Va., Feb. 18, 1933; s. Walter Francis and Evelyn Virginia (Riggleman) W.; m. Rosemary Winter, Sept. 5, 1964; children: Leslie Anne, Walter Francis III. BS, U. Richmond, 1954, JD, 1966. Bar: Va. 1966, D.C. 1974. Assoc. Hunton and Williams, Richmond, 1966-74, ptnr., 1974—. Contbr. articles to profl. jours. 1st lt. U.S. Army, 1955-57. Mem. ABA (chmn. real property com. sect. gen. practice 1995—, dep. chair urban, state and local govt. com. 1995—, sect. gen. practice), Va. Bar Assn., Richmond Bar Assn., D.C. Bar Assn., Phi Beta Kappa, Phi Delta Phi. Home: 8901 Tresco Rd Richmond VA 23229-7725 Office: Hunton & Williams Riverfront Plaza East Twr 951 E Byrd St Richmond VA 23219-4040

WITTBRODT, EDWIN STANLEY, consultant, former bank executive, former air force officer; b. Flint, Mich., Aug. 13, 1918; s. Stanley Frank and Marie (Ross) W.; m. Joan Helen Miller, Apr. 22, 1950; children: Stephanie Rita, Candace Lee, Edwin Stanley. Student, Gen. Motors Inst. Tech., 1936-38, Grad. Sch. Dept. Agr., 1950-51, Indsl. Coll. Armed Forces, 1961-62, George Washington U., 1962, U. So. Calif., 1963-64. Joined U.S. Army, 1941, commd. 2d lt., 1942; advanced through grades to brig. gen. USAF, 1968; various assignments U.S., 1941-49; budget officer Hdqrs. USAF, 1949-53, 56-61; dir. budget and acctg. Hdqrs. N.E. Air Command, Nfld., 1953-56; comptroller space systems div. Los Angeles, 1962-64; comptroller aero., systems div. Wright-Patterson AFB, 1964-66; asst. comptroller USAF, 1966-67; dir. acctg. and fin. Hdqrs. USAF, 1967-68; asst. comptroller air force for acctg. and fin., comdr. Air Force Acctg. and Fin. Ctr., Denver, 1968-71; v.p. systems Cen. Bank Denver, 1971-81, v.p. info. resources mgmt., 1981-84; dir. Computer Congenerics Corp. Colo., Hasa Corp. Co-chmn. Combined Fed. Campaign, Denver, 1968-87; Hon. dir. USO, Denver, 1968-71, mem. council, 1971-87 . Decorated D.S.M., Legion of Merit, Soldier's medal, Commendation medal with oak leaf cluster; recipient Gen. Jimmy Doolittle Disting. Fellow award, Flint No. Alumni Assn. Disting. Fellow award, 1990, Treas. Dept. Pioneer in Elec. Commerce award, 1995. Mem. Am. Soc. Mil. Comptrollers (past pres. Washington chpt., nat. v.p. 1968-70, pres. Denver chpt. 1971-72), Assn. Govt. Accountants, Assn. Mil. Banks (dir. 1974-84), Am. Inst. Banking, Denver C. of C. (chmn. mil. affairs com. 1979-82), Aurora C. of C. (mil. affairs coun. 1987—), Air Force Assn. (v.p. N. Colo. 1971-72, pres. Silver and Gold chpt. 1972-73, state treas. 1976-83, pres. Mile High chpt. 1987-88). Club: Columbine Country. Home: 10 Niblick Ln Columbine Valley CO 80123 *I have adopted two attitudes that I believe assisted me in all of my undertakings: (1)—that of being what I call a "responsible non-conformist" and (2)—"no problems—just opportunities.".*

WITTBRODT, FREDERICK JOSEPH, JR., automotive designer; b. Detroit, Feb. 6, 1955; s. Frederick Joseph Sr. and Hilda Lottie (Neubert) W.; m. Deborah Carrie Kay, Apr. 11, 1992; stepchildren: Angela Defer, Michael Defer II; children from previous marriage: Robin Lynn, Daniel Joseph. Grad., Philpot Sch. Automotive Body Drafting, Royal Oak, Mich., 1977, Entech. Engring., Troy, Mich., 1984. Designer Modern Engring Co.-Design, Troy, Mich., 1977-78, Detroit Indsl. engring., Troy, Mich., 1978-80, Engring Tech., Ltd., Troy, Mich., 1980-86, Pioneer Engring., Dearborn, Mich., 1986, APD, Dearborn, Mich., 1988-89, Mega-Tech. Engring., Warren, Mich., 1989-90, Uni-Tech, Madison Heights, Mich., 1990-91, Harman at Harvard, Southfield, Mich., 1991; sr. automotive designer Lincoln Tech. at Schlegel, Madison Heights, 1991-92; sr. designer, surface devel. specialist Resource Techs. at Harvard Industries, Farmington Hills, Mich., 1992-95; sr. designer, surface devel. specialist, resource tech. Brytax-Rainford, Inc., Marysville, Mich., 1996—; owner Wittbrodt Design Co., Chesterfield, Mich. Mem. NRA, Internat. Platform Soc. Avocations: rifle and bow hunting, 4x4 wheeling, fishing, boating. Home: 52286 Lexington Ln Chesterfield MI 48051-2182

WITTCOFF, HAROLD AARON, chemist; b. Marion, Ind., July 3, 1918; s. Morris and Bessie (Pruss) W.; m. Dorothy Brochin, 1946; 2 sons. A.B. magna cum laude, DePauw U., 1940; Ph.D., Northwestern U., 1943; grad., Advanced Mgmt. Program, Harvard U., 1964. With Gen. Mills, Inc., Mpls., 1943-79; head chem. research dept. Gen. Mills, Inc., 1952-56, Dir. chem. research, 1956-67, v.p., dir. chem. research and devel., 1967-69, v.p., dir. corp. research, 1969-79; dir. research and devel. Koor Chems., Beer Sheva, Israel, 1979-82; dir. process evaluation and research planning Chem Systems, Tarrytown, N.Y., 1982-85; sci. adviser Chem. Systems Internat., Tarrytown, N.Y., 1985—; adj. prof. chemistry U. Minn., 1973-82. Author: The Phosphatides, 1951, Industrial Organic Chemistry: A Perspective 2 vols. 1980; Pharmaceutical Chemicals in Perspective, 1989, Industrial Organic Chemicals, 1996. Recipient Minn. award Am. Chem. Soc., 1976. Mem. Phi Beta Kappa, Sigma Xi, Phi Eta Sigma. Patentee in field. Home: Box 307 Scarborough Manor Scarborough NY 10510

WITTE, MARLYS HEARST, internist, educator; b. N.Y.C., 1934. MD, NYU Sch. Medicine, 1960. Intern N.C. Meml. Hosp., Chapel Hill, 1960-61; resident Bellevue Hosp. Ctr., N.Y.C., 1961-63; fellow NYU Hosp., Washington U., St. Louis, 1964-66; prof. surgery U. Ariz., 1965-69, 69—; attending internist Ariz. Health Sci. Ctr., Tucson, 1965-69, 69—. Rsch. fellow Am. Heart Assn., 1995-96. Mem. AAAS, Am. Hosp. Assn., Alpha Omega Alpha. Office: U Ariz Coll Medicine 1501 N Campbell Ave Tucson AZ 85724-0001

WITTE, MERLIN MICHAEL, oil company executive; b. Los Angeles, Mar. 28, 1926; s. Anthony A. and Julia (Macke) W.; m. Donna Patricia Hurth, Jan. 22, 1949; children: James Anthony, Daniel Michael, Catherine Ann, Michael Leon, Robert Joseph, Joseph William, Anne Marie, William Benson, Janet Mary. B.A., Loyola U., Los Angeles, 1949. With IRS, U.S. Treasury Dept., 1949-51; investment, tax mgr. McCulloch Motors Corp., also Robert P. McCulloch, 1951-55; pres., gen. mgr., dir. McCulloch Oil Corp., Los Angeles, 1956-80; pres., dir. Merlin Assocs., Inc., Los Angeles, 1980—, M.M. Witte & Assocs., Inc., Los Angeles, 1980—; mgr., chief exec. United Oil Producers, Los Angeles, 1984-86; bd. dirs. Kent Fin. Svcs., Inc., Search Exploration, Inc.; bd. dirs., chmn. McCulloch Energy, Inc., 1991-95; co-chmn. The Am. Drilling Co., L.L.C., 1995—. Mem. bd. regents Loyola Marymount U., LA., 1991—. Served with USAAF, 1944-45. Mem. Ind. Oil and Gas Producers Assn., Ind. Petroleum Assn., Western, West Cen. Tex. oil and gas assns., Town Hall, Bel-Air Country Club (pres. 1990-91), PGA West Golf Club.

WITTEBORT, ROBERT JOHN, JR., lawyer; b. Chgo., Dec. 29, 1947; s. Robert John and Marguerite (Shaughnessy) W. B.A., Yale U., 1969; J.D., Notre Dame U., 1974. Bar: Ill. 1974, U.S. Dist. Ct. (no. dist.) Ill. 1974, U.S. Ct. Appeals (7th cir.) 1975, U.S. Tax Ct. 1977, U.S. Ct. Mil. Appeals 1982. Assoc. Hopkins & Sutter, Chgo., 1974-77; gen. counsel, asst. dir. Ill. Housing Devel. Authority, Chgo., 1977-82; ptnr. Chapman and Cutler, Chgo., 1982-90; sr. ptnr. Law Offices Robert J. Wittebort, Jr., 1990—; co-founder, exec. v.p. Chgo. Bldg. Svcs., Inc., 1990—. Contbg. editor: Business Law, 4th edit., 1977. Contbr. Notre Dame Lawyer, 1974. Bd. dirs. Music of the Baroque, Metropolitan Housing Devel. Corp., Chgo. Served to comdr. USNR, 1969—. Mem. Nat. Assn. Bond Lawyers, Naval Order U.S. (vice comdr.-gen.), Ill. Commandery Naval Order U.S. (comdr. 1987-88), Lambda Alpha. Republican. Clubs: Chgo., Saddle & Cycle (Chgo.).

WITTEN, DAVID MELVIN, radiology educator; b. Trenton, Mo., Aug. 16, 1926; s. Buford Isom and Mary Louise (Melvin) W.; m. Netta Lee Watkins, Dec. 23, 1950; children—David Melvin, II, Michael Lee. Student, Trenton Jr. Coll., 1943-44, 46-47; A.B., Washington U., St. Louis, 1950, M.D., 1954; M.S. in Radiology, Mayo Grad. Sch. Medicine, U. Minn., 1960. Diplomate: Am. Bd. Radiology. Intern Virginia Mason Hosp., Seattle, 1954-55; practice medicine specializing in family medicine Trenton, Mo., 1955-57; fellow in radiology Mayo Clinic/Mayo Found., Rochester, Minn., 1957-60; cons. in diagnostic roentgenology Mayo Clinic, 1960-70; instr. Mayo Grad. Sch. Medicine, Rochester, 1960-66; asst. prof. radiology Mayo Grad. Sch. Medicine, 1966-70; pvt. practice medicine specializing in radiology Aberdeen, Wash., 1970-71; clin. assoc. prof. U. Wash., 1970-71; prof. diagnostic radiology, chmn. dept. diagnostic radiology U. Ala., Birmingham, 1971-82; diagnostic radiologist in chief Univ. Hosp., Birmingham, 1971-82; prof., chmn. dept. radiology U. Mo., Columbia, 1982-87, prof. emeritus, 1987—; pres. U. Ala. Health Services Found., 1973-75. Author: Atlas of Tumor Radiology-The Breast, 1969, Clinical Urography, 1977; contbr. articles on radiology of breast cancer, urologic and gastrointestinal disease to profl. jours.; mem. editorial bd. Am. Jour. Roentgenology, 1976-87, Applied Radiology, 1978-87, Urologic Radiology, 1979-87, Radiographics, 1983-87. Served with USNR, 1944-46. Fellow Am. Coll. Radiology; mem. Radiol. Soc. N.Am., Am. Roentgen Ray Soc., AAAS, Soc. Genitourinary Radiology (pres. 1981-82), Assn. Univ. Radiologists, AMA, Mo. Radiol. Soc. (pres. 1988-89), Mo. State Med. Assn., Can. Assn. Radiologists (hon.), Audubon Soc. (editor The Bluebird (Mo.) chpt. 1990-95). Home: 601 Covered Bridge Rd Columbia MO 65203-9562 Office: Univ Mo Health Scis Ctr 1 Hospital Dr Columbia MO 65201-5276

WITTEN, LOUIS, physics educator; b. Balt., Apr. 13, 1921; s. Abraham and Bessie (Perman) W.; m. Lorraine Wollach, Mar. 27, 1949 (dec. 1987); children: Edward, Celia, Matthew, Jesse; m. Francis L. White, Jan. 2, 1992. B.E., Johns Hopkins U., 1941, Ph.D., 1951; B.S., NYU, 1944. Research assoc. Princeton U., N.J., 1951-53; research assoc. U. Md., College Park, 1953-54; staff scientist Lincoln Lab., MIT, 1954-55; assoc. dir. Martin Marietta Research Lab., Balt., 1955-68; prof. physics U. Cin., 1968—; trustee Gravity Research Found. Editor: Gravitation: An Introduction to Current Research, 1962, Relativity: Procs. of Relative Conf. in Midwest of 1969, 1970, Symposium on Asymptotic Structure of Space-Time, 1976; patentee in field; contbr. numerous articles to sci. jours. Served to 1st lt. USAF, 1942-46. Fulbright lectr. Weismann Inst. Scis., Rehovot, Israel, 1963-64. Fellow Am. Phys. Soc.; mem. Am. Math. Soc., Internat. Astron. Union, AAAS. Office: Univ Cincinnati Dept Physics Cincinnati OH 45221

WITTEN, MARK LEE, lung injury research scientist, educator; b. Amarillo, Tex., June 23, 1953; s. Gerald Lee and Polly Ann (Warren) W.; m. Christine Ann McKee, June 10, 1988; 1 child, Brandon Lee. BS in Phys. Sci., Emporia State U., 1975; PhD, Ind. U., 1983. Postdoctoral fellow U. Ariz., Tucson, 1983-88; instr. in medicine Harvard Med. Sch., Boston, Mass., 1988-90; rsch. assoc. prof. U. Ariz., Tucson, 1990—; cons. Ames Life Scis. Space Sta. program NASA; grant cons. USAF, Washington, 1991—. Contbr. articles to profl. jours. Grantee USAF, 1991—, Tng. grant Dept. of Def., 1992—, NIH, 1991—, Upjohn Pharm., 1992, Dept. of Army, 1993. Mem. AIAA, Am. Physiol. Soc., Soc. Critical Care Medicine, Am. Thoracic Soc., N.Y. Acad. Scis., Soc. Toxicology. Methodist. Achievements include first animal model of cigarette smoke exposure to show cigarette smoke increases lung permeability, animal model of passive cigarette smoke, to demonstrate pulmonary edema in a microgravity model. Office: U Ariz Dept Pediatrics AHSC 1501 N Campbell Ave Tucson AZ 85724

WITTEN, THOMAS JEFFERSON, JR., mathematics educator; b. Welch, W.Va., Feb. 10, 1942; s. Thomas Jefferson and Gladys Marium (McMeans) W.; m. Barbara Phyllis Honaker, Feb. 20, 1965; children: Thomas Jefferson III, Rebecca A. Dye, Timothy A., Stephanie L. Dye. BS in Edn., Concord Coll., Athens, W.Va., 1965; MA in Edn., W.Va. U., Morgantown, 1971. Cert. tchr., Va., W.Va. Tchr. math. McDowell County Schs., Gary (W.Va.) High Sch., 1965-71, asst. prin., 1971-73; asst. prin. inst. Tazewell County Schs., Richlands (Va.) High Sch., 1973-87; secondary supr. Jackson County Schs., Ripley, W.Va., 1987-88; asst. prof. math. Southwest Va. Community Coll., Richlands, 1988—; math. cons. S.W. Va. C.C. Computer Math. Grant Project, Richlands, 1988-90; coord. S.W. Va. Tech Prep Consortium, 1992—. Mem. sch. bd. Tazewell (Va.) County Schs., 1990-91, 95—; faculty senate pres. South Va. C.C., 1992-94. Recipient K-8 Tchr. Improvement grant, 1992-93. Mem. Va. C.C. Assn., Mountain Math Alliance (chmn. 1909—), PTA (life, pres. 1979-81), Richlands Rotary (pres. 1989-91), Masons (jr. deacon 1966-68), Shriners. Democrat. Methodist. Avocations: painting, cross-stitch, reading, computers, old cars, writing. Home: 737 Terry Dr Richlands VA 24641-2616 Office: SW Va C C Box SVCC Richlands VA 24641

WITTENBERG, JON ALBERT, accountant; b. Valparaiso, Ind., Mar. 22, 1939; s. Fred E. and Elizabeth (DeWaal) W.; m. Joann S. Zachwieja, May 13, 1967; children: Brad, Glen, Pam. BS, Ind. U., 1961. CPA, Ill. Auditor Ernst & Young, Chgo., 1961-66; fin. analyst Amoco Chems., Chgo., 1966-69; contr. Nat. Van Lines, Broadview, Ill., 1969-76, Consol. Millinerey, Chgo., 1976—. Mem. Am. Inst. CPA's, Ill. Soc. CPA's, Inst. Mgmt. Accts. Home: 1297 W New Britton Dr Hoffman Estates IL 60195-1764 Office: Consol Millinerey Co 18 S Michigan Ave Ste 605 Chicago IL 60603-3206

WITTER, RICHARD LAWRENCE, veterinarian, educator; b. Bangor, Maine, Sept. 10, 1936; s. John Franklin and Verna Harriet (Church) W.; m. Joan Elizabeth Denny, June 30, 1962; children—Jane Katherine, Steven Franklin. B.S., Mich. State U., 1958, D.V.M., 1960; M.S., Cornell U., 1962, Ph.D., 1964. Rsch. veterinarian Agrl. Rsch. Svc., U.S. Dept. Agr., East Lansing, Mich., 1964-75, dir. Avian Disease and Oncology Lab., 1975—; clin. prof. pathology Mich. State U., East Lansing, 1965—. Contbr. articles to profl. jours. Recipient Disting. Alumni award Coll. Vet. Medicine, Mich. State U., 1985, Disting. Service award USDA, 1985. Mem. AVMA, Am. Assn. Avian Pathologists (P.P. Levine award 1967, 81, 88, 92, Upjohn Achievement award 1992), Poultry Sci. Assn. (CPC Internat. award 1976), Mich. Vet. Med. Assn., World Vet. Poultry Assn. (B. Rispens rsch. award 1983). Lodge: Kiwanis. Avocations: piano, hunting, fishing, gardening. Home: 3880 Sheldrake Ave Okemos MI 48864-3646 Office: Avian Disease and Oncology Lab 3606 E Mt Hope Rd East Lansing MI 48823-5338

WITTHUHN, BURTON ORRIN, university official; b. Allentown, Pa., Aug. 22, 1934; s. Ray Arthur and Mae Marcella (Kline) W.; m. Patricia King, June 24, 1961; children: Jonathan, Andrew. BS, Kutztown (Pa.) U., 1956; MEd, Pa. State U., 1962, PhD, 1968. Tchr. Allentown (Pa.) Pub. Schs., 1956-63; teaching asst., assoc. Pa. State U., University Park, 1963-66, research asst., 1965-66; asst. prof. Ohio State U., Columbus, 1967-70; prof., chmn. dept. geography Edinboro (Pa.) State Coll., 1970-79, assoc. v.p. acad. affairs, 1980-83; provost, v.p. acad. affairs Edinboro Univ. of Pa., 1984-88; provost, v.p. acad. affairs Western Ill. U., Macomb, 1988-93, acting pres., 1993, provost, v.p. acad. affairs, 1994—; vis. rsch. prof. Nat. Taiwan Normal U., 1978; cons. Project Africa/Carnegie-Mellon U., Pitts., 1967-70; mem. mid. states evaluation team Griffiss AFB, Utica, N.Y., 1987, Cortland (N.Y.) U., 1962; mem. mid. states periodic rev. team, Phila., 1986; mem. mid. states evaluation team in conjunction with Am. Optometric Assn. accreditation visit SUNY Sch. Optometry, 1987; mem. evaluation team Pa. Dept. Edn., U. Pitts., 1988; mem. accreditation team U. Calif. Coll. Optometry, Berkeley, 1990, Ferris State U., Big Rapids, Mich., 1991, U. Houston, 1992; mem. mid. states evaluation team Indiana U. of Pa., 1995; cons., core evaluator North Cen. Assn., 1994—; vice chmn. Quad Cities Grad. Ctr., 1991—; mem. nat. screening com. for Africa, Inst. of Internat. Edn., 1994, 95. Author: Discovery in Geography, 1976; mem. editl. bd. Pa. Geographer, Chronicle of CQI; contbr. chpts. to books in field. Mem. Edinboro Planning & Zoning Commn., 1973-77. Recipient Disting. Alumnus award Kutztown U., 1990; Fulbright Hays fellow, Ethiopia, Kenya, Uganda, 1965. Mem. Nat. Coun. Geog. Edn. (exec. bd. 1977-80, mem. award com. for region IV 1981—), Pa. Coun. Geog. Edn. (exec. sec. 1976-79, pres. 1975-76, Outstanding Prof. award 1978), Bishops Com. Democrat. Episcopalian. Lodge: Rotary (pres. Edinboro club 1972-73). Avocations: reading, golf, photography, model constrn. Home: 1106 Bayberry Ln Macomb IL 61455 Office: Western Ill U Sherman Hall Adams St Macomb IL 61455

WITTICH, BRENDA JUNE, religious organization executive, minister; b. Muncie, Ind., Dec. 19, 1946; d. Plano Brentie and Norma June (Huggins) Gossett; m. Chester Edward Wittich, Dec. 24, 1980; 1 child, September Leigh Noonan. Lic., Morris Pratt Inst. Assn., 1979, postgrad., 1983-86. Ordained minister Nat. Spiritualist Assn. of Churches, 1986. Pastor Fifth

Spiritualist Ch., St. Louis, 1988—. Co-author, editor: National Spiritualist Association Churches Public Relations Handbook, 1992; co-author booklet: Spiritualism - Pathway of Light, 1992; contbr. articles to Nat. Spiritualist Mag. Mem. St. Louis Pub. Sch. Clergy Leaders Forum, 1991-92, Tchrs. for Nat. Spiritualist Assn. of Chs. Ednl. Ctr.-Psychology and Parlimentary Procedures. Mem. Nat. Hemlock Soc., Nat. Spiritualist Assn. of Chs. (trustee 1990-92, supt. pub. rels. 1990-94, v.p. bd. trustees 1992-94, pres. bd. trustees 1994), Inst. Noetic Scis. Avocations: travel, reading. Home: 3903 Connecticut St Saint Louis MO 63116-3905 Office: Nat Spiritualist Assn Chs 13 Cottage Row PO Box 217 Lily Dale NY 14752 *Idealism is not dead, it lies dormant within all people. It is the responsibility of those of us who possess it to assist awakening it in others. We must dream our lofty dreams and see them fulfilled.*

WITTICH, JOHN JACOB, retired college president, educational administrator, corporation consultant; b. Huntley, Ill., Nov. 13, 1921; s. John and Eva (Karl) W.; m. Leah Elliott, Apr. 2, 1944; children: Karen Ann Zvonar, Jane Ellen Tock, John Elliott. B.A., DePauw U., 1943, LL.D. (hon.), 1971; M.A., U. N.Mex., 1949; Ph.D., Stanford U., 1952; L.H.D. (hon.), Ill. Coll., 1979; D.P.S. (hon.), MacMurray Coll., 1980. Tchr. Albuquerque High Sch., 1948-49; teaching asst. Stanford, 1949-51; asst. prof. psychology Coll. of Pacific, Stockton, Calif., 1951-52; dean of admissions, dir. scholarships, assoc. prof. DePauw U., Greencastle, Ind., 1952-61; exec. dir. Coll. Center of Finger Lakes, Corning, N.Y., 1961-63, Coll. Student Personnel Inst., Claremont, Calif., 1963-68; dir. grad. studies in student pers. Claremont Grad. Sch., 1963-68; pres. MacMurray Coll., Jacksonville, Ill., 1968-80; program dir. Fla. Assn. Colls. and Univs., 1980-84; dir. higher edn. program Stetson U., 1981-88; v.p. Capital Formation Counselors, Inc., Belleaire Bluffs, Fla., 1983—. Contbr. articles to popular and profl. jours. Mem. exec. com. Divsn. Higher Edn., Ctrl. Ill. Conf. of United Meth. Ch., 1968-80; mem. exec. com. Fedn. Independent Ill. Colls. and Univs. and Assoc. Colls. Ill.; mem. non-pub. adv. com. Ill. Bd. Higher Edn., 1972-78; mem. Nat. Merit Scholarship Selection Com., 1956, 61; cons. Calif. Gov.'s Conf. on Edn., 1965, on Youth, 1966; trustee Fla. Endowment for Humanities, 1982-85; presdl. counsellor Stetson U., 1987—; bd. dirs. DeLand House Next Door, 1990-94; adv. com. West Volusia County Hosps., 1992—. With USMC, 1943-46, PTO. Recipient Alumni citation DePauw U., 1994; Rockefeller fellow Aspen Inst. for Humanistic Studies, 1979. Mem. AAUP, APA, Am. Coll. Pers. Assn. (commn. chmn.), Nat. Assn. Coll. Admissions Counselors (exec. bd. 1955-58), Cen. States Coll. Assn. (exec. com. 1969-77, sec.-treas. 1970-77), 4th Marine Divsn. Assn., Sigma Chi.

WITTING, CHRIS J., electrical manufacturing executive; b. Cranford, N.J., Apr. 7, 1915; s. Nicholas and Anne (Begasse) W.; B.S., N.Y. U., 1941; grad. Am. Inst. Banking; student Fordham Law Sch.; D.Eng. (hon.), Clarkson Coll. Tech.; m. Grace Orrok, Oct. 8, 1938; children—Leland James, Anne Kristin, Nancy Jane, Chris J. Exec. asst. Guaranty Trust Co., 1933-36, N.Y. Trust Co., 1936-39; mgr. Price Waterhouse & Co., 1939-41; comptroller, treas. U.S.O. Camp Shows, Inc., 1941-46; mng. dir. Allen B. DuMont Labs., Inc., 1946-53; pres. Westinghouse Broadcasting Co., 1953-54, group v.p. and gen. mgr. consumer products group, Westinghouse Electric Corp., 1954-64; v.p. exec. asst. to chmn. and pres. Internat. Tel.& Tel. Corp., 1964-65; pres., chief exec. officer, dir. Crouse-Hinds Co., Syracuse, N.Y., 1965-75, chmn., chief exec. officer, 1975-82; vice chmn. bd. Cooper Industries Inc., Houston. Chmn. Pub. Auditorium Authority of Pitts. and Allegheny County, 1963-64; chmn. bd. trustees Syracuse U., 1975-93. Mem. Nat. Electric Mfrs. Assn. (chmn. bd. govs., bd. dirs.), Electronic Industries Assn. (bd. govs. 1961-62, dir. 1960-63), Nat. Planning Assn. (nat. council), Am. Mgmt. Assn. (mem. mktg. planning council), Elec. Mfrs. Club, Met. Devel. Assn. Syracuse and Onondaga County, N.Y. (dir.). Clubs: Athletic, Union League, Century, Onondaga Country, Athletic (Syracuse). Home: 518 Bradford Pky Syracuse NY 13224-1804 Office: State Tower Bldg Syracuse NY 13202

WITTLER, SHIRLEY JOYCE, former state official, state commissioner; b. Ravenna, Nebr., Oct. 10, 1927; d. Earl William and Minnie Ethel (Frink) Wade; m. LeRoy F. Wittler, Dec. 31, 1946; children: Julie Diane, Barbara Liane. Student, U. Nebr., 1944-47. Real estate saleswoman Harrington Assocs., Lincoln, Nebr., 1965-69; real estate broker Tom Searl Realty, Inc., Cheyenne, Wyo., 1970-76; dep. state treas. Wyo., 1976-78; state treas., 1979-83; chmn. state tax commn. and bd. equalization State of Wyo., 1985-90; ret., 1990. Pres. LWV, Lincoln, 1965-69; bd. dirs. LWV Wyo., 1970-72; fin. chmn. Republican Central Com. Laramie County, Wyo., 1974-76; chmn. Laramie County Pres. Ford Com., 1976; Rep. precinct committeewoman, 1972-77; mem. Laramie County Library Bd., 1976, Community Devel. Adv. Bd., 1974-77. Mem. Cheyenne Bd. Realtors (pres. 1976, Cheyenne Realtor of Yr. 1974), Women's Civic League (treas. 1974, legis. chmn. 1975-76). Lutheran. Home: 5022 Hoy Rd Cheyenne WY 82009-4850

WITTLICH, GARY EUGENE, music theory educator; b. Belleville, Ill., Dec. 3, 1934; s. Marvin Oscar W. and Erma Carrie (Garlich) Jackson Wittlich; m. Barbara L. Casey, Jan. 4, 1958 (div. Feb. 1969); children: M. Kent, Kristi L.; m. Mildred Elizabeth Read, Mar. 17, 1971. B.M.Ed., So. Ill. U., 1957, M.Mus., 1959; Ph.D., U. Iowa, 1969. Asst. prof. music Upper Iowa U., Fayette, 1959-63; prof. music, grad. studies in music theory Ind. U., Bloomington, 1975-94, assoc. dean Office of Info. Tech., 1995—, dir. of computing Sch. of Music, 1989-95; Meadows disting. vis. prof. music So. Meth. U., Dallas, 1982-83; vis. prof. U. Mich., Ann Arbor, 1974; dir. Ctr. for Profl. Devel. in Music Tech., CMS/ATMI, 1995—; cons. U. Del. Music Videodisc Series, NEH, 1982-85; mem. music test com. Ednl. Testing Svc., Princeton, N.J., 1983-85, chmn., 1986-90. Author: (with C. Lee Humphries) Ear Training: An Approach Through Music Literature, 1974, (with others) Aspects of Twentieth-Century Music, 1975, (with J. Schaffer and L. Babb) Microcomputers and Music, 1986, (with D. Martin) Tonal Harmony for the Keyboard, 1988. Served with U.S. Army, 1957, 61-62. NSF grantee Ind. U., 1970; fellow Inst. for Acad. Tech., 1992. Mem. Assn. for Tech. in Music Instrn. (founding), Coll. Music Soc. (bd. mem. for theory 1987-89), Soc. Music Theory (exec. bd. 1982-85, pres. 1988-91). Home: 3101 David Dr Bloomington IN 47401-4472 Office: Sch Music Ind U Bloomington IN 47405

WITTLINGER, TIMOTHY DAVID, lawyer; b. Dayton, Ohio, Oct. 12, 1940; s. Charles Frederick and Dorothy Elizabeth (Golden) W.; m. Diane Cleo Dominy, May 20, 1967; children: Kristine Elizabeth, David Matthew. BS in Math., Purdue U., 1962; JD with distinction, U. Mich., 1965. Bar: Mich. 1966, U.S. Dist. Ct. (ea. dist.) Mich. 1966, U.S. Ct. Appeals (6th cir.) 1968, U.S. Supreme Ct. 1971. Assoc. Hill Lewis (formerly Hill, Lewis, Adams, Goodrich & Tait), Detroit, 1965-72, ptnr., 1973—, head litigation dept., 1976—; mem. profl. assistance com. U.S. Dist. Ct. (ea. dist.) Mich., 1981-82. Mem. house of deps. Episc. Ch., N.Y.C., 1979—; vice chmn. Robert Whitaker Sch. Theology, 1983-87; sec. bd. trustees Episc. Ch., Diocese of Mich., Detroit, 1983—, sec. conv. Episc. Diocese Mich., 1990—, mem., sec. Episcopal nat. econ. justice implementation com., 1988—, mem. Episc. nat. exec. coun., 1991—; active Nat. Episc. Jubilee Minstry Com., Nat. Episc. Coalition for Social Witness and Justice, Fifth Province Episc. Ecclesiastical Ct. Appeal; bd. dirs. Episc. Student Found., U. Mich., 1990-93; chair Grubb Inst. Behavioral Studies Ltd., Washington, 1986—. Mem. ABA, State Bar Mich., Nat. Bd. Trial Advocacy (cert.), Engring. Soc. Detroit. Home: 736 N Glenhurst Dr Birmingham MI 48009-1143 Office: Hill Lewis 255 S Woodward Ave Birmingham MI 48009-6182

WITTMANN, OTTO, art museum executive; b. Kansas City, Mo., Sept. 1, 1911; s. Otto and Beatrice Knox (Billingsley) W.; m. Margaret Carlisle Hill, June 9, 1945; children—William Hill, John Carlisle. Student, Country Day Sch., Kansas City; A.B., Harvard U., 1933; postgrad., 1937-38, postgrad. Carnegie scholar, summer 1937; LL.D., U. Toledo; D.F.A., Hillsdale Coll., Bowling Green State U., U. Mich., Kenyon Coll., Skidmore Coll. Curator prints Nelson Gallery Art, Kansas City, 1933-37; instr. history of art Emerson Sch., Boston, 1937-38; curator Hyde Collection, Glens Falls, N.Y., 1938-41; instr. history of art Skidmore Coll., Saratoga Springs, N.Y., 1938-41; asst. dir. Portland (Oreg.) Mus. Art, 1941; asso. dir. Toledo Mus. Art, 1946-59, trustee, 1958—, dir., 1959-76, dir. emeritus, 1977—; v.p., cons., art advisor, 1977—; trustee, cons. Los Angeles County Mus. Art, 1977-78; vice chmn., trustee, cons. J. Paul Getty Trust, 1977—; organizer exhbns. art activities Am. museums USIA, 1953-55; editorial cons. Gazette des Beaux Arts; vice chmn. Nat. Collection Fine Arts Commn.; bd. dirs. Toledo Trust Co.; cons. Clark Art Inst., 1990—. Editorial chmn. Toledo Mus. Catalogue of European Paintings and Guide to Collections; writer numerous museum catalogues, profl. articles. Founding mem. Nat. Council Arts; mem. mus. panel NEH; chmn. adv. panel Nat. Found. Arts and Humanities; mem. art adv. panel IRS; mem. nat. arts accessions com. U.S. embassies; mem. U.S.-ICOM Nat. Com.; former sec. gen. com. pour Musées du Verre, ICOM; founding mem. Ohio Arts Council; sponsor Nat. Trust Sch., Attingham, Shropshire, Eng. Served to maj. AUS, USAAF, OSS, 1941-46. Decorated officer Legion of Honor, France, officer Order Orange Nassau, Netherlands, comdr. Arts and Letters France; comdr. Order of Merit Italy). Fellow Museums Assn. (Eng.); mem. Intermus. Conservation Assn. (pres. 1955-56, trustee), Harvard Soc. Contemporary Art (co-dir. 1931-33), Assn. Art Mus. Dirs. (pres. 1961-62, 71-72), Am. Assn. Museums (former v.p., Disting. Service to Mus. award 1987), Coll. Art Assn., Archeol. Inst. Am., Internat. Inst. for Conservation of Hist. and Artistic Works, Soc. Archtl. Historians, Verien der Freunde Antiker Kunst, Am. Soc. French Legion Honneur, Alliance Francaise de Toledo (trustee), Phi Kappa Phi. Episcopalian (vestryman). Clubs: Traveller's (London); Century Assn. (N.Y.C.); Toledo, Harvard (pres. 1956-57), Rotary (pres. 1963-64). Home: 300 Hot Springs Rd Apt 163 Montecito CA 93108-2065 also: J Paul Getty Trust 401 Wilshire Blvd Santa Monica CA 90401-1455

WITTMER, JAMES FREDERICK, preventive medicine physician, educator; b. Carlinville, Ill., Dec. 30, 1932; s. Franklin Benjamin and Eva Caroline (Zihlman) W.; m. Juanita Lou Wilkey, June 29, 1962; children: Ellen, Carol, Nancy. MD, Washington U., St. Louis, 1957; MPH, Harvard U., 1961. Diplomate Am. Bd. Preventive Medicine. Intern U. Va. Hosp., Charlottesville, 1857-58; commd. capt. USAF, 1958, advanced through grades to col., 1971; ret., 1979; dean allied health U. Tex. Health Sci. Ctr., San Antonio, 1979-80; asst. med. dir. Conoco Oil Co., Ponca City, Okla., 1980-81; assoc. med. dir. Mobil Oil Corp., N.Y.C., 1981-83; dir. health, environ. and safety ITT, N.Y.C., 1983-95, corp. v.p., 1990-95; clin. prof. medicine Cornell U. Med. Coll., N.Y.C., 1984—; lectr. environ. medicine NYU, N.Y.C., 1984—; adj. prof. U. Tex. Sch. Pub. Health, Houston, 1987—; nat. coord. com. on clin. preventive svcs. USPHS, 1994—. Mem. med. and ins. com. Pres.'s Com. on Employment People with Disabilities, Washington, 1986-94, chmn., 1986-90. Fellow ACP, Am. Coll. Occupational and Environ. Medicine (bd. dirs. 1990—, sec. 1992-94), Am. Coll. Preventive Medicine, Aerospace Med. Assn., N.Y. Acad. Medicine; mem. AMA, Tex. Occupational Med. Assn., Physicians Sci. Soc. Avocations: running, skiing, boating. Home and Office: 159 Sabine Rd Boerne TX 78006-6217

WITTNER, LOREN ANTONOW, lawyer, former public relations executive; b. N.Y.C., May 2, 1938; s. Henry Warren and Miriam Margo (Antonow) W.; m. Judith Ginsberg, June 21, 1959 (div. Sept. 1972); children: Jennifer Leslie, Elizabeth Anne; m. Dianna Marks, Apr. 2, 1975. AB, Columbia U., 1958; JD, Harvard U., 1961. Bar: N.Y. 1961, Ill. 1966. Assoc. O'Dwyer & Bernstien, N.Y.C., 1961-62, Emil & Kobrin, N.Y.C., 1962-66; assoc. Antonow & Fink, Chgo., 1966-70, ptnr., 1970-77; rep. of Sec. U.S. Dept. Commerce, Chgo. and Washington, 1977-81; exec. v.p. Daniel J. Edelman, Inc., Chgo., 1981-90; ptnr. Winston & Strawn, Chgo., 1990-94; dir. client svcs. Lewis and Roca, Phoenix, 1994—; chmn. Midwest region Fed. Regional Council, 1978-79. Served with USAR, 1961-65. Mem. ABA. Avocation: classical music.

WITTREICH, JOSEPH ANTHONY, JR., English language educator, author; b. Cleve., July 23, 1939; s. Joseph Anthony and Mamie (Pucel) W. BA, U. Louisville, 1960, MA, 1961; PhD, Western Res. U., 1966. Faculty U. Wis., 1966-78; prof. English U. Md., 1978-88; disting. prof. English The Grad. Ctr. CUNY, 1988—, exec. officer English program, 1990-96; vis. prof. Calif. State U., L.A., 1972, U. Md., 1977, Brown U., 1978, Brandeis U., 1981, Grad. Ctr. CUNY, 1987, Queens Coll. CUNY, 1992, Hunter Coll. CUNY, 1994, Inst. Renaissance and Eighteenth-Century Studies, Folger Shakespeare Library, 1979. Author: The Romantics on Milton, 1970, Calm of Mind, 1971, Milton and the Line of Vision, 1975, Angel of Apocalypse, 1975, Visionary Poetics, 1979, Composite Orders, 1983, Image of That Horror, 1984, Interpreting Samson Agonistes, 1986, Feminist Milton, 1987. Nat. Endowment for Humanities grantee, 1974, 86; Nat. Endowment for Humanities-Huntington Library grantee, 1976; Guggenheim fellow, 1978. Mem. MLA, Renaissance Soc. Am., Milton Soc. Am. (pres. 1979, honored Miltonist 1993), Internat. Assn. Profs. English. Democrat. Roman Catholic. Home: 25 Central Park W Apt 2D New York NY 10023-7206 Office: CUNY Grad Ctr 33 W 42nd St New York NY 10036-8003

WITTROCK, MERLIN CARL, educational psychologist; b. Twin Falls, Idaho, Jan. 3, 1931; s. Herman C. and Mary Ellen (Baumann) W.; m. Nancy McNulty, Apr. 3, 1953; children: Steven, Catherine, Rebecca. BS in Biology, U. Mo., Columbia, 1953, MS in Ednl. Psychology, 1956; PhD in Ednl. Psychology, U. Ill., Urbana, 1960. Prof. grad. sch. edn. UCLA, 1960—, founder Ctr. Study Evaluation, chmn. div. ednl. psychology, chmn. faculty, exec. com.; univ. com. on disting. teaching; fellow Ctr. for Advanced Study in Behavioral Scis., 1967-68; vis. prof. U. Wis., U. Ill., Ind. U., Monash U., Australia; bd. dirs. Far West Labs., San Francisco; chmn. com. on evaluation and assessment L.A. Unified Sch. Dist.; mem. nat. adv. panel for math. scis. NRC of NAS, 1988-89; chmn. nat. bd. Nat. Ctr. for Rsch. in Math. Scis. Edn., chmn. charges com. UCLA; adv. bd. Kauffman Found., Kansas City, Mo., 1995—; bd. dirs. Western Edn. Lab. for Edn. Rsch. Author, editor: The Evaluation of Instruction, 1970, Changing Education, 1973, Learning and Instruction, 1977, The Human Brain, 1977, Danish transl., 1980, Spanish transl., 1982, The Brain and Psychology, 1980, Instructional Psychology: Education and Cognitive Processes of the Brain, Neuropsychological and Cognitive Processes of Reading, 1981, Handbook of Research on Teaching, 3d edit., 1986, The Future of Educational Psychology, 1989, Research in Learning and Teaching, 1990, Testing and Cognition, 1991, Generative Science Teaching, 1994, Metacognitiion 1995. Capt. USAF, 1953-55. Recipient Thorndike award for outstanding psychol. rsch., 1987, Disting. Tchr. of Univ. award UCLA, 1990; Ford Found. grantee. Fellow AAAS, APA (pres. divsn. ednl. psychology 1984-85, assn. coun. 1988-91, award for Outstanding Svc. to Ednl. Psychology 1991, 93, Disting. Svc. award for svc. to sci. adv. coun.), Am. Psychol. Soc., (charter fellow), Am. Ednl. Rsch. Assn. (chmn. ann. conv., chmn. publs. 1980-83, assn. coun. 1986-89, bd. dirs. 1987-89, chmn. com. on ednl. TV 1989—, Outstanding Contbns. award 1986, Outstanding Svc. award 1989); mem. Western Edn. Lab. for Edn. Rsch. (bd. dirs.), Phi Delta Kappa. Office: UCLA 3022 Moore Hall Los Angeles CA 90095

WITTRUP, RICHARD DERALD, health care executive; b. Marne, Iowa, Oct. 2, 1926; s. Otis Kermit and Ruby Beatrice (Olsen) W.; m. Marilyn Eleanor Sorensen, June 7, 1949; children: Kenton Lawrence, Alan Scott, Eleanor Elizabeth. BA in Econs., U. Mo., 1951; MBA, U. Chgo., 1955. Adminstrv. asst. U. Chgo. Hosp., 1952-57; adminstr. U. Ky. Hosp., Lexington, 1957-68; asst. exec. v.p. Brigham Women's Hosp., Boston, 1968-69, exec. v.p., 1970-78; adminstr. Herman Smith Assocs. Internat., Jeddah, Saudia Arabia, 1978-80, mng. dir., 1981-88, v.p. profl. affairs, 1980-88; asst. to pres. and CEO Henry Ford Health System, Detroit, 1988-93, corp. v.p., 1993—. Sgt. U.S. Army, 1945-47, Italy. Fellow ACHE; mem. Am. Hosp. Assn., Healthcare Execs. Study Soc. Baptist. Office: Henry Ford Health System 1 Ford Pl Detroit MI 48202-3450

WITTSTEIN, EDWIN FRANK, stage and film production designer; b. Mt. Vernon, N.Y., Apr. 7, 1929; s. Nathan Harry and Miriam (Goldman) W. Student, Parsons Sch. Design, 1946-50; BS, NYU, 1950; postgrad., Cooper Union, 1950-52. Stage designer Dramatic Workshop prodn. The Inspector General, 1947; set designer Gertrude Stein's Yes Is for a Very Young Man; set and costume designer Ounga Opera, Phila., 1950, (opera) The Celebrated Jumping Frog of Calaveras County, Venice, Italy, 1953, The Transposed Heads, 1958, The Fantasticks, 1960 (still running); designer Broadway prodn. Kean, 1961; set and costume designer The Gondoliers, N.Y.C. Opera, 1963, The Knack (directed by Mike Nichols), 1964, The Marriage of Figaro, N.Y.C. Opera, 1965, The Amen Corner, 1965, Happy Birthday Wanda June, Enter Laughing, 1965, The Room, A Slight Ache, 1965, The Yearling, 1965, Serjeant Musgrave's Dance, 1966 (Obie award 1966), You Know I Can't Hear You When the Water's Running, 1967, set designer Merchant of Venice, Shakespeare Festival Conn., 1967, As You Like It, Richard II, Shakespeare Festival Conn., 1968, The Man in the Glass Booth, 1968, The Basement, The Tea Party, Celebration, 1969, (for Cin. Playhouse) The Miser, Volpone, The Good Woman of Setzuan, Angel Street, He Who Gets Slapped, 1968-70, The Country Wife, Shakespeare Theatre, Conn., 1973, Ulysses in Nightown, 1974 (Tony award nomination 1974, Maharam award 1974), The Torchbearers, 1978, The Aspern Papers, 1978, Love's Labors Lost, 1983, Berkshire Theatre Festival, 1988, Tusitala, 1988, Tete a Tete, 1989, The Hasty Heart, 1990, Trains, 1991, (sets, costumes 30th anniversary tour) The Fantasticks, 1990, Sarah, Plain and Tall, 1991 (Emmy nomination 1991), Colette Collage, 1991, March of the Falsettos, 1991, Falsettoland, 1991, (prodn. designer Hallmark Hall of Fame TV) An American Story, 1992, (prodn. designer Hallmark Hall of Fame TV) Skylark, 1993, (prodn. designer Hallmark Hall of Fame TV) A Place for Annie, 1993, (set designer off-Broadway) I Do! I Do!, 1996; designer TV shows Armstrong Circle Theatre, The Tonight Show with Steve Allen, NBC operas Cosi Fan Tutte, La Traviata, La Boheme, Boris Godounov, Cavalleria Rusticana, Blithe Spirit, The Diary of Anne Frank, Camino Real, The Royal Family, The Prince of Homburg; prodn. designer TV series The Adams Chronicles (Emmy nomination 1975); designer TV films A Memory of Two Mondays, 1971, For Ladies Only, 1982, Legs, 1982, Samson and Delilah, 1983, Heartsounds, 1984; designer TV spl. Echoes in the Darkness, 1987; designer films Bananas, 1971, Play It Again Sam, 1971, The Seven-Ups, 1972; art dir. films Smile, 1975, Fame, 1979; prodn. designer film Endless Love, 1981; set and costume designer (ballet) Coppelia, 1992. Home: 339 E 87th St New York NY 10128-4801

WITUCKI, JANET MARIE, nursing educator; b. Stevens Point, Wis., Nov. 27, 1946; d. Joseph John and Victoria Rose Tylka; m. Elmer Andrew Witucki, Aug. 19, 1967; 1 child, William James. Diploma, St. Joseph's Sch. Nursing, 1967; BSN, Ball State U., 1991, MSN, 1994. Staff nurse Meml. Hosp., Wausau, Wis., 1967-69; charge nurse, insvc. dir. Colonial Manor, Wausau, 1969-73, The Willows, Alexandria, Ind., 1979-81; allied health instr. North Ctrl. Tech. Inst., Wausau, 1973-79; staff nurse Cmty. Hosp., Anderson, Ind., 1981-85; instr., allied health coord. Ivy Tech. State Coll., Muncie, Ind., 1985-93; dir. practical nursing program Ivy Tech. State Coll., Muncie, 1993-94; mem. nursing faculty Ball State U., Muncie, 1994—; bd. dirs. Day Star Alzheimer Adult Day Care Ctr., Muncie, 1993—; presenter in field. Mem. Ind. State Nurses Assn. (1st v.p. dist. 6), Nat. League Nursing, Mid State Dist. Nurses Assn. (past pres.), Ball State U. Nursing Alumni (bd. dirs. 1994—), Sigma Theta Tau. Avocations: reading, travel. Home: RR1 4980 Beechmont Dr Anderson IN 46012 Office: Ball State U Sch Nursing University Ave Muncie IN 47306

WITWER, SAMUEL WEILER, SR., lawyer; b. Pueblo, Colo., July 1, 1908; s. Samuel W. and Lulu (Richmond) W.; m. Ethyl L. Wilkins, Aug. 14, 1937; children: Samuel Weiler III, Michael Wilkins, Carole Ann Witwer Dalton, David R. PhB, Dickinson Coll., 1930, LLD, 1970; JD, Harvard, 1933; LLD, Simpson Coll., 1955, U. Ill., 1971, John Marshall Law Sch., 1976; LHD, DePaul U., 1971; JD, Lake Forest Coll., 1971. Bar: Ill. 1933. Since practiced in Chgo.; now mem. firm Witwer, Poltrock & Giampietro; spl. asst. Ill. Atty. Gen., 1971; dir. Harvard Law Soc. Ill.; state laureate Lincoln Acad. Ill., 1974, vice chancellor, 1984—. Contbr. articles on constl. law and govt. to legal publs. Ill. chmn. U.S.O., 1958-63; citizens com. U. Ill.; mem. Bd. Social and Econ. Relations, Methodist Ch. (gen.), 1954-60, Council World Service and Fin., 1960-64; mem. jud. council Supreme Ct. of United Methodism, 1964-72; Chmn. Ill. Com. Constl. Revision, 1950-55; pres. 6th Ill. Constnl. Conv., 1969-70; State chmn. Ill. Citizens for Eisenhower-Nixon, 1956; v.p. United Republican Fund of Ill.; Rep. candidate U.S. senate, Ill., 1960; Pres. bd. trustees Dickinson Coll., 1964-79, hon. pres. bd., 1980—; trustee Northwestern Meml. Hosp. Recipient 1st Disting. Svc. medal of Ill., 1970, Citizen Fellow award Inst. Medicine Chgo., 1973; named A Chicagoan of Yr., Chgo. C. of C., 1954, 68, The Chicagoan of Yr., 1970; Chicagoan of Yr., Chgo. Press Club, 1971, Ill. Man of Yr., Ill. News Broadcasters, 1970; subject of biographies A Political Biography of Samuel W. Witwer of Illinois (Gertz and Gilbreth), 1984, Quest for a Constitution, 1984. Mem. Am. Law Inst. (dir.), ABA, Ill. Bar Assn. (citation civic service 1972), Chgo. Bar Assn. (bd. mgrs. 1944-46), Chgo. Council on Fgn. Relations (past dir.), Chgo. Urban League (past dir.), Chgo. Sunday Evening Club (trustee emeritus), Union League (1st Disting. Pub. Svc. award 1955), Legal Club (Chgo.), Comml. Club, Law Club, Omicron Delta Kappa, Sigma Chi (Significant Sig award). Republican. Methodist. Home: 111 Abingdon Ave Kenilworth IL 60043-1201 Office: 125 S Wacker Dr Ste 2700 Chicago IL 60606-4546

WITWER, SAMUEL WEILER, JR., lawyer; b. Chgo., Aug. 5, 1941; s. Samuel Weiler and Ethyl Loraine (Wilkins) W.; m. Susan P. Stewart, Sept. 18, 1971; children: Samuel Stewart, Michael Douglas. AB with honors, Dickinson Coll., 1963; JD, U. Mich., 1966. Bar: Ill. 1967, U.S. Dist. Ct. (no. dist.) Ill. 1967, U.S. Ct. Appeals (7th cir.) 1972, U.S. Supreme Ct. 1973, U.S. Ct. Appeals (6th cir.) 1985, U.S. Dist. Ct. (ea. dist.) Mich., 1987. Assoc. Witwer, Moran, Burlage & Atkinson, Chgo., 1967-74, ptnr., 1974—; mem. Fed. Trial Bar Admissions Com. No. Dist. Ill., 1982—. Governing mem. Chgo. Zool. Soc., 1986-90; trustee United Meth. Homes and Services, Chgo., 1974—, Dickinson Coll., Carlisle, Pa., 1976—; mem. Cook County Home Rule Commn., Chgo., 1974-75; chmn. Agy. Appeals Com. Chgo., 1975-78; atty. Glenview Park Dist., 1982—; spl. asst. atty. gen. Auditor Gen. Ill., 1984-92. Mem. ABA, Meth. Bar Assn. (pres. 1972-73), Chgo. Bar Assn., Ill. Bar Assn., Law Club of Chgo., Sigma Chi, Phi Delta Phi. Republican. Methodist. Club: Union League. Home: 1330 Overlook Dr Glenview IL 60025-5166 Office: Witwer Poltrock & Giampletro 125 S Wacker Dr Chicago IL 60606-4402

WITZGALL, CHRISTOPH JOHANN, mathematician; b. Hindelang, Bavaria, Germany, Feb. 25, 1929; came to U.S., 1959; s. Otto and Hanna (Schulte-Liese) W.; m. Elizabeth Bingham, Oct. 10, 1964; children: John Chandler, Hanna Elizabeth, George Matheus. PhD in Maths., Universitat Munich, 1958. Rsch. assoc. Princeton (N.J.) U., 1959-61, U. Mainz, Germany, 1961; postdoctoral RAND Corp., Santa Monica, Calif., 1961, Argonne Nat. Lab., Joliet, Ill., 1962; mathematician Nat. Bur. of Stds., Washington, 1962-66, Boeing Scientific Rsch. Labs., Seattle, 1966-73, Nat. Inst. Stds. and Tech., Gaithersburg, Md., 1973—; acting chief ops. rsch. div. Nat. Inst. Standards and Tech., Gaithersburg, Md., 1979-82; vis. prof. U. Tex., Austin, 1971, Universitat Wurzburg, Germany, 1972, U. Md., College Park, 1977, Johns Hopkin's U., Balt., 1985. Co-author: Convexity and Optimization in Finite Dimensions, 1970. Mem. AAAS, Informs, Soc. for Indsl. and Applied Maths., Am. Math. Soc. Office: Nat Inst Stds and Tech Gaithersburg MD 20899

WITZIG, WARREN FRANK, nuclear engineer, educator; b. Detroit, Mar. 26, 1921; s. Arthur Judson and Mary (Bender) W.; m. Bernadette Sullivan, Mar. 31, 1942; children: Eric, Leah, Marc, Lisa Witzig Davidson. B.E.E., Rensselaer Poly. Inst., 1942; M.S., U. Pitts., 1944, Ph.D., 1952. Registered profl. engr., Pa., Washington. Research engr. Westinghouse Research, Pitts., 1942-48; mgr. reactor physics, engr. Bettis Atomic, Pitts., 1948-60; cofounder, sr. v.p., dir. NUS Corp., Washington, 1960-67; head dept. nuclear engring. Pa. State U., 1967-87, emeritus, 1987—; cons. nuclear engr. utilities industry; chmn. Pa. Gov.'s Com. on Atomic Energy Devel., 1970-80; mem. Saxton safety com., 1970-72; mem. waste com. Atomic Indsl. Forum, 1971-73; mem. adv. com. Dept. Energy, 1980-82; mem. ops. rev. com. Tex. Utility; mem. nuclear safety and compliance com., bd. dirs. GPU, 1983-92; mem. nuclear oversight com. PSE&G, 1983-91; mem. accrediting bd. Inst. Nuclear Power Ops., 1992—; mem. safety rev. bd. TVA, 1986-91; chmn. Westinghouse Nuclear Safety and Environ. Commn., 1988-93; chmn. safety audit bd. Centichem., 1989. Designer S5W submarine reactor, 1956-60. Mem. bd. mgmt. YMCA, 1955-64. Fellow AAAS, Am. Nuclear Soc. (mem. exec. com. edn. div., past chmn. nat. com. on public info., chmn. nuclear engring. dept. head com. 1980); mem. Am. Phys. Soc., IEEE (past chmn. nuclear eng. and plasma div.), Sigma Xi, Eta Kappa Nu, Pi Kappa Alpha, Sigma Pi Sigma (Power Engring. Educator spl. citation). Presbyterian (elder). Achievements include design of S5W submarine reactor; criticality engineer on Nautilus maiden voyage; developed continuing and long distance education in nuclear engineering. Home: 1330 E Park Hills Ave State College PA 16803-3244 Office: Pa State U 231 Sackett Bldg University Park PA 16802

WIWCHAR, MICHAEL, bishop; b. Komarno, Manitoba, Canada, May 9, 1932. ordained priest June 28, 1959. Pastor St. John the Baptist Church, Newark, NJ, 1990-93; bishop Diocese of St. Nicholas of Chicago for the Ukrainians, 1993—. Office: Chancery Office 2245 W Rice St Chicago IL 60622*

WIXOM, WILLIAM DAVID, art historian, museum administrator, educator; b. Phila., July 17, 1929; s. Clinton Wood and Beatrice Rachel (Hunt) W.; BA, Haverford (Pa.) Coll., 1951; MA, Inst. Fine Arts NYU, 1963; m. Nancy Coe, Aug. 8, 1959; 3 children. Asst. curator to curator medieval and renaissance decorative arts Cleve. Mus. Art, 1958-78, chief curator early western art, 1979; chmn. dept. medieval art and The Cloisters, Met. Mus. Art, N.Y.C., 1979—; adj. assoc. prof. history of art Case Western Res. U., Cleve., 1967-78, adj. prof., 1978; adj. prof. N.Y.U., 1981-82; mem. adv. council for Snite Mus. Art Notre Dame U., 1974-95. Bd. dirs. Internat. Ctr. Medieval Art, N.Y.C., 1971-82, pres., 1971-74. Belgium-Am. Ednl. Found. fellow, 1962; Nat. Endowment Arts grantee, 1973; fellow Pierpont Morgan Library, 1979—; J. Paul Getty Mus. Guest Scholar, 1996. Fellow Soc. of Antiquaries of London; mem. Coll. Art Assn. (dir. 1979-83), Medieval Acad. Am., Internat. Center Medieval Art. Quaker. Author: Treasures from Medieval France, 1967; Renaissance Bronzes from Ohio Collections, 1975; contbg. author The Royal Abbey of Saint Denis in the Time of Abbot Suger, 1981, The Treasury of San Marco, 1985; Gothic and Renaissance Art in Nuremberg, 1986, Festschrift Gerhard Bott, 1987, Hommage à Hubert Landais, 1987, The Cloisters, Studies in Honor of the Fiftieth Anniversary, 1992, Festschrift Gerhard Schmidt, 1994; contbr. articles in field to profl. jours. Office: Cloisters Fort Tryon Park New York NY 10040

WIXON, RUFUS, retired accounting educator; b. Cherokee County, Iowa, Nov. 27, 1911; s. Rufus and Stella Maude (Mathews) W.; m. Doris Elizabeth Hunter, Oct. 28, 1939; children: Marjorie Jeanne, Joanne Elizabeth, Kathryn Ann. B.S.C., U. Iowa, 1933, M.A., 1935; Ph.D., U. Mich., 1945. Staff accountant I.B. McGladrey & Co., Cedar Rapids, Iowa, 1933-34; instr. accounting U. N.D., 1935-36; staff accountant Edward Gore & Co., Chgo., 1936-37; instr. accounting Wayne U., 1937-41; lectr. econs. U. Mich., 1941-45, asst. prof. econs., 1945-47; prof. accounting, chmn. dept. U. Buffalo, 1947-49, U. Pa., 1949-65; prof. accounting Fla. Inst. chair accountancy U. Fla., Gainesville, 1965-66; prof. accounting U. Pa., Phila., 1966-80, emeritus prof., 1980—; assoc. chief, specialist accounting U. Pa.-U. Karachi Project, Karachi, Pakistan, 1955-57; Cons. Office Asst. Sec. Def. (comptroller), 1958-60; prof. IMEDE, Mgmt. Devel. Inst., Lausanne, Switzerland, 1961-62; accounting editorial bd. Found. Press. Author: (with W.A. Paton, R.L. Dixon) Problems and Practise Sets for Essentials of Accounting, 1949, Budgetary Control, 1952, rev., 1961, Principles of Accounting, (with R.G. Cox), 1961, 2nd edit., 1969; Editor: Accountant's Handbook, 5th edit, 1970. Mem. Am. Acad. Polit. and Social Sci., Am. Accounting Assn. (chmn. com. standards accounting instrn., v.p. 1959), Am. Econ. Assn., Controllers Inst. Am., Order of Artus, Beta Gamma Sigma, Beta Alpha Psi, Phi Kappa Phi, Alpha Kappa Psi, Alpha Tau Omega. Club: Springhaven. Home: 1343 W Baltimore Pike D-116 Granite Farms Estates Wawa PA 19063 Office: U Penn Wharton Sch Philadelphia PA 19104

WLEUGEL, JOHN PETER, manufacturing company executive; b. Hoyanger, Sogn, Norway, July 1, 1929; s. Johan and Helga (Faye) W.; m. Leonor Abaroa, Dec. 1959; children—Jan Andrew, Cecilia Maria. B.A., U. Copenhagen, 1953; M.B.A., U. Toronto, 1957. With Belgium Machine Tool Assn., 1953-54; with Massey-Ferguson Ltd., Toronto, 1954-71, treas., 1968-71, also dir. several subs.; sr. v.p. Bata Ltd., Toronto, also bd. dirs.; dir., officer several subsidiaries (Bata Shoe Orgn.), Don Mills, Ont., Can., 1972-89; exec.-in-residence Schulich Sch. Bus., York U., North York, Can., 1990—; bd. dirs. Internat. UNP Holdings Ltd., Toronto, Ont. Can., Advanced Material Resources Ltd., The Canadian Coun. for the Americas. Mem. Financial Execs. Inst. Club: University (Toronto). Home: 5 Campbell Crescent, North York, ON Canada M2P 1P1 Office: York U, Schulich Sch Bus, 4700 Keele St, North York, ON Canada M3J 1P3

WOBBLETON, JUDY KAREN, artist, educator; b. Williamston, N.C., Aug. 31, 1947; d. Lloyd Thomas and Lillian Edith (Hudson) Letchworth; m. Albert Virgil Wobbleton Jr., Apr. 7, 1968; children: Olivia Elizabeth, Virgil Alan. Clk. Beaufort County Hosp., Washington, N.C., 1965-68; ins. supr. Mercy Hosp., Sacramento, 1968-72; adminstrv. asst. hosp. svcs. Fairbanks (Alaska) Meml. Hosp., 1972-75; basketry artist Williamston, 1983—; instr. basketry N.C. Basketmakers, 1984-94, Wayne C.C., Goldsboro, N.C., 1986-91, Wayne County Arts Coun., Goldsboro, 1990-91; co-founder A.C. Basketmakers, 1984. Contbg. artist: The Basket Book, 1988, Basketmaker's Baskets, 1990, Craft Works in The Home, 1990. Troop leader Girl Scouts U.S., Goldsboro, 1983-88, svc. unit mgr., 1987-91; active Roanoke Arts & Crafts Guild, 1991-96. Recipient 2d Pl. award Wilson Arts Coun., 1987, 3d Pl. award Martin County Arts Coun., 1992. Mem. N.C. Basketmakers Assn. (hon., bd. dirs. 1984-96, membership chmn. 1984-87, pres. 1990-94, mem. conv. rev. com. 1994-96), Goldweavers Basketry Guild (hon.). Avocations: reading, cooking, painting. Home and Office: Baskets By Judy 1325 Oakview Rd Williamston NC 27892

WOBST, FRANK GEORG, banker; b. Dresden, Germany, Nov. 14, 1933; came to U.S., 1958, naturalized, 1963; s. Robert Georg and Marianne (Salewsky) W.; m. Joan Shuey Firkins, Aug. 24, 1957; children: Franck Georg, Ingrid, Andrea. Student, U. Erlangen, 1952-54, U. Goettingen, 1954-58, Rutgers U., 1964. With Fidelity American Bankshares, Inc., Lynchburg, Va., 1958-74, exec. v.p., dir., 1974-85; chmn., chief exec. officer, dir. Huntington Nat. Bank, 1974-85, chmn. exec. com., 1986—; chmn., chief exec. officer, dir. Huntington Bancshares, Inc., 1974—. Mem. Greater Columbus C. of C., Am. Inst. Banking, Assn. Res. City Bankers, Robert Morris Assos., Newcomen Soc. Club: Scioto Country. Home: 129 N Columbia Ave Columbus OH 43209-1414 Office: Huntington Bancshares Inc 41 S High St PO Box 1558 Columbus OH 43287*

WOBUS, REINHARD ARTHUR, geologist, educator; b. Norfolk, Va., Jan. 11, 1941; s. Reinhard Schaffer and Oral (Phares) W.; m. Sheridan Whitcher, Mar. 18, 1967; children: Erik Reinhard, Cameron Wright. BA, Washington U., St. Louis, 1962; MA, Harvard U., 1963; PhD, Stanford U., 1966. Asst. prof. geology Williams Coll., Williamstown, Mass., 1966-72, assoc. prof., 1972-78, prof., 1978-85, Edna McConnell Clark prof. geology, 1985—, dept. chmn., 1988—; geologist U.S. Geol. Survey, Denver, 1967-86; vis. prof. Colo. Coll., Colorado Springs, 1976, 82-83, Colo. State U., Ft. Collins, summers, 1977-84; staff geologist Colo. Outdoor Edn. Ct., Florissant, 1983; co-founder Keck Twelve-Coll. Geol. Consortium. Contbr. maps and articles on Precambrian geology of So. Rocky Mountains to profl. jours. Danforth fellow, 1962, Woodrow Wilson felow, 1962, NSF fellow, 1962-66. Fellow Geol. Soc. Am.; mem. Am. Geophys. Union, Nat. Assn. Geology Tchrs., Coun. on Undergrad. Rsch., Colo. Sci. Soc., Mineral Soc. Am., Phi Beta Kappa, Sigma Xi. Current work: Petrology and geochronology of Precambrian igneous and metamorphic rocks and mid-Tertiary volcanic rocks, so. Rocky Mountains. Subspecialties: Petrology, Geology. Home: 20 Grandview Dr Williamstown MA 01267-2528 Office: Williams Coll Dept Geology Williamstown MA 01267

WODLINGER, MARK LOUIS, broadcast executive; b. Jacksonville, Fla., July 13, 1922; s. Mark H. and Beatrice Mae (Boney) W.; m. Marilyn Stone-Birk; children: Kevin, Michael, Stephen, Mark. BS, U. Fla., 1943. Salesman Sta. WQUA, Moline, Ill., 1948; mgr. Sta. WOC-AM-FM-TV, Davenport, Iowa, 1949-58; v.p. Sta. WMBD-TV, Peoria, Ill., 1959-61; v.p., gen. mgr. Sta. WZZM-TV, Grand Rapids, Mich., 1962-63, Sta. KMBC-TV, Kansas City, Mo., 1963-69; pres. Intermedia, Kansas City, 1969-73; builder, owner comml. radio stas. Swaziland, Africa; operator Radio Malawi, Blantyre, and Marknews TV and Radio News Bur., Nairobe, Kenya, 1971-74; owner, pres. Sta. KBEQ, Kansas City, 1973-77; owner Sta. WCJX-FM, Miami, 1985-86, Sta. WIXI-FM, Naples and Ft. Myers, Fla., 1986-95, Sta. KKLO-AM, Leavenworth, Kans., 1982-92, Sta. KCWV, Kansas City, Mo., 1982-90, TV-5, Hit Video USA, Satellite Music Network, Houston, 1985-88; owner SMR-2-way radio/telephone, Naples, Fla., 1993—, San Francisco, 1993—; chmn. bd. dirs. Wodlinger Broadcasting Co., Naples, 1978—; ptnr. Wireless Cable, Naples, 1990—; owner, chmn. bd. dirs. KABELTEL KFT, Budapest, Hungary, Sopron, Hungary, Nagykanizsa, Hungary, Papa, Hungary, Szombathely, Hungary, Kecskemet, Kaposvar, Hungary, Salgotarjan, Hungary, 1991—, comml. FM Radio Ikva, Sopron, 1993—, Hungary comml. FM Radio Zalaegerszeg, Hungary, 1995—, comml. FM Radio Kecskemet, Hungary, 1995—, comml. FM Love Radio 97.8, Tallinn, Paide, Rakvere, Tartu, Sindi, Viliandi and Marjamaa, Estonia, 1993—, comml. FM Love Radio 67.07, Riga, Latvia, 1994—; ptnr., chmn. bd. dirs. wireless cable TV Ukrainian-Am. Broadcasting, Kiev, Ukraine, 1990—, comml. TV Channel 7, 1990—, comml. FM Radio 69.89, Kiev, 1992—; owner, ptnr. comml. FM Radiocentras, Vilnius, Lithuania, 1992—; ptnr. joint mktg. AT&T Paradyne, Largo, Fla., 1992—, Bellcore, Morristown, N.J., 1995—; owner, ptnr., chmn. bd. dirs. real estate devel., Croatia, 1991—; owner outdoor advt. billboards, Tallinn, Estonia, 1993—; owner, ptnr. real estate devel., Hungary, 1991—. Bd. dirs. Kansas City Philharm., Kansas City Civic Coun., Naples YMCA; mem. Conservancy, Naples Civic Assn. Served to lt. USN, 1941-45. Mem. Nat. Assn. Broadcasters, Mo. Assn. Broadcasters, Broadcast Pioneers. Republican. Episcopalian. Clubs: Kansas City, Univ., Vanguard, Carriage, Port Royal, Naples Yacht, Houston Yacht, White Lake Yacht (Whitehall, Mich.). Lodge: Rotary. Home: 800 Galleon Dr Naples FL 33940-7646 Office: 3355 Tamiami Trl N Naples FL 33940-4165

WOELFEL, JAMES WARREN, philosophy educator; b. Galveston, Tex., Aug. 16, 1937; s. Warren Charles and Mary Frances (Washinka) W.; m. Sarah Chappell Trulove, Nov. 24, 1982; children by previous marriages: Skye Caitlin, Allegra Eve, Sarah Judith; stepchildren: Ann Marie and Paul Trulove. BA, U. Okla., 1959; MDiv, Episcopal Div. Sch., Cambridge, Mass., 1962; MA, Yale U., 1964; PhD, U. St. Andrews, Scotland, 1967. Asst. prof. philosophy and religion U. Kans., Lawrence, 1966-70, asst. prof. philosophy, 1970-71, assoc. prof. philosophy and religion, 1971-75, prof. philosophy and religious studies, 1975-88, prof. philosophy, 1988—, acting chmn. dept. religious studies, 1983-84, dir. Western civilization program, 1985—; manuscript reader for various presses, jours. Author: Bonhoeffer's Theology, 1970, Borderland Christianity, 1973, Camus: A Theological Perspective, 1975 (republished as Albert Camus on the Sacred and the Secular, 1987), Augustinian Humanism, 1979, The Agnostic Spirit as a Common Motif in Liberal Theology and Liberal Scepticism, 1990; editor (with Sarah Chappell Trulove) and contbr.; Patterns in Western Civilization, 1991; contbr. numerous articles, essays, revs. to profl. publs. Danforth grad. fellow Episcopal Div. Sch., Cambridge, Mass., 1959-62, U. St. Andrews, 1962-63, 65-66, Yale U., New Haven, 1963-65; Fulbright scholar U. St. Andrews, 1962-63; grantee NEH, Exxon Found., Mellon Found., Menninger Found., Inst. for Ecumenical and Cultural Research. Mem. Am. Acad. Religion, Highlands Inst. for Am. Religious Thought, Phi Beta Kappa. Democrat. Avocations: piano; walking. Home: 808 Alabama St Lawrence KS 66044-3942 Office: U Kans Western Civilization Program 2106 Wescoe Hall Lawrence KS 66045-2178

WOELFEL, JOSEPH DONALD, communications educator; b. Buffalo, June 3, 1940; s. Richard Joseph and Elizabeth Lillian (Graeber) W.; children: Charles, Joseph, Johanna, Evan, Alaina, Alec. BS in Sociology, Canisius Coll., 1962; MA in Sociology, U. Wis., 1963, PhD in Sociology, 1968. Asst. prof. sociology U. Ill., Urbana, 1968-72; assoc. prof. communications Mich. State U., East Lansing, 1972-78; prof. communications SUNY, Albany, N.Y., 1978-89; prof., chair communications SUNY, Buffalo, N.Y., 1989—; pres. The Galileo Co., Amherst, N.Y., 1978—; dir. rsch. Terra Rsch. Computing Co., Birmingham, Mich., 1990—; cons. Agy. Internat. Devel., Albany Rsch. Svcs., Almeth Rsch., Am. Mktg. Assn., Arbitron, ASG, Blue Cross/Blue Shield Mich., others. Author: Communication and Science, 1992, 94, What's Wrong With This Picture?, 1995, Variational Principles of Communication, 1995, (with others) The Measurement of Communication Process: Galileo Theory and Method, 1980; editor Systemsletter, 1983-85; editor-in-chief RAH Press, 1995—; assoc. editor Human Communication Rsch., 1976, 79, Communication Quar., 1977-83, Informatologia Jugoslavia, 1985—; cons. editor Am. Sociol. Rev., Am. Jour. Sociology, Rural Sociology, Jour. Cross Cultural Rsch., Human Orgn., Human Communication Rsch., Communication Rsch.; contbr. chpts. in books and articles to profl. publs. Bd. dirs. WBFO, Buffalo, 1991-92. Sr. fellow East-West Communication Inst., Honolulu, 1977-83, Faculty fellow Rockefeller Inst. Govt., 1985—; Richard W.D. Nicholas Agrl. Sci. scholar U. Melbourne, 1986; recipient Pres.'s award for Excellence in Rsch., SUNY, 1983, Fulbright award Conf. Dubrovnik, 1983. Mem. AAAS, N.Am. Classification Soc., N.Y. Acad. Scis., Internat. Soc. Network Analysis, Neural Network Soc., Psychometric Soc., Soc. Scientific Study of Communication. Office: U Buffalo Dept Communication 332 MFAC-Fillmore Buffalo NY 14261

WOELFEL, STACEY WILLIAM, news director; b. St. Louis, Aug. 5, 1959; s. William Michael and Betty Lee (Smith) W.; m. Rebecca Laine Gardner, Aug. 15, 1981; children: Alexander Gardner, Lauren Smith. B Journalism, U. Mo., 1981, MA, 1990. Photographer, editor WESH-TV, Orlando, Fla., 1981-84, field producer, 1984-85, assignment editor, 1985-86; exec. assignment editor KOMU-TV/U. Mo., Columbia, 1986-89, asst. news dir., 1989-91, news dir., 1991—. Recipient News awards Orlando Press Club, 1983, 84, AP Broadcasters of Fla., 1984, Mo. Broadcasters, 1992, Kansas City Press Club, 1992. Mem. NATAS, Radio-TV News Dirs. Assn. Office: KOMU TV Highway 63 S Columbia MO 65201

WOELFFER, EMERSON SEVILLE, artist; b. Chgo., July 27, 1914; s. George K. and Marguerite (Seville) W.; m. Diane Anderson, Dec. 7, 1945. Student, Art Inst. Chgo., 1935-38; B.F.A., Inst. Design, Chgo., 1949; PhD (hon.), New Sch. for Social Rsch., 1991, Otis Parsons Sch. Design, L.A., 1993, Otis Parson's Art Inst., 1993, New Sch. Social Rsch., Otis Sch. head painting dept. Otis Art Inst., Los Angeles, 1974—; artist in residence. One-man shows include Paul Kantor Gallery, Beverly Hills, Calif., 1953, 60, Poindexter Gallery, N.Y.C., 1958, 61, Primus-Stuart Gallery, L.A., 1961, Santa Barbara (Calif.) Mus. Art, 1964, Quay Gallery, San Francisco, 1967, Honolulu Acad. Arts, 1970, Jodi Scully Gallery, L.A., 1972, 73, Newport Harbour Art Mus., Newport Beach, Calif., 1974, Phillips Collection, Washington, 1975, Gruenebaum Gallery, N.Y.C., 1978, New Orleans Mus. Art, 1987, Wenger Gallery, L.A., Manny Silverman Gallery, L.A., 1991, 93, Parsons Sch. Design, L.A., 1992, Otis Art Inst., James Corcoran Gallery, 1993, Hyundai Art Gallery, Seoul, Korea, 1995; traveling exhbn. at Modern Art Mus., New Delhi, India, 1988, collages of 1987-89 Manny Silverman Gallery, L.A.; two-person show Harcourt Gallery, San Francisco, 1990; exhibited in group shows at UCLA, 1987-88; represented in permanent collections British Mus., Art Inst. Chgo., Whitney Mus. Am. Art, Mus. Modern Art, N.Y.C., L.A. County Mus. Art, Washington Gallery Modern Art, Wight Galleries of UCLA, San Francisco Mus. Art, Bauhaus Archives, Berlin, Smithsonian Archives Am. Art, Washington, Santa Fe Mus. Art, Seattle Art Mus., Biblioteque Nationale, Paris, Acad. Arts and Sci., N.Y., also numerous others. Grantee Guggenheim Found., 1968-69, NEA, 1974, Pollock Krasner, 1986, Greenburger Found., 1988. Home: 475 Dustin Dr Los Angeles CA 90065-5023

WOELFLEIN, KEVIN GERARD, banker; b. Haverhill, Mass., Feb. 9, 1933; s. John Henry and Helen Margaret (Hoar) W.; m. Ann Buckley, Sept. 9, 1957; children: Karl G., Luise A., Andrew B., Peter H. B.S., MIT, 1954; M.B.A., U. Pa., 1958, postgrad., 1959-65. Venture analyst Atlas Chem. Industries, Wilmington, Del., 1959-66; economist Fed. Res. Bank Phila., 1966-67; asst. v.p. 1st Nat. Bank Chgo., 1967-70, v.p., 1970-72; v.p., gen. mgr. (Tokyo br.), 1972-75; pres., chief exec. officer, dir. UBAF Arab Am. Bank, N.Y.C., 1975-81; pres., chief operating officer, dir. Am. Security Bank, Washington, 1981-83; pres., dir. Mass. Co., Inc., Boston, 1983-86; pres. U.S. Capital Investments Co., Greenwich, Conn., 1983—; chmn. bd. Conn. Bancorp, Inc., also bd. dirs.; chmn. bd. Norwalk (Conn.) Bank, 1990-92, also bd. dirs. Bd. dirs. Small Bus. High Tech. Inst., 1982-85; mem. exec. com. MIT Enterprise Forum, Washington, 1982-85; mem. MIT Corp. vis. com. Ctr. for Internat. Studies; mem. adv. council U.S.-Japan Study Ctr., Johns Hopkins U. Sch. Advanced Internat. Studies, 1982-85; trustee Convent of Sacred Heart, Greenwich, Conn., 1977-81; mem. U.S.-Saudi Arabian Joint Commn. on Econ. Cooperation, 1982-84. Served to lt. U.S. Army, 1954-56. Recipient Corp. Leadership award MIT, 1980; Knight of Malta, Fed. Assn., 1984. Mem. Riverside Yacht Club, Columbia Country Club. Office: US Capital Investments Co 2 Greenwich Plz Ste 100 Greenwich CT 06830-6353

WOERNER, ROBERT LESTER, landscape architect; b. Rochester, N.Y., Jan. 31, 1925; s. William John and Loretta Bertha (Hettel) W.; m. Mary Jane Warn, May 12, 1952; children: Jane Marie, Anne Louise. B.S., SUNY Coll. Forestry, Syracuse, 1949. Cert. landscape architect, Wash., Idaho. Draftsman N.A., Rotunno Landscape Architects, Syracuse, 1947-49; landscape architect Park Dist., Plan Commn., Yakima, Wash., 1949-50; asst. supt. parks Spokane Park Dept., Spokane, Wash., 1950-56; dir. Denver Bot. Gardens, 1956-58; pvt. practice landscape architect Spokane, 1959—; chmn. bd. registration Landscape Architects State of Wash., 1976-78; pres. Council Landscape Archtl. Registration Bds., 1978-79. Mem. Zoning Bd. Adjustment, Spokane, 1983; mem. Urban Design Com., 1983; mem. Capitol Campus Design Adv. Com., 1982-94. Cpl. U.S. Army, 1943-45, ETO. Recipient Indsl. Landscaping Award Am. Assn. Nurserymen, Lincoln Bldg., Spokane, 1966; recipient Cert. of Merit Wash. Water Power, 1967, State Indsl. Landscaping award Wash State Nurserymen's Assn., Wash. Water Power, 1968. Fellow Am. Soc. Landscape Architects (pres. 1979-80, Disting. Svc. award 1976). Republican. Roman Catholic. Lodge: Kiwanis.

WOESSNER, FREDERICK T., composer, pianist; b. Teaneck, N.J., July 23, 1935; s. Fred and Bertha W.; m. Lise, Feb. 14, 1960 (div. 1973); children: Betty, Allison. Student, Peabody Conservatory of Music, Balt., 1960-61; MBA, NYU, 1968; MA, Calif. State U., Los Angeles, 1975; pvt. study with, David Diamond, Charles Haubiel, Albert Harris. Owner Al-Fre-Bett Music, Los Angeles, 1980—. Composer (for orch.) Nursery Song, Variations on an Irish Air, Reflections for Strings, Fanfare for Winds, String Quartet, Concerto for piano improvisations and orch., Secret Gospels (Cantata), Sonic studies for Piano I Elegy for Trumpet and Winds, (music for films) Sky Bandits, Gunbus, Pale Horse, Pale Rider, The Curb Your Appetite Diet, Centerfold, (title music for TV) Actors Forum, (for stage) From Berlin to Broadway, Oh Atlantis, Kurt, Lil Nell, Another Town, Victorian Atmospheres; composer and pianist, album-film/video, Vincent Moreaux, His Finest Hour In My Forest Cathedral, Songs from the Sea; rec. artist Sonic Arts and Repertoire Records. Pres. bd. dirs. Inst. for Recording and Multimedia Arts; mem. bd. govs.Music and the Arts Found. of Am., Inc. Mem. ASCAP, Nat. Acad. Recording Arts and Scis., Dramatists Guild, Soc. Composers and Lyricists, Am. Fedn. Musicians, Am. Soc. Music Arrangers and Composers (treas. 1978—), Composers and Arrangers Found. Am. (sec.). Democrat. Office: Al-Fre-Bett Music PO Box 45 Los Angeles CA 90078-0045

WOESTE, JOHN THEODORE, academic administrator; b. Alexandria, Ky., June 28, 1934; s. Theodore John and Ruth Elizabeth (Kinstler) W.; m. Martha Helen Messmer, Aug. 11, 1956; children: Shan, Keith, Lori, John, Jennifer, Troy. BS, U. Ky., 1956; MS, U. Wis., 1963, PhD, 1967. Asst. county agt. Ky. Coop. Extension Service, Owen County, 1956-57; county extension agt. Ky. Coop. Extension Service, Richmond, 1959-62; area adminstr. Ky. Cooperative Extension Service, Lexington, 1966-69; dist. extension dir. U. Wis., Madison, 1969-72; asst. dir. Wis. Coop. Extension Service, Madison, 1972-76; dean, dir. of extension U. Fla. Inst. Food and Agrl. Scis., Gainesville, 1976—. Mem. sch. bd. Middleton (Wis.)-Cross Plains Dist., 1973; supr. Alacua Soil and Water Conservation Dist., Gainesville, 1980; bd. dirs. Fla. State Fair, Tampa, 1976—, Fla. 4-H Found., Gainesville. Recipient Disting. Service award USDA, Washington, 1987; named Outstanding Citizen Middleton-West Towne Rotary, Middleton, 1974. Mem. Nat. Assn. Nat. Assn. State Colls. and Land Grant Univs. (chmn. extension section 1984-85, senator 1988-91), Nat. Extension Com. (joint coun. 1991-94, strategic planning coun. 1992-96), Epsilon Sigma Phi (State Disting. Service award), Gamma Sigma Delta, Alpha Gamma Rho. Democrat. Roman Catholic. Lodge: Kiwanis, Rotary. Avocations: fishing, coaching youth basketball, baseball, lector. Home: 4410 NW 16th Pl Gainesville FL 32605-3408 Office: U Fla Agriculture Extension 1038 McCarty Hall Gainesville FL 32611

WOESTENDIEK, (WILLIAM) JOHN, JR., columnist; b. Winston-Salem, N.C., Sept. 5, 1953; s. William John Sr. and Josephine (Pugh) W.; m. Jennifer Ann Swartz, Sept. 1, 1979; 1 child, Joseph Yoon Tae. BJ, U. N.C., 1975. Reporter Ariz. Daily Star, Tucson, 1975-78; reporter, asst. city editor, city editor Lexington (Ky.) Herald-Leader, 1978-81; reporter Phila. Inquirer, 1981-90; nat. corr. West Coast bur. Phila. Inquirer, Newport Beach, Calif., 1990-93; reporter Phila. Inquirer, 1994-96, columnist, 1996—. Recipient Paul Tobenkin Meml. award Columbia U., 1984, Nat. Headliners award Press Club Atlantic City, 1987, Pulitzer Prize for Investigative Reporting Columbia U., 1987, Ernie Pyle award, 1994, Best Feature Story award Ky. Press. Assn., 1978, Best Investigative Story award Ky. Press Assn., 1979, Nat. Arc of Excellence Nat. Assn. Retarded Citizens, 1984, Best News Reporting First Place award AP Mng. Editors Pa., 1985, Sigma Delta Chi award for Feature Writing, 1994; John S. Knight fellow Stanford U., 1988-89. Office: The Phila Inquirer PO Box 8263 Philadelphia PA 19101-8263

WOETZEL, DAMIAN ABDO, ballet dancer, educator; b. Newton, Mass., May 17, 1967; s. Robert Kurt and Sheila Marilyn (Barry) W. Grad. high sch., Holllywood, Calif., 1983. Prin. dancer L.A. Ballet, 1983-85; mem. corps de ballet N.Y.C. Ballet, 1985-88, soloist, then prin. dancer, 1989—; Dir. ballet program New York State Summer School for the Arts, Saratoga Springs, N.Y., 1994—; dancer, choreographer New York City Opera, 1994-95. Performed in Jerome Robbins' Four Seasons Dance at a Gathering; Goldberg Variations, Glass Pieces, Interplay, Other Dances; Balanchine's La Sonnambula, Stars and Stripes, Mozariana, Ballo della Regina, Tarantella, The Nutcracker, La Source,Coppelia, Donizetti Variations, Raymonda Variations, Martin's the Sleeping Beauty, Jeu de Cartes, Musical Offering, Paulenc Sonata, Les Petits Riens, The Waltz Project; also Tschaikovsky's Pas de Deux; danced in N.Y.C. Ballet's Balanchine Celebration, 1993, danced in film George Balanchine's The Nutcracker, 1993; choreographed Ebony Concerto, 1994, Glazounov Pas de Deux, 1994; danced in Alexander Borodin's opera Prince Igor, 1994. Recipient 1st prize Commemorative award Nat. Ballet Achievement Fund, Phila., 1984. Avocations: carpentry, gardening, guitar playing, surfing. Office: NYC Ballet Inc NY State Theater Lincoln Ctr Plz New York NY 10023

WOFFORD, HARRIS LLEWELLYN, former senator, national service executive; b. N.Y.C., Apr. 9, 1926; s. Harris Llewellyn and Estelle (Gardner) W.; m. Emmy Lou Clare Lindgren, Aug. 14, 1948 (dec. Jan. 1996); children: Susanne, Daniel, David. BA, U. Chgo., 1948; study fellow, India, 1949, Israel, 1950; LLB, Yale U., 1954; LL.B., Howard U., 1954. Bar: D.C. 1954, U.S. Supreme Ct. 1958, Pa. 1978. Asst. to Chester Bowles, 1953-54; law assoc. Covington & Burling, Washington, 1954-58; legal asst. to Rev. Theodore Hesburgh, Commn. on Civil Rights, 1958-59; assoc. prof. Notre Dame Law Sch., 1959-60, on leave, 1961-66; asst. to Sen. Kennedy, 1960; spl. asst. to Pres. Kennedy, 1961-62; spl. rep. for Africa, dir. Ethiopian program U.S. Peace Corps, 1962-64; assoc. dir. Peace Corps, Washington, 1964-66; pres. Coll. at Old Westbury, SUNY, 1966-70, Bryn Mawr (Pa.) Coll., 1970-78; counsel firm Schnader, Harrison, Segal and Lewis, Phila. and Washington, 1979-86; chmn. Pa. Dem. State Com., 1986; sec. labor and industry Commonwealth of Pa., 1987-91; U.S. senator from Pa., 1991-95; vis. lectr. Howard Law Sch., 1956. Author: It's Up to Us, 1946, (with Clare Wofford) India Afire, 1951, Of Kennedys and Kings, 1980; editor: Embers of the World, 1970; co-editor: Report of the U.S. Commission on Civil Rights, 1959. Mem. Coun. Fgn. Rels., 1968—; co-chmn. Com. for Study of Nat. Svc., 1977-80; mem. U.S. Adv. Com. on Nat. Growth Policy Processes, 1975-76; trustee The Am. Coll. , Bryn Mawr, 1975-83; mem. coun. U.S.-South Africa Leader Exch. Program, 1971-87; bd. dirs. Internat. League for Human Rights, 1979—, pres., 1980—; bd. dirs. Pub. Interest Law Ctr. Phila., 1978-87; trustee Martin Luther King Ctr. for Nonviolent Social Change, 1983-87; governing coun. Wilderness Soc., 1983-87. With USAF, 1944-45. Mem. ABA. Roman Catholic. Office: Corporation for Nat Svc 1201 New York Ave NW Washington DC 20525 Office: Corp for Nat Svc 1201 New York Ave NW Washington DC 20525

WOGAN, GERALD NORMAN, toxicology educator; b. Altoona, Pa., Jan. 11, 1930; s. Thomas B. and Florence E. (Corl) W.; m. Henrietta E. Hoenicke, Aug. 24, 1957; children: Christine F., Eugene E. BS, Juniata Coll., 1951; MS, U. Ill., 1953, PhD, 1957. Asst. prof. physiology Rutgers U., New Brunswick, N.J., 1957-61; asst. prof. toxicology MIT, Cambridge, 1962-65, assoc. prof., 1965-69, prof. toxicology, 1969—, head dept. applied biol. scis., 1979-88, prof. chemistry, 1989—, dir. divsn. toxicology, 1988—; cons. to nat. and internat. govt. agys., industries. NIH grantee, 1963—. Mem. edit. bd. Cancer Rsch., 1971-79, Applied Microbiology, 1971-79, Chem.-Biol. Interactions, 1975-78, Toxicology, Environ. Health, 1974-84, Jour. Nat. Cancer Inst., 1988—; contbr. articles and revs. to profl. jours. Recipient Disting. Alumni award U. Ill. Fellow Am. Acad. Microbiology; mem. AAAS, NAS, Inst. Medicine, Am. Assn. Cancer Rsch., Am. Soc. Pharmacology and Exptl. Therapeutics, Am. Soc. Microbiology, Soc. Toxicology, Am. Inst. Nutrition, Sigma Xi. Office: MIT Divsn of Toxicology 77 Massachusetts Ave Rm 16-333 Cambridge MA 02139-4301

WOGAN, ROBERT, broadcasting company executive; b. N.Y.C., Oct. 13, 1925; s. Robert and Johanna (Hilderbrandt) W.; m. Phyllis Jayn Volz, Nov.

21, 1965 (div. 1991); children—Robert, Stephen. Grad. pub. schs. Page NBC, 1943, asst. mgr. guest relations, 1945-46, night announcer, sec., 1946, asst. supr. announcing, 1946-47; asst. supr. announcing NBC (prodn. div.), 1947-48, night adminstrv. asst., 1948-50, supr. network program operations, 1950-55, Eastern radio program and prodn. mgr., 1955-63, exec. producer "Monitor" program, 1963-65, v.p. radio network programs, 1965-73; exec. producer spl. programs NBC Radio Network, 1973-75, regional mgr. affiliate relations, 1975-81, regional dir. affiliate relations, 1981-89; regional mgr. Westwood One Cos., 1989—, Mut. Broadcasting System, 1989—, NBC Radio Network, 1989—, Talknet Programs, 1989—; exec. producer conv. entertainment, coordinator NBC/Mus. of Broadcasting to preserve history radio data. Exec. producer X Minus One radio program, 1974-75. Mem. Nat. council Boy Scouts Am., 1970—; chmn. Radio com. United Hosp. Fund, 1972. Served with AUS, 1944-45. Recipient Radio-TV All-Am. of Year award for Experiment in Drama, 1963, Gabriel award for pub. service programming, 1967, Freedoms Found. award, 1972, Peabody awards for "Monitor", 1972, for "Project I Experiment", 1973. Mem. Broadcast Pioneers, Internat. Radio and TV Soc. Home: 360 W 22nd St New York NY 10011-2600 Office: 30 Rockefeller Plz New York NY 10112 also: 1700 Broadway New York NY 10019-5905 also: 1775 S Jefferson Davis Hwy Arlington VA 22202

WOGEN, WARREN RONALD, mathematics educator; b. Forest City, Iowa, Feb. 19, 1943; s. Milford N. and Olive A. (Sime) W.; m. Sherry D., Aug. 23, 1969; children—Shannon, Lori. A.B., Luther Coll., 1965; M.A. in Math., Ind.U., 1967, Ph.D. in Math., 1969. Prof. math. U. N.C., Chapel Hill, 1969—. Contbr. articles to profl. jours. Mem. Am. Math. Soc. Office: U NC Math Dept. Chapel Hill NC 27599-3250

WOGLOM, ERIC COOKE, lawyer; b. Bklyn., Mar. 14, 1943; s. Joseph F. and Rita Mary (Cooke) W.; m. Joshan Robin Levitsky, May 11, 1968; children—Peter Douglas, Brian Stewart. B.A., Yale U., 1964; LL.B., U. Pa. 1967. Bar: N.Y. 1968, U.S. Patent and Trademark Office 1970, U.S. Ct. Appeals (9th cir.) 1972, U.S. Ct. Appeals (2d cir.) 1973, U.S. Dist. Ct. (so. and ea. dist.) N.Y. 1974, U.S. Supreme Ct. 1974, U.S. Ct. Appeals (7th cir.) 1980, U.S. Ct. Appeals (Fed. cir.) 1982. With Fish & Neave, N.Y.C., 1967—, sr. ptnr., 1976—; mem. intellectual property adv. com. U.S. Dist. Ct. Del. Served with U.S. Army, 1967. Mem. ABA, Am. Intellectual Property Law Assn., Assn. Bar City N.Y. (past chair com. on patents), N.Y. Law Inst., N.Y. Intellectual Property Law Assn. (past chair com. on econ. matters effecting the profession), N.Y. State Bar Assn. Republican. Roman Catholic. Clubs: Yale of N.Y.C., Shelter Island Yacht. Home: 430 North St Harrison NY 10528-1118 Office: Fish & Neave 1251 Avenue Of The Americas New York NY 10020-1104

WOGSLAND, JAMES WILLARD, retired heavy machinery manufacturing executive; b. Devils Lake, N.D., Apr. 17, 1931; s. Melvin LeRoy and Mable Bertina (Paulson) W.; m. Marlene Claudia Clark, June 1957; children: Karen Lynn, Steven James. BA in Econs., U. Minn., 1957. Various positions fin. dept. Caterpillar Tractor Co., Peoria, Ill., 1957-64, treas., 1976-81; mgr. fin. Caterpillar Overseas S.A., Geneva, 1965-70, sec.-treas., 1970-76; dir.-pres. Caterpillar Brasil S.A., São Paulo, 1981-87; exec. v.p. Caterpillar, Inc., Peoria, 198-90, also bd. dirs., vice-chmn., 1990-95; bd. dirs. First of Am. Bank Corp., Kalamazoo, Protection Mut. Ins. Co., Park Ridge, Ill., Cipsco, Inc., Springfield, Ill. Mem. adv. bd. St. Francis Hosp., Peoria, 1987-95; bd. dirs. Peoria Area Cmty. Found., 1986-92; trustee Eureka Coll., 1987-95. Sgt. USAF, 1951-55. Mem. Hayden Lake Golf and Country Club. Republican. Presbyterian. Home: 9675 Easy St Hayden Lake ID 83835-9526

WOHL, DAVID, humanities educator, college dean-theatre director; b. Washington, Nov. 28, 1950; s. Joseph Gene and Carol (Weiss) W.; children: Isaac, Gabriele. BA, Clark U., 1972; MA, U. Conn., 1975; PhD, Kent State U., 1988. Staff asst. Am. Theatre Assn., Washington, 1975-76; prof. W.Va. State Coll., Institute, 1976-79, chmn. dept. comm., 1979-88, dean divsn. arts and humanities, 1988—; artistic dir. Charleston (W.Va.) Stage Co., 1991—; gen. mgr. Porthouse Theatre Festival, Cuyahoga Falls, Ohio, 1984-85; cons. U. South Ala., Mobile, 1988; bd. dirs., treas., pres. Southeastern Theatre Conf., 1993—; co-dir. W.Va. Gt. Tchrs. Stage dir. Kanawha Players, 1978—, Nutmeg Summer Playhouse, 1975-76, W.Va. Theatre Festival, Charleston Playhouse; prodr.: (films) Chillers, 1985, Strangest Dreams, 1990, Paradise Park, 1992 (Gold medal Houston Internat. Film Festival 1992, 1st place award Chgo. Film Festival 1992); contbr. articles to theatre jours. Bd. dirs. Kanawha Arts Alliance, Charleston, 1979-81, Kanawha Players, 1982-85; pres. W.Va. Theatre Conf., 1987-89; v.p. Arts Advocacy W.Va., 1994—. NEH Fellow, 1977, 80; Dept. Edn. teaching fellow, 1976-77. Mem. Am. Soc. for Theatre Rsch., Assn. for Theatre in Higher Edn., Speech Comm. Assn. Home: 1411 Summit Ln Charleston WV 25302-2639 Office: W Va State Coll PO Box 28 Institute WV 25112-0028

WOHL, RONALD H., management consultant, writing and editorial expert; b. Washington, Sept. 3, 1942; s. Bernard Carl and Martha (Aberbach) W.; m. Myrna Zelda Chevelier, June 27, 1965; children: Jennifer Lynn, Amy Beth. Student, Fla. State U., 1960-62; BA in Anthropology, George Washington U., 1965; postgrad., George Washington U. Law Sch., 1965-67, Am. U., Washington, 1969-74. Cert. mgmt. cons. Asst. to regional credit mgr. Sears, Roebuck & Co., Bethesda, Md., 1966-67; supr. payroll & ins. Montgomery Coll., Rockville, Md., 1967-71; supr. program info. & analysis Nat. Rural Elec. Coop. Assn., Washington, 1971-74; employee benefits comms. cons. Wyatt Co., Washington, 1974-77; pres. R.H. Wohl & Assocs./In Plain English, Gaithersburg, Md., 1977—; columnist Gazette Newspapers, Gaithersburg, 1987, Montgomery Jour., Rockville, 1989-90; bd. dirs. Braille Tech., LLC, 1995. Mem. editl. bd., author Employers Guide to Managed Health Care, 1994—, Civic Action Handbook, 1994—. Precinct chair Montgomery County Dems., 1978—; Dem. candidate for Md. Ho. of Dels., Annapolis, 1986; chmn. Commn. on Humanities, Montgomery County Md., 1987—; dir. North Potomac (Md.) Citizens Assn., 1988-95; citizen mem. Comty. Policing Steering Com., Montgomery County, Md., 1992—; tchr. Am. Jewish history and comparative religion; bd. dirs. Temple Beth Ami Brotherhood, Rockville, 1981-95, pres. 1990-92. Mem. Am. Assn. Home Based Bus. (nat. bd. dirs.), Inst. for Mgmt. Cons. (v.p. mem. Washington D.C. chpt. 1994-95). Home: 14501 Antigone Dr North Potomac MD 20878-2484 Office: R H Wohl & Assocs/ In Plain English PO Box 3300 Gaithersburg MD 20885-3300

WOHLER, JEFFERY WILSON, newspaper editor; b. Eugene, Oreg., Dec. 30, 1947; s. Benjamin Otto and Mildred Martha (Wilson) W.; m. Kandis Brewer, May 4, 1974 (div. 1985); m. Mary Lou Fletcher, Aug. 30, 1986; 1 child, Kennedy Read. BS in Journalism, U. Oreg., 1970. Staff writer Oreg. Jour., Portland, 1970-76, suburban editor, 1976-78, asst. city editor, 1978-80, city editor, 1980-82; dep. metro. editor The Oregonian, Portland, 1982-84, sports editor, 1984-92, editor, voice info. svcs., 1992—. Mem. Assoc. Press Sports Editors (v.p. 1989-91, pres. 1991-92), City Club of Portland (com. chair). Avocations: golf, reading. Home: 7610 NE Sacramento St Portland OR 97213-6043 Office: Oregonian 1320 SW Broadway Portland OR 97201-3469

WOHLFORD, JAMES GREGORY, pharmacist; b. Virginia, Minn., Nov. 4, 1956; s. James Hoover and Jeanne Katherine (Imgrund) W. AA, Indian River C.C., Ft. Pierce, Fla., 1977; BS in Pharmacy, U. Fla., 1981; MBA, Fla. Inst. Tech., 1987; PhD in Pharmacy, Southeastern U. Health Sci., 1994. Registered pharmacist, Fla., Ala. Rsch. asst. U. Fla., Gainesville, 1979-81; pharmacist Lawnwood Med. Ctr., Ft. Pierce, 1981—. Mem. Fla. Soc. Hosp. Pharmacists, Am. Soc. Hosp. Pharmacists. Roman Catholic. Avocations: snow skiing, scuba diving, water skiing. Home: 4250 N A 1 A Apt 904 Fort Pierce FL 34949-8340 Office: Lawnwood Regional Med Ctr PO Box 188 Fort Pierce FL 34954-0188

WOHLGELERNTER, BETH, organization executive; b. N.Y.C., Jan. 30, 1956; d. Maurice Nathaniel and Esther Rachel (Feinerman) W. BA, Barnard Coll., 1977. Exec. aide to pres. Barnard Coll., N.Y.C., 1977-80; spl. asst. to pres. The Commonwealth Fund, N.Y.C., 1980-81; asst. to chief exec. officer/pres. Mary McFadden, Inc., N.Y.C., 1981-84; exec. adminstr. The Donna Karan Co., N.Y.C., 1984-90; exec. dir. Hadassah, The Women's Zionist Orgn. Am., Inc., N.Y.C., 1990—; comm. adv. coun. AT&T, 1992—. Bd. dirs., v.p. N.Am. Conf. on Ethiopian Jewry, N.Y.C., 1981-85, bd. advisors, 1985—; bd. govs. Lincoln Sq. Synagogue, N.Y.C., 1988-94, bd. trustees, 1994—; bd. trustees United Israel Appeal, 1991—. Office: Hadassah The Women's Zionist Orgn Am Inc 50 W 58th St New York NY 10019-2500

WOHLGEMUTH, JOHN HAROLD, solid state physicist; b. N.Y.C., Dec. 20, 1946; s. Harold V. and Joan G. (Purvey) W.; m. Bethany H. Hubbard, June 23, 1973; children: Edward J., Robert B. BS, Rensselaer Poly. Inst., 1968; PhD, Rensseler Poly. Inst., 1973. Post-doctoral rsch. U. Waterloo, Ont., Can., 1973-75, U. Pa., Phila., 1975-76; mgr. advanced devel. Solarex, Rockville, Md., 1976-83; dir. rsch. & devel. Solarex, Frederick, Md., 1986—; mgr. solid sci. group Cabot Corp., Billerica, Md., 1983-86; U.S. del. Internat. Electrotechnical Commn., Geneva, 1986—. Author IEEE Photovoltaic Specialist Conf., 1988, 90, 91, 93, 94, 95. Mem. IEEE, Am. Physical Soc., Materials Rsch. Soc. Methodist. Home: 5215 Fairgreen Way Ijamsville MD 21754-9634 Office: Solarex 630 Solarex Ct Frederick MD 21703-8624

WOHLGENANT, RICHARD GLEN, lawyer; b. Porterville, Calif., Dec. 2, 1930; s. Carl Ferdinand and Sara Alice (Moore) W.; m. Teresa Joan Bristow, Dec. 27, 1959; children: Mark Thomas, Tracy Patrice, Timothy James. B.A., U. Mont., Missoula, 1952; LL.B., Harvard U., Cambridge, Mass., 1957. Bar: Colo. 1957, U.S. Dist. Ct. Colo. 1957. Assoc. Holme Roberts & Owen LLC, Denver, 1957-62; ptnr./mem. Holme Roberts & Owen, Denver, 1962—. Bd. dirs. Adopt-A-Sch., Denver, 1976-80, St. Joseph Found., Denver, 1990-93, Denver Com. Coun. Fgn. Rels., Japanese-Am. Soc. Colo., Rocky Mountain chpt. U.S. Mex. C. of C. Mem. ABA, Colo. Bar Assn., Denver Bar Assn., Am. Coll. Real Estate Lawyers, Univ. Club, Law Club, City Club. Republican. Roman Catholic. Home: 300 Ivy St Denver CO 80220-5855 Office: Holme Roberts & Owen LLC 1700 Lincoln St Denver CO 80203-4501

WOHLLEBEN, RUDOLF, microwave and antenna researcher; b. Bad Kreuznach, Germany, June 4, 1936; s. Georg Konrad and Kathrin (Lellbach) W.; m. Walburg Groehler, Aug. 27, 1967 (div. Nov. 1982); children: Niclas-Jakob, Philipp-Andreas; m. Rosemarie Rudloff, Dec. 21, 1982; stepchildren: Viola Ehrenheim, Mathias Ehrenheim. BSEE, diploma in elec. engrng., U. Karlsruhe, Germany, 1958, Tech. U. Munich, 1960; MSEE, Tech. U. Munich; D of Engrng., Tech. Hochschule, Aachen, Germany, 1969. R & D engr. Forschungsinst. HF-Physik, Rolandseck, Rhein, Germany, 1961-64; rsch. and teaching asst. Inst. Tech. Electronics RWTH, Aachen, 1964-70; group leader antennas and electronics divsn. Max-Planck Inst. for Radioastronomie, Bonn, Germany, 1971—; lectr. U. Kaiserslautern, Germany, 1980—; cons. H. Schilling GmbH, Weiskirchen, Germany, 1969-71, Nuffield Obs., Manchester, Eng., 1975, ESA-ESTEC, Noordwijk, The Netherlands, A.N.T., Backnang, Elekluft, Bonn, Space Rsch. Inst., Moscow, R. Hirschmann-Antennen, Esslingen, Phys. Inst. of U. of Cologne. Author, editor: Corps Alemannia/Karlsruhe in 250 Semstern, 1988; co-author: Antennas for Elliptical Polarization and its Measuring Techniques, 1968, Farfield Pattern Simulation of Linear Array Antennas on the Analog Computer, 1970, Interferometry in Radioastronomy and Radar Techniques, 1991, Interferometrie in Radioastronomie u. Radartechnik, 1973; contbr. 62 articles to sci. jours.; discoverer: (with Dirk Fiebig) beam squint of a radially displaced fed paraboloid reflector antenna, 1990. Recipient Th. Heuss medal, German Liberal Party, 1990. Mem. Informationstechnische Gesellschaft, Corps Alemannia, Weinheimer Verband Alter Corpsstudenten (chmn. 1995-97). Mem. Free Democrat Party. Avocations: 16-millimeter film amateur, piano, soccer, gardening, genealogy. Office: Max-Planck Inst Radioastronomie, Auf dem Huegel 69, D-53121 Bonn Germany

WOHLSCHLAG, DONALD EUGENE, zoologist, marine ecologist, educator emeritus; b. Bucyrus, Ohio, Nov. 6, 1918; s. Herman Albert and Agnes Mae (Canode) W.; m. Elsie Marjorie Baker, June 5, 1943; children: William Eugene, Nancy Sue, Sarah Ann. BS, Heidelberg Coll., 1940; PhD, Ind. U., 1949. Research assoc. in zoology U. Wis., 1948-49; asst. prof. biol. scis. Stanford U., 1949-56, assoc. prof., 1956-64, prof., 1964-65; prof. zoology and marine scis. U. Tex., Aransas, 1965-86; prof. emeritus zoology and marine scis. U. Tex., Port Aransas, 1986—; dir. Marine Sci. Inst., 1965-70; mem. U.S. Marine Subcom. for Internat. Biol. Program, 1966-71; mem. com. on ecol. research interocean-canal Nat. Acad. Scis., 1969-70; mem. Tundra Biome Panel, NSF, 1971-74; mem. water ecosystems com. Inst. Ecology, 1974-76. Contbr. numerous articles on arctic, antarctic and Gulf Coast fish ecol. research to profl. publs.; editor: Contbns. in Marine Sci, 1974-88. Served to 1st lt. USAAF, 1942-46. Recipient Antarctic medal NSF, 1965; NSF grantee, 1955-70; NOAA grantee, 1976-79; Office Naval Research grantee, 1952-54; Tex. Dept. Water Resources grantee, 1975-79. Fellow AAAS, Am. Inst. Fisheries Research Biologists, Arctic Inst. N. Am., Explorers Club; mem. Am. Fisheries Soc., Am. Soc. Limnology and Oceanography, Am. Soc. Zoologists, Am. Soc. Ichthyology and Herpetology, Ecol. Soc. Am. (pres. Western sect. 1965), Estuarine Research Fedn. (dir. 1976-78), Gulf Estuarine Research Soc. (pres. 1976-78), Sigma Xi. Home: 625 E Ave C Port Aransas TX 78373 Office: U Tex Port Aransas Marine Lab Port Aransas TX 78373 *Maintain the habitat; preserve the species, humans included.*

WOHLTMANN, HULDA JUSTINE, pediatric endocrinologist, diabetologist; b. Charleston, S.C., Apr. 10, 1923; d. John Diedrich and Emma Lucia (Mohrmann) W. B.S., Coll. Charleston, 1944; M.D., Med. U. S.C., 1949. Diplomate Am. Bd. Pediatrics. Intern Louisville Gen. Hosp., 1949-50; resident in pediatrics St. Louis Children's Hosp., 1950-53; mem. faculty Washington U. Sch. Medicine, St. Louis, 1953-65, instr., 1953-58, asst. prof., 1958-65, postdoctoral fellow biochemistry, 1961-63; assoc. prof. pediatrics, head pediatric endocrinology Med. U. S.C., Charleston, 1965-70, prof., 1970-90, prof. emeritus, 1990—. Bd. dirs. Franke Home, Charleston, 1975—, treas., 1989-91; mem. adv. bd. for ethics ctr. Newberry (S.C.) Coll., 1989—; trustee Luth. Theol. So. Sem., 1991—. Mem. Am. Pediatric Soc., Ambulatory Pediatric Assn., Endocrine Soc., Am. Diabetes Assn., Am. Acad. Pediatrics, Am. Fedn. Clin. Rsch., Midwest Soc. Pediatric Rsch., So. Soc. Pediatric Rsch., S.C. Diabetes Assn. (bd. dirs. 1970-86, pres. 1970-73, 84-85, v.p., 1982-83, Profl Svc. award 1977), Lawson Wilkins Endocrine Soc., Sugar Club. Lutheran. Contbr. articles to sci. jours. Home: 280 N Hobcaw Dr Mount Pleasant SC 29464-2562

WOIT, ERIK PETER, corporate executive, lawyer; b. Riga, Latvia, Mar. 10, 1931; s. Walter E. and Sigrid (Radzins) W.; m. Bonnie Jean Ford, June 16, 1953; children: Peter Gordon, Steven Ford. A.B., Allegheny Coll., 1953; J.D., Harvard U., 1956. Bar: N.Y. 1959, U.S. Supreme Ct., 1971. Asso. firm Mudge, Stern, Baldwin & Todd, N.Y.C., 1956-57, 60-62; asst. sec., internat. counsel Richardson-Merrell, Inc., 1962-71; sec., gen. counsel Amerace Corp., N.Y.C., 1971-73, v.p., group exec., 1973-74, pres. ESNA div., 1974-77, sr. v.p. adminstrn., chief adminstrv. and chief fin. officer, 1977-83; sr. v.p. Orient Express Hotels, Inc., N.Y.C., 1983—, also bd. dirs.; chmn. Sea Containers Am. Inc., 1984—; sr. v.p. Sea Containers Ltd., 1987—; participant Dept. Def. Joint Civilian Orientation Conf., 1994. Served to capt. USMCR, 1957-60. Mem. ABA, Assn. Bar City N.Y., Sigma Alpha Epsilon. Clubs: Harvard, Sky (N.Y.C.), 21 Club Inc. (N.Y.C.) (pres. 1995—). Home: 559 West Rd New Canaan CT 06840-2512 Office: 1155 Avenue Of The Americas New York NY 10036-2711

WOITACH, RICHARD, conductor, pianist; b. Binghamton, N.Y., July 27, 1935; s. Peter T. and Ester L. (Karkula) W.; m. Theresa Ballester, June 29, 1957 (div.); children—Paul, Karl; m. Jeryl E. Metz, Apr. 16, 1976. B.M., Eastman Sch. Music, 1956. Asst. condr. Met. Opera, N.Y.C., 1959-68; assoc. condr. Met. Opera, 1973—; guest lectr. in music Ind. U., 1972; music dir. Wolf Trap Opera Co., 1981-87; mem. faculty Juilliard Sch. Music, 1987; pres. New Artists Coalition Inc., 1986-87. Recs. with London Symphony for Saturn, 1980, with Regina Reshik for Epic, 1969, with Theresa Stratas for Nonesuch, 1982, with Jon Vickers for Centre discs, 1985; solo piano recs. on Opus One Label, 1967, 71; contbg. editor Opera Quar., 1983-89. Home: 697 W End Ave New York NY 10025-6823 Office: care Met Opera Lincoln Center New York NY 10023

WOIWODE, LARRY (ALFRED WOIWODE), writer, poet; b. 1941. Writer in residence U. Wis., 1973-74; vis. prof. SUNY, Binghamton, 1983-85, prof., dir. creative writing program, 1985-88. Author: What I'm Goint to Do, I Think, 1969 (with others) Poetry North, 1970, Beyond the Bedroom Wall, 1975, (verse) Even Tide, 1977, Poppa John, 1981, Born Brothers, 1988, The Neumiller Stories, 1989. Recipient Award of Merit Am. Acad. of Arts and Letters, 1995. Office: c/o Michael di Capua Books Farrar Straus & Giroux 19 Union Sq W New York NY 10003*

WOJCICKI, ANDREW ADALBERT, chemist, educator; b. Warsaw, Poland, May 5, 1935; s. Franciszek Wojcicki and Janina (Kozlowa) Hoskins; m. Marba L. Hart, Dec. 21, 1968; children: Katherine, Christina. BS, Brown U., 1956; PhD, Northwestern U., 1960; postdoctoral fellow, U. Nottingham, Eng., 1960-61. Asst. prof. chemistry Ohio State U., Columbus, 1961-66, assoc. prof., 1966-69, prof., 1969—, acting chmn., 1981-82; assoc. chmn. Ohio State U., 1982-83, 84-86; vis. prof. Case Western Res. U., 1967, U. Bologna, Italy, 1988; vis. researcher U. Coll. London, 1969; sr. U.S. scientist Alexander von Humboldt Found., Mulheim/Ruhr, Germany, 1975-76; vis. scholar U. Calif.-Berkeley, 1984. Contbr. articles to profl. and scholarly jours. Guggenheim fellow U. Cambridge (Eng.), 1976; recipient Disting. Teaching award Ohio State U., 1968, Humboldt Sr. award Humboldt Found., 1975, 76. Mem. Am. Chem. Soc. (Columbus sect. award 1992), Royal Chem. Soc., Sigma Xi, Phi Lambda Upsilon. Home: 825 Greenridge Rd Columbus OH 43235-3411 Office: Ohio State U 120 W 18th Ave Columbus OH 43210-1106

WOJCICKI, STANLEY GEORGE, physicist, educator; b. Warsaw, Poland, Mar. 30, 1937; came to U.S., 1950; s. Franciszek and Janina (Kozlow) W.; m. Esther Denise Hochman, Nov. 17, 1961; children: Susan Diane, Janet Maia, Anne Elizabeth. A.B., Harvard U., 1957; Ph.D., U. Calif., Berkeley, 1962. Physicist Lawrence Radiation Lab., Berkeley, 1961-66; asst. prof. physics Stanford U., 1966-68, assoc. prof., 1968-74, prof., 1974—, chmn. dept., 1982-85, dep. dir. Superconducting Supercollider Central Design Group, 1984-89; chmn. Stanford Linear Accelerator Center Exptl. Program Adv. Com., 1979-81; chmn. High Energy Physics Adv. Panel, 1990-96. Assoc. editor Phys. Rev. Letters for Exptl. High Energy Physics, 1978-80. Recipient Alexander von Humboldt Sr. Am. Scientist award, 1981; NSF fellow, 1964-65; Sloan Found. fellow, 1968-72; Guggenheim fellow, 1973-74. Fellow Am. Phys. Soc. Office: Stanford U Physics Dept Stanford CA 94305

WOJCIK, ANTHONY STEPHEN, computer science educator; b. Chgo., Sept. 18, 1945; s. Casimir Anthony and Elizabeth Anne (Hudak) W.; m. Paula Jean Valaitis, Aug. 16, 1969; children: Laura Anne, Jeffrey Anthony. BS in Math., U. Ill., 1967, MS in Math., 1968, PhD in Computer Sci., 1971. Asst. prof. dept. computer sci. Ill. Inst. Tech., Chgo., 1971-76, assoc. prof. dept. computer sci., 1976-81, chmn. dept. computer sci., 1978-84, prof. dept. elec. and computer engring., 1984-86, prof. dept. computer sci., 1981-86; mem. tech. staff Bell Labs., Naperville, Ill., 1974; scientist in residence Argonne (Ill.) Nat. Lab., 1981, resident assoc., 1982-85, 86—, vis. scientist, 1985-86; prof. computer sci. Mich. State U., East Lansing, 1986—, chmn. dept. computer sci., 1986-95. Named Outstanding Young Man of Am., 1981-82. Mem. IEEE (chmn. midwestern area com. 1975-78), Assn. Computing Machinery. Roman Catholic. Office: Mich State U Dept Computer Sci East Lansing MI 48824

WOJCIK, CASS, decorative supply company executive, former city official; b. Rochester, N.Y., Dec. 3, 1920; s. Emil M. and Casimira C. (Krawiecz) W.; student Lawrence Inst. Tech., 1941-43, Yale U., 1943-44, U.S. Sch. for European Personnel, Czechoslovakia, 1945; m. Lilliam Leocadia Lendzion, Sept. 25, 1948; 1 child, Robert Cass. Owner, Nat. Florists Supply Co., Detroit, 1948-88, Nat. Decorative, Detroit, 1950—; co-owner Creation Center, Detroit, 1955-60; cons.-contractor hort.-bot. design auto show displays, TV producers, designers and decorators. Mem. Regional Planning and Evaluation Council, 1969-75; city-wide mem. Detroit Bd. Edn., 1970-75; commr. Detroit Public Schs. Employees Retirement Commn., until 1975; mem. Area Occupational Ednl. Commn., Ednl. Task Force; chmn., grand marshal Ann. Gen. Pulaski Day Parade, Detroit, 1970, 71; mem. Friends of Belle Isle; mem. Nat. Arboretum Adv. Council, U.S. Dept. Agr., 1982-83; mem. pastoral coun. Archidiocese of Detroit, 1983-86, 88-92; v.p. rsch. Barna Coll., Ft. Lauderdale, Fla.; vice chmn. 13th Congl. Dist. Rep. Party Mich., 1987-91; elected to 1988 electoral coll. Served with U.S. Army, 1944-46. Decorated Bronze Star; recipient citation Polish-Am. Congress, 1971, Art in Park 3d prize City of Oakland Park, Fla. Mem. S.E. Mich. Coun. Govts., Mich., Nat. sch. bd. assns., Big Cities Sch. Bd. Com., Nat. Coun. Great Cities Schs., Mcpl. Finance Officers Assn. U.S., Nat. Coun. Tchr. Retirement, Central Citizens Com. Detroit, Internat. Platform Assn., Mich. Heritage Coun., Nat. Geog. Soc. Roman Catholic. Club: Polish Century (Detroit). Home: 1729 SW 14th Ct Fort Lauderdale FL 33312-4109

WOJCIK, LAWRENCE A., lawyer; b. Chgo., Apr. 4, 1951. BS with high honors, De Paul U., 1973, LLM in Taxation, 1981; JD, Northwestern U., 1977. Bar: Ill. 1977; CPA., Ill. Ptnr. Keck, Mahin & Cate, Chgo. Mem. ABA, AICPA, Ill. Soc. CPA, Chgo. Bar Assn., Ill. State Bar Assn., Fed. Cir. Bar Assn., Seventh Cir. Bar Assn. Office: Keck Mahin & Cate 77 W Wacker Dr Ste 4900 Chicago IL 60601-1629*

WOJCIK, MARTIN HENRY, foundation development official; b. Chgo., May 10, 1948; s. Henry Martin and Mary Lorraine (Naughton) W. B.S., Ill. Inst. Tech., 1970; M. in Humanities, Bonn U., W. Ger., 1975. Price adminstr. R.R. Donnelley & Sons., Chgo., 1970-72; dir. devel. Citizens for a Better Environment, Milw., 1976-79; pres. Citizens for a Better Environment, Chgo., 1979-85, bd. dirs., 1979-85, 89—; chmn. bd. dirs. Citizens for a Better Environment, 1990-91; dir. found. relations Northwestern U., Evanston, Ill., 1987-89; dir. corp. and found. rels. Mayo Found., Rochester, Minn., 1989—; mem. policy adv. com. Ill. EPA, Springfield, 1980-82. Bd. dirs. Rochester Civic Theatre, 1991—, pres. bd. dirs. 1994-95; mem. adv. panel Minn. State Arts Bd., 1995. Mem. Ill. Inst. Tech. Alumni Assn. Roman Catholic. Home: 535 19th St NW Rochester MN 55901-4901 Office: Mayo Found Med Edn and Rsch Rochester MN 55905

WOJEWODSKI, STAN, JR., artistic director, dean. MFA, Cath. U. of Am. Artistic dir. Ctr. Stage, Balt., 1977-91, Yale Repertory Theatre, 1991—; dean Yale Sch. of Drama, 1991—; tchr. Hammerstein Ctr. for Theater Studies, Columbia U.; advisor Theater Cornell; bd. dirs. Theatre Comms. Group; mem. theater panel Nat. Endowment for Arts. Dir.: Hamlet, The Baltimore Waltz, On the Verge, Edward the Second (Yale Repertory Theatre), The Countess Cathleen (Abbey Theatre, Dublin, Ireland), On the Verge, Volpone (Guthrie Theater), Don Quixote de la Jolla, The Heliotrope Bouquet by Scott Joplin and Louis Chauvin (La Jolla Playhouse), Much Ado About Nothing (Settle Repertory Theatre); staged David Mamet's Oleanna; dir. Williamstown Theatre Festival, Old Globe Theatre, San Diego, Hudson Guild Theatre, N.Y., Berkshire Theatre Festival. Office: Yale Repertory Theatre Box 208244 Yale Sta 222 York St New Haven CT 06520-8244

WOJNILOWER, ALBERT MARTIN, economist; b. Vienna, Austria, Feb. 3, 1930; came to U.S., 1939; s. Theodore and Lissy (Koppel) W.; m. Sue Freudenfels, Apr. 6, 1952; children: Daniel, Michael, Joel, Samuel. A.B., Columbia U., 1951, A.M., 1951, Ph.D., 1960. Economist Fed. Res. Bank of N.Y., N.Y.C., 1951-62; assoc. economist First Nat. City Bank of N.Y.C., N.Y.C., 1962-63; chief economist The First Boston Corp., N.Y.C., 1964-86, sr. advisor, 1986—; cons. Rep. Nat. Bank of N.Y., N.Y.C., 1980—; adj. prof. fin. NYU Grad. Sch. Bus. Adminstrn., N.Y.C., 1961-66. Author: The Quality of Business Loans, 1960; co-author: Financial Institutions and Markets, 1970, 2d edit., 1981. Recipient A.A. Green prize Columbia Coll., 1951. Mem. Am. Fin. Assn. (bd. dirs. 1979-81), Am. Econ. Assn., Phi Beta Kappa. Democrat. Jewish. Office: The Clipper Group Corp 12 E 49th St New York NY 10017

WOJTYLA, KAROL JOZEF See JOHN PAUL, HIS HOLINESS POPE, II

WOLANDE, CHARLES SANFORD, corporate executive; b. Chgo., July 25, 1954; s. Sam C. and Marie Helene (Riccio) W.; m. Marian Helene Gillespie, Nov. 10, 1985; children: Eric, Jill, Patrick. B St. Mary's Coll., Winona, Minn., 1976. Lab. tech. Jefferson Electric, Bellwood, Ill., 1976-73; pres. Comark, Inc., Glendale Heights, Ill., 1978—; also CFO Comark, Inc., Bloomingdale, Ill. Named High Tech. Entrepreneur of the year Peat, Marwick, Mitchell, Chgo., 1987. Mem. C. of C. Glendale Heights. Republican. Roman Catholic. Avocations: golf, bowling, skiing. Home: 937 Fox

Glen Dr Saint Charles IL 60174-8808 Office: Comark Inc 471 Brighton Dr # 600 Bloomingdale IL 60108-3102

WOLANER, ROBIN PEGGY, magazine publisher; b. Queens, N.Y., May 6, 1954; d. David H. and Harriet (Radlow) W.; m. Steven J. Castleman, 1992; 1 child, Terry David. BS in Indsl. and Labor Rels., Cornell U., 1975. Sr. editor Viva Mag., N.Y.C., 1975-76; editor Impact Mag., N.Y.C., 1976-77; circulation mgr. Runner's World Mag., Mountain View, Calif., 1977-79; cons. Ladd Assocs., San Francisco, 1979-80; gen. mgr. Mother Jones Mag., San Francisco, 1980-81, pub., 1981-85; founder, pub. Parenting Mag., San Francisco, 1985-91, pres., 1991-92; v.p. Time Pub. Ventures, 1990-96; pres., CEO Sunset Pub. Corp., 1992-95; trustee Muir Investment Fund, 1991-94. Mem. bd. advisor U. Calif. Grad. Sch. Journalism, Berkeley, 1991-96; bd. dir. Bay Area Coun., 1992-95, Party Am. Inc., 1995—, Med. Self Care Inc., 1996—, Ifusion Com. LLC, 1996—. Jewish. Office: 2240 Hyde St San Francisco CA 94109

WOLANIN, BARBARA ANN BOESE, art curator, art historian; b. Dayton, Ohio, Dec. 12, 1943; d. William Carl and Elisabeth Cassell (Barnard) Boese; m. Thomas R. Wolanin, June 11, 1966 (div. 1980); children: Peter Michael, Andrew Thomas. AB, Oberlin Coll., 1966, AM, 1969; MAT, Harvard U., 1967; PhD, U. Wis., 1981. Dir. children's art classes Allen Art Mus., Oberlin, Ohio, 1967-68; art tchr. Lorain (Ohio) Pub. Schs., 1968-69, Newton (Mass.) Pub. Schs., 1969-71; teaching asst. U. Wis., Madison, 1972-74; asst. prof. art history Trinity Coll., Washington, 1978-83, James Madison U., Harrisonburg, Va., 1983-85; curator U.S. Capitol, Architect of the Capitol, Washington, 1985—; guest curator Pa. Acad. of Fine Arts, Phila, 1980-83. Author exhbn. catalog Arthur B. Carles, 1983, others; contbr. articles to profl. jours. Woodrow Wilson fellow, 1967, Kress fellow U. Wis., 1974, Smithsonian fellow, 1976; recipient Faculty Devel. award James Madison U., 1985. Mem. Women's Caucus for Art, Am. Assn. Mus., Coll. Art Assn., Am. Inst. for Conservation, Phi Beta Kappa (pres. Trinity Coll. 1982-83). Democrat. Episcopalian. Home: 4347 Brandywine St NW Washington DC 20016-4542 Office: US Capitol Office Capitol Architect Washington DC 20515

WOLANIN, THOMAS RICHARD, federal government official; b. Detroit, Dec. 1, 1942; s. Chester Richard and Helen Theresa (Luszki) W.; children: Peter, Andrew. BA magna cum laude, Oberlin Coll., 1965; MA, Harvard U., 1970, PhD, 1972. Staff dir. subcom. on labor-mgmt. rels. House Edn. and Labor Com., 1975-77, dep. staff dir. subcom. on select edn., 1977-78; exec. asst. to pres. NYU, 1981-82; analyst Senate Budget Com., 1982-83; staff dir. subcom. on investigations House P.O. and Civil Svc. Com., 1983-85, 87-91; staff dir. subcom. on postsecondary edn. House Edn. and Labor Com., 1978-81, 85-87;, 91-93; dep. ast. sec. legis. and congl. affairs U.S. Dept. Edn., Washington, 1993—; instr. govt. Oberlin Coll., 1967-69; teaching fellow in govt. Harvard U., 1969-70; asst. prof. polit. sci. U. Wis., Madison, 1971-78; congl. fellow Office of Congressman Frank Thompson, Jr., 1971-72; rsch. specialist Spl. Com. on Labor, House Edn. and Labor Com., 1972; cons. Nat. Commn. on Student Fin. Assistance, ERIC Clearinghouse on Higher Edn., Antioch U.; mem. Task Force on Student Loan Options, Nat. Assn. Ind. Colls. and Univs., adv. com. Nat. Study Debt Study, Lilly Found., Am. Coun. Edn. Author: Presidential Advisory Commissions: Truman to Nixon, 1975; co-author: Congress and the Colleges: Higher Education in National Politics, 1976; contbr. articles to profl. jours. Woodrow Wilson fellow, 1965-66, Harvard Grad. prize fellow, 1965-67, 69-71; guest scholar The Brookings Instn., 1970, Congl. fellow, 1971-72, Ford Found. travel and student grantee, 1972-73, 73-74, Spencer fellow Nat. Acad. Edn., 1975-81, acad. specialist grantee USIA, 1990. Mem. Am. Polit. Sci. Assn., Polish Am. Arts Assn. Washington, Polish Am. Congress, Congl. Fellowship Alumni Assn., Phi Beta Kappa. Democrat. Roman Catholic. Avocations: military history, Polish history, literature. Office: Legis & Congl Affairs Office US Dept Edn 600 Independence Ave SW Washington DC 20202-0004

WOLAS, HERBERT, lawyer; b. Bronx, N.Y., June 27, 1933; s. Irving and Mary (Kessner) W.; m. Annette Rudolph, Aug. 20, 1957; children: Cherise, Collette, Claudine. AA, UCLA, 1953, BA, 1954, JD, 1960. Bar: Calif. 1961. Since practiced in L.A. Served with F.A. AUS, 1955-56. Office: 1875 Century Park E Ste 2000 Los Angeles CA 90067-2521

WOLBRINK, DONALD HENRY, landscape architect, city planner; b. Ganges, Mich., May 13, 1911; s. Isaac M. and Ruby (Payne) W.; m. Florence Theresa Stack, Dec. 24, 1938; 1 child, Gretchen. B.A., U. Mich., 1932, M. Landscape Design, 1933. Landscape architect Nat. Park Service, Washington, 1934-41; landscape architect C.E., Omaha, 1941-44; assoc. Bartholomew Assocs., Honolulu, 1946-58, ptnr., 1958-64; pres. Donald Wolbrink, Honolulu, 1964-87, ret., 1989; dir. emeritus First Fed. Savs. and Loan, Honolulu; chmn. bd. Hawaii Architects and Engrs., Honolulu, 1979-84 (project dir. Melbourne strategy plan 1972-73); dir. Interplan, Melbourne, Australia, 1972-80. Co-author Hawaii State Law (land use law), 1961, sociophysical planning process, 1980; dir. (book) Tourism Standards, 1972. Bd. dirs. Oahu Devel. Conf., Honolulu, 1975-86 (project dir. 9 prin. Micronesian Islands 1961-75), C. of C., Honolulu, 1971-73, Downtown Improvement Assn., Honolulu, 1973-79; pres. Foresight, Inc., Honolulu, 1972-85. Served to lt. USN, 1944-46. Recipient Victorian Archtl. award Royal Australian Inst., 1977, Disting. Service award Engring. Assn. Hawaii, 1983, Spl. Achievement award Am. Plan Assn., 1990. Fellow ASCE, Am. Soc. Landscape Architects (trustee 1960-66, 77-78, merit award Hawaii chpt. 1983); mem. Am. Inst. Cert. Planners, Nat. Hist. Planning Pioneer Am., Inst. Consulting Planners. Avocation: photography. Home: 900 W Alpine Way Shelton WA 98584

WOLBRINK, JAMES FRANCIS, real estate investor; b. Charles City, Iowa, Sept. 8, 1942; s. Richard William and Anna (Bult) W.; m. Karen Ann Dunkerly, June 18, 1966. BS in Indsl. Engring., Iowa State U., 1966, postgrad., 1968-72. Cert. assn. exec. Tech. writer/editor Lawrence Radiation Lab., Livermore, Calif., 1966-67; editor, head engring. publs. Engring. Research Inst., Iowa State U., Ames, 1967-70; mng. dir., edn. and publs. Am. Inst. Indsl. Engrs., Norcross, Ga., 1971-83; commodities broker Clayton Brokerage, 1983-85; now pres. Wolbrink Properties, 1983—. Named Outstanding Young Alumnus Iowa State U., 1977. Mem. Sandy Springs Optimist Club (pres. 1989-90), Optimist Internat. (gov. Ga. dist. 1994-95), Delta Chi. Home and Office: 4520 Northside Dr NW Atlanta GA 30327-4548

WOLCHKO, MATTHEW JOHN, architect; b. Passaic, N.J., Jan. 10, 1961; s. John Stephen and Irene Wolchko; m. Marie Elena Theresa Malady, Feb. 15, 1992; 11 child, Katherine. BS in Architecture, Pa. State U., 1983; MArch, Ariz. State U., 1985. Registered architect, N.J.; lic. profl. planner, N.J.; cert. Nat. Coun. Archtl. Registration Bds.; notary pub., N.J. Draftsman Walter Kawecki, Montclair, N.J., 1984; rsch. asst. Coll. Architecture Ariz. State U., 1984-85; profl. intern Swanke, Hayden, Connell, N.Y.C., 1984; draftsman The Aybar Partnership, Ridgefield, N.J., 1985-89, ptnr., 1990—; presenter in field various confs. and workshops. Contbg. author: The Computability of Design, 1987. Mem. Three Saints Russian Orthodox Ch.; mem. Garfield (N.J.) Planning Bd., 1986-90, chmn., 1988-90; mcpl. rep. N.J. State Devel. and Redevel. Master Plan; mcpl. contact N.J. State Green Acres Program-Passaic River/Dundee Dam Hist. Park; mem. Garfield Zoning Bd. of Adjustment, 1994—; active Nat. Ry. Hist. Soc., Anthracite R.R. Hist. Soc. Mem. Architects League of No. N.J. (trustee 1996). Home: 65 Bergen St Garfield NJ 07026-2111 Office: Aybar Partnership 605 Broad Ave Ridgefield NJ 07657-1604

WOLCK, WOLFGANG HANS-JOACHIM, linguist, educator; b. Koenigsberg, Germany, Sept. 19, 1932; came to U.S., 1963; s. Walter Erich and Margarete (Brettschneider) W.; m. Carolyn Ann Burch, June 18, 1966. Student, Birkbeck Coll., London, 1956; Staatsexamen, Christian Albrecht U., Kiel, Germany, 1960; Ph.D., J.W. Goethe U., Frankfurt, Germany, 1963. Instr. German and Latin Liverpool (Eng.) Inst., 1957-58; instr. Albert Ludwig U., Freiburg, Germany, 1964-65; asst. prof. Ind. U., Bloomington, 1966-69; assoc. prof. linguistics SUNY-Buffalo, 1970-74, prof., 1975—, chmn. dept., 1977-87, 89-91, dir. Latin Am. Studies program, 1972-76; research fellow Instituto de Estudios Peruanos, Lima, Peru, 1976-77; advisor Ministry of Edn., Lima, 1972, 82-83; rsch. prof. Belgian Nat. Sc. Found., 1991—; cons. Fischer-Price Toys, Inc., East Aurora, N.Y., 1980—; hon. prof. San Marcos Nat. U., Lima, 1972; mem. Fulbright Nat. Screening Com., 1993—, E.C. Scientific Com. Linguistic Minorities, 1993—. Author: Phonematische Analyse der Sprache von Buchan, 1965, Pequeño Breviario Quechua, 1987; co-author: Interkulturelle Mehrsprachigkeit, 1991; editor: The Social Dimension of Dialectology, 1976, The Fifth LACUS Forum, 1979, International Handbook on Contact Linguistics, 1996. Founding mem. Peru Earthquake Relief Com., Washington, 1972; field rep. United Way Campaign, Buffalo, 1977-81. Recipient Bronze medal Mazaryk U., Brno, Czech Republic, 1971; Fulbright grantee, 1963-64. Mem. Am. Dialect Soc., Linguistic Soc. Am., Societas Linguistica Europea, Linguistic Assn. Can. and U.S., Am. Assn. Applied Linguistics, Ctr. for Cognitive Sci., Centre for Multilingual Rsch., Sociedad Boliviana de Linguistica (hon.), Ellicottville Ski Club (dir. 1988-94). Home: 611 Skinnersville Rd Buffalo NY 14228-2505 Office: SUNY 685 Baldy Hall Buffalo NY 14260-1030

WOLCOTT, JOHN WINTHROP, III, corporate executive; b. Balt., Dec. 3, 1924; s. John Winthrop, Jr. and Dorothy C. (Fraser) W.; m. Elizabeth Thelin Hooper, Apr. 24, 1948 (div. 1985); children: John Winthrop IV, Elizabeth T., Katherine C.; m. Karen E. Jones, Oct. 1, 1985; 1 child, Oliver Lund. B.Indsl. Engring., Gen. Motors Inst., 1951. Registered profl. engr., Ohio. With Gen. Motors Corp., 1946-53, Weatherhead Co., Cleve., 1957-60; v.p. H.K. Porter Co., Inc., Pitts., 1960-64; pres., dir., CEO Ametek, Inc., N.Y.C., 1964-66; v.p. Am. Machine & Foundry Co., 1966-77, group exec. process equipment group, 1967-70; exec. v.p. ops., dir. AMF, Inc., 1970-77; pres., chief exec. officer, dir. Transway Internat. Corp., N.Y.C., 1978-86, chmn. bd., 1982-86; bd. dirs. Fleet Aerospace Inc. Served with USCGR, 1943-46. Mem. Soc. Colonial Wars, Md. Club (Balt.), Brook Club (N.Y.C.). Episcopalian. Home: 210 Carrsbrook Dr Charlottesville VA 22901-1004

WOLCOTT, OLIVER DWIGHT, international trading company executive; b. Marshfield, Oreg., Oct. 17, 1918; s. Dwight Oliver and Agnes Beatrice (Kunkel) W.; m. Valborg K. Rasmussen, Mar. 22, 1942; 1 child, John Oliver. BS, U. Calif., 1940; MBA, Stanford U., 1942. With Chemurgic Corp., 1943-50, pres., 1947-50; with subs. W.R. Grace & Co., 1950-60, v.p., 1958-60; with Balfour Guthrie & Co., San Francisco, 1961-77; from v.p. to pres. Balfour Guthrie & Co., 1964-77; dir. Barclays Bank Calif., 1974-88, chmn., 1979-85; dir. Wilson & Geo., Meyer & Co., 1981-92, Bd. Trade San Francisco, 1969-77. Mem. Pacific-Union Club. Address: 3773 Terra Grenada Dr Walnut Creek CA 94595

WOLCOTT, ROBERT WILSON, JR., consulting company executive; b. Phila., Nov. 20, 1926; s. Robert Wilson and Alice (Huston) W.; m. Margaret Hoopes, June 24, 1949; children: Allyn M., Anne H. BSCE, Princeton U., 1948. V.p., gen. mgr. Internat. Mill Service div. IU Internat. Corp., Phila., 1963-65, pres., 1965-70; group v.p. IU Internat. Corp., Phila., 1970-82, exec. v.p., 1982-88; cons. Phila., 1988—. Bd. dirs. The Church Farm. Sch., Exton, Pa., 1981—, Zool. Soc. Phila., 1983—. Mem. Am. Iron & Steel Inst., AIME. Clubs: Merion Cricket (Haverford, Pa.); Gulph Mills Golf (King of Prussia, Pa.); Phila. Home: 236 Atlee Rd Wayne PA 19087-3836 Office: 125 Strafford Ave Ste 130 Wayne PA 19087-3318

WOLCOTT, SAMUEL H., III, investment banker; b. Boston, June 1, 1935; s. Samuel H. and Mary (Weld) W.; m. Nora Bradley, Dec. 28, 1960; 1 child, Natalie. A.B., Harvard U., 1957. Ptnr. J. Barth & Co., San Francisco, 1961-70; exec. v.p. Dean Witter Reynolds, N.Y.C., 1970-87, E.F. Hutton, 1987-88, Dean Witter Reynolds, N.Y.C., 1988—. Office: Dean Witter Reynolds 2 World Trade Ctr Fl 65 New York NY 10048-0203

WOLD, DAVID C., bishop. Bishop of Southwestern Wash. Evang. Luth. Ch. in Am., Tacoma. Office: Synod of Southwestern Washington 420 121st St S Tacoma WA 98444-5218

WOLD, FINN, biochemist, educator; b. Stavanger, Norway, Feb. 3, 1928; came to U.S., 1950, naturalized, 1957; s. Sverre and Herdis (Rasmussen) W.; m. Bernadine Moe, June 13, 1953; children—Eric Robert, Marc Sverre. Student, U. Oslo, 1946-50; M.S., Okla. State U., 1953; Ph.D., U. Calif. at Berkeley, 1956. Research asso. U. Calif. at Berkeley, 1956-57; asst. prof. biochemistry U. Ill., Urbana, 1957-62; asso. prof. U. Ill., 1962-66; prof. biochemistry U. Minn. Med. Sch., Mpls., 1966-74; prof. biochemistry U. Minn., St. Paul, 1974-81, head dept., 1974-79; Robert A. Welch prof. chemistry U. Tex. Med. Sch., Houston, 1981—; vis. prof. Nat. Taiwan U., 1971, Rice U., 1974, Amademia Sinica, Taiwan, 1990, U. Tromso, Norway, 1991-94; cons. in field. Author, contbg. author books; mem. edit. bd. Jour. Biol. Chemistry, 1974-79, 81-86, Biochemistry, 1974-83, Protein Sci., 1995—; contbr. articles to profl. jours. Fulbright fellow, 1950; John Simon Guggenheim fellow, 1960-61; recipient Lalor Found. Research award, 1958, NIH research career devel. award, 1961-66. Mem. AAAS, Am. Soc. Biochemistry and Molecular Biology (councilor 1978-81, sec. 1992-95), Am. Chem. Soc. (councilor 1980-83, chmn. divsn. biol. chemistry 1985-86), Protein Soc. (pres. 1989-91), Biochem. Soc. (London). Office: U Tex Med Sch PO Box 20708 Houston TX 77225-0708

WOLD, JOHN SCHILLER, geologist, former congressman; b. East Orange, N.J., Aug. 31, 1916; s. Peter Irving and Mary (Helff) W.; m. Jane Adele Pearson, Sept. 28, 1946; children: Peter Irving, Priscilla Adele, John Pearson. AB, St. Andrews U., Scotland and Union Coll., Schenectady, 1938; MS, Cornell U., 1939; LLD (hon.), U. Wyo., 1991. Dir. Fedn. Rocky Mountain States, 1966-68; v.p. Rocky Mountain Oil and Gas Assn., 1967, 68; mem. Wyo. Ho. of Reps., 1957-59; Wyo. Republican candidate for U.S. Senate, 1964, 70; mem. 91st Congress at large from, Wyo.; chmn., CEO Wold Trona Co., Inc.; pres., chmn. Wold Oil & Gas Co.; ret. Wold Nuclear Co., Wold Mineral Exploration Co., Casper, Wyo.; founding pres. Wyo. Heritage Soc.; founder Central Wyo. Ski Corp.; chmn. Wyo. Natural Gas Pipeline Authority, 1987-91; chmn. bd. Nuclear Exploration and Devel. Corp., Mineral Engring. Co. Contbr. articles to profl. jours. Chmn. Wyo. Rep. Com., 1960-64, Western State Rep. Chmns. Assn., 1963-64; mem. exec. com. Rep. Nat. Com., 1962-64; chmn. Wyo. Rep. State Fin. Com.; Active Little League Baseball, Boy Scouts Am., United Fund, YMCA, Boys Clubs Am.; former pres. bd. trustees Casper Coll.; trustee Union Coll. Served to lt. USNR, World War II. Named Wyo. Man of Yr. AP-UPI, 1968; Wyo. Mineral Man of Yr., 1979, Wyo. Heritage award, 1992; named Benefactor of Yr., Nat. Coun. for Resource Devel., 1993. Mem. Wyo. Geol. Assn. (hon. life, pres. 1956), Am. Assn. Petroleum Geologists, Ind. Petroleum Assn. Am., AAAS, Wyo. Mining Assn., Sigma Xi, Alpha Delta Phi. Episcopalian (past vestryman, warden). Home: 1231 W 30th St Casper WY 82604-4738 Office: Mineral Resource Ctr 139 W 2d St Casper WY 82601

WOLD, ROBERT LEE, architect, engineer; b. Oak Park, Ill., Oct. 20, 1931; s. Leaman A. and Helen Wold; m. Susan J. Olmstead, Dec. 18, 1854; children: Kyle, Eric, Karla. MArch with high honors, U. Ill., 1954. Registered architect, Ill., Mich., Fla., Pa., S.C., Mass. Designer DeLeuw Cather Co., Chgo., 1949-53; architect Perkins & Will, Chgo., 1954-55, Donker Assocs., Grand Rapids, Mich., 1957-59, Wold, Bowers, De Shane & Covert, Grand Rapids, 1960-76; prin. Robert Lee Wold & Assocs., Grand Rapids, 1976-94. Prin. works include Walker City Ctr., Kent Community Hosp. (AIA Design award 1972), Grand Valley State U. Campus Ctr. (AIA Design award 1975), First of Am. Bank Bldg. (AIA Design award 1983), Grand Valley State Downtown Campus (AIA Design award 1989). 1st lt. Corps of Engrs., U.S. Army, 1955-56. Recipient Gold medal Mich. Soc. Architects, 1982. Fellow AIA; mem. Rotary. Home: 3 Newhall Hilton Head Island NC 29928 Office: Tower Pinkster Titus Wold Inc 678 Front Ave NW Grand Rapids MI 49504-5323

WOLD, WILLIAM SYDNEY, molecular biology educator; b. Pine Falls, Manitoba, Can., Feb. 12, 1944; came to U.S., 1974; s. Roy and Nellie (Yurchison) W.; m. Susan Ann Lees, Dec. 30, 1967; m. Loralee Jane, William Guy, Jessica Ann, Jonathan Evered. BSc, U. Manitoba, 1965, MSc, 1968, PhD, 1973. Postdoctoral fellow St. Louis U., 1973-75, instr., 1975-76, from asst. prof. to prof. molecular biology, 1976-92, prof., chmn. dept. molecular microbiology and immunology, 1992—; reviewer's res. NIH, Washington, 1990—. Contbr. articles to Cell Jour., CRC Critical Revs. in Immunology, Molecular Biology and Medicine; assoc. editor jour. Virology, 1990—. NIH grantee, 1980—. Mem. AAAS, Am. Soc. Microbiology, Am. Soc. Virology, Internat. Soc. Antiviral Rsch. Achievements include discovery and characterization of human adenovirus proteins that counteract host immunosurveillance and that modulate virus-cell interactions by stimulating growth factor signal transduction. Office: St Louis U Molecular Microbiology & Immunology 1402 S Grand Saint Louis MO 63104

WOLDEGABRIEL, GIDAY, research geologist; b. Mai Misham/Adwa, Tigray, Ethiopia, Sept. 3, 1955; came to U.S., 1982; s. Giday WoldeGabriel and Mislal Mesfin; m. Almaz Berhane Tesfamichael, Jan. 15, 1994. BS in Geology with honors, Addis Ababa (Ethiopia) U., 1978, MS in Geology, 1980; PhD in Geology, Case Western Res. U., 1987. Lectr. geology Addis Ababa U., 1980-82; dir.'s postdoctoral fellow Los Alamos (N.Mex.) Nat. Lab., 1987-90, contractor/collaborator, 1990-92, mem. tech. staff, 1992—. Author: (with others) Water Rock Interaction: Low-Temperature Environments, 1992; contbr. articles to profl. jours. Mem. Am. Geophysical Union. Avocations: running, camping, skiing, body building, swimming. Home: 45 Paige Cir Los Alamos NM 87544-3638 Office: Los Alamos Nat Lab EEES-1/MS D462 Los Alamos NM 87545

WOLDT, GERALD D. (JAY WOLDT), nurse anesthetist; b. Chippewa Falls, Wis., May 30, 1943; s. D.C. and Blanche A. (Patrie) W.; children: Michael B., Eve A. Diploma in Nursing, St. Mary's Sch. Nursing, Wausau, Wis., 1965; diploma, Tripler Army Sch. Anesthesia, Honolulu, 1970; BSN, Med. Coll. Ga., 1977; MSN, Oreg. Health Sci. U., 1980. Cert. RN anesthetist. Staff nurse operating rm. Fitzsimons Hosp., Denver, 1966-67; commd. U.S. Army, 1966, advanced through grades to lt. col., 1981; staff anesthetist 93d Evac Hosp., Vietnam, 1970-71, 27th Surg. Hosp., Vietnam, 1971; clin. instr., staff anesthetist Madigan Army Hosp., Tacoma, Wash., 1971-72; staff anesthetist Munson Army Hosp., Leavenworth, Kans., 1972-76; chief anesthetist Dwight D. Eisenhower Hosp., Augusta, Ga., 1976-78, 2d Gen. Hosp., Landstuhl, Germany, 1980-83; nurse anesthesia cons. 7th MEDCOM, Germany, 1980-83; chief anesthetist, clin. instr. DeWitt Army Hosp., Ft. Belvoir, Va., 1983-87; staff anesthetist Potomac Hosp., Woodbridge, Va., 1986-91; dir. nurse anesthesia Mary Washington Hosp., Fredericksburg, Va., 1991-95; dir. nurse anesthesia Fredericksburg (Va.) Ambulatory Surgery Ctr., 1996—; co-facilitator death and dying seminars, 1980-83; lectr. in field. Mem. Am. Assn. Nurse Anesthetists, Sigma Theta Tau. Roman Catholic. Avocations: reading, racquetball, tennis, walking, painting. Home: One Charleston Ct Stafford VA 22554

WOLDT, HAROLD FREDERICK, JR., newspaper publishing executive; b. Atlanta, July 4, 1947; s. Harold Frederick and Dorothy R. (Lansdowne) W.; m. Lisa Diane Neves; children: Lauren Rae, Katherine Neves. BS in Journalism, So. Ill. U., 1969. Classified advt. rep. Chgo. Tribune, 1969-70, classified automobile staff mgr., 1970-72; nat. advt. sales rep. Chgo. Tribune newspapers, N.Y.C., 1972-74, city circulation mgr., 1974-77; nat. circulation mgr. Chgo. Tribune, 1977-80, circulation mgr., 1980-84; v.p., circulation dir. News & Sun Sentinel Co., Ft. Lauderdale, Fla., 1985; circulation mgr. Newsday, Inc., L.I., N.Y., 1985-86; circulation dir. Newsday, Inc., Melville and L.I., N.Y., 1986-88, v.p., circulation dir., 1988—; with Distbn. Systems. Am. subs. of Newsday, Inc., 1988-94; v.p. circulation Newsday and Distbn. Systems Am., subs. Newsday, Inc., Melville, 1994—; speaker, participant Am. Press Inst.; bd. dirs. Abilities Health and Rehab. Svcs. (Nat. Ctr. for Disability Svcs.), Albertson, L.I., N.Y., 1992—. Bd. dirs. Robert R. McCormick Boys Club, Chgo., 1980-81; chmn. United Way campaign, Chgo. Tribune, 1980. Mem. Am. Pubs. Newspaper Assn. (circulation and readership com. 1988-93), Internat. Circulation Mgrs. Assn. (pres. 1991-92), Alpha Delta Sigma, Tau Kappa Epsilon. Office: Newsday Inc 235 Pinelawn Rd Melville NY 11747-4226

WOLENSKY, MICHAEL K., lawyer; b. Chattanooga, Aug. 16, 1946; s. Gabriel Albert and Irene (Northcutt) W.; m. Sandra Joy Silverman, Aug. 10, 1969; 1 child, David G. BME, Ga. Inst. Tech., 1967; JD, Am. U., 1971. Bar: Va. 1971, Fla. 1972, D.C. 1972, Ga. 1981, U.S. Supreme Ct. 1974. Patent examiner U.S. Patent Office, Washington, 1968-71; trial atty. SEC, Miami, Fla., 1971-75; chief enforcement atty. SEC, San Francisco, 1975-77; asst. gen. counsel SEC, Washington, 1977-82; regional adminstr. SEC, Atlanta, 1982-87; of counsel Kilpatrick & Cody, Atlanta, 1987-90; ptnr., chmn. litigation dept. Kutak Rock, Atlanta, 1990—; arbitrator Nat. Assn. Securities Dealers, N.Y.C., 1987—, Am. Arbitration Assn., Atlanta, 1988—. Contbr. articles to profl. publs. Mem. ABA, Atlanta Bar Assn. Avocations: tennis, coaching youth sports. Office: Kutak Rock 4400 Ga-Pacific Ctr 133 Peachtree St Atlanta GA 30303

WOLF, ALFRED, rabbi; b. Eberbach, Germany, Oct. 7, 1915; came to U.S., 1935, naturalized, 1941; s. Hermann and Regina (Levy) W.; m. Miriam Jean Office, June 16, 1940; children: David B., Judith C. (dec.), Dan L. BA, U. Cin., 1937; MHL, Hebrew Union Coll., 1941; DD, 1966; PhD, U. So. Calif., 1961; DHL, U. Judaism, 1987, Loyola Marymount U., 1990. Ordained rabbi, 1941. Rabbi Temple Emanuel, Dothan, Ala., 1941-46; S.E. regional dir. Union Am. Hebrew Congregations, 1944-46; Western regional dir. Union Am. Hebrew Congregations, Los Angeles, 1946-49; rabbi Wilshire Blvd. Temple Los Angeles, 1949-85, rabbi emeritus, 1985—; dir. Skirball Inst. on Am. Values of Am. Jewish Com., 1985-95; founding dir., 1996—; lectr. U. So. Calif., 1955-69, Hebrew Union Coll., Jewish Inst. Religion, Calif., 1963-65, 74; lectr. religion Seven Seas div. Chapman Coll., 1967; adj. prof. theology Loyola U. Los Angeles, 1967-74; lectr. sociology Calif. State U., Los Angeles, 1977; co-chair First Nationwide Conf. for Cath. Jewish and Protestant seminiaries, Chgo., 1993. Author: (with Joseph Gaer) Our Jewish Heritage, 1957, (with Monsignor Royale M. Vadakin) Journey Of Discovery - A Resource Manual for Catholic-Jewish Dialogue, 1989; editor Teaching About World Religions: A Teacher's Supplement, 1991. Mem. camp commn. adminstrv. com. Camp Hess Kramer, 1951—; mem. L.A. Com. on Human Rels., 1956-72, mem. exec. bd., 1960—, chmn., 1964-66, hon. mem., 1972—; pres. Anytown U.S.A., 1964-66; mem. United Way Planning Coun. Bd., chmn., 1974-78; mem. youth adv. com. NCCJ, 1968-72, exec. bd., 1972-93; founding pres. Interreligious Coun. So. Calif., 1970-72; chmn. clergy adv. com. L.A. Sch. Dist., 1971-81; chmn. Nat. Workshop on Christian-Jewish Rels., 1978; bd. govs. Hebrew Union Coll., bd. alumni overseers, 1972—; mem. L.A. 2000 Com., 1986-89, The 2000 Partnership, 1989-95, Berlin Sister City Com., L.A., 1987-89; bd. dirs. Jewish Fedn. Coun., 1978-85, bd. govs., 1985—; bd. dirs. Jewish Family Svc. L.A., sec., 1978-80. Recipient Samuel Kaminker award as Jewish educator of year Western Assn. Temple Educators, 1965, John Anson Ford Human Relations award County Commn. on Human Relations, 1972, 90, Harry Hollzer Meml. award Los Angeles Jewish Fedn. Council, 1978, Volpert Community Service award, 1986, Community Service award United Way of Los Angeles, 1980, Leadership award Los Angeles Bd. Edn., 1981, Service to Edn. award Associated Adminstrs. Los Angeles, 1983, Pub. Service award Jewish Chautauqua Soc., 1986, N.Am. Interfaith Leadership award Nat. Workshop for Christian-Jewish Rels., 1990. Mem. Bd. Rabbis So. Calif. (pres.), Am. Jewish Com. (exec. com. Los Angeles chpt., Max Bay Meml. award 1986), Central Conf. Am. Rabbis (exec. bd., mem. commn. on Jewish edn. 1970-72, treas. 1975-79, chmn. interreligious activities com. 1975-79, hon. mem. 1991—), Pacific Assn. Reform Rabbis (pres.), So. Calif. Assn. Liberal Rabbis (pres.), Synagogue Council Am. (mem. com. interreligious affairs), Alumni Assn. Hebrew Union Coll.-Jewish Inst. Religion, Town Hall, Los Angeles World Affairs Council, U. So. Calif. Alumni Assn. Home: 3389 Ley Dr Los Angeles CA 90027-1315 Office: Skirball Inst on Am Values 635 S Harvard Blvd Los Angeles CA 90005-2586

WOLF, ALFRED PETER, research chemist, educator; b. N.Y.C., Feb. 13, 1923; s. Josef and Margarete (Kunst) W.; m. Elizabeth H. Gross, June 15, 1946; 1 child, Roger O. B.A., Columbia U., 1944, M.A., 1948, Ph.D., 1952; Ph.D. (hon.), U. Uppsala, (Sweden), 1983, U. Rome, 1989. Chemist Brookhaven Nat. Lab., Upton, N.Y., 1951, chemist with tenure, 1957-64, sr. chemist, 1964—, chmn. chemistry dept., 1982-87; adj. prof. chemistry Columbia U., N.Y.C., 1953-83; vis. lectr. U. Calif., Berkeley, 1964; cons. Philip Morris, Inc., Richmond, Va., 1966-91, NIH, Bethesda, Md.; cons., advisor IAEA, Vienna, Austria; advisor Italian NRC, Rome, 1959—, Atomic Rsch. Inst., Julich, Germany, 1981-90; rsch. prof. psychiatry NYU, 1988—. Author: Synthesis of 11C, 18F and 13N Labelled Radiotracers for Biomedical Application, 1982; contbr. numerous articles to profl. jours.; patentee in field; editor: Jour. Labelled Compounds and Radiopharms., Radiochimica Acta. Served with AUS, 1943-46. Recipient JARI award Pergamon Jours., 1986, The Javits Neurosci. Investigator award, 1986, Georg V. Hevesy Meml. medal Georg V. Hevesy Found. Nuclear Medicine, 1986, disting. sci. award Inst. Clin. PET, 1996. Mem. NAS, Am. Chem. Soc. (Nuclear Applications in Chemistry award 1971, Esselen award 1988),

Chem. Soc. (U.K.), Soc. Nuclear Medicine (1982 Paul Aebersold award, pres. radiopharm. council 1980, George Hevesy award 1991), German. Chem. Soc. Home: PO Box 1043 Setauket NY 11733-0803 Office: Brookhaven Nat Lab Dept Chemistry Upton NY 11973

WOLF, ARON S., psychiatrist; b. Newark, Aug. 25, 1937; B.A., Dartmouth Coll., 1959; M.D., U. Md., 1963; married; children: Jon, Lisa, Laurie. Intern, U. Md. Hosp., Balt., 1963-64; resident in psychiatry Psychiat. Inst., U. Md. Hosp., Balt., 1964-67, chief resident, 1966-67; practice medicine specializing in psychiatry, Anchorage, 1967—; dir. Springfield Hosp. Alcoholic Clinic, Balt., 1966-67; psychiat. cons. Levindale Hebrew Home and Infirmary, Balt., 1966-67, McLaughlin Yough Center, Anchorage, 1969-72; mem. staff Providence Hosp., chief psychiatry sect., 1977-81, 94; mem. staff Humana Hosp., Alaska, Kodiak Island Hosp., Palmer Valley Hosp., Valdez Community Hosp., Bethel Community Hosp., Cordova Alaska Hosp.; mem. staff Charter North Hosp., exec. com., 1984-86; staff psychiatrist Langdon Psychiat. Clinic, 1970-71; ptnr. Langdon Clinic, Anchorage, 1971—, clinic pres., 1981-95; clin. prof. U. N.Mex., 1991—; med. dir. Cordova Community Mental Health Ctr., 1976-80, 84—, ptnr., dir. comprehensive substance dependence program Breakthrough, 1989; assoc. adminstrn. Med. Affairs Providence Hosp., Anchorage, 1995; cons. Alaska Native Med. Ctr., 1975-77, Woman's Resource Ctr., Anchorage, 1977-81; instr. dept. psychology U. Alaska, Anchorage, 1968-75; assoc. clin. prof. psychiatry U. Alaska, Fairbanks, 1974-85, clin. prof., 1985—; assoc. clin. prof. U. Wash., 1974-85, clin. prof., 1985—, clin. prof. psychiatry Sch. Medicine U. N.Mex.; participant weekly mental health TV talk show, Anchorage, 1970—; guest lectr. to various profl. and civic groups, 1967—. Vice pres. Greater Anchorage Area Borough Sch. Bd., 1971-72, pres., 1973-74; pres. Chugach Optional Sch. Parent Adv. Bd., 1976-77; mem. med. adv. com. Alaska Kidney Found., 1977-82; mem. Alaska Gov.'s Mental Health Adv. Bd., 1976-84, chmn., 1983; mem. Gov's. Task Force on Criminally Committed Patients, 1980—; bd. dirs. Greater Anchorage Drug Mgmt. Group, 1972-73. Served with M.C., USAF, 1967-70. Recipient Wendell-Muncie award Md. Med. Soc., 1967; diplomate Am. Bd. Psychiatry and Neurology, Am. Bd. Forensic Psychiatry. Fellow Am. Psychiat. Assn. (pres. Alaska dist. br. 1975, sec. Alaska br. 1984-85, del. assembly 1975-81, 86, 89-93, area III chmn. assembly procedures com. 1982—, nat. planning com. 1981, nat. membership com. 1981-86, 89—, chmn. confidentiality com., 1986—, recorder of assembly 1984-85, chmn. 1988, Alaska del., 1986—, chair nat. membership com. 1992—); mem. Am. Acad. Psychiatry and Law (mem. ethics com., 1987) , Am. Soc. Law and Medicine, Soc. Air Force Psychiatrists, ACLU, AMA (chmn. mental health com. 1971-75, medicine and law com. 1980-81), Alaska Med. Assn., N.Y. Acad. Scis., Am. Assn. of Med. Adminstrn. Contbr. articles on psychiatry to profl. jours. Home: 8133 Sundi Dr Anchorage AK 99502-4144 Office: 4001 Dale St Anchorage AK 99508-5459

WOLF, ARTHUR HENRY, museum director; b. New Rockford, N.D., June 18, 1953; s. Louis Irwin and Vivian Joyce (Grinde) W.; m. Holly M. Chaffee, Oct. 18, 1984. BA in Anthropology, U. Nebr., 1975; MA, U. Ariz., 1977. Lab. asst., acting curator anthropology U. Nebr. State Mus., Lincoln, 1973-75; rsch. asst. Ariz. State Mus., Tucson, 1975-77; curator of collections Sch. Am. Rsch., Santa Fe, N.Mex., 1977-79; dir. Millcent Rogers Mus., Taos, N.Mex., 1979-87, Nev. State Mus. and Hist. Soc., Las Vegas, 1988-92, Mus. of Rockies, Bozeman, Mont., 1992—; speaker in field; cons. Pueblos of Zuni, Picuris, San Ildefonso and Taos. Contbr. articles and revs. to profl. jours. Trustee Kokopelli Archeol. Rsch. Fund, Bozeman, 1992—; active Mont. Ambs. Recipient Young Alumnus award U. Nebr. Lincoln, 1990. Mem. Am. Assn. Mus. (bd. dirs. 1994—, vis. com. roster 1989—), Rotary, Assn. Sci. Mus. Dirs. Avocations: travel, reading, music. Home: 1718 S Black #A Bozeman MT 59715 Office: Mus of Rockies Montana State U Bozeman MT 59717

WOLF, BARRY, genetics, pediatric educator; b. Chgo., June 19, 1947; s. Bert D. and Toby E. (Urkoff) W.; m. Gail Harriet Ross, Oct. 2, 1971; children: Michael Loren, Bryan Phillip. BS, U. Ill., 1969; MD, U. Ill. Coll. Medicine, 1974; PhD, U. Ill., 1974. Diplomate Am. Bd. Pediatrics, Med. and Biochem. Genetics. Intern, resident in pediatrics Childrens Meml. Hosp., Northwestern U., Chgo., 1974-76; fellow Yale U. Sch. Medicine, New Haven, Conn., 1976-78; prof. human genetics Med. Coll. Va., Richmond, 1978—, vice chair for rsch. dept. pediatrics, 1996—. Author over 140 jour. articles and book chpts. dealing with inherited disorders of metabolism and biochem. genetics, specifically disorders of biotin metabolism. Recipient E. Mead Johnson award for pediatric rsch. Am. Acad. Pediatrics, 1988, Borden award in nutrition Am. Inst. Nutrition, 1987, Outstanding Scientist of Va. award Va. Sci. Mus., 1986, Ounce of Prevention award Action for Prevention of Va., 1985. Mem. Am. Soc. Clin. Investigation, Soc. Pediatric Rsch., Soc. for Inherited Metabolic Diseases (bd. dirs.), Am. Soc. Clin. Nutrition, Am. Inst. Nutrition, Soc. for the Study of Inborn Errors of Metabolism, Am. Soc. Human Genetics. Avocations: oriental cloisonne. Office: Med Coll Va Dept Human Genetics PO Box 980033 Richmond VA 23298

WOLF, CHARLES, JR., economist, educator; b. N.Y.C., Aug. 1, 1924; s. Charles and Rosalie W.; m. Theresa van de Wint, Mar. 1, 1947; children: Charles Theodore, Timothy van de Wint. B.S., Harvard U., 1943, M.P.A., 1948, Ph.D. in Econs., 1949. Economist, fgn. service officer U.S. Dept. State, 1945-47, 49-53; mem. faculty Cornell U., 1953-54, U. Calif., Berkeley, 1954-55; sr. economist The Rand Corp., Santa Monica, Calif., 1955-67; head econs. dept. The Rand Corp., 1967-81; dean The Rand Grad. Sch., 1970—; sr. economist, 1981—; sr. fellow Hoover Inst., 1988—; corp. fellow in internat. econs., 1996—; bd. dirs. Fundamental Investors Fund, Capital Income Builder Fund, Am. Capital Fund, Capital World Growth Fund; mem. adv. com. UCLA Clin. Scholars Program; mem. exec. com. Rand Ctr. for Russian and Eurasian Studies; lectr. econs. UCLA, 1960-72; mem. adv. bd. grad. sch. pub. policy Carnegie-Mellon U., 1992—. Author: The Costs and Benefits of the Soviet Empire, 1986, Markets or Governments: Choosing Between Imperfect Alternatives, 1988, 93, (with others) The Impoverished Superpower: Perestroika and the Soviet Military Burden, 1990, Linking Economic Policy and Foreign Policy, 1991, Promoting Democracy and Free Markets in Eastern Europe, 1992, Defense Conversion and Economic Reform in Russia and Ukraine, 1994; contbr. articles to profl. jours. Mem. Assn. for Public Policy Analysis and Mgmt. (pres. 1980-81), Am. Econs. Assn., Econometric Soc., Coun. on Fgn. Rels., Internat. Inst. Strategic Studies London. Clubs: Cosmos (Washington); Riviera Tennis (Los Angeles); Harvard (N.Y.). Office: RAND Grad Sch Policy Studies 1700 Main St Santa Monica CA 90401-3208

WOLF, CHARLES BENNO, lawyer; b. Chgo., Apr. 16, 1950; s. Ludwig and Hilde (Mandelbaum) W.; m. Sarah Lloyd, Sept. 1, 1973; children: Walter Ludwig, Peter Barton. AB, Brown U., 1972; JD, U. Chgo., 1975. Bar: Ill. 1975, U.S. Dist. Ct. (no. dist.) Ill. 1975, U.S. Ct. Appeals (4th, 5th, 6th, 7th, 8th, 9th, 10th, and 11th cirs.) 1985, U.S. Supreme Ct. 1985. Ptnr. Vedder, Price, Kaufman & Kammholz, Chgo., 1975—. Co-author: ERISA Claims and Litigation, 10th edit., 1995; contbr. articles to profl. jours. Mem. ABA, Chgo. Bar Assn., Internat. Found. Employee Benefit Plans. Office: Vedder Price Kaufman & Kammholz 222 N La Salle St Ste 2600 Chicago IL 60601-1003

WOLF, CHARLOTTE ELIZABETH, sociologist; b. Boulder, Colo., Sept. 14, 1926; d. Marion Guy and Ethel Eugenia (Thomas) Rosetta; m. René A. Wolf, Sept. 3, 1952; children: Christopher Robin, Michele Renee. B.A., U. Colo., 1949, M.A., 1959; Ph.D., U. Minn., 1968. Lectr. sociology U. Md., Tokyo, 1959-62, Turkey, 1965-67; instr. St. Mary Coll., Leavenworth, Kans., 1962-63; teaching asst. U. Minn., 1963-65; asst. prof. Colo. State U., 1968-69, Colo Woman's Coll., 1969-74; assoc. prof. sociology Ohio Wesleyan U., Delaware, 1974-80, prof., 1980, chmn. dept. sociology and anthropology, 1974-83; prof., chairperson dept. sociology and social work Memphis State U., 1983-92, prof. emeritus, 1992—. Author: Garrison Community: A Study of an Overseas American Military Colony, 1969, Southern Town/Two Communities, 1993; adv. editor Sociological Inquiry, 1988—, mem. bd. editors, 1990— ; contbr. chpts. to books and social sci. encys., articles to profl. jours.; mem. editorial bd. dirs. Sociological Spectrum, 1989-92. Recipient Ohio Wesleyan Outstanding Rsch. award, 1982, Faculty Devel. Leave Memphis State U., 1987-88; Mellon rsch. grantee, 1977, Shell Oil Co. grantee, 1978; Memphis State Ctr. for Humanities fellow, 1990. Mem. ACLU (bd. dirs. Memphis chpt. 1988—), AAUP (chpt. pres.), Am. Sociol. Assn. (chmn. com. status women 1974-76, nominations com. 1982-84), Soc. Study Social Problems (chair budget, audit and fin. com. 1975-79, treas. 1979-81), Western Social Sci. Assn. (exec. coun. 1974-77), Pacific Sociol. Assn., So. Sociol. Soc. (nominating com. 1987—, membership com. 1986-87), Mid South Sociol. Assn. (chair local arrangements 1986-87, awards com.), Sociologists Women in Soc. (chair nominations com. 1971-73, chair nominations com. South 1987-88), Soc. for Study Symbolic Interaction (C.H. Cooley award com. 1985-86, publs. com. 1989-92, chair George Herbert Mead publs. com. 1989-92, award com. 1988-89, mem. George Herbert Mead award com. 1994-95), North Ctrl. Sociol. Assn. (v.p. 1983-84), NOW (pres. Denver 1970-71, nat. bd. dirs. 1971-73, Woman of Yr. Denver chpt., chair nat. rsch. com. 1971-74), Memphis Bus. and Profl. Women's Network (exec. bd. 1991-93). Democrat. Home: Rock Creek Ranch Mc Coy CO 80463

WOLF, CONSTANCE SLOGGATT, art educator; b. Merrick, N.Y., June 25, 1959; d. Arthur Hastings Sloggatt and Dorothea Mae (Green) Sloggatt-Rush; m. Charles Robert Wolf. BFA in Painting, Pratt Inst., 1982; MFA in Painting, L.I. U., 1987; studies in edn., art and computers, 1990—. Asst. tchr. Usdan Ctr. for Performing & Creative Arts, Wheatley Heights, N.Y., summer 1986; asst. painting tchr. L.I. U., Greenvale, N.Y., 1985-87; asst. to dir. Fine Arts Mus. L.I., Hempstead, N.Y., 1987-89; art instr. Huntington (N.Y.) Twp. Art League, summer 1991, 94, 95; secondary art tchr. Northport (N.Y.)-East Northport Sch. Dist., 1991—; presenter conf. N.Y. State Art Tchrs. Assn., 1994; coord. ednl. resource Women Artists Visual Resource Collection, 1994-95, Student Portfolio on Laser Disc, 1994-95, Portfolio on CD ROM. One woman show Northport (N.Y.) Cmty. Gallery, 1994. Sponsor, co-sponsor Nat. Art Honor Soc., Northport H.S., 1992-93, 93-94, 94-95, 95-96, 96—; instr. religious edn. Old First Ch., Huntington, 1990-91. Recipient mini grant Western Suffolk Tchrs. Ctr., 1994-95. Mem. NOW, Nat. Art Edn. Assn., Nat. Mus. for Women in Arts, Huntington Twp. Art League (instr.), N.Y. State Art Tchrs. Assn., Girls, Inc. Avocations: painting. Office: Northport-E Northport Sch D Art Dept Laurel Hill Rd Northport NY 11768

WOLF, CYNTHIA TRIBELHORN, librarian, library educator; b. Denver, Dec. 12, 1945; d. John Baltazar and Margaret (Kern) Tribelhorn; m. H.Y. Rassam, Mar. 21, 1969 (div. Jan. 1988); children: Najma C., Yousuf J.; adopted children: Leonard Joseph Lucero, Lakota E. Rassam-Lucero. BA, Colo. State U., 1970; MLS, U. Denver, 1985. Cert. permanent profl. librarian, N.Mex. Elem. tchr. Sacred Heart Sch., Farmington, N.Mex., 1973-78; asst. prof. library sci. edn. U. N.Mex., Albuquerque, 1985-90, dir. libr. sci. edn. divsn., 1989-90; pres. Info. Acquisitions, Albuquerque, 1990—; libr. dir. Southwestern Coll., Santa Fe, 1992-94; mem. youth resources Rio Grande Valley Libr. Sys., Albuquerque, 1994—; fine arts resource person for gifted edn. Farmington Pub. Schs., 1979-83; speaker Unofficial Mentorships & Market Research, 1992—. Mem. Farmington Planning and Zoning Commn., 1980-81; bd. dirs. Farmington Mus. Assn., 1983-84; pres. Farmington Symphony League, 1978. Mem. ALA, N.Mex. Library Assn., LWV (bd. dirs. Farmington, 1972-74, 75, pres.). Avocations: mixed media graphics design, market research, creative approaches to personal journals. Office: Rio Grande Valley Libr Sys Albuquerque NM 87000

WOLF, DALE EDWARD, state official; b. Kearney, Nebr., Sept. 6, 1924. BSc, U. Nebr., 1945; PhD in Agronomy and Weed Control, Rutgers U., 1949. With Dept. Agr., 1946; assoc. prof. agronomy Rutgers U., 1949; with E.I. duPont de Nemours & Co., Inc., from 1950, dir. agrichem. mktg., then gen. mgr. biochem. dept., 1972-79; v.p. biochems., also chmn. bd. subs. Endo Labs., Inc., Wilmington, Del., from 1979; group v.p. Agrl. Products, Wilmington, Del., from 1983; dir. Del. Devel. Office, Dover, 1987-89; lt. gov. of Del. Dover, 1989-93; gov. State of Del., Dover, 1993; sr. internat. cons. Mezzullo & McCandlish Law Firm, 1993—; chmn. Daynel Internat. LLC, 1996. Co-author: Principles of Weed Control, 1951. Bd. dirs. Del. chpt. ARC, 1975; gen. campaign chmn. United Way Del., 1978, also bd. dirs.; gen. campaign chmn. Girls Club Del., 1987; chmn. Del. Found. for Literacy, 1993—. 1st lt. AUS, 1943-46. Decorated Bronze Star, Purple Heart. Mem. Nat. Agrl. Chem. Assn. (chmn. 1981-83), Pharm. Mfrs. Assn. (dir.), Masons, Sigma Xi, Alpha Zeta.

WOLF, DAVID, lawyer; b. Boston, July 11, 1927; s. Ezekiel and Ray (Cohen) W.; m. Maxine Laura Bunnin, June 29, 1963; children—Eric E., Douglas R., James A. BA, U. Mass., 1949; LLB, Harvard U., 1952; postgrad., Northeastern U., 1952-55. Bar: Mass. 1952, U.S. Patent Office 1952, U.S. Ct. Customs and Patent Appeals 1955, U.S. Supreme Ct. 1958, U.S. Ct. Appeals (fed. cir.) 1983. Ptnr. Wolf, Greenfield & Sacks, P.C., Boston, 1952—; Watercolor artist; exhibited various local shows; holder of 13 U.S. letters patents in various arts. Watercolor artist; exhibited various local shows; holder of 12 U.S. letters patents in various arts. Bd. dirs. Newton Country Players, 1964-67, Killington East Homeowners Assn., pres. 1992—; mem. Com. for Accuracy in Mid. East Reporting in Am., 1989—, bd. dirs., 1990, gen. counsel, 1993—; mem. Am. Jewish Congress, 1990-92. Recipient various awards for art. Mem. Am. Patent Law Assn. (lectr. trademark trial adv. programs 1986-89), Lic. Execs. Soc., U.S. Trademark Assn., Harvard Law Sch. Alumni Assn., Boston Patent Law Assn. (pres. 1976), New Eng.-Israel C. of C. (v.p., bd. dirs. 1984-96), Hadassah Men's Assn., B'nai B'rith, Free Sons Israel, Alpha Epsilon Pi. Office: Wolf Greenfield & Sacks PC Fed Res Plz 600 Atlantic Ave Boston MA 02210-2211

WOLF, DON ALLEN, hardware wholesale executive; b. Allen County, Ind., June 18, 1929; s. Ellis Adolphus and Bessie Ruth (Fortman) W.; m. Virginia Ann Lunz, Oct. 8, 1949; children—Rebecca, Donna, Richard, Lisa. Student exec. course, Ind. U., 1969. With Hardware Wholesalers Inc., Fort Wayne, Ind., 1947—; purchasing mgr. Hardware Wholesalers Inc., 1957—, v.p., gen. mgr., 1967-80, pres., 1980-92; ret., 1992; bd. dirs. Ft. Wayne Nat. Bank, Clarcor. Pres., bd. dirs. Big Brothers, Fort Wayne, 1973-74; nat. pres. Big Brothers Soc. Am., 1977-80. Mem. Nat. Wholesale Hardware Assn. (dir. 1977—, pres. 1984-85, named Hardware Wholesaler of Year 1973, 85), Ind. State C. of C. (dir.). Republican. Lutheran. Office: Hardware Wholesalers Inc PO Box 868 Fort Wayne IN 46801-0868 also: 6502 Nelson Rd Fort Wayne IN 46803-1920*

WOLF, DUANE CARL, microbiologist; b. Forsyth, Mo., Apr. 7, 1946; s. Deward Carl and Mary Catherine (Collins) W. BS, U. Mo., 1968; PhD, U. Calif., Riverside, 1973. Asst. prof. dept. agronomy U. Md., College Park, 1973-78; assoc. prof. dept. agronomy U. Ark., Fayetteville, 1979-81; prof. dept. agronomy U. Ark., 1981—; presenter in field at nat. meetings. Contbr. articles to profl. jours.; author, co-author rsch. reports at regional meetings; co-author 5 book chpts. Fellow Am. Soc. Agronomy (chair environ. quality sect. 1988), Soil Sci. Soc. Am. (chair microbiol. biochem. sect. 1994); mem. AAAS, Am. Soc. Microbiology, Vietnam Vets. Am., Sigma Xi, Gamma Sigma Delta. Office: U Ark Dept Agronomy Fayetteville AR 72701

WOLF, EDWARD DEAN, electrical engineering educator; b. Quinter, Kans., May 30, 1935; s. Ezra Lawrence and Zora Blanche (Jamison) W.; m. Marlene Kay Simpson, Aug. 12, 1955; children: Julie Christine, LeAnn Cynthia, Shelly Diane. Student, Kans. State U., 1953; BS magna cum laude, McPherson Coll., 1957; PhD, Iowa State U., 1961; postgrad., Princeton U., 1961-62, U. Calif.-Berkeley, 1968. Mem. tech. staff Rockwell Internat. Sci. Ctr., Thousand Oaks, Calif., 1963-65; mem. tech. staff, sr. mem. tech. staff Hughes Research Labs., Malibu, Calif., 1965-67, 67-72, sect. head, 1972-78, sr. scientist, 1974-78; dir. Nat. Nanofabrication Facility, Cornell U., Ithaca, N.Y., 1978-88, prof. elec. engring., 1978-90, prof. emeritus, 1991—; dir. Office Technology Access and Bus. Assistance Cornell U., Ithaca, N.Y., 1995—; co-owner, pres. Biolistics, Inc., 1986-89; cons. Dept. Def., 1978, 81-82, various indsl. cos., 1978—; mem. univ. adv. com. Semiconductor Rsch. Corp., Research Triangle, N.C., 1982-84, ad hoc com. NAS, 1977-79, steerinc com. European Microcircuits Engring. Conf., 1976-78; guest prof. Tech. U., Vienna, 1987; vis. fellow Trinity Coll, Cambridge (Eng.) U., 1986-87; fgn. fellow Erwin Schrodinger Soc., Vienna, 1987; bd. dirs. Phyton, Inc., Cornell Rsch. Found. Editorial bd.: IEEE Spectrum, 1983-85; contbr. numerous articles on microminiaturization to profl. jours.; patentee in field. Named outstanding young man of Am., 1966. Fellow Am. Inst. Chemists, IEEE; mem. Bohmische Phys. Soc. (sci. me.), Am. Phys. Soc., Am. Vacuum Soc., Electron Microscopy Soc. Am., Sigma Xi, Phi Lambda Upsilon. Republican. Home: 1691 Taughannock Blvd Trumansburg NY 14886-9120 Office: Cornell U 167 Biotech Bldg Ithaca NY 14853

WOLF, EDWARD LINCOLN, physics educator; b. Cocoa, Fla., Nov. 22, 1936; s. Norman Lincoln and Harriet (Burgess) W.; m. Carol Joyce Euwema, June 15, 1958; children: Douglas Wakefield, David Lincoln. BA, Swarthmore Coll., 1958; PhD, Cornell U., 1964. Postdoctoral fellow U. Ill. Dept. Physics, Urbana, 1964-66; research assoc. Eastman Kodak Co., Rochester, N.Y., 1967-75; prof. physics Iowa State U., Ames, 1975-85; head dept. physics, prof. Polytechnic U., Bklyn., 1986—;, 1986-95; prof. physics Polytechnic U., Bklyn., 1986—; sr. vis. fellow Cavendish Lab. U. Cambridge, U.K., 1973-74; vis. prof. U. Pa., Phila., 1982. Author: Principles of Electron Tunneling Spectroscopy, 1985; editor: Materials and Mechanisms of Superconductivity, 1985. Fellow Am. Phys. Soc.; mem. Phi Beta Kappa, Sigma Xi. Presbyterian. Avocations: jogging, cycling, music. Office: Polytechnic U Dept Physics Six Metrotech Ctr Brooklyn NY 11201-2990

WOLF, EMIL, physics educator; b. Prague, July 30, 1922; naturalized U.S. citizen, 1967; BSc, U. Bristol, Eng., 1945, PhD, 1948; DSc, U. Edinburgh, Scotland, 1955; D. honoris causa, U. Groningen, 1989, U. Edinburgh, 1990, Palacky U., Czechoslovakia, 1992. Rsch. asst. observatory Cambridge U., Eng., 1948-51; rsch. asst., lectr. math. and physics U. Edinburgh, 1951-54; rsch. fellow theoretical physics U. Manchester, Eng., 1954-59; vis. rsch. scientist Courant Inst. NYU, 1957; assoc. prof. optics U. Rochester, N.Y., 1959-61; prof. physics U. Rochester, 1961—, prof. optics, 1978—, Wilson prof. optical physics, 1987—; Guggenheim fellow, vis. prof. U. Calif. at Berkeley, 1966-67; vis. prof. U. Toronto, 1974-75. Author: (with M. Born) Principles of Optics, 1959, (with L. Mandel) Optical Coherence and Quantum Optics, 1995; editor: Progress in Optics, Vol. I-XXV, 1961-96, (with L. Mandel) Selected Papers on Coherence and Fluctuations of Light, 2 vols., 1970, various confs.; contbr. articles to profl. jours. Recipient Marconi medal Italian Nat. Rsch. Coun., 1987, Gold medal Czechoslovak Acad. Scis., 1991, medal Union of Czechoslovak Mathematicians and Physicists, 1991, Gold medal Palacky U., Olomouc, Czechoslovakia, 1991. Fellow Optical Soc. Am. (Frederic Ives medal 1977, Max Born award 1987, dir.-at-large 1972-74, v.p. 1976, pres. 1978, hon. mem.), Am. Phys. Soc., Brit. Inst. Physics, Am. Inst. Physics (governing bd. 1977-78), Franklin Inst. (Albert A. Michelson medal 1980), Optical Soc. India (hon.), Optical Soc. Australia (hon.). Office: U Rochester Dept Physics and Astronomy Rochester NY 14627

WOLF, ERIC ROBERT, anthropologist, educator; b. Vienna, Austria, Feb. 1, 1923; came to U.S., 1940, naturalized, 1943; s. Arthur George and Maria (Ossinovski) W.; m. Kathleen Bakeman, Sept. 24, 1943; children: John David, Daniel Jacob; m. Sydel Finfer Silverman, Mar. 18, 1972. B.A., Queens Coll., 1946; Ph.D. (Viking Fund fellow), Columbia U., 1951; DL (hon.), U. Mich., 1992; D.h.c., U. Vienna, 1993. Asst. prof. U. Ill., 1952-55, U. Va., 1955-58; vis. asst. prof. Yale U., 1958-59; assoc. prof. U. Chgo., 1959-61; prof. U. Mich., Ann Arbor, 1965-71, chmn. dept. anthropology, 1970-71; disting. prof. Herbert H. Lehman Coll. and Grad. Ctr., CUNY, 1971-92, disting. prof. emeritus, 1992—; field work, P.R., 1948-49, Mexico, 1951-52, Italy, 1960-61. Author: Sons of the Shaking Earth, 1958, Peasants, 1968, Peasant Wars of the Twentieth Century, 1969, Europe and the People Without History, 1982. Served with AUS, 1943-45. Decorated Silver Star; recipient Career award NIH, 1964-69, J.S. Staley prize Sch. for Am. Rsch., Santa Fe 1988, Kevin Lynch award MIT, 1989; Guggenheim fellow, 1960-61; sr. fellow NEH, 1973-74; MacArthur Found. fellow, 1990. Fellow NAS, Am. Acad. Arts and Scis, Nat. Acad. Scis.; mem. Am. Anthrop. Assn. Home: 4 Blueberry Hl Irvington NY 10533-1402

WOLF, FRANK R., congressman, lawyer; b. Philadelphia, Pa., Jan. 30, 1939; m. Carolyn Stover; children: Frank, Virginia, Anne, Brenda, Rebecca. B.A., Pa. State U., 1961; LL.B., Georgetown U., 1965. Bar: Va., D.C. Legis. asst. former Congressman Edward G. Biester, Jr., 1968-71; asst. to Sec. of Interior Rogers B. Morton, 1971-74; dep. asst. sec. for Congl. and Legis. Affairs, Dept. Interior, 1974-75; mem. 97th-104th Congresses from 10th Va. dist., Washington, 1981—; mem. appropriations com., chmn. transp. subcom., mem. TPS and fgn. affairs subcom. Served with USAR. Republican. Presbyterian. Office: US Ho of Reps 241 Cannon Hse Office Bldg Washington DC 20515-4610

WOLF, FREDERIC EASTMAN, retired lawyer; b. Wauseon, Ohio, Apr. 10, 1909; s. Fred H. and Lillian (Eastman) W.; m. Elaine Merrifield Huffman, Mar. 9, 1934 (dec. 1954); children: Mary Lynn Wolf Thompson, Myrna Elizabeth Wolf Malec, Michael A.; stepchildren: G. Scott Huffmann, B. Bruce Huffmann; m. Gertrude Powell Treece, Dec. 4, 1954 (dec. 1969); 1 dau., Jill Joanne; 1 stepson, Ian E. Treece; m. Frances Clock Brown, Jan. 19, 1973 (dec. 1987); 1 stepson, David. B.A., U. Mich., 1930, J.D., 1932. Bar: Ohio 1932. With Smith, Beckwith, Ohlinger & Froelich, Toledo, 1932-38; partner Beckwith, Ohlinger, Koles & Wolf, Toledo, 1939, Ohlinger, Koles, Wolf & Flues, Toledo, 1940-42; chief rent atty. Toledo rent area OPA, 1942-46; ptnr. Ohlinger, Koles & Wolf, Toledo, 1946-62, Eastman & Smith, Toledo, 1963-89; ret., 1989. Contbr. articles to profl. jours.; Bd. editors: U. Mich. Law Rev., 1931-32. Mem. ABA, Ohio Bar Assn., Mich. Bar Assn., Toledo Bar Assn., Masons, Barristers, Order of Coif, Phi Beta Kappa, Phi Eta Sigma, Phi Kappa Phi, Delta Theta Phi. Home: PO Box 10032 Toledo OH 43699-0032

WOLF, FREDRIC M., educational psychologist; b. Canton, Ohio, Aug. 7, 1945; s. Wayne S. and Anita (Manheim) W.; m. Leora DeLelys Lucas, Sept. 29, 1985; children: Jacob M. Claire D., Adam C.N. BS, U. Wis., 1967; postgrad. Law Sch. Georgetown U., 1967-68; MEd, Kent State U., 1977, PhD, 1980. Instr. math. Cuyahoga C.C., Cleve., 1978-79; rsch. assoc. behavioral scis. Northeastern Ohio U. Med. Coll., Rootstown, 1979-80; rsch. assoc. med. edn. Ohio State U. Coll. Medicine, Columbus 1980-82, clin. asst. prof. pediatrics, 1981-82; asst. prof. postgrad. medicine U. Mich. Med. Sch., Ann Arbor, 1982-87, assoc. prof. 1987-93, prof. 1993—; assoc. dir. edn. Mich. Diabetes Rsch. & Tng. Ctr., Ann Arbor, 1982-84; acting dir. 1984-85; vis. fellow U.K. Cochrane Ctr.; vis. scholar Green Coll., U. Oxford, Eng.; cons. Office Technology Assessment, U.S. Congress, 1987—; dir. Learning Resource Ctr. & Lab. Computing, Cognition, & Clin. Skills, 1990—; cons. Office Rsch. U.S. Dept. Edn., 1986—; cons. Nat. Heart Lung and Blood Inst. NIH, Bethesda, Md., 1985—, Nat. Inst. Deafness & Other Comm. Disorders, Small Bus. Innovation Rsch. Program; cons. NSF, NRC, NAS. Author: Meta-analysis: Quantitative Methods for Research Synthesis, 1986; co-editor: Software for Health Sciences Ednucation: A Resource Catalog, 1994; book rev. editor Medical Decision Making, Editorial Boards: Evaluation & the Health Professions, Medical Decision Making; contbr. articles to profl. jours. Vol. Peace Corps, L.Am., 1969-72. Grantee Mich. Dept. Pub. Health, 1984-86, Spencer Found., 1983-84, NIH, 1985—. Fellow APA, Am. Psychol. Soc., Royal Statis. Soc.; mem. AAAS, Am. Ednl. Rsch. Assn., Am. Statis. Assn., Midwestern Ednl. Rsch. Assn. (v.p. 1984-85, pres. 1986-87), Soc. Behavioral Medicine, Soc. Med. Decision Making, Sigma Xi. Office: U Mich Dept Postgrad Medicine G1208 Towsley Ctr Box 0201 Ann Arbor MI 48109-0201

WOLF, G. VAN VELSOR, JR., lawyer; b. Balt., Feb. 19, 1944; s. G. Van Velsor and Alice Roberts (Kimberly) W.; m. Ann Holmes Kavanagh, May 19, 1984; children: George Van Velsor III, Timothy Kavanagh (dec.), Christopher Kavanagh, Elisabeth Huxley. BA, Yale U., 1966; JD, Vanderbilt U., 1973. Bar: N.Y. 1974, Ariz. 1982, U.S. Dist. Ct. (so. dist.) N.Y. 1974, U.S. Dist. Ct. Ariz. 1982, U.S. Ct. Appeals (2d cir.) 1974, U.S. Ct. Appeals (9th cir.) 1982. Agrl. advisor U.S. Peace Corps, Tanzania and Kenya, 1966-70; assoc. Milbank, Tweed, Hadley & McCloy, N.Y.C., 1973-75; vis. lectr. law Airlangga U., Surabaya, Indonesia, 1975-76, U. Ariz. 1990, Vanderbilt U., 1991, U. Md., 1994, Ariz. State U., 1995; editor in chief Environ. Law Reporter, Washington, 1976-81; cons. Nat. Trust for Historic Preservation, Washington, 1981; assoc. Lewis & Roca, Phoenix, 1981-84, ptnr., 1984-91; ptnr. Snell & Wilmer, Phoenix, 1991—. Bd. dirs. Ariz. div. Am. Cancer Soc., 1985—, sec. 1990-92, vice chmn. 1992-94, chmn., 1994—. Editor: Toxic Substances Control, 1980; contbr. articles to profl. jours. Bd. dirs. Phoenix Little Theater, 1983-90, chmn., 1986-88. Mem. ABA (vice chmn. SONREEL commn. state and regional environ. coop.), Assn. Bar City N.Y., Ariz. State Bar Assn. (coun. environ. & nat. res. law sect. 1988-93, chmn. 1991-92), Maricopa County Bar Assn., Ariz. Acad., Union Club (N.Y.C.), Univ. Club (Phoenix). Office: Snell & Wilmer 1 Arizona Ctr Phoenix AZ 85004-0001

WOLF, GARY HERBERT, architect; b. Lansing, Mich., July 15, 1950; s. Herbert C. and Margaret Wolf; m. Bonnie L. Grad, June 21, 1980; children: Alexander, Theodore. BA, Cornell U., 1972; M Archtl. History, U. Va., 1974; MArch, Princeton U., 1978. Assoc. Graham Gund Archs., Inc., Cambridge, Mass., 1983-87; prin. Adams & Wolf Archs., Inc., Belmont, Mass., 1987-91, Gary Wolf Archs., Inc., Boston, 1991—; dir. design Heliotrope, Providence, R.I., 1993—; mem. other archtl. firms, preservation orgns. and other instns. including constrn. mgmt. dept. Harvard U., Michael Graves Arch., Nat. Register Historic Places, 1974-83; vis. critic Harvard U. Grad. Sch. Design, Cambridge, Mass.; thesis advisor Boston Archtl. Ctr.; guest juror R.I. Sch. Design, Providence, Mass. Inst. Tech., Cambridge. Prin. archtl. works include Tree-House Porch, Brookline, Mass., 1987-88, 66 Leonard St., Belmont, Mass., 1988, Autumn Leaves House, Weston, Mass., 1988-94, Synectics Bldg. Restoration, Cambridge, Mass., 1987-88, 90-91, Mus. of Our Nat. Heritage Renovations, New Galleries and Meeting Hall, Lexington, Mass., 1993-96, Brookline Music Sch., 1991-94; designer Zephr Hammock, Glass Curtain Lamp, other objects; contbr. articles to profl. jours. Recipient Thomas Jefferson Meml. Found. Scholarship U. Va., 1972-74, Merit award Internat. Conceptual Furniture Competition, Progressive Archiecture Mag., 1980, 1st pl. Great Am. Facades Design Competition, 1990, Builder's Choice Design awards, 1991, 92, 93, Good Design Disting. Product award Chgo. Athenaeum: Mus. Architecture and Design, 1994, Gold Indsl. Design Excellence award Bus. Week/Indsl. Design Soc. Am., 1994, Best Products award Time Mag., 1994. Mem. AIA, Am. Assn. Mus., Nat. Trust Historic Preservation, Boston Soc. Archs. (past chair membership com.). Office: Gary Wolf Archs 145 Hanover St Boston MA 02108-2402

WOLF, GARY WICKERT, lawyer; b. Slinger, Wis., Apr. 19, 1938; s. Leonard A. and Cleo C. (Wickert) W.; m. Jacqueline Weltzin, Dec. 17, 1960; children: Gary, Jonathan. B.A.A., U. Minn., 1960, J.D. cum laude, 1963. Bar: N.Y. 1964, U.S. Ct. Appeals (2d cir.) 1969, U.S. Dist. Ct. (so. dist.) N.Y. 1969, U.S. Supreme Ct. 1971. Assoc. Cahill, Gordon & Reindel, N.Y.C., 1963-70, ptnr., 1970—; dir. Southwestern Pub. Svc. Co. Trustee Newark Acad. Livingston (N.J.), 1989-95. Mem. N.Y. State Bar Assn. (com. on securities regulation), Anglers Club (N.Y.C.), Downtown Assn. (N.Y.C.), Mashomack Fish and Game Club (Pine Plains, N.Y.). Home: Pleasantville Rd New Vernon NJ 07976 Office: Cahill Gordon & Reindel 80 Pine St New York NY 10005-1702

WOLF, HANS ABRAHAM, retired pharmaceutical company executive; b. Frankfurt, Fed. Republic Germany, June 27, 1928; came to U.S., 1936, naturalized, 1944; s. Franz Benjamin and Ilse (Nathan) W.; m. Elizabeth J. Bassett, Aug. 2, 1958; children: Heidi Elizabeth, Rebecca Anne, Deborah Wolf Streeter, Andrew Robert. AB magna cum laude, Harvard U., 1949, MBA, 1955; PhB, Oxford U., 1951. Math instr. Tutoring Sch., 1946-47; statis. research Nat. Bur. Econ. Research, N.Y.C., 1948-49; researcher Georgetown U., 1951-52; confidential aide Office Dir. Mut. Security, Washington, 1952; analyst Ford Motor div. Ford Motor Co., Dearborn, Mich., summer 1954; foreman prodn. M&C Nuclear Inc., Attleboro, Mass., 1955-57; asst. supt. prodn. Metals & Controls Corp., Attleboro, 1957-59, mgr. product dept., 1959-62, controller, 1962-67; asst. v.p., controller materials and services group Tex. Instruments Inc., Dallas, 1967-69, treas., v.p., 1969-75; v.p., fin., chief fin. officer Syntex Corp., Palo Alto, Calif., 1975-78, exec. v.p., 1978-86, vice chmn., chief adminstrv. officer, 1986-92, vice chmn., 1992-93, also bd. dirs., 1986-93; bd. dirs. Clean Sites, Inc., Alexandria, Va., Tab Products Co., Palo Alto, Calif., chmn., 1995—; bd. dirs. Network Equipment Techs., Redwood City, Calif., Satellite Dialysis Ctrs., Inc., Redwood City, Hyal Pharms., Missisauga, Ont. Author: Motivation Research—A New Aid to Understanding Your Markets, 1955. Mem. Norton (Mass.) Sch. Bd., 1959-62, chmn., 1961-62; pres., bd. dirs. Urban League Greater Dallas, 1971-74; bd. dirs. Dallas Health Planning Coun., mem. community adv. com., 1973-75; bd. dirs., pres. Children's Health Coun. of the Mid Peninsula; cubmaster Boy Scouts Am., 1976-78; elder United Ch. Christ, 1970-73, vice chmn. gen. bd., 1970-71, moderator, 1978-80; trustee Pacific Sch. Religion, 1986-94, chmn., 1990-94; trustee World Affairs Coun. San Francisco, 1986-92, 94—; dir. Tech Mus. San Jose. With USAF, 1952-53. Mem. Am. Mgmt. Assn. (planning council fin. div. 1970-76), Phi Beta Kappa.

WOLF, HAROLD ARTHUR, finance educator; b. Lind, Wash., Feb. 10, 1923; s. Edward and Olga (Limert) W.; March 23, 1961; children: Mark, Suellen. B.A., U. Oreg., 1951; M.A., U. Mich., 1952, Ph.D., 1958. Instr. Lehigh U., 1955-56; economist Prudential Life Ins. Co., Newark, 1957-58; asst. prof. fin., money, banking U. Colo., 1958-60, assoc. prof., 1961-64, prof., 1965-68; prof. fin. U. Tex., Austin, 1969—; pvt. practice consulting for fin. instns., 1960—. Author: Personal Finance, 1978, 8th edit., 1989, Managing Your Money, 1977, Personal Financial Planning, 8th edit., 1989, alternate edit., 1991, 2nd alternate edit., 1992. Served with U.S. Navy, 1941-47. Mem. Am. Economic Assn., Am. Fin. Assn., So. Fin. Assn. Home: 7004 Edgefield Dr Austin TX 78731-2926 Office: Dept Finance University of Texas Austin TX 78712

WOLF, HAROLD HERBERT, pharmacy educator; b. Quincy, Mass., Dec. 19, 1934; s. John I. and Bertha F. (Sussman) W.; m. Joan Z. Silverman, Aug. 11, 1957; children: Gary Jerome, David Neal. B.S., Mass. Coll. Pharmacy, 1956; Ph.D., U. Utah, 1961; LLD (hon.), U. Md., 1994. Asst. prof. pharmacology Coll. Pharmacy Ohio State U., 1961-64, assoc. prof., 1964-69, prof., 1969-76, Kimberly prof., 1975-76, chmn. div. pharmacology, 1973-76; dean Coll. of Pharmacy, U. Utah, Salt Lake City, 1976-89, prof. pharmacology, 1989—, dir. Anticonvulsant Drug Devel. Program, 1989—; vis. prof. U. Sains Malaysia, 1973-74; mem. Nat. Joint Commn. on Prescription Drug Use, 1976-80; mem. NIH rev. com. Biomed. Rsch. Devel. Grant Program, 1978-79; external examiner U. Malaya, 1978, 92, 96, U. Sains Malaysia, 1980. Contbr. articles in field of central nervous system pharmacology and field of pharm. edn. Recipient Alumni Achievement award Mass. Coll. Pharmacy, 1978, Disting. Faculty award U. Utah, 1989, Rosenblatt prize, 1989, Disting. Alumnus award Coll. Pharmacy, U. Utah, 1991. Fellow AAAS, Acad. Pharm. Scis.; mem. Am. Soc. Pharmacology and Exptl. Therapeutics, Am. Pharm. Assn. (task force on edn. 1982-84), Am. Assn. Colls. of Pharmacy (pres. 1977, Disting. Pharmacy Educator award 1988, scholar in residence 1989, chmn. commn. on implementing change in pharmacy edn. 1989-92, 95-96), Am. Soc. Hosp. Pharmacists (commn. on goals 1982-84), Am. Coun. on Pharm. Edn. (bd. dirs. 1985-88), Soc. Neurosci. Jewish. Home: 4512 Bruce St Salt Lake City UT 84124-4720 Office: Univ Utah Coll Pharmacy Salt Lake City UT 84112

WOLF, IRVING, clinical psychologist; b. New Haven, Aug. 7, 1924; s. Samuel and Annie W.; m. Elizabeth Pennington Haughey, Aug. 1, 1949; children: Susan, Richard, Robert, William. A.B., Boston U., 1949, A.M., 1951, Ph.D., 1954. Diplomate Am. Bd. Profl. Psychology. Clin. psychologist VA Hosp., Brockton, Mass., 1954-57; clin. psychologist Mass. Gen. Hosp., Boston and research assoc. Harvard Med. Sch., 1957-59; prof. psychology, chmn. doctoral program clin. psychology, dir. fed. relations Boston U., 1959-75; vis. Fulbright prof. U. Philippines, Manila, 1965-66; dir. Nat. Ctr. Alcohol Edn., Washington, 1974; div. dir., sr. exec. Nat. Inst. Alcohol Abuse and Alcoholism, HEW, 1976-80; prof. psychology, sr. exec. Fed. Exec. Inst., Charlottesville, Va., 1981-85; pvt. practice, 1986-88; clin. dir. Devereux Found., Rutland, Mass., 1989-92; clin. assoc. Am. Geriatric Svcs., Rockland, Mass., 1992-95, Advanced Health Systems, 1996—. Author articles in field. Served with AUS, 1943-46. Named Disting. Alumnus Boston U. Coll. Liberal Arts, 1974. Fellow Am. Psychol. Assn.; mem. Eastern Psychol. Assn., Sr. Exec. Assn., Fed. Exec. Inst. Alumni Assn., Phi Beta Kappa. Home: 20 Pickwick Way Wayland MA 01778-3800

WOLF, JACK KEIL, electrical engineer, educator; b. Newark, Mar. 14, 1935; s. Joseph and Rosaline Miriam (Keil) W.; m. Toby Katz, Sept. 10, 1955; children—Joseph Martin, Jay Steven, Sarah Keil. B.S., U. Pa., 1956; M.S.E., Princeton, 1957, M.A., 1958, Ph.D., 1960. With R.C.A., Princeton, N.J., 1959-60; asso. prof. N.Y. U., 1963-65; from asso. prof. to prof. elec. engring. Poly. Inst. Bklyn., 1965-73; prof. dept. elec. and computer engring. U. Mass., Amherst, 1973-85; chmn. dept. U. Mass., 1973-75; Stephen O. Rice prof. Ctr. Magnetic Rec. Research, dept. elec. engring. and computer sci. U. Calif.-San Diego, La Jolla, 1985—; mem. tech. staff Bell Telephone Labs., Murray Hill, N.J., 1968-69; prin. engr. Qualcomm Inc., San Diego, 1985. Editor for coding IEEE Transactions on Information Theory, 1969-72. Served with USAF, 1960-63. NSF sr. postdoctoral fellow, 1971-72; Guggenheim fellow, 1979-80. Fellow IEEE (pres. info. theory group 1974, co-recipient info. theory group prize paper award 1975, co-recipient Comm. Soc. prize paper award 1993), Nat. Acad. Engring.; mem. AAAS, Sigma Xi, Sigma Tau, Eta Kappa Nu, Pi Mu Epsilon, Tau Beta Pi. Achievements include research on information theory, communication theory, computer/communication networks, magnetic recording. Home: 8529 Prestwick Dr La Jolla CA 92037-2025

WOLF, JAMES ANTHONY, insurance company executive; b. Washington, May 10, 1945; s. Arthur William and Marie Antoinette (Dalton) Wolf; m. Sheila Marie Regan, June 27, 1968; children: Jayne Ann, Elizabeth. BS in Fin. cum laude, Boston Coll., 1967. Mktg. rep. IBM, Newark, N.J., 1967-68, Boston, 1970-78; mktg. mgr. IBM, N.Y.C., 1978-81; 2nd v.p. Tchrs. Ins. & Annuity Assn., N.Y.C., 1981-82, v.p., 1982-85, sr. v.p., 1985—. Served to sgt. U.S. Army, 1968-70, Vietnam. Mem. Am. Mgmt. Assn. Republican. Roman Catholic. Home: 233 Ridge Common Fairfield CT 06430-7010 Office: Tchrs Ins & Annuity Assn Am 730 3rd Ave New York NY 10017-3206

WOLF, JOHN STEVEN, construction executive, land developer; b. Portsmouth, Ohio, Sept. 4, 1947; s. John Andrew and Betty Lee Wolf; A.S. in Civil Engring. Tech., Ohio Coll. Applied Sci., 1967; B.S. in Civil Engring., Ohio U., 1975. Project engr. Columbus & So. Ohio Electric Co., 1974-75; staff project engr. Goodyear Atomic Corp., Piketon, Ohio, 1975-78; constrn. mgr., project engr. Am. Electric Power Service Corp., Lancaster, Ohio, 1978-83; project mgr. F. and P. Mgrs., Inc., Columbus, Ohio, 1983-85, Target Constrn. Co., Columbus, 1985-91; area mgr. Sherman R. Smoot Co., Indpls., 1991-93; dir. constrn. Pizzuti Devel., Inc., Columbus, 1993—; panel mem., speaker, seminars and classes in mgmt. and constrn. related areas. Served with U.S. Army, 1968-69; Vietnam. Decorated Army Commendation medal (2), Combat Infantry badge; registered profl. engr., Ohio, Ind. Nat. Soc. Profl. Engrs., Ohio Soc. Profl. Engrs, Ind. Soc. Profl. Engrs. Methodist. Club: Masons, Scottish Rite, Shriners. Home: 510 Wickham Way Gahanna OH 43230-2233 Office: Ste 1900 250 E Broad St Columbus OH 43215

WOLF, JOSEPH ALBERT, mathematician, educator; b. Chgo., Oct. 18, 1936; s. Albert M. and Goldie (Wykoff) W. BS, U. Chgo., 1956, MS, 1957, PhD, 1959. Mem. Inst. for Advanced Study, Princeton, 1960-62, 65-66; asst. prof. U. Calif., Berkeley, 1962-64, assoc. prof., 1964-66, prof., 1966—, Miller research prof., 1972-73, 83-84; prof. honorario Universidad Nacional de Cordoba, Argentina, 1989; vis. prof. Rutgers U., 1969-70, Hebrew U., Jerusalem, 1974-76, Tel Aviv U., 1974-76, Harvard U., 1979-80, 86. Author: Spaces of Constant Curvature, 1967, 72, 74, 77, 84, Unitary Representations on Partially Holomorphic Cohomology Spaces, 1974, Unitary Representations of Maximal Parabolic Subgroups of the Classical Groups, 1976, Classification and Fourier Inversion for Parabolic Subgroups with Square Integrable Nilradical, 1979; co-editor, author: Harmonic Analysis and Representations of Semisimple Lie Groups, 1980, The Penrose Transform and Analytic Cohomology in Representation Theory, 1993; editor Geometriae Dedicata, Math Reports, Jour. of Math. Systems, Estimation and Control, Letters in Math. Physics, Jour. of Group Theory in Physics; contbr. articles to profl. jours. Alfred P. Sloan rsch. fellow, 1965-67, NSF fellow, 1959-62; recipient Médaille de l'Université de Liège, 1977, Humboldt prize, 1995. Mem. Am., Swiss math. socs. Office: U Calif Dept Math Berkeley CA 94720

WOLF, JOSEPH GORDON (PEPE LOBO), marketing communicator, television producer; b. Ft. Sill, Okla., Apr. 23, 1944; s. Gordon Joseph Wolf and Amanda Roth Block; 1 child, Harrison; m. Celeste Miles, Dec. 25, 1992. BA, Yale U., 1966; MBA, Columbia U., 1968. Photographer Bldg. News Inc., L.A., 1973-74; free-lance photojournalist L.A., 1975; mag. editor Fluor Corp., L.A., 1976-77; mag. editor TRW, L.A., 1978-79, with mktg. comms., 1980—; TV producer and dir. Lobo Prodns., L.A., 1980—. Producer, dir. film Three Miles High, 1981, tapes Gt. American, 1983, CRWTH, 1983, TV shows Space Sta., 1985, Lost or Last Frontier, 1986, TV series Space Capsules, 1987, tapes Craig Internat., 1989, O'Hare Com. and Cont., 1992, Hits!, 1993; photojournalist. Vol. Peace Corps., Columbia, S.Am., 1968-70. Recipient CINE Golden Eagle, U.S. Internat. Film and Video Festival Silver Screen awrd, others. Mem. Bus. Mktg. Assn. (bd. dirs. 1992—), Am. Def. Preparedness Assn., Navy League of U.S. (life), Assn. U.S. Army, Armed Forces Comms. and Electronics Assn., Air Force Assn. Republican. Jewish. Avocations: skiing, snow-boarding, scuba diving. Home: 2304 Gardner Pl Glendale CA 91206-3013 Office: TRW R2/1028 One Space Park Redondo Beach CA 90278

WOLF, JULIUS, medical educator; b. Boston, Aug. 15, 1918; s. Herman and Rose (Kurgan) W.; m. Irene H. Bechtloff, May 4, 1945; children—Maritja Ann, Miriam Jeanne, Brenda Joyce. S.B., Boston U., 1940, M.D., 1943. Intern L.I. Coll. Hosp., 1943-44, resident, 1944-45; resident Bronx VA Hosp., 1947-48, sect. chief medicine, chief gastroenterology sec., chief med. service, 1948-72, chief staff, 1970-90; assoc. dean Mt. Sinai Med. Ctr., N.Y.C., 1974-90; assoc. prof. medicine Columbia Coll. Phys. and Surg., 1961-67; prof. medicine Mt. Sinai Sch. Medicine, 1968—. Chmn. VA Lung Cancer Group, 1962-75. Served to capt. AUS, 1943-45. Fellow ACP. Home: 315 Covert Ave New Hyde Park NY 11040-5436

WOLF, KARL EVERETT, aerospace and communications corporation executive; b. Hartford, Conn., Aug. 19, 1921; s. Carl Fred and Anna (Voss) W.; m. Lola Sue Stoner, Aug. 1, 1948; children: Paula R., Gloria J., Glenn K. B.S., U.S. Mil. Acad., 1943; J.D., U. Pa., 1953; S.J.D., George Washington U., 1963. Bar: D.C. 1953, Conn. 1953, U.S. Supreme Ct. 1960, Calif. 1971, Mich. 1975. Commd. 2d lt. U.S. Army, 1943, advanced through grades to lt. col., 1959, ret., 1963; assoc. counsel Philco. Corp., Phila., 1963-73; v.p., gen. counsel Ford Aerospace Corp., Detroit, 1973-88; ret., 1988; mem. adv. bd. Bur. Nat. Affairs, Fed. Contract Reports, Washington, 1963-73. Author: State Taxation of Government Contractors, 1964. Decorated Silver Star, Bronze Star; Croix de Guerre (Belgium). Mem. ABA, Fed. Bar Assn., Calif. Bar Assn. Home: 535 Dunnegan Dr Laguna Beach CA 92651-1432

WOLF, LESLEY SARA, lawyer; b. N.Y.C., Jan. 15, 1953; d. Herbert and Ardelle (Brush) W.; m. Dhiya El-Saden; children: Jordan, Evan. BA, Sarah Lawrence Coll., 1975; JD, U. Va., 1978. Bar: Calif. 1978. Assoc. Gibson, Dunn & Crutcher, L.A., 1978-86, ptnr., 1987—. Bd. dirs. L.A. Arts Coun., 1990-91, Franciscan Health Ctr., 1992-94. Office: Gibson Dunn & Crutcher 333 S Grand Ave Los Angeles CA 90071-1504

WOLF, LEWIS ISIDORE, lawyer; b. Bklyn., June 8, 1933; s. Ephraim and Rachel (Dunajevsky) W.; m. Ruth Ullmann; children: Sara S., Joseph J. BA, Bklyn. Coll., 1954; JD cum laude, Bklyn. Law Sch., 1957; LLM, NYU, 1967. Bar: N.Y. 1958, U.S. Dist. Ct. (so. and ea. dists.) N.Y. 1961, U.S. Ct. Appeals (2d cir.) 1964, U.S. Supreme Ct. 1964. Pvt. practice law, N.Y.C., 1958—; atty. and mng. atty. Cosmopolitan Mut. Ins. Co., 1958-77, atty. of record, 1977-81; mem. Smith, Mazure, Director, Wilkins, Young, Yagerman & Tarallo, P.C., N.Y.C., 1981—; arbitrator N.Y. County Civil Ct. With N.Y. N.G., 1957-63. Mem. ABA, N.Y. State Bar Assn., N.Y. County Lawyers Assn., Am. Arbitration Assn. (arbitrator accident claims tribunal). Office: 111 John St New York NY 10038

WOLF, MARK LAWRENCE, federal judge; b. Boston, Nov. 23, 1946; s. Jason Harold and Beatrice (Meltzer) W.; m. Lynne Lichterman, Apr. 4, 1971; children: Jonathan, Matthew. BA cum laude, Yale U., 1968; JD cum laude, Harvard U., 1971; hon. degree, Boston Latin Sch., 1990. Bar: Mass. 1971, D.C. 1972, U.S. Supreme Ct. 1976. Assoc. Surrey, Karasik & Morse, Washington, 1971-74; spl. asst. to dep. atty. gen. U.S. Dept. Justice, Washington, 1974-75, spl. asst. to atty. gen., 1975-76; dep. U.S. atty. U.S. Dept. Justice, Boston, 1981-85; from assoc. to ptnr. Sullivan & Worcester, Boston, 1977-81; judge U.S. Dist. Ct. Mass., Boston, 1985—; lectr. Harvard U. Law Sch., Cambridge, Mass., 1990—; adj. prof. Boston Coll. Law Sch., 1992. Bd. dirs. Albert Schweitzer Fellowship, Boston, 1974—, pres., 1989—; chmn. John William Ward Fellowship, Boston, 1986—. Recipient cert. appreciation U.S. Pres., 1975, Disting. Service award U.S. Atty. Gen., 1985. Mem. Boston Bar Assn. (council 1982-85), Am. Law Inst. Office: US Dist Ct McCormack PO & Courthouse Rm 1900 Boston MA 02109*

WOLF, MARTIN EUGENE, lawyer; b. Balt., Sept. 9, 1958; s. Eugene Bernard and Mary Anna (O'Neil) W.; m. Nancy Ann Reinsfelder, May 9, 1980; children: Matthew Adam, Allison Maria, Emily Elizabeth. BA, Johns Hopkins U., 1980; JD, U. Md., 1991. Bar: Md. 1991, U.S. Dist. Ct. Md. 1992, U.S. Ct. Appeals (4th cir.) 1992, U.S. Ct. Appeals (2d cir.) 1993. Mgmt. trainee Giant Foods, Inc., Landover, Md., 1980-82, dept. mgr., 1982-83, ops. analyst, 1983-86, fin. coord., 1986-89; law clk. Piper & Marbury, L.L.P., Balt., 1989-91, assoc., 1991-96; prin. Law Office of Martin E. Wolf, Abingdon, Md., 1996—; dir. Giant Food Fed. Credit Union, Landover, 1984-89; pres. Stalagmite Properties, Ltd., Abingdon, Md., 1995—; teaching asst. U. Md. Sch. Law, Balt., 1992-94; adj. prof. U. Md. Law Sch., Balt., 1996—. Mem. ABA, Md. State Bar Assn., Harford County Bar Assn., Harford County Bar Found. (Vol. Svc. award 1992, 94). Republican. Roman Catholic. Avocations: Lacrosse, hockey. Home: 11 Mitchell Dr Abingdon MD 21009

WOLF, MARY CAHN, YMCA association volunteer; b. Chgo., Apr. 1, 1929; d. Morton David and Elizabeth (Hofeller) Cahn; m. Stephen Louis Wolf, Jan. 29, 1955; 1 child, Matthew Stephen. BA, Rockford Coll., 1951. Bd. dirs. YWCA, N.Y.C., 1966-73; nat. bd. dirs. YWCA U.S.A., 1973-85, asst. treas. nat. bd. dirs., 1976-79, 1st v.p. nat. bd. dirs., 1982-85, del. triennial convs., 1967-85; vis. del. World YWCA Coun., Singapore, 1983; UN NGO rep. World YWCA, 1985—. N.Y. State Dem. commiteewoman, 1960-64; mem. The Mt. Sinai Hosp. Aux. Bd., 1970—, pres., 1976-81; founding mem., pres. Playwrights Horizons, N.Y.C., 1974-76; active World Svc. Coun., 1980—; vol. NGO Forum, Decade Women, Nairobi, 1985; trustee Mt. Sinai Hosp., 1976-81; bd. dirs. New Alternatives Children, N.Y., 1982—. Named hon. mem. nat. bd. dirs. YWCA U.S.A., 1991. Mem. Cosmopolitan Club, Women's City Club. Reform Jewish. Avocations: music, theatre, photography, literature, travel.

WOLF, MILTON ALBERT, economist, former U.S. ambassador, investor; b. Cleve., May 29, 1924; s. Sam and Sylvia (Davis) W.; m. Roslyn C. Zehman, June 23, 1948; children: Leslie Eric, Caryn Sue, Nancy Gail, Sherri Hope. BA in Chemistry and Biology, Ohio State U., 1948; BS in Civil Engring. summa cum laude, Case Inst. Tech., 1954; MA in Econs., Case Western Res. U., 1973, PhD in Econs., 1993, LHD (hon.), 1980; LLD (hon.), Cleve. State U., 1980. Pres. Zehman-Wolf Constrn. Co., Cleve., 1948-76; U.S. ambassador to Austria, 1977-80; Disting. professorial lectr. in econs. Case Western Res. U., 1981-87; chmn. Milton A. Wolf Investors, 1980—; bd. dirs. Am. Greetings Corp., Town and Country Trust; U.S. del. UN conf. on Sci. and Tech. for Devel., 1979; U.S. del. dedication of UN Internat. Ctr., Vienna, 1979; host Salt II Summit, Vienna, 1979; trustee Cleve. Clinic; chmn. Fulbright Commn. for Austria, 1977-80. Trustee, chair Ohio State U.; trustee Case Western Res. U., Cleve. Orch.; vice chmn. Coun. Am. Ambs.; chmn. Am. Austrian Found.; pres. Am. Jewish Joint Distbn. Com.; life trustee Mt. Sinai Med. Ctr., Cleve.; mem. econ. adv. task force Carter Presdl. Campaign, 1976; mem. Carter Inauguration Com.; nat. fin. chmn. John Glenn Presdl. Campaign, 1983-84; dir. transition Gov. Celeste, State of Ohio, 1982-83; nat. trustee United Israel Appeal, United Jewish Appeal, Coun. Jewish Fedns.; trustee United Way Svcs.; life trustee Park Synagogue, Cleve.; past pres., life trustee Jewish Cmty. Fedn., Cleve. With USAAF 1943-48. Recipient Gt. Golden medal of honor with sash Republic of Austria, 1980, Gt. Golden medal of State Province of Salzburg, Republic of Austria, 1979, Eisenman award Jewish Cmty. Fedn. Cleve., 1990, Internat. Humanitarian award Raoul Wallenberg Com., 1995. Mem. Am. Econ. Assn., Cleve. Engring. Soc., Cleve. Builders Assn., Coun. Fgn. Rels., Fgn. Policy Assn., Acad. Polit. Sci., Cleve. Com. World Affairs, UN Assn.- U.S. (bd. govs.), Tau Beta Pi. Jewish. Home: 19200 S Park Blvd Shaker Hts OH 44122-1857 Office: 25700 Science Park Dr Beachwood OH 44122-7312

WOLF, NEAL LLOYD, lawyer; b. Chgo., Feb. 8, 1949; s. Ira and Bettye (Brainin) W.; m. Caren Ellen Mirsky, June 11, 1972 (div. Apr., 1995); children: Michael Elliot, Brian Martin. AB magna cum laude, Princeton U., 1970; JD, U. Chgo., 1974. Bar: Ariz. 1974, U.S. Dist. Ct. Ariz. 1974, U.S. Ct. Appeals (9th cir.) 1975, Ill. 1983, U.S. Dist. Ct. (no. dist.) Ill. 1983, U.S. Ct. Appeals (7th cir.) 1983, U.S. Ct. Appeals (8th cir.) 1985, U.S. Supreme Ct., 1985, U.S. Dist. Ct. (no. dist.) Tex., 1990. Ptnr. Lewis and Roca, Phoenix, 1974-83, Winston & Strawn, Chgo., 1983-86, 89—, Ross & Hardies, Chgo., 1986-89. Mem. ABA. Avocations: golf, reading, movies, tennis. Office: Winston & Strawn 35 W Wacker Dr Chicago IL 60601-1614

WOLF, PETER MICHAEL, investment management and land planning consultant, educator, author; b. New Orleans, Dec. 6, 1935; s. Morris and Ruth (New) W.; m. Alessandra Cantey, July 3, 1967; children—Phelan Godchaux, Alexis Ambler. B.A., Yale U., 1957; M.A., Tulane U., 1963; Ph.D., NYU, 1968. Ptnr. Wolf and Co., New Orleans, 1958-62; assoc. Wilbur Smith & Assocs., N.Y.C., 1968-70; faculty mem. NYU, 1966-67, Pratt Inst., N.Y.C., 1968-70; adj. prof. Cooper Union, N.Y.C., 1971-87; chmn. bd. fellows and mem. faculty Inst. Architecture and Urban Studies, N.Y.C., 1972-82; prin. Peter Wolf Assocs., N.Y.C., 1970—; organizer of exhbns. Mus. Modern Art, N.Y.C., 1969; writer exhbns. Whitney Mus. Art, N.Y.C., 1970; contbr. exhbns. Mus. Modern Art, N.Y.C., 1973, Albany Inst Art, 1975. Author: Land in America: Its Value, Use and Control, 1981; On Streets, 1979; The Future of the City: New Directions in Urban Planning, 1974; The Evolving City, Urban Design Proposals by Ulrich Franzen and Paul Rudolph, 1974. Trustee Guild Hall, East Hampton, N.Y., 1981-86, Van Allen Inst., 1995—, Godchaux Res. Plantation Fund (pres. 1994—). NEA Fellow, 1979; Graham Found. Fellow, 1967-68, 93-94; Fulbright Fellow, 1965-66; Ford Found. grantee, 1971-74. Recipient Charles B. Shattuck award Nat. Research and Edn. Trust Fund, 1983. Mem. Am. Inst. Cert. Planners. Avocation: tennis. Home: 325 W End Ave New York NY 10023-8135 Office: 7 W 36th St New York NY 10018-7911

WOLF, ROBERT B., lawyer; b. Phila., Aug. 18, 1914; s. Morris and Pauline (Binswanger) W.; children—Edwin David, Virginia. B.A., Haverford Coll., 1936; LL.B., Harvard, 1939. Bar: Pa. 1939. Ptnr. Wolf, Block, Schorr & Solis-Cohen, 1940-43, 46-56, 57-85, of counsel, 1985—; gen. counsel FHA, Washington, 1956-57; instr. humanities Haverford Coll., 1948-49, 71-72. Chmn. mayor's coordinated housing improvement program, Phila., 1951, Phila. Youth Svcs. Coordinating Com., 1978-84; past chmn. Pa. Com. Crime and Delinquency; mem. juvenile adv. com. Pa. Commn. on Crime and Delinquency, 1976-86; ct. master Phila. Youth Study Ctr., 1989-91; trustee Benjamin Franklin Found., Berlin, Germany, 1955-56. 1st lt. inf. AUS, 1943-45; office Asst. Sec. War, 1945-46. Mem. Am., Pa., Phila. bar assns., Phi Beta Kappa. Home: 2101 Harts Ln Conshohocken PA 19428-2416 Office: Wolf Block Schorr & Solis-Cohen Packard Bldg Philadelphia PA 19102

WOLF, ROBERT HOWARD, advertising executive, marketing consultant; b. N.Y.C., Feb. 11, 1942; s. Charles and Dorothy (Goldstein) W.; m. Rebecca Helene Beck, Feb. 26, 1978; children—Jessica Leigh, Caroline Beth. B.A., Long Island U., 1964; M.B.A., Adelphi U., 1967. Mktg. mgr. Lever Bros, N.Y.C., 1967-70; mgmt. supr Wells, Rich, Greene, N.Y.C., 1971-77, sr. v.p., mng. dir., 1978-81; sr. v.p., gen. mgr. Kenyon & Eckhardt, Los Angeles, 1981-83; exec. v.p., gen. mgr. Chiat/Day Advt., N.Y.C., 1983-87, pres., chief exec. officer, vice chmn., 1987-89; chmn., CEO Chiat/Day N.Am., N.Y.C., 1989-95; pres. Bob Wolf Co., Beverly Hills, Calif., 1995—; bd. dirs. Jenny Craig Inc., United Way L.A. Mem. El Caballero Country Club. Home: 9817 Hythe Ct Beverly Hills CA 90210-1016 Office: Bob Wolf Co 468 N Camden Dr Beverly Hills CA 90210

WOLF, ROBERT THOMAS, lawyer; b. N.Y.C., Apr. 14, 1936; s. Simon and Rose (Salzhauer) W.; divorced; 1 child, Lisa Eve. BS in Econs., U. Pa., 1955; LLB, Bklyn. Law Sch., 1963. Bar: N.Y. 1964. Asst. corp. counsel City of N.Y., 1970-80; ptnr. Weinberger & Wolf, Bronx, N.Y., 1980-83, Weinberger, Wolf, Rodrigues & Malach, Bronx, 1983-87, Weinberger, Wolf & Malach, Bronx, 1987-88, Wolf & Malach, Bronx, 1988-90; sole practice Bronx, 1990—. With U.S. Army, 1957-59. Mem. N.Y. State Bar Assn., Bronx County Bar Assn., Assn. Trial Lawyers Am., N.Y. State Trial Lawyers Assn. Avocations: sports, reading, swimming, Spanish literature and conversation. Office: 327 E 149th St Bronx NY 10451-5601

WOLF, ROSALIE JOYCE, financial executive; b. Southampton, N.Y., May 8, 1941; d. Saul and Anne W.; m. Milton Stern, May 15, 1979; 1 dau., Dina G. Pruzansky. A.B., Wellesley Coll., 1961; M.A. in Math, Northwestern U.,

1962. With Mobil Oil Corp., N.Y.C., 1962-77; asst. treas. internat. Mobil Oil Corp., to 1977; v.p. venture capital group Donaldson, Lufkin, Jenrette, N.Y.C., 1977-79; asst. corp. contr. Internat. Paper Co., N.Y.C., 1979—, treas., 1981-86; prin., chief fin. officer Aldrich, Eastman & Waltch Inc., Boston, 1986-89; mng. dir. pvt. equity Merchant Banking Group, Bankers Trust Co., N.Y.C., 1989-93; treas., chief investment officer The Rockefeller Found., N.Y.C., 1994—; dir., mem. compensation com. Narragansett Capital Corp., 1983-86. Durant scholar Wellesley Coll., 1961. Mem. Fin. Women's Assn. N.Y., Women's Forum, Phi Beta Kappa.

WOLF, STEPHEN M., airline executive; b. Oakland, Calif., Aug. 7, 1941. BA, San Francisco State U., 1965. Various positions Am. Airlines, Los Angeles, 1965-79, v.p. western div., 1979-81; sr. v.p. mktg. Pan Am. World Airlines, N.Y.C., 1981-82; pres., chief operating officer Continental Airlines, Houston, 1982-83; pres. Republic Airlines, Mpls., 1984-85, pres., chief exec. officer, 1985-86; chmn., pres., chief exec. officer Tiger Internat., Los Angeles, 1986-87; chmn., pres., chief exec. officer UAL Corp. and United Airlines, Chgo., 1987-92, chmn., CEO, 1992-94, former pres., dir.; adviser Air France, 1994-96; chmn., CEO USAIR Inc, Arlington, Va., 1996—; bd. dirs. Air Transport Assn., Bus. Roundtable, Washington, conf. bd. N.Y. Internat. Air Transport Assn., Geneva, World Travel and Tourism Coun., London. Bd. dirs. Alzheimer's Disease and Related Disorders Assn., Chgo., Art Inst., Chgo., Chgo. Symphony Orch., Muscular Dystrophy Assn., Rush-Presbyn.-St. Luke's Med. Ctr., Chgo., J.L. Kellogg Sch. Bus. Adv. Coun., Northwestern U. Trustee Northwestern U., mem. bus. adv. com. Transportation Ctr. Office: USAIR Inc 2345 Crystal Dr Arlington VA 22227*

WOLF, STEWART GEORGE, JR., physician, medical educator; b. Balt., Jan. 12, 1914; s. Stewart George and Angeline (Griffing) W.; m. Virginia Danforth, Aug. 1, 1942; children: Stewart George III, Angeline Griffing, Thomas Danforth. Student, Phillips Acad., 1927-31, Yale U., 1931-33; A.B., Johns Hopkins U., 1934, M.D., 1938; M.D. (hon.), U. Göteborg, Sweden, 1968. Intern N.Y. Hosp., 1938-39, resident medicine, 1939-42, NRC fellow, 1941-42; rsch. fellow Bellevue Hosp., 1939-42, clin. assoc. vis. neuropsychiatrist, 1946-52; rsch. head injury and motion sickness Harvard neurol. unit Boston City Hosp., 1942-43; asst., then assoc. prof. medicine Cornell U., 1946-52; prof., head dept. medicine U. Okla., 1952-67, Regents prof. medicine, psychiatry and behavioral scis., 1967—, prof. physiology, 1967-69; dir. Marine Biomed. Inst., U. Tex. Med. Br., Galveston, 1969-78; dir. emeritus Marine Biomed. Inst., U. Tex. Med. Br., 1978—, prof. medicine univ., also prof. internal medicine and physiology med. br., 1970-77; prof. medicine Temple U., Phila., 1977—; v.p. med. affairs St. Luke's Hosp., Bethlehem, Pa., 1977-82; dir. Totts Gap Inst., Bangor, Pa., 1958—; supr. clin. activities Okla. Med. Rsch. Found., 1953-55, head psychosomatic and neuromuscular sect., 1952-67, head neuroscis. sect., 1967-69; adv. com. Space Medicine and Behavioral Scis., NASA, 1960-61; cons. internal medicine VA Hosp., Oklahoma City, 1952-69; cons. (European Office), Paris, Office Internat. Rsch., NIH, 1963-64; mem. edn. and supply panel Nat. Adv. Commn. on Health Manpower, 1966-67; mem. Nat. Adv. Heart Coun., 1961-65, U.S. Phamacopeia Scope Panel on Gastroenterology, Regent Nat. Libr. Medicine, 1965-69; chmn., 1968-69; mem. Nat. Adv. Environ. Health Scis. Coun., 1978-82; exec. v.p. Frontiers Sci. Found., 1967-69; mem. sci. adv. bd. Muscular Dystrophy Assns. Am., Inc., 1974-91, chmn., 1980-89; mem. gastrointestinal drug adv. com. FDA, 1974-77; bd. Internat. Cardiology Fedn.; mem. bd. visitors dept. biology Boston U., 1978-88; mem. vis. com. Ctr. for Social Rsch., Lehigh U., 1980-90; chmn. adv. com. Wood Inst. on History of Medicine, Coll. Physicians, Phila., 1980-90, mem. program com. Coll. Physicians, 1990-91; dir. Inst. for Advanced Studies in Immunology and Aging, 1988—. Author: Human Gastric Function, 1943, The Stomach, 1965, Social Environment and Health, 1981, others; adv. editor Internat. Dictionary Biology and Medicine, 1978—; editor in chief Integrative Physiol & Behavioral Sci.: The Official Jour. of Pavlovian Soc., 1990—. Pres. Okla. City Symphony Soc., 1956-61; mem. Okla. Sch. of Sci. and Math. Found., 1961—. Recipient Disting. Svc. Citation U. Okla., 1968, Dean's award for disting. med. svc., 1992; Horsley Gantt medal Pavlovian Soc., 1987, Hans Selye award Am. Inst. Stress, 1988, Rsch. award Carolinska Inst., Stockholm, 1994, Wilém Laufberger medal Acad. Scis. of Czech Republic, Citation for sci. and humanitarian achievement The J.E. Purkyně Bohemian Med. Assn. Fellow Am. Psychiat. Assn. (disting., trustee 1992—, Hofheimer prize for rsch. 1952); mem. AMA (coun. mental health 1960-64), Am. Soc. Clin. Investigation, Am. Clin. and Climatol. Assn. (pres. 1975-76), Assn. Am. Physicians, Am. Psychosomatic Soc. (pres. 1961-62), Am. Gastroent. Assn. (rsch. award 1943, pres. 1969-70), Am. Heart Assn. (chmn. com. profl. edn., com. internat. program, awards), Coll. Physicians Phila., Collegium Internat. Activitas Nervosae Superioris (exec. com. 1992—, pres. 1994), Philos. Soc. Tex., Sigma Xi, Alpha Omega Alpha, Omicron Delta Kappa. Club: Cosmos (Washington). Home: 1430 Totts Gap Rd Bangor PA 18013-9716 Office: Totts Med Rsch Labs Bangor PA 18013

WOLF, WERNER PAUL, physicist, educator; b. Vienna, Austria, Apr. 22, 1930; came to U.S., 1963, naturalized, 1977; s. Paul and Wilhelmina Wolf; m. Elizabeth Eliot, Sept. 23, 1954; children: Peter Paul, Mary-Anne Githa. BA, Oxford (Eng.) U., 1951, DPhil, 1954, MA, 1954; MA (hon.), Yale U., 1965. Rsch. fellow Harvard U., 1956-57; Fulbright travelling fellow, 1956-57; Imperial Chem. Industries rsch. fellow Oxford U., 1957-59, univ. demonstrator, lectr., 1959-62; lectr. New Coll., 1957-62; faculty Yale U., 1963—, prof. physics and applied sci., 1965-76, dir. grad. studies dept. engring. and applied sci., 1973-76, Becton prof., 1976-84, chmn. dept. engring. and applied sci., 1976-81, chmn. council engring., 1981-84, Raymond J. Wean prof. engring. and applied sci., prof. physics, 1984—, dir. undergrad. studies dept. applied physics, 1987-94, dir. grad. studies coun. engring., 1989, chmn. dept. applied physics, 1990—, chair commn. on econ. status of faculty, 1990-92; dir. ednl. affairs, 1994—; cons. Dupont Exptl. Sta., Wilmington, Del., 1957, Hughes Aircraft, Culver City, Calif., 1957, GE Rsch. Lab., Schenectady, N.Y., 1960, Mullard Rsch. Labs., Salfords, England, 1961, IBM, Yorktown Heights, N.Y., 1962-66, Brookhaven Nat. Lab., 1966-80, GE R & D Ctr., Schenectady, 1966—; vis. prof. Technische Hochschule, Munich, Germany, 1969; Sci. Research Council sr. vis. fellow Oxford U., 1980, 84; vis. fellow Corpus Christi Coll., 1984, 87; mem. program com. Conf. Magnetism and Magnetic Materials, 1963, 65, 86, chmn., 1968, mem. adv. com., 1964-65, 70-76, 85-88, chmn., 1972, steering com., 1970-71, conf. gen. chmn., 1971; mem. organizing, program coms. Internat. Congress on Magnetism, 1967, internat. program com., 1978-79, planning com., 1979-85; vis. physicist Brookhaven Nat. Lab., 1966, 68, vis. sr. physicist, 1970, research collaborator, 1972, 74, 75, 77, 80; mem. vis. com. dept. phys./sci. U. Del., 1980, 84, 86; mem. NATO Advanced Study Inst. Program Com., 1983, 85, internat. adv. bd. Yamada Conf. XXV on Magnetic Phase Transitions, 1990. Editor: CASE Reports, 1988-90; contbr. papers on magnetic materials and low temperature physics. Alexander von Humboldt Found. sr. U.S. scientist awardee, 1983; vis. guest fellow Royal Soc. London, 1987. Fellow IEEE, Am. Phys. Soc. (edn. com. 1977-80, program dir. Indsl. Grad. Intern Program 1978-79, chmn. fellowship com., Div. Condensed Matter Physics 1981-83); mem. Conn. Acad. Sci. and Engring., Yale Sci. and Engring. Assn. (Meritorious Svc. award 1985). Home: 37 Apple Tree Ln Woodbridge CT 06525-1258 Office: Yale U Dept Applied Physics PO Box 208284 New Haven CT 06520-8284

WOLF, WILLIAM MARTIN, computer company executive, consultant; b. Watertown, N.Y., Aug. 29, 1928; s. John and Rose (Emrich) W.; m. Eileen Marie Jolly, Aug. 19, 1952 (div. 1974); children: Rose, Sylvia, William. BS, St. Lawrence U., 1950; MS, U. N.H., 1951; postgrad., U. Pa., 1951-52, MIT, 1952-55. Programmer digital computer lab. MIT, Cambridge, Mass., 1952-54; pres. Wolf R & D Corp., Boston, 1954-69, Wolf Computer Corp., Boston, 1969-76, Planning Systems Internat., Boston, 1976-81, Micro Computer Software Inc., Cambridge, 1981-88, Tech. Acquisition Corp., Boston, 1989-91, Planning Internat., Inc., Boston, 1989-94, Wolfsort Corp., Boston, 1989—; chmn. Wolf & McManus, Brookline, Mass., 1995—; dir., exec. dir. Tech. Capital Network MIT, 1992-94; co-founder, pres. Assn. Ind. Software Cos., Washington, 1965-67, Design Sci. Inst., Phila., 1969-73, Nat. Coun. Profl. Svc. Firms, Washington, 1970-75; seminar leader MIT Sloan Sch., Cambridge, 1970; co-founder, bd. dirs. Harbor Nat. Bank, Boston. Author computer program; inventor management system, orbit calculator, sorting method. Co-founder X-10 Orgn., Boston, 1962; trustee Addison Gilbert Hosp., Gloucester, Mass., 1963; v.p. Young Pres. Orgn., Boston, 1970; overseer Mus. Sci., Boston, 1989—; mem. Computer Mus. Named Outstanding Young Man in Boston, Jaycees, 1962; recipient Speaker's award Data Processing Mgmt. Assn., 1966. Mem. World Bus. Coun., MIT Club (Alumni award 1991), Boston Computer Soc., Forty-Niners.

WOLFART, H.C., linguistics scholar, author, editor; b. Lindau im Bodensee, Germany, 1943. Grad. (BA equivalent), Albert-Ludwigs-U., Freiburg im Breisgau, Fed. Republic Germany, 1964; MA, Cornell U., 1967, Yale U., 1966; M.Phil., Yale U., 1967, PhD, 1969. Lectr. U. Alta., Edmonton, Can., 1967-68; asst. prof. U. Man., Winnipeg, Can., 1969-72; assoc. prof. U. Manitoba, Winnipeg, Can., 1972-77, prof., head anthropology dept., 1977-78, prof., coord. linguistics program, 1978-87, prof., head linguistics dept., 1987-93, U. Disting. Prof., head linguistics dept., 1993—. Author: Plains Cree: A Grammatical Study, 1973, (with F. Pardo) Computer Assisted Linguistic Analysis, 1973, (with J.F. Carroll) Meet Cree: A Guide to the Cree Language, 2d edit., 1981, (with D.H. Pentland) Bibliography of Algonquian Linguistics, 1982; editor: essays in Alongquian Bibliography in Honour of V.M. Dechene, 1984; editor and translator: (told by L. Beardy) pisiskiwak kâ-pîkiskwêcik/Talking Animals, 1988, (told by Nêhiyaw/Glecia Bear, co-edited and co-translated with F. Ahenakew wanisinwak iskwêsisak/Two Little Girsl Lost in the Bush, 1991; editor Linguistic Studies Presented to John L. Finlay, 1991, (told by Nêhiyaw/Glecia Bear and others, co-edited and co-translated with F. Ahenakew) kôhkominawak otâcimowiniwâwa / Our Grandmothers' Lives as Told in their Own Words, 1992, (co-edited and co-translated with F. Ahenakew) kinêhiyâwiwininaw nêhiyawêwin / The Cree Language is Our Identity: The LaRonge Lectures of Sarah Whitecalf, 1993; mem. editl. bd. Actes du Congrès des Algonquinistes, 1982-94, Revue canadienne de linguistique, 1983-86; assoc. editor (supplements) Algonquin and Iroquoian Linguistics, 1985—; gen. editor Sociètè d'Edition de textes algonquiens, 1985—. Recipient Rh Inst. award in the humanities, 1980; fellow Studienstiftung des deutschen Volkes, 1966-67, Can. Coun./Social Scis. and Humanities Rsch. Coun., 1975-76, 82-83, 86-96. Fellow Philol. Soc., Royal Soc. of Can.; mem. Assn. canadienne de linguistique, Societas Linguistica Europaea, Linguistic Assn. Gt. Britain, Linguistic Soc. Am., Soc. for the Study of Indigenous Langs. of Ams., Soc. for Mesopotamian Studies, Rupert's Land Rsch. Ctr., British Assn. Can. Studies, Oxford Bibliog. Soc., Friends of Bodleian, Henry Sweet Soc. Office: Linguistics Dept, U Manitoba, Winnipeg, MB Canada R3T 2N2

WOLFBEIN, SEYMOUR LOUIS, economist, educator; b. Bklyn., Nov. 8, 1915; s. Samuel and Fanny (Katz) W.; m. Mae Lachterman, Mar. 1, 1941; children: Susan Lois, Deeva Irene. B.A., Bklyn. Coll., 1936; M.A., Columbia U., 1937, Ph.D., 1941. Research assoc. U.S. Senate Com. on Unemployment and Relief, 1938; economist, div. research WPA, 1939-42; economist Bur. Labor Statistics, Dept. Labor, 1942-45, chief occupational outlook div., 1946-49, chief div. manpower and productivity, 1949-50, chief div. manpower and employment, 1950-59, dep. asst. sec. labor, 1959-67; dir. Office Manpower, Automation and Tng., 1962-67, spl. asst. to sec. labor for econ. affairs, 1965-67; dean Sch. Bus. Adminstrn., Temple U., Phila., 1967-78; Joseph A. Boettner prof. bus. adminstrn. Sch. Bus. Adminstrn., Temple U., 1978-85; dean Temple U. in Japan, 1983-85; pres. T/W/O, 1986—; prof. econs. Am. U., Washington; dir. Lincoln Bank of Phila. Author: Decline of a Cotton Textile City, 1942, The World of Work, 1951, Employment and Unemployment in the U.S.--A Study of American Labor Force, 1964, Employment, Unemployment and Public Policy, 1965, Education and Training for Full Emplyment, 1967, Occupational Information: A Career Guidance View, 1968, Emerging Sectors of Collective Bargaining, 1970, Work in American Society, 1971, Manpower Policy: Perspectives and Prospects, 1973, Labor Market Information for Youth, 1975, Men in the Pre-Retirement Years, 1977, Establishment Reporting in the U.S., 1978, The New Labor Force, 1988, America's Service Economy, 1988, The Older Worker, 1988, Working and Not Working in the U.S.A., 1989, The Temporary Help Supply Industry, 1989, In the Year 2000: A New Look, 1990, Our Industrial Future, 1990, Our Occupational Future, 1990, To the Year 2000-- and Beyond: The World of Work, 1992, The Job Outlook in the U.S.A., 1994, Women at Work: A New Look, 1995, Education and Training for Work, 1996, Part Time Work in the U.S.A., 1996; contbr. numerous articles to profl. and tech. jours. Mem. commn. on human resources Nat. Acad. Scis.; mem. adv. com. NSF; bd. mgrs. Springarden Coll.; v.p. World Trade Council; mem. Mayor's Adv. Council on Employment, Phila.; bd. dirs. Jewish Employment and Vocat. Service. Served with U.S. Army, 1944-45. Recipient alumni award of honor Bklyn. Coll., 1954; Distinguished Service award Dept. Labor, 1955, 61. Fellow Am. Statis. Assn., AAAS; mem. Md. Civic Assn. (pres. Bannockburn 1957-59), Washington Statis. Soc. (pres.), Data Mgmt. Processing Assn. (hon. life), Am. Statis. Assn. (chmn. social statistics sect. 1956-57), Nat. Vocational Guidance Assn. (Eminent Career award 1970, chmn. occupational research com.), D.C. Guidance and Personnel Assn. (trustee). Home: E 706 Parktowne 2200 Benjamin Franklin Pky Philadelphia PA 19130 *Every year that goes by underscores the major common denominator to successful career development in America: the need to be responsive to social and economic change.*

WOLFBERG, MELVIN DONALD, company executive, optometrist, former college president, consultant; b. Altoona, Pa., June 24, 1926; s. Max Alex and Claire (Schiffman) Wolfberg; m. Audrey Iris Koch, Apr. 26, 1952; children: Debra Lynn, Michael Alex, Daniel Ben; m. Linda Diane Machesic, Dec. 4, 1979. OD, Pa. Coll. Optometry, Phila., 1951; D of Ocular Sci. (hon.), New England Coll. Optometry, 1989, Ill. Coll. Optometry, 1990. Lic. optometrist, Pa. Pvt. practice and ptnr. optometric practice Selinsgrove, Pa., 1951-79; pres. Pa. Coll. Optometry, Phila., 1979-89, chmn. bd., 1976-79; v.p. profl. rels. Bausch and Lomb, Rochester, N.Y., 1991-95; pres. In Vision Inst., Boston, 1991-95; cons. to sec. HEW, Washington, 1970-77; dir. Better Vision Inst., N.Y.C., 1960-80. Mem. Selinsgrove City Coun., 1961-62; pres. Selinsgrove Community Chest, 1957; chmn. Optometrists Rep. Nat. Com., 1972, 76; chmn. Nat. Inter-Profl. Health Coun., Washington, 1972-77; dir. Univ. City Sci. Ctr., Phila., 1980-87; adv. com. Coun. Higher Edn., Commonwealth Pa., 1980-89. Served with U.S. Army, 1944-46, ETO. Decorated Purple Heart, Bronze Star, Silver Star; named Man of Yr. Central Pa. Optometric Soc., 1964, Alumnus of Yr. Pa. Coll. Optometry, 1970; recipient Carel C. Koch Meml. medal, 1989. Fellow Am. Acad. Optometry (pres. 1985-86); mem. Pa. Assn. Colls. and Univs. (exec. com. 1982-89, sec.-treas. 1985-88, vice chmn. 1988-89), Pa. Optometric Assn. (pres. 1959-61, Optometrist of Yr.), Am. Optometric Assn. (pres. 1969-70, Disting. Svc. award 1994), Pa. Coll. Optometry Alumni Assn. (pres. 1957), Beta Sigma Kappa.

WOLF-CHASE, GRACE ANNAMARIE, astronomer, astrophysicist; b. N.Y.C., Dec. 12, 1957; d. Franz and Ruth Anna (Schnabel) Wolf; m. Dennis Arthur Chase, Apr. 25, 1994; 1 child, Jaclyn Ruth Chase. AB, Cornell U., 1981; PhD, U. Ariz., 1992. Undergrad. rsch./teaching asst. Cornell U., Ithaca, N.Y., 1980-81; grad. rsch./teaching asst. U. Ariz., Tucson, 1981-86; telescope operator Nat. Radio Astronomy Obs., Kitt Peak, Ariz., 1986-90; instr. astronomy lab. U. Ariz., Tucson, 1990-91; lectr. astronomy U. Nev., Las Vegas, 1993; postdoctoral fellow NASA/Ames Rsch. Ctr., Moffett Field, Calif., 1994—; pub. lectr. Flandrau Sci. Ctr., U. Ariz., Tucson, 1990-92; lectr. astronomy camp Steward Obs., Tucson, 1991-92; presenter in field. Contbr. articles to sci. jours. including Astron. Jour., Astrophys. Jour., Bull. of the Am. Astron. Soc., CO: 25 Years of Millimeter-wave Spectroscopy, book rev. to Nature mag. Nat. Rsch. Coun. fellow NAS, 1994-95. Nat. Rsch. Coun. fellow NAS, 1994-95. Mem. Am. Astron. Soc., Planetary Soc. Avocations: figure skating, science fiction, swimming, weightlifting, flying. Office: NASA/Ames Rsch Ctr Mail Stop 245-6 Moffett Field CA 94035

WOLFE, AL, marketing and advertising consultant; b. Wyo., May 3, 1932; s. Clyde A. and Margaret V. (Joyce) W.; m. F. Carilouise, 1957 (div. 1994); children: Kirk, Kelley, Alison. B.A. in Psychology, U. Wyo., 1958. Product mgr., merchandising mgr. Gen. Mills, Mpls., 1958-62; asst. mktg. dir., v.p., account supr. Compton Advt., Chgo. and N.Y.C., 1963-66; v.p., account supr., exec. v.p., gen. mgr. Wells Rich Greene, N.Y.C., 1967-76; exec. v.p., dir. N.W. Ayer ABH Internat., N.Y.C., 1976-81; mng. dir., pres., bd. dirs. DDB Needham Worldwide, Chgo., 1981-87, pres. U.S. Div., 1987-88; pres. Al Wolfe Assocs., Inc., Mktg. and Advt. Cons., Sedona, Ariz., 1989—; bd. dirs. Clorox Co., Oakland, Calif., Dolphin Software, Inc., Lake Oswego, Oreg. Bd. dirs. U. Wyo. Found., pres., 1993-94; past pres. bd. dirs. U. Wyo. Art Mus.; chmn. Sedona Med. Ctr. Found.; bd. dirs. Sedona Acad.; trustee Heard Mus., Phoenix; bd. dirs. Sedona Cultural Park. Recipient Disting. Alumnus award U. Wyo. 1981. Mem. Econ. Club (Chgo.), Sedona 30 Club. Home: 405 Manzanita Dr Sedona AZ 86336-4002 Office: Al Wolfe Assocs Inc PO Box 2367 Sedona AZ 86339-2367

WOLFE, ALBERT BLAKESLEE, lawyer; b. Parkersburg, W.Va., Apr. 6, 1909; s. William Henry and Katharine (White) W.; m. Beatrice Ewan, Oct. 23, 1942 (dec. Nov. 1986); children: Katharine Ward, Diana Ewan Wolfe Larkin. Grad., Hill Sch., 1927; A.B., Princeton U., 1931; LL.B., Harvard U., 1934. Bar: Mass., W.Va. 1934. Assoc. Rackemann, Sawyer & Brewster, Boston, 1934-40; partner Rackemann, Sawyer & Brewster, 1940-74, of counsel, 1974—; pres. Parkersburg Property Mgmt. Co., 1956-78. Chmn. Cambridge Hist. Commn., 1963-73; mem. Mass. Hist. Commn., 1963-73; pres. Keystone Fund (charitable fund), W.Va., 1951-89; trustee Marietta Coll., 1961-74, life assoc., 1974—; trustee Nat. Trust for Historic Preservation, 1970-79; dir. Longfellow's Wayside Inn, 1972-89. Served to lt. comdr. USNR, 1942-45. Fellow Am. Bar Found. (life), Mass. Bar Found. (life); mem. ABA (chmn. real property, probate and trust law sect. 1968-69), Mass. Bar Assn., W.Va. Bar Assn., Am. Law Inst. (adviser model land devel. code 1963-76), Mass. Hist. Soc., Soc. Colonial Wars, Colonial Soc. Mass., Harvard Club Boston, Abstract Club Boston (pres. 1963-73), Harvard Faculty Club, Harvard Faculty Club (pres. 1963-73). Home: Old Harrisville Rd 311 Rivermead Rd Peterborough NH 03458 also: High Wells Old Harrisville Rd Dublin OH 03444 *Conservation of resources—natural, cultural, and human, can, since space explorations have held a mirror to earth, be seen as the greatest challenge humankind has ever faced. We need more than ever before to understand all facets of human history, and to transcend allegiances to territory, home, country, ideology, religious sect, and even family, and to see all earth as home, and each and every man and woman, no matter how different from us, as a fellow sharer of the human experience. Building bridges of mutual understanding becomes ever more important.*

WOLFE, ALBERT J., agency administrator, researcher; b. Long Branch, N.J., June 30, 1955; s. Albert J. and Gretchen (Gehlhaus) W. BA, Duquesne U., 1977; MA, U. Akron, 1985; MPA, Rutgers U., 1994. Chief Bur. of Mcpl. Inf. N.J. State League of Municipalities, Trenton, 1983—. Author: A History of Municipal Government in New Jersey Since 1798, 1990, The Faulkner Act: New Jersey's Optional Municipal Charter Law, 2d edit., 1993, There's Trouble in River City: The Dynamics of Local Regulation of New Technologies, 1988, Police Compensation in New Jersey: Who Says Crime Doesn't Pay?, 1992, New Jersey's Five Traditional Forms of Municipal Government, 1996. Office: NJ State League Municipalities 407 W State St Trenton NJ 08618

WOLFE, BARBARA L., economics educator, researcher; b. Phila., Feb. 15, 1943; d. Manfred and Edith (Heimann) Kingshoff; m. Stanley R. Wolfe, Mar. 20, 1965 (div. Mar. 1978); m. Robert H. Haveman, July 29, 1983; children: Jennifer Ann Wolfe, Ari Michael Wolfe. BA, Cornell U., Ithaca, N.Y., 1965; MA, U. Pa., 1971; PhD, U Pa., 1973. Asst. prof. Bryn Mawr (Pa.) Coll., 1973-76; rsch. assoc. Inst. Rsch. on Poverty, Madison, 1976-77, dir., 1994—; from asst. prof. to assoc. prof. U. Wis., Madison, 1977-88; prof., 1988—; resident scholar NIAS, Wassenear, The Netherlands, 1984-85; vis. scholar Russell Sage Found., N.Y., 1991-92. Co-author: Succeeding Generations, 1994; editor: (book) Role of Budgetary Policy in Demographic Transitions, 1994, contbr. articles to profl. jours. Active Commn. on Children with Disabilities, Washington 1994-95, Tech. Adv. Panel Social Security, Washington, 1994-95. Recipient Best Article of Yr. award Rev. Income and Wealth, 1992, Fulbright award Coun. Internat. Exch. of Scholars, 1984. Mem. Am. Econ. Assn. (bd. com. 1989-92, exec. bd. 1996—). Office: U Wis Inst Rsch on Poverty 1180 Observatory Dr Madison WI 53706

WOLFE, CAMERON WITHGOT, SR., federal judge; b. San Francisco, Aug. 14, 1910; s. Frederick Lee and Edythe (Turnor) W.; m. Jean Brown, Aug. 15, 1936; children: Cameron Jr., Bruce McLaren, Robert Reese. AB, Stanford U., 1931; LLB, U. Calif., Berkeley, 1934. Bar: Calif. 1934, U.S. Dist. Ct. (no. dist.) Calif. 1934, U.S. Ct. Appeals (9th cir.) 1934. Dep. dist. atty. Alameda County, Oakland, Calif., 1936-42; ptnr. Feruhoff & Wolfe, Oakland, 1946-75; bankruptcy judge U.S. Cts., Oakland, 1975-93; adj. prof. U. Calif., Berkeley, 1946-51. Lt. commdr. USN, 1942-46. Mem. Nat. Conf. Bankruptcy Judges, Calif. State Bar Assn., Alameda County Bar Assn., Phi Beta Kappa. Avocations: teaching, gardening, golf, boating. Home: 522 Blair Ave Piedmont CA 94611-3757 Office: Bankruptcy Ct PO Box 2070 Oakland CA 94604-2070

WOLFE, CAMERON WITHGOT, JR., lawyer; b. Oakland, Calif., July 7, 1939; s. Cameron W. and Jean (Brown) W.; m. Frances Evelyn Bishopric, Sept. 2, 1964; children: Brent Everett, Julie Frances, Karen Jean. AB, U. Calif.-Berkeley, 1961, JD, 1964. Bar: Calif. 1965, U.S. Dist. Ct. (no. dist.) Calif. 1965, U.S. Ct. Appeals (9th cir.) 1965, U.S. Tax Ct. 1966, U.S. Ct. Claims 1977, U.S. Ct. Appeals (3d cir.) 1980, U.S. Ct. Appeals (fed. cir.) 1983, U.S. Supreme Ct. 1986 . Assoc., then ptnr. Orrick, Herrington & Sutcliffe, San Francisco, 1964—; bd. dirs. Crowley Maritime Corp.; mem. steering com. Western Pension Conf. Pres. League to Save Lake Tahoe, 1979, 80; chmn. League to Save Lake Tahoe Charitable Trust, 1966-91, Piedmont Ednl. Fund Campaign, 1982-83; pres. Piedmont Ednl. Found., 1986-90; bd. dirs. Yosemite Fund., 1993—. Served with U.S. Army, 1957, with USAR, 1957-65. Mem. ABA (mem. taxation com.), Calif. State Bar, San Francisco Bar Assn., Order of Coif, Phi Beta Kappa. Clubs: Pacific Union (San Francisco); Claremont Country (Oakland, Calif.). Home: 59 Lakeview Ave Piedmont CA 94611-3514 Office: Orrick Herrington & Sutcliffe 400 Sansome St San Francisco CA 94111-3308

WOLFE, CHARLES MORGAN, electrical engineering educator; b. Morgantown, W.Va., Dec. 21, 1935; s. Slidell Brown and Mae Louise (Maness) W.; children—David Morgan, Diana Michele. B.S.E.E., W.Va. U., Morgantown, 1961, M.S.E.E., 1962; Ph.D., U. Ill., 1965. Research assoc. U. Ill., Urbana, 1965; mem. staff MIT Lincoln Lab., Lexington, Mass., 1965-75; prof. elec. engring Washington U., St. Louis, 1975—, Samuel C. Sachs prof., 1982-90, dir. semicondr. research lab., 1979-90; cons. MIT Lincoln Lab., 1975-76, Fairchild Semicondr., Palo Alto, Calif., 1975-76, Air Force Avionics Lab., Dayton, Ohio, 1976-79, U. Ill., 1983-85. Author: Physical Properties of Semiconductors, 1989; editor: Gallium Arsenide and Related Compounds, 1979; contbr. articles to profl. jours., chpts. to books. Served as sgt. USMC, 1955-58. Fellow IEEE (field awards com. 1984-87, Jack A. Morton award 1990); mem. NAE, AAAS, AAUP, Electrochem. Soc. (Electronics divsn. award 1978). Office: Washington U Campus Box 1127 Saint Louis MO 63130-1127

WOLFE, DAVID LOUIS, lawyer; b. Kankakee, Ill., July 24, 1951; s. August Christian and Irma Marie (Nordmeyer) W.; m. Gail Lauret Fritz, Aug. 25, 1972; children: Laura Beth, Brian David, Kaitlin Ann. BS, U. Ill., 1973; JD, U. Mich., 1976. Bar: Ill. 1976, U.S. Dist. Ct. (no. dist.) Ill. 1976. Assoc., Gardner, Carton & Douglas, Chgo., 1976-82, ptnr., 1983—; lectr. estate planning Aid Assn. for Lutherans SMART Program, Chgo., 1980-84; lectr. Ill. Inst. Continuing Legal Edn., Chgo. Bar Assn., Lake Shore Nat. Bank, Ill. State Bar Assn. Contbr. articles to legal publs. Recipient Recognition award Ill. Inst. Continuing Legal Edn., 1981-84. Mem. ABA (sects. on taxation, corp. banking and bus. law 1981—, lectr.), NFL Players Assn. (cert. contract advisor 1983—), NCAA (cert. contract advisor), Chgo. Assn. Commerce and Industry (employee benefit subcom. 1983—), Ill. State Bar Assn. (employee benefits sect. council, 1986—, recognition award 1983), Phi Kappa Phi, Beta Alpha Psi, Beta Gamma Sigma, Sigma Iota Lambda, Phi Eta Sigma. Office: Gardner Carton & Douglas 321 N Clark St Ste 3300 Chicago IL 60610-4714

WOLFE, DEBORAH CANNON PARTRIDGE, government education consultant; b. Cranford, N.J.; d. David Wadsworth and Gertrude (Moody) Cannon; 1 son, Roy Partridge. BS, N.J. State Coll.; MA, EdD, Tchrs. Coll., Columbia U.; postgrad., Vassar Coll., U. Pa., Union Theol. Sem., Jewish Sem. Am.; hon. doctorates, Seton Hall U., 1963, Coll. New Rochelle, 1963, Morris Brown U., 1964, Glassboro/Rowan Coll., 1965, Bloomfield Coll., 1988, Monmouth Coll., 1988, William Paterson Coll., 1988; LLD (hon.), Kean Coll., 1981; LHD (hon.), Stockton State Coll., 1982; LLD (hon.), Jersey City State Coll., 1987, Centenary Coll., William Paterson Coll., 1989, Tuskegee U., 1989, Glassboro State Coll., 1985, Tuskegee U., 1989, St. Peter's Coll., 1989, Rider Coll., 1989, Georgian Court Coll., 1990; DSc (hon.), Stevens Inst. Tech., 1991; LLD (hon.), Rutgers U., 1992, Thomas Edison Coll., 1992; DSc, U. Med. and Dentistry N.J., 1989. Former prin., tchr. pub. schs. Cranford, also Tuskegee, Ala.; faculty Tuskegee Inst., Grambling Coll., NYU, Fordham U., U. Mich., Tex. Coll., Columbia U.; supervision and adminstrn. curriculum devel., social studies U. Ill., summers;

prof. edn., affirmative action officer Queens Coll.; prof. edn. and children's lit. Wayne State U.; edn. chief U.S. Ho. of Reps. Com. on Edn. and Labor, 1962—; Fulbright prof. Am. lit. NYU; U.S. rep. 1st World Conf. on Women in Politics; chair non-govtl. reps. to UN (NGO/DPI exec. com.), 1983—; editl. cons. Macmillan Pub. Co.; cons. Ency. Brit.; adv. bd. Ednl. Testing Svc.; mem. State Bd. Edn., 1964-94; chairperson N.J. Bd. Higher Edn., 1967-94; mem. nat. adv. panel on vocat. edn. HEW; mem. citizen's adv. com. to Bd. Edn., Cranford; mem. Citizen's Adv. Com. on Youth Fitness, Pres.'s Adv. Com. on Youth Fitness, White House Conf. Edn., 1955, White House Conf. Aging, 1960, White House Conf. Civil Rights, 1966, White House Conf. on Children, 1970, Adv. Coun. for Innovations in Edn.; v.p. Nat. Alliance for Safer Cities; cons. Vista Corps, OEO; vis. scholar Princeton Theol. Sem., 1989—; active Human Rels. Coun., N.J., 1994—; vis. prof. U. Ill., U. N.C., Wayne State U.; theologian-in-residence Duke U.; mem. trustee bd. Sci. Svc. Contbr. articles to ednl. publs. Bd. dirs. Cranford Welfare Assn., Cmty. Ctr., 1st Bapt. Ch., Cranford Cmty. Ctr. Migratory Laborers, Hurlock, Md.; trustee Sci. Svc., Seton Hall U., bd. regents; mem. Pub. Broadcasting Authority, N.J. Commn. on Holocaust, 1996—, Tuskegee U. Alumni, 1995, N.J. Conv. of Progressive Baptists, 1995; sec. Kappa Delta Pi Ednl. Found.; mem. adv. com. Elizabeth and Arthur Schlesinger Libr., Radcliffe Coll., trustee Edn. Devel. Ctr., 1965—; assoc. min. 1st Bapt. Ch.; chair Human Rels. Commn., 1995. Recipient Woman of Yr. award Delta Beta Zeta, Woman of Yr. award Morgan State Coll., Medal of Honor, DAR, 1990, Disting. Svc. medal Nat. Top Ladies of Distinction, 1991, Disting. Svc. award nat. Assn. State Bds. Edn., 1992, 94, Disting. Svc. to Edn. award N.J. Commn. on Status of Women, 1993, Svc. to Children award N.J. Assn. Sch. Psychologists, 1993, Disting. Medal award U. Medicine and Dentistry N.J., Union Coll., citationn N.J. State Coun. on Vocat. Edn., 1994, citation N.J. State Bd. Edn., 1994, Women Who Make a Difference award Zonta Internat., 1996, Minister's Appreciation award Progressive Nat. Baptist Convention, 1996. Mem. NEA (life), ASCD (rev. coun.), AAAS (chmn. tchr. edn. com.), LWV, NCCJ, AAUW (nat. edn. chmn.), AAUP, NAACP (Medal of Honor 1994), Coun. Nat. Orgns. Children and Youth, Am. Coun. Human Rights (v.p.), Nat. Panhellenic Coun. (dir.), Nat. Assn. Negro Bus. and Profl. Women (chmn. spkrs. bur., Nat. Achievement award 1958), Nat. Assn. Black Educators (pres.), N.Y. Tchrs. Assn., Am. Tchrs. Assn., Fellowship So. Churchmen, Internat. Reading Assn., Comparative Edn. Soc., Am. Acad. Polit. and Social Sci., Internat. Assn. Childhood Edn., Nat. Soc. Study Edn., Am. Coun. Edn. (commn. fed. rels.), Nat. Alliance Black Educators (pres.), Internat. Platform Assn., Ch. Women United p., mem. exec. com.), UN Assn.-U.S.A. (exec. com.), N.J. Fedn. Colored Women's Clubs, Delta Kappa Gamma (chmn. world fellowship com.), Kappa Delta Pi (chmn. ritual com., mem. ednl. found., 1980—, laureate 1990, scholarship named in her honor, citation 1994), Pi Lambda Theta, Zeta Phi Beta (internat. pres. 1954, chmn. edn. found. 1974—, Monore Twp., N.J. chair human rels. commn., Achievement award Atlantic region). Home: 326 Nantuckett Ln Jamesburg NJ 08831-1704 Office: NJ State Bd Higher Edn 20 W State St Trenton NJ 08608-1206 *I feel I am extremely fortunate to have been born into a family where love of God and love of knowledge have been major concerns. The knowledge we have sought has not been 'knowledge for knowledge's sake' but 'knowledge to improve society and the world'. I have always felt that 'God power' linked with 'Brain power' was the greatest force in the world and I knew that in order to achieve such strength one must work diligently and constantly. Because knowledge changes so rapidly this quest for wisdom must be eternal. Hence I hope I'm still learning and growing for education must be involved from 'the womb to the tomb'.*

WOLFE, EDWARD WILLIAM, II, music educator, composer; b. Albuquerque, Sept. 24, 1946; s. Edward William and Mary Ellen (Gabriele) W.; m. Nancy Jean Brown, Aug. 16, 1980. B in Music Edn., U. N.Mex., 1968, MA, 1973. Cert. tchr., N.Mex., Calif. Tchr. Grant Jr. High Sch., Albuquerque, 1970-75, Manzano High Sch., Albuquerque, 1974-75, Hoover Mid. Sch., Albuquerque, 1975-77, San Dimas (Calif.) High Sch., 1977-85; instr. music Calif. Poly. State U., Pomona, Calif., 1984; tchr. Bonita High Sch., LaVerne, Calif., 1985-89, Lone Hill Mid. Sch. and Feeders, San Dimas, Calif., 1989—; tchr. Hummingbird Music Camp, Jemez, N.Mex., 1970-76; cons. BUSD, San Dimas, 1980—; presenter jazz edn. SCSBOA fall conf., 1995. Author: The Language of Music, 1974, rev. 1993; composer Quartet for Horns, 1967, Oboe Sonata, 1967, Trio for Flute, Violin and Horn, 1968, Caverna, 1972, Quintet for Brass, 1993, numerous compositions and jazz arrangements, 1972—. Mem. Task Force on Mid. Sch. Reform, 1990. Recipient award Juvenile Justice Commn. City of San Dimas, 1984, 93; named to BUSD Hall of Fame, 1991. Mem. Music Educators Nat. Conf. (adjudicator 1969-77, 80—, v.p. dist. 7 1972, pres. 1975-76), Calif. Music Educators Assn. (task force on mid. sch. reform 1990, Outstanding Music Edn. cert. 1991), Nat. Assn. Jazz Educators (adjudicator 1980—, treas. N.Mex. chpt. 1972), Calif. Tchrs. Assn., So. Calif. Sch. Band and Orch. Assn., Bonita United Teaching Assn., Phi Mu Alpha. Avocation: model railroader. Home: 817 S Dumaine Ave San Dimas CA 91773-3808 *Personal philosophy: America's children need and deserve the best we can provide in education. They have tried to do what we have demanded of them and by so doing have in many instances forfeited the very thing that is required for their emotional and physical growth. They have missed their childhood along with all its wonder and opportunities for healthy learning. As a muisc educator, I have dedicated my life to the pursuit of educational excellence for my students. To this end I Will continue to try to provide a loving atmosphere for their emotional growth, a challenging course of study for their intellectual stimulation and a promise of success for their all important self image. I'll endeavor to provide the best I can with the hope that after I'm gone, they will do the same.*

WOLFE, ELLEN DARLENE, librarian, elementary school educator; b. Mattoon, Ill., Dec. 16, 1952; d. Floyd Dale and Irma Jane (Hensley) Robinson; m. Walter Ray Wolfe, Mar. 12, 1994; children: Gregory David, William Scott, Joseph Dean, Brian Matthew, Joshua Paul. BS, Ind. State U., 1987. Cert. elem. educator, Ill. Reading tchr. Marshall (Ill.) Community Dist. 2, 1987-91; law libr. Robinson (Ill.) Correctional Ctr., 1991-94; libr. Palestine (Ill.) Cmty. Unit Sch. Dist. # 3, 1994—; libr. City of Marshall, 1986—; dir. summer camp Clark County Handicapped Assn., Marshall, 1988—; law libr. Robinson Correctional Ctr., 1991. Coord. Jr. youth group St. Mary's Cath. Ch. Mem. Correctional Edn. Assn., Home Ext. Club, Kappa Delta Pi, Phi Delta Kappa. Roman Catholic. Home: RR 1 Box 27 Palestine IL 62451-9705 Office: Robinson Correctional Ctr PO Box 1000 Robinson IL 62454-0919

WOLFE, ETHYLE RENEE (MRS. COLEMAN HAMILTON BENEDICT), college administrator; b. Burlington, Vt., Mar. 14, 1919; d. Max M. and Rose (Saiger) W.; m. Coleman Hamilton Benedict, Dec. 4, 1954. B.A., U. Vt., 1940, M.A., 1942; postgrad., Bryn Mawr Coll., 1942-43; Ph.D., N.Y. U., 1950; LHD (hon.), CUNY, 1989; LittD (hon.), Iona Coll., 1989. Teaching fellow U. Vt., 1940-42; research fellow Latin Bryn Mawr (Pa.) Coll., 1942-43; instr. classics Bklyn. Coll., 1947-49, instr. classical langs., 1949-54, asst. prof., 1954-59, assoc. prof., 1960-68, prof., 1968—, acting chmn. dept. classics and comparative lit., 1962-63, chmn. dept., 1967-72; dean Bklyn. Coll. (Sch. Humanities), 1971-78; exec. officer Humanities Inst. Bklyn. Coll., 1980-89, provost and v.p. for acad. affairs, 1982-88, provost emeritus, 1989—; mem. exec. com., chmn. com. on undergrad. affairs, com. on univ.-wide programs CUNY faculty senate; mem. study group AAAS, 1987-89; dir. Fund for Improvement of Postsecondary Edn.-funded Ctr. for Core Studies, 1987-88; co-chair senate report, Chancellor's Coll. Prep. Initiative, 1991; mem. exec. com for publ.: The Liberal art of science: Agenda for Action:, dir. Nat. Core Visitors Programs, 1985-89. Asso. editor: Classical World, 1965-71; co-editor: The American Classical Review, 1971-76; contbr. articles to jours. in field. Ethyle R. Wolfe Inst. for the Humanities Bklyn. Coll. named in honor, 1989; mem. Columbia U. Seminar in Classical Civilization. Recipient Kirby Flower Smith award, 1939, Goethe prize U. Vt., 1940, Alumni Achievement award U. Vt., 1985, Charles Frankel prize NEH, 1990; named to Hall of Honor U. Vt., 1991; named Disting. U. Faculty Sen. Emeritus, CUNY, 1992; NEH grantee, 1971, 1982-84, Andrew W. Mellon Found. grantee, 1984-88. Mem. Am. Philol. Assn., Archeol. Inst. Am., Vergilian Soc. Am., Classical Assn. Atlantic States (exec. com.), Am. Soc. Papyrologists, N.Y. Classical Club (past pres.), Phi Beta Kappa (past pres. Rho chpt., pres. 1988-90). Home: 360 W 22nd St New York NY 10011-2600 Office: Bklyn Coll Bedford Ave # H Brooklyn NY 11222

WOLFE, EVA AGNES, retired educator; b. Stockport, Iowa, Jan. 13, 1910; d. Marion S. and Hattie Florence (Webber) Munson; m. Donald Earl Wolfe, 1937; 1 child, Sharon Dawn. BA, Iowa Wesleyan U., 1951; student, U. Minn., 1928-89, State U. Iowa, 1928, 29, 30. Tchr. rural schs. Van Buren County, Stockport, 1929-30; grade sch. tchr. Van Buren County, Keosauqua, Iowa, 1930-37, Pleasant Lawn Consol. Sch., Mt. Pleasant, Iowa, 1946-50; tchr. home econs., English Danville (Iowa) Consol. High Sch., 1951-60; tchr. home econs. West Burlington (Iowa) Pub. Schs., 1961-74; ret., 1974. Mem. Am. Assn. Ret. Persons. Mem. DAR, AAUW, Henry County Ret. Tchrs. (pres. 1976-78), Daus of Nile, Order of Eastern Star, White Shrine, Alpha Xi Delta. Democrat. Methodist. Avocations: music, reading, sewing, dancing, exercise. Home: 11202 N Madison Dr Sun City AZ 85351-4040 also: 507 S Walnut St Mount Pleasant IA 52641-2427

WOLFE, GEORGE C., theater director, producer, playwright; b. Lexington, Ky., 1954. BA, Pomona Coll.; MFA, NYU. Prodr. N.Y. Shakespeare Festival, N.Y.C., 1993—; bd. dirs. Young Playwrights Festival, N.Y.C. Works include: (writer, lyricist) Paradise!, 1985; (writer, dir.) The Colored Museum, 1986 (Elizabeth Hull-Kate Warriner award Dramatists Guild 1986), Jelly's Last Jam, 1992 (Joe A. Callaway award Stage Dirs. and Choreographers Found. 1993, Drama Desk award); (librettist) Queenie Pie, 1987; (scene contbr.) Urban Blight, 1988; curator Festival of New Voices, 1990, 92; (adaptor, dir.) Spunk, 1990 (Obie award for best dir. 1990); (dir. plays) Caucasian Chalk Circle, 1990, Angels in America, 1992, (Tony award for best dir. in a play 1993), Twilight: Los Angeles, 1992, Perestroika, 1993 (Tony award nominee for best dir. 1994), Blade to the Heat, 1994, The Tempest, 1995; actor: A Delicate Balance, 1996 (Best Leading Actor Tony 1996). Grantee Rockefeller Found., Nat. Endowment for Arts, Nat. Inst. Musical Theatre; recipient Hull-Warriner award, Audleco awards (2), The George Oppenheimer/Newsday award, CBS-FDG New Play award, NYU Disting. Alumni award, HBO/USA Playwrights award, Person of Yr. award Nat. Theatre Conf., Spl. Achievement award Audleco, Spirit of the City award, LAMBDA award; named A Living Landmark, N.Y. Landmarks Conservancy. Mem. Dramatists Guild (mem. exec. bd.). Office: NY Shakespeare Festival Joseph Papp Pub Theater 425 Lafayette St New York NY 10003-7010

WOLFE, GEORGE CROPPER, private school educator, artist, author; b. New Orleans, Sept. 6, 1933; s. Howard Edward and Amaryllis (Brannen) W.; m. Catherine Vasterling, June 2, 1955; children: David, Michael, Philip. BA in Fine Art, La. State U., 1956; MEd, U. New Orleans, 1972, MS in Urban Planning, 1975; postgrad., Tex. Tech U., Junction, 1986-93. Cert. tchr. art, social studies, La. Elem. tchr. Live Oak Manor Sch., Waggaman, La., 1962-65; tchr. art Isidore Newman Sch., New Orleans, 1965—. Author: 3-D Wizardry (also video), Papier Maché Plaster and Foam, 1995; contbr. articles to profl. jours. Served with USCG, 1956-58. Recipient Telly award for video how-to, 1996. Mem. Nat. Art Edn. Assn. (La. Art Educator of Yr. 1990), La. Art Edn. Assn. (pres. 1978-79), Kappa Delta Pi, Phi Delta Kappa (v.p., Rsch. award 1996). Home: 342 Jefferson St Natchitoches LA 71457

WOLFE, GERALDINE, administrator; b. Monticello, Ark., Mar. 29, 1944; d. John Wesley and Hazeline (Daniels) Fisher; 1 child, Arin. BA, Keuka Coll., 1965; MA, Mt. Holyoke Coll., 1967; MSEd, Elmira Coll., 1981; cert. ednl. adminstrn. SUNY-Brockport, 1985; PhD Cornell U., 1988. Tchr. biology and health Corning Sch. Dist., N.Y., 1967-90; asst. prof. SUNY, Plattsburgh, 1990-93; adminstr. Saranac Lake Ctrl. Sch. Dist., 1993-96; asst. supt. Schenectady City Sch. Dist., 1996—. Mem. Mid. States Evaluation Team, 1985; chmn. bd. trustees Friendship Bapt. Ch., Corning, 1984-90. Oslo scholar U. Oslo, 1964. Mem. N.Y. State Profl. Health Educators Assn., Women in Ednl. Adminstrn., LWV, Sigma Xi, Sigma Lambda Sigma. Democrat. Club: Cosmopolitan (officer 1979-81) (Elmira). Mem. allocations com. United Way, 1982-90; mem. edn. com. Planned Parenthood, 1984-90. Mem. NAACP, ASCD, Nat. Assn. Sec. Sch. Prins., Am. Assn. Sch. Adminstrs., Nat. Alliance Black Sch. Educators, N.Y.S. Assn. for Computers and Technologies in Edn., N.Y.S. Assn. Compensatory Educators, N.Y. State Coun. Sch. Supts., Cornell Edn. Soc., Jr. League of Elmira, Rotary Club of Saranac Lake, Delta Kappa Gamma, Phi Delta Kappa. Avocations: tennis; cross countryskiing; travel; piano; reading. Home: 7 Forest Hills Dr Elmira NY 14905-1107 Office: Schenectady City Sch Dist 108 Education Dr Schenectady NY 12303

WOLFE, GREGORY BAKER, international relations educator; b. Los Angeles, Jan. 27, 1922; s. Harry Norton and Laura May (Baker) W.; m. Mary Ann Nelson, June 15, 1946; children: Gregory Nelson, Laura Ann, Melissa Helene. A.B., Reed Coll., 1943; M.A., Fletcher Sch. Law and Diplomacy, 1947, Ph.D., 1961; Dr. honoris causa, U. Autonoma de Guadalajara, Mex., 1984; D.H.L., Southeast Coll. Osteo. Medicine, Miami, Fla., 1985. With internat. div. Arthur D. Little, Inc., Cambridge, Mass., 1951-57; dir. Greater Boston Econ. Study Com., 1957-61; dir. Latin Am. program Com. Econ. Devel., 1961-64; dir. intelligence and rsch. for Am. republics State Dept., 1964-68; pres. Portland State U., 1968-74; dean Sch. Internat. Svc. Am. U., Washington, 1975-79; pres. Fla. Internat. U., Miami, 1979-86; prof. internat. rels. Fla. Internat. U., 1979—; vis. scholar Cambridge U., Eng., 1986-87; sr. cons. Orion Comml. Realty Inc., 1991—; fed. negotiator Joint Transp. Com. Washington 1962-66. Contbr. articles to profl. jours. Chmn. bd. trustees Internat. Fine Arts Coll., 1993—; bd. dirs. Chopin Found. U.S., Inc., 1988-96, Concert Assn. Fla., Inc., 1988—, Am. Coll. Madrid, 1994—; founding chmn. Brickell Ave. Lit. Soc., 1988-96; bd. dirs. Endicott Coll. Ctr., Mex., 1996—. Recipient Fla. Internat. Ctr. award, 1980, Leonard Abess award, 1984, Orden del Merito Civil, King of Spain, 1986, Fulbright lectr., Ecuador, 1989.

WOLFE, HAROLD JOEL, lawyer, business executive; b. Toronto, Ont., Can., July 21, 1940; s. Max and Beatrice Irene (Albert) W.; m. Carole S. Wolfe, Aug. 17, 1967; 3 children. B.Commerce, U. Toronto, 1963, LL.B., 1966. Mem. firm Goodman & Carr (Barristers), Toronto, 1968-69; with Oshawa Group Ltd., Toronto, 1970—; corp. v.p. real estate Oshawa Group Ltd., 1971—, also dir. Mem. Law Soc. Upper Can. Office: Oshawa Group Ltd, 302 East Mall, Toronto, ON Canada M9B 6B8

WOLFE, HARRIET MUNRETT, lawyer; b. Mt. Vernon, N.Y., Aug. 18, 1953; d. Lester John Francis Jr. and Olga Harriet (Miller) Munrett; m. Charles Briant Wolfe, Sept. 10, 1983. BA, U. Conn., 1975; postgrad., Oxford U. (Eng.), 1976; JD, Pepperdine U., 1978. Bar: Conn. 1979. Assoc. legal counsel, asst. sec. Citytrust, Bridgeport, Conn., 1979-90; v.p., sr. counsel, asst. sec. legal dept. Shawmut Bank Conn., N.A., Hartford, 1990—; mem. govt. rels. com. Electronic Funds Transfer Assn., Washington, 1983—. Mem. Conn. Bar Assn. (mem. legis. com. banking law sect.), ABA, Conn. Bankers Assn. (trust legis. com.), Guilford Flotilla Coast Guard Aux., U.S. Sailing Assn., Phi Alpha Delta Internat. (Frank E. Gray award 1978, Shepherd chpt. Outstanding Student award 1977-78). Home: 26 Farm View Dr Madison CT 06443-1631 Office: Shawmut Bank Conn NA 777 Main St Hartford CT 06115-2000

WOLFE, JAMES RONALD, lawyer; b. Pitts., Dec. 10, 1932; s. James Thaddeus and Helen Matilda (Corey) W.; m. Anne Lisbeth Dahle Eriksen, May 28, 1960; children: Ronald, Christopher, Geoffrey. B.A. summa cum laude, Duquesne U., 1954; LL.B. cum laude, NYU, 1959. Bar: N.Y. 1959. Assoc. Simpson, Thacher & Bartlett, N.Y.C., 1959-69, ptnr., 1969-95, counsel, 1996—. Co-editor: West's McKinney's Forms, Uniform Commercial Code, 1965. Served to 1st lt. U.S. Army, 1955-57. Mem. ABA, N.Y. State Bar Assn., Assn. of Bar of City of N.Y., Am. Judicature Soc., N.Y. Law Inst. Republican. Roman Catholic. Home: 641 King St Chappaqua NY 10514-3807 Office: Simpson Thacher & Bartlett 425 Lexington Ave New York NY 10017-3903

WOLFE, JANICE KAY, oncological nurse; b. Cedar Rapids, Iowa, Sept. 13, 1942; d. Francis Demerlin Brown and Lora Elizabeth Miller; m. Lincoln Louis Marburger Jr., Oct. 4, 1960 (dec. Aug. 18, 1972); children: Rhonda, Lora, Helen Phillip, Carmen; m. Clifford G. Wolfe, Apr. 11, 1992. Diploma in nursing, Kirkwood Coll., 1977, ADN, 1982. RN, Iowa, Ariz. Supr. staff nurses Long Term Care Ctr., Marion, Iowa, 1977-79; staff nurse ICU Mercy Hosp., Cedar Rapids, 1979-80; hematology/oncology nurse U. Iowa Hosp. and Clinics, Iowa City, 1982-92; clin. nurse Indian Health Svc., USPHS, Winslow, Ariz., 1992—, HIV-AIDS coord. and counselor, 1994—. Lutheran. Avocations: horseback riding, piano. Home: 210 Papago Blvd Winslow AZ 86047-2024

WOLFE, JEAN ELIZABETH, medical illustrator, artist; b. Newark, Oct. 3, 1925; d. Arthur Howard and Ethel (Harper) Wolfe; BS, Russell Sage Coll., 1947; student Pratt Inst., 1949-50; grad. diploma U. Rochester Sch. Medicine and Dentistry, 1955; postgrad. (W.B. Saunders fellow), U. Pa., 1955-56, U. Pa., 1980, 95; MFA in Painting, U. Pa., 1973, MA (hon.), 1973. Cert. Med. Illustrator. Exhibitor, Pratt Inst. Galleries, Bklyn., 1958, N.Y. Med. Coll., 1958, Assn. Med. Illustrators, 1961-86, 90, AMA, N.Y.C., 1965, Phila., 1965, A.C.S., Atlantic City, 1965, Rsch. Study Club L.A., 1966, Phila. Art Alliance, 1967, 73, U. Pa. Alumni Ophthal. Assn., 1967-68, N.J. Med. Soc., 1968, Cayuga Mus. History and Art, 1968, Pensacola Art Ctr., 1969, FAA Aero. Center, Oklahoma City, 1970, Scheie Eye Inst., 1972-75, Assn. Med. Illustrators Traveling Salon, 1978, Moore Coll. Art, 1985, Mus. of Am. Illustration Soc. of Illustrators, 1986, Mutter Mus., Phila. Coll. of Physicians, 1990-92, Axis Gallery, 1992; represented in permanent collections Archives of Med. Visual Resources, Francis A. Countway Med. Libr., Harvard Univ., Mutter Mus., Phila. Coll. Physicians; collection of work donated by Scheie Eye Inst., memoirs and papers housed in The Arthur and Elizabeth Schlesinger Libr. on the History of Women in Am., Radcliffe Coll.; contbg. illustrator Adler's Textbook Ophthalmology, 8th edit., 1969; illustrations in med. books, jours., pharm. house pubs.; instr. Pembroke Coll. Brown U., 1947-49; dept. head Kimberley Sch., Upper Montclair, N.J., 1950-52; freelance med. illustration Studio N.Y. Med. Coll., 1956-60; instr. Pratt Inst., 1958-59; med. artist in ophthalmology, 1960-61, asst. instr. in med. illustration in ophthalmology, 1961-62, instr. in med. illustration in ophthalmology, 1962-65; assoc. in med. illustration U. Pa. Sch. Medicine, 1965-72, tenured sole artist in the hist. of the sch. of medicine, rsch. asst. prof. med. art in ophthalmology, 1972-85, rsch. asst. prof. emeritus, 1985—; independent studio (fine art) painting and med. illustration, 1985—; guest lectr. Johns Hopkins Med. Sch., 1973, NIH; guest artist USAF, Air Force Acad. and NORAD, 1971. Recipient Merit certificate AMA; Appreciation certificate ACS; 1st prize Pensacola Art Ctr., Am. Heart Assn., 1969, Gold medal Graphic Arts Soc. of Del. Valley, 1973. Fellow Assn. Med. Illustrators (emeritus); mem. Assn. Med. Illustrators (Ralph Sweet, Tom Jones awards, gov. 1970—, chmn. nominating com. 1972-73, vice chmn. bd. govs. 1973-74, chmn. bd. 1974-75, selection com., Lifetime Achievement award 1989—, adv. coun. Vesalius Trust 1990—), Soc. Illustrators (cert. merit 1986), Coll. Art Assn., Women's Caucus for Art, Faculty Club of U. Pa. Address: 55 Frazer Rd Beech 222 Malvern PA 19355-1976 also: Scheie Eye Inst 51 N 39th St Philadelphia PA 19104

WOLFE, JOHN, journalist; b. Chgo., Dec. 1, 1951; s. John and Elizabeth Jane (Mordue) W.; m. Ray Ann Kelly, Oct. 4, 1986; children: Caitlin Ann, Terrence Francis. BA, Boston Coll., Chestnut Hill, Mass., 1974. Reporter City News Bur., Chgo., 1976-78, Chgo. Sun Times, 1978-79, Kansas City (Mo.) Times, 1979-81; writer, editor The Associated Press, Chgo., 1981-84; editor Advtg. Age, Chgo., London, N.Y., 1984-93; mng. editor Art & Antiques, N.Y., 1994-95, editor-in-chief, 1995—; freelance writer Chgo. Tribune, 1994, Variety, N.Y., 1994, Playbill, N.Y., 1996. Office: Art & Antiques 3E 54th St New York NY 10022

WOLFE, JOHN THOMAS, JR., university president; b. Jackson, Miss., Feb. 22, 1942; s. John Thomas Sr. and Jeanette (Wallace) W.; children: Wyatt Bardouille, John Thomas Dantzler, David Andrew Dantzler. BEd, Chgo. Tchrs. Coll., 1964; MS, Purdue U., 1972, PhD, 1976. Tchr. English Englewood High Sch., Chgo., 1965-67; linguistics prof. Cuttington Coll., Liberia, West Africa, 1967-69; pres. Wolfe & Assocs., 1970-93; asst. mgr. residence hall Purdue U., West Lafayette, Ind., 1971-75, employee relations mgr., 1975-77; asst. prof. English Fayetteville (N.C.) State U., 1977-82, assoc. prof., 1982-85, coordinator area English and dramatic arts, 1978-83, head div. humaities and fine arts, 1979-84; acad. dean. Ft. Bragg U. Ctr., 1983-85; provost, v.p. for acad. affairs Bowie (Md.) State Coll., 1985-90; pres. Ky. State U., Frankfort, 1990-91; exec. dir. Nat. Rainbow Coalition, 1992-93; pres. Savannah (Ga.) State Coll., 1993—; lectr. Krannert Sch. Mgmt., 1976; mem. N.C. Humanities Commn., 1981-85. Contbr. articles in field. Active N.C. Humanities Com., Greensboro, 1979-83, Arts Coun. Fayetteville, Cumberland, N.C., 1979-85, Minority Bus. Resource Inst. Bd., Landover, Md., 1986—; bd. dirs. Entrepreneurial Devel. Program, Landover, 1986—, Savannah Econ. Devel. Auth., 1994, Savannah Area C. of C., 1994, Savannah Regional Small Bus. Capital Fund, 1994; del. White House Conf. on Librs., 1991; Ga. state rep. Am. Assn. State Colls. and Univs., 1993—. NEH grantee, 1979; Am. Council on Edn. fellow, 1982-83; recipient award Fayetteville Human Relations Commn., 1981. Mem. Nat. Coun. Tchrs. English (pres. Black Caucus 1981-88), Conf. Coll. Composition and Communication (chmn. resolutions com. 1982—), Am. Coun. Edn. (commn. leadership devel. 1995), Kappa Delta Pi, Omega Psi Phi, Alpha Kappa Mu (hon.). Roman Catholic. Avocations: poetry, reading, golfing, long distance motoring. Home: 247 Lyman Hall Rd Savannah GA 31410-1048 Office: Savannah State Coll Office of the Pres PO Box 20444 Savannah GA 31404

WOLFE, JONATHAN A., food wholesaler, retailer. Pres., COO Oshawa Group Ltd., Toronto, Ont., Can. Office: The Oshawa Group Ltd, 302 E Mall, Toronto, ON Canada M9B 6B8

WOLFE, JONATHAN JAMES, pharmacy educator; b. Little Rock, Ark., Mar. 13, 1944; s. Jonathan Edwards and Mary Anne (Murphy) W.; m. Donna Jean Manley, Aug. 13, 1966; 1 child, Robert Jonathan. AB in History and Polit. Sci with honors, Hendrix Coll., 1966; MA in History, U. Va., 1968, PhD in U.S. History, 1971; post grad., Ark. Tech. U., 1973-74; BS in Pharmacy, U. Ark., 1977. Lic. pharmacist. Asst. prof. history and polit. sci Ark. Tech. U., Russellville, Ark., 1970-73; instr. dept. history U. Ark., Little Rock, 1974-85; staff pharmacist The Doctor's Hosp., Little Rock, 1976-78, pharmacy supr., 1978-81; supr. intravenous admixtures Ark. Children's Hosp., Little Rock, 1981-82, pharmacy supr.intensive care satellite, 1982-85; pharmacist Caremark Homecare, Divsn. of Baxter Internat., Little Rock, 1985-88; asst. prof. of pharmacy practice U. Ark. for Med. Sci., Little Rock, 1986-91; pharmacist Little Rock Ambulatory Care Pharmacy, Little Rock, 1989-91; asst. prof. history U. Ark., Little Rock, 1991—; asst. prof. pharmacy practice U. Ark for Med. Sci., Little Rock, 1991—; del. USP Conv., 1995; adv. bd. gov. Winthrop Rockefeller Lectureship, 1990—, chmn., 1994—; state coord. Ark. State Cancer Pain Initiative, 1993. Contbr to profl. jours. Coun. mem. for liberal arts U. Ark., Little Rock, 1983-86; bd. dir., v.p. Little Rock Chamber Mus. Soc., 1992—. Recipient Nat. Achievement award Am. Soc. Hosp. Pharmcists Rsch. and Edn. Found., 1993; Woodrow Wilson fellow Woodrow Wilson Nat. Fellowship Found., 1966, Va.-Wilson fellow U. Va. and Woodrow Wilson Nat. Fellowship Found., 1967, Va.-Danforth fellow U. Va., 1967-70, Summer fellow NEH, 1972; Woodrow Wilson Nat. Fellowship Found. affiliated scholar U. Ark. at Little Rock, 1991. Mem. Ark. Assn. Hosp. Pharmacists (program com. 1987-88, Staff Pharmacist of the Yr. award 1984), History of Medicine Assocs. (bd. dirs. 1991—), Ark. Pharmacists Assn. (ethical affairs com. 1991—, com. chmn.), U. Ark. for Med. Sci. (alumni adv. coun. 1984-93, coun. mem., Meyer Bros. award 1976). Democratic. Roman Catholic. Avocations: chamber music, travel. Home: PO Box 250043 Little Rock AR 72225-0043 Office: U Ark Coll of Pharmacy 4301 W Markham - Slot 522 Little Rock AR 72205-7122

WOLFE, KENNETH L., food products manufacturing company executive; b. 1939; married. B.A., Yale U., 1961; M.B.A., U. Pa., 1967. With Bankers Trust Corp., 1961-62; with Hershey Foods Corp., Pa., 1968—, asst. treas., 1968-70, budget dir., 1970-76, treas., 1976-80, v.p. fin. adminstrn. Hershey Chocolate Co., from 1980, v.p., chief fin. officer, 1981-84, sr. v.p., chief fin. officer, 1984-85, pres., chief operating officer, 1985-93, chmn., CEO, 1994—, also dir. Office: Hershey Foods Corp 100 Crystal A Dr Hershey PA 17033-0810*

WOLFE, LESLIE R., think-tank executive. Exec. dir. Ctr. for Women Policy Studies, Washington, D.C.; pres. Ctr. for Women Policy Studies. Office: Ctr Women Policy Studies 506 Connencticut Ave NW Ste 312 Washington DC 20036-5915*

WOLFE, LILYAN, special education clinical educator; b. N.Y.C., Mar. 17, 1937; d. Alexander and Molly (Springer) Aven; m. Richard Wolfe, June 8, 1957; children: Brian, Stacey. BBA, CUNY, 1957; postgrad., Hunter Coll.,

1962-65; MA, NYU, 1982, postgrad., 1983-85. Cert. tchr., N.J., N.Y.; cert. tchr. of handicapped, N.J. Tchr. PS 101 Manhattan, N.Y.C., 1962-65, Hazlet Twp. (N.J.) Schs., 1976-81; tchr. at risk mother-toddler program U. Medicine and Dentistry N.J., Newark, 1982-85, tchr. therapeutic nursery, 1982-84, head tchr., 1984—. Recipient cert. appreciation, Essex County Child Care Coalition, Newark, 1992. Mem. Nat. Assn. Edn. Young Children, NYU Alumni Assn., Kappa Delta Pi. Avocations: piano, gourmet cooking, travel, reading. Home: 120 Warren Aberdeen NJ 07747-1844 Office: U Medicine and Dentistry NJ Cmty Mental Health Ctr 215 S Orange Ave Newark NJ 07107-3001

WOLFE, MARGARET RIPLEY, historian, educator, consultant; b. Kingsport, Tenn., Feb. 3, 1947; d. Clarence Estill and Gertrude Blessing Ripley; m. David Earley Wolfe, Dec. 17, 1966; 1 child, Stephanie Ripley. BS magna cum laude, East Tenn. State U., 1967, MA, 1969; PhD, U. Ky., 1974. Instr. history East Tenn. State U., 1969-73, asst. prof., 1973-77, assoc. prof., 1977-80, prof., 1980—. Author: Lucius Polk Brown and Progressive Food and Drug Control, Tennessee and New York City, 1908-1920, 1978, An Industrial History of Hawkins County, Tennessee, 1983, Kingsport, Tennessee: A Planned American City, 1987, Daughters of Canaan: A Saga of Southern Women, 1995; contbg. author to books, also introductions to books; contbr. articles to profl. jours. Mem. Tenn. Com. for Humanities, 1983-85, exec. coun. mem., 1984-85; mem. Women's Symphony Com., Kingsport, 1990-95; exec. com. Tenn. Commemorative Woman's Suffrage Commn., 1994-95; mem. state rev. bd. Tenn. Hist. Commn., 1995—. Haggin fellow U. Ky., 1972-73; recipient Disting. Faculty award East Tenn. State U., 1977; East Tenn. State U. Found. rsch. award, 1979, Alumni cert. merit, 1984. Mem. AAUP, ACLU (exec. com. Tenn. 1991-92), NOW, Tenn. State Employees Assn., Am. Studies Assn. (John Hope Franklin Prize com. 1992), Am. Hist. Assn., Orgn. Am. Historians, So. Assn. Women Historians (pres. 1983-84, exec. com. 1984-86), So. Hist. Assn. (com. on the status of women 1987, program com. 1988, interim chair of program com. 1988, mem. com. 1993, 94, 95, nominating com. 1994, chair nominating com. 1995), Smithsonian Assocs., Tenn. Hist. Soc. (editorial bd., 1995—), Coordinating Com. for Women in Hist. Profession, East Tenn. Hist. Soc. (mem. editorial bd. Jour. East Tenn. History), Phi Kappa Phi. Office: ETSU/UT at Kingsport Kingsport TN 37660 also: East Tenn State U Dept History Johnson City TN 37614

WOLFE, MARTHA, elementary education educator; b. Centralia, Ill., Apr. 16, 1944; d. Elmer A. and Dorothy L. (Stonecipher) Krietemeyer; children: Kimberly S., Debora L. BS, So. Ill. U., 1967, MS, 1973, adminstrv. cert., 1987. Cert. elem. tchr., K-12 adminstrn., Ill. Tchr. Title I reading, dir. Cobden (Ill.) Unit Sch. Dist.; presenter in field. Recipient Master Tchr. award Gov. of Ill., 1984. Mem. NEA, Internat. Reading Assn., So. Ill. Reading Assn. (pres., v.p., bd. dirs.), Delta Kappa Gamma (Lambda State scholar 1986). Home: 301 South St Anna IL 62906-1528

WOLFE, MARY JOAN, physician; b. Johnstown, Pa., May 26, 1949; d. Dermot F. and Jean M. (Litzinger) W.; m. Thomas R. Roberts, June 9, 1979; children: Douglas Roberts-Wolfe, Rebecca Roberts-Wolfe. AB in Chemistry, Cornell U., 1971; MD, M.S. Hershey (Pa.) Med. Ctr., 1976. Diplomate Am. Bd. Internal Medicine, Am. Bd. Emergency Medicine. Intern Rochester (N.Y.) Gen. Hosp., 1976-77; resident in internal medicine Westchester County Med. Ctr., Valhalla, N.Y., 1977-79, attending physician emergency dept., 1979-83; practice medicine specializing in internal medicine Ossining, N.Y., 1986—; attending physician emergency room No. Westchester Hosp., Mt. Kisco, N.Y., 1986-89; ind. distributor Biomagnetic Devices, Nikken. Mem. ethics com. Phelps Meml. Hosp., 1994—, mem. bylaws com., 1989-96, chmn., 1996—. Mem. N.Y. Soc. Internal Medicine, Am. Soc. Internal Medicine. Avocations: gardening, camping, swimming, computers. Home: 6 Cecilia Ln Pleasantville NY 10570-1502 Office: 14 Church St Ossining NY 10562-4802

WOLFE, MAURICE RAYMOND, retired museum director, educator; b. Paris (Neuilly), France, Oct. 13, 1924; s. Guy Ellsworth and Genevieve (Plion) W.; m. Warwick Ellen Griffin, Nov. 4, 1955; 1 child, Shavaun. BA, U. Calif. in Sociology, Berkeley, 1948; MA in Sociology, U. Calif., Berkeley, 1952; postgrad. study, U. Paris Sorbonne, 1951; Cert. of Completion Sch. of Edn., U. Calif., Berkeley, 1954, postgrad., 1955. Rsch. asst. dept. of edn. U. Calif., Berkeley, 1949; tchr. of English and history Castlemont H.S., Oakland, Calif., 1954; lectr. in anthropology, philosophy, sociology and edn. U. Md. Overseas, 1956-59; lectr., instr. in philosopy and sociology U. Md., Munich, 1960-62; faculty mem. Merritt Coll., Oakland, Calif., 1962-88; chmn. dept. behavioral scis. Merritt Coll., Oakland, 1967-87; dir. and founder Merritt Coll. Anthropology Mus., Oakland, 1973-88; rsch. assoc. U. Calif. Lowie Mus. of Anthropology, 1985-89; lectr. Personnel Mgmt. for Execs., U.S. Govt. Sponsored, Berkeley, Calif. 1966-67, San Francisco State U. Dept Anthropology, 1967-68, Calif. State U., Hayward, Dept. Sociology, 1970-71; adj. instr. Monterey Peninsula Coll., Dept. Anthropology, 1990, 91, Hartnell Coll., Salinas, Calif. Editor: (jour.) Socioloqus, 1952. Recipient French Govt fellowship, Sorbonne, Paris, 1956; named to list of Great Teachers of Calif., Calif. Assn. Comty. Colls., Santa Barbara, 1984. Home: 33751 Carmel Valley Rd Carmel Valley CA 93924

WOLFE, RALPH STONER, microbiology educator; b. Windsor, Md., July 18, 1921; s. Marshall Richard and Jennie Naomi (Weybright) W.; m. Gretka Margaret Young, Sept. 9, 1950; children: Daniel Binns, Jon Marshall, Sylvia Suzanne. Mem. faculty U. Ill., Urbana, 1953—, prof. microbiology, 1961—; cons. USPHS, Nat. Inst. Gen. Med. Scis. Contbr. microbial physiology rsch. papers to profl. jours. Guggenheim fellow, 1961, 75, USPHS spl. postdoctoral fellow, 1967; recipient Pasteur award Ill. Soc. for Microbiology, 1974, Selman A Waksman Award in Microbiology Nat. Acad. of Sciences, 1995. Mem. NAS (Selman Waksman award in microbiology 1995), Am. Acad. Arts and Scis., Am. Soc. Microbiology (Carski Disting. Teaching award 1971, Abbott Lifetime Achievement award 1996, hon. mem.), Am. Soc. Biol. Chemists. Office: U Ill Dept Microbiology 335 Burrill Hall Urbana IL 61801

WOLFE, RICHARD RATCLIFFE, lawyer; b. Palmyra, Mo., Nov. 29, 1933; s. Francis Dunnan and Marie Ann (Ratcliffe) W.; m. Marilyn Jean McPheron, May 22, 1965; children: Richard Jr., Marie, John, Anne. BS in Engring., Okla. State U., 1955; JD, U. Mich., 1957. Patent atty. Cherry Burrell Corp., Chgo., 1958; designer rocket engring. NASA; tech. asst. U.S. Senate Com. on Aero. and Space Scis., Washington, 1961-64; adminstrv. asst. dir. revenue State of Ill., Springfield, 1964-67, adminstrv. asst. sec. of state, 1967-69; atty. Taylor, Miller, Magner, Sprowl & Hutchings, Chgo., 1969-81, Quinn, Jacobs, Barry & Miller, Chgo., 1981-86, Murchie, Calcutt & Boynton, Traverse City, Mich., 1986—. Author senate report on manned spaced flight program NASA. Dem. nominee 20th dist. U.S. Congress, Ill., 1966. With U.S. Army, 1958-60. Mem. Grand Traverse Yacht Club. Roman Catholic. Avocation: sailing. Office: 539 S Garfield Ave Traverse City MI 49686-3423

WOLFE, ROBERT RICHARD, bioresource engineer, educator; b. Chippewa Falls, Wis., Nov. 9, 1937; s. Lewis Samuel and Bernice (Quale) W.; m. Carol Abrams, June 23, 1974; children: Laura Allene, Richard Kevin. B.S., U. Wis., 1960, M.S., 1961; Ph.D., Purdue U., 1964. Research engr. A.O. Smith Corp., Milw., 1961; research asst. Purdue U., Lafayette, Ind., 1963; asst. prof. U. Wis., Madison, 1964-70; assoc. prof. Rutgers U., New Brunswick, N.J., 1970-77; prof. Rutgers U., 1977—. Contbr. numerous articles to profl. jours. NSF grad. fellow, 1962. Mem. Am. Soc. Engring. Edn., Assn. Environ. Engring. Profs., ASME Machine Vision Soc., IEEE Computer Soc., Am. Soc. Agrl. Engrs. (Jour. Article award 1973, 77, 84, 86), Water Environ. Fedn., Inst. Food Technologists, Instruments Soc. Am., AAUP, Sigma Xi, Tau Beta Pi, Phi Kappa Phi, Alpha Epsilon, Alpha Zeta, Delta Theta Sigma. Home: 31 Wagner Rd Stockton NJ 08559-1413 Office: Rutgers U Dept Bioresource Engri New Brunswick NJ 08903

WOLFE, SHEILA A., journalist; b. Chgo.; d. Leonard M. and Rena (Karn) W. B.A., Drake U. Reporter Chgo. Tribune, 1956-73, asst. city editor, 1973-75, day city editor, 1975-79, city editor, 1979-81, met. coordinator, 1981-83, adminstrv. asst. to mng. editor, 1983—; pres. City News Bur. Chgo. 1986-88, 94-96. Recipient Beck award for outstanding profl. performance Chgo. Tribune, 1979; recipient Disting. Service award Drake U., 1982. Mem. Phi Beta Kappa. Home: 71 E Division St Chicago IL 60610 Office: 435 N Michigan Ave Chicago IL 60611-4001

WOLFE, STANLEY, composer, educator; b. N.Y.C., Feb. 7, 1924; s. Bert S. and Dorothy (Sanders) W.; m. Marguerite Wiberg, Aug. 10, 1960; children: Jeffrey, Madeleine. Student, Stetson U., 1946-47, Henry St. Music Sch., 1947-48; B.S. in Composition, Juilliard Sch. Music, 1952, M.S. in Composition, 1955. Faculty Juilliard Sch., N.Y.C., 1955—; dir. extension div. Juilliard Sch., 1956-89; adj. prof. music Lincoln Ctr. campus Fordham U., 1969-73; lectr. N.Y. Philharmonic Pre-Concert Series, 1985—. Prin. compositions include King's Heart; dance score, 1956, Canticle for Strings, 1957, Lincoln Square Overture, 1958, Symphony Number 3, 1959, String Quartet, 1961, Symphony Number 4, 1965, Symphony Number 5 (Lincoln Center Commn.), 1970, Symphony Number 6, 1981; Violin Concerto, 1987. Served with AUS, 1943-46. Recipient award Am. Acad. and Inst. Arts and Letters, 1990; Guggenheim fellow in composition, 1957; Nat. Endowment for Arts grantee, 1969, 70, 77. Mem. ASCAP, Am. Music Center, Am. Symphony Orch. League (Alice Ditson award 1961), U.S. Chess Fedn. Home: 32 Ferndale Dr Hastings On Hudson NY 10706

WOLFE, THAD ALLISON, air force officer; b. Coulee Dam, Wash., Oct. 26, 1942; s. Clyde Allison and Leona (Ruffner) W.; m. Jill Ann Strathern, June 4, 1964; children: Thori, Christian, Molly. BS in Mil. Sci., USAF Acad., 1964; MSEE, U. Wyo., 1969; grad., Squadron Officer Sch., 1972, Air Command and Staff Coll., 1978, Nat. War Coll., 1985; grad. sr. exec. program in nat. and internat. security, Harvard U., 1992. Commd. 2nd lt. USAF, 1964, advanced through grades to lt. gen., 1993; ops. flight comdr. 6950th Security Wing, RAF Sta. Chicksands, Eng., 1965-66; signals intelligence ops. officer 6994th Security Squadron, Pleiku, South Vietnam, 1966-67; devel. engr. Def. Intelligence Agy., Va., 1969-70; instr. pilot, flight comdr., asst. sect. comdr. Vance AFB, Okla., 1970-74; aircrew tng. Castle AFB, Calif., 1974-75; crew comdr., ops. officer 325th Bombardment Squadron, Fairchild AFB, Wash., 1975-77; readiness analyst, chief of pers. and adminstrn., exec. officer to dir., directorate ops. and readiness Hdqs. USAF, Washington, 1978-81; comdr. 9th Bombardment Squadron, Carswell AFB, Tex., 1981; dep. comdr. for standardization and evaluation 1st Combat Evaluation Group, Barksdale AFB, La., 1982; command ctr. sr. contr. Hdqs. Strategic Air Command, Offutt AFB, Nebr., 1982-84, spl. asst. to comdr. for officer profl. devel., 1988, dep. dir. nat. strategic target list, joint strategic target planning staff, 1988-90; vice comdr., then comdr. 509th Bombardment Wing, Pease AFB, N.H., 1985-88; comdr. Strategic Warfare Ctr., Ellsworth AFB, S.D., 1990-92; asst. dep. dir. for ops. Nat. Security Agy., Ft. George G. Meade, Md., 1992-93; vice comdr. Air Combat Command, Langley AFB, Va., 1993-95; chmn. profl. mil. edn. bd. dirs. Air Combat Command, Langley AFB, 1993-95, chief environ. leadership coun., 1993-95; bd. dirs. Air U., Maxwell AFB, Ala., 1995, Inst. Environ. and Natural Resources, Rsch. and Policy, U. Wyo., Laramie, 1995—. Chmn. membership Boy Scouts Am., Rapid City, S.D., 1991. Decorated D.D.S.M., D.S.S.M., Legion of Merit, Bronze Star, Meriorious Svc. medal with three oak leaf clusters, Air medal, Air Force Commendation medal, Vietnam Svc. medal with svc. star, Republic of Vietnam Campaign medal. Mem. USAF Acad. Assn. of Grads., U. Wyo. Alumni Assn., Air Force Assn., Daedalians. Avocations: reading, sports, antiques, gardening. Office: BHL Capital/ Browning Resources US 3290 Lien St PO Box 505 Rapid City SD 57709

WOLFE, THOMAS KENNERLY, JR., writer, journalist; b. Richmond, Va., Mar. 2, 1931; s. Thomas Kennerly and Helen (Hughes) W.; m. Sheila Berger; children: Alexandra, Thomas. AB, Washington and Lee U., 1951, DLitt (hon.), 1974; PhD in Am. Studies, Yale U., 1957; DFA (hon.), Mpls. Coll. Art, 1971, Sch. of Visual Arts, 1987; LHD (hon.), Va. Commonwealth U., 1983, Southampton Coll. (N.Y.), 1984, Randolph-Macon Coll., 1988, Manhattanville Coll., 1988, Longwood Coll., 1989; DLitt (hon.), St. Andrews Presbyn. Coll., 1990, Johns Hopkins U., 1990, U. Richmond, 1993. Reporter Springfield (Mass.) Union, 1956-59; reporter, Latin Am. corr. Washington Post, 1959-62; city reporter N.Y. Herald Tribune, 1962-66; mag. writer N.Y. World Jour. Tribune, 1966-67; contbg. editor New York mag., 1968-76, Esquire Mag., N.Y.C., from 1977; writer N.Y. Sunday Mag., 1962-66; contbg. artist Harper's Mag., N.Y.C., 1978-81. One-man show of drawings include Maynard Walker Gallery, N.Y.C., 1965, Tunnel Gallery, N.Y.C., 1974; author: The Kandy-Kolored Tangerine-Flake Streamline Baby, 1965, The Electric Kool-Aid Acid Test, 1968, The Pump House Gang, 1968, Radical Chic and Mau-mauing the Flak Catchers, 1970, The Painted Word, 1975, Mauve Gloves and Madmen, Clutter and Vine, 1976, The Right Stuff, 1979 (Am. Book award 1980), In Our Time, 1980, From Bauhaus to Our House, 1981, The Purple Decades: A Reader, 1982, The Bonfire of the Vanities, 1987; editor, contbr. The New Journalism, 1973; contbr. articles to Esquire Mag., others. Recipient Front Page awards for humor and fgn. news reporting Washington Newspaper Guild, 1961, Soc. Mag. Writers award for excellence, 1970, Frank Luther Mott Rsch. award, 1973, Harold D. Vursell Meml. award Am. Acad. and Inst. Arts and Letters, 1980, Columbia Journalism award, 1980, Nat. Sculpture Soc. citation for art history, 1980, John Dos Passos award, 1984, Gari Melchers medal, 1986, Benjamin Pierce Cheney medal Ea. Wash. U., 1986, Washington Irving medal St. Nicholas Soc., 1986, Theodore Roosevelt medal Theodore Roosevelt Assn., 1990, Wilbur Cross medal Yale Grad. Sch. Alumni Assn., 1990, St. Louis Literary award, 1990, Quinnipiac Coll. Pres. award, 1993; named Va. Laureate for Lit., 1977. Office: Farrar Straus & Giroux Inc 19 Union Sq W New York NY 10003-3307

WOLFE, TOWNSEND DURANT, III, art museum director, curator; b. Hartsville, S.C., Aug. 15, 1935; m. Jane Rightor Lee; 1 child, Zibilla Lee; children (by previous marriage): Juliette Elizabeth, Mary Bryan, Townsend Durant. BFA, Atlanta Art Inst., 1958; MFA, Cranbrook Acad. Art, 1959; postgrad, Harvard Inst. Arts Adminstrn., 1970. Instr. Atlanta Art Assn., 1956-59, Memphis Acad. Art, 1959-64, Scarsdale Studio Workshop and Seamen Inst., N.Y.C., 1964-65; dir. Ford Found. Fund for Advancement of Edn. Wooster Community Art Ctr., Danbury, Conn., 1965-68; lectr. art U. Ark., Little Rock, 1969—; dir., chief curator The Ark. Arts Ctr., Little Rock, 1968—; sec. Ark. Arts Ctr. Found., 1973—; pres. Ark. Consortium Arts, 1976-80; pres. Ark. Arts in Edn. Adv. Coun., 1977-79; bd. dirs. Mid-Am. Arts Alliance, 1982-89; mem. adv. bd. Ark. Artists Registry, 1986—, Ark. Repertory Theatre, 1976-84; reviewer Inst. Mus. Svcs., 1984-87, examiner mus. assessment program, 1985-87; overview panel Nat. Endowment for Arts, 1986-88, rev. panel utilization of mus. resources, 1986, grant rev. panel conservation and collection maintenance, 1987; curator 20th Century Am. Sculpture Exhbn., First Ladies' Garden, The White House, 1995. One-man shows include Madison Gallery, N.Y.C., 1961, U. Miss., 1963, Southwestern U., Memphis, 1964, Ark. State U., Jonesboro, 1964, 70; group shows include Ball State Tchrs. Coll., Muncie, Ind., 1959, 63,65, 67, Ann. New Eng. Exhbn., 1966-67, Wadsworth Atheneum, Hartford, Conn., 1967, Audubon Artists, N.Y.C., 1968; represented in permanent collections Ark. State U., Union Planters Nat. Bank, Memphis, Mint Mus. Art, Charlotte, N.C., East Tenn. State U., others; author: Trustee Handbook, 1978, Appraiser Handbook, 1979, Selections from the Permanent Collection of the Arkansas Arts Center Foundation catalogue, 1983, Twentieth Century American Drawings from the Arkansas Arts Center Foundation Collection, 1984, American Drawings, 1986, National Drawings Invitational, 1986, 87, 88, 91, 92, 93, 94, National Objects Invitational, 1987, 88, 89, 91, National Crafts Invitational, 1987, Picasso: The Classical Years 1917-1925, 1987, Carroll Cloar Arkansas Collections, 1987, Revalations Drawing/America catalogue, 1988, The Face, 1988, 90, American Abstract Drawings, 1989, The Figure, 1990, Will Barnet Drawings: 1930-90, 1991, Silverpoint Etc., 1992, Edward Faiers Retrospective, 1994, exhbn. catalogue Memphis Coll. Art. Presdl. appt. Nat. Mus. Svcs. Bd., 1995. Recipient 20 awards for painting, 1958-68, Winthrop Rockefeller Meml. award, 1973, James R. Short award Southeastern Mus. Conf., 1981, Individual Achievement award Ark. Mus. Assn., 1984, Ark. Art Edn. Advocacy award, 1985, Promethean award for excellence in the arts March of Dimes, 1986, Chevalier dans l'ordre des Arts et Lettres, 1988. Mem. Assn. Art Mus. Dirs., Assn. Am. Museums (membership com. 1982-88, accreditation com., sr. examiner 1972—). Democrat. Episcopalian. Office: The Ark Arts Ctr MacArthur Park 9th and Commerce Little Rock AR 72202

WOLFE, WILLIAM JEROME, librarian, English language educator; b. Chgo., Feb. 24, 1927; s. Fred Wiley and Helen Dorothea (Lovaas) W.; m. ViviAnn Lundin O'Connell, June 25, 1960 (div. 1962); 1 child, Lund. AB, U. Chgo., 1948; BA, Roosevelt U., Chgo., 1953; MEd, Chgo. State U., 1963; AA with high honors, Pima C.C., 1992; BA in Art magna cum laude, U. Ariz., 1994. Tchr. English John Marshall High Sch., Chgo., 1956-60; libr. Safford Jr. High Sch., Tucson, Ariz., 1961-71, Santa Rita High Sch., Tucson, 1971-75, Tucson High Sch., 1975-87; tutor Eastside Ctr., Tucson Adult Lit. Vols., 1988—, supr., 1993—. Co-founder Tucson Classic Guitar Soc., 1969-72; docent U. Ariz. Mus. Art, Tucson, 1989—; mem. adv. bd. U. Ariz. Sch. Music, 1995—; singer U. Ariz. Collegium Musicum, Sons of Orpheus Men's Chorus. With U.S. Army, 1945-46, ETO. Mem. Sons of Norway, U. Ariz. Pres. Club, U. Ariz. Hon. Fellows Soc., Nat. Assn. Scholars, Assn. Lit. Scholars and Critics, Amnesty Internat., Human Life Found., Norsemen's Fedn., Phi Kappa Phi. Republican. Mem. Ch. of Christ Scientist. Avocations: poetry writing, drawing, singing, piano, calligraphy. Home: 8460 E Rosewood Tucson AZ 85710 *Through every turn of events, an always reliable and inspiring way to make a pleasing composition out of life consists in joyous thankfulness to the Creator for the love of family, wise counsel of teachers, and kind encouragement of friends.*

WOLFE, WILLIAM LOUIS, optics educator; b. Yonkers, N.Y., Apr. 5, 1931; s. William Louis and Louise Helene (Becker) W.; m. Mary Lou Bongort; children: Carol, Barbara, Douglas. BS in Physics, Bucknell U., 1953; MS in Physics, U. Mich., 1956, MSEE, 1966. Research engr., lectr. U. Mich., Ann Arbor, 1953-66; dept. mgr., chief engr. Honeywell Radiation Ctr., 1966-69; prof. Optical Sci. Ctr., U. Ariz., Tucson, 1969-95; prof. emeritus U. Ariz., Tucson, 1995—. Author: (with others) Fundamentals of Infrared Technology, 1962; (with George J. Zissis) The Infrared Handbook, 1979; series editor: Optical Physics and Engineering; editor: Optical Physics and Engineering, Handbook of Military Infrared Technology; editor-in-chief Infrared Physics; assoc. editor Handbook of Optics, 1995; contbr. articles to profl. jours. Fellow Optical Soc. Am. (many bds. and coms.), Soc. Photo-optical Instrumentation Engrs. (pres., bd. govs., chmn. symposia, exec. com.); mem. IEEE (sr. mem.), Nat. Acad. Sci. (many coms.), Infrared Info. Symposia, Naval Intelligence Adv. Bd. (sci. adv. bd.), Air Force Ad Hoc Electro-Optics Com., Army Research Office Adv. Com., Army Scientific Adv. Bd., Am. Men of Sci., Leaders in Am. Sci., Phi Beta Kappa, Sigma Xi, Omicron Delta Kappa, Pi Mu Epsilon, Sigma Pi Sigma, Phi Eta Sigma. Avocations: vocal music, travel, fishing. Office: U Ariz Optics Dept Tucson AZ 85721

WOLFEN, WERNER F., lawyer; b. Berlin, May 15, 1930; came to U.S., 1939; s. Martin and Ruth Eva (Hamburger) W.; m. Mary Glasier, July 1, 1956; children: Richard, James, Lawrence (dec.). BS, U. Calif., Berkeley, 1950, JD, 1953. Bar: Calif. 1953. Assoc. Irell & Manella, L.A., 1953-57, ptnr., 1957—; co-chmn. exec. com. Irell & Manella. Trustee UCLA Found.; pres. L.A. Goal, 1994—; fin. chmn. Bill Honig for Supt. of Pub. Schs., 1982, 86, 90. Mem. ABA. Democrat. Jewish. Office: Irell & Manella 1800 Avenue Of The Stars Los Angeles CA 90067-4211

WOLFENDEN, RICHARD VANCE, biochemistry educator; b. Oxford, Eng., May 17, 1935; s. John Hulton and Josephine (Vance) W.; m. Anita Gaunitz, May 25, 1965; children: Peter, John. BA, Princeton U., 1956, Exeter Coll., Oxford U., Eng., 1958; MA, Exeter Coll., Oxford U., Eng., 1958; PhD, Rockefeller Inst., 1964. Asst. prof. chemistry Princeton U., N.J., 1964-70; assoc. prof. biochemistry U. N.C., Chapel Hill, 1970-73, prof. biochemistry, 1973-83, alumni disting. prof., 1983—; vis. fellow Exeter Coll., Oxford, 1969; vis. prof. U. Montpellier, France, 1976; mem. molecular biology panel NSF, Washington, 1973-76; mem. bio-organic and natural products study sect. NIH, Washington, 1981-86; cons. Burroughs-Wellcome Co., Research Triangle Park, N.C., 1989—. Mem. editorial bd. Bioorganic Chemistry, 1983—, Biomed. Chem. Letters, 1993—. Fellow AAAS; mem. Am. Chem. Soc., Am. Soc. Biol. Chemists. Democrat. Home: 1307 Mason Farm Rd Chapel Hill NC 27514-4609 Office: U North Carolina Dept Biochemistry Chapel Hill NC 27514

WOLFENSOHN, JAMES DAVID, international public officer; b. Sydney, Australia, Dec. 1, 1933; naturalized, 1980.; s. Hyman and Dora (Weinbaum) W.; m. Elaine Ruth Botwinick, Nov. 26, 1961; children: Sara, Naomi, Adam. BA, U. Sydney, 1954, LLB, 1957; MBA, Harvard U., 1959. Bar: Supreme Ct. of Australia 1957. Ptnr. Ord Minnett (brokers), Australia, 1963-65; mng. dir. Darling & Co. (investment bankers), Australia, 1965-67, J. Henry Schroder Wagg, London, 1968-70; pres. J. Henry Schroder Banking Corp., N.Y.C., 1970-76; exec. dep. chmn., dir. Schroders Ltd., London; prin. exec. officer Schroder Group, London, 1974-77; exec. ptnr. Salomon Bros., N.Y.C., 1977-81; chmn. Salomon Bros. Internat., London, 1977-81; pres., CEO James D. Wolfensohn, Inc., 1981-95; pres. World Bank, 1995—; vis. lectr. fin. U. New South Wales, 1963-66. Contbr. articles to profl. jours. Mem. Australian Olympic Team, 1956; chmn. bd. dirs. John F. Kennedy Ctr. for the Performing Arts, Washington, 1990-95, chmn. emeritus, 1995—; bd. dirs. Met. Opera Assn., 1977-93, Joint Ctr. for Polit. Studies, 1978-88, mem. emeritus, 1988—; trustee Rockefeller Found., 1979-85, Population Coun., 1977-84; trustee Inst. for Advanced Study, Princeton, N.J., 1978—, chmn., 1986—; trustee Brookings Inst., 1983-90, hon., 1990—; trustee Rockefeller U., 1985-94, Howard Hughes Med. Inst., 1987-96; steering com. Bilderberg mtgs., treas. Am. Friends of Bilderberg, Inc., 1985—; pres. Internat. Fedn. Multiple Sclerosis Socs., 1977-83, Carnegie Hall, 1972—, bd. dirs., chmn., 1980-91, chmn. emeritus, 1991; bd. dirs. Nat. Multiple Sclerosis Soc., 1977-82. With Royal Australian Air Force, 1952-57. Recipient Business Com. for the Arts Leadership award, 1994; decorated by govts. of Australia, Germany, France; honored by HM Queen Elizabeth of Eng. with KBE and HM, King of Morocco. Fellow Am. Acad. Arts and Scis.; mem. Coun. on Fgn. Rels., Century Assn., Harvard Club (N.Y.C.), Australian Club (Sydney). Office: The World Bank 1818 H St NW Washington DC 20433

WOLFENSON, AZI U., electrical, mechanical and industrial engineer, consultant; b. Rumania, Aug. 1, 1933; came to Peru, 1937; s. Samuel G. and Polea S. (Ulanowski) W.; m. Rebeca Sterental, Jan. 10, 1983; 1 child, Michael Ben; children by previous marriage: Ida, Jeannette, Ruth, Moises, Alex. Mech., Elec. Engr., Universidad Nacional de Ingenieria, Peru, 1955; MSc in Indsl. Engring., U. Mich., 1966; Indsl. Engr., U. Nacional de Ingenieria, Peru, 1967; PhD in Engring. Mgmt., Pacific Western U., 1983, PhD in Engring. Energy, Century U., 1985, D in Philosophy of Engring. (hon.) World U. Roundtable, Ariz., 1987. Power engr. Peruvian Trading Co., 1956-57; gen. mgr. AMSA Ingenieros S.A., 1957-60; prof. Universidad Nacional de Ingenieria, Peru, 1956-72, dean mech. and elec. engring., 1964-66, dean indsl. engring., 1967-72; dir. SWSA Automotive Parts, Peru, 1954-77; project mgr. Nat. Fin. Corp., Cofide, 1971-73; Peruvian dir. Corporacion Andina de Fomento, CAF, 1971-73; rep. in Peru, CAF, 1973-74; pres. DESPRO cons. firm, 1973-76; exec. pres. Electroperu, 1976-80; cons. engr., 1964—; dir. Tech. Transference Studies, 1971-72. Mem. Superior Coun. Electricity, 1964-66; metal mech. expert for andean group, 1970-71; Nat. Coun. Fgn. Investment and Tech. Transfer, 1972-73; councilman at the Concejo Provincial De Lima, 1969-75; mem. Consultive Coun. Ministry Economy and Fin., 1973-74; pres. Peruvian Jewish Community, 1966-70, Peruvian Hebrew Sch., 1976-78; promoter, co-founder, gen. mgr. La Republica Newspaper, Peru, 1981; pres. PROA project promotion AG, Switzerland, 1982—; chmn. Inst. for the Devel. of the Americas, Inc., Fla., 1993—; co-founder La Republica, 1981, El Popular, 1983, El Nacional, 1985, Todo Sport, 1993, El Chino, 1994, pres. bd. dirs., newspapers; chmn. Inst. Devel. Ams., Inc., Fla., 1993—; chmn. editl. bd. Sport Peru, 1994—. Recipient awards Order Merit for Disting. Svcs., Peru, 1980, Disting. by City Coun. of Huancayo, 1980, Trujillo, 1978, Huaral, 1979, Piura, 1980, Disting. Contbn. award City of Lima, 1970, 71, Disting. Contbn. to Elec. Devel. in Peru, 1979, el Sol Radiante City Hall of Magdalena, Peru, 1995, others; disting. by the American Nuclear Soc. for contbn. to the advancement of nuclear sci. and tech., 1995—; named 1979 Exec., Gente mag., recognition Israel Govt., 1967, Disting. Comision Integracion Electrica Regional, CIER, medal, 1984, Disting. El Sol Radiante award City Hall of Magdalena, Peru, 1995. Fellow Inst. Prodn. Engrs., Brit. Inst. Mgmt.; mem. Colegio Ingenieros Peru, Instituto Peruano de Ingenieros Mecanicos (pres. 1965-66, v.p. 1967, dir. 1969, 70, 76), Asociacion Electrotechnica del Peru, ASME, AIIE (sr.), MTM Assn., Am. Soc. Engring. Edn., Am. Inst. Mgmt. Sci., AAAS, Assn. Mgmt. Sci. (dir. 1968), Asociacion Peruana Avance Ciencia, Inst. Adminstrv. Mgmt., British Inst. Mgmt., Am. Nuclear Soc. (vice chmn. 1988, 90, chmn. Swiss sect. 1991-93, Significant Contbn. to Advancement of Nuc. Sci. award 1995), Alumni Assn. of the Mich., Pacific Western and Century U., United Writers Assn., Swiss Soc. Writers, Swiss Sect. PEN Club Internat., others. Author: Work Communications, 1966, Programmed Learning, 1966, Production Planning and Control, 1968, Transfer of Technology, 1971, National Electrical Development, 1977, Energy and Development, 1979, El Gran Desafio, 1981, Hacia una politica economica alternativa, 1982, The Power of Communications: The Media, 1987. Contbr. articles to newspapers and jours. Clubs: Club der 200, FCL, Hebraica. Home: 3781 NE 208th Ter Miami FL 33180-3835

WOLFENSON, MARV, professional basketball team executive; m. Sandy Wolfenson; children: Ellyn, Ernie, David. Owner Minn. Timberwolves, The N.W. Racquet, Swim & Health Club, 1963—. Office: Minn Timberwolves Target Ctr 600 1st Ave N Minneapolis MN 55403-1400

WOLFERT, RUTH, Gestalt therapist; b. N.Y.C., Nov. 10, 1933; d. Ira and Helen (Herschdorfer) W. BS summa cum laude, Columbia U., 1967, post-grad., 1966-68. Pvt. practice N.Y.C., 1972—; dir. Action Groups, N.Y.C., 1974-76, Gestalt Groups, N.Y.C., 1976—, Chrysalis, N.Y.C., 1996—; mem. faculty, mem. coordinating bd. Women's Interart Ctr., N.Y.C., 1971-75, also bd. dirs.; presenter Stockton (N.J.) State Coll., 1974-75; mem. faculty Inst. for Experiential Learning and Devel., 1988-92, Woodstock U., 1989-91, Gestalt Inst., Atlanta, 1989—; presenter in field. Contbg. author: (booklet) A Consumer's Guide to Non-Sexist Therapy, 1978. Mem. Assn. Humanist Psychology (bd. dirs. ea. regional network 1981-87, pres. 1985-87), N.Y. Inst. Gestalt Therapy (trainer 1979—, chair workshops program 1979-83, co-chair conf. 1983-85, brochure com. 1987-95, interim exec. com. 1988-90, conf. com. 1989-91, v.p. 1993-95), Assn. Transpersonal Psychology (co-chair N.Y. discussion group 1991-92), Assn. Advancement Gestalt Therapy (bd. dirs. 1993—, co-chair Women's Issues in Gestalt Therapy interest group 1993—, conf. com. 1993—). Office: 200 E 32nd St New York NY 10016-6306

WOLFF, ALAN WILLIAM, lawyer; b. Malden, Mass., June 12, 1942; s. Louis K. and Etta (Bernstein) W.; m. Helene N. Novick, Mar. 3, 1965; children: Anna, Jeremy, Ewan. AB, Harvard U., 1963; LLB, Columbia U., 1966. Bar: Mass. 1967, N.Y. 1966, U.S. Supreme Ct. 1971, D.C. 1972, U.S. Ct. Appeals (fed. cir.) 1982, Ct. Internat. Trade 1993. Atty., office of gen. counsel U.S. Treasury Dept., Washington, 1968-73; dep. gen. counsel Spl. Trade Rep. (now U.S. Trade Rep.), Washington, 1973-74, gen. counsel, 1974-76, dep. spl. trade rep. (with rank of ambassador), 1977-79; ptnr. Verner, Liipfert et al, Washington, 1979-85; ptnr. Dewey, Ballantine, Bushby, Palmer & Wood (now Dewey Ballantine), Washington, 1985-92, mng. ptnr., 1992—; mem. Pres.'s Adv. Com. for Trade Negotiations, 1980-82, U.S. Trade Rep.'s Svcs. Policy Adv. Com., 1980-86 (all located in Washington, D.C.); mem. adv. bd. Inst. for Internat. Econ., 1981—, Econ. Strategy Inst., 1990—; nat. adv. bd. Ctr. for Nat. Policy, 1988—; trustee Monterey Inst. Internat. Studies, 1992—; mem. Coun. Fgn. Rels., 1979—. Co-author: The Microelectronics Race, 1987, Steel and the State, 1988, Conflict Among Nations: Trade Policy for the 1990s, 1992; contbr. articles to profl. jours. Mem. ABA, Am. Soc. Internat. Law. Democrat. Unitarian. Office: Dewey Ballantine 1775 Pennsylvania Ave NW Washington DC 20006-4605 also: 1301 Avenue Of The Americas New York NY 10019-6022*

WOLFF, BRIAN RICHARD, metal manufacturing company executive; b. L.A., Dec. 11, 1955; s. Arthur Richard and Dorothy Virginia (Johnson) W.; divorced; children: Ashley Rachael, Taryn Nicole. BSBA, Calif. State U., Chico, 1980; postgrad., U. Phoenix, 1990—. Registered counseling practitioner, Calif., 1996, guidance practitioner, Calif., 1996; ordained min. Progressive Universal Life Ch., 1996. Sales rep. Federated Metals Corp./ASARCO, Long Beach, Calif., 1980-82, dist. sales mgr., 1983-84; sales mgr. Copper Alloys Corp., Beverly Hills, Calif., 1982-83; dir. mktg. Federated-Fry Metals/Cookson, Long Beach, Industry and Paramount, Calif., 1984-87; regional sales mgr. Colonial Metals Co., L.A., 1987-91; nat. sales mgr. Calif. Metal X/Metal Briquetting Co., L.A., 1991-93; sales engr. Ervin Industries, Inc., Ann Arbor, Mich., 1993-95; sales mgr. Southbay Bronze, San Jose, Calif., 1996—; tech. sales mgr. GSP Metals & Chems. Co., 1987-91; cons. sales Calif. Metal Exch., L.A., 1987-91, Atlas Pacific Inc., Bloomington, Calif., 1993—; sales mgr. Southbay Bronze, San Jose, Calif., 1996—. Mem. citizens adv. com. on bus. Calif. Legis., 1983; ordained min. Universal Life, 1996. Mem. Non Ferrous Founders Soc., Am. Foundrymen Soc., Calif. Cast Metals Assn., Steel Structures Painting Coun., Am. Electroplaters Soc., Soc. Die Cast Engrs., NRA. Republican. Presbyterian. Avocations: scuba diving, tennis, freshwater fishing, trap shooting, hunting.

WOLFF, CHRISTIAN, composer, music and classics educator; b. Nice, France, Mar. 8, 1934. A.B., Harvard U., 1955, M.A., 1957, Ph.D., 1963. Instr. classics Harvard U., 1962-65, asst. prof., 1965-71; assoc. prof. classics, comparative lit. and music Dartmouth Coll., Hanover, N.H., 1971-78, prof. classics and music, 1978-80, Strauss prof. music and classics, 1980—; vis. composer Deutscher Akademischer Austauschdient, Berlin, 1974; vis. prof. classics Harvard U., 1980. Author: Ueber form, 1960, Orestes, In Euripides: A Collection of Critical Essays, 1968, On Political Texts and New Music, SONUS, 1980, Euripides in Ancient Writers: Greece and Rome, 1982; contbr. articles to profl. jours.; compositions recorded on Hat Art CD, 1994, Mode CD, 1995. Loeb bequest grantee Harvard U., 1967-68; fellow Ctr. Hellenic Studies, Washington, 1970-71; recipient Music award Am. Acad. and Nat. Inst. Arts and Letters, 1974. Office: Dept of Classics Dartmouth College Hanover NH 03755

WOLFF, CHRISTOPH JOHANNES, music historian, educator; b. Solingen, Germany, May 24, 1940; came to U.S., 1970; s. Hans Walter and Annemarie (Halstenbach) W.; m. Barbara Mahrenholz, Aug. 28, 1964; children: Katharina, Dorothea, Stephanie. Ed., U. Berlin, 1960-63, U. Freiburg, Germany, 1963-65; Dr. Phil., U. Erlangen, Germany, 1966. Lectr. U. Erlangen, 1966-69; asst. prof. U. Toronto, Ont., Can., 1968-70; assoc. prof. musicology Columbia U., 1970-73, prof., 1973-76; prof. musicology Harvard U., 1976—, William Powell Mason prof., 1985—, dept. chmn., 1980-88, 90-91; vis. prof. Princeton U., 1973, 75; hon. prof. U. Freiburg, Germany, 1990—; acting dir. Harvard U. Libr., 1991-92; dean Grad Sch. Arts and Scis., 1992—. Author: Der Stile Antico in der Musik J.S. Bachs, 1968, The String Quartets of Haydn, Mozart, and Beethoven, 1980, Bach Compendium, 7 vols., 1986-89, Bach: Essays on His Life and Music, 1991, Mozart's Requiem, 1994; contbr. numerous articles to profl. jours.; editor: Bach-Jahrbuch, 1974—; critical edits. of music by, Scheidt, Buxtehude, Bach, Mozart, and Hindemith. Recipient Dent medal Royal Mus. Assn., London, 1978. Fellow Am. Acad. Arts and Scis.; Mem. Internat. Musicol. Soc., Am. Musicol. Soc., Gesellschaft fuer Musikforschung. Home: 182 Washington St Belmont MA 02178-3560 Office: Harvard U University Hall 18 Cambridge MA 02138-5723

WOLFF, CHRISTOPHER See KENDALL, CHRISTOPHER

WOLFF, CYNTHIA GRIFFIN, humanities educator, author; b. St. Louis, Aug. 20, 1936; d. James Thomas and Eunice (Heyn) Griffin; m. Robert Paul Wolff, June 9, 1962 (div. 1986); children—Patrick Gideon, Tobias Barrington; m. Nicholas J. White, May 21, 1988. B.A., Radcliffe Coll., 1958; Ph.D., Harvard U., 1965. Asst. prof. English Manhattanville Coll., Purchase, N.Y., 1968-70; asst. prof. English U. Mass., Amherst, 1971-74, assoc. prof., 1974-76, prof., 1976-80; prof. humanities MIT, Cambridge, 1980-85, Class of 1922 prof. lit. and writing, 1985—; mem. exec. com. for Am. lit. MLA, 1979-81; mem. selection bd. Literary Classics Am., 1981—; mem. exec. bd. for fgn. grants Am. Council Learned Socs., 1981-84. Author: (literary criticism) Samuel Richardson, 1972, (literary biography) A Feast of Words: The Triumph of Edith Wharton, 1977, 2d edit., 1995, Emily Dickinson, 1986; bd. editors Am. Quar., 1979-84. AAUW grantee, 1964-65; NEH grantee, 1975-76, 1983-84; Am. Council Learned Socs. grantee, 1984-85. Mem. Am. Studies Assn. Home: 416 Commonwealth Ave Apt 619 Boston MA 02215-2812 Office: MIT Dept Humanities 14N-226 Cambridge MA 02139

WOLFF, DAVID STEPHEN, investments and real estate development executive; b. Phila., Sept. 18, 1940; s. Leo and Carolyn (Hirsch) W.; m. Mary Edna Crawford, Dec. 28, 1972; children: Carolyn Crawford, Elizabeth Brooke. BA, Amherst Coll., 1962; MBA, Harvard U., 1964. V.p. Brookhollow Corp., Dallas, 1965-70; ptnr. Wolff, Morgan & Co., Houston, 1970-85; chmn.bd., pres. Wolff Cos., Houston, 1985—; chmn. bd. Dominion Jaguar-Volvo, 1989—. Chmn. bd. Houston Parks Bd., 1988-90; bd. dirs. Houston Econ. Devel. Coun., 1985-87, Houston C. of C., 1984-85, Harris Galveston Coastal Subsidence Dist., 1976-78; v.p. Houston Grand Opera, 1978-84; trustee Amherst Coll., 1991—. Mem. The Urban Land Inst., Coronado Club, Nantucket Yacht Club. Avocations: cattle ranching, horse farming. Office: Wolff Cos 20 Briar Hollow Ln Houston TX 77027-2802

WOLFF, DEBORAH H(OROWITZ), lawyer; b. Phila., Apr. 6, 1940; d. Samuel and Anne (Manstein) Horowitz; m. Morris H. Wolff, May 15, 1966 (div.); children: Michelle Lynn, Lesley Anne; m. Walter Allan Levy, June 7, 1987. BS, U. Pa., 1962, MS, 1966; postgrad., Sophia U., Tokyo, 1968; JD, Villanova U., 1979; LLM, 1988. Tchr. Overbrook High Sch., Phila., 1962-68; homebound tchr. Lower Merior Twp., Montgomery County, 1968-71; asst. dean U. Pa., Phila., 1975-76; law clk. Stassen, Kostos and Mason, Phila., 1977-78; assoc. Spencer, Sherr, Moses and Zuckerman, Norristown, Pa., 1980-81; ptnr. Wolff Assocs., 1981—; lectr. law and estate planning, Phila., 1980—; Recipient 3d Ann. Community Svc. award Phila. Mayor's Com. for Women, 1984; named Pa. Heroine of Month, Ladies Home Jour., July 1984. Founder Take a Brother Program; bd. dirs. Germantown Jewish Ctr.; high sch. sponsor World Affairs Club, Phila., 1962-68; mem. exec. com., sec. bd. Crime Prevention Assn., Phila., 1965—; bd. dirs. U. Pa. Alumnae Bd., Phila., 1965—, pres. bd. dirs., 1993—, v.p. organized classes, bd. crime prevention; chmn. urban conf. Boys Club Am., 1987; active Hahnaman Brain Tumor Rsch. Bd. Mem. ABA, Pa. Bar Assn., Assn. Trial Lawyers Am., Phila. Bar Assn., Montgomery County Bar Assn., Phila. Women's Network, Bus. Women's Network (pres., bd. dirs.), Crime Prevention Assn. (sec. bd. dirs., v.p. bd. dirs.), Cosmopolitan Club (membership com. Phila.), Lions Club (chmn., pres., bd. dirs., 2nd v.p.). Home and Office: 422 W Mermaid Ln Philadelphia PA 19118-4204

WOLFF, DEE IVONA, artist; b. Springfield, Minn., June 25, 1948; d. Herbert Edmond and Ivona Francis (Steffel) Ricke; m. Leonard Joe Wolff, Aug. 24, 1968. BA, U. Houston, 1971; cert. of art, Glassell Sch., Mus. Fine Arts, Houston, 1976; student, C.G. Jung Ctr., Houston, 1973-85, Oomoto Sch. Traditional Art, Japan, 1984. Fellow MacDowell Colony, Peterborough, N.H., 1987. One-man shows include Galveston (Tex.) Art Ctr., 1977, 90, Covo de Iongh Gallery, Houston, 1977, Watson de Nagy Gallery, Houston, 1978, Watson Gallery, Houston, 1981, 85, Tex. A&M U. Gallery, College Station, 1986, Marvin Seline Gallery, Austin, 1986, 88, Stephen F. Austin U. Gallery, Nacogdoches, Tex., 1987, Diverseworks Artspace, Houston, 1989, 90, Mus. S.E. Tex., Beaumont, 1990, C.G. Jung Ctr., 1990, D'Art, Dallas, 1990; numerous group exhbns. including Art League Houston, 1976, 96, U. Ill., 1977, Moody Gallery, Houston, 1978, Newport Harbor Art Mus., Calif., 1978, Bklyn. Mus., 1979, Witte Meml. Mus., San Antonio, 1979, So. Meth. U., Dallas, 1980, San Antonio Art Inst. Gallery, 1981, Stavanger Kunstforening, Norway, 1982, Waco (Tex.) Art Ctr., 1982, Salzburger Kunstverein, Austria, 1983-84, Houston Art League, 1983, 87, Dallas Pub. Libr., 1983, Mus. Fine Arts, Houston, 1985, Midtown Arts Ctr., Houston, 1985, Galveston Art Ctr., 1986, 92, 93, Aspen (Colo.) Art Mus., 1987, Judy Youens Gallery, Houston, 1987, 91, Mpls. Coll. Art & Design, 1988, Nat. Mus. Women in the Arts, Washington, 1988, Art Mus. SE Tex., Beaumont, 1989, Longview (Tex.) Mus. and Art Ctr., 1989, Lynn Goode Gallery, Houston, 1990, 91, 96, Art Mus. South Tex., Corpus Christi, 1991, 96, Fine Arts Ctr., Lubbock, 1991, 96, Dallas Mus. Fine Arts, 1991, Tex. Fine Arts Assn., 1991, Karen Lanning Gallery, Houston, 1992, Women & Their Work Gallery, Austin, 1992, 96, Hooks-Epstein Gallery, Houston, 1993, 94, U. Tex. Med. Sch., 1993, Diverseworks Artspace, Houston, 1993, C.G. Jung Ctr., Houston, 1995, Houston Lawndale Art Ctr., 1996, Yekaterinburg, St. Petersburg, Russia, Tomsk, Rostovondon, Nizhnily-Novgorod, Russia, 1996, Slover McCutcheon Gallery, Houston; represented in permanent collections Aamoco Corp., Denver, Internat. Materials Mgmt. Engrs., Houston, Wilson Industries, Houston, Marriott Hotels, Jacksonville, Fla., Park Hotel, Charlotte, N.C., Oomoto, Kameoka City, Kyoto, Japan, Enron Corp., Houston, Mus. SE Tex., Art Mus. South Tex., Corpus Christi, Mus. Fine Arts, Houston; commd. St. Philip Presbyn. Ch., Houston, 23 stained glass windows St. Theresea of Lisieux, Sugarland, Tex., Corpus Christi Pub. Libr.; visual design stage sets Kabbalah; subject radio and TV interviews. Bd. dirs. Diverseworks Artspace, Houston, 1989-91, mem. artists adv. bd., 1990-91. Interdisciplinary Arts grantee Nat. Endowment Arts, 1988, Visual Arts Fellowship grantee, 1989; N.Y. State Coun. on Arts grantee, 1989; recipient Spirit of Am. Woman award Houston Performing Arts Soc. and J.C. Penney, 1989. Avocations: reading, yoga, building and fixing things, walking, conversation. Studio: 421 Arlington St Houston TX 77007-2617

WOLFF, DERISH MICHAEL, economist, company executive; b. Boston, May 14, 1935; s. Nathan and Ruth Mae (Derish) W.; m. Maureen Robinson; children: Jeffrey Scott, Hayley Beth. BA, U. Pa., 1957; MBA, Harvard U., 1959. Adminstrv. asst. Sigmund Werner, Inc., Belleville, N.J., 1959-61; devel. economist Louis Berger, Inc., East Orange, N.J., 1961-65, chief economist, 1965-67, v.p., 1968-74, exec. v.p., 1975-82, pres., CEO, 1982—; dir. Louis Berger Internat., Inc., Bronkonsult, CHELBI, Ammann & Whitney; guest lectr. Fgn. Svc. Inst., Newark Inst. Tech., U. Nev., MIT, Harvard U., Rutgers U., U. Denver; mem. Bretton Woods Com., 1987—. Mem. editl. bd. Modern Engrng. Tech, 1978-80, Nat. Devel.-Modern Govt., 1972-79, Constrn. Bus. Review, 1991—. Class chmn. U. Pa. Ann. Giving, 1975-82, class pres., 1982-92; mem. U.S. Presdl. Trade Del. to Japan, 1986; mem. indsl. sector adv. com. Dept. of Commerce, 1988-92; mem. adv. com. U.S. Trade and Devel. Program, 1989-92. Mem. Am. Cons. Engrs. Coun. (chair internat. engrng. com. 1983-85, vice chair 1986-93), Internat. Engrng. and Constrn. Industries Coun. (del. 1986, 87, chmn. 1988-90, Bldg. Futures Coun. 1990—, vice chair 1994—), Ctr. for Strategic and Internat. Studies (steering group/GATT negotiations 1989), Phi Beta Kappa. Jewish. Clubs: Harvard, Penn. Office: Louis Berger Group 100 Halsted St East Orange NJ 07018-2612

WOLFF, EDWARD A., electronics engineer; b. Chgo., Oct. 31, 1929; s. Samuel S. and Lillian P. W.; m. Anna Lee Tishk, June 19, 1951; children: David Steven, Elliot Marvin, Susan Toby. B.S.E.E., U. Ill., 1951; M.S., 1953; Ph.D., U. Md., 1961. Electronic scientist Naval Research Lab., Washington, 1951-54; project engr. Md. Electronic Mfg. Corp., Litton Industries, College Park, Md., 1956-59, Electromagnetic Research Corp., College Park, Md., 1959-61; engrng. mgr. Aero Geo Astro-Keltec Industries/Aiken Industries, Alexandria, Va., 1961-67; v.p. Geotronics, Inc., Falls Church, Va., 1967-71; supervisory electronics engr. NASA Goddard Space Flight Ctr., Greenbelt, Md., 1971—; system mgr. Network TDRS System, 1981-89, MRJ, Inc., Oakton, Va., 1989—; instr. Tex. A&M U., 1962. Author: Spacecraft Technology, 1962, Antenna Analysis, 1966, 2d edit., 1988, Geoscience Instrumentation, 1974, Urban Alternatives, 1975, Microwave Engineering and Systems Applications, 1988. Mem. Md. Gov.'s Sci. Resources Adv. Bd., 1963-67; pres. U.S. Environment and Resources Council, 1972-75; treas. World Evironment and Resources Council, 1975-81. Served with U.S. Army, 1954-56. Fellow IEEE (dir. 1971-72), Washington Acad. Scis.; mem. AIAA, Nat. Soc. Profl. Engrs., Eta Kappa Nu, Sigma Tau, Phi Eta Sigma. Home: 1021 Cresthaven Dr Silver Spring MD 20903-1602 Office: MRJ Inc Oakton VA 22124 *Everything I have done has been with the help of others. In return, as I have acquired management responsibilities, a primary objective has been to help others achieve their goals.*

WOLFF, ELEANOR BLUNK, actress; b. Bklyn., July 10, 1931; d. Sol and Bessie (Schultz) Blunk; m. William Howard Wolff, June 19, 1955; children: Ellen Jill, Rebecca Louise. BA in Edn., Speech and Theatre, Bklyn. Coll., 1972, MS in Spl. Edn., 1975; postgrad., Adelphi U., 1980-81. Cert. tchr., N.Y. Fashion model Garment Ctr., N.Y.C., 1949-50; sec. to v.p. out-of-town/export sales Liebmann Breweries Inc., Bklyn., 1950-58; tchr. N.Y.C. Bd. Edn., Bklyn., 1971-76; sec. to dir. environ. programs, pub. affairs officers, speakers bur. project leader Power Authority State of N.Y., N.Y.C., 1976-85; tchr. Hewlett-Woodmere (N.Y.) Sch. Dist., 1986-89; instr. adult edn. County of Nassau, N.Y., 1986—; actress/model, N.Y., 1992—. V.p. program devel. for youth ctr. Wavecrest Gardens Community Assn., Far Rockaway, N.Y., 1959-63; teen leader Far Rockaway Jewish Ctr. Youth Coun., 1965-68; pres. Parents Assn. P.S. 215Q, Far Rockaway, 1966-67; tutor N.Y. C. Bd. Edn. Sch. Vol. Program, Far Rockaway, 1969-71; chair civic affairs Dem. Club, Far Rockaway, 1961-63; committeewoman Dem. Ctrl. Com., Queens County, N.Y., 1963-64; v.p. membership, mem. constn. com. Nassau County Dem. Women's Caucus, 1988, 89; awards com. Bklyn Coll. Named Mother of Yr. Congregation Shaaray Tefila, Far Rockaway, 1968; recipient Merit award Wavecrest Gardens Community Assn., 1960, Theater Arts Trophy for disting. svc. Bklyn. Coll. Alumni, 1992. Mem. AFTRA, SAG, Nassau Assn. Cmty./ Continuing Edn., Alumni Assn. Bklyn. Coll. (life). Avocations: painting, piano. Home: 29 Princeton Ave Hewlett NY 11557-1521

WOLFF, ELROY HARRIS, lawyer; b. N.Y.C., May 20, 1935; s. Samuel and Rose Marian (Katz) W.; children: Ethan, Anna Louise. A.B., Columbia U., 1957, LL.B., 1963. Bar: N.Y. 1963, D.C. 1969. Assoc. Kaye, Scholer, Fierman, Hays & Handler, N.Y.C., 1963-65; atty.-adviser to commr. FTC, Washington, 1965-67; sr. trial atty. Dept. Transp., 1967-69; assoc. Leibman, Williams, Bennett, Baird & Minow, Washington, 1969-70, ptnr., 1970-72; ptnr. Sidley & Austin, Washington, 1972—; mem. adv. com. on practice and procedure FTC, 1969-71; chmn. adv. com. on procedural reform CAB, 1975. Served to 1st lt. USAF, 1957-60. Mem. ABA (chmn. spring meeting program 1992-94, coun. 1995—), Union Internationale des advocats (chmn. competition law com. 1994—), Monroe Club, Fed. City Club. Office: Sidley & Austin 1722 I St NW Washington DC 20006-3705

WOLFF, FERIDA, author; b. Bklyn., July 7, 1946; d. Sam and Shirley J. (Gootrad) Mevorach; m. Michael L. Wolff, Feb. 3, 1965; children: Stephanie E., Russell S. BA, Queens Coll., Flushing, N.Y., 1967, MS in Edn., 1970; cert. holistic studies, Rosemont (Pa.) Coll., 1992. Tchr. N.Y.C. Bd. Edn., Queens, 1967-68; head tchr. Happy Time Nursery Sch., Queens, 1968-70; freelance writer, 1972-87; instr. yoga adult schs. Camden County (N.J.) Coll., 1990-95; spkr., 1989—; panelist Phila Writer's Conf., 1990, workshop leader, 1993; workshop leader Teen Arts Festival, Camden, N.J., 1993. Author: Pink Slippers, Bat Mitzvah Blues, 1989 (Syndey Taylor honor book), The Woodcutter's Coat, 1992, Danish edit., 1993, French edit., 1993, Seven Loaves of Bread, 1993, The Emporer's Garden, 1994, A Weed is a Seed, 1996, (with Dolores Kozielski) The Toothless Vampire and 99 Other Howl-oween Riddles, 1992, The Halloween Grab Bag., 1993, On Halloween Night, 1994, Spitballs and Spaghetti, 1995, The Bald Beagle, 1996; contbr. articles to profl. jours. Bd. mem., v.p. Friends of the Cherry Hill (N.J.) Free Pub. Libr., 1991-92; scouting coord., troop com. mem. troop 167 Boy Scouts Am., Cherry Hill, 1985-90; libr. vol. coord. Jos. D. Sharp Elem. Sch., Cherry Hill, 1979-87. Mem. Authors Guild, Soc. Children's Book Writers and Illustrators, Penn Laurel Poets, Phila. Children's Reading Round Table (steering com.). Home: 21 Candlewyck Way Cherry Hill NJ 08003-1226

WOLFF, FRANK PIERCE, JR., lawyer; b. St. Louis, Feb. 27, 1946; s. Frank P. and Beatrice (Stein) W.; m. Susan Scallet, May 11, 1984; children: Elizabeth McLane, Victoria Hancox. BA, Middlebury Coll., 1968; JD, U. Va., 1971. Bar: Mo. 1971, U.S. Ct. Appeals (5th cir.) 1974, U.S. Ct. Appeals (8th cir.) 1975, U.S. Supreme Ct. 1975. Ptnr. Lewis, Rice & Fingersh, St. Louis, 1971-90, Bryan Cave LLP, St. Louis, 1990—; bd. dirs. Wood Ceilings, Inc. Bd. dirs. Leadership St. Louis, 1985-88, Washington U. Child Guidance Clinic, St. Louis, 1976-79, Jewish Family and Children's Svc., St. Louis, 1981-83, John Burroughs Sch., 1995—; gen. counsel Mo. Bot. Garden, St. Louis, 1981—, Mo. History Mus. Subdist., St. Louis, 1987—; spl. counsel St. Louis Symphony Soc., 1989—; trustee St. Louis Children's Hosp., 1995—. Capt. USAR, 1968-76. Mem. ABA, Mo. Bar Assn., Bar Assn. Met. St. Louis (chmn. corp. sect. 1984-85), Noonday Club, Westwood County Club (chmn. fin. com. 1989-91, treas. 1989-91, v.p. 1991-93, pres. 1993-95, exec. com. 1989-95). Home: 21 Westwood Country Clb Saint Louis MO 63131-2411 Office: Bryan Cave 1 Metropolitan Sq Saint Louis MO 63102-2750

WOLFF, GEOFFREY ANSELL, novelist, critic, educator; b. L.A., Nov. 5, 1937; s. Arthur Saunders III and Rosemary (Loftus) W.; m. Priscilla Bradley Porter, Aug. 21, 1965; children: Nicholas Hinckley, Justin Porter. Grad., Choate Sch., 1955; student, Eastbourne (Eng.) Coll., 1955-56; BA summa cum laude, Princeton U., 1961; postgrad., Churchill Coll., Cambridge U., Eng., 1963-64. Lectr. in comparative lit. Robert Coll., Istanbul, Turkey, 1961-63; lectr. in Am. civilization Istanbul U., 1962-63; lectr. aesthetics Md. Inst. Coll. Art, 1965-69; vis. lectr. creative arts Princeton (N.J.) U., 1970-71, Ferris prof., 1980, 92; writer-in-residence Brandeis U., Waltham, Mass., 1982-95; prof. English and creative writing U. Calif., Irvine, 1995—; lectr. English lit. Middlebury (Vt.) Coll., 1976, 78; vis. lectr. Columbia U., N.Y.C., 1979, Brown U., Providence, 1981, 88, Boston U., 1981; mem. policy panel in lit. NEA; book critic Esquire mag., 1979-81; founder Golden Horn lit. mag., 1972; vis. prof. Williams Coll., 1994. Author: Bad Debts, 1969, The Sightseer, 1974, Black Sun, 1976, Inklings, 1978, The Duke of Deception, 1979, Providence, 1986; editor: Best American Essays, 1989, The Final Club, 1990, A Day at the Beach, 1992, The Age of Consent, 1995; book editor Washington Post, 1964-69, Newsweek mag., 1969-71, New Times mag., 1974-79; contbr. to mags. Recipient Award in Lit., Am. Acad. of Arts and Letters, 1994, R.I. Gov.'s Arts award, 1992; Woodrow Wilson fellow, 1961-62, 63-64, Fulbright fellow, 1963-64, Guggenheim fellow, 1972-73, 77-78, NEH sr. fellow, 1974-75, NEA fellow, 1979-80, 86-87, Am. Coun. Learned Socs. fellow, 1983-84, Lila Wallace Writing fellow, 1992. Mem. PEN, Princeton Club (N.Y.C.), Colonial CLub (Princeton), Dunes Club. Home: 565 Center St Laguna Beach CA 92651 Office: U Calif-Irvine Program in Writing Dept of English Irvine CA 92717-2650

WOLFF, GRACE SUSAN, pediatrician; b. Rome, N.Y.. MD, Med. Coll. Wis., 1965. Intern St. Vincents Hosp., N.Y.C., 1965-66; resident Columbia-Presby Med. Ctr., N.Y.C., 1967-69; pediatrician Childrens Hosp., Boston, 1969-71, U. Miami (Fla.) -Jackson Meml. Hosp. Office: U Miami-Jackson Meml Hosp PO Box 016960-R76 Miami FL 33101

WOLFF, HERBERT ERIC, banker, former army officer; b. Cologne, Germany, May 24, 1925; s. Hugo and Juanna Anna (Van Dam) W.; m. Alice (Billy) Rafael, Nov. 13, 1946 (dec. July, 1987); children: Karen (dec. Jan., 1992), Herbert E., Allen R. B.A., Rutgers U., 1953; B.S., U. Md., 1957; M.A., George Washington U., 1962; grad., U.S. Army War Coll., 1962, Harvard U., 1979. Commd. 2d lt. U.S. Army, 1945, advanced through grades to maj. gen.; served in Fed. Republic of Germany, Greece, Iran, Republic of Korea, Australia, New Guinea, The Phillipines, Japan and Socialist Republic of Vietnam; dep. dir. ops. NSA-CSS, Ft. Meade, Md., 1973-75; dep. corps. comdr. V. Corps U.S. Army, Frankfurt, Germany, 1975-77; comdr. gen. U.S. Army Western Command U.S. Army, Hawaii, 1977-81; with First Hawaiian Bank, Honolulu, 1981—, sr. v.p., corp. sec.; hon. consul gen. (Dató) U.S. Pacific region Govt. of Malaysia, Honolulu, 1985—. Author: The Man on Horseback, 1962, The Tenth Principle of War, 1964, Public Support, 1964, The Military Instructor, 1968. Mem. exec. bd. Aloha coun. Boy Socuts Am.; bd. dirs. USO, ASYMCA, Girl Scouts of U.S., Hawaii; v.p. Hawaii Com. Fgn. Rels.; pres. Pacific Asian Affairs Coun.; pres. Hawaii Army Mus. Soc. Decorated Bronze Star with V and 3 oak leaf clusters U.S. Army, Air medal (24) U.S. Army, Joint Services commendation medal U.S. Army, Army Commendation medal U.S. Army, Purple Heart, Gallantry Cross with 2 palms, Gallantry Cross with palm and silver star Nat. Order 5th class S. Vietnam, Order Nat. Security Merit Choen-Su S. Korea, D.S.M. with oak leaf clusters (2), U.S. Army, Silver Star with oak leaf cluster U.S. Army, Legion of Merit with 3 oak leaf clusters U.S. Army, D.F.C. U.S. Army, Combat Infantry Badge with two stars; named Citizen of Yr. Fed. Exec. Bd., 1987. Mem. Am. Bankers Assn., Am. Soc. Corps. Secs., Assn. U.S. Army (trustee), 1st Inf. Divsn. Assn., 1st Cav. Divsn. Assn., U.S. Army Mus. Soc. (trustee), Plaza Club (bd. dirs.), Honolulu Country Club, Waialae Country Club, Rotary, Phi Kappa Phi. Office: First Hawaiian Bank PO Box 3200 Honolulu HI 96847-0001 *History is a gift we borrow and hope to pass on. Forget the past and be doomed to repeat it. Remember the past and accept the challenge to convince others.*

WOLFF, IVAN LAWRENCE, venture capitalist; b. Bklyn., Oct. 9, 1944; s. Zachary Henry (dec.) and Gertrude (Abramowitz) W.; m. Susan R. Joseph, June 18, 1967; 1 child, Adam Gregory. B.A., Cornell U., 1966; M.B.A. with distinction, Harvard U., 1968. Cert. fin. analyst. Mktg. mgr. Hughes Aircraft Co., Culver City, Calif., 1968-74; mktg. mgr. M-A Com, Burlington, Mass., 1974-76; div. mgr. customer strategy AT&T, Basking Ridge, N.J., 1976-81; v.p., securities analyst Donaldson, Lufkin, & Jenrette, N.Y.C., 1981-84; sr. v.p., prin. Rothschild, Inc. (Rothschild Venture), N.Y.C., 1984-87, mng. dir., 1987-91; mng. dir. Wolff Assocs., Mountain Lakes, N.J., 1991—. Pres. Cornell Alumni Class, Ithaca, 1981-86, v.p., 1986—; bd. dirs. Smugglers' Notch Condominium Assn., Jeffersonville, Vt., 1982-85. Mem. Inst. Cert. Fin. Analysts. Republican. Office: Wolff Assocs 174 Laurel Hill Rd Mountain Lakes NJ 07046-1217

WOLFF, JESSE DAVID, lawyer; b. Mpls., Aug. 26, 1913; s. Maurice I. and Annalee (Weiskopf) W.; m. Elizabeth Hess, Nov. 22, 1939; children:

Nancy Nicholas, Paula, Daniel Jesse. B.A. summa cum laude, Dartmouth Coll., 1935; J.D., Harvard U., 1938. Bar: N.Y. 1938. Practiced in N.Y.C., 1938—; assoc., then ptnr., to counsel Weil, Gotshal & Manges, 1938-88, 88—, sr. mng. ptnr., 1966-86; past dir., dep. chmn. Sotheby Parke Bernet Group (Eng.); past mem. adv. bd. Sotheby's Inc. Trustee, exec. com. Greatery N.Y. ARC; past mem. exec. com. Salvation Army, N.Y.C. Served with AUS, 1942-45. Mem. ABA, Judge Adv. Gen. Assn. Office: Weil Gotshal & Manges 767 5th Ave New York NY 10153

WOLFF, KURT JAKOB, lawyer; b. Mannheim, Fed. Republic of Germany, Mar. 7, 1936; s. Ernest and Florence (Marx) W.; m. Sanda Lynn Dobrick, Dec. 28, 1958; children: Tracy Ellin, Brett Harris. AB, NYU, 1955; JD, U. Mich., 1958. Bar: N.Y. 1958, U.S. Supreme Ct. 1974, Hawaii 1985, Calif. 1988. Sole practice, N.Y.C., 1958—; assoc. Hays, Sklar & Herzberg, 1958-60; sr. assoc. Nathan, Mannheimer, Asche, Winer and Friedman, 1960-65; sr. assoc. Otterbourg, Steindler, Houston & Rosen, 1965-68, sr. ptnr., 1968-70, dir., treas. 1970—, chmn. bd., 1978-82, chief exec. officer, 1982— ; spl. master N.Y. Supreme Ct., 1977-85; vol. master U.S. Dist. Ct. (so. dist.) N.Y., 1978-82. Lectr., U. Mich. Law Sch.; mem. com. of visitors U. Mich. Law Sch., 1993—; spl. mediator Dept. Disciplinary Com. Appellate Divsn. First Judical Dept., 1991—. Mem. N.Y. State Bar Assn. (lectr.), Am. Arbitration Assn. (arbitrator), N.Y.C. Bar Assn. (arbitration com. 1979-83, state cts. of superior jurisdiction com. 1983-86, mem. com. on legal edn. and admission to the bar, 1991-94), ABA (chmn. ins. com. econs. sect. 1980-82, editor arbitration newsletter, arbitration com. sect. of litigation), Hawaii State Bar Assn., Calif. State Bar Assn., Gen. Arbitration Council Textile Industry N.Y.C., Fed. Bar Council. Contbr. articles to legal jours. Home: 9 Sunset Dr N Chappaqua NY 10514-1633 also: 48-641 Torrito Ct Palm Desert CA 92260 Office: 230 Park Ave New York NY 10169-0075

WOLFF, LARRY F., dental educator, researcher; b. Mankato, Minn., May 25, 1948; m. Charles Harold and Madelyn Catherine (Burns) W.; m. Elizabeth Spencer Thompson, Aug. 7, 1976; children: Adam, Ryan, Sara. BA in Biology, Mankato State U., 1970, M in Biology and Chemistry, 1971; PhD in Microbiology, Northwestern U., 1974; DDS, U. Minn., 1978; M in Periodontology, NYU, 1980; cert. in dentistry, Aarhus (Denmark) Dental Coll., 1979. Rsch. fellow Northwestern U., Chgo., 1972-74; prof. dentistry U. Minn., Mpls., 1980-85, assoc. prof., 1985—, assoc. prof. periodontology, 1985-94. Contbr. articles to profl. jours. Grantee Nat. Inst. Dental Rsch. NIH, 1982—, numerous corps., 1988—. Mem. Am. Acad. Periodontology, Am. Dental Assn., Internat. Assn. Dental Rsch., Internat. Assn. Periodontists, Minn. Dental Assn., Minn. Assn. Dental Rsch. Office: U Minn Sch Dentistry 515 Delaware St SE Minneapolis MN 55455-0348

WOLFF, MANFRED ERNST, medicinal chemist, pharmaceutical company executive; b. Berlin, Feb. 14, 1930; came to U.S., 1933; s. Adolph Abraham and Kate (Fraenkel) W.; m. Helen S. Scandalis, Aug. 1, 1953 (div. 1971); children: Stephen Andrew, David James, Edward Allen; m. Susan E. Hurbert, Jan. 19, 1973 (div. 1975); m. A. Gloria Johnson, Dec. 25, 1982. BS, U. Calif. at Berkeley, 1951, MS, 1953, PhD, 1955. Rsch. fellow U. Va., 1955-57; sr. medicinal chemist Smith, Kline & French Labs., Phila., 1957-60; mem. faculty U. Calif., San Francisco, 1960-82, prof. medicinal chemistry, 1965-82, chmn. dept. pharm. chemistry, 1970-82; dir. discovery rsch. Allergan Labs, Irvine, Calif., 1982-84; v.p. discovery rsch. Allergan Pharms., Irvine, 1984-89; v.p. R & D Immunopharmaceutics Inc., San Diego, 1989-91, sr. v.p. R & D, 1991-95; pres. Technipharm Cons., Laguna Beach, Calif., 1995—; adj. prof. medicinal chemistry U. So. Calif., 1982—; elected mem. U.S. Pharm. Conv. Com. of Revision, 1990—. Editor: Burger's Medicinal Chemistry and Drug Discovery, 5th edit., 1995-96; asst. editor Jour. Medicinal Chemistry, 1968-71; mem. editl. bd. Medicinal Chemistry Rsch., 1991-95; contbr. articles to profl. jours. Fellow AAAS, Am Assn. Pharm. Scientists; mem. Am. Chem. Soc., Licensing Execs. Soc. Patentee in field.

WOLFF, PETER ADALBERT, physicist, educator; b. Oakland, Calif., Nov. 15, 1923; s. Adalbert and Ruth Margaret W.; m. Catherine C. Carroll, Sept. 11, 1948; children: Catherine Mia, Peter Whitney. AB in Physics, U. Calif., Berkeley, 1945, PhD in Physics, 1951. Rsch. scientist Lawrence Radiation Lab., 1951-52; staff scientist Bell Telephone Lab., Murray Hill, N.J., 1952-63; dept. head, dir. electronic rsch. lab. Bell Telephone Lab., 1964-70; prof. physics U. Calif., San Diego, 1963-64; prof. physics, head solid state and atomic physics div., assoc. dir. Material Sci. Ctr. MIT, Cambridge, 1970-76, prof. physics, 1976-89, prof. emeritus, 1994—; dir. rsch. lab. of electronics MIT, 1976-81; dir. Francis Bitter Nat. Magnet Lab., 1981-87; dir. Draper Lab. Contbr. articles to profl. jours. Served with C.E. U.S. Army, 1945-46. Fellow Nippon Electric Co. Rsch. Inst., Princeton, 1989-94. Mem. Am. Phys. Soc., Am. Acad. Arts and Scis.

WOLFF, ROBERT JOHN, biology educator; b. Marquette, Mich., Jan. 22, 1952; s. Lee Stewart and Mary Joyce (Hamel) W.; m. Marcia Lynn Beugel, May 17, 1974. BA, Hope Coll., 1974; MA, Western Mich. U., 1976; PhD, U. Wis., Milw., 1985. Assoc. prof. biology Trinity Christian Coll., Palos Heights, Ill., 1980—; exec. dir. Associated Colls. of the Chgo. Area, 1994—; summer faculty DuSable Inst. Environ. Studies, Mancelona, Mich., 1986-87; faculty rsch. participant Argonne (Ill.) Nat. Lab., 1989—; vis. asst. prof. U. Ill., Chgo., 1990; sci. edn. cons. Sch. Dist. 161, Homewood, Ill., 1990—; exec. dir. Associated Colls. Chgo. Area. Author: Environmental Science in Action, 1993; contbr. numerous rsch. papers to jours., articles to gen. interest publs. Grantee Smithsonian Instn., Washington, 1985, Morton Arboretum, Lisle, Ill., 1985-87; Field assoc. Field Mus. Natural History, Chgo., 1991. Mem. Am. Arachnological Soc. (chair elections com. 1989, 90), Am. Soc. Zoologists (edn. com. 1990—), Associated Colls. of Chgo. Area (chair biology div. 1983-84, 88-89), Sigma Xi. Mem. Ref. Ch. in Am. Achievements include research in biology and conservation of spiders and other invertebrates. Home: 29 Sorrento Dr Palos Heights IL 60463-1752 Office: Trinity Christian Coll 6601 W College Dr Palos Heights IL 60463-1768

WOLFF, ROBERT PAUL, philosophy educator; b. N.Y.C., Dec. 27, 1933; s. Walter Harold and Charlotte (Ornstein) W.; m. Cynthia Griffin, June 9, 1962 (div. 1986); children: Patrick Gideon, Tobias Barrington; m. Susan Gould, Aug. 25, 1987. AB, Harvard U., 1953, MA in Philosophy, 1954, PhD, 1957. Instr. Harvard U., 1958-61; asst. prof. philosophy U. Chgo., 1961-63; vis. lectr. Wellesley Coll., 1963-64; assoc. prof. philosophy Columbia, 1964-69, prof., 1969-71; prof. philosophy U. Mass., Amherst, 1971-92, prof. Afro-Am. studies and philosophy, 1992—; grad. program dir. doctoral program in Afro-Am. Author: Kant's Theory of Mental Activity, 1963, A Critique of Pure Tolerance, 1965, Political Man and Social Man, 1966, Kant: A Collection of Critical Essays, 1967, Poverty of Liberalism, 1968, The Ideal of the University, 1969, In Defense of Anarchism, 1970, Philosophy: A Modern Encounter, 1971, The Autonomy of Reason, 1973, About Philosophy, 1975, 6th edit., 1995. Exec. dir. Harvard-Radcliffe Alumni/ae Against Apartheid, 1988-90; pres., exec. dir. Univ. Scholarships for South African Students, 1990—; co-dir. inst. advanced study in humanities U. Mass., 1992—, grad. program dir. Doctoral Program in Afro-Am. Studies, 1996—. Home: 107 Buffam Rd Amherst MA 01002-9723

WOLFF, SANFORD IRVING, lawyer; b. Chgo., Apr. 13, 1915; s. Herbert Barron and Libby (Levey) W.; m. Ann Barry, Mar. 21, 1970; children—Paul, David, Laura. BA, Knox Coll., 1936; grad., John Marshall Law Sch., U. Chgo., 1940. Bar: Ill. 1940, N.Y. 1973. Pvt. practice Chgo. and N.Y.C., 1945—; chief exec. AFTRA, AFL-CIO, N.Y.C., 1968-85; of counsel Becker, London & Kossow, N.Y.C., 1985—; chief exec. and counsel Am. Guild of Musical Artist, AFL-CIO, 1988-93. Trustee Harris Sch., Chgo. Served with AUS, 1940-45. Decorated Combat Inf. badge, Purple Heart, Bronze Star with cluster, Silver Star. Mem. ABA, Chgo. Bar Assn. Office: 1841 Broadway New York NY 10023-7603

WOLFF, SHELDON, radiobiologist, educator; b. Peabody, Mass., Sept. 22, 1928; s. Henry Herman and Goldie (Lipchitz) W.; m. Frances Faye Farbstein, Oct. 23, 1954; children: Victor Charles, Roger Kenneth, Jessica Raye. B.S. magna cum laude, Tufts U., 1950; M.A., Harvard U., 1951, Ph.D., 1953. Teaching fellow Harvard U., 1951-52; sr. research staff biology div. Oak Ridge Nat. Lab., 1953-66; prof. cytogenetics U. Calif., San Francisco, 1966—, dir. Lab. Radiobiology and Environ. Health, 1983-95; vis. prof. radiation biology U. Tenn., 1962, lectr., 1953-65; cons. several fed. sci. agys.; mem. health and environ. rsch. adv. com. U.S. Dept. Energy, 1986—, chmn., 1987-95; co-chmn. Joint NIH/Dept. Energy Subcom. on Human Genome, 1989-94. Editor: Chromosoma, 1983—; assoc. editor: Cancer Research, 1983—; Editorial bd.: Radiation Research, 1968-72, Photochemistry and Photobiology, 1962-72, Radiation Botany, 1964-86, Mutation Research, 1964—, Caryologia, 1967—, Radiation Effects, 1969-81, Genetics, 1972-85; Contbr. articles to sci. jours. Recipient E.O. Lawrence meml. award U.S. AEC, 1973. Mem. Genetics Soc. Am., Radiation Rsch. Soc. (counselor for biology 1968-72, Failla lectr. 1992, medal 1992), Am. Soc. Cell Biology, Environmental Mutagen Soc. (coun. 1972—, pres. 1980-81, award 1982), Internat. Assn. Environ. Mutagen Socs. (treas. 1978-85), Sigma Xi. Democrat. Home: 41 Eugene St Mill Valley CA 94941-1717 Office: U Calif Lab Radiobiology San Francisco CA 94143

WOLFF, SIDNEY CARNE, astronomer, observatory administrator; b. Sioux City, Iowa, June 6, 1941; d. George Albert and Ethel (Smith) Carne; m. Richard J. Wolff, Aug. 29, 1962. BA, Carleton Coll., 1962, DSc (hon.), 1985; PhD, U. Calif., Berkeley, 1966. Postgrad. research fellow Lick Obs, Santa Cruz, Calif., 1969; asst. astronomer U. Hawaii, Honolulu, 1967-71, assoc. astronomer, 1971-76; astronomer, assoc. dir. Inst. Astronomy, Honolulu, 1976-83, acting dir., 1983-84; dir. Kitt Peak Nat. Obs., Tucson, 1984-87, Nat. Optical Astronomy Observatories, 1987—; dir. Gemini Project Gemini 8-Meter Telescopes Project, 1992-94. Author: The A-Type Stars--Problems and Perspectives, 1983, (with others) Exploration of the Universe, 1987, Realm of the Universe, 1988, Frontiers of Astronomy, 1990; contbr. articles to profl. jours. Trustee Carleton Coll., 1989—. Rsch. fellow Lick Obs. Santa Cruz, Calif., 1967; recipient Nat. Meritorious Svc. award NSF, 1994. Mem. Astron. Soc. Pacific (pres. 1984-86, bd. dirs. 1979-85), Am. Astron. Soc. (coun. 1983-86, pres.-elect 1991, pres. 1992-94). Office: Nat Optical Astronomy Obs PO Box 26732 950 N Cherry Ave Tucson AZ 85719-4933

WOLFF, STEVEN ALEXANDER, arts and entertainment consultant; b. N.Y.C., July 18, 1957; s. Joel Charles and Joan (Mittlemark) W.; m. Gail English Loflin, June 12, 1988; children: Jessica Sadye, Ian Charles. BA in Econs., SUNY, Brockport, 1978; MFA in Theatre Adminstrn., Yale U., 1981. Cert. mgmt. cons. Cons. Artec Cons., N.Y.C., 1981-83; mgr. Theatre Projects Cons., N.Y.C., 1983-88; sr. v.p., prin. Hill Arts & Entertainment/AMS/ArtSoft Mgmt. Svcs., Guilford, Conn., 1988-91; pres., founder AMS Planning & Rsch. Corp., Fairfield, Conn., 1991—, Audience Insight LLC, Fairfield, 1996—; pres. Audience Insight LLC, Fawfield, Conn., 1996—; lectr. in field. Major projects include Aronoff Ctr. for Arts, Cin., Calif. Ctr. for Arts, Escondido, Metro-Dade Arts Ctr., Miami; contbr. articles to profl. jours. Recipient Cert. of Honor, ARC (nat. chpt.), 1978. Mem. Internat. Soc. Performing Arts Adminstrs., Internat. Downtown Assn., Assn. Performing Arts Presenters. Avocation: competitive offshore sailing. Office: AMS Planning & Rsch Corp 2150 Post Rd Fairfield CT 06430-5669

WOLFF, TOBIAS (JONATHAN ANSELL WOLFF), author; b. Birmingham, Ala., June 19, 1945; s. Arthur Saunders and Rosemary (Loftus) W.; m. Catherine Dolores Spohn, 1975; children: Michael, Patrick, Mary Elizabeth. BA, Oxford Univ., 1972, MA, 1975; MA, Stanford Univ., 1978. Mem. faculty Stanford (Calif.) U., Goddard Coll., Plainfield, Vt., Ariz. State U., Tempe, Syracuse (N.Y.) U.; reporter Washington Post. Author: In the Garden of the North American Martyrs, 1981 (St. Lawrence award for fiction 1982), The Barracks Thief, 1984 (PEN/Faulkner award for fiction 1985), Back in the World, 1985, This Boy's Life: A Memoir, 1989 (L.A. Times Book prize 1989), In Pharaoh's Army: Memories of the Lost War, 1994 (Esquire-Volvo-Winterstone's award, Eng. 1994); editor: Matters of Life and Death: New American Stories, 1983, The Stories of Anton Chekhov, 1987, Best American Short Stories, 1994, The Vintage Book of Contemporary American Stories, 1994. Recipient Wallace Stegner fellowship in creative writing, 1975-76; Nat. Endowment for the Arts fellowship in creative writing, 1978, 85; Mary Roberts Rinehart award, 1979; Ariz. Coun. on Arts and Humanities fellowship in creative writing, 1980, Guggenheim fellowship, 1982; Rea award, 1989; Whiting Writer's award, 1989, Lila-Wallace-Reader's Digest award, 1993, Lyndhurst Found. award, 1994. Office: Syracuse Univ Dept of English Syracuse NY 13244-0002

WOLFF, VIRGINIA EUWER, writer, secondary education educator; b. Portland, Oreg., Aug. 25, 1937; d. Eugene Courtney and Florence Evelyn (Craven) Euwer; m. Art Wolff, July 19, 1959 (div. July 1976); children: Anthony Richard, Juliet Dianne. AB, Smith Coll., 1959; postgrad., Goddard Coll., Warren Wilson Coll., L.I. U., Portland State U., Lewis & Clark Coll. Cert. tchr., Oreg. Tchr. The Miquon Sch., Phila., 1968-72, The Fiedel Sch., Glen Cove, N.Y., 1972-75, Hood River Valley (Oreg.) H.S., 1976-86, Mt. Hood Acad., Govt. Camp, Oreg., 1986—; 2d violinist Quartet con brio, Portland, 1989—. Author: Probably Still Nick Swansen, 1988, The Mozart Season, 1991, Make Lemonade, 1993. Violinist Mid-Columbia Sinfonietta, Hood River, 1976—, Oreg. Sinfonietta, Portland, 1988—. Recipient Young Adult Book award Internat. Reading Assn., 1989, PEN U.S.A. Ctr. West, 1989, Best Young Adult Book of Yr. award Mich. Libr. Assn., 1993, Child Study Children's Book award Bank Street Coll., 1984, Oreg. Book award Oreg. Lit. Arts, 1994. Mem. Soc. Children's Book Writers/Illustrators (Golden Kite 1994), Chamber Music Soc. Oreg. Avocations: chamber music, swimming, hiking, playing violin, gardening. Office: Curtis Brown Ltd care Marilyn E Marlow 10 Astor Pl New York NY 10003-6935

WOLFF, WILLIAM F., III, investment banker; b. N.Y.C., Apr. 12, 1945; s. William F. Jr. and Nancy (Wimpfheimer) W.; m. Phyllis Fox, June 1, 1969; children: Kenneth, Jonathan, Gillian. BA, U. Mich., 1967; JD, Columbia U., 1970, MBA, 1971. Bar: N.Y. 1970. V.p. Salomon Bros., Inc., N.Y.C., 1971-78; prin. Morgan Stanley & Co., N.Y.C., 1978-83; mng. dir. Lehman Brothers, N.Y.C., 1983—. Trustee St. David's Sch., N.Y.C., 1985—, Nat. Glaucoma Trust, 1992—. Mem. Univ Club (N.Y.), Ocean Beach Club (Elberon, N.J.) (trustee 1985-89). Office: Lehman Bros Three World Fin Ctr New York NY 10285

WOLFF, WILLIAM I., surgeon, educator; b. N.Y.C., Oct. 24, 1916; s. Julius Louis and Matilda (Brick) W.; m. Lillian Myrick, June 30, 1952 (div. 1967); children: Richard, Deborah, David, Alan, Lisa, Mitchell, George, Rebecca, Barbara; m. Rita T. Smith, Feb. 15, 1972. BS, NYU, 1936; MD, U. Md., 1940. Diplomate Am. Bd. Surgery, Am. Bd. Thoracic Surgery. Intern Cornell U. divsn. Bellevue Hosp., 1940-42, resident specializing in chest surgery Columbia U. divsn., 1942-43; resident, chief Bronx Vets. Hosp., 1946-48; chief thoracic surgery Deshon Vets. Hosp., 1949; practice medicine specializing in surgery N.Y.C., 1950—; assoc. prof. surgery NYU, N.Y.C., 1960—; dir. surgery Beth Israel Med. Ctr., N.Y.C., 1962-76; prof. surgery Mt. Sinai Sch. Medicine, N.Y.C., 1965—; 1st disting. lectr. soc. Am. Gastrointestinal Surgeons, 1987; vis. prof. or invited guest lectr. over 40 med. schs. univ. ctrs., over 150 tchg. hosps., numerous nat. and internat. cancer confs. in U.S., Eng., South Africa, Kenya, Israel, Mex., Can., USSR, France and P.R. Contbr. over 120 articles to med. jours., chpts. to books. Served to maj. M.C. AUS, 1943-46, ETO. Mem. ACS, Am. Coll. Gastroenterology (bd. govs.), Am. Assn. for Thoracic Surgery, Soc. Thoracic Surgeons (founding), Soc. for Surgery Alimentary Tract, Am. Coll. Chest Physicians, Am. Gastroenterologic Assn., Internat. Soc. Surgery, Internat. Cardiovasc. Surg. Soc., N.Y. Surg. Soc. (pres. 1980-81), N.Y. Acad. Medicine (chmn. sect. on surgery), Assn. Alumni Bellevue Hosp. (pres. 1982), Aspetuck Valley Country Club. Achievements include early contributor to subject of cardiac resuscitation by ccardiac message; originator of scientific procedure of colonoscopy and removal of colonic polyps. Avocations: gardening, ballet, tennis, theatre. Office: 44 Gramercy Park N New York NY 10010-6310

WOLFFE, ALAN PAUL, molecular embryologist, molecular biologist; b. Burton-on-Trent, Staffordshire, Eng., June 21, 1959; s. Ronald and Mildred (Hasbury) W.; m. Elizabeth Jane Hall, Aug. 21, 1982. BA with honors in Biochemistry, Oxford U., 1981; PhD, MRC London, 1984. Postdoctoral fellow Carnegie Instn., Balt., 1984-86, prin. investigator, 1987; prin. investigator, asst. prof. Nat. Inst. Diabetes and Digestive and Kidney Diseases, Bethesda, Md., 1988-90; assoc. prof. Nat. Inst. Diabetes and Digestive and Kidney Diseases, Bethesda, 1990; chief lab. molecular embryology Nat. Inst. Child Health and Human Devel., Bethesda, 1990—, prof., 1992—; ad hoc reviewer NSF, 1989-92, molecular biology study sect. NIH, 1990; mem. biologyical scis. study sect. NIH, 1991—; mem. biochemistry program panel NSF, 1992-93; chmn. meeting Chromatin Structure and Transcription Fedn. Am. Socs. Exptl. Biology, 1993. Author: Chromatin: Structure and Function, 1992; contbr. articles. Fellow Rsch. Coun. Predoctoral Rsch., 1981-84, European Molecular Biology Orng., 1984-86; grantee Am. Cancer Soc., 1987, Fogarty Internat. Ctr., 1991, NIH, 1992, NSF, 1993. Mem. AAAS, Am. Assn. Cancer Rsch., Am. Soc. Microbiology, Am. Soc. Cell Biology, Brit. Soc. Devel. Biology, Biochemical Soc. (U.K.). Achievements include major contributions to elucidating role of nucleic acid packaging proteins (histones for DNA, Y-box proteins for RNA) in regulating gene expression (transcription of DNA, translation of RNA). Office: Nat Inst Child Health & Human Devel Molecular Embryol Lab Rm B1A13 9000 Rockville Pike Bldg 6 Bethesda MD 20892-0001

WOLFGANG, BONNIE ARLENE, musician, bassoonist; b. Caribou, Maine, Sept. 29, 1944; d. Ralph Edison and Arlene Alta (Obetz) W.; m. Eugene Alexander Pridonoff, July 3, 1965 (div. Sept. 1977); children: George Randall, Anton Alexander, Stephan Eugene. MusB, Curtis Inst. Music, Phila., 1967. Soloist Phila. Orch., 1966; soloist with various orchs. U.S., Cen. Am., 1966-75; prin. bassoonist Phoenix Symphony, 1976—, with Woodwind Quintet, 1986—. Home: 9448 N 106th St Scottsdale AZ 85258-6056

WOLFGANG, JAMES STEPHEN, history educator, minister; b. Indpls., Dec. 8, 1948; s. James Harold and Alma Jean (Cowgill) W.; m. Bette Ashworth, June 5, 1969; children: Lesley Dawn, Lindsay Brooke. BA, Ind. Wesleyan U., 1970; MA, Butler U., 1975; MDiv, So. Bapt. Theol. Sem., 1978; MA, Vanderbilt U., 1990. Ordained min., Ch. of Christ, 1969. Minister Expwy. Ch. of Christ, Louisville, 1975-79, Danville (Ky.) Ch. of Christ, 1979-96; instr. history U. Ky., Lexington, 1994—; vis. prof. Internat. Christian U., Vienna, Austria, 1990; vis. instr. Redlands Coll. Brisbane, Australia, 1993; instr. history Lexington C.C., 1993-95. Mem. editl. adv. bd. Louisville Courier-Jour., 1994-95; news reader Sta. WUKY-FM, 1994—; contbr. articles to profl. jours. Pres. PTA Danville Ind. Schs., 1983, 86, 91. Recipient Grosswirth-Salny award Mensa Ednl. Rsch. Found., 1990, Lester London award, 1991. Mem. Am. Hist. Assn., Am. Soc. Ch. History, Orgn. Am. Historians, So. Hist. Assn., Mensa (Bluegrass chpt., bd. govs. 1990-94), Hospice (Heritage chpt., bd. dirs. 1993—, v.p. 1994—). Home: 803 Sunset Dr Danville KY 40422-1156 Office: U Ky 1743 Patterson Tower Lexington KY 40506-0027

WOLFGANG, MARVIN EUGENE, sociologist, criminologist, educator; b. Millersburg, Pa., Nov. 14, 1924; s. Charles T. and Pauline (Sweigard) W.; m. Lenora D. Poden, June 1, 1957; children: Karen Eleanor, Nina Victoria. B.A., Dickinson Coll., Carlisle, Pa., 1948; M.A., U. Pa., 1950, Ph.D., 1955. Instr., asst. prof. Lebanon Valley Coll., 1948-52; instr. to prof. sociology U. Pa., Phila., 1952—; chmn. dept. U. Pa., 1968-72, prof. sociology and law, 1972—; also dir. Sellin Ctr. for Studies in Criminology and Criminal Law; vis. prof., fellow Churchill Coll., U. Cambridge, Eng., 1968-69; cons. Rand Corp.; Chmn. rev. com. on crime and delinquency NIMH, 1971-73; rsch. dir. Nat. Commn. on Causes and Prevention of Violence, 1968-69; commr. Nat. Commn. on Obscenity and Pornography, 1968-70. Author: Patterns in Criminal Homicide, 1958, Crime and Race, 1964, (with T. Sellin) The Measurement of Delinquency, 1964, (with F. Ferracuti) The Subculture of Violence, 1967, Crime and Culture, 1968, (with L. Radzinowicz) Crime and Justice, 3 vols, 1971, rev. edit., 1977, (with T. Sellin, R. Figlio) Delinquency in a Birth Cohort, 1972, (with R. Figlio, T. Thornberry) Criminology Index, 2 vols, 1975, Evaluating Criminology, 1978, (with N. Weiner) Criminal Violence, (with R. Figlio et al) National Survey of Crime Severity, 1986, (with T. THornberry and R. Figlio) From Boy to Man: From Delinquency to Crime, 1987, (with N. Weiner) Violent Crime, Violent Criminals, Pathways to Criminal Violence, 1988, (with P. Tracy and R. Figlio) Delinquency Careers in Two Birth Cohorts, 1990, (with D. Nevares and P. Tracy) Delinquency in Puerto Rico: The 1970 Birth Cohort Study, 1991. Chmn., bd. dirs. Thomas Skelton Harrison Found.; chmn. Eisenhower Found. With AUS, 1943-45, ETO. Recipient Fulbright rsch. award, 1957-58, Hans von Hentig award World Soc. Victimology, 1988; Guggenheim fellow, 1957-58, 68-69. Mem. Am. Philos. Soc., Am. Acad. Arts and Scis., Internat. Soc. Criminology, Am. Soc. Criminology (past pres., rsch. award 1960, Edwin Sutherland award 1989), Am. Acad. Polit. and Social Sci. (pres.), Pa. Prison Soc. (bd. dirs., past pres.). Home: 4106 Locust St Philadelphia PA 19104-3509 Office: Am Acad Polit & Social Sci 3937 Chestnut St Philadelphia PA 19104-3110

WOLFINGER, RAYMOND EDWIN, political science educator; b. San Francisco, June 29, 1931; s. Raymond Edwin and Hilda (Holm) W.; m. Barbara Kaye, Aug. 8, 1960; 1 son, Nicholas Holm. A.B., U. Calif.-Berkeley, 1951; M.A., U. Ill., 1955; Ph.D., Yale U., 1961. Asst. prof. polit. sci. Stanford (Calif.) U., Calif., 1961-66; assoc. prof. Stanford U., Calif., 1966-70, prof., 1970-71; prof. U. Calif.-Berkeley, 1971—, Heller prof. polit. sci., 1995—; dir. U. Calif. Data Archive and Tech. Assistance, 1980-92; chmn. bd. overseers Nat. Election Studies, Ann Arbor, Mich., 1982-86. Author: The Politics of Progress, 1974, (with others) Dynamics of American Politics, 1976, 80, (with Steven J. Rosenstone) Who Votes, 1980, (with others) The Myth of the Independent Voter, 1992; mem. editorial bd. Brit. Jour. Polit. Sci., 1980-84, Am. Polit. Sci. Rev., 1985-88. Bd. dirs. S.W. Voter Rsch. Inst. Inc., San Antonio, 1988-96, Consortium of Social Sci. Assns., 1987-93, pres. 1988-90. 1st lt. U.S. Army, 1951-53. Fellow Ctr. for Advanced Study in Behavioral Scis., 1960-61; Guggenheim fellow, 1965; Ford Found. faculty research fellow, 1970-71. Fellow Am. Acad. Arts and Scis.; mem. Am. Polit. Sci. Assn. (sec. 1981-82), AAUP (council 1981-84), Western Polit. Sci. Assn. (v.p. 1988-89, pres. 1989-90). Democrat. Office: U Calif Dept Polit Sci Berkeley CA 94720

WOLFLE, DAEL LEE, public affairs educator; b. Puyallup, Wash., Mar. 5, 1906; s. David H. and Elizabeth (Pauly) W.; m. Helen Morrill, Dec. 28, 1929 (dec. July 1988); children: Janet Helen (Mrs. Wilhelm G. Christophersen), Lee Morrill, John Morrill. B.S., U. Wash., 1927, M.S., 1928; postgrad., U. Chgo., summers 1929, 30; Ph.D., Ohio State U., 1931, D.Sc., 1957; D.Sc., Drexel U., 1956, Western Mich. U., 1960. Instr. psychology Ohio State U., 1929-32; prof. psychology U. Miss., 1932-36; examiner in biol. scis. U. Chgo., 1936-39, asst. prof. psychology, 1938-43, assoc. prof., 1943-45; on leave for war work with Signal Corps, 1941-43; with OSRD, 1944-45; exec. sec. Am. Psychol. Assn., 1946-50; dir. commn. on human resources and advanced tng. Assoc. Research Councils, 1950-54; exec. officer AAAS, 1954-70; editor Sci., 1955, pub., 1955-70; prof. pub. affairs U. Wash., Seattle, 1970-76; prof. emeritus U. Wash., 1976—; mem. sci. adv. bd. USAF, 1953-57; mem. def. sci. bd. Dept. Def., 1957-61; mem. adv. council on mental health NIMH, 1960-64; mem. nat. adv. health council USPHS, 1965-66; mem. commn. on human resources NRC, 1974-78; mem. adv. bd. Geophys. Inst., Fairbanks, Alaska., 1970-93, chmn. adv. bd., 1972-81. Author: Factor Analysis to 1940, 1941, Science and Public Policy 1959, The Uses of Talent, 1971, The Home of Science, 1972, Renewing a Scientific Society, 1989; editor: America's Resources of Specialized Talent, 1954. Trustee Russell Sage Found., 1961-78, Pacific Sci. Cent. Found., 1962-80, Biol. Scis. Curriculum Study, 1980-85; chmn. bd. J. McK. Cattell Fund, 1962-82. Named Alumnus Summa Laude Dignatus, U. Wash., 1979. Mem. AAAS, (pres. Pacific divsn. 1991-92, exec. com. 1990—), AAUP, APA, Am. Acad. Arts and Scis. (exec. com. western sect. 1985-92), Sigma Xi. Home: 4545 Sand Point Way NE Apt 805 Seattle WA 98105-3932 Office: U Wash Grad Sch Pub Affairs Seattle WA 98195

WOLFLEY, ALAN, corporate executive; b. Rockford, Ill., Dec. 23, 1923; s. Chester E. and Lois (Karlson) W.; m. Joanne Higgins, Jan. 6, 1945; children: C. Alan, Susan (Mrs. Peter M. Baumgartner), E. William. B.A. cum laude, Middlebury (Vt.) Coll., 1947; M.B.A., Harvard U., 1949. Budget supr. Merck & Co., Rahway, N.J., 1949-52; asst. to treas. Standard Vacuum Oil Co., 1952-59; asst. treas. Parke-Davis & Co., 1959-64; v.p. finance Cardorundum Co., 1964-68; v.p. finance, dir. Scovill Mfg. Co., 1968-71; exec. v.p., mem. exec. com., dir. Cerro Corp., N.Y.C., 1971-76; dir. Southern Peru Copper Co., N.Y.C., 1973-77, Marmon Group, Inc., Chgo., 1977-86; pres., dir. Greenley Energy Corp., 1978-88; U.S.A. rep. Coenco Corp., 1989—. Mem. nat. council Salk Inst., 1979-86. Served to capt. USAAF, World War II. Decorated Silver Star, D.F.C., Air medal, Purple Heart. Mem. Harvard (N.Y.C.), Wee Burn Country Club (Darien, Conn.), Pine Valley Golf Club (Clementon, N.J.), Landsdowne Club (London, Eng.), Chi Psi. Republican. Methodist. Home: 22 Canaan Close New Canaan CT 06840-4928 Office: Coenco Corp PO Box 218 New Canaan CT 06840-0218

WOLFMAN, BERNARD, lawyer, educator; b. Phila., July 8, 1924; s. Nathan and Elizabeth (Coff) W.; m. Zelda Bernstein, Dec. 25, 1948 (dec. Oct. 1973); children: Jonathan L., Brian S., Dina A.; m. Toni A. Grotta, June 12, 1977. AB, U. Pa., 1946, JD, 1948; LLD (hon.), Jewish Theol. Sem., 1971, Capital U., 1990. Bar: Pa. 1949, Mass. 1976. Mem. law firm Wolf, Block, Schorr & Solis-Cohen, Phila., 1948-63; prof. law U. Pa. Law Sch., 1963-76, dean, 1970-75, Kenneth W. Gemmill prof. tax law and tax policy, 1973-76, chmn. Faculty Senate, 1969-70; Fessenden prof. law Harvard U., 1976—; vis. prof. Stanford U. Law Sch., summer 1982, NYU Law Sch., 1987-88; Irvine lectr. Cornell U. Law Sch., 1980; Halle lectr. Case Western Res. U. Law Sch., 1983, Sugarman lectr., 1989; Cleve. State U. Sch. Law, 1983; Altheimer lectr. U. Ark. Sch. Law, Little Rock, 1994; mem. editl. bds. law divsn. Little Brown & Co., Jour. Corp. Taxation; gen. counsel AAUP, 1966-68, mem. coun., 1979-82; cons. to ind. counsel Lawrence E. Walsh (Iran-Contra prosecution), 1987-89; mem. adv. group to commr. internal revenue, 1966-67; cons. tax policy U.S. Treasury Dept., 1963-68, 77-80; chmn. Task Force Univ. Governance, U. Pa., 1968-70; mem. steering com. IRA project Adminstrv. Conf. U.S., 1974-80; vice chmn. bd. advs. NYU-IRS Continuing Profl. Edn. Project, 1981-85; mem. legal activities policy bd. Tax Analysts, 1974—; mem. exec. com. Fed. Tax Inst. New Eng., 1976—. Author: Federal Income Taxation of Corporate Enterprise, 1971, 3d edit., 1990, (with J. Holden and D. Schenk) Ethical Problems in Federal Tax Practice, 1981 3d edit. 1995, (with J. Holden and K. Harris) Standards of Tax Practice, 1991, 3d edit. 1995; sr. author: Dissent Without Opinion: The Behavior of Justice William O. Douglas in Federal Tax Cases, 1975; contbr. articles to profl. jours. Adv. com. Commn. Philanthropy and Pub. Needs, 1973-75; mem. Phila. regional council Pa. Gov.'s Justice Commn., 1973-75; trustee Found. Center, N.Y.C., 1970-76, Fedn. Jewish Agys. Greater Phila., 1968-74; bd. dirs. Phila. Lawyers Com. Civil Rights Under Law, 1970-74, Phila. Defender Assn., 1955-69; mem. Nat. Lawyers Adv. Council of Earl Warren Legal Tng. Program. Served with AUS, 1943-45. Fellow Am. Bar Found., Am. Coll. Tax Counsel (regent 1st cir.); mem. ABA (past chmn. com. on taxation, coun. sect. individual rights and responsibilities 1978-82, coun. sect. taxation 1982-85), Am. Law Inst. (cons. fed. income tax project 1974—), ACLU (nat. dir. 1973-75), Order of Coif (exec. com. 1982-91, v.p. 1986-89, pres. 1989-91), Phi Beta Kappa. Home: 229 Brattle St Cambridge MA 02138-4623 Office: Law Sch Harvard U Cambridge MA 02138

WOLFMAN, BRUNETTA REID, education educator; b. Clarksdale, Miss., Sept. 4, 1931; d. Willie Orlando and Belle Victoria (Allen) Reid Griffin; m. Burton Wolfman, Oct. 4, 1952; children: Andrea, Jeffrey. BA, U. Calif., Berkeley, 1957, MA, 1968, PhD, 1971; DHL (hon.), Boston U., 1983; DP (hon.), Northeastern U., 1983; DL (hon.), Regis Coll., 1984, Stonehill Coll., 1985; DHL, Suffolk U., 1985; DET (hon.), Wentworth Inst., 1987; AA (hon.), Roxbury Community Coll., 1988. Asst. dean faculty Dartmouth Coll., Hanover, N.H., 1972-74; asst. v.p. acad. affairs U. Mass., Boston, 1974-76; acad. dean Wheelock Coll., Boston, 1976-78; cons. Arthur D. Little, Cambridge, Mass., 1978; dir. policy planning Dept. Edn., Boston, 1978-82; pres. Roxbury C.C., Boston, 1983-88, ACE sr. assoc., 1988-94, NAWE sr. assoc., 1994—; assoc. v.p. acad. affairs George Washington U., Washington, 1989-92, prof. edn., 1992-96, prof. edn. emeritus, 1996—; pres. bd. dirs. Literacy Vols. of Capitol Region; mem. comm. com. bd., pub. rels. com. LVA, Inc.; bd. dirs. Am. Coun. Edn., Harvard Cmty. Health Plan. Author: Roles, 1983; contbr. articles to profl. jours. Bd. overseers Wellesley (Mass.) Coll., 1981; bd. dirs. Boston-Fenway Program, 1977, Freedom House, Boston, 1983, Boston Pvt. Industry Coun., 1983, NCCJ, Boston, 1983, co-chmn.; bd. overseers Boston Symphony Orch.; trustee Mus. Fine Arts, Boston; councilor Coun. on Edn. for Pub. Health. Recipient Freedom award NAACP No. Calif., 1971, Amelia Earhart award Women's Edn. and Indsl. Union, Boston, 1983; Sr. scholar Nat. Assn. Women in Edn. Mem. Am. Sociol. Assn., Assn. Black Women in Higher Edn., D.C. Sociol. Soc., Greater Boston C. of C. (edn. com. 1982), Cosmos Club (Washington), Pi Lambda Theta, Alpha Kappa Alpha (Humanitarian award 1984), Phi Delta Kappa (pres. GW chpt.). Home: 657 Commercial St Provincetown MA 02657 Office: George Washington U 2134 G St NW Washington DC 20037-2797

WOLFMAN, EARL FRANK, JR., surgeon, educator; b. Buffalo, Sept. 14, 1926; s. Earl Frank and Alfreda (Peterson) W.; m. Lois Jeannette Walker, Dec. 28, 1946; children—Nancy Jeannette, David Earl, Carol Anne. BS cum laude, Harvard U., 1946; MD cum laude, U. Mich., 1950. Diplomate Am. Bd. Surgery. Intern U. Mich., Ann Arbor, 1950-51, asst. resident in surgery, 1951-52, resident in surgery, 1954-55, from jr. clin. instr. surgery to assoc. prof., 1955-66, asst. to dean, 1960-61, asst. dean, 1961-64; practice medicine specializing in surgery, 1957—, Sacramento, 1966—; prof. surgery Sch. Medicine, U. Calif., Davis, 1966—, chmn. dept. surgery, 1966-78, assoc. dean, 1966-76; mem. staff, chief surg. svcs. Sacramento (Calif.) Med. Ctr., 1966-78. Contbr. articles to profl. jours. Served to lt. M.C. USNR, 1952-54. Fellow ACS; mem. AMA (del. 1987—), Ctrl. Surg. Soc., Western Surg. Soc., Sacramento Surg. Soc., Pacific Coast Surg. Soc., Calif. Acad. Medicine, Frederick A. Coller Surg. Soc., Pan Am. Med. Assn., Soc. Surgery Alimentary Tract, Am. Assn. Endocrine Surgeons, Sacramento Med. Soc., Yolo Med. Soc., Calif. Med. Assn. (trustee 1991—), Am. Soc. Gen. Surgeons, Comstock Club. Methodist. Home: 44770 N El Macero Dr PO Box 3086 El Macero CA 95618 Office: U Calif-Davis Sch Medicine Dept Surgery 4301 X St Sacramento CA 95817-2214

WOLFMAN, IRA JOEL, editor, writer; b. Oct. 7, 1950; s. Aaron and Beatrice Ruth (Perlo) W.; m. Julia Diamant, June 24, 1979 (dec. 1982); m. Ronda Small, Dec. 20, 1991. B.A. cum laude, SUNY, Albany, 1971. News editor Washington Park Spirit, Albany, N.Y., 1971-73; sr. editor Smash mag., N.Y.C., 1975-76, Circus mag., N.Y.C., 1976-79; assoc. editor 3-2-1 Contact mag., N.Y.C., 1979-80; editor Sesame St Parents' Newsletter, N.Y.C., 1980-83; editor in chief Enter mag., N.Y.C., 1983-85, Sesame St. mag., Parents Guide, 1990-94; v.p., editor-in-chief Adult Consumer mags. Children's Television Workshop, N.Y.C., 1994—; newsletter editor Found. for Grandparenting, Mt. Kisco, N.Y., 1984-87; editor Am. Writer, 1988-89; freelance writer and editor, contbr. to Travel & Leisure, Architectural Record, Metropolis, N.Y. Daily News, Ms., Spy, 1985—. Author: Do People Grow on Family Trees? Genealogy for Kids and Other Beginners, 1991, My World and Globe, 1991. N.Y. State Legis. Corrs. scholar, 1970. Jewish.

WOLFMAN JACK (ROBERT WESTON SMITH), radio personality; b. Bklyn., Jan. 21, 1938; s. Anson Weston and Rosmond (Small) S.; m. Lou Lamb, May 5, 1961; children: Joy Rene, Tod Weston. Grad. high sch., L.I., N.Y.; 1st class lic., Nat. Acad. Broadcasting, Washington. Radio personality, salesman, sta. mgr. Universal Broadcasting, Shreveport, La. and Mpls.; radio personality, salesman, owner U.S. rights Sta. XERF, Del Rio, Tex., 1961-65; radio personality, sta. mgr., owner U.S. rights Sta. XERB, Rosarito Beach, Calif., 1966-71; radio personality Armed Forces Radio, 1970-86, Sta. KDAY, Los Angeles, 1971-73, Sta. WNBC, N.Y.C., 1973-74, 1976-77; first English-speaking radio personality in Japan Sta. FM-Tokyo, 1975-77; radio personality syndicated on 2,177 stations in 53 fgn. countries, 1973—; tv personality-host The Midnight Special, L.A., 1973-82, The Wolfman Jack Show, 24 countries and U.S., 1978-79, The Disco Awards Special, 1979; appears as actor 26 U.S. network tv shows, 1974—; tv personality-host The Rock'N' Roll Palace, 1988—. Appeared in films American Graffiti, 1973, Hanging on a Star, 1976, Dead Man's Curve, 1977, Motel Hell, 1980, Mortuary Academy, 1987; author: Have Mercy!, 1995, (with Byron Laursen) Have Mercy--Confessions of the Original Rock 'n' Roll Animal. Mem. AFTRA, SAG, AGVA, Alliance Can. Cinema, TV and Radio Artists, Rhythm and Blues Found. Republican. Episcopalian. Subject of 18 U.S. pop/rock songs including Clap for the Wolfman by The Guess Who, Living on the Highway by Freddie King, and Wolfman Jack by Todd Rundgren. *Died July 1, 1995.*

WOLFORD, DENNIS ARTHUR, hospital administrator; b. Ft. Wayne, Ind., Aug. 8, 1946; s. Donald Arthur and Madelyn Marie (Howell) W.; m. Margaret Bearden, June 19, 1986; children: Jack Douglas, Michele. B.S. in Bus. Adminstrn., Tusculum Coll., 1968. Auditor, U.S. GAO, Washington, 1968-70; exec. mgr. Irene Byron Hosp., Fort Wayne, 1970-73; asst. adminstr. McCray Meml. Hosp., Kendallville, Ind., 1973-78, adminstr., 1978-84, Macon County Gen. Hosp., Lafayette, Tenn., 1984—. Pres. Cole Ctr. Family YMCA, Kendallville, 1982-84; pres. bd. dirs. Tenn. Vocat. Tng. Ctr., 1989-93. Fellow Am. Coll. Healthcare Exec.; mem. Healthcare Fin. Mgmt. Assn., Kendallville C. of C. (bd. dirs. 1981-83), Macon County C. of C. (pres. bd. dirs. 1992-93), Rotary (v.p. 1992, pres. 1993). Republican. Lutheran. Avocations: swimming, racquetball, volleyball, skiing, traveling. Home: 105 Sonoma Dr Lafayette TN 37083-3154 Office: Macon County Gen Hosp PO Box 378 Lafayette TN 37083-0378

WOLFRAM, STEPHEN, physicist, computer company executive; b. London, Aug. 29, 1959; came to U.S., 1978; Degree, Eton Coll., 1976, Oxford U., 1978; PhD in Theoretical Physics, Calif. Inst. Tech., 1979. With Calif. Inst. Tech., Pasadena, 1979-82, Inst. for Advanced Study, Princeton, N.J., 1983-86; prof. physics, math, computer sci. U. Ill., Champaign, 1986—; pres., CEO Wolfram Rsch. Inc., Champaign, 1987—. Author: Theory and Applications of Cellular Automata, 1986, Mathematica, 1988, Cellular Automata and Complexity, 1994; editor jour. Complex Systems, 1987—. Fellow MacArthur Found., 1981. Office: Wolfram Rsch Inc 100 Trade Center Dr Champaign IL 61820

WOLFRAM, THOMAS, physicist; b. St. Louis, July 27, 1936; s. Ferdinand I. and Audrey H. (Calvert) W.; m. Eleanor Elaine Burger, May 22, 1965; children: Michael, Gregory, Melanie, Susan, Steven. BA, U. Calif., Riverside, 1959, PhD in Physics, 1963; MA in Physics, UCLA, 1960. Dir. divsn. physics and chemistry; Engr. Atomics Internat., Canoga Park, Calif., 1960-63; mem. tech. staff N.Am. Aviation Corp. Sci. Ctr., Thousand Oaks, Calif., 1963-68; group leader in solid state physics Rockwell Internat. Sci. Ctr., Thousand Oaks, 1968-72, dir. div. physics and chemistry, 1972-74; prof. physics, chmn. dept. physics and astronomy U. Mo., Columbia, 1974-83; dir. phys. tech. divsn. AMOCO Corp., 1983-87; v.p., gen. mgr. AMOCO Laser Co., 1987-95; bus. cons., 1995—; cons. in field. Editor: Inelastic Electron Tunneling Spectroscopy, 1978; contbr. rsch. articles to numerous publs. in field. Recipient Disting. Prof. award Argonne Univs. Assn., 1977. Fellow Am. Phys. Soc. Office: Amoco Laser Co 1251 Frontenac Rd Naperville IL 60563-1750 *Crisis is the catalyst for constructive change.*

WOLFSCHMIDT, WILLI See FLINT, WILLIS WOLFSCHMIDT

WOLFSHEIMER, RONALD MILTON, financial services executive; b. Washington, July 24, 1952; s. Frank and Lois (Baer) W.; m. Janet Rosen; children: Chad, Jacob. BS, Ind. U., 1974. Audit staff Arthur Andersen & Co., Washington, 1974-76; audit supr. Alexander Grant & Co., Washington, 1976-79; sr. v.p. Calvert Group, Ltd., Bethesda, Md., 1979-95, CFO, 1995—; bd. dirs. Calvert Adminstrv. Svcs. Co., Bethesda, 1980—. Home: 11402 Duryea Dr Potomac MD 20854-3115 Office: Calvert Group Ltd 4550 Montgomery Ave Ste 1000N Bethesda MD 20814-3343

WOLFSON, AARON HOWARD, radiation oncologist, educator; b. Nashville, May 13, 1955; s. Sorrell Louis and Jacqueline Adele (Falis) W.; m. Adrienne Sue Mates, Dec. 16, 1979; children: Alexis Ellyn, Andrew Lane. BA, U. Fla., 1978, MD, 1982. Diplomate Am. Bd. Radiology. Intern internal medicine Jackson Meml. Hosp., Miami, Fla., 1982-83; staff physician Pub. Health Svc., Miami, 1983-85; pvt. practice Palm Beach Gardens, Fla., 1985-86; resident in radiation oncology Med. Coll. Va., Richmond, 1986-89; instr. radiation oncology U. Miami Sch. Medicine, 1989-91, asst. prof., 1991—. Contbr. articles to profl. jours. Bd. dirs. Children's Home Soc., Ft. Lauderdale, Fla., 1993—, Temple Beth Israel, Sunrise, Fla., 1994—; mem. spkrs. bur. U. Miami, 1993—; vol. spkr. Broward County Schs., 1990—. Sylvester Cancer Ctr. grantee, 1992. Mem. Gynecologic Oncology Group, Radiation Therapy Oncology Group, Am. Soc. Therapeutic Radiology and Oncology, Temple Beth Israel Men's Club (v.p. 1993—). Jewish. Achievements include research on malignant tumors of the uterus. Avocations: bridge, tennis, reading science fiction. Office: Univ of Miami 1475 NW 12th Ave # D-31 Miami FL 33136-1002

WOLFSON, HAROLD, public relations consultant; b. Pawtucket, R.I., Oct. 3, 1926; s. Samuel and Dora (Kasindorf) W.; m. Marian A. Granrud, Oct. 9, 1953; children: Nancy C. Jenne, Peter G. BA, Yale U., 1949. Feature writer N.Y. Jour.-Am., N.Y.C., 1949-55; v.p. Ruder & Finn Inc., N.Y.C., 1955-63; pres. Rubenstein, Wolfson & Co., N.Y.C., 1963-89; pub. rels. cons. Larchmont, N.Y. Served with USN, 1944-46. Mem. Pub. Relations Soc. Am. (chmn. pub. relations com. N.Y. chpt. 1984-86). Home and Office: 20 Iselin Ter Larchmont NY 10538-2631

WOLFSON, IRWIN M., insurance company executive; b. Bronx, N.Y., May 29, 1937; s. Herman M. and Kate (Greenstein) W.; m. Pauline S. Frechtel, Dec. 25, 1962; children: Fran M., Lisa G. BS in Econs., NYU, 1960. Owner/CEO Wolfson Agency, Yonkers, N.Y., 1973—; instr., owner Successful Adult Fin. Seminars, Yonkers, 1990—. Mem. operating bd. Child Abuse Prevention Ctr., White Plains, N.Y., 1990—. Sgt. U.S. Army, 1960-66. Recipient Achievement award Congressman Elliot Engel, 1992, proclamation From T. Zaleski (Mayor) City of Yonkers, 1992, letter of Recognition from M. Cuomo (Governor) N.Y. 1992; Irwin M. Wolfson Day proclaimed by A. O'Rourk (County Exec.) N.Y. 1992. Mem. Yonkers Nat. Exch. Club (pres. 1990-91, N.Y. dist. dir. 1991-95, N.Y. dist. pres. 1996). Home: 11-4 Jackson Ave Scarsdale NY 10583-3104 Office: Wolfson Agency 475 Tuckahoe Rd Yonkers NY 10710-5707

WOLFSON, LARRY M., lawyer; b. Springfield, Ill., June 12, 1947; m. Cynthia Sherwood, 1972; children: Sharon Eve, Rachel Beth, Anna Faye. BSBA, Northwestern U., 1969; JD cum laude, U. Mich., 1974. Bar: Ill. 1974. Ptnr. Jenner & Block, Chgo. Mem. ABA, Ill. State Bar (lectr. Comml. Banking and Bankruptcy Law Edn. Series 1990), Chgo. Bar Assn., Chgo. Coun. Lawyers, Comml. Law League Am., Am. Bankruptcy Inst. Office: Jenner & Block 1 E Ibm Plz Chicago IL 60611

WOLFSON, LAWRENCE AARON, hospital administrator; b. Chgo., July 11, 1941; s. Norman William and Doris D. (Brownstein) W.; m. Cheryl Jean Vogel, Feb. 6, 1987; children: Marc David, Sara Elizabeth, Aaron Michael, Ryan Anthony, Ashley Michelle. BA in Biology, Ind. U., South Bend, 1973, MBA, 1980. Sales rep. Gen. Med. Corp., South Bend, 1973-75, Hoechst-Roussel Pharmaceuticals, Somerville, N.J., 1975-79; purchasing agt. Simon Bros., Inc., South Bend, 1979-81; purchasing mgr. Ingalls Meml. Hosp., Harvey, Ill., 1981-83; dir. purchasing Community Hosp., Munster, Ind., 1983-86; corp. purchasing mgr. Columbus-Cuneo-Cabrini Med. Ctr., Chgo., 1986-88; materials mgmt. cons. South Western Med. Ctr., Chgo., 1988-91; asst. dir. materials mgmt. Michael Reese Hosp. and Med. Ctr., Chgo., 1989-91; dir. material mgmt. Regional Med. Ctr. at Memphis, 1991—; mem. editorial bd. Hosp. Material Mgmt. Quarterly, Aspens Pubs. Cubmaster Cub Scouts, South Bend, 1976-78, Cub Scouts, Cordova, 1995—. With USN, 1961-71. Mem. Am. Soc. Hosp. Materials Mgmt., Healthcare Materials Mgmt. Soc. (regional rep. 1984, cert. profl. in health care material mgmt., Material Mgr. of Yr. 1995), Nat. Assn. Purchasing Mgmt., Am. Soc. Clin. Pathologists (affiliate), Am. Legion, B'nai Brith (pres. 1980-81). Jewish.

WOLFSON, MARK ALAN, investment and business educator; b. Chgo., Sept. 25, 1952; s. Jack and Maribelle (Simen) W.; m. Sheila Rae Aronesti, Aug. 3, 1975; children: Laura Rachel, Charles Michael. BS in Acctg. and Fin., U. Ill., 1973, M Acctg. Sci., 1974; PhD in Acctg., U. Tex., 1977. Asst. prof. Stanford (Calif.) U., 1977-81, assoc. prof., 1981-85, prof. acctg., 1985-87, Joseph McDonald prof., 1987-92, assoc. dean, 1990-93; Dean Witter prof., 1992—; v.p. Keystone Inc., 1995—; prin. Arbor Investors, 1995—; Ford Found. vis. assoc. prof. U. Chgo., 1981-82; Thomas Henry Carroll vis. prof. Harvard U., Boston, 1988-89; cons. Fin. Acctg. Stds. Bd., Norwalk, Conn., 1985, 89-92; rsch. assoc. Nat. Bur. Econ. Rsch., Cambridge, Mass., 1988—; mem. steering com. Ctr. Econ. Policy Rsch., Stanford, 1990—; mem. task force Fed. Home Loan Bank Bd., 1989; bd. dirs. Investment Tech. Group, Jefferies Group, L.A., New Am. Holdings (Robert M. Bass Group); bd. advisors FEP Capital; gen. ptnr. P & PK Family Ltd. Partnership. Mem. editorial bd. Jour. Acctg. and Econs., Jour. Acctg. Rsch., Jour. Acctg., Auditing and Fin., Jour. Corp. Fin., Rev. Acctg. Studies; contbr. articles to profl. jours. Recipient Pomerance prize Chgo. Bd. Options Exch., 1981, Disting. Tchg. award Stanford U., 1990, Notable Contbn. to Lit. award AICPA-Am. Acctg. Assn., 1990, 92, Wildman award, 1991; named Disting. Accountancy Alumnus, U. Ill., 1989. Mem. Acctg. Rschrs. Internat. Assn., Am. Acctg. Assn., Am. Fin. Assn., Am. Econ. Assn., Am. Taxation Assn. Jewish. Office: Arbor Investors Ste 300 2400 Sand Hill Rd Menlo Park CA 94025

WOLFSON, MICHAEL GEORGE, lawyer; b. Chgo., Sept. 1, 1938; s. A. Lincoln M. Weingarten and Brina (Nelson) W.; m. Rita Sue Parsont, Sept. 11, 1966; children: Bethany Lynne, Sara Wynne, Deborah Kay. Student, MIT, 1956-58; BA, U. Chgo., 1961, JD, 1964, postdoctoral, 1964-65. Bar: Ill. 1964, N.Y. 1969. Assoc. Cravath, Swaine & Moore, N.Y.C., 1965-71, Brown, Wood, Fuller, Caldwell & Ivey, N.Y.C., 1971-73; ptnr. Brown & Wood (and predecessor firm Brown, Wood, Fuller, Caldwell & Ivey), N.Y.C., 1974—. Woodrow Wilson fellow, 1961; Ford Found. fellow in internat. trade and devel., 1965. Fellow Am. Bar Found.; mem. ABA. Avocations: reading, photography, running, cross-country skiing. Office: Brown & Wood 1 World Trade Ctr New York NY 10048-0557

WOLFSON, WARREN DAVID, lawyer, specialty retail store company executive; b. Syracuse, N.Y., Mar. 2, 1949; s. Isaiah Wolfson and Rosalind (Rothman) Gingold; separated; children: Scott E., Tara N., Lynn T. BSBA, Boston U., 1970; JD, Syracuse U., 1974. Bar: N.Y. 1975, U.S. Tax Ct. 1975, U.S. Ct. Claims 1975, U.S. Ct. Appeals (2d cir.) 1975. Assoc., Hancock & Estabrook, Syracuse, 1974-80; sec. Fay's Inc., Liverpool, N.Y., 1980—, gen. counsel, 1981—, v.p., 1983-89, sr. v.p., 1989—; bd. dirs. Syracuse Label Co., Inc; bd. dirs. Drug Quiz Show, Inc. Bd. dirs., sec., treas. Fay's Found., Liverpool, 1982—; mem. adv. coun. Inst. for Sensory Rsch., Syracuse U., 1991—; bd. dirs. Jewish Home of Ctrl. N.Y. Mem. ABA, Am. Corp. Counsel Assn., Nat. Assn. Chain Drug Stores (mem. govtl. affairs com.), Lafayette Country Club. Office: Fay's Inc 7245 Henry Clay Blvd Liverpool NY 13088-3523

WOLGIN, DAVID LEWIS, psychology educator; b. Elizabeth, N.J., Oct. 17, 1945. BA, Rutgers U., 1967; MA, Vanderbilt U., 1968; PhD, Rutgers U., 1973. Postdoctoral fellow Inst. for Neurological Sci., U. Pa., Phila., 1973-74; rsch. assoc. U. Ill., Urbana, 1974-75; asst. prof. Fla. Atlantic U., Boca Raton, 1975-79, assoc. prof., 1979-85, prof., 1985—, dir. Inst. for the Study of Alcohol and Drug Dependence, 1986—. Author: (with others) Hunger: Basic Mechanisms and Clinical Implications, 1976, The Expression of Knowledge, 1982, Psychoactive Drugs: Tolerance and Sensitization, 1989; contbr. articles to profl. jours. Pres. Synagogue Inverrary-Chabad, Lauderhill, Fla., 1981-92; dir. Boca Raton Synagogue, 1995—, v.p. 1996—. Rsch. grantee Nat. Inst. on Drug Abuse, 1990—. Mem. Soc. for Neurosci., N.Y. Acad. Sci., Soc. for Stimulus Properties Drugs, Soc. for the Study Ingestive Behavior, European Behavioural Pharmacology Soc., Ea. Psychol. Assn., Internat. Behavioral Neurosci. Soc. (charter). Office: Fla Atlantic U Dept Psychology Boca Raton FL 33431

WOLICKI, ELIGIUS ANTHONY, nuclear physicist, consultant; b. Buffalo, May 10, 1927; s. Karol Thaddeus and Katarzyna (Garbus) W.; m. Wilma Pitsenbarger, Aug. 28, 1954; children: Karol, Ann, Stasia, Stefanie. BS magna cum laude, Canisius Coll., 1946; PhD in Nuclear Physics, U. Notre Dame, 1950. Postdoctoral rsch. assoc. in nuclear physics, dept. physics State U. Iowa, Iowa City, 1950-52; rsch. physicist Van de Graaff Br. Naval Rsch. Lab., Washington, 1952-55, head charged particles reactions sect. Van de Graaff Br., 1955-66, assoc. div. supt. nuclear sci. and tech. div., 1966-84; program area reviewer for hardness assurance Dept. Def. Nuclear Agy., Washington, 1976-84, program area reviewer for single event upsets, 1981-84; chmn. Air Force NASA Hardness Assurance Com., 1979-90; pres. Wolicki Assocs. Inc., Alexandria, Va., 1984-94. Contbr. articles to jours., chpts. to books; patentee in field. Recipient Centennial award U. Notre Dame, 1965, Meritorious Civilian Svc. award Naval Rsch. Lab., 1971. Fellow IEEE (best paper award conf. on nuclear and space radiation effects 1987), Am. Phys. Soc. Roman Catholic. Achievements include early research on ion beam analysis of surfaces; ion implantation; radiation effects in electronic devices, SDI neutral particle beams; early work on single event upsets of microcircuits by cosmic rays in space. Avocations: travel, tennis, theater, music composition. Home and Office: 1310 Gatewood Dr Alexandria VA 22307-2032

WOLIN, ALFRED M., federal judge; b. Orange, N.J., Sept. 17, 1932; s. George and Juliet (Rosenstock) W.; m. Jane Zapiekov, Mar. 27, 1960; children: Roger, Marc. BA, U. Mich., 1954; LLB, JD, Rutgers U., 1959. Pvt. practice Elizabeth, N.J., 1960-80; judge Union County Dist. Ct., Elizabeth, N.J., 1980-85, Union County Superior Ct., Elizabeth, N.J., 1985-87, U.S. Dist. Ct., Newark, N.J., 1987—; atty. Roselle Bd. Adjustment, 1965-74; legis. aide to Senator Matthew J. Rinaldo, N.J. Senate, 1970-72; spl. asst. prosecutor Union County, 1970; congl. field rep. 12th congl. dist., 1972-79; mcpl. prosecutor Town of Westfield, N.J., 1973-74. Chief staff atty. Union County Legal Aid Soc., 1964-74; mem. Union County Ethics Com., sec., 1970-78, exec. com. Statewide Speedy Trial Com., Conf. Presiding Criminal Judges, Criminal Practice Com.; active Temple Emanuel, Jewish Fedn. Cen. N.J. SPC 2 U.S. Army, 1954-56, Germany. Mem. ABA, Am. Judicature Soc., N.J. Bar Assn. (judicial selection, discipline of the bar, lawyer referral coms.), Union County Bar Assn. (sec. 1970-74, pres. elect 1975, pres. 1976, judicial appointments com.), Fed. Judges Assn. Jewish. Office: US Dist Ct 50 Walnut St 367 US Courthouse Newark NJ 07101 *Notable cases include: (as judge) presided over trademark rights suit involving Procter & Gamble vs. Revlon, 1990, which alleged that Revlon's creation of Ivory Coast shampoo infringed on name of Procter & Gamble's Ivory soap. The suit was settled for an undisclosed amount.**

WOLIN, JEFFREY ALAN, artist. AB, Kenyon Coll., 1972; MFA, Rochester Inst. Tech., 1977. Represented by Catherine Edelman Gallery, Chgo.; photographer City of Kalamazoo (Mich.) Police Dept., 1973-74; asst. prof. photography Ind. U., Bloomington, 1980-86, assoc. prof. photography, 1986-92, prof., 1993—; head photographics svcs. George Eastman House, Rochester, 1976-80; adj. instr. photography U. Rochester, 1978-80. Exhbns. include Ryerson Photog. Are Ctr., Toronto, Can., 1978, New Eng. Sch. Photography, Boston, 1979, Northlight Gallery, Tempe, Ariz., 1980, 88, Israel Mus., Jerusalem, 1980, George Eastman House, Rochester, 1981, 82, Boston Visual Arts Union, 1983, Ind. State Mus., Indpls., 1985, Seattle Arts Mus., 1986, Chgo. Cultural Ctr., 1986, 87, J.B. Speed Art Mus., Louisville, 1987, Silver Image Gallery, Columbus, Ohio, 1987, Marianne Deson Gallery, Chgo., 1988, Burden Gallery, N.Y., 1988, Nexus Contemporary Art Ctr., Atlanta, 1988, 89, Exposure Gallery, Orleans, Mass., 1988, Images Gallery, Cin., 1989, New Harmony (Ind.) Gallery Contemporary Art, 1989, Catherine Edelman Gallery, Chgo., 1989, 91, 92, 93, 94, San Francisco Camerawork, 1990, U. Oreg. Mus. Art, Eugene, 1990, 92, Sol Mednick Gallery, Phila., 1991, Mus. Contemporary Photography, Chgo., 1991, 92, Blue Sky Gallery, Oreg. Ctr. for Photog. Arts, Portland, 1992, Mus. Fine Arts, Houston, 1992, L.A. County Art Mus., 1992, Opsis Gallery, N.Y.C., 1992, Mus. Modern Art, N.Y.C., 1992, Ctr. Creative Photography, Tucson, 1993, Robert Klein Gallery, Boston, 1994, Fuller Mus. Art, Brockton, Mass., 1994, Nelson-Atkins Mus. Art, Kansas City, 1994, Mpls. Mus. Am. Art, St. Paul, 1995, others; permanent collections include Seattle Arts Mus., San Francisco Mus. Modern Art, Northlight Gallery, Mus. Modern Art, N.Y., Mus. Contemporary Photography, Chgo., Mus. Fine Arts, Houston, L.A. County Art Mus., Kalamazoo (Mich.) Inst. Art, Internat. Mus. Photography at George Eastman House, Ctr. Creative Photography, Tucson, Can. Ctr. for Architecture, Montreal, others. Visual Artist fellow NEA, 1988, 92, Master Artist fellow Ind. Arts Commn., 1991, John Simon Guggenheim fellow, 1991, ArtsLink fellow to Czechoslovakia, 1994, U.S./France fellow Cité Internationale des Arts-Paris, 1994. Subject of books and articles. Home: 2504 Poplar Ct Bloomington IN 47401

WOLIN, NEAL STEVEN, lawyer; b. Chgo., Dec. 9, 1961; s. Harry S. and Doris (Wacker) W. BA summa cum laude, Yale U., 1983; MSc, U. Oxford, Eng., 1985; JD, Yale U., 1988. Bar: Ill. 1989, D.C. 1989. Adj. asst. prof. of law Bklyn. Law Sch., 1989; law clk. U.S. Judge Eugene H. Nickerson, Bklyn., 1988-89; assoc. Wilmer, Cutler & Pickering, Washington, 1989-90; spl. asst. to dirs. ctrl. intelligence Webster Gates & Woolsey, 1990-93; dep. legal adviser Nat. Sec. Coun. The White House, 1993-94; exec. asst. to the nat. sec. adviser The White House, 1994-95; dept. gen. counsel U.S. Dept. Treasury, 1995—. Coker Teaching fellow Yale Law Sch., 1987-88, Henry fellow, Henry Trust, U. Oxford, 1983-84. Mem. Coun. on Fgn. Rels., Phi Beta Kappa. Home: 4601 Connecticut Ave NW # 318 Washington DC 20008-5700

WOLINS, JOSEPH, artist; b. Atlantic City, Mar. 26, 1915; s. Morris and Rebecca (Katerinska) W.; m. Selma Lazaar, Dec. 7, 1957; children: Richard Lazaar, David Lazaar, John Wolins, Sarah Wolins. Student, Nat. Acad.

Design, 1931-35. Painter with Fed. art projects, 1934-41; tchr. South Shore Art Sch., Rockville Center, N.Y., 1950-55, 92d St. YMHA, N.Y.C., 1960, Bklyn. Mus. Art Sch., 1961-62, Long Beach (N.Y.) High Sch., 1962-68; pvt. classes, 1961—. One-man shows include Contemporary Arts Gallery, N.Y.C., Bodley Gallery, N.Y.C., Silvermine Guild, Norwalk, Conn., Slater Mus., Norwich, Conn., Agra Gallery, Washington; exhibited in group shows at Everson Mus., Syracuse, N.Y., World's Fair, N.Y.C., 1939, J.B. Neumann Gallery, N.Y.C., Toledo Mus., Corcoran Art Gallery, U. Ill. Mus., Pa. Acad. Fine Art, Whitney Mus., Sao Paolo Mus. Modern Art, Norfolk (Va.) Mus., Smithsonian Instn., Butler Art Inst., Youngstown, Ohio, Met. Mus. Art, N.Y.C.; represented in permanent collections Met. Mus. Art, Norfolk Mus., Albert Gallery at St. Joseph's (Mo.) U., Ball State Mus. Art, Muncia, Ind., Fiske U. Art Gallery, Mobile, Mus. in Ein Horod, Israel, Butler Art Inst., Nat. Mus. Am. Art, Washington, Slater Mem. Mus., Norwich, Conn., Wichita (Kans.) Art Mus., Everson Mus. of Art, Syracuse, New Brit. Mus. Art, Conn., Boca Raton Art Mus., Fla., also pvt. collections. Grantee Mark Rothko Found., 1971; recipient Painting award Audubon Artists, 1976, Painting award Nat. Inst. Arts and Letters, 1976, Painting award Am. Soc. Contemporary Artists, 1976. Mem. Audubon Artists, Am. Soc. Contemporary Artists. Address: 463 West St New York NY 10014-2010

WOLINSKY, EMANUEL, physician, educator; b. N.Y.C., Sept. 23, 1917; s. Jacob and Bertha (Siegel) W.; m. Marjorie Claster, Nov. 15, 1946; children: Douglas, Peter. B.A., Cornell U., 1938, M.D., 1941. Diplomate Am. Bd. Med. Microbiology. Intern, resident medicine N.Y. Hosp., 1943-45; bacteriologist Trudeau Lab., Saranac Lake, N.Y., 1947-56; mem. faculty Case Western Res. U. Sch. Medicine, 1956—, prof. medicine, 1968-88, prof. pathology, 1981-88, prof. emeritus, 1988—; dir. microbiology Cleve. Met. Gen. Hosp., 1959-91, acting dir. dept. pathology, 1980-86, chief div. infectious diseases, 1961-83. Co-editor Textbook of Pulmonary Diseases, 5th edit., 1993; Asso. editor: Am. Rev. Respiratory Diseases, 1973-79; Contbr. articles to profl. jours., textbooks. Mem. Tb panel U.S.-Japan Co-op. Med. Sci. Program, 1969-75. Recipient Crystal Cross award Ohio Thoracic Soc., 1995, Louis Weinstein award Clin. Infectious Diseases, 1995. Mem. Am. Soc. Microbiology, Am. Thoracic Soc. (Trudeau medal 1986), Infectious Diseases Soc. Am., Phi Beta Kappa, Alpha Omega Alpha. Home: 24761 S Woodland Rd Cleveland OH 44122-3327 Office: Met Health Med Ctr 2500 Metrohealth Dr Cleveland OH 44109-1900

WOLINSKY, LEO C., newspaper editor. BA in Journalism, U. So. Calif., 1972. Journalist, 1972—; staff writer L.A. Times, 1977-86, dep. chief Sacramento bur., 1987-89, city editor, 1990, Calif. polit. editor, 1991, metro editor, 1994—. Office: Los Angeles Times Times Mirror Sq Los Angeles CA 90053

WOLINTZ, ARTHUR HARRY, physician, neuro-ophthalmologist; b. Bklyn., May 30, 1937; s. Louis and Celia (Ragofsky) W.; m. Carol Sue Bergstein, Nov. 28, 1963; children: Robyn Joy, Ellen Sharon. Student, NYU, 1955-58; MD summa cum laude, SUNY, Bklyn., 1962; postgrad., Columbia U., 1967-68. Diplomate Am. Bd. Psychiatry and Neurology, Am. Bd. Ophthalmology; licensee Nat. Bd. Med. Examiners, U. State of N.Y. Intern Maimonides Hosp., Bklyn., 1962-63, jr. resident in medicine, 1963-64; resident Nat. Inst. Neurol. Diseases and Blindness, Bethesda, Md., 1964-66; chief resident Mt. Sinai Hosp., N.Y.C., 1966-67; clin. asst. prof. neurology Downstate Med. Ctr. SUNY, Bklyn., 1968-69, resident in ophthalmology, 1969-71, from asst. prof. to prof., 1971—, prof. clin. ophthalmology and clin. neurology, 1977—, interim chief ophthalmology, 1983, acting regional chmn. dept. ophthalmology, 1984, disting. tchg. prof., 1995—; chmn. dept. ophthalmology, 1987-96; asst. neurologist Presbyn. Hosp., N.Y.C., 1967-68; instr. neuropathology Coll. Physicians and Surgeons Columbia U., N.Y.C., 1967-68; instr. neurology Mt. Sinai Sch. Medicine, N.Y.C., 1967-68; assoc. dir. neurology Maimonides Med. Ctr., Bklyn., 1968-69; asst. neurologist Coney Island Hosp., Bklyn., 1968-69; vis. neurologist Kings County Hosp. Ctr., Bklyn, 1968-69; chief div. ophthalmology and neuro-ophthalmology Kingsbrook Jewish Med. Ctr., Bklyn., 1971, sec. med. and dental staff 1976-77, v.p. 1978-79, pres. 1980-81, dir. ophthalmology 1981; attending physician State Univ. Hosp., Bklyn., 1971, Kings County Hosp. Ctr., Bklyn., 1971; cons. Luth. Med. Ctr., Beth Israel Med. Ctr., Brookdale Hosp. Med. Ctr., Bklyn., L.I. Coll. Hosp., Bklyn., Maimonides Med. Ctr., Cath. Med. Ctr. Bklyn. and Queens, Bklyn. VA Hosp. Author: Essentials of Clinical Neuro-Ophthalmology, 1976; contbr. chpts. to sci. textbooks and handbooks, articles to profl. jours. Treas. Flatbush Jewish Ctr., Bklyn. With USPHS 1964-66. Recipient J. Eugene Chalfin Meml. Lecture award Alumni Assn. State Univ.-Kings County, 1981, Tchr. of Yr. award dept. ophthalmology Interfaith Med. Ctr., 1988. Fellow ACP, ACS, Am. Acad. Ophthalmology and Otolaryngology, Am. Acad. Neurology; mem. AMA, Med. Soc. County Kings, Med. Soc. State N.Y., Bklyn. Ophthal. Soc., N.Y. Acad. Medicine, AAAS, Am. Acad. Neurology, Alumni Assn. SUNY (Master Tchr. award 1987, pres.-elect 1989, pres. 1990-91), Oddfellows, Alpha Omega Alpha. Avocations: Torah reader, cantor. Home and Office: 100 Ocean Pky Brooklyn NY 11218-1755

WOLITARSKY, JAMES WILLIAM, securities industry executive; b. Tarrytown, N.Y., Feb. 19, 1946; s. Edward and Beulah (Kemmet) W.; divorced; children: James Jr., Matthew. BA, Franklin & Marshall Coll., 1968; MBA, NYU, 1973. Auditor Hertz, Herson & Co., N.Y.C., 1970-73; comml. loan officer The Phila. Nat. Bank, 1973-76; chief fin. officer Almo Electronics Corp., Phila., 1976-80; dir. budget and control Paine Webber Inc., N.Y.C., 1981-82, dir. mktg. adminstrn., 1982-83, dir. mut. funds and asset mgmt., 1983-84; sr. v.p., dir. product mgmt. Phila. Nat. Bank, 1984-86; exec. v.p., chief fin. officer The Moseley Holding Corp., N.Y.C., 1986-87; pres., chief exec. officer Moseley Securities Corp., N.Y.C., 1987-88; exec. v.p. Gruntal Fin. Corp., N.Y.C., 1988-91; chief fin. officer, bd. dirs. Janney Montgomery Scott Inc., Phila., 1991—; bd. dirs. Phila. Depository Transfer Corp., Addison Capital Shares, Inc., treas.; treas. Addison Capital Mgmt. Corp. Bd. dirs. Cliveden of Nat. Hist. Trust, Inc. Sgt. U.S. Army, 1968-70. Decorated Bronze Star, Vietnam Cross of Gallantry. Mem. Securities Industry Assn. Episcopalian. Club: Phila. Racquet, Phila. Country. Avocations: fishing, skiing, tennis, golf. Home: 49 Oak Knoll Dr Berwyn PA 19312-1282 Office: Janney Montgomery Scott Inc 1801 Market St Philadelphia PA 19103-1628

WOLITZER, STEVEN BARRY, investment banker; b. Bklyn., Mar. 14, 1953; s. Philip and Regina (Wurm) W.; m. Joyce Sue Lindower, Dec. 7, 1985; children: David Joel, Scott Richard, Rachel. BS, NYU, 1973; MBA, Harvard U., 1977. CPA, N.Y. Mng. dir. Lehman Bros. Inc., N.Y.C., 1977—. Home: 250 E 87th St Apt 21B New York NY 10128-3120 Office: Lehman Bros Inc 3 World Fin Ctr New York NY 10285

WOLKEN, JEROME JAY, biophysicist, educator; b. Pitts., Mar. 28, 1917; s. Abraham I. and Dina (Lando) W.; m. Dorothy O. Mallinger, June 19, 1945 (dec. 1954); children: Ann A., Jonathan; m. Tobey J. Holestein, Jan. 26, 1956; children: H. Johanna, Erik Andrew. Student, Pa. State U., 1935-36, Duquesne U., 1937-39; BS, U. Pitts., 1946, MS, 1948, PhD, 1949. Rsch. fellow Mellon Inst., 1943-47, Princeton U., 1950-51, Rockefeller Inst., 1951-52; asst. prof. U. Pitts. Sch. Medicine, 1953-57, asso. prof., 1957-61, prof. biophysics physiology, 1962-66; head dept. bioscis. Carnegie Inst. Tech., Pitts., 1964-67; prof. biophysics and bioscis. Carnegie-Mellon U., 1964—, head biophys. rsch. lab., 1964-76; head biophys. rsch. lab. Eye and Ear Hosp., Pitts., 1953-64; rsch. assoc. Carnegie Mus.; guest prof. Pa. State U., 1963, U. Paris, 1967-68, U. Miami (Fla.) Inst. Theoretical Studies, 1966, Univ. Coll., London, 1971, Pasteur Inst., Paris, 1972, AEC, Saclay, France; rsch. fellow Princeton U., 1978; U.S. rsch. fellow Tohoku U., Sendai, Japan, 1988. Author 9 books; editor 2 books; contbr. 120 articles to profl. jours. With USNR, 1941-43. Recipient Career award USPHS, 1962-65. Fellow N.Y. Acad. Scis., AAAS, Optical Soc. Am. (pres. Pitts. sect. 1964-65), Am. Inst. Chemists, Explorers Club; mem. Am. Chem. Soc., Chemists Club N.Y., Am. Inst. Biol. Sci., Biophys. Soc., Soc. Gen. Physiologists, Am. Soc. Cell Biology, Am. Photobiol. Sci., Sigma Xi, Phi Sigma. Achievements include 2 patents for Light Concentrating Lens System. Home: 5817 Elmer St Pittsburgh PA 15232-1915 Office: Carnegie Mellon U Mellon Coll of Sci 4400 5th Ave Pittsburgh PA 15213-2617

WOLKING, JOSEPH ANTHONY, publishing company executive; b. Morris, Minn., May 7, 1934; s. Lawrence William and Tecla Catherine (Loegering) e7W.); m. Kathleen Marie Poehling, Apr. 18, 1959; children: Christopher, Lisbeth, Gregory, Rebecca, Eric. Student, Fordham U., 1952-54; B.A., U. Minn., 1957. With Ojibway Press Inc., Duluth, Minn., 1958-69; asst. to pres. Petroleum Pub. Co. (name changed to PennWell Pub. Co. 1980), Tulsa, 1969; pub. Dental Econs., 1972-75, group v.p., 1975-82, sr. v.p., chief operating officer, 1982-84, exec. v.p., chief operating officer, 1985—, also dir., pres., 1987—, pres., CEO, 1992—. Office: PennWell Pub Co 1421 S Sheridan Rd Tulsa OK 74112-6619

WOLKOFF, EUGENE ARNOLD, lawyer; b. N.Y.C., June 9, 1932; s. Oscar and Jean (Zablow) W.; m. Judith Gail Edwards, Oct. 15, 1967; children—Mandy, Elana, Alexa, Justine. A.B., Bklyn. Coll., 1953; LL.B., St. John's U., 1961. Bar: N.Y. 1962, N.Mex. 1994. Practiced in N.Y.C and Santa Fe; mem. firm Callahan & Wolkoff, N.Y.C., 1965—; bd. dirs. Babylon Enterprises, Inc., Hist. Newspaper Archives, Inc., Data Image Processing Corp.; mem. nat. panel arbitrators Am. Arbitration Assn. Served to lt. col. USAFR, 1953-75. Mem. N.Y. State Bar Assn., N.Mex. Bar Assn., Pi Beta Gamma. Office: 17 Battery Pl New York NY 10004 also: 330 Garfield St Santa Fe NM 87501-2640

WOLL, HARRY J., electrical engineer; b. Farmington, Minn., Aug. 25, 1920; s. Henry L. and Clara M. (Fredrickson) W.; m. Mary V. Cowan, Feb. 15, 1947; children: Daniel, Alice. B.S.E.E., N.D. State U., 1940; postgrad., Ill. Inst. Tech., 1940-41; Ph.D., U. Pa., 1953. With RCA Corp., 1941-85; chief engr. aerospace systems div. RCA Corp., Burlington, Mass., 1963-69; div. v.p. govt. engring. RCA Corp., Moorestown, N.J., 1969-75; div. v.p., gen. mgr. RCA Automated Systems, Burlington, 1975-81; staff v.p., chief engr. RCA Electronic Products and Labs., Princeton, N.J., 1981-85. Chmn. bd. trustees Moore Sch. Elec. Engring., U. Pa.. 1976-90; trustee U. Pa., 1989-91. Recipient 50th Anniversary gold medal Moore Sch. Elec. Engring., U. Pa., 1973. Fellow AAAS, IEEE (past chmn. Phila. sect., past chmn. fellow com.), Aerospace Industries Tech. Council (past chmn.); mem. Sigma Phi Delta, Phi Kappa Phi. Roman Catholic. Patentee in field. Home: PO Box 679 Concord MA 01742-0679

WOLLE, CHARLES ROBERT, federal judge; b. Sioux City, Iowa, Oct. 16, 1935; s. William Carl and Vivian (Down) W.; m. Kerstin Birgitta Wennerstrom, June 26, 1961; children: Karl Johan Knut, Erik Vernon, Thomas Dag, Aaron Charles. AB, Harvard U., 1959; JD, Iowa Law Sch., 1961. Bar: Iowa 1961. Assoc. Shull, Marshall & Marks, Sioux City, 1961-67, ptnr., 1968-80; judge Dist. Ct. Iowa, Sioux City, 1981-83; justice Iowa Supreme Ct., Sioux City and Des Moines, 1983-87; chief judge, 1992—; judge U.S. Dist. Ct. (so. dist.) Iowa, Des Moines, 1987-92, chief judge, 1992—; faculty Nat. Jud. Coll., Reno, 1983—, chief judge 1992—. Editor Iowa Law Rev., 1960-61. Vice pres. bd. dirs. Sioux City Symphony, 1972-77; sec., bd. dirs. Morningside Coll., Sioux City, 1977-81. Fellow Am. Coll. Trial Lawyers; mem. ABA, Iowa Bar Assn., Sioux City C. of C. (bd. dirs. 1977-78). Avocations: sports, art, music, literature. Home: 1601 Pleasant View Dr Des Moines IA 50315-2129 Office: US Dist Judge 103 US Courthouse 123 E Walnut St Des Moines IA 50309-2035

WOLLE, WILLIAM DOWN, foreign service officer; b. Sioux City, Iowa, Mar. 11, 1928; s. William Carl and Vivian Lucille (Down) W.; m. Zanie L. Donahue, Feb. 7, 1992; children from previous marriage: Laila Jean, William Nicholas. B.A., Morningside Coll., 1949; M.Internat. Affairs, Columbia U., 1951. Joined U.S. Fgn. Service, 1951; consular officer Baghdad, Iraq, 1951-52; econ. officer, 1952-53; consular officer Manchester, Eng., 1954-56; trainee Arab lang. and area Beirut, Lebanon, 1957-58; fgn. service officer gen. Aden, So. Yemen, 1958-59; econ. officer Jidda, Saudi Arabia, 1959-62; internat. economist Washington, 1962-64; internat. relations officer, 1964-65; officer in charge Arab-Israeli affairs, 1965-67; detailed Nat. War Coll., 1967-68; counselor polit. affairs Kuwait City, Kuwait, 1968-70; econ. officer, dir. AID, Amman, Jordan, 1970-73; econ. officer Nairobi, 1973-74; ambassador to Oman, Muscat, 1974-78; dir. Middle Eastern/South Asian Research Office, Dept. State, 1978-79; ambassador to United Arab Emirates, 1979-81; adviser internat. affairs Indsl. Coll. Armed Forces, 1982-84; chief sr. officer assignments, Washington, 1984-86. Served with AUS, 1946-47. Recipient Superior Service award Dept. State, 1974, Outstanding Civilian Service award Dept. Def., 1984. Home: 17284 Wexford Loop Dumfries VA 22026

WOLLEN, W. FOSTER, lawyer; b. Union City, N.J., Dec. 24, 1936; s. Ross and Grace (Foster) W.; m. Sheila M. Culkin, Oct. 3, 1964; children: W. Foster, John Ross, Evan, Gillian. AB, Holy Cross Coll., 1958; LLB, U. Va., 1961. Bar: N.Y. 1962, D.C. 1990. Assoc. Shearman & Sterling, N.Y.C., 1962-70, ptnr., 1970-90, mng. ptnr., Washington, 1990-94, sr. v.p., dir. and gen. counsel Bechtel Group, Inc., 1994—. Served with U.S. Army, 1961-62. Fellow Am. Coll. Trial Lawyers (N.Y. chmn. 1987-88); mem. ABA, Bar Assn. City of N.Y. Roman Catholic. Note editor U. Va. Law Rev. Office: Bechtel Group Inc 50 Beale St PO Box 193965 San Francisco CA 94105*

WOLLENBERG, J. ROGER, lawyer; b. N.Y.C., May 1, 1919; s. Harry Lincoln and Gertrude (Arnstein) W.; m. Patricia S. Albright, Jan. 2, 1948; children: Christopher, Meredith, Pamela, Peter, Edward. B.A., U. Calif. at Berkeley, 1939, LL.B., 1942. Bar: Calif. 1946, D.C. 1954. Law clk. U.S. Supreme Ct. Justice William O. Douglas, 1946; with Dept. Justice, 1947-52; asst. gen. counsel FCC, 1952-54; pvt. practice, 1954—; ptnr. Wilmer, Cutler & Pickering, Washington, 1962-91, sr. counsel, 1992—. Mem. Falls Church (Va.) Sch. Bd., 1960-71, chmn., 1962-70; mem. city council City of Falls Church, 1982-88 ; chmn. adv. com. on procedures, U.S. Ct. Appeals, D.C. Cir., 1988-90. Served to lt. USNR, 1942-46. Mem. FCC Bar Assn. (pres. 1965-66), Am. Bar Assn. (ho. of dels. 1967-71). Home: 508 Lincoln Ave Falls Church VA 22046-2621 Office: Wilmer Cutler & Pickering 2445 M St NW Washington DC 20037-1420

WOLLENBERG, RICHARD PETER, paper manufacturing company executive; b. Juneau, Alaska, Aug. 1, 1915; s. Harry L. and Gertrude (Arnstein) W.; m. Leone Bonney, Dec. 22, 1940; children: Kenneth Roger, David Arthur, Keith Kermit, Richard Harry, Carol Lynne. BSME, U. Calif., Berkeley, 1936; MBA, Harvard U., 1938; grad., Army Indsl. Coll., 1941; D in Pub. Affairs (hon.), U. Puget Sound, 1977. Prodn. control Bethlehem Ship, Quincy, Mass., 1938-39; with Longview (Wash.) Fibre Co., 1939—, safety engr., asst. chief engr., chief engr., mgr. container operations, 1951-57, v.p., 1953-57, v.p. ops., 1957-60, exec. v.p., 1960-69, pres., 1969-78, pres., chief exec. officer, 1978-85, pres., chief exec. officer, chmn. bd., 1985—, also bd. dirs.; mem. Wash. State Council for Postsecondary Edn., 1969-79, chmn., 1970-73; mem. western adv. bd. Allendale Ins. Bassoonist SW Washington Symphony. Trustee Reed Coll., Portland, 1962—, chmn. bd. 1982-90. Served to lt. col. USAAF, 1941-45. Recipient Alumni Achievement award Harvard U., 1994. Mem. NAM (bd. dirs. 1981-86), Pacific Coast Assn. Pulp and Paper Mfrs. (pres. 1981-92), Inst. Paper Sci. and Tech. (trustee), Wash. State Roundtable, Crabbe Huson (bd. dirs.). Home: 1632 Kessler Blvd Longview WA 98632-3633 Office: Longview Fibre Co PO Box 606 Longview WA 98632-7391

WOLLERSHEIM, JANET PUCCINELLI, psychology educator; b. Anaconda, Mont., July 24, 1936; d. Nello J. and Inez Marie (Ungaretti) Puccinelli; m. David E. Wollersheim, Aug. 1, 1959 (div. June 1972); children: Danette Marie, Tod Neil; m. Daniel J. Smith, July 17, 1976. AB, Gonzaga U., 1958; MA, St. Louis U., 1960; PhD, U. Ill., 1968. Lic. psychologist, Mont. Asst. prof. psychology, asst. dir. testing and counseling ctr. U. Mo., 1968-71; prof. psychology U. Mont., Missoula, 1971—, dir. chin. psychology, 1980-87; chair Mont. Bd. Psychologists, 1977-78; cons. Mont. State Prison, 1971-85, Trapper Creek Job Corps, 1973—; pvt. practice, Missoula, 1971—. Author numerous rsch. articles. Bd. dirs. Crisis Ctr., Missoula, 1972-73; mem. profl. adv. bd. Head Start, Missoula, 1972-79. Recipient Disting. scholar award U. Montana, 1991. Fellow Am. Psychol. Assn. (bd. dirs. div. clin. psychology 1990-92); mem. Rocky Mountain Psychol. Assn. (pres. 1983-84), Nat. Council Univ. Dirs. Clin. Psychology (bd. dirs., 1982-88). Roman Catholic. Catholic. Home: 105 Greenwood Ln Missoula MT 59803-2401 Office: 900 N Orange St Ste 201 Missoula MT 59802-2998

WOLLERT, GERALD DALE, retired food company executive, investor; b. LaPorte, Ind., Jan. 21, 1935; s. Delmar Everette and Esther Mae W.; m. Carol Jean Burchby, Jan. 26, 1957; children—Karen Lynn, Edwin Del. B.S., Purdue U., 1957. With Gen. Foods Corp., 1959-89; dir. consumer affairs Gen. Foods Corp., White Plains, N.Y., 1973-74; mng. dir. Cottee Foods div. Gen. Foods Corp., Sydney, Australia, 1974-76; gen. mgr. Mexico div. Gen. Foods Corp., Mexico City, 1978-79; pres. Asia/Pacific ops. Gen. Foods Corp., Honolulu, corp. v.p. worldwide coffee and internat. div., 1979-89; ret., 1989; dir. Gen. Foods cos., Japan, Peoples Republic China, Korea, India, Taiwan, Singapore, Philippines. Webelos leader Boy Scouts Am., Mexico City, 1978-79; co. gen. chmn. United Fund campaign, Battle Creek, Mich., 1964-65, White Plains, N.Y., 1972-73. Served with U.S. Army, 1958. Mem. Asian-U.S. Bus. Coun., Oahu Country Club (Hawaii), Venice Golf and Country Club (Fla.), Beacon Hills and Beechwood (Ind.) Club.

WOLLMAN, HARRY, medical educator; b. Bklyn., Sept. 26, 1932; s. Jacob and Florence Roslyn (Hoffman) W.; m. Anne Carolyn Hamel, Feb. 16, 1957; children: Julie Ellen, Emily Jane, Diana Leigh. AB summa cum laude, Harvard Coll., 1954, MD, 1958. Diplomate Am. Bd. Anesthesiology. Intern U. Chgo. Clinics, 1958-59; resident U. Pa., 1959-63, assoc. in anesthesia, 1963-65, mem. faculty, 1965-87, prof. anesthesia, 1970-87, prof. pharmacology, 1971-87, Robert Dunning Dripps prof., chmn. dept. anesthesia, 1972-87; prin. investigator Anesthesia Rsch. Ctr., 1972-78; program dir. Anesthesia Rsch. Tng. Grant, 1972-87; sr. v.p., chief acad. officer, dean Sch. Medicine Hahnemann U., Phila., 1987-92, prof. anesthesiology, 1987-92, prof. pharmacology, 1987-92, univ. prof., 1992—; Mem. anesthesia drug panel, drug efficacy study, com. on anesthesia Nat. Acad. Scis.-NRC, 1970-71, com. on adverse reactions to anesthesia drugs, 1971-72; mem. pharm. and toxicology tng. grants com. NIH, 1966-68, anesthesia tng. grants com., 1971-73, surgery, anesthesia and trauma study sect., 1974-78; chmn. com. on studies involving human beings U. Pa., 1972-76, chmn. clin. practice exec. com., 1976-80. Assoc. editor for revs.: Anesthesiology, 1970-75; Contbr. and editor books. Hon. John Harvard scholar Harvard Coll., 1950-53, Harvard Coll. scholar, 1953-54, Detur award, 1951; NIH rsch. traineeship fellow, 1959-63, Pharm. Mfg. Assn. fellow, 1960-61. Mem. AMA, Pa. Soc. Anesthesiologists (pres. 1972-73), Am. Physiol. Soc., Assn. U. Anesthetists (exec. coun. 1971-74, chmn. scientific adv. bd. 1975-77), Soc. Acad. Anesthesia (chmn. com. fin. resources 1973-77, pres. 1977-78), Am. Soc. Anesthesiologists, Phila. Soc. Anesthesiologists, Pa. Med. Soc., Phila. County Med. Soc., Am. Dental Soc., Anesthesiology (adv. bd. 1985-90), Assn. Med. Coll., Coll. Physicians Phila., Phi Beta Kappa, Sigma Xi. Home: Mus Towers 1801 Buttonwood St Apt 1020 Philadelphia PA 19130 Office: Hahnemann Univ 3508 Market St Ste 201 Philadelphia PA 19104-3316

WOLLMAN, LEO, physician; b. N.Y.C., Mar. 14, 1914; s. Joseph and Sara (Samrick) W.; m. Eleanor Rakow, Aug. 16, 1936 (dec. 1953); children: Arthur Lee, Bryant Lee; m. Charlotte Kornberg Seidman, Oct. 6, 1954 (div. 1969); m. Ellen Hershenson, Mar. 25, 1985. BS, Columbia U., 1934; MS, NYU, 1938; MD, Royal Coll. Edinburgh, 1942; PhD (hon.), Rochdale, 1972; DSc (hon.), U. Mich., 1973. Diplomate Am. Bd. Hypnosis in Ob-Gyn, Nat. Bd. Acupuncture Medicine, Am. Acad. Pain Mgmt., Am. Bd. Psychiatry and Neurology, Am. Bd. Sexology. Intern Cumberland Hosp., Bklyn., 1942-43; resident Leith Gen. Hosp., 1942; practice medicine specializing in ob-gyn Bklyn., 1944-72; in psychiatry, 1972—; mem. staff Maimonides, Coney Island hosps., Bklyn. Hosp. Ctr., Bklyn., Park East, Mt. Sinai hosps., N.Y.C.; med. dir. acupuncture dept. Lexington Health Facility, N.Y.C. Author: Write Yourself Slim, 1976, Eating Your Way to a Better Sex Life, 1983, numerous articles in profl. jours.; editor-in-chief: Jour. Am. Soc. Psychosomatic Dentistry and Medicine, 1968-83; editor newsletter: Soc. Sci. Study Sex; editor: News Bull. of Inst. for Comprehensive Medicine; assoc. editor: Jour. Sex Research; internat. editor: Latin Am. Jour. Clin. Hypnosis; films I Am Not This Body, 1970, StrangeHer, 1971, Let Me Die a Woman, 1978. Pres. Jewish Com. Coun. Greater Coney Island, 1989—. Recipient Jules Weinstein Ann. Pioneer in Modern Hypnosis award, 1964. Fellow Am. Geriatrics Soc., N.Y. Acad. Scis. (life), Acad. Psychosomatic Medicine (sec. 1965), Soc. Clin. and Exptl. Hypnosis (life), Am. Soc. Clin. Hypnosis (life), Soc. Sci. Study Sex (pres. Eastern region 1979-81), Am. Soc. Psychical Research (life), Am. Med. Writers Assn. (life), Internat. Soc. Comprehensive Medicine, Am. Acad. Psychiatry and Neurology, Am. Coll. Sexology; mem. Nat. Geog. Soc. (life), AAAS (council 1971-73), Am. Assn. Social Psychiatry, Am. Soc. Abdominal Surgeons, Internat. Soc. Nonverbal Psychotherapy, N.Y. State Soc. Med. Research, Royal Medico-Psychol. Assn. (Eng.), N.Y. Soc. for Gen. Semantics, Nat. Assn. on Standard Med. Vocabulary (sec. 1964—), Am. Assn. History Medicine, Am. Assn. Study Headache, Am. Acad. Dental Medicine, Am. Assn. Marriage Counselors, Soc. Med. Jurisprudence, Bklyn. Psychol. Assn., Canadian Soc. for Study Fertility, Am. Fertility Soc. (life), Internat. Fertility Assn., Internat. Soc. for Clin. and Exptl. Hypnosis (life), Am. Soc. Psychosomatic Dentistry and Medicine (pres. 1969-72, exec. dir. 1973-83), Assn. Advancement Psychotherapy, Pan-Am. Med. Assn., Andalusian Soc. Sophrology and Psychosomatic Medicine, Brit. Med. Assn., Bklyn. Acad. Medicine, Internat. Soc. Psychoneuroendocrinology, L.I. Hist. Soc.; also hon. mem. numerous fgn. orgns. Address: 3813 Poplar Ave Brooklyn NY 11224-1301 *I have learned that to be busily occupied doing the work I like is to be happy. Doing what you like to do usually results in a job well done. To take pride in one's work is a virtue.*

WOLLMAN, NATHANIEL, economist, educator; b. Phila., May 15, 1915; s. Leon and Rose (Schimmel) W.; m. Lenora Levin, Dec. 25, 1939 (dec. Dec. 1994); children: Stephen, Eric. A.B., Pa. State U., 1936; Ph.D., Princeton U., 1940; LL.D., Colo. Coll., 1972. Instr., asst. prof. Colo. Coll., 1939-48; asso. prof., prof. econs. U. N.Mex., 1948-81, prof. emeritus, 1981—, chmn. dept. econs., 1960-69; dean Coll. Arts and Scis., 1969-81; economist Resources for the Future, 1959-60, 64-65; Chmn. Internat. Environ. Programs Com., 1976-79. Author: (with others) Water Supply and Demand, 1960, Value of Water in Alternative Uses, 1962, Water Resources of Chile, 1968, (with Gilbert Bonem) The Outlook for Water: Quality, Quantity and National Growth, 1971, (with others) Man, Materials and Environment, 1973. Served with USNR, World War II. Mem. Am. Econs. Assn. Home: 7010 Phoenix Ave NE Apt 713 Albuquerque NM 87110-3562

WOLLMAN, ROGER LELAND, judge; b. Frankfort, S.D., May 29, 1934; s. Edwin and Katherine Wollman; m. Diane Marie Schroeder, June 21, 1959; children: Steven James, John Mark, Thomas Roger. BA, Tabor Coll., Hillsboro, Kans., 1957; JD magna cum laude, U. S.D., 1962; LLM, Harvard U., 1964. Bar: S.D. 1964. Sole practice, Aberdeen, 1964-71; justice S.D. Supreme Ct., 1971-85, chief justice, 1978-82; judge U.S. Ct. Appeals (8th cir.), 1985—; states atty. Brown County, Aberdeen, 1967-71. Served with AUS, 1957-59. Office: US Ct Appeals 311 Fed Bldg and US Courthouse 400 S Phillips Ave Sioux Falls SD 57102-0961*

WOLLNER, THOMAS EDWARD, manufacturing company executive; b. Rochester, Minn., Dec. 30, 1936; s. Clarence E. and Grace W. (Day) W.; m. Marlene A. Hanson, July 12, 1958; children: Mark R., Jill M. BA, St. John's U., Collegeville, Minn., 1958; PhD, Wash. State U., 1964. Sr. research chemist tape research 3M Co., St. Paul, 1964-66, research supr., mgr. comml. tape dev. lab., 1966-73, mgr. Cen. Research Labs., 1973-77, dir. Chem. Research Lab., 1977-81, dir. Indsl. and Consumer Sector Research Lab., 1981-84, exec. dir. research and devel. indsl. and consumer sector, 1984-86, v.p. research and devel. indsl. and consumer sector, 1986-87, staff v.p. Corp. Research Labs., 1987—. Served to lt. U.S. Army, 1960. Mem. Am. Chem. Soc., Indsl. Research Inst. (alt. rep.). Office: 3M Co 3M Ctr Bldg 220 4E 01 Saint Paul MN 55144-1000

WOLLPERT, SANDRA COX, horse breeder; b. Phila., July 8, 1950; d. Robert Miller and Audrey Olive (Fullam) Cox; m. Worth Alan Wollpert, Sept. 29, 1973; children: Worth Douglas, Shaunna Lee. BA, Pa. State U., 1971, BS, 1971. Cert. secondary sch. tchr., Pa. Tchr. Cheltenham (Pa.) High Sch., 1972-73; officer Four Seasons Devel. Inc., Ohio, 1975-86; pres. SW Acquisitions and SW Realty Inc., Chardon, Ohio, Blythswood Inc., Chardon; bd. dirs. CW Holding Co., Wilmington, Del., Spruco Investment Co., Wilmington, Diamondtech Inc., Chardon. Author: Cerissa, 1976, Rebel's Honor, 1980, Winter Roses, 1983, Rapture's Fury, 1988. Contbr. Women's Shelter, Lake County, Ohio. Mem. Nat. Trust for Scotland, Arabian Race Com. Ohio (chmn.), Arabian Jockey Club, Deep Springs Trout Club. Avocations: horseback riding, fishing, horse racing, reading, traveling. Home: 12080 Bass Lake Rd Chardon OH 44024-9727 Office: Blythswood Inc 12058 Bass Lake Rd Chardon OH 44024-9461

WOLLUM, ARTHUR GEORGE, II, microbiologist, researcher, educator; b. Chgo., July 26, 1937; s. Arthur George and Hertha (Christensen) W.; m. Karen Hanson, June 18, 1960; children: Steven Arthur, Mark Hanson. BS,

U. Minn., 1959; MS, Oreg. State U., 1963, PhD, 1965. Rsch. assoc. Oreg. State U., Corvallis, 1965-67; asst. prof. microbiology N.Mex. State U., Las Cruces, 1967-71; assoc. prof. N.C. State U., Raleigh, 1971-76, prof., 1976—, head ecology program, 1984-89; vis. prof. Ohio State U., Columbus, 1978-79. Author more than 100 articles and book chpts. on biol. nitrogen fixation, microbial ecology, bioremediation. Fellow Soil Sci. Soc. Am., Am. Soc. Agronomy (divsn. chair, assoc. editor, coms.); mem. Am. Soc. Microbiology, Soc. Am. Forest (assoc. editor Forest Sci.), Soil Sci. Soc. Am. (tech. editor jour.), Sigma Xi, Gamma Sigma Delta. Achievements include advances in the understanding of stress ecology of Bradyrhizobium japonicum and its genetic diversity in soil environments. Office: NC State U Dept Soil Sci Box 7619 Raleigh NC 27695-7619

WOLMAN, J. MARTIN, retired newspaper publisher; b. Elizabeth, N.J., Mar. 8, 1919; s. Joseph D. and Dora (Baum) W.; m. Anne Paley, Sept. 12, 1943; children: Natalie, Jonathan, Ruth Ellen, Lewis Joel. Student, U. Wis., 1937-42. With Wis. State Jour., Madison, 1936-84; pub. Wis. State Jour., 1968-84; pres., gen. mgr. Madison Newspaper, Inc., 1969-84, ret., 1984, dir., 1969—; dir. Lee Enterprises, Inc., 1971-74; treas. Lee Endowment Trusts, 1988—; sec.-treas. Madison Improvement Corp., 1958-62. Treas. Wis. State Jour. Empty Stocking Club, 1948, Children and Youth Services Inc., 1962—; mem. Mayor Madison Adv. Com., 1965; bd. dirs. United Givers Fund, 1960-64, trustee, 1980—; ex-officio Roy L. Matson Scholarship Fund, 1961, Central Madison Com., Madison Art Assn.; trustee Edgewood Coll., Madison, U. Wis. Hosp. and Clinic; chmn. Madison Area Arts Coalition, 1984-85; bd. dirs. Univ. Health Sci. Center, 1975; chmn. U.S. Savs. Bond Met. Wis., 1983; coordinator Barneveld Disaster Fund, Wis., 1985-86; mem. U. Wis. Found., 1968-95; bd. dirs., trustee Wisc. Clin. Cancer Ctr., 1986—; Dir. Wisc. Newspaper Found., 1986-88; v.p., treas. Lee Endowment Found., 1989—. Served with AUS, 1942-46. Named Advt. Man of Year Madison Advt. Club, 1969, Madison Man of Achievement, 1976, Man of Yr. Salvation Army, 1993; recipient Disting. Service award Wis. Newspaper Assn., 1982, Community Service award Inland Daily Press Assn., 1983, Ralph D. Casey Minn. award for Disting. Service in Journalism, 1987, First Ringling Bros. Silver Smile award, 1993, Outstanding Svc. for Youth award, 1995. Mem. Madison C. of C. (dir. 1966-70, 74-84), Inland Daily Press Assn. (dir. 1961-65), Wis. Daily Newspaper League (pres. 1961-65), Wis. Newspaper Assn. (dir. 1977-84). Clubs: B'nai B'rith, Madison. Office: 1901 Fish Hatchery Rd Madison WI 53713-1248

WOLMAN, M. GORDON, geography educator; b. Balt., Aug. 16, 1924; s. Abel and Anna (Gordon) W.; m. Elaine Mielke, June 20, 1951; children: Elsa Anne, Abel Gordon, Abby Lucille, Fredericka Jeannette. Student, Haverford Coll.; AB in Geology, Johns Hopkins U., 1949; MA in Geology, Harvard U., 1951, PhD, 1953. Geologist U.S. Geol. Survey, 1951-58, part-time, 1958—; assoc. prof. geography Johns Hopkins U., Balt., 1958-62; prof. Johns Hopkins, 1962—; chmn. dept. geography and environ. engring., 1958-90, Interim provost, 1987, 90; adv. com. geography U.S. Office Naval Rsch., Oak Ridge Nat. Lab; exec. com. divsn. earth sci. NRC, internat. environ. programs com., environ. studies bd., com. water, com. mineral resources and environ., chmn. nat. commn. water quality policy NAS; chmn. NRC Com. Adv. U.S. Geol. Survey, NAS Commn. Geoscis., Environment and Resources; environ. adv. com. Savannah River Tech. Ctr.; cons. in field. Author: Fluvial Processes in Geomorphology, 1964; Editorial bd.: Science mag. Pres. bd. trustees Park Sch., Balt.; pres. bd. dirs. Sinai Hosp., Balt., Resources for Future, 1980-87; adv. com. Inst. Nuclear Power Ops., 1982-85; active Balt. City Charter Revision Commn., Cmty. Action Com., Balt. With USNR, 1943-46. Recipient Meritorious Contbn. award Assn. Am. Geographers, 1972, Disting. Career award Geomorphology, 1993, D.L. Linton award Brit. Geomorphological Rsch. Group, 1994. Fellow Am. Acad. Arts and Scis.; mem. ASCE, NAS, Am. Geophys. Union (chmn. subcom. sedimentation, pres. hydrol. sect.), Geol. Soc. Am. (v.p. 1983, pres. 1984), Am. Geog. Soc. (councillor 1965-70, Cullum Geog. medal 1989), Washington Geol. Soc., Agrl. Hist. Soc., Md. Acad. Scis. (exec. com. 1970-75), Phi Beta Kappa, Sigma Xi. Home: 2104 W Rogers Ave Baltimore MD 21209-4553 Office: Johns Hopkins U Dept Geography/Environ Engr Baltimore MD 21218

WOLMAN, MARTIN, lawyer; b. Albany, N.Y., Feb. 2, 1937; s. Benjamin S. and Sonya (Kogan) W.; children: Koren M. Wolman-Tardy, Barton T., William B., Brandon S. AB, Brown U., 1958; LLB, U. Calif., Berkeley, 1964. Bar: Calif., 1964, Conn., 1965. Atty. Conn. Bank & Trust Co., Hartford, 1964-67; assoc. Day, Berry & Howard, Hartford, 1967-72, ptnr., 1972—; mem. Conn. Law Revision Commn. Trustee Russell-Sage Coll., Troy, N.Y., 1990, Wadsworth Atheneum, 1994; trustee Kingswood-Oxford Sch., West Hartford, Conn., 1980-93, chmn., 1986-89; bd. dirs. Hartford Hosp., 1991, Inst. of Living, 1994; mem. bd. govs. Hill-Stead Mus., Farmington, Conn., 1990—. Lt. (j.g.) USN, 1958-61. Fellow Am. Coll. Trust and Estate Counsel (chmn. Conn. chpt. 1981-86); mem. Conn. Bar Assn. (chmn. exec. com. probate sect. 1979-82). Office: Day Berry & Howard City Place Hartford CT 06103

WOLMAN, WILLIAM, economist, journalist, broadcaster; b. Montreal, Que., Can.; s. Nathan and Toba (Wexler) W.; m. Ann Livia Colamosca, Jan. 7, 1982; children: John, Flora. BA, McGill U., 1948; PhD, Stanford U., 1957. Asst. prof. econs. Wash. State U., Pullman, 1954-60; v.p. Citicorp, N.Y.C., 1969-71, Argus Rsch. Corp., N.Y.C., 1971-74; chief economist CNBC, Ft. Lee, N.J., 1989—; econs. editor Bus. Week, N.Y.C., 1960-69, sr. editor, 1974-83, editor, 1984-89, exec. editor, 1983-84, chief economist, 1989—. Avocations: skiing, photography. Office: Bus Week 1221 Ave of Americas New York NY 10020-1001

WOLMER, BRUCE RICHARD, magazine editor; b. N.Y.C., Mar. 9, 1948; s. Simon and Elaine (Richelson) Katz; m. Colleen Babington, Nov. 20, 1995. BA, Wesleyan U., Middletown, Conn., 1968; Licence es Lettres, U. Paris (Sorbonne), 1971; MPhil, Johns Hopkins U., 1976; postgrad., Ecole du Louvre, Paris, 1969-71. Rschr. dept. prints Met. Mus. Art, N.Y.C., 1972-73; editor Mus. Modern Art, N.Y.C., 1976-80; assoc. editor ARTnews Mag., N.Y.C., 1980-82, exec. editor, 1982-84; editor-in-chief Art and Antiques Mag., N.Y.C., 1984-85; pvt. art dealer London, Paris, 1986-90; exec. editor Art & Auction Mag., N.Y.C., 1990-94, editor-in-chief, 1994—; Author book, art revs. to N.Y. Observer, Sunday Times (London), ARTS, N.Y.C., Artforum, others. Mem. Reform Club (London). Jewish. Home: 300 W 12th St New York NY 10014 Office: Art & Auction Magazine 440 Park Ave S New York NY 10014

WOLOSHCHUK, CANDACE DIXON, elementary school educator, artist, consultant; b. Joliet, Ill., Jan. 11, 1947; d. Harold Russell and Beatrice Diane (Johnson) Dixon; m. Christopher Ralph Jose, Mar. 1, 1969 (div. Sept. 1982); children: Amy Russell, Jennifer Seavey; m. Thomas Woloshchuk, Dec. 23, 1988; stepchildren: Michael, Debbie, Paul, John. BA in Art, Salem Coll., 1969; postgrad., Merrimac Coll., 1969; MA in Art Edn., U. Hartford, 1977; postgrad., Fitchburg State Coll., 1994. Cert. tchr., Mass., Conn. Art dir. Fred D. Wish Sch., Hartford, Conn., 1969-71; art tchr. Timothy Edwards Jr. H.S., South Windsor, Conn., 1971-72; art coord. Hebron (Conn.) Elem. Sch., Gilead Hill Sch., 1974-78; art tchr. Longmeadow (Mass.) Pub. Schs., 1978-82, Agawan (Mass.) Pub. Schs., 1982-85; visual arts coord. Wilbraham (Mass.) Mid. Sch., 1985—; pres., owner Scholarships Unltd., Monson, Mass., 1992-94; mem. tchr.-trainer program U. Hartford, 1974-78; enrichment, art tchr. Elms Coll., 1988-93. One-women show Garrett Gallery, 1981; group shows include Spencer Arts Ctr., 1993, Craft Adventure Expo '93, 1993 (2nd and 3rd pl. awards), Craft Expo '92, 1992 (2nd pl. award), Wilbraham Pub. Libr., 1992, 93, 94. Chairwomen, mem. Wilbraham Arts Lottery Coun., 1984-88. Recipient Outstanding Visual and Performing Arts Edn. award, Mass. Alliance for Arts Edn., 1988, gold award Am. Sch. Food Svc. Assn., 1987. Mem. ASCD, NAFE, Nat. Art Edn. Assn., Mass. Art Edn. Assn., Mass. Tchrs. Assn., Wilbraham Tchrs. Assn., Am. Craft Coun. Republican. Avocations: sailing, needlepoint, painting, basketweaving. Office: Wilbraham Mid Sch 466 Stony Hill Rd Wilbraham MA 01095-1574

WOLOTSKY, HYMAN, retired college dean; b. N.Y.C., Nov. 27, 1918; s. Max and Bessie (Davis) W.; m. Ruth Schaffel, Mar. 31, 1946; children: Eugene, Paul. BA, CCNY, 1947; MA, Columbia U., 1948, doctoral studies, 1975-80. Cert. social worker. Program dir. Jewish Community Ctr., Portland, Maine, 1949-51; asst. exec. dir. Montgomery County Jewish Community, Chevy Chase, Md., 1951-53; exec. dir. Jewish Community Ctr. of Revere, Mass., 1953-59, YM-YWHA of Brockton, Mass., 1959-61, Mid-Westchester YM & YWHA, Eastchester, N.Y., 1961-65; exec. dir. early childhood ctr. Bank St. Coll. of Edn., N.Y.C., 1965-70, assoc. to provost, 1970-81, assoc. dean, 1981-84; cons. Assn. Mgmt. Svcs., New Rochelle, N.Y., 1984—; field instr. U. Md., College Pk., 1951-53, Boston U. Sch. Social Work, 1954-56, NYU Sch. Social Work, 1965-66, Hunter Coll. Sch. of Social Work, N.Y.C., 1967-70. Co-author: Career Development in Head Start, 1970, Brace Program of Systematic Observation, 1976; producer of videotapes including Experiencias Pre-escolares en Venezuela, 1978; contbr. articles to profl. jours. Trustee Fleetwood Synagogue, Mount Vernon, N.Y., 1963—, Clinton Child Care Assn., N.Y.C., 1970-80, Eastchester Youth Bd., 1961-64. Corp. U.S. Army, 1941-46. Mem. AAUP, Faculty Club Columbia U., Fleetwood Synagogue (pres. 1971-74). Democrat. Jewish. Avocations: travel, film/theatre, literature, museums. Office: Assn Mgmt Svcs 1270 North Ave New Rochelle NY 10804-2629

WOLOWITZ, STEVEN, lawyer; b. Chgo., June 27, 1952; s. Myron and Rose (Gaines) W.; m. Allison Josephy, June 15, 1974; children: Ashley Rose, Jordan Michael. BA with distinction, George Washington U., 1974, JD with honors, 1977. Bar: N.Y. 1978, U.S. Dist. Ct. (so. and ea. dists.) N.Y. 1979, U.S. Ct. Appeals (2d and 7th cirs.) 1984, U.S. Ct. Appeals (5th cir.) 1988, U.S. Supreme Ct. 1988. Assoc. Rosenman & Colin, N.Y.C., 1977-85, ptnr., 1986-88; ptnr. Mayer, Brown & Platt, N.Y.C., 1988—; arbitrator Nat. Futures Assn., 1988—. Contbr. articles to profl. jours. Mem. Phi Eta Sigma, Phi Beta Kappa. Office: Mayer Brown & Platt 1675 Broadway New York NY 10019-6018*

WOLPER, ALLAN L., journalist, educator; b. N.Y.C.; s. Sydelle Wolper; m. Joanna Birnbaum; children: Jill, Richard, Kim. BS, NYU, 1965. Reporter Providence Jour., 1965-67; polit. writer AP, N.Y.C., 1967-69, N.Y. Post, N.Y.C., 1970-63; writer, producer WABC Eyewitness News, N.Y.C., 1974-75; editor, columnist Soho Weekly News, N.Y.C., 1974-82; host, writer, producer of Right to Know Suburban Cablevision and N.J. Network, Sta. WNYC-TV, N.Y.C., Newark and Avenel, N.J., 1982-89; host, producer series on media Right to Know Right to Know syndicated pub. radio series on the media, Newark, 1989—; prof. journalism Rutgers U., 1978-92; assoc. prof. journalism Rutgers U., Newark, 1992—, prof., 1995—. Host, producer, writer documentary The Marielitos, 1984, Hillside: Desegregation, 1985, Impact, 1988, TV spl. The First Amendment, 1989 (Brechner award 1995); columnist Sports Media, Washington Journalism Rev., 1980-82, media N.J. Reporter, Princeton, 1982-85; contbg. writer Campus Journalism Editor and Pub. Mag., 1987—; contbr. articles to profl. jours. With U.S. Army, 1961-63. Recipient best pub. affairs program award Internat. TV and Video Festival, 1985, Nat. Cable TV Assn., 1986, award for cable excellence, 1986, 3 Aces award Nat. Cable TV, 1985, 86, Lowell Mellett award Pa. State U., 1985, Alfred I. DuPont award Columbia U., 1985, award in broadcast journalism (1st cable prodr. to win) N.J. Press Assn., 1987, N.J. Bell Enterprise award for best radio documentary, 1992, Best Radio Commentary and Media Nat. Headliner award 1993, Brechner award for magazine, newspaper writing. Mem. AAUP, Soc. Profl. Journalists (chmn. freedom of info. com. Dedline Club N.Y.C. br. 1980, Outstanding Broadcast Journalism award 1984, 87, Disting. Svc. award 1st Place Bicentennial Broadcast Competition 1989, spl. award N.J. Chpt., spl. award N.J. chpt. media criticism 1991, 1st Place Pub. Svc. award Mag. N.J. chpt. 1994, radio documentary 1992, investigative report 1992, winner Joseph Brechner 1st Amendment award 1995). Home: 327 Central Park W New York NY 10025-7631 Office: Rutgers U Journalism Dept Hill Hall Newark NJ 07102

WOLPER, DAVID LLOYD, motion picture and television executive; b. N.Y.C., Jan. 11, 1928; s. Irving S. and Anna (Fass) W.; m. Margaret Dawn Richard, May 11, 1958 (div.); children: Mark, Michael, Leslie; m. Gloria Diane Hill, July 11, 1974. Student, Drake U., 1946, U. So. Calif., 1948. V.p., treas. Flamingo Films, TV sales co., 1948-50, v.p. West Coast Ops., 1954-58; chmn., pres. Wolper Prodns., L.A., 1958—; cons., exec. producer Warner Bros., Inc., 1976—. TV prodns. include Race for Space, Making of the President 1960, 64, Biography series, Story of... series, The Yanks are Coming, Berlin: Kaiser to Khrushchev, December 7: Day of Infamy, The American Woman in the 20th Century, Hollywood and The Stars, March of Time Specials, The Rise and Fall of the Third Reich, The Legend of Marilyn Monroe, Four Days in November, Krebiozen and Cancer, National Geographic, Undersea World of Jacques Cousteau, China: Roots of Madness, The Journey of Robert F. Kennedy, Say Goodbye, George Plimpton, Appointment With Destiny, American Heritage, Smithsonian, They've Killed President Lincoln, Sandburg's Lincoln, Primal Man, The First Woman President, Chico and the Man, Get Christie Love, Welcome Back, Kotter!, Collison Course, Roots, Victory at Entebbe, Roots: The Next Generations, Moviola, The Thorn Birds, North and South Books I, II, III, Napoleon and Josephine, Alex Haley's Queen, Men Of The Dragon, Unwed Father, The Morning After; feature films include The Hellstrom Chronicle, Devil's Brigade, The Bridge at Remagen, If It's Tuesday, This Must Be Belgium, Willy Wonka and The Chocolate Factory, Visions of Eight, This is Elvis, Murder in the First; live spl. events include Opening and Closing Ceremonies 1984 Olympic Games, Liberty Weekend July 3-6, 1986. Trustee L.A. County Mus. Art, Am. Film Inst., L.A. Thoracic and Cardiovascular Found., Boys and Girls Clubs Am., U.S. Golf Assn. Found.; bd. dirs. Amateur Athletic Assn. L.A., L.A. Heart Inst., Acad. TV Arts and Scis. Found., So. Calif. Com. for Olympic Games, U. So. Calif. Cinema/TV Dept.; bd. govs. Cedars Sinai Med. Ctr.; com. mem. U.S. Olympic Team Benefit; mem. adv. com. Nat. Ctr. Jewish Film. Recipient award for documentaries San Francisco Internat. Film Festival, 1960, 7 Golden Globe awards, 5 George Foster Peabody awards, Disting. Service award U.S. Jr. C. of C.; 40 Emmy awards, 145 Emmy nominations Acad. TV Arts and Scis.; Monte Carlo Internat. Film Festival award, 1964, Cannes Film Festival Grand Prix for TV Programs, 1964; Oscar award, 11 Oscar nominations, Jean Hersholt Humanitarian award Acad. Motion Picture and TV Scis., medal of Chevalier The French Nat. Legion of Honor, 1990; named to TV Hall of Fame, 1988. Mem. Nat. Acad. TV Arts and Scis., Acad. Motion Picture Arts and Scis., Producers Guild Am., Caucus for Producers, Writers and Dirs. Office: care Warner Bros Inc 4000 Warner Blvd Burbank CA 91522-0001

WOLPER, MARSHALL, insurance and financial consultant; b. Chgo., Nov. 19, 1922; s. Harry B. and Bessie (Steiner) W.; m. Thelma R. Freedman, April 15, 1957 (div. Oct. 1968); m. Jacqueline N. Miller, Sept. 19, 1969 (div. Jan. 1976); m. Lucee I. G. Lee, Mar. 20, 1985; stepchildren—Robert Insinga, Cyndi Wolper. B.A. in Polit. Sci. and Econs., U. Ill., 1942. Chartered fin. cons. With Kent Products, Chgo., 1946; pres. Marshall Industries, Chgo., 1947-52; with Equitable Life Assurance Soc., 1953-89, nat. honor agt., 1966, nat. sales cons., 1967—; sr. ptnr. Wolper & Katz, 1958—; ptnr. Wolper and Katz Thoroughbred Racing Stable, 1977-86; instr. life underwriting and pensions U. Miami, 1959—; pres. Marshall Wolper Co., 1953—; chmn. bd. M.W. Computer Systems, Inc., 1971-80; pres. Marshall Wolper Pension Sers. Inc., 1978-80, Wolper Ross & Co., 1980-87; lectr. life ins., employee benefit plans, pensions, estate planning to various univs. and spl. meetings; pres. Greater Miami Tax Inst., 1963, Estate Planning Coun. Greater Miami, 1969-70; faculty Practicing Law Inst., 1967—; mem. adv. com., lectr. Inst. on Estate Planning. Author: Medical Entities Taxed as Corporations, 1961, Tax and Business Aspects of Professional Corporations and Associations, 1968; contbr. articles to profl. jours. Bd. dirs. Dade County chpt. ARC, Profl. Selling Inst. Served to 1st lt. AUS, Parachute Infantry, World War II, ETO. Decorated Bronze Star, Purple Heart; recipient Paragon award Equitable Life Assurance Soc., 1972; C.L.U. Mem. Am. Soc. CLUs (pres. Miami chpt. 1963, inst. faculty 1963-65, dir. 1966-67, regional v.p. 1968), The Am. Coll. (joint com. on continuing edn. 1965—), Nat. Assn. Life Underwriters (lectr. 1963, 66, 81), Million Dollar Round Table (life mem., speaker 1962-81, exec. com. 1974-78, pres. 1977), Assn. Advanced Life Underwriting (lectr. 1966, pres. 1972), Am. Soc. Pension Actuaries (dir.), Nat. Assn. Pension Consultants and Adminstrs. (treas.). Office: The Marshall Wolper Co 1546 NE Quayside Ter Miami FL 33138-2208

WOLPERT, EDWARD ALAN, psychiatrist; b. Chgo., Apr. 22, 1930; s. Sol and Dorothy (Greenwald) W.; m. Gloria Adele Yanoff, Mar. 23, 1958; children: Seth Isaac, Andrew Oxman, Edward Greenwald. B.A., U. Chgo., 1950, M.A., 1954, Ph.D., 1959, M.D., 1960. Diplomate: Am. Bd. Neurology and Psychiatry. Intern medicine U. Ill. Research Hosp., 1960-61; resident psychiatry Michael Reese Hosp., 1961-64; dir. clin. services Psychosomatic and Psychiat. Inst., 1966-79, dir. of hosp., 1979-93; clin. assoc. prof. psychiatry U. Chgo. Sch. Medicine, 1972-76, clin. prof. psychiatry, 1976-90; clin. prof. psychiatry U. Ill. Sch. Medicine, 1990-93; prof. psychiatry Rush Med. Coll., 1993—; sr. rsch. scholar Rush Inst. Mental Well-Being, 1993—; cons. Senila Shandman Orthogenic Sch., 1973-96; chmn. Ill. Dept. Mental Health and Devel. Disabilities Rev. Bd. Contbr. articles to profl. jours. Fellow Am. Psychiat. Assn.; mem. AMA, Ill., Chgo. med. socs., Ill. Psychiat. Soc. (pres. 1982-83), AAAS, Am. Psychoanalytic Assn. (certified in psychoanalysis), Assn. for Psychophysiol. Study of Sleep, Am. Psychol. Assn., N.Y. Acad. Scis., George S. Klein Meml. Psychoanalytic Research Forum, Am. Soc. for Clin. Pharmacology and Therapeutics, Chgo. Psychoanalytic Soc., Inst. Medicine Chgo., Wis. Acad. Arts, Letters and Scis. Home: 680 N Lake Shore Dr Apt 1004 Chicago IL 60611-4406 Office: Rush Inst Mental Well Being 1725 W Harrison St Chicago IL 60612-3828

WOLRAICH, MARK LEE, pediatrician. BA, SUNY, Binghamton, 1966; MD, SUNY, Syracuse, 1970. Diplomate Am. Bd. Pediatrics. Pediatric intern SUNY, Syracuse, 1970-71; pediatric resident U. Okla. Health Scis. Ctr., Oklahoma City, 1973-74; pediatric fellowship U. Oreg. Health Scis. Ctr., 1974-76; asst. prof. U. Iowa, 1976-81, assoc. prof., 1981-86, prof., 1986-90; prof. Vanderbilt U., 1990—, dir. divsn. child devel., dir. child devel. ctr., 1990—, dir. ctr. for chronic illnesses and disabilities in children, 1990—; assoc. dir. J.F. Kennedy Ctr. for Rsch. on Edn. and Human Devel., 1990-93; med. supr. U. Iowa Divsn. of Developmental Disabilities, 1980-90; vis. prof. Great Ormond St. Hosp. for Sick Children, London, 1983, U. Cape Town, Rondebosch Cape, South Africa, 1986, Columbus Children's Hosp., Ohio State U., Dept. Pediatrics, 1988; mem. Iowa State Foster Care Rev. Bd. Co-editor Advances in Developmental and Behavioral Pediatrics, 1981-92; cons. editor Am. Jour. on Mental Deficiency; editl. adv. bd. A Guide to Parent Counseling; cons. reviewer Developmental Medicine and Child Neurology, Pediatrics, Nutrition and Behavior, Jour. Pediatrics, Jou. of Social and Personal Relationships, Applied Rsch. in Mental Retardation, Jour. of Clin. Psychology, Jour. Developmental and Behavioral Pediatrics, Clin. Pediatrics, others; contbr. numerous articles to profl. publs.*. Recipient Disting. and Dedicated Svc. award Spina Bifida Assn. of Iowa, 1979, Lou Holloway award for rsch. Health Scis. Edn.; grantee NIMH, 1987-90, 92—, Nat. Inst. on Disability and Rehab. Rsch., 1987-89, 87-88, NIH, 1988-91, 91-94, Iowa Dept. of Human Svcs., 1986-88, 88-89, U. Iowa, 1979, 80-87, United Cerebral Palsy Rsch. and Endl. Found., Inc., 1978-87, 94, Iowa March of Dimes, 1980, Sugar Assn., Inc., 1983, Internat. Life Scis. Inst., 1988-91, W.T. Grant Found., 1989. Fellow Am. Acad. Pediatrics (com., grant 1992—), Am. Acad. Cerebral Palsy and Developmental Medicine; mem. Soc. for Behavioral Pediatrics (pres. 1994-95, program dir. 1990-93), Soc. Developmental Pediatrics, Soc. Pediatric Psychology Assn. (assoc.), Soc. for Pediatric Rsch. (sr.), Am. Acad. Physician and Patient (charter). Office: Vanderbilt U Child Devel Ctr 2100 Pierce Ave Nashville TN 37212-3162

WOLSIFFER, PATRICIA RAE, insurance company executive; b. Indpls., Aug. 15, 1933; d. Charles L. and Dorothy M. (Smith) Bohlsen; m. Edward C. Wolsiffer, Oct. 5, 1956; children: John M., Anderson, Sherry L. Anderson Cooney, Edward J. Wolsiffer. Student, Ind. Central U., 1974-75. Various secretarial positions, 1964-71; with Blue Cross/Blue Shield Ind. (Associated Ins. Cos., Inc.), Indpls., 1971-88, supr. personnel, 1973-76, exec. asst. to pres., 1976-79, corp. sec., 1979-85, exec. asst. to chmn. bd., chief exec. officer, 1985-88, ret. Vol. Hancock Meml. Hosp. Guild. Republican. Presbyterian. Clubs: Order Eastern Star, Daus. of Nile, Ladies Oriental Shrine. Home: 5550 E 100 N Greenfield IN 46140-9445 Office: 120 Monument Cir Indianapolis IN 46204-4906

WOLSON, CRAIG ALAN, lawyer; b. Toledo, Feb. 20, 1949; s. Max A. and Elaine B. (Cohn) W.; m. Janis Nan Braun, July 30, 1972 (div. Mar. 1986); m. Ellen Carol Schulgasser, Oct. 26, 1986; children: Lindsey, Michael and Geoffrey (triplets). BA, U. Mich., 1971, JD, 1974. Bar: N.Y. 1975, U.S. Dist. Ct. (so. and ea. dists.) N.Y. 1975, U.S. Ct. Appeals (2d cir.) 1975, U.S. Supreme Ct. 1978. Assoc. Shearman & Sterling, N.Y.C., 1974-81; v.p., asst. gen. counsel Thomson McKinnon Securities Inc., N.Y.C., 1981-85; v.p., sec., gen. counsel J.D. Mattus Co., Inc., Greenwich, Conn., 1985-88; also bd. dirs. J.D. Mattus Co., Inc. and affiliated cos., Greenwich; v.p., asst. gen. counsel Chem. Bank, N.Y.C., 1988-95; of counsel Williams and Harris, N.Y.C., 1995—; dep. clk. Lucas County Courthouse, Toledo, 1968-69, 71-72. Articles and administrv. editor U. Mich. Law Rev., 1973-74. Mem. ABA, N.Y. State Bar Assn., Assn. of Bar of City of N.Y. (securities regulation com. 1994—), Corp. Bar. Assn. of Westchester and Fairfield, Phi Beta Kappa, Phi Eta Sigma, Pi Sigma Alpha. Avocations: reading, playing piano, fine dining, theater. Home: 41 Bonnie Brook Rd Westport CT 06880-1507 Office: Williams & Harris 20 Exchange Pl New York NY 10005

WOLTER, JOHN AMADEUS, librarian, government official; b. St. Paul, July 25, 1925; s. Amadeus Frank and Marjorie (Wears) W.; m. Joan Patricia Venard, July 6, 1956; children: Mark, Thomas, Matthew, David. Student, Coll. St. Thomas, 1950; BA, U. Minn., 1956, MA, 1965, PhD, 1975; postgrad., Georgetown U., 1957. Officer, seaman Isthmian Lines Inc., N.Y.C., 1943-50, 57-60; marine transp. officer Mil. Sea Transp. Ser., Washington, 1956-57; instr., map libr. U. Minn., 1961-64, asst. to dir. univ. librs., 1964-65, research fellow, 1965-66; asst. prof. Wis. State U., River Falls, 1966-68; asst. chief geography and map. div. Libr. of Congress, Washington, 1968-78, chief, 1978-91, acting dir. pub. svc. and collections MGMT I, 1989-90; cons. in geography, 1991-93; mem. U.S. Bd. Geog. Names, 1969-83, vice chmn., 1980-81, chmn., 1981-83. Rev. editor cartography divsn. Surveying and Mapping, 1971-72; mem. editl. bd. Cartographica, 1971-80, Am. Cartographer, 1974-79, Terrae Incognitae, 1973-75, ACSM Bull., 1974-80, Surveying and Mapping, 1972-80; editl. advisor The Portolan, 1986—; contbg. editor Imago Mundi, 1979-91; contbr. articles to profl. jours. Served with U.S. Army, 1950-52. Libr. of Congress Disting. Svc. award, 1992, Smithsonian Inst. Cert. of award, 1986. Mem. Internat. Geog. Union (U.S. nat. com. 1972-80, 84-88), Internat. Cartographic Assn. (U.S. mem. commn. on history of cartography 1972-76, corr. 1976-92, Assn. Am. Geographers (editorial bd. Annals 1988-92), Spl. Librs. Assn. (sec.-treas. geog.and map div. 1965), Soc. History Discoveries (sec.-treas. 1972-75, coun. 1976-78, v.p. 1983-85, pres. 1985-87), Can. Nautical Rsch. Soc., Am. Congress Surveying and Mapping (chmn. publs. com. 1978-80, Presdl. citation 1985), N.Am. Soc. Oceanic History, N.Mex. Geog. Soc. (bd. dirs., governing bd.), Washington Map Soc., Soc. Nautical Rsch., Gt. Lakes Hist. Soc., Explorers Club, Theta Delta Chi. Home: 5430 Ring Dove Ln Columbia MD 21044-1716

WOLTERINK, LESTER FLOYD, biophysicist, educator; b. Marion, N.Y., July 28, 1915; s. John and Ruth Lavina (Voorhorst) W.; m. Lillian Ruth Nichols, June 30, 1938; children—Charles Paul, Timothy John. A.B., Hope Coll., 1936; M.A., U. Minn., 1940, Ph.D., 1943. Faculty Mich. State U., East Lansing, 1941—; prof. physiology Mich. State U., 1952-84, prof. emeritus, 1984—; asso. scientist AEC, Argonne Nat. Lab., 1948; cons., then biosatellite project scientist Ames Research Center, NASA, 1963-66; Mem. various coms. AEC Conf. on Isotopes in Plant and Animal Research, 1952-59; mem. NASA Manned Space Sta. Commn., 1966; cons. NSF, 1967-70; mem. panel on nitrogen oxides Nat. Acad. Sci./NRC, 1973-75. Contbr. articles to profl. publs., reports to govt. agys. Mem. Mich. Nucleonic Soc. (pres. 1961), Soc. Exptl. Biology and Medicine (sec. Mich. sect. 1961-63), Am. Astronautic Soc. (chmn. San Francisco sect. 1966), AAUP, Am. Inst. Biol. Scis., Am. Physiol. Soc., N.Y. Acad. Scis., IEEE, Biomed. Engring. Soc., Biophys. Soc., Sigma Xi (jr. scientist Mich. State U. 1954). Club: Torch (pres. 1983, sec. 1985-86). Home: 2277 Kewanee Way Okemos MI 48864-2514 Office: Mich State U Dept Physiology East Lansing MI 48824

WOLTERS, CURT CORNELIS FREDERIK, foreign service officer; b. Nymegen, The Netherlands, Mar. 13, 1938; came to U.S., 1957; s. Frederik and Cornelia Johanna (Jansen) W.; m. Sara J. Daughters, June 10, 1962 (div. 1980); children: Gwyneth, Chad; m. Charlotte Cooper, Sept. 22, 1980 (div. 1988); children: Lottena, Cicely; m. Sylvana K. Perry, Apr. 1989; 1 child, Roger. Student, Wash. State U., 1958-61, U. Bonn, Fed. Republic Germany, 1962-63; BA, U. Oreg., 1964, MA, 1966; MBA, U. Washington, 1976; PhD, Pacific Western U., 1989. Asst. sec. Rep. Botswana Govt., Gaborone, 1966-68; program advisor The Ford Found., N.Y.C., 1968-74; sr. rsch. analyst Seattle C. of C., 1974-76; sr. assoc. Inst. Pub. Adminstrn. N.Y., N.Y.C., 1976-78; freelance economist Africa, 1978-79; econ. program officer, diplomat (AID) Dept. State, Washington, 1979—; cons. Inst. for Puget Sound Needs, Seattle, 1975-76, Pacific Cons., Washington, 1976. Contbr. numerous articles to profl. jours.; author project evaluations. Mem. civic action com. Congress of Racial Equality, Eugene, Oreg., 1965-66; vol.

campaign Dixie Lee Ray Gubernatorial Campaign, Seattle, 1976; treas., chmn. fin. com. Internat. Sch. Islamabad, 1989-92. Carnegie Found. fellow, 1964-65, Africa-Asia pub. svc. fellow Maxwell Sch., 1966-68, fellow German Govt., U. Bonn, 1962-63; recipient Air Def. Command Outstanding Achievement award USAF, 1960; Cmty. Svc. award U.S. Embassy, Islamabad, 1992-93, 93-94. Mem. Am. Econ. Assn., Air Force Assn., Wilson Ctr. (assoc. of Smithsonian Instn.), Am. Fgn. Svc. Assn., Holland Am. Club (treas. Greater Seattle area 1975-76), Am. Legion. Office: USAID/Zambia Lusaka Dept of State Washington DC 20521-2310

WOLTERS, OLIVER WILLIAM, history educator; b. Reading, Eng., June 8, 1915; came to U.S., 1964; s. Albert William and Gertrude (Lewis) W.; m. Euteen Khoo, Apr. 25, 1955; children: Pamela Gwyneth, Nigel Christopher. B.A., Lincoln Coll., Oxford U., 1937; Ph.D., Sch. Oriental and African Studies, London, 1961. With Malayan Civil Service, 1938-57; lectr. Sch. Oriental and African Studies, London, 1957-63; prof. S.E. Asian history Cornell U., Ithaca, N.Y., 1964-74, Goldwin Smith prof. S.E. Asian history, 1974-85; ret., 1985. Author: Early Indonesian Commerce, 1967, The Fall of Srivijaya, 1970, History, Culture, and Region in Southeast Asian Perspectives, 1982, Two Essays on Dai-Viet in the Fourteenth Century, 1988; editor: (with others) Southeast Asian History, 1976; sr. editor: The Vietnam Forum, 1985-93. Trustee Breezewood Found., Md., 1964-84. Decorated Officer Order Brit. Empire, 1952; Guggenheim fellow, 1972-73; Bellagio fellow Rockefeller Found., 1982; recipient Disting. Scholarship award Assn. for Asian Studies, 1990. Episcopalian.

WOLTERS, RAYMOND, historian, educator; b. Kansas City, Mo., July 25, 1938; s. Raymond M. and Margaret G. (Reilly) W.; m. Mary McCullough, June 23, 1962; children—Jeffrey, Kevin, Thomas. B.A., Stanford U., 1960; M.A., U. Calif.-Berkeley, 1962, Ph.D., 1967. Instr. dept. history U. Del., Newark, 1965-67, asst. prof., 1967-70, assoc. prof., 1970-75; prof. U. Del., 1975—. Mem. editl. adv. bd. Acad. Am. Ency.; author: Negroes and the Great Depression, 1970, The New Negro on Campus, 1975, The Burden of Brown, 1984, Right Turn, 1996. Fellow NEH, 1971-72, Am. Coun. Learned Socs., 1978-79, Earhart Found., 1989-90; recipient Silver Gavel award ABA. Mem. Am. Hist. Assn., Orgn. Am. Historians, So. Hist. Assn. Home: 20 Bridlebrook Ln Newark DE 19711-2061 Office: U Del History Dept Newark DE 19711

WOLTING, ROBERT ROY, city official; b. Faulkton, S.D., Dec. 29, 1928; s. George and Minnie (Meeter) W.; m. Nancy Catherine O'Brien, Nov. 26, 1953; children: Robert Roy, Linda Marie. Acct. Wolting Implement and Motor Co., Wessington Springs, S.D., 1954-60; city auditor City of Wessington Springs, 1960-64, City of Brookings, S.D., 1964-68; dir. fin. City of Fairbanks, Alaska, 1968-77, city mgr., 1977-79, 90-93, dir. fin., treas., 1984-90; city mgr., 1990-93; elected mem. City Coun., 1994—; city adminstr., clk. City of Union Springs, Ala., 1980-84. Mem. S.D. Retirement Bd., 1966-68. Sgt. USAF, 1950-54. Mem. Alaska Mcpl. Mgrs. Assn., Mcpl. Fin. Officers Assn. (pres. S.D. chpt. 1965-67, sec. Fairbanks chpt. 1976-78, bd. dirs. 1985-90). Democrat. Methodist. Avocation: photography. Home: 431 Le Ann Dr Fairbanks AK 99701-3232 Office: City of Fairbanks 800 Cushman St Fairbanks AK 99701-4632

WOLTZ, HOWARD OSLER, JR., steel and wire products company executive; b. Mt. Airy, N.C., Apr. 2, 1925; s. Howard Osler and Louise (Elliott) W.; m. Joan Elizabeth Moore, Dec. 29, 1949; children: Louise, Joan Woltz Robins, Howard O. III, Edwin Moore. LLB, U. Va., 1948. Bar: N.C., 1948. Ptnr. law firm Mt. Airy, 1948-54; pres., founder Dixie Concrete Products, Inc., Mt. Airy, 1953-69; founder Dixie Exposaic, Inc., Mt. Airy, 1963; pres., chmn. bd. Insteel Industries (formerly Exposaic Industries, Inc.), Mt. Airy, 1969-89, chmn., CEO, 1989-91; v.p., bd. dirs. Quality Mills, Inc., Mt. Airy. Mem. N.C. Ho. of Reps., 1951-53; chmn. Mt. Airy-Surry County Airport Authority, 1987-93; former pres. Greater Mt. Airy United Fund; former chmn. Surry C.C.; vice-chmn. Hospice Surry County; past bd. dirs. Old Hickory Coun. Boy Scouts Am.; bd. dirs. Triad United Meth. Home. Mem. Nat. Concrete Masonry Assn. (pres. 1965), N.C. Concrete Masonry Assn. (pres. 1959), Wire Reinforcement Inst. (chmn. 1982), Am. Wire Producers Assn. (bd. dirs. 1987-91), N.C. State Bar Assn., Mt. Airy C. of C. (Citizen of Yr. 1991). Rotary (past pres. Mt. Airy). Republican. Home: 819 Greenhill Rd Mount Airy NC 27030-9240 Office: Insteel Industries Inc 1373 Boggs Dr Mount Airy NC 27030-2145

WOLTZ, KENNETH ALLEN, consulting executive; b. Phila., Mar. 2, 1943; s. Herman and Florence (Varell) M.; m. Barbara Hand, June 18, 1966; children: Karyn, Diane, Kenneth. BS, U.S. Mil. Acad., 1966; MBA, Xavier U., 1971. Cert. mgmt. cons. Various mgmt. positions GE, Evansdale, Ohio and Bethesda, Md., 1968-73; mgr. systems Xerox Corp., Rochester, N.Y., 1973-75; dir. info. svcs. McGraw Edison, Des Plaines, Ill., 1975-77; mng. dir., mgmt. cons. Peat, Marwick, Mitchell, Chgo., 1977-80; mgmt. cons., CEO, Woltz & Assoc., Inc., Barrington, Ill., 1980—; mgmt. cons. Speaker at various Univs. With U.S. Army, 1966-68. Mem. Soc. Mgmt. Info. Systems, Inst. Mgmt. Cons., West Point Soc. (treas. 1975), Assn. Corp. Growth, Assn. Mgmt. Consulting Firms, Ind. Computer Cons. Assn., Forest Grove Club. Home: RR 2 Barrington Hi IL 60010-9802 Office: Woltz & Assocs Inc Barrington Pl 18-5 E Dundee Rd Barrington IL 60010-7412

WOLVERTON, ROBERT EARL, classics educator; b. Indpls., Aug. 4, 1925; s. Robert N. and Vivian (Lefflar) W.; m. Margaret Jester, Sept. 13, 1952; children: Robert Earl, Laurie Ann, Edwin J., Gary A. AB, Hanover Coll., 1948; MA, U. Mich., 1949; PhD, U. N.C., 1954; LittD, Coll. Mt. St. Joseph on the Ohio, 1977; postdoctoral, Oxford (Eng.) U., 1986. Asst. prof. classics U. Ga., 1954-59; asst. prof. classics, history Tufts U., 1959-62; asst. prof., assoc. prof. classics and humanities, dir. honors program Fla. State U., 1962-67; assoc. prof. classics, assoc. dean U. Ill. Grad. Coll., 1967-69; dean Grad. Sch. and Research; prof. classics Miami U., Oxford, Ohio, 1969-72; pres., prof. classics Coll. Mt. St. Joseph on Ohio, Cin., 1972-77; prof. Miss. State U., Starkville, 1977—, v.p. acad. affairs, 1977-86, prof. classics, 1986—, interim head dept. fgn. langs., 1991-92, head dept., 1992—; vis. lectr. U. Perugia, Italy, 1985; fellow Acad. Adminstrn. Internship Program, 1965-66; field reader U.S. Office Edn.; cons., reviewer North Cen. Assn. Colls. and Schs., So. Assn. Colls. and Schs.; mem. exec. com. Coun. Grad. Schs. U.S., 1970-73; chmn. Midwest Assn. Grad. Schs., 1971; mem. Regents Adv. Com. Grad. Edn., Ohio, 1969-72, chmn., 1971-72; mem. Medford (Mass.) Edn. Coun., 1961-62. Author: Classical Elements in English Words, 1965, An Outline of Classical Mythology, 1966; contbg. translator: A Life of George Washington in Latin Prose (Francis Glass), 1976; editor: (with others) Graduate Programs and Admissions Manual, 1971, 72; contbr. (with others) articles to profl. jours. and encys. Trustee, v.p. Greater Cin. Consortium Colls. and Univs., St. Francis Hosp., Ohio; mem. Cin. coun. on econ. edn.; bd. dirs. Starville Arts Alliance, pres., 1989—, Starkville-Miss. State U. Symphony Assn., 1985—, pres., 1987—, Miss. Opera Assn.; mem. Miss. Com. Humanities, 1982-86, Miss. Arts Commn., 1986-87; pres. coun. of laity St. Mary's of Oxford, 1969-70; mem. Starkville Community Theatre, 1978-79, pres., 1982-82, 82-83; pres. parish coun. St. Joseph Ch., 1979, 89-90; pres. diocesan pastoral coun. Diocese of Jackson, Miss., 1983-84, 86-87. Recipient Outstanding Undergraduate Teaching award Miss. State U., 1990. Mem. Am. Classical League (pres. 1972-76), Am. Philol. Assn. Classical Assn. Middle West and South, Vergilian Soc., Am. Assn. Higher Edn., Assn. Ind. Colls. and Univs. Ohio (sec. 1973-75, vice chmn. 1975-77), Nat. Coun. Chief Acad. Officers (exec. com. 1981-84, chmn. 1983-94), Coun. Basic Edn., Nat. Faculty Humanities Arts and Scis., Acad. Polit. Sci., Ohio Program in Humanities, Golden Key Honor Soc., Cardinal Key Honor Soc., Sigma Chi, Omicron Delta Kappa, Eta Sigma Phi, Phi Kappa Phi (nat. editl. advisor 1984-89), Phi Delta Kappa, Phi Eta Sigma. Home: 102 Colonial Circle Starkville MS 39759-4201

WOLYNES, PETER GUY, chemistry researcher, educator; b. Chgo., Apr. 21, 1953; s. Peter and Evelyn Eleanor (Etter) W.; m. Jane Lee Fox, Nov. 26, 1976 (div. 1980); m. Kathleen Cull Bucher, Dec. 22, 1984; children: Margrethe Cull, Eve Cordelia. AB with highest distinction, Ind. U., 1971; AM, Harvard U., 1972, PhD in Chem. Physics, 1976; DSc (hon.), Ind. U., 1988. Rsch. assoc. MIT, Cambridge, 1975-76; asst. prof., assoc. prof. Harvard U., Cambridge, 1976-80; vis. scientist Max Planck Inst. für Biophysikalische Chemie, Gottingen, Fed. Republic Germany, 1977; assoc. prof. chemistry U. Ill., Urbana, 1980-83, prof., 1983—, prof. physics, 1985—; prof. physics and biophysics U. Ill., 1989—; permanent mem. Ctr. for Advanced Study U. Ill., Urbana, 1989—; William H. and Janet LyCan prof. chemistry Ctr. for Advanced Study U. Ill., Urbana, 1993—; vis. prof. Inst. for Molecular Sci., Okazaki, Japan, 1982, 87; vis. scientist Inst. for Theoretical Physics, Santa Barbara, Calif., 1987, Ecole normale Supérieure, Paris, 1992, Merski lectr. U. Nebr., 1986, Denkewalter lectr., Loyola U., 1986. Contbr. numerous articles to profl. jours. Sloan fellow, 1981-83, J.S. Guggenheim fellow, 1986-87; Beckman assoc. Ctr. for Advanced Study, Urbana, 1984-85. Fellow Am. Phys. Soc., Am. Acad. Arts and Scis.; mem. NAS, AAAS, Am. Chem. Soc. (Pure Chemistry award 1986), N.Y. Acad. Scis., Biophys. Soc., Phi Beta Kappa, Sigma Xi, Phi Lambda Upsilon (Fresenius award 1988), Sigma Pi Sigma, Alpha Chi Sigma. Home: 311 W Oregon St Urbana IL 61801-4125 Office: U Ill Sch of Chem Scis 505 S Mathews Ave Urbana IL 61801-3617

WOLYNIC, EDWARD THOMAS, specialty chemicals technology executive; b. Bklyn., May 29, 1948; s. Edward Joseph and Fortunata Wolynic; m. Loraine Cynthia Ciardullo. BS ChemE, Poly. Inst. N.Y., 1969; MS ChemE, Princeton U., 1972, PhD ChemE, 1974. Staff engr. Union Carbide Corp., Bound Brook, N.J., 1974-75; supr. Union Carbide Corp., Tarrytown, N.Y., 1975-77, mgr. mfg. tech., 1977-82, assoc. dir. tech., 1982-85, dir. tech., 1985-88; v.p. rsch. UOP, Tarrytown, 1988-90; v.p. devel. UOP, Des Plaines, Ill., 1990-92; dir. process R&D Internat. Specialty Products Corp., Wayne, N.J., 1993, v.p. R&D, 1993-95; dir. corp. R&D Engelhard Corp., Iselin, N.J., 1995—. Contbr. tech. articles to profl. jours.; patentee in field. Mem. AIChe, Indsl. Rsch. Inst., Com. Devel. Assn., N.Am. Catalyst Soc. Avocations: fishing, tennis, skiing. Office: Engelhard Corp 101 Wood Ave Iselin NJ 08830-0770

WOLZ, HENRY GEORGE, philosophy educator; b. Kornwestheim, Germany, Sept. 10, 1905; came to U.S., 1930; s. John and Catherin (Pflueger) W.; m. Barbara L. Dertwinkel, Mar. 20, 1955; 1 dau., Ursula. B.S., Fordham U., 1936, M.A., 1938, Ph.D., 1946. Columbia Coll., 1947; Tutor Bklyn. Coll., 1947, Hunter Coll., 1947-49; asst. prof. Wagner Coll., 1947-51; asst. prof. Queens Coll., City U. N.Y., 1951-56, assoc. prof., 1956-64, prof., 1964-76. Author: Plato and Heidegger: In Search of Selfhood, 1981; contbr. numerous articles to profl. jours. Served with AUS, 1942-45. Mem. Am. Philos. Assn., Metaphys. Soc. Am. Home: 25 Ryan St Syosset NY 11791-2129

WOMACH, EMILY HITCH, retired banker and marketing and public relations executive; b. Laurel, Del., Jan. 27, 1927; d. Elon G. and Jennie (Neal) Hitch; m. William S. Womach, Mar. 13, 1943 (Oct. 1982); 1 son, William Richard. Student, Salisbury (Md.) Bus. Inst., 1948; grad. Sch. Fin. Pub. Rels., Northwestern U., 1957; grad. Sch. Fin. Pub. Relations, Am. Inst. Banking, 1958, Stonier Grad. Sch. Banking, Rutgers U., 1968. With Sussex Trust Co., Laurel, 1945-68; sec., asst., cashier Sussex Trust Co., 1956-62, asst. v.p., sec., 1962-67, v.p., sec., 1967-68; adminstrv. asst. to gov. Del., 1968-69; sales rep. Robinson Real Estate, 1969-71; treas. State of Del., 1971-73; also dir. div. treasury dept. finance; v.p., mem. sr. mgmt. Farmers Bank State Del., Wilmington, 1973-76; chmn. bd., pres., chief exec. officer Women's Nat. Bank, Washington, 1976-83; chmn. bd., pres. Internat. Fin. Adv. Svcs., 1983-88; dir. mktg., pub. rels. Asbury Meth. Village, Gaithersburg, Md., 1986-92; pres. First WNB Corp., bank holding co., 1981-83; bd. dirs. Penjerdel Corp.; lectr. in field, 1958—; econ. commentator Spectrum on Economy, WCAV Radio, 1975-76; fin. cons. Past mem. nat. adv. coun. Small Bus. Adminstrn.; mem. Del. Bank Adv. Bd., 1963-71; participant Internat. Workshop Women Leaders in Banking and Fin., Amsterdam and San Remo, Italy. Chmn. budget com., auditor Laurel LWV, 1959-71; bd. dirs. Music at Noon, D.C. Performing Arts Soc., 1978-82; mem. edn. com., also fund drive com. Delmarva Poultry Industry, 1963-66; sec.-treas. Overall Econ. Devel. Program Com., 1967-71; mem. Del. State Small Bus. Adv. Council, 1965-71, Laurel Planning Commn., 1965-68, D.C. Employment Security Bd., 1978-80; v.p. Del. div. Am. Cancer Soc., 1964-68, mem. Del. exec. com. and bd., 1957-71; mem. Sussex County unit bd., 1957-71; bd. dirs. Nat. Capital Area region NCCJ, 1978-81; chmn. Del. Heart Fund, 1972; bd. dirs., treas. Community Fund. Greater Washington, 1978-81; mem. adv. coun. The Women's Inst./Am. U., 1978-83; trustee Wesley Coll., 1973-83. Recipient Outstanding Woman Who Works award Downtown Assn. Memphis, 1964, Merit award Del. Fed. Bus. and Profl. Women's Club, 1966; named Outstanding Citizen of Laurel, Outstanding Person of Yr. in Mktg. Washington Fin. Coun., 1981. Mem. Nat. Assn. Bank Women (v.p. Middle Atlantic div. 1960-61, nat. v.p. 1962-63, nat. pres. 1963-64), Am. Inst. Banking (pres. Sussex chpt. 1958-59), Am. Bankers Assn. (exec. com. savs. div. 1966-67, communication com. mktg. div. 1974-75, mem. adminstrv. com. govtl. rels. coun. 1975-76, 80-83), Del. Bankers Assn. (chmn. pub. rels. com. 1959-63, vice chmn. legis. com.), D.C. Bankers Assn. (adminstrv. coun. 1980-83), Friends of Women's World Banking/USA (pres. 1980-83), Am. Newspaper Women's Club (asso.), Del. C. of C. (dir. 1974-76, Josiah Marvel cup award 1967), Bus. and Profl. Women's Club (pres. Laurel 1951), Am. Acad. Polit. and Social Sci., Internat. Women's Forum, Rehoboth Art League, Nat. Audubon Soc. (bd. dirs. 1985-87), Delta Kappa Gamma (hon.). Democrat. Methodist.

WOMACK, EDGAR ALLEN, JR., technology executive; b. Humboldt, Tenn., Oct. 29, 1942; s. Edgar Allen Sr. and Lucy Opal (George) W.; m. Linda Jane Cochran, Dec. 28, 1963; children: Constance Elaine, Cynthia Lynn. BS, MIT, 1963, MS, 1965, PhD, 1969. Project engr. U.S. Atomic Energy Commn., Washington, 1968-73, br. chief, 1973; div. asst., dir. U.S. Energy Research and Devel. Adminstrn., Washington, 1973-75; program mgr. Babcock and Wilcox Co., Lynchburg, Va., 1975-78, mgr. plant engring., 1978-80, mgr. reactor and fuel mgmt., 1980-82, mgr. field tech. services, 1982-83, v.p. sales and mktg., 1983-85; v.p. R&D Babcock and Wilcox Co., Alliance, Ohio, 1985-93; sr. v.p., chief tech. officer McDermott Internat., New Orleans, 1993—; bd. dirs. Ceramatec Corp., Indsl. Rsch. Industries, Washington, 1989—, pres., 1994-95. Patentee in field. Served to lt. USNR, 1968-70. Hon. Woodrow Wilson Found. fellow. Mem. ASME (ind. adv. bd. 1988—), Am. Mgmt. Assn. (rsch. and devel. coun. 1988-94), Indsl. Research Inst., AAAS, Soc. Sigma Xi. Presbyterian. Avocations: photography, diving, golf. Home: 7412 Jade St New Orleans LA 70124-3539 Office: McDermott Internat Inc PO Box 61961 New Orleans LA 70161-1961

WOMACK, MARY PAULINE, lawyer; b. Chattanooga, Tenn., Dec. 3, 1942; d. Abner and Lucille (Thomas) W. BS, U. Chattanooga, 1964; JD, Woodrow Wilson Coll. Law, 1984. Bar: Ga. 1988, U.S. Dist. Ct. (no. dist.) Ga. 1988. Pvt. practice Atlanta, 1988—. Sec. DeKalb County Dems., 66th dist., regional com. State of Ga. Mem. Ga. Bar Assn., Sigma Delta Kappa (past regional v.p.). Home: 892 Glynn Oaks Dr Clarkston GA 30021-2105 Office: 100 Peachtree St NW Atlanta GA 30303-1906

WOMACK, THOMAS HOUSTON, manufacturing company executive; b. Gallatin, Tenn., June 22, 1940; s. Thomas Houston and Jessie (Eckel) W.; Linda Walker Womack, July 20, 1963 (div. Dec. 1989); children: Britton Ryan, Kelley Elizabeth; m. Pamela Ann Reed, Apr. 20, 1991. BSME, Tenn. Tech. U., Cookeville, 1963. Project engr. U.S. Gypsum Co., Jacksonville, Fla., 1963-65; project mgr. Maxwell House Div. Gen. Foods Corp., Jacksonville, 1965-68; mfg. mgr. Maxwell House Div. Gen. Foods Corp., Hoboken, N.J., 1968-71, div. ops. planning mgr., 1971-73; industry sales mgr. J.R. Schneider Co., Tiburon, Calif., 1973-79; pres. Womack Internat., Inc., Novato, Calif., 1979—, Ceramic Microlight Technologies, LLC, Novato, Calif., 1995—. Holder 4 U.S. patents. Mem. Soc. Tribologists and Lubrication Engrs., Am. Filtration Soc., Soc. Mfg. Engrs., Am. Soc. Chem. Engrs. Avocations: skiing, vintage exotic sports cars. Office: Womack Internat Inc One Digital Dr Novato CA 94949

WOMBLE, WILLIAM FLETCHER, lawyer; b. Winston-Salem, N.C., Oct. 29, 1916; s. Bunyan Snipes and Edith (Willingham) W.; m. Jane Payne Gilbert, Oct. 11, 1941; children: William Fletcher, Jr., Jane Womble Haver, Russell G., Ann Womble Strader. AB, Duke U., 1937, JD, 1939. Bar: N.C. 1939. Assoc. Womble Carlyle Sandridge & Rice P.L.L.C. and predecessors, Winston-Salem, 1939-47; ptnr. Womble Carlyle Sandridge & Rice P.L.L.C. and predecessors, 1947—. Campaign chmn. Forsyth County Community Chest, 1948; mem. N.C. Gen. Statutes Commn., 1953-55; mem. N.C. Bd. Higher Edn., 1955-57, 60-63; mem. N.C. Adv. Budget Commn., 1957-58; mem. N.C. Ho. of Reps., 1953-58, chmn. com. higher edn., 1957, vice chmn. fin. com., 1957; life trustee, past chmn. High Point U.; trustee Winston-Salem State U., 1953-55; past trustee, past pres. Children's Home; bd. dirs. Triad United Methodist Home, 1976-87, 89—, treas., 1975-79, pres., 1979-85; mem. People-to-People Citizen Ambassador Program, 1981, 86; chmn. adminstrv. bd. Centenary United Meth. Ch., 1961-63, chmn. bd. trustees, 1983-85. Served to maj. USAAF, 1941-46. Named Trustee of Yr., Gen. Bd. Global Mins. of United Meth. Ch., Health and Welfare Mins. Dept., 1989. Fellow Am. Bar Found. (life, state chmn. 1984-89, Fifty Yr. award 1995); mem. ABA (ho. of dels. 1978-87, bd. govs. 1982-85, ethics com. 1985-91, chmn. jud. code subcom. 1988-91; exec. coun. Nat. Conf. Bar Pres. 1985-88, resource devel. coun. 1986-92, chair affiliate outreach com. 1994—, coun. mem. sr. lawyers divsn. 1995—), N.C. Bar Assn. (pres. 1966-67, chmn. endowment founders campaign 1986-87, chair sr. lawyers divsn. 1994-95, The Judge John J. Parker award 1984), N.C. State Bar (trustee Interest on Lawyers Trust Accounts 1983-91, vice chmn. 1989-91), Forsyth County Bar Assn.(pers. 1962), Am. Judicature Soc., U.S. Supreme Ct. Hist. Soc., N.C. Supreme Ct. Hist. Soc., Winston-Salem C. of C. (pres. 1960-61), Soc. of Cin., Old Town Club, Twin City Club, Piedmont Club, Rotary (local pres. 1964). Democrat. Methodist. Home: 2027 Virginia Rd Winston Salem NC 27104-2319 Office: Womble Carlyle Sandridge & Rice PO Box 84 1600 So Nat Fin Ctr Winston Salem NC 27102-0084

WOMELDORFF, PORTER JOHN, utility executive; b. Milw., Feb. 26, 1933; s. Virgil Leslie and Leorra (Porter) W.; BSEE, U. Ill., 1954; m. Marilyn Sapp, Jan. 7, 1966; children: John Porter, Michael Wayne. With Ill. Power Co., Decatur, 1954-95, beginning as elec. engr., successively results supr., instrumentation engr., supr. system planning, mgr. planning, 1954-79, v.p., 1979-93, global climate program exec., 1993-95, ret. 1995; pres. Womeldorff Assocs. Ltd., 1995—; mem. Ill. Coal Devel. Bd., 1982—, chair. Chair adv. bd. U. Ill. Coll. Engring., 1986-89; chair sci. com. Global Climate Coalition; lay mem. Central Ill. Ann. Conf., United Methodist Ch., 1968—, lay leader, 1976-79, lay mem. North Central Jurisdictional Conf., 1972—, lay mem. Gen. Conf., 1976—; lay mem. Gen. Bd. Pubs., 1992—. Served to lt. C.E., AUS, 1955-57. Decorated Army Commendation Medal. Mem. Instrument Soc. Am. (v.p. 1971-73, Power Div. Achievement award 1983), IEEE, ASME, U. Ill. Elec. Engring. Alumni Assn. (pres., dir., Outstanding Alumni award 1994), Phi Kappa Phi, Tau Beta Pi, Sigma Tau, Eta Kappa Nu, Alpha Kappa Lambda. Home and Office: 735 Country Manor Dr Decatur IL 62521-2524

WOMER, CHARLES BERRY, retired hospital executive, management consultant; b. Cleve., Mar. 30, 1926; s. Porter Blake and Margaret (Berry) W.; m. Elizabeth Benson, Oct. 7, 1950; children: Richard B., Carol E., John C. M.S. in Hosp. Adminstrn., Columbia U., 1953; B.S. in Mech. Engring., Case Inst. Tech., 1949. Asst. dir. Univ. Hosps., Cleve., 1957-61; assoc. dir. Univ. Hosps., 1961-65, pres., 1976-82; mgmt. cons., 1982-90, ret., 1990; adminstr. Yale-New Haven Hosp., 1965-67, dir., 1968-76, pres., 1976; lectr. Yale U., 1965-78, 87-91; adj. asst. prof. Case Western Res. U., 1976-83; mem. Conn. Commn. on Hosps. and Health Care, 1973-76; bd. dirs. New Haven Savings Bank, 1969-76. Bd. govs. U. New Haven, 1972-76. Served with AUS, 1944-46. Fellow Am. Coll. Healthcare Execs. (life); mem. Am. Hosp. Assn. (chmn. coun. on mgmt. and planning 1977-79), Conn. Hosp. Assn. (trustee 1970-74, pres. 1972-73, Disting. Svc. award 1976), Assn. Am. Med. Colls. (exec. coun. 1974-77, 78-80, treas. 1975-76, chmn. 1979-80, adminstrv. bd. coun. tchg. hosps. 1972-77, chmn. 1975-76). Home: 184 Rimmon Rd Woodbridge CT 06525-1920

WON, KYUNG-SOO, symphony conductor, director; b. Korea, Dec. 4, 1928; m. Hae-Ja (Won). Jan. 9, 1944; children: Alisa, Justin. Mus.M., Cin. Conservatory, 1957; diploma Mozarteum, Salzburg, Austria, protege of Pierre Monteux; postgrad. Ind. U. Cert. tchr., Calif. Formerly prof. Seoul (Korea) Nat. U., music dir. Modesto (Calif.) Symphony, Seoul Philharm. Orch.; music dir., condr. Stockton (Calif.) Symphony; now spl. prof. Kyung-Won U.; violin soloist Cin. Symphony. Soul Philharm., Manila Symphony, Korean Broadcasting System Orch., Korea; guest condr. orchs., London, Berlin, Paris, Vienna, Austria, Ireland, Mexico City, S. Am. cities, Orient. Served with Korean Navy. Recipient Bartok award, Emeel Hermann award, Star award. Mem. Am. Symphony League. Office: Stockton Symphony 37 W Yokuts Ave Ste 4C Stockton CA 95207-5721

WONDER, STEVIE (STEVLAND MORRIS), singer, musician, composer; b. Saginaw, Mich., May 13, 1950; m. Syreeta Wright, 1971 (div. 1972); children: Aisha, Keita, Mumtaz. Student pub. schs. in Detroit until age 12; then transferred to, Mich. Sch. for Blind. Solo singer, Whitestone Bapt. Ch., Detroit, 1959, rec. artist, Motown Records, Detroit, 1963-70; founder, pres. music pub. co., Black Bull Music, Inc., 1970—, Wondirection Records, Inc., 1982—; recs. include Fingertips, 1963, Uptight/Purple Raindrops, 1965, Someday At Christmas/The Miracles of Christmas, 1966, I'm Wondering/Everytime I See You I Go Wild, 1966, I Was Made To Love Her/Hold Me, 1967, Shoo-Be-Doo-Be-Doo-Da-Day/Why Don't You Lead Me To Love, 1968, You Met Your Match/My Girl, 1968, For Once In My Life, I Don't Know Why, My Cherie Amour, Yester-Me, Yester-You, Yesterday, Never Had a Dream Come True, Signed, Sealed, Delivered I'm Yours, Heaven Help Us All, I Wish (Grammy award 1977), Don't You Worry 'Bout a Thing, You Haven't Done Nothin', Boogie on Reggae Woman, (Grammy award 1975), Isn't She Lovely, Sir Duke, Another Star, As You Are the Sunshine of My Life, (Grammy award 1974), Superstition, (Grammy award 1974), Higher Ground, Living For the City, (Grammy award 1975); albums include Little Stevie Wonder: The Twelve-Year Old Genius, 1963, Tribute to Uncle Ray, 1963, Jazz Soul of Little Steve, 1963, At The Beach, 1965, For Once in My Life, 1969, My Cheric Amour, 1970, Talk of The Town, 1970, Portrait, 1976, Uptight, 1966, Down To Earth, 1966, I Was Made To Love Her, 1967, Someday At Christmas, 1967, Stevie Wonder's Greatest Hits, 1968, Music of My Mind, 1972, Innervisions, 1973 (Grammy award 1974), Fulfillingness' First Finale (Grammy award 1975), Songs In the Key of Life, 1976 (Grammy award 1977), Stevie Wonder Live, Where I'm Coming From, 1972, Talking Book, 1972, Journey Through the Secret Life of Plants, 1979, Hotter than July, 1980, Woman in Red (Acad. award, Golden Globe award for single I Just Called to Say I Love You), 1984, In Square Circle (best soul/R&B album of yr., Down Beat mag. Readers' poll) 1986, Characters, 1987, Jungle Fever, 1991, Inner Peace, 1995, numerous others; appeared in films: Bikini Beach, 1964, Muscle Beach Party, 1964; frequent TV appearances include Mike Douglas Show, guest host Saturday Night Live; named (Musician of Year, Down Beat mag. Rock/Blues Poll 1973-75, 77-78, Best Selling Male Soul Artist of Year, Nat. Assn. Rec. Merchandisers 1974), recipient numerous Grammy awards, also numerous awards for best singer/songwriter; Rock Music award 1977, Am. Music award 1978, Am. Video award for best rhythm and blues video for Ebony and Ivory 1982, Inducted Songwriters Hall of Fame 1982. Named to: Rock and Roll Hall of Fame, 1989; recipient Nelson Mandela Courage award, 1991. Office: 4616 W Magnolia Blvd Burbank CA 91505-2731

WONDERS, WILLIAM CLARE, geography educator; b. Toronto, Apr. 22, 1924; s. George Clarence and Ann Mary (Bell) W.; m. Lillian Paradise Johnson, June 2, 1951; children—Karen Elizabeth, Jennifer Anne, Glen William. B.A. with honors, Victoria Coll., U. Toronto, 1946; M.A., Syracuse U., 1948; Ph.D., U. Toronto, 1951; Fil. Dr. h.c., Uppsala U., 1981. Teaching asst. dept. geography Syracuse U., 1946-48; lectr. dept. geography U. Toronto, 1948-53; asst. prof. geography dept. polit. economy U. Alta., 1953-55, assoc. prof. geography, 1955-57, prof., head dept. geography, 1957-67, prof. dept. geography, 1967-87, Univ. prof., 1983—, prof. emeritus, 1987—; vis. prof. geography U. B.C., 1954, U. Okla., 1965-66, St. Mary's U., 1977, U. Victoria, 1989, J.F. Kennedy Inst., Free U. Berlin, 1990; guest prof. Inst. Geography, Uppsala (Sweden) U., 1962-63; rsch. fellow in Geography U. Aberdeen, Scotland, 1970-71, 78; vis. fellow in Can. Studies, U. Edinburgh, Scotland, 1987. Author: Looking at Maps, 1960, The Sawdust Fusiliers, 1991, Norden and Canada-A Geographer's Perspective, 1992, Alaska Highway Explorer, 1994; (with T. Drinkwater et al) Atlas of Alberta, 1969, (with J.C. Muller et al) Junior Atlas of Alberta, 1979; contbr., editor: Canada's Changing North, 1971, The North, 1972, The Arctic Circle, 1976, Knowing the North, 1988; contbr. articles to jours. and encys., chpts. to books. Mem. Nat. Adv. Com. on Geog. Rsch., 1965-69; chmn. Boreal Inst. No. Studies, 1960-62; mem. Can. Permanent Com. on Geog. Names, 1981-94, Alta. Hist. Sites Bd., 1978-83, victim, 1982-83; mem. policy bd. Can. Plains Rsch. Centre, U. Regina (Sask.), 1975-86; mem. adv. bd. Tyrrell Mus. Paleontology, 1984-89; bd. dirs. The Muttart Found., 1986-93, 95—, v.p., 1991-93, mem., 1991—. NSF sr. fgn. scientist fellow, 1965-66; Canada Council leave fellow, 1969-70, 77-78; Nuffield Found. fellow, 1970-71. Fellow Arctic Inst. N.Am., Royal Soc. Can., Royal Can. Geog. Soc.; mem. Can. Assn. Geographers (past pres.), Royal Scottish Geog. Soc., Can. Assn.

Scottish Studies (councillor 1974-77), Scottish Soc. No. Studies, Champlain Soc. (councillor 1981-86), Sigma Xi, Gamma Theta Upsilon.

WONG, CHI-HUEY, chemistry educator; b. Taiwan, Aug. 13, 1948; came to U.S., 1979; m. Yieng-Lii, Mar. 26, 1975; children: Heather, Andrew. BS in Biochemistry, Nat. Taiwan U., 1970, MS in Biochemistry, 1977; PhD in Chemistry, MIT, 1982. Asst. rsch. fellow Inst. Biol. Chemistry Academia Sinica, Taipei, Taiwan, 1974-79; from asst. prof. to prof. chemistry Tex. A&M U., 1983-89; Ernest W. Hahn prof. chemistry Scripps Rsch. Inst., La Jolla, Calif., 1989—; cons. Miles Labs., 1985-88, Dow Chem., 1985-90, G. D. Searle, 1988-90; sci. advisor Amylin, San Diego, 1989-92, Cytel, 1990—; head lab. glycosci. frontier rsch. program Riken, Japan, 1991—. Author: Enzymes in Synthetic Organic Chemistry, 1991; editl. bd. Bicatalysis; contbr. over 250 articles to profl. jours.; patentee in field. Lt. Taiwan Army, 1970-71. Recipient Presdl. Young Investigator in Chemistry award NSF, Washington, 1986; Searle scholar, 1985. Fellow AAAS, Am. Inst. Chemists; mem. Am. Chem. Soc. (Arthur C. Cope scholar award 1993, Internat. Carbohydrate award 1994), Am. Soc. Biochemistry and Molecular Biology, N.Y. Acad. Sci. Office: Scripps Rsch Inst Dept Chemistry 10666 N Torrey Pines Rd La Jolla CA 92037-1027

WONG, CHING-PING, chemist, materials scientist, engineer; b. Canton, China, Mar. 29, 1947; came to U.S., 1966; s. Kwok-Keung and Yun-Kwan (Lo) W.; m. Lorraine Homnack, May 27, 1978; children: Michelle, David. BS in Chemistry, Purdue U., 1969; PhD in Organic/Inorganic Chemistry, Pa. State U., 1975. Postdoctoral scholar Stanford (Calif.) U., 1975-77; mem. rsch. staff AT&T Bell Labs., Princeton, N.J., 1977-82, sr. mem. tech. staff, 1982-87, disting. mem. tech. staff, 1987-92; AT&T Bell Labs. fellow, 1992-96; prof. Sch. of Materials Sci. and Engring., Ga. Inst. Tech., Atlanta, 1996—; assembly, reliability and thermal mgmt. team leader NSF Packaging Rsch. Ctr.; program chmn. 39th Electronic Components Conf., 1989; gen. chmn. 41st Electronic Components and Tech. Conf., 1991; bd. govs. IEEE-Components, Hybrids and Mfg. Tech. Soc., 1987-89, tech. v.p., 1990-91, pres., 1992-93. Author, editor: Polymers for Electronic and Photonic Applications, 1993; contbr. articles to profl. jours. Recipient Outstanding Papers and Contbns. award IEEE-Components, Hybrids and Mfg. Tech. Soc., 1990, 91, 94, 96. Fellow IEEE (Outstanding Sustained Tech. Contbns. award 1995). Achievements include over 38 U.S. and numerous internat. patents for integrated device passivation and encepsulation area; pioneer in application of polymers for device reliability without hermeticity, a new application on electronic device packaging. Home: 11 Wexford Dr Lawrenceville NJ 08648-2023 Office: Ga Inst Tech Sch Materials Sci & Engring 778 Atlantic Dr Atlanta GA 30332-0245 Office: Ga Inst Tech Sch Materials Sci & Engring Atlanta GA 30332-0245

WONG, DAVID, pharmaceutical researcher; b. Canton, China, Oct. 15, 1962; came to the U.S., 1987; s. Ka-Yat and Yeuk-Bing (Lam) W.; m. Yong Kristine Chung, Aug. 29, 1992. BA, U. Tex., 1990, PhD, 1994. Diploma in psychiat. nursing, Hong Kong. Student nurse Hwai Chung Hosp., Hong Kong, 1984-87, psychiat. RN, 1987; co-supr. for undergrad. rsch. U. Tex., Austin, 1991-93, tchg. asst., 1990-94; postdoctoral rsch. CIBUS Pharm., Inc., Redwood City, Calif., 1994-95, scientist, 1995—; cons. Shanghai Materia Medica Med. and Biotech. Inst., 1995—. Recipient Tex. Excellence in Tchg. award Student Coun. Coll. Pharmacy, Austin, 1991, Tex. Excellence in Tchg. award Ex-Student Assn. U. Tex., Austin, 1992, Pen Tchg. Leadership award Fourth Nat. Conf. on Tchg., Asst. Tng. and Employment, Chgo., 1993. Mem. Am. Assn. Pharm. Scientists, Am. Chem. Soc., Hong Kong Nurse's Assn. Home: PO Box 2608 Menlo Park CA 94026 Office: CIBUS Pharm Inc 200D Twin Dolphin Dr Redwood City CA 94065

WONG, DAVID T., biochemist; b. Hong Kong, Nov. 6, 1935; s. Chi-Keung and Pui-King W.; m. Christina Lee, Dec. 28, 1963; children: Conrad, Melvin, Vincent. Student, Nat. Taiwan U., 1955-56; BS, Seattle Pacific U., 1961; MS, Oreg. State U., 1964; PhD, U. Oreg., 1966. Postdoctoral fellow U. Pa., Phila., 1966-68; sr. biochemist Lilly Rsch. Labs., Indpls., 1968-72, rsch. biochemist, 1973-77, sr. rsch. scientist, 1978-89; rsch. advisor, 1990—; adj. prof. biochemistry and molecular biology Ind. U. Sch. Medicine, 1986—, adj. prof. neurobiology, 1991—. Mem. editl. bd. Chinese Jour. Physiology, 1996—; contbr. numerous articles to sci. jours. Alumnus of Growing Vision Seattle Pacific U., 1989. Recipient Scientist of Yr. award, Pres. award Chinese Neuroscience Soc., 1991, Discoverers award Pharm. Mfr. Assn., 1993. Mem. Am. Coll. Neuropsychopharmaeology, Am. Soc. Pharmacology and Exptl. Therapeutics, Internat. Soc. Neurochemistry, Am. Soc. Neurochemistry, Soc. Neurosci. (pres. Indpls. chpt. 1987, 88), Soc. Chinese Bioscientists in Am., Indpls. Assn. Chinese Ams. (pres. 1987), Sigma Xi. Rsch. on biochemistry and pharmacology of neurotransmission; discovery and development of antidepressant drug, Prozac (Fluoxetine) and drug candidates including Tomoxetine, a selective inhibitor of norepinephrine uptake; duloxetine, an inhibitor for uptake of serotonin and norepinephrine; studies of potentially useful substances which activate transmission of norepinephrine, dopamine (Permax (pergolide), an agent for treatment of Parkinson's disease), serotonin, acetylcholine and GABA-neurons; studies of natural products led to the discovery of carboxylic ionophores: Narasin and A204, which increase transport of cations across biomembranes. Office: Lilly Rsch Labs Eli Lilly and Co Lilly Corp Ctr Indianapolis IN 46285

WONG, DAVID YUE, academic administrator, physics educator; b. Swatow, China, Apr. 16, 1934; came to U.S., 1953; s. Fan and Wen (Tsang) W.; m. Katherine Young, Sept. 3, 1960 (div. Mar. 1988); children: Amy, Eric; m. Elizabeth Lewis, Mar. 26, 1988. BA, Hardin Simmons U., 1954; PhD, U. Md., 1957. Theoretical physicist Lawrence Radiation Lab., U. Calif., Berkeley, 1958-59; asst. prof. physics U. Calif., San Diego, 1960-63, assoc. prof., 1963-67, prof., 1967—, chair dept. physics, 1977-80, provost Warren Coll., 1985-94. Alfred P. Sloan fellow, 1966-68. Mem. Am. Inst. Physics.

WONG, GWENDOLYN NGIT HOW JIM, banking executive; b. Chgo., Oct. 9, 1952; d. Vernon K. S. and Yun Soong (Chock) Jim; m. Carey R. Wong, Nov. 10, 1979; children: Jacquelyn C., Brandon R. BEd in Secondary Math., U. Hawaii, 1974; MA in Secondary Math., Columbia U., 1975; postgrad., St. John's U., N.Y.C., 1975-77; MBA, U. San Francisco, 1979. Tng. and devel. analyst and instr. Chase Manhattan Bank, N.Y.C., 1975-77; human resources profl. Crocker Nat. Bank, San Francisco, 1978-82, staff credit rev. dept. contrs. divsn., 1982-85; comml. lender Calif. middle market Wells Fargo Bank/Crocker Nat. Bank, Palo Alto and San Mateo, Calif., 1985-88; mgr. credit dept. San Francisco (Calif.) internat. br. Algemene Bank Nederland N.V., 1988-90; sr. v.p., mgr. credit control and rsch. The Indsl. Bank of Japan, Ltd. San Francisco (Calif.) Agy., 1990—. Treas. United Way of Bay Area; bd. dirs. United Nonprofits Ops., San Francisco Bay coun. Girl Scouts, legis. liaison, coun. trainer, internat. applicants selection com., chair Tri-City Assn., 1991-92, troop leader; bd. dirs. San Francisco Sch. Vols.; chair, founding bd. dirs. Multicultural Initiative, 1991—; v.p. elect program US/China Women's Issues Conf. & NGO Forum, Beijing, White House Briefing, Interagy. Coun. Women. Mem. AAUW (San Mateo br., bd. dirs. 1989-90, 94—, newsletter editor, cmty. programs com., chair couples gourmet interest group, others), Fin. Women's Assn., Assn. Jr. Leagues Internat. Inc. (1st v.p., exec. com. 1993-95, bd. dirs. 1992-95), Jr. League San Francisco, Inc. (adv. mem. bd. dirs. 1992-95, treas. 1990-91, exec. com., bd. dirs. 1990-91, endowment fund com. 1992, others).

WONG, HENRY LI-NAN, bank executive, economist; b. Rangoon, Burma, Nov. 3, 1940; s. Chew King and Jenny (Yu) W.; came to U.S., 1946. m. Laurie Yap, Apr. 11, 1968; children: Rachael S.Y., Remle S.W. BS, Waynesburg Coll., 1965; MS, U. Hawaii, 1968, PhD, 1969. Economist, Econ. Research Service U.S. Dept. Agr., Washington, 1969-70; economist Hawaii Dept. Budget and Fin., Honolulu, 1970-73; dir. Hawaii film office Hawaii Dept. Planning and Econ. Devel., Honolulu, 1973-84; exec. v.p. and chief adminstr., office of chmn. CB Bancshares Inc., Honolulu, 1984—; vice chmn., dir. Hawaii Strategic Devel. Corp., Honolulu, 1991-95; mem. coun. of revenue State of Hawaii, 1995—; v.p., bd. dirs. Friends of East West Ctr., Honolulu, 1983-84. NDEA fellow, 1965-69. Mem. Assn. Film Commrs. (pres. 1980), Am. Econ. Assn., Am. Agrl. Econs. Assn., Hawaii Internat. Film Festival, Chinese C. of C., Hawaii Soc. Corp. Planners, Lanakila Rehab. Ctr. (trustee), Alpha Kappa Psi, Theta Chi. Democrat. Presbyterian. Lodges: Elks, Masons (trustee), Shriners. Office: City Bank City Fin Tower 201 Merchant St Honolulu HI 96813-2929

WONG, JAMES BOK, economist, engineer, technologist; b. Canton, China, Dec. 9, 1922; came to U.S., 1938, naturalized, 1962; s. Gen Ham and Chen (Yee) W.; m. Wai Ping Lim, Aug. 3, 1946; children: John, Jane Doris, Julia Ann. BS in Agr., U. Md., 1949, BS in Chem. Engring., 1950; MS, U. Ill., 1951, PhD, 1954. Rsch. asst. U. Ill., Champaign-Urbana, 1950-53; chem. engr. Standard Oil of Ind., Whiting, 1953-55; process design engr., rsch. engr. Shell Devel. Co., Emeryville, Calif., 1955-61; sr. planning engr., prin. planning engr. Chem. Plastics Group, Dart Industries, Inc. (formerly Rexall Drug & Chem. Co.), L.A., 1961-66, supr. planning and econs., 1966-67, mgr. long range planning and econs., 1967, chief economist, 1967-72, dir. econs. and ops. analysis, 1972-78, dir. internat. techs., 1978-81; pres. James B. Wong Assocs., L.A., 1981—; chmn. bd. dirs. United Pacific Bank, 1988—; tech. cons. various corps. Contbr. articles to profl. jours. Bd. dirs., pres. Chinese Am. Citizens Alliance Found.; mem. Asian Am. Edn. Commn., 1971-81. Served with USAAF, 1943-46. Recipient Los Angeles Outstanding Vol. Service award, 1977. Mem. Am. Inst. Chem. Engrs., Am. Chem. Soc., VFW (vice comdr. 1959), Commodores (named to exec. order 1982), Sigma Xi, Tau Beta Pi, Phi Kappa Phi, Pi Mu Epsilon, Phi Lambda Upsilon, Phi Eta Sigma. Home: 2460 Venus Dr Los Angeles CA 90046-1646 *Personal philisophy: A man's reputation is his most prized possession.*

WONG, JOE, physical chemist; b. Hong Kong, Aug. 8, 1942; arrived in U.S., 1966; s. Po-lim and Mildred (Tam) W.; m. Mei-Ngan, Dec. 20, 1969; children: Glenn, Christina, Theresa. BSc, U. Tasmania, Australia, 1965; BSc with honors, U. Tesmania, Australia, 1966, DSc, 1986; PhD, Purdue U., 1970. Rsch. chemist Electolytic Zinc of Australia, Tasmania, 1966; lectr. in phys. chemistry Electrolytic Zinc of Australia, Tasmania, 1966; rsch. chemist GE R&D Ctr., Schenectady, N.Y., 1970-86; sr. rsch. chemist Lawrence Livermore (Calif.) Nat. Lab., 1986—; adj. prof. chemistry SUNY, Albany, 1981-86; cons. prof. Stanford Synchrotron Rad. Lab., 1993—. Author: Glass: Structure by Spectroscopy, 1976; contbr. articles to profl. jours.; 7 patents in field. Sr. fellowship Sci. and Tech. Agy., 1991; recipient Humboldt Rsch. award Humboldt Found., 1991, RD-100 awards, 1990, 91. Fellow Am. Inst. Chemists; mem. AAAS, Am. Chem. Soc., Am. Phys. Soc., Materials Rsch. Soc., Sigma Xi. Home: 871 El Cerro Blvd Danville CA 94526-2704 Office: Lawrence Livermore Nat Lab PO Box 808 L-369 Livermore CA 94551

WONG, KUANG CHUNG, anesthesiologist; b. Chung King, People's Republic China, Nov. 12, 1936; m. Janny Wu; children: Jade, Shale, Amber, Kaston. BS in Chemistry, Iowa State U., 1959; MS in Pharmacology, State U. Iowa, 1962; PhD in Pharmacology, U. Nebr., Omaha, 1966, MD, 1968. Diplomate Am. Bd. Anesthesiology (assoc. examiner 1979—). Instr. then asst. prof. pharmacology U. Nebr., Omaha, 1965-69; intern Bishop Clarkson Hosp., Omaha, 1968; intern U. Nebr. Coll. Medicine, Omaha, 1968, resident in anesthesia, 1968-69; resident, then fellow U. Wash. Sch. Medicine, Seattle, 1969-70; mem. assoc. grad. faculty U. Nebr., Omaha, 1968-69; asst. to assoc. prof. anesthesiology and pharmacology U. Washington, Seattle, 1970-74; assoc. prof. anesthesiology and pharmacology U. Utah, Salt Lake City, 1974-76, chmn. dept., assoc. prof. anesthesiology and pharmacology, 1976-77, chmn. dept., prof. anesthesiology and pharmacology, 1977—; vis. prof. numerous univs. throughout world, also various hosps.; mem. adv. com. anesthetic and life support drugs FDA, 1982-83; attending anesthesiologist U. Wash. Med. Ctr. and affiliated hosps., Seattle, 1970-74; staff anesthesiologist U. Utah Med. Ctr., Salt Lake City, 1974—; mem. surgery, anesthesia and trauma study sects. NIH, 1982-86. Mem. editorial bd. Anesthesia and Analgesia, 1980-89. Served with U.S. Army, 1955-57. Recipient Dr. Ernest Tibbets Manning Meml. Scholarship, 1965-66, U. Nebr. Upper Regents' Scholarship, 1966-67; grantee NIH, 1969-72, 80-85, Wash. State Heart Assn., 1972-74, Utah Heart Assn., 1975-76, 78-80, U. Utah, 1975-76, 76-77, Knoll Pharm. Co., 1976-79; Riker Labs., Inc., 1976-78, Smith Kline and French, 1979-89. Mem. AMA, Am. Heart Assn., Am. Soc. Anesthesiologists (ad hoc com. self-evaluation 1979), Am. Soc. Clin. Pharmacology and Chemotherapy, Am. Soc. Pharmacology and Exptl. Therapeutics, Assn. Cardiac Anesthesiologists, Assn. Univ. Anesthesiologists, Internat. Anesthesia Rsch. Soc. (trustee 1989—), Salt Lake County Med. Soc., Utah Heart Assn., Utah Med. Soc., Utah Soc. Anesthesiologists, Soc. Acad. Anesthesia Chairmen, Sigma Xi, Alpha Omega Alpha. Office: Univ of Utah Sch of Medicine Dept of Anesthesiology Salt Lake City UT 84132

WONG, MA-LI, psychiatrist; b. Hong Kong; came to U.S., 1985; d. Kowk Keung and Yin Shang (Lau) W.; m. Julio Licinio, Nov. 15, 1985. MD, U. Sao Paulo, Brazil, 1982. Resident in medicine, then neurology U. Sao Paulo Med. Ctr., 1983-85; rsch. assoc. Albert Einstein Coll. Medicine, Bronx, N.Y., 1985-86; resident in psychiatry Albert Einstein Coll. Medicine, 1986-89; rsch. fellow Clin. Neuroendocrinology br. NIMH, Bethesda, Md., 1989-90; chief resident in psychiatry Yale U. Sch. Medicine, New Haven, 1990-91, instr. in psychiatry, 1991-93; vis. scientist clin. neuroendocrinology br. NIMH, Bethesda, Md., 1993—. Contbr. to profl. jours. Mem. N.Y. Acad. Scis., Am. Psychiat. Assn., Am. Fedn. Clin. Rsch., Soc. Neuroscience, Assn. Women Psychiatrists, Endocrine Soc. Avocations: poetry, photography. Office: 8135 N Brook Ln # 907 Bethesda MD 20814

WONG, NANCY L., dermatologist; b. Chung King, China, Aug. 23, 1943; came to U.S., 1947; d. Alice (Lee) Wong; m. Robert Lipshutz; children: Seth, Alison, David. BS magna cum laude, Pa. State U., 1963; MS in Physics, Columbia U., 1965; MD, Jefferson Med. Coll., Phila., 1971. Diplomate Am. Bd. Dermatology. Intern Wilmington Med. Ctr., 1972; resident Jackson Meml. Hosp., Miami, Mount Sinai Med. Ctr., Miami, 1977; physician Kaiser Med. Ctr., Redwood City, Calif., 1987—. NSF fellow, 1963-64, AEC fellow, 1963-64, Woodrow Wilson fellow, 1963-64. Avocations: tennis, music, writing, painting. Office: 910 Maple St Redwood City CA 94063-2034

WONG, PATRICK SECK LAI, chemical engineer; b. Canton, China, Aug. 8, 1936; came to U.S., 1957; s. S.C. and W.S. (Choy) W.; m. Helen Wai Lun Wong, June 26, 1969; children: Julian, Francis, Alex. BSChemE, U. Mich., 1960; MS, MIT, 1962; PhD, Imperial Coll., London, 1967. Rsch. chemist W.R. Grace, Clifton, N.J., 1962-64; rsch. assoc. MIT, Cambridge, Mass., 1967-73; head transport process Alza Corp., Palo Alto, Claif., 1973-79, prin. scientist, 1981-85, dir. producer rsch., 1985-87, sr. dir. rsch., 1987-91, exec. dir. R & D, 1991-94, v.p. rsch., 1994—; v.p. R & D Collins Indls. Co., Hong Kong, 1979-81, Bio-Electro System, Palo Alto, 1988-91. Contbr. articles to Jour. Polymer Sci. (London), AIChemE Jour., Ency. Pharm. Tech. Mem. Am. Chem. Soc., Am. Assn. Pharm. Scientists, Controlled Release Soc., Tau Beta Pi, Sigma Xi. Achievements include over 110 patents for Controlled Drug Delivery, Procardia XL. Office: Alza Corp 950 Page Mill Rd Palo Alto CA 94304

WONG, PO KEE, research company executive, educator; b. Canton City, Kwangtung, China, May 5, 1934; came to U.S., 1959; s. Kum Fun Wong and Wai Chi Lum; m. Ruby Chuen Wah, Aug. 1965; children, Adam, Anita. BS, Taiwan Provincial Cheng Kung U., Tainan, 1956; MS, U. Utah, 1961; PhD Mech. Engring., Calif. Inst. Tech., 1966; PhD in Aeronaut. and Astronaut. Engring., Stanford, 1970. Lic. mech. profl. engr., Taiwan; cert. tchr., Mass. Sr. scientist Lockheed Missile & Space Co., Palo Alto, Calif., 1966-68; lectr. U. Santa Clara, Calif., 1970-71; researcher NASA Ames Rsch. Ctr., Moffet Field, Calif., 1970-71; engr. G.E. Breeder Reactor Dept., Sunnyvale, Calif., 1972-73; specialist engr. Nuclear Svcs. Co., Campbell, Calif., 1973; engr. Stone & Webster Engring. Co., Boston, 1974-76; pres., chief exec. officer Systems Rsch. Co., Somerville, Mass., 1976—; tchr. Boston Public Schs., 1979—. Author, presenter tech. papers; patentee in field. Mem. ASME, AAAS, AIAA, The Math. Assn. of Am., Internat. Platform Assn., Internat. Assn. Structural Mechanics in Reactor Tech., N.Y. Acad. Scis. Achievements include patents in field. Avocations: tennis, table tennis, Chinese chess, Western chess, go-game. Home: 50 Bradley St Somerville MA 02145-2930 Office: Charlestown High Sch 240 Medford St Charlestown MA 02129

WONG, RUTH ANN, nursing administrator; b. Chgo., July 24, 1946; d. Valentine Wally and Sally Sylvia (Poremski) Fronczak; m. James W. Wong, Apr. 20, 1974. Diploma in nursing, St. Mary of Nazareth Sch., 1967; pediatric nurse clinician cert., U. Va., 1973; BA, Occidental Coll., 1977; MPH, UCLA, 1979, perioperative nursing cert., 1990; pub. health nurse cert., Calif. State U., Long Beach, 1982. Cert. PNP. Commd. 2d lt. USAF, 1968, advanced through grades to col., 1994; charge nurse, staff nurse USAF, Barksdale AFB, La., 1968-70, Tachikawa AFB, Japan, 1970-72; charge nurse, staff nurse Kirtland AFB, N.Mex., 1972-74; chief flight nurse 146 Aeromedical Evacuation Squadron, Van Nuys, Calif., 1977-92; chief Air N.G. nursing svcs. Air N.G. Readiness Ctr., Andrews AFB, Md., 1992—; clin. instr. Calif. State U., L.A., 1974-77; field placement supr. grad. program Calif. State U., Northridge, 1981-87; PNP, Children's Hosp., L.A., 1974-77, Headstart Found., East Los Angeles, 1977-80; dir. nursing and health svcs. ARC, Pasadena, Calif., 1980-90, mem. adv. com. nurse asst. tng. program, Washington, 1989-91, ednl. nurse cons., L.A., 1990-92, cons. nurse asst. tng., 1989; perioperative nurse UCLA, 1990-91. Decorated Air Force Commendation medal with one oakleaf cluster, Meritorious Svc. medal, Army Commendation medal. Roman Catholic. Avocations: reading, travel, interior decorating, snow skiing, gardening. Home: 7495 Digby Grn Alexandria VA 22315-5246 Office: Air NG 3500 Fetchet Ave Andrews Air Force Base MD 20762

WONG, SUN YET, engineering consultant; b. Honolulu, Dec. 6, 1932; s. Chip Tong and Shiu Inn (Chang) W.; m. Janet Siu Hung Lau; children: Cathleen, Bryan, Jonathan. BS in Civil Engring. with honors, U. Hawaii, 1954; MS in Civil Engring., Yale U., 1955. Engr. N.Am. Aviation, Downey, Calif., 1955-58; mem. tech. staff Ramo Woolridge Space Tech. Labs., Redondo Beach, Calif., 1958-64; exec. v.p., treas., tech. dir. Mechanics Rsch. Inc., El Segundo, Calif., 1964-77; treas. System Devel. Corp., Santa Monica, Calif., 1977-79; chmn. bd., pres., treas. Applied Rsch. Inc., El Segundo, 1979-81; ind. tech. cons. Rolling Hills Estates, Calif., 1981—; engring. cons. Acurex, Mountain View, Calif., 1983, Ampex, Redwood City, Calif., 1991, Applied Tech., Mountain View, 1983-85, Astron, Mountain View, 1983-85, E Systems, Garland, Tex., 1986-93, Electromech. Systems Inc., Anaheim, Calif., 1984, Hughes, El Segundo, 1992, 94, Intercon, Cerritos, Calif., 1982-84, J.H. Wiggins Co., Redondo Beach, 1982-84, Kodak Datatape, Pasadena, Calif., 1989, Lion Engring., Rancho Palos Verdes, Calif., 1994—, Measurement Analysis Corp., Torrance, Calif., 1984—, MRJ, Fairfax, Va., 1984, Odectics, Anaheim, 1990, Swales & Assocs., Beltsville, Md., 1992-93, Statis. Scis., Inc., Beverly Hills, Calif., 1986, Tompkins and Assocs., Torrance, 1984—, TRW, Redondo Beach, 1984; dir. Lion Engring. Avocation: metal machining. Home and Office: 7 Club View Ln Rolling Hills Estates CA 90274

WONG, VICTOR KENNETH, physics educator, academic administrator; b. San Francisco, Nov. 1, 1938; m. Nancy Wong; children: Cassandra, Pamela, Lianna. BS in Engring. Physics, U. Calif., Berkeley, 1960, PhD in Physics, 1966. Postdoctoral fellow Ohio State U., Columbus, 1966-68; lectr., asst. prof. U. Mich., Ann Arbor, 1968-76, adj. prof. physics, 1992-95; assoc. prof. physics U. Mich., Dearborn, 1976-82, prof. physics, 1982-86, chmn. dept. natural sci., 1980-83, dean Coll. Arts, Sci. and Letters, 1983-86; provost, vice chancellor acad. affairs U. Mich., Flint, 1986-95, prof. physics, 1986—; adj. rsch. scientist U. Mich., 1995—, dir. info. technology for rsch., 1995—. Assoc. editor: Math. Revs., 1980; contbr. articles to profl. jours. Mem. Am. Phys. Soc., Am. Assn. Higher Edn. (1st chmn. Asian caucus 1986-88), Nat. U. Continuing Edn. Assn. (mem. minority com. 1989), North Ctrl. Assn. Colls. and Schs. (cons. evaluation com. 1989—), Am. Coun. Edn. (mem. commn. on minorities in higher edn. 1993-96), Phi Beta Kappa, Tau Beta Pi. Office: Univ Mich Info Tech Divsn 1071 Beal Ave Ann Arbor MI 48109-2103

WONG, WALLACE, medical supplies company executive, real estate investor; b. Honolulu, July 13, 1941; s. Jack Yung Hung and Theresa (Goo) W.; m. Amy Ju, June 17, 1963; children: Chris, Bradley, Jeffery. Student, UCLA, 1960-63. Chmn., pres. South Bay Coll., Hawthorne, Calif., 1965-86; chmn. Santa Barbara (Calif.) Bus. Coll., 1975—; gen. ptnr. W B Co., Redondo Beach, Calif., 1982—; CEO Cal Am. Med. Supplies, Rancho Santa Margarita, Calif., 1986—, Cal Am. Exports, Inc., Rancho Santa Margarita, 1986—, Pacific Am. Group, Rancho Santa Margarita, 1991—; chmn., CEO Alpine, Inc., Rancho Santa Margarita, Calif., 1993—; pres. Bayside Properties, Rancho Santa Margarita, 1993—; bd. dirs. Metrobank, L.A. FFF Enterprises; chmn. bd. 1st Ind. Fin. Group., Rancho Santa Margarita. Acting sec. of state State of Calif., Sacramento, 1982; founding mem. Opera Pacific, Orange County, Calif., 1985; mem. Hist. and Cultural Found., Orange County, 1986; v.p. Orange County Chinese Cultural Club, Orange County, 1985. Named for Spirit of Enterprise Resolution, Hist. & Cultural Found., Orange Country, 1987; recipient resolution City of Hawthorne, 1973. Mem. Westren Accred Schs. & Colls. (v.p. 1978-79), Magic Castle (life), Singapore Club. Avocations: traveling, skiing. Office: Alpine Inc 23042 Arroyo Vis Rancho Santa Margarita CA 92688

WONG, WARREN JAMES, mathematics educator; b. Masterton, N.Z., Oct. 16, 1934; came to U.S. 1964; s. Ken and Jessie (Ng) W.; m. Nellie Gee, May 12, 1962; children: Carole Frances, Andrea. BSc, U. Otago, Dunedin, N.Z., 1955, MSc, 1956; PhD, Harvard U., 1959. Lectr. U. Otago, Dunedin, 1960-64, sr. lectr., 1964; assoc. prof. math. U. Notre Dame, Ind., 1964-68, prof., 1968—. Proceedings editorial bd. Am. Math. Soc., Providence, R.I., 1988-90; contbr. articles to profl. jours. Vestryman St. Michael and All Angels Episcopal Ch., South Bend, 1988-90. Mem. Am. Math. Soc., Math. Assn. Am., Australian Math. Soc. Episcopalian. Office: Dept Math Univ Notre Dame Notre Dame IN 46556-5683

WONG, WILLIE, mayor, automotive executive; b. Mesa, Ariz., Oct. 12, 1948; m. Cobina Wong; children: Kevin, Jeremy. Grad., Ariz. State U. Vice mayor City of Mesa (Ariz.), 1988-90; councilmem., 1990-91; mayor City of Mesa (Ariz.), 1992—; pres. Wilky's Performance Ctr., Mesa, Ariz.; prev. employment with AT&T. Treas. Regional Pub. Transp. Authority; chmn. Williams Redevel. Ptnrship., Maricopa Assn. Govts. Regional Devel. Policy Com.; vice-chmn. Williams Gateway Airport Authority, Mesa Sister Cities; exec. com. League of Ariz. Cities and Towns; bd. dirs. YMCA (past pres.), Child Crisis Ctr., Southwest Pub. Recycling Assn. Named Outstanding Young Man Mesa Leadership, Tng., & Devel. Assn., 1989. Mem. MAG Regional Coun., Econ. Devel. Adv. Bd., Rotary Club-Mesa West. Avocations: baseball, fishing, travel, reading. Home: 1343 E McLellan Mesa AZ 85203 Office: Office of the Mayor 55 N Center St PO Box 1466 Mesa AZ 85211-1466 also: Wilky's Performance Ctr 402 E Main Mesa AZ 85203*

WONG, WING KEUNG, trading, electronics company executive, physician; b. Hong Kong, Jan. 5, 1933; s. Lai Cho Wong and Sut Mui Chung; m. Ban Cho, May 28, 1957; children: Hoi Ling, Hoi Yin. MB, BS, Beijing Med. Coll., 1955. Lic. Med. Coun. Hong Kong. Physician 1st Hosp. of Beijing Med. Coll., 1955-69; with Hosp., Ganshu, China, 1970-73; pvt. practice Hong Kong, 1979-84; dir. Cheung Tai Hong Ltd., Hong Kong, 1974-86, exec. dir., 1987—; dep. chmn. Cheung Tai Hong Holdings Ltd., Bermuda, 1994-95; chmn. bd. dirs. Computime Ltd., Hong Kong, 1979-93; dir. Computime Internat. Ltd., Brit. V.I., 1993-95. Mem. Hong Kong Med. Assn., Dynasty Club, Tower Club. Avocations: travel, music, diving, photography. Office: Cheung Tai Hong Ltd, 31/F Singga Comml Ctr, 144-151 Connaught Rd W Hong Kong Hong Kong

WONG-LIANG, EIRENE MING, psychologist; b. Nassau, Bahamas, Nov. 20, 1961; came to U.S., 1969; d. Menyu and Lim Ming (Chow) Wong; m. Danqing Liang. BA, Trinity U., San Antonio, 1984; PhD, Calif. Sch. Profl. Psychology, 1992. Crisis counselor United Way Crisis Hotline, San Antonio, 1983; lab. asst. Trinity U., 1983; counselor Bayer County Women's Ctr., San Antonio, 1984, Turning Point Juvenile Diversion Project, Garden Grove, Calif., 1985-86; psychol. trainee Wolters Elem. Sch., Fresno, 1987, San Luis Obispo (Calif.) Youth Day Treatment, 1987-88, Calif. Sch. Profl. Psychology Svc. Ctr., Fresno, 1988-89; staff psychologist 314th Med. Ctr., Little Rock, Ark., 1989-93; pvt. practice, clin. psychologist Houston, 1993—. Mem. APA, Am. Soc. Clin. Hypnosis, Internat. Soc. Clin. Hypnosis, Nat. Register Health Svc. Providers in Psychology, Tex. Psychol. Assn., Houston Psychol. Assn., Houston Assn. Clin. Hypnosis (charter, exec.), Psi Chi, Zeta Chi (charter, Trinity U. chpt.). Office: 10101 Southwest Fwy Ste 445 Houston TX 77074-1112

WONG-STAAL, FLOSSIE, medical educator. BA, UCLA, 1968, PhD, 1972. Tchg. asst. UCLA, 1969-70, rsch. asst., 1970-72; post-doctoral fellow U. Calif., San Diego, 1972-73; Fogarty fellow Nat. Cancer Inst., Bethesda, Md., 1973-75; vis. assoc. Nat. Cancer Inst., Bethesda, 1975-76, cancer expert, 1976-78, sr. investigator, 1978-81, chief molecular genetics of hematopoietic cells sect., 1982-89; Florence Seeley Riford chair in AIDS rsch., prof. medicine U. Calif. San Diego, La Jolla, 1990—; vis. prof. Inst. Gen.

Pathology, First U. Rome, Italy, 1985. Mem. editl. bd. Gene Analysis Techniques, 1984—, Cancer Letters, 1984-94, Leukemia, 1987—, Cancer Rsch., 1987, AIDS Rsch. and Human Retroviruses (sect. editor), 1987—, DNA and Cell Biology (sect. editor), 1987—, Microbial Pathogenesis, 1987-90, AIDS: An Internat. Jour., 1987—, Internat. Jour. Acquired Immunodeficiency Syndrome, 1988—, Oncogene, 1988—, Jour. Virology, 1990—; contbr. articles to profl. jours. Recipient Outstanding Sci. award Chinese Med. and Health Assn., 1987, The Excellence 2000 award U.S. Pan Asian Am. C. of C. and the Orgn. of Chinese Am. Women, 1991. Mem. Am. Soc. for Virology (charter), Phi Beta Kappa. Office: Univ California Biology Dept La Jolla CA 92093-5003*

WONHAM, WALTER MURRAY, electrical engineer, educator; b. Montreal, Que., Can., Nov. 1, 1934; m. Vera Anne Hale; children: Marjorie Jane, Cynthia Margaret. B of Engring., McGill U., Montreal, 1956; PhD, U. Cambridge, Eng., 1961. Asst. prof. elec. engring. Purdue U., Lafayette, Ind., 1961-62; rsch. scientist Research Inst. for Advanced Studies, Balt., 1962-64; assoc. prof. Brown U., Providence, 1964-69; rsch. assoc. NASA, Cambridge, Mass., 1967-69, cons., 1969; prof. elec. engring. U. Toronto, Ont., Can., 1970—, J. Roy Cockburn Prof., U. Toronto, 1991—, Cockburn chair, 1991 Author: Linear Multivariable Control: A Geometric Approach, 1974, 3d edit., 1985 (Russian transl. 1980, Chinese transl. 1984); assoc. editor Soc. for Indsl. and Applied Math., Jour. on Control and Optimization, 1965-79, Systems Control Letter, 1981-85. Athlone fellow, Gt. Britain, 1956-58; spl. scholar Nat. Rsch. Coun. Can., 1958-60; sr. postdoctoral resident rsch. assoc. NAS U.S.A., 1967-69. Recipient Brouwer medal Netherlands Math Soc., 1990. Fellow Royal Soc. Can., IEEE (Control Systems Sci. and Engring. award 1987). Office: U Toronto Dept Elec Engring, 35 St George St, Toronto, ON Canada M5S 1A4

WONNACOTT, (GORDON) PAUL, economics educator; b. London, Ont., Can., Mar. 16, 1933; s. Gordon Elliott and Muriel Johnston Wonnacott; m. Donna Elizabeth Cochrane, July 2, 1960; children: David, Ann, Alan, Bruce. BA, U. Western Ont., 1955; MA, Princeton U., 1957, PhD, 1959. Instr., asst. prof. econs. Columbia U., N.Y.C., 1958-62; assoc. prof. then prof. econs. U. Md., College Pk., 1962-91; mem. Pres.'s Coun. Econ. Advisers, 1991-93; Alan Holmes vis. prof. econs. Middlebury Coll., 1994—; mem. rsch. staff Royal Commn. Banking and Fin., Toronto, 1962; sr. staff economist Coun. Econ. Advisers, Washington, 1968-70; assoc. dir. divsn. internat. fin. Fed. Res. Bd., Washington, 1974-75; vis. scholar Office Internat. Monetary Rsch., U.S. Treasury, 1980; econ. adviser to Under Sec. of State, 1990-91. Author: The Canadian Dollar, 1960, 2d rev. edit., 1965, (with R.J. Wonnacott) Free Trade between the United States and Canada: The Potential Economic Effects, 1967, (with H.G. Johnson and H. Shibata) Harmonization of National Economic Policies under Free Trade, 1968, Macroeconomics, 1974, 3d rev. edit., 1984, (with R.J. Wonnacott) Economics, 1979, 4th rev. edit. 1990, Spanish edit., 1981, 3d rev. edit., 1987, (with Y. and C. Crusius) Portuguese edit., 1982, 2d rev. edit., 1985, (with A. Blomquist) Can. edit., 1983, 4th rev. edit., 1994, The United States and Canada: The Quest for Free Trade, 1987; contbr. numerous articles to profl. jours. Fellow Brooking Inst., 1957-58, Ford Found., 1963-64; vis. fellow Inst. Internat. Econs., 1986, 93-94. Mem. Am. Econ. Assn., Can. Econ. Assn. Avocations: skiing, tennis. Home: 10100 Bevern Ln Rockville MD 20854-2130 Office: Middlebury College Dept Econs Middlebury VT 05753

WONNACOTT, RONALD JOHNSTON, economics educator; b. London, Ont., Can., Sept. 11, 1930; s. Gordon and and Muriel (Johnston) W.; m. Eloise Howlett, Sept. 11, 1954; children: Douglas, Robert, Cathy Anne. B.A., U. Western Ont., 1955; A.M., Harvard U., 1957, Ph.D., 1959. Mem. faculty U. Western Ont., London, 1958—, prof. econs., 1964—, chmn. dept., 1969-72; vis. assoc. prof. U. Minn., Mpls., 1961-62; cons. Resources for the Future, Econ. Council Can., Can.-Am. Com., Nat. Planning Assn., C.D. Howe Inst. Author: Canadian-American Dependence: An Interindustry Analysis of Production and Prices, 1961, Canada's Trade Options, 1975, Selected New Developments in International Trade Theory, 1984, The Economics of Overlapping Free Trade Areas and the Mexican Challenge, 1991, (with G.L. Reuber) The Cost of Capital in Canada, 1961, (with Paul Wonnacott) Free Trade Between the U.S. and Canada, 1967, Economics, 1979, 4th edit., 1990, (with Thomas H. Wonnacott) Introductory Statistics, 1969, 5th edit., 1990, Econometrics, 1970, 2d edit., 1979, Regression, 1981. Fellow Royal Soc. Can.; mem. Am. Econ. Assn., Can. Econ. Assn. (pres. 1981), London Hunt Club, Sunningdale Golf Club (Eng.), Hon. Co. Edinburgh Golfers, Craigleith Ski Club. Home: 171 Wychwood Park, London, ON Canada N6G 1S1

WONSER, MICHAEL DEAN, retired public affairs director,; b. Long Beach, Calif., Mar. 12, 1940; s. Franklin Henry and Dorothy Mae (Harris) W.; children: Therice Michele, Sherice Michele, Christopher Franklin; m. Mary L. Van Epps, Dec. 22, 1990. BS, U. Oreg., 1963, MFA, 1965; postgrad., U. Colo., 1976. Instr. Cen. Oreg. Coll., Bend, 1966-68; prof. Adams State Coll., Alamosa, Colo., 1969-91, dir. pub. affairs, 1982-90; pres. Colo. Faculty Com. Trustees, 1980-82. Mem. Chamber Edn. Com., Monte Vista, Colo., 1982-88; pres. Luth. Ch. Alamosa, 1980-85; bd. dirs. Creede Repertory Theatre, 1989-91; mem. Commerce Comm. and Resources Comm., 1995, Cmty. Improvement Commn., Sisters, Oreg., 1996—. Mem. Higher Edn. Assn. of Rockies (pres. Colo. chpt. 1985-88), C. of C. Ambassador (treas. 1982), Alamosa, C. of C. Tourism Bd., Alamosa (chmn. 1987-89), Sisters C. of C. (pres. 1996—, bd. dirs.), Rotary. Republican. Avocations: golf, skiing. Home: 65016 W Highway 20 Bend OR 97701-9186

WOO, MARY ANN, medical educator. BS in Genetics, U. Calif., Davis, 1976; AA in Nursing, Pasadena (Calif.) City Coll., 1980; BS in Nursing, Mt. St. Mary's Coll., L.A., 1985; M Nursing, UCLA, 1988, D Nursing Sci., 1992. Cert. ACLS, critical care nurse, basic cardiopulmonary resuscitation; RN, Calif. Rsch. asst. dept. animal sci. U. Calif., Davis, 1975-76; tchrs. asst. L.A. Unified Sch. Dist., 1976-77, sch. nurse, 1980-81; tutor dept. biology Pasadena (Calif.) City Coll., 1978-80; staf nurse critical care unit Huntington Meml. Hosp., 1981-88; clin. rsch. nurse IV divsn. cardiology UCLA Med. Ctr., 1988-92, clin. rsch. nurse V, 1992-93, lectr., asst. clin. prof., 1993-94, asst. prof., 1994—; Mem. Pacific S.W. Regional Med. Libr. Svc. Task Force, 1988-89, UCLA Sch. Nursing Instrnl. Resources Com., 1990-92, clin. adv. panel on acute myocardial infarction Calif. Hosp. Outcomes Assessment Project, 1992—; external reviewer Alberta Found. for Nursing Rsch., 1992—; mem. com. on computing UCLA, 1994-95, undergrad. program com. Sch. Nursing, 1995—, Sch. Nursing Distance Learning Project, 1995—, Sch. Nursing Virtual Reality Project, 1995—; lectr. various hosps., schs., orgns. Manuscript reviewer Heart and Lung, 1989—, Am. Jour. Critical Care, 1992—, Progress in Cardiovascular Nursing, 1993—, European Heart Jour., 1994—, Am. Jour. Cardiology, 1995—; mem. editl. bd. Heart and Lung: Jour. Critical Care, 1993—; contbr. articles to profl. jours. Recipient Audrienna M. Moseley fellowship award, 1988-92, scholarship Kaiser Found., 1989, Rsch. awards UCLA Sch. Nursing Alumni Assn., 1990, Sigma Theta Tau, Gamma Tau chpt., 1991, Helene Fuld grant, 1990, Critical Care Nursing rsch. grant Hewlett-Packard/AACCN, 1992-93, grants UCLA, 1994, 95, minigrant UCLA, 1995, Office of Instrnl. Devel. award UCLA, 1995. Mem. AACCN (scholarship com. L.A. chpt. 1990-92), Am. Heart Assn. (program com. Coun. on Cardiovascular Nursing, new investigator award 1st pl. 1993, grant-in-aid 1995). Home: 1701 Camino Lindo South Pasadena CA 91030 Office: UCLA Sch Nursing 700 Tiverton Ave Box 951702 Los Angeles CA 90095-1702

WOO, S. B. (SHIEN-BIAU WOO), former lieutenant governor, physics educator; b. Shanghai, China, Aug. 13, 1937; came to U.S., 1955; s. C.K. and Kuo-Ying (Chang) W.; m. Katy K.N. Wu, July 20, 1963; children: Chih-I, Chih-Lan. B.S. in Physics and Math. summa cum laude, Georgetown Coll., Ky., 1956; M.S. in Physics, Washington U., St. Louis, 1962, Ph.D. in Physics, 1964. Prof. physics U. Del., Newark, 1966—; lt. gov. State of Del., Dover, 1985-89; pres. Del. State Senate; chmn. Bd. Pardons; cons. E.I. DuPont Co., Wilmington, Del., 1968, Del. State Coll., Dover, 1980-81. Contbr. articles to profl. jours. Chmn. bd., chief exec. officer Chinese Am. Community Ctr., Hockessin, Del., 1982-83; sec. Asian-Am. caucus Democratic Nat. Conv., 1983—; pres., co-chmn. Gov.'s Internat. Trade Council, 1985—; chmn. Gov.'s task force on High Tech., 1985—. Recipient Highest Achievement award Asian Am. High Tech. Conv., 1985; Army Rsch. grantee, 1972-87, NSF grantee, 1978-81; Inst. fellow Kennedy Sch., Harvard U. Mem. Am. Phys. Soc., AAAS, AAUP (exec. com. nat. council 1974-77), Orgn. Chinese Ams. (bd. dirs. 1977-79, nat. pres. 1990—), Sigma Xi. Home: 5 Farm House Rd Newark DE 19711-7458

WOO, SAVIO LAU CHING, molecular medical geneticist; b. Shaghai, China, Dec. 20, 1944; came to U.S., 1966; s. Kwok-Cheung and Fun-sin (Yu) W.; m. Emily H. Chang, July 14, 1973; children: Audrey C. C., Brian Y.Y. BSc, Loyola Coll., Montreal, Can., 1966; PhD, U. Wash., 1971. Asst. prof. cell biology Baylor Coll. Medicine, Houston, 1975-78, assoc. prof., 1979-83, dir. ctr. for gene therapy, 1991-96, prof., 1984-96, prof. Inst. Molecular Genetics, 1985-96, dir. grad. tng. program cell and molecular biology, 1987-94; assoc. investigator Howard Hughes Med. Inst., Bethesda, Md., 1977-79, investigator, 1979-96; prof., dir. Inst. for Gene Therapy and Molecular Medicine Mount Sinai Sch. Medicine, N.Y.C., 1996—; organizer, 1st chmn. Gordon Conf. on Molecular Genetics, 1985; co-organizer Searle-UCLA Symposium, 1986; organizer 3d Soc. Chinese Bioscientists in Am. Internat. Symposium, 1990; cons. Cooper Lab., Palo Alto, Calif., 1982-84, Zymos Corp., Seattle, 1982-86; sr. sci. advisor Molecular Therapeutics, Inc., West Haven, 1986-92; spl. advisor Gene Medicine, Inc., Woodlands, Tex., 1992-96. Mem. editorial bd. DNA, 1983—, Am. Jour. Human Genetics, 1986-89, Genomics, 1987-95, Biochemistry, 1988-94; U.S. editor: Gene Therapy, 1995—; contbr. over 200 sci. articles to prof. publs. Mem. bd. dirs. March of Dimes Birth Defects Found., Met. Houston chpt., 1979-87. Mem. NIH (study sect. on molecular biology 1983-85, merit award, 1988—), Nat. Inst. Child Health and Human Devel. (bd. sci. counselors 1988-93), Am. Soc. Biol. Chemists, Am. Soc. Cell Biology, N.Y. Acad. Scis., Soc. Study Inborn Errors of Metabolism (D. Noel Raime meml. award 1983).

WOO, SAVIO LAU-YUEN, bioengineering educator; b. Shanghai, China, June 3, 1942; s. Kwok CHong and Fung Sing (Yu) W.; m. Patricia Tak-kit Cheong, Sept. 6, 1969; children: Kirstin Wei-Chi, Jonathan I-Huei. BSME, Chico State U., 1965; MS, U. Wash., 1966, PhD, 1971. Research assoc. U. Wash., Seattle, 1965-70; asst. research prof. U. Calif.-San Diego, La Jolla, 1970-74, assoc. research prof., 1974-75, assoc. prof., 1975-80, prof. surgery and bioengring., 1980-90; vice chmn. for rsch. and dir. MSRC, 1990—; prof. ortho surgery U. Pitts., 1990—, prof. mech. engring., 1990—, Albert B. Ferguson Jr. prof. orthopaedic surgery, 1993—, prof. civil and environ. engring., 1994—, prof. rehab. sci. and tech., 1994—; prin. investigator VA Med. Ctr., San Diego, 1972-90, Pitts., 1990—; cons. bioengr. Children's Hosp., San Diego, 1973-80; cons. med. implant cos., 1978-85; vis. prof. biomechanics Kobe (Japan) U., 1981-82; dir., CEO M&D Coutts Inst. for Joint Reconstrn. and Rsch., 1984-90; mem. sci. adv. com. Whitaker Found., 1986-95, Steadman-Hawkins Sports Medicine Found., 1990—, OsteoArthritis Scis. Inc., 1992-95. Assoc. editor Jour. Biochem. Engring., 1979-87, Jour. Biomechanics, 1978—, Jour. Orthopedic Rsch., 1983-92, Materials Sci. Reports, 1990, Proc. Inst. Mech. Engrs. (Part H), 1990-94; mem. editl. adv. bd. Jour. Orthopedic Rsch., 1993—; internat. adv. bd. Jour. ESSKA, Knee Surgery, Sports Traumatology, Arthroscopy, 1993—; editl. bd. am. Jour. Sports Medicine, 1995—; mem. internat. adv. bd. Jour. Ortho. Sci. Recipient Elizabeth Winston Lanier Kappa Delta award, 1983, 86, awards for excellence in basic sci. rsch. Orthopaedic Rsch. Soc. and Am. Acad. Orthopaedic Surgeons, 1983, 86, 90, 94, O'Donoghue award Am. Orthopaedic Soc. Sports Medicine, 1990, Wartenweiler Meml. Lectureship, 1987, Citation award Am. Coll. Sports Medicine, 1988, Rsch. Career Devel. award NIH, 1977-82, Muybridge medal Internat. Soc. Internat. Biomechanics, 1995; Japan Soc. Promotion of Sci. fellow, 1981. Fellow ASME (sec., chmn. biomechanics com., chmn. honors com. bioengring. divsn., mem. exec. com. 1983-88, sec. 1985-86, chmn. 1986-87, H.R. Lissner award 1991), Am. Inst. Med. and Biol. Engring. (founding fellow, chmn. coll. fellows 1992-94, bd. dirs. 1992-94); mem. NAE, Inst. Medicine NAS, We. Orthopaedic Assn. (hon.), Biomed. Engring. Soc. (bd. dirs. 1984-86), Am. Acad. Orthopedic Surgeons, Orthopaedic Rsch. Soc. (exec. com. 1983-88, chmn. program com. 1983-84, pres. 1985-86), Am. Soc. Biomechanics (pres. 1985-86, sec. 1977-80, exec. com. 1984-87, Giovanni Borelli award 1993), Internat. Soc. Fractures Repair (bd. dirs. 1986-94, v.p. 1987-90, pres. 1990-92), Can. Orthopedic Rsch. Soc. (hon.), European Orthopedic Rsch. Soc., U.S. Nat. Commn. Biomechanics (chmn. 1994—, exec. com. 1988—). Home: 47 Pleasant View Ln Pittsburgh PA 15238-1859 Office: U Pitts Dept Ortho Surg Liliane Kaufmann Bldg 3471 5th Ave Ste 1010 Pittsburgh PA 15213-3221

WOOD, ALLEN JOHN, electrical engineer, consultant; b. Milw., Oct. 1, 1925; s. Alfred John and Kathleen Francis (Welch) W.; m. Barbara Ann Cook, Oct. 29, 1949; children: John Scott, Susan Beth Wood Richmond. BEE, Marquette U., 1949; MS in Elec. Engring., Ill. Inst. Tech., 1951; PhD, Rensselaer Poly. Inst., 1959. Registered profl. engr., N.Y. Engr. Allis Chalmers Mfg. Co., West Allis, Wis., 1949-50; engr. GE, Lynn, Mass., 1951-52; engr. GE, Schenectady, N.Y., 1952-59, sr. engr., 1960-69; mem. tech. staff Hughes Aircraft Co., Culver City, Calif., 1959-60; cons., prin., dir. Power Techs., Inc., Schenectady, N.Y., 1969-91, treas., chief fin. officer, 1989-91; also bd. dirs. Power Techs., Inc., 1969-91; ind. cons., 1991—; adj. prof. Rensselaer Poly. Inst., Troy, 1966—; cons. in field, 1992—. Author: Power System Reliability Calculations, 1973, Power Generation Operation and Control, 1984, 2d edit. 1995; contbr. numerous articles to profl. jours. With U.S. Army, 1942-46, ETO, PTO. Fellow IEEE (life); mem. AAAS, Am. Nuclear Soc. Republican. Mem. Reformed Ch. in Am. Avocations: amateur radio, photography.

WOOD, ARTHUR MACDOUGALL, retired retail executive; b. Chgo., Jan. 27, 1913; s. R. Arthur and Emily (Smith) W.; m. Pauline Palmer, Nov. 17, 1945; children: Pauline, Arthur MacDougall Jr. AB, Princeton U., 1934, LLD (hon.), 1976; LLB, Harvard U., 1937; LHD (hon.), DePaul U., 1977; D in Humanics (hon., Springfield Coll., 1978; HHD (hon.), Beloit Coll., 1981. Bar: Ill. 1937. Atty. Bell, Boyd & Marshall, Chgo., 1937-40; atty. Sears, Roebuck & Co., 1946-52, sec., 1952-59, v.p., 1956-68, dir., 1959-83, comptroller, 1960-62, v.p. charge Pacific Coast ter., 1962-67, v.p. midwestern ter., 1967, pres., 1968-72, chmn., chief exec. officer, 1973-77. Gen. chmn. United Crusade, Los Angeles County, 1966; co-founder Chgo. United, 1975; gov. United Way Am., 1977; trustee Art Inst. Chgo., 1949—, also chmn., 1978-80; life trustee Rush-Presbyn.-St. Luke's Med. Ctr., Chgo.; former trustee Calif. Inst. Tech., U. Chgo.; mem. Chgo. Hort. Soc., trustee, 1992-93; active Pres. Nixon's Labor-Mgmt. Com., 1975, Pres. Coun. Minority Bus. Enterprises, 1970-74. With F.A. AUS; lt. col. USAAF, 1941-45. Decorated Legion of Merit. Mem. Bus. Coun. Office: PO Box 06619 9800 Sears Tower Chicago IL 60606-6619

WOOD, BARBARA ANN, financial executive; b. Davisburg, Mich., June 15, 1945; d. John Eakers and Florence Fay (Adams) Carter; m. Bruce Michael Wood, Nov. 21, 1964; children: Christine Ann Wood-Wall, Michael Nolan. Student, Oakland C.C., Rochester, Mich., 1970. Owner, pres. Keys Tax Svc., Auburn Hills, Mich., 1980-90; divsn. mgr. Advantage Capital Corp., Houston, 1984—, CEO, mem. coun., 1993—; bd. dirs. Chief Pontiac Fed. Credit Union; mem. prodr.'s adv. coun. Advantage Capital Corp. Mem. Internat. Assn. Fin. Planning, Am. Bus. Womens Assn. Republican. Avocations: bicycling, reading, walking, traveling. Office: Comprehensive Investment Sv Ste 102 1899 Orchard Lake Rd Sylvan Lake MI 48320-1775

WOOD, BARBARA LOUISE CHAMPION, state legislator; b. Swampscott, Mass., Jan. 10, 1924; d. John Duncan and Eva Louise (Moore) Champion; m. Newall Arthur Wood, June 12, 1948; children: Gary Duncan, Craig Newall, Brian Scott, Dennis Michael, Joan Wood Unger. Diploma in Nursing, Mary Hitchcock Meml. Hosp. Sch. Nursing, Hanover, N.H., 1945; student, Simmons Coll., 1947-48. RN. Rep., mem. ho. edn. com. Vt. Gen. Assembly, Montpelier, 1981—, vice chmn. edn. com., 1983-87; trustee Vt. State Colls., Waterbury, 1986-90, Gifford Meml. Hosp., Randolph, Vt., 1986—; commr., Vt. rep. Edn. Commn. of the States, Denver, 1981-86. Sch. dir. Bethel Sch. Bd., Vt., 1963-85; mem.-at-large Vt. Sch. Bds. Assn., Montpelier, 1982-85. Served to 2d lt. U.S. Army, 1945-46. Mem. Am. Legion, Vis. Nurse Alliance Vt.-N.H. (bd. dirs. 1991—). Republican. Congregationalist. Clubs: Bethel Woman's (pres. 1976-78); Vt. Fedn. Women's Clubs (dist. pres. 1978-80). Home: Woodland Rd Bethel VT 05032 Office: Vt House of Reps State House Montpelier VT 05602

WOOD, BYARD DEAN, mechanical engineering educator and researcher; b. Cardston, Alta, Can., Mar. 30, 1940; married, 1965; 3 children. BS, Utah State U., 1963, MS, 1966; PhD in Mech. Engring., U. Minn., 1970. Assoc. prof. heat transfer & exptl. methods Ariz. State U., Tempe, 1970-80, prof. mech. engring., 1980—; cons. Solar Energy Rsch. & Edn. Found., 1977—, Solar Rating & Cert. Corp., ERG, Inc. Fellow ASME, Am. Soc. Heating, Refrigeration and Air-Conditioning Engrs. Achievements include research in heat transfer and experimental methods in thermal and photovoltaic solar heating and cooling systems, heat and mass transfer associated with absorption cooling technologies. Office: Ariz State U Mech/Aero Engring Dept Coll Engring & Applied Sciences Tempe AZ 85287-5806

WOOD, CHARLES MARTIN, III, food company executive; b. New Orleans, May 31, 1943; s. Charles Martin and Veva Penick (Miller) W.; m. Daphne Howard Flowers, June 4, 1966. BA, Princeton U., 1965; MBA, Colgate Darden Sch. Bus. Adminstrn., 1970. Dir. product devel. Flowers Industries, Inc., Thomasville, Ga., 1970-71, dir. mktg., 1971-73, dir. fin., 1973-76, v.p. fin., 1976-78, sr. v.p., chief fin. officer, 1978—, dir., 1975—; chmn. bd. Flower Employees Credit League, Thomasville, Ga., 1978; trustee Flowers Industries Retirement Trust, Thomasville, Ga., 1973—; chmn. bus. adv. bd. Valdosta State Coll., Ga., 1980-82. Trustee John D. Archbold Meml. Hosp., Thomasville, Ga., 1977—, chmn., 1994—; dir. Masters of Foxhounds Assn. Am., Boston, 1981—, pres., 1990-93, chmn. Edn. Found., 1993—; jr. warden vestry All Saints Episcopal Ch., Thomasville, 1982; nat. trustee Ducks Unltd., Chgo., 1977-81; state chmn. of yr. Hilton Head, S.C. Served to 1st lt. U.S. Army, 1966-68. Republican. Episcopalian. Clubs: Ivy (Princeton, N.J.); The Brook (N.Y.), Live Oak Hounds (master, huntsman) (1974—). Home: RR 2 Box 191 Monticello FL 32344-9541 Office: Flowers Industries Inc PO Box 1338 US Hwy 19 S Thomasville GA 31799

WOOD, C(HARLES) NORMAN, air force officer; b. Dallas, Mar. 7, 1938; s. Charles Camp Wood and Mary Louise (Wheatley) Ferguson; m. Jerre Louise Jones, June 10, 1961 (div. Sept. 1967); 1 child, Wende Louise; m. Elizabeth Burwell Dillard, June 27, 1969; 1 child, Elizabeth Burwell. BBA, U. Tex., 1960; MPA, Auburn U., 1974. Commd. 2d lt. USAF, 1960, advanced through grades to lt. gen., 1990; electronic warfare officer Strategic Air Command, Kans. and Okinawa, 1962-69; intelligence staff officer Hdqrs. Strategic Air Command, Offutt AFB, Nebr., 1969-72; chief def. analysis br. Hdqrs. Mil. Assistance Command, Saigon, Republic of Vietnam, 1972-73; air staff officer Hdqrs. USAF, Washington, 1974-76; exec. officer Office of Air Force History, Washington, 1976-77; student Nat. War Coll., Washington, 1978-79; dep. comdr. for ops. 544th Strategic Intelligence Wing, Offutt AFB, 1979, wing comdr., 1980; asst. dep. chief of staff intelligence Strategic Air Command, Offutt AFB, 1981-82; exec. dir. Pres.'s Fgn. Intelligence Adv. Bd. The White House, Washington, 1982-83; dep. dir. Nat. Strategic Target List, Joint Strategic Planning Staff, Offutt AFB, 1984; dep. asst. chief of staff intelligence USAF, Washington, 1985; dir. intelligence J-2 Hdqrs. U.S. European Command, Fed. Republic Germany, 1986-87; asst. chief of staff intelligence Air Force Hdqrs., Washington, 1988-90; dir. Intelligence Community Staff, Washington, 1990-92; pres., CEO Armed Forces Comms. and Electronics Assn., Fairfax, Va., 1996—; sr. v.p., gen. mgr. BDM Federal. Decorated D.S.M., Legion of Merit, Def. Superior Svc. medal. Mem. Nat. Mil. Intelligence Assn., Security Affairs Support Assn., Armed Forces Communications and Electronics Assn., Air Force Assn. Republican. Mem. Christian Sci. Ch. Home: 5440 Mt Corcoran Pl Burke VA 22015-2147 Office: Armed Forces Comms and Electronics Assn 4400 Fair Lakes Ct Fairfax VA 22033-3899

WOOD, CHARLES TUTTLE, history educator; b. St. Paul, Oct. 29, 1933; s. Harold Eaton and Margaret (Frisbie) W.; m. Susan Danielson, July 9, 1955; children: Lucy Eaton, Timothy Walker, Martha Augusta, Mary Frisbie. A.B., Harvard, 1955, A.M., 1957, Ph.D., 1962. Investment analyst, trader Harold E. Wood & Co., St. Paul, 1955-56; teaching fellow gen. edn. Harvard, 1959-61, instr. history, 1961-64; mem. faculty Dartmouth, 1964—, prof. history, 1971—, Daniel Webster prof. history, 1980—, Daniel Webster prof. history and comparative lit., 1991—, chmn. dept. history, 1976-79, chmn. dept. comparative lit., 1977; vis. Keeney prof. of history Brown U., 1992-93. Author: The French Apanages and the Capetian Monarchy, 1223-1328, 1966, Philip the Fair and Boniface VIII, 2d edit., 1971, reprint, 1976, Felipe el Hermoso y Bonifacio VIII: Mexico: UTEHA, 1968, The age of Chivalry: Manners and Morals 1000-1450, 1970, The Quest for Eternity, reprint edit., 1983, Joan of Arc and Richard III, 1988, The Trial of Charles I, 1989, Fresh Verdicts on Joan of Arc, 1996; also articles. Chmn. Dresden Bd. Sch. Dirs., 1972-74. Guggenheim fellow, 1986-87; recipient Disting. Service award N.H. Sch. Bds. Assn., 1975; Am. Council Learned Socs. fellow, 1980-81; Am. Bar Found. fellow, 1981-82. Fellow Medieval Acad. Am. (treas. 1989—, fin. com. 1979—, council 1985-87); mem. Am. Hist. Assn. (chmn. nominating com. 1977, Adams prize com. 1976-78), Conf. Brit. Studies, Soc. for French Hist. Studies, N.H. Sch. Bds. Assn. (2d v.p. 1974-75), New Eng. Medieval Conf. (pres. 1978-79), Am. Soc. Legal History, Phi Beta Kappa. Club: St. Botolph (Boston). Home: 7 N Balch St Hanover NH 03755-1502

WOOD, CHARLES W., financial services company executive; b. McAlester, Okla., Nov. 6, 1946; s. Edgar Scott and Jessie Doyle (Ray) W.; m. Maxie Rae Moss, July 3, 1975 (div. July 1988); 1 child, Whitney Rae. AA, Eastern Okla. State Coll., 1966; BS, Okla. State U., 1968. Regional planner Kiamichi Econ. Dist., Wilburton, Okla., 1969-73; state planner Okla. Crime Commn., Oklahoma City, 1973-75, dir. planning, 1975-80, dir., 1980-81; adminstr., mgmt. cons., logistics trainer Okla. Crime Victims Bd., Oklahoma City, 1981-89; registered rep. Waddell and Reed, Inc., Edmond, Okla., 1989-91, dist. mgr., mgmt. trainer, 1991—; mgmt. cons. Author/editor/pub. Victims' Voice newsletter, 1985-91. Recipient Liberty Bell award Okla. Bar Assn., 1985. Mem. Nat. Assn. Victims Compensation (treas. 1983-87, v.p. 1987-89), Jaycees (charter pres. 1970-73), Rotary (treas. 1983-85). Democrat. Ch. of Christ. Avocations: golf, photography, walking, real estate. Office: Waddell and Reed Inc 508 W 15th St Edmond OK 73013

WOOD, CHRISTOPHER L. J., real estate consulting firm executive; b. London, Jan. 20, 1947; came to U.S., 1983; s. Sidney John and Lillian Ballantine (Pollock) W.; m. Pamela Wood, Dec. 14, 1978; 1 child, Alexander Wood. BSC, London U., 1969. Ptnr., dir. Debenham, Tewson & Chinnocks, London, U.S., 1972—. Fellow Royal Instn. Chartered Surveyors; mem. Am. Soc. Real Estate Counselors, St. George's Soc. N.Y., Thames Rowing Club, Union League Club (Phila.). Office: DTZ Debenham Thorpe Internat 20th Flr 560 Lexington Ave Fl 20 New York NY 10022-6828

WOOD, CRAIG BRECKINRIDGE, paleobiologist, natural science educator; b. Washington, Jan. 27, 1943; s. William Ernest Wood and Christina Mae (DeBrito) Phillips; m. Sung He Lee, May 21, 1982; children: William, Violet, Virginia. AB in Geology, U. N.C., 1966; MS in Geology, U. Wyo., 1967; MA in Geology, Harvard U., 1980, PhD in Geology, 1992. Teaching fellow geology, anthropology, biology depts. Harvard U., Cambridge, Mass., 1968-70, 73-74; rsch. assoc. geology dept. Princeton (N.J.) U., 1970-71; geologist Herbert & Assocs. Ltd., Virginia Beach, Va., 1972-73; instr. natural sci. Providence Coll., 1974-79; lectr. biology and geology Asian div. U. Md., Yokota AFB, Japan, 1981-82; asst. prof. natural sci., spl. lectr. geology Providence Coll., 1979-92, assoc. prof. natural sci., 1992—, dir. natural sci. program, 1993-95; Harvard U. exch. scholar dept. paleontology U. Calif., Berkeley, 1988-89; expdn. mem. Rift Valley Rsch. Mission in Ethiopia, Addis Ababa, 1976, Blue Nile region, Ethiopia, 1993, 96; rsch. assoc. in mammalogy Mus. of Comparative Zoology, Harvard U., 1994—. Co-discoverer of "Bodo Man", 1976, first highland mezozoic vertebrates, 1993, first Ethiopian dinosaurs, 1996. Mem. AAAS, Soc. Vertebrate Paleontology, Harvard Club R.I., R.I. Carolina Club (treas.), Humanities Forum of R.I., Sigma Xi, Phi Mu Alpha Sinfonia. Office: Providence Coll Biology Dept Providence RI 02918

WOOD, DAVID CHARLES, lawyer, finance company executive; b. Kansas City, Mo., Aug. 25, 1943; s. Charles O'Brien and Anne Marie (Lohmeyer) W.; m. Rosalie Laitner, Aug. 27, 1966; children: David, Michael, Jennifer. AB in History with honors, U. Mo., 1965, JD, 1968. Bar: Mo. 1968, Iowa 1977. Assoc. Welliver, Porter & Cleaveland, Columbia, Mo., 1968-70; asst. counsel Norwest Fin. Svcs., Inc., Des Moines, 1970-74, asst. gen. counsel, 1974-78, asst. v.p., dir. legal affairs, 1978-79, v.p., gen. counsel, 1979-84, sr. v.p., sec., 1984-88, pres., COO, 1988-94; chmn., CEO, 1995—; also bd. dirs. Norwest Fin. Svcs., Inc., Des Moines; bd. dirs., v.p. Centurion Life Ins. Co., Centurion Casualty Co., Des Moines; v.p. Dial Bank, Sioux Falls, S.D., Dial Nat. Bank, Des Moines; mem. faculty Nat. Installment Banking Sch., U. Colo., Boulder, 1982-83. Mem. bd. editors Mo. Law Rev., 1966-68; contbr. articles to legal publs. Bd. dirs. Des Moines Ballet Assn.,

1989-94, United Way Ctrl. Iowa, 1992-94, Grand View Coll., 1993—, Civic Music Assn., 1993—. Curator's scholar U. Mo., 1961-62, 62-63, Omar E. Robinson Meml. scholar, 1965-66, Law Sch. Found. scholar, 1966-67. Mem. ABA, Iowa Bar Assn., Mo. Bar Assn., Am. Fin. Svcs. Assn. (mem. law com. 1979-84, mem. ops. com. 1988-93), Conf. on Personal Fin. Law (mem. emeritus gen. com.), Iowa Fin. Svcs. Assn. (pres. 1983-87), Metro Bus. Assn. (pres. 1982-83), Phi Eta Sigma. Republican. Methodist.

WOOD, DAVID KENNEDY CORNELL, choreographer, educator; b. Fresno, Calif., Feb. 24, 1925; s. Earl Warner and Elsie Bliss (Kennedy) W.; m. Marni Pope Thomas, Dec. 28, 1958; children—Marina, Raegan, Ellis. B.A., U. Calif., 1945; student, Neighborhood Playhouse, N.Y.C., 1947-48, also other theatre and dance schs. Choreographer Broadway musicals, TV, N.Y.C. Opera Ballet, Met. Opera Ballet, 1950-58; soloist, Hanya Holm Co., 1948-50, soloist, rehearsal dir., Martha Graham Co., 1953-68, prof. dance, U. Calif., 1968—, artistic dir., Bay Area Repertory Dance Co., guest soloist, Belles Artes of Mexico, 1958-59, Sweden Ballet Akademien, 1960-61 (choreographic award Nat. Endowment for Arts 1973-74, 77-78); choreographer: Pre-Amble, 1971, Post Script, 1974, Cassandra, 1974, Changelings, 1970, The Immigrant, 1974, In the Glade, 1977, Jeux, 1978, Prometheus, 1980; Dusty Pools and Puddles, 1983, Rim of Heaven, 1984, Duad, 1985, Nova's prodn. Electrical Super Conductivity, 1986, Quiet Interludes, 1987, Graffitti, 1987, Persephone, 1988, American Decades, 1989, Dojoji, 1993. Served with USNR, 1943-46. Mem. Am. Guild Musican Artists, Actors Equity, AFTRA, Calif. Dance Educators Assn., Am. Assn. Dance Cos. Home: 3090 Buena Vista Way Berkeley CA 94708-2020 *The enjoyment of the act of doing, the willingness to accept the discipline of the moment and an awareness of one's individual growth all contribute to a total sense of achievement as well as a pleasure in it.*

WOOD, DAVID L., entomologist, educator; b. Jan. 8, 1931. BS, SUNY, Syracuse, 1952; PhD, U. Calif., Berkeley, 1960. Lic. forester, Calif. Prof. entomology, emeritis dept. Environ. Sci. Policy, Mgmt. U. Calif., Berkeley, 1970—; lectr., reviewer, cons. in field. Contbr. articles to profl. jours. Recipient Silver medal Swedish Coun. for Forestry and Agril. Rsch., 1983. Fellow Entomological Soc. Can. (Founder's award Lectr. Entomological Soc. Am. 1986, Founder's award Western Forest Insect Work Conf. 1992); mem. AAAS, AIBS, Entomol. Soc. Am., Entomol. Soc. Can., Internat. Soc. Chem. Ecology, Soc. Am. Foresters, Sigma Xi. Home: 26 Hardie Dr Moraga CA 94556-1134 Office: U Calif Divsn Insect Biology Berkeley CA 94720

WOOD, DIANE PAMELA, judge; b. Plainfield, N.J., July 4, 1950; d. Kenneth Reed and Lucille (Padmore) Wood; m. Dennis James Hutchinson, Sept. 2, 1978; children: Kathryn, David, Jane. BA, U. Tex.-Austin, 1971, JD, 1975. Bar: Tex. 1975, D.C. 1978. Law clk. U.S. Ct. Appeals (5th cir.), 1975-76, U.S. Supreme Ct., 1976-77; atty.-advisor U.S. Dept. State, Washington, 1977-78; assoc. law firm Covington & Burling, Washington, 1978-80; asst. prof. law Georgetown U. Law Ctr., Washington, 1980-81, U. Chgo., 1981-88, prof. law, 1988-95, assoc. dean, 1989-92, Harold J. and Marion F. Green prof. internat. legal studies, 1990-95, sr. lectr. in law, 1995—; spl. cons. antitrust divsn. internat. guide U.S. Dept. Justice, 1986-87, dep. asst. atty. gen. antitrust divsn., 1993-95; cir. judge U.S. Ct. Appeals (7th cir.), 1995—. Contbr. articles to profl. jours. Bd. dirs. Hyde-Park-Kenwood Cmty. Health Ctr., 1983-85. Mem. ABA (sec. antitrust and internat. law, chmn. internat. law sect. BIT com., co-chmn. internat. antitrust com., ILP coun. 1989-91, internat. legal scholar officer 1991-93, chmn., antitrust sec. subcom. on internat. unfair trade, vice-chair, sec. internat. antitrust com. 1991, standing com. on law and nat. security 1991-93), Am. Soc. Internat. Law, Am. Law Inst., Internat. Acad. Comparative Law. Democrat.

WOOD, DONALD CRAIG, retired marketing professional; b. Wilmington, Del., June 24, 1937; s. Thomas Henry and Madelyn (Brehm) W.; m. Elizabeth Haring, Apr. 28, 1962; children: Craig Standish, Allison Jean. BA, U. Del., 1959; MBA, Northwestern U., 1967. Sales engr. NVF Corp., Broadview, Ill., 1960-62, Synthane Corp., Morton Grove, Ill., 1962-68; account exec., mgr. sales Donnelley Mktg. subs. Dun and Bradstreet Corp., Oakbrook, Ill., 1968-69; from dir. to v.p. market devel. to v.p. mktg. Donnelley Mktg. subs. Dun and Bradstreet Corp., Stamford, Conn., 1977-1980; from v.p., gen. mgr. to pres. Info. Services Div. Donnelley Mktg. subs. Dun and Bradstreet Corp., Stamford, 1980-86, sr. v.p., 1987-90; v.p., gen. mgr. info. svcs. Triad Systems Corp., Livermore, Calif., 1990-96. Served to 1st lt. U.S. Army, 1959-60. Home: 6 Killdeer Ln Hilton Head Island SC 29928

WOOD, DONALD EURIAH, lawyer; b. Guymon, Okla., May 27, 1935; s. Theodore and Lula Elizabeth (Rider) W.; m. Lynda Sharon Harris, Sept. 30, 1960; children—Donald Craig, Tana Dawn, Kristen Lynn. B.A., Panhandle A. and M. Coll., 1958; LL.B., Okla. U., 1964, J.D., 1970. Bar: Okla. bar 1964. Asst. county atty. Texas County, 1964; county atty., 1965-67; dist. atty. Okla. 1st Jud. Dist., Guymon, 1967—; Mem. adv. com. Okla. Commn. Criminal and Traffic Enforcement Systems, 1972; mem. Gov.'s Commn. Community Affairs and Planning, 1972-75; mem. faculty Panhandle State Coll., 1974-92; mem. Okla. Dist. Atty. Tng. Council, 1976—; mem. Okla. Bur. Narcotics and Dangerous Drugs Commn., 1992—. Served with inf. AUS, 1958-60. Named Okla. Prosecutor of Yr., Assn. Okla. Narcotic Enforcers, 1994-95. Mem. Okla. Bar Assn. (legal ethics com. 1971—), Texas County Bar Assn. (pres. 1966, 1970-71), Nat. Dist. Attys. Assn., Okla. Dist. Attys. Assn. (pres. 1972, exec. com. 1971—), Phi Alpha Delta. Presbyn. Clubs: Elk, Rotarian. Home: 605 Hillcrest Dr Guymon OK 73942-3345 Office: 319 N Main St Guymon OK 73942-4843

WOOD, DONALD FRANK, transportation educator, consultant; b. Waukesha, Wis., Feb. 22, 1935; s. Frank Blaine and Uilah (Mathson) W.; m. Doreen Johnson, July 5, 1968; children: Frank, Tamara. BA, U. Wis., 1957, MA, 1958; PhD, Harvard U., 1970. Transp. planner State of Wis., Madison, 1960-70; prof. San Francisco State U., 1970—. Author: El Camino, 1982, (with others) Motorized Fire Apparatus of the West, 1991, Contemporary Transportation, 1996, Contemporary Logistics, 1996, American Volunteer Fire Trucks, 1993, Commercial Trucks, 1993, International Logistics, 1994, Wreckers & Tow Trucks, 1995; contbr. Ency. Britannica. 2d lt. U.S. Army, 1958. Mem. Coun. of Logistics Mgmt. (chpt. pres. 1975-76), Transp. Rsch. Forum (chpt. pres. 1974), Am. Truck Hist. Soc. Presbyterian. Home: 321 Riviera Cir Larkspur CA 94939-1508 Office: San Francisco State U. Coll Bus San Francisco CA 94132

WOOD, DOUGLAS, author, composer, musician; b. N.Y.C., Dec. 10, 1951; s. James Henry and Joyce Adelle (Wilton) W.; m. Kathryn Ann Sokolowski, May 26, 1973; children: Eric, Bryan. MusB, Morningside Coll., 1973. Tchr. Meriden-Cleghorn (Iowa) Sch., 1973-75, Morris (Minn.) Pub. Schs., 1975-77; speaker at convs. and confs. on wilderness and human spirit. Author: Old Turtle, 1992 (Minn. Book award 1992, named Best Children's Book by Midwest Pubs. 1992, Book of Yr. award Internat. Reading Assn. 1993, ABBY award Am. Booksellers Assn. 1993), Paddle Whispers, 1993, Minnesota: The Spirit of the Land, 1995, Northwoods Cradle Song, 1996, The Windigo's Return, 1996; composer: (album) Earth Songs, Solitary Shores, Deep Woods - Deep Waters, 1996. Named one of Ten Outstanding Young Minnesotans by Minn. Jaycees, 1991. Avocations: canoeing and wilderness exploration, fishing, reading, tennis. Home: 3835 Pine Point Rd Saint Cloud MN 56303-9730

WOOD, EARL HOWARD, physiologist, educator; b. Mankato, Minn., Jan. 1, 1912; s. William Clark and Inez (Goff) W.; m. Ada C. Peterson, Dec. 20, 1936; children: Phoebe, Mark Goff, Guy Harland, Earl Andrew. B.A., Macalester Coll., 1934, D.Sc., 1950; B.S., U. Minn., 1939, M.S., M.B., Ph.D., 1941, M.D., 1942. Teaching fellow physiology U. Minn., 1936-39, instr., 1940; NRC fellow med. scis., dept. pharmacology U. Pa., 1941; instr. pharmacology Harvard Med. Sch., 1942; research asst. acceleration lab. Mayo Aero Med. Unit, 1943; asst. prof. physiology Mayo Found., U. Minn. Grad. Sch., 1944, prof. physiology and medicine, 1950—; staff mem. sect. physiology Mayo Clinic, 1947—; chmn. biophys. scis. unit Mayo Med. Sch.; career investigator Am. Heart Assn., 1961—; Sci. cons. air surgeon USAF Aero Med. Ctr., Heidelberg, Germany, 1946; vis. prof. U. Bern, 1965-66; vis. scientist dept. physiology Univ. Coll., London, 1972-73; rsch. cons. Canadian Air Force, DCIEM, Toronto, 1993-94. Contbr. articles to profl. jours., chpts. to books. Recipient Presdl. certificate of merit, Disting. Lectr. award Am. Coll. Chest Physicians, 1974, Sr. U.S. Scientist Humboldt award Kiel, Fed. Republic Germany, 1985, Phillips Meml. award ACP, 1983, Lucian award for research in cardiovascular diseases McGill U., 1985, Stewart Meml. lectr. Royal Aero. Soc., 1987, Outstanding Achievement award U. Minn., 1991. Fellow Aerospace Med. Assn. (Disting. Research award 1983); mem. Am. Physiol. Soc. (past chmn. circulation group, pres. 1980-81, Daggs award 1995), Am. Soc. Pharmacology and Exptl. Therapeutics, Am., Central socs. clin. investigation, Soc. Exptl. Biology and Medicine, Am. Heart Assn. (Research Achievement award 1973, past chmn. basic sci. sect.), AAAS, Nat. Acad. Medicine Mex., Nat. Acad. Arts and Scis. (Netherlands), Federated Am. Socs. Exptl. Biology (pres. 1981—), German Soc. for Heart and Circulation Rsch., Carl-Ludwig Ehrenmünze, Phi Beta Kappa, Sigma Xi, Alpha Omega Alpha (Outstanding Achievement award 1991). Research, numerous publs. on devel. instrumental techniques and procedures for study heart and circulation in health and disease; applications of these procedures to detection and quantitation of various types of acquired and congenital heart disease, study of effects and compensatory reaction of heart and circulation to various types of circulatory stress. Home: 211 2nd St NW Apt 1918 Rochester MN 55901-3101

WOOD, EDWARD EPHRAIM, JR., park administrator; b. Havre De Grace, Md., Sept. 30, 1946; s. Edward E. Sr. and Phyllis Hopkins Wood; m. Sherry L. Jerkins, Aug. 9, 1969 (div. June 1982); children: Gerald E., Richard J., Sandra D.; m. Jody H. Hewston, Nov. 17, 1984; children: Andrew D., Tobe M. BS in Biology, U. N.Mex., 1970. Rsch. technician Lovelace Found., Albuquerque, 1970-72; pk. ranger Grand Canyon (Ariz.) Nat. Pk., 1972-73, Jefferson Nat. Exp. Mem., St. Louis, 1973, Everglades Nat. Pk., Flamingo, Fla., 1973-75, Padre Island Nat. Seashore, Corpus Christi, Tex., 1975-78; chief interpretation and rsch. mgmt. Lehman Caves Nat. Monument, Baker, Nev., 1978-86; supr. pk. ranger Grand Canyon Nat. Pk., 1986-89; ranger-in-charge Am. Mem. Park, Saipan, MP, 1989-92; supt. War in the Pacific Nat. Historical Park, Agana, Guam, 1992—; co-chmn. Gov. Adv. Commn., Saipan, 1989-92. Editor: Lehman Caves, 2d printing, 1982; contbr. articles to mags. in field of caving and specific Nat. Pk. resources and issues; photographer tourism-related brochures, mags., postcards and notecards. Mem. Saipan Rotary Club, 1989-92, Organist For Guam United Meth. Ch. Avocations: scuba diving, caving, computer graphics, photography. Office: Nat Pk Svc PO Box FA Agana GU 96910

WOOD, ELIJAH, actor; b. Cedar Rapids, Iowa, Jan. 28, 1981. Appeared in films Back to the Future Part II, 1989, Internal Affairs, 1990, Avalon, 1990, Paradise, 1991, Radio Flyer, 1992, Forever Young, 1992, The Adventures of Huck Finn, 1993, The Good Son, 1993, North, 1994, The War, 1994; TV movies include Child in the Night, 1990, Day-O, 1992; also appeared in music video Paula Abdul's Forever Your Girl. Office: William Morris Agency 151 El Camino Beverly Hills CA 90212*

WOOD, ELWOOD STEVEN, III, chemical company executive; b. Norfolk, Va., Mar. 8, 1934; s. Elwood Steven Jr. and Margaret (Schlegel) W.; m. Jean Elizabeth Abbott, Dec. 21, 1961; children: Michael Scott, Tracy Lee. S.B., MIT, 1956, S.M., 1957; M.B.A., U. Pa., 1962. With W.R. Grace & Co., 1961-95; asst. plant mgr. Organic Chems. div. W.R. Grace & Co., Owensboro, Ky., 1964-66; plant mgr. Polyfibron div. W.R. Grace & Co., Adams, Mass., 1966-67; v.p. W.R. Grace & Co., Lexington, Mass., 1967-77; exec. v.p. Constrn. Products div. W.R. Grace & Co., Cambridge, Mass., 1977-82; pres. Polyfibron div., v.p. parent co. W.R. Grace & Co., Lexington, Mass., 1982-95, worldwide GM printing products, 1993-95; ret., 1995. Served to 1st lt. U.S. Army, 1958.

WOOD, EMILY CHURCHILL, gifted and talented education educator; b. Summit, N.J., Apr. 11, 1925; d. Arthur Burdett and Ruth Vail (Pierson) Churchill; m. Philip Warren Wood, June 22, 1946; children: Martha, Arthur, Warren, Benjamin. BA, Smith Coll., 1946; MA in Teaching, Manhattanville Coll., 1971; postgrad., U. Tulsa, 1974-79, Langston U., 1990-92. Cert. tchr. social studies, learning disabilities, elem. edn., econs., Am. history, world history. Tchr. Miss Fines Sch., Princeton, N.J., 1946-47, Hallen Ctr. for Edn., Portchester, N.Y., 1973-74, Town and Country Sch., Tulsa, Okla., 1974-79, Tulsa Pub. Schs., 1979—, Tulsa Jr. Coll., 1990-92, 94; adv. bd. Great Expectations Educators, Tulsa, 1985—; leader colloquia bill of rights Arts and Humanities Coun., Tulsa, 1989; mem. literacy task force Tulsa 2000 Edn. Com., 1990-92; chmn. internat. student exch. Eisenhower Internat. Sch., Tulsa, 1992-94. Author: (with others) Visual Arts in China, 1988, Applauding Our Constitution, 1989, The Bill of Rights: Who Guarantees What, 1993; contbr. articles to profl. jours. Dir. Smith Coll. Alumnae, Northampton, Mass., 1956-59; leader, founder Am. Field Svc., Tulsa, 1982-84; pres., v.p. Booker T. Washington H.S. PTA, Tulsa, 1985; campaign mgr. auditors race Dem. Party, Tulsa, 1988, 92, 94; bd. dirs., nominations chair Sister Cities Internat., Tulsa, 1992—. Named Tulsa Tchr. of Yr. Tulsa Classroom Tchrs. Assn., 1988, Nat. Elem. Tchr. of Yr., Nat. Bar Aux., 1992; recipient Elem. Medal of Excellence, Okla. Found. for Excellence, 1990, Valley Forge Tchrs. medal Freedoms Found., 1992. Mem. Nat. Coun. Social Studies (religion program com. 1984—), DAR, Okla. Edn. Assn., Okla. Coun. Social Studies (pres. 1995, tchr. of yr. 1984), Okla. Bar Assn. (law related com. 1988—, tchr. of yr. 1990), Okla. Coun. Econ. Edn. (state and nat. awards 1981, 89, 92), Kent Place Alumnae Assn. (disting. alumna award 1992). Avocations: reading, swimming, traveling, bicycling. Home: 3622 S Yorktown Pl Tulsa OK 74105-3452

WOOD, ERIC FRANKLIN, earth and environmental sciences educator; b. Vancouver, B.C., Can., Oct. 22, 1947; s. Lorne George and Olga Eugena (Hryvnak) W.; m. Katharine Holding Schwed; children: Eric Alexander, Emily Holding. BASc with hons., U. B.C., 1970; SM, MIT, 1972, MSCE, 1973, ScD, 1974. Rsch. asst. MIT, Cambridge, 1970-73; rsch. scholar Internat. Inst. for Applied Systems Analysis, Vienna, Austria, 1974-76; prof. civil engring. Princeton (N.J.) U., 1976—; EOS sci. steering com. NASA, 1984-87, sci. adv. working group, 1992, land surface processes adv. com., 1985-90, Landsat sci. working group, 1992-93; GCIP sci. steering com. World Climate Rsch. Program, 1993-95. Co-author: An Introduction to Groundwater Contamination from Hazardous Wastes, 1984; assoc. editor: Water Resources Research, 1977-82, Applied Math. and Computation, 1983—, Jour. of Forecasting, 1984—, Rev. in Geophysics, 1988-93; editor (books) Recent Developments in Real-Time Forecasting/Control of Water Resources Systems, 1980, Scale Effects in Hyrology, 1986, Land Surface-Atmospheric Interactions for Climate Models: Observations, Modeling and Analysis, 1990; contbr. numerous articles to profl. jours. Recipient Rheinstein award Princton U., 1980. Fellow Am. Geophys. Union (mem. editl. bd. Water Resources Monographs, 1980-85, exec. mem. hydrology sect. 1984-85, 88-92, 94-95, union fellows com. 1994-98, union meeting com. 1988-90, chmn. remot sensing com., 1988-92, Horton rsch. com. 1992-95, Robert E. Horton award 1988); mem. IFORMS, NAS (com. on flood levee policy), NSF (mem. com. of flood hazard mitigation 1979-80, panel on engring. and global climate change 1991), Am. Meteor Soc. (hydrology com. 1987-90), Brit. Hydrol. Soc. Avocations: squash, sailing, skiing. Office: Princeton U Dept of Civil Engring Princeton NJ 08544

WOOD, EVELYN NIELSEN, reading dynamics business executive; b. Logan, Utah, Jan. 8, 1909; d. Elias and Rose (Stirland) Nielsen; m. Myron Douglas Wood, June 12, 1929 (dec. May 1987); 1 child, Carolyn Wood Evans. BA, U. Utah, 1929, MA, 1947; postgrad., Columbia U., 1956-57. Tchr. Weber Coll., Ogden, Utah, 1931-32; girls counselor Jordan High Sch., Sandy, Utah, 1948-57, tchr. jr. and sr. high schs., 1948-59; instr. U. Utah, 1957-59; founder, originator Evelyn Wood Reading Dynamics, 1959-95; tchr. rapid reading U. Del., 1961; guest lectr. NEA, 1961, Internat. Reading Assn., Tex. Christian U., 1962; faculty Brigham Young U., research specialist for reading, 1973-74. Author, conductor radio programs, 1947; author: (With Marjory Barrows) Reading Skills, 1958, A Breakthrough in Reading, 1961, A New Approach to Speed Reading, 1962, Speed Reading for Comprehension, 1962, also articles. *Died Aug. 26, 1995.*

WOOD, FERGUS JAMES, geophysicist, consultant; b. London, Ont., Can., May 13, 1917; came to U.S., 1924, naturalized, 1932; s. Louis Aubrey and Dora Isabel (Elson) W.; student U. Oreg., 1934-36; AB, U. Calif., Berkeley, 1938, postgrad., 1938-39; postgrad. U. Chgo., 1939-40, U. Mich., 1940-42, Calif. Inst. Tech., 1946; m. Doris M. Hack, Sept. 14, 1946; children: Kathryn Celeste Wood Madden, Bonnie Patricia Wood Ward. Teaching asst. U. Mich., 1940-42; instr. in physics and astronomy Pasadena City Coll., 1946-48, John Muir Coll., 1948-49; asst. prof. physics U. Md., 1949-50; assoc. physicist Johns Hopkins U. Applied Physics Lab., 1950-55; sci. editor Ency. Americana, N.Y.C., 1955-60; aero. and space rsch. scientist, sci. asst. to dir. Office Space Flight Programs, Hdqrs., NASA, Washington, 1960-61; program dir. fgn. sci. info. NSF, Washington, 1961-62; phys. scientist, chief sci. and tech. info. staff U.S. Coast and Geodetic Survey, Rockville, Md., 1962-66, phys. scientist Office of Dir., 1967-73, rsch. assoc. Office of Dir., 1973-77, Nat. Ocean Svc.; cons. tidal dynamics, Bonita, Calif., 1978—; mem. Am. Geophys. Union, ICSU-UNESCO Internat. Geol. Correlation Project 274, Working Group #1-Crescendo Events in Coastal Environments, Past and Future (The Millennium Project), 1988—. Capt. USAAF, 1942-46. Recipient Spl. Achievement award Dept. Commerce, NOAA, 1970, 74, 76, 77. Mem. Sigma Pi Sigma, Pi Mu Epsilon, Delta Phi Alpha. Democrat. Presbyterian. Author: The Strategic Role of Perigean Spring Tides in Nautical History and North American Coastal Flooding, 1635-1976, 1978; Tidal Dynamics: Coastal Flooding, and Cycles of Gravitational Force, 1986, Synergetic Gravitational Forces in Tides and the Solar System, 2 vols., 1996; contbr. numerous articles to encys., reference sources, profl. jours.; writer, tech. dir. documentary film: Pathfinders from the Stars, 1967; editor-in-chief: The Prince William Sound, Alaska, Earthquake of 1964 and Aftershocks, vols. 1-2A and sci. coordinator vols. 2B, 2C and 3, 1966-69. Home: 3103 Casa Bonita Dr Bonita CA 91902-1735

WOOD, FRANK BRADSHAW, retired astronomy educator; b. Jackson, Tenn., Dec. 21, 1915; s. Thomas Frank and Mary (Bradshaw) W.; m. Elizabeth Hoar Pepper, Oct. 5, 1945; children—Ellen, Eunice, Mary, Stephen. B.S., U. Fla., 1936; postgrad., U. Ariz., 1938-39; A.M., Princeton, 1940, Ph.D., 1941; postgrad., U.S. Naval Acad., 1943. Research asso. Princeton, 1946; NRC fellow Steward Obs., U. Ariz., also Lick Obs., U. Calif., 1946-47; asst. prof. U. Ariz., 1947-50; asso. prof. U. Pa., 1950, prof. astronomy, 1954-68, chmn. dept., 1954-57, 58-68; exec. dir. Flower and Cook Obs., 1950-54, dir., 1954-68, Flower prof., 1958-68; prof. astronomy, dir. optical astron. observatories U. Fla., Gainesville, 1968-87, assoc. chmn. dept., 1971-77, prof. emeritus, 1989—; established South Pole obs. sta., U. Fla., 1985—. Author: (with J. Sahade) Interacting Binary Stars, 1978; Editor: Astronomical Photoelectric Photometry, 1953, Present and Future of Telescope of Moderate Size, 1958, Photoelectric Astronomy for Amateurs, 1963; Contbr. articles to profl. jours. Col., aide de camp, gov.'s staff, State of Tenn.; served with USNR, 1941-46. Decorated Air medal; Fulbright fellow Australian Nat. U., 1957-58; NATO sr. fellow in sci. U. Canterbury, Christchurch, New Zealand, 1973; Fulbright fellow Instituto de Astronomia y Fisica del Espacio, Buenos Aires, 1977; recipient plaques of appreciation, Govt. South Korea, 1988, Yonsei U., Korean Astron. Soc. Mem. AAAS (sec. sect. D com. on coun. affairs 1970), Am. Astron. Soc. (coun. 1958-61), Royal Astron. Soc. New Zealand (hon.), Internat. Astron. Union (pres. commn. 42 1967-70, v.p. commn. 38 1979-82, pres. 1982-85), Royal Astron. Soc., Fla. Acad. Sci. (chmn. phys. scis. sect. 1974-75, pres. 1983-84, gold medal 1989), Astron. Soc. Can., Astron. Soc. Pacific, Ret. Officers Assn., Internat. Amateur and Profl. Photoelectric Photometry (hon.), Navy League, Explorers Club, Phi Beta Kappa, Sigma Xi, Phi Kappa Phi. Episcopalian. Home: 714 NW 89th St Gainesville FL 32607-1453 Office: Univ Fla Dept Astronomy Gainesville FL 32611

WOOD, FRANK PREUIT, educator, former air force officer; b. Greenville, Tex., Feb. 28, 1916; s. William L. and Ethel (Preuit) W.; m. Harriet Louise Brawner, Oct. 25, 1941; 1 son, Frank M. B.S. in Elec. Engring, U. Tex., 1939; grad., USAF pilot tng. schs., 1941. Commd. 2d lt. USAAF, 1941; advanced through grades to brig. gen. USAF, 1964; dep. chief staff personnel Air Tng. Command, Randolph AFB, Tex., 1962-66; comdr. Air Force Mil. Tng. Ctr. Lackland AFB, San Antonio, 1966-67; chief Mil. Assistance Adv. Group, Italy, 1967-69; dep. chief staff for personnel Tactical Air Command, Langley AFB, Va., 1969-70; ret., 1970; apptd. asso. dir. Bur. Engring. Research, U. Tex. Coll. Engring., Austin, 1970; dir. Bur. Engring. Research, U. Tex. Coll. Engring., 1971-78. Chmn. bd. equalization City of Austin, 1979—; elder Ctrl. Christian Ch., Austin, 1975-81, chmn. ofcl. bd., 1977; elder Ctrl. Christian Ch., San Antonio, 1985-89, 91-94, 95-98. Decorated Legion of Merit with 4 oak leaf clusters; named Disting. Grad., U. Tex. Coll. Engring., 1968. Club: Headliners (Austin). Home: 7400 Crestway Dr Apt 1003 San Antonio TX 78239-3094

WOOD, GEORGE H., investment executive; b. Kansas City, Mo., Sept. 7, 1946; s. George H. and Helen Lee (Hansen) W. BSBA, U. Mo., 1968, MBA, 1972. Securities analyst Kansas City Life Ins. Co., 1972-75, asst. dir. securities, 1975-76; sr. trust officer Commerce Bank of Kansas City, N.A., 1976-79, v.p., fixed income and portfolio group mgr., 1979-80, v.p., mgr. investment dept., 1980-82, sr. v.p., 1982-88, chief investment officer, 1988-90; mng. dir. Merus Capital Mgmt., 1990-94; v.p. Pacific Investment Mgmt. Co., 1994—. Past bd. dirs., pres. Young Audiences, Inc. With AUS, 1969-71. Chartered fin. analyst . Mem. Inst. Chartered Fin. Analysts (past chmn. curriculum com.), Assn. Investment Mgmt. and Rsch., Fin. Analysts Fedn., San Francisco Soc. Fin. Analysts (bd. dirs.), U. Mo. Alumni Assn., Phi Delta Theta. Home: 2616 Temple Hills Dr Laguna Beach CA 92651-2036 Office: Pacific Investment Mgmt Co 840 Newport Center Dr Newport Beach CA 92660-6310

WOOD, GERALD WAYNE, electrical engineer; b. Lubbock, Tex., June 6, 1956; s. Glendon Waldo and Nelive Ruth (Parker) W. BSEE, Tex. Tech. U., 1979, MSEE, 1984. Engr.-in-tng. Staff mem. BDM Internat., Albuquerque, 1984-89; staff engr. Voss Scientific, Albuquerque, 1989-90; engr. EG&G Mgmt. Systems, Inc., Albuquerque, 1990—. Mem. AAAS, IEEE. Avocations: reading, backpacking. Home: 7709 Ranchwood Dr NW Albuquerque NM 87120-4026 Office: EG&G Mgmt Sys Inc Ste 102 2501 Yale SE Albuquerque NM 87109

WOOD, GINA ELEANE, state agency program administrator; b. Springfield, Mo., Aug. 29, 1959; d. George Henry and Emma (Cook) W. BA in Comm., U. Mo., 1983. With pub. rels. and sales Portland (Oreg.) Observer Newspaper, 1983-85; legis. asst. State Rep. Margaret Carter, Salem, Oreg., 1985-86; exec. dir. Highland Cmty. Svcs./Yaun Youth Care Ctr., Portland, 1986; legis./ops. mgr. Adult and Family Svcs., Salem, 1987-88; mem. gov. staff Gov. Neil Goldschmidt, Salem, 1988-89; regional coord. Child & Youth Commn., Salem, 1989-94; fed. program dir. Commn. Child and Families, Salem, 1994—; cons. Cmty. Rsch. Assocs., Champaign, Ill., 1993—. Precinct com. person Washington County, Portland, Oreg., 1992—; active Oreg. Women's Polit. Caucus, Portland, 1985—, Gov. Task Force on Family Law, Salem, 1993—. Mem. Am. Corrections Assn., Nat. Assn. Blacks in Criminal Justice, Pvt. Industry Coun. (past chair youth com.), Urban League Portland (past chairperson). Democrat. Avocations: reading, theatre, travelling, cooking, jazz music.

WOOD, GLADYS BLANCHE, retired secondary education educator, journalist; b. Sanborn, N.D., Aug. 12, 1921; d. Charles Kershaw and Mina Blanche (Kee) Crowther; m. Newell Edwin Wood, June 13, 1943 (dec. 1990); children: Terry N., Lani, Brian R., Kevin C.; m. F.L. Stutzman, Nov. 30, 1991. BA in Journalism, U. Minn., 1943; MA in Mass Comm., San Jose State U., 1972. Cert. secondary tchr., Calif. Reporter St. Paul Pioneer-Dispatch, 1943-45; editor J.C. Penney Co., N.Y.C., 1945-46; tchr. English and journalism Willow Glen H.S., San Jose, Calif., 1968-87; freelance writer, photographer, 1947—; cons. in field. Named Secondary Journalism Tchr. of Yr. Calif. Newspaper Pubs. Assn., 1977. Mem. AAUW, Soc. Profl. Journalists, Journalism Edn. Assn., Calif. Tchrs. English, Calif. Ret. Tchrs. Assn., Women in Comm., Santa Clara County Med. Assn. Aux., Friends of Libr., Delta Kappa Gamma, Alpha Omicron Pi. Republican. Methodist. Avocations: music, journalism, photography, travel. Home: 14161 Douglass Ln Saratoga CA 95070-5535

WOOD, GORDON STEWART, historian, educator; b. Concord, Mass., Nov. 27, 1933; s. Herbert G. and Marion (Friberg) W.; m. Louise Goss, Apr. 30, 1956; children: Christopher, Elizabeth, Amy. AB, Tufts U., 1955; AM, Harvard, 1959; PhD, Harvard U., 1964. Fellow Inst. Early Am. History and Culture, Williamsburg, Va., 1964-66; asst. prof. Harvard U., Cambridge, Mass., 1966-67; assoc. prof. U. Mich., Ann Arbor, 1967-69; prof. history, Univ. prof. Brown U., Providence, 1969—; Pitt. prof. Cambridge U., 1982-83; bd. trustees Tufts U.; Bancroft lectr. U.S. Naval Acad., 1986; Anson G. Phelps lectr. NYU, 1986; Charles Edmundson lectr. Baylor U., 1987; Samuel Paley lectr. Hebrew U., Jerusalem, 1987; presdl. lecture series on presidency, 1991. Author: The Creation of the American Republic, 1776-1787, 1969,

The Rising Glory of America, 1760-1820, 1971; co-author: The Great Republic, 1977, The Radicalism of the American Revolution, 1992 (Pulitzer Prize for history 1993). Mem. coun. Inst. Early Am. History and Culture, 1980-83; bd. trustees Colonial Williamsburg. With USAF, 1955-58. Recipient Bancroft prize Columbia U., 1970, Disting. Visitor award Australian-Am. Ednl. Found., 1976, Douglass Adair prize, 1984; Emerson prize Phi Beta Kappa, 1992; Sunderland fellow U. Mich. Law Sch., 1990; All Souls Coll. fellow, 1991; Woodrow Wilson Ctr. guest-scholar, 1993-94. Mem. Am. Hist. Assn. (John Dunning prize), Orgn. Am. Historians, Soc. Am. Historians, Nat. Hist. Soc. (chmn. bd. advisors), Soc. Historians of the Early Am. Republic (pres.), Am. Acad. Arts and Scis., Am. Philos. Soc. Home: 77 Keene St Providence RI 02906-1507 Office: 142 Angell St Providence RI 02912-9040

WOOD, HARLINGTON, JR., federal judge; b. Springfield, Ill., Apr. 17, 1920; s. Harlington and Marie (Green) W. A.B., U. Ill., 1942, J.D., 1948. Bar: Ill. 1948. Practiced in Springfield, 1948-69; U.S. atty. So. Dist. Ill., 1958-61; mem. firm Wood & Wood, 1961-69; assoc. dep. atty. gen. for U.S. attys. U.S. dept. Justice, 1969-70; assoc. dep. atty. gen. Justice Dept., Washington, 1970-72; asst. atty. gen. civil div. Justice Dept., 1972-73; U.S. dist. judge So. Dist. Ill., Springfield, 1973-76; judge U.S. Ct. Appeals (7th cir.), 1976—; adj. prof. Sch. Law, U. Ill., Champaign, 1993; disting. vis. prof. St. Louis U. Law Sch., 1996. Chmn. Adminstrv. Office Oversight Com., 1988-90; mem. Long Range Planning Com., 1991-96. Office: US Ct Appeals PO Box 299 600 E Monroe St Springfield IL 62701-0299

WOOD, HOWARD GRAHAM, banker; b. Balt., July 27, 1910; s. Howard and Etta (Graham) W.; m. Florence Tottle, Apr. 2, 1977; children by previous marriage—Robert Graham, Virginia B. Delauney. BA, Johns Hopkins, 1932; LLB, U. Md., 1936. Bar: Md. bar 1936. With First Nat. Bank Md., 1932-85. Author: (with Robert H. Burgess) Steamboats Out of Baltimore, 1969. Mem. Commn. on Revision Balt. City Charter, 1965; treas. S.S. Hist. Soc. Am.; bd. dirs. Presbyn. Home Md. Served to maj. Intelligence Div. AUS, 1942-46. Mem. Phi Beta Kappa, Phi Gamma Delta. Clubs: Elkridge, Johns Hopkins (Balt.). Home: 919 Bellemore Rd Baltimore MD 21210-1206 Office: First Md Bldg Baltimore MD 21202

WOOD, H(OWARD) JOHN, III, astrophysicist, astronomer; b. Balt., July 19, 1938; s. Howard John Jr. and Cara (Loss) W.; m. Austine Barton Read, June 10, 1961 (div. Jan. 1975); children: Cara Loss, Erika Barton; m. Maria Ilona Kovacs, May 22, 1977; 1 child, Andreas M. BA in Astronomy, Swarthmore Coll., 1960; MA, Ind. U., 1962, PhD, 1965. Lectr., asst. prof. then assoc. prof. U. Va., Charlottesville, 1964-70; staff astronomer European So. Obs., Santiago, Chile, 1970-75; Fulbright Rsch. fellow U. Vienna Obs., 1976-78; rsch. assoc. Ind. U., Bloomington, 1978-81; asst. to the dir. Cerro Tololo Inter-Am. Obs., La Serena, Chile, 1982-83; physicist, astronomer NASA/Goddard Space Flight Ctr., Greenbelt, Md., 1984—; advisor, participant Hubble Space Telescope Allen Comm., NASA, Danbury, Conn., 1990; co-chmn. Hubble Space Telescope Ind. Optical Rev. Panel, Columbia, Md., 1990-91; mem. panel The Townes/SAGE Panel-Jet Propulsion Lab., Pasadena, 1991-92. Co-author: Physics of Ap Stars, 1976; contbr. articles to profl. publs. Grantee NSF (10), 1965-82, Am. Astron. Soc., 1978. Mem. Internat. Astron. Union (Commn. 29 1962—), Sigma Xi. Achievements include discovery of Balmer-Line variability of Ap stars; discovery of magnetic fields in southern Ap stars; alignment testing and delivery of the DIRBE photometric cryogenic telescope on the COBE spacecraft; alignment and optical prescription for Hubble Space Telescope while in orbit. Office: NASA/Goddard Space Flight Ctr Code # 717 Greenbelt MD 20771

WOOD, IVAN, JR., lawyer; b. Corpus Christi, Tex., Oct. 1, 1947. AA, Del Mar Jr. Coll., 1967; BBA, U. Tex., 1969, JD, 1972. Bar: Tex. 1972, U.S. Ct. Military Appeals, 1974, U.S. Supreme Ct. 1991. Ptnr. Baker & Hostetler, Houston. Lt. JAGC, USN, 1972-76. Mem. ABA, State Bar Tex., Am. Acad. Hosp. Attys., Nat. Health Lawyers Assn., Beta Alpha Psi, Phi Delta Phi. Office: Baker & Hostetler 1000 Louisiana St Ste 2000 Houston TX 77002-5009*

WOOD, JACALYN KAY, education educator, educational consultant; b. Columbus, Ohio, May 25, 1949; d. Carleston John and Grace Anna (Schumacher) W. BA, Georgetown Coll., 1971; MS, Ohio State U., 1976; PhD, Miami U., 1981. Elem. tchr. Bethel-Tate Schs., Ohio, 1971-73, Columbus Christian Sch., 1973-74, Franklin (Ohio) Schs., 1974-79; teaching fellow Miami U., Oxford, Ohio, 1979-81; cons. intermediate grades Erie County Schs., Sandusky, Ohio, 1981-89, presenter, tchr. insvc. tng. Mem. coun. Sta. WVIZ-TV, 1981-88; assoc. prof. Ashland U., Elyria, Ohio, 1989, dir. elem. edn., 1989—; mem. Lorain County 20/20, mem. strategic planning bd., 1992—; mem. Leadership Lorain County, 1994—; mem. exec. com. Perkins Community Schs., 1981-85; mem. community adv. bd. Sandusky Vols. Am., 1985-89, Sandusky Soc. Bank, 1987-88, vol. Firelands Community Hosp., 1986-87; active Leadership Lorain County, 1994—. Mem. AAUW, ASCD, Am. Businesswomen's Assn. (local pres. 1985), Internat. Reading Assn., Ohio Sch. Suprs. Assn. (regional pres. 1986, state pres. 1986-87), Phi Delta Kappa (local sec. 1985, 86, v.p. 1991-93, pres. 1993—), Phi Kappa Phi, Kappa Delta Pi (local adv. 1991-93). Baptist. Home: 35873 Westminster Ave N Ridgeville OH 44039-1380 Office: Ashland U at LCCC 1005 Abbe Rd N Elyria OH 44035-1613

WOOD, JACK CALVIN, health care consultant, lawyer; b. Greenwood, Ind., Jan. 9, 1933; s. Earl Leon and Gertrude Ruby (Stott) W. A.B., DePauw U., Greencastle, Ind., 1954; J.D., Harvard U., 1961. Bar: Ill. 1961, Tex. 1965, D.C. 1978, Colo. 1983. Assoc. firm Hopkins-Sutter, Chgo., 1961-65; gen. counsel Sisters of Charity Health Care System, Houston, 1965-73; sr. partner firm Wood, Lucksinger & Epstein, Houston, 1973-87, of counsel, 1987-91; of counsel Vinson & Elkins, 1991—; editor-in-chief Topics In Health Care Financing, 1974-94; clin. prof. law St. Louis U. Med. Sch., 1976—; adj. prof. health care adminstrn. Tex. Women's U., 1977—; Pres. St. Joseph Hosp. Found., Houston, 1966-68; chmn. governing com. Am. Bar Assn. Health Law Forum, 1981-84. Author: Financial Management, 1973, Medicare Reimbursement, 1974, Private Third Party Reimbursement, 1975. Served to lt. comdr. USNR, 1954-65. Mem. Am. Soc. Hosp. Attys. (pres. 1974-75), Nat. Health Lawyers Assn. (bd. dirs. 1981-85), Am. Soc. Law and Medicine (bd. dirs. 1981-85). Home: 9216 Cliffwood Dr Houston TX 77096-3511 Office: 9218 Cliffwood Dr Houston TX 77096-3511

WOOD, JACKIE DALE, physiologist, educator, researcher; b. Picher, Okla., Feb. 16, 1937; s. Aubrey T. Wood and Wilma J. (Coleman) Wood Patterson. BS, Kans. State U., 1964, MS, 1966; PhD, U. Ill., 1969. Asst. prof. physiology Williams Coll., Williamstown, Mass., 1969-71; asst. prof. U. Kans. Med. Ctr., Kansas City, 1971-74, assoc. prof., 1974-78, prof., 1978-79; prof., chmn. dept. physiology Sch. Medicine, U. Nev., Reno, 1979-85; chmn. dept. physiology coll. medicine Ohio State U., Columbus, 1985—; cons. NIH, Bethesda, Md., 1982—. Recipient Research Career Devel. award NIH, 1974, Chancellor's award for teaching excellence U. Kans., 1975; named Hon. Citizen City of Atzugi Japan, 1987; Alexander von Humboldt fellow, W.Ger., 1976. Mem. Am. Physiol. Soc. (assoc. editor 1984-96, rsch. award 1986), Soc. Neurosci., Am. Gastroent. Assn., AAAS, Assn. Chairmen Depts. Physiology. Office: Ohio State U Dept Physiology 300 Hamilton Hall 1645 Neil Ave Columbus OH 43210-1218

WOOD, JAMES, supermarket executive; b. Newcastle-upon-Tyne, Eng., Jan. 19, 1930; came to U.S., 1974; s. Edward and Catherine Wilhelmina (Parker) W.; m. Colleen Margaret Taylor, Aug. 14, 1954; children: Julie, Sarah. Grad., Loughborough Coll., Leicestershire, England; hon. LHD, St. Peter's Coll., N.J. Chief food chain Newport Coop. Soc., S. Wales, U.K., 1959-62, Grays Food Coop. Soc., Eng., 1962-66; dir., joint dep. mng. dir. charge retailing Cavenham, Ttd., Hayes, Eng., 1966-80; pres. Grand Union Co., Elmwood Park, N.J., 1973-79; chief exec. officer, dir. Grand Union Co., from 1973, chmn. bd., 1979-80; chmn. bd., CEO Gt. Atlantic & Pacific Tea Co., Inc., 1980—; bd. dirs. Asarco, Inc., Irma Fabrikerne A/S, Denmark, Schering-Plough Corp. Active World USO, UNICEF, United Jersey Bank. With Brit. Army, 1948-50. Mem. Food Mktg. Inst. (bd. dirs.) Roman Catholic. Office: Gt Atlantic & Pacific Tea Co 2 Paragon Dr Montvale NJ 07645-1718*

WOOD, JAMES, broker; b. Mt. Kisco, N.Y., May 2, 1927; s. L. Hollingsworth and Martha (Speakman) W.; m. Frances Randall, May 2, 1953; children: Emily Morris, Stephen H. Grad., Deerfield (Mass.) Acad., 1945; B.A., Haverford (Pa.) Coll., 1950. Mfrs. rep. distbn. fertilizers, 1950-54; with Bank of N.Y., 1954-82, asst. v.p., 1960-61, v.p., 1961-82; broker Prescott Ball & Turben, 1982-93, v.p., 1986-93; broker, v.p. Smith Barney, Mt. Kisco, 1993—; bd. dirs. Trans-Wasatch Co., Park City Consolidated, Oakwood Cemetery, Mt. Kisco. Trustee Bryn Mawr Coll., Jewish Found. for Edn. Women; bd. mgrs. Haverford Coll.; chmn. bd. trustees Am. Bible Soc.; v.p., bd. dirs. Howard Meml. Fund. With USNR, 1945-46. Home: Braewold 153 Wood Rd Mount Kisco NY 10549 Office: Smith Barney 100 S Bedford Rd Mount Kisco NY 10549-3443

WOOD, JAMES ALLEN, lawyer; b. McMinnville, Tenn., Jan. 14, 1906; s. Ira and Emma (Calhoun) W.; m. Eva Beth Sellers, Dec. 28, 1941; 1 son, Eben Calhoun. A.B., U. Tenn., 1929; LL.B., U. Tex., 1934. Bar: Tex. 1934. Tchr. Bolton High Sch., Alexandria, La., 1929-32; since practiced in Corpus Christi; of counsel Wood, Burney, Cohn & Viles and predecessor firms, 1971—; state dist. judge, Corpus Christi, 1941-43; mem. rules adv. com. Supreme Ct. Tex., 1949-86. Author 7 vols. poetry; contbr. articles to profl. jours.; Life on a Warren County Farm (Tenn.) 1906-1923, Early Bench and Bar of Corpus Christi. Bd. dirs. Nueces River Authority, 1972-89, pres., 1981-84, life time hon. dir., 1989—. Lt. USNR, 1943-45. Fellow Am. Coll. Trial Lawyers; mem. ABA, Tex. Bar Assn., Nueces County Bar Assn. (pres. 1941). Home: 458 Dolphin Pl Corpus Christi TX 78411-1514

WOOD, JAMES E., JR., religion educator, author; b. Portsmouth, Va., July 29, 1922; s. James E. and Elsie Elizabeth (Bryant) W.; m. Alma Leacy McKenzie, Aug. 12, 1943; 1 son, James Edward III. BA, Carson-Newman Coll., 1943; MA, Columbia U., 1949; BD, So. Bapt. Theol. Sem., 1947, ThM, 1948; PhD, So. Baptist Theol. Sem., 1957; postgrad., U. Tenn., 1943-44; cert. in Chinese, Yale U., 1949-50; Japanese diploma, Naganuma Sch. Japanese Studies, Tokyo, 1950-51, Oxford U., Eng., 1983; LLD, Seinan Gakuin U., Japan, 1983; LLD (hon.), Capitol U., 1996. Ordained to ministry So. Bapt. Ch., 1942. Pastor So. Bapt. chs., Tenn. and Ky., 1942-48; Bapt. missionary to Japan, 1950-55; prof. religion and lit. Seinan Gakuin U., Japan, 1951-55; prof. history of religions Baylor U., Waco, Tex., 1955-73, dir. honors program, 1959-64; dir. J.M. Dawson Inst. Ch.-State Studies Baylor U., 1980-95, chmn. interdeptl. grad. degree program in ch.-state studies, 1962-73, 80-95, Simon and Ethel Bunn Disting. prof. ch.-state studies, 1980—, chmn. faculty-student Far Eastern exchange program, 1970-72; exec. dir. Bapt. Joint Com. on Public Affairs, Washington, 1972-80; mem. ctrl. panel Bapt. World Alliance Commn. on Religious Liberty and Human Rights, 1965-75, Commn. on Freedom, Justice and Peace, 1976-80; chmn. Bapt. Com. on Bicentennial, 1973-76; mem. So. Bapt. Inter-Agy. Coun., 1972-80, vice chmn., 1975-76, sec. 1976-77; vis. prof. So. Bapt. Theol. Sem., 1974, N.Am. Bapt. Theol. Sem., Sioux Falls, S.D., 1974, 79, Okla. Bapt. U., Shawnee, 1977, Naval Coll. of Chaplains, Providence, 1988—, others; vis. lectr. Ashland (Ohio) Theol. Sem., 1971; Vernon Richardson lectr. U. Bapt. Ch., Balt., 1975, Ea. Bapt. Theol. Sem., Phila., 1975; lectr. First World Congress on Religious Liberty, Amsterdam, 1977, 2d Congress, Rome, 1984, U. Faculty of Law, Warsaw, Poland, 1984, Brigham Young U., 1986, 95, U. Tirana, Albania, 1992, U. Malta, 1994, Austin Coll., 1995, numerous others; chair Internat. Consultation on Relig. Rights and Ethnic Identity, Budapest, 1992; co-chair Internat. Conf. Religious Freedom, Moscow, 1993; mem. internat. adv. bd. World Report on Freedom Conscious Human Rights Ctr., U. Sussex, U.K.; co-chair consultation on Freedom of Conscience and Belief, Moscow, 1993; chair Internat. Consultation Religious Liberty and Social Peace, Malta, 1994; Carver-Barnes lectr. Southeastern Bapt. Theol. Sem., 1981; Asian Found. lectr. Seinan Gakuin U., Japan, 1983; ecumenical consultation on edn. Nat. Coun. Chs., 1974; various other com. coun. positions. Author: A History of American Literature: An Anthology, 1952, (co-author) Church and State in Scripture, History and Constitutional Law, 1958, The Problem of Nationalism, 1969, Nationhood and the Kingdom, 1977, Secular Humanism and the Public Schools, 1986, Reflections on Church and State, 1995; (edited by Derek H. Davis) The Separation of Church and State Defended: Selected Writings of James E. Wood, Jr., 1995, Church-State Relations in the Modern World, 1996; editor: Markham Press Fund, Baylor U. Press, 1970-72; founding editor: Jour. Ch. and State, 1959-73, 80-93, mem. editl. coun., 1973-80; mem. editl. bd. Religion and Public Edn., Religious Freedom Reporter; editor; contbr. numerous profl. pubs. including Religion and Politics, Church and State, others; area editor, contbr. Ency. So. Bapts., 1982; contbr. Changing Trends in Education, 1992, Law, Religion and Human Rights in GLobal Perspective, 1995, Dialogue of Democracy: An American Politics Reader, 1996; contbr. over 300 articles to profl. jours. Sponsor Ams. for Public Schs., 1963-68; bd. dirs. Waco (Tex.) Planned Parenthood, 1966-72, pres., 1971-72; sponsor Christians Concerned for Israel, 1968—, Tex. Conf. Chs. Consultation on Religion and Public Edn., 1971, Nat. Christian Leadership Conf. for Israel, 1978—; pres. Waco area ACLU, bd. dirs. Tex. unit, 1968-72; pres. Nat. Council Religion and Public Edn., 1979-83, exec. com., 1975—, bd. dirs., 1972—; chmn. exec. com. Council Washin Reps. on UN, 1977-80, mem. council exec. com., 1973-80; exec. com. Nat. Coalition on Public Edn. and Religious Liberty, 1973—; mem. religious liberty com. Nat. Council Chs. U.S.A., 1972—, also mem. com. internat. concerns on human rights; Am. rep. Chs. Montreux Colloquium on Helsinki Final Act, 1977; v.p. Waco Conf. Christians and Jews, 1983-86, Internat. Acad. for Freedom of Religion and Belief, 1985-90, pres., 1990—; mem. internat. adv. bd. World Report on Freedom of Conscience, Human Rights Ctr., U. Sussex, Eng.; trustee Internat. Devel. Conf., 1974-80; nat. coun. Am.-Israel Friendship League, 1977—; founder, chmn. Waco Human Rights Week, 1981—; mem. ch. rels. com., U.S. Holocaust Meml. Coun., 1990—. Recipient Disting. Alumnus award Carson-Newman Coll., 1974, Religious Liberty award Alliance for Preservation of Religious Liberty, 1980, Henrietta Szold award Tex. region Hadassah, 1981, Human Rights award Waco Conf. Christians and Jews, 1986, Cir. of Achievement award Baylor U. Mortar Bd., 1991, Religious Freedom Lifetime award Ams. United Ctrl. Tex., 1993; hon. Tex. col., 1969. Mem. Am. Soc. Ch. History, Am. Acad. Religion, Am. Soc. Internat. Law, Am. Soc. Sci. Study of Religion, N. Am. Soc. Ecumenists, NCCJ (ad. com. on ch. state and taxation 1979-85), ACLU, Phi Eta Sigma, Pi Kappa Delta, Alpha Psi Omega. Democrat. Home: 3306 Lake Heights Dr Waco TX 76708-1543 Office: Baylor U PO Box 97308 Waco TX 76798-7308

WOOD, JAMES MICHAEL, lawyer; b. Oakland, Calif., Mar. 22, 1948; s. Donald James and Helen Winifred (Reiman) W.; div.; children: Nathan, Sarah, Ruth. BA, St. Mary's Coll., 1970; JD, U. San Francisco, 1973. Bar: Calif. 1973, U.S. Dist. Ct. (no., cen. and so. dists.) Calif. 1973. Rsch. atty. Alameda County Superior Ct., Oakland, 1973-76; ptnr. Crosby, Heafey, Roach & May, Oakland, 1976—; presenter at profl. confs. Contbr. articles to profl. jours. Chair alumni-faculty devel. fund St. Mary's Coll. Alumni Bd. Dirs., 1990-94. Mem. ABA (litigation sect., health law litigation com., litigation products liability com.), Assn. Trial Lawyers Am. (assoc.), State Bar Calif., Calif. Trial Lawyers Assn. (assoc.), No. Calif. Assn. Def. Counsel, Alameda County Bar Assn., Def. Rsch. and Trial Lawyers Assn., Am. Acad. Hosp. Attys., Am. Soc. Pharmacy Law, Nat. Health Lawyers Assn., Drug Info. Assn. Office: Crosby Heafey Roach & May 1999 Harrison St Oakland CA 94612-3517

WOOD, JAMES NOWELL, museum director and executive; b. Boston, Mar. 20, 1941; s. Charles H. and Helen N. (Nowell) W.; m. Emese Forizs, Dec. 30, 1966; children: Lenke Hancock, Rebecca Nowell. Diploma, Universita per Stranieri, Perugia, Italy, 1962; B.A., Williams Coll., Williamstown, Mass., 1963; M.A. (Ford Mus. Tng. fellow), NYU, 1966. Asst. to dir. Met. Mus., N.Y.C., 1967-68, asst. curator dept. 20th century art, 1968-70; curator Albright-Knox Art Gallery, Buffalo, 1970-73, assoc. dir., 1973-75; dir. St. Louis Art Mus., 1975-80, Art Inst. Chgo., 1980—; vis. com. visual arts U. Chgo., 1980-94; head com. Nat. Endowment Arts. Mem. Intermuseum Conservation Assn. (past pres.), Assn. Art Mus. Dirs. Office: Art Inst Chgo 111 S Michigan Ave Chicago IL 60603-6110

WOOD, JANE, dancer. Attended, Washington Sch. Ballet, Acad. Washington Ballet; studied with Patricia Neary, Geneva Ballet. Dancer Geneva Ballet, until 1978; dancer Ballet West, Salt Lake City, 1978-87, soloist, 1987-89, prin. artist, 1989—. Dance performances include Romeo & Juliet, Sleeping Beauty, Swan Lake, Giselle. Office: Ballet West 50 W 200 S Salt Lake City UT 84101-1642

WOOD, JEANNE CLARKE, charitable organization executive; b. Pitts., Dec. 21, 1916; d. Joseph Calvitt and Helen Caroline (Mattson) Clarke; m. Herman Eugene Wood, Jr., May 6, 1936 (dec.); children: Helen Hamilton (Mrs. John Harry Mortenson), Herman Eugene III. Student, Collegiate Sch. for Girls, Richmond, Va., 1932-33. Asst. to Dr. and Mrs. J. Calvitt Clarke, Christian Children's Fund, Inc., Richmond, 1938-64; founder Children, Inc., Richmond, 1964; pres., internat. dir. Children, Inc., 1964—. Author: (with Helen C. Clarke) In Appreciation: A Story in Pictures of the World-Wide Family of Christian Children's Fund, Inc, 1958, Children's Christmastime Around the World, 1962, Children's Games Around the World, 1962, Children-Hope of the World-Their Needs, 1965, Children-Hope of the World-Their Friends, 1966; Editor: CI News, 1964. Recipient citation Eastern Council Navajo Tribe, 1970, citations Mayor of Pusan (Korea), 1971, citations Mayor of Seoul, 1971, citations Gov. of Kanagawa Prefecture (Japan), 1972, commendation Pres. of U.S., 1972, citation Stephen Philibosian Found., 1975, citation Santa Ana (El Salvador) Dept. Edn., 1975, citation Nat. Sch. for Blind, Dominican Republic, 1982, citation Navajo Tribal Council of Navajo Nation, Window Rock, Ariz., 1982. Office: Children Inc PO Box 5381 1000 Westover Rd Richmond VA 23220-6624 *While there are many things about which we can make no choice in this volatile world where change is constant and sometimes disastrous, it has seemed to me that one can make the choice between accepting things positively or negatively. I have chosen to accept them positively.*

WOOD, JEANNINE KAY, state official; b. Dalton, Nebr., Apr. 22, 1944; d. Grover L. and Elsie M. (Winkelman) Sanders; m. Charles S. Wood, Dec. 7, 1968; children: Craig C., Wendi L. Wood Armstrong. Exec. sec. Idaho Hosp. Assn., Boise, 1966-71; com. sec. Idaho State Senate, Boise, 1976-81, jour. clk., 1981-85, asst. to sec. of senate, 1985-91, sec. of senate, 1991—; pvt. practice typing svc. Boise, 1979-86. Mem. Am. Soc. Legis. Clks. and Secs. (vice chmn. legis. adminstr. com.), Nat. Assn. Parliamentarians, Idaho Assn. Parliamentarians. Methodist. Home: 3505 S Linder Meridian ID 83642 Office: Idaho State Capitol PO Box 83720 Boise ID 83720-0081

WOOD, JOAN KLAWANS, architect; b. Chgo., Dec. 24, 1932; d. Paul H. and Anne (Bronstein) Klawans; m. Henry Austin Wood III, Oct. 5, 1962 (div. Dec. 1982); children: Paul, Joshua, Daniel. BA, U. Chgo., 1953; postgrad., Harvard U., 1954-56; BArch, MIT, 1960. Registered arch., Mass.; cert. arch. Pres. Joan Wood Assocs.-Archs., Inc., Cambridge and Boston, Mass., 1962—; mem., vice-chair Designer Selection Bd., Mass., 1985-89; alt. mem. Zoning Bd. Appeals, Boston, 1987-93, 94—. Prin. works include Coolidge Ice House, WIC and Family Svcs. Bldg., 20 Years of Joan Wood Assocs., 1983, AIA Centennial/Women, Traveling Exhibit, 1988, Boston Soc. Archs. Women in Arch., 1987-91. Mem., former chair Ward 4 Dem. Com., Boston, 1976—, Park Plaza Civic Adv. Com., Boston, 1980-90; mem. Copley Square Design Rev. Com., 1991; active nat. and local Dem. party campaigns, 1960—. Mem. AIA (urban design com. 1979—), New Eng. Women in Real Estate, Boston Soc. Archs. (urban design and homeless com. 1979—), Boston Club. Avocations: politics, baseball, food, visual arts, reading. Office: Joan Wood Assocs Archs Inc 24 Rutland Sq Boston MA 02118-3106

WOOD, JOETTA KAY, special education educator; b. Kirksville, Mo., Sept. 30, 1951; d. Vernon John Wood and Hazel Ellen (Lake) Ammon. BS in Elem. Edn., N.W. Mo. State U., 1973; MS in Spl. Edn., S.W. Mo. State U., 1993. Cert. tchr., Mo. Kindergarten Livingston County Sch., Wheeling, Mo., 1973-75; 1st grade tchr. Mercer (Mo.) Sch., 1975-77, Maysville (Mo.) Sch., 1978-80; learning disabilities tchr. Lakeland Sch., Lowery City, Mo., 1980-81, Tri-County Sch., Jamesport, Mo., 1981-84, Plato (Mo.) Sch., 1981-95; adj. faculty Columbia Coll., 1995. Mem. Coun. for Exceptional Children, Mo. State Tchrs. Assn. Home: PO Box 8 Plato MO 65552-0008 Office: Plato R-5 Sch PO Box A Plato MO 65552-0010

WOOD, JOHN ARMSTEAD, planetary scientist, geological sciences educator; b. Roanoke, Va., July 28, 1932; s. John Armstead and Lillian Cary (Hall) W.; m. Elisabeth Mathilde Heuser, June 12, 1958 (div.); children: Crispin S., Georgia K.; m. Julie Marie Nason, Sept. 9, 1989. B.S. in Geology, Va. Polytech. Inst., 1954; Ph.D. in Geology, Mass. Inst. Tech., 1958; post-doctoral study, U. Cambridge, Eng., 1959-60. Staff scientist Smithsonian Astrophys. Obs., Cambridge, Mass., 1959, 61-62, 65—; research asso. Enrico Fermi Inst. U. Chgo., 1962-65; prof. dept. geol. scis. Harvard, 1976-95; asso. dir. Harvard-Smithsonian Center for Astrophysics, 1981-86; Vice chmn. Lunar Sample Analysis Planning Team, 1971-72. Author: Meteorites and the Origin of Planets, 1968, The Solar System, 1979. Recipient NASA medal for exceptional sci. achievement, 1973, J.L. Smith medal NAS, 1976, G.K. Gilbert award Geol. Soc. Am., 1992. Fellow AAAS, Am. Geophys. Union, Meteoritical Soc. (pres. 1971-72, Leonard medal 1980); mem. NAS, Am. Acad. Arts and Scis., Cosmos Club. Asteroid no. 4736 named in his honor Johnwood. Home: 1716 Cambridge St # 15 Cambridge MA 02138-4343 Office: 60 Garden St Cambridge MA 02138-1516

WOOD, JOHN DENISON, utility company executive; b. Calgary, Alta., Can., Sept. 28, 1931; s. Ernest William and Ellen Gartshore (Pender) W.; m. Christena Isabel; 1 dau., Donna M. BSCE, U. B.C., 1953; MSCE, Stanford U., 1954, PhDCE and Engring. Mechs., 1956. Research asst. in civil engring. and engring. mechs. Stanford U., Palo Alto, Calif., 1953-56; assoc. mgr. dynamics dept. Engring. Mechs. Lab. Space Tech. Labs., Inc., Redondo Beach, Calif., 1956-63; pres., dir. Mechs. Research, Inc., El Segundo, Calif., 1963-66; sr. v.p. engring. and research ATCO Ind., Ltd., Calgary, Alta., 1966-68, sr. v.p. eastern region, 1968-75, sr. v.p. planning, 1975-77; pres., chief exec. officer ATCO Industries N.A., Ltd., Calgary, Alta., 1977-82, ATCOR Resources Ltd., Calgary, 1982-84; pres., chief operating officer Can. Utilities, Ltd., Edmonton, Alta., 1984-88, pres., chief exec. officer, 1988—; bd. dirs. ATCO Ltd., Can. Utilities Ltd., ATCOR Ltd., ATCO Enterprises Inc., Thames Power Ltd., Barking Power Ltd., Vencap Equities Alta. Ltd.; chmn. bd., CEO Can. Western Natural Gas Co. Ltd., Northwestern Utilities Ltd., Alta. Power Ltd., Northland Utilities Enterprises Ltd.; chmn. bd. Frontec Logistics Corp. Co-author: Ballistic Missile and Space Vehicle Systems, 1961. Mem. Pres.'s Club adv. com. U. Alta.; bd. dirs. Jr. Achievement Can., Western Orthopaedic and Arthritis Rsch. Found., Coun. for Can. Unity; bd. govs. Jr. Achievement No. Alta.; mem. adv. coun. Calgary Econ. Devel. Authority, Econ. Devel. Edmonton Bus. Adv. Coun. Athlone fellow, Can. Acad. Engring. fellow. Mem. Engring. Inst. of Can., Sci. Rsch. Soc. Am., Assn. Profl. Engrs. Alta., Sigma Xi, Tau Beta Pi. Baptist. Clubs: Glencoe, Earl Grey, Calgary Petroleum, Mayfair Golf and Country. Avocations: golf, badminton. Office: Can Utilities Ltd, 10035 105th St, Edmonton, AB Canada T5J 2V6 also: Can Western Natural Gas Co Ltd, 909-11 Ave S W, Calgary, AB Canada T2R 1L8*

WOOD, JOHN MARTIN, lawyer; b. Detroit, Mich., Mar. 29, 1944; s. John Francis and Margaret Kathleen (Lynch) W.; m. Judith Anne Messer; children—Timothy Peter, Meagan Anne. B.A., Boston Coll., 1966; J.D., Cath. U. Am., 1969. Bar: D.C. 1970, U.S. Dist. D.C. 1970, U.S. Ct. Appeals (D.C. cir., 3d cir., 4th cir.), U.S. Supreme Ct. 1973. Trial atty. tax div. Dept. Justice, Washington, 1969-73; assoc. Reed Smith Shaw & McClay, Washington, 1973-80, ptnr., 1980—, mng. ptnr., 1989-95, dir. legal personnel, 1995—. Dir. adv. bd. The Salvation Army, Va., Metro Washington; dir. The Franklin Sq. Assn., Leadership Washington, 1993—. Mem. D.C. Bar, Phi Alpha Delta, Delta Sigma Pi. Clubs: Barristers (Washington), Univ. Club, River Bend Golf & C.C. Home: 9490 Oak Falls Ct Great Falls VA 22066-4143 Office: Reed Smith Shaw & McClay 1301 K St NW Washington DC 20005

WOOD, JOSEPH GEORGE, neurobiologist, educator; b. Victoria, Tex., Dec. 8, 1928; s. Harold Robert and Frances Josephine (Marcak) W.; 1 dau., Marian. B.S., U. Houston, 1954, M.S., 1958; Ph.D., U. Tex., Galveston, 1962. Teaching asst. biology U. Houston, 1956-58; instr. anatomy U. Tex. Dental Br., Houston, 1961, Yale U., 1962-63; asst. prof. U. Ark. Med. Sch., Little Rock, 1963-66; assoc. prof. U. Tex., San Antonio, 1966-70; asst. dean acad. devel. U. Tex., 1967-69; prof. and chmn. dept. neurobiology and anatomy U. Tex., Houston, 1970-84; prof. neurobiology and anatomy U. Tex., 1984-88; prof., chmn. dept. anat. sci. U. Okla. Coll. Medicine, 1988-93; dir. Okla. Ctr. Neurosci., 1990-95; ret., 1995; guest prof. dept. pathobiology, cell biol. & Neuroanat U. Minn. Served with AUS, 1954-56. Recipient Basic Sci. Teaching award U. Tex. Houston, 1972, 75, 86, Disting. Alumnus award U. Tex. Med. Br., 1976. Mem. Am. Assn. Anatomists (exec. com.

1974-78), Soc. Neurosci. (exec. com. Houston chpt. 1971-77, pres. 1973-77), Assn. Am. Med. Colls., Cajal Club, Histochem. Soc., Assn. Anatomy Chmn., Tex. Soc. Electron Microscopy (pres. 1970-71, exec. council 1971-79), Houston Neurol. Soc., Sigma Xi (research award 1962), Phi Kappa Phi, Alpha Omega Alpha. Home and Office: 5009 Park Ave Minneapolis MN 55417-1031

WOOD, JOSHUA WARREN, III, lawyer, foundation executive; b. Portsmouth, Va., Aug. 31, 1941; s. Joshua Warren and Mary Evelyn (Carter) W.; m. Marcia Neal Ramsey, Feb. 29, 1964; children: Lauren Elaine, Joshua Warren IV. A.B., Princeton U., 1963; J.D., U. Va., 1971. Bar: Va. 1971, N.J. 1976, U.S. Supreme Ct. 1977, N.Y. 1982. Comml. banking asst. Bankers Trust Co., N.Y.C., 1967-68; assoc. McGuire, Woods & Battle, Richmond, Va., 1971-75; v.p., gen. counsel, sec. The Robert Wood Johnson Found., Princeton, N.J., 1975—; spl. counsel Smith, Lambert, Hicks & Miller, Princeton, 1985-87, Drinker, Biddle & Reath, Princeton, N.J. and Phila., 1987-89; of counsel Lankenau & Bickford, N.Y.C., 1989-92. Mem. editorial bd. Va. Law Rev., 1969-71. Capt. arty. U.S. Army, 1963-67. Decorated Army Commendation medal. Mem. ABA, Princeton Bar Assn., N.Y. Bar Assn., Va. Bar Assn., N.J. Bar Assn., Nat. Health Lawyers Assn., Am. Arbitration Assn. (bd. dirs., mem. panel of arbitrators, task force Mass torts & alternative dispute resolution), Order of Coif, Princeton Club. Office: College Rd PO Box 2316 Princeton NJ 08543-2316

WOOD, KAREN SUE, theatre manager, stage producer, consultant; b. Artesia, Calif., May 14, 1950; d. Frank Leon and Edith Jeanette (DeLong) Wray; m. Lawrence Anthony Wood (div. 1972); 1 child, Kimberly. BA in Theatre Arts, Calif. State U., Fullerton, 1975; MFA in Theatre Mgmt., UCLA, 1977. Assoc. mgr. Huntington Hartford Theatre, L.A., 1978-81; gen. mgr. Sch. Drama, U. So. Calif., L.A., 1986-88, Mark Taper Forum, Ctr. Theatre Group, L.A., 1988—; lectr. dept. theatre Irvine Coll. and UCLA, 1989-93; mgr. theatre co. USIA, Czechoslovakia and Poland, 1988; chair mgmt. com. Music Ctr. Oper. Co., L.A., 1989—, burning tissues com. Theatre L.A., 1992-94; participant Gov.'s Conf. on Arts, Sacramento, 1992-95; founding mem. L.A. Theatre Ctr. Coop., 1992. Producer: (play) Buddies, 1978-79, Uncommon Women and Others, 1982; line producer: 1984 Olympic Arts Festival Theatre du Soleil, 1984, Piccolo Teatro di Milano, 1984, Robert Wilson/King Lear, 1985; assoc. producer 50/60 Vision, 1989-90 (Spl. Prodn. award L.A. Drama Critics Cir. 1989); author: Ambassador Auditorium Box Office Procedures, 1985; also theatre overviews. Trustee, bd. dirs. Odyssey Theatre, L.A., 1980; bd. dirs. Open Fist Theatre, 1995; spkr. Nat. Assn. Schs. of Theatre, 1987. Recipient L.A. Weekly Theatre award, 1979, Dramalogue Theatre award, 1979. Mem. NOW, NAFE, Women in Theatre, Assn. Theatrical Press Agts. and Mgrs., League of Resident Theatres (legue of resident theatres exec. com.), Theatre Commn. Group (charter mem.). Democrat. Office: Ctr Theatre Group Mark Taper Forum 135 N Grand Ave Los Angeles CA 90012-3013

WOOD, KATHERINE, physical education educator; b. Chipley, Fla., Sept. 9, 1958; d. William Lester and Pamela (deBoer) Kitching; m. Jonathan Wood, June 27, 1980; children: Caroline, Victoria. BS, Fla. State U., 1980. Phys. edn. tchr. Longwood (Fla.) Elem. Sch., 1980-82; sci. tchr. Hamilton County Middle Sch., Jasper, Fla., 1982-85, J.L. Wilkinson Middle Sch., Middleburg, Fla., 1985-86; phys. edn. tchr. Holly Hill (Fla.) Middle Sch., 1986-91, Mainland High Sch., Daytona Beach, Fla., 1991—. Co-leader Brownie troop #1171 Spruce Creek Elem. Sch., 1993—. Mem. AAHPERD, Fla. Assn. for Health, Phys. Edn., Recreation, Dance, and Phys. Edn. (co-chair program 1994—, Tchr. of Yr. 1994), NEA. Democrat. Baptist. Avocations: volleyball, light cooking, children. Office: Mainland High Sch 125 S Clyde Morris Blvd Daytona Beach FL 32114-3954

WOOD, KENNETH ARTHUR, retired newspaper editor, writer; b. Hastings, Sussex, Eng., Feb. 25, 1926; came to U.S., 1965; s. Arthur Charles and Ellen Mary (Cox) W.; m. Hilda Muriel Harloe, Sept. 13, 1952. Educated in Eng. Editor Stamp Collector newspaper Van Dahl Publs., Albany, Oreg., 1968-80, editor emeritus, 1980—. Author (ency.) This Is Philately, 1982, (atlas) Where in the World, 1983, Basic Philately, 1984, Post Dates, 1985, Modern World, 1987; author several hundred articles and columns published in the U.K. and U.S.A., 1960—. Served with Brit. Army WW II. Recipient Disting. Philatelist award Northwest Fedn. Stamp Clubs, 1974, Phoenix award Ariz. State Philatelic Hall of Fame, 1979, Disting. Philatelist award Am. Topical Assn., 1979. Fellow Royal Philatelic Soc. (London); mem. Am. Philatelic Soc. (Luff award 1987, Hall of Fame Writers Unit, 1984). Avocations: philately, aviation history, modern history, gardening. Office: Van Dahl Pub PO Box 10 520 E First Albany OR 97321-0006

WOOD, KIMBA M., judge; b. Port Townsend, Wash., Jan. 2, 1944. BA cum laude, Conn. Coll., 1965; MSc, London Sch. Econs., 1966; JD, Harvard U., 1969. Bar: U.S. Dist. Ct. D.C. 1969, U.S. Ct. Appeals D.C. 1969, N.Y. 1972, U.S. Dist. Ct. (ea. and so. dists.) N.Y. 1974, U.S. Ct. Appeals (2d cir.) 1975, U.S. Supreme Ct. 1980, U.S. Dist. Ct. (we. dist.) N.Y. 1981. Assoc. Steptoe & Johnson, Washington, 1969-70; with Office Spl. Counsel, OEO Legal Svcs., Washington, 1970-71; assoc., then ptnr. LeBoeuf, Lamb, Leiby & MacRae, N.Y.C., 1971-88; judge, U.S. Dist. Ct. (so. dist.) N.Y., N.Y.C., 1988—. Mem. ABA (chmn. civil practice, procedure com. 1982-85, mem. coun. 1985-88, jud. rep. 1989-91), N.Y. State Bar Assn. (chmn. antitrust sect. 1983-84), Fed. Bar Coun. (trustee from 1978, v.p., 1984-85), Am. Law Inst. Office: US Dist Ct US Courthouse 500 Pearl St New York NY 10007

WOOD, LARRY (MARY LAIRD), journalist, author, university educator, public relations executive, environmental consultant; b. Sandpoint, Idaho; d. Edward Hayes and Alice (McNeel) Small; children: Mary, Marcia, Barry. BA summa cum laude, U. Wash., 1939, MA summa cum laude, with highest honors, 1940; postgrad., Stanford U., 1941-42, U. Calif., Berkeley, 1946-47; cert. in photography, U. Calif., Berkeley, 1971; postgrad. journalism, U. Wis., 1971-72, U. Minn., 1971-72, U. Ga., 1972-73; postgrad. in art, architecture and marine biology, U. Calif., Santa Cruz, 1974-76, Stanford Hopkins Marine Sta., Santa Cruz, 1977-80. Lifetime secondary and jr. coll. teaching cert., Wash., Calif. Feature writer and columnist Oakland Tribune and San Francisco Chronicle, Calif., 1939—; archtl. and environ. feature and travel writer and columnist San Jose (Calif.) Mercury News (Knight Ridder), 1972-90; teaching fellow Stanford U., 1940-43; dir. pub. rels. 2-counties, 53-parks East Bay Regional Park Dist., No. Calif., 1948-68; pres. Larry Wood Pub. Rels., 1946—; prof. (tenure) pub. rels., mag. writing, journalism, investigative reporting San Diego State U., 1974, 75; disting. vis. prof. journalism San Jose State U., 1976; assoc. prof. journalism Calif. State U., Hayward, 1978; prof. sci. and environ. journalism U. Calif. Berkeley Ext. grad. divsn., 1979—; press del. nat. convs. Am. Geophys. Union Internat. Conf., 1986—, AAAS, 1989—, Nat. Park Svc. VIP Press Tour, Yellowstone after the fire, 1989, Nat. Assn. Sci. Writers, 1989—, George Washington U./Am. Assn. Neurol. Surgeons Sci. Writers Conf., 1990, Am. Inst. Biol. Scis. Conf., 1990, Nat. Conf. Sci. Writers, Am. Heart Assn., 1995, Internat. Cardiologists Symposium for Med./Sci. Writers, 1995, Annenberg Program Electronic Media Symposium, Washington, 1995; EPA del. to USSR and Ea. Europe; expert witness on edn., pub. rels., journalism and copyright; cons. sci. writers interne project Stanford U., 1989—; spl. media guest Sigma Xi, 1990—; mem. numerous spl. press corps; selected White House Spl. Media, 1993—; selected mem., panelist Calif. Environ. Leadership Round Table, 1996—, Duke U. 14th Ann. Sci. Reporters Conf., 1995; internat. press guest Can. Consulate Gen. Dateline Can., 1995, Ministerio delle Risorse Agricole Alimentari e Forestali and Assocs. Conf., 1995; appeared in TV documentary Larry Wood Covers Visit of Queen Elizabeth II. Contbr. over 5,000 articles on various topics for newspapers, nat. mags., nat. and internat. newspaper syndicates including L.A. Times-Mirror Syndicate, Washington Post, Phila. Inquirer, Chgo. Tribune, Miami Herald, Oakland Tribune, Seattle Times, San Francisco Chronicle, Parade, San Jose Mercury News (Nat. Headliner award), Christian Sci. Monitor, L.A. Times/Christian Monitor Worldwide News Syndicate, Washington Post, Phila. Inquirer, Hawaiian Airlines In Paradise and other in-flight mags., MonitoRadio, Sports Illus., Life, Mechanix Illus., Popular Mechanics, Parents, House Beautiful, Am. Home (awards 1988, 89), Archl. Digest, Better Homes and Gardens, Sunset, National Geographic World, Travel & Leisure, Chevron USA/Odyssey (Calif. Pub.'s award 1984), Xerox Edn. Publs., Europe's Linguapress, PSA Mag., Off Duty, Oceans, Sea Frontiers, AAA Westways, AAA Motorland, Travelin', others. Significant works include home and garden columnist and editor, 5-part series Pacific Coast Ports, 5-part series Railroads of the West, series Immigration, Youth Gangs, Endangered Species, Calif. Lighthouse Chain, Elkhorn Slough Nat. Estuarine Res., Ebey's Landing Nat. Hist. Res., Calif. Water Wars, BLM's Adopt a Horse Program, Mt. St. Helen's Eruption, Loma Prieta Earthquake, Oakland Firestorm, Missing Children, Calif. Prison Reform, Columbia Alaska's Receding Glacier, Calif. Underwater Parks, and many others; author: Wonderful U.S.A.: A State-by-State Guide to Its Natural Resources, 1989; co-author over 21 books including: McGraw-Hill English for Social Living, 1944, Fawcett Boating Books, 1956-66, Fodoancisco, Fodor's California, 1982-89, Charles Merrill Focus on Life Science, Focus on Physical Science, Focus on Earth Science, 1983, 87, Earth Science, 1987; contbr. Earth Science 1987; 8 works selected for use by Europe's Woltors-Nordoff-Longman English Language Texts, U.K., Netherlands, 1988; author: (with others) anthology West Winds, 1989; reviewer Charles Merrill texts, 1983-84; book reviewer Profl. Communicator, 1987—; selected writings in permanent collections Oakland Pub. Libr., U. Wash. Main Libr.; environ. works included in Dept. Edn. State of Md. textbook; contbr., author Journalism Quar.; author script PBS/AAA America series, 1992; contbg. editor: Parents. Nat. chmn. travel writing contest for U.S. univ. journalism students Assn. for Edn. in Journalism/Soc. Am. Travel Writers, 1979-83; judge writing contest for Nat. Assn. Real Estate Editors, 1982—; press del. 1st Internat. Symposium Volcanism and Aviation Safety, 1991, Coun. for Advancement of Sci. Writing, 1977—, Rockefeller Media Seminar Feeding the World-Protecting the Earth, 1992, Global Conf. on Mercury as Pollutant, 1992, Earth Summit Global Forum, Rio de Janeiro, 1992; invited Nat. Park Svc. Nat. Conf. Sci. Writers, 1985, Postmaster Gen.'s 1992 Stamps, 1991, Internat. Geophys. Union Conf., 1982-95, The Conf. Bd., 1995, Corp. Comm. Conf., Calif. Inst. Tech.'s Media and Sci. Seminar, 1995, EPA and Dept. Energy Tech. Conf., 1992, Am. Soc. Photogrammetry and Remote Sensing Internat. Conv. Mapping Global change, 1992, N.Y. Mus. Modern Art Matisse Retrospective Press Rev., 1992, celebration 150th anniversary Oreg. Trail, 1993, Coun. Advancement Sci. Writing, 1993, 94, Sigma Xi Nat. Conf., 1988—, PRSA Travel and Tourism Conf., 1993, Internat. Conf. Environment, 1994, 95, Quality Life Europe, Prague, 1994, 14th Ann. Sci. Writers Conf., 1996, Picasso Retrospective, 1996, many others; mem. Gov.'s Conf. Tourism N.C., 1993, 94, 95, Calif., 1976—, Fla., 1987—; press guest 14 U.S. states and 12 fgn. countries' Depts. Tourism, 1986-96. Recipient numerous awards, honors, citations, speaking engagements, including induction into Broadway Hall of Fame, U. Wash., 1984, Broadway Disting. Alumnus award, 1995; citations for environ. writing Nat. Park Svc., U.S. Forest Svc., Bur. Land Mgmt., Oakland Mus. Assn., Oakland C. of C., Chevron USA, USN plaque and citation, best mag. articles citation Calif. Pubs. Assn., 1984; co-recipient award for best Sunday newspaper mag. Nat. Headliners, citation for archtl. features Oakland Mus., 1983; honoree for achievements in journalism Nat. Mortar Bd., 1988, 89; selected as one of 10 V.I.P. press for Yellowstone Nat. Park field trip on "Let Burn" rsch., 1989; named one of Calif.'s top 40 contemporary authors for writings on Calif. underwater parks, 1989, nat. honoree Social Issues Resources Series, 1987; invited V.I.P. press, spl. press guest numerous events worldwide. Mem. Am. Bd. Forensic Examiners, Calif. Acad. Scis., San Francisco Press Club, Nat. Press Club, Pub. Rels. Soc. Am. (charter mem. travel, tourism, environment and edn. divs.), Nat. Sch. Pub. Rels. Assn., Environ. Cons. N.Am., Am. Assn. Edn. in Journalism and Comm. (exec. bd. nat. mag. div. 1978, panel chmn. 1979, 80, author Journalism Quar. jour.), Women in Comm. (nat. bd. officer 1975-77, book reviewer Prof. Communicator), Soc. Profl. Journalists (nat. bd. for hist. sites 1980—), Nat. Press Photographers Assn. (hon. life, cons. Bay Area interne project 1989—, honoree 1995), Investigative Reporters and Editors (charter), Bay Area Advt. and Mktg. Assn., Nat. Assn. Sci. Writers, Calif. Writers Club (state bd., Berkeley bd. 1989—, honoree ann. conv. Asilomar, Calif. 1990), Am. Assn. Med. Writers, Internat. Assn. Bus. Communicators, Soc. Environ. Journalists (charter), Am. Film Inst., Am. Heritage Found. (citation 1986, 87, 88), Soc. Am. Travel Writers, Internat. Oceanographic Found., Oceanic Soc., Calif. Acad. Environ. News Writers, Seattle Advt. and Sales Club (former, Nature Conservancy, Smithsonian Audubon Soc., Nat. Wildlife Fedn., Nat. Parks and Conservation Assn., Calif. State Parks Found., Calif. Environ. Leadership Roundtable, Fine Arts Mus., San Francisco, Seattle Jr. Advt. Club (charter), U. Wash. Comm. Alumni (Sch. Comm. alumni, life, charter mem. ocean scis. alumni, Disting. Alumni 1987), U. Calif., Berkeley Alumni (life, v.p., scholarship chmn. 1975-81), Stanford Alumni (life), Mortar Board Alumnae Assn. (life, honoree 1988, 89), Am. Mgmt. Assn., Nat. Soc. Environ. Journalists (charter), Phi Beta Kappa (v.p., bd. dirs. Calif. Alumni Assn., statewide chmn. scholarship awards 1975-81), Purple and Gold Soc. (planning com., charter, 1995—), Pi Lambda Theta, Theta Sigma Phi. Home: Piedmont Pines 6161 Castle Dr Oakland CA 94611-2737 *A creed I follow is Ralph Waldo Emerson's statement: "Nothing great was ever achieved without enthusiasm."*

WOOD, LARRY JOE, trust banker; b. Corpus Christi, Tex., Jan. 19, 1947; s. Joe Frank and Wilma (Fair) W.; m. Glenna Sue Hutson, Jan. 13, 1979; children: Lawrence Hutson, Bryant McKay. BBA in Fin., Tex. A&I U., 1973; trust mgt. cert., So. Meth. U., 1981. CFP; cert. trust and fin. advisor. Trust asst. Corpus Christi State Nat. Bank, 1974, trust officer, 1975-76; asst. v.p., trust officer Corpus Christi Nat. Bank, 1977-79, v.p., trust officer, 1980; v.p., trust officer Frost Nat. Bank, Corpus Christi, 1981-90; v.p., mgr. investments Ameritrust Tex., Corpus Christi, 1991-92, Tex. Commerce Bank, Corpus Christi, 1993; v.p., trust investments officer Victoria Bank & Trust Co., Corpus Christi, 1994—. Pres. Camp Fire Coun. of Corpus Christi, 1991-93. With USN, 1966-70. Recipient Fin. Leadership award Camp Fire Coun., 1990; named Vol. of Yr. in Leadership, Vol. Ctr., 1994. Mem. Tex. Bankers Assn. (personal trust com. trust divsn. 1978, property mgmt. com. trust divsn. 1979-81), Kiwanis Club of Six Points (bd. dirs. 1978—, pres. 1984-85), Kiwanis Internat. (lt. gov. Tex./Okla. dist. divsn. 4 1987-88), Corpus Christi Estate Planning Coun., Corpus Christi Town Club, Corpus Christi Country Club. Democrat. United Methodist. Avocations: reading, golf. Home: 313 Camellia Dr Corpus Christi TX 78404-2403 Office: Victoria Bank & Trust Co 210 S Carancahua St Fl 6 Corpus Christi TX 78401-3040

WOOD, LAWRENCE CRANE, medical association administrator, educator; b. Phila., May 7, 1935; s. Francis Clark and Mary Louise (Woods) W.; m. Emma Mathis Hollingsworth, Aug. 29, 1959 (div. 1975); children: Lawrence C. Jr., Clinton Tyler; m. Shirley Ann Jacobsen, July 1, 1977; 1 child, Marianna Redd. AB, Princeton U., 1957; MD, U. Pa., 1961. Assoc. physician Mass. Gen. Hosp., Boston; instr. in medicine Harvard U. Med. Sch., Boston; pres., med. dir. Thyroid Found. Am., Boston, 1985—. Author: Your Thyroid: A Home Reference, 1982. Capt. USMC, 1965-68. Mem. ACP, Am. Thyroid Assn., Am. Assn. Clin. Endocrinologists, Mass. Med. Soc., Endocrine Soc. Avocations: fishing, sailing, banjo, guitar. Office: Mass Gen Hosp ACC 635 Parkman St Boston MA 02114

WOOD, LINDA MAY, librarian; b. Fort Dodge, Iowa, Nov. 6, 1942; d. John Albert and Beth Ida (Riggs) Wiley; m. C. James Wood, Sept. 15, 1964 (div. Oct. 1984). BA, Portland State U., 1964; M in Librarianship, U. Wash., 1965. Reference libr. Multnomah County Libr., Portland, Oreg., 1965-67, br. libr., 1967-72, adminstrv. asst. to libr., 1972-73, asst. libr., asst. dir., 1973-77; asst. city libr. L.A. Pub. Libr., 1977-80; libr. dir. Riverside (Calif.) City and County Pub. Libr., 1980-91; county libr. Alameda County Libr., Fremont, Calif., 1991—; adminstrv. coun. mem. Bay Area Libr. and Info. Svcs., Oakland, Calif., 1991—. Chair combined charities campaign County of Alameda, Oakland, 1992; bd. dirs. Inland AIDS Project, Riverside, Calif., 1990-91; vol. United Way of Inland Valleys, Riverside, 1986-87, Bicentennial Competition on the Constitution, 36th Congl. Dist., Colton, Calif., 1988-90. Mem. ALA (CLA chpt. councilor 1992-95), Calif. Libr. Assn. (pres. 1985, exec. com., ALA chpt. councilor 1992-95), Calif. County Librs. Assn. (pres. 1984), League of Calif. Cities (cmty. svcs. policy com. 1985-90), OCLC Users Coun. (Pacific Network del. 1986-89). Democrat. Avocations: folk dancing, opera, reading. Office: Alameda County Libr 2450 Stevenson Blvd Fremont CA 94538-2326

WOOD, MARCUS ANDREW, lawyer; b. Mobile, Ala., Jan. 18, 1947; s. George Franklin and Helen Eugenia (Fletcher) W.; m. Sandra Lee Pellonari, July 25, 1971; children: Edward Alan, Melinda Janel. BA cum laude, Vanderbilt U., 1969; JD, Yale U., 1974. Bar: Oreg. 1974, U.S. Dist. Ct. Oreg. 1974, U.S. Ct. Appeals (9th cir.) 1982. Assoc., then ptnr. Rives, Bonihadi & Smith, Portland, Oreg., 1974-78; ptnr. Stoel Rives and predecessor firms, Portland, 1974—. Pres., bd. dirs. Indochinese Refugee Ctr., Portland, 1980, Pacific Ballet Theatre, Portland, 1986-87; bd. dirs. Outside In, Portland, 1989—. Lt. USNR, 1969-71. Mem. ABA, Phi Beta Kappa. Home: 3707 SW Cullen Blvd Portland OR 97221-3525 Office: Stoel Rives 900 SW 5th Ave Ste 2300 Portland OR 97204-1232

WOOD, MARIAN STARR, publishing company executive; b. N.Y.C., Mar. 30, 1938; d. Edward James and Betty (Starr) Markow; m. Anthony Stuart Wood, Mar. 21, 1963. B.A., Barnard Coll., 1959; postgrad., Columbia U., 1959-64. Teaching asst., lectr. Columbia U., N.Y.C., 1960-64; editor Praeger Pubs., N.Y.C., 1965-71; sr. editor Henry Holt & Co., N.Y.C., 1972-81, exec. editor, 1981-96; assoc. pub. Marian Wood Books, 1996—.

WOOD, MAURICE, medical educator; b. Pelton, Eng., June 28, 1922; came to U.S., 1971; s. Joseph and Eugenie (Lumley) W.; m. Erica Joan Noble, May 1, 1948; children: Roger Lumley, Ashley Michael, Frances Jane. M.B., B.S., U. Durham, Eng., 1945; M.R.C.G.P., Royal Coll. Gen. Practice, London, 1966; F.R.C.G.P., Royal Coll. Gen. Practice, 1975. Diplomate: Am. Bd. Family Practice. Sr. ptnr. med. practice South Shields County, Durham, 1950-71; gen. practice teaching group U. Newcastle, Newcastle-on-Tyne, Eng., 1969-71; gen. clin. asst. dept. psychology-medicine South Shields Gen. Hosp., 1966-71; assoc. prof., dir. research family practice Med. Coll. Va.-Va. Commonwealth U., Richmond, 1971-73, prof., dir. research in family practice, 1973-87, prof. emeritus, 1987—; ; cons. advisor WHO, Geneva, 1979-90, chmn. working party to develop a classification for primary care, 1979-93; exec. dir. N.Am. Primary Care Rsch. Group, Richmond, 1983-93, past pres., pres. emeritus, 1993—; chmn. com. on cmty. oriented primary care Insts. of Medicine, 1982-84. Assoc. editor: Jour. Family Practice, 1976-83. Recipient award for meritorious svc. Va. Acad. Family Physicians, 1976; Maurice Wood award for career achievmeent in primary care rsch. foundind in his honor, 1995. Fellow Royal Coll. Gen. Practitioners, Am. Acad. Family Physicians; mem. Inst. Medicine-Nat. Acad. Sci., Soc. Tchrs. Family Medicine (Curtis Hames Career Research award 1984), Inst. of Medicine, NAS, Ambulatory Sentinel Practice Network, Internat. Primary Care Network (treas., bd. mem.). Episcopalian. Lodge: Rotary. Home: Wintergreen Rt 1 Box 672 Roseland VA 22967 Office: MCV-VCU Dept Family Practice PO Box 251 Richmond VA 23202-0251

WOOD, MICHAEL ALLEN, health care executive; b. Mpls., Apr. 4, 1956; s. Lloyd Allen and Mary Frances (Devereaux) W.; m. Jane Mary Selzer, June 5, 1976; children: Jennifer Elizabeth, Jessica Marie. AAS in Cardiopulmonary Tech., Maryville Coll., St. Louis, 1976; BSBA in Fin., Lindenwood Coll., St. Charles, Mo., 1981, MS in Fin., 1982, MBA in Mktg., 1983. Dir. clin. svcs. Health Cons., Inc., St. Louis, 1976-78; adminstrv. dir. Clasen Home Health Care, St. Louis, 1978-83; v.p. mktg. Biomed. Systems Corp., St. Louis, 1983-84; dir. fin. ARA Med. Rehab. Svcs., St. Louis, 1984-85; pres., CEO St. Louis Mgmt. Group, Inc., 1985—, Physicians Healthcare Network, Inc., 1992—; assoc. prof. Lindenwood Coll., 1984—. Contbr. articles to profl. jours. Bd. dirs. Lindenwood Coll. Bd. Overseers, 1988—; bd. dirs. Lindenwood Coll. Alumni Bd., 1986-90; corp. com. Juvenile Diabetes Found., St. Louis, 1989. Mem. St. Louis Soc. Healthcare Planning and Mktg., Med. Group Mgmt. Assn., Mo. Athletic Club, Alpha Sigma Tau. Roman Catholic. Avocations: golf, racquetball, sporting clays. Office: St Louis Mgmt Group Inc 1023 Executive Pky Dr Saint Louis MO 63141-6323

WOOD, NANCY ELIZABETH, psychologist, educator; d. Donald Sterret and Orne Louise (Erwin) W. B.S., Ohio U., 1943, M.A., 1947; Ph.D., Northwestern U., Evanston, Ill., 1952. Prof. Case-Western Res. U., Cleve., 1952-60; specialist, expert Dept. HEW, Washington, 1960-62; chief of research Pub. Health, Washington, 1962-64; prof. U. So. Calif., Los Angeles, 1965—; learning disabilities cons., 1960-70; assoc. dir. Cleve. Hearing and Speech Ctr., 1952-60; dir. licensing program Brit. Nat. Trust, London. Author: Language Disorders, 1964, Language Development, 1970, Verbal Learning, 1975 (monograph) Auditory Disorders, 1978, Levity, 1980, Stoneskipping, 1989, Bird Cage, 1994. Pres. faculty senate U. So. Calif., 1987-88. Recipient Outstanding Faculty award Trojan Fourth Estate, 1982, Pres.' Svc. award U. So. Calif., 1992. Fellow Am. Speech and Hearing Assn. (elected, legis. council 1965-68), Am. Psychol. Assn. (cert.), AAAS; mem. Internat. Assn. of Scientists. Republican. Methodist. Office: U So Calif University Park Los Angeles CA 90089

WOOD, NATHANIEL FAY, editor, writer, public relations consultant; b. Worcester, Mass., June 23, 1919; s. Henry Fletcher and Edith (Fay) W.; m. Eleanor Norton, Dec. 19, 1945; children: Gary Nathaniel, Janet Ann. BS in Journalism, Bus. Adminstrn., Syracuse U., 1946. Editor, writer various publs., various cities, 1946-51; mng. editor Butane-Propane News, L.A., 1951-52; editor Western Metalworking Mag., L.A., 1952-62; western editorial mgr. Penton Pub. Co. Cleve., L.A., 1962-71; editor Orange County Illustrated, Orange County Bus., Newport Beach, Calif., 1971-72; western editor Hitchcock Pub., L.A., 1972-75; co-owner, mgr. Norton-Wood Pub. Rels. Svcs., Pasadena, Calif., 1975—; editorial dir. Security World, SDM and SCA Mags., Culver City, Calif., 1975-80; mgr. trade show Cahners Pub. and Expo Group, L.A., 1979-82; sr. editor Alarm Installer Dealer Mag., L.A., 1982-89; editor CNC West Mag., Long Beach, Pasadena, Calif., 1982—. Freelance indsl. writer miscellaneous bus. pubs. Organizer Willkie Presdl. Campaign, Syracuse, N.Y., 1940; advisor various GOP campaigns, L.A., Washington, 1940-92; charter mem. Rep. Nat. Com., 1995; nat. adv. bd. Am. Security Coun.; donor L.A. Civic Light Opera; mem., donor L.A. Mus. Art, 1989—; founding mem. Western Heritage Mus., L.A., 1989—; active Met. Opera Guild, Colonial Williamsburg Found., Mus. Natural History L.A. 2nd lt. U.S. Army, 1943-45, PTO. Decorated Purple Heart; recipient Silver, Bronze and Gold medals for Editorial Excellence Gov. of Calif., 1959, 60, 62. Mem. Am. Legion, Scabbard and Blade, L.A. World Affairs Coun., Smithsonian Instn., The Nat. Air and Space Soc., Soc. Profl. Journalists, Alpha Epsilon Rho, Tau Theta Upsilon. Avocations: swimming, boating, tennis, photography, gardening. Home: 1430 Tropical Ave Pasadena CA 91107-1623 Office: Norton-Wood Pub Rels Svcs 1430 Tropical Ave Pasadena CA 91107-1623

WOOD, NEIL RODERICK, real estate development company executive; b. Winnipeg, Man., Can., Aug. 22, 1931; s. Reginald and Pearl (Beake) W.; m. Jean Mitchell Hume, Aug. 10, 1957; children: Barbara, David, John, Brian. B.Com., U. Man., 1952; M.B.A., Harvard U., 1955. Asst. mgr. Ont. real estate investment office Gt. West Life Assurance Co., 1955-59; with Cadillac Fairview Corp. Ltd. (and predecessor), Willowdale, Ont., 1959-61, 63-81; exec. v.p. Cadillac Fairview Corp. Ltd. (and predecessor), 1968-71, pres., 1971-81, vice chmn., 1980-81; pres. N.R. Wood Devel. Co. Ltd., 1982—; exec. v.p., dir. Campeau Corp., 1985-86; bd. dirs. Gentra Inc.; past pres., trustee Internat. Coun. Shopping Ctrs.; past pres. Can. Inst. Pub. Real Estate Cos.; bd. govs. Roy Thompson Hall. Mem. Urban Land Inst., Met. Toronto Bd. Trade, Toronto Club, Rosedale Golf Club, Craigleith Ski Club, Beaumaris Club, Lost Tree Club, Loxahatchee Golf Club, Beacon Hall Club. Home and Office: RR # 3, Newmarket, ON Canada L3Y 4W1

WOOD, PAUL F., national health agency executive; b. Lockport, N.Y., Dec. 7, 1935; s. Dwight Edward and Frances (Fletcher) W.; m. Kathleen Frances Stretton, May 27, 1958; children: Paul S., Richard F. BA, Western Res. Univ., 1964; MA, Kent State U., 1970; PhD, Case Western Res. U., 1975. Assoc. exec. dir. United Way of Stark County, Canton, Ohio, 1967-70; owner Paul Wood Co., N. Canton, Ohio, 1970-86; dir. devel. The Salvation Army, N.Y.C., 1986-90; pres. Nat. Coun. on Alcoholism and Drug Dependence, Inc., N.Y.C., 1990—. Bd. dirs. Fairfield (Conn.) Chorale, 1991-94, Stepping Stones Found., Bedford Hills, N.Y.; fin. com. Westport United Meth. Ch., 1993—. Avocations: sailing, computer programming. Office: Nat Coun On Alcoholism & Drug Dependence 12 W 21st St New York NY 10010-6902

WOOD, PAULA DAVIDSON, lawyer; b. Oklahoma City, Dec. 20, 1952; d. Paul James and Anna Mae (Ferrero) Davidson; m. Andrew E. Wood; children: Michael Paul, John Roland. BS, Okla. State U., 1976; JD, Oklahoma City U., 1982. Bar: Okla. 1983, U.S. Dist. Ct. (we. dist.) Okla. 1983, U.S. Supreme Ct. 1995; cert. pub. mgr. Pvt. practice Oklahoma City, 1984-85; ptnr. Davidson & Wood, Oklahoma City, 1985-87; child support enforcement counsel Okla. Dept. Human Svcs., Oklahoma City, 1987-92, child support adminstr. (IV-D dir.), 1992—; adj. instr. Tech. Inst. Okla. State U., Oklahoma City, 1985. Articles editor Oklahoma City U. Law Rev., 1982. Mem. Okla. Bar Assn. (sec. family law sect. 1987, Golden Gavel award 1987), Nat. Child Support Enforcement Assn. (bd. dirs. 1995), Okla. Child Support Enforcement Assn., S.W. Regional Child Support Enforcement

Assn. (pres. 1996), Nat. Assn. State Child Support Enforcement Adminstrs., Western Interstate Child Support Enforcement Coun. (sec. 1995). Republican. Roman Catholic. Office: Okla Dept Human Svcs PO Box 53552 Oklahoma City OK 73152-3552

WOOD, QUENTIN EUGENE, oil company executive; b. Mechanicsburg, Pa., Mar. 5, 1923; s. Lloyd Paul and Greta (Myers) W.; m. Louise Lowe, Apr. 14, 1958. B.S., Pa. State U., 1948. Petroleum engr. Quaker State Oil Refining Corp., Parkersburg, W.Va., 1948-52; chief engr. Quaker State Oil Refining Corp., Bradford, Pa., 1952-55; mgr. prodn. Quaker State Oil Refining Corp., 1955-68; v.p. prodn. Quaker State Oil Refining Corp., Oil City, Pa., 1968-70; exec. v.p. Quaker State Oil Refining Corp., Oil City, 1970-73, pres., chief ops. officer, 1973-75; pres., chief exec. officer Quaker State Oil Refining Corp., 1975-82, chmn., chief executive officer, 1982-88, chmn. bd., 1988-90, dir., 1990-93; bd. dirs. Pa. Mfrs. Ins. Co.; chmn. industry tech. adv. com. U.S. Bur. Mines, 1960-70, Penn Grade Tech. Adv. Com., 1955-69, Pa. Oil and Gas Conservation Commn., 1961-71. Trustee Pa. State U., 1976-94, pres., 1985-87. 1st lt. USAAF, 1943-46. Mem. Am. Inst. Metall. Engrs., Pa. Grade Crude Oil Assn. (dir.), Pa. Oil Producers Assn. (past pres., dir. Bradford dist.), Am. Petroleum Inst. (dir.), Nat. Petroleum Refiners Assn. (dir.). Home: 1402 Spinnakers Reach Dr Ponte Vedra Beach FL 32082-4414 Office: Quaker State Corp Oil Creek Station Box G Oil City PA 16301

WOOD, R. STEWART, bishop; b. Detroit, June 25, 1934; s. Raymond and Marjorie Wood; m. Kristin Lie Miller, June 25, 1955; children: Lisa, Raymond, Michael. AB, Dartmouth Coll., 1956; MDiv, Va. Theol. Seminary, 1969; MA in Counseling and Sociology, Ball State U., 1973; postgrad., Va. Seminary. Ordained to diaconate and priesthood Episc. Ch., 1959. Vicar Episc. Ch., Seymour and Bean Blossom, Ind.; assoc. rector Grace Ch., Muncie, Ind., rector, 1966-70; exec. dir. Episc. Community Svcs., Indpls., 1970-76; rector All Saint's Episc. Ch., Christ Ch., Glendale, Ind., 1976-84, St. John's Ch., Memphis, 1984-88; elected Bishop Coadjutor Diocese Mich., Detroit, 1988-89, diocesan bishop, 1990—; dir. summer camps, conf. ctr.; dep. Gen. Conv. 1970, 73, 76, 82; exec. coun. Coalition for Ordination of Women, bd. dirs. Avocations: camping, golf, tennis, photography, motorcycling. Office: 4800 Woodward Ave Detroit MI 48201-1310

WOOD, RAYMUND FRANCIS, retired librarian; b. London, Nov. 9, 1911; came to U.S., 1924; s. George S. and Ida A. (Lawes) W.; m. Margaret Ann Peed, Feb. 26, 1943; children: Paul George, Gregory Leo, David Joseph. AB, St. Mary's U., Balt., 1931; MA, Gonzaga U., 1939; PhD, UCLA, 1949; MS in Libr. Sci., U. So. Calif., L.A., 1950. Instr. English U. Santa Clara (Calif.), 1939-41; rehab. officer VA, L.A., 1946-48; reference libr. Fresno (Calif.) State Coll., 1950-66; prof. libr. sci. UCLA, L.A., 1966-77, prof. emeritus, 1977—, from asst. dean to assoc. dean Grad. Sch. Libr. & Info. Sci., 1970-77. Author: California's Agua Fria, 1952, Life and Death of Peter Lebec, 1954, The Saints of the California Landscape, 1987; co-author: Librarian and Laureate: Ina Coolbrith of California, 1973, many others. Vol. driver ARC, Van Nuys, Calif., 1977—; pres. Friends of the Encino/Tarzana Br. Libr., Tarzana, Calif., 1977-80, Jedediah Smith Soc., Stockton, Calif., 1987-90, knight comdr. Order of St. Gregory, 1994. With U.S. Army, 1942-46, ETO. Travel grantee Am. Book Found., 1964, Del. Amo Found., 1974. Mem. ALA (book reviewer 1974—), Calif. Libr. Assn. (many offices), Mariposa County Hist. Assn. (life), Oral History Assn. (life), Fresno County Hist. Soc. (editor 1959-66), Westerners L.A. Corral (editor of Brand Book 1982). Democrat. Byzantine Catholic. Avocations: lecturing, writing, reading, traveling. Home: 18052 Rosita St Encino CA 91316-4217

WOOD, RICHARD COURTNEY, library director, educator; b. Spartanburg, S.C., Aug. 8, 1943; s. Herman Alva and Mildred Eloise (Porter) W.; m. Amy Louise Black, Aug. 16, 1974. BA, U. Tex., 1966; MLS, U. S.C., 1977. Head cataloging Wofford Coll. Libr., Spartanburg, 1969-78; hosp. libr. John Peter Smith Hosp., Ft. Worth, 1978-80; reference libr. Tex. Coll. Osteo. Medicine, Ft. Worth, 1980-82, assoc. dir. libr., 1982-91; dir. librs., assoc. prof. Sch. Medicine, Tex. Tech U. Health Scis. Ctr., Lubbock, 1991—; cons. Tarrant County Med. Libr. Assn., Fort Worth, 1978-82, 84, Med. Plaza Hosp., Fort Worth, 1979-82, Grand Prairie (Tex.) Community Hosp., 1980-81, Cook-Fort Worth Children's Hosp., 1988—. Patron Kimball Art Mus. Fort Worth, 1987—; spokesman Neighborhood Assn., Fort Worth, 1989; vis. exec. United Way, Fort Worth, 1990. Mem. Dallas-Tarrant County Consortium (chmn. 1980-81), Metroplex Consortium Health Scis. (chmn. 1980-81), South Cen. Regional Group, Med. Libr. Assn. (chmn. osteo. librs. sect. 1986-87), South Cen. Acad. Med. Librs. (bd. dirs. 1991—), Nat. Network Librs. Medicine (bd. dirs. South Cen. region 1991-93), Deutsche Gesellschaft für Heereskunde, Sigma Tau Delta. Republican. Presbyterian. Avocations: languages, travel, history, gardening, music. Home: 1805 Bangor Ave Lubbock TX 79416-5518 Office: Libr of Health Scis Tex Tech U Scis Ctr Lubbock TX 79430

WOOD, RICHARD D., JR., retail executive; b. 1938. BS in Commerce, U. Va., 1961; LLB, U. Pa., 1964. With Montgomery McCracken Walker & Rhoads, 1964-68; v.p., counsel Wawa Inc., Media, Pa., 1968-74, exec. v.p., 1974-79, pres., CEO, 1979—. With USMC, 1964-68. Office: Wawa Inc Red Roof 260 W Baltimore Pike Media PA 19063-5620*

WOOD, RICHARD J., academic administrator. A.B., Duke U., 1959; B.D., Union Theol. Sem., 1962; M.A., Yale U., 1963, Ph.D., 1965. Pres. Earlham Coll., Richmond, Ind., 1985—. Office: Earlham Coll Office of President Richmond IN 47374

WOOD, RICHARD ROBINSON, real estate executive; b. Salem, Mass., Nov. 8, 1922; s. Reginald and Irene Margaret (Robinson) W.; m. Pamela Vander Wiele, Mar. 8, 1951 (div. Apr. 1969); children: Christopher Robinson, Bryant Cornelius, Marcella Wood Mackenzie; m. Jane Philbin, Sept. 19, 1970. AB, Harvard Coll., 1944; postgrad., Mass. Inst. Tech., 1947-48. V.p. Hunneman & Co., Boston, 1959-72; trustee, sec. Mass. Real Estate Investment Trust, Boston, 1967-69; trustee Suffolk Franklin Savings Bank, 1967-74; pres., chmn. Continential Real Estate Equity, Boston, 1972-74; exec. v.p. ITEL Real Estate Corp., San Francisco, 1974-75; v.p. Baird & Warner, Chgo., 1976-80; pres., chmn. Renwood Properties, Inc., Peabody, Mass., 1981—; v.p., dir. Common Goal Capitol Group, Balt., 1986—; gen. ptnr. Common Goal Mortgage Fund, Balt., 1986—; v.p., bd. dirs. St. Katherines Care Ctrs., 1990—; pres., chmn. ILCO Properties, Chgo., 1981-87; mem. Coun. for Rural Housing and Devel., 1988—; trustee 19 Chauncy St. Trust, 1995—, Inst. for Responsible Housing Preservation, 1994—. Mem. Mayor's Citizen Adv. Bd., Boston, 1965-67; pres. Boston Rep. city Com., 1965-67; committeeman, treas. Mass. Rep. State Com., Boston, 1964-72; mem. Coun. for Rural Housing and Devel., 1988—. With Med. Corps U.S. Army, 1943-44. Mem. Nat. Leased Housing Assn., Harvard Club Boston, Longwood Cricket Club, Harvard Club of N.Y. Avocations: tennis, skiing. Home: 19 Chauncy St Cambridge MA 02138-2549 Office: Renwood Properties Inc 100 Corp Pl Ste 403 Peabody MA 01960

WOOD, ROBERT COLDWELL, political scientist; b. St. Louis, Sept. 16, 1923; s. Thomas Frank and Mary (Bradshaw) W.; m. Margaret Byers, Mar. 22, 1952; children—Frances, Margaret, Frank Randolph. AB, Princeton U., 1946; MA, Harvard U., 1947, MPA, 1948, PhD, 1950; LLD or DHL (hon.), St. Bonaventure Coll., U. Pitts., 1965, Bklyn. Poly. Inst., 1966, Princeton U., 1969, Rhode Island Coll., U. Mass., 1970, Worcester Poly. Inst., 1971, U. Maine, 1972, Hokkaido U., Japan, 1975, North Adams Coll., 1977, Boston U., 1978, Stonehill Coll., 1979. Assoc. dir. Fla. Legis. Reference Bur., Tallahassee, 1949-51; mgmt. orgn. expert U.S. Bur. Budget, Washington, 1951-54; lectr. govt. Harvard U., 1953-54, asst. prof., 1954-57; asst. prof. polit. sci. MIT, 1957-59, assoc. prof., 1959-62, prof., 1962-66, head dept., 1965-66, 69-70; undersec. HUD, Washington, 1966-68; sec. HUD, 1969; chmn. Mass. Bay Transp. Authority, Boston, 1969-70; dir. Harvard U.-MIT Joint Center for Urban Studies, Cambridge, 1969-70; pres. U. Mass., 1970-77; supt. Boston Public Schs., 1978-80; prof. U. Mass., Boston, 1981-83; Henry Luce prof. Dem. Instns. and the Social Order Wesleyan U., Middletown, Conn., 1983-93, John E. Andrus prof. govt., 1993; prof. emeritus U. Mass., Boston, 1994—; sr. fellow McCormack Inst. Pub. Affairs, U. Mass., Boston. Author: Suburbia, Its People and Their Politics, 1958, Metropolis Against Itself, 1959, 1400 Governments, The Political Economy of the New York Region, 1960, The Necessary Majority, Middle America and Urban Crisis, 1972, Whatever Possessed the President? Academic Experts and Presidential Policy, 1960-88, 1993; (with others) Schoolmen and Politics, 1962, Government and Politics of the U.S, 1965; author, editor: Remedial Law: When Courts Become Administrators, 1990. Trustee Coll. Bd., 1979-83, Kettering Found., 1971-76; mem. Commn. on Acad. Health Ctrs. and Economy New Eng.; bd. dirs. Lincoln Inst. Land Policy, 1976-80; chmn. Inst. for Resource Mgmt., 1982-84, 20th Century Task Force Fed. Ednl. Policy, 1983, Conn. Gov.'s Coalition on Adult Literacy, 1986-89; mem. Gov.'s Commn. on Quality and Integrated Edn., 1989-90. Served with inf. AUS, World War II, ETO. Decorated Bronze Star; recipient Hubert H. Humphrey award, 1985. Fellow Am. Acad. Arts and Scis., Am. Polit. Sci. Assn. (Career Achievmenet award 1989), Cosmos Club Washington, Phi Beta Kappa.

WOOD, ROBERT ELKINGTON, II, financial services company executive; b. Houston, May 7, 1938; s. Robert Whitney and Elizabeth Cushing (Neville) W.; m. Susan Mayer, Jan. 5, 1963; children: Katherine Hardwick, Elizabeth Neville. BA, Princeton U., 1960. Various merchandising and oper. positions Sears, Roebuck & Co., Chgo., 1960-78, various other positions, 1978-85; chmn., chief oper. officer Sears Consumer Fin. Corp. (subs. Dean Witter), Riverwoods, Ill., 1985-88; sr. exec. v.p., chief adminstrv. officer Dean Witter Fin. Svcs. Group (subs. Sears, Roebuck & Co.), N.Y.C., 1988—; exec. v.p. mktg & advertising Dean Witter Fin Svcs Group, Riverwoods, Ill.; Trustee Chgo. Dock and Canal Trust, 1985—. Trustee Lyric Opera Chgo., 1980—, Hull House Assn., Chgo., 1972-78, Rehab. Inst. Chgo., 1982—. Republican. Episcopalian. Home: 1430 N Lake Shore Dr Chicago IL 60610-1627 Office: Dean Witter Fin Svcs Group 2500 Lake Cook Rd Ste 600 South Riverwoods IL 60015

WOOD, ROBERT EMERSON, pediatrics educator; b. Jacksonville, Fla., Nov. 15, 1942; s. Waldo E. and Verda V. (von Hagen) W. BS in Chemistry magna cum laude, Stetson U., 1963; PhD in Physiology, Vanderbilt U., 1968, MD, 1970. Bd. cert. pediatrics; bd. cert. pediatric pulmonology. Intern in pediatrics Duke U. Med. Ctr., Durham, 1970-71, resident in pediatrics, 1971-72; fellow pediatric pulmonology Case Western Res. U., Cleve., 1974-76, asst. prof. pediatrics, 1976-82, assoc. prof. pediatrics, 1982-83; assoc. prof. pediatrics, chief divsn. pediatric pulmonary medicine Dept. Pediatrics, U. N.C., Chapel Hill, 1983-88, prof. pediatrics, chief divsn. pediatric pulmonary medicine, 1988—; dir. pediat. ICU, 1984-86, dir. Ctr. Pediat. Bronchology, 1994—. Mem. editorial bd.: Pediatric Pulmonology, 1992—, Jour. Bronchology, 1993—; contbr. chpts. to books and articles to profl. jours. Lt. comdr. USPHS, 1972-74. Named Grad. fellow Danforth Found., 1963-68, Med. Scientist fellow Life Ins. Med. Rsch. Found., 1965-70, Clin. Rsch. fellow Cystic Fibrosis Found., 1974-76. Mem. Am. Bronchesophagological Assn., Am. Assn. for Bronchology, Soc. for Pediatric Rsch., Am. Thoracic Soc., N.C. Pediatric Soc. Office: U NC CB # 7220 Pediat Pulmonary Medicine Chapel Hill NC 27599-7220

WOOD, ROBERT WINFIELD, retired science administrator, biophysicist; b. Detroit, Mich., Dec. 31, 1931. BS, U. Detroit, 1953; MA, Vanderbilt U., 1955; PhD Biophysics, Cornell U., 1961. Sci. fellow Nat. Inst. Gen. Medicine, 1961-62; radiation physicist AEC, 1962-73; dir. phys. and tech. rsch. divsn.Office of Health and Environmental Rsch. U.S. Dept. Energy, Washington, 1973-91, dir. med. applications and biophysics dvsn., 1991-94. Recipient Presidential Meritorious Rank award, 1990, Meritorious Svc. award Dept. Energy, 1990. Mem. Health Physics Soc., Radiation Rsch. Soc., Sigma Chi. Office: Office Health & Environ Rsch U S Dept Energy Mail Stop Er # 70 Gtn Washington DC 20585

WOOD, RONALD, musician; b. London, June 1, 1947. Owner Woody's on the Beach (nightclub), Miami, 1987—. Guitarist and bassist with Jeff Beck Group, 1966-69, Faces, 1969-75, Rolling Stones, 1975—, New Barbarians, 1979; solo albums include Gimme Some Neck, 1979; albums (with Rolling Stones) Black and Blue, 1976, Love You Live, 1977, Some Girls, 1978, Sucking in the Seventies, 1981, Emotional Rescue, 1979, Tattoo You, 1981, Still Life, 1982, Undercover, 1983, Between the Sheets, 1985, Dirty Work, 1986, Rewind, 1986, Steel Wheels, 1988, Flashpoint, 1991, Voodoo Lounge, 1994 (Grammy award Best Rock Album); (with Faces) Long Player, A Nod's As Good As A Wink..., To a Blind Horse, Ooh-La-La; (with Small Faces) First Step, Ogden's Nut Gone Flake, There Are But Four Small Faces, 1991, All or Nothing, 1992; (solo) I've Got My Own Album To Do, Now Look; films include Let's Spend the Night Together, 1982, Digital Dreams, 1983. *

WOOD, RUTH DIEHM, artist, design consultant; b. Cleve., July 31, 1916; d. Ellis Raymond and Frances Helen (Peshek) Diehm; m. Kenneth Anderson Wood, Sept. 14, 1937. Student, Spencerian Bus. Coll., 1935-36, John Huntington Inst., 1936, Cleve. Inst. Art, 1934-37, 45. Legal sec. Klein, Diehm & Farber, Attys., Cleve., 1936-37; freelance graphic designer Bailey Meter Co., Wickliffe, Ohio, 1967; interior design cons., lectr. One-woman shows include Artist & Craftsmen Assn., Cleve., 1949, Art Colony, Cleve., 1953, Women's City Club, Cleve., 1955, Cleve. Inst. Art Alumni, 1954, Malvina Freedson Gallery, Lakewood, Ohio, 1965, Intown Club, Cleve., 1953, Studio Inn, Painesville, Ohio, 1955, Little Gallery, Chesterland, Ohio, 1961, Hospitality Inn, Willoughby, Ohio, 1965, Coll. Club Cleve., 1965, Lakeland Community Coll., Mentor, Ohio, 1979, Holden Arboretum, Mentor, 1981, Fairmount Fine Arts Ctr., Russell, Ohio, 1992; represented in 12 nat. juried shows, 28 regional and local mus., many pvt. collections. Recipient 1st prize Oil Still Life, Cleve. Mus. Art, 1945, Grumbacher Merit award Lakeland Fla. Internat., 1952, Artistic Achievement award Gates Mills, 1973, numerous other awards; certs. of award in Nyumon and Shoden, Ikenobo Sch. Floral Art, Kyoto, Japan. Mem. Cleve. Inst. Art Alumni, Artists and Craftsmen, Geauga Artists, Women in the Arts. Republican. Mem. Seventh-Day Adventist. Avocations: travel, ikenobo floral art. Home and Studio: Kenwood Designers 11950 Sperry Rd Chesterland OH 44026-2225

WOOD, SAMUEL EUGENE, college administrator, psychology educator; b. Brotherton, Tenn., Aug. 16, 1934; s. Samuel Ernest and Daisy J. (Jernigan) W.; m. Helen J. Walker, June 2, 1956; children: Liane Wood Kelly, Susan Wood Benson, Alan Richard; m. Ellen Rosenthal Green, Sept. 8, 1977; stepchildren: Bart M. Green, Julie Alice Green. BS in English and Music, Tenn. Tech. U., 1961; M in Edn. Adminstrn., U. Fla., 1967, D in Edn., 1969. Asst. prof. edn. W.Va. U., 1968-70; asst. prof. edn. U. Mo., St. Louis, 1970-75, mem. doctoral faculty, 1973-75; dir. rsch. Ednl. Devel. Ctr., Belleville, Ill., 1976-81; prof. psychology Meramec Coll., St. Louis, 1981-94; pres. Higher Edn. Ctr., St. Louis, 1985—; prof. psychology Lindenwood Coll., 1995—; exec. dir. Edn. Opportunity Ctrs., St. Louis, 1985—, Project Talent Search, St. Louis, 1991—; bd. commrs. Pub. TV Com., St. Louis, 1985—; planning com. St. Louis Schs., 1985-90; adminstr. German-Am. student exch. program Internat. Bus. Students, 1985—; sponsor Higher Edn. Ctr. Internat. Edn. Coun., 1985—; co-founder, pres. Higher Edn. Cen. Cable TV Channel, Sta. HEC-TV, St. Louis, 1986; v.p. St. Louis County Cable TV Commn., 1991—. Musician, composer with USN Band, 1956-59; composer A Nautical Musical Comedy, A Child's Garden of Verses in Song, 1979; numerous poems set to music; co-author: (with Ellen Green Wood) (textbook) The World of Psychology, 1993, 2d edit., 1996, Can. edit., 1996; contbr. articles to ednl. and sci. jours. Served with USN, 1955-59. US Office Edn. grantee 1976-81, 85—. Mem. Internat. Edn. Consortium (bd. dirs. 1985-91), Phi Kappa Phi. Democrat. Baptist. Avocations: writing, reading, music composition and performance. Home: 5 Sona Ln Saint Louis MO 63141-7742 Office: Higher Edn Ctr 8420 Delmar Blvd Ste 504 Saint Louis MO 63124-2180

WOOD, SHARON, mountaineer; b. Halifax, N.S., Can., May 18, 1957; d. Stan and Peggy Wood. LLD (hon.), U. Calgary, 1987. Climbed peaks Mt. McKinley (Alaska), Mt. Logan (Can.), Mt. Aconcagua (Argentina), Mt. Makalu (Himalayas), Mt. Everest (Himalayas, 1st N.Am. woman to climb); Can. Light Everest Expedition, 1986; lectr. in field. Recipient Tenzing Norgay Trophy, 1987. Address: Box 1482, Canmore, AB Canada T0L 0M0

WOOD, STEPHEN, minister. Dir. Native Am. Ministry Dist. of the Christian and Missionary Alliance. Office: 10454 S Hyacinth Pl Highlands Ranch CO 80126

WOOD, STEPHEN WRAY, educator, legislator, minister; b. Winston Salem, N.C., Oct. 6, 1948; s. D.W. and Annie Lee (Harris) W.; m. Starr Smith, June 18, 1978; children: Allyson, Joshua. BTh., John Wesley Coll., 1970; BA, Asbury Coll., 1973; MA, U. N.C., 1979; DMin, Luther Rice Sem., Fla., 1980; MDiv, Houston Grad. Sch. Theology, 1990. Ordained to ministry Soc. of Friends, 1980. Asst. dean, asst. prof. John Wesley Coll., High Point, N.C., 1975-81; assoc. pastor Glenwood Friends Ch., Greensboro, N.C., 1979-81; pastor Deep River Friends Ch., High Point, 1981-84, Battle Forest Friends, 1986-92; adj. prof. Luther Rice Sem.; assoc. prof. Houston Grad. Sch. Theology; pres. Triad Christian Counseling, Greensboro, 1979. Contbr. articles to religious jours., Dictionary of N.C. Biography; composer, singer religious music. Trustee John Wesley Coll., High Point, 1981—; bd. dirs. Friends Ctr.-Guilford Coll., Greensboro, 1982-89; vice chmn. Guilford County Rep. Party, N.C., 1981-85; mem. N.C. State Ho. Reps., 1985-86, 89-90, 90-91, 92-93, 94-95; chaplain High Point Jaycees. With U.S. Army, 1970-71; capt. N.C. State Militia. Mem. BMI (affiliate songwriter 1978—). Avocations: golf, book collecting, reading. Office: PO Box 5172 High Point NC 27262 *I often reflect upon the maternal advice proffered me as a child, "Steve, if at first you don't succeed, try, try again." We may be down but not out. There is no such thing as the good old days because the future is just as bright as the promises of God. We conquer by continuing.*

WOOD, THOMAS E., lawyer; b. L.A., Apr. 20, 1939; s. Louis Earl and Youda (Hays) W.; m. Sally Ann, June 22, 1963; children: Julia E. and Melissa H. BA, Amherst Coll., 1961; LLB, U. Pa., 1966. Bar: Pa. 1966. Assoc. Drinker Biddle & Reath, Phila., 1966-72, ptnr., 1972—. Chmn. Easttown Zoning Hearing Bd., Easttown Twp., Pa., 1976—. Mem. Phila. Club. Office: Drinker Biddle & Reath 1000 Westlakes Dr Ste 300 Berwyn PA 19312-2409

WOOD, VIVIAN POATES, mezzo soprano, educator, author; b. Washington, Aug. 19, 1923; d. Harold Poates and Mildred Georgette (Patterson) W.; studies with Walter Anderson, Antioch Coll., 1953-55, Denise Restout, Saint-Leu-La-Fôret, France and Lakeville, Conn., 1960-62, 64-70, Paul A. Pisk, 1968-71, Paul Ulanowsky, N.Y.C., 1958-68, Elemer Nagy, 1965-68, Vyautas Marijosius, 1967-68; MusB Hartt Coll. Music, 1968; postgrad. (fellow) Yale U., 1968; MusM (fellow), Washington U., St. Louis, 1971, PhD (fellow), 1973. Debut in recital series Internat. Jeunesse Musicals Arts Festival, 1953, solo fellowship Boston Symphony Orch., Berkshire Music Ctr., Tanglewood, 1964, St. Louis Symphony Orch., 1969, Washington Orch., 1949, Bach Cantata Series Berkshire Chamber Orch., 1964, Yale Symphony Orch., 1968; appearances in U.S. and European recitals, oratorios, operas, radio and TV, 1953-68; appeared as soloist in Internat. Harpsichord Festival, Westminister Choir Coll., Princeton, N.J., 1973; appeared as soloist in meml. concert, Landowska Ctr., Lakeville, 1969; prof. voice U. So. Miss., Hattiesburg, 1971—, asst. dean Coll. Fine Arts, 1974-76, acting dean, 1976-77; guest prof. Hochschule für Musik, Munich, 1978-79; prof. Italian Internat. Studies Program, Rome, 1986; Miss. coord. Alliance for Arts Edn., Kennedy Ctr. Performing Arts, 1974—; mem. Miss. Gov.'s Adv. Panel for Gifted and Talented Children, 1974—; mem. 1st Miss. Gov.'s Conf. on the Arts, 1974—; bd. dirs. Miss. Opera Assn. Author: Polenc's Songs: An Analysis of Style, 1971. Recipient Young Am. Artists Concert award N.Y.C., 1955; Wanda Landowska fellow, 1968-72. Mem. Miss. Music Tchrs. Assn., Nat. Assn. Tchrs. of Singing, Music Tchrs. Nat. Assn., Am. Musicology Soc., Golden Key, Mu Phi Epsilon, Delta Kappa Gamma, Tau Beta Kappa (hon.), Pi Kappa Lambda. Democrat. Episcopalian. Avocation: sailing. Office: U So Miss Sch Music South Pt # 8264 Hattiesburg MS 39406-9539

WOOD, WAYNE W., state legislator; b. Janesville, Wis., Jan. 21, 1930. Grad. high sch., Janesville. Formerly builder, contractor, factory worker; mem. Janesville City Coun., 1972-76, pres., 1974-75; mem. Wis. Ho. of Reps., Madison, 1976—; mem. criminal justice and corrections com., rules com., ways and means com., 1985—, vice chmn., 1989-95, mem. state affairs com., 1987—. Mem. State VTAE Bd., 1975-76; mem. Coun. of State Govts. Legis. Oversight Task Force, 1983, Janesville Housing Authority, 1971-77; former mem. Children's Svc. Soc. Adv. Bd., Rock County Sr. 4-H Coun., Sinnissippi Coun. Boy Scouts Am. Mem. UAW. Home: 2429 Rockport Rd Janesville WI 53545-4445

WOOD, WENDY DEBORAH, filmmaker; b. N.Y.C., Oct. 4, 1940; d. John Meyer and Marion Emily (Peters) W.; m. William Dismore Chapple, Dec. 7, 1963; 1 child, Samuel Eliot. BA cum laude, Vassar Coll., 1962; MA, Stanford U., 1964. Teaching asst. Stanford U., 1962-64; photographer, film editor Bristol (Eng.) U., 1964-66, asst. dir. Internat. Conf. Film Schs., 1966; rsch. asst. biology dept. U. Conn., Storrs, 1970-72; sr. media specialist Aetna Life & Casualty Co., Hartford, Conn., 1972-89; media writer, prodr., dir. U. Conn. Ctr. for Media and Tech., Storrs., 1989—; pres. Chapple Films, Inc., 1972—. Films include: Yankee Craftsman, 1972; Alcoholism, Industry's Costly Hangover, 1974; Draggerman's Haul, 1975; Flight Without Wings, 1977; Auto Insurance Affordability (2 awards), 1981; Where Rivers Run to the Sea (award), 1981; Our Town is Burning Down (6 awards), 1982; Wellness at the Worksite, 1984 (4 awards); Welcome to the Aetna Institute, 1985 (4 awards); Aenhance, 1989 (3 awards). Mem. peer rev. com. Conn. Commn. Higher Edn, 1992—. Recipient CINE Golden Eagle award Council on Internat. Non-theatrical Events, 1972, 76, 84, 1st Place award Indsl. Photography, 1974, cert. Outstanding Creativity U.S. TV Commls. Festival, 1974, EFLA award Am. Film Festival, 1974, 76, Dir's. Choice award Sinking Creek Film Festival, 1975, award Columbus Film Festival, 1975, award Excellence Life Ins. Advtrs. Assn., 1975, Silver Screen award U.S. Indsl. Film Festival, 1976, 81, 1st place award Conn. Film Festival, 1977, 1st prize Nat. Outdoor Travel Film Festival, 1978, 1st pl. Houston Film Festival, 1982, CINE Golden Eagle, 1982, 84, award Am. Film Festival, 1982, N.Y. Film Festival, 1982, 83, Silver CINDY award Assn. Visual Communicators, 1985, others. Bd. dirs. Windham Regional Arts Council, 1987, 88, 89; mem. jury N.Y. Internat. Video and Film Festival. Mem. Info. Film Producers Am. (nat. dir., pres. chpt. 1981-82, Cindy award 1971, 72, 81, 82, 85, 87), Internat. Quorum Motion Picture Producers, Audio Visual Communicators (pres. Conn. chpt. 1985, treas. 1988). Democrat. Quaker. Home: 604 Phoenixville Rd Chaplin CT 06235-2211 Office: U Conn Media Ctr # U-1 Storrs CT 06269

WOOD, WILLIAM JEROME, lawyer; b. Indpls., Feb. 14, 1928; s. Joseph Gilmore and Anne Cecilia (Morris) W.; m. Joann Janet Jones, Jan. 23, 1954; children: Steven, Matthew, Kathleen, Michael, Joseph, James, Julie, David. Student, Butler U., 1945-46; AB with honors, Ind. U., 1950, JD with distinction, 1952. Bar: Ind. bar 1952. Mem. firm Wood, Tuohy, Gleason, Mercer & Herrin (and predecessor), Indpls., 1952—; bd. dirs. Grain Dealers Mut. Ins. Co., Indpls., Am. Income Life Ins. Co., Waco, Tex.; gen. counsel Ind. Cath. Conf.; city atty., Indpls., 1959-60; instr. Ind. U. Sch. Law, 1960-62. Author: Indiana Pastors' Legal Handbook, 2nd edit., 1992, Realtors' Indiana Legal Handbook, 2d edit., 1991. Mem. Ind. Corp. Survey Commn., 1963—, chmn., 1977-86; mem. Ind. Corp. Law Study Commn., 1985-87; mem. Ind. Non Profit Corp. Law Study Commn., 1989-91; past bd. dirs. Alcoholic Rehab. Center, Indpls., Indpls. Lawyers' Commn., Community Svc. Coun. Indpls. Served with AUS, 1946-48. Recipient Brotherhood award Ind. region NCCJ, 1973. Mem. Ind. Bar Assn. (award 1968, sec. 1977-78), Indpls. Bar Assn. (pres. 1972-73, coun. bd. mgrs. 1992-93), Indpls. Bar Found., St. Thomas More Legal Soc. (pres. 1970), Indpl. Lit. Club (pres. 1973-74). Democrat. Roman Catholic. Home: 3619 E 75th Pl Indianapolis IN 46240-3674 Office: 3400 Bank One Ctr Tower Indianapolis IN 46204-5134

WOOD, WILLIS BOWNE, JR., utility holding company executive; b. Kansas City, Mo., Sept. 15, 1934; s. Willis Bowne Sr. and Mina (Henderson) W.; m. Dixie Gravel, Aug. 31, 1955; children: Bradley, William, Josh. BS in Petroleum Engring., U. Tulsa, 1957; grad. advanced mgmt. program, Harvard U., 1983; JD (hon.), Pepperdine U., 1996. Various positions So. Calif. Gas Co., L.A., 1960-74, v.p. then sr. v.p., 1975-80, exec. v.p., 1983-84; pres., CEO Pacific Lighting Gas Supply Co., L.A., 1981-83; sr. v.p. Pacific Enterprises, L.A., 1984-85, exec. v.p., 1985-89, pres., 1989-91, pres., CEO, 1991-92, chmn., pres., CEO, 1992-93, chmn., CEO, 1993—; bd. dirs. Gt. Western Fin. Corp., Gt. Western Bank, L.A.; dir. Automobile Club So. Calif.; trustee U. So. Calif.; bd. visitors Rand Grad. Sch. Trustee, vice chmn. Harvey Mudd Coll., Claremont, Calif., 1984—; trustee, chmn. Calif. Med. Ctr. Found., L.A., 1983—; trustee, past pres. S.W. Mus., L.A., 1983—; bd. dirs. L.A. World Affairs Coun.; dir., past chmn. bus. coun. for Sustainable Energy Future, 1994—. Mem. Soc. Petroleum Energy Engrs., Am. Gas Assn., Pacific Coast Gas Assn. (past bd. dirs.), Pacific Energy Assn., Calif.

Bus. Roundtable, Calif. State C. of C. (bd. dirs.), Nat. Assn. of Mfrs. (bd. dirs.), Hacienda Golf CLub, Ctr. Club, Calif. Club. Republican. Office: Pacific Enterprises 633 E 5th St Ste 5400 Los Angeles CA 90013-2109

WOODALL, DAVID MONROE, research engineer; b. Perryville, Ark., Aug. 2, 1945; m. Linda Carol Page, June 6, 1966; 1 child, Zachary Page. B.A., Hendrix Coll., 1967; M.S., Columbia U., 1968; Ph.D., Cornell U., 1974. Registered profl. engr., N.Mex. Nuclear engr. Westinghouse Corp., Pitts., 1968-70; asst. prof. U. Rochester, N.Y., 1974-77; asst. prof. U. N.Mex., Albuquerque, 1977-79, assoc. prof., 1979-83, prof., 1984-86, chair dept., 1980-83; group physics mgr. Idaho Nat. Engring. Lab., Idaho Falls, 1986-92; cons. to govt. Contbr. articles to sci. jours. Grantee NSF, Office Naval Research, others. Mem. Am. Phys. Soc., Am. Nuclear Soc. (chpt. chair 1982-83), IEEE. Office: Univ Idaho Engring Expt Station Coll Engring Moscow ID 83844-1011

WOODALL, JACK DAVID, manufacturing company executive; b. Ferndale, Mich., Aug. 1, 1936; s. William John and Florence Gladys (Feyen) W.; m. Janice Tracy Lanier, July 6, 1958; children: David Lanier, Kevin Langford, Elizabeth Tracy, Matthew Thomas. BS in Bus., Stetson U., 1958; MS in Internat. Affairs, George Washington U., 1969. Commd. 2d lt. U.S. Army, 1958, advanced through grades to lt. gen., 1989; comdr. 1st Brigade, 2d Inf. Div., Camp Casey, Republic of Korea, 1978-79; chief officer distbn. Mil. Pers. Ctr., Alexandria, Va., 1979-81, dir. plans and ops., 1981-82; chief plans and policy Allied Forces So. Europe, Naples, Italy, 1982-84; asst. div. comdr. 4th Inf. Div., Colorado Springs, Colo., 1984-86; comdg. gen. Berlin Brigade, 1986-87; dep. comdg. gen. V Corps, Frankfurt, Fed. Republic Germany, 1987-88; comdg. gen. 2d Inf. Div., Camp Casey, Korea, 1988-89, U.S. Army Japan, IX Corps, Camp Zama, 1989-92; pres. Innovative Tech., Brooksville, Fla., 1992—. V.p. West Pacific Girl Scouts Japan, Republic of Korea, The Philippines, 1989-92, Far East coun. Boy Scouts Am., 1990-92. Recipient Disting. Alumni award Stetson Alumni Assn., 1985, numerous mil. awards. Mem. Assn. U.S. Army (chpt. pres. 1986-88), Greater Hernando County C. of C. (dir.), Barnett Banks of the Sun Coast (dir.). Avocation: jogging.

WOODALL, LEE, professional football player; b. Carlisle, Pa., Oct. 31, 1969. Student, U. Pa. Linebacker San Francisco 49'ers, 1994—. Selected to Pro Bowl, 1994. Achievements include member of San Francisco 49'ers Super Bowl XXIX Champions, 1994. Office: San Francisco 49'ers 4949 Centennial Blvd Santa Clara CA 95054

WOODALL, LOWERY A., hospital administrator; b. Lincoln County, Miss., June 10, 1929; s. Clem and Ruth (Smith) W.; m. Pat Pack; children: Linda Woodall Sullivan, Lowery A., Margaret Michelle Rowell. BS, U. So. Miss., 1951; postgrad. Baylor U., 1956, U. Chgo., 1959. Bus. mgr. Miss. Bapt. Hosp., Jackson, 1953-56, adminstrv. asst., 1956-58, asst. adminstr., 1958-62; exec. dir. Forrest Gen. Hosp., Hattiesburg, Miss., 1962—; dir. Blue Cross/Blue Shield, Jackson, 1975—, Hattiesburg Community Blood Ctr.; pres., dir. AAA Ambulance Service, Inc., 1967—; past chmn. Southeastern Hosp. Conf. 11-state, 1981-82, Miss. Hosp. Assn., Jackson, 1970-71. Bd. dirs. Indsl. Park Commn., Hattiesburg, 1981—; mem. Forrest County Indsl. Bd., Hattiesburg, 1972—, pres. 1972-73. Named Exec. of Yr., Sales and Mktg. Assn., 1977, Profl. Secs. Internat., 1981; Hub award Community Leaders, 1981; Liberty award South Central Miss. Bar Assn., 1982; recipient Disting. Svc. Award for Excellence, Southeastern Hosp. Conf., 1992. Fellow Am. Coll. Hosp. Adminstrs. Baptist. Lodge: Rotary (pres. 1978-79). Home: 1 Bristol Ln Hattiesburg MS 39402-2368 Office: Forrest Gen Hosp PO Box 16389 Hattiesburg MS 39404-6389

WOODALL, SAMUEL ROY, JR., trade association executive; b. July 8, 1936; s. Samuel Roy W.; m. Jane Marvin Brock, Aug. 5, 1958; children—Samuel Roy III, Lawrence B., Claiborne A., George G. B.A., U. Ky., 1958, LL.B., 1962; postgrad. (Woodrow Wilson fellow), Yale U., 1959. Bar: Ky. bar 1962. Atty. Ky. Dept. Ins., 1962-64, gen. counsel, 1965-66; commr. ins. Commonwealth Ky., 1966-68; assoc. firm Wyatt, Grafton and Sloss, Louisville, 1968-69; ptnr. Wyatt, Grafton and Sloss, 1969-72; pres. Western Pioneer Life Ins. Co. (and predecessors), Louisville, 1972-76; asst. to pres. Am. Life & Accident Ins. Co., Louisville, 1976-80; pres. Nat. Assn. Life Cos., Washington, 1980-93; v.p. and chief counsel state rels. Am. Coun. Life Ins., Washington, 1993—; guest instr. ins. law U. Louisville, 1968-69. Note editor: U. Ky. Law Rev, 1961-62. Pres. Citizen's Met. Planning Council, Louisville, 1970-71; chmn. City of Louisville Riverfront Commn., 1970-75, Ky. Heritage Commn., 1964-77; bd. dirs. Bingham Child Guidance Clinic, Louisville, 1969-76, Youth Performing Arts Council, 1979-80. Recipient Sullivan medallion U. Ky., 1958; named 1 of Ky.'s 3 Outstanding Young Men Ky. Jr. C. of C., 1968. Mem. ABA, Ky. Bar Assn., D.C. Bar Assn., Fedn. Ins. Counsel, Phi Beta Kappa, Phi Alpha Delta (pres. chpt. 1961-62). Home: 2851 29th St NW Washington DC 20008-4111 Office: Am Coun Life Ins 1001 Pennsylvania Ave NW Washington DC 20004-2505

WOODALL, WILLIAM LEON, retired insurance executive; b. Kirby, Ark., July 29, 1923; s. Ocie Doan and Hazel Cornelia (Paslay) W.; m. Patricia Ann Reese, Sept. 30, 1950; children: Michael Reese, David William, Stacy Ann. BS, Miami U., Oxford, Ohio, 1947. CPCU. Home office underwriter Ohio Casualty Group Ins. Cos., Hamilton, 1947-52, underwriter Mpls. br. office, 1952-53, field rep., Des Moines, 1953-54, underwriter Detroit br. office, 1962-64, mgr. Indpls. br. office, 1964-68, company v.p., Hamilton, 1968-77, sr. v.p., 1977-84, exec. v.p., sec., 1984-88, pres., chief oper. officer, 1988-91, also bd. dirs.; ptnr. Cady Ins. Agy., Burlington, Iowa, 1954-62. Republican. Methodist. Lodge: Elks. Home: 910 Macewen Dr Osprey FL 34229-9293

WOODARD, ALFRE, actress; b. Tulsa, Nov. 8, 1953; m. Roderick Spencer; 2 adopted children. Student, Boston U. Appeared in (films) Remember My Name, 1976, Health, Cross Creek, 1983 (Acad. award nomination), Extremities, 1986, Scrooged, 1988, Mandela, 1988, Miss Firecracker, 1989, Grand Canyon, 1991, The Gun in Betty Lou's Handbag, 1992, Passion Fish, 1992, Heart and Souls, 1993, Rich in Love, 1993, Bopha!, 1993, Blue Chips, 1994, Crooklyn, 1994, How to Make an American Quilt, 1995, (TV series) Tucker's Witch, 1982-83, Sara, 1985, St. Elsewhere, 1985-87, Hill Street Blues (Emmy award for guest appearance in drama series 1984), L.A. Law (Emmy award for guest appearance in drama series 1987), (TV spls.) For Colored Girls Who Have Considered Suicide/When the Rainbow is Enuf, Trial of the Moke, Words by Heart, (TV films) A Mother's Courage: The Mary Thomas Story, Child Saver, Ambush Murder, Freedom Road, 1979, Sophisticated Gents, 1981, The Killing Floor, Unnatural Causes, 1986, Mandela, 1987, The Child Saver, Sweet Revenge, 1990, Blue Bayou, 1990, Bopho, 1993, (plays) For Colored Girls Who Have Considered Suicide, When the Rainbow is Enuf, (off-Broadway plays) A Map of the World, 1985, A Winter's Tale 1989, So Nice They Named Twice, Horatio. Recipient Emmy awards for guest appearance in drama series. Office: ICM 8942 Wilshire Blvd Beverly Hills CA 90211-1934*

WOODARD, ALVA ABE, business consultant; b. Roy, N.Mex., June 28, 1928; s. Joseph Benjamin and Emma Lurania (Watkins) W.; m. Esther Josepha Kaufmann, Apr. 5, 1947 (div. Sept. 1991); children: Nannette, Gregory, Loreen, Arne, Mark, Kevin, Steven, Curtis, Marlee, Julie, Michelle; m. Margaret Adele Evenson, Oct. 1, 1994. Student, Kinman Bus. U., 1948-49, Whitworth Coll., 1956, Wash. State U., 1953-54. Sec.-treas., dir. Green Top Dairy Farms, Inc., Clarkston, Wash., 1948-52; v.p., treas., sec., dir. ASC Industries, Inc. (subs. Gifford-Hill and Co.), Spokane, Wash., 1953-75; dir. Guenther Irrigation, Inc., Pasco, Wash., 1966-71; mng. dir. Irrigation Rental, Inc., Pasco, 1968-75, Rain Chief Irrigation Co., Grand Island, Nebr., 1968-75; sec., dir. Keeling Supply Co., Little Rock, 1969-72; pres., dir. Renters, Inc., Salt Lake City, 1971-75, Woodard Western Corp., Spokane, 1976-86, Woodard Industries, Inc., Auburn, Wash., 1987-90; cons. Woodard Assocs., Spokane, Wash., 1985—; pres., dir. TFI Industries, inc., Post Falls, Idaho, 1989-90; v.p., sec., treas., dir. Trans-Force, Inc., Post Falls, 1989-90, TFI Computer Scis., Inc., Post Falls, 1989-90. Newman Lake (Wash.) Rep. precinct committeeman, 1964-80; Spokane County del. Wash. Rep. Conv., 1968-80. Mem. Adminstrv. Mgmt. Soc. (bd. dirs. 1966-68), Optimists. Avocations: fishing, theater, golf, reading, dancing. Home and Office: 921 E 39th Ave Spokane WA 99203

WOODARD, CAROL JANE, educational consultant; b. Buffalo, Jan. 19, 1929; d. Harold August and Violet Maybelle (Landsittel) Young; m. Ralph Arthur Woodard, Aug. 19, 1950; children—Camaron Jane, Carsen Jane, Cooper Ralph. BA, Hartwick Coll., 1950; MA, Syracuse U., 1952; PhD, SUNY, Buffalo, 1972; LHD (hon.), Hartwick Coll., 1991; postgrad., Bank St. Coll., Harvard U. Cert. tchr., N.Y. State. Tchr. Orchard Park, N.Y., 1950-51, Danville, Ind., 1951-52, Akron, N.Y., 1952-54; dir. Garden Nursery Sch., Williamsville, N.Y., 1955-65; tchr. Amherst (N.Y.) Coop. Nursery Sch., 1967-69; asst. prof. early childhood edn. SUNY, Buffalo, 1969-72; lab. demonstration tchr. and student teaching supr. SUNY, 1969-76, assoc. prof., 1972-79, prof., 1979-88, prof. emeritus, 1988—; co-dir. Consultants in Early Childhood, 1988—; cons. Lutheran Ch. Am., Villa Maria Coll., Buffalo Pub. Schs., Buffalo Mus. Sci., Headstart Tng. Programs, Erie Community Coll., N.Y. State Dept. Edn., numerous workshops.; cons. sch. systems, indsl. firms, pubs., civic orgns. in child devel.; vis. prof. The Netherlands and East China Univ., Shanghai, People's Republic of China; sci. trainer The Wright Group, 1995. Author 7 books for young children, 2 textbooks in field; co-author: Physical Science in Early Childhood, 1987; co-author nat. curriculum for ch. sch. for 3-yr.-olds; author: (booklet) You Can Help Your Baby Learn; author/coord. TAKE CARE child protection project, 1987; contbr. chpts. to books, articles to profl. jours. Trustee Hartwick Coll., Oneonta, N.Y., 1978-87; cons. EPIC Birth to Three Program, 1992; design cons. indoor playground Noah's Ark Jewish Ctr., Buffalo, 1992; sites project coord. Buffalo Pub. Schs., 1994-96; student tchg. supervisor SUNY, Fredonia, 1994—. Mem. Nat. Assn. Edn. Young Children, Early Childhood Edn. Council Western N.Y., Assn. Childhood Edn. Internat., Phi Delta Kappa, Pi Lambda Theta. Home: 1776 Sweet Rd East Aurora NY 14052-3028

WOODARD, CLARA VERONICA, nursing home official; b. Bayonne, N.J.; d. William George and Lula (Langston) Yelverton; m. John Henry Woodard; children: John Michael, Stephen Jay. Grad., Bayonne Hosp. Sch. Nursing, 1951, Manhattan Sch. Radiology, 1953, NYU-Bellevue Med. Ctr., 1955, Valencia Community Coll., Orlando, Fla. RN, N.J., Fla. Head nurse Bayonne Hosp., 1949-50; office nurse Dr. D.G. Morris, Bayonne, 1951-52; pvt. duty nurse Christ Hosp and Bayonne Hosp., 1954-58; tchr. kindergarten, Nuremburg, Fed. Republic Germany, 1972-73; ICU-CCU nurse Holy Spirit Hosp., Camp Hill, Pa., 1973-74; head nurse Orlando Gen. Hosp., 1974-76, house supr., 1976-78; dir. nurses Winter Park (Fla.) Care Ctr., 1980-83; Medicare coord. Pinar Terrace Manor, Orlando, 1987-92, clin. instr., 1992—, house supr., nurse mgr. Alzheimer unit, 1993—; instr. Valencia Coll., Orlando, Fla. Named Employee of Yr. and Employee of Month, Orlando Gen. Hosp., 1980, Employee of Month, Winter Park Care Ctr., 1983. Mem. NAFE, Nat. League Negro Women. Democrat. Roman Catholic. Avocations: poetry, short stories, public speaking, theology. Home: 2931 De Brocy Way Winter Park FL 32792-4505 Office: Pinar Terrace Manor 7950 Lake Underhill Rd Orlando FL 32822-8229

WOODARD, CLARENCE JAMES, manufacturing company executive; b. Conde, S.D., May 8, 1923; s. Wayne W. and Sarah (Halley) W.; m. Patricia Ann Roberts, Jan. 12, 1946; children—Charles D., Sarah H., Scott D., Thomas J. Student, Stanford U., 1941-43; BS with honors in Mech. Engring, Calif. Inst. Tech., 1944; LHD (hon.), John F. Kennedy U., 1986. Pres. Baldwin-Lima-Hamilton Co., Los Angeles, 1946-53; with Rucker Co., Oakland, Calif., 1953-77, chmn. bd., chief exec. officer, 1965-77; office of chmn., cons. to bd. dirs., dir., mem. audit and fin. coms. NL Industries, Inc., N.Y., 1977-82; pres., chief exec. officer Woodard Industries, Inc., San Francisco, 1982—; chmn. Woodard Found., San Francisco; past chmn. West Coast exec. council Nat. Indsl. Conf. Bd.; past chmn. exec. com., bd. dirs., audit com. Delta Calif. Industries, San Francisco; bd. dirs. Informatics Inc., Los Angeles, Systron Donner Corp., Concord, Calif. Bd. dirs., trustee U. Calif. Sch. Bus. Adminstrn., Berkeley; mem. nat. council Salk Inst., La Jolla, Calif.; vice chmn. bd. regents John F. Kennedy U., Orinda, Calif.; chmn. Calif. Found. for the Retarded, Oakland; life nat. trustee Boys Clubs Am., N.Y.C.; bd. dirs., pres. Oakland Boys Clubs; bd. dirs. Children's Hosp., Oakland; trustee Orinda Found.; bd. dirs., vice chmn. United Way, San Francisco; bd. dirs. exec. com. chmn., chmn. fin. com. San Francisco Mus. Modern Art; donor Woodard treatment rm. St. Luke Hosp., San Francisco. Served to lt. USNR, 1943-46. Endowed Woodard Chair in Mech. Engring. at Stanford U.; Patricia R. Woodard Disting. Lecture Series on Cancer, St. Francis Hosp., San Francisco, donor New Patient Pavilion, Children's Hosp. of Oakland; named Man of Yr., Easter Seal Soc., 1986, Am. Cancer Soc., 1989, Episcopal Charities, 1991. Mem. ASME (life), Am. Petroleum Inst., Inst. Environ. Scis., Tau Beta Pi. Clubs: Pacific Union, St. Francis Yacht, Villa Taverna, Commonwealth (San Francisco); Claremont Country, Lakeview (Oakland); Orinda Country; Les Ambassadeurs (London). Office: PO Box 742 Orinda CA 94563-9999

WOODARD, HAROLD RAYMOND, lawyer; b. Orient, Iowa, Mar. 13, 1911; s. Abram Sylvanus and Grace Lenora (Brown) W.; m. Clara F. Jarrell, Apr. 30, 1986; stepchildren: Walter J., Turner J., Laurel C. BS, Harvard U., 1933, LLB, 1936. Bar: Ind. 1936. Pvt. practice with firm and predecessor Woodard, Emhardt, Naughton, Moriarty & McNett, Indpls., 1936—; lawyer, 1936-46; ptnr. Woodard, Emhardt, Naughton, Moriarty & McNett, Indpls., 1950—; adj. prof. patent law Sch. Law Ind. U., Indpls., 1957-88. Lt. USNR, 1942-46. Named Sagamore of the Wabash, Gov. of Ind., 1991. Fellow Am. Coll. Trial Lawyers; mem. ABA, Ind. 7th Cir. Bar Assn. (past pres.), Am. Patent Law Assn., Lawyers Assn. Indpls. (past pres.), Ind. U. Sch. Law-Indpls. Alumni Assn. (1st hon. mem.), Columbia Club (past pres.), Woodstock Club (past pres.), Univ. Club (past pres.), 100 Club (past pres.). Methodist. Office: Woodard Emhardt Naughton Moriarty & McNett 3700 Bank One Tower Indianapolis IN 46204-5137

WOODARD, JOHN ROGER, urologist; b. Hawkinsville, Ga., Dec. 18, 1932; s. John Alton and Mary Louise (Williams) W.; m. Inga Lou Harper, Sept. 3, 1955; children: John Roger, Susan, Stephen, Honor. Student, Emory U., Atlanta, 1950-53; M.D., Med. Coll. Ga., Augusta, 1957. Diplomate: Am. Bd. Urology. Intern in surgery Med. Coll. Va., 1957-58, resident in surgery, 1958-59; resident in urology N.Y. Hosp.-Cornell Med. Center, 1959-63; postgrad. fellow in pediatric urology Great Ormand St. Hosp. for Sick Children, London, 1963-64; instr. surgery, surgeon to outpatients N.Y. Hosp.-Cornell Med. Center, 1964; asso. in surgery Emory U., 1964-68; asso. prof. surgery U. Ala. Med. Center, 1968-69; prof. urol. surgery, dir. pediatric urology Emory U., 1969—; chief urology Henrietta Egleston Hosp. for Children., 1970—; numerous vis. professorships. Contbr. articles to sci. jours., chpts. to med. textbooks. Fellow ACS (bd. govs. 1986-92), Am. Acad. Pediatrics (chmn. urology sect. 1987-88); mem. AMA, Med. Assn. Atlanta (bd. dirs. 1986-89), Med. Assn. Ga., Soc. Pediatric Urology, Am. Urol. Assn., Am. Assn. Gen. Urol. Surgeons, Soc. Pediatric Urol. Surgeons, Nat. Urol. Forum, Cherokee Town and Country Club. Home: 10 Prescott Walk Atlanta GA 30307 Office: 1901 Century Blvd NE Ste 14 Atlanta GA 30345-3300

WOODARD, JOSEPH LAMAR, law librarian, law educator; b. Auburndale, Fla., Dec. 28, 1937; s. Wilbur Allen and Florence Virginia (Ladd) W.; m. Eleanor Eugenia Cummings, Aug. 7, 1964; children: Robert Edward, James Frederick. BA, U. Fla., 1959, J.D., 1962; MS in Libr. Sci., Columbia U., 1964. Bar: Fla. 1962, U.S. Dist. Ct. (mid. dist.) Fla. 1970. Asst. reference libr. Columbia U., N.Y.C., 1962-64; asst. libr.Cahill, Gordon, Reindel and Ohl, N.Y.C., 1964-65; law libr. Tulane U., 1965-69; ptnr. Schuh, Schuh and Woodard, St. Petersburg, Fla., 1969-71; law librarian Stetson U., 1971—, prof. law, 1979—. Pres. Tampa Bay Library Consortium, 1981, 88-89. Served with USAR, 1957-63. Mem. Fla. Bar, Am. Assn. Law Librs. (sec.-treas. S.E. chpt. 1975-78), Pinellas Pub. Lib. Coop. (sec.-treas. 1993-94, pres. 1994-95). Republican. Presbyterian. Office: 1401 61st St S Saint Petersburg FL 33707-3246

WOODARD, ROBERT E., bishop. Bishop, Ch. of God in Christ, S.E. Tex., Houston.

WOODBERRY, PAUL FRANCIS, real estate executive; b. Boston, Dec. 23, 1927; s. Ronald S. and Elsie E. (Carney) W.; m. Margery Ann Brennan, May 7, 1955; children: Laura, Seth, Lesley, Sarah, Sturgis. B.A., Dartmouth Coll., 1949, M.B.A., 1950. Group exec. W.R. Grace & Co., N.Y.C., 1955-69; pres. Winston Industries, Birmingham, Ala., 1969-70; v.p. Alleghany Corp., N.Y.C., 1970-76, now dir.; exec. v.p. Centex Corp., Dallas, 1976-86; chief fin. officer, exec. v.p., dir. BF Enterprises, Inc., San Francisco, 1986—, also bd. dirs.; cons. Alleghany Corp., 1991—. Bd. dirs. Alleghany Corp., Alleghany Properties Inc., World Minerals, Inc., URC Holdings Co., BF Enterprises, Inc. 1st lt. USAF, 1951-55. Decorated Air medal, Commendation medal. Republican. Roman Catholic. Club: University (N.Y.C.). Home: 1855 Tularosa Rd Lompoc CA 93436-9643 Office: PO Box 639 Lompoc CA 93438

WOODBRIDGE, HENSLEY CHARLES, retired foreign languages educator, librarian; b. Champaign, Ill., Feb. 6, 1923; s. Dudley Warner and Ruby Belle (Mendenhall) W.; m. Annie Emma Smith, Aug. 28, 1953; 1 dau., Ruby Susan Woodbridge Jung. A.B., Coll. William and Mary, 1943; M.A., Harvard, 1946; Ph.D., U. Ill., 1950, M.S. in L.S. 1951; student, U. Nacional de Mexico, summer 1941, 45; D.Arts, Lincoln Meml. U., 1976. Corr. Worldover Press, Mexico, 1945; instr. French and Spanish U. Richmond, 1946-47; teaching asst. U. Ill., 1948-50; reference librarian Ala. Poly. Inst., 1951-53; librarian Murray (Ky.) State Coll., 1953-65; Latin-Am. bibliographer, asso. prof. fin. langs. So. Ill. U., Carbondale, 1965-71, prof., 1971-93, prof. emeritus, 1993—. Author: (with Paul Olson) Tentative Bibliography of Ibero-Romance Linguistics, 1952, Jesse Stuart: a bibliography, 1960, (with Gerald Moser) Rubén Darío y el Cojo ilustrado, 1964, (with John London and George Tweney) Jack London: a bibliography, 1966, rev. edit., 1973, Jesse Stuart and Jane Stuart: a bibliography, 1969, rev. edit., 1979, Rubén Darío: A selective critical bibliography, 1975, Rubén Darío: una bibliografía selectiva, clasificada y anotada, 1975, Benito Pérez Galdós: A selective annotated bibliography, 1975, (with David Zubatsky) Pablo Neruda: An Annotated Bibliography of Biographical and Critical Studies, 1988; co-author: Printing in Colonial Spanish America, 1976; editor Ky. Library Assn. Bull, 1959-60, Ky. Folklore Record, 1963-64, Am. Assn. Tchrs. Spanish and Portuguese-Scarecrow Press Bibliographical Series; contbg. editor: Am. Book Collector, 1965-73; assoc. editor: Hispania, 1967-81; editor, pub.: Jack London Newsletter, 1967-91; mem. editorial bd.: Modern Lang. Jour, 1971-73, Hispanic Linguistics, 1983—; co-editor: (with Dan Newberry) Basic List of Latin American Materials in Spanish, Portuguese and French, 1975; co-compiler: (with Annie Woodbridge) The Collected Short Stories of Mary Johnston, 1982, Spanish and Spanish American Literature: An Annotated Guide to Selected Bibliographies, 1983, Guide to Reference Works for the Study of the Spanish Language and Literature, 1987, 96; contbr. to: Ency. Info. and Library Scis., vol. 36, Cambridge History of Latin American Literature. Mem. Ky. Folklore Soc., Medieval Soc. Am., Cervantes Soc. Am., MLA, Am. Assn. Tchrs. Spanish and Portuguese, Bibiog. Soc. Am., Ky. Hist. Soc., Instituto de estudios madrilenos, Asociación española de bibliografía, Hispanic Soc. Am. (corr.). Club: Filson. Home: 1804 W Freeman St Carbondale IL 62901-2106

WOODBRIDGE, JOHN MARSHALL, architect, urban planner; b. N.Y.C., Jan. 26, 1929; s. Frederick James and Catherine (Baldwin) W.; m. Sally Byrne, Aug. 14, 1954; children: Lawrence F., Pamela B., Diana B.; m. Carolyn Kizer, Apr. 8, 1975. B.A. magna cum laude, Amherst Coll., 1951; M.F.A. in Architecture, Princeton U., 1956. Designer John Funk, architect, San Francisco, 1957-58; designer, asso. partner Skidmore, Owings & Merrill, San Francisco, 1959-73; staff dir. Pres.'s Adv. Council and Pres.'s Temporary Commn. on Pennsylvania Ave., Washington, 1963-65; exec. dir. Pennsylvania Ave. Devel. Corp., Washington, 1973-77; lectr. architecture U. Calif., Berkeley; vis. prof. U. Oreg., Washington U., St. Louis. Co-author: Buildings of the Bay Area, 1960, A Guide to Architecture in San Francisco and Northern California, 1973, Architecture San Francisco, 1982, San Francisco Architecture, 1992. Chmn. Commn. on Architecture Episc. Ch. Recipient Fed. Design Achievement award Nat. Endowment for Arts, 1988; Fulbright scholar to France, 1951-52. Fellow AIA; mem. Nat. Trust Historic Preservation, Soc. Archtl. Historians, Phi Beta Kappa. Democrat. Episcopalian. Home and Office: 19772 8th St E Sonoma CA 95476-3803

WOODBRIDGE, LINDA, English language educator; b. Chelsea, Mass., Mar. 23, 1945; d. Richard Lord and Viola Beatrice (MacDougall) Taylor; married; children: Dana Louise, Rachel Amelia. BA with honors, UCLA, 1966, MA, 1968, PhD, 1970. Asst. prof. U. Alta., Edmonton, Can., 1970-76, assoc. prof. English, 1976-82, prof., 1982-94, chmn. dept., 1986-89; prof. Penn. State U., Pa., 1994—. Author: Women and the English Renaissance, 1984, The Scythe of Saturn: Shakespeare and Magical Thinking, 1994, numerous articles; compiler: Shakespeare: A Selective Bibliography, 1987; co-editor True Rites & Maimed Rites: Ritual and Anti-Ritual in Shakespeare and His Age, 1992. Rsch. grantee Social Sci. and Humanities Rsch. Coun. Can., 1980, 91-94, 94—. Mem. MLA, Shakespeare Assn. Am. (v.p. 1991-92, pres. 1992-93), Assn. Can. U. Tchrs. of English, Renaissance Soc. Am. Office: Penn State U 117 Burrowes Bldg University Park PA 16802-6200

WOODBURN, RALPH ROBERT, JR., lawyer; b. Haverhill, Mass., Nov. 3, 1946; s. Ralph Robert and Josephine Marie (McClure) W.; m. Janet M. Smith, Sept. 15, 1985. BA, Mich. State U., 1967; JD, Harvard U., 1972; LLM, Boston U., 1981. Bar: Mass. 1972, U.S. Tax Ct. 1987. Assoc. Bowers, Fortier & Lakin, Boston, 1972-76; ptnr., assoc. Haussermann, Davison & Shattuck, Boston, 1976-83; ptnr. Palmer & Dodge, Boston, 1983—; tchr. Harvard Ctr. for Lifelong Learning, Cambridge, Mass., 1986-89; chmn. Wellesley Cable Access Bd., 1993-95. Contbr. articles to Boston Bar Jour. and Estate Planning. Treas. Exeter Assn. of New Eng., Boston, 1985-89, v.p., 1989-91, pres., 1991-93. Fellow Am. Coll. Trust and Estate Counsel; mem. ABA, Boston Bar Assn. (chmn. probate legislation 1983-93), Brae Burn Country Club (Newton, Mass.), Harvard Club of Boston. Home: 25 Cypress Rd Wellesley MA 02181-2918 Office: Palmer & Dodge 1 Beacon St Boston MA 02108-3106

WOODBURY, ALAN TENNEY, lawyer; b. Milw., July 7, 1943; s. Isaiah Tenney and Maxine Arvilla (Hooper) W.; m. Deborah Carson Eayre, Jan. 27, 1968; children: Jeffrey Tenney, Alison Eayre. BA, Bowdoin Coll., 1965; JD, Temple U., 1968. Bar: Pa. 1968; CLU, ChFC. Atty. Fidelity Mut. Life Ins. Co., Phila., 1968-74, assoc. counsel, 1974-76, asst. v.p., assoc. counsel, 1976-78, 2nd v.p., assoc. counsel, 1978-79, 2nd v.p., sec., assoc. counsel, 1979-84; v.p., sec., assoc. counsel Fidelity Mut. Life Ins. Co., Radnor, Pa., 1984-91, sr. v.p., sec., gen. counsel, 1991-93, sr. v.p. ins. coun., 1994—. Mem. ABA, Phila. Bar Assn., Assn. Life Ins. Counsel. Republican. Office: Fidelity Mut Life Ins Co 250 King Of Prussia Rd Wayne PA 19087-5220

WOODBURY, LAEL JAY, theatre educator; b. Fairview, Idaho, July 3, 1927; s. Raymond A. and Wanda (Dawson) W.; m. Margaret Lillian Swenson, Dec. 19, 1949; children: Carolyn Inez (Mrs. Donald Hancock), Shannon Margaret (Mrs. Michael J. Busenbark), Jordan Ray, Lexon Dan. BS, Utah State U., 1952; MA, Brigham Young U., 1953; PhD (Univ. fellow), U. Ill., 1954. Teaching asst. U. Ill., 1953; assoc. prof. Brigham Young U., 1954-61; guest prof. Colo. State Coll., 1962; asst. prof. Bowling Green State U., 1961-62; asso. prof. U. Iowa, 1962-65; producer Ledges Playhouse, Lansing, Mich., 1963-65; prof. speech and dramatics, chmn. dept. Brigham Young U., 1966-70, assoc. dean Coll. Fine Arts and Communications, 1969-73, dean Coll. Fine Arts and Communications, 1973-82; vis. lectr. abroad; bd. dirs. Eagle Systems Internat.; bd. dir. workshop Fedn. for Asian Cultural Promotion, Republic of China; dir. European study tour. Author: Play Production Handbook, 1959, Mormon Arts, vol. 1, 1972, Mosaic Theatre, 1976, also articles, original dramas; profl. actor PBS and feature films. Chmn. gen. bd. drama com. Young Men's Mut. Improvement Assn., 1958-61; bd. dirs. Repertory Dance Theatre, Utah ARC; chmn. Utah Alliance for Arts Edn.; mem. adv. coun. Utah Arts Festival; missionary LDS Ch., N.Y.C., 1994. With USN, 1942-46. Recipient Creative Arts award Brigham Young U., 1971, Disting. Alumni award, 1975, Tchr. of Yr. award, 1988, Excellence in Rsch. award, 1992, Disting. Svc. award, 1992. Mem. Rocky Mountain Theatre Conf. (past pres.), Am. Theatre Assn. (chmn. nat. com. royalties 1972—, mem. fin. com. 1982—), NW Assn. Univs. and Colls. (accrediting officer), Am. Theatre Assn. (v.p. Univ. and Coll. Theatre Assn.), Theta Alpha Phi, Phi Kappa Phi. Home: 1303 Locust Ln Provo UT 84604-3651

WOODBURY, LEE VERNON, health care consultant, physician; b. Florence, S.C., Dec. 18, 1949; s. George Sr. and Melvena Candice (White) W.; m. Bernardette Isabelle Freeman, Aug. 25, 1973 (div.); children: Lee Vernon II, Jenifer Candice Elizabeth. BS, Morehouse Coll., 1973; MD, Med. Univ. S.C., 1977. Diplomate Nat. Bd. Med. Examiners. Intern Richland Meml. Hosp., Columbia, S.C., 1977-80, resident in internal medicine, 1980; chief med./surg. svcs. S.C. Dept. Mental Health, Columbia, 1984-86, dir. profl. svcs., 1987-88, facility dir., CEO Tucker Ctr., 1988-92, divsn. dir., long term care, 1992-94, cons. spl. projects, 1994—; chmn. Agy. Pharmacy and Therapeutics Com., Columbia, 1988-94; emergency med. cons. Space Shuttle Landing Team, Edwards AFB, Calif., 1981-83; dir. ICU Edwards AFB Hosp., 1981-83; cons. internal medicine S.C. Dept. Mental Health, Columbia, 1986—. Chmn. bd. dirs. Profl. Health Svcs., Columbia, 1987-90; chmn. bd. trustees First N.E. Bapt. Ch., Columbia, 1988-91; chmn. advisor Am. Security Coun. Found., Washington, 1982-89; dir. med. group United Way of Midlands, 1991-92; active NAACP, 1993—, Healthy People-2000, 1992—. Maj. USAF, 1980-84. Recipient Recognition award Am. Security Coun. Found., 1983. Mem. S.C. State Employees Assn. (bd. dirs. 1988—). Avocations: computer engring. and design, tennis, basketball, photography, music. Office: SC Dept Mental Health Office Occupl Health/Safety 2100 Bull St Columbia SC 29202

WOODBURY, MARION A., insurance company executive; b. Wilmington, N.C., 1923; m. Alice Battey Bryson; children—Sheldon, Marion A., Frank, Spencer, Alice. Student, U. N.C., 1949; LLB, Woodrow Wilson Coll., 1956. With exec. tng. program Chubb and Son, N.Y.C., 1949; asst. to pres. Bankers Fire & Marine Ins. Co., 1957, exec. v.p. to pres., 1958; v.p. Reins. Corp. of N.Y., 1959-62, exec. v.p., 1962-65, pres., 1965—, also bd. dirs.; chmn. bd., chief exec. officer, dir. United Reins. Corp. N.Y.; bd. dirs. Piedmont Mgmt. Co., Inc., Navigators Ins. Co., POHJOLA A. Ins. Corp.; trustee Coll. of Ins., 1970-75. Served with C.E. U.S. Army, 1945, PTO. Decorated Bronze Star; recipient Good Scout award Greater N.Y. Council Boy Scouts Am., 1977. Mem. Reins. Assn. Am. (chmn. 1974-75, bd. dirs.), U.S. Srs. Golf Assn. Clubs: Wall St. (gov.); Baltrusol Golf. Home: 14 Delegal Rd The Landings Savannah GA 31411 Office: Reins Corp NY 80 Maiden Ln New York NY 10038-4811

WOODBURY, MAX ATKIN, polymath, educator; b. St. George, Utah, Apr. 30, 1917; s. Angus Munn and Grace (Atkin) W.; m. Lida Gottsch, May 30, 1947; children—Carolyn, Max TenEyck, Christopher, Gregory. B.S., U. Utah, 1939; M.S., U. Mich., 1941, Ph.D., 1948; M.P.H., U. N.C., Chapel Hill, 1977. Mem. faculty U. Mich., 1947-49; mem. Inst. for Adv. Study, Princeton, N.J., 1949-50; mem. faculty Princeton U., 1950-52, U. Pa., 1952-54; prin. investigator logistics research project Office Naval Research, George Washington U., 1954-56; faculty NYU, 1956-65; prof. computer sci. Duke U., prof. biomath. Med. Ctr., 1966-88, sr. fellow Ctr. for Study of Aging and Human Devel., 1975—, sr. fellow, sr. scientist Ctr. Demographic Studies, 1985—, prof. emeritus, 1987—; pres. Biomed. Information-processing Orgn., 1961-62, Inst. for Biomed. Computer Research, 1961-71; cons. WHO, UNIVAC, CBS on computer election forecasts, 1952-62, sci. orgns., univs., govt. agys., corps. Contbr. articles to profl. jours. Served with USAAF, 1941-46, MTO. USPHS, NIH grantee, also other govt. agys., 1947—; recipient MERIT award Nat. Inst. on Aging, NIH, June 1, 1988-May 31, 1998. Fellow AAAS, Am. Statis. Assn., Inst. Math. Statistics; mem. numerous sci., profl. socs., Phi Beta Kappa, Sigma Xi, Phi Kappa Phi (inventor of GoM methodology). Home: 4008 Bristol Rd Durham NC 27707-5403 Office: Duke U Ctr Demographics 2117 Campus Dr Durham NC 27708-0408

WOODBURY, RICHARD BENJAMIN, anthropologist, educator; b. West Lafayette, Ind., May 16, 1917; s. Charles Goodrich and Marion (Benjamin) W.; m. Nathalie Ferris Sampson, Sept. 18, 1948. Student, Oberlin Coll., 1934-36; BS in Anthropology cum laude, Harvard U., 1939, MA, 1942, PhD, 1949; postgrad., Columbia U., 1939-40. Archeol. research Ariz., 1938, 39, Fla., 1940, Guatemala, 1947-49, El Morro Nat. Monument, N.Mex., 1953-56, Tehuacan, Mex., 1964; archaeologist United Fruit Co. Zaculeu Project, Guatemala, 1947-50; assoc. prof. anthropology U. Ky., 1950-52, Columbia U., 1952-58; rsch. assoc. prof. anthropology interdisciplinary arid lands program U. Ariz., 1959-63; curator archeology and anthropology U.S. Nat. Mus., Smithsonian Instn., Washington, 1963-69, acting. head office anthropology, 1965-66, chmn. office anthropology, 1966-67; prof., chmn. dept. anthropology U. Mass., Amherst, 1969-73; prof. U. Mass., 1973-81, prof. emeritus, 1981—, acting assoc. provost, dean grad. sch., 1973-74; mem. divsn. anthropology and psychology NRC, 1954-57; bd. dirs. Archaeol. Conservancy, 1979-84, Valley Health Plan, Amherst, 1981-84, Mus. of No. Ariz., 1983-90; liason rep. for Smithsonian Instn., Com. for Recovery of Archeol. Remains, 1965-69; assoc. seminar on ecol. systems and cultural evolution Columbia U., 1964-73; mem. exec. com. bd. dirs. Human Relations Area Files, Inc., New Haven, Conn., 1968-70; cons. Conn. Hist. Commn., 1970-72. Author (with A.S. Trik) The Ruins of Zaculeu, Guatemala, 2 vols., 1953, Prehistoric Stone Implements of Northeastern Arizona, 1954, Alfred V. Kidder, 1973, Sixty Years of Southwestern Archaeology, 1993; editor: (with I.A. Sanders) Societies Around the World (2 vols.), 1953, (with others) The Excavation of Hawikuh, 1966, Am. Antiquity, 1954-58, Abstracts of New World Archaeology; editor-in-chief: Am. Anthropologist, 1975-78; mem. editorial bd.: Am. Jour. Archeology, 1957-72. Mem. sch. com., Shutesbury, Mass., 1979-82, chmn., 1980-82, bd. assessors, 1982-85; chmn. finance com. Friends of Amherst Stray Animals, 1983-85. With USAF, 1942-45. Fellow Mus. No. Ariz., 1985. Fellow AAAS (coun. rep. Am. Anthrop. Assn. 1971-63, com. on desert and arid zones rsch. Southwest and Rocky Mountains divsn. 1958-64, vice-chair 1962-64, com. arid lands 1969-74, sec. 1970-72), Am. Anthrop. Assn. (exec. bd. 1963-66, A.V. Kidder award 1989), Archeol. Inst. Am. (exec. com. 1965-67); mem. Soc. Am. Archeology (treas. 1953-54, pres. 1958-59, chmn. fin. com. 1987-89, Fiftieth Anniversary award 1985, Disting. Svc. award 1988), Ariz. Archeol. and Hist. Soc., Archeol. Conservancy (life), Sigma Xi. Office: U Mass Dept Anthropology Machmer Hall Amherst MA 01003

WOODBURY, STEPHEN ABBOTT, economics educator; b. Beverly, Mass., Oct. 25, 1952; s. Stephen E. and Barbara (Sandberg) W.; m. Susan Pozo, May 29, 1982 (div. June 1992); 1 child, Ricardo Pozo. AB, Middlebury (Vt.) Coll., 1975; MS, U. Wis., 1977, PhD, 1981. Asst. prof. of econs. Pa. State U., University Park, 1979-82; asst. prof. of econs. Mich. State U., East Lansing, 1982-88, assoc. prof. econs., 1988-94; prof. econs., 1994—; sr. economist W.E. Upjohn Inst., Kalamazoo, Mich., 1984—; dep. dir. Fed. Adv. Coun. on Unemployment Compensation, Washington, 1993-94, cons., 1994-96; cons. U. Hawaii/State of Hawaii, Honolulu, 1991—, State of Mich. Task Force, Lansing, 1989-90, U.S. Dept. Labor, Washington, 1988, European Communities Commn., Brussels, 1987-88; vis. prof. U. Stirling, Scotland, 1992; vis. scholar Fed. Res. Bd., Washington, 1992. Author: Tax Treatment of Benefits, 1991; (with others) Access to Health Care, 1992; editor Rsch. in Employment Policy; contbr. articles to profl. jours. Recipient Rsch. grants William H. Donner Found., 1991, U.S. Dept. Health and Human Svcs., 1985, and U.S. Dept. Labor, 1995. Mem. Am. Econ. Assn., Am. Statis. Assn., Assn. for Evolutionary Econs., Econometric Soc., Indsl. Rels. Rsch. Assn., Midwest Econs. Assn. (1st v.p. 1993-94), Ea. Econ. Assn., Soc. Labor Economists, Am. Law and Econs. Assn. Office: Mich State Univ Dept Econs Marshall Hall East Lansing MI 48824

WOODCOCK, DAVID GEOFFREY, architect, educator; b. Manchester, Eng., May 28, 1937; s. Herbert Edwin and Constance Mary (Bristol) W.; m. Kathleen Mary Bishop, Oct. 1, 1960 (dec. 1964); 1 child, Jonathan Alfred; m. Valerie Frances Gubbins, July 4, 1964; children: Frances Mary, Penelope Jane. BA with 1st class honors in Architecture, U. Manchester, 1960, D in Town Planning, 1966. Chartered architect, U.K.; registered architect, Tex. Lectr. U. Manchester, 1961; asst. prof. Tex. A&M U., College Station, 1962-66, assoc. prof., 1970-76, prof., 1976—; sr. lectr. Kent. Inst. Art & Design, Canterbury, England, 1966-70; pvt. practice, College Station, 1980—, Canterbury, 1966-70. Bd. dirs. Opera and Performing Arts Soc. Tex. A&M U., 1980-83, 88-91, pres., 1993-94, adv. bd. Hammons Sch. Architecture Drury Coll., Mo., 1990-93, Savannah (Ga.) Coll. Arts and Design/Architecture, 1987-93; active Episc. Diocese Tex. Archtl. Commn., 1987—. Recipient Rsch. Excellence award Tex. Hist. Commn., 1991, Romieniec award for archtl. edn. Tex. Sch. Architecture, 1995. Fellow AIA; mem. Royal Inst. Brit. Architecture, Assn. for Preservation Tech. Internat. bd. dirs. 1990—), Nat. Coun. for Preservation Edn. (bd. dirs.), Assn. Collegiate Schs. Architecture (regional dir. 1981-84, Disting. Prof. 1991). Avocations: drawing, creative and gifted education, choral singing. Office: Tex A&M U Dept Architecture College Station TX 77843

WOODCOCK, JANET, federal official; b. Washington, Pa., Aug. 29, 1948; d. John and Frances (Crocker) W.; m. Roger Henry Miller, Nov. 16, 1981; children: Kathleen Miller, Susanne Miller. BS cum laude, Bucknell U., 1970; MD, Northwestern U., Chgo., 1977. Diplomate Am. Bd. Internal Medicine. Intern Hershey Med. Ctr./Pa. State U., 1977-78, resident in internal medicine, 1978-80, chief resident in medicine, 1980-81; fellow in rheumatology U. Calif./VA Med. Ctr., San Francisco, 1982-84; instr. medicine divsn. rheumatology and immunology VA Med. Ctr., San Francisco, 1984-85; med. officer divsn. biol. investigational new drugs Ctr. for Biologics Evaluation and Rsch./FDA, Rockville, Md., 1986-87, group leader divsn. biol. investigational new drugs, 1987-88, dep. dir. divsn. biol. investigational new drugs, 1988, dir. divsn. biol. investigational new drugs, 1988-90; dir. Ctr. for Drug Evaluation and Rsch./FDA, Rockville, Md., 1994—; acting dep. dir. Ctr. for Biologics Evaluation and Rsch., FDA, Rockville, Md., 1990-92, dir. office of therapeutics rsch. and rev., 1992-94; dir. Ctr. for Drug Evaluation and Rsch., FDA, Rockville, 1994—; instr. medicine, asst. prof. divsn. gen. internal medicine Hershey Med. Ctr./Pa. State U., 1981; analytical chemist rsch. divsn. A.B. Dick Co., Niles, Ill., 1971-73. Nat. Merit scholar Bucknell U., 1966, Pa. State scholar, 1966; Rsch. fellow Am. Rheumatism Assn.; VA Investigator grantee, 1985. Mem. Alpha Omega Alpha, Alpha Lambda Delta. Office: Dept Health & Human Service Center Drug Evaluation & Research 9200 Corporate Blvd Rockville MD 20850-3229

WOODCOCK, KENNETH ROBERT, global power company executive; b. Kearny, N.J., July 25, 1943; s. Robert John and Gertrude (Jamieson) W.; m. Dorothy Hackney MacColl, Sept. 25, 1971; children: Laura Jamieson, Elizabeth MacColl. BSME, Lehigh U., 1965; MBA, U. Pitts., 1966. Devel. engr. E.I. Du Pont De Nemours & Co., Wilmington, Del., 1966-67; environ. cons. TRW Systems Group, Washington, 1969-71; staff engr. U.S. EPA, Washington, 1971-74; assoc. asst. adminstr. U.S. Fed. Energy Adminstrn., Washington, 1974-77; exec. asst. U.S. Dept. Energy, Washington, 1977-81; project mgr. The AES Corp., Arlington, Va., 1981-84, v.p., 1984-87, sr. v.p., 1987—. Trustee St. Patrick's Episcopal Day Sch., Washington, 1982-86, Nat. Cathedral Sch., 1987-94, Washington Concert Opera, 1994—; chpt. mem. Washington Nat. Cathedral, 1992-94; coun. mem. Phillips Collection, 1994. 2d lt. USPHS, 1967-69. Mem. Chevy Chase Club, Dunes Club, Point Judith Country Club. Avocations: reading, tennis, platform tennis, boating, skiing. Home: 2621 Foxhall Rd NW Washington DC 20007-1126 Office: The AES Corp 1001 19th St N Arlington VA 22209-1722

WOODCOCK, LEONARD, humanities educator, former ambassador; b. Providence, Feb. 15, 1911; s. Ernest and Margaret (Freel) W.; m. Sharon Lee Tuohy, Apr. 14, 1978; children—Leslie, Janet, John. Ed., St. Wilfred's Coll.; student, Wayne State U., 1928-30, Walsh Inst. Accountancy, Detroit, 1928-30; numerous hon. degrees. Staff rep. internat. union UAW, 1940-46, adminstrv. asst. to pres., 1946-47, regional dir., 1947-55, internat. v.p., 1955-70, pres., 1970-77, pres. emeritus, 1977—; chief of mission with rank of amb. U.S. Liaison Office, Peking, 1977-79; amb. to People's Republic of China, 1979-81; adj. prof. U. Mich., 1981—; bd. dirs. ATC Internat. Inc., Houston, Nat. Commn. U.S. China Rels.; dynamometer operator Continental Aviation & Engring. Co., 1947. Bd. govs. emeritus Wayne State U., 1970. Mem. Am.-China Soc. (bd. dirs.). Home: 2404 Vinewood Blvd Ann Arbor MI 48104-2768

WOODCOCK, RICHARD BEVERLEY, health facility administrator; b. Leeds, Yorkshire, Eng., June 7, 1945; arrived in Can., 1948; s. Stanley Walter and Jessica Stretton (Coyne) W.; children: Matthew, Christopher, Jeffrey, Lindsay. Honors BA in Bus. Adminstrn., Waterloo (Ont.) Luth. U., 1970. Cert. hosp. adminstr. Dir. fin. Northwestern Gen. Hosp., Toronto, 1973-76; asso. adminstr. Brantford Gen. Hosp., Ont., 1976-81, pres., 1982—; sec., treas. Brantford Gen. Hosp. Found., 1977—. Fellow Am. Coll. Healthcare Execs., Can. Coll. Health Svc. Execs., Rotary (bd. dirs. Brantford chpt. 1981-84, Paul Harris fellow Rotary Internat.). Avocations: alpine skiing, boating. Office: Brantford Gen Hosp, 200 Terrace Hill St, Brantford, ON Canada N3R 1G9

WOODDELL, PHILO GLENN, fine arts educator, radio broadcaster and producer; b. Hutchinson, Kans., Sept. 3, 1941; s. Philo Davis and Jean Elise Wooddell. B of Music Edn., Southwestern Coll., Winfield, Kans., 1963; MM, Crane Sch. Music, Potsdam, N.Y., 1985; MA, NYU, 1989. Cert. in music and speech edn., N.Y. Tchr., chmn. fine arts/humanities dept. Jeffersonville (N.Y.)-Youngsville Ctrl. Sch. Dist. 1, 1965—; local host N.P.R.'s Morning Edit., WJFF-FM, prodr., host Sunday Brunch, Music of the Cinema; mem. programming and adv. bds. Radio Catskill, also pres. bd. trustees, 1991-92, v.p. bd. trustees, 1993; film composer, moderator Universal City, Calif.; clinician on film music NOMA, N.Y.C.; music and media clinician Western Heritage Mus., Glendale/Burbank, Calif.; mem. adv. com. Cities as Sch. Bldg. Leadership Team; media clinician Tisch Sch. of the Arts, N.Y.C., 1994; soundtrack moderator UCLA, 1995. Dir. profl. and semi-profl. prodns. for dinner, proscenium, exptl. and children's theatre; performed with Central City (Colo.) Opera Assn., Kansas City Starlight Theatre, Dallas Summer Musicals, N.P.R. Playhouse; shows at various Catskill resorts; vocalist with Phila. Orch., Saratoga Performing Arts Ctr., Saratoga Springs, N.Y.; voice over/narration experience; editor The Collegian; contbr. articles to profl. jours. Founder Sullivan County (N.Y.) Help Line; founder, bd. dirs. Sullivan County Festival of the Arts Program. Mem. Am. Guild of Variety Artists, Music Educators Nat. Conf., Am. Choral Dirs. Assn., Am. Film Inst. (charter), Arts Alliance Assn., Arts in Edn. Assn., N.Y. State United Tchrs., Sullivan County Dramatic Workshop, N.Y. State Music Educators Assn., Soc. for Preservation of Film Music, Lions Club Internat., Phi Mu Alpha Sinfonia. Home: 50 Durr Rd # 88 Jeffersonville NY 12748-0088 Office: Sta WJFF-Radio Catskill PO Box 797 Jeffersonville NY 12748-0797

WOODE, MOSES KWAMENA ANNAN, scientist, medical and chemistry educator; b. Takoradi, Ghana, June 27, 1947; came to U.S., 1981; s. Emmanuel Kwamena and Georgina Aba (Arthur) W.; m. Eunice Adjaottor, Aug. 24, 1974; children: Linda-Marie, Timothy. BS in Chemistry and Math., U. Ghana, Legon, Accra, 1971, BS in Chemistry with honors, 1972, MS in Chemistry; PhD in Chem. Crystallography, Sch. Tech. and Medicine, London, 1978. Assoc. prof. med. edn. and chemistry U. Va., Charlottesville, 1986-93, dir. Assisting Students Achieve Med. Degrees, 1987—, asst. dean, acad. support, 1988-91, assoc. dean acad. support and strategic programs, 1992—, rsch. assoc. prof. chemistry, assoc. prof. ob-gyn., 1986-93, prof. med. edn., ob-gyn. rsch. prof. chemistry, 1993—. Contbr. articles to profl. jours. Grantee NIH, 1987—, Robert Wood Johnson Found., 1988—, U.S. Dept. HHS, 1990—. Fellow Am. Inst. Chemists; mem. APHA, ACA, Am. Crystallographic Assn., Sigma Xi. Achievements include design of academic enrichment programs at high school, college and medical school levels; contribution to understanding of structure-function relationships of biologically important molecules and liquid crystals. Office: U Va Sch Medicine PO Box 446 Charlottesville VA 22902-0446

WOODEN, JOHN ROBERT, former basketball coach; b. Martinsville, Ind., Oct. 14, 1910; s. Joshua Hugh and Roxie (Rothrock) W.; m. Nellie C. Riley, Aug. 8, 1932; children: Nancy Anne, James Hugh. B.S., Purdue U., 1932; M.S., Ind. State U., 1947. Athletic dir., basketball and baseball coach Ind. State Tchrs. Coll., 1946-48; head basketball coach UCLA, 1948-75; lectr. to colls., coaches, business. Author: Practical Modern Basketball, 1966, They Call Me Coach, 1972; Contbr. articles to profl. jours. Served to lt. USNR, 1943-46. Named All-Am. basketball player Purdue U., 1930-32, Coll. Basketball Player of Yr., 1932, to All-Time All-Am. Team Helms Athletic Found., 1943, Nat. Basketball Hall of Fame, Springfield (Mass.) Coll., as player, 1960, as coach, 1970, Ind. State Baksetball Hall of Fame, 1962, Calif. Father of Yr., 1964, 75, Coach of Yr. U.S. Basketball Writers Assn., 1964, 67, 69, 70, 72, 73, Sportsman of Yr. Sports Illustrated, 1973, GTE Acad. All-Am., 1994; recipient Whitney Young award Urban League, 1973, 1st ann. Velvet Covered Brick award Layman's Leadership Inst., 1974, 1st ann. Dr. James Naismith Peachbasket award, 1974, medal of excellence Bellarmine Coll., 1985, Sportslike Pathfinder award to Hoosier with extraordinary svc. on behalf of Am. youth, 1993, GET All Am. Acad. Hall of Fame, 1994, 40 for the Age award Sports Illustrated, 1994, the 1st Frank G. Wells Disney award for role model to youth, 1995, Disting. Am. award Pres. Reagan, 1995, Svc. to Mankind award Lexington Theol. Sem., 1995, NCAA Theodore Roosevelt Sportsman award, 1995. *I have tried to live the philosophy of my personal definition of success which I formulated in the middle thirties shortly after I entered the teaching profession. Not being satisfied that success was merely the accumulation of material possessions or the attainment of a position of power or prestige, I chose to define success as "peace of mind which can be attained only through the self-satisfaction that comes from knowing you did your best to become the best that you are capable of becoming.".*

WOODEN, REBA FAYE BOYD, guidance counselor; b. Washington, Ind., Sept. 21, 1940; d. Lester E. and Opal M. (Burch) Boyd; m. N. Nuel Wooden, Jr., Dec. 23, 1962 (div. 1993); children: Jeffrey Nuel, Cynthia Faye. BA, U. Indpls., 1962; MS, Butler U., 1968, Ind. U., 1990. Cert. tchr., counselor, Ind. Tchr. Mooresville (Ind.) High Sch., 1962-66; tchr. Perry Meridian High Sch., Indpls., 1974-92, counselor, 1992—; part-time instr. Ind. U.-Purdue U. at Indpls., 1994-95. Named Outstanding High Sch. Psychology tchr. APA, 1987. Mem. NEA, Ind. State Tchrs. Assn., Perry Edn. Assn. Methodist. Avocations: reading, travel. Home: 113 Severn Dr Greenwood IN 46142-1880 Office: Perry Meridian High Sch 401 W Meridian School Rd Indianapolis IN 46217-4215

WOODFIELD, CLYDE VERNON, senator; b. Hot Springs, Ark., Feb. 11, 1932; s. Ozy V. and Bessie L. (Robertson) W.; m. Sharon Jean McCoy, Mar. 1, 1966; children: John, David, Kelly, Michael. BBA, U. So. Miss., 1955; postgrad., U. Ark., U. So. Miss. Owner, operator Sahara Motel, Gulfport, Miss., Woodfield Farms, Gulfport; asst. mayor City of Gulfport; mem. Ho. of Reps., Jackson, Miss., 1967-71, 82-86; mem. Miss. State Senate, Jackson, 1987—, vice chmn. rules com., 1993—, chmn. bus. and fin. instns. com., 1993—. Bd. dirs. Salvation Army, 1983, Cheshire Home, 1992-94, Natural Sci. Found., 1993; pres. Arts Fair for Handicapped, 1992; mem. exec. bd. Miss Teen USA, 1991-94. Mem. Masons, Shriners. Home: Woodfield Farms 11452 County Farm Rd Gulfport MS 39503 Office: Miss State Senate PO Box 1018 Jackson MS 39215-1018

WOODFORD, ARTHUR MACKINNON, library director, historian; b. Detroit, Nov. 23, 1940; s. Frank Bury and Mary-Kirk (MacKinnon) W.; children: Mark, Amy; m. Reneé Ann Skuba, Apr. 25, 1990; stepchildren: Brandon, Christopher. Student, U. Wis., 1958-60; BA in History, Wayne State U., 1963; AM in LS, U. Mich., 1964. Libr. Detroit Pub. Libr., 1964-74; asst. dir. Grosse Pointe (Mich.) Pub. Libr., 1974-77; dir. St. Clair Shores (Mich.) Pub. Libr., 1977—. Author: All Our Yesterdays, 1969, Detroit and Its Banks, 1974, Detroit: American Urban Renaissance, 1979, Charting The Inland Seas, 1991, Tonnancour, 1994. Mem. Mich. Libr. Assn. (v.p. 1988-89), Gt. Lakes Maritime Inst., Prismatic Club Detroit (pres. 1982), Algonquin Club (treas. 1983-93). Methodist. Avocations: tennis, bridge, reading, model shipbuilding. Home: 22401 Lakeland St Saint Clair Shores MI 48081-2323 Office: Saint Clair Shores Pub Libr 22500 E Eleven Mile Rd Saint Clair Shores MI 48081-1399

WOODHOUSE, DERRICK FERGUS, ophthalmologist; b. Sutton, Surrey, U.K., May 29, 1927; s. Sydney Carver and Erica (Ferguson) W.; m. Jocelyn Laira Perry, Mar. 9, 1957; children: Karen Tace, Iain Kenrick, Gillian Erica. BM, BCh., Oxford U., Eng., 1951; DO, London Coll., 1956. Intern in medicine, surgery, ophthalmology St. Thomas Hosp., Plymouth, Exeter Hosps., London, 1952-53; registrar in ophthalmology Birmingham (Eng.) Eye. Hosp., 1958-60; sr. registrar in ophthalmology Bristol (Eng.) Eye Hosp., 1960-63; cons. eye surgeon Wolverhampton & Midland Counties Eye Infirmary, Eng., 1963-89; staff opthalmologist Liverpool Hosp., NSW, Australia, 1989—. Contbr. articles to profl. jours.; author: Ophthalmic Nursing, 1980. Mem. Wolverhampton Health Authority, 1970-77; treas. Ophthalmic Nursing Bd., 1970-84, chmn., 1984-88. With RAF, 1953-57. Recipient Gold medal, Nepal Med. Assn., 1989. Fellow Royal Coll. Surgeons, Royal Soc. Medicine, Royal Coll. Ophthalmologists; mem. Irish Coll. Ophthalmologists, Brit. Computer Soc., N.Y. Acad. Scis. Mem. Soc. of Friends.

WOODHOUSE, JOHN FREDERICK, food distribution company executive; b. Wilmington, Del., Nov. 30, 1930; s. John Crawford and Anna (Houth) W.; m. Marilyn Ruth Morrow, June 18, 1955; children: John Crawford II, Marjorie Ann Woodhouse Purdy. BA, Wesleyan U., 1953; MBA, Harvard U., 1955. Bus. devel. officer Can. Imperial Bank of Commerce, Toronto, Ont., 1955-59; various fin. positions Ford Motor Co., Dearborn, Mich., 1959-64, Cooper Industries, Inc., Mount Vernon, Ohio, 1964-67; treas. Houston, 1967-69, Crescent-Niagara Corp., Buffalo, 1968-69; exec. v.p., chief fin. officer Sysco Corp., Houston, 1969-71, pres., chief operating officer, 1972-83, pres., chief exec. officer, 1983-85, chief exec. officer, chmn. bd., 1985—, mem. exec. and fin. coms., also bd. dirs.; bd. dirs. Shell Oil Co., Winrock Internat.; dir. Harvard Bus. Sch. Assocs., 1995—. Chmn. Mich. 16th dist. rep. Club, 1962-64; treas. Cooper Industries Found., 1967-69; trustee Wesleyan U., 1976-92, vice-chmn., 1986-92; ruling elder Presbyn. Ch.; bd. trustees Mt. Holyoke Coll., South Hadley, Mass., 1996—. Mem. Nat. Am. Wholesale Grocer's Assn. (bd. dirs. 1990—, vice chmn. 1992, chmn. 1994—), Internat. Foodservice Distbrs. Assn. (bd. dirs. 1988—), Houston Soc. Fin. Analysts, Fin. Execs. Inst., Harvard Bus. Sch. Club (bd. dirs.), Sigma Chi. Avocations: backpacking, canoeing, tennis. Office: Sysco Corp 1390 Enclave Pky Houston TX 77077-2025

WOODHULL, JOHN RICHARD, electronics company executive; b. LaJolla, Calif., Nov. 5, 1933; s. John Richard Woodhull and Mary Louise (Fahey) Hostetler; m. Barbara Adams; children: Elizabeth A., John A. BS in Engring. Physics, U. Colo., 1957, MS in Applied Math., 1960. Engr. Space Tech. Labs. (now TRW Systems), Redondo Beach, Calif., 1960-63; mgr., engr. Northrop Corp., Hawthorne, Calif., 1964; mem. tech. staff Logicon, Inc., San Pedro, Calif., 1964-69, pres., chief exec. officer, Torrance, Calif., 1969—, also bd. dirs.; instr. physics U. Colo., 1959-60; bd. dirs. 1st Fed. Fin. Corp. Bd. mgrs. San Pedro (Calif.) and Peninsula YMCA; bd. dirs. Los Angeles YMCA, 1985—, Sunrise Med., Torrance, 1986—. With USN, 1956-59. Mem. Chief Execs.' Orgn., World Bus. Coun., Nat. Indsl. Security Assn. (bd. dirs. 1986—). Avocations: sailboat racing, tennis, skiing. Office: Logicon Inc 3701 Skypark Dr Ste 200 Torrance CA 90505-4712*

WOODHULL, NANCY JANE, foundation executive; b. Perth Amboy, N.J., Mar. 1, 1945; d. Harold and May (Post) Cromwell; m. William Douglass Watson, Sept. 24, 1976; 1 child, Tennessee Jane. Student, Trenton State Tchrs. Coll., 1963-64. Dept. editor News Tribune, Woodbridge, N.J., 1964-73; reporter Detroit Free Press, 1973-75; mng. editor Times-Union, Rochester, N.Y., 1975-80, Democrat & Chronicle, Rochester, 1980-82; mng. editor USA Today, Arlington, Va., 1982-83, sr. editor, 1983-87; pres. Gannett New Media, Washington, 1986-90, Gannett News Svc., Washington, 1988-90; exec. v.p., editor-in-chief So. Living Mags., Birmingham, Ala., 1990-92; pres. Nancy Woodhull & Assoc., Inc., Washington and Pittsford, N.Y., 1991-92; scholar-in-residence U. Rochester, N.Y., 1992-96; chmn. bd. Peabody Radio and TV awards; trustee The Freedom Forum; co-chair Women, Men & Media, Washington, 1989—; mem. adv. bd. New Direction For News U. Mo., 1989—; mem., chair bd. Nat. Women's Hall of Fame, Seneca Falls, N.Y., 1990-96; mem. adv. bd. Knight Ctr. for Specialized Journalism U. Md., 1993—; vice chair Internat. Women's Media Found., Washington, 1996—; exec. dir. Media Studies Ctr., N.Y., 1996—, sr. v.p., Arlington, Va., 1996—. Office: Media Studies Ctr 580 Madison Ave New York NY 10022

WOODHULL, PATRICIA ANN, artist; b. Gary, Ind., Nov. 24, 1924; d. John Joseph and Georgia Mildred (Voorhis) Harding; m. Bradley Allen Woodhull, May 8, 1948; children: Leslie, Marcia, Clarisse. BS in Clothing Design, Purdue U., 1946; life teaching credential, Calif. State U., Fullerton, 1978. Social worker County Dept. Lake County and Bartholomew County, Gary and Columbus, Ind., 1946-50; home demonstrator Pub. Svc. Co. Ind., Columbus, 1950-53; substitute tchr. Fullerton (Calif.) H.S. Dist., 1968-73; children's art and drama tchr. Fullerton Cmty. Svcs., 1973-85; children's pvt. art tchr. Fullerton, 1990-93; art tchr. Montessori Sch., Fullerton, 1990-91; art/drama tchr. creative arts program Fullerton Pub. Schs., 1972-89; founder, dir. Players Improv Theatre Group, Fullerton, Calif. One woman shows include Fullerton City Libr., 1992, William Carlos Gallery, Fullerton, 1992, 93, Whittier (Calif.) City Hall, 1993, Muckinthaler Ctr., Fullerton, 1993, Brookhurst Ctr., Anaheim, 1993, Whitier Libr. Show, 1994; exhibited in group shows at Whittier Art Gallery, 1991, Hillcrest Art Show, Creative Arts Ctr., Burbank, Calif., 1991, Bidge Gallery City Hall, L.A., 1992, The Art Store, Fullerton, 1992, Women Painters West, 1993, New England Fine Arts Inst., Boston, 1993; represented in pvt. collections. Recipient Spl. award Orange County Fair, Costa Mesa (Calif.) County Fair, 1985; 3rd pl. award Hillcrest Whittier (Calif.) Show, 1990, 2nd award West Coast Collage

Show, Lancaster, Calif., 1989, Evelyn Nunn Miller award Women Painters West, Torrance, Calif., 1994. Mem. Nat. League Am. Pen Women (pres. Orange County 1993), Women Painters West, Pan Hellenic Orange County (pres. 1994), Alpha Chi Omega (pres. local chpt. 1993). Republican. Avocations: designing knitwear, reading, music. Home: 1519 E Harmony Ln Fullerton CA 92631-2015

WOODHURST, ROBERT STANFORD, JR., architect; b. Abbeville, S.C., July 12, 1921; s. Robert Stanford and Eva (Ferguson) W.; m. Dorothy Ann Carwile, Aug. 4, 1945; 1 son, Robert Stanford III. BS in Architecture, Clemson U., 1942. Registered arch., S.C., Ga. Designer Harold Woodward, Arch., Spartanburg, S.C., 1946-47; assoc. architect F. Arthur Hazard, Arch., Augusta, Ga., 1947-54; ptnr. Woodhurst & O'Brien, Architects, Augusta, 1954-83, Woodhurst Partnership, 1983—; v.p. Southeastern Architects and Engrs., Inc., Augusta, 1964-83; lectr. history architecture N. Augusta Community Coll.; mem. nat. exam. com. Nat. Council Archtl. Regis. Bds.; pres. Ga. State Bd. Archs. Chmn. Augusta-Richmond County Planning Commn., 1966-68; trustee Hist. Augusta, Inc.; active Mayor's Adv. Com., 1965-68; mem. Augusta Bldg. Code Bd. Appeals, 1955-58. Served to capt. U.S. Army, 1942-45. Decorated Air medal with 7 oak leaf clusters; Croix de Guerre avec palms (France); prisoner ofwar, Germany. Fellow AIA (Bronze medal 1942); mem. Ga. Assn. AIA (pres. 1977, Bronze medal 1977, Rothchild Silver Medal 1987), Soc. Archtl. Historians, Nat. Council Archtl. Registration Bds., Augusta Country Club, Pinnacle Club, Elks. Democrat. Baptist. Designed and built: 1st Baptist Ch., Augusta, Univ. Hosp. Med. Ctr., Augusta, Peabody Apts. and Irvin Towers, Augusta, W. Lake Country Club, Augusta, Med. Library, Med. Coll. Ga., Library Voorhees Coll., Denmark, S.C., Ambulatory Care Ctr., Univ. Hosp., Augusta, Married Students Apartments, Med. Coll. Ga., Covenant Presbyn. Ch., Augusta, Student Ctr. Voorhees Coll., Pres.' Home Voorhees Coll., others. Home: 810 Dogwood Ln Augusta GA 30909-2704 Office: Woodhurst Partnership 607 15th St Augusta GA 30901-2601

WOODIN, MARTIN DWIGHT, retired university system president; b. Sicily Island, La., July 7, 1915; s. Dwight E. and Gladys Ann (Martin) W.; m. Virginia Johnson, Sept. 7, 1939 (dec.); children: Rebecca Woodin Johnson, Pamela Woodin Fry, Linda Woodin Middleton; m. Elisabeth Wachalik, Oct. 5, 1968. B.S., La. State U., 1936; M.S., Cornell U., 1939, Ph.D., 1941; L.H.D. (hon.), U. New Orleans, 1985. Faculty La. State U., 1941-85, prof. agrl. econs., head dept., 1957-59; dir. resident instrn. Coll. Agr., 1959-60; dean La. State U. at Alexandria, 1960-62; exec. v.p. La. State U. System, Baton Rouge, 1962-72; pres. La. State U. System, 1972-85; Cons. agr. and planning, Nicaragua, Taiwan, Thailand. Contbr. articles to profl. jours. Dep. dir. La. Civil Def. Agy., 1961-72; v.p., exec. com. United Givers Baton Rouge; sec. La. State U. Found., 1962-72; mem. La. Constn. Revision Commn., Arts and Humanities Coun. of Greater Baton Rouge; mem. pres.'s coun. Nat. Assn. State Univs., 1972-85; mem. coun. trustees Gulf South Rsch. Inst., 1972-85; pres. Coun. So. Univs., 1975-76. With USNR, 1942-46, PTO. Named Alumnus of Yr., La. State U., 1985; named to Order of Jose Cecilio Del Valle, Republic of Honduras, 1985. Mem. Am. Agrl. Econ. Assn., Am. Mktg. Assn., VFW, Am. Legion (post comdr.), Internat. House, So. Assn. Land Grant Colls. and State Univs. (pres. 1977-78, 83-84), Elks, Rotary, Sigma Xi, Omicron Delta Kappa, Phi Kappa Phi (pres.), Beta Gamma Sigma, Phi Eta Sigma, Gamma Sigma Delta, Alpha Zeta, Pi Gamma Mu, Acacia. Presbyterian. Home: 234 Court St Baton Rouge LA 70810-4801

WOODING, PETER HOLDEN, interior and industrial designer; b. N.Y.C., Nov. 15, 1940; s. Edmund von Richen and Barbara (Holden) W.; m. Joanna Stypula; 1 child, Robert. BS in Design, U. Mich., 1963; student, Art Ctr. Coll., Los Angeles, 1962. Designer Herman Miller Co., Ann Arbor, 1962-63; account designer Gen. Electric Co., Louisville, 1963-71; design dir. Research and Design Inst., Providence, 1971-76, prin., 1976-78; owner, dir. Peter Wooding Design Assocs., Providence, 1978—; lectr., critic RISD, 1976—, Taipei Inst. Tech.; mem. juries for internat. design competitions, 1985-92; head U.S. del. Internat. Design Congress, Amsterdam, 1987, Nagoya, Japan, 1989, U.S. del. to Hungary USIA, U.S. del. USSR/USA Designers Esch., del. to Ljubljana, Yugoslavia, 1991. Contbr. articles to various profl. jours. Bd. dirs. Leuthi-Peterson Camps for Internat. Understanding, Switzerland, 1978-79; pres. Worldesign Found., 1989-90. Recipient I.D. Designers Choice, 1974, Hatch award Boston Art Dirs. Club, 1981, Am. Inst. Graphic Arts award, 1981, Designer's Choice award Indsl. Design Mag., 1982, Idea award in environments, 1989, Internat./Inter-Design on Environ., 1992. Fellow Indsl. Designers Soc. Am. (pres. 1987-88, exec. v.p. 1985-86, chmn. 1988-90); mem. Human Factors Soc., Am. Soc. Interior Designers (interior design project award 1991, 1st place nat. competition award 1991). Avocations: running, biking, travel. Home: 28 Arnold St Providence RI 02906-1002 Office: 369 Ives St Providence RI 02906-3926*

WOODING, WILLIAM MINOR, medical statistics consultant; b. Waterbury, Conn., Aug. 24, 1917; s. George Lee and Ella Elizabeth (Asher) W.; m. Nina C. Peaslee, May 30, 1940; children: Barbara Lee Wooding Bose, Elizabeth Ann Wooding Kontur. B Chem. Engring. cum laude, Poly. Inst. Bklyn., 1953. Lab. asst. Am. Cyanamid Co., Stamford, Conn., 1941-44, chemist, 1945-50, rsch. chemist, 1950-56, rsch. adminstrv. svcs. coord., 1956-57; asst. chief chemist Revlon Rsch. Ctr., N.Y.C., 1957-60, assoc. rsch. dir., 1960-65; assoc. rsch. dir. Carter-Wallace, Inc., Cranbury, N.J., 1965-67, dir. tech. svcs., 1967-75; dir. statis. svcs. Carter-Wallace, Inc. and Wallace Labs., Cranbury, 1975-82; cons. med. statis. and clin. trials BioStatistics, Swanton, Vt., 1982—; instr. Stat-a-Natrix Inst., Edison, N.J., 1983-86. Author: Planning Pharmaceutical Clinical Trials, 1994. Home and Office: BioStatistics RR 1 Box 4690 Maquam Shore Swanton VT 05488-9736

WOODLAND, IRWIN FRANCIS, lawyer; b. New York, Sept. 2, 1922; s. John James and Mary (Hynes) W.; m. Sally Duffy, Sept. 23, 1954; children: Connie, J. Patrick, Stephen, Joseph, William, David, Duffy. BA, Columbia U., 1948; JD, Ohio State U., 1959. Bar: Calif. 1960, Wash., 1991, U.S. Dist. Ct. (cen. dist.) Calif. 1960, U.S. Dist. Ct. (no. dist.) Calif. 1962, U.S. Dist. Ct. (so. dist.) Calif. From assoc. to ptnr. Gibson, Dunn & Crutcher, L.A., 1959-88; ptnr. Gibson, Dunn & Crutcher, Seattle, 1988—; Bd. dirs. Sunlaw Energy Corp., Vernon, Calif. With USAF, 1942-45, ETO. Mem. ABA, Calif. Bar Assn., L.A. Bar Assn., Wash. State Bar Assn., Fed. Energy Bar Assn., Am. Mgmt. Assn., Phi Delta Phi, Jonathan Club, Bel Air Bay Club. Roman Catholic.

WOODLE, E. STEVE, transplant surgeon; b. Texarkana, Ark., Jan. 7, 1954; m. Linda Metzger, Sept. 7, 1979; three children. BS summa cum laude, Tex. A&M U., 1976; MD magna cum laude, U. Tex., 1980. Diplomate Am. Bd. Surgery, Am. Coll. Surgeons. Asst. prof. surgery Washington U. Sch. Medicine, St. Louis, 1990-92; asst. prof. surgery & immunology U. Chgo., 1992—; com. mem. Ctr. for Biol. Evaluation and Rsch., FDA, Washington, 1994—. Contbr. over 70 articles to med. and sci. jours. Mem. Am. Soc. Transplant Surgeons, Internat. Transplantation Soc., numerous others. Office: U Chgo Dept Surgery MC 5027 5841 S Maryland Chicago IL 60637

WOODLEY, DAVID TIMOTHY, dermatology educator; b. St. Louis, Aug. 1, 1946; s. Raoul Ramos-Mimosa and Marian (Schlueter) W.; m. Christina Paschall Prentice, May 4, 1974; children: David Thatcher, Thomas Colgate, Peter Paschall. AB, Washington U., St. Louis, 1968; MD, U. Mo., 1973. Diplomate Am. Bd. Internal Medicine, Am. Bd. Dermatology, Nat. Bd. Internal Medicine. Intern Beth Israel Med. Ctr., Mt. Sinai Sch. Medicine, N.Y. Hosp., Cornell U. Sch. Medicine, N.Y.C., 1973-74; resident in internal medicine U. Nebr., Omaha, 1974-76; resident in dermatology U. N.C., Chapel Hill, 1976-78, asst. prof. dermatology, 1983-85, assoc. prof. dermatology, 1985-88; prof. medicine, co-chief div. dermatology Cornell U. Med. Coll., N.Y., 1988-89; prof. and vice chair dept. dermatology Stanford U., 1989-93, Northwestern U., 1993—; research fellow U. Paris, 1978-80; expert NIH, Bethesda, Md., 1983-89; prof., assoc. chmn. dermatology Stanford U Sch. Medicine, 1989-93; chmn. dermatology Sch. Medicine Northwestern U., 1993—. Contbr. chpts. to books and articles in field to profl. jours. Mem. Potomac Albicore Fleet, Washington, 1982-83, Friends of the Art Sch., Chapel Hill, 1983—, Jungian Soc. Triangle Area, Chapel Hill, 1983—. Fellow Am. Acad. Dermatology; mem. Dermatology Found., Am. Soc. for Clin. Research, Soc. Investigative Dermatology, ACP (assoc.), Assn. Physican Poets, Am. Soc. for Clin. Investigation, 1988. Home: 503 W Barry Ave Chicago IL 60657-5416 Office: Northwestern U Med Sch Dept Dermatology 303 E Chicago Ave Chicago IL 60611

WOODLOCK, DOUGLAS PRESTON, judge; b. Hartford, Conn., Feb. 27, 1947; s. Preston and Kathryn (Ropp) W.; m. Patricia Mathilde Powers, Aug. 30, 1969; children: Pamela, Benjamin. BA, Yale U., 1969; JD, Georgetown U., 1975. Bar: Mass. 1975. Reporter Chgo. Sun-Times, 1969-73; staff mem. SEC, Washington, 1973-75; law clk. to Judge F.J. Murray, U.S. Dist. Ct. Mass., Boston, 1975-76; assoc. Goodwin, Procter & Hoar, Boston, 1976-79, 83-84, ptnr., 1984-86; asst. U.S. atty., Boston, 1979-83; judge U.S. Dist. Ct., Boston, 1986—; instr. Harvard U. Law Sch., 1980, 81; mem. U.S. Jud. Conf. Com. on Security, Space and Facilities, 1987-95; chmn. New Boston Fed. Courthouse Bldg. Com., 1987—. Contbr. articles to profl. jours. Articles editor Georgetown Law Jour., 1973-75. Chmn. Commonwealth of Mass. Com. for Pub. Counsel Services, 1984-86, Town of Hamilton Bd. Appeals, 1978-79. Recipient Dir.'s award U.S. Dept. Justice, 1983, Thomas Jefferson award for Pub. Architecture, AIA, 1996. Mem. ABA, Mass. Bar Assn., Boston Bar Assn., Am. Law Inst., Am. Judicature Soc., Am. Bar Found. Office: US Dist Ct McCormack PO & Courthouse Rm 1502 Boston MA 02109

WOODMAN, HAROLD DAVID, historian; b. Chgo., Apr. 21, 1928; s. Joseph Benjamin and Helen Ruth (Sollo) W.; m. Leonora Becker; children—Allan James, David Edward. B.A., Roosevelt U., 1957; M.A., U. Chgo., 1959, Ph.D., 1964. Lectr. Roosevelt U., 1962-63; asst. prof. history U. Mo., Columbia, 1963-66; assoc. prof. U. Mo., 1966-69, prof., 1969-71; prof. Purdue U., West Lafayette, Ind., 1971—, Louis Martin Sears disting. prof., 1990—; chmn. Com. on Am. Studies, 1981-94. Author: Conflict and Consensus in American History, 1966, 9th rev. edit., 1996, Slavery and the Southern Economy, 1966, King Cotton and His Retainers, 1968, Legacy of the American Civil War, 1973, New South-New Law, 1995; mem. editorial bd. Jour. So. History, 1972-75, Wis. Hist. Soc., 1972-76, Bus. History Rev., 1971-77, Agrl. History, 1976-82, Am. Hist. Rev., 1981-84, Jour. Am. History, 1985-88. Served with U.S. Army, 1950-52. Recipient Otto Wirth award Roosevelt U., 1990; Woodrow Wilson Internat. Center for Scholars fellow, 1977; Social Sci. Rsch. Coun. faculty grantee, 1969-70; Nat. Humanities Ctr. Fellow, 1983-84. Mem. Am. Hist. Assn., Orgn. Am. Historians, Econ. History Assn., Agrl. History Soc. (pres. 1983-84, Everett E. Edwards award 1963), Soc. Am. Historians, Bus. History Conf. (pres. 1981-82), Ind. Assn. Historians (pres. 1983-84), So. Hist. Assn. (exec. coun. 1982-85, Ramsdell award 1965, pres. 1995-96). Home: 1100 N Grant St West Lafayette IN 47906-2460 Office: Purdue U Dept History West Lafayette IN 47907

WOODMAN, HARRY ANDREWS, retired life insurance company executive, consultant; b. Orange, N.J., June 15, 1928; s. Harry Andrews and Mildred Amelia (Woods) W.; m. Betty Jo Pulsford, July 1, 1950; children: Richard Cushman, Andrea Ellen, Lynn Adele, Thomas Gordon. BA, Amherst Coll., 1950. With N.Y. Life Ins. Co., N.Y.C., 1950-89, 2d v.p., 1968-71, v.p., 1971-89; pvt. practice underwriting, actuarial cons. Cos Cob, Conn., 1989—. With USN, 1952-53. Mem. Soc. Actuaries, Home Office Life Underwriters Assn. (former pres.). Home and Office: 58 N Old Stone Bridge Rd Cos Cob CT 06807-1510

WOODMAN, WALTER JAMES, lawyer; b. Talara, Peru, Jan. 21, 1941; s. Walter James and Nora Carmen (Wensjoe) W.; m. Ruth Meyer, Dec. 19, 1970; children: Justin Meyer, Jessica Hilary. BA, U. Miami, 1964; JD, So. Meth. U., 1967. Bar: Tex. 1967, La. 1980, U.S. Dist. Ct. (no. dist.) Tex. 1967, U.S. Dist. Ct. (wwe. dist.) La. 1979, U.S. Dsit. Ct. (ea. dist.) Tex. 1983, U.S. Dist. Ct. (mid. dist.) La. 1988, U.S. Dist. Ct. (ea. dist.) La. 1989, U.S. Ct. Appeals (5th cir.) 1968, 81, U.S. Supreme Ct. 1971. Lawyer Dallas, 1967-72, Waxahachie, Tex., 1972-79; lawyer in sole practice Shreveport, La., 1979—; bd. dirs. N.W. La. Legal Svcs., Shreveport, 1993-96. Author book revs. and articles. Candidate Tex. Ho. of Reps., 1972; bd. dirs. Gov.'s Pan Am. Commn., BatonRouge, 1993-96. Mem. The North La. Civil War Roundtable. Home: Nonesuch Farm 12250 Ellerbe Rd Shreveport LA 71115 Office: 9045 Ellerbe Rd Ste 102 Shreveport LA 71106-6799

WOODMAN, WILLIAM E., theater, opera and television director; b. N.Y.C.; s. William E. and Ruth (Cornwall) W. BA, Hamilton Coll.; MFA, Columbia U. Stage mgr. Am. Shakespeare Festival, Stratford, Conn., 1957-61; co-producer Robin Hood Theater, Arden, Del., 1961-64; drama educator (founding mem.) Julliard Sch. Lincoln Ctr. Drama Div., N.Y.C., 1968-73; artistic dir. Goodman Theater, Chgo., 1973-78; drama educator U. So. Calif., 1993, Hamilton Coll., 1994, Circle in the Square Theatre Sch., 1995. Dir. The Freedom of the City (Brian Friel) on Broadway and at the Goodman Theatre, Chgo.; producer, dir. premieres by Edward Bond, Sam Shepard, Christopher Hampton, David Rabe, Studes Terkel, others; dir. ABC ARTS Cable TV Long Day's Journey into Night, 1982, Shakespeare Video Richard II, Romeo and Juliet, The Tempest 1981-83, Phila. Drama Gild, 1981-94, Dramski Teatar, Skopje, Yugoslavia, Buried Child, 1987, Man & Superman, Roundabout Theatre, N.Y.C., 1988, (PBS American Playhouse) The Diaries of Adam & Eve, 1988, Saint Joan, Repertory Theatre of St. Louis, 1989, The Lighthouse, Chgo. Opera Theatre, 1990, Die Fledermaus, June Opera Festival of N.J., 1990, Moon for the Misbegotten, Mo. Repertory, 1990, Cocktail House, Syracuse Stage, 1990, The Miser, Who's Afraid of Virginia Woolf, Playmaker's Repertory Co., 1991-92, The Gigli Concert, Court Theatre, 1992, The Tempest, Shakespeare in the Park, Westerly, R.I., 1992, The Glass Menagerie, Vt. Stage Co., 1994, Twelfth Night, Syracuse Stage, 1995. Served with U.S. Army, 1954-56. Mem. Dirs. Guild of Am., Soc. Stage Dirs. and Choreographers. Office: 205 W End Ave Apt 29S New York NY 10023-4851

WOODRELL, FREDERICK DALE, health care executive; b. St. Charles, Mo., Sept. 4, 1954; s. Robert Lee and Jeananne Monique (Daily) W.; m. Brenda Kay Justice, Aug. 10, 1974; children: Sara, Grace, Evan. BS in Acctg., Emporia State U., 1976; MPA, U. Mo., 1977. Cons. Robert Brown Consulting, Kansas City, 1976-78; asst. adminstr. Lee's Summit (Mo.) Community Hosp., 1978-79; asst. adminstr. Leesburg (Fla.) Regional Med. Ctr., 1979-82, adminstr., 1982-86; pres., CEO Ctrl. Fla. Heathcare Devel., Leesburg, Fla., 1986-92; dir. U. Miss. Hosp. & Clinic, Jackson, Miss., 1992—; healthcare exec. and cons. Quorum Health Resources, Nashville, 1979—. Active Friends of Children's Hosp., Jackson, 1992—; chmn. Assn. Retarded Citizen, Lake Tavares, Fla., 1990-92. Named Lake County Citizen of Yr. by Orlando (Fla.) Sentinal, 1988. Mem. Am. Hosp. Assn., Am. Coll. Healthcare Execs., Jackson Rotary. Avocations: golf, reading, horseback riding, fishing. Home: 2164 Brackenshire Cir Jackson MS 39211-5836 Office: U Hosps & Clinics U Miss Med Ctr 2500 N State St Jackson MS 39216-4500*

WOODRESS, JAMES LESLIE, JR., English language educator; b. Webster Groves, Mo., July 7, 1916; s. James Leslie and Jessie (Smith) W.; m. Roberta Wilson, Sept. 28, 1940. A.B., Amherst Coll., 1938; A.M., NYU, 1943; Ph.D., Duke U., 1950; LittD, U. Nebr., 1995. News editor Sta. KWK, St. Louis, 1939-40; rewriteman, editor UPI, N.Y.C., 1940-43; instr. English, Grinnell (Iowa) Coll., 1949-50; asst. prof. English, Butler U., Indpls., 1950-53; asso. prof. Butler U., 1953-58; asso. prof. English, San Fernando Valley (Calif.) State Coll., 1958-61, prof., 1961-66, chmn. dept., 1959-63, dean letters and scis., 1963-65; prof. English, U. Calif.-Davis, 1966-87, chmn. dept., 1970-74; vis. prof. Sorbonne, Paris, 1974-75, 83. Author: Howells and Italy, 1952, Booth Tarkington: Gentleman from Indiana, 1955, A Yankee's Odyssey: The Life of Joel Barlow, 1958, Dissertations in American Literature, 1957, 62, 68, Willa Cather: Her Life and Art, 1970, 75, 81, American Fiction 1900-50, 1974, Willa Cather: A Literary Life, 1987; editor: Eight American Authors, 1971, American Literary Scholarship: An Annual, 1965-69, 75-77, 79, 81, 87, Critical Essays on Walt Whitman, 1983, Cather's The Troll Garden, 1983, (with Richard Morris) Voices from America's Past, anthology, 1961-62, 75. Served to lt. AUS, 1943-46. Ford Fund for Advancement Edn. fellow, 1952-53; Guggenheim fellow, 1957-58; Fulbright lectr. France, 1962-63; Fulbright lectr. Italy, 1965-66; recipient Hubbell medal, 1985. Mem. MLA (sec. Am. Lit. group 1962-63), AAUP, Phi Beta Kappa. Address: 824 Sycamore Ln Davis CA 95616-3225 Office: U Calif Dept English Davis CA 95616

WOODRICK, ROBERT, food products executive. CEO D W Food Ctrs., Grand Rapids, Mich. Office: D&W Food Ctrs PO Box 878 Grand Rapids MI 49588-0878

WOODRING, DEWAYNE STANLEY, religion association executive; b. Gary, Ind., Nov. 10, 1931; s. J. Stanley and Vera Luella (Brown) W.; m. Donna Jean Wishart, June 15, 1957; children: Judith Lynn (Mrs. Richard Bigelow), Beth Ellen (Mrs. Thomas Carey). B.S. in Speech with distinction, Northwestern U., 1954, postgrad. studies in radio and TV broadcasting, 1954-57; M.Div., Garrett Theol. Sem., 1957; L.H.D., Mt. Union Coll., Alliance, Ohio, 1967; D.D., Salem (W.Va.) Coll., 1970. Asso. youth dir. Gary YMCA, 1950-55; ordained to ministry United Methodist Ch., 1955; minister of edn. Griffith (Ind.) Meth. Ch., 1955-57; minister adminstrn. and program 1st Meth. Ch., Eugene, Oreg., 1957-59; dir. pub. relations Dakotas area Meth. Ch., 1959-60, dir. pub. relations Ohio area, 1960-64; adminstrv. exec. to bishop Ohio East area United Meth. Ch., Canton, 1964-77; asst. gen. sec. Gen. Council on Fin. and Adminstrn., United Meth. Ch., Evanston, Ill., 1977-79; assoc. gen. sec. Gen. Council on Fin. and Adminstrn., 1979-84; exec. dir., chief exec. officer Religious Conf. Mgmt. Assn., 1982—; mem. staff, dept. radio svcs. 2d assembly World Coun. Chs., Evanston, 1954; vice-chmn. commn. on entertainment and program North Ctrl. Jursidictional Conf., 1968-72, chmn., 1972-76; mem. commn. on gen. conf. United Meth. Ch., 1972-93, bus. mgr., exec. dir., 1976-93, mem. divsn. interpretation, 1969-72; chmn. comm. commn. Ohio Coun. Chs., 1961-65; mem. exec. com. Nat. Assn. United Meth. Found., 1958-72; del. World Meth. Conf., London, Eng., 1966, Dublin, Ireland, 1976, Honolulu, 1981, Nairobi, 1986, Singapore, 1991, Rio de Janeiro, Brazil, 1996; exec. com. World Meth. Coun., 1986—; del. White House Conf. on Travel and Tourism, 1995; bd. dirs. Ohio East Area United Meth. Found., 1967-78, v.p., 1967-76; chmn. bd. mgrs. United Meth. Bldg., Evanston, 1977-84; lectr., cons. on fgn. travel; Marriott Customer Leadership Forum, Red Lion Hotels and Inss Customer adv. bd. Creator: nationally distbd. radio series The Word and Music; producer, dir.: TV series Parables in Miniature, 1957-59. Adviser East Ohio Conf. Communications Commn., 1968-76; pres. Guild Assocs., 1971—; trustee, 1st v.p. Copeland Oaks Retirement Ctr., Sebring, Ohio, 1969-76; bd. dirs. First Internat. Summit on Edn., 1989. Recipient Cert. Meeting Profl. award, 1985, Cert. Expt. Mgr. award, 1988; named to Ky. Cols., 1989, Conv. Liaison Coun. Hall of Leaders honoree, 1994. Mem. Am. Soc. Assn. Execs., Ind. Soc. Assn. Execs. (Mtg. Planner of Yr. award 1990), Mtg. Profl. Internat., Conv. Liaison Coun. (bd. dirs., past chmn.), Def. Orientation Conf. Assn. (chaplain), Ind. Conv. visitors Assc. (bd. dirs., 1996-99) Cert. Mtg. Profls. (bd. dirs. 1983-91), Internat. Assn. Exposition Mgmt., Found. for Internat. mtgs. (bd. dirs.).Marriott cust. leadsp. forum, red Lion Hotels Inns cust. adv. bd. Home: 7224 Chablis Ct Indianapolis IN 46278-1540 Office: 1 RCA Dome St 120 Indianapolis IN 46225-1023

WOODRING, JAMES H., lawyer; b. Johnstown, Pa., 1942. BA, Dickinson Coll., 1964; LLB, Yale U., 1967. Bar: Ohio 1967. Atty. Squire Sanders & Dempsey, Cleve.; prop. James H Woodring Law Firm. Mem. ABA, Cleve. Bar Assn., Ohio State Bar Assn. Office: James H Woodring Law Firm 23450 Wimbeldon Rd Cleveland OH 44114*

WOODRING, MARGARET DALEY, architect, planner; b. N.Y.C., Mar. 29, 1933; d. Joseph Michael and Mary (Barron) Daley; m. Francis Woodring, Oct. 25, 1954 (div. 1962); m. Robert Bell, Dec. 20, 1971; children: Ward, Lissa, Gabrielle, Phaedra. Student, NYU, 1959-60; BArch, Columbia U., 1966; MArch, Princeton U., 1971. Registered architect; cert. planner. Architect, planner various firms, N.Y.C.; environ. design specialist Rutgers U., New Brunswick, N.J., 1966-68; programming cons. Davis & Brody, N.Y.C., 1968-71; planning cons. William H. Liskamm, San Francisco, 1971-74; mgr. planning Met. Transp. Commn., Oakland, Calif., 1974-81; dir. Internat. Program for Housing and Urban Devel. Ofcls. Ctr. for Environ. Design Rsch. U. Calif., Berkeley, 1981-89; prin. Woodring & Assocs., San Rafael, Calif., 1989—; adj. lectr. dept. architecture U. Calif., Berkeley, 1974-84; founder New Horizons Savs. Assn., San Rafael, 1977-79; cons. U.S. Agy. for Internat. Devel., Washington, 1981-89; mem. jury Nat. Endowment Arts, others. Chair Bicentennial Com., San Rafael, 1976; bd. dirs. Displaced Homemakers Ctr., Oakland, 1981-84; pres. Environ Design Found., San Francisco, 1984-90. William Kinne Travel fellow Columbia U., 1965-66; Richard King Mellon fellow Princeton U., 1968-70. Mem. AIA (chair urban design com. San Francisco chpt. 1980-81), Am. Inst. Cert. Planners, Urban Land Inst., Soc. for Internat. Devel. (pres. San Francisco chpt. 1980-83), World Affairs Coun., Internat. World Congress on Land Policy. Avocations: hiking, gardening, reading, race walking. Home: 226 Magnolia Ave San Rafael CA 94901-2244 Office: Woodring & Assocs 938 B St San Rafael CA 94901-3005

WOODRUFF, BRUCE EMERY, lawyer; b. Mason City, Iowa, June 23, 1930; s. Frederick Bruce and Grace (Emery) W.; m. Carolyn Clark, Aug. 18, 1956; children: David C., Douglas B., Lynn M., Daniel R. BS in Bus., U. Ill., 1952; JD, Washington U., St. Louis, 1959. Bar: Mo. 1959, D.C. Dist. Ct. (ea. dist.) Mo. 1959, U.S. Ct. Appeals (8th cir.) 1960, U.S. Supreme Ct. 1979. Assoc. Armstrong, Teasdale, Schlafly, Davis & Dicus, St. Louis, 1959-65; ptnr. Armstrong Teasdale, Schlafly & Davis (and predecessor firms), St. Louis, 1966-95, counsel, 1996—; prin. counsel St. Louis C. of C., 1962-89; bd. dirs. Christian Health Svcs. Devel. Corp., St. Louis, BJC Health Sys., St. Louis, Cass. Comml. Corp., Cass Bank & Trust Co., Rainbow Village, Inc., Group Health Plan; city atty., Kirkwood, Mo., 1986. Named Kirkwood Citizen of Yr., 1983. Mem. ABA (banking law com.), Mo. Bar Assn., Bar Assn. Met. St. Louis, Am. Acad. Healthcare Attys. Republican. Presbyterian. Clubs: Algonquin (Glendale, Mo.); Noonday (St. Louis (bd. dirs. 1988-91). Avocations: golf, swimming, sailing, photography. Home: 333 Dickson Ave Saint Louis MO 63122-4631 Office: Armstrong Teasdale Schlafly & Davis 1 Mel Nor Ln Ste 2600 Saint Louis MO 63125-5329

WOODRUFF, C(HARLES) ROY, professional association executive; b. Anniston, Ala., Sept. 27, 1938; m. Kay Carolyn Jernigan, June 26, 1962; children: Charles R. Jr., Earl David. BA, U. Ala., 1960; BD, So. Bapt. Theol. Sem., 1963, PhD in Psychology of Religion and Pastoral Care, 1966. Lic. profl. counselor, Va. Asst. pastor Ft. Mitchell Bapt. Ch., South Ft. Mitchell, Ky., 1960-63; Protestant chaplain Silvercrest Hosp., New Albany, Ind., 1963-66; dir. dept. pastoral care and edn. Bryce State Hosp., Tuscaloosa, Ala., 1966-71; assoc. prof., chaplain supr. dept. patient counseling Med. Coll. Va., Richmond, 1971-76; assoc. prof., chmn. dept. psychology of religion and pastoral care Midwestern Bapt. Theol. Sem., Kansas City, Mo., 1976-78; exec. dir. Peninsula Pastoral Counseling Ctr., Newport News, Va., 1978-88, Am. Assn. Pastoral Counselors, Washington, 1988—; lecturing fellow Interpreter's House, Lake Junaluska, N.C., 1968-78; pastoral counselor, clin. supr. Psychol. Clinic, U. Ala., Tuscaloosa, 1969-71; adj. staff mem. The Counseling Inst., Kansas City, 1976-78. Author: Alcoholism and Christian Experience, 1968; (with others) Alcohol, In and Out of the Church, 1968, Work Adjustment: The Goal of Rehabilitation, 1973, Pastoral Theology and Ministry, Key Resources, 1983, The Dictionary of Pastoral Care and Counseling, 1990; also articles. Apptd. by Gov. of Va. to Bd. Profl. Counselors, Commonwealth of Va., 1987-95 (chmn. 1993-95); mem. Nat. Mental Health Leadership Forum, 1990-93. United Meth. Ch. Gen. Bd. Christian Social Concerns grantee, 1965; So. Bapt. Theol. Sem. teaching fellow, 1965-66. Fellow Coll. Chaplains of Am. Protestant Hosp. Assn.; mem. Assn. for Clin. Pastoral Edn. (cert. supr.), Assn. Couples for Marriage Enrichment (cert.). Home: 10827 Burr Oak Way Burke VA 22015-2416 Office: Am Assn Pastoral Counselors 9504A Lee Hwy Fairfax VA 22031-2303

WOODRUFF, DONALD B., art director, production designer. Prodn. designer: (films) Barbarosa, 1982; art dir.: (films) Ruthless People, 1986, Harry and the Hendersons, 1987, Jaws-the Revenge, 1987, Who's That Girl?, 1987, The Naked Gun: From the Files of Police Squad!, 1988, Fletch Lives, 1989, The Hunt for Red October, 1990, For the Boys, 1991. Office: care Art Directors Guild 11365 Ventura Blvd Ste 315 Studio City CA 91604-3148

WOODRUFF, FAY, paleoceanographer, geological researcher; b. Boston, Jan. 23, 1944; d. Lorande Mitchell and Anne (Fay) W.; m. Alexander Whitehill Clowes, May 20, 1972 (div. Oct. 1974); m. Robert G. Douglas, Jan. 27, 1980; children: Ellen, Katerina. RN, Mass. Gen. Hosp. Sch. Nursing, Boston, 1965; BA, Boston U., 1971; MS, U. So. Calif., 1979. Rsch. assoc. U. So. Calif., L.A., 1978-81, rsch. faculty, 1981-96; keynote spkr. 4th Internat. Symposium on Benthic Foraminifera, Sendai, Japan, 1990. Contbg. author: Geological Society of America Memoir, 1985; contbr. articles to profl. jours. Life mem. The Nature Conservancy, Washington, 1992; bd. dirs. Friends of Friendship Park, 1995-96. NSF grantee, 1986-88, 88-91, 91-

94. Mem. Am. Geophys. Union, Geol. Soc. Am., Internat. Union Geol. Scis. (internat. commn. on stratigraphy, subcommn. on Neogene stratigaphy 1991-92), Soc. Woman Geographers (sec. So. Calif. chpt. 1990-96), Soc. Econ. Paleontologists and Minerologists (sec., editor N.Am. Micropaleontology sect. 1988-90), Oceanography Soc. (chpt. mem.), Sigma Xi. Episcopalian. Avocation: birding. Office: U So Calif Dept Geol Scis Los Angeles CA 90089-0740

WOODRUFF, GENE LOWRY, nuclear engineer, university dean; b. Greenbrier, Ark., May 6, 1934; s. Clarence Oliver and Avie Ercilla (Lowry) W.; m. Marylou Munson, Jan. 29, 1961; children—Gregory John, David Reed. B.S. with honors, U.S. Naval Acad., 1956; M.S. in Nuclear Engring., MIT, 1963, Ph.D. in Nuclear Engring., 1966. Registered profl. engr., Wash. Asst. prof. nuclear engring. U. Wash., Seattle, 1965-70, assoc. prof., 1970-76, prof., 1976-93, chmn. dept., 1981-84, dir. nuclear engring. labs., 1973-76, dean Grad. Sch., 1984-93, prof. chem. engring. environ. studies, 1989—; vice-chair, chair-elect Grad. Record Exam., 1991-92, chair, 1992-93; cons. to govt. and industry. Contbr. numerous articles to sci. and tech. jours. Served to lt. USN, 1956-60. Mem. Nat. Soc. Profl. Engrs. (Achievement award 1977), Am. Nuclear Soc. (Achievement award 1977, chmn. honors/awards com. 1981-84, nat. program com. 1971-75, exec. com. fusion div. 1976-80, vice chmn. edn. div. 1983-84, Arthur Holly Compton award 1986), Am. Soc. Engring. Edn., Assn. Grad. Schs. (v.p./pres.-elect 1990-91, pres. 1991-92). Democrat. Home: 2700 123rd Ave SE Bellevue WA 98005-4147 Office: University of Washington Box 351750 Seattle WA 98195-1750

WOODRUFF, HARRISON D., JR., principal. Prin. Keith Valley Middle Sch., Horsham, Pa. Recipient Blue Ribbon award U.S. Dept. Edn., 1990-91. Office: Keith Valley Mid Sch 227 Meetinghouse Rd Horsham PA 19044-2119

WOODRUFF, HOWARD CHARLES, biomedical researcher; b. Phila., Oct. 5, 1912; s. Howard Anson and Mary Ann (Neely) W.; m. Hildred Morris Levy; children: Charlotte Leib, Harriet Spizzirri. BS, U. Pa., 1932, postgrad., 1933-37; postgrad., U. Munich, Germany, 1937-38; PhD, U. Fla., 1950. Polymer devel. staff GE Co., Schenectady, N.Y., 1944-48, Johnson Wax Co., Racine, Wis., 1948-52, Napko Corp., Houston, 1952-68; viral rschr. Viral Rsch. Co., Houston, 1968-78, Viral Tech. Inc., Des Plaines, Ill., 1980-94; cons. Atomic Energy Commn.-Plant Constrn. Author: Organization Essentials, 1967, Treatment and Diagnosis of AIDS, 1991. With British Intelligence, 1943-45. Mem. N.Y. Acad. Sci. (hon.). Achievements include patents for radiation reactive polymers, polymers developing resistance, polyglycerides and polyglycerides, heat cure acrylic polymers. Avocation: archery. Home: 800 S River Rd Des Plaines IL 60016

WOODRUFF, JOHN DOUGLAS, non-profit association administrator, retired air force officer; b. Bonham, Tex., Feb. 12, 1944; s. Alexander Campbell and Lois Kathryn (Turner) W.; m. Carol Lynne Thompson, June 11, 1966; children: Keith Byron, Jill Marie, David Kent. BS in Sociology/Psychology, East Tex. State U., 1966; grad. with distinction, AFROTC, 1966; MS in Edn., U. So. Calif., 1970; grad. with distinction, Air Command and Staff Coll., 1977; USAF exch. student, U.S. Army War Coll., 1980-81. Commd. 2d lt. USAF, 1966; advanced through grades to col. USAF Air Rescue Svc., 1990; comdr. USAF Air Rescue Svc., McClellan AFB, Calif., 1990-93; vice comdr. 314th Airlift Wing, Little Rock, 1993-95; field svc. manager ARC, Little Rock, 1995—; adj. instr. psychology Golden Gate U., Pope AFB, N.C., 1975-76; com. chmn. Sec. of Air Force's Blue Ribbon Panel on Space, Maxwell AFB, Ala., 1988. Contbr. articles to USAF mag. Mil. sponsor for civic leader program Mil. Affairs Com., Abilene, Tex., 1982-83, Logstar Civilian Hon. Comdr. Program, Sacramento, 1990-93; mem. Cmty. Coun., Jacksonville, Ark., 1993-95. Decorated Legion of Merit with 2 oak leaf clusters, Meritorious Svc. medal with 3 oak leaf clusters, Air Force Commendation medal. Mem. Air Force Assn. (Citation of Honor 1989), Airlift/Tanker Assn., Air Rescue Assn., Jolly Green Pilots Assn., Order of Daedalians. Episcopalian. Avocations: antique refinishing and restoration, military history. Home: 7305 Yuma Ct North Little Rock AR 72116-4359 Office: Amer Red Cross 401 S Monroe Little Rock AR 72205

WOODRUFF, JUDY CARLINE, broadcast journalist; b. Tulsa, Nov. 20, 1946; d. William Henry and Anna Lee (Payne) W.; m. Albert R. Hunt, Jr., Apr. 5, 1980; children: Jeffrey Woodruff, Benjamin Woodruff, Lauren Ann Lee. Student, Meredith Coll., 1964-66; B.A., Duke U., 1968. News announcer, reporter Sta. WAGA-TV, Atlanta, 1970-75; news corr. NBC News, Atlanta, 1975-76; White House corr. NBC News, Washington, 1977-83; anchor Frontline, PBS documentary series, 1983-90; corr. MacNeil-Lehrer News Hour, PBS, Washington, 1983-93; anchor and sr. corr. CNN, Washington, 1993—; mem. bd. advisors Henry Grady Sch. Journalism, U. Ga., 1979-82; bd. visitors Wake Forest U., 1982-89; mem. bd. advisors Benton Fellowship in Broadcast Journalism, U. Chgo., 1984-90, Knight Fellowship in Journalism, Stanford U., 1985—; trustee Duke U., 1985—; founding bd. dirs. Internat. Women's Media Found., 1989—. Author: This is Judy Woodruff at the White House, 1982. Mem. Commn. on Women's Health, The Commonwealth Fund. Recipient award Leadership Atlanta, Class of 1974, Atlanta chpt. Women in Comms., 1975, Edward Weintal award for excellence in fgn. policy reporting, 1987, Joan Shorenstein Barone award for series on def. issues, 1987, Helen Bernstein award for excellence in journalism N.Y. Pub. Libr., 1989, Pres.'s award Nat. Women's Hall of Fame, 1994, CableAce award for best newscaster, 1995, Allen H. Neuharth award for excellence in journalism, 1995. Mem. NATAS (Atlanta chpt. Emmy award 1975), White House Corrs. Assn. Office: Cable News Network 820 1st St NE Washington DC 20002-4243

WOODRUFF, KAY HERRIN, pathologist, educator; b. Charlotte, N.C., Sept. 22, 1942; d. Herman Keith and Helen Thelma (Tucker) Herrin; m. John T. Lyman, May 3, 1980; children: Robert, Geoffry, Carolyn. BA in Chemistry, Duke U., 1964; MD, Emory U., 1968. Diplomate Am. Bd. Pathology (trustee 1993—). Medicine and pediat. intern U. N.C., Chapel Hill, 1968-69, resident in anatomic pathology, 1969-70; chief resident in anatomic pathology, instr. U. Okla., Oklahoma City, 1970-71, fellow in electron microscopy-pulmonary pathology, instr., 1971-72; chief resident in clin. pathology U. Calif., San Francisco, 1972-74, asst. clin. prof. dept. anatomic pathology, 1974-91, assoc. clin. prof., 1991—; chief electron microscopy VA Hosp., San Francisco, 1974-75, attending clin. cons. dept. anatomic pathology, 1986—; pvt. practice, San Pablo, Calif., 1981—; pres. med. staff Brookside Hosp., San Pablo, 1994, med. dir. Regional Cancer Ctr., 1995—; assoc. pathologist Children's Hosp., San Francisco, 1979-81, St. Joseph's Hosp., San Francisco, 1977-79; cons. pathologist Lawrence Berkeley (Calif.) Lab., 1974-93; med. dir. Bay Area Tumor Inst. Tissue Network, San Pablo, 1989—; asst. clin. prof. pathology health and med. scis. program U. Calif., Berkeley and U. Calif., San Francisco Joint Med. Program, 1985-91, assoc. clin. prof., 1991—, others. Contbr. articles and abstracts to med. jours. Mem. exec. bd. Richmond (Calif.) Quits Smoking, 1986-90, Bay Area Tumor Inst., Oakland, Calif., 1987—; mem. exec. bd. Contra Costa unit Am. Cancer Soc., Walanut Creek, Calif., 1985-87, mem. profl. edn. com., 1985—, mem. pub. edn. com., 1985-86, mem. task force on breast health Calif. div., 1992-93; mem. transfusion adv. com. Irwin Meml. Blood Bank, San Francisco, 1977-83; chmn. transfusion adv. com. Alameda Contra County Blood Bank, 1989-92; commr. Calif. Bd. Med. Quality Assurance, 1978-80. Recipient young investigator award Am. Lung Assn., 1975-77; Outstanding Svc. awards Am. Cancer Soc., 1986, 87, Disting. Svc. award, 1988; Disting. Clin. Tchg. award U. Calif., San Francisco and Berkeley Joint Med. Program, 1987, Outstanding Tchg. award, 1988, Excellence in Basic Sci. Instrn. award, 1990, Excellence in Tchr. Clin. Scis. award, 1993; cert. of recognition Cmty. Svc. Richmond, 1989. Mem. AMA, Coll. Am. Pathologists (editl. bd. CAP Today 1986-90, bd. govs. 1990-96, chair coun. on practice mgmt. 1994), Am. Med. Women's Assn. (exec. bd. 1984-87, regional bd. govs. 1984-87), No. Calif. Women's Med. Assn. (pres. 1982-84), Calif. Soc. Pathologists (bd. dirs. 1988-90), No. Calif. Oncology Group, South Bay Pathology Soc., Am. Assn. Blood Banks, Calif. Med. Assn., Alameda-Contra Costa County Med. Soc., Am. Soc. Clin. Pathology, Calif. Pathology Soc. Avocations: classical piano, bicycle touring, distance running, reading, wind surfing. Office: Brookside Hosp Dept Pathology 2000 Vale Rd San Pablo CA 94806-3808

WOODRUFF, MARGARET SMITH, lawyer; b. Kansas City, Mo.; d. Arthur Bremner and Berendina (Teeuwen) Smith; m. Charles Lawrence Woodruff; children: Anne Teeuwynn, Paul Lawrence. AB, Mt. Holyoke Coll., 1963; MS in Libr. Sci., Drexel U., 1966; JD cum laude, Villanova U., 1977. Bar: Pa. 1977, U.S. Dist. Ct. (ea. dist.) Pa., U.S. Ct. Appeals (3d and 6th crcts.), U.S. Supreme Ct. 1980. Law clk. to Hon. John P. Fullam U.S. Dist. Ct. (ea. dist.) Pa., 1978; ptnr. Schnader, Harrison, Segal & Lewis, Phila., 1977—; participant seminars for Pa. Conf. of State Trial Judges, Pittsburgh, 1993, Pa. Bar Inst., Phila., Harrisburg, Pitts. and Allentown, Pa., 1988, 91. Co-author: The Expert Witness: Law and Practice, 1993; contbr. articles to law revs. and jours. Mem. ABA, Pa. Bar Assn., Phila. Bar Assn., Order of Coif. Home: 9265 Germantown Ave Philadelphia PA 19118-2618 Office: Schnader Harrison Segal & Lewis 1600 Market St Ste 3600 Philadelphia PA 19103-7240

WOODRUFF, MARTHA JOYCE, home health agency executive; b. Unadilla, Ga., Jan. 3, 1941; d. Metz Loy and Helen (McCorvey) Woodruff. BA, Shorter Coll., 1963; MA, U. Tenn.-Knoxville, 1972. Tchr., Albany H.S. (Ga.), 1963-69; instr. U. Tenn.-Knoxville, 1970-72; asst. prof. Valdosta State Coll. (Ga.), 1972-76; coord. Staff Builders, Atlanta, 1976-78; pres., owner Med. Pers. Pool, Knoxville, 1978-93; owner, pres. Priority Healthcare Svcs, Knoxville, 1993—, Pers. Pool of Knoxville, Inc., 1985-87; mem., adviser Owners Adv. Coun., Pers. Pool of Am., Ft. Lauderdale, Fla., 1980-82. active Altzheimers Assn. Mem. Nat. Coun. on Aging, Nat. Assn. for Adult Daycare, Exec. Women Internat. (bd. dirs. Knoxville chpt.), East Tenn. Women's Polit. Caucus, Tenn. Assn. Home Care, Nat. Assn. Homecare, Knoxville C. of C. (com. for cost containment 1982-85), Blount County C. of C. (retirement com. 1983, mem. indsl. rels. com. 1983). Republican. Methodist.

WOODRUFF, NEIL PARKER, agricultural engineer; b. Clyde, Kans., July 25, 1919; s. Charles Scott and Myra (Christian) W.; m. Dorothy Adele Russ, June 15, 1952; children—Timothy C., Thomas S. B.S., Kans. State U., 1949, M.S., 1953; postgrad., Iowa State U., 1959. Agrl. engr. Agrl. Research Service, Dept. Agr., Manhattan, Kans., 1949-63; research leader Agrl. Research Service, Dept. Agr., 1963-75; cons. engr. Manhattan, 1975-77; civil engr. Kans. Dept. Transp., Topeka, 1977-79; prof., mem. grad. faculty Kans. State U., civil engr. facilities planning, 1979-84; mem. sci. exchange team to Soviet Union, 1974; with W/PT Cons., 1984—. Contbr. articles to tech. jours. and books. Fellow Am. Soc. Agrl. Engrs. (Hancor Soil Water Engring. award 1975); mem. Sigma Xi, Gamma Sigma Delta. Home and Office: 12906 W Blue Bonnet Dr Sun City West AZ 85375-2538

WOODRUFF, THOMAS ELLIS, electronics consulting executive; b. Stockton, Calif., Feb. 8, 1921; s. Ennis Casselberry and Gracella (Scotford) W.; m. Doris Elaine Walters, Jan. 14, 1947 (div. Aug. 1962); children: Mary Ann Woodruff Mahaffy, Martha Lee; m. Ruth Elizabeth Craik, Feb. 25, 1964; 1 child, Robert Peter; stepchildren: Gordon Lee Vickers, Barbara Ann Vickers, Mary Jean Vickers. AA, Stockton Jr. Coll., 1941; BSEE, U. Calif., Berkeley, 1943. Registered profl. engr., Calif. Engr. GE, Syracuse, N.Y., 1944-47; staff engr. Hughes Aircraft Co., Culver City, Calif., 1947-56; mgr. electronics design Sanders Assocs., Nashua, N.H., 1956-58, chief engr. preliminary design, 1958-60, mgr. spl. programs div., 1960-62, corp. dir. systems, 1962-65, v.p., gen. mgr. corp. systems group, 1965-73, v.p. antisubmarine weapons and communications, 1966-72, dir., 1968-70, sr. dir., 1970-76, v.p. gen. mgr. ocean systems group, 1972-76, v.p. sci. and tech., 1976-88, corp. cons., 1989—; v.p. Sanders Nuclear Corp., Nashua, 1966-71; mem. adv. com. Def. Intelligence Agy., Washington, 1978-83; joint adv. com. MIT Lincoln Lab., Bedford, Mass., 1988-89; cons. Superconductor Tech., Inc., Santa Barbara, Calif., 1988—, Oryx, Inc., Paramus, N.J., 1989—, Sanders/Lockheed, 1988-91, ret. 1992. Patentee, co-patentee 14 inventions in electronics for computers, control systems, video displays, submarine detection devices, others. Mem. IEEE (sr.). Republican. Avocations: skiing, photography, motorcycling, swimming. Home and Office: 8 Berkeley St Nashua NH 03060-2309

WOODRUFF, TOM, JR., special effects designer; b. Williamsport, Pa., Jan. 20, 1959; s. Thomas Howard and Shirley Joanne (Boyer) W.; m. Tami H. Spitler, Aug. 22, 1981; children: David Thomas, Taylor Jon, Connor Boyer. BA (cum laude), Lycoming Coll., 1980. Artist, technician Burman Studios, Van Nuys, Calif., 1983; co-designer, artist Stan Winston Studio, Inc., Northridge, Calif.; designer, ptnr. Amalgamated Dynamics, Inc., Chatsworth, Calif., 1988—. Designer and performer (film) Tremors, 1989, Alien III, 1990; co-designer (film) The Santa Clause, 1994, Demolition Man, 1993, Wolf, 1993; co-designer, performer (film) Pumpkinhead, 1987, Leviathan, 1988, Alien Nation, 1988, Death Becomes Her, 1992 (Academy award Visual Effects 1993), Jumanji, 1995, Mortal Kombat, 1995; dir., writer (short film) The Demon with 3 Tales, 1987; lab technician (film) Predator, 1987; artist and performer (Film) Monster Squad, 1986, The Terminator, 1985, Aliens, 1986, (TV) Amazing Stories, 1986. Office: Amalgamated Dynamics Inc 21604 Marilla St Chatsworth CA 91311-4123

WOODRUFF, TRUMAN O(WEN), physicist, emeritus educator; b. Salt Lake City, May 26, 1925; s. Wilford Owen and Evelyn (Ballif) W.; m. Ambrosia Lydia Solaroli, Sept. 14, 1948 (dec. June 1991); m. Patricia O'Keefe Vincent, Sept. 23, 1995. AB, Harvard U., 1947; BA, Oxford (Eng.) U., 1950; PhD, Calif. Inst. Tech., 1955. Nat. scholar Harvard, 1942-44, 46-47, Sheldon traveling fellow, 1947-48; Rhodes scholar Oxford U., 1948-50; Dow Chem. Co. fellow, Howard Hughes fellow Calif. Inst. Tech., 1950-54; research asso. physics U. Ill., 1954-55; physicist Gen. Elec. Research Lab., 1955-62; prof. physics Mich. State U., 1962-85, prof. emeritus, 1985—, chmn. dept., 1972-75; sr. scientist research labs. Hughes Aircraft Co., Malibu, Calif., 1986-87; cons. in physics Los Angeles, 1987—; vis. prof. Scuola Normale Superiore, Pisa, Italy, 1982—. Contbr. articles to sci. jours. Served with USNR, 1944-46. Fulbright fellow U. Pisa, 1968-69. Fellow Am. Phys. Soc.; mem. Assn. Harvard Chemists, Phi Beta Kappa, Sigma Xi. Office: 11 Thornwood Irvine CA 92714-3227

WOODRUFF, VIRGINIA, writer, broadcast journalist; b. Morrisville, Pa.; d. Edwin Nichols and Louise (Meredith) W.; m. Raymond F. Beagle Jr. (div.); m. Albert Plaut II (div.); 1 child, Elise Meredith. Student, Rutgers U. News corr. Sta. WNEW-TV Metromedia, N.Y.C., 1967; nat., internat. critic-at-large Mut. Broadcasting System, 1968-75; lectr. Leigh Bur., 1969-71; byline columnist N.Y. Daily Mirror, N.Y.C., 1970-71; first Arts critic Teleprompter and Group W Cable TV, 1977-84; host/producer The First Nighter N.Y. Times Primetime Cable Highlight program, 1977-84; pres., chief exec. officer Starpower, Inc., 1984-91; affiliate news corr. ABC Radio Network, N.Y.C., 1984-86; pres. Promarket People Inc., 1991-93; S.W. contbg. corr. Am. in the Morning, First Light, Mut. Broadcasting System, 1992; S.W. freelance corr. Voice of Am., USIA, 1992—; perennial critic Off-Off Broadway Short Play Festival, N.Y.C., 1984—; was 1st Woman on 10 O'Clock News, WNEW-TV, 1967. Contbg. feature writer Vis a Vis mag., 1988-91. Mem. celebrity panel Arthritis Telethon, N.Y.C., 1976. Selected episodes of First Nighter program in archives N.Y. Pub. Libr., Billy Rose Theatre Collection, Rodgers and Hammerstein Collection, Performing Arts Rsch.Ctr. Mem. Drama Desk. Presbyterian. Clubs: National Arts, Dutch Treat.

WOODRUFF, WANDA LEA, elementary education educator; b. Woodward, Okla., May 2, 1937; d. Milton Casper and Ruth Arlene (Bradshaw) Shuck; m. William Jennings Woodruff, Aug. 18, 1962; children: Teresa Kaye, Bruce Alan, Neal Wayne. BS, Northwestern State U., 1959; MA in Edn., Olivet Nazarene U., 1973. Cert. K-8th grade tchr. Anthony (Kans.) Pub. Schs., 1959-60, transition class tchr., 1960-61, 1st grade tchr., 1961-62; 5th grade tchr. Versailles (Ky.) Pub. Schs., 1962-63; 1st grade tchr. Bradley (Ill.) Elem. Schs., 1968-93; presch. vol. Concern Ctr., Bartlesville, Okla., 1994—. Com. chmn. Bus. and Profl. Women, Anthony, 1959-62; sec. com. PTA, Anthony, 1959-63, Bradley (Ill.) PTA, 1968-93. Recipient grant for edn. First of Am. Bank, 1991-92, 92-93. Mem. Bartlesville Pilot Club Internat. (edn./patriotism chairperson 1994-95, dir. 1995-96, mem. com. Spl. Olympics 1995-96, pres-elect 1996—). Avocations: jogging, reading, baking, working with children and young people. Home: 2373 Mountain Rd Bartlesville OK 74003-6926

WOODRUM, CLIFTON A., III, lawyer, state legislator; b. Washington, July 23, 1938; s. Clifton A. Jr. and Margaret (Lanier) W.; m. Emily Abbitt, Aug. 10, 1963; children—Robert, Meredith, Anne. A.B., U. N.C., 1961; LL.B., U. Va., 1964. Bar: Va. 1964, U.S. Dist. Ct. (we. dist.) Va. 1964, U.S. Ct. Appeals (4th cir.) 1968, U.S. Supreme Ct. 1970. Assoc. Dodson, Pence & Coulter, Roanoke, Va., 1964-68; ptnr. Dodson, Pence, Viar, Woodrum & Mackey, 1968-95, counsel Dodson, Prince & Viar, 1995—; mem. Va. Ho. of Dels., 1980—. Chmn. 6th Dist. Democratic Com., Va., 1972-76; mem. State Water Commn., 1981—; State Crime Commn., 1982—, chmn. 1995—; chmn. Med. Malpractice Study, Va., 1984-85. Mem. ABA, Assn. Trial Lawyers Am., Va. Bar Assn., Roanoke Bar Assn. Episcopalian. Home: 2641 Cornwallis Ave SE Roanoke VA 24014-3339 Office: Dodson Pence & Viar PO Box 1371 Roanoke VA 24007-1371

WOODRUM, PATRICIA ANN, librarian; b. Hutchinson, Kans., Oct. 11, 1941; d. Donald Jewell and Ruby Pauline (Shuman) Hoffman; m. Clayton Eugene Woodrum, Mar. 31, 1962; 1 child, Clayton Eugene, II. BA, Kans. State Coll., Pittsburg, 1963; MLS, U. Okla., 1966. Br. libr. Tulsa City-County Libr. System, 1964-65, head brs., 1965-66, head reference dept., 1966-67, chief extension, chief pub. svc., 1967-73, asst. dir., 1973-76, exec. dir., 1976—; bd. dirs. Local Am. Bank Tulsa. Mem. editorial bd. Jour. of Library Administration. Active Friends of Tulsa Libr., Leadership Tulsa Alumni; regent UCT/RSC, Tulsa. Recipient Disting. Libr. award Okla. Libr. Assn., 1982, Leadership Tulsa Paragon award, 1987, Women in Comm. Newsmaker award, 1989, Outstanding Alumnus award U. Okla. Sch. Libr. Info. Studies, 1989, Headliner award Tulsa Press Club, 1996; inducted into Tulsa City-County Libr. Hall of Fame, 1989, Okla. Womens Hall of Fame, 1993. Mem. ALA, Pub. Libr. Assn. (pres. 1993-94), Okla. Libr. Assn. (pres. 1978-79, Disting. Libr. award 1982, Meritorious Svc. award 1996), Tulsa C. of C. Democrat. Episcopalian. Avocations: backpacking, swimming, gardening. Office: Tulsa City-County Libr 400 Civic Ctr Tulsa OK 74103-3857

WOODRUM, ROBERT LEE, executive search consultant; b. Merkel, Tex., Mar. 3, 1945; s. Bill and Norma (Shea) W.; m. Linda Mary Larkin, July 20, 1968; children: Jennifer, Michael. BA, Calif. State U., Northridge, 1967; postgrad., U. Okla., 1974. Press sec. U.S. Senate, Washington, 1977-78; dir. pub. affairs U.S. Office Personnel Mgmt., Washington, 1979-80; pres. Corp. Communications, Washington, 1980-82; v.p. Norton Simon Inc., N.Y.C., 1982-83; spl. asst. to the commr. NFL, N.Y.C., 1983-84; exec. dir. Ritz Paris Hemingway Award, 1984-87; pres. Ritz Paris Internat., 1984-86; sr. v.p. AmBase Corp., 1986-91; v.p., ptnr. Korn/Ferry Internat., N.Y.C., 1991—; advisor USIA, Washington, 1980-93, ARC, 1983, White House Vets. Com., 1979-80. Trustee N.Y.C. Meals on Wheels, Inc. Lt. comdr. USN, 1968-77. Decorated Navy Achievement medal (2). Mem. N.Y. Sky Club. Home: 6 Plumbridge Ln Hilton Head Island SC 29928-3360 Office: Korn/Ferry Internat 237 Park Ave New York NY 10017-3142

WOODS, BARBARA A. SHELL, psychotherapist; b. Banner Elk, N.C., June 11, 1939; d. Oscar Ketron and Mamie Maruja (Perry) Shell; m. James Wesley Woods, May 7, 1966; children: Jonathan Scott, Eric Jason. BS in Bus. Mgmt., East Tenn. State U., 1961; MA in Counseling and Devel., George Mason U., 1983, postgrad., 1985-88. Cert. clin. mental health counselor, mediator, Va.; nat. cert. counselor, nat. cert. career counselor; lic. profl. counselor, Va. Office asst. vet. affairs East Tenn. State U., Johnson City, 1958-61; sec. purchasing dept. U. Tenn., Knoxville, 1961-62; social worker I and II Tenn. Welfare Dept., Knoxville, 1962-66; daycare coord. Econ. Opportunity of Atlanta, 1966-67; child welfare worker Forsyth County Dept. of Welfare, Winston Salem, N.C., 1967-68; dir., tchr. Woodland Pre-Sch., Alexandria, Va., 1975-78; pers. mgmt. Woodward & Lothrup, Tyson's Corner, Va., 1983; career coord. Nat. Bd. for Cert. Counselors, Alexandria, 1984; counselor, trainer The Women's Ctr. of Northern Va., Vienna, Va., 1985-90; counseling dir. The Women's Health Connection, Vienna, 1990-92; trainer, counselor City of Falls Ch. Youth At Risk Program, Falls Church, 1993-94; dir./owner Change & Growth Consulting, Tyson's Corner and Woodbridge, Va., 1984—. Zoning chairperson West Springfield (Va.) Civic Assn., 1980-82; citizen mem. Fairfax County Citizens Planning Task Force, Springfield, 1979-82. Scholarship Am. Legion, 1957. Mem. ACA, No. Va. Chpt. clin. Counselors (chairperson 1990-92, Appreciation award 1992), Va. Clin. Counselor (regional rep. 1990-92), Nat. EAP Assn. (sec. 1989-90), Met. Area Career/Life Planning Network (founder, Appreciation award 1985), Va. Counselors Assn. Methodist. Avocations: gardening, crafts, decorating, reading. Office: Change and Growth Cons 1334 G St Woodbridge VA 22191-1603

WOODS, BRUCE WALTER, editor, poet; b. Dunkirk, N.Y., Apr. 13, 1947; s. Walter Gerald Woods and Alma (Johnson) Rice. B.A., SUNY-Fredonia, 1969. Assoc. editor Dirt Rider, Canoga Park, Calif., 1972, editor, 1972-75; exec. editor Dirt Bike, Encino, Calif., 1975-76, editor, 1976; asst. editorial dir. Daisey Pub., Encino, Calif., 1976-78; editor The Mother Earth News, Hendersonville, N.C., 1978-87; editor-in-chief The Mother Earth News and Am. Country, Hendersonville, N.C., 1987-94; assoc. publ. Writer's Digest, Cin., 1994-95; editor Writer's Yearbook, Cin.; assoc. pub. Writer's Digest; editl. dir. Popular Woodworking. Author: From the Carp of Good Hope, 1970, How Far?, 1971, Food, 1973, Fieldbook, 1976; editor: Back Country Handbook, 1979, Chui! A Guide to the African Leopard, 1994. Avocations: hunting; fishing; bicycling; motorcycling. Office: F&W Pubs Writer's Digest 1507 Dana Ave Cincinnati OH 45207-1056

WOODS, CYNDY JONES, junior high educator, researcher; b. Phoenix, Oct. 26, 1954; d. Glenn Billy and Helen Marie (Harrison) Jones; m. Clifford R. Woods, Apr. 3, 1975; children: Sean, Kathleen, Connor. AA in English, St. John's Coll., 1974; BA in English, Ariz. State U., 1992, M in Secondary Edn., 1994. Cert. secondary tchr., c.c. instr., Ariz. Tchr. grades 6-8 John R. Davis Sch., Phoenix, 1993; tchr. grade 7 Thomas J. Pappas Sch., Phoenix, 1994—; adj. faculty English and lit. Rio Salado C.C., 1995—; treas. martin Luther Sch. Bd., Phoenix, 1995—. Author: (poetry) Dance on the Horizons, 1993, The Sound of Poetry: Best Poems of 1995, Across the Universe, 1996; contbr. articles to profl. jours. Mem. St. Francis Xavier Sch. Bd., Phoenix, 1995; v.p. City/County Child Care Bd., Phoenix, 1988-92; youth group advisor Mt. Calvary Luth. Ch., Phoenix, 1988—. Mem. Ariz. Edn. Assn., Brophy Coll. Prep. Mother's Guild, Xavier Coll. Prep. Mother's Guild. Democrat. Avocations: computers, homeless issues, at-risk issues, volleyball, writing. Home: P O Box 27575 Phoenix AZ 85061 Office: Thomas J Pappas Sch 413 N 7th Ave Phoenix AZ 85007

WOODS, DANIEL JAMES, lawyer; b. Bklyn., Nov. 12, 1952; s. James J. and Elinor (Masten) W.; m. Kathryn Anne Morris, Dec. 27, 1974; children: Meghan M., Alexandra K., Shauna E. AB cum laude, U. So. Calif., 1974, JD, 1977. Bar: Calif. 1977, U.S. Dist. Ct. (cen., ea., so., and no. dists.) Calif., U.S. ct Appeals (9th cir.) 1978, U.S. Supreme Ct. 1981. Law clk. to judge U.S. Dist. Ct. (ctrl. dist.), Calif., 1977-78; assoc. Brobeck, Phleger & Harrison, L.A., 1978-84, ptnr., 1984—; vol. pro tem L.A. Mcpl. Ct., 1985—, L.A. Superior Ct., 1989—. Mem. ABA (jud. adminstrn. sect.), Maritime Law Assn., Assn. Trial Lawyers Am. (assoc.). Roman Catholic. Avocations: tennis, bicycling, travel. Office: Brobeck Phleger & Harrison 550 S Hope St Los Angeles CA 90071-2627*

WOODS, DAVID FITZWILLIAM, insurance, estate and financial planner; b. Balt., Aug. 2, 1936; s. David Forster and Mona (Thomas) W.; m. Elizabeth Virginia Gans, Oct. 18, 1958; children: David O'Brien, Sarah Woods Bates, Margaret Woods Heffernan, Jennifer Rosalie. BS in Econs., Loyola Coll., Balt., 1964. CLU, ChFC. Agt. Mass. Mut. Life Ins. Co., Springfield, 1966—; prin. Woods & Livingston Fin. Group, Springfield, 1992—; pres. Life and Health and Ins. Found. of Edn., 1995—. Contbr. numerous articles to profl. jours. Trustee, chmn. Baystate Health Systems, Springfield, 1991—, The Am. Coll.; trustee Frank Stanley Beveridge Found., Boca Raton, Fla., 1988—; chmn. Baystate Med. Ctr., Springfield, 1992-94; numerous other civic activities. 1st lt. USAF, 1956-63. Mem. Assn. Life Underwriters (John P. Meehan award 1981), Springfield Assn. Life Underwriters (David F. Woods award 1986), Assn. for Advanced Life Underwriting (dir.), Nat. Assn. of Life Underwriters (pres. 1986-87). Avocations: running, tennis, skiing, hiking, sailing. Office: Woods & Livingston Fin Grp 1500 Main St Ste 604 Springfield MA 01115-0001

WOODS, DAVID LYNDON, publishing and broadcast executive, former federal agency executive; b. San Jose, Calif.; s. Donald Mason and Lynda Rosalia (Mueller) W.; m. Barbara Sue Vacin, June 9, 1956 (div. July 1987); children: Stephanie Lynn Woods Snide, Allison Elizabeth Woods Traba, Roberta Lee, Dana Royce Woods Bunce, Meredith Mason Woods Leech;

divorced. AB, San Jose State Coll., 1952; MA, Stanford U., 1955; postgrad., U. So. Calif., 1962-63; MBA, Rollins Coll., 1965, Oxford (U.K.) U., 1974; PhD, Ohio State U., 1976. Life cert. C.C. tchr., Calif., Fla. Dir. univ. broadcasting Lehigh U., Bethlehem, Pa., 1953-54; mgr. presentations and advtg. Bendix-Pacific divsn. Bendix Corp., North Hollywood, Calif., 1959-60; dir. pub. rels. and advtg. Librascope divsn. GPI, Glendale, Calif., 1961-63; sr. writer-editor Martin Co. subs. Martin-Marietta Corp., Orlando, Fla., 1963-65; head program support br. Navy Dept. Speech Bur., Washington, 1965-70; special asst. to chief naval material Naval Material Command, Washington, 1970-84; dir. Navy sci. and tech. info. Naval Material Command (later at Office Naval Rsch.), Arlington, Va., 1984-93; pres. DaleWood Enterprises, Inc., Middleway, W.Va., 1987—; sec., treas. Capital Access, 1993—; adj. prof. comm. Shepherd Coll., Shepherdstown, W.Va., 1994; prof. bus. and pub. adminstrn. George Washington U., 1975-86; tchr. Stanford (Calif.) U., Lehigh U., Ohio State U., U. Md., U. Va., and numerous other colls. and Univs., 1953-88; bd. dirs. correction naval records Sec. of Navy, Washington, 1980-85; commentator on-air musical host radio Sta. WXVA-AM and FM, Charlestown, W.Va., 1994-95. Author: A History of Tactical Communication Techniques, 1965, 82, (four naval base histories): U.S. Naval and Marine Corps Bases (2 vols.), 1986; editor: Signaling and Communicating at Sea (2 vols.), 1984; author, editor numerous fed. publs.; columnist and contbg. writer State Jour., Charleston, W.Va., 1993-94, Quad State Bus. Jour., Winchester, Va.; contbr. over 150 articles and revs. to numerous jours. Vice-pres. Pimmit Hills (Va.) Civic Assn., 1958-59; chmn. fin. com. Commn. on Aging, Alexandria, 1993; mem. Coun. on Aging of Jefferson County, 1995—; bd. dirs. Nat. Assn. for Uniformed Svcs., Springfield, Va., 1986-91; U.S. del. NATO Congress Internat. Res. Officers, 1984-91, U.S. v.p., 1988-89. Capt. USNR, 1949-87. Recipient Navy Superior Pub. Svc. medal Pentagon, 1986. Mem. Am. Def. Preparedness Assn. (life, adv. and award coms. 1982-88, author 1991-92), U.S. Naval Inst. (life, author 1966—), Naval Res. Assn. (life, nat. v.p. membership 1973-74, dist. pres. 1974-75, 93-94, nat. pub. affairs officer 1966-72, Dist. Svc. award 1976,), Naval Enlisted Res. Assn. (life assoc., pub. 1987-93), Res. Officers Assn. (life, nat. pres. 1985-86, nat. Navy v.p., nat. committeeman, nat. historian, regional coun. chair, dept. pres., dept. v.p., chpt. pres. 1977-84, named to Brigade Vols. 1982), Armed Forces Communication and Electronics Assn. (life, Pres.'s award 1967), Speech Communication Assn. (chair mass comm. divsn. 1970-71, other nat. offices 1966-71), The Res. Network (co-founder, editor 1988—), Sovereign Military Order of Temple of Jerusalem (knight), Army-Navy CLub, Nat. Press Club, Woods Club. Avocations: American musical comedy, bluegrass and old-time banjo music, completing mountain cabin, military signals, history of technology. Office: DaleWood Enterprises Inc PO Box 116 Summit Point WV 25446-0116

WOODS, DENNIS CRAIG, school superintendent; b. Akron, Ohio, Nov. 29, 1946; m. Janice Mary Matvey, Apr. 21, 1971; children: Gregory, Jeffrey, Mark. BA, Brown U., 1968; MA, U. Akron, 1974; postgrad., Ohio State U., 1990—. Job placement specialist Summit County Bd. Edn., Akron, 1971-72; tchr. English, athletic dir. South H.S., Akron, 1972-77; unit prin. Buchtel H.S., Akron, 1977-80; asst. prin. Firestone H.S., Akron, 1980-81, prin., 1987-90; prin. Ellet H.S., Akron, 1981-87; grad. rsch. assoc. Policy Rsch. for Ohio Based Edn., Columbus, 1990-91; asst. dir. Sch. Study Coun. of Ohio, Columbus, 1991-92; supt. Sandy Valley Local Schs., Magnolia, Ohio, 1992—; instructional audit team Sch. Effectiveness Trainers, Columbus, 1992—; presenter adminstr.'s acad. Middletown (Ohio) City Sch. Dist., 1994; presenter Ohio Acad. for Sch. Improvement, Columbus, 1993; site visitor Blue Ribbon Schs. Program, Washington, 1991; presenter in field. Founding mem. Sandy Valley TAP Group, Magnolia, 1993—; advancement chair Troop 50, Boy Scouts Am., Akron, 1986-93; three gallon blood donor ARC, Akron, 1980—. Lt. (j.g.) USNR, 1968-70. Recipient Secondary Prin. award Akron Secondary Prins. Assn., 1985, 89, award Ohio Inst. for Effective Sch. Leadership, 1995.; E.E. Lewis fellow Ohio State U., 1991, Eikenberry scholar, 1990. Mem. ASCD, Horace Mann League, Ohio Assn. Local Supts., Ohio Sch. Bds. Assn., Am. Assn. Sch. Adminstrs., Buckeye Assn. Sch. Adminstrs. (exec. and pub. rels. com. 1995—), Sandy Valley C. of C., Ohio Inst. Effective Sch. Leadership (mem. first cohort 1995), Touchdown Club, Phi Delta Kappa. Avocations: reading, gardening, physical fitness, ornithology. Office: Sandy Valley Local Sch Dist 5362 State Route 183 NE Magnolia OH 44643-8481

WOODS, DONALD DEWAYNE, advertising materials designer/manufacturer; b. Chattanooga, June 17, 1942; s. Wilburn William and Stella Elizabeth (Hooks) W.; m. Wanda Louise Hines, May 29, 1974 (div. Oct. 1989); m. Donna Maria Spanier, Feb. 21, 1992. GED (Gen. Ednl. Devel.), Tex. Camera/reprodn. mgr. Benco Plastics Inc., Knoxville, Tenn., 1964-69; sous chef Cherokee Country Club, Knoxville, 1967-69; auto/screen pressman Gibson Greeting Cards Inc., Cin., 1973-80; plant mgr. Am. Sign Co., Florence, Ky., 1984-86; gen. mgr., co-owner Trans-Acc Graphics, Cin., 1986; owner D & D Enterprises, Cin., 1986—; cons. screen printing Levi Strauss, Cin., 1975-76, Journey Electronics Inc., Mason, Ohio, 1992; designer Screen Printed Products, 1986-89. Author: Screen Printing: Techniques for Point of Sale Merchandise, 1984; co-patentee utilization of night vision device in processing film. Cons., v.p. 7th Step Found., Cin., 1973-78; cons. Cin. Coalition for Homeless, 1992. With U.S. Army, 1960-64, Germany. Recipient Update award Printers Week/Cin. Enquirer, 1989. Mem. Profl. Photographers Assn., Advt. Specialties Assn. (imprinter 1986—), The Planetary Soc., Midwest Screen Printers Assn. (cons. 1978—), Civil War Soc. (participant drama reenactment 1974—). Republican. Mem. Ch. of God. Avocations: photography, boating, Civil War study, genealogy, biblical history. Home and Office: 3300 Gamble Ave Cincinnati OH 45211-5616

WOODS, DONNA SUE, education educator, reading consultant, state agency administrator; b. Springhill, La., Jan. 15, 1954; children: Klaten A., Matthew M., Laura E., Gabriele E. BA, La. Tech U., 1975; MEd, La. State U., 1983; EdD, Okla. State U., 1992. Cert. English, social studies, gifted edn. tchr., La.; cert. English, gifted edn. and reading specialist, Okla. Tchr. English, Grawood (La.) Christian Schs., 1979-80; tchr. spl. edn. Bossier Parish Sch. Bd., Benton, La., 1981-83, curriculum developer, 1990; tchr. gifted Curtis Elem. Sch., Bossier City, La., 1983-88; tchr. lang. arts Elm Grove (La.) Jr. High Sch., 1988-90; teaching asst., univ. rep. Okla. entry yr. assistance Okla. State U., Stillwater, 1990-92, co-dir., instr. 13th ann. reading workshop, 1991, instr. Coll. Vet. Medicine, 1991, developer, dir. student tchr. seminar, 1992; asst. prof. Coll. Edn. Northwestern Okla. State U., Alva, 1992-95; dir. reading and literacy Okla. State Dept. Edn., Oklahoma City, 1995—; adj. instr. Oklahoma City C.C., 1991-92, U. Okla., 1995—; dir. Okla. Nat. Young Readers' Day, 1994, 95-96; presenter in field. Tutor YWCA, Shreveport, La., 1975; supt. youth Sun. schs. 1st Presbyn. Ch., Edmond, Okla., 1991, youth choir dir., 1994—, youth handbells dir., 1995—. Named Favorite Tchr. of Yr., Bossier C. of C., 1987; Centennial scholar Okla. State U. Coll. Edn. Alumni Assn., 1992. Mem. Internat. Reading Assn. (conf. presenter 1996), Okla. Reading Assn. (conf. presenter 1993—), Okla. Early Childhood Tchrs. Assn. (conf. presenter 1991), Alpha Upsilon Alpha (faculty sponsor 1994-95), Kappa Delta Pi, Phi Delta Kappa. Republican. Avocations: reading, music, collecting and repairing antiques, quilting, youth work. Home: 777 E 15th St #160 Edmond OK 73013

WOODS, GEORGE EDWARD, judge; b. 1923; m. Janice Smith. Student, Ohio No. U., 1941-43, 46, Tex. A&M Coll., 1943, Ill. Inst. Tech., 1943; JD, Detroit Coll. Law, 1949. Sole practice, Pontiac, Mich., 1949-51; asst. pros. atty. Oakland City, Mich., 1951-52; chief asst. U.S. atty., Ea. Dist. Mich., 1953-60, U.S. atty., 1960-61; assoc., Honigman, Miller, Schwartz and Cohn, Detroit, 1961-62; sole practice, Detroit, 1962-81; judge, U.S. Bankruptcy Ct., 1981-83, U.S. Dist. Ct. (ea. dist.) Mich., Detroit, 1983—. Served with AUS, 1943-46. Fellow Internat. Acad. Trial Lawyers, Am. Coll. Trial Lawyers; mem. Fed. Bar Assn., State Bar Mich. Office: US Dist Ct 277 US Courthouse 231 W Lafayette Blvd Detroit MI 48226-2719

WOODS, GERALDINE PITTMAN, health education consultant, educational consultant; b. West Palm Beach, Fla.; d. Oscar and Susie (King) Pittman; m. Robert I. Woods, Jan. 30, 1945; children: Jan, Jerri, Robert I. Student, Talladega Coll., 1938-40, D.Sc. (hon.), 1980; B.S. in Zoology, Howard U., 1942; M.A., Radcliffe Coll. and Harvard U., 1943, Ph.D. in Neuroembryology, 1945; D.Sc. (hon.), Benedict Coll., 1977; HHD (hon.), Howard U., 1989; LHD (hon.), Meharry Med. Coll., 1988; DSc (hon.), Fisk U., 1991, Bennett Coll., 1993. Instr. Howard U., Washington, 1945-46; pres. L.A. chpt. Jack and Jill, 1954-56; pres. Aux. to Med., Dental and Pharm. Assn. of So. Calif., 1951-55, state pres., 1955; past mem. local met. bd. YWCA; mem. nat. adv. coun. Gen. Med. Scis. Inst. NIH, 1964-68; mem. gen. rsch. support program adv. com., div. rsch. resources NIH, 1970-73, 77-78. Mem. regional com. Girl Scouts U.S.A., 1969-75, nat. bd., 1975-78; exec. bd. Cmty. Rels. Conf. So. Calif., 1968-72; exec. com. Leadership Conf. Civil Rights, 1967-70; chmn. Def. Adv. Com. Women in Svcs., 1968; mem. air pollution manpower devel. adv. com. EPA, 1973-75; mem. fgn. svcs. officers selection bds. Dept. State, 1967; mem. Calif. Com. on Public Edn.; mem. Calif. Post Secondary Edn. Commn., 1974-78, vice chmn., 1976; chmn. bd. trustees Howard U., 1975-88; chmn. Howard U. Found., 1984-88; trustee Calif. Mus. Found., Atlanta U., 1974-86; bd. dirs. Ctr. for Ednl. Opportunity at Claremont Colls., Robert Wood Johnson Health Policy Fellowships; mem. Inst. Medicine of NAS, 1974—, Nat. Commn. for Cert. of Physicians Assts., 1974-81; initiated Minority Access to Rsch. Careers, also, Minority Biomed. Rsch. Support program NIH; co-chmn. internat. conf. Woman to Woman: Single Parenting from a Global Perspective, 1987; video Re: MARC and MBRS programs A Time for Celebration, 1987; bd. dirs. Charles R. Drew U. Medicine and Sci., 1990-93; founder Head Start, L.A., 1965 (award 1985). Named Woman of Yr. Zeta Phi Beta, 1954, one of 20 Famous Black Scientists Nabisco, Black Woman of Achievement Smithsonian Instn., 1981; recipient Meritorious Achievement award Nat. Med. Assn., Inc., 1979, Leadership Achievement award Nat. Assn. Equal Opportunity in Higher Edn., 1987, awards from Pres.'s Coun. of Youth Opportunity, Iota Phi Lambda, Nat. Pan-Hellenic Coun., Howard U. Alumni Assn., So. Calif. Nat. Assn. Colored Women, Calif. Mus. Found., Ch. Christian Fellowship, NIH, Howard U., Delta Sigma Theta, Delta Headstart, 1985, award Calif. State U., 1993, others; one of honorees Dollars and Sense mag. Salute to Am.'s Top 100 Black Business and Profl. Women, 1985; Morehouse Coll. program Rsch. Extravaganza dedicated to her, 1988; named to Gallery of Honor, Assn. Minority Health Profl. Schs., 1990. Mem. NAACP (life), Nat. Coun. Negro Women (life), Golden Key, Phi Beta Kappa, Delta Sigma Theta (pres. R & D Found. 1983-88, nat. pres. 1963-67, ann. Geraldine P. Woods sci. award for Fed. City Alumnae chpt. established in her honor given to an outstanding scientist, Geraldine Pittman Woods Headstart/State Presch. Ctr. dedicated 1993, Mary Church Ferrell award 1979). Congregationalist.

WOODS, GRANT, state attorney general; m. Marlene Galán; children: Austin, Lauren, Cole. Grad., Occidental Coll., Ariz. State Coll., 1979. Atty. gen. Ariz., 1990—. Founder Mesa Boys and Girls Club. Office: Atty Gen Office 1275 W Washington St Phoenix AZ 85007-2926*

WOODS, GURDON GRANT, sculptor; b. Savannah, Ga., Apr. 15, 1915; s. Frederick L. and Marion (Skinner) W. Student, Art Student's League N.Y.C., 1936-39, Bklyn. Mus. Sch., 1945-46; Ph.D. (hon.), Coll. San Francisco Art Inst., 1966. exec. dir. San Francisco Art Inst., 1955-64; dir. Calif. Sch. Fine Arts, 1955-65; prof. Adlai E. Stevenson Coll., U. Calif. at Santa Cruz, 1966-74; dir. Otis Art Inst., Los Angeles, 1974-77; asst. dir. Los Angeles County Mus. Natural History, 1977-80; Sculptor mem. San Francisco Art Commn., 1954-56; mem. Santa Cruz County Art Commn., Regional Arts Council of Bay Area. Exhibited: N.A.D., 1948, 49, San Francisco Art Assn. anns., 1952-54, Denver Mus. Anns., 1952, 53, Whitney Mus. Ann., 1953, Sao Paulo Biennial, 1955, Bolles Gallery San Francisco, 1969, 70, 72, L.A. Mcpl. Gallery, 1977, San Jose Inst. Contemporary Art (Calif.), Washington Project for the Arts retrospective, 1968-85, Washington, 1985, Retrospective Art Mus. Santa Cruz County, Calif., 1987, d.p. Fong Gallery, 1993, 94, Michael Angelo Gallery, Santa Cruz, 1995; commns. include: cast concrete reliefs and steel fountain, IBM Ctr., San Jose, Calif., fountain, Paul Masson Winery, Saratoga, Calif., McGraw Hill Pubs. (now Birkenstock), Novato, Calif.; work in permanent collection Oakland (Calif.) Mus.; papers in Archives of Am. Art, Smithsonian Instn., Washington. Recipient citation N.Y.C., 1948; prize N.A.D., 1949; Chapelbrook Found. research grantee, 1965-66; Sequoia Fund grantee, 1967; Research grantee Creative Arts Inst., U. Calif., 1968; grantee Carnegie Corp., 1968-69. Mem. Artists Equity Assn (pres. No. Calif. chpt. 1950-52, nat. dir. 1952-55). Address: 133 Seascape Ridge Dr Aptos CA 95003-5890

WOODS, HAROLD BOWDEN, industrial executive; b. Crossplains, Tex., Oct. 31, 1922; s. Plaz Marion and Mamie Elizia (Hensen) W.; m. Laura Frendger; children: Halley, George, Frank, Gary, Mary. BS, U. N. Md., 1965. Commd. 2d lt. USAF, 1942, advanced through grades to col., 1970; aircraft comdr. B-24 USAF, Chia, Burma, India, 1943-45; pilot 68th Fighter Squadron USAF, 1945-53; flight test engr. USAF, Kirtland AFB, N.Mex., 1954; with Security Svc. USAF, Turkey, 1955-59; with Strategic Air Command USAF, 1959-66; with USAF, Vietnam, 1967-69; mgmt. engring. dep. chief staff Tactical Air Command USAF, 1970-73, ret., 1976; CEO Woods Bros. Industries, Inc., Dallas and Ft. Stockton, Tex., 1976—; CEO, sr. mem. bd. dirs. Pinnacle Fin. Group, La Canada, Calif. Contbr. to Keeping an Outpost Alive. Decorated Legion of Merit with 3 oak leaf clusters, DFC with silver cluster and 6 oak leaf clusters, Silver Star, Bronze Star, Air medal with 8 oak leaf clusters. Mem. Air Force Assn., Glider Pilots Assn., Am. Soc. Internat. Law, Order of Daedalions Mil. Pilots, Masons (master). Office: Woods Bros Industries Inc PO Box 22064 El Paso TX 79913

WOODS, HARRIETT RUTH, retired political organization president; b. Cleve., June 2, 1927; d. Armin and Ruth (Wise) Friedman; student U. Chgo., 1945; B.A., U. Mich., 1949; LLD (hon.) Webster U., 1988; m. James B. Woods, Jan. 2, 1953; children: Christopher, Peter, Andrew. Reporter, Chgo. Herald-Am., 1948, St. Louis Globe-Democrat, 1949-51; producer Star. KPLR-TV, St. Louis, 1964-74; moderator, writer Sta. KETC-TV, St. Louis, 1962-64; council mem. University City, Mo., 1967-74; mem. Mo. Hwy. Commn., 1974, Mo. Transp. Commn., 1974-76; mem. Mo. Senate, 1976-84, lt. gov. State of Mo., 1985-89; pres. Inst. for Policy Leadership, U. Mo., St. Louis, 1989-91; pres. Nat. Women's Polit. Caucus, 1991-95; dir. Federal Home Loan Mortgage Corp., 1995—; fellow inst. politics J.F. Kennedy Sch. Govt., Harvard U., 1988. Bd. dirs. LWV of Mo., 1963, Nat. League of Cities, 1972-74; Dem. nominee for U.S. Senate, 1982, 86. Jewish. Office: 1211 Connecticut Ave NW Washington DC 20036-2701

WOODS, HENRY, federal judge; b. Abbeville, Miss., Mar. 17, 1918; s. Joseph Neal and Mary Jett (Wooldridge) W.; m. Kathleen Mary McCaffrey, Jan. 1, 1943; children—Mary Sue, Thomas Henry, Eileen Anne, James Michael. B.A., U. Ark., 1938, J.D. cum laude, 1940. Bar: Ark. bar 1940. Spl. agt. FBI, 1941-46; mem. firm Alston & Woods, Texarkana, Ark., 1946-48; exec. sec. to Gov. Ark., 1949-53; mem. firm McMath, Leatherman & Woods, Little Rock, 1953-80; judge U.S. Dist. Ct. (ea. dist.) Ark., 1980—; referee in bankruptcy U.S. Dist. Ct., Texarkana, 1947-48; spl. assoc. justice Ark. Supreme Ct., 1967-74, chmn. com. model jury instrns., 1973-80; chmn. bd. Ctr. Trial and Appellate Advocacy, Hastings Coll. Law, San Francisco, 1975-76; mem. joint conf. com. ABA-AMA, 1973-78, Ark. Constl. Revision Study Commn., 1967-68. Author treatise comparative fault.; Contbr. articles to legal jours. Pres. Young Democrats Ark., 1946-48; mem. Gubernatorial Com. Study Death Penalty, 1971-73. Mem. ABA, Ark. Bar Assn. (pres. 1972-73, Outstanding Lawyer award 1975), Pulaski County Bar Assn., Assn. Trial Lawyers Am. (gov. 1965-67), Ark. Trial Lawyers Assn. (pres. 1965-67), Internat. Acad. Trial Lawyers, Internat. Soc. Barristers, Am. Coll. Trial Lawyers, Am. Bd. Trial Advocates, Phi Alpha Delta. Methodist. Home: 42 Wingate Dr Little Rock AR 72205-2556 Office: US Dist Ct PO Box 3683 Little Rock AR 72203-3683

WOODS, JAMES DUDLEY, manufacturing company executive; b. Falmouth, Ky., July 24, 1931; s. Alva L. and Mabel L. (Miller) W.; m. Darlene Mae Petersen, Nov. 8, 1962; children: Linda, Debbie, Jeffrey, Jamie. AA, Long Beach City Coll., 1958; BA, Calif. State U.-Fullerton, 1967, postgrad., 1968-70. Mgr. planning and control Baker Internat. Corp., Los Angeles, 1965-68, v.p. fin. and adminstrn. Baker div., 1968-73, corp. v.p., group fin. officer, 1973-76, corp. v.p., 1977, past exec. v.p.; pres., chief exec. officer Baker Internat. Corp., Houston; also dir. Baker Internat. Corp.; pres. Baker Packers, Houston, 1976-77, Baker Oil Tools, Orange, Calif., 1977-87; now chmn., pres., chief exec. officer Baker Hughes Inc., Houston. Served with USAF, 1951-55. Republican. Lutheran. Office: Baker Hughes Inc 3900 Essex Ln Houston TX 77027-5111*

WOODS, JAMES HOWARD, actor; b. Vernal, Utah, Apr. 18, 1947; m. Sarah Marie Owen. Student, MIT, 1965-69. Performances include (Broadway prodns.) Borstal Boy, Trial of the Catonsville 9, Finishing Touches, Moonchildren (Theatre World award), off-Broadway prodn. Saved (Obie award, Clarence Derwent award); (films) The Gambler, 1974, Night Moves, 1975, Alex & the Gypsy, 1976, The Choirboys, 1977, The Onion Field, 1979 (Golden Globe award nomination), The Black Marble, 1980, Eyewitness, 1981, Split Image, 1982, Fast-Walking, 1982, Videodrome, 1983, Against All Odds, 1984, Once Upon a Time in America, 1984, Cat's Eye, 1985, Joshua Then and Now, 1985, Salvador, 1986 (Acad. award nomination, 1987), Best Seller, 1987, Cop, 1988, The Boost, 1988, True Believer, 1989, Immediate Family, 1989, Straight Talk, 1992, Diggstown, 1992, Chaplin, 1992, The Getaway, 1994, The Specialist, 1994, Curse of the Starving Class, 1994, Casino, 1995; (TV miniseries) Holocaust, 1978; (TV movies) All the Way Home, 1971, Footsteps, 1972, A Great American Tragedy, 1972, The Disappearance of Aimee, 1976, Raid on Entebbe, 1977, The Gift of Love, 1978, And Your Name is Jonah, 1979, Badge of the Assassin, 1985, Promise, 1986 (Emmy award, Golden Apple award, Golden Globe award), In Love and War, 1987 (Golden Globe award nomination), (Hallmark TV) My Name Is Bill W. (Emmy award 1989), Citizen Cohn, HBO, 1992 (Emmy nomination, Lead Actor - Miniseries, 1993), Jane's House, 1994, Indictment, 1995; guest on The Simpsons, 1994 (voice only). Mem. Acad. Motion Picture Arts and Scis., Internat. Platform Assn., Players Club, Mountaingate Country Club. Office: ICM 8942 Wilshire Blvd Beverly Hills CA 90211-1934*

WOODS, JAMES ROBERT, lawyer; b. San Francisco, Aug. 3, 1947; s. Robert H. and Grace (Snowhill) W.; 1 child, Heather F. AB with honors, U. Calif., Berkeley, 1969; JD, U. Calif., Davis, 1972. Bar: Calif. 1972, N.Y. 1973, U.S. Dist. Ct. (so. & ea. dists.) N.Y. 1975, U.S. Ct. Appeals (2d cir.) 1975, U.S. Dist. Ct. (no. dist.) Calif. 1984. Assoc. LeBoeuf, Lamb, Leiby & MacRae, N.Y.C., 1972-76; ptnr. Maloney, Chase Fisher & Hurst, San Francisco, 1976-83, leBoeuf, Lamb, Greene & MacRae, San Francisco, 1983—. Co-author: California Insurance Law and Practice; contbr. articles to profl. jours. Office: LeBoeuf Lamb Greene & MacRae 1 Embarcadero Ctr San Francisco CA 94111-3600*

WOODS, JAMES WATSON, JR., cardiologist; b. Lewisburg, Tenn., Feb. 20, 1918; s. James Watson and Sara Frances (Watson) W.; m. Marion Briner, Nov. 26, 1944; children: Diane, James Watson III, Martin Briner. B.A., U. Tenn., 1939; M.D., Vanderbilt U., 1943. Diplomate: Am. Bd. Internal Medicine. Intern, then resident in medicine U. Pa. Hosp., 1943, 44, 46-47, fellow in cardiology, 1947-48; mem. faculty U. N.C. Med. Sch., Chapel Hill, 1953—; prof. medicine U. N.C. Med. Sch., 1964-87, prof. of medicine emeritus, 1987—, chief hypertension unit, 1964—; mem. sr. attending staff N.C. Meml. Hosp. Author papers in field; contbr. chpts. to books. Served as officer M.C., USNR, 1944-46. Fellow ACP; mem. Am. Fedn. Clin. Research, Am. Clin. and Climatological Assn., Council High Blood Pressure Research, Internat. Soc. Hypertension, So. Soc. Clin. Investigation, N.C. Heart Assn. (pres. 1971-72, Bronze medallion 1970, Silver medallion 1972), Sigma Xi, Alpha Omega Alpha, Phi Eta Sigma, Phi Kappa Phi. Democrat. Presbyterian. Home: 631 Quarterstaff Rd Winston Salem NC 27104-1638

WOODS, JOE ELDON, general contractor; b. Hammon, Okla., Apr. 24, 1933; s. Joseph W. and Gertrude E. (Martin) W.; student Ariz. State U., 1955-61; O.P.M. Program Harvard U.., 1984-87; m. Nina Jo Shackelford, July 5, 1952; 1 son, J. Grant. Vice-pres. Kitchell Corp., Phoenix, 1965-69; v.p. devel. Doubletree, Inc., Phoenix, 1969-78; pres., owner Joe E. Woods, Inc., Mesa, Ariz., 1977—; bd. dirs. Price-Woods, Inc., Mesa, 1985—; chmn., bd. dirs. Joe Woods Devel., Mesa, 1986—. Bd. dirs. Mesa United Way, 1983-84; v.p., bd. dirs. East Valley Partnership, Mesa, 1985. With U.S. Army, 1953-55, Korea. Mem. Associated Gen. Contractors, Mesa C. of C. (bd. dirs. 1983-87, chmn. 1985-86, v.p. 1984-85, pres. 1985-86), Harvard Bus. Sch. Republican. Presbyterian. Clubs: Mesa Country, White Mountain Country (Pinetop, Ariz.). Lodge: Rotary. Avocations: golf, fishing, skiing. Office: Joe E Woods Inc 63 E Main St Ste 401 Mesa AZ 85201-7417

WOODS, JOEL GRANT, state attorney general; b. Elk City, Okla., May 19, 1954; s. Joe E. and Nina Jo W.; m. Marlene Galan; children: Austin, Lauren, Cole. BA in Pol. Sci., Occidental Coll., 1976; JD, Ariz. State U., 1979. Bar: Ariz., 1979, U.S. Ct. Appeals (9th cir.), 1985, U.S. Dist. Ct. Ariz., 1985. Atty. Maricopa County Pub. Defender's Office, Phoenix, 1979-82; adminstrv. asst. Office of Congressman John McCain, Mesa, Ariz., 1982-84; pvt. practice law Mesa, 1984-91; atty. gen. State of Ariz., Phoenix, 1991—. Recipient Fair Housing award Ariz. Assn. Realtors, Phoenix, 1991. Fellow Rotary Internat.; mem. Phi Beta Kappa. Republican. Avocations: reading, writing, sports. Office: Office of Atty Gen 1275 W Washington St Phoenix AZ 85007-2926*

WOODS, JOHN ELMER, plastic surgeon; b. Battle Creek, Mich., July 5, 1929; m. Janet Ruth; children: Sheryl, Mark, Jeffrey, Jennifer, Judson. BA, Asbury Coll., 1949; MD, Western Res. U., 1955; PhD, U. Minn., 1966. Intern Gorgas Hosp., Panama Canal Zone, 1955-56, resident in gen. surgery, 1956-57; resident in gen. surgery Mayo Grad. Sch., Rochester, Minn., 1960-65, resident in plastic surgery, 1966-67; resident in plastic surgery Brigham Hosp., Boston, Mass., 1968; fellow, transplant cons. Harvard Med. Sch., Cambridge, Mass., 1969; cons. in gen. and plastic surgery Mayo Clinic, Rochester, 1969—, vice chmn. Dept. Surgery; asst. prof. Mayo Med. Sch., Rochester, 1973-76, assoc. prof., 1976-80, prof. plastic surgery, 1980—, Stuart W. Harrington prof. surgery; vis. prof. Yale Sch. Medicine, New Haven, 1984, Harvard Sch. Medicine, Cambridge, 1984. Contbr. over 200 articles to profl. jours.; also 26 book chpts. and 1 film. Recipient Disting. Mayo Clinician award, 1991. Mem. AMA (council on sci. affairs 1985—), ACS (grad edn. com. 1985—), Am. Bd. Med. Specialties, Am. Bd. Plastic Surgery (sec.-treas. 1985-88, chmn. 1988-89), Am. Soc. Plastic Surgeons Ednl. Fedn. (pres. 1984-85). Avocations: skiing, sailing, reading, the arts. Office: Mayo Clinic E 6-B Plummer N-10 Rochester MN 55905-0001

WOODS, JOHN JOSEPH, school system administrator; b. Syracuse, N.Y., Nov. 10, 1926; s. John Joseph and Agnes C. (Mooney) W.; m. Gertrude B. Fuchs, June 16, 1956 (div. Oct. 15, 1976); m. Ann M. Sorheide, Dec. 16, 1976; children: Gregory, Douglas, Lori, Carrie. BS, SUNY, Rochester, 1981; MS, SUNY, Brockport, 1982; Cert. of Advanced Studies, SUNY, 1982; EdD, U. Rochester, 1987; student, Harvard U., 1988-91. Cert. sch. dist. adminstr., N.Y. Dir. pers. and pub. rels. Alliance Tool Corp., Rochester, N.Y., 1956-78; pres. N.Y. State Sch. Bds. Assn., 1975-76, Woods Pers. Cons. Svcs., 1978-79; sch. supt. Rochester Tooling & Machining Inst., 1979-85; exec. dir. Monroe County Sch. Bds. Assn., Rochester, 1986—; Speaker in field; lectr. U. Rochester, Grad. Sch. of Edn. and Human Devel.; adj. prof., lectr. SUNY Coll. at Brockport; tutor SUNY Empire State Coll. of Rochester; lectr. Rochester Inst. Tech., Roberts Wesleyan Coll.; chmn. Fed. Elem. Secondary Edn. Act Title III State Adv. Coun., 1973-75. Contbr. articles to profl. jours. Trustee grad. sch. edn. U. Rochester, 1990-96. Recipient Scholar fellowship U. Rochester, Monroe County Sch. Bds. Assn. "Good Guy" award. Mem. ASCD, Monroe County Bar Assn. (sch. atty.'s com.), Kappa Delta Pi, Phi Delta Kappa. Home: 626 Rumson Rd Rochester NY 14616-1249

WOODS, JOHN WILLIAM, retired lawyer; b. Ft. Worth, Dec. 10, 1912; s. John George and Eugenia (Smith) W.; m. Gertie Leona Parker, Apr. 15, 1954. B.S., North Tex. State U., 1951, M.Ed., 1952; J.D., St. Mary's U., San Antonio, 1967; postgrad., Fresno State Coll., 1952, West Tex. State U., 1959. Bar: Tex. bar 1966. Tchr. Corcoran, Calif., 1952-53, Pampa, Tex., 1953-63; Tchr. Harlandale Sch. Dist., San Antonio, 1963-67; practicing atty. Amarillo, Tex., 1967-68; county atty. Sherman County, Tex., 1969-72, county judge, 1988, ret.; justice of peace, 1975-88; pvt. practice, Stratford, Tex., 1968-95; ret., 1995. Served to ensign USN, 1930-47, ETO. Mem. Tex. Bar Assn., 69th Jud. Bar Assn., Am. Legion, Masons, Shriners. Democrat. Mem. Disciples of Christ. Home: 2200 W 7th Ave Apt 104 Amarillo TX 79106-6773

WOODS, JOHN WILLIAM, electrical, computer and systems engineering educator, consultant; b. Washington, Dec. 5, 1943; s. John Gill and Margaret (McHugh) W.; m. Harriet Hemmerich, June 17, 1972; children: Anne, Christopher. BSEE, MIT, 1965, MSEE, 1967, PhD, 1970. Sr. rsch. engr. Lawrence Livermore (Calif.) Nat. Lab., 1973-76; asst. prof. Rensselaer Poly. Inst., Troy, N.Y., 1976-78, assoc. prof., 1978-84, prof., 1985—; vis. prof. Delft Tech. U., The Netherlands, 1985; program dir. NSF, Washington, 1987-88; assoc. dir. Ctr. for Image Processing Rsch., 1992—; cons. Kodak, Rochester, N.Y., 1985-86, Johns Hopkins Applied Physics Lab., Laurel, Md., 1987, Calian Comms. Ltd., 1990-91; co-founder Focus Interactive

Tech., Inc., 1993. Co-author: Probability and Random Processes for Engineers, 1986, 2d edit., 1994; editor: Subband Image Coding, 1991; co-editor: Handbook of Visual Communications, 1995; mem. editl. bd. Graphical Models and Image Processing, 1989-93; contbg. author book chpts., articles to profl. jours. Mem. Com. Acad. Excellence, Clifton Park, N.Y., 1984. Capt. USAF, 1969-73. Grantee NSF, Air Force Office Sci. Rsch., Advanced Rsch. Projects Agy., Ctr. Advanced TV Studies, 1978—. Fellow IEEE (editl. bd. Trans. on Video Tech. 1990—); mem. IEEE Signal Processing Soc. (com. chmn. 1983-85, ednl. com. chmn. 1987-93, ad. com. mem. 1986-88, assoc. editor jour. 1979-82, co-chmn. tech. program com. 1st IEEE Internat. Conf. on Image Processing 1994, Best Paper awards 1977, 86, Meritorious Svc. award 1989, Tech. Achievement award 1993). Roman Catholic. Home: 43 Longview Dr Clifton Park NY 12065-2318 Office: Rensselaer Poly Inst ESCE Dept Troy NY 12180-3590

WOODS, LAWRENCE MILTON, airline company executive; b. Manderson, Wyo., Apr. 14, 1932; s. Ben Ray and Katherine (Youngman) W.; m. Joan Frances Van Patten, June 10, 1952; 1 dau., Laurie. B.Sc. with honors, U. Wyo., 1953; M.A., N.Y. U., 1973, Ph.D., 1975; LL.D., Wagner Coll., 1973. Bar: Mont. 1957; C.P.A., Colo., Mont. Accountant firm Peat, Marwick, Mitchell & Co. (C.P.A.'s), Billings, Mont., 1953; supervisory auditor Army Audit Agy., Denver, 1954-56; accountant Mobil Producing Co., Billings, Mont., 1956-59; planning analyst Socony Mobil Oil Co., N.Y.C., 1959-63; planning mgr. Socony Mobil Oil Co., 1963-65; v.p. North Am. div. Mobil Oil Corp., N.Y.C., 1966-67; gen. mgr. planning and econs. North Am. div. Mobil Oil Corp., 1967-69, v.p., 1969-77, exec. v.p., 1977-85, also dir.; pres., chief exec. officer, dir. Centennial Airlines, Inc., 1985-87; pres., dir. Woshakie Travel Corp., 1988—, High Plains Pub. Co. Inc., 1988—; bd. dirs. The Aid Assn. for Lutherans Mutual Funds. Author: Accounting for Capital, Construction and Maintenance Expenditures, 1967, The Wyoming Country Before Statehood, 1971, Sometimes the Books Froze, 1985, Moreton Frewen's Western Adventures, 1986, British Gentlemen in the Wild West, 1989; editor: Wyoming Biographies, 1991; co-author: Takeover, 1980; editor: Wyoming Biographies, 1991; contbr.: Accountants' Encyclopedia, 1962. Bd. dirs. U. Wyo. Research Corp. Served with AUS, 1953-55. Mem. ABA, Mont. Bar Assn., Am. Inst. CPA's, Chgo. Club. Republican. Lutheran. Office: High Plains Pub Co PO Box 1860 Worland WY 82401-1860

WOODS, LINDSAY ELIZABETH, marketing executive; b. Pontiac, Mich., Aug. 2, 1948; d. George Edward Woods and Beth Yvonne (Tucker) Segula. Student, U. Mich., 1966-68; BA in Edn., Lang., Queens Coll., 1970; postgrad., Oakland U., 1975; student, Long Island U., 1981; MBA, U. Phoenix, 1995. French, German instr. Union Free Sch. Dist. #1, Mamaroneck, N.Y., 1970-75; dir. sales Nassau Gold Coast News, Suffolk, N.Y., 1976; exec. v.p. LIN-Z Stables, LTD., Old Westbury, N.Y., 1978-82; chief exec. officer, pres., founder Tyler-Woods, Ltd., Locust Valley, N.Y., 1982—; cons. Murray Electronics, Balt., 1982-83, cons., v.p., bd. dirs. Am. Vet. Products, Ft. Collins, Colo., 1988-90; dir. animal health div. Luitpold Pharms., Inc., Shirley, N.Y. Mem. Standardbred Owners Assn., U.S. Trotting Assn., Old Westbury Horsemans Assn. (v.p. 1980, trustee 1981—), N.Y. State Tchrs. Assn., Nat. Assn. Female Execs. Avocations: community theatre, horse-showing, scuba diving. Address: 704 Baltusrol Way Ruskin FL 33573-6413

WOODS, MARCUS EUGENE, retired electric utility company executive, lawyer; b. Huntington, Ind., June 11, 1930; s. Harry Milton and Birtha Marie (Becker) W.; m. Jean Ann Vickers, Nov. 27, 1965; children: Marcus Eugene, Patrick Douglas, Edith Marie. B.B.A., Marquette U., 1952; J.D., Ind. U., 1960. Bar: Ind., U.S. Dist. Ct. (so. dist.) Ind. 1960, U.S. Ct. Appeals (7th cir.) 1963. Dep. atty. gen. State of Ind., Indpls., 1960-65; atty. Indpls. Power & Light Co., 1965-67, asst. sec., 1967-73, sec., gen. counsel, 1973-85, v.p., 1980-95; sec., gen. counsel IPALCO Enterprises, Inc., 1983-95; ret., 1995; dir. Property and Land Co., Inc., Indpls. Served with USAF, 1952-56. Mem. Ind. State Bar Assn., Indpls. Bar Assn., Edison Electric Inst. (legal com.), Am. Soc. Corp. Secs. Republican. Roman Catholic. Clubs: Athletic; Columbia (Indpls.).

WOODS, NANCY FUGATE, women's health nurse, educator. BS, Wis. State U., 1968; MSN, U. Wash., 1969; PhD, U. N.C., 1978. Staff nurse Sacred Heart Hosp., Wis., 1968, Univ. Hosp., Wis., 1969-70, St. Francis Cabrini Hosp., 1970; nurse clinician Yale-New Haven Hosp., 1970-71; instr. nursing Duke U., Durham, N.C., 1971-72, from instr. to assoc. prof., 1972-78; assoc. prof. physiology U. Wash., Seattle, 1978-82, prof. physiology, 1982-84, chairperson dept. parent and child nursing, 1984-90, prof. dept. parent and child nursing, 1990—; dir. Ctr. Women's Health Rsch., U. Wash., Seattle, 1989—; Pres. scholar U. Calif., San Francisco, 1985-86; cons. USPHS, 1984-85, U. Tex., U. Mont, NIH, 1987, Oreg. Health Sci. U., 1985-87, 87-89, Nat. Ctr. Nursing, 1988, Nordic Inst. Nursing Sci., 1990, U. N.C., Chapel Hill, 1990, 91, U. Ariz., 1991, Mont. State U., 1991, Emory U., Atlanta, 1992. Contbr. articles to profl. jours. Fellow ANA, Am. Acad. Nursing; mem. AAUP, APHA, Am. Coll. Epidemiology, Soc. Menstrual Cycle Rsch. (v.p. 1981-82, pres. 1983-85), Soc. Advanced Women's Health Rsch. Office: U Wash Ctr Womens Health Rsch Sch Nursing Seattle WA 98195

WOODS, PENDLETON, college official, author; b. Ft. Smith, Ark., Dec. 18, 1923; s. John Powell and Mabel (Hon) W.; m. Lois Robin Freeman, Apr. 3, 1948; children: Margaret, Paul Pendleton, Nancy Cox. BA in Journalism, U. Ark., 1948. Editor, asst. pub. mgr. Okla. Gas & Electric Co., Oklahoma City, 1948-69; dir. Living Legends of Okla., Okla. Christian Univ., Oklahoma City, 1969-82, project, promotion dir. Enterprise Square and Am. Citizenship Ctr., 1982-92, dir. Nat. Edn. Program and Am. Citizenship Ctr., 1992—; arbitrator BBB; leader youth seminars in field. Bd. dirs. Campfire Girls Council, Okla. Jr. Symphony (past pres.), Boy Scout Council, Zoo Amphitheater of Oklahoma City, Will Rogers Centennial Commn., Greater Oklahoma City Tree Bank Found.; bd. dirs., co-founder Ctrl. Park Neighborhood Assn.; dir. Okla. for Resource Preservation; chmn. State Directional signage task force; vol. reader Okla. Libr. for the Blind; pres. Okla. Assn. Epilepsy; past pres. Keep Okla. Beautiful; past pres. Oklahoma City Mental Health Clin.; pub. relations chmn. Oklahoma County chpt. A.R.C.; past chmn. Western Heritage award Nat. Cowboy Hall of Fame; past pres., hon. lifetime dir. Variety Health Center; dir. Am. Freedom Council; state pres. Sons Am. Revolution; exec. dir. Oklahoma City Bicentennial Commn.; mem. Okla. Disabilities Coun. Served with AUS, WWII and Korean War; ret. col.; state historian Okla. N.G.; chmn. Oklahoma City Independence Day Parade, mem. exec. com. Oklahoma City Centennial Commn. Named Outstanding Young Man of Year, Oklahoma City Jr. C. of C., 1953; recipient Silver Beaver award Boy Scouts Am., 1963, Wokan award Okla. City Coun. Camp Fire Girls, 1968, Silver medal award of Advt. Fedn. Am., Disting. Community Service award of Neighborhood Devel. and Conservation Ctr, Gold and Silver Patrick Henry Patriotism medals of Mil. Order of the World Wars, 2 Commendation awards Am. Assn. for State and Local History; also 4 honor medals Freedoms Found., Jefferson Davis medal United Daus. of the Confederacy, Okla. Disting. Svc. medal (2), Outstanding Contbn. to Okla. Museums Assn., Okla. Museums Assn., 1987, Outstanding Contbn. to Okla. Tourism award Okla. Dept. Tourism, 1989, 3d Ann. Community Svc. award U. Ark. Alumni Assn., 1992, 5 Who Care award KOCO-TV, 1993, Jefferson award Am. Inst. for Pub. Svc., 1993, Mayor's award in Beautification, 1994, George Washington award Youth Leadership Found., St. Augustine, Fla., 1993. Mem. Soc. Assoc. Indsl. Editors (past v.p.), Advt. Fedn. Am. (past dist. dir.), Central Okla. Bus. Communicators (past pres., hon. life mem.), Okla. Jr. C. of C. (hon. life; past internat. dir.), Okla. Distributive Edn. Clubs (hon. life), Okla. com. employee support for guard and reserve, pub. affairs officer), Oklahoma City Advt. Club (past pres.), Words of Jesus Found. (pres.), Okla. Zool. Soc., Okla. Geneal. Soc. (past pres.), Okla. City chpt. U. Ark. Almuni Assn. (charter pres.), Okla. Lung Assn. (pub. relations com.), Okla. County chpt. Am. Cancer Soc. (dir.), Okla. Travel Industries Assn., Okla. Hist. Soc. (publ. editor), Okla. Heritage Assn. (publ. editor), Oklahoma City Beautiful (publ. editor), Okla. Safety Coun. (publ. editor), Oklahoma County Hist. Soc. (dir., past pres.), 45th Inf. Div. Assn. (past pres.), Mus. Unassigned Lands (chmn.), Mil. Order World Wars (regional comdr., Okla. City comdr., nat. staff), Oklahoma City Hist. Preservation Commn., Oklahoma City Heritage Roundtable, Greater Oklahoma City Clean and Green Coalition, Sigma Delta Chi, Kappa Sigma (nat. commr. publs), Lincoln Park Country (pres.), Am. Ex-Prisoners of War (state comdr.), Okla. Vets Coun. (chmn.). Author: You and Your Company Magazine, 1950, Church of Tomorrow, 1964, Myriad of Sports, 1971, This Was Oklahoma, 1979. Recorded Sounds of Scouting, 1969, Born Grown, 1974 (Western Heritage award Nat. Cowboy Hall Fame), One of a Kind, 1977, The Thunderbird Tradition, 1989; editor Looking Ahead. Home: 541 NW 31st St Oklahoma City OK 73118-7334

WOODS, PHILIP WELLS (PHIL WOODS), jazz musician composer; b. Springfield, Mass., Nov. 2, 1931; s. Stanley J. and Clara (Markley) W.; m. Beverly Berg, 1957 (div. 1973); children: Garth Darryl, Aimee Francesca; m. Jill Goodwin, Dec. 20, 1985; stepchildren: Allisen, Tracey Trotter. Student, Juilliard Sch., N.Y.C., 1948-52; LLD (hon.), East Stroudsberg U., 1994. Alto saxophone and clarinet with Dizzy Gillespie and Quincy Jones, alto saxophone with Benny Goodman, Gene Krupa, Thelonious Monk, Buddy Rich, Charlie Barnet, Michel Legrand, many others; leader European Rhythm Machine, 1968-73, Phil Woods Quartet, 1974-84, Phil Woods Quintet, 1984—; composer Rights of Swing, Three Improvisations, Sonata for Alto and Piano (Four Moods), The Sun Suite, I Remember, Deer Head Sketches, numerous others; recs. with own bands include Rights of Swing, 1971, Phil and Quill (3 albums with Gene Quill), Images (with Michel Legrand) (Grammy award 1976), (with Benny Carter) My Man Benny, My Man Phil, I Remember: A Tribute to Some of the Great Jazz Musicians, 1979, More Live (Grammy award 1982), At the Vanguard (Grammy award 1983), (as the Phil Woods Quintet) Gratitude, Heaven, Bop Stew, All Bird's Children (as Phil Woods' Little Big Band), Evolution, Bouquet, Flash, Real Life; played saxophone on many other recs. including Clark Terry and Ben Webster's Happy Faces, Symbiosis by Bill Evans, A New Album with Lena Horne, Just the Way You Are with Billy Joel, Dr. Wu with Steely Dan; also played on motion picture soundtracks The Hustler, 1961, Blow-Up, 1966, Twelve Angry Men, 1957, It's My Turn, 1980, Boy In A Tree. Co-founder, bd. dirs. Delaware Water Gap (Pa.) Celebration of the Arts, 1978—. Named New Star of 1956 Downbeat mag.; winner Down Beat Critics' Poll, 1975-79, 81-90, 92-93, Down Beat Readers' Poll, 1975-94; recipient Golden Feather award for best group Phil Woods Quartet Downbeat Critics' Poll, 1978, Downbeat Readers Poll award for best acoustic group Phil Woods Quintet, 1988-91, Downbeat Critics' Poll award for best acoustic group Phil Woods Quintet, 1990, Jazz Times Readers Poll award for best alto sax, 1990, 92; elected to Am. Jazz Hall of Fame, 1994. Mem. Am. Fedn. Musicians. Avocations: reading, cooking, movies, computers. Office: PO Box 278 Delaware Water Gap PA 18327-0278

WOODS, PHYLLIS MICHALIK, elementary school educator; b. New Orleans, Sept. 12, 1937; d. Philip John and Thelma Alice (Carey) Michalik; 1 child, Tara Lynn Woods. BA, Southeastern La. U., 1967. Cert. speech and English tchr., libr. sci., La. Tchr. speech, English and drama St. Charles Parish Pub. Schs., Luling, La., elem. tchr., secondary tchr. remedial reading, Chpt. I reading specialist; Wicat tchr. coord.; tchr. cons. St. Charles parish writing project La. State U. Writing Project. Author: Egbert, the Egret, Angel Without Wings; songwriter; contbr. articles and poems to River Parish Guide, St. Charles Herald. Sch. rep. United Fund, St. Charles Parish Reading Assn.; parish com. mem. Young Authors, Tchrs. Who Write; active 4-H. Mem. ASCD, Internat. Reading Assn., St. Charles Parish Reading Coun., Newspaper in Edn. (chmn., historian), La. Assn. Newspapers in Edn. (state com.).

WOODS, REGINALD FOSTER, management consulting executive; b. Charleston, W.Va., Sept. 25, 1939; s. Reginald Foster and Jean Lee (Hill) W.; m. Katharine Terry Norden, May 11, 1963; children: Eric Arthur, Elizabeth Terry, Tracy Lee. BME, Cornell U., 1961, MME, 1962, MBA, 1963. Mktg. specialist Gen. Electric Co., N.Y.C., 1963-64; dir. flight equipment and facilities planning Eastern Airlines, N.Y.C., 1964-70; v.p. planning Butler Internat., Inc., Montvale, N.J., 1970, sr. v.p. fin., 1971-80, exec. v.p., 1980-86, pres., 1986-87; chmn. Mgmt. Resources Group, Inc., Saddle River, N.J., 1987—; pres., ceo The Advantage Ptnrs., Chatham, N.J., 1992-94; bd. dirs. Benedetto, Gartland & Greene, Inc., N.Y.C., DCG Corp., Roseville, Calif., Damon G. Douglas Co., Cranford, N.J., The Advantage Partners, Inc.; pres. DCG Corp., 1994—. Mem. Ridgewood Country Club, Glenmore Country Club.

WOODS, RICHARD DALE, lawyer; b. Kansas City, Mo., May 20, 1950; s. Willard Dale and Betty Sue (Duncan) W.; m. Cecelia Ann Thompson, Aug. 11, 1973; children: Duncan Warren, Shannon Cecelia. BA, U. Kans., 1972; JD, U. Mo., 1975. Bar: Mo. 1975, U.S. Dist. Ct. (we. dist.) Mo. 1975. Assoc. Shook, Hardy & Bacon L.L.P., Kansas City, Mo., 1975-79, ptnr., 1980—; gen. chmn. Estate Planning Symposium, Kansas City, 1985-86; chair Northland Coalition, 1993. Chmn. fin. com. North Woods Ch., Kansas City, 1986-88, 93-96; mem. sch. bd. N. Kansas City Sch. Dist., 1990-96, treas., 1992-96; chmn. planned giving com. Truman Med. Ctr., 1992—; mem. Clay County Tax Increment Fin. Commn., 1990—. Fellow Am. Coll. Trust and Estate Counsel; mem. ABA, KC Bar, Mo. Bar Assn., Kans. City Met. Bar Assn., Lawyers Assn. Kans. City (sec., v.p., pres. young lawyers sect. 1981-84), Kans. City Estate Planning Soc. (bd. dirs. 1985-88, 93-95). Democrat. Office: Shook Hardy & Bacon LLP One Kansas City Place 1200 Main St Kansas City MO 64105-2100

WOODS, RICHARD SEAVEY, accountant, educator; b. Albion, N.Y., Mar. 1, 1919; s. Stanley Taylor and Helen Saxe (Seavey) W.; m. Dorothy Signor Blake, Dec. 19, 1945; children: David Blake, Michael Signor, Martha Seavey, Catherine Hardie. A.B., U. Rochester, 1941; M.B.A., U. Pa., 1947, Ph.D., 1957. C.P.A., Pa. Tchr. English pub. schs. Shortsville, N.Y., 1941-42; instr. accounting U. Pa. Wharton Sch., Phila., 1947-52; asst. prof. U. Pa. Wharton Sch., 1952-58, asso. prof., 1958-64, prof., 1964-87, prof. emeritus, 1987—, asso. chmn. dept., 1961-63, acting chmn., 1961-62, 75-76, chmn., 1963-69. Author: (with O.S. Nelson) Accounting Systems and Data Processing, 1961; cons. editor: Accountant's Handbook, 1970; editor, contbr.: Audit Decisions in Accounting Practice, 1973, Audit Decision Cases, 1973. Served to lt. USNR, 1942-46. Mem. Am. Accounting Assn., Am. Inst. C.P.A.s. Home: 645 Willow Valley Sq J-307 Lancaster PA 17602-4871 Office: Steinberg-Dietrich Hall Univ of Pa Philadelphia PA 19104

WOODS, ROBERT A., chemical company executive. Pres. ICI Americas Inc., Wilmington, Del.; pres. ag products Zeneca Inc., Wilmington, 1993—. Office: Zeneca Inc 1800 Concord Pike PO Box 15458 Wilmington DE 19850-5458*

WOODS, ROBERT ARCHER, investment counsel; b. Princeton, Ind., Dec. 28, 1920; s. John Hall and Rose Erskine Heilman W.; m. Ruth Henrietta Diller, May 27, 1944; children—Robert Archer III, Barbara Diller (Mrs. Gregory Alan Klein), Katherine Heilman (Mrs. John E. Glennon), James Diller. A.B., U. Rochester, 1942; M.B.A., Harvard, 1946. Account exec. Stein Roe & Farnham (investment counsel), Chgo., 1946-53, ptnr., 1954-90; gov. Investment Co. Inst. Trustee U. Rochester; bd. dirs. Chgo. Juvenile Protective Assn., Chgo. Infant Welfare Soc., Chgo. Assn. Retarded Citizens. Served to lt. (s.g.) USNR, 1943-46. Mem. Am. Mgmt. Assn. (trustee 1973), Harvard Bus. Sch. Club Chgo. (pres. 1961), Phi Beta Kappa, Delta Upsilon. Clubs: Univ. Chgo, Chicago, Tower. Home: 470 Orchard Ln Winnetka IL 60093-4222 Office: 1 S Wacker Dr Chicago IL 60606-4614

WOODS, ROBERT EDWARD, lawyer; b. Albert Lea, Minn., Mar. 27, 1952; s. William Fabian and Maxine Elizabeth (Schmit) W.; m. Cynthia Anne Pratt, Dec. 26, 1975; children: Laura Marie Woods, Amy Elizabeth Woods. BA, U. Minn., 1974, JD, 1977; MBA, U. Pa., 1983. Bar: Minn. 1977, U.S. Dist. Ct. Minn. 1980, U.S. Ct. Appeals (8th cir.) 1980. Assoc. Moriarty & Janzen, Mpls., 1977-81, Berger & Montague, Phila., 1982-83; assoc. Briggs and Morgan, St. Paul and Mpls., 1983-84, ptnr., 1984—; adj. prof. William Mitchell Coll. Law, St. Paul, 1985; exec. com., bd. dirs. LEX MUNDI, Ltd., Houston, 1989-93, chmn. bd. 1991-92; bd. dirs. Midwest Asia Ctr., 1993-95, chmn. bd., 1994-95. Author (with others) Business Torts, 1989; sr. contbg. editor: Evidence in America: The Federal Rules in the States, 1987. Mem. ABA, Minn. State Bar Assn., Hennepin County Bar Assn., Ramsey County Bar Assn. (chmn. corp., banking and bus. law sect. 1985-87), Assn. Trial Lawyers Am., Wharton Club of Minn., Phi Beta Kappa. Home: 28 N Deep Lake Rd North Oaks MN 55127-6506 Office: Briggs & Morgan 2400 IDS Ctr 80 S 8th St Minneapolis MN 55402-2100

WOODS, RODNEY IAN, banker; b. Maidstone, Kent, Eng., Feb. 25, 1941; came to U.S., 1965; s. James and Gladys Irene (Radmall) W.; m. Carole Turnbull, Mar. 21, 1970 (div. Jan. 1974); 1 child, Ian Radmall; m. JoAnne Regina Miceli, Sept. 25, 1975; 1 child, Samantha. Acct. supr. Doyle Dane Bernbach, Toronto and N.Y.C., 1966-73; exec. v.p. Siegel & Gale, N.Y.C., 1973-76; mgr. Merrill Lynch, Pierce, Fenner & Smith, N.Y.C., 1976-78; v.p. U.S. Trust Co. N.Y., N.Y.C., 1978-80, sr. v.p., mktg. dir., 1980-87; 1st v.p., dir. mktg. svcs. Merrill Lynch, Pierce, Fenner & Smith, 1987-88; pres., chief exec. officer Merrill Lynch Trust Co., Princeton, N.J., 1988-92; 1st v.p. mktg. eastern divsn. Merrill Lynch Pvt. Client Group, N.Y.C., 1993—; nat. adv. bd. Outward Bound. Bd. dirs. Kane Lodge Found., Madison Square Boys and Girls Club. Mem. St. George's Soc. N.Y. (life), Union League (N.Y.C., bd. govs. 1994-96), Kane (master 1982, dist. dep. grand master 1984-85, trustee 1986—). Republican. Episcopalian. Home: 101 Old Academy Rd Fairfield CT 06430-7161 Office: Merrill Lynch World Fin Ctr N Tower New York NY 10281

WOODS, ROSE MARY, consultant, former presidential assistant; b. Sebring, Ohio, Dec. 26, 1917; d. Thomas M. and Mary (Maley) W. Ed. high sch.; L.D.H., Pfeiffer Coll., 1971. With Royal China, Inc., Sebring, 1935-43, Office Censorship, 1943-45, Internat. Tng. Adminstrn., 1945-47, Herter Com. Fgn. Aid, 1947, Fgn. Service Ednl. Found., 1947-51; sec. to senator, then v.p. Nixon, 1951-61; asst. Mr. Nixon with firm Adams, Duque & Hazeltine, Los Angeles, 1961-63, firm Nixon, Mudge, Rose, Guthrie, Alexander & Mitchell, N.Y.C., 1963-68; exec. asst. to former Pres. Nixon, 1969-75; now consultant. Named 1 of 10 Women of Year Los Angeles Times, 1961, 1 of 75 Most Important Women in Am. Ladies Home Jour., 1971. Home: 1194 W Cambridge St Alliance OH 44601-2169

WOODS, SUSANNE, educator, academic administrator; b. Honolulu, May 12, 1943; d. Samuel Ernest and Gertrude (Cullom) W. BA in Polit. Sci., UCLA, 1964, MA in English, 1965; PhD in English and Comparative Lit., Columbia U., 1970; MA (hon.), Brown U., 1978. Staff Senator Daniel K. Inouye, 1963; asst. editor Rand Corp., Calif., 1963-65; instr. Ventura Coll., Calif., 1965-66; lectr. CUNY, 1967-69; asst. prof. U. Hawaii, 1969-72; asst. prof. English Brown U., Providence, 1972-77, assoc. prof., 1977-83, prof., 1983-93, dir. grad. studies, 1986-88, assoc. dean faculty, 1987-90; v.p., dean Franklin and Marshall Coll., Lancaster, Pa., 1991-95, prof. English, 1991—; vis. assoc. prof. U. Calif., 1981-82; chair exec. bd. NEH-Brown Women Writers Project, 1988—. Author: Natural Emphasis, 1984; gen. editor: Women Writers in English, 1350-1850, 1992—; editor: The Poetry of Aemilia Lanyer, 1993; contbr. numerous articles to profl. jours. and scholarly books; reviewer for various profl. jours., including Renaissance Quar., Jour. of English and Germanic Philology; reader for PMLA Jour., SEL Jour., also others; editorial bd. Hunting Libr. Quar., 1987-90, Ben Jonson Jour., Duquesne U. Press. Pres. Cultural Coun. of Lancaster County, 1993-95, bd. dirs., 1990-95; bd. dirs. Lancaster Gen. Hosp. Found., 1992-95; active various polit. campaigns, 1960-64, 68-76, 84, 92. Bronson fellow, 1976, Huntington Library, 1979-80, 81, Clark Library, 1981, Huntington-NEH, 1984-85, Woodrow Wilson Found., 1968-70. Mem. Am. Council Edn. (R.I. women's coord. 1988-90), MLA (chmn. div. 17th Century English lit. 1982), N.E. MLA (chmn. English Renaissance sect. 1978, Milton sect. 1983), Am. Assn. Higher Edn., Nat. Women's Studies Assn., Renaissance Soc. Am., Milton Soc. (exec. com. 1987-89), Lyrica Soc. (pres. 1987-90), Alpha Gamma Delta. Democrat. Episcopalian. Office: Coll of Wooster Office of President Wooster OH 44691

WOODS, WALTER RALPH, retired agricultural scientist, administrator; b. Grant, Va., Dec. 2, 1931; s. John Wythe and Hazel Gladys (Hash) W.; m. Jacqulyn Rose Miller, Sept. 14, 1953; children: Neal Ralph, Diana Lyn. B.S., Murray (Ky.) State U., 1954; M.S., U. Ky., 1955; Ph.D., Okla. State U., 1957. Instr. animal sci. Okla. State U., 1956-57; asst. prof., then assoc. prof. Iowa State U., 1957-62; assoc. prof., then prof. U. Nebr., 1962-71; prof. animal sci., head dept. Purdue U., 1971-85; dean Kans. State U., Manhattan, 1985-92, dir. Agrl. Expt. Sta., 1985-92, dir. Coop. Ext. Svc., 1987-92; asst. adminstr. for regional rsch. CSRS USDA, Washington, 1993-94; acting dep. adminstr. USDA/CSREES, Washington, 1994-95. Author papers, articles in field. Bd. dirs. Ind. 4-H Found., 1979-81, Kans. 4-H Found., 1987-92; mem. leadership coun. Kans. Value Added Ctr., 1990-92; mem. exec. com. Kans. Rural Devel. Coun., 1990-93; chair Coun. Adminstrv. Head Agr., 1992, Great Plains Agr. Coun., 1990-92. Recipient Disting. Agrl. Alumni award Murray State U., 1969, Meritorious Service award Ind. Pork Producers Assn., 1975. Mem. Am. Soc. Animal Sci. (sec.-treas. Midwest sect. 1979-81, pres. Midwest sect. 1983-84), Sigma Xi, Gamma Sigma Delta. Mem. Disciples of Christ Ch. Home: 8318 Strathmore Ln Roanoke VA 24019

WOODS, WARD WILSON, JR., investment company executive; b. Ann Arbor, Mich., June 27, 1942; m. Priscilla Bacon; children: Katherine, Alexandra. BA, Stanford U., 1964. With constrn. and real estate firm, San Francisco, 1964-66, gen. mgr., 1966-67; with Lehman Bros., N.Y.C., 1967-78, ptnr., 1973-1978; mng. dir. Lehman Bros. Kuhn Loeb Inc., N.Y.C., 1977-78; sr. ptnr. Lazard Freres & Co., N.Y.C., 1978-89; pres., chief exec. officer Bessemer Securities Corp., N.Y.C., 1989—; mng. ptnr. Bessemer Holdings, L.P., N.Y.C., 1989—; chmn. Overhead Door Corp., Stant, Inc., Essex Group; bd. dirs. Freeport McMoRan Inc., Freeport McMollan Copper and Gold Co., Boise Cascade, Kelley Oil and Gas Corp., Bessemer Trust Co. Trustee Boys Club of N.Y.; vice-chmn. Asia Soc.; mem. Coun. on Fgn. Rels.; gov. The Nature Conservancy; bd. visitors Inst. for Internat. Studies Stanford U. Office: Bessemer Securities Corp 630 5th Ave New York NY 10111-0001

WOODS, WILLIAM ELLIS, lawyer, pharmacist, association executive; b. Ballinger, Tex., Sept. 25, 1917; s. Cary Dysart and Gertrude Mae (Ellis) W.; m. Martha Brockman, May 28, 1954. B.S., U. Tex. Sch. Pharmacy, 1938; J.D., Sch. Law, 1953. Bar: Tex. bar 1954, U.S. Supreme Ct 1957. Dir. emergency med. service Tex. State Health Dept., 1942-43, USPHS, 1943-47; asst. dir. Nat. Pharm. Survey Office, 1947-48; with Eli Lilly & Co., 1948-51; first dir. U. Tex. Pharmacy Extension Service, Austin, 1953-54; pvt. practice law Corpus Christi, Tex., 1954-58; asst. to exec. v.p. Nat. Pharm Council, N.Y.C., 1958-64; sec. Nat. Pharm Council, 1964-65; Washington rep., assoc. gen. counsel Nat. Assn. Retail Druggists, 1965-76, exec. v.p., 1976-84, hon. past pres., 1984; presenter testimony on health, pharmacy and small bus. before coms. of U.S. Congress and various fed. agys.; mem. Joint Commn. on Pharmacy Practitioners; chmn. Nat. Small Bus. Legis. Coun., 1981; pres. Nat. Drug Trade Conf., 1981; del. U.S. Pharmacopoeial Conv., 1975, 80. Contbr. articles to pharmacy publs. Recipient Achievement Medal award Alpha Zeta Omega, 1975, Lubin Profl. Pharmacy award U. Tenn., 1982; established Wm. E. Woods Endowed Presdl. Scholarship in Law, U. Tex., 1994. Mem. ABA, Tex. Bar Assn., Law Sci. Acad., Phi Delta Phi, U. Tex. Chancellor's Coun. Methodist. Clubs: Internat., Capitol Hill, Nat. Assn. Execs. (Washington); Can. (N.Y.C.). Home: PO Box 1045 Easton MD 21601-1045

WOODS, WILLIE G., dean, English language and education educator; b. Yazoo City, Miss.; d. John Wesley and Jessie Willie Mae W. BA, Shaw U., Raleigh, N.C., 1965; MEd, Duke U., 1968; postgrad., Pa. State U., 1970, 80-82, Temple U., 1972, U. N.H., 1978, NYU, 1979, Indiana U. of Pa., 1986-88; PhD, Indiana U. of Pa., 1995. Tchr. schs. in N.C. and Md., 1965-69; mem. faculty Harrisburg (Pa.) Area Community Coll., 1969—, assoc. prof. English and edn., 1976-82, prof., 1982-94, sr. prof., 1994—, supr. Writing Ctr., 1975-78, coord. Act 101/Basic Studies Program, 1978-83, dir. Acad. Founds. program 1983-87, asst. dean academ. affairs Acad. Found. and Basic Edn. Div., 1987-89, asst. dean acad. affairs, chmn. social sci., pub. svcs. and basic edn. div., 1989-94, dean social sci., pub. svcs. and basic edn. divsn., 1994—, chmn. dirs. coun., 1981-82; tchr. Community Resources Inst., 1975-90; moderator workshops, cons. in field. Asst. editor Black Conf. Higher Edn. Jour., 1980. Sec., exec. com. People for Progress, 1971-73; bd. mgrs., exec. com. Camp Curtin br. YMCA, 1971-79; bd. dirs. Alternative Rehab. Communities, 1978—; bd. mgrs. Youth Urban Svcs., Harrisburg Area YMCA, 1981-92; bd. dirs. Dauphin Residences, Inc., 1981-88. Kellogg fellow in expanding leadership diversity in cmty. coll. program, 1994-95; recipient cert. of merit for community svcs. City of Harrisburg, 1971, Youth Urban Svcs. Vol. of Yr. award, 1983, Black Student Union award Harrisburg Area Community Coll., 1984. Mem. Pa. Assn. Devel. Educators (chmn. conf. 1980, sec. 1981-82, v.p. 1986-87, pres. 1987-88), Pa. Black Conf. Higher Edn. (Outstanding Svc. award 1980, Central Region award 1982), Nat. Coun. Tchrs. English, Pa. Edn. Assn., Am. Assn. Community and Jr. Colls., Nat.

Coun. on Black Am. (instl. rep. 1983—), AAUP, Alpha Kappa Alpha (Outstanding Svc. award 1983, Basileus award 1984, Ida B. Wells Excellence in Media award 1994, Ivy Honor Roll of Clips award 1994), Alpha Kappa Mu, Phi Kappa Phi. Baptist. Home: 1712 Ft Patton Dr Harrisburg PA 17112-8511 Office: 3300 N Cameron Street Rd Harrisburg PA 17110

WOODS, WINTON D., law educator; b. Balt., Jan. 11, 1938; s. W.D. and Nancy N. W.; m. Barbara Lewis; children: Tad, Adam, Brooke, Lindsy, Jessica. AB Econ./Gov., Ind. U., 1961, JD with distinction, 1965. Bar: Ind., Ariz.; U.S. Supreme Ct. Law clk. U.S. Dist. Ct. (no. dist.) Calif., Sacramento, 1965-67; prof. law U. Ariz., Tucson, 1967—; reporter U.S. Dist. Ariz. Civil Justice Reform Act Com., 1992—; ptnr. NAFTA Arbitration and Mediation Svc., Tucson, 1994—; pres. Law Office Computing, Inc., 1990—; dir. Courtroom of the Future Project, U. Ariz., 1993—. Contbr. articles to profl. jours; author: The Lawyers Computer Book, 1990. Mem. bio-ethics com. UMC, Tucson, 1984—. Recipient Fulbright award, 1979, Educator of Yr. award Internat. Comm. Industry Assn.; fellow NEH, 1972, Nat. Inst. for Dispute Resolution, 1982. Mem. ABA, Ariz. State Bar Assn. Jewish. Avocations: computers, automobiles, photography. Office: Coll of Law U Ariz Tucson AZ 85721

WOODSIDE, DONNA J., nursing educator; b. Ft. Wayne, Ind., Feb. 3, 1940; d. Evan Russell and Helen Bernice (High) Owens; m. Henry W. Schroeder, Nov. 28, 1959 (dec.); children: William Schroeder, Michael Schroeder; m. Robert J. Woodside, Jan. 11, 1974; children: Chris, Tracy. BSN, U. Evansville, 1970; MSN, U. Cin., 1975, EdD, 1981. Cert. diabetes educator, gerontology nurse. Staff nurse Wahiawa (Hawaii) Community Hosp., Health Profl. Agy., Cin.; instr. Bethesda Hosp. Sch. Nursing, Cin.; assoc. prof. U. Cin., 1991; pres. Concepts R & D Inc., 1989—; field nurse Willowbrook Home Health Care, Inc., 1993—. Mem. Am. Assn. Diabetes Educators, Sigma Theta Tau. Home: 2230 Oakleaf Dr Franklin TN 37064-7413

WOODSIDE, FRANK C., III, lawyer; b. Glen Ridge, N.J., Apr. 18, 1944. BS, Ohio State U., 1966, JD, 1969; MD, U. Cin., 1973. Bar: Ohio 1969, Ky. 1991, Mo. 1993, Tenn. 1993; diplomate Am. Bd. Profl. Liability Attys. Mem. Dinsmore & Shohl, Cin.; clin. prof. pediats. U. Cin., 1992—; adj. prof. law U. Cin., 1973-92. Editor: Drug Product Liability, 1985—. Fellow Am. Coll. Legal Medicine, Am. Soc. Hosp. Attys., Soc. Ohio Hosp. Attys.; mem. ABA, Ohio State Bar Assn., Fed. Bar Assn., Internat. Assn. Def. Counsel, Cin. Bar Assn., Def. Rsch. Inst. (chmn. drug and med. svc. com. 1988-91). Office: Dinsmore & Shohl 1900 Chemed Ctr 255 E 5th St Cincinnati OH 45202-4700

WOODSIDE, LISA NICOLE, academic administrator; b. Portland, Oreg., Sept. 7, 1944; d. Lee and Emma (Wenstrom) W. Student Reed Coll., 1962-65; MA, U. Chgo., 1968; PhD, Bryn Mawr Coll., 1972; cert. Harvard U. Inst. for Ednl. Mgmt., 1979; MA, West Chester U., 1994. Mem. dean's staff Bryn Mawr Coll., 1970-72; asst. prof. Widener U., Chester, Pa., 1972-77, assoc. prof. humanities, 1978-83, asst. dean student services, 1972-76, assoc. dean, 1976-79, dean, 1979-83; acad. dean, prof. of humanities Holy Family Coll., Phila., 1983—, v.p., dean acad. affairs, prof. humanities, 1990—; cons. State N.J. Edn. Dept., 1990; accreditor Commn. on Higher Edn., Middle States Assn., 1977-83, 94. Co-author: New Age Spirituality: An Assessment. City commr. for community rels. Chester, 1980-83; mem. Adult Edn. Council Phila. Am. Assn. Papyrology grantee Bryn Mawr Coll.; S. Maude Kaemmerling fellow Bryn Mawr Coll. Mem. Am. Assn. Higher Edn., Coun. Ind. Colls., Eastern Assn. Coll. Deans, Pa. Assn. Colls. and Tchr. Educators, AAUW (univ. rep. 1975-83), Nat. Assn. Women in C. of C., Am. Psychol. Assn., Transpersonal Assn., Audubon Soc., Del. Valley Orienteering, Phi Eta Sigma, Alpha Sigma Lambda, Psi Chi. Home: 360 Saybrook Ln # A Media PA 19086-6761 Office: Holy Family Coll Torresdale Philadelphia PA 19114

WOODSIDE, ROBERT ELMER, lawyer, former judge; b. Millersburg, Pa., June 4, 1904; s. Robert E. and Ella (Neitz) W.; m. F. Fairlee Habbart, July 11, 1931 (dec.); children—William Edward, Robert James, Jane Fairlee; m. Anna C. Woodside, June 27, 1987. A.B., Dickinson Coll., 1926, LL.B., 1928, LL.D. (hon.), 1951. Bar: Pa. 1928. Practiced in Millersburg and Harrisburg, Pa., 1928-42; judge Ct. Common Pleas, Dauphin Co., 1942-51; became atty. gen. Commonwealth of Pa., 1951; judge Superior Court Pa., 1953-65; ptnr. Mette, Evans and Woodside, Harrisburg, 1965-87; ret., 1987; adj. prof. Dickinson Sch. Law, Carlisle, Pa., 1969-87; legislator Pa. State House of Reps., 1932-42, Rep. house leader, 1939, 41; mem. Joint State Govt. Commn., 1939-42; del. 16th congl. dist. Rep. Nat. Conv., 1952; chmn. Pa. Little Hoover Comm.; chmn. Pa. Council Juvenile Ct. Judges, 1947-49. Pres. bd. trustees Pa. Industrial Sch., White Hill, Pa., 1945-55; chmn. on Commn. on Constl. Revision; mem. Pa. Constl. Conv., 1967-68. Mem. Omicron Delta Kappa, Phi Kappa Sigma, Tau Kappa Alpha. Methodist. Clubs: Mason (33 deg., Shriner), Red Man, Royal Arcanum. Home: 351 Union St Millersburg PA 17061

WOODSIDE, WILLIAM STEWART, service company executive, museum official; b. Columbus, Ohio, Jan. 31, 1922; s. William Stewart and Frances (Moorman) W. BSBA, Lehigh U., 1947; MA in Econs, Harvard, 1950. With Am. Can Co., 1950-87, exec. v.p. operations, 1974-75, pres., chief operating officer, 1975-80, CEO, 1980-86, chmn. exec. com., 1987-88; chmn. Sky Chefs, Inc., N.Y.C., 1987—; bd. dirs. Am. Capital. Bd. visitors, chmn. CUNY Grad. Sch. and Univ. Ctr., Acad. Policy Sci.; bd. dirs. Pub. Edn. Fund Network, Fund for N.Y.C. Pub. Edn. Manposer Demonstration and Rsch. Corp.; bd. dirs., past chmn. Inst. Ednl. Leadership; former pres. Whitney Mus. Am. Art; trustee Ctr. Budget and Policy Priorities, Com. for Econ. Devel.; mem. dean's coun. Harvard Sch. Pub. Health. Home: 863 Park Ave New York NY 10021-0342

WOOD-SMITH, DONALD, plastic surgeon; b. Sydney, Australia, June 30, 1931; s. William Frederick and Vera Mary; children: Christina Margaret, Donald William, Phillip Raynor. MB, BS, Sydney U., 1954. Diplomate Am. Bd. Plastic Surgury. Surg. resident Lewisham Hosp., Sydney, 1954-56, Royal Marsden Hosp., 1957-58; resident plastic surgery N.Y. U. Hosp. Med. Center, 1960-64, asst. and assoc. attending surgeon, 1964-92; vis. surgeon Bellevue Hosp., 1964-92; chmn. plastic surgery Manhattan Eye Ear and Throat Hosp., 1975-77; assoc. prof. plastic surgery NYU, 1977-84, prof., 1984-92; surgeon, dir. plastic surgery Manhattan Eye Ear and Throat Hosp., 1977-84; cons. plastic surgeon N.Y. Eye and Ear Infirmary, chmn. dept. plastic and reconstructive surgery, 1984—; prof. plastic surgery Columbia Presbyn. Med. Ctr., 1991—. Author: Nursing Care of the Plastic Surgery Patient, 1967, Cosmetic Facial Surgery, 1973; contbr. articles to med. jours. Fellow ACS, Royal Coll. Surgeons of Edinburgh; mem. Am. Assn. Plastic Surgeons, Am. Soc. Plastic and Reconstructive Surgeons, Am. Soc. Maxillofacial Surgeons, N.Y. Acad. Medicine, Brit. Assn. Plastic Surgeons, N.Y. Athletic Club. Republican. Office: 830 Park Ave New York NY 10021

WOODSON, BENJAMIN NELSON, III, insurance executive; b. Altoona, Kans., June 5, 1908; s. Benjamin Nelson and Mary Ola (Burke) W.; m. Grace Cook, Jan. 25, 1930 (dec. Apr. 1981); 1 child, Mary Burnett Crowell; m. Audrey Haney Watson, Apr. 1, 1983. Student pub. schs. Omaha. Stenographer, salesman, officer Mut. Trust Life Co., Chgo., 1928-37; exec. Life Ins. Mgmt. Rsch. Assocs., Hartford, Conn., 1937-44; exec. v.p. Commonwealth Life, Louisville, 1944-50; mng. dir. Nat. Assn. Life Underwriters/ Life Underwriters Tng. Coun., Washington, 1950-53; pres. Am. Gen. Life, Houston, 1953-72; v.p., then pres., Am. Gen. Corp., Houston, 1954-72, chmn. chief exec. officer, 1972-78, also bd. dirs.; dir. Mitchell Energy & Devel., Houston, 1976—, Am. Capital Mutual Funds, Houston, 1969-96; ptnr., spl. counsel exec. com. John L. Wortham & Son, Houston, 1958—. CLU. Author: More Power to You, 1950; The Set of The Sail, 1968; Simple Truth, 1980, The Best of Woody, 1993; contbr. essays to Life Assn. News, 1937-95. Bd. dirs. Tex. Med. Ctr., Houston, 1981—, Up With People, Tucson, 1972—, Sch. Ins. and Fin. Svcs. Mktg., U. Houston, 1983—, regent, vice chmn. U. Houston, 1977-83; gov. Rice U., Houston, 1962-74, overseer Jones Grad. Sch. Bus., 1977-83, overseer emeritus, 1983—; founder, life trustee Houston Found. for Retarded. Named Disting. Citizen Goodwill Industries, 1973, Man of Yr., Fedn. Ins. Counsel, 1980, Houston Honoree of Yr., NCCJ, 1976; recipient Solomon Huebner Gold award, 1988. Mem. Million Dollar Round Table (life), Nat. Assn. Life Underwriters (John Newton Russell award 1963), Tex. Assn. Life Underwriters, Houston Assn. Life Underwriters, Life Underwriter Tng. Council (founder, life trustee), Life Ins. Mktg. and Research Assn., Houston C. of C. (chmn. 1972-73, named Outstanding Leader 1972). Republican. Mem. Oahu Country (Honolulu); Houston (pres. 1970-72), River Oaks Country (v.p., bd. dirs. 1978-81) Forum (founding chmn. 1979—) (Houston), Metropolitan (N.Y.C.), Woodlands Country. Home: 3711 San Felipe Rd Ste 13-G Houston TX 77019 Office: 2727 Allen Pky Ste 460 Houston TX 77019-2100

WOODSON, DANNY, lawyer; b. St. Louis, June 2, 1949; s. William Melvin Woodson and Wanda Jean (Lucas) Bradford; m. Barbara Ann Cook, Aug. 7, 1971; children: Christopher Allen, Timothy Jon. BS, East Tex. State U., 1970; JD, Tex. Tech. U., 1977. Bar: Tex. 1978, U.S. Dist. Ct. (ea. dist.) Tex. 1979. Assoc. Kenley, Boyland, Hawthorne, Star and Coughlin, Longview, Tex., 1978, Florence and Florence, Hughes Springs, Tex., 1978-83; sole practitioner, Mt. Pleasant, Tex., 1983—; adv. bd. mem. Bowie-Cass Mental Health Svcs., Cass County, Tex., 1981; chmn., adv. bd. mem. Couch Phys. Therapy and Rehab. Svcs., Mt. Pleasant, 1994—. Coach Dixie League Baseball, Mt. Pleasant, 1984, 88, 89, Mt. Pleasant Soccer Assn., 1984-85; chmn. legis. com. Mt. Pleasant C. of C., 1984-85; bd. deacons Trinity Bapt. Ch., Mt. Pleasant, 1986-88. Mem. Cass County Bar Assn. (pres. 1981-82), N.E. Tex. Bar Assn., Titus Cosunty Bar Assn., Tex. Trial Lawyers Assn., Assn. Trial Lawyers of Am. Baptist. Avocations: travel, softball, sports fan. Office: PO Box 399 Mount Pleasant TX 75456-0399

WOODSON, DARREN RAY, professional football player; b. Phoenix, Apr. 25, 1969. Student, Ariz. State U. Safety Dallas Cowboys, 1992—. Named to Sporting News NFL-All-Pro Team, 1994; selected to Pro Bowl, 1994. Mem. Dallas Cowboys Super Bowl XXVII Champions, 1992, Super Bowl XXVIII, 1993. Office: Dallas Cowboys 1 Cowboys Pky Irving TX 75063

WOODSON, HERBERT HORACE, electrical engineering educator; b. Stamford, Tex., Apr. 5, 1925; s. Herbert Viven and Floy (Tunnell) W.; m. Blanche Elizabeth Sears, Aug. 17, 1951; children: William Sears, Robert Sears, Bradford Sears. SB, SM, MIT, 1952, ScD in Elec. Engring., 1956. Registered profl. engr., Tex., Mass. Instr. elec. engring., also project leader magnetics div. Naval Ordnance Lab., 1952-54; mem. faculty M.I.T., 1956-71, prof. elec. engring., 1965-71, Philip Sporn prof. energy processing, 1967-71; prof. elec. engring., chmn. dept. U. Tex., Austin, 1971-81, Alcoa Found. prof., 1972-75, Tex. Atomic Energy Research Found. prof. engring., 1980-82, Ernest H. Cockrell Centennial prof. engring., 1982-93, dir. Center for Energy Studies, 1973-88, assoc. dean devel. and planning Coll. Engring., 1986-87, acting dean, 1987-88, dean' chair for excellence in engring., 1988—; staff engr. elec. engring. div. AEP Service Corp., N.Y.C., 1965-66; cons. to industry, 1956—. Author: (with others) Electromechanical Dynamics, parts I, II, III. Served with USNR, 1943-46. Recipient Fed. Engr. Yr. Awd., Nat Soc. Profl. Engr., 1990. Fellow IEEE (life, pres. Power Engring. Soc. 1978-80); mem. Am. Soc. Engring. Edn., Nat. Acad. Engring., AAAS. Achievements include patents in field. Home: 7603 Rustling Rd Austin TX 78731-1333 Office: U Tex Coll Engineering Austin TX 78712

WOODSON, RODERICK KEVIN, professional football player; b. Fort Wayne, Ind., Mar. 10, 1965. Student, Purdue U. Cornerback Pittsburgh Steelers, 1987—. Named kick returner The Sporting News Coll. All-Am. Team, 1986, Sporting News NFL All-Pro Team, 1989, cornerback, 1990, 92, 93, NFL 75th Anniversary "All Time Team", 1994. Played in Pro Bowl, 1989-93. Office: Pittsburgh Steelers Three Rivers Stadium Pittsburgh PA 15212

WOODSON-HOWARD, MARLENE ERDLEY, former state legislator; b. Ford City, Pa., Mar. 8, 1937; d. James and Susie (Lettrich) Erdley; m. Francis M. Howard; children: George Woodson, Bert Woodson, Robert Woodson, Daniel Woodson, David Woodson. BS, Ind. U. of Pa., 1958; MA, U. South Fla., 1968; EdD, Nova U., 1981. Prof. math. Manatee Community Coll., 1970-82, dir., Inst. Advancement, 1982-86; exec. dir. Manatee Community Coll. Foundation, 1982-86; pres. Pegasus Enterprises, Inc., 1986—; state senator Fla., 1986-90. Candidate for gov. of Fla., 1990; bd. dirs. New Coll. Libr. Assn.; past pres. Manatee Symphony. Mem. Nat. Assn. Women Bus. Owners, Women Owners Network, Manatee C. of C., Sarasota Tiger Bay Club, Kiwanis. Republican. Roman Catholic. Home: 12 Tidy Island Blvd Bradenton FL 34210-3301

WOODSWORTH, ANNE, university dean, librarian; b. Fredericia, Denmark, Feb. 10, 1941; d. Thorvald Ernst and Roma Yrsa (Jensen) Lindner; 1 child, Yrsa Anne. BFA, U. Man., Can., 1962; BLS, U. Toronto, Ont., Can., 1964, MLS, 1969; PhD, U. Pitts., 1987. Edn. libr. U. Man., 1964-65; reference libr. Winnipeg Pub. Library, 1965-67; reference libr. sci. and medicine dept. U. Toronto, 1967-68; med. librarian Toronto Western Hosp., 1969-70; research asst. to chief librarian U. Toronto, 1970-71, head reference dept., 1971-74; personnel dir. Toronto Pub. Library, 1975-78; dir. librs. York U., Toronto, 1978-83; assoc. provost for librs. U. Pitts., 1983-88, assoc. prof., 1988-91; dean Palmer Sch. Libr. and Info. Sci. L.I. U., 1991—; pres. Anne Lindner Ltd., 1974-83; bd. dirs. Population Rsch. Found., Toronto, 1980-83, Ctr. for Rsch. Libraries, 1987-88; mem. rsch. libraries adv. coun. OCLC, 1984-87. Author: The Alternative Press in Canada, 1972, Leadership and Research Libraries, 1988, Patterns and Options for Managing Information Technology on Campus, 1990, Library Cooperation and Networks, 1991, Managing the Economics of Leasing and Contracting Out Information Services, 1993, Reinvesting in the Information Job Family, 1993, The Future of Education for Librarianship: Looking Forward from the Past, 1994. Dir. Sr. Fellows Inst., 1985—; trustee L.I. Librs. Resources Coun., 1993-98. Can. Coun. grantee, 1974, Ont. Arts Coun. grantee, 1974, Coun. on Libr. Resources grantee, 1986, 88, 91, 93; UCLA sr. fellow, 1985. Mem. ALA (com. on accreditation 1990-94, councillor 1993—), Can. Assn. Rsch. Librs. (pres. 1981-83), Assn. Rsch. Librs. (bd. dirs. 1981-84, v.p. 1984-85, pres. 1985-86), Assn. Coll. and Rsch. Librs. (chmn. K.G. Saur award com. 1991-93), Assn. for Libr. and Info. Sci. Edn., N.Y. Libr. Assn., Internat. Soc., Am. Soc. Info. Sci., Archons of Colophon. Office: LI U CW Post Campus Brookville NY 11548

WOODWARD, C. VANN, historian; b. Vanndale, Ark., Nov. 13, 1908; s. Hugh Allison and Bess (Vann) W.; m. Glenn Boyd MacLeod, Dec. 21, 1937 (dec.); 1 child, Peter Vincent (dec.). PhB, Emory U., 1930; MA, Columbia U., 1932; PhD, U. N.C., 1937; hon. doctoral degrees, U. Ark., Brandeis U., Cambridge U., Colgate U., Columbia U., Dartmouth Coll., Dickinson Coll., Emory U., Henderson State U., Johns Hopkins U., U. Mich., U. N.C., Northwestern U., Pa. U., Princeton U., Rhodes Coll., Rutgers U., Tulane U., Washington and Lee U., William and Mary Coll.; hon. doctoral degree, Wesleyan U. Instr. English Ga. Sch. Tech., 1930-31, 1932-33; asst. prof. history U. Fla., 1937-39; vis. asst. prof. history U. Va., 1939-40; assoc. prof. history Scripps Colls., 1940-43; assoc. prof. history Johns Hopkins U., 1946, prof., 1947-61; Commonwealth lectr. U. London, 1954; Harmsworth prof. Am. history Oxford U., 1954-55; Sterling prof. history Yale U., 1961-77, prof. emeritus, 1977—, Jefferson lectr. in humanities, 1978. Author: Tom Watson: Agrarian Rebel, 1938, The Battle for Leyte Gulf, 1947, Origins of the New South, 1951, (Bancroft prize), Reunion and Reaction, 1951, The Strange Career of Jim Crow, 1955, The Burden of Southern History, 1960, American Counterpoint, 1971, Thinking Back, 1986, The Future of the Past, 1989, The Old World's New World, 1991; editor: The Comparative Approach to American History, 1968, Responses of the Presidents to Charges of Misconduct, 1974, Mary Chesnut's Civil War, 1981 (Pulitzer prize 1982), (series) The Oxford History of the United States, 11 vols., 1982—; co-editor: The Private Mary Chesnut, 1984. Served as lt. USNR, 1943-46. Recipient Nat. Acad. Inst. Arts and Letters Lit. award, 1954, Gold medal for history, 1990, Am. Coun. Learned Socs. prize, 1962, Life Work award Am. Hist. Soc., 1986, Life Work Bobst. award, NYU, 1989; Guggenheim Found. fellow, 1946-47, 60-61. Mem. Am. Philos. Soc., Am. Acad. Arts and Letters, Am. Hist. Assn. (pres. 1969), So. Hist. Assn. (pres. 1952), Orgn. Am. Historians (pres. 1968-69, Disting Svc. award 1989), Am. Acad. Arts and Scis. (v.p. 1987-88), Brit. Academy, Royal Hist. Soc., Phi Beta Kappa. Home: 83 Rogers Rd Hamden CT 06517-3533

WOODWARD, DANIEL HOLT, librarian, researcher; b. Ft. Worth, Oct. 17, 1931; s. Enos Paul and Jessie Grider (Butts) W.; m. Mary Jane Gerra, Aug. 27, 1954; children: Jeffrey, Peter. BA, U. Colo., 1951, MA, 1955; PhD, Yale, 1958; MSLS, Cath. U. Am., 1969. Mem. faculty Mary Washington Coll. of U. Va., 1957-72, prof. English, 1966-72, librarian, 1969-72; librarian Huntington Library, Art Collections and Bot. Gardens, San Marino, Calif., 1972-90, sr. rsch. assoc., 1990—. Editor: The Poems and Translations of Robert Fletcher, 1970, The Ellesmere Chances: A New Monochromatic Facsimile, 1996; co-editor: New Ellesmere Chaucer Facsimile, Ellesmere Chaucer: Essays in Interpretation, 2 vols., 1995. Served with AUS, 1952-54. Mem. Bibliog. Soc. Am., Phi Beta Kappa, Beta Phi Mu. Home: 1540 San Pasqual St Pasadena CA 91106-3546 Office: Huntington Libr Art Collections and Bot Gardens 1151 Oxford Rd San Marino CA 91108-1218

WOODWARD, DAVID LUTHER, lawyer, consultant; b. Alexandria, La., Mar. 18, 1942; s. Luther Washburn and Ruby Ellen (Robertson) W.; m. Adeline Myree Peterson, July 12, 1965 (div. 1971); m. Louisette Marie Forget, Nov. 12, 1973. BA, Fla. State U., 1965, JD, 1969; LLM, U. London, 1982. Bar: Fla. 1969, Okla. 1982, Tex. 1987, U.S. Dist. Ct. (mid. and so. dists.) Fla. 1971, U.S. Dist. Ct. (no. and we. dists.) Okla. 1983, U.S. Dist. Ct. (no. dist.) Tex. 1985, U.S. Dist. Ct. (ea. dist.) Wis. 1992, U.S. Ct. of Claims 1970, U.S. Ct. Appeals (fed. and D.C. cirs.) 1970, (5th and 11th cirs.) 1981, (10th cir.) 1982, (9th cir.) 1985, U.S. Tax Ct. 1970, U.S. Ct. Mil. Appeals 1970, U.S. Supreme Ct. 1973. Trial atty. USDA, Washington, 1970; asst. atty. gen. State of Fla., Tampa, 1971-73; ptnr. Rose & Woodward, Tampa, 1973-76; pvt. practice The Law Offices of David Luther Woodward, Tampa, 1976-80; appellate pub. defender State of Okla., 1980-81; instr. U. Okla. Coll. Law, Norman, 1980-81; assoc. Jones, Gungoll, Jackson, Collins & Dodd, Enid, Okla., 1982-84, Brice & Barron, Dallas, 1985-86; pvt. practice Dallas, 1986—; of counsel Kenneth R. Guest & Assocs., Dallas, 1990-91, Sapp & Madden, Dallas and Austin, 1991, Bennett & Kurtzman, Dallas, 1991-93. Contbr. articles to profl. jours. Episcopalian. Office: 222 Turtle Creek Tower 3131 Turtle Creek Blvd Dallas TX 75219-5431

WOODWARD, FREDERICK MILLER, publisher; b. Clarksville, Tenn., Apr. 15, 1943; s. Felix Grundy and Laura Henrietta (Miller) W.;. m. Elizabeth Louise Smoak, Mar. 23, 1967; children: Laura Claire, Katherine Elizabeth. BA cum laude, Vanderbilt U., 1965; postgrad., Tulane U., 1965-70. Manuscript editor U.S.C. Press, Columbia, 1970-73, mktg. dir., 1973-81; dir. U. Press of Kans., Lawrence, 1981—; mem. adv. com. Kans. Ctr. for the Book, Topeka, 1987—; lectr. pub. U. Kans., Lawrence, Kans. State U., Manhattan, 1983—; book judge Western Heritage Ctr., Oklahoma City, 1988. Mem. Assn. Am. Univ. Presses (bd. dirs. 1988-91, pres. 1995-96, past pres. 1996—), Kans. State Hist. Soc. (life), Phi Beta Kappa. Democrat. Avocations: racquetball, reading, music. Home: 2220 Vermont St Lawrence KS 66046-3066 Office: U Press Kans 2501 W 15th St Lawrence KS 66049-3905

WOODWARD, GRETA CHARMAINE, construction company executive, rental and investment property manager; b. Congress, Ohio, Oct. 28, 1930; d. Richard Thomas and Grace Lucetta (Palmer) Duffey; m. John Jay Woodward, Oct. 29, 1949; children: Kirk Jay, Brad Ewing, Clay William. Bookkeeper Kaufman's Texaco, Wooster, Ohio, 1948-49; office mgr. Holland Furnace Co., Wooster, 1948-49; acctg. clk. Columbus and So. Ohio Electric, 1949-50; interviewer, clk. State Ohio Bur. Employment Services, Columbus, 1950-51; clk. Def. Constrn. Supply Ctr. (U.S. Govt.) (formerly Columbus Gen. Depot), 1951-52; treas. Woodward Co., Inc., Reynoldsburg, Ohio, 1963—. Newspaper columnist Briarcliff News, 1960-63. Active Reynoldsburg PTA, 1960-67; Reynoldsburg United Meth. Ch.; mem. women's service bd. Grant Hosp. Avocations: bike riding, crocheting, writing poetry, stock market, financial mags. Office: Woodward Excavating Co Inc 7340 Tussing Rd Reynoldsburg OH 43068-4111

WOODWARD, JAMES HOYT, academic administrator, engineer; b. Sanford, Fla., Nov. 24, 1939; s. James Hoyt and Edith Pearl (Breeden) W.; m. Martha Ruth Hill, Oct. 13, 1956; children: Connie, Tracey, Wade. BS in Aero. Engring. with honors, Ga. Tech. Inst., 1962, MS in Aero. Engring., 1963, PhD in Engring. Mechanics, 1967; MBA, U. Ala.-Birmingham, 1973. Registered profl. engr., Ala. Asst. prof. engring. mechanics USAF Acad., Colo., 1965-67, assoc. prof., 1967-68; asst. prof. engring. mechanics N.C. State U., 1968-69; assoc. prof. engring. U. Ala., Birmingham, 1969-70, assoc. prof., 1973-77, prof. civil engring., 1977-89, asst. v.p., 1973-78, dean engring., 1978-84, acad. v.p., 1984-89; chancellor U. N.C., Charlotte, 1989—; dir. tech. devel. Rust Engring. Co., Birmingham, 1970-73; cons. in field. Contbr. articles to profl. jours. With USAF, 1965-68. Mem. ASCE, ASME, Am. Soc. Engring. Edn., Am. Mgmt. Assn., Sigma Xi. Methodist. Office: U NC Charlotte Office of Chancellor Charlotte NC 28223

WOODWARD, JEFFREY JAMES, arts administrator; b. Fredericksburg, Va., Apr. 9, 1958; s. Daniel Holt and Mary Jane (Gerra) W.; m. Lori Ann Ott; children: Owen Daniel Ott, Samuel Howard Ott. BA, Pomona Coll., 1980; MBA, NYU, 1983. Audience devel. assoc. Mark Taper Forum, L.A., 1983-85; mktg. dir., gen. mgr. Hartford (Conn.) Stage, 1985-90; mng. dir. Northlight Theatre, Evanston, Ill., 1990-91, McCarter Theatre Ctr. for the Performing Arts, Princeton, N.J., 1991—; trustee Artpride, Millburn, N.J., 1992—; on-site evaluator Nat. Endowment for the Arts, Washington, 1993—. Participant Leadership Greater Hartford, 1989. McCarter Theater recipient Tony award for Outstanding Regional Theatre, 1994. Office: McCarter Theat Ctr Perform Arts 91 University Pl Princeton NJ 08540-5121

WOODWARD, JOANNE GIGNILLIAT, actress; b. Thomasville, Ga., Feb. 27, 1930; d. Wade and Elinor (Trimmier) W.; m. Paul Newman, Jan. 29, 1958; children: Elinor Terese, Melissa Stewart, Clea Olivia. Student, La. State U., 1947-49; grad., Neighborhood Playhouse Dramatic Sch., N.Y.C. First TV appearance in Penny, Robert Montgomery Presents, 1952; understudy broadway play Picnic, 1953; appeared in plays Baby Want a Kiss, 1964, Candida, 1982, The Glass Menagerie, Williamstown Theatre Festival, 1985, Sweet Bird of Youth, Toronto, 1988; motion pictures include Three Faces of Eve, 1957 (Acad. award Best Actress, Nat. Bd. Rev. award, Fgn. Press award), Count Three and Pray, 1955, Long Hot Summer, 1958, No Down Payment, 1957, Sound and the Fury, 1959, A Kiss Before Dying, 1956, Rally Round the Flag Boys, 1958, The Fugitive Kind, 1960, Paris Blues, 1961, The Stripper, 1963, A New Kind of Love, 1963, A Big Hand for the Little Lady, 1965, A Fine Madness, 1965, Rachel, Rachel, 1968, Winning, 1969, WUSA, 1970, They Might Be Giants, 1971, The Effect of Gamma Rays on Man-in-the-Moon Marigolds, 1972 (Cannes Film Festival award), Summer Wishes, Winter Dreams, 1973 (N.Y. Film Critics award), The Drowning Pool, 1975, The End, 1978, Harry and Son, 1984, Glass Menagerie, 1987, Mr. & Mrs. Bridge, 1990, Philadelphia, 1993; TV appearances include All the Way Home; TV-film appearances in Sybil, 1976, Come Back, Little Sheba, 1977, See How She Runs, 1978 (Emmy award), Streets of L.A., 1979, The Shadow Box, 1980, Crisis at Central High, 1981, Do You Remember Love?, 1985 (Emmy award), Blind Spot, 1993 (Emmy nomination, Lead Actress - Miniseries, 1993), Breathing Lessons, 1994 (Emmy nomination, Lead Actress - Special, 1994, Golden Globe award, Best Actress); narrator film documentary Angel Dust, TV documentary on Group Theatre, 1989. Co-recipient (with Paul Newman) Kennedy Ctr. Honors for Lifetime Achievement in the Performing Arts. Democrat. Episcopalian. *

WOODWARD, KAREN CALLISON, school system administrator. Supt. Adnerson (S.C.) Sch. Dist. 5. State finalist Nat. Supt. Yr., 1992. Office: Anderson Sch Dist 5 PO Drawer 439 400 Pearman Dairy Rd Anderson SC 29625-3100

WOODWARD, KATHERINE ANNE, secondary education educator; b. Detroit, Apr. 6, 1942; d. Walter E. and Helen (Leuer) Roberts; m. Clifford Edward Woodward, July 1, 1967; children: Ted, Bob, Chris, John-Paul. BA in History, Webster U., 1964; student, St. Louis U., 1966; MA in History, Sam Houston State U., 1991. Cert. tchr., Tex., Mo. Tchr. world history Oxford (Ala.) High Sch., 1967-69; tchr. English Santa Fe Jr. High Sch., Altaloma, Tex., 1969; tchr. world history Jersey Village High Sch., Houston, 1985—. Co-founder, pres. Brazoria County Cay Care, Alvin, Tex., 1970-73; co-founder Cypress Creek Emergency Med. Svc., Houston, 1975. Named Outstanding Young Women in Am., 1976. Mem. ASCD, AAUW (pres. North Harris County 1976-77), Tex. Coun. Social Studies, Cypress-Fairbanks Coun. Social Studies (pres. 1994-95, scholarship 1990), Nat. Coun. Social Studies. Avocations: travel, reading, Dutch painting, music, boating. Office: Jersey Village High Sch 7600 Solomon St Houston TX 77040-2134

WOODWARD, KENNETH EMERSON, retired mechanical engineer; b. Washington, Oct. 30, 1927; s. George Washington and Mary Josephine (Compton) W.; m. Mary Margaret Eungard, Mar. 29, 1956; children:

Stephen Mark, Kristi Lynn. BME, George Washington U., 1949, M Engring. Adminstrn., 1960; MS, U. Md., 1953; PhD, Am. U., 1973. Mech. engr. Naval Rsch. Lab., Washington, 1950-54; value engring. program mgr. Harry Diamond Labs., Washington, 1955-74; sci. adviser U.S. Army Med. Bioengring. R & D Lab., Ft. Detrick, Md., 1974-75; mech. engr. Woolcott & Co., Washington, 1975-90; ret., 1990. Author: Solar Energy Applications for the Home, 1978; contbr. over 25 articles to profl. publs. With U.S. Army, 1946-47. Recipient Dept. of the Army Decoration for Exceptional Civilian Svc., Engring. Alumni Achievement award The George Washington U., Washington, 1987. Mem. ASME, Am. Soc. for Artificial Internal Organs. Republican. Baptist. Achievements include 12 U.S. and 2 foreign patents, development of artifical human heart. Home: 1701 Hunts End Ct Vienna VA 22182-1833

WOODWARD, LESTER RAY, lawyer; b. Lincoln, Nebr., May 24, 1932; s. Wendell Smith and Mary Elizabeth (Theobald) W.; m. Marianne Martinson, Dec. 27, 1958; children: Victoria L. Woodward Eisele, Richard T., David M., Andrew E. BSBA, U. Nebr., 1953; LLB, Harvard U., 1957; LLD (hon.), Bethany Coll., 1974. Bar: Colo., 1957. Assoc. Davis, Graham & Stubbs, Denver, 1957-59, 60-62, ptnr., 1962—; Teaching fellow Sch. Law Harvard U., 1959-60. Bd. dirs. Bethany Coll., Lindsborg, Kans., 1966-74, 87-95, chmn., 1989-92; bd. dirs. Pub. Edn. Coalition, Denver, 1985-92, chmn., 1988-89; mem. Colo. Commn. Higher Edn., Denver, 1977-86, chmn., 1979-81. Mem. ABA, Colo. Bar Assn., Am. Law Inst. Republican. Lutheran. Home: 680 Bellaire St Denver CO 80220-4935 Office: Davis Graham & Stubbs 370 17th St Ste 4700 Denver CO 80202-5647

WOODWARD, RALPH LEE, JR., historian, educator; b. New London, Conn., Dec. 2, 1934; s. Ralph Lee and Beaulah Mae (Suter) W.; m. Sue Dawn McGrady, Dec. 30, 1958; children: Mark Lee, Laura Lynn, Matthew McGrady. A.B. cum laude, Central Coll., Mo., 1955; M.A., Tulane U., 1959, PhD, 1962. Asst. prof. history Wichita (Kans.) U., 1961-62, U. S.W. La., Lafayette, 1962-63; asst. prof. history U. N.C., Chapel Hill, 1963-67; asso. prof. U. N.C., 1967-70; prof. history Tulane U., New Orleans, 1970—; head dept. history Tulane U., 1973-75, chmn. dept. history, 1986-88; dir. Tulane Summer in C. Am., 1975-78; prof. in charge Tulane Jr. Year Abroad, Paris, 1975-76; Fulbright lectr. Universidad de Chile, Universidad Catolica de Valparaiso, Chile, 1965-66, Universidad del Salvador, Universidad Nacional, Buenos Aires, 1968; vis. prof. U.S. Mil. Acad., West Point, N.Y., 1989; regional liaison officer Emergency Com. to Aid Latin Am. Scholars, 1974. Author: Class Privilage and Economic Development, 1966, Robinson Crusoe's Island, 1969, Positivism in Latin America, 1850-1900, 1971, Central America: A Nation Divided, 1976, 2d edit., 1985, Tribute to Don Bernardo de Galvez, 1979, Belize, 1980, Nicaragua, 1983, 2d edit., 1994, El Salvador, 1988, Guatemala, 1992, Rafael Carrera and the Emergence of the Republic of Guatemala, 1993 (Alfred A. Thomas Book award); editor: Central America: Historical Perspectives on the Contemporary Crises, 1988; assoc. editor: Revista del Pensamiento Centroamericano, 1975, Research Guide to Central America and the Caribbean, 1985, Encyclopedia of Latin American History and Culture, 1996; contbg. editor: Handbook of Latin American Studies, 1987-90; series editor: World Bibliographical Series, 1987—; contbr. articles to profl. jours. Served to capt. USMC, 1955-58. Recipient Alfred B. Thomas Book award Southeastern Coun. Latin Am. Studies, 1994; Henry L. and Grace Doherty Found. fellow Tulane U., 1962; named La. Humanist of Yr. La. Endowment for Humanities, 1995. Mem. Am. Hist. Assn. (mem. Conf. L.Am. History, pres. 1989, mem. gen. cou. 1974-76), La. Hist. Assn., Southeastern Conf. L.Am. Studies (program chmn. 1975, pres. 1975-76), L.Am. Studies Assn., Com. on Andean Studies (chmn. 1972-73), Geography and History Acad. Guatemala. Office: Tulane U Dept History New Orleans LA 70118

WOODWARD, RICHARD JOSEPH, JR., geotechnical engineer; b. Pueblo, Colo., Dec. 16, 1907; s. Richard Joseph and Anna Catherine (Earley) W.; m. Mary Irene Campbell, Aug. 29, 1932 (dec.); children: Rita Ann, Sue Marie, Richard Joseph, Patricia Irene. BS, Colo. Coll., 1930; MS, U. Calif., Berkeley, 1947. Naval architect U.S. Navy, 1941-45; lectr. civil engring. U. Calif., Berkeley, 1946-50; ptnr. Woodward-Clyde Cons.'s (and predecessor firms), Oakland, Calif., 1950-53; chmn. bd. Woodward-Clyde Cons.'s (and predecessor firms), 1954-73, chmn. emeritus, 1973—; founding pres. Design Profl.'s Ins. Co., 1972. Co-author: Earth and Earth-Rock Dams, 1963, Drilled Pier Foundations, 1972; Contbr. tech. articles to profl. jours. Mem. state tech. svcs. com. U.S. Dept. Commerce, 1967-70; bd. regents Holy Names Coll., Oakland, 1964-72. Decorated knight magistral grace Sovereign Mil. Order Malta Western Assn.; named Disting. Engring. Alumnus U.Calif.-Berkeley Engring. Alumni Assn., 1983. Fellow ASCE (life mem., chmn. exec. com. soil mechanics and founds. div. 1966-70, Middlebrooks award 1964), Am. Cons. Engrs. Coun. (Past Pres.'s award for outstanding contbns. 1972); mem. Internat. Fedn. Cons. Engrs. (chmn. standing com. profl. liability 1971-76), Structural Engrs. Assn. No. Calif. (bd. dir. 1958-60), Sigma Xi, Chi Epsilon, Delta Epsilon, Kiwanis, Serra Club (Berkeley, Calif.), Athens Club (Oakland, Calif.), Commonwealth Club (San Francisco). Roman Catholic. Home and Office: # 260 3431 Foothill Blvd Oakland CA 94601

WOODWARD, ROBERT FORBES, retired government official, consultant; b. Mpls., Oct. 1, 1908; s. Charles Emerson and Ella (Robertson) W.; m. Virginia Parker Cooke, Feb. 20, 1943 (dec. Jan. 1990); children: Robert Forbes, Mary Cooke. A.B., U. of Minn., 1930; student, George Washington U., 1941; LL.D., U. of Pacific, 1962. Joined U.S. Fgn. Service, 1931; vice consul at Winnipeg, Man., Can., 1932-33; student Fgn. Service Tng. Sch., Dept. of State, Washington, 1933; vice consul Buenos Aires, 1933-36; temp. vice consul Asuncion, Paraguay, 1935; 3d sec. legation and vice consul Bogota, Colombia, 1936-37; vice consul Rio de Janeiro, Brazil, 1937-38; assigned div. Latin Am. Affairs, Dept. State, Washington, 1938-42, 44; 2d sec. of embassy and consul La Paz, Bolivia, 1942-44, dep. chief mission, 1942-44; dep. chief mission Guatemala, 1944-46, Habana, 1946-47; dep. dir. Inter-Am. Affairs, Dept. State, Washington, 1947-49; assigned Nat. War Coll., 1949-50; deputy chief mission Stockholm, Sweden, 1950-52; chief fgn. service personnel Dept. State, 1952-53; dep. asst. sec. state for Inter-Am. Affairs, 1953-54; ambassador to Costa Rica, 1954-58, to Uruguay, 1958-61, to Chile, 1961, to Spain, 1962-65; asst. sec. state for Inter-Am. affairs, 1961-62; adviser to spl. negotiators (Canal Treaties with Panama), 1965-67; interim dir. Office of Water for Peace, 1967; ret., 1968; cons. Dept. State, 1968—, Research Analysis Corp., 1969—, Youth for Understanding, 1972—; acting provost Elbert Covell (Spanish-lang.) Coll., U. of Pacific, Stockton, Calif., 1970; Chmn. U.S. del. Econ. Commn. Latin Am., Santiago, Chile, 1961; vice chmn. U.S. del. Alliance for Progress Conf., Punta del Este, 1961, U.S. del. Fgn. Ministers meeting, Punta del Este, 1962; chmn. U.S. del. Internat. Red Cross Conf., Vienna, 1965; chmn. U.S. del. Conf. for Revision of OAS Charter, Panama, 1966; conducted study on Panama Canal for Dept. Army, Research Analysis Corp., 1971; conducted study on usefulness of UNESCO to U.S. for Dept. State, 1972; coordinator, chief U.S. del. to Working Group with Latin Am. and Caribbean Govts. on transnat. enterprises, 1974-75. Mem. Inter-Am. Comm. on Human Rights, 1972-76, Am. Acad. Diplomacy, Washington Inst. Fgn. Affairs. Recipient Distinguished Service award U. Minn., 1963. Mem. Met. Club, Chevy Chase Club, Sulgrave Club, Ret. Diplomatic and Consular Officers Club. Home: 1642 Avon Pl NW Washington DC 20007-2958

WOODWARD, ROBERT UPSHUR, newspaper reporter, writer; b. Geneva, Ill., Mar. 26, 1943; s. Alfred E. and Jane (Upshur) W.; m. Elsa Walsh, Nov. 25, 1989; 1 child, Tali. B.A., Yale U., 1965. Reporter Montgomery County (Md.) Sentinel, 1970-71; reporter Washington Post, 1971-78, met. editor, 1979-81, asst. mng. editor, 1981—. Author: (with Carl Bernstein) All the President's Men, 1974, The Final Days, 1976, (with Scott Armstrong) The Brethren, 1979, Wired, 1984, Veil: The Secret Wars of the CIA, 1987, The Commanders, 1991, (with David S. Broder) The Man Who Would Be President, 1991, The Agenda: Inside the Clinton White House, 1994. Served with USN, 1965-70. Office: Washington Post Co 1150 15th St NW Washington DC 20071-0001

WOODWARD, STEPHEN RICHARD, newspaper reporter; b. Fukuoka City, Japan, July 27, 1953; came to U.S., 1954; s. Leonard Edwin and Etsuko (Okumura) W.; m. Sandra Elizabeth Richardson, Dec. 31, 1979; children: Daniel Joseph, Elizabeth Etsuko. BA in English, Wright State U., 1975; MA in Journalism, U. Mo., 1979. Advt. coordinator Wright State U., Dayton, Ohio, 1976-77; reporter Kansas City (Mo.) Star, 1979-82; assoc. editor then editor Kansas City Bus. Jour., 1982-83; editor then gen. mgr. Portland (Oreg.) Bus. Jour., 1984-86; exec. bus. editor The Hartford (Conn.) Courant, 1986-87; editor San Francisco Bus. Times, 1987-88; bus. editor The Oregonian, Portland, 1989-93, reporter, 1993—. Recipient 1st Place Investigative Reporting award Assn. Area Bus. Publs., 1983, 1st Place Column Writing award Assn. Area Bus. Publs., 1985. Mem. Investigative Reporters and Editors Inc. Avocations: astronomy, chess, creative writing. Home: 3309 NE Irving St Portland OR 97232-2538 Office: The Oregonian 1320 SW Broadway Portland OR 97201-3469

WOODWARD, SUSAN ELLEN, economist, federal official; b. Loma Linda, Calif., June 14, 1949; d. Frank Colwin and Dollie Dorothy (O'Kane) W.; 1 child, Sonja Stenger Weissman; m. Robert E. Hall, July 20, 1996. BA in Econs., UCLA, 1970, PhD in Mgmt./Fin., 1978. Instr. U. Wash., Seattle, 1975, U. Toronto, 1975-77, UCLA, 1976-83, 84-85, U. Calif., Santa Barbara, 1977-79, U. Rochester (N.Y.), 1983-84; sr. staff economist Coun. Econ. Advisers, Washington, 1985-87; dep. asst. sec., chief economist HUD, Washington, 1987-92; chief economist SEC, Washington, 1992-95; with Cornerstone Rsch., Menlo Park, Calif., 1996—. Mem. Am. Econ. Assn. (editor 1983-87), Am. Fin. Assn. Home: 2122 California St NW # 252 Washington DC 20008-1803 also: 1682 Oak Ave Menlo Park CA 94025 Office: Cornerstone Rsch 1000 El Camino Real Menlo Park CA

WOODWARD, THEODORE ENGLAR, medical educator, internist; b. Westminster, Md., Mar. 22, 1914; s. Lewis Klair and Phoebe Helen (Neidig) W.; m. Celeste Constance Lauve, June 24, 1938; children: William E., R. Craig, Celeste L. Woodward Applefeld. BS, Franklin and Marshall Coll., 1934, DSc (hon.), 1954; MD, U. Md., 1938; DSc (hon.), Western Md. Coll., 1950, Hahnemann U., 1993. Diplomate Am. Bd. Internal Medicine. Asst. prof. medicine U. Md. Sch. Medicine, Balt., 1946-48, assoc. prof., also dir. sect. infectious disease, 1948-54, prof., 1954-83, prof. emeritus, 1983—, chmn. dept., 1954-81; attending physician Balt. VA Med Ctr., 1949—; with Armed Forces Epidemiol. Bd., Washington, 1952-92, mem. commns., 1952-72, pres. bd., 1976-78, 80-92; mem. U.S./Japan Coop. Med. Sci. Program, Washington, 1965—; disting. physician Cen. VA, Washington, 1981-87. Author: Chloramphemicol, 1958, 200 Years of Medicine in Baltimore, 1976, A History of the Department of Medicine, University of Maryland, 1807-1981, 1987, A History of Armed Forces Epidemiological Board, 1940-1990, 1990, Carroll County (Md.) Physicians of the 19th and Early 20th Centuries, 1990, The Armed Forces Epidemiological Board: The History of the Commissions, 1995; contbr. chpts. to textbooks. Life trustee Gilman Sch., Balt., 1955—. Lt. col. Medical Svc. Corp U.S. Army, 1941-46, ETO, PTO. Decorated Order of the Sacred Treasure Gold and Silver Star Govt. of Japan; recipient U.S.A. Typhus Commn. medal Dept. Def., 1945, also Exceptionally Disting. Svc. award, 1990, Outstanding Civilian Svc. medal with oak leaf cluster Dept. Army, 1981. Recipient Disting. Svc. award AMA, 1995. Mem. ACP (master, gov. Md. regent 1969-70, James D. Bruce Meml. award 1970, Disting. Tchr. award 1992), Am. Clin. and Climatol. Assn. (pres. 1969-70), Infectious Disease Soc. Am. (pres. 1976-77, Finland award 1972, Bristol award, Kass award 1991), Inst. Medicine NAS, Elkridge Club (Towson, Md.), Mayo Fellows Assn. (hon.), Hamilton St. Club. Republican. Avocations: photography, gardening, raising wild fowl. Home: 1 Merrymount Rd Baltimore MD 21210-1908 Office: Balt VA Med Ctr 10 N Green St Baltimore MD 21210

WOODWARD, THOMAS AIKEN, lawyer; b. Beatrice, Nebr., June 28, 1933; s. Thomas Aiken and Jessie (Griggs) W.; m. Sara Hubka, Dec. 27, 1962; children: Thomas A., Hewett G. BA, U. Nebr., 1955; JD, U. Mich., 1960; LLM in Taxation, NYU, 1961. Bar: N.Y. 1961, Nebr. 1963, Pa. 1987. Ptnr. Kutak, Rock & Campbell, Omaha, 1969-87; ptnr., chmn. tax dept. Eckert, Seamans, Cherin & Mellott, Pitts., 1987-92; spl. counsel Weller, Wicks & Wallace, Pitts., 1992—. Served to lt. USN, 1955-58. Mem. ABA, N.Y. Bar Assn., Nebr. Bar Assn., Pa. Bar Assn., Allegheny County Bar Assn. Republican. Presbyterian. Office: Weller Wicks & Wallace Benedum Trees Building Ste 1800 Pittsburgh PA 15222-1775

WOODWARD, THOMAS MORGAN, actor; b. Ft. Worth, Sept. 16, 1925; s. Valin Ridge and Francis Louise (McKinley) W.; m. Enid Anne Loftis, Nov. 18, 1950; 1 child, Enid Anne. AA, Arlington State Coll., 1948; BBA, U. Tex., 1951. Motion picture and TV actor, 1955—; numerous TV appearances include Dallas; motion pictures include The Great Locomotive Chase, 1955, Slaughter on 10th Ave., 1957, The Gun Hawk, 1962, Cool Hand Luke, 1966, The Wild Country, 1973, Which Way Is Up, 1977, Speed Trap, 1978, Battle Beyond the Stars, 1980, Girls Just Want to Have Fun, 1985, Dark Before Dawn, 1987, Gunsmoke III, 1991. With USAAF, 1944-45; to capt. USAF, 1951-53. Recipient Golden Boot award Motion Picture and TV Fund, 1988, Golden Lariat award Nat. Western Film Festival, 1988, Lifetime Achievement award in the arts Arlington Tex. Arts Coun., 1994, Lifetime Achievement award for western film acting Wild West Film Festival, 1995; named Disting. Alumnus of Arts U. Tex., 1969; inducted into the Walk of Western Stars William S. Hart Mus., L.A., 1990. Mem. Acad. Motion Picture Arts and Scis., SAR, Pi Kappa Alpha (Disting. Achievement award 1981, inducted into Order of West Range 1988).

WOODWELL, GEORGE MASTERS, ecology research director, lecturer; b. Cambridge, Mass., Oct. 23, 1928; s. Philip McIntire and Virginia (Sellers) W.; m. Alice Katharine Rondthaler, June 23, 1955; children: Caroline Alice, Marjorie Virginia, Jane Katharine, John Christopher. AB, Dartmouth Coll., 1950; AM, Duke U., 1956, PhD, 1958; DSc (hon.), Williams Coll., 1977, Miami U., 1984, Carleton Coll., 1988, Muhlenberg Coll., 1990, Duke U., 1994; Dartmouth Coll., 1996. Mem. faculty U. Maine, 1957-61, assoc. prof. botany, 1960-61; vis. asst. ecologist, biology dept. Brookhaven Nat. Lab., Upton, N.Y., 1961-62; ecologist Brookhaven Nat. Lab., 1965-67, sr. ecologist, 1967-75; founder, dir. Ecosystems Center, 1975-85; dep. and asst. dir. Marine Biol. Lab., Woods Hole, Mass., 1975-76; pres. and dir. Woods Hole Research Ctr., 1985—; lectr. Yale Sch. Forestry, 1967—; chmn. Conf. on Long Term Biol. Consequences of Nuclear War, 1982-83. Editor: Ecological Effects of Nuclear War, 1965, Diversity and Stability in Ecological Systems, 1969, (with E.V. Pecan) Carbon and the Biosphere, 1973, The Role of Terrestrial Vegetation in the Global Carbon Cycle: Measurement by Remote Sensing, 1984, The Earth in Transition: Patterns and Processes of Biotic Impoverishment, 1990, (with K. Ramakrishna) Forests for the Future, 1993, (with F.T. Mackenzie) Biotic Feedbacks in the Warming of the Earth, 1995. Founding trustee Environ. Def. Fund, 1967; founding trustee Natural Resources Def. Coun., 1970, vice chmn., 1974—; founding trustee World Resources Inst., 1982—; bd. dirs. World Wildlife Fund, 1970-84, chmn., 1980-84; bd. dirs. Conservation Found., 1975-77, Ruth Mott Fund, 1984-91, chmn., 1989-91; bd. dirs. Ctr. for Marine Conservation, 1990—; adv. com. TMI Pub. Health Fund, 1980-94. Recipient Joseph Priestley award Dickinson Coll., 1993, Hutchinson medal Garden Club of Am., 1993, Disting. Svc. award Am. Inst. Biol. Scis., 1982. Fellow AAAS, Am. Acad. Arts and Scis.; mem. NAS, Brit. Ecol. Soc., Ecol. Soc. Am. (v.p. 1966-67, pres. 1977-78), Sea Edn. Assn. (bd. dirs. 1980-85), Sigma Xi. Rsch., pub. on structure and function of natural communities, biotic impoverishment, especially ecological effects of ionizing radiation, effects of persistent toxins, world carbon cycle and warming of the earth. Office: Woods Hole Research Ctr Box 296 13 Church St Woods Hole MA 02543-1007

WOODY, CAROL CLAYMAN, data processing executive; b. Bristol, Va., May 20, 1949; d. George Neal and Ida Mae (Nelms) Clayman; B.S. in Math., Coll. William and Mary, Williamsburg, Va., 1971; M.B.A. with distinction (IBM Corp. fellow 1978, Stephen Bufton Meml. Ednl. Found. grantee, 1978-79), Babcock Sch., Wake Forest U., 1979; m. Robert William Woody, Aug. 19, 1972. Programmer trainee GSA, 1971-72; systems engr. Citizens Fidelity Bank & Trust Co., Louisville, 1972-75; programmer/analyst-tng. coordinator Blue Bell, Inc., Greensboro, N.C., 1975-79; supr. programming and tech. services J.E. Baker Co., York, Pa., 1979-82, fin. design supr. bus. systems Lycoming div. AVCO, Stratford, Conn., 1982-83; project mgr. Yale U., 1984—; co-owner Sign of the Sycamore, antiques; mem. Data Processing Standards Bd., 1977, CICS/VS Adv. Council, 1975; speaker Nat. Fuse Conf., 1989, Aion expert systems nat. conf., 1990, bus. sch. Coll. William & Mary, 1994. Mem. Am. Bus. Woman's Assn. (chpt. v.p. 1978-79, Merit award 1978), Nat. Assn. Female Execs. (founder shoreline network 1993), Assn. for System Mgmt., Delta Omicron (alumni pres. 1973-75, regional chmn. 1979-82). Republican. Presbyterian. Author various manuals, contbr. article to profl. jour. Home: PO Box 1450 Guilford CT 06437-0550 Office: PO Box 208276 175 Whitney Ave New Haven CT 06511-7209

WOODY, CLAUDIA LAVERGNE, telecommunications executive, consultant; b. Martinsville, Va., Jan. 30, 1955; d. N. Rees and LaVergne (Tuck) W. BA summa cum laude, Mary Baldwin Coll., 1977; MS, U. Tenn., 1979; MBA, U. Tex., 1989. Asst. basketball coach U. Tenn., Knoxville, 1977-79, asst. athletics dir., 1979-81; asst. athletics dir. U. Tex., Austin, 1981-88, dir. external affairs, asst. dean Coll. Bus., 1988-91; dir. mktg. San Marcos Telephone Co. and San Marcos Telecorp, 1991-93; v.p. mktg. Century Telephone Enterprises, Dallas, 1993—; cons. various univs., 1981—, MacGregor Sporting Goods, Berlin, Wis., 1984-86, Apple Computer, Inc., 1987—; dir., tournament mgr. NCAA Nat. Championships, 1981-88. Mng. editor: Texas: The Business School Mag. (Coun. Advancement and Support Edn. award 1990), 1987-91. Bd. dirs The Vol. Ctr., Austin, 1989-92, Greater Austin Sports Found., 1990-94; bd. dirs., v.p. The Artemis Found., Winter Park, Colo., 1990—; mem. adv. bd. Tex. Ctr. for Legal Ethics and Professionalism, 1994—, Legends of Golf, Austin, 1991-93, San Marcos Incubator, 1992-94, Bus. Sch. S.W. Tex. State U., 1991-94, Rotary Internat., 1994—; mem. Leadership Tex., 1993. Russell scholar, Mary Baldwin Coll., Staunton, Va., 1977; Hilton A. Smith grad. fellow, 1979; recipient The Kozmetsky award U. Tex., Austin, 1989. Mem. Exec. Women Tex. Govt., Coun. Advancement and Support Edn., Coun. Coll. Women Athletics Adminstrs., NAFE, Nat. Soc. Fundraising Execs., Phi Beta Kappa, Omicron Delta Kappa, Psi Chi, Pi Lambda Theta, Kappa Delta Pi, Phi Kappa Phi, Beta Gamma Sigma. Democrat. Avocations: cycling, snow skiing, water skiing, softball. Home: 6206 Stonehill Dr Dallas TX 75240-7836 Office: Century Bus Devel 7502 Greenville Ave Ste 360 Dallas TX 75231-3811

WOODY, DONALD EUGENE, lawyer; b. Springfield, Mo., Mar. 10, 1948; s. Raymond D. and Elizabeth Ellen (Bushnell) W.; m. Ann Louise Ruhl, June 5, 1971; children: Marshall Wittmann, Catherine Elizabeth. BA in Polit. Sci. with honors, U. Mo., 1970, JD, 1973. Bar: Mo. 1973, U.S. Dist. Ct. (we. dist.) Mo. 1973, U.S. Ct. Appeals (8th cir.) 1973, U.S. Supreme Ct. 1987. Assoc. Neale, Newman & Bradshaw, Springfield, 1973-74; ptnr. Taylor, Stafford & Woody, Springfield, 1974-82, Taylor, Stafford, Woody, Cowherd & Clithero, Springfield, 1983-93, Taylor, Stafford, Woody, Clithero & Fitzgerald, Springfield, 1993—. Editor U. Mo. Law Rev., 1973. Chmn. county campaign U.S. senator Thomas Eagleton, Springfield, 1980; committeeman Greene County Dem. Party, Springfield, 1984-86; cons. Children's Home Mayors commn., Springfield, 1985. Mem. ABA, Springfield Metro Bar Assn. (sec. 1977-80, precedure com. 1986, bd. dirs. 1991-93, pres.-elect 1995, pres. 1996), Assn. Trial Lawyers Am., Springfield C. of C. (chmn. performing arts com. 1980-84), Order of Coif, Phi Delta Phi. Avocations: fishing, growing roses, golf, running. Home: 1421 S Ginger Blue Ave Springfield MO 65809-2260 Office: Taylor Stafford et al 1533 E Ridgeview Ste 1000 Springfield MO 65804

WOODY, JOHN FREDERICK, secondary education educator; b. Indpls., Apr. 27, 1941; s. Ralph Edwin and Crystal Oleta (Thomas) W.; m. Nancy Ann Henry, July 7, 1963; children: Michael, Laura. BS in Secondary Sch. Teaching, Butler U., 1963, MS in Edn., 1967, adminstrn. lic., 1979, post-grad., 1991—; postgrad., UCLA, 1980-82, Ind. U., 1990, U. Amsterdam, The Netherlands, 1985, Mont. State U., 1993, Purdue U., 1994. Tchr. Pub. Sch. 90, Indpls., 1963-66, Broad Ripple High Sch., Indpls., 1966-89; tchr., head social studies dept. Arlington H.S., Indpls., 1989—. Author: (resource kits for hist. events) Cram, Inc., 1976-81, (filmstrips) Lowe Sheldrew, 1976-81; contbr. articles to profl. jours. and sch. materials. Sponsor Rep. Nat. Com., 1982—; deacon Heritage Bapt. Ch., 1983—; mem. U.S. Congress German Bundestag Select Com. Ind., 1986-93. Fulbright scholar U.S. Info. Agy., 1985. Mem. ASCD, Nat. Coun. Social Studies, Ind. Coun. Social Studies, Arlington Acad. Com. Avocations: reading, writing, swimming, lifting weights. Home: 7362 Woodside Dr Indianapolis IN 46260-3137 Office: Arlington High Sch 4825 N Arlington Ave Indianapolis IN 46226-2401

WOODY, MARY FLORENCE, nursing educator, university administrator; b. Chambers County, Ala., Mar. 31, 1926; d. Hugh Ernest and May Lillie (Gilliland) W.; diploma Charity Hosp. Sch. Nursing, 1947; BS, Columbia U., 1953, M.A., 1955. Staff nurse Wheeler Hosp., Lafayette, Ala., 1947-48; polio nurse Willard Parker Hosp., N.Y.C., 1949; staff nurse, supr. VA Hosp., Montgomery, Ala., 1950-53; faculty mem., field supr., nursing dept. Tchrs. Coll., Columbia U., N.Y.C., 1955-56; asst. dir. nursing Emory U. Hosp., clin. asst. prof. Emory U. Sch. Nursing, Atlanta, 1956-68; asst. dir., dir. nursing Grady Meml. Hosp., Atlanta, 1968-79; founding dean, prof. Sch. Nursing, Auburn (Ala.) U., 1979-84; assoc. dir., dir. nursing Emory U. Hosp., Atlanta, 1984-93; interim dean Sch. Nursing, Emory U., 1992-93; chmn. Ga. Statewide Master Planning Com. for Nursing and Nursing Edn., 1971-75; faculty preceptor patient care adminstrn. Sch. Public Health, U. Minn., 1977-79; mem. bd. dirs. Wesley Woods Found. & Long Term Hosp., 1994—. Recipient Spl. Recognition, 5th Dist. and Ga. Nurses Assn., 1978, 93, Disting. Achievement in Nursing Svc. award Columbia U. Tchrs. Coll. Alumni Assn., 1992, Jane Van de Vrede Outstanding Svc. to Citizens of Ga. award Ga. League Nursing, Cert. Spl. Recognition award Ga. Nurses Assn., 1993. Fellow Am. Acad. Nursing (charter); mem. Am. Nurses Assn., Nat. League Nursing, Am. Heart Assn., Emory U. Nell Hodgson Woodruff Sch. Nursing Alumni Assn. (hon. 1994), Sigma Theta Tau. Democrat. Chmn. bd. dirs. Am. Jour. Nursing Co., 1978-83. Address: 907 Lenox Hill Atlanta GA 30324-2957

WOOLAM, GERALD LYNN, surgeon; b. Lubbock, Tex., Apr. 16, 1937; s. Rawson Harp and Christine Leta (Rampy) W.; m. Nan Kelly, Feb. 28, 1959; children—Kelly Ann, Gerald Lynn, Gregory Alan. B.A., Tex. Tech. U., 1958; M.D., Baylor U., 1962. Diplomate Am. Bd. Surgery. Intern Parkland Meml. Hosp., Dallas, 1962-63; resident gen. surgery Mayo Clinic and Mayo Grad. Sch. Medicine, U. Minn., Rochester, 1963-67; chief resident asso. in surgery Mayo Clinic and Mayo Grad. Sch. Medicine, U. Minn., 1967-68; practice medicine specializing in surgery Lubbock, 1968—; assoc. clin. prof. surgery Tex. Tech. U. Sch. Medicine, 1972-74, clin. prof., 1975—, prof., interim chmn. dept. surgery, 1980-81. Contbr. articles to profl. jours. Bd. dirs. Community Concert Assn. of Lubbock, 1968-71, 1st United Meth. Ch., Lubbock, 1970-75, 76—, South Plains Health Systems, 1976-81; trustee West Tex. Found., 1971-74. Served with USNR, 1954-62. Recipient Outstanding Clin. Prof. award Tex. Tech. U., 1977. Fellow ACS; mem. AAAS, Priestley Soc. (dir. 1970-73, pres. 1981-82), Lubbock Surg. Soc. (pres. 1972), AMA, Lubbock-Crosby-Garza County Med. Soc. (treas., exec. com. 1971—, pres. 1986), Osler Soc., Am. Cancer Soc. (pres. Lubbock unit 1972-73, pres. Tex. div. 1978-79, nat. del. 1980-88, nat. dir. 1988—), Am. Heart Assn. (pres. Lubbock County div. 1973-74), Tex. Surg. Soc., Soc. Surgery Alimentary Tract, Soc. for Surg. Oncology, Central Assn. Dentists and Physicians, So. Surg. Assn., Sigma Xi, Phi Chi, Alpha Omega Alpha, Phi Kappa Phi, Phi Eta Sigma, Alpha Epsilon Delta. Home: 4007 69th St Lubbock TX 79413-5945 Office: 3702 21st St Lubbock TX 79410-1230

WOOLARD, EDGAR S., JR., chemical company executive; b. Washington, N.C., Apr. 15, 1934; s. Edgar Smith and Mamie (Boone) W.; m. Peggy Harrell, 1956; children: Annette, Lynda. BS, N.C. State U., 1956. Indsl. engr. DuPont, Kinston, N.C., 1957-59, group supr. indsl. engring., 1959-62, supr. mfg. sect., 1962-64, planning supr., 1964-65; staff asst to prodn. mgr. DuPont, Wilmington, Del., 1965-66; product supr. DuPont, Old Hickory, Tenn., 1966-69, engring. supt., 1969-70; asst. plant mgr. DuPont, Camden, S.C., 1970-71; plant mgr. DuPont, Kinston, S.C., 1971-73; dir. products mktg. div. DuPont, Wilmington, Del., 1973-75, mgr. dir. textile mktg. div., 1975-76, mgr. corp. plans dept., 1976-77, gen. dir. products and planning div., 1977-78, gen. mgr. textile fibers, 1978-81, v.p. textile fibers, 1981-83, exec. v.p., 1983-85, vice chmn., 1985-87, pres., COO, 1987-89, chmn., CEO, 1989—, also bd. dirs.; bd. dirs. N.C. Textile Found., Citicorp. Trustee Med. Ctr. Del., N.C. State U., Winterthur Mus. Lt. U.S. Army. Recipient Internat. Palladium medal Soc. Chimie Industrielle (Am. sect.), 1995. Office: DuPont 1007 N Market St Wilmington DE 19898-1226*

WOOLARD, WILLIAM LEON, lawyer, electrical distributing company executive; b. Bath, N.C., Aug. 26, 1931; s. Archie Leon and Pearl Irene (Boyd) W.; m. Virginia Harris Stratton, June 17, 1961; children: William Leon Jr., Margaret Anne. AB, Duke U., 1953, LLB, JD, 1955. Bar: N.C.

1955, U.S. Dist. Ct. (we. and mid. dists.) N.C. 1960. Claims analyst Md. Casualty Co., Charlotte, N.C., 1955-56; dist. mgr. Chrysler Corp., Charlotte, 1956-60; ptnr. Jones, Hewson & Woolard, Charlotte, 1960-86, of counsel, 1986—; pres. Armature Winding Co., Inc., Charlotte, 1970—, also bd. dirs.; v.p. Power Products Mfg. Co., Charlotte, 1970—, also bd. dirs. Mem. adminstrv. bd. 1st United Meth. Ch., Charlotte, 1961-78, trustee, 1984-87; trustee Lawyers Ednl. Found., Charlotte, 1970-78; bd. dirs. Christian Rehab. Ctr., Charlotte, 1972-73, N.C. Eye and Human Tissue Bank, Winston-Salem, 1978-79. Recipient Order of Civil Merit Moran award Republic of Korea, 1990, Disting. Svc. medal Republic of China, 1990, Medal of Friendship Pope John Paul II, 1990, Humanitarian Citizen of Merit medal Republic of China, 1990, Humanitarian medal France, 1990, Outstanding Svc. medal Mayor of Paris, 1990, numerous others; Angier B. Duke scholar Duke U., 1949-53; Carnegie Found. fellow Duke U., 1951-52, Melvin Jones fellow Lions Found., 1978. Mem. ABA, N.C. Bar Assn., N.C. State Bar Assn., 26th Jud. Dist. Bar Assn., Am. Judicature Soc., Lions (pres. Charlotte Cen. club 1972-73, pres., trustee ednl. found. 1973-87, dist. gov., chmn. coun. govs. internat. orgn. 1978-79, internat. bd. dirs. 1981-85, Ambassador of Goodwill award 1983, internat. 3d v.p. 1986-87, 2d v.p. 1987-88, 1st v.p. 1988-89, internat. pres. 1989-90, immediate past pres. 1990-91, chmn. bd. trustee 1990-91), Masons, Shriners, Phi Kappa Sigma, Delta Theta Phi. Avocations: collecting antique and rare books, opera, boating, fishing. Home: 638 Hempstead Pl Charlotte NC 28207-2320 Office: PO Box 32277 Charlotte NC 28232-2277

WOOLDREDGE, WILLIAM DUNBAR, health facility administrator; b. Salem, Mass., Oct. 27, 1937; s. John and Louise (Sigourney) W.; m. Johanna Marie; children: John, Rebecca Wistar. BA, Colby Coll., 1961; MBA, Harvard U., 1964. Staff assoc. Sun Oil Co., Phila., 1964-67; treas. Ins. Co. N.Am., Phila., 1967-72; treas. B.F. Goodrich Co., Akron, Ohio, 1972-84, sr. v.p., 1978-79, exec. v.p., chief fin. officer, mem. mgmt. com., 1979-84; chief fin. officer, exec. v.p., dir. Belden & Blake Corp., North Canton, Ohio, 1984-89; sr. v.p., chief fin. officer, dir. Belden & Blake Oil Prodn., Inc., 1984-89; prin. dir. Carleton Group, Cleve., 1989-92; CFO, v.p. King's Med. Co., Hudson, Ohio, 1993—, also bd. dirs.; bd. dirs. Freeway Corp., Cleve. Bd. dirs. Salvation Army; trustee Children's Hosp. Med. Ctr., Akron. With U.S. Army, 1956-58. Mem. Fin. Execs. Inst. Episcopalian. Club: Country of Hudson. Home: 100 College St Hudson OH 44236-2925 Office: King's Med Co 1920 Georgetown Rd Hudson OH 44236-4060

WOOLDRIDGE, DEAN EVERETT, engineering executive, scientist; b. Chickasha, Okla., May 30, 1913; s. Auttie Noonan and Irene Amanda (Kerr) W.; m. Helene Detweiler, Sept. 1936; children—Dean Edgar, Anna Lou, James Allan. A.B., U. Okla., 1932, M.S., 1933; Ph.D., Calif. Inst. Tech., 1936. Mem. tech. staff Bell Telephone Labs., N.Y.C., 1936-46; co-dir. research and devel. labs Hughes Aircraft Co., Culver City, Calif., 1946-52, v.p. research and devel., 1952-53; pres., dir. Ramo-Wooldridge Corp., Los Angeles, 1953-58, Thompson Ramo Wooldridge, Inc., Los Angeles, also Cleve., 1958-62; research assoc. Calif. Inst. Tech., 1962-79. Author: The Machinery of the Brain, 1963, The Machinery of Life, 1966, Mechanical Man, 1968, Sensory Processing in the Brain, 1979, also articles. Recipient Citation of Honor Air Force Assn., 1950, Raymond E. Hackett award, 1955, Westinghouse Sci. Writing award AAAS, 1963, Disting. Svc. Citation U. Okla, Disting. Alumnus award Calif. Inst. Tech., 1983. Fellow AAAS, Am. Acad. Arts and Sci., Am. Phys. Soc., IEEE, AIAA; mem. Nat. Acad. Scis., Nat. Acad. Engring., Calif. Inst. Assos., Am. Inst. Physics, Phi Beta Kappa, Sigma Xi, Tau Beta Pi, Phi Eta Sigma, Eta Kappa Nu. Address: 4545 Via Esperanza Santa Barbara CA 93110-2319

WOOLEVER, NAOMI LOUISE, retired editor; b. Williamsport, Pa., Sept. 17, 1922; d. Samuel Bruce and Kathryn Elizabeth (Schmidt) W. B.S., Pa. State U., 1944, M.A., 1966, postgrad., 1974-76. Reporter, women's editor Gazette & Bulletin, Williamsport, 1944-53; women's editor Sun-Gazette, Williamsport, 1953-72, assoc. city editor, 1972-74; prof. journalism Williamsport Area Community Coll., 1974-76; nat. editor, mng. editor Grit Pub. Co., Williamsport, 1976-81, editor in chief, 1981-88; career cons. high sch. and coll. journalism classes, Pa. Contbr. articles to profl. jours. Named Woman of Yr., Williamsport Univ. Women, 1967. Mem. Pa. Women's Press Assn. (pres. 1960-62, Pa. Newswoman of Yr. 1958), Nat. Fedn. Press Women (bd. dirs. 1960-62), Soroptimist Club (pres. Williamsport chpt. 1958-60), Univ. Women's Club (pres. 1961-63), Friends of James V. Brown Libr., Williamsport Country Club, Williamsport Woman's Club, Lycoming County Hist. Soc., Clio Club (pres. 1991-93), Phi Kappa Phi, Kappa Tau Alpha, Zeta Tau Alpha. Republican. Mem. United Methodist Ch. Avocations: music, duplicate bridge, photography, sports. Home: 326 N Montour St Montoursville PA 17754-1832

WOOLEY, BRUCE ALLEN, electronics engineer, educator; b. Milw, Oct. 14, 1943; s. Stanley Allen and Viola Beatrice (Lyster) W.; m. Ariel Starr, Sept. 20, 1969; children: Kevin Lyster, Adam David, Eric Allen. B.S., U. Calif.-Berkeley, 1966, M.S., 1968, Ph.D., 1970. Acting asst. prof. U. Calif.-Berkeley, 1969-70; mem. tech. staff Bell Labs., Holmdel, N.J., 1970-84; prof. elec. engring. Stanford U., Calif., 1984—; dir. integrated circuits lab., Stanford U., 1993—; vis. lectr. U. Calif.-Berkeley, 1980; chmn. Internat. Solid-State Circuits Conf., 1981; program chmn. Internat. Symposium VLSI Cirs., 1990. Editor Jour. Solid-State Circuits, 1986-89; contbr. articles to profl. jours.; inventor integrated circuits for communications, arithmetic and tactile sensing. Recipient Univ. medal U. Calif.-Berkeley, 1966; Fortescue fellow, 1966-67. Fellow IEEE; mem. Sigma Xi, Tau Beta Pi, Eta Kappa Nu. Home: 12375 Melody Ln Los Altos CA 94022-3213 Office: Stanford U Ctr for Integrated Systems Dept Elec Engring Stanford CA 94305

WOOLF, KENNETH HOWARD, Architect; b. N.Y.C., Aug. 19, 1938; s. Howard Walter and Elizabeth Ann (Levy) W.; B Arch., Cornell U., 1961; m. Elizabeth Adair Rainwater, July 3, 1965; children—Robert Gregg, Susan Adair, Jennifer Adair. Staff architect Look & Morrison, Architects, Pensacola, Fla., 1965-72; pvt. practice architecture, Pensacola, 1972—; instr. architecture Pensacola Jr. Coll., part-time 1967-76. Chmn., Pensacola Archtl. Rev. Bd., 1970-81; mem. Gulf Breeze Planning Bd., 1976-78; chmn. Pensacola City Bd. Adjustment and Appeals, 1995—. Served with USN, 1961-65. Named Jaycee of Yr., 1970. Mem. AIA (sec. N.W. Fla. chpt. 1976-77, 1977-78, pres. N.W. Fla. 1979-81; Comml. Design Honor award 1975). Prin. works include: Coca-Cola Bottling Co. Plant, Pensacola, 1974, 3 profl. office bldgs. towers, Pensacola, 1976, 84, 92, Bapt. Hosp. addition, 1977, The Village, Housing for Elderly, 1978, 81, Azalea Trace Retirement Cmty. Complex, 1980, Northview Cmty. 1981, Coca-Cola Bottling Plant, Beaumont, Tex., 1983, Episcopal Day Sch., Pensacola, 1993. Mem. AIA (sec. N.W. Fla. chpt. 1976-77, 77-78, pres. N.W. Fla. 1979-81, Comml. Design Honor award 1975), Rotary. Episcopalian. Home: 15 N Sunset Blvd Gulf Breeze FL 32561-4051 Office: 100 W Gadsden St Pensacola FL 32501-3910

WOOLF, MICHAEL E., lawyer; b. Phoenix, Mar. 17, 1949. BS, Ariz. State U., 1971, JD cum laude, 1974. Bar: ariz. 1974. Ptnr. O'Connor, Cavanagh, Anderson, Westover, Killingsworth & Beshears, P.A., Phoenix. Mem. ABA, Scottsdale Bar Assn., Maricopa County Bar Assn., State Bar Ariz. Office: O'Connor Cavanagh Anderson Westover Killingsworth & Beshears 1 E Camelback Rd Ste 1100 Phoenix AZ 85012-2400*

WOOLF, WILLIAM BLAUVELT, retired association executive; b. New Rochelle, N.Y., Sept. 18, 1932; s. Douglas Gordon and Katharine Hutton (Blauvelt) W. A.A., John Muir Jr. Coll., 1951; student, U. Calif. at Berkeley, 1951; B.A., Pomona Coll., 1953; M.A., Claremont (Calif.) Grad. Sch., 1955; Ph.D., U. Mich., 1960. Instr., asst. prof., asso. prof. U. Wash., Seattle, 1959-68; assoc. sec., dir. adminstrn. AAUP, Washington, 1968-79; mng. editor Math. Revs., Am. Math. Soc., Ann Arbor, Mich., 1979-90, acting exec. editor, 1984-85; assoc. exec. dir. Am. Math. Soc., Providence, 1990-96. Bd. dirs. Nat. Child Research Center, Washington, 1975-77; trustee Friends Sch., Detroit, 1985-90, treas., 1986-90. Fulbright Research fellow U. Helsinki, Finland, 1963-64. Fellow AAAS; mem. ACLU (life, treas. Washington 1966-68, bd. dirs. Washtenaw County and Mich. State 1989-90, bd. dirs. R.I. State 1993-95, treas. 1994-95), Am. Math. Soc., Math. Assn. Am. Quaker. Home: 130 Pioneer Dr Port Ludlow WA 98365

WOOLFENDEN, JAMES MANNING, nuclear medicine physician, educator; b. L.A., Nov. 8, 1942. BA with distinction, Stanford U., 1964; MD, U. Wash., 1968. Diplomate Am. Bd. Nuclear Medicine (chmn. credentials com. 1993-94, vice-chmn. examinations com. 1993-95, chmn. exam. com. 1995-96, sec. 1994—), Nat. Bd. Med. Examiners; lic. physician Calif., Ariz., Wash. Med. intern L.A. County-U. So. Calif. Med. Ctr., 1968-69; med. resident West L.A. VA Med. Ctr., 1969-70; nuclear medicine resident L.A. County-U. So. Calif. Med. Ctr., 1972-74; from asst. prof. radiology to assoc. prof. radiology U. Ariz., Tucson, 1974-84, prof. radiology, 1984—; mem. med. staff Univ. Med. Ctr., Tucson, 1974—; cons. VA Med. Ctr., 1974—; cons. med. staff Tucson Med. Ctr., 1975—, Carondelet St. Joseph's Hosp., 1974—, St. Mary's Hosp., Tucson, 1976-90; mem. Nat. Cancer Inst. site visit team NIH, 1976, mem. NHLB Inst. site visit team NIH, 1976, mem. diagnostic radiology study sect., 1993—, chmn., 1995—; mem. med. liaison officer network EPA, 1983—; cons.-tchg. med. staff Kino Comty. Hosp., 1984-94; med. officer Clin. Ctr., NIH, Bethesda, 1984-85; mem. Ariz. Cancer Ctr., U. Ariz., 1988—, sr. clin. scientist Univ. Heart Ctr., 1990—; Ariz. bd. regents U. Ariz. Presdl. Search Com., 1990-91; chmn. Ariz. Atomic Energy Commn., 1979-80, Ariz. Radiation Regulatory Hearing Bd., 1981—; bd. dirs. Calif. Radioactive Materials Mgmt. Forum, 1989—, chmn.-elect, 1993-94, chmn., 1994-95, Western Forum Edn. in Safe Disposal of Low-Level Radioactive Waste, 1990—, vice chmn., 1991-92, chmn., 1992-94. Manuscript reviewer: Noninvasive Med. Imaging, 1983-84, Jour. Nuclear Medicine, 1985—, Investigative Radiology, 1989-94, Archives of Internal Medicine, 1990—; contbr. book chpts.: Diagnostic Nuclear Medicine, 2d edit., 1988, Adjuvant Therapy of Cancer, 1977, Fundamentals of Nuclear Medicine, 1988, others; contbr. articles and book revs. to profl. publs. Mem. Am. Heart Assn. Coun. on Cardiovasc. Radiology. Maj. U.S. Army, 1970-72, Vietnam. Fellow Am. Coll. Nuclear Physicians (long range planning com. 1981-83, govt. affairs com. 1984—, exec. com. 1987-91, sec. 1989-91, parliamentarian 1991-95, treas. 1996—, mem. publs. com. 1993—, chmn. publs. com. 1993-94, and many others); mem. AMA (diagnostic and therapeutic tech. assessment reference panel 1982—), Am. Fedn. Clin. Rsch., Am. Nuc. Soc., Soc. Nuclear Medicine (com. on audit 1992—, bd. trustees 1992—, Bronze medal for sci. exhibit 1984, bd. dirs., sec.-treas. So. Calif. chpt. 1993-95, chmn.-elect 1995—), Assn. Univ. Radiologists, Pima County Med. Soc., Radiol. Soc. N.Am. Office: Ariz Health Scis Ctr 1501 N Campbell Ave Tucson AZ 85724-5068

WOOLFORD, DONNELL, professional football player; b. Balt., Jan. 6, 1966. Student, Clemson U. Cornerback Chgo. Bears, 1989—. Named to Sporting Coll. All-Am. Team, 1988, to Pro Bowl Team, 1993. Office: Chgo Bears Halas Hall 2550 N Washington Rd Lake Forest IL 60045

WOOLHISER, DAVID ARTHUR, hydrologist; b. LaCrosse, Wis., Jan. 21, 1932; s. Algie Duncan and Blanche Lenore (Jasperson) W.; m. Kathryn Brown, Apr. 21, 1957; children: Carl David, Curt Fredric, Lisa Kathryn. B.S. in Agr., U. Wis.-Madison, 1955, BSCE, 1955, PhD, 1962; MS, U. Ariz., 1959. Instr. U. Ariz., Tucson, 1955-58; hydraulic engr. Agrl. Research Service, USDA, Madison, Wis., 1959-61, Columbia, Mo., 1961-63; asst. prof. Cornell U., Ithaca, N.Y., 1963-67; research hydraulic engr. Agrl. Research Service, Ft. Collins, Colo., 1967-81, Tucson, 1981-91, collaborator, 1991-92; vis. scientist Inst. Hydrology, Wallingford, Eng., 1977-78; vis. prof. Imperial Coll., London, 1977-78; faculty affiliate Colo. State U., 1967-84; adj. prof. U. Ariz., 1981-92; vis. prof. Va. Polytech. and State U., 1992, sr. rsch. sci. Colo. State U., 1993—; vis. prof. U. Córdoba, Spain, 1993-94, 96. Contbr. articles to profl. jours. Fellow Am. Geophys. Union (Robert E. Horton award 1983); mem. NAE, ASCE (Hunter Rouse Lectr. 1994, Arid Lands Hydraulic Engring. award 1988), Common Cause. Office: 1631 Barnwood Dr Fort Collins CO 80525-2069

WOOLLAM, JOHN ARTHUR, electrical engineering educator; b. Kalamazoo, Mich., Aug. 10, 1939; s. Arthur Edward and Mildred Edith (Hakes) W.; children: Catherine Jane, Susan June. BA in Physics, Kenyon Coll., 1961; MS in Physics, Mich. State U., 1963, PhD in Solid State Physics, 1967; MSEE, Case-Western Res. U., 1978. Rsch. scientist NASA Lewis Rsch. Ctr., Cleve., 1967-80; prof. U. Nebr., Lincoln, 1979—, dir. Ctr. Microelectronic and Optical Materials Rsch., 1988—; pres. J.A. Woollam co., Inc., Lincoln, 1987—. Editor Jour. Applied Physics Com., 1979-94. Grantee NASA, NSF, USAF, Advanced Rsch. Projects Agy., Physics Com., 1979-94. Fellow Am. Phys. Soc.; mem. Am. Vacuum Soc. (chmn. thin film div. 1989-91). Office: U Nebr Dept Elec Engring 209NWSEC Lincoln NE 68588-0511

WOOLLEN, EVANS, architectural firm executive; b. Indpls., Aug. 10, 1927; s. Evans Jr. and Lydia (Jameson) Ritchey; m. Nancy Clarke Sewell, July 16, 1955 (dec. 1992); children: Ian, Malcolm Sewell. DA, Yale U., 1952, MArch, 1952. Lic. architect Ind., Ala., Conn., Del., Ill., Ky., La., Maine, Mass., N.C., Ohio, Tenn. Chmn. Woollen, Molzan & Ptnrs., Indpls., 1955—; resident Am. Acad. in Rome, spring 1996. Architect Pilot Ctr., Cin. (Nat. HUD 1975), St. Marys Coll. Libr. (Nat. AIA-ALA 1983), Grainger Libr., U. Ill., Urbana, Wartburg Coll. Libr., Waverly, Iowa, Asbury Coll. Libr., Wilmore, Ky. Mem. bd. Ind. State Welfare Bd., 1956-59, Art Assn., 1956-66, Indpls. Capital Improvement Bd., 1965-69. With Signal Corps U.S. Army, 1946-47. Fellow AIA. Democrat. Address: 43 W 43rd St Indianapolis IN 46208-3721 Office: Woollen Molzan & Ptnrs Inc 47 S Pennsylvania St Indianapolis IN 46204-3622

WOOLLEN, THOMAS HAYES, insurance consultant; b. Winston-Salem, N.C., Oct. 6, 1934; s. Junius Wesley and Ruth (Millikan) W.; m. Velva Hayden Whitescarver, Oct. 21, 1960; children: Thomas Hayes Jr., John Carter, Mark Hayden, Velva Hayden. AB, Duke U., 1956. CLU; chartered fin. cons.; registered investment advisor. Regional sales mgr. John H. Harland Co., Atlanta, 1965-75; ins. cons. Planning Cons., Inc., Charlotte, N.C., 1975-81; ins. specialist Merrill Lynch Life Agy., Charlotte, 1981-85; pres. Consol. Cons., Inc., Charlotte, 1985—; mem. steering com. Estate Planners Day Queens Coll., Charlotte, 1988—; bd. dir. N.C. State Bd. CPA Examiners, Raleigh. Ruling elder Covenant Presbyn. Ch., Charlotte, 1980—. Mem. Internat. Assn. Fin. Planners, N.C. Planned Giving Coun., Charlotte Assn. Life Underwriters, Charlotte Estate Planning Coun., Am. Soc. CLU and ChFC (local bd. dirs.), Charlotte Country Club, Charlotte Tower Club. Republican. Avocations: tennis, golf, gardening, writing, reading. Home: 1318 Queens Rd W Charlotte NC 28207-2142 Office: Consol Cons Inc 428 E 4th St Ste 102 Charlotte NC 28202-2434

WOOLLEY, CATHERINE (JANE THAYER), writer; b. Chgo., Aug. 11, 1904; d. Edward Mott and Anna L. (Thayer) W. AB, UCLA, 1927. Advt. copywriter Am. Radiator Co., N.Y.C., 1927-31; freelance writer, 1931-33; copywriter, editor house organ Am. Radiator & Standard San. Corp., N.Y.C., 1933-40; desk editor Archtl. Record, 1940-42; prodn. editor SAE Jour., N.Y.C., 1942-43; pub. relations writer NAM, N.Y.C., 1943-47; condr. workshop on juvenile writing Truro Ctr. for Arts, 1977, 78, 92, Cape Cod Writers Conf., 1990, 91, 92; instr. writing for juveniles Cape Cod Writers Conf., 1965, 66, 92. Author: juvenile books (under name Catherine Woolley) I Like Trains, 1944, rev., 1965, Two Hundred Pennies, 1947, Ginnie and Geneva, 1948, paperback edit., 1988, David's Railroad, 1949, Schoolroom Zoo, 1950, Railroad Cowboy, 1951, Ginnie Joins In, 1951, David's Hundred Dollars, 1952, Lunch for Lennie, 1952 (pub. as L'Incontentabile Gigi in Italy), The Little Car That Wanted a Garage, 1952, The Animal Train and Other Stories, 1953, Holiday on Wheels, 1953, Ginnie and the New Girl, 1954, Ellie's Problem Dog, 1955, A Room for Cathy, 1956, Ginnie and the Mystery House, 1957, Miss Cathy Leonard, 1958, David's Campaign Buttons, 1959, Ginnie and the Mystery Doll, 1960, Cathy Leonard Calling, 1961, paperback edit., 1988, Look Alive, Libby!, 1962, Ginnie and Her Juniors, 1963, Cathy's Little Sister, 1964, paperback edit., 1988, Libby Looks for a Spy, 1965, The Shiny Red Rubber Boots, 1965, Ginnie and the Cooking Contest, 1966, paperback 1979, Ginnie and the Wedding Bells, 1967, Chris in Trouble, 1968, Ginnie and the Mystery Cat, 1969, Libby's Uninvited Guest, 1970, Cathy and the Beautiful People, 1971, Cathy Uncovers a Secret, 1972, Ginnie and the Mystery Light, 1973, Libby Shadows a Lady, 1974, Ginnie and Geneva Cookbook, 1975, adult book Writing for Children, 1990, paperback, 1990; (under name Jane Thayer) The Horse with the Easter Bonnet, 1953, The Popcorn Dragon, 1953, rev. edit. 1989, Where's Andy?, 1954, Mrs. Perrywinkle's Pets, 1955, Sandy and the Seventeen Balloons, 1955, The Chicken in the Tunnel, 1956, The Outside Cat, 1957, English edit., 1958, 83, Charley and the New Car, 1957, Funny Stories To Read Aloud, 1958, Andy Wouldn't Talk, 1958, The Puppy Who Wanted a Boy, 1958, rev., 1986, paperback edition, 1988, French translation Le Petit Chien Qui Voulait Un Garcon, 1991, The Second-Story Giraffe, 1959, Little Monkey, 1959, Andy and His Fine Friends, 1960, The Pussy Who Went To the Moon, 1960, English edit., 1961, A Little Dog Called Kitty, 1961, English edit., 1962, 75, The Blueberry Pie Elf, 1961, English edit., 1962, revised edit., 1994, Spanish edit., 1995, Andy's Square Blue Animal, 1962, Gus Was a Friendly Ghost, 1962, English edit., 1971, Japanese edit., 1982, A Drink for Little Red Diker, 1963, Andy and the Runaway Horse, 1963, A House for Mrs. Hopper; the Cat that Wanted to Go Home, 1963, Quiet on Account of Dinosaur, 1964, English edit., 1965, 74, paperback edit., 1988, Emerald Enjoyed the Moonlight, 1964, English edit., 1965, The Bunny in the Honeysuckle Patch, 1965, English edit., 1966, Part-Time Dog, 1965, English edit. 1966, The Light Hearted Wolf, 1966, What's a Ghost Going to Do?, 1966, English edit. 1972, Japanese edit., 1982, The Cat that Joined the Club, 1967, English edit. 1968, Rockets Don't Go To Chicago, Andy, 1967, A Contrary Little Quail, 1968, Little Mr. Greenthumb, 1968, English edit., 1969, Andy and Mr. Cunningham, 1969, Curious, Furious Chipmunk, 1969, I'm Not a Cat, Said Emerald, 1970, English edit. 1971, Gus Was A Christmas Ghost, 1970, English edit. 1973, Japanese edit., 1982, Mr. Turtle's Magic Glasses, 1971, Timothy And Madam Mouse, 1971, English edit., 1972, Gus And The Baby Ghost, 1972, English edit. 1973, Japanese edit., 1982, The Little House, 1972, Andy and the Wild Worm, 1973, Gus Was a Mexican Ghost, 1974, English edit. 1975, Japanese edit., 1982, I Don't Believe in Elves, 1975, The Mouse on the Fourteenth Floor, 1977, Gus Was a Gorgeous Ghost, 1978, English edit., 1979, Where Is Squirrel?, 1979, Try Your Hand, 1980, Applebaums Have a Robot, 1980, Clever Raccoon, 1981, Gus Was a Real Dumb Ghost, 1982, Gus Loved His Happy Home, 1989; contbr. stories to juvenile anthologies in U.S., Great Britain, France, Germany, and Holland, sch. readers, juvenile mags. Trustee Truro Pub. Libraries, 1974-84; Mem. Passaic (N.J.) Bd. Edn., 1953-56, Passaic Redevel. Agy., 1952-53; pres. Passaic LWV, 1949-52. Named mem. N.J. Literary Hall of Fame, 1987; recipient Phantom Friends Lifetime Achievement award, 1992. Mem. Authors League Am., Friends of Truro Libraries, Truro Hist. Soc., Amnesty Internat. U.S.A., Kenilworth Soc. Democrat. Home: PO Box 71 Truro MA 02666-0071

WOOLLEY, DONNA PEARL, paper, lumber company executive; b. Drain, Oreg., Jan. 3, 1926; d. Chester A. and Mona B. (Cheever) Rydell; m. Harold Woolley, Dec. 27, 1952 (dec. Sept. 1970); children: Daniel, Debra, Donald. Diploma, Drain High Sch. Sec. No. Life Ins. Co., Eugene, Oreg., 1943-44; sec., bookkeeper D & W Lumber Co., Sutherlin, Oreg., 1944, Woolley Logging Co. & Earl Harris Lumber Co., Drain, 1944-70; pres. Woolley Logging Co., 1970—, Smith River Lumber Co., 1970—, Mt. Baldy Mill, 1970-81, Drain Plywood Co., 1970-81, Woolley Enterprises, Inc., Drain, 1973—, Eagle's View Mgmt. Co., Inc., Eugene, 1981—. Bd. dirs. Oreg. Cmty. Found., Portland, Oreg., 1990—, Wildlife Safari, Winston, Oreg., 1986; trustee emeritus U. Oreg. Found., Eugene, 1979—; trustee Linfield Coll. Found., McMinnville, Oreg., 1990—; v.p. Oreg. Trail coun. Boy Scouts Am., Eugene, 1981—; exec. dir. World Forestry Ctr., Portland, 1991—. Recipient Pioneer award U. Oreg., 1982, Econ. and Social Devel. award Soroptimist Club, 1991. Mem. Oreg. Women's Forum, Pacific Internat. Trapshooting Assn., Amateur Trapshooting Assn., Eugene C. of C. (bd. dirs. 1989-92), Arlington Club, Town Club (bd. dirs., pres.), Shadow Hills Country Club, Sunnydale Grange, Cottage Grove/Eugene Rod & Gun Club. Republican. Avocations: golf, travel. Office: Eagle's View Mgmt Co Inc 1399 Franklin Blvd Eugene OR 97403-1979

WOOLLEY, GEORGE WALTER, biologist, geneticist, educator; b. Osborne, Kans., Nov. 9, 1904; s. George Aitcheson and Nora Belle (Jackson) W.; m. Anne Geneva Collins, Nov. 2, 1936; children: George Aitcheson, Margaret Anne, Lawrence Jackson. B.S., Iowa State U., 1930; M.S., U. Wis., 1931, Ph.D., 1935. Fellow U. Wis., 1935-36; mem. staff Jackson Meml. Lab., Bar Harbor, Maine, 1936-49; bd. dirs. Jackson Meml. Lab., 1937-49, v.p. bd., 1943-47, asst. dir. and sci. adminstr., 1947-49, vis. research assoc., 1949—; mem. chief div. steroid biology Sloan-Kettering Inst., N.Y.C., 1949-58, prof. biology, 1949-58; prof. biology Sloan-Kettering Inst. div. Cornell U. Med. Coll., Ithaca, N.Y., 1951—, chief div. human tumor exptl. chemotherapy, 1958-61, chief div. tumor biology, 1961-66; assoc. scientist Sloan-Kettering Inst. Cancer Research, 1966—; health sci. adminstr., program coordinator, head biol. scis. sect. Nat. Inst. Gen. Medical Scis., NIH, 1966-85; cons. Nat. Edn. Service U.S., Washington, 1961—; spl. cons. to Nat. Cancer Inst., NIH, 1956—; Mem. Expert Panel on Carcinogenicity, unio intern. contra cancerum, 1962—; mem. panel com. on growth NRC, 1945-51; mem. several internat. med. congresses. Author chpts. in med. books; mem. editorial bd. Jour. Nat. Cancer Inst., 1947-50. Trustee Dalton Schs., N.Y.C. Fellow AAAS, N.Y. Acad. Sci.; mem. Am. Mus. Natural History, Nat. Sci. Tchrs. Assn. (cons. 1961—), Am. Assn. Cancer Research (dir. 1951-54), Am. Soc. Human Genetics, Mt. Desert Island Biol. Lab., Soc. Exptl. Biology and Medicine, Am. Inst. Biol. Scis., Am. Assn. Anatomists, Am. Genetic Assn., Wis. Acad. Arts Sci. and Letters, Jackson Lab. Assn., Genetics Soc. Am., Environ. Mutagen Soc., Sigma Xi. Clubs: Bar Harbor, Bar Harbor (Maine) Yacht. Achievements include advanced research, teaching and administration in genetics, from the beginnings of the field to present; contributions to fields of cancer, virology, endocrinology and molecular biology. Home: 5301 Westbard Cir Apt 336 Bethesda MD 20816-1427

WOOLLEY, MARY ELIZABETH, research administrator; b. Chgo., Mar. 16, 1947; John Joseph and Ellen Louise (Bakke) McEnerney; m. John Stuart Woolley, Dec. 6, 1969 (div. 1985); children: George Newsom, Nora Ellen; m. Michael Howland Campbell, Jan. 1, 1989. BS, Stanford U., 1969; MA, San Francisco State U., 1972; postgrad., U. Calif., San Francisco and Berkeley, 1974-75. Assoc. dir. Inst. Epidemiology and Behavioral Medicine, San Francisco, 1979-81; adminstr. Med. Rsch. Inst. of San Francisco, 1981-82, v.p., adminstr., 1982-86, v.p., exec. dir., 1986-90; pres. Research! Am., Alexandria, Va., 1990—; cons. in fin. and mgmt. NIH, Bethesda, Md., 1984-92; adj. faculty U. Calif. Sch. Pub. Health, Berkeley, 1983-92, mem. Dean's adv. coun., 1995—; founding mem. Whitehead Inst. Bd. Assocs., 1995—; lectr. to profl. assns. Editor Jour. of Soc. Rsch. Adminstrs., 1986-89, mem. editl. rev. bd., 1989-95; mem. editl. bd. Jour. Women's Health, 1992—, Sci. Comm., 1994—; contbr. articles and editls. to profl. jours. Bd. dirs. Kensington (Calif.) Edn. Found., 1986-89, Enterprise for H.S. Students, 1990-92; mem. capital campaign com. Calif. Shakespeare Festival, 1989-91, v.p. Med. Rsch. Assns. Am., 1993-95. Recipient Silver Touchstone award Am. Hosp. Assn., 1994, Disting. Svc. award Columbia Coll. Physicians and Surgeons, 1994. Mem. AAAS, Assn. Ind. Rsch. Insts. (pres.-elect 1987-89, pres. 1989-90), Soc. Rsch. Adminstrs. (bd. dirs. 1986-90, bd. advisors 1990-93, Hartford-Nicholson Svc. award 1990, Disting. Contbn. to Rsch. Adminstrn. award, 1993), Calif. Biomedical rsch. Assn., (bd. govs. 1986-90), Md. Gov.'s Commn. on Women's Health, 1993—. Democrat. Office: Research! Am 1522 King St Alexandria VA 22314-2717

WOOLLIAMS, KEITH RICHARD, arboretum and botanical garden director; b. Chester, Eng., July 17, 1940; s. Gordon Frank and Margaret Caroline W.; m. Akiko Narita, Apr. 11, 1969; children: Frank Hiromi, Angela Misako. Grad., Celyn Agrl. and Hort. Inst., North Wales, 1955; student, U. Liverpool, various horticultural insts., 1956-59; Kew Cert., Royal Bot. Gardens, Kew, U.K., 1963. Cert. Horticulture Union Cheshire and Lancs. Insts., 1955, Royal Hort. Soc., 1956, 57, 58, Nat. Cert. Horticulture, 1958, Cert. Arboriculture, 1962. Supt. field sta. U. London Queen Mary Coll., Brentwood, Essex, Eng., 1963-65; horticulturist Horizons Ltd., Bermuda, 1965-67; dept. forests, supt. botanic gardens Papua, New Guinea, 1967-68; instr. Eng. staff indsl. cos., Japan, 1968-71; supt., horticulturist Nat. Tropical Bot. Garden, Kauai, Hawaii, 1971-74; horticulturist Waimea Arboretum and Botanical Garden, Haleiwa, Hawaii, 1974-80, dir., 1980—; mem. Pacific islands plant recovery coordinating com. U.S. Fish and Wildlife Svc., 1993—; mem. Hawaii Rare Plant Restoration Group, 1991—. Contbr. articles to profl. jours., New Royal Hort. Soc. Dictionary of Gardening, 1992. Field assoc. botany Bishop Mus., Honolulu, 1981—; bd. dirs. Friends of Honolulu Bot. Gardens, 1980—; v.p., founder Waimea Arboretum Found., 1977—; bd. dirs. Condominium Estate, Wahiawa, Hawaii, 1990—. Mem. Am. Assn. Botanical Gardens and Arboreta, Am. Hort. Soc., Hawaii Audubon Soc., Hawaiian Botanical Soc. (pres. 1979), Internat. Assn. Plant Taxonomists, Royal Hort. Soc., Kew Guild. Avocations: fishing, home repairs, music, reading, travel. Office: Waimea Arboretum & Bot Garden 59-864 Kamehameha Hwy Haleiwa HI 96712-9406

WOOLLS, ESTHER BLANCHE, library science educator; b. Louisville, Mar. 30, 1935; d. Arthur William and Esther Lennie (Smith) Sutton; m.

Donald Paul Woolls, Oct. 21, 1953 (div. Nov. 1982); 1 son, Arthur Paul. AB in Fine Arts, Ind. U., 1958, MA in Libr. Sci., 1962, PhD in Libr. Sci., 1973. Elem. libr. Hammond Pub. Schs., Ind., 1958-65, libr. coord., 1965-67; libr. coord. Roswell Ind. Schs., N.Mex., 1967-70; prof. libr. sci. U. Pitts., 1973—; exec. dir. Beta Phi Mu, 1981-95. Author: The School Library Media Manager, 1995, So You're Going to Run a Library, 1995, Ideas for School Library Media Centers, 1996; editor: Continuing Professional Education and IFLA: Past, Present, and a Vision for the Future, 1993. Fulbright scholar, 1995-96; recipient disting. svc. award Pa. Sch. Librs. Assn., 1993. Mem. ALA (mem. coun. 1985-89, 91-94, 95—), Am. Assn. Sch. Librs. (bd. dirs. 1983-88, pres. 1993-94), Pa. Learning Resources Assn. (pres. 1984-85), Internat. Assn. Sch. Librs. (bd. dirs. 1991—), Internat. Fedn. Libr. Assns. (mem. standing com. sch. librs. sect. 1991—, editor continuing profl. edn. roundtable newsletter). Office: U Pitts Sch Libr and Info Sci Pittsburgh PA 15260

WOOLNER, JOHN ROY, electrical engineer; b. Homestead AFB, Fla., Nov. 6, 1965; s. John Roy and Patricia Jean (Rodney) W. BSEE, So. Ill. U., 1988, postgrad. in elec. engring., 1989—. Registered profl. engr. Ill. Project mgr. EPS Communications, Edwardsville, Ill., 1987-89; design engr. Magnum Techs., Belleville, Ill., 1990; project engr. WSI Techs., St. Louis, 1990-91; sr. engr. Magnum Techs., 1991—; instr. Belleville Area Coll., 1990. Mem. IEEE, Instrument Soc. Am. Avocations: Karate, hunting, gardening, fishing.

WOOLSEY, DAVID ARTHUR, leasing company executive; b. Oakland, Calif., Nov. 27, 1941; s. Stanley Arthur Woolsey and Jane Bernadette (Gallagher) Woolsey-Weyler; m. Kathleen Marie McDonnell, June 26, 1965; children: Anne C., Matthew J., Jane K. BS, U. San Francisco, 1963; MBA, U. Calif., Berkeley, 1965. Mgr. lease and spl. projects financing Kaiser Aluminum & Chem. Corp., Oakland, Calif., 1965-68; v.p. U.S. Leasing Internat., Inc., San Francisco, 1968-78; exec. v.p. GATX Capital Corp., San Francisco, 1978, exec. v.p., 1982-88, also bd. dirs.; exec. v.p. Orix U.S.A. Corp., 1988—, also bd. dirs. Mem. Equipment Leasing Assn. Am. (bd. dirs.), Orinda Country Club (Calif., pres. 1981), Commonwealth Club (Calif). Republican. Roman Catholic. Home: 40 Charles Hill Rd Orinda CA 94563-1523 Office: ORIX USA Corp 1 Bush St Ste 250 San Francisco CA 94104-4408

WOOLSEY, FREDERICK WILLIAM, retired journalist, music critic; b. Miles City, Mont., Oct. 7, 1919; s. Fred W. and Louise (Gaylord) W.; m. Mary Lou Hubbard, Apr. 27, 1957 (dec. June 1976); m. Jane R. Towery, Oct. 15, 1983. B.J., U. Mo., 1943. Radio news writer Sta. KXOK, St. Louis, 1943; telegraph desk The Times, Shreveport, La., 1946; reporter, features writer Nashville Tennessean, 1947-55, night city editor, 1955; reporter, rewrite desk Louisville Times, 1956-65, music critic, 1960-85; feature writer Courier-Jour. Sunday mag., 1965-85. Author: radio series Tall Tales of Tenn; folklore, Sta. WSM, Nashville, 1954-55; contbr. articles to journalism anthologies. Mem. Louisville Human Rights Com., 1960; chmn. pub. rels. com. City-County Human Rels. Commn., 1961-62; mem. Ky. Civil Liberties Union, 1956—; bd. dirs. Louisville Urban League, 1958-68, Widowed Persons Svc., 1978-80, Louisville Chamber Music Soc., 1982—, U. Louisville Libr. Assocs.; co-founder, exec. bd. Friends of U. Louisville Sch. Music, 1991-93. With USAF, 1943-46. Recipient certificate of merit for mag. writing Am. Bar Assn., 1974. Democrat. Episcopalian. Home: 2416 Dundee Rd Louisville KY 40205-2047

WOOLSEY, JOHN MUNRO, JR., lawyer; b. N.Y.C., Apr. 22, 1916; s. John M. and Alice B. (Bacon) W.; m. Ledlie Laughlin, Dec. 27, 1948; children: John, Alice, Henry, Mary. B.A., Yale U., 1938, LL.B., 1941. Bar: N.Y. 1941, Mass. 1947. Assoc. Debevoise, Stevenson, Plimpton & Page, N.Y.C., 1941-42; with Bd. Econ. Warfare, Washington, 1942; with firm Herrick & Smith and predecessor firms, Boston, 1946-86, ptnr., 1956-83, of counsel, 1984-86; of counsel Palmer & Dodge, 1986—; with Office of U.S. Chief of Counsel, Nürnberg Trials, Germany, 1945-46. Former pres. Trustees of Reservations, Shady Hill Sch. Served to lt. USNR, 1942-46. Decorated Order of White Lion (Czechoslovakia). Mem. Am. Antiquarian Soc., Am. Law Inst., Tavern Club, Century Club (N.Y.C.). Office: Palmer & Dodge One Beacon St Boston MA 02108

WOOLSEY, KATHLEEN MARGARET, psychotherapist; b. Peoria, Ill., May 3, 1947; d. Bernard George and Margaret Helen (Moran) Maxwell; m. E. Baird Woolsey, July 13, 1969 (div. 1989); children: Nathan B., Alexandria B.; m. John Richard Enzminger, Apr. 18, 1992. BA, U. Iowa, 1969; MA, Bradley U., 1987. Pvt. practice Pekin, Ill., 1989—; AIDS counselor Peoria City/County Health Dept., 1994—, AIDS support group facilitator, 1987-91; grief counselor Woolsey Funeral Home, Pekin, 1988-89. Bd. dirs. YWCA, Pekin, 1972-75; pres. Pekin Meml. Hosp. League, 1978. Mem. Am. Psychol. Assn. (assoc.). Republican. Methodist. Avocations: horseback riding, reading, tennis, golf. Home: 16875 Springfield Rd Pekin IL 61554-8666 Office: 110 N 5th St Ste 217 Pekin IL 61554-3306

WOOLSEY, LYNN, congresswoman; b. Seattle, Nov. 3, 1937. BA, U. San Francisco, 1980. Mem. 103rd-104th Congresses from 6th Calif. dist., 1993—; mem. Ho. Reps. coms. on budget, & econ. & edml. opportunity. Office: US House of Reps 439 Cannon Bldg Washington DC 20515-0003*

WOOLSEY, R. JAMES, lawyer; b. Tulsa, Sept. 21, 1941; s. Robert James and Clyde (Kirby) W.; m. Suzanne Haley, Aug. 15, 1965; children—Robert Nathaniel, Daniel James, Benjamin Haley. B.A. with great distinction, Stanford U., 1963; M.A. (Rhodes scholar), Oxford (Eng.) U., 1965; LL.B., Yale U., 1968. Bar: Calif. bar 1969, D.C. bar 1970. Program analyst Office Sec. Def., Washington, 1968-70, NSC, Washington, 1970; gen. counsel Com. Armed Services, U.S. Senate, 1970-73; assoc. firm Shea & Gardner, Washington, 1973-77; ptnr. Shea & Gardner, 1979-89; ambassador and U.S. rep. to negotation on conventional armed forces in Europe, 1989-91; ptnr. with Shea & Gardner, 1991-93; dir. Central Intelligence, Washington, 1993-95; ptnr. Shea & Gardner, 1995—; undersec. of navy, 1977-79; advisor U.S. del. SALT, Helsinki and Vienna, 1969-70. Mem. Pres.'s Commn. on Strategic Forces, 1983-84, Fed. Ethics Law reform, 1989; Blue Ribbon Commn. on Defense Mgmt., 1985-86; del.-at-large Soviet Arms Talks, Geneva, 1983-86; trustee Stanford U., 1972-74, Regent Smithsonian Instution, 1989-93; dir. Martin Marietta, 1991-93, British Aerospace Inc., 1992-93, Fairchild Industries, 1984-89, Titan Corp., 1983-89, DynCorp, 1988-89, USF&G, 1995—, Sun Healthcare Group, Inc., 1995—, Yurie Systems Corp., 1996—. Served with U.S. Army, 1968-70. Mem. Council Fgn. Relations, Phi Beta Kappa. Presbyterian. Office: Shea & Gardner 1800 Massachusetts Ave NW Washington DC 20036

WOOLSEY, ROBERT EUGENE DONALD, mineral economics, mathematics and business administration educator; b. Fort Worth, Oct. 31, 1936; s. Eugene Ralph W. and Ruby Ruth (White) Binder Woolsey; m. Ronita Elaine Packer, Sept. 17, 1958; children: Wysandria W.W., Darrell E. B.A., U. Tex., 1959, M.A., 1967, Ph.D., 1969. Staff mem. Sandia Corp., Albuquerque, 1966-68; assoc. dir. Computer Center U. Tex., Austin, 1968-69; assoc. prof. math. Colo. Sch. Mines, Golden, 1969-72, prof. math., 1972-74, prof. mineral econs., 1974-79, prof., head dept., 1979-81, MAPCO Found. prof., 1981-84, prof., program dir. Ops. Rsch./Mgmt. Sci. program divsn. econs. & bus., 1988—; vis. coll. Colo. Women's Coll., Denver, 1979-81; adj. prof. U. Waterloo, Ont., Can., 1972—, Instituto Technologico de Monterrey, Nuevo Leon, Mexico, 1974—, U. Witwatersrand, Johannesburg, S. Africa, 1984—; vis. prof. dept. engring. U.S. Mil. Acad., West Point, N.Y., 1986-87; prof. core faculty Walden U., 1990—; bd. dirs. Southland Energy Corp., Tulsa, New Tech. Devel. Co., Inc., Vancouver, B.C., Can. Author: Operations Research for Immediate Application, 1975, Applied Management Science, 1980; editor: Transactions of the Institute of Industrial Engineering, 1981-84, Production and Inventory Management, 1984—, Interfaces, 1975-82, Jour. Ops. Mgmt., 1986-87; contbr. articles to profl. jours. Pres. Rocky Mountain Fire Brigade, Inc., Golden, Colo., 1972-83. Served to capt. USAF, 1959-62. Named tchr. of yr. Standard Oil Ind., 1972,96; recipient 1st Harold Larnder Meml. prize Can. Operational Rsch. Soc., 1986, Disting. Civilian Svc. medal U.S. Dept. Army, 1987, Comdrs. medal, 1991, Outstanding Civilian Svc. medal, 1995; named Hon. Col. 115 Engr. Regiment U.S. Army, 1987. Fellow Am. Inst. Decision Sci. (v.p. 1981-83); mem. Inst. Mgmt. Scis. (council 1976-78, pres. 1986-87), Inst. Indsl. Engrs. (sr. mem., editor 1981-84), Ops. Rsch. Soc. Am. (editor 1975-82), Newcomen Soc. Republican. Episcopalian. Home: 1826 Smith Rd Golden CO 80401-1756 Office: Colo Sch Mines Dept Math Golden CO 80401

WOOSLEY, RAYMOND, pharmacology and medical educator; b. Ky., Oct. 2, 1942; m. Julianne B. BS, Western Ky. U., 1964; PhD, U. Louisville, 1967; MD, U. Miami, 1973. Med. lic. Tenn. 1976, D.C. 1988. Intern, resident Vanderbilt U. Hosp., Nashville, 1973-76; sr. pharmacologist, dir. rsch. Meyer (Glaxo) Labs., Ft. Lauderdale, Fla., 1968-71; instr. dept. medicine, pharmacology Vanderbilt U., Nashville, 1976-77, asst. prof., 1977-79, assoc. prof., 1979-84, assoc. dir. clin. rsch. ctr., 1981-88, prof., 1984-88; prof. pharmacology, medicine, chmn. dept. pharmacology Georgetown U. Sch. Medicine, Washington, 1988—, also chief divsn. clin. pharmacology, 1988-94; dir. Inst. for Cardiovascular Scis., Washington, 1995—; researcher in field. Author: Clinical Application of Zinc Metabolism, 1975, Cardiovascular Pharmacology and Therapeutics, 1994; contbr. chpts. to books and articles to profl. jours. NIH Predoctoral fellow NIH, 1964-67, postdoctoral fellow U. Louisville, 1967-68, Vanderbilt U., 1976-77, Am. Coll. Clin. Pharmacology fellow, 1974; Ogden scholar Western Ky. U., 1960-64; recipient Cancer Devel. award in Clin. Pharmacology Pharm. Mfrs. Assn. Found., 1977-80. Fellow Am. Coll. Clin. Pharmacology, Am. Coll. Physicians, Am. Heart Assn. (coun. clin. cardiology 1985—); mem. Am. Soc. Pharmacology & Exptl. Therapeutics (clin. pharmacology exec. com. 1981-92), Am. Fedn. Clin. Rsch., Am. Soc. Clin. Pharmacology and Therapeutics (Rawls-Palmer award 1990), Am. Bd. Clin. Pharmacology, Assn. Med. Sch. Pharmacology (pres. 1996—). Office: Georgetown U Sch Medicine Dept Pharmacology 3900 Reservoir Rd NW Washington DC 20007-2195

WOOSNAM, IAN HAROLD, professional golfer; b. St. Martins, Shropshire, U.K., Mar. 2, 1958; s. Harold and Joan Woosnam; m. Glendryth Mervyn Pugh, Nov. 12, 1983; children: Daniel Ian, Rebecca Louise, Amy Victoria. Ed., St. Martins Modern Sch. Profl. golfer, 1976—; tournament winner News of the World under 23 match-play, 1979, Cacharel under 25 Championship, 1982, Swiss Open, 1983, Silk Cut Masters, 1983, Scandinavian Enterprise Open, 1984, Zambian Open, 1985, Lawrence Batley TPC, 1986, 555 Kenya Open, 1986, Hong Kong Open, 1987, Jersey Open, 1987, Cepsa Madrid Open, 1987, Bell's Scottish Open, 1987, 90, Lancome Trophy, 1987, 93, Suntory World Match-Play Championship, 1987, 90, World Cup (Wales) Team and Individual, 1987, Million Dollar Challenge, 1987, Volvo PGA Championship, 1988, Carrols Irish Open, 1990, 91, 92, Epson Grand Prix, 1990, U.S. Masters, 1991, USF&G Classic, 1991, PGA Grand Slam of Golf, 1991, World Cup Individual, 1991, Murpheys English Open, 1993, Air France Cannes Open, 1994, Brit. Masters, 1994, Johnnie Walker Classic, 1996, Heineken Classic, 1996; ranked 1st Sony world rankings, 1991, Ryder Cup Team Mem., 1983, 85, 87, 89, 91, 93, 95. Avocations: snooker, sports, water skiing.

WOOSTER, ROBERT, history educator; b. Beaumont, Tex., Aug. 27, 1956; s. Ralph Ancil and Edna Lee (Jones) W.; m. Catherine Cox, 1992. BA, Lamar U., 1977, MA, 1979; PhD, U. Tex., 1985. Scholar in residence Tex. State Hist. Assn., Liberty, 1985-86; asst. prof. Corpus Christi (Tex.) State U., 1986-90, assoc. prof., 1990-95, prof., 1995—. Author: Soldiers, Sutlers and Settlers (Bates award 1987), U.S. Military and Indian Policy, 1988, History of Fort Davis, 1990, Nelson A. Miles and The Twilight of the Frontier Army, 1993; editorial adv. bd. Southwestern Hist. Quar., Austin, Tex., 1989—. Dep. dir. U.S. Mil. Acad./ROTC fellowship U.S. Mil. Acad., West Point, N.Y., 1990. Mem. Tex. State Hist. Assn., Western Hist. Assn., Orgn. Am. Historians. Democrat. Home: 4600 Ocean Dr Apt 708 Corpus Christi TX 78412-2543 Office: Texas A&M Univ 6300 Ocean Dr Corpus Christi TX 78412-5503

WOOSTER, WARREN S(CRIVER), marine science educator; b. Westfield, Mass., Feb. 20, 1921; s. Harold Abbott and Violet (Scriver) W.; m. Clarissa Pickles, Sept. 13, 1948; children: Susan Wooster Allen, Daniel, Dana Wooster Pawka. Sc.B., Brown U., 1943; M.S., Calif. Inst. Tech., 1947; Ph.D., UCLA, 1953. From research asst. to prof. Scripps Instn. Oceanography, U. Calif., 1948-73; dir. UNESCO Office Oceanography, 1961-63; dean Rosenstiel Sch. Marine Atmospheric Sci., U. Miami, 1973-76; prof. marine studies and fisheries U. Wash., Seattle, 1976-91, prof. emeritus, 1992; dir. Inst. Marine Studies U. Wash., 1979-82. Contbr. to books, profl. jours. Served with USNR, 1943-46. Fellow Am. Geophys. Union, Am. Meterol. Soc.; mem. Sigma Xi. Office: U Wash Sch Marine Affairs 3707 Brooklyn Ave NE Seattle WA 98105-6715

WOOTAN, GERALD DON, osteopathic physician, educator; b. Oklahoma City, Nov. 19, 1944; s. Ralph George and Corrinne (Loafman) W. BA, Cen. State U., Edmond, Okla., 1970, BS, 1971; MEd, Cen. State U., 1974; MB, U. Okla., Oklahoma City, 1978; DO, Okla. State U., 1985. Dir. mfg. engring. lab. GE, Oklahoma City, 1965-70; counseling psychologist VA Hosp., Oklahoma City, 1970-76; physician asst. Thomas (Okla.) Med. Clin., 1978-81; pvt. practice, Jenks, Okla., 1986—; intern Tulsa Regional Med. Ctr., 1985-86; assoc. prof. Okla. State U. Coll. Osteo. Medicine, 1986-95, with Springer Clinic, 1995—; sec. Springer Clinic Inc., Tulsa, 1990-91; chmn. gen. practice quality assurance Tulsa Regional Med. Ctr., 1989-91; v.p. New Horizons Counseling Ctr., Clinton, Okla., 1977-81; sr. aviation med. examiner FAA, Tulsa, 1991—; pres. S.W. Diagnostics, Inc., Tulsa, 1989-91, Okla. Edn. Found. Osteo. Medicine, Tulsa, 1988-89; pres., trustee Tulsa Long Term Care Authority. Contbr. articles to profl. jours.; patentee for human restraint. Advancement chmn., chmn. Eagle bd. rev. Boy Scouts Am., Tulsa, 1987-88; trustee Tulsa Long Term Care Authority, 1988-91; trustee Tulsa Community Found. for Indigent Health Care, Inc., 1988-91. With USN, 1962-64. Named Clin. Preceptor of Yr., U. Okla., 1980, Outstanding Alumni award Okla. State U. Coll. Osteo. Medicine, 1990. Mem. Am. Osteo. Assn., Okla. Osteo. Assn., Tulsa Dist. Osteo. Soc. (pres. 1991-92), Am. Acad. Physician Assts., Am. Coll. Gen. Practitioners, Okla. Acad. Gen. Practitioners (v.p.), Am. Coll. Osteo. Family Physicians (bd. cert. 1993, pres. Okla. chpt. 1993-94), Okla. State U. Coll. Osteo. Medicine Alumni Assn. (pres. 1988-89). Avocations: scuba diving, aviation medicine. Home: 4320 E 100th St Tulsa OK 74137-5305 Office: Jenks Health Team 324 W Main St Jenks OK 74037-3747

WOOTEN, CECIL AARON, religious organization administrator; b. Laurel, Miss., June 3, 1924; s. Cecil A. and Alice (Cox) W.; m. Helen Moss, Apr. 4, 1947; children: Michael, Margaret, Martin, Marsha, Mark. B.S. in Mech. Engring, U. Ala., 1949. With CBI Industries, 1941—, bd. dirs., 1965-83; mng. dir. CBI Constructors Ltd., London, 1957-62; mgr. (Houston sales dist.), 1962-64; v.p., mgr. corp. services Oak Brook, Ill., 1968-69; sr. v.p.-gen. sales mgr., 1969-78; sr. v.p. comml. devel. Chgo. Bridge & Iron Co. (subs. CBI Industries), 1978-79; sr. v.p. corp. adminstrn. CBI Industries, Oak Brook, 1980-83; dir. devel. Christian Family Services, Gainesville, Fla., 1983-86, Denver Ch. of Christ, 1986-88, Boston Ch. of Christ, 1988-92; pres. Internat. Chs. of Christ, Inc., L.A., 1994—; bd. dirs. Oak Brook (Ill.) Bank. Former trustee Elmhurst (Ill.) Coll.; former bd. sponsors Good Samaritan Hosp., Downers Grove, Ill. Served to 1st lt. AUS, 1943-46. Mem. ASME, Nat. Soc. Profl. Engrs. Lodge: Rotary. Home: 3902 Quailwood St Moorpark CA 93021-3194 Office: Internat Chs of Christ Ste 1750 3530 Wilshire Blvd Los Angeles CA 90010-2328

WOOTEN, FRANK THOMAS, research facility executive; b. Fayetteville, N.C., Sept. 24, 1935; s. Frank Thomas and Katherine (McRae) W.; m. Linda Walker, July 14, 1962; children: Laurin Walker, Patrick Thomas, Ashley Tripp. BSEE, Duke U., 1957, PhD, 1964. Engr. Corning Glass Works, Raleigh, N.C., 1964-66; engr. Research Triangle Inst., Research Triangle Park, N.C., 1966-68, mgr. biomed. engring., 1968-75, exec. asst. to pres., 1975-80, v.p., 1980-89, pres., 1989—. Contbr. articles on semiconductors and biomed. engring. to profl. publs., 1966-83; patentee semiconductors tech. Bd. dirs. N.C. Biotech. Ctr., 1989—, MCNC, 1989-94; corp. mem. Nat. Inst. Statis. Scis., 1990—. Served to lt. (j.g.) USN, 1957-59. Shell fellow, 1961; recipient Disting. Engring. Alumnus award Duke U., 1991. Mem. IEEE, Assn. for Advancement Med. Instrumentation (chmn. com. on aerospace tech. 1971-77), Ballistic Missile Def. Orgn. (tech. application rev. panel 1990-94). Baptist. Office: Research Triangle Inst PO Box 12194 3040 W Cornwallis Rd Research Triangle Park NC 27709

WOOTEN, FREDERICK (OLIVER), applied science educator; b. Linwood, Pa., May 16, 1928; s. Frederick Alexander and Martha Emma (Guild) W.; m. Jane Watson MacPherson, Aug. 30, 1952; children: Donald, Bartley. BS in Chemistry, MIT, 1950; PhD in Chemistry, U. Del., 1955. Sr. scientist Lawrence Livermore (Calif.) Lab., 1957-72; prof. applied sci. U. Calif., Davis, 1972—, chmn. dept. applied sci., 1973-93; vis. prof. physics Drexel U., Phila., 1964, Chalmers Tech. H.S., Goteborg, Sweden, 1967-68, Heriot-Watt U., Edinburgh, Scotland, 1979, Trinity Coll., Dublin, Irelans, 1986, Mich. State U., East Lansing, 1993, Boston U., 1996; vis. scholar in math. U. Mass., Amherst, 1991; staff physicist All-Am. Engring. Co., Wilmington, Del., 1955-57; cons. in field. Author: Optical Properties of Solids, 1972. Mem. AAAS, Am. Phys. Soc., N.Y. Acad. Scis., Sigma Xi. Home: 2328 Alameda Diablo Diablo CA 94528 Office: Univ Calif Dept Applied Sci Davis CA 95616

WOOTEN, JAMES TERRELL, journalist; b. Detroit, July 13, 1937; s. J.R. and Clara Charlene (Richmond) W.; m. Katherine Joanne Richardson, Aug. 26, 1958 (dec. 1978); children: Karen, Kristen, Katie, Elizabeth; m. Patience Jean O'Connor, Sept. 27, 1980; 1 dau., Jacqueline DeLacie O'Connor. B.A., Bethel Coll., McKenzie Tenn., 1958; B.D., Presbyn. Theol. Sem., Memphis, 1961. Reporter Huntsville Times, Ala., 1965-68, N.Y. Times, N.Y.C, 1968-73, 74-78; columnist Phila. Inquirer, 1973-74; writer Esquire mag., N.Y.C., 1978-79; nat. corr. ABC News, Washington, 1979—. Author: Soldier, 1972, Dasher, 1978. Recipient Ernie Pyle Meml. award Scripps-Howard, 1974; recipient Blue Pencil award Columbia U., 1979. Office: ABC News Washington Bur 1717 Desales St NW Washington DC 20036-4401

WOOTTON, ALAN J., physics educator; b. June 16, 1948; came to U.S., 1981, naturalized.; BSc in Physics and Math., London U., 1969, PhD in Physics, 1973. Rsch. asst. Royal Holloway Coll., London U., 1971-74; rsch. asst. Culham Lab. U.K. Atomic Energy Authority, Eng., 1974-77, sr. sci. officer, 1977-81; exptl. physicist fusion energy divsn. Oak Ridge (Tenn.) Nat. Lab., 1981-84; dir. TEXT, assoc. dir. exptl. rsch. Fusion Rsch. Ctr. U. Tex., Austin, 1084-93, prof. physics, 1990—, dir. Fusion Rsch. Ctr., 1993—; mem. internat. sci. com. for transport, chaos and plasma physics workshops, 1994—; mem. adv. panel exptl. divsn. MIT, 1991-94; mem. edge theory com. Dept. Energy, 1992-93; mem. sci. adv. com. Internat. Sch. Plasma Physics Piero Caldirola, Italian Soc. Physics, 1992; organizer confs. in field. Contbr. over 100 articles to sci. jours., over 150 conf. procs., chpts. to books. Mem. Am. Phys. Soc. (exec. com. divsn. plasma physics 1991, paper slection com.). Office: U Tex Fusion Rsch Ctr Austin TX 78712

WOOTTON, JOHN FRANCIS, physiology educator; b. Penn Yan, N.Y., May 31, 1929; s. John Edenden and Margaret Eliza (Smith) W.; m. Joyce Albertine Mac Mullen, Aug. 28, 1959; children: J. Timothy, David M., Barbara H., Bruce C. BS, Cornell U., 1951, MS, 1953, PhD, 1960. Grad. rsch. asst. Cornell U., Ithaca, N.Y., 1956-60; post doctoral fellow U. Coll., London, 1960-62; from asst. prof. to assoc. prof. dept. physiology Cornell U., 1962-70, prof. dept. physiology, 1970—, assoc. dean Grad. Sch., 1980-83; grad. faculty rep. field of physiology Cornell U., 1990-92, 93—; vis. scientist MRC Molecular Biology, Cambridge, Eng., 1969-70, Nat. Inst. Med. Rsch., London, 1985-86, 92-93; teporary sr. rsch. assoc. Stanford (Calif.) U., 1977-78. Contbr. articles to profl. jours. 1st lt. USAR, 1954-56. Rsch. and Travel grantee NIH, USDA Burroughs Wellcom Fund, Med. Rsch. Coun., Cornell Biotech. Program. Mem. AAAS, Am. Soc. Biochemistry, Molecular and Cell Biology, Am. Chem. Soc., Biophys. Soc., Sigma Xi (v.p., pres. Cornell chpt.). Avocations: travel, choral singing, gardening, art, fishing. Office: Cornell U Dept Physiology T8-022 Veterinary Rsch Tower Ithaca NY 14853-5908

WOOTTON, ROBERT RAY, lawyer; b. Binghamton, N.Y., Nov. 3, 1952; s. Earle Edwards and Alburta (Andre) W.; m. Carol Ann Jansto; m. Oct. 8, 1982; children: Anne Andre, Samuel Earle, Nathaniel John. BA, Yale U., 1974, JD, 1979; BPhil, Oxford U., 1976. Bar: Ill. 1979, U.S. Dist. Ct. (no. dist.) Ill. 1979. Assoc. Sidley & Austin, Chgo., 1979-86, ptnr., 1986-89, 92—; tax legis. counsel U.S. Treasury Dept., 1989-91; adj. prof. sch. law Northwestern U., Chgo., 1988-89. Office: Sidley & Austin 1 First National Plz Chicago IL 60603

WORCESTER, ANNE PERSON, sports association executive; married. Degree in Econs. with honors, Duke U., 1982. Tournament coord. racquet sports divsn. Internat. Mgmt. Group, 1983-84; dir. corp. sales Lipton Championships, 1985-86, head corp. sales Phila. men's tennis tournament, 1986-87; tournament mgr. tennis events Lipton Championships, Spain, 1987-88; dir. worldwide ops. Va. Slims Tennis, 1988-91; mng. dir. Women's Tennis Coun., 1991-94; CEO WTA Tour, 1994—. Named one of Most Powerful Women in Tennis, Tennis Week Mag., 1993, one of Power 25, Racquet Mag., 1994, 95. Office: WTA Tour 1266 E Main St 4th Fl Stamford CT 06902-3546

WORCESTER, DONALD EMMET, history educator, author; b. Tempe, Ariz., Apr. 29, 1915; s. Thomas Emmet and Maud (Worcester) Makemson; m. Barbara Livingston Peck, July 5, 1941; children: Barbara Livingston and Elizabeth Stuart (twins), Harris Eugene. AB, Bard Coll., 1939; MA, U. Calif., 1940, PhD, 1947. Lectr. Calif. Coll. Agr., Davis, 1946, U. Calif., 1947; asst. prof. U. Fla., 1947-51, assoc. prof., 1951-55, head dept., 1955-59, prof. history, 1955-63; chmn. dept. history Tex. Christian U., 1963-72, Lorin A. Boswell prof. history, 1971-80, Ida and Cecil Green emeritus tutor, 1981-94; vis. prof. U. Madrid, 1956-57; chmn. bd. Univ. Press Mgrs., 1961-63. Author: The Interior Provinces of New Spain, 1786, 1951, (with Wendell G. Schaeffer) The Growth and Culture of Latin America, 1956, 2d edit., 1971, Sea Power and Chilean Independence, 1962, Spanish edit., 1971, The Three Worlds of Latin America, 1963, (with Maurice Boyd) American Civilization, 1964, (with Robert and Kent Forster) Man and Civilization, 1965, Makers of Latin America, 1966, Brazil: From Colony to World Power, 1973; editor: Forked Tongues and Broken Treaties, 1975, Bolivar, 1977, The Apaches: Eagles of the Southwest, 1979, German edit., 1982, The Chisholm Trail: High Road of the Cattle Kingdom, 1981, Pioneer Trails West, 1985, The Spanish Mustang: From the Plains of Andalusia to the Prairies of Texas, 1986, The Texas Cowboy, 1986, The Texas Longhorn: Relic of the Past, Asset of the Future, 1987, (fiction) The War in the Nueces Strip, 1989, A Visit from father and other Tales of the Mojave, 1990, Brazos Scout, 1991, Man on Two Ponies, 1992, Gone to Texas, 1993, Western Horse Tales, 1994; also children's books; mng. editor: Hispanic Am. Hist. Rev, 1960-65; editor TCU Monographs in History and Culture, 1966-73; mem. edit. bd. The Am. West. Served to lt. comdr. USNR, 1941-45. Recipient Golden Spur award Western Writers Am., 1975, 80; C.L. Sonnichsen Book award, 1985. Mem. Western Hist. Assn. (v.p. 1973-74, pres. 1974-75), Western Writers Am. (v.p. 1972-73, pres. 1973-74, Saddleman award 1988), N.Mex. Hist. Soc., Westerners Internat. (dir. 1975-80, pres. 1978, 79), Tex. Inst. Letters, Phi Beta Kappa, Phi Alpha Theta (pres. 1960-62). Home: 9321 Bear Creek Rd Aledo TX 76008-4004 Office: Texas Christian U Dept History Fort Worth TX 76129

WORD, ELIZA SWITZER, critical care nurse, administrator; b. Staunton, Va., June 3, 1946; d. Emily Virginia Switzer; m. Herman Lee Word, Nov. 7, 1972; 1 child, Herman Lee. Diploma, Roanoke (Va.) Meml. Hosp., 1966; BSN, Lynchburg (Va.) Coll., 1988. Nurse VA Med. Ctr., Salem, Va., Community Hosp., Roanoke, Roanoke Meml. Hosp.; critical care nurse VA Med. Ctr., Salem, nurse mgr. oper. rm. Mem. ANA. Home: 2611 Hillendale Dr NW Roanoke VA 24017-1115

WORDEN, ALFRED MERRILL, former astronaut, research company executive; b. Jackson, Mich., Feb. 7, 1932; s. Merrill Bangs and Helen Crowell) W.; m. Jill Lee Hotchkiss, July 9, 1982; children: Merrill Ellen, Alison Pamela, Tamara Lynn. BS, U.S. Mil. Acad., 1955; MS in Aeros., Astronautical and Instrumentation Engring., U. Mich., 1963, DSc in Astronautical Engring., 1972. Commd. 2nd lt. USAF, 1955, advanced through grades to lt. col., 1971; stationed at Andrews AFB, Md., 1956-61, U. Mich., 1961-63, Farnborough, Eng.; with RAF, 1963-65; instr. Aerospace Rsch. Pilots Sch., Edwards AFB, Calif., 1965-66; astronaut Manned Spacecraft Ctr., NASA, Houston, 1966-72; command module pilot Apollo XV, 1971; sr. aerospace engr., test pilot, dir. systems studies divsn. Ames Rsch. Ctr., Moffett Field, Calif., 1972-75, ret., 1975; v.p. High Flight Found., Colorado Springs, Colo., 1975—; pres. MW Aerospace, Inc., 1985—, Jet Electronics and Tech., Inc., 1990-93; staff v.p. BF Goodrich Aerospace, Brecksville, Ohio, 1993—. Author: poetry Hello Earth-Greetings from Endeavour, 1974; children's book A Flight to the Moon, 1974. Bd. dirs. Boys' Clubs Am., Palm Beach County, Salvation Army. Inducted into Mich. Aviation Hall of

Fame, 1990. Mem. AIAA, Soc. Exptl. Pilots, Am. Astron. Soc., Explorers Club, Circumnavigators Club. Episcopalian (sr. warden 1969-71). Office: BF Goodrich Rsch Ctr 9921 Brecksville Rd Brecksville OH 44141-3201

WORDEN, ELIZABETH ANN, artist, comedy writer, singer; b. Karnes City, Tex., Nov. 8, 1954; d. Alan Walker and Mary Paralee (Long) W. BS in Comms., U. Tex., 1977. Disc jockey, newsperson KMMK Radio, McKinney, Tex., 1978, KPBC Radio, Irving, Tex., 1979-80, KDNT Radio, Denton, Tex., 1980-81, KJIM Radio, Ft. Worth, 1981-82, KPBC Radio, Irving, 1983, KRYS Radio, Corpus Christi, Tex., 1984; owner Worden Industries, Corpus Christi, Tex.; represented by Abney Gallery, N.Y.C., 1995—. Executed paintings for Am. Embassy, Bogota, Colombia; one-woman shows include Art Ctr., Corpus Christi, 1990; exhibited in groups shows at Tex. A&M, Corpus Christi, 1986, 92, Galeria Chapparal, Corpus Christi, 1988, New Eng. Fine Art Inst., Boston, 1993, Am. Embassy, Bogota, Colombia; numerous paintings in pvt. collections. Mem. Art Ctr. Corpus Christi. Mem. Nat. Assn. of Fine Artists, Tex. Fine Arts Assn. Avocations: writing fiction and poetry, acting, photography, reading. Home and Office: Worden Industries 3842 Brookhill Dr Corpus Christi TX 78410-4404

WORDEN, KATHARINE COLE, sculptor; b. N.Y.C., May 4, 1925; d. Philip Gillette and Katharine (Pyle) Cole; m. Frederic G. Worden, Jan. 8, 1944; children: Rick, Dwight, Philip, Barbara, Katharine. Student Potters Sch., Tucson, 1940-42, Sarah Lawrence Coll., 1942-44. Sculptor; works exhibited Royce Galleries, Galerie Francoise Besnard (Paris), Cooling Gallery (London), Galerie Schumacher (Munich), Selected Artists Gallery, N.Y.C., Art Inst. Boston, Reid Gallery, Nashville, Weiner Gallery, N.Y.C., Boston Athanaeum, House of Humor and Satire, Gabrovo, Bulgaria, 1983, Newport Bay Club, 1984; pvt. collections Grand Palais (Paris), Dakar and Bathurst, Africa; dir. Stride Rite Corp., 1980-85; occupational therapist psychopathic ward Los Angeles County Gen. Hosp., 1953-57; Headstart vol., Watts, Calif., 1965-67; tchr. sculpture Watts Towers Art Center, 1967-69; participant White House Women Doers Luncheon meeting, 1968; dir. Cambridgeport Problem Center, Cambridge, Mass., 1969-71; mem. Jud. Nominating Commn., 1976-79; bd. overseers Boston Mus. Fine Arts, 1980-83; bd. govs. Newport Seamens Ch. Inst., 1989-91; trustee Comm. Rsch., Miami, Fla., 1960-69, chmn. bd., 1966-69; trustee Newport Art Mus., 1984-86, 92-94, Jamestown Cmty. Theatre, 1994—, Newport Health Found., 1986-91, Hawthorne Sea Fund, 1990-93; bd. dirs. Boston Center for Arts, 1976-80, Child and Family Svcs. of Newport County, 1983-90, 91—. Mem. Common Cause (Mass. adv. bd. 1971-72, dir. 1974-75), Mass. Civil Liberties Union (exec. bd. 1973-74, dir. 1976-77). Home: 24 Fort Wetherill Rd Jamestown RI 02835-2908

WORDSWORTH, JERRY L., wholesale distribution executive; b. 1944. With MBM, Rocky Mount, N.C., 1966—, chmn., pres. Office: MBM PO Box 800 Rocky Mount NC 27802*

WORELL, JUDITH P., psychologist, educator; b. N.Y.C.; d. Moses and Dorothy Goldfarb; m. Leonard Worell, Aug. 11, 1947 (div.); children: Amy, Beth, Wendy; m. H.A. Smith, Mar. 23, 1985. BS magna cum laude, Queens Coll., 1950; MA, Ohio State U., 1952, PhD in Clin. Psychology, 1954; DHL (hon.), Colby-Sawyer Coll., 1993. Research assoc. Iowa Psychopathic Hosp., Iowa City, 1957-59; research assoc. Okla. State U., 1960-66; asst. prof. U. Ky., Lexington, 1969-71; assoc. prof. U. Ky., 1971-75, prof. ednl. and counseling psychology, 1976—, dir. counseling psychology tng. program, 1980-93, chairperson dept. ednl. and counseling psychology, 1993—. Author: (with C.M. Nelson) Managing Instructional Problems, 1981; (with W.E. Stilwell) Psychology for Teachers and Students, 1981; Psychological Development in the Elementary Years, 1982; (with Fred Danner) The Adolescent as Decision-maker: Applications to Development and Education, 1989, (with Pam Remer) Feminist Perspectives in Therapy: An Empowerment Model for Women, 1992; assoc. editor Jour. Cons. and Clin. Psychology, 1976-79, mem. editorial bd., 1984-89; assoc. editor Psychol. Women Quar., 1984-89, editor, 1989-95; mem. editorial bd. Sex Roles, 1984—, Psychol. Assessment, 1991—, Clin. Psychology Rev., 1991—, Women and Therapy, 1992—; cons., reviewer 10 jours.; contbr. articles to profl. jours. Named U. Ky. Campus Woman of Yr., 1976, Outstanding Univ. Grad. prof., 1991, Disting. Ky. psychologist, 1990; USPHS fellow, 1953; NIMH rsch. grantee, 1962-69. Fellow APA (pres. Clin. Psychology of Women 1986-88, chmn. com. state assn. rels. 1982-83, fellow selection divsn. 35 com. 1983-84, policy and planning bd. 1989-92, publs. and communications bd. 1992—, chair 1996—, chair jours. com., Disting. Leader for Women in Psychology 1990), Ky. Psychol. Assn. (pres. 1981-82, rep. at large 1995—), Southeastern Psychol. Assn. (exec. coun. mem.-at-large, pres.-elect 1993-94 pres. 1994-95), Am. Women in Psychology, Phi Beta Kappa. Home: 3892 Gloucester Dr Lexington KY 40510-9729 Office: U Ky Dept Ednl and Counseling Psychology 235 Dickey Hall Lexington KY 40506

WORENKLEIN, JACOB JOSHUA, lawyer; b. N.Y.C., Oct. 1, 1948; s. Abraham and Cela (Zyskind) W.; divorced; children: David, Daniel, Laura; m. Cindy Sternkler, Feb. 26, 1995. BA, Columbia U., 1969; MBA, JD, NYU, 1973. Bar: N.Y. 1974. Assoc. Milbank, Tweed, Hadley & McCloy, N.Y.C., 1973-81, ptnr., 1982-93, chmn. firm planning com., 1988-90, mem. exec. com., 1990-93, sr. advisor to exec. com., 1993-94; mng. dir., group head of global project fin. group Lehman Bros., N.Y.C., 1993—; mem. investment banking mgmt. com. Lehman Bros., 1993—; mem. adv. coun. Amoco Power Resources Corp., 1995—. Mem. editl. bd. Jour. Project Fin., 1996—; contbr. articles to profl. jours. Pres. Old Broadway Synagogue, N.Y.C., 1978—; trustee Fedn. Jewish Philanthropies, N.Y.C., 1984-86; bd. overseers United Jewish Appeal-Fedn. Jewish Philanthropies, 1987, chmn. lawyers divsn. major gifts, 1989-91, chmn. lawyers divsn., 1991-93, bd. dirs., 1991—; trustee Jewish Cmty. Rels. Coun. N.Y., 1995—. Office: Lehman Bros 3 World Fin Ctr 200 Vesey St Fl 16 New York NY 10281-1009

WORGUL, BASIL VLADIMIR, radiation scientist; b. N.Y.C., June 30, 1947; s. John and Stephanie (Litwin) W.; m. Kathleen R. Hennessey, June 14, 1969; children: Ronald Adam, Suzanne Kathleen. BS, U. Miami, Fla., 1969; PhD, U. Vt., 1974. Rsch. assoc. Columbia U., N.Y.C., 1975-78, asst. prof., 1979-84, assoc. prof., 1984-90, dir. Eye Radiation & Environ. Rsch. Lab., 1984—, prof., 1990—; cons. Nat. Coun. on Radiation Protection, Washington, 1988—, Internat. Com. on Radiation Protection, 1988—, NASA, 1990-92; dir. Residents Basic Sci., Dept. Ophthalmology, Columbia U., 1983-92; Am. dir. Ukranian Am. Chernobyl Ocular Study. Co-organizer Citizens to Preserve Warwick, N.Y., 1986. NIH grantee, 1977—, NASA grantee, 1987—, Dept. Energy grantee, 1990—, DNA grantee, 1992—; Robert McCormick Rsch. scholar, 1987-88. Mem. AAAS, Assn. for Rsch. in Vision and Ophthalmology, Radiation Rsch. Soc., Acad. Scis. Ukraine (fgn.), N.Y. Acad. Scis., Soc. Gen. Physiologists, Am. Soc. for Cell Biology, Internat. Assn. Ocular Toxicology. Achievements include definition of the mechanism of radiation cataract development; discovery of Terminal Body-a cellular organelle; description of the preferred dynamic reorientation of the mitotic spindle in an adult epithelium. Office: Columbia U 630 W 168th St New York NY 10032-3702

WORK, BRUCE VAN SYOC, business consultant; b. Monmouth, Ill., Mar. 20, 1942; s. Robert M. and Evelyn (Rusken) W.; m. Janet Kay Brown, Nov. 12, 1966; children: Bruce, Terra. B.A., Monmouth Coll., 1964; B.S., U. Mo.-Rolla, 1966; postgrad., U. Chgo., 1978-79. Registered profl. engr., Ill. Various mgmt. positions Midcon Corp. (and subs.), 1966-79; pres. Indsl. Fuels Corp., Troy, Mich., 1979-85, Costain Coal Inc., Troy, Mich., 1985-89; pvt. practice small bus. cons., 1989-92; bus. cons. Wallis Oil Co., 1992—. Mem. various coms. Cuba United Meth. Ch. Mem. Detroit Athletic Club, Forest Lake Country Club, Blue Key. Office: 1732 Lakeshore Dr Cuba MO 65453-9684 *One of the keys to success is to treat everyone as you would want to be treated, equally and with respect. People are the key to your success.*

WORK, CHARLES ROBERT, lawyer; b. Glendale, Calif., June 21, 1940; s. Raymond P. and Minna M. (Fricke) W.; m. Linda S. Smith, Oct. 4, 1965 (div.); children: Matthew Keehn, Mary Lucila Landis, Benjamin Reed; m. Veronica A. Haggart, Apr., 1985, 1 child, Andrew Haggart. BA, Wesleyan U., 1962; JD, U. Chgo., 1965; LLM, Georgetown U., 1966. Bar: D.C. 1965, Utah 1965. Asst. U.S. atty. D.C., 1966-73; dep. adminstr. law enforcement assistance adminstrn., U.S. Dept. Justice, 1973-75; ptnr. Peabody, Lambert & Meyers, Washington, 1975-82, McDermott, Will & Emery, Washington, 1982—. Recipient Rockefeller Pub. Service award 1978. Mem. D.C. Bar (pres. 1976-77). Office: McDermott Will & Emery 1850 K St NW Washington DC 20006-2213

WORK, HENRY HARCUS, physician, educator; b. Buffalo, Nov. 11, 1911; s. Henry Harcus and Jeannette (Harcus) W.; m. Virginia Codington, Oct. 20, 1945 (dec. Nov. 1991); children—Henry Harcus III, David Codington, William Bruce, Stuart Runyon. A.B., Hamilton Coll., Clinton, N.Y., 1933; M.D., Harvard, 1937. Intern, resident Boston Children's Hosp., 1937-40, Emma P. Bradley Home Providence, 1940, Buffalo Children's Hosp., 1940-42, N.Y. Hosp., 1945-47; psychiat. services adviser, chief U.S. Children's Bur., Washington, 1948-49; assoc. prof. pediatrics U. Louisville, 1949-55; mem. faculty UCLA, 1955-72, prof. psychiatry and pub. health, 1966-72; chief profl. svcs. Am. Psychiat. Assn., Washington, 1972-83; clin. prof. George Washington U., Georgetown U., Uniformed Svcs. U. of Health Scis., U. Md., 1973—. Author: A Guide to Preventive Child Psychiatry, 1965, Minimal Brain Dysfunction: A Medical Challenge, 1967, Psychiatric Emergencies in Childhood, 1967, Crisis in Child Psychiatry, 1975, also articles. Served to capt. AUS, 1942-45. Recipient Simon Wile Award, Amer. Acad. of Child and Adolescent Psychiatry, 1994. Mem. So. Calif. Psychiat. Assn. (pres. 1966-67), Am. Orthopsychiat. Assn. (v.p. 1968-69), Am. Coll. Psychiatry (sec.-gen. 1979-93), Group for Advancement of Psychiatry (pres. 1982-85). Home: 4986 Sentinel Dr Apt 504 Bethesda MD 20816

WORK, WILLIAM, retired association executive; b. Ithaca, N.Y., Aug. 10, 1923; s. Paul and Helen Grace (Nicholas) W.; m. Jane Noel Magruder, Nov. 26, 1960; children—Paul Magregor, Jeffrey William. AB, Cornell U., 1946; MA, U. Wis., 1948, PhD, 1954; D Arts (hon.), Eastern Mich. U., 1986; LLD (hon.), Emerson Coll., 1987. Cert. assn. exec. Instr., asso. dir theatre Purdue U., 1948-50; from instr. to prof., dir. theatre Eastern Mich. U., 1951-63; exec. sec. Speech Communication Assn., Annandale, Va., 1963-88, ret., 1988; mem. faculty U. Wis., 1950-51, So. Ill. U., 1959; cons., reader, review panelist U.S. Office Edn., 1966-71; del. White House Conf. Children, 1970; pres. Alliance Assn. Advancement Edn., 1977, Coun. Communication Socs., 1974-77; past. mem. AAAS, AAUP, Internat. Communication Assn., Internat. Inst. Communications. Contbr. articles, revs. profl. jours. Mem. Mich. Cultural Commn., 1959-60; mem. Hastings-on-Hudson (N.Y.) Bd. Edn., 1972-75. Recipient Alex Drier award, 1962. Mem. Phi Kappa Phi. Democrat. Unitarian. *If, as George Santayana wisely noted, those who cannot remember the past are condemned to repeat it, then it must be equally true that those who fail to prepare for the future are condemned to endure it.*

WORKMAN, GEORGE HENRY, engineering consultant; b. Muskegon, Mich., Sept. 18, 1939; s. Harvey Merton and Bettie Jane (Meyers) W.; Asso. Sci., Muskegon Community Coll., 1960; B.S.E., U. Mich., 1966, M.S.E., 1966, Ph.D., 1969; m. Vicki Sue Hanish, June 17, 1967; children—Mark, Larry. Prin. engr. Battelle Meml. Inst., Columbus, Ohio, 1969-76; pres. Applied Mechanics Inc., Longboat Key, Fla., 1976—; instr. dept. civil engring. Ohio State U., 1973, 82. Served with USN, 1961-64. Named Outstanding Undergrad. Student, Engring. Mechanics dept. U. Mich., 1965-66, Outstanding Grad. Student, Civil Engring. dept., 1968-69. Registered profl. engr., Ohio. Mem. Am. Acad. of Mechanics, ASME, ASCE, Nat. Soc. Profl. Engrs., Sigma Xi, Chi Epsilon, Phi Kappa Phi, Phi Theta Kappa. Congregationalist. Contbr. tech. papers to nat. and internat. confs. Home and Office: 3431 Bayou Ct Longboat Key FL 34228-3028

WORKMAN, KAYLEEN MARIE, special education educator; b. Paola, Kans., Aug. 25, 1947; d. Ralph I. and Pearl Marie (Shults) Platz; m. John Edward Workman, Aug. 10, 1980; children: Andrew Ray, Craig Michael. BS in Edn., Emporia State U., 1969, MS in Edn., 1983. Tchr. English/speech Lincoln (Kans.) High Sch., 1969-70, substitute tchr., 1970-71; substitute tchr. Hudson (Wis.) Sch. Dist., 1971-72; tchrs. aide learning disabilities Park Forest South (Ill) Jr. High Sch., 1977-78; learning disabilities/English instr. George York Sch., Osawatomie, Kans., 1978—; supr. Loose Ends Clown Troop, 1988-91; presenter in field. Author of poems. Com. mem., sec. Cub Scouts, Osawatomie, 1987-88, com. mem. Boy Scouts Am., 1988-91, sec., 1990-91; forensics judge Osawatomie H.S. Forensics Team, 1991-92; hunter's safety instr. Osawatomie Sportsman's Club, 1982-86; mem. Osawatomie Cmty. Band, 1990-92. Mem. Osawatomie-NEA (v.p. 1982-83, 93-94, pres. 1983-84, 94-95, sec. 1986), Kans.-NEA (Sunflower uniserv adminstrv. bd. 1985, Sunflower uniserv coord. coun.), Learning Disabilities Assn., Delta Kappa Gamma. Avocations: hunting, fishing, collecting Santa Clauses, writing poetry, shopping. Office: York Sch at Osawatomie St Hosp PO Box 500 Osawatomie KS 66064-0500

WORKMAN, MARGARET LEE, state supreme court justice; b. May 22, 1947; d. Frank Eugene and Mary Emma (Thomas) W.; m. Edward T. Gardner III; children: Lindsay Elizabeth, Christopher Workman, Edward Earnshaw. AB in Polit. Sci., W.Va. U., 1969, JD, 1974. Bar: W.Va. 1974. Asst. counsel to majority, pub. works com. U.S. Senate, Washington, 1974-75; law clk. 13th jud. cir., W.Va. Ct., Charleston, 1975-76, judge, 1981-88; pvt. practice Charleston, 1976-81; justice W.Va. Supreme Ct. Appeals, Charleston, 1989—, chief justice, 1993. Advance person for Rosalyn Carter, Carter Presdl. Campaign, Atlanta, 1976. Democrat. Episcopalian. Office: State Supreme Ct 317 State Capitol Charleston WV 25305-0001

WORKMAN, NORMAN ALLAN, accountant, graphic arts consultant; b. Boston, Apr. 20, 1918; s. William Horace and Estelle Emily (Hanlon) W.; m. Harriet Patricia Banfield, AAug. 1, 1946; children: Stephen, Mark, Brian, Patricia. Student, Coll. William and Mary, 1938-39; BS in Econs. magna cum laude, Bowdoin Coll., 1941. CPA, Oreg. Staff acct. Lybrand Ross Bros. & Montgomery, Boston, 1941-43, Whitfield Stratford & Co., Portland, Oreg., 1946-51; ptnr. Workman, Shephard & Co., CPAs, Portland, 1951-60; sole practitioner Portland, 1961—. Newsletter columnist Good Impressions, 1993—. Chmn. bd. Sylvan Sch., Portland, 1956-57; pres. Doernbecher Children's Hosp. Found., Portland, 1963-85, Bowdoin Club Oreg., Portland, 1963—; trustee Oreg. Episcopal Schs., Portland, 1974-76. Lt. (j.g.) Supply Corps, USNR, 1944-46. Mem. AICPA, Inst. Mgmt. Accts. (pres. Portland chpt. 1954-55), Oreg. Soc. CPA's, Pacific Printing and Imaging Assn., Arlington Club, Multnomah Athletic Club, Phi Beta Kappa. Avocations: bird hunting, fishing, horticulture. Home: 4381 SW Fairview Blvd Portland OR 97221-2709 Office: 1750 SW Skyline Blvd Portland OR 97221-2545

WORKMAN, WILLIAM DOUGLAS, III, former mayor; b. Charleston S.C., July 3, 1940; s. William Douglas, Jr. and Rhea (Thomas) W.; BA, The Citadel, 1961; grad. U. S.C., 1993; m. Marcia Mae Moorhead, Apr. 23, 1966; children: William Douglas IV, Frank Moorhead. Reporter, Charleston News & Courier, 1965-66, Greenville (S.C.) News, 1966-70; tchr., adminstr., dean allied health scis. Greenville Tech. Coll., 1967-75; exec. asst. to Gov. of S.C., Columbia, 1975-78; mktg. exec. Daniel Internat. Corp., Greenville, 1978-90, dir. of facilities Fluor Daniel, 1991-93; v.p. S.C. ops. Piedmont Natural Gas, 1994—; mayor City of Greenville, 1983-95. Chmn. Greenville County Rep. Conv., 1980, 82, 87, 89, 91, S.C. 4th Congl. Dist. Rep. Conv., 1980, 82, 84; chmn. S.C. Rep. Conv., 1984, 89, vice chmn., 1982, 87; Rep. nominee U.S. Congress 4th Dist. S.C., 1986; mem. S.C. Adv. Commn. on Intergovtl. Rels., 1990—; bd. dirs. S.C. Appalachian Coun. of Govts., 1991-95; mem. Mcpl. Assn. S.C. 1981-95 (bd. dirs., 1990—, pres., 1993-94); trustee Sch. Dist. Greenville County, 1969-75, also vice chmn.; bd. dirs. YMCA Camp Greenville, 1973-83, 90-95, chmn., 1975; chmn. S.C. Health Coordinating Coun., 1976-78; founder S.C. Literacy Assn., treas., 1969-73; mem. Greenville City Council, 1981-83; mem. Southern Growth Policies Bd., 1992—, S.C. Adv. Commn. on Intergovtl. Rels., 1991—. Served with AUS, 1962-64; lt. col. Res. Decorated Army Commendation medal with 2 oak leaf clusters, Legion of Merit; named Outstanding State Chmn., S.C. Jaycees, 1969; Order of Palmetto, 1978. Mem. Res. Officers Assn., Assn. U.S. Army, Am. Legion. U.S. Conf. Mayors, Southeastern Gas Assn., Nat. Mgmt. Assn. (mgr. yr. award Greenville chpt. 1985), Newcomen Soc. (S.C. com.), S.C. Downtown Devel. Assn. (bd. dirs.), Greenville Country Club, Greenville-Piedmont Citadel Club (past pres.), Greenville City Club (bd. dirs.), Poinsett Club, Greenville adv. bd. Nat. Bank of S.C. Home: 30 Craigwood Rd Greenville SC 29607-3652 Office: PO Box 1905 Greenville SC 29602

WORLEY, BLAND WALLACE, banker; b. Kinston, N.C., Aug. 14, 1917; s. Bland W. and Ida Ruth (Gooding) W.; m. Ada Harvey, June 28, 1941; children: Anne, Ada, Bland W. B.S., U. N.C., 1938; grad. exec. program, 1955; grad., Grad. Sch. Banking, Rutgers U., 1954. Insp. Hooper Holmes Bur., Greensboro, N.C., 1938-39; mgr. CIT Corp., Salisbury, N.C., 1939-42; mgr. time payment dept. Wachovia Bank & Trust Co., High Point, N.C., 1946-50; v.p., also High Point office exec. Wachovia Bank & Trust Co., 1951-56; sr. v.p. charge Wachovia Bank & Trust Co. (Greensboro operations), 1956-69; exec. v.p. charge statewide banking div. Wachovia Bank & Trust Co., Winston-Salem, N.C., 1969-70, also dir.; vice-chmn., dir., 1970-75; past trustee Wachovia Realty Investments; former CEO, dir. Barclays Am. Corp., chmn., 1976-84; dir., chmn. First Fed. Savs. & Loan Assn., Charlotte, N.C.; dir. Culp Inc., High Point, N.C.; past vol. chmn. for N.C. U.S. Savs. Bond Program. Past chmn. nat. exec. com. for vol. state chmn. 1969-77; pres. Greater Greensboro United Fund, 1975-77; past treas., mem. nat. exec. bd. Boy Scouts Am., 1970-85; past bd. dirs. N.C. Citizens Assn.; bd. dirs. N.C. Coun. Mgmt. and Devel., 1979-84; bd. dirs., past pres. Bus. Found. of N.C.; trustee, former chmn. bd. trustees Greensboro Coll.; past trustee Atlantic Christian Coll., Wilson, N.C.; past bd. visitors Guilford Coll., Greenboro; trustee U. N.C., Charlotte, 1981-85. Named High Point Young Man of Yr., 1953, Outstanding Young Businessman N.C., 1958; recipient Silver Beaver, Silver Antelope, Silver Buffalo awards Boy Scouts Am., Disting. Citizens award N.C. Citizens for Bus. and Industry, 1987. Mem. N.C. Bankers Assn. (past pres.), Nat. Consumer Fin. Assn., Greensboro C. of C. (past pres., disting. citizen award 1968), Greater Charlotte C. of C. (chmn. 1980-81), Piedmont Club, Old Town Country Club. Home: 1244 Arbor Rd Apt 232 Winston Salem NC 27104-1136

WORLEY, GORDON ROGER, retail chain financial executive; b. Arlington, Nebr., Oct. 13, 1919; s. Carl H. and Zella E. (Ludwig) W. B.S., U. Nebr., 1945; M.B.A., Northwestern U., 1956. C.P.A., Ill. With Aldens, Inc., Chgo., 1940-67; asst. treas. Aldens, Inc., 1956-57, v.p., treas., 1957-67; v.p., controller Gamble-Skogmo, Inc., Mpls., 1967; v.p. fin. Montgomery Ward & Co., Inc., 1967-68; exec. v.p. fin. Montgomery Ward & Co., Inc., Chgo., 1975-83; also dir.; v.p. fin. Marcor Inc., Chgo., 1968-75; also dir. Marcor Inc.; dir. Signature Fin./Mktg. Inc., Montgomery Ward Ins. Group, Ill. Power Co., Decatur, Axia, Inc, Stein, Roe & Farnham Funds, Am. Mgmt. Systems, Inc., Arlington, Va. Bd. dirs. Northwestern Meml. Hosp.; trustee Garrett-Evang. Theol. Sem., chmn., 1984-89; mem. and vice chmn. Ill. Capital Devel. Bd., 1973-77; mem. Nat. Commn. on Electronic Fund Transfers, 1975-77. Served with USAAF, 1943-46. Mem. Conf. Bd. Coun. of Fin. Execs., Fin. Execs. Inst., Nat. Retail Mchts. Assn., Execs. Club, Econ. Club, Mid-Am. Club, Chgo. Club, Oak Park Country Club, Hole-In-The-Wall Club (Naples, Fla.). Methodist.

WORLEY, JANE LUDWIG, lawyer; b. Reading, Pa., Sept. 4, 1917; d. Walter Schearer and Marion Grace (Johns) L.; m. Floyd Edwin Worley, Oct. 30, 1946 (dec. Jan. 1982); children: Laetitia Anne, Thomas Allen, Christopher Ludwig. AB, Bryn Mawr Coll., 1938; JD, Temple U., 1942. Bar: Pa. 1943, U.S. Dist. Ct. (ea. dist.) Pa. 1980, U.S. Supreme Ct. 1968. Assoc. Richardson Moss & Richardson, Reading, 1943-48; pvt. practice Wernersville, Pa., 1948—; sec., bd. dirs. Worley Lumber Co. Inc., Wernersville, 1955—. Sec. Friends of Reading Mus. Art, 1986-91; sec. Berks County chpt. ARC, 1986-87, v.p., 1987-91. Mem. ABA, Pa. Bar Assn., Berks County Bar Assn., DAR, Jr. League Reading. Republican. Mem. United Ch. of Christ. Avocations: antique and art collecting, travel. Office: 551 W Penn Ave Wernersville PA 19565-1417

WORLEY, LLOYD DOUGLAS, English language educator; b. Lafayette, La., Sept. 11, 1946; s. Albert Stiles and Doris (Christy) W.; m. Maydean Ann Mouton, Apr. 4, 1966; children: Erin Shawn, Albert Stiles II. BA, U. SW La., 1968, MA, 1972; PhD, So. Ill. U., 1979. Ordained priest, Liberal Cath. Ch. Tchr. Lafayette H.S., 1969-74; vis. asst. prof. dept. English So. Ill. U., Carbondale, 1979-80; asst. prof. dept. English Pa. State U., DuBois, 1980-87; assoc. prof., assoc. dir. composition dept. English U. No. Colo., Greeley, 1987-88, prof. dept. English, 1988—; acting dir. Writing Component Ctr. Basic Skills, So. Ill. U., 1980. Editor: Ruthven Literary Bull., 1988-92; contbr. book chpts., articles. Rector Parish of St. Albertus Magnus, sec-treas. Am. Province; mem. Am. Clerical Synod Chpt. Decorated Knight Cmdr. Order of Merit St. Angilbert, 1993, Prelate Comdr. Order of Noble Companions of Swan, 1993, Grand Chamberlain, 1995, Knight Order of Guadalupe, 1995, Knight Comdr. Justice Sovereign Order St. John, Knight Grand Cross of Bear of Alabona, 1995; created hereditary Baron of Royal and Serene House of Alabona-Ostrogojsk by HRSH Prince William I Fedn. of Princes of Holy Roman Empire-in-Exile, 1993. Fellow Philalethes Soc.; mem. ASCD, Internat. Assn. for Fantastic in Arts (divsn. head Am. Lit. 1987-93), Lord Ruthven Assembly (pres. 1988-94), Conf. Coll. Composition and Commn., Nat. Coun. Tchrs. English, Am. Conf. Irish Studies, Sigma Tau Delta (bd. dirs. 1990—, high plains regent various states 1992—), Masons (century lodge #190), Order of DeMolay (chevalier, corss of honor, legion of honor), Knights Holy Sepulchre (Sov. Grand Master), Rose & Crox Martinist Order (pres. premier nat. coun.). Democrat. Office: 2644 11th Ave # D-109 Greeley CO 80631-8441

WORLEY, MARVIN GEORGE, JR., architect; b. Oak Park, Ill., Oct. 10, 1934; s. Marvin George and Marie Hyancinth (Donahue) W.; B.Arch., U. Ill., 1958; m. Maryalice Ryan, July 11, 1959; children—Michael Craig, Carrie Ann, Alissa Maria. Project engr. St. Louis area Nike missile bases U.S. Army C.E., Granite City, Ill., 1958-59, architect N.Cen. div. U.S. Army C.E., Chgo., 1960; architect Yerkes & Grunsfeld, architects, Chgo., 1961-65, asso., 1965; asso. Grunsfeld & Assos., architects, Chgo., 1966-85.; prin. Marvin Worley Architects, Oak Park, Ill., 1985—. Dist. architect Oak Park Elementary Schs., Dist. 97, 1973-80. Mem. Oak Park Community Improvement Commn., 1973-75; mem. exec. bd. Oak Park Council PTA, 1970-73, pres., 1971-72. Served with AUS, 1959. Mem. AIA (corporate), Chgo. Assn. Commerce and Industry, Oak Park-River Forest C. of C. Office: 37 South Blvd Oak Park IL 60302-2777

WORLEY, ROBERT WILLIAM, JR., lawyer; b. Anderson, Ind., June 13, 1935; s. Robert William and Dorothy Mayhew (Hayler) W.; m. Diana Lynn Matthews, Aug. 22, 1959; children: Nathanael, Hope Hillegas. BS in Chem. Engring., Lehigh U., 1956; LLB, Harvard U., 1960. Bar: Conn. 1960, Fla. 1977, U.S. Supreme Ct. 1966. Assoc. then ptnr. Cummings & Lockwood, Stamford, Conn., 1960-91; gen. counsel Consol. Asset Recovery Corp. sub. Chase Manhattan Corp., Bridgeport, Conn., 1991-94; v.p., sr. assoc. counsel The Chase Manhattan Bank, N.A., N.Y.C., 1994—. Mem. trustees com. on bequests and trusts Lehigh U., 1979—; mem. Conn. Legis. Task Force on Probate Court System, 1991-93; chmn. Greenwich Arts Council, 1981-82; v.p., bd. dirs. Greenwich Choral Soc., 1962-77, 80, mem., 1960—; bd. dirs. Greenwich Ctr. for Chamber Music, 1981-85, Greenwich Symphony, 1986-89; commr. Greenwich Housing Authority, 1972-77; past mem. Republican Town Com. Greenwich; mem. bldg. com. for sr. ctr. Greenwich Bd. Selectmen, 1980-81. Served to capt. JAGC, AUS, 1965. Mem. ABA, Conn. Bar Assn. (exec. com. probate sect. 1980), Fla. Bar Assn., Stamford Bar Assn. (sec.), Greenwich Bar Assn. Republican. Christian Scientist. Club: Landmark, Harvard Boston. Home: 316 Sound Beach Ave Old Greenwich CT 06870-1932 Office: The Chase Manhattan Bank Legal Dept 39th Fl 270 Park Ave New York NY 10017-2070

WORMAN, HOWARD JAY, physician, educator; b. Paterson, N.J., May 21, 1959; s. Louis and Dora (Rubin) W. BA, Cornell U., 1981; MD, U. Chgo., 1985. Diplomate Am. Bd. Internal Medicine. Intern N.Y. Hosp., N.Y.C., 1985-86, resident, 1986-87; guest investigator Rockefeller U., N.Y.C., 1987-90; asst. prof. Mt. Sinai Sch. Medicine, N.Y.C., 1990-94; asst. attending physician Mt. Sinai Hosp., N.Y.C., 1990-94; asst. prof. Coll. Physicians and Surgeons Columbia U., N.Y.C., 1995—; asst. attending physician Presbyn. Hosp., N.Y.C., 1995—. Mem. editl. bd. Hepatology, Frontiers in Biosci.; contbr. articles to profl. jours. Recipient Physician-Scientist award NIH, 1987-92; Charles E. Culpeper scholar in Med. Scis., 1994-95. Mem. AAAS, ACP, Am. Chem. Soc., Am. Fedn. Clin. Rsch. (Trainee award in clin. rsch. 1989, Henry Christian award 1990), Am. Soc. Cell Biology, Am. Assn. Study of Liver Diseases, N.Y. Acad. Scis. (vice chmn. biol. scis. sect. 1992-93, chmn. 1993-94), Hon. Order Ky. Cols., Phi Beta Kappa. Democrat. Jewish. Avocations: music, reading. Office: Columbia U Coll Physicians & Surgeons 630 W 168th St New York NY 10032-3702

WORMAN, LINDA KAY, nursing administrator; b. Buffalo, N.Y., Sept. 28, 1959; d. Robert Kindig and Winifred (Hostetter) W. BSN, Emory U., 1980; MPH, U. N.C., 1986. RN; cert. lactation cons.; cert. advanced nursing adminstr. Staff nurse SICU U. Hosp., Cleve., 1980-81; staff nurse labor and delivery Med. Ctr., Columbus, Ga., 1981; dep. prin. tutor Macha (Africa) Mission Hosp., 1981-85; staff nurse neurosci. ICU Duke U. Hosp., Durham, N.C., 1985-86; nurse mgr. maternal-child Woodland (Calif.) Meml. Hosp., 1986-88; nurse mgr. obstetrics Pa. State U. Hosp., Hershey, 1988-94; v.p. nursing svcs. Jersey Shore (Pa.) Hosp., 1994—. Rape and domestic violence crisis vol. Harrisburg YWCA, 1992-94. Mem. Am. Orgn. of Nurse Execs., Pa. Perinatal Assn. (bd. dirs. 1989-94). Home: 8 Spruce Dr Lock Haven PA 17745-1037 Office: Jersey Shore Hosp 1020 Thompson St Jersey Shore PA 17740

WORMAN, RICHARD W., insurance company executive, state senator; b. Noble County, Ind., July 3, 1933; s. William D. and Leah M. W.; m. Marna Jo Neuhouser, Sept. 29, 1951; children—Terry Jo, Renny, Denny, Rex, Tammy. Buyer, Neuhouser Poultry, Leo, Ind., 1951-53; salesman Allen Dairy, Ft. Wayne, Ind., 1953-57; with Nationwide Ins. Co., Columbus, Ohio, 1951-88, dist. sales mgr.; owner Securance Ins., 1990—; mem. Ind. Ho. of Reps., 1972-76, Ind. Senate, 1978—; trustee, assessor County of Allen, Ind., 1970-72. C.L.U. Mem. Life Underwriters Assn., Republican. United Methodist. Clubs: Lions (past pres.), Mason (past master), Shriner, Elks, Optimist. Office: PO Box 320 Leo IN 46765-0320

WORMWOOD, RICHARD NAUGHTON, retired naturalist; b. Old Forge, N.Y., May 21, 1936; s. F. Earl Hill-Wormwood and Eleanor Bardou-Naughton; m. Michele Gano-Kenney (div.); children: Anneene, Chauncey; m. Donna Rhodes-Harrington, Jan. 30, 1983; one stepchild, Melissa Harrington Goucher. Student, Rochester Inst. Tech., 1955, Harper Coll., 1956, Russell Sage Coll., 1957, New Paltz Art Coll., 1958, N.Am. Sch. Conservation, 1972-74, N.Y. State Police Acad., 1974, Herkimer C.C., 1977-78. Dir. Tailored Ski Instruction, 1965-79; interpretive naturalist Adirondack Naturalist Explorations, Warrensburg, N.Y., 1980-91; with Adirondack Park Agency, Newcomb, N.Y., 1991; miniature craftsman Adirondack Rustic Miniatures, Chestertown, N.Y., 1991-95; with Omni/Sagamore, Lake George, N.Y., 1992-93; Wormwood Wild Ventures/Adirondack Eco-tour Adventure Guides, Lake George, N.Y., 1994—; gadfly Pro Ski Instructors of Am., 1965-68. Author: Wilderness Option, 1979, Adirondak Frontier, 1982, Finding Sasquatch, 1982, Adirondack Naturalist, 1989. Civil rights activist, Greenwich Village, Mexico City, 1957; founder Adirondack Naturalist Fellowship, 1991, Conservatory of Naturism, 1995. Avocations: wilderness walking and canoeing, nature photography and videography. Home: Loon Lake Adirondacks Chestertown NY 12817

WORNER, LLOYD EDSON, retired college president; b. Mexico, Mo., Sept. 13, 1918; s. Lloyd Edson and Letitia (Owen) W.; m. Mary Haden, Aug. 24, 1945; children: Linda Lou, Mary Susan. Student, Washington and Lee U., 1936-38, LL.D., 1972; A.B., Colo. Coll., 1942, LL.D., 1981; postgrad., Princeton U., 1942-43; M.A., U. Mo., 1944, Ph.D., 1946, L.H.D. (hon.), 1983; L.H.D. (hon.), U. No. Colo., 1975. Instr. history Colo. Coll., 1946-47, asst. prof., 1947-50, assoc. prof., 1950-55, prof., dean coll., 1955-63, pres., 1963-81, pres. emeritus, 1981—. Trustee emeritus Fountain Valley Sch.; bd. visitors Mo. Mil. Acad. Congregationalist. Home: 1985 Mesa Rd Colorado Springs CO 80904-1812

WORNER, THERESA MARIE, physician; b. Breckenridge, Minn., Feb. 19, 1948; d. William Daniel and Elizabeth (Stelten) W.; m. Martin Herbst, Mar. 24, 1979. AB, St. Theresa Coll., 1970; MD, U. Minn., 1974. Diplomate Am. Bd. Internal Medicine. Rotating intern Kings County Hosp., Bklyn., 1974-75, resident medicine, 1975-77; fellow VA Med. Ctr., Bronx, N.Y., 1977-78; chief med. sect. Alcoholism treatment program VA Med. Ctr., Bronx, 1978-87; asst. prof. medicine Mt. Sinai Sch. Medicine, N.Y.C., 1984-87; mem. faculty Postgrad. Ctr., 1985-90; physician in charge alcoholism svcs. L.I. Coll. Hosp., Bkyn., 1987-92; assoc. prof. clin. medicine SUNY, Health Sci. Ctr., Bkyn., 1988—; dir. rsch. 32BJ Health Fund, 1992—; clin. assoc. prof. Pub. Health Cornell U. Med. Coll., 1996—; pres./founder Alcohol. Info, 1995; advisor Patient Care Mag., 1984—. Referee Hepatology, 1986, Jour. Study Alcohol, 1984—, Substance Abuse, 1992—, Alcoholism: Clinical and Exptl. Rsch., 1992—, Drug and Alcohol Dependence, 1993—, Drug Therapy, 1994—; contbr. numerous articles to profl. jours. Active Bronx Bot. Garden, Mus. Modern Art, Met. Mus. Art, Mus. Natural History, Bklyn. Mus. Art, Turtle Bay Civic Assn., Bklyn. Lyric Opera, Empire State Opera, Amato Opera. Grantee Child Welfare Adminstrn., 1991, 92, 93; recipient Physicians Recognition award AMA, 1984, 89, 91, 96, Cert. of Merit Govt. Employees Ins. Co., 1986, PACT Intern Site award, 1991, 92. Fellow ACP; mem. AAAS, Am. Med. Soc. on Alcoholism and Other Drug Dependence, Am. Soc. Internal Medicine, Am. Assn. for Study Liver Diseases (Travel award 1978), N.Y. Acad. Scis., Rsch. Soc. on Alcoholism, Internat. Soc. Biologic Rsch. in Alcoholism. Home: 322 E 50th St New York NY 10022-7902 Office: Rsch Dept 32BJ Health Fund 13th fl 101 Ave of Americas New York NY 10013

WORRELL, ALBERT CADWALLADER, forest economics educator; b. Phila., May 14, 1913; s. Pratt Bishop and Bertha May (Cadwallader) W.; m. Helen Haffner Diefendorf, July 31, 1937; children: Kathleen Worrell Weigel, Frederick Strayer, Nancy WorrellShumaker. B.S., U. Mich., 1935, M.F., 1935, Ph.D., 1953. Asso. prof. U. Ga., 1947-55; asso. prof. Yale, 1955-63, prof. forest econs., 1963-67; Edwin Weyerhaeuser Davis prof. forest policy, 1967-83, Edwin W. Davis prof. emeritus, 1983—; forest economist U.N. Econ. Commn. for Latin Am., Santiago, Chile, 1960-61; guest prof. U. Freiburg, Germany, 1970. Author: Economics of American Forestry, 1959, Principles of Forest Policy, 1970, Unpriced Values, 1979. Mem. Soc. Am. Foresters. Home: 134 Meadowbrook Dr Nacogdoches TX 75964-6568

WORRELL, ANNE EVERETTE ROWELL, newspaper publisher; b. Surry, Va., Mar. 7, 1920; d. Charles Gray and Ethel (Roache) Rowell; student Va. Intermont Coll., 1939, LittD (hon.), 1991; LittD (hon.), U. Richmond, 1965; m. Thomas Eugene Worrell, Sept. 12, 1941; 1 son, Thomas Eugene. Founding stockholder Worrell Newspapers Inc., 1949, v.p., dir., 1969-73; pres. Bristol Newspapers, Inc., Va., pubs. Bristol Herald-Courier, Bristol Va.-Tennessean, 1979—; v.p., sec. Worrell Investment Co., Charlottesville, Va. Pres., Bristol Jr. League, 1959; bd. dirs. The Corp. for Thomas Jefferson's Poplar Forest Found., Friends of Bacon's Castle, Va. Hist. Soc.; trustee Va. Intermont Coll., 1973—, Preservation Alliance Va., Assn. for the Preservation of Va. Antiquities; chmn. Centennial Campaign, 1982—; active State Rev. Bd., Bayly Mus., Friends of Bacon's Castle. Named Outstanding Alumna, 1981. Mem. DAR (Shadwell chpt.), Nat. Trust for Hist. Preservation. Clubs: Contemporary, Farmington Country. Episcopalian. Home: Seven Sunset Circle Farmington Charlottesville VA 22901 Office: Pantops PO Box 5386 Charlottesville VA 22905-5386 also: Bristol Newspapers Inc 320 Morrison Blvd Bristol VA 24201-3812

WORRELL, AUDREY MARTINY, geriatric psychiatrist; b. Phila., Aug. 12, 1935; d. Francis Aloysius and Dorothy (Rawley) Martiny; m. Richard Vernon Worrell, June 14, 1958; children: Philip Vernon, Amy Elizabeth. MD, Meharry Med. Coll., 1960. Diplomate Am. Bd. Psychiatry and Neurology. Intern Misericordia Hosp., Phila., 1960-61; resident SUNY-Buffalo Affiliated Hosp., 1961-63, Buffalo Psychiat. Ctr., 1963-64; dir. capitol region Mental Health Ctr., Hartford, Conn., 1974-77; acting regional dir. Region IV, State Dept. Mental Health, 1976-77; asst. chief psychiatry VA Med. Ctr., Newington, Conn., 1977-78, acting chief psychiatry, 1978-79, chief psychiatry, 1978-80; dir. Capitol Regional Mental Health Facilities, Hartford, Conn., 1980-87; clin. prof. psychiatry U. Conn., 1981-87; commr. State Dept. Mental Health, Hartford, 1981-86; CEO and med. dir. Vista Sandia Hosp., Albuquerque, 1986-88; dir. consultation liason Lovelace Med. Ctr., Albuquerque, 1988-89, geriatric psychiatry, 1989-93, dir. geriatric psychiatry Charter Hosp., Albuquerque, 1993—, St. Joseph Med. Sys., Albuquerque, 1994—. Contbr. articles to profl. jours. Bd. dirs. Transitional Services, Buffalo, 1973-74, ARC, Buffalo, 1973-74, Child and Family Services, Hartford, 1972-73; co-chmn. United Way/Combined Health Appeal, State of Conn., 1983, 84; active Child Welfare Inst. Adv. Bd., Hartford, 1983—, Conn. Prison Bd., Hartford, 1984-85. Recipient Leadership award Conn. Council Mental Health Ctrs., 1983; Outstanding Contbn. award to Health Services YWCA, Hartford, 1983; chmn. Gov.'s Task Force on Mental Health Policy, 1982-85; mem. Gov.'s Task Force on Homeless, 1983-85. Mem. New Eng. Mental Health Commrs. Assn., Am. Med. Women's Assn., Conn. Assn. Mental Health and Aging, Conn. Coalition for Homeless Inc., Conn. Rehab. Assn., Am. Assn. Psychiat. Adminstrs., Am. Hosp. Assn., AMA, Am. Orthopsychiat. Assn., Am. Pub. Health Assn., Assn. Mental Health Adminstrs., Hosp. and Community Psychiatry Service, Corporators of Inst. of Living of Hartford, Am. Psychiat. Assn., Conn. Psychiat. Soc., NASMHPD (sec., bd. dirs. 1982-86), Am. Coll. Psychiatrists, Am. Coll. Mental Health Adminstrs.

WORSECK, RAYMOND ADAMS, economist; b. Providence, Mar. 25, 1937; s. Wilford Howe and Florence Marie (Dillmann) W.; m. Mary Elizabeth Lottes, July 15, 1972; children: Andrew Wilford, David Edward. BS in Math., St. Louis U., 1959, MA in Econs., 1970. Registered rep. N.Y. Stock Exchange. Commodity analyst Longstreet-Abbott & Co., St. Louis, 1959-65, dir. basic rsch., 1965-67; sr. price analyst Doane Agrl. Svc., St. Louis, 1967-69; dir. commodity rsch. A.G. Edwards & Sons, Inc., St. Louis, 1969-85, mgr. econ. rsch., 1985—, chief economist, 1989—. Mem. Am. Econs. Assn., Nat. Assn. Bus. Economists (chpt. pres. 1984-85), Fin. Analysts Soc. (bd. govs. St. Louis chpt. 1994-95), St. Louis Com. on Fgn. Rels., Futures Industry Assn. (nat. pres. rsch. divsn. 1983-84), Pub. Securities Assn. (econs. adv. com.), St. Louis Soc. Fin. Analysts (bd. govs.). Avocations: history, music, cycling. Home: 331 Elm Valley Dr Saint Louis MO 63119-4574 Office: AG Edwards & Sons Inc 1 N Jefferson Ave Saint Louis MO 63103-2205

WORSHAM, BERTRAND RAY, psychiatrist; b. Atkins, Ark., Feb. 14, 1926; s. Lewis Henry and Emma Lavada (Burris) W.; m. Margaret Ann Dickson, June 4, 1947 (div. 1960); children: Eric Dickson, Vicki Gayle; m. Lynne Ellen Reynolds, Aug. 27, 1976; children: Mary Ellen Clarice, Richard Andrew (dec.). BA, U. Ark., 1951; MD, U. Ark., Little Rock, 1955. Intern Hillcrest Med. Ctr., Tulsa, 1955-56; resident in psychiatry Menninger Sch. Psychiatry, Topeka, 1956-59; pvt. practice, 1959-78; clin. instr. U. Okla. Sch. Medicine, 1965-78; coord. drug and alcohol treatment unit Washington D.C. VA Med. Ctr., 1978-84; med. dir. Norman divsn. Okla. State Vets. Ctr., 1984-89; psychiat. cons. Comty. Counselling Ctr., Oklahoma City, 1989—; cons. Oklahoma City Vets. Hosp., 1959-72, State Dept. Pub. Health, 1960-65; dir. Cmty. Mental Health Ctr., Shawnee, Okla., 1965-72; mem. staff Coyne Campbell Hosp., 1960-78, Bapt. Med. Ctr., 1960-78, Mercy Health Ctr., 1960-78, Deaconess Hosp., 1963-78, Dr.'s Gen. Hosp., 1963-78, Presbyn. Hosp., 1962-78, U. Health Sci. Ctr., 1962-78, Children's Meml. Hosp., 1968-78, Oklahoma City VA Hosp., 1960-78, Washington D.C. Va. Hosp., 1978-84, Okla. Vets. Ctr., Norman, 1984-89. Mem. Civil Disaster Com., Oklahoma City, 1966, USN League, Okla., 1972—. With USAF, 1944-46; capt. USNR, 1957-86, ret. Fellow Menninger Found., Charles F. Menninger Found.; mem. AMA, Am. Psychiat. Assn. (Okla. dist. br. 1959-78, 84—), Assn. Mil. Surgeons of U.S., Ret. Officers Assn., World Fedn. for Mental Health, Internat. Platform Assn., Washington Psychiat. Assn., No. Va. Mental Health Assn., Masons (32 degree). Republican. Episcopalian. Avocations: golf, church activities. Home: 9915 N Kelley Ave Oklahoma City OK 73131-2022 Office: Comty Counseling Ctr 1140 N Hudson Ave Oklahoma City OK 73103-3918 *Man's ability to do goal-directed work is his greatest asset. And as results add together he more nearly approaches an infinitely profound civilization.*

WORSLEY, JAMES RANDOLPH, JR., lawyer; b. Rocky Mount, N.C., July 28, 1924; s. James Randolph and Helen Marie (Killian) W.; m. Cornelia Cheston, Feb. 11, 1956; children: Cornelia Worsley Newell, Julia Worsley Neilson, Charlotte Cheston Worsley. BS, E. Carolina U., 1944; postgrad., Harvard U., 1944-45, LLB, 1949. Bar: N.C. 1949, D.C. 1949. Assoc. Klagsbrunn, Hanes & Irwin, Washington, 1949-54; ptnr. Ober, Kaler, Grimes & Shriver (and predecessor firm), Washington, 1955-94, coun., 1995—. Chmn. Md. Potomac Water Authority, 1969-71, Montgomery County (Md.) Charter Revision Commn., 1967; mem. pastoral coun. Archdiocese of Washington, 1975-78; bd. dirs. Madeira Sch., Greenway, Va., 1975-81. Fellow Am. Bar Found.; mem. Chevy Chase Club, Met. Club. Democrat. Roman Catholic. Avocations: sailing, tennis. Home: 11 Quincy St Chevy Chase MD 20815-4226 Office: Ober Kaler Grimes & Shriver 1401 H St NW Ste 500 Washington DC 20005-3324

WORTH, GARY JAMES, communications executive; b. Berkeley Township, N.J., Dec. 13, 1940; s. Melvin Raymond and Viola Vista (Landis) W. Student, Trenton State Coll., 1964, Palm Beach Jr. Coll., 1958-59. Dir. sta. relations MBS, Inc., N.Y.C., 1972; v.p. sta. relations MBS, Inc., 1972; exec. v.p. MBS, Inc., Washington, 1972-79; mem. exec. com. MBS, Inc., 1978-79; v.p. Mut. Reports, Inc., Washington, 1972-79; dir. Mut. Reports, Inc., 1972-79; v.p., dir. WCFL, Inc., Chgo., 1979, Mut. Radio N.Y., Inc., N.Y.C., 1979; pres. Robert Wold Co. Inc. and subs. Wold Communications, Inc., L.A., 1980-85, also dir.; pres., chief exec. officer, dir. WesternWorld Inc. and subs. WesternWorld TV, L.A., 1986-93, The Video Tape Co., North Hollywood, Calif., 1987—; sec. dir. WesternWorld Video Inc., L.A., 1986-87; chmn., CEO, dir. Starcom TV Svcs., Inc., 1993-96; chmn., CEO Starcom Entertainment, Inc., 1993—. Producer, dir.: USAF movie Assignment McGuire. Served to capt. USAF, 1960-66, Vietnam. Decorated Air Force Commendation medal, Armed Forces Expeditionary medal.; recipient Chief Herbert H. Almers Meml. award Bergen County (N.J.) Police Acad., 1972. Mem. Nat. Assn. Broadcasters, Nat. Assn. TV Program Execs., Nat. Informercial Mktg. Assn. Methodist.

WORTH, GEORGE JOHN, English literature educator; b. Vienna, Austria, June 11, 1929; came to U.S., 1940, naturalized, 1945; s. Adolph and Theresa (Schmerzler) W.; m. Carol Laverne Dinsdale, Mar. 17, 1951; children: Theresa Jean (Wilkinson), Paul Dinsdale. AB, U. Chgo., 1948, MA, 1951; PhD, U. Ill., 1954. Instr. English U. Ill., Urbana, 1954-55; faculty U. Kans., Lawrence, 1955—, assoc. prof., 1962-65, prof. English lit., 1965-95; prof. emeritus English, 1995—; asst. chmn. dept. U. Kans., Lawrence, 1961-62, assoc. chmn., 1962-63, acting chmn., 1963-64, chmn., 1964-79. Author: James Hannay: His Life and Work, 1964, William Harrison Ainsworth, 1972, Dickensian Melodrama, 1978, Thomas Hughes, 1984, Great Expectations: An Annotated Bibliography, 1986; editor: (with Harold Orel) Six Studies in Nineteenth Century English Literature and Thought, 1962, The Nineteenth Century Writer and His Audience, 1969, (with Edwin Eigner) Victorian Criticism of the Novel, 1985. Mem. AAUP, MLA, Dickens Fellowship, Internat. Assn. U. Profs. English, Dickens Soc., Midwest Victorian Studies Assn., Rsch. Soc. for Victorian Periodicals. Office: U Kans Dept English Wescoe Hall Lawrence KS 66045-2115

WORTH, IRENE, actress; b. Nebr., June 23, 1916. B.Edn., U. Calif. at Los Angeles, 1937; pupil, Elsie Fogarty, London, 1944-45. Formerly tchr. Debut as Fenella in: Escape Me Never, N.Y.C., 1942; Broadway debut as Cecily Harden in: The Two Mrs. Carrolls, 1943; London debut in The Time of Your Life, 1946; following roles, mostly on London stage, include Anabelle Jones in Love Goes to Press, 1946; Ilona Szabo in: The Play's The Thing, 1947; as Eileen Perry in: Edward my Son, 1948; as Lady Fortrose in: Home is Tomorrow, 1948; as Mary Dalton in: Native Son, 1948; title role in: Lucrece, 1948; as Olivia Raines in: Champagne for Delilah, 1949; as Celia Coplestone in: The Cocktail Party, 1949, 50; various roles with Old Vic Repertory Co., London, including Desdemona in Othello; Helena in Midsummer Night's Dream and Lady Macbeth in Macbeth; also Catherine de Vausselles in: The Other Heart, tour to S. Africa, 1952; as Portia in: The Merchant of Venice, 1953; found. mem. Shakespeare Festival Theatre, Stratford, Ont., Can., 1953; as Helena in: All's Well That Ends Well; Queen Margaret in: Richard III, London; appeared as Frances Farrar in: A Day by the Sea, 1953-54; leading role in: The Queen and the Rebels, 1955, Hotel Paradiso, 1956; as Mary Stuart, 1957, The Potting Shed, 1958; Albertine Prine in: Toys in the Attic, 1960 (Page One award); mem., Royal Shakespeare Co., 1962-64; including world tour King Lear, 1964; star: Tiny Alice, N.Y.C., 1964, Aldwych, 1970; Noel Coward trilogy Shadows of the Evening; Hilde in: A Song at Twilight; Anna-Mary in: Come into the Garden Maud (Evening Standard award); Hesione Hushabye in: Heartbreak House (Variety Club Gt. Britain award 1967); Jocasta in: Oedipus, 1968; Hedda in: Hedda Gabler, 1970; with internat. Co., Theatre Research, Paris and Iran, 1971; leading role in: Notes on a Love Affair, 1972; Mme. Arkadina in: The Seagull, 1973; Gertrude in: Hamlet; Mrs. Alving in: Ghosts, 1974; Princess Kosmonopolis in: Sweet Bird of Youth, 1975-76 (Jefferson award, Tony award); Lina in: Misalliance, 1976; Mme. Ranevskaya in: The Cherry Orchard, 1977 (Drama Desk award); Kate in: Old Times, 1977, After the Season, 1978, Happy Days, 1979, Eyewitness, 1980, Coriolanus, 1988, Lost In Yonkers, (Tony award, 1991), Valentina in The Bay at Nice-Royal Nat. Theatre, 1986, Irene Worth's Edith Wharton on tour, 1994; films include; role of Leonie in: Orders to Kill, 1958 (Brit. Film Acad. award), The Scapegoat, 1958, King Lear, 1970, Nicholas and Alexandra, 1971, Rich Kids, 1979, Eyewitness, 1981, Death Trap, 1982, Fast Forward, 1985, Lost in Yonkers, 1993, also numerous radio, TV appearances, Eng., Can., U.S., including; Stella in: The Lake; Ellida Wangel in: The Lady from the Sea (Daily Mail Nat. TV award), also Candida, Duchess of Malfi, Antigone, Prince Orestes, Variations on a Theme, The Way of the World, The Displaced Person; (with Brit. Broadcasting Co.) Coriolanus, 1984; poetry recitals, recs.; (recipient Whitbread Anglo-Am. award outstanding actress 1967). Decorated comdr. Brit. Empire (hon.). Address: Internat Creative Mgmt care Sam Cohn 40 W 57th St Fl 6 New York NY 10019-4001

WORTHAM, DEBORAH LYNNE, school system director, principal; b. Chgo., May 13, 1949; d. Leon Cabot and Bessie (Summers) Smith; m. Chester Hopes Wortham, Jan. 29, 1972; children: Shelley Sharon, Chester Hopes III. BS, U. Wis., 1972; MS, Morgan State U., 1981. Tchr., reading tchr., support tchr. Balt. City Pub. Schs., 1972-87, asst. prin., 1988-90, prin. Samuel Coleridge Taylor Sch., 1990-94, dir. efficacy, 1994—; program facilitator Balt. Schs.-Johns Hopkins U., 1987-88; dean of edn. Higher Dimensions Learning Ctr., Balt., 1985—. Author: Teaching by Signs and Wonders, 1992. Recipient Mayor's Citation for Volunteerism, Balt., 1982, Am. Best Elem. Sch. for Significant Improvement award Redbook Mag., 1993, 95; cited Administrator's Class Act, Channel II TV, Balt., 1991. Mem. ASCD, Phi Delta Kappa, Alpha Kappa Alpha. Democrat. Pentecostal. Office: Balt City Pub Schs Bd Edn 200 E North Ave Baltimore MD 21202-5910

WORTHAM, MAXINE ALLINE, early childhood education executive director; b. Jackson, Tenn., June 23, 1947; d. Wilie and Alline (Hayes) W. BS, Lane Coll., 1968; MS, Ill. State U., 1973, PhD, 1985. Adminstrv. endorsement and superintendency. Math/sci. tchr. Roosevelt & Trewyn Sch., Peoria, Ill., 1968-72; spl. edn. tchr. Lincoln Elem., Peoria, 1973-76, tchr. grade 6, 1976-78; dean of students Manual H.S., Peoria, 1978-86; adminstrv. asst. Blaine Sumner Middle Sch., Peoria, 1986-87; prin. Glen Oak Primary, Peoria, 1987-88; dir. pers. Peoria (Ill.) Pub. Schs., 1988-89, exec. dir. pers., 1989-91, exec. dir. primary schs., 1991-92; pres. bd. Ill. Assn. Sch., Coll. and Univ. Staff, 1992-93. Author: The Constitutionality of the Illinois Public Schools Finance System, 1985. Pres. bd. dirs. Tri-County Urban League, Peoria, 1983-84; fellow Edn. Policy Fellowship Program, 1985-86; mem. adv. bd. Peoria (Ill.) Pub. Libr., 1986-89, Salvation Army, Peoria, 1987-93, Ctrl. Ill. Light Co., Peoria, 1991-94; bd. mem. Peoria (Ill.) Assn. Retarded Citizen, 1994—; pres. Tri-Urban League Guild; steward Ward Chapel African Meth. Episc. Ch. Recipient Martin Luther King Jr. Leadership award Southside Pastors Assn., Peoria, 1989, Profl. award YWCA, Peoria, 1989; named Outstanding Young Women in Am., 1983. Mem. Alpha Kappa Alpha, Delta Kappa Gamma (v.p.), Phi Delta Kappa, Rotary. Methodist. Home: 6908 N Michele Ln Peoria IL 61614-2625 Office: Peoria Pub Schs 3202 N Wisconsin Ave Peoria IL 61603-1260

WORTHAM, THOMAS RICHARD, English language educator; b. Liberal, Kans., Dec. 5, 1943; s. Tom and Ruth (Cavanaugh) W. AB, Marquette U., 1965; PhD, Ind. U., 1970. From asst. prof. to assoc. prof. UCLA, 1970-82, prof., 1982—, vice-chmn. and dir. undergrad. studies, 1993—; vis. prof. Am. lit. U. Warsaw, Poland, 1976-77; sr. rsch. fellow Am. Coun. of Learned Socs., 1983-84. Editor: James Russell Lowell's The Biglow Papers: A Critical Edition, 1977, Letters of W. D. Howells, vol. 4, 1892-1901, 1983, The Early Prose Writings of William Dean Howells, 1853-1861, 1990; asst. editor Nineteenth-Century Fiction, 1971-75, mem. adv. bd., 1976-83, co-editor, 1983-86; co-editor Nineteenth-Century Literature, 1986-95, editor, 1995—. Regent's faculty fellow in the humanities U. Calif., 1971; travel grantee Nat. Endowment for the Humanities, 1985-86, 88-89; grants-in-aid of rsch. Am. Philos. Soc., 1976, 81. Mem. Modern Lan. Assn. of Am. (Norman Foerster prize com. of Am. Lit. sect. 1973, chmn. Pacific coast region, com. on manuscript holdings of Am. Lit. sect. 1972-78, mem. Hubbell prize com. of Am. Lit. sect. 1989-91), Am. Studies Assn., Ralph Waldo Emerson Soc. (bd. dirs. 1992-95). Republican. Episcopalian. Avocations: breeding and training Arabian horses. Office: U Calif Dept English 405 Hilgard Ave Los Angeles CA 90024-1301

WORTHEN, JOHN EDWARD, academic administrator; b. Carbondale, Ill., July 15, 1933; s. Dewey and Annis Burr (Williams) W.; m. Sandra Damewood, Feb. 27, 1960; children: Samantha Jane, Bradley Edward. BS in Psychology (Univ. Acad. scholar), Northwestern U., 1954; MA in Student Pers. Adminstrn., Columbia U., 1955; EdD in Adminstrn. in Higher Edn. (Coll. Entrance Exam. Bd. fellow), Harvard U., 1964; PhD (hon.), Yeungnam U., Daegu, Korea, 1986. Dean of men Am. U., 1959-61; dir. counseling and testing and asst. prof. edn., 1963-66, asst. to provost and asst. prof., 1966-68, acting provost and v.p. acad. affairs, 1968, assoc. provost for instrn., 1969, v.p. student affairs, 1970-75, v.p. student affairs and adminstrn., 1976-79; pres. Ind. U. of Pa., 1979-84, Ball State U., Muncie, Ind., 1984—; cons. to public schs. Aviator USN, 1955-59. Mem. Am. Assn. Counseling and Devel., Rotary Internat., Phi Delta Kappa, Kappa Delta Pi, Ind. C. of C., Ind. Bus. Modernization and Tech. Corp.

WORTHEY, CAROL, composer; b. Worcester, Mass., Mar. 1, 1943; d. Bernard Krieger and Edith Lilian (Cramer) Symonds; m. Eugene Worthey III, June 1969 (div. 1980); 1 child, Megan; m. Raymond Edward Korns, Sept. 21, 1980. BA in Music Composition, Columbia U., 1965; grad., Dick Grove Sch. Music., L.A., 1979; grad. filmscoring prog., UCLA, 1978; music studies with Darius Milhaud, Walter Piston, Elliot Carter, Vincent Persichetti, Grant Beglarian, Karl Korte, Otto Luening, Eddy Lawrence Manson, Dick Grove; studied, RISD, 1948-54, Columbia U., 1965. Sr. composer, arranger Celebrity Ctr. Internat. Choir, Hollywood, Calif., 1985—. Composer, arranger The Hollywood Chorale; composer ballets Athena, 1963, The Barren, 1965; composer, lyricist, librettist full-length musical The Envelope Please, 1988; composer piano works performed in France, Italy, Germany, Can., U.S. and Eng. by Mario Feninger, 1982; composer Pastorale performed in Mex., 1994, Neighborhood of the Heart, 1994, (choir) Unquenchable Light, 1993; composer film score The Special Visitor, 1992; compositions performed at Aspen Music Festival, 1963, Carnegie Hall, 1954, Dorothy Chandler Pavilion, 1986-89; appeared as singer-songwriter on L.A. Songwriter's Showcase, 1977; arranger Merv Griffin Show, 1981, The Night Before Christmas, L.A. Children's Theatre, 1988-91, Capistrano Valley Symphony, 1994, Very Old Merry Old Christmas, Dorothy Chandler Pavillion, 1994, Judge, 1994; author: Treasury of Holiday Magic, 1992, (poems) The Lonely Wanderer Comes Home, 1994; art work exhibited RISD, 1952, Folk and Craft Mus., L.A., 1975, 1st Internat. Art Exhibit Celebrity Ctr. Pavillion, 1992; cable TV show: Neighborhood of the Heart, 1995, 96. Vol. performer various childcare ctrs., old folks homes, etc.; judge Composer's Competition, Inner City Cultural Ctr., 1995. Recipient Silver Poet award World of Poetry, 1987, 2nd place winner, 1st BarComposers and Songwriters Competition for "Fanfare for Joy & Wedding March", 1990, Golden Poet award World of Poetry, 1992. Mem. Nat. Assn. Composers, USA, Broadcast Music Inc., Nat. Acad. Songwriters, Songwriters and Composers Assn., Toastmasters Internat., Film Adv. Bd. Jewish. Avocations: gourmet cooking, films, macrame, creative writing, calligraphy.

WORTHING, CAROL MARIE, minister; b. Duluth, Minn., Dec. 27, 1934; d. Truman James and Helga Maria (Bolander) W.; children: Gregory Alan Beatty, Graydon Ernest Beatty. BS, U. Minn., 1965; Master of Divinity, Northwestern Theol. Seminary, 1982; D of Ministry, Grad. Theol. Found., Notre Dame, Ind., 1988; MBA in Ch. Mgmt., Grad. Theol. Found., Donaldson, Ind., 1993. Secondary educator Ind. (Minn.) Sch. Dist., 1965-78; teaching fellow U. Minn., 1968-70; contract counselor Luth. Social Svc., Duluth, 1976-78; media cons. Luth. Media Svcs., St. Paul, 1978-80; asst. pastor Messiah Luth. Ch., Fargo, N.D., 1982-83; vice pastor Messiah Luth. Ch., Fargo, 1983-84; assoc. editor Luth. Ch. Am. Ptnrs., Phila., 1982-84; editorial assoc. Luth. Ptnrs. Evang. Luth. Ch. Am., Phila. and Mpls., 1984—; parish pastor Resurrection Luth. Ch., Pierre, S.D., 1984-89; assoc. pastor Bethlehem Luth. Ch., Cedar Falls, Iowa, 1989-90; exec. dir. Ill. Conf. Chs., Springfield, 1990-96, Tex. Conf. of Chs., 1996—; mem. pub. rels. and interpretation com. Red River Valley Synod, Fargo, 1984-86, mem. ch.

devel., Pierre, 1986-87; mem. mgmt. com. office comm. Luth. Ch. in Am., N.Y.C., Phila., 1984-88; mem. mission ptnrs. S.D. Synod, 1988, chmn. assembly resolutions com., 1988; mem. pre-assembly planning com., ecumenics com., chmn. resolutions com. N.E. Iowa Synod, 1989-90; mem. ch. and society com., 1990-96; ecumenical com., 1995-96; Luth. Ecumenical Rep. Network, 1995-96; Cen. and So. Ill. Synod,; nat. edn. cons. Am. Film Inst., Washington, 1967-70; chaplain state legis. bodies, Pierre, 1984-89. Author: Cinematics and English, 1967, Peer Counseling, 1977, Tischrede Lexegete, 1986, 88, 90, Way of the Cross, Way of Justice Walk, 1987, Introducing Collaboration as a Leadership Stance and Style in an Established Statewide Conference of Churches, 1993. Co-facilitator Parents of Retarded Children, 1985; bd. dirs. Countryside Hospice, 1985; cons. to adminstrv. bd. Mo. Shores Women's Ctr., 1986. Mem. NAFE, Nat. Assn. Ecumenical Staff (chair of site selection com. 1991-92, chair of scholarship com. 1993-94, mem. profl. devel. com. 1993-94, chair program planning com. 1996, bd. dirs. 1995-96), Pierre-Ft. Pierre Ministerium (v.p. 1986-87, pres. 1987-88). Democrat. Avocations: writing prose and poetry, concerts, theater, art, photography. Home: 3816 S Lamar Blvd #3816 Austin TX 78704 Office: Tex Conf Chs 6633 Hwy 290 E Ste 200 Austin TX 78723-1157 *Ecumenism is, I believe, about full coherence between our ecclesiology and our ethics. The Spirit of God calls the church to come together for a compassionate purpose: to respond to all who suffer, so that the world might be transformed into God's own vision of peace, justice, and love.*

WORTHINGTON, GEORGE RHODES, naval officer; b. Louisville, July 11, 1937; s. William Bowman and Elizabeth (Frost) W.; m. Sydna Anne Alexander, Mar. 28, 1981 (div. Oct. 1990); children: Rhodes Ballard, Graham Rankins, Greer Anne. BS, U.S. Naval Acad., 1961; postgrad., USMC, Quantico, Va., 1975-76, Nat. War Coll., 1978-79. Commd. ensign USN, 1961, advanced through grades to rear adm., 1989; communications officer USS Halsey Powell USN, San Diego, 1961-63, flag lt., aide comdr. cruiser-destroyer Flotilla Seven, 1963-65; exec. officer Underwater Demolition Team Eleven USN, Coronado, Calif., 1965-68; ops. officer USS Strong USN, Charleston, S.C., 1969-71; exec. officer Naval Spl. Warfare Group USN, Saigon, Vietnam, 1971-72; comdg. officer Seal Team One USN, Coronado, 1972-74; naval attache Def. Attache Office USN, Phnom Penh, Cambodia, 1974-75; comdg. officer Undersea Warfare Group One USN, Coronado, 1976-78; program sponsor Office of Chief of Naval Ops. USN, Washington, 1979-85; comdr. Naval Spl. Warfare Group One USN, Coronado, 1985-87; chief of staff Spl. Ops. Command Europe USN, Stuttgart, Fed. Republic Germany, 1987-88; dep. asst. sec. of def. (spl. ops.) Def. Dept., Washington, 1988-89; comdr. Naval Spl. Warfare Command, Coronado, 1989-92; mktg. agent, cons. PIDEAC Inc., Coronado, 1992—; cons. IFG Ltd., Vantage Systems, Inc., Burdeshaw Assoc., Inc., v.p. IBD, Inc. Decorated D.S.M., Legion of Merit (2), Def. Superior Svc. medal, Meritorious Svc. medal, Navy Combat Action ribbon. Mem. Mayflower Soc. D.C., Naval Acad. Alumni Assn., Naval Inst., (past pres.), Navy League San Diego, MILMEC, Army-Navy Club, Army-Navy Country Club. Republican. Episcopalian. Avocations: masters swimming, skiing, sport parachuting. Address: Adella Ave # 4 Coronado CA 92118

WORTHINGTON, JANET EVANS, academic director, English language educator; b. Springfield, Ill., Jan. 30, 1942; d. Orville Ray and Helen May (Tuxhorn) Evans; m. Gary H. Worthington; children: Rachael Allene, Evan Edmund, Adam Nicholas Karl. Student, Blackburn Coll., 1960-62; BA in English Lang. and Lit., U. Chgo., 1965; MA in English, U. Iowa, 1969; PhD in English Edn., Fla. State U., 1977; postgrad., W. Va. Inst. Tech., 1981-82, Rensselaer Poly. Inst., 1984. Teaching. fellow Fla. State U., Tallahassee, 1971-72, grad. assistant, 1972-73; coord. lang. arts rsch. Piedmont Schs. Project, Greer, S.C., 1973-76; English instr. Woodrow Wilson High Sch., Beckley, W.Va., 1976-77; Reading specialist, adj. instr. in English W. Va. Inst. Tech., Montgomery, W.Va., 1977-78; asst. prof. W.Va. Inst. Tech., Montgomery, 1979-82, assoc. prof., 1983-87, prof. English, 1987-88; dir. W.Va. Inst. Tech., Oak Hill, 1988-90; tech. writing program coord. Community and Tech. Coll. W.Va. Inst. Tech., Montgomery, 1983-88; dir. continuing edn. Nicholls State U., Thibodaux, La., 1990—; tech. writing cons., various bus., 1986—, Dept. of Mines, State of W.Va., 1980-81; reading cons. Dept of Mines, 1980-81, Mt. Hope (W.Va.) High Sch., 1980-81, Reading Tchrs. Study Group, Kanawha County, W.Va., 1981-83; project mgr. Dept. of Mines, State of W.Va., 1981-83, Dept. of Nat. Resources, State of W.Va., 1984-85; involved in curriculum devel. for various depts., W.Va. Inst. Tech., 1973-90, Raleigh County Schs., Beckley, W.Va., Piedmont Schs. Project, Greer, S.C., English and reading instr. Upward Bound Program, W.Va. Inst. Tech., 1980-85; adj. instr. W.Va. Coll. Grad. Studies, 1979, 81, 83. Author (with William Burns): Practical Robotics: Systems, Interfacing, and Applications, 1986, (with A.B. Somers): Candles and Mirrors: Response Guides for Teaching Novels and Plays in Grades Six through Twelve, 1984, Response Guides for Teaching Children's Books, 1979; editorial bd.: W.Va. Community Coll. Jour.; reviewer: Macmillan Pub. Co. texts, 1985; editor: Diamond Shamrock, 1985; co-producer, host (TV series): About the Author; contbr. numerous articles to profl. jours.; participated in numerous presentations. Mem. W.Va. Community Coll. Assn.; bd.dirs., Curtain Callers, 1979-89, Fayette Fine Arts Coun., 1986-87; promotions chair, W.Va. Children's Book award com., 1984-85. Mem. AAUW (recording sec. 1983-85, pres. 1985—), Assn. for Tchrs. of Tech. Writing, Nat. Assn. for Devel. Edn., Soc. for Tech. Comm. Home: 112 E Garden Dr Thibodaux LA 70301-3750 Office: Nicholls State U Continuing Edn PO Box 2011 Thibodaux LA 70310

WORTHINGTON, MELVIN LEROY, minister, writer; b. Greenville, N.C., June 17, 1937; s. Wilbur Leroy and Alma Lee (Braxton) W.; m. Anne Katherine Wilson, Sept. 12, 1959; children: Daniel Edward, Lydia Anne. Diploma, Imperial Detective Acad., Cin., 1965; B.Bibl.Edn., Columbia Bible Coll., S.C., 1959; B.Th., Luther Rice Sem., Jacksonville, Fla., 1967, B.Div., 1969, M.Th., 1970, D.Th., 1974; M.Ed., Ga. State U.-Atlanta, 1979. Ordained to ministry, Central Conf. Free Will Baptists, 1957. Pastor Union Chapel Free Will Bapt. Ch., Chocowinity, N.C., 1959-62, Palmetto Free Will Bapt. Ch., Vanceboro, N.C., 1959-62, First Free Will Bapt. Ch., Darlington, S.C., 1962-66, Wesconnett Free Will Bapt. Ch., Jacksonville, Fla., 1967; pastor First Free Will Bapt. Ch., Amory, Miss., 1967-72, Albany, Ga., 1972-79; exec. sec. Nat. Assn. Free Will Bapt., Inc., Nashville, 1979—, chmn. Sunday Sch. bd., 1975-77, asst. moderator, 1977-79, chmn. grad. study com., 1976-77; clk. S.C. State Assn. Free Will Bapt., Florence, 1966-67; asst. moderator Ga. State Assn. Free Will Bapt., Moultrie, 1973-74, moderator, 1975-79; pres. Ga. Bible Inst., Albany, 1978. Editor in chief: Contact mag., 1979—, author editorial, 1980—; contbr. articles to profl. jours. Adv. bd. Nat. Fedn. Decency, 1985; nat. bd. dirs. Christian Leaders for Responsible TV, 1986. Mem. Evang. Press Assn., Religious Conf. Mgmt. Assn. (dir. 1983, v.p. 1986, pres. 1989-92), Nashville C. of C., Future Farmers Am. (N.C. Farmer degree 1955, Am. Farmer degree 1957). Democrat. Home: 3308 Timber Trail Dr Antioch TN 37013-1011 Office: Nat Assn Free Will Bapt Inc 5233 Mount View Rd Antioch TN 37013-2306 *The basic principle which has guided, governed and guarded my life has been a burning desire to find, follow and finish the will of God.*

WORTHLEY, HAROLD FIELD, minister, educator; b. Brewer, Maine, Nov. 3, 1928; s. Herbert Morrison and Aline May (Field) W.; m. Barbara Louise Bent, June 25, 1955; children—Susan Louise Field, Laura May, David Bruce. A.B., Boston U., 1950, M.A., 1951; S.T.B., Harvard Div. Sch., 1954, S.T.M., 1956, Th.D., 1970. Ordained to ministry United Ch. of Christ, 1954. Minister Congl. chs., Maine, N.H., Mass., 1951-62; assoc. prof. religion and chaplain Wheaton Coll., Norton, Mass., 1963-77; exec. sec., archivist Congl. Christian Hist. Soc., Boston, 1971—; librarian Congl. Library, Boston, 1977—; editor Bull. of Congl. Library, 1976—, Hist. Intelligencer, 1980-86. Author: Inventory of the Records of the Particular Churches of Massachusetts, 1620-1805, 1970; contbr. articles to profl. jours. Fellow Pilgrim Soc., Congl. Christian Hist. Soc.; mem. United Ch. of Christ Hist. Council. Home: 14 Mansfield Ave Norton MA 02766-2212 Office: The Congregational Libr 14 Beacon St Boston MA 02108-3704

WORTHY, FRED LESTER, computer science educator; b. Greeley, Colo., Mar. 8, 1936; s. William and Gladys (Walburn) W.; m. Susan Worthy, June 4, 1963; children: Michael (dec.), Nina E. BS in Math., Colo. State Coll., 1959; MA in Physics, Colo. State U., 1965; cert. computer sci., Clemson U., 1978; student Computer Tchrs. Inst., Ctrl. State U., Edmond, Okla., 1989-90. Physics tchr. Littleton (Colo.) H.S., 1959-63, King H.S., Tampa, 1963-65; prof. physics Ga. So. Coll., Statesboro, 1965-66; rsch. USAF (NASA), Tullahoma, Tenn., 1966-68; prof. physics Bapt. Coll., Charleston, S.C., 1968-78; registrar, asst. dean Bapt. Coll., Charleston, 1969-70; prof. computer sci. Charleston So. U., 1978—; bus. cons. Charleston, 1981—; dir. Developed Creative Physics Labs. for H.S. as part of Self-Paced Physics, 1962-63, Established Hands-On Computer Curriculum, 1979-86, Hands-On Teaching Labs. for Computers Across the Curriculum, 1987-93; developer new physics labs. for coll. NSF, Bapt. Coll., Charleston, 1970-72. Author: Twenty-Five Self-Paced Computer Laboratories, 1986-93. Chmn., deacon Summerville (S.C.) Bapt. Ch., 1978-85; chmn. judge com. Miss Charleston-Miss America, Charleston, 1992—; mem. Miss S.C. Judges List, 1991—. Avocation: photography. Home: 104 Three Iron Dr Summerville SC 29483-2937

WORTHY, JAMES AGER, former professional basketball player; b. Gastonia, N.C., Feb. 27, 1961; m. Angela Worthy. Grad., U. N.C., 1985. Basketball player L.A. Lakers, 1982-94. Named to Sporting News All-Am. First Team, 1982; named MVP, NCAA Divsn. I Tournament, 1982, MVP, NBA playoffs, 1988, mem. All-Star team, 1986-92; mem. NCAA Divsn. I Championship Team, 1982, NBA All-Rookie Team, 1983. Mem. NBA Championship Teams, 1985, 87, 88. *

WORTHY, JAMES CARSON, management educator; b. Midland, Tex., Jan. 8, 1910; s. James Arthur and Minnie (Gressett) W.; m. Mildred Leritz, June 20, 1934; 1 dau., Joan (Mrs. Robert Wood Tullis). Student, Northwestern U., 1929-33; AB, Lake Forest Coll., 1952, LLD (hon.), 1961; LLD, Chgo. Theol. Sem., 1960; LittD (hon.), Sangamon State U., 1991. Employment mgr. Schuster & Co., Milw., 1936-38; mem. personnel staff Sears, Roebuck & Co., Chgo., 1938-50; dir. employee relations Sears, Roebuck & Co., 1950-53, asst. to chmn. bd., 1955, vice pres. pub. relations, 1956-61; v.p. Cresap, McCormick & Paget, 1962-72; prof. Sangamon State U., Springfield, Ill., 1972-78, J.L. Kellogg Grad. Sch. Mgmt. Northwestern U., Evanston, Ill., 1978—; asst. dep. adminstr. NRA, Washington, 1933-36; asst. sec. commerce, 1953-55; Industry mem. spl. panel WSB, 1952; mem. President's Com. on Govt. Contracts, 1953-55, President's Commn. on Campaign Costs, 1961-62; Mem. Ill. Bd. of Higher Edn., 1967-69. Bd. dirs. Nat. Merit Scholarship Corp., 1958-63; mem. exec. bd. Indsl. Relations Research Assn., 1952-54; pres. Sears-Roebuck Found., 1956-61; trustee Latin Sch. Chgo., 1968-72, Chgo. Theol. Sem., 1953-73; dir. Selected Am. Shares, 1961-79,Comml. Credit Co., 1975-81, Control Data Corp., 1979-87, William C. Norris Inst., 1987—; co-chmn. Ill. Citizens for Eisenhower-Nixon, 1952; v.p. United Rep. Fund of Ill., 1955-59, pres., 1959-60, exec. com., 1961-72; mem. Nat. Rep. Finance Com., 1958-60; del. Rep. Nat. Conv., 1960; pres. Republican Citizens League Ill., 1961-62. Fellow Acad. Mgmt. (Dean of Fellows 1987-90), Internat. Acad. Mgmt.; mem. Commercial Club, Univ. Club (Chgo.), Indian Hill Club (Winnetka, Ill.). Congregationalist. Home: 23 Calvin Cir Evanston IL 60201-1911 Office: Northwestern U JL Kellogg Grad Sch Mgmt Evanston IL 60201

WORTHY, K(ENNETH) MARTIN, lawyer; b. Dawson, Ga., Sept. 24, 1920; s. Kenneth Spencer and Jeffrie Pruett (Martin) W.; m. Eleanor Vreeland Blewett, Feb. 15, 1947 (dec. July 1981); children: Jeffrie Martin, William Blewett; m. Katherine Teasley Jackson, June 17, 1983. Student, The Citadel, 1937-39; B.Ph., Emory U., 1941, J.D. with honors, 1947; MBA cum laude, Harvard U., 1943. Bar: Ga. 1947, D.C. 1948. Assoc. Hopkins & Sutter (formerly Hamel & Park), Washington, 1948-51, ptnr., 1952-69, 72-90, sr. counsel, 1991—; asst. gen. counsel Treasury Dept., 1969-72; chief counsel IRS, 1969-72; dir. Beneficial Corp., 1977-96, emeritus, 1996—; mem. Nat. Coun. Organized Crime, 1970-72; cons. Justice Dept., 1972-74. Author: (with John M. Appleman) Basic Estate Planning, 1957; contbr. articles to profl. jours. Del. Montgomery County Civic Fedn., 1951-61, D.C. Area Health and Welfare Coun., 1960-61; mem. coun. Emory U. Law Sch., 1976—, chmn., 1993-95; trustee Chelsea Sch., 1981—, St. John's Coll., Annapolis, Md. and Santa Fe, 1987-93, 95—, Sherman Found., Newport Beach, Calif., 1991—; chmn. dept. fin. Episcopal Diocese, Washington, 1969-70; fellow Aspen Inst., 1982-92. Capt. AUS, 1943-46, U.S. Army, 1951-52. Recipient Army Commendation Ribbon, 1945, Treasury Exceptional Svc. award and medal, 1972, IRS Commrs. award, 1972, Disting. Alumnus award Emory U., 1992. Fellow Am. Bar Found., Am. Coll. Tax Counsel (bd. regents 1980-88, chmn. 1985-87), Atlantic Coun. (counselor); mem. ABA (coun. taxation sect. 1965-69, 72-75, chmn. 1973-74, del. Nat. Conf. Lawyers and CPAs 1981-87, ho. of dels. 1983-89, chmn. audit com. 1985-90), Fed. Bar Assn. (nat. coun. 1969-72, 77-79), Ga. Bar Assn., D.C. Bar, Am. Law Inst., Nat. Tax Assn., Am. Tax Policy Inst. (trustee 1989—), Chevy Chase Club, Met. Club, Sea Island Club, Harvard Club N.Y.C., Phi Delta Theta, Phi Delta Phi, Omicron Delta Kappa. Home: PO Box 30264 189 W Gascoigne 18th Ave Sea Island GA 31561 also: 604 Somerset House II 5610 Wisconsin Ave Chevy Chase MD 20815-4415 Office: Hopkins & Sutter 888 16th St NW Fl 7 Washington DC 20006-4103

WORTHY, PATRICIA MORRIS, municipal official, lawyer; b. Fort Benning, Ga., May 28, 1944; d. Walter and Ruby Mae (Lovett) Morris. AA, Queensborough Community Coll., 1964; BA, Bklyn. Coll., 1966; JD, Howard U., 1969. Bar: D.C. 1971. Trial atty. NLRB, Washington, 1969-71; dep. gen. counsel ACTION, Washington, 1971-74; assoc. Dolphin, Branton, Stafford & Webber, Washington, 1974-77; dep. asst. sec. for regulatory functions HUD, Washington, 1977-80; adj. prof. Howard U. Sch. Law, 1979-92; chmn. D.C. Pub. Service Commn., 1980-91, Washington Met. Area Transit Commn., 1980-91; chief of staff Office of Mayor Sharon Pratt Kelly, Washington, 1991-92; vis. prof. law Howard U., Washington, 1992—; bd. dirs. Anacostia Econ. Devel. Corp.; chmn. D.C. Jud. Nomination Commn.; mem. adv. bd. Afro-Am. Datanamics, Inc. Bd. dirs. Nat. Black Child Devel. Inst., 1975-80; chmn. Occupl. Safety and Health Bd., Washington, 1979-80; trustee WETA-TV Channel 26. Mem. ABA, Nat. Conf. Black Lawyers, Nat. Conf. Bar Examiners (multistate profl. responsibility com. 1986-89), World Peace Through Law (chairperson young lawyers sect. 1973-75). Office: Howard U Sch Law Van Ness & Connecticut Ave NW Washington DC 20001

WORTIS, AVI See AVI

WORTLEY, GEORGE CORNELIUS, government affairs consultant, investor; b. Syracuse, N.Y., Dec. 8, 1926; s. George C. and Arlene (Hirsh) W.; m. Barbara Jane Hennessy, May 13, 1950; children: George C. IV, Ann Wortley Lavin, Elizabeth Wortley Ring. B.S., Syracuse U., 1948. Newspaper pub., pres. Manlius Pub. Corp., Fayetteville, N.Y., 1950-92; pres. Nat. Editorial Found., 1968-73; mem. 97th-100th Congresses from 27th N.Y. Dist., 1981-89, mem. Banking, Fin. and Urban Affairs com., mem. Select Com. on Aging, Select Com. on Children, Youth and Family; pvt. bus. cons., investor Washington, 1989—, Sunrise Holdings, Inc., Washington, 1993—; pres. Am. Newspapers Reps., 1966-68. Pres. Hiawatha coun. Boy Scouts Am., 1972-75; mem. Nat. Commn. on Hist. Publs. and Records, 1977-80, Fayetteville Sr. Citizen Housing Commn., 1977-80; mem. allocations com. United Way of Ctrl. N.Y., 1979-81; mem. pub. rels. com. St. Camillus Health Care Ctr., 1971-78; mem. fed. legis. com. Am. Lung Assn., 1974-77; bd. dirs. Crouse-Irving Meml. Hosp. Found., 1975-87, pres. 1979-81; bd. dirs. Am. Heart Assn., N.Y., 1960-80, chmn. pub. rels. com., 1970-74, chmn. legis. com. 1977, mem. fund raising adv. com., 1974-79; trustee Cazenovia Coll., 1981-94; bd. dirs. Onondaga Hist. Assn., 1980-90; dir. Global Leadership Inst., 1987—. Served with MMR, USNR, WWII. Recipient Silver Beaver award Boy Scouts Am., 1973, Silver Antelope award, 1981. Mem. Nat. Newspaper Assn. (legis. com. 1976-80), Greater Syracuse C. of C. (dir. 1979-81), Upstate Coun. Indsl. Editors, LeMoyne Coll. Pres.'s Assocs., Syracuse U. Alumni Asn. (nat. treas. 1973-77), Chavaliers du Testabin, Cosmos Club, Century Club, Georgetown Club, Lions, KC, Kappa Sigma (pres. 1957-59). Republican. Roman Catholic. Office: 1350 I St NW Ste 200 Washington DC 20005-3305

WORTMAN, RICHARD S., historian, educator; b. N.Y.C., Mar. 24, 1938; s. Joseph R. and Ruth (Nacht) W.; m. Marlene Stein, June 14, 1960; 1 child, Leonie. B.A., Cornell U., 1958; M.A., U. Chgo., 1960, Ph.D., 1964. Instr. history U. Chgo., 1963-64, asst. prof., 1964-69, asso. prof., 1969-76, prof., 1976-77; prof. history Princeton U., 1977-88, dir. Russian studies, 1982-88; prof. history Columbia U., 1988—; trustee Nat. Council for Soviet and Eastern European Research, 1983-89; sr. fellow Harriman Inst., 1985-86. Author: The Crisis of Russian Populism, 1967, The Development of a Russian Legal Consciousness, 1976, (with Leopold Haimson and Ziva Galili) The Making of Three Russian Revolutionaries: Voices from the Menshevik Past, 1987, Scenarios of Power: Myth and Ceremony in Russian Monarchy, vol. I, 1995. Social Sci. Research Council grantee, 1975-76; Guggenheim fellow, 1981-82. Mem. Am. Assn. Advancement Slavic Studies (pres. Mid-Atlantic Slavic Conf. 1982-83), AAUP., Am. Hist. Assn. Home: 410 Riverside Dr Apt 91 New York NY 10025-7924

WORTON, RONALD GIBERT, geneticist, educator; b. Winnipeg, Man., Can., Apr. 2, 1942; s. William Keller and Winnifred Pitt (Barber) W.; m. Helen Margaret Dixon, June 4, 1966; 1 child, Scott Robert. BS with honors, U. Man., 1964, MS, 1965; PhD, U. Toronto, 1969; Doctorate honoris causa, U de Louvain, Belgium, 1991. Asst. prof. U. Toronto, 1973-80, assoc. prof., 1980-84, prof., 1985-96; dir. rsch. Ottawa (Ont., Can.) Gen. Hosp., 1996—; prof. dept. medicine U. Ottawa, 1996—; staff geneticist, Hosp. for Sick Children, Toronto, 1971-85, sr. scientist rsch. inst., 1984—, geneticist-in-chief, 1985—. Contbr. articles to profl. jours.; patentee in field. Decorated Order of Can.; recipient internat. award Gairdner Found., 1989, award of distinction Muscular Dystrophy Assn. Can., 1989, Mead Johnson award, 1991. Fellow Royal Soc. Can. (Centenary medal 1990), Can. Coll. Med. Geneticists (bd. dirs. 1980-85), Am. Soc. Human Genetics (chmn. program com. 1984-87, bd. dirs. 1988-91), Genetics Soc. Can., Can. Soc. for Cell Biology. Avocations: skiing, curling. Home: 1772 Rhodes Cres, Ottawa Ontario, Canada K1H 5T2

WORTZEL, MURRAY N., library consultant, educator; b. Bklyn., July 1, 1923; s. Alex and Anna (Weintraub) W. AB, Stanford U., 1946; MLS, Columbia U., 1963, cert., 1974. Cashier, bookstore mgr. Sch. Social Work Columbia U., NYC, 1950-63; asst. to social sci. libr. Hunter Coll., NYC, 1963-64; social sci. libr., instr. Hunter Coll., Bronx, 1964-66; reference libr. Herbert H. Lehman Coll. CUNY, Bronx, 1967-79, asst. prof., 1970-80, periodicals libr., assoc. prof., 1981-89; ret., 1989; guest lectr. Baruch Coll. CUNY, 1979; libr. U.S. Ops. CUNY/Lehman-Hiroshima Coll., 1990-91. Referee articles in social scis. for Spl. Librs. Jour., N.Y., 1970-78; contbr. articles to profl. jours. Co-planner, moderator program on The Homeless: On the Streets, in Transit and in Stats., Spl. Librs. Assn., N.Y.C., 1989; vol. Kurt Weill Found. for Music Archives, 1989—; planner, participant Spl. Libr. Assn. program on the history and future of the social sci. div.'s Health and Human Svcs. Roundtable, Pitts., 1990; pres. Leonard Eisner Meml. Com., Inc., 1992—. Faculty fellow Lehman Coll., CUNY, Bronx, 1965-66. Mem. ALA (numerous coms.), AAAS, Spl. Librs. Assn. (chmn. social sci. divsn. 1974-75, archivist 1978—, book rev. editor 1982-89, sec.-treas. 1988-90. Disting. Svc. award N.Y. chpt. 1987, Hall of Fame inductee 1989, Profl. Excellence award Edn. Divsn. 1993), Soc. Work Librs. Group (coord coun. of social work edn., paper presenter 1989, co-planner author forums 1990—), Social Welfare History Group (co-chmn.), N.Y. Acad. Sci., Sigma Xi, Kappa Delta Pi. Avocation: music of Kurt Weill. Home: 401 1st Ave Apt 11C New York NY 10010-4009

WORZEL, JOHN LAMAR, geophysicist, educator; b. West Brighton, S.I., N.Y., Feb. 21, 1919; s. Howard Henry and Marie Alma (Wilson) W.; m. Dorothy Crary, Nov. 22, 1941; children: Sandra, Howard, Richard, William P. B.S. in Engring. Physics, Lehigh U., 1940; M.A. in Geophysics (grad. resident scholar), Columbia U., 1948, Ph.D., 1949. Research assoc. Woods Hole (Mass.) Oceanographic Inst., 1940-46; geodesist Columbia U., N.Y.C., 1946-48; research assoc. Columbia U., 1948-49, instr. geology, 1949, asst. prof., 1950-52, assoc. prof., 1952-57, prof., 1957-72; asst. dir. Lamont Geol. Obs., Palisades, N.Y., 1951-64; acting dir. Lamont Geol. Obs., 1964-65, assoc. dir., 1965-72; prof., dep. dir. earth and planetary scis. div. Marine Biomed. Inst., U. Tex. Med. Br., Galveston, 1972-74; acting dir. geophys. lab. Marine Sci. Inst., 1974-75, dir. geophys. lab., 1975-79; also prof. geol. sci. dept. U. Tex. at Austin, 1972-79; adj. prof. Rice U., 1974-78; ret., 1979; Bd. dirs. Palisades Geophys. Inst., 1970—, treas., 1970-74, pres., 1974—. Bd. dirs. Rockland County council Boy Scouts Am., 1964-72. Recipient USN Meritorious Pub. Service citation Dept. of Navy, 1964; Guggenheim Found. fellow, 1963. Fellow Internat. Assn. Geodesy, Am. Geophys. Union, Geol. Soc. Am.; mem. Soc. Exploration Geophysicists (chmn. com. 1974-76, v.p. 1978-79), Pi Mu Epsilon, Tau Beta Pi. Republican. Lutheran. Research on gravity and seismic refraction and reflection at sea, sound transmission of sea water. Home: Apt A-308 8117 Blue Heron Dr E Wilmington NC 28405

WÖSSNER, MARK MATTHIAS, business executive; b. Berlin, Oct. 14, 1938; m. Anna Hvastija, Mar. 30, 1991. Dr. Ing., Tech. U., Karlsruhe, Germany, 1968. Mgmt. asst. Bertelsmann, Gütersloh, Germany, 1968; with tech. works mgmt. Bertelsmann/Mohndruck, Gütersloh, Germany, 1970, tech. dir., 1972, gen. mgr., 1974; exec. mem. Bertelsmann, Gütersloh, 1976, bd. dir., dep. chmn., 1981, pres., chief exec. officer, 1983. Office: Bertelsmann AG, Postfach 111, 33311 Güetersloh Germany

WOSZCZYK, WIESLAW RICHARD, audio engineering educator, researcher; b. Czestochowa, Poland, Jan. 9, 1951; arrived in Can., 1974; s. Waclaw Konstanty and Krystyna Maria (Malek) W.; m. Trudy Elizabeth Erickson, Dec. 28, 1978; children: Jake, Magda. MA, State Acad. Music, Warsaw, Poland, 1974; PhD, Chopin Acad., Warsaw, 1984. Rsch. asst. McGill U., Montreal, Can., 1974-75; recording engineer Basement Recording Co. Inc., N.Y.C., 1975-76; sound dir. Harry Belafonte Enterprises Inc., N.Y.C., 1977; chief engr. Big Apple Recording Studios, N.Y.C., 1976-78; asst. prof. McGill U., Montreal, 1978-84, chmn. grad. studies in sound recording, 1979—, assoc. prof., 1984-91, full prof., 1991—; tech. dir. McGill Records, Montreal, 1987—; owner, cons. Sonologic Registered, Montreal, 1988—; chmn. internat. conf. TV Sound Today and Tomorrow, 1991; vis. prof. Bang and Olufsen A/S, Denmark, 1994. Recording engr. over 50 records and films, 1975-85; prodr. over 30 compact discs, 1985—; mem. rev. bd. Jour. Audio Engring., 1992; contbr. articles to profl. jours. Recipient Grand Prix du Disque award Can. Coun. for Arts, 1978, Bd. Govs. award Audio Engring. Soc., 1991; Major Rsch. SSHRC grantee Rsch. Coun. Can., 1986, 93; Indsl. grantee Sony Classical, 1992, Bruel & Kjaer, 1991. Mem. Audio Engring. Soc. (gov., chmn. membership com., 1991—), Acoustical Soc. Am., Sigma Xi. Roman Catholic. Achievements include 3 patents on audio transducers; major rsch. on the design and application of transducers for music recording, auditory design in sound recording, multi-channel sound recording, reprodn. and audio-visual interactions. Office: McGill U Faculty Music, 555 Sherbrooke St W, Montreal, PQ Canada H3A 1E3

WOTEKI, CATHERINE ELLEN, nutritionist; b. Fort Leavenworth, Kans., Oct. 7, 1947; d. Joseph Jeremiah and Catherine (Costello) O'Connor; m. Thomas Henry Woteki, June 7, 1969. BS, Mary Washington Coll., 1969; MS, Va. Poly. Inst. and State U., 1971, PhD, 1973. Registered dietitian. Asst. prof. Drexel U., Phila., 1975-77; project dir. Congl. Office of Tech. Assessment, Washington, 1977-80; group leader USDA, Washington, 1980-83; dep. dir. Nat. Ctr. for Health Statis., Washington, 1983-90; dir. Food and Nutrition Bd., Washington, 1990-93; dep. assoc. dir. for sci. Office of Sci. and Tech. Policy, Washington, 1994—. Contbr. over 43 articles to profl. jours. Named Outstanding alumna Va. Poly. Inst. and State U., 1987; recipient Elijah White award Nat. Ctr. for Health Statis., 1987, Spl. Recognition award USPHS, 1987, Staff Achievement award Inst. of Medicine, 1991. Mem. Am. Inst. Nutrition, Am. Dietetic Assn. Coun. on Rsch., Inst. Food Technologists, Am. Pub. Health Assn. Office: Office Sci and Tech Policy 0E0B Washington DC 20500

WOTIZ, JOHN HENRY, chemist, educator; b. Ostrava, Czech Republic, Apr. 12, 1919; came to U.S., 1939, naturalized, 1944; s. Berthold B. and Bertha (Kauder) W.; m. Kathryn Erdody, Feb. 23, 1945; children: Anita, Karen, Vivian. Student, Czech Polytechnicum, Prague, 1937; B.S., Furman U., 1941; M.S., U. Richmond, 1943; Ph.D., Ohio State U., 1948. Instr. U. Pitts., 1948-50, asst. prof., 1950-54, assoc. prof., 1954-57; group leader research center Diamond Alkali Co., Painesville, Ohio, 1957-59; sr. group leader Diamond Alkali Co., 1959-62; prof., chmn. chemistry dept. Marshall U., Huntington, W.Va., 1962-67, So. Ill. U., Carbondale, 1967-68; prof. So. Ill. U., 1968-89, prof. emeritus, 1989—; Nat. Acad. Scis. vis. prof., USSR, 1969, Eastern Europe, 1972; vis. prof., lectr., East Asian and Pacific Ocean countries, 1974, Japan, 1982, Gt. Britain, Fed. Republic Germany, Norway, Sweden, Czechoslovakia, Poland, Hungary, 1987, Peoples Republic China, 1988, Can., India, 1990; past cons. Air Reduction Co., Watson Standard Co.; pres. Glenview Press, Carbondale, Ill. Editor: The Kekulé Riddle: A Challenge for Chemists and Psychologists, 1993. contbr. articles to profl. jours. Served as lt., Chem. Corps AUS, 1946-48. Recipient Univ. gold medal Vysoká Škola Báňská in Ostrava, Czech Republic, 1992. Mem. Am. Chem. Soc. (chmn. div. history of chemistry 1979-80, chmn. of So. Ill. Section, 1992, bd. dirs. Ctr. for History of Chemistry, Internat. Dexter award for outstanding contbns. to history of chemistry 1982), History of Sci. Soc., AAUP, Am. Contract Bridge League, Sigma Xi. Unitarian-Universalist. Home: 903 S Glenview Dr Carbondale IL 62901-2438

WOTMAN, STEPHEN, dentistry educator; b. N.Y.C., Aug. 5, 1931; s. Jacob Abraham and Rose (Aronson) W.; m. Joyce Ruth Greenberg (div. 1983); children: Russell (dec.), Joshua; m. Sara Dedman Rouse. Student, Franklin and Marshall Coll., 1948-51; DDS, U. Pa., 1956. Pvt. practice dentistry West Nyack, N.Y., 1959-70; rsch. asst., then instr. div. stomatology Sch. Dental and Oral Surgery, Columbia U., N.Y.C., 1962-68, asst. clin. prof. div. preventive dentistry, 1968-70, assoc. prof., 1970-81, spl. asst. to dean, 1970-74, asst. dean for adminstrn. and planning, 1974-77, coord. for dental sch. reconstruction, 1975-77, acting dir. Office of Edn. and Behavioral Scis., 1975-79; assoc. prof. dentistry in pub. health, asst. dean for acad. affairs Sch. Pub. Health, Columbia U., 1981-85, acting dean Sch. Pub. Health, acting assoc. dean faculty of medicine, 1985-86, assoc. dean. pub. health and dental and oral surgery, 1986-87; prof. community dentistry Case Western Res. U., Cleve., 1987—, dean Sch. Dentistry, 1987-88, prof. epidemiology and biostats, dir. MPH degree program, 1993—. Author: (with others) Dental Fluorosis in Diseases of the Mouth and Jaw, 1969, Diseases of the Salivary Glands, 1976, The Pennsylvania Experiment, 1985; contbr. articles to profl. jours. V.p., trustee Bd. Edn. Ramapo Cen. Sch., Spring Valley, N.Y., 1964-70; chmn. bd. trustees Rockland Country Day Sch., Congers, N.Y., 1977-79. Capt. U.S. Army, 1956-58. Recipient Meritorius Svc. award Rockland County Dental Soc., 1975; named to Pierre Fauchard Acad., 1988; grantee Nat. Inst. Dental Rsch., 1968-72, Nat. Heart and Lung Inst., NIH, 1971-75, Sch. Dental and Oral Surgery Columbia U., 1974, U. Pa., 1977, 78, Cleve. Found., 1987, 88, others. Mem. ADA, AAAS, Am. Pub. Health Assn., Ohio Dental Assn., Cleve. Dental Assn., Internat. Assn. Dental Rsch., Ohio Pub. Health Assn., Sigma Xi, Omicron Kappa Upsilon. Rsch. interest in salivary chemistry in systemic diseases such as hypertension, cystic fibrosis, also, health adminstrn. planning in acad. instns., health policy and ambulatory care. Home: 13415 Shaker Blvd Cleveland OH 44120-1548 Office: Case Western Reserve U Sch Dentistry Cleveland OH 44106-2624*

WOTRING, MELANIE JEAN See HASTINGS, MELANIE JEAN

WOTT, JOHN ARTHUR, arboretum and botanical garden executive, horticulture educator; b. Fremont, Ohio, Apr. 10, 1939; s. Arthur Otto Louis and Esther Wilhelmina (Werth) W.; children: Christopher, Timothy, Holly. BS, Ohio State U., 1961; MS, Cornell U., 1966, PhD, 1968. Mem. staff Ohio State Coop. Extension Svc., Bowling Green, 1961-64; rsch. asst. Cornel U., Ithaca, N.Y., 1964-68; prof. Purdue U., West Lafayette, Ind., 1968-81; prof. Ctr. Urban Horticulture U. Wash., Seattle, 1981—; assoc. dir. Ctr. Urban Horticulture U. Wash., Seattle, 1990-93; dir. arboreta Washington Park Arboretum, Seattle, 1993—. Contbr. numerous papers to profl. jours. Mem. Am. Soc. Horticultural Sci. (com. chmn. 1967-82), Am. Assn. Botanic Gardens and Arboreta, Internat. Plant Propagators Soc. (pres. 1984, sec.-treas. 1985—). Avocations: music, antiques. Office: Washington Park Arboretum U Wash Box 358010 Seattle WA 98195-8010

WOUK, HERMAN, writer; b. N.Y.C., May 27, 1915; s. Abraham Isaac and Esther (Levine) W.; m. Betty Sarah Brown, Dec. 9, 1945; children: Abraham Isaac (dec.), Nathaniel, Joseph. AB with gen. honors, Columbia U., 1934; LHD (hon.), Yeshiva U., 1954; LLD (hon.), Clark U., 1960; LittD (hon.), Am. Internat. Coll., 1979; PhD (hon.), Bar-Ilan U., 1990. Writer radio programs for various comedians N.Y.C., 1935; asst. writer weekly radio scripts comedian Fred Allen, 1936-41; Presdl. cons. to U.S. Treasury, 1941; vis. prof. English Yeshiva U., 1952-57; scholar-in-residence Aspen Inst. Humanistic Studies, 1973-74. Author: novels: Aurora Dawn, 1947, The City Boy, 1948, Slattery's Hurricane, 1949, The Caine Mutiny, 1951 (Pulitzer Prize award for fiction 1952), Marjorie Morningstar, 1955, Youngblood Hawke, 1962, Don't Stop the Carnival, 1965, The Winds of War, 1971, War and Remembrance, 1978, Inside, Outside, 1985 (Washingtonian Book award 1986), The Hope, 1993, The Glory, 1994; dramas: The Traitor, 1949, The Caine Mutiny Court-Martial, 1953; comedy: Nature's Way, 1957; non-fiction: This is My God, 1959; screenplays for TV serials: The Winds of War, 1983, War and Remembrance, 1986. Trustee Coll. of V.I., 1961-69; bd. dirs. Washington Nat. Symphony, 1969-71, Kennedy Ctr. Prodns., 1974-75. Exec. officer U.S.S. Southard USNR, 1942-46, PTO. Recipient Richard H. Fox prize, 1934, Columbia U. medal for Excellence, 1952, Alexander Hamilton medal, 1980, U. Calif.-Berkeley medal, 1984, Golden Plate award Am. Acad. Achievement, 1986, USN Meml. Found. 'Lone Sailor' award, 1987, Yad Vashem KaZetnik award, 1990. Mem. Naval Res. Assn., Dramatists Guild, Authors Guild, Internat. Platform Assn. (Ralph Waldo Emerson award 1981), PEN. Jewish. Clubs: Bohemian (San Francisco); Cosmos, Metropolitan (Washington); Century Assn. (N.Y.C.). Office: care BSW Literary Agy 3255 N St NW Washington DC 20007-2845

WOVSANIKER, ALAN, lawyer, educator; b. Newark, Mar. 19, 1953; s. Harold and Sally (Gooen) W.; m. Susan Orme, Aug. 23, 1987. AB, Brown U., 1974; JD, Harvard U., 1977. Bar: N.J. 1977. Law clk. to presiding judge U.S. Dist. Ct. N.J., Camden, 1977-78; ptnr. Lowenstein, Sandler, Kohl, Fisher & Boylan, Roseland, N.J., 1978—; adj. prof. Seton Hall Law Sch., 1988—, Rutgers U. Law Sch., 1989—; mem. dist. ethics com. Supreme Ct. Contbr. articles to profl. jours. Mem. exec. com. N.J. chpt. Anti-Defamation League. Mem. Essex County Bar Assn. (chmn. banking law com. 1994, trustee 1996—). Office: Lowenstein Sandler Et Al 65 Livingston Ave Roseland NJ 07068-1725

WOWCHUK, ROSANN, provincial legislator; b. Swan River, Man., Can., Aug. 15, 1945; d. Wasyl and Mary (Pilipchuk) Harapiak; m. Silvestor Wowchuk, June 5, 1965; children: Kimberlie, Pamela, Michael. Cert. in teaching, Man. Tchr.'s Coll., Winnipeg, 1964. Tchr. Cowan, Man., 1964-66; farmer with husband Winnipeg, 1965—; substitute tchr. various schs., 1966-84; polit. organizer Man. New Dem. Party, Winnipeg, 1986-90; elected mem. Man. Govt., Winnipeg, 1990—. Mcpl. councillor Local Govt. Dist. of Mountian, Swan River, 1982-90. Roman Catholic. Office: Manitoba Legislature, Legis Bldg, Winnipeg, MB Canada R3C OV8

WOYCZYNSKI, WOJBOR ANDRZEJ, mathematician, educator; b. Czestochowa, Poland, Oct. 24, 1943; came to U.S., 1970; s. Eugeniusz and Otylia Sabina (Borkiewicz) W.; m. Elizabeth W. Holbrook; children: Lauren Pike, Gregory Holbrook, Martin Wojbor. MSEE, Wroclaw (Poland) Poly., 1966; PhD in Math., Wroclaw U., 1968. Asst. prof. Inst. Math. Wroclaw U., 1968-72, assoc. prof., 1972-77; prof. dept. math. Cleve. State U., 1977-82; prof., chmn. dept. math. and stats. Case Western Res. U., Cleve., 1982-91, dir. Ctr. for Stochastic and Chaotic Processes in Sci. and Tech., 1989—; rsch. fellow Inst. Math. Polish Acad. Scis., Warsaw, 1969-76; postdoctoral fellow Carnegie-Mellon U., Pitts., 1970-72; vis. assoc. prof. Northwestern U., Evanston, Ill., 1976-77; vis. prof. Aarhus (Denmark) U., 1972, U. Paris, 1973, U. Wis., Madison, 1976, U. S.C., 1979, U. N.C., Chapel Hill, 1983-84, Gottingen (Germany) U., 1985, 91, U. NSW, Sydney, Australia, 1988, Nagoya (Japan) U., 1992, 93, 94, U. Minn., Mpls., 1994. Dep. editor in chief: Annals of the Polish Math. Soc., 1973-77; assoc. editor Chemometrics Jour., 1987-94, Probability and Math. Stats., 1988—, Annals of Applied Probability, 1989—, Stochastic Processes and Their Applications, 1993—; co-editor: Martingale Theory and Harmonic Analysis in Banach Spaces, 1982, Probability Theory and Harmonic Analysis, 1986, Nonlinear Waves and Weak Turbulence, 1993, Nonlinear Stochastic PDE's: Hydrodynamic Limit and Burgers' Turbulence, 1995, IN a Reporter's Eye: The Life of Stefan Bonach, 1996; author: (monograph) Martingales and Geometry in Banach Spaces I, 1975, part II, 1978; co-author: Random Series and Stochastic Integrals: Single and Multiple, 1992. Rsch. grantee NSF, 1970, 71, 76, 77, 81, 87—, Office of Naval Rsch., 1985-96. Fellow Inst. Math. Stats.; mem. Am. Math. Soc., Am. Statis. Assn., Polish Math. Soc. (Gt. prize 1972), Polish Inst. Arts and Scis., Racquet Club East, Rowfant Club. Roman Catholic. Avocations: tennis, music, skiing, sailing, rare books collecting. Home: 3296 Grenway Rd Cleveland OH 44122-3412 Office: Case Western Res U Dept Statistics Cleveland OH 44106

WOYTOWITZ, PETER JOHN, mechanical engineer; b. Balt., Nov. 9, 1953; s. Peter John and Anna Mae (Zink) W.; m. Cristina Guevarra, Oct. 12, 1985; children: Christopher John, Phillip Charles. BSME, U. Md., 1976; MS in Engring., Santa Clara U., 1980; degree in engring., Stanford U., 1985; PhD, Santa Clara U., 1993. Registered profl. engr. Calif. Stress engr. Boeing Comml. Airplane Co., Seattle, 1977-78; engr. rsch. & devel. Ford Aerospace and Communications Corp., Palo Alto, Calif., 1978-83; sr. engr. Anamet Labs., Inc., San Carlos, Calif., 1983-85; sr. mech. engr. Failure Analysis Assocs., Menlo Park, Calif., 1985-93; v.p., prin. engr. Engring. Mechanics Tech., San Jose, Calif., 1993—; lectr. San Jose State U., 1985-88, 93—, Santa Clara (Calif.) U., 1993—; book reviewer McGraw-Hill, 1993; jour. reviewer Mechanism & Machine Theory, 1993. Co-author: Optimization of Structural Systems, 1991. Mem. ASME (v.p. student chpt. 1975), AIAA, Am. Acad. Mechs., Pi Tau Sigma. Roman Catholic. Home: 318 Farley St Mountain View CA 94043 Office: Engring Mechanics Tech # 166 4340 Stevens Creek Blvd San Jose CA 95129

WOZNIAK, DEBRA GAIL, lawyer; b. Rockford, Ill., Oct. 3, 1954; d. Richard Michael and Evalyn Louise Wozniak. BA, U. Nebr., 1976, JD, 1979. Bar: Nebr. 1980, Iowa 1980, Ill. 1982. CPCU. Asst. legal counsel Iowa Ho. of Reps., Des Moines, 1980-81; mng. atty. Rapp & Gilliam, Des Moines, 1981; from asst. counsel to counsel and asst. dir. Alliance of Am. Insurers, Schaumburg, Ill., 1981-87; from asst. counsel to counsel StateFarm Ins. Cos., Bloomington, Ill., 1987—. Mem. Nebr. Bar Assn., Iowa Bar Assn. Avocation: antiques. Office: State Farm Ins Cos One State Farm Plz Bloomington IL 61710

WRAASE, DENNIS RICHARD, utilities company executive, accountant; b. Washington, Mar. 15, 1944; s. Richard Harold and Esther Morelle (Cowan) W.; m. Cecilia Anne Kirby, Dec. 30, 1987; children: Richard Reid, Elisabeth Kirby. BS, U. Md., 1966; MS, George Washington U., 1975. CPA, Md. Acct. Exxon Corp., Balt., 1966-70; fin. analyst Exxon Corp., Houston, 1970-74; mgr. fin. systems Potomac Electric Power Co., Washington, 1974-78, asst. comptr., 1978-81, dir. computer and gen. svcs., 1981-83, comptr., 1983-92, v.p., 1986-89, sr. v.p., 1989—; CFO, 1996—; CEO Potomac Capital Investment, 1996—. Pres. Olney Jaycees, Md., 1978; bd. dirs., v.p. Nat. Capital area Boy Scouts Am., Washington, 1987—, Better Bus. Bur., Washington Bd. Trade. With USAR, 1967-73. Mem. Am. Inst. CPAs, Fin. Execs. Inst. Democrat. Lutheran. Office: Potomac Electric Power Co 1900 Pennsylvania Ave NW Rm 800 Washington DC 20068-0001

WRAGG, ALAN, publishing executive. Pub. The Cable Guide, N.Y.C. Office: TVSM Inc 475 Fifth Ave New York NY 10017-6273*

WRANGHAM, RICHARD WALTER, anthropology educator; b. Leeds, Yorkshire, Eng., Nov. 8, 1948; came to U.S., 1980; s. Geoffrey Walter and Dorothy Joan (Boyle) W.; m. Elizabeth Alison Ross, May 31, 1980; children: Ross Geoffrey, David Wilberforce, Ian Arthur. MA in Zoology, Oxford (Eng.) U., 1970; PhD in Zoology, Cambridge (Eng.) U., 1975. Lectr. Harvard U., Cambridge, Mass., 1976-77, prof., 1989—; rsch. fellow King's Coll., Cambridge U., 1977-80; asst. prof. U. Mich., Ann Arbor, 1980-84, assoc. prof., 1984-89; sci. trustee Leakey Found., San Francisco, 1980-84; pres. Dolphins of Shark Bay Rsch. Found., Albuquerque, 1987-90, dir. Kibale Chimpanzee Project, Uganda, 1987—; trustee Digit Fund, Denver, 1990—. MacArthur Found. fellow, 1987. Home: 11 Divinity Ave Cambridge MA 02138-2019 Office: Harvard U Peabody Mus 11 Divinity Ave Cambridge MA 02138-2019

WRAY, CECIL, JR., lawyer; b. Memphis, Nov. 19, 1934; s. Thomas Cecil and Margaret (Malone) W.; m. Gilda Gates, Sept. 11, 1964; children: Christopher A., Kathleen Wray Baughman. Student, U. Va., 1952-53; BA magna cum laude, Vanderbilt U., 1956; LLB, Yale U., 1959. Bar: Tenn. 1959, N.Y. 1961, U.S. Supreme Ct. 1964. Registered counseil juridique, France, 1978-82. Law clk. to justice Tom C. Clark U.S. Supreme Ct., Washington, 1959-60; assoc. Debevoise & Plimpton, N.Y.C., 1960-67, ptnr., 1968—; resident ptnr. Debevoise & Plimpton, Paris, 1976-79. Co-author: Innovative Corporate Financing Techniques, 1986. Pres. Search & Care, Inc., N.Y.C., 1981-87, Episcopal Charities, N.Y.; vestryman St. James' Ch., N.Y.C., 1982-87, warden, 1988-94; mem. bd. trustees Fondation des Etats-Unis, Paris, 1976-79; bd. dirs. East Side Community Ctr., Inc., Hudson Highlands Music Festival. Fellow Am. Coll. Investment Counsel (trustee 1981-86, pres. 1983-84); mem. ABA, Am. Law Inst., N.Y. State Bar Assn., Assn. Bar City N.Y., Internat. Bar Assn., Union Internat. Avocats, Am. Soc. Internat. Law, Coun. Fgn. Rels., Ausable Club (St. Huberts, N.Y.), Union Club, Century Club, Order of Coif, Phi Beta Kappa. Episcopalian. Home: 47 E 88th St New York NY 10128-1152 Office: Debevoise & Plimpton 875 3rd Ave New York NY 10022-6225

WRAY, GERALDINE SMITHERMAN (JERRY WRAY), artist; b. Shreveport, La., Dec. 15, 1925; d. David Ewart and Mary Virginia (Hoss) Smitherman; m. George Downing Wray, June 24, 1947; children: Mary Virginia Hill, Deanie Galloway, George D. Wray III, Nancy Armistead. BFA with honors, Newcomb Art Sch., Tulane U., 1946. One woman shows include Don Batman Gallery, Kansas City, Mo., 1982, Gallery II, Baton Rouge, 1985, McNeese Coll., Lake Charles, La., 1987, Dragonfly Gallery, Shreveport, La., 1987, Barnwell Garden and Art Ctr., Shreveport, 1988, 95, Southdown Mus., Houma, La., 1989, La. State U., Shreveport, 1991, WTN Radio Station, Shreveport, 1993, The Cambridge Club, Shreveport, 1993, Centerary Coll., 1993, Northwestern State U., Natchitoches, La., 1995, Goddard Mus., Ardmore, Okla.,1996; Group shows include Waddell's Gallery, Shreveport, 1990, 91, Water Works Gallery, Dallas, 1990, Southwestern Watercolor Show, 1991 (D'Arches award), Masur Mus. Exhibition (honorable mention 91, 92), 1991, 92, Bossier Art Ctr., Bossier City, La., 1992, Irving Art Assn. (honorable mention), 1992, Leon Loard Gallery, Montgomery, Ala., 1993, Ward-Nasse Gallery, N.Y.C., 1993, Soc. Experimental Artists Internat. (1st. place, honorable mention), 1993, Palmer Gallery, Hot Springs, Ark., 1994, Art Expo, N.Y.C., 1996, Carson Gallery, Dallas, Billinglsey Gallery, Pensacola, Fla., Hummingbird Gallery, Ft. Worth, Tex. Art chmn. Jr. League, Shreveport, 1955-60; bd. dirs. Holiday-in-Dixie Cotillion, Shreveport, 1974-76. Mem. Nat. Watercolor Soc. (signature mem. 1994, 96), Southwestern Watercolor Soc. (signature mem. 1991), La. Watercolor Soc. (signature mem. 1990), La. Artists Inc. (elected mem.). Episcopalian. Avocation: tennis. Home: 573 Spring Lake Dr Shreveport LA 71106-4603

WRAY, GILDA GATES, foundation administrator; b. Washington, Jan. 15, 1943; d. Samuel Eugene and Philomene (Asher) Gates; m. Cecil Wray, Jr., Sept. 11, 1964; children: Christopher, Kathleen Wray Baughman. BA cum laude, Smith Coll., 1964; MA in Internat. Affairs, Columbia U., 1966. Exec. dir. Horizon Concerts, N.Y.C., 1981-87; from program officer to sr. program officer Charles Hayden Found., N.Y.C., 1987-92, v.p., 1992—, trustee, 1993—; bd. dirs. Hudson Valley Shakespeare Festival; mem. rels. com. N.Y. Regional Assn. Grantmakers, 1990-93. Trustee Brearley Sch., N.Y.C., 1979-88, Yorkville Civic Coun., N.Y.C., 1979-81; bd. mgrs. N.Y. Jr. League, 1973-76, 79-81; chmn. grants com. St. James Ch., N.Y.C., 1979-87, mem .gov. com. Babcock-Michel Fund, 1988-92; mem. adv. bd. DeKay Found., N.Y.C., 1991—; mem. gov. bd. Fgn. Policy Assn., N.Y.c., 1982-90; trustee Adirondack Mus., 1994—. Mem. Cosmopolitan Club (bd. govs. 1992-95). Episcopalian. Avocations: hiking, tennis, skiing, gardening, reading. Office: Charles Hayden Found One Bankers Trust Plz 130 Liberty St New York NY 10006-1105

WRAY, ROBERT, lawyer; s. George and Ann (Moriarty) W.; m. Lila Keogh (dec.); children: Jennifer, Edward, Hillary. BS, Loyola U., 1957; JD, U. Mich., 1960. Bar: D.C., Ill. 1960. Assoc. Hopkins & Sutter, Chgo., 1964-69; gen. counsel Agy. for Internat. Devel., 1969-71; sr. counsel TRW, Inc., 1972-73, Export-Import Bank of the U.S., 1974-79; prin. Robert Wray Assocs., 1979-86; internat. ptnr. Pierson, Ball & Dowd, 1986-87; prin. Robert Wray Assocs., 1988—; spec. counsel Graham & James, 1988—. Recipient medal of superior honor Dept. of State. Mem. ABA, Fed. Bar Assn., Am. Soc. Internat. Law, Internat. Bar Assn., Coun. for Excellence in Govt., Bretton Woods Com., Met. Club, Talbot Country Club, Annapolis Yacht Club. Office: Robert Wray Assocs 2000 M St NW Washington DC 20036-3307

WRAY, THOMAS JEFFERSON, lawyer; b. Nashville, July 17, 1949; s. William Esker and Imogene (Cushman) W.; m. Susan Elizabeth Wells, Aug. 19, 1972; children: William Clark, Caroline Kell. BA, Emory U., 1971; JD, U. Va., 1974. Bar: Tex. 1974, U.S. Dist. Ct. (so., no. and ea. dists.) Tex. 1976, U.S. Ct. Appeals (5th and 11th cirs.) 1976, U.S. Supreme Ct. 1987. Assoc. Fulbright & Jaworski, L.L.P., Houston, 1974-82; ptnr. Fulbright & Jaworski, Houston, 1982—. Mem. ABA, Houston Bar Assn., Houston Mgmt. Lawyers Forum (chmn. 1981-82), Houston Club, Briar Club, Phi Beta Kappa. Republican. Episcopalian. Home: 3662 Ella Lee Ln Houston TX 77027

WRAY, WILLIAM HURBERT, English educator; b. Callaway, Va., Feb. 23, 1940; s. William Oscar and Nana B. (Holt) W. AA in Edn., Ferrum (Va.) Coll., 1959; BS in Edn., Radford U., 1964, MS in Edn., 1974; EdD, Kensington U., 1979; BA, Georgetown U. Cert. post grad. collegiate profl. Tchr. Franklin County (Va.) Pub. Schs., Rocky Mt., Va., 1961-94; exch. tchr. U.S. Office Edn., Sweden, 1963-64; prof. of English Upper Iowa U., Fayette, 1974-84; prof. English and Psychology St. Joseph Coll., Portland, Maine, 1984-88; prof. English, Fine Arts ECPI Computer Ctr., Roanoke, Va., 1994; organist Copper Hill (Va.) Ch. of Brethern; piano tchr. Leeds Music, Inc., Roanoke, Va., 1968-74. Ordained Elder Presbyn. Ch., Callaway, Va., 1969. Nominated Va. Tchr. of Yr., Richmond, 1993. Mem. NEA, Va. Edn. Assn., Franklin County Edn. Assn., Nat. Coun. Tchrs. of English, Am. Guild Organists. Democrat. Mem. Ch. of Brethren. Avocations: coin collecting, stamp collecting, antiques, auctions, music, travel. Home: RR 1 Box 92 Callaway VA 24067-9712

WREFORD, DAVID MATHEWS, magazine editor; b. Perth, Australia, Dec. 17, 1943; emigrated to Can., 1966; s. Peter Mathews and Mary Lichfield (Edquist) W.; m. Donna Diane Campbell, Sept. 28, 1970; children—Elizabeth Mary, Catherine Anne. B.Sc. in Agr. with honours, U. Western Australia, 1966. Field editor Southam Bus. Publns. Ltd., Winnipeg, Man., Can., 1967-73; field editor Country Guide, Public Press Ltd., Milton, Ont., 1973-75; editor Country Guide, United Grain Growers Ltd., Winnipeg, 1975—. Mem. Man. Inst. Agrologists, Agrl. Inst. Can., Canadian Fedn. Farm Writers and Broadcasters. Mem. Ch. of Eng. Home: 294 Elm St, Winnipeg, MB Canada R3M 3P3 Office: United Grain Growers Ltd, PO Box 6600, Winnipeg, MB Canada R3C 3A7 also: Toronto-Dominion Centre 25th Fl, 201 Portage Ave, Winnipeg, MB Canada R3C 3A7

WREGE, JULIA BOUCHELLE, tennis professional, physical education educator; b. Charleston, W.Va., Apr. 11, 1944; d. Dallas Payne and Mary Louise (Hagan) Bouchelle; m. Douglas Ewart Wrege, July 13, 1968; children: Dallas Ewart, Shannon Bouchelle. B.S. in Physics, Ga. Inst. Tech., 1965, M.S. in Physics, 1967. Systems analyst GE Apollo Systems, Daytona Beach, Fla., 1967-68; med. scientist Space Instruments Research, Atlanta, 1968-70; head tennis profl. Riverside Tennis Club, Atlanta, 1971-72, Am. Adventures, Roswell, Ga., 1972-75, Hampton Farms Tennis Club, Marietta, Ga., 1975-79; head women's tennis coach Ga. Inst. Tech., Atlanta, Ga., 1979-86, 91-92; v.p. Sirius Software, Inc., 1988—; instr. physics So. Coll. Tech., 1990—; stadium chmn., umpire, referee USTA, Atlanta, 1977—. Author: Tournament Manual, 1977, 3d edit., 1989; co-developer software TMS Tennis Tournament, 1989. Pres. Dickerson Mid. Sch. Parent-Tchr.-Student Assn., Marietta, Ga., 1982-85. Named Umpire of Yr., Ga. Tennis Assn., 1978, So. Tennis Assn., 1978; Ga. Tennis Coach of Yr., Assn. Intercollegiate Athletics for Women-Ga. Tennis Coaches Assn., 1981, 82, 83. Mem. U.S. Profl. Tennis Assn. (pres. 1980), U.S. Tennis Assn., Intercollegiate Tennis Coaches Assn., Ga. Tennis Assn. (pres. 1976-81, 94—, v.p. 1974-76, 91-92), Atlanta Lawn Tennis Assn., Atlanta Profl. Tennis Assn., Alpha Xi Delta, Sigma Pi Sigma. Republican. Episcopalian. Home: 1366 Little Willeo Rd Marietta GA 30068-2135

WREN, HAROLD GWYN, arbitrator, lawyer, legal educator; b. Big Stone Gap, Va., May 19, 1921; s. James H. and Jessie M. (Reeve) W.; m. Beryl E. Bird, Nov. 20, 1948; children: James H., II, Geoffrey G. A.B., Columbia U., 1942, LL.B., 1948; J.S.D., Yale U., 1957. Bar: N.Y. 1948, Okla. 1956, Tex. 1959, Ky. 1983. Assoc. firm Willkie Farr & Gallagher, N.Y.C., 1948-49; assoc. prof. law U. Miss., Oxford, 1949-54; prof. law U. Okla., Norman, 1954-57, So. Meth. U., Dallas, 1957-65, Boston Coll., 1965-69; dean, prof. law Lewis and Clark Law Sch., Portland, Oreg., 1969-72, U. Richmond, Va., 1972-76; prof. law U. Louisville, 1976-81, dean, 1976-81; arbitrator Am. Arbitration Assn., 1958—, Fed. Mediation and Conciliation Service, 1958—; of counsel Voyles and Johnson, P.S.C., Louisville, 1991—. Author: Creative Estate Planning, 1970, Problems in Corporate Changes, 1958, Problems in Texas Estates, 1961, (with Gabinet and Carrad). Tax Aspects of Marital Dissolution, 1987, (with Glascock) The Of Counsel Agreement, 1991. Served to capt. USNR, 1942-80. Fulbright scholar, 1953-54. Fellow Am. Coll. Trust and Estate Counsel, Am. Coll. Tax Counsel, Am. Bar Found. (life); mem. ABA, Louisville Bar Assn., Conversation Club, Order of Coif, Phi Beta Kappa, Phi Kappa Phi. Democrat. Episcopalian. Home: 5944 Ashwood Bluff Dr Louisville KY 40207 Office: Ste 500 100 N 6th St Louisville KY 40202

WREN, ROBERT JAMES, aerospace engineering manager; b. Moline, Ill., May 12, 1935; m. Jordis Wren; children: James, Patrick, Kiley. BSCE, U. Tex., 1956; MSCE, So. Meth. U., 1962; doctoral candidate, U. Houston. Registered profl. engr. Tex. Engring. aide Ctrl. Power and Light Co., Corpus Christi, 1954; sta. clk. City of Austin (Tex.) Power Plant, 1954-55; assoc. engr., hydraulic engr. U.S. Bur. of Reclamation, Austin, 1955-57; structural test engr. Gen. Dynamics, Ft. Worth, 1957-62; sr. structural dynamics engr., mgr. vibration and acoustic test facility NASA-Manned Spacecraft Ctr., Houston, 1962-63, 63-66, head exptl. dynamics sect., 1965-70; mgr. Apollo Spacecraft 2TV-1 CSM Test Program, 1966-68, Apollo Lunar Module-2 Drop Test Program, 1968-70; mgr. structural design space sta., space base, lunar base, mars mission NASA-Manned Spacecraft Ctr., Houston, 1970-73; mgr. structural design and devel., space shuttle carrier aircraft-747 NASA Johnson Space Ctr., Houston, 1973-74, mgr. structural div. space shuttle payload systems, 1974-84; mgr. engring. directorate for space shuttle payload safety NASA-Johnson Space Ctr., Houston, 1984—, alternate chmn. space shuttle payload safety review panel, 1990—. Pres. Friendswood Little League Baseball, 1980-83; bd. dirs. Bay Area YMCA, Houston, 1982—, chmn., 1983-84. Recipient Sustained Superior Performance award NASA, Personal Letter of Commendation, George Low NASA Apollo Program, Outstanding Svc. award NASA, Group Achievement awards NASA; Paul Harris fellow Rotary. Mem. Space Ctr. Rotary (dir., treas., sec., v.p. 1979-85, pres. 1985-86, Rotary dist. 5890/govt. rep. 1986-87, area coord. 1987-89, zone leader 1988-89, gov.'s aide 1989-90, chmn. dist. assembly 1989-90, 93-94, fin. com. 1989-91, Rotary Nat. award for Space Achievement Found./co-founder, bd. dirs. 1984—), Rotary World Health Found. Plastic Surgery for Children (co-founder, bd. dirs. 1985—), Rotary Space Meml. Found. (co-founder, bd. dirs. 1986—). Methodist. Avocations: snow and water skiing, running, scuba diving, tennis, sailing. Home: PO Box 1466 Friendswood TX 77549-1466 Office: NASA Johnson Space Ctr Houston TX 77058

WRENN, JAMES JOSEPH, East Asian studies educator; b. New Haven, Conn., July 7, 1926; s. James Joseph and Mariea (Enright) W.; m. Harriet Huddleston Calhoun, July 7, 1953; children: Annemarie Wrenn-Bessmer, James Joseph, Michael Enright, Christopher David. BA, Yale U., 1953, PhD, 1964. Lectr. in Chinese Grad. Sch., Yale U., New Haven, 1961-62, Brown U., Providence, 1962-64; asst. prof. Brown U., 1964-67, assoc. prof. linguistics, 1967-73, prof., 1974-91, co-chmn. East Asian Studies, 1987-95, dir. Ctr. for Lang. Studies, 1987-90. Contbr. articles to profl. jours. Platoon sgt. USMCR, 1944-46, PTO, 1950-52, Korea. Fgn. area fellow Ford Found., Republic of China, 1958-59. Mem. AAUP, MLA, Am. Council Tchrs. Fgn. Langs., Assn. Asian Studies, Chinese Lang. Tchrs. Assn. Club: Faculty. Home: 22 Rhode Island Ave Providence RI 02906-5506 Office: Brown U Brown Sta Box 1850 Providence RI 02912

WRIGHT, ABRAHAM, English language educator, college lecturer; b. Wedgefield, S.C., June 6, 1946; s. Glen and Marion (Green) W. BA, Morris Coll., 1969; MA, Howard U., 1974. Advanced Profl. English Secondary Level, Md. English tchr. North Dist. H.S., Varnville, S.C., 1969-70, Howard County Pub. Schs. Sys., Columbia, Md., 1974—; English lectr. Prince George's C.C., Largo, Md., 1974—. Sec. The Consultation on Church Union, Princeton, N.J., 1992—; mem., bd. trustees The Intern. Coun. of Cmty. Churches, Mokena, Ill., 1986— (sec. 1991—). With U.S. Army, 1970-72, Korea. Mem. Howard County (Md.) Tchrs. Assn., 1974—, Md. State Tchrs. Assn., 1974—, NEA, 1974—. Democrat. Avocations: reading, editing, shopping for old furniture. Home: 1912-3 Rosemary Hills Dr Silver Spring

MD 20910 Office: Oakland Mills HS 9410 Kilimanjaro Rd Columbia MD 21045

WRIGHT, ALFRED GEORGE JAMES, band symphony orchestra conductor, educator; b. London, June 23, 1916; came to U.S., 1922, naturalized, 1936; s. Alfred Francis and Elizabeth (Chapman) W.; m. Bertha Marie Farmer, Aug. 6, 1938; children: Adele Marie Wright Needham, Cynthia Elaine Wright Williams; m. Gladys Violet Stone, June 28, 1953. BA, U. Miami, 1937, MEd, 1947; PhD (hon.), Troy State U., 1980. Dir. music Miami Sr. High Sch., 1938-54; prof., head dept. bands Purdue U., Lafayette, Ind., 1954-85; founder, condr. U.S. Coll. Wind Band Tours, 1971—; pres. Internat. Music Tours, Inc.; v.p., exec. sec. Music Tour Svcs., Inc.; dir. pre-race pageant Indpls. 500 Mile Automobile Race, 1957-82; mem. adv. coun. Performing Arts Abroad, 1972—; chmn. N.Am. Band Dirs. Coordinating Commn., 1974-75, Nat. H.S. Honors Band, 1975-76, 77—; jury World Music Contest, Holland, 1974, 70, 81, 85; bd. dirs. 500 Festival Assocs., 1961-81; founder, chmn. bd. dirs. Hall of Fame Disting. Band Condrs.; pres. All Am. Hall of Fame Band Found.; chmn. bd., CEO John Philip Sousa Meml. Found., 1979—. Founding condr., Purdue U. Symphony Orch., 1971-81; Author: The Show Band, 1957, Marching Band Fundamentals, 1963, Bands of the World, 1970; marching band editor: Instrumentalist mag, 1953-81; contbr. articles to profl. mags. Mem. bd. advisors Internat. Music Festivals, 1989; bd. dirs. World Assn. Wind Bands and Ensembles Found., 1991-94. Decorated Star of the Order John Philip Sousa; recipient Disting. Svc. award Purdue U., 1993. Mem. Nat. Band Assn. (founder, pres. 1960-63, hon. life pres. 1973), Coll. Band Dirs. Nat. Assn., Am. Sch. Band Dirs. Nat. Assn., Japan Marching Band Assn. (hon. bd. dirs. 1971-77), Big Ten Band Dirs. Assn. (pres. 1977), Am. Bandmasters Found. (bd. dirs. 1987-89), Am. Bandmasters Assn. (pres. 1979-80), Nat. Acad. Wind and Percussive Arts (founder, chmn. 1961-81), Phi Mu Alpha, Kappa Kappa Psi (Disting. Svc. award 1981), Phi Beta Mu. Home and Office: 345 Overlook Dr West Lafayette IN 47906-1249

WRIGHT, ANDREW, English literature educator; b. Columbus, Ohio, June 28, 1923; s. Francis Joseph and Katharine (Timberman) W.; m. Virginia Rosemary Banks, June 27, 1952; children: Matthew Leslie Francis, Emma Stanbery. A.B., Harvard U., 1947; M.A., Ohio State U., 1948, Ph.D., 1951. Prof. English lit. U. Calif., San Diego, 1963—; chmn. dept. lit. U. Calif., 1971-74; dir. U. Calif. Study Center, U.K. and Ireland, 1980-82; vis. prof. U. Queensland, Australia, 1984, Colegio de la Frontera Norte, San Antonio del Mar, Baja, Calif., 1991-92. Author: Jane Austen's Novels: A Study In Structure, 1953, Joyce Cary: A Preface to His Novels, 1958, Henry Fielding: Mask and Feast, 1965, Blake's Job: A Commentary, 1972, Anthony Trollope: Dream and Art, 1983; Fictional Discourse and Historical Space, 1987; contbg. author numerous books, articles to profl. jours.; editorial bd. Nineteenth Century Fiction, 1964-86. Bd. dirs. Calif. Coun. Humanities, 1983-87. Guggenheim fellow, 1960, 70; Fulbright Sr. Research fellow, 1960-61. Fellow Royal Soc. Lit.; mem. MLA, Jane Austen Soc., Athenaeum (London), Trollope Soc., Santayana Soc., Phi Beta Kappa. Home: 7227 Olivetas Ave La Jolla CA 92037-5335 Office: U Calif San Diego Dept Lit La Jolla CA 92093-0410

WRIGHT, ANTONY POPE, research chemist; b. Charlottesville, Va., Apr. 28, 1943; s. David McCord and Caroline J. (Jones) W.; m. Judith A. Brown, Apr. 26, 1975; children: Christopher W., David M., Simon K., Amy E. BSc, McGill U., Montreal, Que., Can., 1963; PhD, U. Wis., 1973. Chemist Stauffer Wacker Silicones, Adrian, Mich., 1967-70; scientist Dow Corning Corp., Midland, Mich., 1973—; vis. fellow U. Durham, Eng., 1989-90. Contbr. chpt. to book. Lt. (j.g.) USNR, 1963-67. Fellow Royal Soc. Chemistry; mem. Am. Chem. Soc. Achievements include patents in fields of catalysis, organofluorine and organosilane/silicone products and synthesis; co-discovery of the Wright West Rearrangement in Organosilicon Chemistry, the telomerization of diiodochlordtrifluorethylene in organofluorine chemistry. Home: 7300 N Jefferson Rd Rhodes MI 48652-9602 Office: Dow Corning Corp PO Box 995 Midland MI 48686

WRIGHT, BARBARA EVELYN, microbiologist; b. Pasadena, Calif., Apr. 6, 1926; d. Gilbert Munger Wright and Leta Luella (Brown) Deery. AB, Stanford U., 1947, MA, 1948, PhD, 1951. Biologist NIH, Bethesda, Md., 1953-61; assoc. biochemist Mass. Gen. Hosp., Boston, 1961-69; asst. prof. microbiology Harvard Med. Sch., Boston, 1966-75, assoc. prof., 1975-82; rsch. dir. Boston Biomed. Rsch. Inst., 1967-82; rsch. prof. divsn. biol. scis. U. Mont., Missoula, 1982—; dir. Stella Duncan Rsch. Inst., Missoula, 1982—; cons. Miles Lab., Elkhart, Ind., 1980-84. Author: Critical Variables in Differentiation, 1973; editor: Control Mechanisms in Respiration and Fermentation, 1963; contbr. articles to profl. jours. Grantee NIH, NSF, 1991-96. Mem. AAAS (pres. Pacific divsn. 1984-85), Am. Soc. for Microbiology (Nat. Found. for Microbiology lectr. 1970, divsnl. lectr. 1978), Am. Soc. Biol. Chemists. Avocations: board sailing, skiing, kayaking. Home: 1550 Trotting Horse Ln Missoula MT 59801-9220 Office: U Mont DBS Missoula MT 59812

WRIGHT, BETTY REN, children's book writer; b. Wakefield, Mich., June 15, 1927; d. William and Revena Evelyn (Trezise) W.; m. George Albert Frederiksen, Oct. 9, 1976. BA, Milw.-Downer Coll., 1949. With Western Pub. Co., Inc., 1949-78, mng. editor Racine Editl., 1967-78. Author numerous juv. and jr. novels, including The Doll House Murders, 1983, Christina's Ghost, 1985, The Summer of Mrs. MacGregor, 1986, A Ghost in the Window, 1987, The Pike River Phantom, 1988, Rosie and the Dance of the Dinosaurs, 1989, The Ghost of Ernie P., 1990, A Ghost in the House, 1991, The Scariest Night, 1991, The Ghosts of Mercy Manor, The Ghost of Popcorn Hill, 1993, The Ghost Witch, 1993, A Ghost Comes Calling, 1994, Out of the Dark, 1995, also numerous picture and ednl. books; contbr. fiction to mags. Recipient alumni svc. award Lawrence U. (merged with Milw.-Downer Coll.), numerous awards for books, including Mo. Mark Twain award, 1986, 96, Tex. Bluebonnet award, 1986, 88, Young Readers award Pacific N.W. Libr. Assn., 1986, Reviewer's Choice Booklist, Ala. Young Readers award, 1987, Ga. Children's Choice award, 1988, Ind. Young Hoosier Book award, 1989, Children's Choice Book/Internat. Reading Assn.-CBS, 1984, S.C. Children's Choice award, 1995, Okla. Sequoyah Children's Choice award, 1988, 95. Mem. AAUW, Allied Authors, Coun. for Wis. Authors (juv. book award 1985, 96), Phi Beta Kappa. Avocations: reading, travel. Home and Office: 611 47th Ave Kenosha WI 53144-1021

WRIGHT, BLANDIN JAMES, lawyer; b. Detroit, Nov. 29, 1947; s. Robert Thomas and Jane Ellen (Blandin) W.; m. Kay Emons Heideman, Aug. 28, 1969; children: Steven Blandin, Martha Kay. BA, U. Mich., 1969; JD, Dickinson Law Sch., 1972; LLM in Taxation, NYU., 1973; MS in Taxation with honors Am. U., 1992. Bar: Pa. 1973, Fla. 1976, U.S. Tax Ct. 1977, D.C. 1979, U.S. Supreme Ct. 1979, Va. 1984, N.Y. 1991. CPA, Tex., Va. Atty. Office Internat. Ops., Nat. Office IRS, Washington, 1973-76; tax dir. Intairdril Ltd., London, 1976-78; tax atty. Allied Chem. Corp., Houston, 1978-79; v.p., gen. counsel Assoc. Oiltools, Inc., London, 1979-82, v.p. taxes, gen. counsel J. Lauritzen (USA), Inc., Charlottesville, Va., 1982-85; sole practice, Charlottesville, 1985-88; ptnr. Richmond & Fishburne, Charlottesville, 1988-90; of counsel, 1990-91; tax counsel Mobil Oil Corp., N.Y.C., 1990, Fairfax, Va., 1990—; officer Pamaco Partnership Mgmt. Corp., Va., 1986-91, CRW Energy Corp., 1986-90, Transp. & Tourism Internat., Inc., 1986—, Hotsprings Assocs., Inc., 1989-91, MDM Hotels, Inc., 1992—, Internat. Shipping & Resorts, Inc., 1992—, United Holdings Ltd., 1993—, Cruise and Resorts Internat., Inc., 1994—; bd. dirs. Blandin J. Wright, P.C., Internat. Shipping Adv. Svcs., Inc.; bd. dirs. T.T.I. Corp. Contbr. articles to profl. jours. Coach Charlottesville Youth Soccer, Baseball and Basketball, 1984-89; coach London Youth Baseball, 1982. Mem. ABA, Fairfax County Bar Assn., Am. Arbitration Assn. (arbitrator 1985—), AICPA, Tex. Soc. CPAs, Va. Soc. CPAs, Farmington Country Club, Beta Gamma Sigma. Roman Catholic. Home: 1560 London Rd Charlottesville VA 22901-8880 Office: Queen Charlotte Sq 12010 Johns Pl Fairfax VA 22033-4646 also: 3225 Gallows Rd Ste 3a916 Fairfax VA 22031-4872

WRIGHT, BOB, editor. Office: The Copley Press Inc 350 Camino De La Reina San Diego CA 92108-3003

WRIGHT, BOB, broadcasting executive; b. Rockville Center, N.Y., Apr. 23, 1943; m. Suzanne Werner, Aug. 26, 1967; children: Kate, Christopher, Maggie. A.B. in History, Coll. Holy Cross, 1965; LL.B., U. Va., 1968. Bar: N.Y. 1968, Va. 1968, Mass. 1970, N.J. 1971. With Gen. Electric Co., 1969-70, 73-80, gen. mgr. plastics sales dept., 1978-80; law sec. to chief judge U.S. Dist. Ct., N.J., 1970-73; pres. Cox Cable Communications, Atlanta, 1980-83; exec. v.p. Cox Communications, 1980-83; v.p., gen. mgr. housewares, audio and cable TV ops. GE, 1983-84; pres., chief exec. officer GE Fin. Svcs. Inc., 1984-86, NBC, N.Y.C., 1986—. Office: NBC Inc 30 Rockefeller Plz New York NY 10112

WRIGHT, BURTON, sociologist; b. Detroit, Jan. 31, 1917; s. Burton and Hazel Marie (Thomas) W.; A.A., C.Z. Coll., 1944; B.A., U. Wash., Seattle, 1947, M.A., 1949; Ph.D., Fla. State U., 1972; m. Marie Fidelis Gallivan, Jan. 26, 1942; children: Burton III, Catherine Margaret (dec.). Enlisted U.S. Navy, 1937, commd. and advanced through grades to comdr., 1957; dir. Naval Res. Recruiting, 1960-64; ret., 1964; mem. faculty U. Wash., 1947-49, Northwestern U., summers 1956-59, George Washington U., Washington, 1954-60, Rollins Coll., Winter Park, Fla., 1966-69; cons. Ford Found., 1951, Dept. Air Force, 1955, U.S. Army Chem. Corps, 1956; prof. dept. sociology U. Central Fla., Orlando, 1972-82, prof. emeritus, 1982-89; ret., 1989; vis. prof. Troy State U., Dothan; dir. Am. Sociol. Assn. Nat. Honors Program, 1981-89. Decorated Navy Commendation medal. Fellow Am. Anthrop. Assn.; mem. Am. Sociol. Assn. (membership com. 1983-86), Soc. Psychol. Study Social Problems, AAUP, Am. Acad. Arts and Scis., Soc. Study Social Problems, So. Sociol. Soc., North Central Sociol. Soc. Roman Catholic. Club: Univ. (Winter Park). Author: (with John P. Weiss and Charles M. Unkovic) Perspective: An Introduction to Sociology, 1975; (with Vernon Fox) Criminal Justice and the Social Sciences, 1978; (with John P. Weiss) Social Problems, 1980. Home: 502 Dunleith Blvd Dothan AL 36303-2936

WRIGHT, C. T. ENUS, college administrator; b. Social Circle, Ga., Oct. 4, 1942; s. George and Carrie Mae (Enus) W.; m. Mary Stephens, Aug. 9, 1974. B.S., Fort Valley State U. (Ga.), 1964; M.A., Atlanta U., 1967; Ph.D., Boston U., 1977. Tchr., Ga. Pub. Schs., Social Circle, 1965-67; mem. faculty Morris Brown Coll., Atlanta, 1967-73, div. chmn., 1973-77; program dir., asst. provost Eastern Wash. U., Cheney, 1977-81; v.p. academic affairs Talladega Coll. (Ala.), 1981-82; pres. Cheyney U. Pa., Cheyney, 1982-85; v.p. and provost Fla. Meml. Coll., 1985-89; exec. dir. Internat. Found. and Coord. African-African Am. Summit, 1989; cons. and lectr. in field. Author: (booklet) The History of Black Historical Mythology, 1980; contbr. articles to profl. jours. Commnr., Wash. Pub. Broadcasting, Olympia, 1980-84; exec. com. Boy Scouts Am., Phila., 1982—. Human Relations scholar, 1969, Nat. Teaching fellow Boston U., 1971. Mem. Am. Assn. Colls. and Univs. (coms. 1982—), Am. Hist. Assn. (coms. 1970—), Assn. Study Afro-Am. Life & History (coms. 1965—), Nat. Assn. Equal Opportunity in Higher Edn. (coms. 1982—), NEA (coms. 1965—). Am. Baptist. Clubs: Lions (Cheyney, Wash. (v.p. 1979-81)); Tuscan; Atlanta Constitution. Office: Intl Found 5122 E Shea Blvd Ste 2098 Scottsdale AZ 85254-4687

WRIGHT, CALEB MERRILL, federal judge; b. Georgetown, Del., Oct. 7, 1908; s. William Elwood and Mary Ann (Lynch) W.; m. Katherine McAfee, Nov. 29, 1937; children: Thomas Merrill, William Elwood, Scott McAfee, Victoria. BA, Del. U.; LLB, Yale U., 1933. Bar: Del. 1933. Solo practice Georgetown, 1933-55; U.S. dist. judge Del. Dist., 1955-57, chief judge, 1957-73, sr. judge, 1973—. Mem. Del., Sussex County bar assns., Am. Judicature Soc., Am. Law Inst., Kappa Alpha. Republican. Presbyterian. Club: Wilmington. Home: Cokesbury Village C20 726 Loveville Rd Hockessin DE 19707-1515 Office: US Dist Ct 844 N King St # 34 Wilmington DE 19801-3519

WRIGHT, CAMERON HARROLD GREENE, electrical engineer; b. Quincy, Mass., Jan. 21, 1956; s. Frederick Herman Greene and Dorothy Louise (Harrold) W.; m. Robin Michele Rawlings, May 14, 1988. BSEE summa cum laude, La. Tech. U., 1983; MSEE, Purdue U., 1988; PhD, U. Tex., 1996. Registered profl. engr., Calif. Commd. 2d lt. USAF, 1983, advanced through grades to major, 1995; avionics design engr. USAF Avionics Lab., Wright-Patterson AFB, Ohio, 1983-86; divsn. chief space test range space divsn. USAF, L.A. AFB, 1988-90, dir. advanced satellite systems, 1990-91; instr. elec. engring. USAF Acad., Colorado Springs, 1991-93, asst. prof., 1996—; mem. exec. com. Nat. Aerospace and Electronics Conf., Dayton, Ohio, 1983-86. Contbr. articles to profl. jours.; reviewer profl. jours.; co-author, editor: An Introduction to Electrical Engineering, 1994. Coord. tech. career motivation Dayton Sch. Dist., 1983-86; speaker engring. careers Colorado Springs Middle Sch., 1991-93; vol. computer/network cons. Project Transitions Hospice, Austin, Tex., 1995—. Mem. IEEE (sr.), Air Force Assn. (life, dir. L.A. Young Astronaut program 1988-91, Officer of Yr. 1991), Am. Soc. for Engring. Edn. Achievements include development of unique process to detect incoming missile warheads for Strategic Defense Initiative, robotic laser system for eye surgery. Office: U Tex Austin ENS 610 Austin TX 78712

WRIGHT, CHARLES ALAN, lawyer, law educator, author; b. Phila., Sept. 3, 1927; s. Charles Adshead and Helen (McCormack) W.; m. Mary Joan Herriott, July 8, 1950 (div. Jan. 1955); 1 child, Charles Edward; m. Eleanor Custis Broyles Clarke, Dec. 17, 1955; children: Henrietta, Cecily; stepchildren: Eleanor Custis Clarke, Margot Clarke. BA, Wesleyan U., Middletown, Conn., 1947; LL.B., Yale U., 1949; LHD (hon.), Episcopal Theol. Sem. S.W., 1992. Bar: Minn. 1951, Tex. 1959. Law clk. to Hon. Charles E. Clark, U.S. Ct. Appeals (2d cir.), New Haven, 1949-50; asst. prof. law U. Minn., Mpls., 1950-53, assoc. prof., 1953-55; assoc. prof. law U. Tex., Austin, 1955-58, prof., 1958-65, McCormick prof., 1965-80, Bates prof., 1980—; Arthur Goodhart vis. prof. legal sci. Cambridge (Eng.) U., 1990-91, Hayden W. Head regents chair, 1990-91; vis. prof. U. Pa., 1959-60. Harvard U., 1964-65, Yale U., 1968-69; vis. fellow Wolfson Coll., Cambridge U., 1984; reporter study div. of juridstiction between state and fed. cts. Am. Law Inst., 1963-69; mem. adv. com. on civil rules Jud. Conf. U.S., 1961-64, standing com. on rules of practice and proc., 1964-76, 87-93; cons., counsel for Pres., 1973-74; mem. com. on infractions NCAA, 1973-83, chmn., 1978-83, chmn. adminstrv. rev. panel, 1993-94; mem. permanent com for Oliver Wendell Holmes Devise, 1975-83; mem. Commn. on Bicentennial of U.S. Constn., 1985-92. Author: Wright's Minnesota Rules, 1954, Cases on Remedies, 1955, (with C.T. McCormick and J.H. Chadbourn) Cases on Federal Courts, 9th edit., 1992, Handbook of the Law of Federal Courts, 5th edit., 1994, (with H.M. Reasoner) Procedure-The Handmaid of Justice, 1965, Federal Practice and Procedure: Criminal, 2d edit., 1982, (with A.R. Miller) Federal Practice and Procedure: Civil, 1969-73, 2d edit. (with A.R. Miller and M.K. Kane), 1983—, (with A.R. Miller and E.H. Cooper) Federal Practice and Procedure: Jurisdiction and Related Matters, 1975-82, 2d edit., 1986—, (with K.W. Graham and V.J. Gold) Federal Practice and Procedure: Evidence, 1977—; mem. editorial bd. Supreme Ct. Hist. Soc. Yearbook, 1987-93—. Trustee St. Stephen's Episc. Sch., Austin, Tex., 1962-66, St. Andrew's Episc. Sch., Austin, 1971-74, 77-80, 81-84, chmn. bd., 1973-74, 79-80; trustee Capitol Broadcasting Assn., Austin, 1966—, chmn. bd., 1969-90; trustee Austin Symphony Orch., 1966—, mem. exec. com., 1966-70, 72-83, 86—; trustee Austin Choral Union, 1984-90, Austin Lyric Opera Soc., 1986—; bd. dirs. Am. Friends of Cambridge (Eng.) U., 1994—. Hon. fellow Wolfson Coll. Cambridge U., 1986—. Mem. ABA (commn. on standards jud. adminstrn. 1970-77), AAAS, Am. Law Inst. (coun. 1969—, 2d v.p. 1987-88, 1st v.p. 1988-92, pres. 1993—), Am. Bar Found. (Rsch. award 1989), Inst. Jud. Adminstrn., Am. Judicature Soc., Philos. Soc. Tex., Am. Friends Cambridge U. (bd. dirs. 1994—), Country Club, Tarry House Club, Headliners Club, Ridge Harbor Yacht Club, Barton Creek Lakeside Club (Austin), Century Club, Yale Club (N.Y.C.), Mid Ocean Club (Bermuda). Republican. Episcopalian. Avocations: reading and reviewing mysteries, railroads, fishing, coaching Legal Eagles (intramural touch football team). Home: 5304 Western Hills Dr Austin TX 78731-4822 Office: U Tex Sch Law 727 E 26th St Austin TX 78705-3224

WRIGHT, CHARLES EDWARD, lawyer; b. Portland, Oreg., Mar. 21, 1906; s. Archibald Robert and Grace May (Springer) W.; m. Elisabeth Knowlton Strong, Oct. 28, 1937; children—Frederick Pares, Hilda Wright Rhodes, Elisabeth Wright Ritchie. A.B., Yale U., 1929, LL.B., 1932. Assoc. firm Platt, Platt, Fales, Smith & Black, Portland, 1933-37; sr. atty. Seattle regional office SEC, 1937-43; practice in Portland, 1943—; partner firm Bullivant, Wright, Johnson, Pendergrass and Hoffman, 1947-90; ptnr. Bullivant, Houser, Bailey, Pendergrass & Hoffman, 1990-94; retired, 1994. Bd. dirs. Portland Jr. Symphony; trustee, v.p. Catlin Hillside Schs. Mem. ABA, Oreg. Bar Assn., Am. Judicature Soc., Travelers Aid Soc. (dir. 1946), Portland Art Assn. (past dir.), Oreg. Yale Alumni Assn. (pres. 1961), City Club (past dir.). Home: 7226 NW Penridge Rd Portland OR 97229-6806

WRIGHT, CHARLES PENZEL, JR., English language educator; b. Pickwick Dam, Tenn., Aug. 25, 1935; s. Charles Penzel and Mary Castleman (Winter) W.; m. Holly McIntire, Apr. 6, 1969; 1 child, Luke Savin Herrick. B.A., Davidson (N.C.) Coll., 1957; M.F.A., U. Iowa, 1963; postgrad., U. Rome, 1963-64. Mem. faculty U. Calif., Irvine, 1966-83; prof. English U. Calif., 1976-83; mem. faculty U. Va., Charlottesville, 1983—; Fulbright vis. prof. N.Am. lit. U. Padua, Italy, 1968-69; disting. vis. prof. U. Degli Studi, Florence, Italy, 1992. Author: The Dream Animal, 1968, The Grave of the Right Hand, 1970, The Venice Notebook, 1971, Hard Freight, 1973, Bloodlines, 1975, Colophons, 1977, China Trace, 1977, Wright: A Profile, 1979, The Southern Cross, 1981, Country Music: Selected Early Poems, 1982, The Other Side of the River, 1984, Zone Journals, 1988, Halflife, 1988, Xionia, 1990, The World of the 10,000 Things, 1990, Chickamauga, 1995, Quarter Notes, 1995; trans.: The Storm and Other Poems (Eugenio Montale), 1978, Orphic Songs (Dino Campana), 1984. Served with AUS, 1957-61. Recipient Pen Translation Prize, 1979, Nat. Book award for poetry, 1983, citation in poetry Brandeis U. Creative Arts Awards, 1987, Merit medal Am. Acad. and Inst. Arts and Letters, 1992, Ruth Lilly Poetry prize, 1993; Fulbright scholar, 1963-65; Guggenheim fellow, 1976, Ingram Merrill fellow, 1980, 93. Mem. Fellowship of So. Writers, Am. Acad. Arts and Letters. Home: 940 Locust Ave Charlottesville VA 22901-4030 Office: English Dept Univ Va Charlottesville VA 22901

WRIGHT, CHATT GRANDISON, academic administrator; b. San Mateo, Calif., Sept. 17, 1941; s. Virgil Tandy and Louise (Jeschien) W.; children from previous marriage: Stephen Brook, Jon David, Shelley Adams; m. Janice Teply, Nov. 28, 1993. Student, U. Calif., Berkeley, 1960-62; BA in Polit. Sci., U. Calif., Davis, 1964; MA in Econs., U. Hawaii, 1968. Instr. econs. U. Hawaii, Honolulu, 1968-70; mgr. corp. planning Telecheck Internat., Inc., Honolulu, 1969-70; economist State of Hawaii, Honolulu, 1970-71; adminstr. manpower City & County of Honolulu, 1971-72; bus. adminstr., dean. Hawaii Pacific U., Honolulu, 1972-74, v.p., 1974-76, pres., 1976—; bd. dirs. Hawaii Visitors Bur. Commr. City and County of Honolulu Manpower Area Planning Commn., 1976-82; Mayor's Salary Commn. City of County of Honolulu, 1977-80; ethics commr. Honolulu City Ethics Commn., 1978-84; coun. mem. City and County of Honolulu Labor Market Adv. Coun., 1982-84; bd. dirs. Hawaii Econ. Devel. Corp., 1980-84; trustee Queen's Med. Ctr., Honolulu, 1986-92, Honolulu Armed Svcs. YMCA, 1984-86, Hawaii Maritime Ctr., 1990-92; chmn. bd. trustees Hist. Hawaii Found., 1994-95, mem., 1990—; mem. adv. bd. Cancer Rsch. Ctr. Hawaii, 1987; trustee St. Andrew's Priory Sch., 1994—; bd. member, Hawaii visitors bureau, 1995; Advisory bd. member CEE, 1996—; bd. dirs. Downtown Improvement Assn., 1988—; bd. govs. Hawaii Med. Libr., 1989-92; mem. adv. bd. Aloha coun. Boy Scouts Am., 1991—; trustee Molokai Gen. Hosp., 1991-92. With USN, 1967-80. Recipient Pioneer award Pioneer Fed. Savs. Bank, 1982. Mem. Am. Assn. Higher Edn., Assn. Governing Bds. Univs. and Colls., Japan-Am. Soc. Honolulu, Social Sci. Assn., Nat. Assn. Intercollegiate Athletics (vice chair NAIA coun. of pres. 1994, mem. NAIA coun. of pres. 1985—), Hawaii Joint Coun. Econ. Edn. (bd. dirs. 1982-88), Western Coll. Assn. (exec. com. 1989-92), Hawaii Assn. Ind. Colls. and Univs. (chmn. 1986), Hawaii C. of C., Sales and Mktg. Execs. Club Honolulu, Outrigger Canoe Club, Pacific Club (Honolulu), Plaza Club (bd. govs. 1992—), Dahu Country Club, Rotary (Paul Harris fellow 1986). Republican. Episcopalian. Avocations: hunting, fishing, reading, travel. Office: Hawaii Pacific U Office Pres 1166 Fort Street Mall Honolulu HI 96813-2708

WRIGHT, CONNIE SUE, special education educator; b. Nampa, Idaho, Aug. 26, 1943; d. Ruel Andrew and Renabel Carol (Graham) Farwell; m. Roger R. Wright, July 5, 1968; 1 child, Jodi C. BA, N.W. Nazarene Coll., 1967; MA in Spl. Edn., Boise State U., 1990. Cert. elem. tchr. grades kindergarten through 8th, cert. spl. edn. tchr. grades kindergarten through 12th, Idaho. Tchr. 3rd and 4th grades Vallivue Sch. Dist. 139, Caldwell, Idaho, 1967-69; tchr. 2nd grade Nampa Sch. Dist. 131, 1969-70; tchr. 3rd grade Caldwell Sch. Dist. 132, 1970-73; tchr. spl. edn. grades kindergarten through 3rd Hubbard Elem. Sch., Kuna (Idaho) Joint Sch. Dist. 3, 1985-92; tchr. adolescents CPC Intermountain Hosp. of Boise, 1992-93; tchr. spl. edn. Pioneer Elem. Sch., Meridian, Idaho, 1993—; mem. Internat. Edn. Conf. Between Russia and U.S., 1994. Libr. Horizon's Reading Coun., 1990-91. Named Tchr. Yr. Pioneer Elem. Sch., 1994-95. Mem. Coun. for Exceptional Children, Coun. for Learning Disabilities, Internat. Reading Assn. (Idaho coun.), Delta Kappa Gamma Soc. Internat. (Omicron chpt.). Avocations: reading, doll making, computers.

WRIGHT, DAVID BURTON, retired newspaper publishing company executive; b. Fowler, Ind., Aug. 29, 1933; s. Claude Matthew and Rose Ellen (Lavelle) W.; m. Geraldine F. Gray, May 9, 1964; children—David Andrew, Anne Kathleen. A.B., Wabash Coll., 1955. C.P.A., Ind. Audit staff George S. Olive & Co. C.P.A.s, Indpls., 1958-63, mgmt. cons., 1963-65; controller Herff Jones Co., Indpls., 1965-69, corp. controller, asst. sec., 1970-71; asst. bus. mgr. Indpls. Newspapers Inc., 1971-77, asst. sec., treas., 1975-93, bus. mgr., 1977-93, v.p., 1982-93; asst. sec., treas. Central Newspapers Inc., Indpls., 1975-79, sec., treas., 1979-89; asst. sec., treas. Muncie Newspapers Inc., Ind., 1975-93; mem. St. Francis Hosp. Adv. Bd., Indpls., 1983—. Sec. St. Francis Hosp. Adv. Bd., 1986-87, v.p., 1987-91, pres., 1991-93. Served with U.S. Army, 1956-58. Mem. Ind. Assn. CPAs, Indpls. Econ. Club, KC. Roman Catholic. Home: 6713 Forrest Commons Blvd Indianapolis IN 46227-2396

WRIGHT, DAVID L., food and beverage company executive; b. Wenatchee, Wash., Mar. 12, 1949; s. Franklin Sven and Mary Elizabeth (Collins) W.; m. Karen Sue Rice, Mar. 28, 1981; children: Kara, Erin, Jonathan, Anna Catherine. BA, U. Calif., Davis, 1971. Chief of rsch. dept. of benefit payments State of Calif., Sacramento, 1972-75; profl. staff mem. com. on agr. U.S. Ho. Reps., Washington, 1975-77; adminstrv. asst. Rep. William C. Wampler, Washington, 1977-81; spl. asst. for legis. affairs to Pres. The White House, Washington, 1981-84; dir. govt. affairs Pepsico Inc., Purchase, N.Y., 1984-87; v.p., govt. affairs Pepsico, Inc., Purchase, N.Y., 1987—; bd. dirs., exec. com. Pub. Affairs Coun., Washington, 1995—. Dir., v.p. Nat. Conf. State Legislatures Found., Denver, 1989—. Capt. USAR, 1971-79. Mem Capitol Hill Club, Redding Country Club. Republican. Office: Pepsico Inc 700 Anderson Hill Rd Purchase NY 10577-1403

WRIGHT, DEIL SPENCER, political science educator; b. Three Rivers, Mich., June 18, 1930; s. William Henry and Gertrude Louise (Buck) W.; m. Patricia Mae Jaffke, Aug. 22, 1953; children: David C., Mark W., Matthew D., Lois L. BA, U. Mich., 1952, M in Pub. Adminstrn., 1954, PhD, 1957. Asst. prof. polit. sci. Wayne State U., Detroit, 1956-59; from asst. to assoc. prof. U. Iowa, Iowa City, 1959-67; assoc. prof. U. Calif., Berkeley, 1965-66; prof. U. N.C., Chapel Hill, 1967-83, alumni disting. prof., 1983—; Carl Hatch vis. prof. U. N.Mex., Albuquerque, 1987; adj. prof. U. Okla., Norman, 1972—; lectr. USIA, Washington, various dates; cons. Office Mgmt. and Budget, Washington, 1979-80. Author: Understanding Intergovernmental Relations, 3d edit., 1988; editor: Federalism and Intergovernmental Relations, 1984; contbr. over 60 articles to various polit. sci. and pub. adminstrn. jours. Mem. dir's. adv. com. NIH, Bethesda, Md., 1970-74, N.C. Coun. on State Goals and Policies, Raleigh, 1973-77, N.C. State Internship Coun., Raleigh, 1985-93. Internat. Inst. Mgmt. research fellow, Berlin, 1977. Mem. Nat. Acad. Pub. Adminstrn., AAAS, Am. Polit. Sci. Assn., Am. Soc. Pub. Adminstrn., Midwest Polit. Sci. Assn., Policy Studies Orgn., So. Polit. Sci. Assn. (pres. 1981-82). Republican. Methodist. Lodge: Rotary (bd. dirs. Chapel Hill club 1981, 84, 90). Home: 204 Velma Rd Chapel Hill NC 27514-7641 Office: U North Carolina Dept Polit Sci Campus Box 3265 Chapel Hill NC 27599-3265

WRIGHT, DONALD CONWAY, editorial cartoonist; b. Los Angeles, Jan. 23, 1934; s. Charles C. and Sally (Olberg) W.; m. Rita Rose Blondin, Oct. 1, 1960 (dec. June 1968); m. Carolyn Ann Jay, Feb. 5, 1969. Student, Fla. pub. schs. Staff photographer, copy boy Miami News, Fla., 1952-56, graphics editor, 1958-60, polit. cartoonist, 1960-63, editorial cartoonist, 1963—; with The Palm Beach Post, West Palm Beach, Fla., 1989—; syndicated by Washington Star Syndicate, 1970, N.Y. Times Syndication Sales Service, 1976-82,

Chgo. Tribune Co. Syndicate, 1982—; prod. animated cartoons for nat. TV distbn. Newsweek Broadcasting Service, 1978, for "Sunday" Today Show, NBC, 1987, 88; lectr. Miami-Dade Community Coll., 1985. Author: Wright On!, 1971, Wright Side Up, 1981; co-author: Gang of Eight, 1985; exhibited in one-man shows at Inst. for Contemporary Art, Fla. State U., Tallahassee, 1982, Lowe Art Mus., U. Miami, Coral Gables, Fla., 1979, U. Miami Lowe Art Mus., 1968; group show, Dayton, Ohio, 1969; represented in permanent collection Syracuse U., N.Y.; created theme artwork From the Hip (Dino De Laurentiis), 1987. Bd. overseers Emerson Coll., Boston U., 1976-79; AUS 1956-58. Recipient Outstanding Young Man in Communications Media award Young Democrats Fla., 1965, award Nat. Cath. Press, 1965, citation Freedoms Found., Valley Forge, Pa., 1966, Pulitzer prize, 1966, 80, Sch. Bell award Fla. Edn. Assn., 1968, Grenville Clark Editorial Page Cartoon award The Stanley Found. Iowa, 1969, Scripps-Howard Edward J. Meeman Conservation award Scripps-Howard Found., 1971, 1st place award Fla. Better Newspaper Daily Contest Fla. Press Assn., 1972, 1st prize Population Inst. Cartoon Contest Awards, N.Y.C., 1975, Editorial Category award Population Inst. Cartoon Contest Awards, N.Y.C., 1975, Nat. Headliner award Press Club Atlantic City, N.J., 1980, Tom Wallace award Inter Am. Press Assn., 1983, 86, 90, Robert F. Kennedy Meml. Journalism award, Washington, 1983, 88, 1st recipient Cox Newspapers award, 1988, David Brinkley award Barry U., 1989. Mem. Overseas Press Club Am. (awards 1969, 72, 80, 82, 85, 92), Nat. Cartoonists Soc. (Reuben award 1985, 86), Soc. Profl. Journalists (award for disting. svc. in journalism 1978, 90). Democrat. Office: The Palm Beach Post 2751 S Dixie Hwy West Palm Beach FL 33405-1233

WRIGHT, DONALD EUGENE, retired librarian; b. Boulder, Colo., July 25, 1930; s. Kelley E. and Iva Bell (Winkle) W.; m. Verna Venetta Vorpahl, June 18, 1953 (dec.); children: Sara, Amy, John Kelley. A.B., U. Colo., 1952; A.M., U. Denver, 1953. Library asst. U. Colo., 1948-52, Denver Pub. Library, 1952; reference asst. Ft. Wayne (Ind.) Pub. Library, 1953, Detroit Pub. Library, 1953-56; dir. N. Platte (Nebr.) Pub. Library, 1956-58; library cons. Nebr. Pub. Library Commn., 1958-60; asst. dir. Lincoln (Nebr.) City Libraries, 1960-61; dir. project to aid small pub. libraries ALA, 1961-63, exec. sec. reference services div., 1963-64, exec. sec. trustee assn., 1963-64; chief bur. library services Conn. Dept. Edn., 1964-65; assoc. state librarian, also chief library devel. Ill. State Library, Springfield, 1965-67; librarian Evanston (Ill.) Pub. Library, 1967-92; adminstrv. librarian Niles (Ill.) Pub. Library Dist., 1992-93; ret., 1993; interim dir. OakPark (Ill.) Pub. Libr., 1995—; Chmn. Gov. Nebr. Conf. Library Trustees, 1958; co-chmn. for Ill. White House Conf. on Library and Info. Svc., 1977-78, vice chmn. nat. task force, 1985, nat. transition team, 1992. Contbr. profl. jours. Mem. Nebr. Library Assn. (bd. dirs. 1958-61, pres. elect 1961), ALA (life, pres. library adminstrn. div. 1978-79), Ill. Library Assn. (pres. 1972). Presbyterian. Clubs: Rotary; University (Evanston). Home: 1715 Chancellor St Evanston IL 60201-1513

WRIGHT, DONALD FRANKLIN, newspaper executive; b. St. Paul, July 10, 1934; s. Floyd Franklin and Helen Marie (Hansen) W.; m. Sharon Kathleen Fisher, Dec. 30, 1960; children: John, Dana, Kara, Patrick. BME, U. Minn., 1957, MBA, 1958. With Mpls. Star & Tribune Co., 1958-77, research planning dir., then ops. dir., 1971-75, exec. editor, 1975-77; exec. v.p., gen. mgr. Newsday, Inc., L.I., 1977-78, pres., chief operating officer, 1978-81; pres., chief operating officer Los Angeles Times, 1981-87; sr. v.p. Times Mirror Co., Los Angeles, 1988—. Hon. mem., former vice chmn. Claremont Grad. Sch. and Univ. Ctr.; vice chmn. L.A. Area coun. Boy Scouts Am., 1989—, past chmn., v.p. western region, past pres. area IV; bd. dirs. Assocs. Calif. Inst. Tech., U. Minn. Found.; past bd. dirs. United Way Long Island, Calif.;. Mem. Am. Newspaper Pubs. Assn. (past chmn. telecom. com. and prodn. mgmt. com.), U. Minn. Alumni Assn., City Club Bunker Hill. Presbyterian. Office: Los Angeles Times Times Mirror Co Times Mirror Sq Los Angeles CA 90053

WRIGHT, DOUGLAS TYNDALL, civil engineering educator, executive, former university administrator; b. Toronto, Oct. 4, 1927; s. George C. and Etta (Tyndall) W.;. B.A.Sc. with honors in Civil Engring, U. Toronto, 1949; M.S. in Structural Engring, U. Ill., 1952; Ph.D. in Engring, U. Cambridge, 1954; D.Eng. (hon.), Carleton U., 1967; LL.D. (hon.), Brock U., 1967, Concordia U., 1982; D.Sc. (hon.), Meml. U. Nfld., 1969; DHL (hon.), Northeastern U., 1985, U. Waterloo, 1995; D.Univ. (hon.), Strathclyde U., Glasgow, 1989; D de L'Université, Compiegne U., France, 1991; D Univ. (hon.), Université de Sherbrooke, 1992; DSc, McMaster U., 1993, Queen's U., 1993; LLD (hon.), U. Waterloo, 1995. Lectr. dept. civil engring. Queen's U., 1954-55, asst. prof., 1955-58, assoc. prof., 1958; prof. civil engring. U. Waterloo, 1958-67, chmn. dept. civil engring., 1958-63, dean engring., 1959-66; chmn. Ont. Com. on Univ. Affairs Govt. of Ont., 1967-72; chmn. Ont. Commn. Post-Secondary Edn., Toronto, 1969-72, dep. provincial sec. for social devel., 1972-79; dep. minister culture and recreation, 1979-80; pres. U. Waterloo, Ont., Ont., 1981-93; prof. engring. U. Waterloo, Ont., 1981—; vis. prof. Universidad Nacional Autónoma de Mexico, 1964, 66, Université de Sherbrooke, 1966-67; cons. engr. Netherlands and Mexican Pavilions Expo, 1967, Olympic Sports Palace, Mexico City, 1968, Ont. Place Dome and Forum, 1971; tech. advisor Toronto Skydome, 1984-92; dir. ElectroHome Ltd., Bell Can., London Life Ins. Co., London Ins. Group, Com Dev Ltd., Geometrica Inc., Visible Decisions, Inc., Meloche, Monnex, Inc., Global Med. Net Inc., Can. Inst. for Advanced rsch., RIM Ltd., London Guarantee Ins. Co.; mem. Premier's Coun. on Sci. and Tech., Ont., 1985-91, Prime Min.'s Nat. Adv. Bd. for Sci. and Tech., 1985-91; Can. rep. Coun. for Internat. Inst. Applied Sys. Analysis, Laxenburg, Austria; Prime Min.'s personal rep. to Coun. Mins. of Edn., 1990-91. Contbr. articles to profl. jours. Bd. dirs. African Students Found., Toronto, 1961-66; bd. dirs. Ont. Curriculum Inst., 1964-67; bd. govs. Stratford Shakespearian Festival, 1984-86, mem. senate, 1987. Athlone fellow, 1952-54; named Officer of Order of Can., 1991, Chevalier L'Ordre National du Mérite of France, 1992; recipient Gold medal Ont. Profl. Engrs., 1990, Can. Engrs. Gold Medal award Can. Coun. Profl. Engrs., 1992. Engineering Institute of Canada, Sir John Kennedy Medal Award, 1995. Fellow ASCE, Can. Acad. Engring., Engring. Inst. Can. (del. Engrs. Coun. Profl. Devel., N.Y.C. 1961-70); mem. Assn. Profl. Engrs. Province Ont., Internat. Assn. Bridge and Structural Engring., Internat. Assn. Shell Structures, Can. Assn. Latin Am. Studies, Am. Acad. Mechanics, Can. Inst. Internat. Affairs, Can. Inst. Pub. Adminstrn. Clubs: Royal Can. Yacht, Univ. (Toronto). Office: U Waterloo, Engring Dept, Waterloo, ON Canada N2L 3G1

WRIGHT, DOUGLASS BROWNELL, judge, lawyer; b. Hartford, Conn., May 30, 1912; s. Arthur Brownell and Sylvia (Stephens) W.; m. Jane Hamersley, Sept. 24, 1938; children: Jane C., Douglass B., Hamersley S., Elizabeth B., Arthur W. A.B., Yale U., 1933; LL.B., Hartford Coll. Law, 1937. Bar: Conn. 1937. Legal dept. Aetna Life Ins. Co., 1937-39; partner Davis, Lee, Howard & Wright, Hartford, 1939—; lectr. law U. Conn., 1946—; asst. state's atty. State of Conn., 1952-59; judge Conn. Circuit Court, 1959-65, Conn. Superior Ct., 1965—; leader orch. Judge Wright and the Four Wrongs. Author: Connecticut Law of Torts, 1956, Connecticut Legal Forms, 5 vols., 1958, Connecticut Jury Instructions, 3 vols., 1960, 76. Sec., dir. Captioned Films for the Deaf, Inc.; bd. dirs., pres. Am. Sch. for Deaf, 1942—; trustee Hartt Mus. Found., 1949—, Good Will Boys Club Hartford, 1950—; regent U. Hartford; bd. dirs. Vis. Nurse Assn., Newington Home for Crippled Children, Hartford Times Farm, Loomis Sch.; incorporator Conn. Inst. for Blind. Served as lt. USNR, 1942-45. Mem. Phi Beta Kappa, Psi Upsilon. Conglist. Clubs: University (Hartford), Hartford Golf (Hartford), Hartford Tennis (Hartford), 20th Century (Hartford); Coral Beach and Tennis (Bermuda); Hillsboro (Pompano Beach, Fla.). Home: 275 Steele Rd Apt 114A West Hartford CT 06117-2834 Office: 95 Washington St Hartford CT 06106-4406

WRIGHT, EARL JEROME, pastor, bishop; b. Altheimer, Ark., Dec. 10, 1929; s. Frank Lee and Emma Ophelia (Tillman) W.; m. Geraldine Marvel Miller, Aug. 16, 1952; children: Earl Jerome, Michael Ellis, Marvel Sheryl. Grad., William Tyndale Bible Coll., Detroit, 1953; DDiv (hon.), Trinity Hall Div. Sch., 1961. Ordained min. Ch. of God in Christ, 1953. Postal clk. U.S. Post Office, Detroit, 1952-67; pastor Miller Meml. Ch. of God in Christ, Detroit, 1963—; bishop 2d Eccles. Jurisdiction S.W. Mich., Detroit, 1985—; chair adv. com. Bd. of Bishops, 1986—; chmn. ways and means com. Gen. Assembly, 1991—; nat. sec. youth dept. United Nat. Auxs. Conv., 1970-76, nat. registrar, 1976-82. Mem. exec. bd. dirs., NAACP, Detroit, 1983-87; mem. bd. dirs. FEMA, Detroit, 1983—; vice chmn. Mayor's Clergy Com., Detroit, 1987-91. Avocations: fishing, health spa activities, bike riding, horseback riding.

WRIGHT, ELLEN FLORENCE, education consultant; b. Seattle, Aug. 29, 1939; d. Edwin Sherman and Mildred (Redfield) W.; children: Michael Stanley Tetelman, Margaret Elaine. BA in English and Speech, U. Calif., L.A., 1962; MA in Edn., Stanford U., 1965, postgrad., 1970-74. Gen. adminstrv. credential, Calif.; C.C. credential; tchg. credential grades 7-12. Prin. Piedmont (Calif.) H.S., 1978-79; dir. devel. Packard Children's Hosp., Palo Alto, Calif., 1983-85; exec. dir. Peninsula Ctr. for Blind and Visually Impaired, Palo Alto, 1987-90; dir. devel. The Nueva Sch., Hillsborough, Calif., 1990-92; owner Ellen Wright Consulting Co., Menlo Park, Calif., 1992—; mem. Calif. Post Secondary Edn. Commn., Sacramento, 1994—; mem. Western Interstate Commn. for Higher Edn., 1995—; bd. dirs. Alumni Cons. Team Stanford U. Sch. Bus.; bd. dirs. Children's Health Coun., Palo Alto, Garfield Charter Sch.; mem. Com. for Establishment of Academia Content & Performance Standards, 1996—. Mem. Lincoln Club No. Calif., Phi Delta Kappa. Republican. Avocations: sailing, skiing, writing. Office: Bldg 3 Ste 140 3000 Sandhill Rd Menlo Park CA 94025

WRIGHT, ERIN DEAN, graphic design educator; b. Denver, July 24, 1959; s. Elton Stanley and Roxene Roi (Weichel) W.; m. Lisa Dawn Womack, Nov. 25, 1983 (div. Jan. 1988); m. Elizabeth Laura Montgomery, Dec. 12, 1992. BFA, Colo. State U., 1982; MFA, U. Ariz., 1990. Tech. illustrator Woodward-Clyde Cons., Denver, 1982-88; graphic designer, illustrator Tucson, 1988-89; acting asst. prof. La. State U., Baton Rouge, 1989-90, asst. prof., 1990—; panelist Higher Edn. Art Conf., Prescott, Ariz., 1988; cochmn. Resources Pro Bono, Baton Rouge, 1994—; area coord., graphic designer La. State U., Baton Rouge, 1993—, curator Boelts/Carson exhbn., 1994. Artist, designer: (mag. cover) Graffiti, 1988, (trademarks) Comty. Fund for the Arts, 1993, The Epilepsy Assn., 1993, (poster) Boelts/Carson Exhbn., 1994; exhibited works at Soc. Illustration Sch. Comp., N.Y.C., 1989. Bd. dirs. The Epilepsy Assn., Baton Rouge, 1993—. Recipient Citation of Excellence, 7th Dist. Regional Addys, 1993, Addy award Advt. Fedn., 1993, 95; computer animation grantee Coun. on Rsch., La. State U., 1993. Mem. Art Dirs. and Designers Assn. New Orleans, Advt. Fedn. Greater Baton Rouge. Episcopalian. Avocations: mountain biking, backpacking, collecting comic books. Office: La State U 123 Design Ctr Baton Rouge LA 70803

WRIGHT, ERNEST MARSHALL, physiologist, consultant; b. Belfast, Ireland, June 8, 1940; came to U.S., 1965; BSc, U. London, 1961, DSc, 1978; PhD, U. Sheffield, Eng., 1964. Research fellow Harvard U., Boston, 1965-66; from asst. prof. to full prof. physiology UCLA Med. Sch., 1967—, chmn. dept. physiology, 1987—; cons. NIH, Bethesda, Md., 1982—, Senator Jacob K. Javits neurosci. investigator, 1985. Office: UCLA Sch Med Dept Physiology 10833 Le Conte Ave Los Angeles CA 90095-1751

WRIGHT, ETHEL, secondary education educator; b. Apr. 5, 1947; m. James A. Wright, Sept. 26, 1969; children: Cassandra, Hannibal, Omari. BS in English, Alcorn State U., Lorman, Miss., 1970; MS in Edn., Butler U., Indpls., 1975. Tchr. Simmons H.S., Arcola, Miss., 1970-71; tchr. English Indpls. Pub. Schs., 1971—; mem. textbook adoption com. Indpls. Pub. Schs., 1979, liaison for Tchrs. Ctr., mem. film preview com. Clk., Democratic Com., Indpls. Recipient ABCD award Indpls. Pub. Schs., 1985, 92; Gregg and Reed scholar Indpls. Pub. Schs. Mem. NEA, Indpls. Edn. Assn. Avocations: reading, gardening, sewing, growing houseplants, travel.

WRIGHT, EUGENE ALLEN, federal judge; b. Seattle, Feb. 23, 1913; s. Elias Allen and Mary (Bailey) W.; m. Esther Ruth Ladley, Mar. 19, 1938; children: Gerald Allen, Meredith Ann Wright Morton. AB, U. Wash., 1935, JD, 1937; LLD, U. Puget Sound, 1984. Bar: Wash. 1937. Assoc. Wright & Wright, Seattle, 1937-54; judge Superior Ct. King County, Wash., 1954-66; v.p., sr. trust officer Pacific Nat. Bank Seattle, 1966-69; judge U.S. Ct. Appeals (9th cir.), Seattle, 1969—; acting municipal judge, Seattle, 1948-52; mem. faculty Nat. Jud. Coll., 1964-72; lectr. Sch. Communications, U. Wash., 1965-66, U. Wash. Law Sch., 1952-74; lectr. appellate judges' seminars, 1973-76, Nat. Law Clks. Inst., La. State U., 1973; chmn. Wash. State Com. on Law and Justice, 1968-69; mem. com. on appellate rules Jud. Conf., 1978-85, mem. com. on courtroom photography, 1983-85, com. jud. ethics, 1984-92, com. Bicentennial of Constn., 1985-87. Author: (with others) The State Trial Judges Book, 1966; also articles; editor: Trial Judges Jour., 1963-66; contbr. articles to profl. jours. Chmn. bd. visitors U. Puget Sound Sch. Law, 1979-84; mem. bd. visitors U. Wash. Sch. Law, 1989—; bd. dirs. Met. YMCA, Seattle, 1955-72; lay reader Episc Ch. Served to lt. col. USAR, 1941-46, col. Res., ret. Decorated Bronze Star, Combat Inf. badge; recipient Army Commendation medal, Disting. Service award U.S. Jr. C. of C., 1948, Disting. Service medal Am. Legion. Fellow Am. Bar Found.; mem. ABA (coun. div. jud. adminstrn. 1971-76), Fed. Bar Assn. (Disting. Jud. Svc. award 1984), Wash. Bar Assn. (award of merit 1983), Seattle-King County Bar Assn. (Spl. Disting. Svc. award 1984), Appellate Judges Conf., Order of Coif, Wash. Athletic Club, Rainier Club, Masons (33 deg.), Shriners, Delta Upsilon (Disting. Alumni Achievement award 1989), Phi Delta Phi. Office: US Ct Appeals 9th Cir 902 US Courthouse 1010 5th Ave Seattle WA 98104-1179

WRIGHT, FRANK GARDNER, newspaper editor; b. Moline, Ill., Mar. 21, 1931; s. Paul E. and Goldie (Hicks) W.; m. Barbara Lee Griffiths, Mar. 28, 1953; children: Stephen, Jeffrey, Natalie, Gregory, Sarah. B.A., Augustana Coll., Rock Island, Ill., 1953; postgrad., U. Minn., 1953-54. Suburban reporter Mpls. Star, 1954-55; with Mpls. Tribune, 1955-82, N.D. corr., 1955-56, Mpls. City Hall reporter, 1956-58, asst. city editor, 1958-63, Minn. polit. reporter, 1963-68, Washington corr., 1968-72, Washington bur. chief, 1972-77, mng. editor, 1977-82; mng. editor/news Mpls. Star and Tribune, 1982-84, assoc. editor, 1984—; juror for Pulitzer Awards, 1983-84. Chmn. Golden Valley Human Rights Commn., 1965-67; Bd. dirs. Luth. Social Services, Washington. Recipient several Page 1 awards Twin Cities Newspaper Guild, 1950's, 60's, Worth Bingham prize Worth Bingham Meml. Fund, 1971; runnerup Raymond Clapper award for Washington correspondence, 1971; Outstanding Achievement award Augustana Alumni Assn., 1977; citation for excellence in internat. reporting Overseas Press Club, 1985; Minn. SPJ/SDX 1st Place Page One award for in-depth reporting, 1988, MWAP award Human Interest Reporting, 1995. Mem. Am. Newspaper Guild (chmn. Mpls. unit 1961-67, editorial v.p. Twin Cities 1963-67), Minn. AP Editors Assn. (pres. 1981), Phi Beta Kappa. Home: 4912 Aldrich Ave S Minneapolis MN 55409-2353 Office: 425 Portland Ave Minneapolis MN 55488-0001

WRIGHT, FRANKLIN LEATHERBURY, JR., lawyer, banker; b. Phila., Mar. 22, 1945; s. Franklin L. and Victoria M. (Douglas) W.; m. Willette C. Pedrick, June 21, 1969; children: Geoffrey, Stephen. AB, Coll. William and Mary, 1967; JD, Temple U., 1967. Bar: Pa. 1973, D.C. 1978. Atty.-advisor Fed. Home Loan Bank Bd., Washington, 1973-77; asoc. dir. Nat. Assn. Mut. Savs. Banks, Washington, 1977-83; dep. counsel, sr. v.p. Dime Savs. Bank N.Y., Garden City, 1983-85, spl. counsel, 1986—, 1st sr. v.p., 1986-90, exec. v.p., 1987-90, external affairs exec., dep. gen. counsel, 1990-95; external affairs exec., dep. gen. counsel Dime Bancorp Inc. (formerly Dime Savs. Bank N.Y.), N.Y.C., 1990—. Editor Temple U. Law Rev., 1972. Bd. dirs. Family Life Ctr., Garden City, 1987—. With U.S. Army, 1968-70. Mem. Spray Beach Yacht (N.J.). Episcopalian. Office: Dime Bancorp Inc 589 Fifth Ave New York NY 10017

WRIGHT, FRANZ, poet, writer, translator; b. Vienna, Austria, 1953. Translator, author of introduction Rainer Maria Rilke, The Unknown Rilke, 1990; translator modern and contemporary French and German poets; author: (poems) Tapping the White Cane of Solitude, The Earth Without You, Eight Poems, 1981, The One Whose Eyes Open When You Close Your Eyes, 1982, No Siege Is Absolute, 1983, Going North in Winter, 1986, Entry in an Unknown Hand, 1989, Midnight Postscript, 1990, And Still the Hand Will Sleep in Its Glass Ship, 1990, Rorschach Test, 1995, The Night World and the Word Night, 1993; represented in anthologies; contbr. articles to profl. publs. Recipient Witter Bynner Prize for Poetry, 1995, PEN/Voelcker award, 1996; NEA fellow, 1985, 92, Guggenheim fellow, 1989, Whiting fellow, 1991. Office: 38 Francis St Everett MA 02149

WRIGHT, GEARLD LEWIS, mayor, retired educator; b. Lyman, Wyo., Feb. 22, 1933; s. Alton and Ida Mabel (Jensen) W.; m. Lila Lynn Florence, July 16, 1953; children: Jeri Lynn, Alan Kay, Lori Marie, Daryl Wilmer, Merlin Craig, Craig Alton. Diploma in secondary instr., Brigham Young U., 1961, diploma in provisional counseling, 1961. Educator Granite Sch. Dist., Salt Lake City, 1961-87, retired, 1987; mayor West Valley City, Utah; mem. exec. com. Coun. of Govts., Utah Econ. Devel. Corp. Utah, trustee; mem. Pub. Safety Com., Econ. Devel. Com., Utah League Cities, Towns Policy Com., Govs Task Force on Weapons, Nat. League Cities Transp. and Comms. Com., U.S. Conf. Mayors Criminal and Social Justice Com., transp. and comms. com. Pres. Hunter Coun.; mem. Joh Short Feasibility Study Com.; rep. Salt Lake County Assn. Cmty. Couns.; past pres. Jackson Hole Home Owners Assn., Conf. Salt Lake Valley Mayors; active PTA, PTSA; parents adv. com. mem. Primary Children's Med. Ctr., spl. cons., organizer Family Living Seminar; sec., treas. Joseph Thompson Family Orgn.; past. chmn., com. mem. Westfest Internat. Festival. Recipient Dist. Merit award Westview Scouting Dist., West Valley, Utah, 1986. Mem. Wasatch Front Regional Coun. (bd. dirs.). Avocations: sports, history, religion, travel. Home: 5432 Janette Ave West Valley City UT 84120 Office: West Valley City 3600 S Constitution Blvd West Valley City UT 84119

WRIGHT, GLADYS STONE, music educator, composer, writer; b. Wasco, Oreg., Mar. 8, 1925; d. Murvel Stuart and Daisy Violet (Warren) Stone; m. Alfred George Wright, June 28, 1953. BS, U. Oreg., 1948, MS, 1953. Dir. bands Elmira (Oreg.) U-4 High Sch., 1948-53, Otterbein (Ind.) High Sch., 1954-61, Klondike High Sch., West Lafayette, Ind., 1962-70, Harrison High Sch., West Lafayette, 1970-84; organizer, condr. Musical Friendship Tours, Cen. Am., 1967-79; v.p., condr. U.S. Collegiate Wind Band, 1975—; bd. dirs. John Philip Sousa Found. 1984—; chmn. Sudler Cup, 1986—, Sudler Flag, 1982; pres. Internat. Music Tours, 1984—, Key to the City, Taxco, Mex., 1975. Editor: Woman Conductor, 1986—; composer: marches Big Bowl and Trumpets and Tabards, 1987; contbg. editor: Informusica (Spain). Bd. dirs. N. Am. Wildlife Park, Battleground, Ind. 1985. Recipient Medal of the order John Philip Sousa Found., 1988, Star of Order, 1991; 1st woman guest conductor U.S. Navy Band, Washington D.C., 1961, Goldman Band, N.Y.C., 1958, Kneller Hall Band, London, 1975, Tri-State Music Festival Massed Orch., Band, Choir, 1985; elected to Women Bd. Dirs. Hall of Fame of Disting. Women Conductor, 1994. Mem. Am. Bandmasters Assn. (bd. dirs. 1993, 1st woman mem.), Women Band Dirs. Nat. Assn. (founding pres. 1967, sec. 1985, recipient Silver Baton 1974, Golden Rose 1990, Hall of Fame 1995), Am. Sch. Band Dirs. Assn., Nat. Band Assn. (Citation excellence 1970), Tippecanoe Arts Fedn. (bd. dirs. 1986-90), Tippecanoe Fife and Drum Corps. (bd. dirs. 1984), Daughters of Am. Revolution, Col. Dames-Pre Quitanen Chpt., New England Women, Tau Beta Sigma (Outstanding Svc. to Music award 1970), Phi Beta Mu (1st hon. women mem. 1972), North Am. Wildlife Park (bd dirs, 1990—). Avocations: historic preservation, environ. activities.

WRIGHT, GORDON BROOKS, musician, conductor, educator; b. Bklyn., Dec. 31, 1934; s. Harry Wesley and Helen Philomena (Brooks) W.; m. Inga-Lisa Myrin Wright, June 13, 1958 (div. 1979); children: Karin-Ellen Blindenbacher, Charles-Eric, Daniel Brooks. MusB, Coll. Wooster, 1957; MA, U. Wis., 1961; postgrad., Salzburg Mozarteum, 1972, Loma Linda U., 1979; studied with, René Leibowitz, Carl Melles, Wilfred Pelletier, Herbert Blomstedt, Hans Swarowsky. Founder, music dir. Wis. Chamber Orch., 1960-69; music dir. Fairbanks (Alaska) Symphony Orch., 1969-89; prof. music Univ. Alaska, Fairbanks, 1969-89, prof. emeritus, 1989—; founder, music dir. Arctic Chamber Orch., Fairbanks, 1970-89; exec. dir. The Reznicek Soc., Indian, Alaska, 1982—. Guest condr. Philharmonia Hungarica, Philomusica London, Norwegian Radio Orch., Orch. St. Luke's, Anchorage Symphony Orch.; composer: Suite of Netherlands Dances, 1965, Six Alaskan Tone Poems, 1974, Symphony in Ursa Major, 1979 (Legis. award 1979), 1984 Overture, Scott Joplin Suite, 1987, Toccata Festiva, 1992; columnist Alaska Advocate. Founder, bd. dirs. No. Alaska Environ. Ctr., Fairbanks, 1971-78. Served as pvt. AUS, 1957-59. Mem. Am. Musicol. Soc., Royal Musical Assn., Am. Symphony Orch. League, Condr.'s Guild, Arturo Toscanini Soc., Am. Fedn. Musicians, Royal Mus. Assn., Sierra Club (lchmn. Fairbanks Group 1969-71), Friends of Earth-Alaska (bd. dirs. 1978—), Wilderness Soc., Audubon Soc., Alaska Conservation Soc. (editor Rev. 1971-78), Ctr. for Alaskan Coastal Studies (bd. dirs. 1982—). Avocations: hiking, kayaking, collecting books, photography. Home: HC 52 Box 8899 Indian AK 99540-9604

WRIGHT, GORDON PRIBYL, management, operations research educator; b. Crosby, Minn., May 18, 1938; s. Kenneth Eugene and Verla Emily (Pribyl) W.; m. Judith Ann Hill, Aug. 19, 1961; 1 dau., Teresa Ann. B.A., Macalester Coll., 1960; M.A., U. Mass., 1963; Ph.D., Case Western Res. U., 1967. Systems analyst Conn. Gen. Life Ins. Co., Bloomfield, 1960-61; instr. dept. math. U. Mass., 1961-63; statistician, mgmt. scis. group Goodyear Tire & Rubber Co., Akron, Ohio, 1963-64; instr., research asst., ops. research dept. Case Inst. Tech., Cleve., 1964-67; asst. prof. dept. indsl. engring. and mgmt. scis. Technol. Inst., Northwestern U., 1967-70; assoc. prof. mgmt. and statistics Krannert Grad. Sch. Mgmt. and Sch. of Sci., Purdue U., West Lafayette, Ind., 1970-75; assoc. dean Krannert Grad. Sch. Mgmt. and Sch. of Sci., Purdue U., 1979-84, dir. prof., 1982—, Krannert disting. prof., 1982—, dir. of research, 1985-89, dir. doctoral programs, 1985-89; prof., chmn. mgmt., dir. profl. programs Krannert Grad. Sch. Mgmt., Purdue U., 1978-79; Basil Turner prof. mgmt. Purdue U., 1987—; vis. prof. bus. adminstrn. and stats. Amos Tuck Sch. Bus. Adminstrn., Dartmouth Coll., 1976-77; vis. prof. Bradley U.; vis. prof. mgmt. sci. Grad. Sch. Mgmt. UCLA, 1984-85; cons. Okamura Mfg. Co., Yokohama, Japan. Author: (with David G. Olson) Designing Water Pollution Detection Systems, 1974, (with Andrew B. Whinston and Gary J. Koehler) Optimization of Leontief Systems, 1975, (with Herbert M. Moskowitz) An Experiential Approach to Management Science, 1975, Introduction to Management Science, 1979, Statistics for Business and Economics, 1982, (with Frank M. Bass) Stochastic Brand Coice and Brand Switching: Theory Analysis and Description, 1980; contbr. (with Frank M. Bass) articles on ops. research and mgmt. to profl. jours. Served with USAF Res., 1961-67. Recipient Salgo-Noren Found. award for outstanding teaching in bus. adminstrn., 1975; NSF research grantee, 1968-70; Dept. Transp. research grantee, 1972-74; HEW research grantee, 1969-70; Sloan Found. research grantee, 1972-75; Fulbright scholar to Ger., 1986; Vis. Erskine fellowship U. Canterbury, New Zealand, 1985. Mem. Ops. Research Soc. Am., Inst. Mgmt. Scis., Sigma Xi, Beta Gamma Sigma. Home: 136 Seminole Dr West Lafayette IN 47906-2116 Office: Krannert Sch Mgmt Purdue U West Lafayette IN 47907

WRIGHT, GWENDOLYN, art center director, writer, educator; b. Chgo., May 14, 1946; d. William Kemp and Mary Ruth (Brown) W.; m. Paul Rabinow, Nov. 18, 1980 (div. 1982); m. Thomas Bender, Jan. 14, 1985; children: David, Sophia. BA, NYU, 1969; MArch, U. Calif., Berkeley, 1974, PhD, 1980. Assoc. prof. Columbia U., N.Y.C., 1983-87, prof., 1988—; dir. Buell Ctr. for Study Am. Architecture, N.Y.C., 1988-92; cons. Fulbright Scholars, Coun. Internat. Exch. Scholars, Washington, 1988-91. Author: Building the Dream: A Social History of Housing in America, 1980, Moralism and the Model Home, 1981, The History of History in American Schools of Architecture, 1990, The Politics of Design in French Colonial Urbanism, 1991. Fellow Ford Found., 1979-80; Stanford Inst. for Humanities, 1982-83, Mich. Inst. for Humanities, 1991, Getty Ctr. for History of Art and the Humanities, 1992—. Fellow Soc. Am. Historians, N.Y. Inst. for Humanities; mem. Soc. Archtl. Historians, Coll. Art Assn., Am. Hist. Assn., Orgn. Am. Historians. Democrat. Home: 54 Washington Mews New York NY 10003-6608 Office: Columbia U Avery Hall New York NY 10027

WRIGHT, HARRY, III, retired lawyer; b. Lima, Ohio, Apr. 27, 1925; s. Harry Jr. and Marjorie (Riddle) W.; m. Louise Forbes Taylor, Dec. 15, 1956; children: Harry IV, Whitaker Wilson, Priscilla W. Nicholson. Student, The Citadel, 1942-43; B.S., U. Ky., 1948; LL.B., Harvard, 1951. Bar: Ohio 1951. With Porter, Wright, Morris & Arthur, Columbus, 1951—; ptnr. Porter, Wright, Morris & Arthur, 1956-88, of counsel, 1988-95, ret., 1995; adj. prof. law Japan Law Ctr., 1986. Mem. adv. bd. Salvation Army, 1958-74; pres. bd. trustees Six Pence Sch., Columbus, 1965-75; trustee Bradford Coll., 1957-75, pres. bd., 1972-74; trustee Columbus Acad., 1975-81, pres. bd., 1978-80; trustee Columbus Coun. World Affairs, 1979-82 Opera/Columbus, 1980-88, 89-95, Ballet Met., 1987-91; trustee Green Lawn Cemetery, 1992—, Neighborhood Ho., 1993—. With USAF, 1943-46. Mem. ABA (chmn. gen. practice sect. 1976-77, ho. of dels. 1978-87), Ohio Bar Assn. (Supreme Ct. Commn. on CLE 1988-94), Columbus Bar Assn., Columbus Club, Rocky Fork Hunt and Country Club. Episcopalian. Home: 292 N Drexel Ave Columbus OH 43209-1429 Office: 41 S High St Columbus OH 43215-6101

WRIGHT, HARRY FORREST, JR., retired banker; b. Woodbury, N.J., Nov. 9, 1931; s. Harry Forrest and Bertha (Strumpfer) W.; m. Lorraine Catherine McLaughlin, Oct. 16, 1954; children: Harry Forrest III, Lonni Caryn, Gregory William, Douglas Carl. Student, Temple U., 1949-50, Am. Inst. Banking, 1950-52; accounting certificate, Wharton Sch., U. Pa., 1960, asso. degree, 1962. Clk. First Nat. Bank, Phila., 1951-60; asst. comptroller, then asst. v.p. First Pa. Co., 1960- 64; v.p. Md. Nat. Bank, Balt., 1964-66; v.p., comptroller Md. Nat. Bank, 1966-70, sr. v.p., comptroller, 1970-73, exec. v.p., 1973-81, sr. exec. v.p., 1981-89, also bd. dirs., ret., 1989; v.p., treas. Md. Nat. Corp., 1974-77, sr. v.p., 1977-83; exec. v.p., chief fin. officer MNC Fin., Inc., 1983-88, ret., 1989; treas., dir. Md. Nat. Optimation Svcs., Inc., 1969-76, chmn., 1976-79; sec. Md. Switch, Inc., 1976-79; treas., dir. Manab Properties, Inc.; pres., dir. 10 Light St. Corp., 1973-82; affiliate Property Tax Cons., San Diego, 1990—. Treas. Cub Scouts Am., Severna Park, Md., 1965-66, St. Martin's Kindergarten, 1967-72, Bayberry Hill Property Owners Assn., 1985—; bd. dirs. Greater Balt. chpt. Nat. Found. March of Dimes, 1972-89, v.p., 1977-79, pres., 1979-81, chmn., 1981-84; bd. dirs. Nat. Coun. Vols., 1983-85, 89-95, Nat. Fin. Task Force, 1989-95; bd. dirs. Md. Sch. for Blind, 1975—, v.p., 1981-88, pres., 1988-94, chmn. bd., 1994—; chmn. Richard E. Hoover Commn. for Low Vision and Blindness at Greater Balt. Med. Ctr., 1990-92, treas., 1992—. Mem. Bank Adminstrn. Inst. (pres. Balt. 1970-71, state dir. 1971-73, dist. dir. 1977-79), Fin. Execs. Inst. (dir. 1976-78), Sigma Kappa Phi. Club: Mchts. (Balt.) (bd. dirs. 1974-87, v.p. 1976-79, pres. 1979-82). Home and Office: 1314 Saint Josephs Ct Crownsville MD 21032-2129 *Success in life is not measured in material wealth, but in diversity of accomplishment, contribution to social good, and respect from peers, subordinates, and superiors alike. The greatest joys are in children and grandchildren and their growth and achievements, and in teaching them continually to strive harder to be successful and happy.*

WRIGHT, HASTINGS KEMPER, surgeon, educator; b. Boston, Aug. 28, 1928; s. Donald M. and Lucia (Durand) W.; m. Nancy E. Howell, June 19, 1954; children: Mark, Kenneth, Barbara, Donald. AB, Harvard U., 1950, MD, 1954, MA, 1973. Diplomate: Am. Bd. Surgery. Intern Univ. Hosps. Cleve., 1954, resident, 1957-61; asst. prof. surgery Western Res. U., Cleve., 1961-66; assoc. prof. surgery Med. Sch. Yale U., New Haven, 1967-72, prof. Med. Sch., 1972-95; prof. surgery emeritus, 1995—; chief gen. surgery Yale-New Haven Hosp., 1968-79, asst. chief surgery, 1979-95. Author: Complications of GI Surgery, 1972; asst. chief editor Archives of Surgery, Chgo., 1977-89. Capt. U.S. Army, 1955-57. Fellow ACS, Am. Surg. Assn.; mem. Soc. Univ. Surgeons (program dir. 1972), Am. Gastroent. Assn., Soc. Surgery Gastrointestinal Tract. Republican. Episcopalian. Clubs: Mory's Assoc. (New Haven); Yale (N.Y.C.). Home: 35 Wood Rd Branford CT 06405-4935 Office: Yale U Med Sch Dept Surgery 333 Cedar St New Haven CT 06510-3206

WRIGHT, HELEN KENNEDY, professional association administrator, publisher, editor, librarian; b. Indpls., Sept. 23, 1927; d. William Henry and Ida Louise (Crosby) Kennedy; m. Samuel A. Wright, Sept. 5, 1970; 1 child, Carl F. Prince II (dec.). BA, Butler U., 1945, MS, 1950; MS, Columbia U., 1952. Reference libr. N.Y. Pub. Libr., N.Y.C., 1952-53, Bklyn. Pub. Libr., 1953-54; reference libr., cataloger U. Utah, 1954-57; libr. Chgo. Pub. Libr.; asst. dir. pub. dept. ALA, Chgo., 1958-62, editor Reference Books Bull., 1962-85, asst. dir. for new product planning, pub. svcs., 1985—, dir. office for libr. outreach svcs., 1987-90, mng. editor yearbook, 1988—. Contbr. to Ency. of Careers, Ency. of Libr. and Info. Sci., New Book of Knowledge Ency., Bulletin of Bibliography, New Golden Book Ency. Recipient Louis Shores/Oryx Pr. award, 1991. Mem. Phi Kappa Phi, Kappa Delta Pi, Sigma Gamma Rho. Roman Catholic. Home: 1138 W 111th St Chicago IL 60643-4508 Office: ALA 50 E Huron St Chicago IL 60611-2729

WRIGHT, HELEN PATTON, professional society administrator; b. Washington, Jan. 15, 1919; d. Raymond Stanton and Virginia (Mitchell) Patton; m. James Skelly Wright, Feb. 1, 1945 (dec. 1988); 1 son, James Skelly; m. John H. Pickering, Feb. 3, 1990. Student, Sweet Briar Coll., 1936-38; grad., Washington Sch. Secretaries, 1939, Am. U., 1989. Tchr. Washington Sch. Secretaries, N.Y.C., 1939-40; sec. The White House, 1941-43, Am. embassy, London, Eng., 1943-45; asst. to exec. dir. Senate Atomic Energy Com., 1946-47. Author: My Journey, Recollections of the First Seventy Years. V.p., mem. budget and admissions com. United Fund New Orleans, 1960-62; chmn. met. div., campaign; v.p. Dept. Pub. Welfare, Orleans Parish and City New Orleans, 1960-62, Milne Asylum for Destitute Orphan Boys, New Orleans, 1958-62; mem. bd. New Orleans Social Welfare Planning Coun., 1954-62, New Orleans Cancer Soc., 1958-60; v.p. Juvenile Ct. Adv. Com. New Orleans, 1961; successively sec., v.p., pres. Parents' Assn. Metairie Park Country Day Sch., 1956-59; v.p. La. Assn. Mental Health, 1960-62; del. dir. to Nat. Assn. Mental Health, 1960-62; bd. mem. Washington Health and Welfare Coun., 1962-64, Hillcrest Children's Ctr., Washington, 1963-69, D.C. Mental Health Assn., 1962-72, 73-76; bd. dirs. Hospice Care of D.C., 1981-88, 90—, pres., 1986-88; mem. adv. bd. civil commitment project Nat. Ctr. for State Cts., 1981; bd. dirs. Nat. Assn. Mental Health, 1960-66, 67-74, sec., 1968-70, pres.-elect, 1970-71, pres., 1972-73, cons. on assn. film, 1972; mem. Commn. on Mentally Disabled, Am. Bar Assn., 1973-80; chmn. altar guild Christ Ch. Cathedral, New Orleans, 1960, Little Sanctuary of St. Albans Sch., Washington, 1965; pres. Altar Guild, St. Alban's, Chgo., 1976, 77; chmn. Washington com. Nat. Cathedral Assn., 1976, 77, 78, 79, trustee, 1976-90, sec., 1980-83, v.p., 1984-87; bd. dirs. Nat. Ctr. Voluntary Action; mem. task panel Mental Health Problems, Scope and Boundaries, Pres.'s Commn. Mental Health, 1977; mem. tech. rev. com. Md. Psychiat. Rsch. Ctr., 1979-81. Address: 5317 Blackistone Rd Bethesda MD 20816-1822

WRIGHT, HERBERT E(DGAR), JR., geologist; b. Malden, Mass., Sept. 13, 1917; s. Herbert E. and Annie M. (Richardson) W.; m. Rhea Jane Hahn, June 21, 1943; children—Richard, Jonathan, Stephen, Andrew, Jeffrey. AB, Harvard U., 1939, MA, 1941, PhD, 1943; DSc (hon.), Trinity Coll., Dublin, Ireland, 1966, U. Minn., 1996; PhD (hon.), Lund U., Sweden, 1987. Instr. Brown U., 1946-47; asst. prof. geology U. Minn., Mpls., 1947-51, asso. prof., 1951-59, prof., 1959-74, Regents' prof. geology, ecology and botany, 1974-88; dir. Limnological Research Center, 1963-90. Served to maj. USAAF, 1942-45. Decorated D.F.C., Air medal with 6 oak leaf clusters; recipient Pomerance award Archeol. Inst. Am., 1985, Ann. award Sci. Mus. Minn., 1990; Guggenheim fellow, 1954-55, Wenner-Gren fellow, 1954-55. Fellow AAAS, Geol. Soc. Am. (Ann. award archeol. divsn. 1989, Disting. Career award geology and geomorphology divsn. 1992), Soc. Am. Archeology (Fryxell award 1993); mem. NAS, Ecol. Soc. Am., Am. Soc. Limnology, Oceanography, Am. Quaternary Assn. (Career award 1996), Arctic Inst., Brit. Ecol. Soc. Research on Quaternary geology, paleoecology, paleolimnology and environ. archaeology in Minn., Wyo., Sweden, Yukon, Labrador, Peru, eastern Mediterranean. Home: 1426 Hythe St Saint Paul MN 55108-1423 Office: U of Pillsbury 221 Pillsbury Hall 310 Pillsbury Dr SE Minneapolis MN 55455-0219

WRIGHT, HUGH ELLIOTT, JR., association executive, writer; b. Athens, Ala., Nov. 20, 1937; s. Hugh Elliott and Martha Angeline (Shannon) W. A.B., Birmingham-So. Coll., 1959; M.Div., Vanderbilt U., 1962, D.Ministry, 1967; postgrad., Harvard U., 1963. Ordained to ministry Methodist Ch., 1963; pastor Baxter (Tenn.) Meth. Ch., 1963-64; assoc. pastor Waverly Pl. Ch., Nashville, 1965-66; field sec. Tenn. Heart Assn., Nashville, 1964-65; editorial asst. Motive mag., Nashville, 1965-67; Protestant-Orthodox editor Religious News Service, N.Y.C., 1967-75; research fellow Auburn Theol. Sem., N.Y.C., 1976; editor project on mediating structures and public policy Am. Enterprise Inst., 1979-80; coordinator project on ch., state and taxation NAt. Conf. of Christians and Jews, N.Y.C., 1980-83; v.p. for program NCCJ, N.Y.C., 1983-88, sr. v.p., dep. to pres., 1988-91; program cons. N.Y.C., 1992—; cons. Hartford Sem. Found., 1972, United Meth. Bd. Global Ministries, 1975-78, United Meth. Communications, 1979-81; bd. dirs. Internat. Coun. Christians and Jews, DePaul Coll. Law Ctr. on Ch. State Rels., Nat. Coun. Chs. Com. on Religious Liberty, Nat. Coun. Religious and Pub. Edn. Host: Challenge to Faith, Sta. WOR, 1973-77; author: (with R. Lecky) Can These Bones Live, 1969, The Big Little School, 1971, (with R. Lynn) Go Free, 1973, Challenge to Mission, 1973, (with Juanita Wright) Viewers Guide to Six American Families, 1977, (with Howard Butt) At the Edge of Hope, 1978, (with Douglas McGaw) A Tale of Two Congregations, 1980, Holy Company: Christian Heroes and Heroines, 1980, RNS Reporting...Sixty Years of Religious News Service, 1993; editor: (with Robert Lecky) Black Manifesto: Religion, Racism and Reparations, 1969. Recipient award Birmingham Council Indsl. Editors, 1959, Founders medal Vanderbilt U., 1962, Shepherd prize Vanderbilt, 1962, Religious Heritage of Am. award in journalism, 1972, Asso. Ch. Press Feature Article award, 1980. Mem. Authors League and Guild, Am. Acad. Religion, Phi Beta Kappa, Sigma Delta Chi, Alpha Tau Omega, Alpha Psi Omega, Eta Sigma Phi. Democrat. Home: 1346 Midland Ave Bronxville NY 10708-6840 Office: 475 Riverside Dr Ste 300 New York NY 10115-0122

WRIGHT, IDA JOHNSON, state official; b. Cocoa, Fla., June 20, 1933; d. Walter Richard and Ruth Mildred (Fitch) Johnson; m. James Wellington Hunt, July 10, 1954 (div. 1964); 1 child, Mary Evelyn; m. Fred Hamilton Wright, Jr., Nov. 22, 1972 (dec. 1992). AS, Polk C.C., Winter Haven, Fla., 1978, AA, 1980; BS in Mgmt., St. Leo (Fla.) Coll., 1989; MPA, U. South Fla., 1995. Cert. profl. sec., 1976. Sec. U.S. Air Force Civil Svc., Patrick AFB, Fla., 1953-60; exec. sec. GE Co., Patrick AFB, Fla., 1958-63; part-time v.p. Hunt Constrn. Co., Eau Gallie, Fla., 1960-63; exec. sec. to dir. Saturn/Apollo program McDonnell Douglas, Kennedy Space Ctr., Fla., 1964-72; exec. sec. W.R. Grace & Co., Bartow, Fla., 1973-81; sr. exec. sec. to pres. AMAX Chem. Co., Lakeland, Fla., 1981-84; asst. to pres. Allen & Co., Lakeland, Fla., 1985; clk. of commn. Fla. Citrus Commn., Lakeland, 1985—; part-time real estate salesperson Realty World/Griffin Assocs., Bartow, 1981-84; adj. faculty Polk C.C., 1986. Mem. bus. adv. bd. Polk C.C., 1984-85; team leader Paint Your Heart Out-Bartow, 1993-94; vol. Lakeland Reg. Med. Ctr. Auxiliary, 1992—. Mem. Profl. Secs. Internat. (chpt. pres. 1978), Am. Soc. Pub. Adminstrs., Am. Mgmt. Assn., Missile and Space Pioneers, Mosquito Beaters, Pilot Club. Democrat. Baptist. Avocations: reading, walking, decorating. Office: Fla Dept of Citrus 1115 E Memorial Blvd Lakeland FL 33801-2021

WRIGHT, IRVING SHERWOOD, physician, retired educator; b. N.Y.C., Oct. 27, 1901; s. Harry J. and Cora Ann (Hassett) W.; m. Grace Mansfield Demarest, Oct. 15, 1927; children: Barbara Mansfield, Alison Sherwood; m. Lois Elliman Findlay, Oct. 31, 1953. A.B., Cornell U., 1923, M.D., 1926. Diplomate: Am. Bd. Internal Medicine (mem. adv. bd. 1940-49), subcert. in cardiovascular diseases. Intern N.Y. Post Grad. Med. Sch. and Hosp. of Columbia, 1927-29, asst. and assoc. vis. physician, 1929-39, prof. clin. medicine, dir. and exec. officer dept. medicine, 1939-46; asst. physician Bellevue Hosp. (Cornell Div.), 1931-34, assoc., 1934-37; assoc. prof. Cornell Med. Coll. and assoc. attending physician N.Y. Hosp., 1946-48; prof. clin. medicine Cornell Med. Coll., 1948-68, emeritus clin. prof., 1968—; attending physician Drs. Hosp., N.Y.C., 1934-80, N.Y. Hosp., 1948-80; investigator into biomed. problems of aging; hon. staff dept. medicine N.Y. Hosp., 1980—; physician Met. Opera, 1935-62; dir. medicine Cornell Div.) Welfare Hosp. Chronic Disease, 1937-40 (1st pres. its med. bd. 1937-39), cons. physician, 1940-46; cons. to Orange Meml. Hosp., East Orange, N.J., Monmouth Meml. Hosp., Long Branch, N.J., Hackensack (N.J.) Hosp., Mt. Vernon (N.Y.) Hosp.; chief of med. service Army and Navy Gen. Hosp., Hot Springs (Ark.) Nat. Park, 1942-43; cons. in medicine U.S. Army, 6th Service Command, 1944-45, 9th Service Command, 1945; coordinator health survey Am. prisoners of war from Far East, 1945; chmn. Internat. Com. on Blood Clotting Factors, 1954-63, sec. gen., 1963-68; chmn. com. on cerebral vascular diseases NIH, 1961-65; mem. Pres.'s Commn. Heart Disease, Cancer and Stroke, 1966-68; nat. chmn. Commn. Heart Disease Resources, 1968-76. Author and editor numerous books on cardiovascular diseases.; Editor-in-chief: Modern Medical Monographs; Contbr. articles to med. jours. Chmn. Josiah Macy, Jr. Found. Conf. Blood Clotting, 1947-52; Trustee Cornell U., 1960-65. Served as lt. comdr. USNR, 1935-39; lt. col. to col. AUS, 1942-46; civilian cons. in medicine to surgeon gen. U.S. Army, 1946-74; mem. civilian adv. com. to sec. navy, 1946-47. Recipient Albert and Mary Lasker award Am. Heart Assn., 1960, Gold Heart award, 1958, Disting. Service award, 1976; Irving Sherwood Wright professorship in geriatrics at Cornell U. Med. Coll., 1976. Fellow Royal Coll. Physicians (London), ACP (regent, pres. 1965-66, pres. emeritus 1987—), Acad. Medicine (chmn. geriatrics sect. 1976-79, outstanding Contbns. to Sci. and Medicine award medal 1986); mem. Am. Assn. Physicians, AMA (chmn. sect. exptl. med. and therapeutics 1939-40), Am. Heart Assn. (chmn. sect. for study peripheral circulation 1939-40, mem. exec. com., bd. dirs. 1935-57, pres. 1952-53, mem. Nat. Adv. Heart Council 1954-58, 60-61), Cornell U. Med. Coll. Alumni Assn. (pres 1953), NRC (sub-com. cardiovascular diseases 1947-51), Am. Soc. Clin. Investigation, Soc. Exptl. Biology and Medicine, N.Y. Acad. Scis., Am. Geriatrics Soc. (pres. 1971-72, Henderson award 1970, Thewlis award 1974), Am. Fedn. for Aging Research (founding pres. 1980-86, AFAR Distinction award 1987), Harvey Soc., Sigma Xi, Alpha Omega Alpha; corr. mem. of Acad. Columbian de Ciencas Exactas Fisico-Quimicas Y Naturales (Bogota); hon. mem. Royal Soc. Medicine of London, med. socs. Brazil, Chile, Peru, Argentina, Cuba, Switzerland, Sweden and USSR; also hon. faculty of U. Chile. Presbyn (bd. sessions 1935-36). Clubs: Bedford Golf and Tennis; St. Nicholas Society (N.Y.). Home: 25 E End Ave New York NY 10028-7052 *My aim in life has been to improve the quality of medical care in the fields of internal medicine, geriatric cardiovascular diseases by research, teaching at undergraduate, graduate, and international levels, the development of standards and guidelines, and the application of the best of modern knowledge to the care of patients. In light of the technology of recent years I have placed particular emphasis on the role of a primary physician for the patient, who will apply his scientific knowledge with compassion and an understanding of the total illness-including the social and emotional aspects of the patient's problem rather than his disease alone. This, as I see it, is the challenge of the modern physician.*

WRIGHT, J. CRAIG, state supreme court associate justice; b. Chillicothe, Ohio, June 21, 1929; s. Harry and Marjorie (Riddle) W.; m. Jane LaFollette, Nov. 3, 1951; children: Marjorie Jane, Alice Ann. B.A., U. Ky., 1951; LL.B., Yale U., 1954. Ptnr. Wright, Gilbert & Jones, Columbus, 1957-70; judge Franklin County Common Pleas Ct., 1971-84, adminstrv. and presiding judge, 1980-84; assoc. justice Ohio Supreme Ct., Columbus, 1985—. Trustee Columbus Area Coun. on Alcoholism, 1959-83; chmn. bd. House of Hope-Halfway House, Columbus, 1960-68, trustee emeritus; trustee Grace Brethren Ch., Columbus, 1966-81, Worthington Christian Sch., Ohio, 1974-78, St. Anthony's Med. Ctr., Shepherd Hill Hosp. With CIC, U.S. Army, 1955-56. Recipient cert. of excellence Ohio Supreme Ct., 1972-83. Mem. ABA (mem. commn. on impaired lawyers 1988-91, state rep. jud. div. 1975-83), Ohio Bar Assn. (chmn. lawyers assistance com. 1977-84), Ohio Common Pleas Judges Assn. (exec. bd. 1972-83, pres.-elect 1984), Columbus Bar Assn., Am. Judicature Soc., Columbus Country Club, Athletic Club of Columbus. Avocations: golf; duplicate bridge. Home: 443 Country Club Dr Columbus OH 43213-2587 Office: Ohio Supreme Ct 30 E Broad St Fl 2D Columbus OH 43215-3414

WRIGHT, JAMES DAVID, sociology educator, writer; b. Logansport, Ind., Nov. 6, 1947; s. James Farrell and Helen Loretta (Moon) W.; m. Christine Ellen Stewart, July 25, 1987; children: Matthew James, Derek William. BA, Purdue U., 1969; MS, U. Wis., 1970, PhD, 1973. Cert. specialist social policy and evaluation rsch. Asst. prof. sociology U. Mass., Amherst, 1973-76, assoc. prof., 1976-79, prof., 1979-88; Favrot prof. human rels. Tulane U., New Orleans, 1988—. Author/co-author: The Dissent of the Governed, 1976, Under the Gun, 1983, The State of the Masses, 1986, Homelessness and Health, 1987 (commendation Nat. Press Club 1988), Address Unknown: Homeless in America, 1989, The Greatest of Evils: Urban Poverty and the Urban Underclass, 1993, others; editor: (book series) Social Institutions and Social Change, 1984—, (jour.) Social Sci. Rsch. Jour., 1978—; contbr. numerous articles, essays, book chpts. to profl. publs. Mem. Am. Sociol. Assn., Soc. for Study Social Problems. Democrat. Avocations: cooking, gardening, travel.

WRIGHT, JAMES EDWARD, judge; b. Arlington, Tex., Jan. 15, 1921; s. James Robert and Clairette (Smith) W.; m. Eberta Adelaide Slataper, June 25, 1946; 1 child, Patricia Diane Wright Rogers. JD, U. Tex., 1949. Bar: Tex. 1949. Practice in Ft. Worth, 1949-69; city atty. Arlington, 1951-61; judge 141st Dist. Ct., Ft. Worth, 1970-88, sr. dist. judge, 1988—. Served with USAAF, World War II. Paul Harris fellow, 1981; named Disting. Alumnus U. Tex.-Arlington, 1982; named to Mil. Sci. Dept. Hall of Honor, U. Tex.-Arlington, 1985. Fellow Tex. Bar Found. (life); mem. ABA, Ft. Worth-Tarrant County Bar Assn. (pres. 1958-59), Tex. Bar Assn., Sons of the Rep. of Tex., Rotary (pres. Downtown Ft. Worth club 1966-67), Masons (32 deg.), Shriners, Phi Alpha Delta. Baptist. Home: 717 Briarwood Blvd Arlington TX 76013-1502

WRIGHT, JAMES EDWARD, dean, history educator; b. Madison, Wis., Aug. 16, 1939; s. Donald J. and Myrtle (Hendricks) W.; m. Joan Bussah, Sept. 3, 1962 (div.); children: James J., Anne Marie, Michael J.; m. Susan DeBovoise, Aug. 18, 1984. BS, Wis. State U., 1964; MS, U. Wis., 1966, PhD, 1969; MA (hon.), Dartmouth Coll., 1980. From asst. prof. to assoc. prof. history Dartmouth Coll., Hanover, N.H., 1969-80, prof. history, 1980—, assoc. dean faculty, 1981-85, dean faculty, 1989—, acting pres., 1995; sr. historian U. Mid Am., Lincoln, Nebr., 1976-77; humanist-in-residence Colo. Humanities Coun., Georgetown, 1975. Author: Galena Lead District, 1966, Politics of Populism, 1974, Progressive Yankees, 1987; author, co-editor: Great Plains Experience, 1978. Trustee Kimball Union Acad., Meriden, N.H., 1990-94; dir. Sherman Fairchild Found., Greenwich, Conn., 1991—; chair Hanover Dem. Town Com., 1970-74. Cpl. USMC, 1957-60. Danforth fellow, 1964-69, Guggenheim fellow, 1973-74, Charles Warren fellow Harvard U., 1980-81. Mem. Orgn. Am. Historians (chair film, media com. 1983-85), Western History Assn. (chair Caughey prize 1986-87), Phi Beta Kappa (hon.). Home: 7 Quail Dr Etna NH 03750-4404 Office: Dartmouth College Dean of Faculty Hanover NH 03755

WRIGHT, J(AMES) LAWRENCE, lawyer; b. Portland, Oreg., Apr. 12, 1943; s. William A. and Esther M. (Nelson) W.; m. Mary Aileene Roche, June 29, 1968; children: Rachel, Jonathan, Christopher. BBA, Gonzaga U., 1966, JD, 1972; LLM, NYU, 1977. Bar: Wash. 1972, U.S. Ct. Mil. Appeals 1974, U.S. Tax Ct. 1976, U.S. Supreme Ct. 1976. Prin. Halverson & Applegate, P.S., Yakima, Wash., 1972-74, 77—. Mem. St. Elizabeth Hosp. Found., Yakima, 1986-89, Yakima Meml. Hosp. Found., 1990—; pres. fin. bd. St. Paul's Cathedral, Yakima, 1979—; mem. fin. coun. Diocese of Yakima, 1994—; v.p. Apple Tree Racing Assn., 1986-87; bd. dirs. Capital Theatre, Yakima, 1985-95. Capt. U.S. Army, 1966-68, 74-76. Mem. ABA, Wash. Bar Assn., Yakima County Bar Assn., Rotary. Roman Catholic. Avocations: tennis, golf. Office: Halverson & Applegate PS PO Box 22730 311 N 4th St Yakima WA 98907-2715

WRIGHT, JAMES ROSCOE, chemist; b. White Hall, Md., July 7, 1922; s. James Grover and Rose Adele (Hulshart) W.; m. Blanca Zulema Guerrero, June 4, 1950; children: James Alfred, Ronald Keith. B.S. in Edn., Md. State U., Salisbury, 1946; B.S., Washington Coll., 1948; M.S., U. Del., 1949, Ph.D. in Chemistry, 1951; grad., Program Mgmt. Devel., Harvard, 1967, Fed. Execs. Inst., U. Va., 1972. Asst. prof. Trinity U., San Antonio, 1951-52; research chemist S.W. Research Inst., San Antonio, 1951-52, Chevron Research Corp., Richmond, 1952-60; with Nat. Bur. Standards, 1960—; chief bldg. research div., 1967-72, dir. center bldg. tech., 1972-74; dep. dir. Inst. for Applied Tech., 1974-76, acting dir., 1976-78; dep. dir. Nat. Engring Lab., 1978-85; head U.S. del. industralized bldg. to, USSR, 1969; U.S. del. Internat. Union Testing and Rsch. Labs. for Materials and Structures, 1969-74, 75-85, mem. bur., 1970-73, 74-78, 79—, pres., 1971-72, v.p., 1979-82, pres., 1982-85, hon. mem., 1985—; mem. bldg. rsch. adv. bd. NRC, 1976-80; vice chmn., mem. exec. com. U.S. nat. com. Internat. Coun. Bldg. Rsch., Studies and Documentation, 1969-73; rep. Nat. Bur. Standards to Fed. Constrn. Coun., 1967-70; mem. fire coun. Underwriters Labs., 1969-73; mem. U.S.-Egypt working group Tech. Rshc. and Devel., 1976-80; hon. mem. Producers Coun.; guest worker Nat. Bur. Standards, 1985-88; dir., treas. St. Mark Elderly Housing Corp., 1987—; mem. Smithsonian Exhibit Group, 1989—. Author. Served as officer AUS, 1943-46, ETO. Decorated Bronze Star, Purple Heart, Combat Infantry Badge; recipient Gold medal award for exceptional svc. Dept. Commerce, 1975. Mem. Am. Chem. Soc. (emeritus), ASTM (dir. 1977-80, chmn. com. on soc. devel. 1979-80), Chem. Soc. Washington (chmn. auditing com. 1965-66, chmn. profl. rels. and status com. 1964, chmn. long-range planning com. 1967, assoc. editor Capital Chemist 1963-65), Buick Club Am. (bd. dirs. Washington chpt. 1991—, pres. 1990—), Sigma Xi, Kappa Alpha. Patentee in field. Home: 6204 Lone Oak Dr Bethesda MD 20817-1744

WRIGHT, JANE COOKE, physician, educator, consultant; b. N.Y.C., Nov. 30, 1919; d. Louis T. and Corinne (Cooke) W.; m. David D. Jones. A.B., Smith Coll., 1942; M.D. with honors, N.Y. Med. Coll., 1945; Dr. Med. Scis., Women's Med. Coll. Pa., 1965; Sc.D., Denison U., 1971. Intern Bellevue Hosp., N.Y.C., 1945-46, resident, 1946, mem. staff, 1955-67; resident Harlem Hosp., 1947, chief resident, 1948; clin. Cancer Rsch. Found., Harlem Hosp., 1949-52; dir., 1952-55; mem. staff Harlem Hosp., 1949-55; practice medicine specializing in clin. cancer chemotherapy N.Y.C.; mem. faculty dept. surgery Med. Ctr., N.Y. U., N.Y.C., 1955-67; adj. assoc. prof. Med. Ctr., N.Y. U., 1961-67, also dir. cancer chemotherapy services research, 1955-67; prof. surgery N.Y. Med. Coll., N.Y.C., 1967-87, prof. surgery emeritus, 1987—, assoc. dean, 1967-75; mem. staff Manhattan VA Hosp., 1955-67, Midtown, Met., Bird S. Color, Flower-Fifth Ave. Hosps., all N.Y.C., 1967-79, Westchester County Med. Center, Valhalla, N.Y., 1971-87, Lincoln Hosp., Bronx, N.Y., 1979-87; cons. Health Ins. Plan of Greater N.Y., 1962-94; cons. Blvd. Hosp., 1963—, St. Luke's Hosp., Newburgh, N.Y., 1964—; pelvic malignancy rev. com. N.Y. Gynecol. Soc., 1965-66, St. Vincent's Hosp., N.Y.C., 1966—, Dept. Health, Edn. and Welfare, 1968-70, Wyckoff Heights Hosp., N.Y.C., 1969—, NIH, 1971—, others; adv. bd. Skin Cancer Found. Contbr. articles to profl. jours. Mem. Manhattan coun. State Commn. Human Rights, 1949—, Pres.'s Commn. Heart Disease, Cancer and Stroke, 1964-65, Nat. Adv. Cancer Coun. NIH, 1966-70, N.Y. State Women's Coun., 1970-72; bd. dirs. Medico-CARE, Health Svcs. Improvement Fund Inc.; trustee Smith Coll., Northampton, Mass., 1970-80. Recipient numerous awards, including; Mademoiselle mag. award, 1952; Lady Year award Harriet Beecher Stowe Jr. High Sch., 1958; Spirit Achievement award Albert Einstein Sch. Medicine, 1965; certificate Honor award George Gershwin Jr. High Sch., 1967; Myrtle Wreath award Hadassah, 1967; Smith medal Smith Coll., 1968; Outstanding Am. Women award Am. Mothers Com. Inc., 1970; Golden Plate award Am. Acad. Achievement, 1971; Exceptional Black Scientists Poster Ciba Geigy, 1980. Fellow N.Y. Acad. Medicine; mem. Nat. Med. Assn. (edit. bd. jours.), Manhattan Ctrl. Med. Soc., N.Y. County Med. Soc. (nominating com.), AMA, AAAS, Am. Assn. Cancer Rsch. (dir. Rsch. Salute 1971-74), N.Y. Acad. Scis., N.Y. Cancer Soc., Internat. Med. and Rsch. Found. (v.p.), Am. Cancer Soc. (dir. div.), N.Y. Cancer Soc. (pres. 1970-71), Am. Soc. Clin. Oncology (sec. treas. 1964-67), Contin Soc., Sigma Xi, Lambda Kappa Mu, Alpha Omega Alpha. Club: The 400 (N.Y. Med. Coll.). Address: 315 W End Ave New York NY 10023-8158

WRIGHT, JEFF REGAN, civil engineering educator; b. Spokane, Wash., Nov. 25, 1950; s. Harold U. and Gail Virginia (Hodgson) W.; m. Delores Jeanne Finch, Sept. 14, 1972; children: Kelly Hodgson, Myka Kristine. BA, U. Wash., 1975, BS, 1976, MSCE, 1977; PhD, Johns Hopkins U., 1982. Asst. prof. civil engring. Purdue U., West Lafayette, Ind., 1982-86, assoc. prof., 1986-90; prof., 1990—; dir. Ind. Water Resources Rsch. Ctr. Purdue U., West Lafayette, Ind., 1989—; v.p. OMTEK Engring., West Lafayette, 1986—. Author: Expert Systems Applications to Urban Planning, 1989; contbr. numerous articles to profl. publs. Mem. ASCE (editor-in-chief Jour. Infrastructure Sys.), Ops. Rsch. Soc. Am., Inst. Mgmt. Scis. Office: Purdue U WRRC Sch Civil Engring West Lafayette IN 47907-1284

WRIGHT, JEFFREY, actor. stage appearances include (with Arena Stage, Washington D.C.) Les Blancs, She Stoops to Conquer, Juno and the Paycock (with Yale Repertory) Search and Destroy, Playboy of the West Indies, Daylight in the Exile, N.Y. Shakespeare Festival prodn. of Othello, Millenium Approaches, 1993, Angels in America: Perestroika, 1994 (Antoinette Perry award for Featured Actor in a Play 1994); T.V. appearances include The Young Indiana Jones Chronicles, Seperate But Equal; films include Presumed Innocent, 1990, Jumpin' at the Bone Yard, 1991, Basquiat, 1996. *

WRIGHT, JESSE HARTZELL, psychiatrist, educator; b. Altoona, Pa., Sept. 21, 1943; s. Jesse H. and Marion (Stone) W.; m. Susanne Judy Wright, July 9, 1967; children: Andrew, Laura. BS, Juniata Coll., 1965; MD, Jefferson Med. Coll., 1969; PhD, U. Louisville, 1976. Diplomate Am. Bd. Psychiatry and Neurology, Am. Bd. Med. Examiners; lic. psychiatrist, Ky. Asst. prof. U. Louisville, 1975-79, assoc. prof., 1979-87, prof., 1987—; clin. dir. Norton Psychiat. Clinic, Louisville, 1975-83, med. dir., 1983—; resident in psychiatry U. Mich., Ann Arbor, 1970-73; cons. Our Lady of Peace Hosp., Louisville, 1978—, Bapt. Hosp., Louisville, 1979—, Jewish Hosp., Louisville, 1987—. Author first multimedia computer program for psychotherapy, chpts. to books; contbr. articles to prof. jours. Fellow APA; mem. Ky. Psychiat. Assn. (sec. 1979-80, v.p. 1980-81, pres. 1982-83). Avocations: gardening, running, theater, skiing. Home: 15 Indian Hills Trl

Louisville KY 40207-1532 Office: Norton Psychiat Clinic 200 E Chestnut St Louisville KY 40202-1822

WRIGHT, JOHN, classics educator; b. N.Y.C., Mar. 9, 1941; s. Henry and Dorothy (Chaya) W.; m. Ellen Faber, June 16, 1962; children: Jennifer, Emily. B.A., Swarthmore Coll., 1962; M.A., Ind. U., 1964, Ph.D., 1971. Instr. classics U. Rochester, 1968-72, asst. prof., 1972-75; asso. prof. Northwestern U., Evanston, Ill., 1975-77; prof. Northwestern U., 1977-83, John Evans prof. Latin lang. and lit., 1983—, chmn. dept., 1978—. Author: The Play of Antichrist, 1967, Dancing in Chains: The Stylistic Unity of the Comoedia Palliata, 1974, The Life of Cola de Rienzo, 1975, Essays on the Iliad: Selected Modern Criticism, 1978, Plautus: Curculio, Introduction and Notes, 1981, rev. edit., 1993, Ralph Stanley and the Clinch Mountain Boys: A Discography, 1983, The Five-String Banjo Stanley Style, 1984, rev. edit. (Clyde Pharr) Homeric Greek: A Book for Beginners, 1985, It's the Hardest Music in the World to Play: The Ralph Stanley Story in His Own Words, 1987, Traveling the High Way Home: Ralph Stanley and the World of Traditional Bluegrass Music, 1993; album Everything She Asks For, 1993; columnist: Banjo Newsletter; contbr. articles to profl. jours. Fellow Am. Acad. Rome, 1966-68; Nat. Endowment Humanities Younger humanist fellow, 1973-74; named to Honorable Order of Ky. Colonels. Mem. Am. Acad. in Rome Soc. of Fellows, Am. Philol. Assn., Ill. Classical Conf., Petronian Soc., Met. Opera Guild, Chgo. Area Bluegrass Assn., Minn. Bluegrass and Old-Time Music Assn., Internat. Bluegrass Music Assn. (Print Media Personality of Yr. 1994), BMI, Nat. Acad. Recording Arts and Scis. Club: Ralph Stanley Fan. Home: 1137 Noyes St Evanston IL 60201-2633 Office: Northwestern U Dept Classics Evanston IL 60208-2200

WRIGHT, JOHN, film editor. Editor films (with Graeme Clifford and Garth Craven) Convoy, 1978, Separate Ways, 1981, Only When I Laugh, 1981, Frances, 1982, Mass Appeal, 198, Explorers, 1985, (with Mark Roy Warner and Edward A. Warschilka) The Running Man, 1987, Gleaming the Cube, 1989, (with Dennis Virkler) The Hunt for Red October, 1990 (Acad. award nomination for best film editing 1990), (with Steve Mirkovich) Teenage Mutant Ninja Turtles II: The Secret of the Ooze, 1991, Last Action Hero, 1993, Speed, 1994 (Acad. award nomination for best film editing 1994), Die Hard with A Vengeance, 1995, Broken Arrow, 1996, The Rock, 1996; editor TV movies Heartsounds, 1984, My Name Is Bill W., 1989, Sarah, Plain and Tall, 1991. Office: Broder Kurland Webb Uffner Agency 22344 DeGrasse Dr Calabasas CA 91302

WRIGHT, JOHN COLLINS, chemistry educator; b. Oak Hill, W. Va., Aug. 5, 1927; s. John C. and Irene (Collins) W.; m. Margaret Ann Cyphers, Sept. 11, 1949; children: Jeffrey Cyphers, John Timothy, Curtis Scott, Keith Alexander. B.S., W.Va. Wesleyan Coll., 1948, LL.D. (hon.), 1974; Ph.D., U. Ill., 1951; D.Sc. (hon.), U. Ala., 1979, W.Va. Inst. Tech., 1979. Research chemist Hercules, Inc., 1951-57; mem. faculty W.Va. Wesleyan Coll., 1957-64; asst. program dir. NSF, 1964-65; dean Coll. Arts and Scis., No. Ariz. U., 1966-70, W.Va. U., Morgantown, 1970-74; vice chancellor W.Va. Bd. Regents, Charleston, 1974-78; pres. U. Ala., Huntsville, 1978-88, prof. chemistry, 1988—; interim pres. W.Va. Coll. Grad. Studies, Institute, 1975-76; hon. research asso. Univ. Coll., London, Eng., 1962-63; cons. NSF, 1965—, Army Sci. Bd., U.S. Army, 1979-82. Served with USNR, 1945-46. Mich. fellow Center Study Higher Edn., U. Mich., 1965-66. Mem. Am. Chem. Soc., AAAS, Assn. Higher Edn., Am. Assn. State Colls. and Univs. (com. chmn. on sci. and tech. 1987). Office: 4724 Panorama Dr SE Huntsville AL 35801-1215

WRIGHT, JOHN MACNAIR, JR., retired army officer; b. L.A., Apr. 14, 1916; s. John MacNair and Ella (Stradley) W.; m. Helene Tribit, June 28, 1940; children: John MacNair III, Richard Kenneth. B.S., U.S. Mil. Acad., 1940; grad., Airborne Sch., 1947, Strategic Intelligence Sch., 1948; advanced course, Inf. Sch., 1951, Command and Gen. Staff Coll., 1953; M.B.A., U. So. Calif., 1956; grad., Army Logistics Mgmt. Sch., 1957, Advanced Mgmt. Program, U. Pitts., 1959, Nat. War Coll., 1961, Army Aviation Sch., 1965; M.S. in Internat. Affairs, George Washington U., 1973. Enlisted U.S. Army, 1935, comd. 2d. lt., 1940, advanced through grades to lt. gen., 1970; comdr. Battery Wright Corregidor, P.I., 1942; with intelligence div. War Dept. Gen. Staff, 1946-48; mil. attache Am. embassy, Paraguay, 1948-50; bn. comdr. 508th Airborne Regtl. Combat Team, 1951-52; asst. chief of staff for pers. 7th Inf. Div., Korea, 1953, asst. chief staff logistics, 1954; assigned office U.S. Army Chief of Staff, 1956-60; chief staff 8th Inf. Div., 1961-62, asst. chief staff plans and ops. 7th Corps, 1962-63, asst. chief staff plans and ops. 7th Army, 1963-64, asst. div. comdr. 11th Air Assault Div., 1964-65; asst. div. comdr. 1st Cav. Div. (Airmobile) Vietnam, 1965-66; assigned office asst. Chief Staff Force Devel., 1966-67; comdg. gen. U.S. Army Inf. Ctr., 1967-69; comdt. U.S. Army Inf. Sch., 1967-69; comdg. gen. 101st Airborne Div. (Airmobile), Vietnam, 1969-70; controller of the Army Washington, 1970-72; ret., 1973. Dir. R&D Boy Scouts Am., 1973, nat. dir. program, 1974-77, nat. dir. program support, 1977-78; nat. dir. exploring, 1978-81, mem. nat. exploring com., 1981—; pres. Chattahoochee (Ga.) coun. Boy Scouts Am., 1968-69, mem. exec. bd. region 5, 1967-69; mem. nat. coun., 1964-73; tech. adviser Vietnamese Boy Scout Assn., 1965-66; Regent for Life Nat. Eagle Scout Assn., 1988—; exploring chmn. five nations dist. Calif. Inland Empire Coun., 1992—. Decorated D.S.M. with 2 oak leaf clusters, Silver Star with oak leaf cluster, Legion of Merit with oak leaf cluster, D.F.C., Bronze Star with oak leaf cluster, Air medal with 59 oak leaf clusters, Army Commendation medal, Prisoner of War medal, Purple Heart with oak leaf cluster, Combat Inf. badge, Master Parachutist, Sr. Army Aviator, numerous area and campaign ribbons, fgn. decorations; recipient Silver Beaver award Boy Scouts Am., 1961, Silver Antelope award, 1969, Distinguished Eagle Scout award, 1971, Disting. Svc. award Founders and Patriots Am., 1988, Freedoms Found. at Valley Forge Hon. medal, 1992; elected Army Aviation Hall of Fame, 1986. Mem. Assn. U.S. Army, Army Aviation Assn. Am. (pres. 1974-76), 101st Airborne Divsn. Assn., 1st Cavalry Divsn. Assn., SAR (pres. Tex. Soc. 1987-88, pres. Inland Empire chpt. 1992-93, Silver Good Citizenship medal 1984, 87, Meritorious Svc. medal 1986, Patriot, Liberty and Gold Good Citizenship medals 1988), Ret. Officers Assn., West Point Soc., Mil. Order World Wars (Patrick Henry award 1986, 90, comdr. Dallas chpt. 1985-86, vice comdr. dept. ctrl. Calif. 1991-92, comdr. Inland Empire chpt. 1992-93), Nat. Order Founders and Patriots of Am. (sec.-gen. 1986-88, gov. gen. 1988-90, councillor gen. Calif. Soc. 1990-95), Soc. Descendants of Colonial Clergy, Flagon and Tchr. Soc., Soc. Colonial Wars (lt. gov. Calif. soc. 1992—), Sons of the Revolution in State of Calif. (pres. 1993-94), Soc. War of 1812 (dist. dep. pres. gen. 1991—, v.p. Calif. soc. 1993-94, pres. 1994-95), Nat. Huguenot Soc., Soc. Sons and Daus. of Pilgrims, Order Ams. Armorial Ancestry, Soc. Descendents Founders of Hartford, Old Plymouth Colony Descendents, Mil. Order of the Loyal Legion of the U.S., Mil. Order Fgn. Wars of the U.S. (pres. Calif. Soc. 1996-97), Hereditary Order of First Families of Mass., Masons, Shriners, Sojourner, Phi Kappa Phi, Beta Gamma Sigma, Alpha Kappa Psi. Prisoner of war of Japanese, 1942-45. Home: 21227 George Brown Ave Riverside CA 92518-2881

WRIGHT, JOHN PEALE, retired banker; b. Chattanooga, Mar. 27, 1924; s. Robert T. and Margaret (Peale) W.; m. Ruth Garrison, Sept. 11, 1948; children: Margaret Shapard, John Peale, Ruth Garrison, Mary Ivens. Student, Davidson Coll., 1941-43, U. N.C., 1943; B.S. in Phys. Sci, U. Chgo., 1944; M.B.A., Harvard U., 1947. With Am. Nat. Bank & Trust Co., Chattanooga, 1947-82; pres. Am. Nat. Bank & Trust Co., 1962-82, also dir.; dir. spl. projects Third Nat. Corp., Nashville, 1983-85; chmn. bd., dir. Third Nat. Bank of Anderson County, 1980-84. Served to lt. USAAF, 1943-46. Mem. Robert Morris Assocs. (pres. 1968-69), Tenn. Bankers Assn. (bd. dirs., pres. 1973-74). Presbyterian (elder, treas.). Home: PO Box 1667 Santa Rosa Beach FL 32459-1667

WRIGHT, JOHN ROBERT, pathologist; b. Winnipeg, Man., Can., Aug. 18, 1935; came to U.S., 1961, naturalized, 1968; s. Ross Grant and Anna Marie (Crispin) W.; m. Deanna Pauline Johnson, June 25, 1960; children—Carolyn Deanna, David John. M.D. with honors, U. Man., 1959. Diplomate: Am. Bd. Pathology. Intern Winnipeg Gen. Hosp., 1959-60, resident, 1960-61; resident Balt. City Hosp., 1961-63, Buffalo Gen. Hosp., 1963-64; teaching fellow in medicine U. Man., 1960-61; instr. in pathology, Buswell fellow SUNY-Buffalo, 1965-67, prof. pathology, chmn. dept. pathology, 1974—; asst. chief pathology Balt. City Hosps. and; asst. prof. Johns Hopkins U., 1967-74; cons. Roswell Park Meml. Inst., 1975—, bd. visitors, 1981—, interim dir., 1985-86, chmn. bd. visitors, 1987—. Recipient Louis A. and Ruth Siegel Disting. Teaching award SUNY-Buffalo, 1977, 78, 88, Deans award SUNY, 1987. Mem. AMA, AAAS, Coll. Am. Pathologists, Am. Soc. Investigative Pathologists, Am. Soc. Clin. Pathologists, U.S. and Can. Acad. Pathology, Assn. Pathology Chairmen (pres. 1994-96), Am. Heart Assn., Alpha Omega Alpha. Research in amyloidosis and aging, pathology of amyloidosis, characterization of clin. amyloid syndromes. Home: 46 Wynngate Ln Williamsville NY 14221-1840 Office: SUNY 204 Farber Hall Buffalo NY 14214

WRIGHT, JON ALAN, physicist, researcher; b. Tacoma, Wash., Jan. 18, 1938; s. Edward S. and Peggy (Hawley) W.; m. Barbara McCulley, Jan. 27, 1962; children: Jeffrey, Allison, Dana. BS, Cal Tech, 1959; PhD in Physics, U. Calif., Berkeley, 1965. Staff physicist Aerospace Corp., L.A., 1965; postdoctoral physicist U. Calif., San Diego, 1965-67; prof. physics U. Ill., Urbana, 1967-82; dir. Ctr. for Studies of Non-Linear Dynamics, San Diego, 1982—; rsch. physicist U. Calif., San Diego, 1990—; vis. prof. U. Utrecht, Netherlands, 1976; vis. assoc. prof. Stanford U., Palo Alto, Calif., 1973. Contbr. tech. papers to profl. jours. Achievements include specialization in nonlinear dynamics, nonlinear waves, semiclassical methods, ocean waves and remote sensing of ocean. Office: INLS U Calif 0402 San Diego CA 92093-0402

WRIGHT, JOSEPH ROBERT, JR., corporate executive; b. Tulsa, Sept. 24, 1938; s. Joe Robert and Ann Helen (Cech) W. B.S., Colo. Sch. Mines, 1961; M.I.A., Yale U., 1964. Vice pres. Booz, Allen & Hamilton, 1965-71; dep. dir. Bur. Census, Dept. Commerce, 1971-72; dep. adminstr. Social and Econ. Statis. Adminstrn., 1972-73, acting asst. sec. econ. affairs, 1973; asst. sec. adminstr. Dept. Agr., 1973-76; pres. Citicorp Retail Inc. and Retail Consumer Services Inc., N.Y.C.; v.p. Citicorp, Inc., 1976-81; dep. sec. Dept. Commerce, Washington, 1981-82; dep. dir. Office Mgmt. and Budget, Washington, 1982-88; chmn. Pres.'s Council on Integrity and Efficiency, 1982-89; chmn. Pres.'s Coun on Mgmt. Improvement, 1984-89; dir. Office Mgmt. and Budget, 1988-89; exec. v.p., vice chmn. W.R. Grace & Co., N.Y.C., 1989-94; chmn. Grace Environ., Inc., 1989-94, Avic Group Internat., 1995—, Jefferson Ptnrs., 1995—; bd. dirs. Travelers Corp., 1990—, Harcourt, Brace, Jovonavich, Inc., 1990-91, W.R. Grace & Co., 1989-91, Canonie Environ., Inc., 1989-94, Grace Energy, Inc., 1990-94, Productora de Papeles, S.A., 1991-94, La Posta Recycling Ctr., Inc., 1992-94, Nat. Assn. Mfg.; bd. advs. Baker & Taylor, 1992—, Netmatics, 1996—, Deswell Industries, Inc., 1995—, Ardshiel, Inc., 1990-94; fed. co-chmn. Coastal Plains Regional Commn., 1981-82, Four Corners Regional Commn., 1981-82, New Eng. Regional Commn., 1981-82, Old West Regional Commn., 1981-82, Pacific N.W. REgional Commn., 1981-82, S.W. Border Regional Commn., 1981-82; ptnr. Gulfstream Capital, 1995—, Austin Trading Co., 1995—. Mem. adv. bd. Coun. for Excellence in Govt., 1988-96, The Jefferson Group, 1993—; trustee Hampton U., 1990—. 1st lt. AUS, 1963-65. Recipient Pres.'s Citizens award and medal, 1989; named Govt. Exec. of Yr., Govt. Computer News Mag., 1988, medal disting. achievement Colo. Sch. Mines, 1985. Mem. Young Pres. Orgn., Nat. Acad. Pub. Adminstrn., Colo. Sch. Mines Alumni Assn., Pres.'s Export Coun., Chief Execs. Orgn., World Bus. coun., Reagan Alumni Assn., Palm Beach (Fla.) Golf and Polo Club, Banyon Country Club (Fla.), Sky Club (N.Y.C.). Home: 2 Ocean Ln Lake Worth FL 33462-3337 Office: 2100 W Sample Rd Ste 300 Pompano Beach FL 33064 also: Jefferson Capital 1341 G St NW Washington DC 20005 also: Avic Group Internat 599 Lexington Ave New York NY 10022

WRIGHT, JUDITH MARGARET, law librarian, educator; b. Jackson, Tenn., Aug. 16, 1944; d. Joseph Clarence and Mary Catherine (Key) Wright; m. Mark A. Johnson, Apr. 17, 1976; children—Paul, Michael. B.S., Memphis State U., 1966; M.A., U. Chgo., 1971; J.D., DePaul U., 1980. Bar: Ill. 1980. Librarian Oceanway Sch., Jacksonville, Fla., 1966-67; program dir. ARC, South Vietnam, 1967-68; documents and reference librarian D'Angelo Law Library, U. Chgo., 1970-74, reference librarian, 1974-77, dir., lectr. in law, 1980—; mem. adv. bd. Legal Reference Svcs. Quar., 1981—. Mem. ABA, Am. Assn. Law Libraries, Chgo. Assn. Law Libraries. Democrat. Methodist. Home: 5525 S Harper Ave Chicago IL 60637-1829

WRIGHT, JUDY, occupational health nurse, program director; b. Sewickley, Pa., July 12, 1924; d. Frank Allen and Ethel Cecilia (Cook) LaRoy; m. Robert James Wright, June 27, 1946; children: Judith Ann, Jo Ann. Diploma in nursing, Shadyside Hosp., Pitts., 1945. RN, Pa. Coord. admissions D.T. Watson Rehab. Hosp., Sewickley, rehab. coord., coord. employee health-lymphedema program. Contbr. articles to nursing jours. Mem. Assn. Rehab. Nurses (sec. SW chpt.), Nat. Rehab. Assn., Am. Congress Rehab. Medicine, Internat. Lymphology Soc., Oncology Nursing Soc. Home: RR 2 Box 292 New Brighton PA 15066-9613

WRIGHT, KATIE HARPER, educational administrator, journalist; b. Crawfordsville, Ark., Oct. 5, 1923; d. James Hale and Connie Mary (Locke) Harper; BA, U. Ill., 1944; MEd, 1959; EdD, St. Louis U., 1979; m. Marvin Wright, Mar. 21, 1952; 1 dau., Virginia K. Jordan. Elem. and spl. edn. tchr. East St. Louis (Ill.) Pub. Schs., 1944-65, dir. Dist. 189 Instructional Materials Program, 1965-71, dir. spl. edn. Dists. 188, 189, 1971-77, asst. supt. programs, 1977-79; interim supt. East St. Louis Sch. Dist. 189, 1993-94; adj. faculty Harris/Stowe State Coll., 1980; mem. staff St. Louis U., 1989—; interim supt. Dist. 189 Schs., 1994—; cons. to numerous workshops, seminars in field; mem. study tour People's Republic of China, 1984. Mem. Ill. Commn. on Children, 1973-85, East St. Louis Bd. Election Commrs.; pres. bd. dirs. St. Clair County Mental Health Center, 1970-72, 87— (award 1992); bd. dirs. River Bluff coun. Girl Scouts U.S., 1979—, nat. bd. dirs., 1981-84; bd. dirs. United Way, 1979—, Urban League, 1979—, Provident Counseling Ctr., 1995—; pres. bd. trustees East St. Louis Pub. Library, 1972-77; pres., bd. dirs. St. Clair County Mental Health Ctrs., 1987; adv. bd. Magna Bank; charter mem. Coalition of 100 Black Women; mem. coordinating council ethnic affairs Synod of Mid-Am., Presbyn. Ch. U.S.A; charter mem. Metro East Links Group; charter mem. Gateway chpt. The Links, Inc.; Ill. Minority/Female Bus. Coun., 1991—; mem. State of Ill. Corrections Sch. Bd. Author: Delta Sigma Theta/East St. Louis Chapter History, 1992. Recipient Lamp of Learning award East St. Louis Jr. Wednesday Club, 1965, Outstanding Working Woman award Downtown St. Louis, Inc., 1967, Ill. State citation for ednl. document Love is Not Enough, 1974, Delta Sigma Theta citation for document Good Works, 1979, Girl Scout Thanks badge, 1982, award Nat. Coun. Negro Women, 1983, Community Svc. award Met. East Bar Assn., 1983, Journalist award Sigma Gamma Rho, Spelman Coll. Alumni award, 1990, A World of Difference award, 1990, 91, Edn. award St. Louis YWCA, 1991, SIU-E-Kimmel award, 1991, St. Clair County Mental Health award, 1992, Gateway East Metropolitan Ministry Dr. M.L. King award, 1993, Nat. Coun. Negro Women Black Women Leader of the Year, 1995, Disting. Alumni award U. Ill., 1996; named Woman of Achievement, St. Louis Globe Democrat, 1974, Outstanding Adminstr. So. region Ill. Office Edn., 1975, Woman of Yr. in Edn. St. Clair County YWCA, 1987, Nat. Top Lady of the Yr., 1988; named to Vashon High Sch. Hall of Fame, 1989, Citizen Ambassador, South Africa, 1996. Mem. Am. Libraries Trustees Assn. (regional v.p. 1978-79, 92, nat. sec. 1979-80), Ill. Commn. on Children, Mensa, Council for Exceptional Children, Top Ladies of Distinction (pres. 1987-91, nat. editor 1991—, journalism award 1992, Media award 1992), Delta Sigma Theta (chpt. pres. 1960-62), Kappa Delta Pi (pres. So. Ill. U. chpt. 1973-74), Phi Delta Kappa (Service Key award 1984, chpt. pres. 1984-85), Iota Phi Lambda, Pi Lambda Theta (chpt. pres. 1985-87). Republican. Presbyterian. Club: East St. Louis Women's (pres. 1973-75). Contbr. articles to profl. jours.; feature writer St. Louis Argus Newspaper, 1979—. Home: 733 N 40th St East Saint Louis IL 62205-2138

WRIGHT, KENNETH BROOKS, lawyer; b. Whittier, Calif., June 5, 1934; s. Albert Harold and Marian (Schwey) W.; m. Sandra Beryl Smith, June 20, 1959; children: Margo Teresa, Daniel Brooks, John Waugh. B.A. cum laude, Pomona Coll., 1956; J.D., Stanford U., 1960. Bar: Calif. 1961, U.S. Supreme Ct. 1979. Assoc., then ptnr. Lawler, Felix & Hall, 1961-77; ptnr. Morgan, Lewis & Bockius, Los Angeles, 1978—; teaching team leader Nat. Inst. Trial Advocacy, 1978-80; mem. governing com. Calif. Continuing Edn. of Bar, 1973-77, chmn., 1975-76; nat. panel arbitrators Am. Arbitration Assn., 1970—; lectr. ABA Sect. Litigation Nat. Inst., 1979-86; bd. dirs. L.A. Internat. Comml. Arbitration Ctr. Chmn. bd. editors: Am. Bar Jour, 1977-81. Pres. Pomona Coll. Alumni Assn., 1970-71; pres. Campbell Hall Sch., 1973-74, bd. dirs., vice chmn., 1994—, parent tchr. coun., 1975—; counsel Vol. League San Fernando Valley, 1979-81; chmn. sect. adminstrn. of justice Town Hall of Calif., 1970-71; sr. warden Episcopal Ch., 1973-74. Served with U.S. Army, 1956-57. Mem. ABA (dir. programs litigation sect. 1977-81, mem. coun. 1982-88, mem. standing com on comm. 1978-88, chmn. 1987-88, chmn. sect. book pub. com. 1986-89, pres. fellows young lawyers 1985-86, bd. dirs. 1980-89), Internat. Bar Assn., Assn. Bus. Trial Lawyers (chair com. alt. dispute resolution 1991-93, bd. dirs. 1993-96), Am. Law Inst., Am. Bar Found., Am. Bd. Trial Advs., So. Calif. Def. Counsel, Def. Rsch. Inst., State Bar Calif. (mem. gov. com. continuing edn. of the bar 1972-77, chmn. 1975-76), Conf. Barristers (exec. com. 1966-69, 1st v.p. 1969), L.A. County Bar Assn. (com. on judiciary 1981-83, chmn. continuing legal edn. adv. com. 1989-91, vice-chmn. continuing legal edn. com. 1991-93, bd. dirs. L.A. Lawyers 1989-94), L.A. County Bar Found. (bd. dirs., trustee 1993—, mem. exec. com. internat. sect. 1996—), U.S. Supreme Ct. Hist. Soc., Jonathan Club, Chancery Club, Phi Beta Kappa. Republican. Avocations: skiing, tennis. Home: 3610 Longridge Ave Sherman Oaks CA 91423-4918 Office: Morgan Lewis & Bockius 801 S Grand Ave Fl 22 Los Angeles CA 90017-4613

WRIGHT, KENNETH OSBORNE, retired astronomer; b. Ft. George, B.C., Can., Nov. 1, 1911; s. Charles Melville and Agnes Pearl (Osborne) W.; m. Margaret Lindsay Sharp, Sept. 25, 1936 (dec. June 1969); 1 child, Nora Louise Wright Osborne; m. Jean May MacLachlan, Mar. 21, 1970. B.A., U. Toronto, Ont., Can., 1933, M.A., 1934; Ph.D., U. Mich., 1940; D.Sc. (hon.), Nicholas Copernicus U., Torun, Poland, 1973. With Dominion Astrophys. Obs., Victoria, B.C., 1936-84, asst. dir., 1960-66, dir., 1966-76, guest worker, 1976-84; hon. prof. physics U. Victoria, 1965-80, bd. govs., 1973-75; lectr. U. B.C., 1943-44; spl. lectr. in astronomy U. Toronto, 1959-60; research asso. Mt. Wilson and Palomar Obs., 1962; chmn. asso. com. on astronomy NRC Can., 1972-74. Decorated Can. Centennial medal. Fellow Royal Soc. Can.; mem. Internat. Astron. Union, Am. Astron. Soc., Can. Astron. Soc., Royal Astron. Soc. Can. (Gold medal 1933), Royal Astron. Soc., Astron. Soc. Pacific., Round Table, Rotary. Mem. United Ch. of Can. Research, publs. in field. Home: #202 1375 Newport Ave, Victoria, BC Canada V8S 5E8

WRIGHT, KIETH CARTER, librarian, educator; b. Billings, Mont., Nov. 11, 1933; s. Donald DeWitt and Isabella Sarah W.; children from previous marriage: Cynthia Jean, Elizabeth Anne. BA, Willamette U., 1955; MDiv, Union Theol. Sem., N.Y.C., 1958; MS In Libr. Scis, Columbia U., 1968, D of Libr. Scis., 1972. Chaplain intern Big Spring (Tex.) State Hosp., 1958-59; pastoral care worker N.C. Bapt. Hosp., Winston-Salem, N.C., 1960-64; adminstr. Nat. Council Chs., N.Y.C., 1964-70; librarian Gallaudet U., Washington, 1972-75; mem. faculty Cath. U. Am., Washington, 1976; dean Dept. Libr. and Info. Studies U. Md., College Park, 1977-79; chmn. dept. libr. sci. and ednl. technology Sch. Edn. U. N.C., Greensboro, 1980-86, prof. Sch. Edn., 1986—. Author: Library and Information Services for Handicapped Individuals, 1979, 3d edit., 1989, Workstations and Local Area Networks for Libraries, 1990, Serving Disabled, 1991, The Challenge of Technology, 1993, Computer-related Technologies in Library Operation, 1995. Office Edn. grantee, 1992-94. Mem. ALA. Home: 1605 Bearhollow Rd Greensboro NC 27410-3501 Office: U NC Sch Edn Greensboro NC 27412-5001

WRIGHT, LAURALI R. (BUNNY WRIGHT), writer; b. Saskatoon, Sask., Can., June 5, 1939; d. Sidney Victor and Evelyn Jane (Barber) Appleby; m. John Herbert Wright, Jan. 6, 1962 (separated 1986); children: Victoria Kathleen, Johnna Margaret. Student, Carleton U., 1958-59, U. B.C., 1960, 62-63, U. Calgary, 1970-71, Banff Sch. Fine Arts, 1976; MA, Simon Fraser U., Burnaby, B.C., Can., 1995. Reporter Saskatoon Star-Phoenix, 1968-69, Calgary Albertan, 1969-70; reporter, columnist Calgary Herald, 1970-76, 1970-76, asst. city editor, 1976-77; freelance writer Calgary, 1977—. Author: (novels) Neighbours, 1979 (New Alta. novelist award Alta Culture and Multiculturalism 1978), The Favorite, 1982, Among Friends, 1984, The Suspect, 1985 (Edgar Allen Poe award Mystery Writers Am. 1986), Sleep While I Sing, 1986, Love in the Temperate Zone, 1988, A Chill Rain in January, 1989 (Arthur Ellis award Crime Writers Can. 1990), Fall From Grace, 1991, Prized Possessions, 1993, A Touch of Panic, 1994, Mother Love, 1995. Mem. Writers Union Can., Authors' Guild of U.S., Internat. P.E.N., Mystery Writers of Am., Authors League Am., Periodical Writers Assn. Can., Writers Fedn. B.C. Avocations: gardening, reading, movies, theater, concerts, jogging. Office: Virginia Barber Lit Agy Inc 101 Fifth Ave New York NY 10003-1008

WRIGHT, LAWRENCE A., federal judge; b. Stratton, Maine, Dec. 25, 1927; m. Avis Leahy, 1953; children: Michael, David, James, Stephen, Douglas. BA, U. Maine, 1953; JD, Georgetown U., 1956; LLM, Boston U., 1962. Bar: D.C. 1956, Maine 1956, Mass. 1968, Vt. 1971. Sr. trial counsel chief counsel office IRS, Boston, 1958-69; tax commr. State of Vt., 1969-71; ptnr. Gravel, Shea & Wright Ltd., Vt., 1971-84; judge U.S. Tax Ct., Washington, 1984—. 2d lt. U.S. Army, 1945-48; ret. col. JAG, USAR, 1978. Decorated Legion of Merit, others. Home: 1844 Northbridge Ln Annapolis MD 21401-6575 Office: US Tax Ct 400 2nd St NW Washington DC 20217-0001

WRIGHT, LILYAN BOYD, physical education educator; b. Upland, Pa., May 11, 1920; d. Albert Verlenden and Mabel (Warburton) Boyd; B.S., Temple U., 1942, M.Ed., 1946; Ed.D., Rutgers U., 1972; m. Richard P. Wright, Oct. 23, 1942; 1 child, Nicki Wright Vanek. Tchr. health and phys. edn. Woodbury (N.J.) High Sch., 1942-43, Glen-Nor High Sch., Glenolden, Pa., 1944-46, Chester (Pa.) High Sch., 1946-54; chmn. women's dept. health and phys, edn. Union (N,J.) High Sch., 1954-61; with Trenton State Coll., 1961-90, head women's program health and phys. edn., 1967-77, chmn. dept. health, phys. edn. and recreation, 1977-86, adj. faculty mem. 1990-92, prof. emeritus, 1991—; mem. N.J. State Com. Div. Girls and Women's Sports, 1958-80; chmn. New Atlantic Field Hockey Sectional Umpiring, 1981-85; chmn. New Atlantic Field Hockey Assn., 1985-90; with recreation after sch. program Newport Counseling Ctrl, 1992-93. Active Chester United Fund; water safety, first aid instr.; vestry Ch. Epiphany, Newport, N.H., 1992—, sr. warden, 1995—; vestry St. Luke's Episcopal Ch., 1988-91; trustee Olive Pettis Libr., Goshen, 1992—; dist. ednl. improvement team for Goshen-Lempster Sch. Dist., 1995—. ARC Scholarship in her honor N.J. Athletic Assn. Girls, 1971; named to Hall of Fame, Temple U., 1976. Recipient U.S. Field Hockey Assn. award, 1989, named Nat. Honorary Field Hockey Umpire. Mem. AAHPERD (chmn. Eastern Dist. Assn. Div. Girls and Women's Sports, sec. to council for services Eastern dist. 1979-80, chmn. 1980-81, chmn. com. on aging and adult devel. of ea. dist. 1993—, N.J. rep. to council for convs. 1984-85, Honor Fellow award 1986), N.J. AHPER (pres. 1974-75, past pres. 1975-76, v.p. phys. edn. div., parliamentarian 1990—, Disting. Service and Leadership award 1969, 93, Honor Fellow award 1977, Presdl. Citation award 1993, 95, Disting. Leadership award 1994), N.J. Women's Lacrosse Assn. (umpiring chmn. 1972-76), Nat. Assn. Phys. Edn. in Higher Edn., Eastern Assn. Phys. Edn. Coll. Women, North Jersey, Ctrl. Jersey bds. women's ofcls., Am., Pa. (v.p. 1953-54), Chester (pres. 1949-54) fedns. tchrs., U.S. Field Hockey Assn. (exec. com., chair honorary umpire award com. 1992), North Jersey Field Hockey Assn. (past pres.), N.H. Field Hockey Umpires' Assn., No. New Eng. Lacrosse Officials Bd., U.S. Women's LaCrosse Assn. (Honorary and Emeritus Umpiring Rating award), Kappa Delta Epsilon, Delta Psi Kappa (past pres. Phila. alumni chpt.), Kappa Delta Pi. Home: PO Box 239 Goshen NH 03752

WRIGHT, MARK KEMPER, marketing executive; b. Cleve., Aug. 17, 1955; s. Hastings Kemper and Nancy (Howell) W.; m. Martha Steele, Sept. 24, 1988; children: Douglas, Catherine. BA, Northwestern U., 1981; MBA, Vanderbilt U., 1984. Mktg. analyst Lettuce Entertain You, Chgo., 1977-80; regional mktg. mgr. Shoney's, Nashville, 1980-83; dir. mktg. Eric Ericson and Assocs. Advt., Nashville, 1983-85, v.p. mktg., 1985—; pres. Signa subs. Eric Mktg. Comms., Nashville, 1987-93; founder, prin., bd. dirs. Inforum, Inc., Nashville; mem. Owen Grad. Sch. entrepreneurial studies task force Vanderbilt U., 1995. Inventor healthcare planning, mktg. software. Author, founder newspaper polls, 1984-88, televised polit. exit polls, 1987-88; mktg. cons. United Way, 1984-93, chmn. rsch. and planning task force, 1989-90; mktg. cons. Meharry Med. Sch., Nashville, 1987-90, Fisk U., Nashville, 1985-86; primary author Greater Nashville 2000 Econ. Community Devel. Mktg. Plan, 1989. Community Coalition of Minority Health award, 1989. Republican. Episcopalian. Avocations: mountain climbing, hiking, tennis. Home: 9226 Fox Run Dr Brentwood TN 37027-7444 Office: Ericson Mktg Comms 1130 8th Ave S Nashville TN 37203

WRIGHT, MARSHALL, retired manufacturing executive, former diplomat; b. El Dorado, Ark., July 14, 1926; s. John Harvey and Helen Vaughan (Williams) W.; m. Mable Olean Johnson, Sept. 12, 1950 (dec. June 1989); children: William Marshall, Jefferson Vaughan; m. Lind Groseclose Vaughan, Mar. 31, 1990. Student, U. Ark., 1946-48, Cornell U., 1957-58; B.S. in Fgn. Service, Georgetown U., 1951. Joined U.S. Fgn. Service, 1953; vice consul Egypt, 1953-55; adminstrv. officer Can., 1956; econ. officer Burma, 1958-60; polit. officer Thailand, 1966-67; spokesman for State Dept., 1964-66; country dir. for Philippines, 1969; sr. mem. NSC, 1967-68, dir. long range planning, 1970-72; asst. sec. state for congl. relations, 1972-74; sr. fellow Nat. War Coll., 1969-70; v.p. govt. affairs Eaton Corp., 1974-76, v.p. pub. affairs, 1976-80, v.p. corp. affairs, 1980-91. Chmn. Cleve. ARC; trustee Cleve. Orch., Cleve. Inst. Music; chmn. Cleve. Com. Fgn. Rels.; vice chmn. Govtl. Rsch. Inst.; mem. Conf. Bd. Pub. Affairs Rsch. Coun., MAPI, Pub. Affairs Coun.; bd. dirs. Cleveland Town Hall, Bus. Industry Polit. action Com. With USMC, 1944-46. Recipient Meritorious Service award State Dept., 1966, Distinguished Service award, 1972. Mem. Am. Fgn. Svc. Assn., Columbia Country Club, Met. Club, Dacor, Mayfield Country, Union, Moss Creek Golf Club. Home (summer): 304 Corning Dr Cleveland OH 44108-1014 Home (winter): Moss Creek Plantation 80 Toppin Dr Hilton Head SC 29926

WRIGHT, MARY JAMES, multimedia instructional designer; b. Charlottesville, Va., Aug. 20, 1946; d. Harry Beech and Virginia Allen (Root) James; m. Paul Sims Wright, July 26, 1969; children: Christopher Brennan, Keith Allen. BA summa cum laude, Mary Washington Coll., 1968; MA, Northwestern U., 1969; postgrad., Trinity Coll., 1981, Gallaudet U., 1991. Instr. drama and speech Mary Washington Coll., Fredericksburg, Va., 1969-71, Charles County Community Coll., La Plata, Md., 1973-79; arts and media coord. Charles County Arts Coun., La Plata, 1973-82, Gen. Smallwood Mid. Sch., Indian Head, Md., 1980-82, No. Va. Community Coll., Annandale, 1982-84; computer-based learning specialist USDA Grad. Sch., Washington, 1984-85, U.S. Army Engr. Sch., Ft. Belvoir, Va., 1985-87, Battelle Meml. Inst., Columbus, Ohio, 1987-88; videodisc designer Kendrick & Co., Washington, 1988-90; instrnl. design mgr. The Discovery Channel, Bethesda, Md., 1990-93; instnl. design mgr. Edunetics Corp., Arlington, Va., 1994-95; interactive multimedia designer and developer Smart House, Ltd. Partnership, Upper Mralboro, Md., 1990; project mgr., instl. designer Toby Levine Comms., Inc., 1990—. Author, dir.: Story-Theatre for Children, 1979; contbr. articles to profl. jours.; pub. classroom guides for nat. media products: PBS, Discovery Channel, Nat. Geographic. Pres. Am. Christian Television System of No. Va., Action for Women, Charles County AAUW; sign lang. interpreter Deaf Ministry. Nat. Danforth fellow 1969; recipient Achievement award Dept. of Army, 1986, Kendrick & Co., 1989; recipient Outstanding Arts Programming award Md. Dept. Parks and Recreation, 1980, Silver and Bronze Cindy awards Cinema in Industry and Edn., 1992, Red Ribbon Am. Film & Video Assn. Festival, Special Jury award Houston Internat. Film Festival, 1992, Gold award Nebr. Interactive Media, 1993. Mem. ASCD, Internat. Interactive Courseware Soc. (Mark of Excellence award 1992), Assn. for Devel. Computer-Based Instrn. Systems (coord. spl. interest groups D.C. chpt. 1989-90), No. Va. Registry Interpreters for the Deaf, Mortar Bd., Alpha Psi Omega, Alpha Phi Sigma. Home and office: 4302 Rolling Stone Way Alexandria VA 22306-1225

WRIGHT, MICHAEL GEORGE, science administrator, research metallurgist; b. Bristol, U.K., Apr. 15, 1939; m. Fiona E. Crozier; children: Craig, Graeme. BS, U. Wales, 1960; MSc, McMaster U, 1964. Metallurgist GE-Simon Carves Atomic Energy Group, Kent, U.K., 1960-62, Inland Steel Co., Ind., 1964-66; rsch. sci. Atomic Energy Can. Ltd., Pinawa, Man., Can., 1966-77, br. mgr., 1977-82, sr. adv. and asst., 1982-84, mgr. engring. divsn., 1984-86, gen. mgr., 1986-90; v.p. ops., 1990-94, gen. mgr. nuclear ops., 1994—. Office: Atomic Energy of Can Ltd, Chalk River Labs, Chalk River, ON Canada KOJ IJO

WRIGHT, MICHAEL WILLIAM, wholesale distribution, retailing executive; b. Mpls., June 13, 1938; s. Thomas W. and Winifred M. Wright. B.A., U. Minn., 1961, J.D. with honors, 1963. Ptnr. Dorsey & Whitney, Mpls., 1966-77; sr. v.p. Supervalu Inc., Mpls., 1977-78; pres., chief operating officer Super Valu Stores, Inc., Mpls., 1978—, chief exec. officer, 1981—, chmn., 1982—; bd. dirs., past chmn. Fed. Res. Bank, Mpls.; bd. dirs. Norwest Corp., Honeywell, Inc., The Musicland Group, Shopko, Inc., S.C. Johnson & Co., Inc., Cargill, Inc., Internat. Ctr. for Cos. of the Food Trade and Industry, Food Mktg. Inst., Nat. Am. Wholesale Grocers Assn., Inc.; vice chmn. Food Mktg. Inst. 1st lt. U.S. Army, 1964-66. Office: Supervalu Inc PO Box 990 Minneapolis MN 55440

WRIGHT, MILDRED ANNE (MILLY WRIGHT), conservator, researcher; b. Athens, Ala., Sept. 9, 1939; d. Thomas Howard and Anne Louise (Ashworth) Speegle; m. William Paul Wright, Nov. 20, 1965; children: Paul Howard, William Neal. BS in Physics, U. Ala., Tuscaloosa, 1963. Rschr. in acoustics Wyle Labs., Huntsville, Ala., 1963-64; tchr. physics, English Huntsville H.S., 1964-67; ptnr. Flying Carpet Oriental Rugs, Florence, Ala., 1974—; adj. mem. faculty U. North Ala., Florence, 1988, lectr. Inst. for Learning in Retirement, 1991—. Columnist Times Daily, 1992—; photojournalist, writer River Views Mag., 1993—; contbr. articles to profl. jours. (1st pl. award 1986, 87). Pianist, organist Edgemont Meth. Ch., Florence, 1987-90; mem. steering com. Melton Hollow Nature Ctr., Florence, 1990—, Design Ala., Florence, 1991, River Heritage Discovery Camp, 1993—; mem. River Heritage Com., Florence, 1991—; accompanist Shoals Boy Choir, Muscle Shoals, Ala., 1992-93; bd. dirs. Heritage Preservation, Inc., 1989—, pres., 1990-92, 96—, treas., 1995-96; bd. dirs. Tenn. Valley Hist. Soc., pres., 1991-95, Ala. Preservation Alliance, treas., 1993—, Florence Main St. program, 1992-94, Maud Lindsay Free Kindergarten, Frank Lloyd Wright Rosenbaum House Found., Inc., 1992—, Gen. Joseph Wheeler Home Found., 1994—, treas., 1995—, Friends of the Ala. Archives, 1995—, sec., 1995—; mem. adv. coun. Human Environ. Scis. Dept.; mem. Coby Hall steering com. U. North Ala., 1992—, Kennedy-Douglass Ctr. Arts; adv. bd. Waterloo Mus., 1995—; newsletter editor Gen. Joseph Wheeler Home Found., 1995—; mem. Cahaba Adv. Bd., State of Ala., 1996—; mem. adv. bd. Florence Children's Mus., 1995—; exhibit chmn. Tenn. Valley Art Assn., 1996—. Recipient Disting. Svc. award Ala. Hist. Commn., 1991, Outstanding Svc. award Edgemont Meth. Ch., 1990, Capital award Heritage Preservation, Inc., 1992, Merit award Ala. Preservation Alliance, 1995. Mem. Ala. Writers' Conclave (Creative Works award 1986, 87), Ala. Hist. Assn., Ala. Archeol. Soc., Natchez Trace Geneal. Soc., Colbert County Hist. Landmarks Found., Nat. Trust for Hist. Preservation, Tennessee Valley Art Assn. (exhibit chmn. 1995—), La Grange Living History Assn., Trail of Tears Assn., Firenze Club (past pres., pres. 1996—), Optimist Club, Sigma Pi Sigma. Avocations: bridge, photography, travel, discovering old buildings, gardening. Home: PO Box 279 Florence AL 35631-0279

WRIGHT, MINTURN TATUM, III, lawyer; b. Phila., Aug. 7, 1925; s. Minturn T. and Anna (Moss) W.; m. Nonya R. Stevens, May 11, 1957; children: Minturn T., Richard S., Robert M., Marianne F. BA, Yale U., 1949; LLB, U. Pa., 1952. Bar: Pa. 1953, U.S. Ct. Appeals (3d cir.) 1953, U.S. Supreme Ct. 1962. Law clk. U.S. Ct. Appeals (3d cir.), 1952-53; assoc. Dechert, Price & Rhoads, Phila., 1953-61, ptnr., 1961-95, chmn., 1982-84; bd. dirs. Penn Va. Corp., Phila. Contributionship, Vector Security Co. Inc., Cotiga Devel. Co.; vis. prof. U. Pa. Law Sch., 1965-69, 93—. Contbr. articles to profl. jours. Trustee Acad. Nat. Scis. Phila., 1958—, chmn., 1976-81, vice chmn., 1995—; trustee Hawk Mountain Sanctuary Assn., chmn. bd. dirs., 1992—, Rare Ctr., The Nature Conservancy (Pa. chpt.). Served with U.S. Army, 1943-46. Mem. ABA, Pa. Bar Assn., Phila. Bar Assn., Nat. Coal Lawyers Assn., Eastern Mineral Law Assn. (trustee), Phila. Club, Milldam Club. Episcopalian. Office: Dechert Price & Rhoads 4000 Bell Atlantic Tower 1717 Arch St Philadelphia PA 19103-2713

WRIGHT, MURIEL DEASON See WELLS, KITTY

WRIGHT, NORMAN HAROLD, lawyer; b. N.Y.C., Mar. 7, 1947; s. Donald H. and Georgianna (Reinert) W.; m. Julie K. Angert, May 29, 1971; children: Zane H., Anne V. BS in Engring., U. Toledo, 1969; JD, Creighton U., 1978. Bar: Nebr. 1978, U.S. Ct. Appeals (8th cir.) 1978, U.S. Supreme Ct. 1989. Engr. E.I. DuPont de Nemours & Co., Inc., Columbus, Ohio, 1969-72, El Paso, Tex., 1972-75; assoc. Fraser, Stryker, Vaughn, Meusey, Olson, Boyer & Bloch, P.C., Omaha, 1978-83, ptnr., 1984—; dir. Nebr. Tax Rsch. Coun., Lincoln, 1989—. Author: Nebraska Legal Forms, Real Estate, 1983. Chmn. bd. Am. Diabetes Assn., Omaha, 1991; bd. trustees Trinity Cathedral Episcopal Ch., Omaha, 1986-89. Mem. ABA, Nebr. Bar Assn., Inst. Property Taxation, Nebr. Tax Forum, Cosmopolitan Club (sec. 1990-92, pres. 1995). Republican. Episcopalian. Avocations: golf, skiing, baseball. Home: 8910 Frances St Omaha NE 68124-2041 Office: Fraser Stryker Vaughn Meusey Olson Boyer & Bloch PC 409 S 17th St Ste 500 Omaha NE 68102-2609

WRIGHT, OLGA, artist, aesthetician; b. Mangum, Okla., Feb. 6, 1932; m. George Wayne Polly, Jr., Aug. 21, 1956. Student, N.Y. Art Students League, 1959; BS, Arts and Industries U., Kingsville, Tex., 1962. Owner Olga Wright Aesthetics, Corpus Christi, Tex., 1937—. One-woman shows include Centenial Mus., 1978. Recipient Best of Show award Dimension Show, 1977, Best Oil of Show award, 1977, 79, All Membership Show of Art Ctrs. Artfest '96. Mem. Art Ctr. Corpus Christi, Art Assn., Art Guild, Pastel Soc., South Tex. Art League, Water Color Soc. South Tex. Avocations: photography, philately, writing, botany, jewelry making. Home: 4238 Estate Dr Corpus Christi TX 78412-2429 Office: Olga Wright Aesthetics 4238 Estate Dr Corpus Christi TX 78412-2429

WRIGHT, SIR (JOHN) OLIVER, retired diplomat; b. U.K., Mar. 6, 1921; m. Lillian Marjory Osborne, Sept. 19, 1942; children: Nicholas, John, Christopher. Ed., Solihull Sch., Christ's Coll., Cambridge, Eng.; D.H.L. (hon.), U. Nebr., 1983; LL.D., Rockford Coll., 1984. Joined Diplomatic Service, 1945; Brit. ambassador to Denmark, 1966-69, to Fed. Republic Germany, 1975-81, to U.S., 1982-86; vis. prof. U. S.C.; dir. Berkeley Hotel; dir. Enviromed P.L.C.; Tobin Lewin vis. prof. Wash. U., St. Louis. Trustee Brit. Mus., 1986-91; bd. dirs. Brit. Council; chmn. Anglo-Irish Encounter, 1986-91. With Royal Navy, 1941-45. Decorated D.S.C., knight grand cross Royal Victorian Order, knight grand cross Order of St. Michael and St. George, grand cross German Order of Merit; named hon. fellow Christ's Coll., 1981; Clark fellow, Cornell U., 1987. Mem. German C. of C. London (pres.). Club: Travellers' (London). Avocations: theatre; gardening.

WRIGHT, PATRICK E., grain company executive; b. 1936. With Owensboro (Ky.) Grain Co., 1955—, now pres. Office: Owensboro Grain Co 719 E 2nd St Owensboro KY 42303-3301*

WRIGHT, PETER MELDRIM, lawyer; b. Charlottesville, Va., Apr. 10, 1946; s. David McCord and Caroline Wallace (Jones) W.; m. Astrid Gabriella Mercedes Sandberg, June 4, 1972; children: David Habersham, Christian Langdon. AB, U. Ga., 1967, JD, 1972. Bar: Ga. 1972, U.S. Dist. Ct. (no. dist.) Ga. 1972. Assoc. Jones, Bird & Howell, Atlanta, 1972-77, ptnr., 1977-82; ptnr. Alston & Bird, Atlanta, 1982—. Author: A Survey of State Blue Sky Laws Applicable to Tax Exempt Bonds, 1987, Long Term Care Facilities, Chapter 7 of Health Care Corporate Law—Facilities and Transactions, 1996. Sec. Atlanta coun. Soc. Colonial Wars in Ga., 1975-88, dep. gov., 1989-91; mem. Soc. Clin. Ga., Savannah, historian, 1996—. Mem. ABA, Ga. Bar Assn., Atlanta Bar Assn., Nat. Assn. Bond Lawyers (chmn. blue sky laws and legal investment law coms. 1982-85, bd. dirs. 1985-86), Ga. Hist. Soc. (bd. curators 1993-94, sec. 1994—), Oglethorpe Club (Savannah, Ga.), St. Andrew's Soc. Savannah. Home: 3502 Woodhaven Rd NW Atlanta GA 30305-1011 Office: Alston & Bird 1 Atlantic Ctr 1201 W Peachtree St NW Atlanta GA 30309-3400

WRIGHT, RANDOLPH EARLE, retired petroleum company executive; b. Brownsville, Tex., Dec. 22, 1920; s. William Randolph and Nelle Mae (Earle) W.; m. Elaine Marie Harris, May 9, 1943; 1 son, Randolph Earle. B.S., U. Tex., 1942. With Texaco Inc., 1946-82; mgr. gas div. Texaco Inc., Houston, 1968-70; gen. mgr. producing dept. Texaco Inc., 1970-71, v.p. gas dept., 1971-82; v.p., sr. officer Texaco Inc., Houston, 1972-80; past pres., dir. Sabine Pipe Line Co.; v.p., asst. to pres. Texaco U.S.A., 1980-82, ret., 1982; past v.p. Texaco Mineral Co.; past chmn. engring. found. adv. council U. Tex., Austin. Past mem. exec. bd. Sam Houston Area council Boy Scouts Am.; past bd. dirs., past pres. Jr. Achievement S.E. Tex.; past bd. dirs. Houston Symphony Soc., Tex. Research League, Houston C. of C.; past trustee U. St. Thomas; trustee S.W. Research Inst. Served with USNR, World War II. Mem. Tex. Research League. Clubs: Lakeside.

WRIGHT, RICHARD G., optical and health care company executive; b. Syracuse, N.Y., Mar. 11, 1934; s. Herbert G. and Marguerite (Wood) W.; m. Barbara Ann Lutzy, Aug. 18, 1954; children: Linda, Richard Jr., Pamela, Michelle, Craig. Student, Colgate U., 1953-54; BS, Syracuse U., 1957. Dir. mktg. soft contact lens div. Am. Optical Co., Southbridge, Mass., 1976-79, gen. mgr. soft contact lens div., 1979-81; exec. v.p. Barnes-Hind div. Revlon, Inc., N.Y.C., 1981-83, pres., 1983-85; pres. Revlon Vision Care Internat., N.Y.C., 1985-86; pres., COO Foster-Grant Corp., Leominster, Mass., 1986-89; pres., CEO Xenon Vision Inc., Princeton, N.J., 1989-91; v.p., gen. mgr. Storz Instruments, Co. divsn. Am. Cyanamid Co., 1991-94; chmn., CEO Celgene Corp., Warren, N.J., 1994—. Home: 90 Stone Run Rd Bedminster NJ 07921 Office: Celgene Corp 7 Powder Horn Dr Warren NJ 07059

WRIGHT, RICHARD JOHN, business executive; b. Bklyn., June 17, 1951; s. David Francis and Mary Catherine W.; m. Linda Marie Green, May 24, 1975; children: Sean, Bridget. B.S. in Physics with honors, Bates Coll., 1973; M.B.A., Rutgers U., 1974. C.P.A. Mgr. Coopers & Lybrand, N.Y.C., 1975-81; chief fin. officer Drexel Burnham Lambert, N.Y.C., 1981-92; pres., dir. DP Investments G.P. Corp., N.Y.C., 1992—; pres. DPI-A Corp., N.Y.C., 1992—, DPI-B Corp., N.Y.C., 1992—; mng. dir. Viking Group, Ltd., Whitredge Capital, L.P. Mem. AICPA, Fin. Exec. Inst., N.Y. State Soc. CPAs, Williams Club, Spring Lake Bath and Tennis Club. Office: DP Investments GP Corp 450 Lexington Ave New York NY 10017-3911

WRIGHT, RICHARD NEWPORT, III, civil engineer, government official; b. Syracuse, N.Y., May 17, 1932; s. Richard Newport and Carolyn (Baker) W.; m. Teresa Rios, Aug. 23, 1959; children—John Stannard, Carolyn Maria, Elizabeth Rebecca, Edward Newport. B.C.E., Syracuse U., 1953, M.C.E. (Parcel fellow), 1955; Ph.D., U. Ill., 1962. Jr. engr. Pa. R.R., Phila., 1953-55; instr. civil engring. U. Ill., Urbana, 1957-62; asst. prof. U. Ill., 1962-65, assoc. prof., 1965-70, prof., 1970-74, adj. prof., 1974-79; chief structures sect. Bldg. Research div. U.S. Bur. Standards, Washington, 1971-72; pres. Internat. Council for Bldg. Research, Studies and Documentation, 1983-86; dep. dir. tech. Ctr. Bldg. Tech., 1972-73, dir., 1974-91; dir. Bldg. and Fire Rsch. Lab., 1991—. Contbr. articles to profl. jours. Pres. Montgomery Village Found., 1989-90, bd. dirs., 1985—. Served with AUS, 1955-57. Named Fed. Engr. of Yr. Nat. Soc. Profl. Engrs., 1988. Fellow ASCE, AAAS. Home: 20081 Doolittle St Montgomery Village MD 20879-1354 Office: Dept of Commerce Nat Inst Standards & Tech Bldg and Fire Research Labs Gaithersburg MD 20899

WRIGHT, RICHARD OSCAR, III, pathologist, educator; b. La Junta, Colo., Aug. 9, 1944; s. Richard O. Sr. and Frances R. (Curtiss) W.; m. Bernale Trout, May 31, 1969; children: Lauren Diane, Richard O. IV. BS in Biology, Midwestern State U., 1966; MS in Biology, U. Houston, 1968; DO, U. Health Sci., 1972. Cert. anatomic pathology and lab. medicine Am. Osteo. Bd. Pathology. Sr. attending pathologist Normandy Met. Hosps., St. Louis, 1977-81; sr. attending pathologist Phoenix (Ariz.) Gen. Hosps., 1981—, dir. med. edn., 1989-92; clin. asst. prof. pathology Coll. Osteo. Medicine, Pomona, Calif., 1985—; clin. instr. pathology Ohio U. Coll. Osteo. Medicine, Athens, 1976-77; clin. asst. prof. pathology Kirksville (Mo.) Coll. Osteo. Medicine, 1985-87; vis. lectr. pathology New Eng. Coll. Osteo. Medicine, Biddeford, Maine, 1989-92; cons. pathologist Phoenix (Ariz.) Indian Med. Ctr., 1992-94; adv. bd. Inter Soc. Coun. Pathology, Chgo., 1992—. Active Ariz. Rep. Party, Phoenix, Rep. Nat. Com., Washington; chmn. bd. trustees Phoenix (Ariz.) Gen. Hosp., 1994-95; ex-occicio, mem. bd. trustees, 1995—. Recipient Mead-Johnson award Nat. Osteo. Assn., 1975. Fellow Am. Osteo. Coll. Pathologists (pres. 1989-90, bd. govs. 1984-91), Coll. m. Pathologists; mem. Ariz. Osteo. Med. Assn. Ariz. Soc. Pathologists, Century Club Alumni Assn., AAAS, Alpha Phi Omega, Rho Sigma Chi, Psi Sigma Alpha. Presbyterian. Office: Anatomic Pathology Assoc 19829 N 27th Ave Phoenix AZ 85027-4001

WRIGHT, ROBERT, broadcast executive. Office: NBC 30 Rockefeller Plz New York NY 10112

WRIGHT, ROBERT JOSEPH, lawyer; b. Rome, Ga., Dec. 13, 1949; s. Arthur Arley and Maude T. (Lacey) W.; m. Donna Ruth Bishop, Feb. 18, 1972; children: Cynthia Ashley, Laura Christine. BA cum laude, Ga. State U., 1979; JD cum laude, U. Ga., 1983. Bar: GA. 1983, U.S. Dist. Ct. (no. dist.) Ga. 1983, U.S. Dist. Ct. (mid. dist.) Ga. 1985. Assoc. Craig & Gainer, Covington, Ga., 1983-84, Heard, Leverett & Adams, Elberton, Ga., 1984-86; gen. counsel Group Underwriters, Inc., Elberton, 1987—. Editorial staff Ga. Jour. Internat. and Comparative Law, 1981-82. Mem. State Bar Ga. (sec. legal econs. sect. 1987-88, chmn. legal econs. sect. 1988-90), Order of the Coif, Masons, Phi Alpha Delta. Baptist. Home: 1030 E Canyon Creek Ct Watkinsville GA 30677-1500

WRIGHT, ROBERT PAYTON, lawyer; b. Beaumont, Tex., Feb. 15, 1951; s. Vernon Gerald and Huberta Read (Nunn) W.; m. Sallie Chesnutt Smith, July 16, 1977; children: Payton Cullen, Elizabeth Risher. AB, Princeton U., 1972; JD, Columbia U., 1975. Bar: Tex. 1975. Ptnr. Baker & Botts, L.L.P., Houston, 1975—. Author: The Texas Homebuyer's Manual, 1986. Mem. State Bar Tex. (chmn. coun. real estate, probate, trust law sect. 1994-95), Houston Bar ASsn. (chmn. real estate sect. 1989-90), Tex. Coll. Real Estate Lawyers, Houston Real Estate Lawyers Coun., Houston Club (mem. com. young mems. 1987). Episcopalian. Office: Baker & Botts LLP 910 Louisiana St Houston TX 77002

WRIGHT, ROBERT ROSS, III, law educator; b. Ft. Worth, Nov. 20, 1931; m. Susan Webber; children: Robert Ross IV, John, David, Robin. BA cum laude, U. Ark., 1953, JD, 1956; MA (grad. fellow), Duke U., 1954; SJD (law fellow), U. Wis., 1967. Bar: Ark. 1956, U.S. Supreme Ct. 1968, Okla. 1970. Instr. polit. sci. U. Ark., 1955-56; mem. firm Forrest City, Ark., 1956-58; partner firm Norton, Norton & Wright, Forrest City, 1959; asst. gen. counsel, asst. sec. Crossett Co., Ark.; atty. Crossett div. Ga.-Pacific Corp., 1960-63; asst. sec. Pub. Utilities Co., Crossett, Triangle Bag Co., Covington, Ky., 1960-62; mem. faculty law sch. U. Ark., 1963-70; asst. prof., dir. continuing legal edn. and research, then asst. dean U. Ark. (Little Rock div.), 1965-66, prof. law, 1967-70; vis. prof. law U. Iowa, 1969-70; prof. U. Okla., 1970-77; dean U. Okla. (Coll. Law); dir. U. Okla. (Law Center), 1970-76; vis. prof. U. Ark., Little Rock, 1976-77; Donaghey Disting. prof. U. Ark, 1977—; Ark. commr. Nat. Conf. Commrs. Uniform State Laws, 1967-70; past chmn. Com. Uniform Eminent Domain Code; past mem. Com. Uniform Probate Code, Ark. Gov.'s Ins. Study Comm.; chmn. Gov. Commn. on Uniform Probate Code; chmn. task force joint devel. Hwy. Research Bd.; vice chmn. Okla. Jud. Council, 1970-72, chmn., 1972-75; chmn. Okla. Center Criminal Justice, 1971-76. Author: Arkansas Eminent Domain Digest, 1964, Arkansas Probate Practice System, 1965, The Law of Airspace, 1968, Emerging Concepts in the Law of Airspace, 1969, Cases and Materials on Land Use, 3d edit., 1982, supplement, 1987, 4th edit., 1991, Uniform Probate Code Practice Manual, 1972, Model Airspace Code, 1973, Land Use in a Nutshell, 1978, 2d edit., 1985, 3d edit., 1994, The Arkansas Form Book, 1979, 2d edit., 1988, Zoning Law in Arkansas: A Comparative Analysis, 1980; contbr. numerous articles to legal jours. Mem. Little Rock Planning Commn., 1978-82, chmn., 1982. Named Ark. Man of Year Kappa Sigma, 1958. Fellow Am. Law Inst., Am. Coll. Probate Counsel (acad.); mem. ABA (chmn., exec. coun. gen. practice sect., former chmn. new pubs. editl. bd., sect. officers conf.), Ark. Bar Assn. (exec. coun. 1985-88, ho. of dels., life mem., chmn. eminent domain code com., past mem. com. new bar ctr., past chmn. preceptorship com., exec. com. young laywers sect.), Okla. Bar Assn. (past vice-chmn. legal internship com., former vice-chmn. gen. practice sect.), Pulaski County Bar Assn., Ark. Bar Found., U. Wis. Alumni Assn., Duke U. Alumni Assn., U. Ark. Alumni Assn., Order of Coif, Phi Beta Kappa, Phi Alpha Delta, Omicron Delta Kappa. Episcopalian. Home: 249 Pleasant Valley Dr Little Rock AR 72212-3170 Office: U Ark Law Sch 1201 McAlmont St Little Rock AR 72202-5142

WRIGHT, ROBIN, actress; b. 1966; d. Fred W., children: Dylan Frances, Hopper Jack. Television appearances include The Yellow Rose, 1983-84, Santa Barbara, 1984-87 (Emmy awards Best Ingenue in a Daytime Drama series 1985-87); films include Hollywood Vice Squad, 1986, The Princess Bride, 1987, State of Grace, 1990, Denial, 1991, The Playboys, 1992, Toys, 1992, Forrest Gump, 1994, The Crossing Guard, 1995, Moll Flanders, 1995, Loved, 1996. Office: Care CAA 9830 Wilshire Blvd Beverly Hills CA 90212-1804

WRIGHT, RODNEY H., architect; b. Valparaiso, Ind., June 2, 1931; s. George and Lena May (Cahoon) W.; m. Sydney Sullivan Goelitz, Feb. 16, 1966; children by previous marriage: Weston, Julie-An; stepchildren: Louise Goelitz, Ann Marie Goelitz, Thomas Goelitz. Grad. high sch. With various archtl. firms, 1953-60, pvt. practice architecture, 1960—; architect Hawkweed Group Ltd., Chgo., 1978-85; sole propr. Rodney Wright, Architect; lectr Northwestern U., 1971; keynote speaker First Solar Symposium, Sao Paulo, Brasil, 1976; presenter 1987 European Conf. on Architecture, Munich, 1st/2d conf. How Successful Directors Manage, 1986-93; speaker for various child care mtgs. and workshops. Author: Hawkweed, 1975, Passive Solar House Book, 1980, Urban Brickyard, Saving Energy Serving Children, 1993. Bd. dirs. Lake County Urban League, 1961-69, chmn., 1961-65; bd. dirs. Uptown Devel. Ctr., Chgo., 1969-73. With U.S. Army, 1950-53. Design fellow Nat. Endowment for Arts, 1975; recipient award U. Wis./Early Childhood Edn. Conf. Fellow AIA (chpt. dir. 1971, co-chmn. task force 1 1969-72, mem. nat. com. community devel. ctrs. 1970-72). Pioneer in design of passive solar and superinsulated bldgs. Research design of child care environments, including use of color, equipment, natural nonpolluting materials. Address: RR 4 Box 175A Osseo WI 54758-8962

WRIGHT, ROSALIE MULLER, newspaper and magazine editor; b. Newark, June 20, 1942; d. Charles and Angela (Fortunata) Muller; m. Lynn Wright, Jan. 13, 1962; children: James Anthony Meador, Geoffrey Shepard. BA in English, Temple U., 1965. Mng. editor Suburban Life mag., Orange, N.J., 1960-62; assoc. editor Phila. mag., 1962-64, mng. editor, 1969-73; founding editor Womensports mag., San Mateo, Calif., 1973-75; editor scene sect. San Francisco Examiner, 1975-77; exec. editor New West mag., San Francisco and Beverly Hills, Calif., 1977-81; features and Sunday editor San Francisco Chronicle, 1981-87, asst. mng. editor features, 1987-96; v.p. and editor-in-chief Sunset Mag, Menlo Park, Calif., 1996—; tchr. mag. writing U. Calif., Berkeley, 1975-76; participant pub. procedures course Stanford U., 1977-79; chmn. mag. judges at conf. Coun. Advancement and Support of Edn., 1980, judge, 1984. Contbr. numerous mag. articles, critiques, revs., Compton's Ency. Mem. Am. Assn. Sunday and Feature Editors (treas. 1984, sec. 1985, 1st v.p. 1986, pres. 1987), Am. Newspaper Pubs. Assn. (pub. task force on minorities in newspaper bus. 1988-89, Chronicle minority recruiter 1987-94), Internat. Women's Forum, Internat. Women's Media Found., Calif. Soc. Newspaper Editors, Women's Forum West (bd. dirs. 1993—, sec. 1994). Office: Sunset Magazine 80 Willow Rd Menlo Park CA 94025 *Keep a sharp eye out for talent, recognize it and reward it, and everyone profits.*

WRIGHT, SCOTT OLIN, federal judge; b. Haigler, Nebr., Jan. 15, 1923; s. Jesse H. and Martha I. Wright; m. Shirley Frances Young, Aug. 25, 1972. Student, Central Coll., Fayette, Mo., 1940-42; LLB, U. Mo., Columbia, 1950. Bar: Mo. 1950. City atty. Columbia, 1951-53; pros. atty. Boone County, Mo., 1954-58; practice of law Columbia, 1958-79; U.S. dist. judge Western Dist. Mo., Kansas City, from 1979. Pres. Young Democrats Boone County, 1950, United Fund Columbia, 1965. Served with USN, 1942-43; as aviator USMC, 1943-46. Decorated Air medal. Mem. ABA, Am. Trial Lawyers Assn., Mo. Bar Assn., Mo. Trial Lawyers Assn., Boone County Bar Assn. Unitarian. Clubs: Rockhill Tennis, Woodside Racquet. Lodge: Rotary (pres. Columbia 1965). Office: US Dist Ct US Courthouse 811 Grand Blvd Ste 741 Kansas City MO 64106-1909

WRIGHT, STEPHEN GAILORD, civil engineering educator, consultant; b. San Diego, Aug. 13, 1943; s. Homer Angelo and Elizabeth Videlle (Ward) W.; m. Ouida Jo Kennedy; children: Michelle, Richard. BSCE, U. Calif., Berkeley, 1966, MSCE, 1967, PhD CE, 1969. Prof. civil engring. U. Tex., Austin, 1969—. Contbr. numerous tech. papers & research reports, 1969—. Mem. ASCE. Republican. Presbyterian. Home: 3406 Shinoak Dr Austin TX 78731-5739 Office: U Tex Dept Civil Engring Austin TX 78712

WRIGHT, SUSAN WEBBER, judge; b. Texarkana, Ark., Aug. 22, 1948; d. Thomas Edward and Betty Jane (Gary) Webber; m. Robert Ross Wright, III, May 21, 1983; 1 child, Robin Elizabeth. BA, Randolph-Macon Woman's Coll., 1970; MPA, U. Ark., 1972, JD with high honors, 1975. Bar: Ark. 1975. Law clk. U.S. Ct. Appeals 8th Circuit, 1975-76; asst. prof. law U. Ark.-Little Rock, 1976-78, assoc. prof., 1978-83, prof., 1983-90, asst. dean, 1976-78; dist. judge U.S. Dist. Ct. (ea. dist.) Ark., Little Rock, 1990—; vis. assoc. prof. Ohio State U., Columbus, 1981, La. State U., Baton Rouge, 1982-83; mem. adv. com. U.S. Ct. Appeals 8th Circuit, St. Louis, 1983-88. Author: (with R. Wright) Land Use in a Nutshell, 1978, 2d edit., 1985; editor-in-chief Ark. Law Rev., 1975; contbr. articles to profl. jours. Mem. ABA, Ark. Bar Assn., Pulaski County Bar Assn., Ark. Assn. Women Lawyers (v.p. 1977-78). Episcopalian. Office: US Courthouse 600 W Capitol Ave Ste 302 Little Rock AR 72201-3323

WRIGHT, THEODORE PAUL, JR., political science educator; b. Pt. Washington, N.Y., Apr. 12, 1926; s. Theodore Paul and Margaret (McCarl) W.; m. Susan Jane Standfast, Feb. 18, 1967; children: Henry Sewall, Margaret Standfast, Catherine Berrian. BA magna cum laude, Swarthmore Coll., 1949; MA, Yale U., 1951, PhD, 1957. Instr. govt. Bates Coll., Lewiston, Maine, 1955-57; asst. prof., 1957-64, assoc. prof., 1964-65; assoc. prof. polit. sci. Grad. Sch. Public Affairs, SUNY, Albany, 1965-71, prof., 1971-95; prof. emeritus SUNY, Albany, 1995—. Author: American Support of Free Elections Abroad, 1964; contbr. articles on Indian Muslims and Pakistan to profl. jours., chpts. to books. Trustee Am. Inst. Pakistan Studies, 1973-82. Served with USNR, 1944-46. Carnegie intern Indian civilization U. Chgo., 1961-62; Fulbright rsch. prof. India, 1963-64; Am. Inst. Indian Studies rsch. fellow India, 1969-70; Am. Coun. Learned Socs. grantee on South Asia in London, 1974-75; Am. Inst. Pakistan Studies/Fulbright rsch. fellow, Pakistan, 1983-84, Fulbright lectr., 1990-91. Mem. South Asian Muslim Studies Assn. (pres. 1988—), Assn. Asian Studies (chmn. N.Y. Conf. on Asian Studies 1988-89), Dutch Settlers Soc. of Albany (pres. 1988-90), Adirondack Mountain Club, Phi Beta Kappa (chpt. pres. 1992-93), Phi Delta Theta. Republican. Unitarian. Home: 27 Vandenburg Ln Latham NY 12110-1190 Office: SUNY Albany Grad Sch Pub Affairs Milne Hall Albany NY 12222

WRIGHT, THEODORE ROBERT FAIRBANK, biologist, educator; b. Kodaikanal, Tamil Nadu, India, Apr. 10, 1928; s. Horace Kepler and Adelaide Caskey (Fairbank) W.; m. Eileen Marie Yongen, Jan. 6, 1951. ABin Biology, Princeton U., 1949; MA in Biology, Wesleyan U., 1954; PhD in Zoology, Yale U., 1959. Asst. professor biology Johns Hopkins U., Balt., 1959-65; assoc. prof. biology U. Va., Charlottesville, 1965-75, prof. biology, 1975-95; prof. emeritus, 1995—; vis. scientist Max Planck Inst. for Biology, Tubingen, 1975-76, Devel. Biology Ctr., U. Calif., Irvine, 1982. Editor: The Genetics and Biology of Drosophila, vol. 2a-c, 1978, vol. 2d, 1980, Genetic Regulatory Hierarchies in Development, 1990; co-editor: Advances in Genetics, 1988-92. With U.S. Army, 1950-52. NIH postdoctoral fellow Max Planck Inst. for Biology, Tubingen, Fed. Republic Germany, 1958-59; NSF grantee, 1967-72, 90-93; NIH grantee, 1972-93; Am. Cancer Soc. grantee, 1988-90. Fellow AAAS; mem. AAUP, Genetics Soc. Am., Soc. for Devel. Biology, Va. Acad. Sci., Sigma Xi. Office: U Va Dept Biology Gilmer Hall Charlottesville VA 22903-2477

WRIGHT, THOMAS HENRY, bishop; b. Wilmington, N.C., Oct. 16, 1904; s. John Maffitt and Josie Young (Whitaker) W.; m. Hannah Hagans Knowlton, Dec. 1, 1937; children—Thomas Henry, Hannah K., James K., John M. A.B., U. of South, 1926, D.D., 1946; B.D., Va. Theol. Sem., Alexandria, Va., 1930, D.D., 1946; D.D., Washington and Lee U., 1940, U. N.C., 1965. Clk. Standard Oil Co. of N.J., Wilmington, 1926-27; ordained to ministry P.E. Ch., 1929, nat. acting sec. of coll. work, 1933-34; Episcopal chaplain U. of N.C., 1931-32, Va. Mil. Inst., 1934-41, Washington and Lee U., 1934-41; rector Robert E. Lee Meml. Ch., Lexington, Va., 1934-41; dean Grace Cathedral, San Francisco, 1941-43; rector St. Mark's Ch., San Antonio, Tex., 1943-45; consecrated bishop of Diocese of East Carolina, St. James Ch., Wilmington, N.C., Oct. 1945; Pres. of Province.; U.S. rep. to World Christian Student Fed. Meeting, Holland, 1932; Regional dir. Ch. Soc. for Coll. Work; asso. mem. Forward Movement Commn., P.E. Ch.; chmn. overseas dept. Nat. Council of Episcopal Ch. Contbr. to jours. Trustee U. of South. Mem. Sigma Nu (former grand chaplain), Sigma Upsilon, Alpha Phi Epsilon; hon. mem. Omicron Delta Kappa. Democrat. Address: The Bishop's House 1625 Futch Creek Rd Wilmington NC 28405-9377

WRIGHT, THOMAS JAMES, chemical company executive; b. Livingston, Mont., June 13, 1932; s. William James and Mary Doreen (Smyth) W.; m. Sandra Gray Church, Jan. 29, 1962; children: James Bland, Jacqueline Doreen. BS in Metall. Engring., Mont. Sch. Mines, 1959. With minerals research lab. N.C. State U., Ashville, 1959-64; project engr. Texasgulf, Inc., Aurora, N.C., 1964-65, process engr., 1965-67, mill supt., 1967-71, acid plant supt., 1971-73, asst. gen. mgr., 1975-78; gen. mgr. Texasgulf Chems. Co., Aurora, 1978-79; sr. v.p. prodn. Texasgulf Chems. Co., Raleigh, N.C., 1979-81, pres., 1981-89; pres., coo, now exec. v.p. Texasgulf Chems. Co. (acquired by PCS Phosphate), 1989—; plant mgr. Agrico Chem. Co., South Pierce, Fla., 1973-75; bd. dirs. Texasgulf, Inc., Stamford, Conn., Elf Aquitaine, Inc., Stamford, Compania Exploradora Del Istmo, Mexico City. Served with U.S Army, 1954-56. Mem. Am. Mining Congress, N.C. Engring. Found. (past bd. dirs.), Sulphur Inst. (bd. dirs.), Fertilizer Inst. (bd. dirs.), Phosphate Chem. Export Assn. (bd. dirs.), Potash and Phosphate Inst. (past bd. dirs.), Internat. Fertilizer Assn., N.C. Water Resources Rsch. Inst., Farm Care U.S.A., Raleigh C. of C. Roman Catholic. Clubs: North Ridge Country, MacGregor Downs Country, Capital City (Raleigh). Avocation: golf. Office: PCS Phosphate PO Box 30321 Raleigh NC 27622-0321*

WRIGHT, THOMAS WILLIAM DUNSTAN, architect; b. Rome, Jan. 12, 1919; s. Charles Will and Helen Bree (Dunstan) W.; m. Penelope Ladd, Aug. 6, 1942 (dec. June 1988); children: Peter W.D., Felicity Wright Evans, Alegra; m. Anita Robbins Gordon, Dec. 30, 1995. AB, Harvard U., 1941, MArch, 1950. Designer Joseph Saunders (architect), Alexandria, Va., 1950; assoc. Leon Brown (architect), Washington, 1950-53; ptnr. firm Brown and Wright, Washington, 1953-80; sole propr. Thomas W. D. Wright, FAIA, Architects, 1980—; pres. Wright & Rubin Architects, P.C., 1985-89, Wright & Heyne Architects, 1990-91; prin. Thomas W.D. Wright, FAIA, Washington, 1991—; past mem. Old Georgetown bd. U.S. Commn. Fine Arts; past 1st v.p. D.C. Commn. Arts; past mem. D.C. Commrs. Planning and Urban Renewal Adv. Council; arbitrator Am. Arbitration Assn. Served to lt. comdr. USNR, 1941-46. Am. Sabre Fencing champion, gold medallist sr. age group (70-74); mem. U.S. Sr. Fencing Team, gold medallist sabre 70, 1995. Fellow AIA (past pres. Washington Met. chpt., past nat. chmn. com. on Nat. Capital City, past mem. com. on design, com. on housing); mem. Soc. Archtl. Historians, Nat. Assn. Intergroup Relations Ofcls., Nat. Assn. Housing and Redevel. Ofcls., Nat. Com. against Discrimination in Housing, ACLU. Democrat. Clubs: Cosmos (Washington), Harvard (Washington). Home: 7500 Exeter Rd Bethesda MD 20814-6108 Office: 1400 20th St NW Washington DC 20036-5906 *Since the essential origin of creativity is knowing the sources, then the fundamental source of design is the human being—its body, its mind, its senses and reactions, individually and collectively.*

WRIGHT, VERNON HUGH CARROLL, bank executive; b. Bronxville, N.Y., Sept. 24, 1942; s. Dudley Hugh and Helen Margurite (Carroll) W. m. Lucy Hiss Babb, June 7, 1966; children: Dudley Hugh II, Katherine Babb. BS in acctg., U. Balt., 1969. Sr. v.p. Maryland Nat. Bank, Balt., 1969-90, 91, MNC Fin., Balt., 1990-91; vice chmn., chief corporate fin. officer MBNA Am. Bank, N.A., Newark, Del., 1991—; bd. dirs. MBNA Am. Bank, Newark, Del.; exec. v.p., chief corp. fin., chmn. exec. v.p., chief corp. fin. officer MBNA Corp. With USN, 1962-66. Avocations: farming, teaching. Office: MBNA Am Bank NA West Lamington Wilmington DE 19884-0785

WRIGHT, VICKI LYNN, gifted and talented education educator; b. Sioux Falls, S.D., Sept. 20, 1956; d. Victor Eugene and Thenetta Lou (Lancaster) Nield; m. John Albert Paul Wright, July 28, 1979. BA in Art and Spanish, Augustana Coll., Sioux Falls, 1978, MA in Gifted Edn., 1990. Tchr. art Sioux Falls Pub. Schs., 1982-87, gifted edn. tchr., 1987-92; gifted edn. tchr. West Des Moines (Iowa) Cmty. Schs., 1992—. Innovative Project grantee Sioux Falls Pub. Schs., 1991-92; Artists in Schs./Cmty. New Residency Program grantee Iowa Arts Coun., 1993; Iowa Arts Coun. program grantee, 1993-95. Mem. ASCD, NEA, Iowa Edn. Assn., West Des Moines Edn. Assn. (bldg. rep. 1993-94). Avocations: computers, cruising the Internet, computer graphics, reading, telecomputing. Office: Crossroads Elem Sch 1050 50th St West Des Moines IA 50266-4902

WRIGHT, WALTER AUGUSTINE, III, lawyer; b. Newton, Mass., Feb. 9, 1957; s. Walter A. Jr. and Charlotte T. 9Doucette) W.; m. Elizabeth A. Heger, July 4, 1981; children: John Walter, Gregory, Charlotte, Sarah. BA magna cum laude, Tufts U., 1979, MA in Polit. Sci., 1980; JD magna cum laude, Boston Coll., Newton, 1983. Bar: Mass. 1983, U.S. Dist. Ct. Mass. 1983, U.S. Ct. Appeals (1st cir.) 1983. Owner, mgr. Wright Contracting, Needham, Mass., 1976-81; dir. corp. rels. Gen. Scis. Corp., Needham, 1979-81; assoc. Rich May Bilodeau & Flaherty, P.C., Boston, 1983-90, mem., shareholder, 1990—; chmn. bd. Alberca, Inc., Boston, 1992-93; chmn., pres. MapleCrest Group, Inc., Needham Heights, Mass., 1993—; mng. gen. ptnr. MapleCrest Fund I, Boston, 1995—; asst. sec. EV Environ., Inc., Southport, Conn., 1991—, Environ. Data Resources, Inc., Southport, Conn., 1989—, Hunter Environ. Svcs., Inc., Southport, 1986-93; cons. on numerous start-up cos. Mem. State Adv. Com. for Spl. Edn., Mass. Dept. Edn., Boston, 1974-76; mem. Needham Sch. Com., 1978-81; mem. Needham Dem. Town Com.; bd. dirs. Needham Little LEague, 1993—; founder Rookie League, 1993—; founder Rookie League, 1993—; mem. St. Bartholomew Pastoral Coun.; cons. numerous polit. campaigns. Recipient award for dedicated svc. Needham Sch. Com., 1981; honors scholar Tufts U., 1974-80, Adelman scholar, 1982. Mem. ABA, Mass. Bar Assn., Village Club (svc. award 1992). Roman Catholic. Avocations: political consulting, venture capital, public speaking, family, baseball. Home: 121 Thornton Rd Needham MA 02192-4354 Office: Rich May Bilodeau & Flaherty 294 Washington St Boston MA 02108-4608

WRIGHT, WILEY REED, JR., lawyer; b. Seattle, Jan. 31, 1932; s. Wiley Reed and Gertrude Ellen (Datson) W.; m. Sally Harrison Clarke, 1955 (div. 1963); children: Wiley III, Margaret, Andrew; m. Roberta Hostinsky, Oct. 18, 1963; children: Cathryn, Amy, Susan. BS in Commerce, Washington and Lee U., 1954, LLB, 1956. Bar: Va. 1956, U.S. Dist. Ct. (ea. dist.) Va. 1956, U.S. Ct. Appeals (4th cir.) 1956, U.S. Supreme Ct. 1993. Law clk. to hon. judge U.S. Dist. Ct., Alexandria, Va., 1958-59; ptnr. Clarke, Richard, Moncure & Whitehead, Alexandria, 1959-68; judge corp. and cir. cts. Alexandria, 1968-79, chief judge cir. ct., 1979-84; ptnr. Hazel & Thomas P.C., Alexandria, 1984-96; mem. at large Va. State Bar Coun., 1984-90; mem. Jud. Coun. Va., 1982-84, vice chmn. jud. conf. Va., 1980-82. Assoc. editor: Virginia Circuit Judges Benchbook, 1987. Legal counsel to Alexandria C. of C., 1984-88. 1st lt. U.S. Army, 1956-58. Fellow Am. Bar Found., Va. Law Found.; mem. ABA, Va. Bar Assn., Alexandria Bar Assn., 4th Cir. Conf., George Mason Inns of Ct., Boyd-Graves Conf., Phi Delta Phi, Omicron Delta Kappa. Avocations: boating, fishing, biking. Home: PO Box 358 Lively VA 22507 Office: Jams/Endispute 700 11th St NW Ste 450 Washington DC 20001

WRIGHT, WILLARD JUREY, lawyer; b. Seattle, Feb. 25, 1914; s. Raymond Garfield and Elizabeth (McPherson) W.; m. Alice Ostrander, Dec. 27, 1939 (dec. Dec. 1969); children: Susan, Alice, Rosemary, Raymond Garfield II; m. Katharyn Stubbs Little, July 18, 1970; children: Anne, Gwendolyn, Kathy. AB with honors, Princeton, 1936; cert., Woodrow Wilson Sch. Pub. and Internat. Affairs, 1936; JD with honors, U. Wash., 1939; grad., Navy. Lang. Sch., U. Colo., 1944. Bar: Wash. 1939, U.S. Dist. Ct. 1939, U.S. Ct. Appeals (9th cir.) 1958, U.S. Supreme Ct. 1954. Editor Wash. Law Rev., 1937-39; practice of law Wash., 1939—; partner Wright, Innis, Simon & Todd, Seattle, 1939-69, Davis, Wright, Todd, Riese & Jones, 1969-85; counsel Davis Wright & Jones, 1986-89, Davis Wright Tremaine, Seattle, 1990—; spl. asst. atty. gen. State of Wash., 1953; acting prof. fed. income taxation U. Wash. Law Sch., 1956; pres. Assoc. Vintners, Inc., 1979-81; pres. 1223 Spring St. Owners Assn., 1986-93; officer, dir. or gen. counsel various U.S. bus. corps.; chmn. King County Rep. Rules Com., 1950-58; chmn. 37th Dist. Rep. Orgn., 1949-52; del. Rep. Nat. Conv., Chgo., 1952. Contbr. articles to profl. jours. Trustee Seattle Found., 1954-63, pres., 1961-63, Seattle Com. Fgn. Rels., 1959-62, Lakeside Sch., 1938-67, pres., 1951-55, hon. trustee, 1967—; trustee Princeton U., 1957-61; vis. com. U. Wash. Coll. Bus. Adminstrn., 1963-70, U. Wash. Law Sch., 1974-78; pres. U. Wash. Ann. Fund, 1973-74, U. Wash. Law Sch. Found., 1974-75; trustee Helen Bush Parkside Sch., 1946-63, pres., 1959-62; dir. Seattle Times Co., 1968-89; mem. governing bd. Univ. Hosp., Seattle, 1978-87, chmn., 1980-82; sec., trustee Seattle Art Mus., 1958-88, hon. trustee, 1988—; vestryman Epiphany Episcopal Ch., 1959-64, 68-70, 73-76, 89-92, sr. warden 1970, 74-76, chancellor 1976-95, trustee ch. pension fund, N.Y., 1970-76. Lt. USNR, 1943-46. Recipient Vivian Carkeek prize U. Washington Law Sch., 1939, Disting. Svc. award Lakeside Sch., 1964, Bishop's Cross Diocese of Olympia, 1977, Crown award Epiphany Episcopal Ch., 1994, Disting. Alumnus award Lakeside Sch., 1980. Fellow Am. Bar Found., Am. Coll. Trust and Estate Counsel; mem. ABA, Wash. State Bar Assn. (chmn. real estate, probate and trusts sect. 1958-61), Seattle-King County Bar Assn. (trustee 1955-58, 64-67, pres. 1966-67), Am. Judicature Soc., Nat. Assn. Estate Planning Councils (dir. 1969-71), Estate Planning Council Seattle (pres. 1968-69, dir.), Alumni Assn. U. Wash. Law Sch. (pres. 1957-58), Seattle World Affairs Council (charter trustee, sec. 1949-57), Urban League Seattle (trustee 1956-60, 68-70, pres. bd. trustees 1956-58), Order of Coif, Princeton Quadrangle Club (pres. 1935-36), Seattle Golf Club (sec., trustee 1968-71), Phi Delta Phi. Home: 1630 43rd Ave E # 1022 Seattle WA 98112-3222 Office: Davis Wright Tremaine Century Sq Seattle WA 98101

WRIGHT, WILLIAM BIGELOW, financial executive; b. Rutland, Vt., Dec. 21, 1924; s. Earl Smith and Christine (Bigelow) W.; m. Polly Pardee, Aug. 27, 1949; children: Christine, Henry, John, Lucy. Graduated, Phillips Exeter Acad., 1943; AB, Princeton U., 1950. With Chubb & Son, N.Y.C., 1950-53; various positions Am. Internat. Group, N.Y.C., Havana, Tokyo, Seoul, Hong Kong, 1953-57; asst. to the pres. Johnson & Higgins, Caracas, Venezuela, 1957-63; pres. Marble Bank, Rutland, 1968-83; chmn. bd. Marble Bank, Marble Fin. Corp., Rutland, 1983-94, Marble divsn. Albank, Rutland; bd. dirs. Bunbury Co., Princeton, N.J. Vice pres., treas. Windham Found., Grafton, Vt.; sch. commr. City of Rutland, 1966-75; chmn. Vt. Blue Cross and Blue Shield, 1980-83; pres. Northeast chpt. 10th Mountain Divsn. Assn., 1993-95; trustee, treas. Green Mountain Coll., Poultney, Vt.; pres. Princeton Alumni Assn. of Vt., 1989—; trustee Calvin Coolidge Meml. Found., Plymouth, Vt., 1992—. With U.S. Army, 1943-46; ETO. Mem. Ivy Club, Princeton Club N.Y.C., Alumni Coun. Princeton U. (exec. com. 1992-95, v.p., exec. com. Class of '47 1992—). Republican. Congregationalist. Avocations: skiing, golfing, sailing, traveling. Home: RR 2 Box 7564 Mendon VT 05701 Office: Albank Marble Divsn PO Box 978 Rutland VT 05702-0978

WRIGHT, WILLIAM CARLOS, financial planner; b. Detroit, Oct. 8, 1929; s. Hugh H. and Opal L. (Early) W.; m. Patty L. Whitford, Aug. 26, 1951; children: Kendall H., Robert C., Kimm L. BS, Ctrl. Mich. U.; postgrad., U. Mich., CFP Coll. CFP, securities prin. With Consumers Power Co., 1952-76; pres. Complete Fin. Planning, Flint, Mich., 1976—. Chmn. Goodwill Industries, Flint; past pres. Flint Bd. Edn., Flint Indsl. Execs. Mem. Inst. CFPs, Flint Area C. of C. (chmn. bd.), Mich. State C. of C. (vice chmn.), Warwick County Club, Internat. Assn. Fin. Planning, Rotary (Paul Harris fellow 1991). Office: Complete Fin Planning 2337 Stonebridge Dr Flint MI 48532-5407

WRIGHTON, MARK STEPHEN, chemistry educator; b. Jacksonville, Fla., June 11, 1949; s. Robert D. and Doris (Cutler) W.; children: James Joseph, Rebecca Ann. BS, Fla. State U., 1969; PhD, Calif. Inst. Tech., 1972; DSc (hon.), U. West Fla., 1983. Asst. prof. chemistry MIT, Cambridge, 1972-76, assoc. prof., 1976-77, prof., 1977-95, Frederick G. Keyes prof. chemistry, 1981-89, head dept. chemistry, 1987-90, Ciba-Geigy prof. chemistry, 1989-95, provost, 1990-95; prof., chancellor Washington U., St. Louis, 1995—; bd. dirs. Ionics, Inc., Helix Tech. Corp., OIS (Optical Imaging Sys.), Inc. Author: Organometallic Photochemistry, 1979; editor books in field; cons. editor, Houghton-Mifflin. Trustee Mo. Bot. Garden, St. Louis Symphony. Recipient Herbert Newby McCoy award Calif. Inst. Tech., 1972, Disting. Alumni award, 1992, E.O. Lawrence award Dept. Energy, 1983, Halpern award in photochemistry, N.Y. Acad. Scis., 1983, Fresenius award Phi Lambda Upsilon, 1984, Dreyfus tchr.-scholar, 1975-80; Alfred P. Sloan fellow, 1974-76, MacArthur fellow, 1983-88. Fellow AAAS; mem. Am. Acad. Arts and Scis., Am. Chem. Soc. (award in pure chemistry 1981, award in inorganic chemistry 1988), Electrochem. Soc. Office: Washington Univ Office of Chancellor 1 Brookings Dr Box 1192 Saint Louis MO 63130

WRIGHT-RIGGINS, AIDSAND F., III, religious organization executive. Exec. dir. ABC Bd. of Nat. Ministries, Valley Forge, Pa. Office: ABC Bd of Nat Ministries PO Box 851 Valley Forge PA 19482-0851

WRIGLEY, ELIZABETH SPRINGER (MRS. OLIVER K. WRIGLEY), foundation executive; b. Pitts., Oct. 4, 1915; d. Charles Woodward and Sarah Maria (Roberts) Springer; BA U. Pitts., 1935; BS, Carnegie Inst. Tech., 1936; m. Oliver Kenneth Wrigley, June 16, 1936 (dec. July 1978). Procedure analyst U.S. Steel Corp., Pitts., 1941-43; rsch. asst. The Francis Bacon Found., Inc., Los Angeles, 1944, exec., 1945-50, trustee, 1950—, dir. rsch., 1951-53, pres., 1954—, dir. Francis Bacon Libr.; mem. adv. coun. Shakespeare Authorship Roundtable, Santa Monica, Calif.; mem. regional Fine Arts adv. coun. Calif. State Poly. U., Pomona. Mem. ALA, Calif. Libr. Assn., Renaissance Soc. Am., Modern Humanities Rsch. Assn., Cryptogram Assn., Alpha Delta Pi. Presbyn. Mem. Order Eastern Star, Damascus Shrine. Editor: The Skeleton Text of the Shakespeare Folio L.A. (by W.C. Arensberg), 1952. Compiler: Short Title Catalogue Numbers in the Library of the Francis Bacon Foundation, 1958; Wing Numbers in the Library of the Francis Bacon Foundation, 1959; Supplement To Francis Bacon Library Holdings in the STC of English Books, 1967; (with David W. Davies) A Concordance to the Essays of Francis Bacon, 1973. Home: 4805 N Pal Mal Ave Temple City CA 91780-4129 Office: Francis Bacon Libr 655 N Dartmouth Ave Claremont CA 91711-3960

WRIGLEY, ROBERT ERNEST, museum director, ecologist; b. Buenos Aires, Argentina, May 2, 1943; s. Ernest and Eva (Muir) W.; m. Gail Trueman, May 20, 1967 (dec. 1984); children: Mark E., Robert A.; m. Arlene Dahl, May 24, 1986. BS, McGill U., Montreal, Que., Can., 1965; MS, McGill U., 1967; PhD, U. Ill., 1970. Curator Man. (Can.) Mus. of Man and Nature, Winnipeg, 1970-80; mus. dir. Man. (Can.) Mus. of Man and Nature, 1980-86, dir. rsch. and collections, 1986-88; assoc. prof. Natural Resources Ins. U. Man., 1988-89; dir. Oak Hammock Marsh Interpretive Ctr., Stonewall, Can., Can., 1989-95; curator Assiniboine Park Zoo, Winnipeg, Can., 1996—; bd. dirs. Ft. Whyte Centre, Winnipeg, 1983-90, Friends of Assiniboine Park Conservatory, 1988—. Author: 12 books including Reptiles and Amphibians, 1989, Mammals in North America , 1986, Large Mammals, 1984 (Gold award 1984), Manitoba's Big Cat, 1982; mng. editor Manitoba Nature, 1972-82; contbr. articles to profl. jours. Mem. Manitoba Conservation Awards Ecological Resources and Endangered Species Com., 1982-91. Mem. Am. Soc. Mammalogists, The Can. Field-Naturalist, Ducks Unlimited Can., Cactus and Succulent Soc. Am., Manitoba Naturalists Soc. Avocations: natural history book and stamp collecting, collecting beetles, raising succulent plants and fish. Home: 505 Boreham Blvd, Winnipeg, MB Canada R3P 0K2 Office: Assiniboine Park Zoo, 2355 Corydon Ave, Winnipeg, MB Canada

WRIGLEY, WILLIAM, corporation executive; b. Chgo., Jan. 21, 1933; s. Philip Knight and Helen Blanche (Atwater) W.; m. Alison Hunter, June 1, 1957 (div. 1969); children: Alison Elizabeth, Philip Knight, William Jr.; m. Julie Burns, Nov. 28, 1981. Grad., Deerfield Acad., 1950; B.A., Yale, 1954. With Wm. Wrigley Jr. Co., Chgo., 1956—, v.p., 1960-61, pres., CEO, 1961—, also bd. dirs.; dir. Wrigley Philippines, Inc., The Wrigley Co. (N.Z.) Ltd., Wrigley Co. (Australia) Pty. Ltd., The Wrigley Co. (H.K.) Ltd., The Wrigley Co. (P.N.G.) Pty. Ltd., Wrigley & Co. Ltd., Japan, Wrigley Poland S.P.Z.O.O., Wrigley Chewing Gum Co. Ltd., China, Wrigle d.o.o., Slovenia, Wrigley Romania SRL, The Wrigley Co. (Thailand) Ltd. Wrigley de Mexico S.A., The Wrigley Co. Ltd., England, Wrigley Enterprises, Inc.; chmn., dir. Wrigley Co., S.A., Spain, Wrigley T.O.O., Russia, Wrigley (Cayman) Ltd., Wrigley Ltd.; trustee, chmn., mem. pension com., mem. fin. com., mem. com. non-mgmt. dirs., mem. nominating com. Wm. Wrigley Jr. Co. Found.; bd. dirs. Texaco Inc.; bd. dirs., exec. com., chmn. Santa Catalina Island Co.; chmn., bd. dirs., mem. corp. issues com, mem. nominating com. Am. Home Products Corp.; dir. Grocery Mfrs. Am. Bd. dirs. Wrigley Meml. Garden Found.; life trustee Northwestern Meml. Hosp.; benefactor, mem. Santa Catalina Island Conservancy; trustee. CEO adv. bd., mem. devel. com. U. So. Calif. Lt. (j.g.) USNR, 1954-56, lt. comdr. Res., 1956-77. Mem. Navy League U.S., Chgo. Hist. Soc. (hon. life), Field Mus. Nat. Hist. (life), Art Inst. Chgo. (life), Cowboy Artists Am. Mus. (founding), Wolf's Head Soc., U. So. Calif. Oceanographic Assocs. (hon. life), Catalina Island Mus. Soc. (life), The Calif. Club, Saddle and Cycle Club, Racquet Club, Chgo. Yacht Club, Tavern Club, Comml. Club, 410 Club (co-chmn.), Catalina Island Yacht Club (hon. life), Tuna Club Santa Catalina Island, L.A. Yacht Club, Lake Geneva Country Club (Wis.), Lake Geneva Yacht Club, Brook Club (N.Y.C.), Delta Kappa Epsilon.

WRINKLE, JOHN NEWTON, lawyer; b. Chattanooga, July 31, 1929; s. John Stuart and Anne (Ownbey) W.; m. Louise Rucker Agee, Feb. 1, 1958; children: Anne Blair, Margaret Rucker. BA, Vanderbilt U., 1951; LLB, Yale U., 1955. Bar: Ala. 1955, U.S. Dist. Ct. (no. dist.) Ala. 1956, U.S. Ct. Appeals (5th cir.) 1958, U.S. Ct. Appeals (11th cir.) 1981, U.S. Tax Ct. 1957. Assoc. White, Bradley, Arant, All & Rose, Birmingham, Ala., 1955-63; ptnr. Bradley, Arant, Rose & White, 1963-92, counsel, 1993—; coord. prelaw students Birmingham So. Coll., 1989—. Trustee Birmingham Symphony Assn., 1970-79, 80-83, Episcopal Found. Jefferson County, 1994—; mem. bd. advisors St. Andrew's Sewanee Sch., 1985—. With USAF, 1951-52. Disting. fellow Birmingham-Southern Coll., 1995—. Fellow Am. Coll. Trust and Estate Counsel; mem. ABA, So. Employee Benefits Conf. (steering com. 1970-73), Birmingham Bar Assn., Assn. of Bar of City of N.Y., Birmingham Com. Fgn. Rels., Redstone Club, Mountain Brook Club, Country Club of Birmingham, Summit Club, Knickerbocker Club (N.Y.C.), Yale Club (N.Y.C.), Phi Beta Kappa, Phi Alpha Delta. Episcopalian. Home: 2 Beechwood Rd Birmingham AL 35213-3914 Office: Bradley Arant Rose & White 2001 Park Pl Ste 1400 Birmingham AL 35203-2747

WRIST, PETER ELLIS, pulp and paper company executive; b. Mirfield, Eng., Oct. 9, 1927; arrived in Can., 1952; s. Owen and Evelyn (Ellis) W.; m. Mirabelle Harley, Sept. 3, 1955; children: Denise Wrist Parson, Philip, Lydia Wrist Schweizer, Richard; m. Kathryn Idelson. BA, Cambridge (Eng.) U., 1948, MA, 1952; MS, London U., 1952; cert. advanced mgmt. program, Harvard U., 1967; DSc (hon.), U. B.C., 1993. Rsch. physicist Brit. Paper & Bd. Industry Rsch. Assn., Kenley, Eng., 1949-52, Que. North Shore Paper Co., Baie Comeau, Can., 1952-56; rsch. physicist Mead Corp., Dayton, Ohio, 1956-60, assoc. dir. rsch., 1960-61, dir. rsch., 1961-66, mgr. rsch. and engring., 1966-68, v.p. rsch. and engring., 1968-72, v.p. tech., 1972-83; exec. v.p. Pulp and Paper Research Inst. Can., Pointe Claire, Que., 1983-86; pres., chief exec. officer Pulp and Paper Rsch. Inst. Can., Pointe Claire, Que., 1986-94, dep. chmn. bd., 1994-95; ret., 1994; chmn. prize selection com. Marcus Wallenberg Found.; chmn. Nat. Coun. for Air and Stream Improvement, 1972-75; past mem., chmn. rsch. adv. com. Inst. Paper Chemistry, 1971-83. Contbr. articles to profl. jours. Fellow Tech. Assn. Pulp and Paper Industry (bd. dirs. 1971-74, v.p. 1975-77, pres. 1977-79, Engring. award 1969, Gold medal 1983); mem. Can. Pulp and Paper Assn. (tech. sect., Howard Smith award 1954, Weldon Gold medal 1956), N.Y. Acad. Sci. Avocations: sailing, gardening. Home: 7778 SE Country Estates Way Jupiter FL 33458-1042

WRISTON, WALTER BIGELOW, retired banker; b. Middletown, Conn., Aug. 3, 1919; s. Henry M. and Ruth (Bigelow) W.; m. Barbara Brengle, Oct. 24, 1942 (dec.); 1 dau., Catherine B.; m. Kathryn Ann Dineen, Mar. 14, 1968. B.A. with distinction, Wesleyan U., Middletown, Conn., 1941; LL.D., Wesleyan U., 1984; postgrad., Ecole Francaise Middlebury, Vt., 1941, Am. Inst. Banking, 1946; M.A., Fletcher Sch. Internat. Law and Diplomacy, 1942; LL.D., Lawrence Coll., 1962, Tufts U., 1963, Brown U., 1969, Columbia U., 1972, Morehouse Coll., 1985; D.C.S., Pace U., 1974, St. John's U., 1974; D.H.L., Lafayette Coll., 1975; LL.D., Fordham U., 1977; D.C.S., N.Y. U., 1977. Officer spl. div. Dept. State, Washington, 1941-42; jr. insp. comptrollers div. Citibank (N.A.), 1946-50, asst. cashier, 1950-52, asst. v.p., 1952-54, v.p., 1954-58; sr. v.p., 1958-60, exec. v.p., 1960-67, pres., 1967-70, chmn., 1970-1984, also dir.; bd. dirs. York Internat. Corp., Tandem Computers Inc., United Meridan Corp., ICOS Corp., AEA Investors Inc., Bio-

Rsch. Labs. Ltd., Cygnus, Inc., WMNB Acquisitions Corp., Vion Pharms., Inc.; trustee Rand Corp., 1973-83; mem. Nat. Commn. on Productivity, 1970-74, Nat. Commn. for Indsl. Peace, 1973-74; chmn. Pres.' Econ. Policy Adv. Bd., 1982-89. Author: Risk and Other Four-Letter Words, 1986, The Twilight of Sovereignty, 1992. Life gov. N.Y. Hosp.; trustee Manhattan Inst. for Policy Rsch. Inc. Served with AUS, 1942-46. Mem. Bus. Coun., Links Club, Univ. Club, River Club, Sky Club, Met. Club (Washington), Palm Beach Bath and Tennis Club, Ocean Club Fla. Office: Citicorp Ctr 425 Park Ave 3rd Fl New York NY 10022

WRITER, SHARON LISLE, secondary education educator; b. L.A., Aug. 29, 1939; d. Harlan Lawerance and Emma Mae (Cordery) Lisle; m. Robert Vincent Writer, Dec. 30, 1961; children: Martin Carl, Cynthia Louise, Brian Robert, Scott Andrew. BS, Mt. St. Marys Coll., 1961; MS in Sci. Edn., Calif. State U., Fullerton, 1989; postgrad., U. Calif., Irvine, 1987, Colo. Sch. Mines, 1994. Cert. secondary tchr., Calif. Tchr. St. Mary's Acad., L.A., 1961-62, Escambia High Sch., Pensacola, Fla., 1962-63; rsch. asst. U. So. Calif., L.A., 1964-65, U. Calif., Irvine, 1965-66; tchr. aide Cerro Villa Jr. High Sch., Villa Park, Calif., 1975-76, tchr., 1976-88; tchr. Villa Park High Sch., 1988—, mentor tchr., 1990—; tchr. of yr. com. Orange (Calif.) Unified Sch. Dist., 1992, supt. adv. coun., 1990—, curriculum sci. com., 1991—. Active Villa Park Womens League, 1975—, Assistance League of Orange, 1991—; project leader, county coord. Orange County 4-H Assn., Anaheim, Calif., 1975-84; bd. sec. Orange County Sci. Fair, 1986-91, awards chmn., 1991-94, pres., 1994—. Recipient Outstanding Sci. Tchr. award Orange County Sci. Tchrs. Assn., 1993; named Tchr. of Yr. Villa Park High Sch., 1990, 94, Outstanding Coach Orange County Sci. Olympiad, 1990, 92, 94, 96, Calif. State Sci. Olympiad, 1987. Mem. NSTA (conv. hospitality com. 1989, 90, hospitality co-chair 1994 nat. conv.), Am. Chem. Soc., Calif. Sci. Tchr. Assn., Orange County Sci. Educators Assn. (Disting. Sci. Tchr. award 1993). Roman Catholic. Avocations: tennis, swimming, water skiing, needlepoint. Home: 18082 Rosanne Cir Villa Park CA 92667-6431 Office: Villa Park High School 18042 Taft Ave Villa Park CA 92667-4148

WROBLE, ARTHUR GERARD, lawyer; b. Taylor, Pa., Jan. 21, 1948; s. Arthur S. and Sophia P. Wroble; m. Mary Ellen Sheehan, Nov. 19, 1977; children: Sophia Ann, Sarah Jean, Stacey Margaret. BSBA with honors, U. Fla., 1970, MBA, 1971, JD, 1973. Bar: Fla. 1973, U.S. Ct. Appeals (5th cir.) 1974, U.S. Ct. Appeals (11th cir.) 1981, U.S. Dist. Ct. (so. dist.) Fla. 1974, U.S. Dist. Ct. (mid. dist.) Fla. 1982, U.S. Dist. Ct. (no. dist.) Fla. 1986, U.S. Army Ct. Mil. Rev. 1989, U.S. Ct. Mil. Appeals, 1990, U.S. Supreme Ct., 1976. Ptnr. Burns, Middleton, Farrell & Faust (now Steel, Hector, Davis, Burns & Middleton), Palm Beach, Fla., 1973-82; ptnr. Wolf, Block, Schorr & Solis, Cohen, Phila. and West Palm Beach, Fla., 1982-87, Scott, Royce, Harris & Bryan, P.A., Palm Beach, 1987-89, Grantham and Wroble, P.A., Lake Worth, 1989-92; prin. Arthur G. Wroble, P.A., West Palm Beach, 1992—; mem. 15th Jud. Cir. Ct. Nominating Commn., 1979-83; mem. U. Fla. Law Ctr. Council, 1981-84, U.S. Magistrate Merit Selection Panel, So. dist. Fla., 1987; mem. adv. bd. alternative sentencing program Palm Beach County Pub. Defender's Office; adj. instr. bus. law Coll. of Boca Raton (now Lynn U.), 1988. Contbr. articles to profl. jours. Served to lt. col. JAG, USAR, 1990-91. Named Eagle Scout, Boy Scouts Am., 1962. Mem. ABA, Fla. Bar (bd. govs. young lawyers sect. 1979-83, bd. govs. 1985-89), Palm Beach County Bar Assn. (pres. young lawyers sect. 1978-79, bd. dirs. 1979-81, sec.-treas. 1981-83, pres. 1984-85), Fla. Bar Found. (bd. dirs. 1990-93), Fla. Assn. Women Lawyers, Fla. Council Bar Assn. Pres. (bd. dirs. 1986-92), Guild Cath. Lawyers Diocese Palm Beach, Inc. (pres. 1980-81, bd. dirs. 1981—, Monsingnor Jeremiah P. O'Mahoney Outstanding Lawyer award 1993), Legal Aid Soc. Palm Beach County, Inc. (bd. dirs. 1981—), Univ. Fla. Alumni Assn. Palm Beach County Club (pres. 1983-84), Kiwanis (pres. 1980-81, pres. West Palm Beach found. 1989—, dir. 1981—, Citizen of Yr. 1994), KC (grand knight 1978-79). Roman Catholic. Home: 7645 Clarke Rd West Palm Beach FL 33406-8709 Office: 1615 Forum Pl West Palm Beach FL 33401-2320

WROBLESKI, JEANNE PAULINE, lawyer; b. Phila., Feb. 14, 1942; d. Edward Joseph and Pauline (Popelak) W.; m. Robert J. Klein, Dec. 3, 1979. BA, Immaculata Coll., 1964; MA, U. Pa., 1966; JD, Temple U., 1975. Bar: Pa. 1975. Pvt. practice law, Phila., 1975—; ptnr. Kohn, Swift & Graf, P.C., Phila.; lectr. on bus. law Wharton Sch., Phila. Mem. Commn. on Women and the Legal Profession, 1986-89; v.p. Center City Residents' Assn. Eisenhower Citizen Amb. del. to Soviet Union. Bd. dirs. South St. Dance Co., Women in Transition; bd. dirs., mem. exec. com. Temple Law Alumni; del. to Moscow con. on law and econ. coop., 1990; del. to jud. conf. for 3d cir. U.S. Ct. Appeals, 1991; mediator U.S. Dist. Ct. (ea. dist.) Pa., 1996. Rhea Liebman scholar, 1974. Mem. AAUW, ABA, Pa. Bar Assn., Phila. Bar Assn. (chmn. women's rights com. 1986, com. on jud. selection and reform 1986-87, chmn. appellate cts. com. 1992, bus. cts. task force), Pa. Acad. Fine Arts, Nat. Mus. Women in the Arts, Am. Judicature Soc., Jagiellonian Law Soc., Alpha Psi Omega, Lambda Iota Tau. Democrat. Clubs: Lawyers, Founders, Peale, Penn. Office: Kohn Swift & Graf PC 2400 One Reading Ctr 1101 Market St Philadelphia PA 19107-2934

WROBLEY, RALPH GENE, lawyer; b. Denver, Sept. 19, 1935; s. Matthew B. and Hedvig (Lyon) W.; m. Madeline C. Kearney, June 13, 1959; children: Kirk Lyon, Eric Lyon, Ann Lyon. BA, Yale U., 1957; JD, U. Chgo., 1962. Bar: Mo. 1962. With Bell Telephone Co., Phila., 1957-59; assoc. Stinson, Mag & Fizzell, Kansas City, Mo., 1962-65, mem. 1965-88; ptnr. Bryan, Cave, McPheeters & McRoberts, Kansas City, 1988-92; ptnr., exec. com. Blackwell, Sanders, Matheny, Weary & Lombardi, 1992—. Bd. dirs. Human Resources Corp., 1971; mem. Civic Coun. Kansas City, 1986—; chmn. Pub. Housing Authority of Kansas City, 1971-74; vice chmn. Mayor's Adv. Commn. on Housing, Kansas City, 1971-74; bd. govs. Citizens Assn., 1965—, vice chmn., 1971-75, chmn., 1978-79; bd. dirs. Coun. on Edn., 1975-81, v.p., 1977-79; bd. dirs., pres. Sam E. and Mary F. Roberts Found., 1974-96; founder, pres. 1974—; trustee Clearinghouse for Mid Continent Founds., 1977-96, chmn. 1987-89; bd. dirs. Bus. Innovation Ctr., 1984-91, vice-chmn. 1987-91, adv. bd. dirs., 1993—, Midwest Regional Adv. Bd. Inst. Internat. Edn., 1989-93, Internat. Trade Assn., 1989-92, v.p., 1990; former chmn. bd. dir. Mid-Am. Coalition on Healthcare, 1991-95. Mem. Mo. Bar Assn. Republican. Presbyterian (elder). Club: Yale (pres. 1969-71, outstanding mem. award 1967). Home: 1015 W 67th Ter Kansas City MO 64113-1942 Office: 2300 Main St Kansas City MO 64108-2415

WROBLOWA, HALINA STEFANIA, electrochemist; b. Gdansk, Poland, July 5, 1925; came to U.S., 1958, naturalized, 1970; MSc, U. Lodz (Poland), 1949; PhD, Warsaw Inst. Tech., 1958; 1 dau., Krystyna Wrobel-Knight. Chmn. dept. prep. studies U. Lodz, 1950-53; adj. Inst. for Phys. Chemistry, Acad. Scis., Warsaw, Poland, 1958-60; dep. dir. electrochemistry lab. Energy Inst., U. Pa., Phila., 1960-67, dir. electrochemistry lab., 1968-75; prin. research scientist Ford Motor Co., Dearborn, Mich., 1978-91; pvt. practice cons., 1991—; chmn. Gordon Rsch. Conf. Served with Polish Underground Army, 1943-45. Decorated Mil. Silver Cross of Merit with Swords. Mem. Electrochem. Soc., Internat. Electrochem. Soc., Mensa, Sigma Xi. Contbr. chpts. to books, articles to profl. jours., patent lit.

WRONG, DENNIS HUME, sociologist, educator; b. Toronto, Nov. 22, 1923; s. Humphrey Hume and Mary Joyce (Hutton) W.; m. Elaine L. Gale, Nov. 24, 1949 (div. Oct. 1965); 1 child, Terence Hume; m. Jacqueline Conrath, Mar. 26, 1966. BA, U. Toronto, 1945; PhD, Columbia U., 1956. Tchr. Princeton U., 1949-50, Rutgers U., 1950-51, U. Toronto, 1954-56, Brown U., 1956-61; mem. grad. faculty New Sch. Social Research, 1961-63; prof. sociology, chmn. dept. Univ. Coll., NYU, 1963-65; prof. sociology NYU, 1966-94, prof. emeritus, 1994—; vis. prof. U. Nev., 1965-66; vis. fellow Oxford U., 1978. Author: American and Canadian Viewpoints, 1955, Population, 1956, 59, Population and Society, 1961, 67, 77, Skeptical Sociology, 1976, Power: Its Forms, Bases and Uses, 1979, 88, 95, Class Fertility Trends in Western Nations, 1980, The Problem of Order: What Unites and Divides Society, 1994, 95; editor: Social Research, 1961-64, (with Harry L. Gracey) Readings in Introductory Sociology, 1967, 72, 77, Contemporary Sociology: A Journal of Reviews, 1972-74, Max Weber, 1970; mem. editl. bd. Dissent, 1966—; contbg. editor Partisan Rev., 1981-87. Guggenheim fellow, 1984-85, Woodrow Wilson Internat. Ctr. for Scholars fellow, 1991-92. Mem. Am. Sociol. Assn., Eastern Sociol. Soc. Home: 144 Drakes Corner Rd Princeton NJ 08540-7519 Office: NYU Dept Sociology Washington Sq N New York NY 10003

WRONSKI, STANLEY PAUL, education educator; b. Mpls., Apr. 8, 1919; s. John and Katherine (Kotvis) W.; m. Geraldine Breslin, May 27, 1943; children: Linda A., Mary Jo Tewinkel, Sandra J., John S., Paul S. BS in Edn., U. Minn., 1942, MA, 1947, PhD, 1950. Counselor Bur. Vet. Affairs U. Minn., Mpls., 1946-47, instr. Coll. Edn., 1948-49; tchr. Marshall High Sch., Mpls., 1947-48; asst. prof. Ctrl. Wash. Coll., Ellensburg, 1950-51; from asst. to assoc. prof. Boston U., 1951-57; from assoc. prof. to prof. Mich. State U., East Lansing, 1957-84, prof. emeritus, 1984—; advisor Ministry of Edn., Bangkok, Thailand, 1964-66; pres. New Eng. Assn. Social Studies Tchrs., Boston, 1955-56, Mich. Coun. for Social Studies, 1960-61, Nat. Coun. for Social Studies, 1974. Co-author: Teaching Social Studies in High School, 1958, 73, Modern Economics, 1964, School and Society, 1964, Social Studies and Social Sciences, 1986. Active U.S. Nat. Commn. for UNESCO, Washington, 1974-76, mil. adv. coun. Ctr. for Def. Info., Washington, 1988—; pres. Greater Lansing UN Assn., 1986-88, chair Mich. UN at Fifty Planning Com., 1995. Comdr. USN, 1942-64. Recipient Internat. Educator award Pacific Rim Consortium, 1992, Glen Taggart award Mich. State U., 1995; named Outstanding Social Studies Educator, Social Studies Tchr. Jour., 1981. Mem. NEA (life), Nat. Peace Found. (charter), Univ. Club (charter), Mich. U. Nat. Fifty com. (chair, 1995). Avocations: golf, reading, volunteer work. Home: 4520 Chippewa Dr Okemos MI 48864-2008 Office: Mich State U Sch of Edu Erickson Hall East Lansing MI 48824

WROTEN, WALTER THOMAS, lawyer; b. Stockton, Calif., Dec. 29, 1950; s. Walter Thomas Wroten and Ellen Amelia (Richards) Israel; m. Georgia Ann Sowers, Jan. 21, 1979 (div. Nov. 1988); m. Mary Alice Ficek, Aug. 1995. AA, Am. River Coll., 1974; BA, U. Calif., Berkeley, 1976; JD, U. No. Calif., 1988. Bar: Calif. 1991, U.S. Dist. Ct. (ea. dist.) Calif. 1991. Pres., CEO Wroten Internat., Sacramento, 1976-83; assoc. Law Office Dan Sullivan, Sacramento, 1991-92; pvt. practice Sacramento, 1992—. Mem. ABA, Am. Trial Lawyers Assn., Calif. Trial Lawyers Assn., Capitol City Trial Lawyers Assn., Sacramento County Bar Assn., San Joaquin County Bar Assn. Democrat. Office: 901 H St Ste 200 Sacramento CA 95814-1808

WROTH, JAMES MELVIN, former army officer, computer company executive; b. Lincoln, Nebr., Feb. 2, 1929; s. Charles M. and Reba (Sharp) W.; m. Donna Mae Benson, June 4, 1951 (dec.); children: Mark, David S., Mary E. Bannon; m. Molly B. Mullan, June 15, 1975; stepchildren: Edward H. Mullan (dec.), Philip C. Mullan. B.S., U. Nebr., 1951; M.B.A., Syracuse U., 1963; postgrad., F.A. Sch., 1957, Command and Gen. Staff Coll., 1962, Armed Forces Staff Coll., 1967, Army War Coll., 1968; grad., Advanced Mgmt. Program, Harvard, 1972. Commd. 2d lt. U.S. Army, 1951, advanced through grades to brig. gen., 1973; 40th inf. divsn. Korea, 1952-53; instr. A.A.A. Sch., Ft. Bliss, Tex., 1954-56; with 3d Inf. Div., Ft. Benning, Ga. and, Germany, 1957-61, Office Chief of Staff, U.S. Army, 1963-66; comdg. officer 1st Bn. 31st Arty., Korea, 1967; exec. asst. to asst. sec. Army, 1968-70; exec. officer I Field Force Vietnam Arty., 1970; comdg. officer 52d Arty. Group, Vietnam, 1971; with Office Dep. Chief Staff for Personnel, Dept. Army, 1972-75; comdg. gen. VII Corps Arty. and Augsburg Germany Mil. Community, 1975-77; comdr. 2d ROTC region, Ft. Knox, Ky., 1977-79; ret., 1979; v.p., dir. mgmt. scis. ops. Gen. Research Corp., McLean, Va., 1979-82; group v.p Info. Systems & Network Corp., Bethesda, Md., 1982-93; chmn., pres. J-Tech, Inc., White Stone, Va., 1993—. Trustee Washington Adventist Hosp. Found., 1989-93. Decorated D.S.M., Legion of Merit, Bronze Star, Air Medal with V device, Army Commendation medal; Vietnamese Gallantry Cross with palm.; Recipient John J. Pershing award, 1951, 40 and 8 award, 1951, F.A. Assn. award, 1950. Mem. Nat. Soc. Pershing Rifles (past nat. comdr.), Alpha Kappa Psi, Beta Gamma Sigma. Home: RR 2 Box 4320 White Stone VA 22578-9802 Office: PO Box 1287 White Stone VA 22578-1287

WROTH, L(AWRENCE) KINVIN, lawyer, educator; b. Providence, July 9, 1932; s. Lawrence Counselman and Barbara (Pease) W.; m. Susan Collins, May 2, 1958 (div. 1972); children: Ann K., Caroline D., Eliza H.; m. Deborah Bethell, Aug. 10, 1972; 1 dau., Katharine L.; stepchildren—John H., David H., Elizabeth T. and Sarah B. Zobel. B.A., Yale U., 1954; LL.B., Harvard U., 1960. Bar: Mass. 1960, Maine 1974. Teaching fellow, asst. prof. law Dickinson Sch. Law, 1960-62; rsch. assoc. Harvard U., 1962-64; assoc. prof. law U. Maine Sch. Law, Portland, 1964-66; prof. U. Maine Sch. Law, 1966-96; assoc. dean Sch. Law U. Maine, 1977-78, acting dean, 1978-80, dean, 1980-90; dean, prof. Vt. Law Sch., 1996—; rsch. fellow Charles Warren Center Studies in Am. History, Harvard U., 1968-74; cons. civil and probate procedure, profl. and jud. responsibility, and ct.-bar rels. Maine Supreme Jud. Ct., 1967—; cons. civil and criminal procedure and evidence Vt. Supreme Ct., 1969—. Author: (with R.H. Field and V.L. McKusick) Maine Civil Practice, 2d edit., 1970; editor-in-chief: Province in Rebellion, 1975; editor: (with H.B. Zobel) Legal papers of John Adams, 1965; reporter: Vermont Rules of Civil Procedure, 1971, Vermont Rules of Criminal Procedure, 1974, Maine Rules of Probate Procedure, 1980, (with J. Dooley) Vermont Rules of Evidence, 1982, Maine Code of Judicial Conduct, 1993, Vermont Code of Judicial Conduct, 1994. Pres. Greater Portland Landmarks, Inc., 1966-69, adv. trustee, 1969-85; adv. coun. Nat. Trust Hist. Preservation, 1967-70; bd. dirs. Maine Bar Found., 1983-89, sec., 1983-86, v.p., 1987, pres., 1988, fellow, 1991; bd. dirs. Pine Tree legal Assistance Inc., 1985-96; mem. bd. dirs. Nat. Assn. IOLTA Programs, Inc., 1988-90; bd. dirs. Portland Symphony Orch., 1990, v.p. for ops. and resources, 1991-95, pres., 1995-96; mem. Maine Commn. on Legal Needs, 1989-90, Commn. to Study Future of Maine's Cts., 1991-93. Recipient Littleton-Griswold prize Am. Hist. Assn., 1966, Howard H. Dana award Maine Bar Found., 1991, Justice Louis Scolnik award Maine Civil Liberties Union, 1992, Herbert Harley award Am. Judicature Soc., 1994. Fellow Am. Bar Found.; mem. ABA, Maine Bar Assn. (Disting. Svc. award 1990), Am. Law Inst., Colonial Soc. Mass., Mass. Hist. Soc. Office: Vt Law Sch Chelsea St PO Box 96 South Royalton VT 05068

WRUBLE, BERNHARDT KARP, lawyer; b. Wilkes-Barre, Pa., Mar. 21, 1942; s. Maurice and Ruth Yvonne (Karp) W.; m. Judith Marilyn Eyges, Nov. 16, 1968 (div. 1987); children: Justine, Vanessa, Alexis; m. Jill Diamond, Nov. 24, 1990; children: Mattia, Austin. BA in Polit. Sci., Williams Coll., Williamstown, Mass., 1963; LLB, U. Pa., 1966; postgrad., NYU, 1972-74, Harvard U., 1978. Bar: U.S. Dist. Ct. (so. dist.) N.Y. 1969, U.S. Dist. Ct. (ea. dist.) N.Y. 1972, U.S. Ct. Appeals (2d cir.) 1972, U.S. Supreme Ct. 1972, U.S. Ct. Appeals (7th cir.) 1974, U.S. Ct. Appeals (D.C. and 4th cirs.) 1984, U.S. Ct. Appeals (5th cir.) 1985, U.S. Ct. Appeals (11th cir.) 1986. Law clk. to presiding judge U.S. Ct. Appeals (3d cir.), 1966-67; assoc. Simpson, Thacher & Bartlet, N.Y.C., 1968-73; ptnr. Simpson, Thatcher & Bartlett, N.Y.C., 1974-77; prin. dep. gen. counsel U.S. Dept. Army, Washington, 1977-79; dir. Office Govt. Ethics, Washington, 1979; exec. asst. to sec. and dep. sec. U.S. Dept. Energy, Washington, 1979-81; dir. Pres.'s Interagy. Coal Export Task Force, Washington, 1980-81; ptnr. Verner, Liipfert, Bernhard, McPherson and Hand, Washington, 1981—. Bd. dirs. Epilepsy Found. Am., 1983, chmn., 1991. Mem. ABA, D.C. Bar Assn., N.Y. State Bar Assn., Williams Coll. Alumni Assn. (pres. Washington chpt. 1986-91), Williams Coll. Soc. Alumni Assn. (exec. com. 1988-91). Democrat. Office: Verner Liipfert Bernhard McPherson and Hand 901 15th St NW Ste 700 Washington DC 20005-2301

WRUBLE, BRIAN FREDERICK, investment company executive; b. Kalamazoo, Apr. 18, 1943; s. Milton and Rose Muriel (Nathanson) W.; m. Susan Roberta Shifrin, June 23, 1968 (div. Oct. 1984); children: Amy Carolyn, Jordan Todd; m. Kathleen Wilson Bratton, Apr. 20, 1985; 1 child, Henrietta Zane Bratton. BEE, Cornell U., 1965, MEE, 1966; MBA with distinction, NYU, 1976. Field engr. Sperry Corp., Lake Success, N.Y., 1966-69; v.p. Alliance One Instl. Services, Inc., N.Y.C., 1970-76, H. C. Wainwright and Co., Inc., N.Y.C., 1976-77, Wainwright Securities, Inc., N.Y.C., 1977; v.p., co-mgr. fundamental equities research Smith Barney, Harris Upham & Co., N.Y.C., 1977-79; exec. v.p. chief fin. ops. Equitable Life Assurance Soc. U.S., N.Y.C., 1979-92; chmn., pres., chief exec. officer Equitable Capital Mgmt. Corp., N.Y.C., 1985-92; chief investment officer Equitable Life Assurance Soc. U.S., N.Y.C., 1991-92; pres. chief oper. officer, dir. Delaware Mgmt. Holdings, Inc., 1992-95; pres., CEO The Delaware Group, 1992-95; pres., chief oper. officer Delaware Mgmt. Co., 1992-95; chmn. Delaware Distributors, Inc., 1992-95; chmn., chief exec. officer Delaware Svc. Co., Inc., 1992-95; gen. ptnr. Odyssey Ptnrs., L.P., N.Y.C., 1995—; chmn., pres. Equitable Realty Assets Corp., Atlanta, 1983-92; v.p., dir. TELMARI, Inc., N.Y.C., 1982-83, Equitable Variable Life Ins. Co., 1987-92; chmn. Equico Capital Corp., N.Y.C., 1984-92, CEO Equitable Gen. of Okla., Oklahoma City, 1985-86; bd. dirs. Advanced System Applications Inc., 1985-87, Frye Copysystems Inc., N.Y.C., 1988-90, Supermkts. Gen. Corp., 1990-92, The Jackson Lab., Inc., 1990—; trustee Equitable Retirement Plans, N.Y.C., 1980-86, Inst. Advanced Study, 1992—; gov. Assn. Investment Mgmt. and Rsch., 1992—; pres. Hudson River Trust, 1991-92, Equitable Funds, 1991-92. Vice chmn. Boys Choir of Harlem, N.Y.C., 1984-92; bd. dirs. Harlem Youth Devel. Found., 1989-92, Corp. Ptnrs. Phila. Art Mus., 1992-95, vice chmn., 1993-95; bd. govs. Jerome Levy Econ. Inst., 1990—. Recipient Heroes award Boys Choir Harlem, 1990, Founders award, 1993. Mem. IEEE, Assn. Investment Mgmt. and Rsch., Phila. Soc. Security Analysts, Inst. CFAs (CFA, vice chmn. 1993-94, chmn. 1994-95, bd. trustees rsch. found. 1994-95, assoc. editor CFA Digest 1983—), Phila. C. of C. (bd. dirs. 1992-95, mem. exec. com. 1993-95). Republican. Jewish. Avocations: running, skiing, sailing, amateur radio. Office: Odyssey Ptnrs LP 31 W 52d St New York NY 10019

WRUCK, ERICH-OSKAR, foreign language educator, administrator; b. Gr. Kroessin/Pomerania, Germany, Oct. 29, 1928; came to U.S., 1952, naturalized, 1954; s. Erich Albert and Erna (Kroening) W.; m. Esther Emmy Schmidt, Oct. 3, 1953; children: Eric Gordon, Karin Esther, Krista Elisabeth. BA magna cum laude, Rutgers U., 1959, MA, 1961, PhD, 1969. Asst. instr. Rutgers U., New Brunswick, N.J., 1959-62; asst. prof. Davidson Coll., N.C., 1962-69, assoc. prof., 1969-73, prof., chmn. dept. German, 1983-87, dir. Davidson Abroad Program, Marburg, Fed. Republic German, 1966-67, 71-72, Jr. Year Abroad Program, Wuerzburg, Fed. Republic Germany, 1986-87, 89-92 (ret. 1994). Served to 1st lt. U.S. Army, 1953-57, to col. USAR, 1986. Recipient Meritorious Service medal Dept. Army, 1983, 86, 88; inducted into Arty. OCS Hall of Fame, 1996. Mem. Goethe Gesellschaft, Freies Deutsches Hochstift, Schiller Gesellschaft (charter mem.), Goethe Soc. of N. Am., Soc. for German Am. Studies, Julius Maximilians medal U. Wuerzburg, 1987. Republican. Lutheran. Avocations: painting, photography, soaring, skiing, running.

WRUCKE-NELSON, ANN C., elementary school educator; b. Mankato, Minn., Nov. 5, 1939; d. G.F. and Dorothy (Thomas) Wrucke; children: Chris, Dor-Ella. BS, Mankato State U., 1961; MLA, So. Meth. U., 1974; postgrad., U. Minn., 1963, Tex. Woman's U.; EdD in Early Childhood Edn., Tex. Woman's U., 1992. Cert. elem., kindergarten, bilingual-ESL, history tchr., Tex. Tchr. Rochester (Minn.) Pub. Schs., Christ the King Sch., Dallas; dir., tchr. Norway Christian Presch., Dallas; Every Student Learns Lang. program kindergarten tchr. Dallas Ind. Sch. Dist.; tchr. summer session Tex. Woman's U., 1991; presenter in field. Producer video: A Year of Language Learning, 1990. Sunday sch. tchr. Holy Trinity Ch. Recipient Tchr. of Yr. award, 1989, Tex. TESOL scholarship, 1994; Bill Martin Literacy Conf. scholar; named ESL Tchr. of Yr., 1991. Mem. Assn. for Childhood Edn. Internat., So. Assn. on Children Under Six, Tchrs. English to Speakers Other Lang., Tex. Tchrs. English to Speakers Other Lang., Dallas Assn. for Edn. of Young Child.

WU, GARY G., petroleum engineer, consultant; b. Beijing, People's Republic of China, Oct. 28, 1960; came to U.S., 1985; s. Baoshan Wu and Fengzi Yu; m. Ding Zhu, Dec. 27, 1992; children: Woody, Andrew. BS in Petroleum, China Petroleum U., Beijing, 1982; MS in Petroleum, U. Tex., 1988, PhD in Petroleum, 1992. Registered profl. engr., Tex. Process engr. China Oil Devel. Co., Beijing, 1982-83; project mgr. China Nat. Offshore Oil Co., Beijing, 1983-85; rsch. asst. U. Tex., Austin, 1986-90; rsch. engr. Texaco Inc., Houston, 1990-91; rsch. asst. U. Tex., Austin, 1991-92; project scientist Texaco Inc., Houston, 1992—; reservoir engring. cons. PEC Inc., Houston, 1993—; cons. U. Tex., Austin, 1993-94. Contbr. articles to profl. jours. and procs. Mem. Soc. Petroleum Engrs. (assoc. mem., chmn. student chpt. 1988-89, author procs. 1994). Achievements include research in geochemical modeling software "Netreac," PC-Windows software "Simtools." Avocations: skiing, soccer, swimming, micro-computers. Home: 19831 Emerald Springs Houston TX 77094 Office: Texaco-EPTD 3901 Briarpark Houston TX 77042

WU, GUOYAO, nutrition, physiology, and animal science educator; b. China, July 28, 1962; s. Fanjiu Wu and Meixiao Huang; m. Yan Chen, Aug. 7, 1995. BS in Animal Sci., South China Agrl. U., 1982; MS in Animal Nutrition, Beijing (People's Republic of China) Agrl. U., 1984; MS in Animal Biochemistry, U. Alberta, Can., 1986, PhD in Animal Biochemistry, 1989; postgrad. in metabolism/diabetes, McGill U., Mont., Can., 1989-91; postgrad. in biochemistry, Meml. U. Nfld., Can., 1991. Grad. teaching asst. U. Alberta, 1985-88; postdoctoral rschr. Royal Victoria Hosp., McGill U., 1989-91, Meml. U. Newfoundland, 1991; asst. prof. dept. animal sci. and faculty nutrition Tex. A&M U., College Station, 1991-96; assoc. prof. Tex. A&M U., 1996—. Reviewer Amino Acids, Am. Jour. Clin. Nutrition, Am. Jour. Physiology, Can. Jour. Physiology and Pharmacology, Diabetes, Diabetologia, Jour. Nutrition, Jour. Nutritional Biochemistry, Jour. Cellular Physiology, Metabolism, Can. Diabetes Assn., Med. Rsch. Coun. Can., U. Toronto Banting and Best Ctr., Can.; editl. advisor Biochem. Jour., 1993-96; contbr. articles to profl. jours. Grantee Tex. A&M U., 1992—, Ajinomoto Inc., Japan, 1992, USDA, 1992—, Houston Livestock Show and Rodeo, 1992-95, Am. Heart Assn., 1995—; nat. scholarship for grad. studies abroad Ministry Edn. China, 1984-86, grad. tchg. assistantship U. Alta., 1985-88, dissertation fellowship, 1989, Ctr. Rsch. Fund award, 1988, Andrew Stewart Grad. prize, 1989, U. Alberta, Can. Rsch. Inst. fellowship Royal Victoria Hosp., 1988, fellowship Can. Diabetes Assn., 1989, Med. Rsch. Coun. Can. fellow, 1989-91. Mem. AAAS, Am. Diabetes Assn., Am. Inst. Nutrition, Am. Physiol. Soc., Am. Soc. Animal Sci., Biochem. Soc. U.K., Can. Soc. Nutritional Scis., Juv. Diabetes Found. Internat. (grantee 1992-94). Home: 4707 Shoal Creek Dr College Station TX 77845 Office: Tex A&M Univ Dept Animal Sci College Station TX 77843

WU, HARRY PAO-TUNG, librarian; b. Jinan, Shandong, China, May 1, 1932; came to U.S., 1960; s. James Ching-Mei and Elizabeth Hsiao (Lu) W.; m. Irene I-Len Sun, June 23, 1961; children: Eva Pei-Chen, Walter Pei-Liang. BA, Nat. Taiwan U., Taipei, 1959; student Ohio State U., 1962; MLS, Kent State U., 1966.. Archive and library asst. Taiwan Handicraft Promotion Center, Taipei, 1959-60; student asst. Kent State U. Library, 1960-61; reference librarian Massillon (Ohio) Pub. Library, 1964-65, acting asst. dir., 1965, asst. dir., head adult services, 1966; dir. Flesh Pub. Library, Piqua, Ohio, 1966-68; dir. St. Clair County Library System, Port Huron, Mich., 1968—; founder and dir. Blue Water Library Fedn., Port Huron, 1974—; pres. Mich. Library Film Circuit, Lansing, 1977-79; mem. St. Clair County Literacy Project Com., 1986—; bd. dirs. Blue Water Reading Coun., 1987-88, Mich. Waterways council Girl Scouts U.S.A., Port Huron, 1985-86; bd. dirs. United Way St. Clair County, Mich., 1990-91; bd. trustees Libr. Mich., 1992—. Mem. Am., Mich. (chmn. library systems roundtable 1974-75) library assns., Am. Mgmt. Assn., Assn. Ednl. Communications and Tech., Detroit Suburban Librarians Roundtable, Chinese-Am. Librarians Assn. Clubs: Port Huron Internat. (pres. 1988), Rotary (dir. 1972-74, 88-90, Paul Harris fellow 1988). Home: 1518 Holland Ave Port Huron MI 48060-1511 Office: 210 Mcmorran Blvd Port Huron MI 48060-4001

WU, HSIU KWANG, economist, educator; b. Hankow, China, Dec. 14, 1935; came to U.S., 1952, naturalized, 1963; s. Kao Cheng and Edith (Huang) W.; m. Kathleen Gibbs Johnson, Aug. 17, 1968. Grad., Lawrenceville Sch., 1954; A.B., Princeton U., 1958; M.B.A., U. Pa., 1960, Ph.D., 1963. Prof., group coordinator fin., econs. and internat. bus. Boston U., 1968-72; prof., chmn. fin., econs. and legal studies faculty U. Ala., 1972-81, Lee Bidgood prof. fin. and econs., 1978—, Ala. Banker Edn. Found. Banking Chair prof., 1973-78; econ. adviser Office of Comptroller of Currency, U.S. Treasury, 1966-69, 75-80; dir. Ala. Fed., 1984-88; dir. SECOR Bank FSB, 1988-93, chmn. bd., 1992-93; cons. instl. investor study SEC, 1969-70; mem. com. examiners undergrad. program for counseling and evaluation test in bus. Ednl. Testing Service, 1971, 77. Co-editor: Elements of Investments, 2d rev. edit, 1972; Contbr. articles to law and econ. jours. Sloan Faculty fellow Sloan Sch. Mgmt., Mass. Inst. Tech., 1965-66. Mem. Am. Econ. Assn., Am. Fin. Assn., Am. Statis. Assn., Fin. Mgmt. Assn. Home: 3332 Arcadia Dr Tuscaloosa AL 35404-4361 Office: U Ala Coll Commerce Tuscaloosa AL 35487

WU, JAMES CHEN-YUAN, aerospace engineering educator; b. Nanking, China, Oct. 5, 1931; came to U.S., 1953, naturalized, 1963; s. Chien Lieh and Cheng-Ling (Hsia) W.; m. Mei-Ying Chang, Sept. 7, 1957; children—Alberta Yee-Hwa, Norbert Mao-Hwa. Student, Nat. Taiwan (Formosa) U., 1949-52; BS, Gonzaga U., 1954; postgrad., Columbia U., 1954; MS (univ. fellow), U. Ill., 1955, PhD, 1957. Engr. Wah Chang Corp., N.Y.C., 1954; researcher Mass. Inst. Tech. at Cambridge, 1957; asst. prof. Gonzaga U., Spokane, Wash., 1957-59; research specialist Douglas Aircraft Co., 1959-65, group leader, 1960-61, supr., 1961-62, br. chief, 1963-65; prof. aerospace engring. Ga. Inst. Tech., 1965—; cons. N.Am. Aviation Co., Geophys. Tech. Corp., European Atomic Energy Commn., Ispra, Italy, European Atomic Energy Commn. (research center), U.S. Army Research Office, Durham, S.C. Contbr. articles to profl. jours. Chmn. bd. dirs. Chinese-Am. Inst. Recipient profl. achievement award Douglas Aricraft Co., 1963, Outstanding Tchrs. award Gonzaga U., 1959; Asso. fellow Am. Inst. Aeros. and Astronautics. Mem. Am. Soc. Engring. Sci. (founding), Soc. Indsl. and Applied Math. (vice-chmn. Pacific N.W. 1958-59), Am. Astron. Soc. (sr.), Am. Phys. Soc., Nat. Assn. Chinese Ams. (pres. Atlanta chpt.), Sigma Xi, Tau Beta Pi, Sigma Alpha Nu. Office: Sch Aerospace Engring Georgia Inst Tech 48967 Ventura Dr Fremont CA 94539

WU, JING-JYI, foundation administrator; b. I-Lan, Taiwan, May 3, 1939; s. Jan-Loo and Jing-Yeh (Chen) W. BA, Nat. Chengchi U., Taipei, Taiwan, 1962; PhD, U. Minn., Mpls., 1967. Lectr. Queens Coll. N.Y., 1967-68; asst. prof. Yeshiva (N.Y.) U., 1968-72; adj. assoc. prof. CCNY, 1972; prof., adj. prof. Nat. Chengchi U., Taipei, 1972—; artistic dir. Lanling Theater Workshop, Taipei, 1980—; exec. dir. Found. for Scholarly Exch., Taipei, 1977—; cons. Chiang Ching-Kuo Found. for Internat. Scholarly Exch., Taipei, 1989—, co-dir. Asian-Am. Repertory Theater at LaMaMa E.T.C., N.Y., 1970-72; external assessor Hong Kong Rsch. Grants Coun., 1993; TV host Chinese TV Svc., Taipei, 1973-85. Author: Four Great Dreams of the Youth, 1980 (Best Seller List), The Initial Experiment of Langling Theater Workshop, 1982, The Search for Self-Identity, 1992; co-author, choreographer: (play) Won-Ton Soup, 1969. Mem. Nat. Cultural Coun., Taiwan, 1992—; mem. bd. Nat. Cultural Arts Found., 1995—; com. mem. arts edn. com. Ministry of Edn., Taiwan, 1988—; bd. mem. Straits Exch. Found., Taiwan, 1990-93; bd. chmn. Christian Children's Fund, Chinese Children's Fund, Taiwan, 1979-85, 91-94. Effective teaching and rsch. grantee Harvard-Yenching Inst., 1974; Fulbright scholar of theater arts U.S. State Dept., 1976; recipient Disting. award for Scholarly Contbn. Chinese United Assns. of Edn., Taiwan, 1990. Mem. Chinese Theater Assn. (bd. mem. 1990—), Chinese Creativity Assn. (bd. mem., standing com. 1992—), Chinese Guidance Assn. (bd. mem. 1990—). Avocations: travel, theater, dance, reading. Office: Found Scholarly Exch, 1-A Chuan-Chow St 2nd fl, Taipei 100, Taiwan

WU, LI-PEI, banker; b. Changhwa, Taiwan, Sept. 9, 1934; came to U.S., 1968; s. Yin-Su and Chiao-Mei (Hsiao) W.; m. Jenny S. Lai, Mar. 24, 1963; children: George T., Eugene Y. BA, Nat. Taiwan U., 1957; MBA, Kans. State U., Ft. Kays, 1969; Comml. Banking Exec. Program, Columbia U., 1974. Staff acct., asst. controller, asst. v.p., v.p. Nat. Bank Alaska, Anchorage, 1969-73, v.p. controller, 1973-76, sr. v.p. chief fin. officer, 1976-78; chmn. exec. com. Alaska Nat. Bank of the North, Anchorage, 1978-79, chief adminstrv. officer, 1979-80, pres., 1980-81; pres., chief exec. officer Gen. Bank, Los Angeles, 1982-84, chmn., pres, chief exec. officer, 1984—; fin. cons. alaska '84, 1981-82, Western Airlines, Los Angeles, 1981-82, Microsci. Internat. Corp., San Jose, Calif., 1986-87; bd. dirs. Simons, Li & Assocs., Ft. Collins, Colo. Pres. Taiwanese United Fund, 1991. Recipient Outstanding Entrepreneur award Nat. Assn. Investment Cos. Mem. Taiwanese Am. Citizens League (life mem., pres.). Avocations: reading, sports. Office: Gen Bank 800 W 6th St Los Angeles CA 90017-2704

WU, NELSON IKON, art history educator, author, artist; b. Peking, China, June 9, 1919; came to U.S., 1945, naturalized, 1956; s. Aitchen K. and Lu-Yü (Yang) W.; m. Mu-lien Hsüeh, Dec. 1, 1951; children: Chao-ming, Chao-ting, Chao-ping, Chao-ying. B.A., Nat. Southwest Asso. U., Kunming, China, 1942; M.A., Yale U., 1949, Ph.D., 1954. Instr. Nat. S.W. Asso. U. Kunming, China, 1942-43; asst. prof. history of art San Francisco State Coll., 1954-55; instr. Yale U., 1955-59, asst. prof., 1959-65; prof. history of art and Chinese culture Washington U., St. Louis, 1965-68, Edward Mallinckrodt Disting. Univ. prof., 1968-84, emeritus, 1984—, chmn. dept. art and archaeology, 1969-70; founder-adviser Asian Art Soc. Washington U., St. Louis, 1972—; fellow Davenport Coll., Yale, 1956-65; vis. prof. Tokyo U., 1972; Founder art festivals Yenling Yeyuan Picnic, 1952-65, Ashiya Seminar, Japan, 1966-67. Cinematographer, assoc. dir., editor motion picture The Flop, 1952; dir., writer music The Finger Painting of Wu Tsai-yen, 1955; author: (pseudonym Lu-ch'iao): Wei-yang Ko (Song Never to End, voted Most Profoundly Influential Book of 1950's by readers of China Times, 1991), 1959 (over 50 printings), Tung Ch'i-ch'ang: Apathy in Government and Fervor in Art, 1962, Chinese and Indian Architecture: City of Man, Mountain of God, and Realm of Immortals, 1963 (Italian and German transls.), Jen-tzu Tales, 1974, over 20 printings, Ch'an-ch'ing-shu, 1975, over 10 printings; contbg. author: Renditions, 1976, (with Kohara and Ch'en) Hsu/Wei and Tung Ch'i-ch'ang, Tokyo, 1978, Chinese garden design Yanling Yeyuan, 1951—; contbr. to Artibus Asiae, 1966, River Styx, 1980, 81, 82, St. Louis Post-Dispatch, 1988, China Times, 1988, 89, 92, 95, China Times Weekly, 1992, United Daily News, 1995, 96; adv. editor Tsing-hua Jour. Chinese Studies, 1982—; exhibited at Faculty Show, Washington U., 1985, St. Louis Art Mus., 1985; featured on PBS show Living Treasures, 1987. Trustee Yale-in-China Assn., 1959-65; hon. trustee Nankai Sch., Tientsin, China, 1993. Tsing-hua Research fellow, 1954-55; Morse fellow Yale, 1958-59; Am. Council Learned Socs. fellow, 1958-59; Guggenheim Found. fellow, 1965-66; Fulbright research scholar, 1965-67; research scholar Kyoto U., Japan, 1965-67; Nat. Endowment for Humanities sr. fellow, 1972; New Haven Art Festival Lit. award, 1960; Calligraphy prize Ashiya, Japan, 1966; Living Treasures plaque St. Louis Older Adult Services and Info. System, 1985; hon. in Taipei, Taiwan at a conf. on contemporary Chinese lit., 1990. Mem. St. Louis Chinese Soc. (pres. 1969-70), League of Chinese Americans (dir. 1974-77). Home: 6306 Waterman Ave Saint Louis MO 63130-4707 also: 1530 Notch Rd Cheshire CT 06410-1970

WU, OLIVIA SHAO-TUNG, editor, writer; b. Shanghai, People's Republic of China, Jan. 10, 1949; d. Tingfen and Polly Ding Ching (Wong) W.; m. Dec. 16, 1972; 1 child, Erling St. Clair. BA, Careton Coll., 1969. Adj. piano instr. U. N.C., Chapel Hill, 1973-74; pvt. practice music tchr. Chapel Hill, 1973-82; caterer Moveable Feast, Chapel Hill, 1977-82; cooking tchr. Olivia Wu Sch. of Cooking, Chapel Hill, 1977-79; mgr., owner La Patissere, Chapel Hill, 1979-82; food editor, restaurant reviewer Daily Herald, Chgo., 1988—. Author: The Grand Wok Cookbook, 1984 (Toastmaster award 1984). Democrat. Avocations: dancing, running, badminton, softball. Office: Paddock Publs 217 W Campbell St Arlington Heights IL 60005-1411 Office: Chicage Sun-Times 401 N. Wabash St Chicago IL 60611

WU, PAN, electrical engineer; b. Hefei, Anhui, China, Dec. 12, 1955; came to U.S., 1983; s. S.H. and S.W. (Pan) Wu; m. Li Yan, July 25, 1983; children: Patrick, Leo. BSEE, U. Sci. and Tech. of China, Hefei, 1982; MSEE, Oreg. State U., Corvallis, 1987; PhD in Elec. Engring., Portland State U., 1993. Grad. asst. Portland (Oreg.) State U., 1987-91, adj. instr., 1990; sr. design engr. Intel Corp., Aloha, Oreg., 1991-94; mem. tech. staff AT&T Bell Labs., Allentown, Pa., 1994—; cons. Top-Vu Tech. Inc., New Brighton, Minn., 1990-91. Contbr. articles to profl. jours. Bd. dirs. Lehigh Valley chpt. Orgn. Chinese Ams. Textronix Found. fellow, Beaverton, Oreg., 1991, Jorgenson scholar for sci. Portland State U., 1992. Mem. IEEE, Eta Kappa Nu. Achievements include the design of the GaAs and CMOS transconductance amplifiers and transdonductance-C filters in the early stage; and patents for research and development of the CPU of Intel's 100 MHz Pentium microprocessor and the cable interface chips in AT&T's communications systems. Office: AT&T Bell Labs 555 Union Blvd Rm 23r-143G Allentown PA 18103-1229

WU, RAY JUI, biochemistry educator; b. Peking, China, Aug. 14, 1928; came to U.S., 1949, naturalized, 1961; s. Hsien and Daisy (Yen) W.; m. Christina Chan, Aug. 11, 1956; children: Albert, Alice. B.S., U. Ala., 1950; Ph.D., U. Pa., 1955. Asso. mem. Pub. Health Research Inst. City of N.Y., 1957-66; asso. prof. biochemistry, molecular and cell biology Cornell U., Ithaca, N.Y., 1966-72; prof. Cornell U., 1972—, chmn. sect., 1975-79; vis. rsch. scientist Stanford U., 1965-66; NSF sr. fellow MRC Lab., Cambridge, Eng., 1971; vis. assoc. prof. MIT, 1972. Contbr. chpts. to books, articles to profl. jours. NIH grantee, 1960—; NSF grantee, 1967—; Am. Cancer Soc. grantee, 1976—; Rockefeller Found grantee, 1985—. Mem. Am. Soc. Biol. Chemists, Am. Chem. Soc., AAAS, Academia Sinica, Internat. Soc. Plant Molecular Biology. Democrat. Home: 111 Christopher Cir Ithaca NY 14850-1701 Office: Cornell U Biotechnology Bldg Ithaca NY 14853

WU, SHI TSAN, educator, science research administrator; b. Nanchang, Kiangxi, Peoples' Republic of China, July 31, 1933; came to U.S., 1957; s. Shu Zee and Duan Ming (Pao) W.; m. Mai San Kao, Sept. 4, 1964; children: Cheyenne, Roselind, Patricia. BS in Mech. Engring., Nat. Taiwan U., 1955; MS in Mech. Engring., Ill. Inst. Tech., 1959; PhD in Aerospace Engring., U. Colo., 1967. Various teaching positions, 1955-64; asst. rsch. prof. Rsch. Inst., Huntsville, Ala., 1967-69, assoc. prof. mech. engring., 1969-72, prof. mech. engring., 1972—, founder, dir. Ctr. Space Plasma and Aeronomic Rsch., 1986—, Disting. prof., 1990—; vis. scientist High Altitude Obs. Nat. Ctr. for Atmospheric Rsch., summers 1969, 72, 73, rsch. asst., 1964-67; vis. prof. U. Sci. & Tech. of China, 1982—, Wu-Han U., 1982—, LaTrobe U., Melbourne, Australia, 1975-76; PhD thesis examiner Tel Aviv U., 1982; cons. Battelle Rsch. Lab., 1978—, various labs. Dept. Commerce, 1974—, Wyle Labs., Huntsville, Ala., 1970-75, Northrup Corp., Huntsville, 1969-74; project specialist Chinese Provincial U. Devel. Project, World Bank, 1989—, others; participant Solar Maximum Yr. Workshops in Australia, People's Republic of China, Ireland, USSR (chmn. various coms.). Corr. editor Acta Astrophysica Sinica, 1985; contbr. articles to profl. jours. Recipient Wright Gardner award Ala. Acad. Sci., 1986; Fulbright-Hays scholar Australia, 1975-76; NSF fellow U. Colo., 1971. Fellow AIAA (dir. Miss. sect. 1980-82, 1987—, chmn. various local and nat. coms. and confs., Martin Schilling award, 1987, Herman Orberth award, 1983); mem. Ctr. for Space Sci. and Applied Tech., Chinese Acad. Sci (hon. 1990), NASA (sec. Adv. Solar Obs. Sci. Working Group 1981—, chmn. various coms. and confs.), ASME (modeling & simulation com. Solar Energy div. 1979—), Internat. Coun. Sci. Unions (various coms.), Sigma Xi (pres. 1974-76, sec. 1972-74, named Researcher of Yr. 1979, Outstanding Svc. award 1977). Office: U Ala-Ctr Space Plasma & Aeronomic Rsch Engring Bldg Huntsville AL 35899

WU, TAI TE, biological sciences and engineering educator; b. Shanghai, China, Aug. 2, 1935; m. Anna Fang, Apr. 16, 1966; 1 son, Richard. M.B., B.S., U. Hong Kong, 1956; B.S. in Mech. Engring, U. Ill., Urbana, 1958; S.M. in Applied Physics, Harvard U., 1959, Ph.D. in Engring. (Gordon McKay fellow), 1961. Rsch. fellow in structural mechanics Harvard U., 1961-63; rsch. fellow in biol. chemistry Harvard U. (Med. Sch.), 1964, rsch. assoc., 1965-66; rsch. scientist Hydronautics, Inc., Rockville, Md., 1962; asst. prof. engring. Brown U., Providence, 1963-65; asst. prof. biomath. Grad. Sch. Med. Scis., Cornell U. Med. Coll., N.Y.C., 1967-68; assoc. prof. Grad. Sch. Med. Scis., Cornell U. Med. Coll., 1968-70; assoc. prof. physics and engring. scis. Northwestern U., Evanston, Ill., 1970-73, prof., 1973-74, prof. biochemistry and molecular biology and engring. scis., 1973-85, acting chmn. dept. engring. scis., 1974, prof. biochem., molecular biology, cell biology and biomed. engring., engring. scis., applied math., 1985-94, prof. biochemistry, molecular biology, cell biology, biomed. engring., 1994—. Author: (with E.A. Kabat and others) Variable Regions of Immunoglobulin Chains, 1976, Sequences of Immunoglobulin Chains, 1979, Sequences of Proteins of Immunological Importance, 1983, Sequences of Proteins of Immunological Interest, 1987, 5th edit., 1991; editor: New Methodologies in Studies of Protein Configuration, 1985; contbr. articles to profl. jours. Recipient progress award Chinese Engrs. and Scientists Assn. So. Calif., Los Angeles, 1971; C.T. Loo Scholar, 1959-60; NIH Research Career Devel. awardee, 1974-79. Mem. Am. Soc. Biochem. & Molecular Biology, Biophys. Soc., Chgo. Assn. Immunology, Sigma Xi, Tau Beta Pi, Pi Mu Epsilon. Office: Dept Biochem Molecular & Cell Biology Northwestern U Evanston IL 60208

WU, TAI TSUN, physicist, educator; b. Shanghai, China, Dec. 1, 1933; came to U.S., 1950, naturalized, 1964; s. King Ching and Wei Van (Tsang) W.; m. Sau Lan Yu, June 18, 1967. B.S., U. Minn., 1953; S.M., Harvard U., 1954, Ph.D., 1956. Jr. fellow Soc. Fellows Harvard U., 1956-59, asst. prof., 1959-63, assoc. prof., 1963-66, Gordon McKay prof. applied physics, 1966—, prof. physics, 1994—; mem. Inst. Advanced Study, Princeton, 1958-59, 60-61, 62-63; vis. prof. Rockefeller U., 1966-67; sci. assoc. Deutsches Elektronen-Synchrotron, Hamburg, Ger., 1970-71, 82-83; Kramers prof. U. Utrecht, Netherlands, 1977-78; sci. assoc. CERN, Geneva, Switzerland, 1977-78, 86—. Author: (with Ronold W.P. King) Scattering and Diffraction of Waves, 1959, (with Barry M. McCoy) Two-Dimensional Ising Model, 1973, (with Ronold W.P. King, Glenn S. Smith and Margaret Owens) Antennas in Matter: Fundamentals, Theory and Applications, 1981, (with Hung Cheng) Expanding Protons: Scattering at High Energies, 1987, (with Raymond Gastmans) The Ubiquitous Photon: Helicity Method for QED and QCD, 1990, (with Ronold W.P. King and Margaret Owens) Lateral Electromagnetic Waves: Theory and Applications to Communications, Geophysical Exploration, and Remote Sensing, 1992. Recipient Alexander von Humboldt award, 1985; Putnam scholar, 1953; fellow A.P. Sloan Found., 1960-66; fellow NSF, 1966-67; Guggenheim Found., 1970-71. Mem. Am. Acad. Arts and Sci., Sigma Xi, Eta Kappa Nu, Tau Beta Pi. Home: 35 Robinson St Cambridge MA 02138-1403 Office: Harvard U Physics Dept 204B Pierce Hall Cambridge MA 02138-2901 *A person's strength is, simultaneously, his weakness.*

WU, TUNG, curator, art historian, art educator, artist; b. Foochow, Fukien, China, Dec. 10, 1940; came to U.S., 1965; s. Chin-Wen and Jingrong (Chen) W.; m. Ying Chin, July 16, 1974. BA, Normal U., Taipei, Taiwan, 1962; postgrad., U. Mich., 1967-70, Harvard U., 1979—. Rsch. asst. Nat. Palace Mus., Taichung, Taiwan, 1962-65; photographer Archive U. Mich., 1966-68; rsch. asst. Cleve. Mus. Art, 1968, Nelson-Atkins Mus. Art, Kansas City, Mo., 1969; rsch. fellow Mus. Fine Arts, Boston, 1971-79, asst. curator, 1980-85, assoc. curator, 1985-86, curator Asian art, 1986-92, Matsutaro Shoriki curator Asian art, 1992—; teaching asst. U. Kans., Lawrence, 1969, Harvard U., 1978; vis. lectr. Harvard U., Cambridge, Mass., 1975, Emmanuel Coll., Boston, 1992, Simmons Coll., Boston, 1993; advisor Chinese Inst. Am., N.Y.C., 1985—, Chinese Cultural Found., San Francisco, 1985-87; cons. Project Emperor-One, Boston, 1983-86; panelist mus. program NEA, 1995. Mem. Nat. Com. on U.S.-China Rels., Washington, 1985—; mem. Nat. Devel. Seminar Taipei, 1989, 92.; advisor dept. Asian trade art Peabody Mus., Salem. Mass., 1991—; trustee W.A. Compton Found. Oriental Arts; mem. Nat. Edn. Reform, Taipei, 1994. Nat. Mus. History fellow (Taipei), 1984—; grantee Freer Found. U. Mich., 1968, Ford Found., Kansas City, 1969, Smithsonian Instn., Washington, 1978. Mem. Taoist Soc. Japan, Soc. Chinese Kunqu Opera, Soc. Chinese Calligraphy. Office: Mus Fine Arts Asiatic Dept 465 Huntington Ave Boston MA 02115-5519

WU, WAYNE WEN-YAU, artist; b. Tachia, Taiwan, Republic of China, Oct. 5, 1935; s. K.C. Kau and Chin-Fong (Chen) W.; m. Amy Hsueh, Dec. 25, 1961; children: Ingrid, Judy, David. BA in Fine Arts, Taiwan Normal U., 1959. Supr. art edn. ctr. Taichung (Taiwan) Libr., 1970-74; instr. fine arts dept. Taiwan Normal U., Taipei, 1973-74; instr. paintings Hunter Mus. of Art, Chatanooga, Tenn., 1980-92; artist, paintings instr. Wayne Wu's Art Studio, Atlanta, 1994—. Represented in 20 solo shows including Taiwan Mus. of Art, 1995, and over 100 group shows. Mem. Am. Watercolor Soc. Home: 2415 Hamptons Passage Alpharetta GA 30202-7411

WU, WILLIAM, lawyer, dentist; b. Hong Kong, Nov. 29, 1952; s. Hou-I and Mei Ching (Chen) W.; m. Lucia Chiang, Aug. 3, 1980; children: Winona, Eunice, Malinda. BA magna cum laude, SUNY, Buffalo, 1975; DDS, Temple U., 1979, JD cum laude, 1992. Bar: Pa. 1992, N.J. 1993. Pvt. practice dentistry, Phila., 1979—; pvt. practice law, Bryn Mawr, Pa., 1992—. Mem. editl. adv. bd. Dental Econs., 1988-89; contbr. articles to legal and dental jours. Bd. dirs. Asian Am. Coun. Greater Phila., 1980-82, United Comtys. S.W. Phila., 1984-89, Phila. Chinatown Devel. Corp., 1985-89, On-Lok House, residence for elderly, 1986—; mem. adv. bd. Fellowship Commn., Phila., 1981-84; trustee United Way Southeastern Pa., 1987-90; pres. Chinese Benevolent Assn. Greater Phila., 1985—. Office: 131 N 9th St Philadelphia PA 19107-2410

WU, WILLIAM LUNG-SHEN (YOU-MING WU), aerospace medical engineering design specialist, foreign intelligence analyst; b. Hangchow, Chekiang Province, China, Sept. 1, 1921; came to U.S., 1941, naturalized, 1955; s. Sing-Chih and Mary (Ju-Mei) Wu. AB in Biochemistry, Stanford U., 1943, MD, 1946; MS in Chemistry and Internal Medicine, Tulane U., 1955; diploma, U.S. Naval Sch. Aviation Medicine, Pensacola, Fla., 1956, USAF Sch. Aviation Medicine, USAF Aerospace Med. Ctr., 1961; cert. of tng. in aviation medicine, U. Calif., Berkeley, 1962, 1964. Diplomate Am. Bd. Preventive Medicine, Am. Bd. Internal Medicine, Am. Bd. Psychiatry, Am. Bd. Pathology. Gen. rotating intern U. Iowa Hosps., Iowa City, 1945-46; resident Lincoln (Nebr.) Gen. Hosp., 1946-47, resident in pathology, 1947-48; resident in pathology Bryan Meml. Hosp., Lincoln, 1947-48; fellow, instr. in internal medicine Tulane U., New Orleans, 1948-54; asst. vis. physician Charity Hosp. and Hutchinson Meml. Teaching and Diagnostic and Cancer Detection Clinics, New Orleans, 1948-51, vis. physician, 1951-54; staff physician Holderman (Army) Hosp., Napa, Calif., 1958; staff physician Aviation Space and Radiation Med. Group Gen. Dynamics/Convair, San Diego, 1958-61; aerospace med. specialist, med. monitor for Life Sciences Sect. Gen. Dynamics/Astronautics, San Diego, 1961-65; aerospace med. and bioastronautics specialist Lovelace Found. for Med. Edn. and Rsch., Albuquerque, 1965-68; staff physician Laguna Honda Hosp., San Francisco, 1968-74; ret.; staff physician Kaiser-Permanente Hosp. all-night med. clinic, San Francisco, 1971-73; safety rep. and med. examiner U.S. Civil Aeronaut. Adminstrn., 1959; med. examiner Fed. Aviation Adminstrn., 1961; expert witness in forensic medicine and/or medicolegal jurisprudence for cts. Author 8 books and 100 tech. papers in field. Active mem. Planning, Rsch. and Devel. Commn. Redwood City; bd. dirs. Legal Aid Soc. Santa Clara County, U.S. Congl. Adv. Bd., Am. Security Coun. Found., Little House Sr. Multipurpose Ednl. Ctr.; Life Fellow Royal Soc. of Lichtenstein, Zurich, Switzerland, Oxford Club (N.Y. and Fla.), Royal Coll. of Heraldry. Comdr., flight surgeon M.C., USN, 1954-57. Recipient Gold medal Internat. Inst. Cmty. Svc., 1976, J. Edgar Hoover Gold Disting. Pub. Svc. award Am. Police Hall of Fame, 1991, Albert Einstein Bronze medal Universal Intelligence Data Bank Am., 1986, Cambridge Gold medal, Dedication Insignia. Fellow San Diego Biomed. Rsch. Inst. (bd. dirs. 1961-65, sec. of fellows 1961-62, chmn. of fellows 1963), Inst. Environ. Scis. (chmn. specifications and standards com.), AIAA (mem. nominating com. San Diego sect., plant rep. life sci. sect. 1963-65); mem. IEEE (vice chmn. San Diego chpt. profl. tech. group on biomed. electronics 1962-65), N.Y. Acad. Scis., Internat. Univ. Found. (hon. pres.), Internat. Acad. Found. (hon. registrar-sec.), Computer Club, Sigma Xi, U.S. Naval Inst. (life), Naval League of U.S. West-pac (life), Conss. Nat. Resource Ctr. Network. Achievements include research of theroetical aspects of cold catalyzed hydrogen fusion nuclear-rocket warm super-conductor hyper-magnetic, hydrogen-fusion space stations; patentee S(RAM-PANT)S. Home: 250 Budd Ave Apt 219 Campbell CA 95008

WU, XIN DI, research physicist; b. Fenghui, China, Apr. 7, 1963; m. Ruoyi Zhou, 1991. BS, Fudan U., 1982; PhD in Physics, Rutgers U., 1989. L. Robert Oppenheimer fellow Los Alamos (N.Mex.) Nat. Lab., 1989-91, staff, 1991—. Mem. Math. Rsch. Soc., Am. Phys. Soc. Office: Los Alamos Nat Lab PO Box 1663 Los Alamos NM 87544-0600*

WU, YING CHU LIN SUSAN, engineering company executive, engineer; b. Beijing, June 23, 1932; came to U.S., 1957; d. Chi-yu and K.C. (Kung) Lin; m. Jain-Ming Wu, June 13, 1959; children: Ernest H., Albert H., Karen H. BSME, Nat. Taiwan U., 1955; MS in Aero. Engring., Ohio State U., 1959; PhD in Aeros., Calif. Inst. Tech., 1963. Sr. engr. Elecro-Optical Systems, Inc., Pasadena, Calif., 1963-65; asst. prof. aero. engring. U. Tenn. Space Inst., Tullahoma, 1965-67, assoc. prof., 1967-73, prof., 1973-88; adminstr. Energy Conversion R&D Programs, Tullahoma, 1981-88; pres., chief exec. officer ERC, Inc., Tullahoma, 1987—; presdl. appointee adv. bd. Nat. Air and Space Mus., Smithsonian Inst., 1993—. Contbr. over 90 articles to profl. jours. Mem. Better Sch. Task Force, Tullahoma, 1985-86; founding mem. Tullahoma Edn. Found. for Excellence; trustee Rochester Inst. Tech., 1992-94; mem. adv. com. NASA Aeronautics, 1994—. Recipient Chancellor's Rsch. award U. Tenn., 1978, Outstanding Educator of Am. award, 1973, 75; Amelia Earhart fellow, 1958, 59, 62, Plasmadynamics and Lasersaward Am. Inst. of Aeronautics and Astronautics, 1994. Fellow ASME, AIAA (assoc., chmn. Tenn. sect., H.H. Arnold award 1984, Plasmodynamics and Lasers award 1994); mem. Soc. Women Engrs. (life mem., achievement award 1985), Rotary, Sigma Xi (chmn. U. Tenn. Space Inst. club). Office: ERC Inc PO Box 417 Tullahoma TN 37388-0417 Address: 5605 Onyx Dr Rocklin CA 95677-4741

WU, ZHOULING, physics educator; b. Anhui, China, Nov. 2, 1964; came to U.S., 1992; BS, Tsinghua U., 1985; PhD, Chinese Acad. of Sci., 1990. Guest scientist Free U., Berlin, 1990-91, Alexander von Humboldt fellow, 1991-92; vis. prof. Wayne State U., Detroit, 1992-94; prof. Ea. Mich. U., Ypsilanti, 1994—. Contbr. articles to profl. jours. Recipient Dakeng Optics Rsch. award Chinese Acad. of Scis., 1989; DFG Rsch. fellowship German Rsch. Soc., 1990, AvH Rsch. fellowship Alexander von Humboldt Found., 1991. Mem. Optical Soc. of Am., Am. Phys. Soc., Am. Physics Tchrs. Soc., Am. Vacuum Soc. Achievements include research in the field of thin film physics and applied optics. Office: Dept Physics/Astronomy Ea Mich Univ 303 Strong Hall Ypsilanti MI 48197

WUDL, FRED, chemistry educator; b. Cochabamba, Bolivia, Jan. 8, 1941; came to U.S., 1958; s. Robert and Bertha (Schorr) W.; m. Linda Raimondo, Sept. 2, 1967. BS, UCLA, 1964, PhD, 1967. Postdoctoral rsch. fellow Harvard U., 1967-68; asst. prof. dept. chemistry SUNY, Buffalo, 1968-72; mem. tech. staff AT&T Bell Labs., Murray Hill, N.J., 1972-82; prof. chemistry and materials U. Calif., Santa Barbara, 1982—. Recipient arthur C. Cope scholar award Am. Chem. Soc., 1993, Award for Chemistry of Materials, 1996, Natta medal Italian Chem. Soc., 1994, Wheland medal U. Chgo., 1994. Fellow AAAS. Office: U Calif Dept Chemistry Santa Barbara CA 93106

WUDUNN, SHERYL, journalist, correspondent; b. N.Y.C., Nov. 16, 1959; d. David and Alice (Mark) W.; m. Nicholas D. Kristof, Oct. 8, 1988. BA, Cornell U., Ithaca, N.Y., 1981; MBA, Harvard U., 1986; MPA, Princeton U., 1988. Lending officer Bankers Trust Co., N.Y.C., 1981-84; intern reporter Wall St. Jour., L.A., 1986; bus. reporter South China Morning Post, Hong Kong, 1987; corr. N.Y. Times, Beijing, 1989-93, Tokyo, 1995—. Coauthor: China Wakes, 1994. Recipient Pulitzer Prize for fgn. reporting, 1990, George Polk award L.I. U., N.Y., 1990, Hal Boyle award Overseas Press Club, 1990. Avocations: aerobics, singing. Office: NY Times Asahi Shumbun Bldg, 3-2 Tsukiji 5-chome, Chuo-ku Tokyo 104-11, Japan Head Office: NY Times 229 W 43rd St New York NY 10036-3913

WUEBBELS, THERESA ELIZABETH, visual art educator; b. Breese, Ill., Nov. 8, 1950; d. Wilson Theodore and Selma Maria (Haake) W. BA, Notre Dame Coll., St. Louis, 1972; postgrad., Boston Coll., 1976-79, Pembroke State U., 1988. Teaching nun Sch. Sisters of Notre Dame, St. Louis, 1969-80; art tchr. Cathedral Sch., Belleville, Ill., 1972-76, Sacred Heart Sch., Fort Madison, Iowa, 1976-80; missionary sister Little Sisters of Jesus, 1980-87; art tchr. Balden County Schs., Clarkton, N.C., 1989—; visual art tchrs. coord. Bladen County Schs., Elizabethtown, N.C., 1991—. Coord. Celebration of the Arts Festival for Bladen County, 1992—; task force mem. founding Clarkton Sch. Discovery, Clarkton, N.C., 1993-94. Named Tchr. of Yr. Clarkton Sch. of Discovery, 1992-93, 93-94, 94-95. Mem. N.C. Art Edn. Assn., Nat. Art Edn. Assn., Visual Art Guild. Roman Catholic. Avocations: fossils, shells, pottery, cats, nature. Home: 653 Poe Elkins Rd Clarkton NC 28433-7243 Office: Clarkton Sch Discovery PO Box 127 Clarkton NC 28433-0127

WUENSCH, BERNHARDT JOHN, ceramic engineering educator; b. Paterson, N.J., Sept. 17, 1933; s. Bernhardt and Ruth Hannah (Slack) W.; m. Mary Jane Harriman, June 4, 1960; children: Stefan Raymond, Katrina Ruth. SB in Physics, MIT, 1955, SM in Physics, 1957, PhD in Crystallography, 1963. Rsch. fellow U. Bern, Switzerland, 1963-64; asst. prof. ceramics MIT, Cambridge, 1964-69, assoc. prof. ceramics, 1969-74, prof., 1974—, TDK chair materials sci. and engring., 1985-90, dir. Ctr. Materials Sci. and Engring., 1988-93, acting dept. head dept. materials sci. and engring., 1980; vis. prof. Crystallographic Inst., U. Saarland, Fed. Republic Germany, 1973; physicist Max Planck Institut für Festkorperforschung, Stuttgart, Fed. Republic Germany, 1981; mem. U.S. nat. com. for crystallography NRC, NAS, 1980-82, 89-94; mem. N.E. regional com. for selection of Marshall Scholars, 1970-73, chmn., 1974-80. Co-editor: Modulated Structures, 1979, Neutron Scattering in Materials Science, 1995; adv. editor Physics and Chemistry of Minerals, 1976-85; assoc. editor Can. Mineralogist, 1978-80; editor Zeitschrift fuer Kristallographie, 1981-88. Ford Found.

postdoctoral fellow, 1964-66. Fellow Am. Ceramic Soc. (Outstanding Educator award 1987), Mineral. Soc. Am.; mem. Am. Crystallographic Assn., Mineral. Assn. Can., Materials Rsch. Soc., Electrochem. Soc. Episcopalian. Home: 190 Southfield Rd Concord MA 01742-3432 Office: MIT Rm 13-4037 77 Massachusetts Ave Cambridge MA 02139-4307

WUERL, DONALD W., bishop; b. Pittsburgh, Nov. 12, 1940; s. Francis J. and Mary A. (Schiffhauer) W. BA, Cath. U. Am., 1962; MA, Cath. U. Am., Rome, 1963; ThM, Pontifical Gregorian U., Rome, 1967; ThD, Pontifical U. St. Thomas, Rome, 1974; DD (hon.), Duquesne U., 1989, Washington and Jefferson Coll., 1990; HLD (hon.), La Roche Coll., 1990; LHD (hon.), St. Vincent Coll., 1992. Ordained priest Roman Cath. Ch., 1966. Asst. pastor, parochial vicar St. Rosalia Ch., Pitts., 1967-69; sec. to Cardinal John Wright Congregation for Clergy, Rome, 1969-79; vice-rector St. Paul Sem., Pitts., 1980-81, rector, 1981-85; Ord. aux. bishop of Seattle, titular bishop of Rosmarkaeum, 1986, bishop of Pittsburgh, 1988—; sec. to Bishop of Pitts., 1967-69; lectr. Duquesne U., Pitts., 1968-69, 80-85, Pontifical U. St. Thomas, 1975-79; lectr. adult theology program Diocese of Pitts., 1967-69, dir. Inst. Continuing Edn. for Priests, 1982-84, assoc. gen. sec., 1985; ofcl. Congregation for Clergy, Rome, 1969-79; mem. alumni bd. govs. Cath. U. Am., 1977-84, vice-pres. for religious, 1981-82; exec. sec. to Papal rep. for Study of Sems. in U.S., 1982-85. Author: The Forty Martyrs, 1971, Fathers of the Church, 1975, The Catholic Priesthood Today, 1976, A Visit to the Vatican, 1981, The Church and Her Sacraments: Making Christ Visible, 1990; co-author: The Teaching of Christ: A Catholic Catechism for Adults, 1976, rev., 1984, 91, abridged, 1979, study guide, 1977, A Catholic Catechism, 1986; contbg. author: New Catholic Ency.; contbr. articles to religion publs.; author religious cassette programs. Recipient Disting. Pennsylvanian award Gannon U., 1989, Brotherhood award NCCJ, 1991, Treee of Life award Jewish Nat. Fund, 1992, Disting. Alumni award Cath. U. Am., 1992; named Vectors/Pitts. Man of Yr. in religion, 1988. Mem. Am. Cath. Hist. Assn., Cath. Theol. Soc. Am., Fellowship Cath. Scholars, Acad. Romana Universale, Phi Kappa Theta (Man of Achievement award 1988). Office: Diocese of Pitts 111 Blvd Of The Allies Pittsburgh PA 15222-1618*

WUHL, CHARLES MICHAEL, psychiatrist; b. N.Y.C., Sept. 24, 1943; s. Isadore and Sali (Ackner) W.; m. Gail; children—Elise, Amy. M.D., U. Bologna, 1973. Diplomate Am. Bd. Psychiatry and Neurology. Intern, N.Y. Med. Coll., 1975-76, resident in psychiatry, 1976-77; fellow in child psychiatry Columbia Presbyn. Med. Center, 1977-78; practice medicine specializing in psychiatry and child psychiatry, Englewood, N.J., 1978—; attending staff, mem. faculty N.Y. Med. Coll.; psychiatrist NYU, also asst. clin. prof. psychiatry NYU Sch. Medicine. Contbr. to Psychosocial Aspects of Pediatric Care, 1978, World Book Ency., 1980—. Mem. Am. Psychiat Assn., AMA, Am. Acad. Child Psychiatry. Office: 163 Engle St Englewood NJ 07631-2530

WULBERT, DANIEL ELIOT, mathematician, educator; b. Chgo., Dec. 17, 1941; s. Morris and Anna (Greenberg) W.; children: Kera, Noah. BA, Knox U., 1963; MA, U. Tex., Austin, 1964, PhD, 1966. Research assoc. U. Lund (Sweden), 1966-67; asst. prof. U. Wash., Seattle, 1967-73; prof. U. Calif.-San Diego, La Jolla, 1973—; vis. prof. Northwestern U., Evanston, Ill., 1977. Contbr. articles in field. Office: U Calif San Diego Dept Math # 0112 La Jolla CA 92093

WULF, JANIE SCOTT MCILWAINE, gifted and talented education educator; b. Smithfield, Va., Mar. 30, 1934; d. Porter O'Brien and Claire (Bennett) Scott; m. Harro Biner Wulf, Sept. 22, 1962; children: Susan, Thomas, Katherine, Jane. BS, Longwood Coll., Farmville, Va., 1955; MEd in Guidance, George Mason U., Fairfax, Va., 1975; postgrad., U. Va. Cert. home econs., upper elem. tchr., guidance counselor, g/t cert., Va. Tchr. kindergarten Faith Luth. Day Sch., Arlington, Va.; tchr. home econs. Annandale High Sch., Fairfax; tchr. sci. Chesterfield County Pub. Schs., Chester; tchr. English gifted and talented edn. Fairfax County Pub. Schs., Fairfax, also middle sch. team leader, 1990-91; team leader, supervising tchr. Fairfax County Frost Sch., 1990-95. Mem. Va. Edn. Assn., Va. Assn. Tchrs. English, Va. Mid. Sch. Assn., Am. Fedn. Tchrs., Fairfax County Fedn. of Tchrs.

WULF, JEROLD W., manufacturing executive; b. 1930. With Andersen Corp., Rayport, Minn., 1958—, pres., CEO, 1990—. Office: Andersen Corp 100 4th Ave N Rayport MN 55003

WULF, MELVIN LAWRENCE, lawyer; b. N.Y.C., Nov. 1, 1927; s. Jacob and Vivian (Hurwitz) W.; m. Deirdre Howard, Dec. 18, 1962; children: Laura Melissa, Jane Miranda. B.S., Columbia U., 1952, LL.B., 1955. Bar: N.Y. 1957. Asst. legal dir. ACLU, 1958-62, legal dir., 1962-77; Distinguished vis. prof. Hofstra Law Sch., 1975, spl. prof. law, 1976-77; mem. firm Clark Wulf & Levine, 1978-83, Beldock, Levine & Hoffman, 1983—. Author articles. Served to lt. (j.g.) USNR, 1955-57. Ford Found. fellow, 1967. Home: 340 Riverside Dr New York NY 10025-3423 Office: 99 Park Ave New York NY 10016

WULF, WILLIAM ALLAN, computer information scientist, educator; b. Chgo., Dec. 8, 1939; s. Otto H. and Helen W. (Westermeier) W.; m. Anita K. Jones, July 1, 1977; children: Karin, Ellen. BS, U. Ill., 1961, MSEE, 1963; PhD in Computer Sci., U. Va., 1968. Prof. computer sci. Carnegie-Mellon Univ., Pitts., 1968-81; chmn., chief exec. officer Tartan Labs., Pitts., 1981-87; AT&T prof. computer sci. Univ. Va., Charlottesville, 1988—; asst. dir. Nat. Sci. Found., Washington, 1988-90; chair bd. on computer sci. and telecommunications NRC; bd. dirs. Baker Engrs., Beaver, Pa.; cons. various computer mfrs. Author: Fundamental Structures of Computer Science, 1981. Bd. dirs. Pitts. High Tech. Coun., 1982-88; trustee Charles Babbage Inst. Fellow IEEE, AAAS, Assn. Computing Machinery (coun.); mem. NAE, Am. Acad. Arts & Scis. Avocations: woodworking, photography. Office: U Va Dept Computer Sci Charlottesville VA 22903

WULF, WILLIAM ARTHUR, lawyer; b. Mpls., Apr. 11, 1945; s. Robert W. and Margaret A. (Rogers) W.; m. Kathleen D. Inzeo, Jan. 4, 1969; children: Robert, Amy, Paula, Maureen. BS in History, U. Wis., 1967; JD, Marquette U., 1971. Bar: Wis. 1971, U.S. Dist. Ct. (we. dist.) Wis. 1971, U.S. Dist. Ct. (ea. dist.) Wis. 1994. Part-time city atty. City of Merrill, 1971-75; assoc. Sazama & Wulf, S.C., Merrill, 1971-79; pvt. practice Merrill, 1979-83; ptnr. Ament, Wulf & Frokjer, Merrill, 1983—; trial specialist Nat. Bd. Trial Advocacy. Past chmn. United Way; bd. dirs. local hosp. fund. With USNG, 1969-75. Mem. Nat. Orgn. Social Security Reps., State Bar Wis., Lincoln County Bar Assn. (past sec.-treas., v.p., pres.), Optimists, KC. Roman Catholic. Avocations: skiing, sailing, golf. Office: Ament Wulf & Frokjer PO Box 626 Merrill WI 54452

WULFF, HARALD P., chemicals executive. Pres., ceo Henkel Corp., Gulph Mills, Pa. Office: Henkel Corp 2200 Renaissance Blvd King Of Prussia PA 19406*

WULFF, JOHN KENNETH, controller; b. L.A., Oct. 15, 1948; s. Kenneth A. and Grace L. (Pinkerton) W.; m. Linda Carol Coffman, June 20, 1970; children: Kenneth E., J. Christopher, Jason D. BS, U. Pa., Phila., 1971. CPA, Conn. Staff acct. Peat Marwick & Co. and predecessors, N.Y.C., 1971-74; mgr. Peat Marwick & Co. and predecessors, 1974-77; ptnr. Peat Marwick Main & Co. and predecessors, 1977-87; dep. contr. Union Carbide Corp., Danbury, Conn., 1987-88, v.p., contr., 1988-95, v.p., CFO, treas., contr., 1995—. Mem. Fin. Execx. Inst., AICPA, and vairous other profl. orgns.

WÜMPELMANN, KNUD AAGE ABILDGAARD, clergyman, religious organization administrator; b. Odense, Denmark, Aug. 7, 1922; s. Heinrich Christian and Helga P.P. (Abildgaard) W.; m. Karen M. Petersen, Aug. 23, 1947; children: Jørgen, Mogens. BD, Cen. Bapt. Theol. Sem., Kansas City, Kans., 1953, MRE, 1954; DD (hon.), William Jewell Coll., Liberty, Mo., 1985. Ordained to ministry Bapt. Union Denmark, 1948. Asst. pastor Jetsmark Bapt. Ch., Denmark, 1947-50; asst. pastor København Meml. Ch., Copenhagen, 1950-55, min., 1955-64; gen. sec. Bapt. Union Denmark, Copenhagen, 1964-80; sec., treas. European Bapt. Fedn., Copenhagen, 1980-89; regional sec. for Europe Bapt. World Alliance, Copenhagen, 1980-89; pres. Bapt. World Alliance, McLean, Va., 1990-95. Author: Vi tror, 1966; editor: Baptistsamfundene i Rwanda-Burundi, 1968. Recipient Disting. Svc. award Ctrl. Bapt. Theol. Sem., Scroll of Honor, Bapt. Theol. Sem., Rüschlikon-Zürich, Switzerland, 1991. Home: Villavej 8, DK-4340 Toelloese Denmark Office: Bapt World Alliance 6733 Curran St Mc Lean VA 22101-3804

WUNDER, CHARLES C(OOPER), physiology and biophysics educator, gravitational biologist; b. Pitts., Oct. 2, 1928; s. Edgar Douglas and Annabel (Cooper) W.; m. Marcia Lynn Barnes, Apr. 4, 1962; children: E(dgar) Douglas, David Barnes, Donald Charles. A.B. in Biology, Washington and Jefferson Coll., 1949; M.S. in Biophysics, U. Pitts., 1952, Ph.D. in Biophysics, 1954. Assoc. U. Iowa, Iowa City, 1954-56, asst. prof. physiology and biophysics, 1956-63, assoc. prof. physiology and biophysics, 1963-71, prof. physiology and biophysics, 1971—; cons. for biol. simulation of weightlessness U.S. Air Force, 1964; vis. scientist Mayo Found., Rochester, Minn., 1966-67. Author: Life into Space: An Introduction to Space Biology, 1966; also chpts., numerous articles, abstracts. Recipient Research Career Devel. award NIH, 1961-66; AEC predoctoral fellow U. Pitts., 1951-53; NIH spl. fellow, 1966-67; grantee NIH, NASA. Mem. Am. Physiol. Soc., The Biophys. Soc. (charter), Aerospace Med. Assn., Iowa Acad. Sci. (chmn. physiology sect. 1971-72, 83-84, 96—, co-chmn. 1982-83, 95-96), Soc. Exptl. Biology and Medicine, Am. Soc. Biomechanics (founding), Aerospace Physiologist Soc., Iowa Physiol. Soc. (pres.-elect 1965-66),. Presbyterian. Achievements include the establishment of chronic centrifugation as an approach for investigating gravity's role as a biological determinant. Home: 702 W Park Rd Iowa City IA 52246-2425 Office: U Iowa BSB Iowa City IA 52242

WUNDERLICH, ALFRED LEON, artist, art educator; b. Salem, Oreg., June 26, 1939; s. Joseph Anthony and Anna Margaret (Meyer) W.; children: Annelise, Jonathan Resor. Cert., Cooper Union, 1961; B.F.A., Yale U., 1962, M.F.A., 1968. Dir. visual studies program Hopkins Ctr., Dartmouth Coll., Hanover, N.H., 1965-66; asst. prof. art Hopkins Ctr., Darmouth Coll., Hanover, N.H., 1966-74; assoc. prof. R.I. Sch. of Design, Providence, 1983-94; prof. R.I. Sch. of Design, Providence, 1994—; adj. lectr. Hunter Coll. CUNY, 1973, adj. prof., vis. artist Pahlavi U., Shiraz Iran, 1978, vis. artist U. Edinburgh, Scotland, Edinburgh Internat. Arts Festival, 1973, Kansas City Art Inst., Art Inst. Chgo., Ohio State U., 1986, Carnegie Mellon U., 1987; fine arts advisor Inst. for Internat. Edn.; mem. U.S. Art in Space team, met with Soviet Artists Union team, Moscow, 1990; owner, artistic dir. GAS-523 project to fly aboard NASA Space Shuttle, 1997. One-man shows Dartmouth Coll., 1969, Kyoto, Japan, 1969, Pahlavi U., 1978, Kwanghow Mus., Canton, China, 1979, Chang-tu Mus., Szechwan, China, 1978, MIT, 1981, Swarthmore Coll., 1985; group exhbns. Harvard U. 1995, MIT 1996, also numerous other group exhbns.; represented in permanent collections Mus. Modern Art, N.Y.C., Art Inst. Chgo., Yale U. Art Gallery, Nat. Gallery Scotland, 1st Nat. Bank Boston, Dartmouth Coll., Smithsonian-Cooper Hewitt Mus., Stanford U. Art Mus., also others. Recipient Bocour Color award, 1960; Yale ALumni fellow, 1962-63; Yaddo fellow, 1973; Dartmouth Faculty fellow, 1968; Fulbright grantee to India, 1963-64; Dartmouth Coll. research grantee, 1970-72; SUNY research grantee, 1983. Home: 151 Pratt St Providence RI 02906-1412 Office: RISD 2 College St Providence RI 02903-2717

WUNDERLICH, BERNHARD, physical chemistry educator; b. Brandenburg, Germany, May 28, 1931; came to U.S., 1954, naturalized, 1960; s. Richard O. and Johanne (Wohlgefahrt) W.; m. Adelheid Felix, Dec. 28, 1953; children: Caryn Cornelia, Brent Bernhard. Student, Humboldt U., Berlin, Germany, 1949-53, Goethe U., Frankfurt, Germany, 1953-54, Hastings Coll., 1954-55; Ph.D., Northwestern U. 1957. Instr. chemistry Northwestern U., Evanston, Ill., 1957-58; instr. chemistry Cornell U., Ithaca, N.Y., 1958-60, asst. prof., 1960-63; assoc. prof. phys. chemistry Rensselaer Poly. Inst., Troy, N.Y., 1963-65, prof. phys. chemistry, 1965-88, prof. emeritus, 1988—; prof. chemistry U. Tenn., Knoxville, 1988—; Disting. scientist div. chemistry Oak Ridge Nat. Lab., 1988—; cons. E.I. duPont de Nemours Co., 1963-88; dir. Lab. for Advanced Thermal Analysis; rsch. in solid state of linear high polymers. Author: Macromolecular Physics, Vol. 1, 1973, Vol. 2, 1976, Vol. 3, 1980, Thermal Analysis, 1990; author computer and audio courses on Crystals of Linear Macromolecules and Thermal Analysis; contbr. over 450 articles to profl. jours.; mem. editl. bd. Chemistry, 1965-68, Makromolekulare Chemie, Jour. Thermal Analysis; mem. adv. bd. Jour. Polymer Sci., Macromolecules, 1984-88, Polymers for Advanced Tech., Macromolecular Sci., Phys. Recipient Humboldt award, 1987-88, award for applied chem. thermodynamics Swiss Soc. for Thermal Analysis and Calorimetry, 1993, TA Instruments award Internat. Conf. Thermal Analysis and Calorimetry, 1996. Fellow Am. Phys. Soc., N.Am., Thermal Analysis Soc. (Mettler award in thermal analysis 1971); mem. Am. Chem. Soc. Home: 200 Baltusrol Dr Knoxville TN 37922-3707 Office: U Tenn Dept Chemistry Knoxville TN 37996

WUNDERLICH, RENNER, film producer, cinematographer; b. St. Louis, May 5, 1947; s. Harry Joseph and Erlynne (Renner) W.; m. Margaret Lazarus; children: Michael, Matthew. BA, Boston Coll., 1968. Prodr., dir., cinematographer, editor Cambridge (Mass.) Documentary Films, 1974—; freelance videographer and sound tech. NBC, ABC, CBS, PBS, BBC and ind. prodrs., 1984—. Prodr., dir., cinematographer, editor: (TV show) Mr. Goodman, 1972-73, (documentaries) Taking Our Bodies Back, 1974, Rape Culture, 1975, Eugene Debs and the American Movement, 1977, Killing Us Softly, 1978, Pink Triangles, 1982, Calling the Shots, 1982, 91, The Last Empire, 1986, Still Killing Us Softly, 1987, Hazardous Inheritance, 1991, Not Just a Job, 1991, Life's Work, 1993, Defending Our Lives, 1993 (Academy Award, Best Documentary Short Subject 1994). Recipient Silver Hugo award Chgo. Internat. Film Festival, 1972, Red Ribbon award Am. Film and Video Festival, 1983, 92, 1st Pl. award Nat. Coun. Family Rels. Film and Video Festival, 1984, 93, Blue Ribbon award Am. Film and Video Festival, 1986, 87, 91, Bronze Apple award Nat. Ednl. Film and Video Festival, 1988, 1st Pl. award Chicagoland Ednl. Film and Video Festival, 1988, Chris award Columbus Internat. Film Festival, PASS award Nat. Coun. Crime and Delinquency, 1993, Silver Apple award Nat. Ednl. Film and Video Festival, 1991, Cert. of Merit, AAAS, 1991, Silver placque Chgo. Internat. Film Festival, 1993, Outstanding Film of Yr. award New England Film and Video Festival, 1993, Exceptional Merit in Media award Nat. Women's Polit. Caucus, 1994. Mem. Acad. Motion Picture Arts and Scis. Avocation: electric cars. Office: Cambridge Documentary Films PO Box 385 Cambridge MA 02139

WUNDERLICH, RICHARD LEE, financial manager, investment advisor; b. Cleve., Apr. 16, 1951; s. Richard Lee and Rose Elisabeth (Heyman) W.; m. Candace Irene Gargus, Apr. 27, 1988. BBA, Cleve. State U., 1977. Mng. ptnr. Wunderlich, Rauckhorst & Co., Cleve., 1983-86; v.p. Wunderlich, Shine & Co. CPAs, Cleve., 1985-87; pres. Dimensional Agy., Inc., Cleve., 1985-88; v.p. Finalco Group, Inc., McLean, Va., 1987-88; pres. Agiotage Group Inc./Master Planning Systems, Cleve., 1988—; v.p. Diamonds & Wunder Farm, Cleve., 1992—; bus. mgr. Ohio Diagnostic Imaging, Inc., Cleve., 1993—; securities cons. Colonial Penn Group Inc., Phila., 1988-90. Served with USN, 1970-74. Mem. AICPA, Registry Fin. Planning Practitioners, Ohio Soc. CPAs, Inst. CFPs, Internat. Assn. for Fin. Planning. Republican. Avocations: sport horses, motorcycling, photography. Office: Agiotage Group Inc North Benton OH 44449

WUNDERMAN, JAN DARCOURT, artist; b. Winipeg, Man., Can., Jan. 22, 1921; d. Rene Paul and Georgette Marie (Guionet) Darcourt; m. Frank Joseph Malina, 1938 (div. 1945); m. Lester Wunderman (div. 1967); children: Marc, Geroge, Karen Renee. BFA, Otis Art Inst., L.A., 1942. One man show Easthampton Guild Hall, L.I., 1977; represented in numerous permanent pub., corp. and pvt. collections including Zimmerli Mus., Nat. Assn. of Women Artists, Rutgers U., 1994. Recipient Ohashi award Pan Pacific Exhbn., Tokyo and Osaka, 1962, Emily Lowe award 1965, J.J. Akston Found. prize, 1965, Canaday Meml. prize, 1979, Marian De Solo Mendes prize, 1981, Charles Horman Meml. prize, 1983, Amelia Peabody award Nat. Assn. Women, 1991, Grumbacher Gold medal of honor, 1992, Doris Kreindler award 1992. Mem. Nat. Assn. Women Artists (medal of honor 1966, Marcia Brady Tucker award 1965, E. Holzinger prize 1966, Jane C. Stanley prize 1977, Marge Greenblatt award 1990, Amelia Peabody award 1991), Am. Soc. Contemporary Artists (corr. sec. 1977-78, Bocour award 1980, Elizabeth Erlanger Meml. award 1990, Kreindler award 1992), Contemporary Artists Guild (rep. by Denise Bibro Fine Art N.Y.C.). Avocations: history, travel. Studio: 41 Union Sq W Rm 516 New York NY 10003-3208

WUNNICKE, BROOKE, lawyer; b. Dallas, May 9, 1918; d. Rudolph von Falkenstein and Lulu Lenore Brooke; m. James M. Wunnicke, Apr. 11, 1940; (dec. 1977); 1 child, Diane B. BA, Stanford U., 1939; JD, U. Colo., 1945. Bar: Wyo. 1946, U.S. Dist. Cty. Wyo. 1947, U.S. Supreme Ct. 1958, Colo. 1969. Pvt. practice law, 1946-56; ptnr. Williams & Wunnicke, Cheyenne, Wyo., 1956-69; of counsel Calkins, Kramer, Grimshaw & Harring, Denver, 1969-73; chief appellate dep. atty. Dist. Atty's Office, Denver, 1973-86; of counsel Hall & Evans L.L.C., Denver, 1986—; adj. prof. law U. Denver Coll. of Law, 1978—; lectr. Internat. Practicum Inst. Denver, 1978—; panelist Judicial Resolutions. Author: Ethics Compliance for Business Lawyers, 1987; co-author: Standby Letters of Credit, 1989, Corporate Financial Risk Management, 1992, Legal Opinion Letters Formbook, 1994, 95, UCP 500 and Standby Letters of Credit-Special Report, 1994, Supplement, 1995, Standby and Commercial Letters of Credit, 1996; columnist Letters of Credit Report; contbr. articles to profl. jours. Pres. Laramie County Bar Assn., Cheyenne, Wy., 1967-68; Dir. Cheyenne C. of C., Cheyenne, Wy., 1965-68. Recipient awards for Outstanding Svc., Colo. Dist. Attys. Coun., 1979, 82, 86, Disting. Alumni award U. Colo. Sch. of Law, 1986, 93, Lathrop Trailblazer award Colo. Women's Bar Assn., 1992. Fellow Colo. Bar Found. (hon.); mem. ABA, Wyo. State Bar, Denver Bar Assn. (trustee 1977-80), Colo. Bar Assn., Am. Arbitration Assn. (nat. panel, regional panel large complex cases), William E. Doyle Inn of Ct. (hon.), Order of Coif, Phi Beta Kappa. Republican. Episcopalian. Avocations: reading, writing, teaching, lecturing. Office: Hall & Evans L L C 1200 17th St Denver CO 80202-5800

WUNSCH, CARL ISAAC, oceanographer, educator; b. Bklyn., May 5, 1941; s. Harry and Helen (Gellis) W.; m. Marjory Markel, June 6, 1970; children—Jared, Hannah. S.B., MIT, 1962, Ph.D., 1967. Asst. prof. phys. oceanography MIT, Cambridge, 1967-70; assoc. prof. MIT, 1970-75, prof., 1975-76, Cecil and Ida Green prof., 1976—, Sec. of Navy rsch. prof., 1985-89, head dept. earth and planetary scis., 1977-81; sr. vis. fellow U. Cambridge, Eng., 1969, 74-75, 81-82; sr. vis. scientist Geophys. Fluid Dynamics Lab., Princeton, 1993-94; vis. rschr. CNES/CNRS, Toulouse, France, 1994; cons. NSF, NAS, JPL. Author: The Ocean Circulation Inverse Problem, 1996; co-author: Ocean Acoustic Tomography, 1995; assoc. editor Jour. Phys. Oceanography, 1977-80, Revs. of Geophysics and Space Physics, 1981-85; co-editor: Evolution of Physical Oceanography, 1981; editor Cambridge U. Press Monographs on Mechanics and Applied Mathematics, 1984-88; contbr. articles to profl. jours. Recipient Tex. Instruments Found. Founders prize, 1975, Huntsman prize Bedford Inst. Oceanography and Govt. of N.S., Can., 1988, Pub. Svc. medal NASA, 1993, Fulbright sr. scholar, 1981-82; Guggenheim fellow, 1981-82. Fellow Am. Geophys. Union (James R. Macelwane award 1971, Maurice Ewing medal 1990), Am. Meterol. Soc., Royal Astron. Soc., Am. Acad. Arts and Scis.; mem. NAS (chmn. bd. ocean studies 1991-94), Soc. Indsl. and Applied Math., Oceanography Soc. Home: 78 Washington Ave Cambridge MA 02140-2708 Office: Dept Earth Atmospheric & Planetary Scis MIT Cambridge MA 02139

WUNSCH, JAMES STEVENSON, political science educator; b. Detroit, Sept. 27, 1946; s. Richard Ellis and Jane Rolston (Stevenson) W.; m. Lillian C. Richards, Mar. 29, 1969 (div. Feb. 1983), 1 child, Kathryn; m. Mary Gayle Gundlach, Aug. 19, 1983; children: Hallie, Hannah. BA, Duke U., 1968; MA, Ind. U., 1971, PhD, 1974. Rsch. fellow U. Ghana, Accra, 1971-72; asst. prof. Creighton U., Omaha, 1974-78, assoc. prof., 1978-86, prof. polit. sci., 1986—, chmn. dept., 1983-93; social sci. analyst and cons., Ghana, Liberia, Kenya, Sudan, Thailand, Philippines, USAID, Washington, 1978-80; vis. assoc. prof. Ind. U., Bloomington, 1985-86; sr. project mgr. Assocs. in Rural Devel., Burlington, Vt., 1987-88, cons., Bangladesh, Zambia, Nigeria, South Africa, Swaziland, Botswana, 1985—; USIA Disting. lectr., South Africa, 1993. Author: The Failure of the Centralized State, 1990, (monograph) Rural Development, Decentralization and Administrative Reform, 1988; contbr. articles to profl. jours., chpts. to books. Bd. dirs. Omaha Symphony Chorus, 1977-78, Nebr. Choral Arts Soc., 1982-96, Voices of Omaha, 1982-85, Trinity Cathedral, Omaha, 1980-83; participant Leadership Omaha, 1982-83; mem. Omaha Com. Fgn. Rels., 1975-95; mem. govt. affairs com. Greater Omaha C. of C., 1980-85; mem. issues and interests com. Nebr. Rep. party, 1984-88; mem. Leadership Omaha Program, 1982-83. Recipient R.F. Kennedy Quality Tchg. award Creighton U., 1985, Burlington No. award, 1992, Dean's award for excellence in tchg., 1994; rsch. award NSF, NEH, USAID, USIA; Fulbright-Hays fellow in Ghana, 1971-72, Internat. Affairs fellow N.Y. Coun. Fgn. Rels., 1978-79. Mem. ASPA, Am. Polit. Sci. Assn., Midwest Polit. Sci. Assn., African Studies Assn., Internat. Studies Assn., Phi Beta Kappa, Pi Sigma Alpha, Phi Beta Delta. Republican. Episcopalian. Avocations: vocal music, camping, cross-country skiing. Home: 1631 N 53rd St Omaha NE 68104-4947 Office: Creighton U Dept Polit Sci 30th And California Omaha NE 68178

WUNTCH, PHILIP SAMUELS, journalist, film critic; b. Austin, Tex., Aug. 2, 1945; s. David and Lillian (Samuels) W.; m. Mimi West, Apr. 27, 1986. BA in Journalism, So. Meth. U., 1968. Journalist, entertainment writer Dallas Times Herald, 1968-69; entertainment writer Dallas Morning News, 1969-74, film critic, 1974—. Contbr. articles to World Book Year Book, 1981—. Avocation: constant reading. Office: Dallas Morning News PO Box 655237 Dallas TX 75265-5237

WUORINEN, CHARLES PETER, composer; b. N.Y.C., June 9, 1938; s. John Henry and Alfhild (Kalijarvi) W. BA, Columbia U., 1961, MA, 1963; DMus (hon.), Jersey City State Coll., 1971. Lectr. Columbia U., 1964-65, instr., 1965-69, asst. prof., 1969-71, co-dir. Group Contemporary Music, 1962—; vis. lectr. Princeton U., 1967-68, New Eng. Conservatory, 1968-71, Yale U., 1983; adj. lectr. U. South Fla., 1971-72; faculty Manhattan Sch. Music, 1972-79, U. So. Calif., 1981; artistic dir., chmn. Am. Composers Orch., 1973-87; composer-in-residence Ojai Festival, 1975, Santa Fe Chamber Music Festival, 1993; San Francisco Symphony, 1984-89; condr. Cleve. Orch., 1976, Finnish Radio Orch., 1979, Helsinki Philharm., 1979; disting. prof. Rutgers U., 1984—; vis. prof. SUNY, Buffalo, 1989-94, NYU, 1990. Author: Simple Composition; mem. editorial bd. Perspectives of New Music; bd. mem. Composers Recs. Inc., 1962-89; composer numerous works including Music for Orchestra, 1956, Be Mery All That Be Present, mixed chorus, 1957, Concert for Four Trombones, 1960, Madrigale Spirituale, 1960, Turetzky Pieces, 1960, Evolutio: organ, 1961, Evolution Transcripta for chamber orch., 1961, Tiento Sobre Cabezon, 1961, Concert for Double Bass Alone, 1961, Trio No. 1 for flute, cello and piano, 1961, Invention for percussion quintet, 1962, Octet, 1962, Duuiensela for cello and piano, 1962, Bearbeitungen über das Glogauer Liederbuch, 1962, The Prayer of Jonah, 1962, 2d Flute Trio: Piece for Stefan Wolpe, 1962, Chamber Concerto for cello and 10 players, 1963, Piano Variations, 1963, Flute Variations, 1963, Composition for violin and 10 instruments, 1964, Chamber Concerto for flute and 10 players, 1964, Orchestral and Electronic Exchanges, 1965, Composition for oboe and piano, 1965, Chamber Concerto for oboe and 10 players, 1965, Super Salutem for male voices and instruments, 1964, Piano Concerto, 1966, The Bells for carillon, 1966, Bicinium, 2 oboes, 1966, Janissary Music for 1 percussionist, 1966, Harpsichord Divisions, 1966, Making Ends Meet for piano four-hands, 1966, John Bull: Salve Regina Versus Septem, 1966, Duo for violin and piano, 1967, The Politics of Harmony: A Masque, 1967, String Trio, 1968, Flute Variations II, 1968, Time's Encomium (electronic), 1969, Adapting to the Times for cello and piano, 1969, The Long and the Short for violin, 1969, Contrafactum for orch., 1969, Nature's Concord trumpet and piano, 1969, Piano Sonata, 1969, Ringing Changes for percussion, 1970, A Song, 1970, Tuba Concerto, 1970, A Message to Denmark Hill, 1970, Cello Variations, 1970, String Quartet, 1971, Canzona for 12 instruments, 1971, Grand Bamboula for string orch., 1971, Amplified Violin Concerto, 1972, Harp Variations, 1972, Bassoon Variations, 1972, Violin Variations, 1972, On Alligators for 8 instruments, 1972, Speculum Speculi for 6 players, 1972, Third Trio for flute, cello and piano, 1973, 12 Short Pieces for piano, 1973, Grand Union for cello and drums, 1973, Arabia Felix for 6 Instruments, 1973, Second Piano Concerto, 1974, Fantasia for violin and piano, 1974, Reliquary for Igor Stravinsky for orch., 1975, The W. of Babylon (opera), 1975, TASHI, 1975, Hyperion for 12 instruments, 1975, Cello Variations 2, 1975, 2d Piano Sonata, 1976, Percussion Symphony, 1976, The Winds, 1977, Fast Fantasy for cello and piano, 1977, Archangel for trombone and string quartet, 1977, Six Pieces for violin and piano, 1977, Six Songs for two voices, Wind Quintet, Self Similar Waltz for piano, Ancestors for chamber ensemble, 1978, Two-Part

Symphony, 1978, Archaeopteryx for bass trombone and chamber ensemble, 1978, The Magic Art, A Masque for chamber orch, 1979, Fortune for 4 instruments, 1979, 2d String Quartet, 1979, The Celestial Sphere for chorus and orch., 1979, Psalm 39 for baritone and guitar, 1979, Percussion Duo, 1979, Joan's for 5 instruments, 1979, Blue Bamboula for piano, 1980, Capriccio for piano, 1981, Horn Trio, 1981, Short Suite for orch., 1981, Trio for bass instruments, 1981, New York Notes for 6 players, 1982, Mass, 1982, Divertimento for alto sax and piano, 1982, Divertimento for string quartet, 1982, Spinoff for violin, double bass and congas, 1983, Trio for violin, cello and piano, 1983, Third Piano Concerto, 1983, Rhapsody for violin and orch., 1984, Concertino, 1984, Crossfire for orch., 1984, Movers and Shakers for orch., 1984, Bamboula Squared for orch. and computer-generated sound, 1984, Natural Fantasy for organ, 1985, Horn Trio Continued, 1985, Trombone Trio, 1985, Prelude to Kullervo for tuba and orch., 1985, Double Solo for Horn Trio, 1985, Fanfare for the Houston Symphony, 1986, The Golden Dance for orch., 1986, Third Piano Sonata, 1986, Third String Quartet, 1987, Galliard for chamber orch., 1987, Bamboula Beach for orch., 1987, FIVE: Concerto for amplified cello and orch., 1987, Sonata for violin and piano, 1988, Bagatelle for piano, 1988, Ave Christe for piano, 1988, Another Happy Birthday for orch., 1988, Machault Mon Chou for orch., 1988, String Sextet, 1989, Twang for soprano and piano, 1989, A Solis Ortu for chorus, 1989, Genesis for chorus and orch., 1989, Astra for orch., 1990, Delight of the Muses for orch., 1991, Missa Brevis, 1991, A Winter's Tale for Soprano and Six Instruments, 1992, Microsymphony, 1992, Missa Renovata for Chorus and Orch., 1992, Saxophone Quartet, 1992, Concerto for Saxophone Quartet and Orch., 1993, The Mission of Virgil for orch., 1993, Percussion Quartet, 1994, Piano Quintet, 1994, Christes Crosse, 1994, Lightenings VIII, 1994, Guitar Variations, 1994, Sonata for Guitar and Piano, 1995, The Great Procession, 1995, Katz Fugue for piano, 1995. Recipient Philharmonic Young Composers award, 1954; Bennington Composers Conf. scholar, 1956-60; Bearns prize, 1958-59, 61; MacDowell Colony fellow, 1958; Alice M. Ditson fellow, 1959; Arthur Rose teaching fellow, 1960; Broadcast Music-Student Composers award, 1959, 61, 62, 63; Lili Boulanger Meml. award, 1963; Festival fellow Santa Fe Opera, 1962; Festival fellow World's Fair Music and Sound, 1962; commd. by Koussevitzky Found., 1964, Berkshire Music Center, 1963, Fromm Found., 1963-71, Ford Found., 1962, Orch. of Am., 1958, Columbia U., 1956, Washington and Lee U., 1964, Fine Arts Quartet, 1969, Naumberg Found., 1971, U. South Fla., 1972, Nat. Opera Inst., 1973, Light Fantastic Players, 1973, N.Y. State Council on the Arts, 1974, N.Y. Philharm., 1974, Balt. Chamber Music Soc., 1974, Buffalo Philharm., 1974, Ojai Festival, 1974, Contemporary Chamber Ensemble, 1974, TASHI, 1974, Beethoven Festival, Bonn, 1978, Albany Symphony, 1981, San Francisco Symphony, 1984, 86, 88, 89, Cleve. Orch., 1984, Balt. Symphony, 1984, Houston Symphony, 1986, N.Y.C. Ballet, 1987, 90, Libr. of Congress, 1988, New World Symphony, 1987, Chamber Music Soc. Lincoln Ctr., 1989, 92, Am./ Soviet Youth Orch., 1990, Phila. Orch., 1992, Beethorenhalle Orch., Bonn Mönchengladbach and Ludwig Forum, Germany; grantee Nat. Inst. Arts and Letters, 1967, Nat. Endowment Arts, 1974, 76; Guggenheim fellow, 1968, 72; Ingraham Merrill fellow, 1972, Rockefeller Found. fellow, 1979, 80, 81, John D. and Catherine T. MacArthur fellow, 1986-91; recipient Pulitzer prize, 1970, Brandeis U. creative arts award, 1970, Creative Artists Pub. Svc. award, 1976; Arts and Letters award Finlandia Found., 1976, Koussevitzky Internat. Rec. award, 1970, 72. Mem. AAAS, AAAL, Am. Soc. Univ. Composers, Am. Composers Alliance (bd. dirs.), Am. Music Ctr. (bd. dirs.), Internat. Soc. Contemporary Music (bd. dirs.), Am. Acad. Arts and Scis., Phi Beta Kappa. Office: care Howard Stokar Mgmt 870 W End Ave New York NY 10025-4948

WURMAN, RICHARD SAUL, architect; b. Phila., Mar. 26, 1935; s. Morris Louis and Fannie (Pelson) W.; m. Gloria Nagy; children: Joshua, Reven, Vanessa, Anthony. BArch (T.P. Chandler fellow), U. Pa., MArch with highest honors; DFA (hon.), U. of the Arts, 1994; LHD (hon.), Art Ctr College of Design, 1995. Mem. faculty N.C. State U., Raleigh, 1962-64, 77, Washington U., St. Louis, 1965, Princeton U., 1965-67, Cambridge (Eng.) U., 1967-68, N.Y.C. program Cornell U., 1968-70, CCNY, 1968-70, UCLA, 1976, U. So. Calif., 1976; prof. architecture, dean Sch. Environ. Design, Calif. State Poly. U., Pomona; chmn. dept. Otis/Parsons, Los Angeles; with Archtl. Office Louis I. Kahn, London, 1960-62; chmn. dept. environ. design Otis Parsons Calif.; crwnding dir. Group Environ. Edn., 1968; bd. dirs. Internat. Design Conf., Aspen, Colo., 1970—, chmn., 1972; co-chmn. 1st Fed. Design Assembly, 1973; trustee Center Bldg. Edn. Programs, 1976—; dep. dir. Phila. Office Housing and Community Devel., 1977; bd. dirs., chmn., creative dir. TED Confs.-Tech. Entertainment Design Conf., 1984—, Kobe, Japan, 1992, Monterey, Calif., 1994—, Med. Comm. Conf., Charlestown, S.C., 1995; pres. Access Press Ltd., The Understanding Bus., 1981-91; designer exhbns., cons. in field; vis. scholar MIT, 1993—, RISD, 1995—. Author 53 books including The Notebooks and Drawings of Louis I. Kahn, The Nature of Recreation, Urban Atlas, Man Made Philadelphia, Aspen Visible, Our Man Made Environment; also author 27 vols. ACCESS travel and info. guidebook series; editor: What Will Be Has Alway Been: The Words of Louis I. Kahn, Information Anxiety, Follow the Yellow Brick Road, The Wall Street Journal Guide to Understanding Money and Markets, Fortune Guide to Understanding Personal finance, 1992, USATLASN, The Newport Guide, 1995, Information Architects, 1996; DE contbr. articles to profl. jours.; retrospective exhbn. AXIS Design Gallery, Tokyo, 1991. Recipient Thornton Oakley medal, 1954, Arthur Spayd Brookes Gold medal, 1958, Kevin Lynch award MIT, 1991; Graham fellow, 1966, 76; T.P. Chandler fellow, 1968; fellow Guggenheim Found., 1969; fellow Rockefeller Bros. Fund, 1972; fellow Nat. Endowment Arts, 1970, 73, 74, 76, 79-80; fellow World Econ. Forum, Davos, Switzerland, 1994; grantee Fels Found., 1970; grantee Ednl. Facilities Lab., 1972, 74; grantee Rohm & Haas Co., 1976. Fellow AIA (medal 1958); mem. Am. Inst. Graphic Artists (v.p., bd. dirs. 1985), Alliance Graphique Internat. Address: The Orchard 180 Narragansett Ave Newport RI 02840-6929

WURMFELD, SANFORD, artist, educator; b. N.Y.C., Dec. 6, 1942; s. Charles Jacob and Esther (Witzling) W.; m. Rella Stuart-Hunt, Dec. 11, 1971; children: Jeremy Philip, Treva. BA in Art with honors, Dartmouth Coll., 1964; ind. study, Rome, 1964-65. Lectr. Hunter Coll., N.Y.C., 1967-72, asst. prof., 1972-77, assoc. prof., 1977-80, chmn. dept. art, 1978—, prof. art, 1980—; vis. artist lectr. Calif. State Coll., Hayward, Cooper Union, N.Y., Bard Coll., Arondale-on-Hudson, N.Y., Livingston Coll., New Brunswick, N.J., 1973, SUNY, Fredonia, 1971, Drexel U., Phila., 1970, Whitney Mus., 1982, Met. Mus. Art, 1987, Princeton U., 1990, The Slade Sch. U. Coll., London, 1991, Chelsea Coll. Art, London, 1991, Whitney Mus., 1992, Hochschule der Kurst, Berlin, 1995. One man shows include Susan Caldwell Gallery, Inc., N.Y., 1978, Bard Coll. Invitational Exhibit, 1977, Susan Caldwell Gallery, 1976-77, Galarie Denise Rene, 1974, Rockefeller Meml. Gallery, Fredonia, N.Y., 1971, Tibor de Nagy Gallery, 1968, Bryant Park, N.Y., Fischbach Gallery, 1969; group shows include Mus. Modern Art, N.Y., 1968, Grank Palais, Paris, 1968, Kunsthaus, Zurich, 1968, Tate Gallery, London, 1968, Ft. Worth Art Ctr., 1969, Galerie de Gestlo, Kunstfair, Basel Switzerland, 1970, 72, Columbia Film Festival, 1973, Galerie Denise Rene, 1974, Hopkins Ctr. Galleries, 1974, Lehigh U., 1976, Susan Caldwell Gallery, 1977-79, Toni Birckhard Gallery, Cin., 1980, Carnegie Internat., 1983, Shangha Exhbn. Hall Shanghai, China, 1986, Long Beach Mus. of Art, Calif., 1989, William Paterson Coll. of N.J., 1990, Hallwells Contemporary Arts Ctr., Buffalo, 1991, Louis Stern Fine Arts, L.A., 1995, Andre Zarre Gallery, N.Y., 1996, others; represented in permanent collections at Met. Mus. Art., N.Y., Guggenheim Mus., N.Y., SUNY, Fredonia, Cen. Trust Co., Cin., Am. Telephone and Telegraph, N.Y., Baxter Travenol Labs., Deerfield, Ill., Gen. Electric Corp., Fairfield, Conn., Sprengler Mus., Hanover, Fed. Republic of Germany, City of Hannover, Fed. Republic of Germany, Shreve, Lamb, & Harmon Corp., N.Y., Silkscreeners Guild, W. Ger., Warner Nat. Corp., Cin., U. N.C., William Hayes Ackland Meml. Art Ctr., Chapel Hill, others; contbr. articles to profl. jours. Recipient Ames award Dartmouth Coll., 1964; fellow Guggenheim Found., 1974, Nat. Endowments for the Arts Individual Artist's, 1987-88; CUNY faculty rsch. grantee. Home: 18 Warren St New York NY 10007-1066 Office: Hunter Coll Dept Art 695 Park Ave New York NY 10021-5024

WÜRSIG, BERND GERHARD, marine biology educator; b. Barsinghausen, Hanover, Fed. Republic of Germany, Nov. 9, 1948; s. Gerhard Paul and Charlotte Annemarie (Yorkowski) W.; m. Melany Anne Carballeira, Nov. 19, 1969; children: Kim, Paul. BS, Ohio State U., 1971; PhD, SUNY, Stony Brook, 1978. Postdoctoral researcher U. Calif., Santa Cruz, 1978-81; prof. Moss Landing (Calif.) Marine Labs., 1981-89; dir. Marine Mammal Lab. Tex. A&M U., Galveston, 1989—; govt. cons. Minerals Mgmt. Service, Washington, 1980—. Contbr. articles to profl. jours.; contbr. seven-part miniseries to TV on lives of dolphins, dolphin problems induced by humans, also Discovery Channel show on Life of B. Würsig; co-author: The Hawaiian Spinner Dolphin, 1994, Whales, Dolphins and Porposes, 1995. Recipient Dean's award for excellence in teaching, 1986, Alban-Heiser award for excellence in Tex. conservation rsch. Zool. Soc. Houston, 1991, Student Body award for most effective tchr. Tex. A&M U., 1994-95. Mem. Marine Mammal Soc. (pres. 1991-93), N.Y. Acad. Scis., Soc. Cryptozoology, Am. Behavior Soc., Am. Mus. Natural History, Soc. Archimedes. Club: Explorers (N.Y.C.) (fellow of research). Avocations: photography, diving, airplane piloting, skiing, hiking. Home: 2304 Dixie Woods Dr Pearland TX 77581-5744 Office: Tex A&M U Marine Mammal Rsch Program 4700 Ave U Bldg 303 Galveston TX 77551

WURSTER, CHARLES FREDERICK, environmental scientist, educator; b. Phila., Aug. 1, 1930; s. Charles Frederick and Helen B. (Schmittberger) W.; m. Eva M. Tank-Nielsen, Aug. 26, 1970; children: Steven Hadley, Nina F., Erik Frederick. SB, Haverford Coll., 1952; MS, U. Del., 1954; PhD, Stanford U., 1957. Teaching asst. U. Del., 1952-54; research asst. Stanford U., 1954-57; Fulbright fellow Innsbruck, Austria, 1957-58; research chemist Monsanto Research Corp., 1959-62; research assoc. biol. scis. Dartmouth Coll., 1962-65; asst. prof. biol. scis. SUNY, Stony Brook, 1965-70; assoc. prof. environ. scis. Marine Scis. Rsch. Ctr., 1970-94, prof. emeritus, 1994—; vis. prof. Macquarie U., Sydney, Australia, 1988; founding trustee, sec., mem. exec. com. Environ. Def. Fund, Inc., 1967—; mem. adminstr's. pesticide policy adv. com. EPA, 1975-78. Contbr. numerous articles to profl. publs. Fellow AAAS; mem. Defenders of Wildlife (dir. 1975-84, 87-96), Nat. Parks and Conservation Assn. (trustee 1970-79). Research on DDT, PCBs, other chlorinated hydrocarbons, effects on phytoplankton, birds; relationship between environmental sciences and public policy; instrumental in banning several insecticides, including DDT, Dieldrin and Aldrin. Ecol. tourism. Office: SUNY Marine Scis Research Ctr Stony Brook NY 11794-5000

WURSTER, DALE ERWIN, pharmacy educator, university dean emeritus; b. Sparta, Wis., Apr. 10, 1918; s. Edward Emil and Emma Sophia (Steingraeber) W.; m. June Margaret Peterson, June 16, 1944; children: Dale Eric, Susan Gay. BS, U. Wis., 1942, PhD, 1947. With faculty U. Wis. Sch. Pharmacy, 1947-71, prof., 1958-71; prof., dean N.D. State U. Coll. Pharmacy, 1971-72, U. Iowa Coll. Pharmacy, Iowa City, 1972-84, prof., 1972—, interim dean, 1991-92, dean emeritus, 1984—; George B. Kaufman Meml. lectr. Ohio State U., 1968; cons. in field; phys. sci. adminstr. U.S. Navy, 1960-63; sci. adv. Wis. Alumni Rsch. Found., 1968-72; mem. revision com. U.S. Pharmacopoeia, 1961-70, pharmacy rev. com. USPHS, 1966-72. Contbr. articles to profl. jours., chpts. to books; patentee in field. With USNR, 1944-46. Recipient Superior Achievement citation Navy Dept., 1964, merit citation U. Wis., 1976; named Hancher Finkbine Medallion Prof. U. Iowa, 1984; recipient Disting. Alumni award U. Wis. Sch. Pharmacy, 1984. Fellow Am. Assn. Pharm. Scientists (founder, sponsor Dale E. Wurster Rsch. award 1990—, Disting. Pharm. Sci. award 1991); mem. Am. Assn. Colls. Pharmacy (exec. com. 1964-66, chmn. conf. tchrs. 1960-61, vis. scientist 1963-70, recipient Disting. Educator award 1983), Acad. Pharm. Scis. (exec. com. 1967-70, chmn. basic pharmaceutics sect. 1965-67, pres. 1975, Indsl. Pharm. Tech. award 1980), Am. Pharm. Assn. (chmn. sci. sect. 1964-65, Rsch. Achievement award 1965), Wis. (Disting. Service award 1971), Iowa Pharmacists Assn. (Robert G. Gibbs award 1983), Wis. Acad. Scis., Arts and Letters, Soc. Investigative Dermatology, Rumanian Soc. Med. Sci. (hon.), Am. Found. Pharm. Edn. (bd. grants 1987-92), Ea. Va. Med. Sch. Contraceptive Rsch. and Devel. Program (tech. adv. com. 1989—), Am. Assn. Pharm. Scientists (Disting. Scientist award 1991), Sigma Xi, Kappa Psi (past officer), Rho Chi, Phi Lambda Upsilon, Phi Sigma. Home: 16 Brickwood Knls NE Iowa City IA 52240-9144

WURTELE, CHRISTOPHER ANGUS, paint and coatings company executive; b. Mpls., Aug. 25, 1934; Valentine and Charlotte (Lindley) W.; m. Heather Campbell (div. Feb. 1977); children: Christopher, Andrew, Heidi; m. Margaret Von Blon, Aug. 21, 1977. BA, Yale U., 1956; MBA, Stanford U., 1961. V.p. Minn. Paints, Inc. (merged with Valspar Corp. 1970), Mpls., 1962-65, exec. v.p., 1965, pres., CEO, 1973-96, chmn., 1996—; dir. Gen. Mills Inc., Donaldson Co., Bemis Co., IDS Mutual Fund Group. Mem. adv. coun. Grad. Sch. Bus. Stanford U.; bd. dirs. Bush Found., Walker Art Ctr. With USN, 1956-59. Mem. Am. Bus. Conf., Mpls. Club, Nat. Paint & Coatings Assn. (bd. dirs.). Episcopalian. Home: 2409 E Lake Of The Isles Pky Minneapolis MN 55405-2479 Office: Valspar Corp 1101 S 3rd St Minneapolis MN 55415-1211

WURTELE, MORTON GAITHER, meteorologist, educator; b. Harrodsburg, Ky., July 25, 1919; s. Edward Conrad and Emily Russell (Gaither) W.; m. Zivia Syrkin, Dec. 31, 1942; children—Eve Syrkin, Jonathan Syrkin. S.B., Harvard, 1940; M.A., UCLA, 1944, Ph.D., 1953. Asst. prof. meteorology Mass. Inst. Tech., Cambridge, 1953-58; asso. prof. meteorology U. Calif. at Los Angeles, 1958-64, prof., 1964—, chmn. dept., 1971-76; vis. prof. U. Buenos Aires, 1962, U. Jerusalem, 1965; cons. in field. Prin. contbr.: Glossary of Meteorology; co-editor: Progress in Desert Research; contbr. articles to profl. jours. Trustee Univ. Corp. for Atmospheric Rsch.; pres., dir. Sage Resources, Inc. With USNR, 1940-41. Fulbright grantee, 1949-50, 65; NATO sr. fellow, 1961-62. Fellow Am. Meteorol. Soc.; mem. Am. Profs. for Peace in Middle East (nat. exec. 1974—), Royal Meteorol. Soc., Am. Geophys. Union, Phi Beta Kappa, Sigma Xi. Club: Harvard So. Calif. Home: 432 E Rustic Rd Santa Monica CA 90402-1114 Office: UCLA Meterology Dept Los Angeles CA 90024-1565

WURTMAN, JUDITH JOY, research scientist; b. Bklyn., Aug. 4, 1939; d. Alexander Mordecai and Jeanette Teicher Hirschhorn; m. Richard Jay Wurtman; children: Rachael, David. BA, Wellesely (Mass.) Coll., 1959; MA in Biology Edn., Harvard U., 1960; PhD, George Washington U., 1973. Tchr. Malden Sch. System, 1959-60; rsch. asst. Microbiol. Assocs., Bethesda, Md., 1962-67; exhibit researcher Boston Mus. Sci., 1973-74; asst. prof. Newton (Mass.) Coll., 1974-76; postdoctoral fellow dept. nutrition MIT, Cambridge, 1976-78, rsch. scientist dept. nutrition, dept. brain and cognitive sci., 1987—; mem. scientific adv. bd. NutriSystem, Phila., 1988-89, Interneuron Pharms., Boston, 1989—; bd. dirs. Walden Labs. Author: Eating Your Way Through Life, 1979, The Carbohydrate Craver's Diet, 1983, The Carbohydrate Craver's Diet Cookbook, 1984, Managing Your Mind and Mood Through Food, 1987; editor: Nutrition and the Brain (8 vols.), 1983—, The Serotonin Solution, 1996. Mem. Am. Inst. Nutrition, Am. Dietitic Assn., Am. Soc. for Clin. Nutrition, Boston Soc. Psychiatry and Neurology, Soc. for Light Treatment and Biol. Rhythms, Sigma Xi (MIT chpt.). Office: MIT Dept of Brain and Cognitive Scis E25-604 Cambridge MA 02139

WURTMAN, RICHARD JAY, physician, educator, inventor; b. Phila., Mar. 9, 1938; s. Samuel Richard and Hilda (Schreiber) W.; m. Judith Joy Hirschhorn, Nov. 15, 1959; children: Rachael Elisabeth, David Franklin. A.B., U. Pa., 1956; M.D., Harvard U., 1960. Intern Mass. Gen. Hosp., 1960-61, resident, 1961-62, fellow medicine, 1965-66, clin. assoc. in medicine, 1985—; research assoc., med. research officer NIMH, 1962-67; mem. faculty MIT, Cambridge, 1967—, prof. endocrinology and metabolism, 1970-80, prof. neuroendocrine regulation, 1980-84, Cecil H. Green disting. prof., 1994—; dir. Clin. Rsch. Ctr., MIT, Cambridge, 1985—; prof. neuroscience MIT, 1984-94; lectr. medicine Harvard Med. Sch., 1969—; prof. Harvard-MIT Divsn. Health Scis. and Tech., 1978—; sci. dir. Ctr. for Brain Scis. and Metabolism Charitable Trust, 1981—; invited prof. U. Geneva, 1981; Sterling vis. prof. Boston U., 1981; mem. small grants study sect. NIMH, 1967-69, preclin. psychopharmacology study sect., 1971-75; behavioral biology adv. panel NASA, 1969-72; coun. basic sci. Am. Heart Assn., 1969-74; rsch. adv. bd. Parkinson's Disease Found., 1972-80, Am. Parkinson's Disease Assn., 1978—; com. phototherapy in newborns NRC-Nat. Acad. Scis., 1972-74, com. nutrition, brain devel. and behavior, 1976, mem. space applications bd., 1976-82; mem. task force on drug devel. Muscular Dystrophy Assn., 1980-87; chmn. life scis. adv. com. NASA, 1979-82; chmn. adv. bd. Alzheimer's Disease Assn., 1981-84; assoc. neuroscis. rsch. program MIT, 1974-82; chmn. life scis. adv. bd. USAF, 1985—; Bennett lectr. Am. Neurol. Assn., 1974; Flexner lectr. U. Pa., 1975; founder, chmn. sci. adv. bd. Interneuron Pharms., Inc., 198—; Hans Lindler Meml. lectr. Weizmann Inst., 1993. Author: Catecholamines, 1966; (with others) The Pineal, 1968; editor: (with Judith Wurtman) Nutrition and the Brain, Vols. I and II, 1977, Vols. III, IV, V., 1979, Vol. VI, 1983, Vol. VII, 1986, Vol. VIII, 1990, also numerous other articles and books; mem. editl. bd. Endocrinology, 1967-73, Jour. Pharmacology and Exptl. Therapeutics, 1968-75, Jour. Neural Transmission, 1969-88, Neuroendocrinology, 1969-72, Metabolism, 1970-80, Circulation Research, 1972-77, Jour. Neurochemistry, 1973-82, Life Scis., 1973-81, Brain Rsch., 1977—; holder of approximately 40 U.S. patents on new treatments for diseases and conditions. Recipient Alvarenga prize and lectureship Phila. Coll. Physicians, 1970, CIBA-Geigy Drew award in Biomed. Rsch., 1982, Roger Williams award in Preventive Nutrition, 1987, Roger J. Williams award in Preventive Medicine, 1989, NIMH Merit award, 1989—, Internat. Prize for Modern Nutrition, 1989, Hall of Fame Disting. Alumni award Ctrl. H.S. Phila., 1992; Disting. lectr. Purdue U., 1984; Rufus Cole lectr., Rockefeller U., 1985; Pfizer lectr. NYU Med. Sch., 1985; Grass Fedn. lectr. U. Ga., 1985, Alan Rothballer Meml. lectr., N.Y. Med. Coll., Valhalla, N.Y., 1989, Gretchen Kerr Green lectr in the neuroscis., 1989; Wellcome Vis. Prof. Washington State U., Pullman, 1989; Julius Axelrod Disting. lectr. in neurosci., CUNY, 1990, Sigma Tau Found. lectr. on aging, Rome, 1990, Disting. lectr. in neurosci. La. State U., 1991, McEwen lectr. Queen's U., Ont., 1991; Plenary lectr. 3d Internat. Symposium on Microdialysis, 1993; Hans Lindner Meml. lectr. Weizmann Inst., 1993. Mem. Am. Soc. Clin. Investigation, Endocrine Soc. (Ernst Oppenheim award 1972), Am. Physiol. Soc., Am. Soc. Biol. Chemists, Am. Soc. Pharmacology and Exptl. Therapeutics (John Jacob Abel award 1968), Am. Soc. Neurochemistry, Soc. Neuroscis., Am. Soc. Clin. Nutrition, Am. Inst. Nutrition (Osborne & Mendel award 1982). Club: Harvard (Boston). Home: 300 Boylston St Boston MA 02116-3923 Office: Mass Inst Tech 45 Carleton St # E25-604 Cambridge MA 02142-1323

WURTZ, ROBERT HENRY, physiologist, scientist; b. St. Louis, Mar. 28, 1936; s. Robert Henry and Alice Edith (Popplwell) W.; m. Sally Smith, Dec. 20, 1958 (div.); children: William, Erica; m. Emily Otis, Apr. 23, 1983. AB, Oberlin Coll., 1958; PhD, U. Mich., 1962. Rsch. assoc. Com. for Nuclear Info., St. Louis, 1962-63; fellow Sch. Medicine, Washington U., 1962-65; rsch. psychologist NIH, Bethesda, Md., 1965-66, physiologist, 1966-78, chief lab. sensorimotor rsch., 1978—; vis. scientist Cambridge U., Eng., 1975-76. Editor: Neurobiology of Saccadic Eye Movement, 1989. Recipient Karl Spencer Lashley award Am. Philos. Soc., 1995. Fellow AAAS; mem. NAS, Am. Acad. Arts and Scis., Soc. Neurosci. (pres. 1991), Am. Physiol. Soc., Assn. for Rsch. in Vision and Opthalmology, Soc. Exptl. Psychologists. Office: NIH Nat Eye Inst 9000 Rockville Pike Bethesda MD 20892-0001

WURTZEL, ALAN HENRY, television executive; b. N.Y.C., Jan. 29, 1947; s. Sam and Bernice (Weinstein) W.; m. Susan Warner, Dec. 20, 1970; children: Joanna, Caroline. BA, CUNY, Queens, 1967; MA, U. Mich., 1969; PhD, NYU, 1974. Asst. prof. Queens Coll. of CUNY, N.Y.C., 1970-75, U. Ga., Athens, 1975-78; mgr. social research ABC-TV, N.Y.C., 1978-81, v.p. broadcast standards and practices, 1981-88, sr. v.p. mktg. and research services, 1988-1993, sr. v.p. news mag. and longform programming, 1993—; sr. v.p. news mag. and longform programming Good Morning America, 1995—. Author: Television Production, 1978, 4th edit., 1995. Office: ABC News 47 W 66th St New York NY 10023-6201

WURTZEL, ALAN LEON, retail company executive; b. Mount Vernon, N.Y., Sept. 23, 1933; s. Samuel S. and Ruth (Mann) W.; m. Irene C. Rosenberg, Oct. 9, 1988; children from previous marriage: Judith Halle, Daniel Henry, Sharon Lee. AB, Oberlin Coll., 1955; postgrad., London Sch. Econ., 1955-56; LLB cum laude, Yale, 1959. Bar: Conn. 1959, D.C. 1960, Va. 1968. Law clk. Chief Judge David L. Bazelon, U.S. Ct. Appeals, D.C., 1959-60; assoc. Fried, Frank, Harris, Shriver & Kampelman, Washington, 1960-65; legisl. asst. to Senator Joseph Tydings, 1965-66; with Cir. City Stores, Inc. (formerly Wards Co., Inc.), Richmond, 1966—, v.p., 1968-70, pres., 1970-83, chief exec. officer, 1973-86, chmn., 1983-94; vice chmn., 1994—; pres. NATM Buying Corp., 1978-86; pres. Operation Independence, 1987-88; bd. dirs. Office Depot, Inc., Boca Raton, Fla., Dollar Tree Stores, Norfolk, Va., Nat. Alliance of Bus., Washington; mem. Nat. Skills Stds. Bd. Bd. visitors Va. Commonwealth Ednl. U., 1985-92; trustee Oberlin Coll.; dir. Washington Ednl. Television Assn.; pres. Jewish Community Fedn., Richmond, 1983-85. Mem. Va. State Bd. Edn., Gov.'s Econ. Adv. Coun. Office: 2134 R St NW Washington DC 20008-1907 Office: Cir City Stores Inc 9950 Mayland Dr Richmond VA 23233-1463

WURZBURG, RICHARD JOSEPH, healthcare executive; b. Chicago, Ill., Mar. 12, 1947; s. Max and Babette (Strasburger) W.; m. Ruth Lea Goldhaber, Apr. 8, 1979; children: Jeffrey Joseph, Robert Ian. BJ, U. Mo., 1970; MBA, U. Pa., 1972. Comml. banking asst. 1st Nat. Bank Chgo./ Continental Ill. Nat. Bank Chgo., 1972-75; sr. product mgr. Citicorp Subs., St. Louis, 1975-77; v.p. CNA Health Plans, chgo., 1977-82; exec. v.p. Bank Adminstrn. Inst., Rolling Meadows, Ill., 1982-85; sr. v.p. 1st Fed. Savs. and Loan, Rochester, N.Y., 1985-86; pres., CEO Partners Health Plan, South Bend, Ind., 1986-94; chmn. Partners Health Adminstrs., Inc., South Bend, 1992-94; pres. Michiana Healthnet, South Bend, 1994; COO N.Am. Med. Mgmt. Tex., Houston, 1995—. Trustee Temple Beth-El, South Bend, 1990-95, chmn. endowment com. 1990-95; mem. adv. bd. Jr. League, 1992-95. Mem. Knollwood Country Club, Summit Club (bd. dirs. 1993-95), St. Joseph Valley Jewish Fedn. (dir. 1993-95, v.p. 1994-95). Avocations: golf, reading. Office: NAm Med Mgmt Tex 1235 N Loop W Ste 450 Houston TX 77008

WURZBURGER, WALTER SAMUEL, rabbi, philosophy educator; b. Munich, Germany, Mar. 29, 1920; s. Adolf W. and Hedwig (Tannenwald) W.; m. Naomi C. Rabinovitz, Aug. 19, 1947; children—Benjamin W., Myron I., Joshua J. BA, Yeshiva U., 1944, DD (hon.), 1987; MA, Harvard U., 1946, PhD, 1951. Ordained rabbi, 1944. Rabbi Congregation Chai Odom, Boston, 1944-53, Shaarei Shomayim Congregation, Toronto, Ont., Can., 1953-67; rabbi Shaaray Tefila Congregation, Lawrence, N.Y., 1967-94, Rabbi emeritus, 1994—; editor Tradition, N.Y.C., 1961-87; columnist Toronto Telegram, 1957-67; adj. assoc. prof. philosophy Yeshiva U., 1967-80, adj. prof., 1980—. Author: Ethics of Responsibility, 1994; editor: A Treasury of Tradition, 1967; contbg. editor Sh'ma; contbr. articles to profl. jours., chpts. to books, Ency. Judaica, Ency. of Religion, Ency. of Bioethics. Mem. exec. com. United Jewish Welfare Funds of Toronto, 1965-67; past chmn. commn. on adoptions, synagogue commn., trustee Fedn. Jewish Philanthropies N.Y.; bd. dirs. Union Orthodox Jewish Congregations Am.; chmn. com. on interreligious affairs Synagogue Coun. Am., 1973-75, 83-87, pres., 1981-83, hon. pres., 1983-85; mem. interfaith com. United Community Funds of Toronto, 1960-67; v.p. synagogue commn. Fedn. Philanthropies, 1973-75; mem. nat. adv. com. United Jewish Appeal Am., 1971-78. Recipient Nat. Rabbinic Leadership award Union Orthodox Jewish Congregations Am., 1983, Samuel Belkin Lit. award Yeshiva Coll. Alumni Assn., 1994. Mem. Rabbinical Coun. Am. (past pres.), Rabbinical Coun. Can. (past pres.). Home: 138 Hards Ln Lawrence NY 11559-1315

WURZEL, LEONARD, retired candy manufacturing company executive; b. Phila., Feb. 4, 1918; s. Maurice L. and Dora (Goldberg) W.; m. Elaine Cohen, Aug. 18, 1949; children—Mark L., Lawrence J. B.S., Washington and Jefferson Coll., 1939; M.B.A., Harvard, 1941. With Loft Candy Corp., Long Island City, N.Y., 1946-64; v.p. Loft Candy Corp., 1949-56, exec. v.p., 1956-57, pres., 1957-64, dir., 1949-64; chmn., dir. Calico Cottage Candies, Inc., 1964-94; ret., 1994; mayor Village of Sands Point, N.Y., 1989—. Capt. Adj. Gen.'s Dept., AUS, 1941-46. Decorated Bronze Star. Mem. Assn. Mfrs. Confectionery and Chocolate (bd. dirs., past pres., chmn.), Candy Chocolate and Confectionery Inst. (bd. dirs., treas.), Retail Confectioners Internat. (bd. dirs., past pres.). Home: 25 Woodland Dr Sands Point NY 11050-1136 Office: Tibbits Ln Sands Point NY 11050-0109

WURZEL, MARY V., past association executive; b. Newport, R.I., July 17, 1918; d. William James and Mary Josephine (Dennis) Veach; m. Edward Milton Wurzel, Sept. 2, 1945; children: William D., David L., Edward Michael, Donald J., James D. BA, Brown U., 1939. Pres. Ex-Ptnrs. of Servicemen/Women for Equality, Alexandria, Va., 1984-90, 92-94. Docent Kennedy Ctr.; alumni chair Brown U., Providence, R.I.; Navy Arlington Lady. Home: 203 Yoakum Pkwy # 903 Alexandria VA 22304-3723

WUSSLER, ROBERT JOSEPH, broadcasting executive, media consultant; b. Newark, Sept. 8, 1936; s. William and Anna (MacDonald) W.; children:

Robert Joseph, Rosemary, Sally, Stefanie, Christopher, Jeanne. BA in Communication Arts, Seton Hall U., 1957, LLD (hon.), 1976; LLD (hon.), Emerson Coll., 1976. With CBS News, N.Y.C., 1957-72; v.p., gen. mgr. Sta. WBBM-TV, Chgo., 1972-74; v.p. CBS Sports, N.Y.C., 1974-76, pres., 1977-78; pres. Sta. CBS-TV, N.Y.C., 1976-77, Pyramid Enterprises Ltd., N.Y.C., 1978-80; exec. v.p. Turner Broadcasting System Inc., Atlanta, 1980-87, sr. exec. v.p., from 1987, bd. dirs.; pres. Atlanta Sports Teams, Inc., 1981-87; pres., chief exec. officer COMSAT Video Enterprises, Inc., Washington, 1989-92; pres. Wussler Group, 1992—; chmn. bd. dirs. Nat. Acad. TV Arts and Scis., 1986-90; bd. dirs. Atlanta Hawks Ltd., Atlanta Braves Nat. League Baseball Club, Inc.; co-owner Denver Nuggets, NBA, 1989-92. Bd. regents Seton Hall U., 1978-84; trustee Marymount Manhattan Coll., 1977-81. Recipient Emmy awards, numerous other nat. and internat. news and sports awards. Mem. Dirs. Guild Am., Internat. Radio and TV Soc., Ariz. Heart Inst., Cable Advt. Bur., Nat. Cable TV Assn. (satellite network com.), European Broadcasting Union. Roman Catholic.

WUSTENBERG, WENDY WIBERG, public affairs specialist, consultant; b. Faribault, Minn., Sept. 30, 1958; d. George Lyman and Ruth Elizabeth (Morris) Wiberg; m. William Wustenberg, Nov. 11, 1989; children: Russell Morris, Lauren Ruth. BA in Journalism, U. Minn., 1977-83. Dir. comms., press sec. Office Gov. Quie, St. Paul, 1980-83; sr. prodr. news and pub. affairs Twin Cities Pub. TV, St. Paul, 1983-88; chief of staff Minn. House Reps., St. Paul, 1990; CFO, mng. ptnr. Issue Strategies Group, St. Paul, 1988-92; cons. Wustenberg and Assocs., Farmington, MN, 1992—; trustee Farmington Sch. Bd., 1993—; dir. Cmty. Action Coun., Apple Valley, Minn., 1991-93; pres. SOAR, Inc., Rosemount, Minn., 1990—; adj. prof. Metro. State U., St. Paul, 1986—; lobbyist State of Minn., St. Paul, 1992—. Author: Families and Sexuality, 1983; creative dir.: (avt. campaign) Environmental Trust Fund, 1988 (Assn. Trends award 1988); contbr. articles to profl. jours. Minn. exec. dir. Bush/Quayle Campaign, Bloomington, 1992; instr. Courage Ctr. Alpine Skiers, Welch, Minn., 1988; trustee The Carpenter Found. and Carpenter Nature Ctr., 1995—. Recipient Nat. Promotion award Corp. for Pub. Broadcasting, Washington, 1986, 87, Local Documentary and Outreach award, 1987, J.C. Penney award U. Mo. Journalism Sch., 1987; finalist TV Acad. awards Nat. Acad. TV Arts and Scis., N.Y.C., 1986; named Adult Educator of Yr., Mo. Valley Assn. Adult Edn., 1986; named Disting. Alumni, U. Minn., 1994. Mem. Minn. Sch. Bds. Assn. (del.), Minn. Alumni Assn., Order Eastern Star. Republican. Avocations: equestrian training, gardening, golf, furniture restoration, cooking.

WUTHNOW, ROBERT, sociology educator; b. Sterling, Kans., June 23, 1946; s. Victor Robert and Kathryn Clare (Huey) W.; m. Sara Margery Wilcox, June 15, 1968; children—Robyn Elizabeth, Kathryn Brooke, Joel Robert. B.S., U. Kans., 1968; Ph.D., U. Calif, Berkeley, 1975. Instr. U. Ariz., Tucson, 1974-76; asst. prof. Princeton (N.J.) U., 1976-79, assoc. prof., 1979-84, prof. sociology, 1984-92, Gerhard R. Audlinger prof. social scis., 1992—; bd. trustees Princeton U. Press, 1985-89; bd. advisors Princeton Religion Research Ctr., 1979—; cons. Gallup Orgn., 1980—. Author: The Consciousness Reformation, 1976, Experimentation in American Religion, 1978, Meaning and Moral Order, 1987, The Restructuring of American Religion, 1988, The Struggle for America's Soul, 1989, Communities of Discourse, 1989, Acts of Compassion, 1991, Rediscovering the Sacred, 1992, Christianity in the 21st Century, 1993, Sharing the Journey, 1994, Producing the Sacred, 1994, God and Mammon in America, 1994, Learning to Care, 1995; co-author: Adolescent Prejudice, 1975, Cultural Analysis, 1984. Spl. career fellow Ford Found., 1969-72; William Paterson preceptor Princeton U., 1976-79. Mem. Am. Sociol. Assn., Soc. for Sci. Study of Religion (exec. council 1979-80). Home: 4 Highland Rd Princeton NJ 08540-4710 Office: Princeton U Dept Sociology 2N2 Green Hall Princeton NJ 08544

WYANT, CORBIN A., newspaper publisher; m. Donna Lee Humphrey, Oct. 5, 1963; children: Mrs. Blair Milliken, Corbin W., Beth Ashley. BA, Bucknell U., 1958; student Grad. Sch. Journalism, Pa. State U., 1973-74. Reporter/photographer Daily Leader-Times, Kittanning, Pa., 1958-69, advt. sales rep., circulation mgr., 1960-61, co-pub., gen. mgr., 1961-73; pres. Daily Dispatch, Douglas, Ariz., 1965-73; pub. Daily Herald News, Punta Gorda, Fla., 1974-76; v.p., gen. mgr. Naples (Fla.) Daily News, 1977-85, pub., 1985—, pres., 1986—. Former treas. and founder Mental Health Clinic Armstrong County, Pa.; former bd. dirs. Mental Health and Mental Retardation Assn. Armstrong and Ind. Counties, Med. Ctr. Hosp., Punta Gorda, Fla.; former chmn. Armstrong County Airport Authority; former v.p., bldg. chmn. YMCA Charlotte County; elder First Presbyn. Ch., Naples, Fla.; asst. coach Babe Ruth Baseball, Naples, 1983; coach Little League, Nples, 1979; bd. dirs. Naples Philharm., Inc., 1987—, Cmty. Concert Assn., 1978-84; mem. adv. bd. Salvation Army, Naples, 1987—; v.p. Collier Cultural Ctr., Inc., 1978-82, YMCA Collier County, 1977-87. Mem. Fal. Press Assn. (bd. dirs. 1986-92, pres. 1993-94, chmn. 1994-95), Fla. Newspaper Advt. Network (founder, bd. dirs. 1987—), Econ. Devel. Coun. Collier County (bd. dirs. 1995—), Edison Cmty. Coll. Endowment Corp. (bd. dirs. 1994—), Gulf Coast Sailing Assn., Collier Athletic Club, Forum Club Collier County (pres. 1988-89), Rotary (pres. Naples 1982-83). Office: Naples Daily News 1075 Central Ave Naples FL 33940-6237

WYATT, DORIS FAY CHAPMAN, English language educator; b. Del Rio, Tex., July 12, 1935; d. Cecil Cornelius and Lola Wade (Veazey) Chapman; m. Jimmy Trueman Wyatt, June 2, 1956 (div. Nov. 1977); children: Abra Natasha Smith, Kent Colin Wyatt, Garrett Bret Wyatt. BS in Edn., S.W. Tex. State U., 1956; MA in English, U. North Tex., 1969; MA in Counseling, East Tenn. State U., 1983. Cert. profl. tchr. career ladder III, Tenn.; cert. marriage and family therapist. Elem. tchr. Clover Pk. Pub. Schs., Tacoma, 1957-58; jr. high reading tchr. Levelland (Tex.) Pub. Schs., 1964-67; tchr. English Denton (Tex.) Pub. Schs., 1967-70; tchr. reading & English Vets. Upward Bound, East Tenn. State U., Johnson City, 1981-87; tchr. English Johnson City (Tenn.) Pub. Schs., 1970—; beauty cons. Mary Kay Cosmetics, Johnson City, 1971-95; adj. faculty mem. Tusculum Coll., Greeneville, Tenn., 1993—; pine plantation owner. Area dir. People-to-People Student Ambassador Program, Washington County, Tenn., 1975-94, tchr.-leader, Johnson City, 1974-84. Named to Nat. Dean's list, 1982-83. Mem. NEA, AAUW, Johnson City Edn. Assn. (pres., bd. dirs. 1989-90), Tenn. Edn. Assn., Nat. Coun. Tchrs. English, Assembly on Lit. for Adolescents, Alpha Delta Kappa (pres. 1994-96), Phi Kappa Phi. Democrat. Methodist. Avocations: people, travel, photography, reading. Home: 1805 Sundale Rd Johnson City TN 37604-3023 Office: Johnson City Pub Schs Sci Hill High Sch John Exum Pky Johnson City TN 37604-4553

WYATT, FOREST KENT, university president; b. Berea, Ky., May 27, 1934; s. Forest E. and Almeda (Hymer) W.; m. Janice Collins, Mar. 4, 1956; children: Tara Janice Wyatt Mounger, Elizabeth Pharr Wyatt Mitchell. BS in Edn., Delta State U., Cleveland, Miss., 1956; MEd, U. So. Miss., 1960; EdD, U. Miss., 1970; postgrad., Harvard Inst. Ednl. Mgmt., 1975. Instr., coach Univ. Mil. Sch., Mobile, Ala., 1956-60; tchr., adminstr. Bolivar County dist. schs., Cleveland, Miss., 1960-64; alumni sec. Delta State U., 1964-69, adminstrv. asst. to pres., dir. adminstrv. services, assoc. prof. edn., 1969-75, pres., 1975—; dir. Grenada Bank. Contbr. articles to profl. jours. Past bd. dirs. United Givers Fund, Cleveland Beautification Commn.; past bd. dirs., past v.p. Miss. Com. for Humanities, Delta Area coun. Boy Scouts Am. Friends of State Libr. Commn.; past chmn. Indsl. Devel. Found.; past pres. Cleveland Crosstie Arts Coun.; past trustee So. Bapt. Theol. Sem.; past bd. dirs. Miss. Econ. Coun.; past pres. Gulf South Conf.; bd. dirs. Southeastern Regional Vision for Edn. With U.S. Army, 1957-58. Recipient Kossman award for Outstanding Community Svc. C. of C., 1987. Mem. Miss. Assn. Educators, Am. Coun. on Edn. (mem. com. on govtl. rels.), Am. Coun. on Tchrs. Edn., Miss. Assn. Sch. Adminstrs., Am. Assn. State Colls. and Univs. (chmn. athletic com., com. governance, com. profl. devel. task force on athletics), NCAA (coun., past chmn. student-athlete adv. com., pres's. commn., gender equity com., exec. dir. search com., chmn. athletics cert. study com. divsn. II), Miss. Assn. Colls. (past pres.), So. Assn. Colls. and Schs. (Commn. on Colls.), Inter-Alumni Coun., Cleve. C. of C. (past pres.), Cleve. Country Club (dir.), Lions, Phi Delta Kappa, Omicron Delta Kappa, Kappa Delta Pi. Address: Delta State U Cleveland MS 38733

WYATT, GERARD ROBERT, biology educator, researcher; b. Palo Alto, Calif., Sept. 3, 1925; came to Can., 1935; s. Horace Graham and Mary Aimee (Strickland) W.; m. Sarah Silver Morton, Dec. 19, 1951 (dec. Mar. 1981); children—Eve Morton, Graham Strickland, Diana Silver; m. Mary Evelyn Rogers, Mar. 16, 1985. B.A., U. B.C., Can., 1945; postgrad, U. Calif.-Berkeley, 1946-47; Ph.D., Cambridge U., 1950. Research scientist Can. Dept. Agr., Sault Ste. Marie, Ont., 1950-54; asst. prof. biochemistry Yale U., New Haven, 1954-60, assoc. prof., prof. biology, 1960-73; prof. biology Queen's U., Kingston, Ont., 1973-94, prof. emeritus, 1994—; sci. dir. Insect Biotech Can., 1990-93. Contbr. articles to profl. jours. Guggenheim fellow, 1956; Killam Research fellow, 1985. Fellow Royal Soc. Can.; mem. Can. Soc. Cell Biology, Am. Entomol. Soc. Avocation: natural history. Home: 114 Earl St, Kingston, ON Canada K7L 2H1 Office: Queen's Univ, Dept Biology, Kingston, ON Canada K7L 3N6

WYATT, JAMES FRANK, JR., lawyer; b. Talladega, Ala., Dec. 1, 1922; s. James Frank and Nannie Lee (Heaslett) W.; m. Rosemary Barbara Slone, Dec. 21, 1951; children: Martha Lee, James Frank III. B.S., Auburn U., 1943; J.D., Georgetown U., 1949, postgrad., 1950. Bar: D.C. 1949, Ala. 1950, Ill. 1953, U.S. Supreme Ct 1953. Atty. Office Chief Counsel, IRS, 1949-51; tax counsel Universal Oil Products Co., Des Plaines, Ill., 1951-63; asst. treas. Universal Oil Products Co., 1963-66, v.p. fin., treas., 1966-75; treas. CF Industries, Inc., Long Grove, Ill., 1976-78; v.p. fin., treas. CF Industries, Inc., 1978-82; assoc. Tenney & Bentley, 1983-85, Arnstein, Gluck, Lehr, Barron & Milligan, 1985-88; pvt. practice, 1989—; dir. 1st Nat. Bank, Des Plaines. Village trustee, Barrington, Ill., 1963-75; bd. dirs. Buehler YMCA, Barrington Twp. Republican Orgn., 1963—; pres. Barrington Area Rep. Workshops, 1962-63. Served to capt., Judge Adv. Gen. Corps AUS, 1944-47. Mem. Tax Execs. Inst. (v.p. 1965-66, chpt. pres. 1961-62), Fed., Am., Chgo. bar assns., Barrington Home Owners Assn. (pres. 1960-61), Newcomen Sco., Assn. U.S. Army, Scabbard and Blade, Phi Delta Phi, Sigma Chi. Episcopalian. Clubs: Barrington Hills Country; Economics, University (Chgo.). Home: 625 Concord Pl Barrington IL 60010-4508 Office: 200 Applebee St Barrington IL 60010-3063

WYATT, JAMES LESLIE, III, university president; b. Aug. 24, 1945; m. Jeanne Cogburn, 1968; children: Cathey and Will (twins), Betsy. BA, Abilene Christian U., 1968; BFA, U. Tex., Austin, 1969, MFA, 1971, PhD in Edn., 1974. Asst. dean Coll. Fine Arts, instr. art U. Tex., Austin, 1971-75, assoc. dean Coll. Fine Arts, asst. prof. art, 1975-77; dean Coll. Fine Arts, assoc. prof. U. Ark., Little Rock, 1977-83, vice chancellor for univ. advancement, assoc. prof. art, 1983-88; vice chancellor for exec. affairs, prof. art history U. Miss., 1988-95; pres. Ark. State U., State University, 1995—; speaker and presenter in field. Exhibited art work in solo shows at Gardner Galley, Abilene, Tex., 1969, Huntington Gallery, U. Tex., 1970, The Clean Well-Lighted Place Gallery, Austin, 1971; group shows include DuBose Gallery, Houston, Contemporary Gallery, Dallas, U. Ark. Little Rock; contbr. articles to profl. jours. Recipient awards, fellowships and grants. Office: Ark State U PO Box 10 State University AR 72467-0010

WYATT, JAMES LUTHER, drapery hardware company executive; b. Williamsburg, Ky., May 13, 1924; s. Jesse Luther and Grace Edwina (Little) W.; m. Barbara Christman, Aug. 28, 1946; children—Linda Lou, William Charles Christman (dec.). B.S., U. Ky., 1947, M.S., 1948; Sc.D., Mass. Inst. Tech., 1952. Registered profl. engr., Ohio, Pa. Devel. engr. titanium div. Nat. Lead Co., Sayreville, N.J., 1948-50; tech. mgr., head, dept. metall. engring., mgr. new products Horizons, Inc., Cleve., 1953-57; cons., asso. Booz, Allen & Hamilton, N.Y.C., 1957-61; v.p. program devel. Armour Research Found., Chgo., 1961-63; v.p. new product devel. Joy Mfg. Co., Pitts., 1963-67; v.p. corp. devel. Nat. Gypsum Co., Buffalo, 1967-69, Max Factor & Co., Hollywood, Calif., 1969-71; pres. Wyatt & Co., 1971—, Jimbabs, Inc., 1983—, Ambassador Industries, Inc., Los Angeles, 1988—; U.S. del. 1st World Metall. Congress. Contbr. tech., mgmt. papers to profl. lit. Mem. Pompano Beach Power Squadronm, adminstr. officer, 1991, exec. officer, 1992, comdr., 1993; chmn. bd. trustees Meth. Ch., 1992, mem. fin. com., 1993, mem. adminstrv. bd. Lt. col. USAAF, 1942-46. Mem. AIME, Am. Soc. Metals, Sigma Phi Epsilon, Alpha Chi Sigma. Clubs: Econs. (Chgo.), Execs. (Chgo.); Univ. (N.Y.C.); Calif. Yacht. Patentee in field. Home: 510 NE Golden Harbour Dr Boca Raton FL 33432-2942 Office: Bunker Hill Twr Ste 507 800 W First St Los Angeles CA 90012

WYATT, JOE BILLY, academic administrator; b. Tyler, Tex., July 21, 1935; s. Joe and Fay (Pinkerton) W.; m. Faye Hocutt, July 21, 1956; children: Joseph Robert, Sandra Faye. B.A., U. Tex., 1956; M.A., Tex. Christian U., 1960. Systems engr. Gen. Dynamics Corp., 1956-65; mgr. Digital Computer Lab., 1961-65; dir. computer ctr., assoc. prof. computer sci. U. Houston, 1965-72; dir. Office Info. Tech. Harvard U., 1972-76, sr. lectr. computer sci., 1972-82, v.p. adminstrn., 1976-82; chancellor Vanderbilt U., Nashville, 1982—; mem. faculty Kennedy Sch. of Harvard U., 1976-82; bd. dirs., chmn. com. on math/sci., Am. Coun. of Edn.; bd. dirs. Reynolds Metals Co., SONAT Corp., Advanced Networking and Sys. Corp. Author (with others) Financial Planning Models for Colleges and Universities, 1979; editor-in chief: Jour. Applied Mgmt. Systems, 1983; contbr. articles to profl. jours.; patentee in field of data processing. Trustee Harvard U. Press, 1976-83, pres., 1975-76, chmn. bd., 1976-79; trustee EDUCOM, Princeton, N.J., 1973-81, Leadership Nashville, 1983-93; bd. dirs. Nashville Inst. Arts, 1982-83, Ingram Industries, 1990—; chmn. adv. com. IST, NSF, 1978-85; vice chmn. bd. Mass. Tech. Devel. Corp., Boston, 1977-83; mem. Coun. Competitiveness; fellow Gallaudet Coll., 1981-83; mem. alumni bd. dirs. Harvard Bus. Sch., 1982-92. Recipient award for exemplary leadership CAUSE, Hilton Head, S.C., 1982, Nat. Tree of Life award Jewish Nat. Fund, 1988; named Outstanding Tennessean Gov. of Tenn., 1986. Fellow AAAS; mem. IEEE, Assn. Am. Univs. (chair exec. com. 1990-91), Hosp. Corp. Am. (bd. dirs. 1984-89), Nat. Assn. Ind. Colls. and Univs. (policy bd. 1980-82), Am. Coun. edn. (chair adv. com. on tech. edn. 1980-81, bd. dirs. 1990-92), Assn. Computing Machinery (pres. Dallas and Ft. Worth chpt. 1963-65), U. Rsch. Assn. (bd. trustees 1988—), So. U. Rsch. Assn., Inc. (chmn. coun. pres. 1988-89), Bus. Higher Edn. Forum (exec. com. 1990-93), Aircraft Owners and Pilots Assn., Nashville C. of C. (bd. dirs. 1983-86, pres.-elect 1995), Experimental Aircraft Assn. (pres. adv. com.), Govt. Univ. Industry Rsch. Roundtable, Sigma Xi, Beta Gamma Sigma, Phi Beta Kappa (hon.), Harvard Club (N.Y.C.). Methodist. Office: Vanderbilt U Office of Chancellor 211 Kirkland Hall Nashville TN 37240

WYATT, JOSEPH LUCIAN, JR., lawyer, author; b. Chgo., Feb. 21, 1924; s. Joseph Lucian and Cecile Gertrude (Zadico) W.; m. Marjorie Kathryn Simmons, Apr. 9, 1954; children: Daniel, Linn, Jonathan. AB in English Lit. with honors, Northwestern U., 1947; LLB, Harvard U., 1949. Bar: Calif. 1950, U.S. Dist. Ct. (cen. dist.) Calif. 1950, U.S. Ct. Appeals (9th cir.) 1950, U.S. Tax Ct., U.S. Supreme Ct. 1965. Assoc. firm Brady, Nossaman & Walker, L.A., 1950-58; ptnr. Brady, Nossaman & Walker, L.A., 1958-61; pvt. practice L.A., 1961-71; sr. mem. Cooper, Wyatt, Tepper & Plant, P.C., L.A., 1971-79; of counsel Beardsley, Hufstedler & Kemble, L.A., 1979-81; ptnr. Hufstedler & Kaus, L.A., 1981-85; sr. of counsel Morrison & Foerster, L.A., 1995—; mem. faculty Pacific Coast Banking Sch., Seattle, 1963-92, Southwestern Grad. Sch. Banking, 1988-89; adviser Am. Law Inst., 1988—, Restatement, Trusts 3d. Author: Trust Administration and Taxation, 4 vols., 1964—; editor: Trusts and Estates, 1962-74. Lectr. continuing legal edn. programs, Calif. and Tex.; trustee Pacific Oaks Coll. and Children's Sch., 1969—; counsel, parliamentarian Calif. Democratic party and presdl. conv. dels., 1971—; mem. Calif. State Personnel Bd., 1961-71, v.p., 1963-65, pres., 1965-67; bd dirs. Calif. Pub. Employees Retirement System, 1963-71. Served with USAAF, 1943-45. Fellow Am. Coll. of Trust and Estate Counsel; mem. ABA, Internat. Acad. Estate and Trust Law (treas.), Am. Law Inst., Calif. Bar Assn. (del. state conf. 1956, 62-67), L.A. Bar Assn. (trustee 1956). Democrat. Christian Scientist. Avocations: poetry, fishing. Home: 1119 Armada Dr Pasadena CA 91103-2805

WYATT, LENORE, civic worker; b. N.Y.C., June 12, 1929; d. Benedict S. Rosenfeld and Ora (Copel) Kanner; m. Bernard D. Copeland, May 17, 1953 (dec. March 1968); children: Harry (dec.), Robert (dec.); m. C. Wyatt Unger, Mar. 26, 1969 (dec. Feb. 1992); 1 child, Amy Unger; m. F. Lowry Wyatt, Sept. 12, 1992. Student, Mills Coll., 1946-48; BA, Stanford U., 1950, MA, 1952; postgrad., NYU, 1952-53. Instr. Stanford U., Palo Alto, Calif., 1952, Hunter Coll., N.Y.C., 1952-53, Calif. State U., Sacramento, 1956-60, U. Calif., Davis, 1965-69; property mgr. Unger, Demas & Markakis, Sacramento, 1974-83; former actress and model. Pres. Sacramento Opera Assn., 1972-73; treas. Sacramento Children's Home, 1990-92, v.p., 1992—; former mem. bd. dirs. Sutter Hosp. Aux., Sutter Hosp. Med. Rsch. Found., Sacramento Symphony League, Temple B'nai Israel Sisterhood, Sacramento chpt. Hadassah, Sacramento Children's Home Guild; active Sacramento Opera Assn., Crocker Soc. of Crocker Art Gallery, Sacramento Symphony Assn., Sacramento Reportory Theater Assn.; founding mem. Tacoma Communities Art Sch.; mem. Temple Beth El of Tacoma. Mem. Joint Adventure Investment Club, Am. Contract Bridge League, Sacramento Pioneer Assn., Stanford U. Alumni Assn. (past bd. dirs. Sacramento) Sutter Club, Kandahar Ski Club, Sutter Lawn Tennis Club, DelPaso Country CLub (capt. women's golf 1983), Tacoma Country and Golf Club, Maui Country Club, Wash. Athletic Club, Tacoma Club. Republican. Jewish. Avocations: golf, duplicate bridge.

WYATT, MARY JEAN (M.J. WYATT), public relations executive. Acct. exec. Burson-Marsteller; acct. supr. Rowland Co.; acct. exec., acct. supr. Manning, Selvage & Lee, 1980-85, v.p., dep. group mgr., 1985-86; v.p., group mgr. Ketchum, 1986-87, sr. v.p., 1988, sr. v.p., group mgr., dir. healthcare, 1989-90; pres. Ruder Finn Healthcare, 1990—. Bd. dirs. Nat. Hemophilia Found. Mem. Am. Med. Writers Assn., Women in Comm. Inc. Office: Ruder Finn Inc 301 E 57th St New York NY 10022-2900*

WYATT, OSCAR SHERMAN, JR., energy company executive; b. Beaumont, Tex., July 11, 1924; s. Oscar Sherman Sr. and Eva (Coday) W.; m. Lynn Sakowitz; children: Carl, Steven, Douglas, Oscar Sherman III, Brad. BS in Mech. Engring., Tex. Agrl. and Mech. Coll., 1949. With Kerr-McGee Co., 1949, Reed Roller Bit Co., 1949-51; ptnr. Wymore Oil Co., 1951-55; founder Coastal Corp., Corpus Christi, Tex., 1955; now chmn. bd., CEO Coastal Corp., Houston. Served with USAAF, World War II. Office: Coastal Corp Coastal Tower 9 E Greenway Plz Houston TX 77046

WYATT, RICHARD JED, psychiatrist, educator; b. Los Angeles, June 5, 1939; children: Elizabeth, Christopher, Justin. BA, Johns Hopkins U., 1961, MD, 1964; MD (hon.), Ctrl. U. Venezuela, 1977. Intern in pediat. Western Res. U. Hosp., Cleve., 1964-65; resident in psychiatry Mass. Mental Health Ctr., Boston, 1965-67; with NIMH, 1967—, asst. dir. intramural rsch., 1977-87, chief neuropsychiatry br., chief Neurosci. Ctr., 1972—; clin. prof. psychiatry Stanford U. Med. Sch., 1973-74, Duke U. Med. Sch., 1975—, Uniformed Svcs. Sch. Medicine, 1980—, Columbia U., 1987—; practice medicine specializing in psychiatry Washington, 1968—; cons. Psychiatry Shelter Program for the Homeless, Columbia U., 1987—; mem. sci. adv. bd. Nat. Alliance for Rsch. Schizophrenia and Depression, 1991. Mem. editl. bd. Advances in Neurosci., 1989, Harvard Rev. Psychiatry, 1992; assoc. prodr. PBS spls. To Paint the Stars, Moods in Music. Recipient A.E. Bennett award Soc. Biol. Psychiatry, 1971, Psychopharm. award APA, 1971, Superior Achievement award USPHS, 1980, Dean award Am. Coll. Psychiatrists, McAlpin Rsch. Achievement award Nat. Mental Health Assn., 1986, Media award for To Paint the Stars, 1991, Arthur P. Noyes award Commonwealth of Pa., 1986, Arieti award Am. Acad. Psychoanalysts, 1989, Robert L. Robinson award for Moods in Music, 1990, Mental Health Bell Media award for Moods in Music, Mental Health Assn. Atlanta, 1991. Fellow Am. Psychiat. Assn. (task force on local arrangements 1991—), Am. Coll. Neuropsychopharmacology (nominating com. 1991, Efron award 1983); mem. AMA, Washington Psychiat. Assn. Office: NIMH Neurosci Ctr Rm 536 WAW Bldg St Elizabeth Hosp Washington DC 20032-2698

WYATT, ROBERT LEE, IV, lawyer; b. Las Cruces, N.Mex., Mar. 9, 1964; s. Robert Lee III and Louise Carole (Bard) W. BS, Southeastern Okla. State U., 1986; JD, U. Okla., 1989. Bar: Okla. 1989, U.S. Dist. Ct. (we. dist.) Okla. 1990, U.S. Ct. Appeals (10th cir.) 1990, U.S. Dist. Ct. (no. dist.) Okla. 1991, U.S. Ct. Appeals (8th cir.) 1991, U.S. Supreme Ct. 1993. Intern Okla. State Bur. Investigation, Oklahoma City, 1988-89, guest lectr., 1989; dep. spl. counsel Gov. of Okla., 1995; atty. Jones, Wyatt & Roberts, Enid, Okla., 1989—. Mem. ABA (mem. criminal & litigation sects.), Okla. Bar Assn. (mem. ins., family and litigation sects.), Garfield County Bar Assn., Okla. Criminal Def. Lawyers Assn., Nat. Inst. for Trial Advocacy, Phi Delta Phi, Alpha Chi. Democrat. Baptist. Home: 4911 Ridgedale Dr Enid OK 73703-4602 Office: Jones Wyatt & Roberts 114 E Broadway Enid OK 73701

WYATT, ROBERT ODELL, journalism educator; b. Jackson, Tenn., Feb. 7, 1946; s. Odell and Sera Mae (Mebane) Wyatt. BA, U. of the South, 1968; MA, Northwestern U., 1970, PhD, 1973; MS, U. Tenn., 1977. Asst. to assoc. prof. U. Tenn., Nashville, 1973-79; assoc. prof. Mid. Tenn. State U., Murfreesboro, 1979-84, prof., 1984—, dir. Office Communication Rsch., 1989—; vis. prof. comm. U. Caen, France, 1994; cons. in comm.; mem. Pulitzer Prize Jury, 1980, 85, 91, 93, chair jury, 1985, 91, 93; rsch. cons. Freedom Forum First Amendment Ctr., Vanderbilt U. Author: Free Expression and the American Public, 1991 (Sigma Delta Chi award for rsch. on journalism 1992); editor book sect. The Nashville Tennessean, 1978-93; contbr. articles to profl. jours. Mem. Soc. Profl. Journalists, Assn. for Edn. in Journalism and Mass Comm., Internat. Comm. Assn., Am. Assn. Pub. Opinion Rsch., Speech Comm. Assn. Democrat. Episcopalian. Home: 2008 Hackberry Ln Nashville TN 37206 Office: Middle Tenn State U PO Box 391 Murfreesboro TN 37133-0391

WYATT, WILSON WATKINS, JR., finance association and public relations executive; b. Louisville, Dec. 3, 1943; s. Wilson Watkins Sr. and Anne (Duncan) W.; m. Jane Clay, Aug. 15, 1964 (dec. 1975); children: Carol, Wilson III, Sarah Wyatt. Student, U. of the South, 1961-65. Reporter The Courier-Jour., Louisville, 1965-67; pub. rels. account exec. Doe-Anderson Advt., Louisville, 1967-68; account exec. Zimmer-McClaskey-Lewis, Louisville, 1968-70; ptnr. Bennett & Wyatt Pub. Rels., Louisville, 1970-71; state rep., vice chair appropriations and revenue com. Ky. Gen. Assembly, Frankfort, 1969-71; exec. dir. Louisville Cen. Area Inc., 1971-77; dir. corp. affairs and communications Brown & Williamson Tobacco Corp., Louisville, 1977-82; v.p. pub. policy BATUS Inc., Washington, 1982-86; v.p. corp. affairs BATUS Inc., Louisville, 1986-90; sr. v.p. corp. affairs PNC Fin. Corp., Pitts., 1990-92; sr. v.p. corp. comm. and govt. rels. The Travelers Cos., Hartford, 1992-94; exec. dir., CEO Am. Acad. of Actuaries, Washington, 1995—; lead U.S. def. pub. rels. activities against hostile takeover for B.A.T. Industries, U.K., 1989-90; chmn. Travelers Found., 1991-94, Travelers Good Govt. Com., 1992-94. Mem. youth adv. com. Atlantic Inst., 1967-68; del. North Atlantic Treaty Assn. Young Leaders Conf., 1967; chmn. Leadership Effort for All Dems., Ky., 1967-68; regional campaign coord. for Robert F. Kennedy, Ky.-Ind., 1968; mem. Pres.'s Forum, Washington, 1988-91; trustee Conn. Policy Econ. Commn., 1992-95; mem. exec. com. Hartford Downtown Coun., 1992-94; mem. adv. bd. Dem. Leadership Coun., Washington. Named one of Outstanding Young Men in Am., Ky. Jaycees, 1973. Mem. Pub. Rels. Seminar, The Vice Pres.'s Forum, Pub. Affairs Rsch. Coun. (conf. bd. 1986-95), Pub. Affairs Coun. (bd. dirs. 1982—, exec. com. 1982-86), Speakers Club (Washington), Greater Hartford C. of C. (exec. com. 1992-94), Hartford Stage (bd. dirs. 1993-95). Avocations: boating, photography, writing, tennis. Office: Am Acad Actuaries 1100 Seventeenth St NW 7th Fl Washington DC 20036

WYATT-BROWN, BERTRAM, historian, educator; b. Harrisburg, Pa., Mar. 19, 1932; s. Hunter and Laura Hibbler (Little) Wyatt-B.; m. Anne Jewett Marbury, June 30, 1962; children: Laura (dec.), Natalie. B.A., U. of South, 1953, LL.D. (hon.), 1985; B.A. with honours, King's Coll., Cambridge (Eng.) U., 1957, M.A., 1961; Ph.D., Johns Hopkins U., 1963. Mem. faculty Colo. State U., Ft. Collins, 1962-64, U. Colo., Boulder, 1964-66; mem. faculty Case Western Res. U., Cleve., 1966-83; prof. history Case Western Res. U., 1974-83; Richard J. Milbauer prof. history U. Fla., Gainesville, 1983—; Fleming lectr. La. State U., Baton Rouge, 1995; vis. prof. U. Wis.-Madison, 1969-70. Author: Lewis Tappan and the Evangelical War Against Slavery, 2d edit., 1971, Southern Honor: Ethics and Behavior in the Old South, 1982, paperback edit., 1983, Yankee Saints and Southern Sinners, 1985, paperback edit., 1990, Honor and Violence in the Old South, 1986; The House of Percy: Honor, Melancholy and Imagination in a Southern Family, 1994, 96, The Literary Percys: Family History, Gender, and the Southern Imagination, 1994; also articles; editor: The American People in the Antebellum South, 1973. Served to lt. USNR, 1953-55. Grantee Am. Philos. Soc., 1968-69, 72-73, NEH, summer 1975; Guggenheim fellow, 1974-75; assoc. Woodrow Wilson Internat. Ctr. Scholars, 1975; fellow Davis Ctr. Princeton U., 1977-78, NEH fellow, 1985-86, NEH fellow Nat. Humanities Ctr., 1989-90; recipient Ramsdell award So. Hist. Assn., 1971, History prize Ohio Acad. History, 1983, ABC/Clio, 1989, Jefferson Davis Meml. prize for History, 1983; finalist Am. Book award and Pulitzer prize for History, 1983; Commonwealth Fund lectr. Univ. Coll., London, 1985,

Lamar lectr. Mercer U., 1993, Webb lectr. U. Tex., Arlington, 1994. Mem. Orgns. Am. Historians (exec. coun. 1990-93), Soc. Am. Historians, So. Hist. Assn. (exec. coun. 1994—), Soc. for History Early Am. Republic (pres. 1995-96), Phi Beta Kappa, Phi Alpha Theta (History prize 1983). Episcopalian. Home: 3201 NW 18th Ave Gainesville FL 32605-3705

WYCHE, BRADFORD WHEELER, lawyer; b. Greenville, S.C., Feb. 22, 1950; s. C. Thomas and Harriet Durham (Smith) W.; m. Carolyn Diane Smock, July 1, 1978; children: Charles Denby Smock, Jessica Kaye. AB in Environ. Sci., Princeton U., 1972; MS in Natural Resource Mgmt., Yale U., 1974; JD, U. Va., 1978. Bar: S.C. 1978, U.S. Dist. Ct. S.C. 1978, U.S. Ct. Appeals (4th cir.) 1978. Ptnr. Wyche, Burgess, Freeman & Parham, Greenville, 1979—. Contbr. articles to profl. jours. Mem. S.C. Gov.'s Coun. on Natural Resources, Columbia, 1983-84, Pendleton Place, Greenville, 1984-88, S.C. Coastal Coun., 1986-95; pres. Warehouse Theatre, Greenville, 1982-83, Greenville's Symphony Assn., 1989-90; chair Greenville Cmty. Found., 1994. Mem. S.C. Bar Assn. Avocations: tennis, piano, whitewater kayaking. Home: 312 Raven Rd Greenville SC 29615-4248 Office: Wyche Burgess Freeman & Parham PO Box 728 44 E Camperdown Way Greenville SC 29602

WYCHE, CYRIL THOMAS, lawyer; b. Greenville, S.C., Jan. 28, 1926; C. Granville and Mary (Wheeler) W.; m. Harriet Smith, June 19, 1948; children: Sara McCall, Bradford Wheeler, Mary Frances. BE, Yale U., 1946; LLB, U. Va., 1949. Bar: S.C. 1948, U.S. Dist. Ct. S.C. 1950, U.S. Ct. Appeals (4th cir.) 1952, U.S. Ct. Claims 1964, U.S. Supreme Ct. 1970. Ptnr. Wyche, Burgess, Freeman & Parham, P.A., Greenville, S.C., 1948—. Pres., bd. dirs. YMCA, Greenville, 1960; pres. Greenville Little Theatre, 1965, Arts Festival Assn., Greenville, 1970, Greenville Community Corp., 1976—; bd. dirs. Greater Greenville C. of C., 1980. Served with USN, 1943-46. Named Environmentalist of Yr., State of S.C., 1979; recipient Conservation award Gulf Oil Corp., 1983. Mem. ABA, S.C. Bar Assn., Greenville County Bar Assn., Am. Judicature Soc.one of our Nationwide recipients of the nature conservancy Oak Leaf awards, 1995; Nat.recipient of the Alexander Calder Conservation award presented by the Conservantion fund in partnership with union camp Corp, 1996; the order of the Palmetto, the highest award for public svs. in SC, 1996. Presbyterian. Avocations: skiing, scuba diving, piano, tennis, white water canoeing. Office: Wyche Burgess Freeman & Parham 44 E Camperdown Way PO Box 10207 Greenville SC 29603

WYCHE, MARGUERITE RAMAGE, realtor; b. Birmingham, Ala., May 30, 1950; d. Raymond Crawford and Marguerite Getaz (Taylor) Ramage; m. Madison Baker Wyche III, Aug. 7, 1971; children: Madison Baker IV, James Ramage. BA cum laude, Vanderbilt U., 1972. Lic. broker, S.C., also cert. real estate specialist, grad. Real Estate Inst. Real estate agt. Slappey Realty Co., Albany, Ga., 1973-76, McCutcheon Co., Greenville, S.C., 1973-76; real estate agt. Furman Co., Greenville, 1985-87, broker's assoc., 1987-95; v.p., broker in charge The Furman Co. Residential LLC, Greenville, 1995—; v.p. The Furman Co. Residential LLC, 1996. Bd. dirs. Christ Ch. Episcopal Sch., Greenville, 1979-82, 86-89, chmn. bd. visitors, 1992-93; bd. dirs., cmty. v.p. Jr. League of Greenville, 1983, state pub. affairs chair S.C. Jr. League, 1984; mem. Greenville Cmty. Planning Coun., 1983; bd. dirs., chmn. long range planning com. Meals on Wheels, Greenville, 1990-93; mem. Palmetto Soc.-United Way of Greenville, 1992—; mem. elves workshop com. Children's Hosp., Greenville, 1992-93; mem. Greenville Tech. Found. Bd., 1995—. Mem. Greenville Bd. Realtors, Million Dollar Club (life), Vanderbilt Alumni Assn., Christ Ch. Episcopal Sch. Alumni Assn. (pres., bd. dirs. 1980-81), Mortar Board, Delta Delta Delta. Republican. Episcopalian. Avocations: golf, skiing, gardening, hiking, travel. Home: 134 Rockingham Rd Greenville SC 29607-3621 Office: The Furman Co 252 S Pleasantburg Dr Ste 100 Greenville SC 29607-2547

WYCHE, SAMUEL DAVID, sportscaster; b. Atlanta, GA, Jan. 5, 1945; m. Jane Wyche; children—Zak, Kerry. B.A., Furman U., 1966; Masters degree, U. S.C. Profl. football player Continental Football League, Wheeling Ironmen, 1966; profl. football player Cin. Bengals, 1968-70, Washington Redskins, 1971-73, Detroit Lions, 1974-75, St. Louis Cardinals, 1976, Buffalo Bills, 1976; owner sporting goods store, Greenville, S.C., 1974-92; asst. coach San Francisco 49ers, 1979-82; head coach Ind. U., Bloomington, 1983, Cin. Bengals, 1984-91, Tampa Bay (Fla.) Buccaneers, 1992-95; sports analyst NBC Sports, Tampa, 1996—. Named Coach of Yr. NFL, 1988, Nat. Football League, 1988. Office: Sam Wyche Inc 334 Blanca Ave Tampa FL 33606

WYCKOFF, E. LISK, JR., lawyer; b. Middletown, N.J., Jan. 29, 1934; m. Elizabeth Ann Kuphal; children: Jenny Adele, Edward Lisk III. B.A., Duke U., 1955; J.D., U. Mich., 1960. Ptnr. Kramer, Levin, N.Y.C.; lectr. Practising Law Inst., 1970—, World Trade Inst., various profl. and bus. orgns. in U.S. and abroad; spl. counsel N.Y. State Bankers Assn., 1974—; counsel N.Y. State Senate Com. Housing and Urban Renewal, 1969-71, N.Y. State Senate Com. Judiciary, 1963-64, Com. Affairs of the City of N.Y., 1962; mem. N.Y.C. Mayor's Taxi Study Commn., 1967. Directing editor, commentator West's McKinney's Forms on Estates and Trusts, 1974—; mng. editor, 1982-84; commentator McKinney's Not-For-Profit Corp. law, 1993—; contbr. articles to profl. jours. Bd. dirs., pres. 1652 Wyckoff House and Assn., Inc., 1982—; trustee Soc. for Preservation of L.I. Antiquities, 1988—, N.Y.C. Hist. House Trust, 1993—, Inner-City Scholarship Fund., Inc. 1993—, The Bard Ctr. Bard Coll., 1994—; trustee, pres. Homeland Found., 1989—; bd. advisors Wildlife Conservation Soc., 1993—; mem. Concilium Socalium to Vatican Mus., 1991—; papal hon. Knight Commr. of Order of St. Gregory The Great, 1995. Fellow Am. Coll. Trust and Estate Counsel, Am. Bar Found.; mem. ABA (chair com. on internat. property, estate and trust of law sect. real property, probate and trust law, taxation 1991—), Internat. Fiscal Assn., Internat. Bar Assn., N.Y. State Bar Assn. (exec. com. tax sect., chmn. com. income taxation estates and trusts 1976-80, com. internat. estate planning 1980—), Assn. of Bar of City of N.Y. (mem. com. lectures and continuing edn., com. trusts, estates and surrogate cts. 1970-73, com. corp. Clubs: Holland Soc., St. Nicholas Soc., Knickerbocker, Racquet and Tennis (N.Y.C.), Mashomack Fish and Game Preserve, Pine Plains, N.Y., Essex (Conn.) Yacht Club. Avocations: tennis, sailing. Office: Kramer Levin Naftalis 919 3rd Ave New York NY 10022

WYCLIFF, NOEL DON, journalist, newspaper editor; b. Liberty, Tex., Dec. 17, 1946; s. Wilbert Aaron and Emily Ann (Broussard) W.; m. Catherine Anne Erdmann, Sept. 25, 1982; children: Matthew William, Grant Erdmann. BA, U. Notre Dame, 1969. Reporter Houston Post, 1970-71, Dayton (Ohio) Daily News, 1972-73, Seattle Post-Intelligencer, 1978, Dallas Times-Herald, 1978-79, Chgo. Sun-Times, 1981-85; reporter, editor Chgo. Daily News, 1973-78; editor N.Y. Times, N.Y.C., 1979-81, editorial writer, 1985-90; dep. editor editorial page Chgo. Tribune, 1990-91, editor editorial page, 1991—; occasional instr. journalism Columbia Coll., Chgo., Roosevelt U., Chgo. Woodrow Wilson fellow, 1969. Mem. Am. Soc. Newspaper Editors, Nat. Assn. Black Journalists, Nat. Assn. Minority Media Execs. Roman Catholic. Office: Chicago Tribune 435 N Michigan Ave Chicago IL 60611-4001

WYCOFF, ROBERT E., petroleum company executive; b. Tulsa, 1930; married. B.S.M.E., Stanford U., 1952, M.S.M.E., 1953. With Atlantic Richfield Co., L.A., 1953—, various engring. and mgmt. positions, 1957-70, mgr. western region Internat. div., 1971-73, v.p., resident mgr. Alaska region N.Am. Producing div., 1973-74, corp. planning v.p., 1974-77, sr. v.p. planning and fin., 1977-80, exec. v.p., 1980-84, chief corp. officer, 1984, vice chmn., 1985, pres., chief operating officer, 1986-93, also dir.; chmn. Lyondell Petrochem. Co., Houston. Mem. ASME, Am. Petroleum Inst. Office: Atlantic Richfield Co PO Box 2579 515 S Flower St Los Angeles CA 90071*

WYDEN, RONALD LEE, senator; b. Wichita, Kans., May 3, 1949; s. Peter and Edith W.; m. Laurie Oseran, Sept. 5, 1978; 1 child, Adam David. Student, U. Santa Barbara, 1967-69; A.B. with distinction, Stanford U., 1971; J.D., U. Oreg., 1974. Campaign aide Senator Wayne Morse, 1972, 74; co-founder, co-dir. Oreg. Gray Panthers, 1974-80; dir. Oreg. Legal Services for Elderly, 1977-79; instr. gerontology U. Oreg., 1976, U. Portland, 1980, Portland State U., 1979; mem. 97th-104th Congresses from 3d Oreg. dist., Washington, D.C., 1981—; mem. Commerce com., subcom. telecom. and fin., health and environment, small bus. com.; U.S. Senator from Oreg. 1996—. Recipient Service to Oreg. Consumers award Oreg. Consumers League, 1978, Citizen of Yr. award Oreg. Assn. Social Workers, 1979, Significant Service award Multnomah County Area Agy. on Aging, 1980; named Young Man of Yr. Oreg. Jr. C. of C., 1980. Mem. Am. Bar Assn., Iowa Bar Assn. Democrat. Jewish. Office: 259 Russell Senate Bldg Washington DC 20510*

WYDICK, RICHARD CREWS, lawyer, educator; b. Pueblo, Colo., Nov. 1, 1937; s. Charles Richard and Alice (Marsh) W.; m. Judith Brandli James, 1961; children—William Bruce, Derrick Cameron. B.A., Williams Coll., 1959; LL.B., Stanford U., 1962. Bar: Calif. bar 1962. Asso. firm Brobeck, Phleger & Harrison, San Francisco, 1966-71; mem. faculty U. Calif. Law Sch., Davis, 1971—; prof. law U. Calif. Law Sch., 1975—, dean, 1978-80. Author: Plain English for Lawyers, 3d edit., 1994. Served to capt. USAR, 1962-66. Office: Sch Law U Calif Davis CA 95616

WYDLER, HANS ULRICH, lawyer, banker, accountant; b. Hamburg, Germany, Nov. 11, 1923; came to U.S., 1927, naturalized, 1932; s. John Joseph and Grethe Adolfine (Heitmann) W.; m. Susan Gail Hart, Sept. 1, 1965; children: Hans Laurence, Steven Courtney. BS, Ohio State U., 1944, BME with honors, 1947; BIE with honors, 1949; MS, MIT, 1948; LLB, Harvard U., 1951. Bar: Mass. 1951; registered profl. engr. Mass. Atty., systems engr., trustee Louis J. Hunter Assocs., Boston, 1951-57; asst. v.p. Chem. Bank, N.Y.C., 1958-64; v.p. Mfrs. Nat. Bank Detroit, 1964-65; sr. v.p. Security Nat. Bank, Huntington, N.Y., 1973-74; internat. and tax atty., acct. Hans U. Wydler, N.Y.C., 1966—; dir. Volume Mdse., Inc., Buning Internat. Inc., 1977-84. With USN, 1944-46. Mem. Acad. Polit. Sci. (life), ABA, N.Y. County Lawyers Assn., ASME. Home and Office: 945 5th Ave New York NY 10021-2655

WYER, JAMES INGERSOLL, lawyer; b. Denver, June 9, 1923; s. William and Katherine (Rolfe) W.; m. Joan Best Connelly, Aug. 13, 1960; children: Joan Connelly Tatnall, Peter Ford, June Wyer Nugent. B.A., Yale U., 1945, LL.B., 1949. Bar: N.Y. 1950, N.J. 1987. Assoc. Dewey, Ballantine, Bushby, Palmer & Wood, N.Y.C., 1949-56, Am. Cyanamid Co., Wayne, N.J., 1956; v.p., gen. counsel Am. Cyanamid Co., 1973-86; of counsel Robinson, St. John & Wayne, Newark, 1987—; bd. dirs. TherMold, Inc., William Penn Life Ins. Co. N.Y., PharmGenics, Inc. Bd. dirs. Nat. Legal Ctr. for the Pub. Interest. Served with USNR, 1943-46. Mem. Assn. Gen. Counsel (1st v.p. 1982-84, pres. 1985-86), ABA, Assn. of Bar of City of N.Y., Atlantic Legal Found. (chmn. 1986—). Republican. Clubs: Jupiter Island (Hobe Sound, Fla.); Seabright (N.J.) Beach, Seabright Lawn, Tennis and Cricket (Rumson, N.J.); Coral Beach and Tennis (Bermuda), Hobe Sound (Fla.) Yacht. Office: Robinson St John & Wayne 2 Penn Plz E Newark NJ 07105-2246

WYER, WILLIAM CLARKE, insurance executive; b. Portland, Maine, Dec. 8, 1946; s. John A. and Evelyn (Clarke) Petruccelli; m. Barbara D. Judge; 1 child, Melissa K. AAS, Corning (N.Y.) Community Coll., 1968; postgrad., Russell Sage Coll., 1969. Dir. pub. rels. N.Y. State Rep. Com., 1968-71; exec. asst. to co-chmn. Rep. Nat. Com., 1972; asst. to pres. Rollins Internat. Co., 1972-74; spl. asst., campaign dir. to U.S. Senator William V. Roth, Jr., Del., 1975-77; exec. asst. to U.S. Congressman Thomas B. Evans, Jr., Del., 1977-78; pres. Del. C. of C., 1978-89; mng. dir. Wilmington 2000, Inc., 1993-95; sr. v.p. Blue Cross Blue Shield of Del., 1995—; pres. Allnation Life Ins. Co., 1995—; pres. Wyer Group Inc., 1993—; bd. dirs. Beneficial Nat. Bank, Artesian Resources Corp. Board dirs. Port Wilmington Maritime Soc., 1978—; mem. adv. bd. Nature Conservancy; trustee Goldey Beacon Coll., Med. Ctr. of Del. Found. Mem. Del. C. of C. (life, hon. sr. coun.), Rodney Square Club (founding bd. govs.), Univ. and Whist Club, Northport Yacht Club (Maine chpt.), Ocean Reef Club (Key Largo, Fla.). Republican. Methodist. Home: 1980 Superfine Ln Apt 501 Wilmington DE 19802-4913

WYETH, ANDREW, artist; b. Chadds Ford, Pa., July 12, 1917; s. Newell Converse and Carolyn (Bockius) W.; m. Betsy Merle James, May 15, 1940; children: Nicholas, James Browning. Educated pvt. tutors; DFA (hon.), Colby Coll., Maine, 1954, Harvard U., 1955, Dickinson Coll., 1958, Swarthmore Coll., 1958, Nasson Coll., 1963, U. Md., U. Del., Northeastern U., Temple U., 1964; LHD (hon.), Tufts U., 1963; DFA (hon.), Princeton U., 1965; LHD (hon.), Franklin and Marshall Coll., 1965, Lincoln U., 1966, Amherst Coll., 1967; DFA (hon.), Bowdoin Coll., 1970; LHD (hon.), Ursinus Coll., 1971; DFA (hon.), U. Pa., 1972; LHD (hon.), West Chester U., 1984; DFA (hon.), Dartmouth Coll., 1984, Bates Coll., 1987; LHD (hon.), U. Vt., 1988. Artist, landscape painter, 1936—; first one-man show William Macbeth Gallery, N.Y.C., 1937, first solo exhbn. ever held in White House, 1970, first exhbn. by living Am. artist Royal Acad. Arts, London, 1980; exhibited Doll & Richards, Boston, 1938, 40, 42, 44, Cornell U., 1938, Macbeth Gallery, 1938, 41, first tempera show, 1943, 45, Currier Gallery, Manchester, N.H., 1939, room of watercolors, Art Inst. Chgo., 1941; room at Realist and Magic Realist show, Mus. Modern Art, N.Y.C., 1943; one-man exhbn., M. Knoedler & Co., N.Y.C., 1953, 58, Mass. Inst. Tech., Cambridge, 1960, Fogg Art Mus., William Farnsworth Library and Mus., 1963, Helga Pictures at numerous art museums, other univs. and museums; also exhbns. Arnot Mus., Elmira, N.Y., 1986, Seibu-Pisa, Tokyo, 1986, Kenesaw (Ga.) Mus. Art, 1986, Thomasville (Ga.) Art Ctr., 1987, Acad. of the Arts of USSR, Leningrad, 1987, Acad. of the Arts USSR, Moscow, 1987, Nat. Gallery of Art, Washington, 1987, Corcoran Gallery Art, Washington, 1987, An American Vision: Three Generations of Wyeth Art, various mus., 1987, Dallas Mus. Art, 1987, Mus. Fine Arts, Boston, 1988, Terra Mus. Am. Art, Chgo., 1988, Mus. Fine Arts, Houston, 1988, Setagaya Art Mus., Tokyo, 1988, L.A. County Mus. Art, L.A., 1988, Palazzo Reale, Milan, Italy, 1988, Fitzwilliam Mus., Cambridge, Eng., 1988, Fine Arts Mus. San Francisco, 1988, Brandywine River Mus., Chadds Ford, Pa., 1988, Detroit Inst. Arts, k1989, Sezon Mus. Art, Tokyo, 1991, Heckscher Mus., Huntington, N.Y., 1989, Gilcrease Mus., Tulsa, 1989, Portland (Maine) Mus. Art, 1989, Nukaga Gallery, Japan, 1990, Marcelle Fine Art Inc., N.Y.C., 1990, Takuji Kato Modern Art Mus., Tokyo, 1991, Takuji Kato Modern Art Mus., Chichibu City, Japan, 1991, Jacksonville (Fla.) Art Mus., 1992, Portland (Maine) Mus. Art, 1993, Farnsworth Art Mus., Rockland, Maine, 1994, San Francisco Mus. Modern Art, 1995, Charles and Emma Frye Art Mus., 1995; represented in permanent collections Met. Mus. Art, Nat. Gallery Art. Awarded 1st prize Wilmington Soc. Fine Arts, 1939, Obrig prize Am. Watercolor Soc., 1945, award of Merit, Am. Acad. Arts and Letters and Nat. Inst. Arts and Letters, 1947, 1st prize in watercolor Nat. Acad., 1946, Gold medal Nat. Inst. Arts and Letters, 1965, George Walter Dawson Meml. medal Phila. Watercolor Club, 1957, Mellon Gold medal of Achievement Pa. Artists Exhibit, Ligonier Valley, Pa., 1958, Arts Festival award and Citation for bringing dignity to Am. art Phila. Mus. Art, 1959, Percy M. Owens Meml. award Fellowship of Pa. Acad. Fine Arts, Phila., 1960, Presdl. Medal of Freedom, 1963, citation LaSalle Coll., Phila., 1965, Gold medal of honor Pa. Acad. Fine Arts, 1966, Carnegie Inst. award, award for excellence 1st award recognize outstanding performance in arts, Washington Coll., Chestertown, Md., 1976; Gold medal Nat. Arts Club, 1978, first Am. artist awarded Presdl. award Gold Congl. medal, 1988. Mem. Am. Watercolor Soc. (certificate of merit 1962), Nat. Inst. Arts and Letters, Soviet Acad. Arts (hon.), Academie des Beaux-Arts, Chester County Art Assn. (dir.), Audubon Soc. (dir.), N.Y. Watercolor Soc., Wilmington Soc. Fine Arts, Phila. Watercolor Club (dir.), Washington Watercolor Club (dir.), Balt. Watercolor Club (dir.), Am. Acad. Arts and Letters. (Nat. Academician elect May 1945, Gold medal preeminence in painting 1965), Am. Acad. Arts and Scis., Royal Soc. Painters and Watercolours (London). Office: care Frank E Fowler PO Box 247 Lookout Mountain TN 37350-0247*

WYETH, JAMES BROWNING, artist; b. Wilmington, Del., July 6, 1946; s. Andrew and Betsy (James) W.; m. Phyllis Overton Mills, Dec. 12, 1968. Privately tutored. One man shows include: M. Knoedler & Co., N.Y.C., 1966, William A. Farnsworth Mus., Rockland, Maine, 1969, Coe Kerr Gallery, N.Y.C., 1974, Brandywine River Mus., Chadds Ford, Pa., 1974, Joslyn Art Mus., Omaha, 1976, Pa. Acad. Fine Arts, 1980, Greenville County Art Mus., Greenville, S.C., 1981, Amon Carter Mus., Ft. Worth, 1981, Anchorage Fine Arts Mus., 1983; touring exhbn. An American Vision: Three Generations of Wyeth Art, various mus. worldwide, 1987—. Mem. stamp adv. com. U.S. Postal Service, 1969—; mem. Nat. Endowment for Arts, 1972—; bd. govs. Nat. Space Inst., 1975—. Served with Del. Air N.G., 1966-71. Office: care Frank E Fowler PO Box 247 Lookout Mountain TN 37350-0247*

WYGANT, FOSTER LAURANCE, art educator; b. Dayton, Ohio, Oct. 30, 1920; s. Harold F. and M. Esther (Weber) W.; m. Rae E. Hoyt, 1 child, Nancy Laura. Profl. diploma, Juilliard Sch. Music, 1942; B.A., Columbia U., 1949, M.A., 1956, Ed.D., 1959; postgrad., Am. Art Sch., Art Students League, 1951-53. Clarinetist Dallas Symphony and free-lance clarinetist N.Y.C., 1945-47, publicity, fund-raising positions, and free-lance artist, 1952-56, tchr. art, pub. schs., 1956-59; asst. prof. Montclair State Coll., N.J., 1959-63, assoc. prof., 1963-68; prof. art edn. U. Cin., 1968-87, chmn. dept., 1968-84, dir. Sch. Art Edn. and Art History, 1984-86, emeritus prof., 1987—; vis. sr. lectr. Leeds Coll. Art, Eng., 1966; regional chmn. Scholastic Awards Program, 1968-84; chmn. Action for Arts in Ohio Schs., 1974-75. Author: Art in American Schools in the Nineteenth Century, 1983, School Art in ?American Culture 1820-1970, 1993; editor, prin. author: Standards for Art Teacher Preparation Programs, 1979, Principles, Purposes and Standards for School Art Programs, 1982; contbr. numerous articles to profl. jours. Served with U.S. Army, 1941-45. N.Y. State and Juilliard Sch. Music scholar, 1939-41; Kellogg Found. fellow Columbia U., 1955-56. Mem. Nat. Art Assn. (nat. dir. higher edn. divsn. 1975-79, Recognition award 1980, Disting. Svc. award 1982, Disting. fellow 1995), Ohio Art Edn. Assn. (pres. 1972-74), Seminar for Rsch. in Art Edn., Coun. for Policy Studies in Art Edn., Am. Fedn. Musicians. Home: 3562 Interwood Ave Cincinnati OH 45220-1824

WYGOD, MARTIN J., pharmaceuticals executive; b. N.Y.C.. BS, N.Y.U., 1961. Chmn., pres., chief exec. officer Medco Containment Inc., Montvale, N.J., 1983-94; chmn. Synetic, Inc., Elmwood Park, N.J., 1994—. Office: Synetic Inc 669 River Dr Ctr 2 Elmwood Park NJ 07407-1361 Office: National RX Services Inc PA 5073 Ritter Rd Mechanicsburg PA 17055-6921*

WYKES, EDMUND HAROLD, retired insurance company executive; b. Newcastle-on-Tyne, Eng., July 19, 1928; s. Cyril Edmund and Sylvia (Glover) W.; m. Joan Nightingale, Oct. 1, 1955; children—Julie, Christopher. LL.B., Durham U., 1949; postgrad., Gibson and Weldon Coll. Law, 1953. Bar: Ont. 1958. Solicitor H.E. Ferens & Son, Durham City, Eng., 1953-57; sec., counsel Imperial Life Assurance Co. of Can., Toronto, 1971-77, gen. counsel, sec., 1977-80, v.p., gen. counsel, sec., 1980-91, v.p., sec., 1991-93; ret., 1993. Solicitor Supreme Ct. Eng., 1953. Served with RAF, 1949-51. Mem. English Law Soc., Assn. Life Inst. Counsel, Am. Soc. Corp. Secs. Inc. Home: 86 Wimbleton Rd, Etobicoke, ON Canada M9A 3S5

WYKOFF, FRANK CHAMPION, economics educator; b. Oakland, Calif., Feb. 20, 1942; s. Victor Clifton and Clarisse (Champion) W.; m. Jane Pierpont Humphreys, Sept. 11, 1965; children: Victor Clifton, Elisabeth Pierpont. AB, U. Calif., Berkeley, 1963, MA, 1965, PhD, 1968. Instr. U. Calif., Berkeley (part-time), 1964-68, 74; prof. econs. Pomona Coll., Claremont, Calif., 1968—, Elden Smith prof., 1979—; dir. Ctr. for Study of Economics; vis. prof. U. B.C., Vancouver, 1976-77; fin. economist U.S. Treasury Dept., Washington, 1972-73; cons., 1973-81; instr. U. Wis.-Madison, 1971; speaker Found. for Am. Communications, 1982—; expert cons. GAO, Washington, 1980—. Author: Macroeconomics, 1981, Understanding Economics Today, 1986; editor Econ. Inquiry Jour. Faculty fellow GAO, 1980; fellow Brookings Instn., 1972-73, NSF, 1976; faculty fellow Haynes Found., 1969, 71; fellow Ford Found., 1968, 70. Mem. Am. Econ. Assn., Western Econ. Assn., Inst. on Advanced Econs. for Journalists (dir. FACS). Home: 1001 Richmond Dr Claremont CA 91711-3351 Office: Pomona Coll Econ Inquiry 109 Seaver North 645 N College Ave Claremont CA 91711

WYLE, EWART HERBERT, clergyman; b. London, Sept. 12, 1904; s. Edwin and Alice Louise (Durman) W.; B.A., U. Louisville, 1930; B.D., Lexington Theol. Sem., 1933; postgrad. Louisville Presbyn. Theol. Sem., Temple U., 1933-35; D.D., Tex. Christian U., 1953; m. Prudence Harper, June 12, 1959; 1 son, Ewart Herbert. Ordained to ministry Christian Ch., 1935; pastor First Ch., Palestine, Tex., 1935-37, First Ch., Birmingham, Ala., 1937-41, First Ch., Tyler, Tex., 1944-54, Country Club Ch., Kansas City, Mo., 1954-59; minister Torrey Pines Ch., La Jolla, Calif., 1959-79, minister emeritus, 1979—. Bd. dirs. Scripps Meml. Hosp., pres., 1980-81. Served as chaplain, maj., AUS, 1941-44. Mem. Mil. Order World Wars, Am. Legion, Tau Kappa Epsilon, Pi Kappa Delta. Clubs: Masons (32 deg.), Shriners, Rotary, LaJolla Beach and Tennis. Home: 8850 N La Jolla Scenic Dr La Jolla CA 92037-1608

WYLE, FREDERICK S., lawyer; b. Berlin, Germany, May 9, 1928; came to U.S., 1939, naturalized, 1944; s. Norbert and Malwina (Mauer) W.; m. Katinka Franz, June 29, 1969; children: Susan Kim, Christopher Anthony, Katherine Anne. B.A. magna cum laude, Harvard U., 1951, LL.B., 1954. Bar: Mass. 1954, Calif. 1955, N.Y. 1958. Teaching fellow Harvard Law Sch., 1954-55; law clk. U.S. Dist. Ct., No. Dist. Calif., 1955-57; assoc. firm Paul, Weiss, Rifkind, Wharton & Garrison, N.Y.C., 1957-58; pvt. practice San Francisco, 1958-62; spl. asst. def. rep. U.S. del. to NATO, Paris, 1962-63; mem. Policy Planning Council, Dept. State, Washington, 1963-65; dep. asst. sec. def. for European and NATO affairs Dept. Def., Washington, 1966-69; v.p. devel., gen. counsel Schroders, Inc., N.Y.C., 1969-71; atty., cons. Schroders, Inc., 1971-72; chief exec. officer Saturday Rev. Industries, Inc., San Francisco, 1972-76; individual practice law San Francisco, 1976—; internat. counsel to Fed. States Micronesia, 1974-82; cons. Rand Corp., Dept. of Def., Nuclear Regulatory Commn.; trustee in bankruptcy, receiver various corps since 1974. Contbr. to: Ency. Brit, 1972, also articles in profl. publs., newspapers. Served with AUS, 1946-47. Mem. World Affairs Coun., Internat. Inst. Strategic Studies, Phi Beta Kappa. Office: 2500 Russ Bldg 235 Montgomery St San Francisco CA 94104-2902

WYLIE, EVAN BENJAMIN, civil engineering educator, consultant, researcher; b. Donavon, Sask., Can., Jan. 14, 1931; came to U.S., 1950; s. Mansel and Florence (Riddell) W.; m. Frances Eleanor Miller, Feb. 4, 1955; children—Brian Douglas, Scott Cameron, Karen Louise. B.S. in Civil Engring., U. Denver, 1953; M.S. in Civil Engring., U. Colo., 1955; Ph.D. in Civil Engring., U. Mich., 1964. Registered profl. engr., Mich. Engr. Ford Motor Co. of Can., Toronto, Ont., 1956-59; asst. prof. civil engring. U. Denver, 1959-62; asst. prof. civil engring. U. Mich., Ann Arbor, 1965-66, assoc. prof. civil engring., 1966-70, prof. civil engring., 1970—, chmn. dept. civil engring., 1984-90, chmn. dept. civil and environ. engring., 1991-94. Author: (with V.L. Streeter) Hydraulic Transients, 1967, Fluid Mechanics, 1975, 8th edit., 1985, Fluid Transients, 1978, Fluid Transients in Systems, 1993. Fellow ASME, ASCE; mem. Am. Soc. Engring. Edn., Internat. Assn. Hydraulic Rsch. Republican. Avocations: tennis; skiing; woodworking. Home: 1070 Chestnut St Ann Arbor MI 48104-2824 Office: Univ Mich Dept Civil Environ Engring Ann Arbor MI 48109-2125

WYLLIE, PETER JOHN, geologist, educator; b. London, Feb. 8, 1930; came to U.S., 1961; s. George William and Beatrice Gladys (Weaver) W.; m. Frances Rosemary Blair, June 9, 1956; children: Andrew, Elizabeth (dec.), Lisa, John. B.Sc. in Geology and Physics, U. St. Andrews, Scotland, 1952, B.Sc. with 1st class honours in Geology, 1955, Ph.D. in Geology, 1958, D.Sc. (hon.), 1974. Glaciologist Brit. W. Greenland Expdn., 1950; geologist Brit. N. Greenland Expdn., 1952-54; asst. lectr. geology U. St. Andrews, 1955-56; research asst. geochemistry Pa. State U., State College, 1956-58, asst. prof. geochemistry, 1958-59, asso. prof. petrology, 1961-65, acting head, dept. geochemistry mineralogy, 1962-63; research fellow chemistry Leeds (Eng.) U., 1959-60, lectr. exptl. petrology, 1960-61; prof. petrology geochemistry U. Chgo., 1965-77, Homer J. Livingston prof., 1978-83, chmn. dept. geophys. scis., 1979-82, master phys. scis. collegiate div., asso. dean coll., asso. dean phys. scis. div., 1972-73; chmn. div. geol. and planetary scis. Calif. Inst. Tech., Pasadena, 1983-87, prof. geology, 1987—; chmn. commn. exptl. petrology high pressures temperatures Internat. Union Geol. Scis.; mem. adv. panel earth scis. NSF, 1975-78, chmn. adv. com. earth scis. div., 1979-82; mem. U.S. Nat. Com. on Geology, 1978-82; mem. U.S. Nat. Com. Internat. Union Geodesy and Geophysics, 1980-84, U.S. Nat. Com. Geochemistry, 1981-84; chmn. com. on objectives in solid-earth scis. NRC, 1988-93. Author: The Dynamic Earth, 1971, The Way the Earth Works, 1976; editor: Ultramafic and Related Rocks, 1967; chmn. editorial & writing com. Solid-Earth Sciences and Society, 1993; editor Jour. Geology, 1967-83; editor-in-chief Minerals Rocks (monograph series), 1967—. Served with RAF, 1948-49. Recipient Polar medal H.M. Queen Elizabeth, Eng.; Quantrell award, 1979; Wollaston medal Geol. Soc. London, 1982, Abraham-Gottlob-Werner-

Medaille German Mineral. Soc., 1987. Fellow Am. Acad. Arts and Sci., Royal Soc. London, Edinburgh Geol. Soc. (corr.), Mineral Soc. Am. (pres. 1977-78, award 1965), Am. Acad. Scis. (fgn. assoc.), Am. Geophys. Union, Indian Geophys. Union (fgn.), Nat. Acad. Sci. India (fgn.), Russian Acad. Scis. (fgn.), Russian Mineral. Soc. (fgn., hon.), Indian Nat. Sci. Acad. (fgn.), Geol. Soc. Am.; mem. Mineral. Soc. Gt. Britain and Ireland (hon.), Internat. Mineral Assn. (2d v.p. 1978-82, 1st v.p. 1982-86, pres. 1986-90), Internat. Union of Geodesy and Geophysics (v.p. 1991-95, pres. 1995-99). Office: Calif Inst Tech Geol Planetary Scis 17 # 25 Pasadena CA 91125

WYLLY, BARBARA BENTLEY, performing arts association administrator; b. Bala-Cynwyd, Pa., June 10, 1924; d. William Henry and Virginia (Barclay) Bentley; m. William Beck Wylly, Apr. 26, 1947; children: Virginia Wylly Johnson, Barbara L., Thomas C. II. A, Briarcliff Jr. Coll., 1943. Pres. bd. dirs. Hillside Hosp. Inc., Atlanta, 1982, mem. adv. coun., 1982—; pres. Atlanta Symphony Assocs., 1975-76, mem. adv. bd., 1976—; chmn. bd. dirs. Ctr. for Puppetry Arts, Atlanta, 1988—. Republican. Episcopalian. Avocations: walking, reading, music. Home: 940 Foxcroft Rd NW Atlanta GA 30327-2622 Office: Ctr Puppetry Arts 1404 Spring St NW Atlanta GA 30309-2820

WYLY, CHARLES JOSEPH, JR., corporate executive; b. Lake Providence, La., Oct. 13, 1933; s. Charles Joseph and Flora (Evans) W.; m. Caroline Denmon; children: Martha, Charles Joseph III, Emily, Jennifer. B.S., La. Tech. U., 1956. Sales rep. IBM Service Bur. Corp., 1956-64; v.p. Wyly Corp., Dallas, 1964-65, exec. v.p., 1965-69, pres., 1969-73, chmn. exec. com., 1973-76, dir., 1964-76, dir. 1964-76; vice chmn. bd. Earth Resources Co., 1968-80; vice chmn. bd. dirs. USACafes, Inc. (Bonanza Internat., Inc.), 1968-89, Sterling Software, Inc., Michaels Stores, Inc.; chmn. Tex. High-Speed Rail Authority, 1990-91, Maverick Capital. Mem. Pres.'s Advisory Council on Mgmt. Improvement, 1970-73; vice-chmn. Devel. Council So. Methodist U. Found. Sci. and Engring., 1970-71; Mem. Republican Nat. Fin. Com., 1970—; Bd. dirs. Dallas County United Way Fund; pres. Dallas Theater Center., 1972-79. Mem. Am. Mgmt. Assn., Pi Kappa Alpha, Omicron Delta Kappa, Delta Sigma Pi, Beta Gamma Sigma. Clubs: City, Crescent, Park City, Brookhollow (Dallas). Office: 8080 N Central Expy Ste 1100 Dallas TX 75206-1806

WYMAN, DAVID SWORD, historian, educator; b. Weymouth, Mass., Mar. 6, 1929; s. Hollis Judson and Ruth (Sword) W.; m. Mildred Louise Smith, Sept. 13, 1950; children: James Nayler, Teresa Carol. AB, Boston U., 1951; EdM, Plymouth State Coll., 1961; AM, Harvard U., 1962, PhD, 1966; DHL (hon.), Hebrew Union Coll. Jewish Inst. Religion, 1986, Yeshiva U., 1988. Various positions, 1951-57; tchr. pub. schs. Tilton, N.H., 1957-60; tchr. pub. high sch. Penacook, N.H., 1960-61; prof. history U. Mass., Amherst, 1966-91, Josiah DuBois prof. history, 1986-91, Josiah DuBois prof. emeritus, 1991—, chmn. Judaic Studies Program, 1977-78, 82-84; acad. advisor Simon Wiesenthal Ctr., L.A., 1983—; nat. coun. Nat. Christian Leadership Conf. for Israel, 1986, numerous radio and TV appearances; historian advisor to films. Author: Paper Walls: America and the Refugee Crisis, 1938-41, 1968, The Abandonment of the Jews: America and the Holocaust, 1941-45, 1984 (Anisfield-Wolf award 1984, Stuart Bernath award 1984, Theodore Saloutos book award 1984, Present Tense Lit. award 1984, Boston Hadassah Myrtle Wreath award 1985, Nat. Jewish Book award 1985); editor: America and the Holocaust, 13 vols. documents, 1989-90; contbr. articles to profl. jours., chpts. to books. Recipient Chancellor's medal, U. Mass., 1986, Achievement award Isaac M. Wise Temple, Cin. 1986, Humanitarian award Bklyn. Holocaust Meml. Com., 1986; elected to Boston U. Collegium Disting. Alumni, 1986; Woodrow Wilson fellow, 1961-62, 65-66; grantee Social Sci. Rsch. Coun., 1969-70, Am. Coun. Learned Socs., 1969-70, Charles Warren Ctr. at Harvard U., 1969-70. Mem. Soc. for Am. Baseball Rsch., N.H. Hist. Soc., Friends Hist. Assn., Phi Beta Kappa. Avocations: baseball, greyhounds as pets, local N.H. history. Home: 61 Columbia Dr Amherst MA 01002-3105

WYMAN, JAMES THOMAS, petroleum company executive; b. Mpls., Apr. 9, 1920; s. James Claire and Martha (McChesney) W.; m. Elizabeth Winston, May 6, 1950; children: Elizabeth Wyman Wilcox, James Claire, Steven McChesney. Grad., Blake Prep. Sch., Mpls., 1938; B.A., Yale U., 1942. With Mpls. Star and Tribune, 1946-50; advt. mgr. Super Valu Stores, Inc., Eden Prairie, Minn., 1951-54; store devel. mgr. Super Valu Stores, Inc., 1955-56, gen. sales mgr., 1956-57, sales v.p., 1957-60, dir., 1959-87, exec. v.p., 1961-64, pres., chief exec. officer, 1965-70, chmn. exec. com., 1970-76, ret., 1976; chmn. bd., bd. dirs. Marshall & Winston, Inc. Served to lt. (s.g.) USNR, World War II. Clubs: Minneapolis; Woodhill Country (Wayzata). Home: 2855 Woolsey Ln Wayzata MN 55391-2752 Office: 1105 Foshay Tower Minneapolis MN 55402

WYMAN, JAMES VERNON, newspaper executive; b. Brockton, Mass., Nov. 17, 1923; s. George Dewey and Christine Laverne (Skinner) W.; m. Viola Marie Bousquet, June 24, 1950; children—J. Vernon, Douglas Phillip, Carolyn Anne. Student, Northeastern U., Boston, 1946-48; B.S. in Journalism, Boston U., 1951. With Providence Jour.-Bull., 1951-95, asst. city editor, 1960-63, city editor, 1963-74, exec. city editor, 1974, metro mng. editor, 1974-79, exec. news editor, 1979-85, dep. exec. editor, 1985-88, v.p., exec. editor, 1989-95. Served with AUS, 1942-46, PTO. Recipient Yankee Quill award, 1989. Mem. New Eng. AP News Execs. Assn. (past pres.), AP Mng. Editors Assn., New Eng. Soc. Newspaper Editors, Acad. New Eng. Journalists (past dir.), New Eng. Newspaper Assn., Sigma Delta Chi (past pres. New Eng. chpt.). Roman Catholic. Home: 6 Barway Ln Cumberland RI 02864-4914 *Success comes in many packages and is gauged in myriad ways. But it must be most rewarding when it can be measured in terms of simple, effective service to others—in terms of sincere endeavors to foster hope and to ignite the human spirit in those around you.*

WYMAN, JANE (SARAH JANE FULKS), actress; b. St. Joseph, Mo., Jan. 4, 1914; d. R. D. and Emme (Reise) Fulks; m. Myron Futterman, 1937; m. Ronald Reagan, 1940 (div. 1948); children: Maureen Reagan Revell, Michael; m. Fred Karger (div.). Student, U. Mo., 1935. Formerly radio singer, chorus girl in movie musicals, actress. Chorus girl: Gold Diggers of 1937; actress: (featured roles) films My Man Godfrey, 1936, Brother Rat, 1938, Lost Weekend, 1945 (Acad. award nomination), The Yearling, 1946 (Acad. award nomination), Johnny Belinda, 1948 (Acad. award winner), Stage Fright, 1950, The Glass Menagerie, 1950, The Blue Veil, 1951 (Acad. award nomination), Magnificient Obsession, 1954 (Acad. award nomination), All That Heaven Allows, 1956, Miracle in the Rain, 1956, Holiday for Lovers, 1959, Pollyanna, 1960, Bon Voyage, 1962, How to Commit Marriage, 1969; TV shows Fireside Theater, 1955, Jane Wyman Theater, Falcon Crest, 1981-90 (recipient Golden Globe awardBest Actress in Series-Drama, 1984). Address: PO Box 42126 Los Angeles CA 90042-0126*

WYMAN, LOUIS CROSBY, judge, former senator, former congressman; b. Manchester, N.H., Mar. 16, 1917; s. Louis Eliot and Alice Sibley (Crosby) W.; m. Virginia Elizabeth Markley, Aug. 20, 1938; children—Jo Ann, Louis Eliot. B.S. with honor, U. N.H., 1938; LL.B. cum laude, Harvard U., 1941. Bar: Mass. bar 1941, N.H. bar 1941, D.C. bar 1947, Fla. bar 1957. Asso. firm Ropes, Gray, Best, Coolidge & Rugg, Boston, 1941-42; mem. firm Wyman, Starr, Booth, Wadleigh & Langdell, Manchester, N.H., 1949-52; gen. counsel to U.S. Senate investigating com., 1946; sec. to U.S. Senator Styles Bridges, 1947; counsel to joint congl. com. on Fgn. Econ. Cooperation, 1948-49; atty. gen. N.H., 1953-61; legis. counsel to gov. N.H., 1961; partner Wyman, Bean & Stark, Manchester, 1957-78; asso. justice Superior Ct. N.H., 1978—; mem. 88th, 90th-94th congresses from 1st dist. N.H., mem. com. appropriations, subcom. on def.; apptd. U.S. senator, 1974; chmn. N.H. Commn. on Interstate Cooperation; mem. Jud. Council of N.H.; chmn. Nat. Com. on Internal Security, 1958-61. Served as lt. USNR, 1942-46. Fellow Am. Coll. Trial Lawyers; mem. ABA (chmn. standing com. jurisprudence and law reform 1961-63), Mass. Bar Assn., N.H. Bar Assn., Fla. Bar Assn., D.C. Bar Assn., Nat. Assn. Attys. Gen. U.S. (pres. 1957), Phi Kappa Phi, Theta Chi, Kappa Delta Pi. *In a mixed up world each person needs a goal—something he or she can strive for, work toward and measure progress against. Mine has always been to try to help make this world a better place to live for all—with dignity, privacy, security and reasonable comforts. Toward greater progress in this goal I forsook the practice of law for years of public service during which it was more clearly possible to do much for people. Less money but more action if you will. Throughout everything in life it is vital to believe in something greater than man alone and to seek guidance from prayer. Faith that sincere effort will be rewarded, if not in this life in the next, also helps.*

WYMAN, RALPH MARK, corporate executive; b. Usti, Czechoslovakia, Feb. 7, 1926; came to U.S., 1941, naturalized, 1946; s. Hans and Stella (Parnas) W.; m. Lotte Ann Novak, Oct. 25, 1947; 1 dau., Leslie Andrea Wyman Cooper. Student, Upper Can. Coll., 1942, Bucknell U., 1942-43; B.S. in Bus. Adminstrn., NYU, 1945; postgrad., Columbia U., 1945-46. Asst. mgr. export dept. Liebermann Waelchi & Co., Inc., N.Y.C., 1946-47; trainee White Weld Co. (investment brokers), 1947-48; v.p. H.O. Canfield Co., 1948-65, vice chmn. bd., 1965-79, dir., 1953-79; dir. Pantasote Inc., 1960-89, vice chmn. bd., 1967-89; mng. partner United Eagle Mgmt. Co., Eagle Mgmt. Co., 1960—; pres. Veritas Co., 1960—; dir., chmn. Eagle Capital Internat. LLC, 1985—; dir., vice chmn. Affiliate Artists, Inc., 1971-88. Pres. Panwy Found.; bd. dirs. United Way of Greenwich, 1980-86; bd. dirs. Kids in Crisis, Greenwich, 1993—, sec., 1995; trustee Princeton Theol. Sem., 1976—. Mem. Greenwich Country Club, Lambda Chi Alpha. Presbyterian (elder, trustee Synod of N.E. 1974-76). Home: Baldwin Farms North Greenwich CT 06831 Office: Greenwich Office Park 9 10 Valley Dr Greenwich CT 06831

WYMAN, RICHARD VAUGHN, engineering educator, exploration company executive; b. Painesville, Ohio, Feb. 22, 1927; s. Vaughn Ely and Melinda (Ward) W.; m. Anne Fenton, Dec. 27, 1947; 1 son, William Fenton. B.S., Case Western Res. U., 1948; M.S., U. Mich., 1949; Ph.D., U. Ariz., 1974. Registered profl. engr., Nev.; registered geologist, Ariz., Calif.; lic. water right surveyor, Nev. Geologist N.J. Zinc Co., 1949, 52-53, Cerro de Pasco Corp., 1950-52; chief geologist Western Gold & Uranium, Inc., St. George, Utah, 1953-55, gen. supt., 1955-57, v.p., 1957-59; pres. Intermountain Exploration Co., Boulder City, Nev., 1959-93; tunnel supt. Reynolds Electric & Engring. Co., 1961-63, mining engr., 1965-67; asst. mgr. ops. Reynolds Electric and & Engring. Co., 1967-69; constrn. supt. engr. Sunshine Mining Co., 1963-65; lectr. U. Nev., Las Vegas, 1969-73, assoc. prof., 1973-80, dept. chmn., 1976-80, prof., 1980-92, prof. emeritus, 1992—, chmn. dept. civil and mech. engring., 1984-90, chmn. dept. civil and environ. engring., 1990-91; mineral rep. Ariz. Strip Adv. Bd., 1976-80, U.S.B.L.M.; mem. peer rev. com. Nuclear Waste Site, Dept. Energy, Las Vegas, 1978-82; pres. Ariz. Juno Resources, Boulder City, 1980-83, v.p., 1990—; pres. Wyman Engring. Cons., 1987—; cons. Corp. Andina de Fomento, Caracas, Venezuela, 1977-78; v.p. Comstock Gold, Inc., 1984-93; program evaluator Accreditation Bd. for Engring. and Tech., 1995—. Contbr. articles to profl. jours. Sec. Washington County Republican Party, Utah, 1958-60; del. Utah Rep. Conv., 1958-60; scoutmaster Boy Scouts Am., 1959-69. Served with USN, 1944-46. Fellow ASCE (edn. divsn. 1990, local rep. nat. conv. Las Vegas 1990), Soc. Econ. Geologists (life); mem. AIME (chmn. So. Nev. sect. 1971-72, dir. 1968—, sec.-treas. 1974-92, chmn. Pacific S.W. Minerals Conf. 1972, gen. chmn. nat. conv. 1980, Disting. Mem. award 1989), Assn. Engring. Geologists (dir. S.W. sect. 1989-91), Am. Inst. Minerals Appraisers, Nev. Mining Assn. (assoc.), Assn. Ground Water Scientists and Engrs., Arctic Inst. N.Am. (life), Am. Soc. Engring. Edn., Sigma Xi (pres. Las Vegas sect. 1986-91), Phi Kappa Phi (pres. U. Nev. Las Vegas chpt. 100 1982-83), Sigma Gamma Epsilon. Congregationalist. Home: 610 Bryant Ct Boulder City NV 89005-3017 Office: Wyman Engring PO Bxo 60473 Boulder City NV 89006-0473

WYMAN, ROBERT J., biology educator, neurophysiologist, neurogeneticist; b. Syracuse, N.Y., June 8, 1940; s. Ralph M. and Selma (Franklin) W. A.B., Harvard U., 1960; M.S., U. Calif.-Berkeley, 1963, Ph.D., 1965; M.A. hon., Yale U., 1980. Math. analyst Tech. Research Group, Syosset, N.Y., 1959; NSF research fellow Calif. Inst. Tech., Pasadena, 1966; asst. prof. biology Yale U., New Haven, 1966-71, assoc. prof., 1971-80, prof., 1980—; vis. scientist Nobel Inst., Stockholm, 1970-71, Med. Research Council, Cambridge, Eng., 1974, Biozentrum, Basel, Switzerland, 1977; bd. sci. advs. MicroGeneSys Corp., New Haven. Contbr. articles to profl. jours. Bd. dirs. Urban League Conn., Nat. Abortion Rights Action League, Planned Parenthood of Conn.; bd. sponsors Nat. Com. for Effective Congress; mem. Fedn. Am. Scientists. Harvard Club scholar, 1956-60; NIH predoctoral fellow, 1960-65; NSF postdoctoral fellow, 1966; NASA research grantee NASA, 1968-70, NIH research grantee, 1967—, NSF grantee, 1986—. Mem. Soc. Neurosci., Internat. Brain Rsch. Orgn., Soc. Exptl. Biology, Genetics Soc. Am., Conn. Acad. Arts and Scis. (coun.), Sigma Xi. Home: 233 Mansfield Grove Rd New Haven CT 06512 Office: Yale U Biology Dept New Haven CT 06520-8103

WYMAN, STANLEY MOORE, radiologist; b. Cambridge, Mass., Aug. 3, 1913; s. John Palmer and Lelia (Moore) W.; m. Jessie Elinor Brooks, July 23, 1945 (dec. Apr. 1978); children—Stephen Brooks, Jean Wyman Beebe, Martha Wyman Bermingham, Barbara Wyman Samett; m. Evelyn S. Stigger, Apr. 26, 1980. A.B., Harvard, 1935, M.D., 1939. Radiologist Mass. Gen. Hosp., Boston, 1946-68, 76-80; vis. radiologist Mass. Gen. Hosp., 1969-76, sr. radiologist, 1980—; cons. U.S. Naval Hosp., Chelsea, Mass., 1961-74; clin. prof. radiology Harvard Med. Sch., 1978-82, emeritus clin. prof. radiology, 1982—; Cons. radiol. tng. com. NIH. Contbr. articles to profl. jours. Served to maj., M.C. AUS, 1942-46. Decorated Bronze Star. Mem. AMA (former del.), Radiol. Soc. N.Am. (past pres., Gold medal 1974), Am. Coll. Radiology (pres. 1970-71, gold medal 1971), Am. Roentgen Ray Soc. (Silver medal 1952), New Eng. Roentgen Ray Soc. (hon. mem. past pres.), Mass. Radiol. Soc. (past pres.), Mass. Med. Soc. (pres. 1981-82), Aesculapian Club, Harvard Club (Boston), Economy Club (Cambridge, Mass.) (pres. 1989-90). Home: 987 Memorial Dr Cambridge MA 02138-5737 Office: Mass Gen Hosp Boston MA 02114

WYMAN, WILLARD G., headmaster. Headmaster Thacher Sch., Ojai, Calif. Office: Thacher Sch 5025 Thacher Rd Ojai CA 93023-9001

WYMAN, WILLIAM GEORGE, musician; b. London, Oct. 24, 1936; m. Mandy Smith (div. 1992); 1 child from previous marriage, Stephen; m. Suzanne Accosta, Apr. 1993; children: Katharine, Jessica. Owner Ripple Records, Ripple Music, Ripple Publs., Ripple Prodns.; owner Sticky Fingers restaurant, London. Bassist with musical group, The Rolling Stones, 1962-92; albums include: 12 x 5, 1964, The Rolling Stones Now, 1965, Out of Our Heads, 1965, December's Children, 1965, Big Hits, 1966, Aftermath, 1966, Got Live If You Want It, 1967, Between the Buttons, 1967, Their Satanic Majesties Request, 1967, Flowers, 1967, Beggar's Banquet, 1968, Through the Past Darkly, 1969, Let it Bleed, 1969, Get Yer Ya Yas Out, 1970, Sticky Fingers, 1971, Hot Rocks: 1964-1971, 1972, Exile on Main Street, 1972, More Hot Rocks (Big Hits & Fazed Cookies), 1972, Goats Head Soup, 1973, It's Only Rock n' Roll, 1974, Made in the Shade, 1975, Metamorphosis, 1975, Black and Blue, 1976, Love You Live, 1977, Some Girls, 1978, Sucking in the Seventies, 1981, Tattoo You, 1981, Still Life, 1981, Undercover, 1983, Rewind: 1971-1984, Between the Sheets, 1985, Dirty Work, 1986, Emotional Rescue, 1988, Steel Wheels, 1989, Flashpoint, 1991, Voodoo Lounge, 1994, (with Charlie Watts, Andy Fairweather-Low, Chris Rea, Paul Rogers, Jimmy Page) Willie and the Poor Boys, 1985, (with Gary Brooker) Willie and the Poor Boys Live, 1985, numerous others; solo recs. include Stone Alone, Monkey Grip, Bill Wyman, Stuff; films Sympathy for the Devil, 1970; Gimme Shelter, 1970, Ladies and Gentlemen the Rolling Stones, 1974, Let's Spend the Night Together, 1982, Digital Dreams, 1983, Rolling Stones in IMAX Larger Than Live; composer: (soundtrack) Green Ice; author: photographs Chagall Mediterrané, 1984, (with Ray Coleman) Stone Alone: The Story of a Rock 'n' Roll Band, 1991; contbr. photographs to Chagall's World. Avocations: archeology, writing. Address: care Ripple Prodns Ltd, 344 Kings Rd, London SW3 5UR, England

WYNAR, BOHDAN STEPHEN, librarian, author, editor; b. Lviv, Ukraine, Sept. 7, 1926; came to U.S., 1950, naturalized, 1957; s. John I. and Euphrosina (Doryk) W.; m. Olha Yarema, Nov. 23, 1992; children: Taras, Michael, Roxolana, Yarynka. Diplom-Volkswirt Econs., U. Munich, Germany, 1949, Ph.D., 1950; M.A., U. Denver, 1958. Methods analyst, statistician Tramco Corp., Cleve., 1951-53; freelance journalist Societ Econs., Cleve., 1954-56; adminstrv. asst. U. Denver Librs., 1958-59, head tech. svcs. div., 1959-62; assoc. prof. Sch. Librarianship, U. Denver, 1962-66; dir. div. libr. edn. State U. Coll., Geneseo, N.Y., 1966-67; dean Sch. Libr. Sci. State U. Coll., Geneseo; prof. State U. Coll., 1967-69; pres. Libraries Unlimited Inc., 1969—. Author: Soviet Light Industry, 1956, Economic Colonialism, 1958, Ukrainian Industry, 1964, Introduction to Bibliography and Reference Work, 4th edit, 1967, Introduction to Cataloging and Classification, 8th edit, 1992, Major Writings on Soviet Economy, 1966, Library Acquisitions, 2d edit, 1971, Research Methods in Library Science, 1971, Economic Thought in Kievan Rus', 1974; co-author: Comprehensive Bibliography of Cataloging and Classification, 2 vols., 1973, Ukraine: A Bibliographic Guide to English Language Publications, 1990; editor Ukrainian Quar., 1953-58, Preliminary Checklist of Colorado Bibliography, 1963, Studies in Librarianship, 1963-66, Research Studies in Library Science, 1970—, Best Reference Books, 3d edit., 1985, 4th edit., 1992, Colorado Bibliography, 1980; gen. editor: American Reference Books Ann., 1969—; editor: ARBA Guide to Subject Encyclopedias and Dictionaries, 1985, ARBA Guide To Biographical Dictionaries, Reference Books in Paperback, An Annotated Guide, 2d edit., 1976, 3rd edit., 1991, Dictionary of Am. Library Biography, 1978, Ukraine-A Bibliographic Guide to English-Language Publications, 1990, International Writings of Bohdan S. Wynar 1949-1992, 1993, Recommended Reference Books for Medium-Sized and Small Libraries, 1981—; co-editor, contbr. Ency. Ukraine, 1955—;editor Library Sci. Ann., 1984-90. Bd. dirs., mem. exec. bd. ZAREVO, Inc. Mem. ALA (pres. Ukrainian Congress com. br., Denver 1976), Colo. Library Assn., N.Y. Library Assn., Am. Assn. Advancement Slavic Studies (pres. Ukrainian Research Found. 1976-90), AAUP, Ukrainian Hist. Assn. (exec. bd.), Sevčenko Societe Scientifique (Paris), Ukrainian Acad. Arts and Scis. (N.Y.C.). Office: Librs Unltd Inc 6931 S Yosemite St Englewood CO 80112-1415

WYNDRUM, RALPH W., JR., communications company executive; b. N.Y.C., Apr. 20, 1937; s. Ralph W. and Virginia M. (Woolley) W.; m. Meta Schmidt, Apr. 23, 1960; children: Dorothy, Jeanne, Ralph, Joan. B.S., Columbia U., 1959, M.S. in Elec. Engring., 1960, M.S. in Bus. Adminstrn., 1978; Sc.D., NYU, 1963. Mem. tech. staff Bell Labs., Murray Hill, N.J., 1963-65; supr. exploratory circuit design Bell Labs., 1965-69; head loop transmission tech. dept. Bell Labs., Holmdel and Whippany, N.J., 1969-79; head advanced loop transmission systems dept. Bell Labs., Whippany, 1979-87, head internat. loop systems dept., 1987, dir. systems analysis ctr., 1987-90, dir. quality process ctr., 1990-92, dir. quality, engring., software and techs., 1993-94; v.p. AT&T World Svcs., 1994—, dir. process engr. ctr., 1995—; v.p. tech. realization AT&T Labs., 1996—; adj. prof. N.J. Inst. Tech., 1965, Stevens Inst. Tech., 1980-88. Contbr. articles to profl. jours. Fellow IEEE (bd. dirs. 1988-90, v.p. pubs. 1990-91, President's Leadership award 1991); mem. IEEE Comm. Soc. (chmn. conf. bd. 1981-87), Sigma Xi, Eta Kappa Nu, Beta Gamma Sigma. Republican. Roman Catholic. Patentee in field. Home: 35 Cooney Ter Fair Haven NJ 07704-3001 Office: AT&T Labs Rm 31324 Holmdel NJ 07733

WYNER, AARON DANIEL, mathematician; b. N.Y.C., Mar. 17, 1939; s. Alvin and Mary (Jacobson) W.; m. Nusha Zukerman, June 9, 1963; children—Tamar, Abraham, Dena, Yael. BS, Queens Coll., 1960, Columbia U., 1960; MS, Columbia U., 1961, PhD, 1963. Asst. prof. elec. engring. Columbia U., 1963; mem. tech. staff Bell Labs., Murray Hill, N.J., 1963—; head comm. analysis rsch. dept. Bell Labs., 1974-93; adj. and vis. prof. Columbia U., Polytech. U., Technion, Haifa, Israel, Weizmann Inst. Sci., Rehovot, Israel., Princeton U. Assoc. editor: IEEE Transactions on Info. Theory, 1970-72, editor-in-chief, 1983-86. Guggenheim Found. fellow, 1966. Fellow IEEE (past pres. Info. Theory Soc., Centennial medal 1984, Claude Shannon award), AAAS; mem. Internat. Sci. Radio Union (chmn. U.S. commn. on signals and sys. 1987-90, vice-chmn. internat. commn. 1990-93), Nat. Acad. Engring. Patentee in field. Home: 33 Oakview Ave Maplewood NJ 07040-2213 Office: Bell Labs 600 Mountain Ave New Providence NJ 07974-2008

WYNER, JUSTIN L., laminating company executive; b. Boston, Aug. 6, 1925; s. Rudolph H. and Sara G. Wyner; m. Genevieve Gloria Geller, July 3, 1955; children: George Michael, Daniel Mark, James Henry. BS cum laude, Tufts Coll., 1946; MBA, Harvard U., 1948. Chmn. bd. Shawmut Mills div. R.H. Wyner Assocs., West Bridgewater, Mass. Mem. Brookline Rep. Town Com., 1964—; trustee Beth Israel Hosp., Boston, 1966—, mem. fin. com., 1972-80; trustee Temple Israel, Boston, 1964—, pres., 1979-82, chmn. bd. mgrs., 1983-94; trustee Am. Jewish Hist. Soc., 1987—, pres., 1992—; trustee Hebrew Coll., 1967—, chmn. cultural affairs com., 1977-78, trustee Temple Kehillath Israel, 1967—; trustee Combined Jewish Philanthropies, Boston, 1966—, bd. mgrs., 1989—; trustee Roxbury Latin Sch., 1985-89; moderator Town of Brookline, Mass., 1970-82, 91-94, chmn. fin. com., 1961-64; nat. chmn. Reps. for Eugene McCarthy, 1968; chmn. Brookline United Fund, 1960; pres. Jewish Community Rels. Coun., 1971-73, mem. adminstrv. com., 1967—; dir. Brookline Taxpayer's Assn., 1956-61, Brookline Community Coun., 1957-61; gov. Hebrew Union Coll.-Jewish Inst. Religion, 1987-92; bd. dirs. Mass. div. Am. Cancer Soc., 1987—; pres. Hebrew Free Loan Soc. Boston, 1972-88; active various other civic and religious orgns. Mem. Nat. Assn. for Textile Tech. (nat. bd. govs. 1970-73), Nat. Knitwear Mfrs. Assn. (past dir., bd. dirs., present hon. life dir.), New Bedford Yacht Club, Harvard (Boston and N.Y.C.), Belmont Country Club, Thorny Lea Golf Club, Norfolk Trout. Avocations: sailing, amateur radio, golf. Home: 830 Newton St Chestnut Hill MA 02167-2643 Office: Shawmut Mills 208 Manley St West Bridgewater MA 02379-1044

WYNER, YEHUDI, composer, pianist, conductor, educator; b. Calgary, Alta., Can., June 1, 1929; s. Lazar and Sarah Naomi (Shumiatcher) Weiner; m. Nancy Joan Braverman, Sept. 16, 1951 (div. 1967); children: Isaiah, Adam, Cassia; m. Susan M. Davenny, June 15, 1967. Diploma, Juilliard Sch. Music, 1946; A.B., Yale U., 1950, B.Mus., 1951, M.Mus., 1953; M.A., Harvard U., 1952. Vis. assoc. prof. Hofstra Coll., 1959; lectr. Queens Coll., N.Y.C., 1959-60; instr. Hebrew Union Coll., N.Y.C., 1957-59; music dir. Westchester Reform Temple, N.Y.C., 1959-68; asst. prof. theory Yale U., 1963-69, assoc. prof. theory, 1969-77, chmn. composition dept., 1969-73; prof. music SUNY, Purchase, 1978-89, dean music, 1978-82; faculty Berkshire Music Ctr., 1975-85; faculty Tanglewood Music Ctr. (formerly Berkshire Music Ctr.), 1975—; vis. prof. composition Cornell U., 1987 Ziskind vis. prof. composition Brandeis U., 1987-88, Walter Naumburg prof. composition, dir. contemporary ensemble, 1989—; vis. prof. Harvard U., 1991-93, 96-97. Mus. dir., New Haven Opera Soc., 1968-77, Turnau Opera Assn., 1961-64; mem., Bach Aria Group, 1968—; composer-condr., Tanglewood, 1961; composer-in-residence, Santa Fe Chamber Music Festival, 1982, Am. Acad. in Rome, spring 1991; composer: Two Chorale Preludes for Organ, 1951, Partita for Piano, 1952, Dance Variations for Wind Octet, 1953, rev., 1959, Psalm 143, chorus, 1952, Sonata for Piano, 1954, Concert Duo for Violin and Piano, 1955-57, Dedication Anthem, 1957, Serenade for Seven Instruments, 1958, Passover Offering, 1959, Three Informal Pieces for Violin and Piano, 1961, Friday Evening Service for Cantor, Chorus, Organ, 1963, Incidental Music for play The Old Glory, 1964, Torah Service with Instruments, 1966, Da Camera for Piano and Orch, 1967, Cadenza for Clarinet and Harpsichord, 1969, De Novo for cello and small ensemble, 1971, Liturgy for the High Holidays, 1971, Three Short Fantasies for Piano, 1963-71, Songs, 1950-79, Canto Cantabile for Soprano and Concert Band, 1972, music for play The Mirror, 1972-73, Memorial Music for Soprano and 3 Flutes, 1971-73, Intermedio for Soprano and String Orchestra, 1974, Wedding Music, 1976, Dances of Atonement for Violin and Piano, 1976, Fragments from Antiquity; 5 songs for soprano and symphony orch., 1978; Piano Quartet, 1980, All the Rage for flute and piano, 1980; Processionals and Marches, 1979, 80, Tanz and Maissele, 1981, On This Most Voluptuous Night, 1982, Passage for 7 Instruments, 1983, Wind Quintet, 1984, String Quartet, 1985, Composition for Viola and Piano, 1987, Toward the Center for piano, 1988, Sweet Consort for flute and piano, 1988, Leonardo Vincitore for 2 sopranos, string bass and piano, 1988, O To Be a Dragon, four songs for women's chorus and piano, 1989, Trapunto Junction for brass trio and percussion, 1991, Changing Time for small ensemble, 1991, New Fantasies for piano, 1991, Amadeus' Billiard for small ensemble, 1991, Il Cane Minore for 2 clarinets and bassoon, 1992, Wedding Dances: From the Notebook of Suzanne de Venné, 1993, Post Fantasies for Piano, 1993, Prologue and Narrative for cello and orch., 1994, Song Cycle for soprano, baritone and piano, Restaurants, Wines-Bistros, Shrines, 1994, More Fantasies for Piano, 1994, Lyric Harmony for orch., 1995. Recipient Inst. Arts and Letters grant, 1961, Brandeis Creative Arts award, 1963; commns. from Yale U., 1958, Mich. U., 1959, Fromm Found., 1960, Koussevitzky Found. at Library Congress, 1960, Ford Found., 1971, Yale Band, Yale Repertory Theater, Cantilena Chamber Players, Aeolian Chamber Players, Santa Fe Chamber Music Festival, Collage of Boston, N.Y. Woodwind Quintet, Frank Taplin project, NEA Consortium, Boston Symphony Chamber Players, Atlantic Sinfonietta, Carnegie Hall Am. Composers Orch., RNCM

Manchester Internat. Cello Festival; Rome Prize fellow, 1953-56; Alfred E. Hertz fellow U. Calif., 1953-54; Guggenheim fellow, 1960, 76-77; NEA grantee, 1976. Mem. Internat. Soc. Contemporary Music (mem. bd.), Am. Composers Alliance (exec. bd.), Am. Music Center (exec. bd.). Office: Music Dept Brandeis U Waltham MA 02254

WYNETTE, TAMMY, singer; b. Red Bay, Ala., May 5, 1942; d. William Hollis Pugh; m. George Jones, Sept. 1968 (div.); m. George Richey, 1978; children: Gwen, Jackie, Tina. Former beauty operator. Rec. artist Epic Records, 1967—; regular appearances on Grand Ole Opry; tours U.S., Can., Europe; recs. include: Womanhood, Stand By Your Man, Run Woman Run, 1970, Woman to Woman, 1974, Womanhood, 1978, Crying In The Rain, 1981, Sometimes When We Touch, 1985, From the Bottom of my Heart, 1986, Higher Ground, 1987, Next To You, 1989, Heart Over Mind, 1990, Best Loved Hits, 1991, (with others) Tears of Fire: The 25th Anniversary Collection, 1992; author autobiography Stand By Your Man, 1982. Named Female Vocalist of Year Country Music Assn., 1968, 69, 70.

WYNGAARDEN, JAMES BARNES, physician; b. East Grand Rapids, Mich., Oct. 19, 1924; s. Martin Jacob and Johanna (Kempers) W.; m. Ethel Vredevoogd, June 20, 1946 (div. 1977); children: Patricia Wyngaarden Fitzpatrick, Joanna Wyngaarden Gandy, Martha Wyngaarden Krauss, Lisa Wyngaarden Rolland, James Barnes Jr. Student, Calvin Coll., 1942-43, Western Mich. U., 1943-44; MD, U. Mich., 1948; DSc (hon.), U. Mich. and Med. Coll. of Ohio, 1984, U. Ill., 1985, George Washington U., 1986; PhD (hon.), Tel Aviv U., 1987; DSc. (hon.), U. S.C., West Mich. U., 1989. Diplomate: Am. Bd. Internal Medicine. Intern Mass. Gen. Hosp., Boston, 1948-49; resident Mass. Gen. Hosp., 1949-51; vis. investigator Pub. Health Rsch. Inst., N.Y.C., 1952-53; investigator NIH, USPHS, Bethesda, Md., 1953-56; asso. prof. medicine and biochemistry Duke U. Med. Sch., 1956-61, prof., 1961-65; vis. scientist Inst. Biologie-Physieochemique, Paris, 1963-64; prof., chmn. U. Pa. Med. Sch., 1965-67; physician-in-chief Med. Svc. Hosp. U. PA., Phila., 1965-67; Frederic M. Hanes prof., chmn. dept. medicine Duke U. Sch. of Medicine, Durham, N.C., 1967-82; physician-in-chief Med. Svc. Duke U. Hosp., Durham, 1967-82; chief of staff Duke U. Hosp., Durham, 1981-82; dir. NIH, Bethesda, MD, 1982-89; assoc. dir. life scis. Office of Sci. and Tech. Policy, Exec. Office of Pres., The White House, 1989-90; dir. Human Genome Orgn., 1990-91; fgn. sec. NAS, 1990-94; prof. medicine, assoc. vice chancellor for health affairs Duke U., Durham, N.C., 1990-94, ret., 1994; mem. staff VA, Durham County Hosps.; sr. assoc. dean internat. med. programs U. Pa., Phila., 1995—; cons. Office Sci. and Tech. Exec. Office of Pres., 1966-72; Mem. Pres.'s Sci. Adv. Com., 1972-73; mem. Pres.'s Com. for Nat. Medal of Sci., 1977-80; mem. adv. com. biology and medicine AEC, 1966-68; mem. bd. sci. counselors NIH, 1971-74; mem. adv. bd. Howard Hughes Med. Inst., 1969-82; mem. adv. council Life Ins. Med. Research Fund, 1967-70; adv. bd. Sci. Yr., 1977-81; vice chmn. Com. on Study Nat. Needs for Biomed. and Behavioral Research Personnel, NRC, 1977-81; bd. dirs. Marion Merrell Dow Corp., Hybridon Corp., Human Genome Scis. Author: (with W.N. Kelley) Gout and Hyperuricemia, 1976; mem. editorial bd. Jour. Biol. Chemsitry, 1971-74, Arthritis and Rheumatism, 1959-66, Jour. Clin. Investigation, 1962-66, Ann. Internal Medicine, 1964-74, Medicine, 1963-90; editor: (with J.B. Stanbury, D.S. Fredrickson) The Metabolic Basis of Inherited Disease, 1960, 66, 72, 78, 83, (with O. Sperling and A. DeVries) Purine Metabolism in Man, 1974, (with L.H. Smith, Jr.) Cecil Textbook of Medicine, 16th edit., 1982, 19th edit., 1992. Bd. dirs. Royal Soc. Medicine Found., 1971-76, The Robert Wood Johnson Found. Clin. Scholar Program, 1973-78. Ensign USNR, 1943-46; sr. surgeon USPHS, 1951-56, rear adm. USPHS, 1982-90. Recipient Borden Undergrad. Research award, U. Mich., 1948, N.C. Gov.'s award for sci., 1974, Disting. Alumnus award We. Mich. U., 1984, Robert Williams award Assn. Profs. Medicine, 1985, Dalton scholar in medicine, Mass. Gen. Hosp., 1950, Richard Schweiker Excellence in Govt. award, 1985, Fedn. of Am. Socs. of Exptl. Biology Pub. Svc. award, 1989, Humanitarian award Nat. Orgn. for Rare Diseases, 1990; Royal Coll. Physicians fellow, 1984. Mem. Am. Rheumatism Assn., Am. Fedn. Clin. Research, So. Soc. Clin. Investigation (pres. 1974, founder's medal 1978), ACP (John Phillips Meml. award 1980), Am. Soc. Clin. Investigation, AAAS, Am. Soc. Biol. Chemists, Assn. Am. Physicians (councillor 1973-77, pres. 1978), Endocrine Soc., Nat. Acad. Scis., Royal Acad. Scis. Sweden, Am. Acad. Arts and Sci., Inst. Medicine, Sigma Xi. Democrat. Presbyterian. Club: Interurban Clinical (Balt.). Avocations: tennis, skiing, painting.

WYN-JONES, ALUN (WILLIAM WYN-JONES), software developer, mathematician; b. Tremadoc, Gwynedd, Great Britain, Aug. 15, 1946; came to U.S., 1976; s. Goronwy Wyn and Mai Jones; m. Jocelyn Ripley, July 29, 1977; 1 stepchild, Electra Truman. BSc with honors, U. Manchester, U.K., 1968; MSc, Univ. Coll. London, 1970. Rsch. engr. Marconi-Elliott Computer Labs., Borehamwood, U.K., 1970-71; asst. tutor math. Poly. North London, 1971-72; programmer CRC Info. Systems, Ltd., London, 1972-76; mgr. devel. Warner Computer (now Warner Ins.), N.Y.C., 1976-80; pres., owner, developer Wallsoft Systems, Inc., N.Y.C., 1982-92, Integrity Systems Corp., N.Y.C., 1980—; software cons. investment banking divsn. Goldman, Sachs & Co., N.Y.C., 1994—; invited speaker at profl. confs. Author, coauthor computer software. Recipient Byte Award Distinction Byte Editors and Columnists, 1988, Readers Choice award Data Based Advisor Readers, 1990, 91. Mem. AAAS, Am. Math. Soc., Math. Assn. Am. Methodist. Achievements include development of template programming in automatic code generation. Home: 609 Columbus Ave Apt 14D New York NY 10024-1436

WYNN, ALBERT RUSSELL, congressman; b. Phila., Sept. 10, 1951; m. Jessie Wynn; 1 child, Gabrielle. BS, U. Pitts., 1973; student, Howard U.; JD, Georgetown U., 1979. Intern African Regional Affairs, U.S. State Dept., 1972-73; exec. dir. consumer protection divsn. Prince George's County, 1977-81; mem. Md. Ho. of Dels., 1982-86; lawyer Albert R. Wynn & Assocs., 1982-86; mem. Md. State Senator from Dist. 25, 1986-92, 103d-104th Congresses from 4th Md. Dist., Washington, 1993—; also regional Dem. whip 103-104th Congresses from 4th Md. Dist., Washington; mem. banking & fin. svcs com., internat. rels. com., Patuxent Inst. reform task force, 1988—, joint com. econ. devel. strategy, 1989—; del. Dem. Nat. Conv. 1984, 88; pres. Metro. Washington coun. consumer agencies. Mem. NAACP legal assistance program, coalition on black affairs, voter registration, edn. coalition, gov.'s task force drunk & drugged driving; 1st vice chmn. legis. black caucus; chmn. Prince George's County black elected officials alliance. Mem. J. Franklin Bourne Bar Assn., Kappa Alpha Psi (past pres.). Democrat. Baptist. Office: US Ho of Reps 418 Cannon House Off Bldg Washington DC 20515-2004

WYNN, COY WILTON, journalist; b. Prescott, Ark., Aug. 9, 1920; s. Ota Gilbert and Kate (Ward) W.; m. Leila Birbari, June 2, 1947. B.A., La. Coll., Pineville, 1941; M.A., La. State U., 1942. Chmn. dept. journalism Am. U., Cairo, Egypt, 1945-47; dir. div. journalism Lehigh U., Bethlehem, Pa., 1947-50; free-lance writer Middle East, 1950-51; corr. AP, Beirut, Lebanon, 1951-55; bur. chief AP, Cairo, 1955-61; corr. Time mag., Rome, 1962-74; chief bur. Time mag., Cairo, 1974-78; chief Rome Bur. Time mag., 1979-85, cons. on Vatican affairs, 1985-91, ret., 1991. Author: Nasser of Egypt: The Search for Dignity, 1959, Keepers of the Keys, 1988; also articles. Former mem. Associazione della Stampa Estera in Italia; hon. trustee John Cabot U., Rome. Named to Hall of Fame Sch. Mass. Comms. La. State U. Roman Catholic. Clubs: American (Rome) (past pres.). Home: 52 Viale Liegi, Rome Italy 00198

WYNN, JOHN CHARLES, clergyman, retired religion educator; b. Akron, Ohio, Apr. 11, 1920; s. John Francis and Martha Esther (Griffith) W.; m. Rachel Linnell, Aug. 27, 1943; children: Mark Edward, Martha Lois Borland, Maryan Kay Ainsworth. BA, Coll. Wooster, 1941; BD, Yale U., 1944; MA, Columbia U., 1963, EdD, 1964; DD, Davis and Elkins Coll., 1958. Ordained to ministry Presbyn. Ch., 1944. Student asst. pastor Trinity Luth. Ch., New Haven, 1943-44; assoc. minister First Presbyn. Ch., Evanston, Ill., 1944-47; pastor El Dorado, Kans., 1947-50; dir. family edn. and research United Presbyn. Bd. Christian Edn., Phila., 1950-59; prof. Colgate Rochester/Bexley Hall/Crozer Theol. Sem., 1959-85, prof. emeritus, 1985—; pvt. practice family therapy; adj. prof. U. Rochester, San Francisco Theol. Sem., St. Bernard's Sem., Wesley Theol. Sem.; postdoctoral fellow Cornell U., 1973-74, St. John's U., 1980; lectr. Sch. Continuing Edn. Johns Hopkins U.; mem. summer faculty Union Theol. Sem., N.Y.C.; del. study conf. World Coun. Chs., 1953, 57, 64, 65, 67, 75, 80; lectr. 5 univs., Republic of South Africa, 1968; chmn. com. on sexuality in human cmty. U.P. Ch.; vol. mem. chaplaincy staff Charlestown Care Ctr., Balt. Author: How Christian Parents Face Family Problems, 1955, Pastoral Ministry to Families, 1957, Families in the Church, A Protestant Survey, 1961, Christian Education for Liberation and Other Upsetting Ideas, 1977, Family Therapy in Pastoral Ministry, 1982 (rev. and expanded as Family Therapy in Pastoral Ministry: Counseling for the Nineties, 1991), The Family Therapist, 1987; Editor: Sermons on Marriage and Family Life, 1956, Sex, Family and Society in Theological Focus, 1966, Sexual Ethics and Christian Responsibility, 1970; Contbr. articles to mags. and religious jours. Bd. dirs. Presbyn. Life, Planned Parenthood League Rochester and Monroe County, Family Service Rochester, Pastoral Counseling Ctr. Fellow Am. Assn. Marriage and Family Therapy (approved supr.); mem. Religious Edn. Assn., Nat. Coun. Chs. of Christ in U.S.A. (chmn. com. family life 1957-60), Nat. Coun. Family Rels., Family Svc. Assn. Am., Rochester Coun. Chs. (dir.). Address: 717 Maiden Choice Ln Apt 523 Catonsville MD 21228-6116

WYNN, KARLA WRAY, artist, agricultural products company executive; b. Idaho Falls, Idaho, Oct. 1, 1943; d. Wiliam and Elma (McCowin) Lott; m. Russell D. Wynn, June 7, 1963 (div. 1996); children: Joseph, Jeffrey, Andrea. Student, Coll. of Holy Names, 1962-63, Providence Coll. Nursing, 1962-63; BFA, Idaho State U., 1989; postgrad., Alfred U., 1993. Co-owner R.D. Wynn Farms, American Falls, Idaho, 1963-96, office mgr., 1975-84; co-owner Redi-Gro Fertilizer Co., American Falls, 1970-96, office mgr., 1980-84; pres. Lakeside Farms, Inc. (name now Redi-Gro Fertilitzer Inc.), American Falls, 1975-96; artist, 1990—; owner Blue Heron, Pocatello, Idaho, 1991-96. Watercolor paintings and ceramic clay sculptures exhibited at various art shows and galleries. Buddhist.

WYNN, KENNETH RICHARD, design and furnishings company executive; b. Utica, N.Y., June 22, 1952; s. Michael and Zelma (Kutner) W.; children: Jennifer, Ashley, Michael. B.A. in French Lit., Swarthmore Coll., 1973; M.B.A. in Fin., U. Nev., 1977. Dir. purchasing Golden Nugget, Inc., Las Vegas, 1973—, v.p. design and constrn., 1977—; pres. Atlandia Design. Mem. devel. planning group property Swarthmore Coll. (Pa.), 1983—. Recipient Harvard Club award (Syracuse), 1969. Republican. Jewish. Office: Atlandia Design 3260 Industrial Rd Las Vegas NV 89109-1132

WYNN, ROBERT E., retired career officer, electronics executive; b. Dallas, Jan. 31, 1942; s. Wendell W. and Thelma (Smart) W.; m. Lavenia K. Davis, Mar. 25, 1972; children: Leslie, Lauren. Bachelors degree, West Point, 1964; MEE, U. Tenn., 1971. Commd. 2d lt. U.S. Army, 1964, advanced through grades to commdg. gen., 1990; chief comm. Ops. Divsn. 5th Signal Command, Heidelberg, Germany, 1979-81; chief of staff 5th Signal Command, Worms, Germany, 1984-85; chief plans and programs, dep. chief staff Ops. and Plans DCS for OPS and PLANS, Washington, 1981-84; comdr. 2d Signal Brigade, Mannheim, Germany, 1986-88, U.S. Army Info. Systems Command/Tng. Doctrine Command, Ft. Monroe, Va., 1988-90; commdg. gen. 7th Signal Command, Ft. Ritchie, Md., 1990-92, U.S. Army Info. Systems Engring. Command, Ft. Huachuca, Ariz., 1992—; ret., 1995; mgr. C3 sys. Electrospace sys., Inc., Richardson, Tex., 1995—. Decorated Bronze Star, Legion of Merit, Silver Order of Mercury. Mem. Assn. U.S. Army Assn. Grads. (life), Armed Forces Comm. and Electronics Assn. (life, bd. dirs.), Sky Soldier (life, 173d airborne brigade), Signal Corps Regiment (life). Avocations: golf, tennis. Home: 703 Laredo Cir Allen TX 75002-5444

WYNN, STEPHEN A., hotel, entertainment facility executive; b. 1941; married. Pres., chief exec. officer Best Brands, Inc., 1969-72; chmn. bd. dirs., pres., CEO Mirage Resorts Inc. (formerly Golden Nugget Inc.), 1973—. Office: Mirage Resorts Inc 3400 Las Vegas Blvd S Las Vegas NV 89101 Office: G N L V 3260 Industrial Rd Las Vegas NV 89109-1132*

WYNN, THOMAS JOSEPH, judge, educator; b. Chgo., Aug. 30, 1918; s. Phillip H. and Delia B (Madden) W.; m. Bernadette L. Lavelle, Apr. 17, 1948; children: Thomas Joseph, John P. AB, DePaul U., 1941, JD, 1942. Bar: Ill. 1942. Spl. investigator Phoenix & Murphy, Chgo., 1942; pvt. practice law Chgo., 1946-59; ptnr. Wynn & Ryan, Chgo., 1959-79; assoc. judge Cir. Ct. Cook County, Ill., 1979-83, judge chancery div. mechanic's lien sect., 1983—; lectr. bus. law Latin Am. Inst., Chgo., 1946-47; mem. faculty Coll. Commerce, DePaul U., Chgo., 1947—, assoc. dean Evening div., 1957-73, prof., 1972-79, part-time faculty, 1979-83, adj. prof. bus. law, 1983—; asst. atty. gen. Ill., 1957-58; bd. dirs., gen. counsel Suburbanite Bowl, Inc., 1958-79; gen. legal counsel Chgo. Consortium Colls. and Univs., GM Tool Corp.; pres., bd. dirs. Metroplex Leasing and Financing, Inc. Candidate for alderman Chgo. City Coun., 1951; candidate for judge Mcpl. Ct. Chgo., 1956; exec. sec., bd. dirs. Ill. Good Govt. Inst., 1958-79; mem. adv. bd. to dean Coll Law DePaul U., 1992—. Ensign-lt. (S.G.) USNR, 1942-46. Mem. Ill. Bar Assn., Chgo. Bar Assn. (mem. arbitration and alternative dispute resolution com., civil practice coms., mem. internat. law com., mem. judiciary com.), Ill. Judges Assn. (com. mandatory arbitration alt. dispute resolution, com. pubs.), Assn. Univ. Evening Colls. (past chmn.), Am. Bus. Law Assn. (pres. 1972-73), Am. Real Estate and Urban Econs. Assn., Chgo. Area Evening Deans and Dirs. Assn., U.S. Adult Edn. Assn., Ill. Adult Edn. Assn., Am. Right-of-Way Assn. (advisor chmn., nat. ednl. com., 1963-64), St. Vincent DePaul Soc., DePaul Law Alumni Assn. (past pres.), Smithsonian Inst., Pres.'s Club, (DePaul U. 1986—), Blue Key, Gamma Eta Gamma, Beta Gamma Sigma, Delta Mu Delta. Home: 225 S Rohlwing Rd Palatine IL 60067-6441 Office: Cir Ct Cook County Daley Civic Ctr Chicago IL 60606

WYNNE, BRIAN DOUGLAS, lawyer; b. L.A., Oct. 15, 1967; s. Robert Jay and Marlene (Friedman) W.; m. Suzanne Kahn, Aug. 3, 1991; 1 child, Jacob Kahn Wynne. BA, U. Calif., Santa Barbara, 1989; JD, Southwestern U., 1992. Bar: Calif. 1992, U.S. Dist. Ct. (ctrl. dist.) Calif. 1993. Legal extern family law dept. L.A. Superior Ct., L.A., 1992; atty. Trope and Trope, L.A., 1992—. Mem. Beverly Hills Bar Assn., L.A. County Bar Assn. Avocations: golf, skiing, travel. Office: Trope and Trope Ste 801 12121 Wilshire Blvd Los Angeles CA 90025

WYNNE, BRIAN JAMES, former association executive, consultant; b. N.Y.C., Dec. 2, 1950; s. Bernard and Dolores (Doyle) W. Student, Institute des Sciences Politiques, Paris, 1970-71; B.A., Coll. Holy Cross, 1972; M.A., U. So. Calif., 1974. Mem. staff Exec. Cons., Inc., McLean, Va., 1974-76; prin., 1976-78; exec. dir. Indsl. Designers Soc. Am., Washington, 1978-88; cons. to various non-profit orgns.; dir. Worldesign 85, founder Worldesign Found. Mem. Am. Soc. Assn. Execs., Indsl. Designers Soc. Am. (hon.), Phi Sigma Iota. Home: 5200 N Ocean Blvd Fort Lauderdale FL 33308-3037

WYNNE, BRUCE, tribal administrator, artist; b. Wellpinit, Wash., June 14, 1944; s. William and Gertrude (Flett) W.; m. Marie Jacob (dec. Sept. 1970); m. Mary Eaves, Apr. 1, 1973; children: John (dec.), Angela, Duane, Jena. Grad., Inst. Am. Indian Arts, Santa Fe, 1964; BFA, U. Colo., 1975. Exhibits designer Heard Mus., Phoenix, 1968-70; asst. dir. Indian Ednl. Opportunity Program U. Colo., Boulder, 1970-73; prof. artist, primarily in sculpture, 1975-84; mem. Spokane Indian Tribal Coun., 1984—, vice chmn., 1985-87, tribal chmn., 1989—. Exhibited in shows, including Scottsdale Nat. Indian Arts Exhbn., 1967, 75, 76, Red Cloud Nat. Indian Art Exhibit, Pine Ridge, S.D., 1970, Heart Mus., 1971, 75, 76, Santa Fe Indian Art Market, 1975, Gallup (N.Mex.) Intertribal Exhbn., 1976, Philbrook Ann. Indian Arts Exhbn., Tulsa, 1976, 77, Native Am. Ctr. for Living Arts, Niagara Falls, N.Y., 1980; represented in collections including Heard Mus., Philbrook Art Ctr., Diamond L. Found., Snyder, Tex., Buffalo Bill Mus. and Western Art Ctr., Cody, Wyo. Mem. Pres. Clinton Transition Team, 1992-94; mem. N.W. Portland Area Indian Health Bd.; mem. Wash. State Gov.'s Adv. Com. on Social and Health Svcs., 1992—. Mem. Affiliated Tribes of N.W. Indians (pres. 1991—), Nat. Congress of Am. Indians (v.p. 1991—, bd. dirs., mem. health com.), Upper Columbia United Tribes (chmn. 1989-94), Inland Tribal Consortium. Office: Spokane Bus Coun PO Box 477 Wellpinit WA 99040-0477 Office: Spokane Tribe of Indians Alex Sherwood Meml Ctr 6208 Ford Wellpinit Rd Wellpinit WA 99040-9700

WYNNE, JAMES EARL, lawyer; b. Chgo., Sept. 3, 1950; s. Conrad Joseph and Irene F. (Spengler) W.; m. Cathy Mantay, July 27, 1974; children: Alison Laurel, Ashley Erin, Michael James. BA in Econs., Mich. State U., 1972; JD, Ill. Inst. Tech.-Chgo.-Kent, 1975. Bar: Ill. 1975, Mich. 1978, U.S. Dist. Ct. (no. dist.) Ill. 1975, U.S. Dist. Ct. (ea. dist.) Mich. 1978, U.S. Ct. Appeals (6th cir.) 1985. Atty. Coghlan & Joyce, Chgo., 1975-78, Milmet & Vecchio, Detroit, 1978-83; ptnr. Milmet & Vecchio, 1983-86, Butzel Long, Detroit, 1986—; hearing panelist Mich. Atty. Discipline Bd., Detroit, 1987—; adj. prof. trial advocacy U. Detroit Law Sch., 1989—. Author: (with others) Tolling Statues of LImitation, 1988, (with another) REmedies of Buyers and Sellers under the UCC. Mem. ABA, Am. Trial Lawyers Assn., Chgo. Bar Assn., Mich. Bar Assn., Detroit Bar Assn. Republican. Roman Catholic. Club: Detroit Golf. Avocations: golf, home renovation. Office: Butzel Long 150 W Jefferson Ave Ste 900 Detroit MI 48226-4415

WYNNE, JOHN OLIVER, newspaper, broadcast and cable executive; b. Norfolk, Va., July 6, 1945; s. Oliver Jr. and Margaret (Klasman) W.; m. Susan Stribling (Snodgrass), Dec. 23, 1972; children: John Oliver Jr., Lee Stribling (dec.), Bradford Annan. BA, Princeton U., 1967; JD, U. Va., 1971. Bar: Va. 1971. Atty. Willcox, Savage, Lawrence, Dickson & Spindle, Norfolk, 1971-74; corp. sec. Landmark Comm., Inc., Norfolk, 1974-77, v.p. broadcast and cable, 1977-78; v.p., gen. mgr. Sta. KNTV-TV subs. Landmark Comm., Inc., Norfolk; pres. broadcasting and video enterprises Landmark Comm., Inc., 1980-90, COO, pres. newspapers and broadcasting group, 1990-91, pres., CEO, 1991—; chmn. The Weather Channel, 1981—, The Travel Channel, 1992—; bd. dirs. Cabletelevision Advt. Bur., N.Y.C., 1983-90. Trustee Norfolk Acad., 1980—; trustee Va. Found. for Ind. Colls., 1990—; bd. dirs., vice chmn. Children's Health System, Inc., Norfolk, 1987-93; chmn. Jr. Achievement, Norfolk, 1987; chmn. capital campaign South Hampton Rds. United Way, Norfolk, 1986. Served with U.S. Army, 1968-74. Mem. Nat. Cable TV Assn. (bd. dirs. 1988—), Harbor Club. Episcopalian. Club: Harbor (Norfolk). Avocations: golf, tennis, skiing, walking, reading. Office: Landmark Communications Inc 150 W Brambleton Ave Norfolk VA 23510-2018

WYNNE, JOHNNY CALVIN, university dean, plant breeding researcher; b. Williamston, N.C., May 17, 1943; s. James Harry and Rachel Loraine (Ayers) W.; m. Diane Louise Sawyer, 1961 (div. Feb. 1989); children: Debbie Ann, Donna Carol; m. Jacqueline Crawford Creech, Nov. 25, 1989; children: John Christopher, James Alexander. BS, N.C. State U., 1965, MS, 1968, PhD, 1974. Instr. crop sci. dept. N.C. State U., Raleigh, 1968-74, asst. prof., 1974-78, assoc. prof., 1978-83, prof., 1983-91, acting tchg. adminstr., 1987-89, head dept., 1989-91, assoc. dean, dir. N.C. agr. rsch. svc., 1992—. Recipient rsch. award Nat. Peanut Coun., 1992. Fellow AAAS, Am. Peanut Rsch. and Edn. Soc. (pres. 1990, Bailey award 1977); mem. Crop Sci. Soc. Am., Coun. for Agrl. Sci. and Tech., So. Assn. Expt. Sta. Dirs. (chmn. 1994), Sigma Iota Rho. Office: N Carolina State Univ PO Box 7643 Raleigh NC 27695

WYNNE, LYMAN CARROLL, psychiatrist; b. Lake Benton, Minn., Sept. 17, 1923; s. Nels Wind and Ella C. (Pultz) W.; m. Adele Rogerson, Dec. 22, 1947; children: Christine, Randall, Sara, Barry, Jonathan. War certificate, Harvard, 1943, MD, 1947, PhD in Social Psychology, 1958; MD (hon.), Oulu U., Finland, 1989. Med. intern Peter Bent Brigham Hosp., Boston, 1947-48; grad. fellow social relations Dept. Harvard, 1948-49; resident neurology Queen Square Hosp., London, Eng., 1950; resident psychiatry Mass. Gen. Hosp., Boston, St. Elizabeth's Hosp., Washington, also NIMH, 1951-54; psychoanalytic tng. Washington Psychoanalytic Inst., 1954-60, teaching analyst, 1965-72; cons., investigator WHO, 1965—; staff NIMH, 1954-57, chief sect. family studies, 1957-61, chief adult psychiatry br., 1961-72; mem. faculty Washington Sch. Psychiatry, 1956-72; prof. U. Rochester Sch. Medicine and Dentistry, 1971—, chmn. dept. psychiatry, 1971-77, dir. div. family programs, 1971-83; psychiatrist-in-chief Strong Meml. Hosp., Rochester, N.Y., 1971-77; vis. lectr. Am. U., Beirut, Lebanon, 1963-64. Chmn. bd. dirs. Family Process; mem. editorial adv. bd. Jour. Nervous and Mental Diseases; sr. editor: The Nature of Schizophrenia, 1978; editor: The State of the Art in Family Therapy Research; co-editor: Psychosocial Intervention in Schizophrenia, 1983, Children at Risk for Schizophrenia, 1984, The Language of Family Therapy, 1985; sr. editor Systems Consultation, 1986. Chmn. AAMFT Rsch. & Edn. Found., 1992-94. Med. dir. USPHS, 1961-72; mem. NRC, 1969-72. Recipient Commendation medal USPHS, 1965; Hofheimer prize Am. Psychiat. Assn., 1966; Frieda Fromm-Reichmann award Am. Acad. Psychoanalysis, 1966; Meritorious Service medal USPHS, 1966; Stanley Dean award Am. Coll. Psychiatrists, 1976; McAlpin Research Achievement award, 1977, Disting. Achievement in Family Therapy Research, Am. Family Therapy Assn., 1981; Disting. Research Achievement award Assn. Marriage and Family Therapy, 1982, Disting. Profl. Contbn. award Am. Assn. for Marriage and Family Therapy, 1985, Disting. Contbn. to Family Therapy award Am. Family Therapy Assn., 1989. Fellow Am. Psychiat. Assn. (life), Am. Acad. Psychoanalysis; mem. Am. Psychosomatic Soc. (mem. council 1969-72), Psychiat. Research Soc., Western N.Y. Psychoanalytic Soc. (pres. 1986-87), Am. Coll. Psychoanalysts, Am. Family Therapy Assn. (pres. 1986-87), Am. Assn. for Marriage and Family Therapy (bd. dirs. 1992-94), Am. Psychoanalytic Assn., Assn. for Clin. Psychosocial Rsch. (coun. 1984-91). Home: 17 Tobey Brk Pittsford NY 14534-1819 Office: Strong Meml Hosp Rochester NY 14642-8409

WYNNE-EDWARDS, HUGH ROBERT, entrepreneur, scientist; b. Montreal, Que., Can., Jan. 19, 1934; s. Vero Copner and Jeannie Campbell (Morris) W.-E.; married; children from previous marriages: Robin Alexander, Katherine Elizabeth, Renée Elizabeth Lortie, Krista Smyth, Jeannie Elizabeth, Alexander Vernon. B.Sc. with 1st class honors, U. Aberdeen, Scotland, 1955; M.A., Queen's U., 1957, Ph.D., 1959; D.Sc. (hon.), Meml. U., 1975. Registered profl. engr. B.C., 1995—. With Geol. Survey Can., 1958-59; lectr. Queen's U., Kingston, Ont., 1968-72, asst. prof., then assoc. prof., 1961-68, prof., head dept. geol. scis., 1968-72; prof., then Cominco prof., head dept. geol. scis. U. B.C., Vancouver, 1972-77; asst. sec. univ. br. Ministry of State for Sci. and Tech., Ottawa, 1977-79; sci. dir. Alcan Internat. Ltd., Montreal, 1979-80, v.p. R&D, chief sci. officer, 1980-89; CEO Moli Energy Ltd., Vancouver, 1989-90; pres. Terracy Inc., Vancouver, 1989—; sci. advisor Teck Corp., Vancouver, 1989-91; pres., CEO B.C. Rsch. Inc., Vancouver, 1993—; advisor Directorate Mining and Geology, Uttar Pradesh, India, 1964, Grenville project Que. Dept. Natural Resources, 1968-72; vis. prof. U. Aberdeen, 1965-66, U. Witwatersrand, Johannesburg, South Africa, 1972; UN cons., India, 1974, SCITEC, 1977-78; mem. sci. adv. com. CBC, 1980-84; mem. Sci. Coun. Can., 1983-89, Nat. Adv. Bd. on Sci. and Tech., 1987; indsl. liaison com. UN Ctr. for Sci. and Tech. in Devel., 1982-84; vice chmn. tech. adv. group Bus. Coun. for Sustainable Devel., Geneva, 1991; mem. Nat. Biotech. Adv. Coun., 1995—. Bd. dirs. Royal Victoria Hosp., Montreal, 1984-89; dir. Soc. Quebecoise d'initiatives petroliére, 1983-87; dir. CS Resources Ltd., 1993—; dir. Atomic Energy Can. Ltd., 1996—. Decorated officer Order of Can., 1991; recipient Spendiarov prize 24th Internat. Geol. Congress, Montreal, 1972. Fellow Can. Acad. Engring., Royal Soc. Can.; mem. Can. Rsch. Mgmt. Assn. (vice chmn. 1982-84, chmn. 1984-85, assn. medal 1987), Univ. Club (Montreal). Mem. United Ch. Avocations: tennis, skiing, carpentry. Office: Terracy Inc, 2030 27th St, West Vancouver, BC Canada V7V 4L4 also: BC Rsch Inc, 3650 Wesbrook Mall, Vancouver, BC Canada V6S 2L2

WYRICK, CHARLES LLOYD, JR., publisher, writer, editor; b. Greensboro, N.C., May 5, 1939; s. Charles Lloyd and Edythe Ellen (Ellis) W.; m. Constance Michelle Hooper, Aug. 22, 1964; children—Charles Lloyd, III, Christopher Conrad Hooper. B.A., Davidson (N.C.) Coll., 1961; M.F.A., U. N.C., 1967. Instr. Stephens Coll., Columbia, Mo., 1964-66; asst. head programs div. Va. Museum, Richmond, 1966-68; exec. dir. Assn. Preservation Va. Antiquities, Richmond, 1968-70; pres. Research & Restoration, Inc., Richmond, 1970-73; dir. Del. Art Mus., Wilmington, 1973-79, Gibbes Mus. Art, Charleston, S.C., 1980-86; pres. Wyrick & Co., Charleston, 1986—, Dixie Media, Inc., Charleston, 1989—; editor, pub. "Omnibus", 1989-94; mem. Richmond Commn. Archt. Rev., 1969-72, New Castle County (Del.) Hist. Rev. Bd., 1975-88, also vice chmn.; mem. Bd. Archtl. Rev. City of Charleston, 1988-94, chmn., 1992-94; mem. Charleston Consortium on Higher Edn.; cons. in field. Author: "The 17th Street Market", 1972; contbr. articles to profl. jours. Bd. visitors Davison Coll., 1974-77; chmn. Econs. of Amenities City of Charleston, 1978, S.C. Coastal Conservation League, 1989-94; bd. dirs. Charleston Area Arts Coun., 1989-91, Friends of Charleston County Courthouse, 1989-94, Pub. Art Trust, 1988-90; adv. com. S.C. Dept. Natural Resources, 1992—. Recipient 1st award spl. column writing Va. Press Assn., 1973. Mem. Assn. Am. Pubs., Pubs. Assn. of South (bd. dirs. 1990-92, pres. 1991-92), S.C. Acad. Authors (bd. dirs. 1990-92), Carolina

Yacht Club. Home: 34 Legare St Charleston SC 29401-2336 Office: 1-A Pinckney St Charleston SC 29401-2626

WYRICK, PRISCILLA BLAKENEY, microbiologist; b. Greensboro, N.C., Apr. 28, 1940; d. Carnie Lee and Prestine (Blakeney) W. BS in Med. Tech., U. N.C., Chapel Hill, 1962; MS in Bacteriology, U. N.C., 1967, PhD in Bacteriology, 1971. Technologist Clin. Microbiology Lab., N.C. Meml. Hosp., Chapel Hill, 1962-64; asst. supr. Clin. Microbiology Lab., N.C. Meml. Hosp., 1964-65, supr., 1965-66; sci. staff fellow Nat. Inst. Med. Rsch., Mill Hill, London, 1971-73; asst. prof. dept. microbiology U. N.C. Sch. Medicine, Chapel Hill, 1973-79; assoc. prof. U. N.C. Sch. Medicine, 1979-88, prof., 1988—. Grantee, NIH. Mem. Am. Acad. Microbiology, Am. Soc. Microbiology (pres. N.C. br. 1981-82, chmn. div. gen. med. microbiology 1981-82), AAAS, Soc. Infectious Diseases, Sigma Xi. Office: U NC Sch Medicine CB 7290 816 FLOB Chapel Hill NC 27599

WYRSCH, JAMES ROBERT, lawyer, educator, author; b. Springfield, Mo., Feb. 23, 1942; s. Louis Joseph and Jane Elizabeth (Welsh) W.; m. B. Darlene Wyrsch, Oct. 18, 1975; children: Scott, Keith, Mark, Brian, Marcia. BA, U. Notre Dame, 1963; JD, Georgetown U., 1966; LLM, U. Mo., Kansas City, 1972. Bar: Mo. 1966, U.S. Ct. Appeals (8th cir.) 1971, U.S. Supreme Ct. 1972, U.S. Ct. Appeals (10th cir.) 1974, U.S. Ct. Appeals (5th cir.) 1974, U.S. Ct. Mil. & Appeals 1978, U.S. Ct. Appeals (6th cir.) 1982, U.S. Ct. Appeals (11th cir.) 1984, U.S. Ct. Appeals (7th cir.) 1986, U.S. Ct. Appeals (4th cir.) 1990. Assoc. Wyrsch, Atwell, Mirakian, Lee and Hobbs, P.C. and predecessors, Kansas City, Mo., 1970-71, of counsel, 1972-77, ptnr., 1978—, pres., shareholder, 1988—; adj. prof. U. Mo., 1981—; mem. com. instrns. Mo. Supreme Ct., 1983—. Capt. U.S. Army, 1966-69; named to Who's Who in Kansas City Law, Kansas City Bus. Jour., 1991, 1994; recipient Joint Svcs. Commendation medal U.S. Army, 1969, U. Mo. Kansas City Svc. award Law Found., 1991-92. Fellow Am. Coll. Trial Lawyers, Am. Bar Found.; mem. ABA, Am. Arbitration Assn. (panel arbitrators), Mo. Bar Assn. (vice chmn. criminal law com. 1978-79), Kansas City Bar Assn. (chmn. anti-trust com. 1981), Assn. Trial Lawyers Am., Am. Bd. of Trial Advocates (adv.), Nat. Assn. Criminal Def. Attys., Mo. Assn. Criminal Def. Attys. (sec. 1982), Phi Delta Phi, Country Club of Blue Springs. Democrat. Roman Catholic. Co-author: Missouri Criminal Trial Practice, 1994; contbr. articles to profl. jours. Home: 1501 Sunnycreek Ln Blue Springs MO 64014 Office: Wyrsch Atwell Mirakian Lee & Hobbs PC 1101 Walnut St Fl 13 Kansas City MO 64106-2122

WYRTKI, KLAUS, oceanography educator; b. Tarnowitz, Germany, Feb. 7, 1925; came to U.S., 1961; s. Wilhelm and Margarete (Pacharzina) W.; m. Helga Kocher, June 6, 1954 (div. 1970); children: Undine, Oliver; m. Erika Maassen. PhD magna cum laude, U. Kiel, Germany, 1950. With German Hydrographic Inst., Hamburg, 1950-51; German Rsch. Coun. postdoctoral rsch. fellow U. Kiel, 1951-54; head Inst. Marine Rsch., Djakarta, Indonesia, 1954-57; sr. rsch. officer, then prin. rsch. officer div. fisheries and oceanography Commonwealth Sci. and Indsl. Rsch. Orgn., Sydney, Australia, 1958-61; assoc. rsch. oceanographer, then rsch. oceanographer Scripps Instn. Oceanography, U. Calif., 1961-64; prof. oceanography U. Hawaii, Honolulu, 1964—; chmn. North Pacific Expt., 1974-80, com. on climate changes and ocean Internat. Assn. Phys. Scis. of the Oceans; mem. Spl. Com. on Ocean Rsch. Working Group on Prediction of El Nino, Sci. Working Group on Topography Expt., panel on climate and global change NOAA. Author: El Nino—The Dynamic Response of the Equatorial Pacific Ocean to Atmospheric Forcing, 1975; editor: Oceanographic Atlas of the International Indian Ocean Expedition, 1988; mem. editl. bd. Jour. Phys. Oceanography, 1971-79. Recipient Excellence in Rsch. award U. Hawaii, 1980, Rosenstiel award U. Miami, 1981. Fellow Am. Geophys. Union (Maurice Ewing medal 1989), Am. Meteorol. Soc. (Harald Ulrick Sverdrup Gold medal 1991), Deutsche Meteorologische Gesellschaft (Albert Defant medal 1992). Office: U Hawaii 1000 Pope Rd Honolulu HI 96822-2336

WYSCHOGROD, EDITH, philosophy educator; b. N.Y.C.; d. Morris and Selma Shurer; m. Michael Wyschogrod, Mar. 9,1955; children: Daniel, Tamar. AB, Hunter Coll., 1957; PhD, Columbia U., 1970. Prof. philosophy Queens Coll., Flushing, N.Y., 1967-92; J. Newton Rayzor prof. philosophy and religious thought Rice U., Houston, 1992—. Author: Emmanuel Levinas: The Problem of Ethical Metaphysics, 1974, Spirit in Ashes, 1985, Saints and Postmodernism, 1990; co-editor: Lacan and Theological Discourse, 1989. Nat. Humanities Ctr. fellow, 1981, Woodrow Wilson Ctr. fellow, 1987-88, Guggenheim fellow, 1995-96. Mem. Am. Acad. Religion (pres. 1992-93). Office: Rice University PO Box 1892 6100 South Main Houston TX 77251

WYSE, LOIS, advertising executive, author; b. Cleve.; d. Roy B. Wohlgemuth and Rose (Schwartz) Weisman; m. Marc Wyse (div. 1980); m. Lee Guber (dec. 1988). Pres. Wyse Advt. Inc., N.Y.C., 1951—; bd. dirs. Consol. Natural Gas, Pitts.; ptnr. City & Co. Author 56 books; contbg. editor Good Housekeeping; syndicated columnist Wyse Words. Trustee Beth Israel Med. Ctr., N.Y.C. Mem. Woman's Forum (bd. dirs.), PEN. Office: Wyse Advt Inc 24 Public Sq Cleveland OH 44113-2201

WYSE, ROGER EARL, physiologist; b. Wauseon, Ohio, Apr. 22, 1943. BS in Agr., Ohio State U., 1965; MS, Mich. State U., 1967, PhD in Crop Sci., 1969. Fellow Mich. State U., 1969-70; plant physiologist Agr. Rsch. Svc. USDA, 1970-86; dean of rsch. Cook Coll. Rutgers U., 1986-92; dean, dir. Coll. Agr. and Life Sci. U. Wis., Madison, 1992—. Recipient Arthur Flemming award, 1982. Mem. AAAS, Am. Soc. Plant Physiol., Am. Soc. Agronomy, Am. Soc. Crop Sci. Office: Univ of Wisconsin Wisconsin Agr Experiment Sta 140 Agricultural Hall Madison WI 53706

WYSE, ROY, labor union administrator; b. Sept. 18, 1932; m. Pat Wyse; 5 children. With assembly plant Ford Motor Co., Liberty, Mo., from 1951; with UAW, 1951—, sec. Local 249, 1972-79, internat. rep., regional auditor, 1979-86, asst. dir. Region 5, 1986-89, dir. Region 5, 1989-95, nat. sec.-treas., 1995—, also dir. nat. aerospace dept., 1995—. Past mem., past pres. Orrick (Mo.) Bd. Edn.; mem. Orrick City Coun. Address: UAW Pub Rels & Pubs Dept 8000 E Jefferson Ave Detroit MI 48214

WYSE, WILLIAM WALKER, lawyer; b. Spokane, Wash., July 20, 1919; s. James and Hattie (Walker) W.; m. Janet E. Oswalt, Jan. 30, 1944; children: Wendy L., Scott C., Duncan E. AB, U. Wash., 1941; JD, Harvard U., 1948. Bar: Oreg. 1948. Pvt. practice Portland; ptnr. Stoel, Rives, Boley, Jones & Gray, 1953-88; pres. Wyse Investment Services, 1988—; past dir. Treasureland Savs. and Loan Assn.; past trustee, sec. Pacific Realty Trust; past trustee Holladay Park Plaza. Bd. dirs. Cmty. Child Guidance Clinic, 1951-57, pres., 1956-57; chmn. ctrl. budget com. United Fund, 1958-60; 1st v.p. United Good Neighbors; chmn. bd. dirs. Portland Sch. Bd., 1959-66; bd. dirs. Oreg. Symphony Soc., 1965-74, 93—, pres., 1968-70; pres. Tri-County Cmty. Coun., 1970-71; bd. dirs. Portland Mental Health Assn.; bd. dirs., sec. Oreg. Parks Found. Mem. ABA, Oreg. Bar Assn., Multnomah County Bar Assn., Am. Coll. Real Estate Lawyers, Univ. Club, Arlington Club, Portland City Club (past gov.), Wauna Lake Club, Delta Upsilon. Republican. Presbyterian. Home: 3332 SW Fairmount Ln Portland OR 97201-1446 Office: 806 SW Broadway Portland OR 97205-3333

WYSER-PRATTE, JOHN MICHAEL, lawyer; b. Paris, Sept. 4, 1936; came to U.S., 1950; s. Eugene John and Marguerite (von Prattes) W.-P.; m. Jean Doughty Templeton, Aug. 22, 1964 (div. Jan. 1976); children: Michèle Marguerite, Renée Christine; m. Maryse Sislian, Jan. 23, 1976; 1 child, Anne Catherine. BA, Coll. of the Holy Cross, 1958; JD, Georgetown U., 1963; cert. in internat. law studies, U. Geneva, 1964, Institut Universitaire des Hautes Etudes Internationales. Bar: N.Y. 1965, U.S. Ct. Appeals (2d crct.) 1974, U.S. Dist. Ct. (so. and ea. dists.) N.Y. 1975. Assoc. Coudert Bros., N.Y.C., 1964-71, ptnr., 1972-86; ptnr. Schnader, Harrison, Segal & Lewis, N.Y.C., 1987-95, Ross & Hardies, N.Y.C., 1995—; rsch. asst. Inst. for Internat. Trade Law, Georgetown U. Law Ctr., 1962-63; guest lectr., seminar speaker local C. of C.s, France, 1986—; guest speaker ann. Round Table Groupement des Industries Françaises Aéronautiques et Spatiales, Paris, 1986-92. Capt. USMC, 1958-62, USMCR, 1962-71. Schulte Zur Hausen fellow, 1963-64. Mem. ABA, Union Internationale des Avocats, Assn. Bar City of N.Y., French-Am. C. of C. (U.S.), Paris Am. Club. Republican. Roman Catholic. Office: Ross & Hardies Park Ave Towers 65 E 55th St New York NY 10022

WYSK, RICHARD A., engineering educator, researcher; b. Holyoke, Mass., Sept. 22, 1948; s. Stanley and Sophia Dorothy (Mazurowski) W.; m. Caryl Lynne Ray, Jan. 18, 1969; children: Richard Patrick, Rebecca Jeanne, Robyn Caryl. BS in Indsl. Engring. & Ops. Rsch., U. Mass., 1972, MS in Indsl. Engring. & Ops. Rsch., 1973; PhD in Indsl. Engring., Purdue U., 1977. Prodn. control mgr. Gen. Electric, Erie, Pa., 1973-75; rsch. analyst Caterpillar Tractor, Inc., Peoria, Ill., 1975-76; assoc. prof. Va. Polytechnic Inst., Blacksburg, 1977-83; prof. Pa. State U., State College, 1983-90; dir. Inst. Mfg. Systems, College Station, 1990-94; Royce Wisenbaker chair Tex. A&M U., College Station, 1990-94; William Lionhard chair in engring. William Leonhard chair in engring., State College, 1995—. Co-author: A Study Guide for the P.E. in I.E., 1982, An Intro to Automated Proc. Plan., 1985, Modern Manufacturing Process Engineering, 1989, Computer-aided Manufacturing, 1991 (Book-of-the-Yr. award Inst. Indsl. Engrs. 1992, E. Eugene Merchant Mfg. Textbook award Soc. Mfg. Engrs. 1992). Pks. commr. Montgomery County Pks. & Recreation, Blacksburg, 1982-83; adv. mem. Inst. Systems Rsch. U. Md., 1991—. With U.S. Army, 1969-71, Vietnam. Decorated Army Commendation medal with 2 oak leaf clusters. Fellow Inst. Indsl. Engrs. (chpt. pres. 1990—, Region III Award of Excellence 1982, D. Baker award 1993); mem. Soc. Mfg. Engrs. (sr., Outstanding Young Mfg. Engr. 1981), Engring. Accreditation Commn. (commr. 1990-92), Sigma Xi. Avocations: racquetball, basketball. Office: Pa State U 207 Hammond Bldg State College PA 16802-1401

WYSKOWSKI, BARBARA JEAN, lawyer; b. Jersey City, Feb. 20, 1967; d. Robert Louis and Barbara Joan (Dabrowski) W. BA, Rutgers U., New Brunswick, N.J., 1988; JD, Rutgers U., Camden, 1992. Bar: N.J., U.S. Dist. Ct. N.J., 1993. Law clk. Kevin William Kelly, Esq., Brick, N.J., 1989, Monke & Marriot, Sea Girt, N.J., 1990, Ann Segal, Esq., Voorhees, N.J., 1991; rsch. asst. Sch. Law Rutgers U., Camden, 1991-92; pro bono atty. Ocean-Monmouth Legal Svcs., Toms River, N.J., 1993-94; pvt. practice Manasquan, N.J., 1993—; cons. in field; lectr. in field. Advocate Women Against Abuse, Phila., 1989-90; pres. Amnesty Internat., 1989-92. Mem. ABA, N.J. State Bar Assn. (mem. lawyer to lawyer cons. network 1993-95), Ocean County Bar Assn., So. Monmouth Bd. Realtors. Roman Catholic. Avocations: surfing, running, skating. Home: Royal Court Apts I 5 Wall Rd Spring Lake NJ 07762 Office: Ste 103 2517 Hwy 35 Bldg M Manasquan NJ 08736

WYSLOTSKY, IHOR, engineering company executive; b. Kralovane, Czechoslovakia, Dec. 22, 1930; s. Ivan and Nadia (Alexiew) W.; came to U.S., 1958, naturalized, 1961; M.E., Sch. Aeros., Buenos Aires, Argentina, 1955; m. Marta Farion, 1983; children: Katria, Bohdan, Roman, Alexander. Design engr. Kaiser Industries, Buenos Aires, 1955-58; cons. design engr., Newark, 1959-64; chief engr. Universal Tool Co., Chgo., 1964-69; pres. CBC Devel Co., Inc., Chgo., 1969-74; pres. TEC, Inc., Chgo., 1972-83; pres. REDEX Corp., 1983-89, chmn. 1993—; engring. adviser to bd. Biosystems Insts., Inc., La Jolla, Calif. Co-founder Ukrainian Univ. Studies, U. Ill.; co-founder, pres. Am. Ukrainian Bus. Coun., 1991-93; mem. Ukrainian working com. Ctr. Strateqic Internat. Studies, Washington. Vis. com. mem. Harvard U. Mem. Packaging Inst. U.S.A., Am.-Israeli C. of C. (v.p.), Brit. Engring. Assn. River Plate. Mgmt. adv. bd. Modern Plastics Publs. Patentee in field. Home: 6133 N Forest Glen Ave Chicago IL 60646-5015 Office: 860 East State Pky Schaumburg IL 60170

WYSOCKI, BOLESLAW A(NTONI), psychologist, educator; b. Poland, June 10, 1912; s. Wladyslaw and Wiktoria (Mizia) Wysocki; student U. Cracow, U. Edinburgh (Scotland), Cambridge (Eng.) U., Oxford (Eng.) U., 1932-48; Ph.D., U. London (Eng.), 1954. Came to U.S., 1952, naturalized, 1958. Dir. edn. Ministry Edn., Gt. Britain, 1948-52; counselor, tchr. Marquette U., Milw., 1952-55; asso. prof. psychology Alliance (Pa.) Coll., 1955-57, Merrimack (Mass.) Coll., 1957-60, Regis (Mass.) Coll., 1960-62; prof. psychology Newton (Mass.) Coll., 1962-75, Boston Coll., 1975—. Clin. work mental instns., 1952—. Served as mil. psychologist Polish Army, 1943-48. Mem. Am., Mass., Brit. psychol. socs., Polish Inst. Arts and Scis. in Am., AAUP. Contbr. articles to profl. jours. Home: 240 Brattle St Cambridge MA 02138 Office: Boston Coll Dept Psychology Mcguinn Hall Chestnut Hill MA 02167

WYSOCKI, F(ELIX) MICHAEL, lawyer; b. Phila., Sept. 12, 1947; s. Felix and Helen (Kuzmik) W.; m. Lois Barbara Abramson, Aug. 23, 1970; 1 child, Dana. BA with highest distinction, George Washington U., 1969; JD cum laude, U. Pa., 1972. Bar: Pa. 1972, U.S. Dist. Ct. (ea. dist.) Pa. 1972. Assoc. Goodis, Greenfield, Henry, Shaiman & Levin, Phila., 1972-75, Garfinkel & Volpicelli, Phila., 1975-79; ptnr. Garfinkel & Volpicelli, 1979-80, Rawle & Henderson, Phila., 1980-86, Saul, Ewing, Remick & Saul, Phila., 1987—; lectr. Pa. Bar Inst. Bd. dirs., pres. Radnor A Better Chance. Mem. ABA, Pa. Bar Assn., Phila. Bar Assn. (vice chmn. real property sect. 1988, chmn. real property sect. 1989, bd. govs. 1989, exec. com. real property sect.), Phi Beta Kappa. Avocations: reading, running, cycling, skiing, tennis. Office: Saul Ewing Remick & Saul 3800 Centre Sq W Philadelphia PA 19102

WYSS, DAVID ALEN, financial service executive; b. Ft. Wayne, Ind., Nov. 14, 1944; s. Alen G. and Anne W. (Winicker) W.; m. Grace H. Hawes, June 11, 1966; children: Sarah J., Alen D. BS, MIT, 1966; PhD, Harvard U., 1971. Economist Fed. Res., Washington, 1970-74, sr. economist, 1975-77; advisor Bank Eng., London, 1974-75; sr. staff economist Council Econ. Advisers, Washington, 1977-79; v.p. DRI Ltd., London, 1979-83; rsch. dir. DRI/McGraw Hill, Lexington, Mass., 1983—. Contbr. numerous articles to profl. jours. Mem. Am. Econ. Assn., Am. Statis. Assn., Nat. Assn. Bus. Economists. Office: DRI/McGraw Hill 24 Hartwell Ave Lexington MA 02173-3103

WYSS, JOHN BENEDICT, lawyer; b. Evanston, Ill., Nov. 23, 1947; s. Walther Erwin and Caroline Nettie (Benedict) W.; m. Joanne P. Comstock, Oct. 22, 1994; children: John Christian, Kirsten Dunlop. BS in Physics summa cum laude, Stanford U., 1969; JD, Yale U., 1972. Bar: Calif. 1972, D.C. 1974, U.S. Supreme Ct. 1976. Trial atty. antitrust div. U.S. Dept. Justice, Washington, 1972-74; assoc. Kirkland & Ellis, Washington, 1974-78, ptnr., 1978-83; ptnr. Wiley, Rein & Fielding, Washington, 1983—. Mem. ABA, Phi Beta Kappa. Office: Wiley Rein & Fielding 1776 K St NW Washington DC 20006-2304

WYSS, NORMA ROSE TOPPING, counselor, supervisor, educator, writer; b. Wautoma, Wis., Jan. 7, 1919; d. Eugene Leonard Topping and Sylvia Maude (Attoe-Dumond) Topping Schubert; m. Werner Oscar Wyss; children: Werner Oscar II (dec.), Christine Camille (dec.), Melanie Rose (dec.), Sylvia Ann (dec.). Diploma, Waushara Normal, 1939; BA in Elem. Edn., Fla. State U., 1949, MS, 1960; postgrad., U. Md., 1964; PhD in Social Change and Counselling, Walden U., 1986; grad., Inst. Children's Lit., West Redding, Conn., 1993. Cert. employment counselor and supr. Tchr. Hoeft Sch., Berlin, Wis., 1939-40, Escambia County Sch. Bd., Pensacola, Fla., 1946-66; area I counselor supr. Fla. State Dept. of Labor, Pensacola and Tallahassee, 1966-79; freelance writer N.Y.C., 1986-90; field interviewer Arbitron, Laurel, Md., 1985-88; counselor Career Mgmt. Specialists, 1994-95. Author: Core Counseling: The Christian Faith and the Helping Relationship: A Paradigm of Social Change, 1990; children's short stories. Communicant mem., usher, greeter, cantor, pre-marriage counselor, good shepherd o-chmn. Luth. Ch. of the Resurrection, Pensacola, Fla. Mem. Am. Counseling Assn., Nat. Assn. Ret. Tchrs., Escambia Educators (life), Fla. Ret. Educators (life), DAR (treas. Pensacola chpt. 1988-90, Alpha Delta Kappa (1st pres. Fla. Alpha chpt. 1953), Kappa Delta Pi. Democrat. Avocations: conchology, reading, playing organ, water color, oil painting. Office: 4629 Petra Circle Pensacola FL 32526-1132

WYTON, ALEC, composer, organist; b. London, Aug. 3, 1921; came to U.S., 1950, naturalized, 1968; s. Gilbert and Jessie (Burrage) W.; m. Mary Thornton Broman; children: Vaughan, Richard, Patrick, Christopher. B.A., Oxford U., 1945, M.A., 1949; Mus.D. (hon.), Susquehanna (Pa.) U., 1970. Asst. organist Christ Church Cathedral, Oxford U., 1943-46; organist St. Mathews Ch., Northampton, Eng., 1946-50, Christ Church Cathedral, St. Louis, 1950-54, Cathedral St. John the Divine, N.Y.C., 1954-74, St. James's Ch., N.Y.C., 1974-87, St. Stephen's Ch., Ridgefield, Conn., 1987—; chair dept. music Manhattan Sch. Music, 1984-93; adj. prof. music Union Theol. Sem., N.Y.C., 1960-73; chmn. dept. ch. music Manhattan Sch. Music, 1984-93; coord. standing commn. on ch. music Episcopal Ch., 1974-85. Composer numerous pieces.; Contbr. articles to profl. jours. Served with Brit. Army, 1941-42. Fellow Royal Coll. Organists, Am. Guild Organists (hon. fellow, pres. 1964-69), Royal Canadian coll. Organists, Royal Acad. Music, Royal Sch. Ch. Music. Republican. Episcopalian. Home: 75 Danbury Rd Apt B-1 Ridgefield CT 06877-4042

WYVILL, J. CRAIG, research engineer, program director; b. Washington, May 8, 1951; s. Andrew J. and Rach. C. Wyvill; m. Peggy T. Wyvill. BSME, Ga. Tech, 1973; MBA, Ga. State U., 1981. Registered profl. engr., Ga., Va. Energy systems engr. Union Carbide Corp., Charleston, W.Va., 1973-75; project officer EPA, Washington, 1975-79; rsch. engr. Ga. Tech Rsch. Inst., Atlanta, 1979—, dir. agrl. tech. rsch. program, 1982—. Mem. ASME, Soc. Mfg. Engrs. (chpt. chmn. 1990, 93-94), Inst. Food Technologists, Ga. Agribus Coun. Office: Ga Inst Tech Ga Tech Rsch Inst Marc Bldg Rm 335 Atlanta GA 30332-0823

XENAKIS, STEPHEN NICHOLAS, psychiatrist, army officer; b. Washington, July 5, 1948; s. Stanley Steve and Mary Alexandria (Poulos) X.; m. Mary Elizabeth Boddie, Jan. 19, 1974; children: Nicholas John, Lea Elizabeth. AB, Princeton U., 1970; MD, U. Md., Balt., 1974; postgrad., Balt.-D.C. Psychoanalytic Inst., 1972-75, Armed Forces Staff Coll., 1984-85, U.S. Army War Coll., 1989-90. Diplomate Am. Bd. Psychiatry and Neurology. Commd. U.S. Army, 1972, advanced through grades to brig. gen., 1994; resident U. Md., Balt., 1974; intern Letterman Army Med. Ctr., Presidio of San Francisco, 1974-75, resident in psychiatry, 1975-78; fellow in child and adolescent psychiatry Letterman Army Med. Ctr., U. Calif., San Francisco, 1978-80; chief dept. psychiatry Darnell Army Community Hosp., Ft. Hood, Tex., 1980-82; div. surgeon 1st Cav. Div., Ft. Hood, Tex., 1982-84; chief child, adolescent, family psychiatry Eisenhower Army Med. Ctr., Ft. Gordon, Ga., 1985-86, dep. comdr. clin. svcs., dir. med. edn., 1986-89; comdr. Blanchfield Army Community Hosp., 1990-93; project mgr. AMEDD Vanguard, Fairfax, Va., 1993, TRICARE S.E., Augusta, Ga., 1994-95; cmdg. gen. Southeast Regional Command Eisenhower Army Med. Ctr., Ft. Gordon, Ga., 1995—; clin. prof. Uniformed Svcs. of Health Scis., Bethesda, Md., 1985—, Med. Coll. of Ga., Augusta, 1985—; lectr., author Porter Lecture, 1989. Contbr. articles to profl. jours. Bd. dirs. Augusta Regional AIDS Coun., 1987-89. Fellow Am. Acad. and Adolescent Psychiatry, Am. Psychiat. Assn., Am. Coll. Physician Execs., Assn. Mil. Surgeon U.S. Greek Orthodox. Office: Commander Eisenhower Army Med Ctr Fort Gordon GA 30905

XIDIS, KATHLEEN O'CONNOR, history educator; b. Fort Wayne, Ind., May 17, 1939; d. John Arthur and Harriet Sloan (Stimmel) O'C.; m. Robert D. Xidis, Dec. 28, 1972; 1 child, Elizabeth Claire. BA, St. Mary's Coll., Notre Dame, Ind., 1961; MA, Ind. U., 1964, PhD, 1970. Secondary tchr. Bishop Noll H.S., Hammond, Ind., 1961-63; legis. asst. U.S. Ho. of Reps., Washington, 1965-66; faculty Johnson County C.C., Overland Park, Kans., 1970—; reader for advanced placement tests in U.S. history Ednl. Testing Svc., Princeton, N.J., 1990, 91, 92, 95. Author: Hints and Help for History Students, 1994; co-author: Writing in History Class: A Guide for College Students, 1991. Mem. Am. Hist. Assn., Orgn. Am. Historians, Tomahawk Soc., Nat. Soc., Children of the Revolution (sr. pres. 1991—), Nat. Coun. for History Edn. (charter mem.), DAR (Quivira Crossing chpt.). Home: 10220 Long St Lenexa KS 66215-1826 Office: Johnson County CC 12345 College Blvd Overland Park KS 66210-1283

XIE, GANQUAN, mathematician, computational geophysical scientist, educator; b. Changsha, Hunan, People's Republic of China, July 2, 1943; s. Shuming Xie and Sumen Liu; m. Jianhua Li, Sept. 29, 1969; children: Feng, Lee. BCS, Hunan U., ChangSha City, 1966; PhD, SUNY, 1984; postdoctoral rsch., NYU, 1984-86. Asst. prof. Hunan Computer Research Inst., 1967-80; vice-chmn. Soc. Computational Math., Hunan, 1979-81; postdoctoral research Courant Inst. Math., N.Y.C., 1984—; prof., dir. Hunan Computer Rsch. Tech. Inst., 1987-88; staff scientist Lawrence Berkely lab., 1991—; chmn. Chinese Computational Math. Soc., 1986-88; vis. rscher SUNY, 1989; vis. prof. KSU, 1990. Mem. editorial com. Jour. Computational Math., Beijing, 1987-88; inventor in field; contbr. to profl. jours. Nat. Sci. Found. grantee, 1986-87, recipient Chinese Scientific prize, 1978. Mem. Soc. Indsl. Applied Math., SEG (Soc. of Exploration Geophysicists), AGU (Am. Geophys. Union). Avocations: applied math., numerical inversse tomography of the seismic exploration and electromagnetic exploration. Home: 1413 Glendale Ave Berkeley CA 94708-2027 Office: Lawrence Berkeley Lab Bldg 90 Earth Scis Divsn Berkeley CA 94720

XIONG, JEAN Z., artist, consultant; b. Beijing, China, Nov. 1, 1953; came to U.S., 1983.; d. Xian-Li and Zhang Yao (Zhu) Xiong; m. Charles C. Feng, Apr. 12, 1989. Grad., Shu Zhou (China) Inst., 1977; MFA, Acad Art Coll., San Francisco, 1986. Freelance artist/instr. Beijing, 1978-81; design artist First Impressions Advt., Reno, 1986; computer artist Visual Dynamics, San Francisco, 1988-89, Mediagenic, Menlo Park, 1989-91; leader artist Tecmagik Inc., Redwood City, Calif., 1992-94; computer artist Electronic Arts, San Mateo, Calif., 1995—; cons. entertainment software devel., Calif., 1991-92, 94-95; artist Electronic Arts, San Mateo, 1995—. One-woman shows San Francisco, 1984, 85, Monterey, Calif., 1984; exhbns. in Hong Kong, China, 1979, 80, 81. Recipient prize of Excellence Nat. Youth Artist Assn., 1980, Artist Assn., Hong Kong, 1981; scholar Acad. Art Coll., 1983-86. Mem. Mus. Modern Art, Tradtional Chinese Inst. (Beijing). Office: 1601 Maxine Ave San Mateo CA 94401-3451

XUE, LAN, engineering educator; b. Beijing, China, June 25, 1959; s. Futang and Jingmei (Yu) X.; m. Xiaoping Li, Apr. 3, 1985; 1 child, Dyland Mooching. BSME, Changchun Inst. Optics, 1982; MS in Tech. Systems Mgmt., SUNY, Stony Brook, 1986, MS in Policy and Mgmt., 1987; PhD in Engring. and Pub. Policy, Carnegie Mellon U., 1991. Instr., researcher Changchun (People's Republic of China) Inst. Optics, 1982-85; rsch. and teaching asst. SUNY, Stony Brook, 1985-87, Carnegie Mellon U., Pitts., 1987-91; asst. prof. George Washington U., Washington, 1991—; cons. Capital Iron & Steel Co., Beijing, 1993, Tangshan (China) Iron & Steel Co., 1993, The World Bank, 1994, NIST, 1994-95; lectr. in field. Contbr. articles to profl. jours. Dilthy fellow George Washington U., 1993; recipient Pride award George Washington U., 1995, Stephen Lee award Carnegie Mellon U., 1991, Short Term Enrichment Program award AAAS, 1989, Chinese Econ. Rsch. fellowship Washington Ctr. for China Studies, 1996. Mem. IEEE Soc. on Engring. Mgmt., Chinese Econ. Soc., Chinese Profl. Forum (pres. 1993-94), Tech. Transfer Soc. (bd. dirs. 1994—), Inst. Mgmt. Sci., Am. Soc. for Engring. Edn., Chinese Assn. for Sci. & Tech. (pres. Washington chpt. 1995—). Avocations: reading, table tennis, tai-chi, travel. Office: George Washington U Dept Engring Mgmt Washington DC 20052

YABLANS, FRANK, film company executive, motion picture producer; b. N.Y.C., Aug. 27, 1935; s. Morris and Annette Y.; m. Ruth Edelstein, Dec. 21; children: Robert, Sharon, Edward. Student, CCNY, U. Wis. Salesman, Warner Bros., 1956-58; br. mgr. Walt Disney Prodns., 1958-66; v.p. Filmways Prodns., 1966-69; successively v.p. sales, v.p. marketing, exec. v.p., pres. Paramount Pictures Corp., N.Y.C., 1969-75; pres. Frank Yablans Presentations, Inc., N.Y.C., 1975—; dir. Dirs. Co., Cinema Internat. Corp.; chmn. bd. MGM/UA Entertainment Co., 1983-85; founder Northstar Entertainment, 1985—; pres. Epic Records, 1989—; pres., chief exec. officer Nova Internat. Films, Inc. Films include Silver Streak, 1976, The Other Side of Midnight, 1977, The Fury, 1978, (also co-author screen play) North Dallas Forty, 1979, Mommie Dearest (producer, co-author screen play), Monsignore, 1982, The Star Chamber, 1983, Kid Co, 1983, Boy and Cell, 1989, Lisa, 1990. Chmn. entertainment div. Fedn. Jewish Philanthropies; bd. dirs. Boys' Clubs Am., Will Rogers Hosp.; trustee Am. Film Inst. Served with AUS, 1954-56. Decorated commendatore Repubblica Italiana. Mem. Variety Club Internat. (chmn.), Motion Picture Assn. (dir.). Club: Fairview Country.

YABLON, JEFFERY LEE, lawyer; b. Chgo., June 28, 1948; s. Robert R. and Faye I. (Goldberg) Y.; m. Jean C. LaPrade, Apr. 17, 1983. BA with honors, U. Wis., 1970; JD, Stanford U., 1973. Bar: Calif. 1974, D.C. 1975. Law clk. to Judge Cynthia Holcomb Hall, U.S. Tax Ct., Washington, 1973-75; Fulbright scholar U. Florence, Italy, 1975-76; assoc. Covington & Burling, Washington, 1976-80, Lee, Toomey & Kent, Washington, 1980-82; assoc. Shaw, Pittman, Potts & Trowbridge, Washington, 1982-84, ptnr., 1984—. Contbr. articles to legal jours. Bd. dirs. Am. Friends Hebrew U.,

Washington, 1991—. Mem. ABA, State Bar Calif., D.C. Bar. Jewish. Office: Shaw Pittman Potts & Trowbridge 2300 N St NW Washington DC 20037-1122

YABLON, LEONARD HAROLD, publishing company executive; b. N.Y.C., June 3, 1929; s. Philip A. and Sarah (Herman) Y.; m. Carol Sydney Torgan, June 8, 1950 (dec. Aug. 1995); children: Scott Richard, Bonnie Michele. BS, L.I. U., 1950; MBA, CCNY, 1969. CPA, N.Y. Acct., 1950-63; exec. v.p., dir. Forbes Inc., N.Y.C., 1963—; pres. Sangre de Cristo Ranches, Fiji Forbes; v.p. Forbes Investors Adv. Inst.; pres. Forbes Trinchera; sec.-treas. Forbes Found.; pres. Forbes Europe. Home: Pleasant Ridge Rd Harrison NY 10528 Office: 60 5th Ave New York NY 10011-8802

YACKEL, JAMES WILLIAM, mathematician, academic administrator; b. Sanborn, Minn., Mar. 6, 1936; s. Ewald W. and Marie E. (Heydlauff) Y.; m. Erna Beth Seecamp, Aug. 20, 1960; children: Jonathan, Juliet, Carolyn. BA, U. Minn., 1958, MA, 1960, PhD, 1964. Rsch. instr. dept. math. Dartmouth Coll., Hanover, N.H., 1964-66; asst. prof. dept. stats. Purdue U., West Lafayette, Ind., 1966-69, from assoc. prof. to prof., 1969-76, assoc. dean sci., 1976-87; vice chancellor acad. affairs Purdue U. Calumet, Hammond, Ind., 1987-90, chancellor, 1990—; rsch. mathematician Inst. Def. Analysis, Washington, 1969. Author: Applicable Finite Mathematics, 1974; editor Statistical Decision Theory, 1971; contbr. articles to profl. jours. Fellow AAAS; mem. Am. Math. Soc., Math. Assn. Am., Inst. Math. Stats. Research on Ramsey's theorem and finite graphs, stochastics processes, density estimation. Office: Purdue U Calumet Office of Chancellor Hammond IN 46323

YACKLE, ALBERT REUSTLE, aeronautical engineer; b. Willow Grove, Pa., May 13, 1922; s. Albert J. and Marion D. (Reustle) Y.; m. Ruth E. Everett, Sept. 18, 1948; children: Linda McCann, Tom, Brad. BS in Mech. Engring. Aeronautical Option, Pa. State U., 1943. Registered profl engr., Calif. Structures engr. Ea. Aircraft, 1944; structures engr. Kellett Aircraft Corp., 1946-48, chief structures engr., 1950-60; structures engr. Chase Aircraft, 1948-50; advanced design and program mgr. Lockheed Aircraft Corp., 1960-91; ret., 1991; cons. Huntington Med. Rsch. Inst., Pasadena, Calif., 1991-94. Contbr. tech. papers to profl. jours. Lt. (j.g.) USN, 1944-46. Fellow (assoc.) AIAA; mem. Am. Helicopter Soc. Achievements include 2 patents in rigid rotor helicopters. Home: 5105 Quakertown Ave Woodland Hills CA 91364-3538

YACKTMAN, DONALD ARTHUR, financial executive, investment counselor; b. Chgo., Sept. 12, 1941; s. Victor and Matilda (Chamberlain) Y.; m. Carolyn I. Zuppann, June 15, 1965; children:Donald, Stephen, Jennifer, Melissa, Brian, Robert, Michael. B.S., U. Utah, 1965; M.B.A., Harvard U., 1967. Chartered investment counselor. Trainee, Continental Bank, Chgo., 1967-68; assoc. Stein Roe & Farnham, Chgo., 1968-74, ptnr., 1974-82; pres. Selected Am. Shares; sr. v.p. Prescott Asset Mgmt., 1982-92; pres. Yacktman Asset Mgmt. Co. and Yacktman Fund, 1992—; mem. exec. bd. N.W. Suburban coun. Boy Scouts Am., 1984—; young men's pres. Ch. Jesus Christ Latter Day Saints. Mem. Fin. Analysts Soc. Office: Yacktman Asset Mgmt Co 303 W Madison St Ste 1925 Chicago IL 60606-3308

YACONETTI, DIANNE MARY, business executive; b. Chgo., Dec. 16, 1946; d. Anthony and Dora Marie (Mazzoni) Pontillo. Student, Mallinckrodt Coll., 1984-85; Advanced Mgmt. Program, Harvard U., 1990. Various positions Brunswick Corp., Skokie, Ill., 1964-80, mgr. legal support services, 1980-83, asst. sec., 1984-86, corp. sec., 1986-88, v.p. adminstrn., corp. sec., 1988—; bd. dirs. The Lambs, Libertyville, Ill. Mem. Am. Soc. Corp. Secs. Roman Catholic. Office: Brunswick Corp 1 N Field Ct Lake Forest IL 60045-4811

YACOUB, IGNATIUS I., university dean; b. Dwar Taha, Syria, Jan. 5, 1937; came to U.S. 1978; s. Immanuel and Martha (Kharma) Y.; m. Mary Haddad, Sept. 14, 1961; children—Hilda, Lena, Emile. A.B., Middle East Coll., Beirut, Lebanon, 1960; M.A., Pacific Union Coll., Angwin, Calif., 1964; Ph.D., Claremont Grad. Sch., Calif., 1976. Dean studies Middle East Coll., Beirut, Lebanon, 1967-73, 75-78; dir. dept. edn. Afro-Mideast div. Seventh-Day Adventist Ch., 1970-73, dir. dept. pub. affairs, 1975-78; prof., chmn. dept. bus. econs. Southwestern Union Coll., Keene, Tex., 1978-80; prof., chmn. dept. bus. and econs. Loma Linda U., Riverside, Calif., 1980-86, dean Sch. of Bus. and Mgmt., 1986-90; prof. mgmt., 1995—; dean Sch. Bus. and Mgmt., La Sierra U., Riverside, Calif., 1990-95; prof. adminstrn. and mgmt. Loma Linda (Calif.) U., 1995—; bd. dirs. Riverside Nat. Bank. Mem. Exec. 2000 Coun. Riverside Cmty. Hosp. Found., 1991-95. Recipient Gov.'s Appreciation award, Lions Club, Lions Club award, Beirut, cert. Appreciation Exec. 2000 Coun. Mem. Am. Mgmt. Assn., Acad. Mgmt., Greater Riverside C. of C. (Svc. award), Corona C. of C. Seventh-day Adventist. Home: 2722 Litchfield Dr Riverside CA 92503-6213

YACOVONE, ELLEN ELAINE, banker; b. Ithaca, N.Y., Aug. 4, 1951; d. Wilfred Elliott and Charlotte Frances (Fox) Drew; m. Richard Daniel Yacovone, June 2, 1979; stepchildren: Christopher Daniel, Kimberly Marie. Student Broome Community Coll., 1973-80; cert. Inst. Fin. Edn., Chgo., 1974. Sec. to exec. v.p. Ithaca Savs., N.Y., summer 1968; mortgage clk. Citizens Savs. Bank, 1968-69; with Lincoln Bank, Van Nuys, Calif., 1970-71; asst. bookkeeper Henry's Jewelers, Binghamton, N.Y., 1971-74; teller, br. supt., br. mgr. First Fed. Savs., Binghamton, N.Y., 1974-82, v.p., cen. regional sales mgr., 1982-86, dist. sales mgr., 1986-88; br. mgr. Great Western Bank, Pensacola, Fla., 1988-89, v.p., regional mgr. San Diego east region, 1989-95; br. v.p. Gateway Ctr., San Diego, 1995—, North Park, 1996—; owner, operator EYE Shirts, 1995—. Mem. Gov.'s Commn. on Domestic Violence, Albany, N.Y., 1983-87; bd. dirs. S.O.S. Shelter, Inc., Endicott, N.Y., 1979-88, pres., 1982-83, treas., 1985-86; vol. United Way of Broome County, Binghamton, 1976-88, Sta. WSKG Pub. TV, Conklin, N.Y., 1974-88; mem. Found. State U. Ctr. at Binghamton; bd. dirs. Interfaith Shelter Network, San Diego, 1992—, Schs. of Success and the San Diego Innovative Presch. Project, 1995—, San Diego Urban League, 1995—, Black Econ. Task Force, 1995—. Named Woman of Achievement, Broome County Status of Women Coun., 1981. Mem. Triple Cities Bus. and Profl. Women (pres. 1979-81, young careerist award 1977), Sales and Mktg. Execs., Broome County C. of C., Broome County Bankers Assn. (bd. dirs. 1979-88, pres. 1983-84), Inst. Fin. Edn. (bd. dirs. 1976-88, pres. 1984-85, winner N.Y. State speech contest 1984), The Catfish Club. Republican. Methodist. Avocations: exercise, hand painting wearables and wood, wood working, gardening, needlecrafts. Home: 602 Myra Ave Chula Vista CA 91910-6230 Office: Great Western Bank 3921 30th St San Diego CA 92104

YACOWITZ, HAROLD, biochemist, nutritionist; b. N.Y.C., Feb. 17, 1922; s. Louis and Clara (Kurtzberg) Y.; m. Ann Ruth Barnett, Dec. 31, 1941; children: Caryn R., Richard S., Suzanne Yacowitz Dragan. BS, Cornell U., 1947, M in Nutritional Sci., 1948, PhD, 1950. Rsch. biochemist Parke-Davis Inc., Detroit, 1950-51; assoc. prof. Ohio State U., Columbus, 1951-55; head nutrition rsch. dept. Squibb Inst. for Med. Rsch., New Brunswick, N.J., 1955-59; dir. rsch. Nopco Chem. Co. Inc., Harrison, N.J., 1959-61, Amburgo Co. Inc., Phila., 1961-80; rsch. assoc. Fairleigh Dickinson U., Madison, N.J., 1961-80; pres., dir. rsch. Dr. H. Yacowitz & Co., Piscataway, N.J., 1961—, Animal Identification & Marking Systems Inc., Piscataway, 1982—; pres. Peninsula Investment & Devel. Inc., Cambridge, Md., 1961—; pres., bd. dirs. rsch. Drug Delivery Devices Inc., Piscataway, 1991—. Contbr. articles to profl. jours.; patentee in field. Leader Boy Scouts Am., Ithaca, N.Y., 1946-50, Piscataway, 1955-59. With U.S. Army, 1943-46, ETO, PTO. Grange League Fedn. fellow Cornell U., 1947-48, Robert Gould rsch. fellow, Cornell U., 1949-50, Coun. on Arteriosclerosis fellow Am. Heart Assn., 1970. Fellow N.Y. Acad. Scis. (chmn. sect. biology and medicine 1972-76); mem. Am. Chem. Soc., Am. Inst. Nutrition, Am. Assn. Lab. Animal Scientists, Exptl. Investors Club (New Brunswick, pres. 1955-59). Jewish. Avocations: gardening, sailing, fishing, swimming. Office: Animal Ident Marking Syst Inc 221 2nd Ave Piscataway NJ 08854-3519

YADEKA, THEOPHILUS ADENIYI, administrator; b. Ibadan, Nigeria, Apr. 16, 1939; came to U.S., 1971; s. Joshua A. and Alice (Opawole) Y.; m. Julianah M., Aug. 23, 1965; children: Olatunde, Mofoluke, Ayoola, Mobolaji, Adedoja. Diploma, S.D.A. Nursing Sch., 1965, SUNY, 1972; BS in Healthcare Adminstrn., St. Francis Coll., 1976; MS in Healthcare & Nursing Adminstrn., L.I. U., 1977. Prin. hosp. adminstr. Ministry Health/State Hosp. Mgmt. Bd., Ibadan, Nigeria, 1978-85; asst. chief hosp. adminstr. State Hosps. Mgmt. Bd., Ibadan, Nigeria, 1985-89; supr. nursing Lincoln Hosp., Bronx, N.Y., 1977-78, asst. DON, 1989-90; asst. DON Bronx Lebanon Hosp. Ctr., 1990—; charge and staff nurse Met. City Hosp., N.Y.C., 1965-77, St. Barnabas Hosps., N.Y.C., 1965-77. Mem. Am. Coll. Hosp. Adminstrs., Am. Coll. Nursing Home Adminstrs., Inst. Health Svc. Adminstrs. Nigeria. Home: 2420 Morris Ave Apt 4J Bronx NY 10468-6629 Office: Bronx Lebanon Hosp Ctr Bronx NY 10457

YADEN, SENKA LONG, biology educator; b. Apr. 21, 1935; s. Takojungba and (Medemmakla) Y.; m. Theola Thedford, Dec. 4, 1982. BS, Wilson Coll., Bombay, 1956; MS, U. Bombay, 1958; PhD, U. Minn., 1965. Teaching asst. biology U. Minn., Mpls., 1961-65; assoc. prof. biology Jarvis Christian Coll., Hawkins, Tex., 1967-75, chair sci. div., 1976-78, prof. biology, 1979-81; sr. sci. assoc. dept. pharmacology Tex. Coll. Osteo. Medicine, Ft. Worth, 1981-84; assoc. prof. sci. Parker Coll., Irving, Tex., 1985-86; assoc. prof. biology Talladega (Ala.) Coll., 1987-88; prof. biology, chair dept. biology Wiley Coll., Marshall, Tex., 1988-91; dir. health careers opportunity program health human svcs., 1989-92; prof. biology Tex. Coll., Tyler, 1993—. Pres. Naga-Am. Found., 1989—. Home: 3712 Lexington Dr Tyler TX 75701-6717 Office: Tex Coll 2404 N Grand Ave Tyler TX 75702-1962

YAFFE, BARBARA MARLENE, journalist; b. Montreal, Que., Can., Mar. 4, 1953; d. Allan and Ann (Freedman) Y.; m. Wilson E. Russell, Aug. 30, 1985. Student, McGill U., 1970-73; BA, U. Toronto, 1974; B in Journalism, Carleton U., 1974. Reporter Montreal Gazette, 1975-76, Toronto Globe and Mail, 1976-79; reporter, columnist Toronto Globe and Mail, Halifax, N.S., 1979-81; TV bur. chief CBC-TV, St. Johns, Nfld., 1981-84, Edmonton, Alta., 1983; reporter Toronto Globe and Mail, St. John's, 1984-86; editor Sunday Express, St. John's, 1987-88; editor Vancouver Sun, 1988-93, columnist, 1993—. Recipient Gov. Gen.'s award Roland Michener Found., 1977. Jewish. Office: c/o Vancouver Sun, 2250 Granville St, Vancouver, BC Canada V6H 3G2

YAFFE, DAVID PHILIP, lawyer; b. Waukegan, Ill., Jan. 31, 1952; s. Robert M. Yaffe and Ruth David Rickard; m. Deborah M.P. Yaffe, 1976; children: Andrea, Alicia. BA, Johns Hopkins U., 1974; JD with honors, George Washington U., Washington, 1977. Bar: Va. 1977, D.C. 1978, U.S. Dist. Ct. (4th and 9th cir.). Assoc. Duncan & Allen, Washington, 1977—, mng. ptnr., 1988-94. Contbr. articles to profl. jours. Nat. chair Second Decade Soc., Johns Hopkins U., Balt., 1993-94; co-pres. Agudus Achim Congregation, Alexandria, Va., 1993-95. Mem. ABA (SONREEL, vice chmn. electric power com. 1993—), Fed. Energy Bar Assn., Univ. Club. Avocation: golf. Home: 4528 Sleaford Rd Annandale VA 22003

YAFFE, JAMES, author; b. Chgo., Mar. 31, 1927; s. Samuel and Florence (Scheinman) Y.; m. Elaine Gordon, Mar. 1, 1964; children: Deborah Ann, Rebecca Elizabeth, Gideon Daniel. Grad., Fieldston Sch., 1944; B.A. summa cum laude, Yale U., 1948. Prof. Colo. Coll., Colo. Springs, 1968—; dir. gen. studies Colo. Coll., 1981—. Author: Poor Cousin Evelyn, 1951, The Good-for-Nothing, 1953, What's the Big Hurry?, 1954, Nothing But the Night, 1959, Mister Margolies, 1962, Nobody Does You Any Favors, 1966, The American Jews, 1968, The Voyage of the Franz Joseph, 1970, So Sue Me!, 1972, Saul and Morris, Worlds Apart, 1982, A Nice Murder for Mom, 1988, Mom Meets Her Maker, 1990, Mom Doth Murder Sleep, 1991, Mom Among the Liars, 1992; play The Deadly Game, 1960, (with Jerome Weidman) Ivory Tower, 1967, Cliffhanger, 1985; also TV plays, stories, essays, revs. Served with USNR, 1945-46. Recipient Nat. Arts Found award, 1968. Mem. P.E.N., Authors League, Writers Guild of Am., Dramatists Guild, A.A.U.P., Mystery Writers of Am., Phi Beta Kappa. Jewish. Club: Elizabethan (Yale). Avocations: music, bridge, movies. Address: 1215 N Cascade Ave Colorado Springs CO 80903-2303 Office: Colo Coll Off Dir Gen Studies Colorado Springs CO 80903

YAFFE, SUMNER JASON, pediatrician, research center administrator, educator; b. Boston, May 9, 1923; s. Henry H. and Ida E. (Fisher) Y.; m. Anita Yaffe; children: Steven, Kris, Jason, Noah, Ian, Zachary. A.B., Harvard U., 1945, M.A., 1950; M.D., U. Vt., 1954. Diplomate Am. Bd. Pediatrics. Intern Children's Hosp., Boston, 1954-55, resident, 1955-56; resident in pediatrics St. Mary's Hosp., London, 1956-57; instr. pediatrics Stanford U., Palo Alto, Calif., 1959-60, asst. prof., 1960-63; assoc. prof. pediatrics SUNY-Buffalo, 1963-66, prof., 1966-75, adj. prof. biochem. pharmacology, 1968-75, acting chmn. dept. pediatrics, 1974-75; prof. pediatrics and pharmacology U. Pa., Phila., 1975-81; dir. Ctr. for Research for Mothers and Children, NIH, Bethesda, Md., 1981—; clin. prof. pediatrics Georgetown U. Med. Ctr., 1986, Johns Hopkins Hosp., 1986; attending physician Palo Alto-Stanford Hosp., 1959-63; attending physician Children's Hosp., Buffalo, 1963-75, Phila., 1975-81; vis. prof. pharmacology Karolinska Inst., Stockholm, 1969-70; dir. Pediatric Renal Clinic, Stanford Med. Ctr., 1960-63; dir. newborn nursery service Palo Alto-Stanford Hosp., 1960-63, program dir. Clin. Research Ctr. for Premature Infants, 1962-63; dir. Clin. Research Ctr. for Children Children's Hosp., Buffalo, 1963-70, dir. Poison Control Ctr., 1967-75, dir. div. clin. pharmacology, Phila., 1975-81; program cons. Nat. Inst. Child Health and Human Devel., NIH, 1963-71, mem. tng. grant com., 1963-65, mem. reproductive biology com., 1965-67; mem. adv. panel on maternal and child health WHO, Geneva, 1970—; liaison rep. drug research bd. NRC, 1971-75, com. on drug dependence, 1972-75, mem. com. on problems of drug safety, 1972-75; mem. adv. panel in pediatrics U.S. Pharmacopeia, 1970—, in toxicology, 1974-75; cons. Am. Found. for Maternal and Child Health, Inc., 1973—; pres. Maternal and Child Health Research Found., Children's Hosp., 1974—; Wall Meml. lectr. Children's Hosp., Washington, 1968—; Dr. W.E. Upjohn lectr. Can. Med. Assn., 1974; Louisville pediatric lectr. Sch. Medicine U. Louisville, 1974; William N. Creasy vis. prof. clin. pharmacology SUNY, 1976; advisor Internat. Childbirth Assn. Greater Phila., 1979-83; guest lectr. Dept. Pediatrics Georgetown U. Hosp., Washington, 1988—; lectr. in pediatrics Johns Hopkins Sch. Medicine, Balt., 1988—. Author: Clinics in Perinatology, 1974, Drug Assessment: Criteria and Methods, 1979, Pediatric Pharmacology, 1980, 2d edit. 1992; co-author: (with R. Galinsky) Clinical Therapeutics, 1978; editor: (with R. H. Schwartz) Drug and Chemical Risks to the Fetus and Newborn, 1980, (with G.G. Briggs, T.W. Bodendorfer, R.K. Freeman) Drugs in Pregnancy and Lactation, A Reference Guide to Fetal and Neonatal Risk, 1983, 2d edit., 1986, 4th edit., 1994, (J.V. Aranda) Pediatric Phyarmacology, 2nd edit., 1993; mem. editorial bd. Pediatric Alert, 1977—, Pharmacology, 1977—, Devel. Pharmacology and Therapeutics, 1979—; mem. editorial adv. bd. Drug Therapy, 1979—; cons. editor Clin. Pharmacokinetics, 1977; co-editor Developmental Pharmacology, 1979-94; contbr. chpts. to profl. books., articles to profl. jours. Served with U.S. Army, 1943-44. Recipient Lederle Med. Faculty award Lederle Found., 1962; Fulbright scholar, 1956-57. Fellow Acad. Pharm. Scis.; mem. AMA (com. on drugs 1963-68), Am. Acad. Pediatrics (chmn. com. on drugs 1967-76), AAUP, Am. Coll. Clin. Pharmacology and Chemotherapy, Am. Fedn. for Clin. Rsch., Am. Pediatric Soc., Am. Pharmaceutics Assn., Am. Pub . Health Assn., Am. Soc. for Clin. Pharmacology and Therapeutics (chmn. sect. on pediatric pharmacology 1977-83), Am. Soc. Pharmacology and Exptl. Therapeutics, Fedn. Am. Socs. for Exptl. Biology, Perinatal Rsch. Soc., Soc. for Pediatric Research, Sigma Xi, Alpha Omega Alpha. Home: 6417 Tilden Ln Rockville MD 20852-3742 Office: Nat Inst of Child Health & Human Devel 6100 Executive Blvd Bethesda MD 20892-7510

YAGER, HUNTER, advertising executive; b. Bklyn., Sept. 29, 1929; s. Jules and Lucille (Kornblum) Y.; m. Gertrude Kathryn Johnson, Feb. 17, 1960; children—Leslie Jeanne, Andrew Hunter, Phoebe Hildreth. BA, N.Y. U., 1950; MBA, Harvard U., 1955. Copywriter Donahue & Coe, Inc., N.Y.C., 1951-53; account exec. Foote, Cone & Belding, N.Y.C., 1955-58; account exec., account supr., v.p., mgmt. supr., exec. v.p. mgmt. com. Grey Advt., Inc., N.Y.C., 1958-85; dir. Grey Advt., Ltd., Can., 1970-79; mktg. and advt. cons., 1985-91, retired, 1992; dir. Vicorp Restaurants, Inc.; instr. mktg. NYU, 1961-62. Dir., sec., mem. exec. com., devel. com., mktg. com. Chamber Music Soc. of Lincoln Ctr., 1986-90; dir., mktg. com. Manhattan Theatre Club, 1987-92; bd. dirs., pres. West Lyon Farm Condominium Assn., Greenwich, Conn., 1985-90; v.p. Powder Mill Owners Assn., Londonberry, Vt.; bd. dirs. Harvard Bus. Sch. Club, Fairfield County, 1986-91; trustee exec. bd. Manchester Music Festival, 1993-95. Mem. Camp Rising Sun Alumni Assn., Harvard Bus. Sch. Alumni Assn. (bd. dirs. 1993—), Harvard Club. Home: West Fields RR 2 Box 3190 Manchester VT 05255

YAGER, JOHN WARREN, retired banker, lawyer; b. Toledo, Sept. 16, 1920; s. Joseph A. and Edna Gertrude (Pratt) Y.; m. Dorothy W. Merki, July 25, 1942; children: Julie M., John M. AB, U. Mich., 1942, JD, 1948. Bar: Ohio 1948. Pvt. practice law Toledo, 1948-64; trust officer Toledo Trust Co., 1964-69; v.p., trust officer Fifth Third Bank, 1969-91; sec. First Ohio Bancshares, Inc., 1980-85; ret. Pres. Toledo Met. Park Dist., 1971-85, Neighborhood Health Assn., 1974-75, councilman, Toledo, 1955-57, 60-61, mayor, 1958-59; bd. dirs. Toledo-Lucas County Library, 1968-70, Riverside Hosp., Downtown Toledo Assn.; past pres. Toledo Legal Aid Soc., Toledo Council Chs., Toledo Mcpl. League, Econ. Opportunity Planning Assn., Toledo, Com. on Relations with Toledo, Spain. Maj. USMC, 1942-46, 50-52. Decorated Bronze Star; named one of 10 Outstanding Young Men in Toledo, 1952, 54, 55. Mem. Toledo Bar Assn., Delta Tau Delta. Home: 29301 Bates Rd Perrysburg OH 43551-3808

YAGER, JOSEPH ARTHUR, JR., economist; b. Owensville, Ind., Apr. 14, 1916; s. Joseph Arthur and Edna (Pratt) Y.; m. Virginia Estella Beroset, Sept. 2, 1938; children: Thomas, Martha. A.B., U. Mich., 1937, J.D., 1939, M.A., 1940; grad., Nat. War Coll., 1955. Economist OPA, 1942-44; economist State Dept., 1946-47, chief China research br., 1949-50; chief div. research for State Dept., Far East, 1952-57; attaché U.S. consulate gen., Canton, China, 1947-48; consul U.S. consulate gen., Hong Kong, 1950-51; econ. counselor Taipei, 1957-59; dep. chief of mission, 1959-61; dir. Office Chinese Affairs, 1961, Office East Asian Affairs, 1961-63; mem. Policy Planning Council, 1963-66, vice chmn., 1966-68; dep. dir. internat. and social studies div. Inst. Def. Analyses, 1968-72; sr. fellow Brookings Instn., 1972-83, guest scholar, 1983-86; resident cons. Sci. Applications Internat. Corp., 1986-89, sr. fellow, 1989—. Author: Transforming Agriculture in Taiwan, 1988, Prospects for Nuclear Weapons Proliferation in a Changing Europe, 1992; co-author: Energy and U.S. Foreign Policy, 1974, New Means of Financing International Needs, 1978, Military Equation in Northeast Asia, 1979, Nonproliferation and U.S. Foreign Policy, 1980, International Cooperation in Nuclear Energy, 1981, Energy Balance in Northeast Asia, 1984, Energy Policy Experience of Asia Countries, 1987. Served in AUS, 1944-45. Mem. Phi Delta Phi, Delta Tau Delta. Home: 10006 Woodhill Rd Bethesda MD 20817-1218 Office: Sci Applications Internat Corp 1710 Goodridge Dr Mc Lean VA 22102-3701

YAGER, VINCENT COOK, banker; b. Chgo., June 15, 1928; s. James Vincent and Juanita (Cook) Y.; m. Dorothy Marie Gallagher, Sept. 28, 1957; children: Susan Marie, Sheila Ann. B.A., Grinnell Coll., 1951. Asst. cashier Chgo. Nat. Bank, 1954-60, Harris Trust & Savs. Bank, Chgo., 1960-63; v.p. comml. loan dept. Madison Bank & Trust, Chgo., 1963-68; v.p. fin. Cor-Plex Internat. Corp., Chgo., 1968-70; pres., chief exec. officer, dir. First Nat. Bank of Blue Island, Ill., 1970-89; pres., CEO, dir. Great Lakes Fin. Resources, Inc., Matteson, Ill., 1982—; vice-chmn., dir. Bank of Matteson, Ill., 1992—; chmn. GL Mortgage Corp., Wheeling, Ill. Mem. adv. bd. St. Francis Hosp., Blue Island, others. With U.S. Army, 1951-53, ETO. Mem. Robert Morris Assocs. (pres. chpt. 1981-82), Bankers Club of Chgo. Mem. United Ch. of christ. Clubs: Midlothian Country; Econ. of Chgo. Lodge: Rotary. Home: 1032 S Rand Rd Villa Park IL 60181-3145 Office: Gt Lakes Fin Resources Inc 4600 Lincoln Hwy Matteson IL 60443-2315

YAGER, WALTER STUART, aerospace engineer; b. Calmar, Iowa, Mar. 31, 1936; s. Walter Douglas and Eldie Charolette (Grundland) Y.; m. Elizabeth Lee Sunbarger, Aug. 31, 1958; children: Ellen Denise Yager Brandon, Douglas Lee. BS in Aero. Engring., U. Okla., 1959; MS in Aerospace Mech. Engring., Air Force Inst. Tech., 1967. Engr. Northrup Aircraft, Hawthorne, Calif., 1959; commd. 2d lt. USAF, 1959, advanced through grades to col., 1980, ret., 1985; engr., dir. Martin Marietta, Denver, 1985—; mem. Titan II Mishap Investigation, Little Rock, 1978; pres. Def. Meteorol. Satellite Mishap Investigation, L.A., 1980. Active Civilian/Mil. Coun., Cape Canaveral, Fla., 1978-81. Decorated Legion of Merit. Mem. AIAA (sr.), Air Force Assn. Avocations: golf, bridge. Home: 1071 E Phipps Pl Highlands Ranch CO 80126

YAGIELA, JOHN ALLEN, dental educator; b. Washington, July 23, 1947; s. Stanley and Kathryn Marie (Gilkeson) Y.; m. Dolores Jean Mitchell, Mar. 21, 1970; children: Gregory, Leanne. Student, U. Calif., Riverside, 1965-67; DDS, UCLA, 1971, postgrad., 1982-83; PhD in Pharmacology, U. Utah, 1975. Diplomate Am. Dental Bd. Anesthesiology. Asst. prof. dentistry Emory U., Atlanta, 1975-78, assoc. prof., 1978-82; assoc. prof. UCLA, 1982-83, prof., 1983—, assoc. dean acad. and adminstrv. affairs, 1984-89; cons. Astra Pharm. Products Inc., Worcester, Mass., 1982—, VA Wadsworth divsn., L.A., 1983-92, Gen. Med. Co., L.A., 1988—, ADA, Chgo., 1991—. Co-author: Regional Anesthesia of the Oral Cavity, 1981, Local Anesthesia of the Oral Cavity, 1995; co-editor: Pharmacology and Therapeutics for Dentistry, 3d edit., 1989; editor Anesthesia Progress, 1990-95, The Pulse, 1996—; contbr. articles on dental therapeutics to profl. jours. Recipient Award of Achievement Am. Coll. Dentists, 1971; Regents scholar UCLA, 1968-71; Alpha Omega award, 1971. Fellow Am. Dental Soc. Anesthesiology; mem. ADA, AASS, Internat. Assn. Dental Rsch. (sec.-treas. PTTG group 1984-88, pres.-elect 1989-90, pres. 1990-91), Am. Assn. Dental Schs. (chmn. pharmacology therapeutics sect. 1983), Am. Soc. Dentist Anesthesiolgists (v.p. 1995-96), Omicron Kappa Upsilon. Methodist. Avocations: photography, hiking. Home: 23918 Stagg St West Hills CA 91304 Office: UCLA Sch Dentistry Ctr for Health Scis Los Angeles CA 90095

YAGODA, HARRY NATHAN, system engineering executive; b. Bklyn., May 19, 1936; s. Hyman and Sylvia (Yoskowitz) Y.; m. Myrna Rita Hirschel; children: Michelle Robin, Randi Noelle. BSEE, CUNY, 1958; MSEE, NYU, 1960; PhDEE, Poly. U. N.Y., 1963. Registered profl. engr. 19 states including N.Y., N.J., Calif. Mem. tech. staff AT&T Bell Labs., Whippany, N.J., 1958-62; assoc. prof. engring. Poly. U. N.Y., Bklyn., 1962-70; pres. Computran Systems Corp., Hackensack, N.J., 1970—. Named Disting. Alumnus, Poly. U. N.Y., 1980. Fellow Inst. Transp. Engring. (bd. dirs. 1982-84). Home: 75 Anderson Dr Wayne NJ 07470-2650 Office: Computran Systems Corp 100 1st St Hackensack NJ 07601-2124

YAGYU, KUNIYOSHI, surgeon; b. Asa, Japan, Nov. 3, 1950; s. Yukihiko and Kazuko (Murata) Y.; m. Noriko Ohara, Dec. 8, 1985; children: Mitsuyoshi, Eriko. MD, U. Tokyo, 1976, DMS, 1986. Intern U. Tokyo Hosp., 1976-77, sr. resident, 1981-82, assoc., 1982-86, instr., 1989-93, asst. prof., 1993—; staff dept. surgery Tokyo Welfare Pension Hosp., 1977-79, Japanese Red Cross Soc. Med. Ctr., Tokyo, 1979-81; staff surgeon Kanagawa Children Med. Ctr., Yokohama, Japan, 1986-87; scholar Alexander von Humboldt Found. Hannover (Germany) Med. Sch., 1987-89. Co-author: Surgical Diagnosis, 1988, Current Therapy in Cardiovascular Disease, 1996. Recipient Tech. award Nikkei BP Inc., 1996; grantee-in-aid for sci. rsch. Ministry of Edn., Sci. and Culture, Japan, 1990, 92. Mem. N.Y. Acad. Sci., AAAS, Transplantation Soc., Am. Heart Assn., Internat. Soc. for Artificial Organs, Internat. Soc. for Heart and Lung Transplantation. Avocations: jogging, skiing, painting, sculpture. Home: 2-21-3 Ekoda Aoba-ku, Yokohama 225, Japan Office: U Tokyo Cardiothoracic Surg, 7-3-1 Hongo Bunkyo-ku, Tokyo 113, Japan

YAHR, MELVIN DAVID, physician; b. N.Y.C., Nov. 18, 1917; s. Isaac and Sarah (Reigelhaupt) Y.; m. Felice Turtz, May 9, 1948; children—Carol, Nina, Laura, Barbara Anne. A.B., N.Y. U., 1939, M.D., 1943. Diplomate: Am. Bd. Psychiatry and Neurology (pres.). Intern Lenox Hill Hosp., N.Y.C., 1943-44; resident Lenox Hill Hosp., also Montefiore Hosp., Bronx, N.Y., 1947-48; staff Columbia, 1948-73, asso. prof. clin. neurology, 1957-62, prof. neurology, 1962-70, H.H. Merritt prof. neurology, 1970-73, asst. dean grad. medicine, 1959-67, assoc. dean, 1967-73; asst. neurologist N.Y. Neurol. Inst., 1948-53, assoc. attending neurologist, 1953-60, attending neurologist, 1960-73; Goldschmidt prof. neurology, chmn. dept. neurology Mt. Sinai Med. Center, 1973-92; Aidekman Family Prof. Neurological Rsch., 1992—; exec. dir. Parkinson's Disease Found., 1957-73; panel neurologist N.Y.C. Bd. Edn., 1958-59; mem. com. evalutation drugs in neurology NIH, 1959-60, panel mem. neurol. study sect., 1959-80; mem. com. revisions U.S. Pharmacopea. Assoc. editor: Internat. Jour. Neurology; editor-in-chief Jour. Neural Transmission, 1989—; Archives Neurology, 1964-89. Fellow Am. Acad. Neurology, N.Y. Acad. Medicine, Harvey Soc.; mem. A.M.A. (chmn.

com. neurol. disorders in industry), Am. Neurol. Assn. (sec.-treas. 1959-68, pres. 1969), Assn. Research Nervous and Mental Disease, N.Y. State Neurol. Soc., New York County Med. Soc., Am. Epilepsy Soc., Eastern Assn. Electroencephalographers. Office: Mt Sinai School of Med City U Clin Ctr Rsch Parkinson's 5 E 98th St Box 1139 New York NY 10029-6504

YAKAN, MOHAMAD ZUHDI, political science educator; b. Tripoli, Lebanon, Aug. 28, 1938; came to U.S., 1988; s. Zuhdi Rasheed and Habibah (Shaaban) Y.; m. Sibylle Nickle, Apr. 8, 1988. HS, Internat. Coll., Beirut, Lebanon, 1956; BA, Am. U. Beirut, 1959; MA, A.U.B., Beirut, 1961; PhD, U. Mich., 1965. Asst./acting mgr. Prodeco/Pub. Rels.-Mktg., Beirut, 1965-71; asst. prof. Beirut U. Coll., 1965-71; lectr. law faculty Lebanese U., Beirut, 1966-71; asst. prof., dir. devel. and rel. Beirut U. Coll., 1971-88; lectr. Wayne State U., Detroit, 1988-89, Henry Ford Coll., Dearborn, Mich., 1988-89; v.p., gen. mgr. internat. I.A.S. Group, San Diego, 1989-90; lectr. U. San Diego, 1990-91; adj. prof. U.S. Internat. U., San Diego, 1991-93, assoc. prof., 1994—. Author: Lebanon and Challenges of Future, 1978, Political Authority in Lebanon, 1979, Hijrah Calendar, 1981; editor: Lebanese Constitutional Issues, 1975, Roman Law and Muslin Shari'a, 1975, Diwan Al-Mu'atamid Bin Abbad, 1975, Diwan Al-Shafi'e, 1981, Diwan Al-Baghdadi, 1983, Constitutional Law and Political Systems, 1982; co-editor: documents on Lebanon's Political System, 1975; author more than 100 articles and papers. Founding mem. Salwa Nassar Found., Beirut, 1970, Lebanese Polit. Sci. Assn., Beirut, 1959, Lebanese Assn. for Human Rights, Beirut, 1985, Internat. Coun. for Muslim-Christian Dialogue, Beirut, 1985. Recipient H.B. Earhart Found. award, 1965. Mem. Am. Polit. Sci. Assn., Middle East Inst. (assoc. Middle East rsch. and info. project), Acad. Polit. Sci., Western Polit. Sci. Assn., Acad. Polit. and Social Sci., Middle East Studies Assn., Fgn. Policy Assn., UN Assn., Internat. Studies Assn., World Affairs Coun. San Diego. Avocations: research, reading. Home: 9051 Westmore Rd San Diego CA 92126 Office: USIU Dept Liberal & Interdisciplinary Studies 10455 Pomerado Rd San Diego CA 92131-1717

YALCINTAS, M. GÜVEN, medical physicist; b. Milas, Turkey, Apr. 11, 1946; came to U.S., 1968; s. Kazim and Samiye Yalcintas; 1 child, Banu. BS in Physics, Ankara U., 1967; MS in Health Physics, U. Rochester, 1971, PhD in Med. Physics, 1974. Dir. EGE MEd. Sch., Izmir, Turkey, 1975-76, EMI Med., Chgo., 1976-77; group leader Oak Ridge (Tenn.) Nat. Lab., 1977-88; dir. tech. transfer Lockheed Martin, Oak Ridge, 1988-93, dir. tech. transfer of environ. techs. HAZWRAP, 1993—; adj. prof. radiation biology Tenn. Tech U.; adj. prof. environ. scis. Tusculcum Coll., adv. bd. environ. sci. program. Contbr. articles to profl. jours. Lt. Turkish Army, 1975-76. Mem. Am. Nuclear Soc. chmn. 1986—, newsletter editor), East Tenn. Health Physics Assn., Health Physical Soc. Avocations: soccer, chess, writing, boating, skiing. Home: 208 Toqua Greens Ln Loudon TN 37774 Office: Martin Marietta Box 2009 MS 7173 Oak Ridge TN 37831

YALDEN, MAXWELL FREEMAN, Canadian diplomat; b. Toronto, Ont., Can., Apr. 12, 1930; s. Frederick and Marie (Smith) Y.; m. Janice Shaw, Jan. 28, 1952; children: Robert, Cicely (dec.). B.A., Victoria Coll., U. Toronto, 1952; M.A., U. Mich., 1954, Ph.D., 1956; D.U. (hon.), U. Ottawa, 1982. With Can. Dept. External Affairs, 1956-69, asst. undersec. state, 1969-73, dep. minister communications, 1973-77, commr. ofcl. langs., 1977-84; Can. amb. to Belgium and Luxembourg, 1984-87; chief Can. Human Rights Comms., Ottawa, 1987—. Office: Canadian Human Rights Commission, 320 Queen St #1300, Ottawa, ON Canada K1A 1E1

YALE, JEFFREY FRANKLIN, podiatrist; b. Derby, Conn., Jan. 18, 1943; s. Irving and Bernice (Blume) Y.; m. Lenore Bernsley, Apr. 23, 1987; children: Brian Joseph, Andrew Malcolm, Owen Slade. Student, U. Fla., 1960-62; D of Podiatric Medicine, Ill. Coll. Podiatric Medicine, 1966. Diplomate Am. Bd. Podiatric Surgery, Am. Bd. Podiatric Orthopedics, Am. Bd. Med. Quality Assurance and Utilization Rev. Surg. resident Highland Gen. Hosp., Oakland, Calif., 1966-67; capt. U.S. Army Med. Svc., Fort Ord, Calif., 1967-71; instr. masters level Quinnipiac Coll., Hamden, Conn., 1981; cons. surgeon VA Med. Ctr., West Haven, Conn., 1982—; chmn. podiatric surgery Griffin Hosp., Derby, Conn., 1974—; assoc. clin. prof. U. Osteo. Health Scis., Des Moines, 1982—; chmn. Podiatric Medicine Test Com. Nat. Bd. Podiatric Med. Examiners, 1977-94; pres. Ct. Examining Bd. in Podiatry, 1979, Am. Acad. Podiatric Sports Medicine, 1986; pres. Yale Podiatry Group, P.C., Ansonia, Conn., 1976—; bd. dirs. Podiatry Ins. Co. Am., Brentwood, Tenn., also chmn. underwriting com.; editl. adv. bd. Am. Podiatric Med. Assn., 1992-95. Author: Firm Footings For the Athlete, 1984, The Arthritic Foot, 1984, Yale's Podiatric Medicine, 3d edit., 1987; contbr. numerous sci. articles to profl. jours. Corporator Griffin Hosp., Derby, Conn., 1982. Capt. U.S. Army, 1967-71. Fellow Am. Acad. Podiatric Sports Medicine, Am. Assn. Hosp. Podiatrists, Am. Coll. Foot and Ankle Surgeons; mem. New Haven County Podiatric Med. Assn., Conn. Podiatric Med. Assn., Am. Podiatric Med. Assn., Conn. Pub. Health Assn., Am. Pub. Health Assn. Jewish. Avocations: marble collecting, swimming, gardening. Home: 18 Inwood Rd Woodbridge CT 06525-2558 Office: Yale Podiatry Group PC 364 E Main St Ansonia CT 06401-1904

YALE, SEYMOUR HERSHEL, dental radiologist, educator, university dean, gerontologist; b. Chgo., Nov. 27, 1920; s. Henry and Dorothy (Kulwin) Y.; m. Muriel Jane Cohen, Nov. 6, 1943; children: Russell Steven, Patricia Ruth. B.S., U. Ill., 1944, D.D.S., 1945, postgrad., 1947-48. Pvt. practice of dentistry, 1945-54, 56—; asst. clin. dentistry U. Ill., 1948-49, instr. clin. dentistry, 1949-53, asst. prof. clin. dentistry, 1953-54, assoc. prof. dept. radiology Coll. Dentistry, 1956, prof., head dept. Coll. Dentistry, 1957-65, adminstrv. asst. to dean Coll. Dentistry, 1961-63, asst. dean Coll. Dentistry, 1963-64, acting dean Coll. Dentistry, 1964-65, dean, 1965-87, dean emeritus, 1987—; also mem. grad. faculty dept. radiology Coll. Medicine U. Ill., Chgo., prof. dentistry and health resources mgmt. Sch. Pub. Health, 1987—; sr. dental dir. Dental Care Plus Mgmt. Corp., Chgo.; pres., dir. dental edn. Dental Care Plus Mgmt. Ednl. Svcs., Ltd.; health care facilities planner; dir. tng. Dental Technicians Sch., U.S. Naval Tng. Ctr., Bainbridge, md., 1954-56; mem. subcom. 16 Nat. Com. on Radiation Protection; mem. Radiation Protection Adv. Bd., State of Ill., 1971, City of Chgo. Health Sys. Agy.; founder Ctr. for Rsch. in Periodontal Disease and Oral Molecular Biology, 1977; organizer, chmn. Nat. Conf. on Hepatitis-B in Dentistry, 1982; organizer, dir. Univ. Taskforce Primary Health Care Project, U. Ill., Chgo.; chmn. U. Ill.-U. Stockholm-U. Gothenberg Conf. on Geriatrics, 1985; dir. planning AMVETS/UIC Tchg. Nursing Home Project, 1987-91; co-sponsor 1st Egyptian Dental Congress, 1984; adj. prof. Ctr. for Exercise Sci. and Cardiovasc. Rsch., Northeastern Ill. U., Chgo., 1991, Northwestern U. Sch. Dentistry Divsn. Behavioural Scis., Evanston, Ill., 1996—. Editor-in-chief Dental Care Plus Mgmt. Digest, 1995—. Bd. dirs., co-benefactor (with wife) World Heritage Mus., U. Ill., Urbana, 1985; mem. Hillel Bd., U. Ill.-Chgo.; life mem. (with wife) Bronze Circle of Coll. Liberal Arts, U. Ill., Urbana; mem. (with wife) Pres.' Council, U. Ill. Recipient centennial research award Chgo. Dental Soc., 1959; Distinguished Alumnus award U. Ill., 1973; Harry Sicher Meml. Lecture award Am. Coll. Stomologic Surgeons, 1983. Fellow Acad. Gen. Dentistry (hon.), Am. Coll. Dentists; mem. Ill. Dental Soc. (mem. com. on radiology), Chgo. Dental Soc., Internat. Assn. Dental Rsch., Am. Acad. Oral Roentgenology, Am. Dental Assn., Odontographic Soc. Chgo. (Award of Merit 1982), Council Dental Deans State Ill. (chmn.), N.Y. Acad. Scis., Gerontol. Soc. Am., Pierre Fauchard Acad. (Man of Yr. award Ill. sect. 1988), Am. Pub. Health Assn., Gerontol. Soc. Am., Omicron Kappa Upsilon, Sigma Xi, Alpha Omega (hon.). Established (with wife) collection of Coins of Ottoman Empire and Related Mohammedan States and supplemental antique map collection at World Heritage Mus. Home: 155 N Harbor Dr Chicago IL 60601-7328 Office: 25 E Washington St Chicago IL 60602

YALEN, GARY N., insurance company executive; b. N.Y.C., May 17, 1942; s. Sidney Leo and Mildred (Epstein) Y.; m. Rena Lynn Gear, Nov. 3, 1968; children—Robert, Lesley. BEE, Rensselaer Poly. Inst., 1964; MBA, U. Mich., 1965. Chartered fin. analyst. Mktg. engr. N.Y. Telephone Co., N.Y.C., 1965-69; security analyst Merrill Lynch, N.Y.C., 1969-74; security analyst Irving Trust Co., N.Y.C., 1974-80, research dir., 1980-83, sr. v.p., chief investment officer, 1983-87, exec. v.p., 1987-89; exec. v.p. Bank of N.Y., 1989-90; chief investment officer, exec. v.p. Fortis Asset Mgmt. (formerly Amev), 1990-95; pres., chief investment officer Fortis Advisers, 1995—. Served with U.S. Army, 1966-68, Vietnam. Mem. N.Y. Soc. Security Analysts, Beta Gamma Sigma. Avocations: golf, bridge. Home: 175 Nancy Ln Wyckoff NJ 07481-2522 Office: Fortis Advisers One Chase Manhattan Plz New York NY 10005

YALMAN, ANN, judge; b. Boston, June 9, 1948; d. Richard George and Joan (Osterman) Y. BA, Antioch Coll., 1970; JD, NYU, 1973. Trial atty. Fla. Rural Legal Svcs., Immokalee, Fla., 1973-74; staff atty. EEO, Atlanta, 1974-76; pvt. practice Santa Fe, N.Mex., 1976—; part time U.S. magstrate, N. Mex., 1988-96. Commr. Met. Water Bd., Santa Fe, 1986-88. Mem. N.Mex. Bar Assn. (commr. Santa Fe chpt. 1983-86). Home: 441 Calle La Paz Santa Fe NM 87501-2821 Office: 304 Catron St Santa Fe NM 87501-1806

YALOW, ROSALYN SUSSMAN, medical physicist; b. N.Y.C., N.Y., July 19, 1921; d. Simon and Clara (Zipper) Sussman; m. A. Aaron Yalow, June 6, 1943; children: Benjamin, Elanna. A.B., Hunter Coll., 1941; M.S., U. Ill., Urbana, 1942, Ph.D., 1945; D.Sc. (hon.), U. Ill., Chgo., 1974, Phila. Coll. Pharmacy and Sci., 1976, N.Y. Med. Coll., 1976, Med. Coll. Wis., Milw., 1977, Yeshiva U., 1977, Southampton (N.Y.) Coll., 1978, Bucknell U., 1978, Princeton U., 1978, Jersey City State Coll., 1979, Med. Coll. Pa., 1979, Manhattan Coll., 1979, U. Vt., 1980, U. Hartford, 1980, Rutgers U., 1980, Rensselaer Poly. Inst., 1980, Colgate U., 1981, U. So. Calif., 1981, Clarkson Coll., 1982, U. Miami, 1983, Washington U., St. Louis, 1983, Adelphi U., 1983, U. Alta. (Can.), 1983, SUNY, 1984, Tel Aviv U., 1985, Claremont (Calif.) U., 1986, Mills Coll., Oakland, Calif., 1986, Cedar Crest Coll., Allentown, Pa., 1988, Drew U., Madison, N.J., 1988, Lehigh U., 1988; L.H.D. (hon.), Hunter Coll., 1978; DSc. (hon.), San Francisco State U., 1989, Technion-Israel Inst. Tech., Haifa, 1989; DSc (hon.), Med. Coll. Ohio Toledo, 1991; L.H.D. (hon.), Sacred Heart U., Conn., 1978, St. Michael's Coll., Winooski Park, Vt., 1979, Johns Hopkins U., 1979, Coll. St. Rose, 1988, Spertus Coll. Judaica, Chgo., 1988; D. honoris causa, U. Rosario, Argentina, 1980, U. Ghent, Belgium, 1984; D. Humanities and Letters (hon.), Columbia U., 1984; DSc (hon.), Fairleigh Dickinson U., 1992, Conn. Coll., 1992, Smith Coll., Northampton, Mass., 1994, Union Coll., Schenectady, 1994. Diplomate: Am. Bd. Scis. Lectr., asst. prof. physics Hunter Coll., 1946-50; physicist, asst. chief radiosotope service VA Hosp., Bronx, N.Y., 1950-70, chief nuclear medicine, 1970-80, acting chief radioisotope service, 1968-70; research prof. Mt. Sinai Sch. Medicine, CUNY, 1968-74, Disting. Service prof., 1974-79, Solomon A. Berson Disting. prof.-at-large, 1986—; Disting. prof.-at-large Albert Einstein Coll. Medicine, Yeshiva U., 1979-85, prof. emeritus, 1986—; chmn. dept. clin. scis. Montefiore Med. Ctr., Bronx, 1980-85; N.J., 1992, Northampton, Mass.; cons. Lenox Hill Hosp., N.Y.C., 1956-62, WHO, Bombay, 1978; sec. U.S. Nat. Com. on Med. Physics, 1963-67; mem. nat. com. Radiation Protection, Subcom. 13, 1957; mem. Pres.'s Study Group on Careers for Women, 1966-72; sr. med. investigator VA, 1972-92, sr. med. investigator emeritus, 1992—. Co-editor: Hormone and Metabolic Research, 1973-79; editorial adv. council: Acta Diabetologica Latina, 1975-77, Ency. Universalis, 1978—; editorial bd.: Mt. Sinai Jour. Medicine, 1976-79, Diabetes, 1976, Endocrinology, 1967-72; contbr. numerous articles to profl. jours. Bd. dirs. N.Y. Diabetes Assn., 1974. Recipient VA William S. Middleton Med. Research award, 1960; Eli Lilly award Am. Diabetes Assn., 1961; Van Slyke award N.Y. met. sect. Am. Assn. Clin. Chemists, 1968; award A.C.P., 1971; Dickson prize U. Pitts., 1971; Howard Taylor Ricketts award U. Chgo., 1971; Gairdner Found. Internat. award, 1971; Commemorative medallion Am. Diabetes Assn., 1972; Bernstein award Med. Soc. State N.Y., 1974; Boehringer-Mannheim Corp. award Am. Assn. Clin. Chemists, 1975; Sci. Achievement award AMA, 1975; Exceptional Service award VA, 1975; A. Cressy Morrison award N.Y. Acad. Scis., 1975; sustaining membership award Assn. Mil. Surgeons, 1975; Distinguished Achievement award Modern Medicine, 1976; Albert Lasker Basic Med. Research award, 1976; La Madonnina Internat. prize Milan, 1977; Golden Plate award Am. Acad. Achievement, 1977; Nobel prize for physiology/medicine, 1977; citation of esteem St. John's U., 1979; G. von Hevesy medal, 1978; Rosalyn S. Yalow Research and Devel. award established Am. Diabetes Assn., 1978; Banting medal, 1978; Torch of Learning award Am. Friends Hebrew U., 1978; Virchow gold medal Virchow-Pirquet Med. Soc., 1978; Gratum Genus Humanum gold medal World Fedn. Nuclear Medicine or Biology, 1978; Jacobi medallion Asso. Alumni Mt. Sinai Sch. Medicine, 1978; Jubilee medal Coll. of New Rochelle, 1978; VA Exceptional Service award, 1978; Fed. Woman's award, 1961; Harvey lectr., 1966; Am. Gastroenterol. Assn. Meml. lectr., 1972; Joslin lectr. New Eng. Diabetes Assn., 1972; Franklin I. Harris Meml. lectr., 1973; 1st Hagedorn Meml. lectr. Acta Endocrinologica Congress, 1973; Sarasota Med. award for achievement and excellence, 1979; gold medal Phi Lambda Kappa, 1980; Achievement in Life award Ency. Brit., 1980; Theobald Smith award, 1982; Pres.'s Cabinet award U. Detroit, 1982; John and Samuel Bard award in medicine and sci. Bard Coll., 1982; Disting. Research award Dallas Assn. Retarded Citizens, 1982, Nat. Medal Sci., 1988; Abram L. Sachar Silver Medallion Brandeis U., Waltham, Mass., 1989, Disting. Scientist of Yr. award ARCS, N.Y.C., 1989, Golden Scroll award The Jewish Advocate, Boston, 1989, spl. award Clin. Ligand Assay Soc., Washington, 1988, numerous others. Fellow N.Y. Acad. Scis. (chmn. biophysics div. 1964-65), Am. Coll. Radiology (asso. in physics), Clin. Soc. N.Y. Diabetes Assn.; mem. Nat. Acad. Scis., Am. Acad. Arts and Scis., Am. Phys. Soc., Radiation Research Soc., Am. Assn. Physicists in Medicine, Biophys. Soc., Soc. Nuclear Medicine, Endocrine Soc. (Koch award 1972, pres. 1978), Am. Physiol. Soc., (hon.) Harvey Soc., (hon.) Med. Assn. Argentina, (hon.) Diabetes Soc. Argentina, (hon.) Am. Coll. Nuclear Physicians, (hon.) The N.Y. Acad. Medicine, (hon.) Am. Gastroent. Assn., (hon.) N.Y. Roentgen Soc., (hon.) Soc. Nuclear Medicine, Phi Beta Kappa, Sigma Xi, Sigma Pi Sigma, Pi Mu Epsilon, Sigma Delta Epsilon, Tau Beta Pi. Office: VA Hosp 130 W Kingsbridge Rd Bronx NY 10468-3992

YALOWITZ, KENNETH SPENCER, ambassador; b. Chgo., May 28, 1941; s. Henry and Audrey (Socol) Y.; m. Judith Gold, 1963; 1 child, Andrew Seth. BS, U. Wis., 1962; MA in Polit. Sci., Columbia U., 1964; cert., Russian Inst., 1965. Career fgn. svc. officer Sr. Fgn. Svc. U.S. Dept. State, 1966—; fgn. affairs analyst Bur. Intelligence and Rsch. Dept. State, 1966, with Arms Control and Disarmament Agy.; econ. officer at U.S. Embassy Dept. State, Moscow, 1975-77; comml. attache at embassy Dept. State, The Hague, The Netherlands; dep. dir. Office Internat. Econ Affairs, Bur. Internat. Orgn. Affairs Dept. State, Washington, 1980; dep. dir. econs. affairs Office of Soviet Union Affairs Dept. State, 1982-84, econ. counselor U.S. Mission to NATO, dir. Office of Australia and New Zealand Affairs, Bur. East Asian and Pacific Affairs, 1989-91; min. counselor for econ. affairs U.S. Embassy Dept. State, Moscow, 1991-93, acting dep. chief of mission U.S. Embassy, 1992-93; U.S. amb. to Belarus Fgn. Svc., Dept. State, Minsk, 1994—; congl. fgn. affairs fellow Am. Polit. Sci. Assn., 1985; with Bur. East/West Trade Dept. Commerce; area studies chmn. for the states of the former Soviet Union Sch. Area Studies Fgn. Svc. Inst., Washington, 1993-94; vis. prof. internat. rels. Indsl. Coll. of the Armed Forces, 1988. Woodrow Wilson fellow Woodrow Wilson Nat. Fellowship Found., 1962. Mem. Am. Fgn. Svc. Assn., Am. Polit. Sci. Assn. Office: US Amb Minsk Belarus US Dept State Washington DC 20521-7010

YAMABE, SHIGERU, medical educator; b. Tokyo, July 7, 1923; s. Hiroshi and Jyo (Mihara) Y.; m. Takako Naoi, Apr. 2, 1967; 1 child, Yoko. MS, Osaka (Japan) U., 1946, PhD, 1952. Lectr. Osaka U. Med. Sch., 1953-58; prof. Kobe Coll., Nishinomiya, Japan, 1958-89, hon. prof., 1989—; system dir. Drug Rsch. System Internat., Kobe, 1989—; rsch. exec. mbr. Osaka Seijinbyo Med. Ctr., Higashinariku, Osaka, Japan, 1991—; vis. lectr. Tokyo U., Kyoto (Japan) U., 1966-84; vis. prof. dept. microbiology London Hosp. Med. Coll., 1978—, Case Western Res. U., Cleve., 1982, 84, Harvard Med. Sch., Boston, 1988-89; hon. vis. lectr. London Hosp. Med. Coll., 1990—; invited lectr. U. Paris VI, 1992—; vis. sr. scientist Inst. Pathology, Oxford, 1992—; vis. prof. Grad. Sch. Pub. Health U. Pitts., 1993—; sr. sci. advisor Taiho Pharm. Co., Tokyo, 1991—. Author: Bioenergetics, 1968 (award 1970); editor: Research and Development of New Drugs, 1994; internat. jour. editor Antiviral Chemistry and Chemotherapy, 1993—, Jour. Chemotherapy, 1988—; drug designer, inventor Tazobactam antibiotic, 1991, Zaltoprofen anti-inflammatory drug, 1993; 40 patents for cancer and AIDS drugs. Fellow Royal Soc. Medicine; active mem. N.Y. Acad. Sci. Avocation: poetry. Home: 1-2-7 Kamokogahara, Higashinada, Kobe 658, Japan Office: ESS, Hotel Okura Kobe Chuo-ku, Kobe 650, Japan

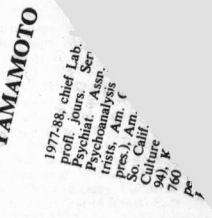

YAMADA, KENNETH MANAO, cell biologist; b. Mpls., Sept. 18, 1944; s. Paul Manao and Masaye (Uriu) Y.; m. Susan Jane Sleeper, July 1, 1973. BA in Biol. Scis., Stanford U., 1966, PhD in Biol. Scis., 1971, MD, 1972. Intern Mary's Help Hosp./Seton Med. Ctr., Daly City, Calif., 1972-73; commd. lt. USPHS, 1974, advanced t[illegible] Cancer Inst., Bethesda, M[illegible] Bethesda, Md., 1990—; m[illegible] external adv. com. Howar[illegible] Conf. on Fibronectin, 1[illegible] Anderson Hosp., 1988; [illegible] Med. Sch., 1988. C[illegible] Postdoctoral fellow U. [illegible] Luke and Jacob Davi[illegible] Cell Biology (coun. m[illegible] Biology, Internat. So[illegible] Cancer Rsch. Assn. ([illegible] (Undergrad. Rsch. awa[illegible] 30 Rm 421 30 Convent Dr Bethe[illegible]

YAMADA, SHINICHI, mathematician, computer [illegible] Nagoya, Japan, Jan. 10, 1937; s. Umekichi and Nami (Kawa[illegible] Atsuyo Yamamoto, Oct. 10, 1964; 1 child, Atsushi. BS, U. Tokyo, [illegible] DSc, 1988; SM, Harvard U., 1970. System analyst Nippon Univac Co., Tokyo, 1959-70, tech. advisor, 1970-90; lectr. Keio U., Tokyo, 1980-85, Waseda U., Tokyo, 1982—, Chiba U., 1989—, prof. dept. info. sci. Hirosaki U., Japan, 1990-93, prof. dept of information scis., Science U. of Tokyo, 1993—. Author: Sciences of Information Processing, 1984, Micro-Prolog Collection, 1986, Kowalski Logic for Problem Solving, 1987, Encyclopedia of Artificial Intelligence, 1988, Encyclopedia of Computer Systems, 1989, Encyclopedia of MathematicalInformation Sciences, 1996. Mem. editorial staff Info. Processing Soc. Japan, 1983-87; contbr. articles to profl. jours. Mem. IEEE, AAAS, Am. Math. Soc., Math. Soc. Japan, Assn. Symbolic Logic, Assn. Computing Machinery, N.Y. Acad. Scis. Clubs: Harvard of Japan. Home: 821-19 Nishi-Fukai, Nagareyama-Shi Chiba 270-01, Japan Office: Sci U Tokyo Dept Info Sci, Yamasaki 2641 Noda City, Chiba 278, Japan

YAMADA, TADATAKA, internist; b. Tokyo, June 5, 1945. MD, NYU, 1971. Intern Med. Coll. Va. Hosps., Richmond, 1971-72, resident in internal medicine, 1972-74; gastrointestinal fellow UCLA, 1977-79; prof. medicine U. Mich., Ann Arbor; mem. staff U. Mich. Hosp., Ann Arbor. Mem. AAAS, ACP, AAP, AGA, ASCI, IOM. Office: U Mich Gastrointestinal Peptide Rsch 3101 Taubman Ctr Ann Arbor MI 48109-0368*

YAMADA, TOSHIKATSU AUGUSTINE, academic administrator, mechanical engineer; b. Nagoya, Aichi, Japan, Jan. 23, 1923; s. Etsujiro and Yuki (Takeuchi) Y.; m. Chizuko Shirota, Nov. 22, 1956; children: Takahisa, Chieko. B in Engring., Nagoya (Japan) U., 1948, D in Engring., 1977. Asst. Nagoya (Japan) U., 1963-66; asst. prof. Toyota Coll. Tech., Japan, 1966-70, prof., 1970-87; pres. Aichi Coll. Tech., Gamagori, Japan, 1987—. Author: Milling With Plain Milling Cutters, 1977, Under The Beautiful Purple-Blue Flag, 1987. Mem. ASME, Japan Soc. Mech. Engrs., Gamagori (Japan) Internat. Assn. (dir. 1992—, v.p. 1994—). Avocations: classical music, tea ceremonies, bird watching, Judo. Home: 3-8-10 Wakamuzu, Chikusa Nagoya 464, Japan Office: Aichi Coll Tech, 50-2 Manori Nishihasama, Aichi Gamagori 443, Japan

YAMAGUCHI, KRISTI TSUYA, ice skater; b. Hayward, Calif., July 12, 1971; d. Jim and Carole (Doi) Y. Gold medalist, Figure Skating Albertville Olympic Games, 1992; U.S. Skating champion, 1992, World Skating champion, 1991, 1992, World Junior champion, 1988, world prof. figure skating champion, 1994. Recipient Women First award YWCA, 1993. Avocations: tennis, rollerblading, reading, and dancing. Address: U.S. Figure Skating Assn. 20 1st St Colorado Springs CO 80906-3624*

YAMAKAWA, ALLAN HITOSHI, academic administrator; b. San Francisco, Oct. 18, 1938; s. Victor Tadashi and Alice Tsugie (Sato) Y.; m. Nancy Ann Habel, Apr.17, 1977 (div. Mar 1987); children: Bryan Allan, David Scott. BS, Roosevelt U., 1962, MEd, 1970. Tech. svcs. dir. audio visual libr. Roosevelt U., Chgo., 1958-60; dean, exec. dir. Ency. Britannica Schs., Inc., Chgo., 1960-67; curriculum svcs. dir. Field Enterprises Newspaper Div., Chgo., 1967-70; edn. svcs. dir. Chgo. Tribune Co., 1970-76; tng. svcs. dir. Dialogue Systems Inc., N.Y.C., 1976-79; orgn. devel. dir. U. Ill., Chgo., 1979—; cons., trainer Can. Daily Newspaper Pub. Assn., Toronto, 1973-84, Am. Newspaper Pub. Found., Reston, Va., 1972-80, Gifted Students Found. Dallas, 1974-75; cons. Cedars Sinai Med. Ctr., Beverly Hills, Calif., 1983—, W. K. Kellogg Found., 1987—. Author: Handbooks of Teaching Methods, 1974, Communicate, 1975, Catalysts For Change, 1976, Evaluation of Senior Administrators, 1994; patentee experiential learning method. Instr. ARC, Chgo., 1954-85; bd. dirs. Edison Regional Gifted Ctr. Sch., Chgo., pres., 1989-93; dist. program chmn. Boy Scouts Am., 1985—. Mem. ASTD, ASCD, Soc. Programmed and Automated Learning, Toastmasters (pres. 1974-76). Avocations: photography, computer programming, electronics, pyrotechnics, film production. Office: Univ Ill 1524(G) W Pratt Blvd Chicago IL 60626

YAMAKAWA, DAVID KIYOSHI, JR., lawyer; b. San Francisco, Jan. 25, 1936; s. David Kiyoshi and Shizu (Negishi) Y. BS, U. Calif., Berkeley, 1958, JD, 1963. Bar: Calif. 1964, U.S. Supreme Ct. 1970. Prin. Law Offices of David K. Yamakawa Jr., San Francisco, 1964—; dep. dir. Cmty. Action Agy., San Francisco, 1968-69; dir. City Demonstration Agy., San Francisco, 1969-70; mem. adv. coun. Calif. Senate Subcom. on the Disabled, 1982-83, Ctr. Substance Abuse and Mental Health Svcs. Adminstrn. U.S. Dept. Health and Human Svcs., 1995—; chmn. cmty. residential treatment system adv. com. Calif. Dept. Mental Health, 1980-85, San Francisco Human Rights Commn., 1977-80; pres. Legal Assistance to the Elderly, 1981-83; 2d v.p. Nat. Conf. Social Welfare, 1983—; v.p. Region IX, Nat. Mental Health Assn., 1981-83; vice-chmn. Mt. Zion Hosp. and Med. Ctr., 1986-88; bd. dirs. United Neighborhood Ctrs. of Am., 1977-83, ARC Bay Area, 1988-91, Mt. Zion Inst. on Aging, 1993—, v.p., 1994—; bd. trustees Mt. Zion Med. Ctr., U. Calif., San Francisco, 1993—; chmn. bd. trustees United Way Bay Area, 1983-85; chief fin. officer Action for Nature, Inc., 1987—; v.p. Friends of Legal Assistance to the Elderly, 1984—; bd. dirs. Ind. Sector, 1986-92, Friends of the San Francisco Human Rights Commn., 1980—, CFO, 1980-85, vice chmn., 1985-94, CFO, 1994—, La Madre de los Pobres, 1982—, v.p., 1994—, Nat. Concilio Am., 1987—, Hispanic Community Found. of the Bay Area, 1989—, legal coun., 1989—; bd. dirs., pres. Non-Profit Svcs., Inc., 1987—, sec., 1987-90, chmn., 1990—; pres. Coun. Internat. Programs, San Francisco, 1987-89; mem. citizens adv. com. San Francisco Hotel Tax Fund Grants for the Arts Program, 1991—. Recipient John B. Williams Outstanding Planning and Agy. Rels. vol. award United Way of the Bay Area, 1980, Mortimer Fleishhacker Jr. Outstanding Vol. award United Way, 1985, Spl. Recognition award Legal Assistance to the Elderly, 1983, Commendation award Bd. Suprs. City and County of San Francisco, 1983, cert. Honor, 1985, San Francisco Found. award, 1985, 1st Mental Health Awareness award Mental Health Assn. San Francisco, 1990; David Yamakawa Day proclaimed in San Francisco, 1985. Mem. ABA (Liberty Bell award 1986), Internat. Inst. San Francisco (bd. dirs., 1989-95, pres. 1990-93). Office: 582 Market St Ste 410 San Francisco CA 94104-5305

YAMAMOTO, HARRY YOSHIMI, research institute director, educator; b. Honolulu, Nov. 26, 1933; s. Isami and Takeno (Morita) Y.; m. Millie Y. Wakugawa, Jan. 31, 1957; children: Craig A., Joanne V. BS, U. Hawaii, 1955; MS, U. Ill., 1958; PhD, U. Calif., 1962. Prof. U. Hawaii, Honolulu, 1961—; dir. Hawaii Inst. Tropical Agr. and Human Resources, Honolulu, 1993—; cons. HYCON, Honolulu, 1970—; bd. dirs. Hawaii Biotechnology Group, Inc., Honolulu, 1983—. Contbr. rsch. articles to profl. jours. Rsch. grantee NSF, USDA, DOE industry. Mem. Am. Soc. Plant Physiology, Am. Chem. Soc., AAAS. Office: U Hawaii at Manoa Hawaii Inst of Tropical Agr and Human Re Honolulu HI 96822

YAMAMOTO, JOE, psychiatrist, educator; b. Los Angeles, Apr. 18, 1924; s. Zenzaburo and Tomie (Yamada) Y.; m. Maria Fujitomi, Sept. 5, 1947; children: Eric Robert, Andrew Jolyon. Student, Los Angeles City Coll., 1941-42, Hamline U., 1943-45; B.S., U. Minn., 1946, M.B., 1948, M.D., 1949. Asst. prof. dept. psychiatry, neurology, behavioral sci. U. Okla. Med. Center, 1955-58, asst. prof., 1958-60; assoc. prof. dept. psychiatry U. So. Calif. Sch. Medicine, Los Angeles, 1961-69; prof. U. So. Calif. Sch. Medicine, 1969-77, co-dir. grad. edn. psychiatry, 1963-70; prof. UCLA, 1977—; dir. Psychiat. Outpatient Clinic, Los Angeles County-U. So. Calif. Med. Center, 1958-77; dir. adult ambulatory care services UCLA Neuropsychiat. Inst.,

...r Cross Cultural Studies. Contbr. articles in field to ...d to capt., M.C. U.S. Army, 1953-55. Fellow Am. ... (life), Pacific Rim Coll. Psychiatrists, Am. Acad. ... trustee, mem. exec. com., pres. 1978-79), Am. Coll. Psychia-... rthopsychiat. Assn. (pres.-elect 1993-94, pres. 1994-95, past ... Assn. for Social Psychiatry (trustee 1981-84, v.p. 1984-86); mem. ... Psychoanalytic Inst. and Soc. (pres. 1972-73), Soc. for Study of ... and Psychiatry, Group for Advancement Psychiatry (bd. dirs. 1992- ... appa Phi, Alpha Omega Alpha. Office: UCLA Neuro-psychiat Inst ... Westwood Plz Los Angeles CA 90024-1754 *Learning about the diverse ... ples of America, I have been fascinated with how we can be Asian, ... ispanic, Black, European, and Native American and still identify with our national values. We value our freedom, individual rights and our ability to be someone different but equal. In mental health also there is a need for recognition of cultural differences and the need of treatment response to the individual.*

YAMAMOTO, KAORU, psychology, education educator; b. Tokyo, Mar. 28, 1932; came to U.S., 1959; s. Saburo and Hideko (Watanabe) Y.; m. Etsuko Hamazaki, Apr. 6, 1959 (div. 1986); m. Carol-Lynne Moore, Oct. 4, 1986; children: Keita Carey Moore, Kiyomi Lynne Moore. BS in Engring., U. Tokyo, 1953; MA, U. Minn., 1960, PhD, 1962. Engr. Toppan Printing Co., Tokyo, 1953; engr., rsch. chemist Japan Oxygen Co., Tokyo, 1954-57, 58-59; asst. prof. Kent (Ohio) State U., 1962-65; from asst. to assoc. prof. U. Iowa, Iowa City, 1965-68; prof. Pa. State U., University Park, 1968-72, Ariz. State U., Tempe, 1972-87, U. Colo., Denver, 1987—; vis. prof. U. Minn., Mpls., 1974, Simon Fraser U., Burnaby, B.C., Can., 1984, U.Victoria, B.C., 1986, U. Wash., Seattle, 1987, Zhejiang Normal U., Jinhua, China, 1991; Fulbright lectr. U. Iceland, 1985. Author: The Child and His Image, 1972, Their World, Our World, 1993; author, editor: 6 books; co-author: Beyond Words, 1988; editor Am. Ednl. Rsch. Jour., 1972-75, Ednl. Forum, 1984-92; contbr. chpts. to books and articles to profl. jours. Landsdowne scholar U. Victoria, 1985. Fellow APA; mem. Am. Sociol. Assn., Am. Anthrop. Assn., Motus Humanus. Avocations: winter sports, travel, classical music, reading. Office: U Colo Denver Box 106 PO Box 173364 Denver CO 80217-3364

YAMAMOTO, KEITH ROBERT, molecular biologist, educator; b. Des Moines, Feb. 4, 1946. BS, Iowa State U., 1968; PhD, Princeton U., 1973. Asst. prof. biochemistry U. Calif., San Francisco, 1976-79, assoc. prof., 1979-83, prof., 1983—, vice chmn. dept., 1985—, dir. biochemistry and molecular biology program, 1988—; mem. genetic biology rev. panel NSF, Washington, 1984-87; chmm. molecular biology study sect. NIH, Bethesda, Mdf., 1987-90, mem. nat. adv. coun. for human genome rsch., 1990-91. Co-author: Gene Wars: Military Control over the New Genetic Technologies, 1988; co-editor: Transcriptional Regulation, 1992 ; assoc. editor Jour. Molecular Biology, 1988—, editor Molecular Biology of the Cell, 1991—. Mem. Com. for Responsible Genetics, Boston, 1989—; testifier hearings on biol. warfare com. on govtl. affairs U.S. Senate, Washington, 1989. Recipient Gregory Pincus medal Worchester Found. for Exptl. Biology, 1990; Dreyfus tchr.-scholar, 1982-86. Fellow Am. Acad. Arts and Scis.; mem. AAAS, NAS (panel on sci. responsibility and conduct of rsch. 1990-91), Protein Soc., Am. Soc. for Cell Biology (coun. 1991-92), Am. Soc. for Biochemistry and Molecular Biology (publs. com. 1990-93), Am. Soc. for Devel. Biology. Home: 332 Douglass St San Francisco CA 94114-2452 Office: U Calif San Francisco Dept Biochemistry 513 Parnassus Ave San Francisco CA 94122-2722

YAMAMOTO, MICHAEL TORU, journalist; b. San Francisco, July 9, 1960; s. Harry Naoto and Noriko (Yoshitomi) Y.; m. Marianne Chin, Oct. 9, 1993. BA Psychology, San Francisco State U., 1981, BA Journalism, 1981. Editor San Francisco State U. Phoenix, 1980; news editor Hayward (Calif.) Daily Rev., 1979-80, Long Beach (Calif.) Press-Telegram, 1981; nat. desk editor L.A. Times, 1981-85; night news editor L.A. Times, Washington, 1986-87, investigative projects editor, 1988; dep. city editor San Francisco Chronicle, 1989-92, exec. projects editor, 1993, city editor, 1993—; adj. prof. Am. U., Washington, 1987, Calif. State U. at Northridge, Calif., 1984-85; vis. faculty mem. Am. Press Inst., Reston, Va., 1994, Poynter Inst. for Media Studies, St. Petersburg, Fla., 1995, San Francisco Unified Sch. Dist., 1994; fellow Coro Found., San Francisco, 1990-91. Recipient Dow Jones Newspaper Fund scholarship, Princeton, N.J., 1980. Mem. Asian Am. Journalism Assn., White House Corr. Assn., Soc. Profl. Journalists., World Affairs Coun. Office: San Francisco Chronicle 901 Mission St San Francisco CA 94103

YAMAMOTO, TAMOTSU, art educator, artist, architectural illustrator; b. Kyoto, Japan, Jan. 28, 1946; came to U.S., 1972; s. Kyuichi Mitsuyori and Koume Yamamoto; m. Selene Rate Hunter, July 18, 1977. BFA, Kyoto U. Fine Arts, 1969, MFA, 1971; postgrad. diploma, Sch. Museum Fine Arts, Boston, 1975, 76. Prin. Yamamoto Archtl. Illustration, Boston, 1976—; prof. Mt. Ida Coll., Newton, Mass., 1994—; adj. prof. Chamberlayne Jr. Coll., 1979-88, Mass. Coll. Art, 1983-88, Boston Archtl. Ctr., 1988—, Wentworth Inst. Tech., 1994—. Contbr. Architecture in Perspective, vol. 4, 1989, vol. 7, 1992, vol. 8, 1993, vol. 9, 1994, Architecture in Perspective: Retrospective, 1992, Architectural Rendering, 1992, The Art of Architectural Illustration, 1994, KAPA Retrospective, 1995; exhbns. include Mus. Fine Arts, Kyoto, 1966-71, 72, Gallery 16, Kyoto, 1969, Hartford Mus. Fine Arts, 1972, Ctr. Advanced Visual Studies, Cambridge, Mass., 1972, 75, Avant Garde Festival N.Y., 1975, 78, Boston Mus. Fine Arts, 1977, Charles River, Cambridge, 1978, Artists Found., 1978, 80, Tokyo Express, 1981, JARA ann. exhbn., Tokyo, Nagoya and Osaka, Japan, 1986—, Chgo. Art Inst., 1989, Nev. Mus. Art, Reno, 1990, John B. Aird Gallery, Toronto, 1990, Japan Archtl. Renderers Assn. Japan Inst. Architects Nat. Conv., Kobe, 1993, Robert W. Woodruff Arts Ctr., Atlanta, 1993, Gwenda Jay Gallery, Chgo., 1993, World Conv., Chgo., AIA NeoCon93, The Internat. Architects, AIA Chpt. Gallery, San Francisco, Architecture II Gallery, U. Manitoba, Can., Design Exch., Toronto, 1992, Boston Archtl. Ctr., 1994, AIA Nat. Conv., L.A., 1994, Coll. Art and Design, Detroit, 1994, Chgo. Architecture Found., 1994, Contract Design Ctr., San Francisco, 1994, Galerie Aaedes, Berlin, AIA Nat. Conv., Atlanta, ACSA European Conf., Lisbon, Portugal, 1995, Chgo. Archtl. Found., Boston Archtl. Ctr., Mt. Ida Coll., Newton, Mass., 1996; contbr. articles to profl. jours. Recipient Excellence in Design award Boston Soc. Architects, 1973, Comp. Winning award Internat. Archtl. Artist, 1989, 92, 93, 94. Mem. Am. Soc. Archtl. Perspectivists (treas. exec. bd. dirs. 1989-93, adv. coun. 1994—, internat. coord., pres.), Japan Archtl. Renderers Assn. (hon.), Inst. Contemporary Arts, Boston Archtl. Ctr. (grantee faculty expense fund 1994). Avocations: golf, ski, classical experimental music. Home: 15 Sleeper St Boston MA 02210-1225

YAMANE, GEORGE MITSUYOSHI, oral diagnosis and radiology educator; b. Honolulu, Aug. 9, 1924; s. Seigi and Tsuta (Moriwaki) Y.; m. Alice Matsuko Nemoto, July 6, 1951; children: Wende Michiko, Linda Keiko, David Kiyoshi. Student, U. Hawaii, 1944; A.B., Haverford Coll., 1946; D.D.S., U. Minn., 1950, Ph.D., 1962. Teaching, research asst. U. Hawaii, Honolulu, 1943-44; teaching asst. div. oral pathology, oral diagnosis Sch. Dentistry, U. Minn., Mpls., 1951-53; asst. prof. oral pathology Coll. Dentistry U. Ill., Chgo., 1957-59; dir. tissue lab. Sch. Dentistry U. Wash., Seattle, 1960-63; asst. prof. oral pathology Sch. Dentistry U. Wash., 1959-63; grad. faculty mem. U. Minn., Mpls., 1963-70; prof., chmn. div. oral diagnosis, oral medicine and oral roentgenology U. Minn., 1963-70; prof., chmn. dept. oral diagnosis and radiology Dental Sch. Univ. of Medicine and Dentistry of N.J., 1970-83; prof. dept. biodental sci. Dental Sch. Coll. of Medicine and Dentistry of N.J., 1983-88, assoc. dean research and postgrad. programs, 1976-79, dir. div. oral and pathobiology, 1988-92, prof. dept oral pathology, biology and diagnosis sci., 1988-92, prof. emeritus, 1992—; cons. Children's Orthopedic Hosp. and Med. Ctr., Seattle, 1960-63, VA Hosp., American Lake, Wash., 1961-63, Mpls., 1964-70; cons. Minn. State Dept. Health, 1965-70, Wyo. State Bd. Health, 1966-70. Contbr. articles to med. and dental jours. Served with AUS. USPHS fellow, 1953-55; recipient Nell S. Talbot Instructorship award Coll. Dentistry U. Ill., 1958; Excellence in Teaching award U. Medicine and Dentistry N.J., 1984, Exceptional Merit award U. Medicine and Dentistry N.J., 1986. Fellow Am. Acad. Oral Pathology, AAAS, Am., Internat. colls. dentists, N.J. Acad. Medicine; mem. Am. Dental Assn., Orgn. Tchrs. Oral Diagnosis (sec.-treas. 1970-73, pres. 1974-75), Am. Acad. Periodontology, Internat. Assn. Dental Research, Am. Assn. Dental Schs., Sigma Xi (pres. Newark chpt. 1985), Omicron Kappa Upsilon, Xi Psi Phi.

YAMANE, STANLEY JOEL, optometrist; b. Lihue, Kauai, Hawaii, Mar. 13, 1943; s. Tooru and Yukiko (Miura) Y.; m. Joyce Mitsuko Tamura; children—Stanley Tooru Aiichi, Karen Margaret. B.S. in Optometry, Pacific U., 1966, O.D., 1966. Diplomate Am. Acad. Optometry. Practice optometry Waipahu, Hawaii, 1967-73; ptnr. with Dr. Dennis M. Kuwabara, 1973-81; ptnr. Drs. Kuwabara & Yamane, Optometrists, Inc., Waipahu, 1981-91; with br. office Drs. Kuwabara & Yamane, Optometrists, Inc., Honolulu; with DBA Eye Care Assocs. of Hawaii, Honolulu, 1989-91; dir. profl. affairs Vistakon, Inc., 1991-92; v.p. profl. affairs Vistakon Inc., 1992—; lectr., cons. in field; sec.-treas. Hawaii Bd. Examiners in Optometry, 1975-76, v.p., 1976-78, pres., 1978-80; mem. adj. faculty Coll. Optometry, Pacific U., 1977-91, Pa. Coll. Optometry, 1981-91, So. Coll. Optometry, 1982-91, U. Mo., St. Louis, 1990-91; bd. dirs. Hawaii Vision Svc. Plan, 1984-91. Cons. editor Optometric Mgmt. Jour., 1981-91, Contact Lens Forum Jour., 1987-91, editor, 1991; contbr. articles to profl. jours. Bd. mgrs. Leeward Oahu Br. YMCA, 1967-70, Hi-Y advisor, 1967-71, mem. Century Club, 1967-91, bd. mgrs. West Oahu Br., 1971-78, gen. chmn. sustaining membership, 1976; 2d v.p. August Ahrens Elem. Sch. PTA, 1969; mem. Leeward Mental Health Adv. Council, 1975-76, Friends of Waipahu Cultural Garden Park Found., 1976—, Aloha council Boy Scouts Am., 1976-91; mem. bus. adv. council Waipahu High Sch., 1976-81, Parent-Tchr.-Community Adv. Council, 1978-80; bd. dirs. Central/Leeward unit Am. Cancer Soc., 1977-80, pub. edn. dir., 1978-79, v.p., 1979-80, founder, chmn. Celebrity Auction, 1980, dir. Oahu Baseline Survey, 1978; bd. dirs. Barbers Point council Navy League Am., 1981-85; profl. bd. advisors U. Houston Inst. for Contact Lens Research. Recipient Merit award Nat. Eye Research Found., 1974, Disting. Service award, 1976. Fellow Am. Acad. Optometry (cornea and contact lens diplomate, vice chair cornea and contact lens sect. 1992-94, chair cornea and contact lens sect. 1994—, sec., 1990-92, vice chair ethics com. 1991-92, corp. support for Jour. com. 1981, chair diplomate awards com. 1988-90), AAAS, Am. Optometric Assn. (ann. congress del. 1978, pub. health com. 19738, optometric paraoptometric personnel com. 1978-79, contact lens project team 1979-80, task force on R&D 1984-87, contact lens sect. coun. 1988-92, sec., 1989-90, vice chair 1990-91, chair elect 1991-92, numerous coms.), Leeward Oahu Jaycees (Disting. Service award 1969, Top Outstanding Young Man award 1975), Hawaii State Jaycees, Am. Optometric Found. (bd. dirs. 1981-91 , chmn. task force clin. research 1981-83, nominations com. 1982, treas. 1985-86, sec., 1987-88, pres.-elect, 1988-89, pres. 1989-90), Am. Pub. Health Assn., Better Vision Inst., Coll. Optometrists in Vision Devel., Hawaii Optometric Assn. (corr. sec. 1968-70, state newsletter editor 1968-70, rec. sec. 1971, 2d v.p. 1972, pres. 1974-75; Man of Yr. 1975, Optometrist of Yr. 1979), Internat. Optometric & Optical League, Internat. Soc. Contact Lens Rsch., Brit. Contact Lens Assn., Japan Contact Lens Acad., Nat. Assn. of the Professions, Nat. Eye Research Found. (fellow Internat. Orthokeratology sect.; editorial bd. Contacto Jour. 1979, contact lens cert. com. 1981-85), Nat. Fedn. Ind. Bus., Optometric Cons. in Contact Lens Optometric Extension Program Found. (chmn. study group 1969-70, state dir. 1971-73), Optometric Hist. Soc., Optometric Polit. Action Coms., Soc. Contact Lens Specialists, Hawaii Assn. Children with Learning Disabilities, Hawaii Assn. Intellectually Gifted Children (pub. relations chmn. 1st Ann. State Conf. 1975, legis. lobbyist 1975-76), Waipahu Bus. Assn. (bd. dirs. 1974-78, chmn. pub. relations 1974-75, legis. lobbyist 1974-75, pres. 1974-75), Nat. Acad. Practice in Optometry (mem.-at-large on exec. com., disting. practitioner in optometry). Democrat. Baptist. Home: 8609 Autumn Green Dr Jacksonville FL 32256-9560 Office: Vistakon Inc Vp Profl Affairs 4500 Salibury Rd Ste 300 Jacksonville FL 32216-0954

YAMAOKA, SEIGEN HARUO, bishop; b. Fresno, Calif., Aug. 21, 1934; s. Haruichi and Rika (Ogawa) Y.; m. Shigeko Masuyama, Apr. 3, 1966; children—Jennifer Sae, Stacy Emi. B.A., Calif. State U.-Fresno, 1956; M.A., Ryukoku U., Kyoto, Japan, 1961; M.R.E., Pacific Sch. Religion, Berkeley, Calif., 1969, D.Min., 1979. Ordained to ministry Buddhist Chs. Am., 1961. Minister Oakland Buddhist Ch., Calif., 1964-71; registrar Inst. Buddhist Studies, Berkeley, 1969-71, lectr., mem. Curriculum com., 1969-81, pres., 1981—; minister Stockton Buddhist Temple, Calif., 1971-81; treas. No. Calif. Radio Ministry, 1975-76; cons. ethnic studies Stockton Unififed Sch. Dist., 1974-76; chmn. Buddhist Chs. Am. Ministers Assn., 1979-81; bishop Buddhist Chs. Am., San Francisco, 1981—, research com., 1970-79; English sec. Ministerial Assn., 1972-75; assoc. in doctrinal studies Hokyo, Kyoto, 1974; mem. Bd. Buddhist Edn., 1975; vice chmn. No. Calif. Ministers Assn., 1976; trustee Numata Ctr. for Buddhist Translation and Research, Buddhist Dharma Kyokai Soc. of Am. Author: Compassion in Encounter, 1970, Teaching and Practice Jodo Shinshu, 1974, Jodo Shinshu: Religion of Human Experience, 1976, Meditation-Gut-Enlightenment... Way of Hara, 1976, Awakening of Gratitude in Dying, 1978; editor, advisor, writer: Dharma School Teachers Guide, 1979. World advisor Thanksgiving Sq., Dallas; eccleseastical endorsing agt. for Buddhists chaplains Dept. of Def. Mem. Japan Karate Fedn., Shinshu Acad. Soc., San Francisco-Japanese Am. Citizens League, Calif. State U.-Fresno Alumni Assn., Pacific Sch. Religion Alumni Assn., Internat. Assn. Shin Buddhist Studies, Internat. Translation Ctr. Kyoto, Hongwanji Bishops Council Kyoto. Home: 37 Waterloo Ct Belmont CA 94002-2936 Office: Buddhist Chs of Am 1710 Octavia St San Francisco CA 94109-4341

YAMARONE, CHARLES ANTHONY, JR., aerospace engineer, consultant; b. Bronxville, N.Y., Oct. 30, 1936; s. Charles Anthony and Mildred (La Manna) Y.; m. Catherine MacMullan, May 31, 1957; children: Charles Anthony III, Thomas, Stephen, Mark, James. BSEE, Manhattan Coll., 1958. Design engr. Gen. Precision Inc., Pleasantville, N.Y., 1958-62; engr. supr. Jet Propulsion Lab., Calif. Inst. Tech., Pasadena, 1962-69, sect. mgr., 1969-76, data processing mgr., 1976-80, project mgr., 1980-. Recipient Astronautique medal Assn. Aeronautique et Astronautique de France, 1992, medal Ctr. Nat. d'Etudes Spatiales, 1994, Outstanding Leadership medal NASA, 1993. Mem. Am. Geophys. Union, Am. Inst. for Advancement of Science. Office: Jet Propulsion Lab Topex Project Office 4800 Oak Grove Dr Pasadena CA 91109-8001

YAMASAKI, YUKUZO, lawyer; b. Yamaguchi, Japan, Oct. 12, 1924; s. Bunsaburo and Yasuko (Ueda) Y. m. Keiko Furubayashi, Aug. 15, 1961; children: Takao, Chiyo. BA, Tokyo U., 1952; M of Comparative Law, So. Meth. U., 1965. Assoc. Shozawa & Nagashima (name now Nagashima & Ohno), Tokyo, 1961-72; trainee Kaye,Scholer,Fierman, Hayes & Handler, N.Y.C., 1965-66; sr. ptnr. Yamasaki Law & Patent Office, Tokyo, 1972—. Author: Digest of Japanese Patent Infringement Cases 1966-68, 1970; contbr. articles to Jour. of Assn. Internat. pour Protection Propriété Indsl. Mem. Indsl. Property Coun. of the Patent Office, Tokyo, 1991—. Recipient commendation Ministry Internat. Trade Industry. Mem. First Tokyo Bar Assn., Japanese Bar Assn. (chmn. intellectual property com. 1989-90), Patent Attys. Assn. of Japan, Inter-Pacific Bar Assn. (chmn. intellectual property com. 1991-93), Japanese Br. Assn. Internat. Protection Propriété Indsl. (councillor, commendation 1986). Home: 2-20-21 Higashi, Kunitachi 186, Japan Office: Yamasaki Law & Patent Office, 1-11-28 Nagatacho, Chiyoda 100, Japan

YAMASHITA, WESLEY FARRELL, lawyer; b. Las Vegas, July 17, 1955; s. Kiyoshi and Mary (Sato) Y.; m. Bonnie Jean Hull, Dec. 28, 1977; children: Nicholas, Nathan, Brent, Amy, Anne. BS cum laude, Brigham Young U., 1978, JD, 1982. CPA, Utah; Bar: Utah 1982, U.S. Dist. Ct. Utah 1982, Nev. 1986, U.S. Dist. Ct. Nev. 1986, U.S. Tax Ct. 1986. Acct. Squire & Co., Orem, Utah, 1981-84; contr., counsel Sommerset Corp., Provo, Utah, 1984-85, Ron Lewis Constrn., Moapa, Nev., 1985; assoc. Mills Gibson & Waite, Las Vegas, 1986-89, Clark Greene & Assocs., Las Vegas, 1989—; mem. supr. com. Moapa Valley Fed. Credit Union, Overton, Nev., 1987-90, chmn., 1993. Author, lectr. course materials Nat. Bus. Inst., 1992—. Scoutmaster, asst. scoutmaster, com. mem. Boy Scouts Am., Boulder Dam Area Coun., 1987—. Mem. ABA, Clark County Bar Assn. Republican. Mem. Ch. of LDS. Avocations: sports, reading. Home: 1695 N Whitmore PO Box 1355 Overton NV 89040 Office: Clark Greene & Assocs Ltd 3770 Howard Hughes Pkwy #195 Las Vegas NV 89109

YAMATO, KEI C., international business consultant; b. Honokaa, Hawaii, Sept. 21, 1921; s. Kango and Shizuka (Tanaka) Y.; m. Sherrie Keiko Inamine; children: Karen, Marla, Kei Tracy. B.A., U. Hawaii, 1946; LL.B., Yale, 1950; DD, World Christianship Ministries, 1994. Ordained to ministry Ind. Universal Ch. of God, 1994. Pres. Internat. Bus. Mgmt. Co., 1950; founder Pacific-Asia Bus. Council, 1950; pres. Orchids of Hawaii Internat., Inc., 1951, Polynesian Products, Inc., Holiday Promotions Internat., Inc., 1952, Orchawaii Internat. Travel Corp., 1962, Pacific Area Landscaping, Inc., 1970—, Hawaii Hort. Enterprises, Inc., 1970—, Agrisystems, Inc., 1971-95; minister Ind. Universal Ch. God, Honolulu, 1995—; v.p., dir. Sperry & Hutchison Travel Awards, Inc., 1964, Copley Internat. Corp., 1967; all N.Y.C.; pres. Internat. Cons. Co., 1968, Asia-Pacific Corp., 1968; chmn. Asia Internat. Group of Cos., Asia Internat. Cons.; mng. dir. Internat. Cons. Assocs., 1993; universal cons. svcs. God's Universal Ch. and Ministries. Bd. dirs. Internat. Execs. Assn., World Trade Club N.Y.C., Sales Execs. Club N.Y.C.; mem. Regional Export Expansion Council, U.S. Dept. Commerce; organizer Asia Pacific Inst.; pres. Saudi Arabia Pacific Asia Bus. Council, Arab Assian Assocs. Served to 1st lt. AUS, World War II, ETO. Decorated Silver Star, Purple Heart with 2 oak leaf clusters. Mem. Advt. Club N.Y.C., Nat. Indsl. Conf. Bd., Profl. Mgmt. Cons. Assn. Am., Sales Promotion Execs. Assn., Chgo. Execs. Club, Sales and Marketing Execs. Internat., N.Y. Hort. Soc., Asia Soc., Japan Soc., Am. Mgmt. Assn. (lectr.), 442d Regimental Combat Team Assn., Landscape Contractors Assn. Hawaii, Gen. Contractors Assn. Hawaii, Friends East-West Center, East-West Philosophers Conf., Hawaii Assn. Nurserymen, Hawaii Bot. Soc., Honolulu Execs. Assn., U. Hawaii Alumni Assn., Navy League, Nat. Fedn. Ind. Bus., Am. Assn. Nurserymen, Pacific Area Travel Assn., Assn. U.S. Army, Hawaii Visitors Bur., Hawaii C. of C., U.S. Arab C. of C., Saudi Arabia Bus. Council. Clubs: Rotary, Bankers. Home: PO Box 781 Honolulu HI 96808

YAMAYEE, ZIA AHMAD, engineering educator, dean; b. Herat, Afghanistan, Feb. 2, 1948; came to U.S., 1974; s. Sayed and Merjan Ahmad. BSEE, Kabul (Afghanistan) U., 1972; MSEE, Purdue U., 1976, PhD, 1978. Registered profl. engr., Calif., Wash. Mem. faculty of engring. Kabul U., 1978; engr. Systems Control, Inc., Palo Alto, Calif., 1979-81; sr. engr. Pacific N.W. Utilities, Portland, Oreg., 1981-83; assoc. prof. elec. engring. Clarkson U., Potsdam, N.Y., 1983-85; assoc. prof. Gonzaga U., Spokane, 1985-87, dean Sch. Engring., 1988—; prof., chair elec. engring. dept. U. New Orleans, 1987-88; part-time rsch. engr. La. Power and Light Co., New Orleans, 1987-88; sr. cons. Engring. and Cons. Svcs., Spokane, 1989—. Contbr. articles, reports to profl. jours. Bd. dirs. Wash. State Math., Engring. Sci. Achievement, Seattle, 1989—; mem. Spokane Intercollegiate Rsch. and Tech. Inst. Adv. Coun., 1990—. NSF grantee. Mem. Am. Soc. Engring. Edn., IEEE (sr.). Office: University of Portland 5000 N Willamette Blvd Portland OR 97203

YAMIN, DIANNE ELIZABETH, judge; b. Danbury, Conn., June 4, 1961; d. Raymond Joseph and Linda May (Bucko) Goetz; m. Robert Joseph Yamin, Sept. 3, 1988; children: Samantha Blythe, Rebecca Anne. AB, Lehigh U., 1983; JD, Mercer U., 1986. Bar: Conn. 1986, U.S. Dist. Ct. Conn. 1989. Lawyer Gerald Hecht & Assocs., Danbury, 1986-92; judge State Conn., Danbury, 1991—; atty. Yamin & Yamin, Danbury, 1992—; chmn. ethics com. Conn. Probate Assembly, 1994—; mem. Conn. Coun. on Adoptions, 1992—, Conn. Probate Assembly, 1991—. Bd. dirs. Big Brothers/Big Sisters, Danbury, 1987-94; dir. Lions Club Danbury, 1993-94; dir. Conn. Brass Soc., Inc., 1991—, Friends of Tarrywile Park, Inc., Danbury, 1993—. Recipient outstanding young citizen award Conn. Jaycees, 1994, pro bono award Conn. Legal Svcs., 1993. Mem. ABA, Conn. Bar Assn., Conn. Health Lawyers Assn., Danbury Bar Assn., Omicron Delta Kappa. Republican. Roman Catholic. Avocations: ballet, volunteerism, travel, outdoor activities. Home: 8 Johnson Dr Danbury CT 06811 Office: 155 Deer Hill Ave Danbury CT 06810

YAMIN, MICHAEL GEOFFREY, lawyer; b. N.Y.C., Nov. 10, 1931; s. Michael and Ethel Y.; m. Martina Schaap, Apr. 16, 1961; children: Michael Jeremy, Katrina. AB magna cum laude, Harvard U., 1953, LLB, 1958. Bar: N.Y. 1959, U.S. Dist. Ct. (so. dist.) N.Y., U.S. Dist. Ct. (ea. dist.) N.Y., U.S. Ct. Appeals (2d cir.) 1960, U.S. Supreme Ct. 1967. Assoc. Weil, Gotshal & Manges, N.Y.C., 1958-65; sr. ptnr. Colton, Hartnick, Yamin & Sheresky, N.Y.C., 1966-93; sr. ptnr. Kaufmann, Feiner, Yamin, Gildin & Robbins, N.Y.C., 1993—. Bd. trustees Gov.'s Com. Scholastic Achievement, 1976—; chmn. Manhattan Community Bd. 6, 1986-88, mem., 1974-88; mem. Manhattan Borough Bd., 1986-88; bd. trustees Rockland County Soc. Prevention of Cruelty to Children, 1979—. Served as lt. USNR, 1953-55, Korea. Mem. ABA, N.Y. State Bar Assn., Assn. Bar City N.Y., Fed. Bar Coun., Am. Fgn. Law Assn. (Am. Branch), Internat. Law Assn., Societe de Legislation Comparee, Internat. Bar Assn. Clubs: Harvard Faculty (Cambridge, Mass.); Harmonie, Harvard (N.Y.C.) (trustee N.Y. Found. 1981—, sub-chmn. schs. and scholarships com. 1972-93, bd. mgrs. 1985-88, 93—, chair house com. 1992-95, v.p. 1995—), Harvard Alumni Assn. (elected dir. 1995—). Home: 206 E 30th St New York NY 10016-8202 Office: 777 3rd Ave New York NY 10017

YAMMINE, RIAD NASSIF, oil company executive; b. Hammana, Lebanon, Apr. 12, 1934; s. Nassib Nassif and Emilie (Daou) Y.; came to U.S., 1952, naturalized, 1963; m. Beverly Ann Hosack, Sept. 14, 1954; children: Kathleen Yammine Gross, Cynthia Yammine Rotman, Michael. BS in Petroleum Engring., Pa. State U., 1956; postgrad. Advanced Mgmt. Program, Harvard U., 1977. Registered profl. engr., Ohio. Engr. Trans-Arabian Pipe Line Co., Saudi Arabia, 1956-61; with Marathon Pipe Line Co., 1961-75, mgr. Western div., Casper, Wyo., 1971-74, mgr. Eastern div., Martinsville, Ill., 1974-75; mktg. ops. div. mgr. Marathon Oil Co., 1975-83; pres. Marathon Pipeline Co., 1983-84; v.p. supply and transp. Marathon Petroleum Co., 1984-88, dir., 1984-90; pres. EMRO Mktg. Co., 1988—; bd. dirs. Marathon Oil Co.; also officer, bd. dirs. various subs. Patentee in field. Trustee, Wright State Univ. Found.; past trustee, Fisk U. Mem. ASME, Am. Petroleum Inst. Republican. Club: Findlay Country. Home: 200 Penbrooke Dr Findlay OH 45840 Office: 539 S Main St Findlay OH 45840-3242 also: 500 Speedway Dr Enon OH 45323-1056

YAMNER, MORRIS, lawyer; b. Passaic, N.J., Sept. 5, 1938; s. Sam and Edna (Halpern) Y.; 1 child, Laura; m. Gail Garber, Oct. 23, 1975; children: Laura, Amy, Lisa. BS in Bus., Ohio State U., 1959; JD, Georgetown U., 1962. Bar: N.J. 1962, N.Y. 1983. Law sec. Superior Ct., Somerville, N.J., 1962-63; dep. atty. gen. Atty. Gen. Office, Trenton, N.J., 1963-66; ptnr. Cole, Yamner & Bray, Paterson, N.J., 1966-90, Sills, Cummis, Newark, 1990—. Bd. dirs. Jewish Fedn., Clifton, N.J., 1985—, YM/YMHA, 1980—. Mem. Daus. of Miriam (bd. dirs. 1985—), Preakness Hills Country Club (bd. dirs. 1992—). Office: Sills Cummis 1 Riverfront Plz Newark NJ 07102-5401

YAN, CHONG CHAO, pharmacology, toxicology and nutrition researcher; b. Qing Jiang, Jiangsu, China, Oct. 16, 1963; came to the U.S., 1993; s. Mao Liang Yan and Gui Ying Ding; m. Yun Sun, July 28, 1988; 1 child, Jenny. BSc, Nanjing (China) Med. Coll., 1985; MS, Chinese Acad. Preventive Med., Beijing, 1988, MD/PhD, 1992. Rsch. fellow dept. metabolism and pathol. biochemistry Inst. Superiore di Sanità, Rome, 1990-92; rsch. fellow dept. gastroenterology U. Modena, Italy, 1992-93; rsch. assoc. dept. pharmacology U. Ariz., Tucson, 1993-95, asst. sci. investigator dept. pharmacology, 1995—; rschr. Chinese Acad. Preventive Medicine, Beijing, 1985-90. Contbr. articles to profl. jours. Mem. Internat. Soc. Toxinology, Soc. Exptl. Biology and Medicine, Soc. Toxicology. Avocations: driving, swimming, table tennis, volleyball. Office: Dept Pharmacology Univ Ariz Tucson AZ 85724

YAN, SAU-CHI BETTY, biochemist; b. Hong Kong, Nov. 25, 1954; d. Ming Yan and Choo-Chen Woo; m. Victor J. Chen, Feb. 29, 1980; 1 child, Heidi I. BS, Ctrl. Mo. State U., 1975; PhD, Iowa State U., 1980. Postdoctoral fellow St. Paul-Ramsey Med. Ctr., 1980-82; postdoctoral fellow med. sch. U. Tex., Houston, 1982-84; sr. biochemist Eli Lilly & Co., Indpls., 1985-88, sr. scientist, 1989-93, sr. rsch. scientist, 1993—. Patentee in field; contbr. articles to profl. jours. Bd. dirs. A Children's Habitat, Indpls., 1994. Mem. AAAS, Am. Soc. Biochemistry, Molecular Biology, Protein Soc., Soc. Chinese Bioscientists Am. Office: Eli Lilly & Co DC1543 307 W Mccarty St # Dc1543 Indianapolis IN 46225-1235

YANAGISAWA, SAMUEL TSUGUO, electronics executive; b. Berkeley, Calif., Feb. 18, 1922; s. Jusaku George and Mitsuyo (Mochizuki) Y.; m. Fernande Gerardine Renar, July 10, 1952; children: Shane Henry, Steven Kim, Ian Gerard. B.S. with honors in Elec. Engring., U. Calif.-Berkeley, 1942. Product line mgr. Machlett Labs. Inc., Springdale, Conn., 1943-63; v.p. ops. Warnecke Electron Tubes, Inc., Des Plaines, Ill., 1963-67; with

Varo Inc., Garland, Tex., 1968-87, pres., 1971-84, chief exec. officer, 1974-85, chmn., 1976-87, also bd. dirs., ret., 1987; pres. Yanagisawa & Assocs., Dallas, 1989—; dir. Republic Bank, Garland; mem. Army Sci. Bd., 1986-90. Contbr. articles to profl. jours.; patentee electron devices. bd. dirs. So. Meth. U. Found. for Sci. and Engring.; mem. adv. coun., chmn. bd. visitors McDonald Obs., U. Tex., Austin; mem. adv. coun. Communities Found. of Tex.; bd. dirs. Dallas Council on World Affairs; adv. coun. Sch. Engring, U. Tex. at Dallas. Served to lt. AUS, 1945-46. Mem. IEEE (sr.), AAAS, Am. Def. Preparedness Assn., U.S. Night Vision Assn., Soc. Info. Display, Am. Electronic Assn., Am. Vacuum Soc., Assn. U.S. Army, Assn. Old Crows, Japanese Am. Citizens League, Nat. Japanese Am. Hist. Soc., Phi Beta Kappa, Sigma Xi, Tau Beta Pi, Eta Kappa Nu. Office: Yanagisawa & Assocs 7708 Chalkstone Dr Dallas TX 75248-5320

YANAGITANI, ELIZABETH, optometrist; b. Ogden, Utah, Nov. 24, 1953; d. Katsuyoshi and Yaeko (Watanabe) Y. AS, Weber State Coll., Ogden, Utah, 1974; BA magna cum laude, U. Utah, 1976; OD, Pacific U., Forest Grove, Oreg., 1980. Externship Tripler Army Med Ctr., Schofield Barracks, Hawaii, 1979; staff optometrist Gen. Med., San Diego, 1984-89, San Ysidro Health Ctr., Calif., 1985-87, 91—, Logan Heights Family Health Ctr., San Diego, 1989-91; assoc. of pvt. office Chula Vista, Calif., 1985—; asst. instr. Am. Bus. Coll., San Diego, 1982. Recipient Gates Meml. award Nat. Eye Rsch. Found., 1980; scholar Weber State Coll., 1972-73, U. Utah, 1975, Project award Beta Sigma Kappa, 1980. Mem. San Diego County Optometric Soc. (v.p. 1985), Calif. Optometric Soc. (del. to leadership conf. 1985), Achievement Through Vision/COVD (pres. 1990), Phi Kappa Phi. Avocations: travel, photography.

YANCEY, ASA GREENWOOD, SR., physician; b. Atlanta, Aug. 19, 1916; s. Arthur H. and Daisy L. (Sherard) Y.; m. Carolyn E. Dunbar, Dec. 28, 1944; children: Arthur H. II, Carolyn L., Caren L., Asa Greenwood Jr. BS, Morehouse Coll., 1937, ScD (hon.), 1991; MD, U. Mich., 1941; ScD (hon.), Howard U., 1991. Diplomate Am. Bd. Surgery. Intern City Hosp., Cleve., 1941-42; resident Freedmen's Hosp., Washington, 1942-45, U.S. Marine Hosp., Boston, 1945; instr. surgery Meharry Med. Coll., 1946-48; chief surgery VA Hosp., Tuskegee, Ala., 1948-58; chief surgery of Hughes Spalding Pavilion, 1958-72; pvt. practice specializing in surgery Atlanta, 1958-86; med. dir. Grady Meml. Hosp., Atlanta, 1972-89; mem. staff Hughes Spalding Hosp., St. Joseph Hosp., Emory U. Hosp., up to 1986-88; asst. prof. surgery Emory U., 1958-72, assoc. prof., 1972-75, prof. surgery, 1975-86, prof. emeritus, 1986—, assoc. dean Emory U. Sch. Medicine, 1972-89; clin. prof. surgery Morehouse Sch. Medicine, 1985—. Contbr. articles to profl. jours. Mem. Atlanta Bd. Edn., 1967-77, Fulton-De Kalb Hosp. Authority; trustee Body for Grady Meml. Hosp., 1989-93. 1st lt. M.C., AUS, 1942. Fellow ACS, Am. Surg. Assn.; mem. Nat. Med. Assn. (1st v.p. 1988-89, trustee 1960-66, editorial bd. jour. 1964-80), Inst. Medicine of NAS, So. Surg. Assn. Baptist. Home and Office: 2845 Engle Rd NW Atlanta GA 30318-7216

YANCEY, ELEANOR GARRETT, retired crisis intervention clinician; b. Ga., Oct. 24, 1933; adopted d. Overton LaVerne Garrett; m. Robert Grady Yancey, Nov. 10, 1961 (div. Apr. 1968); children: Katherine La Verne, David Shawn. Student, High Mus. Art Inst., 1952-53, Ga. State U., 1953-55, 78; BA, La Grange Coll., 1958. Social worker, case worker Fulton County Dept. Family and Children's Svcs., Atlanta, 1957-61; asst. tchr. Atlanta (Ga.) Bd. Edn., 1973-85; mental health crisis intervention clinician Dekalb County Bd. Health, Decatur, 1985-95, acting dir. crisis intervention, 1988-90; ret., 1995. Performed summer stock, 1969-70. Performed with Rogers & Co., 1969, 70; band booster pres. Henry Grady High Sch., Atlanta, 1977-78, v.p. PTA, 1978-79; pres. PTA Morningside Elem. Sch., Atlanta, 1977; grand juror Dekalb County, Decatur, 1983; active Sesquicentennial Celebration of Ala. Statehood. Mem. Kappa Kappa Iota (Lambda chpt. state pres. 1987-88, Eta pres. local chpt. 1992—). Democrat. Avocations: drawing, gardening, travel, music. Home: 3425 Regalwoods Dr Doraville GA 30340-4019

YANCEY, JIMMIE ISAAC, marketing professional; b. Ripley, Miss., Dec. 11, 1935; s. Charlie Edward and Overa (Wilbanks) Y.; m. Jonell Smith, Mar. 1, 1958; children: Angela Jo, Jamie Lorraine, Cynthia Overa, Melanie Ann. BS, Miss. State U., 1963, MBA, 1966. Editor univ. rels. Miss. State. U., Starkville, 1963-65, editor coll. bus., 1965-66; editor Miss. Extension Svc., Starkville, 1966-67, Nat. Cotton Coun., Memphis, 1967-71; pub. rels. dir. Cotton Inc., Raleigh, N.C., 1971, Am. Soybean Assn., Hudson, Iowa, 1971-78; gen. mgr. Prog. Farmer Network, Starkville, 1978-86; owner, mgr. Yancey Agrl. Network, Starkville, 1986—; mktg. cons. Wyffel's Hybrids, Inc., Atkinson, Ill., 1987-93. Bd. dirs. Agri-Bus. Edn. Found.; sr. adv. com. Coll. Bus. and Industry, Miss. State U. Mem. Nat. Agrl. Mktg. Assn., (pres. 1986-87, Meritorious Svc. award 1986), Nat. Assn. Farm Broadcasters, Am. Advt. Fedn., Starkville C. of C. (venture capital com. 1990), Am. Soybean Assn. (Mertorious Svc. award 1974, Broadcaster of Yr. 1984), Hudson C. of C. (pres. 1972, Iowa chpt.), Nat. Alliance of Ind. Corp. Cons., Miss. Rotary, Pres.'s Club. Presbyterian. Avocations: gardening, fishing. Office: Yancey Agrl Network PO Box 1850 PO Box 1850 Starkville MS 39759-7000

YANCEY, RICHARD CHARLES, investment banker; b. Spokane, Wash., May 28, 1926; s. George R. and M. Ruth (Yenney) Y.; m. Mary Anne Shaffer, Feb. 5, 1956; children: Leslie, Jennifer, Richard C. Jr. BA in Econs., Whitman Coll., Walla Walla, Wash., 1949; MBA with distinction, Harvard U., 1952. Assoc. Dillon, Read & Co. Inc., N.Y.C. 1952-63; v.p. Dillon, Read & Co., Inc., N.Y.C., 1963-75, mng. dir., 1975-89, dir., 1990; sr. adv., 1992; ret. Dillon, Read & Co., Inc., N.Y.C., 1992; bd. dirs. Composite Group Mut. Funds, Spokane, Wash., Ad Media Corp. Advisors, inc., N.Y.C., The Score Bd., Inc., Cherry Hill, N.J., Capmac Holdings, Inc., N.Y.C., Fiberite, Inc., Tempe, Ariz.; former mem. partnership bd. Whittle Comms. L.P., Knoxville, Tenn. Former bd. overseers Whitman Coll.; former trustee, former pres. Plymouth Ch. of Pilgrims, Bklyn.; former trustee N.Y. Infirmary-Beekman Downtown Hosp. Served with USNR, 1944-46, PTO. Mem. N.Y. Soc. Security Analysts, Harvard Club, Met. Club, N.Y.C., Pilgrims of the U.S. Republican. Home: 42 Monroe Pl Brooklyn NY 11201-2603 Office: Dillon Read & Co Inc 535 Madison Ave Fl 15 New York NY 10022-4212

YANCEY, ROBERT EARL, JR., oil company executive; b. Ashland, Ky., June 16, 1945; s. Robert E. Sr. and Estelline (Tackett) Y.; m. Nina McGee, June 16, 1962; children: Rob, Yvonne, Elizabeth. BS in Chem. Engring., Cornell U., 1967. Sr. v.p., group operating officer; supt. Catlettsburg (Ky.) Refinery, 1976-79; exec. asst. Ashland (Ky.) Petroleum Co., 1979-80, group v.p., 1980-81, sr. v.p., 1981-86, pres., 1986—; sr. v.p., group operating officer Ashland Inc., 1988—. Republican. Avocations: golf, hunting, fishing. Home: 504 Amanda Furnace Dr Ashland KY 41101-2193 Office: Ashland Petroleum Co PO Box 391 Ashland KY 41105-0391

YANCEY, WALLACE GLENN, insurance company executive; b. Langdale, Ala., Sept. 8, 1930; s. Wallace Odell and Nellie Leigh (Roughton) Y.; m. Betty Jo Carden, June 1, 1956; children—Angela, Susan, Reed. B.S. in Bus. Adminstrn., Auburn U., 1956. Sales rep. Arkwright Mut. Ins. Co. (formerly Arkwright-Boston Ins. Co.), Birmingham, Ala., 1957-59; sales rep. Arkwright Mut. Ins. Co. (formerly Arkwright-Boston Ins. Co.), Atlanta, 1960-61; br. mgr. Arkwright Mut. Ins. Co. (formerly Arkwright-Boston Ins. Co.), N.Y.C., 1961-64; regional sales mgr. Arkwright Mut. Ins. Co. (formerly Arkwright-Boston Ins. Co.), Atlanta, 1964-68; v.p. mktg. Arkwright Mut. Ins. Co. (formerly Arkwright-Boston Ins. Co.), Waltham, Mass., 1975-79, sr. v.p., 1979-88, exec. v.p., 1988—; v.p., gen. mgr. Hobbs Group, Inc. (formerly Hobbs Brook Agy., Inc.), Waltham, 1969-75, pres., chief exec. officer, 1985—; pres., chief exec. officer HPR Ltd., Bermuda, Arkwright Mgmt. Corp, Hamilton, Bermuda; exec. v.p. Arkwright Mut. Ins. Co., Waltham, 1988—. Comdr. Acton Minutemen, Mass., 1978-79; bd. dirs. Acton Youth Hockey Assn., 1973-75. Served with USN, 1948-52, Korea. Republican. Congregationalist. Home: 110 Whitman St Stow MA 01775-1371 Office: Arkwright Mut Ins Co 225 Wyman St Waltham MA 02154-1209

YANCIK, JOSEPH JOHN, government official; b. Mt. Olive, Ill., Dec. 1, 1930; s. Joseph John and Anna (Gubach) Y.; m. Rosemary Panich, Feb. 19, 1955; children—Geri Anne, Ellen Marie. BS, U. Ill., 1954; MS in Mining Engring., Mo. Sch. Mines, 1956; PhD, U. Mo., Rolla, 1960. Mining research engr. St. Joe Lead Co., Bonne Terre, Mo., 1955-58; mgr. research and devel. Monsanto Co., St. Louis, 1960-70; asst. dir. mining U.S. Bur. Mines, Washington, 1970-77; v.p. research Nat. Coal Assn., Washington, 1977-82; pres. Bituminous Coal Research, Inc., Washington, 1980-82; dir. Coal Export Office U.S. Dept. Commerce, Washington, 1982-84; dir. Office of Energy Internat. Trade Adminstrn., Washington, 1984-95; pvt. practice Mc Lean, 1995—; cons. energy in internat. trade and investment; dir. energy affairs U.S.-Russia Bus. Coun., Washington, 1996—. Contbr. articles to profl. jours. Served with C.E. U.S. Army, 1950-52. Recipient Alumni Achievement award U. Mo.-Rolla, 1975, Silver Medal award U.S. Dept. Commerce, 1986, Gold Medal award Dept. Commerce, 1992. Mem. Cosmos Club (Washington). Roman Catholic. Home and Office: 1703 James Payne Cir Mc Lean VA 22101-4223

YANDELL, CATHY MARLEEN, foreign language educator; b. Anadarko, Okla., Dec. 27, 1949; d. Lloyd O. and Maurine (Dunn) Y.; m. Mark S. McNeil, Sept. 7, 1974; children: Elizabeth Yandell McNeil, Laura Yandell McNeil. Diplome d'etudes, Inst. des Professeurs de Français à l'Etranger, Sorbonne, 1970; BA, U. N.Mex., 1971; MA, U. Calif., Berkeley, 1973, PhD, 1977. Teaching asst. U. Calif., Berkeley, 1971-75, acting instr., 1976-77; asst. prof. Carleton Coll., Northfield, Minn., 1977-83, assoc. prof., 1983-89, prof. French, 1989—; chair commn. on the status of women Carleton Coll., Northfield, 1983-85, ednl. policy com., 1985-86, 96—, romance langs. and lits., 1990-94, pres. of faculty, 1991-94, Bryn-Jones disting. tchg. prof. humanities, 1996—. Contbr. to Art & Argumentation: The Sixteenth Century Dialogue, 1993, French Texts/American Contexts: French Women Writers, 1994; editor: Pontus de Tyard's Solitaire Second, ou prose de la musique, 1980; contbr. articles to profl. jours. Active exec. com., then mem. Amnesty Internat., Northfield, 1980—. Regents' Travelling fellow U. Calif. at Berkeley, 1975-76; Faculty Devel. grantee Carleton Coll., 1988, 91; NEH Rsch. fellow., 1994-95. Mem. MLA (del. 1989-92). Democrat. Avocations: dance, music, hiking, biking, cross-country skiing. Home: 514 5th St E Northfield MN 55057-2220 Office: Carleton College 1 N College St Northfield MN 55057-4001

YANDERS, ARMON FREDERICK, biological sciences educator, research administrator; b. Lincoln, Nebr., Apr. 12, 1928; s. Fred W. and Beatrice (Pate) Y.; m. Evelyn Louise Gatz, Aug. 1, 1948; children: Mark Frederick, Kent Michael. A.B., Nebr. State Coll., Peru, 1948; M.S., U. Nebr., 1950, Ph.D., 1953. Research asso. Oak Ridge Nat. Lab. and Northwestern U., 1953-54; biophysicist U.S. Naval Radiol. Def. Lab., San Francisco, 1955-58; asso. geneticist Argonne (Ill.) Nat. Lab., 1958-59; with dept. zoology Mich. State U., 1959-69; prof., asst. dean Mich. State U. (Coll. Natural Sci.), 1963-69; prof. biol. scis. U. Mo., Columbia, 1969—, dean Coll. Arts and Scis., 1969-82, research prof., dir. Environ. Trace Substances Research Ctr., 1983-93, dir. Alzheimer's Disease and Related Disorders Program, 1994—; research prof., dir. Environ. Trace Substances Research Ctr. and Sinclair Comparative Medicine Research Farm, Columbia, 1984-94; prof. emeritus, 1994—; Trustee Argonne Univs. Assn., 1965-77, v.p., 1969-73, pres., 1973, 76-77, chmn. bd., 1973-75; bd. dirs. Coun. Colls. Arts and Scis., 1981-82; mem. adv. com. environ. hazards VA, Washington, 1985—, chmn. sci. coun., 1988—, chmn. of com., 1990—. Contbr. articles to profl. jours. Trustee Peru State Coll., 1992. Served from ensign to lt. USNR, 1954-58. Recipient Disting. Svc. award Peru State Coll., 1989. Fellow AAAS; mem. AAUP (Robert W. Martin acad. freedom award 1971), Am. Inst. Biol. Sci., Environ. Mutagen Soc., Genetics Soc. Am., Radiation Research Soc., Soc. Environ. Toxicology and Chemistry. Home: 2405 Ridgefield Rd Columbia MO 65203-1531 Office: U of Mo 521 Clark Hall Columbia MO 65211

YANDLE, STEPHEN THOMAS, law school dean; b. Oakland, Calif., Mar. 7, 1947; s. Clyde Thomas and Jane Walker (Hess) Y.; m. Martha Anne Welch, June 26, 1971. BA, U. Va., 1969, JD, 1972. Bar: Va. 1972. Asst. dir. admissions U. Va. Law Sch., Charlottesville, 1972-76; from asst. to assoc. dean Northwestern U. Sch. Law, Chgo., 1976-85; assoc. dean Yale U. Law Sch., New Haven, 1985—. Served to capt. U.S. Army, 1972. Mem. Law Sch. Admission Coun. (programs, edn. and prelaw com. 1978-84), Assn. Am. Law Schs. (chmn. legal edn. and admissions sect. 1979, nominations com. 1987, chmn. adminstrn. of law schs. sect. 1991), Nat. Assn. for Law Placement (pres. 1984-85, co-chair Joint Nat. Assn. com. on placement 1986-88). Office: Yale U Sch Law PO Box 208215 New Haven CT 06520-8215

YANEY, GEORGE, history educator; b. Teaneck, N.J., Oct. 30, 1930; s. Arthur J. and Frances (Levings) Y.; m. Ann Hinrichs, June 7, 1952; children: Brian, Dale, Carolyn, Tara. B in Mgmt. Engring., Rensselaer Poly. Inst., 1952; MA, U. Colo., 1956; PhD, Princeton U., 1961. Instr. Coll. Wooster, Ohio, 1957-58; prof. history U. Md., College Park, 1960—. Author: Systematization of Russian Government, 1973, Urge to Mobilize, 1982, World of the Manager, 1994. Served to capt. USMC, 1952-54, Korea. Rsch. fellow Harvard U., 1969-70, fellow Slavic Rsch. Ctr., U. Hokkaido, Japan, 1990-91; Fulbright grantee, 1975, 77, 85, Internat. Rsch. Exchanges Bd. grantee 1965, 75, 77, 85, 89. Home: 7303 Baylor Ave College Park MD 20740-3001 Office: Univ of Maryland Dept Of History College Park MD 20742

YANG, BAIYIN, adult education educator; b. Changshu, Jiangsu, China, Mar. 17, 1962; came to U.S., 1992; s. Zongde Yang and Fengyin Gu; m. Xiaoping Lu, Dec. 14, 1987; 1 child, Zhuowei. BS, Nanjing U., 1982; M Continuing Edn., U. Sasktchewan, Can., 1992; PhD, U. Ga., 1996. Lectr. The Chinese Acad. Scis., Nanjing, 1982-87, coord. tng. and devel., 1987-90; computer lab. advisor U. Saskatchewan, Saskatoon, 1990-92; stat. cons. U. Ga., Athens, 1993—; rsch. asst. U. Ga., 1992—, tchg. asst. summer 1992; rsch. asst. U. Saskatchewan, 1990-91. Contbr. articles to profl. jours. Mem. Am. Ednl. Rsch. Assn., Am. Assn. Adult and Continuing Edn., ASTD, Kapp Delta Pi. Office: Dept Adult Edn U Ga Tucker Hall Athens GA 30602

YANG, CHEN NING, physicist, educator; b. Hefei, Anhwei, China, Sept. 22, 1922; married, 1950; 3 children. BSc, SW Assoc. U., China, 1942; PhD in Physics, U. Chgo., 1948; DSc (hon.), Princeton U., 1958, Polytech. Inst. Bklyn., 1965, U. Wroclaw, 1974, Gustavus Adolphus Coll., 1975, U. Md., 1979, U. Durham, Eng., 1979, Fundan U., China, 1984, Eidg Technische Hochschule, Switzerland, 1987, Moscow State U., 1992. Instr. physics U. Chgo., 1948-49; mem. Inst. Advanced Study, Princeton, N.J., 1949-66, prof., 1955-66; Albert Einstein prof. physics, dir. inst. theoretical physics SUNY, Stony Brook, 1966—; bd. trustees Woods Hole Oceanographical Inst., 1962-78, Rockefeller U., 1970-76, Salk Inst., 1978-79; mem. governing coun. Courant Inst. Math. Sci., 1963—; mem. sci. adv. com. IBM, 1966-71; chmn. divsn. particles & fields Internat. Union Pure & Applied Physics, 1972-76; chmn., fachbeirat Max Planck Inst. Physics, Munich, 1980-83; disting. prof.-at-large Chinese U., Hong Kong. Recipient Bower Achievement in Sci. award and prize Franklin Inst., 1994, Nobel prize in Physics, 1957, Rumford prize, 1980, Nat. medal sci., 1986, Liberty award, 1986, Benjamin Franlin medal, 1993. Mem. NAS (chmn. panel theoretical physics 1965, chmn. physics surv. com. 1965), Am. Philosophical Soc., Royal Spanish Acad. Sci., Polish Acad. Sci., Royal Soc. London, Russian Acad. Sci. Research in theoretical physics. Office: SUNY Stony Brook Inst Theoretical Phys Stony Brook NY 11794-3840

YANG, CHIN-PING, chemist, engineering educator; b. Penghu Hsien, Taiwan, Republic of China, Dec. 25, 1931; s. Yee Yang and Chi Chao; m. Ye-ho Hwang, Oct. 10, 1961; children: Chung-Sheng, Chung-Chen, Chung-Cheng. BS in Chemistry, Taiwan Normal U., Taipei, Republic of China, 1956; M. Engring., Tokyo U., 1973; D. Engring., Tokyo Inst. Tech., 1986. Chmn., prof. chem. engring. dept. Tatung Inst. Tech., Taipei, 1970-89, prof. chem. engring. dept., 1990—; chmn. grad. sch. chem. engring. Tatung Inst. Tech., Taipei, 1980-89; cons. Tatung Co., Taipei, 1963—. Contbr. articles to profl. jours.; patentee in field. Mem. Am. Chem. Soc., Japan Chem. Soc., Chinese Chem. Soc., Soc. Polymer Sci. Japan, Soc. Chinese Inst. Chem. Engrs. Home: 126-1 Chien St Shihlin, Taipei Taiwan Office: Tatung Inst of Tech, 40 Chungshan N Rd 3d Sec, Taipei Taiwan

YANG, EDWARD S., electrical engineering educator; b. Nanking, Peoples Republic of China, Oct. 16, 1937; s. Joseph L. and York-Shih (Lung) Y.; m. Ruth Chu; children: David K., Grace S. BS, Nat. Cheng-Kung U., Taiwan, 1957; MS, Okla. State U., 1961; PhD, Yale U., 1966. Engr. IBM Corp., Poughkeepsie, N.Y., 1961-63; asst. prof. elec. engring. Columbia U., N.Y.C., 1965-70, assoc. prof., 1970-75, prof., 1975—, chmn. dept., 1987-89, 93—. Author: Fundamental Semiconductor Devices, 1978, Microelectronic Devices, 1988; contbr. over 150 articles to profl. jours. Fellow IEEE. Office: Columbia U Dept Of Elec Engring New York NY 10027

YANG, HENRY T., university chancellor, educator; b. Chungking, China, Nov. 29, 1940; s. Chen Pei and Wei Gen Yang; m. Dilling Tsui, Sept. 2, 1966; children: Maria, Martha. BSCE, Nat. Taiwan U., 1962; MSCE, W.Va. U., 1965; PhD, Cornell U., 1968; Doctorate (hon.), Purdue U., 1996. Rsch. engr. Gilbert Assocs., Reading, Pa., 1968-69; asst. prof. Sch. Aeros. and Astronautics, Purdue U., West Lafayette, Ind., 1969-72, assoc. prof., 1972-76, prof., 1976-94, Neil A. Armstrong Disting. prof., 1988-94, sch. head, 1979-84; dean engring. Purdue U., 1984-94; chancellor U. Calif., Santa Barbara, 1994—; mem. sci. adv. bd. USAF, 1985-89; mem. aero. adv. com. NASA, 1985-89; mem. engring. adv. com. NSF, 1988-91; mem. mechanics bd. visitors ONR, 1990-93; mem. def. mfg. bd. DOD, 1988-89, def. sci. bd., 1989-91; mem. acad. adv. bd. Nat. Acad. Engring., 1991-94; mem. tech. adv. com. Pratt & Whitney, 1993-95; bd. dirs. Space Industries Internat., 1993-95; mem. Naval Rsch. Adv. Com., 1996—. Recipient 12 Best Tchg. awards Purdue U., 1971-94, Centennial medal Am. Soc. Engring. Edn., 1993. Fellow AIAA, ASEE; mem. NAE, Academia Sinica. Home: University House University Calif Santa Barbara CA 93106 Office: Chancellor's Office U California Santa Barbara CA 93106

YANG, JEFFREY CHIH-HO, magazine editor, publisher, featured columnist; b. Bklyn., Mar. 14, 1968; s. David Chang-Sing and Bailing (Wu) Y. BA, Harvard U., 1989. Publicity dir. Asian CineVision, N.Y.C., 1990-91; asst. editor Village Voice, N.Y.C., 1991-92, featured columnist, 1992—; editor in chief A. Magazine, N.Y.C., 1989-94, editor-in-chief, pub., 1994—; CEO, pres. Metro East Publs., Inc., N.Y.C., 1994—; guest lectr. CUNY, Princeton U., 1993—. Mem. Asian Am. Journalists Assn. (bd. dirs. N.Y.C. chpt.). Office: Metro East Pubs Inc 220 Lafayette St Ste 400 New York NY 10012

YANG, RALPH TZU-BOW, chemical engineering educator, researcher; b. Chung King, China, Sept. 18, 1942; came to U.S., 1965, naturalized, 1976; s. Chen Pei and Wei (Gee) Y.; m. Frances H. Chang, Dec. 23, 1972; children—Michael, Robert. BS, Nat. Taiwan U., 1964; MS, Yale U., 1968, PhD, 1971. Rsch. assoc. Argonne Nat. Lab., Ill., 1972-73; sci. Aluminum Co. of Am., Pitts., 1973-74; group leader Brookhaven Nat. Lab., Upton, N.Y., 1974-78; assoc. prof. SUNY-Buffalo, 1978-82, prof., 1982—, chmn. chem. engring. dept., 1990-95; Praxair prof. chem. engring., chair, 1993-95, prof., chmn. chem. engring. dept. U. Mich., 1995—; cons. in field. Author: Gas Separation by Adsorption Processes, 1987. Contbr. articles to profl. jours. Patentee in field. Research grantee NSF, 1980—, Dept. Energy, 1980—, Alcoa Found., 1979-81. Fellow Am. Inst. Chem. Engring. (William H. Walker award for excellence in contbn. to chem. engring. lit., 1991); mem. Am. Chem. Soc. (Ind. Engring. Chem. Rsch. jour. adv. bd 1991-93), Am. Carbon Soc. (adv. bd. 1985—), Am. Soc. Engring. Edn., Internat. Adsorption Soc. (adv. bd. Jour. of Adsorption 1993—), Adsorption Sci. and Tech. (adv. bd. 1986—). Office: U Mich Dept Chem Engring Ann Arbor MI 48109

YANG, SHANG FA, biochemistry educator; b. Tainan, Taiwan, Nov. 10, 1932; came to U.S., 1959, naturalized, 1971; s. Chian-Zuei and En-Liu (Lu) Y.; m. Eleanor Shou-yuan, Sept. 16, 1964; children: Albert, Bryant. BS, Nat. Taiwan U., 1956, MS, 1958; PhD, Utah State U., 1962. Rsch. assoc. U. Calif., Davis, 1962-63, NYU Med. Sch., N.Y.C., 1963-64, U. Calif.-San Diego, La Jolla, 1964-65; asst. biochemist U. Calif.-Davis, 1966-69, assoc. biochemist, 1969-74, prof., biochemist, 1974—, chmn., 1989-90 ; prof. Hong Kong U. Sci. & Tech., 1994—; spl. rsch. fellow Academia Sinica, Taipei, 1995—; vis. prof. U. Konstanz, Germany, 1974, Nat. Taiwan U., Taipei, 1983, U. Cambridge, Eng., 1983, Nagoya U., Japan, 1988-89. Assoc. editor Jour. Plant Growth Regulation, 1981—; mem. editl. bd. Plant Physiology, 1974-92, Plant Cell Physiology, 1987-91, Plant Physiology and Biochemistry, 1988—, Acta Phytophysiologica Sinica, 1988—. Recipient Campbell award Am. Inst. Biol. Sci., 1969; Guggenheim fellow, 1982; recipient Internat. Plant growth Substance Assn. Research award, 1985, Wolf prize agriculture, 1991, Outstanding Rsch award Am. Soc. Horticultural Sci., 1992. Mem. NAS, Academia Sinica, Am. Soc. Biochemistry and Molecular Biology, Am. Soc. Plant Physiologists (chmn. Western sect. 1982-84). Home: 1118 Villanova Dr Davis CA 95616-1753 Office: U Calif Dept of Vegetable Corps Davis CA 95616

YANG, TONY TIEN SHENG, engineering educator; b. Tainan, Formosa, May 26, 1928; came to U.S., 1957; s. Tsang and Shih Y. (Cheng) Y.; m. Hsiu-Ying Tsai, Aug. 7, 1959; 1 son, Joseph. B.S., Nat. Taiwan U., 1953; M.S., U. Okla., 1959, Ph.D., 1968. Registered profl. engr., D.C. Md., Okla. Project engr. Okla. Dept. Hwys., Oklahoma City, 1958-66, sr. structural engr., 1968-70; prof., chmn. civil and mech. engring. program Fed. City Coll., Washington, 1970-73, prof., chmn. engring. and computer sci. dept., 1973-78; prof., chmn. civil and mech. engring. dept. U. D.C., Washington, 1978-86, prof. civl engring., 1987—. Mem. ASCE, Am. Soc. Engring. Edn., Am. Concrete Inst. Home: 6108 Beech Tree Dr Alexandria VA 22310-2240 Office: 4200 Connecticut Ave NW Washington DC 20008-1174

YANG, WEN-CHING, chemical engineer; b. Taipei, Taiwan, Nov. 11, 1939; came to U.S., 1964; s. Ting-Lien and Ho (Lee) Y.; m. Rae Tien, Aug. 24, 1968; children: Evonne R., Peter T. BSChemE, Nat. Taiwan U., Taipei, 1962; MSChemE, U. Calif., Berkeley, 1965; PhD in Chem. Engring., Carnegie Mellon U., 1968. Sr. engr. rsch. and devel. ctr. Westinghouse Electric Co., Pitts., 1968-76, fellow engr., 1976-93, adv. engr. sci. and tech. ctr., 1993—; instr. U. Pitts., 1980, 83; chair rsch. rev. panel Office Fossil Energy, Dept. Energy, Washington, 1990. Author: (with others) Encyclopedia of Fluid Mechanics, 1986, 92; editor spl. vol. Powder Tech. jour., 1987; contbr. over 75 papers to sci. jours. Lt. Army Tank Corp., 1962-63. Fellow AIChE (programming chair and sec. group 3, editor 4 symposium series vols. 1987-88, 92-93, sec. particle tech. forum 1993—, Fluidized Processes Recognition award 1993); mem. Am. Chem. Soc., Chinese Am. Chem. Soc. (pres. Pitts. chpt. 1994), Orgn. Chinese Am. Achievements include patents in field; development of widely-used correlations and design equations in pneumatic transport and fluidization areas. Avocations: Chinese calligraphy, painting, tennis, gardening. Home: 236 Mount Vernon Dr Export PA 15632-9035 Office: Westinghouse Electric Co Sci & Tech Ctr 1310 Beulah Rd Pittsburgh PA 15235

YANG, WILOX, physicist; b. Canton, China, May 25, 1922; s. Shaw Hong and Ah Han (Lee) Y.; m. Constance Lee Bycofski, Jan. 20, 1960 (dec. June 1964); m. Janet D. Smith, Mar. 23, 1966; children—Eleanor, Lisa, Lori. B.Sc., Huachung U., Wuchang, China, 1947; M.Sc., Poly. Inst. N.Y., 1963, Ph.D., 1974. Mem. staff Princeton-Penn Accelerator, Princeton (N.J.) U., 1962-69; mem. staff high energy physics research U. Pa., Phila., 1969-75; engring. physicist Fermilab, Batavia, Ill., 1975—. Mem. Am. Phys. Soc., N.Y. Acad. Sci., Sigma Xi. Democrat. Club: Sigma Xi. Contbr. articles to profl. jours. Home: 30w113 Lindenwood Ct Warrenville IL 60555-1351 Office: Fermi Nat Accelerator Lab PO Box 500 Batavia IL 60510-0500

YANG, YANG, research scientist; b. Kaohsiung, Taiwan, Nov. 7, 1958; came to U.S., 1985; s. Shun-Wen and Huang-Yin Yang; m. Danmei Lee, May 30, 1987. BS in Physics, Nat. Cheng Kung U., 1982; MS in Physics, U. Mass., 1988, PhD in Physics, 1992. Rsch. asst. U. Mass., Lowell, 1989-91; rsch. assoc. U. Calif., Riverside, 1991-92; rsch. scientist UNIAX Corp., Santa Barbara, Calif., 1992—. Contbr. articles to profl. jours. Mem. Am. Phys. Soc., Material Rsch. Soc. Office: UNIAX Corp 6780 Crotona Dr Santa Barbara CA 93117

YANG, ZHEN, research scientist; b. Shenyang, Liaoning, People's Republic of China, Aug. 16, 1959; came to U.S., 1992; s. Gue-Fu Yang and Jing-Ren Han; m. Su-Ling Lu, Aug. 10, 1986; 1 child, Lu-Ning. BS in Pharm. Chemistry, Shenyang Coll. Pharmacy, 1982, MS in Pharm. Chemistry, 1986; PhD in Organic Chemistry, Chinese U. of Hong Kong, 1992. Asst. engr. Pharm. Factory of Baoto, Inner Mongolia Autonomous Region, China, 1982-83; teaching asst. pharm. dept. Shenyang Coll. Pharmacy, 1986-89; rsch. asst. Chinese U. of Hong Kong, 1989, teaching asst., 1989-92; rsch. scientist Scripps Rsch. Inst., La Jolla, Calif., 1992—. Contbr. articles to profl. jours. Fellow Hong Kong Jockey Club, 1989-92. Achievements include patents for strategy for ABC taxoid analogs, synthesis of taxol and taxol analogs, total synthesis of brenetoxin B and Zaragozic Acid. Home: 3717 Nobel Dr #1106 San Diego CA 92122-9999 Office: The Scripps Rsch

Inst Dept Chemistry MB 10A 10666 N Torrey Pines Rd La Jolla CA 92037-1027

YANKEE, MARIE, educator, publishing executive; m. J.R. Yankee, June 6, 1956; children: Michael, David, Stephen, Jennifer. Diploma Montessori edn., Montessori Inst. Am., 1968; MS, Southeastern U., Greenville, S.C., 1980, PhD, 1981. Chief exec. officer The Fernhaven Studio, Los Angeles, 1966—, Montessori Ednl. Environment, Los Angeles, 1974—, Yankee Montessori Mfg., L.A., 1980-86; pres. Internat. Montessori Inst. Tchr. Ednl. Programs, Sage, Calif., 1980—; rsch. editor Edn. Systems Pub., L.A., 1982—; dir. EEI, Inc., L.A., 1987—; cons. Calif. pub. schs., 1976; prof. Univ. Coll. Vancouver. Author: Montessori Curriculum, 1985, Reading Program, 1981, Science for Preschool, 1981, Geography for Preschool, 1982. Mem. Am. Montessori Soc., Montessori Inst. Am. Home: 38395 Trifone Rd Hemet CA 92544-9693 Office: Edn Systems Pub PO Box 536 Hemet CA 92546-0536

YANKWICH, PETER EWALD, chemistry educator; b. L.A., Oct. 20, 1923; s. Leon Rene and Helen (Werner) Y.; m. Elizabeth Pope Ingram, July 14, 1945; children: Alexandra Helen Yankwich Capps, Leon Rene II, Richard Ingram. BS, U. Calif., Berkeley, 1943, PhD, 1945. Mem. sci. staff Radiation Lab., U. Calif., Berkeley, 1944-48; faculty U. Calif., 1947-48; mem. faculty U. Ill., Urbana, 1948-88, prof. chemistry, 1957-88; head div. phys. chemistry U. Ill., Urbana, 1962-67, v.p. acad. affairs, 1977-82; Mem. Adv. Coun. on Coll. Chemistry, 1961-68; NSF Sr. Postdoctoral fellow, 1960-61, exec. officer Directorate for Sci. and Engring. Edn., 1985-90, Directorate for Edn. and Human Resources, 1990-92, sr. staff assoc., 1992—. Mem. Urbana Bd. Edn., 1958-73. Fellow AAAS, Am. Phys. Soc.; mem. Am. Chem. Soc. (chmn. phys. chemistry div. 1971-72, chem. edn. planning and coordinating com. 1974-77, chmn. edn. commn. 1977-81, bd. dirs. 1982-91), Phi Beta Kappa, Sigma Xi. Home: 4512 4th Rd N Arlington VA 22203-2343

YANNAS, IOANNIS VASSILIOS, polymer science and engineering educator; b. Athens, Apr. 14, 1935; s. Vassilios Pavlos and Thalia (Sarafoglou) Y.; m. Stamatia Frondistou (div. Oct. 1984); children: Tania, Alexis. AB, Harvard U., 1957; SM, MIT, 1959; MS, Princeton U., 1965, PhD, 1966. Asst. prof. mech. engring. MIT, Cambridge, 1966-68, duPont asst. prof., 1968-69, assoc. prof., 1969-78, prof. polymer sci. and engring. dept. mech. engring., 1978—, prof., dept. materials sci. and engring., 1983—; prof. Harvard-MIT Div. Health Scis. and Tech., Cambridge, 1978—; vis. prof. Royal Inst. Tech., Stockholm, 1974. Mem. editorial bd. Jour. Biomed. Materials Rsch., 1986—, Jour. Materials Sci. Materials Medicine, 1990—, Tissue Engineering, 1994—; contbr. over 100 tech. articles. to profl. jours.; 13 patents in field. Recipient awards for design of first successful artificial skin for treatment of massively burned patients, including Founders award Soc. for Biomaterials, 1982, Clemson award Soc. for Biomaterials, 1992, Fred O. Conley award Soc. Plastics Engrs., 1982, award in medicine and genetics Sci. Digest/Cutty Sark, 1982, Doolittle award Am. Chem. Soc., 1988; fellow Pub. Health Svc., Princeton U., 1963, Shriners Burns Inst., Mass. Gen. Hosp., Boston, 1980-81. Fellow Am. Inst. Chemists, Am. Inst. Med. and Biol. Engrs. (founding mem.), Biomaterials Sci. and Engring.; mem. Inst. Medicine of Nat. Acad. Scis. Office: MIT Bldg 3-334 77 Massachusetts Ave Cambridge MA 02139-4301*

YANNI, JOHN MICHAEL, pharmacologist; b. St. Mary's, Pa., Nov. 3, 1952; s. John Paul and Regina (Emmert) Y.; m. Nancy Jane Reedy, Sept. 22, 1979; children: Susan Elizabeth, Jennifer Ruth, Steven Reedy. BS, Allegheny Coll., 1974; MS, Va. Commonwealth U., 1979, PhD, 1982. Biologist A.H. Robins Co., Richmond, Va., 1980-82, sr. rsch. biologist, 1982-86, rsch. assoc., 1986-88; group leader Eastman Kodak Co., Rochester, N.Y., 1988-90; asst. dir. Alcon Labs., Inc., Fort Worth, 1990-92, dir., 1992-93, sr. dir., 1993—. Contbr. articles to profl. jours. Alden scholar Allegheny Coll., 1974. Mem. Am. Soc. Pharmacology and Exptl. Therapeutics, N.Y. Acad. Sci., Assn. for Rsch. in Vision and Ophthalmology, Soc. for Leukocyte Biology. Achievements include patents in area of allergy; described thromboxane A2's muco-secretory effect; identified antiallergic potential of Arylalkly-heterocyclic amines; discovered potential drugs (opatanol, emedine) for treatment of ocular allergy; described secretory response of human conjunctival mast cells. Office: Alcon Labs Inc 6201 S Freeway Fort Worth TX 76134

YANNUCCI, THOMAS DAVID, lawyer; b. Springfield, Ohio, Mar. 30, 1950; s. David Marion and Patricia (Wilson) Y.; m. Lisa Marie Copeland, June 30, 1972; children: Teresa, Andrea, Thomas D. Jr. AB, U. Notre Dame, 1972, JD, 1976. Bar: Ohio 1977, U.S. Ct. Appeals (D.C., 1st, 2d, 5th, 7th, 8th, 11th and 10th cirs.) 1980, U.S. Supreme Ct. 1980, D.C. 1981. Law clk. to presiding justice U.S. Ct. Appeals (D.C. cir.), Washington, 1976-77; trial atty. U.S. Dept. Justice, Washington, 1977-80; ptnr. Kirkland & Ellis, Washington, 1980—. Editor-in-chief U. Notre Dame Law Rev., 1975-76. Roman Catholic. Office: Kirkland & Ellis 655 15th St NW Ste 1200 Washington DC 20005-5701*

YANNUZZI, WILLIAM A(NTHONY), conductor; b. Balt., July 30, 1934; s. Carmine and Maria Rosaria (Capparelli) Y. A.B. cum laude, Johns Hopkins U., 1957, M.A., 1958; M.A., St. Johns Coll., Santa Fe, 1969. Tchr. French Balt. City Coll., 1958-66; mem. faculty Peabody Conservatory, 1977—. Asst. condr., Balt. Opera Co., Inc., 1962-73; music dir., 1973—. Served with U.S. Army, 1951-54. Mem. Phi Beta Kappa. Office: Balt Opera Co Inc 1202 Maryland Ave Baltimore MD 21201-5561

YANOFF, MYRON, ophthalmologist; b. Phila., Dec. 21, 1936; s. Jacob and Lillian S. (Fishman) Y.; m. Karin Michelle Lindblad, Aug. 8, 1980; 1 dau., Alexis A.; children by previous marriage: Steven L., David A., Joanne M. A.B., U. Pa., 1957; M.D., 1961. Prof. ophthalmology and pathology U. Pa. Med. Sch., Phila.; William F. Norris and George E. de Schweinitz prof. ophthalmology, chmn. dept., dir. Scheie Eye Inst., 1977-86; chmn., prof. ophthalmology Med. Coll. Pa. and Hahnemann U., Phila., 1988—; 1st exchange vis. prof. U. Vienna, 1992. Author: Ocular Pathology, Textbook of Ophthalmology; contbr. articles to profl. jours. Served to maj. M.C. USAR. Recipient Humboldt award, 1988. Mem. Am. Ophthalmic Soc., Verhoeff Soc., Am. Acad. Ophthalmology (Sr. Honor award 1995). Office: Hahnemann U Feinstein Bldg Dept Ophthalmology Broad & Race Sts Philadelphia PA 19102

YANOFSKY, CHARLES, biology educator; b. N.Y.C., Apr. 17, 1925; s. Frank and Jennie (Kopatz) Y.; m. Carol Cohen, June 19, 1949, (dec. Dec. 1990); children: Stephen David, Robert Howard, Martin Fred; m. Edna Crawford, Jan. 4, 1992. BS, CCNY, 1948; MS, Yale U., 1950, PhD, 1951, DSc (hon.), 1981; DSc (hon.), U. Chgo., 1980. Rsch. asst. Yale U., 1951-54; asst. prof. microbiology Western Res. U. Med. Sch., 1954-57; mem. faculty Stanford U., 1958—, prof. biology, 1961—, Herzstein prof. biology, 1966—, career investigator Am. Heart Assn., 1969-95. Served with AUS, 1944-46. Recipient Lederle Med. Faculty award, 1957; Eli Lilly award bacteriology, 1959; U.S. Steel Co. award molecular biology, 1964; Howard Taylor Ricketts award U. Chgo., 1966; Albert and Mary Lasker award, 1971; Townsend Harris medal Coll. City N.Y., 1973; Louisa Gross Horwitz prize in biology and biochemistry Columbia U., 1976; V.D. Mattia award Roche Inst., 1982; medal Genetics Soc. Am., 1983; Internat. award Gairdner Found., 1985; named Passano Laureate Passano Found., 1992. Mem. NAS (Selman A. Waksman award in microbiology 1972), Am. Acad. Arts and Scis., Genetics Soc. Am. (pres. 1969, Thomas Hunt Morgan medal 1990), Am. Soc. Biol. Chemists (pres. 1984), Royal Soc. (fgn. mem.), Japanese Biochem. Soc. (hon.). Home: 725 Mayfield Ave Stanford CA 94305-1016 Office: Stanford U Dept Of Biological Sci Stanford CA 94305

YANOWITCH, MICHAEL H., lawyer; b. Phila., Jan. 23, 1949. BA cum laude, Yale U., 1973; MBA with honors, U. Chgo., 1976, JD with honors, 1977. Bar: Ill. 1977, N.Y. 1984; CPA Ill. Law clerk to Hon. Harlington Wood U.S. Ct. Appeals 7th cir., 1977-78; ptnr. Sidley & Austin, N.Y.C. Mem. Order Coif, Beta Gamma Sigma. Office: Sidley & Austin 875 3rd Ave New York NY 10022-6225*

YANTIS, RICHARD WILLIAM, investments executive; b. Tipp City, Ohio, Nov. 19, 1923; s. Guy Everett and Frances (Barnhart) Y.; m. Marjorie Louise Gray, May 11, 1943; children: Cheryl Ann, Sandra Lee, Susan Elizabeth. Student, U. Dayton, 194142. Regional mgr. Gen. Finance Corp., Chgo., 1946-53; v.p. Fruehauf Trailer Finance Co., Detroit, 1953-56; pres. Delta Acceptance Corp., Ltd., London, Ont., Can., 1956-64; exec. v.p., dir. Avco Corp., Greenwich, Conn., 1965-73; pres. Avco Community Developers, Inc., La Jolla, Calif., 1973-75; cons. Avco Community Developers, Inc., 1975-80; pres. Cathedral Mortgage Co., Inc., Palm Springs, Calif., 1980-82. Served with USNR, 1941-45. Clubs: Masons, Shriners, Seven Lakes Country; London, London Hunt and Country. Home: 331 Westlake Ter Palm Springs CA 92264-5534

YAO, DAVID DA-WEI, engineering educator; b. Shanghai, China, July 14, 1950; came to U.S., 1983, naturalized, 1990; s. William Kang-Fu and Nancy Yun-Lan (Lu) Y.; m. Helen Zhi-Heng Chen, Jan. 31, 1979; children: Henry, John. MASc, U. Toronto, Ont., Can., 1981, PhD, 1983. Assoc. prof. systems engring. Harvard U., Cambridge, Mass., 1986-88; asst. prof. indsl. engring. and ops. rsch. Columbia U., N.Y.C., 1983-86, prof., 1988—, Thomas Alva Edison prof., 1992—; acad. visitor AT&T Bell Labs., Holmdel, N.J., 1989, T.J. Watson Rsch. Ctr., IBM, Yorktown, N.Y., 1990—. Co-author: Monotone Structure in Discrete-Event Systems, 1994; editor: Stochastic Modeling and Analysis of Manufacturing Systems, 1994; contbr. more than 100 articles to sci. jours. including Maths. Ops. Rsch., Jour. of Assn. Computing Machinery, Advances in Applied Probability, 1983—. Recipient Presdl. Young Investigator award NSF, Washington, 1987-92, Guggenheim fellow John Simon Guggenheim Meml. Found., N.Y.C., 1991-92. Mem. IEEE, Soc. Indsl. and Applied Math., Ops. Rsch. Soc. Am. (George Nicholson prize 1983). Achievements include development of theory of algebraic structures in discrete-event systems, theory of stochastic convexity and its applications in queuing networks, stochastic network models for computer integrated manufacturing systems, methodologies in the optimization and control of stochastic discrete-event systems. Home: 1261 Underhill Ave Yorktown Heights NY 10598-5718 Office: Columbia U Engring Dept 302 Mudd Bldg New York NY 10027-6699

YAO, JAMES TSU-PING, civil engineer; b. Shanghai, China, July 7, 1933; came to U.S. 1953; s. C.C. and Mae Jane (Wang) Y.; m. Anna Lee, June 14, 1958; children: Tina Lee, Timothy H.J., Shana Lynn. BSCE, U. Ill., 1957, MSCE, 1958, PhD, 1961. Registered profl. engr. Tex., N.Mex. Postdoctoral preceptor Columbia U., N.Y.C., 1964-65; asst. prof. civil engring. U. N.Mex., Albuquerque, 1961-64, assoc. prof., 1965-69, prof., 1969-71; prof. Purdue U., W. Lafayette, Ind., 1971-88, asst. head dept. civil engring., 1983-88, asst. dean grad. sch., 1984-87; prof. Tex. A&M U., College Station, 1988—, head dept. civil engring., 1988-93. Editor Jour. Structural Engring., 1990-92. Recipient Max Planck Rsch. award Alexander Von Humboldt Found., 1990, Civil Engring. Disting. Alumnus award, U. Ill., Urbana, 1991, Centennial medallion Am. Soc. Engring. Edn., 1993. Fellow ASCE (State-of-the-Art of Civil Engring. award 1973, 83, Alfred M. Freudenthal medal 1990, Richard R. Torrens award 1992, Pres.'s medal 1995). Avocations: volleyball, paperfolding. Office: Tex A&M Univ Dept Civil Engring College Station TX 77843-3136

YAPLE, HENRY MACK, library director; b. Vicksburg, Mich., May 30, 1940; s. Henry J. and Pauline B. (Spencer) Y.; m. Marilyn Lou Bales, Dec. 31, 1971; children: Sean H., Kendra S. BA in English with hons., Kalamazoo Coll., 1963; MA, U. Idaho, 1966; postgrad., U. d'Aix-Marseille, France, 1965-66, U. Toronto, 1966-69; MLS, W. Mich. U., 1972. Order libr. Mich. State U., E. Lansing, 1972-74, humanities bibliographer, 1974-78; acquisitions libr. U. Wyo., Laramie, 1978-87; libr. dir. Whitman Coll., Walla Walla, Wash., 1987—; Mem. Wyo. Coun. for the Humanities, 1982-86. U. Toronto scholar, 1966-69; Rotary fellow, 1965, 66; U. Wyo. rsch. grantee, 1982, 86. Mem. ALA, Wyo. Libr. Assn. (pres. 1984-85), Nat. Ski Patrol System (sr. patroller 1978—, nat. #6946 1988), Wash. Libr. Assn., Northwest Assn. of Pvt. Colls. and U. Librs. (pres. 1987-88, 94-95), Rotary (Walla Walla), Beta Phi Mu. Avocations: book collecting, skiing, kayaking. Home: 1889 Fern St Walla Walla WA 99362-9393 Office: Whitman Coll Office Libr 345 Boyer Ave Walla Walla WA 99362-2067

YARBOROUGH, N. PATRICIA, human resources educator, human resources executive; b. Beckville, Tex., Dec. 7, 1936; d. James Lamar and Del (Davis) Y. BMus, North Tex. State U., 1958, EdD, 1969; MEd, U. Md., 1963; LLD (hon.) Teikyo Post U., 1993. Edn. cons. Prentice-Hall, Inc., Englewood Cliffs, N.J., 1963-65; tchr. Dallas Ind. Sch. Dist., 1965-67, supr. music, 1968-69, coordinator staff devel., 1969-70; dean instrn. Mountain View Coll. of Dallas County Community Coll. Dist., 1976-77, chmn. div. humanities, 1970-73, dean instrn. and student devel., 1973-76; v.p. instrn. Brookhaven Coll. of Dallas County Community Coll. Dist., 1977-80; pres. Mattatuck Community Coll., Waterbury, Conn., 1980-82; v.p. human resources and corp. rels, Scovill Inc., Scovill World Hdqrs., Waterbury, Conn., 1982-86; pres. Teikyo Post U., Waterbury, 1986-91, also trustee; v.p. human resources and pub. rels. UNR Industries, Inc., Chgo., 1991-93; pres. Yarborough Assocs., 1993—; proposal evaluator NEH, 1981; corporator The Banking Ctr. Bd. dirs. St. Mary's Hosp., Waterbury, 1981—, Conn. Pub. Broadcasting, Mattatuck Mus.; pub. mem. Conn. Humanities Council, NEH, 1982-84; bd. dirs. ARC, Waterbury chpt., 1982-85. U.S. Office Edn. grantee, N. Tex. State U., 1967. Mem. Sigma Alpha Iota, Alpha Chi, Phi Kappa Lambda.

YARBOROUGH, WILLIAM CALEB, former professional stock car race driver; b. Timmonsville, S.C., Mar. 27, 1939. Named Grand Nat. Champion Nat. Assn. Stock Car Auto Racing, 1976. Winner Atlanta 500, 1967, 68, 74, Cam 2 Motor Oil 400, 1977, Capital City 400, 1976, Carolina 500, 1975, Daytona 500, 1968, 77, 83, 84, Mason-Dixon 500, 1969, Nat. 500, 1973, So. 500, 1968, 73, 74, 78, Va. 500, 1974, 77, Wilkes 400, 1974, Winston Western 500, 1974; champion Winston Cup, 1976-78, many others. Office: care Nat Assn Stock Car Auto Racing 1801 Volusia Ave Daytona Beach FL 32114-1215*

YARBOROUGH, WILLIAM GLENN, JR., military officer, forest farmer, defense and international business executive; b. Rock Hill, S.C., June 21, 1940; s. William Glenn and Bessie (Rainsford) Y.; m. Betsy Gibson, Jan. 24, 1969; children: Bill, Clinton, Frank, Elizabeth. BS, U. S.C., 1961, MBA, 1969; postgrad. Command and Gen. Staff Coll., 1970, Naval War Coll., 1979, Colgate-Darden Grad. Bus. Sch., U. Va., 1983. Commd. to U.S. Army, advanced through grades to col., 1980; co. and troop comdr. and squadron staff officer, Vietnam, Europe, 1961-71, strategist, Washington, 1971-73, chief of assignments, Office Personnel Mgmt., Mil. Personnel Ctr., Washington, 1973-76; comdr. 1st Squadron, 1st Cavalry, Europe, 1976-78; chief of staff and spl. asst. to chief of staff 1st Armored Div., Europe, 1978; br. chief Office of Chief of Staff, Washington, 1979-80; exec. to dep. commanding gen. Material Devel. and Readiness Command, Washington, 1980-81; mil. dep. for asst. sec. for research, devel. and acquisition, Washington, 1981-85; army mktg. dir. Grumman Corp., Bethpage, N.Y., 1990-93; corp. v.p. Allied Rsch. Corp., Vienna, Va., 1993—; bd. dirs. Carleton Techs. Decorated Silver Star, Bronze Star medal with 4 oak leaf clusters and V device, Purple Heart. Mem. Assn. U.S. Army (George Washington chpt., v.p. membership), Am. Legion, Armed Forces Communications and Electronics Assn., U.S. Army Armor Assn., SAR, Am. Def. Preparedness Assn. (bd. dirs. N.Y. chpt.), Purple Heart VFW Soc., Army-Navy Club, Army Navy Country Club, Belle-Meade Country Club, Tower Club.

YARBOROUGH, WILLIAM PELHAM, writer, lecturer, retired army officer, consultant; b. Seattle, May 12, 1912; s. Leroy W. and Addessia (Hooker) Y.; m. Norma Mae Tuttle, Dec. 26, 1936; children: Norma Kay (dec.), William Lee, Patricia Mae. BS, U.S. Mil. Acad., 1936; grad., Command and Gen. Staff Coll., 1944, Brit. Staff Coll., 1950, Army War Coll., 1953. Commd. 2nd lt. U.S. Army, 1936, advanced through grades to lt. gen., 1968, ret., 1971; various assignments U.S. Army, U.S., Philippines and ETO, 1936-42; exec. officer Paratroop Task Force, North Africa, 1942; comdr. 2d Bn., 504th Par. Inf. Regt., 82d Airborne Div., Sicily invasion, 1943, 509th Parachute Inf., Italy and France, 1943-44; comdg. officer 473 Inf., Italy, 1945; provost marshal 15th Army Group, ETO, 1945, Vienna Area Command and U.S. Forces, Austria, 1945-47; mem. staff, faculty U.S. Army Info. Sch., 1948-49; operations officer, gen. staff Joint Mil. Assistance Adv. Group, London, Eng., 1951-52; mem. faculty Army War Coll., 1953-56, 57; dep. chief Mil. Assistance and Adv. Group, Cambodia, 1956-57; comdg. officer 66th CIC Group, Stuttgart, Germany, 1958-60, 66th M.I. Group, Stuttgart, 1960; comdg. gen. U.S.A. Spl. Warfare Ctr.; also comdt. U.S. Army Spl. Warfare Sch., Ft. Bragg, 1961-65; sr. mem. UN Command Mil. Armistice Commn., Korea, 1965; asst. dep. chief staff DCSOPS for spl. operations Dept. Army, Washington; chmn. U.S. delegation Inter-Am. Def. Bd., Joint Brazil U.S. Def. Commn., Joint Mexican-U.S. Def. Commn.; Army mem. U.S. sect. permanent Joint Bd. on Def., Can.-U.S. Def. Commn., Washington, 1965; asst. chief of staff intelligence Dept. Army Washington, 1966-68; comdg. gen. I Corps Group, Korea, 1968-69; chief staff, also dep. comdr.-in-chief U.S. Army, Pacific, Hawaii, 1969-71. Contbr. Internat. Mil. and Def. Ency., 1993, MacMillan Ency. of the Am. Mil., 1994; William P. Yarborough collection papers and artifacts donated to Mugar Meml. Librs., Boston U. Decorated Disting. Svc. medal with three oak leaf clusters, Silver Star, Legion of Merit with three oak leaf clusters, Bronze Star, Joint Svc. Commendation medal with oak leaf clusters, Croix de Guerre with Palm (France), Cross for Valor and Diploma (Italy), Order of Merit Second Class (Korea), Order of Ulchi (Korea). Fellow Co. Mil. Historians, Explorers Club; mem. Kiwanis Club. Home: 160 Hillside Rd Southern Pines NC 28387-6727

YARBRO, JAMES WESLEY, financial executive; b. Woodbury, Tex., Mar. 30, 1920; s. Daniel Fore and Annie Belle (Hunt) Y.; m. Mary Elise Alderdice, Aug. 17, 1944; children: Suzanne Elise, James Wesley Jr., Rosemary. BS, North Tex. State Coll., 1940. CPA, Tex. Instr. high sch. Crane, Tex., 1940-42; aviator USN, South Pacific Theater, 1942-45; internal revenue agt. U.S. Treasury Dept., Ft. Worth, 1946-51; asst. sec.-treas., tax mgr. So. Prodn. Co., Ft. Worth, 1951-57; with Tex. Pacific Coal & Oil Co., Ft. Worth, 1957-63, fin. v.p., bd. dirs., 1959-63; fin. v.p. King Resources Co., Denver, 1963-66; fin. v.p., sec.-treas. Western Co. N.Am., Ft. Worth, 1967-69; pvt. practice fin. svc. Ft. Worth, 1969-88; ret., 1988. Lt. USNR, 1942-45. Mem. AICPAs, Tex. Soc. CPAs, Ind. Petroleum Assn. Am., Petroleum Club Ft. Worth, Rotary. Christian Ch. Home: 1417 Westover Ln Fort Worth TX 76107-3547

YARBROUGH, JOHN WILLIAM, secondary school educator; b. Dallas, June 2, 1946; s. Lonnie Jordan and Emma Joe (Robinson) Y. BA in History, U. North Tex., 1968; M in Liberal Arts, So. Meth. U., 1987; postgrad., U. Tex., Arlington, 1986, U. Dallas, 1990, U. Dallas. Cert. tchr., Tex. Tchr. Delay Mid. Sch., Lewisville, Tex., 1971-73; tchr., advanced placement dir. Lewisville H.S., 1973-80, Casady Sch., Oklahoma City, Okla., 1980-82, Episcpal Sch. Dallas, 1982-85; tchr. W.T. White H.S., Dallas, 1985-86; tchr., dept. chair James Madison H.S., Dallas, 1986-92; tchr. Stockard Mid. Sch., Dallas, 1992-93, Holmes Mid. Sch., Dallas, 1993—; cons. Am. history S.W. Region of Coll. Bd., Austin, Tex., 1979-81; panelist Luther Quincentenary, U. North Tex., Denton, 1984; participant Advanced Placement Workshop, Southwestern Region Coll. Bd., 1990, 92, Inst. for Tchrs. of Talented Students, Carleton Coll., 1992, 95, Coop. Learning in the Social Studies, Nat. Coun. for the Social Studies, 1993, Architecture in the Classroom, Nat. Trust for Historic Preservation, 1994. Del. Tex. Dem. State Conv., 1972-94. Woodrow Wilson Nat. Found. fellow U. Tex., Dallas, 1995. Mem. ASCD, Nat. Coun. for the Social Studies, Am. Hist. Assn., Dallas Coun. for the Social Studies, Orgn. Am. Historians, Tex. Coun. for the Social Studies. Avocations: reading, music. Office: OW Holmes Classical Acad and Mid Sch 2001 E Kiest Blvd Dallas TX 75216-3326

YARBROUGH, MARILYN VIRGINIA, lawyer, educator; b. Bowling Green, Ky., Aug. 31, 1945; d. William Ottoway Yarbrough and Merca Lee (Hardin) Toole; m. Walter James Ainsworth, Sept. 3, 1967 (div. Oct. 1980); children: Carmen Virginia, Carla Renee; m. David A. Didion, Dec. 31, 1987. BA, Va. State U., 1966; JD, UCLA, 1973. Bar: Calif. 1973, Kans. 1982. Instr. Boston Coll. Law Sch., Newton, Mass., 1975-76; prof. law U. Kans., Lawrence, 1976-87, assoc. vice chancellor, 1983-87; prof. Law Sch. U. Tenn., Knoxville, 1987-93; dean Law Sch U. Tenn., Knoxville, 1987-91; William J. Maier Jr. chair law W.Va. U., Morgantown, 1991-92; prof. U. N.C. Law Sch., Chapel Hill, 1992—, assoc. provost, 1994—. Editor in chief Black Law Jour. 1972-73; contbr. articles to profl. jours. Bd. dirs. Knox County Endl. Enrichment Fund, Knoxville, 1989-92, Knoxville Housing Partnership, 1989-92, United Way of Knoxville, 1990-92; trustee Law Sch. Admission Coun., pres., 1986-88; trustee Webb Sch. of Knoxville, 1988-91, Kenyon Coll.; mem. Pulitzer Prize Bd., 1990—. Mem. ABA (reporter Am. Law Inst.-ABA com. continuing profl. edn. 1988-90, sect. legal edn. and admissions to bar 1989-94), Poynter Inst. for Media Studies (adv. bd. 1984-90, bd. dirs. 1990-92). Democrat. Mem. United Ch. of Christ. Home: PO Box 9221 Chapel Hill NC 27515-9221

YARBROUGH, MARTHA CORNELIA, music educator; b. Waycross, Ga., Feb. 8, 1940; d. Henry Elliott and Jessie (Sirmans) Y.; B.M.E., Stetson U., 1962; M.M.E., Fla. State U., 1968, Ph.D., 1973. Choral dir. Ware County High Sch., Waycross, Ga., 1962-64, Glynn Acad., Brunswick, Ga., 1964-70; asst. choral dir. Fla. State U., 1970-72; cons. in music Muscogee County Sch. Dist., Columbus, Ga., 1972-73; cons. in tchr. edn. Psycho-Edno. Cons., Inc., Tallahassee, 1972-73; asst. prof. music edn., dir. univs. choruses and oratorio soc. Syracuse U., 1973-76, assoc. prof. music edn., 1976-83, prof., 1983-86, acting asst. dean Coll. Visual and Performing Arts, 1980-82, acting dir. Sch. Music, 1980-82, chmn. music edn., 1982-86; prof. music La. State U., Baton Rouge, 1986—, coordinator music, edn., 1986—, Haymon prof. of Music, 1995—; artist in residence Sch. Music U. Ala., Tuscaloosa, 1989-90. Chair exec. com. Music Edn. Rsch. Coun., 1992-94. Mem. Music Educators Nat. Conf. (sr. rschr. award, 1996), N.Y. State Sch. Music Assn., Am. Ednl. Research Assn., Soc. Research Music Edn. (mem. exec. com. 1988-90, program chair 1990-92, chair, 1992-94), AAUP, Pi Kappa Lambda, Phi Beta, Kappa Delta Pi. Co-author: Competency-Based Music Education, 1980; mem. editorial com. Jour. Research in Music Edn.; contbr. articles to profl. jours., chpts. in books. Office: Sch Music La State U Baton Rouge LA 70803

YARD, RIX NELSON, former athletic director; b. Ocean County, N.J., July 1, 1917; s. George Rix and Lena (Nelson) Y.; m. Adra Gehrett, Sept. 12, 1941; children: Rix Nelson, Constance. BS, U. Pa., 1941, MS, 1947, EdD, 1956. Tchr. Swissvale (Pa.) High Sch., 1946; instr., asst. football coach, head basketball coach Denison U., 1947-49, chmn. dept. phys. edn., dir. athletics, lacrosse coach, 1953-63; asst. football coach U. Pa., 1949-53; dir. athletics Tulane U., 1963-76, prof. phys. edn., 1968-82, prof. emeritus, 1982—, dir. club and intramural sports, 1976-82, also adminstr. phys. edn. major program. Pres. New Orleans Football Hall of Fame, 1965-76; Vice pres. Granville (Ohio) Bd. Edn., 1961-63; asst. fire chief Granville Vol. Fire Co., 1958-63; mem. Granville Zoning Com., 1961; Bd. dirs. New Orleans chpt. A.R.C. Served with USNR, 1941-46; ret. capt. Res. Named Nat. Lacrosse Coach of Yr., 1963; named to Sports Hall of Fame Denison U., 1983, Ohio Lacross Hall of Fame, 1995. Mem. Nat. Collegiate Athletic Assn. (chmn. TV com. 1958, 60, rep. to Sugar Bowl 1964-78, chmn. ins. com. 1971-76, chmn. acad. and testing requirements com.), Nat. Assn. Coll. Dirs. Athletics (exec. com.); (named to Hall of Fame 1977); Mem. Navy League (dir. New Orleans chpt.). Club: New Orleans Quarterback (dir. 1967-78). Home: 6 Roberts Landing Dr Poquoson VA 23662-1026

YARDE, RICHARD FOSTER, art educator; b. Boston, Oct. 29, 1939; s. Edgar St. Clair and Enid (Foster) Y.; m. Susan Donovan, July 8, 1967; children: Marcus, Owen. BFA in Painting cum laude, Boston U., 1962, MFA, 1964. Asst. prof. art Boston U., 1965-71; assoc. prof. art Wellesley Coll., 1971-76; vis. assoc. prof. Amherst Coll., 1976-77, Mt. Holyoke Coll., 1980-81; vis. artist Mass. Coll. Art, 1977-91; prof. art U. Mass., Boston, 1981-90, Amherst, 1990—; visual arts panelist Mass. Coun. Art and Humanities, 1976-78; bd. overseers Inst. Contemporary Art, Boston, 1991—. Exhibited in one-man shows Studio Mus. in Harlem, San Diego Mus., Balt. Mus.; exhibited in group shows Newport (R.I.) Art Mus., NAD, Mass. Cultural Coun. Recipient Alumni award for disting. contbn. to arts Boston U., 1987, Chancellor's award for disting. scholarship U. Mass., Boston, 1984, Acad. award in art Am. Acad. Arts and Letters, 1995; Nat. Endowment for Arts fellow, 1976, other awards. Office: U Mass Amherst Fine Arts Ctr Amherst MA 01003

YARDIS, PAMELA HINTZ, computer consulting company executive; b. N.Y.C., Sept. 23, 1944; d. Edward F. and Isabella (Sawers) Hintz; m. J.A. Yardis, Apr. 2, 1966 (div. July 1980); children: Bradley, Brent, Tricia, Todd, Ryan, Kara, Melissa. BA, Bethany Coll., 1966; MA, Columbia U., 1983, MEd, 1983. Cert. mgmt. cons. Tchr. Yonkers (N.Y.) Pub. Schs., 1966-68; cons. PHY, Inc., Stamford, Conn., 1978-83; account exec. Mgmt. Systems,

Stamford, 1982-84; sr. account exec., cons. Mgmt. Dynamics, Yonkers, 1984-86; v.p. GMW Assn., Inc., N.Y.C., 1986-87; pres. Chestnut Hill Cons. Group, Inc., Stamford, 1987—. Chmn. Mayor's Commn. Prevention Youth Drug and Alcohol Abuse, Stamford, 1986-91; mem. Dem. Cen. Com., Stamford, 1984—; bd. dirs., pres. Alcohol and Drug Coun., Inc., Conn. Communities for Drug Free Youth, Childcare, Inc., Youth Shelter. Recipient Gov.'s Cmty. Svc. award, 1988, Golden Rule award J.C. Penney, Bravo award YWCA, 1992, Women of Enterprise award SBA & Avon, Inc., 1993, Sacian award S.W. Area Commerce and Bus., 1994. Mem. Women in Mgmt. (v.p. 1986-88, Ann. Recognition award), Data Processing Mgmt. Assn., Advt. Rsch. Found., Inst. Mgmt. Cons. (pres. Fairfield Westchester chpt. 1990-93, chmn. 1993-94, fellow 1995, nat. bd. dirs., chmn. 1993-95), Sales and Mktg. Execs. (bd. dirs.). Presbyterian. Avocations: travel, camping, politics. Home: 125 Chestnut Hill Rd Stamford CT 06903-4029 Office: Chestnut Hill Cons Group PO Box 15755 Stamford CT 06901-0755

YARDLEY, JOHN FINLEY, aerospace engineer; b. St. Louis, Feb. 1, 1925; s. Finley Abna and Johnnie (Patterson) Y.; m. Phyllis Steele, July 25, 1946; children: Kathryn, Robert, Mary, Elizabeth, Susan. B.S., Iowa State Coll., 1944; M.S., Washington U., St. Louis, 1950. Structural and aero. engr. McDonnell Aircraft Corp., St. Louis, 1946-55, chief strength engr., 1956-57; project engr. Mercury spacecraft design, 1958-60; launch ops. mgr. Mercury and Gemini spacecraft, Cape Canaveral, Fla., 1960-64; Gemini tech. dir. Mercury and Gemini spacecraft, 1964-67; v.p., dep. gen. mgr. Eastern div. McDonnell Douglas Astronautics, 1968-72, v.p., gen. mgr., 1973-74, pres., 1981-88, sr. corp. v.p., 1989, ret.; assoc. adminstr. for manned space flight NASA, Washington, 1974-81. Served to ensign USNR, 1943-46. Recipient Achievement award St. Louis sect. Inst. Aerospace Scis., 1961, John J. Montgomery award, 1963, Pub. Service award NASA, 1963, 66 ; profl. achievement citation Iowa State Coll., 1970, Spirit of St. Louis medal, 1973, Alumni citation Washington U., 1975, Disting. Achievement citation Iowa State U., 1976, Presdl. citation as meritorious exec. Sr. Exec. Service, 1980, NASA Disting. Service medal, 1981, Goddard Meml. trophy, 1983, Achievement award Washington U. Engring. Alumni, 1983, Elmer A. Sperry award, 1986; named Engr. of Yr. NASA, 1982; Von Karman Astronautics Lectureship award, 1988. Fellow AIAA (Goddard award 1982), Am. Astronautical Soc. (Space Flight award 1978); mem. Internat. Acad. Astronautics, NASA Alumni League (bd. dirs.), Nat. Acad. Engring., Nat. Space Club (bd. govs.), Tau Beta Pi, Phi Kappa Phi, Phi Eta Sigma, Phi Mu Epsilon. Presbyterian. Home: 14319 Cross Timbers Ct Chesterfield MO 63017-5718

YARDLEY, JONATHAN, journalist, columnist; b. Pitts., Oct. 27, 1939; s. William Woolsey and Helen (Gregory) Y.; m. Rosemary Roberts, June 14, 1961 (div. 1975); children: James Barrett, William W. II.; m. Susan L. Hartt, Mar. 23, 1975. AB, U. N.C., Chapel Hill, 1961; DHL (hon.), George Washington U., 1987. Writer N.Y. Times, 1961-64; editorial writer, book editor Greensboro (N.C.) Daily News, 1964-74; book editor Miami (Fla.) Herald, 1974-78, Washington Star, 1978-81; book critic, columnist Washington Post, 1981—. Author: Ring: A Biography of Ring Lardner, 1977, Our Kind of People: The Story of an American Family, 1989, Out of Step: Notes from a Purple Decade, 1991, States of Mind: A Personal Journey Through the Mid-Atlantic, 1993; editor: My Life as Author and Editor (H.L. Mencken), 1993. Recipient Pulitzer prize for criticism, 1981, Disting. Alumnus award U. N.C., 1989; Nieman fellow in journalism Harvard U., 1968-69. Episcopalian. Home: 223 Hawthorne Rd Baltimore MD 21210-2503 Office: Washington Post 1150 15th St NW Washington DC 20071-0001

YARDLEY, ROSEMARY ROBERTS, journalist, columnist; b. Albertville, Ala., Apr. 1, 1938; d. James Bailey Jr. and Mildred (Smith) Roberts; m. Jonathan Yardley, June 14, 1961 (div. 1975); children: James B., William W. II; m. Donald Arthur Boulton, Apr. 30, 1988. BA, U. N.C., 1960; MA, U. N.C., Greensboro, 1978. Staff writer The Charlotte (N.C.) Observer, 1960-61; editorial asst. The N.Y. Times, N.Y.C., 1962-64; staff writer The Greensboro (N.C.) News and Record, 1974-78, editorial writer, 1978-88, editorial columnist, 1988—; mem. faculty English dept. U. N.C., Greensboro, 1990—. Contbr. articles, book revs. to various publs. Bd. dirs. Weatherspoon Art Mus. U. N.C., Greensboro, 1986—, U. N.C. Journalism Found., 1985-93, Weatherspoon Art Found., 1989—, Friends U. Libr., Greensboro, 1994—, Ea. Music Festival, Greensboro, 1984-88; bd. dirs. English Speaking Union, Greensboro, 1995—. Recipient 2d prize N.C. Press Assn., 1976, 1st prize 1987, 2d prize 1995; John S. Knight fellow Stanford U., 1980-81; Bosch Found. travel fellow, 1990, Atlantik Bruke Found. travel fellow, 1988. Democrat. Presbyterian. Home: 223 Elmwood Dr Greensboro NC 27408-5829 Office: The Greensboro News and Record 200 E Market St Greensboro NC 27401-2910

YARGER, SAM JACOB, dean, educator; b. Pontiac, Mich., Oct. 8, 1937; s. Ralph And Eva L. (Little) Y.; m. Gwen Polk (div. 1982); 1 child, Mark Alan; m. Sally K. Mertens. BS in Elem. Edn., Eastern Mich. U., 1959; MA in Sch. Psychology, U. Mich., 1962; PhD in Ednl. Psychology, Wayne State U., 1968. Asst. prof. Oakland (Mich.) Community Coll., 1967-68, U. Toldeo, 1968-71; assoc. prof. Syracuse (N.Y.) U., 1971-77, prof., 1977-84, assoc. dean, 1980-84; dean, prof. U. Wis., Milw., 1984-92, U. Miami, Fla., 1992—; rschr. Assessment Pre-Vocat. Skills Mentally Retarded Youth, 1964-65, Tchr. Attitude Change in REls. to Program Input, 1968, Leader Behavior in a Task Oriented Setting in Relation to Group Activity, 1968, Attitudes Inner-City Residents Toward Ednl. Programs and Tchrs., 1970, Dimensions Tchr. Ctr. Movement in Am. Edn., 1972-75, Dimensions Field Derived Content in Tchr. Edn. Programs, 1973-75, Nat. Study Inservice Edn., 1976-77, Nat. Study Preservice Edn., 1976-77, Nat. Study Preservice Edn., 1976-77, Nat. Study Federally-Funded Tchr. Ctr., 1979-82, Nat. Study Tchr. Edn., 1985-94; developer, dir. tchr. edn. programs, various U.S. locations; mem., chmn. various univs. coms.; cons., spkr. in field. Author: Improving Teacher Education, 1978, Documenting Success - A Guidebook for Teacher Centers, 1979, Inservice Teacher Education, 1980; author monographs; contbr. articles to profl. jours., chpts. to books. Mem. Am. Ednl. Rsch. Assn. (assoc. editor 1983-85, chair elect Orgn. Instl. Affiliates 1994-95), Am. Assn. Colls. for Tchr. Edn. (bd. dirs. 1984-87, exec. com. 1985-87). Office: U Miami Sch Edn PO Box 248065 Coral Gables FL 33124-8065

YARINGTON, CHARLES THOMAS, JR., surgeon, administrator; b. Sayre, Pa., Apr. 26, 1934; s. C.T. and Florence (Hutchinson) Y.; m. Barbara Taylor Johnson, Sept. 28, 1963; children: Leslie Anne, Jennifer Lynne, Barbara Jane. AB, Princeton, 1956; MD, Hahnemann Med. Coll., 1960; grad., Army Command and Gen. Staff Coll., 1969, Air War Coll., 1973, Indsl. Coll. Armed Forces, 1974. Intern Rochester (N.Y.) Gen. Hosp., 1960-61; resident Dartmouth Hosp., 1961-62, U. Rochester Strong Meml. Hosp., 1962-65; instr. otolaryngology U. Rochester Sch. Medicine, 1962-65; asst. prof. surgery W.Va. U. Sch. Medicine, 1967-68; assoc. prof., chmn. dept. otorhinolaryngology U. Nebr. Med. Center, 1968-69, prof., chmn. dept. otorhinolarygology, 1969-74; clin. prof. otolaryngology U. Wash., Seattle, 1974—; clin. prof. surgery Uniformed Services U. Health Scis., Bethesda, 1985—; chief otolaryngology Virginia Mason Med. Ctr., Seattle, 1978-88, 92-95, chief dept. surgery, 1988-91; surgeon Mason Clinic, Seattle, 1996—; Cons. Surg. Gen. USAF, Hunter Group Med. Mgmt. Cons., 1996—; pres. Virginia Mason Rsch. Ctr., Seattle, 1983-85; trustee Mason Clinic, 1988-91; adv. coun. Nat. Inst. Neurol. Diseases, Communicative Diseases, Stroke of NIH, Bethesda, Md., 1986-90; bd. dirs. Virginia Mason Hosp., Mirginia Mason Med. Ctr., bd. govs., 1989—. Author books and articles in field.; Mem. editorial bd. Aviation, Space, Environ. Med. Jour., Otol. Clinics of N. Am., Mil. Medicine, Otolaryngology-Head and Neck Surgery. Trustee Seattle Opera Assn., 1983-89. Served to maj., M.C. AUS, 1965-67; brig. gen. USAF Res., to 1986. Decorated D.S.M., Legion of Merit; named Commdr. Venerable Order St. John (Gt. Britain), Companion with Star, Order Orthodox Hospit, Republic of Cypress; recipient Sir Henry Wellcome medal, 1984. Fellow ACS, Royal Soc. Medicine, Am. Acad. Otolaryngology (Barraquer Meml. award 1968, mem. standing com., bd. govs. 1982-88, Honor award 1974); mem. Am. Broncho-Esophagological Assn. (council, treas. 1982-86, pres. 1987-88), Am. Laryngol. Assn., Pacific Coast Soc. Ophthalmology and Otolaryngology (coun., pres. 1987-88), Soc. Med. Cons. to Armed Forces, Am. Soc. Head and Neck Surgery, N.W. Acad. Head and Neck Surgery (pres. 1984-86), Am. Soc. Otology, Rhinology and Laryngology (v.p. 1992-93), Res. Officers Assn. (pres. Seattle chpt., nat. officer), Pan-Pacific Surg. Assn., AMA, Sons of Revolution (pres. Wash. 1985-87), Seattle Yacht Club, Princeton Quadrangle Club, RAF Club (London), Cosmos Club (Washington), Rainier Club (Seattle), Sigma Xi. Office: Mason Clinic 1100 9th Ave Seattle WA 98101-2756

YARIV, AMNON, electrical engineering educator, scientist; b. Tel Aviv, Israel, Apr. 13, 1930; came to U.S., 1951, naturalized, 1964; s. Shraga and Henya (Davidson) Y.; m. Frances Pokras, Apr. 10, 1972; children: Elizabeth, Dana, Gabriela. B.S., U. Calif., Berkeley, 1954, M.S., 1956, Ph.D., 1958. Mem. tech. staff Bell Telephone Labs., 1959-63; dir. laser research Watkins-Johnson Co., 1963-64; mem. faculty Calif. Inst. Tech., 1964—, Thomas G. Myers prof. elec. engring. and applied physics, 1966—; chmn. bd. ORTEL Inc. Author: Quantum Electronics, 1967, 75, 85, Introduction to Optical Electronics, 1971, 77, 89, Theory and Applications of Quantum Mechanics, Propagation of Light in Crystals. Served with Israeli Army, 1948-50. Recipient Pender award U. Pa., Harvey prize Technion, Israel, 1992. Fellow IEEE (Quantum Electronics award 1980), Am. Optical Soc. (Ives medal 1986), Am. Acad. Arts and Scis.; mem. NAS, NAE, Am. Phys. Soc. Office: 1201 E California Blvd Pasadena CA 91125-0001

YARKONY, GARY MICHAEL, physician, researcher; b. N.Y.C., May 22, 1953; m. Kirsten Kohlmeyer; children: Judith, Rachel, Seth, Lauren. BA in Biology, SUNY, Buffalo, 1974; MD, SUNY, Syracuse, 1978; Master in Mgmt., Northwestern U., 1994. ;. Intern, then resident in physical medicine, rehab. Northwestern U., Chgo., 1978-81, chief resident dept. rehab. medicine, 1980; asst. dir. head trauma program Rehab. Inc. Chgo., 1981-84, attending staff, 1981-94; v.p. clin. program devel. Schwab Rehab. Hosp., Chgo., 1994—; clin. prof. sect. orthopaedic surgery and rehab. medicine U. Chgo. Med. Ctr., 1995—, clin. prof. dept. surgery and neurology, 1995—; attending physician Northwestern Meml. Hosp., Chgo., 1984-94; assoc. prof. dept. rehab. medicine Northwestern U. Med. Sch., 1985-94; adj. assoc. prof. Pritzker Inst. for Med. Engring., Ill. Inst. Tech., 1991—; dir. rehab. Midwest Regional Spinal Cord Injury Care Sys., Chgo., 1984-94. Contbr. articles to profl. jours. and chpts. to book. Fellow Am. Acad. Physical Medicine and Rehab.; mem. Assn. Academic Physiatrists, Am. Spinal Injury Assn., Internat. Med. Soc. Paraplegia, Internal Rehab. Medicine Assn., Phi Beta Kappa, Phi Eta Sigma. Office: Schwab Rehab Hosp 1401 S California Ave Chicago IL 60608-1612

YARLOW, LORETTA, art museum director; b. N.Y.C., Sept. 26, 1948; d. Albert and Sylvia (Seligsohn) Y.; m. Gregory Salzman, June 5, 1977; children: Nina, Alexander. BA, Sarah Lawrence Coll., 1970; EdM, Harvard U., 1971. Curator Inst. Contemporary Art, Boston, 1972-74; co-dir. Yarlow/Salzman Gallery, Toronto, Ont., Can., 1974-84; dir./curator Art Gallery York U., Toronto, 1988—. Office: Art Gallery York U, 4700 Keele St, North York, ON Canada M3J 1P3

YARMOLINSKY, ADAM, educator; b. N.Y.C., Nov. 17, 1922; s. Avrahm and Babette (Deutsch) Y.; m. Harriet Leslie Rypins, 1945 (div. 1981); children: Sarah Franklin, Tobias, Benjamin, Levi, Matthew Jonas; m. Jane Cox Vonnegut, 1984 (dec.); m. Sarah Ames Ellis, 1990. AB, Harvard U., 1943; LLB, Yale U., 1948. Bar: N.Y. 1949, D.C. 1952; U.S. Supreme Ct. 1955. Law clk. to Judge C.E. Clark U.S. Ct. Appeals (2d cir.), 1948-49; assoc. Root, Ballantine, Harlan, Bushby & Palmer, N.Y.C., 1949-50; law clk. to Justice Stanley Reed U.S. Supreme Ct., 1950-51; assoc. Cleary, Gottlieb, Friendly & Ball, Washington, 1951-55; dir. Washington office Fund for the Republic, Inc., 1955-56, sec., 1956-57; pub. affairs editor Doubleday & Co., Inc., 1957-59; cons. pvt. founds., 1959-60, spl. asst. sec. of def., 1961-64; dep. dir. Pres.'s. Anti-Poverty Task Force, 1964; chief U.S. Emergency Relief Mission to Dominican Republic, 1965; prin. dep. asst. sec. def. for internat. security affairs, 1965-66; prof. law Harvard U.; mem. inst. politics John F. Kennedy Sch. Govt., 1966-72; (on leave, 1970-72); chief exec. officer Welfare Island Devel. Corp., 1971-72; Ralph Waldo Emerson univ. prof. U. Mass., 1972-77; counselor ACDA, 1977-79; of counsel Fort & Schlefer, Washington, 1979—; prof. policy scis. grad. program U. Md. Balt. County, Balt., 1985-93, acting provost, 1986-87, provost, 1987-93; regents prof. pub. policy U. Md. System, 1993—; lectr. Am. U. Law Sch., 1951-56, Yale U. Law Sch., 1958-59; adj. prof. Georgetown U. Law Ctr., 1984-85; cons. Office Tech. Assessment, 1974-77; mem. gov.'s adv. coun. Mass. Comprehensive Health Planning Agy., 1972-76; nat. adv. com. Inst. for Rsch. on Poverty, 1972-77; mem. adv. coun. inter-univ. seminar on Armed Forces and Soc.; mem. Governing Coun. Wye Faculty Seminar; moderator Aspen Inst. Exec. Seminars, 1976—, Troutbeck Ednl. Leadership Program, 1984—, Oxford Aspen Seminars, 1986-89. Author: Recognition of Excellence, 1960, The Military Establishment, 1971, Paradoxes of Power, 1983; also articles in periodicals; editor: Case Studies in Personnel Security, 1955, Race and Schooling in the City, 1980, The Economist, London, 1956-60; (with Nicholas Farnham) Rethinking Liberal Education, 1995. Trustee Bennington Coll., 1984—, chmn., 1986-88; trustee Robert F. Kennedy Meml., Vera Inst. Justice, 1967—, New Directions Edn. Fund, 1979-82, Ctr. for Nat. Policy, 1984—, Am. Sch. Tangiers, 1979-89, Ocean Rsch. and Edn. Soc., 1980-85, Coalition for Nat. Svc., 1986—, Coun. Econ. Priorities, 1990-93, Hospice Care of D.C., 1990—, vice chair Ind. Sector, 1980-84, 89-95, chmn. gov. rels. com., 1989-92, vice chmn. bd., 1994-95; trustee Com. for Nat. Security, 1983, chmn. bd., 1986-91; chmn. bd. Lawyers Alliance for World Security, 1995—, PACT, 1995—. Recipient Disting. Pub. Svc. medal Dept. Def., 1966. Fellow Am. Acad. Arts and Scis.; mem. Assn. Bar City of N.Y. (chmn. com. sci. and law 1984-87), Am. Law Inst. (life), Hudson Inst., Internat. Inst. Strategic Studies, Inst. Medicine of NAS (charter mem., coun. 1970-77, com. on human rights 1978-89), Coun. on Fgn. Rels., Century (N.Y.C.), Cosmos (D.C.). Office: UMBC 5401 Wilkens Ave Baltimore MD 21228-5329

YARNALL, D. ROBERT, JR., entrepreneur, investor; b. Phila., Feb. 11, 1925; s. D. Robert and Elizabeth (Biddle) Y.; m. Rie Gabrielsen, June 24, 1954 (dec. Oct. 1980); children: Joan, Sara, Kristina; m. Anne Gates, July 3, 1982; stepchildren—Sarah, Michael, Amy Gates. B.M.E., Cornell U., 1948. Mech. engr. Westinghouse Electric Co., Phila., 1947; dir. relief mission to Poland Am. Friends Service Com., 1948-49; with Yarnall Waring Co. (name changed to Yarway Corp. 1965), Phila., 1949-86, v.p., 1957-62, pres., chief exec. officer, 1962-78, chmn. bd., 1968-86; founder, chmn. bd. Envirite Corp., Plymouth Meeting, Pa., 1975—; dir. James G. Biddle Co., Plymouth Meeting, Pa., 1957-78, chmn. bd., 1976-78; dir. Fed. Res. Bank of Phila., 1965-72, dep. chmn., 1971-72; dir. S.K.F. Industries, King of Prussia, Pa., Quaker Chem. Co., Phila., Meritor Fin. Group (PSFS), Keystone Internat. Inc., Houston; Cons. UN Indsl. Devel. Orgn. mission to, Indonesia, 1968; exec.-in-residence on faculty Centre d'Etudes Industrielles, Geneva, Switzerland, 1971-72; Bd. dirs. World Affairs Council, Pa., 1957-61, 64-68, 74—, chmn. bd., 1978-80. Trustee Internat. House, Phila., chmn., 1972-76; trustee U. Pa., 1981—, Phila Art Mus., 1978—, Greater Phila. Partnership, 1975—; trustee St. John's Coll., Annapolis, Md., 1975-86, vice chmn., 1978-82; bd. dirs. Pa. Environ. Council, 1976—, WHYY, Phila., Greater Phila. First Corp., 1984-86, Chestnut Hill Hosp., 1986—. Served with Am. Field Service with Brit. Army, World War II. Mem. ASME, Chief Execs. Orgn. Clubs: Philadelphia, Union League, Divotee Golf (Phila.). Home: 6706 Springbank Ln Philadelphia PA 19119-3713 Office: Envirite Corp Plymouth Meeting PA 19462

YARNELL, JEFFREY ALAN, regional credit executive; b. Columbus, Ohio, Oct. 23, 1941; s. Russell Lester and Grace Wilma (Adams) Y.; m. Carroll Ginevra Meier, July 6, 1982; children: Natalie, Brian. Student, Ohio State U., 1963. Cert. credit exec. Nat. Assn. Credit Mgmt. Teller Huntington Nat. Bank, Columbus, Ohio, 1965-66; credit mgr. janitrol divsn. Midland Ross, Columbus, 1966-68; asst. credit mgr. Marlite divsn. Masonite, Dover, Ohio, 1968-72; v.p., gen. credit mgr. wholesale fl. coverings Carson Pirie Scott, Chgo., 1972-88; regional credit mgr. Ga.-Pacific Corp., Des Plaines, Ill., 1988—; bd. dirs. Chgo.-Midwest Credit Mgmt. Assn., 1991-94. Author: Credit Manual, 1978. Advisor Jr. Achievement, Dover, Ohio, 1969-70; mem. Toastmasters Internat., Columbus, Ohio, 1965-67; councilor Boy Scouts Am., Palos Heights, Ill., 1980-81. With USNR, 1963-65. Mem. Chgo.-Midwest Credit Mgmt. Assn. (bd. dirs. 1991-94). Republican. Lutheran. Avocations: golf, skiing, chess, reading, stock market analysis, bowling. Office: Ga Pacific Corp 2300 Windy Ridge Pkwy SE Atlanta GA 30339

YARNELL, MICHAEL ALLAN, lawyer; b. Chgo., Sept. 10, 1944; s. Howard Winfred and Mary Elizabeth (Card) Y.; m. Karen Alice Hockenyos, June 12, 1971 (div. Mar. 1994); children: Sarah Munro, Jacob Rainey; m. Kristina Louise Renshaw, July 17, 1996. BS, Ariz. State U., 1967; JD with honors, U. Ill., 1971. Bar: Ariz. 1971. Ptnr. Streich, Lang, Weeks & Cardon, Phoenix, 1971-91, also bd. dirs.; mem. Myers, Barnes & Jenkins, Phoenix, 1991; judge Maricopa County Superior Ct., Phoenix, 1991—. Author: Ins and Outs of Foreclosure, 1981, 9th edit., 1996; projects editor Law Rev. U. Ill. Law Forum, 1970; contbr. articles to profl. jours. Chairperson Phoenix Children's Theatre, 1987. 1st lt. U.S. Army, 1971-72, Korea. Fellow Ariz. Bar Found.; mem. ABA, Am. Judicature Assn., Maricopa Bar Assn., State Bar Ariz. (Outstanding Contbn. to Continuing Legal Edn. award 1988), Order of Coif, Phi Kappa Phi. Republican. Avocations: computers, small boat sailing, white water rafting. Office: Maricopa County Superior Ct 101 W Jefferson St Phoenix AZ 85003-2205

YARNELL, RICHARD ASA, anthropologist; b. Boston, May 11, 1929; s. Sidney Howe and Floy Mae (Wilson) Y.; m. Meredith Jean Black; children—Karen Lyn, Anne Chesson, William Sidney, Susan Lynn. Student, Tex. A&M Coll., 1946-47; B.S., Duke U., 1950; M.A., U. N.Mex., 1958; Ph.D., U. Mich., 1963. Mem. faculty Emory U., Atlanta, 1962-71, asso. prof., 1967-71; mem. faculty U. N.C., Chapel Hill, 1971—, prof. anthropology, 1975-94, prof. emeritus, 1994—. Contbr. papers, reports to profl. jours., books. With USAF, 1951-55. Fellow AAAS; mem. Soc. for Econ. Botany, Soc. Ethnobiology, Southeastern Archaeol. Conf., Soc. Am. Archaeology (Fryxell medal 1992). Office: U NC Dept Anthropology Clb 3115 Chapel Hill NC 27514

YAROSEWICK, STANLEY J., academic administrator, physicist; b. Epping, N.H., Sept. 10, 1939. BS, U. N.H., 1961; MS, Clarkson Coll. Tech., 1963, PhD in Physics, 1966. Asst. prof. physics Clarkson Coll. Tech., Potsdam, N.Y., 1966-69, assoc. prof. physics, 1969-74; prof. physics West Chester (Pa.) Univ., 1974-87, v.p. acad. affairs, provost, 1987-94, interim pres., 1991-92; pres. Keene (N.H.) State Coll., 1994—. Mem. Am. Assn. Physics Tchrs., Am. Assn. State Colls. and Univs. Office: Keene State Coll Keene NH 03431

YAROWSKY, JONATHAN R., lawyer; b. Kansas City, Mo., May 23, 1949. AB summa cum laude, U. Mich., 1971; MS, Cornell U., 1974; JD, UCLA, 1977. Teaching instr. Cornell U., Ithaca, N.Y., 1972-74; summer assoc. Fed. Pub. Defender's Office, L.A., 1975; assoc. Rosenfeld, Meyer & Susman, Beverly Hills, Calif., 1976, Covington & Burling, 1977-82; majority counsel House Judiciary Subcom. on Econ. and Comml. Law, Washington, 1982-90; gen. counsel House Com. on Judiciary, Washington, 1991-95; spl. counsel to the Pres. The White House, Washington, 1995—. Chief comment editor UCLA Law Rev., 1977. Mem. Nat. Commn. on Crime. Mem. Phi Beta Kappa. Office: The White House 486 Old Exec Office Bldg Washington DC 20506

YARROW, PETER, folksinger; b. N.Y.C., May 31, 1938. B.A., Cornell U. Mem. group: Peter, Paul, and Mary, 1962—, also solo performer, recording artist, Warner Bros.: albums with Peter, Paul, and Mary include: Peter, Paul, and Mary, Moving, In the Wind, In Concert, A Song Will Rise, See What Tomorrow Brings, Peter, Paul, and Mary Album, Album 1700, Late Again, Peter, Paul & Mommy, 10 Years Together: The Best Of, Reunion, Peter, Paul & Mommy, Too (Emmy nominee 1993), No Easy Walk to Freedom, Lifelines; solo album: Peter, 1972, That's Enough for Me, 1973, Hard Times, 1975, Love Songs, 1975; on Broadway appearance: Peter, Paul, and Mary "From Bleecker to Broadway", 1986; TV spls. include: Reunion, Holiday Concert, Peter, Paul & Mommy, Too, Lifelines (PBS). Bd. dirs. Newport Folk Found., Kerrville (Tex.) Folk Festival, Ctr. for Global Edn., Augsberg Coll. Recipient Emmy nominee for "Puff the Magic Dragon", 1979, Citizen Action Leadership award, Vista, 1979, Alfred Lowenstein award, 1982, Hospice Care of R.I. award, 1987, Nat. Emergency Civil Liberties Com. award, 1988, Interlochen Disting. Alumnus Arts award, 1992, Conn. Hospice award, 1993, Grammy award for prodr. Peter Paul & Mommy, too, 1994, Kate Wolf Meml. award for the World Folk Music Assn., 1994.

YARWOOD, DEAN LESLEY, political science educator; b. Decorah, Iowa, Mar. 17, 1935; s. Harold Nicholas and Elsie Mabel (Roney) Y.; m. Elaine Delores Bender, Sept. 2, 1956; children: Lucinda, Kent, Keith, Douglas, Dennis. BA, Iowa U., 1957; MA, Cornell U., 1961; PhD, U. Ill., 1966. Tchr. social studies, acting jr. high prin. Mid-Prairie Community Sch., Wellman, Iowa, 1957-59; asst. prof. Coe Coll., Cedar Rapids, Iowa, 1963-66, U. Ky., Lexington, 1966-67; asst. prof. U. Mo., Columbia, 1967-70, assoc. prof., 1970-78, prof., 1978—, dir. grad. studies dept. polit. sci., 1970-72, 88, 94—, chmn. dept. polit. sci., 1988-91, Frederick A. Middlebush prof. polit. sci., 1992-95. Editor: The National Administrative System: Selected Readings, 1971, Public Administration, Politics, and the People: Selected Readings for Managers, Employees and Citizens, 1987; author, co-author numerous articles in polit. sci. jours. Recipient Bradish Meml. scholarship, 1953-57, Iowa Merit scholarship, 1956-57, Woodrow Wilson fellowship, 1959-60, James Garner fellowship, 1961-62, Woodrow Wilson Dissertation fellowship, 1962-63. Mem. Am. Soc. Pub. Adminstrn. (chmn. sect. on pub. adminstrn. edn. 1986-87, publs. com. 1986-89, com. on orgnl. rev. and evaluation 1995, Ctrl. Mo. chpt. coun. 1979-80, pres. 1980-81, ex-officio mem. coun. 1981-83), Am. Polit. Sci. Assn., Midwest Polit. Sci. Assn., So. Polit. Sci. Assn., Mo. Polit. Sci. Assn. (v.p. 1990-91, pres. 1991-92), Mo. Inst. for Pub. Adminstrn. (coun. 1976-77, v.p. 1977-78, pres. 1978-79), Phi Beta Kappa. Home: 304 Mumford Dr Columbia MO 65203-0230 Office: U Mo Dept Polit Sci 314 Professional Bldg Columbia MO 65211

YARYAN, RUBY BELL, psychologist; b. Toledo, Apr. 28, 1938; d. John Sturges and Susan (Bell) Y.; m. John Frederick Buenz, Jr., Dec. 15, 1962 (div. 1968). AB, Stanford U., 1960; PhD, U. London, 1968. Lic. clin. psychologist; diplomate Am. Bd. Psychology. Rsch. dir., univ. radio and tv U. Calif., San Francisco, 1968-70; dir. delinquency coun. U.S. Dep. Justice, Washington, 1970-73; evaluation dir. Office of Criminal Justice Planning, Sacramento, Calif., 1973-76; CAO project mgr. San Diego (Calif.) County, 1977-92; dir. devel. svcs. Childhelp USA, Woodland Hills, Calif., 1992-94; rsch. coord. Neuropsychiat. Inst. and Hosp. UCLA, 1986-87; exec. dir. Centinela Child Guidance Clinic, Inglewood, Calif., 1987-89; clin. dir. Nat. Found. Emotionally Handicapped, North Hills, Calif., 1990-93; pvt. practice Beverly Hills, Calif., 1973—; psychologist Sr. Psychology Svcs., North L.A. County, 1994—; cons. White House Conf. Children, Washington, 1970; mem. Nat. Adv. Com. Criminal Justice Standards and Goals, Washington, 1973; clin. affiliation UCLA Med. Ctr. Contbr. articles to profl. jours.; chpts. to books and monographs in field. Chair Human Svcs. Commn., City of West Hollywood, Calif., 1986; first vice-chair United Way/Western Region, L.A., 1988; mem. planning-allocations-rsch. coun. United Way, San Diego, 1980-82. Grantee numerous fed., state and local govt. orgns. Mem. Am. Psychol. Assn., Western Psychol. Assn., Calif. Psychol. Assn., Am. Orthopsychiat. Assn., Am. Profl. Soc. on Abuse of Children, Phi Beta Kappa. Episcopalian. Avocations: painting, music, theatre, writing, reading. Office: 337 S Beverly Dr Ste 107 Beverly Hills CA 90212-4307

YARYMOVYCH, MICHAEL IHOR, manufacturing company executive; b. Bialystok, Poland, Oct. 13, 1933; came to U.S., 1951, naturalized, 1956; s. Nicholas Joseph and Olga (Kruczowy) Y.; m. Roxolana Abramiuk, Nov. 21, 1951; children—Tatiana, Nicholas. B.Aero. Engring., NYU, 1955; M.S. in Engring. Mechanics, Columbia U., 1956, D. Engring. Sci., 1969. Dep. asst. sec. research and devel. U.S. Air Force, Washington, 1967-70; dir. AGARD, NATO, Paris, 1970-73; chief scientist U.S. Air Force, 1973-75; asst. adminstr. field ops. ERDA, 1975-77; v.p. engring. N.Am. aerospace ops. Rockwell Internat. Corp., Seal beach, Calif., 1977-81; v.p. advanced systems devel. Rockwell Internat. Corp., El Segundo, Calif., 1981-86, v.p., assoc. dir. Sys. Devel. Ctr., 1986—; mem. Air Force Sci. Adv. Bd., 1990—; chmn. NATO Adv. Group for Aerospace R&D, 1994—; cons. in field. Author papers in field. Translator Russian books and periodicals. Recipient Exceptional Civilian Svc. award Dept. Air Force, 1968, 73, 75, 94, Disting. Svc. award ERDA, 1977; Guggenheim fellow, 1956-58. Fellow AIAA (dir., pres., gen. chmn. ann. meeting 1978); mem. Air Force Assn., Nat. Mgmt. Assn., Nat. Security Industries Assn., AAAS, Am. Astronautical Soc., Aerospace Industry Assn., Internat. Acad. Astronautics (v.p. sci. programs). Office: Rockwell Internat Sys Devel Ctr 2800 Westminster Ave Seal Beach CA 90740-5606

YASHER, MICHAEL, accountant; b. United, Pa., Aug. 17, 1928; s. Michael and Mary (Sasik) Y.; m. Margaret Jean Wallace, June 23, 1956 (dec. July 12, 1987); 1 child, Michael. BS, Penn State U., 1956; diploma, Air

Command & Staff Coll., 1972, Nat. Defense U., 1977; MA, Ctrl. Mich. U., 1983. CPA, D.C.; cert. profl. contract mgr., D.C. Commd. USAF, 1948, advanced through grades to; commd. 2d lt. U.S. GAO, Washington, 1956-84; advanced through grades to col. Haskins & Sells, CPAs, Phila.; ret. USAF, 1988; mem. appropriations com. U.S. House of Reps., 1978-79; acct. to the comptroller U.S. Air Materials Command, 1979-83; acct., cons. E. K. Williams Co., Silver Spring, Md., 1985—. Contbr. numerous papers and articles to profl. publs. Treas. Boy Scouts Am., Rockville, Md., 1970s; bd. dirs. Sr. Softball Assn., Montgomery County, Md., 1993-94; pres. Leisure World (Md.) Billiards Club, 1994; commr., organizer Senior Softball League, 1994, Montgomery County, Md., 1994. Col. USAF, 1948-88, Korea. Recipient Bronze medal for softball Md. Sr. Olympics, 1992, 1994, Gold medal, 1994, Bronze medal for volleyball, 1995, Silver medal for Softeball, 1995, Meritorious Svc. award U.S.G.A.O., 1975, Data Systems Design Ctr. Outstanding Officer Mobilization Augmentee, 1978, 14 military decorations and others. Mem. AICPA, Res. Officers Assn., Billiards Club, Am. Legion. Democrat. Roman Catholic. Avocations: coin collecting, sports. Home: 1507 Interlachen Dr Apt 318 Silver Spring MD 20906-5625 Office: E K Williams Co 1700 Elton Rd Silver Spring MD 20903-1701

YASHON, DAVID, neurosurgeon, educator; b. Chgo., May 13, 1935; s. Samuel and Dorothy (Cutler) Y.; children—Jaclyn, Lisa, Steven. B.S. in Medicine, U. Ill., 1958, M.D., 1960. Diplomate Am. Bd. Neurol. Surgery. Intern U. Ill., 1961, resident, 1961-64, asst. in neuroanatomy, 1960; clin. instr. neurosurgery U. Chgo., 1965-66; asst. prof. neurosurgery Case Western Res U., Cleve., 1966-69; assoc. prof. neurosurgery Ohio State U., Columbus, 1969-74, prof., 1974-89, prof. emeritus, 1989—; mem. staff St. Ann's Hosp., Children's Hosp., Park Med. Ctr.; cons. Med. Research and Devel. Command, U.S. Army; mem. Neurology B Study Sect NIH. Author: Spinal Injury; contbr. articles to med. jours. Served as capt. U.S. Army, 1960-68. Fellow Royal Coll. Surgeons Can. (cert.), A.C.S.; mem. AMA, Am. Physiol. Soc., Congress Neurol. Surgeons, Am. Assn. Anatomists, Canadian, Ohio neurosurg. socs., Am. Assn. Neurol. Surgeons, Research Soc. Neurol. Surgeons, Acad. Medicine Columbus and Franklin County, Soc. for Neurosci., Soc. Univ. Surgeons, Am. Acad. Neurology, Assn. for Acad. Surgery, Am. Acad. Neurol. Surgery, Am. Assn. for Surgery of Trauma, Central Surg. Soc., Ohio Med. Soc., Columbus Surg. Soc., Sigma Xi, Alpha Omega Alpha. Office: Park Med Ctr 1492 E Broad St Ste 1201 Columbus OH 43205-1546

YASNYI, ALLAN DAVID, communications company executive; b. New Orleans, June 22, 1942; s. Ben Z. and Bertha R. (Michalove) Y.; BBA, Tulane U., 1964; m. Susan K. Manders; children: Benjamin Charles, Evelyn Judith, Brian Mallut. Free-lance exec. producer, producer, writer, actor and designer for TV, motion picture and theatre, 1961-73; producer, performer The Second City; dir. fin. and adminstrn. Quinn Martin Prodns., Hollywood, Calif., 1973-76, v.p. fin., 1976-77, exec. v.p. fin. and corp. planning, 1977; vice chmn., CEO QM Prodns., Beverly Hills, Calif., 1977-78, chmn. bd., CEO, 1978-80; pres., CEO The Synapse Communications Group, Inc., 1981—; exec. dir., adj. prof. U. So. Calif. Entertainment Tech. Ctr., 1994—; participant IC IS Forum, 1990—; exec. prodr. first live broadcast combining Intelsat, Intersputnik, The Voice of Am., and The Moscow World Radio Svc., 1990; resource guest Aspen Inst. Exec. Seminars, 1990; chmn. bd. dirs. Found. of Global Broadcasting, Washington, 1987-93. Trustee Hollywood Arts Coun., 1980-83; exec. v.p., trustee Hollywood Hist. Trust, 1981-91; bd. dirs. Internat. Ctr. for Intergative Studies, N.Y.C., 1988-92; bd. dirs. Asthma and Allergy Foun. Am., 1981-85. Logistical combat officer U.S. Army, 1964-66, Viet Nam. Named to Tulane U. Hall of Fame. Mem. Acad. TV Arts and Scis., Inst. Noetic Scis., Hollywood Radio and TV Soc., Hollywood C. of C. (dir., vice-chmn. 1978-93), Screen Actors Guild, Assn. Transpersonal Pyschology (keynote speaker 1988). Office: 4132 Fulton Ave Sherman Oaks CA 91423-4340

YASSIN, ROBERT ALAN, museum administrator, curator; b. Malden, Mass., May 22, 1941; s. Harold Benjamin and Florence Gertrude (Hoffman) Y.; m. Marilyn Kramer, June 9, 1963; children: Fredric Giles, Aaron David. BA (Rufus Choate scholar), Dartmouth Coll., 1962; postgrad., Boston U., 1962-63; M.A., U. Mich., 1965, postgrad. (Samuel H. Kress Found. fellow), 1968-70, Ph.D. candidate, 1970; postgrad (Ford Found. fellow), Yale U., 1966-68. Asst. to dir. Mus. Art U. Mich., 1965-66, asst. dir., 1970-72, asso. dir., 1972-73, acting dir., 1973, instr. dept. history of art, 1970-73; co-dir. Joint Program in Mus. Tng., 1970-73; chief curator Indpls. Mus. Art, 1973-75, 87-89, acting dir., 1975, dir., 1975-89; exec. dir. Tucson Mus. Art, 1990—; adj. prof. Herron Sch. Art Ind. U./Purdue U., 1975-89. Contbr. to mus. publications. Mem. Ariz. Hist. Soc., Ariz. Mus. Assn., Tucson Mus. Assn., Tucson Arts Coalition., Tucson Downtown Adv. Coun. Mem. Am. Assn. Mus. (bd. dirs. Internat. Coun. Mus. 1986-89), Assn. Art Mus. Dirs., Coll. Art Assn. Am., Intermus. Conservation Assn. (chmn. exec. com. 1977-78), Tucson C. of C. (cultural affairs com., econ. devel. com.), Nat. Trust Historic Preservation, Rotary. Jewish. Home: 3900 N Calle Casita Tucson AZ 85718-7204 Office: Tucson Mus Art 140 N Main Ave Tucson AZ 85701-8218

YASSKY, LESTER, lawyer, banker; b. N.Y.C., July 19, 1941; s. Leo and Ida (Tauss) Y.; m. Harriet Anne Rose, June 30, 1963; children—David, Evan, Rachel. B.A., Columbia U., 1963; LL.B., Harvard U., 1966. Bar: N.Y. 1967. Assoc. Shea & Gould, N.Y.C., 1966-75; ptnr. Shea & Gould, 1975-90; sec. Toys "R" Us, Inc., Paramus, N.J., 1978-90; sr. v.p., gen. counsel Dai-Ichi Kangyo Bank, Ltd., 1990—. Mem. ABA, N.Y.C. Bar Assn., N.Y. State Bar Assn., Phi Beta Kappa. Democrat. Avocations: sports; travel. Office: Dai-Ichi Kangyo Bank Ltd 1 World Trade Ctr New York NY 10048-0202

YASTOW, SHELBY, lawyer. Sr. v.p., gen. counsel, sec. McDonald's Corp., Oak Brook, Ill. Office: Mc Donalds Corp 1 Croc Dr Hinsdale IL 60521*

YASTRZEMSKI, CARL MICHAEL, former baseball player, public relations executive; b. Southampton, N.Y., Aug. 22, 1939; m. Carolann Casper, Jan. 30, 1960. Student, Notre Dame U.; B.S. in Bus. Adminstrn., Merrimack Coll. Second baseman, shortstop Raleigh (N.C.), Carolina League, 1959; outfielder Mpls. (Am. Assn.), 1960; left fielder Boston Red Sox (Am. League), 1961-83, cons., instr., 1983—; with Eaton Vance Corp., Boston, 1968—, Kahn's & Co. (subs. Sara Lee Corp.), Cincinnati, 1978—. Chosen most valuable player Carolina League, 1959; chosen most valuable player Am. League, 1967; inducted into Baseball Hall of Fame, 1989. Mem. Am. League All-Star Team, 1963, 65-77, 79, 83. Office: Eaton Vance Corp 24 Federal St Fl 5 Boston MA 02110-2507

YASUDA, HIROTSUGU KOGE, chemical engineering professor; b. Kyoto, Japan, Mar. 24, 1930; s. Mitsuo and Kei (Niwa) Y.; m. Gerda Lisbeth Schmidtke, Apr. 6, 1968; children: Ken Eric, Werner Akira, Lisbeth Kay. BSChemE, Kyoto U., 1953; MS in Polymer Chemistry, SUNY, Syracuse, 1959, PhD in Polymer and Phys. Chemistry, 1961. Rsch. assoc. Ophthalmic Plastic Lab., Mass. Eye & Ear Infirmary, Boston, 1962-63; head biomaterial sect. eye rsch. Cedar-Sinai Med. Ctr., L.A., 1963-65; vis. scientist Royal Inst. Tech., Stockholm, 1965-66; sr. chemist Rsch. Triangle Inst., Rsch. Triangle Pk., N.C., 1966-72, mgr. Polymer Rsch. Lab., 1972-78; prof. chem. engring. U. Mo., Rolla, 1978-88, dir. Thin Films Inst., 1974-88; prof. chem. engring. U. Mo., Columbia, 1988—, chmn. dept., 1988-90, dir. Ctr. for Surface and Plasma Techs., 1989—. Author: Plasma Polymerization, 1985. Home: 1004 Lake Point Ln Columbia MO 65203-2900 Office: U Mo Ctr for Surface Sci and Plasma Tech Columbia MO 65211

YASUFUKU, SACHIO, electrical engineer, educator; b. Qingdao, China, Nov. 11, 1929; (parents Japanese citizens); s. Kozo and Takie (Suematsu) Y.; m. Yoko Kikutani, Dec. 16, 1958. BS, Nagoya (Japan) U., 1952, D Engring., 1979. Rschr. Furukawa Electric Co., Ltd., Yokohama, Japan, 1952-63, prodn. engr., 1963-65; rsch. leader Furukawa Electric Co., Ltd., Hiratsuka, Japan, 1965-72; sr. specialist Toshiba Corp. Yokohama, Kawasaki, Japan, 1972-79, chief specialist, 1979-89; adj. prof. Tokyo Denki U., 1989—. Contbr. articles to profl. publs.; patentee in field. Recipient nat. award for invention Japan Inst. Invention and Innovation, 1963, 23 nat. awards for progress of elec. machinery Japan Elec. Mfrs., 1974. Fellow IEEE (sec. Tokyo chpt. Elec. Insulation Soc. 1980-83, chmn. 1984-86, regional editor Elec. Insulation mag. 1988-91, contbg. editor 1992—); mem. AAAS, N.Y. Acad. Scis. Roman Catholic. Avocation: travel. Home: 520 3-1 Higashi Kugenuma, Fujisawa Kanagawa 251, Japan Office: Tokyo Denki U, 2-2 Nishiki-cho Kanda, Chiyoda-ku Tokyo 101, Japan

YATES, ALBERT CARL, academic administrator, chemistry educator; b. Memphis, Sept. 29, 1941; s. John Frank and Sadie L. (Shell) Y.; m. Ann Young; children: Steven, Stephanie, Aerin Alessandra, Sara Elizabeth. B.S., Memphis State U., 1965; Ph.D., Ind. U., 1968. Research assoc. U. So. Calif., Los Angeles, 1968-69; prof. chemistry Ind. U., Bloomington, 1969-74; v.p. research, grad. dean U. Cin., 1974-81; exec. v.p., provost, prof. chemistry Washington State U., Pullman, 1981-90; pres. Colo. State U., Fort Collins, 1990—; chancellor Colo. State U. System, Fort Collins, 1990—; mem. grad. record exam. bd. Princeton (N.J.) U., 1977-80, undergrad. assessment program council, 1977-81; cons. NRC, 1975-82, Office End., HEW, 1978-80; mem. exec. council acad. affairs NASULGC, 1983-87, ACE, 1983-87,. nat adv. council gen. med. scis. NIH, 1987—. Contbr.: research articles to Jour. Chem. Physics; research articls to Phys. Rev.; research articles to Jour. Physics, Phys. Rev. Letters, Chem. Physics Letters. Served with USN, 1959-62. Recipient univ. and State honors and awards. Mem. Am. Phys. Soc., Am. Chem. Soc., AAAS, Nat. Assn. State Univs. and Land Grant Colls. (mem. exec. council academic affairs), Am. Council Edn. (mem. exec. com. academic affairs), Sigma Xi, Phi Lambda Upsilon. Home: 1744 Hillside Dr Fort Collins CO 80524-1965 Office: Colo State U 102 Administration Bldg Fort Collins CO 80523

YATES, CHARLES RICHARDSON, former arts center executive; b. Atlanta, Sept. 9, 1913; s. Presley Daniel and Julia (Richardson) Y.; m. Dorothy Malone, May 20, 1944; children: Dorothy Y. Kirkley, Charles R., Sarah F., J. Comer. B.S. with honors, Ga. Inst. Tech., 1935. With 1st Nat. Bank Atlanta, 1935-47, asst. v.p., 1940-47; with Joshua L. Baily & Co., Inc., Atlanta, 1947-60; v.p. Joshua L. Baily & Co., Inc., 1956-60; v.p. finance Atlantic Coast Line R.R. Co. and L. & N. R.R. Co., 1960-67; v.p. Seaboard Coast Line R.R. Co., 1967-71, v.p. finance, 1971-73; v.p. finance L. & N. R.R. Co., 1967-73; pres. Atlanta Arts Alliance, 1973-83; trustee Profile Fund I, Sacramento; dir. Technology Park/Atlanta. Trustee Ga. Tech. Found., Woodruff Arts Ctr. Served with AUS, 1941-42; lt. USNR, 1942-46. Mem. Ga. C. of C. (dir., pres. 1965-67), East Lake Golf Club (pres. 1995—), Augusta Nat. Club (sec.), Atlanta Athletic Club, Peachtree Golf Club, Capital City Club, Royal and Ancient Golf Club. Episcopalian.

YATES, DAN CHARLES, insurance company official; b. Spring Valley, Ill., Oct. 14, 1952; s. Earl John Jr. and Charlotte Elaine (Sandberg) Y.; m. Margaret Mary McBride, Mar. 1, 1980; 1 child, Keith. B Bus. in Fin., Western Ill. U., 1977. CPCU. Claims adjuster G.A.B. Bus. Svcs., Kansas City, Mo., 1978-80; claims mgr. Dodson Group, Kansas City, 1980—; mem. conf. com. Property Loss Rsch. Bur., Schaumburg, Ill., 1994-96, vice chair, 1994-95, chair, 1995-96; adv. coun. midwest region Nat. Assn. Ind. Ins. Adjusters, 1986-89, mem. Credit Com. for Bee Dee Co. Credit Union, 1992— (pres., chair 1994—). Vol. Jr. Achievement. With U.S. Army, 1972-74. Mem. Kansas City Property Claims Assn. (pres. 1992). Avocations: bowling, basketball, blood donor. Office: Dodson Group 9201 State Line Rd Kansas City MO 64114

YATES, DAVID JOHN C., chemist, researcher; b. Stoke-on-Trent, Staffordshire, Eng., Feb. 13, 1927; came to U.S., 1958; s. Eric John and Beatrice Victoria (Street) Y.; m. Natalie Chmelnitsky, June 22, 1983. B.S. with honors, U. Birmingham, U.K., 1949; Ph.D., U. Cambridge, Eng., 1955, Sc.D., 1968. Rsch. physicist Kodak Labs., Wealdstone, London, 1949-50; rsch. chemist Brit. Ceramic Rsch. Assn., Stoke-on-Trent, 1950-51; rsch. assoc. dept. colloid sci. U. Cambridge, 1951-58; lectr. Sch. Mines and dept. chemistry Columbia U., N.Y.C., 1958-60; sr. rsch. fellow Nat. Phys. Lab., Teddington, U.K., 1960-61; rsch. assoc. corp. labs. Exxon Rsch. and Engring., Annandale, N.J., 1961-86; rsch. prof. dept. of chem. engring. Lafayette Coll., Easton, Pa., 1986-87; rsch. prof. dept. materials sci. Rutgers U., Piscataway, N.J., 1987-88; cons. San Diego, 1988—. Contbr. over 70 articles to profl. jours., chpts. to books; 13 U.S. patents, numerous fgn. patents. Fellow Inst. of Physics (U.K.), Royal Soc. Chemistry (U.K.), N.Y. Catalysis Club (chmn. 1966-67). Club: N.Y. Catalysis (chmn. 1965-66). Avocations: photography, bicycling, gliding, travel, sports cars.

YATES, ELLA GAINES, library consultant; b. Atlanta, June 14, 1927; d. Fred Douglas and Laura (Moore) Gaines; m. Joseph L. Sydnor (dec.); 1 child, Jerri Gaines Sydnor Lee; m. Clayton R. Yates (dec.). A.B., Spelman Coll., Atlanta, 1949; M.S. in L.S, Atlanta U., 1951; J.D., Atlanta Law Sch., 1979. Asst. br. librarian Bklyn. Pub. Library, 1951-54; head children's dept. Orange (N.J.) Pub. Library, 1956-59; br. librarian E. Orange (N.J.) Pub. Library, 1960-69; med. librarian Orange Meml. Hosp., 1967-69; asst. dir. Montclair (N.J.) Pub. Library, 1970-72; asst. dir. Atlanta-Fulton Pub. Library, 1972-76, dir., 1976-81; dir. learning resource ctr. Seattle Opportunities Industrialization Ctr., 1982-84; asst. dir. adminstrn. Friendship Force, Atlanta, 1984-86; state librarian Commonwealth of Va., 1986-90; library cons. Price Waterhouse, 1991; adv. bd. Library of Congress Center for the Book, 1977-85; cons. in field; vis. lectr. U. Wash., Seattle, 1981-83; mem. Va. Records Adv. Bd., 1986-90; mem. Nagara Exec. Bd., 1987-91. Contbr. to profl. jours. Vice chmn. N.J. Women's Coun. on Human Rels., 1957-59; chmn. Friends Fulton County Jail, 1973-81; bd. dirs. United Cerebral Palsy Greater Atlanta, Inc., 1979-81 Coalition Against Censorship, Washington, 1981-84, YMCA Met. Atlanta, 1979-81, Exec. Women's Network, 1979-82, Freedom To Read Found., 1979-85, Va. Black History Mus., Richmond, 1990-91; sec., exec. dir. Va. Libr. Found. Bd., 1986-90. Recipient meritorious svc. award Atlanta U., 1977, Phoenix award City of Atlanta, 1980, Serwa award Nat. Coalition 100 Black Women, 1989, Black Caucus award, 1989, disting. svc. award Clark-Atlanta U., 1991, ednl. support svc. award Tuskegee Airmen, 1993; named profl. woman of yr. NAACP N.J., 1972, outstanding chum of yr., 1976; named outstanding alumni Spelman Coll., 1977, named to alumni hall of fame, 1995. Mem. ALA (exec. bd. 1977-83, commn. freedom of access to info.), NAACP, Southeastern Libr. Assn., Nat. Assn. Govt. Archives and Records Adminstrn. (exec. bd. 1987-91), Delta Sigma Theta. Baptist. Home and Office: 1171 Oriole Dr SW Atlanta GA 30311-2424

YATES, ELSIE VICTORIA, retired secondary English educator; b. Newport, R.I., Dec. 16, 1916; d. Andrew James and Rachel Agnes (Sousa) Tabb; m. George Herman Yates, July 12, 1941 (div. Apr. 1981); children: Serena, George Jr., Michael, Elsie French, David. AB in English and History, Va. Union U., 1938; postgrad., U. R.I., 1968-73, Salve Regina U., 1968-73. Life cert. in secondary English and reading specialist, R.I. Reading specialist grades 7 and 8 title I Newport (R.I.) Sch., 1971-74, secondary English educator, 1975-87; ret., 1987. Mem. adult com. Young Life, Newport, 1981-93; active Newport (R.I.) Substance Abuse Force, 1989-93; chmn. multicultural curriculum com. New Visions for Newport (R.I.) Schs., 1991-94; mem. edn. com. Swinburne Sch., Newport, 1992-94. Recipient Outstanding Ednl. Contbn. Under Title I award U.S. Office Edn., Bur. Sch. Sys., 1976, Presdl. citation Nat. Edn. Assn. R.I., 1987, Appreciation for Svc. award Cmty. Bapt. Ch., Newport, 1988, Outstanding Svc. award in field of edn. to the youth in cmty. Queen Esther Chpt. 2, Newport, 1992. Mem. R.I. Ret. Tchrs. Assn., Newport Ret. Tchrs. Assn. Baptist. Avocations: reading, handicrafts, community activities. Home: 8 Bayside Vlg Apt A Newport RI 02840-1321

YATES, ELTON G., retired petroleum industry executive; b. Slidell, La., July 31, 1935; s. Elton O. and Leona E. (Sollberger) Y.; m. Jo Ellen Levy, Apr. 11, 1955; children—Sherlyn, Michele, Steven. B.S. in Petroleum Engring, La. State U., 1957. Petroleum engr. Texaco Inc., various locations, 1957-68; dist. engr. Texaco Inc., Corpus Christi, Tex., 1968-70; div. devel. engr. Texaco Inc., Houston, 1970-71; coordinator joint ops. Texaco Inc., N.Y.C., 1971-75; pres., gen. mgr. Texaco Iran, London, 1975-77; asst. gen. mgr. producing Eastern Hemisphere Texaco Inc., N.Y.C., 1977-78; gen. mgr. producing Harrison, N.Y., 1978-79, corp. v.p., dept. head producing, 1979-82; div. pres. Texaco Oil Trading and Supply, 1981-82; pres. Texaco Middle East/Far East, 1982-84, Texaco Latin Am./West Africa, 1984-87; corp. sr. v.p. Texaco Inc., White Plains, N.Y., 1987-94, ret., 1994; bd. dirs. numerous Texaco Inc. Co. subs., Coast Guard Found.; former dir. Arabian Am. Oil Co.; dir. Caltex Corp. and Amoseas. Mem. dean's adv. coun. Coll Engring. La. State U. Elected to La. State U. Coll. Engring. Hall of Distinction. Mem. Soc. Petroleum Engrs. of AIME, 25 Yr. Club of Petroleum Industry, Country Club of N.C., Country Club of Darien (Conn.), Country Club of Pinehurst (N.C.), Phi Epsilon Tau. Methodist.

YATES, JERE EUGENE, business educator, management consultant; b. Memphis, Apr. 4, 1941; s. Emmett Eugene and Naomi Christine (Whitfield) Y.; m. Carolyn Kay Hall, June 8, 1962; children: Camille, Kevin, Brian. BA, Harding U., 1963, MTh, MA, 1966; PhD, Boston U., 1968. Instr. Harding U., Searcy, Ark., 1967-69; prof. bus. Pepperdine U., Malibu, Calif., 1969—; cons. Hughes Aircraft Co., L.A., 1973—, Allied-Signal Corp., North Hollywood, Calif., 1985-90, Pacific Physican Svcs., 1988-96, Med Ptnrs./Mullikin, 1996—. Author: Managing Stress, 1979 (membership book award, 1979); contbr. articles to profl. jours. Mem. AAUP, Acad. Mgmt., UCP/Spastic Children's Found. (bd. dirs., exec. com.), Orgnl. Behavior Teaching Soc., North Ranch Country Club. Republican. Mem. Ch. of Christ. Office: Pepperdine U Business Dept 24255 Pacific Coast Hwy Malibu CA 90263

YATES, JOHN MELVIN, ambassador; b. Superior, Mont., Nov. 25, 1939; s. Leon Glen and Violet May (McPheeters) Y.; m. Peggy Maureen Simpson, Mar. 26, 1961 (dec. Apr. 1986); children: Catherine Diener, John Simpson, Maureen Cole, Paul Marion, Leon Gregory; m. Mary Barbara Carlin, Jan. 30, 1988. A.B., Stanford U., 1961; M.A., Fletcher Sch. Law and Diplomacy, 1962, M.A.L.D., 1963, Ph.D., 1972. Fgn. service officer U.S. Dept. State, Washington, 1964—, Algiers, Algeria, 1964-66, Blantyre, Malawi, 1967-68, Bamako, Mali, 1969-71, New Delhi, India, 1973-75, Ankara, Turkey, 1975-77, Libreville, Gabon, 1977-80, Washington, 1971-73, 80-82; U.S. amb. to Republic of Cape Verde U.S. Dept. State, 1983-86; counselor for polit. affairs U.S. Dept. State, Manila, 1986-89; dep. chief of mission U.S. Dept. State, Lagos, Nigeria, 1989-91; dep. chief of mission U.S. Dept. State, Kinshasa, Zaire, 1991-93, chief of mission, 1993-95; amb. to Republic of Benin U.S. Dept. State, Cotonou, 1995—. Recipient Presdl. award for sustained superior accomplishment in conduct of fgn. policy. Mem. Am. Fgn. Service Assn. Office: Cotonou Dept State Washington DC 20521-2120

YATES, JOHN THOMAS, JR., chemistry educator, research director; b. Winchester, Va., Aug. 3, 1935; s. John Thomas and Kathryn (Barnett) Y.; m. Kerin Joyce Narbut, Oct. 18, 1958; children: Geoffrey, Nathan. BS, Juniata Coll., 1956; PhD, MIT, 1960. Asst. prof. chemistry Antioch Coll., Yellow Springs, Ohio, 1960-63; NRC fellow, research chemist Nat. Bur. Standards, Washington, 1963-66; R.K. Mellon prof. chemistry U. Pitts., 1982—, dir. Surface Sci. Ctr., 1982—; co-dir. materials rsch. ctr. U. Pitts., 1994, R.K. Mellon prof. chemistry and physics, 1994—. Co-author: The Surface Scientist's Guide to Organometallic Chemistry, 1987; co-editor: Vibrational Spectroscopy of Molecules on Surfaces, 1987, Chemical Perspectives of Microelectronic Materials, Vol. 131; assoc. editor: Studies in Surface Science and Catalysis, 1986; series editor: Methods of Surface Characterization, 1987; bd. editors Ann. Rev. Phys. Chemistry, 1983-85, Jour. Phys. Chemistry, 1983-88, Jour. Chem. Physics, Jour. Catalysis, Chem. Revs., Langmuir, Surface Sci., Applications of Surface Sci., Accounts Chem. Rsch.; co-editor Langmuir; contbr. revs. and articles to profl. jours.; inventor desorption spectrometer, 1981. Sherman Fairchild Disting. scholar Calif. Inst. Tech., 1977-78; recipient Silver medal Dept. Commerce-Nat. Bur. Stds., 1973, Stratton award, 1981, Gold medal Dept. Commerce Nat. Bur. Stds., 1981, Pres.'s Disting. Rsch. award U. Pitts., 1989, Proctor & Gamble award, 1989, Alexander von Humboldt Sr. Rsch. award, 1994. Fellow Am. Phys. Soc. (bd. dirs. divsn. chem. physics 1991—, chmn. divsn. chem. physics 1989), Am. Vacuum Soc. (chmn. surface sci. divsn. 1973, 92, trustee 1975, bd. dirs. 1982-85, M.W. Welch award 1994, fellow 1994); mem. NAS, Am. Chem. Soc. (chmn. divsn. colloid and surface chemistry, Langmuir lectr. 1979, Kendall award in colloid of surface chemistry 1986, Morley prize Cleve. chpt. 1990, Peter Debyb lectr. Cornell U. 1993). Office: U Pitts Surface Sci Ctr Dept Chemistry Pittsburgh PA 15260

YATES, KATHLEEN BARRETT, newspaper executive; b. Washington, July 28, 1954; d. William Kirby and Beatrice Mabel (Robinson) Y.; m. Peter Andrew Troop, July 6, 1986; children: Jay Robinson, Tora Ballad. BA, Trinity Coll., 1976; MBA, Stanford U., 1981. Economist Gordian Assocs., Washington, 1976-79; asst. to pub. San Jose (Calif.) Mercury News, 1981-82, dir. fin., 1982-86, sr. v.p., gen. mgr., 1988—; asst. to pres. Knight Ridder Inc., Miami, Fla., 1986-88. Trustee San Jose Repertory Theater, 1984-86, San Jose Mus. of Art, 1988-90, Sta. KTEH Pub. TV, San Jose, 1988—, Health Dimension, Inc., San Jose, 1989—. Recipient Twin award YWCA, 1985. Office: San Jose Mercury News 750 Ridder Park Dr San Jose CA 95131-2432

YATES, LINDA SNOW, communications executive; b. St. Louis, July 20, 1938; d. Robert Anthony Jerrue and June Alberta (Crowder) Armstrong; m. Charles Russell Snow, Nov. 26, 1958 (div. 1979); children: Cathryn Louise, Christopher Armstrong, Heather Highstone, Sean Webster; m. Alan Porter Yates, July 22, 1983. BBA, Auburn U., 1973, MEd, 1975, postgrad. Cert. profl. sec. Div. head placement div. Solutions Group, Atlanta, 1981-83; employment coord. Fulton Fed. Savs., Atlanta, 1983-84; owner, recruiter Data One, Inc., Atlanta, 1984-85; ops. mgr. Talent Tree Temporaries, Atlanta, 1985-87; legal asst., sec. Rice & Keene, Atlanta, 1987-90; legal word processing asst. Kilpatrick & Cody, Atlanta, 1990-94; pres., owner Power Comm., Hilton Head, S.C., 1994—; adj. instr. DeKalb C.C., Atlanta, 1980-84, Mercer U., Atlanta, 1981-82; instr. bus. So. Union State Jr. Coll., Valley, Ala., 1974-75; legal sec. Swift, Currie, McGhee & Hiers, Atlanta, 1979-80, Samford, Torbert, Denson & Horsley, Opelika, Ala., 1969-71. Columnist Neon News Flash, 1995. Mem. Paralegal Assn. Beaufort County (charter mem., sec. 1993-94), Women Bus. Owners, Nat. Assn. Pers. Cons., Internat. Soc. Poets (Disting. mem., Internat. Poet of Merit 1996), Phi Delta Kappa. Republican. Episcopalian. Avocations: golf, writing, international travel. Home: 234 Tennis Villas Fripp Island SC 29920 also: PO Box 2441 Cashiers NC 28717 Office: 33 Office Park Rd 4A-127 Hilton Head Island SC 29928-4612

YATES, MARGERY GORDON, elementary education educator; b. Walton, N.Y., July 3, 1910; d. McClellan Gordon and Marcia Beulah (Ramsdell) Gordon-Strahl; m. James McKendree Yates, Aug. 11, 1933; 1 child, Sally. BS, U. Houston, 1943, MS, 1948; MA, Stanford U., 1952. Tchr. Baldwin (N.Y.) Sch. Dist., 1928-34, Houston Sch. Dist., 1943-48; supr. primary edn. Watsonville (Calif.) Sch. Dist., 1948-53; edn. cons. San Mateo County Office Edn., Redwood City, Calif., 1953-58; supr. primary edn. Jefferson Elem. Sch. Dist., Daly City, Calif., 1958-65; tchr. Hillsborough (Calif.) Sch. Dist., 1965-75; instr. U. Houston, 1956, San Jose State Coll., 1957. Mem. AAUW (edn. area rep. 1987-88, 89-90, 91-92, 92-93, 93-94, Fellowship award honoree 1991), Burlingame Music Club (pres. 1992-93, 93-94), Commonwealth Club Calif., Alpha Delta Kappa (corr. sec. Calif. state bd. 1981-82, Gamma Beta chpt. pres. 1971-74, treas. 1985-89, 94—). Republican. Mem. Ch. Christian Sci. Avocations: gardening, edn., community support, travel, music, dance, theater. Home: 2731 Summit Dr Burlingame CA 94010-6039

YATES, MICHAEL FRANCIS, management consultant; b. N.Y.C., Feb. 9, 1946; s. John Berchmans and Jane Ann (Gretz) Y.; student Canisius Coll., 1963-64; B.A., U. Buffalo, 1968; m. Christine Mary Dallos, Jan. 14, 1967; children—Erik Michael, Alison. Mgmt. trainee, dept. mgr. Sears, Roebuck & Co., Buffalo, 1968-69; cons. Rothman & D'Alessandro, Inc., N.Y.C., 1969-71; sr. cons. Martin & Segal & Co., Inc., N.Y.C., 1971-75, A.S. Hansen, Inc., N.Y.C., 1975-78; exec. v.p. A.M. D'Alessandro & Co., Inc., North Haledon, N.J., 1978-81; mng. dir., Alexander & Alexander Consulting Group, Inc., Lyndhurst, N.J., 1981—. Pres. Lincoln Sch. PTA, 1975-77; chmn. Bethlehem Twp. Econ. and Indsl. Devel. Bd., 1980-83; pres. Bethlehem Twp. Republican Club, mem. Hunterdon County com.; mem. Republican Nat. Com. Mem. Am. Mgmt. Assn., Am. Compensation Assn., Soc. Human Resource Mgmt., Adminstrv. Mgmt. Soc., Aircraft Owners and Pilots Assn. Home: 519 Lannon Ln Glen Gardner NJ 08826-3817 Office: 125 Chubb Ave Lyndhurst NJ 07071-3504

YATES, PATRICIA ANN HENNING, nursing director; b. French Camp, Miss., Aug. 11, 1939; d. Dotson Sidney and Elsie (Armstrong) Henning; m. Jesse Morris Yates; children: Gail, Jesse, Cynthia, Renee, Cristelle. LPN, N.W. Jr. Coll.; ADN, Miss. Delta Jr. Coll. RN, Miss.; CNA; lic. nursing home adminstr.; cert. BTLS, ACLS; cert. healthcare risk mgmt. Dir. nursing North Panola Hosp. & Nursing Home, Sardis, Miss., 1976-84, Montfort Jones Hosp., Kosciusko, Miss., 1987-88, Quitman County Hosp. & Nursing

Home, Marks, Miss., 1989—. Mem. ANA, Am. Orgn. Nurse Execs., Miss. Hosp. Assn., orgn. Nurse Execs. (bd. dirs.), Soc. for Risk Mgmt. Democrat. Baptist. Avocations: fishing, reading. Home: RR 3 Box 170 Batesville MS 38606-9803 Office: Quitman County Hosp & Nursing Home 340 Getwell St Marks MS 38646-9785

YATES, PATRICIA ANN THOMPSON, elementary school educator; b. Louisville, Feb. 22, 1942; d. Albert Gregory and Eleanor (Bloemer) Thompson; m. Ronald Anthony Yates, Aug. 24, 1963; children: Robert Eric, Kristin Yates Sutton, Kurt Daniel. BA, Aquinas Coll., Grand Rapids, Mich., 1963; MEd, Xavier U., Cin., 1976. Cert. reading specialist (K-12), reading supr. Remedial reading tchr. Cin. Pub. Schs., 1977—; asst. coord. The Olympus Ctr., Cin., 1992—; cons. Cin. Ctr. for Developmental Disorders, 1995—. Author: Root Word Program, 1990. Bd. dirs. Ohio Valley br. Orton Dyslexia Soc., Cin., 1989—; ednl. adv. com. edn. dept. Coll. Mount St. Joseph, Cin., 1990-94. U. Cin. grantee, 1988. Mem. Internat. Reading Assn. Avocations: reading, tennis, sewing. Office: The Olympus Ctr 38 E Hollister St Cincinnati OH 45219

YATES, PETER, director, producer; b. Ewshoot, Surrey, England, July 24, 1929; s. Robert L. and Constance Yates; m. Virginia Pope; 3 children. Student, Royal Acad. of Dramatic Art. Entered film industry, 1956. Films directed: Summer Holiday, 1962, One Way Pendulum, 1964, Robbery, 1966, Bullitt, 1968, John and Mary, 1969, The Hot Rock, 1971, The Friends of Eddie Coyle,1972, for Pete's Sake, 1973, The Deep, 1976, Krull, 1982, Eleni, 1985, Suspect,1987, An Innocent Man, 1989; dir., producer Murphy's War, 1970, Mother, Jugs and Speed, 1975, Breaking Away, 1979 (nominated Acad. award 1980), Eyewitness, 1980, The Dresser, 1983 (nominated Acad. award 1984), The House on Carroll Street, 1986, Year of the Comet, 1991, Roommates, 1994. Mem. Acad. Motion Pictures Arts & Scis., Dirs. Guild Am., Garrick Club.

YATES, ROBERT DOYLE, anatomy educator; b. Birmingham, Ala., Feb. 28, 1931; s. James William, Jr. and Mildred (Doyle) Y.; m. Jane Congleton, 1955; children: Robert Lee, Pamela C. BS, U. Ala., 1954, MS, 1956, PhD, 1959. Student anatomy dept. U. Ala., Birmingham, postdoctoral fellow, 1959-60; with U. Tex., Galveston, 1961-72; prof. anatomy Tulane U. Med. Sch., New Orleans, 1972—, chmn. dept. anatomy, 1972—; vis. investigator Harvard U. Med. Sch., Boston, 1962-63, Yale U. Med. Sch., New Haven, 1965-67. Mem. editorial bd.: Am. Jour. Anatomy, Anat. Record; contbr. articles to profl. jours. and chpts. to books. Vestryman Trinity Episc. Ch., Galveston, 1965-68; vestryman, jr. warden Trinity Episc. Ch., New Orleans, 1985-89, sr. warden, 1989-92. With inf. U.S. Army, 1960-61. Recipient numerous awards NIH, 1965-72, Research Career Devel. award, Golden Apple teaching award AMA Student Assn., 1971. Mem. Am. Assn. Anatomists (chmn. nominating com. 1980, sec.-treas. 1988-96), Internat. Fedn. Assn. Anatomists (treas. 1989—), Assn. Anatomy Cell Biology and Neurobiology Chairpersons (sec.-treas. 1976—), Am. Soc. Cell Biology. Republican. Avocations: tennis, stained glass, beveled glass, hunting. Office: Tulane U Sch of Medicine 1430 Tulane Ave New Orleans LA 70112-2699

YATES, ROBIN DAVID SEBASTIAN, Chinese history educator; b. Oxford, Eng., July 30, 1948; came to U.S., 1970; s. Joseph Ronald St. John and Mary Violet (Eliot) Y.; m. Grace Sieugit Fong, June 29, 1991. BA, Oxford U., 1970, MA, 1974; MA, U. Calif., Berkeley, 1975; PhD, Harvard U., 1980. Lectr. Harvard U., Cambridge, Mass., 1980-82; asst. prof. MIT, 1983-84; asst. prof. Harvard U., Cambridge, Mass., 1984-87, assoc. prof., 1987-88, Harris K. Weston assoc. prof. humanities, 1988-89; Burlington No. Found. prof. Asian studies Dartmouth Coll., Hanover, N.H., 1989-93, chair Asian studies program, 1992-93; prof. Chinese history McGill U., Montreal, Que., Can., 1993—, dir. Ctr. East Asian studies, 1993—, chmn. dept. East Asian studies, 1993—, mem. senate, 1995—; cons. Nova, WGBH, Terra Nova TV, Discovery Channel, Project Emperor I, Voyager Co., FilmRoos. Author: Washing Silk: The Life and Selected Poetry of Wei Chuang (834-910), 1988, (with W. Joseph Needham) Science and Civilisation in China, Vol. 5, Part 6, 1994; mem. editl. bd. China Rev. Internat., 1993—. Fellow NEH, 1982-83, Am. Coun. Learned Socs., 1988-89, Com. on Scholarly Comm., China NSF, 1992, Chiang Ching-Kuo Found., 1994-95, Soc. Sci. Human Rsch. Coun., 1996—. Mem. Assn. for Asian Studies (pres. New Eng. regional conf. 1990-91, bd. dirs., chair China and Inner Asia Coun. 1991-93). Achievements include discovery of earliest representation of a gun in the world in Buddhist cave temple. Avocations: gardening, cooking. Office: McGill U Ctr East Asian Studies, 3434 McTavish, Montreal, PQ Canada H3A 1X9

YATES, SHIRLEY JEAN, educator; b. St. Louis, Oct. 3, 1949; d. Norman William and Wilma (Bratton) M.; m. Joseph Hans Sturm, June 24, 1972 (div. June 1980); m. Robert A. Yates, June 2, 1984 (dec. 1993). BA, Harris Tchrs. Coll., 1970; M in Bus. Mgmt., Webster U., 1981. Cert. adminstrv. specialist; cert. gifted tchr. Educator St. Louis Pub. Schs., 1970—; tchr. gifted lang. arts McKinley Classical Jr. Acad., St. Louis, Mo. vol. abused neglected infants Salvation Army, St. Louis, 1986-92; mem. Dem. Nat. Com., Washington, 1993—, St. Clair NOW, Belleville, Ill., 1991—. Scholarship Parson's Blewett, 1981, 86, 94; recipient Pub. Svc. award Dept. of Justice, 1991, 92. Mem. NOW. Democrat. Roman Catholic. Avocations: bowling, golf, gardening, reading. Office: McKinley Classical Jr Acad 2156 Russell Blvd Saint Louis MO 63104-2607

YATES, SIDNEY RICHARD, congressman, lawyer; b. Chicago, Ill., Aug. 27, 1909; s. Louis and Ida (Siegel) Y.; m. Adeline Holleb, June 24, 1935; 1 child, Stephen R. Ph.B., U. Chgo., 1931, J.D., 1933. Bar: Ill. bar 1933. Practiced as sr. mem. Yates & Holleb; asst. atty. Ill. State Bank Receiver, 1935-37; asst. atty. gen. attached as traction atty. Ill. Commerce Commn., 1937-40; mem. 80th-87th, 89th-104th Congresses from 9th Dist. Ill., 1949-62, 1965—; ranking minority mem. Appropriations subcoms. on the Interior; U.S. del. UN Trusteeship Council with rank of ambassador. Served to lt. USN, 1944-46. Recipient Joseph Henry medal Smithsonian Instn., 1995. Mem. Am., Ill. State, Chgo. bar assns., Am. Vets. Com., Chgo. Council Fgn. Relations, Decalogue Soc. Lawyers. Democrat. Jewish. Clubs: City, Bryn Mawr Country. Office: US House of Reps 2109 Rayburn House Bldg Washington DC 20515-1309*

YATSEVITCH, GRATIAN MICHAEL, retired army officer, diplomat, engineer; b. Kiev, Russia, Nov. 16, 1911; s. Michael Gratian and Margaret (Thomas) Y.; A.B., Harvard U., 1933, M.A., 1934, postgrad. (J.B. Woodworth fellow), 1935-40; m. Barbara Stewart Franks, July 2, 1973; children by previous marriage—Gael Yatsevitch McKibben, Peter, Kara, Gratian. Mining engr. Zlot Mines Ltd., also Beshina Gold Mines Ltd. of London in Yugoslavia, 1935-40, mgr. gold mine, 1936-40; commd. 2d lt. field arty.-U.S. Army, 1933, advanced through grades to col., 1951; chief cannon and aircraft armament br. devel. prodn. cannon, Office of Chief of Ordnance, 1940-45; mil. attache, Moscow, 1945-46; U.S. del. Allied Control Commn., Sofia, Bulgaria, 1946-47; mil. attache, Sofia, 1947-49; attache and spl. asst. to U.S. Amb., Turkey, 1952-53, Iran, 1957-63; sr. staff officer, Washington, 1950-52, 53-57; ret., 1969; hon. chmn. Star Trading and Marine Co., Washington; econ. cons. Middle E. Decorated Legion of Merit with oak leaf cluster. Clubs: Met. (Washington); Carlton, Lansdowne (London); Camden Yacht. Contbr. articles on arty. and mineral. subjects to mags. Home: Easterly Shermans Pt Camden ME 04843 Office: 1050 17th St NW Ste 450 Washington DC 20036-5503

YAU, KEVIN KAM-CHING, astronomer; b. Hong Kong, July 11, 1959; came to U.S., 1992; s. Ching-Fat and Ping-Kiu (Leung) Y.; m. Florence Wai-Chung Liu, Aug. 22, 1987; children: Stephanie, Cherrymay. BS in Physics, U. Liverpool, Eng., 1982; MS in Astrophysics, U. Durham, Eng., 1984, PhD in Astronomy, 1988. Sr. rsch. asst. U. Durham, 1987-92; postdoctoral fellow Jet Propulsion Lab., Pasadena, Calif., 1992-94, mem. tech. staff, 1994—. Coauthor: Halley's Comet in History, 1985; contbr. articles to profl. jours. Rsch. scholar U. Durham, 1984-87; awardee Victor Nadarov Fund, Royal Astron. Soc., 1983. Fellow Royal Astron. Soc.; mem. Internat. Astron. Union, Am. Astron. Soc. Achievements include expert status on the long-term motion of cometary orbits; successfully determining the past orbit of comet Halley and Swift-Tuttle and identified their returns from hist. records back to 200 B.C.; co-discoverer of the 164 BC return of Halley's comet from Babylonian clay tablets; world authority on the application of early astronomical observations to solve contemporary problems in astronomy. Office: Jet Propulsion Lab MS 230-101 4800 Oake Grove Dr Pasadena CA 91109

YAU, SHING-TUNG, mathematics educator; b. Swatow, China, Apr. 4, 1949; came to U.S., 1969; m. Yu-Yun Kuo; children: Isaac, Michael. PhD, U. Calif., Berkeley, 1971; PhD (hon.), Chinese U. Hong Kong, 1980, Harvard U., 1987. Mem. Inst. Advanced Study, Princeton, N.J., 1971-72; asst. prof. math. SUNY, Stony Brook, 1972-73; prof. math. Stanford (Calif.) U., 1974-79, Inst. Advanced Study, Princeton, 1979-84, U.Calif.-San Diego, La Jolla, 1984-87, Harvard U., Cambridge, Mass., 1987—; vis. prof., chair math. dept. U. Tex., Austin, 1986; spl. chair Nat. Tsing Hua U., Hsinchu, Taiwan, 1991—; Wilson T.S. Wang Disting. Vis. Prof. Chinese U. Hong Kong, 1991—. Contbr. numerous articles to profl. publs. Named Honorable prof., Fudan U. China, Academia Sinica China; recipient Sr. Scientist award, Humboldt Found. fellow, 1985; Crafoord prize 1994, recipient Veblen prize, 1981, Fields medal, 1982, Certy prize, 1980. Mem. NAS, AAAS, N.Y. Acad. Scis., Acad. Arts and Scis. Boston, Am. Math. Soc., Am. Phys. Soc., Soc. Indsl. Applied Math. Office: Harvard U Dept Math 3d Fl Sci Ctr 1 Oxford St Cambridge MA 02138-2901

YAU, STEPHEN SIK-SANG, computer science and engineering educator, computer scientist, researcher; b. Wusei, Kiangsu, China, Aug. 6, 1935; came to U.S., 1958, naturalized, 1968; s. Pen-Chi and Wen-Chum (Shum) Y.; m. Vickie Liu, June 14, 1964; children: Andrew, Philip. BS in Elec. Engring, Nat. Taiwan U., China, 1958; MS in Elec. Engring, U. Ill., Urbana, 1959, PhD, 1961. Asst. prof. elec. engring. Northwestern U., Evanston, Ill., 1961-64, assoc. prof., 1964-68, prof., 1968-88, prof. computer scis., 1970-88, Walter P. Murphy prof. Elec. Engring. and Computer Sci., 1986-88, also chmn. dept. computer scis., 1972-77; chmn. dept. elec. engring. and computer sci. Northwestern U., 1977-88; prof. computer and info. sci., chmn. dept. U. Fla., Gainesville, 1988-94; prof. computer sci. and engr., chmn. Ariz. State U., 1994—; conf. chmn. IEEE Computer Conf., Chgo., 1967; symposium chmn. Symposium on feature extraction and selection in pattern recognition Argonne Nat. Lab., 1970; gen. chmn. Nat. Computer Conf., Chgo., 1974, First Internat. Computer Software and Applications Conf., Chgo., 1977; Trustee Na. Electronics Conf., Inc., 1965-68; chmn. organizing com. 11th World Computer Congress, Internat. Fedn. Info. Processing, San Francisco, 1989; gen. co-chmn. Internat. Symposium on Autonomous Decentralized Systems, Japan, 1993, gen. chmn., Phoenix, 1995. Editor-in-chief Computer mag., 1981-84; assoc. editor Jour. Info. Scis., 1983—; editor IEEE Trans. on Software Engring., 1988-91; contbr. numerous articles on software engring., distributed and parallel processing systems, computer sci., elec. engring. and related fields to profl. publs.; patentee in field. Recipient Louis E. Levy medal Franklin Inst., 1963, Golden Plate award Am. Acad. of Achievement, 1964, The Silver Core award Internat. Fedn. Info. Processing, 1989, Spl. award, 1989. Fellow IEEE (mem. governing bd. Computer Soc. 1967-76, pres. 1974-75, dir. Inst. 1976-77, chmn. awards com., 1996—; Richard E. Merwin award Computer Soc. 1981, Centennial medal 1984, Extraordinary Achievement 1985, Outstanding Contbn. award Computer Sci. Soc. 1985), AAAS, Franklin Inst.; mem. Assn. for Computing Machinery, Am. Fedn. Info.-Processing Socs. (mem. exec. com. 1974-76, 79-82, dir. 1972-82, chmn. awards com. 1979-82, v.p. 1982-84, pres. 1984-86; chmn. Nat. Computer Conf. Bd. 1982-83), Am. Soc. Engring. Edn., Sigma Xi, Tau Beta Pi, Eta Kappa Nu, Pi Mu Epsilon. Office: AZ State U Computer Sci & Eng GWC 206 Tempe AZ 85287-5406

YAU, TE-LIN, corrosion engineer; b. Ton-Chen, Anhuei, China, Apr. 9, 1945; s. Chiu-Ho and Chih (Yang) Y.; m. Jue-Hua Tsai, Mar. 19, 1979; children: Kai-Huei, Ian-Huei, Jean-Huei. BS in Engring. Sci., Cheng Kung U., Taiwan, 1969; MS in Engring. Sci., Tenn. Technol. U., 1972; PhD in Metall. Engring., Ohio State U., 1979. Mech. engr. Taiwan Shipbuilding Corp., Keelung, Taiwan, 1970-71; corrosion group head Teledyne Wah Chang, Albany, Ore., 1979—; cons. Fontana Corrosion Ctr., Ohio State U., Columbus, 1979. Author: ASTM STP, 1984, 85, 86, 90, 92, 95, ASM Metals Handbook, 1987, ASM Stress Corrosion Cracking, 1992; contbr. over 60 articles to profl. jours. Mem. Nat. Assn. Corrosion Engrs. Internat. (chmn. T-5A-38 task group on reactive metals 1993—), Electrochem. Soc., TAPPI, Sigma Xi. Achievements include a patent on novel liquid metal seal on zirconium or hafnium reduction apparatus; devel. of new applications for reactive metals, improving the performance of reactive metals by employing metall., electrochem. and mech. techs. Home: 1445 Belmont Ave SW Albany OR 97321-3765 Office: Teledyne Wah Chang Albany 1600 Old Salem Rd NE Albany OR 97321-4548

YAVITZ, BORIS, business educator and dean emeritus; b. Tbilisi, USSR, June 4, 1923; came to U.S., 1946, naturalized, 1950; s. Simon and Miriam (Mindlin) Y.; m. Irene Bernhard, July 17, 1949; children—Jessica Ann, Judith, Emily. M.A., Cambridge (Eng.) U., 1943; M.S., Columbia U., 1948, Ph.D., 1964. Economic cons. Jewish Agy. for Palestine, N.Y.C., 1948-49; mgmt. cons. Werner Mgmt. Cons., Larchmont, N.Y., 1949-54; owner, mgr. Simbar Devel. Corp., N.Y.C., 1954-61; faculty Columbia U., N.Y.C., 1964-94; prof. mgmt. Columbia U., 1964-94; dean Columbia U. (Grad. Sch. Bus.), 1975-82, Paul Garrett prof. pub. policy and bus. responsibility, 1982-94; dep. chmn., dir. Fed. Res. Bank N.Y., 1976-82; dean emeritus, Paul Garrett prof. emeritus Columbia U., 1994—; prin. Lear, Yavitz & Assocs. L.L.C., 1995—; bd. dirs. J.C. Penney Co. Inc., Barnes Group Inc., Israel Discount Bank of N.Y., Crane Co., Medusa Corp.; trustee Am. Assembly, N.Y.C., 1975-82; vice chmn. The Inst. for the Future, 1984—; bd. govs. Media and Soc. Seminars, 1983-84; mem. nat. adv. coun. W. Averill Harriman Inst. Advanced Study of Soviet Union, 1983—; chmn. Nat. Assn. Corp. Dirs. Blue Ribbon Commn. on Corp. Governance. Author books; contbr. articles in field to profl. jours. Served to lt. British Royal Navy, 1943-46. Mem. ASME, Inst. Mgmt. Sci. Home and Office: Old Canoe Place Rd Hampton Bays NY 11946

YAWORSKI, JOANN, reading skills educator; b. Phillipsburg, N.J., Oct. 11, 1956; d. Michael and Cecilia (Ruchala) Y. BA, Pa. State U., 1977; MEd, Millersville U., 1982; postgrad., U. Houston, 1984, Lehigh U., 1988-90; PhD, SUNY, Albany, 1996. Cert. tchr. Russian lang., Russian area studies, reading specialist, elem edn., Tex., N.J., Pa., N.Y. Reading tutor Ephrata (Pa.) Sr. H.S., 1980-81; tchr. Am. History/World Cultures Linden Hall Sch., Lititz, Pa., 1981-82; tchr., Russian lang. Spring Branch Sch. Dist., Houston, Tex., 1982-85; dir. devel. reading Green Mountain Coll., Poultney, Vt., 1989-95; tchg. asst. dept. reading U. Albany (N.Y.), SUNY, 1995-96; SUNY, Albany, 1995-96; presenter 28th and 29th ann. confs. Coll. Reading and Learning Assn. Mem. U.S. Figure Skating Assn. Democrat. Roman Catholic. Avocations: instructing skiing and ice skating, precision team ice skating, ice dancing, ballet. Home: 81 Lake Ave #6 Saratoga Springs NY 12866 Office: SUNY Dept Reading Edn 333 Albany NY 12222

YBARRA, KATHRYN WATROUS, systems engineer; b. Middletown, Conn., Aug. 7, 1943; d. Claude Philip Jr. and C. Lyle (Crook) Watrous; m. Norman L. Adams (div.); children: Cynthia Anne Leonard, Suzette Mae Gross, Daniel Joseph Adams; m. Raul M. Ybarra, Dec. 11, 1976; stepchildren: Esther Ingram, Yolanda Ybarra, Lisa Ybarra. BA in Computer Sci., U. Tex., 1985. Scientific programmer Tracor, Inc., Austin, 1978-86; tech. staff engr. Honeywell, Inc. Comml. Avionics, Phoenix, 1986—. Mem. Friends of Phoenix Libr., v.p. Juniper chpt., 1996. Mem. RTCA (spl. com. # 147, Traffic Alert and Collision Avoidance Sys. II, chair requirements working group 1991—, leadership citation 1995). Roman Catholic. Achievements include 5 patents for algorithms related to aircraft tracking systems for collision avoidance. Home: 3360 W Phelps Rd Phoenix AZ 85023

YE, JOE, electrical engineer, consultant; b. Shanghai, July 12, 1967; came to U.S., 1990; s. Yong-Lie and Hui-Fen (Young) Y. BS, U. Sci. and Tech. China, 1989; MS, Pa. State U., 1994. Product engr., tech. liaison Corning Corp.-China TV Program, Shanghai, 1989-90; rsch. asst. Pa. State U., State College, 1991-93, 94; product engr. GM Corp., Anderson, Ind., 1994—; cons. Zybron, Dayton, Ohio, 1992—. Recipient grant Dept. Def. Advanced Agy., 1993, 1st prize for social work Nat. Edn. Bur., China, 1988. Mem. Am. Ceramic Soc., Internat. Elec., Electronics Engring. Soc. Achievements include development of smart materials for sensor and actuator. Avocations: music, football, traveling, reading. Home: 1863 Lake Lila Dr Apt 12-A5 Ann Arbor MI 48105

YEAGER, ANDREA WHEATON, editor; b. Baytown, Tex., Apr. 17, 1951; d. Virgil Jerry Jr. and Billy Ruth (Leslie) Wheaton; m. Danny Rhea Bowen, Feb. 21, 1976 (div. Sept. 1985); m. Hubert Allen Yeager Jr., Dec. 21, 1985; 1 child, Elyssa Mae. BA in Teaching, Sam Houston State U., Huntsville, Tex., 1973. Assoc. editor The Houstonian, Sam Houston State U., Huntsville, Tex., 1970-73; reporter The Orange (Tex.) Leader, 1973-74, lifestyle editor, 1974-78; editor The Suburbia Reporter, Houston, 1978-79; copy editor The Houston Chronicle, 1979-81, features copy desk chief, 1981-85; copy editor The Sun Herald, Biloxi, Miss., 1986-88, features editor, 1988-91, mng. editor, 1991—. Crisis vol. Gulf Coast Women's Ctr., Biloxi, 1991—; bd. dirs. Am. Heart Assn., Bulfport, 1990-92, Boys & Girls Clubs of Gulf Coast, Biloxi, Crimestoppers, Internat. Tng. in Comm.; mem. Leadership Gulf Coast Class, 1991-92, class rep., 1995—; pres. Altrusa Internat. of Biloxi, 1993—; mem. nutrition adv. bd. Gulfport Sch. Dist./Am. Cancer Soc., 1993—. Mem. La.-Miss. AP Mng. Editors (pres. 1995-96), Harrison County Home Econs. Coun. (v.p. 1991—), Miss. Press Assn., Pub. Rels. Assn. Miss., Gayfers Career Club. Republican. Methodist. Avocations: dance, reading, needle arts, computers, travel. Home: 12297 Windward Dr Gulfport MS 39503-5501 Office: The Sun Herald 205 Debuys Rd Gulfport MS 39507-2838

YEAGER, CAROLINE HALE, radiologist, consultant; b. Little Rock, Sept. 5, 1946; d. George Glenn and Crenor Burnelle (Hale) Y.; m. William Berg Singer, July 8, 1978; children: Adina Atkinson Singer, Sarah Rose Singer. BA, Ind. U., Bloomington, 1968; MD, Ind. U., Indpls., 1971. Diplomate Am. Bd. Radiology; med. lic. State of Calif. Intern Good Samaritan Hosp., Los Angeles, 1971-72; resident in radiology King Drew Med. Ctr. UCLA, Los Angeles, 1972-76; dir. radiology Hubert Humphrey Health Ctr., Los Angeles, 1976-77; asst. prof. radiology UCLA, Los Angeles, 1977-84; asst. prof. radiology King Drew Med. Ctr. UCLA, Los Angeles, 1977-85, dir. ultrasound, 1977-84; ptnr. pvt. practice Beverly Breast Ctr., Beverly Hills, Calif., 1984-87; cons. Clarity Communications, Pasadena, Calif., 1981—; pvt. practice radiology Claude Humphrey Health Ctr., 1991-93; dir. sonograms and mammograms Rancho Los Amigos Med. Ctr., 1993-94; trustee Assn. Teaching Physicians, L.A., 1976-81; cons. King Drew Med. Ctr., 1984, Gibraltar Savs., 1987, Cal Fed. Inc., 1986, Medical Faculty At Home Professions, 1989—, Mobil Diagnostics, 1991-92, Xerox Corp., 1990-91, Frozen Leopard, Inc., 1990-91. Author: (with others) Infectious Disease, 1978, Anatomy and Physiology for Medical Transcriptionists, 1992; contbr. articles to profl. jours. Trustee U. Synagogue, Los Angeles, 1975-79; mem. Friends of Pasadena Playhouse, 1987-90. Grantee for innovative tng. Nat. Fund for Med. Edn., 1980-81. Mem. Am. Inst. Ultrasound in Medicine, L.A. Radiology Soc. (ultrasound sect.), Nat. Soc. Performance and Instrn. (chmn. conf. Database 1991, publs. L.A. chpt. 1990, info. systems L.A. chpt. 1991, dir. adminstrn. L.A. chpt. 1992, Outstanding Achievement in Performance Improvement award L.A. chpt. 1990, bd. dirs. 1990-93, Pres. award for Outstanding Chpt. 1992, v.p. programs 1993), Stanford Profl. Women L.A. Jewish. Avocations: geneology, writing, humor. Home and Office: 3520 Yorkshire Rd Pasadena CA 91107-5440

YEAGER, CHARLES WILLIAM, lawyer, newspaper publisher; b. Frederick, Md., Sept. 18, 1921; s. Ralph A. and Ina Jane (Nuckles) Y.; m. Charlotte L. Matthews, Nov. 26, 1958; children: Gretchen A. Murphy, Kristin A. Bridge, Charles W. Yeager Jr., Matthew R. Yeager. BA, W.Va. U., 1943; LLB, U. Va., 1948. Bar: W.Va. 1948, Fla. 1969, U.S. Supreme Ct. 1968. Ptnr. Steptoe & Johnson, Charleston, W.Va., 1948-93; of counsel Rose and Atkinson, Charleston, 1993—. Pub., editor The Nicholas CHronicle. Maj. U.S. Army, 1942-46. Democrat. Office: Nicholas Chronicle 603 Church St Summersville WV 26651-1411

YEAGER, DAVID P., management consultant; b. 1953. Grad., U. Dayton, 1975; Masters, U. Chgo., 1988. With affiliated cos. Hub Group, Inc., 1975—; vice chmn. bd. Hub Group, Inc., Lombard, Ill., 1985—. Office: Hub Group Inc 377 E Butterfield Rd Lombard IL 60148-5615*

YEAGER, ERNEST BILL, physical chemist, electrochemist, educator; b. Orange, N.J., Sept. 26, 1924; s. Ernest Frederick and Olga (Wittwer) Y. BA, Montclair State Coll., N.J., 1945; LLD (hon.), Montclair State Coll., 1983; MS in Chemistry, Case Western Res. U., 1946; PhD in Phys. Chemistry, Western Res. U., 1948. Instr. Case Western Res. U., 1948-51, asst. prof., 1951-56, assoc. prof., 1956-58, prof. chemistry, 1958-83, Frank Hovorka prof. chemistry, 1983-90, prof. emeritus, 1990—, acting chmn. dept. chemistry, 1964-65, chmn. dept. chemistry, 1969-72, chmn. faculty senate, 1972-73; dir. Case Ctr. for Electrochem. Scis. (now called Ernest B. Yeager Ctr. for Electrochem. Scis.), 1976-91; vis. prof. U. Southampton, Eng., 1968; cons. Union Carbide Corp., 1954-85, Inst. Def. Analyses, 1963-66, 91-92, NASA, 1964-68, Argonne Nat. Lab., 1965-67, Gen. Motors Corp., 1969-76, Eveready Battery Co., 1985-93; mem. com. undersea warfare NRC, 1961-73; adv. bd. Office Critical Tables, 1964-69, mem. phys. scis. div., 1968-73; mem. power panel Advanced Research Project Agy., 1972-75; chmn. Gordon Research Conf. Electrochemistry, 1966; mem. internat. commn. electrochemistry Internat. Union Pure and Applied Chemistry, 1971-76; mem. vis. com. Brookhaven Nat. Lab., 1979-81; mem. adv. com. on USSR-Eastern Europe Nat. Acad. Sci., 1979-85; mem. com. on battery materials tech. Nat. Materials Adv. Bd., 1980-81, mem. com. on fuel cells, 1981-83; mem. rev. com. chem. tech. div. Argonne Nat. Lab., 1984-88; mem. com. on electrochem. aspects of energy conservation and prodn. Nat. Materials Adv. Bd. NRC, 1985-86; mem. advanced fuel cell working group Dept. Energy, 1984; mem. com. on electrochem. aspects of energy conservation and prodn. of the nat. materials adv. bd. NRC, 1985-86; mem. NSF com. for internat. programs., 1988-91; mem. bd. visitors Chemistry Div. Office of Naval Rsch., 1988-90. Editor: Transactions of the Symposium on Electrode Processes, 1959, 66, Techniques of Electrochemistry, Vol. I, 1972, Vol. II, 1973, Vol. III, 1977, Comprehensive Treatise of Electrochemistry, Vol. I, 1980, Vols. II, III, IV, 1981, Vols. V, VI,VII, 1983, Vols. VIII, IX, X, 1984, Electrochemistry in Industry: New Directions, 1982; mem. editorial bd. Jour. Advanced Energy Conversion, 1964-66; sect. editor Electrochem. Acta, 1972-76; contbr. articles to profl. jours. Elder area Presbyn. ch. Coffin fellow 1947-48, NATO sr. fellow, 1968; recipient Ann. Tech. award Cleve. Tech. Socs. Coun., 1954, Ann. award Chem. Professions, 1967-68, Ann. Alumni citation Montclair State Coll., 1968, Commendation cert. USN, 1972; named Case Ctr. for Electrochem. Scis. renamed Ernest B. Yeager Ctr. for Electrochem. Scis. in his honor, 1994. Fellow AAAS; mem. AAUP, Acoustical Soc. Am. (v.p. 1969-70, Biennial award), Electrochem. Soc. (hon., v.p. 1962-65, pres. 1965-66, Acheson medal 1980, Heise award Cleve. sect. 1965, de Nora medal 1992), Am. Chem. Soc. (Morley medal 1981), Soc. Applied Spectroscopy (pres. Cleve. chpt. 1953-54), Internat. Soc. Electrochemists (hon., v.p. 1967-69, pres. 1969-70), Optical Soc. Am., Chem. Soc. London, Sigma Xi (pres. Case Western Res. U. chpt. 1959-60). Home: Judson Park Apt 506 2181 Ambleside Rd Cleveland OH 44106

YEAGER, JANICE SKINNER, library director; b. Corbin, Ky., July 3, 1945; d. Raymond and Eula (Reeves) Skinner; m. Thomas A. Yeager, Nov. 11, 1988. BA, Berea Coll., (1966); MLS, U. Ky., 1969. Cert. libr., Ind. Extension libr. Rock County Libr. Systems, Janesville, Wis., 1969-71; serial bibliographer Ohio State U. Librs., Columbus, 1971-74; adminstr. Arrowhead Libr. System, Janesville, 1974-85; asst. dir. Monroe County Pub. Libr., Bloomington, Ind., 1985-91, assoc. dir. support svcs., 1991—; adj. instr. Ind. U., Bloomington, 1987. Mem. ALA (coun. 1995—), AAUW (named to ednl. found. program 1985, pres. Bloomington br. 1989-91), Ind. Libr. Fedn. (sec. 1990-91, bd. dirs. 1992—), South Cen. Ind. Pers. Assn. (sec. 1987, pres. 1988), Stone Hills Libr. Network (pres. 1990-91), Network Career Women (sec. 1986), Pub. Libr. Assn. (pres. pub. libr. sys. sect. 1982-83). Office: Monroe County Pub Libr 303 E Kirkwood Ave Bloomington IN 47408-3534

YEAGER, LILLIAN ELIZABETH, nurse educator; b. Bainbridge, Ga., Dec. 23, 1943; d. Earnest and Lottie (Brown) Martin; m. Thomas Stephen Yeager, May 26, 1973 (dec. Oct. 1993); 1 child, Michelle. BSN, Tuskegee U., 1964; MSN, Wayne State U., 1972. RN, Ky., Ind., Mich. Staff/charge nurse John Andrew Hosp., Tuskegee Institute, Ala., 1964-65; instr. nursing Tuskegee U., 1965-69; sr. instr. Harper Hosp. Sch. Nursing, Detroit, 1969-73; staff nurse Met. Hosp., Detroit, 1970-72; asst. prof. nursing Ind. U. Southeast, New Albany, 1973-79, assoc. prof. nursing, 1979—, acting asst. dean Sch. of Nursing, 1990-91; cons. nursing process VA Med. Ctr., Louisville, Ky., 1987-88; cons. clin. recognition Floyd Meml. Hosp., New Albany, 1989-90. Prodr., presenter (video) Patient Education, 1993. Mem. fertilization overview com. Alliant Hosps., Louisville, 1982-95; bd. dirs. Frazier Rehab. Ctr., Louisville, 1981—; mem. Louisville Urban League, 1992—; mem. dept. evangelism Dicoese of Ky.-Episcopal, Louisville, 1992—. Recipient VA Appreciation award VA Med. Ctr., Louisville, 1986, FACET Excellence in Teaching award Office of Pres., Ind. U., 1990, Outstanding Contbns. to Nursing award Jefferson C.C., Louisville, 1992, Univ. Svc. award Coun. Nursing Faculty Ind. U. Sch. Nursing, 1993. Mem. ANA, Ind. State Nurses Assn. (1st v.p. 1986-88, 95—, treas. 1988-92), N.Am. Nursing Diagnosis Assn., Kyanna Black Nurses Assn., Sigma Theta Tau, Chi Eta Phi, Delta Sigma Theta. Democrat. Home: 4604 Lincoln Rd Louisville KY 40220-1069 Office: Ind U Sch Nursing Southeast Campus 4201 Grant Line Rd New Albany IN 47150-2158

YEAGER, MARK L., lawyer; b. Chgo., Apr. 7, 1950. BA, U. Mich., 1972; JD, Northwestern U., 1975. Bar: Ill. 1975, Fla. 1985. Ptnr. McDermott, Will & Emery, Chgo., 1975—. Mem. ABA (vice-chmn. Robinson-Patman Act com.).

YEAGER, PHILLIP CHARLES, transportation company executive; b. Bellevue, Ky., Nov. 15, 1927; s. Ferd A. and Helen (Koehler) Y.; m. Joyce E. Ruebusch, June 2, 1951; children: David P., Debra A. Yeager Jensen, Mark A. BA, U. Cin., 1951. Warehouse mgr. Pure Carbonic Co., Cin., 1950-52; trace clk., rate clk., asst. office mgr. Pa. R.R., Chgo., 1952-56; salesman Pa. R.R., Kansas City, Mo., 1956-59; asst. dir. Trailvan Pa. R.R., Phila., 1959-65; div. sales mgr. Pa. R.R., Milw., 1965-68; dir. Trailvan Penn-Ctrl. R.R., N.Y.C., 1968-71; pres. Hub City Terminals, Chgo., 1971-85; chmn. The Hub Group, Chgo., 1985—; bd. dirs. 30 Hubcity terminals. Cpl. U.S. Army, 1946-47. Recipient Achievement award Intermodal Transp. Assn., 1991, Harry E. Salzberg medallion for outstanding achievement in transp.; named Chgo. Transp. Man of Yr., Chgo. Transp. Assn., 1990. Mem. N.Y. Traffic Club, Chgo. Traffic Club. Republican. Lutheran. Avocations: golf, biking, swimming. Office: The Hub Group Inc 377 E Butterfield Rd Ste 700 Lombard IL 60148-5659*

YEAKEL, JOSEPH HUGHES, clergyman; b. Mahanoy City, Pa., Mar. 12, 1928; s. Claude Harrison and Florence Mae (Hughes) Y.; m. Lois Josephine Shank, Mar. 26, 1948; children—Claudia Jo, Joseph Douglas, Joanna Irene, Mary Jo, Jody Lucile. A.B., Lebanon Valley Coll., 1949, D.D. (hon.), 1968; M.Div., United Theol. Sem., 1952; LL.D. (hon.), Otterbein Coll.; S.T.D. (hon.), Keuka Coll. Ordained to ministry United Methodist Ch., 1952; student asst. pastor Euclid Ave. Evang. United Brethren Ch., Dayton, Ohio, 1949-52; asst. pastor Otterbein Evang. United Brethren Ch., Hagerstown, Md., 1952-55; pastor Messiah Evang. United Brethren Ch., York, Pa., 1955-61, Meml. Evang. United Brethren Ch., Silver Spring, Md., 1961-63; asst. sec. Gen. Bd. Evangelism, Evang. United Brethren Ch., 1963-65, exec. sec., 1965-68; gen. sec. Gen. Bd. Evangelism United Meth. Ch., Nashville, 1968-72; bishop N.Y. West area United Meth. Ch., 1972-84, bishop Washington area, 1984—. Served with USNR, Seabees, 1945-46, PTO. Home: 8684 Doves Fly Way Laurel MD 20723-1248 Office: 9226 Colesville Rd Silver Spring MD 20910-1658

YEARGIN-ALLSOPP, MARSHALYN, medical epidemiologist, pediatrician; b. Greenville, S.C., May 17, 1948; d. Grady Andrew and Willie Mae (Blocker) Yeargin; m. Ralph Norman Allsopp, Apr. 5, 1975; children: Timothy Chandler, Whitney Marisha. Student Bennett Coll., 1964-66; BA, Sweet Briar Coll., 1968; MD, Emory U., 1972. Diplomate Am. Bd. Pediatrics. Intern Montefiore Hosp., Bronx, N.Y., 1972-73, resident, 1973-75; instr. pediatrics Albert Einstein Coll. Medicine, Bronx, 1975-77, asst. prof. pediatrics, 1977-78, 80-81; pediatrician Montefiore-Morrisania Comprehensive Health Care Ctr., Bronx, 1975-78, Louise Wise Adoption Agy., N.Y.C., 1975-80, Children's Evaluation and Rehab. Ctr., Rose F. Kennedy Ctr., Bronx, 1980-81; officer USPHS, 1981—, comdr., 1983—; epidemiologic intelligence surveillance officer birth defects br. Ctrs. for Disease Control, Atlanta, 1981-83, preventive medicine resident, 1982-84, med. epidemiologist, 1984—; pediatric cons. Clayton County Early Intervention Program, Jonesboro, Ga., 1983—; med. dir. Easter Seal Presch. Program, Atlanta, 1981-83; physician Com. on Handicapped, N.Y.C., 1979-81, United Cerebral Palsy Program, Bronx, 1980-81. Bd. overseers Sweet Briar Coll., 1981-89; bd. dirs. Neighborhood Arts Ctr., Atlanta, 1984-87; mem. prevention edn. com. Retarded Citizens, Atlanta, 1984—; mem. fundraising campaign Greater Atlanta YWCA, 1985; bd. trustees Pace Acad., 1986—; co-chmn. Minority Atlanta Families in Ind. Schs., Inc., 1986—; chair, Bd. dirs. profl. adv. com. Cerebral Palsey Ctr., Reach, Inc., Atlanta, 1988—; Recipient Disting. Alumna award, Sweet Briar Coll., 1992. mem. State of Ga. Interagy. Coun. for Edn. of the Handicapped Act., 1988—. Fellow Am. Acad. Pediatrics, Am. Acad. Cerebral Palsy and Devel. Medicine; mem. AMA, Atlanta Med. Assn., Jack and Jill of Am., Phi Beta Kappa, Delta Sigma Theta. Office: Ctrs for Disease Control 1600 Clifton Rd NE Atlanta GA 30329-4018

YEARIAN, MASON RUSSELL, physicist; b. Lafayette, Ind., July 5, 1932; married; three children. BS, Purdue U., 1954; MS, Stanford U., 1956, PhD in Physics, 1961. Rsch. assoc. physics U. Pa., 1959-61; from asst. prof. to assoc. prof. Stanford (Calif.) U., 1961-71, prof. physics, 1971—, dir. High Energy Physics Lab., 1973—. Office: Stanford U WW Hanson Exptl Physics Lab Stanford CA 94305-4085*

YEARLEY, DOUGLAS CAIN, mining and manufacturing company executive; b. Oak Park, Ill., Jan. 7, 1936; s. Bernard Cain and Mary Kenny (Howard) Y.; m. Elizabeth Anne Dunbar, Feb. 8, 1958; children: Sandra, Douglas Jr., Peter, Andrew. BMetE, Cornell U., 1958; postgrad., Harvard U., 1968. Engr. welding Gen. Dynamics, Groton, Conn., 1958-60; dir. rsch., project engr. Phelps Dodge Copper Products, Elizabeth, N.J., 1960-68; mgr. ops. Phelps Dodge Internat. Co., N.Y.C., 1968-71; v.p. ops. Phelps Dodge Tube Co., L.A., 1971-73; exec. v.p. Phelps Dodge Cable and Wire Co., Yonkers, N.Y., 1973-75; pres. Phelps Dodge Brass Co., Lyndhurst, N.J., 1975-79; pres. Phelps Dodge Sales Co., N.Y.C., 1979-82, v.p. mktg., 1979-82; sr. v.p. Phelps Dodge Corp., N.Y.C., 1982-87, exec. v.p., 1987-89, chmn., CEO, 1989-91; chmn., pres., CEO Phelps Dodge Corp., Phoenix, 1991—, also bd. dirs.; bd. dirs. USX Corp., Pitts., J.P. Morgan and Co., Inc. and Morgan Guaranty Trust Co., N.Y.C., Lockheed Martin Corp., Calabasas, Calif., So. Peru Copper Co. Mem. Ariz. Econs. Coun., 1989—, Conf. Bd., 1989—; bd. dirs. Am. Grad. Sch. Internat. Mgmt., 1990-92, Phoenix Symphony, 1988-94; chmn. Arts Coalition, 1989-90; trustee Phoenix Art Mus., 1994—. Mem. Nat. Elec. Mfrs. Assn. (bd. dirs. 1983-92), Internat. Copper Assn. (bd. dirs. 1987—, chmn. 1990—), Am. Mining Congress (vice chmn.), Copper Devel. Assn. (chmn. 1989-93, dir. 1993—), Nat. Assn. Mfrs. (bd. dirs. 1988-94), Bus. Roundtable, Bus. Coun., Skyu Club, Echo Lake Country Club, Paradise Valley Country Club, Ariz. Club, Blind Brook Country Club. Republican. Congregationalist. Avocations: tennis, golf, classical music. Home: 8201 N Via De Lago Scottsdale AZ 85258-4215 Office: Phelps Dodge Corp 2600 N Central Ave Phoenix AZ 85004-3050

YEARWOOD, DONALD ROBERT, oil and shipping executive; b. Bklyn., Sept. 16, 1939; s. John Kirton and Helen Agnes (Schoenaker) Y.; m. Marie Louise Piovano, Oct. 20, 1962; children: Adam, Christopher, Jennifer, Katherine. Student, Bklyn. Coll., 1958; BS in Marine Engring., U.S. Mcht. Marine Acad., 1961; postgrad., Cooper Union for Advancement Sci. & Art, 1963; MBA in Mgmt., CUNY, 1968; postgrad., World Trade Inst., 1980, NYU, 1994. Cert. marine engr., U.S. Coast Guard, 1961. Marine engr. Cities Svc. Oil Co., at sea, 1961-62; sr. project engr. M. Rosenblatt & Son, Inc., N.Y.C., 1962-65; mgr. Mgmt. Info. Systems John J. McMullen Assocs., N.Y.C., 1965-70, v.p. mgmt. scis., 1972-75; v.p., gen. mgr. Pacific Marine Corp., Tokyo, 1970-72; pres. Pacific Marine Corp., N.Y.C., 1976-78; cons. Inter-Maritime Group, Geneva, 1978-81; pres. Am. Trading Transp., N.Y.C., 1981-89; sr. v.p. Am. Trading & Prodn., Balt., 1989-92; chmn., CEO, Attransco Inc., N.Y.C., 1992—, also bd. dirs.; adj. prof. St. John's U., 1979-81; chmn. Shoreline Mut., Bermuda. Author: Graduate Records Exam: Business, 1967; patentee liquified natural gas inventions. Chmn. U.S. Mcht. Marine Acad. Found., Kings Point, N.Y., 1988-89; bd. visitors Mass. Maritime Acad., 1986—. Lt. USN, 1961-67. Mem. Soc. Naval Archs. and Marine Engrs., Nat. Cargo Bur., Soc. Marine Port Engrs., Am. Bur. Shipping, U.S. Mcht. Marine Acad. Alumni Assn. (exec. v.p., pres. 1994-95, Outstanding Profl. Achievement award 1986, Meritorious Alumni Svc. award 1986, Disting. Svc. award 1991), N.Y. Yacht Club, Harbor Hills Yacht Club.

YEARWOOD, TRISHA, country music singer, songwriter; b. Monticello, Ga., 1964; m. Chris Latham (div.); m. Robert Reynolds, May 21, 1994. Degree in Music Bus., Belmont Coll. Intern MTM Records, demo singer, commercial jingles singer; recording artist MCA Records. Albums include Trisha Yearwood, 1991 (platnium), Hearts in Armor, 1992 (Grammy nomination: Best Country Female Vocal, 1994 for "Walkaway Joe"), The Song Remembers When, 1993; back-up vocalist Garth Brooks albums; opening act Garth Brooks Tour, 1991; TV appearances on TNN American Music Shop. Named Best New Country Artist by Am. Music Awards, 1992, Top New Female Vocalist by Acad. Country Music, 1992; first female in country music history to have debut single reach #1 on charts with She's in Love with the Love, 1991. Office: MCA Records Internat 70 Universal City Plz Universal City CA 91608

YEATES, ZENO LANIER, retired architect; b. Atlanta, Jan. 9, 1915; s. Zeno Epps and Louise (Ames) Y.; m. Elsie Lankford, June 12, 1947; children—Zeno Ames, Arthur Lankford, Laura. B.S. in Civil Engring, Miss. State U., 1937; B.Arch., U. Pa., 1942, M.Arch., 1976. Asso. J. Frazer Smith & Assos., Memphis, 1947-57; partner Zeno Yeates & Assos., Memphis, 1957-63; pres. Yeates & Gaskill, Inc. (Architects), Memphis, 1963-79, Yeates Gaskill Rhodes (Architects, Inc.), 1980-85; ret., 1983; chmn. Tenn. Br. Arch. and Engring. Examiners, 1963-67; vol. Internat. Exec. Svc. Corp.; designer 11 hosps. in S.Am., Ctrl. Am., Eastern Europe. Fellow AIA (dir. 1975-77); mem. Tenn. Soc. Architects (pres. 1958), Constrn. Specifications Inst. Presbyterian. Clubs: Kiwanis (Memphis), Univ. (Memphis). Home: 2992 Gardens Way Memphis TN 38111-2647

YEATMAN, HARRY CLAY, biologist, educator; b. Ashwood, Tenn., June 22, 1916; s. Trezevant Player and Mary (Wharton) Y.; m. Jean Hansford Anderson, Nov. 24, 1949; children—Henry Clay, Jean Hansford. A.B., U. N.C., Chapel Hill, 1939, M.A., 1942, Ph.D., 1953; student, Cornell U., summer 1937. Asst. prof. biology U. of South, Sewanee, Tenn., 1950-54; asso. prof. U. of South, 1954-60, prof., 1960—, Kenan prof., 1980—, chmn. dept., 1972-76, elderhostel tchr., 1987-88; vis. prof. marine biology Va. Inst. Marine Sci., Gloucester Point, summer 1967; cons. Smithsonian Instn., Sci. Applications, Inc., La Jolla, Calif., Ctrs. for Disease Control, Atlanta, WHO, Ecol. Analysts, Inc., Balt., Duke Power Co., Charlotte, N.C. Contbr. articles to profl. jours. Served with AUS, 1942-46. Gen. Edn. Bd. fellow, 1941-42; Brown Found. fellow, 1984. Fellow AAAS; mem. Soc. Systematic Biology (charter), Soc. Limnology and Oceanography (charter), Soc. Ichthyology and Herpetology, Tenn. Acad. Sci., Am. Micros. Soc., Am. Ornithologists Union, Tenn. Ornithol. Soc., Tenn. Archeol. Soc., Nat. Speleological Soc., Blue Key, Phi Beta Kappa, Sigma Xi, Omicron Delta Kappa, Sigma Nu. Republican. Episcopalian. Home: Jumpoff Rd PO Box 356 Sewanee TN 37375 Office: Woods Lab Sewanee TN 37383-1000

YEATMAN, HOYT, special effects expert, executive. BA, UCLA, 1977. Mem. spl. effects crews for various movies; mem. animation and spl. effects teams NBC-TV, N.Y.C.; mem. prodn. team Paramount Pictures; co-founder, v.p., supr. visual effects Dream Quest Images, Simi Valley, Calif.; guest speaker, U.S. and overseas. Visual effects works include: (TV) Laugh-In Spls., Buck Rogers, Battlestar Gallactica, (movies) Close Encounters of the Third Kind, The Abyss (Oscar 1989), Star Trek: The Motion Picture, (projects) Michael Jackson's Moonwalker, John Badham's Blue Thunder, Short Circuit, Steven Spielberg's Amazing Stories; also dir. TV commls. for Proctor & Gamble, Taco Bell. Office: Dream Quest Images 2635 Park Center Dr Simi Valley CA 93065-6212

YEATS, ROBERT SHEPPARD, geologist, educator; b. Miami, Fla., Mar. 30, 1931; s. Robert Sheppard and Carolyn Elizabeth (Rountree) Y.; m. Lillian Eugenia Bowie, Dec. 30, 1952 (dec. Apr. 1991); children: Robert Bowie, David Claude, Stephen Paul, Kenneth James, Sara Elizabeth; m. Angela M. Hayes, Jan. 7, 1993. B.A., U. Fla., 1952; M.S., U. Wash., 1956, PhD, 1958. Registered geologist, Oreg., Calif. Geologist, petroleum exploration and prodn. Shell Oil Co., Ventura and Los Angeles, Calif., 1958-67; Shell Devel. Co., Houston, 1967; assoc. prof. geology Ohio U., Athens, 1967-70; prof. Ohio U., 1970-77; prof. geology Oreg. State U., Corvallis, 1977—; prof. oceanography Oreg. State U., 1991—, chmn. dept., 1977-85; geologist U.S. Geol. Survey, 1968, 69, 75; Glomar Challenger scientist, 1971, co-chief scientist, 1973-74, 78; mem. Oreg. Bd. Geologist Examiners, 1981-83; chmn. Working Group 1 Internat. Lithosphere Program, 1987-90; mem. geophysics study com. NRC, 1987-94; chmn. task force group on paleoseismology Internat. Lithosphere Program, 1990—; chmn. subcom. on Himalayan active faults Internat. Geol. Correlation Program, Project 206, 1984-92; researcher on Cenozoic tectonics of So. Calif., Oreg., New Zealand and Pakistan; active faults of Calif. Transverse Ranges, deep-sea drilling in Ea. Pacific; vis. scientist N.Z. Geol. Survey, 1983-84, Geol. Survey of Japan, 1992, Inst. de Phys. du Globe de Paris, 1993. Mem. Ojai (Calif.) City Planning Commn., 1961-62, Ojai City Council, 1962-65. 1st lt. U.S. Army, 1952-54. Named Richard H. Jahns Disting. Lectr. in Engring. Geology, 1995; Ohio U. rsch. fellow, 1973-74; grantee NSF, U.S. Geol. Survey. Fellow AAAS, Geol. Soc. Am. (chmn. structural geology and tectonics divsn. 1984-85, Cordilleran sect. 1988-89, assoc. editor bull. 1987-89); mem. Am. Assn. Petroleum Geologists (Outstanding Educator award Pacific sect. 1991), Am. Geophys. Union, Seismol. Soc. Am., European Union of Geoscis., Oreg. Acad. Sci. Home: 1654 NW Crest Pl Corvallis OR 97330-1812 Office: Oreg State U Dept Geoscis Corvallis OR 97331

YEAW, MARION ESTHER, retired nurse; b. Chgo., June 13, 1926; d. Clarence Yates and Olga Sophia (Gorling) Y. BSN, U. Mich., 1949; MEd, Mills Coll., Oakland, Calif., 1965. Cert. tchr. in nursing, Calif. Staff nurse U. Mich. Hosp., Ann Arbor, 1949-51; instr. pediatric nursing Kaiser Found. Sch. Nursing, Oakland, 1951-76, 1976-78; instr. pediatric nursing Contra Costa Community Coll., San Pablo, Calif., 1976-78, Merritt C.C., Oakland, Calif.; dir. staff devel. Waters Edge Inc., Alameda, Calif., 1978-89; retired, 1989. Mem. AAUW, Bus. and Profl. Women's Club (Woman of Achievement award 1988), Alumnae Assn. U. Mich. Sch. Nursing, Mills Coll. Alumni Assn. Lutheran. Home: 1601 Broadway # 6 Alameda CA 94501-3050

YEAZELL, RUTH BERNARD, English language educator; b. N.Y.C., Apr. 4, 1947; d. Walter and Annabelle (Reich) Bernard; m. Stephen C. Yeazell, Aug. 14, 1969 (div. 1980). BA with high honors, Swarthmore Coll., 1967; MPhil (Woodrow Wilson fellow), Yale U., 1970, PhD, 1971. Asst. prof. English Boston U., 1971-74, UCLA, 1975-77, assoc. prof., 1977-80, prof., 1980-91, Yale U, 1991—, dir. grad. studies, 1993—, Chace family prof., 1995—. Author: Language and Knowledge in the Late Novels of Henry James, 1976, Death and Letters of Alice James, 1981, Fictions of Modesty: Women and Courtship in the English Novel, 1991; assoc. editor Nineteenth-Century Fiction, 1977-80; editor: Sex, Politics, and Science in the 19th Century Novel, 1986, Henry James: A Collection of Critical Essays, 1994. Woodrow Wilson fellow, 1967-68, Guggenheim fellow, 1979-80, NEH fellow, 1988-89, Pres.'s Rsch. fellow U. Calif., 1988-89. Mem. MLA (exec. coun. 1985-88), English Inst. (supervising com. 1983-86). Office: Yale U Dept English New Haven CT 06524

YEE, ALBERT HOY, retired psychologist, educator; b. Santa Barbara, Calif., June 14, 1929; children: Lisa Diane, Hoyt Brian, Cynthia Rae. B.A., U. Calif., Berkeley, 1952; M.A., San Francisco State U., 1959; Ed.D., Stanford U., 1965. Post-doctoral research fellow U. Oreg., Eugene, 1966-67; assoc. prof. edn. U. Wis., Madison, 1967-70, prof., 1970-73; prof. ednl. psychology, dean grad. studies and research Calif. State U., Long Beach, 1973-79, originating founder Grad. Ctr., 1974; prof. edn. U. Mont., 1979-83, dean Sch. Edn., 1979-82; sr. lectr. psychology Chinese U. of Hong Kong, 1985-89; dean, prof. psychology Am. Coll., Singapore; sr. lectr. psychology Nat. U., Singapore, 1989-90; dir. program U. Md., Hongkong, 1990; disting. vis. prof. ednl. psychology spl. adviser coll. grad. studies and internat. programs Marist Coll., 1990-92; prof. ednl. psychology Fla. Internat. U., Miami, 1992-94; chmn. 1st Fed. Adv. Com. for Asian and Pacific Island Ams., Bur. Census, 1976-81. Author: Man, Society and the World, 1968; co-author: Comprehensive Spelling Instruction: Theory, Research and Application, 1971; editor: Social Interaction in Educational Settings, 1971, Perspectives on Management Systems Approaches to Education: A Symposium, 1973, Search for Meaning, 1984, A Study on Possible Future Developments for Hong Kong: Strategic Planning and Innovations, 1985, A People Misruled: Hong Kong and the Chinese Stepping-Stone Syndrome, 1989, 2d edit., 1992; editor: East Asian Higher Education: Traditions and Transformatinos, 1994. With AUS, 1952-55, Korea, Japan. Recipient Civic Commendation Madison, 1973; sr. Fulbright lectr. Tokyo and Tamagawa Univs., Japan; also 1st Fulbright scholar to People's Republic China, 1972. Fellow AAAS, Nat. Conf. Research in English, Am. Psychol. Assn. , Am. Psychol. Soc.; mem. Calif. Coll. and Univ. Faculty Assn. (founder 1961), Am. Ednl. Research Assn., Chinese Hist. Soc. Am. and Orgn. of Chinese Americans (Bicentennial speaker), Asian-Am. Psychol. Assn. (pres. 1979-82, jour. editor 1981-82), Brit. Psychol. Soc., Hong Kong Psychol. Soc.

YEE, ALFRED ALPHONSE, structural engineer, consultant; b. Honolulu, Aug. 5, 1925; s. Yun Sau and Kam Ngo (Lum) Y.; m. Janice Ching (div.); children: Lailan, Mark, Eric, Malcolm, Ian; m. Elizabeth Wong, June 24, 1975; children: Suling, Trevor, I'Ling. BSCE, Rose Hulman Inst. Tech., 1948, Dr. of Engring. (hon.), 1976; MEng in Structures, Yale U., 1949. Registered profl. engr., Hawaii, Calif., Guam, Fla., Tex., Minn., Ohio., Northern Mariana Islands. With civil engring. dept. Dept. Pub. Works, Terr. of Hawaii, Honolulu, 1949-51; structural engr. 14th Naval Dist., Pearl Harbor, Hawaii, 1951-54; pvt. practice structural engring. cons. Honolulu, 1954-55; structural engring. cons. Park & Yee Ltd., Honolulu, 1955-60; pres. Alfred A. Yee & Assocs. Inc., Honolulu, 1960-82; v.p., tech. adminstr. Alfred. A. Yee div. Leo A. Daly, Honolulu, 1982-89; pres. Applied Tech. Corp., Honolulu, 1984—. Patentee in concrete tech., land and sea structures; contbr. articles to profl. jours. Served with U.S. Army, 1946-47. Named Engr. of Yr., Hawaii Soc. Profl. Engrs., 1969, one of Men Who Made Marks in 1970, Honolulu, 1970. Fellow Yale Engring. Assn.; mem. Nat. Acad. Engring., Prestressed Concrete Inst. (Martin P. Korn award 1965), NSPE, Soc. Naval Architects and Marine Engrs., Fla. Engring. Soc., Internat. Assn. Bridge and Structural Engring., Post-Tensioning Inst., ASCE (hon.), Am. Concrete Inst. (hon.). Avocations: golfing, swimming. Office: 1441 Kapiolani Blvd Ste 810 Honolulu HI 96814-4404

YEE, BEN, import-export business executive; b. Seattle, June 16, 1946; s. Sam and Gertrude (Jue) Y. BA in Mktg. and Bus., Seattle Coll., 1980; BA in Hotel and Restaurant Mgmt., Wash. State U., Pullman, 1982. Importer/exporter, distbr. Internat. Distbr. and Svcs., San Francisco, 1980-86; import/export cons., direct factory contact in China By Enterprises, Inc., Seattle, 1986—, pres., 1986-92, CEO, 1992—; bd. dirs. World Trade Inst., Seattle. Patentee Create-A-Lite; speaker in field. Bd. dirs. Chinese Am. U., Seattle, 1993—. Mem. World Trade Ctr., China Trade Rels. Orgn. Home: 23110 30th Ave S Des Moines WA 98198-7287 Office: By Enterprise Inc PO Box 68305 Seattle WA 98168

YEE, DAVID, chemist, pharmaceutical company executive; b. Albany, N.Y., Sept. 26, 1948; s. Fook On and King Sau (Seto) Y.; m. Vivien Chee-Nan Yeo, May 11, 1974; children: Daniel Ming-dao, Peter Ming-de. BS (cum laude), Rensselaer Polytech. Inst., 1970; MS, Cornell U., 1973, PhD, 1978. Fellow Max Planck Inst. for Exptl. Medicine, Göttingen, Germany, 1978-80; rsch. assoc. Harvard U., 1980-85; rsch. dir. Advance Biofactures Corp., Lynbrook, N.Y., 1985—. Contbr. articles to profl. jours. including Analytical Chemistry, Jour. of Molecular Evolution, Biochemistry, Hoppe-Seyler's Zeitschrift für Physiologische Chemie, FEBS Letters, European Jour. Biochemistry; patentee in field. Mem. AAAS, Am. Chem. Soc., Am. Sci. Affiliation, N.Y. Acad. Scis. Avocations: chess, music, philately, reading. Office: 35 Wilbur St Lynbrook NY 11563

YEE, EDMOND, church administrator. Exec. dir. Committee for Multicultural Ministries of the Evangelical Lutheran Church, Chgo. Office: Evangelical Lutheran Church Am 8765 W Higgins Rd Chicago IL 60631-4101

YEE, ROBERT DONALD, ophthalmologist; b. Peking, China, Feb. 21, 1945; came to U.S., 1947, naturalized, 1947; s. James and Marian Y.M. (Li) Y.; m. Linda Margaret Neil, June 28, 1968; children—Jillian Neil, Allison Betram. A.B., Harvard U., 1966, M.D., 1970. Diplomate Am. Bd. Ophthalmology. Intern, U. Rochester, N.Y., 1970-71; resident in ophthalmology Jules Stein Eye Inst., UCLA, 1971-74; fellow in neuro-ophthalmology Nat. Eye Inst., Bethesda, Md., 1974-76; chief ophthalmology Harbor-UCLA Med. Ctr., Torrance, Calif., 1976-80; asst. prof. ophthalmology Sch. Medicine, UCLA, 1976-78, assoc. prof., 1978-82, prof., 1982-87; prof., chmn. dept. ophthalmology Ind. U. Sch. Medicine, Indpls., 1987—. Mem. editorial bd. Investigative Ophthalmology and Visual Sci., 1982—, von Graefe's Archives of Ophthalmology, 1983-89. Author numerous med. research papers. Served as lt. comdr. USPHS, 1974-76. Fulbright scholar, 1966; NIH grantee, 1976—; Dolly Green Research scholar, 1984-86; Feldman endowed chair ophthalmology UCLA, 1984-87. Fellow Am. Acad. Ophthalmology, Am. Coll. Surgeons; mem. Assn. Research in Ophthalmology and Vision (chmn. eye movement sect. 1981, 87—), Ind. Acad. Opthalmology, Calif. Med. Assn., Los Angeles County Med. Assn., Ind. Med. Soc., Indpls. Ophthal. Soc., Phi Beta Kappa, Alpha Omega Alpha. Office: Ind U Med Ctr 702 Rotary Cir Indianapolis IN 46202-5133

YEE, STEPHEN, airport executive. Adminstrv. asst. health dept. City of L.A., 1958-63, sr. adminstrv. asst. dept. airports, 1963-72, fed. aid coord., 1972-75, project mgr., 2d level roadway and terminal improvements, airport facilities planner, 1975-83, staff asst. to bd. airport commrs., 1983-85, airport mgr. L.A. Internat. Airport, 1985—. Office: Los Angeles Intl Airport Los Angeles Dept of Airports 1 World Way Los Angeles CA 90045-5803*

YEGGE, ROBERT BERNARD, lawyer, college dean emeritus, educator; b. Denver, June 17, 1934; s. Ronald Van Kirk and Fairy (Hill) Y. A.B. magna cum laude, Princeton U., 1956; M.A. in Sociology, U. Denver, 1958, J.D., 1959. Bar: Colo. 1959, D.C. 1978. Ptnr. Yegge, Hall and Evans, Denver, 1959-78; with Harding & Ogborn successor to Nelson and Harding, 1979—; prof. U. Denver Coll. Law, 1965—, dean, 1965-77, dean emeritus, 1977—; asst. to pres. Denver Post, 1971-75; v.p., exec. dir. Nat. Ctr. Preventive Law, 1986-91. Author: Colorado Negotiable Instruments Law, 1960, Some Goals; Some Tasks, 1965, The American Lawyer: 1976, 1966, New Careers in Law, 1969, The Law Graduate, 1972, Tomorrow's Lawyer: A Shortage and Challenge, 1974, Declaration of Independence for Legal Education, 1976. Mng. trustee Denver Ctr. for Performing Arts, 1972-75; chmn. Colo. Coun. Arts and Humanities, 1968-80, chmn. emeritus, 1980—; mem. scholar selection com. Henry Luce Found., 1975—; Active nat. and local A.R.C., chmn. Denver region, 1985-88; trustee Denver Symphony Soc., Inst. of Ct. Mgmt., Denver Dumb Friends League, 1992—, Met. Denver Legal Aid Soc., 1994—, Colo. Acad.; trustee, vice chmn. Nat. Assembly State Arts Agys.; vice chmn. Mexican-Am. Legal Edn. and Def. Fund, 1970-76. Recipient Disting. Svc. award Denver Jr. C. of C., 1965; Harrison Tweed award Am. Assn. Continuing Edn. Adminstrs., 1985, Alumni Faculty award U. Denver, 1993. Mem. Law and Soc. Assn. (life, pres. 1965-70), ABA (chmn. lawyers conf. 1987-88, chmn. accreditation commn. for legal assistant programs 1980-90, standing com. legal assts. 1987-92, standing com. delivery legal svcs. 1992-95, com. on Gavel award 1995—, del. to jud. adminstrn. coun. 1989-95), Colo. Bar Assn. (bd. govs. 1965-77), Denver Bar Assn., D.C. Bar Assn., Am. Law Inst., Am. Judicature Soc. (bd. dirs. 1968-72, 75-85, Herbert Harley award 1985), Am. Acad. Polit. and Social Sci., Am. Sociol. Assn., Assn. Am. Law Schs., Order St. Ives, Phi Beta Kappa, Beta Theta Pi, Phi Delta Phi, Alpha Kappa Delta, Omicron Delta Kappa. Home: 3472 S Race St Englewood CO 80110-3138 Office: Harding & Ogborn 1200 17th St Ste 1950 Denver CO 80202-5810

YEGGY-DAVIS, GERALDINE MARIE, elementary reading and special education educator; b. Riverside, Iowa, July 25, 1922; d. Henry Clair and Mary Maurine (Bigley) Yeggy; m. Henry Louis Davis, Dec. 28, 1976. BA, Marycrest Teikyo U., Davenport, Iowa, 1947; MA, U. Detroit, 1970; postgrad., UCLA; Ednl. Specialist degree, Western Ill. U., 1976; PhD in Reading Edn., La Salle U., 1995. Cert. permanent tchr., ednl. adminstr., reading specialist, learning disabilities, Iowa. Primary tchr. numerous sch. systems, including, Davenport, Ottumwa, Iowa, Ft. Madison, Des Moines, Mpls., Rock Island, Ill.; reading specialist, primary tchr. Chpt. I, Davenport Community Schs.; tchr. spl. edn. Child Devel. Inc., Milan, Ill.; pres. Child Devel. Inc., Milan, Ill.; administrator C.O.P.E. Tutoring Sch., Milan, Ill.; workshop presenter curriculum of perceptual/conceptual experiences program; adminstr. C.O.P.E. tutorial sch. for primary children with learning disabilities, Milan, Ill. Contbr. numerous publs. for children. Bd. dirs. Quad-Cities Spl. Persons Encounter Christ (S.P.E.C.); active Illowa Dog

Trainers. Recipient Ind. U. Sch. Project award for Effective Teaching of Reading, 1983, Golden Apple award Scott County, 1991; fellow Wall St. Jour., 1964. Mem. NEA, ASCD, Nat. Coun. Tchrs. Math., Internat. Reading Assn., Ill. State Edn. Assn., Iowa Reading Assn., Miss. River Band Reading Assn., Nat. Learning Disabilities Assn., Ill. Learning Disabilities Assn., Early Childhood Edn. Assn. Home: 509 33rd Ave W Milan IL 61264-3753 Office: COPE Tutoring Sch Annex Bldg 3 12 W First St Milan IL 61264

YEGULALP, TUNCEL M., mining engineer, educator; b. Konya, Turkey, Nov. 5, 1937; came to U.S., 1963; s. Faik Suleyman and Selma Safiye (Karatay) Y.; m. Sevinc Guneri, July 5, 1963; children—Ali, Serdar. B.S., Tech. U., Istanbul, 1961; D.Engring. Sci., Columbia U., 1968. Mining engr. M.T.A., Ankara, Turkey, 1961-63, chief feasibility studies group, 1971; research engr. Mobil Research, Paulsboro, N.J., 1967-69; chief systems cons. Sisag Ltd., Ankara, 1971-72; asst. prof. Columbia U., N.Y.C., 1972-75, assoc. prof. Henry Krumb Sch. Mines, 1975-85, prof., 1985—; dir. N.Y. Mining and Mineral Resources Inst. Rsch., 1987—; elected permanent mem. U.S. del. World Mining Congress, 1993. Author articles in field. Served to 2d lt. C.E. Turkish Army, 1969-71. Internat. AEC fellow, Vienna, 1963; Krumb fellow, Columbia U., 1964, Campbell fellow, 1965. Mem. AIME, Inst. Mgmt. Scis., Ops. Research Soc. Am., Turkish Studies Assn., Sigma Chi. Moslem. Office: Columbia U 805-1 SWM New York NY 10027

YEH, CHAI, electrical engineer, educator; b. Hangchow, China, Sept. 21, 1911; came to U.S., 1933, naturalized, 1956; s. Yun Ching and Ai Hwa (Ho) Y.; m. Ida Chiang, June 20, 1936; children—Yin, Jen. B.S., Chekiang U., Hangchow, 1931; Ph.D., Harvard U., 1936. Prof. elec. engring. Pei Yang U., Tientsin, China, 1936-37, Tsing Hwa U., Peking, China, 1937-48; chmn. dept. elec. engring. Tsing Hwa U., 1945-47; vis. prof. elec. engring. U. Kans., 1948-56; prof. elec. and computer engring. U. Mich., Ann Arbor, 1956-81, prof. emeritus, 1981—. Author: Handbook of Fiber Optics, Theory and Applications, 1990, Applied Photonics, 1994; contbr. articles to profl. jours. Elected to Internat. Directory Disting. Leadership, 1994. Mem. IEEE, Sigma Xi. Home: Apt F 364 1111 Alvarado Ave Davis CA 95616-0806 Office: U Mich Dept Engring Ann Arbor MI 48109

YEH, GEORGE CHIAYOU, engineering company executive; b. Chiayi City, Taiwan, Oct. 3, 1926; came to U.S., 1953; s. Chinshyang and Teauchai (Auyang) Woo; m. Lillian Rueieng How, Dec. 27, 1957; children: Bryan V., Katherine A., Christine J., Maximillian S. BS, Nat. Taiwan U., Taipei, 1950; DEng., U. Tokyo, 1953; MS, U. Toronto, Ont., Can., 1955, PhD, 1957. Lectr. Japan Tech. Fedn., Tokyo, 1952-53; assoc. prof. chem. engring. Auburn (Ala.) U., 1957-61; assoc. prof. chem. engring. Villanova (Pa.) U., 1961-63, prof. chem. engring., 1963-91, prof. emeritus, 1991—, asst. v.p. academic affairs, dir. rsch. and patent affairs, 1973-79; pres. Thermodyne Corp., Newtown Square, Pa., 1992—, Hammo Inc., Newtown Square, 1992—; dir. rsch. Rising Sun Engring. Co., Ala., 1958-61; cons. Thiele Kaoline Co., Ga., 1959-62, Ingersol-Rand Co., N.Y., 1975-78; prin. investigator NASA, Tex., 1967-73. Contbr. articles to profl. jours.; patentee (75) in field, U.S. and fgn. countries. Mem. bd. overseers Soc. of Friends, Westtown, 1968—; bd. dirs. Westtown Sch., 1984-85. Recipient Cert. of Appreciation NASA, 1968, 69, 70, Meritorious Svc. award United Inventors and Scientists Am., 1976, Letters of Appreciation White House & Nuclear Power Regulatory Commn., 1979. Fellow Am. Inst. Chemists (chmn. 1972-76, Meritorious Svc. award 1972), Tau Beta Pi (Disting. Engr. award 1968). Avocations: oil painting, gardening, Bonsai. Office: Thermodyne Corp PO Box 442 Newtown Square PA 19073-0442

YEH, GREGORY SOH-YU, physicist, educator; b. Shanghai, Peoples Republic of China, Apr. 11, 1933; came to the U.S., 1953; BS, Holy Cross U., 1957; MS, Cornell U., 1960; PhD, Case Inst. Tech., Cleve., 1966. Rsch. physicist Goodyear, Akron, Ohio, 1960-61; sr. rsch. physicist Gen. Tire, Akron, 1961-64; asst. prof. U. Mich., Ann Arbor, 1967-69, assoc. prof., 1969-72, prof., 1972—; vis. scientist Ford Motor Co., Dearborn, Mich., 1970, Dow Corning, Midland, Mich., 1981; vis. prof. U. Calif., Berkeley, 1982, U. Ulm, Germany, 1973, 83. Avocations: photography, skiing. Office: U Mich Physics Dept Dow Bldg 3042 Ann Arbor MI 48109

YEH, HSU-CHONG, radiology educator; b. Taipei, Taiwan, Mar. 30, 1937; came to U.S., 1973; s. Ping-Hui and Ah-Chu (Chuang) Y.; m. Cha-Pying Yeh, Sept. 26, 1964; children: David, Benjamin. MD, Nat. Taiwan U., Taipei, 1962. Diplomate Am. Bd. Radiology. Rotating intern U. Alberta Hosp., Edmonton, Can., 1964-65; resident in diagnostic radiology Montreal (Can.) Gen. Hosp., McGill U., 1969-72, fellow in diagnostic ultrasound, 1972-73; mem. active med. staff Soldier's Meml. Hosp., Campbellton, N.B., Can., 1967-69; assoc. Mt. Sinai Sch. Medicine, N.Y.C., 1973-75, asst. prof. radiology, 1976-78, assoc. prof., 1979-86, prof., 1986—; cons. radiology VA Hosp., Bronx, N.Y., 1977-87. Author: Radiology of the Adrenals, 1982; contbg. author: Frontiers in Liver Disease, 1981, Ultrasound Annual, 1985, Ultrasonography of the Urinary Tract, 1991, Surgical Management of Urologic Disease, 1991; contbr. articles to med. jours. 2d lt. Armored Corps, Taiwan Army, 1962-63. Fellow Soc. Radiologists in Ultrasound, Royal Coll. Physicians and Surgeons Can.; mem. Am. Inst. Ultrasound in Medicine, Radiol. Soc. N.Am. (sci. exhibit award 1988-91), Computerized Radiology Soc., Am. Roentgen Ray Soc. (sci. exhibit award 1988), N.Y. Roentgen Ray Soc. Avocations: fine art painting, sculpture, jogging, movies. Office: Mt Sinai Med Ctr One Gustave L Levy Pl New York NY 10029-6574

YEH, K. H., bank executive; b. Taipei, Taiwan, Republic of China, Feb. 1, 1932; m. Hsiu-Mei Yeh Tsang. BA, Nat. Taiwan U., 1954. Exec. v.p. Hwa Nan Comml. Bank, Ltd., Taiwan, 1955-81; pres. Banking Inst. Republic China, 1981-88; CEO Fin. Info. System Group Ministery Fin., Taiwan, 1984-88; pres. Chang Hwa Comml. Bank Ltd., Taiwan, 1988-94; chmn. Taipeibank, Taipei, 1994—. Author: Theory and Practice of Lending Management, 1980; editor: Practice of Bank's Consumer Loan, 1983. Recipient Disting. Fin. Staffer award Ministry Fin., Taipei, 1974. Mem. Banker's Assn. Taiwan (chmn. 1988-92), Banker's Assn. Taipei (chmn. 1992), Taiwan U. Alumni Assn. (mng. dir. Taipei chpt. 1994), Taiwan U. Alumni Club, Taipei Yuen-Shan Club. Home: 3 Fl No 432 Chi Lin Rd, Taipei 104, Taiwan Office: Taipeibank, 50 Sec 2 Chung Shan N Rd, Taipei 104, Taiwan

YEH, PAUL PAO, electrical and electronics engineer, educator; b. Sung Yang, Chekiang, China, Mar. 25, 1927; came to U.S., 1956, naturalized, 1963; s. Tsung Shan and Shu Huan (Mao) Y.; m. Beverley Pamela Eng, May 15, 1952; children: Judith Elaine, Paul Edmond, Richard Alvin, Ronald Timothy, Cheryl Quan-Hang. Student, Nat. Cen. U., Nanking, China, 1946-49; BSEE, U. Toronto (Ont., Can.), 1951; MSEE, U. Pa., 1960, PhD, 1966. Registered profl. engr., Ont. Design engr. Can. Gen. Electric Co., Toronto, 1951-56; asst. prof. SUNY, Binghamton, 1956-57; sr. engr. H.K. Porter, ITE & Kuhlman, Phila. and Detroit, 1957-61; assoc. prof. N.J. Inst. Tech., Newark, 1961-66; supr. rsch. and devel. N.Am. Rockwell, Anaheim, Calif., 1966-70; sr. R&D engr. Lockheed Advanced Devel. Co., Burbank, Calif., 1970-72, 78-89; mem. tech. staff The Aerospace Corp., El Segundo, Calif., 1972-78; chief scientist Advanced Systems Rsch., Pasadena, Calif., 1989—; cons. Consol. Edison Co., N.Y.C., 1963-64, Pub. Svc. Elec. and Gas Co. N.J., 1965-66, Zhejiang Sci. and Tech. Exch. Ctr. with Fgn. Countries, 1995—; sr. lectr. State U. Calif., Long Beach, 1967-73; vis. prof. Chung Shan Inst. Sci. and Tech., 1989-92, Tsinghua U., 1993—, S.E. U., 1994—, Zhejiang U., 1994—; cons. prof. Northwestern Poly. U., 1993—, Shanghai U., 1994—; hon. prof. Beijing U. Aeros. and Astronautics, 1993—, Zhejiang U. Sci. and Tech., 1994—; rschr. power sys. design and control, 1951-66; investigator R&D Stealth tech. electronic warfare, avionics, nuclear hardening, anti-submarine warfare. Recipient Achievement award for anti-submarine warfare/magnetic anomaly detection sys. Lockheed Corp. Mem. IEEE (sr., life), Nat. Mgmt. Assn., Am. Def. Preparedness Assn., Assn. Old Crows, Chinese Am. Engring./Sci. Assn. So. Calif. (pres. 1969-71), Nat. Ctrl. U. Alumni Assn. (pres. 1977), Nat. Security Indsl. Assn., Beijing Assn. for Sci. and Tech. Exchs. with Fgn. Countries, (hon. dir.), Assn. Profl. Engrs. of Ont., N.Y. Acad. Scis., Air Force Assn., Zhejiang Assn. for Sci. and Tech. Exchs. with Fgn. Countries (advisor), Armed Forces Comms. and Electronics Assn., U.S. Naval Inst. Republican. Presbyterian. Achievements include patent for Non-Capacitive Transmission Cable. Home: 5555 Via De Campo Yorba Linda CA 92687-4916 Office: Advanced Systems Rsch Inc 33 S Catalina Ave Ste 202 Pasadena CA 91106-2426

YEH, RAYMOND WEI-HWA, architect, educator; b. Shanghai, China, Feb. 25, 1942; came to U.S., 1958, naturalized, 1976; s. Herbert Hwan-Ching and Joyce Bo-Ding (Kwan) Y.; m. Hsiao-Yen Chen, Sept. 16, 1967; children—Bryant Po Yung, Clement Chung-Yung, Emily Su-Yung. B.A., U. Oreg., 1965, B.Arch., 1967; M.Arch., U. Minn., 1969. Cert. Nat. Coun. Archtl. Registration Bds.; registered architect, Okla., Calif., Hawaii. Draftsman, designer various archtl. firms, 1965-68; design architect Ellerbe Architects, St. Paul, 1968-70; v.p., dir. design Sorey, Hill, Binnicker, Oklahoma City, 1973-74; prin. architect Raymond W.H. Yeh & Assos., Norman, Okla., 1974-80; asst. prof. to prof. U. Okla., Norman, 1970-79; head dept. architecture, prof. Calif. Poly. State U., San Luis Obispo, 1979-83; dean Coll. Architecture U. Okla., Norman, 1983-92; prin. architect W.H. Raymond Yeh, Norman, 1983-93; dean sch. architecture U. Hawaii at Manoa, Honolulu, 1993—; profl. adviser Neighborhood Conservation and Devel. Center, Oklahoma City, 1977 79. Works include: St. Thomas More U. Parish and Student Center, Norman, Summit Ridge Center Retirement Community, Harrah, Okla., (recipient Nat. Design award Guild Religious Architecture 1978). Bd. dirs. Internat. Alumni Assn., 1978-80. Nat. Endowment for Arts fellow, 1978-79. Fellow AIA (dir., pres. Okla. chpt. 1986, design awards, nat. com. chmn. 1989); mem. Calif. Coun. Archtl. Edn. (dir., pres. 1982-83), Okla. Found. for Architecture (founding chair bd. 1989-90), Asian Soc. Okla. (award of Excellence 1992). Presbyterian. Office: U Hawaii Manoa Sch Architecture Honolulu HI 96813

YEH, TSUNG, orchestral conductor; b. Shanghai, People's Republic China, May 17, 1950; came to U.S., 1981; s. Zu-Jiu and Ren-Qing (Zhang) Ye; m. Sau-Lan Wong, Apr. 8, 1983; 1 child, Mona. B. Music, The Mannes Coll. Music, 1983; postgrad., Yale U., 1983-84. Exxon/Arts Endowment condr. St. Louis Symphony Orch., 1984-87; prin. condr. St. Louis Youth Orch., 1986-87; resident condr. Fla. Orch., Tampa and St. Petersburg, Fla., 1987-89; music dir., condr. South Bend (Ind.) Symphony Orch., 1988—; prin. guest condr. Albany (N.Y.) Symphony Orch., 1991—; guest condr. Rochester (N.Y.) Philharm., 1987, Minn. Orch., Mpls., 1987, Traverse (Mich.) Symphony Orch., 1989, Taiwan (Republic of China) Symphony Orch., 1989, San Francisco Symphony Orch., 1989, Albany (N.Y.) Symphony Orch., 1990, Taipei (Republic of China) Symphony Orch., 1991, Hong Kong Philharm. Orch., 1991. Mem. Fischoff Chamber Music Assn. (bd. dirs. 1989—), Am. Symphony Orch. League, Conductors' Guild. Office: South Bend Symphony Orch PO Box 267 South Bend IN 46624-0267

YEH, WILLIAM WEN-GONG, civil engineering educator; b. Szechwan, China, Dec. 5, 1938; s. Kai-Ming and Der-Chao (Hu) Y.; m. Jennie Pao, Mar. 25, 1967; children: Michael, Bobby. B.S.C.E., Nat. Cheng-Kung U., Taiwan, 1961; M.S.C.E., N.Mex. State U., 1964; Ph.D. in Civil Engring., Stanford U., 1967. Acting asst. prof. Stanford U., 1967; asst. research engr. UCLA, 1967-69, asst. prof. civil engring., 1969-73, assoc. prof., 1973-77, prof., 1977—, chmn. dept., 1985-88; cons. Office of Hydrology, UNESCO, Paris, 1974, Jet Propulsion Lab., Pasadena, Calif., 1975-78, U.S. Bur. Reclamation, Phoenix, 1977-81, Dept. Water and Power, São Paulo, Brazil, 1981-83, Rockwell Internat., 1983-88, U.S. AID, 1987-91, Met. Water Dist. of So. Calif., 1989—. Contbr. numerous articles to scholarly jours. Recipient Disting. Faculty award UCLA Engring. Alumni Assn., 1975; recipient Engring. Found. Fellowship award United Engring. Trustees, 1981, numerous research grants including NSF, 1967—. Fellow Am. Geophys. Union (Robert E. Horton award 1989), ASCE (editor Jour. Water Resources Planning and Mgmt. 1988-93, Julian Hinds award 1994), Am. Water Resources Assn. Home: 822 Hanley Ave Los Angeles CA 90049-1914 Office: U Calif 5732 B BH 405 Hilgard Ave Los Angeles CA 90095

YELLE, RICHARD WILFRED, artist, designer; b. Attleboro, Mass., July 22, 1951; s. Joseph Edward and Margaret Jeanne (Hickland) Y.; divorced; 1 child, Scott Richard. BFA, Mass. Coll. Art, 1974; MFA, RISD, 1976; MA, NYU, 1983. Prin. Richard Yelle Design, N.Y.C., 1976—; co-founder, dir. N.Y. Exptl. Glass Workshop (now Urban Glass), N.Y.C., 1977-80; dir. Clayworks Studio Workshop, N.Y.C., 1978-80; co-founder, pub. Craft International. Mag., N.Y.C., 1980-83; adminstr. Mus. Mile, N.Y.C., 1982-84; asst. v.p. Mass. Coll. Art, Boston, 1984-86; chmn. product design Parsons Sch. Design, N.Y.C., 1986—; panelist Nat. Endowment for Arts, Washington, 1983, site visitor, 1983-84; clk. Mass. Coll. Art Found., Boston, 1985-86. Exhibited in numerous glass art and design shows; in permanent collections Met. Mus. Art, N.Y.C., Mus. Fine Arts, Boston, others; founder, editor Glass mag., 1978-81, mem. editorial bd., 1981—. Recipient Disting. Alumnus award NYU, 1984; RISD teaching fellow, 1974-76. Mem. Glass Art Soc., Am. Craft Coun., Urban Glass (chmn. 1980-85, bd. dirs.), Indsl. Designers Soc. Am. Office: Parsons Sch Design Product Design Dept 66 5th Ave New York NY 10011-8802

YELLEN, JANET LOUISE, government official, economics educator; b. Bklyn., Aug. 13, 1946; d. Julius and Anna Ruth (Blumenthal) Y.; m. George Arthur Akerlof, July 8, 1978; 1 child, Robert Joseph. BA in Econs. summa cum laude, Brown U., 1967; PhD, Yale U., 1971. Asst. prof. econs. Harvard U., Cambridge, Mass., 1971-76; lectr. London Sch. Econs. and Polit. Sci., Washington, 1978-80; asst. prof. econs. Sch. Bus. Adminstrn., U. Calif., Berkeley, 1980-82, assoc. prof., 1982-85, prof. Haas Sch. Bus., 1985—, Bernard T. Rocca Jr. prof. internat. bus. and trade, 1992—; cons. div. internat. fin., Bd. Govs. of FRS, Washington, 1974-75, economist trade and fin. studies sect., 1977-78, mem., 1994—; rsch. fellow MIT, Cambridge, 1974; cons. Congl. Budget Office, 1975-76, mem. panel econ. advisers, 1993—; rsch. affiliate Yale U., New Haven, 1976; mem. adv. panel in econs. NSF, 1977-78, 91-92; mem. Brookings Panel on Econ. Activity, 1987-88, 90-91, sr. adviser, 1989—; Yrjö Jahnsson Found. lectr. on macroecon. theory, Helsinki, 1977-78; mem. Coun. on Fgn. Rels., 1976-81. Author: (monograph) (with Arrow and Shavell) The Limits of the Market in Resource Allocation, 1977; assoc. editor Jour. Econ. Perspectives, 1987-91; contbr. articles to profl. jours. Hon. Woodrow Wilson fellow, 1967, grad. fellow NSF, 1967-71, Guggenheim fellow, 1986-87; grantee NSF, 1975-77, 90-94. Mem. Am. Econ. Assn. (adv. com. to Pres. 1986-87, nominating com. 1988-90), Phi Beta Kappa. Home: 3201 Leland St Chevy Chase MD 20815 Office: Bd Govs of FRS 20th and E St NW Washington DC 20551*

YELLEN, LINDA, film director, writer, producer; b. Forest Hills, N.Y., July 13; d. Seymour and Bernice (Mittelman) Y. BA magna cum laude, Barnard Coll.; MFA in Film, Columbia U., PhD in Lang., Lit. and Communications. Mem. film faculty Columbia U., N.Y.C., Barnard Coll., Yale U., CUNY; prin. Chrysalis-Yellen Prodns., Inc., N.Y.C., 1982—; pres. The Linda Yellen Co., N.Y.C., 1988—; represented by William Morris Agy. Producer, dir.: (films) Prospera; Come Out, Come Out; Looking Up, 1978; exec. producer (film) Everybody Wins, 1989; producer, dir., co-writer (film) Prisoner Without a Name, Cell Without A Number, NBC-TV, 1984 (Peabody award, Writers Guild nominee for best screenplay); exec. producer, producer (CBS network spls.): Hard Hat and Legs, 1980; Mayflower: The Pilgrims Adventure, 1979; Playing For Time, 1981 (Emmy award for best dramatic spl., Peabody award, Christopher award); exec. producer, producer, co-writer (CBS network spl.) The Royal Romance of Charles and Diana, 1982; exec. producer, producer (TV movies): Second Serve: The Renee Richards Story, CBS-TV, 1986 (Luminous award), Liberace, CBS-TV, 1988; exec. producer Hunt for Stolen War Treasures, syndicated TV, 1989, Sweet Bird of Youth, NBC-TV, 1989; dir., writer, prodr. Chantilly Lace, 1993, Parallel Lives, 1994, The End of Summer, 1995, (Showtime); contbr. articles to N.Y. Times, Village Voice, Interview, Hollywood Reporter. Mem. Dirs. Guild Am. (exec. council), Writers Guild Am., Acad. TV Arts and Scis., Women in Film.

YELLIN, THOMAS GILMER, broadcast executive; b. N.Y.C., Jan. 2, 1953; s. David and Carol Lynn (Gilmer) Y.; m. Anne Locksley, July 30, 1982; children: Chloe Locksley Yellin, Isabel Locksley Yellin. BA, Harvard U., 1975. Producer Sta. WQED, Pitts., 1975-76; assoc. producer CBS Reports, CBS News, N.Y.C., 1976-80, sr. producer, 1985-89; producer, then sr. producer Nightline ABC News, N.Y.C., 1980-84, sr. producer ABC World News Tonight, 1984-85; sr. producer West 57th mag. CBS News, N.Y.C., 1985-89; exec. producer Peter Jennings Reporting ABC News, N.Y.C., 1989-92, exec. producer Day One Mag., 1992—. Office: Day1One 147 Columbus Ave 8th FL New York NY 10023

YELLIN, VICTOR FELL, composer, music educator; b. Boston, Dec. 14, 1924; s. Mendl and Sarah (Fell) Y.; m. Isabel Joseph, May 26, 1948; 1 son, David. A.B. cum laude, Harvard U., 1949, A.M., 1952, Ph.D., 1957. Teaching fellow Harvard U., Cambridge, Mass., 1952-56; asst. prof. NYU, N.Y.C., 1956-58, assoc. prof., 1961-64, prof., 1964—; asst. prof. Williams ., Williamstown, Mass., 1958-60; assoc. prof. Ohio State ., Columbus, 1960-61; coordinator N.Y. Metro-Fulbright-Hayes Vis. Scholars, 1978-82; mem. editorial adv. bd. Am. Music. Composer: (opera) Abaylar, 1974 (song cycle) Dark of the Moon, 1986; conductor: Mrs. H.H.A. Beach's Grand Mass in E-flat, N.Y.C., 1982; author: Chadwick, Yankee Composer, 1990, Bye Bye Blues Variations for Violin and Piano, Tully Hall, N.Y.C., 1992; contbr. Early Melodrama in Am., The Aethiop, Orchestral Restoration. Served with U.S. Army, 1943-46, ETO. Recipient grant Nat. Endowment Humanities, 1978. Mem. Am. Musicol. Soc., Sonneck Soc. Home: 52 Washington Mews New York NY 10003-6608 Office: NYU 100 Washington Sq E New York NY 10003-6656

YELTON, ELEANOR O'DELL, retired reading specialist; b. Maryville, Tenn., Jan. 21, 1929; d. Rondie Bliss and Maxie (Williams) O'Dell; m. Doran Yelton, Aug. 26, 1951; children: Doran II, Marshall, David, Holly. BS, East Tenn. State U., 1951. Cert. tchr., Fla. Tchr. Rozelle Sch., Memphis, 1952-55; tchr. English Clay High Sch., Green Cove Springs, Fla., 1963-66, reading specialist, 1986-96; reading specialist The Bolles Sch., Jacksonville, Fla., 1966-84; chair adv. coun. Clay High Sch., Green Cove Springs, 1991-92. Author: (newsletters) PERKS, 1990 (Secondary Reading Coun. Fla. award 1991), Parents' Link, 1993. Mem. Internat. Reading Assn., Fla. Reading Assn., Secondary Reading Coun. Fla., Clay County Acad. Excellence, Clay County Reading Coun. (founder Books for Babies program Humana Hosp. 1990, pres. 1990-91, Literacy award 1995). Avocations: traveling, reading, computers. Home: 3977 Susan Dr Green Cove Springs FL 32043

YEMMA, JOHN, newspaper editor. Fgn. editor Boston Globe. Office: Globe Newspaper Co 135 Morrissey Blvd Boston MA 02107

YEN, JEFFREY HSING-GAN, chemical engineer; b. Taipei, Republic of China, Mar. 29, 1949; came to U.S., 1974; s. Cheng and Chuing-Yao (Tan) Y.; m. Helene Heui Ling Lin, May 24, 1987; children: Richmond, Debbie, Colleen, Calvin. BSChemE, Nat. Taiwan U., 1972; MSChemE, Carnegie-Mellon U., 1976, PhDChemE, 1979. Sr. rsch. engr. Mobil R&D Co., Paulsboro, N.J., 1979-85; sr. engr. Pennwalt Corp., King of Prussia, Pa., 1985-89; prin. engr. Elf Atochem, King of Prussia, 1989—; program chmn. Elf Process Tech. Conf., 1994, 95. Author more than 30 tech. papers and presentations. Mem. AIChE (area chmn. 1992, mem. liaison rsch. and new tech. 1993, dir. fuels and petrochems. divsn. 1995—, meeting program chair fuels and petrochems. divsn. 1996—). Achievements include design of high thermal-flux reactors; invention of sour gas well technology, bi-modal zeolitic cracking processes, cost effective heavy metal treatment. Home: Rd # 1 Box 218C Hendrickson Mill Rd Swedesboro NJ 08085 Office: Elf Atochem 900 1st Ave King Of Prussia PA 19406

YEN, SAMUEL S(HOW)-C(HIH), obstetrics and gynecology educator, reproductive endocrinologist; b. Beijing, Feb. 22, 1927; s. K.Y. and E.K. Yen; children: Carol Amanda, Dolores Amelia, Margaret Rae. BS, Cheeloo U., China, 1949; MD, U. Hong Kong, 1954, DSc, 1980. Diplomate Am. Bd. Ob-Gyn (bd. examiners 1973-78), Am. Bd. Reproductive Endocrinology (bd. examiners 1976-82). Intern Queen Mary Hosp., Hong Kong, 1954-55; resident Johns Hopkins U., Balt., 1956-60; assoc. prof. reproductive biology Case Western Res. U., Cleve., 1970—; prof. ob-gyn U. Calif., San Diego, 1972-83, chmn. dept. reproductive medicine, 1972-83, prof. reproductive medicine, 1983—; dir. reproductive endocrinology U. Calif. Med. Ctr., San Diego, 1983—, W.R. Persons chair, 1987; assoc. dir. obstetrics Univ. Hosp., Cleve., 1968-70; DeGroof lectr., 1987; Van Campenhaut lectr. Can. Fertility and Andrology Soc., 1995. Editor: Reproductive Endocrinology Physiology, Pathophysiology and Clinical Management, 1978, 2d rev. edit., 1986, 3d edit., 1991; mem. editorial bd. Endocrine Revs., 1984—. Recipient Axel Munthe Found. award, 1982, Simpson medal U. Edinburgh, Scotland, 1996; Oglebay fellow, 1968-69. Fellow Royal Coll. Ob-Gyn., Royal Coll. Obstetricians and Gynecologists (ad eundem, London); mem. NAS Inst. Medicine, Assn. Am. Physicians, Soc. for Gynecol. Investigation (pres. 1981, Disting. Scientist award 1992), Endocrine Soc. (Rorer Clin. Investigator award 1992). Office: U Calif-San Diego Reproductive Medicine # 0633 La Jolla CA 92093

YEN, TEH FU, civil and environmental engineering educator; b. Kun-Ming, China, Jan. 9, 1927; came to U.S., 1949; s. Kwang Pu and Ren (Liu) Y.; m. Shiao-Ping Siao, May 30, 1959. BS, Cen. China U., 1947; MS, W.Va. U., 1953; PhD, Va. Poly. Inst. and State U., 1956; hon. doctoral degree, Pepperdine U., 1982, Internat. U. Dubna, Russia, 1996. Sr. research chemist Good Yr. Tire & Rubber Co., Akron, 1955-59; fellow Mellon Inst., Pitts., 1959-65; sr. fellow Carnegie-Mellon U., Pitts., 1965-68; assoc. prof. Calif. State U., Los Angeles, 1968-69; assoc. prof. U. So. Calif., 1969-80, prof. civil engring. and environ. engring., 1980—; hon. prof. Shanghai U. Sci. and Tech., 1986, U. Petroleum, Beijing, 1987, Daqing Petroleum Inst., 1992; cons. Universal Oil Products, 1968-76, Chevron Oil Field Rsch. Co., 1968-75, Finnigan Corp., 1976-77, GE, 1977-80, United Techs., 1978-79, TRW Inc., 1982-83, Exxon, 1981-82, DuPont, 1985-88, Min. Petroleum, Beijing, 1982—, Biogas Rsch. Inst.-UN, Chengdu, 1991. Author numerous tech. books; contbr. articles to profl. jours. Recipient Disting. Svc. award Tau Beta Pi, 1974, Imperial Crown Gold medal, Iran, 1976, Achievement award Chinese Engring. and Sci. Assocs. So. Calif., 1977, award Phi Kappa Phi, 1982, Outstanding Contbn. honor Pi Epsilon Tau, 1984, Svc. award Republic of Honduras, 1989, award in Petroleum Chem. Am. Chem. Soc., 1994, Kapitsa Gold medal Russian Fedn., 1995. Fellow Royal Chem. Soc., Inst. Petroleum, Am. Inst. Chemists; mem. Am. Chem. Soc. (bd. dirs. 1993, councillor, founder and chmn. geochemistry divsn. 1979-81, Chinese Acad. Scis. (standing com.), Acad. Scis. Russian Fedn. (academician, fgn. mem.). Home: 2378 Morslay Rd Altadena CA 91001-2716 Office: U So Calif University Park KAP 224A Los Angeles CA 90089

YEN, WILLIAM MAO-SHUNG, physicist; b. Nanking, Kiangsu, China, Apr. 5, 1935; came to U.S., 1952; s. Wanli and Jane Hsanlin (King) Y.; m. Delane Robinson, Aug. 16, 1968 (div. May 1974); m. Laurel Frances Curtis, Aug. 18, 1978; 1 child, Jane Luhsan Bess. BS, U. Redlands, 1956; PhD, Washington U., 1962. Rsch. assoc. Stanford (Calif.) U., 1962-65; asst. prof. U. Wis., Madison, 1965-68, assoc. prof., 1968-72, prof., 1972-90, ret., 1990; Graham Perdue prof. U. Ga., Athens, 1986—; cons. Lawrence Livermore (Calif.) Nat. Labs., 1975-84, Argonne (Ill.) Nat. Labs., 1976-82, Rosemount Corp., Eden Prairie, Minn., 1988—. Editor: Laser Spectroscopy of Solids I, 1981, II, 1988, Dynamical Processes in Disordered Solids, 1989; contbr. more than 190 articles to scholarly and profl. jours. Washington U. fellow, 1960, J.S. Guggenheim Found. fellow, 1979, Fulbright Sr. fellow, 1995; recipient Sr. U.S. Scientist award A.V. Humboldt Found., 1985, 90; named hon. prof. U. St. Antonio de Abad, Cusco, Peru, 1983, hon. prof. Inst. Physics, Acad. Sinica, 1995. Fellow AAAS, Am. Physical Soc., Optical Soc. Am.; mem. Electro Chem. Soc., Sigma Xi. Achievements include pioneering establishment of laser spectroscopy as a tool to study optical properties of solids. Home: 180 River Oak Way Athens GA 30605-2677 Office: U Ga Dept Physics and Astronomy Athens GA 30602

YENKIN, BERNARD KALMAN, coatings and resins company executive; b. Columbus, Ohio, Dec. 2, 1930; s. Abe I. and Eleanore G. (Weiner) Y.; m. Miriam Schottenstein, Mar. 31, 1957; children: Leslie Mara, Jonathan, Allison Katsev, Amy. BA, Yale U., 1952; MBA, Harvard U., 1954. V.p. Yenkin-Majestic Paint Corp., Columbus, 1968-77, pres., 1977-85, chmn. bd., 1985—. Pres. Columbus Jewish Fedn., 1980-82, Pro Musica Chamber Orch., Columbus, 1983-85, Columbus Torah Acad., 1977-79; bd. v.p. Jewish Ednl. Svc. N.Am., N.Y.C., 1991-95. Recipient Mayor's award for Vol. Svc. City of Columbus, 1984, Young Leadership award Columbus Jewish Fedn., 1965. Mem. Yale Club of Cen. Ohio (pres. 1979-81), Yale Club of N.Y., U. Club (Columbus). Office: Yenkin-Majestic Industries 1920 Leonard Ave Columbus OH 43219-2514

YENSON, EVELYN P., lottery official; b. Johannesburg, Republic of South Africa, Dec. 20, 1944; came to U.S., 1963; d. T. and P.F. Yenson; children: Megan Y. Sun, Elliot H. Sun. BA, Coll. New Rochelle, 1967; MA, U. Wis., Milw., 1968. Planner/evaluator Seattle Pub. Schs., 1971-73; dir. planning divsn., various other positions Dept. Cmty. Devel., Seattle, 1973-83; planning dir. Seattle Ctr., 1983-84; pvt. practice as cons. Seattle, 1984-85; dir., dep.

commr. Expo '86, Vancouver, B.C., Can., 1985-86; dir. Wash. State Lottery, Olympia, 1987—; presenter in field. Mem. Mcpl. League Bd., Seattle, 1991-92; bd. dirs. Seattle Arts Commn., 1989-93, Camp Brotherhood, Seattle, 1994—, treas., 1995; bd. dirs. Leadership Tomorrow; sec. bd. dirs. Sunhill, Inc., Seattle. Mem. N.Am. Assn. State and Provincial Lotteries (pres. 1991-93, past pres.), Intertoto (bd. dirs.). Roman Catholic. Avocations: arts, music, swimming, golfing, walking. Home: 2350 34th Ave S Seattle WA 98144-5554 Office: Wash State Lottery PO Box 43001 Olympia WA 98504-3001

YEO, RON, architect; b. Los Angeles, June 17, 1933; s. Clayton Erik and Rose G. (Westman) Y.; m. Birgitta S. Bergkvist, Sept. 29, 1962; children: Erik Elov, Katarina Kristina. B.Arch., U. So. Calif., 1959. Draftsman Montierth & Strickland (Architects), Long Beach, Calif., 1958-61; designer Gosta Edberg S.A.R. Arkitekt, Stockholm, 1962; partner Strickland & Yeo, Architects, Garden Grove, Calif., 1962-63; pres. Ron Yeo, Architect, Inc., Corona del Mar, Calif., 1963—; cons., lectr. in field. Archtl. works include Garden Grove Civic and Community Center, 1966, Hall Sculpture Studio, 1966, Garden Grove Cultural Center, 1978, Gem Theater, 1979, Festival Amphitheatre, 1983, Los Coyotes Paleontol. Interpretive Ctr., 1986. Mem. Orange County Planning Commn., 1972-73, 1975-76; chmn. Housing and Community Devel. Task Force, 1978, Orange County Fire Protection Planning Task Force, City of Newport Beach City Arts Commn., 1970-72; pres. Orange County Arts Alliance, 1980-81. Fellow AIA; mem. Constrn. Specifications Inst. Democrat. Office: Ron Yeo FAIA Architect Inc 500 Jasmine Ave Corona Del Mar CA 92625-2308

YEO, RONALD FREDERICK, librarian; b. Woodstock, Ont., Can., Nov. 13, 1923; s. Frederick Thomas and Jugertha Aleda (Vansickle) Y.; m. Margaret Elizabeth Horsley, Oct. 12, 1953; children: Joanne, Peter. BA, U. Toronto, 1948, BLS, 1966; LLD (hon.), U. Regina, 1990. Mgr. book dept. Am. News Co., Toronto, 1948-53; sales mgr., dir. Brit. Book Service, Toronto, 1953-63; mgr. trade div. Collier-Macmillan Can., Ltd., Toronto, 1963-65; pub. services coordinator North York (Ont.) Pub. Library, 1966-71; chief librarian Regina (Sask.) Pub. Library, 1971-88; mem. Nat. Library Adv. Bd., 1982-87, chmn., 1986-87. Served with RCAF, 1942-45. Recipient Silver Jubilee medal, 1977. Mem. Can. Libr. Assn. (pres. 1978-79), Can. Assn. Pub. Librs. (chmn. 1975-76), Sask. Libr. Assn., Adminstrs. of Large Pub. Librs. (chmn. 1973-74), Kiwanis (pres. Regina chot. 1981-82).

YEOMANS, DONALD KEITH, astronomer; b. Rochester, N.Y., May 3, 1942; s. George E. and Jessie (Sutherland) Y.; m. Laurie Robyn Ernst, June 20, 1970; children: Sarah, Keith. BA, Middlebury (Vt.) Coll., 1964; MS, U. Md., 1967, PhD, 1970. Supr. Computer Scis. Corp., Silver Spring, Md., 1973-76; rsch. astronomer Jet Propulsion Lab., Pasadena, Calif., 1976-92, supr., 1993—; discipline specialist Internat. Halley Watch, 1982-89; prin. investigator NASA Comet Mission, 1987-91, Near-Earth Asteroid Rendezvous Mission, 1994—. Author: Comet Halley: Once in a Lifetime, 1985, The Distant Planets, 1989, Comets: A Chronological History of Observation, Science, Myth, and Folklore, 1991. Recipient Space Achievement award AIAA, 1985, Exceptional Svc. medal NASA, 1986, Achievement award Middlebury Coll. Alumni, 1987; named NASA/JPL Sr. Rsch. Scientist, 1993. Mem. Internat. Astron. Union, Am. Astron. Soc., Astron. Soc. Pacific. Democrat. Presbyterian. Avocations: tennis, history of astronomy. Office: Jet Propulsion Lab 4800 Oak Grove Dr #301-150G Pasadena CA 91109-8001

YEOMANS, DONALD RALPH, Canadian government official, consultant; b. Toronto, Ont., Can., Mar. 25, 1925; s. Ralph and Louise (Weismiller) Y.; m. Catherine Simpson Williams, May 13, 1950; children: Patricia Ann, Nancy Louise, Jane Elizabeth. B.A.Sc., U. Toronto, 1947. Registered profl. engr., Ont.; cert. mgmt. acct. Mem. Bur. of Govt. Orgns., Ottawa, Ont., 1962-64; dep. sec. Treasury Bd., Ottawa, 1964-69; asst. dep. minister Dept. Supply and Services, Ottawa, 1969-75; assoc. exec. dir. Anti-Inflation Bd., Ottawa, 1975-76; asst. dep. minister Dept. Nat. Health-Welfare, Ottawa, 1976-77; commr. Correctional Services of Can., Ottawa, 1977-85; chmn. Tariff Bd., 1985-89; spl. advisor Can. Jud. Centre, 1989-92; mem. bd. govs. Carleton U., 1980-93, chmn., 1989-91; spl. advisor Royal Com. Govt. Orgns., 1961, Royal Com. Fin. Accountability, 1977; assoc. Cons. and Audit Can., 1992—; exec. counsellor Pub. Svc. Commn., 1990-95; mem. bd. govs. Can. Comprehensive Audit Found., 1989-94; mem. ind. adv. com. Auditor Gen. Can., 1989-95; chmn. Coun. Adminstrv. Tribunals, 1986; chmn. Coun. Chairs Ont. Univs., 1991-93; mem. Expert Com. on AIDS in Prisons, 1992-94; chmn. awards com. Am. Correctional Assn., 1992—. Recipient Centennial medal Govt. Can., 1967, Jubilee medal Govt. Can., 1977, E.R. Cass award Am. Corr. Assn., 1991; Australian Commonwealth fellow, 1985. Fellow Soc. Mgmt. Accts. Can (pres. 1977); mem. Assn. State Correctional Adminstrs (pres. 1983), Inst. Pub. Adminstrn. Can. (pres. 1974). Clubs: Five Lakes (pres. 1975); Canadian (Ottawa, pres. 1978). Home and Office: 310 Clemow Ave, Ottawa, ON Canada K1S 2B8

YEOSOCK, JOHN JOHN, army officer; b. Wilkes-Barre, Pa., Mar. 18, 1937; s. John A. and Elizabeth B. (Petras) Y.; m. Betta Lynn Hoffner, July 20, 1960; children—John John, Elizabeth John. BS in Indsl. Engring., Pa. State U., 1959; MS in Ops. Rsch., U.S. Naval Postgrad. Sch., Monterey, Calif., 1969; postgrad., Nat. War Coll., 1976. Commd. officer U.S. Army, 1959, advanced through grades to lt. gen.; brigade comdr. 194th Armored Brigade, Ft Knox, Ky., 1978-80; chief of staff 1st Cavalry div. U.S. Army, Ft. Hood, Tex., 1980-81, asst. div. comdr., 1983-84; project mgr. Saudi N.G., Riyadh, Saudi Arabia, 1981-83; dep. chief of staff ops. Forces Command., Atlanta, 1984-86; comdr. 1st Cavalry Div., Ft. Hood, 1986-88; asst. dep. chief of staff for ops. The Pentagon, Washington, 1988-89; comdr. 3d Army and dep. comdg. gen. Forces Command, Ft. McPherson, Ga., 1989—&; comdr. U.S., U.K., French Army Forces, Kuwaiti Theater Ops., Desert Storm, Saudi Arabia, 1990-91; internat. cons., 1993—. Decorated D.S.M. (3), Legion of Merit (2), Bronze Star, French Legion of Honor, King Faisal award Class II, King Abdul Aziz medal Class II (Saudi Arabia), Combat Infantryman badge; recipient Nat. Vets. award, 1994, AUSA Inspiration award Atlanta, 1992; named Outstanding Engring. Alumnus, Pa. State U., 1990, Disting. Alumni, 1992, Disting. Alumnus, Valley Forge Mil. Acad., 1994; named to Pi Kappa Phi Hall of Fame. Mem. Wilkes-Barre C. of C. (hon., Achievement award 1991). Home: 411 Taberon Rd Peachtree City GA 30269-3215

YEP, WALLEN LAI, import/export company executive, author; b. Stockton, Calif., July 23, 1943; s. Hong Wey and Kim Chin Gee Y.; m. Yong Sun Hwang, June 12, 1970; 1 child, Lisa Suk Kyung. AA, Coll. of San Mateo, 1972; BA, Calif. State U., San Francisco, 1975; certificate in contract administrn., U. Calif., Berkeley, 1975; MBA, Golden Gate U., 1977. Cert. profl. cons. to mgmt. Nat. Br. Profl. Mgmt. Cons. Contract price analyst U.S. Army Procurement Agy., Korea, 1969; base supply supr. AAEOI, Korea, 1970-71; staff-advisor In-Change Group, Korea, 1971; administrv. svcs. supr. Far West Lab., San Francisco, 1971-74; assoc. administr. Met. Transp. Commn., Berkeley, 1974-84; prin. W. Yep Internat. Cons., Piedmont, Calif., 1985—; instr. Asian mktg. and internat. bus. mgmt. Lincoln U., 1978-83; guest panelist East Indian experience in N. Am. symposium U. Calif., Berkeley, So. East Asian Studies, 1978; speaker internat. symposium econ. cooperation and fgn. trade, Taiyuan, Shanxi Province, China, 1984; internat. speaker in field. Author: Occupational Certification and Licensing Handbook, 1978, Hidden Fallacies of Foreign Market Data, 1979, Financial Status of the PRC, Wage Differentials in PRC, Consumer Value Analysis, Who Are You, 1994, Sequel, 1994. Co-chmn. North Beach Chinatown Youth Svcs. Ctr., 1977-86; hon. adv. bd. Mission Coaltion, 1977-79; pres. Internat. Ctr. Tech. Assistance and Devel.; adv. East Bay Local Devel. Corp., 1977; mem. Oakland (Calif.) Unified Sch. Dist. Affirmative Action Purchasing adv. com. , 1978; mem. Pres. adv. bd. West Coast Christian Coll., 1983; Presdl. invitation to be del. Calif.-White House/Nat. Gov.'s conf. fgn. trade and export promotion, Seattle, 1979. Served with U.S. Army, 1967-69. Named Outstanding Young Men of Am. Jaycees, 1980; recipient Citizen of the Day award KABL Radio, 1978. Mem. Nat. Assn. Purchasing Mgmt. (cert. purchasing mgr.), No. Calif. Purchasing Mgmt. Assn., Oakland World Trade Assn., Assn. of MBA Execs., Calif., Golden Gate Alumni Assns., Nat. Contract Mgmt. Assn. (cert. profl. contracts mgr.). Office: PO Box 21011 Piedmont CA 94620-1011

YERBY, ALONZO SMYTHE, health services administrator, educator; b. Augusta, Ga., Oct. 15, 1921; s. Rufus Garvin and Wilhelmina Ethlyn (Smythe) Y.; m. Monteal Monica May, Sept. 17, 1943; children—Mark, Lynne, Kristen. B.S., U. Chgo., 1941; M.D., Meharry Med. Coll., 1946; M.P.H., Harvard, 1948. Diplomate: Am. Bd. Preventive Medicine. Intern Coney Island Hosp., Bklyn.; resident in preventive medicine Health Ins. Plan N.Y., 1950-53; exec. dir. med. services N.Y.C. Dept. Health; med. welfare adminstr. N.Y.C. Dept. Welfare, 1960-65; commr. of hosps. N.Y.C., 1965-66; prof. health services adminstrn. Harvard Sch. Pub. Health, Boston, 1966-82; dep. asst. sec. health for intergovtl. affairs Dept. Health and Human Services, Washington, 1980-81; prof., dir. div. health services adminstrn. Uniformed Services U. of Health Scis., Bethesda, Md., 1982—; cons. Bur. Family Services, Nat. Center Health Services Research, HEW, WHO; mem. Nat. Adv. Commn. on Health Manpower, 1966-67, HEW Adv. Com. on Relationships with State Health Agys., 1963-66, Nat. Profl. Standards Rev. Council, 1978-80; vis. scientist USA-USSR Exchange Program, 1967, 79. Author: Community Medicine in England and Scotland, 1976. Served with AUS, 1943-46. Fellow Am. Pub. Health Assn.; mem. Am. Coll. Preventive Medicine, Inst. Medicine of Nat. Acad. Scis., N.Y. Acad. Medicine. Club: Harvard (N.Y.C.). Home: 466 Park Dr # 1 Boston MA 02215-3750

YERGIN, DANIEL HOWARD, writer, consultant; b. Los Angeles, Feb. 6, 1947; s. Irving H. and Naomi Y.; m. Angela Stent, Aug. 10, 1975; children: Alexander George, Rebecca Isabella. BA with first class honors, Cambridge U., Eng., 1968, MA, 1970, PhD, 1974; PhD (hon.), U. Mo., 1980, U. Houston, 1994. Contbg. editor New York mag., 1968-70; research fellow Harvard U., Cambridge, Mass., 1974-76; lectr. bus. sch. Harvard U., 1976-79, lectr. Kennedy Sch. Govt., 1979-83; research assoc. Harvard U., Cambridge, 1983—; pres. Cambridge Energy Research Assoc., Cambridge, 1982—, also chmn., sec. energy task force on strategic energy R&D; mem. policy adv. com. Program on U.S.-Japan Rels., Harvard U.; mem. bd. energy experts Dallas Morning News; mem. internat. panel advisors Asia-Pacific Petroleum Conf.; fellow World Econ. Forum, Davos. Author: Shattered Peace: The Origins of the Cold War and the National Security State, 1977, rev. edit., 1990, The Prize: Epic Quest for Oil, Money and Power, 1991 (Pulitzer Prize for non-fiction 1992); co-author: Cold War, 1977, Energy Future, 1979, Global Insecurity, 1982, Future of Oil Prices: Perils of Prophecy, 1984, Russia 2010: And What It Means for the World, 1993; contbg. editor Atlantic Monthly, 1977-83. Mem. adv. bd. Solar Energy Rsch. Inst., Golden, Colo., 1979-81; sec. Energy Adv. Bd. Fellow Univ. Consortium for World Order Studies, 1974-75, Rockefeller Found., 1975-79, German Marshall Fund, 1980-81; Marshall scholar Cambridge U., 1974. Fellow Atlantic Inst. Internat. Affairs; mem. PEN, Lehrman Inst. (assoc.), Coun. on Fgn. Rels., Nat. Petroleum Coun., Internat. Assn. for Energy Econs., Am. Hist. Assn., Am. Polit. Assn., Royal Inst. Internat. Affairs, Assn. Marshall Scholars (bd. dirs. 1988-91), U.S. Energy Assocs. (bd. dirs.), Offshore No. Seas Found. Internat. Coun., The Nature Conservancy (Last Great Places com.), Yale Club (N.Y.C.), Harvard Club (N.Y.C.). Office: Cambridge Energy Rsch Assocs 20 University Rd Ste 450 Cambridge MA 02138-5756

YERKES, DAVID NORTON, architect; b. Cambridge, Mass., Nov. 5, 1911; s. Robert Mearns and Ada (Watterson) Y.; m. Catharine Noyes, Oct. 7, 1939 (dec. 1969); 1 dau., Catharine; m. Sarah Hitchcock Satterlee, July 9, 1972. B.A., Harvard U., 1933; M.F.A., Yale U., 1935. Draftsman, designer Chgo. and Washington, 1937-39, Deigert & Yerkes and Assos., Washington, 1945-69, David N. Yerkes & Assos., Washington, 1970-80, Yerkes, Pappas and Parker, 1980-83; Mem. panel archtl. advisers Nat. Commn. Fine Arts, 1961-63, 79-82; vice chmn. Presdl. Inaugural Parade Com., 1965. Prin. works include Voice of America Studios, Washington, 1958, Nat. Arboretum Hdqrs. Bldg. Am. Embassy, Somalia, also Madeira Sch. Auditoriu, 1969; 4 stas. Washington subway sys., 1971-81, hdqrs., Nat. Trust Historic Preservation, Washington, 1977, suite, Time, Inc., Washington, 1980, also various schs., labs; paintings exhibited in New Eng. and Washington. Served to capt. AUS, 1943-45. Firm recipient numerous regional and nat. awards; recipient Kemper award AIA, 1972. Fellow AIA (bd. dirs. 1965-68, v.p. 1968-69, chmn. nat. honor awards jury 1966, chmn. Reynolds Meml. award jury 1969, pres. found. 1974-76). Home: 1527 30th St NW Washington DC 20007-3088

YERKES, SUSAN GAMBLE, newspaper columnist; b. Evanston, Ill., Sept. 5, 1959; d. Charles Tyson and Darthea (Campbell) Higgins. BA in Liberal Arts (hon.), U. Austin, 1974; MA in Mass Comms., Wichita State U., 1976. Pub. affairs dir. anchor KAKE-TV, Wichita, Kans., 1977-81; freelance writer pub. rels. YS Comms. Global, 1981-84; metro columnist San Antonio Light, 1986-93; lifestyle columnist S.A. Express News, San Antonio, 1993—; radio TV host WOAI-AM, San Antonio, 1993—; nat. assn. broadcast editls., Boston, 1978-81. Recipient 1st Place Column Writing Nat. Press Women, 1988. Mem. Internat. Women's Forum, Women in Comm., Pub. Rel. Soc. Am., Phi Beta Kappa. Episcopalian. Avocations: horseback riding, travel, reading, friends. Home: 7711 Broadway # 29B San Antonio TX 78209 Office: San Antonio Express News Ave E 3rd St San Antonio TX 78205

YERMAN, FREDRIC WARREN, lawyer; b. N.Y.C., Jan. 8, 1943; s. Nat W. and Tina (Barotz) Y.; m. Ann R. Rochlin, May 31, 1965; children: Emily, Deborah. BA, CUNY, 1963; LLB, Columbia U., 1966. Bar: N.Y. 1967. Assoc. Kaye, Scholer, Fierman, Hays & Handler, N.Y.C., 1966-74, ptnr., 1974—, chmn. exec. com., 1990-92; bd. dirs. Lawyer's Com. for Civil Rights under Law, N.Y. Bd. dirs. United Way Tri-State, N.Y., Legal Aid Soc., N.Y.C.; chmn. Jewish Bd. Family and Children Svcs., N.Y.C., 1994—. Fellow Am. Coll. Trial Lawyers. Home: 31 Sheridan Rd Scarsdale NY 10583-1523 Office: Kaye Scholer Fierman Hays & Handler 425 Park Ave New York NY 10022-3506

YERRID, C. STEVEN, lawyer; b. Charleston, W.Va., Sept. 30, 1949; s. Charles George and Audrey Faye Yerrid; m. Vee West, Aug. 23, 1985. BA in History and Polit. Sci., La. State U., 1971; JD, Georgetown U., 1975. Bar: Fla. 1975, Va. 1975, U.S. Supreme Ct. 1979, D.C. 1984. Aide U.S. Senator Ellender, Washington, 1971-73; lobbyist Am. Hosp. Assn., Washington, 1973-75; ptnr. Holland & Knight, Tampa, Fla., 1975-86; pres. Stagg, Hardy & Yerrid, Tampa, 1986-89, Yerrid, Knopik & Valenzuela, Tampa, 1990—; lobbyist Am. Optometric Assn., 1972-73. Mem. ABA, Va. Bar Assn., D.C. Bar Assn., Fla. Acad. Trial Lawyers (bd. dirs. 1989—), Fla. Bar Assn. (chmn. admiralty law com. 1984-85, bd. cert. com. 1988-91, vice chmn. 1989-91), Southeastern Admiralty Law Inst., Am. Judicature Soc., Assn. Trial Lawyers Am. (sustaining), Am. Bd. Trial Advocates (advocate), Maritime Law Assn. (proctor), Bd. Cert. Civil Trial Lawyers, Nat. Bd. Trial Advocacy, Harbour Island Athletic Club, Centre Club, Tampa Club. Democrat. Avocations: skiing, swimming, fishing. Office: Yerrid Knopik & Valenzuela 101 E Kennedy Blvd Ste 2160 Tampa FL 33602-5147

YERUSHALMI, YOSEF HAYIM, historian, educator; b. N.Y.C., May 20, 1932; s. Leon and Eva (Kaplan) Y.; m. Ophra Pearly, Jan. 4, 1959; 1 child, Ariel. B.A., Yeshiva U., 1953; M.Hebrew Lit., Jewish Theol. Sem. Am., 1957, DHL (hon.), 1987; M.A., Columbia, 1961, Ph.D., 1966; M.A. (hon.), Harvard, 1970; LHD (hon.), Hebrew Union Coll., 1996. Instr. Jewish history Rutgers U., New Brunswick, N.J., 1963-66; asst. prof. Hebrew and Jewish History Harvard, 1966-70, prof., 1970-78, Jacob E. Safra prof. Jewish history and Sephardic civilization, 1978-80, chmn. dept. near eastern langs. and civilizations, 1978-80; Salo Wittmayer Baron prof. Jewish history, culture and soc., and dir. Center for Israel and Jewish Studies, Columbia U., 1980—. Author: From Spanish Court to Italian Ghetto: isaac Cardoso, A Study in Seventeenth-Century Marranism and Jewish Apologetics, 1971, Haggadah and History, 1975, The Lisbon Massacre of 1506, 1976, Zakhor: Jewish History and Jewish Memory, 1982, Freud's Moses: Judaism Terminable and Interminable, 1991, Ein Feld in Anatot: Versuche uber judische Geschichte, 1993, Diener von Königen und nicht Diener von Dienern: Einige Aspekte der politischen Geschichte der Juden, 1995; author (in Hebrew): Spinoza on the Survival of the Jews, 1983; contbr. articles to profl. publs. on Spanish and Portuguese Jewry and history of psychoanalysis; chmn. publs. com. Jewish Publ. Soc., 1972-84; pres. Leo Baeck Inst., 1986-91. Bd. dirs. Conf. Jewish Social Studies, Psycho analytic Research and Devel. Fund, Editorial Bd., History and Memory. Recipient Newman medal CUNY, 1975, Nat. Jewish Book award, 1983, 92,Ansley award Columbia U. Press, 1968, medal of achievement in history Nat. Found. for Jewish Culture,1995; Kent fellow, 1963, travel fellow Nat. Found. for Jewish Culture, 1964, fellow NEH, 1976-77, Rockefeller fellow in humanities, 1983-84, Guggenheim fellow, 1989-90. Fellow Am. Acad. Jewish Research, Am. Acad. Arts and Scis., Academia Portuguesa da História (hon.). Home: 450 Riverside Dr New York NY 10027-6821 Office: Columbia University 511 Fayerweather Hall 116th St & Broadway New York NY 10027

YESAWICH, PETER CHARLES, advertising executive; b. Ithaca, N.Y., Oct. 28, 1950; s. Paul Joseph Jr. and Elizabeth (Larkin) Y.; divorced; children: Peter Charles, Paul Christopher. BS, Cornell U., 1972, MS, 1974, PhD, 1976; AMP, Yale U., 1994. Dir. rsch. Robinsons, Inc., Orlando, Fla., 1976-78, v.p., 1978-81, exec. v.p., 1981-83; pres., CEO Yesawich, Pepperdine & Brown, Orlando, 1983—; vis. assoc. prof. Cornell U., Ithaca, 1977—, U. Ctrl. Fla., Orlando, 1988—; chmn. Pope Tourism Inst., Orlando, 1988-90. Contbr. articles to profl. jours. Recipient World Travel award Am. Assn. Travel Editors, 1985, Silver Medal award Am. Assn. Advt. Agys., 1992, Adrian award Hospitality Sales and Mktg. Assn. Internat., 1993; named Author of Yr. Cornell Quar., 1986. Mem. Cornell Hotel Soc., Am. Hotel & Motel Assn., Caribbean Hotel Assn., Hotel Sales Mktg. Assn., Am. Mktg. Assn. Avocations: jogging, writing. Office: Yesawich Pepperdine & Brown Ste 600 1900 Summit Tower Orlando FL 32810-5912

YESILADA, BIROL ALI, political science educator; b. Nicosia, Cyprus, Aug. 12, 1956; came to U.S., 1971; s. Ali and Sermin (Mustafa) Y.; m. Susan Diana Lesea, Aug. 20, 1980; children: Sermin, Selin. AB, U. Calif., Berkeley, 1977; MA, San Francisco State U., 1979; PhD, U. Mich., 1984. Vis. asst. prof. U. Mo., Columbia, 1984-85, asst. prof., 1985-91; vis. asst. prof. Middle East Tech. U., Ankara, Turkey, 1987-88; vis. rsch. specialist State Planning Orgn., Ankara, Turkey, 1987-88; assoc. prof. U. Mo., Columbia, 1991—, chair dept. polit. sci., 1994—; pres. Oceania Corp., 1992—; cons. State Planning Orgn., Ankara, 1987-88, Libr. of Congress, Washington, 1988-92, Coun. on Fgn. Rels., N.Y.C., 1990-91, U.S. State Dept. Fgn. Svc. Inst., 1995—, Nat. Intelligence Coun., Washington, 1996, U.S. Inst. Peace, 1996; chair internat. studies adv. com. U. Mo., Columbia, 1992-94. Author, co-editor: Agrarian Reform in Reverse: The Food Crisis in the Third World, 1987, The Political and Socioeconomic Transformation of Turkey, 1993; co-author: The Emerging European Union, 1995; mem. editl. bd. Cyprus Rev. Jour., 1987—, New Perspectives on Turkey, 1987-95; contbr. articles to profl. jours. Bd. dir. U. Mo. Peace Studies, Columbia, 1988-92. Rsch. fellow Am. Coun. Learned Socs. and Social Sci. Rsch. Coun., 1987, Fulbright-Hays, 1982, Turkish Econ. and Social Studies Found. of Eczacibasi Holding, 1995, William T. Kemper fellow for tchng. excellence U. Mo. and Commerce Bank, 1996; recipient Purple Chalk Teaching Excellence award U. Mo., Columbia Arts and Scis. Coll., 1991; rsch. bd. grantee U. Mo., 1996. Mem. Am. Polit. Sci. Assn., European Community Studies Assn., Middle East Studies Assn., Columbia Rotary Club. Muslim. Avocations: jogging, swimming, camping, stamp collecting, ballroom dancing. Home: 1700 Princeton Dr Columbia MO 65203-1851

YESLOW, ROSEMARIE, real estate professional; b. Detroit; d. Karl E. and Madeline E. (Paret) Norberg; widowed; children: Bradford (dec.), Tod, Eric (dec.), Mark. Student, U. Miami, 1947-49; AA in Journalism, Broward Jr. Coll., 1972; student, Fla. Atlantic U., 1973-75; grad., Realtor Inst., 1995. Ins. agt. Wittenstein Ins. Agy., Hollywood, Fla., 1965-75; owner, operator The Karl Motel/Apartments, Hallandale, Fla., 1980—; realtor/assoc. The Keyes Co., Hollywood, 1990-93; realtor, assoc. Ebby Halliday Real Estate, Dallas, 1993—; real estate investor, Hollywood, 1960—. Contbr. articles to profl. jours. Edn. v.p. Nat. Coun. Jewish Women, Hollywood, 1960-66; unit and dept. chmn. LWV, Ft. Lauderdale, Fla., 1960-72; edn. chmn. Dem. Exec. Com., Broward County, Fla., 1976-78; mem. planning and zoning bd. City of Hallandale, 1988-92. Recipient Sch. Bell award Fla. Edn. Assn., 1966. Mem. Nat. Assn. Realtors, Hollywood Bd. Realtors, Hallandale Adult Cmty. Ctr. (adv. com., Cert. of Appreciation 1989), Hallandale Citizens United, Hallandale C. of C. (bd. dirs. 1987-92, Small Bus. Person of Yr. award 1990), Sierra Club. Democrat. Jewish. Avocations: camping, reading, hiking, swimming. Home: 4247 Throckmorton St Dallas TX 75219-2206 Office: Ebby Halliday Real Estate 8333 Douglas Ave Ste 100 Dallas TX 75225-5811

YESNER, DAVID R., anthropology educator; b. Hartford, Conn., Jan. 15, 1948; s. Raymond and Bernice (Lieberman) Y.; m. Kristine June Sanger Crossen, Jun. 9, 1989; 1 child, Daniel Robert Yesner. AB, Cornell U., 1971; MA, U. Conn., 1974, PhD, 1977. Teaching asst. U. Conn., Storrs, Conn., 1973-75; instr. Anchorage C.C., Anchorage, 1975-77; asst. prof. U. So. Maine, Portland, Maine, 1977-81; vis. prof. Mc Gill U., Montreal, Quebec, Can., 1981-82; assoc. prof. U. So. Maine, Portland, Maine, 1982-87; assoc. prof. U. Alaska, Anchorage, 1987-94, prof. anthropology, 1994—; bd. dirs. So. Alaska Mus. Nat. History, Anchorage, 1991—. Editor: (book) As The World Warmed, 1995, Alaska's People, 1995; book rev. editor: Man in the Northeast, 1982-85; contbr. to profl. jours. Mem. Alaska Anthropol. Assn. (editor 1988-91, book review editor 1995), Soc. for Am. Archaeology, Am. Quaternary Assn., Cornell Club of Alaska (alumni mem. 1990-95). Democrat. Jewish. Avocations: Photography, fishing, skiing, camping. Office: U Alaska Dept Anthropology 3211 Providence Dr Anchorage AK 99508-4614

YESTON, MAURY, composer, lyricist, educator; b. Jersey City, Oct. 23, 1945; s. David and Frances (Haar) Y.; m. Anne Sheedy, 1982; children: Jake, Max. BA, Yale U., 1967, PhD, 1974; MA, Clare Coll., Cambridge (Eng.) U., 1972. Assoc. prof. dept. music Yale U., New Haven, 1974-82, dir. undergrad. studies in music, 1976-82; tchr. BMI Mus. Theatre Workshop, 1982—. Composer, lyricist: off-Broadway play Cloud 9 - Music, 1981; Broadway play Nine - The Musical, 1982 (Tony award 1982, Grammy award nominee 1982, Drama Desk award 1982), One Two Three Four Five, 1987, Grand Hotel, 1989 (Tony award nominee 1990), (rec.) Goya: A Life in Song, 1989, December Songs, 1990, Phantom, 1991; composer: Movement for Cello and Orchestra, 1967; author: The Stratification of Musical Rhythm, 1975; author, editor: Readings in Schenker Analysis, 1977. Recipient BMI award, 1982, 89. Office: Flora Roberts 157 W 57th St New York NY 10019-2210

YETMAN, LEITH ELEANOR, academic administrator; b. Kellits, Clarendon, Jamaica, West Indies; came to U.S., 1967; d. 2nd child of 12 children of Percival Augustus and Grace Elizabeth (Anderson) Y.; m. Noel W. Miller, Apr. 8, 1961 (div. 1977); children: Donovan, Jo-Ann, Kirk, Lori-Anne; adopted children: LaFara, Samantha, Brandon Ryan. Attended, Bethlehem Teachers Coll., St. Elizabeth, Jamaica, 1960; BSC, Baruch Coll., 1976; MA, Columbia U., 1978. Cert. tchr., N.Y. Legal sec. various law firms, N.Y.C., 1969-76; instr. Taylor Bus. Inst., N.Y.C., 1977-79; founder, pres., dir. N.Y. Inst. Bus. Tech., N.Y.C., 1981—. Recipient Outstanding Achievement award Baruch Coll. Alumni Assn., 1989; Leith E. Yetman Day proclaimed June 1, 1994 by Manhattan Borough Pres. Mem. Better Bus. Bur. N.Y.C. Office: NY Inst Bus Tech 401 Park Ave S New York NY 10016-8808

YETTER, RICHARD ALAN, engineering educator; b. Trenton, N.J., May 23, 1952; s. Albert Lewis Jr. and Marcella Fern (Snook) Y. BS, Syracuse U., 1974; MS, Cornell U., 1981; MA, Princeton U., 1981, PhD, 1985. Rsch. engr. Ford Motor Co., Dearborn, Mich., 1976-79; profl. rsch. staff Princeton (N.J.) U., 1985-90; rsch. collaborator Brookhaven Nat. Lab., Upton, N.Y., 1983-87; rsch. scientist, lectr. Princeton U., 1990—; cons. Cabot Corp., Ill., 1991, British Oxygen Corp., N.J., 1990-91, U.S. Army & HR Rsch., 1988-92, Rsch. Cottrell & Efthimion Enterprises, N.J., 1989-92. Contbr. chpts. to books and articles to profl. jours.; patentee asymmetric whirl combustion. Exxon Edn. Found. fellow, 1980-84. Mem. SO. Automotive Engrs., Combustion Inst., Pi Tau Sigma, Tau Beta Pi. Avocations: running, tennis, sailing. Office: Princeton U Dept Mech & Aerospace Engring Princeton NJ 08544

YEUNG, ALBERT TAK-CHUNG, civil engineering educator; b. Hong Kong, July 13, 1959; came to U.S., 1984; s. Siu-Hung and Pui-Chan (Lip) Y.; m. Kitman Iris Luk, Jan. 16, 1986; children: Loren Wayne, Ernest Hayes. BSc in Engring., U. Hong Kong, 1982; MS, U. Calif., Berkeley, 1985, PhD, 1990. Registered profl. engr., Tex., civil engr., Hong Kong. Engring. asst. T.H. Chuah & Assocs. Cons. Engrs., Singapore, 1980, Geotech. Control Office, Hong Kong, 1981; staff engr. Binnie & Ptnrs. Internat., Hong Kong, 1982-83, staff resident engr., 1984; lectr. Haking Wong Tech. Inst., Hong Kong, 1983-84; rsch. asst. U. Calif., Berkeley, 1985, 86,

87-89, grad. student instr., 1985-87; rsch. asst. Lawrence Berkeley Lab., 1989; asst. prof. civil engring. Northeastern U., Boston, 1990, Tex. A&M U., College Station, 1991—; asst. rsch. engr. Tex. Transp. Inst., College Station, 1991—; pres. Albert T. Yeung Geotech. Engr., College Station, 1992—; faculty advisor Hong Kong Club, Tex. A&M U., College Station, 1991-93, Asian Am. Assn., 1992-94; spkr. H.S. JETS Club, 1991—. Lead editor: Vertical and Horizontal Deformations of Foundations and Embankments, 2 vols., 1994; co-author: Laboratory Soil Testing for Engineers, 3rd edit., 1994; contbr. articles to profl. jours. Earth Tech. Corp. fellow, Long Beach, Calif., 1987-89; rsch. grantee Tex. Advanced Tech. Program, Tex. Higher Edn. Coord. Bd., Austin, 1992, 94, Tex. Dept. Transp. Coop. Rsch. Program, Austin, 1992, Gulf Coast Hazardous Substance Rsch. Ctr., Beaumont, Tex., 1992, Nat. Coop. Hwy. Rsch. Program, Transp. Rsch. Bd., NRC, Washington, 1993, Energy Resources Program, Tex. A&M U. Sys., 1993; recipient Rsch. Initiation award NSF, Washington, 1992, Select Young Faculty award Tex. Engring. Exptl. Sta., 1993. Mem. AAUP, ASTM (mem. com. D18 on soil and rock and com. D34 on mixed waste 1993—), ASCE (editl. bd. Jour. Geotech. Engring. 1994—, publs. com. geotech. engring. divsn. 1994—, publs. com. geotech. engring. divsn. 1994—, sec. Tex. sect. geotech. com. 1993-94, vice-chair geotech. com. 1994-95, chair geotech. com. 1995-96, Arthur Casagrande Profl. Devel. award 1996), Am. Soc. Surface Mining and Reclamation (com. on containment and mitigation of toxic mine waste 1994—), Am. Soc. Engring. Edn. (Dow Outstanding New Faculty award 1994), internat. Soc. Soil Mechanics and Found. Engring., Hong Kong Instn. of Engrs. (prize 1981, Kumagai prize 1994), Clay Mineral Soc. Achievements include use of electro-kinetics to extract contaminants from fine-grained soil, use of electrophoresis of clay particles to seal leaks in geomembrane liners, use of cone penetration technology to detect and delineate subsurface contamination, use of waste tire chips for highway earth structure construction. Avocations: travel, photography, gardening, sports, collecting. Office: Tex A&M U Dept Civil Engring College Station TX 77843-3136

YEUNG, EDWARD SZESHING, chemist; b. Hong Kong, Feb. 17, 1948; came to U.S., 1965; s. King Mai Luk and Yu Long Yeung; m. Anna Kunkwok Seto, Sept. 18, 1971; children: Rebecca Tze-Mai, Amanda Tze-Wen. AB magna cum laude, Cornell U., 1968; PhD, U. Calif., Berkeley, 1972. Instr. chemistry Iowa State U., Ames, 1972-74; asst prof. Iowa State U., 1974-77, assoc. prof, 1977-81, prof. chemistry, 1981-89, disting. prof., 1989—. Contbr. articles to profl. jours. Alfred P. Sloan fellow, 1974-76; recipient Am. Chem Soc. award in Analytical Chemistry, 1994. Fellow AAAS; mem. Soc. Applied Spectrosci. (Lester Strock award 1990), Am. Chem. Soc. (award in chem. instrumentation 1987, award in analytical chemistry 1994). Home: 1005 Jarrett Cir Ames IA 50014-3937 Office: Iowa State U Gilman Hall Ames IA 50011

YEVICH, ROSEMARIE, analyst; b. Berwick, Pa., Apr. 20, 1948; d. Steven Constantine and Marie Rose (Gafner) Y.; m. Francis Walsh Drislane, June 24, 1978; children: Catherine Marie, Helen Elizabeth, Edward James. BA cum laude, Harvard U., 1968; PhD, Stanford U., 1975. Postdoctoral fellow Rutgers U., New Brunswick, N.J., 1975-77; tchr. Westover Sch., Middlebury, Conn., 1977-80; rsch. assoc. DAS Harvard U. Divsn. Applied Scis., Cambridge, Mass., 1980-83; analyst Harvard U., Cambridge, Mass., 1983—. Co-adaptor, arranger: Great Vespers of B. Ledkovsky, 1976; contbr. articles to profl. sci. jours. Bd. mem. Friends of Nahanton Park, Newton, Mass., 1993. Russian Orthodox. Home: 53 Walden St Newton MA 02160-2133 Office: Harvard U Divsn Applied Scis Cambridge MA 02138

YGLESIAS, HELEN BASSINE, author, educator; b. N.Y.C., Mar. 29, 1915; d. Solomon and Kate (Goldstein) Bassine; m. Bernard Cole, 1938 (div. 1950); children: Tamar Cole, Lewis Cole; m. Jose Yglesias, Aug. 19, 1950 (div. 1992); 1 child, Rafael. Student pub. schs.; LHD (hon.), U. Maine, 1996. Literary editor Nation Mag., 1965-70; adj. assoc. prof. writing Columbia Sch. Arts, N.Y.C., 1973—; vis. prof. creative writing Writers Workshop, U. Iowa, Iowa City, 1980. Author: (novels) How She Died (Houghton Mifflin award), 1972, Family Feeling, 1976, Sweetsir, 1981, The Saviors, 1987, (non-fiction) Starting: Early, Anew, Over and Late, 1978, Isabel Bishop, 1989. Home: HC 64 Box 2075 Brooklin ME 04616-9801

YHOUSE, PAUL ALAN, manufacturing executive; b. Grand Rapids, Mich., June 23, 1949; s. Keith E. and Elaine (Laraway) Y.; m. Elizabeth Orlyk, Aug. 21, 1971. BBA, U. Mich., 1971. With Arthur Andersen & Co., various locations, 1971-76, mgr., 1976-82, ptnr., 1982-91; sr. v.p., CFO Holnam Inc., Dundee, Mich., 1991-93; pres., CEO, 1993—. Active adv. bd. Paton Acctg. Ctr., U. Mich., Ann Arbor. Mem. AICPA (chmn. healthcare com. 1980-91), Fin. Execs. Inst., Mich. Anssn. CPAs. Office: Holnam Inc 6211 Ann Arbor Rd Dundee MI 48131-9527

YIANNIAS, NANCY MAGAS, municipal official; b. Kalamazoo, Feb. 1, 1936; d. George A. and Irene (Callas) Magas; m. Andrew Chris Yiannias, Oct. 20, 1968; 1 child, Chris Andrew. BA, Western Mich. U., 1957; MPH, U. Mich., 1963. Registered sanitarian, Ill. Health educator Stickney Pub. Health Dist., Burbank, Ill., 1966-72, Chgo. Heart Assn., 1972-73; health coord. Village of Elk Grove, Ill., 1974—. Bd. counselors Alexian Bros. Med. Ctr., Elk Grove Village, 1977-93. Mem. Am. Pub. Health Assn., Ill. Pub. Health Assn. (sec. 1981), Soc. Pub. Health Educators, Ill. Soc. Pub. Health Educators (program planning com. 1966), Ill. Environ. Health Assn., N.W. Suburban Access to Care Assn. Home: 1521 Manor Ln Park Ridge IL 60068-1541 Office: Elk Grove Village Dept Health 901 Wellington Ave Elk Grove Village IL 60007

YIANNOPOULOS, ATHANASSIOS NICHOLAS, law educator; b. Thessaloniki, Greece, Mar. 13, 1928; came to U.S., 1953, naturalized, 1963; s. Nicholas A. and Areti T. (Alvanos) Y.; m. Mirta Valdes, May 9, 1982; children—Maria, Nicholas, Alexander, Philip. LL.B., U. Thessaloniki, 1950; M.C.L., U. Chgo., 1954; LL.M. (Walter Perry Johnson fellow in law), U. Calif., Berkeley, 1955, J.S.D., 1956; J.D., U. Cologne, W. Ger., 1961; LLD, U. Thessaloniki, Greece, 1995. Bar: Greece 1958. Mem. faculty La. State U., Baton Rouge, 1958-79; Prof. of comparative law, Eason-Weinmann Tulane U. Law Sch., New Orleans, 1979—; in charge revision La. Civil Code, Law Inst., 1962—. Author: Civil Law Property, 3d edit., 1991, Personal Servitudes, 3d edit., 1989, Predial Servitudes, 1983; (with T. Schoenbaum) Admiralty and Maritime Law, 1984; editor: Louisiana Civil Code, annually, 1980—; contbr. articles to various periodicals Ency. Brit. Pres. Baton Rouge Symphony Assn., 1972-73; bd. dirs. Music Soc., 1961-79. Served to 2d lt. Greek Army, 1950-53. Mem. Order of Phoenix, Am. Acad. Fgn. Law, Internat. Acad. Comparative Law, Am. Law Inst., Phi Alpha Delta. Mem. Greek Orthodox Ch. Club: Baton Rouge City. Office: 662 Sunset Blvd Baton Rouge LA 70808-5081

YIELDING, K. LEMONE, physician; b. Auburn, Ala., Mar. 25, 1931; s. Riley Lafayette and Bertie (Dees) Y.; m. Lerena Wade Hauge, Dec. 7, 1973; children: K. Lemone, Michael Lafon, Teresa Louise, Riley Lafayette, Katrina Elizabeth, Elaine Louise Blodgett, Laura Carlen Blodgett. BS, Ala. Poly. Inst., 1949; MS, U. Ala., 1952, MD, 1954. Intern U. Ala. Med. Center, 1954-55; clin. assoc. Nat. Inst. Arthritis and Metabolic Diseases, NIH, 1955-57, sr. investigator, 1958-64; resident med. service USPHS Hosp., Balt., 1957-58; adj. asst. prof. medicine Georgetown U. Med. Sch., 1958-64; cons. USPHS, 1964-68, 75—; prof. biochemistry, assoc. prof. medicine, chief lab. molecular biology U. Ala. Med. Ctr., Birmingham, 1964-80; prof., chmn. dept. anatomy, prof. medicine U. So. Ala. Coll. Medicine, Mobile, 1980-87; dean grad. sch. U. Tex. Med. Br., Galveston, 1987-95, dean emeritus, 1995—; cons. Am. Heart Assn., Arthritis Found., NIH, NASA. Contbr. to profl. jours., books. Served with USPHS, 1955-64. Grantee USPHS, Am. Cancer Soc., Nat. Found.-March of Dimes, U.S. Army, Am. Inst. Cancer Research. Mem. Am. Soc. Biol. Chemistry, Am. Assn. Cancer Research, Am. Assn. Photobiology, Assn. Research Vision and Ophthalmology, Soc. Exptl. Biology and Medicine, Am. Soc. Pharm. and Exptl. Therapeutics, Am. Assn. Pathologists, So. Soc. Clin. Investigation, Am. Assn. Anatomy, Soc. Toxicology, Sigma Xi.

YIH, CHIA-SHUN, fluid mechanics educator; b. Kweiyang, Kweichow, China, July 25, 1918; s. Ting-Jian and Wan-Lan (Shiao) Y.; m. Shirley Gladys Ashman, Feb. 17, 1949; children: Yiu-Yo, Yuen-Ming David, Weiling Katherine. BS, Nat. Central U., 1942; MS, U. Iowa, 1947, PhD, 1948. Instr. Nat. Kweichow U., 1944-45; instr. math. U. Wis., 1948-49; lectr. U. B.C., 1949-50; assoc. prof. Colo. State U., 1950-52; rsch. engr. U. Iowa, 1952-54, assoc. prof., 1954-56; assoc. prof. U. Mich., Ann Arbor, 1956-58; prof. U. Mich., 1958-68, Stephen P. Timoshenko Disting. univ. prof. fluid mechanics, 1968-88, S.P. Timoshenko Disting. univ. prof. emeritus, 1988—; grad. rsch. prof. U. Fla., 1987-90, grad. rsch. prof. emeritus, 1990—; vis. prof. U. Paris, U. Grenoble, France, 1970-71; Henry Russel lectr. U. Mich., 1974; lectr. Chinese Acad. Sci., Beijing, 1981, von Kármán Inst., Brussels, 1981, Internat. Ctr. of Theoretical Physics, Trieste, Italy, 1994, Cheng Kung U., Tainan, Taiwan, 1995; G.I. Taylor lectr. U. Fla., 1992; hon. prof. U. Hong Kong, 1996—; cons. Huyck Felt Co., 1960-64; trustee Rocky Mountain Hydraulic Lab., 1976-85; attachè de recherche in math. French Govt., 1951-52. Author: Dynamics of Nonhomogeneous Fluids, 1965, Fluid Mechanics, An Introduction to the Theory, 1969, 79, 88, Stratified Flows, 1980; editor: Advances in Applied Mechanics, 1970-82; mem. editl. bd. Advances in Applied Mechanics, Physics of Fluids, 1969-72, SIAM Jour. Applied Math., 1971-72, Ann. Revs. of Fluid Mechanics, 1969-72, Advances in Mechanics of China, Acta Mechanica Sinica, Applied Math. and Mechanics, to 1989, Jour. Hydrodynamics, to 1989; contbr. articles to profl. jours. Recipient Achievement award Chinese Inst. Engrs. N.Y., 1968, Achievement award Chinese Engrs. and Scientists Assn. So. Calif., 1973, Sr. Scientist award Humboldt Found., Fed. Republic Germany, 1977-78, Theodore von Kármán medal ASCE, 1981, Stephen S. Attwood award U. Mich., 1984; sr. postdoctoral fellow NSF, 1959-60, Guggenheim fellow, 1964. Fellow Am. Phys. Soc. (chmn. exec. com. fluid dynamics divsn. 1973-74, Fluid Dynamics prize 1985, Otto Laporte award 1989); mem. U.S. Nat. Acad. Engring., Academia Sinica, Sigma Xi, Pi Mu Epsilon, Tau Beta Pi, Phi Kappa Phi. Home: 3530 W Huron River Dr Ann Arbor MI 48103-9417 Home (winter): 4084 NW 23d Cir Gainesville FL 32605

YIM, SOLOMON CHIK-SING, civil engineering educator, consultant; b. Hong Kong, Sept. 11, 1952; came to U.S., 1972; s. Fuk-Ching and San-Chan (Leung) Y.; m. Lenore S. Hata, Aug. 27, 1983; children: Rachel L., Joshua A. BSCE, Rice U., 1976; MSCE, U. Calif., Berkeley, 1977, MA in Math., 1981, PhD in Civil Engring., 1983. Rsch. asst. U. Calif., 1976-83, vis. lectr., 1983-84, vis. assoc. prof., 1993-94; sr. rsch. engr. Exxon Prodn. Rsch. Co., Houston, 1984-87; asst. prof. civil engring. Oreg. State U., Corvallis, 1987-91, assoc. prof., 1991—; cons. engr., 1977—; mem. ship structures com. NRC, 1990—; mem. grad. fellowship com. in sci. and engring. Dept. Def., 1989—; sr. vis. scientist Norwegian Coun. for Sci. and Indsl. Rsch., Trondheim, 1994. Fellow Office Naval Rsch., 1988-91; sr. faculty rsch. fellow USN, 1993. Mem. ASCE (publ. com. 1993—), ASME, Soc. Naval Architecture and Marine Engrs., Internation Soc. Offshore and Polar Engrs. (charter, conf. tech. program com. 1992—). Achievements include research in nonlinear stochastic dynamics and chaos of ocean systems, in nonlinear response of structures to earthquakes. Office: Oreg State U Apperson Hall 202 Corvallis OR 97331

YIN, BEATRICE WEI-TZE, medical researcher; b. Taipei, Taiwan, Mar. 9, 1959; came to U.S., 1970; d. Chuan Keun and Ming Hsien (Huang) Y. BS, CUNY, Flushing, 1982, MS, 1988. Rsch. asst. Meml. Sloan-Kettering Cancer Ctr., N.Y.C., 1982—. Inventor Monoclonal antibodies to human gastrointestinal cancers, 1992. Avocations: readings, travel, gardening. Office: Meml Sloan Kettering Cancer Ctr 1275 York Ave New York NY 10021-6007

YIN, FANG-FANG, medical physicist, educator; b. Ningbo, Zhejiang, China, Sept. 14, 1958; came to U.S., 1985; s. Shisheng Yin and Xiaoxian Ma; m. Li Sun, Feb. 14, 1986; children: Moli Yin, Lucy Yin. BS, Zhejiang U., 1982; MS, Bowling Green (Ohio) State U., 1987; PhD, U. Chgo., 1992. Lectr. Industry U. of East China, Shanghai, 1982-85; grad. asst. Bowling Green State U., 1985-87; rsch. asst. U. Chgo., 1987-88, researcher, 1989-91; asst./med. physicist U. Rochester, N.Y., 1992-93; sr. instr./med. physicist U. Rochester, 1994—, asst. prof./med. physicist, 1994—; chief Oncologic Imaging Rsch. Lab., Rochester, 1994—. Contbr. articles to profl. jours.; patentee for automated method and system for the detection and classification of abnormal lesions and parenchymal distortions in med. images. Recipient Overman Summer fellowship Bowling Green State U., 1986; rsch. grantee Am. Cancer Soc., 1994, The Whitaker Found., 1995-98. Mem. Am. Assn. Physicists in Medicine. Avocations: tennis, ping pong. Office: Univ Rochester 601 Elmwood Ave # 647 Rochester NY 14642-0001

YIN, GERALD ZHEYAO, technology and engineering executive; b. Beijing, Jan. 29, 1944; came to U.S., 1980; s. Huaixing and Halumi Yin; m. Junling June Yen; 1 child, John Chengjian. BS in Chem. Physics, U. Sci. & Tech. China, Beijing, 1967; postgrad., Beijing U., 1978-80; PhD in Chemistry, UCLA, 1984. Process engr. Lanzhou Oil Refinery, Lanzhou, People's Republic of China, 1968-73; mgr. research staff Chinese Acad. Sciences, Lanzhou, 1973-78; sr. process engr. Intel Corp. Santa Clara TD, Santa Clara, Calif., 1984-86; mgr., staff engr. Lam Rsch. Corp., Rsch. & Devel., Fremont, Calif., 1986-91; mng. dir. Applied Materials, Inc., Santa Clara, Calif., 1991; chief tech. officer Etch Bus. Group. Author: Introducing Orthogonal Design to Semiconductor Industry, 1985; inventor Rainbow oxide etcher, 200mm enhanced Electron Cyclotron Resonance reactor, High Density plasma source for Dielectric Etch and Decoupled Plasma Source and reactors for Conductor Etches. Recipient Nat. Acad. award People's Republic of China, 1979, Nat. Acad. Invention award, People's Republic of China, 1980. Mem. Electrochem. Soc., Am. Chem. Soc., Am. Vacuum Soc., Silicon Valley Chinese Engring. Assn. (founder, first pres.). Achievements include 10 U.S., Japanese and German patents, 16 patent applications pending. Office: Allied Materials Inc 3320 Scott Blvd M/S 1114 Santa Clara CA 95054

YIN, SHIH-JIUN, biochemist; b. Hsuchow, China, Nov. 27, 1946; arrived in Taiwan, 1949; s. Shau-Chian and Hwei-Shan (Wu) Y.; m. Yung-Mei Chen, June 21, 1969; children: Ho-An, Chih-An. BS in Botany, Nat. Chung-Hsing U., Taichung, Taiwan; MS in Biochemistry, Nat. Def. Med. Ctr., Taipei, 1974; PhD in Biochemistry, Ind. U., 1984. Teaching asst. Nat. Chung-Hsing U., Taichung, 1970-72; asst. researcher Tri-Svc. Gen. Hosp., Taipei, 1974-78; from instr. to assoc. prof. Nat. Def. Med. Ctr., Taipei, 1978-88, prof., biochemistry dept., 1989—, biochemistry dept. head, 1990—; chief biochemistry rsch. lab. Tri-Svc. Gen. Hosp., Taipei, 1984—; vis. scientist Karolinska Inst., Stockholm, 1989; vis. prof. Ind. U. Sch. Medicine, Indpls., 1992; speaker in field. Contbr. articles to profl. jours. Lt. Taiwan Air Force, 1969-70. Recipient Excellent Rsch. award Nat. Sci. Coun., 1990-91. Mem. AAAS, Chinese Biochem. Soc. (editl. bd. 1992—), Rsch. Soc. on Alcoholism, Internat. Soc. for Biomed. Rsch. on Alcoholism, European Soc. for Biomed. Rsch. on Alcoholism. Nationalist Party. Avocations: reading, music, hiking, overseas travel. Home: Ln 24 Alley 5 # 75 2F, Ting-Chow Rd 3d Sect, Taipei 100, Taiwan Office: Nat Def Med Ctr Dept Biochem, PO Box 90048, Taipei 100, Taiwan

YIP, CECIL CHEUNG-CHING, biochemist, educator; b. Hong Kong, June 11, 1937; emigrated to Can., 1955; m. Yvette Fung, Oct. 15, 1960; children: Christopher, Adrian. B.Sc., McMaster U., Can., 1959; Ph.D., Rockefeller U., 1963. Research assoc. Rockefeller U., N.Y.C., 1963-64; asst. prof. U. Toronto, Ont., Can., 1964-68, assoc. prof., 1968-74, prof., 1974—, Charles H. Best prof. of med. rsch., 1987-93; chair Banting and Best dept. med. rsch. U. Toronto, Ont., 1990-95; vice-dean rsch. U. Toronto, 1992—. Contbr. sci. articles to publs. Recipient Charles H. Best prize Can. Hoechst Diabetes Workshop, 1972. Mem. AAAS, Am. Soc. Biol. Chemists, Can. Biochem. Soc. Home: 125 Melrose Ave, Toronto, ON Canada M5M 1Y8 Office: Banting and Best Dept Med Rsch, 112 College St, Toronto, ON Canada M5G 1L6

YOAKAM, DWIGHT, country western musician; b. Pikeville, Ky., 1956. Albums include Guitars, Cadillacs, Etc. Etc., 1985, Hillbilly Deluxe, 1987, Buenas Noches From A Lonely Room, 1988, Just Lookin' for a Hit, 1989, If There Was a Way, 1990, This Time, 1993 (2 Grammy nominations); duet with Buck Owens Streets of Bakersfield, 1988 (#1 single); co-prodr. stage appearance Southern Rapture, 1993. Named Top Male Vocalist by Acad. Country Music, 1986.

YOCAM, DELBERT WAYNE, diversified technology company executive; b. Long Beach, Calif., Dec. 24, 1943; s. Royal Delbert and Mary Rose (Gross) Y.; m. Janet McVeigh, June 13, 1965; children—Eric Wayne, Christian Jeremy, Elizabeth Janelle. B.A. in Bus. Adminstrn., Calif. State U.-Fullerton, 1966; M.B.A., Calif. State U., Long Beach, 1971. Mktg.-supply changeover coordinator Automotive Assembly div. Ford Motor Co., Dearborn, Mich., 1966-72; prodn. control mgr. Control Data Corp., Hawthorne, Calif., 1972-74; prodn. and material control mgr. Bourns Inc., Riverside, Calif., 1974-76; corp. material mgr. Computer Automation Inc., Irvine, Calif., 1976-78; prodn. planning mgr. central staff Cannon Electric div. ITT, World hdqrs., Santa Ana, Calif., 1978-79; exec. v.p., COO Apple Computer, Inc., Cupertino, Calif., 1979-91; pres., COO, dir. Textronix Inc., Wilsonville, Oreg., 1992-95; Mem. faculty Cypress Coll., Calif., 1972-79; bd. dirs. Adobe Sys Inc., Mountain View, Calif., 1991—, Oracle Corp., Redwood Shores, Calif., 1992—, Integrates Measurement Sys., Beaverton, Oreg., 1995—, Castelle, Inc., Santa Clara, Calif., 1995—, Sapiens Internat. Corp., 1995—; vice chmn. Tech. Ctr. Innovation, San Jose, Calif., 1989-90. Mem. Am. Electronics Assn. (nat. bd. dirs. 1988-89), Control Data Corp. Mgmt. Assn. (co-founder 1974), L.A. County Heart Assn. (active 1966).

YOCHELSON, BONNIE ELLEN, museum curator, art historian; b. Buffalo, Nov. 6, 1952; d. Samuel and Kathryn (Mersey) Y.; m. Paul Lewis Shechtman, Sept. 3, 1972; children: Emily, Anna. BA in History, Swarthmore Coll., 1974; MA, NYU, 1979, PhD, 1985. Asst. curator dept. prints and drawings Nat. Gallery Art, Washington, 1979-81; lectr. dept. art history U. Pa.q, Phila., 1985-87; curator prints and photographs Mus. of the City of N.Y., 1987-91, cons. curator, 1991—; faculty M of Photography program Sch. Visual Arts, N.Y.C., 1988—; adj. assoc. prof. dept. art history NYU, 1987. Mem. Coll. Art Assn.

YOCHELSON, ELLIS L(EON), paleontologist; b. Washington, Nov. 14, 1928; s. Morris Wolf and Fannie (Botkin) Y.; m. Sally Witt, June 10, 1950; children: Jeffrey, Abby, Charles. BS, U. Kans., 1949, MS, 1950; PhD, Columbia U., 1955. Paleontologist U.S. Geol. Survey, 1952-85, scientist emeritus, 1991; biostratigrapher, specializing in Paleozoic gastropods and minor classes of extinct mollusks; lectr. night sch. George Washington U., 1962-65; rsch. assoc. dept. paleobiology Smithsonian Instn., Washington, 1965—; lectr. Univ. Coll., U. Md., 1966-74; rsch. assoc. Smithsonian Instn., 1967—; lectr. U. Del., 1981; vis. prof. U. Md., 1986-87; organizer N.Am. Paleontol. Conv., 1969, editor proc., 1970-71; Co-editor: Essays in Paleontology and Stratigraphy, 1967; editor: Scientific Ideas of G.K. Gilbert, 1980; editorial bd. Nat. Geog. Rsch. and Exploration; contbr. numerous articles to profl. jours. Co-editor: Essays in Paleontology and Stratigraphy, 1967; editor: Scientific Ideas of G.K. Gilbert, 1980; contbr. numerous articles to profl. jours. Fellow AAAS (chmn. sect. E 1971); mem. Soc. Systematic Zoology (sec. 1961-66, councilor 1973), Internat. Paleontol. Assn. (treas. 1972-76), Paleontol. Soc. (pres. 1976), History of Earth Scis. Soc. (sec.-treas. 1982-85, sec. 1986-87, pres. 1989), N.Am. Paleontol. Conv. (sec.), Sigma Xi. Office: Smithsonian Instn E-305A Mus Natural History Washington DC 20560

YOCHUM, PHILIP THEODORE, retired motel and cafeteria chain executive; b. Quakertown, Pa., Sept. 20, 1924; s. Theodore J. and Margaret (Scheetz) Y.; m. Connie Petrillose, June 23, 1947; children: Cynthia, Philip Theodore. B.S. in Hotel Adminstrn., Cornell U., 1948. Engaged in hotel and restaurant work Quakertown, Pa.; engaged in hotel and restaurant work Ithaca, N.Y., 1948-51; various positions to regional mgr. Slater System, Inc., Balt., 1951-57; asst. v.p. ops. A.L. Mathias Co., Towson, Md., 1957-59; v.p. A.L. Mathias Co., 1959-61, exec. v.p., 1961-65; exec. v.p. (merger A.L. Mathias Co. and Servomation Corp. 1964); pres. Servomation Mathias, Inc. (merger into Servomation Corp., 1974), 1965-74, regional mgr. for food service mgmt. and vending, 1974-76; also dir.; dir. corp. devel. S & S Enterprises (operating Golden Plough Restaurants in Md. and N.J.), 1977-80; dist. mgr. Canteen Corp., Landover, Md., 1980-81; v.p., gen. mgr. Davis Bros., Inc., Hdqrs. Atlanta, 1981-91. Trustee Food Service Execs. Assn. Edn. Trust Fund. Served with AUS, World War II, ETO. Decorated Purple Heart. Mem. Internat. Food Service Execs. Assn. (Food Exec. of Year award Balt. br. 1972, 1990, city chmn. So. region, sec., publicity chmn. Atlanta br.), Food Service and Lodging Inst. (dir.), Cornell Soc. Hotelmen, Ga. Hospitality and Travel Assn., Nat. Restaurant Assn. Home: 158 77th St Avalon NJ 08202-1019

YOCK, ROBERT JOHN, federal judge; b. St. James, Minn., Jan. 11, 1938; s. William Julius and Erma Idella (Fritz) Y.; m. Carla Marie Moen, June 13, 1964; children: Signe Kara, Torunn Ingrid. B.A., St. Olaf Coll., 1959; J.D., U. Mich., 1962; postgrad., U. Strasbourg, France, 1961, Old Dominion Coll., 1964-65, U. Minn., 1966-67. Bar: Minn. 1962, U.S. Supreme Ct. 1965, D.C. 1972. Asso. Thomas, King, Swenson & Collatz, St. Paul, 1966-69; chief counsel Nat. Archives, Office Gen Counsel, GSA, Washington, 1969-70, exec. asst. to adminstr., 1970-72; asst. gen. counsel GSA, 1972-77; trial judge U.S. Ct. Claims, Washington, 1977-82; judge U.S. Claims Ct., Washington, 1982-92, U.S. Ct. Fed. Claims, Washington, 1992—. Served with JAGC USN, 1962-66. Mem. ABA, Minn., Fed., D.C. Bar Assns. Home: 4200 Webster Ct Annandale VA 22003-3424 Office: US Ct Fed Claims 717 Madison Pl NW Washington DC 20005-1011*

YOCKIM, JAMES CRAIG, state senator, oil and gas executive; b. Williston, N.D., Feb. 13, 1953; s. Daniel and Doris (Erickson) Y.; m. Donna Jean Erickson, Apr. 21, 1985; children: Jenna, Ericka. BSW, Pacific Luth. U., 1975; MSW, San Diego State U., 1979. Caseworker Dyslin Boys Ranch, Tacoma, 1975-77; landman Fayette Oil & Gas, Williston, 1980-82; head caseworker, program dir. Pyslin Boys Ranch, 1979-80; owner Hy-Plains Energy, Williston, 1982-87; city fin. commr. City of Williston, 1984-88; therapist Luth. Social Svcs., Williston, 1983-95; senator N.C. State Senate, 1986—; owner James C. Yockim Resources, Williston, 1987—. Dir. Bethel Luth. Found., 1993—; del. N.D. Dem. Conv., 1984, 86, 88, 90, 92, 94, 96; dist. chmn. Dem. Party, Williston, 1988; caucus chmn. Dem. Caucus N.D. State Senate. Recipient Ruth Meiers award N.D. Mental Health Assn., 1989, Legislator of Yr. award N.D. Children's Caucus, 1989; named Outstanding Young North Dakotan N.D. Jaycees, 1988. Mem. NASW. Avocations: racquetball, softball, golf. Home: 1123 2nd Ave E Williston ND 58801 Office: 322 Main Ste 202 PO Box 2344 Williston ND 58802-2344

YOCUM, CHARLES FREDRICK, biology educator; b. Storm Lake, Iowa, Oct. 31, 1941; s. Vincent Cary and Olive Lucille (Cammack) Y.; m. Patricia Joan Bury, Jan. 1, 1981; 1 son, Erik Charles. BS, Iowa State U., 1963; MS, Ill. Inst. Tech., 1968; PhD, Ind. U., 1971. Research biochemist Ill. Inst. Tech. Research Inst., Chgo., 1963-68; grad. fellow Ind. U., Bloomington, 1968-71; postdoctoral fellow Cornell U., Ithaca, N.Y., 1971-73; asst. prof. U. Mich., Ann Arbor, 1973-77, assoc. prof., 1978-82, prof. biol. scis. and chemistry, 1983—, chmn. dept. biology, 1985-91; vis. prof. Mich. State U., East Lansing, 1980-81; cons. NSF, Washington, 1982—. Editorial bd. Plant Physiology, Photosynthesis Research, Biochimica et Biophysica Acta.; contbr. articles to various publs. Fulbright fellow, 1996; rsch. grantee NSF, 1978—, USDA, 1978—; recipient Henry Russel award U. Mich., 1977. Mem. AAAS, Am. Chem. Soc., Am. Soc. Plant Physiologists, Am. Soc. Biol. Chemists, Am. Soc. Photobiology. Avocations: classical music, travel. Office: Dept Biology Univ of Mich Ann Arbor MI 48109-1048

YOCUM, HARRISON GERALD, horticulturist, botanist, educator, researcher; b. Bethlehem, Pa., Apr. 2, 1923; s. Harrison and Bertha May (Meckes) Y. BS, Pa. State U., 1955; MS, Rutgers U., 1961. Horticulture instr. U. Tenn., Martin, 1957-59; biology tchr., libr. asst. high schs., El Paso, Tex., 1959-60; rsch. asst. geochronology lab. U. Ariz., Tucson, 1960-67, rsch. asst. environ. rsch. lab., 1969-76; landscaping supt. Tucson Airport Authority, 1976-82; instr. Pima C.C., Tucson, 1976—. Contbr. articles to profl. jours. Founder Tucson Bot. Gardens, 1964. Mem. Am. Hort. Soc., Men's Garden Club Tucson (pres. 1991), Tucson Cactus & Succulent Soc. (pres. 1991, 92), Internat. Palm Soc. (charter), El Paso Cactus and Rock Club, Tucson Gem & Mineral Soc., Old Pueblo Lapidary Club, Deming Mineral Soc., Nat. Geog. Soc., Ariz.-Sonora Desert Mus., Huachuca Vigilantes, Penn State Alumni Assn., Pa. Club Tucson, Fraternal Order Police Assocs., N.Am. Hunting Club (life), Shriners, Masons, Scottish Rite. Lutheran. Home: 1628 N Jefferson Ave Tucson AZ 85712-4204

YODER, AMOS, university research official; b. Falls City, Nebr., Mar. 2, 1921; s. Amos Howard and Mildred Ann (Johnson) Y.; m. Janet Lee Tatman, June 15, 1946; children: James Amos, Barbara Ann Yoder Gorga, Sally Irene Yoder Ramseyer. BA, Ohio Wesleyan U., 1942; PhD, U. Chgo., 1949. Jr. econs. editor Bd. of Econ. Warfare, Washington, 1942-43; fgn. svc. officer Dept. of State, Washington, 1949-74; Borah Disting. prof. polit. sci. U. Idaho, Moscow, 1974-91; Fulbright prof. Lajos Kossuth U., Debrecen,

Hungary, 1991; rsch. assoc. Mershon Ctr., Ohio State U., Columbus, 1993—; vis. lectr. U. Calif., Davis, 1964-65; Fulbright prof. Fgn. Affairs Coll., Beijing, 1986-87. Author: International Politics and Policymakers Ideas, 1982, The Conduct of American Foreign Policy Since World War II, 1986, World Politics and the Causes of War Since 1914, 1986, The Evolution of the United Nations, 1989, rev. edit., 1993, Communist Systems and Challenges, 1990, Communism in Transition, 1993; guest editor Terrorism-An Internat. Jour., summer 1983; contbr. articles to profl. jours. With USAF, 1943-46. Recipient Commendation ribbon War Dept., 1946, Merit Honor award Dept. State, 1967. Mem. Internat. Studies Assn., Idaho Polit. Sci. Assn. (v.p., pres. 1980-81), Amnesty Internat., Kiwanis (pres. Moscow, Idaho chpt. 1981-82). Democrat. Presbyterian. Home: 127 S Hempstead Rd Westerville OH 43081-2514 Office: Ohio State U Mershon Ctr 1501 Neil Ave Columbus OH 43201-2602 *Whatever success and satisfaction I have attained in my life have been based on playing the games with principles and persistence.*

YODER, ANNA MARY, reading educator; b. Iowa County, Iowa, Nov. 14, 1933; d. Kores M. and Sadie Rebecca (King) Y. BS in Elem. Edn., Ea. Mennonite U., 1959; MA in Linguistics, Hartford Sem. Found., 1968; MA in Curriculum and Instruction, U. Tenn., 1975; postgrad., U. Iowa, 1975-81. Tchr. Am. Sch., Tegulcigalpa, Honduras, 1969-70, Escuela Internat. Sch., San Pedro Sula, Honduras, 1970-75; tchr. bilingual Muscatine (Iowa) Cmty. Schs., 1977-78, tchr., supr. title I, 1978-79; tchr. Escuela Internat. Sch., 1979-80; tchr. home room Muscatine Cmty. Schs., 1980-87, reading tchr., 1987—; nat. dir. adult educators Alfalit Spanish wun of Lit, Honduras, 1963-69. Author/editor: Pre-Cartilla de Alfalit, 1968. Mem. Sisters Cities, Muscatine, 1994, bd. dirs., 1995—. Mem. NEA, Assn. Childhood Edn. Internat., Internat. Reading Assn. Avocations: cats, reading, quilts, volunteer activities. Office: Jefferson Sch 1000 Mulberry Muscatine IA 52761

YODER, BRUCE ALAN, chemist; b. Seward, Nebr., Apr. 29, 1962; s. Elwood John and Elda Raye (Stutzman) Y. BS in Chemistry, Wayne State Coll., 1983. Lab. technician Wayne (Nebr.) State Coll., 1982-83; lab. technician Harris Labs., Lincoln, Nebr., 1984, chemist, 1984; scientist Dorsey Labs., Lincoln, 1984-86, scientist A, 1986-88; product stability analyst Sandoz Pharms., Lincoln, 1988-89, Sandoz Rsch. Inst., Lincoln, 1989-91; mgr. lab. computer ops. Sandoz Pharms., Lincoln, 1991—. Mem. Lancaster County Young Reps., Lincoln, 1988—, co-chmn., 1990-91, pres., 1991-93; mem. Nebr. Fedn. Young Reps., 1988—, mem. exec. com., 1990—; mem. exec. com. Lancaster County Rep. Party, 1990—; mem. Def. Adv. Com. Lancaster County, 1992—; mem. Lincoln Mayor's Cmty. Cabinet, 1992-93; mem. Lincoln City Charter Revision Commn., 1994—; trustee Wayne State Coll. Found., 1991—; advisor Jr. Achievement, 1993—. Recipient Dwight M. Frost, MD award for Overcoming a Phys. Disability Immanuel Rehab. Ctr., 1993, Verdi Smith award for outstanding voluntary contbns. to Lancaster County Rep. Party, 1995-96. Mem. Am. Inst. Chemists, Am. Chem. Soc., Jaycees. Mennonite. Achievements include design of a sample holder for solid dosage forms when using a hunter color instrument, design of a new computer system for Sandoz Pharmaceuticals laboratory computer operations. Home: 2240 Winding Way Lincoln NE 68506-2846 Office: Sandoz Pharms 10401 Highway 6 Lincoln NE 68517-9704

YODER, DAVID E., medical educator, speech-language pathologist; b. Shipshewana, Ind., July 16, 1932; m. Dee Yoder; children:, Lisa, Eric. BA in Speech Comm., Goshen Coll., 1954; MA in Speech Pathology, Northwestern U., 1955; PhD in Speech Pathology and Audiology, U. Kans., 1965. Asst. prof. Colo. State U., Ft. Collins, 1965-68; asst. prof. U. Wis., Madison, 1968-71, assoc. prof., 1971-73, chair dept. comm. disorders, 1973-78, prof., 1973-86; prof. speech and hearing scis. U. N.C., Chapel Hill, 1986—, clin. prof., Sch. Edn., 1986-95, dir. Ctr. Literacy & Disability Studies, 1989-92, assoc. dir. policy studies, 1993—. Co-author: Contemporary Issues in Language Intervention, 1983, Decision Making in Speech-Language Pathology, 1988; co-editor: Language Intervention with the Retarded: Developing Strategies, 1972, Handbook of Speech-Language-Pathology and Audiology, 1988; contbr. numerous articles to profl. jours., chpts. to books; presenter in field of child language disorders, psycholinguistics, autmentative and alternative communication, literacy development, and multicultural awareness; editl. cons. DCCD Pub. of Coun. for Exceptional Children, 1972-74; editl. bd. Topics in Lang. Disorders, 1980-95, Clinics in Communication Disorders, 1991-94; editl. cons. Jour. Speech and Hearing Devel., 1965-72; editor Colo. Speech and Hearing Assn. Jour., 1967-68; editl. cons. Am. Jour. Mental Deficiency, 1972-75; editor Jour. Augmentative and Alternative Communication, 1984-86; contbg. editor Communication Outlook, 1980—. Am. Assn. on Mental Deficiency fellow, 1976; Walker-Bascom prof. in communicative disorders, 1980-86; recipient honors of Wis. Speech-Lang.-Hearing Assn., 1986, Culture for Svc. award Goshen Coll. Outstanding Alumnus, 1992. Fellow Am. Speech and Hearing Assn. (extensive com. work, conv. activity; v.p. for clin. affairs 1979-81, exec. bd. 1983-85, pres. 1984, Honor award 1995), Am. Assn. Mental Retardation (v.p. speech pathology-audiology divsn. 1972-75, v.p. exec.com. 1972-75, extensive com. work and conv. activity), Internat. Soc. Augmentative and Alternative Comms. (bd. dirs. 1982-86, 92-95, extensive conf. work); mem. Internat. Assn. Logopedics and Phoniatrics (chmn. com. augmentative and alternative comm. 1984-90), U.S. Soc. for Augmentative and Alternative Comm. (co-founder, first pres. 1989, exec. bd. 1989-91, bd. dirs. 1990—), N.C. Speech-Hearing-Lang. Assn. (extensive com., conf. and conv. activity), N.C. Augmentative Comm. Assn. (planning com. 1990-93). Office: Univ NC Dept Med Allied Health Prof Speech and Hearing Scis Chapel Hill NC 27599-7120

YODER, EDGAR PAUL, education educator; b. Millersburg, Ohio, June 20, 1946; s. Albert Daniel Yoder and Ella Marie (Bontrager) Erb; m. Deborah Jean Barnhart, June 12, 1971; children: Scott, Suzan. BSA, Ohio State U., 1968, MS, 1972, PhD, 1976. Cert. tchr., counselor, prin., Ohio, Va. Tchr. agr. and sci. Conotton Valley Schs., Bowerston, Ohio, 1968-69, East Holmes Schs., Berlin, Ohio, 1969-72; curriculum specialist Ohio State U., Columbus, 1972-74, project dir., 1974-76; asst. prin. Montgomery County Schs., Blacksburg, Va., 1976-77; asst. prof. Va. Poly. Inst. and State U., Blacksburg, 1977-78; asst. prof. Pa. State U., University Park, 1978-84, assoc. prof. tchr. edn., 1984-94, prof., 1994—, interim dept. head, 1995—; cons. Poland Ministry Edn., Warsaw, 1994, Swaziland Ministry Agr., Mbane, 1985, 87, U. Peredenyia, Kandy, Sri Lanka, 1984. Author text: Ag Supplies and Services, 1974, (with others) Undergraduate Education in Agriculture, 1989, also chpt. to book. Chmn. community svc. Sertoma Internat., Columbus, 1975; asst. dir. Va. HSA Assn., Blacksburg, 1978; sect. chmn. Am. Heart Assn., State College, Va., 1981; pres. Ferguson Twp. PTO, State College, 1983-84; bd. dirs. RAFT Drug Rehab. Ctr., Radford, 1976-78, Nat. Future Farmers Am., Alexandria, Va., 1981-83. Recipient Hon. Degree, Nat. Future Farmers Am., 1983. Mem. Nat. Assn. Coll. Tchrs. Agr. (teacher fellow 1987, Regional Outstanding Teaching award 1992), Am. Assn. Agr. Educators (legis. chmn. 1985), Am. Assn. Ednl. Rsch., Am. Vocat. Edn. Rsch. Assn., Assn. Internat. Agr. and Extension Edn., Phi Delta Kappa, Gamma Sigma Delta (Teaching award of Merit 1987). Avocations: collecting sports memorabilia, restoring antiques, classic cars. Office: Penn State U Coll Agricultural Scis University Park PA 16802

YODER, EDWIN MILTON, JR., columnist, educator, editor, writer; b. Greensboro, N.C., July 18, 1934; s. Edwin M. and Mytrice M. (Logue) Y.; m. Mary Jane Warwick, Nov. 1, 1958; children: Anne Daphne, Edwin Warwick. B.A., U. N.C., 1956; BA, MA (Rhodes scholar), Oxford (Eng.) U., 1958; D.H.L. (hon.), Grinnell Coll., 1980, Elon Coll., 1986; DLitt (hon.), U. N.C., 1993. Editorial writer Charlotte (N.C.) News, 1958-61; editorial writer Greensboro Daily News, 1961-64, assoc. editor, 1965-75; asst. prof. history U. N.C., Greensboro, 1964-65; editorial page editor Washington Star, 1975-81; syndicated columnist Washington Post Writers Group, 1982—; prof. journalism and humanities Washington and Lee U., 1992—. Author: Night of the Old South Ball, 1984, The Unmaking of a Whig, 1990, Joe Alsop's Cold War, 1995; contbr. articles to periodicals. Recipient awards editorial writing N.C. Press Assn., 1958, 61, 66, Walker Stone award Scripps-Howard Found., 1978, Pulitzer prize editorial writing, 1979; Disting. Alumnus award U. N.C., Chapel Hill, 1980. Mem. Nat. Conf. Editorial Writers, Am. Soc. Newspaper Editors. Democrat. Episcopalian. Home: 4001 Harris Pl Alexandria VA 22304-1720

YODER, FREDERICK FLOYD, fraternity executive; b. Wilkinsburg, Pa., Oct. 7, 1935; s. Floyd Elvin and Mary Viola (Stahl) Y. B.S. in Journalism, Ohio U., 1957. Mem. hdqrs. staff Sigma Chi, Evanston, Ill., 1957—, coordinator chpt. visitation and installations program, 1964-72, leadership tng. adminstr., 1962-76, editor mag., 1972-91, dir. comm., 1991-93, dir. alumni participation and cmty. svc., 1994—. Editor The Norman Shield, 1973-91, Sigma Chi Membership Directory, 1977, 87; contbr. articles to interfrat. jours. Served with AUS, 1958. Mem. Coll. Frat. Editors Assn. (past pres., Varner Outstanding Frat. Communicator award, Ford Outstanding Svc. award), Chgo. Headline Club, Soc. Profl. Journalists, Omicron Delta Kappa. Home: 2603 Sheridan Rd Evanston IL 60201-1752 Office: 1714 Hinman Ave Evanston IL 60201-4517

YODER, HATTEN SCHUYLER, JR., petrologist; b. Cleve., Mar. 20, 1921; s. Hatten Schuyler and Elizabeth Katherine (Knieling) Y.; m. Elizabeth Marie Bruffey, Aug. 1, 1959; children: Hatten Schuyler III, Karen Marianne. AA, U. Chgo., 1940, SB, 1941; student, U. Minn., summer 1941; PhD, Mass. Inst. Tech., 1948; D honoris causa, U. Paris VI, 1981; DEngring. (hon.), Colo. Sch. of Mines, 1995. Petrologist Geophys. Lab., Carnegie Instn., Washington, 1948-71, dir., 1971-86, dir. emeritus, 1986—; cons. Los Alamos (N.Mex.) Nat. Lab., 1972—. Author: Generation of Basaltic Magma, 1976; editor: The Evolution of the Igneous Rocks: Fiftieth Anniversary Perspectives, 1979; co-editor Jour. of Petrology, 1959-69; assoc. editor Am. Jour. Sci, 1972-90; contbr. articles to sci. jours. Served to lt. comdr. USNR, 1942-58. Naval Expedition to Siberia, 1945-46. Recipient Bicentennial medal Columbia U., 1954, A.G. Werner medal German Mineral Soc., 1972; named to Disting. Alumni Hall of Fame, Lakewood (Ohio) H.S., 1990; mineral yoderite named in his honor. Fellow Geol. Soc. Am. (coun. 1966-68, A.L. Day medal 1962), Geol. Soc. London (hon. Wallaston medal 1979, Hallimond lectr. 1979), Geol. Soc. South Africa (du Toit lectr. 1987), Am. Acad. Arts and Scis., Mineral. Soc. Am. (coun. 1962-64, 69-73, pes. 1971-72, MSA award 1954, Roebling medal 1992), Am. Geophys. Union (pres. volcanology, geochemistry and petrology sect. 1962-64); mem. NAS (chmn. geology sect. 1973-76, A.L. Day prize and lectr. 1972), Mineral Soc. London (hon.), Geol. Soc. Finland, Russian Mineral Soc. (hon.), Geochem. Soc. (organizer, founding mem., coun. 1956-58), Am. Chem. Soc., Mineral Assn. Can., Washington Acad. Sci., Geol. Soc. Washington, Chem. Soc. Washington, French Soc. Mineralogy and Crystallography (hon.), Am. Philos. Soc. (coun. 1983-85, 94—), Pub. Mems. Assn. of Fgn. Svc. (bd. dirs. 1993-95, v.p. 1994), History of Earth Scis. Soc. (pres. 1995—), SAR, Sigma Xi, Phi Delta Theta (Golden Legion award). Home: 6709 Melody Ln Bethesda MD 20817-3152 Office: Geophys Lab 5251 Broad Branch Rd NW Washington DC 20015-1305

YODER, JOHN CHRISTIAN, state senator, lawyer, insurance company executive; b. Newton, Kans., Jan. 9, 1951; s. Gideon G. and Stella (Hostetler) Y.; m. T. Irene Sanders, Apr. 23, 1984 (div. Nov. 1991). BA, Chapman Coll., Orange, Calif., 1972; JD, U. Kans., 1975; MBA, U. Chgo., 1976. Bar: Kans. 1975, Ind. 1976, D.C. 1985, W.Va. 1991. Assoc. prof. bus. Goshen (Ind.) Coll., 1975-76; chmn. bd. Stone Mill Bakeries, Inc., 1977-81; dist. ct. judge 9th jud. dist. State of Kans., Newton, 1977-80; chmn. bd., v.p., dir. Jay Energy Devel. Co., 1978-81; jud. fellow U.S. Supreme Ct., Washington, 1980-81, spl. asst. to chief justice of the U.S., 1981-83; dir. Asset Forfeiture Office, U.S. Dept. Justice, Washington, 1983-84; pvt. practice, Harpers Ferry, W.Va., 1984—; mem. W.Va. Senate, Charleston, 1993—, minority whip, 1993-94; exec. v.p., dir. Patriot Life Inst. Co., Tampa, Fla., 1985; bd. dirs. Knderhook Oil and Gas Inc., Waukee, Iowa. Rep. nominee for U.S. Senate, 1990, for W.Va. Supreme Ct., 1996. Mem. FBA, W.Va. Bar, D.C. Bar, Ind. Bar Assn., Kans. Bar Assn., U.S. C. of C. (coun. on trends and perspectives 1982-90). Mennonite. Avocations: hiking, bicycling. Home: RR 3 Box 109 Harpers Ferry WV 25425-9728 Office: WVa Senate 1900 Kanawha Blvd E Charleston WV 25305-0002

YODER, LAUREN WAYNE, foreign language educator; b. Newport News, Va., Mar. 9, 1943; s. Lauren Aquilla and Nina Viola (Stemen) Y.; m. Rita Suzanne Frey, June 27, 1964; children—Reinald, Jocelyn. B.A., Eastern Mennonite Coll., 1964; M.A., U. Iowa, 1969, Ph.D., 1973. Tchr. Ecole Secondaire Pedagogique, Kikwit, Zaire, 1966-68; prof. French, dir. Ctr. for Spl. Studies Davidson Coll. Fulbright lectr. U.S. Info. Agy., Paris, 1971-72, Libreville, Gabon, 1980-81; participant NEH summer seminar, Miami, Fla., 1979, Lawrence, Kans., 1991, NEH Inst. Binghamton, N.Y., 1993, country dir. Burundi for Mennonite Ctrl. Com., 1995—. Mem. SAMLA, African Lit. Assn., Caribbean Studies Assn., Assn. Caribbean Studies. Democrat. Mennonite. Avocations: bee-keeping, skiing, gardening, volleyball. Home: PO Box 1604 Davidson NC 28036-1604 Office: Davidson Coll PO Box 1719 Davidson NC 28036-1719

YODER, MARIANNE ELOISE, software developer, consultant; b. Phoenix, Ariz.; d. William Amber and Maryanne King; m. William Ernest Yoder, Dec. 26, 1977. BSN, U. San Francisco, 1972; MS, U. Ariz., 1982, PhD, 1989. RN, Ariz. Nurse U.S. Navy, 1971-80, 91; grad. teaching asst. U. Ariz., Tucson, 1980-82, faculty, 1982-85, grad. rsch. assoc., 1985-90; faculty, dir. coll. health profl. Computer Learning Ctr. No. Ariz. U., Flagstaff, Ariz., 1990-92; software developer Flagstaff, Ariz., 1992—; chair Ariz. state commn. nursing rsch., 1992—; chair of PILOT group, Assn. Devel. of Computer-Based Instructional Systems, Columbus, Ohio, 1990-92. Author: Software Integration Plan Introduction to Nursing Diagnosis, 1992, 2nd edit., 1993, contbg. author: Computer Applications in Nursing Education and Practice, 1993; contbr. articles to profl. jours. Vol. Flagstaff Pub. Libr., 1993—. Recipient Pioneer in Nursing Edn. Informatics award Nurse Educator's Microworld & Fuld, 1994, Meritorious Tchg. Asst. award U. Ariz. Found., 1987. Mem. NLN (exec. bd 1993-97), Ariz. Statewide Coun. on Nursing, Sigma Xi, Sigma Theta Tau (treas. 1970-71), Pi Lambda Theta. Avocations: quilting, skiing, puzzle-making. Home and Office: 1496 W University Heights Dr N Flagstaff AZ 86001-8970

YODER, PATRICIA DOHERTY, public relations executive; b. Pitts., Oct. 30, 1939; d. John Addison and Camella Grace (Conti) Doherty; children: Shari Lynn, Wendy Ann. BA, Duquesne U., 1961. Press sec. U.S. Ho. of Reps., 1965-69; dir. office of pub. info. City of Ft. Wayne, 1973-76; asst. mgr. pub. and corp. communications Mellon Bank N.A., Pitts., 1977-79; v.p. pub. affairs Am. Waterways Operators Inc., Washington, 1980-83; sr. v.p., gen. mgr. 1983-86, exec. v.p., dir. internat. banking, 1989-91, Hill and Knowlton Inc., Pitts.; sr. v.p. corp. and pub. affairs PNC Bank, Pitts., 1987-89; v.p., mgr. corp. pub. rels. and advt. GE Capital, Stamford, Conn., 1991-95; corp. v.p. pub. affairs and comm. GTE Corp., Stamford, 1995—. Trustee Shadyside Hosp., Pressley Ridge Sch., Pitts., Ellis Sch.; bd. dirs. Children's Mus., Civic Light Opera, Pitts. Ballet Theatre, Stamford, (Conn.) Symphony; mem. communications bd. visitors U. Pitts. Recipient Outstanding Woman Bus. & Industry, 1988, Disting. Alumna award Duquesne U., 1996. Mem. Pitts. Field Club, Duquesne Club, Indian Harbor Yacht Club, Century Club of Disting. Duquesne U. Alumni. Roman Catholic. Home: 13 Brownhouse Rd Old Greenwich CT 06870-1502 Office: One Stamford Forum Stamford CT 06904

YODER, RONDA ELAINE, nursing educator; b. Indpls., Oct. 7, 1963; d. Charles Stewart and Sarah Angeline (Pfaff) Bower; m. Robert Paul Yoder, July 22, 1989; children: Robert Andrew, Sarah Elizabeth. BSN, Pensacola Christian Coll., 1985; MSN, Ind. U., Indpls., 1988; DSN, U. Ala., Birmingham, 1994. Emergency staff nurse Westview Hosp., Indpls., 1986-88, West Fla. Regional Med. Ctr., Pensacola, 1988-89; DON Pensacola Christian Coll., 1988-93, mem. nursing faculty, 1993—. Mem. Sigma Theta Tau. Home: 1245 Langley Ave Pensacola FL 32504-8038

YODER, RONNIE A., judge; b. Knoxville, Tenn., July 10, 1937; s. Raymond Abraham and Veryl Hope (Hostetler) Y.; m. Shirley Mae Grimes, June 28, 1961; children: Susan Elizabeth, Mary Amanda, Elizabeth Anne, John Anthony Gerhard. BA in Polit. Sci. with honors, U. Va., 1958, JD, 1961. Bar: Va. 1961, N.Y. 1963, D.C. 1965, U.S. Dist. Ct. D.C. 1965, U.S. Dist. Ct. (so. dist.) N.Y. 1969, U.S. Ct. Claims 1964, U.S. Supreme Ct. 1968. Assoc. Mudge Rose Guthrie & Alexander, N.Y.C. and Washington, 1962-70; of counsel Zuckert Scoutt & Rasenberger, Washington, 1970-72, ptnr., 1972-75; adminstrv. law judge U.S. Dept. Labor, Washington, 1976, CAB, Washington, 1976-84, U.S. Dept. Transp., Washington, 1985—; adminstrv. law judge Nat. Transp. Safety Bd., 1979-80, Maritime Adminstrn., 1983, 86-88, FDIC, 1982-83, SBA, 1983, FAA, 1985—, Fed. Hwy. Adminstrn., 1985—, Fed. R.R. Adminstrn., 1993-95, Rsch. and Spl. Programs Adminstrn., 1991—, Surface Transp. Bd., 1996—. Mem. editorial bd. U. Va. Law Rev., 1959-61; contbr. articles to profl. jours. Sec., co-counsel Capital Headstart, 1966-68; narrator Lincoln Commn., 1985, 86; mem. permanent jud. commn. Nat. Capital Presbytery, 1985-91. Rockefeller fellow, 1961. Mem. ABA (jud. adminstrn. divsn. coun. 1994-95, exec. com. nat. conf. adminstrv. law judges 1980-83, 85-89, 90-96, sec. 1991-92, vice chmn. 1992-93, chmn.-elect 1993-94, chmn. 1994-95, parliamentarian 1991-92, reporter Model Code Jud. Conduct for Fed. Adminstrv. Law Judges 1989, adminstrv. law sect. com. on internat. and comparative adminstrv. law, sect. of sect. officers chmn. task force on participation in profl. assns. by govt. employees 1991-92), FBA, Am. Judicature Soc., Fed. Adminstrv. Law Judges Conf. (exec. com. 1976-81, 85, 87), Nat. Assn. Adminstrv. Law Judges, Va. Bar Assn. (bd. govs. adminstrv. law sect.), Am. Judges Assn., D.C. Bar Assn., SAR, Phi Beta Kappa, Phi Eta Sigma. Home: 1400 Summit Ave Alexandria VA 22302-2735 Office: Dept Transp 400 7th St SW Rm 9228 Washington DC 20590-0001

YODER, SARA ANN, emergency nurse; b. Allensville, Pa., Oct. 24, 1932; d. David E. and Katie E. (Yoder) Y.; m. John R. Yoder, May 11, 1957; children: Edna M., Jennifer R. Diploma, Lewistown Hosp. Sch. Nursing, Pa., 1956. RN, CEN. Oper. rm. nurse Lewistown Hosp., Pa., 1956-58, obstetrics nurse, 1959-65, house supr., 1965-72, nurse emergency dept., 1972—. Mem. Emergency Nurses Assn. (treas. Seven Mountains chpt. 1992-94), Mennonite Health Assn. Republican. Avocations: knitting, reading. Home: 88 Water St Allensville PA 17002

YODER WISE, PATRICIA SNYDER, nurse, educator; b. Wadsworth, Ohio, July 2, 1941; d. Belford Grant and Leona Cora (Mohler) Snyder; m. Robert Thomas Wise, Feb. 17, 1973; children: Doreen Ellen, Deborah Ann. BSN, Ohio State U., 1963; MSN, Wayne State U., 1968; EdD, Tex. Tech U., 1984. Cert. gerontol. nurse and nursing adminstr., RN, Tex., Ohio. Rsch. asst. Wayne State U., Detroit, 1968; ednl. dir. Ohio Nurses' Assn., Columbus, 1968-72; asst. dir. nursing Mt. Clemens (Mich.) Gen. Hosp., 1972-73; assoc. prof., head of nursing Ferris State Coll., Big Rapids, Mich., 1975-77; asst. prof., assoc. prof., dir. continuing edn. U. Colo., Denver, 1977-79; assoc. dean, assoc. prof. Sch. Nursing, Tex. Tech U. Health Scis. Ctr., Lubbock, 1979-86, assoc. dean, prof., 1986-87, interim assoc. dean grad. program, 1986-89, exec. assoc. dean, prof. nursing, 1989-92, interim dean, prof., 1992-93; dean, prof. Sch. Nursing, 1993—; prin. p.t. Wylan Assocs., Lubbock, 1989—; mem. acad. adv. panel on nursing Health and Scis. Network, 1983-92, Nurses Coalition, 1982-92; bd. dirs. RN Polit. Action Com., 1989-93. Editor Jour. Continuing Edn. in Nursing, 1986—. Named Woman of Excellence in Medicine, YWCA, 1996; recipient Am. Jour. Nursing Book of the Yr. award, 1996. Fellow Am. Acad. Nursing; mem. ANA (site visitor continuing edn. 1982-88), Tex. Nurses Assn. (bd. dirs. 1989-93, pres. dist. 18 1987-89, pres. 1995—), Coun. Continuing Edn., Tex. Nurses Found. (pres. 1992-95), Am. Nurses Found. (Tchg. Excellence award), Sigma Theta Tau (grantee). Home: 3713 95th St Lubbock TX 79423-3811

YOE, HARRY WARNER, retired agricultural economist; b. Martinsburg, W. Va., Oct. 20, 1912; s. Horace George and Mary Morrow (Van Metre) Y.; m. Barbara Virginia Fultz, Mar. 22, 1936; children—Harry Warner, Robert Boyd, Paul Michael. B.S., W. Va. U., 1935, grad. study, 1940. Agriculturist U.S. Dept. Agr., Red House Homesteads, W. Va., 1935-38; dir. spl. project U.S. Dept. Agr., Princeton, W.Va., 1938-40; dist. supr. Farm Security Adminstrn. U.S. Dept. Agr., Morgantown, W. Va., 1940-42; econ. cons. Supreme Comdr. Allied Power, Tokyo, Japan, 1947-51; agrl. adminstr. Inter-Am. Affairs, 1951-53; dir. div. Western S.A., ICA, 1953-57; dir. USOM to Haiti, 1957-61, ICA West Indies and Eastern Caribbean Mission, Port-of-Spain, Trinidad, W.I., 1961-62; with AID, Dept. State, Wash., 1962-64; dir. AID mission Georgetown, British Guiana, 1964-68; assoc. mem. firm, dir. econs. and planning div. Miller-Warden-Western, Inc., 1968-69; dir., v.p. Hoskins-Western-Sonderegger, Inc., 1969-82; ret., 1982. Author: Fisheries Cooperatives in Japan, 1950. Served from lt. (j.g.) to comdr. USNR, 1942-46. Recipient commendation for econ. rehab. Yokohama area, Japan U.S. Army, 1946, meritorious award for econ. reforms Japanese Fishing Industry, 1951; spl. commendation ICA, 1953; superior honor award AID, 1967. Mem. Rotary, Alpha Zeta, Pi Kappa Alpha. Episcopalian. Home: RR 3 Martinsburg WV 25401-9803

YOERGER, ROGER RAYMOND, agricultural engineer, educator; b. LeMars, Iowa, Feb. 17, 1929; s. Raymond Herman and Crystal Victoria (Ward) Y.; m. Barbara M. Ellison, Feb. 14, 1953; 1 child, Karen Lynne; m. Laura M. Summitt, Dec. 23, 1971; stepchildren—Daniel L. Summitt, Linda Summitt Canull, Anita Summitt Smith. B.S., Iowa State U., 1949, M.S., 1951, Ph.D., 1957. Registered profl. engr., Ill., Pa., Iowa. Instr., asst. prof. agrl. engring. Iowa State U., 1949-56; assoc. prof. agrl. engring. Pa. State U., 1956-58; prof. agrl. engring. U. Ill., Urbana, 1959-85; head agrl. engring. dept. U. Ill., 1978-85, prof. emeritus agrl. engring., 1985—. Contbr. articles to profl. jours. Patentee in field. Mem. Ill. Noise Task Force, 1974-80. Fellow Am. Soc. Agrl. Engrs. (Massey-Ferguson medalist 1989); mem. Am. Soc. Engring. Edn., Phi Kappa Phi (dir. fellowships, dir. 1971-83, pres. elect 1983-86, pres. 1986-89), Rotary, Moose. Roman Catholic. Home: 107 W Holmes St Urbana IL 61801-6614 Office: 1304 W Pennsylvania Ave Urbana IL 61801-4726

YOGANATHAN, AJIT PRITHIVIRAJ, biomedical engineer, educator; b. Colombo, Sri Lanka, Dec. 6, 1951; came to U.S., 1973; s. Ponniah and Mangay (Navaratnam) Y. BSChemE with honors, Univ. Coll., U. London, 1973; PhDChemE, Calif. Tech. U., 1978. Engring. asst. Shell Oil Refinery, Stanlow, Eng., 1972; teaching asst. Calif. Inst. Tech., 1973-74, 1976, rsch. fellow, 1977-79; asst. prof. Ga. Inst. Tech., 1979-83, assoc. prof., 1983-88, chmn. bioengring. com., 1984-88, prof. chem. engring., 1988—, dir. Bioengring. Ctr., 1989—, prof. mech. engring., 1989—, co-dir. Emory U.-Ga. Tech. Biomed. Tech. Ctr., 1992—, Regents prof., 1994—; adj. assoc. prof. U. Ala., 1985—. Founding fellow Am. Inst. Med. & Biol. Engring., 1992; recipient Edwin Walker prize Brit. Inst. Mech. Engrs., 1988, Humboldt fellowship, 1985, Am. Heart Assn.-Ga. Affiliate Rsch. Investigatorship award, 1980-83, Calif. Inst. Tech. fellowship, 1973-77, Goldsmid Medal and prize Univ. Coll., 1973, 72, Brit. Coun. scholarship, 1971-73. Mem. AICE, ASME, Biomed. Engring. Soc., Am. Soc. Echocardiography (dir. 1987-91). Office: Sch of Chem Engring Ga Tech U Atlanta GA 30332

YOH, HAROLD L., III, company executive; b. L.A., Dec. 22, 1960; s. Harold L. Jr. and Mary Michael (Milus) Y.; m. Sharon Lynn Cructher, Oct. 13, 1984; children: Kristen, Catherine, Samantha. BSME, Duke U., 1983; MBA, U. Pa., 1990. Various positions to v.p., 1983-89; pres. Day Products, Bridgeport, N.Y., 1992-93; sr. v.p. Day & Zimmermann Internat., Phila., 1993-94; pres. Day & Zimmermann Internat.-Process & Indsl., Inc., Phila., 1995—. Office: Day & Zimmermann Internat 1818 Market St 22nd fl Philadelphia PA 19103-3638*

YOH, HAROLD LIONEL, JR., engineering, construction and management company executive; b. Bryn Mawr, Pa., Dec. 12, 1936; s. Harold Lionel and Katherine (Hulme) Y.; m. Mary Michael Milus, June 20, 1959; children: Harold Lionel III, Michael Hulme, Karen Bogart, Jeffrey Milus, William Courtlandt. B.S. in Mech. Engring, Duke, 1958; M.B.A., U. Pa., 1962. Vice pres. H.L. Yoh Co. subs. Day & Zimmerman, Inc., Phila., 1960-63, sr. v.p. div. mgr., 1963-64, pres., 1964-76; v.p. adminstrn. Day & Zimmermann, Inc., Phila., 1961-69, sec., 1966-70, v.p., treas., 1969-76, vice chmn., chief exec. officer, 1976-80, chmn. bd., chief exec. officer, 1980—; also bd. dirs. Day & Zimmermann, Inc.; past pres., past dir. Nat. Tech. Services Assn.; bd. dirs. Continental Bancorp. Greater Phila First Corp. and several other privately held cos. Bd. dirs. Phila. Coll. Arts, Bryn Mawr Civic Assn., Phila. Indsl. Devel. Corp., The Haverford Sch.; past chmn. bd. dirs. Pop Warner Little Scholars; past Pa. State chmn. U.S. Savs. Bonds.; chmn. dean's council Sch. Engring. Duke U., chmn. univ. Greater Phila. Area Capital Campaign; Mid-Atlantic regional chmn. U.S. Olympics. Named Ambassador City of Phila., Silver Knight of D&Z Lone Star chpt. Mgmt. Nat. Mgmt. Assn., 1979-80; recipient Blue Devil award Duke U., Disting. Alumnus award Duke U., Robert Morris award Boy Scouts Am. Mem. ASME, Am. Def. Preparedness Assn. (dir.), Phila. C. of C. (chmn., dir.), Young President's Orgn. (internat. dir.), Phila. Pres.' Orgn., Chief Execs. Orgn., Navy League (life), Newcomen Soc., World Bus. Council, Sigma Nu. Republican. Episcopalian.

Clubs: Union League, Phila. Country (Phila.); Merion Golf (Ardmore, Pa.); University (Washington); Seaview Country (N.J.). Avocations: golf, fishing. Home: 116 Summit House West Chester PA 19382-6518 Office: Day & Zimmermann Inc 1818 Market St. Philadelphia PA 19103*

YOHALEM, HARRY MORTON, lawyer; b. Phila., Jan. 21, 1943; s. Morton Eugene and Florence (Mishnun) Y.; m. Martha Caroline Remy, June 9, 1967; children: Seth, Mark. BA with honors, U. Wis., 1965; JD cum laude, Columbia U., 1969, M in Internat. Affairs., 1969. Bar: N.Y. 1969, D.C. 1981, Calif. 1992, U.S. Supreme Ct. 1985. Assoc. Shearman & Sterling, N.Y.C., 1969-71; asst. counsel to gov. State of N.Y., Albany, 1971-73, counsel office planning svcs., 1973-75; asst. gen. counsel FEA, Washington, 1975-77; mem. staff White House Energy Policy and Planning Office, Washington, 1977; dep. gen. counsel for legal svcs. Dept. Energy, Washington, 1978-80, dep. under sec., 1980-81; ptnr. Rogers & Wells, Washington, 1981-91; gen. counsel Calif. Inst. Tech., Pasadena, 1991—. Editor comments Columbia Jour. Transnat. Law, 1967-68, rsch. editor, 1968-69. Prin. Coun. for Excellence in Govt., Washington, 1990—; pres. Opera Bel Canto, Washington, 1984-87; mem. Lawyers Com. for Arts, Washington, 1981-88; mem. adv. bd. Pasadena Conservatory of Music, Calif., 1994—. Harlan Fiske Stone scholar Columbia U., 1967, 69. Mem. ABA, Calif. Bar Assn., D.C. Bar Assn. Athenaeum, Phi Kappa Phi. Home: 1060 Stoneridge Dr Pasadena CA 91105-2844 Office: Calif Inst Tech 4800 Oak Grove Dr JPL 180-305 Pasadena CA 91109

YOHN, DAVID STEWART, virologist, science administrator; b. Shelby, Ohio, June 7, 1929; s. Joseph Van and Agnes (Tryon) Y.; m. Olivetta Kathleen McCoy, June 11, 1950; children: Linda Jean, Kathleen Ann, Joseph John, David McCoy, Kristine Renee. B.S., Otterbein Coll., 1951; M.S., Ohio State U., 1953, Ph.D., 1957; M.P.H., U. Pitts., 1960. Research fellow, scholar in microbiology Ohio State U., Columbus, 1952-56, prof. virology Coll. Veterinary Medicine, 1969-95, prof. emeritus, 1995—, dir. Comprehensive Cancer Ctr., 1973-88, dep. dir. Comprehensive Cancer Ctr., 1988-94, dir. emeritus Comprehensive Cancer Ctr., 1994—; research assoc., asst. prof. microbiology U. Pitts., 1956-62; assoc. cancer research scientist Roswell Park Meml. Inst., Buffalo, 1962-69; mem. nat. med. and sci. adv. com. Leukemia Soc. Am., 1970-91, trustee, 1971-91; pres. Ohio Cancer Research Assocs., 1982—; mem. cancer research centers rev. com. Nat. Cancer Inst., 1972-77. Pres. bd. deacons North Presbyn. Ch., Williamsburg, N.Y., 1967-68. Recipient Pub. Service award Lions, 1968. Mem. Am. Assn. Cancer Rsch., Am. Soc. Microbiology, Am. Assn. Immunologists, Internat. Assn. Comparative Rsch. on Leukemia and Related Diseases (sec.-gen. 1974-95), Ohio Valley-Lake Erie Assn. Cancer Ctrs. (sec. 1978-95), Sertoma (pres. 1992-93, chmn. bd. dirs. 1993-94, Dist. Sertoman of Yr. award 1987). Home: 974 Willow Bluff Dr Columbus OH 43235 Office: Ohio State U Comprehensive Cancer Ctr 300 W 10th Ave Ste 1132 Columbus OH 43210-1240

YOHN, SHARON A., manufacturing executive; b. Altoona, Pa., Mar. 1, 1952. AS in Retail cum laude, Harcum Jr. Coll. (Pa.), 1972; BSBA, Villanova U., 1976. Dir. overseas ops. Europe and Africa airwalk divsn. Items Internat., Inc., Altoona, Pa., 1987-95, v.p., 1995—. Active ch. choir. Republican. Methodist. Avocations: needlework, sewing, music, performing arts, travel. Office: Items Internat Inc 1540 E Pleasant Valley Blvd Altoona PA 16602-7224

YOHN, WILLIAM H(ENDRICKS), JR., federal judge; b. Pottstown, Pa., Nov. 20, 1935; s. William H. and Dorothy C. (Cornelius) Y.; m. Jean Louise Kochel, mar. 16, 1963; children: William H. III, Bradley G., Elizabeth J. AB, Princeton U., 1957; JD, Yale U., 1960. Bar: Pa. 1961, U.S. Dist. Ct. D.C. 1961. Ptnr. Wells Campbell Reynier & Yohn, Pottstown, 1961-71; mem., chmn. coms. Pa. House of Reps., Harrisburg, 1968-80; ptnr. Binder Yohn & Kalis, Pottstown, 1971-81; judge Montgomery County Ct. of Common Pleas, Norristown, Pa., 1981-91, U.S. Dist. Ct., ea. dist., Pa., 1991—; asst. D.A., Montgomery County D.A. Office, 1962-65; instr. Am. Inst. of Banking, 1963-66. Bd. dirs. Greater Pottstown Drug Abuse Prevention Program, 1970-76, Pottstown Meml. Med. Ctr., 1974-95, chmn., 1984-95. Cpl. USMCR, 1960-66. Mem. Pa. Bar Assn., Montgomery Bar Assn. (bd. dirs. 1967-70). Republican. Office: US Dist Ct 3809 US Courthouse 601 Market St Philadelphia PA 19106-1510

YOKEN, MEL B(ARTON), French language educator, author; b. Fall River, Mass., June 25, 1939; s. Albert Benjamin and Sylvia Sarah (White) Y.; m. Cynthia Stein, June 20, 1976; children: Andrew Brett, David Ryan, Jonathan Barry. B.A., U. Mass., 1960, Ph.D., 1972; M.A.T., Brown U., 1961. Instr. French U. Mass., Dartmouth, 1966-72, asst. prof., 1972-76, assoc. prof., 1976-81 prof., 1981—, dir. French summer study program French Inst., 1981-88; vis. prof. Wheaton Coll., 1987, U. of Montreal, 1981-88, translator New Bedford Superior Ct., New Bedford, Mass., 1985—, Fall River Superior Ct., Fall River, Mass., 1985—; mem. nominating com. Nobel prize for lit., 1972—. Pres. Friends of Fall River Pub. Libr., 1972-80, pres. bd. dirs., 1972-80; pres. New Bedford Pub. Libr., 1980-82, Am. Field Svc., 1985—. Recipient Disting. Svc. award City Fall River, 1974, 80, Excellence in Teaching French award, 1984, 85, Gov.'s citation, 1986, Nat. Disting. Leadership award, 1990, Dist. Svc. award Mass. Foreign Lang. Assn., 1992, Medaille de Vermeil du Rayonnement de la Langue Française, L'Academie Francaise, 1993; Mel Yoken Day proclaimed by Mayor of New Bedford, 1990; Govt. of Que. grantee, 1981-85, 87-89, Can. Embassy grantee, 1986, 87, Southeastern Mass. U. grantee, 1985, 89, 90. Mem. MLA (life), Am. Assn. Tchrs. French (life), Am. Coun. Tchrs. Fgn. Langs., Middlebury Amicale (life), N.E. MLA (coord. 1987-91), New Eng. Fgn. Lang. Assn., Mass. Fgn. Lang. Assn. (bd. dirs. 1985-90, disting. svc. award 1992), N.Y. State Assn. Fgn. Lang. Tchrs., Internat. Platform Assn., Francophone Assn. (v.p. 1990—), Fall River C. of C., Brown U. Alumni Assn. (rep.), Richelieu Internat. Universal Manuscript Soc. (v.p. 1993—). Author: Claude Tillier, 1976, Speech is Plurality, 1978, Claude Tillier (1801-44): Fame and Fortune in His Novelistic Work, 1978, Entretiens Quebecois I, 1986, Entretiens Quebecois II, 1989, Letters of Robert Molloy, 1989, Festschrift in Honor of Stowell Goding, 1993, Entretiens Quebecois III, 1996; contbr. articles to profl. jours. Avocations: traveling, languages, baseball, postcards, meteorology. Home: 261 Carroll St New Bedford MA 02740-1412 Office: U Mass Dartmouth Lang Dept Old Westport Rd North Dartmouth MA 02747-2512

YOKLEY, RICHARD CLARENCE, fire department administrator; b. San Diego, Dec. 29, 1942; s. Clarence Ralph and Dorothy Junese (Sackman) Y.; m. Jean Elizabeth Liddle, July 25, 1964; children: Richard Clarence II, Karin Denise Yokley Dillard. Student, San Diego City Coll., 1967; AS, Miramar Coll., 1975. Cert. fire officer, fire instr., Calif. Disc jockey Sta. KSDS-FM, San Diego, 1966-67; bldg. engr. Consolidated Systems, Inc., San Diego, 1968-72; with Bonita-Sunnyside Fire Dept., Calif., 1972—; ops. chief Bonita-Sunnyside Fire Dept., 1991-93, maintenance officer, 1993—; med. technician Hartson Ambulance, San Deigo, 1978-80, Bay Gen. Hosp. (now Scripps Hosp.), Chula Vista, Calif., 1980-83; chmn. South Bay Emergency Med. Svc., 1988. Contbr. articles to jours., newspapers and mags. Asst. curator Firehouse Mus., San Diego, 1972-89, docent, 1990-93; scoutmaster troop 874 Boy Scouts Am., Bonita, Calif., 1978-79. With USAF, 1962-66. Recipient Heroism and Community Svc. award Firehouse Mag., N.Y.C., 1987, Star News Salutes award Chula Vista Star News, 1987, Golden Svc. award San Diego County Credit Union, 1988. Mem. Internat. Assn. Firefighters (pres. local chpt. 1981-82), Calif. State Firefighters Assn. (dep. dir. so. divsn. 1994—), Calif. Fire Mechanics, San Diego County Fire Prevention Officers (v.p. 1984, pres. 1985), Bonita Bus. and Profl. Assn. (bd. dirs. 1991-93, Historian award 1987), South Bay Commn., Bonita Hist. Mus. (co-founder 1986), Sport Chalet Dive Club (v.p. 1991). Republican. Methodist. Avocations: scuba diving, visit fire departments of foreign countries, collect fire memorabilia, snow skiing. Office: Bonita-Sunnyside Fire Dept 4900 Bonita Rd Bonita CA 91902-1725

YOKUBAITIS, ROGER T., lawyer; b. Wharton, Tex., Jan. 9, 1945. Attended, St. Louis U.; BA, JD, U. Houston, 1969. Bar: Tex. 1969. Ptnr. Carmody & Yokubaitis, L.L.P., Houston. Mem. ABA, Houston Bar Assn., State Bar of Tex., Houston Bankruptcy Conf., Am. Bankruptcy Inst. Office: Carmody Yokubaitis LLP 5718 Westheimer Ste 1010 Houston TX 77057-5732

YOLEN, JANE, author; b. N.Y.C., Feb. 11, 1939; d. Will Hyatt and Isabelle (Berlin) Y.; m. David Wilber Stemple, Sept. 2, 1962; children: Heidi Elisabet, Adam Douglas, Jason Frederic. B.A., Smith Coll., 1960; M.Ed., U. Mass., 1978; LL.D. (hon.), Coll. of Our Lady of the Elms, 1980. Asst. editor This Week mag., 1960; mem. staff Saturday Rev., 1960; asst. editor Gold Medal Books, 1961, Rutledge Press, 1961-63; asst. juvenile editor A.A. Knopf, Inc., 1963-65; free-lance writer, 1965—; lectr. dept. edn. Smith Coll., 1979-84; editor Jane Yolen books, imprint Harcourt Brace Jovanovich, 1988—; tchr. writers confs. Centrum, Cape Cod Writers Conf., Soc. Children's Book Writers, U. Mass.; mem. Mass. Council on Arts, 1974. Author: Pirates in Petticoats, 1963, The Witch Who Wasn't, 1964, The Emperor and the Kite, 1968, Writing Books for Children, 1973, The Girl Who Cried Flowers, 1974, The Hundredth Dove, 1978, The Dream Weaver, 1979, Commander Toad in Space, 1980, The Gift of Sarah Barker, 1981, Touch Magic, 1981, Dragon's Blood, 1982, Tales of Wonder, 1983, Heart's Blood, 1984, Cards of Grief, 1984, Dragonfield, 1985, Merlin's Booke, 1986, The Lullabye Songbook, 1986, Ring of Earth, 1986, Favorite Folktales From Around the World, 1986, Piggins, 1987, Owl Moon, 1987, Three Bears, 1987, A Sending of Dragons, 1987, The Devil's Arithmetic, 1988, Sister Light/Sister Dark, 1988, White Jenna, 1989, Dove Isabeau, 1989, Baby Bear's Bedtime Book, 1990, Tam Lin, 1990, Bird Watch, 1990, Sky Dogs, 1990, Wizard's Hall, 1991, All those Secrets of the World, 1991, Wings, 1991, Hark! A Christmas Sampler, 1991, Encounter, 1992, Briar Rose, 1992, Letting Swift River Go, 1992, What Rhymes with Moon, 1993, Welcome to the Greenhouse, 1993, Honkers, 1993, Here There Be Dragons, 1993, Grandad Bill's Song, 1994, Good Griselle, 1994, The Girl in the Golden Bower, 1994, Old Dame Counterpane, 1994, Old Macdonald's Songbook, 1994, Here There Be Unicorns, 1994, Beneath the Ghost Moon, 1994, The Wild Hunt, 1995, Ballad of the Pirate Queens, 1995, And Twelve Chinese Acrobats, 1995, Water Music, 1995, Among Angels, 1995, Here They Be Witches, 1995, O. Jerusalem, 1996, Welcome to the Sea of Sand, 1996, Passager, 1996, others. Mass. del. Democratic Nat. Conv., 1972; town coordinator Robert Drinan's campaign, 1970; chmn. bd. trustees Hatfield (Mass.) Library, 1978-83. Hobby, Milk and Honey, Sacred Places, Meet the Monsters, 1996—. Mem. Soc. Children's Book Writers (bd. dirs. 1974—), Children's Lit. Assn. (bd. dirs. 1977-79), Sci. Fiction Writers Am. (pres. 1986-88), Nat. Assn. for Preservation and Perpetuation of Storytelling, Authors Guild, Bay State Writers Guild, Western New Eng. Storytellers Guild (founder), Mystery Writers Am., Horror Writers Am. Democrat. Jewish/Quaker. Home: 31 School St Hatfield MA 01038-9701

YOLTON, JOHN WILLIAM, philosopher, educator; b. Birmingham, Ala., Nov. 10, 1921; s. Robert Elgene and Ella Maude (Holmes) Y.; m. Jean Sebastian, Sept. 5, 1945; children: Karin Frances Yolton Griffith, Pamela Holmes Yolton Smith. BA with honors, U. Cin., 1945, MA, 1946; postgrad., U. Calif., Berkeley, 1946-50; DPhil (Fulbright fellow), Balliol Coll., Oxford, Eng., 1952; LL.D. (hon.), York U., 1974; D.Litt. (hon.), McMaster U., 1976. Vis. lectr. philosophy Johns Hopkins U., 1952-53; asst. prof. Princeton U., 1952-57; assoc. prof. Kenyon Coll., 1957-61; prof. U. Md., 1961-63; prof. philosophy York U., Toronto, 1963-78; chmn. dept. York U., 1963-73, acting dean grad. studies, 1967-68, acting pres., 1973-74; prof. philosophy Rutgers U., New Brunswick, N.J., 1978—; dean Rutgers Coll., Rutgers U., 1978-85, John Locke prof. history of philosophy, 1989-92, prof. emeritus philosophy, 1992—; cons. Bertrand Russell Archives, McMaster U., 1973-86. Author: John Locke and the Way of Ideas, 1956, Metaphysical Analysis, 1967, Locke and the Compass of Human Understanding, 1970, Thinking Matter, 1983, Perceptual Acquaintance from Descartes to Reid, 1984, Locke and French Materialism, 1991, Perception and Reality, 1996, other books; gen. editor Clarendon Edit. of Works of John Locke, Oxford U. Press, 1984-92, Blackwell's Companion to the Enlightenment, 1992, Locke Dictionary (Blackwell), 1993, Library of the History of Ideas, 1989—; Concerning Education, 1989, 5 books in field; mem. edtl. bd. jours. in field; v.p., bd. dirs. Jour. of the History of Ideas, 1991—; contbr. articles to profl. jours. Mem. N.J. Com. for Humanities, 1978-85, treas., 1980-85. Am. Council Learned Socs. fellow, 1960-61; Can. Council fellow, 1968-69. Mem. Mind Assn., Can. Philos. Assn., Am. Soc. for 18th Century Studies, Hume Soc.

YONDA, ALFRED WILLIAM, mathematician; b. Cambridge, Mass., Aug. 10, 1919; s. Walter and Theophelia (Naruscewicz) Y.; B.S., U. Ala., 1952, M.A. in Math., 1954; m. Mary Jane McManus, Dec. 19, 1949 (dec.); children—Nancy, Kathryn, Elizabeth, John; m. Peggy A. Terrel, June 22, 1975. Mathematician rocket research Redstone Arsenal, Huntsville, Ala., 1953, U.S. Army Ballistic Research Labs., Aberdeen, Md., 1954-56; instr. math. U. Ala., Tuscaloosa, 1954, Temple U., Phila., 1956-57; asso. scientist, research and devel. div. Avco Corp., Wilmington, Mass., 1957-59; sr. mem. tech. staff RCA, Camden, N.J., 1959-66; mgr. computer analysis and programming dept. Raytheon Co. space and information systems div., Sudbury, Mass., 1966-70, mgr. software systems lab., 1969-70, prin. engr. missiles systems div., 1970-73; mgr. systems analysis and programming GTE Govt. Systems Corp., 1973-77, mgr. software engring. Atlantic ops., 1977-82, sr. mem. tech. staff Command Control & Communications Sector, 1983-91; software systems engr. Yonda Software Systems Cons., 1991—. Pres., Milford Area Assn. Retarded Children, 1970-74; vice-chmn. fin. com. Town of Medway, 1973; bd. dirs. Blackstone Valley Mental Health and Retardation Area, 1970-76; trustee Medway Libraries, 1973-82, chmn., 1974-81. Served with USAAF, 1943-46. Hon. fellow Advanced Level Telecommunications Tng. Center, Ghaziabad, India, 1981. Registered profl. engr. Mem. AAAS, IEEE, Math. Assn. Am., N.Y. Acad. Scis., Sigma Xi, Phi Eta Sigma, Pi Mu Epsilon (pres. Ala. chpt. 1953-54), Sigma Pi Sigma. Contbr. articles to profl. jours. Office: 12 Sunset Dr Medway MA 02053-2008

YONG, RAYMOND NEN-YIU, civil engineering educator; b. Singapore, Apr. 10, 1929; naturalized, 1966; s. Ngim Djin and Lucy (Loh) Y.; m. Florence Lechensky, July 8, 1961; children—Raymond T.M., Christopher T.K. B.A. in Math. and Physics, Washington and Jefferson Coll., 1950; B.S., M.I.T., 1952; M.S., Purdue U., 1954; M.Engring., McGill U., Montreal, Que., Can., 1958, Ph.D., 1960. Mem. faculty McGill U., 1959—, prof. civil engring., 1965—; dir. Geotech Rsch. Ctr., 1973-95; assoc. mem. Ctr. for Medicine, Ethics and Law McGill U., 1991-95; adj. prof. civil engring. U. Fla., Gainesville, 1984—; adj. rsch. prof. civil engring. Carleton U., Ottawa, 1990; disting. rsch. prof. U. Wales, Cardiff. Author: Soil Properties and Behavior, 1975 (Japanese edit. 1977), Introduction to Soil Behavior, 1966 (Japanese edit. 1974), Vehicle Traction Mechanics, 1985, Principles of Contaminant Transport in Soils, 1992 (Japanese edit. 1995). Decorated chevalier Ordre National du Que., 1985; recipient Killam prize Can. Coun., 1985, ASTM Charles B. Dudley award, 1988, Can. Environ. Achievement award, Lifetime Achievement Environment Can., 1991. Fellow Royal Soc. Can., Engring. Inst. Can., Can. Soc. for Civil Engring.; mem. ASCE, ASTM (Charles B. Dudley award 1988), Inst. Civil Engrs., Soc. Rheology, Clay Minerals Soc., Internat. Soc. Terrain-Vehicle Systems (pres. 1993—), Can. Geotech. Soc. (R.F. Legget award 1993). Office: McGill U Dept Civil Engring. and Applied Mechanics, 817 Sherbrooke St w, Montreal, PQ Canada H3A 2K6

YONKMAN, FREDRICK ALBERS, lawyer, management consultant; b. Holland, Mich., Aug. 22, 1930; s. Fredrick Francis and Janet Dorothy (Albers) Y.; m. Kathleen VerMeulen, June 9, 1953 (div. Sept. 22, 1980); children: Sara, Margriet, Nina.; m. Barbara Anne Sullivan, Aug. 22, 1981; 1 child, Fredrick Ryan. B.A., Hope Coll., Holland, 1952; J.D., U. Chgo., 1957. Bar: N.Y. 1958, Mass. 1968, D.C. 1984. With firm Winthrop, Stimson, Putnam & Roberts, N.Y.C., 1957-64; sec., gen. counsel Reuben H. Donnelley Corp., N.Y.C., 1964-66, Dun & Bradstreet, Inc., N.Y.C., 1966-68; mem. law firm Sullivan & Worcester, Boston, 1968-72; gen. counsel Am. Express Co., N.Y.C., 1972-78; exec. v.p. Am. Express Co., 1975-80; pres. Buck Cons., N.Y.C., 1980-81; mgmt. cons. and psychoanalyst, 1981—; counsel Peabody, Lambert & Myers, Washington, 1983-84; chmn. Outward Bound, Inc., 1980-81; mem. bd. and chmn. audit com. Kennecott Corp., 1978-81; adj. prof. law Georgetown U., 1976-78; chmn. Georgetown Internat. Law Inst., 1980-81; vis. com. U. Chgo. Law Sch., 1980-82. Bd. dirs. Washington Campus Program, 1976-81; With AUS, 1952-54. Recipient Silver Anniversary award Nat. Coll. Athletic Assn., 1977. Mem. ABA, N.Y. State Bar Assn., Mass. Bar Assn., Rsch. Soc. for Process Oriented Psychology (Zurich) (diplomate), Union Club (Boston). Presbyterian. Home: 27 Pilgrim Dr Greenwich CT 06831

YONTZ, KENNETH FREDRIC, medical and chemical company executive; b. Sandusky, Ohio, July 21, 1944; s. Kenneth Willard and Dorothy (Kromer) Y.; m. Jean Ann Marshall, July 21, 1962 (div. Aug. 1982); children: Terri, Christine, Michael, Jennifer; m. Karen Glojek, July 7, 1984 (wid. Dec. 1994). BSBA, Bowling Green State U., 1971; MBA, Eastern Mich. U., 1979. Fin. planning mgr. Ford Motor Co., Rawsonville, Mich., 1970-74; fin. mgr. Chemetron Corp., Chgo., 1974-76, pres. fire systems div., 1976-80; pres. electronics div. Allen Bradley Co., Milw., 1980-83, group. pres. electronics, 1983-85, exec. v.p., 1985-86; chmn. bd., pres., chief exec. officer Sybron Corp., Milw., 1986—, also bd. dirs.; bd. dirs. Playtex Corp., N.Y.C., Birg Electronics, St. Louis, Thomson Minwax Co., N.J. Bd. dirs. Boys and Girls Club; founder Karen Youtz Womens Cardiac Awareness Ctr. Mem. Nat. Assn. Mfrs. (bd. dirs.), Bluemound Country Club, Milw. Athletic Club, The Milw. Club (bd. dirs.), Montclair Golf Club, Vintage Club (Indian Wells, Calif.). Roman Catholic. Office: Sybron Corp 411 E Wisconsin Ave Milwaukee WI 53202-4409 *Positive results are seldom achieved from negative thoughts.*

YOOD, HAROLD STANLEY, internist; b. Plainfield, N.J., Feb. 23, 1920; s. Raphael and Netta (Newcorn) Y.; m. Helen H. Hull, Nov. 8, 1941; children: Pamela, Patricia Yood Herskovitz, Paula Yood Peterson, Andrew H. BA, U. Va., 1940, MD, 1943. Intern Syracuse (N.Y.) U. Med. Ctr., 1943; pvt. practice Plainfield, N.J., 1946-91; med. dir. Cen. Jersey Individual Physicians Assn.; staff dept. medicine Muhlenberg Hosp., 1946—, pres. staff, 1980-86, cons., 1991-95, emeritus, 1995—. Contbr. articles to Jour. Med. Soc. N.J., Communication for Ciba, others. Bd. govs. Muhlenberg Regional Med. Ctr., 1980-86, exec. com.; trustee, v.p. United Way Plainfield/Fanwood, 1975-81; bd. dirs. United Way Union County, 1978-81; pres. Jewish Community Ctr., Plainfield, 1970-71; v.p. Jewish Fedn. Cen. N.J., 1971-73, Cen. N.J. Jewish Home for Aged, 1973-80. Capt. M.C. AUS, 1944-45, ETO. Decorated Purple Heart, Croix de Guerre (France), Croix de Guerre (Belgium). Fellow Am. Coll. Gastroenterology (sr.), Am. Coll. Angiography (ret.), Internat. Coll. Angiology (ret.); mem. AMA, Med. Soc. N.J. (governing coun. hosp. med. staff sect. 1983-92, chmn. 1988-90; trustee 1989-90), Union County Med. Soc., Plainfield Area Med. Assn., Am. Coll. Physician Execs., Lions (life). Office: CJIPA 1133 Park Ave Plainfield NJ 07060-3006 *Enjoyment in my profession, pleasure in relationship with patients, a belief in the necessity for civic and community volunteer involvement, a commitment to support causes that aid the unfortunate and do no harm to individuals.*

YOOK, CHONG CHUL, engineering educator; b. Kyngbuk, Sunsan, Korea, Jan. 1, 1926; s. Jae Kyun Yook and Choi (Shoon) Ie; m. Sook Kae Chang, Aug. 15, 1949; children: Myung-Hi, Oak-Soo, Sun-Hi. BS in Engring., Seoul (Republic of Korea) Nat. U., 1950; postgrad., Oak Ridge Inst., Argonne Internat. Inst., 1961, U. Ill., 1962; PhD in Nuclear Engring., Hanyang U., Seoul, 1967. Prof. Chung-Nam Nat. U., Taejon, Republic of Korea, 1957-64, dean Engring. Coll., 1962-64; prof. Hanyang U., 1964-91, prof. emeritus, 1991—; mem. tech. adv. bd. Ministry of Sci. and Tech., Seoul, 1988-90; advisor inspection, testing and examination cons. ITEC Svc. Co., Ltd., Seoul, 1991—. Author: Radiation Safety Handling, 1982, East and West, 1991 (Panel award 1991); patent for applied measuring device of engine ring wear. Mem. energy and resources adv. com. Rep. of Korean Govt., Seoul, 1981-83. Mem. Korean Assn. for Radiation Protection (pres. Seoul chpt. 1977-79), Internat. Radiation Protection Assn. (rep. Netherlands chpt. 1977-80, adv. com. Fed. Republic of Germany 1978-81), Korean Atomic Energy Rsch. Inst. (standing com. Taejon chpt. 1989-90), Korean Radioisotapes Assn. (audit treas. Seoul chpt. 1985-91). Mem. Christian Ch. Avocations: reading, mountain climbing, swimming.

YOON, JI-WON, virology, immunology and diabetes educator, research administrator; b. Kang-Jin, Chonnam, Korea, Mar. 28, 1939; came to U.S., 1965; s. Baek-In and Duck-Soon (Lee) Y.; m. Chungja Rhim, Aug. 17, 1968; children: John W., James W. MS, U. Conn., 1971, PhD, 1973. Sr. investigator NIH, Bethesda, Md., 1978-84; prof., chief div. virology U. Calgary, Alta., Can., 1984—, prof., assoc. dir. diabetes rsch. ctr., 1985-90, prof., dir. diabetes rsch. ctr., 1990—; mem. edit. bd. Annual Review Advances Present Rsch. Animal Diabetes, 1990—, Diabetes Rsch. Clin. Practice, 1989—; scientific coord. 10th Internat. Workshop on Immunology Diabetes, Jerusalem, 1989-90; sr. investigator NIH, 1976-84. Contbg. author: Current Topics in Microbiology and Immunology, 1990, Autoimmunity and Pathogenesis of Diabetes, 1990; contbr. articles to New England Jour. Medicine, Jour. Virology, Sci., Nature, The Lancet, Jour. Diabetes. Rsch. fellow Sloan Kettering Cancer Inst., 1973-74, Staff fellow, Sr. Staff fellow NIH, 1974-76, 76-78; recipient NIH Dir. award, 1984, Heritage Med. Scientist award, Alberta Heritage Found. Med. Rsch., 1984, Lectrship. award, 3d Asian Symposium Childhood Diabetes, 1989, 8th Annual Meeting Childhood Diabetes, Osaka, Japan, 1990, 9th Korean/Can. Heritage award, 1989. Mem. Am. Soc. Immunologists, Am. Diabetes Assn., Am. Soc. Microbiology, N.Y. Acad. Sci., Soc. Virology, Internat. Diabetes Fedn. Baptist. Achievements include first isolation of diabetogenic virus from patients with recent onset of IDDM; first demonstration of prevention of virus-induced diabetes by vaccination with nondiabetogenic virus in animals; discovery that autoimmune IDDM can be prevented by depletion of macrophages in autoimmune diabetic NOD mice, certain viral glycoproteins (rubella virus E2 glycoprotein) can induce organ-specific autoimmune disease; research on molecular identification of diabetogenic viral gene in animal models, discovery of a nontoxic organic compound with no side effects that completely prevents type I diabetes in NOD mice, discovery that bacterial superantigens such as staphylococcal enterotozins (SEC1, SEC3) can prevent autoimmune type I diabetes by activation of CD4+ suppressor T cells in NOD mice; research on the role of cloned T-Cells in the pathogenesis of autoimmune Type I Diabetes at cellular and molecular level. Home: 206 Edgeview Dr NW, Calgary, AB Canada T3A 4W9 Office: Julia McFarlane Diabetes Rsch Ctr, 3330 Hospital Dr NW, Calgary, AB Canada T2N 4N1

YOON, NAE-HYUN, historian, educator; b. Haenam-kun, Korea, June 15, 1939; s. Jae-eyl Yoon and Yong-nam Yi; m. Jeong-oh Kim, Dec. 25, 1964; children: Jang-won, Jin-won, Joo-won. BA, Dankook U., 1965, MA, 1975, LittD, 1978. Asst. prof. coll. lit. Dankook U., Seoul, 1978-81, prof., 1981—, chmn. dept. history, 1982-87, dir. mus., 1989—; vis. scholar Harvard U., Cambridge, Mass., 1979-82; mem. com. cultural assets Ministry of Culture and Athletics, Korea, 1993—; mem. commn. of exam. State Higher Exam. Fgn. Affairs, Korea; mem. com. Jud. Exam., Korea; mem. Ednl. Coun. Korean History. Author: A Study on Shang Dynasty, 1978, Primitive Age of China, 1982, The History of Shang and Chou, 1984 (Ilsuk academic prize 1985), A New Interpretation of Ancient Korean History, 1986 (Book of Today prize 1986), A Study on Ko-Chosen, 1994 (Kumho Acad. prize 1995), The History of China, vol. 1, 1991, vol. 2, 1992, vol. 3, 1995. Mem. Assn. for Asian Studies Inc., Soc. for Study of Early China, Korean Hist. Assn., Soc. for Asian Hist. Studies, Korea Study Soc., Korean Ancient Hist. Soc. Home: 496-4 Pyungchang-dong, Jongro-ku Seoul 110-012, Republic of Korea Office: Dankook U Dept History, 8 Hannam-dong Yongsan-ku, Seoul 140-714, Republic of Korea

YOON, SEWANG, engineering executive; b. Chinhae, Korea, July 28, 1949; came to U.S., 1975; s. Jah Choon and In Soon (Chung) Y.; m. Youngok Byun, Mar. 12, 1975; children: Janice J., Stella J. BS, Seoul (Korea) Nat. U., 1971; MS, UCLA, 1977, PhD, 1980. Mgr. R&D M/A-COM, PHI, Torrance, Calif., 1980-89; v.p. tech. Amonix Inc., Torrance, 1989—. Recipient Meritorious Paper award GOMAC-86, 1986, R & D 100 award for silicon photovoltaic cell, R&D Mag., 1994. Mem. IEEE (assoc.), Sigma Xi. Achievements include design, manufacture and commercialization of a point focus type concentrator solar cell with a record efficiency of 25.5% at 250X concentration, using a point contact cell concept. Office: Amonix Inc 3425 Fujita St Torrance CA 90505

YORBURG, BETTY (MRS. LEON YORBURG), sociology educator; b. Chgo., Aug. 27, 1926; d. Max and Hannah (Bernstein) Gitelman; m. Leon Yorburg, June 23, 1946; children: Harriet, Robert. PhB, U. Chgo., 1945, MA, 1948; PhD, New Sch. Social Rsch., 1968. Instr., Coll. New Rochelle, 1966-67; lectr. City Coll. and Grad. Center, City U. N.Y., 1967-69, asst. prof., 1969-73, assoc. prof. sociology dept., 1973-77, prof., 1978—; rsch. asst. Prof. Clifford Shaw, Chgo. Area Project, 1946-47. Author: Utopia and Reality, 1969, The Changing Family, 1973, Sexual Identity: Sex Roles and Social Change, 1974, The New Women, 1976, Introduction to Sociology, 1982, Families and Societies, 1983, Family Relationships, 1993, Sociological Reality, 1995. Mem. AAAS, Am. Sociol. Assn., Ea. Sociol. Assn., Am.

Coun. Family Rels., N.Y. Acad. Scis. Home: 20 Earley St Bronx NY 10464-1512 Office: CCNY Sociology Dept 138th Convent Ave New York NY 10031-9127

YORDAN, CARLOS MANUEL, foreign service officer; b. P.R., Nov. 27, 1925; s. Nicholas and Octavia (Baez) Y.; m. Hilda Bordas, Aug. 16, 1946; 1 son, Carlos Manuel. Student, Gregg Bus. Coll., 1940-42; M.A. in Polit. Sci., U. Chgo. (corr.), 1960, M.A. in Am. History, 1962. Joined U.S. Fgn. Service, 1947; chief clk. engring. dept. Unifruitco, Dominican Republic, 1944-47; adminstrv. officer State Dept., Santo Domingo, Dominican Republic, 1947-50, Quito, Ecuador, 1950-52; 2d sec., vice consul State Dept., Lima, Peru, 1953-55, Rangoon, Burma, 1956-58, London, 1958-60, Budapest, Hungary, 1960-61, Washington, 1961-65; 1st sec., consul State Dept., Warsaw, Poland, 1965-67, West Berlin, 1967-70, Dublin, 1970-73, Brasilia, Brazil, 1973-77; counselor embassy Santo Domingo, Dominican Republic, 1977-81. Mem. Fgn. Svc. Assn., Royal Dublin Soc., Am. Soc. Natural History, Country Tennis Ctr. Sarasota (Fla.), Tournament Players Club Prestancia. Office: 3697 Gleneagle Dr Sarasota FL 34238-2812

YORINKS, ARTHUR, children's author, writer, director; b. Roslyn, N.Y., Aug. 21, 1953; s. Alexander and Shirley (Kron) Y.; m. Adrienne Berg, Oct. 23, 1983. Writer, tchr. performer Am. Mime Theatre, 1969-79; instr. theatre arts Cornell U., Ithaca, N.Y., 1972-79; assoc. dir. New Works Project, N.Y.C., 1977—; founder, artistic dir. Moving Theatre, N.Y.C., 1979; founder, assoc. artistic dir. The Night Kitchen, N.Y.C., 1990—. Author: (children's books) Sid and Sol, 1977, The Magic Meatballs, 1979, Louis the Fish, 1980 (Sch. Libr. Jour. Best Book Yr. Citation 1980), It Happened in Pinsk, 1983 (Booklist Children's Editor's Choice 1984, Biennale of Illustration plaque 1985), Hey, Al, 1986 (ALA Notable Book citation 1986, Caldecott medal 1987, Ky. Bluegrass award 1988), Bravo Minski, 1988 (Sch. Libr. Jour. Best Book Yr. Citation 1988), Company's Coming, 1988 (ALA Notable Book citation 1986), Oh, Brother, 1989 (Sch. Libr. Jour. Best Book Yr. Citation 1989), Ugh, 1990 (Sch. Libr. Jour. Best Book Yr. citation 1990), Christmas in July, 1991, Whitefish Will Rides Again, 1994, (plays) Six, 1973, The Horse, 1978, Crackers, 1979, The King, 1980, Kissers, 1980, Piece for a Small Cafe, 1981, Piece for a Larger Cafe, 1982, So, Sue Me, 1994, It's Alive!, 1995, The Miami Giant, 1995; (opera librettos) Leipziger Kerzenspiel, 1984, The Juniper Tree, 1985 (music by Philip Glass), The Fall of the House of Usher, 1988 (music by Philip Glass), (screenplay) Sid and Sol, 1982, It's a Miracle, 1991, Usher, 1991, Making Scents, 1993. Office: The Night Kitchen 10 E 53rd St New York NY 10022-5244

YORK, DEREK H., geophysics educator; b. Yorkshire, England, Aug. 12, 1936; married; 1 child. BA, Oxford U., 1957, DPhil, 1960. From lectr. to prof. physics U. Toronto, 1960—; researcher geol. & geochem. lab. U. Nice, France; chmn. subcom. isotope geophysics Nat. Rsch. Coun., 1967. Mem. Am. Geophys. Union, Can. Assn. Physicists. Office: U Toronto Dept Physics, 215 Huron St, Toronto, ON Canada M5S 1A7*

YORK, DONALD GILBERT, astronomy educator, researcher; b. Shelbyville, Ill., Oct. 28, 1944; s. Maurice Alfred and Virginia Maxine (Huntwork) Y.; m. Anna Sue Hinds, June 12, 1966; children: Sean, Maurice, Chandler, Jeremy. BS, MIT, 1966; PhD, U. Chgo., 1971. Rsch. asst. Princeton (N.J.) U., 1970-71, rsch. assoc., 1971-73, rsch. astronomer, 1973-78, sr. rsch. astronomer, 1978-82; assoc. prof. U. Chgo., 1982-86, prof., 1986-92, Horace B. Horton prof. astronomy and astrophysics, 1992—; dir. Apache Point Obs., Astrophys. Rsch. Consortium, Seattle, 1984—, Sloan Digital Sky Survey, 1990—. Contbr. articles to profl. jours. Recipient Pub. Svc. award NASA, 1976; grantee NASA, 1978—, NSF, 1984—. Mem. Internat. Astron. Union, Am. Astron. Soc. (publs. bd. 1980-83). Republican. Avocations: squash, white water canoeing, science history, religion history. Office: 5640 S Ellis Ave Chicago IL 60637-1433

YORK, E. TRAVIS, academic administrator, former university chancellor, consultant; b. Mentone, Ala., July 4, 1922; s. E. Travis and Leila (Hixon) Y.; m. Vermelle Cardwell, Dec. 26, 1946; children: Lisa Carol, Travis Loften. B.S., Auburn U., 1942, M.S., 1946, D.Sc. (hon.), 1982; Ph.D. (research fellow 1946-49), Cornell U., 1949; postgrad., George Washington U., 1957-59; D.Sc. (hon.), U. Fla., 1984. Assoc. prof. agr. N.C. State Coll., 1949-52, prof., 1952-56, head dept. agronomy, 1953-56; Eastern dir. Am. Potash Inst., 1956-59; dir. Ala. Extension Service, Auburn U., 1959-61; adminstr. Fed. Extension Service, U.S. Dept. Agr., 1961-63; provost for agr. U. Fla., 1963-67, v.p. agrl. affairs, 1967-73, exec. v.p., interim pres., 1973-74, Disting. Svc. prof., 1988—; chancellor State U. System of Fla., 1975-80, chancellor emeritus, 1980—. Mem. Am. Food for Peace Coun., 1961-62, Freedom from Hunger Com., 1961-62, Pres.'s. Panel Vocat. Edn., 1961-62; chmn. coun. grad. edn. in agrl. scis. So. Regional Edn. Bd., 1964-66, mem., 1975-80, exec. com., 1978-80, mem. pres. coun., Pres.' Sci. Adv. Coun. Task Force on World Food Problems, 1966-67; mem. senate, exec. com. Nat. Assn. State Univs. and Land Grant Colls., 1967-70; mem. Edn. Commn. of States, 1975-79, steering com., 1977-79, treas., exec. com., 1978-79; bd. dirs. Nat. 4-H Svc. Com., 1963-75, AV Med. Corp., Sante Fe, 1987—; trustee,bd. dirs Hlth Improvement Inc mem., 1996—, exec. com. Nat. 4-H Found., 1968-73; mem.-at-large nat. coun. Boy Scouts Am., 1962-75; dir., pres. Alpha Gamma Rho Edn. Found., 1965-72; bd. dirs. Nat. Ctr. for Voluntary Action, 1970-74; mem. Bd. for Internat. Food and Agrl. Devel., 1980-86, chmn., 1983-86; trustee Escuela Agricola Panamericana, 1980-88, Found. for Agronomic Rsch., 1980-92; tech. adv. com., cons. Group for Internat. Agrl. Rsch., 1983-89; trustee Agronomic Sci. Found., 1989-92. Officer AUS, 1943-45. Recipient B.B. Comer award excellence natural sci. Auburn U., 1942; disting. svc. award Fla. Vet. Med. Assn., 1966; Nat. 4-H Alunbi award, 1967; George Washington honor medal award Freedoms Found., 1967; nat. ptnr. in 4-H award, 1970; disting. faculty award U. Fla., Fla. Blue Key, 1972; E.T. York, Jr. disting. svc. award U. Fla., 1973; honors medal U. Fla. Acad. Scis., 1974; E.T. York svc. award Fla. Bd. Regents, 1983, disting. svc. award Am. Farm Bur., 1991, Rotary Internat., 1994; named to Fla. Agrl. Hall of Fame, 1990, Ala. Agrl. Hall of Honor, 1995. Fellow AAAS, Am. Soc. Agronomy, Soil Sci. Soc. Am., AM. Crop Sci. Soc.; mem. Am. Soc. Hort. Sci. (hon.), Assn. So. Agrl. Scientists (pres. 1968), Blue Key, Rotary (dist. gov. 1981-82, svc. above self award 1993), Sigma Xi, Phi Kappa Phi, Alpha Zeta, Gamma Sigma Delta (internat. disting. svc. award 1973), Omicron Delta Kappa, Phi Delta Kappa, Epsilon Sigma Phi, Alpha Gamma Rho (named to Hall of Fame 1982). Methodist. Address: 4020 SW 78th St Gainesville FL 32608-3608

YORK, GARY ALAN, lawyer; b. Glendale, Calif., Aug. 29, 1943; m. Lois York, 1987; 1 child, Jonathan Alan. BA, Pomona Coll., 1965; LLB, Stanford U., 1968. Bar: Calif. 1969. Ptnr. Dewey Ballantine, L.A., 1985-95, Buchalter, Nemer, Fields & Younger, L.A., 1995—; instr. law sch. UCLA, 1968-69. Bd. editors Stanford Law review, 1966-68. Mem. ABA (chmn. real estate fin. com., real property probate and trust sect. 1987-89, chmn. usury com. 1992-93), L.A. County Bar Assn. (chmn. real estate fin. sect. 1993-96), State Bar of Calif., Am. Coll. Real Estate Lawyers. Office: Buchalter Nemer Fields & Younger 601 S Figueroa St Los Angeles CA 90017

YORK, HERBERT FRANK, physics educator, government official; b. Rochester, N.Y., Nov. 24, 1921; s. Herbert Frank and Nellie Elizabeth (Lang) Y.; m. Sybil Dunford, Sept. 28, 1947; children: David Winters, Rachel, Cynthia. AB, U. Rochester, 1942, MS, 1943; PhD, U. Calif., Berkeley, 1949; DSc (hon.), Case Inst. Tech., 1960; LL.D., U. San Diego, 1964, Claremont Grad. Sch., 1974. Physicist Radiation Lab., U. Calif., Berkeley, 1943-58, assoc. dir., 1954-58; asst. prof. physics dept. U. Calif., Berkeley, 1951-54, assoc. prof., 1954-59, prof., 1959-61; dir. Lawrence Radiation Lab., Livermore, 1952-58; chief scientist Advanced Rsch. Project Agy., U.S. Dept. Def., 1958; dir. advanced rsch. projects divsn. Inst. for Def. Analyses, 1958; dir. def. rsch. and engring. Office Sec. Def., 1958-61; chancellor U. Calif.-San Diego, 1961-64, 70-72, prof. physics, 1964—, chmn. dept. physics, 1968-69, dean grad. studies, 1969-70, dir. program on sci., tech. and pub. affairs, 1972-88; dir. Inst. Global Conflict and Cooperation, 1983-88, dir. emeritus, 1988—; amb. Comprehensive Test Ban Negotiations, 1979-81; trustee Aerospace Corp., Inglewood, Calif., 1961-87; mem. Pres.'s Sci. Adv. Com., 1957-58, 64-68, vice chmn., 1965-67; trustee Inst. def. Analysis, 1963-96; gen. adv. com. ACDA, 1962-69; mem. Def. Sci. Bd., 1977-81; spl. rep. of sec. def. at space arms control talks, 1978-79; mem. coun. nat. labs. Pres. U. Calif., 1991—; mem. task force future nat. labs. Sec. Emergy, 1994-95; cons. Stockholm Internat. Peach Rsch. Inst.; rschr. in application atomic energy to nat. def. problems of arms control and disarmament, elem. particles. Author: Race to Oblivion, 1970, Arms Control, 1973, The Advisors, 1976, Making Weapons, Talking Peace, 1987, Does Strategic Defense Breed Offense?, 1987, (with S. Lakoff) A Shield in the Sky, 1989, Arms and the Physicist, 1994; also numerous articles on arms or disarmament; bd. dirs. Bull. Atomic Scientists. Trustee Bishop's Sch., La Jolla, Calif., 1963-65. Recipient E.O. Lawrence award AEC, 1962; Guggenheim fellow, 1972, Szilard award Am. Physical Soc., 1994. Fellow Am. Phys. Soc. (forum on physics and soc. award 1976, Leo Szilard award 1994), AAAS; mem. Internat. Acad. Astronautics, Fedn. Am. Scientists (chmn. 1970-71, exec. com. 1969-76, 95—, pub. svc. award 1992), Phi Beta Kappa, Sigma Xi. Home: 6110 Camino De La Costa La Jolla CA 92037-6520 Office: U Calif-San Diego Mail Code 0518 La Jolla CA 92093

YORK, JAMES ORISON, real estate executive; b. Brush, Colo., June 27, 1927; s. M. Orison and Marie L. (Kibble) Y.; m. Janice Marie Sjoberg, Aug. 1, 1959; children: Douglas James, Robert Orison. Student, U. Calif. at Berkeley, 1945-46; B.A. cum laude, U. Wash., 1949. Teaching fellow U. Wash., Seattle, 1950-52; econ. research analyst Larry Smith & Co. (real estate), Seattle and N.Y.C., 1953-60; partner Larry Smith & Co. (real estate), Seattle, 1960-66; pres. Larry Smith & Co. (real estate), San Francisco, 1966-71; pres., chief exec. officer R.H. Macy Properties, N.Y.C., also sr. v.p. planning and devel., dir. R.H. Macy & Co., Inc., 1971-88; pres. James York Assocs. (real estate), 1988—; trustee HRE Properties, Corp. Property Investors; chmn., N.Y.C. retail div. Am. Cancer Soc. Contbg. author: Shopping Towns-USA, 1960. Trustee ICSC Ednl. and Rsch. Found. With USNR, 1945-47. Recipient Disting. Alumnus award U. Wash., 1989. Mem. Am. Soc. Real Estate Counselors, Urban Land Inst., Internat. Real Estate Fedn., Internat. Council Shopping Centers, Phi Beta Kappa, Lambda Alpha. Episcopalian. Clubs: Olympic (San Francisco); American Yacht (Rye, N.Y.); Corinthian Yacht (Seattle); Union League (N.Y.C.); Knights of Malta, Order St. John, Washington Athletic (Seattle), Royal Victoria (B.C.) Yacht. Home and Office: 4 Riverstone Laguna Niguel CA 92677-5309

YORK, JAMES WESLEY, JR., theoretical physicist, educator; b. Raleigh, N.C., July 3, 1939; s. James Wesley and Mary Smedes (Poyner) Y.; m. Betty Louise Mattern, Aug. 19, 1961; children: Virginia York Setzer, Guilford Mattern. B.S. with high honors in Physics, N.C. State U., Raleigh, 1962, Ph.D. in Physics, 1966. Asst. prof. N.C. State U., Raleigh, 1965-68; rsch. assoc. Princeton (N.J.) U., 1968-69, lectr., 1969-70, asst. prof., 1970-73; assoc. prof. U. N.C., Chapel Hill, 1973-77, prof. dept. physics, 1977-89, Agnew H. Bahnson, Jr. disting. prof. physics, 1989—, dir. Inst. Field Physics, 1984-90; vis. asst. prof. U. Md., College Park, 1972; prof. associe U. Paris, 1976; vis. scientist Harvard U., Cambridge, 1977; vis. prof. U. Tex., Austin, 1979, 87; spkr. Internat. Symposium on Methods of Differential Geometry in Physics and Mechanics, Warsaw, Poland, 1976; Alfred Schild Meml. lectr. U. Tex., 1979; del. Seventh Internat. Congress on Math. Physics, Boulder, Colo., 1983, Tex. Symposium on Relativistic Astrophysics, Jerusalem, 1984, Marcel Grossman Meeting, Rome, 1985, NATO Advanced Study Inst., Les Houches, France, 1982, Huelva, Spain, 1992, Paris, 1992, Banff, Can., 1992, other internat. and nat. meetings; co-organizer sci. meetings including Neutron stars and pulsars, Princeton, 1969, Spacetime dynamics, Aspen Ctr. for Theoretical Physics, 1981, Classical Problems in Gravitation, 1990, Cosmic Censorship, 1992; mem. com. of visitors physics divsn. NSF, 1991; plenary lectr. Fifth Can. Conf. on Gen. Relativity and Astrophysics, Waterloo, 1993, Directions in Gen. Relativity, College Park, Md., 1993, hon. physics chmn. Cornelius Lanczos Internat. Centenary, Raleigh, N.C., 1993. Mem. editorial bd. Jour. Math. Physics, 1989-92; contbr. chpts. to books, articles to sci. jours. Decorated Companion of St. Patrick, 1960; recipient 3d prize Gravity Rsch. Found.d Essay award, 1975; Ford Found. fellow, 1962-65; Battelle Found. grantee, 1967, NSF postdoctoral fellow, 1969-70, Nat. Rsch. Com. France grantee, 1976, NSF grantee, 1974—, travel grantee, 1971, 76, 83, 84; U.S.A.-Israel Binat. Sci. Found. grantee, 1987-90, 90-93. Fellow Am. Phys. Soc.; mem. AAAS, Internat. Soc. Gen. Relativity and Gravitation, Rotary, Sigma Xi, Phi Kappa Phi, Tau Beta Pi, Sigma Pi Sigma, Pi Mu Epsilon, Phi Eta Sigma. Episcopalian. Avocations: literature, music, sports. Office: U NC Dept Physics and Astronomy Chapel Hill NC 27599-3255

YORK, JOSEPH RUSSELL, media production technician; b. Royal Center, Ind., Oct. 19, 1940; s. William Russell and Naomi (Wellman) Y.; Student Olivet Nazarene Coll., until 1965; BS, Ball State U. student, 1980, MS, 1982; m. Teresa Luanne Ping, June 15, 1963; children: Sherra JoAnn, Kerra SuzAnn, Darren Joseph, Terra LeAnn. Photojournalist, Danville (Ill.) Comml. News, 1961-62, Kankakee (Ill.) Daily Jour., 1963; motion picture dir., editor Calvin Prodns., Inc., Kansas City, Mo., 1965-71, Communico, Inc., St. Louis, 1971-73; editing supr. Premier Film & Rec. Co., Inc., St. Louis, 1973—; producer, dir. TV programming Kans. Fish and Game Commn., 1983—; owner, operator Trinity Prodns., St. Louis, 1963-83; pres. York's Foto Express, Inc., 1986—; asst. libr., prof. humanities and lit. Pratt C.C., 1988—; dir. med. svcs. audio support systems and spl. events Olivet Nazarene U., Bourbonnais. Ill., 1990—; owner, pres. EQ Audio, 1996—, J. York-Wooden Games & Recreation, 1996—. Pastor Ch. of the Nazarene, Selma, Ind. Recipient 1st Pl. award U.S. Indsl. Film Festival, 1972; 2d Pl. award Festival of Ams.-V.I., 1977. Mem. Profl. Photographers Am., Photomarketing Assn. Internat.; Golden Key Nat. Honor Soc. Home: 140 S Country Ct Bourbonnais IL 60914-2113 Office: Olivet Nazarene U 240 E Marsile St Bourbonnais IL 60914-1926

YORK, JOSEPH STAFFORD, secondary gifted and talented education educator; b. Memphis, Oct. 13, 1944; s. Benjamin Preston and Ora Belle (Stafford) Y. BA, Lambuth Coll., Jackson, Tenn., 1966; postgrad., Memphis State U., 1970, St. John's Grad. Inst., Santa Fe, U. Tenn. Cert. English, history and Bible tchr., Tenn. Instr. English, Dyersburg (Tenn.) State Community Coll., Memphis State U.; tchr. English gifted and talented edn. Fayette County Schs., Somerville, Tenn., McNairy County Schs., Adamsville, Tenn.; dep. chief aux. probation officer Juvenile Ct. Memphis and Shelby County; mem. adv. coun. on tchr. edn. and cert. Tenn. Bd. Edn. Author: Handbook for Written Expression, (poem) The Other Side of the Mirror, 1976. Named Tchr. of Yr., Millington (Tenn.) High Sch., 1976, Tenn. SE Dist., 1989, Fayette County Sch. System and Fayette-Ware High Sch., 1989, 90, Outstanding Tenn. Tchr., 1985, Edn. of Yr. Fayette County C. of C., Tenn. Tchr. of Yr., 1991, S.E. Dist. Tenn. Tchr. of Yr., 1990; recipient Excellence in Teaching award U. Tenn. at Knoxville, 1990, 91, 92; charter inductee Nat. Tchrs. Hall of Fame, 1992. Mem. NEA, Nat. Coun. Tchrs. English, Nat. State Tchrs. Yr. (exec. dir. Tenn. chpt. 1991—), Tenn. Coun. Tchrs. English, Conf. on Coll. Composition and Communication, Tenn. Edn. Assn., Assn. Supervision and Curriculum Devel., Fayette County Edn. Assn., McNairy County Edn. Assn., Kappa Delta Pi, Phi Delta Kappa, Kappa Sigma. Home: PO Box 34504 Memphis TN 38184-0504

YORK, MICHAEL (MICHAEL YORK-JOHNSON), actor; b. Fulmer, Eng., Mar. 27, 1942; s. Joseph Gwynne and Florence Edith (Chown) Johnson; m. Patricia McCallum, Mar. 27, 1968. BA with honors in English, Univ. Coll., Oxford U. (Eng.), 1964; DFA (hon.), U. S.C. Profl. debut with Dundee Repertory Theatre, Scotland, 1964; mem. Nat. Theatre Co., London, 1965-66; TV film or miniseries appearances include: Much Ado About Nothing, The Forsyte Saga, Rebel in the Grave, True Patriot, Jesus of Nazareth, 1977, A Man Called Intrepid, 1979, The Phantom of the Opera, 1983, The Master of Ballantrae, 1984, Space, 1985, The Far Country, 1985, Are You My Mother, 1986, Ponce de Leon, 1987, 1987, Till We Meet Again, 1989, The Road to Avonlea, 1991, Gardens of the World, 1993; The Four Minute Mile, The Lady and the Highway Man, 1988, The Heat of the Day, 1988, The Hunt for Stolen War Treasure, 1989, The Night of the Fox, 1990, Duel of Hearts, September, 1995, A Young Connecticut Yankee in King Arthur's Court, 1995; animated films The Magic Paintbrush, 1993; TV appearances: David Copperfield's Christmas, 1994, Teklab, 1994, Fall From Grace, 1994, Not of This Earth, 1995; TV series appearance: Knots Landing, 1987, September, 1994, SeaQuest, 1995, The Naked Truth, 1995; stage appearances include: Any Just Cause, 1967, Hamlet, 1970, Broadway prodns. of Outcry, 1973, Ring Round the Moon, 1975, Bent, 1980, Cyrano de Bergerac, 1981, Whisper in the Mind, 1990, The Crucible, 1991, Someone Who'll Watch Over Me, 1993, Nora, 1993; appeared in motion pictures including: The Taming of the Shrew, 1966, Accident, 1966, Red and Blue, 1967, Smashing Time, 1967, Romeo and Juliet, 1967, The Strange Affair, 1967, The Guru, 1968, Alfred the Great, 1968, Justine, 1969, Something for Everyone, 1969, Zeppelin, 1970, La Poudre D'Escampette, 1971, Cabaret, 1971, England Made Me, 1971, Lost Horizon, 1972, The Three Musketeers, 1973, Murder on the Orient Express, 1974, Great Expectations, 1974, Conduct Unbecoming, 1974, The Four Musketeers, 1975, Logan's Run, 1976, Seven Nights in Japan, The Last Remake of Beau Geste, 1977, The Island of Dr. Moreau, 1977, Fedora, 1977, The Riddle of the Sands, 1978, Final Assignment, 1980, The White Lions, Success is the Best Revenge, 1984, Dawn, 1985, Vengeance, 1986, The Secret of the Sahara, 1987, Imbalances, 1987, Lethal Obsession, 1987, Midnight Cop, 1988, The Return of the Musketeers, 1989, The Long Shadow, 1991, Eline Vere, 1991, Wide Sargasso Sea, 1991, Rochade, 1991, Discretion Assured, Shadow of a Kiss, 1993, Gospa, 1994; radio performances The Dark Tower, 1977, (recipient Peabody award), A Matter of Honor, 1986, Babbitt, 1987, The Crucible, 1988, Are You Now, UTZ, 1989, McTeague, 1992, Make and Break, 1993; recs. include: Mere Christianity, 1982, Anna Karenina, 1985, Don Quixote, 1986, The King Must Die, 1988, British Rock: The First Wave, UTZ, 1989, The Modigliani Scandal, 1989, The Mummy, 1989, Candide, 1989, The Vampire Lestat, 1989, The Berlin Stories, 1990, The Remains of the Day, 1990, City of Joy, 1991, Beyond Love, 1991, Memories, Dreams, Reflections, 1991, A Poet's Bible, 1992, Einstein's Dreams, 1993, Accidentally on Purpose, 1993, The English Patient, 1993, Fortune's Favorite, 1993, The Three Musketeers, 1993, Paradise Lost, 1993, The Book of Psalms, 1994, The Book of Virtues, 1994, The Magic Paw-Paw, 1994; contbr.(books) The Courage of Conviction, 1985, Voices of Survival, 1987; author: Accidentally on Purpose, 1992; (recording) The Rubaiyat of Omar Khayyam, 1995, Aesop's Fables, 1995, The Poetry of Edgar Allen Poe, 1995. Avocations: travel, music, art. Office: ICM 8942 Wilshire Blvd Beverly Hills CA 90211-1934

YORK, RICHARD TRAVIS, art dealer; b. Nashville, Oct. 22, 1950; s. James Samuel and Jeane (Townes) Y. BA, Vanderbilt U., 1972. Dir. Am. art Hammer Galleries, N.Y.C., 1974-76; in charge Am. dept. M. Knoedler & Co., N.Y.C., 1976-77; assoc. Hirschl & Adler Galleries, N.Y.C., 1977-81; dir., owner Richard York Gallery, N.Y.C., 1981—. Author: (exhbn. catalogs) American Folk Art, 1977, The Eye of Steiglitz, 1978 (Arlis award), Buildings Architecture in American Modernism, 1980, Ellen Day Hale, 1981 (Arlis award), The Natural Image: Plant Forms in American Modernism, 1982, An American Gallery, 1986, vols. I & II, 1987, III & IV, 1988, V, 1989, VI, 1990, VII, 1992, Charles G. Shaw: Abstractions of the Thirties, 1987, Will Henry Stevens: A Modernist's Response to Nature, 1987, Joseph Stella: The Tropics, 1988, Joseph Goldyne: Twenty Years of Work, 1992, American Paintings from the Collection of James H. Ricau, 1993, Modernism at the Salons of America, 1922-1936, 1995. Mem. art adv. com. Colby Coll., 1990-94; mem. art adv. panel IRS, 1991—. Mem. Art Dealers Assn. Am. (bd. dirs. 1992-95), William Cullen Bryant Fellows, Met. Mus. of Art, N.Y.C. Office: Richard York Gallery 21 E 65th St New York NY 10021-6524

YORK, THEODORE ROBERT, consulting company executive; b. Mitchel Field, N.Y., May 4, 1926; s. Theodore and Helen (Zierak) Y.; m. Clara Kiefer, Jan. 3, 1952; children: Theodore R. II, Sharon L., Scott K., Krista A. Jarman. BS, U.S. Mil. Acad., 1950; MBA, George Washington U., 1964; MPA, Nat. U., 1984. Commd. 2d lt. USAF, 1950, advanced through grades to col., 1970, ret., 1974; pres. T. R. York Cons., Fairfax, Va., 1974-79, T. R. Cons., San Diego, 1979-85, ULTRAPLECS Intelligent Bldgs., Sandy, Utah, 1991—; dir. Software Productivity Consortium, Herndon, Va., 1985-90. Mem. Loudoun County Rep. Com., Leesburg, Va., 1990-91. Decorated DFC, Air medal (5), Meritorius Svc. medal, Joint Svcs. Commendation medal, Air Force Commendation medal (5). Mem. Internat. Facilities Mgmt. Assn., Intelligent Bldgs. Inst. (advisor), Instituto Mexicana Del Edificios Intelegente (hon.), Office Planners and Users Group, Shriners, Masons. Avocations: computers, electronics. Office: ULTRAPLECS Intelligent Bldg 1289 S Bluff View Dr Sandy UT 84092-5922 *Success is measured in terms of help from others. I believe in building a team to manage any project. Always use the word "we" and forget the word "I" when addressing a successful project and loyalty will follow.*

YORKE, JAMES ALAN, biomathematician; b. Beijing, Aug. 3, 1941; married; eight children. AB, Columbia U., 1963; PhD in Math., U. Md., 1966. From rsch. assoc. to rsch. assoc. prof. Inst. Phys. Sci. and Technology/U. Md., College Park, 1966-72, rsch. prof. math., 1972—; Guggenheim fellow, 1980-81. Mem. AAAS, Am. Math. Soc., Math. Assn. Am., Soc. Indsl. and Applied Math. Office: University of Maryland Inst for Phys Science & Tech College Park MD 20472 Office: Inst Phys Sci & Technology Univ Md College Park MD 20742-2431*

YORKIN, BUD (ALAN YORKIN), producer, director; b. Washington, Pa., Feb. 22, 1926; s. Maurice A. and Jessie (Sachs) Y.; children: Nicole, David. BS in Elec. Engring., Carnegie-Mellon U., 1948; postgrad. in English Lit., Columbia U., 1951; LHD, Washington and Jefferson Coll., 1974. ptnr. Tandem Prodns., Inc., L.A., 1959-74. With engring. staff, NBC, N.Y.C., 1949-50, stage mgr., NBC, 1950-52; assoc. dir. Colgate Comedy Hour, 1952-53; dir. TV shows including Dinah Shore Show, Tony Martin Show, Ernie Ford Show, George Gobel Show, N.Y.C. and L.A., 1948-52; writer, producer, dir. An Evening With Fred Astaire, 1958, Another Evening With Fred Astaire, 1959, Jack Benny spls., 1959; exec. producer TV series All in the Family, 1971-79, Sanford and Son, 1972-77, Maude, 1972-78, Good Times, 1974-79, Diff'rent Strokes, 1978-86, What's Happening, 1976-79, Carter Country, 1977-79, Archie Bunker's Place, 1980-83, The Night They Raided Minsky's, Cold Turkey, Deal of the Century, Blade Runner, also numerous spls.; dir. (films) Come Blow Your Horn, 1965, Never Too Late, 1966, Divorce, American Style, 1967, Inspector Clouseau, 1968; producer, dir. (films) Start the Revolution Without Me, 1970, The Thief Who Came to Dinner, 1971, Twice in a Lifetime, 1985, Arthur on the Rocks, 1988, Love Hurts, 1990, Intersection, 1993. Trustee Am. Film Inst., Mus. Contemporary Art, L.A., Carnegie-Mellon U., Am. Heart Assn., UCLA. Recipient several Emmy awards, Sylvania award, Look award, Dirs. Guild award, Harvard Lampoon's Golden Jester award, Peabody award. Mem. TV Acad. Arts and Scis. (past gov.), Dirs. Guild Am. (gov.). Office: Bud Yorkin Prodns Inc 345 N Maple Dr Ste 206 Beverly Hills CA 90210-3856

YORSZ, STANLEY, lawyer; b. Norwich, Conn., June 5, 1953; s. Stanley and Helen (Chimilewski) Y.; m. Margaret A. McLean, June 14, 1986. BA, Colgate U., 1975; JD, Dickinson U., 1978. Bar: Pa. 1978, U.S. Dist. Ct. (we. dist.) Pa. 1978, U.S. Ct. Appeals (3d cir.) 1980, U.S. Supreme Ct. 1980. Law clk. to judge Pa. Superior Ct., Pitts., 1978-80; assoc. Buchanan Ingersoll P.C., Pitts., 1980-86, ptnr., 1986—. Editor comments Dickinson Law Rev., 1978. Mem. ABA, Allegheny County Bar Assn., Pa. Bar Assn., Rivers Club. Roman Catholic. Avocations: tennis, squash, golf. Office: Buchanan Ingersoll PC 1 Oxford Ctr 301 Grant St Pittsburgh PA 15219

YORTY, SAMUEL, lawyer, former mayor; b. Lincoln, Nebr., Oct. 1, 1909; s. Frank Patrick and Johanna (Egan) Y.; m. Elizabeth Hensel, Dec. 1, 1938 (dec. Fev. 1984; 1 son, William Egan (dec. Oct. 1983); m. Gloria Haig, June 8, 1986. Student law sch., Southwestern U., U. So. Calif., U. Calif. Extension. Bar: Calif. bar 1939. Since practiced in Los Angeles; mem. 82d Congress from 14th Dist. Calif., 83d Congress from 26th Dist. Calif.; mayor Los Angeles, 1961-73; Mem. Calif. State Assembly, 1936-40, 49-50. Served to capt. USAAF, 1942-45. Decorated Encomineda medal Spain; comdr. Finnish Lion; Nat. Order So. Cross Brazil; comdr.'s cross German Order Merit; Gt. Silver Insignia of Honor with Star Austria; Order Civil Merit Korea; Knight Legion of Honor France; Order Homayoun medal Iran; Order Sun of Peru. Republican. Home and Office: 12979 Blairwood Dr Studio City CA 91604-4031

YOSELOFF, JULIEN DAVID, publishing company executive; b. N.Y.C., June 25, 1941; s. Thomas and Sara (Rothfuss) Y.; m. Darlene Starr Carbone, Aug. 6, 1967; children—Michael Ian, Anthony Alexander. B.A., U. Pa., 1962; student, London Sch. Econs., 1962-63; MA, Rutgers U., 1994. With A.S. Barnes and Co., Inc., Cranbury, N.J., 1963-80; dir. Associated Univ. Presses, Inc., 1966—; pres. Rosemont Pub. and Printing Corp., 1985—. Served with AUS, 1964. Mem. Phi Beta Kappa Assos, Phi Beta Kappa. Avocations: amateur radio, photography. Office: 440 Forsgate Dr Cranbury NJ 08512

YOSELOFF, THOMAS, publisher; b. Sioux City, Iowa, Sept. 8, 1913; s. Morris and Sarah (Rosansky) Y.; m. Sara Rothfuss, Apr. 30, 1938; children: Julien David, Mark Laurence; m. Lauretta Sellitti, Apr. 23, 1964; 1 dau.,

Tamar Rachel. A.B., U. Iowa, 1934; Litt.D. (hon.), Bucknell U., 1982; L.H.D. (hon.), Fairleigh Dickinson U., 1982. Chmn. Rosemont Pub. & Printing Corp., 1969—, Associated Univ. Presses, 1969—, Golden Cockerel Press, London, 1979—. Author: A Fellow of Infinite Jest, 1946, (with Lillian Stuckey) Merry Adventures of Till Eulenspiegel, 1944, Further Adventures of Till Eulenspiegel, pub. 1957, The Time of My Life, 1979; Editor: Seven Poets in Search of an Answer, 1944, Voyage to America, 1961, Comic Almanac, 1963, The Man from the Mercury, 1986. Pres. Center for War/Peace Studies, 1977-91. Recipient award of merit Bucknell U., 1975, award of merit U. Del., 1987. Mem. Phi Beta Kappa, Sigma Delta Chi, Delta Sigma Rho. Home: Box 289 68 Cedar Dr Colts Neck NJ 07722-1672 Office: 440 Forsgate Dr Cranbury NJ 08512

YOSHIDA, JAMES ATSUSHI, carbon fiber marketing company executive; b. Ohmiya, Watarai-gun, Mei-ken, Japan, Sept. 6, 1932; came to U.S., 1993; s. Hideo Yoshida and Sumiko (Aya) Murata; m. Sumiko Yoshida, Nov. 23, 1957; children: Linda Emmie Yoshida Wenstrand, Juri Yoshida Kameda. BA, George Pepperdine U., L.A., 1955; MA, U. S.C., 1958. Corp. planning mgr. Mitsui Petrochem, Tokyo, 1958-63; v.p. licensing, Japan rep. Sci. Design Co./Halcon, Tokyo, 1964-70; exec. v.p. mktg. Arco-Sumika Joint Venture, Tokyo, 1971-81; mng. dir. BASF Japan, Tokyo, 1981-92; pres. Toho Carbon Fibers, Palo Alto, Calif., 1993—; mktg. cons. Toho Rayon Co., Tokyo. Home: 8 Versailles Dr Menlo Park CA 94025-4226 Office: 444 High St Palo Alto CA 94301

YOSHIUCHI, ELLEN HAVEN, childbirth educator; b. Newark, Apr. 15, 1949; d. Michael Joseph and Adeline V. (Lindblom) Haven; m. Takeshi Yoshiuchi, Dec. 1, 1973; children: Teri Takumi, Niki Noboru. BA summa cum laude, CUNY, 1980; M Profl. Studies in Human Rels., N.Y. Inst. Tech., 1991. Cert. bereavement svcs. counselor. Pvt. practice childbirth edn., 1983-89; program asst. parent/family edn. St. Luke's/Roosevelt Hosp. Ctr., N.Y.C., 1989-93, mem. faculty parent/family edn. program, 1990—; mem. faculty Family Ctr. at Riverdale Neighborhood House, Bronx, N.Y., 1991—; mem. perinatal bereavement com. St. Luke's/Roosevelt Hosp. Ctr., N.Y.C., 1989—; mem. bd. trustees Pan Asian Repertory Theater, N.Y., 1996—. Editor ASPO/N.Y.C. News, 1983-86; contbr. articles to profl. jours. Bd. trustees Pan Asian Repertory Theatre, N.Y.C., 1996—. Fellow Am. Coll. Childbirth Educators; mem. ACA, Internat. Childbirth Edn. Assn., Assn. Specialists in Group Work, N.Y. State Perinatal Assn., Am. Soc. for Psychoprophylaxis in Obstetrics/Lamaze (cert. tchr., pres. N.Y.C. chpt. 1987-91, nominating com. 1991-93, dir. ednl. program 1991-93).

YOSHIZUMI, DONALD TETSURO, dentist; b. Honolulu, Feb. 18, 1930; s. Richard Kiyoshi and Hatsue (Tanouye) Y.; BS, U. Hawaii, 1952; DDS, U. Mo., 1960, MS, 1963; m. Barbara Fujiko Iwashita, June 25, 1955; children: Beth Ann E., Cara Leigh S., Erin Yuri. Clin. instr. U. Mo. Sch. Dentistry, Kansas City, 1960-63; pvt. practice, Santa Clara, Calif., 1963-70, San Jose, Calif., 1970—. With USAF, 1952-56. Mem. Am. Dental Assn., Calif. Dental Assn., Santa Clara County Dental Soc., Omicron Kappa Upsilon, Delta Sigma Delta. Contbr. articles to profl. jours. Home: 5054 Parkfield Ave San Jose CA 95129-3225 Office: 2011 Forest Ave San Jose CA 95128

YOSHIZUMI, TERRY TAKATOSHI, medical physicist; b. Osaka, Japan, July 2, 1949; came to U.S., 1975; s. Akira and Fumie Yoshizumi; m. Rebecca P. Peterson; 1 child, Alexander J. BS, Ehime U., Japan, 1973; MS, UCLA, 1975, U. Cin., 1977; PhD, U. Cin., 1980. Rsch. fellow Sloan-Kettering Inst., N.Y.C., 1980-81; chief radiation safety officer The Bklyn. Hosp., 1981-82; instr. U. Cin., 1982-83; asst. prof. W.Va. U., Morgantown, 1983-87, Howard Univ. Coll. Medicine, Washington, 1987-90; radiation safety officer Va. Conn. Health Care Sys., 1990—; assoc. rsch. scientist Yale U. Sch. of Medicine, New Haven, 1991-96, lectr., 1996—. Author: (with others) Physics of Nuclear Medicine, 1984; contbr. articles to profl. jours. including Physics Medicine and Biology, Jour. of Nuclear Medicine, Nuclear Med. Biology, Health Physics. Sloan-Kettering Ins./Cornell Grad. Sch. Med. Scis. postdoctoral fellow, 1980-81, Soc. Nuclear Medicine student rsch. fellow, 1980; U. Cin. scholar, 1975-80. Mem. Am. Coll. Radiology, Health Physics Soc., Am. Assn. of Physicists in Medicine. Office: Va Conn Health Care Sys 950 Campbell Ave West Haven CT 06516

YOSKIN, JON WILLIAM, II, insurance company executive; b. Phila., Oct. 16, 1939; s. Lewis William and Louise (Houck) Y.; m. Dorothea James, Sept. 25, 1961 (div. Mar. 1992); children: Nicholas, Dorothea, Maurice P.; m. Elizabeth Anne Groves, Sept 26, 1992. Pvt. practice Phila., 1959-74; sr. v.p. Middle Atlantic Gen. Investment Co., Phila., 1974-80; exec. v.p. Transatlantic Life Assurance Co., Phila., 1980-85, Meritor Life Ins. Co., Phila., 1985-88; owner, CEO Tri-Arc Fin. Svcs., Phila., 1988—; chmn. Remedium Ins. Co. Ltd., Bermuda, 1996—; bd. dirs. Nat. Media Corp.; chmn., CEO Remedium Ins. Co., Ltd., Bermuda, 1996—. bd. mem. Concerto Soloist, Phila., 1990-92; mem. Spl. Olympics Adv. Com. Mem. Nat. Assn. Life Underwriters, Nat. Assn. Ins. Brokers (bd. dirs.), Profl. Assn. Ins. Agts., Sons of Am. Revolution, Mil. Order Loyal Legion of U.S. Republican. Episcopalian. Avocation: big game hunting. Home: 1606 Pine St Philadelphia PA 19103-6711 Office: Tri-Arc Fin Svcs PO Box 6745 983 Old Eagle School Rd Ste 616 Wayne PA 19087

YOSKOWITZ, IRVING BENJAMIN, lawyer, manufacturing company executive; b. Bklyn., Dec. 2, 1945; s. Rubin and Jennie Y.; m. Carol L. Magil, Feb. 11, 1973; children: Stephen M., Robert J. BBA, CCNY, 1966; JD, Harvard U., 1969; postgrad., London Sch. Econs., 1971-72. Bar: N.Y. 1970, D.C. 1970, Conn. 1982. Programmer IBM, East Fishkill, N.Y., 1966; systems analyst Office Sec. Def., Washington, 1969-71; asso. firm Arnold & Porter, Washington, 1972-73; atty. IBM, 1973-79; regional counsel IBM, Bethesda, Md., to 1979; dep. gen. counsel United Technologies Corp., Hartford, Conn., 1979-81; v.p. and gen. counsel United Technologies Corp., 1981-86, sr. v.p., gen. counsel, 1986-90, exec. v.p., gen. counsel, 1990—; bd. dirs. BBA Group, PLC, 1995—. Mem. editorial bd. Harvard Law Rev., 1968-69. With U.S. Army, 1969-71. Knox fellow, 1971-72. Mem. ABA, Am. Corp. Counsel Assn. (bd. dirs. 1982-85), Assn. Gen. Counsels. Office: United Techs Corp United Techs Bldg Hartford CT 06101

YOSOWITZ, SANFORD, lawyer, metal sales and fabricating executive; b. Cleve., July 26, 1939; s. Joseph and Esther (Moss) Y.; m. Ruth A. Goodman, June 24, 1962; children: Jeffrey Seth, Mark Robert, Chari Beth. B.S., Ohio State U., 1961; J.D., Case Western Res. U., 1964. Bar: Ohio 1964. Assoc. Lane, Krotinger & Santora, Cleve., 1964-66; law practice Cleve., 1966-69; corp. atty., asst. sec. Alcan Aluminum Corp., Cleve., 1969-73, sr. atty., asst. sec., 1979-80, v.p., gen. counsel, sec., 1980—; also dir. Alcan Aluminum Corp.; div. counsel Alcan Bldg. Products, Cleve., 1973-79; sec./treas. Nikkei N.Am. Aluminum, Inc., 1992—; lectr. Ohio Legal Ctr. Inst., 1969-70, Greater Cleve. Bar Assn., 1972—; adv. bd. Can.-U.S. Law Inst. Editor-in-chief: Western Res. Law Rev., 1963-64; pub., editor: Industrial Concentration, 1979; editorial chmn.: Antitrust Law Jour., 1977-84. Ann. show producer Boy Scouts Am., 1982; auctioneer pub. TV auction, 1974-81, community theatre actor, party entertainment producer and lyricist. Recipient of merit Ohio Legal Ctr. Inst., 1969. Mem. ABA (coun. mem. antitrust law sect. 1984-87), Bar Assn. Greater Cleve. (chmn. corp. law dept. sect. 1973), Ohio Bar Assn., Cuyahoga County Bar Assn., Sigma Alpha Mu. Home: 2585 Larchmont Rd Cleveland OH 44122-1515 Office: Alcan Aluminum Corp 6060 Parkland Blvd Cleveland OH 44124-4185

YOST, LYLE EDGAR, farm equipment manufacturing company executive; b. Hesston, Kans., Mar. 5, 1913; s. Joseph and Alma (Hensley) Y.; m. Erma Martin, July 31, 1938; children: Byron, Winston, Susan, Cameron. B.S. B.A, Goshen Coll., 1937; postgrad., U. Ind., 1940. With St. Joseph Valley Bank, Elkhart, Ind., 1938-41; tchr. Wakarusa (Ind.) High Sch., 1942-45; founder Hesston Corp., Kans., 1947, pres., 1949-83; now chmn. bd. Hesston Corp.; ret., 1991. Bd. dirs., past pres. Farm and Indsl. Equipment Inst.; mem. Gov.'s Com. for Ptnrs. for Progress Kans.-Paraguay; chmn. com. establishing creamery in Uruguay, 1967; mem. State Dept. cultural del. to USSR, 1967; past chmn. pres.'s adv coun. Hesston Coll. (Kans.); chmn. Prince of Peace Chapel, Aspen, Colo. Named Farmarketing Man of Year Nat. Agrl. Advt. and Marketing Assn., 1969; Kansan of Achievement in Bus., 1972; Kansan of Year, 1974. Mem. Alpha Kappa Psi (hon.). Home: 123 Kingsway Hesston KS 67062-9271 Office: PO Box 909 Hesston KS 67062-0909

YOST, NICHOLAS CHURCHILL, lawyer; b. Washington, Aug. 15, 1938; s. Charles Woodruff and Irene Ravitch (Oldakowska) Y.; m. Sandra Moore Rennie; children: Robert, Scott, Daniel. AB, Princeton U., 1960; LLB, U. Calif., Berkeley, 1963. Bar: Calif. 1964, U.S. Supreme Ct. 1972, D.C. 1978. Dep. atty. gen. adminstrv. law Calif. Dept. Justice, 1965-69; counsel Calif. State Environ. Quality Study Coun., 1969-71; dep. atty. gen. in charge environ. unit Calif. Dept. Justice, 1971-77; gen. counsel Coun. Environ. Quality, Exec. Office of Pres., Washington, 1977-81; vis. scholar Environ. Law Inst., Washington, 1981-82; sr. atty. Ctr. for Law in Pub. Interest, Washington, 1982-85; ptnr. Dickstein, Shapiro & Morin, Washington, 1985-94, Sonnenschein Nath & Rosenthal, San Francisco, 1994—; U.S. dir. legal and adminstrv. aspects of environ. protection agreement between U.S. and USSR, 1977-81; dir. Pres.'s Task Force on Global Resources and Environ., 1980-81; mem. U.S. Del. to UN Conf. Environ. and Devel., Rio, 1992; mem. Calif. EPA Blue Ribbon Com. on a Unified Environ. Statute, 1994—. Contbr. articles to profl. jours. Capt. U.S. Army, 1963-65. Mem. ABA (chmn. standing com. on environ. law 1989-91), State Bar Calif. (chmn. com. on environ. 1975-76), D.C. Bar Assn. (co-chmn. environ., energy and natural resources sect. 1985-86, 88-89), Environ. Law Inst. (bd. dirs. 1986-92), UN Assn. L.A. (v.p. 1969-71), UN Assn. Washington (bd. dirs. 1987-93). Home: 901 Powell St Apt 8 San Francisco CA 94108-2024 Office: Sonnenschein Nath 685 Market St Fl 10 San Francisco CA 94105-4200

YOST, PAUL ALEXANDER, JR., foundation executive, retired coast guard officer; b. Phila., Jan. 3, 1929; s. Paul Alexander Sr. and Jeanne Moore (Bailey) Y.; m. Jan Worth, June 2, 1951; children: Linda L., Paul Alexander III, David J., Lisa L., Christopher J. BS, USCG Acad., 1951; MS, U. Conn., 1959; MA, George Washington U., 1964; grad., Naval War Coll., 1964. Commd. ensign USCG, 1951, advanced through grades to adm., 1986; comdr. 8th dist. USCG, New Orleans, 1978-81; chief staff hdqrs. USCG, Washington, 1981-84; comdr. 3d dist., maritime Atlantic def. zone, and Atlantic area USCG, N.Y.C., 1984-86; commandant USCG, Washington, 1986-90, ret., 1990; pres. James Madison Found., Washington, 1990—. Decorated D.S.M. with gold star, Silver Star, Legion of Merit combat "V" with gold star, Meritorious Service Medal. Office: James Madison Meml Fellowship Found 2000 K St NW Washington DC 20006-1809

YOST, WILLIAM ALBERT, psychology educator, hearing researcher; b. Dallas, Sept. 21, 1944; s. William Jacque and Gladys (Funk) Y.; m. Lee Prater, June 15, 1969; children—Kelley Ann, Alyson Leigh. B.A., Colo. Coll., 1966; Ph.D., Ind. U., 1970. Assoc. prof. psychology U. Fla., Gainesville, 1971-77; dir. sensory physiology and perception program NSF, Washington, 1982-83; prof. psychology Loyola U., Chgo., 1977-89, dir. Parmly Hearing Inst., 1977—, prof. hearing scis., 1990—; adj. prof. psychology and otolarynogology Loyola U., Chgo., 1990—; individual expert bio-acoustics Am. Nat. Stds. Inst., 1983—; mem. study sect. Nat. Inst. Deafness and Other Communication Disorders, 1990-94; mem. hearing bioacoustics and biomechanics com. Nat. Rsch. Coun., 1992—. Author: Fundamentals of Hearing, 1977, 84, 94; editor (with others) New Directions in Hearing Science, 1985, Directional Hearing, 1987, Auditory Processing of Complex Sounds, 1987, Classification of Complex Sounds, 1989, Psychoacoustics, 1993; assoc. editor Auditory Neurosci., 1994—; ad hoc reviewer NSF, Air Force Office Sci. Rsch., Office Naval Rsch., 1981—; contbr. chpts. to books, articles to profl. jours. Pres. Evanston Tennis Assn., Ill., 1984, 90. Grantee NSF, 1974—, NIH, 1975—, AFOSR, 1983—. Fellow AAAS, Acoustical Soc. Am. (assoc. editor jour. 1984-91, chair tech. com. 1990—), Am. Speech-Lang.-Hearing Assn.; mem. NAS (exec. com. on hearing bioacoustics, biomechanics 1981-87, chmn. 1993-97), Assn. Rsch. in Otolaryngology (sec.-treas. 1984-87, pres.-elect 1987-88, pres. 1988-89), Acoustics Soc. Am. (chair com. psychol. and physiol. acoustics 1990—), Nat. Inst. Deafness and Other Comm. Disorders (task force, rev. panel 1990—, chmn. 1994), Am. Auditory Soc. (exec. bd. 1993-98). *I am fortunate that I am in an occupation that is so much fun. Teaching and research are very enjoyable. Most days for me are fun.*

YOTHER, MICHELE, publisher; b. Atlanta, Aug. 25, 1965; d. Carole (Spence) Marsh; m. Michael B. Yother, Mar. 17, 1990; 1 child, Christina Michele. BA in acctg. cum laude, Ga. State U., 1990. Asst. v.p. Bank Am., Atlanta, 1986-90; pres. Gallopade Pub. Group, Atlanta, 1990—; pres. Carole Marsh Family Interactive Multimedia, 1993—. Pub. over 2500 children's books, computer disks and activities. Equifax Bus. scholar Ga. State U., 1989. Mem. Women's Nat. Book Assn. (bd. dirs. 1994-95), Bank Am. Club (pres. 1989), Golden Key. Methodist. Home: 359 Milledge Ave SE Atlanta GA 30312-3238 Office: Gallopade Pub Group 359 Milledge Ave SE Ste 100 Atlanta GA 30312-3238

YOTHERS, WENDY LOU, artist, silversmith; b. Grand Rapids, Mich., May 21, 1952; d. Lee W. and Winona (Largen) Y.; 1 child, Douglas Emory Olds. BFA cum laude, U. Mich., 1974; cert., Nat. Coll. Goldsmithing, Lahti, Finland, 1984; MFA (Mgh) with distinction, Guldsmedehojskolen, Copenhagen, 1987. Teaching asst. Tex. Tech. U., Lubbock, 1979-81; lectr. Nat. Coll. Goldsmithing, Lahti, 1982-84; silversmith specializing in restoration, prototype making and prodn. smithing Studio Torben Hardenberg, Copenhagen, 1987, Tiffany & Co., N.Y.C. and Parsipany, N.J., 1993—; silversmith specializing in restoration, prototype making and prodn. smithing Kirk Stieff & Co., Balt., 1988, prototype, model maker, 1989-92. Author: (textbook) Enameling, 1984; exhibited in group shows at Tex. Tech. Mus., Lubbock, 1980, Nat. Inst. Arts and Handcraft, Lahti, 1982, Mus. Applied Art, Hensinki, 1984, Bella Ctr., Copenhagen, 1986, Galleri Metal, Copenhagen, 1986, Gallery Fgn. Ministry, Houses Parliament, Copenhagen, 1986, Galleri Hummeluhre, Jutland, Denmark, 1986, Hotel Sheraton, Goteborg, Sweden, 1986, Frantz Hingelberg Gallery, Arhus, Denmark, 1987, Petur Tryggvi Hjalmarsson Gallery, Reykjavik, Iceland, 1987, Musee des Arts Decoratifs, Paris, 1987-88, Mus. Applied Art, Copenhagen, 1987, Soc. Am. Silversmiths and Soc. Arts and Crafts, Boston, 1990, Soc. Arts and Crafts, 1991, Pritam & Eames, East Hampton, N.Y., 1992, Nat. Mus. Ornamental Metalwork, Memphis, 1992, Worcester (Mass.) Ctr. Crafts, 1992, Nat. Ornamental Metal Mus., Memphis, 1993, Lunt's Design Ctr. Gallery, 1996, Yashiva U. Gallery, 1996, Shreve, Crumy and Lowe Centennial Exhbn., 1996. Grad. rsch. grantee Tex. Tech. U., Lubbock, 1979-80; Rotary Internat. grad. fellow, 1981-82; recipient Cultural award Am. Women's Club, Denmark, 1986, Direcktor Ib Henrickson's Fond stipend, 1985-87. Fellow Soc. Am. Silversmiths. Roman Catholic. Avocations: walking, reading, dancing, art. Home: 90 Oakwood Village #3 Flanders NJ 07836 Office: Tiffany & Co 801 Jefferson Rd Parsippany NJ 07054-3710

YOUMAN, ROGER JACOB, editor, writer; b. N.Y.C., Feb. 25, 1932; s. Robert Harold and Ida (Kellner) Y.; m. Lillian Frank, June 22, 1958; children: Nancy, Laura, Joshua, Andrew. B.A., Swarthmore Coll., 1953. Desk asst. CBS News, N.Y.C., 1953; program editor TV Guide, N.Y.C., 1956; regional editor TV Guide, Memphis, 1956-57, Houston, 1957; asst. programming editor TV Guide, N.Y.C., 1957-60; assoc. editor TV Guide, Radnor, Pa., 1960-65, asst. mng. editor, 1965-72, mng. editor, 1972-76, exec. editor, 1976-79, 80-81, co-editor, 1981-90, editor, 1990-93; editor Panorama, 1979-80; editl. dir. TV Guide On Screen, 1993—; del. U.S.-Soviet Bilateral Info. Talks, 1988, 90. Author: How Sweet It Was, The Television Years; contbr. articles to various publs. Served with AUS, 1954-55. Mem. NATAS, Am. Soc. Mag. Editors. Home: 752 Mancill Rd Wayne PA 19087-2043 Office: TV Guide 4 Corporate Ctr Radnor PA 19088

YOUMANS, JULIAN RAY, neurosurgeon, educator; b. Baxley, Ga., Jan. 2, 1928; s. John Edward and Jennie Lou (Milton) Y.; children—Reed Nesbit, John Edward, Julian Milton. B.S., Emory U., 1949, M.D., 1952; M.S., U. Mich., 1955, Ph.D., 1957. Diplomate: Am. Bd. Neurol. Surgery. Intern U. Mich. Hosp., Ann Arbor, 1952-53; resident in neurol. surgery U. Mich. Hosp., 1953-55, 56-58; fellow in neurology U. London, 1955-56; asst. prof. neurosurgery U. Miss., 1959-62, assoc. prof., 1962-63; assoc. prof. Med. U. S.C., 1963-65, prof., 1965-67, chief div. neurosurgery, 1963-67; prof. U. Calif., Davis, 1967-91; prof. emeritus, 1991—; chmn. dept. neurosurgery U. Calif., 1967-82; cons. USAF, U.S. Army, VA, NRC. Editor: Neurological Surgery, 1973; contbr. articles to profl. jours. No. vice chmn. Republican State Central Com. of Calif., 1979-81. Served with U.S. Navy, 1944-46. Mem. Am. Coll. Surgeons, Am. Assn. Neurol. Surgeons, Am. Assn. Surgery of Trauma, Pan-Pacific Surg. Assn., Western Neurosurg. Soc., Neurosurg. Soc. Am., Soc. Neurol. Surgeons, Soc. Univ. Neurosurgeons, N. Pacific Soc. Neurology and Psychiatry, Royal Soc. Medicine, Am. Trauma Soc., U.S. C. of C., Bohemian Club, Sutter Club, Capital Club of Sacramento, Rotary. Republican. Episcopalian. Office: 502 Mace Blvd Ste 10 Davis CA 95616-4338

YOUN, MYEUNG-RO, painter, educator; b. Chong-Up, Korea, Oct. 14, 1936; s. Moosung Youn and Bonglim Lee; m. Seung-Jae Han, Dec. 18, 1971; children: Kyung-Jin, Eyu-Jin. BFA, Seoul Nat. U., 1960; postgrad., Pratt Graphic Ctr., 1969. Prof. Seoul Nat. U. Coll. Fine Arts, 1972—, dean Coll., 1996; mem. jury Seoul Internat. Print Biennale, 1980, Internat. Biennial Print Exhbn., Taiwan, 1987, Machida-Tokyo, 1993; dir. Visual Art Inst., Seoul Nat. U., 1990-94. One-man shows include Artcore Gallery, L.A., 1984, Hoam Gallery, Seoul, 1991, Sunjae Mus. Fine Art, Kyung-Joo, Korea, 1992, Phak Gallery, Seoul, 1995; exhibited in group shows 3d Biennale de Paris, 1963, XV Bienal of Sao Paulo, 1967, Korean Contemporary Painting, Tokyo, 1968, Internat. Exhbn. Graphic Art, Venice, Italy, 1972, XI Festival internat. de la Peinteur, Gagnes-sur-Mer, France, 1979, Internat. Print Biennial, Ljubljana, 1993, Intergrafia, 1994, Poland, 1994; author: Korean Contemporary Print, 1991. Mem. orgn. com. Kwangju Biennale, 1995—. John D. Rockefeller Found. fellow, 1969; recipient Grand prize 7th Seoul Internat. Print Biennale, 1990. Mem. Korea Fine Arts Assn. (vice dir. 1986-88), Korea Printmakers Assn. (rep. 1973-80). Avocations: music, golf. Home: 412-5 Pyungchang-Dong, Chongro-Ku Seoul 110-012, Republic of Korea Office: Seoul Nat U Coll Fine Arts, San 56-1 Shinlim Dong, Seoul 151-010, Republic of Korea

YOUNG, ALICE, lawyer; b. Washington, Apr. 7, 1950; d. John and Elizabeth (Jen) Y.; m. Thomas L. Shortall, Sept. 22, 1984; children: Amanda, Stephen. AB magna cum laude, Yale U., 1971; JD, Harvard U., 1974. Bar: N.Y. 1975. Assoc. Coudert Bros., N.Y.C., 1974-81; mng. ptnr. Graham & James, N.Y.C., 1981-87; ptnr. Milbank, Tweed, Hadley & McCloy, N.Y.C., 1987-93; ptnr., chair Asia Pacific Practice (U.S.) Kaye, Scholer, Fierman, Hays & Handler, N.Y.C., 1994—; mem. Coun. on Fgn. Rels., 1977—. Contbr. articles to profl. jours. Trustee Aspen (Colo.) Inst., 1988—, Pan-Asian Repertory Theatre, N.Y.C., 1987-90, Lingnan Found., N.Y.C., 1984-91, Asia/Pacific Coun. of The Nature Conservancy, 1995—; mem. bus. com. Met. Mus. Art, N.Y.C., 1989-94, Nat. Com. on U.S.-China Rels., 1993—, U.S.-China Bus. Coun., 1993—, Com. of 100, 1993—, dir. 1995—; mem. bd. overseers visitation com. to Law Sch., Harvard U., 1994—, chair subcom. on grad. program Harvard U., 1996. Named one of 40 Under 40 Crain's Bus., N.Y.C., 1989; Bates fellow Yale U., 1970, NDFL fellow Harvard U., 1967-68; recipient Star award N.Y. Women's Agenda, 1992. Mem. ABA, N.Y. State Bar Assn. (fgn. investment com.), Assn. Bar City N.Y. (spl. com. on rels. with Japanese bar, Union Internat. des Avocats), Nat. Asian Pacific Am. Bar Assn., Asian Am. Bar Assn. N.Y., Harvard Law Sch. Assn. N.Y.C. (trustee 1990-94), Japan Soc. (sec. 1989—), Asia Soc. (pres.'s coun. 1984—). Office: Kaye Scholer Fierman Hays & Handler 425 Park Ave New York NY 10022-3598

YOUNG, ALINE PATRICE, controller; b. Sacramento, Nov. 8, 1957; d. Rene Francis and Patricia May (Taylor) LeFevre; m. Patrick Charles Young, Sept. 6, 1976 (div. Oct. 1979); 1 child, Daniel Alan Young. AA, Fullerton Coll., 1979; BA, Calif State U., Fullerton, 1981; MBA, Pepperdine U., 1988. Mgmt. devel. program Gen. Electric Credit, Anaheim, Calif., 1981-83; credit mgr. Kwikset/Emhart, Anaheim, Calif., 1983-88, Avery Dennison, Azusa, Calif., 1988-90; contr., fin. mgr. Avery Dennison, Monrovia, Calif., 1990-92, site mgr., contr., 1992-95; mgr. advanced cost sys. Allied Signal Inc., Torrance, Calif., 1995—. Chairperson Vision 95 Lutheran High Sch., Orange, Calif., 1993. Mem. Am. Mgmt. Assn., Inst. Mgmt. Accts. Republican. Lutheran. Avocations: skiing, reading, dancing. Office: Allied Signal Aerospace M/Stor 38-2 2525 W 190th St Torrance CA 90504

YOUNG, ANDREW, clergyman, civil rights leader, former mayor, former ambassador, former congressman; b. New Orleans, Mar. 12, 1932; s. Andrew J. and Daisy (Fuller) Y.; m. Jean Childs, June 7, 1954; children—Andrea, Lisa Dru, Paula Jean, Andrew J. III. Student, Dillard U., 1947-48; B.S., Howard U., 1951; B.D., Hartford Theol. Sem., 1955; D.D. (hon.), Wesleyan U., 1970, United Theol. Sem. Twin Cities, 1970; LL.D. (hon.), Wilberforce U., 1971, Clark Coll., 1973, Yale U., 1973, Swarthmore Coll., Atlanta U., others; numerous other hon. degrees. Ordained to ministry Congl. Ch., 1955; pastor in Thomasville, Ga., 1955-57; assoc. dir. dept. youth work Nat. Council Chs., 1957-61; mem. staff So. Christian Leadership Conf., 1961-70, adminstr. citizen edn. program, 1961-64, exec. dir., 1964-70, exec. v.p., 1967-70; now bd. dirs.; mem. 93d-95th Congresses from 5th Ga. Dist.; mem. Rules com.; U.S. ambassador to UN, 1977-79; mayor of Atlanta, 1982-89; co-chmn. Atlanta Com. for the Olympic Games, 1996. Chmn. Atlanta Community Relations Commn., 1970-72; chmn. bd. Delta Ministry of Miss.; bd. dirs. Martin Luther King, Jr. Center for Social Change, Robert F. Kennedy Meml. Found., Field Found., So. Christian Leadership Conf. Recipient Pax-Christi award St. John's U., 1970; Springarn medal.; Medal of Freedom, 1980, French Legion of Honor medal, 1982; co-recipient, Martin Luther King, Jr., Award for Public Svc. (Ebony mag.), 1990. Mem. Ams. Dem. Action. Office: Law Internat Inc 1000 Abernathy Rd NE Atlanta GA 30328-5603

YOUNG, ANDREW BRODBECK, lawyer; b. Phila., Feb. 8, 1907; s. Edward E. and Estelle (Brodbeck) Y.; m. Olive C. Sherley, Apr. 22, 1933; children: Andrew Oliver (dec.), Sherley (Mrs. Paul A. Hollos). A.B., Princeton U., 1928; LL.B., Harvard U., 1931. Bar: Pa. 1931. Ptnr. Stradley, Ronon, Stevens & Young, Phila., 1985-95, assoc., 1995—; v.p., bd. dirs. W.W. Interests (formerly Warren Webster & Co.); bd. dirs. M.A. Bruder & Sons, Inc., Welex Inc., Holmes Investment Co., Phila.; lectr. finance U. Pa., 1939-66; lectr. various tax insts., 1953-81; mem. Mayor's Com. Exec. and Elective Salaries Phila. City Govt., 1959, Mayor's Com. Port Promotion Phila., 1959-63; mem. adv. coun. Phila. Cmty. Renewal Program, 1964-66; chmn., dir. Phila. Indsl. Devel. Corp., 1963-68, pres., 1963-70, chmn., 1970-86; mem. Mayor's Tax Study Commn., 1960, mem. Commr. Internal Revenue's Adv. Group, 1965; voting trustee Phila. Belt Line Ry. Co. Chmn. bd. trustees Mary Jacobs Meml. Libr. Found., Rocky Hill, N.J.; trustee Lovett Found., Michael Bruder Found., Frank Michaels Scholarship Found., Penjerdel Found.; mem. coun. pres.'s advisers LaSalle Coll., 1969-74. With Surgeon Gen.'s Office, AUS, 1942-45. Fellow Am. Bar Found.; mem. ABA (mem. ho. of dels. 1966-70, mem. council tax sect. 1958-70, chmn. sect. 1963-65), Pa. Bar Assn., Am. Law Inst. (tax adv. group, corps.-stockholders project 1957-59), Am. Coll. Tax Counsel, Am. Law Inst. (estate and gift tax project 1964-67), Phila. C. of C. (pres. 1958-60, chmn. bd. 1960-62, dir.), Am. Arbitration Assn. (nat. panel arbitrators), Phi Beta Kappa. Republican. Episcopalian. Clubs: Philadelphia, Sunday Breakfast, Sunnybook Golf, Tunkhannock Creek Assn., Penn, Wilderness, Anglers. Home: 613 Foulkeways Gwynedd PA 19436-1024 Office: 2600 One Commerce Sq 2005 Market St Philadelphia PA 19103-7042

YOUNG, ANN ELIZABETH O'QUINN, historian, educator; b. Waycross, Ga.; d. James Foster and Pearl Elizabeth (Sasser) O'Quinn; student Shorter Coll.; BA, MA, U. Ga., PhD, 1965; m. Robert William Young, Aug. 18, 1968; children: Abigail Ann, Leslie Lynn. Asst. prof. history Kearney (Nebr.) State Coll. (name now U. Nebr. at Kearney 1991), 1965-69, assoc. prof., 1969-72, prof., 1972—; participant Inst. on Islam, Middle East and World Politics, U. Mich., summer 1984, Coun. on Internat. Ednl. Exch., London, 1990, NEH Seminar NYU, 1993, faculty mem. 1985—, sec. 1993-94, pres.-elect 1994-95, pres. 1995—. Mem. NEA, PEO, Phi Alpha Theta, Delta Kappa Gamma (chpt. pres. 1978-79), Phi Mu. Republican. Presbyterian. Contbg. author Dictionary of Georgia Biography; contbr. articles to profl. revs. Office: U Nebr at Kearney Dept History Kearney NE 68849-1285

YOUNG, ARTHUR PRICE, librarian, educator; b. Boston, July 29, 1940; s. Arthur Price and Marion (Freeman) Y.; m. Patricia Dorothy Foss, June 26, 1965; children: John Marshall, Christopher Price. B.A., Tufts U., 1962; M.A.T., U. Mass., 1964; M.S. in L.S., Syracuse U., 1969; Ph.D., U. Ill., 1976. Head reader services, social sci. bibliographer SUNY-Cortland, 1969-72; rsch. assoc. U. Ill. Libr. Rsch. Ctr., Urbana, 1972-75; asst. dean pub. services, assoc. prof. U. Ala., Tuscaloosa, 1976-81; dean librs., prof. U. R.I., Kingston, 1981-89; dir. Thomas Cooper Libr., U. S.C., Columbia, 1989-93; sr. fellow UCLA, 1991; dir. librs. No. Ill. U., DeKalb, 1993—; mem. adj. faculty Syracuse (N.Y.) U., 1970-71, Rosary Coll., River Forest, Ill., 1994—;

pres. Consortium R.I. Acad. and Rsch. Librs., 1983-85; bd. govs. Univ. Press New Eng., 1987-89; mem. exec. bd. Ill. Libr. Computer Sys. Orgn., 1995—; chair Coun. Dirs. State Univ. Librs., 1994-95. Author: Books for Sammies: American Library Association and World War I, 1981, American Library History: A Bibliography of Dissertations and Theses, 1988, Higher Education in American Life, 1636-1986: A Bibliography of Dissertations and Theses, 1988, Cities and Towns in American History: A Bibliography of Doctoral Dissertations, 1989, Academic Libraries: Research Perspectives, 1990, Religion and the American Experience, 1620-1900: A Bibliography of Doctoral Dissertations, 1992, Religion and the American Experience, the Twentieth Century: A Bibliography of Doctoral Dissertations, 1994; editl. bd. various jours. Chair Coun. of Dirs. Ill. State Univ. Librs., 1994-95. Served to capt. USAF, 1964-68. Recipient Berner Nash award U. Ill., 1976. Mem. ALA (chmn. editorial bd.), Assn. Coll. and Rsch. Librs. (publs. in librarianship 1982-88, chmn. Jesse H. Shera Endowment Fund com. 1991-94), S.C. Libr. Assn. (chmn. libr. adminstrn. sect. 1991-92), Assn. Rsch. Librs. (scholarly commn. com. 1991-93), Orgn. Am. Historians, Am. Hist. Assn., Phi Kappa Phi, Beta Phi Mu, Phi Delta Kappa. Episcopalian. Home: 912 Borden Ave Sycamore IL 60178-3200

YOUNG, BARBARA, psychiatrist, psychoanalyst, psychiatry educator, photographer; b. Chgo., Oct. 27, 1920; d. William Harvey and Blanche (DeBra) Y. AB, Knox Coll., 1942; MD, Johns Hopkins U., 1945; grad., Balt. Psychoanalytic Inst., 1955. Intern Univ. Hosps., Iowa City, Iowa, 1945-46, asst. resident in neurologh, 1945-47; asst. resident in psychiatry Phipps Clinic, Johns Hopkins U. Hosp., Balt., 1947-49; staff psychiatrist Perry Point (Md.) VA Hosp., 1949-51; practice medicine specializing in psychiatry/psychoanalysis Balt., 1951—; instr. Johns Hopkins U., 1953-69, asst. prof. psychiatry, 1969—; asst. prof. emeritus, photographer, 1958—; lectr. dept. psychiatry Johns Hopkins U.; lectr. Lucy Daniels Found., Carey, N.C., local psychiat. and social orgns. Works represented in Mus. Modern Art, N.Y.C., Balt. Mus. Art, Santa Barbara (Calif.) Mus. Art, Eastman House, Rochester, N.Y., Yale U. Gallery of Art; photographer: The Plop-A-Lop Tree, 1995. Mem. Am. Psychoanlytic Assn., Am. Psychiat. Assn., Balt.-Washington Soc. for Psychoanalysis. Democrat. Address: 5307 Herring Run Dr Baltimore MD 21214-1937

YOUNG, BARNEY THORNTON, lawyer; b. Chillicothe, Tex., Aug. 10, 1934; s. Bayne and Helen Irene (Thornton) Y.; m. Sarah Elizabeth Taylor, Aug. 31, 1957; children: Jay Thornton, Sarah Elizabeth, Serena Taylor. BA, Yale U., 1955; LLB, U. Tex., 1958. Bar: Tex. 1958. Assoc. Thompson, Knight, Wright & Simmons, Dallas, 1958-65; ptnr. Rain, Harrell, Emery, Young & Doke, Dallas, 1965-87; mem. firm Locke Purnell Rain Harrell (A Profl. Corp.), 1987—; bd. dirs. Jones-Blair Co. Mem. adv. coun. Dallas Community Chest Trust Fund, Inc., 1964-66; bd. dirs. Mental Health Assn. Dallas County, Inc., 1969-72, Trammell Crow Family Found., 1984-87; trustee Hockaday Sch., Dallas, 1971-77, 90—, chmn. 1994—, Dallas Zool. Soc., 1986-92, Lamplighter Sch., Dallas, 1976—, chmn., 1983-86, St. Mark's Sch., Dallas, 1970—, pres., 1976-78, The Found. for Callier Ctr. and Comm. Disorders, 1988—, Friends of Ctr. for Human Nutrition, 1988—, Shelter Ministries of Dallas Found., 1993—, Dallas Hist. Soc., 1993—; mem. Yale Devel. Bd., 1984-91. Fellow Tex. Bar Found., Dallas Bar Found.; mem. ABA, Tex. Bar Assn., Dallas Bar Assn., Am. Judicature Soc., Order of Coif, Phi Beta Kappa, Pi Sigma Alpha, Phi Gamma Delta, Phi Delta Phi, Dallas Country Club, Dallas County Rep. Men's Club (bd. dirs. 1977-79), Petroleum Club (Dallas), Yale Club (Dallas, N.Y.C.). Home: 6901 Turtle Creek Blvd Dallas TX 75205-1251 Office: Locke Purnell Rain Harrell 2200 Ross Ave Dallas TX 75201-7903

YOUNG, BETTY L., special education/elementary education educator; b. Pitts., Sept. 29, 1938; m. Kenneth R. Young; children: Kenneth M., Dawn L. Pustay, Wendy A. Essex, Patrick A. Student, LaRoche Coll., 1970-71; BS in Edn./Spl. Edn., Slippery Rock U., 1975, postgrad., 1976—; postgrad., Carlow Coll., 1991. Tchr. Allegheny Intermediate Unit, Pitts., 1985-88, Carlynton Sch. Dist., Carnegie, Pa., 1989—; dir. unit Camp Starburst for the Emotionally Disabled, Pitts., 1986-88. Mem. Perry Hwy. Presch. Bd., Slippery Rock Alumni Assn. Avocations: walking, biking, physical fitness, arts and crafts. Home: 490 Brown Rd Wexford PA 15090-8401

YOUNG, BLESS STRITAR, lawyer; b. Mar. 17, 1947. Student, Marietta Coll., 1965-68; BA, Temple U., 1969, JD, 1973. Bar: Pa. 1973, U.S. Dist. Ct. (ea. dist.) Pa. 1975, D.C. 1978, U.S. Ct. Appeals (D.C. cir.) 1978, N.Y. 1979, U.S. Supreme Ct. 1979, Calif. 1983, U.S. Dist. Ct. (no. dist.) Calif. 1983, U.S. Dist. Ct. (so. and cen. dists.) Calif. 1985. Assoc. Arthur S. Kafrissen & Assocs., Phila., 1973-74; atty. Bell of Pa., Phila., 1974-77, AT&T, N.Y.C., 1977-83; gen. atty. AT&T, San Francisco, 1983-87, L.A., 1987-88; ptnr. Fulbright & Jaworski, L.A., 1988—; judge pro tem Contra Costa County Superior Ct., Martinez, Calif., 1985-87, L.A. Mcpl. Ct., 1988—. Atty. Vol. Lawyers for Arts, N.Y.C., 1977-83. Named one of Outstanding Young Women Am., 1977. Mem. ABA (sect. litigation, labor and employment commn., chairperson trade secrets litigation subcom. 1994—, co-chair ERISA and Employee Benefits litigation subcom. 1992-94, editor Model Jury Instructions: Employment Litigation 1994), L.A. Bar Assn. (jud. evaluation com. 1993—, labor and employment sect.), Calif. Bar Assn., Pi Kappa Delta. Office: Fulbright & Jaworski 865 S Figueroa St Los Angeles CA 90017-2543

YOUNG, BRYANT LLEWELLYN, lawyer, business executive; b. Rockford, Ill., Mar. 9, 1948; s. Llewellyn Anker and Florence Ruth Y. AB, Cornell U., 1970; JD, Stanford U., 1974. Bar: Calif. 1974, Nev. 1975, D.C. 1979. Law clk. U.S. Dist. Ct. (no. dist.) Calif., San Francisco, 1974-75; assoc. Dinkelspiel, Pelavin, Steefel & Levitt, San Francisco, 1975-77; White House fellow, spl. asst. to sec. HUD, Washington, 1977-78, spl. asst. to sec., 1978-79, acting dep. exec. asst. for ops. Office of Sec., 1979; dep. gen. mgr. New Community Devel. Corp., 1979, acting gen. mgr., 1979-80; mgmt. cons. AVCO Corp., 1980; spl. asst. to chmn. bd. and chief exec. officer U.S. Synthetic Fuels Corp., Washington, 1980-81, project dir., 1981; pres. Trident Mgmt. Corp., San Francisco, 1981-87; of counsel Pelavin, Norberg, Harlick & Beck, San Francisco, 1981-82, ptnr., 1982-87; mng. ptnr. bus. section Carroll, Burdick & McDonough, San Francisco, 1987-90; founding ptnr. Young, Vogl & Harlick, San Francisco, 1990-93, Young, Vogl, Harlick, Wilson & Simpson, San Francisco, 1993—; pres. Young Enterprises, Inc., 1995—. Mem. pub. affairs com. San Francisco Aid Retarded Citizens, Inc., 1977; U.S. co-chmn. New Towns Working Group, U.S.-USSR Agreement on Cooperation in Field of Housing and Other Constrn., 1979-80; treas., bd. dirs. White House Fellows Found., 1980-84; prin. Coun. Excellence in Govt., Washington, 1986-94; mem. adv. com. Nat. Multi-Housing Coun., 1987-92; mem. Ross Sch. Found., 1994—, sec., 1995—. Mem. ABA (real property, trust and probate law sects.), White House Fellows Assn. (chmn. ann. meeting 1979, del. China 1980), Am. Field Svc. Returnees Assn., Can.-Am. C. of C. No. Calif. (v.p., bd. dirs. 1992—), The Netherlands C. of C. in U.S., Chile-Calif. Found. (mem. exec. com., bd. dirs. 1993—). Office: 425 California St Ste 2500 San Francisco CA 94104-2210

YOUNG, C. CLIFTON, judge; b. Nov. 7, 1922, Lovelock, Nev.; m. Jane Young. BA, U. Nev., 1943; LLB, Harvard U., 1949. Bar: Nev. 1949, U.S. Dist. Ct. Nev. 1950, U.S. Supreme Ct. 1955. Justice Nev. Supreme Ct., Carson City, 1985—, former chief justice, from 1989. Office: Nev Supreme Ct 201 S Carson St Carson City NV 89701

YOUNG, C. W. (BILL YOUNG), congressman; b. Harmarville, PA, Dec. 16, 1930; m. Beverly Angello; children: Pamela Kay, Terry Lee, Kimber, Robert, William, Patrick. Mem. Fla. Legislature, 1960-70, 92nd-104th Congresses from 10th dist. Fla., 1971—; mem. Appropriations com., subcom. Defense, Labor, HHS and Edn., legis.; mem. Fla. Constn. Revision Commn., 1965-67; chmn. So. Hwy. Policy Com., 1966-68; mem. Electoral Coll., 1968; del. Rep. Nat. Conv., 1968, 72, 76, 80, 84, 88. Named Most Valuable Senator, Capitol Press Corps, 1969. Methodist. Office: US Ho Reps 2407 Rayburn Ho Office Bldg Washington DC 20515-0910*

YOUNG, CARL DAVID, engineering educator, biomedical engineer; b. Cullman, Ala., Jan. 26, 1944; s. Ozey Henderson and Ruby Hazel (Mize) Y.; m. Alice Regina Stricklin, Feb. 14, 1962 (div. July 1968); 1 child, Jeffrey David; m. Sylvia Etta Gibson, Apr. 10, 1969 (div. Jan. 1987); 1 child, Brannon David; m. Mairian Janice Stansell Powell, Nov. 24, 1988; children: Karen Lynn Powell Webb, Bethany Jana Powell Hart, William Eric Powell. Assoc. Engring., Chattanooga State Tech., 1967; BS, U. Ala., Birmingham, 1984, MA in Edn., 1986, MS in Biomed. Engring., 1991; BS, Athens State U., 1987. Cert. electronics technician Internat. Soc. Electronics; cert. internal auditor Ala. Indsl. Devel. Tng. Control engr. U.S. Steel, Fairfield, Ala., 1967-82; engring. dept. chair Wallace State Coll., Hanceville, Ala., 1983—; owner C&S Arms, Cullman, Ala., 1984-88. Candidate County Sch. Bd., Cullman, 1986, City Coun., Good Hope, Ala., 1990. Buck sgt. USAF, 1961-65. Mem. NSPE, Am. Soc. Quality Control, Am. Mensa Ltd. Republican. Deism. Avocations: shooting sports, gunsmithing. Office: Wallace State Coll PO Box 2000 Hanceville AL 35077-2000

YOUNG, CHARLES EDWARD, university chancellor; b. San Bernardino, Calif., Dec. 30, 1931; s. Clayton Charles and Eula May (Walters) Y. AA, San Bernardino Coll., 1954; AB, U. Calif., Riverside, 1955; MA, UCLA, 1957, PhD, 1960; DHL (hon.), U. Judaism, L.A., 1969. Congl. fellow Washington, 1958-59; adminstrv. analyst Office of the Pres., U. Calif., Berkeley, 1959-60; asst. prof. polit. sci. U. Calif., Davis, 1960; asst. prof. polit. sci. UCLA, 1960-66, assoc. prof., 1966-69, prof., 1969—, asst. to chancellor, 1960-62, asst. chancellor, 1962-63, vice chancellor, adminstrn., 1963-68, chancellor, 1968—; bd. dirs. Intel Corp.; cons. Peace Corps., 1961-62, Ford Found. on Latin Am. Activities, 1964-66; mem. bd. govs. L.A. Met. Project. Mem. Knight Found. Commn. on Intercollegiate Athletics, Calif. Coun. on Sci. and Tech., NCAA Pres.'s Commn., Coun. for Govt.-Univ.-Industry Rsch. Roundtable and the Nat. Rsch. Coun. Adv. Bd.-Issues in Sci. and Tech., Nat. Com. on U.S.-China Rels., chancellor's assocs. UCLA, coun. trustees L.A. Ednl. Alliance for Restructuring Now; past chair. Assn. Am. Univs., Nat. Assn. State Univs. and Land-Grant Colls.; mem. adminstrv. bd. Internat. Assn. Univs.; bd. govs. Found. Internat. Exchange Sci. and Cultural Info. by Telecommunications, The Theatre Group Inc.; v.p. Young Musicians Found.; bd. dirs. Los Angeles Internat. Visitors Council, Greater Los Angeles Energy Coalition, Los Angeles World Affairs Coun.; trustee UCLA Found. With USAF, 1951-52. Named Young Man of Year Westwood Jr. C. of C., 1962. Fellow AAAS. Office: UCLA Office of Chancellor 405 Hilgard Ave Los Angeles CA 90095

YOUNG, CHARLES RANDALL, software professional; b. Phila., Dec. 18, 1950; s. Charles Calvin and Henrietta Emma (Sorber) Y.; m. Mary Frances Hoey, June 8, 1973. BS with honors in Math., Drexel U., 1973; MS in Computer and Info. Sci., Ohio State U., 1975. Programmer coop Princeton (N.J.) Time Sharing Svcs., 1969-71; grad. tchg. asst. Ohio State U., Columbus, 1973-75; compiler programmer Burroughs, Paoli, Pa., 1975-76; simulation programmer Sperry, Blue Bell, Pa., 1976-78, computer security lead programmer, designer, 1978-84, operating sys. group mgr., 1984-89; disk program devel. mgr. Unisys, Blue Bell, Pa., 1989-91, compiler and posix program mgr., 1991-93, open/oltp program mktg. mgr., 1993-94, superserver and internet product mgr., 1995—. Contbr. articles to profl. jours. Mem. IEEE, Assn. Shareware Profls. Reformed Episcopal. Avocations: swimming, opera, church bass soloist, tennis. Home: 412 Norristown Rd Ambler PA 19002-2737 Office: Unisys PO Box 500 Blue Bell PA 19424-0001

YOUNG, CHRISTOPHER, composer. Scores include (films) The Dorm That Dripped Blood, 1982, Robbie, 1982, The Power, 1983, Savage Hunter, 1984, Highpoint, 1984, Wheels of Fire, 1984, Avenging Angel, 1984, Def-Con 4, 1985, Wizards of the Lost Kingdom, 1985, Barbarian Queen, 1985, Nightmare on Elm Street Part II: Freddy's Revenge, 1985, Godzilla 1985, 1985, Torment, 1986, Getting Even, 1986, Invaders from Mars, 1986, Trick or Treat, 1986, Hellraiser, 1987, Flowers in the Attic, 1987, The Telephone, 1987, Bat-21, 1988, Haunted Summer, 1988, Hellbound: Hellraiser II, 1988, The Fly II, 1989, Hider in the House, 1989, Bright Angel, 1991, The Five Heartbeats, 1991, The Vagrant, 1992, The Dark Half, 1992, Rapid Fire, 1992, Jennifer Eight, 1992, Sliver, 1993, Dream Lover, 1994, Murder in the First, 1995, (TV movies) American Harvest, 1987, Last Flight Out, 1990, Max and Helen, 1990. Address: 1422 Abbot Kinney Rd Venice CA 90291

YOUNG, DALE LEE, banker; b. Palmyra, Nebr., Mar. 13, 1928; s. Mike P. and Grace (Clutter) Y.; m. Norma Marie Shalla, June 18, 1950; children—Shalla Ann, Philip Mike. B.B.A., U. Nebr., 1950. With FirsTier Bank N.A. (formerly First Nat. Bank & Trust Co.), Lincoln, Nebr., 1950-91, cashier, 1966-91, v.p., 1966-76, exec. v.p., 1976-92; sec. ISCO, Inc., Lincoln, 1991—, also bd. dirs.; bd. dirs. Woodmen Accident and Life Co.; sec., bd. dirs. Leasing Corp. Treas. Lincoln City Library Found.; Treas., mem. exec. com. Nebr. Republican Com., 1968—; bd. dirs., v.p. Lincoln Symphony; bd. dirs. Lincoln Community Services, ARC, Lincoln Found.; trustee Bryan Meml. Hosp., 1976-80; mem. Lincoln City Coun., 1991—. Served with AUS, 1946-48, 50-51. Mem. Nebr. Art Assn., Omaha-Lincoln Soc. Fin. Analysts, Lincoln C. of C. (pres.), Theta Xi. Presbyterian. Clubs: Nebraska, Lincoln Country, Univ. Home: 2627 Park Ave Lincoln NE 68502-4023 Office: PO Box 81008 Lincoln NE 68501-1008

YOUNG, DAVID MICHAEL, biochemistry and molecular biology educator, physician; b. Bluffton, Ind., Oct. 11, 1935; s. Eli and Ruth (Comer) Y.; m. Diane Tangeman, Dec. 28, 1957 (div. 1971); children: Peter Michael, Amy Katherine; m. Lucia Virginia Patat, Sept. 2, 1972; children: David Michael II, Allison Amelia. B.S., Duke U., 1957, M.D., 1959. Diplomate: Nat. Bd. Med. Examiners. Intern pediatrics dept. Duke U. Med. Ctr., Durham, N.C., 1958-60; staff scientist Lab Cellular Physiology and Metabolism Nat. Heart Inst., NIH, 1960-62; vis. scientist McCollum-Pratt Inst., Johns Hopkins U., Balt., 1962-63, asst. prof. biology, 1963-64; asst. prof. Harvard U. Med. Sch., Boston, 1965-72, assoc. prof. Biol. chemistry, 1972-79, tutor biochem. scis., 1966-76, mem. grad. program for advanced study in immunology, 1971-76, assoc. chmn. div. med. scis., chmn. program for cell biology, 1972-76; head Lab Phys. Biochemistry Mass. Gen. Hosp., Boston, 1965-79; prof. biochemistry U. Fla. Coll. Medicine, Gainesville, 1979—, prof. medicine, 1979-86, chmn. dept. biochemistry and molecular biology, 1979-81, prof. molecular biology, 1981-86, prof. pediatrics, 1986—; mem. cell physiology study sect. NIH, Bethesda, Md., 1978-82, sect. chmn., 1980; acad. assoc. Nichols Inst., San Juan Capistrano, Calif., 1976—; vis. prof. biology Johns Hopkins U., 1994, 95. Editor-in-chief: Jour. Molecular and Cellular Biochemistry, 1983—; patentee nerve growth factor, nerve growth factor antibody. Served to sr. surgeon USPHS, 1959-63. USPHS spl. fellow, 1962; recipient career devel. award USPHS, 1967-72; NIHresearch grantee, 1964—; grantee John A. Hartford Found., 1968-73. Mem. Am. Soc. Biol. Chemists, Am. Chem. Soc., AAAS, Biophys. Soc., Am. Soc. for Clin. Investigation, Am. Heart Assn. (research allocations com. 1976-79), Am. Soc. for Cell Biology, Alpha Omega Alpha. Home: 2106 NW 27th Ter Gainesville FL 32605-3873 Office: Dept Biochemistry and Molecular Biology Coll Medicine U Fla Gainesville FL 32610

YOUNG, DAVID POLLOCK, humanities educator, author; b. Davenport, Iowa, Dec. 14, 1936; s. Cecil T. and Mary Ella (Pollock) Y.; m. Chloe Hamilton, June 17, 1963 (dec. Feb. 1985); children—Newell Hamilton, Margaret Helen; m. Georgia L. Newman, Dec. 31, 1989. B.A., Carleton Coll., 1958; M.A., Yale, 1959, Ph.D., 1965. Faculty dept. English Oberlin Coll., 1961—, prof., 1973—, Longman prof. of English, 1986—; Translator. Author: Something of Great Constancy: the Art of "A Midsummer Night's Dream", 1965, Sweating Out the Winter, 1969, The Heart's Forest: Shakespeare's Pastoral Plays, 1972, Boxcars, 1973, Work Lights: 32 Prose Poems, 1977, Rilke's Duino Elegies, 1978, The Names of A Hare in English, 1979, (with Stuart Friebert) A Field Guide to Contemporary Poetry and Poetics, 1980, Four T'ang Poets, 1980, (with Stuart Friebert and David Walker) Valuable Nail: Selected Poems of Günter Eich, 1981, (with Dana Hábová) Interferon, or On Theater, Poems by Miroslav Holub, 1982, (with Keith Hollaman) Magical Realist Fiction, 1984; editor: (with Stuart Friebert and David Walker) Field: Contemporary Poetry & Poetics, (with Stuart Friebert) The Longman Anthology of Contemporary American Poetry, 1983, Foraging, 1986, Troubled Mirror: A Study of Yeats's The Tower, 1987, Sonnets to Orpheus, Rainer Maria Rilke, 1987, THe Heights of Macchu Picchu, 1987, Earthshine, 1988, Five T'ang Poets, 1990, The Action to the Word: Structure and Style in Shakespearean Tragedy, 1990, (with Dana Hábová) Vanishing Lung Syndrome Poems by Miroslav Holub, 1990, The Planet on the Desk: Selected and New Poems, 1960-90, 1991, Shakespeare's Middle Tragedies: New Century Views, 1992, The Book of Fresh Beginnings: Selected Poems of Rainer Maria Rilke, 1994, Night Thoughts and Henry Vaughan, 1994, (with Stuart Friebert) Models of the Universe, an Anthology of the Prose Poem, 1995; editor: FIELD, Contemporary Poetry and Poetics, 1969—, contbr. poetry to lit. publs. Recipient U.S. award Internat. Poetry Forum, 1969, Ohio Individual Artist award, 1990; Guggenheim fellow, NEA fellow. Office: Oberlin Coll Dept English Oberlin OH 44074

YOUNG, DAVID WILLIAM, accounting educator; b. L.A., Feb. 8, 1942; s. William Albert and Hilda Mary (Cook) Y.; m. Ernestine M.L. Van Schaik, Oct. 4, 1968 (div. 1975); m. Francesca Michela Larson, Jan. 28, 1984; children: Christian William, Anthony Edwin. BA, Occidental Coll., 1963; MA, UCLA, 1966; D in Bus. Adminstrn., Harvard U., 1977. Systems engr. IBM, Glendale, Calif., 1963-64; asst. to pres. Lundberg Survey, Inc., Hollywood, Calif., 1964-66; program economist U.S. AID, El Salvador, 1966-69; cons. Thomas Goldsmith & Assoc., Cambridge, Mass., 1969-71; mng. dir. Commonwealth Mgmt. Sys., Cambridge, 1971—; assoc. prof. mgmt. Harvard U. Sch. Pub. Health, Boston, 1976-85, cons. faculty mem., 1985—; prof. acctg. and control Boston U. Sch. Mgmt., 1985—, chmn. dept. acctg., 1986-91, dir. acctg. MBA program, 1989-93, dir. inst. acctg. rsch. and edn., 1989-93, dir. health care mgmt. program, 1991-94; mng. dir. The Crimson Group, Cambridge, 1994—; vis. prof. mgmt. control Instituto de Estudios Superiores de la Empresa, Barcelona, Spain, 1984. Author: The Managerial Process in Human Service Agencies, 1979, Financial Control in Health Care, 1984, The Hospital Power Equilibrium, 1985, Management Control in Nonprofit Organizations, 1984, 88, 94, Introduction to Financial and Management Accounting: A User Perspective, 1994; contbr. articles to profl. jours. Trustee Art Inst., Boston, 1990-96, Symmes Hosp., Arlington, 1993-94, Mass. Eye and Ear Infirmary, Boston, 1990-92, Roxbury Comprehensive Comty. Health Ctr., 1983-86; chmn. adv. commn. Mass. Hosp. Payment Sys., 1992-95. Milton Fund fellow Harvard Med. Sch., 1984. Mem. Am. Acctg. Assn., Am. Econ. Assn. Democrat. Office: Boston U Sch Mgmt 704 Commonwealth Ave Boston MA 02215-2441

YOUNG, DAVIS, public relations executive; b. Montclair, N.J., Apr. 12, 1939. BA in Journalism, U. N.C. Acct. extc. Walker & Co., 1963-65; acct. extc. Carr Liggett Adv. Inc., 1965-68, acct. supr., 1968-70, v.p., 1970-75; pres. Young-Liggett Pub. Rels., 1975-88; exec. v.p., dir. Edward Howard & Co., Cleve., 1988-89, pres., COO, 1990—; v.p. Internat. Pub. Rels. Group of Cos., 1986. Recipient Disting. Svc. award Kent State U. Mem. Pub. Rels. Soc. Am. (chmn. nat. com. edn. 1975, pres. Greater Cleve. chpt. 1977, gen. chmn. spring conf., 1982, co-chair nat. conf. 1985, chmn. nat. membership 1986, chmn. nat. conf. 1991, pub. rels. com. 1992, Pres. Citation award). Office: Edward Howard & Co 1 Erieview Plz Fl 7 Cleveland OH 44114-1715*

YOUNG, DENNIS EUGENE, financial services executive; b. Wahoo, Nebr., May 18, 1943; s. Donald W. and Grace B. (Spittgerber) Y.; m. Diane M. Johnson, July 10, 1965; children: Lisa, David, Darren. B.A. magna cum laude, Buena Vista Coll., Storm Lake, Iowa, 1965. With Norwest Fin. Inc., Des Moines, 1965—; treas. Norwest Fin. Corp., Des Moines, 1976—, v.p., chief fin. officer, 1979-83, sr. v.p., treas., 1983—, also bd. dirs.; pres. Norwest Fin. Can., Inc.; treas. Centurion Casualty Co., Des Moines; v.p., treas., bd. dirs. Centurion Life Ins. Co., Des Moines. Trustee, vice chmn. Buena Vista Coll., 1979—; trustee, treas. Des Moines Art Ctr.; bd. govs. Iowa Coll. Found. Mem. Fin. Execs. Inst., Iowa Soc. Fin. Analysts, Nat. Assn. Corp. Treasurers, Des Moines Club, Wakonda (Glen Oaks) Club. Office: Norwest Fin Inc 206 8th St Des Moines IA 50309-3805

YOUNG, DER-LIANG FRANK, civil engineering educator, researcher; b. Chia-Yi, Taiwan, Jan. 4, 1946; s. Wu-Shang and Lee-Rang (Lee) Y.; m. Ching-Ju Yu, Aug. 29, 1971; children: Jacqueline, James. BS, Nat. Taiwan U., 1968, MS, 1971; MS, Calif. Inst. Tech., 1972; PhD, Cornell U., 1976. Registered profl. engr., Ill. Rsch. assoc. Cornell U., Ithaca, N.Y., 1975-76; sr. engr. Harza Engring. Co., Chgo., 1976-81, Nortech Engring. Co., Irvine, Calif., 1981-83; sr. mem. tech. staff Rockwell Internat., Canoga Park, Calif., 1983; assoc. prof. Nat. Taiwan U., 1983-84, prof., 1984—; vis. assoc. prof. Nat. Taiwan U., 1978-79, dir. Hydraulic Rsch. Lab., 1985-91; adj. prof. Centry U., Beverly Hills, Calif., 1982-83; vis. expert Sinotech Engring. Corp., Taipei, 1991-92; examiner Dept. Examination, Taipei, 1988-96; cons. to Gov., Taipei County Govt., 1989-96; advisor Nat. Sci. and Tech. Mus., Kaohsiung, Taiwan, 1986-94. Contbr. articles to books and profl. jours. Judge Outstanding Youth Medal Award, Taipei, 1990-91. Served to 2d lt. Chinese Army, 1968-69. Recipient Disting. Rsch. award Nat. Sci. Coun. Republic of China, 1992-96, Disting. Leadership award Am. Biog. Inst., 1989. Mem. Internat. Assn. for Hydraulic Rsch. (coun. Asian and Pacific div. 1988-95), Am. Geophys. Union, Chinese Inst. Civil and Hydraulic Engrs. (coun. water resources engring. 1985-96). Avocations: swimming, hiking, baseball, fishing, reading. Office: Nat Taiwan U Dept Civil Engring, 1 sec 4 Roosevelt Rd, 10617 Taipei Taiwan

YOUNG, DONALD ALAN, physician; b. Oakland, Calif., Feb. 8, 1939; s. Leo Alan and Pearl Anita (Walker) Y.; children: Jennifer, Karen. B.A., U. Calif., Berkeley, 1960, M.D., 1964. Diplomate Am. Bd. Internal Medicine. Intern, then resident in internal medicine U. Calif. Hosp., San Francisco, 1964-66; resident in internal medicine Parkland Hosp., Dallas, 1966-67; fellow chest diseases U. Calif. Hosp., San Francisco, 1967-68; mem. staff Palo Alto (Calif.) Med. Clinic, 1970-75; med. dir. Am. Lung Assn., 1975-77; scholar adminstrv. scholars program VA, Washington, 1977-80; dep. dir. policy Bur. Program Policy, Health Care Financing Adminstrn. HHS, Washington; exec. dir. Prospective Payment Assessment Commn., Washington, 1984—; clin. instr. U. Calif. Med. Sch., San Francisco, 1968-70, Stanford U. Med. Sch., 1970-75. Trustee Vt. Lung Center; bd. dirs. Mid-Md. Lung Assn. Served with M.C. AUS, 1968-70. Decorated Commendation medal.; Recipient Borden award, 1964. Home: 5495 Vantage Point Rd Columbia MD 21044-2637 Office: 300 7th St SW Suite 301B Washington DC 20024

YOUNG, DONALD E., congressman; b. Meridian, Calif., June 9, 1933; m. Lula Fredson; children—Joni, Dawn. AA, Yuba Jr. Coll., 1952; BA ., Chico (Calif.) State Coll., 1958. Former educator, river boat capt.; mem. Fort Yukon City Council, 6 years, mayor, 4 years; mem. Alaska Ho. of Reps., 1966-70, Alaska Senate, 1970-73, 93rd-104th Congresses from Alaska, 1973—; mem. transp. & infrastructure com., chmn. resources com. With U.S. Army, 1955-57. Republican. Episcopalian. Office: US House of Representatives 2331 Rayburn Bldg Ofc B Washington DC 20515-0005*

YOUNG, DONALD FREDRICK, engineering educator; b. Joplin, Mo., Apr. 27, 1928; s. Oral Solomon and Blanche (Trent) Y.; m. Gertrude Ann Cooper, Apr. 15, 1950; children: Michael, Pamela, Susan, Christopher, David. B.S., Iowa State U., 1951, M.S., 1952, Ph.D., 1956. Research engr. AEC Ames Lab., 1952-55; asst. prof. Iowa State U., Ames, 1955-58, assoc. prof., 1958-61, prof. engring. sci. and mechanics, 1961-74, Anson Marston Disting. prof. engring., 1974—. Author: Introduction to Applied Mechanics, 1972, (with others) Essentials of Mechanics, 1974, (with others) Fundamentals of Fluid Mechanics, 1990, 2d edit., 1994; contbr. articles to profl. jours. Recipient Outstanding Tchr. award Standard Oil, 1971, Faculty citation Iowa State Alumni Assn., 1972, Spl. Recognition award Iowa State U. Rsch. Found., 1988, David R. Boylan Eminent award for rsch., 1995. Fellow ASME (chmn. bioengring. div. 1973-74); mem. Am. Heart Assn., Am. Soc. Engring. Edn., Pi Tau Sigma, Pi Mu Epsilon, Phi Kappa Phi, Sigma Xi. Home: 2042 Prairie Vw E Ames IA 50010-4558 Office: Iowa State U 3023 Black Engr Ames IA 50010

YOUNG, DONALD STIRLING, clinical pathology educator; b. Belfast, N. Ireland, Dec. 17, 1933; s. John Stirling and Ruth Muir (Whipple) Y.; m. Silja Meret; children: Gordon, Robert, Peter. MB, ChB, U. Aberdeen, Scotland, 1957; PhD in Chem. Pathology, U. London, 1962. Terminable lectr. materia medica U. Aberdeen, 1958-59; fellow Postgrad. Med. Sch., U. London, 1959-62, registrar, 1962-64; vis. scientist NIH, Bethesda, Md., 1965-66; chief clin. chemistry service NIH, 1966-77; head clin. chemistry sect. Mayo Clinic, Rochester, Minn., 1977-84; prof. pathology and lab. medicine U. Pa., 1984—; dir. William Pepper Lab. Hosp. of U. Pa., 1984—; past bd. dirs. Nat. Com. Clin. Lab. Standards. Co-editor: Drug Interference and Drug Metabolism in Clinical Chemistry, 1976, Clinician and Chemist, 1979, Chemical Diagnosis of Disease, 1979, Drug Measurement and Drug Effects in Laboratory Health Science, 1980, Interpretation of Clinical Laboratory Tests, 1985, Effects of Drugs on Clinical Laboratory Tests, 1995, Effects of Preanalytical Variables on Clinical Laboratory Tests, 1996. Recipient Dir.'s award NIH, 1977, Gerard B. Lambert award, 1974-75, MDS Health Group award Can. Soc. Clin. Chemists, 1978; Roman lectr. Australian Assn. Clin.

Biochemists, 1979; Jendrassik award Hungarian Soc. Clin. Pathologists, 1985, ATB award Italian Soc. Clin. Biochemistry, 1987. Mem. Am. Assn. Clin. Chemistry (J.H. Roe award Capital sect. 1973, Bernard Gerulat award N.J. sect. 1977, Ames award 1977, Van Slyke award N.Y. met. sect. 1985, J.G. Reinhold award Phila. sect. 1993, past pres.), Internat. Fedn. Clin. Chemists (past pres.), Acad. Clin. Lab. Physicians and Scientists (past exec. com.), Assn. Clin. Biochemists (Ciba-Corning lectr. 1985). Achievements include research in clinical chemistry, optimized use of the clinical laboratory. Home: 1116 Remington Rd Wynnewood PA 19096-4045 Office: Hosp U Pa 3400 Spruce St Philadelphia PA 19104-4283

YOUNG, DOUGLAS, Canadian government official; b. Tracadie, Sept. 20, 1940. Min. transport Canada, 1993-1996, min. human resources development, 1996—. Provincial first elected to N.B. Legislature g.e., 1978, reelected g.e., 1982, 87; apptd. Min. Fisheries and Aquaculture, 1987; elected to the House of Commons g.e., 1988. Office: Human Resource Development, 140 Promenade du Portage, Hull, PQ Canada K1A 0JP also: PO Box 3635, Tracadie, NB Canada E1X 165

YOUNG, DOUGLAS REA, lawyer; b. Los Angeles, July 21, 1948; s. James Douglas and Dorothy Belle (Rea) Y.; m. Terry Forrest, Jan. 19, 1974; 1 child, Megann Forrest. BA cum laude, Yale U., 1971; JD, U. Calif.-Berkeley, 1976. Bar: Calif. 1976, U.S. Dist. Ct. (no. dist.) Calif. 1976, U.S. Ct. Appeals (6th and 9th cirs.) 1977, U.S. Dist. Ct. (cen. dist.) Calif. 1979, U.S. Dist. Ct. Hawaii, U.S. Supreme Ct. 1982. Law clk. U.S. Dist. Ct. (no. dist.) Calif., San Francisco, 1976-77; assoc. Farella, Braun & Martel, San Francisco, 1977-82, ptnr., 1983—; spl. master U.S. Dist. Ct. (no. dist.) Calif., 1977-78, 88, 96; mem. Criminal Justice Act Def. Panel no. dist. Calif.; mem. faculty Calif. Continuing Edn. of Bar, Berkeley, 1982—, Nat. Inst. Trial Advocacy, Berkeley, 1984—, Practicing Law Inst., 1988—, Hastings Coll. of Advocacy, 1985—, adj. prof., 1990; vis. lectr. law Boalt Hall/U. Calif., Berkeley, 1986; judge pro tem San Francisco Mcpl. Ct. 1984—, San Francisco Superior Ct., 1990—. Author: (with Purver and Davis) California Trial Handbook, 2d ed., (with Hon. Richard Byrne, Purver and Davis), 3d edit., (with Purver, Davis and Kerper) The Trial Lawyers Book, (with Hon. Eugene Lynch, Taylor, Purver and Davis) California Negotiation and Settlement Handbook; contbr. articles to profl. jours. Bd. dirs. Berkeley Law Found., 1977-79, chmn., 1978-79; bd. dirs. San Francisco Legal Aid Soc., pres., 1993—, Pub. Interest Clearinghouse, San Francisco, chmn., 1987—, treas. 1988—; chmn., Attys. Task Force for Child Children, Legal Services for Children, 1987—, mem. State Bar Appeciate Law Adv. Commn., 1994—. Recipient award of appreciation Berkeley Law Found., 1983. Mem. ABA (Pro Bono Pub. award 1992), San Francisco Bar Assn. (founding chmn. litigation sect. 1988-89, award of appreciation 1989, bd. dirs. 1990-91), Calif. Acad. Appellate Lawyers, Lawyers Club San Francisco. Democrat. Office: Farella Braun & Martel 235 Montgomery St Ste 3000 San Francisco CA 94104-2902

YOUNG, DOUGLAS RYAN, technology company executive; b. Bronxville, N.Y., Apr. 30, 1945; s. Harold Sydney and Edith Isabelle (Ryan) Y.; m. Anne Honora Sullivan, May 23, 1970; children: Amanda Jennings Young, Christina Crawford Young, Ryan Townsend Young, Kielley Kavanaugh Young. BA, Princeton (N.J.) U., 1967; MBA, NYU, 1978. Various sales, mktg. and planning positions IBM, N.Y., 1970-82; regional mgr. Storage Tech. Corp., N.Y., 1982-84; pres. Unilease Computer Corp., London and N.Y.C., 1984-87; v.p. sale, mktg. and svc. Data Switch Corp., Shelton, Conn., 1987-89; dir. ins. vertical Oracle Corp., N.Y.C., 1989-91; v.p. enterprise mktg. Data Gen. Corp., Westboro, Mass., 1991-94; v.p. mktg. Hitachi Data Sys., Santa Clara, Calif., 1995—. Lt. (j.g.) USN, 1967-70. Avocations: computers, motorcycles, sailing, photography, stunt kite exhibitions. Office: Hitachi Data Sys 750 Central Expy Santa Clara CA 95056

YOUNG, DWIGHT WAYNE, ancient civilization educator; b. Lambert, Okla., Dec. 15, 1925; s. Maurice Leonard and Freda Flora (Polson) Y.; m. Barbara Louise Pirtle, May 25, 1946; children: Terry Wayne, Cecilia Ann. B.A. magna cum laude, Hardin-Simmons U., Abilene, Tex., 1949; Th.M. Dallas Theol. Seminary, 1956; Ph.D., Dropsie Coll., 1955; postgrad., Brown U., 1959-60. Asst. prof. Brandeis U., Waltham, Mass., 1958-63, assoc. prof., 1963-67, 69-72, prof., 1972-87, prof. emeritus, 1987—; cons. Harper & Row Pubs., N.Y.C., 1958-60; vis. prof. Hebrew U., Jerusalem, Israel, 1965, Cornell U., Ithaca, N.Y., 1967-69; chief editor Pirtle Polson Pubs., Gloucester, Mass., 1980—. Author: Coptic Manuscripts from the White Monastery: Works of Shenute, 1993; editor: Studies Presented to Hans Jakob Polotsky, 1981, The Future of Coptic Studies, 1978; contbr. numerous articles and revs. on ancient civiliations to profl. jours. Served with USMC, 1943-46. Recipient Solomon award in Hebrew, Dallas Theol. Seminary, 1951; fellow in Arabic, U. Mich., 1960. Mem. Internat. Assn. for Coptic Studies. Home: 5555 N Sheridan Rd Apt 1102 Chicago IL 60640-1619 Office: Brandeis U Dept Nr Ea Studies South St Waltham MA 02154

YOUNG, EDWIN HAROLD, chemical and metallurgical engineering educator; b. Detroit, Nov. 4, 1918; s. William George and Alice Pearl (Hicks) Y.; m. Ida Signe Sonna, June 25, 1944; children—David Harold, Barbara Ellen. B.S. in Chem. Engring, U. Detroit, 1942; M.S. in Chem. Engring, U. Mich., 1949, M.S. in Metall. Engring, 1952. Chem. engr. Wright Air Devel. Center, Dayton, Ohio, 1942-43; instr. U. Mich., Ann Arbor, 1946-52; asst. prof. U. Mich., 1952-56, assoc. prof., 1956-59, prof. chem. and metall. engring., 1959-89, prof. emeritus chem. and metall. engring., 1989—; Mem. Mich. Bd. Registration for Profl. Engrs., 1963-78, chmn., 1969-70, 72-73, 75-76; mem. Mich. Bd. Registration for Architects, 1963-78. Author: (with L.E. Brownell) Process Equipment Design, 1959; contbr. articles to profl. jours. Dist. commr. Boy Scouts Am., 1961-64; mem. Wolverine coun., 1965-68. With USNR, 1943-46, to capt. Res. ret., 1978. Fellow ASME, ASHRAE, Am. Inst. Chemists, Am. Inst. Chem. Engrs. (Donald Q Kern award 1979), Engring. Soc. Detroit; mem. Am. Chem. Soc., Am. Soc. Engring. Edn., Nat. Soc. Profl. Engrs. (pres. 1968-69, award 1977), Mich. Soc. Profl. Engrs. (pres. 1962-63, Engr. of Year award 1976), Mich. Assn. of Professions (pres. 1966, Distinguished award 1970), Nat. Council Engring. Examiners, Naval Res. Assn., Res. Officers Assn., Sigma Xi, Tau Beta Pi, Phi Kappa Phi, Phi Lambda Upsilon, Alpha Chi Sigma. Republican. Baptist. Home: 609 Dartmoor Rd Ann Arbor MI 48103-4513

YOUNG, ELEANOR LOUISE, retired senior staff nurse; b. Cambridge, Mass., Oct. 10, 1930; d. Allison Homer and Florence May (Sheppard) Jones; m. Joseph Moses, May 6, 1951; children: Catherine, Joseph, Terence, Nora. Student, Mass. Gen. Hosp., Boston, 1949-51; ADS, Massasoit C.C., Brockton, Mass., 1972. Registered nurse, Mass., 1972. RN CCU South Shore Hosp., Weymouth, Mass., 1972-80, sr. staff nurse CCU, 1980-95; retired, 1995; pacemaker instr., 1985-89, quality mgmt. 1988-94, South Shore Hosp., Weymouth, Mass. Mem. Am. Heart Assn., South Shore RN Assn., Alpha Nu Omega. Avocations: travel, knitting, needlepoint.

YOUNG, ESTELLE IRENE, dermatologist; b. N.Y.C., Nov. 2, 1945; d. Sidney D. and Blanche (Krosney) Young. BA magna cum laude, Mt. Holyoke Coll., 1963; MD, Downstate Med. Ctr., 1971. Intern, Lenox Hill Hosp., N.Y.C., 1971-72, resident in medicine, 1972-73; resident in dermatology Columbia Presbyn. Hosp., N.Y.C., 1973-74, NYU Med. Ctr., 1974-75, Boston U. Hosp., 1975-76; asst. dermatologist Harvard U. Health Services, Cambridge, Mass., 1975-76; assoc. staff mem. dermatology Boston U. Med. Ctr., 1976-77; practice medicine specializing in dermatology, Petersburg, Va., 1976—; mem. staff Poplar Springs Hosp., 1976—, Southside Regional Med. Ctr. (formerly Petersburg Gen. Hosp.), 1976—, Cen. State Hosp., 1984—; clin. instr. dept. dermatology Med. Coll. Va., 1976—, asst. clinic prof., 1988-94, assoc. clin. prof., 1994—; sec. med. staff Petersburg Gen. Hosp., 1982—. Fellow Am. Acad. Dermatology; mem. Va. Med. Soc., Va. Dermatology Soc., Tidewater Dermatology Soc. (pres. 1982-83), Physicians for Social Responsiblity (exec. com.), Tidewater Physicians for Social Responsibility (pres. 1990—), Internat. Physicians for Prevention of Nuclear War, Southside Va. Med. Soc., Sigma Xi. Contbr. articles to profl. jours. Home: 2319 Monument Ave Richmond VA 23220-2603 Office: 612A S Sycamore St Petersburg VA 23803-5828

YOUNG, FRANCIS ALLAN, psychologist; b. Utica, N.Y., Dec. 29, 1918; s. Frank Allan and Julia Mae (McOwen) Y.; m. Judith Wadsworth Wright, Dec. 21, 1945; children—Francis Allan, Thomas Robert. B.S., U. Tampa, 1941; M.A., Western Res. U., 1945; Ph.D., Ohio State U., 1949. Instr. Wash. State U., Pullman, 1948-50; asst. prof. Wash. State U., 1950-56, assoc. prof., 1956-61, prof. psychology, 1961-88, dir. primate rsch. ctr., 1957-88, prof., dir. emeritus, 1988—; vis. prof. ophthalmology U. Oreg., Portland, 1964; asst. dir. U. Wash. Regional Primate Ctr., dir. primate field sta., 1966-68; vis. prof. pharmacology U. Uppsala (Sweden) Med. Sch., 1971; vis. prof. optometry U. Houston, 1979-80. Editor: (with Donald B. Lindsley) Early Experience and Visual Information Processing in Perceptual and Reading Disorders, 1970; contbr. chpts. to books, numerous articles to profl. jours. Named Disting. Psychologist State of Wash., Wash. Psychol. Assn., 1973; recipient Paul Yarwood Meml. award Calif. Optometric Assn., 1978; Apollo award Am. Optometric Assn., 1980; Nat. Acad. Sci.-NRC sr. postdoctoral fellow in physiol. psychology U. Wash., 1956-57; research grantee NSF, 1950-53; research grantee USAF, 1965-72; research grantee NIH, 1960-78. Home: 344 NW Webb St Pullman WA 99163-3150 Office: Wash State U Psychology Dept Pullman WA 99164-1170

YOUNG, FRANK EDWARD, federal agency administrator; b. Mineola, N.Y., Sept. 1, 1931; s. Frank E. and Erma F. Y.; m. Leanne Hutchinson, Oct. 20, 1956; children: Lorrie, Debora, Peggy, Frank, Jon. MD, SUNY, 1952; PhD, Case Western Res. U., 1959; DSc (hon.), Roberts Wesleyan Coll., 1983, Houghton Coll., 1984, SUNY, 1986, L.I. U., 1986, Western Bapt. Coll., 1988. Asst. prof. pathology Western Res. U., Cleve., 1962-65; assoc. mem. microbiology Scripps Clinic & Rsch. Found., LaJolla, Calif., 1965-68; assoc. prof. biology U. Calif., San Diego, 1967-70; mem. microbiology & exptl. pathology Scripps Clinic & Rsch. Found., LaJolla, Calif., 1968-70; prof. microbiology and chmn. dept., prof. pathology and radiation biology and biophysics U. Rochester, N.Y., 1970-79, dir. Med. Ctr., 1979-81, dean Sch. Medicine and Dentistry, 1979-84, v.p. for health affairs, 1981-84; commr. FDA, Rockville, Md., 1984-89, dep. asst. sec. for health sci. and environ., 1989-93; dir. office emergency preparedness, 1993—; U.S. rep. WHO exec. bd., Geneva, 1985-88; bd. dirs. High Tech., Rochester, N.Y., 1983-84. Contbr. numerous articles on cloning, gene mapping, gene shuttle vectors, 1970-84; initiator Fed. Regulations rules to increase access to exptl. drugs to desperately ill, 1987-88. Lectr. Christian orgns., 1970—; mem. United Way, Rochester, N.Y., 1982-84, N.Y. State Statutory Adv. Com. on DNA, Albany, N.Y., 1978. Recipient sec.'s spl. citation Dept. Health and Human Svcs., 1989, Surgeon Gen.'s Exemplary Svc. medal, 1988, Disting. Svc. medal Pub. Health Svc., 1986, Edward Mott award, 1985, Surgeon Gen.'s Medallion, 1992. Mem. Inst. Medicine of NAS, AAAS, Am. Acad. Microbiology (bd. govs.). Avocations: fishing, boating, yard work. Office: Office Emergency Prep 5500 Fishers Ln Rm 4-81 Rockville MD 20852-1738

YOUNG, FRANK MITCHELL, musical theater producer; b. Pasadena, Tex., May 22, 1940. Student, U. Tex., 1958, U. Houston, 1960; BA, UCLA, 1963. Asst. condr., singer, stage mgr. Houston Grand Opera, 1963-75; stage mgr. Washington Opera, 1968-71; founder, exec. dir. Theater Under the Stars for Houston Civic Light Opera, 1971—. Debut in Carmen, Houston Grand Opera, 1958; producer 105 mus. prodns., 1968— including 17 Houston premieres, 3 world premieres and 1 Am. premiere. Mem. Nat. Alliance Mus. Theater Producers (pres.), Houston Theater Alliance (v.p.), Houston Cultural Arts Council (theater panel). Office: Theater Under the Stars 4235 San Felipe St Houston TX 77027-2901

YOUNG, FRANK NELSON, JR., biology educator, entomologist; b. Oneonta, Ala., Nov. 2, 1915; s. Frank Nelson and Mary (Loe) Y.; m. Frances Norman, July 2, 1943; children—Elizabeth Von Herrmann, Frank Nelson III. B.S., U. Fla., 1938, M.S., 1940, Ph.D., 1942. Asst. prof. biology U. Fla., Gainesville, 1946-49; asst. prof. Ind. U., Bloomington, 1949-51; assoc. prof. Ind. U., 1951-62, prof., 1963-86, prof. emeritus, 1986—; assoc. Smithsonian Instn., 1989—; rsch. assoc. Fla. Dept. Agriculture. Author: Water Beetles of Florida, 1954; contbr. articles on aquatic insects to profl. jours. Served with U.S. Army, 1942-46, col. Res. ret., 1976. Recipient Phi Sigma medal, 1940; Guggenheim fellow, 1960-61; La. State U. fellow, 1963. Fellow Ind. Acad. Sci., Royal Entomol. Soc.; mem. AAAS, Am. Inst. Biol. Scis. Baptist. Home: 1121 Linden Dr Bloomington IN 47408 Office: 201 Morrison Hall Ind Univ Bloomington IN 47405

YOUNG, GENEVIEVE LEMAN, publishing executive, editor; b. Geneva, Sept. 25, 1930; came to U.S., 1945, naturalized, 1968; d. Clarence Kuangson and Juliana Helen (Yen) Y.; m. Cedric Sun, 1955 (div. 1972); m. Gordon Parks, Aug. 26, 1973 (div. 1979). BA (Wellesley Coll. scholar), Wellesley Coll., 1952. Asst. editor Harper & Row (pubs.), N.Y.C., 1960-62; editor Harper & Row (pubs.), 1962-64, asst. mng. editor, 1964-66, mng. editor, 1966-70; exec. editor J.B. Lippincott Co., N.Y.C., 1970-77; v.p. J.B. Lippincott Co., 1972-77; sr. editor Little, Brown & Co., N.Y.C., 1977-85; editor-in-chief Lit. Guild Am., N.Y.C., 1985-88; v.p., editorial dir. Bantam Books, N.Y.C., 1988-92. Alumna trustee Phillips Acad., Andover, Mass., 1975-78, class agt., 1979-85; mem. Wellesley Bus. Leadership Coun., 989—; mem. Youth Counseling League, 1986—, pres., 1989-96, mem. com. of 100, 1999-93; mem. Literacy Vols. N.Y.C., 1992—, sec., 1996—; mem. Andover Devel. Bd., 1993—; trustee Jewish Bd. Family and Children's Svcs., 1996—. Recipient Alumna Achievement award Wellesley Coll., 1982, Matrix award, 1988. Mem. Assn. Am. Pubs. (exec. coun. gen. pub. div. 1975-78, 85-87, freedom to read comn. 1972-75), Women's Media Group (pres. 1981-82, 2d v.p. 1994—), Century Assn. Home: 30 Park Ave New York NY 10016-3894

YOUNG, GEORGE BERNARD, JR., professional football team executive; b. Balt., Sept. 22, 1930; s. George Bernard and Frances Marie (Kauders) Y.; m. Kathryn M.L. Reddington, Sept. 4, 1965. A.B., Bucknell U., 1952; M.B.A., Loyola U., Balt., 1967; CASE, Johns Hopkins U., 1971. Tchr. history, head football coach Calvert Hall High Sch. and Balt. City Coll., 1953-68; asst. dir. player personnel Balt. Colts, 1968-70, offensive line coach, 1970; dir. player personnel, 1971-73, offensive coordinator, line coach, 1973-74; dir. profl. scouting Miami (Fla.) Dolphins, 1975-79; gen. mgr. N.Y. Football Giants, 1979—, now also v.p. Democrat. Roman Catholic. Office: NY Giants Giants Stadium East Rutherford NJ 07073*

YOUNG, GEORGE CRESSLER, federal judge; b. Cin., Aug. 4, 1916; s. George Philip and Gladys (Cressler) Y.; m. Iris June Hart, Oct. 6, 1951; children: George Cressler, Barbara Ann. A.B., U. Fla., 1938, LL.B., 1940; postgrad., Harvard Law Sch., 1947. Bar: Fla. 1940. Practice in Winter Haven, 1940-41; assoc. firm Smathers, Thompson, Maxwell & Dyer, Miami, 1947; adminstrv., legislative asst. to Senator Smathers of Fla., 1948-52; asst. U.S. atty. Jacksonville, 1952; partner firm Knight, Kincaid, Young & Harris, Jacksonville, 1953-61; U.S. dist. judge No., Middle and So. dists. Fla., 1961-73; chief judge Middle Dist., 1973-81, sr. judge, 1981—; Mem. com. on adminstrn. fed. magistrates system Jud. Conf. U.S., 1973-80. Bd. dirs. Jacksonville United Cerebral Palsy Assn., 1953-60. Served to lt. (s.g.) USNR, 1942-46. Mem. Rollins Coll. Alumni Assn. (pres. 1968-69), ABA (spl. com. on adminstrn. criminal justice), Fla. Bar Assn. (gov. 1960-61), Jacksonville Bar Assn. (past pres.), Am. Judicature Soc., Am. Law Inst., Order of Coif, Fla. Blue Key, Phi Beta Kappa, Phi Kappa Phi, Phi Delta Phi, Sigma Alpha Epsilon. Home: 2424 Shrewsbury Rd Orlando FL 32803-1334 Office: US Dist Ct 635 US Courthouse 80 N Hughey Ave Orlando FL 32801-2231

YOUNG, GEORGE H., III, investment banker; b. Washington, D.C., Feb. 10, 1959; s. George Jr. and Jeanne Marie (Collins) Y. BA (hon) in Internat. Rels., Brown U., 1982; MPhil in Internat. Rels., Magdalene Coll., U. Cambridge, Eng., 1983; MPPM, Yale U., 1987. Assoc. cons. Bain & Co., Boston, 1983-85; assoc. CS First Boston, N.Y.C., 1987-90, v.p., 1990-91, dir., 1992-94; White House fellow U.S. Dept. Treasury, Washington, 1991-92; sr. v.p. Lehman Bros., N.Y.C., 1994—; spkr. in field. Vol. Ch. of the Holy Trinity, N.Y.C., 1990—; application reader White House Fellows Commn., N.Y.C., 1993—; mem. alumni coun. exec. com. Phillips Acad., Andover, Mass., 1994—. Mem. Coun. Fgn. Rels., Harrow Sch. Assn., Oxford & Cambridge Univ. Club, Yale Golf Club. Roman Catholic. Home: 240 Centre St Apt 3D New York NY 10013 Office: Lehman Bros 3 World Fin Ctr New York NY 10285

YOUNG, GORDON ELLSWORTH, composer, organist; b. McPherson, Kans., Oct. 15, 1919; s. Benjamin Warden and Rose Esther (Johnson) Y. Mus.B., Southwestern Coll., 1940, Mus.D., 1960; attended, Curtis Inst. Music, 1944-46; studies with Powell Weaver, Kansas City Conservatory; studies with Joseph Bonnet, Paris. Organist First Meth. Ch., Tulsa, 1940-44; staff organist Radio Sta. KVOO, 1941-44; music writer Tulsa Daily World, 1942-44; organist First Presbyn. Ch., Lancaster, Pa., 1944-48; faculty, glee club dir. Franklin and Marshall Coll., 1946-47; organist Arch St. Presbyn. Ch., Phila., 1949-50, First Presbyn. Ch., Detroit, 1952-72; concert artist. Composer numerous organ, choir, solo voice and instrumental works; performer in 12 fgn. countries; contbr. to Bapt. Hymnal, 1991, Seventh-Day Adventist Hymnal, Hymns for the Family of God; compositions performed and recorded by Christopher Parkening, Feike Asma, Mormon Tabernacle Choir, Crystal Cath. Choir on EMI-Angel, Philips, Goth, Word and Bonneville record labels. Recipient Special Tribute award State of Mich., biographical tribute Nat. Fedn. Music Clubs, 1992. Mem. ASCAP (several awards), Am. Guild of Organists (life, hon.). Republican. Presbyn. Office: PO Box 256 Detroit MI 48231-0256 *A positive attitude in all things makes the whole difference between success and failure in a career.*

YOUNG, HARRISON, II, software development and marketing executive; b. Bklyn., Feb. 11, 1944; s. Harrison and Bobbie Aline (King) Y.; m. Shirley Gene Stanfield, Aug. 31, 1967 (div. Sept. 21, 1992); children: Melanie Marie, Tracy Lea; m. Emelie Martha Mannweiler, Dec. 18, 1993. BBA, Pacific Western U., L.A., 1990; MBA, U. Leicester, Eng., 1993. Cert. computer profl. Sr. systems rep. Info. Systems divsn. RCA, Houston, 1967-70; sr. scientist and program mgr. Tetra Tech Inc., San Diego, 1970-74; co-founder, exec. v.p. and sr. program mgr. Atlantic Analysis Corp., Norfolk, Va., 1974-85; program mgr. Comarco Inc., Anaheim, Calif., 1985-86, v.p., divsn. gen. mgr., 1986-87; pres. Washington-based subs. Comarco Inc., 1987-88; pres., CEO, dir. Comarco Inc., Anaheim, 1985-90; pres., CEO Tetra Tech Systems Integration subsidiary Honeywell, San Diego, 1990-92; pres., COO JWK Internat. Corp., Annandale, Va., 1992-94; pres., CEO Advanced Programming Concepts, Austin, Tex., 1994—. Bd. dirs. Blue Cross Blue Shield of Va., 1976-81. With USN, 1961-67. Mem. Am. Mgmt. Assn., Armed Forces Comms. and Electronics Assn., Nat. Contract Mgmt. Assn., Data Processing Mgmt. Assn., Instrumentation Soc. Am. Avocations: boating, computers, foreign travel. Home: 12633 Pony Ln Austin TX 78727 Office: Advanced Programming Concepts 7004 Bee Caves Rd Austin TX 78746-5065

YOUNG, HARRISON HURST, III, banker; b. Pitts., Dec. 15, 1944; s. Harrison Hurst Jr. and Margaret Ann (Knappen) Y.; m. Susan Parish, Feb. 15, 1969 (div.); m. Kirsty Hamilton, Jan. 29, 1994; 1 child, Angus Harrison Hamilton Young. AB, Harvard U., 1966. Reporter Washington Post, Washington, 1966; lending officer Citibank, N.Y., N.Y., 1971-75; assoc., v.p., prin. Morgan Stanley & Co., Inc., N.Y.C., Bahrain and London, 1975-86; mng. dir. Prudential Securities, Inc., N.Y.C., 1986-89, Dean Witter Reynolds, N.Y.C., 1989-91; dir. divsn. resolutions, chief oper. officer, dep. to chmn. FDIC, Washington, 1991-94; sr. advisor, mng. dir. Morgan Stanley & Co., Inc, Hong Kong and Beijing, 1994—; chief oper. officer, CEO China Internat. Capital Corp., Beijing, 1995—. Served to capt. U.S. Army, 1966-71, Vietnam. Mem. River Club, Brooks's (London), Ladies Recreation Club (Hong Kong), Capital Club (Beijing). Democrat. Episcopalian. Avocation: writing. Office: China Internat Capital Corp 23d Fl, 6 Fuxingmenwai Ave Everbright Bldg, Beijing 100045, China

YOUNG, HOLLY PEACOCK, lawyer, mediator; b. Indpls., Sept. 21, 1949; d. John Edward and Sylvia (Griffith) Peacock; m. Gregory Glenn Young, Sept. 2, 1972; children: Reagan Wheelock, Trevor Griffith. Student Dartmouth Coll., 1969-70; B.A., Conn. Coll., 1971; M.A., U. Tex., 1973; J.D., So. Meth. U., 1982. Bar: Tex. 1983; state water programmer EPA, Dallas, 1973-75, 75-77; asst. mgr. Menlo Sport, Menlo Park, Calif., 1977-79; assoc. Wald, Harkrader & Ross, Dallas, 1983-84; mediator Settlement Cons. Internat., Inc., Dallas, 1993—. bd. dirs. Hindostone Co., Indpls.; with Jour. Air Law and Commerce, 1980-82. Bd. dirs. Montessori Sch. of Park Cities, 1983-87; bd. advisors Cottonwood Gulch Found., 1982-89. Recipient Bronze medal EPA, 1974. Mem. ABA, Tex. Bar Assn., Dallas Bar Assn., Dyslexics CAN. Episcopalian. Home: 4711 Cherokee Trl Dallas TX 75209-1917

YOUNG, HOWARD SETH, chemist, researcher; b. Birmingham, Ala., July 7, 1924; s. Tilden Hendricks and Annie Lou (McGaugh) Y.; m. Anne Reid Maven, Aug. 29, 1945; children: Alice McGaugh, Glenn Reid, Margaret Reid, George Maven, Ralph Hendricks, Elizabeth Anne, Joan McGaugh. BS in Chemistry, Birmingham Southern Coll., 1942; PhD, Brown U., 1948. Chemist Tenn. Eastman Co., Kingsport, 1948-51, sr. rsch. chemist, 1951-62, rsch. assoc., 1963-67, sr. rsch. assoc., 1967-70, dir. engring. rsch., 1970-74; dir. phys. and analytical chemistry rsch. Eastman Chems. Div., Kingsport, 1976-84, asst. dir. rsch., 1984-85, dir. rsch., 1985-89, ret., 1989. Contbr. articles to profl. jours.; patentee in field. Served to corp. U.S. Army, 1945-46. Mem. Am. Chem. Soc., Sigma Xi. Avocations: reading, walking, birdwatching. Home: 1909 E Sevier Ave Kingsport TN 37664-3231

YOUNG, HOWARD THOMAS, foreign language educator; b. Cumberland, Md., Mar. 24, 1926; s. Samuel Phillip and Sarah Emmaline (Frederick) Y.; m. Carol Osborne, Oct. 5, 1949 (div. 1966); children—Laurie Margaret, Jennifer Anne; m. Jennifer Bunker, July 15, 1966 (div. 1980); m. Edra Lee Airheart, May 23, 1981; 1 child, Timothy Howard. B.S. summa cum laude, Columbia U., 1950, M.A., 1952, Ph.D., 1954. Lectr. Columbia U., N.Y.C., 1950-54; asst. prof. Romance langs. Pomona Coll., Claremont, Calif., 1954-60; assoc. prof. Pomona Coll., Claremont, 1960-66, Smith prof. Romance langs., 1966—; vis. prof. Middlebury Program in Spain, Madrid, 1986-87, U. Zaragoza, 1967-68; chief reader Spanish AP Ednl. Testing Service, Princeton, 1975-78, chmn. Spanish lang. devel. commn., 1976-79; mem. fgn. lang. adv. commn. Coll. Bd., N.Y.C., 1980-83; mem. West Coast selection commn. Mellon Fellowships for Humanities, Princeton, 1984-86, European selection com., 1987, 90. Author: The Victorious Expression, 1964, Juan Ramón Jiménez, 1967, The Line in the Margin, 1980; editor: T.S. Eliot and Hispanic Modernity, 1995; contbr. numerous articles and book revs. to profl. jours. Dir. NEH summer seminar for Sch. tchrs., 1993. Served with USNR, 1944-46, ETO. Fellow Del Amo Found., 1960-61, NEH, 1975, 89-90; Fulbright fellow; 1967-68; Rockefeller Study Ctr. scholar, 1976. Mem. MLA, Assn. Tchrs. Spanish and Portuguese, Am. Comparative Lit. Assn., Acad. Am. Poets, Assn. Lit. Scholars and Critics. Home: 447 W Redlands Ave Claremont CA 91711-1638 Office: Pomona Coll Modern Lang Dept 550 Harvard Ave Claremont CA 91711

YOUNG, HUGH DAVID, physics educator, writer, organist; b. Ames, Iowa, Nov. 3, 1930; s. Hugh Surber and Nellie Sibella (Peters) Y.; m. Alice Carroll, June 25, 1960; children: Gretchen Carroll, Rebecca Susan. B.S. in Physics, Carnegie-Mellon U., 1952, M.S. in Physics, 1953, Ph.D. in Physics, 1959, B.F.A. in Music, 1972. Instr. physics Carnegie-Mellon U., Pitts., 1956-59; asst. prof. Carnegie-Mellon U., 1959-65, assoc. prof., 1965-77, prof., 1977—; head dept. natural scis. Margaret Morrison Carnegie Coll., Carnegie-Mellon U., 1962-67, acad. coordinator, lectr. modern engring. mgrs. program, 1966-82; vis. assoc. prof. physics U. Calif., Berkeley, 1967-68, vis. prof. physics, 1974; asst. organist St. Paul's Cathedral, Pitts., 1978-82. Author: Statistical Treatment of Experimental Data, 1962, Fundamentals of Mechanics and Heat, 2d edit., 1974, Fundamentals of Optics and Modern Physics, 2d edit., 1976; (with Sears and Zemansky) College Physics, 7th edit., 1990, University Physics, 8th edit., 1992. Bd. dirs. Renaissance and Baroque Soc., 1980-86. Recipient Ryan teaching award Carnegie Inst. Tech., 1965. Mem. Am. Assn. Physics Tchrs., Am. Phys. Soc., Am. Guild Organists (assoc.). Democrat. Avocations: organ, rock climbing. Home: 5746 Aylesboro Ave Pittsburgh PA 15217-1412 Office: Carnegie-Mellon Univ Dept Physics Pittsburgh PA 15213

YOUNG, J. A., bishop. Bishop of N.W. Okla. Ch. of God in Christ, Lawton. Office: Ch of God in Christ PO Box 844 Lawton OK 73502-0844

YOUNG, J. ANTHONY, entertainment company executive. Student, Edinburgh U., 1967-70. With Arthur Andersen & Co., Glasgow, Scotland, 1970-74, P.A. Mgmt. Cons., Ltd., London, 1974-76; v.p. fin. EMI Films, Inc., 1976-78; with Lorimar Prodns., Inc., Culver City, Calif., 1979-88, past sr. v.p. fin.; former exec. v.p., chief fin. officer Lorimar Telepictures Corp., Culver City; pres. MCA Enterprises Internat. MCA Inc., Universal City, Calif., 1988-93; exec., v.p. ICS Comm. Inc., Century City L.A., 1994—.

YOUNG, J. WARREN, magazine publisher. Pub. Boys Life Mag., Irving, Tex. Office: Boys' Life PO Box 152079 Irving TX 75015-2079

YOUNG, JACK ALLISON, financial executive; b. Aurora, Ill., Dec. 31, 1931; s. Neal A. and Gladys W. Young; m. Virginia Dawson, Jan. 24, 1959;

children: Amy D., Andrew A. BS in Journalism, U. Ill., 1954. CLU; chartered fin. cons.; registered security rep. Advt. writer Caterpillar Tractor Co., 1956-58; ins. agent Equitable Life Assurance Soc., St. Geneva, Ill., 1958—, ins. broker, 1972—; pres. Jack A. Young and Assocs., 1978—; pres. Creative Brokerage, Inc., 1982—; pres., gen. securities prin. Chartered Planning, Ltd.; past trustee Equitable CLU Assn.; past chmn. Equitable Nat. Agents Forum. Bd. dirs. Tri-City Family Services, 1975-83, pres., 1979-81; trustee Delnor-Community Health System, 1985—, chmn., 1988-91; bd. dirs. St. Charles Ctr. Phys. Rehab., 1991—; chmn., pres. Delnor-Community Health Care Found., 1986-88. Served to lt. (j.g.), USN, 1954-56. Named to Equitable Hall of Fame, 1978. Mem. Million Dollar Round Table (life), Am. Soc. C.L.U.s, Am. Coll. C.L.U. Golden Key Soc., Fox Valley Estate Planning Council, Internat. Assn. for Fin. Planning, Inc., Aurora Assn. Life Underwriters (past pres., nat. committeeman), Nat. Assn. Securities Dealers (registered prin.). Club: Geneva Golf (pres. 1994). Home: 18 Campbell St Geneva IL 60134-2732 Office: 28 N Bennett St Geneva IL 60134-2207

YOUNG, JAMES EARL, ceramics educator, educational administrator; b. Chgo., Dec. 20, 1922; s. James Alexander and Ellen (Chedister) Y.; children: Hugh Parker, Katherine Sue. BS, U. Ill., 1948; PhD, State U. N.Y. Coll. Ceramics Alfred U., 1962. Ceramic engr. Republic Steel Co., Chgo., 1948-52; ceramic engr. Armour Research Found., Chgo., 1952-55; research supr. Structural Clay Research Found., Geneva, Ill., 1955-57; research fellow State U. N.Y. Coll. Ceramics at Alfred U., 1957-61, asst. prof., 1961-63, assoc. prof., 1963-67, prof., chmn. dept., 1967-70; dean Coll. Arts and Scis., Rutgers U., Camden, N.J., 1970-73; provost Rutgers U., Newark, 1973-82; exec. dir. Commn. on State Colls. of N.J., 1982-84; prof. Rutgers U., 1984—. Contbr. articles to tech. jours. Served with AUS, 1943-46. Am. Council Edn. fellow acad. adminstrn., 1966-67. Mem. Am. Ceramic Soc. Home: 130 Kingsberry Dr Somerset NJ 08873-4309 Office: PO Box 909 Piscataway NJ 08855-0909

YOUNG, JAMES EDWARD, lawyer; b. Painesville, Ohio, Apr. 20, 1946; s. James M. and Isabel P. (Rogers) Y. BBA, Ohio U., 1968; JD, Ohio State U., 1972. Bar: Ohio 1972; Law clk. to chief judge U.S. Ct. Appeals, Nashville, 1972-73; chief counsel City of Cleve., 1980-81, law dir., 1981-82; assoc. Jones, Day, Reavis & Pogue, 1973-79, ptnr., 1983—. Office: Jones Day Reavis & Pogue 901 Lakeside Ave E Cleveland OH 44114-1116

YOUNG, JAMES FRED, college president; b. Burnsville, N.C., Nov. 11, 1934; s. James Ray and Nina (Briggs) Y.; m. Phyllis Elizabeth Johnson, Apr. 15, 1962; children: Alan James, David Barden, Jane Elizabeth. AA, Mars Hill Coll., 1954; BS, Wake Forest U., 1956; MEd, U. N.C., 1957; EdD, Columbia U., 1964. Tchr. Micaville (N.C.) High Sch., 1957-58; research asst. Columbia U., 1959; prin. Enfield Sch., Halifax County, N.C., 1959-61; asst. supt. Halifax County (N.C.) Schs., 1961-64, Burlington (N.C.) City Schs., 1964-68; supt. Lynchburg (Va.) public schs., 1968-71; dep. supt. public instr. Commonwealth of Va., Richmond, 1971-73; pres. Elon Coll., Elon College, N.C., 1973—; chmn. bd. N.C. Nat. Bank, Burlington.; Bd. dirs. Burlington Day Sch., 1974—, Appalachian Regional Edn. Lab., Charleston, W.Va., 1972-73; chmn. Gov.'s Task Force on Financing Standards of Quality for Public Schs. in Va., 1972-73; sec. exec. com. Ind. Coll. Fund N.C., 1976-78; mem. exec. com. United Ch. of Christ Council for Higher Edn., 1977—. Served with AUS, 1958. Mem. N.C. Edn. Assn. (pres. Halifax County unit 1960-61, Burlington unit 1967-68), N.C. Assn. Ind. Colls. and Univs. (sec. exec. com. 1978—, chmn. 1985-89), Nat. Assn. Intercollegiate Athletics (pres.'s adv. coun. 1977—, com. on eligibility and acad. standards, chmn. coun. pres.'s 1988-90), Internat. Assn. Univ. Pres. (v.p. southeastern region), Alamance County C. of C. (dir. 1974-75). Club: Rotary. Office: Elon Coll Office Pres E Haggard Ave Elon College NC 27244-9344

YOUNG, JAMES HARVEY, historian, educator; b. Bklyn., Sept. 8, 1915; s. W. Harvey and Blanche (DeBra) Y.; m. Myrna Goode, Aug. 25, 1940; children: Harvey Galen, James Walter. B.A., Knox Coll., 1937, D.H.L., 1971; M.A., U. Ill., 1938, Ph.D., 1941; D.Sc., Rush U., 1976. Mem. faculty Emory U., 1941-84, prof. history, 1958-80, Charles Howard Candler prof. Am. social history, 1980-84, prof. emeritus, 1984—, chmn. dept., 1958-66; vis. assoc. prof. Columbia U., 1949-50; mem. nat. adv. food and drug council FDA, 1964-67; mem. Consumers Task Force, White House Conf. on Food, Nutrition and Health, 1969; mem. history life scis. study sect. NIH, 1970-73, 79-80, 91-93, chmn., 1992-93; vis. lectr. Am. Assn. Colls. Pharmacy Vis. Lectrs. Program, 1970-73; cons.-panelist NEH, 1970-83; cons. in history Centers for Disease Control; Logan Clendening lectr. U. Kans. Med. Ctr., 1973; Samuel X. Radbill lectr. Phila. Coll. Physicians, 1978; Beaumont lectr. Yale U., 1980; vis. hist. scholar Nat. Library Medicine, 1986; Harold J. Lawn lectr. U. Minn., 1990; David L. Cowen lectr. Rutgers U., 1990; James Campbell lectr. Rush U., 1992; Waring lectr. Med. U. S.C., 1993. Author: The Toadstool Millionaires, 1961, The Medical Messiahs, 1967, expanded edit., 1992, American Self-Dosage Medicines, An Historical Perspective, 1974, Pure Food: Securing the Federal Food and Drugs Act of 1906, 1989, American Health Quackery: Collected Essays, 1992; editor: (with W.A. Beardslee and T.J.J. Altizer) Truth, Myth and Symbol, 1962, (with T.L. Savitt) Disease and Distinctiveness in the American South, 1988. Served with AUS, 1943-45. FDA rsch. appointee, 1977-85; Carnegie Rsch. grantee, 1947, USPHS grantee, 1960-65, Nat. Libr. Medicine grantee, 1990-94; Faculty fellow Fund Advancement Edn., 1954-55, Social Sci. Rsch. Coun. fellow, 1960-61, Guggenheim fellow, 1966-67. Mem. Am. Hist. Assn., So. Hist. Assn. (pres. 1982), Orgn. Am. Historians, Soc. Am. Historians, Am. Assn. History of Medicine (coun., Fielding H. Garrison lectr. 1979, William H. Welch medal 1982, Continuing Lifetime Achievement award 1992), Am. Inst. History of Pharmacy (coun., hon. pres. 1993-95, Edward Kremers award 1962), Phi Beta Kappa, Sigma Xi, Phi Kappa Phi, Omicron Delta Kappa, Phi Alpha Theta. Congregationalist. Home: 272 Heaton Park Dr Decatur GA 30030-1027

YOUNG, JAMES JULIUS, university administrator, former army officer; b. Fort Ringgold, Tex., Nov. 28, 1926; s. John Cooper and Violet Thelma (Ohl) Y.; m. June Agnes Hillstead, Dec. 17, 1948; children: Robert Michael, Steven Andrew, Patrick James, Mary Frances. B.S., U. Md., 1960; M.H.A., Baylor U., 1962; Ph.D. in Hosp. and Health Adminstrn, U. Iowa, 1969. Commd. 2d lt. U.S. Army, 1947, advanced through grades to brig. gen., 1977; comdr., med. ops. officer, dir. tng. field med. units in European Command, 1949-53; comdr. Mil. Med. Leadership Sch., 1953-54; med. advisor (Nationalist Army of China), 1955-57; asst. adminstr. Fitzsimons Army Med. Center, 1957-60; med. plans and ops. officer (US Forces), Korea, 1962-63; sr. field med. instr., chief field med. service Med. Field Service Sch., 1963-66; dir. health care orgn. and mgmt. analysis Office of Surgeon Gen., 1969-71; dir. med. plans and ops. directorate Office of the Surgeon, Military Assistance Command, Vietnam, 1971-72; exec. officer, chief adminstrv. services Silas Hays Army Hosp., 1973-74; military health analyst, military health care study OMB, Exec. Office of Pres., 1974-76; dep. dir. resources mgmt. and cons. for health care adminstrn. Office of Surgeon Gen., 1976-77; chief Med. Services Corps, U.S. Army and; dir. resources mgmt. Office of Surgeon Gen., 1977-81; ret., 1981; instr. U. Iowa, 1967-69; asst. prof., preceptor Baylor U., 1973-74; vice chancellor for health affairs W.Va. Bd. Regents, Charleston, 1982-87; dean sch. of allied health scis. U. Tex. Health Sci. Ctr., San Antonio, 1987-90, interim dean Sch. Medicine, 1988-89, dean Sch. Medicine, 1989—; cons. to Min. of Health, Republic of Vietnam, 1971-72; adj. prof. Baylor U., 1977-81, George Washington U., 1975-76, W.Va. U., 1986; prof. U. Tex. health Sci. Ctr., San Antonio, 1989—. Contbr. articles to profl. jours. Decorated D.S.M., Legion of Merit, Meritorious Service medal and; others; recipient Walter Reed medallion for service, 1981; Army Med. Dept. medallion for contribution to health service, 1981. Mem. APHA, Coun. Deans, Assn. of Am. Med. Colls., Assn. Mil. Surgeons (chmn. med. svc. sect. 1978), Assn. U.S. Army, Interagy. Inst. Fed. Health Execs., Phi Kappa Tau. Roman Catholic. Home: 1610 Anchor Dr San Antonio TX 78213-1943 Office: U Tex Health Sci Ctr Office Of Dean Med Sch San Antonio TX 78284

YOUNG, JAMES MORNINGSTAR, physician, naval officer; b. Massillon, Ohio, Oct. 28, 1929; s. Ralph Louis and Pauline Louise (Morningstar) Y.; m. Bettylu Jones, July 3, 1952; children: Anne Christine, Mark Andrew, Patricia Jane, Elizabeth Lynne, Judith Pamela, Claudia Dianne; m. Mariette M. Aubuchon, Oct. 11, 1970; children: Gretchen Camille, Jason Paul. AB, Duke U., 1951, MD, 1955. Diplomate Am. Bd. Internal Medicine. Intern Bethesda Naval Hosp., 1955-56, asst. dir. tissue bank, 1956-58, resident, 1958-61; commd. lt. (j.g.) USN, 1955, advanced through grades to lt. comdr., 1961, promoted to temporary rank capt., 1963; White House physician to Presidents Kennedy and Johnson, Washington, 1963-66; staff Oakland (Calif.) Naval Hosp., 1966-69; chief medicine Naval Hosp. Boston, Chelsea, Mass., 1969-74; med. officer Naval Air Sta., South Weymouth, Mass., 1974-75; assoc. clin. prof. medicine Boston U. Sch. Medicine, 1969-75; v.p. med. affairs Mass. Blue Shield/Blue Cross, 1975-87; lectr. Harvard Sch. Pub. Health, 1987-90; sr. advisor Beijing Coll. Traditional Chinese Medicine, 1987-88; med. advisor U.S.-China People's Friendship Assn., Washington, 1988-90; cons. USPHS, Office Asst. Sec. for Health, Nat. Ctr. for Health Svcs., Rsch. and Health Care Tech. Assessment, HHS, 1985-90; v.p. for med. affairs Greenery Rehab. Group, Inc., 1988-90; assoc. med. dir. New. Eng. Rehab. Hosp., 1992-95, chief medicine, 1992-95. Contbr. articles to med. publs. Decorated knight comdr. with star Equestrian Order of the Holy Sepulchre of Jerusalem; named Disting. Citizen of Washington H.S., Massillon, Ohio, 1993. Fellow ACP, AMA, Alpha Omega Alpha, Omicron Delta Kappa, Beta Omega Sigma, Sigma Alpha Epsilon. Home: 340 Chestnut St Newton MA 02165-2951

YOUNG, JAY ALFRED, chemical safety and health consultant, writer, editor; b. Huntington, Ind., Sept. 8, 1920; s. Jacob Phillip and Marie (Skully) Y.; m. Anne Elizabeth Neff, June 29, 1942 (dec. June 1962); children: John, Paul, Cecelia, Michael, Joseph, Andrea, Therese, Gregory, Thomas, Lucy, Margaret, Antonia; m. Mary Ann Owens, Aug. 15, 1962; children: James, Laurence; 4 stepchildren. BS, Ind. U., 1939; AM, Oberlin Coll., 1940; PhD, U. Notre Dame, 1950. Chief chemist Asbestos Mfg. Co., Huntington, Ind., 1941-42; ordnance engr. U.S. War Dept., Washington, 1942-44; from instr. to prof. chemistry King's Coll., Wilkes-Barre, Pa., 1949-69; vis. prof. Carleton U., Ottawa, Ont., Can., 1969-70, Fla. State U., Tallahassee, 1975-77; Hudson prof. Auburn (Ala.) U., 1970-75; mgr. tech. publs. Chem. Mfrs. Assn., Washington, 1977-80; chem. safety and health cons. Silver Spring, Md., 1980—; pro bono cons. Occupational Safety and Health Adminstrn., EPA, Consumer Product Safety Commn., Washington, 1980—. Author: Practice in Thinking, 1958, Chemical Concepts, 1963, Selected Principles of Chemistry, 1963, Arithmetic for Students of Science, 1968, Keys to Chemistry, 1973, Keys to Oxidation-Reduction, 1974, Things That Last, 1977, Fire!, 1977, Actions and Reactions, 1978, Chemistry, A Human Concern, 1978, Kitchen Chemistry, 1980, Improving Safety in the Chemical Laboratory, 1987, 2d edit., 1991, Chemical Safety Manual for Small Businesses, 1989, Developing a Chemical Hygiene Plan, 1990, Safety in Academic Chemistry Laboratories, 1995; contbr. to Ency. Britannica and over 100 articles to profl. jours. Tech. resource person to media and expert witness on chem. hazards, precautions, transp. incidents involving chems. Lt. USNR, 1944-46. Recipient Disting. Chemistry Alumnus award U. Notre Dame, 1968, Excellence in Chemistry Teaching award Mfg. Chemists Assn., 1970. Fellow AAAS; mem. Am. Chem. Soc. (councilor 1963-87, policy com. 1970-81, chmn. div. chem. health and safety 1979-80, chem. health and safety award 1991). Roman Catholic. Avocations: wood and metalworking, gardening. Home and Office: 12916 Allerton Ln Silver Spring MD 20904-3105

YOUNG, JEFFRY JOHN, psychologist, gerontologist, educator, statistician; b. Harvey, Ill., Aug. 23, 1952; s. Harold Joyce and Marion June (Krismer) Y.; m. Rosalind Michelle Lloyd Sheridan, Jan. 25, 1992. Student, St. Patrick's Coll., Mountain View, Calif., 1971-73; BA in Philosophy & Psychology, San Jose State U., 1977, MA in Gen. Psychology, 1978; PhD in Social/Environ. Psychology, Claremont (Calif.) Grad. Sch., 1986. Coord., rsch. assoc. Ctr. for Applied Social Rsch. Claremont Grad. Sch., 1979-86; postdoctoral intern, behavioral scis. svc. sect. L.A. Police Dept., 1986-87; assoc. dir. Ruby Gerontology Ctr. Calif. State U., Fullerton, 1988-91, dir. Gerontology Rsch. Inst., 1989-92, rsch. prof. Sch. Humanities and Social Scis., 1986-93; assoc. dir. Roybal Inst. for Applied Gerontology Calif. State U., L.A., 1991-94, dir. Gerontology Rsch. Ctr., 1991-94; dir. advocacy and demonstration projects Nat. Asian Pacific Ctr. Aging, Seattle, 1994—; adj. asst. prof. Sch. Gerontology, U. So. Calif., L.A., 1991-94; adj. prof. dept. psychology Calif. State U., L.A., 1991-94; co-prin. investigator Alzheimer's Outreach Project Nat. Inst. on Aging, UCLA, 1992-95; cons. health resources and svcs. adminstrn. Alzheimer's Demonstration project East L.A., Calif., 1992-94; project dir. Alzheimer's Disease Rsch. Ctr., Nat. Inst. on Aging, U. So. Calif. and U. Calif., Irvine, 1991-94; dir. Adminstrn. Aging Project, 1994—; prin. investigator Agy. Health Care Policy and Rsch., 1995; facilitator White House Conf. on Aging, 1995; mem. tech. adv. com. Assn. Asian Pacific Health Care Orgns., 1996. Author abstracts, monographs, and articles. Chair adv. bd. com. Rancho Los Amigos Med. Ctr., Downey, Calif., 1993—; touch judge uni. div. So. Calif. Rugby Football Union, 1988-91; pres. Meals on Wheels of Fullerton, Calif., 1993-94; chmn. instl. rev. bd. Calif. State U., L.A., 1994. Recipient Cert. of Recognition, L.A. Police Dept., 1987, Points of Light award, 1992, others; named to Outstanding Young Men of Am., 1986. Mem. APA, Am. Psychol. Soc., Gerontol. Soc. Am., Am. Evaluation Assn. (charter mem.), Am. Bd. Forensic Examiners, N.Am. Mycological Soc. (life), Phi Beta Delta, Sigma Phi Omega (life). Roman Catholic. Avocations: mycology, rare books, rugby, Nordic skiing, microscopy. Home: PO Box 4627 Rolling Bay WA 98061-0627 Office: Nat Asian Pacific Ctr Aging 1511 3rd Ave Ste 914 Seattle WA 98101-1626

YOUNG, JERE ARNOLD, lawyer, management consultant; b. Sinking Spring, Pa., Nov. 29, 1936; s. Herbert M. and Helen (Bock) Y.; m. Constance Werkheiser, June 28, 1958; children—Jere Arnold, Karen Denise, Tracy Lynn. BS in Econs., U. Pa., 1958; JD, Yale U., 1961. Bar: Pa. 1961, U.S. Supreme Ct. 1976. With firm Dechert, Price and Rhoads, Phila., 1961-65; sr. v.p., gen. corp. counsel, sec. Indsl. Valley Bank and Trust Co., Phila., 1965-79; v.p. fin., sec. Tasty Baking Co., Phila., 1980; exec. v.p. SE Nat. Bank of Pa., 1980-82, pres., 1983-84; pres. HP Investors Ltd., 1985-87; chmn., chief exec. officer Hansen Bancorp, Inc., 1988-92; chmn. Hansen Savs. Bank, 1988-92, Hansen Savs. Bank Fla., 1987-92; pres. Capital Adv. Group, Inc., 1992—; bd. dirs. First Comml. Bank of Phila., 1992—. Pres. Radnor Twp. Sch. Authority, 1983. Mem. Del. County Bar Assn. Home: 646 Malin Rd Newtown Square PA 19073-2613 Office: 4 Sentry Pky Ste 325 Blue Bell PA 19422-2311

YOUNG, JERRY WESLEY, animal nutrition educator; b. Mulberry, Tenn., Aug. 19, 1934; s. Rufus William and Annie Jewell (Sweeney) Y.; m. Charlotte Sullenger, July 8, 1959; children: David, Jeretha. BS, Berry Coll., 1957; MS, N.C. State U., 1959, PhD, 1963. Asst. prof. Iowa State U., Ames, 1965-70, assoc. prof., 1970-74, prof. in animal sci. & biochemistry, 1974—. Contbr. articles to profl. jours. Postdoctoral fellow NIH, 1963-65. Mem. Am. Dairy Sci. Assn. (Outstanding Dairy Nutrition Rsch. 1987), Am. Inst. Nutrition, Am. Soc. Animal Sci., Am. Chem. Soc., Sigma Xi, Phi Kappa Phi, Gamma Sigma Delta. Baptist. Office: Iowa State U 313 Kildee Hall Ames IA 50010

YOUNG, JESS R., physician; b. Fairfield, Ill., Feb. 4, 1928; s. Edgar S. and Clara B. (Musgrave) Y.; m. Gloria Wynn, July 10, 1953; children—James C., Patricia A. BS, U. Steubenville, 1951; MD, St. Louis U., 1955. Intern Highland Alameda County Hosp., Oakland, Calif., 1955-56; resident in internal medicine Cleve. Clinic Hosp., 1956-59, mem. staff dept. peripheral vascular disease, 1959—, chmn. dept., 1976-94. Co-author: Leg Ulcer, 1975, Peripheral Vascular Diseases, 1991; contbr. articles to profl. jours., chpts. to books. Served with AUS, 1946-47. Mem. AMA, Am. Heart Assn. (stroke council), Am. Coll. Cardiology, Internat. Cardiovascular Soc., ACP, Am. Fedn. Clic. Research, Ohio Soc. Internal Medicine, Soc. for Vascular Medicine and Rsch., Inter-Urban Club. Methodist. Home: 1503 Burlington Rd Cleveland OH 44118-1216 Office: 9500 Euclid Ave Cleveland OH 44195-0001

YOUNG, JOAN CRAWFORD, advertising executive; b. Hobbs, N.Mex., July 30, 1931; d. William Bill and Ora Maydelle (Boone) Crawford; m. Herchelle B. Young, Nov. 23, 1971 (div.). BA, Hardin Simmons U., 1952; postgrad. Tex. Tech. U., 1953-54. Reporter, Lubbock (Tex.) Avalanche-Jour., 1952-54; promotion dir. Sta. KCBD-TV, Lubbock, 1954-62; account exec. Ward Hicks Advt., Albuquerque, 1962-70; v.p. Mellekas & Assocs., Advt., Albuquerque, 1970-78; pres. J. Young Advt., Albuquerque, 1978—. Bd. dirs. N.Mex. Symphony Orch., 1970-73, United Way of Greater Albuquerque, 1985-89; bd. trustees N.Mex. Children's Found., 1994—. Recipient Silver medal N.Mex. Advt. Fedn., 1977. Mem. N.Mex. Advt. Fedn. (bd. dirs. 1975-76), Am. Advt. Fedn., Greater Albuquerque C. of C. (bd. dirs. 1984), Albuquerque Petroleum Club (membership chmn. 1992-93, bd. dirs. 1993—, sec. 1994—, v.p. 1995—). Republican. Author: (with Louise Allen and Audre Lipscomb) Radio and TV Continuity Writing, 1962. Home: 1638 Tierra Del Rio NW Albuquerque NM 87107 also: 500 Marquette NW Albuquerque NM 87102

YOUNG, JOHN ALAN, electronics company executive; b. Nampa, Idaho, Apr. 24, 1932; s. Lloyd Arthur and Karen Eliza (Miller) Y.; m. Rosemary Murray, Aug. 1, 1954; children: Gregory, Peter, Diana. BSEE, Oreg. State U., 1953; MBA, Stanford U., 1958. Various mktg. and fin. positions Hewlett Packard Co. Inc., Palo Alto, Calif., 1958-63, gen. mgr. microwave divsn., 1963-68, v.p. electronic products group, 1968-74, exec. v.p., 1974-77, COO, 1977-78, pres., 1977-92, CEO, 1978-92; ret., 1992; bd. dirs. Wells Fargo Bank, Wells Fargo and Co., Chevron Corp., SmithKline Beecham Plc. Affymetrix, Inc., Shaman Pharms. Inc., Ciphergen, Novell, Inc. and Gen. Magic; chmn. Smart Valley, Inc. Chmn. ann. fund Stanford U., 1966-73, nat. chmn. corp. gifts, 1973-77, mem. adv. coun. Grad. Sch. Bus., 1967-73, 75-80, Univ. trustee, 1977-87; bd. dirs. Mid-Peninsula Urban Coalition, 1971-80, co-chmn., 1983-85; chmn. Pres.'s Commn. on Indsl. Competitiveness, 1983-85, Nat. Jr. Achievement, 1983-84; pres. Found. for Malcolm Baldrige Nat. Quality Award; mem. Adv. Com. on Trade Policy and Negotiations, 1988-92. With USAF, 1954-56. Mem. Nat. Acad. Engring., Coun. on Competitiveness (founder, founding chair computer systems policy project 1986), Bus. Coun.

YOUNG, JOHN EDWARD, retired lawyer; b. Tulsa, July 11, 1935; s. Russell Edward and Frances Lucille (Wetmore) Y.; m. Mary Moore Nason, Dec. 27, 1966; children: Cynthia Nason, Abigail Brackett. BS with honors, Calif. Inst. Tech., 1956; LLB magna cum laude, Harvard U., 1959. Bar: N.Y. 1961, U.S. Dist. Ct. (so. dist.) N.Y. 1973. Assoc. Cravath, Swaine & Moore, N.Y.C., 1960-67, ptnr., 1968-95; resident ptnr. Cravath, Swaine & Moore, Paris, 1971-73, London, 1990-95. Editor Harvard Law Rev., 1958-59. Sheldon Traveling fellow Harvard U., 1959-60. Mem. ABA, N.Y. State Bar Assn., Assn. of Bar of City of N.Y., Century Assn., Harvard Club of N.Y.C. Democrat. Episcopal. Home: 1088 Park Ave New York NY 10128-1132 Office: Cravath Swaine & Moore 825 8th Ave New York NY 10019-7416

YOUNG, JOHN HARDIN, lawyer; b. Washington, Apr. 25, 1948; s. John D. and Laura Virginia (Gwathmey) Y.; m. Mary Frances (Farley) Crosby. AB, Colgate U., 1970; JD, U. Va., 1973; BCL, Oxford U., Eng., 1976. Bar: Va. 1973, D.C. 1974, U.S. Dist. Ct. (ea. dist.) Va. 1974, U.S. Dist. Ct. D.C. 1974, Internat. Trade Ct. 1974, U.S. Ct. Fed. Claims 1974, U.S. Ct. Appeals (4th, Fed. and D.C. cirs.), U.S. Supreme Ct. 1977. Ptnr. Porter Wright Morris & Arthur, Washington, 1988-92, of counsel, 1992—; gen. counsel The Smoot Corp., 1992—; mem. adv. bd. Antitrust Bull., Jour. Antiturst Law and Econs.; mem. U.S. Sec. State's adv. com. Pvt. internat. Law, 1987-95; chmn. Va. Retirement Sys. Rev. Bd., 1990-94; asst. atty. gen. Commonwealth of Va., 1976-78; mem. master plan task force City of Alexandria, Va., 1987-88, mem. budget and fiscal affairs adv. com., 1989-91; moderator Alexandria Forum, 1993—, Fedn. Forum/TV channel 10, 1989-91; gen. counsel CAPAccess, 1992—. Contbr. articles to profl. jours. and books on litigation, evidence and trial tactics. Gen. counsel Dem. Party of Va., 1993—, state counsel, 1989-92, state counsel dem. predsl. campaign, 1980-96; counsel Gov. Wilder recount, 1989, Gov. Glendenning recount, 1995; nat. chair DNC Conf. of Dem. Counsel, 1995—. Mem. ABA (coun. 1986-89, adminstrv. law sect., chmn. trade regulation and competition com., 1983-86, chair CLE com. 1991-94, chair dispute resolution com. 1994—, vice chair nominating com. 1994-95), Nat. Lawyers Coun., Am. Law Inst., George Mason Am. Inn of Ct. (master), Hon. Soc. Mid. Temple, Comml. Bar Assn. U.K. (overseas mem.), Temple Bar Found. (founding mem., dir.), Phi Alpha Theta (history hons.). Episcopalian. Home: 5146 Woodmire Ln Alexandria VA 22311-1301 Office: 5201 Leesburg Pike Ste 1100 Falls Church VA 22041-3203

YOUNG, JOHN WATTS, astronaut; b. San Francisco, Sept. 24, 1930; s. William H. Y.; m. Susy Feldman; children by previous marriage: Sandra, John. BS in Aero. Engring, Ga. Inst. Tech., 1952; D Applied Sci. (hon.), Fla. Technol. U., 1970; LLD (hon.), Western State U., 1969; DSc (hon.), U. S.C., 1981, Brown U., 1983. Joined USN, 1952, advanced through grades to capt.; test pilot, program mgr. F4 weapons systems projects, 1959-62; then maintenance officer Fighter Squadron 143, Naval Air Sta., Miramar, Calif.; chief astronaut office Flight Ops. Directorate, 1975-87, spl. asst. dir. JSC for engring. ops., safety, 1987-96, comdr. 54-hour, 36-orbit 1st flight of Shuttle Space, 1981, and 10 day orbital shuttle 1st flight Space Lab., 1983, assoc. dir. tech. JSC, 1996—. Decorated DFC (3), D.S.M. (2); recipient NASA Disting. Svc. medal (3), NASA Exceptional Svc. medal (2), NASA Engring. Achievement medal, 1988, NASA Outstanding Leadership medal, 1992, NASA Outstanding Achievement medal, 1994, Congl. Space medal of honor, 1981; named Disting. Young Alumni Svc. award Ga. Tech. Acad. Disting. Engrs., 1994; named to Nat. Aviation Hall of Fame, 1988. Fellow Am. Astronautical Soc. (Flight Achievement award 1972, 81, 83, Space Flight award 1993), Soc. Exptl. Test Pilots (Iven Kincheloe award 1972, 81), AIAA (HAley Astronautics award 1973, 82, 84); mem. Sigma Chi. Astronaut NASA, made 1st two-man 3 orbit flight, Gemini 3, Mar. 1965, Gemini 10 3 day flight, 1966, Apollo 10 8-day flight lunar landing dress rehearsal, 1969, Apollo 16 11 day lunar landing and surface exploration, 1972; dir. space shuttle br., astronaut office, 1973-75. Office: NASA Johnson Space Ctr Houston TX 77058

YOUNG, JOHNNY, foreign service officer; b. Savannah, Ga., Feb. 6, 1940; s. John A. and Eva (Grant) Y.; m. Angelena V. Clark, Sept. 23, 1967; children: David John, Michelle Jeanine. B.S. cum laude in Bus., Temple U., 1966. Chief acct. procurement dept. City of Phila., 1960-67; budget officer Am. Embassy, Tananarivo, Madagascar, 1967-69, gen. services officer, Conakry, Guinea, 1970-72, Nairobi, Kenya, 1972-74; adminstrv. officer, Doha, Qatar, 1974-77, Bridgetown, Barbados, 1977-79, adminstrv. counselor, Amman, Jordan, 1983-85, The Hague, Netherlands, from 1985; career counselor Dept. State, Washington, 1979-81, exec. dir., from 1981; ambassador to Sierra Leone, Freetown, 1990—. Ambassador's rep. Am. Club, Amman, 1983—, Am. Community Sch. Bd., Amman, 1983—. Recipient Group Meritorious award State Dept., 1970, Meritorious Honor, 1975, Cash and Meritorious award, 1983, Meritorious Step Increase award, 1984. Mem. Municipal Fin. Officers Assn. Democrat. Roman Catholic. Office: Am Embassy, Walpole & Siaka Stevens St, Freetown Sierra Leone

YOUNG, JON NATHAN, archeologist; b. Hibbing, Minn., May 30, 1938; s. Robert Nathan Young and Mary Elizabeth (Barrows) Roy; m. Karen Sue Johnson, June 5, 1961 (div. May 1980); children: Shawn Nathan, Kevin Leigh; m. Tucker Heitman, June 18, 1988. BA magna cum laude, U. Ariz., 1960, PhD, 1967; MA, U. Ky., 1962. Archeologist Nat. Park Svc. Southwest Archeol. Ctr., Globe and Tucson, Ariz., 1967-75; exec., camp dir. YMCA of Metro. Tucson, 1976-77; asst. dir. Kit Carson Meml. Found., Taos, N.Mex., 1978; co-dir. Las Palomas de Taos, 1979; archeologist Nat. Forest Svc., Carson Nat. Forest, Taos, 1980—; exec. order cons. U.S. Sec. Interior, 1973-75. Author: The Salado Culture in Southwestern Prehistory, 1967; co-author: Excavation of Mound 7, 1981, First-Day Road Log in Techtonic Development of the Sangre de Cristo Mountains, 1990. Advisor Boy Scouts Am.; active YMCA White Rag Soc.; mem. Kit Carson Hist. Mus. Grantee NEH, 1978; Ariz. Wilson Found., NSF, Ky. Rsch. Found. fellow, 1960-62; Baird Found., Bausch and Lomb, Elks; recipient cert. merit USDA, 1987, 89. Fellow AAAS, Am. Anthrop. Assn., Explorers Club, Royal Anthrop. Inst.; mem. Current Anthropology (assoc.), Ariz. Archaeol. and Hist. Soc., Ariz. Hist. Soc., Coun. on Am.'s Mil. Past, New Mex. Heritage Preservation Alliance, Soc. Hist. Archaeology, Soc. Am. Archaeology, Harwood Found., Millicent Rogers Mus., Taos Archaeol. Soc., Taos County Hist. Soc., Sigma Xi, Phi Beta Kappa, Alpha Kappa Delta, Phi Kappa Phi, Delta Chi. Home: PO Box 2207 Taos NM 87571-2207 Office: Nat Forest Svc Suprs Office 208 Cruz Alta Rd Taos NM 87571-0558

YOUNG, JOSEPH H., federal judge; b. Hagerstown, Md., July 18, 1922; s. J. Edgar and Mabel K. (Koser) Y.; m. Doris Oliver, Sept. 6, 1947; children: Stephen A., William O., J. Harrison. A.B., Dartmouth Coll., 1948; LL.B., U. Va., 1951. Bar: Md. 1951. Assoc. firm Marbury Miller & Evans, Balt., 1951-52; assoc. firm Piper & Marbury, Balt., 1952-58, ptnr., 1958-71, mng. ptnr., 1968-71; judge U.S. Dist. Ct. Md., from 1971, now sr. judge; instr. Johns Hopkins U. (McCoy Coll.), 1954-62. Bd. dirs. Legal Aid Soc. Balt.,

1958-71, CICHA (Health Appeal), 1964-71; bd. dirs. exec. com. Md. div. Am. Cancer Soc., 1958—, chmn. div. bd. dirs. 1969-71, bd. dirs. 1966—, chmn. nat. svcs. com. 1970-73, chmn. exec. com. 1976-77, dir.-at-large 1973-83, vice-chmn. nat. bd. dirs. 1975-77, chmn. nat. bd. 1977-80, chmn. pub. issues com. 1981-83, past officer dir. 1983-90, hon. life mem. 1990—, chmn. world-wide fight com. 1987-90, also mem. trust adv. bd.; mem. oncology adv. coun. Johns Hopkins U.; chmn. com. on campaign orgn. & pub. edn. Internat. Union Contra Cancer, Geneva, Switzerland, 1981-90, mem. fin. com., 1990—, chmn. 1993—, exec. com. 1993—. Decorated Bronze Star, Purple Heart. Recipient Disting. Service Award Am. Cancer Soc., 1983; Dartmouth Coll. Alumni award, 1983; James Ewing Soc. award, 1983. Mem. 4th Circuit Jud. Conf., Assn. Alumni Dartmouth Coll. (pres. 1984-85). Republican. Presbyterian (elder, deacon, trustee). Clubs: Hamilton Street, Rule Day, Lawyers Round Table. Office: US Dist Ct 101 W Lombard St Baltimore MD 21201-2626

YOUNG, JOSEPH LAURIE, architecture educator; b. Huntsville, Tex., Sept. 23, 1924; s. Benjamin Wiley and Margaret (Cater) Y. BArch, U. Tex., 1950; MArch, Ga. Inst. Tech., 1955. Registered architect S.C. Teaching fellow U. Tex., Austin, 1948-50; prof. emeritus architecture Clemson U., S.C., 1950—, Univ. marshall, 1985-88; Hayes Fulbright fellow Middle East Tech. U., Ankara, Turkey, 1963-64; cons. to bus.; artist drawings of hist. bldgs., 1950—; resident prof. Charles E. Daniel Clemson U. Centre Bldg. Rsch. and Urban Study, Genova, Italy, 1985-86, 88-89; dir. Clemson U. Ctr. for Archtl. Study, Coll. of Charleston, S.C., 1988. Elder Ft. Hill Presbyn. Ch. With USNR, 1943-46. Recipient Student Adviser award Clemson U., 1989. Fellow AIA (pres. S.C. chpt. 1971-72, Svc. awards 1969, 71, bd. dir. S.C. chpt. 1966-69); mem. S.C. AIA, Tiger Brotherhood, Rotary Internat., Tau Sigma Delta, Paul Harris Fellow Rotary. Home: 705 Clemson House PO Box 712 Clemson SC 29631

YOUNG, JOSEPH LOUIS, artist; b. Pitts., Nov. 27, 1919; s. Louis and Jennie (Eger) Y.; m. Millicent Goldstein, June 19, 1949; children: Leslie Sybil, Cecily Julie. Grad., Westminster Coll., New Wilmington, Pa., 1941, D. Litt., 1960; Edwin Austin Abbey mural painting scholar, 1949; grad., Boston Mus. Sch. Fine Arts, 1951; Albert H. Whitin traveling fellow, Am. Acad. in Rome, 1951-52. Newspaperman Pitts. and N.Y.C., 1941-43; lectr. Tufts Coll., 1949; painting instr. Boston Mus. Sch., 1950; Idylwild Arts Found., 1959, Brandeis Camp Inst., 1962-74; founder, dir. Joseph Young Mosaic Workshop, 1953—; founding chmn. dept. archtl. arts Brooks Santa Barbara (Calif.) Sch. Fine Arts, 1969-75; head mus. exhibits Bowers Mus., Santa Ana, Calif., 1977-78; head visual arts CETA program, City of Los Angeles, 1978-80; organized internat. sculpture competition for city of Huntington Beach, Calif., 1974; art cons. Allied Arts Commn., City of Huntington Beach, 1973-74; cons. Art in Public Bldgs. Program, Calif. Arts Council, 1976-77; field adminstr. CCA/CETA Program, Los Angeles.; Invited prin. speaker at nat. convs. A.I.A., Am. Craftsmen Council, 4th Congress I.A.P.A., 7th Nat. Sculpture Conf., Council of Am., U. Kans.; lectr. Rome, Venice, Florence (as guest) Italian govt., 1959. Restoration of mosaics from Greek and Roman periods and Della Robbia sculpture, 1972-73; author: A Course in Making Mosaics, 1957, Mosaics, Principles and Practice, 1963, also articles in profl. jours.; pub. mural painting bibliography, 1946; asso. founding editor: Creative Crafts mag, 1960-64; concept and design: ART$MARKET, 1979; work featured 16mm documentary film The World of Mosaic; true fresco, oil and mosiac mural commns. in, Boston, Chgo., Pitts., Los Angeles, survey govt. sponsored mural painting programs, 1951; one man show, Pitts. Arts and Crafts Center, 1950, Falk-Raboff Gallery, Los Angeles, 1953, ten year retrospective exhbn. archtl. art work, Desert Mus., Palm Springs, Calif., 1963, Calif. council A.I.A. Fine Arts Architecture Exhbn., 1964, Nat. Gold Medal Exhbn. of N.Y. Archtl. League, 1951; work reproduced in numerous books, mags., newspapers throughout the world; invited to submit designs for Nebr. State Capitol murals, paintings and mosiacs in numerous pvt. collections; executed mosiac murals Los Angeles Police Facilities Bldg., 1955, Don Bosco Tech. High Sch., 1956, Temple Emanuel, 1957, Southland Shopping Center, 1958, Our Lady of Lourdes Ch., 1959, Cameo residence, Beverly Hills, Calif., 1961, Santa Barbara Stock Exchange, 1960, St. Martins Ch., La Mesa, Calif., 1966, stained glass windows, liturgical art program, Congregation Beth Sholom, San Francisco, 1966, West Apse of Nat. Shrine of Immaculate Conception, Washington, 1966, mosiac arch, Eden Meml. Park, San Fernando, Calif., 1960; commd. to execute mural, Los Angeles County Hall of Records, Shalom Meml. Park, Chgo., B.V.M. Presentation Ch., Midland, Pa., 1961, Hollenbeck Police Sta., Los Angeles, 1963, Beth Emet Temple, Anaheim, Calif., 1963, Temple Sinai, Glendale, Calif., 1963, Sinai Temple, Los Angeles, 1963, Valley Beth Israel, Sun Valley, Calif., 1964, Beth Tikvah, Westchester, Calif., 1964, Belmont High Sch., Los Angeles, 1972; commd. to design and execute 14 bas-relief concrete-mosaic murals for exterior of, Math. Scis. Bldg. at UCLA, bronze sculpture, La Mirada (Calif.) Civic Theatre, 1979; did liturgical art programs for, Congregation B'nai B'rith, Santa Barbara, Temple Beth Torah, Alhambra, Temple Beth Ami, West Covina, Temple Menorah, Redondo Beach, Temple Solael, Canoga Park, Temple Bamidbar, Lancaster, Temple Beth Jacob, Redwood City (all Calif.), other congregations in Calif., concrete bas reliefs, Southgate County Pub. Library, 1973, mosaics for, St. Mary of Angels, Hollywood, Calif., 1973, Triforium polyphonoptic, kinetic tower, Los Angeles Mall, 1969-75; multimedia presentations for, 400th Anniversary Michelangelo, Italian Trade Commn., Casa de Maria, Santa Barbara, Hancock Coll., Santa Maria, Los Angeles County Mus. Art, U. Calif., Los Angeles and Irvine., designs for Holocaust Monument for Pan-Pacific Park in Los Angeles won national competition and dedicated in 1992; appointed to City of West Hollywood Arts Commn.; chmn. Fine Arts Bd., U. of Judaism, L.A.; completed cycle of Stained Glass windows for Ventura County Jewish Community Ctr. devoted to theme of Seven Days of Creation, 12 tribes stained glass for Temple Beth Israel, West Hollywood, Calif., 1991; work subject of restrospective exhbn. at the Jewish Community Galleries, 1986; commd. projects now represented by Yanov & Gold, Ltd. of Los Angeles, Calif. Served with USAAF, 1943-46. Recipient Nat. Army Arts contest award, 1945; Huntington Hartford Found. fellow, 1952-53. Fellow Internat. Inst. Arts and Letters (life); mem. Nat. Soc. Mural Painters (nat. v.p. 1969—), Artists Equity Assn. (pres. So. Calif. chpt. 1956, nat. v.p. 1960), Calif. Confedn. Arts (founding pres. 1976). Home and Studio: Art in Architecture 7917 1/2 Norton Ave Los Angeles CA 90046-5204

YOUNG, KATHERINE ANN, education educator; b. Castleford, Idaho, Apr. 9, 1941; d. Ross and Norna (Scully) Stoner; m. Virgil Monroe Young, Dec. 20, 1964; 1 child, Susan Annette. BS in Elem. Edn., U. Idaho, 1965; MEd, Ea. Washington U., 1969; EdD, Utah State U., 1980. Cert. advanced elem. tchr., Idaho. Tchr. spl. edn. Coeur d'Alene (Idaho) Sch. Dist., 1965-66; tchr. elem. grades Coeur d' Aleue (Idaho) Sch. Dist., 1966-67, Boise (Idaho) Sch. Dist., 1967-88; assoc. prof. edn. Boise State U., 1988-93, prof., 1993—; dir. Alliance of Idaho Geographers/Nat. Geographic Soc., 1993—. Co-author: (resource book) The Story of Idaho Author's, 1977, The Story of Idaho Guide and Resource Book, 1993; author: The Utah Activity Book, 1980, Constructing Buildings, Bridges, and Minds, 1993; cons., contbr. (nat. edn. jour.) Learning, 1991—. Named Idaho Tchr. of Yr., State Dept. of Edn., Boise, 1983; invited to luncheon at White House, Pres. Ronald Reagan, Washington, 1983; Recipient Outstanding Young Educator award Boise Jaycees, 1983; profiled in Idaho Centennial pub., 1990; travel to Japan grantee Rocky Mountain Region Japan Project, 1990. Mem. ASCD, Nat. Coun. for Social Studies, Idaho Law Found., Alliance Idaho Geographers (state coord.). Avocations: travel, reading. Office: Boise State U Dept Tchr Edn 1910 University Dr Boise ID 83725-0001

YOUNG, KENNETH EVANS, educational consultant; b. Toronto, Ont., Can., Mar. 21, 1922; s. John Osborne Wallace and Gwendolyn May (Evans) Y.; m. Mae Catherine Wittenmyer, July 1, 1945; 1 child, Bruce Kenneth. AB, San Francisco State Coll., 1943; MA, Stanford U., 1947, PhD, 1953; LLD (hon.), U. Nev., 1972. Instr. journalism and speech San Francisco State Coll., 1946-48; instr. journalism and English Calif. State Poly. Coll., San Luis Obispo, 1949-50; from asst. prof. to acting dean Coll. Arts and Scis. Kellogg-Voorhis Campus, Pomona, 1951-57; dean faculty U. Alaska, College, 1957-59; fellow in coll. adminstrn. U. Mich., Ann Arbor, 1959-60; exec. v.p. U. Nev., Reno, 1960-64; pres. SUNY, Cortland, 1964-68; v.p., dir. Washington office Am. Coll. Testing Program, 1968-75; pres. Council on Postsecondary Accreditation, Washington, 1975-80; exec. dir. Nat. Univ. Continuing Edn. Assn., Washington, 1980-84; dir. Inst. for Learning in Retirement, Am. U., Washington, 1984-89; sr. assoc., cons. Diane U. Eisenberg Assocs., Washington, 1984-95; chmn. Evans-McCan Group, 1996—. Prin. editor: Understanding Accreditation, 1983; contbr. articles to profl. jours. Sgt. U.S. Army, 1943-45. Republican. Club: Cosmos (Washington). Home: 4200 Cathedral Ave NW Apt 512 Washington DC 20016-4912

YOUNG, KEVIN, track and field athlete. Olympic track and field participant Barcelona, Spain, 1992. Recipient 400m Hurdles Gold medal Olympics, Barcelona, 1992; world recorder holder in 400m hurdles. Address: 13010 Bethany Rd Alpharetta GA 30201-1052*

YOUNG, LAURA, dance educator, choreographer; b. Boston, Aug. 5, 1947; d. James Vincent and Adelaide Janet (Coupal) Y.; m. Anthony Charles Catanzaro, Sept. 26, 1970 (div. Nov. 1981); m. Christopher Edward Mehl, Aug. 23, 1987. Grad. high sch., Cohasset, Mass. Dancer Met. Opera Ballet, N.Y.C., 1971-73; dancer Boston Ballet Co., 1963-65, prin. dancer, 1965-71, 73-89, ballet mistress, 1989-91; guest tchr. Dance Tchrs. Club Boston, 1978-82, Dance Masters Assn., 1979, 90, 92, 93, Walnut Hill Sch., Natick, Mass., 1984-87, 90-91; asst. dir. Boston Ballet II, 1984-86, tchr., dir., 1986-96, dir. summer dance program, 1986-94; 1st hon. mem. Dance Masters Assn., Chpt. 5, 1992; mem. faculty Boston Conservatory, 1990-94; prin. Boston Ballet Sch., 1993—. Choreographer (ballets) Occasional Waltzes, 1984, Albinoni Suite, 1986, Champ Dances, 1987, A Place of Sound and Mind, 1988, Deadlock, 1989, Rumpelstiltskin, 1989. Recipient Leadership award Greater Boston C. of C., 1987; named Disting. Bostonian, Boston's 350th Jubilee Com., 1980. Mem. Am. Guild Mus. Artists, Dance Masters Am. (hon.). Office: Boston Ballet Co 19 Clarendon St Boston MA 02116-6107

YOUNG, LAWRENCE, electrical engineering educator; b. Hull, Eng., July 5, 1925; arrived in Can., 1955; naturalized, 1972; s. Herbert and Dora Y.; m. Margaret Elisabeth Jane, Jan. 5, 1951. B.A., Cambridge U., 1946, Ph.D., 1950, Sc.D., 1963. Asst. lectr. Imperial Coll., London, 1952-55; mem. research staff B.C. Research Council, 1955-63; assoc. prof. U. B.C., Vancouver, 1963-65, prof. dept. elec. engring., 1965-90, prof. emeritus, 1990—. Author: Anodic Oxide Films, 1961; contbr. articles to profl. jours. Recipient Callinan award Dielectrics div. Electrochemical Soc., 1983, Can. Electrochem. Gold medal, 1990. Fellow IEEE, Royal Soc. Can. Office: Dept Electrical Engineering, U BC, Vancouver, BC Canada V6T 1W5

YOUNG, LEO, electrical engineer; b. Vienna, Austria, Aug. 18, 1926; came to U.S., 1953, naturalized, 1958; s. Samuel and Marie Y.; m. Fay Merskey, Jan. 4, 1953 (dec. May 1981); children—Philip Michael, Sarah Anne, Joseph David; m. Ruth Breslow, Jan. 2, 1983. BA, Cambridge U., 1946, MA, 1950; MS, Johns Hopkins U., 1956, D.Engring. (Westinghouse-B.G. Lamme grad. scholar), 1959, D.H.L. (hon.), 1989. Lab. mgr. Decca Radar, Ltd., Surbiton, Eng., 1951-53; adv. engr. Westinghouse Electric Corp., Balt., 1953-60; staff scientist, program mgr. Stanford Research Inst., Menlo Park, Calif., 1960-73; staff cons., asso. supt. Naval Research Lab., Washington, 1973-81; dir. research Office of Undersec. for Def. Research and Engring., Dept. Def., 1981-94; cons. to dir. def. rsch. and engring. Dept. Def., 1994—; bd. dirs. Filtronic-Comtek (U.K.); mem. NSF delegation to Japan, 1995. Author: Microwave Filters, 1964, Systems of Units in Electricity and Magnetism, 1969, Advances in Microwaves, Vols. 1-8, 1966-74, Everything You Should Know About Pensions Plans, 1976; also articles. Fellow AAAS, IEEE (pres. 1980, pres. Microwave Soc. 1969, Microwave prize 1963, Microwave Career award 1988, Disting. Contbns. to Engring. Professionalism IEEE-USA 1993, Pinnacle award 1995); mem. Sigma Xi. Patentee in field. *It has been my goal to serve the public and my belief that engineering and science improve the quality of life. I have enjoyed doing engineering research and am fortunate in receiving recognition.*

YOUNG, LIONEL WESLEY, radiologist; b. New Orleans, Mar. 14, 1932; s. Charles Henry and Ethel Elsie (Johnson) Y.; m. Florence Inez Brown, June 24, 1957; children: Tina Inez, Lionel Thomas, Owen Christopher. BS in Biology, St. Benedict's Coll., Atchison, Kans., 1953; MD, Howard U., 1957. Diplomate Am. Bd. Radiology. Intern Detroit Receiving Hosp., Wayne State Univ. Coll. of Medicine, 1957-58; resident Strong Meml. Hosp., U. Rochester (N.Y.) Med. Ctr., 1958-61; pediatric radiologist, assoc. prof. radiology and pediatrics U. Rochester Med. Ctr., 1965-75; prof. radiology and pediatrics U. Pitts., 1975-86; dir. radiology and pediatrics Children's Hosp. of Pitts., 1980-86; chmn. radiology Children's Hosp. Med. Ctr. of Akron (Ohio), 1986—, Children's Hosp. and Northeastern Ohio U. Coll. Medicine, Rootstown, 1987—; pres. Akron Pediatric Radiologists, 1986—. Lt. comdr. USN, 1961-63. Mem. Am. Coll. Radiology (mem. coun., steering com.), Soc. for Pediatric Radiology. Democrat. Roman Catholic. Avocation: music. Office: Children's Hosp Med Ctr Akron 1472 Rosehill Cres Redlands CA 92373-6527

YOUNG, LOIS CATHERINE WILLIAMS, poet, former reading specialist; b. Wakeman, Ohio, Mar. 10, 1930; d. William McKinley and Leona Catherine (Woods) Williams; m. William Walton Young; children: Ralph, Catherine, William. BS, NYU, 1957; MS, Hofstra U., 1962, profl. diploma, 1967, EdD, 1981; M Pub. Adminstrn., Fla. Internat. U., 1988. Cert. tchr., sch. supr., N.Y., pub. mgmt., Fla. Tchr. Copiague (N.Y.) Schs., 1957-59; research assoc. Columbia and Hofstra Univs., Hempstead, N.Y., 1964-69; tchr. Half Hollow Hills Pub. Schs., Dix Hills, N.Y., 1970-72; instr. Conn. Coll., New London, 1972-73; tchr., supr., reading coordinator Hempstead (N.Y.) Pub. Schs., 1975-85; cons. South African project AID Fla. Meml. Coll., Miami, Fla., 1987-88; clinician Hofstra U., Hempstead, 1962-64; tchr. trainer Amityville (N.Y.) Pub. Schs., 1965, Hofstra Univ., 1982; key speaker Internat. Reading Assn., N.Y., Calif., Caribbean Islands, 1982-86. Author numerous poems. Sec. Nassau County (N.Y.) chpt. Jack and Jill of Am., 1960-62; pres. PTA, Uniondale, N.Y., 1962-68; active Boy Scouts Am., Uniondale, N.Y., 1963-65; bd. dirs. Miami chpt. UN Assn./USA, 1987-92, 1st v.p. 1989-91, Broward Fort Lauderdale chpt., 1993—; active multilateral project, 1987-90; contbr. Procs. South African Project, 1987. Recipient Lifetime Membership award PTA, 1964, rsch. grant N.Y. State Fed. Programs, 1978, Laurel Wreath award Doctoral Assn. of N.Y. Educators, 1982, Cert. of award UN Assn./USA, 1987, 88, Outstanding Achievement award Fla. Internat. U., 1988, Golden Poet award World of Poetry, 1990, 91; fellow Fla. Internat. U., 1987. Mem. Internat. Soc. Poets (life, lifetime adv. panel 1993—, award, Nat. Libr. of Poetry award 1994, 95, Poetry Today 1996), Fla. Internat. U. Alumni Assn., NYU Alumni Assn. (bd. dirs. 1983-90, 2d v.p. 1986-87), Hofstra U. Alumni Assn., Tuskegee Airmen, Inc., Weston (Fla.) Toastmasters Club (charter), Toastmasters Internat., Kappa Delta Pi, Alpha Kappa Alpha, Theta Iota Omega (global affairs com. 1984-86), Phi Delta Kappa. Avocations: creative writing, travel, tennis, radio reading for unsighted, golf. Home: 7187 Crystal Lake Dr W Palm Beach FL 33411

YOUNG, LORETTA (GRETCHEN YOUNG), actress; b. Salt Lake City, Jan. 6, 1913; M. Thomas Lewis (div.). Grad., Ramona Convent, Alhambra, Calif.; student, Immaculate Heart Coll., Hollywood, Calif. Motion picture appearances include Laugh Clown Laugh, 1928, Loose Ankles, 1929, The Squall, 1930, Kismet, 1930, The Devil to Pay, 1930, I Like Your Nerve, 1931, Platinum Blonde, 1932, The Hatchet Man, 1932, Big Business Girl, 1932, Life Begins, 1932, Zoo in Budapest, 1933, Man's Castle, 1933, The House of Rothschild, 1934, Midnight Mary, 1935, The Crusaders, 1935, Clive of India, 1935, Call of the Wild, 1935, Shanghai, 1936, Ramona, 1936, Ladies in Love, 1937, Wife, Doctor and Nurse, 1937, Second Honeymoon, 1938, Four Men and a Prayer, 1938, Suez, 1938, Kentucky, 1938, Three Blind Mice, 1938, The Story of Alexander Graham Bell, 1939, The Doctor Takes a Wife, 1939, He Stayed for Breakfast, 1940, Lady from Cheyenne, 1941, The Men in Her Life, 1941, A Night to Remember, 1942, China, 1943, Ladies Courageous, 1944, And Now Tomorrow, 1944, The Stranger, 1945, Along Came Jones, 1946, The Perfect Marriage, 1946, The Farmer's Daughter, 1947 (Acad. award 1947), The Bishop's Wife, 1948, Rachel and the Stranger, 1948, Come to the Stable, 1949, Cause for Alarm, 1951, Half Angel, 1951, Paula, 1952, Because of You, 1952, It Happens Every Thursday, 1953, others; appeared in TV series Loretta Young Show (Emmy awards 1954, 56, 59, Acad. Television Arts & Scis.), 1953-61, in TV films Christmas Eve (Golden Globe Award for best actress in a TV movie), 1986, Lady in a Corner, 1989; stage appearance in An Evening with Loretta Young, 1989. Active in Cath. charity orgns. Roman Catholic. *

YOUNG, LOWELL SUNG-YI, medical administrator, educator; b. Honolulu, Dec. 5, 1938. AB, Princeton U., 1960; MD, Harvard U., 1964. Di;omate Am. Bd. Internal Medicine with subspecialty in infectious diseases. Intern, jr. asst. resident, sr. asst. resident med. divsn. Bellevue Hosp. and Meml. Hosp., N.Y.C., 1964-67; fellow in medicine Cornell U. Med. Coll., 1965-67; epidemic intelligence officer bacterial diseases br. Nat. Communicable Disease Ctr., Atlanta, 1967-69, chief spl. pathogens sect., 1968-69; spl. postdoctoral rsch. fellow Nat. Inst. Allergy and Infectious Diseases, 1969-70; rsch. fellow in medicine Meml. Hosp./Cornell U. Med. Coll., 1969-70; clin. asst. physicisn infectious disease svc. dept. medicine Meml. Hosp., 1970-72, assoc. dir. microbiology lab., 1971-72; instr. in medicine Cornell U. Med. Coll., 1970-72; asst. clinician Sloan-Ketterin Inst. for Cancer Rsch., 1971-72; adj. prof. pharmacy U. of Pacific, San Francisco, 1989—; mem. microbiology and invectious diseases adv. com. Nat. Inst. Allergy and Infectious Diseases, 1981-85, mem. allergy and immunology rsch. com., 1975-79; mem. staff Calif. Pacific Med. Ctr., Mt. Zion Hosp. and Med. Ctr., U. Calif., San Francisco; mem. sci. adv. bd. Am. Found. for AIDS Rsch. Mem. editl. bd. Infection, Infectious Diseases in Clin. Practice, Diagnostic Microbiology and Infectious Diseases, Antomicrobial Agts. and Chemotherapy, Infection and Immunity; contbr. numerous articles to profl. jours., chpts. to books. Recipient Alexander D. Langmuir prize Epidemic Intelligence Svc., 1970, Garrod medal Brit. Soc., 1992. Fellow ACP (mem. med. self-assessment com.), Infectious Diseases Soc. Am. (councillor 1983-85); mem. Am. Soc. for Clin. Investigation, Am. Fedn. for Clin. Rsch., Am. Soc. for Microbiology, Western Soc. for Clin. Rsch., Internat. Immunocompromised Host Soc., Brit. Soc. Antimicrobial Chemotherapy. Office: Calif Pacific Med Ctr Kuzell Inst 2200 Webster St Ste 305 San Francisco CA 94115-1821

YOUNG, LUCY CLEAVER, physician; b. Wheeling, W.Va., Aug. 8, 1943. B.S. in Chemistry, Wheaton Coll. (Ill.), 1965; M.D., Ohio State U., 1969. Diplomate Am. Bd. Family Practice, Bd. of Ins. Medicine. Rotating intern Riverside Meth. Hosp., Columbus, Ohio, 1969-70; resident Trumbull Meml. Hosp., Warren, Ohio, 1970-71; practice medicine specializing in family practice, West Chicago, Ill., 1971-73, Paw Paw and Mendota, Ill., 1973-78; co-founder and med. dir. Wholistic Health Ctr. of Mendota, 1976-78; asst. med. dir. Met. Life Ins. Co., Gt. Lakes Head Office, Aurora, Ill., 1979-80; med. dir. Commonwealth Life Ins. Co., Louisville, 1980-85; assoc. prof. U. Ill. Abraham Lincoln Sch. Medicine, 1976-79; faculty monitor MacNeal Meml. Hosp. Family Practice Ctr. (Ill.), 1979-80; faculty preceptor U. Louisville Family Practice Dept., 1981-85; Locum Tenens Family Practice for Kron Med. Corp. of Chapel Hill, N.C., 1986-89; physician Red Bird Mission & Med. Ctr., Beverly, Ky., 1989-90; family practice floater Ochsner Clinic satellites, New Orleans, 1990—; clin. faculty preceptor La. State U. Sch. Medicine, 1992—; mem. staffs Central DuPage Hosp., Winfield, Ill., 1971-73, Mendota Community Hosp., 1973-80. Vol. Red Bird Med. Ctr., 1985—. Fellow Am. Acad. Family Practice; mem. Christian Med. and Dental Soc. (del. to House 1995—). Home: PO Box 0730 Madisonville LA 70447-0730 Office: Ochsner Clinic 1514 Jefferson Hwy New Orleans LA 70121-2429

YOUNG, MARGARET ALETHA MCMULLEN (MRS. HERBERT WILSON YOUNG), social worker; b. Vossburg, Miss., June 13, 1916; d. Grady Garland and Virgie Aletha (Moore) McMullen; BA cum laude, Columbia Bible Coll., 1949; grad. Massey Bus. Coll., 1958; MSW, Fla. State U., 1965; postgrad. Jacksonville U., 1961-62, Tulane U., 1967; m. Herbert Wilson Young, Aug. 19, 1959. Dir. Christian edn. Eau Claire Presbyn. Ch., Columbia, S.C., 1946-51; tchr. Massey Bus. Coll., Jacksonville, Fla., 1954-57, office mgr., 1957-59; social worker, unit supr. Fla. div. Family Svcs., St. Petersburg, 1960-66, dist. casework supr., 1966-71; social worker, project supr., program supr. Project Playpen, Inc., 1971-81, pres. bd., 1982-83, cons., 1986-89; pvt. practice family counselor, 1982—; mem. coun. Child Devel. Ctr., 1983-89; mem. transitional housing com., Religious Community Svcs., 1984-90. Mem. Acad. Cert. Social Workers, Nat. Assn. Social Workers (pres. Tampa Bay chpt. 1973-74), Fla. Assn. for Health and Social Services (pres. chpt. 1971), Nature Conservancy, Eta Beta Rho. Democrat. Presbyn. Rotary Ann (pres. 1970-71). Home: Presbyterian Home CMR 13 201 W 9th North St Summerville SC 29483-6721

YOUNG, MARGARET BUCKNER, civic worker, author; b. Campbellsville, Ky.; d. Frank W. and Eva (Carter) Buckner; m. Whitney M. Young, Jr., Jan. 2, 1944 (dec. Mar. 1971); children: Marcia Elaine, Lauren Lee. BA, Ky. State Coll., 1942, MA, U. Minn., 1946. Instr. Ky. State Coll., 1942-44; instr. edn. and psychology Spelman Coll., Atlanta, 1957-60; dir. emeritus N.Y. Life Ins. Co.; alt. del. UN Gen. Assembly, 1973. Mem. pub. policy com. Advt. Coun. Trustee emerita Lincoln Ctr. for Performing Arts; chmn. Whitney M. Young, Jr. Meml. Found., 1971-92; trustee Met. Mus. Art, 1976-90; bd. govs. UN Assn., 1975-82; bd. visitors U.S. Mil. Acad., 1978-80; dir. Philip Morris Cos., 1972-91. Author: The First Book of American Negroes, 1966, The Picture Life of Martin Luther King, Jr., 1968, The Picture Life of Ralph J. Bunche, 1968, Black American Leaders-Watts, 1969, The Picture Life of Thurgood Marshall, 1970, pub. affairs pamphlet.

YOUNG, MARILYN RAE, former school system adminstrative secretary, mayor; b. Muskegon, Mich., Dec. 29, 1934; d. Albert Henry Cribley and Mildred Ida (Johnson) Raby; m. Peter John Young, May 21, 1955; children: Pamela Lynn Young-Walker, Lane Allen. Grad. high sch., Calumet City, Ill., 1952. Dep. pub. fiduciary Yuma County, Ariz., 1979-83; adminstrv. sec. Yuma Sch. Dist. One, 1983-95; councilman City of Yuma, 1990-93, mayor, 1993—. Pres. bd. dirs. Behavioral Health Svcs. of Yuma, 1979-90; vice chmn. Yuma Planning and Zoning Commn., 1985-89; v.p. bd. dirs. Children's Village, Yuma, 1983-89; lay leader Trinity United Meth. Ch., 1986—; grad. Yuma Leadership Inc., 1985, treas. bd. dirs., 1986-89; participant Ariz. Women's Town Hall, 1989, various Yuma County Town Halls, 1987-93; adv. bd. mem. Friends of KAWC; chmn. Yuma Pub. Safety Police Bd., 1990—, Yuma Fire Pub. Safety Bd., 1990—, Yuma Youth Leadership Com., 1991-95; mem. allocation panel United Way, 1991-93; charter mem. Friends of Roxaboxen; active H.S. Ad Hoc Com., 1991—; exec. bd. mem. Yuma Met. Planning Orgn., 1990—, Western Ariz. Coun. of Govts., 1990—; corp. bd. dirs. Greater Yuma Econ. Devel., 1990-95; hon. chmn. Yuma County San Luis Rio Colo. Commn., 1990—; mem. Nat. League of Cities FAIR Com., 1990—, Binational Border Health Task Force, 1990—, resolution com. League of Ariz. Cities and Towns, 1990—, mem. com. U.S. Conf. of Mayors, 1990—. Mem. Yuma County C. of C. (mem. mil. affairs com. 1988-90). Avocations: community involvement, reading, travel, needlework. Home: 1288 W 18th St Yuma AZ 85364-5313 Office: City of Yuma 180 W 1st St Yuma AZ 85364-1407

YOUNG, MARVIN OSCAR, lawyer; b. Union, Mo., Apr. 4, 1929; s. Otto Christopher and Irene Adelheide (Barlage) Y.; m. Sue Carol Mathews, Aug. 23, 1952; children: Victoria Leigh, Kendall Marvin. A.B., Westminster Coll., 1951; J.D., U. Mich., 1954; LLD, Westminster Coll., 1989. Bar: Mo. 1954. Practice law firm Thompson, Mitchell, Thompson Douglas, St. Louis, 1954-55, 57-58; atty. Mo. Farmers Assn., Columbia, 1958-67; exec. v.p. First Mo. Corp., Columbia, 1965-68; v.p. ops. MFA-Central Coop., Columbia, 1967-68; v.p., gen. counsel, sec. Peabody Coal Co., St. Louis, 1968-82; gen. counsel Peabody Holding Co., Inc., St. Louis, 1983-85; also dir., sec. subs. and affiliates Peabody Coal Co.; ptnr. Gallop, Johnson & Neuman, St. Louis, 1986—, chmn. corp. dept., 1988-90, chmn. energy dept., 1990—; city atty. Warson Woods, Mo., 1990—; speaker at legal insts. Assoc. editor Mich. Law Rev., 1953-54; contbr. articles to profl. jours. Pres. Warson Woods PTA, 1974-75; trustee Met. Sewer Dist. St. Louis, 1974-80, chmn. 1978-80; mem. Mo. Energy Coun., 1973-77, Mo. Environ. Improvement and Energy Resources Athority, 1983-87, vice chmn. 1986-87; trustee Eastern Mineral Law Found., 1983—; pres. Alumni Assn. Westminster Coll., Fulton, Mo., 1978-80, trustee coll., 1977—, exec. com., 1978—, chmn. 1986-90; chmn. Churchill Meml. and Libr., Fulton, 1992—; mem. Chancellor's Coun. Adv. Bd. U. of Mo., St. Louis, 1992—; mem. lawyers adv. coun. Gt. Plains Legal Found., Kansas City, Mo., 1976-84; mem. Rep. Com. Boone County, Mo., 1962-68, chmn. legis. dist. com., 1962-64, 66-68; alt. del. Rep. Nat. Conv., 1968; pres. Clayton Twp. Rep. Club, 1973-77; sr. warden Episc. Ch., 1988-89. Served to capt. USAF, 1955-57. Recipient alumni award of merit, 1972; Churchill fellow, 1990; named Coal Lawyer Yr. Nat. Coal Assn., 1994. Mem. ABA, Mo. Bar Assn., Bar Assn. Met. St. Louis, Barristers Soc., Round Table Club of St. Louis, John Marshall Rep. Lawyers Club (pres. 1977), Mo. Athletic Club, Rotary (bd. dirs. St. Louis club 1993-95), Masons, Order of Coif. Home: 555 Flanders Dr Saint Louis MO 63122-1617 Office: Gallop Johnson & Neuman LC 101 S Hanley Rd Ste 1600 Saint Louis MO 63105-3406

YOUNG, MARY ELIZABETH, history educator; b. Utica, N.Y., Dec. 16, 1929; d. Clarence Whitford and Mary Tippit Y. B.A., Oberlin Coll., 1950; Ph.D. (Robert Shalkenbach Found. grantee, Ezra Cornell fellow), Cornell U., 1955. Instr. dept. history Ohio State U., Columbus, 1955-58; asst. prof. Ohio State U., 1958-63, assoc. prof., 1963-69, prof., 1969-73; prof. history U. Rochester, N.Y., 1973—; cons. in field. Author: Redskins, Ruffleshirts, and Rednecks: Indian Allotments in Alabama and Mississippi, 1830-1860, 1961; co-editor, contbr.: The Frontier in Americal Development: Essays in Honor of Paul Wallace Gates, 1969. Recipient Pelzer award Miss. Valley Hist. Assn., 1955, Award Am. Studies Assn., 1982, Ray A. Billington award, 1982; Social Sci. Research Council grantee, 1968-69. Mem. Am. Hist. Assn., Orgn. Am. Historians, Am. Studies Assn., Am. Soc. Ethnic History, Soc. for Historians of the Early Am. Republic, Am. Antiquarian Soc. Home: 2230 Clover St Rochester NY 14618-4124 Office: U Rochester Dept History Rochester NY 14627

YOUNG, MATT NORVEL, JR., university chancellor emeritus; b. Nashville, Oct. 5, 1915; s. Matt Norvel and Ruby (Morrow) Y.; m. Helen Mattox, Aug. 31, 1939; children: Emily Lemley, Matt Norvel III, Marilyn Stewart, Sara Jackson. B.A., Abilene Christian U., 1936; M.A., Vanderbilt U., 1937; Ph.D., George Peabody Coll., Vanderbilt U., 1943; L.H.D., Calif. Coll. Medicine, 1964; LL.D., Lubbock Christian U., 1982, Pepperdine U., 1987. Minister College Ch. of Christ, David Lipscomb Coll., 1941-43, Broadway Ch. Christ, Lubbock, Tex., 1944-57; pres. Pepperdine U., Los Angeles, 1957-71; chancellor Pepperdine U., 1971-84, chancellor emeritus, 1985—, also regent.; chmn. bd. dirs. 21st Century Christian Pub. Co., Nashville; bd. dirs. Imperial Bank, L.A.; co-founder Lubbock Christian U., 1957, Lubbock Children's Home, 1953, Tex. Tech. U. Bible chair, 1950. Author: History of Christian Colleges, 1949, The Church is Building, 1956; co-founder: 21st Century Christian mag., 1938, editor, pub., 1945-76; editor Power for Today, 1955-70, Preachers of Today, Vol. I, 1952, Vol. II, 1959, Vol. III, 1964, Vol. IV, 1970, Vol. V, 1982, Churches of Today, Vol. I, 1960, Vol. II, 1969, Stress is a Killer, 1978. Bd. govs. L.A. County Mus. Natural History, 1960—, trustee, 1970—; bd. dirs. Nat. Coun. on Alcoholism, 1981-83, Calif. M-2 Prisoner Rehab. Assn., 1986-90, Forest Lawn Meml. Parks, Christian Higher Edn. Found.; vice chmn. bd. Union Rescue Mission. Recipient George Washington medal Freedom Found., 1962, 64. Mem. Los Angeles Area C. of C. (dir.), Phi Delta Kappa. Clubs: Bohemian, California. Lodge: Rotary. Home: 24420 Tiner Ct Malibu CA 90265-4705 Office: Pepperdine U Malibu CA 90265

YOUNG, MAURICE ISAAC, mechanical and aerospace engineering educator; b. Boston, Feb. 10, 1927; s. Joseph J. and Alice (Lifshitz) Y.; m. Eleanor Cooper, Sept. 25, 1954; children: Rochelle, Gerald, Rosalind. Student, Worcester Poly. Inst., 1944-45; PhB, U. Chgo., 1949, BS, 1949; MA, Boston U., 1950; PhD, U. Pa., 1960. Sr. dynamics engr. Bell Aircraft Corp., Buffalo, 1951-52; Sr. dynamics engr. Bell Aircraft Corp., Ft. Worth, 1952-53; group engr. Jacobs Aircraft Engine Co., Pottstown, Pa., 1953-54; prin. tech. engr. Piasecki Helicopter and Aircraft Corp., Morton, Pa., 1954-56, Phila., 1956-58; sr. engring. specialist communications and weapons div. Philco Corp., Phila., 1958-61; mgr. applied mechanics Philco Corp., 1958-61; mgr. helicopter research and advanced tech. Vertol Div. Boeing Co., Phila., 1961-68; prof. mech. and aerospace engring. U. Del., 1968-88, prof. emeritus, 1988; mem. internat. organizing com. for modeling and simulation Internat. Assn. Sci. and Tech. for Devel., 1982; cons. Vigyan Rsch. Assocs., Hampton, Va., 1988-90; also cons. in field; NASA-Am. Soc. Engring. Edn. faculty fellow, NASA Langley Rsch. Ctr., 1987. Mem. editorial bd. Powered Lift Aircraft, 1975-83. Served with USAAF, 1946-47. DuPont Faculty fellow, 1969-70; U.S. Army grantee, 1971-76. Fellow AIAA (assoc.); mem. Soc. Engring. Sci., Sigma Xi. Home: 852 Brompton Ct Newport News VA 23608-9344

YOUNG, MERWIN CRAWFORD, political science educator; b. Phila., Nov. 7, 1931; s. Ralph Aubrey and Louise (Merwin) Y.; m. Rebecca Conrad, Aug. 17, 1957; children: Eva Colcord, Louise Conrad, Estelle Merwin, Emily Harriet. BA, U. Mich., 1953; postgrad., Inst. Hist. Rsch. U. London, 1955-56, Inst d'Etudes Politiques, U. Paris, 1956-57; Ph.D., Harvard U., 1964. Asst. prof. polit. sci. U. Wis., Madison, 1963-66, assoc. prof., 1966-69, prof., 1969—, Rupert Emerson prof., 1983; H. Edwin Young prof., 1994; chmn. African Studies Program U. Wis., Madison, 1964-68, chmn. dept. polit. sci., 1969-72, 84-87, assoc. dean Grad. Sch., 1968-71, acting dean Coll. Letters and Sci., 1992-93; vis. prof. Makerere U. Coll., Kampala, Uganda, 1965-66; dean Faculty of Social Sci. Nat. U., Lubumbashi, Zaire, 1973-75; Fulbright prof. U. Dakar, Senegal, 1987-88. Author: Politics in the Congo, 1965, The Politics of Cultural Pluralism, 1976 (Herskovits prize 1977, Ralph Bunche prize 1979), Ideology and Development in Africa, 1982, The African Colonial State in Comparative Perspective, 1994 (Gregory Luebbert prize 1995); co-author: Cooperatives and Development, 1981, The Rise and Decline of the Zairian State, 1985; editor: The Rising Tide of Cultural Pluralism: The Nation-State at Bay?, 1993. Served to 1st lt. U.S. Army, 1953-55. Social Sci. Rsch. fellow, 1967-68, Ford Faculaty fellow, 1967-68, Guggenheim Found. fellow, 1972-73; vis. fellow Inst. for Advanced Study, Princeton, 1980-81; fellow Woodrow Wilson Internat. Ctr. for Scholars, 1983-84. Mem. Am. Polit. Sci. Assn., African Studies Assn. (pres. 1982-83, Disting. Africanist award 1990). Home: 639 Crandall St Madison WI 53711-1836 Office: U Wis Dept Polit Sci North Hall 1050 Bascom Mall Madison WI 53706-1316

YOUNG, MICHAEL EDWARD, composer, music educator; b. San Francisco, June 25, 1939; s. John Davis and Mary Katherine (Polese) Y. BA in Music, U. Wash., 1964, MA in Music, 1966. Organist First Presbyn. Ch., Seattle, 1961-65, St. Paul's Episcopal Ch., Seattle, 1966-70; instr. music Cornish Sch. Allied Arts, Seattle, 1966-70; organist Sts. Peter and Paul Ch., Vancouver, B.C., 1970-74, Cathedral of Our Lady of Lourdes, Spokane, Wash., 1979-83, Messiah Luth. Ch., Spokane, 1988-92; asst. to assoc. prof. music Whitworth Coll., Spokane, 1976—. Composer: Season's Song for Baritone and Piano, 1992, Give Glory, All Creation for Trumpet, Choir and Organ, 1991, A Mountain Symphony for Orchestra, 1987-88, Mountain Sketches, Set 5, 1988, Set 9 for piano, 1994, String Quartet No. 2, 1986, Northwest Images Horn, Cello, Piano, 1981, Serenade to the Mountains for orch., 1995. With U.S. Army, 1957-60. Mem. Am. Guild Organists (assoc.; 25th Creative Ann award 1983), Christian Fellowship of Art Music Composers, Glacier Mountaineering Soc. (charter mem.). Orthodox. Avocations: hiking, photography, mountain climbing. Office: Whitworth Collge Station 1701 Spokane WA 99251

YOUNG, MICHAEL KENT, lawyer, educator; b. Sacramento, Nov. 4, 1949; s. Vance Lynn and Ethelyn M. (Sowards) Y.; m. Suzan Kay Stewart, June 1, 1972; children: Stewart, Kathryn, Andrew. BA summa cum laude, Brigham Young U., 1973; JD magna cum laude, Harvard U., 1976. Bar: Calif. 1976, N.Y. 1985. Law clk. to Judge Benjamin Kaplan, Supreme Jud. Ct. Mass., Boston, 1976-77; law clk. to Justice William H. Rehnquist, U.S. Supreme Ct., Washington, 1977-78; assoc. prof., prof., Fuyo prof. Japanese law Columbia U., N.Y.C., 1978—; dir. Ctr. Japanese Legal Studies Ctr. for Korean Legal Studies, N.Y.C., 1985—; dir. Program Internat. Human Rights and Religious Liberties Columbia U., N.Y.C., 1995—; dep. legal advisor U.S. Dept. State, Washington, 1989-91, dep. under sec. for econ. affairs, 1991-93, amb. for trade and environ. affairs, 1992-93; vis. scholar, mem. law faculty U. Tokyo, 1978-80, 83; vis. prof. Waseda U., 1989; chmn. bd. advisors Japan Soc. Fellow Japan Found., 1979-80; Fulbright fellow, 1983-84. Mem. Coun. Fgn. Rels. Mem. LDS Ch. Avocations: skiing, scuba diving, photography.

YOUNG, MICHAEL WARREN, geneticist, educator; b. Miami, Fla., Mar. 28, 1949; s. Lloyd George and Mildred (Tillery) Y.; m. Laurel Ann Eckhardt, Dec. 27, 1978; children: Natalie, Arissa. BA, U. Tex., 1971, PhD, 1975. NIH postdoctoral fellow Med. Sch., Stanford (Calif.) U., 1975-77; asst. prof. genetics The Rockefeller U., N.Y.C., 1978-83, assoc. prof., 1984-88, prof., 1988—; investigator Howard Hughes Med. Inst., N.Y.C., 1987—; head Rockefeller unit Sci. & Tech. Ctr. Biol. Timing NSF, 1991—; mem. adv. panel on genetic biology NSF, Washington, 1983-87; spl. advisor Am. Cancer Soc., N.Y.C., 1985—; spl. reviewer genetics study sect. NIH, Bethesda, Md., 1990—, mem. cell biology study sect., 1993—. Contbr. articles to profl. jours. Meyer Found. fellow, N.Y.C., 1978-83. Fellow N.Y. Soc. Fellows; mem. AAAS, Genetics Soc. Am., Am. Soc. Microbiologists, N.Y. Acad. Scis., Harvey Soc. Achievements include research on transposable DNA elements, molecular genetics of nerve and muscle development, biological clocks, molecular control of circadian rhythms. Home: PO Box 37 Saddle River NJ 07458-0037 Office: The Rockefeller Univ 1230 York Ave New York NY 10021-6307

YOUNG, MILTON EARL, retired petroleum production company executive; b. San Angelo, Tex., Dec. 3, 1929; s. Edward Earl and Annie Mae (North) Y.; m. Clara Louise Sens, June 1, 1957; children—Vanessa, Bradley. A.A., San Angelo Coll., 1950; B.S. in Petroleum Engring, U. Tex., 1953. Various positions Continental Oil Co., 1953-73; v.p. for prodn., drilling, engring. Tesoro Petroleum Corp., San Antonio, 1973-74, sr. v.p., 1974-85, group v.p. exploration and prodn., 1985-86, retired, 1986. Served with USNR, 1948-49. Mem. Soc. Petroleum Engrs. Republican. Lutheran. Home: 1802 Frazar Rd Sealy TX 77474-8439

YOUNG, MORRIS, electrical engineering consultant; b. Alexandria, Egypt, Aug. 28, 1937; came to U.S., 1949; s. Nessim and Anna Yahia; m. Susan Slater, Dec. 22, 1962; children: Bruce Leonard, Amy Ellen. Student, CUNY, 1953-58, 63-67. Assoc., chief elec. engr. I.M. Robbins P.C., 1973-94; v.p. Joseph R. Loring & Assocs., N.Y.C., 1994—; sr. elec. engr. Lilker Assocs., N.Y.C., 1994-95; with Nassau Tech. Svcs., Wantagh, N.Y., 1995—. Trustee bd. edn. Wantagh Schs., dist. liaison to B.O.C.E.S., chmn. subcom. citizen's adv. com. for capital improvement project, budget adv. com., guest lectr. in indsl. arts dept.; appointee Nassau County Exec. Francis Purcell's Task Force; officer L.I. Planning Coun.; coach, mgr., Am. league pres. Wantagh Little League; chmn. cub pack 185 Boy Scouts Am.; v.p. Wantagh/Seaford Homeowners Assn.; mem. L.I. R.R. Commuter's Coun.; vol. Friends in Svc. to Humanity. Mem. Nat. Soc. Archtl. Engrs., Wantagh Rep. Club, Am. Legion, Jewish War Vets. of the U.S. Home: 3452 Beltagh Ave Wantagh NY 11793-2552 Office: Nassau Tech Svcs 3452 Beltagh Ave Wantagh NY 11793

YOUNG, NANCY, lawyer; b. Washington, Dec. 3, 1954; d. John Young and Byounghye Chang; m. Paul Brendan Ford, Jr., May 28, 1983; children: Paul Brendan III, Ian A., Hunter Chang Young, Jade Augustine Young. BA, Yale U., 1975, MA, 1976; JD, Columbia U., 1979. Bar: N.Y. 1981. Assoc. Simpson Thacher & Bartlett, N.Y.C., 1979-82, Richards O'Neil & Allegaert, N.Y.C., 1982-86; ptnr., chair internat. practice group Richards & O'Neil, N.Y.C., 1986—; lectr. Am. corp. and securities law Tokyo U. Faculty of Law, 1992; bd. dirs. Tsumura Internat. Inc. Contbr. articles to legal publs. Named Internat. Woman of Yr., 1992-93. Mem. ABA (co-chmn. conf. minority ptnrs in corp. majority law firms 1992), Asian-Am. Bar Assn., Assn. Bar of City of N.Y., Internat. Bar Assn., Am. Fgn. Law Assn., Coun. on Fgn. Rels., Fgn. Policy Assn. (bd. govs.), Yale U. Alumni Assn. (bd. govs. 1989-92), Columbia U. Law Sch. Assn. (bd. dirs. 1991-92), Columbia U. Alumni Assn. (bd. dirs. 1991-92), Internat. Lawyers Club. Home: One East End Ave New York NY 10021 Office: Richards & O'Neil 885 3rd Ave New York NY 10022-4834

YOUNG, NEIL, musician, songwriter; b. Toronto, Ont., Can., Nov. 12, 1945; m. Pegi Young; children: Ben, Amber; 1 child (with Carrie Snodgrass), Zeke. Formed rock group Buffalo Springfield (with Stephen Stills), with group until 1968; solo performer, also joined group Crosby, Stills & Nash (became Crosby, Stills, Nash & Young), 1969-70, 74-75; as solo artist and with bank Crazy Horse, 1968-69, 70—. Albums include (with Crosby, Stills, Nash & Young) Déja Vu, 1970, Four-Way Street, 1971, So Far, 1974, American Dream, 1988; (solo albums) Neil Young, 1969, After the Goldrush, 1970, Harvest, 1972, Journey Through the Past, 1972, Time Fades Away, 1973, On the Beach, 1974, Zuma, 1975, American Stars 'n' Bars, 1977, Decade, 1977, Comes a Time, 1978, Hawks and Doves, 1980, Reactor, 1981, Trans, 1983, Neil and The Shocking Pink: Everybody's Rocking, 1983, Old Ways, 1985, Landing on Water, 1986, Freedom, 1989, Harvest Moon, 1992, (4 Grammy nominations), Lucky Thirteen, 1993, Unplugged, 1993; (with Crazy Horse) Everybody Knows This is Nowhere, 1969, Tonight's the Night, 1975, Rust Never Sleeps, 1979, Live Rust, 1979, Life, 1987, Ragged Glory, 1990, Weld, 1991, Arc, 1991, Arc Weld, 1991, Sleeps With Angels, 1994; (with Buffalo Springfield) Buffalo Springfield Again, 1967, Last Time Around, 1968, Retrospective, 1969; (with the Bluenotes) This Note's For You, 1988; (with Stills-Young Band) Long May You Run, 1976; composed film soundtrack Journey Through the Past, 1973, Where the Buffalo Roam, 1980, Human Highway, 1982; writer, dir., performer film Rust Never Sleeps. Academy award nominee, Best Original Song, 1993 (for "Philadelphia" from Philadelphia). Office: Geffen Records 9126 W Sunset Blvd West Hollywood CA 90069-3110

YOUNG, OLIVIA KNOWLES, retired librarian; b. Benton, Ark., Sept. 3, 1922; d. Wesley Taylor and Med Belle (Crawford) Knowles; m. Calvin B. Young, Oct. 6, 1951; 1 child, Brigham Taylor. BA, Tenn. Tech. U., 1942; BS in Libr. Sci., George Peabody Coll. for Tchrs., 1946. Head periodicals and documents dept. Peabody Coll. Library, Nashville, 1946-49; area librarian U.S. Army, Austria, 1949-51; librarian Cairo Pub. Library, Ga., 1955-57, Caney Fork Regional Library, Sparta, Tenn., 1957-58; chief librarian Fort Stewart Ft. Stewart (Ga.) U.S. Army, 1959-63; dir. Watauga Regional Library, Johnson City, Tenn., 1963-70; dir. devel. and extension Tenn. State Library and Archives, Nashville, 1971-82, state librarian and archivist, 1982-85; ret., 1985. Mem. Tenn. Library Assn. (treas. 1970, Honor award 1985), Southeastern Library Assn., ALA, Boone Tree Library Assn. (pres. 1968). Methodist. Club: Altrusa (sec. 1967). Home: PO Box 160444 San Antonio TX 78280-2644

YOUNG, ORAN REED, political scientist, educator; b. Yonkers, N.Y., Mar. 15, 1941; s. John A. and Eleanor (Wiggin) Y.; children: Linda Katrin, Naomi Frankel. AB, Harvard U., 1962; MA, Yale U., 1964, PhD, 1965. Mem. staff Hudson Inst., 1962-64; rsch. assoc. Harvard, 1965; prof. polit. sci. Princeton, 1966-71; prof. govt. U. Tex., Austin, 1972-76; prof. govt. and politics U. Md., College Park, 1976-82; co-dir. Ctr. for No. Studies, 1980-82, dir., 1983-86, sr. fellow, 1986—; sr. fellow Dickey Ctr.; dir. Inst. Arctic Studies, Inst. Internat. Environ. Governance; rsch. prof. govt., prof. environ. studies Dartmouth Coll., 1987—; mem. polar rsch. bd. NRC, 1989—; U.S. del. Internat. Arctic Sci. Com., 1993—. Author: The Intermediaries: Third Parties in International Crises, 1967, Systems of Political Science, 1968, (with others) Neutralization and World Politics, 1968, The Politics of Force: Bargaining During International Crises, 1968, (with others) Political Leadership and Collective Goods, 1971, Bargaining: Formal Theories of Negotiation, 1975, Resource Management at the International Level, 1977, Compliance and Public Authority, A Theory with Applications to International Politics, 1979, Natural Resources and the State: The Political Economy of Resource Management, 1981, Resource Regimes: Natural Resources and Social Institutions, 1982, International Cooperation: Building Regimes for Natural Resources and the Environment, 1989; co-author: The Age of the Arctic: Hot Conflicts and Cold Realities, 1989, Global Environmental Changes: Understanding the Human Dimensions, 1992, Arctic Politics: Conflict and Cooperation in the Circumpolar North, 1992, Polar Politics: Creating International Environment Regimes, 1993, International Governance: Protecting the Environment in a Stateless Society, 1994, The International Political Economy and International Institutions, 1996; sr. editor: World Politics, 1968-76; mem. editl. bd. Internat. Orgn., 1968-76, 90-95. Chmn. com. on the human dimensions of global change NRC, 1989-95; mem. sci. steering com. Human Dimensions of Global Change Programme, 1995. Mem. Internat. Studies Assn., Am. Soc. Polit. and Legal Philosophy, Pub. Choice Soc., Am. Polit. Sci. Assn., Cosmos Club. Home: PO Box 1594 Norwich VT 05055-0663 Office: Dartmouth Coll 6193 Murdough Ctr Hanover NH 03755-3560

YOUNG, PATRICK, writer, editor; b. Ladysmith, Wis., Oct. 19, 1937; s. Rodney and Janice (Wolf) Y.; m. Leah Ruth Figelman, Oct. 8, 1966; 1 child, Justine Rebecca. BA, U. Colo., 1960. Reporter UPI, Washington, 1961-62; journalist USN, 1963-64; staff writer Nat. Observer, Silver Spring, Md., 1965-77; free-lance writer Laurel, Md., 1977-79; mem. sr. staff Pres.'s Commn. on the Accident at Three Mile Island, Washington, 1979; chief sci. and med. writer Newhouse News Svc., Washington, 1980-88; editor Sci. News, Washington, 1988-95; ind. writer, editor, cons., 1995—; sci. writer in residence U. Wis., 1986. Author: Asthma and Allergies, 1980, Drugs and Pregnancy, 1987, Schizophrenia, 1988; co-author: Keeping Young Athletes Healthy, 1991. With USN, 1963-64. Recipient Howard W. Blakeslee award Am. Heart Assn., 1971, Sci. Writing award in physics and astronomy Am. Inst. Physics, 1974, James T. Grady award Am. Chem. Soc., 1977. Mem. Nat. Assn. Sci. Writers, Nat. Press Club.

YOUNG, PAUL ANDREW, anatomist; b. St. Louis, Oct. 3, 1926; s. Nicholas A. and Olive A. (Langford) Y.; m. Catherine Ann Hofmeister, May 14, 1949; children—Paul, Robert, David, Ann, Carol, Richard, James, Steven, Kevin, Michael. B.S., St. Louis U., 1947, M.S., 1953; Ph.D., U. Buffalo, 1957. Asst. in anatomy U. Buffalo, 1953, instr. anatomy, 1957; asst. prof. anatomy St. Louis U., 1957, asso. prof., 1966, prof., 1972—, chmn. dept., 1973—. Author: (with B.D. Bhagat and D.E. Biggerstaff) Fundamentals of Visceral Innervation, 1977, also computer assisted neurological anatomy tutorials; contbr. articles to profl. publs. Recipient Golden Apple award Student AMA, 1974, Teaching award Acad. Sci. St. Louis, 1993. Mem. Am. Assn. Anatomists, Am. Assn. Clin. Anatomists, Soc. Neurosci., Sigma Xi, Alpha Omega Alpha. Office: St Louis U Dept Anatomy & Neurobiology 1402 S Grand Blvd Saint Louis MO 63104-1004

YOUNG, PAUL HOWARD, fiber optics communications engineer, educator; b. Chgo., Sept. 26, 1940; s. Theodore Howard and Dorothy Emma (Davis) Y.; m. Beryl Elaine Cole, July 6, 1981; children: John, James, Sara. BSEE, Calif. State U., San Diego, 1965; MSEE, Calif. State U., San Jose, 1981; PhD in Elec. Engring., LaSalle U., 1995. Cert. secondary and cmty. coll. tchr., Calif.; registered profl. engr., Ariz. Electronic engr. Cubic Corp., San Diego, 1964-70, sr. engr., 1970-74; engring. cons. San Diego, 1974-76; instr. engring. City Coll. San Francisco, 1976-81; assoc. prof. Ariz. State U., Tempe, 1981-90; fiber optics engr., tchr. TACAN Corp., Carlsbad, Calif., 1990—; cons. Hewlett-Packard Corp., Rolm Corp., Motorola, Scottsdale, Ariz., 1985. Author: (text) Electronic Communication Techniques, 1985, 3d edit., 1994; contbr. tech. articles, papers to profl. jours. With USNR, 1960-62. NASA fellow, 1983-84, 86, 87; recipient Grad. Teaching Excellence award, 1989. Mem. NSPE, IEEE (sr.), Am. Soc. for Engring. Edn., Internat. Soc. for Photonics Engring., Nat. Assn. Telecom Engrs. (master cert.), Sierra Club. Avocations: distance running, backpacking, travel. Home: 3523 Brookfield Way Carlsbad CA 92008-7017 Office: TACAN Corp 2330 Faraday Ave Carlsbad CA 92008-7216

YOUNG, PAUL RAY, medical board executive, physician; b. Fairfield, Nebr., June 27, 1932; s. Earl Edward and Louisa May (Saunders) Y.; m. Irene Marie Gray (div. 1971); children: Michael, Susan, Jean, James; m. Faye Elizabeth Hall, Oct. 28, 1972. BA, U. Nebr., Lincoln, 1953; MD, U. Nebr., Omaha, 1958. Diplomate Am. Bd. Family Practice. Intern Rsch. Hosp., Kansas City, Mo., 1958-59; pvt. practice, Raytown, Mo., 1961-67; dir. continuing med. edn. Rsch. Hosp., Kansas City, Mo., 1967-71; assoc. prof. family practice U. Mo. Coll. Medicine, Columbia, 1971-75; chmn. dept. U. Nebr. Coll. Medicine, 1975-80, U. Tex. Med. Br., Galveston, 1980-88; dep. dir. Am. Bd. Family Practice, Lexington, Ky., 1988-90, exec. dir., 1990—; mem. RRC for Family Practice, Chgo., 1976-87, chmn., 1979-87. Founding editor Family Practice Recert., 1979, Jour. Am. Bd. Family Practice, 1987. Pres. Nicholas J. Piscano Meml. Found., Lexington, 1990—. Capt. M.C., USAF, 1959-61. Fellow Am. Acad. Family Physicians; mem. Soc. Tchrs. Family Practice (bd. dirs. 1970-72), Alpha Omega Alpha. Office: Am Bd Family Practice Inc 2228 Young Dr Lexington KY 40505-4219

YOUNG, PAUL RUEL, computer scientist, administrator; b. St. Marys, Ohio, Mar. 16, 1936; s. William Raymond and Emma Marie (Steva) Y.; children: Lisa Robin, Neal Eric. BS, Antioch Coll., 1959; PhD, MIT, 1963. Tchr. math. Harley Sch., Rochester, N.Y., 1957; asst. prof. Reed Coll., 1963-66; NSF postdoctoral fellow in math. Stanford U., 1965-66; asst. prof. computer sci. and math. Purdue U., Lafayette, Ind., 1966-67, assoc. prof., 1967-72, prof., 1972-83; chmn., prof. computing and info. scis., prof. math. U. N.Mex., 1978-79; chmn., prof. computer sci. U. Wash., 1983-88, prof. computer sci. and engring., 1988—; assoc dean engring. U. Wash., Seattle, 1991-94; asst. dir. computer info. scis. and engring. NSF, Arlington, Va., 1994-96; vis. prof. elec. engring. and computer sci. U. Calif.-Berkeley, 1972-73, 82-83; Brittingham vis. prof. U. Wis., Madison, 1988-89; mem. adv. com. computer scis. NSF, 1977-80, chmn., 1979-80. Author: (with Michael Machtey) An Introduction to the General Theory of Algorithms, 1978. NSF and Woodrow Wilson fellow, MIT, 1959, 63. Fellow IEEE (chmn. tech. com. on math. founds. of computing 1981-83), Assn. Computing Machinery; mem. Computing Rsch. Assn. (chmn. 1989-91). Office: U Wash FR-35 Dept Computer Sci & Engring Seattle WA 98195

YOUNG, PAUL WESTIN, structural engineer; b. Bangor, Maine, Feb. 2, 1942; s. Stanley Paul and Linnea Beatrice (Westin) Y.; m. Beverly Ann Henderson, June 10, 1967; children: Erik-Henderson, Leif-Stanton. BSCE, Tufts U., 1965; MSCE, U. Mass., 1968. Registered profl. engr., N.Y., Conn., Mass. Aero. engr. Itek Corp., Lexington, Mass., 1968-70; structural engr. GE Co., Lynn, Mass., 1970-73; pvt. practice Haverhill, Mass., 1973-78; prin., founder Topsfield (Mass.) Engring. Svc., 1978—; lectr., cons. in field. Contbr. articles to profl. jours. Asst. scoutmaster, mem. troop com. Boy Scouts Am., West Newbury, Mass., 1983—; sec. vestry Episc. Ch., West Newbury, 1988-90, sec. men's club Meth. Ch., Salem, N.H., 1978-80; campaign coord. Mass. Rep. Ctrl. Com., Ipswich, 1970. 2d lt. USAF, 1967-68. Mem. ASCE, Am. Inst. Steel Constrn., Earthquake Engring. Rsch. Coun. Achievements include analysis and design innovations for percutaneous anti-migration vena cava filter patent, computer code for nozzle intersections in cylindrical vessels. Home: PO Box 164 7 Kents Ct West Newbury MA 01985 Office: Topsfield Engring Svc 205 Ipswich Rd Topsfield MA 01983

YOUNG, PETER ROBERT, librarian; b. Washington, Aug. 13, 1944; s. Ju Chin and Jane Kathrine (Lybrand) Y.; m. Mary Sue Townsend, Mar. 25, 1978; children: Kathryn, Timothy; children from previous marriage: Robert, Jonathan. AB Philosophy, Coll. Wooster, Ohio, 1966; grad., George Washington U., 1967; MSLS Libr. Svc., Columbia U., 1968. Adminstrv. libr. Am. U. Libr., Washington, 1968; head cataloger, reference libr. Franklin & Marshall Coll. Libr., Lancaster, Pa., 1971-74; asst. libr. pub. svcs. Rice U. Librs., Houston, Tex., 1974-76; asst. dir. Grand Rapids (Mich.) Pub. Libr., 1978; sales support libr. CL Systems Inc., Newtonville, Mass., 1976-78, libr. systems analyst, 1978-80; customer svcs. officer Cataloging Distbn. Svc. Libr. Congress, Washington, 1980-84, asst. chief Marc edit. divsn., 1984-85, chief Copyright Cataloging divsn., 1985-88; dir. acad. info. svcs. The Faxon Co., Westwood, Mass., 1988-89, dir. Faxon Inst. Advanced Studies Scholarly and Sci. Communication, 1989-90; exec. dir. U.S. Nat. Commn. Librs. and Info. Sci., Washington, 1990—; exec. bd. Fed. Libr. and Info. Ctr. com., 1993—; adv. bd. Highsmith Press, 1991—; co chair libr. stats. standard revision com. Nat. Standards Info. Office, 1989-93; libr. adminstrs. devel. program U. Md.; implementation task force libr. data Nat. Ctr. Edn. Stats. U.S. Office Edn., 1988, adv. coun. edn. stats. Office Edn. Rsch. and Improvement, 1990—; lectr. in field. Edit. bd. Serials Review, 1990—; contbr. articles to profl. jours. With U.S. Army, 1968-70, Vietnam. Mem. ALA (pub. policy for pub. librs. com. 1993—, com. rsch. and stats. 1990—, various coms., assns.), Chinese Am. Libr. Assn. (chair pub. rels. com. 1987-88, pres. 1989-90), Ont. Libr. Assn. (planning com., del. mem.), U.S. Nat. Commn. Librs. and Info. Sci. (stats. task force 1988-89). Office: Natl Commission on Libraries 1110 VErmont Ave NW Ste 820 Washington DC 20005-3522

YOUNG, PHILIP HOWARD, library director; b. Ithaca, N.Y., Oct. 7, 1953; s. Charles Robert and Betty Irene (Osborne) Y.; m. Nancy Ann Stutsman, Aug. 18, 1979. BA, U. Va., 1975; PhD, U. Pa., 1980; MLS, Ind. U., 1983. Asst. prof. history Appalachian State U., Boone, N.C., 1980-82; reference asst. Lilly Library, Ind. U., Bloomington, 1982-83; adminstr., info. specialist Ind. Corp. for Sci. & Tech., Indpls., 1983-85; dir. Krannert Meml. Library, U. Indpls., 1985—. Mem. Am. Library Assn., Ind. Libr. Fed., Archaeological Inst. Am., Phi Beta Kappa, Phi Alpha Theta, Beta Phi Mu. Democrat. Methodist. Home: 1944 Patton Dr Speedway IN 46224-5355 Office: U Indpls Krannert Meml Libr 1400 E Hanna Ave Indianapolis IN 46227-3630

YOUNG, PHYLLIS CASSELMAN, music educator; b. Milan, Kans., Oct. 20, 1925; d. Phillip James and Velma (Stewart) Casselman; m. James M. Young, July 14, 1945 (dec. Sept. 1991). MusB with high honors, U. Tex., 1949, MusM, 1950. Tchr. string instruments Kansas City (Kans.) Pub. Schs., 1951-52; prof. cello and string pedagogy U. Tex., Austin, 1953—; dir. U. Tex. String Project, Austin, 1958-93; Parker C. Fielder Regents prof. music U. Tex., Austin, 1991—; presenter numerous workshops and master classes, 1976—. Author: Playing the String Game, 1978, The String Play, 1986; also articles. Mem. Am. String Tchrs. Assn. (state pres. 1972-74, nat. pres. 1978-80, Nat. citation 1974, 82, Disting. Svc. award 1984), European String Tchrs. Assn., Music Educators Nat. Conf., Suzuki Assn. Ams., Tex. Music Educators Assn. Home: 7304 W Rim Dr Austin TX 78731-2043 Office: Sch Music Univ Tex Austin TX 78712

YOUNG, RALPH ALDEN, soil scientist, educator; b. Arickaree, Colo., July 14, 1920; s. Edmond Birdsall and Lottie Opal (Payne) Y.; m. Helen Augusta Claudon, Aug. 28, 1942; children—Gregg, Gayle. B.S., Colo. State U., 1942; M.S., Kans. State U., 1947; Ph.D., Cornell U., 1953. Instr. soils Kans. State U., 1947-48; asst. prof. soils N.D. State U., 1948-50, 53-55, asso. prof., 1955-59, prof., 1959-62; vis. soil chemist U. Calif. at Davis, 1962-63; prof. soil sci., chmn. div. plant, soil and water sci. U. Nev., Reno, 1963-75; assoc. dir. Nev. Agrl. Expt. Sta., 1975-82; prof. soil sci. U. Nev., 1982-84, prof. emeritus, 1985—. Contbr. articles to profl. jours. Served to capt. AUS, 1943-46. Fellow AAAS; mem. Soil Conservation Soc. Am. (pres. chpt. 1968), Am. Soc. Agronomy, Soil Sci. Soc. Am., Western Soil Sci. Soc. (pres. 1972-73), Sigma Xi, Alpha Zeta, Gamma Sigma Delta, Phi Kappa Phi. Home: 2229 Stagecoach Rd Grand Junction CO 81503-2614

YOUNG, RAYMOND GUINN, music educator; b. Morrilton, Ark., Dec. 21, 1932; s. Theodore T. and Vida Mae (Guinn) Y.; m. Barbara Ann Woolcox, Aug. 29, 1953 (div. Nov. 1986); children: Steven Cary, Dale, Michael, Rae Ann; m. Joan Arno, Nov. 20, 1994. MusB, U. Mich., 1955, MusM, 1956. Band dir. Trenton (Mich.) High Sch., 1956-61; asst. band dir., instr. trombone and euphonium U. So. Miss., Hattiesburg, 1961-68, dir. bands, 1968-72; dir. bands La. Tech. U., Ruston, 1972-85, head dept. mus., 1972-88, prof. music, 1988-91; dir. orch. Ruston Civic Symphony, 1975-80; condr. USA Honor Bands, Honolulu, 1975-88; soloist Tokyo Kosei Wind Orch., 1985. Dir. choir Univ. Presbyn. Ch., Ruston, 1973-85. Mem. Am. Bandmaster Assn., La. Bandmaster Assn. (Bandmaster of Yr. 1983), Nat. Band Assn., Coll. Band Dirs. Nat. Assn., Ruston Antique Car Assn. (pres. 1984, 85), Phi Beta Mu, Phi Mu Alpha Sinfonia, Kappa Kappa Psi, Sigma Alpha Iota. Lodge: Masons (illustrious master 1969, 70). Home: 149 Sherlock Herring Rd Purvis MS 39475-3150

YOUNG, RAYMOND HENRY, lawyer; b. Boston, Sept. 28, 1927; s. Raymond H. and Clara Elms (Oakman) Y.; m. Louisa Breda, Sept. 1, 1951; children: Christopher, Pamela, Amy. AB, Yale U., 1947, LLB, 1950. Bar: Mass. 1951. Assoc. Warner, Stackpole, Stetson & Bradlee, Boston, 1950-52; pvt. practice Boston, 1952-64; ptnr. Young & Bayle, Boston, 1964—. Mem. ABA (past sec. sect. real property, probate and trust law, mem. commn. legal problems of the elderly), Am. Coll. Trust and Estate Counsel (mem. joint editorial bd. for uniform probate code), Am. Law Inst. (advisor for restatement property 3d donative transfers), Nat. Commn. on Nat. Probate Ct. Standards, Internat. Acad. Trust and Estate Law (pres.), Mass. Bar Assn., Boston Bar Assn. (past pres.), Boston Estate Planning Coun. (past pres., Estate Planner of Yr. award 1991), Boston Probate and Estate Planning Forum. Home: 122 Garfield St Watertown MA 02172-4916 Office: Young & Bayle 150 Federal St Boston MA 02110-1745

YOUNG, REBECCA MARY CONRAD, state legislator; b. Clairton, Pa., Feb. 28, 1934; d. Walter Emerson and Harriet Averill (Colcord) Conrad; m. Merwin Crawford Young, Aug. 17, 1957; children: Eve, Louise, Estelle, Emily. BA, U. Mich., 1955; MA in Teaching, Harvard U., 1963; JD, U. Wis., 1983. Bar: Wis. 1983. Commr. State Hwy. Commn., Madison, Wis., 1974-76; dep. sec. Wis. Dept. of Adminstrn., Madison, 1976-77; assoc. Wadsack, Julian & Lawton, Madison, 1983-84; elected rep. Wis. State Assembly, Madison, 1985—. Translator: Katanga Secession, 1966. Supr. Dane County Bd., Madison, 1970-74; mem. Madison Sch. Bd., 1979-85. Recipient Wis. Register Deeds Assn. Cert. of Appreciation for Leadership, 1995, Wis. NOW Feminist of Yr. award, 1996. Mem. LWV. Democrat. Avocations: board games, hiking. Home: 639 Crandall St Madison WI 53711-1836 Office: State Legislature-Assembly PO Box 8953 Madison WI 53708-8953

YOUNG, RICHARD, religious organization executive. General secretary suffragan Pentecostal Assemblies of the World, Indpls. Office: Pentecostal Assemblies of the World 3939 Meadows Dr Indianapolis IN 46205-3113

YOUNG, RICHARD, lawyer; b. N.Y.C., June 23, 1919; s. Owen D. and Josephine Sheldon (Edmonds) Y.; m. Janet Nevins, Oct. 2, 1971 (dec. Aug. 1990). AB, St. Lawrence U., 1940, LLD (hon.), 1988; LLB, Harvard, 1947. Bar: N.Y. 1947. Asst., asso. Judge Manley O. Hudson, 1947-60. Bd. editors: Am. Jour. Internat. Law; Contbr. articles to legal jours. Mem. adv. bd. Internat. Law Center, Southwestern Legal Found., Dallas (chmn. 1966-68); trustee St. Lawrence U. Served with AUS, 1942-46. Fellow Royal Geog. Soc.; mem. Am. Soc. Internat. Law, Am. Bar Assn., Am. Geog. Soc., Internat. Law Assn., Phi Beta Kappa Assos., Phi Beta Kappa, Beta Theta Pi, University Club (N.Y.C.). Democrat. Universalist.

YOUNG, RICHARD ALAN, publishing company executive; b. Oak Park, Ill., Mar. 17, 1935; m. Carol Ann Schellinger, June 28, 1958; children: Steven, Karen, Christopher. Student, Colo. Sch. Mines, 1954-56; B.A., U. Iowa, 1958. Chief engr. Cardox Corp., Chgo., 1958-61; asst. chief engr. Goodman Mfg. Co., Chgo., 1961-63; plant and environ. engr. Signode Corp., Glenview, Ill., 1963-68; editor Pollution Engring. Tech. Pub. Co., Barrington, Ill., 1968-81; exec. dir. Nat. Registry of Environ. Profls., 1988—; pub. Cahners Pub. Co., Des Plaines, Ill., 1990-95; dj. prof. George Williams Coll.; mcpl. pollution control adviser and enforcement officer for 24 cities and state govts; ofcl rep. and pollution control expert U.S. Govt. at tech. transfer meetings. Editor 26 books on environ. engring.; pollution engring.; series editor, Marcel Dekker Inc., N.Y.C.; Contbr. articles to profl. jours. Recipient Jesse H. Neal certificate for outstanding editorial writing Am. Bus. Press, Inc., 1971, Outstanding Service award Western Soc. Engrs., Charles Ellet award as Most Outstanding Engr. of Yr. 1970; Environ. Quality award EPA, 1976. Mem. Internat. Assn. for Pollution Control (dir.), Assn. Local Air Pollution Control Ofcls., Am. Soc. Bus. Press Editors (Editl. Excellence award 1980, Design Excellence award 1982), Am. Inst. Plant Engrs. (past nat. chmn. environ. quality), Internat. Congress Environ. Profls. (mng. dir.), Nat. Inst. Hazardous Materials Mgmts. (dir. 1984-88, cert. hazardous materials mgr.), Soc. Environ. Mgmt. & Tech. (nat. dir.). Patentee in field.

YOUNG, RICHARD STUART, technical services executive; b. Southampton, N.Y., Mar. 6, 1927; s. P. Stuart and Myrtle F. (Terrell) Y.; m. Nancy J. Mayer, June 7, 1955; children: Dee Ann, Sandra, Mark. A.B., Gettysburg Coll., 1948, Sc.D., 1966; postgrad., U. N.C., 1951-53; Ph.D., Fla. State U., 1955. With FDA, Washington, 1956-58; with NASA, Army Ballistic Missile Agency, Huntsville, Ala., 1958-59, NASA-Ames Research Center, Moffett Field, Calif., 1960-67; chief exobiology program-hdqrs., chief program scientist Viking NASA, Washington, 1969-77; chief of bioscis. div. NASA Hdqrs., 1975-79; v.p. Rockefeller U., N.Y.C., 1979-82; exec. dir. Am. Soc. Cell Biology, Bethesda, Md., 1982-85; mgr. Mgmt. and Tech. Svcs. Co., Washington, 1985—; sr. scientist Kennedy Space Ctr., Fla., 1987—. Contbr. articles to profl. jours., also books. Served with USN, 1944-46. Mem. Internat. Soc. for Study Origin of Life (sec. 1970-77, v.p. 1977-82). Home: 661 Adams Ave Cape Canaveral FL 32920-2165 Office: MD RES Kennedy Space Center FL 32920

YOUNG, RICHARD WILLIAM, corporate director; b. Ridgewood, N.Y., Oct. 17, 1926; s. Charles Michael and Louise Margaret (Baust) Y.; m. Sheila deLisser, Sept. 11, 1949; children: Christine, Noreen, Brian, Eileen. A.B., Dartmouth Coll., 1946, A.M., 1947; Ph.D., Columbia U., 1950. Sr. rsch. chemist Chemotherapy div. Am. Cyanamid Co., Conn., 1950-56, group leader pesticide chems. Agrl. div., 1956-58, dir. chem. Agrl. div., 1958-60, dir. chem. rsch. cen. rsch. div., 1960-62; asst. dir. rsch. Polaroid Corp., Cambridge, Mass., 1962-69, v.p., 1963-69, sr. v.p. rsch. and devel., 1969-72, sr. v.p., pres. Internat. div., 1972-80, exec. v.p., dir. worldwide mktg., 1980-82; pres. Houghton Mifflin Co., Boston, 1982-85; chmn., CEO Mentor O & O, Inc., Norwell, Mass., 1985-92; bd. dirs. Bay State Milling Corp., Quincy, Mass., Instron Corp., Canton, Mass., Oceantrawl Inc., Seattle, Mentor Corp., Santa Barbara, Calif. Patentee in field. Chmn. bd. trustees Regis Coll., Weston, Mass., Mass. Eye and Ear Infirmary, Boston, Trinitas Found., Quincy; mem. corp. Northeastern U., Boston. Mem. Am. Chem. Soc. Home: 100 Royalston Rd Wellesley MA 02181-1244 Office: Trinitas Found 100 Congress St Quincy MA 02169-0906

YOUNG, ROBERT (GEORGE YOUNG), actor; b. Chgo., Feb. 22, 1907; m. Elizabeth Louise Henderson, 1933; children: Carol Anne, Barbara Queen, Elizabeth Louise, Kathleen Joy. Grad. high sch. pres. Cavalier Prodns., 1947—. Studied and acted with Pasadena Community Playhouse, 4 years; toured in stock, 1931; actor in motion pictures, 1931—; pictures include It's Love Again, Eng., Secret Agent, Eng., The Bride Wore Red, Northwest Passage, Western Union, The Trial of Mary Dugan, H.M. Pulham, Esq., Western Union; radio broadcasts, 1936—; co-star pictures including Mr. and Mrs. North, 1942, And Baby Makes Three, 1949, Bride for Sale, 1949, That Forsythe Woman, 1949, Goodbye My Fancy, 1951, Secret of the Incas, 1954; regular on series Father Knows Best, 1954-62; TV program Window on Main Street, 1961-62; TV series Marcus Welby, M.D, 1969-76; appeared in TV films Vanished, 1971, All My Darling Daughters, 1972, My Darling Daughters' Anniversary, 1973, The Father Knows Best Reunion, 1977, Mercy or Murder?, 1987, Conspiracy of Love, Little Women, Marcus Welby M.D.-A Holiday Affair. Recipient Emmy award, 1956, 1957.

YOUNG, ROBERT A., III, freight systems executive; b. Ft. Smith, Ark., Sept. 23, 1940; s. Robert A. and Vivian (Curtis) Y.; m. Mary Carleton McRae; children—Tracy, Christy, Robert A. IV, Stephen. BA in Econs., Washington and Lee U., 1963. Supr. terminal ops. Ark. Best Freight, Ft. Smith, 1964-65; pres. Data-Tronics Inc, Ft. Smith, 1965-67; sr. v.p. Nat. Bank of Commerce, Dallas, 1967-70; v.p. fin. Ark. Best Corp., Ft. Smith, 1970-73, exec. v.p., 1973, pres., chief operating officer, 1973-88, chief exec. officer, 1988—; pres. ABF Freight Systems, Inc., Ft. Smith, 1979-94; bd. dirs. First Nat. Bank, Ft. Smith, Mosler Corp., Hamilton, Ohio. Pres. United Way, Ft. Smith, 1981; vice chmn. bd. dirs. Sparks Regional Med. Ctr., Ft. Smith, 1995; chmn. bd. trustees Ark. Coll.; bd. dirs. ATA Found., Inc., Ft. Smith Boys Club; chmn. bd. trustees Lyon Coll. Recipient Silver Beaver award Boy Scouts Am. Mem. Am. Trucking Assn. (vice chmn.), Ark. State C. of C. (pres., bd. dirs., chmn.), Phi Delta Theta. Presbyterian. Home: Ark Best Corp P O Box 10048 Fort Smith AR 72917-0048 Office: ABF Freight Systems Inc 3801 Old Greenwood Rd Fort Smith AR 72903 Also: Ark Best Corp 3801 Old Greenwood Rd Fort Smith AR 72903

YOUNG, ROBERT ANTHONY, association director; b. Syracuse, N.Y., May 21, 1943; s. Frank A. and Grace (Farnett) Y. BS, Le Moyne Coll., 1965; MS, Long Beach State Coll., 1966. Exec. dir. Cystic Fibrosis Found., Syracuse, 1974-75; dir. pub. rels. & programs Am. Heart Assn., New Orleans, 1975-76; dir. programs La. State Bar Assn., New Orleans, 1976-84; exec. dir. Am. Coll. Trial Lawyers, Irvine, Calif., 1984—. With USAF, 1966-67. Mem. Am. Soc. Assn. Execs., Nat. Assn. Bar Execs. (leadership award 1986, chmn's. award pub. rels. sect. 1984). Avocations: travel, golf, tennis. Office: Am Coll of Trial Lawyers 8001 Irvine Center Dr Ste 960 Irvine CA 92718-2921

YOUNG, ROBERT CRABILL, medical researcher, science facility administrator, internist; b. Columbus, Ohio, 1940. MD, Cornell U., 1965. Diplomate Am. Bd. Internal Medicine, subspecialty bds. hematology and med. oncology. Intern N.Y. Hosp., N.Y.C., 1965-66, resident, 1966-67; sr. resident Yale-New Haven Med. Ctr., 1969-70; sr. investigator, attending physician med. br. Nat. Cancer Inst., Bethesda, Md., from 1971, chief med. br., 1974-88; pres. Fox Chase Cancer Ctr., Phila., 1988—; clin. prof. medicine Georgetown U., from 1974, assoc. prof., 1976-84; clin. prof. medicine George Washington U., 1984—. Assoc. editor Jour. Clin. Oncology; chmn. editl. bd. Oncology Times. Sr. surgeon USPHS, 1967-69. Fellow ACP; mem. Am. Soc. Hematology, Am. Assn. Cancer Rsch. (pres. 1990), Am. Soc. Clin. Oncology, Am. Cancer Soc. (exec. com. 1995—). Office: Fox Chase Cancer Ctr 7701 Burholme Ave Philadelphia PA 19111-2412

YOUNG, ROBERT DONALD, physicist, educator; b. Chgo., Apr. 20, 1940; s. Robert Joseph and Nellie (Krik) Y.; children: Robert Gerald, Jennifer Ann Young Rolinski; m. BJ Marymont, Feb. 14, 1981; 1 child, Emily Marymont. BS in Physics, Ill. Inst. Technology, 1962; MS in Physics, Purdue U., 1965, PhD in Physics, 1967. Devel. engr. Western Elec., Cicero, Ill., 1962; process engr. Nat. Video Corp., Chgo., 1963; asst. prof. physics Ill. State U., Normal, 1967-73, assoc. prof., 1974-78, prof., 1979—, dir. rsch. Coll. Arts and Scis., 1994-95, assoc. v.p. for rsch., dean grad. studies, 1995—; adj. prof. physics U. Ill., Urbana, 1986—. Contbr. articles to Proceedings Nat. Acad. Sci., Ann. Rev. Biophysics, Phys. Rev. Letters, Chemica Scripta, Jour. Phys. Chemistry, Jour. Chem. Physics, Computers in Physics, Physical Rev., Biophysical Jour. Named Researcher of Yr., Ill. State U., 1989. Mem. Am. Phys. Soc., Am. Chem. Soc., Biophys. Soc., Am. Assn. Physics Tchrs. Achievements include research on glassy properties of proteins, usage of computer techniques in physics education, individualized modular approach in physics education. Home: 4 Turner Rd Normal IL 61761-4218 Office: Grad Sch Ill State Univ Normal IL 61790-4040

YOUNG, ROBERT LERTON, insurance brokerage company executive; b. Columbus, Ohio, Feb. 21, 1936; s. Robert Lerton and Ada Beatrice (Aderholt) Y.; m. Caroline Page Dickey, May 10, 1980. Student, U. Ill., 1953-55, Ohio State U., 1958-60. Mgr. actuarial dept. Gates McDonald & Co., Columbus, 1959-66; dist. mgr. Gates McDonald & Co., Oakland, Calif., 1966-70; v.p., founder Nat. Compensation Services, Inc., Pleasant Hill, Calif., 1970-71; v.p. Fred S. James & Co., Inc., Pleasant Hill and San Francisco, 1971-76; v.p. Sedgwick James, Inc., Chgo., 1976—, chmn. Claims Mgmt. Svcs. divsn., 1985; cons. Los Angeles County Self Ins. Program; mem. adv. com. Calif. Dept. Indsl. Relations; tchr. Calif. Extension, 1970; lectr. Am. Mgmt. Assn. Contbr. articles in field to profl. jours. Mem. Pleasant Hill Youth Commn. Served with U.S. Army, 1955-58. Recipient Service award Chartered Property and Casualty Underwriters, 1971, 75. Mem. Am. Risk and Ins. Assn., Ins. Inst. Am. (risk mgmt. diploma), Am. Soc. Safety Engrs. (indsl. safety diploma), Nat. Coun. Self-Insurers, Internat. Assn. Indsl. Accident Bd. and Commns., Calif. Self-Insurers Assn., Ariz. Self-Insurers Assn., Wash. Self-Insurers Assn., Pa. Self-Insurers Assn., Mass. Self-Insurers Assn., Ga. Self-Insurers Assn., Fla. Self-Insurers Assn., Met. Club (Chgo.), Pinehurst (N.C.) Country Club. Office: Sedgwick James Inc 230 W Monroe St Chicago IL 60606-4703

YOUNG, ROBERT SHERMAN, lawyer; b. Salt Lake City, Oct. 26, 1955; s. Sherman C. and Henrietta (Hatch) Y.; m. Laura Brewer, Sept. 19, 1979; children: Sarah, Amy, Emily, Abbie, Clara, Mary. BA in Fin., U. Utah, 1980, JD, 1983. Bar: Utah 1983, U.S. Ct. Appeals (10th cir.) 1987. With Law Offices Davis S. Young & Robert S. Young, Salt Lake City, 1983-85; corp. and gen. counsel Rocky Mountain Helicopters, Provo, Utah, 1985-95; with Prince, Yeates & Geldzahler, Salt Lake City, 1995—. Scoutleader Boy Scouts Am., Salt Lake City, 1992-93; trustee, pres.-elect Brigham Young Family Assn., Salt Lake City, 1995-96. Mem. ABA, Utah Bar Assn., Lawyer-Pilots Bar Assn. (Utah chmn. 1993), Aviation Ins. Assn. (lectr. 1994). Mem. LDS Ch. Avocations: golf, tennis, basketball, travel, home improvement. Office: Prince Yeates & Geldzahler City Ctr I 175 East 400 South Ste 900 Salt Lake City UT 84111

YOUNG, ROGER AUSTIN, natural gas distribution company executive; b. Boston, Feb. 2, 1946; s. Robert Harris McCarter and Gloria Bond (Tenney) Y.; m. Linda Furste, Sept. 6, 1975; children: Catherine Simms, Geoffrey Furste. B.A., Princeton U., 1968. Systems analyst Orange and Rockland Utilities, Inc., Spring Valley, N.Y., 1968-72; asst. v.p. Bay State Gas Co., Boston, 1972-75, v.p., 1975-80; exec. v.p. Bay State Gas Co., Canton, Mass., 1980-81; pres. Bay State Gas Co., Westborough, Mass., 1981-90, pres., chief exec. officer, 1990—; bd. dirs., mem. exec. com. Inst. Gas Tech.; regional bd. dirs. Baybanks, Inc. Bd. dirs. New Eng. Council. Mem. Am. Gas Assn., New Eng. Gas Assn. (bd. dirs., chmn. 1984-85), Newcomen Soc., Associated Gas Distbrs. Congregationalist. Clubs: The Country (Brookline, Mass.); Colonial (Princeton, N.J.). Home: 125 Mill St PO Box 95 Sherborn MA 01770 Office: Bay State Gas Co 300 Friberg Pky Westborough MA 01581-3900

YOUNG, ROMA SKEEN, lawyer; b. Vancouver, Wash., Feb. 21, 1950; d. Carroll Hallam and Dorothy Elizabeth (Miller) Skeen; m. Robert Hugh Young, Jr., May 20,1978; children: Matthew Hallam, Brian Robert. BA, Sweetbriar Coll., 1971; JD, Georgetown U., 1978. Bar: Pa. 1978. Mem. staff U.S. Senate Energy Com., Washington, 1972-75; lobbyist Marathon Oil Co., Washington, 1975-78; assoc. Pepper, Hamilton & Scheetz, Phila., 1978-84; assoc. Wolf, Block, Schorr and Solis-Cohen, Phila., 1984-89, ptnr., 1989—. Office: Wolf Block Schorr and Solis-Cohen 15th And Chestnut St Fl 12 Philadelphia PA 19102-2625

YOUNG, RONALD FARIS, commodity trader; b. Schenectady, Dec. 17, 1939; s. James Vernon and Dorothy (Girod) Y.; m. Anne Randolph Kendig, Feb. 23, 1963; children: Margaret Randolph Reynolds, Anne Corbin. B.A., U. Va., 1962; M.B.A., Harvard U., 1966. Grain trader Continental Grain Co., 1966-70; pres. Conti-Commodities, Chgo., 1970; v.p. commodity sales DuPont, Glore Forgan, Chgo., 1971-72; self-employed commodity trader Chgo. Bd. Trade, 1972-78; ind. trader Va. Trading Co., 1978-90, pres., 1978-84, dep. chmn., 1984-89; pres. Randolph Ptnrs., Ltd., 1983-91; chmn. bd. Chgo. Bd. Trade, 1978, dir., 1975-77, 80. Bd. dirs. Princeton Fund, 1981-82, Lake Forest Hosp., 1981-84, Lake Forest Country Day Sch., 1981-86. Served with USMCR, 1959-65. Mem. Casino Club, Racquet Club (bd. dirs. 1989—), Onwentsia Club (Lake Forest, Ill., bd. dirs. 1981-90, pres. 1991-93), Everglades Cub (Palm Beach, Fla.), Bath and Tennis Club (Palm Beach, Fla.). Republican. Episcopalian. Home: 1448 N Lake Shore Dr Chicago IL 60610-1625 Office: 141 W Jackson Blvd Unit 1520A Chicago IL 60604-3001

YOUNG, ROY ALTON, university administrator, educator; b. McAlister, N.Mex., Mar. 1, 1921; s. John Arthur and Etta Julia (Sprinkle) Y.; m. Marilyn Ruth Sandman, May 22, 1950; children: Janet Elizabeth, Randall Owen. BS, N.Mex. A&M Coll., 1941; MS, Iowa State U., 1942, PhD, 1948; LLD (hon.), N.Mex. State U., 1978. Tchg. fellow Iowa State U., 1941-42, instr., 1946-47, Indsl. fellow, 1947-48; asst. prof. Oreg. State U., 1948-50, assoc. prof., 1950-53, prof., 1953—, head dept. botany and plant pathology, 1958-66, dean rsch., 1966-70, acting pres., 1969-70, v.p. rsch. and grad. studies, 1970-76, dir. Office for Natural Resources Policy, 1986-90; chancellor U. Nebr., Lincoln, 1976-80; mng. dir., pres. Boyce Thompson Inst. Plant Rsch., Cornell U., Ithaca, N.Y., 1980-86; mem. Commn. on Undergrad. Edn. in Biol. Scis., 1963-68; mem. Gov.'s Sci. Coun., 1987-90; cons. State Exptl. Stas. divsn. USDA; chmn. subcom. plant pathogens, agriculture bd. NAS-NRC, 1965-68; mem. exec. com. study on problems of pest control, 1972-75; mem. exec. com. Nat. Govs.' Coun. on Sci. and Tech., 1970-74; mem. U.S. com. man and biosphere UNESCO, 1973-82; mem. com. to rev. U.S. component Internat. Biol. Program, NAS, 1974-76; mem. adv. panel on postdoctoral fellowships in environ. sci. Rockefeller Found., 1974-78; bd. dirs. Pacific Power & Light Co., 1984-91, Boyce Thompson Inst. for Plant Rsch., 1975-93, Boyce Thompson Southwestern Arboretum, 1981-92, Oreg. Grad. Inst., 1987-94; mem. adv. com. Directorate for Engring. and Applied Sci., NSF, 1977-81; mem. sea grant adv. panel, 1978-80; mem. policy adv. com. Office of Grants, USDA, 1985-86. Trustee Ithaca Coll., 1982-89. Lt. USNR, 1943-46. Recipient Disting. Svc. award Oreg. State U., 1978. Fellow AAAS (exec. com. Pacific div. 1963-67, pres. div. 1971), Am. Phytopathology Soc. (pres. Pacific div. 1957, chmn. spl. com. to develop plans for endowment 1984-86, bd. dirs. 1986-88); mem. Oreg. Acad. Sci., Nat. Assn. State Univs. and Land Grant Colls. (chmn. coun. for rsch. policy and adminstrn. 1970, chmn. standing com. on environment and energy 1974-82, chmn. com. on environment 1984-86), Sigma Xi, Phi Kappa Phi, Phi Sigma, Sigma Alpha Epsilon. Home: 3605 NW Van Buren Ave Corvallis OR 97330-4950

YOUNG, RUSSELL DAWSON, physics consultant; b. Huntington, N.Y., Aug. 17, 1923; s. C. Halsey and Edna (Dawson) Y.; m. Carol Vaughn Jones, Aug. 14, 1954; children: Bessmarie, Gale, Janet, Shari. BS in Physics, Rensselaer Poly. Inst., Troy, N.Y., 1953; PhD in Physics, Pa. State U., 1959. Rsch. assoc. Pa. State U., State College, 1959-61; project leader Nat. Bur. Stds., Gaithersburg, Md., 1961-73, chief optics and micrometrology, 1973-78; chief mech. processing div. Nat. Bur. Stds., Gaithersburg, 1975-80, ind. sys. div. chief, 1980-81, chief mech. prodn. div., 1980-81; pres. R.D. Young Cons., Pasadena, Md., 1981—. Contbr. articles to profl. jours.; inventor in field of instrumentation. 1st lt. Signal Corps, U.S. Army, 1943-46. Recipient Edward V. Condon award Dept. Commerce, 1974, Silver medal 1979, Gaede-Langmuir award 1994, Presdl. citation 1986, Washington Acad. Scis. award 1988. Fellow Internat. Inst. Prodn. Engring. Rsch., Nat. Inst. Standards and Tech.; mem. Am. Vacuum Soc. Avocation: boating. Home: 852 Riverside Dr Pasadena MD 21122-1730

YOUNG, SCOTT, recording tape manufacturer; b. 1946. BS in Bus., U. Fla.; MBA, U. N.C. With Matthews Young and Assocs., 1971-76; exec. v.p., gen. mgr. Music Land, 1977-80; CEO Franklin Music, 1980-84, pvt. cons. to music industry, 1984-86; sr. mktg. exec. Personics Corp., 1986-87; pres., COO Wherehouse Entertainment, Torrance, Calif., 1987-90, pres., CEO, 1990-93, chmn., CEO, 1993—; chmn. Wherehouse Entertainment, Inc., Torrance, 1992-93, chmn., CEO, 1993—. Office: Wherehouse Entertainment PO Box 2831 Torrance CA 90509-2831

YOUNG, SCOTT ALEXANDER, television journalist, author; b. Man., Can., Apr. 14, 1918; s. Percy Andrew and Jean Ferguson Y.; m. Edna Blow Ragland, June 18, 1940; children: Robert, Neil; m. Astrid Carlson Mead, May 20, 1961; children: Deirdre, Astrid; m. Margaret Burns Hogan, May 9, 1980. Grad. high sch.; LittD honoris causa, Trent U., Can., 1990. Columnist Toronto (Ont., Can.) Globe and Mail, 1957-69, 71-80; sports editor Toronto Telegram, 1969-71; TV writer and personality, 1957—; pres. Ascot Prodns. Ltd. Author: Red Shield in Action, 1949, Scrubs on Skates, 1952, reissue, 1985, Boy on Defense, 1953, reissue, 1985, (novel) The Flood, 1956, HMCS, Text for Gilbert Milne's Photos, 1960 (with Astrid Young) (biography) O'Brien, 1967, Silent Frank Cochrane, 1973, (with Punch Imlach) Hockey is a Battle, 1969, (with George Robertson), (novel) Face-Off, 1971, Clue of the Dead Duck, 1962, reissue, 1981, Boy at the Leaf's Camp, 1963, reissue, 1985 (with Astrid Young) (novel) Big City Office Junior, 1964, Scott Young Sports Stories, 1965, The Leafs I Knew, 1966, We Won't Be Needing You, Al, and Other Stories, 1968, (with Leo Cahill) Goodbye Argos, 1973, War on Ice, 1976, Canada Cup of Hockey 1976, 1976 (with Margaret Hogan) Best Talk in Town, 1980 (with Conn Smythe) Memoirs of the Late Conn Smythe, 1981 (with Punch Imlach) Heaven and Hell in the NHL, 1982, (novel) That Old Gang of Mine, 1982, Neil and Me, 1984 (biography) Hello Canada, 1985, Gordon Sinclair-A Life and Then Some, 1987, (novel) Murder in a Cold Climate, 1988, Face-Off in Moscow, 1989, 100 Years of Dropping the Puck, 1989, (short stories) Home for Christmas, 1989, The Boys of Saturday Night, 1990, (with Alan Eagleston) Power Play, 1991, (novel) The Shaman's Knife, 1993, (autobiography) A Writer's Life, 1995, short stories in several anthologies. Mem. Province Ont. Royal Commn. Violence in Communications Industry, 1975-77. Served with Royal Canadian Navy, World War II. Recipient Can. Nat. Newspaper award, 1959, Wilderness award for TV script, 1963, U.S. Eclipse award, 1971; named to NHL Hall of Fame, 1988, Man. Hockey Hall of Fame, 1992. Address: 331 Bland, Cavan, ON Canada L0A 1C0

YOUNG, SEAN, actress; b. Louisville; m. Robert Lujan; 1 child: Rio Kelly Lujan. Grad., Interlochen Arts Acad., Mich., 1978. Actress: (feature films) Jane Austen in Manhattan, 1980, Stripes, 1981, Blade Runner, 1982, Young Doctors in Love, 1982, Dune, 1984, Baby - Secret of the Lost Legend, 1985, No Way Out, 1987, Wall Street, 1987, The Boost, 1988, Cousins, 1989, Fire Birds, 1990, A Kiss Before Dying, 1991, Once Upon a Crime, 1992, Love Crimes, 1992, Fatal Instinct, 1993, Ace Ventura: Pet Detective, 1994, Even Cowgirls Get the Blues, 1994, Dr. Jekyll and Ms. Hyde, 1995; TV appearances include Under the Biltmore Clock, Tender is the Night, Blood and Orchids, 1986, Blue Ice, 1994, Witness to the Execution, 1994. Office: Shonderosa Productions PO Box 20547 Sedona AZ 86341*

YOUNG, SONIA WINER, public relations director, educator; b. Chattanooga, Tenn., Aug. 20, 1934; d. Meyer D. and Rose (Demby) Winer; m. Melvin A. Young, Feb. 24, 1957; 1 child, Melanie Anne. BA, Sophie Newcomb Coll., 1956; M in Ednl. Psychology, U. Tenn.-Chattanooga, 1966. Cert. speech and hearing specialist Am. Speech and Hearing Assn. Speech therapist Chattanooga-Hamilton County Speech and Hearing Ctr., 1961-66, ednl. psychology, 1966-78; staff psychologist Chattanooga Testing and Counseling Services, 1978-80; ins. rep. Mut. Benefit Life Ins. Co., Chattanooga, 1980-84; columnist Chattanooga Times, 1982-84; cmty. affairs reporter Sta. WRCB-TV, Chattanooga, 1983-84; pub. relations and promotions dir. Purple Ladies, Inc., Chattanooga, 1984—; cons. psychology Ga. Dept. Human Resources, also Cheerhaven Sch., Dalton, 1970-78; adj. prof. psychology U. Tenn.-Chattanooga, 1971-80, adj. prof. dept. theatre and speech, 1988—; pres. Speak Out; bd. dirs. M. Young Comm., Vol. Ctr., 1995—, Arthritis Found., 1995—; spl. projects dir. Chattanooga State

Technical C.C., 1995—. Contbg. editor Chattanooga Life and Leisure Mag. Pres. Chattanooga Opera Guild, 1973-74, Chattanooga Opera Assn., 1979-80; bd. dirs., sec. Chattanooga-Hamilton County Bicentenniel Libr., 1977-79; pres. Little Theatre of Chattanooga, 1984-90, bd. dirs., 1974—; v.p. Girls Club, Chattanooga, 1979-80; bd. dirs. March of Dimes, 1988, Chattanooga Symphony Guild, Mizpah Congregation, Chattanooga Area Literacy Council, Chattanooga Cares, 1993—, Tourist Devel. Agy., 1990—; mem. alumni council U. Tenn.-Chattanooga; mem. selection com. Leadership Chattanooga, 1984-86; sec. Allied Arts Greater Chattanooga, 1978-80, residential campaign chmn., 1985; bd. dirs. Chattanooga Ctr. for the Dance, Ptnrs. for Acad. Excellence, 1987—, Chattanooga Mental Health Assn., 1988; chmn. March of Dimes Mother's March, 1988, One of a Kind-the Arts Against AIDS-Chattanooga Cares, 1993, 94; co-chair Am. Heart Assn. Gala, 1994, chmn., 1995; chair Little Theatre Capital Campaign, 1995. Recipient Disting. Citizens award City of Chattanooga, 1975, Steakley award Little Theatre Chattanooga, 1982, Pres. award, 1991, 92, Vol. of Yr., 1995, Woman of Distinction award Am. Lung Assn., 1995, Vol. of Yr. award, 1995, Vol. of Yr. award Chattanooga Cares, 1995. Mem. Phi Beta Kappa (pres. Chattanooga chpt. 1978-79). Jewish. Home: 1025 River Hills Cir Chattanooga TN 37415-5611 Office: U Tenn Theatre & Speech Dept 615 Mccallie Ave Chattanooga TN 37403-2504

YOUNG, STEVEN, professional football player; b. Salt Lake City, Oct. 11, 1961. JD, Brigham Young, 1993. With L.A. Express, USFL, 1984-85, Tampa Bay Buccaneers, 1985-87; quarterback San Francisco 49ers, 1987—. Davey O'Brien Award, 1983, All-America team quarterback, The Sporting News, 1983; Named NFL's Top-rated quarterback, 1991, named NFL MVP The Sporting News, 1992, NFL All-Pro team quarterback, The Sporting News, 1992, Superbowl MVP, 1994. Played in Pro Bowl 1992, 93; highest rated passer NFL, 1991-93. Office: San Francisco 49ers 4949 Centennial Blvd Santa Clara CA 95054-1229*

YOUNG, TAYLOR LYNN, special education administrator, consultant; b. Evansville, Ind., Dec. 7, 1952; s. James Taylor and Luvenia (Welborn) Y.; 1 child, Virginia Melin. BS in Edn., Ea. Ill. U., 1975; MS in Edn., Ill. State U., 1980; PhD in Edn., U. Denver, 1988. Tchr. spl. edn. St. Joseph (Ill.)-Ogden High Sch. Dist. 305, 1975-80; dir. Mid-State Spl. Edn. Coop., Hillsboro, Ill., 1980-81; dir. spl. edn. Mountain Bd. Coop. Svcs., Leadville, Colo., 1981-87; sr. cons. on sch. fin., cons. on spl. edn. Colo. Dept. Edn., Denver, 1987-88; prin. Laremont Sch., Spl. Edn. Dist. Lake County, Gurnee, Ill., 1988-89; dir. edn. Colo. Christian Home, Denver, 1989-92; special edn. tchr. El Paso County Dist. 11, Colo. Springs, Colo., 1992-93, special edn. supr., 1993—; cons. Project Choice, Ill. Bd. Edn., Springfield, 1989-90. Mem. ASCD, Coun. for Exceptional Children, Phi Delta Kappa. Republican. Avocations: golf, travel. Home: 1522 Server Dr Colorado Springs CO 80910-2039 Office: Schl Dist 11 1115 N El Paso St Colorado Springs CO 80910

YOUNG, TERESA GAIL HILGER, adult education educator; b. Modesto, Calif., Mar. 4, 1948; d. Richard George and Jessie Dennie (Dennis) Long; m. Charles Ray Young, June 22, 1974; 1 child, Gregory Paul. BS in Edn., Abilene (Tex.) Christian U., 1970; MEd in Curriculum, Tarleton State U., Stephenville, Tex., 1976; postgrad., Tex. Tech U. Cert. supr., mid-mgmt., supt., Tex. Tchr. sci. Tex. Youth Coun., Gatesville, Gatesville Ind. Sch. Dist.; coord. Edn. and Tng. Ctr., Cen. Tex. Coll., Gatesville; tchr. Tex. Dept. Corrections, Gatesville; conf. presenter. Trustee Jonesboro (Tex.) Ind. Sch. Dist., 1988—. Mem. ASCD, Am. Fedn. Tchrs., Assn. Tex. Profl. Educators.

YOUNG, THOMAS DANIEL, retired humanities educator, author; b. Louisville, Miss., Oct. 22, 1919; s. William Allen and Lula (Wright) Y.; m. Arlease Lewis, Dec. 21, 1941; children: Thomas Daniel, Terry Lewis, Kyle David. B.S., Miss. So. Coll., 1941; M.A., U. Miss., 1948; Ph.D., Vanderbilt U., 1950; postgrad., U. Oxford, 1962, The Sorbonne, 1974. Instr. English U. Miss., 1946-48; asst. Vanderbilt U., Nashville, 1948-50, dean admissions, asst. to vice-chancellor, 1961-64, prof., chmn. dept. English, 1964-72, Gertrude C. Vanderbilt prof. English, 1972-85, Gertrude C. Vanderbilt prof. emeritus, 1985—; asst. prof. English Miss. So. Coll., 1950-51, prof., chmn. dept., 1951-54, dean basic coll., 1954-57; prof. English, dean Delta State Coll., Cleveland, Miss., 1957-61; Pres. So. Lit. Festival Assn., 1952-53; chmn. English commn. Miss. Assn. Coll., 1952-55; coordinator Gen. Edn. Conf., 1953. Author: Jack London and the Era of Social Protest, 1950, The Literature of the South, 1952, rev. edit., 1968, Donald Davidson: An Essay and a Bibliography, 1965, American Literature: A Critical Survey, 1968, John Crowe Ransom; Critical Essays and a Bibliography, 1968, John Crowe Ransom, 1970, Donald Davidson, 1971, The Literary Correspondence of Allen Tate and Donald Davidson, 1974, The New Criticism and After, 1976, Gentleman in a Dustcoat: A Biography of John Crowe Ransom, 1977, The Past in the Present: Studies in the Modern American Novel, 1981, Tennessee Writers, 1981, John Crowe Ransom: An Annotated Bibliography, 1982, The Vocation of Letters in America: The Literary Correspondence of Allen Tate and John Peale Bishop, 1982, Selected Essays of John Crowe Ransom, 1983, Selected Letters of John Crowe Ransom, 1985, Singin' Billy, 1985, (with Louis D. Rubin and others) The History of Southern Literature, Conversations with Malcolm Cowley, 1986, The Lytle-Tate Letters, 1987, Fabulous Provinces: A Memoir, 1988, Modern American Fiction, 1989, Selected Essays, 1990; gen. editor: The Fugitive Bibliographies. Mem. AAUP, South Atlantic MLA (chmn. Am. lit. sect. 1971, chmn. lit. criticism sect. 1969, mem. exec. com. 1969-72), MLA (chmn. So. Lit. sect. 1969, 80, 82), Am. Studies Assn. Lower Miss. (pres. 1956-57), Phi Delta Kappa, Omicron Delta Kappa. Address: PO Box 31 Rose Hill MS 39356-0031

YOUNG, TOMMIE MORTON, social psychology educator, writer; b. Nashville. BA cum laude, Tenn. State U., 1951; MLS, George Peabody Coll. for Tchrs., 1955; PhD, Duke U., 1977; postgrad. U. Okla., 1967, U. Nebr., 1968. Coord., Young Adult Program, Lucy Thurman br. YWCA, 1951-52; instr. edn. Tenn. State U., Nashville, 1956-59; instr., coord. media program Prairie View Coll. (Tex.), 1959-61; asst. prof. edn., assoc. prof. English, dir. IMC Ctr., U. Ark.-Pine Bluff, 1965-69; asst. prof. English and edn., dir. learning lab., N.C. Central U., Durham, 1969-74; prof., dir./chairperson libr. media svcs. and dept. ednl. media, dir. Afro-Am. Family Project, N.C. Agrl. and Tech. State U., Greensboro, 1975—; adj. prof. langs., lit. and philosophy, dir. schs. history project Tenn. State U., Nashville, 1994—; dir. workshops, grants; pres., dir. Ednl. Cons. Svcs. Author: Afro American Genealogy Sourcebook, 1987, Oral Histories of Former All-Black Public Schools, 1991, After School Programs for At-Risk Youth and Their Families, 1994, Sable Scenes, 1996; contbr. poem to Poetry: American Heritage; contbr. rsch. papers, articles to profl. jours. Nat. chmn. Com. to Re-Elect the Pres.; past sec. Fedn. Colored Women's Clubs; bd. dirs. Southwestern div. ARC, Nashville area, 1994—, dir. Volun-Teens; chairperson learning resources com. Task Force Durham Day Care Assn.; bd. dirs., chairperson schs. div. Durham County Unit Am. Cancer Soc.; past mem. adv. bd., bd. dirs. YMCA, Atlanta; chair Guilford County Commn. on Needs of Children; bd. advisors NIH, N.C. Coun. of the Arts; mem. Guilford County Involvement Coun.; chmn. N.C. adv. com. U.S. Civil Rights Com.; mem. exec. planning com. Greensboro. Recipient awards ARC, 1968, 73, NAACP, 1973, HEW, 1978, U.S. Commn. on Civil Rights, 1982; named Disting. Alumni Tenn. State U., 1994. Mem. AAUW (honor award 1983, pres. Greensboro br., chairperson internat. rels. com.), ALA (divsn. coll. and rsch. librs., past chair), NAACP (life, 1st v.p. Durham br., exec. bd. Greensboro br., dir. parent edn./child advocacy program, Woman of Yr. 1992), NEA, Assn. Childhood Ednl. Internat., Comparative and Internat. Edn. Assn., Archives Assoc., Internat. Platform Assn., Nat. Hist. Soc., Greensboro Jr. League (community adv. bd. 1991—), African Am. Gen. Soc. Tenn. (founder 1994), Zeta Phi Beta (chairperson polit. action com. eastern region, nat. grammateus, Polit. and Civic Svc. award 1974, Outstanding Social-Polit. Svc. award 1982, Woman of Yr. 1977), Commn. on Status of Women (Woman of Achievement 1991), Phi Kappa Phi (Disting. State U. Alumni award 1994, Disting Alumni NAFEO award, 1995, Carl Rowan-Oprah Winfrey lectr. Tenn. State U., 1995, Excellence in Journalism award SPJ, 1995, info. officer 1996). Home: PO Box 17684 Nashville TN 37217-0684

YOUNG, TZAY Y., electrical and computer engineering educator; b. Shanghai, China, Jan. 11, 1933; came to U.S., 1958; s. Chao-Hsiung and Chiu-Ming (Chu) Y.; m. Lily Liu, Dec. 27, 1965; children: Debbie Chia-Pei, Arthur Chia-Kai. BS, Nat. Taiwan U., Taipei, 1955; MS, U. Vt., 1959; DEng, Johns Hopkins U., 1962. Rsch. assoc. Johns Hopkins U., Balt., 1962-63; mem. tech. staff Bell Labs., Murray Hill, N.J., 1963-64; asst. prof. Carnegie-Mellon U., Pitts., 1964-68, assoc. prof., 1968-74; prof. elec. and computer engring. U. Miami, Coral Gables, Fla., 1974—, acting chmn. dept., 1988-91, chmn. dept., 1991—; sr. postdoctoral rsch. assoc. NAS, NASA, Goddard Space Flight Ctr., Md., 1972-73. Author: (with T.W. Calvert) Classification, Estimation and Pattern Recognition, 1974; editor: (with K.S. Fu) Handbook of Pattern Recognition and Image Processing, 1986; editor: Handbook of Pattern Recognition and Image Processing, vol. 2, Computer Vision, 1994; also numerous articles. Rsch. grantee NSF, NASA, FHTIC, also indsl. grants. Fellow IEEE (assoc. editor Trans. Computers 1974-76; editorial bd. Trans. Pattern Analysis and Machine Intelligence 1979-84, adv. bd. 1984-90); mem. Sigma Xi, Eta Kappa Ny, Omicron Delta Kappa. Office: U Miami Dept Elec & Computer Engring Coral Gables FL 33124

YOUNG, VERA LEE HALL, educational administrator, association executive; b. Natchitoches, La., Jan. 9, 1944; d. Sidney and Gertrude (Bell) H.; m. Willie L. Young, Aug. 21, 1965 (div. June 1971). BS, Grambling State U., 1967; MS, Bank St. Coll., 1977; PhD with distinction, Century U., 1985. Cert. tchr., La., N.J., N.Y. Ednl. cons. family day care program N.Y.C. Community Sch. Dist. 6; ednl. dir. Leslie Freeman Daycare Ctr., Bklyn., 1973-74; tchr. West N.Y. Bd. of Edn., 1978—; exec. dir., founder Operation Super Inst., Ft. Lee, N.J., 1986—; lectr., tchr., panelist and cons. in field; participant Statewide Child Care Adv. Coun. Conf., N.J., 1980, State Ill. Tchrs. Conf., 1987, U. S.C. Tchrs. Conf., Georgetown, 1989; discussant Speaking for Schools radio program, N.J., N.Y. Author: A Day Care Solution in America: The Learning Center, 1985; contbr. articles to field. Recipient Internat. Order of Merit award (# 320 of 500 world-wide), Internat. Biog. Ctr., Cambridge, Eng.; named Educator or Yr., Black Achievement and Awards, 1988; Dept. Labor grantee, Jerusalem, 1982-83. Mem. NEA, N.J. Edn. Assn. (conf. participant 1987), N.J. Women Bus. Ownership Orgn., Internat. Platform Assn., Internat. Reading Assn., Minority & Women Owned Bus. N.Y., Bank St. Coll. Alumni Assn., Gambling Coll. Alumni Assn. Mem. Dutch Reform Ch. Avocations: reading, travel, sports. Office: Operation Super 229 Main St # 1834 Fort Lee NJ 07024-5709

YOUNG, VERNON ROBERT, nutrition, biochemistry educator; b. Rhyl, Wales, Nov. 15, 1937; married, 1966; 5 children. BS, U. Reading, 1959; diploma in agr., Cambridge U., 1960; PhD in Nutrition, U. Calif., Davis, 1965. Lectr. nutritional biochemistry MIT, Cambridge, Mass., 1965-66, asst. prof. physiology chemistry, 1966-72, assoc. prof., 1972-76, prof. nutritional biochemistry, 1976—; program mgmt. human nutrition competitive rsch. grants program USDA, 1980-81; assoc. program dir. MIT Clin. Rsch. Ctr., Cambridge, Mass., 1985-87; biochemist dept. surgery Mass. Gen. Hosp. & Harvard Med. Sch., Boston, 1987—; sr. vis. scientist USDA Human Nutrition Ctr. Aging, Tufts U., 1988—. Recipient Rank prize in nutrition, 1989. Mem. NAS, Am. Inst. Nutrition (Mead Johnson award 1973, Borden award 1982), Am. soc. Clin. Nutrition (McCollum award 1987), Nutrition Soc., Gerontology Soc. Am., Am. Chem. Soc. Office: MIT Dept Nutritional Biochem Bldg E18 Rm 613 50 Ames St Cambridge MA 02139*

YOUNG, WILLIAM BENJAMIN, special education educator; b. Wichita, Kans., Jan. 30, 1929; s. Ernest William and Florence Belle (McCann) Y.; m. La Vona P., Feb., 1949 (div. 1973); children: Lynda, David, Timothy; m. Patricia Sue Reber, Aug., 1974. Student, Southwestern Coll., Winfield, Kans., 1947-48; B in Gen. Edn., U. Omaha, 1961; MS in Pers. Counseling, Miami U., Oxford, Ohio, 1965; PhD in Exceptional Edn., Adminstrn. and Counseling, Ohio State U., 1972. Cert. elem. and secondary adminstr., tchr., counselor, psychologist, psychometrist, spl. edn., mental retardation, learning disabled/behavior disordered, emotionally handicapped, Ind.; cert. K-12 guidance counselor and edn. leadership, Fla.; lic sexologist, flight instr.; lic. Coast Guard capt. Enlisted USAF, 1948; dir. commd. 2nd lt. commd. 2d lt., 1955; advanced through grades to capt. USAF, 1960, ret., 1966; numerous teaching and counseling positions as civilian, 1966-91; co-owner, instr. Ft. Wayne (Ind.) Ground Schs., 1984-88; marriage and family counselor, pvt. practice, 1966-91; tchr., counselor, behavior specialist Broward County Schs., Ft. Lauderdale, Fla., 1989—; cons., internat. presenter/lectr. learning and behavior problems; adj. prof. grad. spl. edn. Nova U. Mem. ACA, Coun. for Exceptional Children, Coun. Behavior Disorders, Fla. Counseling Assn., 32 degree Masons. Avocations: flying, sailing, traveling, golf, swimming. Home: 2548 Gulfstream Ln Fort Lauderdale FL 33312-4704

YOUNG, WILLIAM DAVID, computer scientist; b. Albuquerque, Nov. 22, 1953; s. Youree Harold and Alma Catherine (Callahan) Y. BS in Math. with honors, U. Tex., 1975, BA in Philosophy with high honors, 1976, MA in Philosophy, 1976, MA in Computer Sci., 1980, PhD in Computer Sci., 1988; postgrad., U. Notre Dame, 1976-77. Rsch. engring. sci. asst., systems analyst U. Tex., Austin, 1978-87; computing rsch. sci. Computational Logic, Inc., Austin, 1987-88, sr. computing rsch. sci., 1988—, also bd. dirs.; part-time instr. Austin C.C., 1978-80, Southwest Tex. State U., San Marcos, 1980-81, 83-86; rsch. sci. Honeywell Secure Computing Tech. Ctr., St. Anthony, Minn., 1984-87; invited lectr., presenter, speaker in field; publ. chair Computer Security Workshop III, 1990, IV, 1991; chmn. panel Symposium Software Analysis, Testing and Verification, 1991, program com., 1991; organizer, chmn. panel computer security founds. Computer Security Workshop II, 1989; bd. dirs. Computational Logic, Inc. Mem. editl. bd. Jour. Computer Security; contbr. articles to profl. jours. papers in field. Mem. IEEE, Assn. Computing Machienry, Abelian Group Investment Club (pres. 1992-96), Phi Beta Kappa, Phi Eta Sigma, Pi Mu Epsilon, Upsilon Pi Epsilon. Home: 2208 Lindell Ave Austin TX 78704-5131 Office: Computational Logic Inc 1717 W 6th St Ste 290 Austin TX 78703-4777

YOUNG, WILLIAM FIELDING, lawyer; b. N.Y.C., Jan. 6, 1948; s. Charles Fielding and Josephine Cope (Roig) Y.; m. Mary Anne Silver, June 13, 1970. BA, U. Va., 1970; JD, Harvard U., 1977. Bar: Va. 1977, U.S. Dist. Ct. (ea. and we. dists.) Va. 1977, U.S. Ct. Appeals (4th cir.) 1977, D.C. 1988, U.S. Dist. Ct. D.C. 1988, U.S. Ct. Appeals (D.C. cir.) 1988. Assoc. Hunton & Williams, Richmond, Va., 1977-85; ptnr. Hunton & Williams, Washington, 1985—, Fairfax, Va., 1985—. Mem. Va. Dist. Export Coun., Richmond, 1983—. Lt. USN, 1970-74. Mem. Va. Bar Assn. (bd. govs. antitrust sect. 1985—, chmn. elect, internat. law sect. 1985-87), Phi Beta Kappa, Downtown Club (Richmond). Democrat. Episcopalian. Home: 1215 Mottrom Dr Mc Lean VA 22101-2721 Office: Hunton & Williams 2000 Pennsylvania Ave PO Box 19230 Washington DC 20036*

YOUNG, WILLIAM GLOVER, federal judge; b. Huntington, N.Y., Sept. 23, 1940; s. Woodhull Benjamin and Margaret Jean (Wilkes) Y.; m. Beverly June Bigelow, Aug. 5, 1967; children: Mark Edward, Jeffrey Woodhull, Todd Russell. A.B., Harvard U., 1962, LL.B., 1967. Bar: Mass. 1967, U.S. Supreme Ct. 1970. Law clk. to chief justice Supreme Jud. Ct., Mass., 1967-68; spl. asst. atty. gen. Mass., 1969-72, chief legal counsel to gov., 1972-74; asso. firm Bingham, Dana and Gould, Boston, 1968-72; ptnr. Bingham, Dana and Gould, 1975-78; assoc. justice Superior Ct., Commonwealth of Mass., Boston, 1978-85; judge U.S. Dist. Ct. Mass., Boston, 1985—; lectr. part time Harvard Law Sch., 1979-90, Boston Coll. Law Sch., Boston U. Law Sch. Served to capt. U.S. Army, 1962-64. Mem. Am. Law Inst., Mass. Bar Assn., Boston Bar Assn., Harvard Alumni (pres. 1976-77). Office: US Dist Ct Rm 1903 McCormack PO & Courthouse Boston MA 02109

YOUNGBERG, ROBERT STANLEY, principal, consultant; b. Chgo., Apr. 21, 1932; s. Holger Raymond and Eva Boyd (Carr) Y.; m. Catherine Jane Fitzpatrick, June 19, 1954; children: Kevin, Melissa, Margo Jenkins, Brian. BS, U. Ill., 1954; MEd, Wayne State U., 1959; PhD, U. Mich., 1975. Tchr. Hanneman-Herman-Dixon, Detroit, 1956-62; counselor Barbour Jr. High/Ruddman Jr. High Sch., Detroit, 1962-67, Redford High Sch., Detroit, 1967-70; prin. mid. sch. Novi, Mich., 1970-79, prin. high sch., 1979-92; pvt. practice edn. cons. Clearwater, Fla., 1992—; site evaluator secondary recognition program U. S. Dept. Edn., Mich. Dept. Edn., 1988-95; immigration and customs inspector U. S. Dept. Justice, 1961-64; summer camp dir. Mich. and Wis., 1965-70; cons. in field. Chmn. citizens adv. com. Sch. Facilities, Detroit, 1958-59; chmn. Citizens Adv. Com. on Mid. Schs., Novi, 1972-74, Citizens Adv. Com. on Humanities and Arts, 1975, Great Cities Sch. Improvement Project, Detroit, 1962-64, Dist. Curriculum Coun., Novi, 1972-80; bd. dirs. Youth Assistance Bd., Novi, 1975-79; site vis. North Ctrl. Assn., 1968-91; bus. cons. Mgmt. Style for Retail Merchants, Novi, 1988-91. With U.S. Army, 1954-56. Mem. Mich. Assn. Sch. Adminstrs., Mich. Assn. Secondary Sch. Prins., Nat. Assn. Secondary Sch. Prins., Nat. ASCD, Kensington Valley Activities Conf. (bd. dirs.), Phi Delta Kappa. Avocations: physical fitness, senior games, racquetball, basketball, track and field events. Office: 2427 Bond Ave Clearwater FL 34619-1204

YOUNGBLOOD, BETTY J., academic administrator; b. Detroit; m. Ralph P. Youngblood; 1 child. BS in Political Sci., Oakland U., Rochester, Mich.; MA in South Asian Studies, U. Minn., PhD in Political Sci. Formerly mem. faculty West Ga. Coll., Tex. Tech U.; various adminstrv. positions Kennesaw State Coll., Marietta, Ga.; v.p. acad. affairs MacMurray Coll., Jacksonville, Ill., Wesley Coll., Dover, Del.; vice chancelllor acad. affairs, dean faculty, prof. polit. sci. U. Wis.-Superior, 1990-91, acting chancellor, 1991-92, chancellor, 1992—; cons., evaluator North Ctrl. Assn. Colls. and Schs. Contbr. articles to profl. jours. Bd. dirs. United Way, Superior. Rsch. grantee for study in N.W. India. Mem. Superior C. of C., Rotary. Office: U Wis-Superior Office of the President 1800 Grand Ave Superior WI 54880-2873

YOUNGBLOOD, ELAINE MICHELE, lawyer; b. Schenectady, N.Y., Jan. 9, 1944; d. Roy W. and Mary Louise (Read) Ortoleva; m. William Gerald Youngblood, Feb. 14, 1970; children: Flagg Khristian, Megan Michele. BA, Wake Forest Coll., 1965; JD, Albany Law Sch., 1969. Bar: Tex. 1970, U.S. Dist. Ct. (no. dist.) Tex. 1971, U.S. Dist. Ct. (so. dist.) Tex. 1972, Tenn. 1978, U.S. Dist. Ct. (mid. dist.) Tenn. 1978. Assoc. Fanning & Harper, Dallas, 1969, Crocker & Murphy, Dallas, 1970-71, McClure & Burch, Houston, 1972-75, Brown, Bradshaw & Plummer, Houston, 1975-76; ptnr. Seligmann & Youngblood, Nashville, 1977-88; atty. Law Offices of Elaine M. Youngblood, Nashville, 1988-94; of counsel Ortale, Kelley Herbert & Crawford, 1994—. Mem. Com. for Women in Govt., Dallas, 1969-71, Law Day com. of Dallas Bar Assn., 1970-71. Mem. ABA, Tex. Bar Assn., Tenn. Bar Assn., Nashville Bar Assn. (fee dispute com. 1990—, vice chmn. 1996, CLE com. 1996), Tenn. Trial Lawyers Assn., Nat. Assn. Women Lawyers, Phi Beta Pi. Republican. Episcopalian. Club: Cable of Nashville (charter). Address: PO Box 198985 200 Fourth Ave N Fl 3 Noel Pl Nashville TN 37219-8985

YOUNGBLOOD, J. CRAIG, lawyer; b. Ft. Worth, July 6, 1947; s. Angus O'Neal and Kathleen (Hill) Y.; m. Linda Gilman, Apr. 17, 1982; children: Jesica Caye, Jaclyn Cristine. Student, Rice U., 1965-66; BA in Polit. Sci. and Math, U. Tex., San Antonio, 1977; JD, U. Tex., Austin, 1980. Bar: Tex. 1982, U.S. Dist. Ct. (so. dist.) Tex. 1982, U.S. Ct. Appeals (D.C., 3rd, 5th and 11th cirs.) 1982, U.S. Ct. Appeals (10th cir.) 1983. Assoc. Vinson & Elkins, Houston, 1981-87, ptnr., 1988—; adv. bd. grad. program in energy and natural resources U. Houston Law Ctr. Mem. Tex. Law Rev.; contbr. chpt. to book; contbr. articles to profl. jours., lectr. in field. Mem. ABA, Tex. Bar Assn., Houston Bar Assn., Fed. Energy Bar Assn., Tex. Law Rev. Assn. Republican. Avocations: hunting, fishing, snow skiing, personal computers. Home: 11 Red Sable Pt The Woodlands TX 77380-2687 Office: Vinson & Elkins 2300 First City Tower 1001 Fannin St Houston TX 77002-6760

YOUNGBLOOD, JOHNNY RAY, pastor; m. Joyce Terrell; 3 children. Grad., Dillard U., D of Ministry (hon.), 1993; MDiv, Colgate-Rochester Sem.; D of Ministry, United Theol. Sem., Dayton, Ohio, 1990; DD (hon.), Boston U., 1993; LHD (hon.), SUNY, 1994. Sr. pastor St. Paul Cmty. Bapt. Ch., Bklyn., 1975—; organizer Eldad-Medad Men's Bible study class St. Paul Cmty. Bapt. Ch., 1987—, sponsor Father's Day Weekend Conf., 1991—, Nehemiah Housing Project, Bklyn. Samuel D. Proctor fellow; book celebrating the life of ministry of Dr. Youngblood, Upon This Rock: The Miracles of A Black Church, authored by Samuel G. Freedman, 1993; chronicled in N.Y. Times, The Charlie Rose Show, CBS Sunday Morning News, ABC's World New Tonight, NBC Nightly News, The McCreary Report, 20/20, and others; recognized in Congl. Record. Office: St Paul Cmty Bapt Ch 859 Hendrix St Brooklyn NY 11207

YOUNGBLOOD, MICHELLE KAREN WOLSTEIN, judge; b. Killeen, Tex., Jan. 14, 1958. BBA, Tex. A&M U., 1980; JD, Baylor U., 1983. Bar: Tex. 1983, U.S. Ct. Appeals (5th, 11th cirs.) 1986, U.S. Supreme Ct., 1986. Asst. city atty. City of Dallas, 1983-85; atty. advisor HUD, Ft. Worth, 1985-87; adminstrv. judge EEOC, Dallas, 1987-93; adminstv. law judge City of Arlington, Tex., 1991—; adj. prof. Tarrant County Jr. Coll., Ft. Worth, 1986—, Dallas Community Coll., 1987—, U. Tex., Arlington, 1992—, Dallas Community Colls., 1991—; pub. spkr. various community orgns. and events, 1983—; profl. mediator/arbitrator, 1990—; mediator Dispute Resolution Svcs.; adj. prof. Weatherford (Tex.) Coll., 1993. Contbr. articles to prof. jours. V.p. Ft. Worth metro chapter Sweet Adelines Internat., 1985—; arbitrator BBB, Ft. Worth, 1986—. Named Woman of the Yr. Meadowbrook Bus. and Profl. Women, Ft. Worth, 1987-88, Outstanding Young Women of Am., 1988, Young Career Women of the Yr., Bus. & Profl. Women, 1989, 91. Mem. Coll. State Bar Tex., Fed. Bar Assn. (pres. Ft. Worth chpt. 1987-88, sec. nat. young lawyers div. 1988—, nat. coun. 1988—), Tarrant County Young Lawyers Assn. (bd. dir. 1986-87), Tarrant County Women's Bar Assn. (bd. dirs. 1986-88), Tarrant County Women's Bar Assn. (bd. dirs. 1986-88), Tarrant County Bar Assn., Tex. Young Lawyers Assn. (Cert. of Spl. Achievement), Bus. and Profl. Women (Young Career Woman of Yr. 1987, 88, 91, Woman of Yr. Meadowbrook-Ft. Worth chpt. 1987). Office: PO Box 8240 Fort Worth TX 76124

YOUNGBLOOD, RICHARD NEIL, columnist; b. Minot, N.D., May 9, 1936; s. Edward Anthony and Helen (Condo) Y.; m. Adele Henley, May 4, 1957 (div. 1983); children: Kent Jay, Ruth Adele, Beth Alise; m. Mary Dinneen, July 14, 1984. BA, U. N.D., 1958. Reporter Grand Forks (N.D.) Herald, 1955-63; reporter Mpls. Star Tribune, 1963-67, asst. city editor, 1967-69, bus./fin. editor, 1969-84, columnist, 1984—. Recipient Excellence award in bus. and fin. journalism John Handcock Mut. Life, 1974; named Newspaper Farm Editor of Yr. Newspaper Farm Editors of Am., 1965. Avocations: reading, crossword puzzles, boating. Office: Mpls Star Tribune 425 Portland Ave Minneapolis MN 55488-0001

YOUNG-BRUEHL, ELISABETH, philosophy educator, psychoanalyst; b. Elkton, Md., Mar. 3, 1946; d. Herbert Gibbons Young and Lois (Williams) Sutton. BA, New Sch. for Social Rsch., 1968, MA, 1974, PhD, 1974. Prof. philosophy Wesleyan U., Middletown, Conn., 1974-91; prof. psychology Haverford (Pa.) Coll., 1992—. Author: Freedom and Karl Jaspers Philosophy, 1981, Hannah Arendt, 1982, Anna Freud, 1988, Mind and The Body Politic, 1989, Freud on Women, 1990, Creative Characters, 1991, Global Cultures, 1994, The Anatomy of Prejudices, 1996. NEH fellow, 1984-85, Guggenheim Found. fellow, 1986-87. Mem. Authors Guild. Democrat. Office: Haverford Coll Haverford PA 19041 also: Inst of PA Hosp Philadelphia PA 19139

YOUNGDAHL, JAMES EDWARD, lawyer; b. Mankato, Minn., Nov. 17, 1926; s. Benjamin Emanuel Lincoln and Livia (Bjorkquist) Y.; children—Jay Thomas Armstrong, Jan Kristi, Lincoln Anders Morton, Sara Lise. Student, Washington U., St. Louis, 1944-45; A.B., U. Mo., 1947; LL.B., U. Ark., 1959. Bar: Ark. bar 1959. Field sec. League for Indsl. Democracy, N.Y.C., 1947-48; nat. rep., asst. regional dir. Amalgamated Clothing Workers Am., CIO and AFL-CIO, St. Louis, Paducah, Ky., New Orleans, 1948-56; since practiced in Little Rock, Memphis, New Orleans and Albuquerque; ptnr. McMath, Leatherman, Woods & Youngdahl, 1959-68, Youngdahl & Larrison, 1968-80, Youngdahl & Youngdahl P.A., 1980—, Youngdahl, Sadin & McGowan, 1985—; instr. labor law U. Ark. Sch. Law, 1963, 69-71, U. Ark. Sch. Law (Ark. Law Sch.), 1964-66; mem. arbitration services adv. com. Fed. Mediation and Conciliation Service, 1978-84. Editor-in-chief: Ark. Law Rev, 1958-59; contbg. editor: Ark. Advocate, 1972-74; contbr. articles to profl. jours. Vice chmn. New Orleans Forum, 1953-54; pres. Ark. Assn. for Mental Health, 1960-61; chmn. Ark. adv. com. U.S. Commn. on Civil Rights, 1962-65; mem. exec. com. So. Regional Council, 1969-74; mem. nat. exec. bd. Workers Def. League, 1965-75; bd. dirs. Voter Edn. Project, Inc., 1971-74. Home: 2046 Royal St New Orleans LA 70116 Office: Ste 201 2929 Coors Blvd NW Albuquerque NM 87120 also: Ste 1805 124 W Capitol Little Rock AR 72203

YOUNGER, JUDITH TESS, lawyer, educator; b. N.Y.C., Dec. 20, 1933; d. Sidney and Kate (Greenbaum) Weintraub; m. Irving Younger, Jan. 21, 1955;

children: Rebecca, Abigail M. B.S., Cornell U., 1954; J.D., NYU, 1958; LL.D. (hon.), Hofstra U., 1974. Bar: N.Y. 1958, U.S. Supreme Ct 1962, D.C. 1983, Minn. 1985. Law clk. to judge U.S. Dist. Ct., 1958-60; asso. firm Chadbourne, Parke, Whiteside & Wolff, N.Y.C., 1960-62; mem. firm Younger and Younger, and (successors), 1962-67; adj. asst. prof. N.Y. U. Sch. Law, 1967-69; asst. atty. gen. State of N.Y., 1969-70; assoc. prof. Hofstra U. Sch. Law, 1970-72, prof., assoc. dean, 1972-74; dean, prof. Syracuse Coll. Law, 1974-75; dep. dean, prof. law Cornell Law Sch., 1975-78, prof. law, 1975-85; vis. prof. U. Minn. Law Sch., Mpls., 1984-85, prof., 1985—; of counsel Popham, Haik, Schnobrich & Kaufman, Ltd., Mpls., 1989-95; cons. NOW, 1972-74, Suffolk County for Revision of Its Real Property Tax Act, 1972-73; mem. N.Y. Gov.'s Panel To Screen Candidates of Ct. of Claims Judges, 1973-74; mem. Minn. Lawyers' Profl. Responsibility Bd., 1991-93. Contbr. articles to profl. jours. Trustee Cornell U., 1973-78. Mem. ABA (council legal edn. 1975-79), Am. Law Inst. (adv. restatement property 1982-84), AAUP (v.p. Cornell U. chpt. 1978-79), N.Y. State Bar Assn., Assn. of Bar of City of N.Y., Minn. Bar Assn. Home: 3520 W Calhoun Pky Minneapolis MN 55416-4657 Office: U Minn Law Sch Minneapolis MN 55455

YOUNGERMAN, JACK, artist, sculptor; b. Louisville, Mar. 25, 1926; s. Guy Arthur and Margaret Anne (Everhart) Y.; m. Delphine Seyrig, July 3, 1950; 1 son, Duncan Pierre. Student, U. N.C., 1944-46; B.A., U. Mo., 1947; postgrad., Ecole des Beaux Arts, Paris, 1947-48. instr. Yale U., New Haven, 1974-75, Hunter Coll., N.Y.C., 1981—, Sch. Visual Arts, N.Y.C., 1981—. One-man shows include Betty Parsons Gallery, N.Y.C., 1958, 60, 61, 64, 65, 68, Paris, 1951, 62, 63, Milan, 1965, Los Angeles, 1963, Worcester Art Mus., 1965, MIT, 1966, Galerie Adrien Maeght, Paris, 1966, Phillips Collections, Washington, 1968, Galerie Denise Rene, Galerie Rive Gauche, Paris, 1973, Pace Gallery, N.Y.C., 1971, 73, 75, Central Park, N.Y.C., 1981, Washburn Gallery, N.Y.C., 1981, 84-87, Guggenheim Mus., 1986, Heland Wetterling Gallery, Stockholm, 1989; exhibited in group shows at Carnegie Internat., 1958, 61, Mus. Modern Art, 1959, Corcoran Mus., Washington, 1958, 63, 79, Kimura Gallery, Tokyo, 1960, Whitney Mus., 1960, 65, 74, 77, 88, 89, Guggenheim Mus., 1961, 64, 66, 81, 82, 86, 88, Art Inst. Chgo., 1962, Mus. Bousmans van Beuningen, Rotterdam, The Netherlands, 1966, Jewish Mus., N.Y.C., 1967, 68, 69, Carnegie Instn., 1971, Hirshhorn Mus., 1980, Haus der Kunst, Munich, W.Ger., 1981, Nat. Gallery Art, Washington, 1981, 83, 89, Found. Nat. des Artes Graphiques et Plastiques, Paris, 1983, Mus. Fine Arts, Budapest, Hungary, 1985, L.A. County Mus. Art, 1986, U.S. Embassy, Moscow, 1988, Szepmuveszeti Muzem, Budapest, 1988, Nat. Gallery of Art, Washington, D.C., 1989, Whitney Mus., N.Y.C., 1989, Ferie Internacional de Arte Contemporaneo, Madrid, Spain, 1991; represented in permanent collections, Mus. Modern Art, N.Y.C., Knox-Albright Mus., N.Y.C., Worcester Art Mus., Smithsonian Instn., Washington, Whitney Mus., Corcoran Mus., Carnegie Inst. Mus. Art, Phillips Collections, Washington, La. Mus. Modern Art, Humlebach, Denmark, New Sch. for Social Rsch., Olympic Sculpture Park, Seoul, S. Korea, Solomon R. Guggenheim Mus., N.Y.C., Univ. Art Mus., Berkeley, Calif., Vassar Coll., Poughkeepsie, N.Y., Yale U. Art Ctr., New Haven, Conn.; stage designs Histoire de Vasco, Paris, 1956; stage design Deathwatch, N.Y.C., 1958. Recipient Nat. Council Arts and Sci., 1966; NEA fellow, 1972; Guggenheim Found. fellow, 1977. Address: 2003 Scuttlehole Rd Bridgehampton NY 11932-0508 Office: Washburn Gallery E 57th St New York NY 10022

YOUNGKEN, HEBER WILKINSON, JR., former university administrator, pharmacy educator; b. Phila., Aug. 13, 1913; s. Heber Wilkinson and Clara (Eastman) Y.; m. Daphne Goodwin, Mar. 28, 1942; children: John R., Richard C. A.B., Bucknell U., 1935; B.S., Mass. Coll. Pharmacy, 1938; M.S., U. Minn., 1940, Ph.D., 1942; student, Harvard Grad. Sch., 1938-39; DSc (hon.), U. R.I., 1992. Asst. biology and pharmacognosy Mass. Coll. Pharmacy, 1935-39; teaching asst. pharmacognosy Coll. Pharmacy, U. Minn., 1939-42; from. instr. to prof. pharmacognosy U. Wash., Seattle, 1942-57; chmn. dept., dir. med. plant lab. U. Wash., 1946-57; prof. pharmacognosy, dean Coll. Pharmacy, U. R.I., 1957-81, v.p. acad. affairs, 1967-68, provost health sci. affairs, 1969-81; vis. prof. U. London, 1970, U. Cairo, Egypt, 1977, 79, 81, 85. Author: (with R. Pratt) Pharmacognosy, 2d edit, 1956, Organic Chemistry in Pharmacy, 1949, Natural Products in Pharmacy; also numerous papers in field. Mem. R.I. Health Care Coordinating Coun., R.I. Gov.'s Justice Commn.; pres. R.I. Health Sci. Edn. Coun., 1976-77; chmn. sect. pharmacognosy/natural products Acad. Pharm. Scis., 1976-77; bd. dirs. R.I. Soc. for Prevention Blindness, Health Data Resources, Inc., R.I. Search; bd. dirs. URI Found., pres. 1984-87. With USNR, 1943-46; now capt. Res. Recipient Edwin L. Newcomb award research pharmacognosy Am. Found. Pharm. Edn., 1951. Fellow Am. Pharm. Assn., Am. Assn. Coll. Pharmacy, AAAS; mem. Soc. Exptl. Biology and Medicine, N.Y. Acad. Sci., Am. Soc. Hosp. Pharmacists, R.I. Pharm. Assn. (Toxicology award 1964, Man of Yr. award 1979, Bowl of Hygeia award 1989), Am. Coll. Apothecary, Soc. Econ. Botany, R.I. Soc. Hosp. Pharmacists, Am. Soc. Pharmacognosy (pres. 1970), Rotarian Club, Sigma Xi, Phi Kappa Phi, Phi Sigma, Rho Chi, Kappa Psi, Phi Kappa Psi. Baptist. Home: 188 Oakwoods Dr Wakefield RI 02879-2533 Office: U RI Coll Pharmacy Kingston RI 02881

YOUNG LIVELY, SANDRA LEE, nurse; b. Rockport, Ind., Dec. 31, 1943; d. William Cody and Flora Juanita (Carver) Thorpe; m. Kenneth Leon Doom, May 4, 1962 (div. 1975); children: Patricia, Anita, Elizabeth, Melissa, Kenny. AS, Vincennes U., 1979, student, U. So. Ind., 1987—. Nursing aide, nurse Forest Del Nursing Home, Princeton, Ind., 1975-80; charge nurse Welborn Bapt. Hosp., Evansville, Ind., 1979-80, 82-83; staff nurse Longview Regional Hosp., Tex., 1980-82; dir. home health Roy H. Laird Meml. Hosp., Kilgore, Tex., 1984-86; med. post-coronary nurse Mercy Hosp., Owensboro, Ky., 1987, Dept. of Corrections charge nurse, Branchville Tng. Ctr., Tell City, Ind, 1987-90; charge nurse dept. mental health Evansville (Ind.) State Hosp., 1990—; staff nurse, asst. dir. Leisure Lodge Home Health, Overton, Tex., 1983-84. Grantee Roy H. Laird Meml. Hosp., 1986. Mem. NAFE, Menniger Found., Vincennes U. Alumni Assn., Internat. Platform Assn. Avocations: writing, research, cake decorating, house plants. Home: 614 Gilmer Rd Apt 251 Longview TX 75604 Office: Evansville State Hosp 3400 Lincoln Ave Evansville IN 47714-0147

YOUNGMAN, HENNY, comedian; m. Sadie Cohen (dec.); children: Gary, Marilyn. Appeared regularly on: radio show Kate Smith, during 1930's, now nightclub and concerts comedian; appears on TV; appeared in: TV series Henny and Rocky, 1955, Joey and Dad, 1975; film Silent Movie, 1976, History of the World, Part I, 1981, The Comeback Trial, 1982, Goodfellows, 1990; recs. include Take My Album...Please, 1978, 128 Greatest Jokes, In Concert, 1987, Bits & Pieces, 1992; author 10 books including: How Do Youe Like ME So Far?, Take My Wife Please, 400 Travelins Salesmen's Jokes, 500 All Time Greatest One-Liners, Don't Put My Name on This Book, Take My Life, Please, Big Book of Insults, 1995. Office: care of Peter Mallon 8051 Shalom Dr Spring Hill FL 34606-6939 *Life should be like a one liner--good to the last word.*

YOUNGMAN, OWEN RALPH, newspaper executive; b. Chgo., Apr. 24, 1953; s. Ralph Elmer and Charlotte Earldine (Ottoson) Y.; m. Linda Ann Erlandson, Aug. 24, 1975. Sportswriter Ashtabula Star-Beacon, Ohio, 1969-71; office clerk Chgo. Tribune, 1971-73, transcriber, 1973-75, copy editor, slotman, 1976-79, copy chief, news editor, 1979-83, dep. sports editor, 1984-86, assoc. met. editor, 1986-88, assoc. features editor, 1988-90, dep. fin. editor, 1990-91, assoc. mng. editor, 1991-93, features editor, 1993-95, mng. editor, features, 1995, dir. interactive media, 1996—. Mem. Evangelical Covenant Ch., Am. Soc. Newspaper Editors, President's Club of North Park Coll., Arts Club of Chgo. Avocations: philately, vocal and instrumental music. Home: 40 Kenmore Ave Deerfield IL 60015-4750 Office: Chicago Tribune 435 N Michigan Ave Chicago IL 60611-4001

YOUNGNER, JULIUS STUART, microbiologist, educator; b. N.Y.C., Oct. 24, 1920; m. Tula Liakakis, 1943 (dec. 1963); children—Stuart, Lisa; m. Rina C. Balter, Aug. 3, 1964. B.A., NYU, 1939; M.S., U. Mich., 1941, Sc.D., 1944. Diplomate: Am. Acad. Microbiology. Teaching asst. dept. microbiology Sch. Medicine, U. Mich., 1941-43, instr., 1946-47; scientist Nat. Cancer Inst., Bethesda, Md., 1949; asst. prof. Virus Research Lab., U. Pitts., 1949-56, asso. prof. dept. microbiology, Sch. Medicine, 1956-60, prof., 1960—; chmn. dept. microbiology Virus Research Lab., U. Pitts. (Sch. Medicine), 1966-85, chmn. dept. microbiology, biochemistry, and molecular biology, 1985-89, Disting. Svc. prof., 1989—; vis. prof. dept. microbiology, Faculty Medicine U. Athens, Greece, 1963; F.G. Novy meml. lectr. Sch. Medicine, U. Mich., 1965; nat. lectr. Found. for Microbiology, 1972-73; 6th ann. Lippard meml. lectr. Coll. Physicians and Surgeons, Columbia U., 1980; mem. study sect. virology and rickettsiology USPHS, NIH, 1965-69; mem. bd. sci. councilors Nat. Inst. Allergy and Infectious Diseases, 1970-74, chmn., 1973-74, mem. task force on virology, 1976-77; mem. clin. a fellowship study sect. NIH, 1979-80; mem. adv. group to microbiology program Am. Inst. Biol. Scis., 1970-73; asso. mem. commn. on influenza Armed Forces Epidemiol. Bd., Dept. Def., 1959-69, mem., 1970-73; com. .on biomed. research and research tng. Am. Assn. Med. Colls., 1973-75; cons. to surgeon gen. Dept. Army, 1973-76. Contbr. chpts. to books, articles to sci. jours. Referee Macy faculty scholar award program Josiah Macy, Jr., Found., 1977; mem. study group immunology and infectious diseases Health Research Services Found., 1959-79, chmn., 1978-79; mem. microbiology and virology study group Am. Cancer Soc., 1981-85, chmn., 1985. Served with U.S. Army, 1944-46; with USPHS, 1947-49. E.I. du Pont de Nemours & Co. ednl. aid grantee, 1973. Fellow Hellenic Soc. Microbiology and Hygiene (hon. fgn.); mem. AAAS, AAUP, Am. Soc. Microbiology (chmn. sect. T 1981—, mem. com. med. microbiology and immunology, bd. pub. and sci. affairs 1981—), Am. Soc. Virology (pres.-elect 1985-86, pres. 1986-87), Soc. for Gen. Microbiology, Am. Assn. Immunologists, Infectious Diseases Soc. Am., Assn. Med. Microbiology Chmn. (pres.), Am. Acad. Microbiology (bd. govs. 1985-91), Am. Type Culture Collection (bd. dirs. 1992-95, chmn. bd. sci. dirs. 1995—), Internat. Soc. Interferon and Cytokine Rsch. (hon.). Office: U Pitts Dept Molecular Genetics & Biochemistry Pittsburgh PA 15261

YOUNG-OSKEY, SUSAN MARIE, elementary education educator; b. Astoria, N.Y., July 30, 1964; d. Thomas Bernard and Carole Marion (Fleming) Y. AA, Suffolk Coll., 1987; BA, Dowling Coll., 1989; MA in Liberal Studies Edn., SUNY, Stony Brook, 1992. Kindergarten asst. tchr. First Steps Sch., East Setauket, N.Y., 1986-88, pre-kindergarten/toddler tchr., 1989-90; kindergarten/pre-kindergarten tchr. Our Lady of Lourdes Sch., West Islip, N.Y., 1990-94, tchr. 1st grade, 1994—. Vol. Rainbow Program Our Lady of Lourdes Parish, 1992. Mem. Reading Specialists Coun. Suffolk (reading specialist 1990-91). Republican. Home: 755 Expressway Dr N Medford NY 11763

YOUNGQUIST, ALVIN MENVID, JR., publisher, editor; b. Toledo, Oct. 9, 1925; s. Alvin Menvid and Elsie W. (Bostock) Y.; m. Judith Jackett, June 13, 1953. B.S., Northwestern U. Sch. Bus., 1950; postgrad., Sch. Journalism, 1951. Editor: Bankers Monthly, Skokie, Ill., 1953-70; editor, pres., pub.: Bankers Monthly, Inc, Northbrook, Ill., 1971-85, cons. editor, 1985—. Served with USNR, 1943-46. Mem. U.S. Power Squadrons (Skokie Valley), U.S. Sailing Assn., White Lake Yacht Club. Republican. Episcopalian. Home and Office: 1410 S Mears Ave Whitehall MI 49461-1737

YOUNGQUIST, ANDREW LANCE, construction executive; b. Newport Beach, Calif., Nov. 30, 1940; s. Vincent R. and Elizabeth (Tebbs) Y.; children: Bill, Jennifer; m. Linda Kay, May 17, 1980. Student, Orange Coast Coll. Pres. Decco Constrn., Orange, Calif., 1970-78; v.p. Capitol Systems, Newport Beach, 1976-77; with Saffell & McAdam, Irvine, Calif., 1977-79; pres. MBK Constrn., Ltd., Irvine, 1979—. Dir. Girl Scout Coun., Orange Empire, Girl Scouts U.S., 1991; bd. mem. Orange County Together. Mem. Nat. Assn. Indsl. Office Pks., Internat. Coun. Shopping Ctrs., Associated Gen. Contractors (bd. mem. Orange County dist.), Bldg. Industry Assn., Balboa Bay Club, Pacific Anglers. Republican. Home: 1851 Braemer Way Newport Beach CA 92660-3724 Office: MBK Constrn Ltd 175 Technology Dr Irvine CA 92718

YOUNGQUIST, WALTER LEWELLYN, consulting geologist; b. Mpls., May 5, 1921; s. Walter Raymond and Selma Regina (Knock) Y.; m. Elizabeth Salome Pearson, Dec. 11, 1943; children: John, Karen, Louise, Robert. BA, Gustavus Adolphus Coll., St. Peter, Minn., 1942; MSc, U. Iowa, 1943, PhD, 1948. Registered profl. geologist, Oreg. Jr. geologist U.S. Geol. Survey, 1943-44; rsch. assoc. U. Iowa, Iowa City, 1945-48; asst. prof. geology U. Idaho, Moscow, 1948-51; sr. geologist Internat. Petroleum Co., Talara, Peru, 1951-54; prof. geology U. Kans., Lawrence, 1954-57, U. Oreg., Eugene, 1957-66; cons. geologist Minerals dept. Exxon Corp., Houston, 1968-73; geothermal cons. Eugene Water & Electric Bd., 1973-92; ind. cons. Eugene, 1992—. Author: Investing in Natural Resources, 1980, Mineral Resources and the Destinies of Nations, 1990, Geodestinies, 1996; co-author: Ordovician Cephalopod Fauna of Baffin Island, 1954. Ensign, USNR, 1944-45. Recipient Lowden Prize in Geology, U. Iowa, 1943. Fellow AAAS, Geol. Soc. Am.; mem. Am. Assn. Petroleum Geologists, Geothermal Resources Coun., N.W. Energy Assn. Lutheran. Avocations: fly-tying, photography, fishing. Office: PO Box 5501 Eugene OR 97405-0501

YOUNGREN, RALPH PARK, architect; b. Cloquet, Minn., Dec. 26, 1924; s. Andrew Frederick and Eunice (Park) Y.; m. Ann Henderson, June 28, 1962; children: Todd Park, Malcolm Park. AB, Harvard U., 1948, BArch, MArch, 1950. Assoc. ptnr. Skidmore, Owings & Merrill, Chgo., 1950-67; pres. Metz, Train, Youngren, Chgo., 1967-84; sr. v.p., dir. design Smith, Hinchman & Grylls, Detroit, 1985-93; sr. cons. designer Smith, Hinchman & Grylis, Detroit, 1994—; archtl. advisor Chgo. Dept. Urban Renewal, 1962. Designer Regenstein Library, Chgo., Rush Med. Coll., Chgo., Beckman Inst., Urbana, Ill., Chrysler Corp., Auburn Hills Corp. Hdqs. Bd. dirs. Greening of Detroit Commn. Staff sgt. U.S. Army, 1943-45, ETO. Fellow AIA (bd. dirs. Chgo. chpt. 1976-78, R.J. Reynolds award 1964), Chgo. Archtl. Found. (trustee 1969-85), Thomas Jefferson Found. (trustee 1972-74), Friends of Modern Art (bd. dirs.), Detroit Inst. Art. Home: 1045 Cedar Bend Dr Ann Arbor MI 48105-2377 Office: Smith Hinchman & Grylls Assoc Inc 150 W Jefferson Ave Ste 100 Detroit MI 48226-4415

YOUNGS, JACK MARVIN, cost engineer; b. Bklyn., May 2, 1941; s. Jack William and Virginia May (Clark) Y.; BEngring., CCNY, 1964; MBA, San Diego State U., 1973; m. Alexandra Marie Robertson, Oct. 31, 1964; 1 child, Christine Marie. Mass properties engr. Gen. Dynamics Corp., San Diego, 1964-68, rsch. engr., 1968-69, sr. rsch. engr., 1969-80, sr. cost devel. engr., 1980-81, cost devel. engring. specialist, 1981—; prin. estimator Martin Marietta Astronautics, 1994-95, Lockheed Martin Astronautics, 1995—. Dist. dir. Scripps Ranch Civic Assn., 1976-79; pres. Scripps Ranch Swim Team, 1980-82; dir., 1986-87; judge Greater San Diego Sci. and Engring. Fair, 1981-92. Mem. Princeton U. Parents Assn. Recipient 5th place award World Body Surfing Championships, 1987, 6th place award, 1988. Mem. AIAA, N.Y. Acad. Scis., Alumni Assn, CUNY, Bklyn. Tech. High Sch. Alumni Assn., Inst. Cost Analysis (cert., charter mem., treas. Greater San Diego chpt. 1986-90), Soc. Cost Estimating and Analysis (cert. cost estimator/analyst, pres. San Diego chpt. 1990-91), Internat. Soc. Parametric Analysts (bd. dirs. San Diego chpt. 1987-90), Nat. Mgmt. Assn. (space systems div. charter mem. 1985, award of honor Convair chpt. 1975), Assn. MBA Execs., San Diego State U. Bus. Alumni Assn. (charter mem. 1986), Scripps Ranch Swim and Racquet Club (dir. 1977-80, treas. 1978-79, pres. 1979-80), Beta Gamma Sigma, Chi Epsilon, Sigma Iota Epsilon. Lutheran. Research in life cycle costing and econ. analysis. Home: 11461 Tribuna Ave San Diego CA 92131-1907 Office: PO Box 85990 San Diego CA 92186-5990

YOUNGS, WILEY JAY, chemistry educator; b. Gouverneur, N.Y., July 5, 1949; s. Randolph Churchill and Beulah Aurelia (Hilton) Y.; m. Claire Adrienne Tessier, Apr. 1, 1978; children: Jessica Tessier, Kelly Lynn. BA in Psychology, SUNY at Albany, 1972; postgrad., State Univ. Coll. at Potsdam, N.Y., 1973-74; PhD, SUNY, Buffalo, 1980. Postdoctoral fellow Northwestern U., Evanston, Ill., 1980-83; asst. prof. chemistry Case Western Res. U., Cleve., 1983-89, assoc. prof., 1989-90; assoc. prof. U. Akron, Ohio, 1990-93, prof., 1993—; cons. Sandoz-AGRO, Chgo., 1993-95. Contbr. numerous articles to profl. jours.; reviewer NSF and PRF rsch. proposals. Mem. Buchtel Coll. Coun. Mem. Am. Chem. Soc. (sec. Cleve. sect. 1989, inorganic topical group chmn. 1988-90), Am. Crystallographic Assn., AAAS. Achievements include patents in field. Office: U Akron Dept Chemistry Akron OH 44329

YOUNGWOOD, ALFRED DONALD, lawyer; b. N.Y.C., Apr. 27, 1938; s. Milton and Lillian (Ginsburg) Y.; m. Judith Goldfarb, June 24, 1963; children: Jonathan David, Stephen Michael. BA magna cum laude, Yale U., 1959; LLB magna cum laude, Harvard U., 1962. Bar: N.Y. 1962, D.C. 1970, U.S. Tax Ct. 1964, U.S. Ct. Appeals (2d cir.) 1969. Law clk. to judge U.S. Dist. Ct. N.Y., 1962-63; assoc. Paul, Weiss, Rifkind, Wharton & Garrison, N.Y.C., 1964-70, ptnr., 1970—. Fulbright scholar, London, 1963-64. Fellow Am. Coll. Tax Counsel; mem. ABA, N.Y. State Bar Assn. (chmn. tax sect. 1978-79, exec. com. 1971—, ho. of dels. 1979-80), Assn. of Bar of City of N.Y. Home: 1125 Park Ave New York NY 10128-1243 Office: Paul Weiss Rifkind Wharton 1285 Ave Of The Americas New York NY 10019-6028

YOUNT, DAVID EUGENE, physicist, educator; b. Prescott, Ariz., June 5, 1935; s. Robert Ephram and Jeannette Francis (Judson) Y.; m. Christel Marlene Notz, Feb. 22, 1975; children—Laura Christine, Gregory Gordon, Steffen Jurgen Robert, Sonja Kate Jeannette. B.S. in Physics, Calif. Inst. Tech., 1957; M.S. in Physics, Stanford U., 1959, Ph.D. in Physics, 1963. Instr. Princeton U., 1962-63, asst. prof. physics, 1963-64, Minn. Mining and Mfg. fellow, 1963; NSF postdoctoral fellow U. Paris, Orsay, France, 1964-65; rsch. assoc. Stanford Linear Accelerator Ctr. Stanford U., 1965-69; assoc. prof. U. Hawaii, 1969-73, prof., 1973—, chmn. dept. physics and astronomy, 1979-85, acting asst. v.p. for acad. affairs, 1985-86, v.p. rsch. and grad. edn., 1986-95. Author: Who Runs the University: The Politics of Higher Education in Hawaii, 1985-92. Mem. Am. Phys. Soc., Undersea and Hyperbaric Med. Soc., Am. Chem. Soc., U.S. Tennis Assn., Sigma Xi. Republican. Lutheran. Achievements include development (with J. Pine) of first high-energy positron beam, (with others) of SLAC two-meter streamer chamber; discovery (with others) of rho (1600) and psi (3772) mesons; development and experimental verification of theoretical model describing the nuclei which initiate bubble formation in aqueous media, including blood and tissue. Home: 5468 Opihi St Honolulu HI 96821-1924 Office: U Hawaii 2505 Correa Rd Honolulu HI 96822-2219 *Actualizing my potential is the central theme of my life. I have the potential to work, to play, to learn, to love, to teach, and to understand. These are not conscious goals so much as forces which motivate my behavior. I work very hard, not for success, but because fulfillment requires an effort. I try to be honest, not as a goal, but because dishonesty interferes with learning, loving, teaching and understanding. I enjoy children, not because I'm an affectionate adult, but because I see that we are involved in the same process.*

YOUNTS, SANFORD EUGENE, university administrator; b. Davidson County, N.C., Aug. 29, 1930; m. Ruth Wilson; children—Gregory Sanford, Leslie Joan. B.S., N.C. State U., 1952, M.S., 1955; Ph.D., Cornell U., 1957. Asst. prof. agronomy U. Md., College Park, 1957-59; eastern agronomist Am. Potash Inst., 1959-60; assoc. prof. N.C. State U., Raleigh, 1960-64; southern regional dir. Potash Inst. N.Am., 1964-67, v.p., 1967-69; dir. rural devel. ctr. U. Ga., Tifton, 1969-72; v.p. for services U. Ga., Athens, 1972—. Editor: (with others) Potassium in Agriculture, 1966, monographs on soil fertility; contbr. articles to profl. jours. Co-chmn., bd. trustees Ctr. for PVO/Univ. Collaboration in Devel., Cullowhee, N.C.; chmn. State Heart Fund Campaign, Ga., 1983, 84; chmn. bd. trustees South-East Consortium, Chapel Hill, N.C., 1981. Named Outstanding Prof., N.C. State U., 1963, Disting. Alumnus, N.C. State U. Coll. Agr. and Life Scis.; recipient Order of May Decoration, Argentine Govt., 1994. Fellow Soil Sci. Soc. Am., Am. Soc. Agronomy, Crop Sci. Soc. Am.; mem. AAAS, Phi Kappa Phi. Lodge: Kiwanis (pres. 1976, disting. pres. 1977). Office: U Ga 300 Old College Athens GA 30602

YOUREE, BEVERLY B., library science educator; b. Jackson, Tenn., Mar. 29, 1948; d. Beverly Durward and Rebecca Wade B.; m. Mack Moore Youree, May 26, 1973; 1 child, Roderick Buford. BA, Union U., 1969; MLS, Peabody Coll., 1970; EdD, Vanderbilt U., 1984. Reserves circulation libr. Mid. Tenn. State U., Murfreesboro, 1970-74, instr. libr. sci., 1974—, mem. faculty senate, 1984-90, sec.-treas., 1987-88; chmn. vis. coms. So. Assn. Evaluation Teams, 1989—; pres. Concerned Faculty and Adminstrv. Women, 1986-90. Contbr. articles to profl. jours. State founder, coord. Tenn. Exhibitors' and Media Profls. Tour; mem. adv. bd. John Wiley & Sons Pub. Co., 1991—; active Middle Tenn. State U.; mem. faculty senate, 1984-90, sec.-treas., 1987-88, mem. unvi. libr. com., 1981-83, sec. 1981-82; mem. ad hoc com. on edn., curriculum svc. and facilities, 1975-76; mem. faculty senate legis. com., 1980-83, sec. 81-83; mem. non-instructional assignment semester com., 1988-90, sec. 88-89, chair 89-90; mem. com. on status of women, 1988-94; mem. grad. coun., 1988-90; active So. Assn. Evaluation Teams, chair vis. coms., 1989, 90, 91, 92, 93, 94; pres. Concerned Faculty and Adminstrv. Women, 1986-90; chmn. Commn. on Status of Women, 1994—. Mem. ALA (mem. state liaison to young adult svcs. divsn. 1988—, mem. outstanding theatre for the college bound list revision com. 1988), NEA, Tenn. Libr. Assn. (chair libr. edn. sect. 1979-80, 88-89, chair vol. state book award com. 1980—, co-chair exhibits for state conv. 1985—, Frances Neal Cheney award 1993), Southeastern Libr. Assn. (sec. sch. libr. sect. 1986-88, chair-elect sch. libr. sect. 1988-90, chair, 1990-92, co-chair exhibits for conv. 1988-90, 90-92), Tenn. Edn. Assn. (sec. higher edn. dept. 1989-93, pres. 1993-95, mem. instructional and prof. devel. commn. 1991-94, past pres. and sec. Middle Tenn. State U. chpt.), Tenn. Assn. Sch., Librs., Middle Tenn. Edn. Assn., Assembly Literature for Adolescents, Soc. Sch. Librs. Internat. (mem. legis. task force 1988-89), Kappa Delta Pi (mem. nominating com. mem. 1991-92, mem. Theta Omicron chpt., treas, 1981—, assoc. counselor 1983-86, counselor 1987-94, Svc. to Edn. award), Phi Delta Kappa. Democrat. So. Baptist. Avocations: knitting, reading, needlepoint. Home: 3567 Castlewood Dr Murfreesboro TN 37129-4605 Office: Middle Tenn State U Dept Ednl Leadership PO Box 184 Murfreesboro TN 37132-0184

YOURZAK, ROBERT JOSEPH, management consultant, engineer, educator; b. Mpls., Aug. 27, 1947; s. Ruth Phyllis Sorenson. BCE, U. Minn., 1969; MSCE, U. Wash., 1971, MBA, 1975. Registered profl. engr., Wash., Minn. Surveyor N.C. Hoium & Assocs., Mpls., 1965-68, Lot Surveys Co., Mpls., 1968-69; site layout engr. Sheehy Constrn. Co., St. Paul, 1968; structural engring. aide Dunham Assocs., Mpls., 1969; aircraft and aerospace structural engr., program rep. Boeing Co., Seattle, 1969-75; engr., estimator Howard S. Wright Constrn. Co., Seattle, 1976-77; dir. project devel. and adminstrn. DeLeuw Cather & Co., Seattle, 1977-78; sr. mgmt. cons. Alexander Grant & Co., Mpls., 1978-79; mgr. project systems dept., project mgr. Henningson, Durham & Richardson, Mpls., 1979-80; dir. project mgmt., regional offices Ellerbe Assocs., Inc., Mpls., 1980-81; pres. Robert Yourzak & Assocs., Inc. Mpls., 1982—; lectr. engring. mgmt. U. Wash., 1977-78; lectr., adj. asst. prof. dept. civil and mineral engring. and mech./indsl. engring. Ctr. For Devel. of Tech. Leadership, Inst. Tech.; mgmt. scis. dept. Sch. Mgmt. U. Minn., 1979-90, bd. adv. inst. tech., 1989-93; founding mem., membership com., mem. Univ. of Minn. com. Minn. High Tech. Coun., 1983-95; speaker in field. Author: Project Management and Motivating and Managing the Project Team, 1984. Chmn. regional art group experience Seattle Art Mus., 1975-78; mem. Pacific N.W. Arts Council, 1977-78, ex-officio adviser Mus. Week, 1976; bd. dirs. Friends of the Rep. Seattle Repertory Theatre, 1973-77; mem. Symphonics Seattle Symphony Orch., 1975-78. Scholar Boeing Co., 1967-68, Sheehy Constrn. Co., summer 1967. Named An Outstanding Young Man of Am., U.S. Jaycees, 1978. Fellow Project Mgmt. Inst. (cert. project mgmt. profl., speaker, founding pres. 1985, chmn., adv. com. 1987-89, bd. dirs. 1984-86, program com. chmn. and organizing com. mem. Minn. chpt. 1984, speaker, project mgr. internat. mktg. program 1985-86, chmn. internat. mktg. standing com. 1986, long range and strategic planning com. 1988-93, chmn., 1992, v.p. pub. rels. 1987-88, ex-officio dir. 1989, 1992, internat. pres. 1990, chmn. bd. 1991, ex-officio chmn. 1992, internat. bd. dirs., chmn. nominating com. 1992); mem. ASTD (So. Minn. chpt.), Am. Cons. Engrs. Coun. (peer reviewer 1986-89), Am. Arbitration Assn. (mem. Mpls. panel of constrn. arbitrators), Minn. Surveyors and Engrs. Soc., ASCE (chmn. continuing edn. subcom. Seattle chpt. 1976-79, chmn. program com. 1978, mem. transp. and urban planning tech. group 1978, Edmund Friedman Young Engr. award 1979, chmn. continuing edn. subcom. 1979-80, chmn. energy com. Minn. chpt. 1980-81, bd. dir. 1981-89, sec. 1981-83, v.p. profl. svcs. 1983-84, v.p. info. svcs. 1984-85, pres. 1986-87, past pres. 1987-89, fellow 1988—, speaker), Inst. Indsl. Engrs. (pres. Twin Cities chpt. 1985-86, chmn. program com. 1983-84, bd. dirs. 1985-88, awards com., chmn. 1984-89, speaker), Cons. Engrs. Council Minn. (chmn. pub. rels. com. 1983-85, vice chmn., 1988, chmn., 1989, program com. chmn. Midwest engrs. conf. and exposition 1985-90, speaker, Honor award 1992), Inst. Mgmt. Cons. (cert. mgmt. cons.), Mpls. Soc. Fine Arts, Internat. Facility Mgmt. Assn., Am. Soc. Engring. Edn., Rainer Club (co-chmn. Oktoberfest), Sierra Club, Chowder Soc., Mountaineers, North Star Ski Touring, Chi Epsilon (life). Office: 7320 Gallagher Dr Ste 325 Minneapolis MN 55435-4510

YOUSUFF, SARAH SAFIA, physician; b. Binghampton, N.Y., Dec. 8, 1960; d. Mohamed and Razia (Sivaramasastry) Y.; m. Donald John Sudy, Aug. 7, 1993. BA in Zoology, U. Tex., Austin, 1982; MD, U. Tex., 1988. Diplomate Am. Bd. Anesthesiology, Am. Bd. Pain Medicine. Fellow in med. mgmt. U. N.C., Chapel Hill, 1992-93; resident in anesthesiology U. Wash., Seattle, 1988-92; staff anesthesiologist Krōn Med., Research Triangle Park, N.C., 1992-94; med. dir. dept. anesthesiology Southwest Hosp., Little Rock, Ark., 1994—; pres. Southwest Anesthesia Assocs., Little Rock, 1994-95; ptnr. Pain Cons. Ark., 1995—; dir. Southwest Pain Mgmt. Clinic, Little Rock, 1995—. capt. USAR, 1990—. Mem. AMA, Am. Soc. Anesthesiology, Am. Coll. Physician Execs., Ark. Med. Soc., Pulaski County Med. Soc. Avocations: photography, international travel, computers, international healthcare. Home: 18 Edenfield Cv Little Rock AR 72212-2667 Office: Southwest Pain Mgmt Clinic 11401 Interstate 30 Little Rock AR 72209

YOUTCHEFF, JOHN SHELDON, physicist; b. Newark, Apr. 16, 1925; s. Slav Joseph and Florence Catherine (Davidson) Y.; A.B., Columbia, 1949, B.S., 1950; Ph.D., U. Calif. at Los Angeles, 1953; m. Elsie Marianne, June 17, 1950; children: Karen Janette, John Sheldon, Mark Allen, Heidi Mary Anne, Lisa Ellen. Ops. analyst Gen. Electric Co., Ithaca, N.Y., 1953-56, cons. engr. Missile & Space Div., Phila., 1956-64, mgr. advanced reliability programs, 1964-72; mgr. reliability and maintainability Litton Industries, College Pk., Md., 1972-73; program mgr. U.S. Postal Service Hdqrs., Washington, 1973—; instr. U. Pa., 1965-66, Villanova U., 1957—. Served to lt. USAAF, 1943-46; to comdr. USNR, 1946—. Registered profl. engr., Calif., D.C. Fellow AAAS, British Interplanetary Soc., Am. Inst. Aero. and Astronautics (asso.); mem. IEEE (sr.), Ops. Research Soc., Research Soc. Am., Am. Math. Soc., Am. Physics Soc., Am. Chem. Soc., Am. Astron. Soc., Am. Geol. Soc., Nat. Soc. Profl. Engrs., Engring. and Tech. Socs. Council Del. Valley (speakers bur.), Res. Officers Assn., Am. Legion. Roman Catholic. Clubs: Explorers (N.Y.C.), Optimists Internat. (pres. Valley Forge chpt. 1970-71). Holder 3 U.S. patents; contbr. articles to profl. jours. and proc. Home: 1400 S Joyce St Apt 540 Arlington VA 22202-1822 Office: L'Enfant Plz Washington DC 20260

YOVICH, DANIEL JOHN, educator; b. Chgo., Mar. 5, 1930; s. Milan D. and Sophie (Dorociak) Y.; m. Anita Barbara Moreland, Feb. 7, 1959; children: Daniel, Amy, David, Julie Ann. Ph.B., DePaul U., 1952; M.A., Governors State U., 1975, M.S., 1976. Cert. reality therapist, cert. profl. mgr., PMA instr. Formulator Nat. Lead Co., 1950-52, 56-59; researcher Montgomery Ward, Chgo., 1959-62; tech. dir. Riley Bros., Inc., Burlington, Iowa, 1962-66, Mortell Co., Kankakee, Ill., 1966-70; exec. dir. Dan Yovich Assos., 1970-79; asst. prof. Purdue U., Hammond, Ind., 1979-84, assoc. prof., 1984-90, prof., 1990—; instr. Army Security Agy. Sch., 1954-56; instr. Napoleon Hill Acad., 1965-66; cons. Learning House, Inc., 1964—; instr. Kankakee C. C. Continuing Edn., 1976; assoc. Hill, Zediker & Assocs. Psychologists, Kankakee, 1975-79; mem adv. bd. Nat. Congress of Inventor Orgns., 1984. Author: Applied Creativity; prdr., moderator: (program) Careers Unlimited, Sta. WCIU-TV, Chgo., 1967; contbr. articles to profl. jours. Mem. community adv. council Governors State U., 1978. Served to 1st lt. AUS, 1952-56. Recipient Outstanding Citizen Award News Pub. Co. Am., 1971, Outstanding Tchr. award Purdue U., 1980, 82, 83, Faculty Service award Nat. U. Continuing Edn. Assn., 1984, Disting. Service award Purdue U.-Calumet Alumni Assn., 1988, Arthur Young award Venture Mag., 1988. Mem. World Future Soc., Nat. Mgmt. Assn., Am. Soc. Tng. and Devel., Am. Soc. Profl. Supervision (exec. sec. 1986), Inventors and Entrepreneurs Soc. Ind. (founder, exec. dir. 1984), Global Intuition Network, Internat. Creativity Network, Infantry Officer Cand. Sch. Alumni Assn. (life), Napoleon Hill Found., Inst. Reality Therapy, Inst. Contemporary Living, Soc. Am. Inventors (life), Am. Legion, K.C. Patentee game Krypto, coating Sanitane. Home: 6736 Waveland Ave Hammond IN 46323-1444 Office: Purdue U (Calumet) 2200 169th St Hammond IN 46323-2068

YOVICICH, GEORGE STEVEN JONES, civil engineer; b. Belgrade, Yugoslavia, June 2, 1929; s. Steven and Draginja (Djurdjevic) Y.; m. Sofija Sckulic, Feb. 3, 1960; 1 son, Steven. B.S. in Civil Engring, High Tech. Sch., Belgrade; M.S.C.E., U. Darmstadt, Germany, 1956; Ph.D. in Bus. and Adminstrn, U. Fla. Registered profl. engr., Ill. and other states. Civil engr. Hollabird & Root, Chgo., 1956-58; bridge engr. Div. Hwys. Ill. Dept. Transp., Chgo., 1958-70; v.p.-project mgr. Arcadia Internat. & Co., Skokie, Ill., 1956-70, chmn. bd., pres., 1970—; chmn. bd. Arcadia Engring. Internat. Inc.; pres. Arcadia Internat. Inc., 1974—; v.p. Hoppmann & Assocs. Inc., Evanston, Ill., 1987—; projects mgr. Midwest, Granite Constrn. Co.; Prof. structural engring. Northwestern U.; prof. math. and structural engring. U. Ill. at Chgo. and Urbana; v.p. Arcadia Nat. Builders; mem. bd. trustees Mchts. Funds Bank, Internat. Bank, Miami, Fla. Legis. asst., mem. hwys. com., mem. traffic safety com., utilities com., r.r. and aviation com., welfare com., Ill. Ho. of Reps., 1970—; advisor Internat. Parliment for Safety and Peace, UN; bd. dirs. Oakton C.C., Skokie, Sch. Dist. 68, Skokie. Maj. AUS, 1954-56. Mem. ASCE, Registered Profl. Engrs. Soc.

YOVITS, MARSHALL CLINTON, computer and information science educator, university dean; b. Bklyn., May 16, 1923; s. Louis Frederick and Rebecca (Gerber) Y.; m. Anita S. Friedman, Aug. 2, 1952; children: Bruce J., Mara F., Steven. B.S., Union Coll., Schenectady, 1944, M.S., 1948; M.S., Yale U., 1949, Ph.D., 1951. Sr. physicist John Hopkins U., 1951-56; physicist electronics br. Office Naval Rsch., Washington, 1956, head info. systems br., 1956-62; dir. Naval Analysis Group, 1962-66; prof., chmn. dept. computer and info. sci. Ohio State U., 1966-78, prof., 1978-79; prof. computer and info. sci. Sch. of Sci., Ind. U., Purdue U., Indpls., 1980—, dean., 1980-93; prof. emeritus Ind. U., Purdue U., Indpls., 1993—; gen. chmn. Computer Sci. conf. NSF, 1973. Editor: (with Scott Cameron) Self-Organizing Systems, Proc. Interdisciplinary Conf., 1960, Large-Capacity Memory Techniques for Computing Systems, 1961 (with George T. Jacobi, Gordon D. Goldstein) Self-Organizing Systems, 1962, (with D.M. Gilford, R.H. Wilcox, E. Staveley, H.D. Lerner) Research Program Effectiveness, 1966, Advances in Computers, Vol. 11, 1971; editor: series Advances in Computers, Vols. 13-40; contbr. rsch. articles to profl. jours. AEC fellow, 1950-51, Indpls. Ctr. Advanced Rsch. fellow, 1988-89; recipient Navy Superior Civilian Service award, 1964; Navy Outstanding Performance award, 1961. Fellow AAAS (chmn. coun. sect. T 1985-88, chmn. 1996), IEEE (computer soc. chmn. awards com. 1989, bd. govs. 1988-89, computer pioneer award 1990), Assn. for Computing Machinery (coun., gen. chmn. computer sci. conf. 1982), EDUCOM (nominating com.), Sigma Xi. Home: 9016 Dewberry Ct Indianapolis IN 46260-1527

YOW, KAY, university athletic coach. Head coach N.C. State U., Raleigh, 1975—. Office: NC State U Box 8501 Case Athletics Ctr Raleigh NC 27695-8501

YOW, THOMAS SIDNEY, III, college administrator; b. Raleigh, N.C., July 12, 1943; s. Thomas Sidney Jr. and Christine (Southerland) Y.; m. Julia Lee Bryson, June 4, 1967; children: Robert, Steve. BA, Meth. Coll., 1966; MDiv, Duke U., 1971, EdD, 1982; DD, Meth. Coll., 1989. Dir. admissions, fin. aid Meth. Coll., Fayetteville, N.C., 1973-77; asst. to pres. Louisburg (N.C.) Coll., 1977-85; pres. Martin Meth. Coll., Pulaski, Tenn., 1985-91, Young Harris (Ga.) Coll., 1991—; bd. dirs. Towns County Bank, Hiawassee, Ga. Bd. dirs. Blue Ridge EMC, Young Harris, Ga., 1994—, Cub Scouts, Louisburg, 1977; mem. commn. on colls. SACS, 1994—; mem. nat. adv. com. Atlanta Com. Olympic Games, 1992-96; mem. Ga. Student Fin. Commn., 1996—. Paul Harris fellow, 1988; Olympic torchbearer, 1996. Mem. Ga. Pvt. Coll. Assn. (pres. 1996—), Towns County C. of C. (bd. dirs. 1992-95). Office: Young Harris Coll Young Harris GA 30582

YRIGOYEN, CHARLES, JR., church denomination executive; b. Phila., Dec. 9, 1937; s. Charles and Erma Mae (Suters) Y.; m. Jeanette Alice Brittingham, Dec. 13, 1958; children: Debra Jean, Charles III. BS in Econs., U. Pa., 1959; BD, Lancaster (Pa.) Theol. Sem., 1962; ThM, Ea. Bapt. Theol. Sem., Phila., 1964; PhD, Temple U., 1973; DD (hon.), Albright Coll., 1987. Ordained to ministry United Meth. Ch., 1960. Pastor various chs. Meth. Ch., Pa., 1958-66; campus min. Meth. Ch., Phila., 1966-68; chaplain, prof. religion Albright Coll., Reading, Pa., 1968-82; gen. sec. Gen. Com. on Archives and History, United Meth. Ch., Madison, N.J., 1982—; vis. scholar Union Theol. Sem., N.Y.C., 1980, adj. prof., 1982-93; adj. prof. ch. history Drew U., Madison, 1982—; adj. prof. Moravian Theol. Sem., Bethlehem, Pa., 1994—; mem. exec. com. World Meth. Coun., 1986—; bd. dirs. Wesley Works Editl. Project. Author: Acts for Our Time, 1987, John Wesley: Holiness of Heart and Life, 1996; editor: Reformed and Catholic, 1978, Catholic and Reformed, 1979, Historical Dictionary of Methodism, 1996, Meth. History Jour., 1982—. Trustee Ocean City (N.J.) Tabernacle Assn. Masland fellow Union Theol. Sem., 1975, 80. Mem. World Meth. Hist. Soc. (gen. sec. 1987—), Wesley Hist. Soc., Wesleyan Theol. Soc., Am. Soc. Ch. History, Charles Wesley Soc. Republican. Home: 2 Hemlock Ln Morristown NJ 07960-6774 Office: Gen Com on Archives and History PO Box 127 Madison NJ 07940

YRIZARRY, ADITA LIVIA, fitness instructor; b. Victorville, Calif.; d. Jose Mercedes and Ada Nivia (Carrasquillo) Y. Fitness instr. cert., U. Tex., 1983; exercise sci. cert., U. Miami, 1987. Cert. aerobic and fitness tng. and step Reebok Aerobic Fitness Assn. Am.; personal tng. crt. Am. Coun. Exercise; cert. group leader Cooper Inst. Aerobic Rsch. Program mgr. Purley Physical, San Antonio, 1980-83; club dir. Broadway Workout, San Antonio, 1983-86; pres., owner Profl. Fitness, Inc., San Antonio, Miami, Tex., Fla., 1986—; cons., step Reebok examiner Aerobic Fitness Assn. Am.; fitness cons. for Med. and Travel Related Fitness Programs; physical tng. dir. Biltmore Hotel Fitness Ctr. and Spa; guest lectr. on fitness and health Jr. High Schs. Tex., Fla.; judge of many aerobics competitions including AAU Team Aerobic Dance, Costa Rica Step Championship, Reebok Nat. Aerobic Championship, Chile Nat. Aerobic Championship; adv. bd. Reebok Internat. CORPS, Muscle Mixes Music Impact Team, Sesamo Prodns. , Santiago, Chile; CEU provider AFAA, Am. Coun. Exercise; spokesperson Exerbar, Spri Products. Presentations include Cen. Am. Conv. Costa Rica, Congress Internat. Aerobics, Valencia, Spain, Body Factory, Madrid, Ctrl. Sportu Bergamo, Italy, Univ Miami, 12th St Gym, Phila., Weston Athletic Club, Ft. Lauderdale, Fla., Fisher Island (Fla.) Spa, Univ. Met., Santiago, Chile. Chmn. Dance for Health Am. Heart Assn., San Antonio, 1983, Workout for Hope, City of Hope, Miami, 1993; vol. Am. Cancer Soc., Miami, 1992—. Recipient 1st place honor Fitness Sanctioning Body, San Antonio, Hon. mention, Am. Heart Assn., San Antonio, 1985, 88. Mem. Nat. Acad. Sports Medicine (cert. personal trainer, cert. instr.). Roman Catholic. Avocations: travel, painting, biking, furniture design, cooking. Home and Office: 1717 N Bayshore Dr Apt 1635 Miami FL 33132-1153

YSSELDYKE, JAMES EDWARD, psychology educator, research center administrator; b. Grand Rapids, Mich., Jan. 1, 1944; 2 children. Student in psychology, Calvin Coll., 1962-65; BA in Psychology, Biology, Western Mich. U., 1966; MA in Sch. Psychology, U. Ill., 1968, PhD, 1971. Lic. consulting psychologist, Minn. Tchr. spl. edn Kent County Juvenile Ct. Ctr., Grand Rapids, 1966-67; research asst. U. Ill. Inst. Research on Exceptional Children, 1969-70, teaching asst. dept. ednl. psychology, 1970; sch. psychology intern Oakland County Schs., Pontiac, Mich., 1970-71; asst. prof. sch. psychology Pa. State U., 1971-75, assoc. prof., 1975; assoc. prof. U. Minn., Mpls., 1975-79, prof., 1979-91, dir. Inst. Research on Learning Disabilities, 1977-83, dir. Nat. Sch. Psychology Inservice Tng. Network, 1977-83; dir. sch. psychology program U. Minn., 1987-93, dir. Nat. Ctr. on Ednl. Outcomes, 1991—; advisor, cons. and researcher in field. Author: (with J. Salvia) Assessment in Special and Remedial Education, 1985, 6th edit., 1995, (with B. Algozzine and M. Thurlow) Critical Issues in Special and Remedial Education, 1992, Strategies and Tactics for Effective Instruction, 1992, (with S.L. Christenson) The Instructional Environment System II, 1993, (with B. Algozzine) Special Education: A Practical Approach for Teachers, 1995; editor: Exceptional Children, 1984-90; assoc. editor: The School Psychologist, 1972-75, mem. editorial bd., cons. editor numerous jours.; contbr. chpts. to books and articles to jours. Dir. Nat. Ctr. on ednl. outcomes, 1991—. Recipient Disting. Teaching award U. Minn., 1988; fellow NIMH, 1967-69; grantee in field. Fellow APA (Lightner Witmer award 1973); mem. ASCD, APA, Am. Ednl. Rsch. Assn., Coun. for Exceptional Children (Rsch. award 1995), Nat. Assn. Sch. Psychologists, Coun. for Ednl. Diagnostic Svcs. Office: Nat Ctr on Ednl Outcomes 350 Elliott Hall 75 E River Rd Minneapolis MN 55455-0280

YU, AITING TOBEY, engineering executive; b. Chekiang, China, Jan. 6, 1921; came to U.S., 1945, naturalized, 1955; s. H.K. and A. (Chow) Y.; m. Natalie Kwok, Nov. 10, 1951; children: Pamela, Leonard T. BS, Nat. Cen. U., Chungking, China, 1943; SM, MIT, 1946; PhD, Lehigh U., 1949; MBA, Columbia U., 1972. Registered profl. engr., Fla. Asst. prof. engring. NYU, 1949-51; design engr. Hewitt-Robins Inc., 1951-54, chief design engr., 1955-58, engring. mgr., 1958-59; dir. systems engring. Hewitt-Robins Inc., Totowa, N.J., 1967-68, v.p. ops., 1968-71; tech. dir. West S.Am. Overseas Corp., N.Y.C., 1959-67; prin. A.T. Yu Cons. Engrs., 1971-72; co-founder, chmn. Orba Corp., Mountain Lakes, N.J., 1972—, now chmn. emeritus. Contbr. articles to profl. jours; patentee in field. Recipient nat. outstanding engring. achievement awards by ASCE, NSPE, AIME, ASME. Mem. NAE, AIME (chmn. minerals processing div., SME pres. 1986), NSPE, Nat. Acad. Forensic Engrs., Nat. Acad. Engring., Sigma Xi. Home: 962 Gullane Dr Cypress Run Tarpon Springs FL 34689 Office: Orba Corp 1250 W Sam Houston Pky S Houston TX 77042-1907

YU, ANTHONY C., religion and literature educator; b. Hong Kong, Oct. 6, 1938; came to U.S., 1956, naturalized, 1976; s. P.C. and Norma (Au) Y.; m. Priscilla Tang, Sept. 18, 1963; 1 son, Christopher Dietrich. B.A., Houghton Coll., 1960; S.T.B., Fuller Theol. Sem., 1963; Ph.D., U. Chgo., 1969. Instr. U. Ill.-Chgo., 1967-68; asst. prof. U. Chgo., 1968-74, assoc. prof., 1974-78, prof., 1978-88, Carl Darling Buck disting. svc. prof. humanities Div. Sch., Dept. East Asian Langs., Comparative Lit. and Civilizations, English, 1988—; assoc. vis. prof. Ind. U., Bloomington, 1975; Whitney J. Oates short-term vis. fellow Princeton U., 1986; Disting. vis. prof. Faculty of Arts, U. Alta., Can., 1992; mem. joint com. on study Chinese civilization Am. Coun. Learned Socs., 1980-86, bd. dirs., 1986-94; regional chmn. Mellon Fellowship in Humanities, 1982-92; bd. dirs. Ill. Humanities Coun., 1995—. Asst. editor Jour. Asian Studies, 1975-78; co-editor Jour. Religion, 1980-89; author, editor: Parnassus Revisited, 1973; editor, translator: The Journey to the West, 4 vols., 1977-83, Essays on The Journey to the West and Other Studies (in Chinese), 1989; co-editor (with Mary Gerhart) Morphologies of Faith: Essays on Religion and Culture in Honor of Nathan A. Scott, Jr., 1990. Recipient Gordon J. Laing prize, 1983; Danforth fellow, 1960-67; Guggenheim fellow, 1976-77; NEH translation grantee, 1977-82; Am. Coun. Learned Socs. sr. fellow, 1986-87; Masterworks Study grante NEH Seminar for Pub. Sch. Tchrs., 1992. Mem. MLA, Assn. for Asian Studies, Am. Acad. Religion (bd. dirs. 1995—), Am. Comparative Lit. Assn., Assn. Lit. Scholars and Critics, Milton Soc. Am., The Arts Club. Home: 950G N Clark St Chicago IL 60610 Office: U Chicago 1025 E 58th St Chicago IL 60637-1509

YU, ELEANOR NGAN-LING, advertising company executive; b. Hong Kong, July 28, 1958; d. Seong Yoon and Esther (Lam) Chan. Student, Oxford U., 1976; BA with honors, U. Ottawa, 1979; MBA, Golden Gate U., 1986. Copywriter, intern Ogilvy & Mather, Ottawa, Can.; asst. account exec. DDB, N.Y.C.; account exec. JWT, N.Y.C.; account supr. Mktg. Group, Phila.; chief exec. officer, pres. AdLand, San Francisco. Mem. com. San Francisco Grandprix Assn., 1988; bd. dirs. Chinatown Youth Ctr., San Francisco, 1986, United Way, San Francisco, 1986, San Francisco C. of C., 1995, Internat. Assn. Advt. Agys., 1995, Asian Am. Arts Found., 1995; mem. San Francisco Econ. Vitality Com., 1994; bd. overseers U. Calif., San Francisco Med./Nursing Sch.; bd. trustees Fielding Inst., 1996; bd. advisors Nat. Asian and Pacific Am. Coalition. Named Entrepreneur of Yr. SBA, 1995, Alumnus of Yr. Golden Gate U., 1995. Mem. NAFE, Asian Bus. Assn. (pres. 1985-86), Pacific Affairs Council (chmn. 1988—), San Francisco C. of C. (mem. bd. dirs. 1994), Golden Gate U. Alumni Assn. (bd. dirs. 1986—), Inter Assn. of Advt. Agy's. Office: AdLand & AdLand Worldwide Penthouse Suites 2728 Hyde St at Beach San Francisco CA 94109

YU, GENRONG, lawyer; b. Shanghai, China, Mar. 17, 1949; came to U.S., 1986; s. Fengwu Yu and Fengyin Hu; m. Xinyin Wei, May 4, 1977; 1 child, Mengchao Yu. BA, Anhui (China) Normal U., 1982; LLM in Internat. Econ. and Maritime Law, Shanghai Maritime Inst., Shanghai, 1985; JD, U. Maine, 1989. Bar: N.Y. Asst. atty. Shanghai Lawyers Office for Maritime Affairs, Shanghai, 1985-86; instr. of Law dept. Internat. Shipping Shanghai Maritime Inst., Shanghai, 1985-86; atty. Healy Baillie, N.Y.C., 1989—; resident ptnr. Healy Baillie, Hong Kong, 1994—; farmer Zongpu People's Commune, Anhui Province, China, 1969-70. Contbr. articles to profl. jours. Flutist Orch. of Anhui Huang Mei Opera Troupe, 1970-78. Mem. ABA, Maritime Law Assn. of U.S., Maritime Law Assn. of the People's Republic of China. Home: 63-16 110th St # 2A Forest Hills NY 11375-1412 Office: Healy & Baillie 29 Broadway New York NY 10006

YU, GEORGE TZUCHIAO, political science educator; b. London, May 16, 1931; s. Wangteh and Ying (Ho) Y.; m. Priscilla Chang, Aug. 11, 1957; children: Anthony, Phillip. A.B., U. Calif., Berkeley, 1954, M.A., 1957, Ph.D., 1961. Asst. prof. polit. sci. U. N.C., Chapel Hill, 1961-65; assoc. prof. polit. sci. U. Ill., Urbana, 1965-70; prof. U. Ill., 1970—, head dept., 1987-92, dir. Ctr. for East Asian and Pacific Studies, 1992—, dir. grad. studies, 1981-85; vis. sr. lectr. polit. sci. Univ. Coll., Nairobi, 1968; chair U.S.-China African Studies Exchange Com., 1985—. Author: The Chinese Anarchist Movement, 1961, 65, Party Politics in Republican China, 1966, China and Tanzania, 1970, China's African Policy, 1975, Intra-Asian International Relations, 1977, Modern China and Its Revolutionary Process, 1985, American Studies in China, 1993, China in Transition, 1994, Asia's New World Order, 1996. Grantee Social Sci. Rsch. Coun., 1967-68, 70-71, NEH, 1978-81, 84-86, Earhart Found., 1976-77, 81-83, 88, Ford Found., 1985-87, 89, 92. Mem. Assn. Asian Studies, African Studies Assn. Office: 702 S Wright St Urbana IL 61801-3631

YU, JEN, medical educator; b. Taipei, Taiwan, Jan. 23, 1943; came to U.S., 1969; s. Chin Chuan and Shiu Lan (Lin) Y.; m. Janet Chen, June 16, 1973; children—Benjamin, Christopher. M.D., Nat. Taiwan U., 1968; Ph.D. in Physiology, U. Pa., 1972. Diplomate Am. Bd. Phys. Medicine and Rehab. Intern. Phila. Gen. Hosp., 1972-73; resident in phys. medicine and rehab. Hosps. U. Pa., 1973-75; asst. prof. dept. phys. medicine and rehab. U. Pa. Sch. Medicine, Phila., 1975-76, U. Tex. Health Sci. Ctr., San Antonio, 1976-79, assoc. prof., 1979-81; prof. dept. phys. medicine and rehab. U. Calif.-Irvine Coll. Medicine, 1981-82, prof., chmn. dept. phys. medicine and rehab., 1982—. Contbr. articles to med. jours. Mem. Am. Acad. Phys. Medicine and Rehab., Am. Congress Rehab. Medicine, Assn. Acad. Physiatrists, Am. Assn. Anatomists, Soc. for Neurosci. Office: U Calif Irvine Med Ctr Dept Phys Medicine and Rehab 101 The City Dr Orange CA 92668-3201

YU, KITSON SZEWAI, computer science educator; b. Toishan, Kwangtung, China, Apr. 4, 1950; came to U.S., 1969; s. Ho Yee and Yin Sang (Chan) Y.; m. Mabel Griseldis Wong, July 15, 1972; 1 child, Robin Roberta Emily. BS, Troy State U., 1974, MS, 1977, BS, 1980. Cert. systems profl.; cert. data processing educator. V.p. Troy (Ala.) Computer Ctr., 1976-81; computer instr. Tory State U., 1980-81, Linn Benton Community Coll., Albany, Oreg., 1981—; dir. real estate program Linn Benton Community Coll., 1985—; mng. broker Kitson Realty, Corvallis, Oreg., 1975—. Vice pres. econ. devel. Daleville C. of C., Ala., 1976; dir. Corvalis Youth Symphony, 1990-93. Mem. Data Processing Mgmt. Assn. (bd. dirs. at large 1982-93, v.p. 1984-85, pres. 1985-86), Greater Albany Rotary (treas. 1985—), Corvallis Multiple Listing Exch. (bd. dirs. 1990-94), Gamma Beta Phi. Home: 2768 NW Wintergreen Pl Corvallis OR 97330-3550 Office: Linn Benton C C 6500 Pacific Blvd SW Albany OR 97321-3755 *Personal philosophy: Ask, when appropriate; Aid, when appreciated.*

YU, ROBERT KUAN-JEN, biochemistry educator; b. Chungking, China, Jan. 27, 1938; came to U.S., 1962; s. Shin-cheng and June Chien-yu (Tsao) Y.; m. Helen Chow, July 1, 1972; children: David S., Jennifer S. BS, Tunghai U., Taiwan, 1960; PhD, U. Ill., 1967; Med.ScD. (hon.), Tokyo, 1980; MA (hon.), Yale U., 1986. Rsch. assoc., instr. Albert Einstein Coll. Medicine, Bronx, 1967-72; asst. prof. Yale U., New Haven, 1973-75, assoc. prof., 1975-82, prof., 1983-88; prof. biochemistry, chmn. dept. Va. Commonwealth U., Richmond, 1988—; mem. study sect. NIH, Washington, 1980-84; mem. Bd. Lab. Svcs., Va., 1994—. Editor: Gangioside Structure Function and Biomedical Potential, 1984, New Trends in Ganglioside Research, 1988; contbr. over 470 articles to profl. publs. Josiah Macy scholar, 1979; grantee NIH, 1975—; recipient Va. Outstanding Scientist of Yr. award, 1995, Jacob Javits award NIH, 1984-91, Alexander von Humboldt award, 1990. Mem. AAAS, Am. Soc. Cell Biology, Am. Soc. Neurochemistry (mem. coun. 1983-86, 91—), Internat. Soc. Neurochemistry, Soc. Neurosci., Am. Soc. Biochemistry and Molecular Biology, Am. Chem. Soc., N.Y. Acad. Sci. Home: 306 Cheswick Ln Richmond VA 23229-7660 Office: Va Commonwealth Univ Medical College Virginia Richmond VA 23298-0614

YU, VICTOR LIN-KAI, physician, educator; b. Mpls., Jan. 9, 1943; s. Robert S.H. and Victoria (Hsiao) Y.; m. Deborah Lin, June 19, 1971; children: Chen Ming, Kwan Ting. BA, Carleton Coll., 1965; MD, U. Minn., 1970. Internship and residency U. Colo., Denver, 1970-72; residency Stanford U., Palo Alto, Calif., 1974, postdoctoral fellow, 1975-77; prof. medicine U. Pitts., 1978—; chmn. bd. sci. counselors NIH, 1986-92; chief infectious disease sect. VA Med. Ctr., Pitts., 1981—; disting. lectr. Am. Soc. Microbiology, 1988; Malia lectr. Shadyside Hosp., 1992; Berris lectr. U. Toronto, 1993; Rubin lectr. Berkshire AHEC. Contbr. rsch. on Legionnaires' disease to sci. publs. Recipient Disting. Rsch. award Am. Legion, 1982, Health Svcs. Rsch. Found., 1984; named disting. scientist Chinese Med. Soc., Taipei, Taiwan, 1988; recipient Gold medal for Outstanding Contbn. to Sci., Fed. Exec. Bd., 1993, Citation of Merit, Allegheny County, Pa., 1993. Fellow ACP; mem. Orgn. Chinese Ams. (officer Pitts. sect. 1978—). Home: 87 Longue Vue Dr Pittsburgh PA 15228-1538 Office: U Pitts Divsn Infectious Disease 501 Kaufmann Bldg Pittsburgh PA 15213

YU, YI-YUAN, mechanical engineering educator; b. Tienjin, China, Jan. 29, 1923; came to U.S., 1947, naturalized, 1962; s. Tsi-Chi and Hsiao-Kung (Wang) Y.; m. Eileen Hsiu-Yung Wu, June 14, 1952; children: Yolanda, Lisa. BS, Tienjin U., 1944; MS, Northwestern U., 1950, PhD, 1951. Prof. mech. engring. (Poly Inst. Bklyn.), 1957-66; cons. engr. Gen. Electric Space Div., Valley Forge, Pa., 1966-70; Disting. prof. aero. engring. (Wichita State U.), 1972-75; mgr. components and analysis Rockwell Internat., Rocketdyne, , Canoga Park, Calif., 1975-79, exec. engr. Energy Systems, 1979-81; dean engring. N.J. Inst. Tech., Newark, 1981-85, prof. mech. engring., 1981-93, prof. emeritus, 1993—; vis. prof. Cambirdge U., 1960; advisor Middle East Tech. U., Ankara, Turkey, 1966; lectr. Gen. Electric Co., 1963-73; mem. ad hoc com. on dynamic analysis USN, 1968-69; cons. internat. adv. panel Chinese U. Devel. Project, 1983, David W. Taylor Naval Ship Rsch. and Devel. Ctr., 1987-88; cons. Atty. Gen.'s Office State N.J., 1982-84. Contbr. Handbook of Engineering Mechanics, 1962; author: Vibrations of Elastic Plates, 1996. Guggenheim fellow, 1959-60; Air Force Office Sci. Research grantee, 1956-66; NASA grantee, 1967-69, 74-75. Fellow AIAA (assoc.), ASME (life); mem. Am. Soc. Engring. Edn., Am. Soc. for Composites, Am. Acad. Mechanics (chmn. com. mech. edn. 1993-94), Sigma Xi, Phi Kappa Phi, Pi Tau Sigma, Tau Beta Pi. Presbyterian. Home: 24 Gordon Rd Essex Fells NJ 07021-1604 Office: 323 King Blvd Newark NJ 07102 *At the end of each day, let everyone of us ask the question: Have I done the best I can this day to make the world a better place to live for myself and for my fellow human beings? As long as the answer is yes, it does not matter whether one is a teacher, farmer, worker, businessperson or homemaker.*

YUAN, SHAO WEN, aerospace engineer, educator; b. Shanghai, China, Apr. 16, 1914; came to U.S., 1934, naturalized, 1954; s. Ti An and Chieh-huang (Chien) Y.; m. Hui Chih Hu, Nov. 5, 1950. B.S., U. Mich., 1936; M.E., Stanford U., 1939; M.S., Calif. Inst. Tech., 1937, Ph.D., 1941. Rsch. engr. Glenn Martin Co., 1942-43; chief of rsch. Helicopter div. McDonnell Aircraft Corp., 1943-45; instr. Washington U., St. Louis, 1944-45; adj. prof. Poly. Inst. Bklyn., 1946-49, assoc. prof., 1949-54, prof., 1954-57; ptnr. von Kármán, Yuan & Arnold Assocs., 1955-63; prof. aerospace engring. U. Tex., 1958-68; prof., chmn. mech. engring. div. George Washington U., 1968-78, chmn. civil, mech. and environ. dept., 1973-78, 80-81, prof. emeritus, 1984; pres. RISE, Inc., 1977-85; Canadair Chair prof. U. Laval, Can., 1957-58; chmn. adv. com. Joint Inst. for Advancement of Flight Sci., 1970-84; hon. prof. Zhejiang U., 1987—; cons. Edo Aircraft Corp., Aerojet Corp., Cornell Aero. Lab., Dept. of Interior, Oak Ridge Nat. Lab., N.Am., Aviation, Inc., Fairchild-Hiller Corp., McDonnell-Douglas Corp., The World Bank; hon. adviser Nat. Center Research of China, Taiwan, 1958-68; chmn., founder 1st U.S.-China Conf. on Energy, Resources, and Environment, 1982; founder Consortium of Univs. for Promoting Grad. Aerospace Studies, 1984; founder Disting. Lecture Series on Founds. of Aerospace Research and Devel., 1986. Author: Foundations of Fluid Mechanics, 1967; Contbr. to: High Speed Aerodynamics and Jet Propulsion series, 1959, Energy, Resources, and Environment: Procs. at 1st U.S.-China Conf., 1982. Recipient Outstanding Achievements award George Washington U., 1981; named Outstanding

Educator of Am., 1970, Outstanding Chinese American, 1983. Fellow AAAS, AIAA; mem. ASME (life), Am. Soc. Engring. Edn., Soc. Engring. Sci. (bd. dirs. 1973-78, pres. 1977), Torchbearers Caltech, Founding Grant Soc. of Stanford U. (charter), John Montieth Soc. of U. Mich. (charter), Sigma Xi, Phi Kappa Phi, Phi Tau Phi, Sigma Gamma Tau, Pi Tau Sigma, Tau Beta Pi, Tau Xi Sigma. Achievements include patents in field. Home: 1400 Geary Blvd Apt 1505 San Francisco CA 94109-6570 *As engineers and scientists, we are concerned with that "something beyond"; consequently, the utmost achievement of an engineer is to create what has never been, for the improvement of quality of life.*

YUAN, SIDNEY WEI KWUN, cryogenic engineer, consultant; b. Hong Kong, July 30, 1957; came to U.S., 1975; s. Chia Chi and Tso Tak (Wong) Y.; m. Katherine K.Y. Dai, Sept. 8, 1981; children: Jacquelyn Kate, Chrystal Sidney. BSc, UCLA, 1980, MSc, 1981, PhD, 1985. Rsch. asst. UCLA, 1980-81, rsch. engr., 1981-85, teaching asst., 1984-85; rsch. scientist Lockheed Missiles & Space Co., Palo Alto, Calif., 1985-96, BEI Electronics, Sylmar, Calif., 1996—; cons. Toyo Sanso Inc., Japan, 1990—, Applied Aerotek Inc., 1991—, Compliance Engring. and Tech., 1992—, Applied Scis. Labs., 1992—; lectr. fundamentals of superconductivity UCLA, 1989. Contbr. over 40 articles on cryogenics, thermodynamics, heat and mass transport to profl. jours. Recipient Nat. Excellence Recognition award Space Found., 1985, Superior Performance Team award Lockheed, 1990. Mem. AIAA (Engr. of Yr. award 1991), Am. Inst. Chem. Engrs. (Indsl. Rsch. award 1994), Cryogenic Soc. Am. (vice chmn. no. Calif.), Sigma Xi, Tau Beta Pi. Republican. Avocations: table tennis, go. Home: 2255 29th St Santa Monica CA 90405 Office: 13100 Telfair Ave San Fernando CA 91342

YUAN, XIAO-JIAN, medical researcher, educator; b. Xintian, Hunan, People's Republic of China, May 9, 1963; s. Tian-Lin Yuan and Li-Hua Chen. MD, Suzhou (China) Med. Coll., 1983; PhD in Physiology, Peking Union Med. Coll., Beijing, 1993; postgrad., U. Md., 1993. Intern Suzhou Med. Coll. Hosp., 1982-83; resident Lanzhou (China) Med. Coll. Hosp., 1983-84; mem. sci. cadre Office Sci. and Tech. Gansu Environ. Protection Bur., Lanzhou, 1984; rsch. assoc. dept. environ. medicine Gansu Inst. Environ. Scis., Lanzhou, 1984-85; postdoctoral fellow dept. physiology and medicine U. Md. Sch. Medicine, Balt., 1988-93, rsch. asst. prof. dept. physiology, 1993-96, rsch. asst. prof. divsn. pulmonary and critical care med., 1993-96, asst. prof., 1996—; lectr. in field; ad hoc reviewer grant applications NIH, 1995-96, study section mem. Am. Heart Assn., 1995-99; ad hoc reviewer rsch. grant applications Wellcome Trust (London), 1995, U.S. Dept. Vets. Affairs, 1995. Author: Olympic Complete Words, 1988; editorial asst. Gansu Assn. Environ. Scis., 1984-85; contbr. articles to profl. jours. Parker B. Francis fellow, 1994-97. Mem. AAAS, Am. Heart Assn. (Md. affiliate rsch. fellow 1990-92, grantee 1990-92, 93-95, Cournand and Comroe Young Investigator award 1995), Am. Physiol. Soc. (Giles F. Filley Meml. award 1995, Rsch. Career Enhancement award 1995), Am. Thoracic Soc., Biophys. Soc., Chinese Assn. Physiol. Sci. (editorial asst. 1987-88), Soc. Chinese Bioscientists in Am., Soc. Biophysicists in A. (Dr. C.W. Dunker award 1993). Home: 2 Wytchwood Ct Apt 202 Baltimore MD 21209-1905 Office: U Md Sch Medicine Div Pulmonary Medicine 10 S Pine St MSTF 800 Baltimore MD 21201

YUAN TSEH LEE, chemistry educator; b. Hsinchu, Taiwan, China, Nov. 29, 1936; came to U.S., 1962, naturalized, 1974; s. Tsefan and Pei (Tasi) L.; m. Bernice Wu, June 28, 1963; children: Ted, Sidney, Charlotte. BS, Nat. Taiwan U., 1959; MS, Nat. Tsinghua U., Taiwan, 1961; PhD, U. Calif., Berkeley, 1965. From asst. prof. to prof. chemistry U. Chgo., 1968-74; prof. U. Calif., Berkeley, 1974—, also former prin. investigator Lawrence Berkeley Lab. Contbr. numerous articles on chem. physics to profl. jours. Recipient Nobel Prize in Chemistry, 1986, Ernest O. Lawrence award Dept. Energy, 1981, Nat. Medal of Sci., 1986, 90, Peter Debye award for Phys. Chemistry, 1986; fellow Alfred P. Sloan, 1969-71, John Simon Guggenheim, 1976-77; Camille and Henry Dreyfus Found. Tchr. scholar, 1971-74, Harrison Howe award, 1983. Fellow Am. Phys. Soc.; mem. NAS, AAAS, Am. Acad. Arts and Scis., Am. Chem. Soc. Office: U Calif Dept Chemistry Berkeley CA 94720*

YUDOF, MARK G., lawyer, educator, academic administrator; b. Phila., Oct. 30, 1944; s. Jack and Eleanor (Parris) Y.; m. Judith Lynn Gomel, July 11, 1965; children: Seth Adam, Samara Lisa. BA, U. Pa., 1965, LLB, 1968. Bar: Pa. 1970, U.S. Supreme Ct. 1974, U.S. Dist. Ct. (we. dist.) Tex. 1975, U.S. Ct. Appeals (5th cir.) 1976, Tex. 1980. Law clk. to judge U.S. Ct. Appeals (5th cir.), 1968-69; assoc. gen. counsel to ABA study FTC, 1969; research assoc. Harvard Ctr. Law and Edn., 1969-70, sr. staff atty., 1970-71; lectr. Harvard Grad. Sch. Edn., 1970-71; asst. prof. law U. Tex., Austin, 1971-74, prof., 1974—, assoc. dean, 1979-84, James A. Elkins Cent. Chair in Law, 1983—, dean, 1984-94, exec. v.p., provost, 1994—, John Jeffers Rsch. Chair in Law, 1991-94; of counsel Pennzoil vs. Texaco, 1987; mem. adv. bd. Inst. for Transnat. Arbitration, 1988—, Am. Jour. Edn., 1991—; chmn. bd. contbrs. to Tex. Lawyer, 1988—; mem. nat. bd. contbrs. Am. Lawyer Newspapers Group, Inc., 1988—; mem. telecomm. infrastructure fund bd. State of Tex. Author: When Government Speaks, 1983 (Scribes Book award 1983, cert. merit ABA 1983), (with others) Educational Policy and the Law, 1992, (with others) Gender Justice, 1986. Mem. Tex. Gov.'s Task Force on Sch. Fin., 1989-90, Tex. Gov.'s Select Com. on Edn., 1988; bd. dirs. Freedom to Read Found., 1989-91; mem. adv. bd. Austin Diagnostic Clinic Cmty., 1989-95; mem. Austin Cable Commn., 1981-84, chmn., 1982; mem. nat. panel on sch. desegregation rsch. Ford Found., 1977-80; mem. state exec. com. Univ. Interscholastic League, 1983-86; mem. rsch. adv. com. Ctr. for Policy Rsch. in Edn., 1985—; bd. dirs. Jewish Children's Regional Svc., 1980-86, Austin Diagnostic Med. Ctr., 1995—; mem. Gov.'s Select Task Force on Pub. Edn., 1995—; mem. Telecomms. Infrastructure Fund Bd., State of Tex., 1995—. Recipient Teaching Excellence award, 1975, Most Meritorious Book award Scribes, 1983, Humanitarian award Austin region NCCJ, 1988, Antidefamation League Jurisprudence award, 1991; fellow Queen Mary and Westfield Coll., U. London. Fellow Tex. Bar Found., Am. Bar Found.; mem. ABA (legal edn. and admissions to bar sect. 1984—), Am. Law Inst., Tex. Bar Assn., Assn. Am. Law Schs. (chmn. law and edn. sect. 1983-84, mem. exec. com. 1988-90), Univ. Club, Headliners Club, Met. Club. Avocation: collecting antique maps. Office: U Tex/ Balcones Rsch Ctr Exec Vice Pres/ Provost MAI 201 Austin TX 78712

YUE, AGNES KAU-WAH, otolaryngologist; b. Shanghai, Peoples Republic China, Dec. 1, 1947; came to U.S., 1967; d. Chen Kia and Nee Yuan (Ying0 ; m. Gerald Kumata, Sept. 25, 1982; children: Julie, Allison Benjamin. BA, Wellesley Coll., 1970; MD, Med. Coll. Pa., 1974; postgrad., Yale U., 1974-78. Intern Yale-New Haven Hosp., 1974-75, resident, 1975-78; fellow U. Tex. M.D. Anderson Cancer Ctr., Houston, 1978-79; asst. prof. U. Wash., Seattle, 1979-82; physician Pacific Med. Ctr., Seattle, 1979-90; pvt. practice Seattle, 1991—. Fellow Am. Acad. Otolaryngology, Am. Coll. Surgeons; mem. Northwest Acad. Otolaryngology. Avocations: sailing, opera, profl. voice, cooking. Office: 1801 NW Market St Ste 410 Seattle WA 98107-3909

YUE, ALFRED SHUI-CHOH, metallurgical engineer, educator; b. China, Nov. 12, 1920; s. Choy Noon-woo and Sze Man-hun (Tom) Y.; m. Virginia Chin-wen Tang, May 21, 1944; children: Mary, Raymond Yuan, John, Ling Tsao, David, Nancy Chang. B.S., Chao-tung U., 1942; M.S., Ill. Inst. Tech., 1950; Ph.D., Purdue U., 1956. Assoc. engr. Taiwan Aluminum Co., 1942-47; instr. Purdue U., 1952-56; research engr. Dow Chem. Co., Midland, Mich., 1956-62; sr. mem. Lockheed, Palo Alto Research Lab., 1962-69; now cons.; prof. engring. and applied sci. U. Calif., Los Angeles, 1969—; hon. prof. Xian Jiao-tong U., China, 1980; cons. LTV Aerospace Co., Lockheed Missile & Space Co., Atlantic Richfield Co.; Sec.-gen. Chinese Culture Assn. in, U.S.A., 1967, also; bd. dirs. Chinese scholar to U.S.A. Fellow AIAA (assoc.); mem. AAAS, AIME, Am. Soc. Metals, Materials Rsch. Soc., Sigma Xi, Sigma Pi Sigma, Tau Beta Pi, Phi Tau Phi (pres. 1978-82). Office: U of Calif Dept Engring Los Angeles CA 90095-1595

YUECHIMING, ROGER YUE YUEN SHING, mathematics educator; b. Mauritius, Feb. 25, 1937; s. James and Marie Yuechiming; m. Renée Bethery, Nov. 9, 1963; children: Françoise, Marianne, Isabelle. BSc with 1st class honours, U. Manchester, Eng., 1964, PhD, 1967. Asst. U. Strasbourg, France, 1967-69; lectr. math. U. Paris VII, 1970—; participant math. confs. and seminars in numerous countries; referee various math. jours. Contbr. over 80 articles on ring theory to sci. jours. of numerous countries. Mem. French Math. Soc., Am. Math. Soc., London Math. Soc., Belgian Math. Soc. Achievements include introduction of concept of p-injective modules, new approaches in ring and module theory leading to a better understanding of von Neumann regular rings, V-rings, self-injective rings and generalizations. Home: 38 rue du Surmelin, 75020 Paris France Office: U Paris VII Unité Mixte, de Recherche 9994 Nat Ctr, Sci Rsch 2 Pl Jussieu, 75251 Paris France

YUELYS, ALEXANDER, former cosmetics company executive; b. Bronx, N.Y., Aug. 12, 1926; s. Dionisyus and Anastasia (Stathes) Y.; m. Nicoletta Lardas, Dec. 9, 1950; 1 son, Jordan. B.A., Hunter Coll., 1950. C.P.A., N.Y. With Arthur Young, 1952-56, Haskins & Sells, 1950-52; with Fabergé, Inc., N.Y.C., 1956-83, exec. v.p., chief fin. officer, dir.; dir. Brut Prodns., Inc., Am. Stage Co. Bd. dirs. St. Michael's Home for Aged, v.p., 1984—. Served with USAAF, 1945-46. Mem. Fin. Execs. Inst., Nat. Assn. Accountants. Home: PO Box 836 Alpine NJ 07620-0836

YUEN, BENSON BOLDEN, airline management consultant, software executive; b. Hong Kong, Nov. 20, 1960; came to U.S., 1968; s. Eugene Howard and Janet (Chan) Y. BSBA in Fin. summa cum laude, U. Cen. Fla., 1983. Mgr. market planning and automation Fla. Express, Inc., Orlando, 1983-85, dir. pricing, 1986-87; dir. customer svc. Seabrook Mktg., Inc., Houston, 1988-91, v.p. customer svc., 1992-94; v.p. consulting svcs. PROS Strategic Solutions, Inc., Houston, 1994-96, sr. v.p. mktg. and consulting svcs., 1996—; cons. airline revenue mgmt., mktg. automation, bus. mgmt., sys. devel. and bus. process engring. to more than 50 airlines and industry-related firms world wide. Designer (software) Passenger Revenue Forecast and Optimization System, 1989, Group Revenue Optimization and Management System Version 3, 1990-94, Version 4, 1995—. Avocations: travel, music. Office: PROS Strategic Solutions 3223 Smith St Ste 100 Houston TX 77006

YUG, BARBARA SANDRA, nursing researcher; b. Milw., May 19, 1938; d. Frank Ronald and Virginia Mary (Nowak) Tandecki; m. Anthony George Yug, June 18, 1960; children: Anthony G., David P., Bryan G. BSN, Marquette U., 1960; MS in Health Svc. Adminstrn., Coll. of St. Francis, Joliet, Ill., 1990. RN, Wis. Staff nurse acute care Nursefinders Inc. and Med. Pers. Pool, Milw., 1985-90; quality assurance, med. UR coord. Wis. Peer Rev. Orgn., Milw. and Madison, 1990-93; hypertension rschr., program coord. Med. Coll. Wis., Zablocki VA Med. Ctr., Milw., 1993—; cert. blood pressure instr. Am. Heart Assn., Milw., 1982-92; blood pressure cert. for rsch. studies Shared Care, Torrance, Calif., 1993, 94; mem. Milw. Blood Pressure Program, 1981-92. Campaign activity worker Common Coun., Brookfield, Wis., 1980; v.p. Lake Shore Jr. Women's Orgn., 1962. Mem. Nat. League for Nursing (advocacy mem.), Marquette U. Women's Orgn., Iota Chi Omega. Avocations: reading, gardening, aerobic exercise, bicycling. Office: Zablocki VA Med Ctr Hypertension Rsch Studies 5000 W National Ave 14A Milwaukee WI 53295

YUHAS, ALAN THOMAS, investment management executive; b. Ashland, Pa., Nov. 27, 1948; s. George Jacob and Elizabeth Jane (Belfonti) Y.; married; children: Daisy Mariella, Alan George. BA, Temple U., 1973, JD, 1980. Statistician Ct. Common Pleas, Phila., 1974-76; mktg. rep. Control Data Corp., Phila., 1976-77; mgr. Chase Econometrics, Bala Cynwyd, Pa., 1977-80; prin. Sparrowhawk Ltd., Phila., 1980-86; prin. Rolland Ross Asset Mgmt., Blue Bell, Pa., 1986—, also bd. dirs.; bd. dirs. RYQ, BIRR, AARR; cons. Gifford Fong Assocs., Walnut Creek, Calif., 1980-83, Fidelity Bank N.A., Phila., 1983-87. Served to sgt. U.S. Army, 1966-69, Vietnam. Mem. Phi Beta Kappa. also: Roll & Ross Asset Mgmt 587 Skippack Pike Ste 400 Blue Bell PA 19422-2158*

YUILL, THOMAS MACKAY, academic administrator, microbiology educator; b. Berkeley, Calif., June 14, 1937; s. Joseph Stuart and Louise (Dunlop) Y.; m. Ann Warnes, Aug. 24, 1960; children: Eileen, Gwen. BS, Utah State U., 1959; MS, U. Wis., 1962, PhD, 1964. Lab. officer Walter Reed Army Inst. Rsch., Washington, 1964-66; med. biologist SEATO Med. Research Lab., Bangkok, Thailand, 1966-68; asst. prof. U. Wis.-Madison, 1968-72, assoc. prof., 1972-76, prof., 1976—, dept. chmn., 1979-82, assoc. dean., 1982-93; dir. Inst. Environ. Studies, 1993—; cons. NIH, Bethesda, 1976-86; chmn. Viral Diseases Panel, U.S.-Japan Biomed. Scis. Program, 1979-86, Am. Com. Arbovirology, 1982—; bd. dirs. Cen. Tropical Agrl. Res. Teaching, Turrialba, Costa Rica, 1988-96. Contbr. chpts. to books, articles to profl. jours. Served to capt. U.S. Army, 1964-66. Recipient grants state and fed. govts., 1968—. Mem. Orgn. Tropical Studies (pres. 1979-85), Wildlife Disease Assn. (treas. 1980-85, pres. 1985-87, editl. bd. 1989—), Am. Soc. Tropical Medicine and Hygiene (editorial bd. 1984-95), Am. Soc. Microbiology, Am. Soc. Virology, Wildlife Soc., Sigma Xi. Avocations: flying; cross-country skiing; music. Office: U Wis Inst Environ Studies 40 Science Hall 550 N Park St Madison WI 53706

YUKEI, HASEBE YOSHIKAZU, religious studies educator; b. Tokyo, July 7, 1929; s. Yoichi Koyu and Shii (Watanabe) H.; m. Reiko H. Nobuta, Oct. 28, 1963. B degree, Komazawa U., Tokyo, 1955, MA, 1957, PhD, 1989. Lectr. Zen culture Shogen Jr. Coll., Minokamo, Gifu, Japan, 1963-65; asst. prof. Aichigakuin U., Nagoya, Aichi, Japan, 1965-75, prof. Buddhist and Zen culture lit., 1975—, dir. univ. libr., 1995—. Author: Introduction to the Studies of Ming and Ching Buddhism, 1979, Historical Studies of Buddhist Orders in the Ming and Ching Dynasties, 1993. Mem. Japanese Assn. Indian and Buddhist Studies, Japanese Assn. for Religious Studies, The Nippon Buddhist Rsch. Assn., Tokai Assn. of Indian and Buddhist Studies, The Japan Art History Soc. Office: Aichigakuin U, 12 Araike, Iwasaki, Nishin-cho, Aichi Japan

YULE, JOE, JR. See ROONEY, MICKEY

YULISH, CHARLES BARRY, public affairs executive; b. Cleve., Oct. 14, 1936; s. Isadore and Minna (Scott) Y.; m. Barbara Pearlman, Aug. 22, 1973 (div. 1983); 1 child, Alexi Jules-Nicholas; m. Cynthia Brown Fleck, Oct. 28, 1995. AA in Govt., U. Fla., 1957; BS in Polit. Sci., Kent State U., 1959; MPA, Syracuse U., 1961; postgrad., NYU, 1961-63, New Sch. Social Rsch., 1963-64. Spl. projects officer U.S. Atomic Energy Commn., Washington and N.Y.C., 1961-63; pub. affairs mgr. Atomic Indsl. Forum, N.Y.C., 1963-66; pres., chief exec. officer Charles Yulish Assocs. Inc., N.Y.C., 1966-83; exec. v.p. Wesley, Brown & Bartle Inc., N.Y.C., 1984-87; vice chmn., ptnr. Holt, Ross & Yulish, Edison, N.J., 1988-92; exec. v.p., mng. dir. E. Bruce Harrison Co., Washington, 1993-95; v.p. corp. comm. U.S. Enrichment Corp., Bethesda, Md., 1995—; bd. dirs. Intermedia News and Feature Svcs. Writer, dir. (film) Energy: We Have the Choices, 1978 (Golden Eagle award); editor: Hard vs. Soft Energy Paths, 1980; author over 60 articles on classical music. Founder, bd. dirs. Serge Koussevitsky Archives Soc., N.Y.C., 1977; bd. dirs. Imperial Russia Hist. Soc., 1986, U.K. and U.S. Friends of Benjamin Franklin. Maxwell fellow Syracuse U., 1960. Mem. Internat. Assn. Pub. Participation Practitioners, Pub. Rels. Soc. Am., Counselors Acad., Soc. Profl. Mgmt. Cons. (cert.). Home: 1438 Q St NW Washington DC 20009-3808

YUN, DANIEL DUWHAN, physician, foundation administrator; b. Chinjoo, Korea, Jan. 20, 1933; came to U.S., 1959, naturalized, 1972; s. Kapryong and Woo Im Yun; m. Rebecca Sungja Choi, Apr. 13, 1959; children: Samuel, Lois, Caroline, Judith. BS, Coll. Sci. and Engring., Yon-Sei U., 1954, MD, 1958; student U. Pa., 1963, PhD Barrington U., 1995. Intern, Quincy (Mass.) City Hosp., 1960; resident and fellow Presbyn.-U. Pa. Med. Ctr., Phila., 1961-65; med. dir. Paddon Meml. Hosp., Nfld., Labrador, Can., 1965-66; dir. spl. care unit Elkins Park (Pa.) Hosp., 1967-79; founder, pres. Philip Jaisohn Meml. Found., Inc., Elkins Park, Pa., 1975-85, also med. dir., trustee; clin. prof. medicine U. Xochicalco, 1978; faculty Med. Coll. Pa.-Hahnemann U. Mem. Bd. Asian Studies Found., U.S. Senatorial Bus. Adv. Bd.; mem. home safety com. Mayor's Commn. on Svcs. to Aging, Phila.; trustee United Way of Southeastern Pa., co-founder Rep. Presdl. Task Force; mem. U.S. Congl. Adv. Bd.; cons. on Korean affairs Phila. City Coun.; hon. mem. adv. coun. Peaceful Unification Policy of Korea; chmn. bd. Korean-Am. Christian Broadcasting of Phila.; mem. Phila. Internat. City Coord. Com.; commr. Pa. Human Rels. Commn., 1991—; founder, pres. Korean Heritage Found., 1991—; amb. City of Phila., 1991. Recipient Phila. award-Human Rights award, 1981, Disting. Community Svc. award Phila. Dist. Atty., 1981, medal of Merit Presdl. Task Force, 1981, Medal of Nat. Order, Republic of Korea, 1984, Nat. Dong Baek medal Republic of Korea, 1987, award City Coun. Phila., 1987, Gov.'s Pa. Heritage awards, 1990, commendation award Pa. Senate, 1991, award Asian Law Ctr., 1991, Republican Senatorial Medal of Freedom, 1994; named to Legion of Honor, The Chapel of Four Chaplains, named Amb. City of Phila., 1991. Mem. AMA, Am. Soc. Internal Medicine, Am. Coll. Cardiology, Am. Heart Assn. (mem. council on clin. cardiology), Pa. Med. Soc., Phila. County Med. Soc., Royal Soc. Health, Am. Coll. Internat. Physicians, World Med. Assn., Fedn. State Med. Bds., Am. Law Enforcement Officers' Assn., Am. Fedn. Police, Internat. Culture Soc. Korea (hon.), Am. Soc. Contemporary Medicine and Surgery. Home: 3903 Somers Dr Huntingdon Valley PA 19006-1913 Office: 60 Township Line Rd Elkins Park PA 19027-2220

YUN, HSING, head religious order; b. Chiangtu, Chiangsu, China, July 22, 1917; came to the U.S., 1980s.; s. Cheng-bao Lee and Yu-ying Liu. Student, Ch'i-hsia Vinaya Sch., 1941, Chiao-shan Buddhist Coll., 1948; PhD (hon.), Oriental U., L.A., 1978. Dir. Hua-ts'ang Temple, Nanjing, China, 1949; Buddhist missionary Lei-yin Temple, Ilan, Taiwan, 1952-66; abbot Fo Kuang Shan, Kaohsiung, Taiwan, 1967-85; master Fo Kuang Shan, Kaohsiung, 1986-91; pres. Hsi Lai U., L.A., 1991—, Buddha's Light Internat. Assn., L.A., 1992—. Avocations: Buddhist lectures and writings.

YUN, SAMUEL, minister, educator; b. Ulsan, Republic of Korea, June 19, 1958; came to U.S., 1984; s. Eungoh and Chanho (Kim) Y.; m. Kyungim Martha Mah, Jan. 10, 1984; children: Miriam, Joseph, Michelle, John. BTh, Yonsei U., Seoul, Republic of Korea, 1980, MTh, 1984; MA in Religion, U. Dubuque, 1985; ThM, Harvard U., 1987; postgrad., Boston U., 1987—. Ordained to ministry Korean Presbyn. Ch. in Am., 1987. Preacher Carmel-Peniel Presbyn. Ch., Rewey, Wis., 1984-85; assoc. pastor, dir. edn. Korean Presbyn. Ch. in Boston, Cambridge, Mass., 1985-88; pastor The Peace Ch., Brockton, Mass., 1988-90, Korean Presbyn. Garden Ch., Hackensack, N.J., 1990-93, Princeton (N.J.) Glory Presbyn. Ch., 1993—; prof., dean acad. affairs Presbyn. Theol. Sem. in Am., Corona, N.Y., 1986-95; sec. gen. Coun. Korean Chs. in New Eng., Boston, 1989-90; rec. sec. Coun. Korean Chs. in N.J., 1991-93. Author: Living the Word, 1990, Living the Prayer, 1994; translator The Black Gold and Isram, 1985. Mem. Am. Acad. Religion, Soc. Bibl. Lit. Home: 9 Sayre Dr Princeton NJ 08540-5804 Office: 115 Sand Hill Rd Monmouth Junction NJ 08852

YUNICH, PETER B., publishing executive; b. N.Y.C., May 9, 1946; s. David Lawrence and Beverly Fay (Blickman) Y.; m. Bonnie Dawn Heiderer, Feb. 17, 1980; children: Whitney, Shannon. BA in Classics, Brown U., 1968; MBA, Harvard U., 1970. Product mgr. Clairol, Inc., N.Y.C., 1970-73; dir. book clubs Doubleday & Co., N.Y.C., 1973-76; exec. v.p. The Charter Co., Jacksonville, Fla., 1977-82; exec. dir. AT&T, Basking Ridge, N.J., 1983-87; pres. Global Transactions Svcs. Co., Basking Ridge, 1987-88, Simon & Schuster Interactive, N.Y.C., 1988—. Home: 7 Highview Ave Basking Ridge NJ 07920-3301 Office: Simon and Schuster 1230 Avenue Of The Americas New York NY 10020-1513

YUNIS, JORGE JOSE, anatomy, pathology, microbiology educator; b. Sincelejo, Colombia, Oct. 5, 1933; s. José and Victoria (Turbay) Y.; m. Malvina Torbay, Jan. 15, 1994; children by previous marriage: George, Olga, Karl, Amira, Omar. MD, Complutense U., Madrid, 1956, PhD, 1957. Gen. practice medicine Barranquilla, Colombia, 1957-59; resident in clin. pathology U. Minn., Mpls., 1959-62, resident in anat. pathology, 1962-64, mem. faculty, 1965-89, prof., 1969-89, dir. grad. studies of lab. medicine, 1969-74, dir. grad. studies of pathology, 1972-74, chmn. human genetics com. for health scis., 1972-77; mem. faculty Hahnemann U., Phila., 1989-92, prof. dept. neoplastic diseases, 1989-92, vice chmn., assoc. dir. Inst. for Cancer and Blood Diseases, 1989-92, dir. Human Genetics and Molecular Biology Div., 1989-92, prof. dept. pathology, 1991-92; prof. depts. anatomy, pathology, microbiology & immunology Thomas Jefferson U. Med. Coll., Phila., 1993—; dir. cancer biol., dept. anatomy, pathology, cell biology Thomas Jefferson U. Med. Col., Phila., 1993—; vis. prof. numerous univs. Author: Human Chromosome Method, 1965, 75, Biochemical Methods in Red Cell Genetics, 1969, Molecular Pathology, 1975, New Chromosomal Syndromes, 1977, Molecular Structure Human Chromosomes, 1977, Esencia Humana, 1995; contbr. more than 250 articles to profl. jours. Named Clin. Prof. of Yr. Harvard Med. Sch., 1987; honored by Colombian Parliament, Bogota, 1986, 93, Colombian Med. Schs. Assn., 1993. Mem. Leukemia Soc. Am. (trustee 1983-88), Colombian Acad. Medicine. Avocations: poetry, literature, photography. Office: Jefferson Med Coll 1020 Locust St Philadelphia PA 19107-6731

YURA, JOSEPH ANDREW, civil engineering educator, consulting structural engineer; b. Hazelton, Pa., Apr. 11, 1938; s. Michael and Anna (Sokol) Y.; m. Joan Marie Seman, Aug. 22, 1964; children: Thomas, Christine, Paul, Elizabeth. B.S., Duke U., 1959; M.S., Cornell U., 1961; Ph.D., Lehigh U., 1965. Registered profl. engr., Tex., Pa., Fla. Asst. prof. Lehigh U., Bethlehem, Pa., 1965-66; asst. prof. U. Tex., Austin, 1966-70, assoc. prof., 1970-75, prof., 1975-82, Warren Bellows prof., 1982—. Recipient Gen. dynamics Teaching award U. Tex., 1972; recipient T.R. Higgins Lectureship award Am. Inst. Steel Constrn., 1974, Hussein M. Alharthy Centennial Professorship award U. Tex., Austin, 1987. Mem. ASCE (Raymond C. Reese Rsch. prize 1991), Structural Stability Rsch. Coun., Rsch. Coun. on Structural Connections, Structural Engrs. Assn. Tex., Am. Soc. for Engring Edn., Phi Beta Kappa, Tau Beta Pi. Democrat. Roman Catholic. Home: 5308 Bull Run Austin TX 78727-6608 Office: U Tex Dept Civil Engring 10100 Burnet Rd Austin TX 78758-4445

YURASKO, FRANK NOEL, judge; b. Rahway, N.J., Dec. 22, 1938; s. Frank H. and Estelle (Trudeau) Y.; m. Mary Byrd, July 23, 1966 (dec. 1991); children—Elizabeth Anne, Suzanne, Frank. B.A., Brown U., 1960; cert. London Sch. Econs., 1961; student Gray's Inn, London, 1960-61; J.D., Yale U., 1964. Bar: N.J. 1964, Fla. 1979, U.S. Dist. Ct. N.J. 1965, U.S. Ct. Appeals (3d cir.) 1980, U.S. Supreme Ct. 1969; cert. civil trial atty., N.J. Judge's law clk. N.J. Dept. Judiciary, Trenton, 1964-66; ptnr. Graham, Yurasko, Golden, Lintner & Rothchild, Somerville, N.J., 1966-80; sole practice, Somerville, 1980—; judge Montgomery Twp. (N.J.) Mcpl. Ct., 1973-84; twp. atty. Hillsborough Twp. (N.J.), 1973—; atty. Green Brook (N.J.) Bd. Adjustment, 1973—. Trustee Gill/St. Bernard Sch., Bernardsville, N.J.; mem. alumni bd. trustees Peddie Sch., Hightstown, N.J. Mem. Am. Judicature Soc., N.J. Bar Assn., Fla. Bar Assn., ABA, Somerset County Bar Assn., Mercer County Bar Assn., Assn. Trial Lawyers Am., Trial Attys. N.J., N.J. Fedn. Planning Ofcls., Nat. Inst. Mcpl. Legal Officers, Middlesex County Trial Lawyers Assn. Office: PO Box 1041 63 Us Highway 206 S Somerville NJ 08876-4102

YURCHENCO, HENRIETTA WEISS, ethnomusicologist, writer; b. New Haven, Mar. 22, 1916; d. Edward and Rebecca (Bernblum) Weiss; m. Basil Yurchenco, June 1936 (div. 1955); 1 child, Peter; m. Irving Levine, 1965 (div. 1979). Student, Yale U., 1935-36; student piano scholarship, Mannes Coll. Music, 1936-38. Radio producer WNYC, WBAI, others, 1939-69; writer, critic, tchr., folk music editor Am. Record Guide and Musical Am., 1959-70; prof. music Coll. City N.Y., 1962-86, Bklyn. Coll., 1966-69, New Sch. for Social Research, 1961-68; co-dir. project for study of women in music, Grad. Ctr. CUNY. Author: A Fiesta of Folk Songs From Spain and Latin America, 1967, A Mighty Hard Road: A Biography of Woody Guthrie, 1970, !Hablamos! Puerto Ricans Speak, 1971; contbr. articles to profl. jours.; 11 field recs. from Mexico, P.R., John's Island, S.C., Guatemala, Ecuador, Morocco, issued by Libr. Congress, Folkways, Nonesuch, Folkways/Smithsonian Global Village; collections in Libr. Congress, Discoteca Hebrew U., Jerusalem, Arais Montana Inst., Madrid, Inst. Nacional Indigenista, Mexico City. Recipient grants-in-aid Am. Philos. Soc., 1954, 56, 57, 65, 67, 89, grants-in-aid CUNY Faculty Research Fund, 1970, 83, 87; NEH grantee, 1984. Mem. Internat. Council Traditional Music (com. on women's studies), Soc. Ethnomusicology, Soc. Asian Music, Sonneck Soc., Internat. Assn. Study of Popular Music, Am. Musicologists Soc. Research in folk, tribal and popular music for Library of Congress, Mexico, Guatemala, P.R., Spain, Morocco, Balearic Islands, John's Island, S.C., Ireland, 1941-83. Home: 360 W 22nd St New York NY 10011-2600 Office: 139th St And Convent Ave New York NY 10031

YURCHUCK, ROGER ALEXANDER, lawyer; b. Amityville, N.Y., June 9, 1938; s. Alexander and Ella Marie (Munley) Y.; m. Sally Ward, Apr. 14, 1961 (div. 1972); children: Scott, Lauren; m. Susan Holland, June 1,

1985. AB cum laude, Northwestern U., 1959; LLB, Harvard U., 1962. Bar: Ohio 1962. Assoc. Vorys, Sater Seymour and Pease, Columbus, Ohio, 1962-68, ptnr., 1969-71, 73—; ptnr. in charge Cin. office Vorys, Sater Seymour and Pease, 1984—; v.p., gen. counsel Fed. Home Loan Mortgage Corp., Washington, 1971-73; vice chmn., bd. dirs. Securities Investors Protection Corp., Washington, 1982-88. Del. Rep. Nat. Conv., 1980, 84. Mem. ABA, Fed. Bar. Assn., Ohio Bar Assn., Phi Beta Kappa. Republican. Episcopalian. Clubs: Queen City (Cin.); Univ. (Columbus). Office: Vorys Sater Seymour and Pease 221 E 4th St Cincinnati OH 45202-4124

YURCISIN, JOHN, church official; m. Ann Popovich, July 16, 1944; 1 child, Ann Melanie. Grad., N.J. State Coll., 1940, Christ the Saviour Sem., 1944. Ordained, 1944. Asst. pastor St. John's Ch., Hawk Run, Pa.; administr. St. Mary's Ch., Clarence, Pa.; pastor Sts. Peter and Paul Ch., Windber, Pa., 1944-52, Christ the Saviour Parish, Johnstown, Pa., 1952; diocesan chancellor; dean Cathedral Parish, Christ the Saviour Sem., 1951-75; elevated to dignity of Protopresbyter, 1962; prof. Orthodox Christian ethics, Carpatho-Russian history and lang., Ch. Slavonic Christ the Saviour Sem.; vicar gen. Am. Carpatho-Russian Orthodox Diocese, 1990—. Editor The Ch. Messenger, 1949-65, A.C.R.Y. Ann. and Ch. Almanac.; contbr. numerous articles and leaflets in field. Decorated Czech. Orthodox Ch.; Carpatho-Russian Studies chair named in his honor. Mem. Orthodox Soc. of Am. Office: 249 Butler Ave Johnstown PA 15906-2137

YUREK, DAVID MAXIMILIAN, neuroscientist, researcher; b. Garfield Heights, Ohio, June 18, 1956; s. Benjamin Frank and Delores Irene (Bogdas) Y.; m. Marjory Mansur; children: David Alexander, Michael Benjamin. BA in Psychology and Biology, U. So. Calif., 1980, PhD in Physiology and Biophysics, 1987. Rsch. technician LTV Techs., Cleve., 1980-82; postdoctoral fellow in neural transplantation and regeneration dept. neurobiology and anatomy sch. medicine U. Rochester, N.Y., 1986-90; asst. prof. dept. surgery/neurosurgery coll. medicine U. Ky., Lexington, 1990—. Reviewer Exptl. Neurology; contbr. articles to profl. jours. Recipient Nat. Sci. Rsch. award NIMH, 1983, Physician Svc. Plan Rsch. award Coll. Medicine, U. Ky., 1992; grantee NIH, 1992—, United Parkinson Found., 1993-94; Neurobehavioral fellow NIMH, 1986, fellow United Parkinson Found., 1989; Woodrow Taylor scholar AARP, 1985. Mem. AAAS, Soc. Neurosci., N.Y. Acad. Scis., Am. Soc. Neural Transplantation. Home: 4321 Buckland Pl Lexington KY 40514-1811 Office: U Ky Coll Medicine 800 Rose St Lexington KY 40536-0001

YURKO, RICHARD JOHN, lawyer; b. Ottawa, Ont., Can., Oct. 30, 1953; came to U.S., 1960; s. Michael and Catherine (Ewanishan) Y.; m. Martha S. Faigen, Apr. 18, 1982; children: Nathan, Daniel. AB summa cum laude, Dartmouth Coll., 1975; JD cum laude, Harvard U., 1979. Bar: Mass. 1979, U.S. Dist. Ct. Mass. 1980, U.S. Ct. Appeals (1st cir.) 1980. Law clk. to Judge James L. King, U.S. Dist. Ct. for So. Dist. Fla., Miami, 1979-80; assoc. Bingham, Dana & Gould, Boston, 1980-85; assoc. Widett, Slater & Goldman, P.C., Boston, 1985-87, shareholder, 1987-92, chmn. litigation dept., 1989-91, hiring ptnr., 1992; shareholder Hutchins, Wheeler & Dittmar, Boston, 1992-94, chmn. litigation dept., 1992-94; shareholder Yurko & Perry, P.C., Boston, 1995—. Contbr. articles to legal jours. Mem. ABA, Mass. Bar Assn., Boston Bar Assn. (chmn. antitrust com.), Phi Beta Kappa. Home: 56 Old Colony Rd Wellesley MA 02181-2844 Office: Yurko & Perry P C 100 City Hall Plz Boston MA 02108

YUROW, JOHN JESSE, lawyer; b. Washington, Jan. 30, 1931; s. Louis and Lauretta (Jedeikin) Y.; m. Bette Hilary Troshinsky, Aug. 1, 1953; children—Michael Jay, Gary Alan, Diane Ruth Yurow Beckwith, Lois Anne. A.B., George Washington U., 1953, J.D., 1958. Bar: D.C. 1958, Mich. 1961. Trial atty. Office Regional Counsel, IRS, Detroit, 1958-62; assoc. Arent, Fox, Kintner, Plotkin & Kahn, Washington, 1962-68, ptnr., 1969—; professorial lectr. in law George Washington U., Washington, 1974-76. Past mem. editorial bd. George Washington U. Law Rev.; contbr. articles on tax subjects to profl. publs. Served with U.S. Army, 1953-55. Mem. D.C. Bar Assn. (chmn. taxation div. 1977-78), ABA, Fed. Bar Assn. (chmn. taxation com. 1972-73), Order of Coif, Phi Delta Phi. Democrat. Club: Indian Spring Country (Silver Spring, Md.). Lodge: B'nai B'rith. Avocations: tennis; travel. Home: 931 Clintwood Dr Silver Spring MD 20902-1724 Office: Arent Fox Kintner Plotkin & Kahn 1050 Connecticut Ave NW Washington DC 20036-5303

YURSO, JOSEPH FRANCIS, engineering manager; b. Hazleton, Pa., July 5, 1930; s. Joseph James and Anna (Payne) Y.; m. Helen Elizabeth Michel, Dec. 17, 1955 (dec. Aug. 1988); children: Joseph Michael, Joanne Elizabeth; m. Barbara Lee Bergen, Apr. 17, 1993. BSME, Pa. State U., 1952; MSME, U.S. Naval Postgrad. U., 1960; hon. degree, Carnegie Mellon U., 1973. Registered profl. engr., Va., Conn. Commd. ens. USN, 1955, advanced through grades to capt., 1975; planning and quality assurance officer, supr. shipbldg. USN, Groton, Conn., 1967-71; ship maintenance officer to comdr. in chief Atlantic Fleet USN, Norfolk, Va., 1971-75; dep. CEO to supr. of shipbldg. conversion and repair USN, Newport News, Va., 1975-77; prodn. officer Norfolk Naval Shipyard USN, Portsmouth, Va., 1977-79; supr. of shipbldg., CEO USN, Groton, Conn., 1979-81; shipyard comdr., CEO Portsmouth Naval Shipyard USN, 1981-84, ret., 1984; group mgr., chief engr. Q.E.D. Sys., Inc., Virginia Beach, Va., 1986—; sr. investigator Naval Sea Sys. Command, Washington, 1974-75, 78-79, 83-84. Contbg. author: Naval Engineering and American Sea Power, 1989; contbr. to profl. publs. Pres. Atlantic Fleet Credit Union, Norfolk, 1974-79, Emmanuel Luth. Ch., Virginia Beach, 1985-87. Recipient Legion of Merit. Mem. ASME, Am. Soc. Naval Engring. (chmn. 1990-91, mem. nat. coun. 1990-92, Presdl. award 1991, 92, Frank G. Law award 1994, nat. v.p. 1993—), Am. Soc. Quality Control (vice chmn. 1991-92, chmn. 1992-95, Presdl. award 1992), Soc. Naval Archs. and Marine Engrs. (chmn. programs 1991-92). Achievements include providing leadership in improving industrial performance of Portsmouth Naval Shipyard, to improve utilization of fleet/U.S. Navy maintenance facilities, introduction of new concepts of quality assurance to U.S. Navy shipbuilding and repair. Home: 4629 Player Ln Virginia Beach VA 23462-4639

YURT, ROGER WILLIAM, medical educator, physician; b. Louisville, June 8, 1945; s. Albert William and Mary Louise (McGrath) Y.; m. Joan A. Terry, Sept. 3, 1971; children: Jennifer, Daniel, Gregory. BS in Biology, Loyola U., New Orleans, 1967; MD, U. Miami, 1972. Diplomate Nat. Bd. Med. Examiners. Intern Parkland Meml. Hosp.-Southwestern Med. Sch., U. Tex.-Dallas, 1972-73, resident in surgery, 1973-74; postdoctoral fellow in medicine Robert B. Brigham Hosp.-Harvard U. Med. Sch., Boston, 1974-77; postdoctoral trainee NIH, 1975-77; resident in surgery, then chief resident in surgery N.Y. Hosp.-Cornell Med. Ctr., N.Y.C., 1977-79, acting dir. Burn Ctr., dir. rsch., 1982-83, dir. Trauma Ctr., 1992—, prof. surgery, 1982-92, prof. surgery, 1992—, The Johnson & Johnson Disting. prof. surgery, 1995—, vice chmn. dept. surgery Cornell U. Med. Coll., 1987—, acting chmn., 1991-93, dir. Burn Ctr., 1995—; acting surgeon-in-chief, The N.Y. Hosp., 1991-93; clin. asst. prof. surgery Uniformed Services U. of Health Sci., Bethesda, Md., 1980-82; clin. asst. prof. gen. surgery Health Sci. Ctr., U. Tex.-San Antonio, 1981-82; chmn. burn com., mem. bd. dirs. Regional Emergency Med. Services of N.Y., 1982-84, mem. trauma ctr. adv. com., 1984—, chmn., 1995—, N.Y. Bklyn. ACS Com. Trauma, 1994—; dir. Mulhearn Research Lab., N.Y.C., 1982—. Editor: Infections in Surgery, 1981-88; contbr. articles to med. jours. Served to maj. M.C., U.S. Army, 1979-82. Grantee United Health Found., 1968-69, NIH, 1984-87; fellow Sch. Medicine, U. Miami, summer 1969-71, USPHS, 1973-75; Irma Hirschl Trust Career Scientist award, 1984-88. Mem. Am. Surg. Assn. Surg. Infection Soc. (charter, chmn. membership com., sec. 1987-90, pres. 1991-92), Assn. Acad. Surgery, Soc. Univ. Surgeons, Internat. Surg. Soc., Am. Assn. for Surgery of Trauma, Ea. Assn. for Surgery of Trauma, Alpha Omega Alpha, Omicron Delta Kappa. Roman Catholic. Office: Cornell U Medical Coll 1300 York Ave New York NY 10021-4805

YUSPEH, ALAN RALPH, lawyer; b. New Orleans, June 13, 1949; s. Michel and Rose Fay (Rabenovitz) Y.; m. Janet Horn, June 8, 1975. B.A., Yale U., 1971; M.B.A., Harvard U., 1973; J.D., Georgetown U., 1978. Bar: D.C. 1978. Mgmt. cons. McKinsey & Co., Washington, 1973-74; adminstrv. asst., legis. asst. Office of U.S. Senator J. Bennett Johnston, Washington, 1974-78; atty. Shaw, Pittman, Potts & Trowbridge, Washington, 1978-79, Ginsburg, Feldman, Weil and Bress, Washington, 1979-82; gen. counsel Com. on Armed Services-U.S. Senate, Washington, 1982-85; ptnr. Preston, Thorgrimson, Ellis & Holman, Washington, 1985-88, Miller & Chevalier, Washington, 1988-91, Howrey & Simon, Washington, 1991—. Editor Law and Policy in Internat. Business jour., 1978-79, Nat. Contract Mgmt. Jour., 1988-92; assoc. editor Pub. Contract Law jour., 1987-91. Chmn. bd. of ethics, City of Balt., 1988-96. 1st lt. USAR, 1971-77. Home: 1812 South Rd Baltimore MD 21209-4506 Office: Howrey & Simon 1299 Pennsylvania Ave NW Washington DC 20004-2400

YUSTER-FREEMAN, LEIGH CAROL, publishing company executive; b. Trenton, N.J., July 23, 1949; d. Leon Carl and Helen Loretta (Wisniewski) Markiewicz; m. Charles Yuster (div. Apr. 1985); stepchildren: Sarah, Elizabeth, Jared, Alexandra; m. Richard N. Freeman; 1 child, Jessica Lee Freeman. Editor R.R. Bowker, N.Y.C., 1971-72, ISBN agy. editorial coord., 1972-78, editorial coord., 1978-79, mgr., AV svcs., 1979-81, mgr., data sources, 1981-83, sr. product mgr., 1983-85, exec. editor, mng. editor, 1985-87, dir. product enhancements, 1987-88, dir. product devel., pub. Ulrich's Database, 1990-91; assoc. pub. Bowker Bus. Rsch., A&I Pub. R.R. Bowker, New Providence, N.J., 1990-91, also pub. Ulrich's Database, 1990-91, pub. Broadcasting & Cable Yearbook, 1991—; mng. dir. Reed Reference Pub., New Providence, 1992-94, v.p. bibliographies, 1994-96, v.p. directories, 1996—; ptnr. Eagle Bakery, Renton, N.J., 1991—. Recipient Climate of Excellence award, Cahners Pub. Co., Newton, Mass., 1987, Cert. of Appreciation, Consortium of Univ. Film Ctrs., Kent, Ohio, 1986. Mem. ALA, Nat. Fedn. of Abstracting and Info. Svcs., Consortium of Coll. and Univ. Media Ctrs., Actors Equity Assn., Am. Rose Soc., Mercer County Bd. Realtors. Democrat. Jewish. Avocations: gardening, dancing, music, kinesiology, community services. Home: 19 Theodora Dr Hillsborough NJ 08876-4723*

YZAGUIRRE, RAUL HUMBERTO, civil rights administrator; b. San Juan, Tex., July 22, 1939; s. Ruben Antonio and Eva Linda (Morin) Y.; m. Audrey H. Bristow, Jan. 2, 1965; children: Regina Dolores, Raul Humberto, Elisa Almalinda, Roberto Hayse, Rebecca Morin, Benjamin Ruben. Student, U. Md., 1963-64; B.S., George Washington U., 1968. Registered med. technologist. Student and community activist, 1963-65; active War on Poverty, 1969-74; founder, exec. dir. Interstate Research Assocs (Hispanic cons. firm), Washington, 1969-73; v.p. Center for Community Change, Washington, 1974; community organizer in S.Tex., 1974; pres. Nat. Council of La Raza, Washington, 1974—; lectr. Harvard U., U. Notre Dame, U. Tex., others.; commr. U.S. Nat. Commn. for UNESCO, 1983—; chmn. bd. dirs. Associated SW Investors, 1976—. Editor-in-chief: Agenda, 1974-81. Co-chmn. Nat. Urban Coalition, 1975-83; co-chmn. Working Com. on Concerns of Hispanics and Blacks, 1979—, sec. ind. sector, 1983-84; sec., chmn. Forum of Nat. Hispanic Orgns., 1976-79; chmn. adv. com. I.N.S.; former trustee Common Cause; co-founder, chmn. Nat. Neighborhood Coalition, 1977—. Served with USAF, 1959-62. Recipient Rockefeller Public Service award, 1979, Common Cause Pub. Service award, 1986. Mem. Am. GI Forum, Hispanic Assn. Corp. Responsibility (co-founder, chmn. bd. dirs.). Democrat. Roman Catholic. Office: Nat Coun La Raza 1111 19th St NW Ste 1000 Washington DC 20036 *The civil rights struggle of the 80's will be the transformation of America to a truly pluralistic society where cultural differences will not only be tolerated, but indeed valued.*

YZERMAN, STEVE, professional hockey player; b. Cranbrook, B.C., Can., May 9, 1965. With Detroit Red Wings, 1983—. Recipient Lester B. Pearson award, 1988-89; named Sporting News NHL Rookie of Yr., NHL All-Rookie Team, 1983-84, 1988-93. Youngest person ever to play in NHL All-Star game, 1984. Office: Detroit Red Wings 600 Civic Center Dr Detroit MI 48226-4408*

ZABAN, ERWIN, diversified manufacturing company executive; b. Atlanta, Aug. 17, 1921; s. Mandle and Sara Unis (Feidelson) Z.; m. Judy Zaban; children: Carol Zaban Cooper, Laura Zaban Dinerman, Sara Kay Franco. Officer Zep Mfg. Co., 1942-62; exec. v.p. Nat. Service Industries, Atlanta, 1962-66, pres., 1966-79, chief exec. officer, 1972-87, chmn., 1975—, also dir.; bd. dir. Engraph, Inc., Wachovia Corp.; elected mem. bd. visitors Berry Coll. Bd. dirs. Atlanta Symphony Orch., 1982, Jewish Home for the Aged, 1985; trustee Atlanta Hist. Soc., 1985. Named Man of Yr. B'nai B'rith, 1977, Father of Yr. Father's Day Coun.; recipient Disting. Svc. award Atlanta Urban League, 1979, NCCJ, 1988, Human Rels. award Anti-Defamation League, 1981, Bd. Govs. award 11-Alive Community Svc. Awards, 1990; named to Ga. State U. Coll. Bus. Adminstrn. Hall of Fame, 1989. Mem. Standard Club, Commerce Club (bd. dirs.). Office: Nat Svc Industries Inc 1420 Peachtree St NE Atlanta GA 30309-3002*

ZABEL, EDWARD, economist, educator; b. Orange, N.J., Oct. 17, 1927; s. Otto and Helen (Katzenberger) Z.; m. Norma Nicholson, June 23, 1956; children: Jeffrey, David, Richard. B.A., Syracuse (N.Y.) U., 1950; M.A., Princeton U., 1953, Ph.D., 1956. Research asst. Princeton U., 1954-56; economist Rand Corp., Santa Monica, Calif., 1956-58; mem. faculty U. Rochester, N.Y., 1958-81; prof. econs. U. Rochester, 1967-81; prof. econs. U. Fla., Gainesville, 1981-83, Matherly prof. econs. and decision scis., 1983—; assoc. editor Mgmt. Sci., 1969-73; bd. editors Applied Econs., 1973—, Applied Econs. Letters, 1993—. Contbr. to profl. jours. Served with AUS, 1945-47. Ford Found. fellow, 1964-65; NSF rsch. grantee, 1960-81. Mem. Am. Econ. Assn., Econometric Soc., Internat. Soc. Inventory Rsch., Western Econ. Assn., Inst. mgmt. Scis., AAUP, Phi Beta Kappa. Democrat. Home: 1926 NW 27th St Gainesville FL 32605-3863 Office: U Fla Dept Econs Gainesville FL 32611

ZABEL, SHELDON ALTER, lawyer, law educator; b. Omaha, Apr. 25, 1941; s. Louis Julius and Anne (Rothenberg) Z.; m. Roberta Jean Butz, May 10, 1975; children: Andrew Louis, Douglas Patrick, Robert Stewart Warren. AB cum laude, Princeton U., 1963; JD cum laude, Northwestern U., 1966. Bar: Ill. 1966, U.S. Supreme Ct. 1976. Law clk. to presiding justice, Ill. Sup. Ct., 1966-67; assoc. Schiff, Hardin & Waite, Chgo., 1967-73, ptnr., 1973—; instr. environ. law Loyola U., Chgo. Mem. bd. dirs. Chgo. Zool. Soc. Mem. ABA, Chgo. Bar Assn., Chgo. Coun. Lawyers, Order of Coif. Jewish. Clubs: Union League, Metropolitan (Chgo.). Avocations: skiing, squash. Office: Schiff Hardin & Waite 7200 Sears Tower 233 S Wacker Dr Chicago IL 60606-6306

ZABEL, VIVIAN ELLOUISE, secondary education educator; b. Randolph AFB, Tex., July 28, 1943; d. Raymond Louis and Dolly Veneta (Lyles) Gilbert; m. Robert Lee Zabel, Feb. 18, 1962; children: René Lynne, Robert Lee Jr., Randel Louis, Regina Louise. BA in English and Speech, Panhandle State U., 1977; postgrad., U. Cen. Okla., 1987-92. Cert. tchr., Okla. Tchr. English, drama, speech, debate Buffalo (Okla.) High Sch., 1977-79; tchr. English, drama, speech Schulter (Okla.) High Sch., 1979-80; tchr. English Morris (Okla.) High Sch., 1980-81; tchr. speech, drama, debate Okla. Christian Schs., Edmond, 1981-82; tchr. English, drama, debate, speech/debate coach Braman (Okla.) High Sch., 1982-83; debate coach Pawhuska (Okla.) High Sch., 1983-84; tchr. English, French, drama, speech and debate coach Luther (Okla.) High Sch., 1984-95; tchr. debate, forensics, yearbook, English, competitive speech Deer Creek H.S., Edmond, Okla., 1995—; dir. drama Nazarene Youth Impact Team, Collinsville, Okla., 1979-81; tchr. H.S. Sunday Sch. class Edmond Ch. of Nazarene, 1991-95; mem. cmty.-sch. rels. com. Luther Pub. Schs., 1991-92, mem. supt.'s adv. com., 1992-94. Editor Potpourri mag., 1975-77; author poetry, short stories. Adult supr. Texas County 4-H, Adams, Okla., 1975-77; double diamond coach NFL; adjudicator and tournament dir. qualifying OSSAA Tournaments. Recipient Disting. Svc. award NFL, 1994. Mem. Nat. Debate Coaches Assn., Nat. Fedn. Interscholastic Speech and Debate Assn., Okla. Speech Theatre Communications Assn., Okla. Coun. Tchrs. Engl. Republican. Nazarene. Home: 2912 Rankin Ter Edmond OK 73013-5344 *Children are our future, yet we are living in an age of throwaway children. We must find a way to save these children, to give them purpose, training, and love so that they have a promising future, and so will we.*

ZABRISKIE, JOHN L., healthcare and agricultural products manufacturing company executive; b. 1940. -. With Merck & Co., Inc., Whitehouse Station, N.J., 1965-93, past exec. v.p., past pres. mfg. divsn.; chmn., CEO Upjohn Co., Kalamazoo, 1993—, also bd. dirs.; pres., CEO Pharmacia & Upjohn, Inc., Staines, U.K. Office: Pharmacia & Upjohn Inc, Knyvett House, The Causeway Staines Middlesex TW18 3BA, United Kingdom

ZABSKY, JOHN MITCHELL, engineering executive; b. Joplin, Mo., Apr. 18, 1933; s. Joseph Anthony and Joan (Lucas) Z. AS, Joplin Jr. Coll., 1953; BSME, U. Mo., 1956; MSME, U. Kans., 1965. Profl. engr., Mo. System engr. Bendix KCD, Kansas City, Mo., 1958-62; rsch. engr. Rocketdyne, Neosho, Mo., 1962-65, Boeing Co., Huntsville, Ala., 1965-66; prin. rsch. engr., scientist Honeywell Inc., St. Paul, 1966-71; chief engr. Pressure Tank & Pipe Fabrication Co., Nashville, 1971-72, Engring. for Industry, Danville, Va., 1972-73; area mgr. fluid machinery Dresser Adv. Tech. Ctr., Irvine, Calif., 1973-85; v.p. ops. ATI, Laguna Niguel, Calif., 1985-93; pres. Cytoprobe, San Diego, 1993-94, v.p. ops., 1994-95; cons. Oral Care Products, L.A., 1990-92, Kleenair Sys., Inc., Irvine, Calif. Patentee in field. Pres. Mpls.-St. Paul Singletons, 1969-72. Mem. AIAA, ASME, Mo. Soc. Profl. Engrs., Soc. Mfg. Engrs. Home: 3640C S Main St Santa Ana CA 92707-5720

ZACCAGNI, JAMES LOUIS, accountant; b. Springfield, Ill., Oct. 12, 1945; s. Louis Paul and Hazel June (Unland) Z.; m. Jennifer G. Zaccagni, Feb. 25, 1978; children: Zachary, Kirsten, Hayden, Amanda. BSBA, So. Ill. U., 1969. CPA, Ill., Tex. Sr. ptnr. Pehlman & Dold CPA's, Springfield, Ill., 1971-85; pvt. practice San Antonio, 1985-88; sr. tax ptnr. Lowrey, Zaccagni & Crider, San Antonio, 1988—. Treas., v.p. Children's Chorus of San Antonio, 1988—; advisor Women's Aglow fellowship, 1988-92, Full Gospel Bus. Men's fellowship Internat., 1992—, pres. and treas., 1989—; treas. Assn. of Spirit Filled fellowship. Mem. Internat. Assn. of Fin. Planners (officer, bd. dirs. 1991—), Tex. Soc. of CPA's (advanced cert. corp. taxation 1994), AICPA, San Antonio Chpt. of CPA's. Avocations: landscaping, music. Office: Lowrey Zaccagni & Crider 14100 San Pedro Ave Ste 300 San Antonio TX 78232-4361

ZACCAGNINO, JOSEPH ANTHONY, hospital administrator; b. New Rochelle, N.Y., June 16, 1946. BA, U. Conn., 1968; MA, Yale U., 1970. Adminstrv. resident Yale-New Haven (Conn.) Hosp., 1970-71, adminstrv. asst., 1971-72, asst. dir., 1972-75, assoc. dir., 1975-77, v.p. adminstrn., 1977-78, exec. v.p., COO, 1978-91, pres., CEO, 1991—. Mem. NEHA, Am. Hosp. Assn. (mem. com. svc.), Conn. Hosp. Assn. (trustee). Office: Yale-New Haven Hosp 20 York St New Haven CT 06510-3220*

ZACCARIA, ADRIAN, utilities executive; b. 1944. BS, U.S. Merchant Marine Acad., 1966. Engr. Raytheon Co., Lexington, Mass., 1967-68, Gen. Dynamics Corp., Falls Ch., Va., 1968-71; with Bechtel Power Corp., San Francisco, 1974—, now pres. Office: Bechtel Power Corp PO Box 193965 50 Beale St San Francisco CA 94105-1813*

ZACCHINO, NARDA, newspaper editor. Assoc. editor L.A. Times, Calif. Office: Los Angeles Times Times Mirror Sq Los Angeles CA 90053

ZACEK, JOSEPH FREDERICK, history educator, international studies consultant, East European culture and affairs specialist; b. Stickney, Ill., Dec. 18, 1930; s. Joseph and Emilie (Dvorak) Z.; m. Judith Ellen Cohen (div. 1975); 1 child, Natalie Ann; m. Jane Perlberg Shapiro; stepchildren: Leslie Helen, Peter Carl. BA summa cum laude, U. Ill., Champaign-Urbana, 1952, MA in History, 1953, PhD in History, 1962; cert., Columbia U. Inst. on East Cen. Europe, 1962. Asst. prof. history Occidental Coll., L.A., 1962-65; asst. prof., dir. Russian & East European Programs UCLA, 1965-68; assoc. prof. SUNY at Albany, 1968-71, dir. Russian & East European Programs, 1968-77, 91-92, prof., 1971—, chair dept. history, 1974-77; mem. selection com. for East Europe Internat. Rsch. and Exch. Bd., Princeton, N.J., 1978-81; nat. bd. cons. NEH, Washington, 1975—; vis. scholar IREX Comenius U., Bratislava, and Charles U., Prague, Czechoslovakia, 1973, Columbia U., 1977-78, U. Ill, Champaign-Urbana, 1987. Author: Palacky: The Historian as Scholar and Nationalist, 1970; editor, co-author: Frantisek Palacky, 1798-1876: A Centennial Appreciation, 1981, The Enlightenment and the National Revivals in Eastern Europe, 1983, The Intimate Palacky, 1984; also numerous periodical articles and chpts. in multi-authored books. With M.I., U.S. Army, 1954-57. Fgn. Area Tng. fellow Ford Found., Columbia U., 1960-62, Sr. Humanities fellow Rockefeller Found., 1977-78, fellow Russian Rsch. Ctr. Harvard U., 1986-91; rsch. grantee Am. Coun. Learned Soc./Soc. Sci. Rsch. Coun., 1965, Am. Philos. Soc., 1968; recipient Comenius medal Govt. of Czech and Slovak Fed. Republic, 1992, Medal of Comenius Pedagogical Inst. in Prague, 1992, Josef Hlávka medal of Czechoslovak Acad. of Scis. in Prague, 1992; also other grad. and postdoctoral awards and grants. Mem. Am. Hist. Assn., Am. Assn. for Advancement Slavic Studies, Czechoslovak History Conf., Slovak Studies Assn., Consortium on Revolutionary Europe, Assn. for Study of Ethnicity and Nationalism, Phi Beta Kappa. Avocations: travel, gardening, music. Office: SUNY Dept History Albany NY 12222

ZACHAR, CHRISTOPHER JOSEPH, lawyer; b. Cedar Rapids, Iowa, Dec. 26, 1964; s. Thomas Joseph and Judith Marie (Smith) Z. BS, Ariz. State U., 1989; JD, U. Ariz., 1992. Bar: Ariz. 1992. Various to law clk. various offices, Chgo., 1989-90, Ariz., 1990-92; ptnr. Zachar & Doughty, P.C., Scottsdale, Ariz., 1992—; futures mgr. Fiesta Bowl, Tempe, 1995. Mem. ATLA, Maricopa County Bar Assn., ABA (student divsn.), Scottsdale Bar Assn. Republican. Avocations: phys. fitness, golf, skiing. Office: Zachar & Doughty PC 3509 E Shea Blvd Ste 111 Phoenix AZ 85028 also: 1515 E Cedar Ave Ste D-3 Flagstaff AZ 86004

ZACHARIA, MATHEW VARIKALAM, educational administrator, management consultant; b. Edathua, Kerala, India, July 9, 1947; came to U.S., 1969; s. Varikalathil Mathew and Annamma (Thomas) Z.; m. Elizabeth Rajeena Cherian, June 13, 1953; children: Manoj Mathew, Melanie Elizabeth. AAS, Manhattan Coll., Bronx, 1971, BS, 1973; MPA, L.I. U., 1990. Adminstrv. dir. Mercy Cmty. Hosp., Port Jervis, N.Y., 1977-86; mgmt. cons. Port Jervis, 1986—; instr. Orange County C.C., Middletown, N.Y., 1990-91; pres. Crossroad Books and Gifts, Port Jervis, 1994—. Mem. sch. bd. Port Jervis City Schs., 1993—; mem. Orange County Christian Coalition, 1993—; Sun. sch. tchr. St. Thomas Marthoma Ch., Yonkers, N.Y., 1987—; organizer Kerala Samajam of Greater N.Y., Manhattan, 1969-70. Mem. Lions. Republican. Avocations: evangelism, Bible reading, touring the Holy Land and Israel. Home: PO Box 196 14 Highland Ave Sparrow Bush NY 12780

ZACHARIAS, DONALD WAYNE, academic administrator; b. Salem, Ind., Sept. 28, 1935; s. William Otto and Estelle Mae (Newlon) Z.; m. Tommie Kline Dekle, Aug. 16, 1959; children: Alan, Eric, Leslie. BA, Georgetown (Ky.) Coll., 1957, LLD (hon.), 1983; MA, Ind. U., 1959, PhD, 1963. Asst. prof. communication and theatre Ind. U., 1963-69; assoc. prof. U. Tex., Austin, 1969-72; prof. U. Tex., 1972-79, asst. to pres., 1974-77; exec. asst. to chancellor U. Tex. System, 1978-79; pres. Western Ky. U., 1979-85, Miss. State U., 1985—; bd. dirs. First Fed. Savs. & Loan Assn., Bowling Green, Ky., Inst. for Tech. Devel., Sanderson Farms, Inc., Miss. econ. Coun. Author: In Pursuit of Peace: Speeches of the Sixties, 1970. Bd. dirs. Greenview Hosp.; pres. Southeastern Conf., 1989-91. With U.S. Army, 1959-60. Named Mississippian of Yr. Data Processing Mgmt. Assn.; recipient Teaching award Ind. U. Found., 1963, Cactus Teaching award U. Tex., 1971, Justin Smith Morrill award U.S. Dept. Agriculture, 1992. Mem. Inst. Tech. Devel. (bd. dirs. 1985-92), Nat. Assn. State Univs. and Land-Grant Colls. (exec. com. 1990-92), Phi Kappa Phi (pres. 1978). Democrat. Episcopalian. Office: Miss State U Office of Pres PO Box J Mississippi State MS 39762

ZACHARIASEN, FREDRIK, physics educator, consultant; b. Chgo., June 14, 1931; s. William Houlder and Ragni (Durban-Hansen) Z.; m. Nancy Walker, Jan. 27, 1957; children—Kerry, Judith. B.S., U. Chgo., 1951; Ph.D., Calif. Inst. Tech., 1956. Instr. MIT, Cambridge, 1955-56; research physicist U. Calif.-Berkeley, 1956-57; asst. prof. physics Stanford U., Calif., 1957-60; prof. Calif. Inst. Tech., Pasadena, 1960—; assoc. dir. Los Alamos Nat. Lab., 1982-83. Author: Structure of Nucleons, 1960; Hadron Physics, 1973; Sound Fluctuation, 1979. Sloan fellow, 1960-64; Guggenheim fellow, 1970. Home: 2235 Villa Heights Rd Pasadena CA 91107-1142 Office: Calif Inst Tech 1201 E California Blvd Pasadena CA 91125-0001

ZACHEM, HARRY M., oil company executive; b. Ironton, Ohio, Aug. 14, 1944; s. Charles Russell and Millie (Norris) Z.; m. Mary M. Hamilton, 1987 ; children: Nancy Kathryn, Mary Elizabeth; m. Mary U. Hamilton, Apr. 1987. BA, U. Ky., 1968; A.M.P., Harvard U., 1985. Supr. Ky. State Govt.,

Frankfort, 1968-71; sales rep. Ashland Oil Inc., Balt., 1972-74; pub. relations rep. Ashland Oil Inc., Ashland, Ky., 1974-75; Washington rep. Ashland Oil Inc., 1975-81, v.p. fed. govt. relations, 1981-86; adminstrv. v.p. Ashland Oil Inc., Ashland, 1986-88; sr. v.p. external affairs Ashland, Inc., 1988—. bd. dirs. Pub. Affairs Council, Washington, 1984—. Mem. Nat. Assn. Mfrs. (bd. dirs. 1992—). Episcopalian. Avocations: golf; tennis; sailing. Office: Ashland Inc PO Box 391 Ashland KY 41105-0391

ZACHER, VALERIE IRENE, interior designer; b. Woodland, Calif., Dec. 12, 1942; d. Albert Richard and Laura Ruth (Mast) Z.; m. William Robert Wallace, June 14, 1964 (div. Oct. 1968); 1 child, Jason Zachery Wallace. BA in Polit. Sci., Stanford U., 1964; AS in Interior Design, West Valley Coll., 1982; cert. TESL, U. Calif. Santa Cruz, Santa Clara, 1994. Owner, operator Artefactorage, Fresno, Calif., 1968-77; owner, designer Viz a Viz, Los Gatos, Calif., 1978-82; facilities project mgr. Nat. Semiconductor, Santa Clara, Calif., 1982-85; project supr. Mervyns, Hayward, Calif., 1985-86; interior designer, project mgr. Charles Schwab & Co., San Francisco, 1986-87; small bus. advisor US Peace Corps, Gaborone, Botswana, 1987-89, Swedish Coop. Ctr., Gaborone, 1989-90; English tchr. YCC Am. Club, Yokohama, Japan, 1992-93; interior design cons. Los Gatos, 1993—; design/facilities cons. Octel Comm. Corp., Milpitas, Calif., 1994—; interior designer Am. Cancer Soc. Designers Showcase, 1994, 95, 96. Avocations: gourmet cooking, gardening, travel. Home and Office: 16721 Madrone Ave Los Gatos CA 95030-4120

ZACHERT, MARTHA JANE, retired librarian; b. York, Pa., Feb. 7, 1920; d. Paul Rodes and Elizabeth Agnes (Lau) Koontz; m. Edward G. Zachert, Aug. 25, 1946; 1 child, Lillian Elizabeth. AB, Lebanon Valley Coll., 1941; MLS, Emory U., 1953; DLS, Columbia U., 1968. Asst. Enoch Pratt Free Library, Balt., 1941-46; head librarian Wood Research Inst., Atlanta, 1947; sch. librarian DeKalb (Ga.) County Schs., 1950-52; head librarian, prof. history of pharmacy So. Coll. Pharmacy, Mercer U., Atlanta, 1952-63; instr. Ga. State Coll., 1962-63, Emory U., summers 1955-59, 1956-57, 59-60; mem. faculty Library Sch., Fla. State U., 1963-78, prof., 1973-78; prof. Coll. Librarianship U. S.C., Columbia, 1973-74, 78-84; vis. fellow Brit. Library, 1980; cons. So. Regional Med. Library, Emory U., 1976-77, Nat. Library Medicine, 1977, others. Assoc. editor: Jour. Library History, 1966-71, 73-76; mng. editor, 1971-73; cons. editor: Jour. Library Adminstrn., 1979-86; contbr. numerous articles to profl. jours. Fellow Med. Libr. Assn.; mem. ALA, Spl. Librs. Assn. (past pres. Fla. chpt., spl. citation 1977, Hall of Fame 1985), Southwestern Libr. Assn. (Hall of Fame 1985), Am. Printing History Assn., Beta Phi Mu (pres. 1974-75). Home and Office: 2018 W Randolph Cir Tallahassee FL 32312-3349

ZACHERT, VIRGINIA, psychologist, educator; b. Jacksonville, Ala., Mar. 1, 1920; d. R.E. and Cora H. (Massee) Z. Student, Norman Jr. Coll., 1937; AB, Ga. State Woman's Coll., 1940; MA, Emory U., 1947; PhD, Purdue U., 1949. Diplomate: Am. Bd. Profl. Psychologists. Statistician Davison-Paxon Co., Atlanta, 1941-44; research psychologist Mil. Contracts, Auburn Research Found., Ala. Poly. Inst.; indsl. and research psychologist Sturm & O'Brien (cons. engrs.), 1958-59; research project dir. Western Design, Biloxi, Miss., 1960-61; self-employed cons. psychologist Norman Park, Ga., 1961-71, Good Hope, Ga., 1971—; rsch. assoc. med. edn. Med. Coll. Ga., Augusta, 1963-65, assoc. prof., 1965-70, rsch. prof., 1970-84, rsch. prof. emeritus, 1984—, chief learning materials divsn., 1973-84, faculty senate, 1976-84, acad. coun., 1976-82, pres. acad. coun., 1983, sec., 1978; mem. Ga. Bd. Examiners Psychologists, 1974-79, v.p., 1977, pres. 1978; adv. bd. Comdr. Gen. ATC USAF, 1967-70; cons. Ga. Silver Haired Legislature, 1980-86, senator, 1987-93, pres. protem, 1987-88, pres., 1989-93, rep., spkr. protem, 1993—; govs. appointee Ga. Coun. on Aging, 1988-96; U.S. Senate mem. Fed. Coun. on the Aging, 1990-93; senator appointee White House Conf. on Aging, 1995. Author: (with P.L. Wilds) Essentials of Gynecology-Oncology, 1967, Applications of Gynecology-Oncology, 1967. Del. White House Conf. on Aging, 1981, 95. Served as ecologist USN, 1944-46;aviation psychologist USAF, 1949-54. Fellow AAAS, Am. Psychol. Assn.; mem. AAUP (chpt. pres. 1977-80), Sigma Xi (chpt. pres. 1980-81). Baptist. Home: 1126 Highland Ave Augusta GA 30904-4628 Office: Med Coll Ga Dept Ob-Gyn Augusta GA 30912 *It's really quite simple—I find, if I wish to be understood or heard, that simplicity is necessary but not ever easy. Simplicity is basic, essential and always the major factor in my search for truth.*

ZACHOS, KIMON STEPHEN, lawyer; b. Concord, N.H., Nov. 20, 1930; s. Stephen and Sophia (Bacogiannis) Z.; m. Anne Colby, July 5, 1959; children: Ellen, Elizabeth, Sarah. BA, Wesleyan U., 1952; JD, NYU, 1955; LLM, Boston U., 1968; LLD (hon.), N.H. Coll., 1992, St. Anselm Coll., 1994. Bar: N.H. 1955, U.S. Dist. Ct. N.H. 1957, U.S. Supreme Ct. 1963. Ptnr. Sheehan, Phinney, Bass & Green, Manchester, N.H., 1957—; White House fellow, spl. asst. to atty. gen. Nicholas deB. Katzenbach, Washington, 1965-66; bd. dirs. New Eng. Tel., Bank of Ireland 1st Holdings Inc., 1st NH Bank Inc., Hitchiner Mfg. Co., Inc., also others. Dep. speaker N.H. Ho. Reps., 1969-74; active various charitable and ednl. orgns. Named Man of Yr., Manchester C. of C., 1985, Disting. Citizen, Boy Scouts Am., 1987, Bus. Leader of Yr., New Hampshire Assn. C of C., 1994; recipient Brotherhood award NCCJ, 1966. Mem. ABA, N.H. Bar Assn. Republican. Greek Orthodox. Avocation: stamp collecting. Home: 2093 Elm St Manchester NH 03104-2316 Office: Sheehan Phinney Bass & Green 1000 Elm St Manchester NH 03101

ZACHRY, HENRY BARTELL, JR., construction company executive; b. 1933; married. BSCE, Tex. A&M U., 1954. With H.B. Zachry Co., San Antonio, 1957—, pres., chief exec. officer, 1965-86, chmn., dir., 1984—. Office: H B Zachry Co PO Box 21130 527 W Harding Blvd San Antonio TX 78221-1810 also: Zachry Inc 527 Logwood Ave San Antonio TX 78221-1738*

ZACK, ARNOLD MARSHALL, lawyer, mediator, arbitrator; b. Lynn, Mass., Oct. 7, 1931; s. Samuel George and Bess Ethel (Freedman) Z.; m. Norma Eta Wilner, Aug. 10, 1969; children: Jonathan Samuel, Rachel Anne. AB, Tufts Coll., 1953; LLB, Yale U., 1956; MPA, Harvard U., 1961. Asst. to Saul Wallen (arbitrator), 1956-63; cons. UN Mission to Congo, 1960, U.S. Peace Corps, 1961-63, Labor Dept., 1962-79, Pres.'s Study Commn. on Nat. Service Corps, 1962-63, U.S. AID, 1963—, Friedrich Ebert Stiftung, 1963-64, Nat. Center for Dispute Settlement, 1968-76; vis. Fulbright lectr. Haile Selassie U., Addis Ababa, 1963-64; referee Nat. R.R.Adjustment Bd., 1964—; mem. faculty Harvard U. Trade Union Program, 1985—; dir.Labor-Mgmt. Inst., Am. Arbitration Assn., 1966-68; full time mediator/arbitrator, Boston, 1968—; bd. dirs. ctr. for socio-legal studies faculty of law U. Natal, 1986-92; mem. Fgn. Svc. Labor Rels. Bd., 1982-84, Presdl. Emergency Bds. 221 and 222; cons. Internat. Labor Orgn., 1961—; chair Essential Industries Dipute Settlement Bd. Bermuda, 1993—; vis. lectr. Yale Law Sch., 1995—; permanent arbitrator, Am. Airlines & APA, Gen. Dynamics, IAM, TWA and Air Line Pilots Assn., TWA and IAM; Yale U. and Fedn. Univ., Procter & Gamble and Ind. Oil and Chem. Workers, Commonwealth Mass., Capital ABC and NABET. Author: Labor Training in Developing Countries, 1964, Ethiopia's High Level Manpower-Analysis and Projections, 1964, Handbook on Grievance Arbitration in the Public Sector, 1974, Handbook on Fact Finding and Arbitration in the Public Sector, 1974, Grievance Arbitration, A Practical Guide, 1977; (with R. Bloch) Arbitration of Discipline and Discharge Cases, 1979, (with R. Bloch) The Agreement in Negotiation and Arbitration, 1983; 2nd Edition, 1995— Arbitration in Practice, 1984, Mediation in the Public Sector, 1985, Grievance Arbitration: Cases on the Merits in Discipline Discharge and Contract Interpretation, 1989, Handbook on Grievance Arbitration: Issues on Procedure and Ethics, 1992; contbr. articles to profl. jours. Recipient Whitney North Seymour medal for oustanding contbn. to arbitration, 1980, Cushing Gavin award, 1986, Mildred Spaulding award, 1987, Disting. Svc. award for arbitration of labor-mgmt. disputes, 1989. Fellow African Studies Assn.; mem. Nat. Acad. Arbitrators (treas. 1972-75, bd. govs. 1977-79, v.p. 1980-82, pres. 1994-95, pres. Rsch. and Edn. Found. 1989-91), Am. Arbitration Assn., Indsl. Rels. Rsch. Assn., Internat. Soc. for Labor Law and Social Securities (bd. dirs.), Harvard Club (Boston), Yale Club (N.Y.C.). Address: 170 W Canton St Boston MA 02118-1216

ZACK, DANIEL GERARD, library director; b. Waukegan, Ill., Oct. 1, 1943; s. Raymond Gerard and Rosanna Marie (Atkinson) Z.; m. Mary Frances Anthony, Aug. 25, 1966; children: Jennifer Lee, Rebecca Jane. BA in Psychology, Western Ill. U., 1967; MS in Libr. Sci., U. Ill., 1975. Editor IBM Corp., Rochester, Minn., 1968-70, Memorex Corp., Mpls., 1970-74; rsch. assoc. Libr. Rsch. Ctr. U. Ill., Urbana, 1974-75; asst. dir. Portage County Pub. Libr., Stevens Point, Wis., 1976-78; dir. Burlington (Iowa) Pub. Libr., 1978-87, Gail Borden Pub. Libr., Elgin, Ill., 1987—. Bd. dirs. Friends of Ill. Librs., 1990—. Mem. ALA, ACLU, Ill. Libr. Assn. (mgr. pub. libr. forum 1991-92, exec. bd. dirs. 1992-95, pub. policy com. 1995—), Pub. Libr. Assn. (intellectual freedom com. 1993—), Kiwanis. Office: Gail Borden Pub Libr Dist 200 N Grove Ave Elgin IL 60120-5505

ZACKHEIM, ADRIAN WALTER, editor; b. N.Y.C., Sept. 19, 1951; s. Albert Alex and Mary Elizabeth (Cooper) Z.; m. Sarah Babst Parsons, Sept. 1, 1985; children: Adrian Alex, David Parsons. BA, Grinnell Coll., 1973; MA, U. Toronto, Ont., Can., 1975. Editor St. Martins Press, N.Y.C., 1977-79; editor Doubleday & Co., Inc., N.Y.C., 1979-84, sr. editor, 1984-85; sr. editor William Morrow & Co., Inc., N.Y.C., 1986-89, sr. editor, v.p., 1989-90, exec. editor, v.p., 1990-91, editorial dir., v.p., 1991-94; publishing dir., v.p. HarperBus., 1994—; exec. editor, v.p. Harper Collins, 1994—. Office: Harper Collins 10 E 53d St New York NY 10022-5244

ZACKHRAS, RUBEN, Marshallese government official. Minister of finance Govt. of the Marshall Islands, Majuro. Office: Govt of Republic of the Marshall Islands Ministry Fin PO Box 2 Majuro MH 96960

ZACKS, GORDON BENJAMIN, manufacturing company executive; b. Terre Haute, Ind., Mar. 11, 1933; s. Aaron and Florence Melton (Spurgeon) Z.; married; children: Catherine E., Kimberly A. B.A., Coll. Commerce, Ohio State U. With R.G. Barry Corp., Pickerington, Ohio, 1955—, exec. v.p., 1964-65, pres., 1965—, chmn. bd., 1979—, now also chief exec. officer, chmn. Mem. Nat. Republican Senatorial Com.; hon. chmn. United Jewish Appeal; bd. dirs. numerous Jewish orgns., locally and nationally. Mem. Chief Exec. Officer Orgn., Am. Mgmt. Assn. Republican. Home: 140 N Parkview Ave Columbus OH 43209-1436 Office: R G Barry Corp 13405 Yarmouth Dr NW Pickerington OH 43147-8493 also: PO Box 129 Columbus OH 43216-0129

ZACKS, SUMNER IRWIN, pathologist; b. Boston, June 29, 1929; s. David and Rose Z.; m. Marilyn Garfinkel, June 28, 1953; children—Nancy Alice, Charles Matthew, Susan Esther. B.A. cum laude, Harvard Coll., 1951, M.D. magna cum laude, 1955; M.A. (hon.), U. Pa., 1975, Brown U., 1977. Diplomate Am. Bd. Pathology. Intern Mass. Gen. Hosp., Boston, 1956; resident Mass. Gen. Hosp., 1956-58; teaching fellow Harvard U., 1956; asst. prof. pathology U. Pa., 1962-64, assoc. prof., 1964-71, prof., 1971-76; prof. pathology Brown U., 1976-89, chmn. pathology, 1977-82; pathologist in chief Miriam Hosp., Providence, R.I., 1976-88, ret., 1989. Author: The Motor Endplate, 1964, 74, Atlas of Neuropathology, 1971; contbr. chpts. to books and articles to profl. jours. Served to capt. USAR, 1958-60. Fellow Am. Coll. Pathology; mem. Histochem. Soc. (sec. 1965-68), Am. Coll. Pathologists, Assn. Am. Pathologists, Am. Soc. Cell Biology, Am. Soc. Neuropathologists, Internat. Acad. Pathology, Sigma Xi.

ZAENGLEIN, WILLIAM GEORGE, JR., lawyer; b. Orange, N.J., Jan. 31, 1929; s. William George Sr. and Elsie May (Traenkle) Z.; m. Elizabeth J. Skinner, Dec. 18, 1954; 1 son, William George, III; m. Joyce A. Moffit, Oct. 18, 1968; 1 son, Eric Hunter. B.A., Yale U., 1952, J.D., 1955. Bar: D.C. 1957, Calif. 1969, U.S. Dist. Ct. (cen. dist.) Calif. 1969. With gen. counsel's office GSA, 1956-59; contract adminstr. Lear Siegler Corp., 1959-63; sr. contract adminstr. Northrop Corp., 1963-66; legal asst. law firm Orange, Calif., 1966-69; v.p., corp. counsel First Am. Title Ins. Co., The First Am. Fin. Corp., Santa Ana, Calif., 1969-77; v.p., sec., corp. counsel First Am. Title Ins. Co., 1977-91; v.p., sec., counsel The First Am. Fin. Corp., 1977-91; retired, 1991; dir. First Am. Trust Co., 1976—. Mem. Orange County Bar Assn., Am. Soc. Corporate Secs., Yale Club of So. Calif., Phi Delta Phi, Chi Phi. Office: First Am Fin Corp 114 E 5th St Santa Ana CA 92701-4642

ZAENTZ, SAUL, motion picture producer; b. Passaic, N.J.. Producer films: One Flew Over the Cuckoo's Nest, 1975 (Oscar for Best Picture), Three Warriors, 1977, Lord of the Rings, 1978, Amadeus, 1984, The Unbearable Lightness of Being, 1988, At Play in the Fields of the Lord, 1991; exec. producer The Mosquito Coast, 1986. Office: Saul Zaentz Co Film Ctr 2600 10th St Berkeley CA 94710-2522

ZAFFARONI, ALEJANDRO C., biochemist, medical research company executive; b. Montevideo, Uruguay, Feb. 27, 1923; came to U.S., 1944; s. Carlos and Luisa (Alfaro) Z.; m. Lyda Russomanno, July 5, 1946; children—Alejandro A., Elisa. B., U. Montevideo, 1943; Ph.D. in Biochemistry, U. Rochester, 1949; Doctorate (hon.), U. Republic, Montevideo, 1983; M.Divinity, Cen. Bapt. Seminary, 1987. Dir. biochem. research Syntex S.A., Mexico City, 1951-54, v.p., dir. research, 1954-56; exec. v.p., dir. Syntex Corp., Palo Alto, Calif., 1956-68; pres. Syntex Labs. Inc., Palo Alto, Calif., 1962-68, Syntex Research, Palo Alto, Calif., 1962-68; founder, co-chmn. ALZA Corp., Palo Alto, Calif., 1968—, also CEO; founder, mem. policy bd. and exec. com. DNAX Research Inst. of Molecular and Cellular Biology, Inc., Palo Alto, Calif., 1980—, chmn., 1980-82; founder, chmn., chief exec. officer Affymax, N.V., Palo Alto, 1989—; chmn. Internat. Psoriasis Research Found., Palo Alto; incorporator Neuroscis. Research Found. MIT, Brookline, Mass.; bd. govs. Weizmann Inst. Sci., Rehovot, Israel; mem. pharm. panel of com. on tech. and internat. econs. and trade issues Nat. Acad. Engring. Office of Fgn. Sec. and Assembly of Engring., Washington; hon. prof. biochemistry Nat. U. Mex., 1957, U. Montevideo, 1959. Contbr. numerous articles to profl. jours.; patentee in field. Recipient Barren medal Barren Found., Chgo., 1974; Pres.'s award Weizmann Inst. Sci., 1978; Chem. Pioneer award Am. Inst. Chemists, Inc., 1979, National Medal of Technology, 1995. Fellow Am. Acad. Arts and Scis., Am. Pharm. Assn.; mem. AAAS, Am. Chem. Soc., Am. Found. Pharm. Edn., Am. Inst. Chemists, Inc., Am. Soc. Biol. Chemists, Inc., Am. Soc. Microbiology, Am. Soc. Pharmacology and Exptl. Therapeutics, Biomed. Engring. Soc., Calif. Pharmacists Assn., Internat. Pharm. Fedn., Internat. Soc. Chronobiology, Internat. Soc. Study of Biol. Rhythms, Soc. Exptl. Biology and Medicine, Sociedad Mexicana de Nutricion y Endocrinologia, Biochem. Soc. Eng., Endocrine Soc., Internat. Soc. Research in Biology of Reproduction, N.Y. Acad. Scis., Christian Legal Soc. (Mo. bd. dirs. 1973—), Tau Kappa Epsilon (internat. pres. 1953-57). *

ZAFREN, HERBERT CECIL, librarian, educator; b. Balt., Aug. 25, 1925; s. Morris and Sadie Mildred (Edlavitch) Z.; m. Miriam Koenigsberg, Feb. 11, 1951; children: Ken, Edie. A.B., Johns Hopkins U., 1944, postgrad., 1946-49; diploma, Balt. Hebrew Coll., 1944, Litt.D. (hon.), 1969; A.M. in Library Sci, U. Mich., 1950. Jr. instr. Johns Hopkins U., Balt., 1947-49; bibliog. searcher Law Libr. U. Mich., Ann Arbor, 1949-50; libr. Hebrew Union Coll.-Jewish Inst. Religion, Cin., 1950-91, prof. Jewish bibliography, 1968-95; prof. emeritus, 1996—; exec. dir. Am. Jewish Periodical Ctr., Cin., 1956-80, co-dir., 1980-96, dir., 1996—; dir. librs. Cin., L.A., N.Y.C., Jerusalem, 1966-94; dir. emeritus librs. Hebrew Union Coll., Jewish Inst. Religion, Cin., 1994—; mem. exec. bd. Jewish Book Council Am., 1979—. Editor Studies in Bibliography and Booklore, 1953—, Bibliographica Judaica, 1969—; compiler: A Gathering of Broadsides, 1967. Served with USN, 1944-46. Mem. Ala, Assn. Jewish Librs. (founder, nat. pres. 1965-66), World Coun. on Jewish Archives (v.p. 1977-81), Assn. Jewish Studies, Spl. Librs. Assn. (pres. Cin. chpt. 1953-54), Coun. Archives and Rsch. Librs. in Jewish Studies (pres. 1974-78, 89-91), Am. Hist. Assn., Israel Bibliophiles, World Union Jewish Studies, AAUP (chpt. pres. 1964-68), Grolier Club (N.Y.C.), Phi Beta Kappa, Beta Phi Mu. Office: Hebrew Union Coll Jewish Inst Religion 3101 Clifton Ave Cincinnati OH 45220-2404

ZAGARE, FRANK COSMO, political science educator; b. Bklyn., June 7, 1947; s. Domenick Joseph and Josephine Ann (Stager) Z.; m. Patricia M. Sclafani, May 26, 1974; children: Catherine, Ann, Elizabeth. BA, Fordham U., 1969; MA, NYU, 1972, PhD, 1977. Asst. prof. Boston U., 1978-87; assoc. prof. SUNY, Buffalo, 1987-91, prof., 1991-94, chmn. dept. polit. sci., 1991-94. Author: Game Theory, 1984, Dynamics of Deterrence, 1987; contbr. articles to profl. publs. MIT/Harvard fellow 1984; grantee U.S. Inst. Peace, 1989-90, NSF, 1992-94. Mem. Am. Polit. Sci. Assn. (coun. mem. conflict processes sect. 1986-89), Internat. Studies Assn., Midwest Polit. Sci. Assn. Home: 123 Morris Ave Buffalo NY 14214-1609 Office: SUNY Buffalo 520 Park Club Ln Buffalo NY 14221-5013

ZAGAROLA, LARRY, accounting firm executive. Mng. ptnr. J.H. Cohn & Co., Roseland, N.J. Office: JH Cohn & Co 75 Eisenhower Pkwy Roseland NJ 07068*

ZAGASKI, CHESTER ANTHONY, JR., author, researcher; b. Manchester, Conn., Mar. 28, 1949; s. Chester Anthony Sr. and Lenora (Zakrszewski) Z.; m. Suzanne M. Celata, Apr. 1979 (div. Apr. 1989); children: Jason Paul, Brian Matthew. BA, U. S.C., 1971; postgrad., Northea. U., Wilbraham, Mass., 1971-72, U. Conn., 1973-75. Career trainee Hartford (Conn.) Ins. Co., 1971; spl. agt. Am. Group, Worcester, Mass., 1973-76; supr. underwriter Interstate Nat./Chgo. Ins., Boston; underwriting mgr. Interstate Nat./Chgo. Ins., Phila., 1977-79; reins. mgr. N.Am. Reins., Phila., 1979-80; asst. v.p. casualty lines Comml. Union Ins. Co., Boston, 1980-82; acct. exec. Frank B. Hall & Co., Boston, 1982-84; surplus lines broker Stewart Smith East (USA), Boston, 1984-86; sr. underwriting cons. CNA Ins. Co., Quincy, Mass., 1986-89; former ind. ins. and risk mgmt. cons. to several prominent firms and groups; cons. Omnium Capital, Montreal, 1st Physicians Ins. Co. Vt.; program participant Deer Island Sentinels; instr., lectr. Inst. Libr. Assn. Boston, Tufts U.; former advisor govt. and bus. groups, including New England Coun., Inc., SBA New England, Commonwealth of Mass., Dept. Environ. Protection, Joint Ins. Com. of Mass. Legis.; provider expert testimony before state and fed. legis. coms., among others. Author: Environmental Risk and Insurance, 1992; contbr. articles to profl. jours. Mem. Quincy City Rep. Com., 1989-91; del. State Conv., Boston, 1990; advisor nat. Bush/Quayle Campaigns, 1989, 92. Mem. Harvard Sq. Script Writers, Cape Cod Writers Ctr. Roman Catholic. Avocation; single parent activities.

ZAGEL, JAMES BLOCK, federal judge; b. Chgo., Mar. 4, 1941; s. Samuel and Ethel (Samuels) Z.; m. Margaret Maxwell, May 27, 1979. BA, U. Chgo., 1962, MA in Philosophy, 1962; JD, Harvard U., 1965. Bar: Ill. 1965, U.S. Dist. Ct. (no. dist.) Ill. 1965, U.S. Supreme Ct. 1970, U.S. Ct. Appeals (7th cir.) 1972. Asst. atty. gen. criminal justice div. State of Ill., Springfield, 1970-77; chief prosecuting atty. Ill. Jud. Inquiry Bd., Springfield, 1973-75; exec. dir. Ill. Law Enforcement Commn., Springfield, 1977-79; dir. Ill. Dept. Revenue, Springfield, 1979-80, Ill. Dept. State Police, Springfield, 1980-87; judge U.S. Dist. Ct. (no. dist.) Ill., Chgo., 1987—. Co-author: Criminal Law and Its Administration, 1989, Cases and Comments on Criminal Procedure, 1992. Named Outstanding Young Citizen, Chgo. Jaycees, 1977 ; recipient Disting. Service Merit award Assn. Commerce and Industry, 1983. Mem. Chgo. Bar Assn., Jud. Conf. of U.S. (codes of conduct com. 1987-92). Office: US Dist Ct 219 S Dearborn St Ste 1978 Chicago IL 60604-1801

ZAGNOLI, ROLAND CANDIANO, management and marketing consultant, pharmacist; b. Highland Park, Ill., Nov. 6, 1931; s. Valerio Walter and Maria Adalgisa (Solignani) Z.; m. Virginia Louise Rizzo, Oct. 7, 1961; children: Roland Christopher, Lisa Louise, Regina Marie, Laurette Rene, Annia Lynn. BS in Pharmacy, U. Mich., 1955; LLB, LaSalle Extension U., 1963; MBA, Harvard U.PP, 1957. RPh, Fla.; registered consulting pharmacist, Fla. Tech. & adminstrv. rotation trainee Abbott Labs., Inc., North Chgo., 1957-59, corp. product mgr., 1959-63; dir. product mgmt. & new mktg. devel. Ross pediatric div. Abbott Labs., Inc., Columbus, Ohio, 1963-65; dir. product mgmt. internat. div. Abbott Labs., Inc., North Chgo., 1965-67; dir. mktg. & sales diagnostics div. Abbott Labs., Inc., North Chgo. & Los Angeles, 1967-70; dual mgr. Amp-Vial project & mfg. hosp. div. Abbott Labs., Inc., North Chgo. & Rocky Mountain, N.C., 1970-73; pres., gen. mgr. Health Care Industries, Inc., Michigan City, Ind., 1973-76, pres., chmn. bd., chief exec. officer, 1976-81; pres., chief exec officer M/PIC Cons., Deltona, Fla., 1982—, Med. Inventors Corp., Orlando, Fla., 1988—; charter mem. Pharmacy Advancement Com. U. Mich., 1976-91; mem. Cen. Fla. Inventors Coun., Orlando, 1984-89; charter mem., bd. advisors Southtech Growth Fund, Ltd., Orlando, 1988-89; advisor Internat. Med. Techs., Winter Springs, Fla., 1989-92. Inventor Dye Pharm. Chem. (tablets dye-coating stability), 1958; patentee, 1959. Charter mem. Cen. Fla. Coun. High Tech., Orlando, 1984-94; gen. chmn. Notre Dame Parish Festival, Michigan City, 1977-79; pres. Evans Scholars Alumni, 1961-62; mem., cons. Mktg. & Mgmt. Ctrl. Fla. Innovation, Corp. 1995—; fund raiser various orgns. Evans Scholar of Yr. Western Golf Assn., 1954; won 8 golf tournament weekend championships at 7 sites in 4 states. Mem. Am. Pharm. Assn., Ctrl. Fla. Soc. Hosp. Pharmacists, Fla. Soc. Hosp. Pharmacists, Cen. Fla. Pharmacy Assn. (v.p. 1990-91), Fla. Pharmacy Assn., Assn. Univ. Tech. Mgrs., Walnut Hill County Club (Columbus), Pottawattamie Country Club (Michigan City), Kiwanis, Rotary, Phi Eta Sigma, Rho Chi. Home and Office: 1936 Saxon Blvd Deltona FL 32725

ZAGON, LAURIE, artist, writer, color consultant; b. N.Y.C., Feb. 4, 1950; d. Jerome and Janet (Rabinowitz) Z.; m. Joseph Sorrentino, Dec. 21, 1991. BFA, Md. Inst. Coll. Art, 1971; MFA, Syracuse U., 1973. Asst. prof. Art CUNY, N.Y.C., 1973-87; color cons. Fieldcrest/Cannon, N.Y.C., 1987-88; nat. speaker Am. Soc. Interior Designers, Washington, 1993—; color, art therapist, Flagstaff, Ariz., 1996, Big Brothers/Big Sisters No. Ariz., 1996. Illustrator (book) It's Never Too Late to Have a Happy Childhood, 1989; one-woman shows include The Nat. Arts Club, N.Y.C., 1989, Gallery 1757, Laguna Beach, Calif., 1991; group exhibits include John Szoke Gallery, N.Y.C., Helio Galleries, N.Y.C., CUNY Abstract Show of Shanghai, China, 1986, L.A. Mcpl. Gallery, 1993, Phoenix Airport Galleries, 1996; co-author: Power of Color, 1995. Color/art therapist for AIDS Children, L.A. Childrens Hosp., 1994; color/art therapist for recovering addicts Capo by the Sea, Dana Point, Calif., 1991, Martin Luther Hosp., Anaheim, 1990. Mem. Nat. Symposium on Healthcare Design (speaker). Home and Office: 1107 Fair Oaks Ave #147 South Pasadena CA 91030

ZAGOREN, ALLEN JEFFREY, surgeon; b. Bklyn., May 17, 1947; s. Max and Harriett (Feldman) Z.; m. Gail Marie Sarcinella, Feb. 20, 1977. BA in Biology, Hofstra U., 1969; DO, Phila. Coll. Osteo. Medicine, 1975. Diplomate Am. Bd. Osteo. Surgery, Nat. Bd. Examiners Osteo.-Med. Surgery. Intern Stratford (N.J.) div. John F. Kennedy Meml. Hosp., 1975-76; resident Cherry Hill (N.J.) Med. Ctr., 1976-80; assoc. prof. surgery U. Medicine and Dentistry, Piscataway, N.J., 1980-82; practice osteo. medicine specializing in surgery Rose Clinic, Des Moines, 1982-94, Capitol Hill Surgery, Des Moines, 1994—; mem. staff Mercy Hosp. Med. Ctr., Des Moines; practice osteo. medicine specializing in surgery Capitol Hill Surgery, Des Moines; chmn. dept. surgery Des Moines Gen. Hosp., 1985-91, Madison County Meml. Hosp., Winterset, Iowa; adj. prof. surgery and nutrition U. Osteo. Medicine; assoc. prof. pharmacy Drake U.; lectr. in field; mem. Nat. Bd. Examiners in Osteo. Medicine and Surgery; mem. surg. rev. com. Bd. Med. Examiners of Iowa, 1996—; med. dir. Wound Care Ctr., 1996, program dir. gen. surgery residency, 1993—. Contbr. articles to profl. jours.; creator videotapes (with others). Bd. dirs. Des Moines Gen. Hosp. Found., sec., 1986—; active Iowa Found. for Med. Care, Nutritional Coun. Iowa; chmn. bd. dirs. Des Moines Gen. Found., 1991-94; trustee Tiffereth Israel Synagogue, 1992. Grantee SKF Labs., Phila., 1986, Norwich (N.Y.) Eaton Labs., 1986, Ross Labs., 1995. Fellow Am. Coll. Osteo. Surgeons (rsch., nutritional support, visual aids coms., chair rsch. com. 1991-92, 1st Prize awards 1982, 83), Am. Coll. Nutrition, Internat. Coll. Surgeons; mem. Am. Osteo. Soc., Am. Soc. Gastrointestinal Endoscopy, Iowa Osteo. Med. Assn. (pres. 1994-95, chmn. constrn. and v.p. bylaws coms. 1992, trustee), Polk County Med. Soc. (treas. 1991-93), Am. Soc. Parenteral and Enteral Nutrition (bd. dirs. 1986, chmn. various coms.), Iowa and Nebr. Soc. Parenteral and Enteral Nutrition (pres. 1990-92), Nat. Wildlife Fedn. (chair com. postgrad. edn. Iowa Health Reform Project 1993), Iowa Health Leadership Consortium (CEO com.), Smithsonian Instn., Airplane Owners and Pilots Assn., Iowa Nebr. Nutrition Soc. (pres. 1990-92). Jewish. Avocations: flying, golf, swimming, skiing, writing. Office: Capitol Hill Surgery 1300 Des Moines St Des Moines IA 50309

ZAGORIA, SAM D(AVID), arbitrator, author, educator; b. Somerville, N.J., Apr. 9, 1919; s. Nathan and Rebecca (Shapiro) Z.; m. Sylvia Bomse, Dec. 21, 1941; children: Paul, Marjorie Zagoria Isacks, Ronald. BL in Journalism, Rutgers U., 1941. With New Brunswick (N.J.) Daily Home News, 1940-41, N.J. Def. Coun., Trenton, 1941-42; Fed. Office Govt. Reports, Newark, 1942; reporter Washington Post, 1946-55; adminstrv. asst. to Senator Clifford P. Case, Washington, 1955-65; mem. NLRB, Washington, 1965-69; dir. Labor-Mgmt. Rels. Svc. U.S. Conf. of Mayors, Washington,

1970-78; mem. U.S. Consumer Product Safety Commn., 1978-84; ombudsman Washington Post, 1984-86; arbitrator, writer, 1986—; Fulbright lectr., Copenhagen, 1987; vis. prof. Fla. Atlantic U., Boca Raton, 1988-91; adj. prof. Wake Forest U., Winston-Salem, N.C., 1993—. Author: Public Workers, Public Unions, 1972, The Ombudsman: How Good Governments Handle Citizens' Grievances, 1988. Campaign mgr. reelection Senator Case, 1960; campaign mgr. race for gov., former Sec. of Labor James P. Mitchell, 1961. With USAAF, 1942-45. Nieman fellow Harvard, 1954. Mem. Common Cause, Nat. Consumers League, Rutgers U. Alumni Assn. Jewish. Home and Office: 2864 Wynfield Crossing Ln Winston Salem NC 27103-6597 also: 3221 S Ocean Blvd Apt 204 Highland Bch FL 33487-2519

ZAGORIN, JANET SUSAN, library and professional development director; b. Lakewood, N.J.; d. Irving C. and Dorothy (Tarshish) Z. BA, Douglass Coll., 1975; MLS, Rutgers U., 1977. Asst. law libr. N.J. Atty. Gen., Trenton, 1977-78; head of reference sect. Cardozo U. Law Sch., N.Y.C., 1978-79; law and legis. svcs. libr. FTC, Washington, 1979-81; dir. of reference Paul Weiss Rifkind, N.Y.C., 1981-82; libr. dir. Riker Danzig Scherer & Hyland, Morristown, N.J., 1982; libr., profl. devel. dir. Baker & McKenzie, N.Y.C., 1982—. Mem. ABA (vice chair standing com. Law Libr. Congress), Fin. Women's Assn. (mem. bd. dirs. 1993-95), Bus. Women's Network, Am. Assn. Law Librs. (chair fgn. comparative internat. law com. 1990-91, vice chair pvt. law librs. 1990-91, chair 1991—, chair com. on recruitment 1991), Spl. Librs. Assn., Ctr. Study of Presidency (adv. bd. 1994—), Asia Soc., Hadassah. Office: Baker & McKenzie 805 3rd Ave New York NY 10022-7513

ZAGORIN, PEREZ, historian, educator; b. Chgo., May 29, 1920; s. Solomon Novitz and Mildred (Ginsburg) Z.; m. Honoré Desmond Sharrer, May 29, 1947; 1 son, Adam. A.B., U. Chgo., 1941; A.M., Harvard U., 1947, Ph.D., 1952. Various positions OWI, U.S. Govt., U.P. Syndicate, CIO, 1942-46; instr. Amherst Coll., 1947-49; lectr. Vassar Coll., 1951-53; from asst. prof. to prof. history McGill U., 1955-65; prof. U. Rochester, 1965—, Joseph C. Wilson prof. history, 1982-90, Joseph C. Wilson prof. history emeritus, 1990—, chmn. dept., 1968-69, acting chmn. dept., 1988-89; vis. prof. Johns Hopkins, 1964-65; Amundsen vis. prof. U. Pitts., 1964; William Andrews Clark Meml. Library prof. UCLA, 1975-76; Thompson lectr. history Vassar Coll., 1987. Author: A History of Political Thought in the English Revolution, 1954, The Court and the Country, 1969, Culture and Politics from Puritanism to the Englightenment, 1980, Rebels and Rulers 1500-1660, 2 vols., 1982, Ways of Lying: Dissimulation, Persecution, and Conformity in Early Modern Europe, 1990, Milton Aristocrat and Rebel: The Poet and His Politics, 1992; co-editor: Philosophy Science and Religion in England 1640-1700, 1991, Guide to Historical Literature, 1994; contbr. numerous articles in hist. jours.; mem. editorial bd. Jour. of the History of Ideas. Sheldon traveling fellow Harvard U., 1949-50, Fulbright fellow 1949-50, faculty rsch. fellow Social Sci. Rsch. Coun., 1958-59, sr. rsch. fellow Folger Shakespeare Libr., 1964-65, fellow Inst. Advanced Study, Princeton, N.J., 1972-73, sr. fellow Nat. Humanities Ctr., 1978-79, fellow Ctr. Advanced Study in Behavioral Scis., 1983-84, Edgar F. Shannon Ctr. for Advanced Studies fellow U. Va., 1994—. Fellow Royal Hist. Soc., Am. Acad. Arts and Scis.; mem. Am. Hist. Assn. (chmn. Gershoy prize com. 1982-84). Home: 2990 Beaumont Farm Rd Charlottesville VA 22901 Office: U Rochester Dept History Rochester NY 14627

ZAGORSKY, CAROL LACCI, information systems project director; b. N.Y.C., Nov. 19, 1942; d. Arthur and Evelyn Marie (Strang) Lacci; m. Eugene Dennis Zagorsky, Jr., May 21, 1983. BBA in Econs., St. John's U., Jamaica, N.Y., 1968. Cert. data processor, quality analyst. Programmer info. systems and services dept. N.Y. Life Ins. Co., N.Y.C., 1967-71, programmer analyst, 1971-74, project leader, 1974-78, project mgr., 1978—, div. head, 1988-89, project dir., 1989—; conf. spkr. Managing Computer Aided Software Engring. Implementation; lectr. NYU, Info. Technols. Inst., 1990-92; instr. Am. Mgmt. Assn.-Total Quality Mgmt. for Mgmt. Info. Sys., 1993-94. Trustee Murray Hill Com., N.Y.C., 1977-79, 85-86, v.p. 1979-85. Mem. Women in Data Processing, Quality Mgmt. Assn. N.Y. (pres. 1991—), Nat. Excelerator Users Group (profl. devel. com.), Met. N.Y. Computer Aided Software Engring. Users Group. Democrat. Episcopalian. Avocations: camping, hiking. Office: NY Life Ins Co 51 Madison Ave New York NY 10010-1603

ZAHARIA, ERIC STAFFORD, developmental disabilities program administrator; b. Pomona, Calif., Aug. 24, 1948; s. Edgar A. and Dorothy (Stafford) Z.; m. Caryle Koentz, Dec. 23, 1967; children: Tye W., Tieg A. BA, Pomona Coll., 1970; MEd, U. Ariz.-Tucson, 1973; PhD, George Peabody Coll., 1978; postgrad., Govt. Execs. Inst. U. N.C., Chapel Hill, 1981. Mental retardation worker Ariz. Tng. Program, Tucson, 1970-71, unit dir., 1971-73; dir. residential svcs. Willmar State Hosp., (Minn.), 1973-76; rsch. asst. Inst. on Mental Retardation and Intellectual Devel., Nashville, 1976-78; dir. mental retardation program svcs. Dept. Mental Health/Mental Retardation, State of Tenn., Nashville, 1978-79; dir. Caswell Ctr., Kinston, N.C., 1979-86; program adminstr. Colo. Div. of Devel. Disabilities, Denver, 1986-90; dir. Utah divsn. Svcs. for People with Disabilities, Salt Lake City, 1990-95; ind. cons. Park City, Utah, 1995—; mem. adj. faculty East Carolina U., Greenville, 1979-86; bd. dirs. Neuse Enterprises Inc., Kinston. Chmn. Big Bros./Sisters Kinston Inc., 1980-83; mem. N.C. Coalition for Community Svc., 1982-85. Mem. Am. Assn. Mental Retardation, Nat. Assn. Supts., Pub. Residential Facilities, Assn. Retarded Citizens, Kinston C. of C. (bd. dirs. 1983-86). Home: 8010 Juniper Dr Park City UT 84060-5370 Office: 120 N 200 W Salt Lake City UT 84103-1550

ZAHL, PAUL FRANCIS MATTHEW, dean; b. N.Y.C., May 24, 1951; m. Mary McLean Cappleman, Dec. 29, 1973; children: John Arthur, David William Franklin, Simeon McLean. Student, U. N.C., 1968-70; AB magna cum laude, Harvard Coll., 1972; MPhil in Theology, U. Nottingham, Eng., 1975; diploma in pastoral studies, St. John's Theol. Coll., Nottingham, 1975; ThD, Eberhard-Karls-Univ., Tübingen, Germany, 1994. Ordained min. Protestant Episcopal Ch., 1976. Deacon in tng. Good Shepherd Episcopal Ch., Silver Spring, Md., 1975-76; curate Grace Ch., N.Y.C., 1976-82; rector St. Mary's Ch., Scarborough, N.Y., 1982-88, St. James' Ch., Charleston, S.C., 1988-92; fellow Episcopal Ch. Found., 1993-95; dean Cathedral Ch. of the Advent, Birmingham, Ala., 1995—; tchr. Gen. Theol. Sem., N.Y.C., 1979-82, The King's Coll., Briarcliff Manor, N.Y., 1985-88, Coll. Charleston, S.C., 1990-92, U. Tübingen, Germany, 1992-93; vis. scholar Wycliffe Hall, Oxford, Eng., 1994-95. Columnist The Anglican Digest, 1986—; contbr. articles to profl. jours. Mem. Phi Beta Kappa. Office: 2017 6th Ave N Birmingham AL 35203

ZAHN, CARL FREDERICK, museum publications director, designer, photographer; b. Louisville, Mar. 9, 1928; s. Fred Joseph and Myrtle (Fulks) Z.; m. Betty Jane Woodrow, Nov. 18, 1950 (div. July 1977); children: Lisa, Karen, Richard; m. Felicitas Magdalena Fuhlrott, July 30, 1979. BA, Harvard Coll., 1948. Asst. in conservation Fogg Art Mus., Cambridge, Mass., 1949-50; with art dept. Benton & Bowles Inc., N.Y.C., 1950-51; design asst. Inst. Contemporary Art, Boston, 1951-56; dir. publs. Mus. Fine Arts, Boston, 1956—; also dir. exhbns., 1995—. exhibitions include: Addison Gallery Am. Art, Andover, Mass., 1959, Am. Inst. Graphic Arts, N.Y.C., 1960—, Rose Art Mus. Brandeis U., Waltham, Mass., 1969; author: Introduction to Hermann Zapf and His Design Philosophy, 1987; co-author Weston's Westons: Portraits and Nudes, 1989. Mem. Am. Inst. Graphic Arts (v.p. 1971-72), Soc. Printers, Bund Deutscher Buchkünstler, Mink Meadows Golf Club, East Chop Tennis Club (bd. dirs. 1970-72), Longwood Cricket Club. Home: 39 Cedarwood Rd Jamaica Plain MA 02130-3021 Office: Mus Fine Arts 479 Huntington Ave Boston MA 02115-5523

ZAHN, DONALD JACK, lawyer; b. Albany, N.Y., Oct. 24, 1941; s. Jerome and Clara (Zinsher) Z.; m. Laurie R. Hyman, Aug. 19, 1966; children: Lawrence, Melissa. AB, NYU, 1963; LLB, Union U., 1966; LLM in Taxation, NYU, 1967. Bar: N.Y. 1966, U.S. Dist. Ct. (no. dist.) N.Y. 1966, U.S. Tax Ct. 1969, U.S. Ct. Appeals (2d cir.) 1970, Tex. 1972, U.S. Ct. Appeals (5th and 11th cirs.). Assoc., Bond, Schoeneck and King, Syracuse, N.Y., 1967-71; ptnr. Haynes and Boone, Dallas, 1971-82, Akin, Gump, Strauss, Hauer & Feld, Dallas, 1982-92; assoc. prof. internat. taxation, fed. income taxation, bus. assns., corp. taxation Tex. Wesleyan Sch. Law , Irving, Tex., 1992—; adj. lectr. Baylor U. Sch. of Law Fed. Income Taxation, 1995; adj. prof. Sch. Law, So. Meth. U., Dallas, 1972-87, 90-91. Trustee, sec. mem. exec. and fin. com., nominating com. Greenhill Sch., Addison, Tex., 1980-90; trustee, chmn. budget com., mem. fin. com. Jewish Fedn. Greater Dallas, 1978-89; trustee, chmn. Found. Jewish Fedn., Dallas, 1980-89; trustee, v.p., pres. Dallas chpt. Am. Jewish Com., 1980-92; mem. Tex. World Trade Council, 1986-87, Dallas Mayor's Internat. Com. Mem. State Bar Tex. (sec. 1982-83, chmn. tax sect. 1984-85, newsletter taxation sect. editor 1980-81), Internat. Bar Assn., Internat. Comte (N. Tex. commn.), Southwestern Legal Found. (adv. bd., treas. Internat. and Comparative Law Ctr., lectr. Acad. in Internat. Law), N.Y. State Bar Assn. Jewish. Office: Tex Wesleyan U Sch of Law 2535 E Grauwyler Rd Irving TX 75061-3410

ZAHN, MARKUS, electrical engineering educator; b. Bergen-Belsen, Germany, Dec. 3, 1946; s. Irving and Maria (Fischer) Z.; m. Linda Ruth Jasen, June 1, 1969; children: Laura Michelle, Daniel Jacob, Jeffrey David, Amy Elizabeth. BSEE, MSEE, MIT, 1968, degree in elec. engring., 1969, ScD, 1970. Prof. elec. engring. U. Fla., Gainesville, 1970-80; prof. MIT, Cambridge, 1980—, dir. VI-A internship program. Author (book) Electromagnetic Field Theory: A Problem Solving Approach, 1979; co-author (videotapes) Demonstrations of Electromagnetic Fields and Energy, 1989. Fellow IEEE. Avocation: stamp collecting. Office: MIT Engring Dept Rm 10-174 Cambridge MA 02135

ZAHN, PAULA, newscaster; b. Feb. 24, 1956; m. Richard Cohen; 1 child, Haley. With Sta. WHDH, Boston, 1983-85; anchor, reporter Sta. KCBS, L.A., 1985-87; co-anchor World News Now ABC News, N.Y.C., 1987-90; co-anchor CBS This Morning CBS News, N.Y.C., 1990—; contbr. CBS news mag. 48 Hours; co-host CBS broadcast Winter Olympics, Albertville, France, 1992. Office: CBS News CBS This Morning 524 W 57th St New York NY 10019-2902

ZAHN, TIMOTHY, writer; b. Chgo., Sept. 1, 1951; s. Herbert William and Marilou (Webb) Z.; m. Anna L. Romo, Aug. 4, 1979; 1 child, Corwin Jame. BA, Mich. State U., 1973; MA, U. Ill., 1975. Author: The Blackcollar, 1983, A Coming of Age, 1984, Cobra, 1985, Spinneret, 1985, Blackcollar: The Backlash Mission, 1986, Cobra Strike, 1986, Triplet, 1987, Deadman Switch, 1988, Cobra Bargain, 1988, Warhorse, 1990, Heir to Empire, 1991, Dark Force Rising, 1992, Star Wars: The Last Command, 1993, Conquerors' Pride, 1994, Conquerors' Heritage, 1995, Conquerors' Legacy, 1996; aso. sci. fiction short stories. Recipient Hugo award nomination for short story World Sci. Fiction Conv., 1983, Hugo award for best novella Cascade Point, 1984, Hugo award nomination short story, 1985. Office: c/o Bantam Books Inc 1540 Broadway New York NY 10036-4039

ZAHND, RICHARD HUGO, professional sports executive, lawyer; b. N.Y.C., July 22, 1946; s. Hugo and Rose (Genovese) Z.; m. Phyllis Beth Workman, Aug. 13, 1978; children: Andrew Richard, Melissa Dawn. A.B., NYU, 1968, J.D., 1971. Bar: N.Y. 1972. Assoc. Paul, Weiss, Rifkind, Wharton & Garrison, N.Y.C., 1971-74; staff atty. Madison Square Garden Corp., N.Y.C., 1974-75; v.p. legal affairs Madison Square Garden Center, Inc., N.Y.C., 1975-79; v.p., gen. counsel Madison Square Garden Corp., N.Y.C., 1979-86; v.p. N.Y. Knickerbockers Basketball Club, N.Y.C., 1979-86, N.Y. Rangers Hockey Club, N.Y.C., 1979-86; ptnr. Morrison & Foerster, N.Y.C., 1986-91; sr. v.p., gen. counsel NHL Enterprises, Inc., N.Y.C., 1992—. Served to capt. U.S. Army, 1972. John Norton Pomeroy scholar NYU Law Sch., 1969; Mortimer Bishop scholar NYU Law Sch., 1969; Judge Jacob Markowitz scholar NYU Law Sch., 1970; recipient Am. Jurisprudence prize NYU Law Sch., 1969. Episcopalian. Office: 1251 Ave Americas Fl 47 New York NY 10020

ZAHNER, MARY ANNE, art educator; b. Dover, Ohio, Mar. 30, 1938; d. Alfred James and Anna Elizabeth (Stewart) Riggle; m. Gordon Dean Zahner, Aug. 27, 1960 (dec. Mar. 1967); 1 child, Anne Colette; m. John Charles Opalek, Aug. 21, 1982. BFA, Ohio U., 1960, MA, 1969; PhD, Ohio State U., 1987. Cert. tchr., Ohio. Instr. art Springfield Twp. Schs., Akron, Ohio, 1960-61, Logan (Ohio) High Sch., 1961-62; instr. art Dover High Sch., 1967-68, chair art dept., 1969-71; teaching asst. Ohio State U., Columbus, 1980-82; from instr. art edn. to asst. prof. U. Dayton, 1971-80, asst. prof., 1982-91, assoc. prof., 1991—; mem. faculty rights, governance and svc. com. U. Dayton, 1992-93, mem. arts series com., 1995—; reviewer Harcourt, Brace, 1993-94. Author: (chpt.) The History of Art Education: Proceedings from the Second Penn. State Conference, 1989; exhibited in group show at Westbeth Gallery, N.Y.C., 1995. Sec. Kettering (Ohio) Arts Coun., 1990, mem., 1988—; mem. discretionary support com. Miami Valley Arts Coun., Dayton, 1992; coord. 3d congl. art contest sponsored by Tony P. Hall, Dayton, 1993, 94, 95. Recipient Best of Show award Canton Art Inst., 1969, Inst. Faculty award The Ohio Partnership for the Visual Arts, 1989. Fellow Ohio Art Edn. Assn. (mem. editl. bd. Ohio Art Edn. Jour. 1986—, editor newsletter Artline 1988, workshop coord. 1992, cons. tchr. insvc. for Dayton Pub. Schs. 1995, Outstanding Art Tchr. western dist. 1992); mem. ASCD, Nat. Art Edn. Assn., Assn. Tchr. Educators, Ohio Alliance for Arts Edn. (bd. dirs.), Univ. Coun. for Art Edn., Phi Delta Kappa, Phi Kappa Phi, Delta Kappa Gamma. Democrat. Presbyterian. Avocations: music, theater, physical fitness. Home: 4429 Wilmington Pike Kettering OH 45440-1934 Office: U Dayton 114 Rike Ctr Dayton OH 45489-1690

ZAHRLY, JANICE HONEA, management educator; b. Ft. Payne, Ala., Sept. 27, 1943; d. John Wiley and Lillian (McKown) Honea. BA, U. Fla., 1964; MBA, U. Ctrl. Fla., 1980; PhD, U. Fla., 1984. Tchr. Hope Mills (N.C.) H.S., 1964-65, Satellite Beach (Fla.) H.S., 1965-69; realtor-assoc. WD Webb Realty, Melbourne, Fla., 1969-70; realtor Aero Realty, Melbourne, 1970-72, Albert J. Tuttle, Realtor, Melbourne, 1972-74; mktg. mgr. Cypress Woods Devel., Orlando, Fla., 1974-76; regional campaign mgr. Pres. Ford Com., 1976; ednl. researcher Peace Corps, Korea, 1976-78; rsch. analyst, tech. writer Rsch. Sys. Inc., Orlando, 1979-80; rsch. asst., lectr. U. Fla., Gainesville, 1980-84; asst. prof. Wayne State U., Detroit, 1984-89; assoc. prof. Old Dominion U., Norfolk, Va., 1989-94, U. N.D., Grand Forks, 1994—; mem. Melbourne Bd. Realtors, 1969-76, orientation chair, 1972, pub. rels. chair, 1973, civic affairs chair, 1973, grievance com., 1975; cons. Wayne County Retarded Persons Assn., Detroit, 1985, Gov.'s Conf. on Women Entrepreneurs, Mich., 1986, Oakland County AAUW Conf. on Women, Mich., 1987, 88, Coll. Bus. and Pub. Adminstrn. Inst. of Mgmt., Old Dominion U., Norfolk, 1990, U.S. Army Corps Engrs., Norfolk, 1990; presenter in field. Contbr. chpts. to books, articles to profl. jours. and procs. Vol. Tidewater AIDS Crisis Task Force, Norfolk, 1990-93, bd. dirs., 1990-92, v.p., 1991, rec. sec., 1992; mem. occupational adv. com. Brevard County Mental Health Ctr., Fla., 1973-74; mem. Brevard County Libr. Bd., 1973-74; bd. dirs. Fla. Dist. 12 Mental Health Bd., 1973-74, sec. 1973-74; bd. dirs. Alachua County Crisis Ctr., Gainesville, 1982-84, chair, 1983-84; vol. Open Door, Detroit, 1986-89; bd. dirs. United Way Grand Forks area, 1996—. Recipient Best Paper award Midwest Soc. for Human Resources/Indsl. Rels., 1989; rsch. fellow Fed. Mogul Corp., 1987-88; rsch. grantee Wayne State U., 1985-89, Old Dominion U., 1990, U. N.D., 1995, 96. Mem. AAUW (bd. dirs. 1974-75), Acad. Mgmt., Assn. for Rsch. on Nonprofit Orgns./Vols., So. Mgmt. Assn., Hampton Rds. Gator Club (co-founder, treas. 1989-91), Alpha Omicron Pi (bd. dirs. alumnae chpt. 1969-73, v.p. 1969-73). Avocations: travel, writing fiction, photography, music. Home: 3424 Cherry St Apt A1 Grand Forks ND 58201-7692

ZAHUMENY, JANET MAE, secondary education educator; b. Rahway, N.J., Mar. 23, 1945; d. Richard Evans and Elsie Mae (Walling) Franklin; m. Edward Zahumeny, Dec. 21, 1966 (div. 1987); 1 child, Carole Ann. BA, Newark State Coll., 1967; MEd, William Paterson Coll., 1990; MA, Kean Coll., 1994. Cert. secondary tchr., N.J. Math. tchr. Hunterdon Cen. High Sch., Flemington, N.J., 1967-68; math., computer tchr. Roselle Park (N.J.) High Sch., 1968—; instr. computers Roselle Park Adult Sch., 1987-88; instr. computer tech. William Paterson Coll., 1992—, U. Calif., Berkeley, 1995—; cons. Gray's Appraisal, Cranford, N.J., 1987; textbook editor Prentice Hall, 1989; computer group asst. Bell Labs., Whippany, N.J., summers 1972-73; chmn. Dist. Computer Study Com., 1988; in svc. tchr. tng, 1988—, 8th grade computer coord., 1988-89; mem. Mid. States Evaluation Team, 1972, 82, 85; liason com. RPHS, 1985—, cooperating tchr. Kean Coll., 1990—, Montclair State U.; adminstrv. asst. to v.p. Alpha Wire, summer 1991—; participant Computing Inst., 1983, Woodrow Wilson Inst., 1991, NSF Inst., 1991; mem. Key Curriculum Press Profl. Devel. Team, 1993—. Mem. Home Page Editorial Bd., Roselle Park Borough Home Page Editorial Bd. Active Cranford PTA, Roselle Park PTSA, Roselle Park Borough Home Page Editl. Bd. Named Outstanding Acad. Tchr., Cittone Inst., Edison, N.H., 1988, Outstanding Tchr., N.J. Gov.'s Recognition Program, 1989, Outstanding Computer/Math. Tchr. Tandy Techs., 1991; recipient Grad. Scholarship Kean Coll., Union, N.J., 1992, Computer Grant award 1993, Presdl. award for excellence in math. tchg., 1994, 95. Mem. NEA, Nat. Coun. Tchrs. Math., Assn. Math. Tchrs. N.J., N.J. Edn. Assn., Roselle Park Edn. Assn., N.J. Assn. for Ednl. Tech., WPC Inst. for Tech. in Math., Mensa, Kean Coll. Alumni Assn., William Paterson Coll. Alumni Assn., Pi Lambda Theta, Kappa Delta Pi, Phi Kappa Phi. Avocations: computers, embroidering, sailing, bowling, bridge. Office: Roselle Park High Sch 185 W Webster Ave Roselle Park NJ 07204

ZAIDI, EMILY LOUISE, retired elementary school educator; b. Hoquiam, Wash., Apr. 20, 1924; d. Burdick Newton and Emily Caroline (Williams) Johnston; m. M. Baqar Abbas Zaidi, June 12, 1949 (dec. Dec. 1983). BA in Edn. and Social Studies, Ea. Wash. State U., 1948; MEd, U. Wash., 1964, EdD, 1974. Tchr. 4th grade Hoquiam Schs., 1948-49; tchr. grades 5-6 Lake Washington Sch. Dist., Kirkland, Wash., 1949-51; tchr. grades 2-3 Port Angeles (Wash.) Schs., 1951-54; tchr. grade 2 Seattle Schs., 1954-55; tchr., reading specialist Northshore sch. Dist., Bothell, Wash., 1955-69, Sacramento City Schs., 1969-87; ret.; mem. Calif. State Instructional Materials Panel, Sacramento, 1975. Mem. Sacramento Opera Assn., 1986—, Sacramento Ballet Assn., 1987—, Sacramento Symphony Assn., 1985—. Fulbright Commn. Exchange Tchr., 1961-62. Mem. Reading Club, Comstock Club. Democrat. Avocations: writing, children's literature, reading, travel. Home: 4230 N River Way Sacramento CA 95864-6055

ZAILLIAN, STEVEN, screenwriter, director; b. Calif., Jan. 30, 1953. BA, San Francisco State U., 1975. Scripts include: The Falcon and the Snowman, 1985, Awakenings, 1990 (Acad. award nominee for best adapted screenplay, 1990), Jack the Bear, 1993, Schindler's List, 1993 (Acad. award best adapted screenplay 1993); co-writer (with Donald Stewart and John Milius) Clear and Present Danger, 1994; scriptwriter, dir.: Searching for Bobby Fisher, 1993.

ZAIMAN, JOEL HIRSH, rabbi; b. Chgo., Mar. 10, 1938; s. Solomon and Ruth (Levy) Z.; m. Ann Shanok, July 1, 1959; children: Elana Beth, Sarina, Ari Lev. BS, DePaul U., 1957; Master of Hebrew Letters, Jewish Theol. Sem., N.Y.C., 1962. Assoc. rabbi Temple Emanu-El, Providence, 1962-73, sr. rabbi, 1973-80; sr. rabbi Chizuk Amuno Congregation, Balt., Md., 1980—; pres. Balt. Bd. Rabbis, 1985-87; 1st v.p. Synagogue Coun. Am., 1988, pres., 1989-91. Contbr. articles to profl. jours. Chmn. edn. com. Solomon Schecter Day Sch., Balt., 1983; bd. dirs. Balt. Bd. Jewish Edn., Md. Commn. on Hereditary and Congenital Disorders, Assoc. Jewish Charities and Welfare Fund, Levindale Hebrew Geriat. Ctr. and Hosp., Balt., 1984—, long range planning com.; v.p. Balt. Jewish Coun., 1992-94, pres., 1994—; chancellors rabbinic cabinet Jewish Theol. Sem.; bd. dirs., patient care adv. com. Sinai Hosp., 1991; bd. dirs., chmn. program com. Inst. Christian and Jewish Studies; adv. coun. Md. Health Care Decisions Act, 1994—. Fellow Pearlstone Inst. Jewish Living (program planning com.); mem. Rabbinical Assembly (exec. council, long range planning com.), United Synagogue Commn. Jewish Edn. (chmn.), Md. Jewish Hist. Soc. (bd. dirs.), Associated Jewish Fedn. Balt. (bd. dirs. 1991—). Home: 7912 Winterset Ave Baltimore MD 21208-3109 Office: Chizuk Amuno Congregation 8100 Stevenson Rd Baltimore MD 21208-1866

ZAIMAN, K. ROBERT, dentist; b. Cin., Oct. 19, 1944; s. Noboru Gary and Toshiko (Matsuyama) Z.; m. Kimberly Ann Sass, Nov. 6, 1976; children: Kara Jean, Matthew Robert. Student, Creighton U., Omaha, 1962-64, DDS, 1968. Asst. prof. Creighton U. Sch. Dentistry, Omaha, 1971-73, assoc. prof., 1973-75; pvt. practice dentistry Omaha, 1971—. Past v.p., bd. dirs. Japanese-Am. Citizens League, Omaha, 1977-86; bd. elders King of Kings Luth. Ch., 1990—. Lt. comdr. USN, 1964-71. Fellow Acad. Gen. Dentistry (pres. 1976-77, nat. del. 1971-76), Acad. Continuing Edn.; mem. ADA, Omaha Dist. Dental Soc. (treas. 1980-85, bd. dirs. 1968—), Nebr. Dental Assn. (del. 1971—), Omaha Study Club (pres.), Delta Sigma Delta (pres. 1973-74). Office: 10841 Q St Ste 109 Omaha NE 68137-3701

ZAINO, RUSSELL B., advertising agency executive, lawyer; b. Louisville, July 10, 1948; s. Louis F. and Mabel (Hickey) Z.; m. Sherrie W. Zaino, Dec. 31, 1975; children: Christine Elizabeth, Jennifer Warren. BS in Commerce, U. Louisville, 1974, JD, 1980. Bar: Ky. Sr. v.p. Liberty Bank, Louisville, 1974-94; pres. The Buntin Group, Louisville, 1994—. Bd. dirs. Ky. Derby Festival, Louisville, 1988—, Louisville Orch., 1995. Staff sgt. U.S. Army, 1967-71, Vietnam. Mem. Ky. Bar Assn., Louisville Bar Assn., Am. Advt. Fedn. (gov.'s coun. 1988-89), Advt. Club Louisville (pres. 1987-88). Avocations: travel, swimming, golf. Home: 2348 Village Dr Louisville KY 40205 Office: The Buntin Group 745 W Main St Louisville KY 40202

ZAISER, KENT AMES, lawyer; b. St. Petersburg, Fla., June 10, 1945; s. Robert Alan and Marion (Brown) Z. AB Duke U., 1967; postgrad. U. Calif.-Berkeley, 1971; JD, U. Fla., 1972. Bar: Fla. 1973, U.S. Dist. Ct. (no. dist.) Fla. 1974, U.S. Supreme Ct. 1978, U.S. Dist. Ct. (so. dist.) Fla. 1980, U.S. Dist. Ct. (mid. dist.) Fla. 1981, U.S. Ct. Appeals (11th cir.) 1981. Rsch. aide Fla. Supreme Ct., Tallahassee, 1973-75, adminstrv. asst. to chief justice, 1975-76; asst. gen. counsel Fla. Dept. Natural Resources, Tallahassee, 1976-80; asst. atty. gen. Fla. Dept. Legal Affairs, Tallahassee, 1980-85; dep. gen. counsel S.W. Fla. Water Mgmt. Dist., Brooksville, 1985-89, gen. counsel, 1989-92; ptnr. Foley and Lardner, Tallahassee, 1992-93; prin. Kent A. Zaiser, P.A., Tallahassee, 1994—; cons. Fla. State Cts. Adminstr., Tallahassee, 1975. Contbg. author: Environmental Regulation and Litigation in Florida, 1980-84. Campaign chmn. Vince Fechtel for State Rep. of Fla., Leesburg, 1972. Mem. Tallahassee Bar Assn., Jefferson County Bar Assn. Democrat. Episcopalian. Club: Governors. Home: 3286 Longleaf Rd Tallahassee FL 32310-6406 Office: PO Box 6045 Tallahassee FL 32314-6045

ZAITZEFF, ROGER MICHAEL, lawyer; b. Detroit, June 25, 1940; s. Peter and Mary (Fedchenia) Z.; m. Amine Erma Wefali, Jan. 30, 1970; children: Zachary, Natasha, Zoe, Peter. BA with high honors and high distinction, U. Mich., 1962; MA with distinction, U. Calif., Berkeley, 1963, JD, 1969. Bar: N.Y. 1970, U.S. Dist. Ct. (so. dist.) N.Y. 1975, U.S. Ct. Appeals (2nd cir.) 1975, D.C. 1985. Assoc. Seward & Kissel, N.Y.C., 1969-77, ptnr., 1977-94; ptnr. Latham & Wakins, N.Y.C., 1994—. Contbr. articles to U. Fla. Law Rev., The Bus. Lawyer, Internat. Bus. Lawyer, Touro Law Rev., Internat. Tax and Bus. Lawyer, Nat. Law Jour. Mem. Tribar Opinion Com., 1990-93. Heller grantee U. Mich., 1962. Mem. ABA, Internant. Bar Assn., Assn. of Bar of City of N.Y., N.Y. State Bar Found., Southwestern Legal Found. (adv. bd.), N.Y. County Lawyers Assn. (spl. com. legal opinions in comml. transactions), Phi Beta Kappa. Office: Latham & Watkins 885 3rd Ave New York NY 10022-4834

ZAJAC, JACK, sculptor, painter; b. Youngstown, Ohio, Dec. 13, 1929; s. John and Elizabeth Z.; m. Corda Eby, Sept. 19, 1956; children: Aaron John, Christian Rafael. Student, Scripps Coll., 1949-53, Am. Acad., in Rome, 1954-55, 57-58, 58-59. prof. art U. Calif., Santa Cruz. One-man shows include San Diego Mus., 1975, Pub. Gardens, Orveito, 1976; works shown in group exhbns. Pitts. Internat., 1955-65, Biennale di Roma, 1968, Stephen Wirtz Gallery, San Francisco, 1984, represented in permanent collections Mus. Modern Art, N.Y.C., Whitney Mus., Hirshorn Mus., Forum Gallery, N.Y.C.. Rome Prize fellow, 1954; Guggenheim fellow, 1959; Am. Acad. Arts and Letters grantee, 1958. Fellow Am. Acad. in Rome; mem. NAD.

ZAJONC, ROBERT B(OLESLAW), psychology educator; b. Lodz, Poland, Nov. 23, 1923; came to U.S., 1949, naturalized, 1953; s. Mieczyslaw and Anna (Kwiatkowska) Z.; m. Donna Benson, June 20, 1953 (div. 1981); children: Peter Clifford, Michael Anton, Joseph Robert; m. Hazel Markus, May 25, 1982; 1 child, Krysia Courcelle Rose. Ph.D., U. Mich., 1955; Dr. hon. causa, U. Louvain, 1984, U. Warsaw, 1989. Asst. prof. psychology U. Mich., 1955-60, assoc. prof., 1960-63, prof., 1963-94, Charles Horton Cooley Disting. prof. psychology, 1983-94, rsch. scientist Inst. for Social Rsch., 1960-83, dir., 1989; prof. psychology Stanford (Calif.) U., 1994—; directeur d'études Maison des Sciences de L'Homme, Paris, 1985-86; vis. prof. U. Oxford, 1971-72. Author: Social Psychology: An Experimental Approach, 1965; editor: Animal Social Psychology, 1970; assoc. editor: Jour. Personality and Social Psychology, 1960-66. Guggenheim fellow, 1978-79; Fulbright fellow, 1962-63; recipient Disting. Prof. award of social sci., 1983. Fellow

AAAS (co-recipient Psychol. prize 1976), APA (Disting. Sci. Contbrn. award 1978), Japan Soc. Promotion of Sci., N.Y. Acad. Scis.; mem. Soc. for Exptl. Social Psychology (Disting. Scientist award 1986), Polish Acad. Scis. (fgn.). Office: Stanford U Dept Psychology Jordan Hall Stanford CA 94305

ZAKANITCH, ROBERT RAHWAY, artist; b. Elizabeth, N.J., May 24, 1935; s. Andrew and Mary Z. Student, Newark (N.J.) Sch. Fine and Indsl. Art, 1954-57. vis. artist, lectr. Sch. Art Inst. Chgo., 1976, U. Calif., San Diego, 1974; lectr. numerous univs. One man shows include Henri Gallery, Alexandria, Va., 1965, Reese Palley Gallery, N.Y.C., 1970, 71, Cunningham Ward, N.Y.C., 1973, 74, Holly Solomon Gallery, N.Y.C., 1977, Robert Miller Gallery, N.Y.C., 1978, 79, 81, 84, 85, 88, Galerie Liatowitsch, Basel, Switzerland, 1978, Galerie Rudolf Zwirner, Cologne, Fed. Republic Germany, 1979, Daniel Templon Gallery, N.Y.C., 1980, Bruno Bischofberger Gallery, Zurich, 1980, James Mayor Gallery, London, 1981, Marcus Gallery, 1984, Inst. Contemporary Art, Phila., 1981, Akira Ikeda Gallery, Nagoya, Japan, 1981, Daniel Templon Gallery, Paris, 1982, 87, 91, McIntosh-Drysdale Gallery, Washington, 1983, Harcus Gallery, Boston, 1984, 87, 89, Delahunty Gallery, Dallas, 1984, Helander/Rubinstein Gallery, Palm Beach, Fla., 1985, 89, Asher Faure Gallery, L.A., 1985, Yares Gallery, Scottsdale, Ariz., 1987, Sidney Janis Gallery, N.Y.C., 1990, Jason McCoy Gallery, N.Y.C., 1994, 1995 (John Simon Guggenheim fellowship grant), Guild Hall, East Hampton, N.Y., 1995, Hirschl & Adler, N.Y.C., 1995, others; group shows include Franklin Gallery, Cornell U., 1978, Va. Mus. Fine Arts, 1979, Palais des Beaux-Arts, Brussels, 1979, Inst. Contemporary Art, U. Pa., 1979, New Mus., N.Y., 1979, Galerie Daniel Templon, Paris, 1980, Nat. Gallery Art, Washington, 1980, Indpls. Mus. Art, 1980, San Francisco Art Inst., 1980, Whitney Mus. Am. Art, N.Y., 1981, Jacksonville Art Mus., 1981, Galeria Civica, Italy, 1982, Mus. Fine Arts, Boston, 1982, Fay Gold Gallery, Atlanta, 1982, High Mus. Art, Atlanta, 1983, Meml. Art Gallery, Rochester, N.Y., 1983, Kuntsmus., Luzern, 1983. Served with U.S. Army, 1958-60. John Simon Guggenheim fellowship grant, 1995. Office: 78 Greene St New York NY 10012-5100

ZAKARIAN, ALBERT, lawyer; b. Pawtucket, R.I., May 3, 1940; m. Barbara Ann Zakarian, May 28, 1967; children: Adam, Dana. BA, Trinity Coll., 1962; LLB, Columbia U., 1965. Bar: Conn. 1965, U.S. Dist. Ct. Conn. 1965, U.S. Ct. Appeals (2d cir.) 1971. Assoc. Day, Berry & Howard, Hartford, Conn., 1968-75, ptnr., 1975—; panelist Conn. Alt. Disp. Resolution, Ctr. for Pub. Resources, 1988—; co-chair Fed. Spl. Masters Program for Dist. of Conn. Contbr. articles to profl. jours. Mem. town com. Simsbury (Conn.) Dems., 1974-86; chmn. Simsbury Human Rels. Commn., 1985. Capt. JAGC USAF, 1965-68, Vietnam. Decorated Bronze Star. Fellow Am. Coll. Trial Lawyers, Am. Bar Found.; mem. Nat. Bd. Trial Advocacy, Am. Bd. Trial Advs. (diplomate), Conn. Bar Assn. (chmn. civil justice sect. 1979-82, fed. judiciary com.), Hartford County Bar Assn. (pres. 1985-86). Democrat. Office: Day Berry & Howard Cityplace Hartford CT 06103

ZAKARIAN, JOHN J., journalist; b. Jerusalem, Oct. 26, 1937; came to U.S., 1957; s. Ivan and Arsha (Aghabekian) Z.; m. Kay Holder, Sept. 14, 1963; children—Paul, David. B.S. in Journalism, So. Ill. U., 1961; M.A. in Mass Communication, U. Iowa, 1965. Reporter AP, Chgo., 1961; reporter Register-Mail, Galesburg, Ill., 1962-64; legis. corr., editorial editor Lindsay-Schaub Newspapers, Decatur, Ill., 1965-69; assoc. editor Herald Traveler, Boston, 1970-71; editorial writer Post-Dispatch, St. Louis, 1971-77; editor editorial page Hartford Courant, Conn., 1977—. Named Alumnus of Yr., So. Ill. U., Carbondale, 1972; recipient Walker Stone Editorial Writing award Scripps-Howard Found., Cin., 1984, 1st prize for Editls. New England Associated Press, 1986, Citation for Excellence Overseas Press Club Am., 1987, Tom Wallace award for Interpretative Commentary Inter Am. Press Assn., 1989; Nieman fellow Harvard U., 1968-69; Am. Leadership Forum, Fellow, founder Hartford and Houston, 1984-85. Mem. Nat. Conf. Editorial Writers (pres. 1976), Am. Soc. Newspaper Editors (mem. internat. press com.). Mem. Armenian Orthodox Ch. Avocations: tennis; chess; gardening; mountain climbing. Office: Hartford Courant 285 Broad St Hartford CT 06115-2500

ZAKHEIM, DOV SOLOMON, economist, government official; b. Bklyn., Dec. 18, 1948; s. Zvi Hirsh and Bella (Rabinowitz) Z.; BA summa cum laude, Columbia U., 1970; student London Sch. Econs., 1968-69; DPhil, Oxford U., 1974; m. Barbara Jane Portnoi, Aug. 20, 1972 (div. 1990); children: Keith Samuel, Roger Israel, Scott Elisha; m. Deborah Bing Lowy, May 26, 1991. Rsch. fellow St. Antony's Coll., U. Oxford, Eng., 1974; asst. to mng. dir. U.K. br. Internat. Credit Bank Geneva, 1974-75; asso. analyst Nat. Security and Internat. Affairs, Congl. Budget Office, Washington, 1975-78, prin. analyst, 1978-81; spl. asst. to asst. sec. def. (internat. security policy) Dept. Def., 1981-82, spl. asst. to under sec. def. (policy), 1982-83; asst. under sec. def. (policy and resources), 1983-85; dep. undersec. def. for planning and resources, 1985-87; exec. v.p. System Planning Corp., Arlington, Va., 1987-90, corp. v.p., 1990—; CEO SPC Internat. Inc., 1988—; cons. to sec. def. and under sec. def. (policy), 1987-93, ABC News, 1991; adj. prof. Nat. Def. U., 1992, Columbia U., 1995, Yeshiva U., 1995-96; guest lectr. War Coll., others. Contbr. articles to profl. jours. V.p. S.E. Hebrew Congregation, Silver Spring, Md., 1978-80; bd. dirs. Yeshiva H.S. of Greater Washington, 1979-82, Young Israel Shomrai Emunah, 1983-85; hon. bd. dirs. Hebrew Acad. of Greater Washington, 1980-82; bd. deps. of Brit. Jews, 1971-72; mem. Chief Rabbi's Chaplaincy Bd., U.K., 1971-72; mem. U.S. Commn. for Preservation of Am.'s Heritage Abroad, 1991-95. Recipient Dirs.'s Award for outstanding svc. Congressional Budget Office, 1979, Disting. Pub. Service medal, Dept. Def., 1986, Bronze Palm to Disting. Pub. Svc. medal Dept. Def. 1987; NSF fellow, 1970-73; Columbia Coll. Kellett fellow, 1974. Mem. Council Fgn. Relations, Internat. Inst. Strategic Studies, U.S. Naval Inst., Royal Inst. Internat. Affairs (U.K.), Soc. Govt. Economists, Phi Beta Kappa. Club: Columbia, Capitol Hill, United Oxford and Cmbridge U. Contbr. articles to profl. jours. Home: 817 Lamberton Dr Silver Spring MD 20902-3038 Office: System Planning Corp 1500 Wilson Blvd Arlington VA 22209-2404

ZAKI, ABDELMONEIM EMAM, dental educator; b. Cairo, Egypt, Dec. 18, 1933; came to U.S., 1959; naturalized, 1976; s. Emam Badr El Din and Fatima Hussein (Kamel) Z. DDS, Cairo U., 1955, MS in Radiology, 1958; MSc in Dentistry, Ind. U., Indpls., 1962; PhD in Anatomy, U. Ill., Chgo., 1969. Dental surgeon Demonstration Tng. Ctr., Qalyb, Egypt, 1955-59; instr., then asst. prof. Cairo U., 1962-67; rsch. asst., assoc. U. Ill., Chgo., 1967-69, asst. prof., 1970-72, assoc. prof., 1972-75, prof. dentistry, 1975—, head dept. oral biology, 1994—; sr. investigator, Nat. Inst. Dental Rsch., Bethesda, Md., 1981-82; cons., Cairo U., Alexandria U., Tanta U., all in Egypt, 1976—. Author: Human Dentition, 1965, rev. edit., 1967; contbr. numerous articles and abstracts to dental publs. Mem. Arab-Am. Anti-Discriminatin Com., Washington. Fellow Internat. Coll. Dentists; mem. Am. and Internat. Assns. Dental Rsch. (officer Chgo. chpt. 1982—), Am. Assn. Anatomists, Electron Microscope Soc. Am., N.Y. Acad. Scis., Chgo. Acad. Sci., Egyptian-Am. Club Chgo., Arab Am. Univ. Grads., Chgo. Health Club, Sigma Xi. Moslem. Office: U Ill Chgo 801 S Paulina St Chicago IL 60612-7210

ZAKIM, DAVID, biochemist; b. Paterson, N.J., July 10, 1935; s. Sam and Ruth (Sorokin) B.; m. Nancy Jane Levine, June 12, 1957 (div. 1976); children: Michael, Eric, Thomas; m. Dagmar Auralia Stanke, July 30, 1978; children: Tamara, Robert. AB in Chemistry, Cornell U., 1956; MD summa cum laude, SUNY, Bklyn., 1961. Diplomate Am. Bd. Internal Medicine. Intern N.Y. Hosp., N.Y.C., 1961-62, asst. resident, 1962-63, fellow, 1963-65; asst. prof. to prof. medicine and pharmacology U. Calif., San Francisco, 1968-83; Vincent Astor Disting. prof. medicine Cornell U. Med. Coll., N.Y.C., 1983—; prof. biochemistry Cornell U. Grad. Sch. Med. Sci., 1983—. Contbr. over 150 articles to profl. jours.; editor: Hepatology: A Textbook of Liver Disease, 1982, 3rd edit., 1996, Disorders of Acid Secretion, 1991; editor series: Current Topics in Gastroenterology, 1985; editor Gastroenterology Medicine Today, 1992—. Capt. U.S. Army, 1965-68. Named Disting. Alumnus, SUNY-Bklyn., 1986. Mem. Am. Assn. Physicians, Am. Soc. Biol. Chemists, Biophysics Soc. Achievements include patent on fusion of proteins with lipid vesicles; demonstration of the lipid-dependence of UDP-glucuronyl transferase; elucidation of mechanism for uptake of fatty acids and bilirubin into cells. Home: 15 Cole Dr Armonk NY 10504-3004 Office: Cornell U Med Coll Medicine-Gastroenterology 1300 York Ave New York NY 10021-4805

ZAKIN, JACQUES LOUIS, chemical engineering educator; b. N.Y.C., Jan. 28, 1927; s. Mordecai and Ada Davies (Fishbein) Z.; m. Laura Pienkny, June 11, 1950; children: Richard Joseph, David Fredric, Barbara Ellen, Emily Anne, Susan Beth. B in Chem. Engring., Cornell U., 1949; MSChemE, Columbia U., 1950; DEng. Sci., NYU, 1959. Chem. engr. Flintkote Research Labs., Whippany, N.J., 1950-51; research technologist, research dept. Socony-Mobil, Bklyn., 1951-53, sr. research technologist, 1953-56, supervising technologist, 1959-62; assoc. prof. chem. engring. U. Mo., Rolla, 1962-65; prof. U. Mo., 1965-77, dir. minority engring. program, 1974-77, dir. women in engring. program, 1975-77; chmn. dept. chem. engring. Ohio State U., Columbus, 1977-94, Helen C. Kurtz prof. chem. engring., 1994—; chmn. sci. manpower and resources com. Coun. Chem. Rsch., 1984-86, mem. governing bd., 1986-89; exec. com., 1988-89; mem. adv. bd. State of Ohio Alternative Fuels, 1992-93; vis. prof. Technion, 1968-69, 94-95, Hebrew U., 1987. Co-editor: Proc. Turbulence Symposium, 1969, 71, 73, 75, 77, 79, 81, 83; contbr. articles to profl. jours. Bd. dirs. Rolla Community Concert Assn., 1966-77, 2d v.p., 1975-77; bd. dirs. Ozark Mental Health Assn., 1976-77; trustee Ohio State Hillel Found., 1981-84, treas., 1984-89, pres., 1989-92; trustee Congregation Beth Tikvah, 1983; bd. trustees Columbus Jewish Fedn., 1989-92; co-chmn. Academics and Scientists for Soviet Refuseniks. With USNR, 1945-46. Recipient Outstanding Rsch. award U. Mo., 1970, Josef Hlavka Meml. medal Czechoslovakian Acad. Sci., 1992; named Outstanding Educator of Yr., Ohio Soc. Profl. Engrs., 1994, Tech. Person of Yr., Columbus Tech. Coun., 1987; Am. Chem. Soc. Petroleum Rsch. Fund Internat. fellow, 1968-69, Socony-Mobil Employee Incentive fellow NYU, 1956-59, Sr. Fulbright Rsch. fellow Technion, 1994-95. Fellow Am. Inst. Chem. Engrs.; mem. Am. Chem. Soc., Soc. of Rheology, Am. Soc. Engring. Edn., Sigma Xi, Phi Lambda Upsilon, Phi Eta Sigma, Alpha Chi Sigma, Tau Beta Pi, Phi Kappa Phi. Jewish. Patentee in field. Office: Ohio State U 140 W 19th Ave Columbus OH 43210-1110

ZAKIN, JONATHAN NEWELL, computer industry executive; b. Suffern, N.Y., Aug. 18, 1949; s. Paul Peter and Shirley Ruth (Friedman) Z.; m. Esther Karlinsky, Jan. 1972 (div. Aug. 1976); m. Andrea Elisabeth Schutze, June 9, 1984; children: Carl Hartwig, Hans Christopher. BS in Mgmt., NYU, 1971; MBA, Harvard U., 1976. Mgr. fin. planning Prudential Lines Inc., N.Y.C., 1971-74, asst. to pres., 1976-77; assoc. J. Henry Schroder Corp., N.Y.C., 1977-78; gen. mgr. Brisk & Kindle Ltd., London, 1978-80; pres. Cosma Internat., Brussels, 1980-84; v.p. sales and mktg. Winterhalter, Inc., Ann Arbor, Mich., 1984-86; exec. v.p. mktg. and sales U.S. Robotics, Inc., Skokie, Ill., 1987—. Mem. Monroe Club, Harvard Club. Avocations: jogging, photography, art collecting. Home: 794 Dean Ave Highland Park IL 60035-4724 Office: US Robotics 8100 Mccormick Blvd Skokie IL 60076-2920*

ZAKKAY, VICTOR, aeronautical engineering educator, scientist; b. Baghdad, Iraq, Sept. 8, 1927; came to U.S., 1946, naturalized, 1956; s. Haron and Massouda Isac (David) Zakkai. B.Ae.E., Poly Inst. Bklyn., 1952, M.Ae.E., 1953, Ph.D.Ae.E., 1959. Research assoc. prof. Poly Inst. Bklyn., 1962-64; assoc. prof. aeronautics NYU, Bronx, 1964-65, prof. aero. and astron. engring., asst. dir. Aero. Lab., 1965-73; prof. applied sci., dir. Antonio Ferri Labs. NYU, Westbury, N.Y., 1973, 75—; chmn. dept. applied sci. NYU, N.Y.C., 1977-84, Astor prof. aero. sci., 1980—; cons. TRW Environ. Engring., Research Triangle Park, N.C., 1980-81, Advanced Tech. Labs., Westbury, 1977-81, b.v. Neratoom, The Hague, Netherlands, 1981—. Editor: (with Olfe) Supersonic Flow, Chemical Processes and Radiation Transfer, 1963; contbr. articles to profl. jours. Mem. AIAA, Sigma Xi, Tau Beta Pi, Sigma Gamma Tau. Home and Office: NYU Barney Building 34 Stuyvesant St New York NY 10003-7506

ZAKS, JERRY, theatrical director, actor; b. Stuttgart, Fed. Republic of Germany, Sept. 7, 1946; came to U.S., 1948, naturalized, 1954; s. Sy and Lily (Gliksman) Z.; m. Jill P. Rose, Jan. 14, 1979; children: Emma Rose, Hannah Lily. AB, Dartmouth Coll., 1967; MFA, Smith Coll., 1969. Guest artist, vis. prof. Dartmouth Coll., 1977, 83-84. Actor: (Broadway plays) Grease, 1974, Once in a Lifetime, 1977, 1940's Radio Hour, 1978, Tintypes, 1980, (off-Broadway plays) including Ensemble Studio Theatre, 1971-81, O'Neill Center, Conn., 1975, Phoenix Theatre, 1976-78, Arena Stage, Washington, 1978, N.Y. Shakespeare Festival, 1975, Manhattan Theatre Club, 1980, Roundabout Theatre, (TV and/or films) including Tuscaloosa's Calling Me, 1979, Attica, 1979; star: (CBS-TV movie) Gentleman Bandit, 1981; appeared in: (TV spl.) Yankee Doodle Dandy, Kennedy Center Tribute to James Cagney, 1980; dir.: (plays, musicals) The Foreigner, 1984 (Obie award 1985), The Marriage of Bette and Boo, 1985 (Obie award 1985, Drama Desk award 1985), (nat. tour) Tintypes, Tap Dance Kid, 1985 (Dramalogue award 1985), Beyond Therapy, Sister Mary Ignatius, Baby with the Bathwater, 1984, House of Blue Leaves, 1986 (Antoinette Perry award), Anything Goes, 1987, Lend Me A Tenor, 1989 (Antoinette Perry award), Six Degrees of Separation, 1990 (Antoinette Perry award), Guys and Dolls, 1992 (Tony award), Smokey Joe's Café, 1994-95 (Tony nomination - Direction of a Musical, 1995) AFunny Thing Happened on the Way to the Forum, 1996 (Tony nomination Best Director of a Musical, 1996); dir. Ensemble Studio, 1978-80, Phoenix Theatre, N.Y.C., 1980-81, Playwrights Horizons, 1981, Phila. Drama Guild, 1981, Denver Ctr. Theater, 1984, N.Y. Pub. Theater, 1984, Assassins, 1990. Bd. dirs. Ensemble Studio Theatre, N.Y.C., 1976—. Mem. AFTRA, Actors Equity Assn., Screen Actors Guild, Soc. Stage Dirs. and Choreographers. Office: St James Theater 246 West 44th St New York NY 10036*

ZAKSHESKE, MARK RICHARD, treasurer; b. Erie, Pa., Apr. 16, 1956; s. Vernon F. and Ruth M. (Merski) Z.; m. Heidi Widmar, July 18, 1981; children: Jennifer, Joseph, Julia. BS, John Caroll U., 1978; MBA, Loyola Coll., 1993. CPA, Ohio. Internal auditor Ameritrust, Cleve., 1978-79, Eaton Corp., Cleve., 1979-80; sr. internal auditor Marshall Field, Cleve., 1980-81; contr. Standard Products Co., Goldsboro, N.C., 1981-88, Haskell of Pitts., Verona, Pa., 1988-90, Stone Indsl., College Park, Md., 1990-95; treasurer Precision Products Group, Inc., Rockford, Ill., 1995—; bd. dirs. Kingship Fed. Credit Union, Balt. Mem. Fin. Mgmt. Assn., KC (warden 1988-94). Republican. Roman Catholic. Avocations: scuba diving, running. Home: 7241 Sentinel Rd Rockford IL 61107-5503 Office: Precision Products Group 4205 Galleria Dr Rockford IL 61111

ZALAZNICK, SHELDON, editor, journalist; b. Bronx, N.Y., Aug. 6, 1928; s. Samuel and Esther Leah (Schneiderman) Z.; m. Vera Altofeldt, Apr. 4, 1953; 1 dau., Andrea. B.A., Univ. Coll. N.Y. U., 1948; M.A., Tchrs. Coll. Columbia, 1950. Tchr. English Benjamin Franklin High Sch., N.Y.C., 1950-52; assoc. editor Newsweek mag., 1952-56; v.p. Manning Pub. Relations Co., 1956-59; sr. editor Forbes mag., 1959-63, mng. editor, 1976-89; founding editor New York mag. sect. N.Y. Herald Tribune, N.Y.C., 1963-64; Sunday editor N.Y. Herald Tribune, 1964-66; staff writer Gen. Learning Corp., 1966-67; assoc. editor Fortune mag., 1967-69; v.p., editorial dir. New York mag., 1969-76. Home: 458 W 246th St Bronx NY 10471-3330

ZALDASTANI, OTHAR, structural engineer; b. Tbilisi, Republic of Georgia, Aug. 10, 1922; came to U.S., 1946; naturalized, 1956; s. Soliko Nicholas and Mariam Vachnadze (Hirsely) Z.; m. Elizabeth Reily Bailey, June 22, 1963; children: Elizabeth, Anne, Alexander. Diplome D'Ingenieur, Ecole Nationale des Ponts et Chaussees, Paris, 1945; Licencie es Scis., Sorbonne, Paris, 1946; MS in Geotech. Engring., Harvard U., 1947, DSc in Aerodynamics, 1950. Registered profl. engr., Mass., R.I., Tenn., Mo., N.H. Mem. faculty Harvard U., Cambridge, Mass., 1947-50; ptnr. Nichols, Norton and Zaldastani, Boston, 1952-63; pres. Nichols, Norton and Zaldastani, Inc., Boston, 1964-76, Zaldastani Assocs., Inc., Boston, 1976-88, chmn., 1988—; Gordon McKay vis. lectr. structural mechanics Harvard U., 1961; trustee, 1st v.p. Mass. Constrn. Industry Bd., 1973-76; mem. Mass. Designer Selection Bd., 1976-80. Contbg. author: Advances in Applied Mechanics, vol. 3, 1953. Patentee sound absorbing block, prestressed concrete beam and deck system. Trustee Wheelock Coll., Boston, 1975-81, mem. corp., 1984—; trustee Boston U. Med. Ctr., 1976—; trustee Brooks Sch., North Andover, Mass., 1986—. Recipient awards from various orgns. and agys. including Prestressed Concrete Inst., Cons. Engrs. Coun. New Eng., Am. Inst. Steel Constrn., Concrete Reinforcing Steel Inst., Dept. Transp., Am. Concrete Inst. Fellow ASCE (Ralph W. Horne award), AIAA (assoc.), Am. Concrete Inst.; mem. Georgian Assn. in the U.S. (pres. 1958-65), Sigma Xi, Harvard Club, Harvard Faculty Club (Cambridge), Somerset Club (Boston), Country Club (Brookline, Mass.), Rolling Rock Club (Ligonier, Pa.). Home: 70 Suffolk Rd Chestnut Hill MA 02167-1218 Office: Zaldastani Assocs Inc 7 Water St Boston MA 02109-4511

ZALESKI, BRIAN WILLIAM, chiropractor; b. Trenton, N.J., Oct. 27, 1962; s. Joseph Rudolph and Roseline (Moore) Z.; m. Petra Gertrude Tucker, Apr. 10, 1983; children: Natasha Reneé, Tatyana Amber. Student, Def. Lang. Inst., Monterey, Calif., 1980-81; BS, Palmer Coll., 1992, D of Chiropractic, 1992. Indsl. disability evaluator, Calif.; qualified med. evaluator, Calif. Grad. rschr. Palmer Coll. of Chiropractice, Davenport, Iowa, 1991-92; chiropractor Peninsula Spinal Care, Daly City, Calif., 1992, Creekside Family Chiropractic, Vacaville, Calif., 1992—; prin. investigator, presenter Internat. Conf. on Spinal Manipulation, 1992. Baseball umpire Iowa High Schs., Davenport, 1989-92, Men's Sr. League, Davenport, 1989-91, No. Calif. Umpires Assn., San Mateo, Calif., 1992; mem. adv. bd. Solano Serve Our Srs. Recipient scholarship Internat. Chiropractors Assn., 1989, 90, Cecil M. Grogan scholarship Palmer Internat. Alumni Assn., 1991, Alma Nielsen scholarship Internat. Chiropractors Assn. Aux., 1991, Student Rsch. grant Palmer Coll. Chiropractic, 1992; named to Dean's List, 1991-92. Mem. Internat. Chiropractors Assn. (coun. on chiropractic pediatrics), Calif. Chiropractic Assn. (net masters com., ins. rels. com.), Assn. for History of Chiropractic, Palmer Internat. Alumni Assn., Napa/Solano Chiropractic Soc. (pres.), Masons, Delta Sigma Chi, Chi Rho Theta. Republican. Office: Creekside Family Chiropractic 3000 Alamo Dr Ste 108 Vacaville CA 95687-6345

ZALESKI, MICHAEL LOUIS, state official, lawyer; b. Kenosha, Wis., Jan. 11, 1941; s. Louis Edward and Lena Louise (Bellotti) Z.; m. Sue Alyce Householder, Nov. 24, 1967; children—Sara, David. B.S. in Psychology, U. Wis., 1963, J.D. in Law, 1966. Bar: Wis. 1966, U.S. Dist. Ct. (we. dist.) Wis. 1966, U.S. Dist. Ct. (ea. dist.) Wis. 1970, U.S. Supreme Ct. 1982. Asst. dist. atty. Dane County, Wis., 1967-70; asst. atty. gen. State of Wis. Madison, 1970-86; atty. Quarles & Brady, Madison, 1986—. Served to capt. JAG, USAR, 1968-72. Mem. Wis. Dist. Attys. Assn. (exec. bd. 1978-86), Roman Catholic. Home: 4710 Deerpath Rd Middleton WI 53562-2324 Office: Quarles & Brady PO Box 2113 1 S Pinckney St Madison WI 53703-2808

ZALEZNIK, ABRAHAM, psychoanalyst, management specialist, educator; b. Phila., Jan. 30, 1924; s. Isadore and Anna (Appelbaum) Z.; m. Elizabeth Ann Aron, June 24, 1945; children: Dori Faith, Ira Harry. AB in econs., Alma Coll., 1945, DLitt (hon.), 1992; MBA, Harvard U., 1947, DCS, 1951; grad., Boston Psychoanalytic Soc. and Inst., 1965. Research asst. Harvard U. Grad. Sch. Bus. Adminstrn., 1947-48, instr., 1948-51, asst. prof., 1951-56, assoc. prof., 1956-61, prof., 1961—, Cahners-Rabb prof. social psychology of mgmt., 1967-83, Konosuke Matsushita prof. leadership, 1983-90, Konosuke Matsushita prof. leadership emeritus, 1990—; research fellow Boston Psychoanalytic Soc. and Inst., 1965-68, mem. faculty, 1972—; pvt. practice psychoanalysis Boston, 1968—; cons. to mgmt.; chmn. bd. King Ranch; vice chmn. bd. Ogden Corp.; bd. dirs. Ardco, Inc., Timberland Co., Le Chateau Stores, Ltd., Freedom Newspapers, Inc., Am. Greetings, Butchers, Inc., TJX Corp. Author: Human Dilemmas of Leadership, 1966, (with Manfred F.R. Kets de Vries) Power and the Corporate Mind, 1975, The Managerial Mystique, 1989, An Executive Guide to Motivating People, 1990, Learning Leadership, 1992; contbr. articles to profl. jours. Trustee Beth Israel Hosp., Boston, 1968—. Served with USNR, 1942-46. Mem. Boston Psychoanalytic Soc., Am. Psychoanalytic Assn. (cert.), Am. Sociol. Assn., Tavern Club (Boston), Belmont Country Club (Mass.). Home: 170 N Ocean Blvd Palm Beach FL 33480 Office: Harvard University Business School Boston MA 02163 also: Ogden Corp 2 Pennsylvania Plz New York NY 10121

ZALINSKI, EDMUND LOUIS GRAY, insurance executive, mutual funds and real estate executive, investor; b. Salt Lake City, Aug. 18, 1915; s. Edward Robins and Agnes (de Schweinitz) Z.; m. Matilde Eleanor Mittendorf, July 15, 1939; children: Nancy Zalinski Johnson, Matilde Zalinski Davidson, Susanne Zalinski Williams. AB, Cornell U., 1937; MBA, Harvard, 1938; PhD summa cum laude, NYU, 1944. Mgr. sales offices N.Y. Life Ins. Co., 1938-47, asst. v.p., 1951-52, 2d v.p., 1953-54, v.p., 1954-55; instr. NYU, 1944-46; 1st mng. dir. Life Underwriter Tng. Coun., 1947-51, pres., 1954, dir., 1951—; exec. v.p. Nat. Assn. Life Underwriters, 1949-51; v.p., chmn. agy. com. John Hancock Mut. Life Ins. Co., Boston, 1955-57; pres., CEO Life Ins. Co. N.Am., 1957-71; pres. dir. INA Life Ins. Co. N.Y., 1968-72; v.p., dir. INA Properties, Inc., INA Trading Corp., Phila. Investment Corp.; dir., chmn. exec. com. Bryn Mawr Trust Co., 1963-88; chmn. Greit Realty Trust, 1966-79; bd. dirs. leasing cos.; bd. dirs. Transwall Corp., B.G. Balmer Co., Integra Life Ins. Corp.; mem. adv. coun. Underwriter Edn. and Tng., 1947-50, Joint Com. on Mmgt. Tng., 1948-51; mem. rsch. adv. com. Life Inst. Agy. Mgmt. Assn., 1951-57; Huebner Found. lectr. Am. Coll., Bryn Mawr, Pa., 1956; mem. vis. com. Grad. Sch. Bus. Adminstrn., Harvard Coll., NYU; trustee Am. Coll. Life Underwriters, 1954-72, chmn. mgmt. edn. com., 1957-72, also chmn. devel. com.; treas., founder, chmn. Life Underwriters Tng. Coun., 1947—, life trustee, 1968—. Author publs. relating to field. Trustee, mem. exec. com., v.p. Phila. Mus. Art, 1965-72; bd. dirs. Bur. Mcpl. Rsch., Phila.; bd. dirs., chmn. exec. com. Pa. Economy League, 1963-72. Recipient Huebner Gold Medal award for professionalism in fin. edn. and tng. Am. Coll., 1993. Mem. Life Inst. Assn. Am. (dir. 1970-72), Ins. Fedn. Pa. (dir., chmn. 1970-72), Newcomen Soc., Loyal Legion, SAR, Cornell Club Phila. (dir.), Harvard Bus. Sch. Club Phila. (past pres.), Merion Cricket Club, Palmbrook Country Club. Home: 100 Grays Ln Apt 401 Haverford PA 19041-1754 also: 9701 W Sandstone Dr Sun City AZ 85351-2058 Office: 410 Lancaster Ave Haverford PA 19041-1329

ZALINSKY, SANDRA H. ORLOFSKY, school counselor; b. Elizabeth, N.J., July 11, 1959; d. Marion E. (Carrajat) Orlofsky; m. Thomas J. Zalinsky, Apr. 12, 1985. BA in Math. & Sci. Edn., Glassboro State Coll., 1981; MA in Adminstrn., Jersey City State Coll., 1985, MA in Counseling, 1990; EdD in Child & Youth Studies, Nova Southeastern U., 1994. Nat. cert. counselor; master addictions counselor. Sr. cam counselor Brick (N.J.) Recreation Dept., 1978-81; tchr. high sch. math. and sci. Brick (N.J.) Twp. Bd. Edn., 1981-88; counselor, cons. pvt. agys., Ocean County, N.J., 1978-81; counselor high sch. Brick Twp. Bd. Edn., 1988—; dept. head guidance Brick Twp. H.S., 1985—; speaker in field. Mem. ASCD (nat. cert. counselor), N.J. Counseling Assn., N.J. Sch. Counselors Assn., N.J. Edn. Assn. (sch. rep. 1981—), Skippers Cove Yacht Club, Phi Delta Kappa. Avocations: sailing, scuba diving, photography, tennis, travel. Home: 20 Davey Jones Way Waretown NJ 08758-2106 Office: Brick Twp Bd Edn 101 Hendrickson Ave Brick NJ 08724-2574

ZALIOUK, YUVAL NATHAN, conductor; b. Haifa, Israel, Feb. 10, 1939; s. Israel Nahum and Ahuda (Nathanson) Z.; m. Susan Marlys Davies, May 5, 1972; children: Eyal, Adam, Tamar. LL.B., Hebrew U., Jerusalem, 1964; student, Rubin Acad. Music, Jerusalem, 1960-63, Guildhall Sch. Music, London, 1965-67. Founder YZ Enterprises, Inc., Maumee, Ohio; apptd. music dir., condr. Raanana Symphonette Orch., Israel, 1996. Condr. Royal Ballet of London, 1966-70; music dir. Opera Studio, Paris, 1973-74, Haifa Symphony, 1975-77; interim chief condr. Edmonton (Alta., Can.) Symphony Orch., 1980-81; music dir., condr. Toledo Symphony Orch., 1980-89, condr. laureate, 1989—; music dir., condr. Raanana Symphonette Israel, 1996—. Recipient 1st prize Am.-Israel Cultural Found. Competition, 1965; 2d prize Internat. Condrs. Competition, Besancon, France, 1966; 1st prize Internat. Condrs. Competition, Besancon, 1967; 1st prize for progressive programming ASCAP, 1984, Entrepreneur of Yr. award, 1992; winner Mitropoulos Condrs. Competition, N.Y.C., 1970. Jewish. Club: Rotary.

ZALK, ROBERT H., lawyer; b. Albert Lea, Minn., Dec. 1, 1944; s. Donald B. and Juliette J. (Erickson) Z.; m. Ann Lee Anderson, June 21, 1969; children: Amy, Jenna. BA, Carleton Coll., 1966; JD, U. Minn., 1969. Bar: Minn. 1969, U.S. Dist. Ct. Minn. 1969. Atty. Popham, Haik, Schnobrich, Kaufman & Doty, Mpls., 1969-72, No. States Power Co., Mpls., 1972-73, Wright, West & Diessner, Mpls., 1973-84, Fredrikson & Byron P.A., Mpls., 1984-94, Zalk & Assocs., Mpls., 1994-95, Zalk & Eayrs, Mpls., 1995—. Fellow Am. Acad. Matrimonial Lawyers bd. mgrs. Minn. chpt. 1989-92), Minn. State Bar Assn. (co-chmn. maintenance guideline com. 1991-94), Hennepin County Bar Assn. (co-chmn. family law sect. 1990-91). Office: Zalk & Eayrs PA Sunset Ridge Bus Park 5861 Cedar Lake Rd Minneapolis MN 55416-1481

ZALL, PAUL MAXWELL, retired English language educator, consultant; b. Lowell, Mass., Aug. 3, 1922; s. Nathan and Bertha (Rubin) Z.; m. Elisabeth Weisz, June 21, 1948; children: Jonathan, Barnaby, Andrew. BA, Swarthmore Coll., 1948; AM, Harvard U., 1950, PhD, 1951. Teaching fellow Harvard U., 1950-51; instr. Cornell U., 1951-55, U. Oreg., 1955-56; research editor Boeing Co., 1956-57; asst. prof. Calif. State Coll., Los Angeles, 1957-61; asso. prof. Calif. State Coll., 1961-64, prof. English, 1964-86; research scholar, cons. to library docents Huntington Library, San Marino, Calif., 1986—; acting chmn. dept. Calif. State Coll., 1969-71; cons. in report writing, proposal preparation and brochures to industry and govt. agys., 1957—. Author: Elements of Technical Report Writing, 1962, Hundred Merry Tales, 1963, Nest of Ninnies, 1970, Literary Criticism of William Wordsworth, 1966, (with John Durham) Plain Style, 1967, Simple Cobler of Aggawam in America, 1969; (with J.R. Trevor) Proverb to Poem, 1970, Selected Satires of Peter Pindar, 1971, Comical Spirit of Seventy Six, 1976, Ben Franklin Laughing, 1980; (with J.A.L. Lemay) Autobiography of Benjamin Franklin, 1981; (with Leonard Franco) Practical Writing, 1978, Norton Critical Edition of Franklin's Autobiography, 1986, Abe Lincoln Laughing, 1983, 95; (with E. Birdsall) Descriptive Sketches, 1984, Mark Twain Laughing, 1985, Being Here, 1987, George Washington Laughing, 1989, Franklin's Autobiography: Model Life, 1989, Founding Mothers, 1991, Becoming American, 1993, Lincoln's Legacy, 1994, Wit and Wisdom of the Founding Fathers, 1996, Blue and Gray Laughing, 1996. Pres. Friends of South Pasadena Library, 1967-70. Served with USAAF, 1942-45, ETO. Am. Philos. Soc. fellow, 1964, 66; John Carter Brown Libr. rsch. grantee, Huntington Libr. rsch. grantee, fellow, 1993. Home: 1911 Leman Ln South Pasadena CA 91030-4628 Office: Calif State Coll Huntington Libr San Marino CA 91108

ZALL, ROBERT ROUBEN, food scientist, educator; b. Lowell, Mass., Dec. 6, 1925; s. Samuel and Sarah (Cohen) Z.; m. Mollie Leah Wiseblood, June 8, 1949; children—Linda Zall Sheffield, Judy Zall Kusek, Jonathan J. B.S., U. Mass., 1949, M.S., 1950; Ph.D., Cornell U., 1968. Gen. mgr. Grandview Dairies, Bklyn. and Arkport, N.Y., 1950-66; dairy industry cons. Ithaca, N.Y., 1966-68; dir. research prodn. Crowley Foods Co., Binghamton, N.Y., 1968-71; prof. food sci. Cornell U., 1971-92; prof. emeritus, 1992—; past trustee Milk Industry Pension and Welfare Fund; dairy industry cons., project dir. EPA-Industry demonstration whey processing plant. Author: (with Bela G. Liptak) Environmental Engineers Handbook, 1972; co-contbr. to Food Processing Waste Management, 1979, Food Processing, 15 vols., 1979, Dairy Microbiology, 1981, rev. edit., 1990; contbr. numerous articles to profl. jours., popular mags. Served with AUS, 1944-46. Recipient Cert. Appreciation EPA, 1975, 79; Howard B. Marlott award N.Y. State Milk and Food Sanitarians. Mem. Internat. Assn. Milk, Food and Environ. Sanitarians, Internat. Dairy Fedn., Inst. Food Technologists, Am. Soc. Agrl. Engrs., Masons, Phi Kappa Phi. Patentee automatic cleaning apparatus, stabilization of milk and improved cheese yield, Rennin-like enzymes from clams, a process for preserving fish and microbial production of acetaldeyde. Home: 54 Woodcrest Ave Ithaca NY 14850-6241 Office: Cornell U Dept Food Sci Stocking Hall Ithaca NY 14853-7201 *Most people I know, never made a success of themselves by just working forty hours a week. It takes hard work, the love of a good wife, and the willingness to accept challenges.*

ZALLEN, HAROLD, corporate executive, scientist, former university official; b. Boston, Apr. 7, 1926; s. Joseph and Lillian L. (Stahl) Z.; m. Eugenia Malone, Aug. 23, 1959. BS in Pharmacy, Northeastern U., Boston, 1951; EdM in Sci. and Math., Boston U., 1954; MS in Organic Synthetic Medicinal Chemistry, Purdue U., 1959, PhD in Analytical Medicinal Chemistry and Nucleonics, 1960. Registered pharmacist, Mass. With USAAF, 1943-46, combat flier, sgt. 487th bomb group, 839th bomb squadron; commd. 1st lt. U.S. Army, 1955, advanced through grades to col., 1986; ret.; mgr. Shoppers World Pharmacy, Inc., Framingham, Mass., 1951-53; asst. prof. phys. sci. Portia Law Sch. Calvin Coolidge Coll., Boston, 1952-54; tchr. physics and chemistry Natick (Mass.) High Sch., 1955-56; grad. instr., asst. radiol. control officer Purdue U., Lafayette, Ind., 1957-58; assoc. prof. chemistry Coll. Pharmacy Mercer U., Atlanta, 1960-61; assoc. prof. to prof., head dept. radiol. scis., dir. Office Radiol. Safety Auburn U., Ala., 1961-66; specialist phys. sci. rsch. div. higher edn. rsch. Bur. Rsch., U.S. Office Edn., 1966-67, head curriculum higher edn. rsch., 1967; head instructional sci. equipment program, assoc. program dir., then dir. spl. projects program NSF, Washington, 1967-72; asst. dean, dir. rsch. and grad. studies Okla. State U., Stillwater, 1972-73, prof. chemistry, 1972-73, rsch. prof. biochemistry and molecular biology, 1973-75; assoc. v.p. for adminstrn. and fin., chief adminstrv. officer Health Scis. Ctr. Campus U. Okla., Oklahoma City and Tulsa, 1973-75; assoc. v.p. for systems planning, procedure devel. and spl. projects, cen. adminstrn. U. Okla., Norman, from 1975; exec. v.p. Acad. World Inc., 1975—; pres. Malone, Zallen & Assocs. div. AcaWorld Corp., Greenville, N.C.; v.p., dir. nuclear div. Vachon, Nix & Assocs., Atlanta; pres., chief exec. officer Computer Profls. Inc., Computer Distbrs. Corp.; pres. Malone Group Internat., Columbus, Ga.; sci. advisor Litton Corp./Army Rsch. Inst., 1991, Omega Tng. Group Inc./GIAT Industries, France, 1992—, Wetzel Internat., Inc., 1994—; chmn. bd. dirs. Cons. Unltd., Columbus, Ga.; analytical chemist Communicable Diseases Ctr. USPHS, Atlanta, 1962; spl. lectr. Radiobiology Inst., NSF, 1963-64; mem. Pres.'s Sci. and Technol. Adv. Commn., Washington; bd. dirs. Internat. Sci. and Engring. Fairs, Sci. Svc., Inc., 1973-85; v.p. Okla. Coll. Osteo. Medicine and Surgery, Tulsa; cons. Okla. State Regents for Higher Edn.; Gov. N.C. primary alt. to So. States Energy Bd., 1984-90, mem. exec. com. bd., 1986; cons. in field. Author 4 books in field, 1986-89; editor, pub. Jour. Internat 6800 Computer Ctr.; contbr. numerous articles to profl. jours. Republican candidate N.C. Gen. Assembly, 1986. Recipient Mayoralty cert. of merit for outstanding svc. and Key to City, City of New Orleans, 1973, Most Outstanding Alumni award Northeastern U., 1996; GE sci. fellow Union U., Schenectady, NY., 1955, fellow Purdue Rsch. Found., 1958, Elks Cancer Soc., 1959, Am. Cancer Soc., 1960. Mem. Am. Chem. Soc. (bd. dirs., chmn. Auburn sect. 1966), Am. Soc. Engring. Edn. (long range planning com.), Nat. Coun. Univ. Adminstrs., Soc. Rsch. Adminstrs. (pres. So. sect. from 1974, chmn. publs. com.), Health Physics Soc., Greenville (N.C.) Area C. of C. (chmn. rsch.), Columbus Club, Rotary (chmn. bull. com. Auburn 1963, bd. dirs. Auburn 1964, bd. dirs. Stillwater 1972-73, Greenville 1981-86, charter pres. Greenville, N.C. Morning club 1986, Paul Harris fellow), MAsons (32 degree), Shriners, Sigma Xi, Phi Lambda Upsilon, Rho Chi, Phi Delta Kappa, Delta Sigma Theta, Beta Phi (past nat. sec.). Baptist. Office: Malone Group Internat PO Box 8767 Columbus GA 31908-8767

ZALTA, EDWARD, otorhinolaryngologist, utilization review physician; b. Houston, Mar. 2, 1930; s. Nouri Louis and Marie Zahde (Lizmi) Z.; m. Carolyn Mary Gordon, Oct. 8, 1971; 1 child, Ryan David; children by previous marriage: Nouri Allan, Lori Ann, Barry Thomas, Marci Louise. BS, Tulane U., 1952, MD, 1956. Diplomate Am. Bd. Quality Assurance and Utilization Rev. Physicians. Intern Brooke Army Hosp., San Antonio, 1956-57; resident in otolaryngology U.S. Army Hosp., Ft. Campbell, Ky., 1957-60; practice medicine specializing in otolaryngology Glendora, West Covina and San Dimas, Calif., 1960-82; ENT cons. City of Hope Med. Ctr., 1961-76; mem. staff Foothill Presbyn.; past pres. L.A. Found. Community Svc., L.A. Poison Info. Ctr., So. Calif. Physicians Coun., Inc.; founder, chmn. bd. dirs. CAPP CARE, INC.; founder Inter-Hosp. Coun. Continuing Med. Edn.; mem. bd. trustees U.S. Pharmacopeial Convention, Inc. Author: (with others) Medicine and Your Money; mem. editorial staff Managed Care Outlook, AAPPO Jour., Med. Interface; mem. editl. adv. bd. Inside Medicaid Managed Care, Disease Management News; contbr. articles to profl. jours. Pres. bd. govs. Glendora Unified Sch. Dist., 1965-71; mem. Calif. Cancer Adv. Coun., 1967-71, Commn. of Californias, L.A. County Commn. on Economy and Efficiency. Served to capt. M.C. AUS, 1957-60. Recipient Award of Merit Order St. Lazarus, 1981. Mem. AMA, Calif. Med. Assn., Am. Acad. Otolaryngology, Am. Coun. Otolaryngology, Am. Assn. Preferred Provider Orgns. (past pres.), Am. Coll. Med. Quality, L.A. County Med. Assn. (pres. 1980-81), Kappa Nu, Phi Delta Epsilon, Glendora CountryClub, Centurion Club, Sea Bluff Beach and Racquet Club; Center Club (Costa Mesa, Calif.), Pacific Golf Club (San Juan, Capistrano). Republican. Jewish. Home: 3 Morning Dove Laguna Niguel CA 92677-5331 Office: West Tower 4000 Macarthur Blvd Ste 10000 Newport Beach CA 92660-2526

ZALUTSKY, MORTON HERMAN, lawyer; b. Schenectady, Mar. 8, 1935; s. Albert and Gertrude (Daffner) Z.; m. Audrey Englebardt, June 16, 1957; children: Jane, Diane, Samuel. BA, Yale U., 1957; JD, U. Chgo., 1960. Bar: Oreg. 1961. Law clk. to presiding judge Oreg. Supreme Ct., 1960-61; assoc. Hart, Davidson, Veazie & Hanlon, 1961-63, Veatch & Lovett, 1963-64, Morrison, Bailey, Dunn, Cohen & Miller, 1964-69; prin. Morton H. Zalutsky, P.C., 1970-76; ptnr. Dahl, Zalutsky, Nichols & Hinson, 1977-79, Zalutsky & Klarquist, P.C., Portland, Oreg., 1980-85, Zalutsky, Klarquist & Johnson, Inc., Portland, 1985-94; Zalutsky & Klarquist, P.C., Portland, 1994—; instr. Portland State U., 1961-64, Northwestern Sch. of Law, 1969-70; assoc. prof. U. Miami Law Sch.; lectr. Practicing Law Inst., 1971—, Oreg. State Bar Continuing Legal Edn. Program, 1970, Am. Law Inst.-ABA Continuing Legal Edn. Program, 1973—, 34th, 37th NYU ann. insts. fed. taxation, So. Fed. Tax Inst., U. Miami Inst. Estate Planning, Southwestern Legal Found., Internat. Foun. Employee Benefit Plans, numerous other profl. orgns. Author: (with others) The Professional Corporation in Oregon, 1970, 82; contbg. author: The Dentist and the Law, 3d edit.; editor-in-chief (retirement plans) Matthew Bender's Federal Tax Service, 1987—; contbr. to numerous publs. in field. Mem. vis. com. U. Chgo. Law Sch. Mem. ABA (vice chair profl. svcs. 1987-89, mem. coun. tax sect. 1987-89, spl. coord. 1980-85), Am. Law Inst., Am. Bar Retirement Assn. (trustee, bd. dirs., vice chair 1990-91, chair 1991-92), A-E-F-C Pension Plan, Multnomah County Bar Assn., Am. Tax Lawyers (charter mem.), Oreg. Estate Planning Coun. Jewish. Home: 3118 SW Fairmount Blvd Portland OR 97201-1466 Office: 215 SW Washington St Fl 3D Portland OR 97204-2636

ZAMBIE, ALLAN JOHN, lawyer; b. Cleve., June 9, 1935; s. Anton J. and Martha (Adamski) Z.; m. Nancy Hall, Sept. 22, 1973. Student, Ohio U., 1953-54; B.A., Denison U., 1957; LL.B., Western Res. U. (now Case Western Res. U.), 1960. Bar: Ohio bar 1960. Asso. firm Hribar and Conway, Euclid, Ohio, 1961-63; staff atty. The Higbee Co., Cleve., 1963-67; asst. sec. The Higbee Co., 1967-69, sec., 1969-74, v.p.-sec., 1974-88, gen. counsel, 1978-88; v.p., sec., gen. counsel The Lamson & Sessions Co., Cleve., 1989-94; of counsel Conway, Marken, Wyner, Kurant & Kern Co., LPA, Cleve., 1994-95; v.p.-sec. John P. Murphy Found., Cleve., 1996—. Trustee Cleve Music Sch. Settlement, pres. bd. trustees, 1980-82; trustee N.E. Ohio affiliate Am. Heart Assn. Served with AUS, 1960-61. Mem. ABA (corp., banking and bus. law sect.), Ohio Bar Assn., Cleve. Bar Assn., Am. Soc. Corporate Secs. (nat. v.p. 1977—). Home: 2953 Litchfield Rd Cleveland OH 44120-1738 Office: Terminal Tower Ste 924 Tower City Ctr Cleveland OH 44113-2203

ZAMBITO, RAYMOND FRANCIS, oral surgeon, educator; b. N.Y.C., Nov. 9, 1926; s. John and Lucy (Mecca) Z.; m. Dorothy M. Sikoryak, Apr. 23, 1960; children: Mary Lucille, Paul Michael, Christine Marie, John Raymond, Michael Sikoryak, Peter Ignatius. Student, Bklyn. Coll., 1943-44; B.S., U. Scranton, 1948; DDS, NYU, 1953, cert. in oral surgery, 1956; MA in Adminstrn. in Higher Edn., Columbia U., 1968, EdD, 1978; MBA in Health Care Mgmt., Adelphi U., 1978; DSc honoris causa, Seton Hall U., 1994. Diplomate Am. Bd. Oral and Maxillofacial Surgery. Intern in oral surgery Kings County Hosp. Ctr., Bklyn., 1956-57; resident in gen. anesthesiology Jewish Chronic Disease Hosp., Bklyn., 1957; resident in oral surgery and anesthesiology Cook County Hosp., Chgo., 1957-59; practice gen. dentistry Kings Park, N.Y., 1953-55, Chgo., 1958-59; oral surgery Bklyn., 1959-61, Williston Park, N.Y., 1961-66, N.Y.C., 1966-68, Jamaica, N.Y., 1968—; asst. dept. of oral and maxillo-facial surgery U. Ill. Coll. Dentistry, 1958-59; instr. Sch. of Dental and Oral Surgery, Columbia U., N.Y.C., 1961-66; chief of svc. in dept. dentistry St. Francis Hosp., Roslyn, N.Y., 1963-66; cons. in oral surgery and dental dept. adminstrn., 1975-85; asst. attending oral surgeon Kings County Hosp. Ctr., Bklyn., 1959-62; attending oral surgeon L.I. Jewish Med. Ctr., New Hyde Park, N.Y., 1962-71; asst. attending oral surgeon Queens Hosp. Ctr., Jamaica, N.Y., 1964-65; assoc. attending oral surgeon Elmhurst (N.Y.) Gen. Hosp. 1965-66; attending oral surgeon and dir. dentistry and oral surgery Lincoln Hosp., 1966-68; asst. prof. of dental surgery Albert Einstein Coll. of Medicine, Yeshiva U., 1966-68, asst. clin. prof., 1968-73; oral surgeon-in-charge Cath. Med. Ctr. of Bklyn., 1968—; cons. in oral and maxillo-facial surgery St. Joseph's Hosp. and Med. Ctr., Paterson, N.J., 1976—; asst. prof. dept. oral surgery and anesthesiology Fairleigh Dickinson U. Sch. of Dentistry, Hackensack, N.J., 1971-72, prof., 1972-89, coordinator dir. hosp. dentistry, 1972-89; adj. assoc. prof. of clin. pharmacy and dentistry Bklyn. Coll. of Pharmacy, 1976-77; cons. oral surgeon Suffolk State Sch., Melville, N.Y., 1965-71; dir. Spl. Dental Clinic for the Handicapped, Bur. of the Handicapped, Cath. Charities, Bklyn., 1973-75. Co-editor: Hospital Dental Practice, A Manual, 1978, Immunology and Infectious Diseases of the Mouth, Head, and Neck, 1991, Manual of Dental Therapeutics, 1991; editor-in-chief Jour. Hosp. Dental Practice, 1973-80; contbr. articles on oral surgery and dental edn. to profl. jours. Lectr. Christian Life Communities movement to secondary schs. and colls., various states, 1962—; tchr. confrat. religious classes, 1964-85; mem. parish coun. St. Gertrude's Roman Cath. Ch., Bayville, N.Y., 1969-72, chmn., 1971-72; founder, chmn. Fedn. Lay Orgns., Diocese of Rockville Centre, 1968-72; pres. David Park Civic Assn., 1966-67; couns. Nat. Coun. Cath. Men, Washington, 1967--72. With USN, 1944-46, capt. Dental Corps, USNR ret. Decorated knight Order of Malta in U.S.; grantee HEW, 1967-70, 85-88. Fellow Am. Coll. of Dentists, Internat. Coll. Dentists, Am. Pub. Health Assn., Am. Dental Soc. of Anesthesiology, L.I. Acad. of Odontology; mem. Am. Soc. of Oral and Maxillofacial Surgeons, Am. Dental Assn. (mem. rev. com. coun. on hosp. and instnl. dental svcs. 1975—, cons. coun. on dental edn. 1973—), N.Y. State Soc. of Oral Surgeons (alt. del. to Am. Soc. Oral Surgeons), Am. Acad. Oral Pathology, Am. Acad. of History of Dentistry, N.Y. State Dental Soc. of Anesthesiology (pres. 1964), Am. Assn. Of Hosp. Dentists, Cath. Dentists Guild (pres. 1955-56), Am. Hosp. Assn. (mem. coun. on profl. svcs. 1976-78), Am. Coll. Oral and Maxillo Facial Surgeons (v.p. 1976-79), Christian Med. Soc., Internat. Assn. of Oral Surgeons, Nat. Fedn. of Christian Life Communities (pres. nat. fedn. 1971-73), del. to internat. gen. assembly in Rome, 1967, Dominican Republic, 1970), Omicron Kappa Upsilon. Home: 603 Bayville Rd Locust Valley NY 1207 Office: Cath Med Ctr Bklyn and Queens 88-25 153rd St Jamaica NY 11432-3731

ZAMBOLDI, RICHARD HENRY, lawyer; b. Kittanning, Pa., Nov. 22, 1941; s. Henry F. and Florence E. (Colligan) Z.; m. Maria Therese Reiser, Aug. 12, 1967; children: Elizabeth M., Richard H. Jr., Margaret B. BBA, St. Bonaventure U., 1963; JD, Villanova U., 1966. Bar: U.S. Dist. Ct. (we. dist.) Pa. 1966, Pa. 1968, U.S. Ct. Appeals (3d cir.) 1970, U.S. Supreme Ct. 1981. Law clk. U.S. Dist. Ct. (we. dist.) Pa., Pitts., 1966-67; atty. Nat. Labor Rels. Bd., Pitts., 1967-68; assoc. Kanehann & McDonald, Allentown, Pa., 1968-69; ptnr. Elderkin Martin Kelly Messina & Zamboldi, Erie, Pa., 1969-90; atty. Knox McLaughlin Gornall & Sennett, Erie, 1990—; Author (student articles) Villanova Law Rev., 1964-65, editor, 1965-66. Mem. Pa. Bar Assn., Erie County Bar Assn. Republican. Roman Catholic. Home: 5223 Clinton St Erie PA 16509 Office: Knox McLaughlin Gornall & Sennett 120 West Tenth St Erie PA 16501

ZAMECNIK, PAUL CHARLES, oncologist, medical research scientist; b. Cleve., Ohio, Nov. 22, 1912; m.; 3 children. AB, Dartmouth Coll., 1933; MD, Harvard U., 1936; DSc (hon.), U. Utrecht, 1966, Columbia U., 1971, Harvard U., 1982, Roger Williams Coll., 1983, Dartmouth Coll., 1988, U. Mass., 1994. Resident Huntington Meml. Hosp. Harvard U., Boston, MA, 1936-37; intern. U. Hosps., Cleve., Ohio, 1938-39; Moseley traveling fellow Harvard U., Boston, 1939-40; Finney-Howell fellow Rockefeller Inst., 1941-42; instr., assoc. prof. Harvard U., 1942-56, Collis P. Huntington prof., 1956-79; dir. J.C. Warren Labs., 1956-79; emeritus prof. oncological medicine Sch. Medicine, 1979—; prin. sci. Worcester Found. Experimental Biology, 1979—; physician Mass. Ge. Hosp., 1956-79; hon. physician Mass. Gen. Hosp., 1979—; vis. fellow dept. chemistry Calif. Tech. U., 1952; vis. Commonwealth scholar U. Cambridge, 1962. Recipient Warren Triennial prize, 1946, 50, James Ewing award, 1962, Borden award, 1965, Am. Cancer Soc. Nat. award, 1968, Passano award, 1970, Nat. medal of sci. NSF, 1991, Hudson Hoagland award, 1992, City of Medicine award, Durham, N.C., 1995, Enterprize 2000 award City of Worcester, Mass., 1996. Mem. NAS, Am. Acad. Arts and Sci., Am. Soc. Biol. Chemists, Am. Assn. Cancer Rsch. (pres. 1964-65), Assn. Am. Physicians, Interurban Club, Peripatetic Club. Office: Worcester Foundation Experimental Biology 222 Maple Ave Shrewsbury MA 01545-2732

ZAMES, GEORGE DAVID, electrical engineer, educator; b. Poland, Jan. 7, 1934; s. Sam Simha and Leona Z.; m. Eva Eisenfarb, July 21, 1964; children: Ethan, Jonathan. B.Eng., McGill U., 1954; Sc.D. in Elec. Engring, MIT, 1960. Asst. prof. MIT, 1960-62, 63-65, Harvard U., 1962-63; sr. scientist NASA, Cambridge, Mass., 1965-71; vis. prof. Technion, Haifa, Israel, 1972-74; prof. elec. engring. McGill U., Montreal, 1974—, Macdonald chair. elec. engring., 1983—. Assoc. editor So. Indsl. and Applied Math. Jour. on Control, 1968-84, Systems and Control Letters, 1981-84, Internat. Math. Assn. Jour. Math. Control and Info., 1983—, Math. of Control Signals and Systems, 1987—; editor at large Jour. Robust and Non-linear Control, 1990—; contbr. articles to profl. jours. Athlone fellow Imperial Coll., London U., 1954-56, Nat. Acad. Scis. Resident Rsch. assoc., 1966-67, Guggenheim fellow, 1965-66, Killam fellow, 1984-86, Sr. fellow Can. Inst. Advanced Rsch., 1984—; recipient Brit. Assn. medal McGill U., 1954, Outstanding Paper award Am. Automatic Control Coun., 1968, Classic Paper citation Inst. Sci. Info., 1981, Outstanding Paper award Control Sys. Soc., 1977, 80, 82, 86, Isaac Walton Killam prize for sci., 1995. Fellow IEEE (Control Sci. Field award 1985), Royal Soc. Can. Home: 4996 Circle Rd, Montreal, PQ Canada H3W 1Z7 Office: McGill U Dept Elec Engring, 3480 University St, Montreal, PQ Canada H3A 2A7

ZAMIR, FRANCES ROBERTA (FRANCES ROBERTA WEISS-SWEDE), principal; b. Bklyn., Nov. 6, 1944; d. Martin and Jean (Roskosky) Swede. BA in English, Calif. State U., Northridge, 1967, MA in Spl. Edn., 1975; MA in Ednl. Adminstrn., Calif. State U., L.A., 1987. Credential adminstrv. svcs., std. elem, spl. edn.-learning handicapped, Calif; cert. resource specialist. Childrens' ctr. tchr. L.A. Unified Sch. Dist., 1966-68, elem. tchr., 1968-76, spl. edn. tchr., 1976-80, resource specialist*tchr., 1980-86, mentor tchr., 1984-86, program specialist/region advisor, 1986-90, asst. prin., 1990-96; owner, ptnr. Best Bet Ednl. Therapy/Tutoring Referral Svc., 1979-81; cons. Academics Plus Tutoring Referral Svc., 1984-86; asst. prof. resource specialist cert. program Calif. State U., Dominguez Hills, 1987-90; instr. early and regular edn. credential program UCLA, 1990—; mem. asst. prin. steering com. L.A. Unified Sch. Dist., Region C, 1992-93; adminstr. portfolio documentation subcom. Adminstrv. Tng. Acad., 1991; sch. site rev. coms. Calif. State Dept. Edn., 1985-87, ad hoc com. on quality indicators, 1985. Mem. Speakers Bur. Commn. on Jews with Disabilities, 1985-86, Assoc. Adminstrs. L.A. Rep. Coun., elem. asst. prin. rep., 1992-94; so. Calif. regional rep. Calif. Assn. Program Specialists, 1988-90. Mem. NEA, Assoc. Adminstrs., L.A. Rep. Coun. (elem. asst. prin. rep. 1992-94), Friends of Calif. State, Calif. Assn. Program Specialists (so. Calif. regional rep. 1988-90), Calif. Assn. Sch. Adminstrs. (spl. edn. com. L.A. chpt. 1985-86, 87-88), Calif. Assn. Resource Specialists (state v.p. and conf. chair 1993-94, state pres. 1984-85, bd. dirs. 1983-86), Calif. Tchrs. Assn., Women in Ednl. Leadership, Kappa Delta Pi, Phi Delta Kappa. Office: L A Unified Sch Dist 450 N Grand Ave Los Angeles CA 90012-2100

ZAMMIT, JOSEPH PAUL, lawyer; b. N.Y.C., May 19, 1948; s. John and Farla (Rudolph) Z.; m. Dorothy Therese O'Neill, June 6, 1970; children: Michael, Paul, Brian. AB, Fordham U., 1968; JD, Harvard U., 1971; LLM, NYU, 1974. Bar: N.Y. 1972, U.S. Dist. Ct. (so. and ea. dists.) N.Y. 1973, U.S. Ct. Appeals (2d cir.) 1973, U.S. Supreme Ct. 1978, U.S. Dist. Ct. (no. dist.) N.Y. 1983, U.S. Ct. Appeals (11th cir.) 1987. Assoc. Reavis & McGrath, N.Y.C., 1971-74; asst. prof. law St. John's U., Jamaica, N.Y., 1974-76, assoc. prof., 1976-78; assoc. Reavis & McGrath, N.Y.C., 1978-79, ptnr., 1979-88; ptnr. Fulbright & Jaworski L.L.P. (formerly Fulbright Jaworski & Reavis McGrath), N.Y.C., 1989—; adj. assoc. prof. St. John's U., Jamaica, 1979-83, adj. prof., 1984—; mem. panel computer arbitrators Am. Arbitration Assn., N.Y.C., 1977—. Bd. editors Computer Law Strategist, 1987—; contbr. articles to profl. jours. Mem. ABA, N.Y. State Bar Assn., Assn. of Bar of City of N.Y. (chmn. com. on computer law 1995—, chmn. comml. liability subcom. 1981-87), Computer Law Assn., Phi Beta Kappa. Office: Fulbright & Jaworski LLP 666 5th Ave New York NY 10103-0001

ZAMMITT, NORMAN, artist; b. Toronto, Ont., Can., Feb. 3, 1931. AA, Pasadena City Coll., 1957; MFA, Otis Art Inst., Los Angeles. One-man shows include Felix Landau Gallery, L.A., 1962, 66, 68, L.A. County Mus. Art, 1977, Corcoran Gallery, Washington, 1978, Flow-Ace Gallery, 1984, Loma Linda U., Riverside, Calif., 1987, Elysium Studio 13, L.A., 1995, 96; included in group shows at L.A. County Mus. Art, 1987, Haags Gemeentemus. Arts, The Hague, 1987, Bronx Mus. Arts, N.Y., 1987, Ace Contemporary Exhbns., L.A., 1988; represented in permanent collections at Libr. of Congress, Corcoran Gallery, Nat. Gallery, Hirschhorn Collection, Washington, Mus. Modern Art, N.Y.C., L.A. County Mus. Modern Art, San Francisco Mus. Modern Art, Larry Aldrich Found. Mus., Conn., Rowland Inst. Sci., Cambridge, Mass., Seattle Art Mus., Stanford U. Hosp., Palo Alto, Calif.; also represented in pvt. collections. Guggenheim fellow, 1968; Pollock-Krasner grantee, 1991. Home: 233 N Wilson Ave Pasadena CA 91106-1422

ZAMORA, MARJORIE DIXON, retired political science educator; b. Farm Randolph, N.Y., Nov. 8, 1933; d. Wendell Hadley and Jessie (Mercer) Dixon; m. Cornelio Raul Zamora, Dec. 20, 1969; 1 child, Daniel Cornelio. BA, Earlham Coll., 1956; MA, U. Ill., 1968; postgrad., U. Ill., Chgo., 1989—. Tchr. Ridge, Sch., Godsman Sch., Stenson Sch., various cities, 1956-62; with U.S. Peace Corps, tchr. Palmares High Sch., Costa Rica, 1963-64; reporter Lerner Newspaper, Chgo., 1965; dormitory counselor U. Ill., Urbana, 1966-68, 86; instr. Chgo. City Coll., 1968-69; prof. polit. sci. Moraine Valley C.C., Palos Hills, Ill., 1969-94, prof. emeritus, 1994—; researcher, Univ. Ill., Chgo., 1985-88. Contbr. articles on Costa Rican polit. bus. cycle and economy, land reform to various publs. in U.S., Cen. Am. Campaign dir. Polit. State Legis., 1974-76. Mem. AAUW, Western Springs Bank and Orch. Assn. (pres. 1990-91), Am. Assn. Retired Persons, State Cmty. Coll. Retirees Assn., Kiwanis (LaGrange, Ill.). Mem. Soc. of Friends. Avocations: skiing, swimming, writing fiction, nonfiction, symphonic music, scuba. Home: 3820 Lawn Ave Western Springs IL 60558-1141

ZAMORANO, WANDA JEAN, secondary education educator; b. Mertzon, Tex., Aug. 11, 1947; d. A.L. and Billie Louise (Byler) Sawyer; married; 1 child, Anna. BS, Sul Ross State Univ., 1970; MEd, Tex. Tech., 1974; EdD, Nova Southeastern U., 1994. Cert. tchr., Tex. Migrant edn. tchr. Balmorhea (Tex.) ISD, 1970-72; reading tchr. Hurst-Euless Bedford (Tex.) ISD, 1972-92; owner cons. firm WZ Enterprizes; cons. Tex. Tech. U., 1980-81; demonstration tchr. Ednl. Svcs. Ctr., Austin, 1975; instr. Richland Coll., Dallas, 1982; mem. nat. faculty Turner Ednl. Svcs. Inc.; adj. prof. Tex. Woman's U.; presneter 67th annual So. N.Mex. Tech. Conf., 1994. Contbr. articles to profl. jours. Active Bedford Jr. High PTA. Named Tchr. of Yr., Bedford, 1984, Most Prominent Educators Tex., 1983, Cable Tchr. of Yr., 1991, Tchr. of Month, Bronco News, 1993; TCI Cable grantee, 1995. Mem. NEA, AAUW (Named USA Today faculty mem.), Hurst-Euless-Bedford Tex. State Tchrs. Assn. NEA (v.p. 1994-95, Internat. Reading Assn., Tex. State Tchr. Assn. (exec. bd.), The Governor's Club (charter), Kappa Delta Pi. Democrat. Avocations: reading, travel, card playing. Home: 2403 Finley Rd Apt 1107 Irving TX 75062-3348 Office: Bedford Jr High 325 Carolyn Dr Bedford TX 76021-4111

ZAMPARELLI, ELSA MARIA JOHANNA ELISABETH, costume designer, art director; b. Dec. 8, 1944; d. Jan Albertus and Maria Johanna (de Jeu) Van de Bovenkamp; m. Robert G. Zamparelli, Aug. 12, 1968 (div. Aug. 1985); m. Steve Kenneth Irish, Aug. 10, 1991; children: André, Mark, Alicia. Costume and set designer: (TV) The Bold and the Beautiful (Emmy award best set decoration 1993, 94); (films) Dances With Wolves (Acad. award nomination 1991), The Last of the Mohicans (Brit. Acad. award nomination 1992), Ace Ventura: When Nature Calls, 1995. Office: Smith Gosnell Nicholson & Assoc PO Box 1166 1515 Palisades Dr Pacific Palisades CA 90272

ZAMPIELLO, RICHARD SIDNEY, metals and trading company executive; b. New Haven, May 7, 1933; s. Sidney Nickolas and Louise Z.; B.A., Trinity Coll., 1955; M.B.A., U. Bridgeport, 1961; m. Helen Shirley Palsa, Oct. 10, 1961; 1 son, Geoffrey Richard. With Westinghouse Elec. Corp., Pitts., 1955-64; exec. v.p. Ullrich Copper Corp., subs. Foster Wheeler, Kenilworth, N.J., 1964-71; sr. v.p. Gerald Metals, Inc., Stamford, Conn., 1971-85; group v.p. Diversified Industries Corp., St. Louis, 1985-90; pres. Plume and Atwood Brass Mill div. Diversified Industries Corp., Thomaston, Conn., 1985-90; pres. Upstate Metals Corp., Canastota, N.Y., 1990—. Mem. ASME, Soc. Mfg. Engrs., AIME. Clubs: Yale, Mining (N.Y.C.); Lake Waramug Country (Washington, Conn.), Washington Country. Home:

Woodbury Rd Washington CT 06793-1814 Office: 20 E Main St Waterbury CT 06702-2302

ZANARDELLI, JOHN JOSEPH, healthcare services executive; b. Monongahela, Pa., July 27, 1950; s. John and Linda (Lazzari) Z.; m. Suzanne King, Jan. 29, 1972; children: Brandon John, Stephen William, Robyn Lynn. AA, Community Coll. Allegheny Cty, Pitts., 1970; AS in Acctg., Community Coll. Allegheny Cty., Pitts., 1991; BS in Edn., California U. Pa., 1972; MPH, U. Pitts., 1979, cert. acct., 1994. Rsch. asst. grad. sch. pub. health U. Pitts., 1973-78; adminstrv. resident Cen. Med. Ctr. & Hosp., Pitts., 1978-79; vice chmn., sec., dir. Allegheny Mountain Health Enterprises, Inc., Oil City, Pa., 1985-88; exec. v.p. Oil City Area Health Ctr., Inc., 1979-88; exec. v.p., chief oper. officer Grane Healthcare, Inc., Pitts., 1988-90; adminstr., chief oper. officer Southwood Psychiat. Hosp., Inc., Pitts., 1990-91; exec. dir. Allegheny Sr. Care, Pitts., Pa., 1991-92; exec. dir., CEO United Meth. Svcs. for the Aging, 1993—; preceptor health adminstrn. program grad. schs. in pub. health and bus. U. Pitts., 1980—; pres. HCPP, Inc., Pitts., 1983—. Fellow Am. Coll. Healthcare Execs. Home: 2997 Greenwald Rd Bethel Park PA 15102-1615 Office: Asbury Heights 700 Bower Hill Rd Pittsburgh PA 15243-2098

ZAND, DALE EZRA, business management educator; b. N.Y.C., July 22, 1926; m. Charlotte Edith Rosenfeld, Oct. 16, 1949; children—Fern, Mark, Karen, Jonathan, Matthew. BEE, Cooper Union, 1945; MBA, NYU, 1949, PhD, 1954. Asst. to v.p. Spectator Bags, 1947-49; v.p. Glo-Cold Co., 1949-50; mem. faculty N.Y. U. Stern Sch. Bus., 1950—, prof. mgmt., 1963—, chmn. dept., 1968—; cons. to industry, 1951—; Bd. dirs. Newfield Exploration Co., Nat. Tng. Labs. Inst. Applied Behavioral Sci. Author: Information, Organization, and Power, 1981, Triadic Leadership, 1996, also articles. Served with USNR, 1945. Ford Found. fellow, 1959-60. Mem. Am. Psychol. Soc., Inst. Mgmt. Sci., Acad. Mgmt., Interant. Assn. Applied Social Scientists. Office: NYU Stern Sch Bus 40 W 4th St # T7 16 New York NY 10012-1118

ZANDE, RICHARD DOMINIC, civil engineering firm executive; b. Battle Creek, Mich., Apr. 29, 1931; s. Dominic and Maria O. (Bombassei) Z.; m. Marilyn Sue Love, Feb. 15, 1958; children: Michael, Michelle, Brent, Patrick. BSCE, Mich. State U., 1955. Registered profl. engr. Ohio, Fla., Ky., W.Va., Mich., Pa., Ind., Ill., N.J., S.C. Prin. Martin & Zande, Columbus, Ohio, 1966-68; chief exec. officer R.D. Zande & Assoc., Columbus, 1968—, Zande Environ. Svc., Columbus, 1988—, Zande-Garrod, Inc., Cin., 1990—; bd. dirs. Franklin County Solid Waste Mgmt. Authority, Columbus, 1985-87; mem. engring. adv. bd. Ohio State U., Columbus, 1988—; mem. small bus. adv. com. Cleve. Fed. Res. Bank, 1992—. Bd. dirs. St. Stephen's Community House, Columbus, 1988—, Bus. Exec. Coun. for the Ctr. for Applied and Profl. Edn., Franklin U., 1990-92, Purchasing Procedures Task Force City of Columbus, Jr. Achievement, 1989-92; dir. small bus. solicitations United Way. Mem. ASCE, NSPE, Ohio Assn. Cons. Engrs., Am. Cons. Engrs. Coun., Greater Columbus Devel. Com., Columbus C. of C. (bd. dirs. 1987-92). Roman Catholic. Home: 901 Bluffview Dr Columbus OH 43235-1776 Office: RD Zande & Assocs Inc 1237 Dublin Rd Columbus OH 43215-1071

ZANDER, ALVIN FREDERICK, social psychologist; b. Detroit, Oct. 13, 1913; s. Hugo Helmuth and Frieda Wilhemenia (Miesler) Z.; m. Patience Clare, Dec. 19, 1939; children—Constance, Christopher, Judith; m. Marion Cranmore, Aug. 11, 1980. BS, U. Mich., 1936, MS in Pub. Health, 1937, PhD, 1942. Asst. dir. research service Boy Scouts Am., N.Y.C., 1943-45; asst. prof. psychology Springfield (Mass.) Coll., 1946-47; prof. psychology, dir. Research Center for Group Dynamics, U. Mich., Ann Arbor, 1959-79; asso. v.p. U. Mich., 1973-80. Author: Group Dynamics, 1953, 3d edit., 1968, Motives and Goals in Groups, 1971, revised edit., 1996, Groups at Work, 1977, Making Groups Effective, 1982, 2d edit., 1994, The Purposes of Groups and Organizations, 1985, Effective Social Action by Community Groups, 1990, Making Boards Effective, 1993. Served with USPHS, 1944-46. U. Chgo. fellow, 1938-39; Fulbright fellow. Oslo, Norway, 1957-58; Japanese Govt. fellow, 1980-81; Gen. Edn. Bd. fellow U. Iowa, 1942. Mem. Am. Psychol. Assn. (div. sec.), Am. Psychol. Soc., Soc. Psychol. Study Social Issues (pres.), Soc. Exptl. Social Psychology. Home: 2841 Ptarmigan Dr # 4 Walnut Creek CA 94595-3136

ZANDER, GAILLIENNE GLASHOW, psychologist; b. Bklyn., Apr. 7, 1932; d. Saul and Anna (Karasik) G.; m. A.J. Zander, Aug. 5, 1952; children: Elizabeth L., Caroline M., Catherine A. MusB, U. Wis., 1953, MS, 1970; PhD, Marquette U., 1984. Diplomate Bd. Forensic Examiners. Music tchr. Wis. Sch. Systems, 1953-65; psychol. asst. Vernon Psychol. Labs., Chgo., 1965-70; psychologist Milw. Pub. Schs., 1970-92, CESA 19, Kenosha, Wis., 1977-78; pvt. practice psychology Milw., 1980—. Fellow Am. Orthopsychiat. Assn.; mem. APA, Wis. Psychol. Assn., Psychologists Assn. in Milw. Pub. Schs. (rep., v.p., pres.), Am. Acad. Pain Mgmt. (diplomate). Home: 13750 Carson Ct Brookfield WI 53005-4989 also: Cooper Resource Ctr 20860 Watertown Rd Waukesha WI 52186-1872

ZANDIN, KJELL BERTIL, management consulting executive; b. Morlanda, Sweden, Mar. 14, 1937; came to U.S., 1975; s. Sven G. and Hildur D. (Johansson) Z.; m. Sonja A. Johansson, Nov. 21, 1964; children: Michael, Christin. MS in Mech. Engring., Chalmers U. of Tech., 1962. Devel. engr. SKF, Gothenburg, Sweden, 1962-64; cons. Maynard MEC AB, Gothenburg, 1964-68; cons. mgr. H.B. Maynard & Co., Inc., Gothenburg, 1969-71, Dusseldorf, Fed. Republic Germany, 1972-75; sr. v.p. H.B. Maynard & Co., Inc., Pitts., 1975—, also ptnr., bd. dirs. Author: MOST Work Measurement Systems, 1980, 2d edit., 1990. Served with Swedish Army, 1957-58. Received First Tech. Innovation award Inst. Indsl. Engrs., 1986. Mem. Inst. Indsl. Engrs. (sr.), Scandinavian soc. Western Pa. Lutheran. Avocations: tennis, golf, skiing. Home: 105 Alleyne Dr Pittsburgh PA 15215-1401 Office: H B Maynard & Co Inc 8 Parkway Center Pittsburgh PA 15220

ZANDMAN, FELIX, electronics executive; b. 1928. PhD, U. Paris The Sorbonne, U. Nancy, France, 1953. With French Nat. Ctr. Sci. Rsch., Paris, 1950-53; with engring. and consulting SNECMA, 1953-57; dir. basic rsch. Tatnall Measuring Systems Co., Phoenixville, Pa., 1957-62; founder, pres., CEO, chmn. bd. Vishay Intertech., Inc., Malvern, Pa., 1962—; also dir. Vishay Intertech., Inc. Office: Vishay Sprague Holdings Corp 678 Main St Sanford ME 04073-2420*

ZANE, RAYMOND J., lawyer, state senator; b. Woodbury, N.J., July 23, 1939; s. Clarence R. and Veronica (Levy) Z.; children—Marybeth, Raymond II, Kenneth. B.S. in Bus. Adminstrn., St. Joseph's U., 1965; J.D., Rutger's U., 1974. Bar: N.J. 1974, N.Y. 1989. Freeholder, Gloucester County, Woodbury, N.J., 1971-73; mem. N.J. Senate, 1973—, dep. asst. minority leader. Mem. N.J. Bar Assn., Gloucester County Bar Assn. Home: 509 Sharp Dr Mickleton NJ 08056-1441 Office: 39 S Broad St Woodbury NJ 08096-7920 Other: NJ State Senate State Capital Trenton NJ 08608

ZANETTI, JOSEPH MAURICE, JR., corporate executive; b. San Francisco, Aug. 3, 1928; s. Joseph Maurice and Lillian Mary (Solari) Z.; m. Marilyn Ruth Parker, Aug. 11, 1956; children: Pamela, Gregory, Geoffrey, Regina. BA, Saint Mary's Coll., 1950; postgrad., U. Calif., Berkeley, 1950-51, 53-55, 56-57; postgrad. in Edn., San Francisco State Coll., 1955-56. Cert. secondary tchr., Calif. Tchr. Piedmont (Calif.) High Sch., 1956-57, Pleasant Hill (Calif.) High Sch., 1957-58; supr. Sandia Labs., Albuquerque, 1958-64; mktg. dir. Ednl. Research Assocs., Albuquerque, 1964-66; exec. asst. Sandia Labs., Albuquerque, 1966-73; pres. U. of Albuquerque, Albuquerque, 1973-75; dir. area devel. Pub. Svc. Co. of N.Mex., Albuquerque, 1975-86; pres., chmn. bd. dirs. Rio Grande Trading Co. Inc., Albuquerque, 1986-88; pres. Foresight, Inc., Albuquerque, 1988-90; v.p. Summa Med. Corp., Albuquerque, 1988-91; sr. v.p. Summa Med. Corp., Vienna, Va., 1991-92; v.p. Systems Support Agy. Inc., Vienna, Va., 1992-93; pres. Complexus, Inc., Albuquerque, N.Mex., 1993—; cons. Pub. Service Co. N.Mex., Albuquerque, 1986-88; ; pres. N.Mex. Internat. Trade and Investment Council Inc., Albuquerque, 1984-89; active Adv. Bd. Coll. and U. Partnership Program, Memphis, 1984—. Chmn. adv. bd. N.Mex. Mus. Natural History, Albuquerque, 1985-90; vice chmn., bd. govs. Albuquerque Tech. Vocat. Inst., 1971-77; mem. Bd. Edn., Albqperque Pub. Schs., 1971-77. Capt. USNR, 1948-83. Mem. Res. Officers Assn. (life), Resource Devel. Com., Albuquerque Pub. Schs. (chmn.). Republican. Roman Catholic.

ZANETTI, RICHARD JOSEPH, editor; b. Weehawken, N.J., Mar. 22, 1939; s. Mario and Lucille (Coco) Z.; m. Norma Diane Nesheim, June 28, 1969; children: Joseph, Michael. BSChemE, Bucknell U., Lewisburg, Pa., 1961, MSChemE, 1964. Technologist Mobil Oil Corp., Bklyn., 1964-66; cofounder ASD Arts, Boston, 1979; dept. editor Chem. Wk. Mag., N.Y.C., 1980-84; assoc. editor Chem. Engring. Mag., N.Y.C., 1984-88, editor-in-chief, 1988—; editorial dir. Chem. and Plastics Info. Svcs., N.Y.C., 1991—; lectr. in field. Producer, dir. documentary film: Standups, 1979; editor Feature Report, Plant Safety, 1988. Cons. Manhattan Coll., Riverdale, N.Y., 1989—. 1st lt. U.S. Army, 1964-65. Mem. Chem. Communications Assn., Drug Chem. and Allied Trade Assn., Tau Beta Pi, Omicron Delta Kappa. Avocations: fiction writing, fishing, stamp collecting. Office: McGraw Hill 1221 Ave Of The Americas New York NY 10020-1001

ZANGERLE, JOHN A., lawyer; b. Lakewood, Ohio, Jan. 24, 1942. BA, Haverford Coll., 1964; JD, Case Western Res. U., 1967. Bar: Ohio 1967. Ptnr. Baker & Hostetler, Cleve. Office: Baker & Hostetler 3200 Nat City Ctr 1900 E 9th St Cleveland OH 44114-3401

ZANGGER, RUSSELL GEORGE, organization executive, flying school executive; b. Larchwood, Iowa, Feb. 22, 1922; s. Charlie and Lina Bell (Sharp) Zangger; m. Marie Unruh, May 24, 1944; 1 child, James Russell. Student pub. schs., Larchwood; DD (hon.), Ch. Gospel Ministries, Chula Vista, Calif., 1981. Farmer, Larchwood, 1944-79; owner, operator Zangger Flying Svc., Larchwood, 1949—; founder, dir. The Remain Intact ORGANization, Larchwood, 1980—. Spokesperson against infant circumcision. Avocation: teaching the meaning of Christianity. Home and Office: The Remain Intact Organization RR 2 Box 86 1917 135th St Larchwood IA 51241-7712

ZANNIERI, NINA, museum director; b. Summit, N.J., Feb. 1, 1955; d. Angelo Joseph and Louise Mary (Brumm) Z.; m. Douglas M. Vogel, Oct. 29, 1994. BA, Boston Coll., 1977; postgrad., Coll. of William & Mary, 1977-78; MA, Brown U., 1980. Curatorial asst. R.I. Hist. Soc., Providence, 1980-81, asst. curator, 1981-83, curator, 1983-86; dir. Paul Revere Meml. Assn., Boston, 1986—. Gen. editor: (exhbn. catalog) Paul Revere: The Man Behind the Myth, 1988; collaborator: (house guide) A Most Magnificent Mansion; project dir.: (exhbn. catalog) Let Virtue Be A Guide To Thee, 1983. Bd. dirs. Freedom Trial Found., Boston, Slater Mill Hist. Site, Pawtucket, R.I. Mem. Am. Assn. Mus.'s, New Eng. Mus. Assn. (curators com. 1984-86, bd. dirs. 1988—), Am. Assn. State and Local History, Phi Beta Kappa. Office: Paul Revere Meml Assn The Paul Revere House 19 North Sq Boston MA 02113-2405

ZANOT, CRAIG ALLEN, lawyer; b. Wyandotte, Mich., Nov. 15, 1955; s. Thomas and Faye Blanch (Sperry) Z. AB with distinction, U. Mich., 1977; JD cum laude, Ind. U., 1980. Bar: Ind. 1980, U.S. Dist. Ct. (so. dist.) Ind. 1980, Mich. 1981, U.S. Dist. Ct. (no. dist.) Ind. 1981, U.S. Ct. Appeals (6th cir.) 1985, U.S. Dist. Ct. (ea. dist.) Mich. 1987. Law clk. to presiding justice Allen County Superior Ct, Ft. Wayne, 1980-81; ptnr. Davidson, Breen & Doud P.C., Saginaw, Mich., 1981—. Mem. ABA, Mich. Bar Assn., Ind. Bar Assn., Saginaw County Bar Assn. Roman Catholic. Home: 547 S Linwood Beach Rd Linwood MI 48634-9432 Office: Davidson Breen & Doud PC 1121 N Michigan Ave Saginaw MI 48602-4762

ZANOTTI, JOHN PETER, broadcasting company executive; b. L.A., June 12, 1948; m. Claudia Jean Haskell, Aug. 8, 1970; children: Jeffrey, Laura, Mark, Christina. AB cum laude, U. So. Calif., 1970; JD magna cum laude, Ariz. State U., 1974. Assoc. corp. dept./pub. fin. O'Melveny and Myers, L.A., 1974-78; corp. dir. legal Harte-Hanks Comms. Inc., San Antonio, 1978-79, asst. sec., 1979-80, v.p. legal, sec., 1980-83; pres. Harte-Hanks Mktg./Cen. Group, Cin., 1983-84; asst. to pres. newspaper divsn. Gannett Co., Inc., Rosslyn, Va., 1984-85; pres., pub. The Cin. Enquirer, 1985-90; CEO, exec. v.p. Phoenix (Ariz.) Newspapers, Inc., 1990-91; pub. The Ariz. Republic, The Phoenix Gazette, 1990-91; pres. TV group Gt. Am. Broadcasting Co., 1991-92, pres., COO, 1992-93; CEO, pres. Citicasters Inc. (formerly Gt. Am. Comms. Co.), Cin., 1993—. Contbr. articles to profl. jours. Trustee Children's Hosp. Med. Ctr., 1989-90, 94—, Johnny Bench Scholarship Fund, 1987-90, 91—, Taft Mus., 1992-93, Xavier U., 1989-90; bd. dirs. Neediest Kids of All, 1986-90, 91—, Ariz. State U. Law Soc., 1990-94; internat. bd. dirs. Just Say No, 1991-92; mem. Walter Cronkite Sch. Journalism and Telecomm. Endowment Com., Ariz. State U., 1990-91, Cin. Bus. Com., 1987-90, Phoenix-40, 1990-91; bd. advisors U. Cin. Coll. Bus. Adminstrn., 1988-90; co-chmn. Last Resort Scholarship Fund, Cin. Youth Collaborative, 1989-90. Mem. Assn. for Maximum Svc. TV, Inc. (bd. dirs. 1992—), Nat. Assn. Broadcasters (bd. dirs. 1994—), TV Operators Caucus, Inc. (bd. dirs. 1993—), State Bar Calif., State Bar Tex., Greater Cin. C. of C. (bd. trustees 1988-90), Cin. Country Club, Commonwealth Club, Queen City Club. Office: Citicasters Inc 1 E 4th St Ste 600 Cincinnati OH 45202

ZANOTTI, MARIE LOUISE, hospital admininstrator; b. Pitts., May 3, 1954; d. Louis Charles and Josephine Rose (Antoniello) Z. BS, U. Pitts., 1976; M of Pub. Health, Yale U., 1980. Adminstrv. asst. Presbyn.-Univ. Hosp., Pitts., 1980-82; dir. Meml. Hosp. Burlington County, Mt. Holly, N.J., 1982-85; accoc. hosp. dir. The Milton S. Hershey Med. Ctr.-Univ. Hosp., Hershey, Pa., 1985-92; assoc. hosp. dir. Latrobe (Pa.)Area Hosp., 1993; workshop presenter Healthcare Fin. Mgmt. Assn., 1988-89. Active Hershey Bus. Assn., 1988—; bd. dirs. Ronald McDonald House, 1991-92, Chestnut Ridge chpt. ARC, 1993—, Med. Alliance Ins. Network, Ltd., 1993—, Latrobe Area C. of C., 1996—. Fellow Am. Coll. Healthcare Execs.; mem. Healthcare Adminstrs. Group (pres. 1989), Hosp. Assn. Pa., Hosp. Coun. Western Pa., Latrobe Area C. of C., Exec. Women Westmoreland County, Yale U. Hosp. Adminstrn., Latrobe Country Club. Avocations: performing arts, sports. Home: 111 Mara Lago St Greensburg PA 15601-9593 Office: Latrobe Area Hosp 121 W 2nd Ave Latrobe PA 15650-1068

ZANUCK, RICHARD DARRYL, motion picture company executive; b. Beverly Hills, Calif., Dec. 13, 1934; s. Darryl F. and Virginia (Fox) Z.; m. Lili Gentle; children: Virginia, Janet; Linda Harrison, Oct. 26, 1969; children: Harrison Richard, Dean Francis; m. Lili Fini, Sept. 23, 1978. Grad., Harvard Mil. Acad., 1952; B.A., Stanford, 1956. Story, prodn. asst. Darryl F. Zanuck Prodns., 1956, v.p., 1956-62; president's prodn. rep. 20th Century-Fox Studios, Beverly Hills, 1962-63; v.p. charge prodn. 20th Century-Fox Studios, 1963-69, pres., 1969-71, dir., 1966-71; chmn. 20th Century-Fox Television, Inc.; sr. exec. v.p. Warner Bros., Inc., 1971-72; co-founder, pres. Zanuck/Brown Co., 1972-88; founder, owner The Zanuck Co., 1989—. Producer: The Sting, 1973 (Acad. award), Jaws, 1975, Jaws 2, 1978, The Island, 1980, Neighbors, 1982, The Verdict, 1983, Cocoon, 1985, Target, 1985, Cocoon, the Return, 1988, Driving Miss Daisy, 1989 (Acad. award, Irving G. Thalberg award 1991), Rush, 1991, Rich in Love, 1992, Clean Slate, 1993, Wild Bill, 1995, Mulholland Falls, 1996. Nat. chmn. Fibrosis Assn., 1966-68; mem. organizing com. 1984 Olympics; trustee Harvard Sch. 2d lt. U.S. Army. Named Producer of Yr., Nat. Assn. Theatre Owners, 1974, '85, Producers Guild Am., 1989; recipient Irving Thalberg award, 1991, Lifetime Achievement award, Producers Guild Am., 1993. Mem. Acad. Motion Picture Arts and Scis. (bd. govs.), Screen Producers Guild, Phi Gamma Delta. Office: 202 N Canon Dr Beverly Hills CA 90210-5302

ZAPAPAS, JAMES RICHARD, pharmaceutical company executive; b. Martinsville, Ind., July 15, 1926; s. James K. and Bertha (Gardner) Z.; m. Patricia A. Ryan, Aug. 30, 1947; children: Marianne Zapapas McGriff, Patricia Zapapas Parry, Gail Zapapas Rodecker, James R., Carol, Julie Zapapas Tepper. BS in Pharmacy, Purdue U., 1947, ScD hon., 1979. Dir. dry products ops. Eli Lilly & Co., Indpls., 1967-70, dir. pers., 1970-73, dir. pers. and pub. rels., 1973-74, v.p. prodn. ops., 1974-75, group v.p., dir., 1976-77, pres. Elizabeth Arden Inc., 1975-76, chmn. bd., 1977-87, ret., 1987; bd. dir., group v.p. Eli Lilly & Co., 1976-86; bd. dir. Am. United Life. Republican. Roman Catholic. Home: 5025 Plantation Dr Indianapolis IN 46250-1638

ZAPEL, ARTHUR L., book publishing executive; b. Chgo., 1921; m. Janet Michel (dec.); children: Linda (dec.), Mark, Theodore, Michelle; m. Cynthia Rogers Pisor, 1986; stepchildren: Dawn, Anthony. BA in English, U. Wis., 1946. Writer, prodr. Westinghouse Radio Stas.; film writer Galbreath Studios, Ft. Wayne; creative dir. Kling Studios, Chgo., 1952-54; writer, prodr. TV commls. J. Walter Thompson Advt., Chgo., 1954-73, v.p. TV and radio prodn., 1954-73; founder, pres. Arthur Meriwether, Inc., 1973-83; pres. Meriwether Pub. Ltd., 1969-90; chmn. Arthur Meriwether, Inc., Meriwether Pub. Ltd., 1990-95; pres. Westcliffe (Colo.) Ctr. for the Arts. Illustrator: 'Twas the Night Before, The Jabberwock; created game A Can of Squirms; wrote plays for ednl. use in schs. and chs.; supr. editing and prodn. 1200 plays and musicals, 1970-95. Founding pres. Art Students League of Colorado Springs, 1992; past pres. Colo. Springs Symphony Coun.; past bd. dirs. Colorado Springs Opera Festival. Recipient numerous awards Freedoms Found., Valley Forge, Art Dirs. Club N.Y., Art Dirs. Chgo., Hollywood Advt., 1960-67, Gold Records Radio Ad Bur., 1959-60, XV Festival Internat. Du Film Publicitaire Venise, 1968, Gold Camera award U.S. Indsl. Film Festival, 1983, Dukane award, 1983, Gold award Houston Internat. Film Festival, 1984. Office: Meriwether Pub Ltd 885 Elkton Dr Colorado Springs CO 80907-3557

ZAPF, HERMANN, book and type designer; b. Nuremberg, Germany, Nov. 8, 1918; s. Hermann and Magdalene (Schlamp) Z.; m. Gundrun von Hesse, Aug. 18, 1951; 1 child, Christian Ludwig. Freelance designer, 1938—; type dir. D. Stempel AG, type foundry, Frankfurt, Fed. Republic of Germany, 1947-56; design cons. Mergenthaler Linotype Co., N.Y.C. and Frankfurt, 1957-74; cons. Hallmark Internat., Kansas City, Mo., 1966-73; v.p. Design Processing Internat. Inc., N.Y.C., 1977-86; prof. typographic computer programs Rochester (N.Y.) Inst. Tech., 1977-87; chmn. Zapf, Burns & Co., N.Y.C., 1987-91; instr. lettering Werkkunstschule, Offenbach, Fed. Republic Germany., 1948-50; prof. graphic design Carnegie Inst. Tech., 1960; instr. typography Technische Hochschule, Darmstadt, Fed. Republic Germany, 1972-81. Author: William Morris, 1948, Pen and Graver, 1952, Manual Typographicum, 1954, 68, About Alphabets, 1960, 70, Typographic Variations, 1964, Orbis Typographicus, 1980, Hora fugit/Carpe diem, 1984, Hermann Zapf and His Design Philosophy, 1987, ABC-XYZapf, 1989, Poetry Through Typography, 1993; designer types, Palatino, Melior, Optima, ITC Zapf Chancery, ITC Zapf Internat., Digiset, Marconi, Digiset Edison, Digiset Aurelia, Pan-Nigerian, URW-Roman and San Serif, Renaissance Roman. Hon. curator Computer Mus., Boston. Recipient Silver medal Brussels, 1962, 1st prize typography Biennale Brno, Czechoslovakia, 1966, Gold medal Type Dirs. Club, N.Y., Frederic W. Goudy award typography Rochester, 1969, Silver medal Internat. Book Exhbn., Leipzig, 1971, Gold medal, 1989; Johannes Gutenberg prize Mainz, Fed. German Republic, 1974, Gold medal Museo Bodoniano, Parma, Italy, 1975, J.H. Merck award, Darmstadt, 1978, Robert Hunter Middleton award, 1987, Euro Design award, 1994; named hon. citizen State of Tex., 1970, hon. royal designer for industry. Mem. Royal Soc. Arts, Am. Math. Soc., Assn. Typographique Internat., Am. Inst. Graphic Arts, Alliance Graphique Internationale, Bund Deutscher Grafik Designer, Internat. Gutenberg Gesellschaft; hon. mem. Type Dirs. Club N.Y.C., Soc. Typographique de France (Paris), Soc. Typographic Arts (Chgo.), Double Crown Club (London), Soc. Scribes and Illuminators (London), Friends of Calligraphy (San Francisco), Soc. Printers (Boston), Soc. Graphic Designers Can., Bund Deutscher Buchkünstler, Grafiska Inst. (Stockholm), Typophiles, Alpha Beta Club (Hong Kong), Soc. of Calligraphy (L.A.), Wynkyn de Worde Soc. (London), Monterey Calligrapher's Guild, Washington Calligraphers Guild, Eesti Kalligraafide Koondis (Tallinn, Estonia), Typographers Internat. Assn., Art Dirs. Club Kansas City, Assocs. Stanford U. Librs., Alcuin Soc. (Vancouver), Goudy Internat. Ctr., Gamma Epsilon Tau.

ZAPPA, GAIL, record producer. Recipient Best Recording Package-Boxed Grammy award, 1996. Office: ICA PO Box 5265 North Hollywood CA 91616*

ZAPPALA, JANET L., television news anchor/reporter; b. L.A., Jan. 6; d. Albert Peter and Maria (Marciona) Z.; 1 child, Bradley. BA, Calif. State U., Northridge, 1976. Reporter KITV, Honolulu, 1977-79; reporter/anchor KFMB-TV, San Diego, 1979-82, KCNC-TV, Denver, 1982-84, KTTV-Fox, L.A., 1987-92, WCAU-TV, Phila., 1993—. Spkr., rep. March of Dimes, Phila., 1994-96; active City of Hope, 1991. Recipient Emmy award Acad. TV Arts and Scis., San Diego, 1980, 81, Golden Mike, Radio and TV News Assn., L.A., 1988. Avocations: piano, skiing, skating, tennis, horseback riding. Office: WCAU-TV City Ave Monument Rd Philadelphia PA 19131

ZAPPALA, STEPHEN A., state supreme court justice; b. 1932; s. Frank and Josephine Zappala. B.A., Duquense U.; LL.B., Georgetown U., 1958. Bar: Pa. 1958. Solicitor Allegheny County, Pitts., 1974-76; judge Ct. of Common Pleas-Allegheny County, 1980-82; assoc. justice Pa. Supreme Ct., 1982—. Served with U.S. Army. Office: Pa Supreme Ct 330 Grant St Pittsburgh PA 15219-2202*

ZAPPE, JOHN PAUL, city editor, educator; b. N.Y.C., July 30, 1952; s. John Paul and Caroline (Pikor) Z.; m. Siobhan Bradshaw, May 30, 1982. AA, Dutchess Community Coll., Poughkeepsie, 1971; BA, Marist Coll., 1973; JD, Syracuse (N.Y.) U., 1978. Reporter Poughkeepsie Jour., 1973-75, Nev. State Jour., Reno, 1979-80; freelance reporter Am. Media Bold, Oakland, Calif., 1981-83; reporter Press-Telegram, Long Beach, Calif., 1983-88, city editor, 1988—, webmaster, 1985—; tchr. Syracuse U., 1976-78, Calif. State U., 1985-87; cons. Am. Media Bold, 1981-83. Chmn. Local 69 Newspaper Guild, Long Beach, 1984-87. Mem. Investigative Editors and Reporters. Office: Press-Telegram 604 Pine Ave Long Beach CA 90844-0003

ZAR, JERROLD H(OWARD), biology educator, statistician; b. Chgo., June 28, 1941; s. Max and Sarah (Brody) Z.; m. Carol Bachenheimer, Jan. 15, 1967; children—David Michael, Adam Joseph. BS, No. Ill. U., 1962; MS, U. Ill., Urbana, 1964, PhD, 1967. NSF fellow marine sci. Duke U. Marine Lab., Beaufort, N.C., 1965; research assoc. dept. zoology U. Ill., Urbana, 1967-68; asst. prof. dept. biol. scis. No. Ill. U., DeKalb, 1968-71; assoc. prof. No. Ill. U., 1971-78, prof., 1978—, chmn. dept. biol. scis., 1978-84, assoc. provost grad. studies and research, dean Grad. Sch., 1984—; vis. scientist Argonne Nat. Lab., 1974; cons. EPA, also other govt. agys. and industries; founder, dir. ENCAP, Inc., 1974-93. Author: Biostatistical Analysis, 1974, 2d edit., 1984, 3d edit., 1996. NIH fellow U. Ill. Urbana, 1965-67. Fellow AAAS; mem. Am. Inst. Biol. Scis., Am. Ornithologists Union, Am. Physiol. Soc., Am. Statis. Assn., Biometric Soc., Cooper Ornithol. Soc., Am. Soc. Zoologists, Ecol. Soc. Am. (cert. sr. ecologist), Nat. Assn. Biol. Tchrs., Nat. Assn. Environ. Profls. (cert. environ. profl.), Wilson Ornithol. Soc. Office: No Ill U Off Dean Grad Sch De Kalb IL 60115-2864

ZARA, LOUIS, author, editor; b. N.Y.C., Aug. 2, 1910; s. Benjamin and Celia (Glick) Rosenfeld; m. Bertha Robbins, Sept. 23, 1930; children: Paul, Philip, Daniel; m. Marlene Brett, Mar. 22, 1958; m. Helen Dillman, Aug. 7, 1987. Student, Hebrew Theol. Coll., 1926-27; ed., Crane Coll., 1927-30, U. Chgo., 1930-31. Chmn. Walt Whitman Fellowship, 1940; Vice pres. Ziff Davis Pub. Co., Chgo., N.Y.C., 1946-61; editor-in-chief Masterpieces, 1950-51, dir. gen. book div., 1959-61; pres. Pub.'s Cons., Inc., N.Y.C., 1955-56, Internat. Communications Corp., N.Y.C., 1955-56; editor in chief gen. trade div. Follett Pub. Co., N.Y.C., 1962-65; editor in chief Mineral Digest, 1969-77; creative dir. George Jensen, Inc., 1974-77; cons. Astro Minerals Ltd., 1968-83. Author: novels Blessed is the Man, 1935, Give Us This Day, 1936, Some for the Glory, 1937, This Land is Ours, 1940, Against This Rock, 1943, Ruth Middleton, 1946, Rebel Run, 1951, In the House of the King, 1952, Blessed is the Land, 1954, Dark Rider, 1961; non-fiction Jade, 1969, Locks and Keys, 1969; also stories, scenarios, radio scripts, dramas, Twentieth Century Fox, 1936, ABC radio-TVshow Stump the Authors, 1945-46; scripts Scattergood Baines, 1941; contbr. fiction, essays and articles to mags. and anthologies, including O'Brien Best Short Stories of 1940. Recipient essay medal Internat. Benjamin Franklin Soc., 1930, Prose award Chgo. Found. Lit., 1940, Daroff Meml. fiction award, 1955. Fellow Royal Numis. Soc., Am. Numis. Soc.; mem. Authors Guild, Melville Soc., Overseas Press Club, Mineral Soc. Am., Macdowell Colony Fellows, Appraisers Soc. Am. (bd. dirs. 1980-87, pres. 1988-90, hon. life 1994), Nat. Commn. Anti-Defamation League (hon. life). Home: 141 E 56th St New York NY 10022-2709

ZARANKA, WILLIAM F., academic administrator, author; b. Elizabeth, N.J., Dec. 22, 1944; s. William A. and Anne M. (Paulauska) Z.; m. Ruth Annalea Falchero; children: Jacob, Philip. BA, Upsala Coll., 1966; MA, Purdue U., 1968; PhD, U. Denver, 1974. Instr. Purdue U., West Lafayette, Ind., summer 1969; asst. prof. U. Pa., Phila., 1975-78; teaching fellow U. Denver, 1969-71, instr. English,, 1969-71, 74-75, asst. prof., dir. creative writing, 1978-84, dean arts and humanities, 1984-89, provost, 1989—.

Author: The Branx X Anthology of Poetry, 1981, The Brand X Anthology of Fiction, 1983, (poetry) A Mirror Driven through Nature, 1981, Blessing, 1986. Fellow Breadd Loaf Writers Conf., 1981. Roman Catholic. Avocation: astronomy. Office: U Denver Office of Provost 2199 S University Blvd Denver CO 80210-4711

ZARB, FRANK GUSTAVE, insurance brokerage executive; b. N.Y.C., Feb. 17, 1935; s. Gustave and Rosemary (Antinora) Z.; m. Patricia Koster, Mar. 31, 1957; children: Krista Ann, Frank, Jr. B.B.A., Hofstra U., 1957, M.B.A., 1962, L.H.D., 1975. Trainee Cities Service Oil Co., N.Y.C., 1957-62; gen. partner Goodbody & Co., N.Y.C., 1962-69; exec. v.p. CBWL-Hayden Stone, Inc. (investment banking), N.Y.C., 1969-71; asst. sec. U.S. Dept. Labor, Washington, 1971-72; exec. v.p. Hayden Stone, Inc., N.Y.C., 1972-73; assoc. dir. Office of Mgmt. and Budget, Washington, 1973-74; asst. to Pres. for Energy Affairs U.S., 1974-77; adminstr. Fed. Energy Adminstrn., Washington, 1974-77; adv. U.S. Congress, 1977-78; gen. ptnr. Lazard Freres & Co., N.Y.C., 1977-88; chmn., pres. chief exec. officer Smith, Barney, Harris, Upham & Co., Inc., N.Y.C., 1988-93; vice chmn., group chief exec. The Travelers Inc., N.Y.C., 1993-94; chmn., pres., CEO Alexander & Alexander Svcs. Inc., N.Y.C., 1994—; bd. dirs. CS First Boston, Inc., Coun. on Fgn. Rels.; former chmn. N.Y. Stock Exch. Nominating Com. Author: The Stockmarket Handbook, 1969, Handbook of Financial Markets, The Municipal Bond Handbook. Mem. bd. trustees Gerald R. Ford Found.; mem. and former chmn. bd. trustees Hofstra U. Recipient Disting. Scholar award Hofstra U., 1974; bus. sch. named in his honor Hofstra U. Mem. Coun. Fgn. Rels. Office: Alexander & Alexander Svcs 1185 Avenue Of The Americas New York NY 10036-2601

ZARCONE, MICHAEL JOSEPH, experimental physicist, consultant; b. Danbury, Conn., Dec. 10, 1950; s. Michael Joseph Zarcone and Mary Elizabeth Belardinelli; children from previous marriage: Cassandra Marie, Sally Marie; m. Sheila Candelario, Feb. 21, 1981; children: Michael Joseph, Christopher Michael. BS in Physics, U. Fairfield U., 1973; MS in Physics, N.Mex. Inst. Mining and Tech., 1984; PhD in Physics, U. Conn., 1989. Rsch. asst. Radon Lab., Socorro, N.Mex., 1983-84, VandeGraaff Accelerator Lab., Storrs, Conn., 1985-89; physics instr. Cen. Conn. State U., New Britain, 1989-90; accelerator tech. fellow Brookhaven Nat. Lab., Upton, N.Y., 1990-91, asst. physicist, 1991-93, physics assoc. II, 1993—; dir. prodn., cons. Corning Costar Corp., Upton, 1994—; cons. corning. Contbr. articles to profl. jours. including Phys. Rev. A, Nuclear Instruments and Methods in Phys. Rsch., Physics Rev. Letters, Atmospheric Environment. Mem. AAAS, Am. Phys. Soc., Sigma Xi. Avocations: mountain climbing, hiking. Home: 17 Jones St East Setauket NY 11733 Office: Brookhaven Nat Lab Bldg 901A Upton NY 11973

ZARE, RICHARD NEIL, chemistry educator; b. Cleve., Nov. 19, 1939; s. Milton and Dorothy (Amdur) Z.; m. Susan Leigh Shively, Apr. 20, 1963; children: Bethany Jean, Bonnie Sue, Rachel Amdur. BA, Harvard, 1961; postgrad., U. Calif., Berkeley, 1961-63; PhD (NSF predoctoral fellow), Harvard, 1964; DS (hon.), U. Ariz., 1990, Northwestern U., 1993, ETH, Zürich, 1993. Postdoctoral fellow Harvard, 1964; postdoctoral research asso. Joint Inst. for Lab. Astrophysics, 1964-65; asst. prof. chemistry Mass. Inst. Tech., 1965-66; asst. prof. dept. physics and astrophysics U. Colo., 1966-68, assoc. prof. physics and astrophysics, asso. prof. chemistry, 1968-69; prof. chemistry Columbia, 1969-77, Higgins prof. natural sci., 1975-77; prof. Stanford U., 1977—, Shell Disting. prof. chemistry, 1980-85, Marguerite Blake Wilbur prof. chemistry, 1987—, prof. physics, 1992—; cons. Aeronomy Lab., NOAA, 1966-77, radio standards physics divsn. Nat. Bur. Standards, 1968-77, Lawrence Livermore Lab., U. Calif., 1974—, SRI, Internat., 1974—, Los Alamos Sci. Lab., U. Calif., 1975—; fellow adjoint Joint Inst. Lab. Astrophysics, U. Colo.; mem. IBM Sci. Adv. Com., 1977-92; chmn. commn. on phys. scis., math. and applications Nat. Rsch. Coun., 1992-95; chmn. bd. dirs. Annual Revs., Inc., 1995—; rschr. and author publs. on laser chemistry and chem. physics. editor Chem. Physics Letters, 1982-85; contbr. and rschr. articles on laser chemistry and chem. physics to profl. jours. Recipient Fresenius award Phi Lambda Upsilon, 1974, Michael Polanyi medal, 1979, Nat. Medal Sci., 1983, Spectroscopy Soc. Pitts. award, 1983, Michelson-Morley award Case Inst. Tech. Case We. Res. U., 1986, ISCO award for Significant Contbns. to Instrumentation for Biochem. Separations, 1990; nonresident fellow Joint Inst. for Lab. Astrophysics, 1970—, Alfred P. Sloan fellow, 1967-69, Christensen fellow St. Catherine's Coll., Oxford U., 1982, Stanford U. fellow, 1984-86. Fellow AAAS, Calif. Acad. Scis. (hon.); mem. NAS (mem. coun., Chem. Scis. award 1991), Nat. Scis. Bd., Am. Acad. Arts and Scis., Am. Phys. Soc. (Earle K. Plyler prize 1981, Irving Langmuir prize 1985), Am. Chem. Soc. (Harrison Howe award Rochester chpt. 1985, Remsen award Md. chpt. 1985, Kirkwood award Yale U. chpt. 1986, Willard Gibbs medal Chgo. chpt. 1990, Peter Debye award in phys. chemistry 1991, Linus Pauling medal 1993, The Harvey prize 1993, Dannie-Heineman Preis 1993, Analytical Chemistry Divsn. award in chem. instrumentation 1995), Am. Philos. Soc., Chem. Soc. London, Phi Beta Kappa. Office: Stanford U Dept Chemistry Stanford CA 94305-5080

ZAREFSKY, DAVID HARRIS, academic administrator, communication studies educator; b. Washington, June 20, 1946; s. Joseph Leon and Miriam Ethel (Lewis) Z.; m. Nikki Sheryl Martin, Dec. 23. 1970; children: Beth Ellen, Marc Philip. BS, Northwestern U., 1968, MA, 1969, PhD, 1974. Instr. communication studies Northwestern U., Evanston, Ill., 1968-73, asst. prof., 1974-77, assoc. prof., 1977-82, prof., 1982—, chmn. dept., 1975-83, assoc. dean Sch. Speech, 1983-88, dean, 1988—. Author: President Johnson's War on Poverty, 1986 (Winans-Wichelns award 1986), Lincoln, Douglas and Slavery, 1990 (Winans-Wichelns award 1991), Public Speaking: Strategies for Success, 1996; co-author: Contemporary Debated, 1983; editor: Rhetorical Movement, 1993; co-editor: American Voices, 1989, Contemporary American Voices, 1992; contbr. articles to profl. jours. Recipient Best Article award So. Speech Communication Assn., 1985, Midwest Forensic Assn., 1988; named Debate Coach of the Year Georgetown U., 1973, Emory U., 1972. Mem. AAUP, Speech Comm. Assn. (pres. 1993, dist. scholar award 1994), Ctrl. State Comm. Assn. (pres. 1986-87), Am. Forensic Assn. (Svc. award 1989), Delta Sigma Rho-Tau Kappa Alpha (Svc. award 1986), others. Democrat. Jewish. Avocations: stamp collecting, reading, travel. Office: Northwestern U 1905 Sheridan Rd Evanston IL 60208-2260

ZAREFSKY, RALPH, lawyer; b. Houston, Apr. 9, 1950. BA cum laude, Northwestern U., 1972; JD, Stanford U., 1976. Bar: Calif. 1976. Law clk. to Hon. Lawrence T. Lydick U.S. Dist. Ct., 1976-78; ptnr. Baker & Hostetler, L.A. Mem. ABA, State Bar Calif., Phi Beta Kappa. Office: Baker & Hostetler 600 Wilshire Blvd Los Angeles CA 90017-3212

ZAREM, ABE MORDECAI, management consulting executive; b. Chgo., Mar. 7, 1917; s. I.H. and Lea (Kaufman) Z.; m. Esther Mariam Moskovitz, Oct. 4, 1941; children: Janet Ruth, David Michael, Mark Charles. B.S. in Elec. Engring, Ill. Inst. Tech., 1939, LL.D. (hon.), 1968; M.S. in Elec. Engring, Calif. Inst. Tech., 1940, Ph.D., 1944; LL.D., U. Calif. at Santa Cruz, 1967. Design engr. very high voltage power transmission system Allis Chalmers Rsch. div., 1944; initiator, group mgr. Microtime & Electro Optical Phys. Rsch., U.S. Naval Test Sta., 1945-48; assoc. dir., mgr. L.A. div. Stanford Rsch. Inst., 1948-56; mem. faculty UCLA, 1956-61; founder, chmn., pres. Electro-Optical Systems, Inc., Pasadena, Calif., 1956-67; v.p. Xerox Corp., L.A., 1963-67, sr. v.p., dir. corp. devel., bd. dirs., 1967-69; mgmt. and engring. cons., 1969-79; founder, chmn. Xerox Devel. Corp., L.A., 1975-80; chmn. strategic bus. planning, techno-econ. and venture capital, pres., owner Abe M. Zarem & Co., 1981—; founder, mng. dir., Frontier Assoc., 1980—; mem. adv. com. competitive tech. program State of Calif., 1989; mem. Calif. Coun. Sci. and Tech., chmn. advanced sci. & tech. programs com. Author: Utilization of Solar Energy, 1963. Traffic and parking commr. City of Beverly Hills, 1971-72, planning commr., 1972-73; Bd. dirs. Music Center Opera Assn., Los Angeles, 1968—; nat. trustee City of Hope; trustee Calif. Inst. Arts, 1973-76. Named Outstanding Young Elec. Engr. in U.S. Eta Kappa Nu, 1948; One of America's Ten Outstanding Young Men U.S. Jr. C. of C., 1950; recipient Albert F. Sperry medal Instrument Soc. Am., 1969. Fellow AIAA, IEEE; sci. mem. (a founder) Solar Energy Soc.; mem. Nat. Acad. Engring. Inventor World's fastest high-speed camera, automatic oscillograph. Home: 9640 Lomitas Ave Beverly Hills CA 90210-3333 *I have always had a Vision, Mission & Series of Strategic Objectives - The principal one having been instilled by loving parents & family who encouraged me. I was born to identify talent and to challenge it to do more than it would have done if it had not met me. I am mentor and tormentor. I build and stretch people.*

ZAREMBKA, PAUL, economics educator; b. St. Louis, Apr. 17, 1942. BS, Purdue U., 1964; MS, U. Wis., 1967, PhD, 1967. Asst. prof. U. Calif., Berkeley, 1967-72; vis. prof. Heidelberg (Fed. Republic Germany) U., 1970-71, Gottingen (Fed. Republic Germany) U., 1972; assoc. prof. SUNY, Buffalo, 1973-76, prof., 1976—, dir. grad. studies dept. econs., 1995—; sr. rsch. officer Internat. Labor Office, Geneva, 1974-77; researcher Louis Pasteur U., Strasbourg, France, 1978-79; Fulbright-Hayes lectr. Coun. Internat. Exchange of Scholars, Poznan, Poland, 1979. Author: Toward a Theory of Economic Development, 1972; editor: Frontiers in Econometrics, 1974, Research in Political Economy, 1977—; co-editor: Essays in Modern Capital Theory, 1976; contbr. articles to profl. publs. Active Buffalo Ctr. chpt. exec. bd. United Univ. Professions, 1981—, pres., 1991-95, grievance officer acad., 1995—; active AFL-CIO Buffalo Labor Coun., 1982-83, 96—, Commn. on Quality Edn. in Buffalo in the 1990s, 1990-91; mem. subcom. on capital appropriations City of Buffalo, 1990—; bd. dirs. United Parents, 1991-94; chair Labor Party, Buffalo. NSF grantee, 1969-72. Office: SUNY Dept Econs 415 Fronczak Hall Buffalo NY 14260

ZAREMSKI, MILES JAY, lawyer; b. Chgo., Aug. 16, 1948; s. Samuel and Ann (Levine) Z.; m. Elena Cinthia Resnik, July 19, 1970; children: Jason Lane, Lauren Devra. BS, U. Ill., 1970; JD, Case Western Res. U., 1973. Bar: Ill. 1973, U.S. Dist. Ct. (no. dist.) Ill. 1973, U.S. Ct. Appeals (7th cir.) 1973, U.S. Supreme Ct. 1977, U.S. Ct. Appeals (8th cir.) 1988. Spl. asst. state's atty. Lake County, Ill., 1980-82; ptnr., co-chair health care practice group Rudnick & Wolfe, Chgo., Tampa, Washington, 1995—; asst. prof. med. jurisprudence U. Health Scis./Chgo. Med. Sch., 1991—; arbitrator, mandatory arbitration programs Cook and Lake Counties, Ill., 1990—. Editor: Medical and Hospital Negligence, 4 vols., 1988, supplement, 1993, 95, 96; columnist Jour. Radiology, 1987-88; contbr. chpts. in books and articles to profl. jours. Oversight com. law sch. Case Western Res. U., Cleve., 1985—; mem. exec. com. law sch. ctr for health care Loyola U., Chgo., 1987-89; mem. lakefront commn. City of Highland Park, Ill., 1982-84; bd. dirs., officer Regional Organ Bank Ill., Chgo., 1986-91; bd. dirs. The Lambs, Libertyville, Ill., 1982-84, Jocelyn Ctr. for Mental Health, 1994—. Named one of Outstanding Young Men in Am., U.S. Jaycees, 1979. Fellow Am. Coll. Legal Medicine (assoc. in law 1973-91, chair legal com. 1996—, editl. bd. Jour. Legal Medicine 1981—, bd. dirs.); mem. ABA (various coms. tort and ins. practice sect., vice chmn. 1979-90, chmn. med. and law com. 1984-85, editor-in-chief Forum 1979-81, spl. com. on med. profl. liability 1985, 91-95, editl. bd. Forum on Health Law 1989-91), Ill. Bar Assn. (1st and 3d prizes 1978-79), Am. Trial Lawyers Assn., Chgo. Trial Lawyers Assn., Chgo. Bar Assn., Lake County Bar Assn., Am. Soc. Law and Medicine (editor-in-chief 1981-83, bd. editors 1983-86), Am. Acad. Hosps. Attys., Am. Soc. Writers on Legal Subjects (scribes), Nat. Health Lawyers Assn., Ill. Assn. Hosps. Attys. Jewish. Avocations: baseball, soccer, coaching athletic teams. Office: Rudnick & Wolfe 203 N LaSalle St Ste 1800 Chicago IL 60601 *Success is a journey; not a destination. "A man may make many mistakes but he isn't a failure until he starts blaming someone else." John R. Wooden.*

ZARET, BARRY LEWIS, cardiologist, medical educator; b. N.Y.C., Oct. 3, 1940; s. Irving Z. and Beatrice (Fader) Zaret; m. Myrna Zimmerman, June 23, 1963; children: Adam L., Elliot C., Owen M. B.S., Queens Coll., 1962; M.D., NYU, 1966; M.A., Yale U., 1982. Diplomate: Am. Bd. Internal Medicine. Intern Bellevue Hosp., N.Y.C., 1966-67, resident, 1967-79; research fellow John Hopkins U., Balt., 1969-71; asst. prof. medicine Yale U., New Haven, 1973-76, assoc. prof. medicine and diagnostic radiology, 1976, chief sect. cardiology, 1978—, assoc. prof. medicine and diagnostic radiology, 1980-82, prof. medicine and diagnostic radiology, 1982-84; Robert W. Berliner prof. medicine Yale U., 1984—, assoc. chair clin. affairs dept. internal medicine, 1994—; mem. staff Yale-New Haven Med. Ctr. Mem. editorial bd. Am. Jour. Cardiology, 1977—, Jour. Am. Coll. Cardiology, 1986-91, 92—, Jour. Cardiac Imaging, 1986—, Circulation, 1993; assoc. editor: Yearbook of Nuclear Medicine, 1980-95; editor-in-chief Jour. Nuclear Cardiology, 1993—; contbr. articles to profl. jours. Recipient Casimir Funk award Soc. Mil. Surgeons, 1973; recipient Herrman Blumgart Pioneer award New Eng. chpt. Soc. Nuclear Medicine, 1978. Fellow Am. Coll. Cardiology, Coun. Clin. Cardiology, Am. Heart Assn., Coun. Circulation, Am. Heart Assn., Am. Physiology Soc.; mem. Am. Soc. Clin. Investigation, Am. Fedn. Clin. Rsch., Assn. Am. Physicians, Soc. Nuclear Medicine, Am. Soc. Nuclear Cardiology, Assn. Univ. Cardiologists, Assn. Profs. Cardiology (pres. 1992), Phi Beta Kappa, Alpha Omega Alpha, Interurban Clin. Club. Jewish. Home: 15 Cassway Rd Woodbridge CT 06525-1214 Office: Yale U Sch Medicine 333 Cedar St # 3fmp New Haven CT 06510-3206

ZARINS, BERTRAM, orthopaedic surgeon; b. Latvia, June 22, 1942; came to U.S., 1946, naturalized, 1956; s. Richard Arthur and Maria (Rozenbergs) Z. A.B. in Chemistry, Lafayette Coll., 1963; M.D., SUNY-Syracuse, 1967. Diplomate Am. Bd. Orthopaedic Surgery. Clin. instr. orthopaedic surgery Harvard Med. Sch., Boston, 1976—, asst. clin. prof., 1982—; orthopaedic surgeon Mass. Gen. Hosp., Boston, 1982-95; assoc. clin. prof. Harvard Med. Sch., Boston, 1995—; chief sports medicine unit Mass. Gen. Hosp., Boston, 1982—; team physician Boston Bruins Hockey Team, 1976—; chmn. edn. com. Sports Medicine council, U.S. Olympic Com., 1980-92; team physician New Eng. Patriots Football Team, 1982—; head physician USA Olympic teams XIV Winter Olympic Games, Sarajevo, 1984. Contbr. articles to profl. jours. Team physician N.E. Revolution profl. soccer team, 1996—. Served to lt. comdr. M.C. USNR, 1973-75. Fellow ACS, Am. Acad. Orthopaedic Surgeons (chmn. com. on sports medicine 1993—), Am. Coll. Sprots Medicine; mem. AMA, Internat. Arthroscopy Assn. (bd. dirs. 1991-95), Arthroscopy Assn. N.Am., N.Am. Trauma Assn. (pres. 1977), Internat. Soc. fo the Knee, Am. Shoulder and Elbow Surgeons, Herodicus Soc., Brookline (Mass.) Country Club. Office: Mass Gen Hosp Ambulatory Care Ctr Ste 514 Boston MA 02114

ZARINS, CHRISTOPHER KRISTAPS, surgery educator, vascular surgeon; b. Tukums, Latvia, Dec. 2, 1943; came to U.S., 1946; s. Richard A. and Maria (Rozenbergs) Z.; m. Zinta Zarins, July 8, 1967; children: Daina, Sascha, Karina. BA, Lehigh U., 1964; MD, Johns Hopkins U., 1968. Surgery residency U. Mich., Ann Arbor, 1968-74; asst. prof. surgery U. Chgo., 1976-79, assoc. prof. surgery, 1979-82, prof. surgery, 1983-93, chief of vascular surgery, 1978-93; prof. surgery, chmn. divsn. vascular surgery Stanford (Calif.) U., 1993—, acting chmn. Dept. of Surgery, 1995—. Author: Essays In Surgery, 1986, Atlas of Vascular Surgery, 1988; editor Jour. of Surg. Rsch., 1982—; contbr. articles to profl. jours. Pres. Latvian Med. Found., Boston, 1991. Lt. comdr. USN, 1974-76. Grantee NIH, NSF. Mem. Am. Surg. Soc., Soc. for Clin. Surgery, Soc. for Vascular Surgery, Internat. Soc. for Cardiovascular Surgery, Soc. of Univ. Surgeons, Latvian Nat. Acad. of Scis., Latvian Vascular Surg. Soc. (pres. 1989). Avocations: triathlons, skiing. Office: Stanford U Med Ctr Divsn Vascular Surgery 300 Pasteur Dr # H3630 Stanford CA 94305-5450

ZARKIN, HERBERT, retail company executive. Exec. vice-pres. Zayre Corp., Framingham, Mass., until 1986; pres. Zayre Corp., HomeClub subs., Framingham, Mass., 1986-88; chmn. Zayre Corp., Zayre Stores div., Framingham, Mass., 1988—; pres., CEO Waban Inc, Natick. Office: Waban 1 Mercer Rd Natick MA 01760*

ZARLE, THOMAS HERBERT, academic administrator. BS, Springfield Coll., 1963; MA, Ohio U., 1965; PhD, Mich. State U., 1970; MPH, Harvard U., 1978. V.p. instl. advancement Bentley Coll., Waltham, Mass., until 1988; pres. Aurora U., Ill., 1988—. Office: Aurora U Office of Pres 347 S Gladstone Ave Aurora IL 60506-4877

ZARLING, JOHN PAUL, mechanical engineering educator; b. Elmhurst, Ill., Mar. 15, 1942; s. Earnie W. and Lorraine M. (Feustel) Z.; m. Fran E. Carlson, Nov. 27, 1965; children: Matthew, John, Katie. BSMechE, Mich. Tech. U., 1964, MSEM, 1966, PhD in EM, 1970. Instr. U. Wis., Madison, 1966-68; asst. prof. U. Wis., Kenosha, 1971-73, assoc. prof., 1973-76; assoc. prof. U. Alaska, Fairbanks, 1976-79, prof., 1979—, assoc. dean, 1986—; asst. vice chancellor U. Wis., 1974-76; prin. Zarling Aero & Engring., Fairbanks, 1978—. Editor conf. procs.; contbr. articles, monographs, procs. to profl. publs. Active Fairbanks Youth Hockey, 1976-83. Mem. ASHRAE, ASME (chmn. Milw. sect. 1975), Am. Soc. Engring. Edn. (bd. dirs. 1986-88). Lutheran. Achievements include patents for Apparatus for Containing Toxic Spills Employing Hybrid Thermosyphon, Thermosyphon Condensate Return Device, Passive-Active Hybrid Thermosyphon. Office: Univ Alaska Sch Engring Dept Mech Engring Fairbanks AK 99775

ZARO, BRAD A., research company executive, biologist; b. San Jose, Calif., Dec. 4, 1949; s. Raymond J. and Irene R. (Cunha) Z.; m. Angela M. Greenan, Nov. 20, 1971; children: Amy C., Kristen E. BA in Zoology, San Jose State U., 1974, MA in Biology, 1981. Chemist, Dept. Drug Metabolism Syntex Rsch., Inc., Palo Alto, Calif., 1976-78, chemist II, Dept. Drug Metabolism, 1978-81, chemist III, Dept. Drug Metabolism, 1981-84, clin. rsch. assoc. I, Inst. of Clin. Medicine, 1984-85, clin. rsch. assoc. II, Inst. of Clin. Medicine, 1985-87, sen. clin. rsch. assoc., Inst. of Clin. Medicine, 1985-87; sen. clin. rsch. assoc. Triton Biosciences, Inc., Alameda, Calif., 1988, mgr. clin. trials, 1988; pres. Clinimetrics Rsch. Assoc., Inc., San Jose, 1988—. Contbr. articles to scholarly jours. Mem. Am. Coll. Clin. Pharmacology, Am. Assoc's. for the Advancement of Sci., Assoc's. of Clin. Pharmacology, Prof. Tech. Cons's. Democrat. Roman Catholic. Avocations: scuba diving, skiing, flying airplanes. Office: Clinimetrics Rsch Assocs 2025 Gateway Pl Ste 403 San Jose CA 95110-1006

ZARR, MELVYN, lawyer, law educator; b. Worcester, Mass., Aug. 29, 1936; m. Gail Sclar, Aug. 29, 1971. A.B., Clark U., 1958; LL.B., Harvard U., 1963. Bar: Mass. bar 1964, Maine bar 1973. Staff atty. NAACP Legal Def. & Edn. Fund, Inc., N.Y.C., 1963-69; co-dir. Mass. Law Reform Inst., Boston, 1970-73; prof. law U. Maine, 1973—; U.S. magistrate, Portland, Maine, 1977-82. Mem. Am. Law Inst. Home: 19 Mckinley Rd Falmouth ME 04105 Office: U Maine Sch Law 246 Deering Ave Portland ME 04102

ZARRELLA, ARTHUR M., superintendent; b. Providence, July 30, 1936; s. Joseph and Flora (Santoro) Z.; m. Ann Miletta, Aug. 19, 1960; children: Matthew, Mark, Chris, Paul. BS, U. R.I., 1960; D of Pedagogy (hon.), R.I. Coll., 1985. Cert. bus. edn., history, social studies, guidance and counseling, critic tchr., secondary sch. prin., secondary sch. asst. prin., supt. of schs. Tchr. bus. edn. Cranston High Sch. West, 1961-62; tchr. bus. edn. Mt. Pleasant High Sch., 1962-65, tchr. social studies, 1965-68; social studies dept. head Ctrl. High Sch., 1968-70, guidance dept. head, 1970-72, student rels. adminstr., 1972-76, prin., 1976-87; prin. Classical H.S., 1987-88, acting asst. supt. for secondary edn., 1988-89, asst. supt. for secondary edn., 1989-90, asst. supt. secondary edn./dep., 1990—, acting supt. schs., 1991-92, supt. of schs., 1992—; asst. coach track and field Mt. Pleasant H.S., 1961-64, head coach track and field, 1964-69; tchr. Brown U., 1970, Providence Coll., 1973-74, 74-75, 86—, advisor adminstrv. internship program, 1976-82; tchr. R.I. Coll., 1980, 82, 95—, social worker practicum supervision U. R.I., 1976-78; advisor adminstrv. internship program Harvard U., 1985-86; cons. The Inst. for Edn. Leadership, Inc., Hartford, 1985; presenter in field, many others. Contbr. articles to profl. jours. Bd. dirs. Mt. Pleasant Little League, 1973-76, treas., 1973-75, pres., 1976; bd. dirs. West End Community Assn., 1976-89, Wiggins Village Tenants Assn., 1980—, Young Vols. of R.I., 1982-84, Urban Edn. Ctr., 1982—, R.I. Leadership Acad., 1983-85, Keep Providenc Beautiful, 1984-85, Providence Edn. Fund, 1985-88, West End Community Ctr., 1986-90, Todd Morsilli Fund, 1987—, chairperson, 1989-91; scholarship chairperson Italian Am. Sports Hall of Fame, 1988-89; others. With USNG, 1959-65. Recipient Delta Sigma Theta Sorority's Comty. Svc. award, 1986, Mayor's citation for comty. svc., 1989, R.I. Ho. of Reps. citation for comty. svc., 1989, Gov.'s citation for comty. svc., 1989, R.I. Senate citation for comty. svc., 1989, Youth Dirs. Assn. Comty. Svc. award, 1989, NAACP Edn. award, 1989, R.I. Ho. of Reps. citation for commitment to substance abuse programs, 1991, Mayor's Citizen citation, 1991, Roberto Clemente Citizen award, 1991, Excellence in Edn. award U. R.I. Alumni Assn., 1996; fellow Danforth Found., 1994—, Annenberg fellow, 1994—. Mem. Nat. Assn. Secondary Sch. Prins., R.I. Assn. Secondary Sch. Prins., R.I. Sch. Adminstrs. Assn., Barnard Club. Roman Catholic. Home: 80 Waller St Providence RI 02908-3822 Office: Dept Supt of Schs 797 Westminster St Providence RI 02903-4018

ZARRO, JANICE ANNE, lawyer; b. Newark, June 30, 1947; d. Samuel James and Elma Dora (Monaco) Z.; m. Bobby C. Wood. BA, Rutgers U., 1969; JD, IIT-Chgo.-Kent Coll. Law, 1973. Bar: Pa. 1974. Counsel jud. com. U.S. Ho. Reps., Washington, 1973-77; profl. staff mem. counsel labor and human resources com. U.S. Senate, Washington, 1977-80; dir. Avon Products, Inc., N.Y.C., 1980-81; dir. Avon Products, Inc., Washington, 1982-86, v.p., 1986-90; pres. The Novus Group, Inc., 1990-92; dir. fed. affairs Mallinckrodt Med., 1992—, v.p., 1993-94; v.p. govt. affairs Worldwide Mallinckrodt Group, 1994—; gen. counsel Nat. Italian-Am. Found., 1989-96, chair bd. trustees, 1996—; mem. Bus. Govt. Rels. Coun., Washington, 1987—. Past chmn. Nat. Capital chpt. Multiple Sclerosis Soc. Recipient Leadership Recognition award Nat. Women's Econ. Alliance, 1984. Mem. ABA, Pa. Bar Assn. Home: 6A W Chapman St Alexandria VA 22301-2502

ZARROW, PHILIP M., electronic assembly process consultant; b. Paterson, N.J., Apr. 9, 1953; s. Frank T. and Barbara E. (Strassman) Z.; m. Golda A. Lechner; children: Joel, Rosalee. BS in Bus. Adminstrn., Rider Coll., 1975. Applications engr./mktg. specialist Argus Internat., Hopewell, N.J., 1975-76; sales engr. Tooltronics, Inc., Glendale, Calif., 1976-78; sales engr., dist. mgr. Universal Instrument Corp., Irvine, Calif., 1978-81; western regional mgr. Test Systems Inc., Tempe, Ariz., 1981-82, Trilog, Inc., Irvine, 1982-83; product mgr., western regional mgr. Excellon-Micronetics, Torrance, Calif., 1983-87; product mgr. Vitronics Corp., Newmarket, N.H., 1987-92; mgr. tech. devel. GSS/Array Tech., San jose, Calif., 1992-94; pres., cons. ITM, Inc., Durham, N.H., 1993—; co-founder, cons. Synergistek Assocs., Round Lake Beach, Ill., 1991-92; dir. ITM, Inc., 1993—; assoc. cons. Teltech, Mpls., 1994—. Co-author: SMT Glossary-Terms & Definitions, 1994; columnist Circuits Assn. Mag., 1995—, mem. editl. adv. bd, 1993-95; contbr. articles to profl. jours. Mem. ISHM, Surface Mount Tech. Assn. (bd. dirs. 1988-91, Mem. Distinction award 1995), Surface Mount Tech. Equipment Mfg. Assn. (chair reflow com. 1990-92). Achievements include research and development of surface mount technology assembly processes; particular expertise in reflow soldering processes, equipment and technology, and component placement; development of reflow and placement equipment classification method and related terminology. Office: ITM Inc PO Box 483 Durham NH 03824

ZARTMAN, DAVID LESTER, animal sciences educator, researcher; b. Albuquerque, July 6, 1940; s. Lester Grant and Mary Elizabeth (Kitchel) Z.; m. Micheal Aline Plemmons, July 6, 1963; children: Kami Renee, Dalan Lee. BS, N.Mex. State U., 1962; MS, Ohio State U., 1966, PhD, 1968. Jr. ptnr. Marlea Guernsey Farm, Albuquerque, 1962-64; grad. rsch. assoc. Ohio State U., Columbus, 1964-68; asst. prof. dairy sci. N.Mex. State U., Las Cruces, 1968-71, assoc. prof., 1971-79, prof., 1979-84; prof., chmn. dept. Ohio State U., Columbus, 1984—; pres. Mary K. Zartman, Inc., Albuquerque, 1976-84; cons. Bio-Med. Electronics, Inc., San Diego, 1984-89, Zartemp, Inc., Northbrook, Ill., 1990, Recom Applied Solutions, 1993—. Contbr. articles to profl. jours.; patentee in field. Recipient State Regional Outstanding Young Farmer award Jaycees, 1963, Disting. Rsch. award N.Mex. State U. Coll. Agr. and Home Econs., 1983; named one of Top 100 Agr. Alumni, N.Mex. State U. Centennial, 1987; spl. postdoctoral fellow NIH, New Zealand, 1973; Fulbright-Hayes lectr., Malaysia, 1976. Fellow AAAS; mem. Am. Dairy Sci. Assn., Am. Soc. Animal Sci., Dairy Shrine Club, Ohio Extension Profs. Assn., Poultry Soc. Am., Sigma Xi, Gamma Sigma Delta, Alpha Gamma Rho (1st Outstanding Alumnus N.Mex. chpt. 1985), Alpha Zeta, Phi Kappa Phi. Home: 7671 Deer Creek Dr Columbus OH 43085-1551 Office: Ohio State U 2029 Fyffe Rd Columbus OH 43210-1007

ZARUBY, WALTER STEPHEN, holding company executive; b. Vegreville, Alta., Can., Mar. 4, 1930; s. William and Annie (Kubon) Z.; m. Margaret Beth Fargey, Sept. 22, 1958; children: Stephen, Jeffrey. B.A.Sc., U. Toronto, 1952. Engr., project mgr. Shell Oil Co. and Shell Can. Ltd., 1952-70; sr. v.p. Westburne Internat. Industries Ltd., Calgary, Alta., 1970-73; pres. Westburne Internat. Industries Ltd., 1973-76, Radium Holdings Ltd., Calgary, 1977-87, Radium Resources Ltd., 1978—, Radium Energy Corp., Las Vegas, Nev., 1981-87; dir. Aberford Resources Ltd., 1981-87; pres. Zaruby & Assocs., Inc., 1987—, Indsl. Minerals Recovery, Inc., 1987—. Mem. Assn. Profl. Engrs., Geologists, and Geophysicists Alta., Assn. Drilling Contractors (bd. dirs. 1971-74). Clubs: Calgary Petroleum, Calgary Golf and Country, Glencoe. Address: 1012 Bel-Aire Dr SW, Calgary, AB Canada T2V 2B9

ZARWYN, BERTHOLD, physical scientist; b. Vienna, Austria, Aug. 22, 1921; came to U.S., 1949, naturalized, 1955; s. Joseph and Bronislawa Regina (Unger) Z.; M.E., Gliwice, Poland, 1946; Sc.D., Munich (W. Ger.) U., 1947; Ph.D., N.Y.U., 1954; Engring. Sc.D., Columbia, 1963. Project engr. Curtiss-Wright Corp., Woodridge, N.J., 1951-55; staff scientist AMF Corp., N.Y.C., 1955-57; chief scientist Link Aviation Co., Binghamton, N.Y., 1957-58; head research staff Am. Bosch-Arma Corp., Garden City, N.Y., 1958-63; corp. cons. Cutler-Hammer Corp., Deer Park, N.Y., 1963-65; chief engr. Bell Aerosystems Corp., Niagara Falls, N.Y., 1965-66; sr. cons. Mitre Corp., Bedford, Mass., 1966-68; spl. asst. to commanding gen., acting chief engr. Hdqrs. U.S. Army Materiel Command, Arlington, Va., 1968-71, chief phys. scis. br., U.S. Army Devel. and Readiness Command, Alexandria, Va., 1971-75, phys. scientist U.S. Army Harry Diamond Labs., Washington, 1975-78; chief system analysis br. U.S. Army Elec. Rsch. and Devel. Command, Adelphi, Md., 1978-79, chief tech. divsn., 1979-81, asst. tech. dir., 1981-85; spl. asst. to dep. chief of staff for tech. and program mgmt. U.S. Army Lab. Command, Adelphi, 1985-87, pres. Pan-Tech. Corp., 1987—; adj. faculty, lectr., cons. in field; dir. Film Microelectronics Co. Inc., Burlington, Mass., 1965-67. Mem. IEEE, Am. Phys. Soc., N.Y. Acad. Scis., Sigma Xi. Editorial bd. Bavarian Soc. Engrs., 1947-49; translation panel Russian Jour. Applied Math. and Mechanics with Pergamon Inst., 1956-57. Inventor nuclear gyroscope, microwave holography, other items. Home and Office: Pan-Tech Corp 7589 Mansfield Hollow Rd Delray Beach FL 33446-3314

ZARZOUR, ROBIN ANN, special education educator; b. Parma, Ohio, Apr. 14, 1964; d. Robert Halim and Rosalie Frances (Ezzie) Z. AAS in Early Childhood Edn., Cuyahoga C.C., 1985; BS in Spl. Edn., Cleve. State U., 1990, MA in Early Childhood Spl. Edn., 1993. Early childhood spl. edn. aide Middleburg Spl. Presch., Middleburg Heights, Ohio, 1983-86; counselor Camp Sunshine, Parma, Ohio, 1986-88; early childhood spl. religious tchr. St. Charles, Parma, Ohio, 1988-89; early childhood spl. edn. tchr. Parma City Sch. System, 1990—. Mem. Cleve. Assn. Mid. Ea. Orgn., 1992—. Recipient Tchr. of Yr. award Cuyahoga Spl. Edn. Svc. Ctr., 1993—. Mem. Coun. for Exception Children, Parma Edn. Assn. (union bldg. rep. 1992—). Democrat. Roman Catholic. Avocations: golf, working out, movies, music.

ZASLOW, JEFFREY LLOYD, syndicated columnist; b. Phila., Oct. 6, 1958; s. Harry and Naomi (Weintraub) Z.; m. Sherry Lynn Margolis, July 4, 1987; children: Jordan Danielle, Alexandra Nicole, Eden Gabrielle. BA with honors, Carnegie-Mellon U., 1980. Reporter/columnist The Orlando (Fla.) Sentinel, 1980-83; staff writer The Wall St. Jour., Chgo., 1983-87; columnist The Chgo. Sun Times, 1987—, USA Weekend mag., 1995—. Author: (with others) You Can Do Something About AIDS, 1988, Tell Me All About It, 1990, Take It from Us, 1994; contbr. feature articles to The N.Y. Times, Reader's Digest, Phila. Inquirer, Boston Globe, Cosmopolitan mag., Glamour, Bus. Week, others; writer of liner notes for singer Don McLean's double-live album, 1983; numerous appearances on TV including ABC's Nightline with Ted Koppel, Good Morning Am., NBC's Today Show, CBS This Morning, Oprah Winfrey Show, The Larry King Show, NBC's Tonight Show, CBS's Saturday Night with Connie Chung; subject of articles in Time, Newsweek, People, Life, Washington Post, others. Jewish. Office: Chgo Sun-Times Inc 401 N Wabash Ave Rm 320 Chicago IL 60611-3532

ZASSENHAUS, HILTGUNT MARGRET, physician; b. Hamburg, Ger., July 10, 1916; came to U.S., 1952, naturalized, 1957; d. Julius and Margret Z. Diploma of Scandinavian Langs., U. Hamburg, 1938; MD, U. Copenhagen, 1952; MD (hon.), Goucher Coll., Towson State U., U. Notre Dame, 1975, U. Md., 1984, Washington Coll., Md., 1984, Western Coll. Md., 1987, U. Md., Balt. County, 1988. With German Dept. Justice, Berlin, 1941-45; secret relief action for Scandinavian polit. prisoners; organizer relief action for German orphans German Dept. Justice, 1945-48; intern, then resident in internal medicine Balt. City Hosp., 1952-54; pvt. practice specializing in internal medicine Balt., 1954—; med. bd. Greater Balt. Med. Center; appointed mem. Md. Council Humanities, 1979—; del. Med. and Chirurgical Faculty of State of Md., 1985-89. Author: biography On Guard in The Dark, 1948; autobiography Walls (Christopher award as best book of year 1975, Best Book of Yr . Book Assn. Evang. Ch. Germany 1981); subject of documentary Woman of Courage, 1989; also articles, essays. Trustee White Rose Found., N.Y., 1988; bd. dirs. Roland Park Country Sch., GBMC, Balt., 1985; bd. dirs. Greater Balt. Medf. Ctr., 1986,; trustee The White Rose Found., N.Y.C., 1988; apptd. hon. senator U. Hamburg, 1990. Decorated knight St. Olav's Order 1st class (Norway); Order Dannebrog 1st class (Denmark), Bundesverdienstkreuz 1st class (Fed. Republic Germany); recipient Danish Red Cross medal, 1948, Norwegian Red Cross medal, 1948, 86, Gold Meml. medal Senate of City of Hamburg, Fed. Republic Germany, 1986, Community Service award Med. Assn. Md., 1986, Gold medal U. Hamburg, 1990; named Outstanding Woman of Year in Balt. County AAUW, 1976; nominated for Nobel Peace Prize, 1974; named to Md. Women's Hall of Fame, 1986; subject of documentary It Mattered to Me, produced by ITV, Yorkshire TV (Eng.), 1981; apptd. hon. sen. U. Hamburg, Fed. Republic Germany, 1990. Mem. Physicians for Social Responsibility (bd. dirs.), Balt. County Med. Soc. Address: 7028 Bellona Ave Baltimore MD 21212-1111 *I know that one person can make the difference. That gives me hope that the walls of hate and prejudice separating man from man one day will fade so that people will cease destroying each other and join to serve life.*

ZATKO, PATRICIA ANN, nursing administrator, geriatrics nurse; b. Buffalo, July 18, 1943; d. Vincent and Florence (Cybulski) Lipka; m. Steven Paul Zatko, Jan. 9, 1965 (dec. Mar. 1984); children: Julie Ann, Steven Paul II, John Vincent. LPN, Boces, 1979; ADN, Trocaire Coll., 1986; BSN magna cum laude, SUNY, Buffalo, 1991. Practical nurse Erie County Med. Ctr., Buffalo, 1979-86, gen. duty nurse, 1986-88, quality rev. nurse, 1988-91, case mgr., 1991—, nursing researcher, 1992. Vol. outreach com. Our Lady of the Blessed Sacrament Ch., Depew, N.Y., 1985—, lector, 1986—, Eucharistic min., bereavement com., grief support group; sec. Citizens for a Greener Depew, 1991, 92; vol. Benedict House. Recipient award Nat. Assn. Counties, 1992. Mem. N.Y. State Nurses Assn. (award 1986), Quality Assurance of Hospice Buffalo, Sigma Theta Tau. Democrat. Roman Catholic. Avocations: crafts, reading, volunteer work, church work. Home: 223 French Rd Depew NY 14043-2162 Office: Erie County Med Ctr 462 Grider St Buffalo NY 14215-3075

ZATKOFF, LAWRENCE P., federal judge; b. 1939; m. Nancy L. Chenhall; four children. BSBA, U. Detroit, 1962; JD cum laude, Detroit Coll. Law, 1966. Bar: Mich., U.S. Supreme Ct. Mem. corp. personnel staff Chrysler Corp., 1962-66; asst. prosecuting atty. Macomb County, Mich.; with Moll, Desenberg, Purdy, Glover & Bayer, Detroit, 1966-68; ptnr. LaBarge, Zatkoff & Dinning, Roseville, 1968-78; probate judge Macomb County, 1978-82; judge Macomb County Cir. Ct., 1982-87, U.S. Dist. Ct. (ea. dist.) Mich., 1986—; part-time faculty Detroit Coll. Law; mem. rep. assembly Mich. State Bar, mem. spl. com. on grievances; appointed assoc. govt. appeal agt. SSS, 1969-72. guest lectr., past mem. scholarship ball com. Macomb County Community Coll.; citizen's adv. bd. Macomb-Oakland Regional Ctr., 1978-79; ex officio mem. Macomb County Youthscope; adv. bd. Met. Detroit chpt. March of Dimes; trustee St. Joseph Hosp. of Mt. Clemens; mem. Selfridge Air NG Base Community Council; Rep. candidate 12th dist. U.S. Congress Mich., 1976, party treas. 12 dist. 1975, exec. com., 1975, chmn. Macomb County exec. com., 1976, del. several nat. and regional Rep. Convs., Macomb County campaign coordinator for U.S. Sen. candidate Marvin Esch, 1976. Mem. ABA, Fed. Bar Assn., Mich. Bar. Assn., Macomb County Bar. Assn. (dir., treas. Young Lawyers sect., past probate ct. liason to bd. dirs., mem. cir. ct. liason com.), Detroit Bar Assn., Am. Judicare Soc., Am. Arbitration Assn., Nat. Orgn. Legal Problems of Edn., Nat. Council Juvenile and Family Ct. Judges, Mich. Probate and Juvenile Ct. Judges Assn. (mental health com.), Nat. Coll. Probate Judges, Mich. Judges Assn., VFW (legal case rep. 1976, spokesman Vietnamese Embassy Paris 1976, judge Voice of Democracy programs 1975, state wide scholarships judge, Voice of Democracy awards 1975, 76, Americanism award 1976, Spl. Recognition award 1978). Clubs: 100, Macomb County 300, Rep. Majority (charter). Office: US Dist Ct 707 US Courthouse 231 W Lafayette Blvd Detroit MI 48226-2719*

ZATUCHNI, GERALD IRVING, physician, educator; b. Phila., Oct. 5, 1933; s. Samuel and Minnie (Pollack) Z.; m. Bette Ruth Christine, June 15, 1958; children: Cheryl Lee, Bettina, Mimi. AB, Temple U., 1954, MD, 1958, MSc, 1965. Diplomate Am. Bd. Obstetrics and Gynecology. Intern Walter Reed Army Hosp, Washington, 1958-59; residency in ob-gyn Temple U. Med. Ctr., Phila., 1962-65; gen. practice medicine Phila., 1965-66; staff assoc. Population Council, N.Y.C., 1966-69; resident advisor Population Council, New Dehli, 1969-71; cons. World Health Orgn., Geneva, 1971-73; regional advisor Population Council, Tehran, Iran, 1973-75; assoc. med. dir. Population Council, N.Y.C., 1975-76; prof. ob-gyn. Northwestern U., Chgo., 1977—; cons. Medico-Legal, 1982—; bd. dirs. Fertility Research Northwestern U. Author books; editor numerous books, jours. Served to capt. USMC, 1958-62. Recipient Phillip Williams prize Phila. Ob. Soc., 1964, Babcock Surg. prize Temple U., 1965; Fertility Research grantee, U.S. Govt., 1981. Fellow Am. Coll. Ob-Gyn.; mem. Soc. Advancement Contraception (pres. 1986). Avocations: painting, sailing, golf, tennis. Office: Prentice Women's Hosp 680 N Lake Shore Dr Ste 1000 Chicago IL 60611-4402

ZAUNER, CHRISTIAN WALTER, university dean, exercise physiologist, consultant; b. Phila., July 21, 1930; s. Philip Walter and Margaret Helen (Gilmor) Z.; m. Betty Ann Schwenk, Feb. 1, 1957; children: Beth, Ward, Joe. BS, West Chester State, 1956; MS, Syracuse U., 1957; PhD, So. Ill. U., 1963. Asst. prof. Temple U., Phila., 1963-65; prof. phys. edn. and medicine U. Fla., Gainesville, 1965-84; dir. Sports Medicine Inst., Mt. Sinai Med. Ctr., Miami Beach, Fla., 1984-87; chmn. exercise sci. Oreg. State U., Corvallis, 1987-94; dean health and human performance East Carolina U., Greenville, N.C., 1994—; cons. in exercise rehab. Hosp. Corp. Am.; cons. in sports medicine State of Kuwait, Arab Gulf; cons. sport sci. curriculum Ministry Edn., Thailand. Contbr. numerous articles to various profl. jours. Served with USN, 1951-54. Grantee U. Fla., 1971, Am. Scandinavian Foun., 1971, Fla. Blue Key, 1978, Nat. Acad. Sci., 1985-86, 88, 90, 94. Fellow Am. Coll. Sports Medicine; mem. Am. Physiol. Soc., N.Y. Acad. Scis., AAHPERD, Sigma Chi. Democrat. Roman Catholic. Office: East Carolina U Sch Health & Human Performance Greenville NC 27858-4353

ZAUSNER, L. ANDREW, lawyer; b. Plainfield, N.J., May 1, 1949; s. Sol and Beatrice (Summer) Z; m. Nancy J. Zausner, Aug. 10, 1990; children: L. Alexander, Samantha Rae. B.A., Boston U., 1971; M.B.A., U. Pa., 1975, J.D., 1975. Bar: Pa. 1975, D.C. 1979, U.S. Supreme Ct. 1979. Mem. firm Blank, Rome, Comisky & McCauley, Phila., 1975-77; atty., adv. legislation Fed. Energy Adminstrn., Washington, 1977; spl. asst. to acting gen. counsel Dept. Energy, Washington, 1977-78; exec. asst. to dep. sec. Dept. Energy, 1978-79; dir. govt. relations Pennzoil Co., 1979-82, v.p. govt. relations, 1982-85; ptnr. Webster & Sheffield, 1985-90, Dickstein, Shapiro & Morin, Washington, 1990—; bd. dirs. Dauphin Deposit Bank and Trust Co., Harrisburg, Pa., chmn. trust and investment com. Home: 8909 Abbey Ter Potomac MD 20854-5434 Office: 2101 L St NW Ste 800 Washington DC 20037-1526

ZAVARIN, EUGENE, forestry science educator; b. Sombor, Yugoslavia, Feb. 21, 1924; came to U.S., 1950; s. Alexey K. and Iya A. (Shepkin) Z.; m. Valentina S. Kusubov, July 15, 1956; children: Ksenya, Sergey, Michael, Nina, Mavrick. BS, U. Goettingen, Fed. Republic Germany, 1949; PhD, U. Calif., Berkeley, 1954. Sr. lab. technician U. Calif., Berkeley, 1952-54; asst. specialist Forest Products Lab., Richmond, Calif., 1954-57, asst. forest product chemist, 1957-62, assoc. forest product chemist, 1962-68, forest product chemist, 1968—; lectr. wood chemistry U. Calif., Berkeley, 1962-75, prof. forestry, 1975-92; prof. forestry emeritus, 1992—; Reviewer grant proposals NSF. Mem. editorial adv. bd. Jour. Wood Chemistry and Tech.; contbr. articles to profl. jours. Fellow NIH, Institut de Chimie des Substances Naturelle, Gif-sur-Yvette, France, 1963; NSF grantee, 1965-67. Fellow Internat. Acad. Wood Sci.; mem. AAAS, Am. Chem. Soc., Sigma Xi. Republican. Avocations: travel, gardening, photography. Home: 280 Edgehill Way San Francisco CA 94127-1005 Office: U Calif Forest Products Lab 1301 S 46th St Richmond CA 94804-4603

ZAVIS, MICHAEL WILLIAM, lawyer; b. Chgo., Apr. 19, 1937; s. Herbert and Ruth (Kanes) Z.; m. Joan Gordon, June 1960; children: Amy Zavis Perlmutter, Cathy. BS, U. Pa., Wharton, 1958; JD, U. Chgo., 1961. Bar. Ill., U.S. Dist. (no. dist.) Ill., U.S. Ct. Appeals (7th cir.). Assoc. Peebles, Greenberg & Keele, Chgo., 1961-63, Greenberger, Krauss & Jacobs, Chgo., 1964-69; ptnr. Goldberg, Weigle, Mallin & Gitles, Chgo., 1969-74, Katten, Muchin & Zavis, Chgo., 1974—; bd. dirs. Ill. Devel. Fin. Authority; mem. adv. com. Sch. Social Svcs. U. Chgo. Editor U. Chgo. Law Rev., 1960-61. Fellow ABA, Ill. State Bar Assn., Chgo. Bar Assn.; mem. Bryn Mawr Country Club (Lincolnwood, Ill.) (past pres.), Standard Club, Boca Rio Country Club. Office: Katten Muchin & Zavis 525 W Monroe St Ste 1600 Chicago IL 60661-3629

ZAWADA, EDWARD THADDEUS, JR., physician, educator; b. Chgo., Oct. 3, 1947; s. Edward Thaddeus and Evelyn Mary (Kovarek) Z.; m. Nancy Ann Stephen, Mar. 26, 1977; children: Elizabeth, Nicholas, Victoria, Alexandra. BS summa cum laude, Loyola U., Chgo., 1969; MD summa cum laude, Loyola-Stritch Sch. Medicine, 1973. Diplomate Am. Bd. Internal Medicine, Am. Bd. Nephrology, Am. Bd. Nutrition, Am. Bd. Critical Care, Am. Bd. Geriatrics, Am. Bd. Clin. Pharm. Intern UCLA Hosp., 1973, resident, 1974-76; asst. prof. medicine UCLA, 1978-79, U. Utah, Salt Lake City, 1979-81; assoc. prof. medicine Med. Coll. Va., Richmond, 1981-83; assoc. prof. medicine, physiology & pharmacology U. S.D. Sch. Medicine, Sioux Falls, 1983-86, Freeman prof., chmn. dept. Internal Medicine, 1987—, chief div. nephrology and hypertension, 1983-88, pres. univ. physician's practice plan, 1992—; chief renal sect. Salt Lake VA Med. Ctr., 1980-81; asst. chief med. service McGuire VA Med. Ctr., Richmond, 1981-83. Editor: Geriatric Nephrology and Urology, 1984; contbr. articles to profl. publs. Pres. Minnehaha div. Am. Heart Assn., 1984-87, pres. Dakota affiliate Am. Heart Assn., 1989-91. VA Hosp. System grantee, 1981-85, 85-88; Health and Human Svcs. grantee Pub. Health Scvs. Rsch. Adminstrn. Bureau Health Profl., 1993—. Fellow ACP, Am. Coll. Chest Physicians, Am. Coll. Nutrition, Am. Coll. Clin. Pharmacology, Internat. Coll. Angiology, Am. Coll. Angiology, Am. Coll. Clin. Pharmacology, Royal Soc. Medicine; mem. Internat. Soc. Nephrology, Am. Soc. Nephrology, Am. Soc. Pharmacology and Exptl. Therapeutics, Am. Physiol. Soc., Am. Inst. Nutrition, Am. Soc. Clin. Nutrition, Am. Geriatric Soc., Westward Ho Country Club. Democrat. Roman Catholic. Avocations: golf, tennis, skiing, cinema, music. Home: 2908 S Duchess Ave Sioux Falls SD 57103-4826 Office: U SD Sch Medicine 1400 W 22nd St Sioux Falls SD 57105-1505

ZAWADA, SANDRA M., protective service official; b. Hartford, Conn., Aug. 12, 1961; d. Chester and Helen (Kywan) Z.; 1 child, Christopher. AS, Post Coll., 1981. Correctional officer Bridgeport Correctional Inst., Dept. Corrections, State of Conn., Bridgeport, 1986-89, Gates Correctional Inst., Dept. Corrections, State of Conn., Niantic, 1989-92; correctional lt. Garner Correctional Inst., Dept. Corrections, State of Conn., Newtown, 1992-94, correctional capt., 1994—. Office: Garner Correctional Inst 50 Nunnawauk Rd Newtown CT 06470-2319

ZAWINUL, JOSEF, bandleader, composer, keyboardist, synthesist; b. Vienna, Austria, July 7, 1932; came to U.S., 1959; s. Josef and Maria (Hameder) Z.; m. Maxine Byars, Mar. 16, 1964; children—Anthony, Erich, Ivan. Student, Realtymnasium, Vienna, 1945-49, Vienna Conservatory Music, 1942-47; Dr. honoris Causa, 1969. Appeared with Vienna Radio Orch., 1952-58, Maynard Ferguson, 1959; mem. Fatty George Band, 1956-58; accompanist Dinah Washington, 1959-61, Joe Williams, 1961; mem. Cannonball Adderley Quintet, 1961-70; recs. with Miles Davis include Bitches Brew, In a Silent Way; founder own group Weather Report, 1970-85, Zawinul Syndicate, 1985—; recs. include: Weather Report, Vitous, 1971, I Sing the Body Electric, 1972, Tale Spinnin', Black Market, 1974, Heavy Weather, 1977, Mr. Gone, 1978,Mysterious Traveler, Night Passage, Sportin Life, Weather Report with Jaco Pastorius, 1981, This is This, 1986, (with Miles Davis), In a Silent Way, 1969, Bitches Brew, 1970, (with Salifkeita) Amen, 1992, (solo) Dialects, Zawinul, (with Zawinul Syndicate) Immigrants, Black Water, 1989, Lost Tribes. Recipient Jazz Record of Year award 5 of 8 albums, 1973-78; named Best Synthesizer player Downbeat mag., 1984, 85, 89. Address: Internat Music Network 2 Main St # FL4 Gloucester MA 01930-5726

ZAWISTOWSKI, STEPHEN LOUIS, psychologist, educator; b. Lackawanna, N.Y., July 28, 1955; s. Louis Henry and Alice Theresa (Bartus) Z.; m. Jane Elaine Clark, May 26, 1979; 1 child, Matthew. BA, Canisius Coll., 1977; AM, U. Ill., 1979, PhD, 1983. Vis. asst. prof. Ind. U., Bloomington, 1983-84, postdoctoral fellow, 1984-85; asst. prof. St. John's U., N.Y.C., 1985-88; sr. v.p. ASPCA, N.Y.C., 1988—. Co-author: Animal Rights Handbook, 1990; co-editor: For Kids Who Love Animals, 1991; contbg. editor Animal Watch Mag.; co-exec. producer (film) Question of Respect, 1990 (silver apple award 1990); bd. editors Psychologists for the Ethical Treatment of Animals, 1988-95; founding co-editor Jour. Applied Animal Welfare Sci.; contbr. articles to profl. jours. Scoutmaster Boy Scouts Am., S.I., 1988—; asst. coach S.I. Youth Soccer, 1986-95; bd. dirs. Nat. Coun. on Pet Population Study and Policy; mem. steering com. N.Y. State Watchable Wildlife Program. Recipient Stan Lesny scholarship Kosciuszki Found., 1977, U. Ill. Grad. fellowship, 1977, Postdoctoral fellowship NSF, 1984; named Psychologist of Yr., Psychologists for Ethical Treatment of Animals, 1989. Mem. Animal Behavior Soc., Order of Arrow, Sigma Xi. Achievements include research in genetics and animal learning. Office: ASPCA 424 E 92nd St New York NY 10128-6804

ZAX, LEONARD A., lawyer; b. Paterson, N.J., July 16, 1950; s. Harry and Shirley Jeanne (Hollander) Z.; m. Helen Kemp, May 25, 1980; children: David Hollander, Laura Alexandra. BA, U. Chgo., 1971; M of City Planning, Harvard U., 1975, JD, 1975. Bar: N.J. 1978, D.C. 1978. Spl. asst. to gen. counsel HUD, 1975-76, spl. asst. to sec. HUD, 1976-77; lectr., mem. faculty Harvard U., Cambridge, Mass., 1977-78; assoc. Fried, Frank, Harris, Shriver & Kampelman, Washington, 1977-82, ptnr., 1982-95; ptnr. Latham & Watkins, 1995—, also chmn. dept. real estate; co-chmn. Mayor's Downtown Housing Commn., Washington, 1986-89, D.C. Enterprise Zones Study Commn., 1986-89; co-chmn. Washington adv. com. Asian Real Estate Assn., Washington, 1991-92. Contbg. author Nat. Law Jour., L.A. Times, Harvard Law Bull., Real Estate Fin. Jour., Jour. RTC Real Estate, Urban Land, Washington Business jour., Washington Post; editor: Real Estate and the RTC: A Guide to Asset Purchases and Contracting, 1990. Trustee Nat. Bldg. Mus., D.C. Preservation League, 1988-95, Greater Washington Rsch. Ctr.; mem. Fannie May nat. adv. com. on real estate devel., Harvard U., 1990-92. Mem. ABA (chmn. com. on housing and urban devel. law 1986-89, steering com. representation of the Homeless Project 1988-91, governing bd. forum com. affordable housing and community devel. 1991-94), D.C. Bar Assn., Urban Land Inst. Home: 4511 28th St NW Washington DC 20008-1035 Office: Latham & Watkins Ste 1300 1001 Pennsylvania Ave NW Washington DC 20004-2505

ZAX, MELVIN, psychologist, educator; b. Cambridge, Mass., Apr. 14, 1928; s. Joseph and Sadie (Kirshner) Z.; m. Ruth Leah Vogel, Apr. 23, 1977; children: Jeffrey S., David B., Jonathan B. A.B., Boston U., 1951, A.M., 1952; Ph.D., U. Tenn., 1955. Clin. psychologist U. Tenn., Knoxville, 1955-56; staff psychologist St. Elizabeths Hosp., Washington, 1956-57; asst. to assoc. prof. psychology U. Rochester, N.Y., 1957-67; assoc. prof. psychology, 1962-67; prof. U. Rochester, N.Y., 1967-93, prof. emeritus, 1993—; pvt. practice, 1973—; chmn. exptl. and spl. tng. rev. com. NIMH, 1970-71. Author: (with G. Stricker) Patterns of Psychopathology, 1963, (with E.L. Cowen) Abnormal Psychology: Changing Conceptions, 1972, (with G.A. Specter) An Introduction to Community Psychology, 1974, (with M. Nichols) Catharsis in Psychotherapy, 1977; editor: (with Stricker) The Study of Abnormal Behavior: Selected Readings, 1964, (with Cowen and E.A. Gardner) Emergent Approaches to Mental Health Problems, 1967, (with D. Dorr and J. Bonner) The Psychology of Discipline, 1983; adv. editor Jour. Cons. and Clin. Psychology, 1965-81; contbr. articles to profl. jours. Served with AUS, 1946-47. NIMH spl. research fellow Psykologisk Inst., Copenhagen, 1966-67. Fellow Am. Psychol. Assn.; mem. Eastern Psychol. Assn., AAUP, Phi Beta Kappa, Sigma Xi, Phi Kappa Phi. Home: 27 Sky Ridge Dr Rochester NY 14625-2167 Office: 625 Panorama Trl Ste 2 Rochester NY 14625-2432

ZAYAS-BAZAN, EDUARDO, foreign language educator; b. Camagüey, Cuba, Nov. 17, 1935; came to U.S., 1962, naturalized, 1969; s. Manuel Eduardo and Aida Modesta (Loret de Mola); m. Carolyn M. Novak, Sept. 12, 1987; children: Eduardo, Elena Maráa. Dr. en Derecho, U. Nat. José, 1958; MS, Kans. State Tchrs.' Coll., 1966. Social worker Cuban Refugee Asst. Program, 1962-64; Spanish tchr. Plattsmouth High Sch., 1964-65, Topeka West High Sch., 1965-66; Spanish instr. Appalachian State U., 1966-68; asst. prof. East Tenn. State U., Johnson City, 1968-73; assoc. prof. East Tenn. State U., 1973-79, prof, 1979—, chmn. fgn. lang. dept., 1973-93. Author: (with P. Ferreiro) Cómo dominar la reducción, 1989, (with G. Fernández de la Torriente) Cómo aumentar su vocabulario 3, Cómo escribir cartas eficaces, 1989, (with N.A. Humbach and José B. Fernández) Nuestro mundo, 1990, (with José Fernáncez) !Arriba!, 1993, (with Carolyn M. Novak) No se qeuivoque con el inglé, 1993, El inglés que usted no sabe que sabe, Priomera y Segunda Serie, 1993; editor: (with Anthony G. Lozano) Del amor a la revolución, 1975, (with L. Suárez) de aquí y de allá, 1980, (with G. J. Fernández Aií somos, 1983; translator: Secret Report on Cuban Revolution, 1981. Pres. Sister Cities Internat., Johnson City, 1971-76. Recipient Disting. Faculty award E. Tenn. State U., 1978. Mem. ACTFL, AAUSC, Am. Assn. Tchrs. Spanish and Portuguese (pres. 1985), Tenn. Fgn. Lang. Teaching Assn. (pres. 1980, Jacqueline Elliott award 1989), Nat. Assn. Cuban-Am. Educators (pres. 1991-93, chair bd. dirs. 1994—), Sigma Delta Pi (Premio Martel 1984), Pi Delta Phi. Home: 2310 David Miller Rd Johnson City TN 37604-3510 Office: East Tenn State U Dept Fgn Langs Johnson City TN 37614

ZAYEK, FRANCIS MANSOUR, bishop; b. Manzanillo, Cuba, Oct. 18, 1920; s. Mansour and Mary (Coury) Z. Student, St. Joseph's Catholic U., Beirut, 1938; D.D., U. Propagation of Faith, 1947, Ph.D., 1947; D.C.L., Lateran U., 1951. Ordained priest Roman Catholic Ch., 1946; rector Maronite Cathedral of Holy Family, Cairo, 1951-56; Oriental sec. to Vatican Apostolic Internunciature; mem. Archdiocesan Tribunal, 1951-56; promoter of justice Sacred Roman Rota, 1956-58; prof. Oriental canon law Internat. Coll. St. Anselm, Rome, 1958-60, Lateran U., Rome, 1960-61; aux. bishop to Cardinal James De Barros Camera; archbishop of Rio de Janeiro, 1962; consecrated maronite bishop, 1962; titular bishop of Callinicum, maronite bishop Rio de Janeiro, 1962-64; presided over First Ann. Maronite Conv., Washington, 1964; first maronite exarch of U.S.A., 1966—, first eparch of St. Maron of Detroit, 1972-77, first eparch of St. Maron of Bklyn., 1977—, given title of archbishop, 1982. Decorated knight comdr. Equestrian Order of Holy Sepulchre of Jerusalem; recipient medal of merit Govt. of Republic Italy, 1966. Address: Eparch of St Maron 294 Howard Ave PO Box 010-360 Staten Island NY 10301

ZAZULIA, IRWIN, retail store executive. Pres., chief exec. officer Hecht's, Arlington, Va. Office: Hecht's 685 N Glebe Rd Arlington VA 22203-2110*

ZBACNIK, RAYMOND ERIC, process engineer; b. Cleve., June 28, 1951; s. Eric Victor and Jeanette Beatrice (Brock) Z. BSChE, Purdue U., 1973; MEChE, Manhattan Coll., 1977; postgrad., Stevens Inst. Tech., 1977-78, Ind. U., Purdue U., 1985. Process engr. Foster Wheeler Corp., Livingston, N.J., 1974-78, sr. process engr., 1979-81, process supr., 1981-84; process engr. Norton Co., Stow, Ohio, 1988-90, Babcock & Wilcox, Barberton, Ohio, 1990—. Mem. AIChE, Am. Chem. Soc., Instn. Chem. Engrs. World Apostolate of Fatima. Roman Catholic. Avocations: prayer, reading, hiking, writing. Home: 4388 Millburn Ave Stow OH 44224-2879 Office: Babcock & Wilcox Utility & Environ Power Divsn 20 S Van Buren Ave Barberton OH 44203-0351

ZBIEGIEN, ANDREA, educator, consultant, educational administrator; b. Berea, Ohio, May 12, 1944; d. Leopold and Anna Meri (Voskovich) Z. BS in Edn., St. John Coll., 1969; MS in Edn., John Carroll U., 1973; MDiv, Grad. Theol. Union, 1986, D of Ministry, 1988. Tchr. jr. high sch. Diocese of Cleve., 1964-76, instr. dept. religious edn., 1971-82, dir. religious edn., 1976-82; diocesan dir. religious edn. Diocese of Toledo, 1982-87; instr. Dept. Christian Formation Diocese of Savannah, Ga., 1987—; dir. religious edn. Diocese of Savannah, 1987—; substitute tchr., Cleve., also Brunswick, Ga., 1976—; cons. Benziger Pub. co., Ohio, 1971-78, Our Sunday Visitor Pubs., 1978-90, Silver, Burdett & Ginn, Savannah, Charleston, St. Augustine, 1988—; adj. prof. St. John U. Grad. Theol. Sem., summers 1978—. Author: RCIA: Parish Team Formation, 1987; producer, author: (videos) RCIA:

Parish Team Formation, 1987; contbr. articles to profl. jours. Facilitator Bishop's Task Force Action for a Change, Cleve., 1969-72; advocate, facilitator Systematic Techniques of Effective Parenting, Huron County, Ohio, 1982-87; advocate Commn. on Children and Youth, Glynn County, Ga., 1989—; vol. Medicine for World's Poor. Recipient scholarship KC, Cleve., 1961-69. Mem. AAUW, ASCD, YWCA, NPCD, Nat. Cath. Edn. Assn., Sisters for Christian Cmty., Ind. Order of Foresters, Golden Isles Fiberarts Guild. Avocations: fiberarts, creative writing, oil painting and sketching. Home: 707A Newcastle St Brunswick GA 31520-8012 Office: SFX Christian Formation Ctr 1116 Richmond St Brunswick GA 31520

ZBORNIK, JOSEPH JOHN, education educator, accounting consultant; b. Chgo., May 30, 1912; s. Joseph and Marie (Skerik) Z.; m. Evelynne Marie Waldon, Aug. 14, 1935; children: Joseph John (dec.), Gail Patricia Frank. BS, U. Ill., 1933, MS in Acctg., 1938; EdD, Loyola U., Chgo., 1961. CPA, Ill.; cert. elem. and secondary tchr., Ill. Tchr. bus. edn. various high schs., Chgo., 1933-1940; sr. field auditor Ill. Dept. Fin., Chgo., 1940-42; tchr. bus. edn. Marshall High Sch., Chgo., 1942-44; instr. Wright Coll., Chgo., 1944-51, chmn. bus. dept., 1951-53; supr. bus. edn. Chgo. Bd. Edn., 1953-58; prin. Goodrich Elem. Sch., Chgo., 1958-61, Austin Evening Sch., Chgo., 1960-65, Brown Elem. Sch., Chgo., 1961-63, Manley Upper Grade Ctr., Chgo., 1963-65, Marshall High Sch., Chgo., 1965-67; supt. dist. 12 Chgo. Pub. Schs., 1967-77; adj. prof. Roosevelt U., Chgo., 1977—; sec. E.F. Felber Co., Maywood, Ill., 1942-83; ptnr. Brook, Zbornik & Assocs., Chgo., 1946-75; Chgo. rep. Ill. State Com., North Cen. Assn. Schs., 1962-67; treas., bd. dirs. Rolling Lns., Countryside, Ill., 1965-84; evaluator CSA scholarships, Berwyn, Ill., 1966—; pres. Dist. Supts. Assn., Chgo., 1971; owner J.J. Zbornik & Assocs., 1975-90. Author: (with others) Public Accounting, 1953, Development of American Business, 1954, Clerical Bookkeeping, 1957; mem. editorial staff LaSalle Extension U., Chgo., 1949-53. Mem. scholarship com. Czechoslovak Soc. Am. Recipient Chicagoland Healthorama Community Service award, 1974, Chgo. Commn. on Human Relations plaque, 1977, Sr. Citizens award mayor City of Chgo., 1985, Man of Yr. Trophy, Archer Brighton Community Conservation Council, 1971, Spl. Appreciation Trophy, Archer Brighton Community Conservation Council, 1977; Zbornik Hall auditorium named in his honor Curie High Sch., 1975. Mem. Nat. Soc. for Study of Edn., Ret. Tchrs. Assn. Chgo. (treas. 1978-92, fin. cons. 1993—). Roman Catholic. Lodge: Kiwanis (pres. 1985-86). Avocations: performing arts, sports, reading. Home: 3219 Clarence Ave Berwyn IL 60402-3558

ZDANIS, RICHARD ALBERT, academic administrator; b. Balt., July 15, 1935; s. Albert Francis and Elsie (Kral) Z.; m. Barbara Rosenberger, June 5, 1955; children: Michael Richard, Carole Lynn. BA, Johns Hopkins U., 1957, PhD in Physics, 1960. Rsch. assoc. Princeton (N.J.) U., 1960-61, instr., 1961-62; asst. prof., then assoc. prof. Johns Hopkins U., Balt., 1962-69, prof., 1969-88, assoc. provost, 1975-79, v.p. for adminstrv. svcs., 1977-79, vice provost, 1979-88; provost Case Western Res. U., Cleve., 1988—; cons. Naval Ordnance Lab., 1967-68, 69-74. Bd. dirs. Great Lakes Mus., Cleve. Edn. Found., Cleve. chpt. ARC, N.E. Ohio Coun. on Higer Edn.; mem. governing coun. Ohio LINK, 1994—. Mem. AAAS, Am. Phys. Soc., Associated Univs. Inc. (bd. dirs.), Assn. Univs. for Rsch. in Astronomy (bd. dirs.). Office: Case Western Reserve Univ Office of Provost 10900 Euclid Ave Cleveland OH 44106-7004

ZDIARA, BRANKO FERDINAND, picture gallery executive; b. Bosanska Gradiska, Switzerland, Feb. 24, 1929; s. Ferdinand and Djoko (Chupkovich) Z.; m. Visic Olga Miodrag, Feb. 6, 1954 (dec. Aug. 13, 1978); children: Md Tatjana, Borislav. Diploma, H.S. Phys. Edn., Belgrade, 1951; Diploma in Tchg., U. Belgrade, Yugoslavia, 1954; diploma, U. Oslo, 1962. Cert. tchr., Yugoslavia. Phys. edn. tchr. Gimnasium, Kraljevo, Yugoslavia, 1951-56, Zemun, Yugoslavia, 1957-58; phys. edn. tchr. Tech. Sch., Belgrade, 1959-60, 63-64; rsch. fellow, superior Fed. Inst. Phys. Culture, Belgrade, 1961-62; mgr. Tech. Sch., Belgrade, 1965-68, Sports Palace, New Belgrade, 1969-70; physiotherapeute Hosp. and Ctr. Thermal, Yverdon, Switzerland, 1971-91; exec. Entreprise Brancomme, Grandson, Switzerland, 1992—; participant XISvesokolski slet Gymnastic Union Yugoslavia, Prague, Czechoslavokia, 1948; mem. rsch. group H.S. of Phys. Edn., Belgrade, 1948-49; observer World Congress Sports Medicine Personnel, Belgrade, 1954, Gimnaestrade, Stuttgart, Germany, 1961; del. to Internat. Soc. Hygiene, Phys. Edn. and Recreation, Paris, 1964; lectr. in field of phys. edn., 1956-64. Contbr. articles to profl. jours. Monitor, coach with gym and sports societies, Yugoslavia, 1951-64; basketball coach Yverdon (Switzerland) Sports, 1975-77. Served with Yugoslavian Infantry, 1944-45. Avocations: writing, painting, sports. Home: Rue de Neuchatel 6, 1422 Grandson Switzerland Office: Entreprise Brancomme, Rue de Neuchatel 6, 1422 Grandson Switzerland

ZEBROSKI, EDWIN LEOPOLD, consulting engineer; b. Chgo., Apr. 1, 1921; s. Peter Paul and Sophie (Rydz) Z.; m. Gisela Karin Rudolph, Sept. 6, 1969; children: Lars, Zoe, Susan, Peggy. BS, U. Chgo., 1941; PhD, U. Calif., Berkeley, 1947. Registered prof. engr., Calif. Project engr. Gen. Electric Co., Schenectady, N.Y., 1947-53; mgr. devel. engring. Gen. Electric Co., San Jose, Calif., 1958-73; mgr. engring. SRI Internat., Menlo Park, Calif., 1954-58, dir. systems and materials dept., 1974-79; dir. nuclear safety analysis ctr. EPRI, Palo Alto, Calif., 1979-81; v.p. engring. INPO, Atlanta, 1981-83; chief nuclear scientist EPRI, 1983-87; dir. risk mgmt. svcs. APTECH Engring. Svcs., Sunnyvale, Calif., 1988—; vis. prof. Purdue U., West Lafayette, Ind., 1977-78; cons. OTA, Washington, 1980, 82-83, Dept. Energy, Washington, 1985-90, panels Nat. Rsch. Coun., 1982-90, Electricite de France, 1986-87, Dept. Interior, Washington, 1987-89, EPRI, Palo Alto, 1988-94, Acad. Sci., USSR, 1987, Juelich Lab., Germany, 1988; mem. commn. engring. edn. NRC, Washington, 1970-73. Contbr. chpts. to books, numerous articles to profl. jours.; patentee in field. Pres. bd. Unitarian Ch., Palo Alto, 1967-68. Recipient Charles A. Coffin award Gen. Electric Co., Schenectady, 1954. Fellow AAAS, Am. Nuclear Soc. (bd. exec. com. 1969-71), Am. Inst. Chemists; mem. NAE (chmn. energy com. 1984-86, chmn. mem. com. 1986-87, policy com. 1995-96), Am. Phys. Soc., Soc. for Risk Analysis. Avocations: safety and risk management, decision analysis, music, writing. Office: APTECH Engring Svcs 1282 Reamwood Ave Sunnyvale CA 94089-2233

ZECCA, JOHN ANDREW, retired association executive; b. Bklyn., June 18, 1914; s. Joseph and Elvira (Orsi) Z.; m. Jean Ann Scott, June 27, 1964; 1 son, John Andrew. Student, Heffley Queensboro Coll., Ridgewood, N.Y., 1931, N.Y. U., 1933-36. Auditor ASCE, 1936-50, comptroller, 1950-60; registered rep. Goodbody & Co., 1960-61; pvt. cons. practice, 1961-64; sec., gen. mgr. United Engring. Trustees, 1965-81; trustee Engring. Index, Inc., 1967-81; sec. Engring. Found., 1965-81. John Fritz Medal Bd. Award, 1965-81; Daniel Guggenheim Medal Bd. Award, 1965-81. Mem. East Side Assn., ASCE, Council Engring. and Sci. Soc. Execs., Am. Soc. Assn. Execs. Home: 15 Hillside Ter Suffern NY 10901-2104

ZECHELLA, ALEXANDER PHILIP, oil company executive, former naval officer; b. Newport, Ky., 1920; s. Nicholas and Cecila (Rizzi) Z.; m. Jean Bary, June 24, 1942; children: Bary, Pamela, Amy. B.S. in Elec. Engring., U.S. Naval Acad., 1942; B.S., Rensselaer Poly Inst., 1947, M.S. in C.E., 1948. Commd. ensign U.S. Navy, 1942, advanced through grades to comdr., 1953, served, 1939-53, destroyer duty World War II, Korean War; design engr. Nuclear Submarine Bettis Atomic Power Lab., Westinghouse Corp., Pitts., 1953-56; various positions in nuclear power reactors Nuclear Submarine Bettis Atomic Power Lab., Westinghouse Corp., 1961-71; pres. Offshore Power Systems subs. Westinghouse Corp., Jacksonville, Fla., 1972-79; corp. v.p. Westinghouse Corp, N.Y.C., 1979-80; design. mgr. Shippingport Power Sta., Pitts., 1956-59; constrn. mgr. prototype nuclear aircraft carrier USS Enterprise, Idaho Falls, Idaho, 1959-61; exec. v.p. Charter Co., Jacksonville, Fla., 1980-84; pres., chief operating officer, chief exec. officer, dir Charter Co., Jacksonville, 1984-85; chmn., pres. Charter Oil Co., Jacksonville, 1980-83; chmn. bd. dirs. Environ. Recovery Group. Trustee St. Vincent's Hosp., Jacksonville, Jacksonville U.; bd. dirs. Tournament Players Championship Charities, Inc.; chmn. St. Vincent's Found., Inc. Mem. Tu Beta Pi, Chi Epsilon. Republican. Episcopalian. Clubs: River, Sawgrass Country. Lodges: Masons; Shriners. Home: 1301 1st St S Jacksonville FL 32250 Office: PO Box 548 251 Levy Rd Atlantic Beach FL 32233-2613

ZECHMAN, EDWIN KERPER, JR., medical facility administrator; b. Harrisburg, Pa., Jan. 22, 1948; married. BA, Shippensburg U., 1970, MA, 1970; M Health Adminstrn., Ohio State U., 1974. Asst. adminstr. Children's Hosp. Med. Ctr., Akron, Ohio, 1974-78, assoc. adminstr., 1978-80; exec. dir. Children's Hosp., New Orleans, 1980-81, Children's Hosp. of Ala., birmingham, 1981-85; pres. Children's Hosp., Pitts., 1985-94; pres., CEO Children's Nat. Med. Ctr., Washington, 1994—. Recipient various cmty. svc. awards. Mem. AMA, Am. Hosp. Assn., Am. Coll. Healthcare Execs. Office: Children's Nat Med Ctr 111 Michigan Ave NW Washington DC 20010-2970*

ZECHMAN, FRED WILLIAM, JR., physiologist, educator, administrator; b. Youngstown, Ohio, Mar. 16, 1928; s. Frederick William and Kathryn S. (Ritz) Z.; m. Nancy Ann Bussard, June 24, 1950; children: Jami Ann, Frederick William III. B.S., Otterbein Coll., 1949; M.S., U. Md., 1951; Ph.D. (Univ. scholar), Duke U., 1957, postgrad. (Univ. fellow), 1956-57. Grad. asst. dept. zoology U. Md., 1949-51; biologist Office Naval Research, Washington, 1951-53; instr. in physiology Duke U., 1953-57; asst. prof. physiology Miami U., Oxford, Ohio, 1957-60; assoc. prof. Miami U., 1960-61; asst. prof. physiology and biophysics U. Ky. Coll. Medicine, 1961-62, assoc. prof., 1963-68, prof. physiology and biophys., 1986-93, chmn. dept. physiology and biophys., research prof., 1980-81, assoc. dean Grad. Sch., 1982-88, vice chancellor research and grad. studies, 1988-90, prof. emeritus, 1993—; vis. prof. U. Hawaii, 1971; bd. dirs. U. Ky. Research Found.; cons., lectr. in field; mem. internat. symposiums. Contbr. articles to profl. publs. Recipient Outstanding Preclin. Teaching award Student AMA, 1968-69, Faculty Sci. Achievement award Ky. Med. Assn., 1971; Am. Physiol. Soc. summer fellow, 1960; USAF grantee, 1960-66, 67-71; NIH grantee, 1966-71, 74-83. Mem. Aerospace Med. Assn., AAAS, Am. Physiol. Soc. (ednl. materials rev. bd. public affairs), Soc. Exptl. Biology and Medicine, Ky. Acad. Sci., Am. Thoracic Soc., Sigma Xi. Home: 6400 Head Rd Wilmington NC 28409-2220

ZECKENDORF, WILLIAM, JR., real estate developer; b. N.Y.C., Oct. 31, 1929; s. William Zeckendorf and Irma (Levy) Kolodin; m. Guri Lie, Feb. 4, 1956 (div. Aug. 1963); children: William Lie, Arthur William; m. Nancy King, Oct. 24, 1963. Student, U. Ariz., 1948-50; LHD (hon.), L.I.U., 1993. Pres. Webb & Knapp, Inc., N.Y.C., 1950-65; chmn. bd. Gen. Property Corp., N.Y.C., 1965-78; mng. gen. ptnr., developer Zeckendorf Co., N.Y.C., 1981—. Chmn. bd. L.I. U., Greenvale, N.Y., 1987-92, trustee, 1959-94, now emeritus. With U.S. Army, 1952-54. Recipient Weizmann Medallion Weizmann Inst. Sci., N.Y., 1985; named Man of Yr. West Side C. of C., N.Y.C., 1984. Mem. Real Estate Bd. N.Y. (bd. govs. 1984-94), Realty Found. N.Y. (bd. dirs. 1976—, Man of Yr. award 1987), Confrerie des Chevaliers du Tastevin (grand senechal 1992—), Commanderie de Bordeaux, Sky Club (N.Y.C.). Republican. Jewish. Home: 770 Lexington Ave 12th Fl New York NY 10021 Office: Zeckendorf Co Inc 245 Park Ave Fl 16 New York NY 10167-0002

ZECKHAUSER, RICHARD JAY, economist, educator; b. Phila., Nov. 1, 1940; s. Julius Nathaniel and Estelle (Borgenicht) Z.; m. Nancy Mackell Hoover, Sept. 9, 1967; children: Bryn Gordon, Benjamin Rennell. A.B., Harvard U., 1962, Ph.D., 1969. Jr. fellow Soc. Fellows Harvard U., 1965-68, mem. faculty, 1968—, prof. polit. econ. Kennedy Sch., 1972—, now Frank P. Ramsey prof. polit. economy; bd. dirs. Recovery Engring., Inc., Johnson-Grace Co., Comm. Group Ins., founder, bd. dirs. Niederhoffer, Cross & Zeckhauser, 1968-84. Co-author: A Primer for Policy Analysis, 1978, Demographic Dimensions of the New Republic, 1981; editor or co-editor: Benefit-Cost and Policy Analysis, 1974, What Role for Government, 1982, Principals and Agents: The Structure of Business, 1985, Am. Soc. Pub. and Pvt. Responsibilities, 1986; Privatization and State-Owned Enterprise: Lessons from the United Kingdom, Canada and the United States, 1988, Strategy and Choice, 1991, Wise Choices, Games, Decisions, and Negotiations, 1996. contbr. more than 150 articles to profl. jours. Fellow Econometric Soc., Assn. for Pub. Policy and Mgmt., Am. Acad. Arts and Scis. Champion numerous regional and nat. contract bridge competitions. Home: 138 Irving St Cambridge MA 02138-1929 Office: Harvard U John F Kennedy Sch Govt 79 JFK St Cambridge MA 02138-5801

ZEDILLO PONCE DE LEÓN, ERNESTO, president of Mexico; b. Mexico City, Apr. 27, 1951; s. Rodolfo Zedillo Castillo and Martha Alicia Ponce de Leon; m. Nilda Patricia Velasco Nuñez; children: Ernesto, Emiliano, Carlos, Nild Patricia, Rodrigo. Student, Instituto Politécnico Nacional, Bradford U., U. Colo.; MA, Yale U., 1977, PhD, 1981. With Partido Revolucionario Institucional, 1971—, Instituto de Estudios Políticos, Económicos y Sociales; econ. rschr. Dirreción Gen. de Programación Económica y Social; lectr. Colegio de Mex., 1978-80; dep. mgr. finance and econ. rsch., advisor to bd. dirs. Banco de Mex.; dep. sec. for planning and budget Govt. Mex., Mexico City, 1985-88, sec. for planning and budget, 1988-92, sec. public edn., 1992-93, pres., 1994—; campaing mgr. presdl. nominee Luis Donald Colosio Partido Revolucionario Institucional, 1993-94. Campaign mgr. Luis Donaldo Colosio. Office: Office of Pres, Los Pinos Puerta No 1, 11109 Mexico City Mexico*

ZEDLER, JOY BUSWELL, ecological sciences educator; b. Sioux Falls, S.D., Oct. 15, 1943; d. Francis H. and Charlotte (Johnson) Buswell; m. Paul H. Zedler, June 26, 1965; children: Emily and Sarah (twins). BS, Augustana Coll., 1964; MS, U. Wis., 1966, PhD, 1968. Instr. U. Mo., Columbia, 1968-69; prof. San Diego State U., 1969—; mem. Nat. Wetland Tech. Com., Water Sci. Tech. Bd. Nat. Rsch. Coun., 1991-94; dir. Pacific Estuarine Rsch. Lab., 1985—, Coastal and Marine Inst., 1991-93; gov. bd. The Nature Conservancy, 1995—. Author: Ecology of Southern California Coastal Wetlands, 1982, Salt Marsh Restoration, 1984; co-author: A Manual for Assessing Natural and Restored Wetlands, 1990, Ecology of Tijuana Estuary, 1992. Fellow San Diego Natural History Mus.; mem. Ecol. Soc. Am. (mem. pub. affairs com. 1988-90), Soc. Wetlands Scientists, Am. Assn. Limnology and Oceanography. Achievements include pioneering studies of impacts of freshwater inflows to coastal wetlands in southwestern U.S. and Australia; contributions to understanding of coastal wetland functioning; development of methods for improving restoration projects in coastal wetlands; identification of shortcomings of ongoing coastal wetland restoration programs. Office: San Diego State U Biology Dept San Diego CA 92182-4614

ZEDROSSER, JOSEPH JOHN, lawyer; b. Milw., Jan. 24, 1938; s. Joseph and Rose (Zollner) Z. AB, Marquette U., 1959; LLB, Harvard U., 1963. Bar: N.Y. 1964, U.S. Dist. Ct. (so. dist.) N.Y. 1966, U.S. Dist. Ct. (ea. dist.) N.Y. 1971, U.S. Ct. Appeals (2d cir.) 1971, U.S. Ct. Appeals (D.C. Cir.) 1975, U.S. Supreme Ct. 1975. Assoc. William G. Mulligan, N.Y.C., 1964-67, Christy, Bauman, Frey and Christy and successors, N.Y.C., 1967-71; dir. community devel. unit Bedford-Stuyvesant Community Legal Svcs. Corp., N.Y.C., 1971-73; assoc. atty. fed. defender svcs. unit Legal Aid Soc., N.Y.C., 1973-74; asst. atty. gen. Environ. Protection Bur., N.Y. State Dept. Law, N.Y.C., 1974-80; regional counsel EPA, N.Y.C., 1980-82; assoc. prof. St. John's U. Sch. Law, N.Y.C., 1982-86; ptnr. Rivkin, Radler, Dunne & Bayh, Uniondale, N.Y., 1986-89, Breed, Abbott & Morgan, N.Y.C., 1989-93, Whitman Breed Abbott & Morgan, N.Y.C., 1993-95; v.p. CPR Inst. for Dispute Resolution, N.Y.C., 1996—. Lectr., contbr. to course handbooks for courses sponsored by Practicing Law Inst. and other assns. Lt. USNR, 1965-74, USAR, 1963-65. Mem. ABA, Assn. of Bar of City of N.Y., N.Y. State Bar Assn. (mem. Environ. Law Sect. Exec. Com.), Alpha Sigma Nu. Roman Catholic. Home: 45 East End Ave Apt 11F New York NY 10028 Office: CPR Inst Dispute Resolution 366 Madison Ave New York NY 10017-3122

ZEFF, OPHELIA HOPE, lawyer; b. Oak Park, Ill., Aug. 19, 1934; d. Bernard Allen and Esther (Levinsohn) Gurvis; m. David Zeff, Dec. 29, 1957 (div. 1983); children: Sally Lyn Zeff Propper, Betsy Zeff Russell, Ellen, Adam; m. John Canterbury Davis, Sept. 18, 1987. BA, Calif. State U., 1956; JD, U. Pacific, 1975. Bar: Calif. 1975. Reporter Placerville (Calif.) Mountain Dem., 1956-57, Salinas Californian, 1957-59; corr. Modesto (Calif.) Bee, 1962-64; atty. ALRB, Sacramento, 1975-76, Yolo County Counsel, Woodland, Calif., 1976-78, Law Office of O.H. Zeff, Woodland, 1978-85; employee rels. officer Yolo County, 1985-87; ptnr. Littler, Mendelson, Fastiff, Tichy & Mathiason, Sacramento, 1987—. Mem. Vallejo (Calif.) Sch. Bd., 1971-74, pres., 1974; mem. Woodland Libr. Bd., 1982; v.p. LWV, Vallejo, 1972; mem. LWV, Sacramento, 1987—. Recipient Am. Jurisprudence Lawyer Coop. Pub., 1974. Mem. Sacramento County Bar, Sacramento Women Lawyers, Indsl. Rels. Assn. No. Calif., Traynor Soc. (life). Democrat. Jewish. Avocations: hiking, skiing, biking, reading, traveling. Office: Littler Mendelson Fastiff Tichy & Mathiason 400 Capitol Mall Fl 16 Sacramento CA 95814-4407

ZEFF, STEPHEN ADDAM, accounting educator; b. Chgo., July 26, 1933; s. Roy David and Hazel (Sex) Z. B.S., U. Colo., 1955, M.S., 1957; M.B.A., U. Mich., 1960, Ph.D., 1962; D in Econs. honoris causa, Turku Sch. Econs. and Bus. Adminstrn., Finland, 1990. Instr. U. Colo., 1955-57; teaching fellow, instr. U. Mich., 1958-61; asst. prof. acctg. Tulane U., New Orleans, 1961-63, assoc. prof., 1963-67, prof., 1967-77, W.R. Irby prof., 1977-78; prof. acctg. Rice U., 1978-79, Herbert S. Autrey prof., 1979—; prof. acctg. U. Limburg, The Netherlands, 1992-95; vis. assoc. prof. U. Calif.-Berkeley, 1964-65, U. Chgo., 1966; vis. prof. Instituto Tecnológico y de Estudios Superiores de Monterrey, Mex., 1969, Victoria U., Wellington, New Zealand, 1976, Harvard U., 1977-78, Northwestern U., 1982, 83, U. Tex.-Austin, 1986, Free U. Amsterdam, 1990, 91, U. Nijenrode, 1994—; spl. lectr., hon. sr. Fulbright scholar Monash U., Australia, 1972. Author: Uses of Accounting for Small Business, 1962, American Accounting Association, Its First 50 Years, 1966, Forging Accounting Principles in Five Countries: A History and an Analysis of Trends, 1972, Forging Accounting Principles in Australia, 1973, Forging Accounting in New Zealand, 1979, Company Financial Reporting: A Historical and Comparative Study of the Dutch Regulatory Process, 1992; editor: Business Schools and the Challenge of International Business, 1968, Asset Appreciation, Business Income and Price-Level Accounting: 1918-1935, 1976, The Accounting Postulates and Principles Controversy of the 1960s, 1982, The U.S. Accounting Profession in the 1890s and Early 1900s, 1988; co-editor: Financial Accounting Theory, Vol. II, 1969; Essays in Honor of William A. Paton: Pioneer Accounting Theorist, 1979, Sourcebook on Accounting Principles and Auditing Procedures 1917-1953, 1984; book rev. editor Acctg. Rev., 1962-66, editor, 1977-82; rev. editor Acctg. Horizons, 1995—; founder, editor Boletín Interamericano de Contabilidad, 1968-71; contbr. articles to profl. jours. Mem. Am. Acctg. Assn. (dir. edn. 1969-71, pres. 1985-86, named Outstanding Acctg. Educator 1988), European Acctg. Assn. (exec. com. 1981—), Tex. Soc. CPAs (hon.), Am. Econ. Assn., Inst. Mgmt. Accts., Fin. Execs. Inst., AAUP. Club: Harvard (N.Y.C.). Home: 4545 Acacia St Bellaire TX 77401-3701 Office: Rice University PO Box 1892 Houston TX 77251-1892

ZEFFIRELLI, FRANCO, theater and film director; b. Florence, Italy, Feb. 12, 1923; s. Ottorino Corsi and Alaide Cipriani. Attended, U. Architecture, Florence.; DHL, U. San Diego, 1980; PhD, U. Tel Aviv, 1993. Actor in Crime and Punishment, 1946, Euridyce, 1947; appeared in film Onorevole Angelina, 1948; set designer for various prodns. of Luchino Visconti, 1949-52, A Streetcar Named Desire, The Three Sisters; dir. (films) The Taming of the Shrew, 1966, Romeo and Juliet, 1967, Brother Sun, Sister Moon, 1971, Filumena, 1977, The Champ, 1979, Endless Love, 1981, I Pagliacci, 1981, La Traviata, 1982, Cavalleria Rusticana, 1986, Otello, 1986, The Young Toscanini, 1988, Hamlet, 1990, Sparrow, 1993, (ballet) Swan Lake, 1985; co-screenwriter, dir.(film) Hamlet, 1990; TV dir. Giorni Di Distruzione, 1966, Fidelio conducted by Leonard Bernstein, 1970, Missa Solemnis of Beethoven conducted by Wolfgang Sawallisch in Basilica of St. Peter in presence of Pope Paul VI, 1970, Jesus of Nazareth (epic film), 1976; numerous operas including Cenerentola, La Scala, 1953, I Pagliacci, 1959, Cavalleria Rusticana, 1959, Lucia Di Lammermoor, Covent Garden, 1959, La Boheme, La Scala, 1963, Falstaff, Met. Opera, 1964, Tosca, Covent Garden, 1965, Norma, Paris Opera, 1965, Anthony and Cleopatra, Met. Opera, 1966, Otello, Met. Opera, 1972, Don Giovanni, Staatsoper, Vienna, 1972, Un Ballo in Maschera, La Scala, 1972, Otello, La Scala, 1976, Carmen, Staatsoper, Vienna, 1978, La Traviata, 1979, 83, Tosca, Met. Opera, 1985, Turandot, 1987, Don Giovanni, 1990, Don Carlo, La Scala, 1992, Aida, Rome Opera, 1993; theater dir. Romeo and Juliet, Old Vic Co., London, 1960, Othello, Stratford-on-Avon, Eng., 1961, Camille, Winter Garden Theatre, N.Y.C., 1962, Who's Afraid of Virginia Woolf?, Festival del Teatro, Venice, and Paris, 1963, Romeo and Juliet, Verona, Italy, Paris, Vienna, Austria, Rome and Milan, Italy, Moscow and Leningrad, 1964, Hamlet, 1964, After The Fall, 1965, Much Ado About Nothing, Old Vic Theatre, 1965, La Lupa, Florence, Rome, Vienna, Zurich, Switzerland, Paris, London and Moscow, 1965, A Delicate Balance, 1966, Black Comedy, 1967, Venti Zecchini D'Oro, 1968, Due Piu Due Non Fanno Quattro, 1969, Sabato, Doemnica, Lunedi, Nat. Theatre, London, 1973, The Dead City, Italy, 1975, Lorenzaccio, Comedie Française, Paris, 1976, Filumena Marturano, Lyric Theatre, London, 1977; author: Zeffirelli by Zeffirelli, 1986. Recipient Liberty award, 1986. Mem. Dirs. Guild Am. Roman Catholic. Address: Via Lucio Volumnio 37, 00178 Rome Italy*

ZEFFREN, EUGENE, toiletries company executive; b. St. Louis, Nov. 21, 1941; s. Harry Morris and Bess (Dennis) Z.; m. Steccia Leigh Stern, Feb. 2, 1964; children: Maryl Renee, Bradley Cruvant. AB, Washington U., 1963; MS, U. Chgo., 1965, PhD, 1967. Research chemist Procter & Gamble Co., Cin., 1967-75, sect. head, 1975-77, assoc. dir., 1977-79; v.p. R & D, Helene Curtis, Inc., Chgo., 1979-95; pres. Helene Curtis USA, Chgo., 1995-96, corp. sr. v.p., 1996—. Co-author: The Study of Enzyme Mechanisms, 1973; contbr. articles to profl. jours.; patentee in field of enzymes and hair care. Mem. AAAS, Am. Chem. Soc., Soc. Cosmetic Chemists, Cosmetic Toiletry and Fragrance Assn. (sci. adv. com. 1979-95, vice chmn. 1984-88, chmn. 1988-90, bd. dirs. 1996—), Indsl. Rsch. Inst., Omicron Delta Kappa. Republican. Jewish. Avocations: tennis, swimming, skiing, reading adventure and espionage novels. Office: Helene Curtis Inc 325 N Wells St Chicago IL 60610

ZEGARELLI, EDWARD VICTOR, retired dental educator, researcher; b. Utica, N.Y., Sept. 9, 1912; s. Frank Anthony and Maria Josephine (Ambroselli) Z.; m. Irene Marie Ceconi, June 17, 1939; children: Edward V., David J., Philip E., Peter J. AB, Columbia U., 1934, DDS, 1937, DSc (hon.), 1983; MS, U. Chgo., 1942. Staff Sch. Dental and Oral Surgery, Columbia U., 1937-78, asst. instr., then successively instr., asst. prof., asso. prof., head diagnosis and roentgenology, 1947-58, chmn. com. dental research, 1956-78, Dr. Edwin S. Robinson prof. dentistry, 1958, prof. dentistry, dir. div. stomatology, 1958-78, acting dean, 1973, dean, 1974-78, dean emeritus, 1979—; Edward V. Zegarelli prof. dentistry, 1993—; chmn. sect. hosp. dental services Columbia-Presbyn. Med. Center; dir. and attending dentist dental service Presbyn. Hosp., 1974-79, also mem. exec. com. of med. bd., 1974-76; police surgeon N.Y.C., 1968-89; chmn. exam. com. N.E. Regional Bd. Dental Examiners, 1969-90; cons. VA, Washington; Weisberger Meml. lectr. Harvard U., 1969, Mershon Meml. lectr., 1970, Ralph L. Spaulding Meml. lectr., 1972; deans com. Montrose VA Hosp.; cons. East Orange, Kingsbridge VA hosps., Westchester Med. Ctr., Valhalla, N.Y., USPHS, Phelps Meml. Hosp., Tarrytown, N.Y., Vassar Bros. Hosp., Poughkeepsie, Bur. Medicine, FDA, Council on Dental Therapeutics; area cons. VA; cons.-lectr. U.S. Naval Dental Sch., Bethesda, Md., 1970-78; pres. N.Y. State Bd. Dental Examiners, 1970-71; chmn. exam. rev. com. N.E. Regional Bd. Dental Examiners, 1969-90; Samuel Charles Miller Meml. lectr., 1976; mem. council deans Am. Assn. Dental Schs., 1973-79; mem. postgrad. edn. com. N.Y.C. Cancer Com.; mem. profl. edn. and grants com. N.Y.C. div. Am. Cancer Soc., 1963-73; chmn. panel on drugs in dentistry NAS, NRC, FDA; mem. N.Y. State Health Research Council, N.Y. Commn. on Health Manpower; chmn. bd. govs. (dental) Gen. Health Ins., N.Y.C. Contbg. author: The Thyroid, Medical Roentgenology, Current Pediatric Therapy, Cancer of Head and Neck; author: (with others) Pharmacotherapeutics of Oral Disease, 1964, Clinical Stomatology, 1966, Diagnosis of Diseases of Mouth and Jaws, 1969, 2d edit., 1978; also articles on mouth, jaw bone disease. Bd. dirs. Hist. Soc. Tarrytowns, 1983, United Way Tarrytowns, 1983, YMCA of Tarrytowns, 1984, Phelps Meml. Hosp. Hospice Agy, 1986. Recipient Austin Sniffen medal 9th Dist. Dental Soc., 1961; Columbia U. Dental Alumni Research award, 1963; Jarvie-Burkhart medal N.Y. Dental Soc., 1970; Samuel J. Miller medal Am. Acad. Oral Medicine, 1976; Henry Spenadel award 1st Dist. Dental Soc., 1979; Man of Yr. award C. of C. Tarrytowns and Irvington, 1983; Man of Achievement award Americans for Italian Migration, 1984; named Disting. Practitioner mem. Nat. Acads. Practice, 1986. Fellow Am. Coll. Dentists (William J. Gies medal 1981), N.Y. Acad. Dentistry, Internat. Coll. Dentists, 9th Dist. Dental Soc.; mem. Am. Acad. Oral Pathology, Am. Assn. for Cancer Edn. (charter), Am. Assn. Dental Examiners (Dentist Citizen of Yr. award 1978), Orgn. Tchrs. Oral Diagnosis, N.Y. Acad. Scis., N.Y. Dental Soc. (chmn. council sci. research 1956-71), Greater N.Y. Acad. Prosthodontics (hon.), Guatemala Dental Soc. (hon.), Am. Dental Assn. (mem. council dental therapeutics 1963-69, vice chmn. 1969), Columbia Dental Alumni Assn.,

William Jarvie Research Soc., Internat. Assn. Dental Research, AAAS, Nat. Italian-Am. Found., Sigma Xi (chpt. pres. 1974-76), Omicron Kappa Upsilon (sec. treas. Columbia chpt. 1944-57, pres. 1959-60), Sigma Phi Alpha., Knight Malta. Lodge: Rotary (pres. 1985-86) (Tarrytown). Home: 120 Gory Brook Rd North Tarrytown NY 10591

ZEHE, ALFRED FRITZ KARL, physics educator; b. Farnstaedt, Halle, Germany, May 23, 1939; came to Mexico, 1990; s. Alfred and Lina Olga (Kuhnt) Z.; m. Ruth Schorrig, July 30, 1960; children: Axel, Peter. MSc, U. Leipzig, Germany, 1964, D Natural Scis., 1969, Habilitation, 1974; D honoris causa, U. Puebla, Mexico, 1980. Researcher U. Leipzig, 1964-68, asst. prof., 1968-71, assoc. prof., 1971-75; prof. Tech. U. Zwickau, Germany, 1975-80, Tech. U. Dresden, Germany, 1980-91; prof. physics U. Puebla, 1991—; dir. dept. math. and scis. Tech. U. Zwickau, Germany, 1975-76; dir. dept. exptl. solid-state physics U. Puebla, 1977-80; dir. vacuum-physics chair Tech. U. Dresden, 1980-90, INTERCONSULT, Mex., Germany, 1994—. Author: Zehe-Roepke Rule for Electromigration, 1985, Microelectronics and ASIC's design, 1994, Industrial Metrology, 1995; editor: Fisica y Tecnologia de Semiconductores, 1982, Compendio Tecnológico para la Práctica Industrial, 1994—; contbr. articles to profl. jours.; patentee in field. Recipient Cincuentenario medal of honor U. PUebla, 1989, Disting. Prof. award Inst. Superior de Informatica, Santo Domingo, 1991; named Disting. Citizen, City Coun., Puebla, 1990. Mem. Phys. Soc. Germany, Phys. Soc. Mex., Math. Soc. Republic Dominicana, Acad. Materials Scis. Mex., Acad. Scis. Republic Dominicana, N.Y. Acad. Scis. Avocations: music, travel, science. Home: Schillerstr 19, 01326 Dresden Germany Office: U Autonoma de Puebla, Apartado Postal # 1505, 72000 Puebla Mexico

ZEHM, STANLEY JAMES, education educator; b. Seattle, Dec. 3, 1936; s. Howard Ernest and Rene (Martin) Z.; m. Andrea Sue Johnson, Oct. 25, 1969; children: Kristofor Michael, Erin Jennifer Zehm Burton. BA, St. Edward's Sem., 1959; MDiv, St. Thomas Sem., 1963; MA in English, Gonzaga U., 1966; PhD in English Edn. with distinction, Stanford U., 1973. Tchr. English Carroll High Sch., Yakima, Wash., 1963-67, McFadden Intermediate Sch., Santa Ana, Calif., 1967-71; supr. student interns, then rsch. asst. Stanford (Calif.) U., 1971-73; prof. edn. Wash. State U., Pullman, 1973-81; dir. curriculum Richland (Wash.) Sch. Dist., 1981-82; asst. supt. Selah (Wash.) Sch. Dist., 1982-86; dean div. edn. and psychology Heritage Coll., Toppenish, Wash., 1987-90; prof. and chair dept. instructional and curricular studies U. Nev., Las Vegas, 1990—; marriage, family and child counselor Graden Grove (Calif.) Counseling Ctr., 1967-71; adv. com. Wash. State Lang. Arts Curriculum Com., Olympia, 1985; adv. bd. Wash. State Arts Commn., Olympia, 1989-90. Co-author: On Being A Teacher, 1993, Classrooms Under the Influence, 1993; contbr. to profl. publs. Bd. Trustees St. Jude's Ranch for Children, Boulder City, Nev., 1993—. Named one of 100 Outstanding English Tchrs., State of Calif., 1968; grantee U.S. Dept. Edn., Dept. Labor, NSF, Nat. Endowment for Humanities. Mem. ASCD, Internat. Reading Assn. (media awards chair 1974-76), Nat. Coun. Tchrs. English, Orange County Tchrs. English (v.p. 1969-70), Phi Delta Kappa. Roman Catholic. Avocations: hiking, theater, reading, botany, poetry. Home: 8116 Lake Hills Dr Las Vegas NV 89128-7090 Office: U Nev Las Vegas Instrnl/Curricular Studies 4505 S Maryland Pky Las Vegas NV 89154-9900

ZEHNER, LEE RANDALL, biotechnologist, research director; b. Darby, Pa., Mar. 15, 1947; s. Warren L. and Alycia G. (Van Riper) Z.; m. Susan D. Hovland, June 23, 1973; children: Adam, Erica. BS in Chemistry, U. Pa., 1968; PhD in Organic Chemistry, U. Minn., 1973. Sr. rsch. chemist Arco Chem. Co., Glenolden, Pa., 1973-78; rsch. group leader Ashland Chem. Co., Dublin, Ohio, 1978-82; mgr. organic rsch. W.R. Grace & Co., Clarksville, Md., 1982-85; dir. biotech. programs Biospherics Inc., Beltsville, Md., 1985—, v.p. sci. svcs., 1991—. Author various tech. publs.; patentee in field. Mem. AIChE, Am. Chem. Soc., Inst. Food Technologists, Am. Mgmt. Assn., N.Y. Acad. Scis. Avocations: swimming, computers, chess. Home: 131 Brinkwood Rd Brookeville MD 20833-2304 Office: Biospherics Inc 12051 Indian Creek Ct Beltsville MD 20705

ZEHR, AMY JO WURCH, elementary education educator; b. Webster City, Iowa, Feb. 16, 1967; d. John William and Vivian Allene (Hassebrock) W. BS, U. Iowa, 1989. Tchr. 4th grade East Union Cmty. Sch., Afton, Iowa, 1989-92; tchr. 3d grade Boone (Iowa) Cmty. Sch., 1992—; conflict mgmt. trainer Boone Cmty. Sch. Dist., 1994—, cons., at-risk com., 1990—, mem. vol. adv. bd., 1993—. Co-author: Math Alternative Assessments, 1994, Language Arts Alternative Assignments, 1994; editor: (video) It's A Wonderful World, 1993-94. Active PTA, Boone, 1989—; tchr. Bible Sch., St. Paul's Luth. Ch., Webster City, 1985, 86; supr. Univ. Parents Care Collective, Iowa City, 1987-88. Cessna scholar, 1985; Teresa Sterns scholar, 1985. Mem. NEA, Iowa State Edn. Assn., Boone Edn. Assn. (assessment team 1994-95), Chi Omega. Avocations: reading, refinishing, water skiing, organ, dance. Home: 1703 130th St Boone IA 50036 Office: Boone Schs Franklin Elem Sch 19th and Crawford Boone IA 50036

ZEHR, CLYDE JAMES, church administrator; b. Valley Ctr., Kans., Oct. 4, 1934; s. John Wesley and Anna Mae (Carithers) Z.; m. Leona Mae Zehr, Nov. 23, 1957; children: Karen Elaine, Mark Wesley. BS, U. Kans., 1957; ThM, Western Evang. Sem., Portland, Oreg., 1961; MBA, Seattle U., 1976. Ordained to ministry Evang. Meth. Ch. Structural engr. Boeing Co., Seattle, 1957-59; pastor Rockwood Evang. Meth. Ch., Portland, 1961-63; missionary OMS Internat., Seoul, Republic of Korea, 1964-80; dir. Christian Leadership Seminars, Kent, Wash., 1980-82; supt. N.W. dist. Evang. Meth. Ch., Kent, 1982-86; gen. supt. Evang. Meth. Ch., Wichita, Kans., 1986—. Author: Study Notes on Leadership, 1982. Trustee Western Evang. Sem., Portland, 1982—. Republican. Office: Evang Meth Ch Hdqrs 3000 W Kellogg Dr Wichita KS 67213-2271

ZEHRING, KAREN, information executive; b. Washington, Dec. 5, 1945; d. Robert William Zehring and Gretchen (Lorenz) Proos; m. George Lang, 1970 (div. 1979); m. Peter Frank Davis, June 10 1979 (div. 1995); children: Jesse, Antonia. BA, U. Denver, 1967; postgrad., Yale U., 1967-68. Assoc. pub. mktg. and sales Instl. Investor Systems, Inc., N.Y.C., 1968-74; co-owner, co-creator Café des Artistes Restaurant, N.Y.C., 1975-79; owner, pub. The Corp. Fin. Letter, N.Y.C., 1976-78; group dir. planning and devel. Bus. Week mag., N.Y.C., 1977-78; owner, pub., exec. editor Corp. Fin. Sourcebook The Corp. Fin. Bluebook, N.Y.C., 1979-84; chmn., pres., pub., editor-in-chief Corp. Fin. mag., N.Y.C., 1986-90; cons. Karen Zehring & Assocs., Castine, Maine, 1990-94; mng. ptnr. Creative Devel. Ptnrs., N.Y.C., 1995—; founder The Fin. Learning Ctr., 1995—. Mem. The Women's Forum, Am. Soc. Mag. Editors, Vt., N.H. Direct Mktg. Assn. Unitarian. Office: Ste 20G 100 W 57th St New York NY 10019-3327

ZEICHNER, OSCAR, historian, educator; b. N.Y.C., Jan. 2, 1916; s. Joseph and Lena (Schaeffer) Z.; m. Florence Koenigsberg, June 27, 1942; children: Barbara Ann, Carolyn Sue. B.A. cum laude, CCNY, 1936; M.A., Columbia U., 1938, Ph.D., 1946. Mem. faculty CCNY, 1936—, prof. history, 1960-76, prof. emeritus, 1976—, asst. dean in charge grad. studies Coll. Liberal Arts and Sci., 1957-63, asso. dean in charge Coll. Liberal Arts and Sci., 1963-68; dean grad. studies CCNY (Coll. Liberal Arts and Sci.), 1968-72; assoc. dean grad. studies CUNY, 1963-68; assoc. Columbia U. Seminar Early Am. History and Culture. Author: Connecticut's Years of Controversy, 1750-76, 1949, 70; editorial bd.: Connecticut Am. Revolution Bicentennial Series Publs.; contbr. articles to profl. jours. Recipient hon. mention J.H. Dunning prize Am. Hist. Assn., 1946. Mem. Assn. for Study Conn. History (pres. 1975-76), Phi Beta Kappa (pres. Gamma chpt. 1971-72). Home: 5500 Fieldston Rd Bronx NY 10471-2533

ZEIDENSTEIN, GEORGE, population educator; b. Pitts., July 29, 1929; s. Max and Sophia (Cohen) Z.; m. Sondra F. Auerbach, Jan. 25, 1953; children: Laura, Louis Peter. B.A., U. Pitts., 1951; J.D. cum laude, Harvard U., 1954. Bar: N.Y. 1954. Pvt. practice N.Y.C., 1954-65; vol. lawyer Lawyers Constl. Def. Com., Holly Springs, Miss., 1964; partner firm Spear and Hill, 1962-65; country dir. Nepal Kathmandu, Peace Corps, 1965-68; regional dir. designate Office E. Asia and Pacific, Washington, 1968; pres. Bklyn. Linear City Devel. Corp., N.Y.C., 1968-69; sr. program officer Asia and Pacific Ford Found., 1969-71, dep. head Asia and Pacific, 1971-72; rep. Ford Found., Bangladesh, 1972-76; pres., trustee Population Council, N.Y.C., 1976-93; disting. fellow Harvard Ctr. Population and Devel. Studies, Cambridge, Mass., 1993—; chmn. Himalayas coun. Asia Soc., 1970-72; assoc. seminar tradition and change in South and S.E. Asia, Columbia U., 1971-73, assoc. seminar on tech. and pub. issues, 1981-85; coun. Overseas Devel. Coun., 1979-93; chmn. Appraisal Group Global Com. Parliamentarians on Population and Devel., 1985-86; bd. visitors Grad. Sch. Pub. Health, U. Pitts., 1988—; advisor to chair Ind. Commn. on Population and Quality of Life, 1993-95. Vice chmn. bd. trustees, chmn. program com. Save the Children Fedn., 1991-95, Internat. Ctr. Rsch. on Women, 1993—; chmn. Internat. HIV/AIDS Alliance, 1993—; bd. dirs. Earthforce, 1993-95; active Britton Woods Com., 1992—. Decorated knight comdr. Order of Lion (Finland, Senegal). Home: 795 East St N Goshen CT 06756-1130 Office: Harvard Ctr Population Devel Studies 9 Bow St Cambridge MA 02138-5103

ZEIDLER, FRANK P., former association administrator, mayor, arbitrator, mediator, fact-finder; b. Milw., Sept. 20, 1912; s. Michael and Clara (Nitschke) Z.; m. Agnes Reinke; children: Clara, Dorothy, Michael, Anita, Mary, Jeannette. Student, Marquette U., 1930, U. Wis. Extension Div., 1930-70, U. Chgo., 1937; LLD (hon.), U. Wis., 1958, St. Olaf Coll., 1988; LHD (hon.), Carthage Coll., 1983, Mt. Mary Coll., 1993, U. Wis.-Milw., 1990. Dir. Milw. Pub. Schs., 1941-48; mayor City of Milw., 1948-60; dir. Wis. Dept. Resource Devel., 1963-64; sec. emeritus Pub. Enterprise Com.; mem. U.S. nat. commn. UNESCO, 1953, 56, 59. Author: Shakespeare's plays in modern verse. Pres. Ctrl. North Cmty. Coun.; past pres., co-editor newsletter Greater Milw. UN Assn.; nat. chmn. Socialist Party U.S.A., 1973-83; Socialist Party candidate for Pres. U.S., 1976; convenor Dem. Socialist Conf.; past pres. Luth. Locial Action Conf.; bd. dirs. Goethe House, Milw., Milw. Theol. Inst.; mem. exec. coun. Luth. Ch. Am., 1980-82; hon. mem. cabinet Interfaith Conf. Greater Milw.; chmn. Norman Thomas Inst. for Peace and Social Justice. Named One of 10 Outstanding Young Men, Nat. Jr. C. of C., 1949; recipient Eugene V. Debs award, 1977. Mem. Am. Arbitration Assn., Milw. World Federalist Assn. (bd. dirs.), Nat. Model R.R. Assn. (founder). Home: 2921 N 2nd St Milwaukee WI 53212-2411

ZEIEN, ALFRED M., consumer products company executive; b. N.Y.C., Feb. 25, 1930; s. Alphonse and Betty (Barthelemy) Z.; m. Joyce Valerie Lawrence, Dec. 26, 1952; children—Scott, Grey, Claudia. B.S., Webb Inst.; M.B.A. postgrad., Harvard U. Group v.p. Gillette Co., Boston, 1973-74, sr. v.p., 1978-81, vice chmn., 1981-90, pres., 1990-91, chmn., chief exec. officer, 1991—; div. gen. mgr. Braun AG, Frankfurt, Federal Republic of Germany, 1974-76, chmn. bd., 1976-78; bd. dirs. Polaroid Corp., Cambridge, Mass., Repligen Corp., Cambridge, Raytheon Corp., Lexington, Mass., Bank of Boston, Mass. Mut. Ins. Co., Springfield. trustee Univ. Hosp., Boston, 1983—. Avocations: sailing; tennis. Home: 300 Boylston St Boston MA 02116-3923 Office: Gillette Co Prudential Towers Bldg Boston MA 02199

ZEIFANG, DONALD P., lawyer; b. Niagara Falls, N.Y., Apr. 13, 1936. BA, U. Notre Dame, 1960; JD, Georgetown U., 1963. Bar: D.C. 1965. Law clk. to Hon. John J. Sirica U.S. Dist. Ct. (D.C. dist.), 1963-65; ptnr. Baker & Hostetler, Washington. Mem. ABA, D.C. bar, Fed. Comm. Bar, Nat. Assn. Broadcasters (v.p. 1973-80, sr. v.p. 1976-80 govt. rels.). Office: Baker & Hostetler Washington Sq Ste 1100 1050 Connecticut Ave NW Washington DC 20036-5303*

ZEIGER, LARRY See KING, LARRY

ZEIGER, SCOTT LESLIE, commercial theater executive; b. Bklyn., Sept. 25, 1960; s. Martin Zeiger and Phyllis Roberta Miller Iampieri; m. Kathleen Marie Ryan, Dec. 4, 1988; 1 child, Joshua Ryan. BA, U. Fla., 1982. Regional mktg. dir. Ringling Bros. Barnum and Bailey Circus, Washington, 1983; dir. mktg. Pace Theatrical Group, Houston, 1983-86, v.p., 1986-89, exec. v.p., 1989-91; pres. Pace Theatrical Group, N.Y.C., 1991—. Exec. prodr.: The Who's Tommy, 1993 (5 Tony awards). Adv. com. Houston Downtown Theatre Dist., 1986-93; bd. dirs. Story Theatre, Ft. Lauderdale, Fla., 1993—. Mem. League of Am. Theatres and Prodrs. (exec. com. 1992—, bd. govs. 1988-92). Jewish. Avocations: travel, exercise, music.

ZEIGLER, ALAN KARL, lawyer; b. Perry, Fla., Oct. 11, 1949; s. Fred Montgomery and Ora Lee (Saunders) Z. BA, Birmingham-So. Coll., 1971; JD, Vanderbilt U., 1974. Bar: Ala. 1975. Clk. to Judge Walter P. Gewin, U.S. Ct. Appeals, Tuscaloosa, Ala., 1974-75; assoc. Bradley, Arant, Rose & White, Birmingham, Ala., 1975; ptnr. Bradley, Grant, Rose & White, Birmingham, Ala., 1981. Episcopalian. Office: Bradley Arant Rose & White 2001 Park Pl Ste 1400 Birmingham AL 35206*

ZEIGLER, BERNARD PHILLIP, electrical and computer engineering educator; b. Montreal, Que., Can., Mar. 5, 1940; came to U.S., 1962; naturalized, 1985; s. Maurice and Sylvia (Filger) Z.; m. Rebecca Robinson, May 1964 (div. 1984); children: Bianca, Noemi; m. Christine Dymek, Aug. 1985; 1 child, Claire. B in Engring. Physics, McGill U., 1962; MEE, MIT, 1964; PhD in Computer Sci., U. Mich., 1969. Asst. prof. computer sci. U. Mich., Ann Arbor, 1970-73, assoc. prof. computer sci., 1973-75; vis. scientist Weizman Inst. Sci., Israel, 1975-80; prof. computer sci. Wayne State U., Detroit, 1981-85; prof. elec. and computer engring. U. Ariz., Tucson, 1985—; cons. Environ. Research lab. U. Ariz., 1986—, Martin Marietta Corp., McDonell Douglas. Author: Theory of Modelling and Simulation, 1976, Multifacetted Modelling and Discrete Event Simulation, 1984, Object-Oriented Simulation of HierarchialModular Models, 1990, Objects and Systems, 1996. With USAF, 1995—. Research grantee, NSF, 1982—, NASA, 1987—. Fellow IEEE. Office: U Ariz Dept ECE Tucson AZ 85721

ZEIGLER, CHARLES E., JR., utility company executive; b. Bogota, N.J., 1925; married. With Pub. Service Co. N.C., Inc., Gastonia, 1946—, v.p., 1956-73, pres., 1973—, chief exec. officer, from 1973, now also chmn. bd.; chmn., pres. PSNC Natural Resources Corp., PSNC Exploration Corp., PSNC Prodn. Corp., PSNC Propane Corp., Tar Heel Energy Corp. Office: Pub Svc Co of NC Inc 400 Cox Rd Gastonia NC 28054-0609*

ZEIGLER, CYNTHIA WALKER, zoological association executive; b. Washington, Feb. 16, 1953; d. Henry Gary and Alma Jane (Eichinger) Walker; m. Frank William Zeigler, Sept. 14, 1984; 1 child, Kelsey Lee Walker. AA in Mass Communications, Miami Dade Community Coll., 1973. Dir. promotion Sportsview, Inc., Miami, Fla., 1975; asst. promotion mgr. Sta. WCIX-TV, Miami, 1975-77; asst. dir. Fla. office CARE, Miami, 1977-85; dir. devel. and membership Zool. Soc. Fla., Miami, 1985-87, asst. exec. dir., 1987-90, dep. dir., 1992—; exec. v.p. Parrot Jungle & Gardens, Miami, Fla., 1990-92; mem. steering com. Pres. Clinton's Summit of Ams., 1994. Producer 12 part TV series Discover Metrozoo, 1986. Chmn. Jr. Orange Bowl, Miami, 1983-90. Named one of Outstanding Young Women Am., 1981. Mem. Nat. Assn. Fundraising Execs., Fla. Assn. Wildlife Rehabilitators (pres. 1977-90), Children's Respiratory and Nutrition Assn. (trustee 1978-91), South Fla. Bus. Communicators (v.p. 1978), Nat. Assn. TV Arts (sec., bd. dirs. 1983, 84). Office: Zool Soc Fla 12400 SW 152nd St Miami FL 33177-1402

ZEIGLER, EARLE FREDERICK, physical education-kinesiology educator; b. N.Y.C., Aug. 20, 1919; s. Clarence Mattison and Margery Christina (Beyerkohler) Shinkle; m. Bertha M. Bell, June 25, 1941; children—Donald H., Barbara A. A.B., Bates Coll., 1940; A.M., Yale U., 1944, Ph.D., 1951; LL.D., U. Windsor, 1975. Assoc. phys. dir., aquatic dir. Bridgeport (Conn.) YMCA, 1941-43; instr. German U. Conn., Storrs, 1943-47; coach, instr. phys. edn. Yale U., 1943-49; asst. prof. U. Western Ont. (Can.), London, 1949-50; prof., chmn. dept. phys., health and recreation edn. U. Western 1949-56; prof., chmn. dept. phys. and health edn. and athletics U. Ont. (Can.), 1950-56, assoc. prof. Sch. Edn.; supr. phys. edn. and athletics U. Mich., Ann Arbor, 1956-63; chmn. dept. phys. edn. Sch. Edn. U. Mich., 1961-63; prof. dept. phys. edn. for men Coll. Phys. Edn., U. Ill., Urbana, 1963-72; head dept. phys. edn. for men, chmn. grad. dept. Coll. Phys. Edn., U. Ill., 1964-68; prof. dept. phys. and health edn. U. Western Ont., London, 1971-89, prof. emeritus, 1989—; dean U. Western Ont. (Faculty of Phys. Edn.), 1972-77. Author: A History of Professional Preparation for Physical Education in the United States, 1951, Administration of Physical Education and Athletics, 1959, The Case Method Approach: An Instructional Manual, 1959, Philosophical Foundations for Physical, Health, and Recreation Education, 1964, A Brief Introduction to the Philosophy of Religion, 1965, (with H.J. VanderZwaag) Physical Education: Progressivism or Essentialism, 1968, Problems in the History and Philosophy of Physical Education and Sport, 1968, (with M.L. Howell and M. Trekell) Research in the History and Philosophy of Physical Education and Sport, 1971, Personalizing Physical Education and Sport Philosophy, 1975, Physical Education and Sport Philosophy, 1977, Issues in North American Physical Education and Sport, 1979, Decision-Making in Physical Education and Athletics, 1982, (with G.W. Bowie) Management Competency Development in Sport and Physical Education, 1983, Ethics and Morality in Sport and Physical Education, 1984, (with J. Campbell) Strategic Market Planning: An Aid to the Evaluation of an Athletics/Recreation Program, 1984 , Assessing Sport and Physical Education: Diagnosis and Projection, 1986, (with G. Bowie and R. Paris) Competency Development in Sport and Physical Education Management, 1988, (with A. Mikalachki and G. Leyshon) Change Process in Sport and Physical Education Management, 1988, Introduction to Sport and Physical Education Philosophy, 1989, Sport and Physical Education: Past, Present, Future, 1990, Professional Ethics for Sport Managers, 1992, Critical Thinking for the Professions of Health, Physical Education, Recreation, and Dance, 1994, A Selected, Annotated Bibliography of Completed Research on Management Theory and Practice in Physical Education and Athletics to 1972, 1995, (with G.W. Bowie) Developing Management Competency in Sport and Physical Education, 1995; author, editor: A History of Sport and Physical Education to 1900, 1973, A History of Physical Education and Sport in the United States and Canada, 1975, (with M.J. Spaeth) Administrative Theory and Practice in Physical Education and Athletics, 1975, History of Physical Education and Sport, 1979, rev. edit., 1988, Physical Education and Sport: An Introduction, 1982, Physical Education and Kinesiology in North America: Professionalism and Scholarly Foundations, 1994; contbr. articles to profl. jours. Recipient Outstanding Tchr. award U. Western Ont., 1987, Disting. Svc. award Internat. Soc. Comparative Phys. Edn. and Sport, 1988; inducted into Univ. Western Ont.'s Wall of Wrestling Fame, 1991, Univ. Western Ont.'s W Club Hall of Fame, 1995; named first Human Movement Scis. and Edn. scholar U. Memphis, 1994. Fellow Am. Acad. Kinesiology and Phys. Edn. (pres. 1981-82, Hetherington award 1989); mem. AAHPERD (Alliance scholar 1977-78, Disting. Svc. award 1979, Honor award 1981, Gulick award 1990), Philosophy Edn. Soc., Internat. Assn. Profl. Schs. Phys. Edn., Can. Assn. Health, Phys. Edn. and Recreation (v.p. 1955-56, v.p. 1983-85, honour award 1975, spl. presentation citation 1986), Am. Philos. Assn., Nat. Assn. Phys. Edn. in Higher Edn., N.Am. Soc. Sport History (life), Philosophic Soc. for Study of Sport (pres. 1974-75), N.Am. Soc. for Sport Mgmt. (founding mem., hon. past pres. 1986-87), Canadian Profl. Schs. Conf. (pres. 1953-55), Ont. Recreation Assn. (v.p. and dir. 1955-56), Soc. Municipal Recreation Dirs. Ont. (Honor award 1956), Phi Epsilon Kappa (life). N.Am. Soc. Sport Mgmt. created the Annual Earle Zeigler Lecture, 1988. Home: 105 8560 Currie Rd, Richmond, BC Canada V6Y 1M2 also: 1177 Sudden Valley Bellingham WA 98226-4818 *Ever since the Platonic tradition split what we once before believed to be a unified organism into mind and body, and then Christianity added a spiritual dimension that shattered a unified concept of the organism even further, purposeful human movement in sport, dance, play, and exercise has been regarded as inferior to so-called intellectual attainments. My life purpose is to work toward redressing that imbalance by promoting a type of education that restores the Greek Classical Ideal.*

ZEIGLER, L(UTHER) HARMON, political science educator; b. Savannah, GA., Mar. 9, 1936; s. Luther H. and Sarah Louise (Betts) Z.; m. Patricia Lynn Duffy, Dec. 20, 1956; children: Michael, Amanda. BA, Emory U., 1957; MA, U. Ill., 1958, PhD, 1960. Asst. prof. Fla. State U., Tallahassee, 1960-61, Emory U., Atlanta, 1961-63, U. Ga., Athens, 1963-64; assoc. prof. U. Oreg., Eugene, 1964-67, prof. dept. polit. sci., 1967-85, chmn., 1982-85; Philip M. Phibbs disting. prof. Am. politics U. Puget Sound, Tacoma, Wash., 1985-92; affiliate prof. U. Wash., 1986-92. Author: The Irony of Democracy, 1970, 10th edit., 1996, Governing American Schools, 1974, Professionals Versus the Public: Attitudes, Commnication and Response in Local School Districts, 1980, American Politics in the Media Age, 1983, Women, Public Opinion and Politics: The Changing Attitudes of American Women, 1984, Pluralism, Corporatism and Confucianism, 1988, The Political Community, 1990, Political Parties in Industrial Democracies, 1992. Fellow Ford Found., 1969; Guggenheim fellow, 1969-70; Fulbright-Hays grantee W. Germ., 1977; sr. scholar Australia, 1978. Mem. Am. Polit. Sci. Assn.

ZEIGLER, VICKI LYNN, pediatrics nurse; b. Hampton, S.C., May 26, 1961; d. Richard Jackson and Miriam Banner (Smith) Z.; m. Paul Crawford Gillette, Feb. 1, 1992. BSN, Med. U. of S.C., 1982, MSN, 1991. RN, S.C.; cert. spl. competency in cardiac pacing for non-physicians N.Am. Soc. Pacing and Electrophysiology. Staff nurse pediatrics Med. U. S.C., Charleston, 1983-85, nurse clinician pediatric cardiology, 1985-91, pediatric arrhythmia/pacemaker case mgr., 1992-94, pediatric arrhythmia nurse specialist, 1994-96; pediat. arrhythmia case mgr. Cook Children's Med. Ctr., Ft. Worth, 1996—; BLS instr. Am. Heart Assn., Columbia, S.C. Contbr. articles to profl. jours. Recipient Young Investigator award Sigma Theta Tau. Mem. AACN, Assn. for Care of Children's Health, North Am. Soc. of Pacing and Electrophysiology, Am. Heart Assn. Coun. of Cardiovascular Nursing, Sigma Theta Tau. Republican. Avocations: sailing, auto racing, reading. Office: Cook Childrens Med Ctr Cardiology Dept 801 7th Ave Fort Worth TX 76104-2796

ZEIKEL, ARTHUR, investment company executive; b. Bronx, N.Y., June 1, 1932; s. Sidney and Dorothy (Einhorn) Z.; m. Terrie Ruth Stoops, Dec. 7, 1960; children: Jeffrey, Jill, Judith. B.B.A., CCNY, 1954; M.B.A., NYU, 1960. Research analyst Ira Haupt Co., N.Y.C., 1958-59; research analyst Blair & Co., N.Y.C., 1959-63; portfolio mgr. Dreyfuss Corp., N.Y.C., 1963-68; pres., dir., chief exec. officer S&P Inter-Capital, N.Y.C., 1968-76; pres. Merrill Lynch Asset Mgmt., Inc., Princeton, N.J., 1976—; exec. v.p., Merrill Lynch & Co. Inc.; pres., Merrill Lynch Investment Mgmt. Inc.; exec. v.p., Merrill Lynch Pierce Fenner & Smith Inc.; pres., trustee, Merrill Lysnch Ready Assets Trust Inc. Author: (with others) Guide to Intelligent Investing, 1977, Investment Analysis and Portfolio Management, 5th edit., 1987; contbr. articles to profl. jours. Served with U.S. Army, 1956-58. Mem. Investment Co. Inst. (bd. govs. 1983—), Fin. Analyst Research Found. (trustee), Fin. Analyst Fedn. Club: Econ. of N.Y. Office: Merrill Lynch Asset Mgmt Inc PO Box 9011 Princeton NJ 08543*

ZEILIG, NANCY MEEKS, magazine editor; b. Nashville, Apr. 28, 1943; d. Edward Harvey and Nancy Evelyn (Self) Meeks; m. Lanny Kenneth Fielder, Aug. 20, 1964 (div. Dec. 1970); m. Charles Elliot Zeilig, Jan. 6, 1974 (div. Dec. 1989); 1 child, Sasha Rebecca. BA, Birmingham-So. Coll., 1964; postgrad., Vanderbilt U., 1971-73. Editorial asst. Reuben H. Donnelley, N.Y.C., 1969-70; asst. editor Vanderbilt U., Nashville, 1970-74; editor U. Minn., St. Paul, 1975; asst. editor McGraw-Hill Inc., Mpls., 1975-76; mng. editor Denver mag., 1976-80; editor Jour. Am. Water Works Assn., Denver, 1981—. Editor, co-pub.: WomanSource, 1982, rev. edit., 1994; contbr. articles to consumer mags. Avocations: travel, reading British and Am. fiction, cooking. Subject of NBC News documentary Women Like Us, 1980. Office: Jour Am Water Works Assn 6666 W Quincy Ave Denver CO 80235-3011

ZEILINGER, ELNA RAE, elementary educator, gifted-talented education educator; b. Tempe, Ariz., Mar. 24, 1937; d. Clayborn Eddie and Ruby Elna (Laird) Simpson; m. Philip Thomas Zeilinger, June 13, 1970; children: Shari, Chris. BA in Edn., Ariz. State U., 1958, MA in Edn., 1966, EdS, 1980. Bookkeeper First Nat. Bank of Tempe, 1955-56; with registrar's office Ariz. State U., 1956-58; piano tchr., recreation dir. City of Tempe; tchr. Thew Sch., Tempe, 1958-61; elem. tchr. Mitchell Sch., Tempe, 1962-74, intern prin., 1976, personnel intern, 1977; specialist gifted edn. Tempe Elem. Schs., Tempe, 1977-86; elem. tchr. Holdeman Sch., Tempe, 1986-89; tchr. grades 1-12 and adult reading, lang. arts, English Zeilinger Tutoring Svc., 1991—; grad. asst. ednl. adminstrn., Iota Workshop coordinator Ariz. State U., 1978; presenter Ariz. Gifted Conf., 1978-81; condr. survey of gifted programs, 1980; reporter public relations Tempe Sch. Dist., 1978-80, Access com. for gifted programs, 1981-83. Author: Leadership Role of the Principal in Gifted Programs: A Handbook, 1980; Classified Personnel Handbook, 1977, also reports, monographs and paintings. Mem. Tempe Hist. Assn., liaison, 1975; mem. Tempe Art League; mem. freedom train com. Ariz. Bicentennial Commn., 1975-76; bd. dirs. Maple Property Owners Assn., 1994—. Named Outstanding Leader in Elem. and Secondary Schs., 1976' Ariz. Cattle Growers scholar, 1954-55; Elks scholar, 1954-55; recipient Judges award Tempe Art League, 1970, Best of Show, Scottsdale Art League, 1976. Democrat. Congregationalist.

ZEILINGER, PHILIP THOMAS, aeronautical engineer; b. David City, Nebr., Feb. 13, 1940; s. Thomas Leroy and Sylvia Dorothy Zeilinger; m. Elna Rae Simpson, June 13, 1970; children: Shari, Chris. AS, Wentworth Mil. Acad., Lexington, Mo., 1959; BSME, Kans. U., 1962. Estimator, engr. Reynolds Electronics and Engring. Co., El Paso, Tex., 1966-68; accessories coord. ITI Garrett, Phoenix, 1974-79, cntrl. access engr., 1968—, controls coord. ITEC, 1983-84, integrated support specialist ITEC, 1984-86, mgr. systems software light helo turbine engring. co. div., 1986-91, FAA designated engr. rep. engine div., 1991—; chmn. Light Helicopter Turbine Engine Company Computer Aided Acquistion and Logistics Working Group. V.p. Indsl. Devel. Authority, Tempe, Ariz., 1979-84; pres. Univ. Royal Garden Homes Assn., Tempe, 1984-90. 1st lt. U.S. Army, 1962-66. Recipient Vol. Svc. award City of Tempe, 1984, Grand Cross of Color, Internat. Order of Rainbow Girls, 1978. Mem. AIAA, Aircraft Owners and Pilots Assn., Explt. Aircraft Assn. (v.p. chpt. 228 1974-79), Masons (master 1990-92, chmn. statewide picnic 1992, Mason of the Yr. 1992). Democrat. Unitarian. Achievements include patent for Airesearch/Garrett. Home: 760 N Sycamore Pl Chandler AZ 85224-6925 Office: 111 34th St Phoenix AZ 85010

ZEILLER, WARREN, former aquarium executive, consultant; b. Weehawken, N.J., Nov. 11, 1929; s. Arthur Herman and Ruth (Preusser) Z.; m. Judith Marion Ricciardi, May 27, 1961; children: Dianne Leigh, Todd Kiersted. B.Sc. in Animal Husbandry, Colo. A&M Coll., 1955; M.A. in Bus., Mich. State U., 1957. Mgmt. trainee Grand Union Co., 1956-58; corp. sec., salesman Art Zeiller Co., Inc., Allendale, N.J., 1958-60; salesman Joseph Abraham Ford Co., Miami, Fla., 1960; with Miami Seaquarium, 1960-85, curator, 1962-85, v.p., gen. mgr., 1977-85, ret., 1985; pres. Images of Art, Inc., Coral Gables, Fla.; exec. dir. Tropical Everglades Visitor Assn., 1988—; lectr., cons. bus., mktg., tourism; TV appearances. Author: Tropical Marine Invertebrates of Southern Florida and the Bahama Islands, 1974, Tropical Marine Fishes of Southern Florida and the Bahama Islands, 1975, Introducing the Manatee, 1992; contbr. articles to profl. jours. Treas. Jr. Orange Bowl Com., 1984-85; mem. adv. bd. Coral Gables War Meml. Youth Ctr., 1973-93, pres., 1981-83; mem. Gov.'s tourism adv. coun. Fla. Hospitality Industry Coun., 1983-84; bd. dirs. Dade Marine Inst.; bd. dirs., pres. Humane Soc. Greater Miami, Inc., 1993-94. Served with USN, 1951-55. Mem. Fla. Attractions Assn. (v.p. 1981-82, pres. 1982-83), Mus. and Art Center, Colo. State U. Alumni Assn., Sigma Chi. Republican. Methodist. Club: Rotary (pres. Coral Gables 1978-79). Patentee surg. cast and cast removal saw. Home: 5016 SW 72nd Ave Miami FL 33155-5529

ZEISEL, STEVEN H., nutrition educator; b. N.Y.C., July 16, 1950. BS in Life Sci., MIT, 1971; MD, Harvard Med. Sch., 1975; PhD in Nutrition/Natural Endocrine, MIT, 1980. Asst. Children's Hosp., Boston, 1980-81; asst. prof. pathology and pediatrics Boston U. Sch. Medicine, 1982-87, assoc. prof., 1987-90, prof., 1990-91; prof. dept. pediatrics U. N.C., Chapel Hill, 1990—, prof., chair dept. nutrition, 1990—; chair med. edn. com. Am. Soc. Clin. Nutrition, 1995—; chair joint membership com. AIN/ASCN, 1992-94; mem. study sect. Clin. Nutrition Rsch. units NIH, 1993-95; del. Assn. AMCCAS, 1991—. Editor-in-chief Jour. Nutritional Biochemistry. Mem. Am. Inst. Nutrition, Am. Soc. Clin. Nutrition, Am. Soc. Parenteral and Enteral Nutrition, Am. Coll. Nutrition, Am. Pub. Health Assn., Soc. Pediatric Rsch. Office: U NC Dept Nutrition # 7400 Sch Pub Health/Sch Medicine McGavran Greenberg Hall Chapel Hill NC 27599-7400

ZEISLER, RICHARD SPIRO, investor; b. Chgo., Nov. 28, 1916; s. Erwin Paul and Ruth Henrietta (Spiro) Z. B.A., Amherst Coll., 1937; postgrad., Harvard U., 1937-38; M.Div., Va. Theol. Sem., 1941. Religious work, 1941-47; owner Richard S. Zeisler & Co. (investments), N.Y.C., 1948—; bd. dirs. PEC Israel Econ. Corp., 1949—. Bd. dirs. Chamber Music Soc., Lincoln Center, 1969—, Skowhegan Sch. Painting and Sculpture, 1983—; trustee Mus. Modern Art, 1979—, mem. com. on painting and sculpture, 1972—, architecture and design com., 1989—; trustee, former v.p. Jewish Bd. Family and Children's Services, N.Y.C., 1951—; past pres. Am. Jewish Com. (N.Y. chpt.); past co-chmn. NCCJ (N.Y. chpt.); mem. com. for dance collection, past chmn. N.Y. Pub. Library, 1967—; mem. creative arts commn. Brandeis U., 1958-94; mem. art adv. com., past chmn. Mt. Holyoke Coll., 1963—; fellow Pierpont Morgan Library, 1963—; governing life mem. Art Inst. Chgo., 1977—, mem. com. on 20th century painting and sculpture, 1981—; life fellow Met. Mus., 1969—; mem. Manhattan Inst., 1990—; mem. adv. coun. Princeton (N.J.) Art Mus., 1993—. Mem. N.Y. Soc. Security Analysts, Am. Coun. on Germany, Asia Soc., U.S.-New Zealand Coun., Ams. Soc., Century Assn. Club (N.Y.C.), Univ. Club (N.Y.C.), Grolier Club (N.Y.C.), Arts Club (Chgo.), Reform Club (London), Econ. of N.Y. Home and Office: 980 Fifth Ave New York NY 10021-0126

ZEIT, RUTH MAE, foundation administrator; b. N.Y.C., May 13, 1945; d. Albert Joseph and Gertrude (Goldberg) Janover; children: Rachael Miriam, Rebecca Madeleine. BA, U. Pa., 1967, postgrad., 1969-70; postgrad., Temple U., 1967-69. Teaching fellow Temple U., Phila., 1967-69, U. Pa., Phila., 1969-70; dir. piano music studio Phila., 1969—; pres. Lupus Found. Del. Valley, Ardmore, Pa., 1983—; Mem. Winner's Ball com. Lupus Found. of Del. Valley, Ardmore, 1986-87, presiding officer, bd. dirs., med. adv. bd., 1983—, prin. organizer Ednl. Symposia, 1983—, prin. organizer patient support groups, 1983—; organizer Lupus Loop Fundraising Marathon Walk/Run; lectr. Prin. coordinator Lupus Found. of Del. Valley Newsletter, 1983—. Liaison with Phila. Mayor Ed Rendell, liaison between Julius Erving and Children's Hosp. of Phila.; coord. Julius Erving Lupus Rsch. Fund; target chmn. Undergrad. Admissions Secondary Sch. Com., U. Pa. Mem. Am. Coll. of Musicians, Sigma Delta Gamma, Music Tchrs. Nat. Assn., Pa. Music Tchrs. Assn. Democrat. Jewish. Avocations: piano, theatre, symphony, movies. Home: 1640 Oakwood Dr Apt W-122 Narberth PA 19072-1232 Office: Lupus Found Delaware Valley 44 W Lancaster Ave Ardmore PA 19003-1339

ZEITLIN, BRUCE ALLEN, superconducting material technology executive; b. N.Y.C., July 31, 1943; s. Lester and Rae (Benson) Z.; m. Amy Joy Kozan, Aug. 29, 1965; children: Laurence, Jessica, Andrea. BS, Rensselaer Poly. Tech., 1965; MS, Stevens Inst. Tech., 1968. Scientist Airco Cen. Rsch. Lab., Murray Hill, N.J., 1965-70; tech. dir. Magnetic Corp. of Am., Waltham, Mass., 1970-72; v.p. IGC/Advanced Supercondrs., Waterbury, Conn., 1985-95, Intermagnetics Gen. Corp., Latham, N.Y., 1986-95; corp. v.p., gen. mgr. APD Cryogenics, a subsidiary of Intermagnetics, Allentown, Pa., 1995—; bd. dirs. Alsthom Intermagnets SA, Paris. Patentee in field. Mem. Am. Phys. Soc. Avocation: astronomy. Office: APD Cryogenics 1833 Vultee St Allentown PA 18103

ZEITLIN, EUGENIA PAWLIK, librarian, educator; b. N.Y.C., Jan. 29; d. Charles and Pauline Pawlik; m. Herbert Zakary Zeitlin, July 3, 1949; children: Mark Clyde, Joyce Therese Zeitlin Harris, Ann Victoria, Clare Katherine. BA in English, Bklyn. Coll., 1945; MA in English, NYU, N.Y.C., 1951; MALS, Rosary Coll., 1968. Teaching credential N.Y., Ariz., Calif., Ill. English tchr. Sea Cliff, L.I., N.Y., 1945-47; English, math. tchr. Merrick (N.Y.) Sch. Dist., 1948-49; English tchr. Wilson Sch. Dist., Phoenix, 1949-50; counselor West Phoenix (Ariz.) High Sch., 1953-56; asst. prof. English Wright Coll., Chgo., 1965-66; asst. prof. English, asst. to v.p. curriculum and instrn. Oakton C.C., Des Plaines, Ill., 1970-76; libr. Pasadena City Coll., L.A. C.C. Dist., L.A., 1979-91. Contbr. articles to profl. jours. Named Northridge City Employee of Yr., 1986. Mem. AAUW (br. pres. Lancaster, Calif. 1958-60), Thoreau Soc. (life), Beta Phi Mu. Avocations: reading, writing, book collecting. Home: 20124 Phaeton Dr Woodland Hills CA 91364-5633

ZEITLIN, HERBERT ZAKARY, retired college president; b. N.Y.C.; s. Leonard and Martha Josephine (Soff) Z.; m. Eugenia F. Pawlik, July 3, 1949; children: Mark Clyde, Joyce Therese Zeitlin Harris, Ann Victoria, Clare Katherine. BS, NYU, 1947, MA, 1949; EdD, Stanford U., 1956. Tchr. Mepham High Sch., Bellmore, N.Y., 1946-47, Nassau County Vocat. Edn. Extension Bd., Mineola, N.Y.; electronics instr., adj. faculty Mephan C.C., 1946-49; tchr., counselor, dir. testing Phoenix Union High Sch. and Coll. Dist., 1949-57; dean eve. coll., prin. high sch. Antelope Valley Union High Sch. and Coll. Dist., Lancaster, Calif., 1957-62; dean instrn. Southwestern Coll., Chula Vista, Calif., 1962-64; pres., supt. Triton Coll., River Grove, Ill., 1964-76; pres., dean West L.A. Coll., 1976-80; pres. Trident Consultants, L.A., mgmt. cons., 1976—; adj. faculty Ariz. State U., Flagstaff, 1953-55, No. Ill. U., DeKalb, 1971-76, U. Calif., Santa Barbara, 1979. Editor in field. Mayor Upper Woodland Hills, Calif. Served with USAAF, 1942-46. Recipient spl. commendation Chgo. Tribune, spl. commendation Richard Ogilvie, former gov. Ill.; Adminstr. of Yr. award Triton Coll. Faculty Assn., 1974; Spl. Achievement award for visionary accomplishment Ill. Sch. Adminstrs. Assn., 1976. Home: 20124 Phaeton Dr Woodland Hills CA 91364-5633 Office: Paramount Properties 21731 Ventura Blvd Woodland Hills CA 91364-1845 *I always felt that being the president of an organization was like being the quarterback on the football team. You had a choice of running with the ball and taking some bruises or passing it to someone who should score. I was lucky most of the time in selecting some very fine receivers.*

ZEITLIN, MARILYN AUDREY, museum director; b. Newark, July 14, 1941; d. Sidney M. and Theresa Feigenblatt) Litchfield; widowed; children: Charles C. Sweedler, Milo Sweedler. Student, Vanderbilt U., 1963-65; AB in Humanities, Harvard U., 1966, MA in Teaching of English, 1967; postgrad., Cornell U., 1971-74. Dir. Ctr. Gallery, Bucknell U., Lewisburg, Pa., 1975-78; Freedman Gallery, Albright Coll., Reading, Pa., 1978-81, Anderson Gallery, Va. Commonwealth U., Richmond, 1981-87; curator, acting co-dir. Contemporary Arts Mus., Houston, 1987-90; exec. dir. Washington Projects for the Arts, 1990-92; dir. Univ. Art Mus., Ariz. State U., Tempe, 1992—; juror Dallas Mus. of Arts, McKnight Awards, Mpls.; grant evaluator IMS; grant evaluator, panelist NEH; lectr., cons. in field. Editor, contbr. essays to art publs. Bd. dirs. Cultural Alliance Washington; curator, commr. for U.S. for 1995 Venice Biennale. Samuel H. Kress fellow, 1972-73. Mem. Assn. Coll. and Univ. Mus. and Galleries (v.p. 1986-88), Am. Assn. Mus., Coll. Art Assn. (U.S. commr. Venice Bieniale 1995). Office: Ariz State U Art Mus PO Box 872911 Tempe AZ 85287-2911

ZEITLIN, MAURICE, sociology educator, author; b. Detroit, Feb. 24, 1935; s. Albert J. and Rose (Goldberg) Z.; m. Marilyn Geller, Mar. 1, 1959; children: Michelle, Carla, Erica. BA cum laude, Wayne State U., 1957; MA, U. Calif., Berkeley, 1960, PhD, 1964. Instr. anthropology and sociology Princeton (N.J.) U., 1961-64, research assoc. Ctr. Internat. Studies, 1962-64; asst. prof. sociology U. Wis.-Madison, 1964-67, assoc. prof., 1967-70, prof., 1970-77, dir. Ctr. Social Orgn., 1974-76; prof. sociology UCLA, 1977—, also research assoc. Inst. Indsl. Relations; vis. prof. polit. sci. and sociology Hebrew U., Jerusalem, 1971-72. Author: (with R. Scheer) Cuba: An American Tragedy, 1963, 1964, Revolutionary Politics and the Cuban Working Class, 1967, 1970, The Civil Wars in Chile, 1984, (with R.E. Ratcliff) Landlords and Capitalists, 1988, Capitalists, 1988, The Large Corporation and Contemporary Classes, 1989; (with J. Stepan-Norris) Talking Union, 1996; Latin Am. editor Ramparts mag., 1967-73; editor-in-chief: Political Power and Social Theory, 1980-90; mem. editorial adv. bd. The Progressive mag., 1985—; editor: (with J. Petras) Latin America: Reform or Revolution?, 1968, American Society, Inc., 1970, 1977, Father Camilo Torres: Revolutionary Writings, 1972, Classes, Class Conflict, and the State, 1980, How Mighty a Force?, 1983, Insurgent Workers: The Origins of Industrial Unionism, 1987. Chmn. Madison Citizens for a Vote on Vietnam, 1967-68; chmn. Am. Com. for Chile, 1973-75; mem. exec. bd. U.S. Com. for Justice to Latin Am. Polit. Prisoners, 1977-84; mem. exec. com. Calif. Campaign for Econ. Democracy, 1983-86. Ford Found. fellow, 1965-67, 70-71; Guggenheim fellow, 1981-82; NSF grantee, 1981, 82; recipient Project Censored award Top Censored Story, 1981; named to Ten Best Censored list, 1978. Mem. Am. Sociol. Assn. (governing council 1977-80, Disting. Contbn. Scholarship award in Pol. Sociology 1992), Internat. Sociol. Assn. (editorial bd. 1977-81), Latin Am. Studies Assn., Orgn. Am. Historians. Democrat. Jewish. *Personal philosophy: "If I am not for myself who will be? and when I am for myself, what am I?" Hillel, the Elder.*

ZEKMAN, PAMELA LOIS (MRS. FREDRIC SOLL), reporter; b. Chgo., Oct. 22, 1944; d. Theodore Nathan and Lois Jane (Bernstein) Z.; m. Fredric Soll, Nov. 29, 1975. B.A., U. Calif. at Berkeley, 1965. Social worker Dept. Public Aid Cook County, Chgo., 1965-66; reporter City News Bur., Chgo., 1966-70, Chgo. Tribune, 1970-75, Chgo. Sun-Times, 1975-81; investigative reporter Sta. WBBM-TV, Chgo., 1981—. Recipient Pulitzer Prize awarded to Chicago Tribune for gen. local reporting on vote fraud series, 1973; Community Service award for vote fraud series UPI, 1972; Feature Series award for nursing home abuses series AP, 1971; Pub. Service award for slumlord series UPI, 1973; Newswriting award AP, 1973; In Depth Reporting award for police brutality series AP, 1974; Investigative Reporting awards Inland Daily Press Assn., 1974, 78; Investigative Reporting award for series on city waste AP, 1975; Pulitzer Prize for pub. service for series on hosp. abuses, 1976; Investigative Reporting award for series on baby selling, 1976; Pub. Service award for series on currency exchange abuses UPI, 1976; Investigative Reporting award for series on abuses in home for retarded children AP, 1977; Soc. Midland Authors Golden Rake award; UPI Public Service award; Ill. AP award; Nat. Headliners Club award; Sweepstakes award for Mirage Tavern investigative project, 1978; Nat. Disting. Service award for series on med. abuses in abortion clinics Sigma Delta Chi, 1979; named Journalist of Yr. No. Ill. U., 1979; recipient George Foster Peabody Broadcasting award, 1982, 85, RTNDA Investigative Reporting award, 1983, DuPont Columbia award 1982, 87. Office: WBBM-TV 630 N Mcclurg Ct Chicago IL 60611-3007

ZEKMAN, TERRI MARGARET, graphic designer; b. Chgo., Sept. 13, 1950; d. Theodore Nathan and Lois (Bernstein) Z.; m. Alan Daniels, Apr. 12, 1980; children: Jesse Logan, Dakota Caitlin. BFA, Washington U., St. Louis, 1971; postgrad, Art Inst. Chgo., 1974-75. Graphic designer (on retainer) greeting cards and related products Recycled Paper Products Co., Chgo., 1970—, Jillson Roberts, Inc., Calif.; apprenticed graphic designer Helmuth, Obata & Kassabaum, St. Louis, 1970-71; graphic designer Container Corp., Chgo., 1971; graphic designer, art dir., photographer Cuerden Advt. Design, Denver, 1971-74; art dir. D'Arcy, McManus & Masius Advt., Chgo., 1975-76; freelance graphic designer Chgo., 1976-77; art dir. Garfield Linn Advt., Chgo., 1977-78; graphic designer Keiser Design Group, Van Noy & Co., Los Angeles, 1978-79; owner and operator graphic design studio Los Angeles, 1979—. Recipient cert. of merit St. Louis Outdoor Poster Contest, 1970, Denver Art Dirs. Club, 1973.

ZELANSKI, PAUL JOHN, art educator, author; b. Hartford, Conn., Apr. 13, 1931; s. John and Sofie (Berkowski) Z.; m. Annette Harding, June 30, 1965; children: John, Noemi, Ruth. Cert., The Cooper Union, 1955; BFA, Yale U., 1957; MFA, Bowling Green (Ohio) State U., 1958. Instr. art North Tex. State U., Denton, 1958-61; prof. art U. Conn., Storrs, 1962—; artist McDowell Art Colony, Peterborough, N.H.; advisor Permanent Pigments; panelist studio talk show Sta. WGHB, Boston, 1963-68; cons. Binnery & Smith; Getty lectr. North Tex. State U., 1989; vis. artist Inst. of Art of Krakow, Poland, 1990, Acad. Visual Arts, Maastricht, 1994; co-chair 3 Nations Student Project, Eng., The Netherlands, USA. Author: Design Principles and Problems, 1984, 2nd edit., 1995, Shaping Space, 1987, 2nd edit., 1995, The Art of Seeing, 1988, 3d edit., 1994, Color, 1989, 2nd edit., 1995; contbr. articles to profl. jours. Mem. com. silver anniversary U. Conn. Sch. Fine Arts, 1985; bd. dirs. Yale U. Art Sch. Alumni Assn., 1979-80. Cpl. U.S. Army, 1952-54. Accademia Italia fellow, 1977. Fellow Am. Commputing Machinery; mem. Computer Art and Design Edn. (chartered), Silvermine Guild Artists, New Eng. Artist Assn. (bd. dirs. 1966-76), Textbooks Authors Am. Roman Catholic. Avocation: reading. Home: 17 Cowles Rd West Willington CT 06279-1705 Office: U Conn # U99 Storrs Mansfield CT 06268

ZELAZO, NATHANIEL K., engineering executive; b. Lomza, Poland, Sept. 28, 1918; came to U.S., June, 1928; s. Morris and Ida (Kachorek) Z.; m. Helene Fishbein-Ret, June 27, 1943; children—Ronald Elliott, Annette Renee. B.S., CUNY, 1940; postgrad., Columbia U., 1940-42, 52-55; M.S.M.E., U. Wis., 1957, DE (hon.), 1986; D. Engring., Milw. Sch. Engring., 1983. Registered profl. engr., Wis., D.C. Vice pres. Norden Ketay (United Tech.), N.Y.C., 1952-55; dir. research devel. Avionics div. J. Oster Corp., Racine, Wis., 1955-59; pres., chief officer Astronautics Corp. Am., Milw., 1959-84, chief exec. officer, 1984—; chmn. bd. Astronautics C.A. Ltd., 1988—, Kearfott Guidance and Navigation Corp., Wayne, N.J., 1988—; v.p. Fgn. Sales Corp., St. Thomas, V.I., 1988—; dir. Astronautics-Kearfott ElectroAutomatica (AKE) Russia. Regent, mem. corp. Milw. Sch. Engring., 1984, bd. dirs., 1980—; mem. engring. adv. coun. Marquette U., Milw., 1984, mem. Pres.'s Exec. Senate; mem. indsl. liaison coun. Coll. Engring. and Applied Sch. U. Wis., Milw.; bd. dirs. Greater Milw. Com. Recipient Employer of Yr. award Dept. Def., 1982, Billy Mitchell Meml. award Air Force Assn., 1977, Small Businessman of Yr. award SBA, 1966, Disting. Svc. award U. Wis., Madison, 1985, ECE Centennial medal U. Wis. Madison, 1991, High Tech. Exporter of Yr. award Wis. Dept. Devel., 1989, Entrepreneur of Yr. award in high tech. Arthur Young, Inc., 1989, Wis. Mfr. of Yr. Spl. award Redlin Browne & Co., 1990, Gov.'s New Product award Wis. Soc. Profl. Engrs., 1993; honoree NCCJ, 1990; named Engr. of Yr., 1985, Engrs. and Scientists Milw. Mem. AIAA, IEEE (Centennial medal 1984), Nat. Soc. Profl. Engrs., Am. Soc. Naval Engrs., Am. Helicopter Soc., Engrs. and Scientists of Milw., Inc., Physics Club Milw., Air Force Assn., Navy League U.S., Armed Forces Communications and Electronics Assn., Am. Technion Soc. (Albert Einstein award 1982), Wis. Clubs: Wisconsin, Milw. Yacht, Milw. Athletic. Avocations: music; sailing; skiing. Home: 1610 N Prospect Ave Milwaukee WI 53202-2491 Office: Astronautics Corp Am 4115 N Teutonia PO Box 523 Milwaukee WI 53201-0523

ZELBY, LEON WOLF, electrical engineering educator, consulting engineer; b. Sosnowiec, Poland, Mar. 26, 1925; came to U.S., 1946, naturalized, 1951; s. Herszel and Helen (Wajnryb) Zylberberg; m. Rachel Kupferminz, Dec. 28, 1954; children: Laurie Susan, Andrew Stephen. BSEE, Moore Sch. Elec. Engring., 1956; MS, Calif. Inst. Tech., 1957; PhD, U. Pa., 1961. Registered profl. engr., Pa., Okla. Mem. staff RCA, Hughes R & D Labs., Lincoln Lab., MIT, Sandia Corp., Argonne (Ill.) Nat. Labs., Inst. for Energy Analysis; mem. faculty U. Pa., 1959-67, assoc. prof., 1964-67; assoc. dir. plasma engring. Inst. Direct Energy Conversion, 1962-67; prof. U. Okla., Norman, 1967-95, dir. Sch. Elec. Engring., 1967-95; ret., 1995; cons. RCA, 1961-67, Moore Sch. Elec. Engring., 1967-68, also pvt. firms. Editor Tech. and Soc. mag., 1990-93; contbr. articles on energy-associated problems and issues to profl. jours. With AUS, 1946-47. Cons. Electrodynamic Corp. fellow Calif. Inst. Tech., 1957, Mpls.-Honeywell fellow U. Pa., 1957-58, Harrison fellow, 1958. Mem. IEEE, Franklin Inst., Sigma Xi, Tau Beta Pi, Eta Kappa Nu, Pi Mu Epsilon, Sigma Tau, Phi Kappa Phi. Home: 1009 Whispering Pines Dr Norman OK 73072-6912 *To learn as much, and to experience as much as possible, without harm to others; read, study, vary professional and recreational activities within constraints of the system.*

ZELDES, JACOB DEAN, lawyer; b. Galesburg, Ill., Dec. 10, 1929; s. Louis Herman and Sophia Ruth (Koren) Z.; m. Nancy S. Zeldes, Aug. 23, 1953; children: Stephen, Kathryn, Amy. BS, U. Wis., 1951; LLB, Yale U., 1957. Bar: Conn. 1957, U.S. Dist. Ct. Conn. 1958, U.S. Ct. Appeals (2nd cir.) 1959, U.S. Supreme Ct. 1960, U.S. Tax Ct. 1966. Ptnr. Zeldes Needle & Cooper PC, Bridgeport, Conn. Lt. (j.g.) USNR, 1951-53, Korea. Fellow Am. Bar Found., Am. Coll. Trial Lawyers. Democrat. Jewish. Avocations: swimming, hiking, travel. Office: Zeldes Needle & Cooper PC 5th Flr 1000 Lafayette Blvd Bridgeport CT 06604-4700

ZELDIN, RICHARD PACKER, publisher; b. Worcester, Mass., Aug. 7, 1918; s. M. and Virginia (Gealt) Z.; m. Virginia Graves, Nov. 25, 1950; children—Elizabeth Ann, Richard Shepherd. BS, West Chester U., Pa., 1942; grad. exec. program bus. adminstrn., Columbia U., 1966. Gen. mgr. profl. and reference book div. McGraw-Hill Book Co., Inc., 1948-68; v.p., publishing dir. Litton Ednl. Pub. Co., Inc., 1968-70; pres. R.R. Bowker Co., 1970-76, Xerox Coll. Pub., Xerox Individualized Pub., 1970-76;; pub. John Wiley & Sons, Inc., 1976-83; v.p. Moseley Assocs. Inc., N.Y.C., 1983—; sec.-treas. sci., tech. and med. book pubs. group Asso. Am. Pubs., 1966-70; mem. adv. com. comml. publs. AEC, 1966-70. Author: A Tennis Guide to the USA, 1980, Business Forms on File, 1984, Personal Forms on File, 1984. Served to lt. USNR, 1942-46. Recipient Disting. Alumni award West Chester U., 1974. Mem. Info. Industry Assn. (sec. 1973—), IEEE, Am. Soc. Info. Sci., Soc. for Scholarly Pub. Clubs: Dutch Treat (N.Y.C.), Pubs. Lunch (N.Y.C.). Home: 20 Fairfield Dr Tinton Falls NJ 07724-3114 Office: Moseley Assocs Inc 270 Madison Ave New York NY 10016-0601

ZELEN, MARVIN, statistics educator; b. N.Y.C., June 21, 1927; m. Thelma Geier, Sept. 10, 1950; children: Deborah, Sandra. BS, CCNY, 1949; MS, U. N.C., 1951; PhD, Am. U., 1957; MA (hon.), Harvard U., 1977. Stat. eng. lab. Nat. Bureau of Standards, 1952-61; assoc. prof. Univ. Md., 1960-61; head, stat. and applied Math. section Nat. Cancer Inst., 1963-66; leading prof. State Univ., Buffalo, N.Y.C., 1967-77; pres. Frontier Sci. and Tech. Rsch. Found., Boston, 1975—; chief div. biostats. Dana Farber Cancer Inst., Boston, 1977—; prof. Harvard U. Sch. Pub. Health, Boston, 1977—; chmn. dept. biostat. Harvard U., 1980-90; vis. prof. Univ. Wis., 1961-63, vis. assoc. prof. Univ. Calif., 1958. Sgt. U.S. Army, 1945-46. Fulbright scholar, 1965-66. Fellow Am. Acad. Arts and Sci., AAAS, Inst. Math. Stats., Am. Statis. Assn.; mem. Internat. Stats. Inst. Home: 230 Eliot St Chestnut Hill MA 02167-1447 Office: Harvard Sch Pub Health 677 Huntington Ave Boston MA 02115-6028

ZELENKOFSKE, PAUL, diversified financial services company executive; b. 1938. CPA. Acct. Murray Axelrod & Co., Ltd., Bala Cynwyd, Pa., 1959-64; pres. Zelenkofske, Axelrod & Co., Ltd., Jenkintown, Pa., 1964—. Office: Zelenkofske Axelrod & Co 101 West Ave Ste 300 Jenkintown PA 19046

ZELENY, MARJORIE PFEIFFER (MRS. CHARLES ELLINGSON ZELENY), psychologist; b. Balt., Mar. 31, 1924; d. Lloyd Armitage and Mable (Willian) Pfeiffer; BA, U. Md., 1947; MS, U. Ill., 1949, postgrad., 1951-54; m. Charles Ellington Zeleny, Dec. 11, 1950 (dec.); children: Ann Douglas, Charles Timberlake. Vocational counseling psychologist VA, Balt., 1947-48; asst. U. Ill. at Urbana, 1948-50, research asso. Bur. Research, 1952-53; chief psychologist dept. neurology and psychiatry Ohio State U. Coll. Medicine, Columbus, 1950-51; research psychologist, cons., Tucson, Washington, 1954—. Mem. Am., D.C. psychol. assns., AAAS, Southeastern Psychol Assn., DAR, Nat. Soc. Daus. Colonial Wars, Nat. Soc. Colonial Dames XVII Century, Nat. Soc. Descendants of Early Quakers, Mortar Bd., Delta Delta Delta, Sigma Delta Epsilon, Psi Chi, Sigma Tau Epsilon. Roman Catholic. Home: 6825 Wemberly Way Mc Lean VA 22101-1534

ZELEZNAK, SHIRLEY ANNE, psychotherapist; b. Ft. Dodge, Iowa; d. Melvin Peter and Illiah Mary (Olson) Hood; m. Donald John Zeleznak, June 14, 1969; children: Kristine Anne, Ryan John. BA, Briar Cliff Coll., 1967; MS in Clin. and Ednl. Psychology and Counseling, Winona State U., 1972. Cert. hypnotherapist, psychotherapist. Secondary tchr. Rochester, Minn., 1969-74; secondary tchr./counselor Mankato, Minn., 1974-77; task force dir. Heart Assn., Mankato, 1978-82; mental health counselor Scottsdale, Ariz., 1985—; tchr. Maricopa County C.C., Scottsdale, 1986-89; motivational speaker, Mankato, 1974-84; sch. cons. Paradise Valley/Scottsdale Sch. Dist., 1987—; bd. dirs. Home Base, Phoenix; psychotherapist St. Maria Goretti Ch., Scottsdale, 1986—; crisis intervention counselor, police dept., Phoenix, 1993—. Author: Series for Junior High Students, 1981 (books), 1982-83 (software programs). Chef A'La Heart, Minn. Heart Assn., Mankato, 1979-81; motivational speaker Gang Awareness, Scottsdale, 1992—. Recipient Appreciation award Minn. Heart Assn., 1981. Mem. Mental Health Counselors, Nat. Ctr. for Learning Disabilities, Am. Counseling Assn., Phoenix Scottish Rite Found., Inst. for Developmental and Behavioral Neurology. Roman Catholic. Avocations: golf, tennis, power walking.

ZELIFF, WILLIAM H., JR., congressman; b. June 12, 1936; m. Sydna Zeliff. BS, Univ. Conn. Exec. DuPont Co., 1959-76; innkeeper; mem. 102nd-104th Congresses from 1st dist. N.H., 1991—; chmn. govt. reform & oversight subcom. on Nat. Security, Internat. Affairs & Criminal Justice; mem. transp. & infrastructure com., small bus. com. Served U.S. Army. Protestant. Office: US House of Reps 1210 Longworth Washington DC 20515-2901*

ZELIKOW, HOWARD MONROE, management and financial consultant; b. Bklyn., Apr. 17, 1934; s. Herman and Mae (Rebell) Z.; m. Doris Brown, June 10, 1956 (div. Aug. 1987); children—Lori Ann Zelikow Florio, Daniel M.; m. Marcie Peskin Rosenblum, Dec. 12, 1987. BA, Dartmouth Coll., 1955, MBA, Amos Tuck Sch., 1956. Acct., Ernst & Ernst, N.Y.C., 1956-61; controller Kratter Corp., N.Y.C., 1961-64; mgr. J.H. Cohn, C.P.A.s, Newark, 1964-65; ptnr. Zelikow & Rebell, CPA's, N.Y.C., 1965-70; v.p. Oxbow Constrn. Corp., Port Washington, N.Y., 1970-76; exec. v.p., treas., chief fin. officer Progressive Ins. Cos., Mayfield Village, Ohio, 1976-87; prin. ZKA Assocs., Cleve., 1987—; ptnr. Kayne Anderson & Co., L.A., 1988—; bd. dirs. Fin. Security Assurance Holding LTD, N.Y.C., The Right Start

Inc., Westlake, Calif. Trustee, Village of Great Neck Estates, Great Neck, N.Y., 1975-76. Mem. AICPA, Fin. Execs. Inst., Oakwood Club, Hillcrest Club, Phi Beta Kappa. Jewish. Home: 3491 Courtland Rd Pepper Pike OH 44122 Office: ZKA Assocs 1800 Avenue of Stars Los Angeles CA 90067

ZELIN, JEROME, retail executive; b. Bklyn., Dec. 24, 1930; s. Isidore and Ida (Roffman) Z.; m. Muriel Altsher, Dec. 18, 1955; children—Dorothy, Michael, Steven. BS magna cum laude, N.Y.U., 1952. Acct. Seymour Schwartz CPA, 1954-57; partner firm Schwartz, Zelin & Weiss CPAs, N.Y.C., 1958-61; vice chmn., pres., exec. v.p., treas., financial v.p., dir. Unishops, Inc. (retail co.), Jersey City, 1961-74; exec. v.p. Masters, Inc., Westbury, N.Y., 1974—. Trustee Temple Sholom of Flatbush. Served with AUS, 1952-54. Mem. N.Y. Soc. CPAs, Am. Inst. CPAs, Beta Gamma Sigma, Tau Alpha Omega. Jewish. Home: 225 Arkansas Dr Brooklyn NY 11234-6901

ZELINSKI, JOSEPH JOHN, engineering educator, consultant; b. Glen Lyon, Pa., Dec. 30, 1922; s. John Joseph and Lottie Mary (Oshinski) Z.; m. Mildred G. Sirois, July 22, 1946; children: Douglas John, Peter David. BS, Pa. State U., 1944, PhD, 1950. Grad. fellow Pa. State U., University Park, 1946-50; project supr. applied physics lab. Johns Hopkins U., Silver Spring, Md., 1950-58; staff scientist Space Tech. Labs. (now TRW, Inc.), Redondo Beach, Calif., 1958-60; head chem. tech. div. Ops. Evaluation Group MIT, Cambridge, 1960-62; prin. rsch. scientist Avco Everett (Mass.) Rsch. Lab., 1962-64; prof. mech. engring. Northeastern U., Boston, 1964-85, prof. emeritus, 1985—; pres. World Edn. Resources, Ltd., Tampa, Fla., 1984—; cons. Avco Everett Rsch. Lab., 1964-71, Pratt & Whitney Aircraft, East Hartford, Conn., 1966-70, Modern Electric Products and Phys. Scis. Co., Inc., Boston, 1980-82, Morrison, Mahoney and Miller, Boston, 1984; vice-chmn., chmn. exec. com. Univ. Grad. Coun., Northeastern U., Boston, 1980-84, dir. mech. engring. grad. program, 1982-85; del. 4th World Conf. Continuing Engring. Edn., Beijing China People to People, Spokane, Wash., 1989. Contbr. articles to profl. jours. Prin. Confraternity Christian Doctrine, Andover, Mass., 1961-64; pres. Andover Edn. Coun., 1962-64; vice chmn. Dem. Town Com., Boxford, Mass., 1980-84. Lt. (j.g.) USNR, 1943-46, PTO. Mem. AAAS, ASME, Am. Chem. Soc., N.Y. Acad. Scis., Combustion Inst. Democrat. Roman Catholic. Achievements include U.S. and foreign patents for coal combustion system for magnetohydrodynamic power generation, for fuel-cooled combustion systems for jet engines flying at high Mach numbers; prediction of optical observables of re-entry vehicles from analysis of decomposition mechanisms of heat-shield materials; invention of high-temperature furnace for production of crystalline graphite; development and verification of a design method for ramjet combustors. Home: Hunters Green 9207 Jubilee Ct Tampa FL 33647-2511

ZELINSKY, DANIEL, mathematics educator; b. Chgo., Nov. 22, 1922; s. Isaac and Ann (Ruttenberg) Z.; m. Zelda Oser, Sept. 23, 1945; children: Mara Sachs, Paul O., David. BS, U. Chgo., 1941, MS, 1943, PhD, 1946. Rsch. mathematician applied math group Columbia U., N.Y.C., 1941-43; instr. U. Chgo., 1943-44, 46-47; Nat. Rsch. Coun. fellow Inst. Advanced Study, Princeton, N.J., 1947-49; from asst. to assoc. prof. dept. math. Northwestern U., Evanston, Ill., 1949-60, prof., 1960-93, prof. emeritus, 1993—, acting chmn. math. dept., 1959-60, chmn., 1975-78; vis. prof. U. Calif. Berkeley, 1960, Fla. State U., Tallahassee, 1963, Hebrew U., Jerusalem, 1970-71, 85, others; vis. scholar Tata Inst., 1979; mem. various coms. Northwestern U.; lectr. in field. Author: A First Course in Linear Algebra, 1968, rev. edit., 1973; contbr. articles to profl. jours. Fulbright grantee Kyoto U., 1955-56, grantee NSF, 1958-80; Guggenheim fellow Inst. Advanced Study, 1956-57, Indo-Am. fellow, 1978-79. Fellow AAAS (mem. nominating com. sect. A 1977-80, chmn. elect sect. A 1984-85, chmn. 1985-86, retiring chmn. 1986-87), Am. Math. Soc. (mem. coun. 1961-67, editor Transactions of A.M.S. 1961-67, mem. various coms., mem. editorial bd. Notices of A.M.S. 1983-86, chmn. editorial bds. com. 1989, chmn. ad hoc com. 1991-92). Jewish. Home: 613 Hunter Rd Wilmette IL 60091-2213 Office: Northwestern U Dept Math Evanston IL 60208

ZELINSKY, PAUL O., illustrator, painter, author; b. Evanston, Ill., Feb. 14, 1953; s. Daniel and Zelda B. (Oser) Z.; m. Deborah M. Hallen, Dec. 31, 1981; children: Anna H., Rachel L. BA summa cum laude, Yale U., 1974; MFA in Painting, Tyler Sch. Art, 1976. Art instr. San Diego State U., 1976; freelance illustrator/author, 1977—. Illustrator: Ralph S. Mouse, 1982, Dear Mr. Henshaw, 1993, More Rootabagas, 1993, Swamp Angel, 1994; illustrator, adapter: Rumpelstiltskin; illustrator, adapter, designer: The Wheels on the Bus, 1990. Recipient Caldecott Honor for Hansel & Gretel, 1985, Rumpelstiltskin, 1987, Swamp Angel, 1995, Best Illustrated Book N.Y. Times Book Rev., N.Y.C., 1981, 85, 94. Mem. Graphic Artists Guild, Children's Illustrators and Authors (charter), Soc. Children's Book Writers and Illustrators, Phi Beta Kappa. Avocations: cooking, reading, child care.

ZELIS, ROBERT FELIX, cardiologist, educator; b. Perth Amboy, N.J., Aug. 5, 1939; s. Felix Andrew and Rita Marie (Jurasz) Z.; m. Gail Ann Heelon, Sept. 10, 1960; children: Robert Felix, Kathleen, Karen, David. B.S. cum laude, U. Mass., 1960; M.D. with honors, U. Chgo., 1964. Diplomate: Am. Bd. Internal Medicine (cardiovascular disease). Intern, then asst. resident in medicine Beth Israel Hosp., Harvard U. Med. Sch., 1964-66; clin. asso. (lt. comdr. USPHS) cardiology br. Nat. Heart Inst., NIH, Bethesda, Md., 1966-68; mem. faculty U. Calif. Med. Sch., Davis, 1968-74; asst. asso. prof. medicine U. Calif. Med. Sch., 1972-74, chief lab. clin. physiology, 1968-74, asst. chief sect. cardiovascular medicine, 1970-74; prof. medicine and cellular/molecular physiology Milton S. Hershey (Pa.) Med. Center, Pa. State U. Coll. Medicine, 1974—, chief div. cardiology, 1974-84, dir. cardiology research, 1984—. Editor: The Peripheral Circulations, 1975; co-editor: Calcium Blockers, 1982; mem. editorial bd. Annals Internal Medicine, 1976-79, Am. Jour. Physiology, 1976-79, Circulation, 1979-82, Am. Heart Jour., 1980-90, Am. Jour. Cardiology, 1983-86, Jour. C.V. Pharmacology, 1991—, Jour. Am. Coll. Cardiology, 1994—; contbr. articles to med. jours. Walter S. Barr fellow, 1960-64; recipient Borden Research award, 1964. Fellow A.C.P., Am. Coll. Chest Physicians, Am. Coll. Cardiology (gov. Eastern Pa. 1977-80); mem. Am. Fedn. Clin. Research (pres. 1977-78), Am. Soc. Clin. Investigation (nat. council 1981-85, v.p. 1984-85), Am. Physiol. Soc., Assn. Am. Physicians, Assn. Univ. Cardiologists, Am. Soc. Pharmacology and Exptl. Therapeutics, Am. Heart Assn. (nat. fellow councils circulation, arteriosclerosis, clin. cardiology and epidemiology, v.p. for community programs 1979-81, award of merit 1983 v.p., exec. com. Pa. 1976-79, pres. Pa. affiliate 1979-80, Charles T. Mears Humanitarian award 1984), Western Soc. Clin. Research, Sigma Xi, Alpha Omega Alpha, Phi Eta Sigma. Roman Catholic. Home: 227 Homestead Rd Hershey PA 17033-1328 Office: MS Hershey Med Ctr Cardiology Divsn Box 850 Hershey PA 17033

ZELL, SAMUEL, transportation leasing company executive; b. Chgo., Sept. 28, 1941; married. BA, U. Mich., 1963, JD, 1966. With Yates Holleb and Michelson, 1966-68; pres. Equity Fin. and Mgmt. Co., 1968—; chmn. Great Am. Mgmt. and Investment Inc., 1981—, also chief exec. officer; also co-chmn. Revco D.S.; chmn. Delta Queen Steamboat Co., New Orleans, 1984—, Eagle Industries Inc.; chmn. Itel Corp., 1985—, bd. dirs. Office: Gt Am Mgmt & Investment Inc 2 N Riverside Plz Lbby 6 Chicago IL 60606-2609*

ZELLER, CLAUDE, physicist, researcher; b. Aulnay, France, Dec. 11, 1940; came to U.S., 1976; m. Elisabeth Kreib, 1962 (div. 1967); 1 child, Frédéric; m. Florence Labour, Oct. 14, 1967; children: Caroline, Elisabeth. PhD, Univ. Nancy, France, 1968. Rsch. physicist Univ. Nancy, France, 1968-76; visiting rsch. faculty Univ. Pa., Phila., 1976-79; sr. physicist Pitney Bowes R&D, Norwalk, Conn., 1979-84, mgr. applied physics, 1984-91; fellow Pitney Bowes, Shelton, Conn., 1992—; adv. bd. CNRS, Paris, 1969-71; sec. scientific bd. Univ. Nancy, 1971-76; cons. Bruker-Spectrospin, Wissembourg, France, 1970-75. Contbr. 76 articles to profl. jours. Recipient sr. fellowship, NATO, 1976. Mem. IEEE, N.Y. Acad. Scis., Am. Phys. Soc., Appalachian Mountain Club, Soc. for Imaging Sci. and Tech., U.S. Jaycees, L'Union Alsacienne (v.p.), Am. Soc. Le Souvenir Français. Roman Catholic. Achievements include pioneer work in electron beam X-Ray microanalysis, early design of soft cast steel electro-magnet yoke for NMR applications, development of advanced materials such as high electrical conductivity intercalated graphite fibers composite materials and very high magnetic permeability amorphous fibers, investigation of the interferences of electronic articles surveillance systems with pacemakers and reporting to international regulatory commissions; 5 patents. Home: 97 Fan Hill Rd Monroe CT 06468-1831 Office: Pitney Bowes Inc 35 Waterview Dr Shelton CT 06484-4301

ZELLER, JOSEPH PAUL, advertising executive; b. Crestline, Ohio, Mar. 19, 1940; s. Paul Edward and Grace Beatrice (Kinstle) Z.; m. Nancy Jane Schmidt, June 17, 1961; children: Laurie, Joe. BA, U. Notre Dame, 1962; MFA, Ohio U., 1963. Mgr.radio/television Drewrys Ltd. USA, Inc., South Bend, Ind., 1963-64; media supr. Tatham-Laird & Kudner, Chgo., 1964-67; v.p. assoc. media dir. J. Walter Thompson Co., Chgo., 1967-77; v.p. media dir, v.p. Campbell-Mithun, Chgo., 1977-80; sr. v.p., dir. media, fin., chmn. media coun. D'Arcy Masius Benton & Bowles, Chgo., 1980-96, sr. v.p., 1996—; chmn. Z Prop, 1986—; dir. circle Desert Caballeros Mus., 1994-96. Pres. Amateur Hockey Assn. Ill., 1985. Mem. Broadcast Pioneers, Chgo. Advt. Club, Moose. Roman Catholic. Avocations: amateur hockey, country music.

ZELLER, MARILYNN KAY, librarian; b. Scottsbluff, Nebr., Mar. 1, 1940; d. William Harold and Dorothy Elizabeth (Wilkins) Richards; m. Robert Jerome Zeller, May 21, 1966; children: Kevin Jerome and Renae Kay. BS, Calvary Bible Coll., 1985; MLS, U. Mo., Columbia, 1989. Cert. libr. File clk. Waddell & Reed, Kansas City, Mo., 1962-65; payroll clk. Century Fin. Co., Kansas City, Mo., 1965-67, Percy Kent Bag Co., Independence, Mo., 1968-70; accounts receivable Swansons on the Pla, Kansas City, 1971-73; clk. casualty ins. Mill Mutuals, Kansas City, 1977-80; registrar's asst. Calvary Bible Coll., Kansas City, 1980-85, libr. asst., 1985-88, asst. libr., 1988-89, head libr., 1989—; chairperson libr. com. Calvary Bible Coll., Kansas City, 1989—; libr. rep. Friends of the Hilda Kroeker Libr., Kansas City, 1989—. Author: History of the Christian Librarian's Association, 1989. Mem. Christian Librarian's Assn., Spl. Librarian's Assn., Mo. Libr. Assn., Am. Libr. Assn. Avocations: walking, reading, crocheting, sewing, swimming. Home: 401 13th Ave N Greenwood MO 64034-9750 Office: Calvary Bible Coll 15800 Calvary Rd Kansas City MO 64147-1303

ZELLER, MICHAEL EDWARD, physicist, educator; b. San Francisco, Oct. 8, 1939; s. Edward Michael and Marie (Eschen) Z.; m. Linda Marie Smith, June 12, 1960; children: Jeffrey, Daniel. B.S., Stanford U., 1961; M.S., UCLA, 1964, Ph.D., 1968. Research assoc. UCLA, 1968-69; instr. physics Yale U., New Haven, 1969-70, asst. prof., 1970-76, assoc. prof., 1976-82, prof., 1982—, chmn., 1989-95. Recipient DeVane medal Phi Beta Kappa, 1980. Fellow Am. Phys. Soc.; mem. N.Y. Acad. Sci., Sigma Xi, Sigma Pi Sigma. Democrat. Jewish. Home: 135 Newton Rd Woodbridge CT 06525-1534 Office: Yale U Physics Dept 260 Whitney Ave New Haven CT 06511-7208

ZELLER, MICHAEL EUGENE, lawyer; b. Queens, N.Y., June 19, 1967; s. Hans Ludwig and Geri Ann (Schottenstein) Z. BA, Union Coll., 1989; JD, Temple Law Sch., 1992; LLM magna cum laude, U. Hamburg, Germany, 1994. Bar: N.Y. 1992, U.S. Dist. Ct. (so. and ea. dists.) N.Y. 1995, N.C. 1996. Fgn. intern Bryan Gonzalez Vargas y Gonzalez Baz, Mexico City, 1990; student law clerk Hon. Jane Cutler Greenspan, Phila., 1990-91; fgn. clerk DROSTE, Hamburg, 1991, fgn. assoc., translator, 1992-94; pres., translator Translations Express, Charlotte, N.C., 1995—; assoc. Internat. and Corp. Law Group of Moore & Van Allen PLLC, Charlotte, 1995—; vol. atty. Children's Law Ctr. Mem. Charlotte World Affairs Coun., Charlotte Mayor's Internat. Cabinet; bd. dirs. Alemannia Soc. Recipient scholarship Fedn. German/Am. Clubs, 1987. Mem. ABA, N.Y. State Bar Assn., N.C. Bar Assn., Mecklenburg County Bar Assn., Gewerblicher Rechtsschutz und Urheberrecht e.V., European Am. Bus. Forum, Am. Translators Assn. Avocations: singing, theater, golf, fictional writing. Office: 100 N Tryon St Fl 47 Charlotte NC 28202-4003

ZELLER, MICHAEL JAMES, psychologist, educator; b. Des Moines, Dec. 3, 1939; s. George and Lila (Fitch) Z. BS, Iowa State U., 1962, MS, 1967. Instr. psychology Mankato (Minn.) State U., 1967-73, asst. prof. psychology, 1974-89, assoc. prof. psychology, 1990—; mem. social sci. edn. coun. Mankato State U., 1976—; ednl. cons. Random House, Scott Foresman, West Pub. Editor: Test Item File to Accompany Introduction to Psychology, 6th edit., 1992; co-author: Test Item File to Accompany Introduction to Psychology, 5th edit., 1989, Test File for Psychology, 3d edit., 1988, Unit Mastery Workbook, 1st edit., 1974, 2d edit., 1976, Test Item File to Accompany Psychology, 1st edit., 1974, 2d edit., 1976, Psychology: A Personal Approach, 1st edit., 1982, 2d edit., 1984; contbr. chpts. to books. With USAR, 1964-70. Mem. APA, Minn. Psychol. Assn., Inter-Faculty Orgn., Midwestern Psychol. Assn., Psi Chi (award 1988). Achievements include development and research on educational materials, methods of instruction and career opportunities for psychology majors. Home: PO Box 1958 Mankato MN 56002-1958 Office: Mankato State U Dept of Psychology MSU 35 PO Box 8400 Mankato MN 56002

ZELLERBACH, WILLIAM JOSEPH, retired paper company executive; b. San Francisco, Sept. 15, 1920; s. Harold Lionel and Doris (Joseph) Z.; m. Margery Haber, Feb. 25, 1946; children: John William, Thomas Harold, Charles Ralph, Nancy. B.S., Wharton Sch., U. Pa., 1942; grad., Advanced Mgmt. Program, Harvard U., 1958. With Crown Zellerbach Corp. and subs., 1946-85; officer, dir. Crown Zellerbach Corp., 1960-85. Mem gen. adv. com. fgn. assistance programs AID, 1965-68; pres. Zellerbach Family Fund. Served as lt. USNR, 1942-46. Mem. Nat. Paper trade Assn. (pres. 1970). Clubs: Villa Taverna (San Francisco), Presidio Golf (San Francisco), Pacific Union (San Francisco), Commonwealth (San Francisco); Peninsula Country (San Mateo, Calif.). Office: 120 Montgomery St Ste 2100 San Francisco CA 94104-4324

ZELLERS, CARL FREDRICK, JR., railway executive; b. Wilmington, N.C., Apr. 25, 1932; s. Carl Fredrick and Bessie Jane (Jackson) Z.; m. Betty B. Burroughs, Dec. 8, 1984; children—Patricia, Carl Fredrick, Pamela. Cert. internal auditor. With Atlantic Coast Line R.R. Co., Wilmington, 1950-62, chief clk., 1958-62; sec.-treas. High Point, Thomasville & Denton R.R. Co. (N.C.), 1963-65; with Fla. East Coast Ry., St. Augustine, 1968—, sec., 1974-76, v.p., 1977—, dir., 1982—, pres. 1992—; pres. Gran Cen. Corp. div. Fla. East Coast Industries, Inc., 1984—, Fla. East Coast Industries, 1995—; bd. dirs. St. Joe Paper Co. Mem. Tax Execs. Inst., Fin. Execs. Inst., Inst. Internal Auditors. Republican. Methodist. Home: 355 Marsh Point Cir Saint Augustine FL 32084-5864 Office: Florida East Coast Industries 1 Malaga St Saint Augustine FL 32084-3580

ZELLMAN, ANDE, editor; b. New Haven, Sept. 6, 1952; s. Seymour Zellman and Lillian Shapiro. BS, Boston U., 1974. Features editor Boston Phoenix, 1978-82; mag. editor Dallas Times Herald, 1982; asst. mag. editor Boston Globe, 1983-85, mag. editor, 1985-94, assoc. editor media devel., 1994—; N.E. judge Livingston Awards (journalism), N.Y., 1988—. Mem. Sunday Mag. Editors Assn. (pres. 1988-90). Office: Boston Globe Mag 135 Morrissey Blvd Boston MA 02107

ZELLNER, BENJAMIN H., astronomer; b. Forsyth, Ga., Apr. 16, 1942; 2 children. BS in Physics, Ga. Inst. Tech., 1964; PhD in Astronomy, U. Ariz., 1970. Rsch. assoc. Lunar & Planetary Lab., U. Ariz., 1970-76, rsch. fellow, 1976-78; rsch. assoc. prof. U. Ariz., Tucson, 1978-85; staff scientist Computer Scis. Corp., Balt., 1985-94; prof. Ga. So. U., Statesboro, 1994—. Rsch. fellow Observatory Paris, 1972-73. Mem. Am. Astron. Soc., Internat. Astron. Union. Achievements include co-discovery of rings of Uranus. Office: Ga So U Dept Physics Statesboro GA 30460

ZELLNER, KENNETH KERMIT, elementary education educator; b. Allentown, Pa., Sept. 4, 1945; s. Mellis Myron and Thelma Amanda (Bortz) Z.; m. Jean Elizabeth Welsh, June 24, 1978; children: Todd Benjamin, Amanda Elizabeth. BS, Kutztown U., 1967, MEd, 1971. Cert. elementary and secondary edn., environ. edn., supervision elementary edn., Pa. Tchr. Parkland Sch. Dist., Allentown, 1967—, environ. lab. cons., 1980-95; cooperating tchr. East Stroudsburg (Pa.) U., 1973-95, Lehigh U., Bethlehem, Pa., 1992-94, sci. camp instr. SMART Ctr., 1993-94; faculty mentor Pa. Gov.'s Sch. of Excellence for Teaching Pa. Dept. Edn., Harrisburg, 1992. Contbr. articles to profl. jours. Mem. little Lehigh watershed curriculum task force Wildlands Conservancy, Emmaus, Pa., 1984-95; mem. newspapers in edn. adv. coun. Allentown Morning Call, 1988-89. Recipient Presdl. Award for Excellence in Sci. and Math. Teaching NSF, 1992, Regional Catalyst award for Excellence in Sci. Teaching Chem. Manufacturers Assn., 1994, Nat. Educators award Milken Family Found., 1994, Congrl. Citation for Outstanding Sci. Teaching Pa. Ho. of Reps., 1994. Mem. Pa. Sci. Tchrs. Assn., Nat. Sci. Tchrs. Assn., Coun. for Elem. Sci. Internat., Assn. Presdl. Awardees in Sci. Teaching, Soc. Elem. Presdl. Awardees, Masons (worshipful master 1985). Republican. Lutheran. Avocations: woodworking, antique and classic cars, snow skiing. Home: 9022 Reservoir Rd Germansville PA 18053-2731 Office: Kernsville Sch 5051 Kernsville Rd Orefield PA 18069-2321

ZELMANOWITZ, JULIUS MARTIN, mathematics educator, university administrator; b. N.Y.C., Feb. 20, 1941; s. Morris and Tillie (Holtz) Z.; m. Joan R. Traubel, June 24, 1962; 1 child, Dawn Michèle. AB, Harvard U., 1962; MS, U. Wis., 1963, PhD, 1966. Asst. prof. U. Calif., Santa Barbara, 1966-73, assoc. prof., 1973-77, prof. maths., 1977—, assoc. vice chancellor acad. affairs, 1985-87, assoc. vice chancellor acad. personnel, 1988—; assoc. prof. Carnegie-Mellon U., Pitts., 1970-71; vis. asst. prof. UCLA, 1969-70, vis. assoc. prof. 1973-74; vis. prof. U. Rome, 1977, McGill U., Montreal, Quebec, 1982-83, 87-88, U. Munich, 1983, 88. Contbr. articles to profl. jours. Sr. rsch. grantee Italian Nat. Rsch. Coun., Rome, 1977, Palermo, 1988; named Milw. Prof. of Maths. The Technion, Haifa, Israel, 1979; Fulbright sr. fellow, Munich, 1983. Mem. Am. Math. Soc., Math. Assn. Am. Home: 3215 Laurel Canyon Rd Santa Barbara CA 93105-2015 Office: U Calif Dept Math Santa Barbara CA 93106

ZELMER, AMY ELLIOTT, health science educator; b. Halifax, N.S., Can., Dec. 20, 1935; d. George Thomas and Annie Caroline (Smart) Elliott; m. A.C. Lynn Zelmer, Dec. 16, 1969; 1 child, JenniferLynne. B.Sc.N., U. Western Ont., 1961; M.P.H., U. Mich., 1963; Ph.D., Mich. State U., 1973. Nurse, health educator N.S. Dept. Public Health, Halifax, 1957-65; dir. health edn. Alta. Dept. Health, Edmonton, 1965-67; asst. prof. extension dept. U. Alta., 1967-72, asst. prof., coordinator continuing edn. Sch. Nursing, 1972-74, dean Faculty Nursing, 1976-80, assoc. v.p. acad., 1980-88; dean Sch. Health Sci., Ctrl. Queensland U., Rockhampton, Australia, 1988-96, prof. health sci., 1992—, hon. prof., 1996—; health edn. specialist S.E. Asia Regional office WHO, New Delhi, 1975-76; cons. Can. Internat. Devel. Agy.; mem. queensland Cen. Region Health Authority, 1991-95. Mem. editorial bd. Qualitative Health Rsch.; Jour. Clin. Rsch. in Nursing; cons. editor: Group and Orgn. Studies, 1976-82. Pres. Edmonton Internat. Aid Soc., 1981. Fellow Royal Coll. Nursing of Australia.; mem. Can. Assn. Univ. Schs. Nursing (pres. 1980-82), Alta. Pub. Health Assn. (pres. 1983-84). Office: Ctrl Queensland U, Rockhampton Queensland 4702, Australia

ZELNICK, CARL ROBERT, Congressional correspondent; b. N.Y.C., Aug. 9, 1940; s. David Isadore and Lillian (Ostrow) Z.; m. Pamela Margaret Sharp, Dec. 30, 1967; children: Eva Michal, Dara Yael, Marni Ruth. B.S., Cornell U., 1961; LL.B., U. Va., 1964. Bar: N.Y. 1965, D.C. 1966. Law assoc. H. Charles Ephraim, Washington, 1966-67; corr./columnist Anchorage Daily News, 1968-76; Assoc. editor Environmental Law Reporter, 1971-72; spl. corr. Christian Sci. Monitor, 1973-77; corr./bur. chief Nat. Pub. Radio, Washington, 1972-76; exec. editor Frost/Nixon Interviews, Washington, 1976-77; dir. news coverage ABC-TV, Washington, 1977-81; dep. bur. chief ABC News, Washington, 1981-82; Moscow bur. chief, corr. ABC News, 1982-84; corr. ABC News, Israel, 1984-86; ABC News Pentagon corr. Washington, 1986-94. Author: Backfire--A Reporter's View of Affirmative Action, 1996; contbr. articles to newspapers and mags. Served with USMC, 1964-65. Recipient Gavel awards Am. Bar Assn., 1969, 74, Du Pont award Columbia U. Sch. Journalism, 1984, Emmy award, 1984, 92. Mem. Council on Fgn. Relations, Radio and TV Corrs. Assn., Internat. Inst. for Strategic Studies, Washington Press Club, Phi Epsilon Pi, Pi Delta Phi. Jewish. Office: ABC News Washington Bureau 1717 DeSales St NW Washington DC 20036-4407

ZELNICK, STRAUSS, entertainment company executive; b. Boston, June 26, 1957; s. Allan Zelnick and Elsa Lee Strauss; m. Wendy Belzberg, 1990; children: Cooper, Lucas. BA summa cum laude, Wesleyan U., Middletown, Ct., 1979; MBA, Harvard U., 1983, JD cum laude, 1983. Bar: N.Y. 1984. Dir. internat. TV Columbia Pictures Internat. Corp., N.Y.C., 1983-85, v.p. internat. TV, 1985-86; sr. v.p. corp. devel. Vestron Inc., Stamford, Conn., 1986-87, exec. v.p., 1987, pres., chief oper. officer, 1988-89; pres., chief oper. officer Twentieth Century Fox, L.A., 1989-93; pres., CEO Crystal Dynamics, Palo Alto, Calif., 1993-95; pres., CEO, BMG Entertainment N.Am., N.Y.C., 1995—. Trustee Wesleyan U., 1992—; mem. contemporary arts coun. Mus. Modern Art, 1989, Young Pres. Orgn.; chmn. Covenant House Calif., 1992-95; bd. dirs. Covenant House, N.Y.C., 1995—. Mem. N.Y. State Bar Assn., Harvard Club, Phi Beta Kappa. Avocations: squash, sailing, skiing. Home: 118 E 65th St New York NY 10021-7007 Office: BMG Entertainment NA 1540 Broadway New York NY 10036-4039

ZELON, LAURIE DEE, lawyer; b. Durham, N.C., Nov. 15, 1952; d. Irving and Doris Miriam (Baker) Z.; m. David L. George, Dec. 30, 1979; children: Jeremy, Daniel. BA in English with distinction, Cornell U., 1974; JD, Harvard U., 1977. Bar: Calif. 1977, U.S. Ct. Appeals (9th cir.) 1978, U.S. Supreme Ct. 1989. Assoc. Beardsley, Hufstedler & Kemble, L.A., 1977-81; assoc. Hufstedler, Miller, Carlson & Beardsley, L.A., 1981-82, ptnr., 1983-88; ptnr. Hufstedler, Miller, Kaus & Beardsley, L.A., 1988-90, Hufstedler, Kaus & Ettinger, L.A., 1990-91, Morrison & Foerster, L.A., 1991—. Editor-in-chief: Harvard Civil Rights-Civil Liberties Law Rev., 1976-77. Vol. atty. ACLU of So. Calif., L.A., 1977—; bd. dirs. N.Y. Civil Liberties Union, 1973-74. Mem. ABA (chmn. young lawyers divsn. pro bono project 1981-83, delivery and pro bono projects com. 1983-85, subgrant competition-subgrant monitoring project 1985-86, chair standing com. on lawyers pub. svc. responsibility 1987-90, chair law firm pro bono project 1989-91, standing com. legal aid and indigent defendants 1991—, chair 1993—), Calif. Bar Assn., L.A. County Bar Assn. (trustee 1989-91, v.p. 1992-93, sr. v.p. 1993-94, pres.-elect 1994-95, pres. 1995—, fed. cts. and practices com. 1984-93, vice chmn. 1987-88, chmn. 1988-89, chmn. judiciary com. 1991-92, chair real estate litigation subsect. 1991-92), Women Lawyers Assn. L.A., Calif. Women Lawyers Assn. Democrat. Office: Morrison & Foerster 555 W 5th St Ste 3500 Los Angeles CA 90013-1080

ZEMAN, JAROLD KNOX, history educator; b. Semonice, Czechoslovakia, Feb. 27, 1926; emigrated to Can., 1948, naturalized, 1955; s. Jaroslav and Jaroslava (Potuckova) Z.; m. Lillian Koncicky, June 18, 1951; children: Miriam, Dagmar, Timothy, Janice. Grad., Charles U., Prague, 1948, Th.Cand., 1948; B.D., Knox Coll., U. Toronto, Ont., Can., 1952; Dr.Theol., U. Zurich, Switzerland, 1966; DD (hon.), McMaster U., Hamilton, Ont., 1985, Acadia U., Wolfville, N.S., 1994. Ordained to ministry Baptist Ch., 1950; pastor in Toronto and Villa Nova, Ont., 1949-59; sec. dept. Can. missions Bapt. Conv., Toronto, 1959-68; prof. ch. history Acadia U., Wolfville, N.S., Can., 1968-91; dir. Acadia Ctr. for Bapt. and Anabapt. Studies, 1991—; vis. prof. Bapt. Theol. Sem., Ruschlikon, Switzerland, 1965, 84, Mennonite Sem., Elkhart, Ind., 1976-77, Regent Coll., Vancouver, B.C., 1979, Gordon-Conwell Theol. Sem., Boston, 1983, Moravian Theol. Sem., Bethlehem, Pa., 1984, Ontario Theol. Sem., Toronto, 1986, 92; guest lectr., U.S., Can.; mem. religious adv. com. CBC. Author: God's Mission and Ours, 1963, The Whole World At Our Door, 1964, The Anabaptists and the Czech Brethren in Moravia, 1526-1628: A Study of Origins and Contacts, 1969, The Hussite Movement and the Reformation in Bohemia, Moravia and Slovakia, 1350-1650, 1977, Baptist Roots and Identity, 1978, Renewal of Church and Society, 1984, Open Doors: Baptists in Canada 1950-90, 1992; co-author: Baptists in Canada 1760-1990: A Bibliograhpy, 1989; numerous articles.; editor: The Believers' Church in Canada, 1979, Baptists in Canada, 1980, Costly Vision, 1988. Mem. Bapt. Fedn. Can. (pres. 1979-82), Am. Hist. Assn., Am. Soc. Ch. History, Soc. Reformation Research, Can. Soc. Ch. History, Czechoslovak Soc. Arts and Scis. Home: PO Box 164, Wolfville, NS Canada B0P 1X0 Office: Acadia U, Chem Dept, Wolfville, NS Canada B0P 1X0

ZEMANIAN, ARMEN HUMPARTSOUM, electrical engineer, mathematician; b. Bridgewater, Mass., Apr. 16, 1925; s. Parsegh and Filor (Paparian) Z.; m. Edna Odell Williamson Zemanian, July 12, 1958; children: Peter, Thomas, Lewis, Susan. BEE, CCNY, 1947; ScD in Engring., NYU, 1953. Registered profl. engr., N.Y. Tutor CCNY, 1947-48; engr. The Maintenance Co., N.Y.C., 1948-52; from asst. to assoc. prof. NYU, 1952-62;

prof. SUNY, Stony Brook, 1962-83, leading prof., 1983--. Author: Distribution Theory and Transform Analysis, 1965, Generalized Integral Transformations, 1968, Relizability Theory for Continuous Linear Systems, 1972, Infinite Electrical Networks, 1991, Transfiniteness for Graphs, Electrical Networks and Random Walks, 1996; co-author: Electronics, 1961; co-editor and co-founder; (rsch. jour.) Circuits, Systems and Signal Processing, 1982—. NSF faculty fellow in sci., 1975-78; recipient Sci. award Armenian Students Assns. Am., 1982; Academician (fgn. mem.) Armenian Acad. Scis., 1990, Academician (fgn. mem.) Armenian Acad. Engr., 1994. Fellow IEEE, Am. Math. Soc., Russian Acad. Natural Scis. (fgn. mem.; Kapitsa Gold medal 1996), Sigma Xi, Tau Beta Pi, Eta Kappa Nu. Democrat. Presbyterian. Office: SUNY Engring Dept Stony Brook NY 11794-2350

ZEMANS, FRANCES KAHN, legal association executive; b. Chgo., May 1, 1943; married; 3 children. BA in zoology, U. Mich., 1965; MA in polit. sci., Northwestern U., 1966, PhD in Polit. Sci., 1972. Instr. dept. politics Lake Forest (Ill.) Coll., 1973-74; instr. dept. polit. sci. Northwestern U., Evaston, Ill., 1974-75; asst. prof. depts. edn. and polit. sci. U. Chgo., 1975-80; dir. edn., rsch. Am. Judicature Soc., Chgo., 1983-85, asst. exec. dir. programs, 1985-87, exec. v.p., dir., 1987—; cons. ABA, 1980; mem. task force on judicial conduct and ethics of spl. commn. on administrn. of justice in Cook County, 1985-88; vis. lectr. Northwestern U., Chgo., 1986; bd. dirs. Cook County Criminal Justice Project, 1987-90; adjudication working group Bureau Justice Assistance, U.S. Dept. Justice, Washington, 1987, 88; mem. task force gender bias in courts, State of Ill., 1988-90;mem. Ill. Judicial Inquiry Bd., 1988-92. Contbr. articles to profl. jours.; mem. editorial bd. Justice System Journal, 1986-90; presenter in field. Bd. dirs. ACLU, Ill., 1978-87; mem. Police Bd. City of Chgo., 1980-87, chair budget com., office of profl. standards com., rules and regulations revision com.; mem. Chgo. crime survey planning com. Chgo. Community Trust, 1984-86, adv. com. govt. assistance project, 1990—; bd. visitors So. Meth. U. Sch. Law, 1987-90. Scholar ABF, 1974-83. Mem. Am. Polit. Sci. Assn., Law and Soc. Assn. (trustee 1980-83). Office: Am Judicature Soc 180 N Michigan Ave Chicago IL 60601-7401

ZEMANS, JOYCE PEARL, art historian, arts administrator; b. Toronto, Ont., Can., Apr. 21, 1940; m. Frederick H. Zemans; children: Deborah, David, Marcia. BA, U. Toronto, 1962, MA in Art History, 1966. Co-chair dept. art history Ont. Coll. Art, Toronto, 1970-71, chair dept. liberal arts, 1973-75; chair dept. visual arts York U., Toronto, 1975-81, univ. prof., 1975-95, dean faculty fine arts, 1985-88, co-dir. MBA program in arts and media adminstrn., faculty adminstrv. studies, 1994—, Robarts chair in Can. studies, 1995-96; dir. Can. Coun., Ottawa, Ont., 1989-92. Author: (book) Jock Macdonald, 1986; (catalogue) J.W.G. Macdonald: The Inner Landscape, 1981, Christopher Pratt, 1985, Kathleen Munn and Edna Tacon: New Perspectives on Modernism, 1989; (career series) Art, 1971; contbr. articles to profl. jours. Bd. dirs. Nat. Coun. Art Adminstrn., 1979-82. Mem. Can. Assn. Fine Art Deans (exec.), Internat. Coun. Fine Art Deans (bd. dirs. 1985-89), Internat. Assn. Art Critics, Univ. Art Assn. Can., Coll. Art Assn., Comité International de l'histoire de l'art, Can., Laidlaw Found. (pres.). Office: York U, Faculty of Fine Arts, Toronto, ON Canada M3J 1P3

ZEMECKIS, ROBERT L., film director; b. Chgo., 1952; m. Mary Ellen Trainor. Ed., U. So. Calif. Cinema Sch. Dir.: (films) I Wanna Hold Your Hand, 1978, Used Cars, 1980, Romancing the Stone, 1984, Back to the Future, 1985, Back to the Future, Part II, 1989, Who Framed Roger Rabbit?, 1988, Back to the Future, Part II, 1989, Back to the Future, PartIII, 1990, Death Becomes Her, 1992, Forrest Gump, 1994 (Best Dir. Acad. award), Contact, 1996; co-screenwriter: 1941, 1979, Trespass, 1992; exec. prodr. : The Public Eye, 1992. Mem. Dirs. Guild Am. also: CAA 9830 Wilshire Blvd Beverly Hills CA 90212-1804*

ZEMEL, JAY NORMAN, electrical engineer, educator; b. N.Y.C., June 26, 1928; s. Leo and Miriam Esther (Schwartz) Z.; m. Jacqueline Eva Lax, July 21, 1950; children: Alan Raymond, Babette Sharon, Andrea Melanie. B.S., Syracuse U., 1949, M.S., 1953, Ph.D., 1956, M.A. (hon.), U. Pa., 1971. Supervisory research physicist U.S. Naval Ordnance Lab., 1954-66; RCA prof. solid state electronics U. Pa., 1966-93, H. Nedwill Ramsey prof. sensor techs., 1993—, chmn. dept. elec. engring., 1973-77, dir. Ctr. for Chem. Electronics, 1979-85, dir. Ctr. for Sensor Tech., 1985-89; vis. prof. Nat. Poly. Inst. Mex., 1971, U. Tokyo, 1978, Naval Research Lab., 1977-78, U. Neuchatel, Switzerland, 1987, U. N.C., Charlotte, 1991-92; vis. scientist Instituto Elettronica dello Stato Solido-Centro Nazionale dela Resercha, Rome, 1985; dir. Advanced Study Inst. on Non-destructive Evaluation in Semicondr. Materials and Devices NATO, 1978, dir. Advanced Study Inst. on Chemically Sensitive Electronic Devices, 1980; mem. com. on sci. and the arts Franklin Inst. Editor in chief: Thin Solid Films, 1972-90; contbr. articles to profl. jours. Recipient Meritorious Civilian Service award Navy Dept., 1958, Sustained Superior Performance award, 1960. Fellow IEEE. Home: 223 Meetinghouse Rd Jenkintown PA 19046-2906 Office: U Pa Moore Sch Elec Engring Philadelphia PA 19104-6314

ZEMEL, NORMAN PAUL, orthopedic surgeon; b. Bklyn., Oct. 15, 1939; s. Nathan M. and Mary (Sklarevsky) Z.; m. Mary P. Kane. BSN, Rutgers U., 1961; MD, Thomas Jefferson Med. Sch., 1965. Bd. cert. orthopaedic surgery with added qualification in hand surgery Am. Bd. Orthopaedic Surgery. Orthopaedic surgery resident Northwestern U., Chgo., 1969-73; hand surgery fellow Boyes Hand Fellowship, L.A., 1973-74; hand surgery physician Boyes, Stark, Ashworth, L.A., 1974-88, Kerlan-Jobe Orthopaedic Clinic, Inglewood, Calif., 1989—; clin. assoc. prof. dept. orthopaedics U. So. Calif. Sch. Medicine, L.A., 1977—. Contbr. chpts. to books and articles to profl. jours. Lt. USNR, 1966-68, Vietnam. Mem. ACS, Am. Acad. Orthopaedic Surgery (bd. councilors), Am. Soc. for Surgery of the Hand, Western Orthopaedic Assn. (pres. L.A. chpt. 1993-94), Soc. Internat. de Orthopedique et de Traumatologie. Avocations: walking, reading, photography. Office: Kerlan-Jobe Orthopaedic Clinic 501 E Hardy St Ste 300 Inglewood CA 90301

ZEMM, SANDRA PHYLLIS, lawyer; b. Chgo., Aug. 18, 1947; d. Walter Stanley and Bernice Phyllis (Churas) Z. BS, U. Ill., 1969; JD, Fla. State U., 1974. Bar: Ill. 1975, Fla. 1975. With fin. dept. Sinclair Oil, Chgo., 1969-70; indsl. rels. advisor Conco Inc., Mendota, Ill., 1970-72; assoc. Seyfarth, Shaw, Fairweather & Geraldson, Chgo., 1975-82, ptnr., 1982—. Bd. dirs. Chgo. Residential Inc., 1993—, pres., 1994-95; mem. Art Inst. Round Table, Chgo., 1993-94. Mem. Ill. State Bar Assn., Fla. State Bar Assn., Univ. Club Chgo. (bd. dirs. 1991-94). Office: Seyfarth Shaw 55 E Monroe St Chicago IL 60603-5702

ZEMMER, JOSEPH LAWRENCE, JR., mathematics educator; b. Biloxi, Miss., Feb. 23, 1922; s. Joseph Lawrence and Hazel (Quint) Z.; m. Joan Kornfield, June 28, 1950; children—Joel Alan, Rachel Lee, Judith Louise. B.S., Tulane U., 1943, M.S., 1947; Ph.D., U. Wis., 1950. Mem. faculty U. Mo., Columbia, 1950—, prof. math., 1961—, chmn. dept., 1967-70, 73-76, prof. emeritus, 1987—; Fulbright lectr. Osmania U., Hyderabad, India, 1963-64. Contbr. articles to profl. jours. Served with AUS, 1944-46. Mem. Am. Math. Soc., Math. Assn. Am. (chmn. Mo. 1960-61), Can. Math. Soc., Phi Beta Kappa, Sigma Xi. Home: 701 Glenwood Ct Columbia MO 65203-2832 Office: U Mo Dept Mathematics Columbia MO 65211

ZEMPLENYI, TIBOR KAROL, cardiologist; b. Part Lupča, Czechoslovakia, July 16, 1916; came to U.S., 1968, naturalized, 1974; s. David Dezider and Irene (Pollak) Z.; m. Hana Bendová, Aug. 13, 1952; 1 son, Jan. MD, Charles U., Prague, Czechoslovakia, 1946, Docent Habilit., 1966; CSc. (PhD), Czechoslovak Acad. Sci., 1960, DSc., 1964. Clin. asst. with dept medicine Prague Motol Clinic, 1946-52; head atherosclerosis rsch. Inst. for Cardiovascular Rsch., Prague, 1952-68; assoc. prof. medicine Charles U., 1966-68; assoc. prof. medicine U. So. Calif., L.A., 1969-75, prof., 1975-92, prof. emeritus, 1992—; attending physician L.A. County- U.So. Calif. Med. Ctr. Author: Enzyme Biochemistry of the Arterial Wall, 1968; editl. bd. Atherosclerosis, 1962-75, Cor et Vasa, 1993—; adv. bd. Advances in Lipid Rsch., 1963-66; contbr. articles to numerous profl. jours. WHO fellow for study in Sweden and Gt. Britain, 1959. Fellow Am. Heart Assn., Am. Coll. Cardiology; mem. Western Soc. for Clin. Rsch., Longevity Assn. (mem. sci. bd.), European Atherosclerosis Group, Italian Soc. for Atherosclerosis (hon.). Office: 3400 Loadstone Dr Sherman Oaks CA 91403-4512

ZEN, E-AN, research geologist; b. Peking, China, May 31, 1928; came to U.S., 1946, naturalized, 1963; s. Hung-chun and Heng-chi'h (Chen) Z. AB, Cornell U., 1951; MA, Harvard U., 1952, PhD, 1955. Research fellow Woods Hole Oceanographic Inst., 1955-56, research asso., 1956-58; asst. prof. U. N.C., 1958-59; geologist U.S. Geol. Survey, 1959-80, rsch. geologist, 1981-89; adj. rsch. prof. geology U. Md., 1990—; vis. assoc. prof. Calif. Inst. Tech., 1962; Crosby vis. prof. MIT, 1973; Harry H. Hess sr. vis. fellow Princeton U., 1981; counselor 28th Internat. Geol. Congress. 1986-89. Contbr. articles to profl. jours. Recipient Maj. John Coke medal Geol. Soc. London, 1992, Outstanding Contbn. to Pub. Understanding of Geology award Am. Geol. Inst., 1994, Thomas Jefferson medal Va. Mus. Natural History Found., 1996. Fellow AAAS, Am. Acad. Arts and Scis., Geol. Soc. Am. (councillor 1985-88, v.p. 1991, pres. 1992, Day medal 1986), Mineral. Soc. Am. (coun. 1975-77, pres. 1975-76, Roebling medal 1991); mem. NAS, Geol. Soc. Washington (pres. 1973), Mineral. Assn. Can. Office: U Md Dept Geology College Park MD 20742

ZENBOPWE, WALTER CADE, III, artist, musician, singer, actor; b. N.Y.C.; s. Walter Cade and Helen (Henderson) Brehon. Student, Arts Students League, Inst. Modern Art. Appeared in (plays) Amen Corner, Hatful of Rain, Jim Pavone & the Buzz Bomb, Mary Mary, Don't Bother I Can't Cope, Harlequinade, The Story of Ulysses, Mateus, Which Way America, Poetry Now Subway Cinema, (films) Cotton Comes to Harlem, Education of Sonny Carson, Claudine, Now, Angel Heart, The Wiz, FX, (T.V.) Joe Franklin Show, Positively Black, Soul, Sammy Davis Telethon, June Rolands, Musical Chairs, Big Blue Marble; one man shows include: Ocean County Coll., 1977, Jackson State U., 1980, Phoenix Gallery, Atlanta, 1982, Olin Mus. Art, Bates Coll., Maine, 1993, others; 2-man shows include: Manchester Inst. Arts and Scis., 1968, Lewiston-Auburn Coll., Maine, 1993, others; 3 man shows include: Suffolk Community Coll., 1987; group shows include Whitney Mus., 1971, Corcoran Gallery, 1972, Black Expo, N.Y.C., 1973, Miss. Mus. Fine Art, 1991, Roanoke (Va.) Mus. Fine Art, 1982, Tampa Mus., 1982, Hunter Mus. Art, 1983, Tucson Mus. Art, 1983, New Eng. Fine Arts Inst., Maine, 1993, Lewiston-Auburn Coll., 1994; represented in permanent collections Fine Arts Mus. South, Bruce Mus., Virginia Beach Art Mus., Rockefeller Found., Peter A. Juley and son Collection, Smithsonian Inst. Nat. Mus. Am. Art, others. Recipient numerous awards for paintings, 1978—, including best in show award Las Olas Art Festival, 1980, Arts Festival Atlanta, 1981, Bruce Mus., 1983, 84, 94, 1st prize, Fine Arts Mus. South, 1982. Mem. SAG, Artists Equity. Avocations: boating, motorcycling, martial arts, fencing, tennis. Home and Studio: 172-03 119th Ave Jamaica NY 11434

ZENGER, JOHN HANCOCK, publishing company executive; b. Salt Lake City, Nov. 13, 1931; s. John H. and L. (Hancock) Z.; m. Dixie Robison, June 1, 1955 (div. 1978); children: Mark R., Robin, Todd R., Blake R., Mitchell R., Drew R.; m. Holly Olsen, June 29, 1979; stepchildren: Roger, Kirk, Lori, Michael. BS, Brigham Young U., 1955; MBA, UCLA, 1957; D in Bus. Adminstrn., U. So. Calif., Los Angeles, 1963. Asst. prof. Grad Sch. Bus. U. So. Calif., L.A., 1966-67; exec. v.p. Blanfield-Smith and Co., Pasadena, Calif., 1965-67; v.p. human resources Syntex Corp., Palo Alto, Calif., 1967-77; pres. Zenger-Miller Inc., Cupertino, Calif., 1977-92; group v.p. Times Mirror Co., San Jose, 1992—. Chmn. Palo Alto Human Rels. Coun., 1961-66. Ford Found. fellow, 1962-63; recipient Disting. Svc. award Brigham Young U., 1983; named to Human Resources Devel. Hall of Fame, 1994. Mem. Am. Soc. Tng. and Devel., Brigham Young U. Alumni Assn. (pres. 1981). Republican. Mormon. Avocation: magic. Home: 27300 Altamont Rd Los Altos Hills CA 94022 Office: 1735 Technology Dr San Jose CA 95110-1313

ZENNER, NICO, air transportation executive; b. Gent, Belgium, Aug. 1, 1964. BS in Commerce and Consular Sci., EHSAL, Brussels, 1989. Regional mgr. Sabena, Singapore, 1991; regional mgr. Sabena, Thailand, 1992; gen. mgr. Sabena, Can., 1993; asst. gen. mgr. Sabena, N.Y.C., 1993—. Office: Sabena 1155 Northern Blvd Manhasset NY 11030-3025

ZENNER, SHELDON TOBY, lawyer; b. Chgo., Jan. 11, 1953; s. Max and Clara (Goldner) Z.; m. Ellen June Morgan, Sept. 2, 1984; children: Elie, Nathaniel. BA, Northwestern U., 1974, JD, 1978. Bar: U.S. Dist. Ct. (no. dist.) Ill. 1978. Assoc. Shadur, Krupp & Miller, Chgo., 1978-80; law clk. to judge U.S. Dist. Ct. (no. dist.) Ill., Chgo., 1980-81; asst. U.S. atty., dep. chief spl. prosecutions div. No. Dist. of Ill., Chgo., 1981-89; ptnr. Katten Muchin & Zavis, Chgo., 1989—; adj. faculty Medill Sch. Journalism, Northwestern U., 1982-89, Sch. of Law, 1986—; instr. Nat. Inst. Trial Attys., 1989—. Mem. Phi Beta Kappa. Office: Katten Muchin & Zavis 525 W Monroe St Chicago IL 60661-3629

ZENOWITZ, ALLAN RALPH, government official; b. Queens Village L.I., N.Y., Apr. 18, 1928; s. Ralph and Ann Louise (Brickman) Z. Student, Trinity Coll., 1947-49; spl. studies, Yale U., 1947, Harvard U., 1948; grad., U.S. Army Armor Sch., 1950; spl. studies, U. Va., 1955, U.S. Naval War Coll., U.S. Army War Coll., Nat. Def. Univ., U.S. Army Command and Gen. Staff Coll.; BA in Govt. and Internat. Rels., U. Conn., 1960; JD, New Eng. Sch. Law, 1964; grad., U.S. Army Quartermaster Sch., 1966, U.S. Army Logistics Mgmt. Coll., 1970. Congl. intern, 1946-47; New Eng. area mgr. F.G. Ludwig Inc., Hartford, Conn., 1953-54; dir. ARZ Pub. Relations and Devel., Hartford, Conn., 1955-56; mgmt. exec. Saks Fifth Ave, N.Y.C., 1956-57; dir. spl. situations Fred Gaertner Jr. & Assoc., mgmt. engrs., bus. cons., N.Y.C., 1957-60; aide to gov. of Mass., 1961-62; state dir. Mass. Civil Def. Agy., Office Emergency Preparedness, 1965-71; chmn. Mass. Emergency Communications Commn.; mem. Mass Radiol. Adv. Protection Coun.; chmn. Mass. Gov's Water Emergency Adv. Com., 1965-71, Mass. Emergency Energy Com., 1970-71; regional dir. U.S. Office of Civil Def., 1971-72, U.S. Def. Civil Preparedness Agy., 1972-79; dir. resources mgmt. Fed. Emergency Mgmt. Agy., Washington, 1980-81, dir. fed. plans, 1981-82, chief Nat. Defense Exec. Res., 1982-83; sr. policy advisor Nat. Emergency Tng. Ctr., 1983-88; spl. asst. for hazardous material mgmt. Office Sec. Def., Washington, 1988-94; sr. policy advisor, exec. officer Fed. Emergency Mgmt. Agy., Washington, 1994—; mem. exec. com. Christian A. Herter chair in internat. relations; mem. policy com. Boston Fed. Exec. Bd., 1971-79; mem. U.S.-Can Civil Emergency Adv. Com., 1971-79; chmn. adv. council New Eng. Sch. Law, Law Enforcement Legal Edn. Program; del. NATO sr. civil emergency com., 1972; cons. Republican Nat. Com., 1964-65; adj. prof. New Eng. Sch. Law, 1965-71; chmn. Dept. Defense Fire Protection Coordinating Com., 1988-91. Mem. Mass. Rep. State Com., 1964-65; mem. Great Barrington Rep. Town Com., 1964-65. Served as 1st lt. AUS, 1950-52; served to col. AUS, brig. gen. (ret.). Recipient White House Citation for outstanding pub. svc., 1967; recipient Disting. Svc. citation Dept. Def., 1971, 91, Commendation medal U.S. Army 1966, 1968, Meritorious Svc. medal U.S. Army, 1976, Legion of Merit U.S. Army, 1977; charter mem. Sr. Exec. Svc. U.S. Govt., 1979. Mem. Am. Acad. Polit. Sci., Am. Polit. Sci. Assn., Am. Soc. Internat. Law,Nat. Emergency Mgmt. Assn. (pres. 1969-70, exec. com. 1968-71, hon. pres. 1971—), Am. Soc. Pub. Adminstrn., U. Conn. Alumni Assn. (pres. greater Washington chpt. 1983-90), Army and Navy Club (Washington). Home: 2555 Pennsylvania Ave NW Washington DC 20037-1613 also: 20 Berkshire Heights Rd Great Barrington MA 01230 Office: 500 C St SW Washington DC 20472-0001

ZENTMYER, GEORGE AUBREY, plant pathology educator; b. North Platte, Nebr., Aug. 9, 1913; s. George Aubrey and Mary Elizabeth (Strahorn) Z.; m. Dorothy Anne Dudley, May 24, 1941; children: Elizabeth Zentmyer Dossa, Jane Zentmyer Fernald, Susan Dudley. A.B., UCLA, 1935; M.S., U. Calif., 1936, Ph.D., 1938. Asst. forest pathologist U.S. Dept. Agr., San Francisco, 1937-40; asst. pathologist Conn. Agrl. Expt. Sta., New Haven, 1940-44; asst. plant pathologist to plant pathologist U. Calif., Riverside, 1944-62, prof. plant pathology, 1962—, prof. emeritus, 1981—, faculty rsch. lectr., 1964, chmn. dept., 1968-73, trustee, 1993-94; cons. NSF, Trust Ty. of Pacific Islands, 1964, 66, Commonwealth of Australia Forest and Timber Bur., 1968, AID, Ghana and Nigeria, 1969, Govt. South Africa, 1980, Govt. Israel, 1983, Govt. Western Australia, 1983, Ministry Agriculture and U. Cordoba, Spain, 1989, Govt. Costa Rica, 1993; mem. NRC panels, 1968-73. Author: Plant Disease Development and Control, 1968, Recent Advances in Pest Control, 1957, Plant Pathology, An Advanced Treatise, 1977, The Soil-Root Interface, 1979, Phytophthora Cinnamomi and the Diseases it Causes, 1980, Phytophthora: Its Biology, Taxonomy, Ecology and Pathology, 1983, Ecology and Management of Soilborne Plant Pathogens, 1984, Compendium of Tropical Fruit Diseases, 1994; assoc. editor: Ann. Rev. of Phytopathology, 1971—, Jour. Phytopathology, 1951-54, also jour. articles. Bd. dirs. Riverside YMCA, 1949-58, Friends of Mission Inn, 1981—, pres., 1991-93, Calif. Mus. Photography, 1988—; pres. Town and Gown Orgn., Riverside, 1962; bd. dirs. Riverside Hospice, 1982-85, pres., 1984-85; bd. dirs. Friends U. Calif. Riverside Botanic Garden, 1985-89, 91-95, pres., 1987-89; bd. trustees U. Calif. Riverside Found., 1993-94. Recipient award of honor Calif. Avocado Soc., 1954, spl. award of honor, 1981; recipient Emeritus Faculty award U. Calif., Riverside, 1991, UCLA Alumnus award, 1996; Guggenheim fellow, Australia, 1964-65, NATO sr. sci. fellow, Eng., 1971; NSF rsch. grantee, 1963, 68, 71, 74, 78; Bellagio scholar Rockefeller Found., 1985. Fellow AAAS (pres. Pacific div. 1974-75), Am. Phytopath. Soc. (pres. 1966, pres. Pacific eiv. 1955, found. bd. dirs. 1987—, v.p. 1991—, award of merit Caribbean div. 1972, award of distinction 1983, Lifetime Achievement award Pacific div. 1991), Explorers Club; mem. NAS, Mycol. Soc. Am., Am. Inst. Biol. Scis., Bot. Soc. Am., Brit. Mycol. Soc., Australasian Plant Pathology Soc., Philippine Phytopath. Soc., Indian Phytopath. Soc., Assn. Tropical Biology, Internat. Soc. Plant Pathology (councilor 1973-78), Pacific Assn. Tropical Phytopathology, Sigma Xi, Gamma Sigma Delta. Home: 708 Via La Paloma Riverside CA 92507-6403

ZENTZ, PATRICK JAMES, artist, rancher; b. Cando, N.D., Jan. 22, 1947; s. Clifford Wayne and Sybil Mae (Dehrer) Z.; m. Susan Grace Hedley, Dec. 7, 1968; children: Keenan, Jesse, Tyson. BA in Biology, Westmont Coll., 1969; MFA in Sculpture, U. Mont., 1974. juror Nev. State Coun. on the Arts Grants Program, Las Vegas, 1989, Nev. State Coun. on the Arts, Artists Fellowship Program, Reno, 1990, Wash State Commn. on the Arts, Olympia, 1992; artist adv. task force Western States Arts Fedn., Portland, 1991; del. Japan-Am. Grassroots Summit, Tokyo and Kyoto, Japan; vis. artist program U. Ill., Carbondale, 1994; lectr. in field. Exhibited in group shows Western State Arts Found., Bklyn. Mus., 1986, No. Ariz. U., 1987, Mont. State U., 1987, Washington Project for the Arts, 1987, Curtis Ctr., Phila., 1987, Aspen Art Mus., 1988, Missoula Mus. of the Arts, 1989, Beall Park Art Ctr., Bozeman, Mont., 1989, John Michael Kohler Art Ctr., 1989, Henry Art Gallery, U. Wash., Seattle, 1989, Seattle Art Mus., 1989, The Ctr. on Contemporary Art, Seattle, 1990, Hockaday Ctr. for the Arts, Kalispell, Mont., Contemporary Arts Mus., Houston, 1990, Boulder Art Ctr., 1991, U. Mont., 1992, Beam Art Gallery, U. Nev., 1992, Internat. Sculpture Ctr., Phila., 1992, Cheney Cowles Mus., Spokane, Wash., 1994, San Antonio Mus. of Art, 1994, Rubelle & Norman Schaffer Gallery, Pratt Inst., Bklyn., 1994, Boise Art Mus., 1995; represented in permanent collections U. Med. Ctr. U. Wash., Seattle, 1990, Richard Tam Alumni Ctr. U. Nev., Las Vegas, 1991, Snake River Correctional Instn., Ontario, Oreg., 1993, Western State Hosp., Ft. Steilecom, Wash., 1993, Salt Palace Renovation and Expansion Project, Salt Lake City, 1994, TRI-MET Westside Light Rail Sys., Portland, 1995. Grantee Art Matters, Inc., 1988, LEF Found., 1992; fellowship Nat. Endowment for the Arts, 1990.

ZEO, FRANK JAMES, technology company executive; b. Springfield, Mass., Jan. 9, 1910; s. Michael and Jennie (Acquavella) Z.; m. Dorothea Louise Duncan, June 27, 1942; children: Virginia D. Coate, Cynthia J. Newell. AB, Yale U., 1932; postgrad., Syracuse U., 1935-37. Cons. Pub. Adminstrn. Svc., Chgo. and Boston, 1938-40; cons. Mass. Taxpayers Found., Boston, 1940-58, exec. v.p., 1959-71; cons. mgmt./pub. affairs Boston, 1971—; ind. distributor Kaire Internat., Inc., Longmont, Colo., 1989—; mktg. assoc. Investment Exch., Calvary, Alta., Can., Scottsdale, Ariz. Bd. dirs. Greater Boston Salvation Army Bd., 1970—, Exec. Svc. Corps of New Eng., Boston, 1982—; chmn. Nat. Taxpayers Conf., Boston, 1970-71; trustee John Hancock Variable Series Trust I, Boston, 1968—; New Eng. peer support coord. Elizabeth Campbell Peer Support Program, Manly, N.S.W., Australia; bd. dirs. Ron Burton Tng. Village, Hubbardston, Mass., 1991—; hon. trustee East Boston Savs. Bank, 1971—, Mass. Taxpayers Found., Boston, 1985—. Lt. Col. USAF, 1942-45. Decorated Legion of Merit. Mem. Govtl. Rsch. Assn. (hon.), Coun. Mem. Yale Club of Boston, Rotary (past pres. Boston club). Congregationalist. Avocations: photography, music, fishing, walking, writing. Home: 90 Naugus Ave Marblehead MA 01945-1552 Office: Lexington Power Mgmt Corp 271 Edgewater Dr Wakefield MA 01880-6215

ZEPF, THOMAS HERMAN, physics educator, researcher; b. Cin., Feb. 13, 1935; s. Paul A. and Agnes J. (Schulz) Z. BS summa cum laude, Xavier U., 1957; MS, St. Louis U., 1960, PhD, 1963. Asst. prof. physics Creighton U., Omaha, 1962-67, assoc. prof., 1967-75, prof., 1975—, acting chmn. dept. physics, 1963-66, chmn., 1966-73, 81-93, coord. allied health programs, 1975-76, coord. pre-health scis. advising, 1976-81; cons. physicist VA Hosp., Omaha, 1966-71; vis. prof. physics St. Louis U., 1973-74; program evaluator Am. Coun. on Edn., 1988—. Contbr. articles and abstracts to Surface Sci., Bull. Am. Phys. Soc., Proceedings Nebr. Acad. Sci., The Physics Tchr. jour., others. Chmn. physics judging com. Greater Nebr. Sci. and Engring. Fair, 1973-85. Recipient Cert. Recognition award Phi Beta Kappa U. Cin. chpt., 1953, Disting. Faculty Svc. award Creighton U., 1987. Mem. AAAS, Am. Phys. Soc., Am. Assn. Physics Tchrs. (pres. Nebr. sect. 1978), Nebr. Acad. Sci. (life, chmn. physics sect. 1985—), Internat. Brotherhood Magicians, Soc. Am. Magicians (pres. assembly #7, 1964-65), KC, Sigma Xi (Achievement award for rsch. St. Louis chpt. 1963, pres. Omaha chpt. 1993-94), Sigma Pi Sigma. Roman Catholic. Office: Creighton U Dept Physics Omaha NE 68178 *The real magic we all have at our disposal - not trickery, not pseudoscience, not spells and incantations - is our ability to comprehend our world, to understand how things behave. Through science we can use that understanding to predict outcomes and exert a measure of control over nature. It's a sacred trust. It makes the scientist a kind of modern day magician.*

ZERBE, ANTHONY, actor; b. Long Beach, Calif.; s. Arthur Le Van and Catherine (Scurlock) Z.; m. Arnette Jens, Oct. 7, 1962; children: Jennet, Jared Le Van. Student, Pomona Coll., 1954-55, Stella Adler Theater Studio, N.Y.C., 1958-60. Pres. prodn. co. Cameo Theater Inc. Actor Fred Miller Theater, Milw., 1962-63, Arena Stage, Washington, 1963-65, Theater Living Arts, Phila., 1965-66, Stratford (Ont., Can.) Theater, 1962, Old Globe Theater, San Diego, 1965-67, 72, Mark Taper Forum, Los Angeles, 1967—, Seattle Repertory Co., 1975—; appeared on Broadway in The Little Foxes, 1981; films include Cool Hand Luke, 1967, Will Penny, 1967, Omega Man, 1970, Liberation of L.B. Jones, 1972, Farewell My Lovely, 1975, Turning Point, 1977, Who'll Stop the Rain, 1978, First Deadly Sin, 1980, Soggy Bottom, U.S.A, 1980, The Dead Zone, 1983, Offbeat, 1985, Steel Dawn, 1987, Private Investigations, 1987; appeared on numerous TV shows, including Harry-O series, 1974-76 (Emmy awd., NATAS, 1976, for continuing performance by a supporting actor in a drama series), Young Riders, 1992-93; TV films include The Priest Killer, 1971, Snatched, 1973, She Lives, 1973, The Healers, 1974, In The Glitter Palace, 1977, Man of Honor, 1980, Attica, 1980, The Return of the Man from UNCLE, 1983 Dream West, 1986, One Police Plaza, 1986; miniseries: George Washington, 1984, North and South, Book II, 1986; one-man show It's All Done With Mirrors, 1977—; (with Roscoe Lee Browne) two-man show Behind the Broken Words, 1977—. Served with USAF, 1959. Recipient Emmy award as best supporting actor Harry-O, 1976. Office: care Susan Smith & Assocs 121 N San Vicente Blvd Beverly Hills CA 90211-2303*

ZERELLA, JOSEPH T., pediatric surgeon; b. Youngstown, Ohio, Mar. 7, 1941; s. Atilio and Ann (Capuzello) Z.; m. Diana Isabelle Talbot, Aug. 5, 1967; children—Ann, Michael, Mark. B.S., Northwestern U., 1962, M.D., 1966. Diplomate Am. Bd. Surgery, Am. Bd. Pediatric Surgery. Intern Med. Coll. Wis., Milw., 1966-67, resident in surgery, 1967-68, 70-73; tng. fellow in pediatric surgery Children's Hosp. Med. Ctr., Cin., 1973-75; staff pediatric surgeon Phoenix Children's Hosp., 1975—; staff Ariz. Children's Hosp., Phoenix, 1975—; pvt. practice medicine specializing in pediatric surgery, Phoenix, 1975—; mem. staff Good Samaritan Hosp., Phoenix, 1975—, sect. chief pediatric surgery, 1979—; mem. staff St. Joseph's Hosp., Phoenix, 1975—, sect. chief pediatric surgery, 1980—; Contbr. articles to profl. jours. Served as capt. U.S. Army, 1968-70. Fellow ACS, Am. Acad. Pediatrics, Am. Pediatric Surg. Assn., Pacific Assn. Pediatric Surgeons. Roman Catholic. Office: Saguaro Children's Surgery Ltd 1301 E Mcdowell Rd Ste 100 Phoenix AZ 85006-2605

ZERETZKE, FREDERICK FRANK H., artist, educator; b. Milw., July 4, 1919; s. Herman and Hertha Hildegarde (Riebow) Z.; m. Marian Louise Elfers, Dec. 7, 1942; children: Frederick J., David L., Mary J., John E. Student, Milw. Art Inst., 1938-39, Layton Sch. of Art, Milw., 1940-41, Rockford (Ill.) Coll., 1947. Art tchr. Burpee Art Gallery, Rockford, Ill., 1946-48; mural artist People's Real Estate Agy., Rockford, 1958, Grace Luth. Ch., Loves Park, Ill., 1960, Sweden House, Rockford, 1972; artist oil meml. young girl First United Presbyn. Ch., Greeley, Colo., 1963; mural artist Linos, Rockford, 1974; art tchr. pvt. studio, Rockford, Ill., 1968-78; art. tchr. pvt. studio, Burlington, Wash., 1978—; artist and tchr. art in nat. def. Camp Callan, San Diego, 1942-43, Rock Valley Coll., Rockford, Ill., 1970-77, Skagit Valley Coll., Mt. Vernon, Wash., 1978-80; water color instr. Daniel Smith Art, Seattle, 1994, 95. Exhibited in Z Studio, Burlington, Vt.; also group shows in art galleries, Wis., Calif., Wash., Ill., Elements Gallery, Bellingham, Wash., 1988-90, Fox Glove Art Gallery, Mt. Vernon, Wash., 1989—, Twisted Willow Gallery, Mt. Vernon, 1993—, Arts and Frame Gallerie, Canyon Lake, Calif., 1993, Arts Coun. Snohomish County, Everett, Wash., 1993; executed mural in Hadamar, Germany, Lino's Italian REstaurant, Rockford, Ill.; pvt. collections include Joseph Stroyan 1978-91, North Whidbey Inn, Oak Harbor, Wash., Kenney Fellers 1990-95 Timbers Restaurant, Sedro-Woolley, Wash., Pastor Karsten Baalson 1983-95. Sec. Loves Park (Ill.) Zoning Bd., 1949-56; mem. Skagit Human Rights Task Force to Protect Fundamental Human Rights Guaranteed in Constitution of U.S., 1996. With U.S. Army, 1941-45, ETO. Scholar Milw. Art Inst., 1939, Layton Sch. Art, 1940; awarded commission for design for Swedish Tour of Sveas Soner Chorus of Rockford, 1965; named Artist of Yr. Winnebago County, 1974. Mem. Tamaroa Water Color Soc. Rockford (hon. lifetime, founder, pres. 1964), Skagit Art Assn. (pres. 1987-88). Mem. Unitarian Ch. Avocations: photography, psychology, travel, hiking, outdoor life. Home: 722 Peterson Rd Burlington WA 98233-2656

ZERIN, STEVEN DAVID, lawyer; b. N.Y.C., Oct. 1, 1953; s. Stanley Robert and Cecilie Paula (Goldberg) Z.; m. Susan Marilyn Wershba, Oct. 13, 1984; children: Alexander James, J. Oliver. BS, Syracuse U., 1974; JD, St. Johns U., 1977. Bar: N.Y. 1978, U.S. Dist. Ct. (so. dist.) N.Y. 1985, U.S. Supreme Ct. 1986. Assoc. Gladstein & Isaac, N.Y.C., 1981-82, Sperry, Weinberg, Wels, Waldman & Rubenstein, N.Y.C., 1982-85; ptnr. Wels & Zerin, N.Y.C., 1985—. Trustee, mem. bd. govs. Daytop Village. Mem. ABA (exec. mem. and lectr. family law sect.), N.Y. State Bar Assn. (exec. com. family law sect.), Assn. of Bar of City of N.Y. Democrat. Home: 200 E 89th St New York NY 10128-4300 Office: Wels & Zerin 600 Madison Ave Fl 22 New York NY 10022-1615

ZERMAN, MAXINE LORAINE, mathematics and science braille consultant; b. Menomonie, Wis., Oct. 18, 1927; d. James and Celia May (Dunahee) Beaver; m. R. P. Allan, Feb. 11, 1945 (div. Aug. 1956); children: Darlene, David (dec.), Daniel; m. Arnold Elwood Zerman, Oct. 29, 1967 (dec. Nov. 1993); stepchildren: Patricia, Gary, Karen (dec.). Student, Milw. Conservatory of Music, 1950-51. Cert. literary braille, math. and sci. braille, math. and sci. braille proofreading. Math. and sci. braille advisor Libr. of Congress/Nat. Libr. Svc. for the Blind and Physically Handicapped, Washington, 1986—; cons. All Braillists, 1985—. Contbr. articles to profl. jours. Named Innovator of the Yr., Fla. Assn. Educators and Rehabilitators, 1991. Mem. Nat. Braille Assn. (math. chmn. 1985-88), Visual Aid Vols. Fla. (pres. 1989-91, editor newsletter 1988-90), Sarasota County Braille Transcribers (pres. 1991-95). Avocations: travel, reading, playing organ, volunteering. Home and Office: 2526 Wisteria St Sarasota FL 34239-4001

ZERNER, MICHAEL CHARLES, chemistry and physics educator, consultant, researcher; b. Boston, Jan. 31, 1940; s. Maurice Bernard and Blanche (Deutsch) Z.; m. Anna Gunilla Fojerstam, May 5, 1966; children: Erik Mark, Emma Danielle. BS, Carnegie Mellon Inst., 1961; MS, Harvard U., 1962, PhD, 1966; postdoctoral U. Uppsala, (Sweden), 1968-70. Asst. prof. U. Guelph (Ont., Can.), 1970-74, assoc. prof., 1974-80, prof., 1980-82, adj. prof., 1982-87; prof. chemistry and physics U. Fla., Gainesville, 1981—, chmn. dept. chemistry, 1988-94; cons. in theoretical chemistry; co-organizer Internat. Sanibel Symposium on Theoretical Chemistry, 1983—. Served to capt. U.S. Army, 1966-68. Recipient cert. U.S. Army Materials Command, 1975, Humboldt prize, 1991-94, Achievement award Internat. Soc. Quantum Bio., 1986; named Fulbright Disting. Prof., 1987; NIH fellow, 1968-70; Grantee NSF, Nat. Sci. and Engring. Rsch. Coun. of Can., Office Naval Rsch. Fellow AAAS, Am. Inst. Physics; mem. Am. Chem. Soc., Sigma Xi, others. Patentee in photoconduction and polymer sci.; co-editor Procs. Internat. Conf. Quantum/Biology and Pharmacology, 1978—; Internat. Congress Quantum Chemistry, 1983—; editor Adv. Quantum Chemistry; assoc. editor Internat. Jour. Quantum Chemistry; contbr. pubs. to profl. lit. Office: U Fla Dept Of Chemistry Gainesville FL 32611

ZERVAS, NICHOLAS THEMISTOCLES, neurosurgeon; b. Lynn, Mass., Mar. 9, 1929; s. Themistocles and Demetra P. (Stasinopoulos) Z.; m. Thalia Poleway, Feb. 15, 1959; children—T. Nicholas, Christopher Louis, Rhea. A.B., Harvard U., 1950; M.D., U. Chgo., 1954. Intern N.Y. Hosp., 1955; resident in neurology Montreal Neurol. Inst., 1956; resident in neurosurgery Mass. Gen. Hosp., Boston, 1958-62; fellow in stereotaxic cerebral surgery U. Paris, 1960-61; asst. attending surgeon, asso. neurosurgery Jefferson Med. Coll., Phila., 1962-67; asso. prof. surgery Harvard U., 1971-77; also chief neurosurg. service Beth Israel Hosp., Boston, 1967-77; prof. surgery Harvard U., 1977—; also chief neurosurg. service Mass. Gen. Hosp., 1977—; Higgins prof. neurosurgery Harvard U., 1987—. Contbr. numerous articles to sci. jours. Chmn. Mass. Coun. Arts and Humanities, 1983-91; trustee Boston Symphony Orch., 1990—, vice chmn., 1993—, pres., 1994. Capt. M.C. AUS, 1956-58. Mem. Am. Acad. Arts and Scis., Am. Acad. Neurol. Surgery (pres. 1990-91), Am. Assn. Neurol. Surgeons, Soc. Neurol. Surgeons, Am. Neurol. Assn., Am. Bd. Neurol. Surgery (chmn. 1990-91), Inst. Medicine Nat. Acad. Scis., Sigma Xi. Home: 100 Canton Ave Milton MA 02186-3507 Office: Mass Gen Hosp 32 Fruit St Boston MA 02114-2620

ZERZAN, CHARLES JOSEPH, JR., gastroenterologist; b. Portland, Oreg., Dec. 1, 1921; s. Charles Joseph and Margaret Cecelia (Mahony) Z.; BA, Wilamette U., 1948; MD, Marquette U., 1951; m. Joan Margaret Kathan, Feb. 7, 1948; children: Charles Joseph, Michael, Kathryn, Paul, Joan, Margaret, Terrance, Phillip, Thomas, Rose, Kevin, Gregory. Commd. 2d. lt., U.S. Army, 1940, advanced through grades to capt., 1945, ret., 1946, re-enlisted, 1951, advanced through grades to lt. col., M.C., 1965; intern Madigan Gen. Hosp., Ft. Lewis, Wash., 1951-52; resident in internal medicine Letterman Gen. Hosp., San Francisco, 1953-56, Walter Reed Gen. Hosp., Washington, 1960-61; chief of medicine Rodriquez Army Hosp., 1957-60, U.S. Army Hosp., Fort Gordon, Calif., 1962-65; chief gastroenterology Fitzsimmons Gen. Hosp., Denver, 1965-66; chief profl. services U.S. Army Hosp., Ft. Carson, Colo., 1967-68; dir. continuing med. edn. U. Oreg., Portland, 1968-73; ptnr. Permanente Clinic, Portland, 1973—; assoc. clin. prof. medicine U. Oreg., 1973—; individual practice medicine, specializing in gastroenterology, Portland, 1968-92; staff Northwest Permanente, P.C., dir., 1980-83. Mem. Portland Com. Fgn. Rels., 1986—, bd. dirs., 1994—. Decorated Legion of Merit, Army Commendation medal with oak leaf cluster; Meritorious Alumnus award Oreg. Health Scis. U., 1990. Diplomate Am. Bd. Internal Medicine. Fellow A.C.P.; mem. Am. Gastroenterol. Assn., Oreg. Med. Assn. (del. Clackamas County), Ret. Officers Assn. Republican. Roman Catholic. Home and Office: 6364 SE Mcnary Rd Portland OR 97267-5119

ZETCHER, ARNOLD B., apparel executive; b. 1940. BA, Washington U., 1962. With Federated Dept. Stores, N.Y.C., 1962-76; chmn. bd., CEO Bonwit Teller, N.Y.C., 1976-80; with Kohl's Corp., N.Y.C., 1980-83; chmn. bd., CEO Kohl's Food Stores, N.Y.C., John Breuner Co., San Ramon, Calif., 1983-86; pres. The Talbot Inc., Hingham, Mass., 1987—. Office: Talbot's Inc 175 Beal St Hingham MA 02043-1501*

ZETTLEMOYER, ALBERT F., computer company executive; b. 1934. Pres. Paramax Sys. Corp. subs. Unisys Corp.; sr. v.p. Unisys Corp., Blue Bell, Pa., exec. v.p., pres. govt. sys. group, 1993—. Office: Unisys Corp Township Ln Union Mtg Rads Blue Bell PA 19422*

ZEUGNER, JOHN FINN, history educator, writer; b. N.Y.C., Oct. 7, 1938; s. Orland Kump and Ethel (Finn) Z.; m. Alice Chatfield Valentine, Sept. 7, 1968; children: Emily Valentine, Maxwell Finn, Laura Ruth. A.B., Harvard U., 1959; M.A., Fla. State U., 1968, Ph.D., 1971. Night mgr. Beach Cart, Sarasota, Fla., 1960-67; asst. prof. history Worcester Poly. Inst., Mass., 1971-74; assoc. prof. Worcester Poly. Inst., 1974-82, prof., 1982—; Fulbright lectr. Osaka U., Kobe U., Japan, 1976-78; vis. prof. Keio U., Tokyo, 1981-83; Bryant Drake guest prof. Kobe Coll., Japan, 1994-95. Contbr. articles, short stores to profl. publs. Served with USCG, 1961-62. Named Paris Fletcher Disting. Prof. Humanities, Worcester Poly. Inst., 1985; grantee NEA, 1970. Mem. Orgn. Am. Historians, Soc. Historians Am. Fgn. Rels., Soc. Historians Tech. Avocations: tennis; chess. Home: 31 William St Worcester MA 01609-2313 Office: Worcester Poly Inst Humanities & Arts Dept Worcester MA 01609

ZEUSCHNER, ERWIN ARNOLD, investment advisory company executive; b. Freiburg, Germany, Nov. 17, 1935; came to U.S., 1936; s. Reinhold Hermann and Helene Barbara (Maas) Z.; m. Christa Elfreide Ellmers, June 20, 1959 (dec. Aug., 1971); children—Peter Erwin, Suzanne Christina, Andrea Ellmers; m. Margaret Anne Finn, Mar. 25, 1972; 1 dau., Elizabeth Nora. B.A. in Econs., Queens Coll., 1957; M.B.A. in Fin, NYU, 1964. Sr. v.p. Chase Manhattan Bank, N.Y.C., 1970-72; sr. v.p., dir. Chase Investors Mgmt. Corp., 1972-80; sr. v.p. Chase Manhattan Corp., 1970-80; ptnr. David J. Greene & Co. (investment advs.), N.Y.C., 1980—. Served to capt. USAF, 1958-60. Mem. N.Y. Soc. Security Analysts (dir.). Home: 1 Middle Dr Manhasset NY 11030-1414 Office: 599 Lexington Ave New York NY 10022-6030

ZEVON, SUSAN JANE, editor; b. N.Y.C., July 23, 1944; d. Louis and Rhea (Alter) Z. BA, Smith Coll., 1966. Asst. editor trends and environments House & Garden, N.Y.C., 1970-80; account supr. Jessica Dee Communications, N.Y.C., 1981-84; editor architecture House Beautiful, N.Y.C., 1985—. Author: Inside Architecture, 1996, (with others) Decorating On The Cheap, 1984. Mem. Archtl. League N.Y., Smith Coll. N.Y. Club (v.p. 1987-88, pres. 1988-89). Avocations: films, lit., gymnastics, art. Office: House Beautiful 1700 Broadway New York NY 10019-5905

ZEVON, WARREN, singer, songwriter; b. Chgo., Jan. 24, 1947; m. Crystal Zevon (div.); 1 child, Ariel; 1 child from previous marriage, Jordan. Folksinger, writer commls., pianist with Everly Bros., 1970-73; albums include Wanted Dead or Alive, 1970, Warren Zevon, 1976, Excitable Boy, 1978 (gold record), Bad Luck Streak in Dancing School, 1980, Stand in the Fire, 1980, The Envoy, 1982, Sentimental Hygiene, 1987, Transverse City, 1989, (with Hindu Love Gods) Hindu Love Gods, 1990, Mr. Bad Example, 1991, Learning to Flinch, 1993, A Quiet Normal Life (the best of Warren Zevon), 1993, Mutineer, 1995; composer: When Johnny Strikes up the Band, Hasten Down the Wind, Werewolves of London, Poor Poor Pitiful Me, Play It All Night Long, Roland the Headless Thompson Gunner. Office: care Virgin Records Am Inc 338 N Foothill Rd Beverly Hills CA 90210-3608

ZHANG, JINGWU, immunologist; b. Shanghai, Feb. 2, 1956; arrived in Belgium, 1986; s. Yuzeng and Xiochin Zhang; m. Ying Chin, Feb. 19, 1986; children: Linda, Peter. MD, Shanghai (China) Med. U., 1984; DSc, U. Brussels, 1990. Lic. MD. Rsch. fellow Dr. Willems Inst., Diepenbeek, Belgium, 1986-90, head dept., 1990—; rsch. assoc. Harvard Med. Sch., Boston, 1991-92; vis. prof. Baylor Coll. Medicine, Houston, 1993; prof. Limburgs U. Ctr., Diepenbeek, 1994—, Shanghai Med. U., 1995. Contbr. articles to profl. jours.; patentee in field. Recipient Rsch. award Am. Multiple Slcerosis Soc., 1990, Achievement award Belgian Soc. Clin. Immunology, 1993, Internat. award Assn. Malattie Rare, 1994. Mem. AAAS, N.Y. Acad. Scis., European Immunology Fedn. Avocations: painting, music, sports. Office: Baylor Coll Medicine Dept Neurology Houston TX 77030

ZHANG, XIAODONG, computer science educator and researcher; b. Beijing, China, July 16, 1958; came to the U.S., 1983; s. Min and Yishan (Jiang) Z.; m. Yan Meng, July 20, 1985; 1 child, Simon. BS, Beijing (China) Poly. U., 1982; MS, U. Colo., 1985, PhD, 1989. Rsch. asst. Beijing (China) Poly. U., 1982-83, Environ. Rsch. Lab., Boulder, Colo., 1983-85, U. Colo., Boulder, 1985-89; tech. staff Toplogix Inc., Denver, 1989; asst. prof. U. Tex., San Antonio, 1989-92, assoc. prof., 1993—, chair computer sci., 1993, dir. high performance computing and software lab., 1993—; vis. scientist Rice U., 1990-91; guest prof. Wuhan U., China; adv. panelist NSF, 1995; program chair 4th Internat. Workshop on Modeling, Analysis and Simulation of Computer and Telecomm. Systems. Co-author: Multiprocessor Performance, 1994; editor Jour. of Parallel Computing, 1994-95; contbr. articles to profl. jours. Recipient Disting. Rsch. Achievement award U. Tex., 1993, Best Paper award 9th Internat. Conf. on Supercomputing, 1995; grantee NSF, 1990—, Southwestern Bell, 1992—, USAF, 1993—, AFOSR, 1995—, ONR, 1995—. Mem. IEEE (sr.; chmn. tech. com. on supercomputing applications), Assn. Computing Machinery (nat. lectr.), Soc. Indsl. and Applied Math. Office: U Tex Computer Sci San Antonio TX 78249

ZHANG, XUMU, chemist, educator; b. E Zhou City, Hubei, China, Oct. 30, 1961; came to U.S., 1985; m. Liping Xiong, July 14, 1986; 1 child, Isadora Y. BS, Wuhan U., 1982; MS, Chinese Acad. Scis., Fuzhou, Peoples Republic of China, 1985; postgrad., U. Calif., San Diego, 1985-87; PhD, Stanford U., 1992. Staff rschr. Chinese Acad. Scis., 1982-85; rsch. asst. Stanford (Calif.) U., 1987-92, postdoctoral fellow, 1992-94; asst. prof. dept. chemistry Pa. State U., University Park, 1994—; cons. Adelphi Tech., Inc., 1993-94. Named Franklin Veatch fellow 1991; grantee: Camille and Henry Dreyfus Found., 1994; recipient DuPont Young Faculty award, 1996, Office of Naval Rsch. Young Investigator award, 1996. Mem. Am. Chem. Soc. Achievements include transition metal catalyzed asymmetric synthesis for chiral drugs. Office: Pa State U Dept Chemistry University Park PA 16802

ZHANG, YOUXUE, geology educator; b. Huarong County, Hunan, China, Sept. 17, 1957; came to U.S., 1983; s. Zaiyi Zhang and Dezhen Wu; m. Zhengjiu Xu; children: Dan, Ray. BS in Geol. Scis., Peking U., Beijing, 1982; MA in Geol. Scis., Columbia U., 1985, MPhil, 1987, PhD in Geol. Scis., 1989. Grad. rsch. asst. Columbia U., N.Y.C., 1983-88; postdoctoral fellow Calif. Inst. Tech., 1988-91; asst. prof. geology U. Mich., Ann Arbor, 1991—. Contbr. articles to profl. jours. Named Young Investigator, NSF, 1994. Mem. Am. Geophys. Union, Geochem. Soc. (F.W. Clarke medal 1993), Mineral. Soc. Am., Sigma Xi. Office: Dept Geol Sci U Mich Ann Arbor MI 48109-1063

ZHANG WEI-QIANG, dancer. Grad. with highest honors, Beijing Dance Acad., 1979; postgrad., Houston Ballet Acad. Prin. dancer Beijing Dance Acad. Ballet Co., 1981-84, Ctrl. Ballet of China, 1984-92, Royal Winnipeg (Man., Can.) Ballet, 1992—; guest artist Houston Ballet, Star Dancers Ballet, Japan, Asami Maki Ballet Co., Universal Ballet Co. of Korea, The Hong Kong Ballet, Goh Ballet, Can., Gala performance in memory of Anton Dolin, London, 1984, 2nd Internat. Ballet Competition Gala, Paris, 1986, 2d Aoyama Ballet Festival, Tokyo, 1988, Gala performance in memory of Prix de Lausanne, Tokyo, 1989, Japan Ballet Festival, Tokyo, 1989, 91, 92, and numerous other festivals and galas. Prin. roles include Giselle, Don Quixote, Swan Lake, Nutcracker, Raymonda, La Fille Mal Gardee, Coppelia, The Leaves Are Fading, The Afternoon of the Faun, Scotch Symphony, Allegro Brillante, Romeo & Juliet, Sleeping Beauty. Recipient Bronze medal 2nd Internat. Ballet Competition, Jackson, Miss., 1982, 2nd prize 4th World Ballet Competition, Osaka, Japan, 1984, Bronze medal 5th Moscow Internat. Ballet Competition, 1985, Highest Honor award 1st Nat. Ballet Competition, Beijing, 1985. Office: Royal Winnipeg Ballet, 380 Graham Ave, Winnipeg, MB Canada R3C 4K2

ZHAO, MEISHAN, chemical physics educator, researcher; b. Shanxian, Shandong, People's Republic of China, Nov. 5, 1958; came to U.S., 1984; s. Zhong Chen Zhao and Ming Rong Zhang; m. Linlin Cai, Sept. 2, 1983; children: Fang, Yuan, Nan. MS in Physics, U. Minn., 1986, PhD in Chem. Physics, 1989. Lectr. physics S.E. U. China, Nanjing, 1982-84; teaching asst., rsch. asst. U. Minn., Mpls., 1984-89; rschr. James Franck Inst. U. Chgo., 1990—. Contbr. articles to profl. jours. Mem. AAAS, Am. Phys. Soc. (internat. editl. bd. Internal. Physics Edn., Chinese ed., 1991-92), N.Y. Acad. Sci. Home: 5642 S Drexel Ave Chicago IL 60637-1418 Office: Univ Chgo James Franck Inst 5640 S Ellis Ave Chicago IL 60637-1433

ZHENG, LISA LIQING, computer programmer; b. Xian, China, May 11, 1966; came to U.S., 1990; d. Youzhong Zheng and Siuping Huang. BSEE, Huazhong U. Sci. & Tech., 1988; MSEE, Purdue U., 1992. Asst. engr. Inst. Electronics Chinese Acad. Scis., Beijing, 1988-90; electronics engr., systems programmer Computer Graphics, Corp., Indpls., 1992-94; programmer Bertelsmann Music Group, Inc., Indpls., 1994—. Avocations: traveling, philately, swimming, bicycling, cooking. Office: Bertlesmann Music Group Inc 6550 E 30th St Indianapolis IN 46219-1102

ZHOU, HUANCHUN, chemist, administrator; b. Shanghai, Oct. 1, 1939; came to U.S., 1985; s. Qingyun and Wanxian (Hu) Z.; m. Qingliang Li, Sept. 5, 1967; 1 child, Fugang. BS equivalent, Fudan U., China, 1962; MS, Shanghai U. Tech., China, 1981; PhD equivalent, U. Fla., 1990. Engr. Wuxi Oil Pump Factory, Jiangsu, China, 1962-67; laborer Wuxi Oil Pump Factory, 1968-74, 1968-74; analytical technician Wuxi Oil Pump Factory, 1974-76; faculty Shanghai U. Tech., 1982-84; rschr. dept. chemistry U. Fla., Gainesville, 1985-91; chemist Fla. Dept. Agr., 1991—; chem. lab. chief Wuxi Oil Pump Factory, 1963-66; chmn. sect. chem. analysis Wuxi Sci-Tech. Assn., 1963-66; lectr. to 201st Am. Chem. Soc. Meeting, 1991. Editor: Wuxi Chem. Analysis and Phys. Test, 1964-66, corr. editor; editor: Jour. Chem. Analysis and Phys. Test, 1964-66; contbr. articles to profl. jours. Co-grantee Office of Naval Rsch., 1991. Achievements include research in determination of phosphorus together with other 6 elements in chrome steel in one solution by using a nonoxidizing acid first in world; searched out of the direct and quantitative relationship between solubility and charges and radii of ions first in world; promotion of simple natural sieve method to prove infinity of prime twins and derivation of simple and most accurate formula in world to estimate number of prime twins; discovered relationship between phase graphs and differential thermal analysis curves; co-developer chemical polymerization polyaniline and polypyrrole on Langmuir-Blodgett trough; discovered method to monitor polymerizations by Langmuir-Blodgett computerized techniques. Home: 7517-C Pitch Pine Cir Tampa FL 33617

ZHOU, KANG-WEI, physics educator; b. Zhongxian, Sichuan, China, June 21, 1935; s. Cheng-Han Zhou and Zhi-Fang Xiong; m. Shi-Fang Dai, Sept. 24, 1961; 1 child, Zhou Bing. B Physics, Sichuan U., Chengdu, China. Asst. lectr. Inner Mongolia U., Huhehaote, China, 1961-71; technician Chengdu 1st radio factory, 1971-78; asst. lectr. Sichuan U., 1979-80, lectr., 1981-85, assoc. prof., 1986-92, prof. physics, 1993—. Author: Diferential and Integral Calculus, 1987; contbr. articles to profl. jours. Recipient sci./tech. award Nat. Edn. Com. of China, 1990, Govt. Sichuan, 1993. Mem. AAAS, Chinese Ctr. of Advanced Sci. and Tech., Internat. Ctr. for Materials Physics, Acad. Sinica, Am. Phys. Soc. Avocations: music, touring. Office: Dept Physics, Sichuan Univ, Chengdu 610064, China

ZHOU, MING DE, aeronautical scientist, educator; b. Zhejiang, China, June 26, 1937; s. Pin Xiang and Ang Din (Xia) Z.; m. Zhuang Yuhua, Aug. 12, 1936; children: Zhengyu, Yan Zhuang. BS, Beijing U. Aeros.-Astronautics, 1962; MS, Northwestern U. Tech., 1967; PhD, Internat. Edn. Rsch. Found., 1992. Tchr. Harbin (China) U. Tech., 1962-64, 67-73; from lectr. to prof. Nanjing (China) U. Aeronautics and Astronautics, 1973-86, 86—; dean bd. postgrad. studies Nanjing (China) U. Aeros. and Astronautics, 1985-89; nationally qualified PhD advisor China, 1989—; rsch. scientist U. Ariz., Tucson, 1991-93, rsch. prof., 1993—; vis. scholar Cambridge (England) U., 1980-82; guest scientist Inst. Exptl. Fluid Mechanics, Göttingen, Germany, 1983-84, 85, 87; sr. vis. scientist Tech. U. Berlin, 1988, 90; rsch. assoc. U. So. Calif., L.A., 1989-90. Author: (with others) Viscous Flows and Their Measurements, 1988, (with others) Introduction to Vorticity and Vortex Dynamics, 1992; mem. editorial com. Chinese Jour. Exptl. Mechanics, 1986-89; contbr. articles to Jour. Fluid Mechanics, Aero. Jour. U.K., Experiments in Fluids, AIAA Jour., Chinese Jour. Aeronautics. Co-recipient Nat. award Progress in Sci. and Tech. first class, Peoples Republic of China, 1985. Mem. AIAA (sr.), Am. Phys. Soc., Chinese Soc. Aeronautics, Chinese Soc. Mechanics (mem. acad. group exptl. fluid mechanics 1986-89), Chinese Soc. Aerodynamic Rsch. (acad. group unsteady flow and vortex control 1985-89). Achievements include patent for techniques and device of artificial boundary layer transition.

ZHU, AI-LAN, opera singer; b. Nanjing, Jiang Su, Peoples Republic of China, Nov. 29, 1956; came to U.S., 1984; d. De-Chang Zhu and Shu-hua Tsao; m. Chai-Lun Yueh, Oct. 30, 1982. MusB, Cen. Conservatory Music, Beijing, 1977; Artist Diploma in Opera, Hartt Sch of Music, U. Hartford, 1986. Appeared in leading opera houses of N.Am.; leading soprano in Tex. Opera Theater, Houston, 1987, Va. Opera Assn., Norfol,, 1987, Opera Theater St. Louis, 1989, PepsiCo Summerfare and European tour, N.Y., 1989, Lyric Opera of Boston, 1990, Glyndebourne Opera Festival, 1990, 91, Lyric Opera of Kansas City, 1990, Caramoor Festival, N.Y., 1990, Chautauqua Opera and Orch., 1990, Opera Pacific, L.A., 1991, Minn. Opera, 1992, Opera Co. Phila., 1992, Mich. Opera Theater, 1993, Austin Lyric Opera, 1993, 94—, Scottish Opera, 1994, Conn. Opera, 1995, Atlanta Opera, 1995, Conn. Opera, 1995, 96, Shanghai Symphony, 1996; European tour Pellèas et Mèlisande, 1992-93; concert singer Chautauqua (N.Y.) Instn., 1987, Liederkranz Found., N.Y.C., 1989; recital The Theatre Musical de Paris, Chatelet, 1991; concert tour with Sherrill Milnes, Beijing, China, 1993. Finalist Luciano Pavarotti internat. vocal competition, Opera Cos. Phila., 1985; recipient 1st prize Sigma Alpha Iota vocal competition, Chautauqua, N.Y., 1986, 5th prize Liederkranz Found. vocal competition, N.Y.C., 1989. Mem. Am. Guild Mus. Artists. Home: 51 King Philip Dr West Hartford CT 06117-2140 Office: Columiba Artists Mgmt 165 W 57th St New York NY 10019-2201

ZHU, BAOJIN, soil chemist; b. Wa Fang Dian City, China, Oct. 6, 1957; came to U.S., 1986; s. Zhenjiang and Silan (Li) Z.; m. Ying He, Aug. 8, 1983; 1 child, Lucy. BS in Soil Sci., Shenyang (China) Agrl. U., 1982, MS in Plant Nutrition, 1984; PhD in Soil Chemistry, U. Wis., 1991. Tchr. Shenyang Agrl. U., 1984-85; rsch. asst. U. Wis., Madison, 1986-91; rsch. assoc. U. Fla., Lake Alfred, 1991-92, Iowa State U., Ames, 1992-94; lead chemist Countrymark Coops. Inc., Indpls., 1994—. Contbr. articles to profl. jours. Recipient Scholarship Ministry of Agr., China, 1986. Mem. Am. Soc. Agronomy, Soil Sci. Soc. Am., Sigma Xi. Achievements include development of a rapid and accurate method for determination of arsenic and selenium in soil and solid wastes; improvement of a Donnan membrane equilibration method for measuring trace metal activities in soil; finding an efficient way to dispose biotechnology byproducts; contucting extensive investigation of selenium and arsenic in soils and sewage sludges in Iowa; avocations: playing tennis, swimming, reading, travel. Home: 5937 Southern Springs Ave Indianapolis IN 46237 Office: Countrymark Coops Inc 950 N Merridian St Indianapolis IN 46204

ZHU, JIANPING, mathematics educator; b. Beijing, People's Republic of China, May 16, 1958; came to U.S. 1986; s. Shunqian and Yuhua (Li) Z.; m. Yan Wang, May 24, 1986; children: Lily Ann, Jimmy Howard. BS, Zhejiang U., Hangzhou, China, 1982; MS, Dalian Inst. Tech., China, 1984; PhD, SUNY, Stony Brook, 1990. Lectr. math. Shanghai Jiaotong U., Shanghai, China, 1984-86; research asst. math. SUNY, Stony Brook, 1986-90; asst. prof. math. Miss. State U., 1990-93, assoc. prof., 1993—; cons. Shanghai Mcpl. Constrn. Corp., 1984-86. Author of 1 book; contbr. articles to profl. jours. SUNY-Stony Brook fellow, 1986-90, rsch. fellow Intel U. Ptnrs., 1992; recipient 2d prize IBM Supercomputing Competition, 1990. Mem. Am. Math. Soc., Soc. of Indsl. and Applied Math. Office: Miss State U Dept Math Mississippi State MS 39762

ZHU, YONG, research scientist; b. Shanghai, Oct. 30, 1947; s. Shuping Chu and Zhiping Wang; m. Shaokui Wang, Apr. 22, 1977; 1 child, Shenke. B of Engr., East China Inst. Chem. Tech., Shanghai, 1981; postgrad., Tianhin Inst. Textile Engring., 1982; PhD in Organic Chemistry, U. Ill., 1992. Laborer Qingdao (China) Cigaratte Manufacture, 1968-72; rsch. asst. Qingdao Inst. Light Industry, 1972-77; asst. prof., head dept. Shandong Inst. Textile Engring., China, 1983-87; vis. scientist U. Ill., Urbana, 1987-88, tchg./rsch. asst., 1988-92, postdoctoral rsch. assoc., 1992-93; scientist Procter and Gamble Far East, Kobe, Japan, 1993-95, Procter and Gamble Co., Cin., 1995—; cons. Qingdao Manufacture of Dyeing Auxiliaries, 1983-87, Jiaonan (China) Manufacture of Fragrances, 1984-87. Contbr. articles to profl. jours. Recipient Edn. scholarship Chinese Edn. Assn., 1987. Mem. Am. Chem. Soc. (vol. in pub. outreach 1991-95), Inter-Am. Photochem. Soc., Chinese Color-Optical Soc., Shandong Textile Engring. Assn. Avocations: sports (volleyball, swimming), music (violin, social dance), travelling.

ZHUKOV, YURI, ballet dancer; b. Leningrad, Russia. Student, A.Y. Vaganova Sch. Choreography, Leningrad. With Kirov Ballet; soloist San Francisco Ballet, 1989-92, prin. dancer, 1992—. Appeared in ballets Nutcracker, Serenade, The Four Temperaments, Handel-a Celebration, The Sleeping Beauty, Swan Lake, Aurora Polaris, Menuetto, The Four Seasons, Variations de Ballet, Vivaldi Concerto Grosso, Dreams of Harmony, The End, Dark Elegies, Rodin, Job, Cinderella, Giselle, Scotch Symphony. Office: San Francisco Ballet 455 Franklin St San Francisco CA 94102-4438

ZIADEH, FARHAT J., Middle Eastern studies educator; b. Ramallah, Palestine, Apr. 8, 1917; s. Jacob and Nimeh Farah Z.; m. Suad Salem, July 24, 1949; children—Shireen, Susan, Rhonda, Deena, Reema. B.A., Am. U., Beirut, 1937; LL.B., U. London, 1940. Bar: Barrister-at-law Lincoln's Inn 1946. Instr. Princeton U., 1943-45, lectr. Oriental studies, 1948-54, asst. prof., 1954-58, asso. prof., 1958-66; magistrate Govt. of Palestine, 1947-48; editor Voice of Am., USIA, 1950-54; prof. U. Wash., Seattle, 1966—; prof., chmn. dept. Near Eastern lang. and lit. U. Wash., 1970-82, dir. Ctr. Arabic Study Abroad, 1983-89; adj. prof. U. Wash. Law Sch., 1978-87, prof. emeritus, 1987—;. Author: Reader in Modern Literary Arabic, 1964, Lawyers, The Rule of Law and Liberalism in Modern Egypt, 1968, Property Law in the Arab World, 1979; contbr. articles to profl. jours. Mem. Middle East Studies Assn. (pres. 1979-80), Am. Oriental Soc. (past pres. western br.), Am. Research Center in Egypt (past bd. govs., exec. com.), Am. Assn. Tchrs. Arabic (past pres.). Eastern Orthodox. Office: Univ Wash Mid Eastern Studies Dept Seattle WA 98195

ZIAKA-VASILEIADOU, ZOE DIMITRIOS, chemical engineer; b. Larissa, Thessalia, Greece, Apr. 15, 1963; came to U.S., 1988; d. Dimitrios J. and Melpomeni D. (Sakellariou) Z.; m. Savvas P. Vasileiadis, Feb. 17, 1985; 1 child, Eugenia-Melina. Diploma in Chem. Engring., Aristotle U. Thessaloniki, Greece, 1987; MS in Chem. Engring., Syracuse U., 1990; PhD in Chem. Engring., U. So. Calif., 1994. Registered profl. engr., European Cmty. Scholar chem. engring. Aristotle U. Thessaloniki, 1982-87; rschr. chem. lab. Exxon Corp., Thessaloniki, 1984, engring. mgr., 1986; fellow Norwegian Ednl. Coun., 1988; scholar Ctr. Indsl. Devel., Greece, 1987-88; rsch. assoc., scholar Syracuse (N.Y.) U., 1988-90; rsch. assoc., fellow U. So. Calif., L.A., 1990-94, adj. prof., 1995; practical trainee Internat. Assn. Exch. Student Engring., Finland, 1985, Israel, 1986; patentee in field. Contbr. articles to AIChE Jour., Chem. Engring. Sci., Jour. Membrane Sci., Separation Sci. and Tech., 5th World Congress Chem. Engring. NATO fellow Greek Govt., Thessaloniki, 1987-88, AXIOS Found. for Worthiness fellow, Torrance, Calif., 1994, CRESPE, COGPS-U. So. Calif. fellow, L.A., 1992, 93, 94. Mem. AIChE, Materials Rsch. Soc., N.Am. Catalysis Soc., Greek Inst. Chem. Engrs. Orthodox Christian. Achievements include research and development of catalytic membrane reactors; design of new separation processes, catalytic and polymeric materials; mathematical modelling of transport and reaction systems; programming and computing processes. Avocations: classical music, swimming, basketball, travel, painting. Home: 1179 W 37th St Apt D Los Angeles CA 90007

ZIAVRAS, SOTIRIOS GEORGE, computer and electrical engineer, educator; b. Athens, Jan. 2, 1962; came to the U.S., 1984; s. George Spyros and Sofia George Z. Diploma in elec. engring., Nat. Tech. U., 1984; MS, Ohio U., 1985; DSc, George Washington U., 1990. Rschr. Riso (Denmark) Nat. Lab., 1983; teaching and rsch. asst. Ohio U., Athens, 1984-85; disting. grad. teaching asst. George Washington U., Washington, 1985-89, rsch. asst., 1986; assoc. prof. N.J. Inst. Tech., Newark, 1990—; rschr. Walter Reed Army Inst. Rsch., Silver Spring, Md., 1987-88; rsch. asst. U. Md., College Park, 1988-89; vis. prof. George Mason U., Fairfax, Va., 1990. Contbr. articles to profl. jours.; assoc. editor: Pattern Recognition Jour., 1994—. Recipient Rsch. Initiation award NSF, 1991. Mem. IEEE (sr.), Assn. for Computing Machinery, N.Y. Acad. Scis. (adv. bd. CIS sect. 1994—), Eta Kappa Nu. Achievements include development of class of high-performance, low-cost interconnection networks for massively parallel computers called reduced hypercubes; introduction of class of multilevel architectures for high-performance multiresolution image analysis. Office: NJ Inst Tech Elec Computer Engring Dept Newark NJ 07102

ZIBART, MICHAEL ALAN, wholesale book company executive; b. Nashville, Mar. 12, 1947; s. Alan Walter and Joy (Hughes) Z.; m. Margaret Anne Boyd, Dec. 27, 1976; children: Emily Joy, Mary Claire. B.A., Vanderbilt U., 1969. Mgmt. trainee Zibart Bros. Books, Nashville, 1961-69; property mgr. Pollack Co., Nashville, 1966-69; buyer Ingram Book Co., Nashville, 1970-75, mgr. trade dept., 1976, v.p., 1976-85, exec. v.p., 1985-88; founder, pres. ProMotion, Inc., Nashville, 1988—. Author: Almanac on Bookselling, 3d edit., 1980; pub. BookPage. Office: ProMotion Inc 2501 21st Ave S # 5 Nashville TN 37212-5626

ZICHEK, SHANNON ELAINE, secondary school educator; b. Lincoln, Nebr., May 29, 1944; d. Melvin Eddie and Dorothy Virginia (Patrick) Z. AA, York (Nebr.) Coll., 1965; BA, U. Nebr., Kearney, 1968; postgrad., U. Okla., Edmond, 1970, 71, 72, 73, 74, 75, U. Nebr., Kearney, 1980, 81, 82, 89, 92. Tchr. history and English, NW High Sch., Grand Island, Nebr., 1948—. Republican. Christian. Home: 2730 N North Rd Grand Island NE 68803-1143

ZICK, JOHN WALTER, retired accounting company executive; b. Highland Park, Ill., Sept. 21, 1925; s. Walter Ernest and Helen Ann (Wiedenhoeft) Z.; m. Mary Ann Sutter, Dec. 11, 1948; children: Sharon, Catherine, John W. B.S., Northwestern U., 1948. With Price Waterhouse, Chgo., 1948-73, N.Y.C., 1973-86; partner Price Waterhouse, 1960-86, partner in charge N.Y.C. office, 1973-76, regional mng. partner, 1976-78, co-chmn., ops., dept. sr. partner, 1978-86. Bd. dirs. Mid-Am. chpt. ARC, 1968-73, Medic Alert Found. U.S., 1994—; founding mem., elder Winnetka (Ill.) Presbyterian Ch., 1956-67; bd. auditors New Trier Twp., Ill., 1969-73; trustee Carnegie Hall Soc. and Corp., 1980—; mem. corp. Greenwich Hosp. Assn., 1980-89. Served with USN, 1943-46. Mem. AICPA (treas. and dir. 1974-77), Ill. Soc. CPAs (pres. 1971-72). Clubs: Pine Valley Golf; Union League (N.Y.C.); Blind Brook; Burning Tree (Washington).

ZICK, LEONARD OTTO, accountant, manufacturing executive, financial consultant; b. St. Joseph, Mich., Jan. 16, 1905; s. Otto J. and Hannah (Heyn) Z.; student Western State U., Kalamazoo; m. Anna Essig, June 27, 1925 (dec. May 1976); children: Rowene (Mrs. A. C. Neidow), Arlene (Mrs. Thomas Anton), Constance Mae (Mrs. Hilary Snell), Shirley Ann (Mrs. John Vander Ley) (dec.); m. 2d, Genevieve Evans, Nov. 3, 1977. Sr. ptnr. firm Zick, Campbell & Rose Accts. and predessor firms, South Bend, Ind., 1928-48; sec.-treas. C. M. Hall Lamp Co., Detroit, 1948-51, pres. 1951-54, chmn. bd., 1954-56; pres., treas., dir. Allen Electric & Equipment Co. (now Allen Group, Inc.), Kalamazoo, 1954-57, pres., treas., dir. The Lithibar Co., Holland, Mich., 1957-61; fin. v.p., treas., dir. Crampton Mfg. Co., 1961-63; mgr. corp. fin. dept. Manley, Bennett, McDonald & Co., Detroit, 1963-68; mgr. Leonard O. Zick & Assocs., Holland, 1968-88; former dir. Eberhard's Foods, Inc., Grand Rapids. Former mem. Mich. Rep. Cen. Com.; trustee YMCA Found., Clearwater, Fla., Adm. Richard E. Byrd Ctr., Boston; vice chmn. Army-Navy Munitions Bd., 1941-42, asst. to vice chmn. War Prodn. Bd., 1941-43. Mem. Nat. Assn. Accts. (past nat. v.p., dir.), Mich. Self Insurers Assn. (past pres.), Fin. Execs. Inst., Stuart Cameron McLeod Soc. (past pres.), Union League (Chgo.), Rotary (Paul Harris fellow). Lutheran. Home: 360 W 40th St Apt 312 Holland MI 49423-4674

ZIEBARTH, E. WILLIAM, news analyst, educator; b. Columbus, Wis., Oct. 4, 1910; s. John and Priscilla (Conrad) Z.; m. Elizabeth Herreid, Dec. 16, 1939; 1 son, John Thomas. B.S., U. Wis., 1933, Ph.M., 1934; Ph.D., U. Minn., 1948, D.H.L. (hon.), 1985. Staff U. of Air, WHA, U. Wis., 1934; instr. speech U. Minn., 1936; acting gen. mgr. sta. WLB, 1944, asso. prof., chmn. dept. speech, 1948, prof., chmn. dept. speech and theatre arts, 1949—, dean summer session, 1954—, dean gen. extension div., 1963-64; dean Coll. Liberal Arts, 1964, interim pres., 1974; cons. for TV World Affairs, 1954; founder, also dir. Min. Sch. of Air, 1938; prodn. mgr. WCCO-CBS, 1945, news analyst, 1947-52, exec. cons., 1948; ednl. dir. central div. CBS network, 1946, cons., 1948-51, spl. fgn., corr., internat. affairs analyst, Scandinavia, So. and Western Europe, 1949, fgn. corr., internat. broadcaster, Scandinavia, Western Europe, Western Asia, 1950, Asiatic analysis, Tokyo, Japan, 1952; exec. v.p., interim gen. mgr. KTCA-TV, KTCI-TV, 1976; exec. v.p., gen. mgr. Twin City Area Pub. TV Corp., 1976-77; radio edn. cons. Hill Found. award study in Soviet Union, 1958, 68; bd. dirs. Midwest Ednl. Television Corp.; trustee Twin City Area TV Corp.; co-chmn. feasibility research Pan-Pacific-Mainland Edn. and Communication Expt. by Satellite, Honolulu, Tokyo, Hong Kong, 1973. Author Six Classic Plays for Radio and How to Produce Them, published in, 1940; contbr.: articles to profl. jours. Mass Media editor Speech Monographs, 1951-53; cons. editor: articles to profl. jours. Central States Speech Jour. Dir. Hennepin County Tb Assn., Minn. Tb and Public Health Asso. Mem. Gov.'s Youth Commn.; mem. Nat. Commn. on Arts and Scis.; Trustee Macalester Coll. Joint winner nat. Peabody award, 1948; recipient citation Nat. English Council, 1949; Radio Council award for distinguished news analysis, 1952, for significant contbns. internat. understanding, 1951; first award Nat. Inst. Edn. by Radio for news interpretation, 1952; Best Commentator award AFTRA, 1955; joint winner Peabody award, internat. affairs, 1960; Nat. Peabody award, 1972; Blakeslee award Nat. Heart Assn., 1972; Mitchell V. Charnley award for Outstanding Contbns. to Broadcast Journalism, 1982; Outstanding Individual award Speech-Communication Assn., 1982; N.W. Area Found. fellow to People's Republic of China, 1976. Mem. Nat. Assn. Edn. by Radio, Fgn. Policy Assn., Minn. Hist. Soc., Nat. Adult Edn. Assn., Nat. Assn. Ednl. Broadcasters and Telecasters, Nat. Soc. Study Communication (Radio council, mass media com.), Central States Speech Assn., Chi Phi, Phi Kappa, Delta Sigma Rho, Phi Delta Kappa, Psi Chi, Alpha Epsilon Rho, Delta Phi Lambda, Lambda Alpha Psi. Clubs: Hesperia, Greyfriars, Campus, Univ. St, Paul. Home: Apt 325 1666 Coffman St Saint Paul MN 55108 Office: N-231 Psychology Elliott Hall # U Minn Minneapolis MN 55455

ZIEBARTH, KARL REX, international transportation consultant; b. Reading, Pa., May 25, 1938; s. Robert Kurt and Leah Evelyn (DuBor) Z.; m. Gisela Hermine Hader, Nov. 13, 1970; children: Viktoria, Alexander, Elena. B.A., Yale U., 1959. Security analyst Bank of N.Y., 1960-63; 2d v.p. Hayden, Stone, Inc., N.Y.C., 1963-70; asst. v.p. Dominick and Dominick, N.Y.C., 1970-71; v.p., sec., treas. Mo.-Kans.-Tex. R.R. Co., Dallas, 1970-78; exec. v.p. fin. Mo.-Kans.-Tex. R.R. Co., 1979-88, also bd. dirs.; pres. Atlantic & Western Mgmt., Irving, Tex., 1990, also bd. dirs.; fin. and transp. cons. Dallas, 1990—; v.p., sec. Iron Rd Railways Inc., 1995—. Trustee Phila. Soc., 1975-78, Dallas Ballet Assn., 1981-86, Am. Enterprise Forum, 1989—. Capt. USAR, 1960-69. Clubs: Racquet (Chgo.); Petroleum (Dallas); Reform (London); Yale (N.Y.C.). Office: 3626 N Hall St Ste 405 Dallas TX 75219-5129

ZIEBARTH, ROBERT CHARLES, management consultant; b. Evanston, Ill., Sept. 12, 1936; s. Charles A. and Marian (Miller) Z.; m. Patience Arnold Kirkpatrick, Aug. 28, 1971; children—Dana Kirkpatrick, Scott Kirkpatrick, Christopher, Nicholas. A.B., Princeton, 1958; M.B.A., Harvard, 1964. With Bell & Howell Co., Chgo., 1964-73; treas., chief fin. officer Bell & Howell Co., 1969-73; mgmt. cons. Ziebarth Co., 1973—; mem. dirs. adv. bd. Arkwright Boston Ins. Co., devel. com. Nat. Assn. Ind. Schs.; bd. dirs. M.B.A. Resources, Inc., Telemedia, Inc., Corp. Resources, Inc., Nordemann Grimm Inc. Assoc. Community Renewal Soc., Citizens Coun. Gateway House; mem. Ill. Bd. Higher Edn., Ill. Joint Edn. Commn.; trustee Choate Sch.; trustee, pres. Latin Sch.Chgo., Chgo. Maternity Ctr.; bd. dirs. Harvard Bus. Sch. Fund, U.S.O., Inc., Prentice Women's Hosp., Northwestern Meml. Corp., Found. for Reproductive Rsch. and Edn., Endowments Inc., Bond Portfolio Endowments Inc. Served to lt. USNR, 1958-62. Mem. Naval Hist. Found., Art Inst. Chgo., Chgo. Hist. Soc., Mus. Modern Art. Presbyn. Clubs: Mid-Am. (Chgo.), Racquet (Chgo.), Saddle and Cycle (Chgo.), Economic (Chgo.), Executives (Chgo.). Office: PO Box 750 Dedham MA 02027

ZIEGAUS, ALAN JAMES, public relations executive; b. Bremerton, Wash., May 8, 1948; s. Alan Moon and Dorothy (Lamont) Z.; m. Constance Jean Carver, 1972; children: Jennifer, Ashley. BJ, San Diego State U., 1970. Staff writer San Diego Tribune, 1972-77; exec. asst. San Diego City Council, 1977-78; v.p. Gable Agy., San Diego, 1978-80; pres. Stoorza, Ziegaus & Metzger, San Diego, 1980—. Mem. planning com. County San Diego, 1980-82; mem. sewage task force City of San Diego, 1986-88, civil svc. com., 1992—; trustee armed forces YMCA, San Diego, 1984—. Recipient Best Investigative Series award AP, 1975. Mem. San Diego Press Club (Best News Story award 1973). Home: 12351 Brassica St San Diego CA 92129-4127 Office: Stoorza Ziegaus & Metzger 225 Broadway Ste 1600 San Diego CA 92101-5018

ZIEGENHAGEN, DAVID M., healthcare company executive; b. Mpls., May 25, 1936; s. Elmer Herbert Ziegenhagen and Margaret Ruth (Mackenzie) Kruger; m. Mary Ange Kinsella, Nov. 26, 1966 (div. Dec. 1982); children: Marc, Eric. BA, U. Minn., 1962. Assoc. dir. Thailand Peace Corps, Bangkok, 1963-65; Thailand program officer Peace Corps, Washington, 1966-67; dir. Western Samoa Peace Corps, Apia, 1967-70; exec. dir. Mental Health Assn. Minn., Mpls., 1970-76; co-founder, pres. Current Newspapers, Inc., Burnsville, Minn., 1975-84; sr. program officer The St. Paul Found., 1982-84; pres. DMZ Assocs., St. Paul, 1983—; exec. dir. Minn. Bd. Med. Practice, St. Paul, 1985-88; CEO, pres. Found. for Health Care Evaluation, Bloomington, Minn., 1988—; field dir. Am Refugee Com., Bangkok, 1979; dir. Health Edn. Rsch. Found., St. Paul, 1993—; mem. Citizens League, Mpls., 1975—, dir., 1988-95; mem. Adminstrs. in Medicine, Washington, 1985-88; dir. Walk-In Counseling Ctr., Washington, 1990—, Ctr. for Clin. Quality Evaluation, 1990—. Mem. Nat. Mental Health Staff Coun. (pres. 1970-76). Avocations: travel, international development, arts. Office: Found for Health Care Evaluation 2901 Metro Dr Ste 400 Minneapolis MN 55425-1558

ZIEGLER, DANIEL MARTIN, chemistry educator; b. Quinter, Kans., July 6, 1927; s. Anton T. and Clara (Weissbeck) Z.; m. Mary Alice Weir, Aug. 19, 1952; children: Daniel L., Paul W., Mary Claire, James M. BS in Chemistry, St. Benedicts Coll., 1949; PhD in Chemsitry, Loyola U., 1955; postdoctoral, U. Wis., 1955-58. Asst. prof. Inst. Enzyme Rsch. U. Wis., Madison, 1958-61; asst. prof. chemistry U. Tex., Austin, 1961-62, assoc. prof. chemistry, 1962-69, prof. chemistry, 1969—, Roger J. Williams Centennial prof. in biochemistry, 1990—. Editor jour. Biol. Chemistry, 1979-83, 85-90, 93—; mem. editl. bd. Analyt. Biochemistry, 1989-91, Arch. Biochem. Biophys., 1966-71; contbr. articles to profl. jours. Recipient Bernard B. Brodie award Am. Soc. Pharmacol. Exptl. Therapy, 1990, Alexander von Humboldt award, Germany, 1991; estab. investigator Am. Heart Assn., 1960-65. Home: 6704 Shoal Creek Blvd Austin TX 78757-4379 Office: U Tex Dept Chemistry & Biochemist Austin TX 78712

ZIEGLER, DELORES, mezzo-soprano; b. Decatur, Ga.; children: Katie, Adam. Grad., Maryville Coll.; postgrad., U. Tenn. Operatic roles include Dorabella in Cosi Fan Tutti, Octavian in Der Rosenkavalier, Dulcinee in Don Quichotte, Cherubino in Le Nozze di Figaro, Rosina in Barber of Seville, Romeo, in I Capuleti e i Montecchi (first singer to sing the role of Romeo in Moscow and San Francisco), Idamante in Idomeneo, Charlotte in Werther, Adalgisa in Norma, Sextus in La Clemenza di Tito; performances with Atlanta Symphony, Bonn Theater der Stadt, Theater der Stadt Koln, La Scala Opera, Paris Opera, Bolshoi Opera, Moscow, Vienna Stattsopera, Phila. Orch., Met. Opera; recs. include Dorabella in Cosi Fan Tutte, EMI, Mozart Requiem, Mozart Great Mass, Atlanta Symphony, Mahler's 8th Symphony Telark Records, Beethoven 9th Symphony, Phila. Orch., EMI, Bach B Minor Mass, Teldek records, Margared in Le Roi d'ys, Erato Disque, title role in Bertoni's Orfeo, Frequenz records, Mozart's Kronenmesse, Deutsch Grammaphon; debut as Dorabella in Cosi fan Tutti, Lyric Opera Chgo., first Carmen at Atlanta Opera; debut at N.Y. Met. as Siebel in Faust, 1990. Office: care Lynda Kay 2702 Crestworth Ln Buford GA 30519-6483 Office: Côté Artists Mngmt Inc 157 W 57th St Ste 803 New York NY 10019-2210

ZIEGLER, DEWEY KIPER, neurologist; b. Omaha, May 31, 1920; s. Isidor and Pearl (Kiper) Z.; m. Mar. 30, 1954; children: Amy, Laura, Sara. BA, Harvard U., 1941, MD, 1945. Diplomate Am. Bd. Psychiatry and Neurology (bd. dirs. 1974-83, exec. com. 1978-82). Intern in medicine Boston City Hosp., 1945-46; asst. resident then chief resident in neurology N.Y. Neurol. Inst.-Columbia U. Coll. Physicians and Surgeons, 1948-51; resident in psychiatry Boston Psychopathic Hosp., 1951-53; asst. chief neurol. service Montefiore Hosp., N.Y.C.; and asst. prof. neurology Columbia U., 1953-55; asst. prof. U. Minn., 1955-56; asso. clin. prof. U. Kans. Med. Sch., 1956-64, chief dept. neurology, 1968-85; prof. U. Kans. Med. Center, 1964-89, prof. emeritus, 1989—; cons. Social Security Adminstrn., 1975—; mem. com. on certification and co-certification Am. Bd. Med. Specialties, 1979-82. Author: In Divided and Distinguished Worlds, 1942; Contbr. numerous articles to profl. jours. Served to lt., j.g., M.C. USNR, 1946-48. Fellow Am. Acad. Neurology (pres. 1979-81, v.p. 1972-73); mem. AMA, Am. Neurol. Assn., Am. Epilepsy Soc. Jewish. Home: 8347 Delmar Ln Shawnee Mission KS 66207-1821 Office: Kans U Med Center 3900 Rainbow Blvd Kansas City KS 66103-2918

ZIEGLER, DONALD EMIL, chief federal judge; b. Pitts., Oct. 1, 1936; s. Emil Nicholas and Elizabeth (Barclay) Z.; m. Claudia J. Chermak, May 1, 1965; 1 son, Scott Emil. B.A., Duquesne U., 1958; LL.B., Georgetown U., 1961. Bar: Pa. 1962, U.S. Supreme Ct. 1967. Practice law Pitts., 1962-74; judge Ct. of Common Pleas of Allegheny County, Pa., 1974-78; judge U.S. Dist. Ct. (we. dist.) Pa., Pitts., 1978-94, chief judge, 1994—. Treas. Big Bros. of Allegheny County, 1969-74. Mem. ABA, Pa. Bar Assn., Allegheny County Bar Assn., Am. Judicature Soc., St. Thomas More Soc. Democrat. Roman Catholic. Club: Oakmont Country. Office: US Post Office & Courthouse 6th Fl Courtroom 12 7th & Grant Sts Pittsburgh PA 15219

ZIEGLER, DONALD ROBERT, accountant; b. Lancaster, Pa., Nov. 15, 1932; s. John Jacob and Esther Mae (McKelly) Z.; m. Suzanne Foster, children: D. Rand, Scott F., Kurt J. B.S. in Econ. Acctg., Franklin and Marshall Coll., 1954. CPA, Pa. Mgr., sr. staff mem. Price Waterhouse, Phila., 1954-67, ptnr. 1967-92, sr. practice ptnr., 1978-92, mng. ptnr. Mid-Atlantic area, 1985-88; vice chmn. Southeast Region, 1988-92; mem. policy bd. Price Waterhouse, N.Y.C., 1980-88, mem. mgmt. com., 1986-92. Author: (with others) Managing and Accounting for Inventories, 1980. Contbg. author various books in field. Trustee Franklin and Marshall Coll., 1983—, alumni exec. coun., 1979-83, devel. com., exec. com. 1995—, chmn. audit com., 1989—, Phila. alumni coun.; trustee Pa. Ballet, 1988-92, 94-95, devel. and fin. coms., vice chmn. bd. trustees, 1989-92, chmn. exec. com., 1989-91. With U.S. Army, 1955-57. Recipient Outstanding Soldier award U.S. Army, 1955, Disting. Svc. Alumni medal Franklin and Marshall Coll, 1991. Mem. AICPA (auditing standards com. 1973-76, chmn. subcom. fraud 1976-80), Pa. Inst. CPAs (Phila. chpt. exec. coun.). Clubs: Rehoboth Beach Country Club; Phila. Aviation (bd. govs. and treas. 1969-90), Royal Blackheath Golf (U.K.). Home: RD 1 700 N Trooper Rd Norristown PA 19403-4502 Office: Price Waterhouse LLP 30 S 17th St Philadelphia PA 19103-4021

ZIEGLER, EARL KELLER, minister; b. Sheridan, Pa., Mar. 4, 1929; s. Abraham Hoffman and Rhoda Bucher (Keller) Z.; m. Vivian Zug Snyder, Aug. 12, 1951; children: Karen Louise Miller, Randall Earl, Doreen Kay Creighton, Michael Wayne, Konne Ziegler Berces, Sulien Nicodemus. BA, Elizabethtown (Pa.) Coll., 1951; MDiv, Bethany Theol. Sem., Chgo., 1954; DDiv, Lancaster (Pa.) Theol. Sem., 1982. Ordained to ministry Ch. of the Brethren, 1950. Pastor Woodbury (Pa.) Congregation, Pa., 1954-60, Black Rock Ch. of Brethren, Brodbecks, Pa., 1960-70, Mechanic Grove Ch. of Brethren, Quarryville, Pa., 1970-83, Atlantic N.E. Dist. Exec., Harrisburg, Pa., 1983-89, Lampeter (Pa.) Ch. of the Brethren, 1989—; moderator Ch. of the Brethren, Elgin, Ill., 1993-94; moderator various dists., Pa., 1959—; mem. Gen. Bd., Ch. of Brethren, 1975-80; chmn. Parish Ministerial Commn., 1979-80; dir. Family Life Inst., 1961, 64, mem. Nat. Korean Cons. Com., 1988-91, Denominational Structure Com., 1990-91, others; adj. prof. ch. history Evang. Sem., Myerstown, Pa., 1988—. Author: Divorce Among the Church of the Brethren Clergy, 1981; contbr. articles to profl. jours. Pres. Manheim Elem. PTA, 1964-65; trustee Elizabethtown Coll., 1965-83; dir. Community Choir, Lineboro, Md., 1966-70; dir. Solanco Community Men's Chorus, Quarryville, 1976-83. Recipient Alumni citation, Elizabethtown Coll. Alumni Assn., 1964, award for Outstanding Ch. Planting in Azua Province of Dominican Republic, 1990, Award of Appreciation, Germantown Ch. of Brethren, 1990. Mem. Lampeter Willow St. Ministerium (pres. 1989-91). Republican. Office: Ch of the Brethren Gen Offices 1451 Dundee Ave Elgin IL 60120-1674 *"You shall have what your faith expects," were the words of Jesus to two blind men. These words challenge the potential within each of us, a faith that conquers, a spirit that soars. Between the possible and the impossible is the measure of one's will.*

ZIEGLER, EKHARD ERICH, pediatrics educator; b. Saalfelden, Austria, Apr. 12, 1940; children: Stefan, Gabriele, Lena. M.D., U. Innsbruck, Austria, 1964. Diplomate: Am. Bd. Pediatrics. Intern U. Innsbruck, 1966-67, resident in pediatrics, 1967-68 70-71, resident in pharmacology, 1964-66, asst. dept. pediatrics, 1970-73; vis. instr. pediatrics U. Iowa, Iowa City, 1968-70, asst. prof. pediatrics, 1973-76, assoc. prof., 1976-81, prof., 1981—; mem. nutrition study sect. NIH, 1988-92. Recipient Nutrition award Am. Acad. Pediactrics, 1988. Mem. Am. Soc. Clin. Nutrition, Soc. Pediatric Research, Soc. Exptl. Biology and Medicine, N.Am. Soc. Pediatric Gastroenterology, Midwest Soc. Pediatric Research, Am. Pediatric Soc., The Nutrition Soc., N.Y. Acad. Scis., Am. Acad. Pediatrics. Club: Univ. Athletic (Iowa City). Office: U Iowa Dept Pediatrics Iowa City IA 52242

ZIEGLER, JACK (DENMORE), cartoonist; b. N.Y.C., July 13, 1942; s. John Denmore and Kathleen Miriam (Clark) Z.; m. Jean Ann Rice, Apr. 20, 1968 (div. 1995); children: Jessica, Benjamin, Maxwell; m. Kelli Joseph, Aug. 1996. B.A. in Communication Arts, Fordham U., 1964. Free-lance cartoonist N.Y.C., 1972—; cartoonist The New Yorker, N.Y.C., 1974—. Author: Hamburger Madness, 1978, Filthy Little Things, 1981, Marital Blitz, 1987, Celebrity Cartoons of the Rich and Famous, 1987, Worst Case Scenarios, 1990, Mr. Knocky, 1993; illustrator: (children's books) Lily of the Forest, 1987, Flying Boy, 1988, Annie's Pet, 1989, Eli and the Dimplemeyers, 1994 (adult books) Waiting Games, 1983, The Joy of Stress, 1984, That's Incurable!, 1984, Modern Superstitions, 1985, The No-Sex Handbook, 1990, There'll Be a Slight Delay, 1991, Byte Me!, 1996. Mem. Cartoonists Assn. (founding mem.), The Glory Boys, Nat. Cartoonists Soc. Democrat.

ZIEGLER, JOHN AUGUSTUS, JR., lawyer; b. Grosse Pointe, Mich., Feb. 9, 1934; s. John Augustus and Monnabell M. Ziegler; divorced; children: John Augustus III, Laura, Lisa, Adeline. AB, U. Mich., JD, 1957. Bar: Mich. 1957. Since practiced in Detroit; assoc. Dickinson, Wright, McKean & Cudlip, 1957-65, ptnr., 1965-68; ptnr. Parsons, Tennent, Hammond, Hardig & Ziegelman, 1969-70, Ziegler, Dykhouse & Wise, 1970-77; pres. Nat. Hockey League, 1977-92, chmn. bd. govs., 1976-78; of counsel Dickinson, Wright, Moon, Van Dusen & Freeman, Detroit, 1992—. Office: 1 Detroit Ctr 500 Woodward Ave Ste 4000 Detroit MI 48226-3423 also: 375 Park Ave Ste 2004 New York NY 10152-2099

ZIEGLER, MICHAEL LEWIS, lawyer; b. N.Y.C., Apr. 27, 1950. BA, SUNY, Albany, 1972; JD, SUNY, Buffalo, 1976; MPH, Columbia U., 1978. Bar: N.Y. 1976. Asst. prof. Columbia U., N.Y.C., 1977-80; ptnr. Epstein Becker & Green, N.Y.C., 1980-88, Bower & Gardner, N.Y.C., 1988-92, LeBoeuf, Lamb, Leiby & MacRae, N.Y.C., 1992—; adj. prof. Columbia U., 1980—, adj. assoc. prof. NYU, 1980—; adj. prof. SUNY Coll. Optometry, 1988—. Bd. dirs., chmn. N.Y. Found. For Ambulatory Care, 1993—; mem., co-chmn. bylaws com. New Leadership Group United Hosp. Fund, 1992—; gen. counsel Ronald MacDonald House of L.I., 1990—; bd. dirs., gen. counsel Care for the Homeless, Inc., 1992—. Named disting. adj. prof. grad. sch. pub. adminstrn. NYU, 1986. Mem. Nat. Health Lawyers Assn., N.Y. Acad. Scis., Assn. Bar N.Y.C. Office: LeBoeuf Lamb Leiby & MacRae 125 W 55th St New York NY 10019-5369*

ZIEGLER, R. W., JR., lawyer, consultant; b. Pitts.; children: Caroline, Gretchen, Jeremy, Benjamin, Phoebe, Polly. Student, Carnegie Tech., U. Pitts.; JD, Duquesne U., 1972. Bar: Pa. 1972, Calif. 1981, U.S. Ct. Appeals (3d cir.) 1977, U.S. Dist. Ct. (no. dist.) Pa. 1972, U.S. Supreme Ct. 1977, U.S. Tax Ct. 1978, Calif. 1982, U.S. Dist. Ct. (9th cir.) 1982. Ptnr. Ziegler & Ombres, Pitts., 1973-79; pres. Ziegler Ross Inc., San Francisco, 1979—; lectr. for Bar Assns. Author: Law Practice Management; editor: Law Office Guide in Computing. Mem. ABA, Am. Mgmt. Assn., Pa. State Bar Assn., Calif. State Bar Assn. Office: Ste 690 1350 Bayshore Hwy Burlingame CA 94010

ZIEGLER, RANDALL KEITH, food service executive; b. Zanesville, Ohio, July 21, 1942; s. Claude M. Jr. and Pearl Pauline (Elliott) Z.; m. Judith Anne Begley, June 12, 1965; children: Dustin Aric, Braeden Keith, McKenzie Anne. BS, Ohio State U., 1965. Sales rep. Lederle Labs. Pharms., Charleston, W.Va., 1965-66; dist. sales mgr. ARA Svcs., Louisville and Dayton, Ohio, 1972-73; mng. dir. Ziegler Foods, Inc., Indpls., 1975-77; v.p.

ARA/ARASERV, Phila., 1977-81, Servomation/Svc. Am., Stamford, Conn., 1981-86; v.p. Fine Host Internat. Corp., Greenwich, Conn., 1986-89, chmn. of bd., 1989—. Capt. USAF, 1966-72. Named Ky. Col., Commonwealth of Ky., 1973; recipient Key Man award Great Falls Jaycees, 1968. Mem. Internat. Assn. Auditorium Mgrs. Found. (named Disting. Allied mem. 1993, bd. dirs. 1986-90, chmn. allied com. 1986-88, chmn. Sports Day 1990—, mem. allied com. 1986—), Nat. Assn. Concessionaires (bd. dirs. 1991—), Blue Ribbon Com. (chmn. 1994-95), Mont. Jaycees (chmn. state mem. 1968), Jaycees (v.p. 1972). Avocations: youth coaching, scuba, family activities. Home: 10 Copper Kettle Rd Trumbull CT 06611-5007 Office: Fine Host Internat Corp 3 Greenwich Office Park Greenwich CT 06831-5115

ZIEGLER, RAYMOND STEWART, architect; b. Colorado Springs, Colo., Aug. 18, 1919; s. Edwin L. and Grace (Stewart) Z.; m. Jolene Baddeley, Aug. 22, 1942; children: John, Richard. Student, Ecole De Beaux Arts, Atelier Winslow, U. Calif., San Francisco Archtl. Club. Ptnr. Allison, Rible, Robinson and Ziegler, Architects, Los Angeles, 1958-69; exec. dir., v.p. Allison, Rible, Robinson and Ziegler an asso. group of Leo A Daly Co., 1969-74; ptnr. Raymond Ziegler Partnership, Architects, 1974-77; pres., chmn. bd. Ziegler Kirven Parrish Architects, 1978-84; pvt. cons. practice Altadena, Calif., 1984—; mem. Calif. adv. bd. Office Architecture and Constrn., 1968-77, chmn., 1971; vis. prof. sch. architecture U. Hawaii, 1987. Bd. dirs. L.A. Beuatiful, 1974-77, 80-86, v.p., 1984, pres., 1985-86, pres.'s coun., 1987-89; bd. dirs. Soc. for Prevention Blindness, 1974-76; hon. lifetime dir. San Gabriel Valley unit Am. Cancer Soc., 1978—, chmn. campaign adv. bd., 1979-80; mem. Untied Way Health Ptnrs. Coun., 1982-85; mem. L.A. County Arhitects Evaluation Commn., 1984-96; chmn. profl. practice sect. com. for 1989 licensing exam. Calif. Bd. Archtl. Examiners. 1st lt. inf. AUS, World War II. Fellow AIA (treas. So. Calif. chpt. 1968-69, bd. dirs. Calif. coun. 1968-69, trustee Ins. Trust of Calif. coun. 1977-81, chmn. 1980-81, bd. dirs. Pasadena and Foothill chpt. 1984, treas. 1985-86); mem. Archtl. Guild (bd. dirs.), Design Profls. Safety Assn. (dir. 1979-85), L.A. C. of C. (bd. dirs. 1972-77), Hist. Soc. Soc. Calif. (bd. dirs. 1982-84, 86-91), Masons, Rotary. Home: 1276 Sunnyoaks Cir Altadena CA 91001-1543

ZIEGLER, RICHARD FERDINAND, lawyer; b. Elizabeth, N.J., Aug. 1, 1949; m. Carolyn Lewis; children: Anna B., David A., Andrew P. D-J. BA in History summa cum laude, Yale u., 1971; JD magna cum laude, Harvard U., 1975. Bar: N.Y. 1976, U.S. Dist. Ct. (so. and ea. dists.) N.Y. 1976, U.S. Dist. Ct. (ea. dist.) Mich. 1982, U.S. Supreme Ct. 1984, U.S. Dist. Ct. (no. dist.) N.Y. 1987. Law clk. to judge U.S. Dist. Ct. (so. dist.), N.Y.C., 1975-76; assoc. Paul, Weiss, Rifkind, Wharton & Garrison, N.Y.C., 1976-77; asst. U.S. atty. U.S. Dept. Justice (so. dist.) N.Y., N.Y.C., 1977-80; assoc. Cleary, Gottlieb, Steen & Hamilton, N.Y.C., 1980-83, ptnr., 1983—. Mem. ABA, Assn. Bar City of N.Y., Fed. Bar Coun., N.Y. State Bar Assn. (chmn. com. on profl. ethics).

ZIEGLER, ROBERT OLIVER, special education educator; b. Cullman, Ala., Sept. 6, 1939; s. Mary Catherine (Taylor) McDonald; adopted Edgar and Kathryn Ziegler; m. Gladys L. Friese, May 3, 1962 (div. Jan. 1970); children: Robert, Edgar, Lesha, Kathy. BS, U. Ala., Tuscaloosa, 1961, MA, 1964, PhD, 1970. Cert. spl. edn. tchr., sch. counselor, music tchr., Ga. Band dir. Phillips Jr. H.S., Mobile, Ala., 1961-62, Wiggins (Colo.) H.S., 1962-63, Eastwood Jr. H.S., Tuscaloosa, 1963-65, McAdory H.S., McCalla, Ala., 1966-70, Calera (Ala.) H.S., 1971-72; prof. music edn. Tift Coll., Forsyth, Ga., 1972-78; jr. H.S. counselor Clayton County Schs., Jonesboro, Ga., 1978-80; elem. sch. counselor Rockdale County Schs., Conyers, Ga., 1980-82; spl. edn. tchr. Henderson Jr. H.S., Jackson, Ga., 1982-87, Clayton County Schs., Jonesboro, Ga., 1987-92, City Schs. of Decatur, Ga., 1992—; clarinetist Mobile (Ala.) Symphony Orch., 1961-62; vis. lectr. Stillman Coll., Tuscaloosa, Ala., 1970-71; prof. grad. sch. Mercer U., Macon, 1972-74; vis. lectr. in music Wesleyan Coll., Macon, Ga., 1975-76; acting head music dept. Tift Coll., Forsyth, Ga., 1976-77; curriculum cons. South Metro Psychoednl. Ctr., Atlanta City Schs., 1989. Contbr. articles to profl. publs. Minister of music, choir dir. United Meth. Ch., 1961-90, lay leader, 1989-94; mem. South Metro Concert Band, Morrow, Ga., 1978—, Tara Wind Band, Jonesboro, Ga., 1987-88. Recipient Cert. of Appreciation United Meth. Ch., 1990, Spl. Mission Recognition award United Meth. Women, 1983; U. Ala. grantee, 1960-61;. Mem. Profl. Assn. Ga. Educators (bldg. rep. 1994-96), Soc. for Preservation and Encouragement of Barber Shop Quartet Singing in Am. (founding, co-dir. Fayetteville chpt. 1990). Avocations: tennis, ragtime piano playing, singing gospel music. Home: 2669 Jodeco Dr Jonesboro GA 30236-5311 Office: City Schs of Decatur 917 S Mcdonough St Decatur GA 30030-4930

ZIEGLER, RONALD LOUIS, association executive, former government official; b. Covington, Ky., May 12, 1939; s. Louis Daniel and Ruby (Parsons) Z.; m. Nancy Lee Plessinger, July 30, 1960; children: Cynthia Lee Charas, Laurie Michelle Albright. Student, Xavier U., 1957-58; BS, U. So. Calif., 1961; DSc (hon.), Mass. Coll. Pharmacy, 1989, L.I. U., 1993. With Procter & Gamble Distbg. Co., 1961; account rep. J. Walter Thompson Co., 1962-68; press dir. Calif. Rep. Central Com., 1961-62; press aide to Richard Nixon in Calif. gubernatorial campaign, 1962; press aide staff Richard Nixon, 1968-69; press sec. to Pres. Nixon, 1969-74, asst. to, 1973-74; mng. dir., sr. v.p. internat. services Syska and Hennessy, Inc., Washington, 1975-80; pres. Nat. Assn. Truck Stop Operators, Alexandria, Va., 1980-87; pres., chief exec. officer Nat. Assn. Chain Drug Stores, Alexandria, 1987—; mem. nat. adv. bd. U. Okla.; adv. coun. Pharm. Found. U. Tex. Bd. dirs. Nat. Coun. on Patient Info. and Edn., Nat. Conf. on Pharm. Assns., Richard Nixon Libr. and Birthplace. Mem. Am. Soc. Assn. Execs., Nat. Retail Fedn. (bd. dirs.), Pharmacists Against Drug Abuse, Assn. White House Press Secs., Nat. Orgn. Rare Disorders, Sigma Chi Alumni. Office: Nat Assn Chain Drug Stores 413 N Lee St Alexandria VA 22314

ZIEGLER, WILLIAM, III, diversified industry executive; b. N.Y.C., June 26, 1928; s. William and Helen (Murphy) Z.; m. Jane Elizabeth Troy, Feb. 22, 1952; children: Melissa Jane, William Troy, Peter Martin, Cynthia Curtis, Helen Matilda, Karl Huttig. B.A., Harvard U., 1950; M.B.A., Columbia U., 1962. Vice pres. GIH Corp., N.Y.C., 1959-64, pres., 1964-95, dir., 1955-95; dir. Am. Maize Products Co., N.Y.C., 1958-95; chmn. bd., dir. Park Ave. Operating Co., Inc., 1958-95; chmn. bd., CEO Swisher Internat. Inc., 1995—; chmn. bd., dir. Swisher Internat. Inc. Bd. dirs. Foresight, Inc., New Haven; trustee Conn. Coll., New London, Conn., 1991-96; pres. E. Matilda Ziegler Found. for Blind; sec. Matilda Ziegler Pub. Co. for Blind; bd. dirs. Maritime Ctr. at Norwalk. Lt. USNR, 1952-54. Mem. Southwestern Area Commerce and Industry Assn. Conn. (dir.). Clubs: N.Y. Yacht, Noroton (Conn.) Yacht. Home: 161 Long Neck Point Rd Darien CT 06820-5815 Office: 20 Thorndal Cir Darien CT 06820

ZIEGLER, WILLIAM ALEXANDER, lawyer; b. N.Y.C., July 15, 1924; s. William Alexander and Sally (Cootes) Z.; m. Glenn Crawley, Feb. 10, 1950; children: Richard S., Daryl A. Henning, Susan G. Barrows, W. Thomas. A.B., Harvard U., 1944, J.D., 1949. Bar: N.Y. 1949, U.S. Tax Ct. 1950, U.S. Dist. Ct. (so. dist.) N.Y. 1949, U.S. Dist. Ct. (ea. dist.) N.Y. 1957, U.S. Dist. Ct. (no. dist.) Ohio 1973, U.S. Dist. Ct. (ea. dist.) Mich. 1983, U.S. Ct. Apppeals (1st cir.) 1963, U.S. Ct. Appeals (2d cir.) 1957, U.S. Ct. Appeals (3d cir.) 1986, U.S. Ct. Appeals (4th cir.) 1979, U.S. Ct. Appeals (5th cir.) 1987, U.S. Ct. Appeals (6th cir.) 1984, U.S. Ct. Appeals (7th cir.) 1992, U.S. Ct. Appeals (8th cir.) 1981, U.S. Ct. Appeals (9th cir.) 1973, U.S. Ct. Appeals (10th and 11th cirs.) 1983, U.S. Ct. Appeals (D.C. cir.) 1972, U.S. Supreme Ct. 1972. Assoc. Sullivan & Cromwell, N.Y.C., 1949-56, ptnr., 1957-89, cons., 1990—; chmn. exec. com., bd. dirs. H.W. Wilson Co., Engring. Info., Inc.; bd. dirs. Std. Comml. Corp.; sec., bd. dirs. H.W. Wilson Found. Mem. Assn. Bar City N.Y., Fgn. Policy Assn. (bd. dirs.), Riverside Country Club (Mont.), Harvard Club of N.Y.C., Harvard Club Fairfield County (bd. dirs.). Office: 125 Broad St New York NY 10004-2400

ZIEHLER, TONY JOSEPH, insurance agent; b. Anderson, Ind., June 20, 1938; s. Joseph Anthony and Julie Ann (Kette) Z.; m. Alice Mae Pattison, Apr. 2, 1956 (div. 1972); children: Susan Z. Brown, Kathryn Z. Dwyer, Jane Z. Bee, Patricia Z. Koty, Michael; m. Barbara Buys Wood, Feb. 28, 1981; stepchildren: David Wayne Wood, Brent Douglas Wood. BSBA, U. Ariz., 1958. CLU. Prin. Ziehler Ins. Group, LLC, Tucson, 1958—. Employee edn. chmn. So. Ariz. Div. Am. Cancer Soc.; co-chmn. Medic-Alert Found., Pima County, Ariz.; chmn. Tucson Festival Soc.; mem. Salpointe High Sch. Found., others. Recipient William Wisdom award U. Ariz., Tucson, 1958. Mem. Greater Tucson Assn. Life Underwriters (pres. 1963-64, Agt. of Yr. 1975), Ariz. Assn. Life Underwriters (pres. 1970-71, Agt. of Yr. 1980), So. Ariz. CLU Soc. (pres. 1968-69), Salvation Army (pres. adv. bd. 1984-85), Univ. of Ariz. Found. (mem. planned giving com.), Rotary, (com. chmn.), Tucson Conquistadores (pres. 1985-86), Los Charros del Desierto, Golden Key Soc., MIllion Dollar Round Table, others. Republican. Avocations: travel, trail riding, Belgian draft horses, mountain hiking, sports. Home: 6000 E Calle De Vita Tucson AZ 85750-1957 Office: Ste B102 6420 E Broadway Blvd Tucson AZ 85710-3536

ZIELINSKI, PAUL BERNARD, grant program administrator, civil engineer; b. West Allis, Wis., Sept. 9, 1932; s. Stanley Charles and Lottie Charlotte (Pliskiewicz) Z.; m. Monica Theresa Beres, July 13, 1957; children: Daniel Paul, Gregory John, Robert Mathias, Sarah Anne. BSCE, Marquette U., 1956; MS, U. Wis., 1961, PhD, 1965. Registered profl. engr., Wis., S.C. Asst. instr. engring. mechanics Marquette U., Milw., 1956-59, asst. prof., 1964-67; instr. civil engring. U. Wis., Madison, 1959-64; from asst. prof. to prof. Clemson (S.C.) U., 1967-78, prof. environ. and systems engring., 1978-82, prof. civil engring., 1982-90, prof. emeritus, 1991—; dir. S.C. Water Resources Rsch. Inst., Clemson, 1978-90; assoc. dir. associateship grant program Nat. Rsch. Coun., Washington, 1990—; cons. Am. Pub. Works Assn., Chgo., 1973-76, Nat. Coun. Examiners of Engring. and Surveying, Clemson, 1973—. Chmn. Clemson City Planning Commn., 1971-74; ex-officio mem. S.C. Water Resources Commn., Columbia, 1978-90. Mem. ASCE, Am. Soc. for Engring. Edn., Sigma Xi. Roman Catholic. Home: 2111 Wisconsin Ave NW Apt 717 Washington DC 20007-2278 Office: Nat Rsch Coun 2201 Constitution Ave NW Washington DC 20418-2907

ZIEMANN, EDWARD FRANCES, food service company executive, sales and marketing professional; b. Chgo., July 3, 1944; s. Edward F. and Ethyle (Ruthenbeck) Z.; m. Linda Magarethe Nakamichi Sowka, July 14, 1952; children: Russell, Jeffrey, Robert, Christina. BA, U. Ill., Chgo., 1967. Cert. foodservice profl. Reservations freight clk. Milw. Road. R.R., Chgo., 1965-66; sales adminstr. Robertson Photo Mechanic, Des Plaines, Ill., 1966-68; v.p. and officer Anetsberger Bros., Inc., Northbrook, Ill., 1968—; mem. Tech. Liaison Com., Chgo., 1990-91. Bd. dirs. Village Improvement Com., Round Lake, Ill.; asst. Catholic Charities, Waukegan, Ill., 1990-91. Mem. Am. Mktg. Assn., Nat. Assn. Food Equipment Manufacture, Bakers Club (century mem.), Moose. Republican. Roman Catholic. Avocations: swimming, golfing, writing, cooking, gardening. Office: Anetsberger Bros Inc 180 Anets Dr Northbrook IL 60062-5452

ZIEMANN, G. PATRICK, bishop; b. Pasadena, Calif., Sept. 13, 1941. Attended, St. John's Coll. and St. John's Sem., Camarillo, Calif., Mt. St. Mary's Coll., L.A. Ordained priest Roman Cath., 1967. Titular bishop, aux. bishop Diocese Santa Rosa, Obba, 1986-92; bishop Diocese Santa Rosa, Santa Rosa, Calif., 1992—. Office: Chancery Office PO Box 1297 547 B St Santa Rosa CA 95401-5249*

ZIEMER, RODGER EDMUND, electrical engineering educator, consultant; b. Sargeant, Minn., Aug. 22, 1937; s. Arnold Edmund and Ruth Ann (Rush) Z.; m. Sandra Lorann Person, June 23, 1960; children: Mark Edmund, Amy Lorann, Norma Jean, Sandra Lynn. B.S., U. Minn., 1960, M.S., 1962, Ph.D., 1965. Registered profl. engr., Mo. Research asst. U. Minn., Mpls., 1960-62; research assoc. U. Minn., 1962; prof. elec. engring. U. Mo., Rolla, 1968-83; prof. elec. engring. U. Colo., Colorado Springs, 1984—, chmn. dept. elec. engring., 1984-93; cons. Emerson Electric Co., St. Louis, 1972-84, Mid-Am. Regional Coun., Kansas City, Mo., 1974, Motorola, Inc., Scottsdale, Ariz., 1980-84, Martin Marietta, Orlando, 1980-81, TRW, Colorado Springs, summer, 1985, Sperry, Phoenix, 1986, Pericle Communications, summer, 1994, Motorola, Schaumburg, 1995. Author: Principles of Communications, 1976, 2d edit., 1985, 3d edit., 1990, 4th edit., 1995, Signals and Systems, 1983, 2d edit., 1989, 3rd edit., 1993, Digital Communications and Spread Spectrum Systems, 1985, Introduction to Digital Communication, 1992, Introduction to Spread Spectrum Communications, 1995; editor: IEEE Jour. on Selected Areas in Communications, 1989, 92, 95, IEEE Communications Mag., 1991. Served to capt. USAF, 1965-68. Scholar Western Electric, 1957-59; trainee NASA, 1962-65. Fellow IEEE; mem. Am. Soc. Engring. Edn., Armed Forces Communications and Electronics Assn., Sigma Xi, Tau Beta Pi, Eta Kappa Nu. Lutheran. Home: 8315 Pilot Ct Colorado Springs CO 80920-4412 Office: Univ Colo PO Box 7150 Colorado Springs CO 80933-7150

ZIENTARA, JAMES EDWARD, stock brokerage executive; b. Hammond, Ind., Mar. 12, 1943; s. Joseph Edward and Leona Dorothy (Poracky) Z.; m. Frances Elizabeth Gehrke, July 30, 1966; children: Amy Elizabeth, Jeffrey Edward. BS in Math., Purdue U., 1966; MBA in Fin., Ind. U., 1970; cert. investment mgmt. analyst, U. Pa., 1989. Tchr. math. Wilbur Wright Jr. High Sch., Munster, Ind., 1966-68; investment advisor trust dept. Continental Ill. Bank, Chgo., 1970-72; sr. investment officer trust dept. SE Bank Trust, Sarasota, Fla., 1972-75; stock broker Dean Witter Reynolds Inc., Bradenton, Fla., 1975—, 1st v.p. investments, 1984—, retirement plan coord., 1985—; grad. asst. Ind. U., Bloomington, 1968. Contbr. Nelson's Guide to Pension Fund Consultants, 1991. Vol. United Way, Bradenton, 1989. Recipient pub. svc. award Am. Radio Relay League, 1965. Mem. Investment Mgmt. Cons. Assn. (new mem. com. 1989), Bradenton C. of C., Bradenton Country Club, Manatee Personal Computer Users Group (founder), Kiwanis. Republican. Avocations: golf, tennis, personal computers, travel. Home: 416 64th Street Ct NW Bradenton FL 34209-1629 Office: Dean Witter Reynolds 1401 Manatee Ave W Bradenton FL 34205-6702

ZIENTARA, SUZANNAH DOCKSTADER, insurance company executive; b. Wichita, Kans., Oct. 1, 1945; d. Ralph Walter and Patricia Ann (Harvey) Dockstader; m. Larry Henry Zientara, Oct. 18, 1975; 1 child, Jillian Sue Zientara Cox. Student, U. Kans., 1963-64; BS in Bus. Edn., Ft. Hays State U., 1968; MEd in Secondary Guidance and Counseling, U. Mo., St. Louis, 1973. CLU. Sec. to supt. Wichita Pub. Schs., 1968-69; tchr. bus. edn. Wichita Heights High Sch., 1969-71, Lindbergh High Sch., St. Louis, 1971-72, Holman Jr. High Sch., St. Louis, 1972-75; guidance counselor Pattonville Heights Jr. High Sch., St. Louis, 1975-79; tchr. data processing Lawrence (Kans.) High Sch., 1979-85; ins. agt. State Farm Ins. Cos., Lawrence, 1985-90; agy. mgr. State Farm Ins. Cos., Tulsa, 1990-95; agy. field exec. State Farm Ins. Cos., Topeka, 1995—; mem. Regional Mgr. Coun., Tulsa, 1992-93; participant Purdue Profl. Mgmt. Inst., West Lafayette, Ind., 1993. Author: Introduction to Data Processing, 1983. Mem. Williams Edn. Fund, U. Kans. Named Outstanding Young Woman of Am., 1974. Mem. Am. Soc. CLU's and ChFC's, USTA, Am. Ski Assn., Topeka C. of C., U. Kans. Alumni Assn., PEO, Shawnee Country Club, Mortar Bd., Pi Omega Pi. Republican. Episcopalian. Avocations: tennis, golf, snow skiing, bridge, music. Home: 3637 SW Kings Forest Rd Topeka KS 66610 Office: State Farm Ins Cos 2930 Wanamaker Dr Ste 6 Topeka KS 66614

ZIERDT, JOHN GRAHAM, JR., transportation company executive; b. Warner Robbins, Ga., July 22, 1943; s. John Graham and Elizabeth (Matthews) Z.; m. Regina Astor, June 18, 1966; children: John III, Karen, Michael. BS in Engring., U.S. Mil. Acad., 1966; MS in Engring., Ariz. State U., 1972. Commd. 2d lt. U.S. Army, 1966, advanced through grades to brig. gen., 1991; battalion comdr. 702d Maintenance Battalion U.S. Army, Camp Casey, Korea, 1984-85; brigade comdr. 46th Support Group U.S. Army, Ft. Bragg, N.C., 1988-89, comdg. gen. 1st Corps Support Command, 1989-91; dir. logistics U.S. Army Forces Command U.S. Army, Atlanta, 1991-95; ret. U.S. Army, 1995; pres., CEO TransCor Am., Inc., Nashville, 1995—. Author: Acquisition Management: The Role and The Reality, 1987. Decorated Legion of Merit with 2 oak leaf clusters, Bronze Star with oak leaf cluster, Disting. Svc. medal; Nat. security fellow Kennedy Sch. Govt., Harvard U., 1986-87. Republican. Roman Catholic. Home: 516 Midway Cir Brentwood TN 37027 Office: TransCor Am Inc 1510 Ft Nesley Blvd Nashville TN 37203

ZIERING, WILLIAM MARK, lawyer; b. New Britain, Conn., Feb. 4, 1931; s. Jacob Max and Esther (Freedman) Z.; m. Harriet Koskoff, Aug. 20, 1958; 1 son, Benjamin. B.A., Yale U., 1952; J.D., Harvard U., 1955. Bar: Conn. 1955, Calif. 1962. Assoc. Koskoff & McMahon, Plainville, Conn., 1959-60; sr. trial atty. SEC, San Francisco, 1960-65; pvt. practice law San Francisco, 1965—; ptnr. Bremer & Ziering, 1972-77; instr. Golden Gate U. Law Sch., San Francisco, 1968-75. Vice pres., bd. dirs. Calif. League Handicapped, 1972—. Served to comdr. USNR, 1955-58. Mem. ABA, Calif. Bar Assn., San Francisco Bar Assn. (past chmn. securities, corps. and banking), Navy League (dir.). Club: Commonwealth. Home: 2027 Lyon St San Francisco CA 94115-1609 Office: 4 Embarcadero Ctr Ste 3400 San Francisco CA 94111-4187

ZIERLER, NEAL, mathematician; b. Balt., Sept. 17, 1926; s. Joseph Nathan and Betsey (Levie) Z.; m. Betty Matsumoto, Dec. 26, 1950 (div. 1981); children: Robert Eugene, Joan Mariye, Ann M. AB, Johns Hopkins U., 1945; AM, Harvard U., 1949, PhD, 1959. Mathematician, physicist Ballistic Rsch. Labs., Aberdeen, Md., 1951; mem. tech. staff instrumentation lab. MIT, Cambridge, Mass., 1952-54; mem. tech. staff Lincoln Lab. MIT, Lexington, Mass., 1954-60; supr. info. processing group of jet propulsion lab. Calif. Inst. Tech., Pasadena, 1960-61; sr. scientist ARCON Corp., Lexington, 1961-62; head sub-dept. process analysis MITRE Corp., Bedford, Mass., 1962-65; tech. staff Ctr. for Comm. Rsch. Inst. Def. Analysis, Princeton, N.J., 1965—. Patentee error-detecting and -correcting devices; contbr. articles to profl. jours. Lt. USN, 1944-46. Fellow IEEE; mem. Am. Math. Soc., Math. Assn. Am. Avocations: tennis, skiing, photography. Office: Inst Def Analysis Ctr Communications Rsch Thanet Rd Princeton NJ 08540-3699

ZIFCHAK, WILLIAM C., lawyer; b. 1948. BA, Harvard U., 1970; JD, Columbia U., 1973. Bar: N.Y. 1974, U.S. Ct. Appeals (2d cir.) 1975, U.S. Ct. Appeals (3d cir., D.C. cir.) 1983, U.S. Dist. Ct. (so. dist.) N.Y. 1984. Ptnr. Kaye, Scholer, Fierman, Hays & Handler, N.Y.C; planning com. NYU Ann. Nat. Conf. Labor, 1991—. Contbr. articles to profl. jours. Mem. ABA (sect. labor and employment law 1975—, subcom. antitrust, RICO and labor rels. law), Assn. Bar City of N.Y. (sec. com. labor and employment law 1984-87), N.Y. State Bar (comml.-fed. litig. sect. co-chair labor and employment law com. 1995—.). Office: Kaye Scholer Fierman Hays & Han 425 Park Ave New York NY 10022-3506

ZIFF, LARZER, English language educator; b. Holyoke, Mass., Oct. 2, 1927; s. Isadore Menden and Sara (Rosenbloom) Z.; m. Ruth Rosalind Geisenberger; children—Joshua, Oliver, Joel, Abigail. Student, Middlebury Coll., 1945-47; M.A., U. Chgo., 1951, Ph.D., 1955; M.A. (hon.), U. Oxford, Eng., U. Pa. Prof. English U. Calif., Berkeley, 1956-73; univ. lectr. Oxford U., Eng., 1973-78; prof. English U. Pa., 1978-81; Caroline Donovan prof. English Johns Hopkins U., Balt., 1981—, chair dept., 1991-95; dir. U. Calif. Edn. Abroad Program, U.K., Ireland, 1969-71; cons. and lectr. in field. Author: The Career of John Cotton, 1962; The American 1890's, 1968; Puritanism in America, 1973; Literary Democracy, 1981; Writing in the New Nation, 1991; also articles, essays in profl. jours.; mem. editorial bds. including ELH, 1981—. Recipient numerous awards for excellence in English including Christian Gauss award, the American 1890's, 1967; Fulbright fellow, 1959-60, fellow Am. Coun. Learned Socs., 1963-64, Newberry Libr., 1964, NEH, 1967-68, Guggenheim fellow, 1977-78, Woodrow Wilson Internat. Ctr. for Scholars, 1986-87; Fulbright Disting. Sr. Lectr., 1993. Fellow Am. Acad. Arts and Scis., Soc. Am. Historians; mem. MLA, Am. Antiquarian Soc., Am. Studies Assn. Office: Johns Hopkins U Dept English Baltimore MD 21218

ZIFF, LLOYD RICHARD, lawyer; b. N.Y.C., Mar. 9, 1942; s. George and Lillian (Gisnet) Z.; m. M. Morrow Cox, Jan. 28, 1967; children: Tina Marie, M. Courtney, Robert G. Grad., Peekskill Mil. Acad.; BA, U. Pa., 1968, JD magna cum laude, 1971. Bar: Pa. 1971, U.S. Supreme Ct. 1975; cert. as arbitrator, 1982—, as mediator, 1992— U.S. Dist. Ct. (ea. dist.) Pa. Assoc. Pepper, Hamilton & Scheetz, Phila., 1971-77, ptnr., 1977-92; founding ptnr. Harkins Cunningham, Phila. and Washington, 1992—; tchg. fellow Sch. Law U. Pa., 1971, lectr., 1981-82; mem. faculty Acad. Advocacy, 1980—; mem. DeVitt implementation com. U.S. Dist. Ct. (ea. dist.) Pa., 1980-84, mem. CLE com., 1985—, chmn. local civil rules adv. com., 1991—, apptd. to adv. group under Civil Justice Reform Act, 1995—; co-chmn. Seminar on Complex Litigation, 1983; invitee Jud. Conf. of 3d Cir., 1986, 89, 91. Contbr. articles to legal jours. Mem. Kent State U. Task Force, Pres.'s Commn. on Campus Unrest, Ohio, 1970; mem. Inter-disciplinary Com. on Child Abuse S.E. Pa., 1973-75; mem. adv. com. Family Resources Ctr., St. Christopher's Hosp. for Children, Phila., 1976; chmn. Phila. Bail Project, 1969; counsel Phila. Vietnam Vets. Meml. Fund, 1985—; mem., bd. dirs. Penndelphia Scholarship Found., 1995—. With U.S. Army, 1965-67. Warwick Found. scholar U. Pa., 1971; Salzburg Seminar fellow Am. Studies-Am. Law and Legal Instns., (Austria), 1978. Mem. ABA, Pa. Bar Assn., Phila. Bar Assn. (chmn. election procedures com. 1976, chmn. spl. com. on admission attys. to fed. practice 1986, chair Fidelity award com. 1987, chair fed. bench bar conf., 1988, chmn. fed. cts. com. 1989), Am. Judicature Soc., U.S. Supreme Ct. Hist. Soc., U.S. Ct. Appeals for the 3d Cir. Hist. Soc., U.S. Dist. Ct. for Ea. Dist. Pa. Hist. Soc., Order of Coif, Chapel of the Four Chaplains, Legion of Honor, The Penn Club of N.Y. Office: Harkins Cunningham 1800 One Commerce Sq Philadelphia PA 19103-7042

ZIFF, MORRIS, internist, rheumatologist, educator; b. N.Y.C., Nov. 19, 1913; s. Benjamin and Ethel (Seldowitz) Z.; m. Jacqueline Mae Miller, Dec. 10, 1978; children: Edward B., David R. BS, NYU, 1934, PhD, 1937, MD, 1948. Intern Bellevue Hosp., N.Y.C., 1948-49, resident in internal medicine, 1949-50, attending physician, 1950-58; asst. prof. medicine NYU, 1954-57, assoc. prof., 1957-58; Ashbel Smith prof. internal medicine U. Tex. Health Sci. Ctr., Dallas, 1958-84, Ashbel prof. emertus internal medicine, 1984—, Morris Ziff prof. rheumatology, 1982—; dir. Harold C. Simmons Arthritis Rsch. Ctr., Dallas, 1983-84; attending physician Parkland Meml. Hosp., Dallas, 1958—; mem. med. staff Zale-Lipshy Univ. Hosp., Dallas, 1989—; cons. Dallas VA Hosp., Brooke Army Hosp., 1964-75, William Beaumont Army Hosp., 1965-76. Contbr. over 250 articles to sci. jours., chpts. to books. Recipient Heberden medal Heberden Soc. London, 1964, Rsch. Career award USPHS, 1962-84, Marchman award Dallas So. Med. Soc., 1968, Disting. Svc. award Arthritis Found., 1968, Disting. Alumni Sci. award NYU, 1966, Carol Nachman prize in rheumatology, 1974, World Internat. Conf. on Inflammation prize, 1986. Fellow ACP; mem. Assn. Am. Physicians, Am. Soc. Clin. Investigation, Am. Assn. Immunologists, Am. Coll. Rheumatology (master, Bunim medal 1982, Gold medal 1988), N.Y. Acad. Medicine (Klemperer medal 1991), Harvey Soc., Phi Beta Kappa, Sigma Xi, Alpha Omega Alpha. Home: 11116 Pinocchio Dr Dallas TX 75229-4031 Office: U Tex Health Sci Ctr Health Sci Ctr 5323 Harry Hines Blvd Dallas TX 75235-9030

ZIFF, PAUL, philosophy educator; b. N.Y.C., Oct. 22, 1920; m. Loredana Vanzetto; 3 children. BFA, Cornell U., 1949, PhD, 1951. Instr. philosophy U. Mich., Ann Arbor, 1952-53; from instr. to asst. prof. Harvard U., Cambridge, Mass., 1953-59; from asst. prof. to assoc. prof. U. Pa., 1959-63; prof. U. Wis., 1964-68, U. Ill., Chgo., 1968-70; Kenan prof. U. N.C., Chapel Hill, 1970-88, prof. emeritus, 1988—; chmn. bd. dirs. Chapel Hill Ctr. Linguistic Rsch.; cons. in field. Contbr. articles to profl. jours. Paul Ziff chair installed in his honor U. N.C., 1994; festschrift Language, Mind and Art pub. in his honor, 1994; grantee Rockefeller Found., spring 1955, Guggenheim Found., Rome, 1962-63. Office: Chapel Hill Ctr for Philosophic Linguistic Rsch 1309 Brigham Rd Chapel Hill NC 27514-3402

ZIFF, WILLIAM BERNARD, JR., publishing executive; b. June 24, 1930; s. William B. and Amelia (Morton) Z.; m. Tamsen Ann Kojis, 1987; children from previous marriage: Dirk Edward, Robert David, Daniel Morton. BA, Rutgers U., 1951; postgrad., Heidelberg U., 1952-53, U. Madrid, 1952-53. Ptnr., then owner and chmn. Ziff Davis Pub. Co., N.Y.C., until 1984; pub. chmn. Ziff Communication Corp., N.Y.C., 1987—. Office: Ziff Bros Investments 153 E 53d St New York NY 10022

ZIFFREN, KENNETH, lawyer; b. Chgo., June 24, 1940. BA, Northwestern U., 1962; JD, UCLA, 1965. Bar; Calif. 1967. Law clerk to Chief Justice Warren, 1965-66; ptnr. Ziffren, Brittenham, Branca & Fischer, L.A. Mem. ABA, State Bar Calif., L.A. County Bar Assn., Beverly Hills Bar Assn., L.A. Copyright Soc. (pres. 1977-78). Office: Ziffren Brittenham Branca & Fischer 2121 Ave of the Stars 32nd Fl Los Angeles CA 90067*

ZIGEL, JAMES M., aircraft manufacturing executive; b. 1947. BA, U. Mo., 1969, JD, 1972. Gen. counsel Astro Industries, 1972-74; atty. U.S. Army Aviation Systems Command, 1974-76; chief counsel NATO, Brussels,

1976-80; asst. gen. counsel Emerson Electric Co., 1980-85; gen. counsel Western Gear Corp., 1985-87; v.p., gen. counsel, sec. Lucas Industries Inc., Reston, Va., 1989—, pres., CEO, 1993. Office: Lucas Industries Inc 11180 Sunrise Valley Dr Reston VA 22091-4367*

ZIGER, STEVEN GARY, architect; b. Washington, Aug. 10, 1955. BS in Architecture, U. Ill., 1977. Registered arch., Md. With RTKL, Balt., 1977-79, Hord, Coplan, Macht, Balt., 1979-84; v.p., founding ptnr. Ziger/Snead Inc. Architects, Balt., 1984—; active Balt. County Design Rev. Panel, State of Md. Archtl. Design Rev. Bd. Mem. adv. bd. Johns Hopkins U. Sch. Continuing Studies; trustee The Woodbourne Ctr., Learning Independence Through Computers, Mus. Contemporary Art, Parks and People; chair mayor's adv. com. on Howard St. Devel. Mem. AIA (pres. Balt. chpt. 1992). Office: Ziger/Snead Inc Architects 1006 Morton St Baltimore MD 21201-5411

ZIGLAR, JAMES W., former federal official, lawyer, investment banker; b. Pascagoula, Miss., Dec. 8, 1945; married; 3 children. BA, George Washington U., 1968, JD, 1972. Bar: Va. 1972, D.C. 1973, N.Y. 1975, Ariz. 1977. Staff asst. Senator James Eastland, Washington, 1964-71; spl. asst. Dept. of Justice, Washington, 1971-72; law clk. to assoc. justice Harry Blackmun U.S. Supreme Ct., Washington, 1972-73; assoc. Mudge, Rose, Guthrie et al, N.Y.C., 1973-77; ptnr. O'Connor, Cavanagh, Anderson et al, Phoenix, 1977-80; sr. v.p. dept. pub. fin. Dillon, Read & Co., N.Y.C., 1980-84; mng. dir. Paine Webber, Inc., Washington, 1984-86, 90—; asst. sec. Dept. of Interior, Washington, 1987-88; mng. dir. Drexel Burnham Lambert Inc., N.Y.C., 1989-90. Bar: Va. 1972, D.C. 1973, N.Y. 1975, Ariz. 1977. Office: Paine Webber Inc 919 18th St NW Ste 650 Washington DC 20005

ZIGLER, EDWARD FRANK, psychologist, educator; b. Kansas City, Mo., Mar. 1, 1930; s. Louis and Gertrude (Gleitman) Z.; m. Bernice Gorelick, Aug. 28, 1955; 1 child, Scott. BA, U. Mo.-Kansas City, 1954; PhD, U. Tex., 1958; MA (hon.), Yale, 1967; DSc (hon.), Boston Coll., 1985; LHD (hon.), Bank St. Coll. Edn., 1989, U. New Haven, 1991, St. Joseph Coll., 1991; PhD (hon.), U. Mo., 1993, CUNY, 1995; Hon. degree, CUNY, 1995; LLD (hon.), Gonzaga U., 1995. Psychol. intern Worcester (Mass.) State Hosp., 1957-59; asst. prof. psychology U. Mo., 1958-59; mem. faculty Yale U., 1959—, prof. psychology and child study center, 1967—, Sterling prof., 1976—, dir. child devel. program, 1961-76, chmn. dept. psychology, 1973-74; head psychology sect. Yale Child Study Center, 1967—; dir. Bush Center in Child Devel. and Social Policy, 1977—; chief Children's Bur. NEW, Washington, 1970-72; cons. in field, 1962—; mem. nat. steering com. Project Head Start, 1965-70, chmn. 15th anniversary Head Start com., 1980; mem. nat. adv. com. Nat. Lab. Early Childhood Edn., 1967-70; nat. rsch. adv. bd. Nat. Assn. Retarded Children, 1968-73; nat. rsch. coun. Project Follow-Through, 1968-70; chmn. adv. com. Vietnamese Children's Resettlement, 1975; mem. Pres.'s Com. on Mental Retardation, 1980; joint appointee Yale U. Sch. Medicine, 1982—, chmn. Yale Infant Care Leave Commn., 1983-85, Parents as Tchrs., 1986—; mem. adv. com. Head Start Quality and Expansion, 1993; mem. adv. com. on svcs. for families with infants and toddlers HHS, 1994. Author, co-author, editor books and monographs; contbr. articles to profl. jours. Served with AUS, 1951-53. Recipient Gunnar Dybwad Disting. scholar in behavioral and social sci. award Nat. Assn. Retarded Children, 1964, 69, Social Sci. Aux. award, 1962, Alumni Achievement award U. Mo., 1965, Alumnus of Yr. award, 1972, C. Anderson Aldrich award Am. Acad. Pediatrics, 1985, Nat. Achievement award Assn. for Advancement of Psychology, 1985, Dorothea Lynde Dix Humanitarian award for svc. to handicapped Elwyn Inst., 1987, Sci. Leadership award Joseph P. Kennedy Jr. Found., 1990, Mensa Edn. and Rsch. Found. award for excellence, 1990, Nat. Head Start Assn. award, 1990 Founders award, 1995, Bldg. dedication Edward Zigler Head Start Ctr., 1990, As They Grow award in edn. Parents mag., 1990, Excellence in Edn. award Pi Lambda Theta, 1991, Friend of Edn. award Conn. Edn. Assn., 1991, Loyola-Mellon Social Sci. award 1991, Pres.'s award Conn. Assn. Human Svcs., 1991, Harold W. McGraw, Jr. prize in edn., 1992, Disting. Achievement in Rsch. award Internat. Assn. Sci. Study of Mental Deficiency, 1992, Disting. Svc. award Coun. Chief State Sch. Officers, 1993, Outstanding Fed. Leadership in Support of Head Start Rsch. Adminstrn. on Children, Youth and Families, 1993, Child and Family Advocacy award Parents as Tchrs. Nat. Ctr., 1994, Nat. Distinction award U. Pa. Edn. Alumni Assn., 1994; named Hon. Commr. Internat. Yr. of Child, 1979. Fellow Am. Orthopsychiat. Assn. (Blanche F. Ittleson award 1989, pres. 1993-94), Am. Psychol. Assn. 9pres. div. 7 1974-75, G. Stanley Hall award 1979, award for disting. contbns. to psychology in pub. interest 1982, Nicholas Hobbs award 1985, award for disting. profl. contbns. to knowledge 1986, Edgar A. Doll award 1986, award for disting. contbn. to cmty. psychology and cmty. mental health 1989); mem. Inst. Medicine of NAS, AAAS, Am. Acad. Mental Retardation (career rsch. award 1982), Soc. Psychol. Study Social Issues (Kurt Lewin Meml. award 1995), Zero to Three (Dolley Madison award 1995), Sigma Xi. Home: 177 Ridgewood Ave North Haven CT 06473-4442 Office: Yale U Dept Psychology PO Box 208205 2 Hillhouse Ave New Haven CT 06520-8205

ZIGLER, TED ALAN, principal; b. Bryan, Ohio, Apr. 29, 1952; s. Olan A. and Patsy A. Zigler; m. Beth E. Auby, Sept. 1, 1973; children: Scott, Amy. EdB, U. Toledo, 1974, EdM, 1977; EdD, U. Cin., 1992. Tchr., coach Montpelier (Ohio) Local Schs., 1974-78; tchr., counselor, coach Bright Local Schs., Mowrystown, Ohio, 1978-79; tchr., coach Margaretta Local Schs., Castalia, Ohio, 1979-84; tchr., coach Northwest Local Schs., Cin., 1984-87, asst. prin. middle sch., 1987-91, asst. prin. H.S., 1991-94; prin. H.S. Southwest Local Schs., Harrison, Ohio, 1994—; instr. U. Cin., Ohio, 1992—, Mt. St. Joseph, Cin.; presenter in field. Mem. Am. Ednl. Rsch. Assn., Midwest Ednl. Rsch. Assn., Nat. Assn. Secondary Sch. Prins., Ohio Assn. Secondary Sch. Adminstrs. Avocations: open wheel racing, college basketball. Office: Wm Henry Harrison HS 960 West Rd Harrison OH 45030

ZIGNAUSKAS, DOROTHY ELIZABETH, special education educator; b. Jersey City, Dec. 8, 1949; d. Sheldon and Rose Lucy (Stabile) Horowitz; m. John A. Zignauskas, May 2, 1982; children: John Jr., Jennifer Rose. BA in Spl. Edn., Jersey City State Coll., 1971, MA in Spl. Edn., 1978. Cert. tchr. handicapped, N.J. Spl. edn. tutor Quitman Street Sch., Newark, 1972-74, tchr. handicapped, 1972-94; tchr. handicapped 18th Ave. Sch., Newark, 1994—. Active mem. Lincroft Sch. PTA, 1987—; leader Girl Scouts U.S., Lincroft, 1994; den mother Boy Scouts Am., Lincroft, 1988-94; food and clothing dr. organizer Quitman St. Sch., 1972-82. Mem. Coun. for Exceptional Children, Children with Attention Deficit Disorder, Living with Attention Deficit Disorder Evenly and Rationally. Republican. Roman Catholic. Avocations: ceramics, sewing, bowling, travel, theater. Office: Newark Bd of Edn 18th Avenue Newark NJ 07108

ZIKAKIS, JOHN P., educator, researcher, biochemist; b. Piraeus, Greece, Sept. 16, 1933; came to U.S., 1958; s. Philip J. and Salome J. (Moshou) Z.; m. Kiki K. Matrozos, Aug. 29, 1958; 1 child, Salome J. Assoc. engr., Pythagoras Coll., Piraeus, 1956; BA, U. Del., 1965, MS, 1967, PhD, 1970. Lab. asst. DuPont de Nemours and Co., Newark, Del., 1959-61; research asst. U. Del., Newark, 1965-70, asst. prof. animal sci. dept., 1970-75, assoc. prof. animal sci. dept., 1975-81, prof. animal sci. dept., coll. marine studies, 1981-89; acad. indust. consultant, 1986—; prof. food sci. U. Del., Newark, 1987-89, prof. emeritus, 1989; v.p. United Chitotechnologies, Inc., Newark, 1989-93; cons. U. Thessaloniki, Greece, 1972-80; vis. prof. U. Panama, 1984-85, sci. advisor, 1985-89; sci. advisor Govt. of Greece, 1972-74; organizer numerous nat. and internat. sci. confs. and symposia over past 23 yrs. Author: Chitin, Chitosan and Related Enzymes, 1984, Advances in Chitin and Chitosan, 1992; mem. editorial bd. Jour. Agr. Food Chemistry, 1983-86; contbr. over 125 articles to profl. jours. Patentee in field. Trustee Riverside Hosp., Wilmington, Del., 1977-84; pres. bd. dirs. Maison Grande Condominium Assn., Inc., Miami Beach, Fla., 1990-92; bd. dirs. Holy Trinity Greek Orthodox Ch., Wilmington, 1971-73; pres. bd. govs. Commondore Condominium Assn., Ft. Lauderdale, Fla., 1993-94. 1st lt. Greek Air Force, 1952-56. Sr. Fulbright scholar, U. Panama, 1984-85; recipient Gold medal and cert. U. Patra, 1973, cert. recognition, commendation for excellence in rsch., edn., pub. svc. Pres. of U. Del., 1977. Mem. AAAS, Am. Chem. Soc. (historian div. agrl. and food chemistry 1980-84, chmn. pub. rels. com. 1980-85, chmn. disting. svc. award com. 1987-88, co-founder, editor div. agrl. and food chemistry membership directory 1980-86, chmn. div. agrl. and food chemistry 1986-87, Disting. Svc. award 1991), N.Y. Acad. Scis., Del. Acad. Sci., Inst. Food Technologists, Am. Inst. Biol. Sci., Am. Chitosci. Soc. (co-founder, trustee, pres. 1989—), Am. Dairy Sci. Assn., Sigma Xi. Avocations: tennis, sailing, swimming, gymnastics. Office: 307 SE 14th St Fort Lauderdale FL 33316-1929

ZIKORUS, ALBERT MICHAEL, golf course architect; b. Needham, Mass., Apr. 9, 1921; s. Walter Peter and Rose Mary (Smith) Z.; m. Charlene Bradstreet Aldrich; 1 child, Michael; m. Joan Gayle Boone, 1979. Student, Mass. State Coll., 1941. Greenskeeper Ould Newbury Golf Course, Newburyport, Mass., 1942, Wellesley (Mass.) Golf Course, 1946, Woodbridge (Conn.) Golf Course, 1948-51; assoc. William F. Mitchell Architect, 1951-52, Orin E. Smith Architect, Southington, Conn., 1953-58. Designed Tunxis Plantation Country Club, Farmington, Conn., Twin Hills Country Club, Longmeadow, Mass., Timberlin Golf Course, Berlin, Conn., Tashua Golf Course, Trumbull, Conn., Segalla Country Club, Amenia, N.Y., others. Sgt. USAF, 1942-46. Mem. Am. Soc. Golf Course Architects. Avocations: swimming, fishing, hiking, hunting, golf. Home/Office: PO Box 187 Canaan ME 04924-0187 Office: PO Box 187 Canaan ME 04924-0187

ZILKHA, EZRA KHEDOURI, banker; b. Baghdad, Iraq, July 31, 1925; came to U.S., 1941, naturalized, 1950; s. Khedouri A. and Louise (Bashi) Z.; m. Cecile Iny, Feb. 6, 1950; children: Elias Donald, Donna Zilkha Krisel, Bettina Louise. Grad., Hill Sch., Pottstown, Pa., 1943; AB, Wesleyan U., Middletown, Conn., 1947; LLD (hon.), Wesleyan U., 1987. Pres. Zilkha & Sons, Inc., N.Y.C., 1956—; pres. 3555 Intermediate Corp., Del., 1991—; bd. dirs. Chgo. Milw. Corp., Chgo., Newhall Land & Farming, Calif., CIGNA Corp., Phila., Cambridge Assocs., Boston, Milw. Land Co., Chgo.; gen. ptnr. Heartland Ptnrs., L.P., Chgo. Chmn. Internat. Ctr. for Disabled, N.Y.C.; trustee Brookings Inst., Washington, Lycée Français, N.Y.C.; trustee emeritus Wesleyan U.; former trustee Spence Sch., N.Y.C. Decorated chevalier Legion d'Honneur, officier Ordre Nat. du Merite (France); recipient Freedom of Human Spirit award Internat. Ctr. for Disabled, 1989. Mem. Coun. Fgn. Rels. Clubs: Racquet and Tennis (N.Y.C.), Knickerbocker (N.Y.C.); Meadow (Southampton, N.Y.); Travellers (Paris), Polo (Paris).

ZILLY, THOMAS SAMUEL, federal judge; b. Detroit, Jan. 1, 1935; s. George Samuel and Bernice M. (McWhinney) Z.; divorced; children: John, Peter, Paul, Luke; m. Jane Greller Noland, Oct. 8, 1988; stepchildren: Allison Noland, Jennifer Noland. BA, U. Mich., 1956; LLD, Cornell U., 1962. Bar: Wash. 1962, U.S. Ct. Appeals (9th cir.) 1962, U.S. Supreme Ct. 1976. Ptnr. Lane, Powell, Moss & Miller, Seattle, 1962-88; judge U.S. Dist. Ct. (we. dist.) Wash., Seattle, 1988—; judge pro tem Seattle Mcpl. Ct., 1972-80. Contbr. articles to profl. jours. Mem. Cen. Area Sch. Council, Seattle, 1969-70; scoutmaster Thunderbird Dist. council Boy Scouts Am. Seattle, 1976-84; bd. dirs. East Madison YMCA. Served to lt. (j.g.) USN, 1956-59. Recipient Tuahku Dist. Service to Youth award Boy Scouts Am., 1983. Mem. ABA, Wash. State Bar Assn., Seattle-King County Bar Assn. (treas. 1979-80, trustee 1980-83, sec. 1983-84, 2d v.p. 1984-85, 1st v.p. 1985-86, pres. 1986-87). Office: US Dist Ct 410 US Courthouse 1010 5th Ave Seattle WA 98104-1130

ZILVERSMIT, DONALD BERTHOLD, nutritional biochemist, educator; b. Hengelo, Holland, July 11, 1919; came to U.S., 1939, naturalized, 1950; s. Herman and Elizabeth (DeWinter) Z.; m. Kitty Fonteyn, June 28, 1945; children: Elizabeth Ann, Dorothy Susan, Sarah Jo. Student, U. Utrecht, Holland, 1936-39, DSc in Phys. Scis. (hon.), 1980; BS, U. Calif., Berkeley, 1940, PhD, 1948. Mem. faculty U. Tenn. Med. Coll., 1948-66, prof., 1956-66; prof. nutrition, prof. biochemistry, molecular and cell biology divs. nutritional sci. and biol. scis. Cornell U., 1966—, prof. emeritus, 1990—; vis. prof. U. Leiden, Holland, 1961-62, Mass. Inst. Tech., 1972-73; vis. fellow Australian Nat. U., Canberra, Australia, 1966; vis. lectr. Venezuela Inst. Sci. Investigations, 1977; career investigator Am. Heart Assn., 1959-89; editor Jour. Lipid Research, 1958-62, Circulation Research, 1962-67, 68-74, Circulation, 1960-65, Biochim. Biophysica Acta, 1969-79, Arteriosclerosis, 1980-90; editor Procs. Soc. Exptl. Biology and Medicine, 1975-87, mem. adv. council, 1978-81; cons. NIH. Editor-in-chief: Jour. of Lipid Research, 1958-61; adv. bd., 1962-72; Contbr. articles to profl. jours. Recipient Borden award, 1976, Disting. Achievement in Nutrition Rsch. award Bristol-Myers Squibb, 1990. Fellow Am. Inst. Nutrition; mem. AAAS, NAS, Am. Physiol. Soc., Am. Soc. Biol. Chemists, Coun. on Arteriosclerosis, Am. Heart Assn. (exec. bd. 1968-70, G. Lyman Duff Meml. award 1978), Soc. Exptl. Biology and Medicine, N.Y. Acad. Scis., Philosophy of Sci. Assn., Soc. Lit. and Sci., Phi Beta Kappa, Sigma Xi. Office: Cornell U Div Nutritional Scis Ithaca NY 14853

ZIMA, MICHAEL DAVID, lawyer; b. St Louis, Aug. 13, 1968; s. Marvin Walter Z. BA, U. Mich., 1990; JD, Ind. U., 1993. Atty. Dist. Coun. IRS, Jacksonville, Fla., 1993—. Author: (short story) The Brook, 1994, The Play, 1994. Mem. Ind. State Bar, Jacksonville Area C. of C. Avocations: tennis, golf, basketball, waterskiing, writing. Home: 9765 Southbrook Dr Apt 3416 Jacksonville FL 32256-0431 Office: Dist Counsel IRS Rm 564 400 W Bay St Jacksonville FL 32202

ZIMAND, HARVEY FOLKS, lawyer; b. N.Y.C., Aug. 28, 1928; s. Savel and Gertrude (Folks) Z.; m. Ingeborg Rockosch, 1963 (div. 1980); children—Patricia Folks, Stephanie Folks; m. Noel French, Apr. 30, 1983. B.A., Colgate U., 1950; postgrad., Oxford U., Eng., 1950; M.A., U. Chgo., 1951; postgrad., Columbia U., 1952-53; LL.B., Yale U., 1957. Bar: N.Y. 1957. Rapporteur Council for Fgn. Relations, N.Y.C., 1952-53; atty. Dept. Navy, Washington, 1956-70; ptnr. Kelley Drye & Warren, N.Y.C., 1970—; dir. Toronto-Dominion Trust Co., N.Y.C. Bd. dirs. Virginia Day Nursery, N.Y.C., 1980-84. Served to cpl. U.S. Army, 1951-53. Fellow N.Y. Bar Found., Am. Coll. Probate Counsel; mem. ABA, N.Y. State Bar Assn., Assn. Bar City of N.Y., Estate Planning Council. Republican. Episcopalian. Clubs: Yale (N.Y.C.); Randolph Mountain (N.H.). Home: 120 E 81st St New York NY 10028-1428 Office: Kelley Drye & Warren LLP 101 Park Ave New York NY 10178*

ZIMBALIST, EFREM, III, publishing company executive. BA in Econs., Harvard U., MBA. Sr. engagement mgr. McKinsey and Co., Inc., L.A.; chmn., CEO, Correia Art Glass, Inc.; asst. to group v.p. newspapers Times Mirror, N.Y.C., 1992-93, v.p. strategic devel., 1993—; pres., CEO, Times Mirror Mags., Inc., N.Y.C. Mem. nat. coun. House Ear Inst.; chmn. emeritus bd. trustees Robert Louis Stevenson Sch. Officer M.I., U.S. Army, 1969-70, Vietnam. Office: Times Mirror Mags Inc Two Park Ave New York NY 10016-5695

ZIMBARDO, PHILIP GEORGE, psychologist, educator, writer; b. N.Y.C., Mar. 23, 1933; s. George and Margaret (Bisicchia) Z.; m. Christina Maslach, Aug. 10, 1972; children: Zara, Tanya; 1 son by previous marriage, Adam. AB, Bklyn. Coll., 1954; MS, Yale U., 1955, PhD, 1959. Asst. prof. psychology Yale U., New Haven, 1959-61, NYU, N.Y.C., 1961-67; vis. assoc. prof. psychology Columbia U., N.Y.C., 1967-68; prof. psychology Stanford (Calif.) U., 1968—; pres. P.G. Zimbardo, Inc., San Francisco. Author: Cognitive Control of Motivation, 1969, Canvassing or Peace, 1970, Psychology and You, 1976, Shyness, What It Is, What To Do About It, 1977, Influencing Attitudes and Changing Behavior, rev. edit., 1977, The Shyness Workbook, 1979, A Parent's Guide to the Shy Child, 1981, The Psychology of Attitude Change and Social Influence, 1991, Psychology and Life, rev. edit., 1996. Pres. Montclair Ter. Assn., 1975—; sr. project advisor Exploratorium, 1993; host, writer, gen. acad. advisor PBS-TV series Discovering Psychology, 1987-90. Ctr. for Advanced Study of Behavioral Scis. fellow, 1971; recipient Peace medal Tokyo Police Dept., 1972, City Medal of Honor, Salamanca, Spain, Disting. Tchr. award Am. Psychol. Found., 1975. Mem. APA (Presdl. citation Discovery Psychology series 1994), AAAS, AAUP, Internat. Congress Psychology, Western Psychol. Assn. (pres. 1983), Ea. Psychol. Assn., Calif. Psychol. Assn. (Disting. Contbn. to Rsch. award 1978), Can. Psyuchol. Assn., Soc. for Psychol. Study of Social Issues, Soc. for Clin. and Exptl. Hypnosis, Sigma Xi, Phi Beta Kappa, Psi Chi. Roman Catholic. Home: 25 Montclair Ter San Francisco CA 94109-1517 Office: Stanford U Psychology Dept Stanford CA 94305 *One of the few virtues of growing up in a poor urban ghetto is the realization that people are the most important resource we have—to be used wisely, well and as often as possible. The second is the tempering of book learning by street wits. The third is to value a career that allows me to contribute to improving the quality of our lives through research and teaching.*

ZIMENT, IRWIN, medical educator; b. England, 1936. MB BChir, Cambridge U., 1961. Intern, resident England, 1961-64, USA, 1964-65; resident Bronx Mcpl. Hosp. Ctr., 1965-66; dir. respiratory therpay Harbor Gen. Hosp., Torrance, Calif., 1968-75; chief medicine Olive View-UCLA Med. Ctr., 1975—, med. dir., 1994—; prof. medicine UCLA Sch. Medicine, 1980—. Contbr. articles to profl. jours. Infectious Disease flelow Wadsworth VA Hosp., L.A., 1966-68. Mem. Am. Thoracic Soc. (clin. problems assembly chmn. 1981-82, coun. chot. reps. 1984-87, resp. bd. mem. advisors 1986-90), Am. Coll. Chest Physicians (steering com. 1987-91, chmn. 1989-91), Nat. Assn. Med. Dirs. Respiratory Care (founding mem., vice pres. 1978, treas. 1979-81, bd. dirs. 1983-89), Calif Thoracic Soc. (pres. 1980-81, various coms. 1970—), L.A. Lung Assn. (various coms. 1969-86). Office: Olive View-UCLA Med Ctr Med Adminstrn Rm 2C138 14445 Olive View Dr Sylmar CA 91342-1495

ZIMET, CARL NORMAN, psychologist, educator; b. Vienna, Austria, June 3, 1925; came to U.S., 1943, naturalized, 1945; s. Leon and Gisela (Kosser) Z.; m. Sara F. Goodman, June 4, 1950; children: Andrew, Gregory. BA, Cornell U., 1949; PhD, Syracuse U., 1953; postdoctoral fellow, Standard U., 1953-55. Diplomate in clin. psychology Am. Bd. Profl. Psychology (trustee 1966-74). Instr., then asst. prof. psychology and psychiatry Yale U., 1955-63; mem. faculty U. Colo. Med. Center, 1963—, prof. clin. psychology, 1965—, head div., 1963—; Mem. Colo. Bd. Psychol. Examiners, 1966-72, Colo. Mental Health Planning Commn., 1964-66; mem. acad. adv. com. John F. Kennedy Child Devel. Center, U. Colo., 1966—; chmn. Council for Nat. Register of Health Service Providers in Psychology, 1975-85, pres., mem. exec. bd. div. psychotherapy, 1970—; chair exec. com. Assn. Psychol. Internship Ctrs., 1988-91. Bd. editors: Jour. Clin. Psychology, 1962—, Jour. Clin. and Cons. Psychology, 1964-73, Psychotherapy, 1967—, Profl. Psychology, 1969-75. With USNR, 1943-46. Recipient Disting. Service award Colo. Psychol. Assn., 1976. Fellow APA (council reps. 1969-72, 73—, bd. dirs. 1985-88, Disting. award for profl. contbn. 1987, div. psychotherapy and div. clin. psychology), Soc. Personality Assessment (pres. 1975-76, bd. dirs., chair gen. psychol. services 1987—); mem. Am. Acad. Clin. Psychology (pres. 1993—), Denver Psychoanalytic (trustee 1968-71), Am. Group Psychotherapy Assn., Med. Sch. Profs. Psychology (pres. 1992-94). Home: 4325 E 6th Ave Denver CO 80220-4939

ZIMET, CAROL, writer; b. Bklyn., May 2, 1922; d. Oscar and Anna (Marcus) Segal; m. Bernard Chesner, June 1945 (div. Nov. 1968); children: Tasha Garfield, Jeffrey Chesner; m. Jesse Zimet, Mar. 1969. Student, Adelphi Coll., 1960-62, Caton Rose Inst. Art, 1962-64. Interior designer Sachs, N.Y.C., 1966-77; cons. lighting 1962-70; lectr. interior design, N.Y., 1967-77. Author: So You Are Going to the Hospital, 1994; author (with others) World of Poetry, 1990, Poems That Will Live Forever, 1992, In the Desert Sun, 1993, Outstanding Poets of 1994, 1994. Vol. ARC, AHRC, IHB. Recipient numerous awards. Mem. Poetry Group of Rockville Ctr. (chair), Barnes and Noble of Carle Place Poetry Group (chair), Internat. Soc. Poetry, Rockville Ctr. Guild for the Arts. Home: 942 Stratford Ct Westbury NY 11590-5823

ZIMKAS, CHARLES PATRICK, JR., space foundation director; b. Scranton, Pa., Sept. 8, 1940; s. Charles Zimkas Sr. and Margaret (Bakunas) Sullick; m. Ursula Frediel Marten; children: Robert L., Uwe F., Michael P., Brian David. Enlisted USAF, advanced through grades to chief master sgt., 1958; dep. chief of staff, personnel adminstrv. div. Aerospace Def. Command, Colorado Springs, Colo., 1971-74; exec. to dep. chief of staff personnel Aerospace Def. Command, Colorado Springs, 1975-80; chief of adminstrn. Air Forces Iceland, Keflavik, 1974-75; first sr. enlisted advisor USAF Space Command, Colorado Springs, 1980-84; ret., 1984; dir. regional devel. Noncommissioned Officers Assn., San Antonio, 1984-86; dir. ops. U.S. Space Found., Colorado Springs, 1986—. Named Air Force Outstanding Airman of Yr., 1978; recipient Air Force Legion Merit. Mem. Noncommd. Officers Assn. (bd. dirs. 1978-84, chmn. bd. dirs. 1982-84, Order of Sword award 1978, Excalibur award 1979), Air Force Assn. (exec. v.p. Lance P. Sijan chpt., medal of merit 1990, 94). Home: 729 Drew Dr Colorado Springs CO 80911-2606 Office: US Space Found 2860 S Circle Dr Ste 2301 Colorado Springs CO 80906-4107

ZIMM, BRUNO HASBROUCK, physical chemistry educator; b. Woodstock, N.Y., Oct. 31, 1920; s. Bruno L. and Louise S. (Hasbrouck) Z.; m. Georgianna S. Grevatt, June 17, 1944; children: Louis H., Carl B. Grad., Kent (Conn.) Sch., 1938; A.B., Columbia U., 1941, M.S., 1943, Ph.D., 1944. Research assoc. Columbia U., 1944; research assoc., instr. Polytech. Inst. Bklyn., 1944-46; instr. chemistry U. Calif. at Berkeley, 1946-47, asst. prof., 1947-50, assoc. prof., 1950-51; vis. lectr. Harvard U., 1950-51; research assoc. research lab. Gen. Electric Co., 1951-60; prof. chemistry U. Calif., La Jolla, 1960-91, prof. emeritus, 1991—. Assoc. editor: Jour. Chem. Physics, 1947-49; adv. bd.: Jour. Polymer Sci, 1953-62, Jour. Bio-Rheology, 1962-73, Jour. Biopolymers, 1963—, Jour. Phys. Chemistry, 1963-68, Jour. Biophys. Chemistry, 1973—. Recipient Bingham Medal Soc. Rheology, 1960, High Polymer Physics prize Am. Phys. Soc., 1963; Kirkwood medal Yale U., 1982. Mem. Biophys. Soc., Am. Soc. Biol. Chemists and Molecular Biologists, Am. Chem. Soc. (Baekeland award 1957), Nat. Acad. Scis. (award in Chem. Scis. 1981), Am. Acad. Arts and Scis., Am. Phys. Soc.

ZIMMAR, GEORGE PETER, publishing executive, psychology educator; b. Chgo., Dec. 31, 1937; s. Peter George and Sofia (Kanellis) Z.; m. Doulie J. Pappas; children: Sofia Corrine, Peter David George. BS in Psychology, Roosevelt U., 1960, MS in Exptl. Psychology, 1961; PhD in Neurosci., SUNY, Buffalo, 1966; postgrad., MIT, 1968. Rsch. assoc. Northwestern U. Med. Sch., Chgo., 1960-61; instr. psychology SUNY, Buffalo, 1962-64; asst. prof. Grinnell (Iowa) Coll., 1965-69; prof., chmn. dept. Briarcliff Coll., Briarcliff Manor, N.Y., 1970-77; editor Praeger Pubs., N.Y.C., 1978-81; sr. editor CBS Pub. Group/Elsevier, N.Y.C., 1981-88; editor-in-chief Rowman & Littlefield Pubs., Totowa, N.J., 1988-89; sr. editor Springer-Verlag, N.Y.C., 1989-92; pres. Youth Edn. Systems, Inc., Scarborough, N.Y., 1985—, also chmn. bd. dirs.; adj. prof. Pace U., Pleasantville, N.Y., 1977, NYU, 1991—; v.p., bd. dirs. McGraw Learning Labs. Inc., Dobbs Ferry, N.Y., 1970-774; bd. dirs. Psychosocial Press, Madison, Conn. Author: Chronology of Wars, 1989; contbr. articles to profl. jours. Pres. Ch. of Our Saviour, Rye, N.Y., 1981-82, bd. dirs., 1973—; capital campaign officer Hackley Sch., Tarrytown, N.Y., 1988. Hillman fellow Roosevelt U., 1961, Sloan Found. fellow, 1968; Cattell grantee Grinnell Coll., 1967. Mem. APA, Am. Psychol. Soc. (charter), Cognite Sci. Soc., Sigma Xi. Greek Orthodox. Office: Youth Edn Systems Inc Scarborough Station Briarcliff Manor NY 10510

ZIMMER, JOHN HERMAN, lawyer; b. Sioux Falls, S.D., Dec. 30, 1922; s. John Francis and Veronica (Berke) Z.; student Augustana Coll., Sioux Falls, 1941-42, Mont. State Coll., 1943; LLB, U. S.D., 1948; m. Deanna Langner, 1976; children by previous marriage: Mary Zimmer Quinlin, Robert Joseph, Judith Maureen Zimmer Rose. Bar: S.D. 1948. Pvt. practice law, Turner County, S.D., 1948—; of counsel Zimmer & Duncan, Parker, S.D., 1992—; states atty. Turner County, 1955-58, 62-64; asst. prof. med. jurisprudence U. S.D.; minority counsel U.S. Senate Armed Services Com. on Strategic and Critical Materials Investigation, 1962-63; chmn. Southeastern Council Govts., 1973-75; mem. U. S.D. Law Sch. adv. council, 1973-74. Chmn. Turner County Rep. Com., 1955-56, 60-74; mem. S.D. Rep. adv. com., 1959-60; alt. del. Rep. Nat. Conv., 1968; pres. S.D. Easter Seal Soc., 1986-87. Served with AUS, 1943-46; PTO. Decorated Bronze Star, Philippine Liberation ribbon. Mem. ABA, Fed., S.D. (commr. 1954-57) Bar Assns., Assn. Trial Lawyers Am., S.D. Trial Lawyers Assn. (pres. 1967-68), VFW, Am. Legion, Phi Delta Phi. Lodges: Elks, Shriners. Home: RR1 PO Box 640 Parker SD 57053 Office: Zimmer & Duncan Law Bldg PO Box 550 Parker SD 57053-0547

ZIMMER, PAUL JEROME, publisher, editor, poet; b. Canton, Ohio, Sept. 18, 1934; s. Jerome Francis and Louise Celina (Surmont) Z.; m. Suzanne Jane Koklauner, Apr. 4, 1959; children: Erik Jerome, Justine Mary. BA, Kent State U., 1959. Assoc. dir. U. Pitts. Press, 1967-78; dir. U. Ga. Press, Athens, 1978-84, U. Iowa Press, Iowa City, 1984—. Author: (poetry) Family Reunion, 1983 (AAAL award 1985), The Great Bird of Love, 1989 (award Nat. Poetry Series 1989), Big Blue Train, 1993, Crossing to Sunlight: Selected Poems, 1996. With U.S. Army, 1954-55. Avocation: collecting antique photography. Home: 420 Fairchild St Iowa City IA 52245-2822 Office: U Iowa Press 119 West Park Rd Iowa City IA 52242

ZIMMER, RICHARD ALAN, congressman, lawyer; b. Newark, N.J., Aug. 16, 1944; s. William and Evelyn (Schlank Rader) Z.; m. Marfy Goodspeed, Dec. 27, 1965; children: Carl William, Benjamin Goodspeed. BA, Yale U., 1966, LLB, 1969. Bar: N.Y. 1971, U.S. Dist. Ct. (so. and ea. dists.) N.Y. 1974, N.J. 1975, U.S. Dist. Ct. N.J. 1975, U.S. Supreme Ct. 1980. Assoc. Cravath, Swaine and Moore, N.Y.C., 1969-75; gen. atty. Johnson & Johnson, New Brunswick, N.J., 1976-91; mem. N.J. Gen. Assembly, 1982-87, chmn. state govt. com., 1986-87; mem. N.J. Senate, 1987-91, 102nd-103rd Congresses from 12th N.J. dist., Washington, D.C., 1991—. Chmn. March of Dimes WalkAmerica, Hunterdon County, N.J., 1984-86; treas. Hunterdon Hospice, Flemington, N.J., 1984-86. Mem. ABA, N.J. State Bar Assn., Hunterdon County Bar Assn. Republican. Home: Locktown-Flemington Rd Flemington NJ 08822-9541 Office: US House of Reps 228 Cannon HOB Washington DC 20515

ZIMMER, STUART, secondary school educator; b. Bklyn., Sept. 20, 1942; s. Joseph and Rose (Sachs) Z.; m. Joan Beth Heyman, June 26, 1965; children: Todd, Ronald. BA, L.I. U., 1964; MA, Bklyn. Coll., 1966. Tchr. area high sch., Bklyn., 1964-67, Canarsie H.S., Bklyn., 1967-77, August Martin H.S., Queens, N.Y., 1977-87, Jamaica (N.Y.) H.S., 1987-95; writer curriculum N.Y.C. Bd. Edn., 1983; presenter numerous workshops and tchg. confs. Author: Government and You, 1985, Economics and You, 1987, Key to Understanding Global Studies, 1988, Key to Understanding U.S. History and Government, 1988, Comprende Tu Mundo, 1989, Los Estados Unidos, 1990, Mastering Global Studies, 1991, Mastering U.S. History and Government, 1992, Mastering Ohio's 9th Grade Citizenship Test, 1993, Mastering Ohio's 12th Grade Citizenship Test, 1994, Ohio: Its Land and Its People, 1994, Historia y Gobierno de los Estados Unidos, 1995, Principios de Economia, 1995, Ohio: It's Neighbors, Near and Far, 1995. Recipient Cert. of Recognition, N.Y.C. Deputy Police Commissioner, 1987, Spl. Achievement citation Am. Flag Inst., N.Y.C., 1987, resolution honoring his many achievements N.Y. State Legislature, Albany, 1989. Mem. Nat. Coun. Social Studies Tchrs., Assn. Tchrs. of Social Studies (assoc. editor publ. 1984-93). Avocations: reading, jogging, stamp collecting. Home: 12 Elmore Pl East Northport NY 11731-5627

ZIMMER, WILLIAM HOMER, JR., retired insurance company executive; b. Cin., Mar. 3, 1930; s. William Homer and Esther Caroline (Krueger) Z.; m. Virginia Louise Avey, June 27, 1951; children: William H. III, Amy Zimmer Schneider. BSBA, Ohio State U., 1952. Staff asst. Cin. Gas & Electric Co., 1952, acct., treas., treas.-sec., v.p. fin., sr. v.p. fin.; vice chmn. Cin. Fin. Corp., 1981-95; ret., 1995; bd. dirs. Alltel Corp., Little Rock. Former trustee Bethesda Hosp. Mem. The Oaks (Sarasota, Fla.), Western Hills Country Club, Double Eagle Country Club (Galena, Ohio), Queen City Club, Masons (33 deg.). Presbyterian. Avocations: golf, fishing, travel. Home: 5883 Countryhills Dr Cincinnati OH 45233-1727

ZIMMERLY, JAMES GREGORY, lawyer, physician; b. Longview, Tex., Mar. 25, 1941; s. George James and Irene Gertrude (Kohler) Z.; m. Nancy Carol Zimmerly, June 11, 1966; children: Mark, Scott, Robin; m. Johanna Bross Huffer, Feb. 14, 1991. BA, Gannon Coll., 1962; MD, U. Md., 1966, JD, 1969; MPH, Johns Hopkins U., 1968. Bar: Md. 1970, D.C. 1972, U.S. Ct. Mil. Appeals 1973, U.S. Supreme Ct. 1973. Ptnr. Acquisto, Asplen & Morstein, Ellicott City, Md., 1970—. Chmn. dept. legal medicine Armed Forces Inst. Pathology, 1971-91; prof. George Washington U., 1972-80; adj. prof. law Georgetown U. Law Ctr., 1972—, Antioch Sch. Law, 1977-80; assoc. prof. U. Md. Sch. Medicine, 1973—; cons. Dept. Def., Dept. Justice, HHS, VA, 1971-91. Fellow Am. Acad. Forensic Scis., Am. Coll. Legal Medicine, (pres. 1980-81), Am. Coll Preventive Medicine; mem. ABA, Md. Bar Assn., Am. Soc. on Law and Medicine, Am. Coll. Emergency Physicians, Md. Med. Soc. Editor: Legal Aspects of Medical Practice, 1978-88, Jour. Legal Medicine, 1975-78, Md. Med. Jour., 1977-88, Lawyers' Med. Ency., 1980-90. Home: 6300 Old National Pike Bluestone Overlook Boonsboro MD 21713 Office: Monumental Life Ins Co 2 East Chase St Baltimore MD 21202

ZIMMERMAN, AARON MARK, lawyer; b. Syracuse, N.Y., Jan. 28, 1953; s. Julius and Sara (Lavine) Z. B.S., Syracuse U., 1974, J.D., 1976. Bar: N.Y. 1977, Pa. 1977, D.C. 1978, S.C. 1978, Fla. 1978, U.S. Dist. Ct. S.C. 1978, U.S. Dist. Ct. (no. dist.) N.Y. Corp. atty., asst. sec. Daniel Internat. Corp., Greenville, S.C., 1977-79; ptnr. Abend, Driscoll & Zimmerman, 1979-81; Zimmerman Law Office, Syracuse, 1981—. Bd. dirs. Syracuse Friends Ametuer Boxing, 1982-92. Mem. Am. Arbitration Assn. (arbitrator), Workers Compensation Com. N.Y. State Bar (exec. com. 1984—), Workers Compensation Assn. of Cen. N.Y. (charter, dir., treas.), N.Y. State Bar, S.C. State Bar, D.C. State Bar, Fla. State Bar, ABA. Lodge: Masons. Home: 602 Standish Dr Syracuse NY 13224-2018 Office: Zimmerman Law Offices 117 S State St Syracuse NY 13202-1103

ZIMMERMAN, BERNARD, lawyer; b. Munich, Bavaria, Fed. Republic Germany, May 31, 1946; came to U.S., 1949; s. Sam and Roza (Spodek) Z.; m. Grace L. Suarez, Oct. 23, 1976; children: Elizabeth, Adam, David, Dara Bylah. AB, U. Rochester, 1967; JD, U. Chgo., 1970. Bar: Calif. 1971, La. 1971, U.S. Supreme Ct. 1975, U.S. Dist. Ct. (no., ea., cen. and so. dists.) Calif., U.S. Dist. Ct. (ea. dist.) La., U.S. Ct. Appeals (9th cir.). Law. clk. chief judge U.S. Dist. Ct. (ea. dist.) La., New Orleans, 1970-71; asst. prof. law La. State U., Baton Rouge, 1971-72; ptnr. Pillsbury, Madison & Sutro, San Francisco, 1972-95; legal cons. 3d Constnl. Conv. Commonwealth of the No. Mariana Islands, Northern Mariana Islands, 1995; U.S. magistrate judge U.S. Dist. Ct. (no. dist.) Calif., 1995—; dep. pub. defender City of San Francisco, 1975; arbitrator U.S. Dist. Ct., San Francisco, AAA; judge pro tem San Francisco Superior and Mcpl. Cts. Bd. dirs., mem. exec. com. San Francisco Lawyers' Com. on Urban Affairs, 1984-95, treas., 1987; mem. regional bd. Anti-Defamation League, 1989-95. Mem. Phi Beta Kappa. Democrat. Jewish. Club: Olympic (San Francisco). Office: 450 Golden Gate Ave San Francisco CA 94102

ZIMMERMAN, BRYANT KABLE, lawyer; b. Mt. Morris, Ill., Nov. 19, 1922; s. Milo D. and Hazel G. (Kable) Z.; m. Harriet Bong, Jan. 20, 1946; children: Paula, Keith, Craig. A.B., Augustana Coll., 1946; student, Washington U., St. Louis, 1942-43; LL.B., Harvard U., 1948. Bar: Calif. 1949. Assoc. counsel McCutchen, Doyle, Brown & Enersen, San Francisco, 1949-63; v.p., gen. counsel FrancoWestern Oil Co., Bakersfield, Calif., 1963-65; sr. v.p., sec., chief legal officer, dir. Guy F. Atkinson Co., South San Francisco, Calif., 1965-88; of counsel Pettit & Martin, San Francisco, 1988-95. Bd. dirs., v.p. Republican Alliance, 1965-74; bd. dirs., sec. Atkinson Found., 1967-88; trustee Willamette U., 1978-90; chmn. Nat. Constrn. Employers Coun., 1985-86, Californians for Compensation Reform, 1984-88; chmn. Coun. on Multiemployer Pension Security, 1983-86. With USAAF, 1942-46. Mem. Nat. Constructors Assn. (bd. dirs. 1980-83, chmn. 1983). Methodist. Home: 75 Del Monte Dr Burlingame CA 94010-6226

ZIMMERMAN, DIANE LEENHEER, law educator, lawyer; b. Newton, N.J., Apr. 16, 1941; d. Adrian and Mildred Eleanor (Booth) Leenheer; m. Earl A. Zimmerman, Sept. 24, 1960 (div. Aug. 1982); m. 2d, Cavin P. Leeman, Feb. 18, 1984. BA, Beaver Coll., Glenside, Pa., 1963; JD, Columbia U., 1976. Bar: N.Y. 1977, U.S. Supreme Ct. 1983. Reporter, Newsweek mag., N.Y.C., 1963-71; spl. features writer N.Y. Daily News, N.Y.C., 1971-73; law clk. U.S. Dist. Ct. (ea. dist.) N.Y., Bklyn., 1976-77; asst. prof. law NYU, N.Y.C., 1977-80, assoc. prof., 1980-82, prof., 1982—; mem. faculty Practicing Law Inst., N.Y.C., 1979, 84, 90, 92, 94; of counsel Skadden, Arps, Slate, Meagher & Flom. Author: fed. ct. report Gender Fairness in Second Cir., 1994—; articles and book rev. editor Columbia Law Rev., 1975-76. Mem. working group on women, censorship and pornography Nat. Coalition Against Censorship. Recipient citation of merit Columbia U. Sch. Journalism, 1972; Kent scholar and Stone scholar, 1973-76; Disting. Lee vis. prof. Coll. William and Mary, 1994. Mem. ABA (vice chmn. tort liability study com. tort and ins. sect. 1986-87, chair 1st amendment rights com. 1989-94), Am. Law Inst., Assn. of Bar of City of N.Y. (chairperson com. civil rights 1981-83), Copyright Soc. USA (trustee 1988-91). Office: NYU Sch Law 40 Washington Sq S New York NY 10012-1005

ZIMMERMAN, DON, film editor. Prodns. include: Coming Home, 1978, Heaven Can Wait, 1978, Uncle Joe Shannon, 1978, Being There, 1979, A Change of Seasons, 1980, Barbarosa, 1982, Rocky III, 1982, Best Friends, 1982, Staying Alive, 1983, Teachers, 1984, Rocky IV, 1985, Cobra, 1986, Over the Top, 1986, Fatal Beauty, 1987, Everybody's All-American, 1988, The Package, 1989, Navy Seals, 1990. Office: The Gersh Agy 232 N Canon Dr Beverly Hills CA 90210-5302

ZIMMERMAN, DON CHARLES, plant physiologist, biochemist; b. Fargo, N.D., Feb. 27, 1934. BS, N.D. State U., 1955, MS, 1959, PhD in Biochemistry, 1964. Rsch. chemist sci. and edn. adminstrn. agrl. rsch. USDA, 1959—, ctr. dir. argl. rsch. svc., 1988—; asst. prof. N.D. State U., 1964-69, adj. prof. biochemistry, 1969—. Mem. AAAS, Am. Soc. Plant Physiology. Office: No Dakota Univ USDA Red River Vly Agrl Rsch Ctr Univ Sta PO Box 5677 Fargo ND 58105

ZIMMERMAN, D(ONALD) PATRICK, lawyer; b. Albany, N.Y., Mar. 20, 1942; s. Bernard M. and Helen M. (Eshelman) Z. Student Lawrenceville Sch., 1960; BA, Rollins Coll., 1964; JD, Dickinson Sch. Law, 1967. Bars: Pa. 1968, U.S. Supreme Ct. 1971. Atty., Legal Aid, 1968-69; pub. defender, Lancaster County, Pa., 1969-72; sole practice, Lancaster, Pa., 1974—; instr. Ct. Common Pleas for Constables, 1976—; solicitor Lancaster County Dep. Sheriff Assn., 1977—, Lancaster County Constable Assn., 1975—; instr. sheriff's dept. Lancaster County for Dep. Sheriffs, 1978—; of counsel to Dep. Sheriff Assn. Pa., 1979-81; spl. counsel Pa. State Constables Assn., 1981; chmn. Bd. Arbitrators Lancaster County, 1975-81; spl. counsel Legislative Com. to Constable Assn. Pa., 1982; mem. pastoral coun. St. Anthony's Catholic Ch., 1995—. Recipient Ofcl. Commendation of Merit, Lancaster County Sheriff's Dept., 1979, Ofcl. Commendation of Merit Fraternal Order Police State Lodge 66, 1985, Outstanding Svc. award, 1987, Disting. Service award Fraternal Order State Police Pa., 1987, Outstanding Leadership award, 1988. Mem. ABA, Am. Trial Lawyers Assn., Pa. Bar Assn., Lancaster County Bar Assn. Author: The Pennsylvania Landlord and Tenant Handbook, 1982, revised edit., 1993; contbr. articles to profl. jours. Office: 214 E King St Lancaster PA 17602-2977

ZIMMERMAN, EDWIN MORTON, lawyer; b. N.Y.C., June 11, 1924; s. Benjamin and Tobie (Fuchs) Z.; m. Caroline Abbot, July 3, 1956; children: Sarah Abbot, Lyle Benjamin, Miriam Appleton. AB, Columbia U., 1944, LLB, 1949. Bar: N.Y. 1949, D.C. 1969, U.S. Supreme Ct 1969. With Hoover Commn. Reorgn. Exec. Br., 1948; law clk. to Hon. Stanley F. Reed U.S. Supreme Ct., 1950-51; law clk. to Judge Simon H. Rifkind U.S. Dist. Ct., 1949-50; pvt. practice law N.Y.C., 1951-59; prof. law Stanford U., 1959-69; with Justice Dept., 1965-69, asst. atty. gen. charge antitrust div., 1968-69; mem. Covington & Burling, Washington, 1969—; Mem. coun. Adminstrv. Conf. U.S., 1975-78; mem. mfg. studies bd. Nat. Acad. Sci., 1983-87. Trustee Textile Mus., 1983—, pres. bd. trustees, 1987—; mem. Folger Poetry Bd., 1990—; mem. adv. bd. Partisan Rev., 1996—. 1st lt. AUS, 1944-46. Mem. ABA, Assn. of Bar of City of N.Y., Am. Law Inst., Coun. Fgn. Rels., Phi Beta Kappa. Home: 1820 Kalorama Sq NW Washington DC 20008-4022 Office: Covington & Burling PO Box 7566 1201 Pennsylvania Ave NW Washington DC 20004-2401

ZIMMERMAN, EVERETT LEE, English educator, academic administrator; b. Lancaster, Pa., Dec. 9, 1936; s. Amos Wanner and Anna (Sensenig) Z.; m. Muriel Laden, Apr. 28, 1963, children: Andrew, Daniel. BA, Bob Jones U., 1958; MA, Temple U., 1961, PhD, 1966. Lectr. Temple U., Phila., 1961-62; instr. Rutgers U., Camden, N.J., 1962-66, asst. prof., 1966-69; asst. prof. U. Calif., Santa Barbara, 1969-72, assoc. prof., 1972-80, prof. English, 1980—, dean, 1988-89. Author: Defoe and the Novel, 1975, Swift's Narrative Satires, 1983, also articles. Dem. committeeman, Phila., 1965-66. Jr. Faculty fellow, 1971, Humanities Inst. fellow, 1975 U. Calif.; NEH grantee, 1986; Guggenheim fellow, 1989-90. Mem. MLA, Am. Soc. 18th Century Studies. Home: 1822 Prospect Ave Santa Barbara CA 93103-1950 Office: U of Calif Dept Of English Santa Barbara CA 93106

ZIMMERMAN, FREDERIC THOMAS, neurologist, researcher, educator; b. Shamokin, Pa., Apr. 12, 1902; s. William Frances and Hattie Roberto (Stahl) Z.; m. Mary Louise Gannon, 1933 (div. 1939); 1 child, Mary Louise. A.B., Bucknell U., 1924; M.D., U. Md., 1928; M.A., Columbia U., 1943. Diplomate Am. Bd. Psychiatry and Neurology. Intern, St. Elizabeth's Hosp., Washington, 1929-31, resident, 1931-34; research asst. Coll. Physicians and Surgeons, N.Y.C., 1941-50; attending neurologist Colombia Presbyn. Hosp., N.Y.C., 1950-60; assoc. clin. prof. N.Y. Med. Coll., N.Y.C., 1954-57; assoc. clin. prof. Coll. Physicians and Surgeons, 1950-60; attending neurologist Bellevue Med. Ctr., N.Y.C., 1976—; cons. in field. Contbr. articles to profl. jours. Park-Davis grantee for treatment of epilepsy, 1952-58; Ciba grantee, 1957-58. Fellow Am. Psychiat. Assn.; mem. Am. Neurol. Assn. (sr.). Avocations: gardening; music; history; art; opera. Home: 20 E 68th St New York NY 10021-5844 Office: 133 E 73d St New York NY 10021

ZIMMERMAN, GAIL MARIE, medical foundation executive; b. Fort Wayne, Ind., June 23, 1945; d. Albert Douglas and Aina Dorothy (Johnson) Z. B.A., U. Puget Sound, 1967. Intelligence analyst CIA, Washington, 1970-72; research asst. Arthur Young & Co., Portland, Oreg., 1972-74; emergency med. service planner Marion-Polk-Yamhill Counties, Salem, Oreg., 1975-76; health cons. Freedman Assocs., Portland, Oreg., 1976-77; legis. asst. U.S. Senator Bob Packwood, Portland, 1977-78; exec. dir. Nat. Psoriasis Found., Portland, 1979—; mem. dermatology panel U.S. Parmacopoeial Conv., 1985-94; lay rep. Nat. Inst. Arthritis, Musculoskeletal and Skin Disease, NIH, 1990-94. Founding bd. dirs. Nat. Abortion Rights Action League, Portland, 1977; pres. bd. dirs. Oreg. Common Cause, Portland, 1977-78. Democrat. Avocations: tennis; flute. Office: Nat Psoriasis Found 6600 SW 92nd Ave Ste 300 Portland OR 97223-7142

ZIMMERMAN, GEORGE OGUREK, physicist, educator; b. Poland, Oct. 20, 1935; s. Charles and Carolin Olga (Fisher) Z.; m. Isa Kaftal, Oct. 4, 1964. B.S., Yale U., 1958, M.S., 1959, Ph.D. (Univ. Wilson fellow 1959-60, D.N. Clark fellow 1959-61), 1963. Research assoc. Yale U., 1962-63; asst. prof. physics Boston U., 1963-68, assoc. prof., 1968-74, prof., 1974—, assoc. chmn. dept. physics, 1971-72, chmn. dept., 1973-83, chmn. faculty coun., 1985-86, dir. honors program in sci. and engring. for HS students, 1978—; mem. staff Nat. Magnet Lab., Cambridge, Mass., 1964, vis. scientist, 1964-70; assoc. physicist U. Calif., San Diego, 1973; vis. scientist Brookhaven Nat. Lab., 1980; vis. scholar Harvard U., 1988, Kamerling Onnes Laboratorium, Leiden, The Netherlands, 1988; pres. Zerres Corp.; participant numerous physics teaching improvement programs for secondary sch. tchrs. and students. Contbr. articles on low temperature physics, phase transitions and superconductivity to profl. jours.; patentee in field. Rsch. Corp. grantee, 1964-65, Air Force Office Sci. Rsch. grantee, 1966-86, NSF grantee, 1975—. Mem. Am. Phys. Soc., N.Y. Acad. Scis., AAAS, Phi Beta Kappa, Sigma Xi. Home: 566 Commonwealth Ave Boston MA 02215-2520 Office: Boston U Dept Physics Boston MA 02215 *Administration is easier than science because in administration one can create one's own reality, while in science reality is unalterable.*

ZIMMERMAN, GIDEON K., minister; b. Lehr, N.D., Aug. 18, 1920; m. Eleanor Pekrul; children: Paul, Mark (dec.), Thomas. Diploma, N.Am. Baptist Sem., Rochester, N.Y., 1943; B.A., Wesley Coll., U. N.D., 1951; postgrad., Bethany Bibl. Sem., 1958-59, Chgo. Lutheran Sem., 1959-61; B.D., N.Am. Bapt. Sem., Sioux Falls, S.D., 1960, D.D. Pastor First Bapt. Ch., Auburn, Mich., 1943-47, Grace Bapt. Ch., Grand Forks, N.D., 1947-51, Temple Bapt. Ch., Milw., 1951-55; gen. sec. dept. Christian edn. N. Am. Bapt. Conf., 1955-68, exec. sec., 1968-79, estate planning counselor, 1979-85. Home: 3721 Bardstown Rd Apt 308 Louisville KY 40218-2261

ZIMMERMAN, HAROLD SAMUEL, retired state senator, newspaper editor and publisher, state administrator; b. Valley City, N.D., June 1, 1923; s. Samuel Alwin and Lulu (Wylie) Z.; m. Julianne Williams, Sept. 12, 1946; children—Karen, Steven, Judi Jean (dec.). B.A., U. Wash., 1947. News editor Sedro-Woolley (Wash.) Courier-Times, 1947-50; editor, pub. Advocate, Castle Rock, Wash., 1950-57; pub. Post-Record, Camas, Wash., 1957-80; assoc. pub., columnist, 1980; assoc. pub., columnist, dir. Eagle Publs., Camas, 1980-88. Mem. Wash. Ho. of Reps., 1967-80; mem. Wash. Senate, 1981-88, Wash. State Environ. Hearings Bd., Lacey, 1988-93. Served with USAAF, 1943-46. Mem. Grange, Sigma Delta Chi, Sigma Chi. Republican. United Methodist. Clubs: Lions, Kiwanis.

ZIMMERMAN, HAROLD SEYMOUR, elementary school educator; b. Bklyn., June 3, 1928. BA, Bklyn. Coll., 1950; MA, So. Ill. U., Edwardsville, 1970; postgrad., various, 1950-90. 8th grade English, Social Studies, Reading tchr. Sherwood Day Sch., Chesterfield, Mo., 1956-64; 7th grade core curriculum, English, Social Studies tchr. Nipher Jr. High Sch., Kirkwood, Mo., 1964-70; 7th grade Social Studies, team teaching tchr. Brittany Woods Sch., University City, Mo., 1971-91; tchr. Russian lit. OASIS, 1995; tchr. Russian Art Oasis, 1996; adj. prof. Russian studies Lindenwood Coll., St. Charles, Mo., 1975—, Washington U., 1972-91; participant 1st U.S./Russia Joint Conf. on Edn., 1994; cons. in field. Author: Facing Issues of Family Living; contbr. articles to profl. jours. Chairperson bd. trustees Indian Meadows subdivsn., Olivette, Mo.; chairperson Youth Commn., Olivette; vol. OASIS, St. Louis Zoo. Mem. NEA, ASCD, Mo. Edn. Assn., Nat. Coun. Social Studies (spl. interest groups psychology, tchr. edn., religion in schs.), Mo. Geog. Alliance Tchr. Cons., People to People, World Coun. of Affairs, Bus. for Russia. Home: 450 E Lockwood Webster Groves MO 63119 *My goal in life is, and was to meet my potential to use for the service of others; a religious commitment.*

ZIMMERMAN, HELENE LORETTA, business educator; b. Rochester, N.Y., Feb. 26, 1933; d. Henry Charles and Loretta Catherine (Hobert) Z. BS, SUNY, Albany, 1953, MS, 1959; PhD, U. N.D., 1969. Cert. records mgr. Bus. tchr., chmn. bus. dept. Williamson (N.Y.) Cen. Sch., 1953-69; asst. prof. U. Ky., Lexington, 1969-70; assoc. prof. bus. Cen. Mich. U., Mt. Pleasant, 1970-74, prof., 1974—. Author General Business, 1977; contbg. author to records mgmt. text book, 1987. Sec. Isabella County Christmas Outreach, Mt. Pleasant, 1983—. Mem. Assn. Records Mgmt. and Adminstrn., Inst. Cert. Records Mgrs. (sec. 1985-89, exam. devel. com. 1993—), Internat. Soc. Bus. Edn. (internat. v.p. English speaking nations 1986-88), Nat. Bus. Edn. Assn., Mich. Bus. Edn. Assn. (bd. dirs. 1985-90, 95—, pres. 1988-89), AAUW (pres. 1984-86), Delta Kappa Gamma (state pres. 1987-89, internat. fin. com. 1990-94). Avocations: travel, crafts. Office: Ctrl Mich U Grawn # 337 Mount Pleasant MI 48859

ZIMMERMAN, HOWARD ELLIOT, chemist, educator; b. N.Y.C., July 5, 1926; s. Charles and May (Cohen) Z.; m. Jane Kirschenheiter, June 3, 1950 (dec. Jan. 1975); children: Robert, Steven, James; m. Martha L. Bailey Kaufman, Nov. 7, 1975 (div. Oct. 1990); m. Peggy J. Vick, Oct. 1991; stepchildren: Peter and Tanya Kaufman. B.S., Yale U., 1950, Ph.D., 1953. NRC fellow Harvard U., 1953-54; faculty Northwestern U., 1954-60, asst. prof., 1955-60; assoc. prof. U. Wis., Madison, 1960-61; prof. chemistry U. Wis., 1961—, Arthur C. Cope and Hilldale prof. chemistry, 1975—; chmn. 4th Internat. Union Pure and Applied Chemistry Symposium on Photochemistry, 1972; organizer, chmn. Organic Photochemistry Symposium at Pacifichem 95, Honolulu, 1995. Author: Quantum Mechanics for Organic Chemists, 1975; mem. editorial bd.: Jour. Organic Chemistry, 1967-71, Molecular Photochemistry, 1969-75, Jour. Am. Chem. Soc., 1982-85, Revs. Reactive Intermediates, 1984-89; contbr. articles to profl. jours. Recipient Halpern award for photochemistry N.Y. Acad. Scis., 1979, Chem. Pioneer award Am. Inst. Chemists, 1986, Sr. Alexander von Humboldt award, 1988, Hilldale award U. Wis., 1988-89, 90. Mem. NAS, Am. Chem. Soc. (James Flack Norris award 1976, Arthur C. Cope Scholar award 1991), Chem. Soc. London, German Chem. Soc., Inter-Am. Photochemistry Assn. (co-chmn. organic div. 1977-79, exec. com. 1979-86), Phi Beta Kappa, Sigma Xi. Home: 1 Oconto Ct Madison WI 53705-4925 Office: U Wis Chemistry Dept 1101 University Ave Madison WI 53706-1322

ZIMMERMAN, HYMAN JOSEPH, internist, educator; b. Rochester, N.Y., July 19, 1914; s. Philip and Rachel (Marine) Z.; m. Kathrin J. Jones, Feb. 28, 1943; children: Philip M., David J., Robert L., Diane E. AB, U. Rochester, 1936; MA, Stanford U., 1938, MD, 1943. Diplomate Am. Bd. Internal Medicine. Intern Stanford (Calif.) U. Hosp., 1942-43; asst. resident in medicine Gallinger Mcpl. Hosp. divsn. George Washington U., Washington, 1946-47, chief resident in medicine, 1947-48, clin. instr. in medicine, 1948-51, prof. Sch. Medicine, 1965-68, 71-79, prof. medicine, gastroenterology Sch. Medicine, 1986-89, prof. emeritus, 1989—; asst. chief of med. svc. VA Hosp., Washington, 1949-51; chief of med. svc. VA Hosp., Omaha, 1951-53, Chgo., 1953-57; chief of liver and metabolic rsch. lab. VA Hosp., Washington, 1965-68; chief of med. svc. VA Hosp., Boston, 1968-71; chief of med. svc. VA Hosp., Washington, 1971-78, sr. clinician, 1978-80, disting. physician, 1984-89; disting. scientist Armed Forces Inst. Pathology, Washington, 1989—; asst. prof. medicine Coll. Medicine U. Nebr., Omaha, 1951-53; assoc. prof. of medicine Coll. of Medicine U. Ill., Chgo., 1953-57; prof., chmn. dept. medicine Chgo. Med. Sch., 1957-65; chmn. dept. of medicine Mt. Sinai Hosp., Chgo., 1957-65; prof. of medicine Sch. of Medicine Boston U., 1968-71; clin. prof. Sch. of Medicine Georgetown U., Washington, 1971-78; sr. clinician VA Hosp., Washington, 1978—; clin. prof. medicine Howard U., 1971-78, Uniformed Svcs. U. Health Scis., 1978—; cons. Clin. Ctr. NIH, Bethesda, 1965—, USN Med. Ctr., Bethesda, 1965—; vis. prof., lectr. numerous hosps. and univs. Author: Hepatotoxicity, 1978; contbr. numerous articles to med. jours.; contbg. editor numerous med. pubs. Maj. AUS, 1943-46. Recipient William Beaumont award for clin. rsch., 1981, Disting. Achievement award Am. Assn. for Study Liver Disease, 1986, gold medal Can. Liver Found., 1989. Fellow ACP (mastership 1993); mem. AMA (mem. coun. on drugs, mem. gastroenterology panel 1968-70), AAAS, AAUP, Am. Soc. Clin. Pharmacology and Therapeutics, Am. Fedn. for Clin. Rsch., Am. Diabetes Assn., Endocrine Soc., Asian-Pacific Assn. for Study of Liver Diseases, Am. Soc. Clin. Investigation, N.Y. Acad. Scis., Cen. Soc. Clin. Rsch., Soc. for Exptl. Biology and Medicine, Am. Gastroenterol. Assn. (named Disting. Educator 1990), Drug Info. Assn., Cosmos Club, Sigma Xi, Alpha Omega Alpha. Jewish. Home: 7913 Charleston Ct Bethesda MD 20817-1421 Office: Armed Forces Inst Path Hepatic Dept Washington DC 20306-6000

ZIMMERMAN, JAMES M., retail company executive; b. 1944. Chmn. Rich's Dept. Store div. Federated Dept. Stores, 1984-88; pres., chief operating officer Federated and Allied Dept. Stores, Cin., 1988—. Office: Federated Department Stores Inc 7 W 7th St Cincinnati OH 45202-2424*

ZIMMERMAN, JAMIE, dancer; b. Portland, Oreg.; m. Nick Bracisco; 1 child, Dakoda. Student, San Jose Dance Theatre. Mem. San Jose Dance Ballet; prin. dancer San Francisco Ballet, 1977-93; tchr. ballet Vacaville, Calif., 1993—; dir. Vacaville Ballet Theatre, 1993—. Performances include New Sleep, In the middle, somewhat elevated, Dreams of Harmony, The Comfort Zone, Nutcracker, Swan Lake (Act II), Eternal Idol, The Tempest, Scherzo, Handel-a Celebration, Menuetto, Ballet d'Isoline, Agon, Theme and Variations, A MidSummer Night's Dream, Cinderella, Manifestiations, Monotones II, Pigs and Fishes, La Sylphide; soloist Aida, 1984; TV appearances include Great Performances/Dance in America broadcast of Cinderella, Romeo and Juliet, The Tempest and A Song for Dead Warriors. Office: San Francisco Ballet 455 Franklin St San Francisco CA 94102-4438

ZIMMERMAN, JEAN, lawyer; b. Berkeley, Calif., Dec. 3, 1947; d. Donald Scheel Zimmerman and Phebe Jean (Reed) Doan; m. Gilson Berryman Gray III, Nov. 25, 1982; children: Charles Donald Buffum and Catherine Elisabeth Phebe (twins); stepchildren: Alison Travis, Laura Rebecca, Gilson Berryman. BSBA, U. Md., 1970; JD, Emory U., 1975. Bar: Ga. 1975, D.C. 1976, N.Y. 1980. Asst. mgr. investments FNMA, Washington, 1970-73; assoc. counsel Fuqua Industries Inc., Atlanta, 1976-79; assoc. Sage Gray Todd & Sims, N.Y.C., 1979-84; assoc. counsel J. Henry Schroder Bank & Trust Co., N.Y.C., 1984-85, asst. gen. counsel, 1986, assoc. gen. counsel, 1987; assoc. gen. counsel, asst. sec. IBJ Schroder Bank & Trust Co., N.Y.C., 1988-90, chief counsel, sec., 1991-93, sr. v.p., gen. counsel, sec., 1993—; asst. sec. IBJ Schroder Leasing Corp., N.Y.C., 1987-90, bd. dirs., sec., 1991—; asst. sec. IBJ Schroder Banking Corp., N.Y.C., 1989-90, chief counsel, sec., 1991-93; asst. sec. IBJ Schroder Internat. Bank, Miami, Fla., 1989-90, sec., 1991—; asst. sec. IBJS Capital Corp., N.Y.C., 1988-90, sec., 1991—; sec. Bonaght Corp., N.Y.C., 1991—; chief legal officer, sec. Execution Svcs., Inc., N.Y.C., 1991-93. Founder, officer ERA Ga., Atlanta, 1977-79; bd. dirs. Ct. Apptd. Spl. Advs., 1988-94. Named one of Outstanding Atlantans, 1978-79. Mem. ABA, Assn. of Bar of City of N.Y., Ga. Assn. Women Lawyers (bd. dirs. 1977-79), Am. Soc. Corp. Secs., Inc., LWV, DAR. Republican. Office: IBJ Schroder Bank & Trust Co 1 State St New York NY 10004-1505

ZIMMERMAN, JO ANN, health services and educational consultant, former lieutenant governor; b. Van Buren County, Iowa, Dec. 24, 1936; d. Russell and Hazel (Ward) McIntosh; m. A. Tom Zimmerman, Aug. 26, 1956; children: Andrew, Lisa, Don and Ron (twins), Beth. Diploma, Broadlawns Sch. of Nursing, Des Moines, 1958; BA with honors, Drake U., 1973; postgrad., Iowa State U., 1973-75. RN, Iowa. Asst. head nurse maternity dept. Broadlawns Med. Ctr., Des Moines, 1958-59, weekend supr. nursing svcs., 1960-61, supr. maternity dept., 1966-68; instr. maternity nursing Broadlawns Sch. Nursing, 1968-71; health planner, community rels. assoc. Iowa Health Systems Agy., Des Moines, 1978-82; mem. Iowa Ho. Reps., 1982-86; lt. gov., Senate pres. State of Iowa, 1987-91; cons. health svcs., grant writing and continuing edn. Zimmerman & Assocs., Des Moines, 1991—; dir. patient care svcs. Nursing Svcs. of Iowa, 1996—; ops. dir. Medlink Svcs., Inc., Des Moines, 1992-96; dir. nurses Nursing Svcs. of Iowa, 1996—. Contbr. articles to profl. jours. Mem. advanced registered nurse practioner task force on cert. nurse mid-wives Iowa Bd. Nursing, 1980-81, Waukee, Polk County, Iowa Health Edn. Coord. Coun., Iowa Women's Polit. Caucus, Dallas County Women's Polit. Caucus; chmn. Des Moines Area Maternity Nursing Conf. Group, 1969-70, task force on sch. health svcs. Iowa Dept. Health, 1982, task force health edn. Iowa Dept. Pub. Instruction, 1979, adv. com. health edn. assessment tool, 1980-81, Nat. Lt. Govs., chair com. on Agrl. and Rural Devel., 1989; Dallas County Dem. Cen. Com., 1972-84; bd. dirs. Waukee Cmty. Sch. Bd., 1976-79, pres. 1978-79; bd. dirs. Iowa PTA, 1979-83, chairperson Health Com., 1980-84; mem. steering com. ERA, Iowa, 1991-92; founder Dem. Activist Women's Network (DAWN), 1992. Mem. ANA, LWV (health chmn. met. Des Moines chpt.), Iowa Nurses Assn., Iowa League for Nursing (bd. dirs. 1979-83), Family Centered Childbirth Edn. Assn. (childbirth instr., advisor), Iowa Cattleman's Assn., Am. Lung Assn. (bd. dirs. Iowa 1988-92), Dem. Activist Women's Network (founder 1992). Mem. Christian Ch. Avocations: gardening, sewing, reading, bridge, breeding British White cattle. Office: Zimmerman & Assocs 7630 Ashworth Rd West Des Moines IA 50266-5859

ZIMMERMAN, JOHN H., communications company executive; b. Akron, Ohio, Oct. 3, 1932; s. Erle C. and Agnes R. (Lower) Z.; m. LaVonne A. Robertson, July 25, 1953; children: Rebecca Zimmerman Brown, J. Jeffrey, Amy Leigh Zimmerman Larimore. B.A. in Econs., Colgate U., 1954; M.B.A., Kent State U., 1962. Dir. labor relations Firestone Tire and Rubber Co., Akron, Ohio, 1975-78, v.p. employee relations, 1978-82; sr. v.p. human resources MCI Communications, Washington, 1982-95; human resource cons., 1996—; adj. prof. Kent State U., 1963-66, U. Akron, 1970-72; mem. U.S. Gov. Commn. on Achieving Necessary Skills, 1990-92; mem. adv. coun. Ctr. for Workplace Excellence; mem. Work Readiness Adv. Com. V.p. Akron-Canton Regional Airport Bd. Trustees, 1981-82; active Nat. Com. Vietnam POW Reemployment, 1972-73; mem. adv. bd. Nat. Urban League, N.Y.C., 1972-83, U. Akron Ctr. Econ. Edn., 1981-82, Nat. Alliance Businessmen Bd., 1973-82; mem. adv. bd. Sch. Bus. and Pub. Mgmt., George Washington U., 1987—; trustee Akron Gen. Med. Ctr., 1981-82, Akron YMCA, 1980-82; chmn. Summit County Pers. Rev. Commn., 1970. Mem. Am. Mgmt. Assn. (mem. HR adv. coun. 1986-93, chair 1991-93, bd. trustees 1991-93), Phi Beta Kappa. Presbyterian. Home: 7272 Evans Mill Rd Mc Lean VA 22101-3423

ZIMMERMAN, JOSEPH FRANCIS, political scientist, educator; b. Keene, N.H., June 29, 1928; s. John Joseph and May Veronica (Gallagher) Z.; m. Margaret Bernardette Brennan, Aug. 2, 1958; 1 child, Deirdre Ann. BA, U. N.H., 1950; MA, Syracuse U., 1951, PhD, 1954. Instr. govt. Worcester Poly. Inst., 1954-55, asst. prof., 1955-57, assoc. prof., 1957-62, prof., 1962-65; lectr. Clark U., Worcester, Mass., 1957-65; prof. polit. sci. SUNY, Albany, 1965—; staff dir. N.Y. State Joint Legis. Com. Transp., 1967-68, rsch. dir., 1968-73; rsch. dir. N.Y. State Select Legis. Com. Transp., 1977-82, Legis. Commn. on Critical Transp. Problems, 1982-95. Author: State and Local Government, 1962, The Massachusetts Town Meeting: A Tenacious Institution, 1967, The Federated City: Community Control in Large Cities, 1972, Pragmatic Federalism, The Reassingment of Functional Responsibility, 1976, (with Frank W. Prescott) The Politics of the Veto of Legislation in New York, 1980, The Government and Politics of the Empire State, 1981, Local Discretionary Authority, 1981, (with Deirdre A. Zimmerman) The Politics of Subnational Governance, 1983, State-Local Relations: A Partnership Approach, 1983, 2d edit., 1995 (CHOICE award as outstandin acad. book, 1984), Participatory Democracy: Populism Revived, 1986, Federal Preemption: The Silent Revolution, 1990, Contemporary American Federalism, 1992, (with Wilma Rule) United States Electoral System: Their Impact Upon Women and Minorities, 1992, (with Wilma Rule) Electoral Systems in Comparative Perspective: Their Impact on Women Minorities, 1994, Curbing Unethical Behavior of Government, 1994, Interstate Relations: The Neglected Dimension of Federalism, 1996; contbr. articles to profl. publs. Pres. Citizens' Plan E Assn., Worcester, 1960-62, Citizens for Neighborhood Improvement Worcester, 1957-59. Served to capt. USAF, 1951-53. Named 1 of 3 Outstanding Young Men Worcester Jr. C. of C., 1959, 61, 1 of 3 Outstanding Young Men Mass, Jr. C. of C., 1961, disting. citizen award Nat. Conf. on Govt., 1986. Mem. Am. Polit. Sci. Assn., Am. Soc. Public Adminstrn., Nat. Mcpl. League. Roman Catholic. Club: German-Am. Social. Home: 82 Greenock Rd Delmar NY 12054-4414 Office: SUNY Grad Sch Public Affairs 135 Western Ave Albany NY 12222

ZIMMERMAN, LEROY S., lawyer, former state attorney general; b. Harrisburg, Pa., Dec. 22, 1934; s. LeRoy and Amelia (Magaro) Z.; m. Mary Augusta Jaymes, Feb. 9; children: Susan A., Mark J., Amy A. BS in Econs., Villanova (Pa.) U., 1956; JD, Dickinson Sch. Law, Carlisle, Pa., 1959; LLD (hon.), Dickinson Sch. Law, 1989. Bar: Pa. 1960. Pvt. practice law, 1960-81; ptnr. Hepford, Zimmerman & Swartz, 1970-81; asst. dist. atty., then dist. atty. Dauphin County, 1963-80; atty. gen. Commonwealth Pa., Harrisburg, 1981-89; sr. ptnr. in charge of Harrisburg office Eckert Seamans Cherin & Mellott, Harrisburg, 1989—; apptd. White Ho. Conf. for a Drug Free Am.; mem., former chmn. exec. working group Fed.-State-Local Prosecutorial Rels.; past pres. Pa. Dist. Attys. Assn. Trustee Dickinson Sch. Law, The Hall Found.; mem. devel. coun. Villanova U.; bd. dirs. Harrisburg Area YMCA, YMCA of the USA. With USAF. Recipient Man of Yr. award Police Chiefs Assn. Southeastern Pa., 1982, Achievement award Nat. Italian-Am. Found., 1983, Pres.'s award Pa. Chiefs Police Assn., 1986. Mem. Nat. Assn. Attys. Gen. (former chmn. criminal law com., mem. anti-trust, asbestos and environ. control coms.), Pa. Dist. Attys. Assn. (past pres.), Phi Alpha Delta, Sons Italy in Am. Republican. Roman Catholic. Club: K.C. Office: Eckert Seamans Cherin & Mellott 213 Market St PO Box 1248 Harrisburg PA 17108*

ZIMMERMAN, LOUIS SEYMOUR, lawyer; b. Houston, Mar. 17, 1949; s. Robert Eugene and Rosalind (Pincoffs) Z.; m. Janet Whaley, Aug. 9, 1975; children: Patrick, Thomas, Frank. BA, Williams Coll., 1971; JD, U. Tex., 1974. Bar: Tex. 1974, U.S. Dist. Ct. (so. and we. dists.) Tex. 1974, D.C. 1974, U.S. Ct. Appeals (5th, 11th and D.C. cirs.) 1974. Law clk. to Hon. judge Owen Cox U.S. Dist. Ct., Corpus Christi, Tex., 1974-76; assoc. Fulbright & Jaworski, Houston, 1976-82; ptnr. Fulbright & Jaworski, Washington, 1983-86, Austin, Tex., 1986—. Office: Fulbright & Jaworski 600 Congress Ave Ste 2400 Austin TX 78701-3234*

ZIMMERMAN, LYDIA, public health nurse; b. McMinnville, Oreg., Jan. 12, 1929; d. Frederick H. and Anna Katarina (Beisel) Koch; m. Howard C. Zimmerman, July 14, 1956; children: Sylvia, Angela, Joan, Garth. Diploma in nursing, Emanuel Hosp. Sch. Nursing, Portland, Oreg., 1949; BSN, U. Wash., 1953; cert. sch. nurse practitioner, UCLA, 1977. RN, Calif.; cert. pub. health nurse; cert. family life educator, sch. nurse. Asst. supr., head nurse surg. Emanuel Hosp., Portland, Oreg., 1949-50; coll. nurse Linfield Coll., McMinnville, Oreg., 1951-52; public health nurse I, sch. nurse, counselor high sch. Lane County Health Dept., Eugene, Oreg., 1953-57, staff nurse, asst. supr. maternal-child, mental health, 1958-63; public health nurse Lucas County Health Dept., Toledo, Ohio, 1967-69; private nurse Shafter, Calif., 1972-74; sch. nurse Rosedale Sch. Dist., Bakersfield, Calif., 1974-76, Beardsley Sch. Dist., Bakersfield, Calif., 1974-80, Panama-Buena Vista Union Sch. Dist., Bakersfield, Calif., 1974—; lctr. Bakersfield Coll., Calif. State Coll., Bakersfield. Mem. APHA, NEA, AAUW, Am. Acad. Nurse Practitioners, Calif. Tchrs. Assn., Nat. Assn. Sch. Nurses (Calif. rep. 1986-87, 87-88), Calif. Sch. Nurses Orgn., Kern County Sch. Nurses Orgn. (co-founder, pres. 1981-83, 91-92), Sex Info. and Edn. Coun. U.S., Nat. Coun. on Family Rels., Ctr. Sci. in Pub. Interest, Calif. Assn. Neurologically Handicapped Children, Assn. Children with Learning Disabilities, Learning Disabilities Assn. Am. (co-founder, pres. Kern County chpt. 1972-74, 76-78, 88—), Am. Hist. Soc. Germans from Russia, Sigma Theta Tau Internat. Congregationalist.

ZIMMERMAN, MARLIN ULRICH, JR., chemical engineer; b. Akron, Ohio, Aug. 2, 1923; s. Marlin Ulrich and Helen (Nelson) Z. BChemE, Johns Hopkins U., 1944; MBA, Harvard U., 1966. Registered profl. engr., Ohio. Jr. engr. Standard Oil Co. (Ohio), Cleve., 1944-46, engr., 1946-48, sr. engr., 1948-49; process engr. Lima (Ohio) refinery Standard Oil Co. (Ohio), 1949-50; group engr. Standard Oil Co. (Ohio), Cleve., 1951-55, group supr., 1956-60, supr. process sys. sect., 1961-63, head acrylonitrile task force, 1961, tech. specialist, 1964-66; mgr. long term planning Norton Co., Worcester, Mass., 1966-69; cons. John Van Der Valk & Assocs., N.Y.C., 1970-73; pvt. practice cons. chem. engr. ammonia-urea Hackensack, N.J., 1974—; head task force to help commercialize Sohio acrylonitrile process. Contbr. articles to profl. jours. Baker scholar, 1966. Mem. AIChE, Johns Hopkins Club. Methodist. Achievements include patent for process improvement of Tosco shale process for oil recovery, patent for pig handling for gasoline blender meter testing loop, others. Avocations: travel, photography, reading, investing, computer programming. Home and Office: 229 Union St Hackensack NJ 07601

ZIMMERMAN, MARTIN E., financial executive; b. Chgo., Jan. 28, 1938; s. Joseph and Sylvea Zimmerman; m. Rita Kalifon, June 20, 1961 (div. 1992); children: Jacqueline, Adam. BSEE, MIT, 1955-59; MBA in Fin., Columbia U., 1961. Dir. market research Nuclear-Chgo., Inc. div. G.D. Searle & Co., 1964-67; pres. Telco Mktg. Services, Inc., Chgo., 1967-74; pres., chmn., chief exec. officer Linc Group, Inc., Chgo., 1975—; pres., CEO Linc Anthem Corp., 1994—. Contbr. numerous articles on leasing to profl. mags. Bd. overseers Columbia U. Grad. Sch. Bus.; trustee Mus. Contemporary Art, Chgo., Ravenswood Med. Ctr., Chgo. Capt. U.S. Army, 1961-63. McKinsey scholar, Kennecott Copper fellow Columbia U., 1959-61. Mem. Equipment Lessors Assn. (bd. dirs.). Clubs: University, Mid-Am. (Chgo.). Avocations: fishing, hunting, skiing, amateur radio. Home: 100 E Bellevue Pl Apt 26D Chicago IL 60611-1125 Office: The Linc Group Inc 303 E Wacker Dr Ste 1000 Chicago IL 60601-5212

ZIMMERMAN, MICHAEL DAVID, state supreme court chief justice; b. Chgo., Oct. 21, 1943; s. Elizabeth Porter; m. Lynne Mariani (dec. 1994); children: Evangeline Albright, Alessandra Mariani, Morgan Elisabeth. BS, U. Utah, 1966, JD, 1969. Bar: Calif. 1971, Utah 1978. Law clk. to Chief Justice Warren Earl Burger U.S. Supreme Ct., Washington, 1969-70; assoc. O'Melveny & Myers, L.A., 1970-76; assoc. prof. law U. Utah, 1976-78, adj. prof. law, 1978-84, 89—; of counsel Kruse, Landa, Zimmerman & Maycock, Salt Lake City, 1978-80; spl. counsel Gov. of Utah, Salt Lake City, 1978-80; ptnr. Watkiss & Campbell, Salt Lake City, 1980-84; assoc. justice Supreme Ct. Utah, Salt Lake City, 1984-93, chief justice, 1994—; co-moderator Justice Soc. Program of Snowbird Inst. for Arts and Humanities, 1991, 92; moderator, Tanner lecture panel dept. philosophy U. Utah, 1994—; faculty Judging Sci. Program Duke U., 1992; bd. dirs. Conf. of Chief Justices, 1995—. Note editor: Utah Law Rev., 1968-69; contbr. numerous articles to legal publs. Mem. Project 2000, Coalition for Utah's Future, 1985—. Named Utah State Bar Appellate Ct. Judge of Yr., 1988; recipient Excellence in Ethics award, Ctr. for Study of Ethics, 1994; participant Justice and Soc. Program of Aspen Inst. for Humanistic Studies, 1988, co-moderator, 1989. Mem. ABA (faculty mem. judges' seminar 1993), Am. Law Inst., Utah Bar Assn., Salt Lake County Bar Assn., Jud. Conf. U.S. (adv. com. civil rules 1985-91), Utah Jud. Coun. (supreme ct. rep. 1986-91), chair 1994—, Utah Constnl. Revisions Commn., Snowbird Inst. for Arts and Humanities (bd. dirs., 1989—), Am. Inns of Ct. VII, Am. Judicature Soc. (bd. dirs. 1995—), Order of Coif, Phi Kappa Phi. Office: Utah Supreme Ct 332 State Capitol Salt Lake City UT 84114-1181

ZIMMERMAN, MICHAEL GLENN, marketing/communications executive; b. Charlotte, N.C., Nov. 22, 1957; s. Glenn Calvin and Phyllis Ann (Miller) Z.; m. MaryBeth O'Neill, Sept. 2, 1989; children: Abbey Marie, Maggie Kathleen. BA in Journalism, Ohio State U., 1980. Acct. supr. Paul Werth Assocs., Columbus, Ohio, 1980-84; acct. mgr. Watt, Roop & Co., Cleve., 1984-85, sr. acct. mgr., 1985-87, v.p., 1987-89, sr. v.p., 1989-92, exec. v.p., dir. client svcs., 1992—; mem. mktg. com. Cleve. regional office Ohio State U., 1990—. Mktg. com. United Way Cuyahoga County, Cleve., 1990—; trustee, devel. chmn., v.p. Ctr. for Mental Retardation, Cleve., 1991—; small bus. alliance Rock & Roll Hall of Fame, Cleve., 1992—. Mem. Am. Advt. Fedn. (Addy award 1989), Pub. Rels. Soc. Am. (Silver Anvil award 1988, 92), Hermit Club Cleve., Elyria Country Club. Republican. Avocations: Ohio State football, arts, travel, gourmet cooking/dining, golf. Home: 3143 Clark Pky Westlake OH 44145-4642 Office: Watt Roop & Co 1100 Superior Ave E Cleveland OH 44114-2518

ZIMMERMAN, NANCY PICCIANO, library science educator; b. Jeannette, Pa., July 29, 1951; d. Daniel Joseph and Helen Elizabeth (Lipinski) Picciano; m. Lee W. Zimmerman, Aug. 10, 1974; children: Matthew, Renée. BA in English, Carlow Coll., Pitts., 1973; MLS in Libr. Sci., U. Pitts., 1974; MS in Computer Edn. and Cognitive Sys., U. North Tex., 1992; PhD in Libr. and Info. Studies, Tex. Woman's U., 1992. Lic. libr. media specialist, K-12, lang. arts/English 7-12. Libr. media specialist Fairfield (Calif.)-Suisun Sch. Dist., 1976-78; reference libr. Pikes Peak Libr. Dist., Colorado Springs, Colo., 1983; libr. media specialist North Pole (Alaska) H.S., 1984-85, Prince William County Schs., Woodbridge, Va., 1985-89; dir. info. retrieval lab. Tex. Woman's U., Denton, 1989-91; adj. prof., rsch. assoc. U. North Tex., Denton, 1991-92; asst. prof. Sch. Info. and Libr. Studies SUNY, Buffalo, 1993—. Nat. stroke and turn ofcl. U.S. Swimming, 1985—. Recipient ALISE rsch. grant award, 1994. Mem. ALA (chair Libr. Rsch. Round Table 1995-96), Am. Assn. Sch. Librs., Internat. Assn. Sch. Librs., N.Y. Libr. Assn., Phi Delta Kappa, Beta Phi Mu (nat. exec. coun. 1994—). Office: SUNY at Buffalo Sch Info & Libr Studies 534 Baldy Hall Box 601020 Buffalo NY 14260-1020

ZIMMERMAN, PAUL ALBERT, retired college president, minister; b. Danville, Ill., June 25, 1918; s. Albert Carl and Hanna Marie (Haffner) Z.; m. Genevieve Emmaline Bahls, June 11, 1944; children—Karmin (Mrs. Raymond Philp), Thomas. Student, Concordia Coll., Ft. Wayne, Ind., 1936-39; B.A., Concordia Sem., St. Louis, 1941, M.Div., 1944; M.A., U. Ill., 1947, Ph.D., 1951; D.D., Concordia Sem., Springfield, Ill., 1975; LLD (hon.), Concordia Coll., Ann Arbor, Mich., 1994. Prof. theology and sci. Bethany Coll., Mankato, Minn., 1944-53; prof. Concordia Tchrs. Coll., Seward, Nebr., 1953-54; pres. Concordia Tchrs. Coll., 1954-61, Concordia Luth. Jr. Coll., Ann Arbor, Mich., 1961-73, Concordia Coll., River Forest, Ill., 1973-83, ret., 1983; pastor St. Luke's Luth. Ch., Harrison, Mich., 1983-88. Author and editor: Darwin, Evolution and Creation, 1959, Rock Strata and the Bible Record, 1971, Creation, Evolution and God's Word, 1972. Chmn. Washtenaw County Red Cross, 1968-70; pres. Ann Arbor Found., 1970-71; mem. Citizens Com. Study Taxation, Ann Arbor, 1972; mem. adv. bd. St. Joseph Mercy Community, 1969-72; chmn. Luth. Ch. Mo. Synod's Bd. for Mission Services, 1982-92, Mission Task Force, 1990-91, adminstrv. asst. pres. Mo. Synod, 1972-73, 93-94, mem. curriculum commn. bd. higher edn., 1963-73, mem. task force constl. revision Mo. Synod, chmn. com. adjudication procedures Mo. Synod. Fellow Creation Rsch. Assn. Lutheran. Home: 2798 Princeton Dr Traverse City MI 49684-9131

ZIMMERMAN, RAYMOND, retail chain executive; b. Memphis, TN, 1933; married. V.p. Service Mdse. Co., Inc., Nashville, from 1959, pres., 1973-1981, chmn., 1981—, now also chief exec. officer, also bd. dirs. Office: Service Merchandise Co Inc 7100 Service Merchandise Dr Brentwood TN 37027-2927*

ZIMMERMAN, RICHARD ANSON, food company executive; b. Lebanon, Pa., Apr. 5, 1932; s. Richard Paul and Kathryn Clare (Wilhelm) Z.; m. Nancy J. Cramer, Dec. 27, 1952; children: Linda Joan, Janet Lee. BA in Commerce, Pa. State U., 1953; LLD, Lebanon Valley Coll., 1992. Asst. sec. Mellon Bank, Harrisburg, Pa., 1956-58; with Hershey (Pa.) Foods Corp., 1958—, asst. to pres., 1965-71, v.p., 1971-76, pres., chief oper. officer, 1976-84, pres., 1984-85, CEO, 1984-95, chmn., 1985-94; ret., 1994; bd. dirs. Lance, Inc., Westvaco Corp., Eastman Kodak Co. Trustee Pa. State U., United Theol. Sem.; mem. United Way Am. Lt USN, 1953-56. Recipient Alumni fellow award Pa. State U., 1978, Disting. Alumni award Pa. State U., 1987, N.C.C.J. Nat. Brotherhood award, 1988. Mem. Alumni Assn. Pa. State U. (pres. 1982-83), Hershey Country Club, Masons, Rotary (pres. Hershey 1973-74), Phi Kappa Psi. Methodist. Office: Hershey Foods Corp PO Box 810 Hershey PA 17033-0810

ZIMMERMAN, RICHARD GAYFORD, journalist; b. Springfield, Ohio, Sept. 3, 1934; s. Charles Ballard and Dorothy Cubitt (Gayford) Z. B.F.A. cum laude, Wittenberg U., 1956; M.A., Am. U., 1958. Freelance writer and polit. cartoonist, 1959-61; wire editor Urbana (Ohio) Daily Citizen, 1960-61; state house corr. Horvitz Newspapers, Mansfield, Lorain, Dover and Willoughby, Ohio, 1962-64, Dayton (Ohio) Jour. Herald, 1964-67; chief state house bur. Cleve. Plain Dealer, 1967-71, reporter Washington bur., 1971-72, chief Washington bur., 1972-77, nat. corr., 1978-85; freelance writer Africa, 1977. Co-author: Ohio Politics, 1994; contbr. articles to various publs. Served with USAF, 1961-62. Recipient award Ohio A.P., 1971, 83, award Ohio Legis. Corrs. Assn., 1968, 69. Mem. Ohio Press Club (trustee 1969), Nat. Press Club (sec. 1974-75, vice chmn. bd. govs. 1975-76, chmn. speakers com. 1979-80, chmn. house com. 1986-88, chmn. forum com. 1990-91, Washington Corr. award 1982), Ohio Legis. Corrs. Assn. (v.p. 1969-70), Beta Theta Pi. Home: 125 10th St SE Washington DC 20003-3922

ZIMMERMAN, ROBERT ALLEN See DYLAN, BOB

ZIMMERMAN, ROBERT EARL, lawyer; b. Kansas City, Mo., Feb. 11, 1928; s. Julius Joseph and Kathryn Bernadine (Highcock) Z.; A.A., Kansas City (Mo.) Jr. Coll., 1947; LL.B., U. Kansas City, 1950; m. Pauline Ann Stephens, Sept. 16, 1950; children: Elaine, David, Mark, Carol. Admitted to Mo. bar, 1950; assoc. firm Madden & Burke, Kansas City, Mo., 1950-51, 53-60; exec. v.p. Stephens Industries, Inc., Kansas City, 1957-63; with Kansas City So. Industries, Inc., 1964-91, successively, atty., gen. atty., asst. gen. counsel, gen. counsel, v.p. and gen. counsel, v.p. law, 1964-82, sr. v.p. law, 1982-91 ; dir. Kansas City So. Ry. Co., La. and Ark. Ry. Co. Served with USMC, 1944-45, with USAF, 1951-53. Mem. ABA, Mo. Bar, Am. Judicature Soc., Kansas City Bar Assn., Lawyers Assn. of Kansas City, Assn. ICC Practitioners. Roman Catholic. Clubs: Hallbrook Farms, Kansas City, Leawood Country, K.C. Died Aug. 9, 1991; buried Mt. Olivet, Kansas City, Mo.

ZIMMERMAN, ROGER JOSEPH, fishery biologist; b. Alice, Tex., Dec. 2, 1941; s. Walter George and Laura Virgie (Heine) Z.; m. Domenica Marie DeCaro, Dec. 28, 1976; children: Kathryn, Robert. BS in Biology, Tex. A&I Coll., 1966, MA in Biology and Geology, 1969; PhD in Marine Scis., U.P.R., Mayaguez, 1979. Tchg. asst. biology dept. U. South Fla., Tampa, 1971; rsch. assoc. marine sci. dept. U. South Fla., St. Petersburg, 1971-73; rsch. assoc. P.R. Nuclear Ctr. U. P.R., 1974-75, grad. fellow, 1975-78, marine benthic ecologist Ctr. for Energy & Environ. Rsch., 1978-81; fishery ecologist fishery mgmt. divsn. NOAA/NMFS Galveston (Tex.) Lab., 1981-91, divsn. chief fishery ecology divsn., 1991-93, lab. dir., 1993—; rsch. fellow U.S. Nat. Mus. Natural History, Smithsonian Instn., Washington and Harbor Beach, Fla., summer 1975, 76; vis. instr. marine biology dept. Tex. A&M U., Galveston, summer 1988, 89; vis. instr. biology dept. Corpus Christi (Tex.) State U., 1986; tchg. asst. biology U. South Fla., 1970; lectr.-counselor Tex. A&I U., 1969, lab. coord., tchg. asst., 1968-69; OAS and U.S. AID advisor to Instuto de Pesca de Ecuador, 1985-88; mem. com. coastal ocean estuarine habitat rsch. planning com. NOAA 1987, sci. adv. com., 1989; chair predator-prey com. S.E. Fisheries Sci. Ctr., 1990-91; coord. climate and global change ecol. sys. and dynamics work group NMFS, 1990, spl. asst. to office of sr. scientist, 1990; mem. sci. adv. com. Galveston Bay project Nat. Estuary Program, 1993-94, mem. mgmt. com. Corpus Christi project, 1994-95; acting dir. SEFSC Galveston lab., 1993; bd. dirs. Gulf of Mex. regional marine rsch. program NMFS-SEFSC, 1992-93; rep. programs on coastal fisheries and estuarine ecology SERSC, 1992-95; cons. advisor in field; adj. wildlife and fisheries dept. and biology dept. Tex. A&M U., dept. biology Corpus Christi State U., dept. marine scis. La. State U., 1985-89, dept. biology U. Houston, 1983-85; presenter workshops in field. Reviewer for jours. in field, including Fishery Bull., Contbns. to Marine Sci., Marine Ecology Progress Series, Jour. Exptl. Marine Biology and Ecology, Marine Biology, Bull. Marine Sci., Jour. Wetlands Ecology and Mgmt., Estuaries, Coastal and Shelf Sci., also various proposals; editl. reviewer SEFSC Galveston Lab., 1984—; contbr. numerous articles to profl. pubs.; author abstracts, revs. in field. Mem. Estuarine Rsch. Fedn., Gulf Estuarine Rsch. Soc., Crustacean Soc., Am. Fisheries Soc., Assn. Marine Labs. of the Caribbean. Office: Nat Marine Fisheries Svc SE Fisheries Sci Ctr 4700 Ave U Galveston TX 77551

ZIMMERMAN, S(AMUEL) MORTON (MORT ZIMMERMAN), electrical and electronics engineering executive; b. Paterson, N.J., Mar. 18, 1927; s. Solomon Zimmerman and Miriam (Feder) Glatzer; m. Marion Patricia Boque, Sept. 15, 1951 (dec. 1993); children: Judy, Suzy, Sharon, Dan; m. Evie Levine, Feb. 24, 1996. Student, Ga. Inst. Tech., 1942-44, 46-48, Oglethorpe U., 1948-51; BSEE, Pacific Internat. U., L.A., 1958. Pres. Comml. Electronics Corp., Dallas, 1954-56, Electron Corp. subs. LTV Corp., 1956-65; chmn. bd., pres. Capital Bancshares, Inc., 1965-66; chmn. bd. Capital Nat. Bank Tampa (formerly Springs Nat. Bank), Fla., 1965, Capital Nat. Bank Miami (name now Peoples Downtown Bank), Fla., 1966, Merc. Nat. Bank Miami Beach (name now Barnett Bank), Fla., 1967, Underwriters Bank & Trust Co. N.Y. (name now Banco Cen.), 1968; chmn. bd., pres. Capital Gen. Corp., 1967, Comml. Tech., Inc., 1977—, Petro Imperial Corp. and subs. DOL Resources and Tech.-Star, Dallas, 1983—; chmn. bd., pres. Tans Exchange Corp., 1965—, Electric & Gas Tech., Inc., 1985—; also chmn. 8 subs. cos.; chmn. bd. Video Sci. Tech., Inc., 1981-92; Interfed. Capital, Inc., 1990—. Patentee: TV camera video amplifier and blanking circuits, electronic thermometer, video x-ray image system and methods, video system and method for presentation and reproduction x-ray film images, electromagnetic radio frequency lighting system, laser display of electronically generated image signal; patent applied for: new tech. for electronic refrigeration system. Petty oficer USN, 1942-45. Recipient Interfaith award City of N.Y. Mem. IEEE, Brookhaven Country Club. Republican. Jewish. Home: 5901 Yardley Ct Dallas TX 75248 Office: Electric & Gas Tech Inc 13636 Neutron Rd Dallas TX 75244-4410

ZIMMERMAN, SCOTT FRANKLIN, lawyer; b. Pitts., June 13, 1935; s. Franklin Prince and Louise (Scott) Z.; m. Judith Kirkpatrick, Aug. 20, 1960; children: Martha, Sarah. BA, Westminster Coll., 1960; LLB, U. Mich., 1963. Bar: Pa. 1963, U.S. Ct. Appeals (3d cir.) 1967, U.S. Ct. Appeals (6th cir.) 1968, U.S. Ct. Appeals (2d cir.) 1972, U.S. Supreme Ct. 1973. Ptnr. Reed Smith Shaw & McClay, Pitts., 1963—; instr. labor econs. Carnegie-Mellon U., Pitts., 1972-78. Trustee Ellis Sch., Pitts., 1987-92. Mem. ABA, Pa. Bar Assn., Allegheny County Bar Assn. Republican. Episcopalian. Clubs: Duquesne, Longue Vue (Pitts.). Avocations: skiing, golf, running, diving. Office: Reed Smith Shaw & McClay James H Reed Bldg 435 6th Ave Pittsburgh PA 15219-1809

ZIMMERMAN, THOM JAY, ophthalmologist, educator; b. Lincoln, Ill., Oct. 5, 1942; s. Kenneth Earl and Georgia Rosemary (Taylor) Z.; m. Tinker Steiner; 1 child, Jessica. BS in Zoology, U. Ill., 1964; MD, U. Ill., Chgo., 1968; PhD in Pharmacology, U. Fla., 1976. Diplomate Nat. Bd. Med. Examiners, Am. Bd. Ophthalmology. Intern St. Lukes Hosp., Chgo., 1968-69; resident U. Fla. Coll. Medicine, Dept. Ophthalmology, Gainesville, 1971-74, corneal fellow, 1974-75, glaucoma fellow, 1976-77; acting chmn. dept. ophthalmology La. State U., New Orleans, 1977; assoc. prof. ophthalmology and pharmacology Ochsner Clinic, New Orleans, 1977-79; prof. pharmacology and toxicology U. Louisville, 1986—, prof., chmn. dept. ophthalmology, 1986—; ophthalmic cons. (glaucoma) USPHS Hosp., New Orleans, 1977-82; cons. Nat. Adv. Eye Council and NEI, 1983; U.S. rep. for exec. com. Pan-Am. Glaucoma Soc., 1983-85; chmn. glaucoma symposium of Nat. Soc. to Prevent Blindness, 1988; guest lectr. numerous profl. socs. and confs. Author 6 books and numerous editorials; contbr. sci. articles to profl. jours.; mem. editorial bd. Jour. Continuing Edn. in Ophthalmology, 1977—, Annals of Ophthalmology, 1978—, Advances in Therapy, 1986—; contbr. book chpts., abstracts. Served with USPHS, 1969-71. Recipient Will F. Lyon award Presbyn.-St. Lukes Hosp., 1969; Robert E. McCormick scholar Research to Prevent Blindness Inc., 1978; grantee Nat. Eye Inst., 1978-84, 85-86; delivered Culler Meml. lecture, Ohio State U., 1986. Fellow Am. Coll. Clin. Pharmacology; mem. AMA (Physician's Recognition award 1971, 73, 75, 77, 79, 81, 83), Assn. for Research in Vision and Ophthalmology,

Am. Soc. for Clin. Pharmacology and Therapeutics, Am. Soc. Contemporary Ophthalmology, Internat. Glaucoma Congress, Am. Acad. Ophthalmology, La.-Miss. Ophthalmology Soc., Research to Prevent Blindness Ophthalmologic Assn., So. Med. Assn., Can. Implant Soc., Ky. Med. Assn., Ky. Acad. Eye Physicians and Surgeons, Louisville Acad. Ophthalmology, Jefferson County Med. Soc., Alpha Omega Alpha. Home: 389 Mockingbird Valley Rd Louisville KY 40207-1337 Office: Univ of Louisville Dept Ophthalmology 301 E Muhammad Ali Blvd Louisville KY 40202-1511

ZIMMERMAN, VICTORIA ANNMARIE, elementary education educator, administrator; b. Salamanca, N.Y., Aug. 23, 1953; d. Benny John and Catherine Theresa (Oliverio) Vecchiarella; children: Alexia, Samuel. AA in Adminstrn., Ctrl. Tex. U., Killeen, 1986, BS, 1988, postgrad. Dept. asst. Ctrl. Tex. Coll., 1988, coll. instr., 1988-89, developer instrnl. materials, 1987-88; supr., tchr. Seneca Nation Johnson O'Malley Program, Salamanca, 1989—; part-time adult edn. tchr. Catt County BOCES, Olean, N.Y., 1994—; mem. adv. bd., office adminstrn. dept. Ctrl. Tex. Coll., 1991—; mem. SHARE, Salamanca, 1991-94; dir. JOM Summer Camp, Salamanca, 1990, 91, 92. Recipient Outstanding Cmty. Svc. award Ft. Hood Youth Activities, 1986, Employee of Yr. award Seneca Nation, 1989-90. Roman Catholic. Avocations: reading, pistol target shooting, drawing, computers, tennis. Home: Bucktooth Run Salamanca NY 14779

ZIMMERMAN, WILLIAM EDWIN, newspaper editor and publisher; b. Bklyn., Feb. 2, 1941; s. George and Ruth (Edelbaum) Z.; m. Teodorina Bello, Dec. 13, 1969; 1 child, Carlota Pastora. BA, Queens Coll., 1962. Pres. Guarionex Press, Ltd., N.Y.C., 1979—; various positions with Am. Banker, N.Y.C., 1962-82, editor, sr. v.p., 1982-89; editor in chief Banking Week, 1986-89; dep. editor. Sunday Bus. sect., The N.Y. Times, 1989; spl. projects editor, editor Student Briefing page Newsday, L.I., N.Y., 1989—. Author: How to Tape Instant Oral Biographies, 1979, A Book of Questions to Keep Thoughts and Feelings, 1984, Make Beliefs, 1987, Life Lines: A Book of Hope, 1990, The Little Book of Joy, 1995, Dogmas: Simple Truths from a Wise Pet, 1995, Make Beliefs for Kids of All Ages, 1996. Mem. Am. Oral History Assn., N.Y. Fin. Writers Assn., Am. Soc. Bus. Writers, Overseas Press Club, Deadline Club, Am. Soc. Bus. Press Editors, Dowtown Athletic Club, N.Y. Athletic Club, Sigma Delta Chi. Democrat. Jewish. Office: Newsday Inc 2 Park Ave New York NY 10016-5603

ZIMMERMAN, WILLIAM IRVING, lawyer; b. Miami Beach, Fla., Dec. 10, 1952; s. S. Robert Zimmerman and Shirley (Munroe) Neivert; m. Felicia Jo French, children: William, Jason, Cyrina, Hunter. BA, Wesleyan U., 1974; JD, U. Miami, 1978. Bar: Fla. 1978, Hawaii 1991. Lawyer William I. Zimmerman Atty. at Law, Pompono Beach, Fla., 1978-90, Captain Cook, Hawaii, 1991-93; lawyer Van Pernis, Smith & Vancil, Kailua-Kona, Hawaii, 1993—; dir. Families in Transition, Kailua-Kona, Hawaii, 1994-95. Pro bono counsel Protect Kohanaiki Ohana, 1991-92; officer, dir. Green Alert, Kailua-Kona, 1992-93; pro bono atty. Hui Hee Nalu o Kona, 1992-94. Named in Am. Leading Lawyers, 1993-94; recipient Cert. Outstanding Excellence, Families in Transition, 1994-95. Mem. Lymans Surf Classic (atty. 1992-94), Ocean Awareness and Preservation. Avocations: surfing, fishing, swimming, camping, spending quality time with family. Home: PO Box 266 Captain Cook HI 96704-0266 Office: William I Zimmerman PO Box 266 Captain Cook HI 96704

ZIMMERMAN, WILLIAM ROBERT, entrepreneur, engineering based manufacturing company executive; b. Cleve., May 11, 1927; s. Irving and Ella (Berger) Z.; m. Nancy Owen, 1963 (div. 1970); 1 child, Amanda; m. Eileen Samuelson, Nov. 11, 1979. BS, MIT, 1948, MS, 1949. Cons. Kurt Salmon Assocs., Washington, 1949-50, A.T. Kearney and Co., Chgo., 1950-52; mill mgr. Am. Envelope Co., West Carrollton, Ohio, 1952-56; exec. v.p. Avery Internat., Pasadena, Calif., 1956-67; pres. Swedlow, Inc., Garden Grove, Calif., 1967-73, Monogram Industries, Inc., Santa Monica, Calif., 1973-78; bd. dirs. Bentley Mills Industry, Calif., Moorhouse Industries, Fullerton, Calif. Council pres. Boy Scouts Am., Painesville, Ohio, 1957-62; exec. com. Jr. Achievement So. Calif., Los Angeles, 1975-77; trustee Los Angeles County Mus. Nat. History, 1987—, Harvey Mudd Coll., Claremont, Calif., 1983—. Republican. Clubs: Calif. (Los Angeles); Valley Hunt, Annendale (Pasadena). Avocations: tennis, jogging. Office: Zimmerman Holdings Inc 2600 Mission St San Marino CA 91108-1676

ZIMMERMANN, GERHARDT, conductor; b. Van Wert, Ohio, June 22, 1945; s. Ervin and Ethel Jane (Allen) Z.; m. Sharon Marie Reher, Mar. 17, 1974; children: Anna Marie, Peter Karl Irum. MusB, Bowling Green State U.; MFA, U. Iowa; student, with James Dixon, Leopold Sipe, Flora Contino, Richard Lert. Tchr. in Genoa (Ohio) Pub. Schs., 1967-70; condr. orch. Augustana Coll., Rock Island, Ill., 1971-72; music dir. Clinton (Iowa) Symphony Orch., 1971-72; asst. prof. music, condr. orchs. Western Ill. U., Macomb, 1972-74; asst. condr. St. Louis Symphony Orch., 1974-78, assoc. condr., 1978-82; music dir., condr. St. Louis Youth Orch., 1975-82, Canton Symphony Orch., 1980—, N.C. Symphony Orch., Raleigh, 1982—; guest condr. Recipient 2d Prize Georg Solti Conducting Competition 1973. Mem. Am. Symphony Orch. League, Nat. Acad. Rec. Arts and Scis., Phi Mu Alpha Sinfonia. Office: NC Symphony Orch Meml Auditorium PO Box 28026 Raleigh NC 27611-8026

ZIMMERMANN, JOHN, financial consultant; b. Milw., June 10, 1937; s. Elmer Harry and Norman Wihelmina (Bergmann) Z.; m. Mary Sue Lankford, Apr. 9, 1959; children: Elizabeth, John Mark. B.B.A., U. Wis., Milw., 1964; M in Banking, Rutgers U., 1984. CPA, Wis., Ga. Audit mgr./research Price Waterhouse & Co., Milw., 1964-73, N.Y.C., 1971-73; asst. v.p., controller First Nat. Bank of Atlanta, 1973-74, v.p., controller, 1974, group v.p., controller, 1974-77, sr. v.p., controller, 1977-84; sr. v.p., controller First Atlanta Corp., 1985-86; exec. v.p., chief operating officer Enterprise Bank Network Inc., Atlanta, 1986-88; cons. to fin. instns., 1990—; bd. dirs. Vinings (Ga.) Bank and Trust, Monogram Credit Card Bank Ga. (subs. GE). Chmn. three yr. capital expansion campaign New Sch., Atlanta, 1984-87, bd. dirs., 1989-91, 94—, also treas.; v.p. adminstrn., fin. and labor United Way Atlanta, 1984-86, mem. goal setting com., 1982, bd. dirs., 1986-88. With USAF, 1955-59. Named Tinker AFB Airman of Quarter, USAF, 1956. Mem. AICPA, Fin. Execs. Inst. (pres. Atlanta chpt. 1982-83, so. area dir. 1985-87), Ga. Soc. CPAs, Wis. Soc. CPAs, Atlanta Athletic Club, Yacht Club. Office: 2160 Fairfax Dr Alpharetta GA 30201

ZIMMERMANN, JOHN PAUL, plastic surgeon; b. Milw., Mar. 9, 1945; s. Paul August and Edith Josephine (Tutsch) Z.; m. Bianca Maria Schaldach, June 13, 1970; children: Veronica, Jean-Paul. BS in Biology, Chemistry, Marquette U., 1966; MD, Med. Coll. Wis., 1970. Diplomate Am Bd. Plastic Surgery. Internship surgery Stanford U. Sch. of Medicine, Calif., 1970-71, residency in gen. surgery, plastic & reconstructive surgery, 1974-79; flight surgeon USAF, 1971-73; fellowship head & neck surgery Roswell Park Meml. Cancer Inst., Buffalo, N.Y., 1977; pvt. practice Napa, Calif., 1979—; dir. Aesthetic Surgery Ctr. of Napa Valley, Calif., 1993—; clinical asst. prof. of plastic surgery Stanford U. Sch. of Medicine, Calif., 1993—; bd. dirs. Interplast, Palo Alto, Calif. (pres., bd. dirs. 1991-94, chmn. bd. dirs. 1994-95). Mem. Am. Soc. Plastic & Reconstructive Surgeons, Am. Soc. Aesthetic Plastic Surgeons, Lipoplasty Soc., Calif. Soc. Plastic Surgeons (bd. dirs.), Calif. Med. Assn., Napa County Med. Assn. Republican. Roman Catholic. Avocations: sailing, golf, direct care of indigent patientsthrough Interplast. Office: 3344 Villa Ln Ste 10 Napa CA 94558

ZIMMERMANN, R. PETER, financial executive; b. Abington, Pa., June 21, 1940; s. Rudolph G. and Josphine (Witt) Zimmermann; m. Mary Elizabeth Kane, Oct. 8, 1971. B.S. in Bus. Adminstrn., Drexel U., 1963. C.P.A. With Ernst & Whinney, Phila., Duesseldorf, Fed. Republic Germany, 1963-71; with Touche Ross & Co., Mexico City, 1971-75; with Touche Ross & Co., N.Y.C., 1975-81, ptnr., 1976-81; v.p., treas. Ford Found., 1981-83; v.p., contr. John Blair & Co., 1983-86; exec. v.p. USGI, Inc., 1987; sr. v.p., chief fin. officer Air Express Internat. Corp., 1988-89; fin. mgmt. cons., 1989-91; CFO Revelation Tech., Inc., 1991-93; v.p., CFO DecisionOne Corp., 1993—. Republican. Clubs: Woodway Country (Darien, Conn.), Merion Golf Club (Ardmore, Pa.). Office: Decision One Corp 50 E Swedesford Rd Frazer PA 19355

ZIMMERMANN, T. C. PRICE, historian, educator; b. Bryn Mawr, Pa., Aug. 22, 1934; s. R.Z. and Susan (Goodman) Z.; m. Margaret Upham Ferris. BA, Williams Coll., 1956, Oxford U., 1958; MA, Oxford U., 1964; AM, Harvard U., 1960, PhD, 1964. Asst. prof. Reed Coll., Portland, Oreg., 1964-67, assoc. prof., 1967-73, prof. history, 1973-77, chmn. dept. history, 1973-75; v.p. acad. affairs Davidson (N.C.) Coll., 1977-86, Charles A. Dana prof. History, 1986—; mem. Oreg. Com. for Humanities NEH, 1971-77; mem. Region 14 selection com. Woodrow Wilson Nat. Fellowship Found., Princeton, N.J., 1967-70. Author: Paolo Giovio: The Historian and the Crisis of Sixteenth-Century Italy, 1995; co-editor of collected works of Paolo Giovio, 1985; contbr. articles to profl. jours. Pres. Am. Alpine Club, N.Y.C., 1979-82, bd. dirs., 1975-83; bd. dirs. Charlotte Opera Assn., N.C., 1980-82, N.C. Outward Bound Sch., Morgantown, 1978-81; bd. advisors Lowell Obs., 1988-93; mem. Rome Prize Jury (Post-Classical Humanistic Studies) Am. Acad. in Rome, 1993. Danforth fellow, 1956-62, Fulbright fellow, Italy, 1962-64, Villa "I Tatti" fellow Harvard U. Ctr., 1970-71; Am. Council of Learned Socs. fellow, N.Y.C., 1975-76. Mem. Am. Hist. Assn., Renaissance Soc. Am., Sixteenth Century Studies Conf., Soc. Italian Hist. Studies, Am. Assn. Italian Studies, Phi Beta Kappa. Office: Davidson College PO Box 1719 Davidson NC 28036-1719

ZIMMERMANN, WARREN, former foreign service officer; b. Phila., Nov. 16, 1934; s. Albert Walter and Barbara (Shoemaker) Z.; m. Corinne Roosevelt Robinson Chubb, Apr. 18, 1959; children: Corinne Alsop, Warren Jr., Elizabeth Zimmermann Metcalfe. BA, Yale U., 1956; BA/MA, Cambridge U., Eng., 1958. Joined Office Fgn. Svc., 1961; consular and polit. officer Am. Embassy, Caracas, Venezuela, 1962-64; student Serbo-Croation lang. Fgn. Svc. Inst., 1964-65; polit. officer Am. Embassy, Belgrade, Yugoslavia, 1965-68; Soviet policy analyst Bur. Intelligence & Rsch., Dept. State, 1968-70; speechwriter to sec. of state Dept. State, Washington, 1970-73; student Russian lang. Fgn. Svc. Inst., Dept. State, 1973; dep. chief, polit. sect. Am. Embassy, Moscow, 1973-75; spl. asst. policy planning Bur. European Affairs, Dept. State, 1975-77; counselor polit. affairs Am Embassy, Paris, 1977-80; dep. chmn. Madrid Conf. on Conf. Security and Cooperation in Europe U.S. Del., 1980-81; dep. chief mission Am. Embassy, Moscow, 1981-84; dep., with rank of amb., to negotiations on nuclear and space arms with Soviet Union U.S. del., Geneva, 1985-86; chmn., with rank of amb., to Vienna Conf. on Conf. Security and Cooperation in Europe U.S. del., Austria, 1986-89; amb. to Yugoslavia, 1989-92; dir. Bur. Refugee Programs Dept. State, Washington, 1992-94; sr. fellow Rand Corp., 1994; sr. fellow Rand, 1994, sr. cons., 1995—; disting. fellow New Sch. Social Rsch., 1994—; vis. prof. Johns Hopkins Sch. Advanced Internat. Studies, 1994—; disting. fellow Sch. Pub. Affairs, U. Md., 1995; Kathryn and Shelby Collum Davis prof. columbia U., 1996—; vis. fellow coun. Fgn. Rels., N.Y.C., 1984-85; chief U.S. del. negotiations Hotline Upgrade Agreement with Soviet Union, 1983-84; Carnegie tchg. fellow Yale U., 1958-59. With U.S. Army, 1959. Mem. Coun. Fgn. Rels., Internat. Inst. Strategic Studies. Democrat. Avocations: history, tennis, skiing, fishing. Home: 96 Interpromontory Rd Great Falls VA 22066

ZIMMET, JESSIE VERELYNN, nurse, trust manager, home designer; b. Garden City, Kans., May 26, 1955; d. Vere Edward and Jessie Nina (Harmon) Z. A in Gen. Sci., Garden City Coll., 1975, ADN, 1977; BSN, Ft. Hays State U., 1982. CCRN; ACLS, instr.; trauma nurse core course provider; neonatal resuscitation program provider. Aide Garden Valley, Garden City, 1975; ICU technician St. Catherine's Hosp., Garden City, 1975-76; PRN flight nurse Life Watch, Wichita, Kans., Amarillo, Tex., 1985; instr. Ft. Hays (Kans.) State U., 1979-80; med. nurse Hadly Regional Med. Ctr., Hays, 1977-83; charge nurse, staff N.W. Tex. Hosp., Amarillo, 1984-94; unit mgr. med. specialty Integrated Health System, Amarillo, 1994-95; High Plains Bapt. Hosp.; house supr. Holy Cross Hosp., Taos, N.Mex., 1995—; PRN CCU High Plains Bapt. Hosp.; spkr. in field. Devel. ventilator wean unit. Mem. San Jacinto Bapt. Ch., Amarillo, 1994; mem. Ulysses (Kans.) 1st Bapt. Ch., 1966. Mem. AACN, NAFE, Emergency Nurses Assn., Intravenous Nurse Soc. Avocations: home designer, builder. Home: 6945 NDCBU Taos NM 87571

ZIMMETT, MARK PAUL, lawyer; b. Waukegan, Ill., July 4, 1950; s. Nelson H. Zimmett and Roslyn (Yastrow) Zimmett Grodzin; m. Joan Robin Urken, June 11, 1972; children: Nora Helene, Lili Eleanor. BA, Johns Hopkins U., 1972; JD, NYU, 1975. Bar: N.Y. 1976, U.S. Dist. Ct. (so. and ea. dists.) N.Y. 1976, U.S. Dist. Ct. (no. dist.) Calif. 1980, U.S. Ct. Appeals (2d cir.) 1980, U.S. Supreme Ct. 1981, U.S. Ct. Appeals (5th cir.) 1986, U.S. Ct. Appeals (9th cir.) 1988. Assoc. Shearman & Sterling, N.Y.C., 1975-83, ptnr., 1984-90; adj. assoc. prof. internat. law NYU, 1986-88. Author: Letters of Credit, New York Practice Guide Business and Commercial Law, 1990; contbr. articles to profl. jours. Mem. ABA (subcom. on letters of credit, com. on uniform comml. code sect. bus. law), N.Y. State Bar Assn., Assn. of Bar of City of N.Y., N.Y. County Lawyers Assn. (com. on bus. bankruptcy law), Citizens Union. Democrat. Jewish. Office: 126 E 56th St New York NY 10022-3613

ZIMMIE, THOMAS FRANK, civil engineer, educator; b. Scranton, Pa., Jan. 24, 1939; s. Thomas and Stella Josephine (Price) Z.; m. Patricia Joyce Kelly, June 8, 1962 (div. 1979); 1 child, David Thomas; m. Judith Anne Braden, July 13, 1989. BSCE, Worcester Poly. Inst., 1960; MSCE, U. Conn., 1962, PhD in Geotech. Engring., 1972. Registered profl. engr., N.Y., Conn. Staff engr. Union Carbide Corp. (Linde div.), Buffalo, 1964-68; profl. engr. Town of Mansfield, Conn., 1968-72; ptnr. Wang and Zimmie Cons., Troy, N.Y., 1973-80; v.p. Arch Engring. Cons., Troy, 1984-88; program dir. NSF, Washington, 1988-90; pres., CEO Civrotech Cons. Engrs., Inc., Troy, 1993—; mem. faculty dept. civil engring Rensselaer Poly. Inst., Troy, 1973—; postdoctoral researcher Norwegian Geotech. Inst., Oslo, 1972-73; geotech. engr. N.Y. Dept. Environ. Conservation, Albany, 1983-85; town engr. Town of North Greenbush, N.Y., 1985-88. Editor: Permeability and Groundwater Contamination, 1981. 1st lt. U.S. Army, 1962-64. Mem. ASCE (Outstanding Svc. award 1986, 87), ASTM (Spl. Svc. award 1980, Charles Dudley award 1984), Transp. Rsch. Bd., Am. Rd. and Transp. Builders Assn. Achievements include research in environmental geotechnology. Home: 39 Zelenke Dr Wynantskill NY 12198-8627 Office: Rensselaer Poly Inst Civil Engring Dept Soil Mechanics Lab Troy NY 12180

ZIMNY, MARILYN LUCILE, anatomist, educator; b. Chgo., Dec. 12, 1927; d. John and Lucile Ruth (Andryske) Z. BA, U. Ill., 1948; MS, Loyola U., Chgo., 1951, PhD, 1954. Asst. prof. anatomy La. State U. Med. Ctr., New Orleans, 1954-59, assoc. prof., 1959-64, prof., 1964-75, prof., acting head, 1975-76, prof., head, 1976—, acting dean sch. grad. studies, 1989-90, dean sch. grad. studies and vice-chancellor for academic affairs, 1990—; vis. prof. anatomy U. Costa Rica Sch. Medicine, 1961, 62; chmn. La. Edn. Quality Support Fund Planning Com., State of La., Bd. Regents, 1993—; mem. So. Regional Edn. Bd., Regional Consortium of State higher Edn. Health Affairs Ofcls., 1993—. Grantee, NIH, 1958-72, 88-89, Arthritis Found., 1969-72, Schlieder Ednl. Found., 1972-75, Frost Found., 1975-78, NSF, 1982-83. Mem. AAAS, Am. Assn. Anatomists (mem. exec. com. 1981-85, program sec. 1990-94), Am. Physiol. Soc., Assn. Anatomy Chmn. (pres. 1983), Electron Microscopic Soc. Am., Am. Assn. Dental Schs. (sect. anat. scis.), Assn. Rsch. in Vision and Ophthalmology, Am./Internat. Assn. Dental Rsch., Omicron Kappa Upsilon, Alpha Omega Alpha. Home: 3330 Esplanade Ave New Orleans LA 70119-3132 Office: La State U Med Ctr Resource Ctr New Orleans LA 70112 *My appreciation for people has been a major factor in attaining my professional goals. Other factors include perseverance in the face of challenge, decision-making, warranted aggressiveness, mental curiosity and dealing openly with friends and colleagues.*

ZIMRING, FRANKLIN E., legal educator, lawyer; b. 1942. B.A., Wayne State U., 1963; J.D., U. Chgo., 1967. Bar: Calif. 1968. Asst. prof. U. Chgo., 1967-69, assoc. prof., 1969-72, assoc. dir. Center for Studies in Criminal Justice, 1971-73, prof., 1972-85, co-dir. Ctr. for Studies in Criminal Justice, 1973-75, dir., 1975-86; prof. law, dir. Earl Warren Legal Inst., Univ. Calif., Berkeley, 1985—. Author: Confronting Youth Crime, 1978; (with Newton) Firearms and Violence in American Life, 1969; (with Hawkins) Deterrence, 1973, (with Frase) Criminal Justice System, 1979, The Changing Legal World of Adolescence, 1982, (with Hawkins) Capital Punishment and the American Agenda, 1986, (with Hawkins) The Scale of Imprisonment, 1991, (with Hawkins) The Search for Rational Drug Control, 1992, (with Hawkins) Incapacitation: Penal Confinement and the Restraint of Crime, 1995. Mem. Am. Acad. Arts and Scis. Office: U Calif Earl Warren Legal Inst Boalt Hall Berkeley CA 94720

ZIMRING, STUART DAVID, lawyer; b. L.A., Dec. 12, 1946; s. Martin and Sylvia (Robinson) Z.; m. Eve Axelrad, Aug. 24, 1969 (div. 1981); m. Carol Grenert, May 24, 1981; children: Wendy Lynn Grenert, Joseph Noah, Matthew Kevin Grenert, Dov Shimon. BA in U.S. History, UCLA, 1968, JD, 1971. Bar: Calif. 1972, U.S. Dist. Ct. (cen. dist.) Calif. 1972, U.S. Dist. Ct. (no. dist.) Calif. 1984; U.S. Supreme Ct., 1994; cert. specialist in estate planning, probate and trust law. Assoc. Law Offices Leonard Smith, Beverly Hills, Calif., 1971-73; ptnr. Law Offices Smith & Zimring, Beverly Hills, Calif., 1973-76; assoc. Levin & Ballin, North Hollywood, Calif., 1976-77; prin. Levin, Ballin, Plotkin, Zimring & Goffin, A.P.C., North Hollywood, 1978-91, Law Offices Stuart D. Zimring, North Hollywood, 1991—; lectr. Los Angeles Valley Coll., Van Nuys, Calif., 1974-82. Author: Inter Vivos Trust Trustees Operating Manual, 1994, Lending to Inter Vivos Trusts—A Guide for Bankers and Their Counsel, 1995, Durable Powers of Attorney for Health Care—A Practical Approach to an Intimate Document, 1995, Reverse Mortgages—An Update, 1996. Bd. dirs. Bet Tzedek, Jewish Legal Svcs., L.A., 1975-88, chmn. legal svcs. com., 1978-82; bd. dirs. Brandeis-Bardin Inst., Simi Valley, Calif., 1976-80; bd. dirs. Bur. Jewish Edn., L.A., 1973-88, chmn. com. on parent and family edn., 1985-87; trustee Adat Ari El Synagogue, L.A., 1982—; bd. dirs. Orgn. for the Needs of the Elderly, 1994, 1st v.p. 1995-96. Recipient Circle award Juvenile Justice Connection Project, L.A., 1989, Wiley W. Manuel award for pro bono legal svcs., 1994, 95. Mem. State Bar Calif., San Fernando Valley Bar Assn. (trustee 1979-86), Nat. Acad. Elder Law Attys. (pres.-elect So. Calif. chpt.). Democrat. Avocations: music, collecting wine, travel, photography. Office: 12650 Riverside Dr North Hollywood CA 91607

ZINBERG, DOROTHY SHORE, science policy educator; b. Boston, Feb. 25, 1928; m. Norman E. Zinberg, 1956 (dec.); children: Sarah, Anne. Student, U. Wis., 1945-47, U. Buffalo, 1947-48; BA, Boston U., 1949, MA, 1958; PhD, Harvard U., 1966. Teaching and research asst. in biochemistry Harvard Med. Sch., Cambridge, Mass., 1949-50, 52-57; research chemist Lever Bros., Cambridge, 1950-52; sr. research asso. Daniel Yankelovich, Inc., N.Y.C., and; Cambridge Center for Research in Behavioral Scis., 1966-68; NSF research sociologist dept. chemistry U. Coll. London, 1968-69; lectr. Harvard U., 1960—, sr. rsch. assoc., 1974—; mem. adv. com. Office Sci. Pers. NRC, Washington, 1971-74, bd. on engring. edn., 1991; spl. adviser Aspen Inst.; vis. scholar NAS, China, 1987; mem. adv. bd. Erik Erikson Inst. for Edn. and Rsch., 1996. Columnist London Times Higher Edn. Supplement, 1993—, N.Y. Times Syndication, 1994. Bd. dirs. Fine Arts Workshop, Provincetown, Mass., 1970-86, internat. sci. exchs. NAS, 1974-77, mem. com. on internat. rels., 1977-80, com. on internat. human resources; chmn. adv. coun. internat. divsn. NSF, 1978-81; mem. coun. Internat. Exch. of Scholars, 1978-81, com. internat. exch. of engrs. NAE, 1987-88, adv. panel Office Tech. Assessment Edn. and Employment of Scientists and Engrs., 1986-88; bd. dirs. on Engring. Edn., NRC, 1990-95; trustee Simon's Rock Coll., 1971-75. Fellow AAAS (com. exch. of scientists with Fed. Republic of Germany 1987, 91, com. on sci. freedom and responsibility 1972-74, com. on opportunities in sci. 1973-76, com. on sci., engring., and pub. policy 1982-88); mem. NAS (com. to evaluate Internat. Sci. and Tech. Ctr. Moscow 1995—), Fedn. Am. Scientists (coun. 1980-85), Coun. on Fgn. Rels., Internat. Sci. Policy Found. (adv. bd. 1988—). Home: 3 Acacia St Cambridge MA 02138-4818 Office: Harvard U JF Kennedy St Cambridge MA 02138

ZINDER, NEWTON DONALD, stock market analyst, consultant; b. N.Y.C., Aug. 12, 1927; s. Paul and Jennie (Feld) Z.; m. Clarice Katz, Dec. 26, 1954; children—Marla, Andrea, Pamela. B.A., NYU, 1948, M.B.A., 1957; M.A., Columbia U., 1949. Securities analyst Ira Haupt & Co., N.Y.C., 1953-60; securities analyst E.F. Hutton & Co., N.Y.C., 1960-63, stock market analyst, 1963-88; stock market analyst Shearson Lehman Bros., N.Y.C., 1988-92; investment cons., 1993—. Served with USN, 1945-46. Mem. Market Technicians Assn. Home: 1734 Roland Ave Wantagh NY 11793-2856

ZINDER, NORTON DAVID, genetics educator, university dean; b. N.Y.C., Nov. 7, 1928; s. Harry Jean and (Gottesman) Z.; m. Marilyn Estreicher, Dec. 24, 1949; children—Stephen, Michael. A.B., Columbia U., 1947; M.S., U. Wis., 1949, Ph.D., 1952. Asst. Rockefeller U., N.Y.C., 1952-56, asso., 1956-58, asso. prof. genetics, 1958-64, prof., 1964—, John D. Rockefeller Jr. prof., 1977—, dean grad. and postgrad. studies, 1993-95; cons. genetic-biology NSF, 1962-66, Office Tech. Assessment, Washington, 1979-81, Chas. Pfizer & Co., 1963-67; chmn. ad hoc com. to rev. viral cancer program Nat. Cancer Inst., 1973-74; mem. vis. com. dept. biology Harvard U., 1975-81, sect. virology Yale U., 1975-83, dept. biochemistry Princeton U., 1975-86; mem. sci. adv. bd. Carter-Wallace Inc., 1982-85, Genetic Systems Corp., 1981-86; mem.adv. com. Alliance Internat. Health Care Trust, 1984— ; trustee Cold Spring Harbor Lab., 1967-85, sec. to bd., 1980-85; chmn. com. to rev. Army chem. weapons stockpile disposal program, NAS/NRC, 1987-91; chmn. program adv. com. on human genome, NIH, 1988-91, other affiliations. Assoc. editor: Virology; sect. editor Intervirology, 1973-90. Recipient Eli Lilly award in microbiology and immunology, 1962, U.S. Steel Found. award in molecular biology, 1966, medal of excellence Columbia U., 1969, award in sci. freedom & responsibility AAAS, 1982; Am. Cancer Soc. scholar, 1955-58. Fellow Am. Acad. Arts and Scis. (coun. 1984-87); mem. NAS (mem. coun. 1988-91, exec. com. Assembly of Life Scis. 1975-78, bd. army sci. and tech. 1981), Soc. Am. Biol. Chemists, Genetics Soc. Am., Am. Soc. for Microbiology, Council Fgn. Relations, Harvey Soc., Sigma Xi. Spl. research in microbial genetics. Home: 450 E 63rd St New York NY 10021-7928 Office: Rockefeller U 1230 York Ave New York NY 10021-6307

ZINE, LARRY JOSEPH, retail executive; b. Williston, N.D., Dec. 12, 1954; s. Joseph and Olga (Hapip) Z.; m. Nancy Jane Brude, Aug. 14, 1976. BBA in Mktg., U. N.D., 1977, MS in Acctg., 1979. CPA, N.D. Grad. teaching asst. U. N.D., Grand Forks, 1978-79, instr., 1979-81; acct. Circle K Corp., Phoenix, 1981-82, tax and audit supr., 1982-84, fin. reporting mgr., 1984-87, v.p. fin. reporting, 1987, chief fin. officer, 1988. Mem. AICPA, Beta Alpha Psi. Avocation: running. Office: Circle K Corp PO Box 52084 Phoenix AZ 85072-2084

ZINGALE, ROBERT G., surgeon; b. Bklyn., Feb. 9, 1957; s. Joseph and Theresa Zingale; m. Christine A. Smith, Oct. 4, 1986; children:Jillian, Kara, Alec. BS cum laude, Pace U., 1979; MD, SUNY, Bklyn., 1983. Diplomate Am. Bd. Surgery, Surg. Crit. Care, Nat. Bd. Med. Examiners. Resident Maimonides Med. Ctr., Bklyn., 1983-88; trauma fellow Coney Island Hosp, Bklyn., 1988-89; attending physician, dir. trauma Huntington (N.Y.) Hosp., 1989—; attending physician Nassau County Med. Ctr., East Meadow, N.Y., 1991—; clin. instr. SUNY, Stony Brook, 1991—; clin. asst. prof. surgery N.Y. Med. Coll./North Shore U. Hosp., Valhalla, 1993—. Contbr. articles to profl. jours. Fellow ACS, Suffolk Acad. Medicine; mem. AMA, Soc. Laparoendoscopic Surgeons, Am. Soc. Gen. Surgeons, N.Y. Met. Breast Cancer Grop, Med. Soc. N.Y., Suffolk County Med. Soc. Office: Huntington Med Group 180 E Pulaski Rd Huntington Station NY 11746-1915

ZINGG, PAUL JOSEPH, university dean; b. Newark, July 22, 1947; s. Carl William Zingg and Dolores Lucking Dulebohn; m. Candace A. Slater, Aug. 9, 1980. BA, Belmont Abbey Coll., Belmont, N.C., 1968; MA, U. Richmond, Va., 1969; PhD, U. Ga., 1974. Prof. St. Bernard's Coll., Cullman, Ala., 1975-77; exec. dean Daniel Hale Williams U., Chgo., 1977-78; vice dean arts and scis. U. Pa., Phila., 1978-83, asst. to pres., 1983-86; cons. U. Calif., Berkeley, 1986; dean liberal arts St. Mary's Coll., Moraga, Calif., 1986-93; dean liberal arts Calif. Poly. State U., San Luis Obispo, 1993-95, provost and acad. v.p., 1995—; vis. instr. history Ga. Coll., Milledgeville, 1971; cons., contbr. on exhibits Oakland Mus., 1992-94; cons., contbr. to PBS-TV documentary film Baseball, 1991-93; editorial cons. U. Nebr. Press, 1994—, others. Author: Pride of the Palestra, 1987, Harry Hooper, 1887-1974: An American Baseball Life, 1993, Runs, Hits and and Era: The Pacific Coast League, 1903-1958, 1995, others; editor, co-author: The Academic Penn, 1986; editor: Contemporary Topics in Applied Ethics, 1984; co-editor, contbr.: Morale, 1996; contbr. numerous articles to profl. jours. Mem. commn. on human resources and social change Nat. Assn. State Univs. and Land-Grant Colls., 1994—; mem. bd. advisors Oakland (Calif.) Mus., 1994—; mem. Ctrl. Coast Performing Arts Ctr. Commn., San Luis Obispo, 1993—; mem. bd. advisors Artemis Theater co., 1993—; bd. dirs. Hearst Art Gallery, Moraga, Calif., 1988-90; NEH summer fellow, 1975, Ctr. for Internat. Study and Rsch. fellow, 1980-82, Am. Coun. on Edn. fellow, 1983-

84; grantee St. Mary's Coll., 1987. 90, 91, 93, NIH, 1987, others. Mem. Orgn. Am. Historians, Soc. for History Edn., N.Am. Soc. for Study of Sport, Am. Studies Assn., Soc. for Am. Baseball Rsch., Am. Coun. on Edn., Assn. Am. Colls. and Univs., Merion Golf Club, U. Calif. Golf Club, Phi Alpha Theta, Phi Beta Delta. Avocations: golf, Labrador retrievers, baseball, hiking. Office: Calif Poly State U Off of Provost San Luis Obispo CA 93407

ZINGMAN, EDGAR ALAN, lawyer; b. N.Y.C., Dec. 26, 1923; s. Louis M. and Sarah (Steinberg) S.; m. Barbara Gold, Dec. 17, 1950; children: Aileen Dale, Margaret Lee, Jonathan Alan. BS, CCNY, 1947; LLB, Yale U., 1950. Bar: N.Y. 1950, Ky. 1950, U.S. Dist. Ct. (ea. and we. dists.) Ky. 1951, U.S. Ct. Appeals (6th cir.) 1952, U.S. Supreme Ct. 1965. Assoc. Wyatt, Grafton & Sloss, Louisville, Ky., 1950-57; ptnr. Wyatt, Tarrant & Combs and predecessor firms, Louisville, 1957—. Bd. dirs. ACLU, N.Y., 1965-70; chmn. bd. dirs. Ky. Civil Liberties Union, 1958-70. Recipient Disting. Svc. award Ky. Hosp. Assn., Louisville, 1978, Am. Hosp. Assn., 1988. Mem. Ky. Assn. Hosp. Attys. (bd. dirs., pres.), Am. Acad. Hosp. Attys. (bd. dirs. 1980-87, pres. 1985), Jefferson Club. Avocations: music, theater, sports, travel, reading. Office: Wyatt Tarrant & Combs 2600 Citizen's Plz Louisville KY 40202

ZINK, CHARLES TALBOTT, lawyer; b. Long Beach, Calif., Oct. 27, 1937; s. William Talbott and Nellie Grace (Hoskins) Z.; m. Deborah Sidney Burks, Nov. 26, 1983. AB, Princeton U., 1959; LLB, U. Va., 1965. Bar: Va. 1965, Ga. 1965. Mng. ptnr. Hansell & Post, Atlanta, 1965-89; ptnr. Jones, Day, Reavis & Poque, Atlanta, 1989-93, Long, Aldridge & Norman, Atlanta, 1993—; lectr. N.W. Ctr. for Profl. Edn., Washington, Atlanta and Tampa, Fla., 1983—; mem. faculty Atlanta Coll. Trial Advocacy, 1985, mem. exec. com., 1984—, pres., 1985, 86. Bd. dirs. Atlanta Humane Soc., 1983—. Lt. (j.g.) USN, 1959-62. Mem. Lawyers Club Atlanta, Atlanta Tax Forum, Capital City Club. Republican. Episcopalian. Office: Long Aldridge & Norman 5300 One Peachtree Ctr Atlanta GA 30308

ZINK, LEE B., academic administrator, economist, educator; b. Salem, Ind., June 7, 1930; s. Otto C. and Lera (Berkey) Z.; m. Patricia Louise Patton, Aug. 16, 1964; children: Kevin Patrick, Barry Lee. BA in Econs. magna cum laude, Ind. U., 1959; PhD in Econs., Okla. State U., 1967. Field rep. GM Acceptance Corp., Louisville, Ky., 1953-54; asst. mgr. Dougherty Motor Sales, Salem, 1954-56; asst. prof. econs. Southeastern State Coll., Durant, Okla., 1964-67; spl. asst. to dir. Tech. Use Studies Ctr. Southwe. State Coll., Durant, Okla., 1964-65, dir., 1965-68, assoc. prof. of Econs., 1967-68; dir., prin. rsch. economist, bur. bus. and econ. rsch. U. N.Mex., Albuquerque, 1968-77; prof. bus. adminstrn. N.Mex. Highlands U., Kirtland, 1974-81; dir. Inst. Applied Rsch. Svcs. U. N.Mex., Albuquerque, 1975—, dir. Nat. Energy Info. Ctr. affiliate/U.S. Dept. Energy, 1978-87, assoc. v.p. rsch., bus. and govt. rels., 1988—; mem. Gov.'s adv. com. statis. standards for Okla., 1964-66, sci. and industry Okla., 1965-66, statewide planning com. implemenation of Tech. Svcs. Act, Okla., 1965-66; cons. majority leader U.S. Ho. Reps., 1964-68, So. Okla. Devel. Assn., 1965-68, Gov. Okla., 1965-68, Kiamichi Econ. Devel. Dist., Okla., 1967-68, N.Mex. Corp. Commn., 1969-74, N.Mex. State Planning Office, 1971, Ohio State U. Evaluation Ctr., 1972, others; mem. Gov.'s adv. com. N.Mex. Dept. Devel., 1971; adv. panel spl. tech. assistance program Office Econ. Opportunity, 1972-74; mem. Albuquerque adv. coun. U.S. Small Bus. Adminstrn., 1974-81, chmn. 1977-79; chmn. Gov.'s Coun. Econ. Advisors, 1975-78; sec. econ. devel. Gov.'s Cabinet, 1975-76, policy advisor, 1976-78; econ. devel. task force We. Interstate Commn. Higher Edn., 1979. Mem. edit. review bd. Review of Regional Economics and Business, 1976-85; bd. edit. contbrs. The Albuquerque Tribune, 1979-82; mem. edit. adv. bd. The Southwest Review of Management and Economics, 1981-85; contbr. articles to profl. jours. Organizing pres. Kiamichi Econ. Devel. Dist., Okla., 1966-67; active Monte Vista Christian Ch., 1968—; exec. dir. N.Mex. Coun. Econ. Edn., 1969-75, chmn. operating com., 1976-86; pres. East Holiday Park Neighborhood Assn., 1978-94; adv. coun. city growth and devel. Greater Albuquerque Leadership Devel. Program, 1980-82; adv. bd. U.S. Armed Svcs., 1980-87; adv. bd. econ. devel. City of Albuquerque, 1980-84; community advisor NCAA Vols. for Youth, 1981-85; mem. Bernalillo county Human Svcs. Coalition, 1982-85; apptd. by Gov.-elect Anaya N.Mex. Jobs Task Force, 1982-83; apptd. chmn. by mayor Better Albuquerque Bond Coms., 1983-87, 93-95; trustee U. Albuquerque, 1983-86; bd. dirs. Nat. Tng. Inst. Cmty. Econ. Devel., 1979-82, Inst. Study Cmty. Econ. Devel., 1980-82, Albuquerque Conv. and Vis. Bur., 1984-87, Consumer Credit Counseling Svc. N.Mex., 1985-94, pres. 1989-90, Better Bus. Bur. N.Mex., 1992—; pres. adv. coun. UNICEF, Albuquerque, 1985-95; mem. employment and tng. needs task force City of Albuquerque, 1987-88; evaluation team Congressman Lujan's South Valley task force, 1987; apptd. chmn. by Mayor Saavedra and city coun. pub. forum com. recycling, 1991. 2d lt. U.S. Army, 1951-53, Germany; lt. col. USAR, 1953-71. Fellow Nat. Defense Edn. Act, 1959-62; grantee Nat. Aeronautics and Space Adminstrn., 1964-68, N.Mex. Dept. Devel., 1968-80, HEW, 1968-76, 1971-72, Bank N. Mex., 1969-77, The Albuquerque Model Cities Agy., 1969-70, Four Corners Regional Commn., 1969-80, U.S. Forest Svc., 1974-77, U.S. Dept. Commerce, 1975-79, 1976—, N.Mex. Energy Resources Bd., 1976-77, The Navajo Nation, 1976-78, U.S. Army Corps. Engrs., 1976-78, U.S. Dept. Energy, 1978-87. Mem. Am. Assembly Collegiate Schs. Bus. (rsch., statis., publs. com. 1976-77, small bus. adminstrn. liasion com. 1976-78), Am. Soc. Info. Sci. (frontier chpt. exec. com. 1972-73, chmn.-elect 1972, chmn. 1973), Assn. Univ. Bus. and Econ. Rsch. (exec. com. 1971-78, v.p. 1975-76, pres. 1976-77), Mid continent Rsch. and Devel. Coun. (bd. dirs. 1965-69), Rocky Mountain States (chmn. bus. rsch. com. 1969-75), Rocky Mountain Coun. Burs. Bus. and Econ. Rsch. (chmn. 1969-77), N.Mex. coun. Econ. Edn. (bd. dirs. 1969-90), Greater Albuquerque C. of C. (end. com. 1968-73, bd. dirs. 1970-76, 78-82, chmn. growth com. 1972, v.p. 1973-74, pres. 1981), Phi Kappa Phi, Phi Beta Kappa (alpha chpt. exec. com., sec. 1973-75), Golden Key (hon.). Democrat. Avocation: pipe organs. Home: 3741 Mount Rainier Dr NE Albuquerque NM 87111-4399 Office: U NMex Inst Applied Rsch Svcs 1920 Lomas Blvd NE Albuquerque NM 87106-2744

ZINMAN, DAVID JOEL, conductor; b. N.Y.C., July 9, 1936; s. Samuel and Rachel Ilo (Samuels) Z.; m. Leslie Heyman (dec.); children: Paul Pierre, Rachel Linda; m. Mary Ingham, May 19, 1974; 1 child, Raphael. B.Mus., Oberlin (Ohio) Conservatory, 1958; M.A., U. Minn., 1961. Asst. to Pierre Monteux, 1961-64; guest condr. U.S. and Europe; music dir. Netherlands Chamber Orch., 1964-77, Rochester (N.Y.) Philharm. Orch., 1974-85; prin. guest condr. Rotterdam Philharm. Orch., 1977-79, chief condr., 1979-82; prin. guest condr., music dir. designate Balt. Symphony Orch., 1983-85, music dir., 1985—; music dir. Tonhalle Orch., Zurich, Switzerland, 1995; adj. prof. Eastman Sch. Music, Rochester. Rec. artist Phillips, Nonesuch, Decca/London, Decca/Argo, Angel/EMI, Telarc, Sony Classical. Recipient Grand Prix du Disque, 1967, 82, Edison award, 1967, 3 Grammy awards, 1990, Grammophone best selling record award, 1993, Grammophone award, 1994, Deutschen Schallplatten prize. Office: Balt Symphony Orch 1212 Cathedral St Baltimore MD 21201-5517

ZINMAN, JACQUES, former insurance agency executive; b. Phila., Nov. 7, 1922; BS, U. Va., 1943; postgrad. U. Pa., 1945. Chmn., The Zinman Group, Ins. Agy., 1950-82. Mem. exec. com. Pa. state Rep. fin. com.; mem. Presdl. Electoral Coll. from Pa., 1972; bd. dirs. Pop Warner Nat. Football League; pres. Lake Agy. of Fla., 1990—. Ensign USNR, 1943-44. Recipient Outstanding Young Man Phila. award Jewish Nat. Fund, 1961. Mem. Variety Club, Theta Delta Chi. Lodge: Masons. Contbr. articles to profl. jours. Office: Lakes Agy of Fla 627 E Atlantic Blvd Pompano Beach FL 33060-6343

ZINN, BEN T., engineer, educator, consultant; b. Tel Aviv, Apr. 21, 1937; came to U.S., 1957; s. Samuel and Fridah (Gelbfish) Cynowicz; children: Edward R., Leslie H. B.S. in Mech. Engring. cum laude, NYU, 1961; M.S. in Mech. Engring., Stanford U., 1962; M.S. in Aerospace Engring., Princeton U., 1963, Ph.D. in Aerospace Engring. and Mech. Scis., 1965. Asst. research Princeton U., 1964-65; asst. prof. Ga. Inst. Tech., Atlanta, 1965-67, assoc. prof., 1967-70, prof., 1970-73, Regents prof., 1973—, Disting. prof., 1990, Davis S. Lewis, Jr. chair Sch. Aerospace Engring., 1992—; research scientist research div. Am. Standard Co., New Brunswick, N.J., summer 1976; cons. Brasilian Space Research Inst., Sao Jose dos Campos, Brazil, Aetna Casualty & Sr. Co., Atlanta. Recipient David Orr Mech. Engring. prize NYU, 1961; recipient Founder's Day NYU, 1961, Cert. of Recognition NASA, 1974; Ford fellow, 1962-63. Fellow AIAA (assoc. editor jour. 1982—), Combustion Inst. (past. pres. Eastern sect.), Nat. Fire Acad. (bd. visitors 1979-82), Am. Tech. Soc. (v.p. Atlanta chpt. 1980-84, pres. 1984-86), Sigma Xi (rsch. award 1969, sustained rsch. award 1976), Tau Beta Pi, Pi Tau Sigma. Office: Ga Inst Tech Aerospace Engring Atlanta GA 30332

ZINN, GROVER ALFONSO, JR., religion educator; b. El Dorado, Ark., June 18, 1937; s. Grover Alfonso and Cora Edith (Saucke) Z.; m. Mary Mel Farris, July 28, 1962; children: Jennifer Anne, Andrew Grover. BA, Rice U., 1959; BD, Duke U., 1962, PhD, 1969; spl. student, U. Glasgow, Scotland, 1962-63. Asst. minister The Barony Ch., Glasgow, 1962-63; instr. in religion Oberlin (Ohio) Coll., 1966-68, asst. prof., 1968-74, assoc. prof., 1974-79, prof., 1979—, Danforth prof. religion, 1986—, chmn. dept. religion, 1980-84, 85-86, 1993-94. Translator: Richard of St. Victor: The Twelve Patriarchs, The Mystical Ark, and Book Three of the Trinity, 1979; co-editor: Medieval France: An Encyclopedia, 1995; mem. editl. bd. Dictionary of Biblical Interpretation; contbr. articles on medieval Christian mysticism and theology. H.H. Powers Travel grantee Oberlin Coll., 1969, 85; Dempster fellow United Meth. Ch., 1965-66, NEH Younger Humanist fellow, 1972-73, Research Status fellow Oberlin Coll., 1972-73, Faculty Devel. fellow Oberlin Coll. 1985, Lilly Endowment fellow U. Pa., 1981-82; recipient ACLS Travel award, 1982. Mem. Medieval Acad. Am. (councillor 1983-86), Am. Soc. Ch. History (coun. mem. 1989-92, 95—), Ecclesiastical History Soc. Democrat. Methodist. Avocations: photography, electronics. Home: 61 Glenhurst Dr Oberlin OH 44074-1423 Office: Oberlin Coll Rice Hall Oberlin OH 44074

ZINN, KEITH MARSHALL, ophthalmologist, educator; b. Bklyn., Oct. 15, 1940; s. Victor Zinn and Eve (Lane) Z.; m. Elaine H. Kirban, Apr. 8, 1979. Student, NYU, Bronx, 1961; M.D., SUNY, Bklyn., 1965. Diplomate Am. Bd. Ophthalmology; lic. physician, N.Y., Calif. Intern St. Lukes Hosp., N.Y.C., 1965-66; research assoc. NIH, Bethesda, Md., 1966-68; post-doctoral fellow Retina Found., Boston, 1968-69; post-doctoral fellow dept. ophthalmology Harvard U. Med. Sch., Boston, 1968; asst. resident to chief resident dept. ophthalmology Mount Sinai Hosp., N.Y.C., 1969-71, ednl. fellow dept. ophthalmology, 1971-72; chief clin. fellow retina service Mass. Eye & Ear Infirmary, Harvard U. Med. Sch., Boston, 1972-73, Heed fellow dept. ophthalmology, 1972-73; research assoc. dept. retina research Retina Found., Boston, 1972-73; mem. faculty Lancaster Post-Grad. Course in Ophthalmology, Harvard U. Med. Sch., Boston, 1970-90; guest faculty dept. ophthalmology Harvard U. Med. Sch., Boston, 1969-84; asst. prof. dept. ophthalmology Mt. Sinai Sch. medicine, N.Y.C., assoc. clin. prof., 1976-80, clin. prof., 1980—; attending ophthalmic surgeon N.Y.C., 1980—; attending ophthalmic surgeon Manhattan Eye Ear & Throat Hosp., N.Y.C., 1981—; surgeon cons. Hosp. Joint Diseases, N.Y.C., 1975-83, Patrolmen's Benevolent Assn., N.Y.C., 1977—; lectr. in field. Author: The Pupil, 1972, Ocular Fine Structure for the Clinician, 1973, The Developing Visual System, 1975, The Retinal Pigment Epithelium, 1975; author-editor: The Retinal Epithelium, 1979, Clinical Atlas of Peripheral Retinal Disorders, 1988; numerous audio-visual teaching progs. in ophthalmology; contbg. editor Mt. Sinai Jour. Medicine, 1975—; assoc. mem. editorial bd. Ophthalmic Surgery, 1980-89; mem. faculty editorial bd. Clin. Opththalmology Update, 1982—; inventor in field. Served to lt. comdr. USPHS, 1966-68. Recipient numerous awards for excellence in medicine, including: Joseph Globus award Mount Sinai Jour. Medicine, 1979, Abraham Kornzweig Teaching award Mount Sinai Sch. Medicine, 1982. Fellow Am. Acad. Ophthalmology, Otolaryngology, ACS, Internat. Coll. Surgeons, Internat. Eye Found., Soc. Eye Surgeons, N.Y. Acad. Medicine, N.Y. Diabetes Assn., N.Y. Heart Assn., N.Y. Soc. Clin. Ophthalmology, Soc. Heed Fellows, Retina Soc., Ophthalmic Soc. U.K., Oxford Ophthal. Congress, Brit. Am. Retinal Group; mem. AMA (Physicians Recognition award 1971, 76, 81, 82, 85), Ophthalmic Laser Surg. Soc. (v.p. 1986-88, pres. 1988-90), Am. Intraocular Lens Implant Soc., N.Y. Acad. Medicine (trustee 1989-90, sec. 1985-86, chmn. ophthalmology sect. 1987-88, David Warfield fellowship com. 1990-92), Am. Bd. Laser Surgery (bd. dirs. 1987—), others. Office: 1044 Fifth Ave New York NY 10028-0108

ZINN, MARCIE LYNN, music educator, pianist; b. Canton, Ill., May 6, 1951; d. Leo G. May and Betty J. (Fanning) Hayes. BS in Piano cum laude, Ill. State U., 1986, MS in Experimental Psychology, 1990; studied piano with Donald Walker, 1986-90. Nat. cert. tchr. of piano, piano pedagogy and theory, Music Tchrs. Nat. Assn. Mgr. Lewistown (Ill.) Plumbing, 1974-80; owner, operator The Musician's Stress Mgmt. Ctr., St. Charles, Ill. Author: (book) Healthy Piano Playing, 1995; contbr. articles to musical edn. jours; columnist: Monthly Music Edn. column in L.A. Family Mag. Mem. Am. Psychol. Assn., Assn. Applied Psychology and Biofeedback, Performing Arts Med. Assn. (assoc.), Mensa, Golden Key, Phi Kappa Lambda. Home: PO Box 682 Saint Charles IL 60174-0682

ZINN, MICHAEL WALLACE, aerospace engineer; b. Washington, Dec. 30, 1962; s. Wallace Bernard and Frances E. AA, Charles County C.C., La Plata, Md., 1983; BS, Tri-State U., Angola, Ind., 1986. Coop student Naval Ordnance Sta., Indian Head, Md., 1980-86; mine decoy engr. Naval Ordnance Sta., Indian Head, 1986-87, airbreathing propulsion engr., 1987-92; airbreathing propulsion engr. Naval Surface Warfare Ctr., Indian Head, 1992—; mem. Joint Army-Navy-NASA-Air Force airbreathing com., expendable engine subcom., Laurel, Md., 1987—; mem. Tech. Coop. Program involved in pyrotechnic aging and degradation Key Tech. Area 421, 1994-96. Author several tech. papers for AIAA and JANNAF. Pres. Port Tobacco Players, Inc., La Plata, Md., 1992-93. Mem. AIAA (sr.), Am. Def. Preparedness Assn. (life), Cruise Missile Assn. Achievements include work on aging surveillance programs for expendable gas turbine engines, on aging properties of expendable engines and solid propellant gas generators; assisted in design of mine clearing line charge solid propellant rocket motor. Home: 4 Somerset St La Plata MD 20646-3923

ZINN, ROBERT JAMES, astronomer, educator; b. Chgo., Aug. 4, 1946; s. Walter Henry and Jean Ann (Smith) A.; m. Graziella Anna di Tullio; children: Gabriele, Annalisa, Giovanni. BS, Case Inst. Tech., 1968; PhD, Yale U., 1974. Carnegie fellow Hale Obs., Pasadena, Calif., 1974-76, Las Campanas fellow, 1976-79; asst. prof. Yale U., New Haven, 1979-82, assoc. prof., 1982-87; prof., 1987—. Mem. Am. Astron. Soc., Internat. Astron. Union. Office: Yale U Dept Astronomy PO Box 208101 New Haven CT 06520-8101

ZINN, WILLIAM, violinist, composer, business executive; b. N.Y.C., Nov. 19, 1924; s. Philip and Anna (Miller) Z.; m. Sophia Kalish, July 11, 1948; children: Karen Louise Heau, David Benjamin. Student, SUNY, 1952-54. Violinist Balt. Symphony, 1944-45, Indpls. Symphony, 1945-46, Ft. Wayne Philharm., 1946-47, Pitts. Symphony, 1947-49, Mpls. Symphony, 1950-51; concertmaster New Britain (Conn.) Symphony, 1968-90, Queens Symphony, 1969-71, Ridgefield (Conn.) Symphony, 1973-76, Chappaqua (N.Y.) Symphony, 1976; soloist with orchs. on records, on radio and in recitals; founder Masterwork Piano Trio, Masterwork Piano Quartet, Classical String Quartet, Zinn's Ragtime String Quartet, Excelsior String Quartet, Queens Festival Orch., Bayside, N.Y., 1965, Assn. Musical William Zinn, Caracas, Venezuela, 1968, Vitametrics of Am., 1976, Internat. Symphony for World Peace, 1978, Big Apple Chamber Pops, 1983, Excelsior Composer's Festival Competition, 1984; tchr. mech. drafting Mondell Inst., 1956; coach ensembles for Chamber Music Assocs., 1973-78; engr. N.Y.C. Bd. Edn. 1951-57, Bodin-Zinn Corp., 1957-58, Chem. Constrn. Corp., 1958-59; pres. Zinn Originals, Inc., 1959-68, Sparx, Inc., Trademark Hall of Fame, Inc., Nice Realty Corp., MFW Restaurant Corp.; co-founder Excelsior Music Pub. Co., Visionary Music Pub. Co., Nat. Music Promotion Agy., Telecommunication Services, 1982, Assoc. Sci. Publs., 1985, Barclay House Pubs., 1985, Excelsior Typographers and Engravers Unltd., 1985, Empco Recs. Internat., 1985, Imperial Editions, 1986, Missing Link Publs., 1986, Krazy Klassics Kompany, 1986, New Age Publs., 1987, Krazy Klassics Komix, 1988, Zinn Pub. Group, 1989, Zinn Communications, 1989, 94, Decca Books, 1993, Arlington House, 1993, Zinn Labs, Inc.; sec.-treas. Spark Industries, Inc., Music Clearing House, 1989, Innovation Records, 1991, Krazy Klassics Records, 1991, Hanover House, 1991; pres. Zinn Labs, Inc., 1994; adj. prof. NYU, 1987—. Author: (with Edward Gordon) Themography, 1947, (with George S. Grosser) Vitametrics I, The Human Formula for Self-Evaluation, 1976, Vitametrics II, The Human Formula for Self-Improvement, 1978, (with George S. Grosser) The Lost Chord, 1981; composer: (perpetual movement for woodwinds, strings and percussion) Chromatique, 1946, Piccolo Concerto, 1948, Violin Concerto, 1950, String Quartet, 1963, (piano solo) Chopinesque, 1965, (ballet) Night Creatures, 1966, Andante for Strings, 1967, Concerto for Octahorn, 1976, The International Anthem For World Peace, 1977, String Symphony, 1977, Romance for French Horn or Viola and Piano, 1981, Concerto for Violin/Viola/Cello/Double Bass and Orch., 1985, Kol Nidrei Meml. for String Quartet or String Orchestra, 1985, six concert duos for violin and viola, 1988, also songs including Mia, 1989, Aloha Hawaii, 1989, The Willows, 1990 (winner Hawaiian Nat. Song Contest 1990), Our Song of Love, 1990, Symphony in Ragtime, 1990, In Old Hawaii, 1991, Christmas in Hawaii, 1991, A Tribute to the Masters for string quartet or string orch. (14 original works in the style of Bach, Vivaldi, Mozart, Beethoven, Brahms, Rossini, Chopin, Schubert, J. Strauss, Jr., Tschaikowksy, Dvorak, Debussy, Mendelssohn, Sousa), 1991, Astroll in a Japanese Garden for violin, cello, harp trio in 24 movements, 1996; arranger numerous operatic arias for string quartet or string orch.; originator Musiphonics, 1981, 24 Paganini caprices for string quartet, 1992, 10 Sousa marches for string quartet, 1992, The Merry Widow Waltz for string quartet or string orch., 1992, Paganini perpetual motion for string quartet, 1992, Mozart Symphony # 40, 1992; arranger 21 Henry Mancini songs for string quartet/string orchestra, 1992, 16 Duke Ellington songs for string quartet/string orchestra, 1993, Gold and Silver Waltz, Skater's Waltz for string quartet and string orchestra, 1993, 7 arias from Porgy & Bess for string quartet/string orchestra, 1994, A Tribute to Fritz Kreisler for violin and piano, 1994, 15 arrangements of Fritz Kreisler orks for String Quartet String Orch., 1994, 12 classic Jewish Favorites for String Quartet/String Orch., 1995, 12 Jewish Songs for String Quartet/String Orch., 1995; pioneer multi-styles of music for string quartet and string orch.; composer over 500 works; developer numerous products for home, personal, automobile and novelty use. Chmn. bd. dirs. Let Us Remember to Remember, 1984. Recipient 41st Hawaiian Nat. Song Contest award, 1990. Mem. ASCAP, Internat. Platform Assn., Nat. Council Women of U.S., Am. Fedn. Musicians, N.Y. Humanist Assn. Home: 35-19 215th Pl Bayside NY 11361-1725

ZINNEMANN, FRED, film director; b. Austria, Apr. 29, 1907; emigrated to U.S., 1929, naturalized, 1937; s. Oskar and Anna (Feiwel) Z.; m. Renee Bartlett, Oct. 9, 1936; 1 child, Tim. Student law, Vienna U., 1925-27; student, Sch. Cinematography, Paris, France, 1927-28; DLitt (hon.), Durham U., U.K., 1964. Asst. cameraman Paris and Berlin, Germany, 1928; asst. dir. to Berthold Viertel, Fox Studio, Hollywood, 1929-30; asst. to Robert Flaherty, 1931. 1st directorial assignment: documentary on Mexican fishermen The Wave, 1934; dir. 16 short subjects for Metro-Goldwyn-Mayer, including Story of Dr. Carver, a series on great physicians including Dr. Semmelweis (Acad. award), also several anti-crime shorts, 1937-41, features including The Seventh Cross, The Search, 1946-47 (Screen Dirs. Guild award), Act of Violence, 1948, The Men, 1949, Teresa, 1950, High Noon, 1951 (Screen Dirs. Guild, N.Y. Film Critics awards), The Member of the Wedding, 1952, Benjy, 1951 (Acad. award best documentary), From Here to Eternity, 1953 (Acad. awards including best picture, best dir., N.Y. Film Critics' Screen Dirs. Guild), Oklahoma !, 1956, A Hatful of Rain, 1957, The Nun's Story, 1958 (N.Y. Film Critic's award), The Sundowners, 1959, Behold a Pale Horse, 1964, A Man for All Seasons, 1966 (Acad. awards best picture, best dir., Dir.'s Guild ann. award , N.Y. Film Critics' award for best film, best dir.); dir. The Day of the Jackal, 1972, Julia, 1976 (3 Oscars, Donatello award 1978), Five Days One Summer, 1982; author: A Life in The Movies, 1992; contbr. to: Ency. Brit.; photo exhibition Victoria & Albert Mus., London, 1992. Co-founder, hon. trustee Artists' Rights Found., 1994. Recipient Golden Thistle award Edinborough Film Festival, 1965, award Moscow Film Festival, 1965, Gold medal City of Vienna, 1967, D. W. Griffith award Dirs. Guild Am., 1971, Donatello (Italy) award, 1976, 3 Golden Globe awards, U.S. Congl. Lifetime Achievement award, 1987, John Huston award Artists Rights Found., 1994; named to Order Arts and Letters, France, 1982. Fellow Brit. Acad. Film and TV (Fellowship award 1978), Brit. Film Inst.; mem. Acad. Motion Picture Arts and Scis., Am. Film Inst. (co-founder 1961, former trustee). Co-founder sch. of neo-realism in Am. motion pictures. Strongly involved in battle for federal laws protecting moral rights of authors. Office: 98 Mount St, London W1Y 5HF, England

ZINNEN, ROBERT OLIVER, general management executive; b. Racine, Wis., June 28, 1929; s. Aloys Henry and Mabel Helen (Holy) Z.; m. Darlene Mary Weyers, Aug. 25, 1956; children: Claudia Jane, Robert O. B.B.A., U. Wis., 1951, J.D., 1956. Bar: Wis. 1956, Ill. 1959, Mass. 1982; CPA, Ill. Tax accountant Price Waterhouse, Chgo., 1956-59; mem. firm Tenney & Bentley, Chgo., 1959-64; assoc. dir. taxes Allstate Cos., Skokie, Ill., 1964-65; v.p. fin. Do-All Co., Des Plaines, Ill., 1965-67; dir. taxes Quaker Oats Co., Chgo., 1967-71; internat. atty. Am. Hosp. Supply Corp., 1971-75; fin. cons. Alexander Proudfoot Co., Chgo., 1975-76; v.p. fin. Milton Bradley Co., Springfield, Mass., 1976-82; co-owner, exec. v.p. Roadmaster Corp., Olney, Ill., 1982-88, cons., 1988—. Mem. Housing and Traffic Commns., Highland Park, Ill., 1963-66; chmn. Congl. Action Com., Springfield; bd. dirs. Assoc. Industries, Mass. Served with U.S. Army, 1951-53. Mem. Toy Mfrs. Am. (bd. dirs. 1984-88), Quail Creek Country Club, Longmeadow Country Club. Republican. Roman Catholic.

ZINNER, MICHAEL JEFFREY, surgeon, educator; b. Miami, Fla., Apr. 2, 1945; s. Doran D. and Eve (Wernicoff) Z.; children: Darren, Daniel. BEE, Johns Hopkins U., 1967; MD, U. Fla., 1971; postgrad., NIH Found. for Edn. in the Scis., Bethesda, Md., 1973-74. Diplomate Am. Bd. Surgery (bd. dirs. 1988—). Intern The Johns Hopkins Hosp., Balt., 1971-72, jr. asst. resident in surgery, 1972-73, sr. asst. resident, 1976-79, asst. chief of svc. in surgery, 1979-80; registrar thoracic surgery Frenchay Hosp., Bristol, Eng., 1977; instr. The Johns Hopkins U. Sch. Medicine, Balt., 1978-80; asst. prof. surgery Downstate Med. Ctr., Bklyn., 1980-83, assoc. prof., 1983-85; assoc. dir. surg. residency program, coord. residency program The Johns Hopkins Med. Instns., Balt., 1985-88, assoc. prof., vice chmn. dept. surgery, 1985-88, prof., 1988; prof., chmn. dept. surgery UCLA Sch. Medicine, 1988-94; mem. staff Kings County Hosp., Bklyn., 1980-85, chief gen. surgery and oncology, 1983-85; mem. staff Balt. VA Hosp., 1985-88, Johns Hopkins Hosp., 1985-88, Wadsworth VA Hosp., L.A., 1988-94; chief of surgery UCLA Med. Ctr., 1988-94; surgeon-in-chief Brigham and Womens Hosp., Boston, 1994—; prof. Harvard Med. Sch., 1994—; ednl. cons. Cath. Med. Ctr., 1981-84; mem. Clin. Rsch. Ctr. Subcom. on Sci. Rev. Protocols, SUNY, Downstate, 1982-84. Contbr. over 100 articles to profl. jours.; lectr. in field. Maj. M.C., U.S. Army, 1973-76. Rsch. grantee NIH, 1982-86, 88—; merit rev. grantee VA, 1988; grantee numerous univers., founds., pharm. cos., 1978—. Fellow ACS (com. on rsch. and edn. 1988); mem. IEEE, NIH (ad hoc, study sect., surgery and biomed. engring. 1986), Am. Fedn. Clin. Rsch., Assn. Acad. Surgery (com. on issues 1980-82, recorder 1982-84, exec. coun. 1982—, pres. 1985-86), Am. Physiol. Soc., Am. Gastroenterol. Assn., Am. Pancreatic Assn., Soc. Univ. Surgeons (com. on publs. 1984-86, com. on edn., 1986-87, exec. coun. 1986—, pres. 1987-88), Soc. Critical Care Medicine, N.Y. Surg. Soc., Gastroenterology Rsch. Group, Surg. Biology Club, Collegium Internationale Chirugiae Digestival, Conjoint Coun. Surg. Rsch., Soc. Surgery of Alimentary Tract, Soc. Clin. Surgery, Alpha Omega Alpha. Avocations: fishing, boating. Office: Brigham and Womens Hosp Dept Surgery 75 Francis St Boston MA 02115-6110

ZINNER, PETER, film editor and director, music editor; b. Vienna, Austria, July 24, 1919; came to U.S., 1940; s. Alfred and Mimy (Kornfeld) Z.; m. Eleanor Zinner, July 24, 1949 (div. Apr. 1955); m. Christa Heutelbeck, Mar. 20, 1959; children: Nicolas Nelken, Katina Andrea. Grad. high sch., Vienna. Apprentice film editor 20th Century Fox Film Studios, Hollywood, Calif., 1943-47; asst. film editor Universal Studios, Hollywood, 1947-49; music film editor MGM Studios, Culver City, Calif., 1949-60; pres. Zinner Internat., Pacific Palisades, Calif., 1970—; 2d unit dir., film editor on Officer and A Gentleman, Parmount Studios. Recipient Acad. award for film editing Deer Hunter, 1978, Brit. Film Acad. award for Deer Hunter, 1978, Emmy awards for War and Remembrance, 1989, Citizen Cohn, 1989, Acad. award nominations for Godfather, 1970-72, for Godfather II, 1974. Democrat. Avocations: skiing, tennis.

ZINSER, ELISABETH ANN, academic administrator; b. Meadville, Pa., Feb. 20, 1940; d. Merle and Fae Zinser. BS, Stanford U., 1964; MS, U. Calif., San Francisco, 1966, MIT, 1982; PhD, U. Calif., Berkeley, 1972. Nurse VA Hosp., Palo Alto, Calif., 1964-65, San Francisco, 1966-69; instr. Sch. Nursing U. Calif., San Francisco, 1966-69; pre-doctoral fellow Nat. Inst. Health, Edn. and Welfare, 1971-72; adminstr. Sch. Medicine U. Wash.,

Seattle, 1972-75, Coun. Higher Edn., State of Ky., 1975-77; prof., dean. Coll. Nursing U. N.D., Grand Forks, 1977-83; vice chancellor acad. affairs U. N.C., Greensboro, 1983-89; pres. Gallaudet U., Washington, 1988, U. Idaho, Moscow, 1989-95; chancellor U. Ky., Lexington, 1995—; bd. dirs. Am. Coun. Edn., Washington; cons. Boeing Aircraft Co., Seattle; chmn. commn. on outreach and tech. transfer; bd. dirs. Nat. Assn. State Univs. and Land Grant Colls. Primary author: (with others) Contemporary Issues in Higher Education, 1985, Higher Education Research, 1988. Bd. dirs. Humana Hosp., Greensboro, 1986-88; v.p., bd. dirs. Ea. Music Festival, Greensboro, 1987-89; trustee N.C. Coun. Econ. Edn., 1985-89, Greensboro Day Sch., 1987-89. Leadership fellow Bush Found., 1981-82. Mem. Am. Assn. Higher Edn., Assn. Am. Colls. (Coun. Liberal Learning), Am. Assn. Univ. Adminstrs., AAUP, AAUW, Pi Lambda Theta, Sigma Theta Tau. Office: U Ky 111 Adminstrn Bldg Lexington KY 40502 Also: U Ky Chancellor's Office 111 Adminstrn Office Lexington KY 40506-0032

ZINSER, WILLIAM EDWARD, neurologist, researcher; b. Charlotte, N.C., May 5, 1955; arrived in Mexico, 1991; s. Guillermo Eduardo and Nellie Marie (Peterson) Z.; m. Susana C. Casillas Zinser, June 2, 1979; children: Luis, Susana, Arturo Javier. BS, Inst. de Ciencias, Mex., 1975; MD, U. Guadalajara, Mex., 1979; degree in Pediatrics, Okla. U., 1985; degree in Neurology, Baylor Coll. Medicine, Houston, 1988. Prof. Inst. de Ciencias, Guadalajara, Mex., 1980-82; asst. prof. U. Fla., Jacksonville, 1988-91; prof. Nat. Autonomous U. Mex., Mexico City, Mex., 1992-94, The Cnological Inst. Superior Edn., Guadalajara, Mex., 1994—; chmn. Neurology Hosp. Sta. M. Chapalita, Guadalajaro, Mex., 1991—; chmn. Pediatric Edn. com. U. Fla., Jacksonville, 1989-91; founding mem. We. Mex. Coll. Neurology. Named Best Jr. Faculty Inst. de Ciencias, Guadalajara, Mex., 1981, U. Fla., Jacksonville, 1989. Mem. Child Neurology Soc., Soc. Neurology. Home: Vina del Mar 1901-1, Guadalajara Mexico Office: Av Nino Obrero 846, Guadalajara Mexico

ZINSSER, WILLIAM KNOWLTON, editor, writer, educator; b. N.Y.C., Oct. 7, 1922; s. William Herman and Joyce (Knowlton) Z.; m. Caroline Fraser, Oct. 10, 1954; children: Amy Fraser, John William. A.B., Princeton U., 1944; L.H.D., Rollins Coll., 1984; Litt.D., Ind. State U., 1985, Wesleyan U., 1988. Feature writer N.Y. Herald Tribune, 1946-49, drama editor, 1949-54, film critic, 1955-58, editorial writer, 1958-59; free-lance writer, 1959—; commentator on NBC-TV Sunday program, 1964-65; columnist Look mag, 1967, Life mag, 1968-72, N.Y. Times, 1977; faculty Yale U., 1971-79, master Branford Coll., 1973-79; gen. editor, Book-of-the-Month Club, 1979-86 . Author: Any Old Place With You, 1957, Seen Any Good Movies Lately?, 1958, Search and Research, 1961, The City Dwellers, 1962, Weekend Guests, 1963, The Haircurl Papers, 1964, Pop Goes America, 1966, The Paradise Bit, 1967, The Lunacy Boom, 1970, On Writing Well, 1976, Writing with a Word Processor, 1983, Willie and Dwike, 1984, Writing to Learn, 1988, Spring Training, 1989, American Places, 1992, Speaking of Journalism, 1994; co-author: Five Boyhoods, 1962; editor Extraordinary Lives, 1986, Inventing the Truth, 1987, Spiritual Quests, 1988, Paths of Resistance, 1989, Worlds of Childhood, 1990, They Went, 1991. Bd. dirs. Bklyn. Mus., 1967-72. Served with AUS, 1943-45, MTO. Clubs: Century Assn, Coffee House. Home: 45 E 62nd St New York NY 10021-8025

ZIOCK, KLAUS OTTO HEINRICH, physics educator; b. Herchen, Germany, Feb. 4, 1925; came to U.S., 1958, naturalized, 1966; s. Samuel and Elisabeth (Bauer) Z.; m. Ursula E. A. Thierbach, May 31, 1952; children—Hans-Joachim, Klaus-Peter, Robert, Michael. Diplom Physiker, U. Bonn, Fed. Republic Germany, 1949, Dr. rer.nat., 1956. Rsch. physicist E. Leybold's Nachfolger, Cologne, Fed. Republic Germany, 1950-54; rsch. assoc. U. Bonn, Fed. Republic Germany, 1956-58; rsch. assoc. Yale U., New Haven, 1958-60, asst. prof. physics, 1960-62; assoc. prof. physics U. Va., Charlottesville, 1962-72, prof. physics, 1972—. Author: Basic Quantum Mechanics, 1969; contbr. numerous articles to profl. jours.; patentee in field. Recipient Humboldt prize Alexander von Humboldt Stiftung, 1978. Mem. Am. Phys. Soc.

ZIOLKOWSKI, JAN MICHAEL, medievalist educator; b. New Haven, Nov. 17, 1956; s. Theodore J. and Yetta (Goldstein) Z.; m. Elizabeth Ann Hillenius; children: Saskia Elizabeth, Ada Margaret, Yetta Joy. AB summa cum laude, Princeton U., 1977; PhD, U. Cambridge, Eng., 1982; MA (hon.), Harvard U., 1987. Asst. prof. Harvard U., Cambridge, Mass., 1981-84, John L. Loeb assoc. prof. of the humanities, 1984-87, prof. medieval Latin and comparative lit., 1987—. Editor Comparative Literature Studies. Fellow Guggenheim Found., 1987-88, ACLS, 1986, Rome Prize fellow, Am. Acad. in Rome, 1980-81; Marshall scholar, 1977-80. Mem. Medieval Acad. Am. (councillor 1991-94), Phi Beta Kappa. Home: 930 Centre St Newton MA 02159-1266 Office: Harvard Univ Dept. Medieval Latin/Liter Cambridge MA 02138

ZIOLKOWSKI, THEODORE JOSEPH, comparative literature educator; b. Birmingham, Ala., Sept. 30, 1932; s. Miecislaw and Cecilia (Jankowski) Z.; m. Yetta Bart Goldstein, Mar. 26, 1951; children: Margaret Cecilia, Jan Michael, Eric Josef. AB, Duke U., 1951, AM, 1952; student, U. Innsbruck, Austria, 1952-53; PhD, Yale U., 1957. Instr., then asst. prof. Yale U., New Haven, 1956-62; assoc. prof. Columbia U., N.Y.C., 1962-64; prof. Germanic langs. and lit. Princeton (N.J.) U., 1964-69, chmn., 1973-79, Class of 1900 prof. modern langs., 1969—, prof. comparative lit., 1975—, dean Grad. Sch., 1979-92; vis. prof. Rutgers U., 1966, Yale U., 1967, 75, CUNY, 1971, Bristol U., 1987, U. Munich, 1992; vis. scholar U. Ctr. in Va., 1971, Piedmont U. Ctr., N.C., 1971; Dancy Meml. lectr. U. Montevallo, 1973; Christopher Longest lectr. U. Miss., 1979; Patten Found. lectr. Ind. U., 1980; vis. lectr. Österreichische Akademie der Wissenschaften, 1992; chmn. N.Y. State Doctoral Evaluation Program in German, 1975-80; nat. rev. panel for U.S. Nat. Grad. Fellows Program, 1985-87, 91—; chmn. overseers vis. com. on German Harvard U., 1982-88; mem. selection com. for Bennett award, 1988; with German-Am. Acad. Coun., 1993—. Author: Hermann Broch, 1964, The Novels of Hermann Hesse, 1965, Hermann Hesse, 1966, Dimensions of the Modern Novel, 1969, Fictional Transfigurations of Jesus, 1972 (James Russell Lowell prize for criticism), Disenchanted Images, 1977, Der Schriftsteller Hermann Hesse, 1979, The Classical German Elegy, 1980, Varieties of Literary Thematics, 1983, German Romanticism and Its Institutions, 1990, Virgil and the Moderns, 1993' also articles and revs.; editor: Hermann Hesse, Autobiographical Writing, 1972, Hermann Hesse, Stories of Five Decades, 1972, Hesse: A Collection of Critical Essays, 1972, Hermann Hesse, My Belief: Selected Essays, 1974, Hermann Hesse, Tales of Student Life, 1976, Hermann Hesse, Pictor's Metamorphoses and Other Fantasies, 1982, Hermann Hesse, Soul of the Age: Selected Letters, 1891-1962, 1991; mem. editl. bd. Germanic Rev., 1962—, Publs. MLA, 1971-75, Arbitrium, 1983—, 17th Century Studies, 1985—, Germanistik, 1987—; mem. editl. bd. Priceton U. Press, 1972-75, trustee, 1982-95; translator (with Yetta Ziolkowski): The Poetics of Quotation (Herman Meyer) 1968, Herman Hesse: A Pictorial Biography, 1975. Chmn. N.Y. State Humanities Screening Com., 1996. Recipient Howard T. Behrman award for disting. achievement in humanities, 1978, Wilbur Lucius Cross medal Yale U., 1982, Goethe Inst. gold medal, 1987, Henry Allen Moe prize in humanities, 1988; Fulbright rsch. grantee, 1958-59, grantee Am. Philos. Soc., 1959, NEH grantee, 1978, Guggenheim fellow, 1964-65, Am. Coun. Learned Socs. fellow, 1972, 76; resident fellow Bellagio Study Ctr., 1993. Mem. MLA (exec. coun. 1976-77, pres. 1985), Acad. Lit. Studies, Am. Comparative Lit. Assn., Am. Acad. Arts and Scis., Assn. Lit. Scholars and Critics, Authors Guild, Am. Assn. Tchrs. German (hon. life), Yale Grad. Sch. Assn. (pres. 1974-76), Assn. Grad. Schs. (v.p. 1989-90, pres. 1990-91), Heinrich von Kleist Gesellschaft, Goethe-Gesellschaft, Novalis-Gesellschaft, Internat. Vereinigung für Germanistik (exec. coun. 1985-95, treas. 1990-95), Am. Philos. Soc. (councillor 1991—), Göttingen Akademie der Wissenschaften, Austrian Akademie der Wissenschaften, Phi Beta Kappa. Home: 36 Bainbridge St Princeton NJ 08540-3902 Office: Princeton U 230 E Pyne Bldg Princeton NJ 08544

ZIOMEK, JONATHAN S., journalist, educator; b. Newport News, Va., July 28, 1947; s. Stanley Walter and Joy Carmen (Schmidt) Z.; m. Rosalie Ziomek, Aug. 14, 1977; children: Joseph, Jennifer; 1 stepchild, Daniel. BA in Sociology, U. Ill., 1970, MS in Journalism, 1982. Reporter, feature writer, Sun. fin. editor Chgo. Sun-Times, 1970-78; press sec. Robert Ash Wallace for U.S. Senate campaign, Chgo., 1979-80; asst. prof. Medill Sch. Journalism, Northwestern U., Evanston, Ill., 1983-88; dir. grad. editl. programs Medill Sch. Journalism/Northwestern U., Evanston, Ill., 1988—, asst. dean, assoc. prof., 1994—; presenter workshops. Contbr. articles to various mags.; editor: Chgo. Journalist Newsletter, 1991-93. Participant Internat. Visitors Ctr., Chgo., 1988—; fact-finder USIA, Bulgaria and Yugoslavia, 1990. Mem. Assn. for Edn. in Journalism and Mass Communications, Soc. Profl. Journalists, Nat. Assn. Sci. Writers, Headline Club. Home: 2149 Hartrey Ave Evanston IL 60201-2571 Office: Northwestern Univ Medill Sch Journalism Evanston IL 60208

ZION, ROGER H., consulting firm executive, former congressman; b. Escanba, Mich., Sept. 17, 1921; s. Herschel G. and Helen (Hutchinson) Z.; m. Marjorie Knauss, Feb. 20, 1945; children—Gayle, Scott, Randy. B.A., U. Wis., 1943; postgrad., Grad. Sch. Bus. Adminstrn., Harvard, 1944-45. With Mead Johnson & Co., 1946-66, dir. tng. and profl. relations, 1965-66; internat. marketing mgmt. cons., 1966; mem. 90th-93d congresses from 8th Dist. Ind.; chmn. Republican Task Force on Energy and Resources; pres. Resources Devel., Inc. (cons.), Washington, 1975—. Author: Keys to Human Relations in Selling, 1963, The Hallowed Howls of Congress, 1994, The Republican Challenge, 1995. Vice pres. Buffalo Trace council Boy Scouts Am., 1961; Bd. dirs., chmn. Evansville (Ind.) chpt. ARC, 1960-65. Served to lt. USNR, 1943-46, PTO. Named Toastmaster Evansville Press Gridiron dinner, 1963; recipient Citizen of Month award New Image Com. of Evansville's Future, 1962. Mem. VFW, Am. Legion, Nat. Sales and Marketing Execs. Assn. (pres. Evansville 1962), Wabash Valley Assn., AMVETS (life), Rotary (dir. Evansville club 1964), Evansville Country Club (dir. 1960-65), Alpha Delta Phi (pres. Wis. chpt. 1941-43). Republican. Congregationalist. Home: 834 Plaza Dr Evansville IN 47715-6936 Office: 412 1st St SE Washington DC 20003-1804

ZIPERSKI, JAMES RICHARD, lawyer, trucking company executive; b. Milw., May 27, 1932; s. George Felix and Louise (Medema) Z.; m. Patricia Jean Hoag, June 28, 1958; children: Jean Marie, David Carrington, James Patrick. BS, Marquette U., 1953, JD, 1957. Bar: Wis. 1957, U.S. Supreme Ct., 1967, U.S. Ct. Appeals, 1978. Resident counsel Schwerman Trucking Co., Milw., 1957—, sec., 1962—, exec. v.p. corp., 1977-80, exec. v.p., 1980-86; exec. v.p., corp. and sec. Evergreen Holding Corp. (parent co. Schwerman Trucking Co.), Milw., 1987—, also bd. dirs. Served with AUS, 1953-55. Mem. Transp. Lawyers Assn., Westmoor Country Club, Kiwanis, Alpha Kappa Psi, Phi Delta Phi. Home: 2110 N Swan Blvd Milwaukee WI 53226-2644 Office: Evergreen Holding Corp PO Box 736 611 S 28th St Milwaukee WI 53215-1201

ZIPES, DOUGLAS PETER, cardiologist, researcher; b. White Plains, N.Y., Feb. 27, 1939; s. Robert Samuel and Josephine Helen (Weber) Z.; m. Marilyn Joan Jacobus, Feb. 18, 1961; children: Debra, Jeffrey, David. B.A. cum laude, Dartmouth Coll., 1961, B.Med. Sci., 1962; M.D. cum laude, Harvard Med. Sch., 1964. Diplomate Am. Bd. Internal Medicine (mem. subsplty. bd. cardiovascular disease 1989—, chmn., 1995—, chmn. com. cert. in clin. cardiac electrophysiology 1989-96). Intern, resident, fellow in cardiology Duke U. Med. Ctr., Durham, N.C., 1964-68; vis. scientist Masonic Med. Research Lab., Utica, N.Y., 1970-71; asst. prof. medicine Ind. U. Sch. Medicine, Indpls., 1970-73, assoc. prof., 1973-76, prof., 1976-94, prof. pharmacology and toxicology, 1993—, disting. prof. medicine, 1994—; dir. Divsn. of Cardiology Krannert Inst. Cardiology, Ind. U. Sch. Medicine, 1995—; cons.; mem. cardiology adv. com. NIH, 1991-94. Author: Comprehensive Cardiac Care, 7th edit., 1991; editor: Slow Inward Current, 1980, Cardiac Electrophysiology and Arrhythmias, 1985, Nonpharmacological Therapy of Tachyarrhythmias, 1987, Cardiac Electrophysiology From Cell to Bedside, 1990, 2d edit., 1994; co-editor: Treatment of Heart Diseases, 1992, Abiation of Cardiac Arrhythmias, 1994, Antiarrhythmic Therapy: A Pathophysiologic Approach, 1994; mem. editl. bd. Circulation, 1974-78, 83—, Am. Jour. Cardiology, 1979-82, 88—, Am. Jour. Medicine, 1979-90, Jour. Am. Coll. Cardiology, 1983, Am. Heart Jour., 1977—, PACE, 1977—, Circulation Rsch., 1983-90, Am. Jour. Noninvasive Cardiology, 1985-89, Jour. Electrophysiology, 1987-89, Cardiovascular Drugs and Therapy, 1986-93, Japanese Heart Jour., 1989—, Jour. Cardiovascular Pharmacology and Therapeutics, 1994—, Jour. Cardiovascular Pharmacology, 1995—, Cardiovascular Therapeutics, 1995, Current Clin. Trials, 1995; editor-in-chief: Progress in Cardiology, 1988-92, Jour. Cardiovascular Electrophysiology, 1990—, Cardiology in Rev., 1992—, Contemporary Treatments of Cardiovascular Disease, 1996; contbr. numerous articles to med. pubs.; patentee cardioverter, elec. prevention of arrhythmia, discrimination of atrial fibrillation and fixation of implantable devices. Pres., bd. dirs. Indpls. Opera Co., 1983-85; mem. study sect. NIH, Washington, 1977-81; mem. nat. merit rev. bd. VA, 1982-85, Cardiology Adv. Com. NHLBL, 1991-94, chmn. steering com. AVID. Recipient Disting. Achievement award Am. Heart Assn., 1989. Fellow ACP, Am. Coll. Cardiology (chmn. ACC/AHA subcom. to assess EP studies, chmn. young investigators award com. 1988-94, trustee 1992—, mem. nominating com. 1993, Disting. Scientist award 1996), Am. Heart Assn. (exec. com. 1980-88, sci. sessions program 1983-86, 96—, chmn. various coms., chmn. 1995, bd. dirs. Internat. Cardiology Found. 1993—, bd. dirs. 1994—, chmn. emergency cardiac care com.); mem. Am. Soc. Clin. Investigation, Assn. Univ. Cardiologists (v.p. 1994, pres. 1995), Assn. Am. Physicians, Am. Physiol. Soc., Cardiac Electrophysiology Soc. (pres. 1985-86), N.Am. Soc. Pacing and Electrophysiology (pres. 1988-90, trustee 1990—, Disting. Scientist award 1995), InterAm. Soc. Cardiology (1st v.p. 1995—), Ind. Cardiac Electrophysiology Soc. (founder). Home: 10614 Winterwood Carmel IN 46032-9688 Office: Ind U Sch Medicine 1100 W Michigan St Indianapolis IN 46202-5208

ZIPF, WILLIAM BYRON, pediatric endocrinologist, educator; b. Dayton, Ohio, Mar. 20, 1946; s. Robert Eugene and Merium (Murr) Z.; m. Joanne Fisher, Sept. 20, 1969; children: William Byron Jr., Thanda Lynn, Robert E. II. BA, Denison U., 1968; MD, Ohio State U., 1972. Diplomate Nat. Bd. Med. Examiners, Am. Bd. Pediatrics, Am. Bd. Pediatric Endocrinology. Intern in pediatrics Mott Children's Hosp./U. Mich., Ann Arbor, 1972-73, resident in pediatrics, 1973-75, clin. fellow in pediatric endocrinology, 1975-76, rsch. fellow, 1976-78; asst. prof. dept. pediatrics and physiology Ohio State U., Columbus, 1978-83, assoc. prof., 1983-89, prof., 1989—; dir. clin. study ctr. Children's Hosp./Ohio State U., Columbus, 1982—, vice-chmn. dept. pediatrics, 1989—, dir. pediatric endocrinology, 1990—. Contbr. chpts. on endocrine diseases of children to books, articles to profl. jours. Grantee NIH, 1980-84, Cystic Fibrosis Found., 1987-92. Fellow Am. Acad. Pediatrics, Nat. Med. Bd.; mem. Soc. Pediatric Rsch., Endocrine Soc., Lawson Wilkins Soc. Pediatric Endocrinolgoy. Achievements include discovery of endocrine abnormalities associated with conditions of altered nutrition in children; definition of role of pancreatic peptide abnormalities in specific appetite disorders. Office: Childrens Hosp 700 Childrens Dr Columbus OH 43205-2666

ZIPP, JOEL FREDERICK, lawyer; b. Shaker Heights, Ohio, Feb. 12, 1948; s. Jack David and Eleanor Adele Z.; m. Elizabeth Ann Frieden, Dec. 4, 1976; 1 child, Carlyn Leigh. BS, U. Wis., 1970, MS, 1972; JD, Case Western Res. U., 1975. Bar: Ohio 1975, D.C. 1976, U.S. Ct. Claims, 1976, U.S. Ct. Appeals (D.C. cir.) 1976, U.S. Ct. Appeals (5th cir.) 1979, U.S. Ct. Appeals (11th cir.) 1983, U.S. Supreme Ct. 1983. Trial atty. Fed. Energy Regulation Com., Washington, 1975-79, asst. dir. office of enforcement, 1979; assoc. Morley, Caskin & Generelly, Washington, 1979-80, ptnr., 1981—; gen. counsel, sec. Portland Natural Gas Transmission Sys., 1993—. Notes editor Energy Law Jour., 1990—; contbr. articles to profl. jours. Bd. dirs. Westmoreland Children's Ctr., Washington, 1986-88. Smithsonian fellow, 1969. Mem ABA, Fed. Energy Bar Assn. (bd. dirs., past com. chair 1992, 93 ann. meetings). Jewish. Avocations: sailing, skiing, running. Home: 9216 Burning Tree Rd Bethesda MD 20817-2251 Office: Morley Caskin 1225 I St NW Washington DC 20005-3914

ZIPPER, HERBERT, symphony conductor; b. Vienna, Austria, Apr. 27, 1904; came to U.S., 1946; s. Emil and Regina (Westreich) Z.; m. Trudl Dubsky, Oct. 1, 1939 (dec. July, 1976). Master diploma, Vienna State Acad. for Music and Drama, Vienna, 1926. Prof. Conservatory of Düsseldorf, Fed. Republic Germany, 1931-33; apptd. by Pres. Sergio Osmeñ-a of Philippines as mem. com. for cultural rehab. of Philippines, 1946; lectr. New Sch. for Social Research in opera, symphony, and composition, 1947-52; exec. dir. Nat. Guild Community Mus. Schs., 1967-72; music cons. JDR 3d Fund, N.Y.C.; projects dir. U. So. Calif. Sch. Performing Arts, Los Angeles, 1972-80; invited guest condr. and tchr. conducting and composition People's Republic of China, 1981. Asst. condr. Wiener Burgtheater, 1923-25, condr. Vienna Madrigal Assn., 1927-29, opera condr. Stadtheater Ingolstadt, Bavaria, 1929-30, condr. Mcpl. Music Soc., 1931-33; guest condr. in various cities of Europe, 1933-37; instrumental in found. and orgn. of Vienna Concert Orch., composed mainly of musicians who fled Germany, 1934; composed music for polit. satires in Paris, 1939; mus. dir. Manila Symphony Orch. and head Acad. Music of Manila, 1939-42; gave 130 symphony concerts for armed forces and civilians, 1945-46; mus. dir. Bklyn. Symphony Orch., 1947-50; Fine Arts Quartet Concert series, Chgo., Wilmette, Ill., 1960-67; condr. summer season, Manila Symphony Orch., 1951-69; dir. Community Music Ctr. North Shore, 1953-67, condr. Chgo. Businessmen's Orch., 1955-62, condr. 26 symphony concerts in Beijing, Tienjin and Guangzhou, Peoples Republic China, 1981, 4 months 1982, condr. orchs. in 4 cities, Peoples Republic China, 4 months, 1984; condr. concerts in Beijing, Jinan, Tianjin, Qingdao, Peoples Republic China, 1986, Beijing and Shenyang, China, 1988, Beijing and Changchun, 1989, Beijing Cen. Philharm., Orch. Concerts, 1990; condr. Cen. Philharm. of China, Philharm. Chamber Orch., Radio Broadcast Orch., Beijing, 1991, concerts with Tianjin Philharmonic, 1993; opened Styrian Automn, Graz, Austria, 1988, Zipper's Biography, 1992, Chinese edition, 1992, German edition, 1993; composer revision of choral works by old masters and own choral arrangements, 1948-49; German version of Ernst Toch's opera The Last Tale, 1964. Chmn. Philippine fellowship project, 1966; pres. Nat. Guild Community Music Schs., 1957-62, exec. dir. 1967-72; project dir. U. So. Calif. Sch. of Performing Arts, 1972-80. Prisoner Dachau and Buchenwald concentration camps, 1938-39. Recipient Louis S. Weiss Meml. prize New Sch. of Social Research, N.Y., 1954, Presdl. award medal and citation Pres. of Philippines, 1959, Austrian Cross Honor for Sci. and Art, 1966, Silangan award U. East Manila, Philippines, 1977, Samuel Rosenbaum Meml. award Nat. Guild Community Schs. Arts, Golden Honor Insignia for important achievements Govt. Vienna, Austria, 1993. Reorganized orch. after imprisonment by Japanese and work in underground, 1945. Home: 1091 Palisair Pl Pacific Palisades CA 90272-2459

ZIPPIN, CALVIN, epidemiologist, educator; b. Albany, N.Y., July 17, 1926; s. Samuel and Jennie (Perkel) Z.; m. Patricia Jayne Schubert, Feb. 9, 1964; children: David Benjamin, Jennifer Dorothy. AB magna cum laude, SUNY, Albany, 1947; ScD, Johns Hopkins U., Balt., 1953. Rsch. asst. Sterling-Winthrop Rsch. Inst., Rensselaer, N.Y., 1947-50; instr. biostats. Sch. Pub. Health, U. Calif., Berkeley, 1953-55; asst. to full rsch. biostatistician Sch. Medicine U. Calif., San Francisco, 1955-67, asst. prof. preventive medicine, 1958-60, prof. epidemiology, 1967-91, prof. emeritus, 1991—; vis. assoc. prof. stats. Stanford U., 1962; adv. WHO, 1969—; vis research worker Middlesex Hosp. Med. Sch., London, 1975; various coms. Am. Cancer Soc. and Nat. Cancer Inst., 1956—; faculty adviser Regional Cancer Centre, Trivandrum, India, 1983—; cons., lectr., vis. prof. in field. Co-author book, book chpts.; author or co-author papers primarily on biometry and epidemiology of cancer; editorial advisor Jour. Stats. in Medicine, Boston, 1981-86. Mem. Dem. Ctrl. Com., Marin County, Calif., 1994—. Recipient Disting. Alumnus award SUNY, Albany, 1969, also awards, fellowships and grants for work in cancer biometry and epidemiology. Fellow Am. Statis. Assn., Am. Coll. Epidemiology, Royal Statis. Soc. Gt. Britain; mem. Biometric Soc. (mem. internat. coun. 1978-81, pres. Western N.Am. region 1979-80), Calif. Cancer Registrars Assn. (hon.), Internat. Assn. Cancer Registries (hon.), B'nai B'rith (pres. Golden Gate lodge 1970-71, pres. Greater San Francisco Bay area coun. 1974-75), Phi Beta Kappa, Sigma Xi, Delta Omega. Home: 4 Warren Ct Tiburon CA 94920-1117 Office: Univ Calif Dept Epidemiology San Francisco CA 94143-0746

ZIPPRODT, PATRICIA, costume designer. B.A., Wellesley Coll.; student, Art Inst. Chgo., Art Students League N.Y., Fashion Inst. Tech. Asst. to various theatre designers; lectr., condr. master classes Yale U., Harvard U., others; vis. lectr. theatre arts NYU; prof. theatre arts Brandeis U., 1985-93; founding mem. Nat. Theater for the Deaf. Designer: (Broadway mus.) Fiddler on the Roof, 1964 (Tony award 1964), Cabaret, 1966 (Tony award 1966), Zorba, 1968 (Drama Desk award 1968), 1776, 1969 (Drama Desk award 1969, Joseph P. Maharam award 1970), Pippin, 1972 (Drama Desk award 1973), Mack and Mable, 1974, Chicago, 1975, King of Hearts, 1978, Alice in Wonderland, 1982 (Joseph P. Maharam award 1983), Smile, 1983, The Accidental Death of an Anarchist, 1984, Sweet Charity, 1985 (Tony award 1986), Big Deal, 1986, Shogun: The Musical, 1990 (Drama Desk award 1990, Joseph P. Maharam award 1990), My Fair Lady, 1993; (Broadway plays) A Period of Adjustment, 1962, Little Foxes, 1967, Plaza Suite, 1968, Scratch, 1971, All God's Chillun' Got Wings, 1975, Poor Murderer, 1976, Kingdoms, 1981, Fools, 1981, Brighton Beach Memoirs, 1983, The Glass Menagerie, 1983, Macbeth, 1988, Cat on a Hot Tin Roof, 1989, My Favorite Year, 1992; (off-Broadway plays) Our Town, 1960, The Balcony, 1960, Camino Real, 1961, Oh Dad Poor Dad Etc., 1962, A Man's a Man, 1963, The Blacks, 1962; (Guthrie Theatre) Waiting for Godot, 1973, Don Juan, 1982 (Joseph P. Maharam award 1983), The Bacchae, 1987; (Nat. Actors Theatre) The Crucible, 1991-92, Hotel Paradiso, 1991-92, The Master Builder, 1991-92, Little Hotel On The Side, 1992, School for Scandal, 1994, Picasso At The Lapin Agile, 1995; (Boston Opera) Madam Butterfly, 1962, Hippolyte E Aricie, 1966, The Rise and Fall of the City of Mahagonny, 1972; (New York City Opera) Katerina Ismailova, 1967, The Flaming Angel, 1968, Naughty Marietta, 1978; (Guggenheim Mus., N.Y.C.) The Mother of Us All, 1972; (Julliard Opera) Lord Byron, 1973; (Met. Opera) Tannhaüser, 1977, The Barber of Seville, 1982; (Am. Repertory Theatre, Cambridge, Mass.) The Fall of the House of Usher, 1988; (Am. Ballet Theatre) Les Noces, 1969, The Leaves are Fading, 1975, Estuary, 1982, Coppélia, 1991; (New York City Ballet) Watermill, 1972, Dybbuk Variations, 1974, The Sleeping Beauty, 1991; (Houston Ballet) Helgi Tommasen, 1985; (Ballet Hispanico) Cada Noche Tango Jnez de Castro Tres Cantos, 1988; (films) The Graduate, 1967; (television spls.) Anne Bancroft Spl., CBS, 1970, June Moon, WNET, 1973, The Glass Menagerie, ABC, 1973, Alice in Wonderland, WNET, 1983, Chrysler Skating, 1992; (nat. tours) Bette Midler, 1976, Ben Vereen, 1983; designer, advisor: The Seagull (St. Petersburg, Russia), Anna Christie (Beijing, China); exhibitor design sketches Wright-Hepburn, London, 1966, Capicorn Gallery, N.Y.C., 1968, Mus. City N.Y., 1972, U. Calif.-San Diego, 1974, Toneelmuseum, Amsterdam, The Netherlands, 1975, U.S. Internat. Theatre Inst. traveling exhibit, 1974-78, N.Y. City Ballet, 1994. Recipient award for spl. costumes NATAS, 1970, spl. award New Eng. Conf., 1973, Ritter award Fashion Inst. Tech., 1977, Disting. Career award S.E. Theatre Conf., 1985; inductee Theater Hal of Fame, 1992. Mem. United Scenic Artists, Costume Designers Guild, Motion Picture Acad. Arts and Scis. Address: 29 King St New York NY 10014-4966

ZIRBES, MARY KENNETH, social justice ministry coordinator; b. Melrose, Minn., Sept. 4, 1926; d. Joseph Louis and Clara Bernadine (Petermeier) Z. BA in History and Edn., Coll. St. Catherine, 1960; MA in Applied Theology, Sch. Applied Theology, Berkeley, Calif., 1976. Joined Order of St. Francis, Roman Cath. Ch., 1945. Tchr. Pub. Grade Sch., St. Nicholas, Minn., 1947-52; prin. Holy Spirit Grade Sch., St. Cloud, Minn., 1953-59, St. Mary's Jr. High Sch., Morris, Minn., 1960-62; coord. Franciscan Mission Team, Peru, South America, 1962-67, Franciscan Missions, Little Falls, Minn., 1967-70; dir. St. Richard's Social Ministry, Richfield, Minn., 1971-80, Parish Community Devel., St. Paul, Mpls., Minn., 1980-85; councillor gen. Franciscan Sisters of Little Falls, 1960-62, 67-70; asst. dir. Renew-Archdiocese of St. Paul-Mpls., 1986-89; coord. Parish Social Justice Ministry-Archdiocese of St. Paul-Mpls., 1990-93; minister Franciscan Assocs., 1993—; leader of team on evangelical life Franciscan Sisters of Little Falls, 1994—; co-developer Assn. of Pastoral Ministers, Mpls., St. Paul, 1979-81, Compañeros/Sister Parishes-Minn. and Nicaragua, 1984-89, Minn. Interfaith Ecology Coalition, 1989-92. Author: Parish Social Ministry, 1985, (manual) Acting for Justice, 1992. Organizer Twin Cities Orgn., Mpls., 1979-80; bd. dirs. Franciscan Sisters Health Care, Inc., Little Falls, 1990-93, Rice-Marion Residents Assn., St. Paul, 1991-92. Named Outstanding chair Assn. Pastoral Ministers, 1981; recipient Five Yrs. of Outstanding Svc. award Companeros, 1989. Mem. Assn. Pastoral Ministers (chair 1979), Amnesty Internat., Voices for Justice-Legis. Lobby, Audubon Soc., Network, Minn. Interfaith Ecology Coalition, Franciscan Sisters of Little Falls. Avocations: water color painting, birding, golf, reading history and biography. Office: Franciscan Sisters 116-8th Ave SE Little Falls MN 56345

ZIRILLI, FRANCESCO, mechanical engineer, engineering educator; b. Buenos Aires, Apr. 23, 1956; s. Giuseppe and Giuseppa (Nucifora) Z.; m. Joanne A. Long, July 8, 1994; 1 child, Kristen Long. BSME, Clarkson U., Potsdam, N.Y., 1977, MSME, 1979, PhD in Mech. Engring., 1985. Assoc. engr. GE Co., Schenectady, N.Y., 1978-80; cons. engr. Stress Tech., Inc.,

Rochester, N.Y., 1983-84; project mgr. Xerox Corp., Rochester, 1984—; sr. lectr. U. Rochester, 1986—. Contbr. articles to profl. jours. Mem. ASME, TAPPI, Pi Tau Sigma. Achievements include 2 patents. Avocations: stamp collecting, woodworking, travel, reading. Office: Xerox Corporation 800 Phillips Rd #139-20A Webster NY 14580

ZIRIN, HAROLD, astronomer, educator; b. Boston, Oct. 7, 1929; s. Jack and Anna (Buchwalter) Z.; m. Mary Noble Fleming, Apr. 20, 1957; children: Daniel Meyer, Dana Mary. A.B., Harvard U., 1950, A.M., 1951, Ph.D., 1952. Asst. phys. scientist RAND Corp., 1952-53; lectr. Harvard, 1953-55; research staff High Altitude Obs., Boulder, Colo., 1955-64; prof. astrophysics Calif. Inst. Tech., 1964—; staff mem. Hale Obs., 1964-80; chief astronomer Big Bear Solar Obs., 1969-80, dir., 1980—; U.S.- USSR exchange scientist, 1960-61; vis. prof. Coll. de France, 1986, Japan Soc. P. Sci., 1992. Author: The Solar Atmosphere, 1966, Astrophysics of the Sun, 1987; co-translator: Five Billion Vodka Bottles to the Moon, 1991; adv. editor: Soviet Astronomy, 1965-69; editor Magnetic and Velocity Fields of Solar Active Regions. Trustee Polique Canyon Assn., 1977-90. Agassiz fellow, 1951-52; Sloan fellow, 1958-60; Guggenheim fellow, 1960-61. Mem. Am. Astron. Soc., Internat. Astron. Union, AURA (dir. 1977-83). Home: 1178 Sonoma Dr Altadena CA 91001-3150 Office: Calif Inst Tech Big Bear Solar Observatory 40386 N Shore Dr Big Bear City CA 92314-9672

ZIRIN, JAMES DAVID, lawyer; b. N.Y.C., Jan. 10, 1940; s. Morris and Kate (Sapir) Z.; m. Marlene Hess, May 18, 1990. AB with honors, Princeton U., 1961; JD with honors, U. Mich., 1964. Bar: N.Y. 1965, U.S. Supreme Ct. 1978. Asst. U.S. atty. U.S. Dist. Ct. (so. dist.) N.Y., N.Y.C., 1967-70; assoc. Breed, Abbott & Morgan, N.Y.C., 1965-67, 70-72, ptnr., 1972-93; ptnr. Brown & Wood, N.Y.C., 1993—. Contbr. articles to Lincoln Times, Forbes, Barron's, N.Y., Newsday, N.Y. Law Jour. Bd. dirs. Legal Aid Soc., N.Y.C., 1984-89, exec. com., 1986-89. Lt. USNR, 1965-70. Fellow Am. Coll. Trial Lawyers; mem. Fed. Bar Coun. (v.p. 1982-84), Assn. of Bar of City of N.Y., University Club. Republican. Office: Brown & Wood One World Trade Ctr New York NY 10048

ZIRKEL, DON, public information official; b. Ozone Park, N.Y., Aug. 13, 1927; s. George Henry and Frances Anna (Neumann) Z.; m. Marie Margaret Greene, June 28, 1952; children: Jeanne Zirkel O'Connell, Barbara Zirkel Dempsey, Joseph, Thomas, Mary Zirkel Pacifico, Anne Zirkel-Hagopian, John, Paul, Timothy. Student, Fordham U., 1948-50; B.A., St. John's U., 1955. Mem. editorial staff Cath. newspaper The Tablet, Bklyn., 1948-85; editor Cath. newspaper The Tablet, 1968-85; exec. staff N.Y. State Div. Human Rights, 1985-92; dir. pub. info. Ctr. for Devel. Disabilities, Woodbury, N.Y., 1992—; lectr. in field. Contbr. articles to Cath. newspapers, mags. Rsch. asst. to Congressman James J. Delaney, 1961-63, Congressman Hugh L. Carey, 1963-65; bd. dirs. Citizens for Ednl. Freedom, Cath. Interracial Coun. Intercommunity Ctr. for Justice and Peace. With AUS, 1950-52. Recipient Best News Story award Cath. Press Assn., 1957, Americanism award Cath. War Vets., 1961, Worldmission award U.S. Mission Secretariat, 1963. Roman Catholic (lector 1966—, Eucharistic minister 1973—, ordained deacon 1979). Club: K.C. (State award 1973). Home: 34 Fountain St Hicksville NY 11801-3120 Office: Ctr Devel Disabilities 72 S Woods Rd Woodbury NY 11797-1024

ZIRKEL, GENE, computer science and mathematics educator; b. N.Y.C., Dec. 2, 1931; s. George Henry and Frances Anna (Neumann) Z.; m. Patricia Lou McCormick, Apr. 15, 1968; 1 child, George Stephen. BS, St. John's Coll., Bklyn., 1953; MA, St. John's U., Queens, N.Y., 1960; MS, N.Y. Inst. Tech., 1984. Tchr. Mt. St. Michael's H.S., Bronx, N.Y., 1955-56, Cardinal Hayes H.S., Bronx, 1956-60; chair math. Marist H.S., Bayonne, N.J., 1960-62, prin., 1966-67; tchr. Aquinas H.S., Augusta, Ga., 1962; chair theology Archbishop Molloy H.S., Queens, 1962-66; prof. Nassau C.C., Garden City, N.Y., 1967—; lectr. Marist Coll., Poughkeepsie, N.Y., 1959-66, Adelphi U., Garden City, 1973-74; com. create nat. exam Math Assn. Am.; founder New Horizon Learning Ctr. Co-author: Understanding Statistics, 1972, Beginning Statistics, 1976, Program CSI, 1990, Understanding Fortran 77 & 90, 1994; contbr. articles to profl. jours.; columnist Standard Deviations. Union rep. Labor and Religion Coalition, L.I., N.Y., 1980s; Cath. chaplain Nassau C.C., vol. parish outreach poor, homeless and hungry; vol. Habitat for Humanity. Recipient Best Articles of 1976 award Matyc Jour. (Math. & Computer Edn.); NSF scholar, 1960. Fellow Dozenal Soc. (chmn. bd. dirs. 1991-92, pres. 1977-88, v.p. 1988-90); mem. Nat. Coun. Tchrs. Math. (life). Democrat. Avocation: swimming. Home: 6 Brancatelli Ct West Islip NY 11795-2502 Office: Nassau Community Coll 1 Education Dr Garden City NY 11530-6719

ZIRKIND, RALPH, physicist; b. N.Y.C., Oct. 20, 1918; s. Isaac and Zicel (Lifshitz) Z.; m. Ann Goldman, Nov. 22, 1940; children: Sheila Zirkind Knopf, Elaine Zirkind Gorman, Edward I. B.S., CCNY, 1940; M.S., Ill. Inst. Tech., 1945; postgrad., George Washington U., 1946-47; Ph.D., U. Md., 1950; D.Sc., U. R.I., 1968. Physicist Navy Dept., 1945-50, chief physicist, 1951-60; physicist Oak Ridge Nat. Lab., 1950-51, Advanced Research Project Agy., Washington, 1960-63; prof. Poly. Inst. Bklyn., 1963-70, U. R.I., Kingston, 1970-72; adj. prof. U. R.I., 1972—; physicist Advanced Research Projects Agy., Arlington, Va., 1972-74; cons. Advanced Rsch. Projects Agy., and industry, Arlington, 1974—; lectr. U. Md., 1948-50, George Washington U., 1952-53, U. Mich., 1966; cons. ACDA, Jet Propulsion Lab., Calif. Inst. Tech. Contbg. author: Jet Propulsion Series, 1952, FAR Infrared Properties of Materials, 1968; editor: Electromagnetic Sensing of Earth, 1967; mem. editorial bd.: Infrared Physics, 1963—; contbr. articles profl. jours. Recipient Meritorious Civilian Svc. award Navy Dept., 1957, Meritorious Civilian Svc. award Dept. Def., 1970, Outstanding Educator of Am. medal, 1972, Maj. Contbn. award BMDO/AIAA, 1994. Mem. Am. Phys. Soc., N.Y. Acad. Scis., Sigma Xi, Sigma Pi Sigma, Eta Kappa Nu. Home: 820 Hillsboro Dr Silver Spring MD 20902-3202 Office: 4001 Fairfax Dr Ste 700 Arlington VA 22203-1618

ZIRKLE, LEWIS GREER, physician, executive; b. Pittsfield, Mass., July 23, 1940; s. Lewis Greer and Vivian (Shaw) Z.; m. Sara K. Zirkle, Aug. 24, 1963; children: Elizabeth, Molly, Julie. BS, Davidson Coll., 1962; MD, Duke U., 1966. Intern Duke U. Hosp., 1966-67, resident, 1968-73; resident U.S. Army, Shriner's Hosp., 1967-68; pvt. practice Richland, Wash., 1973—; bd. dirs. Orthopedics Overseas, chmn. program in Vietnam, 1992—. Contbr. articles to profl. jours. Maj. U.S. Army, 1968-73. Presbyterian. Avocations: reading, sports. Home: 2548 Harris Ave Richland WA 99352-1638 Office: NW Orthopedics 875 Swift Blvd Richland WA 99352-3513

ZIRSCHKY, JOHN H., federal government official; b. Fullerton, Calif., July 6, 1957; m. Natalie Ziegler; 2 children. BS in Civil Engring., U. Tenn.; MS in Engring., Utah State U.; PhD, Clemson U. Registered profl. engr., S.C. Rsch. asst. Utah Water Rsch. Lab. Utah State U., Logan, 1978-80; engr. Ecology & Environment, Inc., Kansas City, Kans., 1980-82, ERM-Southeast, Inc., Atlanta, 0984-89, Dames and Moore, Atlanta, 1989-90; rsch. engr. Clemson U., 1982-84; legis. asst. Office Sen. James M. Jeffords, Washington, 1990-93; profl. staff mem. Senate Com. Environment and Pub. Works, Washington, 1993-94; acting asst. sec., prin. dep. asst. sec. Dept. of Army, Washington, 1994—. Contbr. more than 40 articles to profl. pubs. Mem. ASCE, Water Environment Fedn., Pub. Water Supply Coun., Am. Water Works Assn., Sigma Xi, Tau Beta Pi, Chi Epsilon. Office: Dept of the Army Civil Works The Pentagon Washington DC 20310-0103

ZISCH, WILLIAM E., technical services executive. V. chmn. Science Applications Internat. Corp., San Diego. Office: Sci Applications Internat 10260 Campus Point Dr San Diego CA 92121-1522*

ZISCHKE, DOUGLAS ARTHUR, foreign service officer; b. Sioux Falls, S.D., May 24, 1929; s. Arthur Gustav and Alice Minetta (Wedeking) Z.; m. Janice Mae Kuehnemann, June 8, 1957; children: Mark Douglas, Deborah Jan, Todd Lincoln. B.S. in Journalism, U. Wis., 1951, M.S. cum laude, 1952. Joined U.S. Fgn. Svc., 1957; tech. editor Forest Svc., Madison, 1955-57; asst. info. officer USIS, Montevideo, Uruguay, 1957-58, La Paz, Bolivia, 1958-59; asst. cultural affairs officer, br. pub. affairs officer Mexico, 1960-65; info. specialist Washington, 1965-67; pub. affairs officer Tegucigalpa, Honduras, 1967-69; dep. pub. affairs officer Buenos Aires, Argentina, 1969-71; pub. affairs officer Guatemala, Guatemala, 1971-74; assigned to U.S. Army War Coll., 1974-75; dep. pub. affairs officer Am. embassy Tehran, Iran, 1975-78; cultural coord. USICA, Washington, 1979-80; internat. cons., 1980-86; fgn. affairs advisor State Dept., 1986—. Author monograph. Bd. dirs. Boy Scouts Am; dir. Lutheran Ch. 1973-74. Served with Signal Corps, AUS, 1953-55.

ZISKIN, LAURA, film producer. Co-founder Frogwood Films. Films include: (assoc. prodr.) Eyes of Laura Mars, 1978; (prodr.) Murphy's Romance, 1985, No Way Out, 1987, D.O.A., 1988, Everybody's An American, 1988, The Rescue, 1988, What About Bob?, 1991, The Doctor, 1991, Hero, 1992; (exec. prodr.) Pretty Woman, 1990; producer: To Die For, 1995. *

ZISMAN, BARRY STUART, lawyer; b. N.Y.C., Sept. 18, 1937; s. Harry and Florence Rita (Tucker) Z.; m. Maureen Frances Brumond, Dec. 30, 1979; children: Michael Glenn, Marlene Ann. AB, Columbia U., 1958, JD, 1961. Bar: D.C. 1962, N.Y. 1965, Tex. 1986, U.S. Dist. Ct. (ea. and so. dists.) N.Y. 1967, U.S. Ct. Appeals (D.C. cir.) 1967, U.S. Dist. Ct. (no. and so. dists.) Tex. 1986, U.S. Ct. Appeals (5th cir.) 1988, U.S. Supreme Ct. 1967. With U.S. Govt., 1962-66; pvt. practice Syosset, N.Y., 1966-71; sr. counsel CBS Inc., N.Y.C., 1972-75; asst. gen. counsel, asst. sec. M. Lowenstein & Sons, N.Y.C., 1975-79; gen. counsel Grumman Allied Indsl. Inc., Bethpage, N.Y., 1979-83; asst. gen. counsel Grumman Corp., Bethpage, 1982-83; sr. atty. FDIC, Dallas, 1984-87; of counsel Arter & Hadden, Dallas, 1987-88, ptnr., 1988; ptnr. Winstead, McGuire, Sechrest & Minick, Dallas, 1988-90, Arter & Hadden, Dallas and Washington, 1990-91, Rubinstein & Perry, Dallas, 1991-94, The Zisman Law Firm, P.C., Dallas, 1994—; advisor in field; vice-chmn. Assn. of Bank and Thrift Receivership Coun. Editor and author: Banks and Thrifts: Government Enforcement and Receivership Law, 1991. With U.S. Army, 1961-62. Home and Office: 905 Murl Dr Irving TX 75062-4441

ZISMAN, LAWRENCE S., internist; b. 1959. MD, Albert Einstein Coll. Medicine, 1987. Postdoctoral fellow U. Colo. Health Sci. Ctr. Recipient Clinician Scientist award Am. Heart Assn., 1995-96. Office: U Colo 5483 E Utah Pl Denver CO 80222-3948

ZISSMAN, LORIN, marketing research, consulting company executive; b. Phila., July 13, 1930; s. Charles Louis and Sarah (Axelman) Z.; m. Beverly Ann Zissman, June 23, 1957 (div. Sept. 1987); children: Nancy Zissman Peters, Jonathan, Eric, Amy; m. Carole Winokur, Oct. 16, 1988. BA, Temple U., 1951. Rsch. analyst Benson & Benson, Princeton, N.J., 1955-56; pres. Opinion Rsch. Corp., ORC Caravan Surveys, Princeton, 1956-69; v.p. Response Analysis Corp., Princeton, 1969-70; pres. Total Rsch., Inc., Princeton, 1970-75; pres. Total Rsch. Corp., Princeton, 1975-86, pres., chief exec. officer, 1986-93, chmn., chief exec. officer, 1993—. Mem. Am. Mktg. Assn. (chmn. standards and practices com. 1973-74), Coun. Am. Survey Rsch. Orgns., Am. Assn. Pub. Opinion Rsch., Am. Contract Bridge League, Princeton Community Players, Villagers Barn Theatre. Jewish. Avocations: theatre, softball, tennis, ping pong, bridge. Home: 7F Marten Rd Princeton NJ 08540-1634 Office: Total Rsch Corp Princeton Corp Ctr 5 Independence Way Princeton NJ 08540-6627

ZITO, JAMES ANTHONY, retired railroad company executive; b. Oak Park, Ill., Feb. 5, 1931; s. Bruno and Concetta (Kalasardo) Z.; m. Mary B. De Stasio, July 9, 1983; children: Antony, Antonia. Student, Elmhurst Coll., 1956-57; sr. exec. program, Stanford U., 1981. Sr. v.p. ops. Chgo. & North Western Transp. Co., 1976-90, also bd. dirs.; former chmn. A.A.R. Op. Transp. Co.; pres. Z&B Inc., Campbell St. R.E. Corp. With USCG, 1951-53. Mem. St. Charles Country Club, KC. Home: 1655 Persimmon Dr Saint Charles IL 60174-1328

ZITO, MICHAEL ANTHONY, advertising and graphics design typesetting company owner; b. San Diego, Feb. 25, 1957; s. Richard and Margaret Jane (Greggs) Z. Student, El Paso C.C., 1976-77, Grossmont Coll., 1977-78. Emergency med. technician E&E Ambulance Svc., Colorado Springs, Colo., 1972-73; psychiat. technician Alvarado Hosp., San Diego, 1975-78; surg. technician, orderly Eisenhower Osteopathic Hosp., Colorado Springs, 1973-75; mktg. mgr. Calif. Dept. Forestry Fire Fighters, San Diego, 1978-79; mktg. rep. Mort Fin. Svcs., San Diego, 1980-81, Mil.-Civil Svc. Yellow Pages, San Diego, 1983-84; nuclear technician San Onofre (Calif.) Nuclear Power Plant, 1982-83; mktg. rep. Stas. XPRS, XHRM, KMLO, 1982-84; pres. Discount Yellow Pages, San Diego, 1984-87, 3-D Advt. Graphics and Typesetting Co., San Diego, 1987—; nat. coord. Robbins Rsch. Internat., La Jolla, Calif., 1993-94. Actor TV documentary and movies, San Diego, 1987 (award Nat. Movie Arts Festival and Movies 1988). Instr. YMCA/USO, 1971-72. Recipient award Nat. Movie Arts Festival, 1988. Roman Catholic. Avocations: beekeeping, musician, snow skiing, swimming, photography.

ZITO, ROBERT JOHN AMADEUS, lawyer; b. N.Y.C., Sept. 11, 1956; s. Joseph J. and Phyllis A. (Esposito) Z.; m. Dana Sabine Cole, July 4, 1992. BA, Tulane U., 1978; JD, NYU, 1981. Bar: N.Y. 1985, U.S. Dist. Ct. (so. and ea. dists.) N.Y. 1983, (no. dist.) 1993, U.S. Ct. Appeals (2nd cir.) 1988, U.S. Tax Ct. 1984, U.S. Supreme Ct. 1988. Assoc. LaRossa Cooper, N.Y.C., 1981-85, Spengler Carlson, N.Y.C., 1985-90; ptnr. Zito & Assocs., N.Y.C., 1990-91, Sullivan Donovan, N.Y.C., 1991-93, Tanner Propp & Farber, N.Y.C., 1993—; advisor Ch. of Incarnation, N.Y.C., 1994. Maj. N.Y. Guard, 1991—. Recipient Bklyn. Achievement award The Bklyn. (N.Y.) Dems., 1994, N.Y. Guard Achievement medal, 1995. Mem. ABA, N.Y. Bar Assn., Fed. Bar Coun., Columbian Coun., Ancient Chpt. RAM, Holland Lodge F & AM, Knights Templar. Democrat. Episcopalian. Avocation: musical instruments. Office: Tanner Propp & Farber 99 Park Ave New York NY 10016

ZITRIN, ARTHUR, physician; b. Bklyn., Apr. 10, 1918; s. William and Lillian (Elbaum) Z.; m. Charlotte Marker, Oct. 4, 1942; children—Richard Alan, Elizabeth Ann. B.S., City Coll. N.Y., 1938; M.S., N.Y. U., 1941, M.D., 1945; certificate psychoanalytic medicine, Columbia, 1955. Diplomate: Am. Bd. Psychiatry and Neurology. Research fellow animal behavior Am. Museum Natural History, 1939-42; intern King County Hosp., 1945-46; resident psychiatry Bellevue Hosp., 1948-51; instr. physiology Hunter Coll., N.Y.C., 1948-49; mem. faculty N.Y.U. Sch. Medicine, 1949—, professor psychiatry, 1967—; mem. staff Bellevue Hosp., N.Y.C., 1951—; dir. psychiatry Bellevue Hosp., 1955-68, N.Y.C. Dept. Hosps., 1962- 64; pvt. practice, 1949—; attending psychiatrist Univ. Hosp., N.Y.C.; cons. psychiatrist Manhattan Va Hosp. Author papers in field. Served to capt., M.C. AUS, 1946- 48. Fellow Am. Psychiat. Assn. (life), N.Y. Acad. Medicine; mem. AMA, N.Y. Soc. Clin. Psychiatry (pres. 1966- 67), Am. Psychoanalytic Assn. (life), Sigma Xi, Alpha Omega Alpha. Home: 56 Ruxton Rd Great Neck NY 11023-1529 Office: 550 1st Ave New York NY 10016-6481

ZIV, ISRAEL, orthopedic surgeon; b. Tel Aviv, Israel, Nov. 23, 1948; came to U.S., 1990; s. Zvi and Yula-Yocheved (Maliniak) Z.; m. Liora Vardi, Sept. 25, 1969; children: Amir-Baruch, Dotan, Elad. MD, Hebrew U., Jerusalem, 1972; DSc, Technion, Haifa, Israel, 1989. Lic. physician, N.Y., Nebr, Israel; lic. orthopaedic surgeon, Israel; lic. Ednl. Coun. Fgn. Med. Grads. Intern Govt. Mcpl. Hosps., Tel Aviv, 1972-73; rsch. fellow Mt. Sinai Hosp., Toronto, Ont., Can., 1976; resident orthopedic surgery U. Toronto, 1976-81; clin. fellow Hosp. Sick Children, Toronto, 1981-82; orthopaedic surgeon Israel Def. Forces Rehab. Centre, Haifa, 1982-84; instr. dept. biomed. engring. Technion, Israel Inst. Tech., 1984; lectr., sr. lectr. orthopaedic surgery Hebrew U. and Hadassah Med. Sch., 1984-92; staff orthopaedic surgeon VA Med. Ctr., Buffalo, 1991-92, chief orthopaedic sect., 1992—; prof., dir. orthopaedic rsch. SUNY, Buffalo, 1990—; adj. prof. dept. biophysics SUNY, Buffalo, 1991—, dept. mech. engring., 1992—, dept. biomaterials Sch. Dentistry, 19936. Contbr. articles to profl. jours. Capt. Israel Def. Forces, 1973-76. Ralph Levitz fellow Technion, 1985; grantee Hebrew U. and Hadassah, 1985, Deborah Rosenlicht and Dorothy Sillman Fund for Osteoarthritis, 1986, VA, 1992-93, 94—, Johnson & Johnson Orthopaedics, 1992-93, Howmedica and Housler Assocs., Inc., 1993, The Whitaker Found., 1993-95. Fellow Royal Coll. Physicians and Surgeons (Can.); mem. Internat. Rsch. Soc. Orthopaedic Surgery and Traumatology, Ea. Orthopaedic Assn., Orthopaedic Rsch. Soc., Acad. Orthopaedic Assn., Israel Orthopaedic Soc., Acad. Medicine Toronto. Avocation: squash. Office: SUNY at Buffalo Dept Orthopaedic Surgery 162 Farber Ln Buffalo NY 14221-5754

ZIVARI, BASHIR, architect, industrial designer; b. Bklyn., Aug. 13, 1961; s. Farajollah and Ingeborg Elfriede (Brügmann) Z.; m. Pamela Lorraine Ray, Feb. 17, 1990. M Indsl. Design with distinction, Pratt Inst., 1991, BArch, 1984. Registered architect, N.Y. With Russo & Sonder Architects, N.Y.C., 1984-88; pvt. practice architecture, N.Y.C., 1988; asst. designer Lee Harris Pomeroy Architects, N.Y.C., 1988-91; project mgr. The Phillips Janson Group Architects, N.Y.C., 1991—. Designs in permanent collections of Mus. Modern Art, N.Y.C., Cooper-Hewitt Mus., N.Y.C.; patentee for modular stool. Recipient 2d place Shaw-Walker furniture competition, 1987; Roscoe awards for outstanding achievement in product design Interior Design mag., 1993, best of category award for children's furniture, 1993; gold award for consumer product Businessweek mag. and Indsl. Design Soc. Am., 1994. Mem. Baha'i Faith. Avocation: squash. Home: 309 Carroll St Brooklyn NY 11231-4901

ZIVLEY, WALTER PERRY, lawyer; b. Mineral Wells, Tex., Aug. 5, 1931; s. Walter Perry Sr. and Jane (Beeler) Z.; m. Nancy Campbell, Feb. 5, 1955; children: Bruce, Claire Zivley Baker, Lisa Zivley Trujillo, Walter Perry Jr. BBA, So. Meth. U., 1953, LLB, 1955. Bar: Tex. 1955, U.S. Dist. Ct. (so. and ea. dists.) Tex., U.S. Ct. Appeals (5th cir.), U.S. Tax Ct., U.S. Supreme Ct. Assoc. Hutcheson, Taliafeno and Hutcheson, Houston, 1955-62, ptnr., 1962; ptnr. Liddell, Sapp, Zivley, Hill and LaBoon L.L.P., Houston, 1963—; bd. dirs. Tex. Commerce Bank W. Ctrl., Houston. Pres. Open Door Mission Found., Inc., Houston, 1992. Fellow Am. Coll. Trust and Estate Coun.; mem. ABA, State Bar Tex. (real estate probate and trust sect., chmn. 1975-76), Houston Bar Assn. Republican. Presbyterian. Avocations: hunting, tennis, golf. Office: Liddell Sapp Zivley Hill and LaBo 3400 Tex Commerce Towers Houston TX 77002

ZIZIC, THOMAS MICHAEL, physician, educator; b. Milw., Dec. 9, 1939; s. Michael Mitchell Zizic and Dorothy (Batas) Ciric; m. Karen Owens, June 15, 1962 (div. Sept. 1967); m. Martha Ann Ardos, Nov. 22, 1967; children: Lara Ann, Kristine Michelle. BS, U. Wis., 1961; MD, Johns Hopkins U., 1965. Intern Johns Hopkins Hosp., Balt., 1965-66, asst. resident, 1966-67, fellow in internal medicine, 1969-71, instr. dept. medicine, 1971-73, asst. prof. medicine, 1971-81, assoc. prof. medicine, 1981—; pvt. practice, Balt., 1988—; co-dir. Chesapeake Osteoporosis Ctr., Balt., 1988—; dir. med. affairs Murray Electronics, 1993—; v.p. med. quality care Physicians Quality Care, 1995—; pres. U.S. Osteoporosis Network, Inc., 1996—; cons. in field. Contbr. numerous articles and abstracts to profl. jours. V.p. Md. chpt. Arthritis Found., Balt., 1976-77; chmn. Md. Commn. on Arthritis and Related Diseases, 1986-90. Fellow Am. Coll. Rheumatology, 1986; Md. Soc. Rheumatic Diseases (pres. 1975-76), D.C. Rheumatism Assn., Balt. City Med. Soc., Johns Hopkins Hosp. Med. Soc., Arthritis Found. (fellow 1971-73, v.p. 1976-77, med. and sci. com. 1977-79, chmn. profl. edn. com. 1977-78, govtl. affairs com. 1979-83), Phi Beta Kappa, Phi Kappa Phi, Phi Eta Sigma. Avocations: skiing, tennis. Office: 5601 Loch Raven Blvd Baltimore MD 21237 *Give 100% today. We have only the present. Plan for the future but don't live inthe future. The future never comes. We have only today.*

ZIZZA, SALVATORE J., diversified company executive; b. Francofonte, Italy, Nov. 19, 1945; came to U.S., 1956; s. Carmelo and Gregoria (Mazzarino) Z.; m. Deborah Ann Bright, Sept. 24, 1983; children: Robert Carl, Gregory Thomas, Christopher John. B.A. in Polit. Sci., St. John's U., 1967, M.B.A., 1972. Asst. mgr. Chem. Bank, N.Y.C., 1967-71; asst. sec. Am. Bank & Trust Co., N.Y.C., 1972-73; pres. Mortgagee Affiliates, N.Y.C., 1973-78; owner, pres. Zizza & Co. Ltd., N.Y.C., 1978—; pres., chief operating officer, dir. Nico, Inc., N.Y.C., 1978—, Lehigh Group Inc., N.Y.C., 1985—; chmn. Initial Acquisition Corp., The Bethlehem Corp.; dir. Gabelli, Equity-Growth-Asset Funds, Multimedia and Convertible Securities. Bd. govs. Columbus Citizens Com., N.Y.C., 1980; bd. dirs. Nat. Italian Am. Found., Washington, 1986. Mem. Young Mortgage Bankers Assn., Real Estate Bd. of N.Y., Young Pres. Orgn. Roman Catholic. Avocations: skiing; tennis; reading.

ZIZZO, ALICIA, concert pianist; b. N.Y.C., Apr. 2, 1945; d. Spiro and Christine (Corda) Theodoratos; m. Thomas Edward Zizzo; children: Peter, Claudia. BA, Hofstra U., 1965; postgrad., C.W. Post U., 1975, L.I. U., 1976, Mannes Coll. Music. performed Eastern Europe; lectr. in field. Debut as concert pianist N.Y.C.; performed in major concert halls throughout Europe, named as one of the great Am. pianists in the world; one of few Am. artists invited to perform by Ea. Bloc countries Europe; discovered lost manuscripts of George Gerswhin's classical music; first pianist to record George Gershwin's Rhapsody in Blue and Concerto in "F" from orignial manuscripts; recorded reconstructed fragments of lost George Gershwin manuscipts of Lullaby and original piano score of his opera Blue Monday; created first authentic version of Preludes and Rhapsody in Blue, Warner Bros. Publs., 1995, Gershwin/21220 Edits.; feature artist Vienna and other major internat. concert series and symphony orchs.; recordings for Pro-Arte Records, Fanfare Records, Mastersound Records; music publ. by Warner Bros. Publs.; recordings include Virtuoso Piano Fantasies-Works by Chopin, The Gershwin Manuscripts, Picwick Internat. Records, London, Debussy, et. al. Address: care Jeffrey James Arts Cons 316 Pacific St Massapequa Park NY 11762 Office: Jeffrey James Arts Consulting 316 Pacific St Massapequa Park NY 11762-1807 Office: c/o Allegro Imports 12630 NE Mary St Portland OR 97230-1059

ZLATKIS, ALBERT, chemistry educator; b. Pomorzany, Poland, Mar. 27, 1924; came to Can. 1927, U.S., 1949, naturalized, 1959; s. Louis and Zisel (Nable) Z.; m. Esther Shessel, June 15, 1947; children: Debra, Lori, Robert. B.A.Sc., U. Toronto, 1947, M.A.Sc., 1948; Ph.D., Wayne State U., 1952. Rsch. chemist Shell Oil Co., Houston, 1953-55; asst. prof. chemistry U. Houston, 1955-58, assoc. prof., 1958-63, chmn. chemistry dept., 1958-62, prof. chemistry, 1963—; adj. prof. chemistry Baylor Coll. Medicine, 1975—; tour speaker Am. Chem. Soc., 1961, 63, 66, South Africa Chem. Inst., 1971, USSR Acad. Scis., 1973, Polish Acad. Scis., 1977; chmn. Internat. Symposium on Advances in Chromatography, 1963—. Author: Practice of Gas Chromatography, 1967, Preparative Gas Chromatography, 1971, Advances in Chromatography, 25 vols., 1963-88, A Concise Introduction to Organic Chemistry, 1973, High Performance Thin-Layer Chromatography, 1977, 75 Years of Chromatography—A Historical Dialogue, 1979, Instrumental HPTLC, 1980, Electron Capture—Theory and Practice in Chromatography, 1981; contbr. articles to profl. jours.; mem. editorial bd. Jour. High Resolution Chromatography, Jour. Chromatograpic Science, Chromatographia, Jour. Chromatography. Recipient Analyst of Yr. award Dallas Soc. Analytical Chemistry, 1977, Tswett Meml. medal USSR Acad. Scis., 1980, Tswett Chromatography medal, 1983, NASA Tech. award, 1975, 80, NASA Patent award, 1978, Disting. Tex. Scientist award Tex. Acad. Sci., 1985, James L. Waters Pioneers in Devel. Analytical Instrumentation award, 1990; grantee USPHS, 1966, NASA, 1964-76, Welch Found., 1969, AEC, 1967, NSF, 1978, EPA, 1979, U.S. Army Rsch. Office, 1982, Gulf Coast Hazardous Substance Rsch. Ctr., 1989, Tex. Advanced Rsch. Program, 1991. Mem. Am. Chem. Soc. (chmn. S.E. Tex. sect. 1964, award in chromatography 1973, S.W. regional award 1988), Groupement pour l'Avancement des Méthodes Spectrographiques (France), Sigma Xi, Phi Lambda Upsilon. Home: 22 Sandalwood Dr Houston TX 77024-7122

ZLATOFF-MIRSKY, EVERETT IGOR, violinist; b. Evanston, Ill., Dec. 29, 1937; s. Alexander Igor and Evelyn Ola (Hill) Z.-M.; m. Janet Dalbey, Jan. 28, 1976; children from previous marriage—Tania, Laura. B.Mus., Chgo. Mus. Coll., Roosevelt U., 1960; M.Mus., Roosevelt U., 1961. Mem. faculty dept. music Roosevelt U., Chgo., 1961-66; founding mem., violinist, violist Music of the Baroque, 1971—. Violinist orch. Lyric Opera of Chgo., 1974—; concert master, pers. mgr., 1974—, violinst, violist, Contemporary Chamber Players U. Chog., 1964-82, solo violinist, Bach Soc., 1966-83; violist, violinist, Lexington String Quartet, 1966-81; rec. artist numerous recs., radio-TV and films; solo violinist appearing throughout U.S. Recipient Olive Ditson award Franklin Honor Soc., 1961. Mem. Nat. Acad. Rec. Arts and Scis. Republican. Roman Catholic. Home: 41 W 743 Hughes Rd Elburn IL 60119 Office: Lyric Opera Chgo 20 N Wacker Dr Chicago IL 60606-2806

ZLATOPER, RONALD JOSEPH, career officer; b. Cleve., Mar. 21, 1942; s. Joseph M. and Ann Rose (Bayda) Z.; m. Barry Lane Oliver, Aug. 8, 1970; children: Ashley D., Michael J. BS in Math., Rensselaer Poly. Inst., 1963; MSA, George Washington U., 1970; MS in Mgmt., MIT, 1975. Commd. ensign USN, 1963, advanced through grades to admiral, 1994; disting. grad.

Naval War Coll., Newport, R.I., 1973; program coord. Office of Chief of Naval Ops., Washington, 1975-77; comdg. officer Attack Squadron 85, Naval Air Sta., Oceana, Va., 1978-81; exec. asst. Office of Program Appraisal, Sec. of Navy, Washington, 1981-82; comdr. Airwing One on USS America, Norfolk, Va., and Indian Ocean, 1982-83; mil. asst. to Sec. Def. Office of Sec. Def., Washington, 1983-85; Airwing comdr. Carrier Airwing 15, San Diego and Indian Ocean, 1986-87; chief of staff U.S. 7th Fleet, Yokosuka, Japan, 1987-88; dir. distbn. Naval Mil. Pers. Command, Washington, 1988-90; comdr. Carrier Group 7, San Diego and Persian Gulf, 1990-91; chief of naval pers. Bur. Pers., Washington, 1991-94; comdr.-in-chief U.S. Pacific Fleet, 1994—. Contbr. articles on naval strategy to profl. jours. Bd. dirs. Ptnrs. in Edn., Navy Pers. Command, Washington, 1988-90, Armed Forces Retirement Home, Washington, 1991-94, Navy Marine Corps Relief Soc., Washington, 1991-94; vol. So Others Might Eat, Washington, 1988-90; nominating chair U.S. Naval Inst., 1993-94; exec. coun. Boy Scouts Am., 1994—; bd. dirs. Hawaii Red Cross, 1994—; active Honolulu Coun. on Fgn. Rels., 1994—, Honolulu-Pacific Fed. Exec. Bd., 1994—. Decorated D.F.C., D.S.M., Legion of Merit with two oak leaf clusters, Meritorious Svc. medal. Mem. Assn. Naval Aviation, Naval Inst., Pi Kappa Phi (treas. 1963). Roman Catholic. Avocations: reading, running, basketball, skiing, tennis. Home: 37 Makalapa Dr Honolulu HI 96818-3110 Office: 250 Makalapa Dr Honolulu HI 96818

ZLOCH, WILLIAM J., federal judge; b. 1944. Judge U.S. Dist. Ct. (so. dist.) Fla., Ft. Lauderdale, 1985—. Office: US Dist Ct 299 E Broward Blvd Fort Lauderdale FL 33301-1944

ZLOTOLOW-STAMBLER, ERNEST, real estate executive, architectural executive; b. Buenos Aires, Sept. 27, 1943; came to U.S., 1981; m. Laura I. Chotti; children: Dan A., Vanessa E., Paul J. BA, Buenos Aires Nat. Coll., 1960; cert. architecture, U. Buenos Aires, 1968. Lic. architect; registered profl. engr., Argentina. Prof. U. Buenos Aires, 1964-81; mng. ptnr. Zlotolow, Chotti & Assocs., Buenos Aires, 1968-81; pres. Imparsa Corp., Buenos Aires, 1970-86; mng. ptnr. Archeting Assocs., Buenos Aires, 1970-81; prof. U. Belgrano, Buenos Aires, 1976-80; v.p. Playa de la Gruta Corp., Montevideo, Uruguay, 1976-78; project mgr. Kravco Corp., King of Prussia, Pa., 1981-84; chmn. Zlotolow-Evantash-Reider Ltd., Southeastern, Pa., 1985—; pres. Meridian Real Corp., Wayne, Pa., 1985—, U.S.E.S. Corp., 1989—; gen. ptnr., One Jenkintown (Pa.) Sta. Assocs., 1984-89. Contbr. articles to profl. publs. Paul Harris fellow, 1987, Guy Gundaker fellow, 1990, Paul Vaughan fellow, 1991. Mem. AIA, Urban Land Inst., Nat. Trust Historic Preservation, Pa. Soc. Architects, Sociedad Ctrl. Arquitectos (Argentina), Rotary (pres. 1990-91, chmn. charitable found. 1990-91), Gundaker Found. (bd. dirs. 1992—, v.p. 1996—), Green Hills Landowners Assn. (bd. dirs. 1994—). Avocations: boating, macroeconomics, computer science. Office: Meridian Real Corp PO Box 623 Southeastern PA 19399-0623

ZLOWE, FLORENCE MARKOWITZ, artist; b. Allentown, Pa.; d. Morris and Anna (Mandel) Markowitz; m. Irwin Zlowe, May 1, 1936. Student, Pa. Mus. Coll. Art, Phila., 1929-33; fine arts courses, NYU, 1950-53. One woman show, Charles Z. Mann Gallery, N.Y.C., 1968, Community Gallery, N.Y.C., 1978; exhibited in group shows, Nat. Acad., Riverside Mus., N.Y., Nat. Arts Club, Pen and Brush Club, Lever House, Jersey City Mus., Norfolk (Va.) Mus., Fort Lauderdale (Fla.) Mus., Joe and Emily Lowe Mus., Fla.; represented in permanent collections, Norfolk Mus., Fort Lauderdale Mus., Joe and Emily Lowe Mus., Wilson Pub. Co., N.Y.C., Phila. Mus. Art, Butler Inst. Am. Art, Minn. Mus. Art, St. Paul, Cooper-Hewitt Mus. Design, Smithsonian Instn., N.Y.C., Tweed Mus., Duluth, Minn., Evansville (Ind.) Mus., Lakeview (Ill.) Center Arts and Scis., Ga. Mus. Art, Athens, Slater Meml. Mus., Norwich, Conn. Mem. Am. Soc. Contemporary Artists (dir., treas.), N.J. Soc. Painters and Sculptors, Nat. Assn. Women Artists (1st prize ann. 1958, 12 additional awards for oils 1958-84), League Present Day Artists, Artists Equity Assn. N.Y. Home: 440 E 57th St New York NY 10022-3045 Studio: 41 Union Sq W New York NY 10003-3208

ZOBACK, MARK DAVID, geophysicist, educator; b. N.Y.C., Apr. 13, 1948; s. Larry and Minnie (Greenberg) Z.; m. Mary Lou Chetlain, Sept. 15, 1973; children: Eli Matthew, Megan Lacey. BS, U. Ariz., 1969; MS, Stanford U., 1973, PhD, 1975. Geophysicist Amoco Prodn. Co., Ft. Worth, Tex., 1969-71; rsch. geophysicist U.S. Geol. Survey, Menlo Park, Calif., 1975-84; prof. geophysics Stanford (Calif.) U., 1984—, chair dept., 1992—; chair coord. com. Continental Sci. Drilling, 1990—; cons. in field. Editor 4 books; patentee in field; contbr. articles to profl. jours. Postdoctoral fellow Nat. Rsch. Coun., 1975; recipient Sr. Sci. award von Humboldt Found., 1991. Fellow AAAS, Geol. Soc. Am.; mem. Am. Geophys. Union (pres. techondophysics sect. 1989-90). Home: 716 Garland Dr Palo Alto CA 94303-3603 Office: Stanford U Dept Geophysics Mitchell Bldg Stanford CA 94305

ZOBEL, DONALD BRUCE, botany educator; b. Salinas, Calif., July 17, 1942; s. Bruce John and Barbara June (Lemon) Z.; m. Priscilla Fay Matthews, July 9, 1966; children: Cheryl, Gregory. BS, N.C. State U., 1964; MA, Duke U., 1966, PhD, 1968. Asst. prof. Oreg. State U., Corvallis, 1968-74, assoc. prof., 1974-82, prof., 1982—; vis. rschr. Taiwan Forestry Rsch. Inst., Taipei, 1976-77; Fulbright lectr. Tribhuvan U., Kathmandu, Nepal, 1984-85; Indo-Am. fellow, Kumaun U., NainiTal, India, 1991. Author: Ecology, Pathology and Management of Port-Orford-cedar (Chamaecyparis lawsoniana), 1985, A Practical Manual for Ecology, 1987; contbr. articles to profl. jours. Grantee NSF, 1974-77, 80-84, 94—. Mem. AAAS, Ecol. Soc. Am., NW Sci. Assn. (trustee 1980-83), Internat. Assn. for Ecology, Brit. Ecol. Soc. Republican. Mem. Christian Ch. Home: 2310 NE Seavy Cir Corvallis OR 97330-4231 Office: Oreg State U Dept Botany & Plant Pathol 2082 Cordley Hall Corvallis OR 97331-2902

ZOBEL, HILLER BELLIN, judge; b. N.Y.C., Feb. 23, 1932; s. Hiller and Harriet Selma (Bellin) Z.; m. Deborah Bethell, June 21, 1958; children—John H., David H., Elizabeth T., Sarah B.; m. Rya S. Weickert, Nov. 23, 1973. B.A. cum laude, Harvard U., 1953, LL.B., 1959; postgrad., Oxford U., 1956. Bar: Mass. 1959, U.S. Ct. Appeals 1960, U.S. Dist. Ct. 1960, U.S. Supreme Ct. 1966. Assoc. firm Bingham, Dana & Gould, Boston, 1959-67; research assoc. Harvard U., 1962-63; assoc. prof. Boston Coll. Law Sch., 1967-69, prof., 1969-79; assoc., counsel firm Hill & Barlow, Boston, 1971-72; partner, counsel firm Brown, Rudnick, Freed & Gesmer, Boston, 1972-79; assoc. justice Mass. Superior Ct., 1979—; reporter Mass. Advisory Com. on Rules of Civil Procedure; spl. asst. atty. gen. Commonwealth of Mass.; spl. counsel Mass. Dept. Pub. Utilities. Author: The Boston Massacre, 1970, 96, (with J.W. Smith) Massachusetts Rules of Practice, 1974-81, (with S.N. Rous) Doctors and the Law, 1993; editor: (with L.K. Wroth) Legal Papers of John Adams, 1965; contbr. articles to profl. jours. Served with U.S. Navy, 1953-55. Recipient Am. Hist. Assn. Littleton-Griswold prize, 1966. Fellow Soc. Am. Historians; mem. Am. Law Inst., Mass. Hist. Soc., Colonial Soc. Mass., Am. Antiquarian Soc., Mass. Bar Assn., Boston Bar Assn., Maritime Law Assn. U.S., Am. Soc. Legal History (v.p. 1970-71), Nat. Conf. State Trial Judges (exec. com. 1990-93). Democrat. Jewish. Office: Superior Ct Boston MA 02108

ZOBEL, LOUISE PURWIN, author, educator, lecturer, writing consultant; b. Laredo, Tex., Jan. 10, 1922; d. Leo Max and Ethel Catherine (Levy) Purwin; m. Jerome Fremont Zobel, Nov. 14, 1943; children: Lenore Zobel Harris, Janice A., Robert E., Audrey Zobel Dollinger. BA cum laude, Stanford U., 1943, MA, 1976. Cert. adult edn. and community coll. tchr., Calif. Freelance mag. writer and author Palo Alto, Calif., 1942—; writer, editor, broadcastor UP Bur., San Francisco, 1943; lectr. on writing, history, travel No. Calif., 1964—; lectr., educator U. Calif. campuses, other colls. and univs., 1969—; writing cons. to pvt. clients, 1969—; editorial asst. Assn. Coll. Unions Internat., Palo Alto, 1972-73; acting asst. prof. journalism San Jose State U., 1976; keynote speaker, seminar leader, prin. speaker at nat. confs. Author: (books) The Travel Writer's Handbook, 1980, (paperback), 1982, 83, 84, 85, rev. edit., 1992; author, narrator (90 minute cassette) Let's Have Fun in Japan, 1982; contbr. articles to anthologies, nat. mags. and newspapers; writer advertorials. Bd. dirs., publicity chair Friends of Palo Alto Libr., 1985—; officer Santa Clara County Med. Aux., Esther Clark Aux., others; past pres. PTA. Recipient award for excellence in journalism Sigma Delta Chi, 1943, awards Writers Digest, 1967-75, 94, Armed Forces Writers League, 1972, Nat. Writers Club, 1976. Mem. Am. Soc. Journalists and Authors, Travel Journalists Guild, Internat. Food, Wine and Travel Writers Assn., Pacific Asia Travel Assn., Calif. Writers Club (v.p. 1988-89), AAUW (v.p. 1955-57, Nat. writing award 1969), Stanford Alumni Assn., Phi Beta Kappa. Avocations: travel, reading, writing, photography. Home and Office: 23350 Sereno Ct Unit 30 Cupertino CA 95014-6543

ZOBEL, ROBERT LEONARD, state government official; b. Reedsburg, Wis., July 28, 1935; s. Leonard Walter and Kathryn Jennifer (Cleveland) Z.; m. Faith Minnie Weatherwax, Aug. 5, 1961; children: Karl, Paul, Mary. BS in Fin., U. N.D., 1961. Investment banker Loewi & Co., Milw., 1961-65; bank examiner State of Wis., Madison, 1965-68, dir. investment bd., 1968—; mem. adv. bd. Merrill Lynch Capital, N.Y.C., Madison Fund, Boston, Zell/Chillmack, Chgo., Hancock Internat., Boston, Horizon Ptnrs., Milw.; mem. stockholder rep. bd. Burdick, Milton/Madison, A.C. Equipment, Milw.; bd. dirs. Trak Internat., Port Washington, Pa Vera, Madison; presenter nat. and internat. profl. assns., seminars, others. Mem. owners' com. Olympia Resort, Oconomowoc, Wis.; coach youth soccer, Baseball and basketball orgns.; lay min. area United Meth. Ch.; participant mission projects, including ch. bldg., Vulcain, Costa Rica, Rio Claro, Costa Rica, Prince Town, Trinidad, Portsmouth, Dominica, hosp. and sch. rehab., Bo, Sierra Leone, Maua, Kenya, Santa Cruz, Bolivia, Cochabamba, Bolivia, Gomay, St. Vincent; vol. Salvation Army. With USN, 1956-58. Mem. Elks. Avocations: mission work, golf, tennis, reading, public speaking. Home: 5312 Healy Ln Monona WI 53716-2519 Office: Wis Investment Bd 121 E Wilson St Madison WI 53703-3455

ZOBEL, RYA WEICKERT, federal judge; b. Germany, Dec. 18, 1931. A.B., Radcliffe Coll., 1953; LL.B., Harvard U., 1956. Bar: Mass. 1956, U.S. Dist. Ct., Mass., 1956, U.S. Ct. Appeals (1st cir.) 1967. Assoc. Hill & Barlow, Boston, 1967-73; assoc. Goodwin, Procter & Hoar, Boston, 1973-76, ptnr., 1976-79; U.S. dist. judge of Mass. Boston, 1979—; dir. Fed. Jud. Ctr., Washington, 1994—. Mem. ABA, Boston Bar Assn., Am. Bar Found., Mass. Bar Assn., Am. Law Inst. Office: Fed Judicial Ctr Thurgood Marshall Fed Bldg One Columbus Cir NE Washington DC 20002

ZOBELL, KARL, lawyer; b. La Jolla, Calif., Jan. 9, 1932; s. Claude E. and Margaret (Harding) ZoB.; m. Barbara Arth, Nov. 22, 1968; children: Bonnie, Elizabeth, Karen, Claude, Mary. Student, Utah State U., 1949-51, Columbia U., 1951-52; AB, Columbia U., 1953, student of law, 1952-54; JD, Stanford U., 1958. Bar: Calif., 1959. Assoc., lawyer Gray, Cary, Ames and Frye, San Diego, 1959-64, ptnr., lawyer, 1964—, chmn., 1989-90; dir., officer San Diego Digital Multimedia Assn., San Diego, 1994; bd. dirs., founder La Jolla (Calif.) Bank and Trust Co.; v.p. bd. dirs. Geisel-Seuss Enterprises, Inc. Trustee La Jolla Town Coun., 1962-87, chmn. bd. trustees, 1967-68, pres. 1976-77, 80-81, v.p., 1986-87; trustee La Jollans Inc., 1964-80, founder, 1964, pres. 1965-68, 73-76, 78-79, Dr. Seuss Found., 1992—, James C. Copley Charitable Found., 1992—; mem. charter rev. com. City San Diego, 1968, 73; chmn. City of San Diego Planning Commn., 1988-93; trustee La Jolla Mus. Art, 1964-72, San Diego Mus. Contemporary Art, 1990-92; pres. 1967-70, bd. dirs Scripps Meml. Hosp. Found., 1980-84, bd. overseers, Stanford Law Sch., 1977-80, U. Calif., San Diego, 1974-76. Served to lt. USCG, 1954-57. Fellow Am. Coll. Trust and Estate Counsel; mem. ABA, Calif. Bar, La Jolla Beach and Volleyball Club (pres. 1982—), La Jolla Beach and Tennis Club, Lambda Alpha. Republican. Home: Po Box 1 1555 Coast Walk La Jolla CA 92037-3731 Office: Gray Cary Ames & Frye 1200 Prospect St Ste 575 La Jolla CA 92037-3608

ZOBRIST, BENEDICT KARL, library director, historian; b. Moline, Ill., Aug. 21, 1921; s. Benedict and Lila Agnas (Colson) Z.; m. Donna Mae Anderson, Oct. 23, 1948; children: Benedict Karl II, Markham Lee, Erik Christian. AB, Augustana Coll., Rock Island, Ill., 1946; postgrad., Stanford U., 1946-47; MA, Northwestern U., 1948, PhD, 1953; postgrad., U. Ill., 1961, Tunghai U., Taiwan, 1962, Columbia U., 1962-63, Fed. Exec. Inst., Charlottesville, Va., 1974, Hebrew U., Israel, 1978; LHD, Avila Coll., 1995. Manuscript specialist in recent Am. history Library of Congress, Washington, 1952-53; asst. reference librarian Newberry Library, Chgo., 1953-54; command historian Ordnance Weapons Command, Rock Island Arsenal, 1954-60; prof. history, chmn. dept. Augustana Coll., 1960-69, asst. dean faculty, 1964-69, assoc. dean, dir. grad. studies, 1969; asst. dir. Harry S. Truman Libr., Independence, Mo., 1969-71; dir. Harry S. Truman Libr., 1971-94; exec. sec. Harry S. Truman Libr. Inst., Independence, 1971-94; mem. steering com. Harry S. Truman Statue Com., Independence, 1973-76; dir., regent Harry S. Truman Good Neighbor Award Found., 1974—; mem. Independence Truman Award Commn., 1975-94, Mo. Hist. Records Adv. Bd., 1978—; adj. prof. history U. Mo.-Kansas City, 1975—, Ottawa U., Kansas City, 1977-94, U. Mo. St. Louis, 1987-94; chmn. Independence Commn. Bicentennial of U.S. Constitution, 1987, Uptown Independence, Inc., 1989-94; mem. adv. coun. Truman Little White House State Historic Site, Key West, Fla., 1987-94. Contbr. articles, revs. to profl. jours. Trustee Heritage League of Greater Kansas City, 1981—, Liberty Meml. Assn., Kansas City, Mo., 1990—, Black Archives Mid-Am., Inc., Kansas City, 1992-94; mem. Truman Nat. Centennial Com., 1982-84. Served with AUS, 1942-46. Recipient Outstanding Alumni Achievement award Augustana Coll., 1975, Bronze Good Citizenship medal Kans. SAR, 1986, People's Choice award Independence (Mo.) Neighborhood Councils, 1987, Mid-Am. Regional Council award for contbns. to met. community, 1987, Citizen Achievement award Black Archives of Mid-Am., 1988, Silver Good Citizenship medal Mo. SAR, 1988, Special Recognition award City of Independence, 1988, Outstanding Civic Leader in Independence, 1989, Gold Medal of Honor DAR, 1990, Spl. Commendation award Nat. Park Svc., 1993; named World Citizen of Yr. by Kans. City Mayor's UN Day Com., 1994. Mem. AAUP, Am. Hist. Assn., Jackson County (Mo.) Hist. Soc. (v.p. 1972-82, 93-95), Orgn. Am. Historians, Assn. Asian Studies, Am. Assn. State, Local History, Soc. Am. Archivists, U.S. Power Squadron, Am. Legion, La Societe des 40 Hommes et 8 Chevaux, VFW. Home: 71B T St Lake Lotawana MO 64086-9728

ZOBRIST, GEORGE WINSTON, computer scientist, educator; b. Highland, Ill., Feb. 13, 1934; s. George H. and Lillie C. (Augustin) Z.; m. Freida Groverlyn Rich, Mar. 29, 1955; children: Barbara Jayne, George William, Jean Anne. B.S., U. Mo., 1958, Ph.D., 1965; M.S., Wichita State U., 1961. Registered profl. engr., Mo., Fla. Electronic scientist U.S. Naval Ordnance Test Sta., China Lake, Calif., 1958-59; research engr. Boeing Co., Wichita, 1959-60; instr. Wichita State U., 1960-61; assoc. prof. U. Mo., Columbia, 1961-69, U. So. Fla., Tampa, 1969-70; chmn. elec. engring. dept. U. Miami, Coral Gables, Fla., 1970-71; prof. U. South Fla., Tampa, 1971-72, 73-76; prof., chmn. dept. elec. engring. U. Toledo, 1976-79; dir. computer sci. and engring. Samborn, Steketee, Otis, Evans, Inc., Toledo, 1979-82; prof. computer sci. Grad. Engring. Ctr. U. Mo.-Rolla, St. Louis, 1982-85; prof. computer sci. U. Mo., Rolla, 1985—, chmn. dept., 1994—; rsch. prof. U. Edinburgh, Scotland, 1972-73; lectr. U. Western Cape, South Africa, 1995 summer; cons. Wilcox Electric Co., Bendix Corp., both Kansas City, Mo., 1966-68, ICC, Miami, 1970-71, Def. Comm. Agy., Washington, 1971, 72, U.S. Naval Rsch. Labs., Washington, 1971, Med. Svc. Bur., Miami, 1970-71, NASA, Kennedy Space Ctr., Fla., 1973-76, 88, 89, 93, 94, Prestolite Corp., Toledo, 1977-79, IBM, Lexington, Ky., 1983-86, Wright-Patterson AFB, Ohio, 1986, PAFB, Fla., 1987, McDonnell Douglas, Mo., 1989, Digital Systems Cons., Mo., 1989, Oak Ridge Nat. Labs., 1992. Author: Network Computer Analysis, 1969, Progress in Computer Aided VLSI Design, 1988-90; editor: Internat. Jour. Computer Aided VLSI Design, 1989-91, Object Oriented Simulation IEEE Press, 1996, Computer Sci. and Computer Engring. Monograph series, 1989-91, Internat. Jour. of Computer Simulation, 1990—, VLSI Design, 1992—; contbr. articles to profl. jours. Served with USAF, 1951-55. Named Young Engr. of Yr. ctrl. chpt. Mo. Soc. Profl. Engrs., 1967; NSF summer fellow, 1962, 64; NASA, IBM, DOE, UES/AFOSR, McDonnell Douglas rsch. grantee, 1967-88. Mem. IEEE (sr.), Soc. Computer Simulation, Am. Legion, Rotary, Sigma Xi, Tau Beta Pi, Phi Eta Sigma, Eta Kappa Nu, Pi Mu Epsilon, Upsilon Pi Epsilon. Home: 12030 Country Club Dr Rolla MO 65401-7469 Office: U Mo-Rolla Dept Computer Sci Rolla MO 65409

ZOCHOLL, STANLEY ERNEST, electronics executive; b. Phila., July 23, 1929; s. Hugo Ernest and Elsa Elizabeth (Peterson) Z.; m. Edith Ruth Wolf, Aug. 23, 1952; children: Susan Louise, Joanne Edith, Carol Lynn. BSEE, Drexel U., 1958, MSEE, 1973. Various positions ITE Cir. Breaker Co., Phila., 1955-69; sr. devel. engr. Gould-Brown Boveri, Phila., 1969-81; protection engr. BBC Brown Boveri, Horsham and Allentown, Pa., 1981-87; dir. tech. Westinghouse ABB Power T&D Co. (name changed to ABB Power T&D Co., Inc. 1989), Allentown, 1987-91; disting. engr. Schweitzer Engring. Labs., 1991—. Patentee in field. Fellow IEEE (power system relay com. 1985—, instr. seminars 1988-89, Best Paper award Trans. 1988). Home and Office: 71 E Rambler Dr Southampton PA 18966-2034

ZODHIATES, SPIROS GEORGE, association executive; b. Cyprus, Mar. 13, 1922; came to U.S., 1946, naturalized, 1949; s. George and Mary (Toumazou) Z.; m. Joan Carol Wassel, Jan. 10, 1948; children: Priscilla Zodhiates Barnes, Lois Zodhiates Jenks, Philip, Mary. Student, Am. U., Cairo, 1941-45; B.Th., Shelton Coll., 1947; M.A., N.Y. U., 1951; Th.D., Luther Rice Sem., 1978. Ordained to ministry Gen. Assn. Regular Baptist Chs., 1947; gen. sec., now pres. Am. Mission to Greeks (name changed to AMG Internat. 1974), Chattanooga, N.J., 1946—; pres. Am. Mission to Greeks (name changed to AMG Internat. 1974), 1965—. Author: numerous Bible-study books and booklets including Behavior of Belief, 1959, the Pursuit of Happiness, 1966, To Love is to Live, 1967, Getting the Most Out of Life, 1976, Life After Death, 1977, Hebrew Greek Key Study Bible, 1984, Complete Word Study New Testament, 1991 (Gold Medallion 1993), Complete Word Study Dictionary: New Testament, 1992, Complete Word Study Old Testament, 1994; editor in chief: (Greek) Voice of the Gospel, 1946, Pulpit and Bible Study Helps, 1975—. Served with Brit. Army, 1943-46. Recipient Gold Cross Greek Red Cross, 1951; decorated Order Brit. Empire. Home: 8927 Villa Rica Cir Chattanooga TN 37421-1506 Office: AMG Internat 6815 Shallowford Rd Chattanooga TN 37421-1755

ZOELLER, DONALD J., lawyer; b. Queens Village, N.Y., Mar. 18, 1930; s. Henry Adolph and Marion Elizabeth (Brodie) Z.; m. Susan Josephine Campisi, Sept. 3, 1955; children—Paul Joseph, Jean Marie, Diane Marie. A.B., Fordham Coll., 1951; LL.B., Fordham Sch. Law, N.Y.C., 1958. Bar: N.Y. 1959, D.C. 1967. Law clk. to judge U.S. Dist. Ct. (so. dist.) N.Y., N.Y.C., 1958-59; assoc. Mudge Rose Guthrie Alexander & Ferdon, N.Y.C., 1959-68, ptnr., 1968-95, exec. ptnr., 1991-95; chmn. exec. com. Mudge Rose Guthrie Alexander & Ferndon, N.Y.C., 1995; chmn. liquidation com. Carter, Ledyard & Milburn, N.Y.C., 1995—, counsel, 1995—; chmn. liquidation com. Mudge, Rose, Genturel, Alexander & Ferdon, N.Y.C., 1995—, counsel, 1995—; adj. prof. law Fordham U. Law Sch., 1989—; lectr. in field. Contbr. articles to legal publs. 1st lt. U.S. Army, 1951-53, Korea. Mem. ABA, N.Y. State Bar Assn., Bar Assn. City of N.Y., Nassau County Bar Assn., Inst. Jud. Adminstrn., Am. Judicature Soc. Republican. Roman Catholic. Avocations: skiing; swimming; tennis; reading. Office: Carter Ledyard & Milburn Alexander & Ferdon 2 Wall St New York NY 10005 *Notable cases include: Matsushita Electric Indsl. co. Ltd. et al vs. Zenith Radio Corp. et al, 475 U.S. 574, 89 L. edit. 2d 538, 106, s.ct. 1438.*

ZOELLER, FUZZY, professional golfer; b. New Albany, Ind., 1952. Professional golfer, 1973—; PGA tour victories include San Diego Open, 1979, Masters, 1979, Colonial Nat., 1981, Heritage Classic, 1983, U.S. Open, 1984, Bay Hill Classic, 1985, AT&T Pro Am., 1986, Heritage Classic, 1986, Anheuser-Busch Classic, 1986. Office: care PGA Tour Ponte Vedra Beach FL 32082*

ZOELLER, JACK CARL, financial executive; b. Buffalo, Feb. 26, 1949; s. Ronald Carl and Margaret Lillian (Wademan) Z.; m. Kathryn Louise Helmke, Apr. 25, 1981; children: Andrew, Alexander, Charles (dec.). BS, U.S. Mil. Acad., 1970; M of Pub. Policy, Harvard U., 1972; M of Letters, Oxford (Eng.) U., 1974. Program budget officer Army Chief of Staff's Office, Pentagon, Washington, 1978-80; v.p. E.F. Hutton & Co., Inc., N.Y.C., 1982; pres. E.F. Hutton Indemnity Group, N.Y.C., 1983-85, Capital Risk Mgmt., Iselin, N.J., 1985-87; exec. v.p., bd. dirs. Comfed Mortgage Co., Lowell, Mass., 1987-88, pres., 1988-91; pres. ComFed Savs. Bank, Lowell, 1990-91; chmn. chief exec. officer ComFed Bancorp., Cambridge, Mass., 1990-95; pres. The Zoeller Group, Washington, 1993—; bd. dirs. N.Am. Health Plans, Inc., Amherst, N.Y., 1995—; pres. N.Am. Fin. Corp., 1995—. Mem. exec. com. Lowell Devel. and Fin. Corp., 1989-91, class gift com. U.S. Mil. Acad., 1990—; youth sports coach, 1990—. Served to Capt. U.S. Army, 1970-80. Decorated Meritorious Svc. medals; Rhodes scholar Oxford U., 1972. Mem. West Point Soc. N.Y. (bd. govs. 1985-87), West Point Soc. D.C., Fed. Nat. Mortgage Assn. (N.E. regional adv. bd. 1990-91), New Eng. Hist. Geneal. Soc., Soc. Mayflower Descs. Home: 2810 31st St NW Washington DC 20008-3523 Office: North Am Fin Corp 1919 Gallows Rd Ste 900 Vienna VA 22182

ZOELLER, JANICE L., magazine editor; b. N.Y.C., Apr. 12, 1954; d. Albert S. Jr. and Betty (Hurley) Bagley; m. William A. Zoeller, Oct. 14, 1989; 1 child, Jacqueline Ann. BA, Queens Coll., 1977; MBA, N.Y. Inst. Tech., 1983. Editor Dental Lab. Rev., Harcourt Brace Jovanovich, N.Y.C., 1977-81; sr. editor Am. Druggist, Hearst Corp., N.Y.C., 1981-92, editor-in-chief, 1995—; editor Supermarket Pharmacy, Fairchild Publs., N.Y.C., 1992-95. Mem. N.Y. Bus. Press Editors (pres. 1986-89). Lutheran. Avocation: scuba diving. Office: Hearst Corp 1790 Broadway New York NY 10019

ZOELLICK, ROBERT BRUCE, corporate executive, lawyer; b. Evergreen Park, Ill., July 25, 1953; s. William T. and Gladys (Lenz) Z.; m. Sherry Lynn Ferguson, June 28, 1980. BA with honors, Swarthmore Coll., 1975; M Pub. Policy, JD magna cum laude, Harvard U., 1981. Bar: D.C. 1981. Spl. asst. to asst. atty. gen. criminal div. U.S. Dept. Justice, Washington, 1978-79; pvt. practice law, 1981-82; law clk. to Judge Patricia M. Wald, U.S. Ct. Appeals for D.C. Cir., Washington, 1982-83; v.p., asst. to chmn. and chief exec. officer of bd. Fannie Mae, Washington, 1983-85; from spl. asst. to Dep. Sec., Dep. Asst. Sec. for Fin. Instns. Policy, to counselor to sec. and exec. sec. U.S. Treasury Dept., Washington, 1985-88; dir. campaign isues George Bush for Pres., Washington, 1988; counselor of Dept. with rank under sec. U.S. Dept. State, Washington, 1989-92, under sec. for econ. and agrl. affairs, 1991-92; dep. chief of staff, asst. to Pres. White House, Washington, 1992-93; exec. v.p., gen. counsel Fannie Mae, Washington, 1993—. Decorated Knight Comdr.'s Cross (for work on German unification, Germany); recipient Alexander Hamilton award U.S. Treasury Dept., 1988, Disting. Svc. award U.S. State Dept, 1992; fellow Luce Found., Hong Kong, 1980. Mem. D.C. Bar Assn., Phi Beta Kappa.

ZOELLNER, JAMIE L., critical care nurse; b. Cumming, Ga., Sept. 18, 1963; d. James H. and Reba (Mills) Z. AS and AA with honors, Polk Community Coll., 1989; BSN with honors, U. Fla., 1993; MSN, Duke U., 1994. RN, CCRN, Fla., N.C., S.C.; cert. ACLS, adult NP, critical care CNS. Staff nurse surg. ICU Lakeland (Fla.) Regional Med. Ctr., 1988-95; nurse practitioner cardiothoracic surg. svcs. GSRMC, Myrtle Beach, S.C., 1995—. Mem. ACCN, SCCM, Sigma Theta Tau, Phi Kappa Phi.

ZOELLNER, ROBERT WILLIAM, chemistry educator; b. Marshfield, Wis., May 30, 1956; s. Willard Rudolph and Marie Martha (Prihoda) Z.; m. Barbara Moore, Feb. 5, 1983; children: Joan Moore, Thaddeus Barak. BS, St. Norbert Coll., De Pere, Wis., 1978; PhD, Kans. State U., 1983. Postdoctoral assoc. Cornell U., Ithaca, N.Y., 1983-84; vis. scientist U. Aix-Marseille (France) III, 1984-85; asst. prof. No. Ariz. U., Flagstaff, 1986-92, assoc. prof., 1992—; sabbatical assoc. Istituto per lo Studio della Stereochimica Consiglio Nazionale delle Ricerche, 1994-95. Mem. AAAS, Am. Chem. Soc., Internat. Coun. on Main Group Chemistry, N.Y. Acad. Scis., N.D. Acad. Sci., Wis. Acad. Sci., Arts and Letters, Sigma Xi, Alpha Chi Sigma, Phi Lambda Upsilon. Office: No Ariz U Dept Chemistry PO Box 5698 Flagstaff AZ 86011-5698

ZOFFER, H. JEROME, business educator, university dean; b. Pitts., July 23, 1930; s. William and Sarah Leah (Fisher) Z.; m. Maye Rattner, July 19, 1959; children: Gayle Risa, William Michael. BBA, U. Pitts., 1952, MA, 1953, PhD, 1956; CPCU, Am. Inst., Phila., 1954. Sales and mgmt. cons., 1952-60; instr. Sch. Bus. Adminstrn., U. Pitts., 1953-56; asst. prof. Sch. Bus. Adminstrn. U. Pitts., 1956-59, assoc. prof. Joseph M. Katz Grad. Sch. Bus., 1959-66, prof. Sch. Bus. Adminstrn., Grad. Sch. Bus., 1966—, chmn. dept. real estate and ins., 1958-60, dir. spl. studies, 1960-62, asst. dean for acad. affairs, 1962-65, assoc. dean for adminstrn., 1965-68, dean Grad. Sch. Bus., 1968—; bd. dirs. Pennwood Savs. Bank, Homestate Pa. Growth Fund, The Enterprise Corp.; Ford Found. fellow in applied math. U. Pa., Phila., 1961-62; mem. visitation com. Am. Assembly Collegiate Schs. of Bus., 1972-96, mem. standards com., 1974-78, mem. exec. com., 1975-87, chmn. accreditation rsch. com., 1974-84, v.p. bd. dirs., 1984-85, pres., 1985-86, chmn. Mid. State Evaluation Accrediting Teams, 1967-85. Author: The History of Automobile Liability Insurance Rating: 1900-1958, 1959; also monographs.; contbr. articles to profl. jours. Bd. dirs., v.p. Leadership Inst. for Community Devel., 1968-73, Allegheny chpt. Epilepsy Found. Am., 1971-77; bd. dirs. Pitts. Dist. Export Coun., 1974-77; bd. govs. Internat. Ins. Seminars, Inc., 1968-77; pres. Temple Sinai Congregation, 1979-81; mem. festival bd. Three Rivers Art Festival, 1988-93; mem. steering com. Leadership Pitts., 1986-91; sec. Am. Jewish Com., 1993-95; bd. dirs. Student Cons. Project, U. Pitts., 1970-96, Consortium for Coop. and Competitiveness, 1986-96, Moral Force in the Workplace, 1986-96; investment com. United Jewish Fedn., 1992-95. Named Man of Yr. in Edn., Vectors Pitts., 1986, Disting. Alumnus, 1989, U. Pitts. Alumni Assn. Mem. Soc. Psychol. Study Social Issues, Mid. Atlantic Assn. Colls. Bus. Adminstrn. (pres. 1972-73), Am. Assn. Univ. Adminstrs. (exec. com. 1971-79, pres. 1975-77, dir. 1980-83, pres. found. 1983-95), Univ. Club (bd. dirs. 1988-94, sec. 1990-91, v.p. 1991-92, pres. 1992-93), Omicron Delta Gamma, Beta Gamma Sigma (pres. Beta chpt. 1964-68). Home: 5620 Aylesboro Ave Pittsburgh PA 15217-1402 Office: U Pitts Pitts Campus Katz Grad Sch Bus Pittsburgh PA 15260

ZOGHBY, GUY ANTHONY, lawyer; b. Mobile, Ala., Sept. 30, 1934; s. Herbert Michael and Laurice (Haik) Z.; m. Verna Madelyn Antoine, Mar. 2, 1957 (dissolved); children: Guy Anthony II, Madelyn A., Gregory M.; m. Judy-ann EcKberg, Jan. 2, 1976. AB in English, Spring Hill Coll., 1955; JD, U. Cin., 1963; cert., U.S. Army JAG Sch., 1964. Bar: Ohio 1963, Ala. 1965, Calif. 1978, Pa. 1988. Commd. 2d lt. U.S. Army, 1955, advanced through grades to capt., 1963, various assignments, 1955-63; dep. staff JAG 11th Air Assault Div., Ft. Benning, Ga., 1963-64, 1st Cav. Div., 1964-65; atty. office of v.p. and gen. counsel IBM, Armonk, N.Y., 1965-67, staff atty., 1967-69, sr. atty., 1969-71; regional counsel IBM, Bethesda, Md., 1972-73; corp. staff counsel IBM, London, 1973-77; div. counsel IBM, Armonk, N.Y., 1977-80, mng. atty., 1980-83, group counsel, from 1983; now v.p., gen. counsel PPG Industries Inc., Pitts.; v.p., gen. counsel, 1987-93; sr. v.p., gen. counsel PPG Industries Inc., Pitts., 1994—; lectr. profl. seminars. Editor U. Cin. Law Rev., 1962-63. Bd. dirs. Allegheny A.R.C., 1989—, Am. Judicature Soc., 1988—, pres. 1993-95; bd. dirs. Assn. Gen. Counsel, 1987, Pitts. Civic Light Opera, 1992—; Am. Law Inst., 1992—, The Duquesne Club, 1988; mem. bd. visitors U. Cin. coll. Law, 1986—. Decorated Commendation medal with one oak leaf cluster; recipient Lawrence Maxwell prize U. Cin. Mem. Am. Corp. Counsel Assn. (cir. 1982—, exec. com. 1982-88, chmn. 1987—), Order of Coif. Roman Catholic. Office: PPG Industries Inc 1 Ppg Pl Pittsburgh PA 15272-0001

ZOGRAFI, GEORGE, pharmacologist, educator; b. N.Y.C., Mar. 13, 1936; married; 4 children. BS, Columbia U., 1956; MS, U. Mich., 1958, PhD in Pharm. Chemistry, 1961; DS (hon.), Columbia U., 1976. Asst. prof. pharmacology Columbia U., N.Y.C., 1961-64; from asst. prof. to assoc. prof. U. Mich., Ann Arbor, 1964-72; rsch. fellow Am. Found. Pharm. Edn., 1970-71; Pheiffer rsch. fellow Utrecht (The Netherlands) U., 1970-71; prof. pharmacology U. Wis., Madison, 1972—, dean, 1975-80. Mem. AAAS, NAS (Inst. Medicine), Am. Pharm. Assn. (Ebert prize 1984), Am. Chem. Soc., Am. Assn. Pharm. Scientists, Internat. Pharm. Fedn., Internat. Assn. Colloid and Interface Scientists, Am. Inst. Hist. Pharm., Sigma Xi. Office: U Wis Sch Pharmacology 425 N Charter St Madison WI 53706*

ZOHDI, MAGD ELDIN, engineering educator; b. Cairo, Apr. 18, 1933; came to U.S., 1964, naturalized, 1971; s. Ismail Abdella and Nemat (Rizk) Z.; diploma Cairo U., 1954, B.S., 1962; M.S., U. Kan., 1965; Ph.D., Okla. State U., 1969; m. Omnia Elmenshawy, Sept. 17, 1964; children—Tarek, Mona. With Maintenance Machinery, Cairo, 1954-60; instr. Cairo U., 1962-64; grad. teaching asst. Okla. State U., Stillwater, 1966-69; asso. prof. La. State U., Baton Rouge, 1969-75, prof., 1977-95; pres. Am. Contracting and Trading Corp., Baton Rouge, 1978, Quality Contracting Inc.; mem. U.S. Engrng. Adv. Com. to State of Qatar. Fulbright scholar, 1964; recipient Excellence in Undergrad. Teaching award Standard Oil Found., 1971; Presdl. Honor award Okla. State U., 1968; Outstanding Educators of Am. award 1972; Disting. Faculty fellow La. State U. Sys., 1985. Mem. Soc. Mfg. Engrs., Am. Inst. Indsl. Engrs., Am. Mil. Engrs., Sigma Xi, Tau Beta Pi. Contbr. articles to profl. jours., chpts. to tech. textbooks. Achievements include application of mathematical programming for optimization of air to ground gunnery design and effectiveness. Home: 5050 S Chalet Ct Baton Rouge LA 70808-4839 Office: La State Univ 3132 Cedar Ave Bldg Baton Rouge LA 70805-7877

ZOHN, HARRY, author, educator; b. Vienna, Austria, Nov. 21, 1923; came to U.S., 1940, naturalized, 1945; s. Abraham Leon and Adele (Awin) Z.; m. Judith Ann Gorfinkle, Sept. 3, 1962; children: Steven David, Marjorie Eve. BA, Suffolk U., Boston, 1946; MA in Edn., Clark U., 1947; AM, Harvard U., 1949, PhD, 1952; LittD (hon.), Suffolk U., 1976. Credit investigator Credit Bur. Greater Boston, 1941-46; tchg. fellow in German Harvard U., 1947-51; mem. faculty Brandeis U., 1951—, prof. German, 1967—, chmn. dept. Germanic and Slavic langs., 1967-77, 87-90, chmn. Sch. Humanities coun., 1978-79, chmn. grad. program in lit. studies, 1981-84; exec. dir. Goethe Soc. New England, 1963-68. Author: Wiener Juden in der deutschen Literatur, 1964, Karl Kraus, 1971, German edit., 1990, Jüdisches Erbe in der österreichischen Literatur, 1986, Amerikanische, "Thirty-Eighters" aus Wien als doppelte Kulturträger, 1994, Austriaca and Judaica, 1995; editor: Liber Amicorum Friderike Zweig, 1952, Wie sie es sehen, 1952, Schachnovelle, 1960, Men of Dialogue, 1969, Der farbenvolle Untergang, 1970, Greatness Revisited, 1971, Deutschland, Deutschland über alles, 1972, The Saints of Qumran, 1977, Germany?, Germany!, 1990, Aus dem Tagebuch eines Emigranten, 1992; transl. books by Theodor Herzl, Kurt Tucholsky, Karl Kraus, Jacob Burckhardt, Walter Benjamin, Gershom Scholem, Alex Bein, Andrè Kaminski, Fritz Molden, Manès Sperber, Hermann Langbein, others; mem. editl. bd. Modern Austrian Lit., Cross Currents; gen. editor (series) Austrian Culture. Mem. adv. com. fgn. langs. Commonwealth Mass., 1961-64; trustee Suffolk U., 1978-81, 83—. Decorated officer's cross Order Merit (Fed. Republic Germany) 1960; Cross of Honor for Sci. and Art (Republic of Austria) 1984; Gold Medal of Honor, City of Vienna, 1994; recipient Art prize Wolfgang Altendorf Cultural Found., 1991. Mem. Am. Assn. Tchrs. German (pres. Mass. chpt. 1954-59), Am. PEN Ctr., Austro-Am. Assn. Boston (chmn. bd. dirs. 1965—), Internat. Stefan Zweig Soc. (v.p. 1957-90), Internat. Arthur Schnitzler Assn. (v.p. 1978—), Austrian PEN Club, Internat. Franz Werfel Soc. (chmn. bd. dirs. 1995—), PEN Ctr. German-Speaking Writers Abroad, New Eng. MLA (past sec.-treas., chmn. Mass. chpt., bd. dirs.). Home: 48 Davis Ave Newton MA 02165-1924 Office: Brandeis U Shiffman Hall Waltham MA 02254-9110

ZOHN, MARTIN STEVEN, lawyer; b. Denver, Oct. 22, 1947; s. William and Alice (Lewis) Z.; m. Carol Falender, June 6, 1980; children: David Joseph, Daniel Robert. BA, Ind. U., 1969; JD, Harvard U., 1972. Bar: Calif. 1972, Ind. 1973, U.S. Ct. Claims 1980, U.S. Supreme Ct. 1980, U.S. Ct. Appeals (9th cir.) 1981. Assoc. Cadick, Burns, Duck & Neighbors, Indpls., 1972-77, ptnr., 1977-80; ptnr. Pacht, Ross, Warne, Bernhard & Sears, Inc., L.A., 1980-86, Shea & Gould, L.A., 1986-89, Proskauer Rose Goetz & Mendelsohn, L.A., 1989—; pres. Indpls. Settlements, Inc., 1977-79. Mem. Fin. Lawyers Conf., L.A. County Bar Assn. (exec. com. prejudgment remedies sect. 1985-92), Beverly Hills Bar Assn. (exec. com. bus. law sect. 1985-92), Phi Beta Kappa.

ZOHNY, A. Y., law educator, business educator, consultant, international development consultant; b. Cairo, May 13, 1946; s. Younis Zohny and Dawlat Hussein; m. Patricia Trobian, Aug. 20, 1983; 1 child, Josephine. BS, El Shorta Acad., Cairo, 1969; LLB, Ain Shams U., Cairo, 1969; MA in Political Sci., Bloomsburg U., 1976; PhD in Pub. and Internat. Affairs, U. Pitts., 1984. Assoc. prof. European Divsn. U. Md., Heidelberg, West Germany, 1987-88; assoc. prof. bus. adminstrn., dir. Inst. for Internat. Devel. & Strategic Studies Southeastern U., Washington, D.C., 1988-90; prof. bus. law and bus. adminstrn. Strayer Coll., Washington, D.C., 1990—; CEO, pres. Middle East Devel. Sci. Inst., Hanover, Md., 1992—; faculty assoc. Johns Hopkins U., Balt., 1994—; sr. advisor Ednl. Mission Embassy of Saudi Arabia, Washington, D.C., 1985-86; internat. devel. cons. World Bank MSDA. Author: (book) Politics, Economics and Dynamics of Development Administration, 1988. Recipient scholarship Bloomsburg U., 1975-76; fellow U. Pitts., 1979-84. Mem. Congress of Political Economists, Acad. of Management. Democrat. Avocations: swimming, horseback riding. Office: Strayer Coll Alexandria Campus 2730 Eisenhower Ave Alexandria VA 22314

ZOIS, CONSTANTINE NICHOLAS ATHANASIOS, meteorology educator; b. Newark, Feb. 21, 1938; s. Athanasios Konstantinos and Asimina (Speros-Blekas) Z.; m. Elyse Stein, Dec. 26, 1971; children: Jennifer, Jonathan. BA, Rutgers U., 1961; MS, Fla. State U., 1965; PhD, Rutgers U., 1980. Draftsman Babcock and Wilcox Corp., Newark, 1956; designer Foster Wheeler Corp., Carteret, N.J., 1956; instr. Rutgers U., New Brunswick, N.J., 1961-62; grad. asst. Fla. State U., Tallahassee, 1962-65; rsch. meteorologist Nat. Weather Svc., Garden City, L.I., N.Y., 1965-67; prof. Kean Coll. N.J., Union, 1967—; founder meteorology program Kean Coll., N.J.; cons. Connell, Foley and Geiser, Roseland, N.J., 1986-88; chmn. Kean Coll. All-Coll. Promotion com., 1991-93. Author, editor: Papers in Marine Science, 1971; author: Observation of the Newark N.J. Nocturnal Heat Island and Its Consideration in Terms of a Physical Model, 1980, Dynamical and Physical Oceanography, 1988, Atmospheric Dynamics: Exercises and Problems, 1988, Climatology Workbook, 1988, Weather Map Folio, 1989; contbg. author: Outcomes Assessment at Kean College of N.J., 1992, Synoptic Meterology-Exercises and Readings, Vols. 1-3, 1995. Mem. AAAS, Nat. Weather Assn., Am. Meteorol. Soc. (pres. N.J. chpt. 1980-81), N.Y. Acad. Scis. (vice chmn. atmospheric scis. sect. 1986-87, chmn. 1987-88, adv. com. atmospheric sci. sect., 1988—), N.J. Marine Scis. Consortium, Phi Beta Kappa. Republican. Greek Orthodox. Avocations: guitar, banjo, fishing, baseball, snorkeling. Home: 2798 Carol Rd Union NJ 07083-4831 Office: Kean Coll of NJ Dept Meterology Morris Ave Union NJ 07083-7117 *I tried!.*

ZOLA, GARY PHILLIP, religious educational administrator, rabbi,; b. Chgo., Feb. 17, 1952; m. Stefani Paula Rothberg; children: Amanda Roi, Jorin Benjamin, Jeremy Micah, Samantha Leigh. BA in Am. History with distinction, U. Mich., 1973; MA in Counseling Psychology, Northwestern U., 1976; PhD in Am. Jewish History, Hebrew Union Coll., Cin., 1991. Ordained rabbi, 1982. Dir. informal edn. and youth activities Temple Israel, Mpls., 1973-74; regional youth dir., asst. camp dir. Olin-Sang-Ruby Union Inst., UAHC, Chgo., 1974-77; student pulpit B'nai Israel Congregation, Williamson, W.Va., 1978-79; mem. student pulpit Anshe Sholom Congregation, Olympia Fields, Ill., 1979-80, Columbus Hebrew Congregation, Columbus, Ind., 1981-82; rabbi for high holy days Chgo. Jewish Experience, Chgo., 1982—; nat. dir. admissions Hebrew Union Coll.-Jewish Inst. Religion, Cin., 1982-89, nat. dean admissions and student affairs, 1989-91, nat. dean admissions, student affairs and alumni rels., 1991—; del. Emerging Leaders Conf., Am. Coun. for Internat. Leadership, 1989, 91; bd. dirs. Am. Jewish Com., Cin., 1982—, mem. exec. com., 1984—; bd. dirs. Hillel U. Cin., 1991—, Jewish Fedn., Cin., 1993—; pres. Greater Cin. Bd. Rabbis, 1993—, Jewish Cmty. Rels. Coun., (bd. dir.,1994—); founding mem. Kehillah of Cin., Jewish Think Tank. Author: Isaac Harby of Charleston, 1994; editor: Hebrew Union College--Jewish Institute of Religion--A Centennial History, 1875-1975, (Michael A. Meyer), 1992, Women Rabbis: Exploration and Celebration, 1996; contbr. numerous scholarly articles to profl. jours.; mem. editl. bd. Reform Judaism. bd. dirs. ethics com. Jewish Hosp., Cin.; life mem. N.Am. Fedn. Temple Youth; active NCCJ. Mem. Ctrl. Conf. Am. Rabbis, Orgn. Am. Historians, Assn. Jewish Studies, So. Jewish Hist. Soc., Am. Jewish Hist. Soc., N.Am. Fedn. Temple Youth (life). Office: Hebrew Union Coll Jewish Inst Religion 3101 Clifton Ave Cincinnati OH 45220-2404

ZOLBER, KATHLEEN KEEN, nutrition educator; b. Walla Walla, Wash., Dec. 9, 1916; d. Wildie H. and Alice (Johnson) Keen; m. Melvin L. Zolber, Sept. 19, 1937. BS in Foods and Nutrition, Walla Walla Coll., 1941; MA, Wash. State U., 1961; PhD, U. Wis., 1968. Registered dietitian. Dir. food service Walla Walla Coll., 1941-50, mgr. coll. store, 1951-59, asst. prof. food and nutrition, 1959-62, assoc. prof., 1962-64; assoc. prof. nutrition Loma Linda (Calif.) U., 1964-72, prof. nutrition, 1973-91, dir. dietetic edn., 1967-84, dir. dietetics Med. Ctr., 1972-84, dir. nutrition program, 1984-91; retired. Mead Johnson grantee, 1965-67; recipient Alumna of Yr. award Walla Walla Coll., 1977; Delores Nyhus award Calif. Dietetic Assn., 1978. Mem. Am. Dietetic Assn. (pres. 1982-83, Copher award 1992), Am. Pub. Health Assn., AAUP, Omicron Nu, Delta Omega. Home: PO Box 981 Loma Linda CA 92354-0981

ZOLL, PAUL MAURICE, cardiologist; b. Boston, July 15, 1911; s. Hyman and Molly (Homsky) Z.; m. Janet F. Jones, Oct. 28, 1939; children—Ross Holman, Mary Janet; m. Ann Blumgart Gurewich, Jan. 2, 1981. A.B. summa cum laude, Harvard, 1932, M.D., 1936. Intern Beth Israel Hosp., Boston, then Bellevue Hosp., N.Y.C., 1936-39; practice medicine, specializing in cardiology Boston, 1939-94; med. research Beth Israel Hosp., 1939—, asst. in medicine to physician, 1947—; med. research Harvard Med. Sch., 1939—, research fellow in medicine to clin. prof. medicine, 1941—; cons. cardiology Boston hosps. Assoc. editor: Circulation, 1956-65; contbr. articles to med. jours. Served from 1st lt. to maj. M.C. AUS, 1941-45. Decorated Legion of Merit; recipient John Scott award City of Phila., 1967; Eugene Drake Meml. lectr. and award Maine Heart Assn., 1968; 1st Wenckebach Meml. lectr. Groningen, Netherlands, 1973; Albert Lasker award for clin. med. research, 1973; Polytechnic/Wunsch award in biomed. engrng., 1980; Tex. Heart Inst. medalist and Ray C. Fish awardee, 1981; Paul Dudley White award Mass. Heart Assn., 1985; named Man of Year Boston Latin Sch., 1974, Pioneer in Cardiac Pacing and Electrophysiology, N.Am. Soc. Pacing and Electrophysiology, 1989, medal Cardiostim Soc., 1990. Mem. Mass. Med. Soc., Am. Heart Assn. (award of merit 1974, 92), Am. Fedn. Clin. Research, Assn. Am. Physicians, N.Am. Soc. Pacing and Electrophysiology, Internat. Cardiac Pacing Soc., Phi Beta Kappa, Sigma Xi. Pioneer electric cardiac pacemaker, 1952, cardiac monitor, 1955, external countershock defibrillator, 1956. Home: 261 Brookline St Newton Centre MA 02159-3139 Office: Beth Israel Hosp 330 Brookline Ave Boston MA 02215-5400

ZOLLAR, JAWOLE WILLA JO, art association administrator; b. Kansas City, Kans., Dec. 21, 1950; d. Alfred Jr. and Dorothy Delores Zollar; 1 child, Elizabeth Herron. BA in Dance, U. Mo., Kansas City, 1975; MFA in Dance, Fla. State U., 1979. Faculty Fla. State U., Tallahassee, 1977-80; artistic dir. Urban Bush Women, N.Y.C., 1984—. Recipient N.Y. Dance and Performance award, 1992; named Outstanding Alumni U. Mo.-Kansas City, 1993; Mankato State U. Worlds of Thought Resident scholar, 1994; Nat. Endowment of Arts Choreography fellow, 1992, 93, 94. Mem. Dance U.S.A., Assn. of Am. Cultures, Internat. Assn. of Blacks in Dance. : 339 15th St Brooklyn NY 11215 Office: Urban Bush Women 225 Lafayette St Ste 201 New York NY 10012 Also: care IMG Artists 22 E 71st St New York NY 10021-4911

ZOLLAR, NIKKI MICHELE, state agency administrator; b. Chgo., June 18, 1956; d. Lowell M. and Doris J. (Lowe) Z.; m. William A. Von Hoene, Jr., June 18, 1983; children: William Lowell Von Hoene, Branden Tracey. BA, Johns Hopkins U., 1977; JD, Georgetown U., 1980. Fed. jud. law clk. U.S. Dist. Ct. (no. dist.) Ill., Chgo., 1980-81; assoc. Lafontant, Wilkins, Jones & Ware, Chgo., 1981-83, Kirkland & Ellis, Chgo., 1983-85; chmn., sec. Chgo. Bd. Election Commrs., 1987-90; dir. Ill. Dept. Profl. Regulation, Chgo., 1991—. Trustee Cmty. Youth Creative Learning Experience; mem. women's coun. Chgo. Hear Assn.; mem. Chgo. com. Solidarity with So. Africa; mem. women's bd. Jackson Park Hosp. (award); active Chgo. Urban League, Nat. Coalition of 100 Black Women. Recipient outstanding achievement award YWCA, Washington Park YMCA, youth svc. bd. Beatrice Caffrey Found., David C. Hilliard award Chgo. Bar Assn., 1988-89, Kizzy award Revlon Corp./Kizzy Scholarship Fund, African Am. Women's Achievement award Columbia Coll., Martin Luther King Jr. award for dedicated leadership Boy Scouts Am., outstanding young profl. award Chgo. Urban Profls., svc. and leadership award United Negro Coll. Fund, outstanding achievement cert. Ill. State Atty. Appellate Svc. Commn., African Am. history maker award Gov. Jim Edgar; named one of 100 outstanding black bus. and profl. women in U.S. Dollars and Sense mag. Mem. Ill. Women in Govt., Women Execs. in State Govt., Alpha Gamma Pi. Mem. United Ch. of Christ. Avocation: long distance running. Office: Ill Dept Profl Regulation 320 W Washington St Springfield IL 62786

ZOLNO, MARK S., lawyer. BA Polit. Sci., No. Ill. Univ., 1965; JD, John Marshall Law Sch., 1978; MA cum laude Internat. Rels., Universidad de las Américas, Mexico, 1974. Bar: Ill. 1978, U.S. Dist. Ct. (no. dist.) Ill. 1979, U.S. Ct. Internat. Trade 1979, U.S. Ct. Appeals (fed. cir.) 1979. With U.S. Customs Svc., Dept. Commerce, U.S. Trade Rep's. Office, Internat. Trade Commn., Fed. Trade Commn., FDA; ptnr. Katten Muchin & Zavis, Chgo., 1988—; past chmn. Chgo. Bar Assn. Customs and U.S. Trade Law Com.; lectr. in field. Contbr. articles to profl. jours. Office: Katten Muchin & Zavis 525 W Monroe St Ste 1600 Chicago IL 60661-3629

ZOLOMIJ, ROBERT WILLIAM, landscape architect, consultant; b. Phila., Oct. 13, 1942; s. William and Anna (Sikacz) Z.; m. Joanne M. Volk, Oct. 2, 1965; children: Nancy Lyn, Christopher John; m. Nancy S. Helfferich, Nov. 21, 1992. BS in Landscape Architecture, Pa. State U., 1965; M Landscape Architecture, U. Ill., 1971. Lic. landscape arch., Ill. Site planner Bucks County Planning Commn., Doylestown, Pa., 1965-67; assoc. prof. U. Ill., Urbana, 1968-78; sr. landscape arch. Skidmore Owings & Merrill, Chgo., 1978-79; sr. assoc. Barton-Aschman Assocs., Evanston, Ill., 1979-84; v.p. Harland Bartholomew Assocs., Northbrook, Ill., 1984-86; ptnr. Land Design Collaborative, Inc., Evanston, 1986—. Co-author: Time Saver Standards for Landscape Architects, 1988. Univ. fellow U. Ill., 1967. Fellow Am. Soc. Landscape Archs. (chpt. treas. 1986-88, v.p. 1988-90, pres. 1990-92). Avocations: golf, travel, reading, woodworking. Home: 3429 Harrison St Evanston IL 60201-4953 Office: Land Design Collaborative 1563 Sherman Ave Evanston IL 60201-4421

ZOLOTOW, CHARLOTTE SHAPIRO, author, editor; b. Norfolk, Va., June 26, 1915; d. Louis J. and Ella F. (Bernstein) Shapiro; m. Maurice Zolotow, Apr. 14, 1938 (div. 1969); children: Stephen, Ellen. Student, U. Wis., 1933-36. Editor children's book dept. Harper & Row, N.Y.C., 1938-44; sr. editor Harper & Row, 1962-70; v.p., assoc. pub. Harper Jr. Books, 1976-81; editorial cons., editorial dir. Charlotte Zolotow Books, 1982-90; pub. emerita, advisor Harper Collins Children's Books, 1991—; tchr. U. Colo. Writers Conf. on Children's Books, U. Ind. Writers Conf.; also lectr. children's books. Author: The Park Book, 1944, Big Brother, 1960, The Sky Was Blue, 1963, The Magic Words, 1952, Indian Indian, 1952, The Bunny Who Found Easter, 1959, In My Garden, 1960, But Not Billy, 1947, 2d edit, 1983, Not a Little Monkey, 1957, 2d edit., 1989, The Man With The Purple Eyes, 1961, Mr. Rabbit and the Lovely Present, 1962, The White Marble, 1963, A Rose, A Bridge and A Wild Black Horse, 1964, 2d edit., 1987, Someday, 1965, When I Have a Little Girl, 1965, If It Weren't for You, 1966, 2d edit., 1987, Big Sister, Little Sister, 1966, All That Sunlight, 1967, When I Have A Son, 1967, My Friend John, 1968, Summer Is, 1968, Some Things Go Together, 1969, The Hating Book, 1969, The New Friend, 1969, River Winding, 1970, 79, Lateef and His World, 1970, Yani and His World, 1970, You and Me, 1971, Wake Up and Goodnight, 1971, William's Doll, 1972, Hold My Hand, 1972, 2d edit., 1987, The Beautiful Christmas Tree, 1972, Janie, 1973, My Grandson Lew, 1974, The Summer Night, 1974, 3d edit. 1991, The Unfriendly Book, 1975, It's Not Fair, 1976, 2d edit., 1987, Someone New, 1978, Say It, 1980, If You Listen, 1980, 2d edit. 1987, The New Friend, 1981, One Step, Two ..., 1981, The Song, 1982, I Know a Lady, 1984, Timothy Too!, 1986, Everything Glistens, Everything Sings, 1987, I Like to be Little, 1987, The Poodle Who Barked at the Wind, 1987, The Quiet Mother and the Noisy Little Boy, 1988, Something's Going to Happen, 1988, This Quiet Lady, 1992, The Seashore Book, 1992, Snippets, 1992, The Moon was the Best, 1993, Peter and the Pigeons, 1993, others; compiler An Overpraised Season, Early Sorrow. Recipient Harper Gold award for editorial excellence, 1974, Kerlan award U. Minn., 1986, Corp. award for children's books Lit. Market Pl., 1990, Silver medallion U. So. Miss., 1990, Tribute for Far Reaching Contbn. to Children's Lit., ALA, 1991. Mem. PEN, Authors League. Home: 29 Elm Pl Hastings Hudson NY 10706-1703 Office: 10 E 53d St New York NY 10022-5244

ZOMBER, BEVERLY LOUISE, medical, surgical, geriatric and psychiatric nurse, educator; b. Evergreen Park, Ill., June 24, 1945; d. Louis and Irene (Cloud) Z. BA, DePaul U., 1967; MA, Northwestern U., 1969; ADN, Fla. Keys Community Coll., 1990. RN, Fla. Ins. claims specialist R.R. Retirement Bd., Chgo., 1969-77; Medicare specialist Social Security Adminstrn., Key West, Fla., 1979-88, L.A., 1979-88; mental health technician Guidance Clinic of Middle Keys, Marathon, Fla., 1988-90; staff/charge nurse Marathon Manor Convalescent Ctr., 1990-92; med.-surg. staff nurse, team leader Mariner's Hosp., Tavernier, Fla., 1992; staff nurse/counselor Marathon Comprehensive Psychiat. Clinic, 1992—; area dir. Nursing Unlimited, Inc., Marathon, 1993; mktg. dir., mem. adj. faculty, cons. Nursing Unltd., Florida Keys, Fla., 1992; owner, pres. Forms Inc., 1992—; instr. English lit., composition and creative writing Fla. Keys. C.C., Marathon, 1993—; instr. practical nursing Monroe County Sch. System, Fla. Keys, 1993—; dir. nursing Griswold Spl. Care, Fla. Keys, 1993-96. Former chmn. Inter-Agy. Coun. Monroe County, Fla. Ill. State scholar 1963-67, DePaul U. scholar, 1963-67. Mem. ANA, Fla. Nurses Assn., Marathon Bus. and Profl. Women.

ZONANA, VICTOR, lawyer, educator; b. Zagazig, Egypt, Aug. 28, 1940; s. Isaac A. and Fortunee (Cohen Beyda) Z.; m. Mary Linda Haynie, Aug. 22, 1964; children: David A., Nancy B. BS in Econs., Hofstra U., 1961; LLB, NYU, 1964, LLM, 1966. Assoc. Kaye, Scholer, Fierman, Hays & Handler, N.Y.C., 1966-69; prof. NYU, 1969-80, adj. prof., 1981—, Charles S. Lyon vis. prof., 1994; dep. tax legis. counsel U.S. Dept. Treasury, 1975-76; cons. to asst. commr. IRS, 1975, office of chief counsel, 1994; counsel, ptnr. Kaye, Scholer, Fierman, Hays and Handler, N.Y.C., 1980-87, Arnold & Porter, N.Y.C., 1988—; prof. Bklyn. Law Sch., 1996—. Mem., chmn. adv. bd. NYU Tax Inst. Fellow Am. Coll. Tax Counsel; mem. ABA, N.Y. State Bar Assn. (co-chmn. com. on fgn. activities of U.S. taxpayers, chmn. com. on depreciation and investment credit, co-chmn, com. tax acctg. matters, com. tax policy). Office: Arnold & Porter 399 Park Ave New York NY 10022-4614 also: Bklyn Law Sch 250 Joralemon St Brooklyn NY 11201

ZONANA, VICTOR F., government agency official, writer, communications executive; b. N.Y.C., Mar. 3, 1954; s. Felix and Nelly Z. BA, Dartmouth Coll., 1975. Staff writer Wall St. Jour., Phila. and San Francisco, 1975-85; spl. writer L.A. Times, San Francisco and N.Y.C., 1985-93; dep. asst. sec. pub. affairs U.S. Dept. Health and Human Svcs., Washington, 1993—. Recipient John Hancock award Outstanding Journalism, 1993. Mem. Soc. Profl. Journalists, Nat. Lesbian and Gay Journalists Assn. (founder 1991), Phi Beta Kappa. Home: 3835 S St NW Washington DC 20007-2118 Office: Dept Health and Human Svcs 200 Independence Ave SW Washington DC 20201-0004

ZONDLER, JOYCE EVELYN, kindergarten educator; b. Jersey City, N.J., June 28, 1952; d. Vincent Roger and Marta (Gruber) Hohmann; m. Kenneth P. Zondler, June 20, 1976 (div.). BA, Jersey City State Coll., 1974, MA, 1981. Cert. elem., early childhood tchr., N.J. Kindergarten tchr. Robert Fulton Sch., North Bergen, N.J., 1974—; mem. curriculum rev. coms. for math. and sci. North Bergen Schs., 1993—, for lang. arts, 1992-93, mem. report card rev. com. Mem. exec. bd. Fulton Sch. PTA, 1976-86, sec., 1978-80, v.p. 1980-82, treas. 1982-86. Recipient Gov.'s Recognition award, 1991. Mem. North Bergen Edn. Assn. (sec. 1989-91, v.p. 1991-93, pres. 1993—). Democrat. Roman Catholic. Office: Robert Fulton Sch 7407 Hudson Ave North Bergen NJ 07047-5607

ZONIS, MARVIN, political scientist, educator; b. Boston, Sept. 18, 1936; s. Leonard and Clara (Barenberg) Z.; m. Lucy Salenger, Jan. 3, 1976; children by previous marriage-Nadia E. Leah; 1 stepdaughter, Brix E. Smith. A.B., Yale U., 1958; postgrad., Harvard Grad. Sch. Bus., 1958-59; Ph.D., M.I.T., 1968; candidate, Inst. for Psychoanalysis, Chgo., 1977-85. Mem. faculty U. Chgo., 1966—, assoc. prof. and prof. behavioral scis., 1973-89—, prof. Grad. Sch. Bus., 1989—; dir. U. Chgo. (Center for Middle Eastern Studies), 1976-79; pres. Marvin Zonis and Assocs., Internat. Cons., 1991—; cons. in field; chmn. com. on Middle East Am. Coun. Learned Socs.-Social Sci. Rsch. Coun., 1970-76; pres. Am. Inst. Iranian Studies, 1969-71; bd. dirs. CNA Fin. Corp. Author: The Political Elite of Iran, 1971, Khomeini, The Islamic Republic of Iran, and the Arab World, 1987, Majestic Failure: The Fall of the Shah, 1991, The East European Opportunity: The Complete Business Guide and Source Book, 1992; contbr. articles to profl. jours. Served with USAF, 1959-60. Recipient Quantrell award for excellence in teaching U. Chgo., 1979. Office: U. Chicago 5828 S University Ave Chicago IL 60637-1515 *Psychoanalytic approaches to the study of political phenomena open new vistas to understanding as well as facilitating the design of U.S. policy.*

ZOOGMAN, NICHOLAS JAY, lawyer; b. N.Y.C., Apr. 2, 1947; s. Morris William and Hannah (Stern) Z.; m. Carla Ganz, June 7, 1970; children: Sarah Elizabeth, Peter William. BA, NYU, 1967; MA, Harvard U., 1969, JD, 1973. Bar: N.Y. 1974, U.S. Dist. Ct. (so. and ea. dists.) N.Y. 1974, U.S. Ct. Appeals (2d cir.) 1975, U.S. Supreme Ct. 1979, U.S. Dist. Ct. (ea. dist.) Mich. 1988, U.S. Ct. Appeals (D.C. cir.) 1990, U.S. Ct. Appeals (6th cir.) 1993. Assoc. Donovan Leisure Newton & Irvine, N.Y.C., 1973-75; ptnr. Anderson Kill Olick & Oshinsky, N.Y.C., 1976—. Mem. ABA, N.Y. State Bar Assn., Assn. Bar City N.Y., Phi Beta Kappa, Pi Sigma Alpha. Office: Anderson Kill Olick & Oshinsky 1251 Avenue Of The Americas New York NY 10020-1104

ZOOK, DONALD ROY, church financial administrator; b. Tunkhannock, Pa., Dec. 11, 1934; s. Roy William and Mary Alice (Pote) Z.; m. Anna Ruth Kline, Nov. 23, 1957; children: David, Esther, Lester. BS in Acctg., Elizabethtown Coll., 1955; MBA, Pa. State U., 1972; EdD in Bus. Edn., Temple U., 1980. CPA, Pa.; cert. fin. planner. Missionary Brethren in Christ Missions, Zimbabwe, 1955-71; prof. acctg. Messiah Coll., Grantham, Pa., 1972-82; area dir. P-W CPA Rev. Courses, Mount Joy, Pa., 1974—; exec. dir. Brethren in Christ Missions, Mount Joy, 1982-90; CEO Jacob Engle Found., Grantham, Pa., 1990—; bd. dirs. chmn. bd. trustees pension fund Brethren in Christ Ch. Contbr. numerous articles to profl. jours. Mem. Am. Mgmt. Assn., Pa. Inst. CPA's (mem. com. sch. and coll. relations 1975-77), Am. Inst. CPA's, Nat. Assn. Accts. (cert. Disting. Performance, 1979). Avocations: reading, tennis. Office: Jacob Engle Found PO Box 290 Grantham PA 17027-0290

ZOOK, ELVIN GLENN, plastic surgeon, educator; b. Huntington County, Ind., Mar. 21, 1937; s. Glenn Hardman and Ruth (Barton) Z.; m. Sharon Kay Neher, Dec. 11, 1960; children—Tara E., Leigh A., Nicole L. B.A., Manchester Coll., 1959; M.D., Ind. U., 1963. Diplomate Am. Bd. Surgery, Am. Bd. Thoracic Surgery, Am. Bd. Plastic Surgery. Intern Meth. Hosp., Indpls., 1963-64; resident in gen. and thoracic surgery Ind. U. Med. Center, Indpls., 1964-69; resident in plastic surgery Ind. U. Hosp., Indpls., 1969-71; asst. prof. plastic surgery Ind. U. Hosp., 1971-73; asso. prof. surgery So. Ill. U., Springfield, 1973-75; prof. So. Ill. U., 1975—, chmn. div. plastic surgery, 1973—; mem. staff Meml. Med. Center, St. Johns Hosp., Springfield. Contbr. articles to med. jours. Mem. AMA, Assn. Acad. Surgery, Am. Soc. Plastic and Reconstructive Surgery (sec. 1988-91, v.p. 1991-92, pres.-elect 1992-93, pres. 1993-94), Midwestern Soc. Plastic and Reconstructive Surgery (pres. 1986-87), ACS, Sangamon County Med. Soc. (pres. 1987), Am. Cleft Palate Assn., Am. Assn. Plastic Surgery (trustee 1987-90), Plastic Surgery Rsch. Coun. (chmn. 1981), Am. Burn Assn., Ill. Surg. Soc., Am. Soc. Surgery Hand (coun.), Am. Bd. of Plastic Surgery (sec.-treas. 1988-91, chmn. 1991-92), Am. Soc. Aesthetic Plastic Surgery, Am. Soc. Surgery of Trauma, Assn. Acad. Chmn. Plastic Surgery (pes. 1986-87), Am. Surg. Assn., RRC for Plastic Surgery, Sangamo Club, Springfield Med. Club, Island Bay Yacht Club. Presbyterian. Clubs: Sangamo, Springfield Med, Island Bay Yacht. Home: 42 Hazel Dell Springfield IL 62707-9507 Office: 800 N Rutledge St Springfield IL 62702-4911 *Do the best possible in all that is possible.*

ZOOK, KAY MARIE, nursing administrator; b. O'Neill, Nebr.; d. Roy W. and Elsie B. Carroll; m. Larry A. Zook; children: David, Debra Zook Wickizer. Diploma, Mary Lanning Sch. Nursing, Hastings, Nebr., 1955; BS, Hastings Coll., 1957; MS, St. Francis Coll., Joliet, Ill., 1984. RN, Nebr., Minn., Colo. Instr. nursing Mary Lanning Meml. Hosp., Hastings; instr. med.-surg. nursing Bryan Meml. Hosp., Lincoln, Nebr.; asst. DON Lincoln Gen. Hosp.; charge nurse St. Luke's Hosp., Duluth, Minn.; edn. coord. Rose Med. Ctr., Denver; v.p. patient svcs. St. Joseph Hosp., Denver, 1973—. Author: (bulletin) A New Threat to Health Care Delivery: The Nursing Shortage, 1988. Mem. Denver Leadership Forum, 1987. Fellow The Wharton Sch. U. Pa., Phila., 1985. Mem. Am. Orgn. Nurse Execs., Colo. Soc. Nurse Execs., Colo. League Nursing. Office: St Joseph Hosp 1835 Franklin St Denver CO 80218-1126

ZOOK, RONALD Z., school system administrator. Supt. Parkrose Sch. Dist. # 3, Portland, Oreg. Recipient Nat. Superintendent of the Yr. awd., Oregon, Am. Assn. of School Administrators, 1993. Office: Parkrose Sch Dist 3 10636 NE Prescott St Portland OR 97220-2648

ZOOK, THERESA FUETTERER, gemologist, consultant; b. Barberton, Ohio, Mar. 12, 1919; d. Charles Theodore and Ethel May (Knisely) Fuetterer; m. Donovan Quay Zook, June 21, 1941; children: Theodore Alan, Jacqueline Deborah Zook Cochran. AB, Ohio U., 1941; MA in Pub. Adminstrn., Am. U., 1946. Adminstrv. intern Nat. Inst. Pub. Affairs, Washington, 1941-42; mgmt. intern U.S. Dept. Agr., Washington, 1941-42; adminstrv. analyst Office Emergency Mgmt., Washington, 1942-43, Office Price Adminstrn., Washington, 1943-45; founder Zook and Zook Cons., Arlington, Va., 1945-47; tchr. ancient history and U.S. govt. Fairfax County (Va.) Pub. Schs., 1963-64; founder, pres. Associated Gem Consulting Lab., Alexandria, 1974—, Alpha Gate Crafts Ltd., Alexandria, 1977—; color cons. Internat. Com. on Color in Gems, Bangkok, Thailand, 1983. Author: Directory of Selected Color Resources Annotated Guide, 1982, Reunion of Descendants of David and Magdalena (Blough) Zook, 1983, Basic Machine Knitting, 1979; contbr. articles to profl. jours. Bd. dirs. Am. Embassy Com. on Edn., Montevideo, Uruguay, 1972; co-founder Workshop of Arts, Santiago, Chile, 1958; mem. Nat. Trust for Hist. Preservation, Nat. Mus. Women in Arts, Nat. Mus. Am. Indian, Am. Horticulture Soc., Textile Mus. Fellow Gemmological Assn. of Gt. Britain (diplomate); mem. AAUW, DAR, Nat. Geneal. Soc., Inter-Soc. Color Coun. (chmn. com. color in gemstones 1982-84, Appreciation cert. 1984), Accredited Gemological Assn. (co-founder, v.p.). Avocations: garden design, knitting, fabric creation, genealogy, music. Home: PO Box 6310 Alexandria VA 22306-0310

ZOON, KATHRYN EGLOFF, biochemist; b. Yonkers, N.Y., Nov. 6, 1948; d. August R. and Violet T. (Pollock) Egloff; BS, Rensselaer Poly. Inst., 1970; PhD Johns Hopkins U., 1975; m. Robert A. Zoon, Aug. 22, 1970; children: Christine K, Jennifer R. Interferon rsch. fellow NIH, Bethesda, Md., 1975-77, staff fellow, 1977-79, sr. staff fellow, 1979-80; sr. staff fellow div. biochem. biophysics Bur. Biologics, FDA, Bethesda, 1980-83; rsch. chemist divsn. biochem. biophysics, 1983-84, rsch. chemist divsn. virology, 1984-88, rsch. chemist div. cytokine biology, Ctr. for Biologics Evaluation and Rsch., FDA, 1988—, div. dir., 1989-92; dir. Ctr. for Biologics Evaluation and Rsch., 1992—; lectr. NIH, 1994, Reigelman Lecturship, 1994. N.Y. State Regents fellow, 1970; Person of the Yr. award Biopharm, 1992, 95, Pub. Svc. award Genetic Engring. News, 1994; Presdl. Meritorious Exec. Rank award, 1994. Mem. Am. Soc. Biochemistry and Molecular Biology, Internat. Soc. Interferon Rsch., Internat. Soc. Cytokine Rsch. Roman Catholic. Contbr. numerous articles on research in biol. chemistry to sci. jours.; sect. editor Jour. Interferon Research, 1980—. Office: CBER 1401 Rockville Pike Rockville MD 20852-1428

ZOPF, PAUL EDWARD, JR., sociologist; b. Bridgeport, Conn., July 9, 1931; s. Paul Edward and Hilda Ernestine (Russell) Z.; m. Evelyn Lanoel Montgomery, Aug. 5, 1956; 1 child, Eric Paul. B.S., U. Conn., 1953; M.S., U. Fla., 1955, Ph.D., 1966. Asst. prof. sociology Guilford Coll., Greensboro, N.C., 1959-66, assoc. prof., 1966-70, prof., 1970-72, Dana prof. sociology, 1972-93; Dana prof. sociology emeritus, 1993—; cons. local govt. agys. Author: North Carolina: A Demographic Profile, 1967, Demography: Principles and Methods, 1970, 76, Principles of Inductive Rural Sociology, 1970, Profile of Women in Greensboro: 1990, 1977, Sociocultural Systems, 1978, Cultural Accumulation in Latin America, 1980, Population: An Introduction to Social Demography, 1984, Income and Poverty Status of Women in Greensboro, 1985, America's Older Population, 1986, American Women in Poverty, 1989, Mortality Patterns and Trends in the United States, 1992; editor Guilford Coll. Self-Study Accreditation Report; contbr. articles to profl. jours. Recipient Teaching Excellence award Guilford Coll., 1978; grantee Kenan Found., 1970-79, Guilford Coll., 1979—. Mem. Am. Acad. Polit. and Social Sci., Am. Sociol. Assn., Internat. Union Sci. Study Population, So. Sociol. Soc., Rural Sociol. Soc., Population Reference Bur. Quaker. Home: 815 George White Rd Greensboro NC 27410-3317 Office: Guilford Coll Dept Sociology Greensboro NC 27410 *In my role as professor, researcher and author, I have oriented my activities to the service of students, my institution, my professional discipline, and various community agencies. I have found that pursuing various professional processes that I enjoy and can handle adequately, is the real reward. Honors, if they come, are a by-product of that pursuit; they would be elusive and perpetually inadequate if they were the principal reason for my efforts.*

ZORE, EDWARD JOHN, insurance company investment executive; b. Milw., July 5, 1945; s. Joseph F. and Marie A. Z.; m. Diane Widemshek, Aug. 19, 1967; children: Annemarie, Kathryn. B.S., U. Wis.-Milw., 1968, M.S., 1970. Exec. v.p., CFO, chief investment officer Northwestern Mut. Life Ins. Co., Milw., 1969—. Republican. Roman Catholic. Home: 129 W Miller Dr Mequon WI 53092-6189 Office: Northwestern Mutual Life Ins Co 720 E Wisconsin Ave Milwaukee WI 53202-4703

ZORIO, JOHN WILLIAM, financial services executive; b. Fayetteville, W.Va., Nov. 17, 1946; s. Nelson and Zelma (Simpson) Z.; m. Mary Ann Helen Dombrowski, Aug. 13, 1966; children: Jennifer Susan, Jonathan David. BSBA in Econs., Concord Coll., 1968. CLU, ChFC. Field underwriter N.Y. Life Ins. Co., McLean, Va., 1971-73, asst. gen. mgr., 1974-79; gen. mgr. N.Y. Life Ins. Co., Cin., 1980-83; v.p. N.Y. Life Ins. Co., N.Y.C., 1984-85; gen. mgr. N.Y. Life Ins. Co., Cleve., 1986-89; sr. v.p, N.Y. Life Ins. Co., Chgo., 1989-95; mng. ptnr. N.Y. Life Ins. Co., Rosemont, Ill., 1995—. Sgt. U.S. Army, 1969-71. Republican. Roman Catholic. Avocations: woodworking, reading, sports. Home: 540 Turicum Rd Lake Forest IL 60045-3366 Office: NY Life Ins Co 5600 N River Rd Ste 800 Rosemont IL 60018

ZORITCH, GEORGE, dance educator, choreographer; b. Moscow, June 6, 1917; came to U.S., 1936; s. Serge and Helen (Grunke) Z. Diploma Lady Deterding's Russian Sch., Paris, 1933. Mem. Ida Rubinstein Ballet Co., Paris, 1933-34, Pavlova's Co., West Indies, Australia, India, Egypt and Eng., 1934-35, Col. de Basil's Ballet Russe de Monte-Carlo, U.S.A., S. Am., Europe, 1936-38; soloist Denham Ballet Russe de Monte-Carlo, U.S.A., Can., S. Am., Europe, 1938-42; prof., mem. dance faculty com. fine arts U. Ariz., 1973-87; actor, dancer plays, musicals, concert tours, Broadway and throughout U.S., S. Am., Europe, 1943-50: actor 17 movies in Hollywood, Calif. and Rome; premier danseur noble Grand Ballet du Marquis de Cuevas, Europe, Africa, S.Am., 1951-57, Denham Ballet Russe de Monte Carlo, U.S.A., 1957-62; founder George Zoritch Sch. Classical Ballet, West Hollywood, Calif., 1963-73; fine arts prof., mem. com. on dance, U. Ariz., Tucson, 1973-87, ret.; freelance engagements, 1973—. Editor records: George Zoritch for Classical Ballet, 1962-65. Recipient Key to Jacksonville (Fla.) Mayor Hans G. Tantzler Jr., 1968, The Bolshoi Theatre Medallion of Merit award IV Internat. Ballet Competition-Moscow, 1981, Ariz. Dance Treasures award Ariz. Dance Arts Alliance and Ariz. State U. Dept. Dance, 1992, Merit award Acad. of Choreographic Sch. A. Vaganova, 1993, Vaslav Nijinsky Medallion of Merit award The Consulate Gen. of Republic of Poland, 1994, Diaghilev House Silver Medallion of Merit award Sixth Dance Competition of Paris, 1994; named Amb. San Antonio World's Fair. Mem. Ariz. Dance Arts Alliance (hon. life mem.), Phoenix Ballet Guild (hon. mem.), Nat. Soc. Arts and Letters (Medallion of Merit award Valley of Sun chpt. 1990).

ZORKO, MARK A., financial executive; b. Cleve., Mar. 11, 1952; s. Frank A. and Dorothy E. (Bever) Z.; m. Sue A. Langdon, Sept. 6, 1975; children: Jennifer, Andrew. BS in Acctg., Ohio State U., 1976; MBA in Mgmt. Info Systems, U. Minn., 1977. CPA; cert. practicioner in inventory mgmt. Sr. staff cons. Arthur Andersen & Co., Mpls., 1978-80; fin. mgr. Honeywell, Inc., Mpls. and Brussels, 1980-87; corp. contr. Zenith Data Systems Corp., St. Joseph, Mich., 1987-91; CFO Inverness Castings Group, Inc., Bangor, Mich., 1991-93; v.p. fin., sec., CFO Comptronix Corp., Guntersville, Ala., 1993-94; v.p., CFO Western Res. Products, Inc., Nashville, 1995—; bd. dirs. Intellimedia Corp. Treas., bd. dirs. United Way, St. Joseph, 1988-93. Sgt. USMC, 1970-73. Mem. AICPA, Fin. Execs. Inst., Nat. Assn. Corp. Treas., Am. Prodn. and Inventory Control Soc., Minn. Soc. CPAs. Methodist. Avocations: sailing, skiing, golf, hockey, soccer. Home: 9301 Grist Mill Ct Brentwood TN 37027 Office: Western Res Products Inc 435 Calvert Dr Nashville TN 37066

ZORN, ERIC JOHN, newspaper columnist; b. New Haven, Jan. 6, 1958; s. Jens Christian and Frances (Barnhart) Z.; m. Johanna Wolken, Nov. 2, 1985; 1 child, Alexander. BA, U. Mich., 1980. With Chgo. Tribune, 1980—, met. reporter, 1985-86, columnist, 1986—; instr. Northwestern U. Medill Sch. Journalism, Evanston, Ill., 1985-89. Co-author: Murder of Innocence, 1990. Avocation: old-time square dance caller. Office: Chgo Tribune PO Box 25340 435 N Michigan Ave Chicago IL 60611-4001

ZORNES, MILFORD, artist; b. Camargo, Okla., Jan. 25, 1908; s. James Francis and Clara Delphine (Lindsay) Z.; m. Gloria Codd, 1935; 1 son, Franz Milford; m. Patricia Mary Palmer, Nov. 8, 1942; 1 dau., Maria Patricia. Student, Otis Art Inst., Los Angeles, 1929, Pomona Coll., 1930-34. Instr. art Pomona Coll., 1946-50; art dir. Vortox and Padua Hills Theatre, Claremont, 1954-66. Exhibited, Calif. Watercolor Soc., Met. Mus., Am. Watercolor Soc., Corcoran Gallery, Bklyn. Mus., Denver Mus., Cleve. Mus., L.A. Mus., Brooks Gallery, London, Bombay Art Assn., Chgo. Art Inst., Butler Mus., Gallery Modern Masters, Washington, Santa Barbara (Calif.) Mus., Cin. Mus., Laguna (Calif.) Art Gallery, Oklahoma City Mus., Springville (Utah) Mus.; represented in permanent collections at L.A. Mus., White House Collection, Met. Mus., Pentagon Bldg., Butler Mus., UCLA, Nat. Acad., San Diego Mus., L.A. County Fair, Home Savs. and Loan Assn., L.A., Corcoran Gallery, Washington; mem. art com., Nat. Orange Show, San Bernardino, Calif., 1963-65; author: A Journey to Nicaragua, 1977, The California Style: California Watercolor Artists, 1925-1955, 1985; subject of book by Gordon McClelland: Milford Zornes, Hillcrest Press, 1991. Served with U.S. Army, 1943-45, CBI. RecipientPaul Prescott Barrow award Pomona Coll., 1987, David Prescott Burrows award, 1991, A Most Disting. Citizen award So. Utah State Coll., 1988, Am. Artist Achievement award Am. Artist Mag., 1994. Mem. NAD, Am. Watercolor Soc., Southwestern Watercolor Soc., Watercolor West, Nat. Watercolor Soc., Utah Watercolor Soc. Address: PO Box 176 Orderville UT 84758-0176 *It has been my effort in life to have awareness: not to have all knowledge because no one can encompass all knowledge; not to have only wealth or only success, because there is no dimension of completeness of wealth or success; not to achieve complete goodness, because goodness and right are relative; not to enjoy the epitomy in taste because taste is a gratification of self alone; but rather to seek and achieve understanding of relative values and a concept of the completeness of life. With this as my effort and my inner goal, I find success within the areas of my limited abilities, my meager knowledge, and my frail grasp of the infinite.*

ZORNOW, DAVID M., lawyer; b. N.Y.C., Mar. 31, 1955; s. Jack and Marion (Gilden) Z.; m. Martha Malkin, July 21, 1985; children: Samuel Morris, Hannah Jane, Ethan Lewis. AB summa cum laude, Harvard U., 1976; JD, Yale U., 1980. Bar: N.Y. 1981, U.S. Ct. Appeals (3d cir.) 1982, U.S. Dist. Ct. (so. dist.) N.Y. 1983, U.S. Ct. Appeals (2d cir.) 1984, U.S. Dist. Ct. D.C. 1989, U.S. Ct. Appeals (D.C. cir.) 1989, U.S. Dist. Ct. Ariz. 1990, U.S. Dist. Ct. (ea. dist.) N.Y. 1993. Law clerk to Judge Herbert J. Stern U.S. Dist. Ct. N.J., Newark, 1980-82; assoc. Kramer Levin Kamin Nessen & Frankel, N.Y.C., 1982-83; asst. U.S. atty. so. dist. N.Y. U.S. Atty.'s Office, N.Y.C., 1983-87; assoc. counsel Office Ind. Counsel-Iran/Contra Investigation, Washington, 1987-89; ptnr. Skadden Arps Slate Meagher & Flom, N.Y.C., 1989—; chmn. N.Y.C. Civilian Complaint Rev. Bd., 1994—; vis. faculty Trial Advocacy Workshop Harvard Law Sch., Cambridge, Mass., 1988. Mem. ABA (com. on white collar crime), Fed. Bar Coun., Assn. of Bar of City of N.Y., N.Y. Assn. Criminal Def. Lawyers, N.Y. Coun. Def. Lawyers. Office: Skadden Arps Slate Meagher & Flom 919 3rd Ave New York NY 10022

ZORNOW, WILLIAM FRANK, historian, educator; b. Cleve., Aug. 13, 1920; s. William Frederick Emil and Viola (Schulz) Z. A.B., Western Res. U., 1942, A.M., 1944, Ph.D., 1952. Vice pres., treas. Glenville Coal & Supply Co., Real Value Coal Corp., Zornow Coal Corp., 1941-45; dep. clk. Probate Ct., Cuyahoga County, Ohio, 1941-43; prodn. planning engr. Hickok Elec. Instrument Co., Cleve., 1943-46; teaching asst. Western Res. U., 1944-47; instr. U. Akron, 1946-47, Case Inst. Tech., 1947-50, Washburn U., 1950-51; lectr. Cleve. Coll., 1948-49; asst. prof. Kans. State U., 1951-58; asst. prof. history Kent (Ohio) State U., 1958-61, asso. prof., 1961-66, prof. history, 1966—; perpetual hon. fellow Harry S. Truman Libr. Inst., Independence, Mo.; collection corr. Berkshire Loan and Fin. Co., Painesville (Ohio) Security Credit Acceptance Corp., Mentor, Ohio, 1951-60; cons. Karl E. Mundt Library, Dakota State Coll., Madison, S.D.; presenter 1st coll. arts and scis. faculty lecture series Kent State U., 1962. Author: Lincoln and the Party Divided, 1954, rev. edit., 1972, Kansas: A History of the Jayhawk State, 1957, America at Mid-Century, 1959; author: (with others) Abraham Lincoln: A New Portrait, 1959, Kansas: The First Century, 1956; contbr. articles to encys. and profl. jours.; editor: Shawnee County (Kans.) Hist. Bull, 1950-51; abstractor: America: History and Life: Historical Abstracts, 1964—. Mem. Dir.'s Circle Cleve. Mus. Art, 1989—, Cleve. Clin. Found., 1992—, Soc. Fellows. Faculty rsch. grantee Kans. State U., 1955-57, Kent State U., 1960-64. Mem. AAAS, AAUP, Soc. Fellow of Cleve. Clinic Found., Am. Acad. Polit. and Social Sci., Am. Assn. State and Local History (award of merit 1958), Am. Hist. Assn., Orgn. Am. historians, Ohio Acad. History (chmn. awards com.), Ohio Hist. Soc. (libr. adv. com. 1969—), Ohio Soc. N.Y., Ctr. Study of Presidency, Acad. Polit. Sci., Lincoln Fellowship of Wis., Sierra Club San Francisco, Delta Tau Delta (4-star coun. 1992—), Pi Gamma Mu, Phi Alpha Theta, Phi Delta Kappa. Home: 7893 Middlesex Rd Mentor OH 44060-7617 Office: Kent State U 305 Bowman Dr Kent OH 44240-4507

ZOROWSKI, CARL FRANK, engineering educator, university administrator; b. Pitts., July 14, 1930; s. Stanley and Mary Josephine (Kozuch) Z.; m. Sarah Jane Crossley, Aug. 7, 1954 (dec. 1983); children: Kathleen Ann, Karl Alan, Kristine Alaine; m. Louise Parrish Lockwood, Apr. 13, 1985. BSME, Carnegie Inst. Tech., 1952, MSME, 1953, PhD, 1956. Instr. Carnegie Inst. Tech., Pitts., 1952-56, asst. prof., 1956-61, assoc. prof., 1961-62; prof. mech. and aero. engring. dept. N.C. State U., Raleigh, 1964-66, R.J. Reynolds Industries prof., 1966—, assoc. dept. head, 1964-72, dept. head, 1972-79, assoc. dean acad. affairs Sch. Engring., 1979-85, dir. Integrated Mfg. Systems Inst., 1986-92, dept. head, 1992-93; dir. Succeed/NSF Coalition, 1993—, assoc. dean acad. affairs, 1993-94. Served to 2d lt. USAR, 1952-58. Recipient research award Sigma Xi, 1967. Fellow ASME (Richards Meml. award 1975); mem. Am. Soc. Engring. Edn. (Western Electric award 1968), Fiber Soc. (Achievement award 1970). Contbr. pubs. to profl. jours.; patentee in field. Home: 103 Windyrush Ln Cary NC 27511-9758 Office: NC State U PO Box 7901 Raleigh NC 27695

ZORTHIAN, BARRY, communications executive; b. Kutahia, Turkey, Oct. 8, 1920; naturalized 1930; s. Herbert Peter and Annaly (Markarian) Z.; m. Margaret Aylaian, June 6, 1948; children: Gregory Jannig, Stephen Arnak. BA, Yale U., 1941; LLB, N.Y. U., 1953; LLD (hon.), Ind. Inst. Tech., 1970. Bar: N.Y. 1953. Newspaper reporter, 1936-42, newspaper and radio reporter, 1947-48; news and policy editor USIA, 1948-56, program mgr. Voice of Am., 1956-61; dep. pub. affairs. officer USIS, India, 1961-64; min.-counselor for info. Am. Embassy, Vietnam, 1964-68; v.p. Time, Inc., 1969-79, v.p. govt. affairs, 1974-79; pres. Time-Life Broadcast, 1969-73, Washington/Balt. Regional Assn., 1979-81; sr. v.p. Gray and Co., Washington, 1981-84; ptnr. Alcalde & Fay, Arlington, Va., 1984—. Bd. dirs. Am. U. of Armenia, Internat. Coll. of Beirut, Armenian Gen. Benevolent Union. With USMCR, 1942-46; col. Res. ret. Mem. Coun. on Fgn. Rels., Am. Fgn. Svc. Assn., Bus.-Govt. Rels. Coun., Marine Corps Res. Officers Assn. Conglist., Century Assn. (N.Y.C.) Club, Congl. Country (Washington) Club, Burning Tree (Washington) Club, Met. (Washington) Club. Home: 4201 Cathedral Ave NW Apt 405E Washington DC 20016-4914 Office: Alcalde & Fay 2111 Wilson Blvd Ste 850 Arlington VA 22201-3001

ZOSIKE, JOANIE FRITZ, theater director, actor; b. Bklyn., July 6, 1949; d. Nathan and Gloria S. (Greenberg) Hieger; m. Godson E. Zosike, Dec. 12, 1995. BA in Theatre, NYU, 1980. Co-founder, actor, devel. dir. Protean Forms Collective, N.Y.C., 1986-88; mng. dir., actor Living Theatre, N.Y.C., 1990—; co-dir. DADAnewyorkDADA; bd. dirs. Gathering of Tribes; writer-in-residence Women's Theatre Project at ATA, N.Y. Author: (stage prodns.) You Told Me That the Carousel Was Crystal, Frames, Inside, 12 Steps to Murder; author: (with Hanon Reznikov) ...And Then The Heavens Closed; actress (stage prodns.) Not in My Name, Anarchia, Mysteries and Smaller Pieces, Utopia, Rules of Civility, Humanity, Body of God, I and I, The Tablets, Poland 1931, Midsummer Night's Dream, Mother! I'm Pregnant!, Visions of Paradise, 12 Steps to Murder, No Nukes at Liberty, Mother Courage, Daily Activity of Slaves, Greetings from the Abyss, (solo performances) All Right So I AM the Earth, Harpies Complex, Ereshkigal's Peg, Fritzgabriel Cabaret, Alen Mak Festival (Bulgaria), Festival des Politisches Liedes (Germany), (films) Mass and Masses, Human Flesh, (TV) The Gong Show; vocalist (radio show) Women on the Edge of Time; contbr. Between Ourselves: Letters Between Mothers and Daughters (edited by Karen Payne), Women in American Theatre (edited by Helen Krich Chinoy and Linda Walsh Jenkins); contbr. poetry and articles to artistic jours. Vol. N.Y.C. War Tax Resistance, N.Y.C. Peoples Life Fund. Action-Vista grantee; recipient Artists Residency award Edward Albee Found., 1982. Mem. War Resisters League. Office: The Living Theatre 800 W End Ave Ste 5-a New York NY 10025-5467

ZOSS, ABRAHAM OSCAR, chemical company executive; b. South Bend, Ind., Feb. 17, 1917; s. Harry and Fannie (Friedman) Z.; B.S. in Chem. Engring., U. Notre Dame, 1938, M.S., 1939, Ph.D., 1941; m. Betty Jane Hurwich, Dec. 24, 1939; children: Roger, Joel, Hope Zoss Schladen; m. 2d, Magda Szanto, May 26, 1978. With Gen. Aniline & Film Corp., Easton, Pa., 1941-47, tech. mgr., Linden, N.J., 1947-55, plant mgr., 1955-57; mgr. mfg. adminstrn., chem. div. Minn. Mining & Mfg. Co., St. Paul, 1957-58, prodn. mgr. chem. div., 1958-60; v.p. Photek Inc., West Kingston, R.I., 1960-62; asst. corp. tech. dir. Celanese Corp., N.Y.C., 1962-65, corp. tech. dir., 1965-66, corp. dir. comml. devel., 1966-69; v.p. corp. devel. Tenneco Chems., Inc., N.Y.C., 1969-71, Universal Oil Products Co., Des Plaines, Ill., 1971-72; group v.p. Engelhard Industries div. Engelhard Minerals & Chem. Corp., Murray Hill, N.J., 1972-74, v.p. bus. devel., 1974-77; v.p. corp. devel. CPS Chem. Co., Inc., Old Bridge, N.J., 1977, dir., v.p., chief adminstrv. officer, 1978-84; pres. Bus. Devel. Internat., N.Y.C., 1984—; mem. field info. agy. Office Tech. Svc., Commerce Dept., Europe, 1946; teaching asst. U. Notre Dame, 1939-41. Mem. Met. Mus. Art, N.Y.C., Mus. Modern Art, N.Y.C. Recipient Centennial Sci. award U. Notre Dame, 1965, accredited Profl. Chemist, 1980. Fellow Am. Inst. Chemists, AAAS; mem. Am. Chem. Soc., Am. Inst. Chem. Engring., N.Y. Acad. Scis., Comml. Devel Assn., Colloqium Cons. Strategy, Soc. Chem. Industry, Tech. Transfer Soc., Soc. Plastics Engrs., Societe de Chimie Industrielle (pres. Am. sect.), Chemists Club (N.Y.C.). Contbr. articles to profl. pubs. Patentee in field. Home and Office: 45 East End Ave Ste 11D New York NY 10028

ZOTALEY, BYRON LEO, lawyer; b. Mpls., Mar. 18, 1944; s. Leo John and Tula (Koupis) Z.; m. Theresa L. Cassady, Sept. 7, 1969; children: Nicole, Jason, Krisanthy. BA in Psychology, U. Minn., 1966; MATC, Coll. St. Thomas, St. Paul, 1968; JD, William Mitchell Coll. of Law, 1970. Bar: Minn. 1970, U.S. Dist. Ct. Minn. 1971, U.S. Ct. Appeals (8th cir.) 1972, U.S. Supreme Ct. 1975. Pres. LeVander, Zotaley, Vander Linden & Rydland, Mpls., 1970—; arbitrator Minn. No Fault Panel, 1974—; cons. Marthe Properties, Mpls., 1980-90, Theron Properties, Mpls., 1985—. Bd. dirs. Minn. Consumer Alliance, 1994-95; mem. adv. bd. Beniloe-St. Margarets Jr. H.S., 1993-95. Mem. ABA, ATLA, Minn. Bar Assn., Hennepin County Bar Assn., Minn. Trial Lawyers Assn. (chmn. Amicus Curiae com. 1980-87, bd. govs. 1982-93, mem. exec. com. 1987-89, emeritus, 1994—). Home: 5504 Parkwood Ln Minneapolis MN 55436-1728 Office: LeVander Zotaley Vander Linden & Rydland 720 Northstar W Minneapolis MN 55402

ZOX, LARRY, artist; b. Des Moines, May 31, 1937; s. Oscar and Mildred (Friedman) Z.; m. Jean Marilyn Glover, July 19, 1965; children: Melinda, Alexander Cassidy. Student, Okla. U., 1955-56, Drake U., 1957, Des Moines Art Center, 1955-57. vis. critic Cornell U., summer 1967; faculty (Sch. Visual Arts), 1967-68, 69-70, 70-76, Yale, summer, 1972, Kent State U., summer 1974. Exhibited one man shows at Am. Gallery, N.Y.C., 1962, Kornblee Gallery, N.Y.C., 1964-66, 68, 69, 70, 71, Andre Emmerich Gallery, 1973, 75, 76, Whitney Mus. Am. Art, 1973, Galerie Rocke, Cologne, Germany, 1968, Janie C. Lee Gallery, Houston, 1974, Hokin Gallery, Bay Harbor Islands, Fla., 1981, Meridith Long & Co., Houston, 1981, Hokin Gallery, Palm Beach, 1981, Salander-O'Reilly Galleries, N.Y., 1982, Rubiner Gallery, West Bloomfield, Mich., 1985, 90, Images Gallery, Toledo, 1986, 90, 91, Percival Gallery, Des Moines, 1987, 89, 91, Marsh Gallery U. Richmond, Va., 1992, Robert Strin-St. Louis, Mo., 1992, C.S. Schulte Gallery, Millburn, N.J., 1993-94, Gallery One Toronto, Can., others; exhibited group shows at

Am. Gallery, 1963, Am. Fedn. Art, 1963-65, Mus. Modern Art, N.Y.C., 1964, Albright-Knox Art Gallery, Buffalo, 1964, Washington Gallery Modern Art, 1964, Gallery Modern Art, N.Y.C., 1965, Tibor de Nagy, N.Y.C., 1965, ann., Whitney Mus., N.Y.C., 1965-70, one-man retrospective, 1973, Art Inst. Chgo., 1965, Kornblee Gallery, 1966, Guggenheim Mus., N.Y.C., 1966, Expo Am. Pavilion, 1967, Palm Springs Desert Mus., 1973, Daniel Templon Gallery, Paris, 1975, Andre Emmerich Gallery, 1975, Andre Emmerich Gallery, N.Y., 1975, Edmonton (Alta., Can.) Art Gallery, 1977, Old Vanderbilt Mansion, Old Brookville, N.Y., 1979, Allen Rubiner Gallery, Royal Oak, Mich., 1980, Meredith Long & Co., N.Y., 1980, Md. Inst. Coll. Art, Balt., 1980, Meredith Long & Co., Houston, 1980, Mus. Fine Arts, Boston, 1981, Solomion R. Guggenheim Mus., N.Y., 1981, Salander-O'Reilly Gallery, N.Y., 1981, St. Lawrence U., 1985, Rubiner Gallery, West Bloomfield, 1986, Percival Gallery, Des Moines, 1987, Gallery of Art, 1988, Charles H. MacNider Mus., 1988, Sioux City Art Ctr., 1988, Des Moines Art Ctr., 1988, Blanden Meml. Art Mus., 1988, Muscatine Art Ctr., 1988, C.S. Shulte Gallery, N.Y. and N.J., 1991, others; represented in permanent collections Am. Republic Ins. Corp., Des Moines, J. & L. Hudson Co., Detroit, Joseph H. Hirshhorn Mus., U.S. Steel Corp., Mus. Modern Art, N.Y.C., Philip Johnson Collection, Dallas Mus. Fine Arts, Des Moines Art Center, Met. Mus. Art, N.Y.C., Indpls. Mus., Whitney Mus.; artist in residence, Juniata Coll., Huntingdon, Pa., 1964, U. N.C., 1967. Recipient Nat. Council Arts award, 1969; Guggenheim fellow, 1967.

ZRAKET, CHARLES ANTHONY, systems research and engineering company executive; b. Lawrence, Mass., Jan. 9, 1924; s. Habib and Martha (Beshara) Z.; m. Shirley Ann Camus, Oct. 13, 1961; children: David C., Suzanne M., Elizabeth A., Caroline A. BSEE, Northeastern U., Boston, 1951; SMEE, MIT, 1953; PhD in Engring. (hon.), Northeastern U., 1988. Mem. rsch. staff digital computer lab. MIT, 1951-53, group leader digital computer lab., Lincoln Lab., 1953-58; tech. dir., then sr. v.p. MITRE Corp., Bedford, Mass. and McLean, Va., 1958-78, exec. v.p., chief oper. officer, 1978-86, pres., chief exec. officer, 1986-90; trustee MITRE; bd. dirs. Kennedy Sch. Govt. Harvard U., 1990-94, Alpha Industries, Wyman-Gordon Corp. Contbr. articles to Science, Daedalus, IEEE Jours; co-editor: Managing Nuclear Operations. Trustee Northeastern U., Computer Mus. With AUS, 1943-46. Decorated Bronze Star, Purple Heart with oak leaf cluster, Combat Inf. badge; named Disting. Corp. Leader MIT, 1985, Dept. Def. Medal for Disting. Pub. Svc., 1990. Fellow AAAS, IEEE, AIAA (Reed Aeros. award 1993), Am. Acad. Arts and Scis.; mem. NAE, Sigma Xi, Tau Beta Pi, Eta Kappa Nu. Home: 71 Sylvan Ln Weston MA 02193-1027

ZRULL, JOEL PETER, psychiatry educator; b. Detroit, Jan. 10, 1932; s. Arthur Benjamin and Mildred (Bazy) Z.; m. Nancy Jane Eichenlaub, June 19, 1954; children: Mark Christian, Lisa Carol. BA with honors, U. Mich., 1953, MD, 1957. Diplomate Am. Bd. Psychiatry, Am. Bd. Child Psychiatry. From instr. to assoc. prof. psychiatry U. Mich. Med. Sch., Ann Arbor, 1962-73; prof., chief child psychiatry Med. Coll. Ohio, Toledo, 1973-75, prof., chmn. dept. psychiatry, 1975—; cons. Monroe (mich.) County Intermediate Sch. Dist., 1961—; pres. Associated Physicians MCO, Inc., Toledo, 1983-84, 87-90; chief of staff Med. Coll. Hosps., Toledo, 1984-86; mem. com. on cert. in child psychiatry Am. Bd. Psychiatry and Neurology, 1986-91, chmn. 1990-91. Editor: Adult Psychiatry: New Directions in Therapy, 1983; contbr. articles to profl. jours. Grantee NIMH, 1974-76, Ohio Dept. Mental Health, 1978-86. Fellow Am. Psychiat. Assn. (life), Am. Acad. Child and Adolescent Psychiatry (chmn. com. tng. 1984-87, chmn. comm. memls. and awards 1992-95), Am. Coll. Psychiatrists, Am. Orthopsychiat. Assn.; mem. AMA, Soc. Profs. of Child and Adolescent Psychiatry (sec. treas. 1989-92, pres.-elect 1992-94, pres. 1994-96). Roman Catholic. Avocations: tennis, bridge, golfing. Home: 6133 W Wyandotte Rd Maumee OH 43537-1334 Office: Med Coll Ohio PO Box 10008 Toledo OH 43699

ZSCHAU, MARILYN, singer; b. Chgo., Feb. 9, 1944; d. Edwin Arthur Eugene and Helen Elizabeth (Kelly) Z. BA in Radio, T.V., Motion Pictures, U. N.C.; ed. Juilliard Sch. Music, opera theatre with Christopher West, voice with Florence Page Kimball, also studied with John Lester. Toured with Met. Nat. Co., 1965-66; debut, Vienna Volksoper, in Die Tote Stadt, 1967, Vienna Staatsoper, in Ariadne auf Naxos, 1971; with N.Y.C. Opera from 1978; debut Met. Opera, in La Boheme, 1985, La Scala, in Die Frau ohne Schatten, 1986, Royal Opera, Covent Garden; has toured and sung in many countries. Office: Janice Mayer & Assocs 201 W 54th St Ste 1C New York NY 10019

ZSIGMOND, VILMOS, cinematographer, director; b. Szeged, Hungary, June 16, 1930; came to U.S., 1957, naturalized, 1962; s. Vilmos and Bozena (Illichmann) Z.; children: Julia, Susi. MA, U. Film and Theater Arts, Budapest, Hungary, 1955. Free-lance cinematographer for numerous comls., also ednl., documentary and low-budget feature films, 1965-71; now dir., cinematographer on commls. (winner several nat. and internat. awards); feature films, 1971—; films include McCabe and Mrs. Miller, 1971; Images, 1972, Deliverance, 1972, The Long Goodbye, 1973, Scarecrow, 1973, Cinderella Liberty, 1973, The Sugarland Express, 1974, Obsession, 1976, Close Encounters of the Third Kind, 1977 (Acad. award 1977), The Last Waltz, 1978, The Rose, 1978, The Deerhunter, 1978 (Acad. award nomination and Brit. Acad. award), Heavens Gate, 1979, The Border, 1980, Blow Out, 1980, Jinxed, 1981, Table for Five, 1982, The River, 1983 (Acad. award nomination), No Small Affair, 1984, Real Genius, 1985, Witches of Eastwick, 1986, Journey to Spirit Island, 1988, Fatman and Little Boy, 1989, Two Jakes, 1989, Bonfire of the Vanities, 1990, Stalin, 1991 (CableAce award, Direction of Photography and/or Lighting Direction in a Dramatic/Theatrical Special/Movie or Miniseries, ASC award, Emmy award), Sliver, 1992; dir. The Long Shadow, 1992, Intersection, 1993, Maverick, 1993, The Crossing Guard, 1994, Assassins, 1995, The Ghost and the Darkness, 1996. Mem. Acad. Motion Picture Arts and Scis., Dirs. Guild, Am. Soc. Cinematographers. Office: Feinstein & Shorr 16133 Ventura Blvd Ste 800 Encino CA 91436-2409

ZUBE, ERVIN HERBERT, landscape architect, geographer, educator; b. Milw., Apr. 24, 1931; s. Ervin Louis and Germaine Emma (Petersen) Z.; m. Margaret Jean Pew, June 19, 1954; 1 child, Eric Carl. BS, U. Wis.-Madison, 1954; MLA in Landscape Architecture, Harvard u., 1959; postgrad., FAAR, Am. Acad., Rome, 1961; PhD in Geography, Clark U., 1973. Asst. to dean of men U. Wis., Madison, 1953-54, Asst. prof., 1961-64; asst. prof. U. Calif., Berkeley, 1964-65; prin. Zube and Dega Assocs. Landscape Architects, Madison, Wis., 1961-64; pres. Rsch., Planning and Design Assocs., Amherst, 1966-70; prof., dept. head U. Mass., Amherst, 1965-72, dir. environ. research inst., 1972-77; dir. sch. Renewable Natural Resources U. Ariz., Tucson, 1977-83, prof. landscape architecture, 1983-84, 87—, chmn. landscape resources divsn., 1984-87; adj. prof. geography, regional devel. U. Ariz., 1985—; sr. Fulbright Hays Disting. prof. U. Ljubljana, Yugoslavia, 1979; Lansdowne vis. geography scholar U. Victoria, 1986; mem. Nat. Commn. on Rsch. and Resources Mgmt. Policy, Nat. Pk. Sys., 1988-89; lectr. in field; mem. exec. bd. Ency. on Environ., 1991-94; chairperson GAP analysis peer rev. panel U.S. Fish and Wildlife Svcs., Nat. Biol. Survey, 1993. Author, editor 11 books; editorial bd. Landscape Rsch., 1974—, Landscape Jour., 1981—, Jour. Archtl. and Planning Rsch., 1983—, Landscape Ecology, 1987-92, New Eng. Landscape, 1987-91, Landscape and Urban Planning, 1988—, Environ. Psychology, 1990—, Jour. Planning Lit., 1990—, Society and Natural Resources, 1991-93; contbr. articles to profl. jours., chpts. to books. Trustee Hubbard Ednl. Trust, 1969—; bd. dirs. Tucson Bot. Garden, 1981-83, 85-87, Ariz. Sonora Desert Mus., Tucson, 1981-85, 86-89, pres., 1987-88, mem. adv. coun., 1985-86, Rsch. Ranch Found., Elgin, Ariz., 1981-93, v.p., 1989-90, pres., 1990-92; active U.S. MAB program, Project 13, 1977-88, chair, 1980-86, mem. U.S. Nat. Com., 1980-83. Fellow NATO, Eng., 1977, NEA, 1983-84, Udall Ctr. for Studies in Pub. Policy fellow, 1992-93; scholar Harvard U., 1983-84. Fellow Am. Soc. Landscape Archs. (chmn. coun. edn. 1973-75, dir. profl. practice inst. 1982-87, chmn. 1986-87, Bradford Williams medal 1981, rsch. honor award 1982, ASLA medal 1995); mem. Nat. Archtl. Accrediting Bd. (dir. 1978-80), Internat. Coun. for Exch. Scholars (mem. adv. com. in arch. and city planning chairperson 1979-82), Eisenhower Consortium Western Environ. Forestry Rsch. (v.p. rsch. 1979-82), Environ. Design Rsch. Assn. (dir. 1982-85, chmn. 1984-85), Assn. Am. Geographers, S.W. Pks. and Monuments Assn. (bd. dirs. 1985-94, 95—, v.p. 1986-89, pres. 1989-92), Landscape Arch. Found. (bd. dirs. 1989-91, Alfred Lagasse medal 1992), Rincon Inst. (bd. advisors 1990—, chairperson 1994—), Nat. Pks. and Conservation Assn. (sci. adv. com. 1991-95, coun. advisors 1993-95), Nat. Pk. Coop. Assocs. (bd. dirs. 1993—, v.p. 1994—). Office: U Ariz 325 Bio Sci E Tucson AZ 85721

ZUBKOFF, MICHAEL, medical educator; b. N.Y.C., June 2, 1944; s. Harry and Catherine (O'Brien) Z.; children: Steven, Joel, Lisa; m.Leslee Ann Cohen, 1991. BA, Am. Internat. Coll., 1965, LLD (hon.), 1981; MA, Columbia U., 1966, cert. Internat. Fellow program, 1967, PhD, 1969; MA (hon.), Dartmouth Coll., 1980. Research assoc. conservation human resources Columbia U., N.Y.C., 1967-69; assoc. prof. health econs., assoc. chmn. dept. family and community health Meharry Med. Coll., Nashville, 1968-75; assoc. prof. econs. Vanderbilt U., Nashville, 1970-75; prof. econs. and mgmt. Amos Tuck Sch. Bus., chmn. dept. community and family medicine Med. Sch. Dartmouth Coll., Hanover, N.H., 1975—; mem. inst. medicine Nat. Acad. Scis., 1982—, mem. assembly engrs. inst. med. com. on tech. and health care, 1977-79, grad. med. ednl. nat. adv. com., 1977-81, com. on grad.-med. edn. programs for mil. services Nat. Acad. Scis., 1980-82., nat. research council commn. on human resources Nat. Acad. Scis., 1980-84, com. on aging soc. Nat. Acad. Scis., 1984—; corr. com. human rights Nat. Acad. Scis., 1983—, nat. rsch. coun. com. computer tech. and svc. sector productivity Nat. Acad. Scis., 1991—; instr. econs. Harvard U., Yale U., and ColumbiaU., 1967-69. Co-author: Urban Health Services: The Case of New York, 1971, Consumer Incentives for Health Care, 1974, Health: A Victim of Cause of Inflation, 1976, Framework for Government Intervention in the Health Sector, 1978, Hospital Cost Containment: Selected Notes for Public Policy, 1979; contbr. numerous articles to profl. jours. Fellow Woodrow Wilson Found., 1965-67, Fulbright Found., 1967-68, USPHS, 1968-69. Mem. Am. Econ. Assn., Am. Pub. Health Assn. Home: RR 1 Fairlee VT 05045-9801 Office: Dartmouth Med Sch Dept of Community & Family Med Strasenburgh Hall HB 7250 Hanover NH 03755

ZUBROFF, LEONARD SAUL, surgeon; b. Minersville, Pa., Mar. 27, 1925; s. Abe and Fannie (Freedline) Z.; BA, Wayne State U., 1945, MD, 1949. Diplomate Am. Bd. Surgery. Intern Garfield Hosp., Washington, 1949-50, resident in surgery, 1951-55, chief resident surgery, 1954-55; pvt. practice medicine specializing in surgery, 1958-76; med. dir. Chevrolet Gear and Axle Plant, Chevrolet Forge Plant, GM, Detroit, 1977-78, divisional med. dir. Detroit Diesel Allison div., 1978-87, regional med. dir. GM, 1987-89; ret., 1989; bd. trustees LeVine Found.; mem. staff Hutzel Hosp., Detroit Meml. Hosp.; chief of surgery, chief profl. svcs. N.E. Air Command, Pepperell AFB, Newfoundland. With USAF, 1956-58. Fellow ACS; mem. Acad. Surgery Detroit, Coll. Occupational and Environ. Medicine, Mich. Occupational Med. Assn. (pres. 1990-91), Detroit Occupational Physicians Assn. (former pres.), Masons (33 degree), Phi Lambda Kappa. Home and Office: 22511 Bellwood Dr South Southfield MI 48034

ZUCARO, ALDO CHARLES, insurance company executive; b. Grenoble, France, Apr. 2, 1939; s. Louis and Lucy Zucaro; m. Gloria J. Ward, Oct. 12, 1963; children: Lucy, Louis, Faye. BS in Acctg, Queens Coll., N.Y.C., 1962. C.P.A., N.Y., Ill. Ptnr. Coopers & Lybrand (and predecessor), Chgo. and N.Y.C., 1962-76; exec. v.p., chief fin. officer Old Republic Internat. Corp., Chgo., 1976-81, pres., 1981—, chief exec. officer, 1990—, also chmn. bd. dirs., 1993—, chmn. of the bd., 1993—; pres., bd. dirs. Old Republic Life Ins. Co., Old Republic Life of N.Y., Old Republic Ins. Co., Internat. Bus. and Merc. Reassurance Co., Republic Mortgage Ins. Co., Old Republic Nat. Title Ins. Co., Home Owners Life Ins. Co. Editor: Financial Accounting Practices of the Insurance Industry, 1975, 76. Mem. AICPAs. Roman Catholic. Office: Old Republic Internat Corp 307 N Michigan Ave Chicago IL 60601

ZUCCHERO, ROCCO, communications specialist; b. Chgo., Dec. 19, 1956; s. Rocco and Rosaria Francesca (Patellaro) Z.; m. Patricia Anne Howard, May 19, 1990. AA, U. Ill., Chgo., 1977. Outside plant tech. Ameritech, Chgo., 1981—. Home: 8107 Leawood Ln Woodridge IL 60517-4125

ZUCCO, RONDA KAY, addictions program manager; b. Peoria, Ill., Apr. 3, 1960; d. Richard Leon Zucco. BA, So. Ill. U., 1981. Cert. addictions profl.; internat. cert. alcohol and drug counselor. Counselor Spl. Supportive Svcs., So. Ill. U., Carbondale, 1981-83; substance abuse counselor Interventions, Chgo., 1984-86; addictions counselor Parkside at BroMenn, Bloomington, Ill., 1986-89; dir. continuing care/sr. counselor Fla. Hosp. (formerly Parkside), Orlando, Fla., 1989-95, cmty. rels. rep. Ctr. for Psychiatry, 1995; addictions program mgr. Charter Behavioral Health Sys., Kissimmee, Fla., 1995—; tng. instr. for group facilitation Parkside/Fla. Hosp., 1989-95; presenter seminars in field, bd. dirs. Ill. Cert. Bd. Addiction Profls., Bloomington, 1986-89. Vol. ARC, Cardondale, 1978-81, crisis hotline Jackson County Cmty. Mental Health Ctr., Cardondale, 1981, Alliance for the Mentally Ill Greater Orlando, 1995—, Coalition for the Homeless, Orlando, 1995—; active AIDS Spkr.'s BUr., BroMenn Healthcare, Blomington, Ill., 1986-89. State of Ill. Gen. Assembly scholar, 1977-81. Mem. Am. Mktg. Assn., Am. Assn. for Counseling and Devel., Am. Mental Health Counselors Assn., Fla. Alcohol and Drug Abuse Assn., Fla. Prevention Assn., Nat. Businesswomen's Leadership Assn., C. of C. Greater Orlando, Kappa Delta Pi, Chi Sigma Iota. Avocations: reading, running, swimming and diving, tennis, theater. Home: 10600 Bloomfield Dr Apt 311 Orlando FL 32825

ZUCK, ALFRED CHRISTIAN, consulting mechanical engineer; b. Ridgefield, N.J., Dec. 16, 1924; s. Frederick William and Margaret Christine (Umland) Z.; m. Vilma Hudson, May 6, 1951; children: Allyson, Jon, Randall. M.E., Poly. Inst. Bklyn., 1960. Registered profl. engr., 21 states including N.Y.; nat. council engring. examiners; lic. profl. planner, N.J. From designer to sr. v.p. Syska & Hennessy, Inc., N.Y.C., 1946-78; prin. Edwards & Zuck (P.C.), N.Y.C., 1978-91, ret., 1991; mem. nat. panel Am. Arbitration Assn, Nat. Council Engring. Examiners. Served with AUS, 1943-46; to 1st lt. USAF, 1951-52; to capt. N.J. Air N.G., 1947-56. Decorated Bronze Star (2). Fellow Am. Cons. Engrs. Council (past mem. Nat. Ethical Practices Com.); mem. NSPE, N.Y. State Soc. Profl. Engrs. (past chmn. profl. engrs. in pvt. practice program), Am. Soc. Mil. Engrs., Nat. Council Engring. Examiners, N.Y. Assn. Cons. Engrs. (past v.p., bd. dirs.), ASHRAE, N.Y. Bldg. Congress. (bd. govs.). Lutheran. Club: N.Y. Athletic. Home: 444 Weymouth Dr Wyckoff NJ 07481-1217 Office: Edwards & Zuck PC 330 W 42nd St New York NY 10036-6902

ZUCK, ALFRED MILLER, association executive; b. East Petersburg, Pa., Aug. 27, 1934; s. Walter Newton and Mary (Miller) Z.; m. Geraldine Connelly, July 21, 1957; children: Susan, David. BA, Franklin and Marshall Coll., 1957; MPA, Syracuse U., 1958. Dir. fed. program Presdl. Commn. on Youth Opportunities, Washington, 1967-68; dir evaluation Employment and Tng. Adminstrn., Dept. Labor, Washington, 1968-70, dir adminstrn. and mgmt., 1970-75; comptroller U.S. Dept. Labor, Washington, 1975-77; exec. dir. Commn. on Exec., Legis. and Jud. Salaries, Washington, 1980; asst. sec. Dept. Labor, Washington, 1977-83, acting sec., 1981; asst. adminstr. EPA, Washington, 1983; exec. dir. Nat. Assn. Schs. of Pub. Affairs and Adminstrn., Washington, 1983—; pres. Internat. Inst. Adminstrv. Scis., Brussels, 1989-92, Am. Consortium for Internat. Pub. Adminstrn., Washington, 1984-89; bd. dirs. Pub./Pvt. Venture, Inc., Phila., 1984-90. Recipient Presdl. Disting. Exec. award Pres. of U.S., 1980; Disting. Alumni award Franklin and Marshall Coll., 1980. Fellow Nat. Acad. Pub. Adminstrn. (trustee 1989—, chmn. bd. trustees 1993—); mem. Phi Beta Kappa. Office: NASPAA 1120 G St NW Ste 730 Washington DC 20005-3801

ZUCKER, ALEXANDER, physicist, administrator; b. Zagreb, Yugoslavia, Aug. 1, 1924; came to U.S., 1939; s. William and Bertha (Klopfer) Z.; m. Joan-Ellen Jamieson, Nov. 28, 1953; children: Rebecca, Claire, Susannah. B.A., U. Vt., Burlington, 1947; M.S., Yale U., New Haven, 1948, Ph.D., 1950. Physicist Oak Ridge Nat. Lab., Tenn., 1950-60, assoc. dir. electro-nuclear div., 1972-75, dir. heavy ion project, 1988, assoc. dir. phys. scis., 1973-88, acting lab. dir., 1988; assoc. dir. for nuclear techs. Oak Ridge Nat. Lab., 1989-93; exec. dir., environ. studies bd. NAS-NAE, Washington, 1970-72; mem. U.S. del. to USSR on Peaceful Uses of Atomic Energy, 1963; Ford prof. physics U. Tenn., Knoxville, 1968-73; U.S. del. to Pugwash Conf., 1971; research coordination council Gas Research Inst., Chgo., 1978-85; com. Army manpower Nat. Research Council, Washington, 1982-83; adv. panel on technologies to reduce U.S. materials import vulnerability Office of Technology Assessment, Washington, 1982-85; council on energy engring. research Dept. of Energy, Washington, 1983—; industry, nat. lab. steel initiative White House, Washington, 1984. Editor Internat. Jour. Nuclear Sci. Applications, 1980—; cons. editor Ency. and Yearbook of Sci. and Tech. McGraw-Hill Pub. Co., 1989; mem. editorial bd. Science, 1981-82; contbr. articles to profl. jours. Guggenheim fellow, 1966-67; Fulbright-Hays Research scholar, 1966-67. Fellow Am. Phys. Soc., AAAS, Sigma Xi; mem. ASME, Nat. Acad. Scis. (nuclear physics del. to People's Republic of China 1979), Internat. Union Pure and Applied Physics (mem.-at-large U.S. nat. com. 1976-78). Research in nuclear physics with heavy ions and protons; accelerators, especially cyclotrons; materials research programs, especially high-temperature materials and surfaces; nuclear power reactors, especially gas-cooled reactors; research reactor with ultra high neutron flux. Office: Oak Ridge Nat Lab PO Box 2008 Oak Ridge TN 37831-2008

ZUCKER, ALFRED JOHN, English educator, academic adminstrator; b. Hartford, Sept. 25, 1940; s. Samuel and Rose (Zucker) Z.; AA, L.A. Valley Coll., 1960; AB in English, UCLA, 1962, AB in Speech, MA in English, 1962, MA in Speech, 1963, PhD, 1966, postgrad., UCLA, U. So. Calif., Harvard U.; m. Sallie Lea Friedheim, Dec. 25, 1966; children—Mary Anne, John James, Jr., James Patrick, Patrick Jonathan, Anne-Marie Kathleen, Kathleen Mary. Lectr. English, Los Angeles City Coll., 1963-68; prof. English, philosophy, chmn. div. humanities Los Angeles Southwest Coll., 1968-72, chmn. English dept., 1972-74, asst. dean instruction, 1974—; prof. English El Camino Coll., 1985—; prof. English L.A. Valley Coll., 1989—. Mem. Los Angeles Coll. Dist. Senate, 1969—. Mem. Los Angeles Coll. Tchrs. Assn. (dir.), Calif. Jr. Coll. Assn., Calif. Tchrs. Assn., AAUP, World Affairs Coun., Mensa, Phi Beta Kappa, Phi Delta Kappa (pres. U. Calif. at Los Angeles chpt. 1966-67, v.p. 1967-68), Tau Alpha Epsilon. Lodge: KC. Contbr. articles to profl. jours. Office: 5800 Fulton Ave Van Nuys CA 91401-4062

ZUCKER, DAVID, director; b. Milw., Oct. 16, 1947. co-founder (with Jerry Zucker and Jim Abrahams) Kentucky Fried Theatre, Madison, WI, 1969, then Los Angeles, CA, 1972. Co-screenwriter: Kentucky Fried Movie, 1977; co-screenwriter, co-dir.: Airplane!, 1980; co-exec. prodr, co-dir., co-screenwriter: Top Secret, 1984, The Naked Gun, 1988, The Naked Gun 2 1/2: The Smell of Fear, 1991, The Naked Gun 33 1/3: The Final Insult, 1994; co-dir.: Ruthless People, 1986; co-exec. prodr.: Brain Donors, 1992; TV series: Police Squad!, 1982; TV spls.: Our Planet Tonight, 1987. Office: Zucker Bros Prodns Sony Studios 10202 Washington Blvd Culver City CA 90232-3119

ZUCKER, HOWARD ALAN, pediatric cardiologist, intensivist, anesthesiologist; b. N.Y.C., Sept. 6, 1959; s. Saul and Phyllis (Goldblatt) Z.. BS, McGill U., Montreal, Quebec, Can., 1979; MD, George Washington U., 1982. Diplomate Am. Bd. Pediatrics, subspecialties in pediatric critical care, pediatric cardiology, Am. Bd. Anesthesiology, subspecialty in anesthesia critical care. Pediatric intern Johns Hopkins Hosp., Balt., 1982-83, pediatric resident, 1983-85; anesthesiology resident Hosp. of U. Pa., Phila., 1985-87; pediatric critical care fellow Children's Hosp. of Phila., 1987-88; asst. prof. anesthesiology and pediatrics Yale U. Sch. Medicine, New Haven, Conn., 1988-90; pediatric cardiology fellow Children's Hosp., Harvard Med. Sch., Boston, 1990-92; asst. prof. pediatrics and anesthesiology Columbia U. Coll. Physicians and Surgeons, N.Y.C., 1992—; pediat. dir. ICU, dir. pediatric transport Columbia Presbyn. Med. Ctr. Babies & Children's Hosp. N.Y., N.Y.C., 1992—; involved with crew tng. of NASA Space Shuttle STS-1 Mission, 1978-80; rsch. affiliate, Man-vehicle Lab, MIT. Chmn. bd. Terre Verte Found., Inc. Named Person of Week ABC World News Tonight, 1993. Fellow Am. Acad. Pediatrics, Am. Coll. Cardiology, Am. Coll. Chest Physicians; mem. AMA, Am. Soc. Anesthesiologists, Am. Heart Assn., Soc. Critical Care Medicine. Jewish. Achievements include research in adaptation to zero gravity, cardiac critical care chmn. of bd. Terre Certe Found., Inc. Home: 100 Winston Dr Apt 12G Cliffside Park NJ 07010-3240 Office: Columbia Presbyn Med Ctr Babies & Childrens Hosp NY 3959 Broadway New York NY 10032-1537

ZUCKER, JERRY, producer, director; b. Milw., Mar. 11, 1950. Student, U. Wis. co-founder Ky. Fried Theatre. Films include: Kentucky Fried Movie, 1977 (co-screenwriter, actor), Rock 'n' Roll High School, 1979 (2nd unit dir.), Airplane!, 1980 (co-dir., co-screenwriter), Top Secret, 1984 (co-dir., co-screenwriter), Ruthless People, 1986 (co-dir.), The Naked Gun, 1988 (exec. prodr., co-screenwriter), Ghost, 1990 (dir.), The Naked Gun 2 1/2: The Smell of Fear, 1991 (exec. co-prodr.), Brain Donors, 1992 (co-exec. prodr.), My Life, 1993 (co-prodr.), The Naked Gun 33 1/3: The Final Insult, 1994 (co-exec. prodr.), First Knight, 1995 (dir.).

ZUCKER, JERRY, energy systems manufacturing executive; b. Tel-Aviv, Israel, Aug. 24, 1946; came to U.S., 1952, naturalized, 1958; s. Leon and Zipora (Shlifkovitz) Z.; m. Anita Goldberg, June 21, 1970; children: Jonathan Michael, Andrea Michelle, Jeffrey Mark. BS, U. Fla., 1968, MEE, 1972. Electronics design engr. Vital Industries, Inc., Gainesville, Fla., 1968-71; devel. engrng. group dir. Cons. Engrs., Inc., Gainesville, 1971-73; supt. process engrng. and tech. services Hudson Pulp & Paper Corp., Palatka, Fla., 1973-78; dir. mfg. and tech. services Raybestos Manhattan, Inc., North Charleston, S.C., 1978-82; chmn. bd., chief exec. officer InterTech Group, Inc.; bd. dirs. High Tech. Coatings Corp., Advanced Chem. Techs., Inc., Tighitco, Inc., Ecosys, Inc., Polymer Group, Inc., FiberTech Group, Inc., ConX Inc., Tycon Inc., Worthington Products Inc., Aerospace Def. Inc., Technetics Group, Inc., Thantex, Inc., Global Golf, Inc., Fabrene, Inc., Polymer Group, Inc., Daramic, Inc., RemGrit Corp.; cons. phosphate mining, pulp and paper and sugar industries. Bd. dirs. Roper Hosp., Trident United Way, Charleston Jewish Fedn., pres., Hotline Inc. (crisis intervention), Hebrew Benevolent Soc., Hebrew Orphan Soc., Orgn. Rehab. Tng., S.C. Aquarium; pres. Synagogue Emanuel. Mem. TAPPI (mem. nat. elec. engring. com. 1977—), IEEE, Am. Chem. Soc. Jewish. Numerous patents in electrochem., mech., chem. fields. Contbr. articles to tech. jours. Home: 16 Buckingham Dr Charleston SC 29407-3455 Office: The InterTech Group Inc PO Box 5205 4838 Jenkins Ave North Charleston SC 29405

ZUCKER, JOY ALLISON, television executive producer; b. Ridgewood, N.J., Mar. 9, 1965; d. Martin David and Rona Lee (Rubin) Z. BA, U. Md., 1986. Stage mgr. ABC Sports, N.Y.C., 1983-86, ABC News, Washington, 1986-88, USA Today on TV, Rosslyn, Va., 1988-90; prodr. Mizlou Sports News Network, Rosslyn, Va., 1990; prodr., reporter Nostalgia TV, Alexandria, Va., 1991; prodr. Newschannel 8, Springfield, Va., 1991—, exec. prodr., 1994; stage mgr., asst. dir. Raycom/Jefferson Pilot Teleprodns., 1984-95. Bd. dirs. Dist. Spl. Olympics, 1995—. Recipient Dateline award Soc. Profl. Journalists, 1995. Mem. NATAS (bd. govs., Emmy award 1994). Jewish. Avocations: scuba diving, cooking, dancing, cycling, aerobic exercise. Home: 3152-C Anchorway Ct Falls Church VA 22042

ZUCKER, NORMAN LIVINGSTON, political scientist, educator, author; b. N.Y.C., Aug. 1, 1933; s. George Meyer and Beatrice Lillian (Livingston) Z.; m. Naomi Judith Flink, June 25, 1961; children: Sara, George. B.A., Rutgers U., 1954, M.A., 1956, Ph.D., 1960. Asst. prof. polit. sci. Tufts U., Medford, Mass., 1962-66; asso. prof. polit. sci. U. R.I., Kingston, 1966-69; prof. U. R.I., 1969—; cons. Select Commn. on Immigration and Refugee Policy, 1980; manuscript cons. to pubs. Author: George W. Norris: Gentle Knight of American Democracy, 1966, The American Party Process, 1968, The Coming Crisis in Israel: Private Faith and Public Policy, 1973, The Guarded Gate: The Reality of American Refugee Policy, 1987, Desperate Crossings: Seeking Refuge in America, 1996; cons. editor World Affairs, 1975-84; assoc. editor Jour. Refugee Studies, 1987—; contbr. articles and revs. to profl. jours., chpts. to books. Wurzweiler Found. grantee, 1963; Am. Philos. Soc. grantee, 1964; Rockefeller Found. fellow in human rights, 1980. Mem. Internat. Polit. Sci. Assn., Am. Polit. Sci. Assn., New Eng. Polit. Sci. Assn., AAUP. Office: U RI Dept Polit Sci Kingston RI 02881

ZUCKER, ROBERT A(LPERT), psychologist; b. N.Y.C., Dec. 9, 1935; s. Morris and Sophie (Alpert) Z.; m. Martine Latil; children: Lisa, Alex, Eleanor; m. Kristine Ellen Freeark, Mar. 10, 1979; 1 child, Katherine. B.C.E., CCNY, 1956; postgrad., UCLA, 1956-58; Ph.D., Harvard U., 1966. Lic. psychologist, Mich. From instr. to asst. prof. psychology Rutgers U., 1963-68; from asst. prof. to assoc. prof. to prof. Mich. State U., 1968-94; prof. psychology in psychiatry and psychology U. Mich., 1994—, dir. Alcohol Rsch. Ctr., 1994—, dir. substance abuse divsn. dept. psychiatry, 1994—; vis. prof. U. Tex., Austin, 1975; vis. rsch. prof. psychology in psychiatry U.

Mich., 1990-91; vis. scholar Nat. Inst. Alcohol Abuse and Alcoholism, 1980; dir. clin. tng. Mich. State U., 1982-94; lectr. Nebr. Symposium on Motivation, 1986; cons. in field. Editor: Further Explorations in Personality, 1981, Personality and the Prediction of Behavior, 1984, The Emergence of Personality, 1987, Studying Persons and Lives, 1990, Personality Structure in the Life Course, 1992, The Development of Alcohol Problems: Exploring the Biopsychosocial Matrix of Risk, 1994, Alcohol Problems Among Adolescents: Current Directions in Prevention Research, 1995; contbr. chpts. and articles to profl. publs. Bd. dirs. Nat. Coun. on Alcoholism-Mich., 1978-82; mem. Psychosocial Initial Rev. Group, Nat. Inst. Alcohol Abuse and Alcoholism, 1989-92. Fellow AAAS, APA, APS, Am. Orthopsychiat. Assn.; mem. Midwestern Psychol. Assn., Ea. Psychol. Assn., Soc. Personology, Soc. Life History Rsch. in Psychopathology. Office: Univ Mich 400 E Eisenhower Pky Ann Arbor MI 48108-3318 *Clinical psychology has always appealed to me because of its concern about human trouble as well as for its scientific commitment. Clinical involvement can serve as a counterpoint to scientific and scholarly activity; a firm grounding in the datum of everyday experience is critical to the evolution of the science as well as the profession of psychology.*

ZUCKER, STEFAN, tenor, writer, editor, radio broadcaster; b. N.Y.C. BS, Columbia U., 1967; postgrad., NYU, 1967-72. Freelance tenor concerts and operas in U.S. and Europe, 1965—; tenor RCA Records, N.Y.C., 1972-77; guest singer radio and TV programs, U.S. and Europe, 1975—; radio producer, host WKCR-FM, N.Y.C., 1980-94; opera critic N.Y. Tribune, 1983-84; philosophy lectr. Coll. Ins., N.Y.C., 1972. Record producer including Rossini's Rivals: Music By Then-Famous, Now-Obscure, Italian Composers, 1984; restorer films of opera singers, 1987—; singer, producer, stage dir., adminstr. various operas, 1967—; editor Opera Fanatic mag., 1986—; contbr. articles to Internat. Dictionary of Opera, Opera News, The Opera Quar., Am. Record Guide, Opera Fanatic, News World, Professione Musica, others. Pres. Bel Canto Soc., Inc., 1985—; Named Worlds Highest Tenor by Guinness Book of World Records, 1979—; subject of record Stefan Zucker: The World's Highest Tenor, 1981. Mem. NYU Philosophy Assn. (pres. 1969-72, v.p. 1968), Music Critics Assn., Assn. Furtherment Bel Canto (pres. 1967-80). Office: Bel Canto Soc Inc 11 Riverside Dr New York NY 10023-2504

ZUCKER, WILLIAM, retired business educator; b. Bridgeport, Conn., July 21, 1917; s. Meyer and Ida Lena (Elovitz) Z.; m. Kathlyn Saltman, Jan. 16, 1944; children—Peter Bayard, Alison Beth, Jeremy Michael, David Laurence. A.B., Johns Hopkins U., 1938; AM, Harvard U., 1940, PhD, 1951. Sec. Commerce and Industry Assn. of N.Y., N.Y.C., 1944-59; v.p. Downtown Lower Manhattan Assn., N.Y.C., 1959-64; pres. Southeastern Pa. Econ. Devel. Corp., Phila., 1964-73; adj. prof. Wharton Sch. U. Pa., Phila., 1972-83, assoc. dir. Entrepreneurial Ctr., Wharton Sch., 1973-83, dir. exec. edn. Wharton Sch., 1977-83, dir. Wharton Real Estate Ctr., 1983-88, Meshulam Riklis prof. creative mgmt. Wharton Sch., 1983-88; prof. emeritus U. Pa., 1988—; pres. Adviserv Co., Phila., 1993-94; lectr. CCNY, 1956-58; vis. prof. Grad. Sch. Bus. Columbia U., 1988-91. Author: Local Development Corporations, 1980, REITS, 1975; editor Real Estate Fin. Jour., 1985—; contbr. articles to profl. jours. Mem. New Canaan Bd. Edn., Conn., 1961-64, New Canaan Bd. Fin., 1958-61. Democrat. Jewish. Home: Cathedral Village 600 E Cathedral Rd # L105 Philadelphia PA 19128-1933 Office: U Pa 2000 Steinberg Dietrich Hal Philadelphia PA 19104

ZUCKERBERG, DAVID ALAN, pharmaceutical company executive; b. Bklyn., Sept. 11, 1946; s. Murray and Selma (Gold) Z.; m. Doris Tavel, May 23, 1971; children: Stephen A., Jonathan P. BS ChemE, Poly. Inst. Bklyn., 1968; MS in Biochemistry, Fairleigh Dickinson U., 1975. Process devel. engr. Procter & Gamble, Cin., 1968-70; with research and devel. Beecham, Clifton, N.J., 1970-77; with research and devel. Block Drug Co., Jersey City, 1977-86, v.p. quality assurance, quality control, 1986-91, v.p. tech. svcs., 1991—; lectr. in chemistry St. Thomas Aquinas Coll., Sparkill, N.Y., 1978-88. Contbr. articles to profl. jours. Mem. New City Jewish Ctr. Mem. Am. Chem. Soc., Am. Inst. Chem. Engrs., Internat. Assn. Dental Rsch., Non-prescription Drug Mfrs. Assn. (mfg. controls com. 1986-90). Republican. Home: 32 Roslyn Ln New City NY 10956-3643 Office: Block Drug Co Inc 257 Cornelison Ave Jersey City NJ 07302-3113

ZUCKERBERG, ROY J., investment banking executive; b. N.Y.C., July 21, 1936; s. Sam and Gertrude R. (Rabstein) Z.; m. Barbara Hope Schwam, June 21, 1959; children: Lloyd P., Dina R. B.S., Lowell Tech. Inst., 1958. Vice pres. The Zuckerberg Co., Copiague, N.Y., 1959-67; with Goldman, Sachs & Co., N.Y.C., 1967—, v.p. securities sales, 1972, gen. ptnr., 1977, co-head securities sales div., 1988-89, co-head equities div., mem. mgmt. com., 1990—. Trustee L.I. Jewish Med. Ctr., 1981-89, vice chmn., 1989—; trustee Brandeis Sch., 1979-86, ARC Greater N.Y., 1992—, Jewish Communal Fund, 1992—; bd. dirs. The Brookdale Found., 1985—, Am. Jewish Joint Distbn. Com. Inc., 1992—; trustee The Bklyn. Mus., 1987-94; mem. bd. overseer Albert Einstein Coll. Medicine Yeshiva U., 1989—. Clubs: Harmonie, Woodmere, Mashomack. Home: 1249 Veeder Dr Hewlett NY 11557-2512 also: 435 E 52nd St New York NY 10022-6445 Office: Goldman Sachs & Co One New York Plaza fl 50 New York NY 10004*

ZUCKER-FRANKLIN, DOROTHEA, medical scientist, educator; b. Berlin, Aug. 9, 1930; came to U.S., 1949; d. Julian and Gertrude (Feige) Zucker; m. Edward C. Franklin, May 15, 1956 (dec. 1982); 1 child, Deborah Julie. BA, Hunter Coll., 1952; MD, N.Y. Med. Coll., 1956. Diplomate Am. Bd. Internal Medicine. Intern Phila. Gen. Hosp., 1956-57; resident in internal medicine Montefiore Hosp., N.Y.C., 1957-59, postdoctoral fellow in hematology, 1959-61; with Med. Sch. NYU, N.Y.C., 1962—, prof. Med. Sch., 1974—, dir. lab., 1966—; asst. attending physician Montefiore Hosp., 1961-65; assoc. attending physician Univ. Hosp., 1968-74, attending physician, 1974—; assoc. attending physician Bellevue Hosp., 1968-74, attending physician, 1974—; cons. physician Manhattan (N.Y.) VA Hosp., 1970—, PHS Agy. for Healthcare Policy and Rsch., 1992—; sci. adv. bd., rev. panel Israel Cancer Rsch. Fund, 1982—; mem. U.S.-Israel Binat. Sci. Found., 1980—; bd. dirs. Henry M. and Lillian Stratton Found., Inc., 1987—; AID related Rsch. Rev. Com. NIHLB, 1986-90; mem. allergy immunol. com. NIH, 1974-80, pathological tng. com. NIH, 1971-74, Health Resource Coun., N.Y.C., 1971-74, blood products com. FDA, 1981-87. Mem. editl. bd. Blood, 1973-76, 80-86, Jour. Reticuloendothelial Soc., 1964-74, 80—, Am. Jour. Pathology, 1979—, Blood Cells, 1980—, Ultrastructural Pathology, 1979, Am. Jour. Medicine, 1981—, Hematology Oncology, 1982—, Jour. Immunology, 1986—; author: (with others) The Physiology and Pathology of Leukocytes, 1962, Atlas of Blood Cells, Function and Pathology, 1981, 2d edit., 1989, Amyloidosis, 1990; contbr. 250 articles to sci. publs., and 10 chpts. to med. textbooks. Recipient Career Devel. award NIH, 1965-70; NIH rsch. grantee, 1970—; postdoctoral fellow in electromicroscopy NYU, 1962-63. Fellow N.Y. Acad. Scis.; mem. Inst. Medicine NAS, Am. Fedn. Clin. Rsch., Am. Soc. Clin. Investigation, Am. Assn. Physicians, Am. Soc. Hematology (pres. 1995, chairperson subcom. on leukocyte physiology 1977, chairperson subcom. on immunohematology 1984, exec. coun. 1985—, advanced learning resources com. 1987—), Soc. Exptl. Biology and Medicine, Am. Soc. Exptl. Biology, Am. Soc. Immunologists, Am. Soc. Cell Biology, Reticuloendothelial Soc. (pres. program and nominating coms. 1984-85), N.Y. Soc. Electron Microscopists (pres. 1962, 84-85), N.Y. Soc. for Study of Blood. Office: NYU Med Ctr 550 1st Ave New York NY 10016-6481

ZUCKERKANDL, EMILE, molecular evolutionary biologist, scientific institute executive; b. Vienna, Austria, July 4, 1922; came to U.S., 1975; s. Frederic and Gertrude (Stekel) Z.; m. Jane Gammon Metz, June 2, 1950. M.S., U. Ill., 1947; Ph.D., Sorbonne, Paris, 1959. Postdoctoral research fellow Calif. Inst. Tech., Pasadena, 1959-64; research dir. CNRS, Montpellier, France, 1967-80, dir. Ctr. Macromolecular Biochemistry, 1965-75; pres. Linus Pauling Inst., Palo Alto, Calif., 1980-92, Inst. Molecular Med. Scis., Palo Alto, Calif., 1992—; cons. in genetics Stanford U., 1963, vis. prof., 1964; vis. prof. U. Del., 1976. Contbg. author: Evolving Genes and Proteins, 1965; co-author: Genetique des Populations, 1976; editor Jour. Molecular Evolution, 1971—. Decorated Order of Merit (France). Fellow AAAS; mem. Societe de Chimie Biologique, N.Y. Acad. Scis., Internat. Soc. Study Origin of Life. Home: 565 Arastradero Rd Apt A Palo Alto CA 94306-4339 Office: Inst Molecular Med Scis 460 Page Mill Rd Palo Alto CA 94306-2025

ZUCKERMAN, BARRY, medical educator. Prof., chmn. dept. pediatrics Boston U. Sch. Medicine; mem. Nat. Commn. on Children, Carnegie Commn. on Mtg. the Needs of Young Children.; bd. dirs. Zero to Three, Nat. Ctr. for Clin. Infant Programs, Nat. Ctr. Children in Poverty. Recipient Nat. Leadership Award Children's Def. Fund, 1994. Office: Boston City Hosp Dept Peds Dowling 3 S Boston MA 02215

ZUCKERMAN, MARTIN HARVEY, personnel director; b. N.Y.C., Feb. 20, 1942; s. Merwin and Helen (Weinstein) Z.; m. Joyce S. Harris, July 26, 1969; children: Lyle, Evan. BA, NYU, 1963; JD, St. John's U., 1965; LLM, NYU, 1966. Bar: N.Y. 1966. Field atty. Nat. Labor Relations Bd., N.Y.C., 1966-70; sr. atty. Simpson, Thatcher & Bartlett, N.Y.C., 1970-80; v.p. compensation and benefits Chemical Banking Corp. (formerly Mfrs. Hanover Trust Co.), N.Y.C., 1980-1983, sr. v.p., asst. personnel dir., 1983-85, exec. v.p., personnel dir., 1985-92; exec. v.p., pers. dir. Chem. Banking Corp. (formerly Mfrs. Hanover Trust Co.), 1992—; mem. mgmt. com. Chem. Banking Corp., 1994—; mem. adv. coun. on human resources mgmt. The Conf. Bd., 1992—. Trustee Drs. Hosp., 1984-92, Beth Israel Hosp., 1987—, Employee Benefit Rsch. Inst., 1989—; treas. Puerto Rican Legal Def. and Edn. Fund, Inc., mem. exec. com., 1985—. Mem. N.Y. State Bar Assn., N.Y. County Lawyers Assn.

ZUCKERMAN, MORTIMER BENJAMIN, publisher, editor, real estate developer; b. Montreal, Que., Can., June 4, 1937; came to U.S., 1961, naturalized, 1977; s. Abraham and Esther Z. B.A. in Econs. and Polit. Theory with 1st class honors, McGill U., Montreal, 1957, LL.B. with honors, 1961; M.B.A. with distinction, U. Pa., 1962; LL.M., Harvard U., 1962. Sr. v.p. Cabot, Cabot & Forbes, Boston, 1965-69; chmn. bd. Boston Properties Co., 1970—; pres., chmn. bd. Atlantic Monthly Co., Boston, 1980—; chmn., editor-in-chief U.S. News & World Report; chmn., co-pub. N.Y. Daily News; dir., exec. com. Stride Rite Corp., 1970-83; dir. Property Capital Trust Co., 1979-80, RET Income Found., 1976-79; public interest dir. Fed. Home Loan Bank of Boston, 1972-73; lectr., then assoc. prof. Harvard U. Grad. Sch. Design, 1966-74; vis. lectr. city and regional planning Yale U., 1967-69. Pres. bd. trustees Sidney Farber Cancer Inst., Boston, 1980; trustee Mus. Sci., 1980, Beth Israel Hosp., 1975, Ford Hall Forum, 1979-83, Urban Inst., Russell Sage Found., 1985-86; chmn. bd. visitors Boston U. Sch. Medicine, 1978-79; adv. bd. Ctr. Strategic and Internat. Studies; adv. bd. Wharton Sch.; bd. dirs. Wolf Trap Found., Tennis Hall of Fame. Mem. Coun. on Fgn. Rels., Internat. Inst. Strategic Studies. Clubs: Harvard (Boston and N.Y.C.); Harmonie (N.Y.C.). Office: New York Daily News 220 E 42nd St New York NY 10017-5806 Office: US News & World Report 2400 N St NW Washington DC 20037-1196*

ZUCKERMAN, RICHARD ENGLE, lawyer, law educator; b. Yonkers, N.Y., Aug. 2, 1945; s. Julius and Roslyn (Ehrlich) Z.; m. Denise Ellen Spoon, July 14, 1968; children: Julie Ann, Lindsay Beth. BA, U. Mich., 1967; JD cum laude, Southwestern U., 1974. Bar: Calif. 1974, Mich. 1976, Nev. 1986, U.S. Dist. Ct. (ea. and we. dists.) Mich. 1977, U.S. Ct. Appeals (6th cir.) 1977, U.S. Ct. Appeals (9th cir.) 1982, U.S. Ct. Appeals 2d and 7th cirs.) 1994, U.S. Tax Ct. 1980, U.S. Supreme Ct. 1985. Spl. atty. organized crime and racketeering sect. U.S. Dept. Justice, Detroit, 1974-77; sr. ptnr. Raymond, Rupp, Wienberg, Stone & Zuckerman, P.C., Troy, Mich., 1977-87, Honigman, Miller, Schwartz & Cohn, Detroit, 1987—; adj. prof. Detroit Coll. Law, 1978—; mem. Mich. Atty. Grievance Commn., 1995—. Served to lt. USN, 1967-71, Vietnam. Mem. ABA (grand jury com. criminal justice sect.), Mich. Atty. Grievance Commn. (supreme ct. nominee 1995—), Fed. Bar Assn. (chmn. criminal law sect. Detroit chpt. 1985-90, bd. dirs. 1985-94, co-chair criminal def. atty. com. 1955—), Knollwood Country Club (West Bloomfield, Mich.), Std. Club, Am. Inns Ct. (master of bench 1995—). Republican. Jewish. Office: Honigman Miller Schwartz & Cohn 2290 First National Bldg Detroit MI 48226

ZUCKERMAN, STUART, psychiatrist, educator; b. Syracuse, N.Y., Feb. 18, 1933; s. George and Cassie (Kolsan) Z. Student, U. Kans., 1950-51; BS, U. Ala., 1954; DO, Phila. Coll. Osteo. Medicine, 1958. Diplomate Am. Osteo. Bd. Neurology and Psychiatry, Am. Nat. Bd. Psychiatry, Am. Coll. Forensic Medicine, Bd. Forensic Medicine, Bd. Forensic Examiner; cert. correctional health profl. Rotating intern Hosps. Phila. Coll. Osteo. Medicine, 1958-59; psychiat. fellow, resident Phila. Mental Health Clinic, 1959-62, Psychoanalytic Studies Inst., Phila., 1959-62; chief resident, 1962; chief div. neuropsychiatry Grandview Hosp., Dayton, Ohio, 1962-65; asst. med. dir., chief children's and adolescent's unit N.J. State Hosp., Ancora, 1967-70; chief outpatient dept. Atlantic City, 1970-72; practice specializing in neuropsychiatry Atlantic City, 1965—; founding prof. psychiatry, chmn. dept. Ohio U. Coll. Osteo. Medicine, Athens, 1976-77; clin. prof. Ohio U. Coll. Osteo. Medicine, 1977—; mem. faculty U. Pa. Sch. Medicine, Phila. Coll. Osteo. Medicine, 1972-76; lectr. U. Pa., 1977-79; prof. dept. psychiatry, charter faculty Sch. Medicine, Marshall U., 1977-78, clin. prof., 1979-80; clin. prof. N.Y. Coll. Osteo. Medicine, 1979—; chief mental hygiene VA Hosp., Huntington, W.Va., 1978-79; liaison psychiatrist, acting chief VA Med. Center, Perry Point, Md., 1979-80; med. dir. Mental Health Clinic of Ocean County, Toms River, N.J., 1980-85, Ventnor Mental Health Ctr., Atlantic City; chief psychiatrist N.J. Dept. Corrections So. State Correctional Facility, 1985—; attending psychiatrist Atlantic City, Shore Meml., Kessler Meml., Washington Meml., Atlantic County Mental hosps., 1965-76; attending psychiatrist, asst. dir. dept. psychiatry Phila. Gen. Hosp., 1972-76; med. dir. Shawnee Mental Health Center, (Adams, Lawrence, Scioto counties), Portsmouth, Ohio, 1977-78; cons. psychiatrist Athens Mental Health and Mental Retardation Ctr., 1976-77, Scioto Meml., So. Hills, Mercy hosps., Portsmouth, 1977-78, Lansdowne Cmty. Mental Health Center, (Greenup, Carter counties), Ashland, Ky., 1977-78, Atlantic City Med. Ctr., 1984—, Cmty. Meml. Hosp., Toms River, N.J., 1984-91, So. Ocean County Hosp., Manahawkin, N.J., 1984-91, Paul-Kimball Med Ctr., Lakewood, N.J., 1984—, Obleness Meml. Hosp., Clin. Services of Athens, Vinton, Hocking Counties, Hudson Health Ctr., Ohio U., 1976077; cons. Bayside State Prison, Leesburg, N.J., 1989-94, Atlantic County Justice System, Mays Landing, N.J., 1992-93, child study spl. svcs. S. Jersey sch. systems; chmn. profl. adv. com. Atlantic County Mental Health Bd., 1969-71; mem. nominating com. Mental Health Assn., Atlantic County, 1972-75; exam. psychiatrist Jersey Police and Fire depts.; mem. Atlantic County Mental Health Bd.; mem. profl. adv. com. N.J. Dept. Corrections; cons. N.J. Dept. Pub. Advocate. Mem. adv. bd. Osteo. Physician, 1975—; assoc. editor Bull. Am. Coll. Neuropsychiatrists, 1963-70, Jour. Corr. Health; contbr. articles to profl. jours. Bd. dirs. Atlantic County Family Svcs. Assn., 1968-74, Cape May County Drug Abuse Coun., 1973-76, Nat. Comm. Correctional Health Care, 1988—; mem. Ventnor City Beautification Com. Fellow Am. Coll. Forensic Psychiatry, Am. Coll. Neuropsychiatrists (bd. reps.), Am. Acad. Disability Evaluating Physicians (charter), Acad. Medicine N.J.; mem. AMA (Physicians Recognition award 1985—), AAUP, Am. Bd. Forensic Examiners (cert. 1994), Am. Coll. Forensic Medicine (bd. cert. 1996), World Psychiat. Assn., Am. Psychiat. Assn., N.J. (confidentiality, pub. psychiatry com., gen. hosp. psychiatry com., law com., mkgt. benefits com.) Psychiat. Assn., Am. Assn. Psychiatrists in Alcohol and Addictions (founder), Am., N.J. pub. health assns., Am. Osteo. Assn. (hosp. inspection team 1971-75, bd. reps.), Am. Assn. CMHC Psychiatrists, Am. Assn. Psychiatrists in Pvt. Practice, Internat. Assn. Med. Specialists, Am. Soc. Law and Medicine, Am. Acad. Clin. Psychiatrists, Corp. Advancement Psychiatry, Am. Med. Writers A., Nat. Council Community Mental Health Ctrs., Met. Coll. Mental Health Assn., Am. Soc. Criminology., South Jersey Neuropsychiat. Soc., Psychiat. Outpatients Ctrs. Am., Am. Coll. Legal Medicine, Acad. Psychiatry and Law (pub. info. com., edn. com., internat. affairs com.), Am. Acad. Forensic Scis., Am. Assn. Acad. Psychiatry, Am. Coll. Emergency Physicians, Am. Acad. Psychotherapists, Am. Assn. Mental Deficiency, Am. Assn. Psychiat. Services for Children, Acad. Psychosomatic Medicine, N.J. (chmn. com. on confidentiality), Fla. assns. osteo. physicians and surgeons, N.J. Hosp. Assn., Am. Vocat. Assn., Am. Assn. Group Therapy, Assn. Mil. Surgeons U.S., Nat. Assn. VA Physicians, Am. Assn. Psychiat. Adminstrs., Am. Assn. Adolescent Psychiatry, World Med. Assn., Am. Assn. Mental Health Adminstrs., Am. Assn. Gen. Hosp. Psychiatrists, Human Factors Soc., Orthopsychiat. Assn., Am. Physicians Fellowship, Assn. for Research Nervous and Mental Diseases, Atlantic County Osteo. Med. Soc. (pres. 1970-72), N.J. Assn. Mil. Surgeons U.S. (v.p.), Am. Assn. Correctional Health Care, Am. Coll. Forensic Psychiatry (diplomate 1984), charter mem. Soc. of Correctional Physicians. Home: 6700 Atlantic Ave Ventnor City NJ 08406-2618 Office: Ventnor Mental Health Ctr Ventnor City NJ 08406

ZUCKERT, DONALD MACK, marketing executive; b. N.Y.C., Apr. 3, 1934; s. Sidney L. and Doris (Mack) Z.; m. Susan Liefter; children: Andrew, Timothy. AB in Govt. with honors, Bowdoin Coll., 1956; LLB, NYU, 1959. Bar: N.Y., Conn. 1960. With Ted Bates Worldwide, Inc., N.Y.C., 1960-87; pres. Ted Bates U.S. Affiliate Group, N.Y.C., 1974-83, Ted Bates Advt./N.Y., N.Y.C., 1983-86; chmn., chief exec. officer Ted Bates Worldwide, Inc., 1986-87; pres. Backer Spielvogel Bates Worldwide Inc., N.Y.C., 1987; chmn., chief exec. officer Arcature Corp., Stamford, Conn., 1989-95; vice chmn. Draft Direct Worldwide, N.Y.C., 1996—; bd. dirs. Calif. & Wash. Co., San Bruno, Calif., Suanti Ltd., Manchester, N.H., F.S.G.S. Inc., Stamford, Conn., Rattlesnake Holdings, Inc., Wilmington, Del. Bd. govs., trustee Bowdoin Coll., Brunswick, Maine; nat. overseer Strawbery Banke Mus., Portsmouth, N.H. Served to capt. AUS, 1956-57. Mem. Innis Arden Golf Club (Old Greenwich, Conn.), Westworth by the Sea Country Club (New Castle, N.H.), New Castle Yacht Club, River Club (N.Y.C.), Alpha Tau Omega. Office: DraftDirect Worldwide 633 3rd Ave New York NY 10017

ZUCKMAN, HARVEY LYLE, law educator; b. Mpls., Apr. 14, 1934; s. George and Elizabeth (Polinsky) Z.; m. Charlotte Anne Snyder, Jan. 27, 1962; children: Jill Belinda, Beth Nancy, Michael Scott. A.B., U. So. Calif., 1956; LL.B., NYU, 1959. Bar: Calif. 1960, D.C. 1973, U.S. Supreme Ct. 1963. Atty. civil div. appellate sect. U.S. Dept. Justice, Washington, 1963-67; prof. law St. Louis U., 1967-70, Columbus Sch. Law of Cath. U. Am., 1970—; dir. Inst. for Communications Law Studies Columbus Sch. Law, Cath. U. Am., 1981—; adj. prof. communications Am. U., 1976-81; cons. Bur. Nat. Affairs., 1974-81. Producer: Am. Law Inst.-ABA Legal Edn. TV series, 1973-74; co-author: Mass Communications Law, 1977, 4th edit., 1994; editor ABA newsletter Comm. Lawyer, 1981-86. Served with U.S. Army Judge Adv. Gen., 1960-63. Mem. ABA (forum com. on comm. law, co-chmn. nat. celebration of 200th anniversary of 1st amendment 1991), D.C. Bar Assn. (chairperson com. on continuing legal edn. 1975-83), Fed. Comm. Bar Assn., Am. Law Inst., Assn. Am. Law Schs. (sects. family law and mass comm.). Democrat. Office: Cath U Am Columbus Sch Law Leahy Hall Washington DC 20064

ZUEHLKE, RICHARD WILLIAM, technical communications consultant, writer; b. Milw., June 17, 1933; s. Harold Babcock and Phoebe Blanche (Frykman) Z.; m. Carol Sue Yates, Dec. 26, 1955; children: Kenneth Richard, William Woodfill, Deanne Elizabeth. B.S., Lawrence Coll., 1955; Ph.D., U. Minn., 1960. Instr. chemistry Lawrence U., 1958-62, asst. prof., 1962-68; Eliphalet Remington prof. chemistry U. Bridgeport, 1968-79, chmn. dept., 1968-73; vis. prof. U. R.I., 1976-77, 79-80, assoc. marine scientist, 1980-85; owner, pres. The Right Connection, Inc., 1983-91; pres. TetraR Cons., Inc., 1985-88; cons. Kimberly-Clark Corp., 1960-62, United Illuminating Co., 1969-75, Chem. Specialties Corp., 1970-73, Sperry Remington Corp., 1976-79; NSF Sci. Faculty fellow U. Pitts., 1966-67; asst. to dir. Gordon Rsch. Confs., 1990-94; cons., writer in field. Fellow Am. Inst. Chemists; mem. Am. Chem. Soc., AAAS, Sigma Xi, Sigma Phi Epsilon. Congregationalist. Lodge: Rotary. Home: 1410 South Rd Wakefield RI 02879-7641 Office: 1410 South Rd Wakefield RI 02879-7641

ZUETEL, KENNETH ROY, JR., lawyer; b. L.A., Apr. 5, 1954; s. Kenneth Roy Sr. and Adelle Francis (Avant) Z.; m. Cheryl Kay Morse, May 29, 1976; children: Bryan, Jarid, Christopher, Lauren. BA, San Diego State U., 1974; JD, U. San Diego, 1978. Bar: Calif. 1978 U.S. Ct. Appeals (9th cir.) 1979, U.S. Dist. Ct. (ctrl. dist.) Calif. 1979, U.S. Dist. Ct. (so. and no. dists.) Calif. 1980, U.S. Dist. Ct. (ea. dist.) 1981. Clk. to fed. Judge Martin Pence U.S. Dist. Ct. Hawaii, Honolulu, 1978-79; assoc. litigation Buchalter, Nemer, L.A., 1979-83, Thelen, Marrin, L.A., 1983-88; ptnr. Hammond, Zuetel & Cahill, Pasadena, Calif., 1988—; superior ct. arbitrator L.A. Superior Ct., 1982-90, superior ct. settlement officer, 1988-93; judge pro temp L.A. Mcpl. Ct., 1983—, L.A. Superior Ct., 1989—; guest lectr. Loyola U. Sch. Law, 1986—; CEB lectr. Author: Civil Procedure Before Trial, 1992; cons. editor: Cal. Civ. Proc., 1992; contbr. articles to profl. jours. Recipient Recognition award L.A. (Calif.) Bd. Suprs., 1988. Mem. State Bar Calif. (mem. adv. com. continuing edn. 1985-88, trial practice subcom. 1985-88, disciplinary examiner 1986), Los Angeles County Bar Assn. (chair trial atty. project 1982-83, mem. L.A. del. conf. of dels. 1986—, chair L.A. del. conf. of dels. 1995, exec. com. barristers 1984-88, superior ct. com. 1985-88, civil practice com. 1992-94, exec. com. litigation sect. 1989-90), Pasadena Bar Assn., Inns of Ct. (barrister L.A. chpt. 1991-92), Phi Beta Kappa, Phi Kappa Phi, Phi Alpha Theta, Pi Sigma Alpha. Republican. Presbyterian. Home: 567 Willow Springs Ln Glendora CA 91741 Office: Hammond Zuetel & Cahill 180 S Lake Ave #540 Pasadena CA 91101

ZUFRYDEN, FRED S., academic administrator, marketing educator, researcher; b. Grenoble, France, June 13, 1943; came to U.S., 1956; s. Henri and Cecile (Frymer) Z.; m. Toby Marlene Levin, Dec. 24, 1967; 1 child, Ryan. B.A. in Math., UCLA, 1965, M.B.A., 1966, Ph.D. in Bus. Adminstrn., 1971. Rsch. engr. mil. ops. and systems analysis group N.Am. Aviation, Inc., L.A., 1966-67; rsch. assoc. resources rsch. dept. Planning Rsch. Corp., L.A., 1967-68; ops. rsch. specialist data systems div. Litton Systems, Inc., L.A., 1968-70; asst. prof. dept. mgmt. scis. Sch. Bus. and Econs., U. Calif., Northridge, 1970-71; asst. prof. dept. mktg. Grad. Sch. Bus. U. So. Calif., L.A., 1971-75; assoc. prof. U. So. Calif., 1975-82, prof., 1982—, Ernst Hahn prof. mktg., 1991—, chmn. mktg. dept., 1987-90, rsch. dir. internat. bus. econs. and rsch. Grad. Sch. Bus., 1983—. Mem. editorial bd. Jour. Advt. Rsch., 1981—, Mktg. Sci., 1979—, Jour. Mktg., 1978—; mem. cons. and planning com. Mktg. Sci. Jour., 1979; referee Jour. Mktg. Rsch., Mgmt. Sci., Decision Sci., Jour. Internat. Rsch. in Mktg.; mem. abstract writing staff International Abstracts in Operations Rsch./Mgmt. Sci., 1973; contbr. articles to profl. jours. including Jour. Mktg. Rsch., Mktg. Sci., Jour. Operational Rsch. Soc., Mgmt. Sci., Decision Scis., Jour. Mktg., Jour. Advt. Rsch., Jour. Internat. Rsch. in Mktg., Jour. Royal Statis. Soc., Interfaces, Rsch. in Mktg., Jour. of Mktg. Rsch. Soc., Jour. of Bus., others. Rsch. grantee U. So. Calif., 1973, 75, 76, 77, 78, A.C. Nielsen Co., 1988-90. Mem. Am. Mktg. Assn. (cert. recognition 1974), Ops. Rsch. Soc. Am., Inst. Mgmt. Sci., Omega Rho, Beta Gamma Sigma.

ZUHDI, NAZIH, surgeon; b. Beirut, May 19, 1925; came to U.S., 1950; s. Omar and Lutfiye (Atef) Z.; children by previous marriage: Omar, Nabil; m. Annette McMichael; children: Adam, Leyla, Zachariah. BA, Am. U., Beirut, 1946, MD, 1950. Diplomate Am. Bd. Surgery, Am. Bd. Thoracic Surgery. Intern St. Vincent's Hosp., S.I., N.Y., 1950-51, Presbyn.-Columbia Med. Ctr., N.Y.C., 1951-52; resident Kings County SUNY Med. Ctr., N.Y.C., 1952-56; fellow SUNY Downstate Med. Ctr., Bklyn., 1953-54; resident Univ. Hosp., Mpls., 1956; resident Univ. Hosp., Oklahoma City, 1957-58, practice surgery specializing in cardiovascular and thoracic, 1958-87, practice in heart transplantation, lung transplantation and heart-lung transplantation, 1985—; founder, dir. Transplantation Inst. Bapt. Med. Ctr., 1984—, transplantation surgeon in chief Bapt. Hosp., Oklahoma City; founder, chmn. Okla. Cardiovascular Inst., Oklahoma City, 1983-84, Okla. Heart Ctr., Oklahoma City, 1984-85. Contbg. author Cardiac Surgery, 1967, 2d edit., 1972; contbr. articles to profl. jours.; developer numerous med. devices, techniques, rsch. and publs. on cardiopulmonary bypass, internal hypothermia, assisted circulation, heart surgery and transplantation of thoracic organs; developer heart-lung machines; designer, use of exptl. plastic bypass hearts; originator use of banked citrated blood for cardiopulmonary bypass for open heart surgery, of clin. non-hemic primes of heart-lung machines producing intentional hemodilution, at present, the universally accepted principle of cardiopulmonary bypass for partial and total body perfusion; researcher in cardiovascular studies. Named Hon. Citizen, Brazil; named to Okla. Hall of Fame, 1994; Muslim scholar, lectr.; NCCJ Humanitarian honoree, 1996. Fellow ACS; mem. AMA, Am. Thoracic Soc., Okla. Thoracic Soc., So. Med. Assn., Okla. Med. Assn., Internat., Coll. Angiology, Am. Coll. Chest Physicians, Oklahoma City C. of C., Oklahoma County Med. Soc., Oklahoma City Clin. Soc., Okla. Surg. Assn., Oklahoma City Surg. Soc., Southwestern Surg. Congress, Am. Coll. Cardiology, Am. Soc. Artificial Internal Organs, Soc. Thoracic Surgeons (founder mem.), Am. Assn. for Thoracic Surgery, Internat. Cardiovascular Soc., Okla. State Heart Assn., Osler Soc., So. Thoracic Surg. Assn., Lillehei Surg. Soc., Internat. Soc. Heart Transplantation, Dwight Harken's Founder's Group Cardiac Surgery, Internat. Soc. Cardiothoracic Surgery (Japan, founder), Am. Soc. Transplant Surgeons, Milestones of Cardiology of Am. Coll. Cardiology, Okla. City Golf and Country Club, Okla. Hall of Fame. Achievements include first banked citrated blood for cardiopulmonary bypass for open heart surgery; invention of clinical non-hemic primes of heart-lung machines producing intentional hemodilution. Home: 7305 Lancet Ct Oklahoma City OK 73120-1430

ZUHLKE, MARYBETH, elementary school curriculum consultant, educator; b. Kenosha, Wis., Jan. 16, 1946; d. Charles Casmir and Elizabeth (Mulich) Safransky; m. Lee VanLunduyt, Aug. 24, 1968 (div. 1985); children: Kyle, Ravi; m. Tom Zuhlke, Sept. 9, 1990. Student, U. Dallas, 1965-67; BS, U. Wis., Whitewater, 1968; MS, U. Wis., Milw., 1973, postgrad., 1988-89; postgrad., Marquette U., 1978-81. Cert. elem. tchr., prin., coord. instruction, Wis. Tchr. second grade Kenosha Unified Sch. Dist., 1968-70, community liaison tchr., 1974-79, dissemination specialist, 1979-82, curriculum cons., 1982—; cons. Conn. Facilitator, North Haven, 1984-86, South Ocean Internat. Sch., Datong, China, 1995-96; prin. McKinley Elem. Sch., Kenosha, 1988-89. Co-author: Kenosha Model Kindergarten Manual, 1985, Kenosha Model Math. Manual, 1986; editor: Kenosha Model Language Experience, 1979. Mem. Racine (Wis.) Arts Coun., 1980—. Mem. ASCD, Internat. Reading Assn., Parent Edn. and Childhood Assn. (exec. bd. 1976-83), Inst. of World Affairs, Wis. State and Fed. Specialists (newsletter editor 1986-87), Assn. Wis. Sch. Administrs., Phi Delta Kappa. Avocations: reading, cross-country skiing, nature. Home: 1419 Crabapple Dr Racine WI 53405-1703 Office: Kenosha Unified Sch Dist Parkside Kenosha WI 53142

ZUICHES, JAMES JOSEPH, academic administrator; b. Eau Claire, Wis., Mar. 24, 1943; s. William Homer and Bronnie Monica (Stich) Z.; m. Carol Ann Kurilo, Aug. 19, 1967; children: James Daniel, Joseph Kurilo. BA in Philosophy, U. Portland, 1967; MS in Sociology, U. Wis., 1969, PhD in Sociology, 1973. Instr., asst. prof., assoc. prof. sociology Mich. State U., East Lansing, 1971-82, prof., 1982; assoc. program dir. in sociology NSF, Washington, 1979-80, program dir. in sociology, 1980-82; assoc. dir. rsch. Cornell U., Ithaca, N.Y., 1982-86; assoc. dean Coll. Agr. and Home Econs., Wash. State U., Pullman, 1986-94, dir. Agrl. Rsch. Ctr., 1986-94; program dir. food sys. and rural devel. W.K. Kellogg Found., Battle Creek, Mich., 1994-95; dean Coll. Agr. and Home Econs. Wash. State U., Pullman, 1995—; mem. adv. subcom. NSF, 1977-79; sci. adv. com. USDA Nat. Rsch. Initiative, Washington, 1992-93; com. on future land grant univ. bd. on agr., NRC, Washington, 1994-96; pub. Wash. Land and People Mag., 1987-92. Co-editor: The Demography of Rural Life, 1993; contbr. articles to profl. jours. Pres., bd. dirs. Edgewood Village Children's Ctr., East Lansing, 1978-79. Recipient sustained superior performance award NSF, 1981; rsch. grantee NIMH, 1973, ERDA, 1978. Fellow AAAS; mem. Rural Sociol. Soc. (pres. 1992-93, editor 50th Anniversary Rsch. Series, 5 vols. 1988-93), Am. Sociol. Assn., Population Assn. Am. Roman Catholic. Avocations: skiing, swimming, hiking, reading.

ZUICK, DIANE MARTINA, elementary education educator; b. Gary, Ind., May 19, 1951; d. Arnold and Matilda (Chaimovitz) Herskovic; m. Norman Robert Zuick, Aug. 12, 1973; children: Scott, Amy. BS in Edn., Ind. U., 1972, MS in Edn., 1974. Tchr. 5th grade George L. Myers Sch., Portage, Ind., 1972-73, tchr. 3d grade, 1973-83, tchr. 1st grade, 1983-90, tchr. 2d grade, 1990—; mem. prime time com. Portage Twp. Schs., 1991—, mem. reading curriculum com., 1987-88, mem. devel. com., 1983-85; mem. adv. K'ton Ton Pre-Sch., Highland, Ind., 1984-86. Chair sch. bd. Congregation Beth Israel, Hammond, Ind., 1993-95, mem. sch. bd., 1992-95, mem. exec. bd., 1994—; mem. B'nai B'rith, Hammond, 1993—, mem. dist. bd. govs., 1995—. Recipient Ind. Dept. Instrn. Prime Time award, 1988, 89; Portage Twp. Schs. grantee, 1993, 94. Mem. NEA, Ind. State Tchrs. Assn., Portage Assn. Tchrs., Tchrs. Applying Whole Langs., Internat. Reading Assn., Ind. U. Alumni Assn. Avocations: reading, travel, piano, nature, music. Home: 58 Cedar Ln Schererville IN 46375-1107 Office: Portage Twp Schs 6240 US Highway 6 Portage IN 46368-5057

ZUIDEMA, GEORGE DALE, surgeon; b. Holland, Mich., Mar. 8, 1928; s. Jacob and Reka (Dalman) Z.; m. Joan K. Houtman, June 2, 1953; children: Karen Sue, David Jay, Nancy Ruth, Sarah Kay. A.B., Hope Coll., 1949, D.Sc. (hon.), 1969; M.D., Johns Hopkins U., 1953. Diplomate: Am. Bd. Surgery. Intern Mass. Gen. Hosp., 1953-54, asst. resident surgeon, then chief resident surgeon, 1954, 57, 58, 59; asst. prof. surgery, then assoc. prof. U. Mich. Sch. Medicine, 1960-64; prof. surgery, dir. dept. Johns Hopkins Sch. Medicine; also surgeon in chief Johns Hopkins Hosp., 1964-84; prof. surgery, vice provost med. affairs U. Mich., 1984-94; Cons. Walter Reed Army Med. Center, Sinai Hosp., Balt., Balt. City Hosp., Clin. Center of NIH; chmn. Study on Surg. Services for U.S., 1970-75. Editor: (with O.H. Gauer) Gravitational Stress in Aerospace Medicine, 1961; (with G.L. Nardi) Surgery-A Concise Guide to Clinical Practice, 1961, 4th edit., 1982; (with R.D. Judge and F. Fitzgerald) Physical Diagnosis, 1963, 4th edit., 1982; (with W.F. Ballinger and R.B. Rutherford) Management of Trauma, 1968, 3d edit., 1979, 4th edit., 1985; (with L. Schlossberg) Atlas of Human Functional Anatomy, 1977, 2d edit., 1980, 3d edit., 1986, Shackelford's Surgery of the Alimentary Tract, 4th edit., 1996; editor Jour. Surg. Rsch., 1966-72, assoc. editor, mem. editl. bd., 1972—; mem. editl. bd. Surgery Ann., 1968—, Surgery, 1970—, co-editor in chief, 1975—. Bd. dirs. Md. divsn. Am. Cancer Soc., 1964-68; trustee William Beaumont Hosp., Royal Oak, Mich., Hope Coll., Holland, Mich. Capt. M.C., USAF, 1954-56. John and Mary R. Markle scholar academic medicine, 1961-66; recipient Henry Russell award U. Mich., 1963. Fellow ACS, Royal Coll. Surgeons Ireland (hon.); mem. Assn. Am. Med. Colls., Ctrl. Soc. Clin. Rsch., Soc. Univ. Surgeons, Am. Surg. Assn., So. Surg. Assn., Soc. Clin. Surgery, Soc. Vascular Surgery, Internat. Cardiovascular Surgery, Halsted Soc., Nat. Inst. Medicine, Assn. Acad. Surgeons (pres. 1967-69), Allen O. Whipple Soc., Coun. on Grad. Med. Edn., Phi Beta Kappa, Tri Beta, Alpha Omega Alpha. Home: 11 Haverhill Ct Ann Arbor MI 48105-1406 Office: U Mich M4100 Med Sci I Ann Arbor MI 48109-0608

ZUK, JUDITH, botanic garden administrator. Ceo and pres. Bklyn Botanic Garden, Brooklyn, N.Y., 1980—. Office: Brooklyn Botanic Garden 1000 Washington Ave Brooklyn NY 11225-1008

ZUKER, MICHAEL, biomathematician; b. Montreal, Que., Can., Apr. 1, 1949; s. Norman and Edith (Diamond) Z.; m. Barbara Ann Boness, Dec. 24, 1978; children—Sandra Esther, Leslie Susan. B.Sc., McGill U., Montreal, Que., Can., 1970; Ph.D., MIT, 1974. Rsch. officer NRC Can., Ottawa, Ont., 1974-94; fellow Can. Inst. for Advanced Rsch., 1988-94; assoc. prof. Inst. for Biomed. Computing Washington U., St. Louis, 1994—; vis. scholar Stanford U., 1991-92. Assoc. editor: Bull. Math. Biology, 1984-86; mem. editl. bd. Computer Applications in Biosci., Gene Combis; contbr. rsch. articles to profl. jours. Recipient Silver medal Royal Conservatory of Music, Toronto, 1962; Prince of Wales scholar McGill U., Montreal, Que., Can., 1969; Woodrow Wilson fellow, 1970. Mem. AAAS, Soc. Math. Biology. Avocations: piano playing, windsurfing, cycling. Home: 435 Oakley Dr Saint Louis MO 63105 Office: Washington U Inst for Biomed Computing 700 S Euclid Ave Saint Louis MO 63110-1012

ZUKERMAN, MICHAEL, lawyer; b. Bklyn., Oct. 3, 1940; s. Charles Morris and Gertrude Ethel Zukerman; m. Claire J. Goldsmith, June 25, 1961 (div. 1986); children: Steven, Amy; m. Elaine DeMasi, Nov. 21, 1986; children: Jaclyn, Laura. BS, U. Fla., 1961; LLB, St. John's U., 1964; LLM, NYU, 1966. Bar: N.Y. 1965, Pa. 1983, U.S. Tax Ct. 1984. Credit analyst, loan officer Franklin Nat. Bank, 1964-66; assoc. Jaffin, Schneider, Kimmel & Galpeer, N.Y.C., 1966-67; ptnr. Zukerman, Licht & Friedman and predecessors, N.Y.C., 1967-79, Baskin & Sears, P.C., N.Y.C., 1979-85, Graubard, Moskowitz, Dannett, Horowitz & Mollen, 1985-86, Gersten, Savage, Kaplowitz & Zukerman, 1986-89; of counsel Olshan, Grundman, Frome & Rosenzweig, 1990-95; of counsel Graham & James, 1995—; pres. First Ptnrs. Credit Corp., N.Y.C., 1988-93, exec. v.p. Brookhill Group, 1986-88, Real Mark Adv. Corp., 1993—; mem. bd. dirs. Interjurist LTD, internat. law firm, 1986—. Contbg. editor Real Estate Taxation and Acctg., 1988-93; lectr. on various subjects, 1986—. Contbr. articles to profl. jours. Trustee Temple Beth Torah, Melville, N.Y., 1972-80; bd. dirs. Dayton Mgmt. Corp., 1974—, Suffolk Jewish Community Planning Bd., Hauppague, N.Y., 1982-85, WATSCO, Inc., Am. Vending Assocs., 1983-86; trustee, treas. YMHA Suffolk County, Hauppague, 1980-85; co-chmn. bus. adv. coun. Town of Greenburgh, 1992; bd. dirs. Congregation Bnai Elohim, 1994, 2d v.p., 1995. Mem. ABA. Home: 6 Thomas St Scarsdale NY 10583-1031 Office: Graham & James 885 3d Ave 24th Flr New York NY 10022-1106

ZUKERMAN, MORRIS E., investment banker; b. Vineland, N.J., June 13, 1944; s. Nathan Z.; m. Karen D. Solomon, Dec. 5, 1971; children: Laura B., Sarah B., Alexandra W. Diploma, Phillips Acad., Andover, Mass., 1962; BA, Harvard Coll., 1966; MBA (with high distinction), Harvard Grad. Sch. Bus. Adminstrn., 1970; MA (with honors), Cambridge (Eng.) U., 1968. Economist Internat. Bank for Reconstrn. and Devel., Washington, 1968-70, U.S. Office Mgmt. and Budget, Washington, 1970-72; mng. dir. Morgan Stanley & Co. Inc., N.Y.C. and L.A., 1972-88; pres. M. E. Zukerman & Co. Inc., N.Y.C., 1988—. Trustee Phillips Acad. Andover, 1984-88, Jackson Lab., Bar Harbor, Maine, 1988-90, The Spence Sch., N.Y.C., 1989-93; bd. dirs. L.A. Music Ctr. Opera, 1986-90; vis. com. on faculty recruitment, Harvard U. Sch. of Arts and Scis., 1990-92. Mem. Harvard Club N.Y.C., University Club (N.Y.C.), Regency Club (L.A.), Oxford & Cambridge U. Club (London). Avocation: African affairs. Office: M E Zukerman & Co Inc 535 Madison Ave Fl 19 New York NY 10022-4212*

ZUKERMAN, PINCHAS, concert violinist, violist, conductor; b. Tel Aviv, July 16, 1948; came to U.S., 1962; s. Yehuda and Miriam (Lieberman) Z.; m. Eugenia Rich, May 26, 1968 (div.); children: Natalia, Arianna; m. Tuesday Weld, 1985. Student, Juilliard Sch. Music, 1965-68; MusD (hon.), Brown U., 1989. Ind. concert violinist, 1968—. With impresario, Sol Hurok, 1967-76; condr., soloist English Chamber Orch., 1974, Mostly Mozart Festival, N.Y.C., 1975; guest condr., soloist Los Angeles Philharm., Boston Symphony, Phila. Orch., N.Y. Philharm.; music dir. South Bank Festival, London, 1978-80, St. Paul Chamber Orch., 1980-87; prin. festival condr. Dallas Internat. Summer Music Festival, 1990—; prin. guest condr. Dallas Symphony, 1993—; toured with Isaac Stern; mem. trio with Daniel Barenboim and Jacqueline du Pre; (rec. artist) CBS, EMI, Philips Classics labels, RCA Victor Red Seal, BMG Classics. Winner Internat. Levintritt Competition, 1967. Office: care Shirley Kirshbaum & Assoc 711 West End Ave-5 KN New York NY 10025

ZUKOSKI, CHARLES FREDERICK, surgeon, educator; b. St. Louis, Jan. 26, 1926; s. Charles F. Jr. and Bernadine (Edom) Z.; m. Elizabeth Paull Jacob, May 9, 1953; children: Helen, Charles, Robin, Ann. BS, U. N.C., 1947; MD, Harvard U., 1951. Diplomate Am. Bd. Surgery. Intern Roosevelt Hosp., N.Y.C., 1951-52; resident Univ. Hosp., Birmingham, Ala., 1955-58; asst. chief VA Hosp., Birmingham, 1958-59; rschr. Med. Coll. Va., Richmond, 1959-61; asst. prof. Vanderbilt U. Med. Ctr., Nashville, 1961-68; assoc. prof. Coll. Medicine U. N.C., Chapel Hill, 1968-69; prof. surgery Coll. Medicine U. Ariz., Tucson, 1969-95, prof. emeritus dept. surgery Coll. Medicine, 1995—; chief surg. svc. VA Hosp., Tucson, 1990-95. Contbr. 85 articles to profl. publs. Capt. USAF, 1953-55. Fellow NIH, 1959-61, 66-67, Josia Macy Found., 1976-77. Fellow ACS, Am. Surg. Assn.; mem. Soc. Univ. Surgeons, So. Surg. Assn. Achievements include research on immunosuppressive drugs. Home: 1901 E Miraval Cuarto Tucson AZ 85718

ZUKOWSKI, WALTER HENRY, administrative science educator; b. Worcester, Mass., Sept. 28, 1914; s. Frank B. and Helen (Jankowska) Z.; m. Lucille Kathryn Pinette, Dec. 26, 1955; 1 dau., Mary L.A. B.B.A., Clark U., 1948, A.M., 1949, Ph.D., 1956. Instr. Worcester Poly. Inst., 1949-50, Clark U., 1951-52; mem. faculty Colby Coll., Waterville, Maine, 1952—; prof. adminstrv. sci. Colby Coll., 1965-73, Wadsworth prof. adminstrv. sci., 1973-82; emeritus Wadsworth prof. adminstrv. sci., 1982—; chmn. dept. adminstrv. sci. Colby Coll., 1958-80; asst. prof. La. State U. (C.Z. br.), summers 1952-54; vis. prof. Rockefeller Found. grantee Al-Hikma U., Baghdad, Iraq, 1958-59, Robert Coll., Istanbul, Turkey, 1965-66; vis. prof., cons. ednl. policy Iranzamin Coll., Tehran, Iran, 1972-73; cons. in field. Mem. platform com. Maine Republican Party, 1964. Served with USAAF, 1942-46. Mem. Am. Finance Assn., Am. Econ. Assn., Am. Accounting Assn. Home: PO Box 402 Waterville ME 04903-0402

ZUKOWSKY, JOHN ROBERT, curator; b. N.Y.C., Apr. 21, 1948; s. John and Mary (Charchan) Z. BA, Hunter Coll., 1971; MA, SUNY, Binghamton, 1974, PhD, 1977. Archtl. archivist Hudson River Mus., Yonkers, N.Y., 1974-76; archtl. archivist Art Inst. Chgo., 1978-81, architecture curator, 1981—; mem. Historic Sites Adv. Council, Springfield, Ill., 1982-83, Landmarks Preservation Council, Chgo., 1982-83; jury mem. Honor awards AIA, Washington, 1987. Co-author: Hudson River Villas, 1985, The Sky's the Limit Chicago Skyscrapers, 1990, Austrian Architecture and Design, 1991; co-author, editor: Mies Reconsidered, 1986, Chicago Architecture: 1872-1922, 1987, Chicago Architecture and Design, 1923-93, 1993, The Many Faces of Modern Architecture, 1994, Karl Friedrich Schinkel, 1781-1841: The Drama of Architecture, 1994, Building for Air Travel: Architecture and Design for Commercial Aviation, 1996; editor: A System of Architectural Ornament (Louis H. Sullivan), 1990; contbr. articles to profl. jours. Decorated Chevalier des arts and lettres (France), Ritter Kreuz 2d class, Austria; recipient Honig award Chgo. chpt. Am. Soc. Appraisers, 1989; postdoctoral rsch. fellow NEH, 1977-78, Rsch. fellow, NEA, 1991. Mem. AIA (hon., Disting. Svc. award Chgo. chpt. 1986), Arts Club Chgo. Office: Art Inst Chgo Dept Architecture 111 S Michigan Ave Chicago IL 60603-6110

ZULCH, JOAN CAROLYN, retired medical publishing company executive, consultant; b. Great Neck, N.Y., Apr. 10, 1931; d. Walter Howard and Edna Ruth (Howard) Z. B.S. in Biology, Allegheny Coll., 1952; postgrad., Hunter Coll., 1954. Med. sec. E.R. Squibb & Sons, N.Y.C., 1952; with Macmillan Pub. Co., N.Y.C., 1952-88, editorial asst. med. dept., 1952-56, asst. editor med. dept., 1956-58, editor med. dept., 1958-61, med. editor coll. and profl. div., 1961-75, sr. editor medicine, coll. and profl. div., 1975-78, exec. editor med. books, profl. books div., 1978-79, editor-in-chief, 1979-80, asst. v.p., editor-in-chief profl. books div., 1980-82; v.p., pub. med., nursing, health sci. dept. Macmillan Pub. Co., 1982-85, v.p., pub. med. books, sci., tech., med. dept., 1985-88, cons. med. pub., 1989—. Recipient Best Illustrated Med. Book award Assn. Med. Illustrators, 1977, Outstanding Book in Health Sci. award Assn. Am. Pubs., 1982. Mem. AAAS, AAUW, Post Libr. Assn., L.I.U. (rec. sec. 1990-93, exec. coun. 1990—), Friends of Locust Valley Libr. (pres. 1991-93, 94—, treas. 1993-94), Alpha Gamma Delta, Delta Sigma Rho. Republican. Home and Office: 36 Wood Ln Lattingtown PO Box 547 Locust Valley NY 11560-0547

ZULKER, CHARLES BATES, broadcasting company executive; b. Pleasantville, N.J., Dec. 20, 1926; s. William John and Virginia (Carr) Z.; m. Virginia Wright, June 24, 1949; children: Connie Lee, Timothy Scott Charles. Adminstrv. officer Princeton (N.J.) U., 1950-60; asst. mgr. Sta. WPEL, Montrose, Pa., 1960-65; gen. mgr. Sta. WCHR, Trenton, N.J., 1965—. Trustee Princeton Evang. Fellowship, 1973-83; bd. council Word of Life Internat., Schroon Lake, N.Y., 1974-82; mem. exec. bd. Upper Makefield Community Assn., 1972-79. With U.S. Army, 1945-46. Mem. Wooden Canoe Heritage Assn. of Am., Nat. Religious Broadcasters, Nat. Assn. of Broadcasters. Office: Woodside Rd Yardley PA 19067

ZULKEY, EDWARD JOHN, lawyer, author; b. Chgo., June 10, 1948; s. Edward M. and Virginia (Domecki) Z.; m. Janice Buren, Aug. 12, 1972; children: Claire, Jack. BA, Northwestern U., 1970; JD, U. Ill., 1973. Bar: Ill. 1973, Ariz. 1990, U.S. Ct. Appeals (7th cir.) 1973, U.S. Dist. Ct. (no. dist.) Ill. 1973, U.S. Dist. Ct. (no. dist.) Ariz. 1990. Ptnr., gen. counsel Baker & McKenzie, Chgo., 1973—. Contbr. articles to profl. jours. Named to Order of the Coif, 1973. Mem. ABA (co-chair legal malpractice of ins. coverage), Internat. Assn. Def. Counsel. Avocations: Am. history, running, sailing, guitar. Office: Baker & McKenzie 1 Prudential Plz 130 E Randolph St Chicago IL 60601

ZUMBRUN, ALVIN JOHN THOMAS, law and criminology educator; b. Balt., Aug. 9, 1926; s. Orrell Sylvester Tilton and Mary Kathryn (Sprinkle) Z.; m. Marianne Jane Nolan, Aug. 26, 1950; children: Mary Susan, Alvin J.T. Jr., Steven M., Diane, MaryAnn, Mary Kathleen. BA, U. Md., 1952, MA, 1956; MEd in Spl. Edn., Coppin State U., 1972, MEd in Adminstrn., 1974; JD, U. Balt., 1970. Probation officer Supreme Bench of Balt., 1950-52; budget and program dir. Cmty. Chest, Balt., 1953-55; mng. dir. Criminal Justice Commn., Balt., 1956-59; exec. dir., criminologist Md. Crime Investigating Com., Balt., 1960-96; dept. chmn., prof. criminal justice Catonsville (Md.) C.C., 1968-94; dept. chmn., dir. grad. program, prof. criminal justice U. Balt., 1974-76; adj. prof. criminal justice U. Md., Hood Coll., Coppin State U., Md. State Police Acad., Balt. County Police Acad., 1969—; mem. adv. bd. U. Balt. Criminal Justice Program, 1976-94; cons. Am. Edn. Assn., Washington, 1980—; mem. senate Catonsville C.C., 1970-83. Author: Maryland Crime Report, 5 vols., 1959-94, Directory of Criminal Justice Agencies, 22 vols., 1962-94, Civil Disturbance Riots of 1968, 69, also rsch. in field. Mem. scholarship com. Md. Troopers Assn., Pikesville, 1990-93; mem. adv. bd. articulation com. U. Md., College Park, 1977-94; lay pres., mem. coun. Salem Luth. Ch., Catonsville, 1956-59, 65-68. Lt. (j.g.) USN, 1943-50. Recipient Superior Pub. Svc. award Afro Am. Newspaper, 1962, Excellence in Teaching award Md. State Bd. C.C.s, 1987, Superior Ednl. Svcs. award Balt. County Police Chief, 1994, Gov.'s citation for ednl. achievements Gov. of Md., 1994, Hon. Trooper 25 Yrs. Acad. Teaching Md. State Police, 1995. Mem. VFW, Md. Acad. Criminal Justice Profs. (pres. 1971-94), Internat. Soc. Criminology, Nat. Dist. Attys. Assn., Internat. Assn. Chiefs of Police, Maplewoods Homeowners Assn. (pres. 1995—). Avocations: walking, biking, family activities, world travel. Home: 438 Maple Forest Rd # 9349 Catonsville MD 21228-0349

ZUMBRUNNEN, DAVID ARNOLD, mechanical engineering educator, consultant; b. Salt Lake City, Sept. 3, 1955; s. Lynn David and Anne Cecilia Z.; m. Elizabeth Buck. B in Mech. Engring., U. Minn., 1977; MS in Mech. Engring., Purdue U., 1984, PhD in Mech. Engring., 1988. Registered profl. engr., Ind., S.C. Rsch. asst. Purdue U., West Lafayette, Ind., 1982-83, rsch. fellow, asst., 1985-88; staff engr. MPR and Assocs., Washington, 1983-85; assoc. prof. Clemson (S.C.) U., 1988—. Lt. USN, 1977-82. Presdl. Faculty fellow The White House/NSF, 1992—. Mem. ASME, AIAA, Soc. of Mfg. engrs., Soc. of Plastics engrs. Avocations: rowing, tennis, jogging, bicycling. Office: Clemson U Dept Mech Engring Clemson SC 29634-0921

ZUMETA, BERTRAM WILLIAM, retired economist; b. Rutherford, N.J., Jan. 18, 1919; s. Arthur H. and Bertha A. (Cook) Z.; m. Ruth Spencer Astbury, Apr. 1, 1943; children: William Mark, David Cook. A.B., Franklin and Marshall Coll., 1940; postgrad., U. Pa., 1946-50, 52-53. Lectr., instr. econs. and stats. Wharton Sch. U. Pa., 1945-51, 53-63; economist Fed. Res. Bank of Phila., 1959-66, Phila. Electric Co., 1966-70; sr. v.p., economist 1st Pa. Bank, 1970-72, asst. to pres., 1972; v.p., economist First Pa. Corp., 1973-74, sr. v.p., economist, 1974-78; exec. v.p., economist First Pa. Bank and First Pa. Corp., Phila., 1978-80; sr. lectr. mgmt. Wharton Sch., U. Pa., 1980-81; bd. govs. Pa. Economy League, 1979-83; mem. U.S. Sec. of Commerce's Econ. Adv. Bd., 1967-68, Pa. Gov.'s Econ. Adv. Coun., 1967-70, 74-76. Served to comdr. USNR, 1942-45, 51-53. Home: 511 Foulkeways Gwynedd PA 19436

ZUMWALT, ELMO RUSSELL, JR., retired naval officer; b. San Francisco, Nov. 29, 1920; s. Elmo Russell and Frances Z.; m. Mouza Coutelais-du-Roche; children: Elmo Russell, James Gregory, Ann F., Mouzetta C. B.S. with distinction, U.S. Naval Acad., 1942; student, Naval War Coll., 1952-53, Nat. War Coll., 1961-62; LL.D., Villanova U., 1972, U. N.C., 1975, Nat. U., 1979; L.H.D., U.S. Internat. U., 1973; Dr. Pub. Service, Central Mich. U., 1974; D.Sc., Mich. Tech. U., 1979. Commd. ensign U.S. Navy, 1942, advanced through grades to adm., 1970; served with U.S.S. Phelps, 1942-43, U.S.S. Robinson, San Francisco and South Pacific, 1943-44; exec. officer U.S.S. Saufley, 1945-46; exec. officer, navigator U.S.S. Zellars, 1946-48; asst. prof. naval sci. U. N.C., Chapel Hill, 1948-50; comdg. officer U.S.S. Tills, 1950-51; navigator U.S.S. Wisconsin, Korea, 1951-52; head shore and overseas bases sect. Navy Dept., Washington, 1953-55; comdr. destroyer U.S.S. Isbell, 1955-57; lt. detailer Navy Dept., Washington, 1957; spl. asst. for naval personnel to Asst. Sec. Navy, Washington, 1957-58; exec. asst., sr. aide Office Asst. Sec. Navy, 1958-59; comdr. Frigate U.S.S. Dewey, 1959-61; desk officer for France, Spain and Portugal Office Sec. Def., 1962-63, dir. arms control and contingency planning for Cuba, 1963; exec. asst., sr. aide Sec. of Navy, 1963-65; comdr. Cruiser Destroyer Flotilla, 1965-66; dir. chief naval ops. systems analysis group Washington Office Chief Naval Ops.; dep. sci. officer Center Naval Analyses, 1966-68; comdr. U.S. Naval Forces Vietnam, chief naval adv. group Vietnam, 1968-70; chief naval ops. Washington, 1970-74; pub. gov. Am. Stock Exchange, 1979-85; dir. Transway Internat., Inc., 1976-85, RMI, Inc., 1983-86, Am. Bldg. Maintenance Industries, 1995, Navistar Internat. Corp., Gifford-Hill & Co., Inc., 1979-86, Unicorp Am. Corp., 1994; pres., chief exec. officer, dir. Am. Med. Bldgs., Inc., Milw., 1977-79; vice chmn. bd. Am. Med. Bldgs., Inc., 1980-83, chmn., chief exec. officer, 1983-85, chmn., 1985—; pres. Admiral Zumwalt & Cons., Inc., 1979-86, Admiral Zumwalt & Cons. Inc., 1980—; bd. dirs. Aeronca, Inc., Fleet Aerospace, Inc., NL Industries, Inc. Dallas Semiconductor; vis. prof. Vanderbilt U., 1974-75, U. Nebr., 1975, Whittier Coll., 1975; mem. bd. govs. Am. Stock Exch., 1978-84; chmn. Phelpe-Stokes Fund, 1985-93. Author: On Watch, 1976, My Father My Son, 1986. Dem. candidate for U.S. Senate, 1976; chmn. Nat. Marrow Donor Program, 1988-94, Ethics and Pub. Policy Ctr., 1988—. Decorated D.S.M. with Gold Star, Legion of Merit with Gold Star, Bronze Star with combat V, Navy Commendation medal with combat V; Philippine Republic Presdl. citation; Vietnamese Chuong My medal 1st Class; Nat. Order Vietnam 3d class; Vietnamese Navy Disting. Service Order 1st class. Address: 1000 Wilson Blvd Ste 3105 Arlington VA 22209-3901

ZUMWALT, RICHARD DOWLING, flour mill executive; b. Amarillo, Tex., Dec. 1, 1912; s. Richard Dowling and Cora Bell (Pate) Z.; m. Florine Anita Nelson, Oct. 23, 1938; 1 dau., Alexandra Anita (Mrs. Klaus Schwabe). Extension student, Tex. Tech. Coll., 1931, Dallas Coll., 1949. With J. C. Crouch Grain Co., 1931-44; with Burrus Mills, Inc., Dallas, 1944-83, exec. v.p., 1956-64, pres., 1964-83; sec.-treas. Zumwalt Inc., 1973—; ret. gen. mgr. Burrus milling dept. Cargill, Inc.; past pres. Bulgur Assos., Washington, Dallas Grain Exchange. Mem. Millers Nat. Fedn., Tex. Mfrs. Assn. (past dir.). Home: 7353 Blairview Dr Dallas TX 75230-5416

ZUMWALT, ROGER CARL, hospital administrator; b. Eugene, Oreg., Oct. 26, 1943; s. Robert Walter and Jean Elaine (Adams) Z.; m. Sharon Marlene Ryan, Aug. 22, 1970; children: Kathryn Nicole, Timothy Robert. Student, Boise State U., 1963-65; BA, Western Oreg. State Coll., 1969; postgrad., U. Iowa, 1969-71; MA cum laude, Oreg. State U., 1973. Adminstr. Coulee Cmty. Hosp., Grand Coulee, Wash., 1973-75, Eastmoreland Hosp., Portland, Oreg., 1975-81; hosp. surveyor Am. Osteo. Assn., Chgo., 1977—; exec. dir. Cmty. Hosp., Grand Junction, Colo., 1981—; speaker numerous local and nat. presentations, subjects including healthcare, hosp. mktg./success/costs, 1981—; CEO Cmty. Med. Plz., 1984—, Cmty. Health Care Providers Orgn., 1986—, Cmty. Hosp. Found., 1988—. Newspaper columnist, 1973-75; contbr. articles, presentations to profl. publs. Commr. Multnomah County Health Care Commn., Portland, 1978-81; health cons. Grant County Housing Auth., Grand Coulee, 1974-75; mem. pk. bd. City of Tigard, Oreg., 1976-78; caucus rep. Mesa County Rep. Party, Grand Junction, 1988; mem. adv. com., pres.'s office Mesa State Coll., Grand Junction, 1989; bd. dirs. Hospice of Grand Valley, Grand Junction, 1992—, mem. devel. com., 1993—, vice chmn. bd. dirs., 1994—. Fellow Coll. Osteo. Healthcare Execs. (bd. dirs. 1985-88, pres. 1987, examiner 1989—, Disting. Svc. award 1989); mem. Am. Osteo. Healthcare Assn. (bd. dirs. 1987—, treas. 1992-93, 1st v.p. 1994—, 2d v.p. 1993-94, vice chairperson 1994-95, chairperson-elect 1995-96, chmn. 1996—), Am. Osteo. Assn. (ex-officio mem. bd. dirs.), Bur. Healthcare Facilities Accreditation (v.p. 1994), Joint Commn. on Am. Healthcare Orgn. (task force on small and rural accreditation 1994—), Colo. Hosp. Assn. (bd. dirs. 1987-92), Grand Valley Hospice (bd. dirs. 1992—), Mountain States Vol. Hosp. Assn. (bd. dirs. 1984—, exec. com. 1991—, v.p. 1993, vice chmn. bd. dirs. 1992—), Western Coll. Ind. Practice Assn. (Medicine Mauls Measles com., fin. com. 1991-92), Western Colo. Health Care Alliance (bd. dirs. 1989-94, v.p. 1992, chmn. bd. dirs. 1993, past chmn. bd. dirs. 1994), Mesa County Mental Health Assn. (bd. dirs. 1988-89, 91-92), Grand Junction C. of C. (bd. dirs. 1991-93), Rotary, Masons, Shriners (pres. Grand Junction club 1989, bd. dirs. El Jebel 1986-90, 1st v.p. Western Colo. club 1989). Republican. Methodist. Avocations: golf, camping, fishing, hunting. Home: 2515 Snowmass Ct Grnd Junction CO 81503-1752 Office: Community Hosp 2021 N 12th St Grand Junction CO 81501-2980

ZUMWALT, ROSS EUGENE, forensic pathologist, educator; b. Goodrich, Mich., July 18, 1943; s. Paul Lawrence and Lila Ann (Birky) Z.; m. Theresa Ann Schar, Sept. 12, 1970 (div. Apr. 1988); children: Christopher Todd, Tenley Ann; m. Cheryl Lynn Willman, Sept. 4, 1988; 1 child, David Willman Zumwalt. BA, Wabash Coll., 1967; MD, U. Ill., 1971. Diplomate in anat. and forensic pathology Am. Bd. Pathology. Intern, resident in pathology Mary Bassett Hosp., Cooperstown, N.Y., 1971-73; resident in anat. and forensic pathology Southwestern Med. Sch., Dallas, 1973-76; asst. med. examiner Dallas County, Dallas, 1974-76; staff pathologist, dir. labs. Naval Regional Med. Ctr., Camp Lejeune, N.C., 1976-78; dep. coroner Cuyahoga County, Cleve., 1978-80, Hamilton County, Cin., 1980-86; assoc. prof. pathology U. Cin. Sch. Medicine, 1980-86; prof. pathology U. N.Mex. Sch. Medicine, Albuquerque, 1987—; chief med. investigator Office of Med. Investigator, Albuquerque, 1991—; trustee Am. Bd. Pathology, Tampa, Fla., 1993—. Lt. comdr. USN, 1976-78. Fellow Am. Acad. Forensic Scis., Coll. Am. Pathologists; mem. AMA, Nat. Assn. Med. Examiners (bd. dirs. 1984—, pres. 1995-96), Am. Soc. Clin. Pathologists, Am. and Can. Acad. Pathologists. Avocation: golf. Office: Office of Med Investigator 700 Camino de Salud Albuquerque NM 87131 Also: 819 El Alhambra Cir NW Albuquerque NM 87107-6301

ZUNG, THOMAS TSE-KWAI, architect; b. Shanghai, China, Feb. 8, 1933; came to U.S., 1937, naturalized, 1954; 1 child, Thomas Bates. Student Drew U., 1950-51, (Rose scholar) Va. Poly. Inst., 1951-53, Columbia U., 1955-57; BArch, U. Mich., 1960; MS in Design Sci. (student R. Buckminster Fuller), Internat. Coll., 1982. Project architect Edward Durell Stone, architect, N.Y.C., 1958, 60-65; architect, Cleve., 1967—; pres. Buckminster Fuller, Sadao and Zung, architects, 1979—; prin. archtl. works include City Cleve. Pub. Utilities Bldg., Cleve. State U. Sports Center Dome, Mayfran, Inc., Sawmill Creek Lodge, U. Akron Guzzetta Hall, music, speech and theater arts center, Alumni Center Bowling Green State U., U. Akron Master Plan-West, City of East Cleveland, Superior Euclid beautification plan, student recreation ctr. at Bowling Green State U., Glenville Public Libr., campus bldg. Tex. Wesleyan Coll., recreation, health and phys. edn. bdg. Wittenberg U., Medina Res. Park Office, arena, health, phys. edn. complex U. Akron, Dyke Coll., Lima State Prison, Cleve. Children's Christian Home, State of Ohio Pre-Release Ctr. Cleve., Lorain-Grafton State Prison, Mayfield High Sch., Asian Village Project, Cleve. Metroparks Tropical Rainforest Bldg., Student Union Wittenberg U., YWCA Salem Ohio, China Internat. Trade Ctr. People's Rep. China, additions to Cleve. Hopkins Internat. Airport, Ohio State U. Coll. of Dentistry-Postle Hall and Hist. Costume and Textile Mus., Columbus, Western Res. Psychiat. Hosp., Ohio, Trumbull State Prison; patentee in field. Task force chmn. Greater Cleve. Growth Assn., 1970; mem. Coun. Human Rels., 1972, Leadership Cleve. Class '77; cubmaster local Boy Scouts Am., 1977-79; bd. dirs. Buckminster Fuller Inst., 1983—, Pearl S. Buck Found., 1989—, hist. house com. Pearl S. Buck House, cons. architect; trustee Pace Assn., 1970-73, Karamu House, 1974-80, Cleve. Inst. Music, 1979—, Ohio Arts Coun., 1982-84, Chinese Cultural Assn., 1980-84; vestryman St. Christopher-by-River, 1980-83. Served with Signal Corps, U.S. Army, 1953-55. Decorated 4 medals; recipient Design award Cleve. chpt. AIA, 1972, Korean Inst. Constrn. Tech., 1984; Anicka Design award U. Mich., 1959, Sr. design prize, 1960; Pub. Works award State of Ohio, 1971, Ohio Valley ABC Design Excellence award Wittenberg U. Student Union, 1989, others. Mem. AIA (dir. Cleve. chpt. 1980, design award 1989), Am. Soc. Planning Ofcls., English Speaking Union (trustee 1972-75), Ohio Soc. Architects, Ohio Assn. Minority Architects and Engrs. (trustee 1982—), Hermit Club, City Club (dir. 1972-74, v.p. 1974), Rotary. Office: Buckminster Fuller Sadao & Zung 13000 Shaker Blvd Cleveland OH 44120-2063

ZUNIGA, FRANCISCO, sculptor, graphic artist; b. San Jose, Costa Rica, Dec. 27, 1912. prof. sculpture and art La Emerelda, Mexico City, 1938-70. Works exhibited at Internat. Art Fair, Basel, Switzerland, 1951, Gallery Modern Art, Scottsdale, Ariz., 1966, Mus. Modern Art, Mexico City, 1969, Phoenix Art Mus., 1972, 74, Nat. Mus. Art, Tokyo, 1974-75, Oakland (Calif.) Mus., 1977; commd. monument State Govt. Morelita, Mex., 1960, monument Adolpho Lopez Mates, Mex., 1960, Allegory to Youth fountain Dept. Pub. Works, Mex., 1964; represented in permanent collections Hirschorn Mus. Sculpture Garden, Washington, Met. Mus., N.Y.C., Mus. Modern Art, N.Y.C., Inst. Nat. Bellas Artes, Mex., Nat. Mus. Modern Art, Kyoto, Japan. Recipient First prize Ann Salon Sculpture, Mex., 1957, first prize sculpture Diego Rivera-2, Internat. Biennal Patinging, 1960. Office: c/o Brewster Gallery 41 W 57th St New York NY 10019

ZUNKER, RICHARD E., insurance company executive; b. 1938. BS, U. Wis., 1964. With Employers Ins. Wausau, Wis., 1964-69, Northwestern Nat. Investors Life, 1969-75; with Safeco Life Ins. Co., Seattle, 1975—, pres., also bd. dirs. With U.S. Army, 1956-58. Office: Safeco Life Ins Co PO Box 34690 Seattle WA 98124-1690*

ZUNZ, OLIVIER JEAN, history educator; b. Paris, July 19, 1946; s. Jean R. and Monique M. (Blin) Z.; m. Christine M. Crommen, July 3, 1970; children: Emmanuel, Sophie. Licence in history and geography, U. Paris X, 1968, M in History, 1969; Doctorat-ès-Lettres, U. Paris I, Panthéon-Sorbonne, 1982. Scientist Ctr. Nat. de la Recherche Scientifique, Paris, 1976-78; asst. prof. dept. history U. Va., Charlottesville, 1978-83, assoc. prof., 1983-88, prof., 1988—; vis. prof. Ecole des Hautes Etudes en Scis., Sociales, Paris, 1985—; dir. seminar for Coll. Tchrs. NEH, 1989, 92. Author: The Changing Face of Inequality: Urbanization, Industrial Development, and Immigrants in Detroit, 1880-1920, 1982, Making America Corporate, 1870-1920, 1990; co-author: Reliving the Past: The Worlds of Social History, 1985; co-editor: (with David Ward) The Landscape of Modernity: Essays on New York City, 1900-1940, 1992; mem. editorial bd. Revs. in Am. History, 1990—; contbr. articles, book revs. to profl. jours. Jr. fellow Mich. Soc. Fellows, 1973-76, John Simon Guggenheim Meml. Found. fellow, 1986-87; grantee U. Mich.-Ford Found. Population Devel. Fund, 1974-76, NSF, 1976-78, NEH, 1979-81, 84-87; also recipient numerous rsch. grants. Mem. Am. Hist. Assn., Orgn. Am. Historians. Home: 1368 Hilltop Rd Charlottesville VA 22903-1225 Office: U Va Dept History Randall Hall Charlottesville VA 22903-3284

ZUPCOFSKA, PETER F., lawyer; b. Boston, Feb. 18, 1952; s. Patrick P. and Josephine M. (Gnoza) Z. BA magna cum laude, Boston Coll., 1973, JD, 1976. Bar: Mass. 1977, U.S. Supreme Ct. 1994. Asst. register Norfolk divsn. Probate and Family Ct., Dedham, Mass., 1976-83; assoc. Burns & Levinson, Boston, 1983-88, ptnr., 1989; of counsel Bingham, Dana & Gould, Boston, 1989-92, ptnr., 1992—; mem. Commonwealth Mass. Dept. Social Svcs. No. Code adv. com., 1986-89; lectr. in field. Co-author: Motions and Cases in Family Law Trial Advocacy, Family Law Trial Inst.: Problems and Cases, 1992; author: Drafting Documents to Support a Divorce Action, 1994; contbr. chpt. to Massachussetts Family Law Manual, 1994; contbr. articles to profl. jours. Mem. Law and Child Devel. Project Boston Coll., 1974-76; apptd. to Probate and Family Ct. pretrial subcom., 1995—; participant Probate and Family Ct. Lawyer for the Day Project, 1990-96; bd. dirs. Boston Coll. Alumni, 1993-95; mem. Boston Coll. Law Sch. Alumni Coun., 1991-95, Pres. Cir., 1991—, Dean's Coun., 1986—, Leadership Gifts Com., 1987-90, chmn. Alumni Assn. Law Day, 1989, co-chmn. Class 1976 5th Yr., 10th Yr., 15th Yr. Reunion com.; vol. Hole in the Wall Gang Camp, Ashford, Conn., 1991, benefit com., 1992-94; co-chmn. Boston Benefit, 1995, 96. Fellow Mass. Bar Found. (life); mem. ABA (family law sect. 1978—, exec. mem. adoption com. 1982-83, vice-chmn. 1980-82, Merit cert. 1981-83), Mass. Bar Assn. (family law sect. 1983—, co-chmn. Norfolk probate and family ct. bench bar com. 1988-89, Cert Appreciation 1988-89), Boston Bar Assn. (family law sect. 1989—), Boston Estate Planning Coun., Mass. Continuing Legal Edn. (curriculum adv. com., family law 1990-93, 95—). Home: 85 Dartmouth St Boston MA 02116 Office: Bingham Dana & Gould 150 Federal St Boston MA 02110-1745

ZUPKO, ARTHUR GEORGE, consultant to drug industry, retired college administrator; b. Yonkers, N.Y., Nov. 22, 1916; s. George and Julia (Tutko) Z.; m. Lillian Belle Cosner, Dec. 20, 1947; 1 child, Arthur Maynard. Student, N.Y. U., 1936-38; B.S., U. Fla., 1942; M.S., Purdue U., 1948, Ph.D., 1949; D.Sc. (hon.), L.I. U., 1979. Research asst. Burroughs Wellcome Co., Tuckahoe, N.Y., 1936-38; asst. prof., assoc. prof., prof. St. Louis Coll. Pharmacy, 1949-55, assoc. dean, 1955, dean, 1956-60; provost Bklyn. Coll. Pharmacy, L.I. U., 1960-73, pres., 1973-76; pres. Arnold and Marie Schwartz Coll. Pharmacy and Health Scis., 1976-79, pres. emeritus, 1979—; bd. dirs. MedPhone, Inc., U.S. Adapted Names, Biofine Pharm.; mem. bd. pharmacy cons. Chas. Pfizer & Co. Author: (with Otto Ruhmer) Contributions of Jews to Pharmacy, 1959, Drug Interactions, 1979; Contbr. articles to profl. jours. Spl. gifts Bklyn. chpt. Am. Cancer Soc., 1963; solicitor ARC, 1962-63; merit badge counselor Hutchinson-Bronx River council Boy Scouts Am., 1963-64; solicitor United Fund, 1961-65; mem. Narcotic Addiction Centers Com., 1960-65; bd. dirs. Korean-Am. Found., Tb and Respiratory Assn., Bklyn.; mem. spl. com. Cooley's Anemia Found. Served with U.S. Army, 1934-36; Served with USNR, 1942-46. Decorated Bronze Star medal. Fellow Am. Found. Pharm. Edn.; mem. Am. Pharm. Assn. (hon. chmn. bd. trustees 1988), Am. Coll. Apothecaries, N.Y. State Pharm. Soc. (hon. pres.), Kings County Pharm. Soc., N.Y. Acad. Pharmacy, AAAS, N.Y. Acad. Sci., Sigma Xi, Rho Chi, Phi Kappa Phi, Phi Lambda Upsilon, Delta Sigma Theta, Alpha Zeta Omega. Home: 402 Santa Helena Ln Fort Myers FL 33903-1507

ZUPKO, RAMON, composer, music professor; b. Pitts., Nov. 14, 1932; s. Michael E. and Frances E. (Bartek) Z.; m. Vonette Sarche, Sept. 14, 1969; 1 child, Mischa. BS in Music, Juilliard, 1956, MS in Music, 1957. Asst. prof. music Chgo. (Ill.) Musical Coll., 1967-71; prof. music Western Mich. Univ., Sch. Music, Kalamazoo, 1971—. Recipient composition fellowship Guggenheim Found., 1982, Composers awards Am. Acad. & Inst. of Arts and Letters, N.Y., 1982, Disting. Faculty award Mich. Assn. Governing Bds., Lansing, 1984, Composers awards NEA, Washington, 1978-80, 85, Koussevitzky Found. award 1981, Disting. Faculty scholar award Western Mich. U., 1983, Kennedy-Friedheim award, Washington, 1980. Mem. Am. Composers Alliance, Phi Kappa Phi. Avocations: biking, photography. Home: RR 1 Kalamazoo MI 49009-9801 Office: Sch Music Dalton Ctr Western Mich U Kalamazoo MI 49008

ZURAV, FRANCES STALFORD, special education educator; b. Newark, Dec. 16, 1929; d. William and Anna (Bader) Stalford; m. David B. Zurav, Mar. 18, 1951; children: Ilene Halprin, Edward H. BS, Syracuse U., 1951; MA, Newark State U., 1966. Cert. clin. competence, speech pathologist, N.J. Speech pathologist Cerebral Palsy Ctr., Morristown, N.J., 1965-66; specialist speech-lang. Bd. Edn., Plainfield, N.J., 1966—. Mem. Am. Speech-Lang.-Hearing Assn., N.J. Speech-Lang.-Hearing Assn. (legis. com. 1972-74), Union County Speech-Lang.-Hearing Assn. Home: 1 Archbridge Ln Springfield NJ 07081-2702

ZURAWSKI, VINCENT RICHARD, JR., biotechnology company executive, research scientist; b. Irvington, N.J., June 10, 1946; s. Vincent Richard and Norma Mary (Alliston) Z.; m. Mary R. Stanziola, Aug. 18, 1968; children: Daniel Vincent, John Alliston. B.A., Montclair State Coll., 1968; Ph.D., Purdue U., 1973. Postdoctoral research fellow chemistry dept. Purdue U., West Lafayette, Ind., 1974; rsch. fellow dept. medicine Harvard Med. Sch., Boston, 1975-78, instr. dept. medicine, 1978-79; rsch. fellow dept. medicine Mass. Gen. Hosp., Boston, 1975-79; co-founder Centocor, Inc., Malvern, Pa., 1979, v.p., tech. dir., 1979-82, sr. v.p., tech. dir., 1982-83, exec. v.p., tech. dir., 1983-86, corporate sec., 1981-86, sr. v.p. tech. affairs, 1986-87, sr. v.p., chief scientific officer, 1987-93; founder, pres., chief exec. officer Apollon Inc., 1992—; lectr. Harvard Med. Sch., Boston, 1985-92; vis. prof. Radiumhemmet and Karolinska Hosp., Stockholm, 1988; mem. adv. com. devel. rsch. in cancer diagnostics Nat. Cancer Inst., 1988-89; mem. biotechnology adv. com. Ea. Tech. Coun., 1992—; bd. dirs. Pa. Biotechnology Assn., 1993—. Contbr. articles to profl. jours. and chpts. to books; assoc. editor Jour. Clin. Lab. Analysis, 1986-87; adv. editor Nuclear Med. Communications, 1986—; patentee in field; pioneer in clin. applications of monoclonal antibodies. With USAR, 1969-76. NIH postdoctoral fellow, 1976-78; Med. Found. research fellow, 1978-79; NIH grantee, 1985, 87-90. Mem. AAAS, Am. Assn. Cancer Rsch., Am. Chem. Soc., Am. Soc. Microbiology, Am. Soc. for Biochemistry and Molecular Biology, Am. Assn. Immunologists. Office: Apollon Inc 1 Great Valley Pky Malvern PA 19355-1423

ZURHEIDE, CHARLES HENRY, consulting electrical engineer; b. St. Louis, May 9, 1923; s. Charles Henry and Ollie C. (Kirk) Z.; m. Ruth M. Plueck, June 25, 1949; children—Barbara Anne, Pamela S. B.S. in Elec. Engring, U. Mo., Columbia, 1944. Registered profl. engr., Mo. Distbn. engr. Laclede Power & Light Co., St. Louis, 1944-45; sub-sta. engr., then indsl. engr. Union Electric Co., St. Louis, 1945-51; chief elec. engr. Fruin-Colnon Contracting Co., St. Louis, 1951-54; a founder, treas., v.p. Smith-Zurheide, Inc., St. Louis, 1954-65; pres. Zurheide-Herrmann, Inc., St. Louis, 1965—, chmn. bd., 1988—; chmn. Elec. Code Rev. Commn., St. Louis, 1965-96, Mo. Bd. Profl. Engrs., 1977-82, St. Louis Indsl. Devel. Commn., 1965-67; mem. adv. panel region 6 GSA, 1977—; plan commn., City of Ferguson, Mo., 1966-73; tech. adv. com. St. Louis C. of C., 1977. Recipient Distinguished Service in Engring. award U. Mo., 1976. Fellow Am. Cons. Engrs. Council; mem. Mo. Soc. Profl. Engrs. (Engr. of Year award 1970), Cons. Engrs. Council Mo., IEEE, Illuminating Engring. Soc., Engrs. Club St. Louis, Tau Alpha Pi. Clubs: Norwood Hills Country, Mo. Athletic. Home: 25 Lake Pembroke Dr Saint Louis MO 63135-1210 Office: Zurheide-Herrmann Inc 4333 Clayton Ave Saint Louis MO 63110-1621

ZURIER, ROBERT BURTON, medical educator, clinical investigator; b. Passaic, N.J., Feb. 19, 1934; s. Milton and Lillian (Matzner) Z.; m. Catherine Elizabeth Miers, June 3, 1962; 1 child, Adam Wheaton. BS, Rutgers U., 1955; MD, U. Tex. Southwestern Med. Ctr., Dallas, 1962; MA (hon.), U. Pa., 1981. Intern, then resident in medicine Boston City Hosp., 1962-64; fellow in medicine St. Lukes Hosp., N.Y.C., 1964-66; fellow in rheumatology NYU, 1970-73; pvt. practice internal medicine Holden, Mass., 1967-70; asst. prof. medicine U. Conn., Farmington, 1973-76, assoc. prof., 1976-80; prof., chief. rheumatology U. Pa., Phila., 1980-91; prof. medicine, dir. rheumatology div. U. Mass. Med. Ctr., Worcester, 1991—. Served to capt. USAR, 1956-68. Guggenheim Found. fellow, 1986. Mem. AAAS, Am. Coll. Rheumatology, Am. Soc. Clin. Investigation, Interurban Clin. Club (pres. 1989-90). Office: U Mass Med Ctr 55 Lake Ave N Worcester MA 01655-0002

ZURKOWSKI, PAUL GEORGE, information company executive; b. Milw., Nov. 8, 1932; s. Stanley Frank and Martha (Bednarz) Z.; m. Margaret Ann Becker, July 9, 1960; children: Paul Coleman, Pamela Carol, Patricia Christine, Peggy Catherine, Paula Claire, Peter Christopher. B.A., U. Wis., Whitewater, 1954; LL.B., U. Wis., Madison, 1957. Bar: Wis. 1957, U.S. Supreme Ct. 1961. Publisher Our Ads (shopping guide), Palmyra, Wis., 1950-55; investigator legal firm Swingen & Stern, Madison, 1955-58; atty. HHFA, Washington, 1958; examiner ICC, 1958-59; congl. legis. asst., 1959-61, 64-69; individual legal practice, also congl. home sec. Madison, 1961; exec. dir. Info. Industry Assn., Washington, 1969; pres. Info. Industry Assn., 1972-89, Ventures in Info., Chevy Chase, Md., 1989—; bd. dirs. Herner & Co. Pub. Holy Redeemer News, 1984-87, Today's Parish, 1987-90, Our Parish Times, 1990—, Family Beach Times, 1995—; editor Chatter, Rock Creek Coun., KC, 1993—. Pres. Parish Cmty. Svcs. Inc., Md., 1991—; founder, lifetime mem. Cath. Bus. Network, 1993, past pres., 1993-94, sec., 1994—. Served with AUS, 1957, officer USAR, 1961-64. Decorated Army Commendation medal; recipient Disting. Alumni Svc. award U. Wis., Whitewater, 1974, Outstanding Svc. award, CNB, 1994; named to Info. Industry Hall of Fame, 1988. Office: 8027 Ellingson Dr Chevy Chase MD 20815-3029

ZUSPAN, FREDERICK PAUL, obstetrician, gynecologist, educator; b. Richwood, Ohio, Jan. 20, 1922; s. Irl Goff and Kathryn (Speyer) Z.; m. Mary Jane Cox, Nov. 23, 1943; children: Mark Frederick, Kathryn Jane, Bethany Anne. BA, Ohio State U., 1947, MD, 1951. Intern Univ. Hosps., Columbus, Ohio, 1951-52; resident Univ. Hosps., 1952-54; resident Western Res. U., Cleve., 1954-56, Oblebay fellow, 1958-60, asst. prof., 1958-60; chmn. dept. bo-gyn. McDowell (Ky.) Meml. Hosp., 1956-58, chief clin. svcs., 1957-58; prof., chmn. dept. ob-gyn. Med. Coll. Ga., Augusta, 1960-66; Joseph Boliver DeLee prof. ob-gyn., chmn. dept. U. Chgo., 1966-75; obstetrician, gynecologist in chief Chgo. Lying-In Hosp., 1966-75; prof., chmn. dept. ob-gyn. Ohio State U., Columbus, 1975-87, R.L. Meiling prof. ob-gyn. Sch. Medicine, 1984-90, prof. emeritus, 1991—. Founding editor Lying In, Jour. Reproductive Medicine; editor-in-chief Am. Jour. Ob-Gyn. and Ob-Gyn. Reports, (with Lindheimer and Katz) Hypertension in Pregnancy, 1976, Current Developments in Perinatology, 1977, (with Quilligan) Operative Obstetrics, 1981, 89, Manual of Practical Obstetrics, 1981, 90, Clin. and Exptl. Hypertension in Pregnancy, 1979-86, (with Rayburn) Drug Therapy in Ob-Gyn., 1981, 3rd edit., 1992; editor: (with Christian) Controversies in Obstetrics and Gynecology; contbr. articles to med. jours., chpts. to books. Pres. Barren Found., 1974-76. With USNR, 1942-43; 1st lt. USMCR, 1943-45. Decorated DFC, Air medal wth 10 oak leaf clusters. Mem. Soc. Gynecol. Investigation, Chgo. Gynecol. Soc., Am. Assn. Ob-Gyn., Columbus Ob-Gyn. Soc. (pres. 1984-85), Am. Acad. Reproductive Medicine (pres.), Am. Coll. Obstetricians and Gynecologists, Assn. Profs. of Gynecology and Obstetrics (pres. 1972), South Atlantic Assn. Obstetricians and Gynecologists (Found. prize for rsch. 1962), Ctrl. Assn. Ob-Gyn. (cert. of merit, rsch. prize 1970), Am. Soc. Clin. Exptl. Hypnosis (exec. sec. 1968, v.p. 1970), Soc. Gynecol. Investigation, Internat. Soc. Study of Hypertension in Pregnancy (pres. 1981-83), Am. Gynecology and Obstetrics Soc. (pres. 1986-87), Soc. Perinatal Obstetrics, Perinatal Rsch. Soc., Sigma Xi, Alpha Omega Alpha, Alpha Kappa Kappa. Home: Upper Arlington 2400 Coventry Rd Columbus OH 43221-3754 *The strength of our nation rests in the quality of our offspring. Every fetus has the privilege of being wellborn.*

ZUSSY, NANCY LOUISE, librarian; b. Tampa, Fla., Mar. 4, 1947; d. John David and Patsy Ruth (Stone) Roche; m. R. Mark Allen, Dec. 20, 1986. BA in Edn., U. Fla., 1969; MLS, U. So. Fla., 1977, MS in Pub. Mgmt., 1980. Cert. librarian, Wash. Ednl. evaluator State of Ga., Atlanta, 1969-70; media specialist DeKalb County Schs., Decatur, Ga., 1970-71; researcher Ga. State Libr., Atlanta, 1971; asst. to dir. reference Clearwater (Fla.) Pub. Libr., 1972-78, dir. librs., 1978-81; dep. state libr. Wash. State Libr., Olympia, 1981-86, state libr., 1986—; chmn. Consortium Automated Librs., Olympia, 1982—; cons. various pub. librs., Wash., 1981—; exec. officer Wash. Libr. Network, 1986-90; v.p. WLN (non-profit orgn.), 1990-93. Contbr. articles to profl. jours. Treas. Thurston-Mason Community Mental Health Bd., Olympia, 1983-85, bd. dir., 1982-85; mem. race com. Seafair Hydroplane Race, Seattle, 1986—, mem. milk carton derby team, 1994—. Mem. ALA, Assn. Specialized and Coop. Libr. Agys. (legis. com. 1983-86, chmn.. 1985-87, vice chmn. state libr. agys. sect. 1985-86, chmn. 1986-87, chmn. govt. affairs com. Libr. Adminstrn. and Mgmt. Assn., 1986-87), Freedom To Read Found. (bd. dirs. 1987-91), Chief Officers of State Libr. Agys. (bd. dirs.-at-large 1987-90, v.p., pres.-elect 1990-92, pres. 1992-94), Wash. Libr. Assn. (co-founder legis. planning com. 1982—, fed. rels. coord. 1984—), Fla. Libr. Assn. (legis. and planning com. 1978-81), Pacific N.W. Libr. Assn., Rotary (bd. dirs. 1995—), Phi Kappa Phi, Phi Beta Mu. Avocations: hiking, barbershop chorus/quartet, hydroplane boat racing, cross country skiing. Home: 904 E Bay Dr NE # 404B Olympia WA 98506-3970 Office: Wash State Libr PO Box 42460 Olympia WA 98504-2460

ZUSY, CATHERINE, curator; b. Washington, May 4, 1958; d. Frederick John and Mary Jane (Lloyd) Z.; m. Samuel Conant Kendall, Sept. 6, 1992. BA, Bucknell U., 1981; MA in History Mus. Studies, SUNY, Oneonta, 1984. Curator of edn. Deland (Fla.) Mus., 1981-82; asst. curator State Capital Pub. Mus., Guthrie, Okla., 1982-83; rsch. asst., dept. Am. decorative arts Mus. Fine Arts, Boston, 1985-87; curator decorative arts The Bennington (Vt.) Mus., 1988-91; chief curator N.H. Hist. Soc., Concord, N.H., 1991-95; lectr. L.A. County Mus. Arts, M. H. de Young Mus., San Francisco, Mus. Fine Arts, Boston, others. Author: Highlights from the Bennington Museum, 1989, Norton Stoneware and American Redware: The Bennington Museum Collection, 1992; contbr. author to catalogues; contbr. articles to profl. jours. Sec. N.H. Visual Arts Coalition, 1992-94; mem. steering com. N.H. Save Outdoor Sculpture, 1992-94; mem. selection com. N.H. % for Art Program, 1994-95. Hist. Deerfield Summer fellow, 1981, Nat. Mus. Act and Norse Found. fellow, 1983-84, Louise du Pont Crowninshield Rsch. fellow Winterthur Mus., 1990; grantee Am. Ceramic Cir., 1993-95; recipient Charles F. Montgomery award Decorative Arts Soc., 1993.

ZUU-CHANG HONG, engineering educator; b. Bei-Kun, Yuan-Lin, Taiwan, Apr. 25, 1942; s. San-Lin and Fei-Rien (Jih) H.; m. Sue-Jane Chen, Jan. 15, 1974 (div. Apr. 1979); children: Grace Shau-Wei Hong, Chao-I Hong; m. Hsiu-Ching Chen, Apr. 14, 1982; children: Chao-Tien Hong, Chao-Hun Hong, Chao-Min Hong. BS, Nat. Taiwan U., 1968; MS, U. Calif., Davis, 1971; PhD, U. Ill., 1975. Assoc. to full prof. dept. mech. engring. Nat. Taiwan U., Taipei, 1975-80, prof., 1982-85; prof. and head dept. mech. engring. Nat. Taiwan Inst. Tech., Taipei, 1980-82; prof., dean Coll. Engring., Nat. Cen. U., Chungli, Taiwan, 1985-88, prof., 1988-94, dept. dir. Taipei del. to Internat. Astronautical Fedn., 1991-94; cons. Chun-San Inst. Sci. and Tech., Lung-Tan, Tao-Yuan, 1981-93, Taiwan Inst. Econ. Rsch., Taipei, 1989-94; prof.-in-charge Automatic Control Lab., Taiwan U., 1976, Computational Fluid Dynamic Lab. Cen. U., 1985; dep. dir. Taipei del. to Internat. Astron. Fedn. Congress, 1991, 92, 93, 94. Editor-in-chief Jour. of Chinese Soc. of Mech. Engring., 1979-89, Trans. of Aero. and Astronautical Soc. of Republic of China, 1994—; editor-in-chief: (book) Experiments for Mechanical Engineering, 1983; contbr. articles to profl. jours., publs. With Chinese Navy, ROTC, 1968-69. Recipient Disting. Rsch. award Nat. Sci. Coun., Taipei, 1991-92; Disting. Prof., Nat. Cen. U., Chung-Li, 1989, Disting. Paper of Yr. Soc. of Theoretical and Applied Mechanics, Tainan, 1982. Mem. Chinese Inst. Engrs. (Disting. Paper of Yr. 1979), Chinese Soc. Mech. Engrs. (bd. dirs. 1980-85, Disting. Paper of Yr. 1984, 86), Chinese Soc. Aeros. and Astronautics (bd. dirs. 1986-93, 95—), Welding Soc. of Rep. of China (bd. dirs. 1986—), Chinese Soc. of Automation (bd. dirs. 1992—, vice chmn. 1994—), Soc. Mfg. Engrs. (chmn. Taipei chpt. 1993-94, Internat. Astronaut. Fedn. Congress (dep. dir. Taipei delegation 1991-94), others. Achievements include patent in field. Home: Lane-16 Wen-Chou St 5th Fl # 11, Taipei 10616 Taiwan Republic of China Office: Nat Ctrl Univ, Dept Mech Engring, 32054 Chung-Li Taiwan

ZWAHLEN, FRED CASPER, JR., journalism educator; b. Portland, Oreg., Nov. 11, 1924; s. Fred and Katherine (Meyer) Z.; m. Grace Eleanor DeMoss, June 24, 1959; children: Molly, Skip. BA, Oreg. State U., 1949; MA, Stanford U., 1952. Reporter San Francisco News, 1949-50; acting editor Stanford Alumni Rev., Palo Alto, Calif., 1950; successively instr. journalism, news bur. asst., prof. journalism, chmn. journalism dept. Oreg. State U., Corvallis, 1950-91, prof. emeritus, 1991—; Swiss tour guide, 1991—; corres. Portland Oregonian, 1950-67. Author: (with others) Handbook of Photography, 1984. Coord. E.E. Wilson Scholarship Fund, 1964—; active budget com. Corvallis Sch. Dist., 1979. Recipient Achievement award Sch. Journalism U. Oregon, 1988. Mem. Assn. for Edn. in Journalism and Mass Communications (conv. chmn. 1983, pres.' award 1988), Oreg. Newspaper Pubs. Assn. (bd. dirs. 1980-85, student loan fund named in his honor 1988), Soc. Profl. Journalists (nat. svc. citation 1988), Corvallis Country Club, Shriners, Masons, Elks, Moose, Eagles, Delta Tau Delta. Republican. Presbyterian. Avocations: photography, sightseeing, travel. Home: 240 SW 7th St Corvallis OR 97333-4551 Office: Oreg State U Dept Student Activities Corvallis OR 97331

ZWASS, VLADIMIR, computer scientist, educator; b. Lvov, USSR, Feb. 3, 1946; came to U.S., 1970, naturalized, 1979; s. Adam and Friderike (Getzler) Z.; m. Alicia Kogut, Apr. 24, 1977; 1 child, Joshua Jonathan. M.S., Moscow Inst. Energetics, 1969; M.Ph., Columbia U., 1974, Ph.D., 1975. Mem. profl. staff IAEA, Vienna, Austria, 1970; asst. prof. computer sci. Fairleigh Dickinson U., 1975-79, assoc. prof., 1979-84, prof., 1984—, prof. computer sci. and mgmt. info. systems, 1990—, chmn. com. computer sci., 1976—; cons. U.S. Govt., Met. Life Ins. Co., Citibank, Diebold Group; seminar assoc. Columbia U., 1986—; speaker nat. and internat. meetings. Author: Introduction to Computer Science, 1981, Programming in Fortran, 1981, Programming in Pascal, 1985, Programming in Basic, 1986, Management Information Systems, 1992; editor-in-chief Jour. Mgmt. Info. Sys., 1983—, Jour. Electronic Commerce, 1996—; contbr. articles to profl. jours. and publs., Ency. Britannica, N.Y. Times, chpts. to books. Columbia U. fellow, 1970-71; Helena Rubinstein Found. scholar, 1971-75; grantee USN, other agys. Mem. IEEE, Assn. Computer Machinery, Assn. for Info. Sys., Sigma Xi, Eta Kappa Nu. Home: 19 Warewoods Rd Saddle River NJ 07458 Office: Dept Computer Sci Fairleigh Dickinson U Teaneck NJ 07666

ZWEBEN, MURRAY, lawyer, consultant; b. Elizabeth, N.J., May 9, 1930; s. Jacob and Anna (Katz) Z.; m. Elaine Tinkelman, Nov. 22, 1950 (div. Apr. 1974); children: M. Lisa, Marc Samuel, John Eric, Harry T.; m. Anne Waggoner, Apr. 23, 1974; 1 child, Suzanne Grady. BS, Albany (N.Y.) State U., 1952, MS, 1953; LLB, George Washington U., 1959. Sec. to parliamentarian U.S. Senate, Washington, 1956-59, asst. parliamentarian, 1963-75, parliamentarian, 1975-81, parliamentarian emeritus, 1983—; law clk. U.S. Claims Ct., Washington, 1959-60; atty. Columbia Gas Systems, N.Y.C., 1960-63; pvt. practice, Washington, 1981-84; cons. atty. Nossaman, Guthmar, Knox & Elliott, Washington, 1984-86, of counsel, 1986—; cons. atty. Elliott, Zweben & Steelman, Washington, 1986-90, Elliott & Zweben, Washington, 1990-96. Lt. USN, 1953-56. Avocation: tennis. Home: 4010 Highwood Ct NW Washington DC 20007-2131 Office: The Willard # 1800 1455 Pennsylvania Ave NW Washington DC 20004

ZWEBEN, STUART HARVEY, information scientist, educator; b. Bronx, N.Y., Apr. 21, 1948; s. Max D. and Ruth (Schwartz) Z.; m. Rochelle T. Small, June 13, 1971; 1 child, Naomi. BS, CUNY, 1968; MS, Purdue U., 1971, PhD, 1974. Systems analyst IBM Corp., Kingston, N.Y., 1969-70; asst. prof. Ohio State U., Columbus, 1974-80, from vice chmn. to acting chmn. computer sci. dept., 1982-84, assoc. prof., 1980-92, prof., 1992—; chmn. Ohio State U., 1994—; pres. Computing Scis. Accreditation Bd., Stamford, Conn., 1989-91, v.p. 1987-89, sec.-treas. 1986-87; sec.-treas. Fedn. on Computing in the U.S., Washington, 1992. Contbr. articles to profl. jours. Rsch. grantee NSF, 1981-83, 88-90, 91-93, 93-96, Army Rsch. Office, 1980-83, Dept. Edn., 1983-85, Applied Info. Tech. Rsch. Ctr., 1990-91; equipment grantee AT&T Bell Labs, 1984, 86-88. Mem. AAUP, IEEE Computer Soc. (assoc. editor 1990—), Assn. for Computing Machinery (pres. 1994-96, v.p. 1992-94, coun. mem. 1982-88, chpt. bd. chmn. 1982-85, publications bd. 1988-92, fin. com. 1990-92, constn. and bylaws chmn. 1988-92, Recognition of Svc. award 1980, 85, 87, 88). Avocations: sports, philately. Office: Ohio State U Computer Scis 2015 Neil Ave Columbus OH 43210-1210

ZWEIBEL, JOEL BURTON, lawyer; b. N.Y.C., Feb. 7, 1935; s. Jacob and Ruth (Fleischner) Z.; m. Lynn Herzog (dec. Nov. 1984); children: Jane, Emily; m. Chrystine Marie Trichter. BBA, CCNY, 1955; LLB, Yale U., 1958. Bar: N.Y. 1959. Ptnr. Kaye, Scholer, Fierman, Hays & Handler, N.Y.C., 1969-79, Gelberg & Kronovet, N.Y.C., 1979-81, Kramer, Levin, Nessen, Kamin & Frankel, N.Y.C., 1981-90, O'Melveny & Myers, N.Y.C., 1990—; lectr. 2d Ann. Uniform Comml. Code Law Inst., 1968. Author: Creditors' Rights Handbook, 1980; co-author: Herzog's Bankruptcy, 6th edit., 1980; contbr. articles to profl. jours. Recipient award Bankruptcy and Reorgn. div. Fedn. United Jewish Appeal, 1989. Mem. ABA, Assn. of Bar of City of N.Y. (chmn. com. on bankruptcy and corp. reorgn. 1981-84), Nat. Bankruptcy Conf. (chmn. com. on avoiding powers 1983—, treas. 1991—), Beta Gamma Sigma. Avocations: art, theatre, music, photography. Office: O'Melveny & Myers 153 E 53rd St New York NY 10022-4602

ZWEIFEL, DAVID ALAN, newspaper editor; b. Monroe, Wis., May 19, 1940; s. Cloyence John and Uva Lorraine (Skinner) Z.; m. Sandra Louise Holz, Sept. 7, 1968; children: Daniel Mark, Kristin Lynn. BJ, U. Wis., 1962. Reporter The Capital Times, Madison, Wis., 1962-71, city editor, 1971-78, mng. editor, 1978-83, editor, 1983—. V.p. Alliance for Children and Youth, Madison, 1983—; bd. dirs. United Cerebral Palsy Dane County, Madison, 1984-91. Lt. U.S. Army, 1963-65; col. USNG, ret. Named Investigative Reporter of Yr. Madison Press Club, 1972. Mem. Am. Soc. Newspaper Editors (com. freedom info.), Wis. AP (pres. 1987-88), Wis. Freedom Info. Coun. (pres. 1986—), Wis. N.G. Assn. (trustee 1975-81), U. Wis. Alumni Assn., Elks. Avocations: running, bowling, book collecting. Home: 5714 Tecumseh Ave Monona WI 53716-2964 Office: The Capital Times PO Box 8060 Madison WI 53708-8060

ZWEIFEL, DONALD EDWIN, automobile dealer, civic affairs volunteer; b. L.A., Nov. 30, 1940; s. Robert Fredrick and Eugenia Bedford (White) Z.; m. Donna Jean Croslin; 1 son, Phillip Matthew. Student, Orange Coast Coll., 1963-67, 90-92, U. Calif., Irvine, 1968-70, Western State U. Coll. Law, 1973, Irvine U. Coll. Law, 1974-75, Rancho Santiago Jr. Coll., 1988, Chapman U., 1989, 93—; grad., Aviation Ground Sch., 1990; student, USAF Air U., 1994-95. Cert. Student Pilot, 1989. Devel. tech. Hughes Aircraft, Newport Beach, Calif., 1963-64; co-founder Sta. KUCI-FM, Irvine, Calif., 1970; owner, mgr. Zweifel Jaguar Car Sales and Svc., Santa Ana, Calif., 1975-76; pres. Zweifel & Assocs. Inc., Santa Ana, 1977-86, Zweifel South Coast Exotic Cars, Orange, Calif., 1987—. Co-author: Challenge 2000, Regaining the America's Cup, 1996; editor: (coll. textbook) The Dream Is Alive, Space Flight and Operations In Earth Orbit. Vol. emergency coord. emergency mgmt. div. Orange County Fire Dept., 1985-87, Navy Relief Soc., 1993, CAP Squadron, 1993, sr. programs officer, 1993-94, asst. transp. officer Calif. Wing Hdqrs., 1994-95, Group VII Facilities officer, 1994-95, squadron pers. officer, 1993-95, Calif. wing rep. to Orange County Vol. Orgns. Active in Disaster, ARC, 1994-95, Calif. wing vol. Office Emergency Svcs., Calif., 1994-96, grad. Squadron Leadership Sch., 1993, Wings Supply Officers Sch., 1995; program coord. Young Astronaut Coun., 1989-90; cadet CAP, USAF auxiliary, Long Beach, Calif., 1953-60, 62-64; mem. Orange County Homeless Issues Taskforce, 1994-95, Orange County Homeless Svc. Providers for the Reuse of Marine Corps Air Sta., Tustin, Calif., 1994—; mem. restoration adv. bd., chmn. operable unit # 1 subcom. Marine Corps Air Sta., El Toro, Calif., 1994—; apptd. to CalEPA DTSC Adv. Group Mil. Base Closure, 1995—, CalEPA Dept. Toxics & Substances Control Adv. Group rep. El Toro Local Redevel. Authority, 1996—; vol. mediator Victim-Offender Reconciliation program, 1995—; mem. So. Calif. Vol. Orgns. Active in Disaster, restoration adv. bd. MCAS Tustin, 1994—. With Army N.G., 1958-59. Recipient 6 certs. achievement Fed. Emergency Mgmt. Agy., 1989-96, 2 certs. appreciation CAP, 2 certs commendation, 1994. Mem. Air Force Assn. (vice-chmn. civilian recruitment Calif. state membership com. 1988-89, 90-91, v.p. membership, Gen. Doolittle chpt. bd. dirs. 1987-89, 90-92, Exceptional Svc. award Gen. Jimmy Doolittle chpt. 1988, 91, Calif. Meritorious Svc. award 1988), Calif. Assn. for Aerospace Edn. (fellow), Marine Corps Hist. Found. (life), Aerospace Edn. Found. (Gen. Jimmy Doolittle fellow 1988, Gen. Ira Eaker fellow 1989, Pres.'s award 1988), U.S. Naval Inst., AIAA (Cert. of Appreciation 1989, L.A. chpt. hist. com. 1989), Marine Corps Assn. (assoc.), Navy League, Gulf & Vietnam Vet. Hist.-Strategic Studies Assn. (cons., co-founder, trustee 1983—, exec. dir.), Am. Def. Preparedness Assn., Exptl. Aircraft Assn., Assn. of Old Crows, U.S. Marine Corps Combat Correspondents Assn. (affiliate), Confederate Air Force (col. 1989, adj. 1st Composite Group detachment 1989), Aircraft Owners and Pilots Assn., World Affairs Coun. Orange County. Avocations: sailing, bicycle racing, traveling, flying. Home and Office: Gulf & Vietnam Vets Hist Assn 2110 W Larkspur Dr Orange CA 92668

ZWEIFEL, RICHARD GEORGE, curator; b. L.A., Nov. 5, 1926; s. Harold Charles and Kathleen Marguerite (Garland) Z.; m. Frances Ann Wimsatt, July 30, 1956; children: Matthew Karl, Kenneth Paul, Ellen Katrina. B.A., UCLA, 1950; Ph.D., U. Calif. at Berkeley, 1954. Mem. staff Am. Mus. Natural History, N.Y.C., 1954-89, chmn. curator dept. herpetology, 1968-80, curator emeritus, 1989—; sci. attaché Gondwana, 1974-75. Served with AUS, 1945-46. Mem. Soc. Study Evolution, Am. Soc. Ichthyologists and Herpetologists. Home: PO Box 354 Portal AZ 85632-0354

ZWEIG, GEORGE, physicist, neurobiologist; b. Moscow, May 20, 1937; came to U.S., 1938; s. Alfred and Rachael (Frölich) Z. BS in Math., U. Mich., 1959; PhD in Physics, Calif. Inst. Tech., 1963. NAS-NRC fellow European Orgn. for Nuclear Rsch., Geneva, 1963-64; asst. prof. physics Calif. Inst. Tech., Pasadena, 1964-66, assoc. prof., 1966-67, prof., 1967-83; staff mem. Los Alamos (N.Mex.) Nat. Lab., 1981-85, fellow, 1985—; founder, pres. Signition, Inc., Los Alamos, 1985—; vis. prof. physics U. Wis., Madison, 1967-68; mem. Jason div. Inst. for Def. Analysis, Arlington, Va., 1965-72. Recipient MacArthur prize MacArthur Found., 1981, Disting. Alumnus award Calif. Inst. Tech., 1984; Alfred P. Sloan Found. fellow in physics, 1966-74, in neurobiology, 1974-78. Mem. IEEE, AAAS, Am. Math. Soc., Am. Phys. Soc., Assn. for Rsch. in Otolaryngology. Discoverer quarks, 1963; creator continuous wavelet transform for signal processing, 1975, active model of coclear mechanics, 1987. Office: LANL MS B276 PO Box 1663 Los Alamos NM 87544-0600

ZWEIMAN, BURTON, physician, scientist, educator; b. N.Y.C., June 7, 1931; s. Charles and Gertrude (Levine) Z.; m. Claire Traig, Dec. 30, 1962; children: Amy Beth, Diane Susan. AB, U. Pa., 1952, MD, 1956. Diplomate Am. Bd. Internal Medicine, Am. Bd. Allergy & Immunology. Intern Mt. Sinai Hosp., N.Y.C.; Hosp. U. Pa., Bellevue Hosp. Ctr. Hosp. U. Pa., Bellevue Hosp. Center, 1957-60; fellow NYU Sch. Medicine, 1960-61; mem. faculty dept. medicine U. Pa. Sch. Medicine, Phila., 1963—; prof. medicine, chief allergy and immunology divsn. U. Pa. Sch. Medicine, 1975—; cons. U.S. Army, NIH; co-chmn. Am. Bd. Allergy and Immunology, 1979-81. Editor Jour. Allergy Clin. Immunology, 1988-93; contbr. articles to med. jours. Served with M.C., USNR, 1961-63. Allergy Found. Am. fellow, 1959-61. Fellow ACP, Am. Acad. Allergy, Asthma and Immunology (past pres.); mem. Am. Assn. Immunologists, Am. Fedn. Clin. Rsch., Phi Beta Kappa, Alpha Omega Alpha. Office: U Pa Sch Medicine 512 Johnson Pavilion 36th and Hamilton Walk Philadelphia PA 19104-1999

ZWERDLING, ALEX, English educator; b. Breslau, Germany, June 21, 1932; came to U.S., 1941, naturalized, 1946; s. Norbert and Fanni (Alt) Z.; m. Florence Goldberg, Mar. 23, 1969; 1 son, Antony Daniel. B.A., Cornell U., 1953; postgrad. (Fulbright scholar), U. Munich, Germany, 1953-54; M.A., Princeton U., 1956, Ph.D., 1960. Instr. English Swarthmore Coll., 1957-61; asst. prof. English U. Calif., Berkeley, 1961-67; assoc. prof. U. Calif., 1967-73, prof., 1973-86; prof. English U. Calif., Berkeley, 1988—; chmn. grad. studies U. Calif., 1985-86; univ. prof. George Washington U., 1986-88; vis. prof. Northwestern U., 1977; dir. edn. abroad program U. Calif., London, 1996—; mem. advanced placement exam. com. Ednl. Testing Svc., 1975-79; mem. fellowship panel Nat. Endowment for Humanities, 1977-82, 84-87, Nat. Humanities Ctr., 1989-90; fellow Ctr. for Advanced Study in Behavioral Scis., 1964-65. Author: Yeats and the Heroic Ideal, 1965, Orwell and the Left, 1974, Virginia Woolf and the Real World, 1986; mem. adv. com. PMLA, 1978-82. Am. Coun. Learned Socs. fellow, 1964-65; NEH fellow, 1973-74; Guggenheim fellow, 1977-78; Woodrow Wilson Ctr. fellow, 1991-92, fellow Nat. Humanities Ctr., 1992-93. Mem. MLA (chmn. 20th Century Brit. lit. div. 1969-70, 85-86). Office: U Calif Dept English Berkeley CA 94720

ZWERDLING, DAVID MARK, psychiatrist; b. Detroit, Jan. 13, 1944; s. Joseph and Alice (Granoff) Z.; m. Martha A. Teitelbaum, May 29, 1977; children: Celia T., Maury T. (dec.), JoLillian T. BA, Harvard U., 1965; JD, U. Chgo., 1969; MD, Yale U., 1975. Bd. cert. psychiatry and child/adolscent psychiatry. Asst. clin. prof. psychiatry George Washington U., Washington, 1980—; assoc. staff Childrens Nat. Med. Ctr., Washington, 1980—; psychiatrist child, adolscent and adult pvr. ptactice, Silver Spring, Md., 1980—; staff psychiatrist Cmty. Psychiat. Clinic, Inc., Montgomery County, Md., 1980-88, med. dir. Wheaton office, 1988-93, med. dir., 1993—; mem. adv. bd. Ctr. for Divorcing Families, Inc., Rockville, Md., 1990-93. Author: (with others) Psychiatric House Calls, 1988. Pres. Forest Glen Park Citizens Assn., Silver Spring, 1983, 84; mem. Zwerdling Meml. Program Social Justice com. Temple Sinai, Washington. Mem. Am. Psychiat. Assn., Am. Acad. Child/Adolscent Psychiatry. Office: Cmty Psychiat Clinic Inc 2424 Reedie Dr Silver Spring MD 20902

ZWERLING, GARY LESLIE, investment bank executive; b. N.Y.C., Aug. 6, 1949; s. Seymour Joseph and Evelyn Rhoda (Posner) Z.; m. Marierose Miraglia, Aug. 25, 1974; children: Cara Marisa, Craig Harris. BEngring., SUNY, Stony Brook, 1970; MBA, SUNY, Albany, 1972. V.p. Chase Manhattan Bank, N.Y.C., 1972-78; gen. ptnr. Goldman, Sachs & Co., N.Y.C., 1978—. Mem. N.Y. One to One Sponsoring Group, Heritage Soc. of A Living Meml. to the Holocaust-Mus. Jewish Heritage. Mem. Thoroughbred Owners and Breeders Assn. Jewish. Avocation: skiing. Office: Goldman Sachs & Co 85 Broad St New York NY 10004-2434

ZWERVER, PETER JOHN, linguistics educator; b. Grouw, Friesland, The Netherlands, Sept. 3, 1942; came to U.S., 1959; m. Margot Anne Otters, July 16, 1978. AA in Fgn. Langs., Cerritos Coll., 1963; BA in German and English, Calif. State U., Long Beach, 1963; MA in Edn., Azusa Pacific U., 1971; PhD in Edn., Pacific Western U., 1980; PhD in Linguistics, Clayton U., 1988; BS in Liberal Studies, SUNY, Albany, 1989; BA in Archtl. Arts, Clayton U., 1995. Cert. standard elem., jr. high sch. and gen. secondary tchr., Calif.; cert. in standard supervision and adminstrv. svcs. grades kindergarten through 12, Calif. Tchr. math. and woodworking Monrovia (Calif.) Unified Sch. Dist., 1966—; assoc. prof. applied linguistics Pacific Western U., L.A., 1984-92, prof., 1992—; v.p. adminstrv. svcs. Am. M & N U., Metairie, La., 1993—; fellow in community arts and architecture Am. Coastline U., New Orleans, 1989; mem. acad. adv. coun. Pacific Western U., 1984—; chmn. acad. coun. Am. Coastline U., 1988—. Editor jour. Internat. Inst. for Ind. Scholarship, Pacific Western U., 1983-87; contbg. author: Poetic Voices of America, 1993; columnist Foothill Inter-City Newspapers, 1983-86. Pres. Monroe Sch. PTA, 1975, Santa Anita Family Svc., Monrovia, 1982, Arcadian Christian Sch., Arcadia, Calif., 1974. Recipient Hon. Svc. award Nat. Congress of Parents and Tchrs., 1976. Mem. NEA, Nat. Assn. Scholars, Calif. Tchrs. Assn., Monrovia Tchrs. Assn., Doctorate Assn. N.Y. Educators, Phi Beta Kappa, Phi Delta Kappa (rsch. rep. U. So. Calif. chpt. 1990-91, Rsch. award 1987, Intrnat. Svc. Key, 1993). Avocations: woodworking, attending concerts, museums, architecture, reading.

ZWICK, BARRY STANLEY, newspaper editor, speechwriter; b. Cleve., July 21, 1942; s. Alvin Albert and Selma Davidowna (Makofsky) Z.; m. Roberta Joan Yaffe, Mar. 11, 1972; children: Natasha Yvette, Alexander Anatol. BA in Journalism, Ohio State U., 1963; MS in Journalism, Columbia U., 1965. Copy editor Phila. Inquirer, 1964; night news editor Detroit Free Press, 1965-67; West Coast editor L.A. Times/Washington Post News Svc, 1967-77; makeup editor L.A. Times, 1978—; adj. prof. U. So. Calif., L.A., 1975-77. Author: Hollywood Tanning Secrets, 1980. NEH profl. journalism fellow Stanford U., 1977-78. Jewish. Avocations: photography, jet skiing, snowmobiling. Office: LA Times Times Mirror Sq Los Angeles CA 90012

ZWICK, CHARLES J., think-tank executive. Chmn. of the board Carnegie Endowment for International Peace, Washington, D.C. Office: Carnegie Endowment Internat Peace 2400 N St NW Washington DC 20037-1153*

ZWICK, EDWARD M., director, producer, scriptwriter; b. Chgo., Oct. 8, 1952; s. Allen and Ruth Ellen (Reich) Z.; m. Lynn Liberty Godshall, Oct. 24, 1982. BA, Harvard U., 1974; MFA, Am. Film Inst., 1976. Editor, feature writer The New Republic, Rolling Stone, 1972-74; co-founder Bedford Falls Prodn. Co. Writer, prodr., dir.: (TV series) Family, 1976-80 (Humanitas prize 1980), (TV spl.) Spl. Bull., 1983 (Emmy award for outstanding drama spl. 1983, Dir. Guild award 1983, Writers Guild award 1983, Humanitas prize 1983); dir.: (TV movies) Paper Dolls, 1982, Having It All, 1982, Extreme Close-Up, 1990, (films) About Last Night, 1986, Glory, 1989, Leaving Normal, 1992, Legends of the Fall, 1994, Coverage Under Fire, 1995; co-creator, exec. prodr.: (with Marshall Herskovitz) Thirtysomething, 1987-91 (Emmy award for outstanding drama series 1988), Dream Street, 1989, My So-Called Life, 1994-95; author: Literature and Liberalism, 1975. Office: ICM 8942 Wilshire Blvd Beverly Hills CA 90211-1934

ZWIEP, DONALD NELSON, mechanical engineering educator, administrator; b. Hull, Iowa, Mar. 18, 1924; s. Daniel and Nellie (De Stigter) Z.; m. Marcia J. Hubers, Sept. 3, 1948; children: Donna J., Mary N., Joan L., Helen D. BSME, Iowa State Coll., 1948, MSME, 1951; DEng (hon.), Worcester Polytech. Inst., 1965. Registered profl. engr., Mass. Design engr. Boeing Airplane Co., 1948-50, sr. tool engr., summer 1953, summer faculty asso., 1955; asst. prof. Colo. State U., 1951-56, assoc. prof., 1956-57; cons. engr. aviation div. Forney Mfg. Co., 1956-57; prof., head dept. mech. engring. Worcester Polytech. Inst., 1957-88, acting head mgmt. engring., 1974-76, chmn. Mfg. Engring. Application Ctr., 1981-88, acting provost, v.p. acad. affairs, 1988-90, prof., dept. head emeritus, 1990—; constrn. engr. U.S. C.E., summer 1954; cons. engr., acting chief engr. J.J. Malir, Inc., summer 1956. Chmn. bd. trustees James F. Lincoln Arc Welding Found., 1976—. Served as pilot USAAF, World War II, CBI; lt. col. USAFR; cons. and ednl. specialist. Fellow ASME (life, v.p. edn. 1972-74, pres. 1979-80); mem. Am. Soc. Engring. Edn. (life, pres. Colo. State U. chpt. 1954-55, treas. Rocky Mountain sect. 1955, nat. bd. dirs. 1974-75), Am. Assn. Engring. Socs. (chair coun. pre-coll. edn.), Am. Welding Soc., Soc. Mfg. Engrs., Torch Club, Sigma Xi, Omicron Delta Kappa, Tau Beta Pi, Sigma Tau, Pi Tau Sigma. Methodist. Home: 47 Birchwood Dr Holden MA 01520-1937 Office: Worcester Poly Inst 100 Institute Rd Worcester MA 01609-2247

ZWILICH, ELLEN TAAFFE, composer; b. Miami, Fla., Apr. 30, 1939; d. Edward Porter and Ruth (Howard) Taaffe; m. Joseph Zwilich, June 22, 1969 (dec. June 1979). MusB, Fla. State U., 1960, MusM, 1962; D Mus. Arts, Juilliard Sch., 1975; studies with Roger Sessions and Elliott Carter; MusD (hon.), Oberlin Coll., 1987, Converse Coll., 1994; LHD (hon.), Manhattanville Coll., 1991, Marymount Manhattan Coll., 1994, N.Y. New Sch., Mannes, 1995. composer in residence Santa Fe Chamber Music Festival, 1990, Am. Acad. Rome, 1990; first Composer's Chair, Carnegie Hall, 1995. Premiere, Symposium for Orch., Pierre Boulez, N.Y.C., 1975, Chamber Symphony and Passages, Boston Musica Viva, Richard Pittman, 1979, 82. Symphony 1, Gunther Schuller, Am. Composers Orch., 1982; violinist Am. Symphony, N.Y.C., 1965-73; composer: Sonata in Three Movements, 1973-74; String Quartet, 1974; Clarino Quartet, 1977; Chamber Symphony, 1979; Passages (for Soprano and Chamber Ensemble), 1981; String Trio, 1982; Symphony 1:3 Movements for Orch., 1982 (Grammy nomination New World Records, 1987); Divertimento, 1983; Einsame Nacht, 1971; Emlekezet, 1978; Im Nebel, 1972; Passages for Soprano and Orch., 1982; Trompeten, 1974; Fantasy for Harpsichord, 1983; Intrada, 1983; Prologue and Variations, 1983; Double Quartet for Strings, Chamber Music Soc. of Lincoln Ctr., 1984; Celebration for Orch., Indpls. Symphony, John Nelson, 1984; Symphony #2 (Cello Symphony) San Francisco Symphony, Edo De Waart, 1985, Symphony #2 Louisville Orch. recording, L.L. Smith (Grammy nomination 1991); Concerto Grosso 1985, Handel Festival Orch., Steven Simon, 1986; Concerto for Piano and Orch., Detroit Symphony, Gunther Herbig, Marc-André Hamelin, 1986; Images for 2 Pianos and Orch., Nat. Symphony Orch., F. Machetti, 1987; Tanzspiel, Peter Martins N.Y.C. Ballet, 1987; Praeludium Boston chpt. AGO, 1987; Trio for piano, violin and cello; Kalichstein, Laredo, Robinson trio, 1987; Symbolon, Zubin Mehta and the N.Y. Philharm., Leningrad and Moscow (USSR), N.Y.C. (Koussevitsky Internat. Rec. award nominee 1990), 1988; concerto for trombone and orch. J. Friedman, Sir Georg Solti, Chgo. Symphony, 1989, concerto for trombone and orch. Christian Lindberg, James De Priest, Malmö Symphony, concerto for flute and orch. D.A. Dwyer, Seija Ozawa, Boston Symphony, 1990, quintet for clarinet and string quartet David Schiffrin, Chamber Music N.W., 1990; concerto for oboe and orch. John Mack, Christoph von Dohnanyi, Cleve. Orch., 1991; concerto for bass trombone strings, timpani and cymbals Chgo. Symphony Orch. Ch. Vernon, Daniel Barenboim, 1991; concerto for violin, violoncello and orch. Jaime Laredo, Sharon Robinson, Louisville Orch., L. Smith, 1991; Immigrant Voices Peter Leonard, St. Lukes Orch., N.Y. Internat. Festival ot the Arts Chorus, Ellis Island, 1991, concerto for flute and orch, D.A. Dwyer, J. Sedares, London Symphony Orch., 1992, Symphony # 3 (Grammy nominee 1993), J. Ling, N.Y. Philharmonic, 1993, concerto for bassoon and orch., Nancy Goeres, Lorin Maazel, Pitts. Symphony, 1993, concerto for horn and string Orch., David Jolley, Rochester Philharm., L.L. Smith., 1993, Fantasy for Orch., JoAnn Falletta, Long Beach Symphony Orch., 1994, American Concerto, 1994, A Simple Magnificat, 1994; New World Records: Music By Ellen Taaffe Zwilich; N.Y. Philharm. conducted by Zubin Mehta. Recipient Elizabeth Sprague Coolidge Chamber Music prize, 1974, Gold medal G.B. Viotti, Vercelli, Italy, 1975, citation Ernst von Dohnanyi, 1981, Pulitzer prize, 1983, Composers award Lancaster Symphony Orch., Arturo Toscanini Music Critics award, 1987, Alfred I. DuPont award, 1991; Martha Baird Rockefeller Fund rec. grantee, 1977, 79, 82, Guggenheim fellow, 1981. Mem. AAAL, Am. Fedn. Musicians (hon. life), Am. Music Ctr. (bd. dirs., v.p. 1982-84), Am. Composers Orch. (bd. dirs.), Am. Acad. Arts and Letters (Acad. award 1984, elected 1992), MacDowell Colony (bd. dirs.), Fla. Artists Hall of Fame, Carnegie Hall Composer's Chair. Home: 600 W 246th St Bronx NY 10471-3611 Office: care Music Assocs Am 224 King St Englewood NJ 07631-3026

ZWINGE, RANDALL JAMES HAMILTON See **RANDI, JAMES**

ZWIRN, ROBERT, architect, architecture educator; b. N.Y.C., Apr. 6, 1948; m. Sharon Kay Hansen, Mar. 19, 1972 (div. Sept. 1979); m. Carolyn Marie Pione, Feb. 20, 1994. BS, Rensselaer Poly. Inst., 1968, BArch, 1969; MArch, U. Oreg., 1970; JD, U. Ala., Montgomery, 1975. Registered architect, Ala., Ohio, La. Asst. prof. architecture Auburn (Ala.) U., 1970-78, assoc. prof., 1978-79; vis. fellow Princeton (N.J.) U., 1979-81; architect I.M. Pei & Ptnrs., N.Y.C., 1981-84; prof. architecture Miami U., Oxford, Ohio, 1984—, chmn. dept., 1984-92; dir. Sch. Architecture La. State U., Baton Rouge, 1994—; chair Coun. of Acad. Heads, La. State U., 1994-95, mem. strategic planning com., 1994-95; exec. com. Univ. Senate, Miami U., 1993-94; archtl. advisor City of Forest Park, Ohio, 1989-90. Contbr. biographies to Ency. Architecture. Numerous archtl. commns., 1976—. Mem. Future of Oxford, 1988-89. Miami U. Sch. Fine Arts grantee, 1988; NEH summer stipend grantee UCLA, 1994. Mem. Assn. Collegiate Schs. Arch. (nat. bd. dirs., bd. dirs. East Cen. region 1986-89, co-editor 1989, co-chair ann. adminstr.'s meeting, co-chair adminstrv. conf. 1996), Archs. Soc. Ohio (bd. dirs. 1988-89, Profl. Devel. award 1990). Democrat. Jewish. Avocation: gardening. Office: La State U Sch Architecture Baton Rouge LA 70808

ZWISLOCKI, JOZEF JOHN, neuroscience educator, researcher; b. Lwow, Poland, Mar. 19, 1922; came to U.S., 1951; s. Tadeusz and Helena (Moscicki) Z.; m. Ruth Gerber, Oct. 29, 1945 (div. May 1954); m. Sylvia Claire Goldman, July 11, 1954 (dec. July 17, 1992); m. Jadwiga M. Morrison, Dec. 2, 1993. Diploma, Fed. Tech. Inst., Zurich, Switzerland, 1944, Sc.D., 1948; D. honoris causa, U. Adam Mickiewicz, Poznán, Poland, 1991. Research asst. dept. otolaryngology U. Basel, Switzerland, 1945-51; research fellow psychoacoustic lab. Harvard U., Cambridge, Mass., 1951-57; dir. Bioacoustic Lab. Syracuse U., N.Y., 1958-63, founder, dir. Lab. of Sensory Communication, 1963-73, founder dir. Inst. for Sensory Research, 1973-84, prof. neurosci., 1984-88, Disting. prof. neurosci., 1988-92; Disting. rsch. prof. Inst. for Sensory Rsch. Syracuse U., 1992, prof. communicative disorders dept. spl. edn. Sch. Edn., 1982-92; research prof. SUNY Health Sci. Ctr. at Syracuse, 1967—; affiliate prof. bioengring. L.C. Smith Coll. Engring., Syracuse U., 1986-92; Carhart Meml. lectr. Am. Auditory Soc., 1992; mem. exec. coun. Com. Hearing, Bioacoustics and Biomechanics, NRC, Washington, 1965-68, chmn., 1967-68; mem. rev. panel on communicative scis. NIH, Bethesda, Md., 1966-70, chmn., 1969-70; mem. Communicative Disorders Program Project rev. com. NIH, Bethesda, 1971-75; chmn. Bd. Sci. Advs. Ctr. Health Scis., U. Wis., Madison, 1975-78. Inventor acoustic ear simulator, acoustic bridge, layered earplugs; contbr. articles to profl. jours. Recipient Faculty Research award Syracuse chpt. Sigma Xi, 1973, Internat. Ctr. Ricerche e Studi Amplifon prize, 1976, Chancellor's citation, Syracuse U., 1980, Javits Neurosci. Investigator award NIH, 1984, Kwiek medal Acoustics Inst., A. Mickiewicz U., Poland, 1991, medal Acoustical Soc. Poland, 1991, Hugh Knowles prize Northwestern U., 1992. Fellow Acoustical Soc. Am. (chmn. tech. com. on psychol. and physiol. acoustics 1962, 63, exec. coun. 1982-85, recipient 1st Bekesy medal 1985, chmn. long-range planning com. 1983-86, nominating com. 1986-87, mem. com. on tutorials 1988-91, com. on meetings 1988-91, chmn. spring meeting, 1989), Am. Speech and Hearing Assn., The Polish Inst. of Arts and Scis. of Am.; mem. NAS, Internat. Soc. Audiology (v.p. 1967-72), Internat. Union of Physiol. Scis. (commn. on auditory physiology 1982-89), Internat. Union Pure and Applied Physics (Commn. on Acoustics 1982-89), Collegium Oto Rhino Laryngologicum Amicitiae Sacrum, Assn. for Research in Otolaryngology (award of merit 1988), Hearing Research (edit. bd.). Clubs: Drumlins Tennis, Onondaga Ski (Syracuse). Avocations: skiing, tennis, trout fishing, inventions.

ZWOYER, EUGENE MILTON, consulting engineering executive; b. Plainfield, N.J., Sept. 8, 1926; s. Paul Ellsworth and Marie Susan (Britt) Z.; m. Dorothy Lucille Seward, Feb. 23, 1946; children: Gregory, Jeffrey, Douglas. Student, U. Notre Dame, 1944, Mo. Valley Coll., 1944-45; BS, U. N.Mex., 1947; MS, Ill. Inst. Tech., 1949; PhD, U. Ill., 1953. Mem. faculty U. N.Mex., Albuquerque, 1948-71, prof. civil engring., dir. Eric Wang Civil Engring. Rsch. Facility, 1961-70; rsch. assoc. U. Ill., Urbana, 1951-53; owner, cons. engr. Eugene Zwoyer & Assocs., Albuquerque, 1954-72; exec. dir., sec. ASCE, N.Y.C., 1972-82; pres. Am. Assn. Engring. Socs., N.Y.C., 1982-84; exec. v.p. T.Y. Lin Internat., San Francisco, 1984-86, pres., 1986-89; owner Eugene Zwoyer Cons. Engr., 1989—; chief oper. officer, treas. Polar Molecular Corp., Saginaw, Mich., 1990, exec. v.p., 1991-92. Trustee Small Bus. Research Corp., 1976-80; trustee Engring. Info., Inc., 1981-84; internat. trustee People-to-People Internat. 1974-86; v.p. World Fedn. Engring. Orgns., 1982-85. Served to lt. (j.g.) USN, 1944-46. Named Outstanding Engr. of Yr. Albuquerque chpt. N.Mex Soc. Profl. Engrs., 1969, One Who Served the Best Interests of the Constrn. Industry, Engring. News Record, 1980; recipient Disting. Alumnus award the Civil Engring. Alumni Assn. at U. Ill., 1979, Disting. Alumnus award Engring. Coll. Alumni Assn., U. N.Mex., 1982, Can.-Am. Civil Engring. Amity award Am. Soc. Civil Engrs., 1988, Award for Outstanding Profl. Contbns. and Leadership Coll. Engring. U. N.Mex., 1989. Mem. AAAS, ASCE (dist. bd. dirs. 1968-71), NSPE, Am. Soc. Engring. Edn., Am. Concrete Inst., Nat. Acad. Code Adminstrn. (trustee, mem. exec. com. 1973-79), Engrs. Joint Coun. (bd. dirs. 1978-79), Engring. Soc. Commn. on Energy (bd. dirs. 1977-82), Sigma Xi, Sigma Tau, Chi Epsilon. Home: 6363 Christie Ave Apt 1326 Emeryville CA 94608-1940 Office: 1172 San Pablo Ave Ste 200C Berkeley CA 94706-2245

ZYLANOFF, PHILLIPA LOUISE, anesthesiologist; b. Indpls., Feb. 2, 1943; d. Joseph David Zylanoff and Phillipa (Schreiber) Moore; divorced;

children: Gwendolynn, Ann, Daniel, Aliza, Tamar. BS, Calif. State U., Hayward, 1966; MD, Med. Coll. Pa., 1972. Diplomate Am. Bd. Anesthesiology. Asst. prof. U. Calif., Davis, 1977-79; staff anesthesiologist New Iberia (La.) Parish Hosp., 1979-81; pvt. practice anesthesiology Moorehead, Ky., 1981-84; asst. prof. U. S. Ala., Mobile, 1985-87; dir. anesthesiology Randolph Hosp., Asheboro, N.C., 1987-90; pvt. practice anesthesiology Detroit, 1990—. Contbr. articles to profl. jours. Course dir. Mich. affiliate Am. Heart Assn. Mem. AMA, Mich. Soc. Anesthesiologists, Mich. State Med. Soc., Wayne County Med. Soc. (peer review com. 1991-93), Soc. Cardiovascular Anesthesiologists (presenter 1987). Republican. Jewish. Avocations: gardening, scuba diving, music. Home: 17311 Beechwood Ave Franklin MI 48025-5523

ZYLBERBERG, ABRAHAM LIEB, lawyer; b. Lodz, Poland, Apr. 21, 1947; came to U.S., 1959; s. Israel Jacob and Sara (Gartman) Z.; m. Harriet Ellen Shapiro, Sept. 5, 1977; 1 child, David. BA, U. Chgo., 1969; JD, U. Mich., 1973. Bar: N.Y. 1974. Assoc. Sullivan & Cromwell, N.Y.C., 1973-79; ptnr. Sage, Gray, Todd & Sims, N.Y.C., 1980-87, Hughes, Hubbard & Reed, N.Y.C., 1987-89, White & Case, N.Y.C., 1989—. Mem. Assn. Bar City N.Y. Home: 1105 Park Ave New York NY 10128-1200 Office: White & Case 1155 Avenue Of The Americas New York NY 10036-2711

ZYLIS-GARA, TERESA GERARDA, soprano; b. Landwarow, Poland, Jan. 23, 1935; married; 1 child. Student conservatories. Debut, Cracow, Glyndebourne (Eng.) Opera, 1965, Paris Opera, 1966, San Francisco Opera, Met. Opera, 1968, Salzburg (Austria) Festival, leading soprano, Deutsche Opera am Rhein, appearances with, Vienna Staatsopera, Royal Opera House-Covent Garden, London, Munich (W.Ger.) Staatsoper, Hamburg (W.Ger.) Staatsoper, La Scala, Milan, Italy, also opera houses of Berlin, Brussels, Paris, San Francisco and Chgo., Teatro Colon, Buenos Aires, Bolshoi-Moscow, soprano soloist with, Boston Symphony Orch., N.Y. Philharm. Orch., Los Angeles Philharm., Cleve. Orch., guest artist on radio and TV in, Europe and U.S.; rec. artist: Angel, Deutsche Grammophon and, Seraphim records; prin. roles in: Il Trovatore; Un Ballo in: Maschera; Desdemona in: Otello; Marschallin in: Der Rosenkavalier; also title role in: Tosca. Winner contest Assn. German Broadcasters, Internat. Singing Competition, Munich, 1960; recipient Prime Minister's prize, 1979, Mozart gold medal, Mexico City, Polish Nat. award. Fellow Kosciuszko Found., Frederic Chopin Found. Office: c/o Hamburg State Opera, Grosse-Theaterstasse 34, D-2000 Hamburg 36, Germany Address: 16A Blvd de Belgique, Monaco-Ville Monaco *L'artiste face a l'oeuvre est comme le roseau dans le vent: c'est lui qui doit plier. La musique est l'expression universelle de l'ame d'un peuple.*

ZYLSTRA, STANLEY JAMES, farmer, food company executive; b. Hull, Iowa, Dec. 18, 1943; s. Jerald S. and Dora (Te Slaa) Z.; m. Ruth Eileen Van Batavia, Jan. 3, 1964; children: Rachel Ann, Carl Dean. BA, Northwestern Coll., 1965; MA, Univ. S.D., 1969. Math tchr., counselor Boyden-Hull Sch., 1965-73; farmer Hull, 1970—; dir. Land O'Lakes, Mpls., 1985—, chmn. bd. dirs., 1988—. Mem. Kiwanis (pres. 1974-75). Republican. Mem. Reformed Church in America. Home: RR 1 Box 200 Hull IA 51239-9763 Office: Land O'Lakes Inc 4001 Lexington Ave N Saint Paul MN 55126-2934

ZYWICKI, ROBERT ALBERT, electrical distribution company executive; b. Chgo., Sept. 23, 1930; s. Martin Albert and Margaret Irene (Mackowski) Z.; m. Barbara Joan Hagerty; children: Robert, Cheryl, Cindy, Carrie. B in Commerce, Northwestern U., 1966. Teller Chgo. Title and Trust Bank, Chgo., 1949-50; painter Getz Molding Co., Chgo., 1950-51; purchasing agt. Woodworker's Tool Works, Chgo., 1953-54; serviceman Addressograph Multigraph, Chgo., 1954-55; mem. Chgo. Fire Dept., 1955-62; v.p. Anixter Bros. Inc., Skokie, Ill., 1955-87; co-owner A-Z Industries, Northbrook, Ill., 1987-92, A-Z Anicom (formerly A-Z Industries), Northbrook, Ill., 1992—. Served as cpl. U.S. Army, 1951-53. Mem. Am. Legion (comdr.). Republican. Roman Catholic. Avocations: thoroughbred horse racing, classical music, baseball card collecting, tennis. Home: 1330 Sprucewood Ln Deerfield IL 60015-4771 *Love your family, respect your friends and co-workers, value your customers and suppliers. Always keep each in its proper perspective. Most of all, remember - love, value and respect are all two-way streets.*